VIDEO & DVD GUIDE 2003

Mick Martin
and Marsha Porter

Contributing Editor:
Derrick Bang

BALLANTINE BOOKS • NEW YORK

A Ballantine Book
Published by The Ballantine Publishing Group
 Published in the United States by The Ballantine Publishing Group, a division of Random House, Inc., New York, and simultaneously in Canada by Random House of Canada Limited, Toronto. This is the eighth revised edition of *Video Movie Guide 1995* published in 1994 by Ballantine Books.

Ballantine and colophon are registered trademarks of Random House, Inc.

www.ballantinebooks.com

Mass Market edition ISBN 0-345-44991-6
Trade Paperback edition ISBN 0-345-44992-4

Cover design by Dreu Pennington-McNeil
Cover photos supplied by Globe Photos, Inc.

Manufactured in the United States of America

Revised Edition: September 2002

10 9 8 7 6 5 4 3 2 1

CONTENTS

DERRICK TRIBBLE and WILLIAM GLINES, RESEARCH EDITORS

CHIEF CONTRIBUTORS

R. SCOTT BOLTON

JASON B. DAMRON

M. FAUST

JIM LANE

JOHN LARSEN

ROCHELLE O'GORMAN

BOB POLUNSKY

RICH GARRISON

ED GRANT

MARK HALVERSON

TIM HAYES

TOM TOLLEY

LORI J. TRIBBLE

ROBERT YOUNG JR.

DEDICATED TO THE MEMORY OF BILL CRETER AND SIMON MACMILLAN

CONTENTS

DERRICK TRIBBLE and WILLIAM GLINES,
RESEARCH EDITORS

CHIEF CONTRIBUTORS

R. SCOTT BOLTON

JASON B. DAMRON

M. FAUST

JIM LANE

JOHN LARSEN

ROCHELLE O'GORMAN

BOB POLUNSKY

RICH GARRISON

ED GRANT

MARK HALVERSON

TIM HAYES

TOM TOLLEY

LORI J. TRIBBLE

ROBERT YOUNG JR.

DEDICATED TO THE MEMORY OF
BILL CRETER
AND SIMON MACMILLAN

FOREWORD/INTRODUCTION

Welcome to the newly christened *Video & DVD Guide*. We feel it is long overdue to acknowledge the revolutionary advancements brought to home movie viewing by this technical marvel. DVDs enhance the watching of movies like no other achievement before. It is now the preferred way of enjoying video entertainment in the comfort of one's own home, allowing its owners to truly create a home theater environment.

You hold in your hands the most comprehensive critical guide to movies on video available. Where other movie-review books contain films that may never be released to video stores, *Video & DVD Guide (VDG)* concentrates only on what you can rent at your local shop or purchase through the mail. Even so, that still puts this eighteenth annual edition at more than 18,000 titles.

Video & DVD Guide is also a book written by people who love movies *for* people who love movies. We treat this annual publication like some kind of holy quest, searching out obscure titles and oddball distributors in order to pack *VDG* with as many titles as possible. This is why you'll find more B-movies, foreign films, old-time and spaghetti Westerns, TV movies, direct-to-video releases, silent films, and TV series covered here than in any other movie guide.

As in previous years, we have covered all the major movie releases available in stores as well as several months' worth of upcoming titles, which we reviewed while they were in theatrical release. Also, we have gone backward as much as forward, catching up on whatever obscure or previously unreleased titles we may have missed in earlier editions. We honestly believe that you cannot find a more complete critical review of entertainment on video.

In past years, reviews in *VDG* have been broken down into genre categories. Now, by popular demand, we are listing all movies together in word-by-word alphabetical order. As our readers have pointed out, so many movies today mix genres—horror with comedy, science fiction with mystery, for example—there are no clear-cut categories anymore. So we decided it was time to put an end to the confusion.

To help you find movies reviewed in this book, we have several features: a cast index, a director index, an index of Academy Award winners, and a complete alphabetical listing of alternate titles at the back of the book. Alternate titles have been listed so that a film like *The Christmas Tree,* for example, can be found under its video title, *When Wolves Cry,* in the text, and so on. In addition, a bullet (•) has been placed next to each new review. If a movie is available on DVD, it is so indicated. We have included everything available at the time of this edition's publication. DVD releases, however, come out on a regular, weekly basis, so we cannot claim to be complete and up-to-date.

A few readers have expressed dismay because we reevaluate films from edition to edition. We feel this is necessary. A good movie might catch us on a bad day or vice versa and lead to a less-than-objective analysis. Some of the better-known film critics balk at being considered consumer guides, but that is exactly what we strive to be. Not everyone is going to like everything. But if a film has merit, even if we don't particularly care for it, we have strived to call attention to its attributes. We want this book to be, given the capriciousness of opinion, the most accurate and useful critical guide to movies.

This is why we rate genre movie against genre movie. For example, dramas are rated against dramas, Westerns against Westerns, and so on. There is no way the John Wayne/Johnny Mack Brown B-plus Western, *Hell Town,* could be compared with *Lawrence of Arabia,* for example, so we try to keep things in perspective.

Our rating system runs from five stars to a turkey. A five-star movie is a must-see; a four-star rating means it's well worth watching. The desirability of a film with a lesser rating depends on how much one likes a particular type of motion picture or a movie star. A turkey by any other name is still a bad movie, which is why we give at least a two-star rating to so-bad-they're-good movies, such as *Plan 9 from Outer Space* and *Robot Monster.* If a film is particularly offensive even though it has a big-name star, we want you to know why. Likewise, if a little-known gem has special attributes, we've done our best to call your attention to them.

When a film has been rated G, PG, PG-13, R, X, or NC-17 by the Motion Picture Association of America (MPAA), we have noted it. Only theatrically released films distributed after November 1967 were considered by the MPAA ratings board, so we have attempted to indicate the potentially objectionable content in films released before then, as well as in unrated made-for-cable and direct-to-video products. These ratings are confusing at times, so, wherever appropriate, we have explained them.

Please see the section entitled TO ORDER VIDEOS for a list of companies that specialize in selling and renting videos.

We welcome comments from our readers, but can only answer those that come with a self-addressed, stamped envelope. Our mailing address is Video & DVD Guide, P.O. Box 189674, Sacramento, CA 95818. Or you may e-mail us at bang@dcn.davis.ca.us. Check out our ongoing Web site at *www.videodvdguide.com* hosted by Derrick Tribble. Until next year, happy viewing!

TO ORDER VIDEOS

Video & DVD Guide (VDG) is meant to function as a viewing guide to what is available in video stores for rent and a buyer's guide to titles available by mail order. As with books, some movies may go "out of print" and become unavailable for purchase. A number of video companies have gone out of business in the last two years. However, many videos that can no longer be purchased still can be found for rent in many stores. So we do not delete any titles.

A number of Disney titles are released for a brief period of time and then placed on moratorium, which means you can find them for viewing purposes at a rental store, but cannot currently buy them—although they will be rereleased eventually. More and more video companies are using this approach. Other titles that were available at one time exist in some kind of never-never land now, as rights have been transferred from one company to another.

Still others, like *The Gods Must Be Crazy* and *The Final Countdown*, were pulled by their respective distributors and currently are not available for purchase. But they were available on video at one time, so we include them in our book. After all, Richard Lester's *Three* (and *Four*) *Musketeers* was rereleased, so anything can happen.

We regret any inconvenience a reader might have in attempting to buy a particular title listed in this book. However, as much as we would like to help, we do not have the time or resources to find movies for readers who want to buy them. But help is available.

Mike Antonaros has graciously agreed to answer letters from *VDG* readers about the availability and price of desired movies. Write to him at Dickens Video, 5325 Elkhorn Boulevard #292, Sacramento, CA 95842, or call toll free at (800) 228-4246.

Readers interested in buying their favorite movies on video cannot order them directly from the distributor, which is why we do not list video companies in the book. Instead, we have found a number of mail-order houses that sell and rent videos.

There are other sources for movies on video, but we have not dealt personally with any of them. We welcome comments from readers on whether we should or should not list them in the book.

Most of the following mail-order companies carry a line of recent video releases in addition to their specialty:

Classic, foreign, silent, and contemporary films for rent and for sale: Facets Multimedia, 1517 Fullerton Avenue, Chicago, IL 60614, (800) 331-6197.

Rental outlets: Home Video Festival, P.O. Box 2032, Scranton, PA 18501-9952, (800) 258-FILM; Video Library, 7157 Germantown Avenue, Philadelphia, PA 19119, (800) 669-7157. Eddie Brandt's Saturday Matinee, 6310 Colfax Avenue, North Hollywood, CA 91606, (818) 506-4242 or (818) 506-7722.

Various: Columbia House Video Club, 1400 North Fruitridge Avenue, Terre Haute, IN 47812-9621, (800) 544-4431; Critics' Choice Video, P.O. Box 549, Elk Grove Village, IL 60009-0549; Value Video International, P.O. Box 22565, Denver, CO 80222; the National Film Board of Canada, (800) 542-2164.

Classic and creaky oldies (many of which are in the public domain): Video Classic, P.O. Box 293, White River Junction, VT 05001-0293, (802) 295-4903; Outre Products, P.O. Box 1900, Evanston, IL 60204, (847) 866-7155; Discount Video, P.O. Box 7122, Burbank, CA 91510; Video Yesteryear, Box C, Sandy Hook, CT 06482; Blackhawk Films, 15959 Triumph Street, Commerce, CA 90040-1688; Hollywood Attic, 138 Fifth Avenue, Pelham, NY 10803; Foothill Video Inc., P.O. Box 547, Tujanga, CA 91043, (818) 353-8591; Grapevine Video, P.O. Box 46161, Phoenix, AZ 85063, (602) 245-0210; Mike LeBell's Video, 75 Fremont Place, Los Angeles, CA 90005, (213) 938-3333.

Cult, foreign, classic, independent, and out-of-print: Kim's Video & Music, 350 Bleecker St., New York, NY 10014, (212) 675-8996.

Canadian and specialty titles: The National Film Board of Canada, (800) 542-2164 (from the United States and elsewhere); or (800) 267-7710 (from Canada).

1950s TV shows: Shokus Video, P.O. Box 3125, Chatsworth, CA 91313.

Horror films: Sinister Cinema, P.O. Box 4369, Medford, OR 97501-0168, (541) 773-6860; Something Weird, P. O. Box 33664, Seattle, WA 98133, (206) 361-3759.

B Westerns: Boyd Magers, Video West, 1312 Stagecoach Road SE, Albuquerque, NM 87123.

Serials: Stokey's Serials, P.O. Box 426, Selden, NY 11784.

For Beta tapes: Absolute Beta Movies, P.O. Box 130, Remington, VA 22734, (540) 439-3259.

The Internet is, of course, becoming an increasingly popular source for video sales. We've tried to be careful with our endorsements here, as many companies spring up and disappear in a matter of months or years, but we do feel comfortable with these three sites: www.reel.com, www.videoexpress.com, and www.kencranes.com.

In Canada: Videomatica, Ltd., 1859 West 4th Avenue, Vancouver, B.C. V6J-1M4, (604) 734-0411 (for rentals), (604) 734-5752 (for sales), (800) 665-1469 (toll free in Canada only).

A number of these companies have 35mm or 16mm copies of old fright flicks or shoot-'em-ups from which they make their copies. Quality can vary greatly depending on the condition of the original print and the integrity of the company itself. We have seen videos that were obviously duplicated from other videos instead of an original print. So let the buyer beware. The list of mail-order houses in *VDG* is purely a service for our readers and does not constitute an endorsement on the part of the authors or the publisher. Good luck!

ACKNOWLEDGMENTS

The authors are grateful to a number of wonderful people without whose help *Video & DVD Guide (VDG)* would not be a reality. Health-and-nutrition expert Cary Nosler (a.k.a. Captain Carrot) planted the seed. Our first editor, Marilyn Abraham, helped define the book's form and nurture its growth, and our current editor, Patricia Peters, is a consistent source of support, sage advice, and inspiration.

Derrick Bang, a founding contributor, is the entertainment editor for *Davis Enterprise* as well as the host/producer/writer of the *Cable Connection* TV series. He continues to play an important role in the yearly creation of *VDG* as consulting editor.

Research editors Derrick Tribble and William Glines serve as our source points. Derrick and Bill keep our staff up on the latest films to hit video. In addition, Bill is our number-one fact checker.

Our chief contributors, a splendid crew of film critics, movie buffs, and historians, have also contributed greatly to this tome. Allow us to introduce them:

R. Scott Bolton appears each week on AM 1520 KVTA as "Scott the Video Guy" and has just published his first novel, *Killed by Death*. For more information, visit his Web site at *www.rscottbolton.com*.

Jason B. Damron has been in the video industry since 1983. His family owned two video stores in Northern California for fourteen years. Soon after the second location closed, he went to work for the sales department at the very same video products distributor that his family bought from all those years. Jason is a huge proponent of DVD, and his CA license plate even reads "DVD GUY."

M. Faust has written about movies and video over the past twenty years for numerous publications, including *Movies on TV*, *Video* magazine, the *Motion Picture Guide*, FamilyWonder.com, and the *Buffalo News*. He is also the owner of Mondo Video, the coolest video store in upstate New York.

Tim Hayes is a freelance writer and a B-film buff. His reviews have appeared in *The Ottowa Citizen*.

Mark Halverson and Jim Lane share film-critic duties at the *Sacramento News and Review*. They have been reviewing movies for more than twenty years.

John Larsen has been the film and video editor of the *Ventura County Reporter* for twenty-five years. He reviews for numerous publications and radio stations including the *Pasadena Weekly* and KVTA Talk Radio. His Web site, www.lightviews.com is a popular site for fans of video, DVD, and film. In addition, he is a screenwriter and script doctor whose latest projects include *School Girl Zombies*, *My Generation*, and *Bad Boys of Cell Block Seven*. He is also responsible for bringing R. Scott Bolton, another main contributor, into the fold.

Rochelle O'Gorman reviews videos for *Pulse!* magazine and is a nationally syndicated audiobook critic whose reviews can be found in the *Los Angeles Times, Boston Globe, New York Post*, and on audiobookscafe.com. She has been writing about film, video, and audiobooks for eighteen years.

Classic-films expert Bob Polunsky is the film critic for San Antonio's KENS-TV, WOAI-AM, and KAJA-FM.

Motion-picture historian and collector Tom Tolley is another founding contributor whose amazing knowledge of movies has been a key factor in shaping this book.

Lori J. Tribble is an independent video producer, assistant media specialist at a Sacramento, CA hospital, and a film buff.

Another chief contributor since the beginning, Robert Young Jr., is the author of *Roscoe "Fatty" Arbuckle,* a biography of the life and career of the silent-comedy star, and last year appeared on A&E's *Biography* special on the great clown. He also wrote *Movie Memo,* a short history of the MGM studios, ghosted the autobiography of Sessue Hayakawa, and was a contributing editor for *American Classic Screen.*

In addition, Jack Garner, Rich Garrison, Ed Grant, Gayna Lamb-Bang, Harvey Burgess, Devin Davis, Jean Fournier, Paul Freeman, Bob Holman, Chris Hunter, Scott Hunter, David Linck, Boyd Magers, Bill MacLeod, Craig Modderno, Bill O'Brien, Linda Rajotte, Mike Reynolds, Vicki and Mark Sazaki, Bob Shaw, Bill Smith, Lisa Smith-Youngs, Bob Strauss, and John Tibbetts also wrote reviews.

VDG is dedicated to the memory of Bill Creter, a lifelong movie buff whose knowledge of the history of movies, sage advice, and warm heart will be sorely missed.

Thanks also to our families for their support and patience. Eileen and Chuck Porter, Hada Martin, Matt and Norma Condo, and Diane Martin have pitched in to help on numerous occasions. Even Francesca Martin has done her bit.

We'd also like to thank Mike and Betty Antonaros, Louise Braverman, Norton Buffalo, Keith Burton, Tayen Chen, Henry Chung, Joe and Nancy Cunningham, Bernard Dauphinais, Jim Dixon, Fred Dodnick, Betsy Flagler, Stan Goman, Caron Harris, Carol Johnson, David Johnson, Alix Krijgsman, Bob Kronenberg, Stacey Mendonca, Clara Ogden, Steve Palmer, Gary Quattrin, Marcia Raphael, Helen Rees, Michael Riesenberg, Colette Russen, Russ Solomon, Jon Souza, Roger Sperberg, Jerry and Karen Sterchi, Milos Strehlik, Steven Taveira, Walter von Hauffe, Tami Walker, and Bob Wilkins.

A

A COEUR JOIE (HEAD OVER HEELS) Sixties fluff about a woman torn between two men. Original title in its American release: *Two Weeks in September*. In French with English subtitles. 89m. **DIR:** Serge Bourguignon. **CAST:** Brigitte Bardot, Laurent Terzieff. **1967**

A LA MODE ★★★ A French teenager (Ken Hegelin) becomes apprenticed to an eccentric Jewish tailor and dreams of success in the world of fashion design. This lightweight, easygoing, coming-of-age comedy profits from good performances, especially by Jean Yonne as the old tailor, and from its witty, satirical jabs at the flashy world of haute couture. In French with English subtitles. Rated R for sexual scenes and mild profanity. 81m. **DIR:** Remy Duchemin. **CAST:** Ken Hegelin, Jean Yonne, Francois Hautesserre, Florence Darel, Maurice Benichou. **1993**

A NOS AMOURS ★★★ This winner of the Cesar (French Oscar) for best film of 1983 examines the life of a working-class girl of 15 (Sandrine Bonnaire) who engages in one sexual relationship after another. In French with English subtitles. Rated R for nudity. **DIR:** Maurice Pialat. **CAST:** Sandrine Bonnaire, Dominique Besnehard, Maurice Pialat. **1983**

A NOUS LA LIBERTE ★★1/2 Louis and Emile are two prisoners who plan an escape. Only Louis gets away and, surprisingly, he becomes a rich, successful businessman. There are some slapstick segments, and many believe that this film was the inspiration for Charlie Chaplin's *Modern Times*. In French with English subtitles. B&W; 87m. **DIR:** René Clair. **CAST:** Raymond Cordy, Henri Marchand. **1931**

AARON LOVES ANGELA ★★★ This Harlem love affair features a black youth (Kevin Hooks) falling for a sweet Puerto Rican girl (Irene Cara). Their relative innocence contrasts with the drug-dealing violence around them. Rated R for violence and profanity. 99m. **DIR:** Gordon Parks Jr. **CAST:** Moses Gunn, Kevin Hooks, Irene Cara, Ernestine Jackson, Robert Hooks. **1975**

ABBOTT AND COSTELLO GO TO MARS ★★1/2 The comedy team was getting a little tired when they made this movie, which has become a cult favorite. It's set in space, but the plot is the same as a TV sitcom. B&W; 78m. **DIR:** Charles Lamont. **CAST:** Bud Abbott, Lou Costello, Mari Blanchard, Jack Kruschen, Horace McMahon, Martha Hyer, Robert Paige, Anita Ekberg. **1953**

ABBOTT AND COSTELLO IN HOLLYWOOD ★★ Lesser Abbott and Costello effort has Bud and Lou trying to make it big as movie stars. Best scenes occur early in the film, with Lou playing a barber. B&W; 83m. **DIR:** S. Sylvan Simon. **CAST:** Bud Abbott, Lou Costello, Frances Rafferty, Robert Stanton. **1945**

ABBOTT AND COSTELLO IN THE FOREIGN LEGION ★★★1/2 Lou Costello inadvertently buys a slave girl in the Sahara just because he waved at the girl flirting with him. Watch for some of the team's funniest routines. B&W; 79m. **DIR:** Charles Lamont. **CAST:** Bud Abbott, Lou Costello, Walter Slezak, Patricia Medina, Douglass Dumbrille. **1950 DVD**

ABBOTT AND COSTELLO MEET CAPTAIN KIDD ★★ One of Abbott and Costello's few color films, this is strictly preschooler fare. The boys get chased around uncharted islands, pirate ships, etc., by the infamous Captain Kidd, as portrayed by Charles Laughton, who makes every effort to retain his dignity. 70m. **DIR:** Charles Lamont. **CAST:** Bud Abbott, Lou Costello, Charles Laughton, Hillary Brooke, Leif Erickson. **1952**

ABBOTT AND COSTELLO MEET DR. JEKYLL AND MR. HYDE ★★★1/2 Fun mixture of comedy and horror has the team up against the smooth Dr. Jekyll and the maniacal Mr. Hyde. One of the boys' better films of the 1950s. Boris Karloff is in top form in the dual role, and don't miss the hilarious scene in which Lou is turned into a mouse! B&W; 77m. **DIR:** Charles Lamont. **CAST:** Bud Abbott, Lou Costello, Boris Karloff. **1953**

ABBOTT AND COSTELLO MEET FRANKENSTEIN ★★★★ For Bud Abbott and Lou Costello, this film meant a resurgence of popularity after a slow fall from favor as the 1940s box-office champs. Yet it never compromises the characters of Dracula (Bela Lugosi), the Wolfman (Lon Chaney Jr.), or the Frankenstein monster (Glenn Strange). B&W; 83m. **DIR:** Charles Barton. **CAST:** Bud Abbott, Lou Costello, Lon Chaney Jr., Bela Lugosi, Glenn Strange. **1948**

ABBOTT AND COSTELLO MEET THE INVISIBLE MAN ★★ Bud and Lou are private eyes hired by a prizefighter to clear him of his manager's murder. The fighter injects himself with a serum that renders him invisible and helps Lou kayo his opponents in the ring before the real murderer is exposed. B&W; 82m. **DIR:** Charles Lamont. **CAST:** Bud Abbott, Lou Costello, Arthur Franz, Nancy Guild, Adele Jergens, Sheldon Leonard, William Frawley. **1951**

ABBOTT AND COSTELLO MEET THE KEYSTONE KOPS ★★★1/2 A boon for nostalgia buffs, this film features pie-in-the-face director Mack Sennett and three of the surviving Keystone Kops in a climactic chase scene. B&W; 78m. **DIR:** Charles Lamont. **CAST:** Bud Abbott, Lou Costello, Maxie Rosenbloom, Lynn Bari, Mack Sennett, Harold Goodwin, Heinie Conklin, Hank Mann, Carol Costello. **1955**

ABBOTT AND COSTELLO MEET THE KILLER, BORIS KARLOFF ★★★ Second in the duo's *Abbott and Costello Meet*... series, brought on by the tremendous popularity of their *Frankenstein* send-up the year before. In this enjoyable outing, Bud and Lou match wits with Boris Karloff, in classic form as a sinister swami doing away with his enemies at a posh hotel. B&W; 84m. **DIR:** Charles Barton. **CAST:** Bud Abbott, Lou Costello, Boris Karloff, Lenore Aubert, Gar Moore, James Flavin. **1949**

ABBOTT AND COSTELLO MEET THE MUMMY ★★ Final (and overdue) entry in the seven-year cycle of "horror comedies" pitting Abbott and Costello against Universal Pictures' monster stable. Not without amusing moments, but mostly, the same tired vaudeville routines are dragged out as the boys flee two mummies—one real, one fake—in Egypt. B&W; 79m. **DIR:** Charles Lamont. **CAST:** Bud Abbott, Lou Costello, Marie Windsor, Richard Deacon. **1955 DVD**

ABBOTT AND COSTELLO SHOW, THE (TV SERIES) ★★★ Set in Hollywood, this comedy series depicts Bud Abbott's and Lou Costello's efforts to improve their financial situation. Though the comics appear somewhat weary and the humor is often forced, enough of the gags work to make the episodes worth a glance. Many of Abbott and Costello's classic routines are incorporated into the shows, boosting the slim plots. 53m. **DIR:** Various. **CAST:** Bud Abbott, Lou Costello, Sidney Fields, Hillary Brooke, Joe Besser. **1952–1954 DVD**

ABDUCTED ★★1/2 This is not as sleazy as the video box art would have you believe. A backwoods jogger (Roberta Weiss) is abducted by a crazed mountain man and taken back to his cabin. Nothing new, but some good chase scenes. Not rated, but has violence, profanity, and adult subject matter. 87m. **DIR:** Boon Collins. **CAST:** Roberta Weiss, Lawrence King Phillip, Dan Haggerty. **1985**

ABDUCTED II ★★1/2 Less a sequel than a remake, this time with three young lovelies terrorized by mountain man Lawrence King. Rated R for violence and nudity. 91m. **DIR:** Boon Collins. **CAST:** Jan-Michael Vincent, Dan Haggerty, Raquel Bianca, Lawrence King. **1994**

ABDUCTION ★★ This film comes across as a cheap exploitation of the Patty Hearst kidnapping. It includes theories that may or may not be true. As in the real incident, Patty is kidnapped from the house she shares with her boyfriend. Rated R for profanity, violence, nudity, and sex. 100m. **DIR:** Joseph Zito. **CAST:** Gregory Rozakis, Leif Erickson, Dorothy Malone, Lawrence Tierney. **1975 DVD**

ABE LINCOLN IN ILLINOIS ★★★★ Based on Sherwood Anderson's Broadway play, this is a reverent look at the early career and loves of the sixteenth president. As contrasted to John Ford's *Young Mr. Lincoln*, this is a more somber, historically accurate, and better-acted version. B&W; 110m. **DIR:** John Cromwell. **CAST:** Raymond Massey, Ruth Gordon, Gene Lockhart, Mary Howard. **1934**

ABEL GANCE'S BEETHOVEN ★★★★ Originally titled *Un Grand Amour de Beethoven*, this contains some of Abel Gance's finest work with sound, especially in the scene at the Heiligenstadt Mill when Beethoven first begins to lose his hearing. In French with English subtitles. B&W; 116m. **DIR:** Abel Gance. **CAST:** Harry Baur, Annie Ducaux. **1937**

ABERRATION 🦃 A bunch of rubber lizards attacks a young couple in their cabin in the hills. Dullsville. Rated R for language and gore. 93m. **DIR:** Tim Boxell. **CAST:** Pamela Gidley, Simon Bossell, Valery Nikolaev. **1997**

ABIGAIL'S PARTY ★★★★★ A superb slice of acerbic British social commentary. Beverly is a gin-sodden shrew with middle-class aspirations, who holds a small get-together for the neighbors. This movie is like an English version of *Who's Afraid of Virginia Woolf*, a group of adults congregate, imbibe vast amounts of alcohol, and squirm-inducing disaster ensues. 105m. **DIR:** Mike Leigh. **CAST:** Alison Steadman. **1977**

ABILENE TOWN ★★★ Cattlemen and homesteaders are at loggerheads in the 1870s in this fast-paced shoot-'em-up. Randolph Scott is the trusty tall man with the star. Edgar Buchanan is sly, as always. B&W; 89m. **DIR:** Edwin L. Marin. **CAST:** Randolph Scott, Ann Dvorak, Rhonda Fleming, Lloyd Bridges, Edgar Buchanan. **1946**

ABOMINABLE DR. PHIBES, THE ★★★1/2 Stylish horror film features Vincent Price in one of his best latter-day roles as a man disfigured in a car wreck taking revenge. Rated PG-13. 93m. **DIR:** Robert Fuest. **CAST:** Vincent Price, Joseph Cotten, Hugh Griffith, Terry-Thomas. **1971**

ABOMINABLE SNOWMAN OF THE HIMALAYAS, THE ★★★ The writer and director of the British *Quatermass* series worked on what is probably the only intelligent yeti movie. Peter Cushing and Forrest Tucker are a botanist and an exploitative promoter (American, of course) searching for the legendary giant creatures in Nepal. B&W; 85m. **DIR:** Val Guest. **CAST:** Peter Cushing, Forrest Tucker, Maureen Connell. **1957**

•ABOUT ADAM ★★★★ Enchanting romantic Irish comedy stars a lovely Kate Hudson as Lucy Owens, a Dublin care singer who has just met Adam, the man of her dreams, well played by Stuart Townsend. When Lucy introduces Adam to her family, including sisters Laura and Alice, his charm wins them over, perhaps too well. It's not long before Adam is juggling the romantic overtures of all three sisters, all the while trying to decide whether or not to marry Lucy. Sharp production values and a winning cast turns this regional comedy into a universal valentine. Rated R for adult situations and language. 97m. **DIR:** Gerard Stembridge. **CAST:** Stuart Townsend, Kate Hudson, Frances O'Connor, Charlotte Bradley. **2000 DVD**

ABOUT LAST NIGHT . . . ★★★★ A slick adaptation of David Mamet's play, *Sexual Perversity in Chicago*. Demi Moore and Rob Lowe meet for a one-night stand and then realize they *like* each other. Jim Belushi and Elizabeth Perkins turn in solid performances, but the film belongs to Moore. Rated R for nudity and explicit adult situations. 113m. **DIR:** Edward Zwick. **CAST:** Rob Lowe, Demi Moore, James Belushi, Elizabeth Perkins, George DiCenzo. **1986 DVD**

ABOVE AND BEYOND ★★★1/2 Good account of the secret training led by Paul Tibbets (Robert Taylor) to prepare for the first atomic-bomb attack on Hiroshima. Bogs down some when dealing with his home life, but overall a fine biographical drama. Jim Backus has a cameo as General Curtis E. LeMay. B&W; 122m. **DIR:** Melvin Frank. **CAST:** Robert Taylor, Eleanor Parker, James Whitmore, Larry Keating, Jeff Richards, Jim Backus. **1952**

ABOVE SUSPICION (1943) ★★★★ Newlyweds Joan Crawford and Fred MacMurray, while honeymooning on the Continent at the outbreak of World War II, innocently become involved in espionage. Conrad Veidt, who died before the movie was released, steals every scene in which he appears. Not rated, but good family entertainment. B&W; 90m. **DIR:** Richard Thorpe. **CAST:** Joan Crawford, Fred MacMurray, Conrad Veidt, Basil Rathbone, Reginald Owen. **1943**

ABOVE SUSPICION (1994) ★★★1/2 In a positively spooky precursor to the accident that would end his career, Christopher Reeve stars as a dedicated cop who becomes crippled during a bust gone sour. Confined to a wheelchair and clinically depressed, he begins to question the wisdom of staying alive. Ah, but things are not as they seem in this deliciously twisty script from Jerry Lazarus, W. H. Macy, and Steven Schachter. You'll be guessing to the last frame—this one's very clever. Rated R for nudity, violence, profanity, and simulated sex. 92m. **DIR:** Steven Schachter. **CAST:** Christopher Reeve, Joe Mantegna, Kim Cattrall, Edward Kerr, Geoffrey Rivas, Finola Hughes, William H. Macy. **1994**

ABOVE THE LAW ★★★1/2 Director Andrew Davis, who gave credibility to Chuck Norris in *Code of Silence*, teams up with karate expert Steven Seagal (who cowrote the story and coproduced with Davis) for this tough, action-filled cop thriller. Seagal is a Chicago cop and Vietnam veteran who takes on the CIA. The result is a strong entry for action buffs. Rated R for lots of violence, profanity, and drug use. 97m. **DIR:** Andrew Davis. **CAST:** Steven Seagal, Pam Grier, Sharon Stone, Daniel Faraldo, Henry Silva. **1988 DVD**

ABOVE THE RIM ★★1/2 Two brothers clash as they try to influence a morally struggling young man in this Manhattan melodrama about inner-city crime, broken dreams, and one high-school athlete's attempt to climb out of the dangerous Harlem street scene. The laws and rhythms of the street are brought to life by a magnetic cast, but this bold bite out of the dark side of the Big Apple has a familiar taste to it. Rated R for violence and language. 96m. **DIR:** Jeff Pollack. **CAST:** Duane Martin, Leon, Tupac Shakur, Bernie Mac, Marlon Wayans. **1994**

ABRAHAM ★★★1/2 Abraham and Sarah prove their faith by obeying a divine command to undertake a difficult journey to the Promised Land and later to sacrifice son Isaac. Handsome production values and a fine cast. Not rated. 150m. **DIR:** Joseph Sargent. **CAST:** Richard Harris, Barbara Hershey, Maximilian Schell, Vittorio Gassman. **1994**

ABRAHAM LINCOLN ★★★★ A milestone in many ways, this episodic film is legendary director Griffith's first "talkie," Hollywood's first sound biography of an American, the first attempt to cover Lincoln's life from cradle to grave, and the first about the martyred president to include the Civil War. Walter Huston's peerless performance in the title role dominates throughout. B&W; 91m. **DIR:** D. W. Griffith. **CAST:** Walter Huston, Una Merkel, Kay Hammond, Ian Keith, Hobart Bosworth, Jason Robards Sr., Henry B. Walthall. **1930**

ABRAXAS GUARDIAN OF THE UNIVERSE ★★ A renegade alien peace officer flees to Earth and impregnates a young woman, only to be caught and sent to prison. Five years later he escapes and returns to Earth to engage in countless, violent chase scenes. Not rated; contains violence. 87m. **DIR:** Damien Lee. **CAST:** Jesse Ventura, Marjorie Bransfield, Sven-Ole Thorsen. **1992 DVD**

ABSENCE OF MALICE ★★★★ Sally Field is a Miami reporter who writes a story implicating an innocent man (Paul Newman) in the mysterious disappearance—and possible murder—of a union leader in this taut, thoughtful drama about the ethics of journalism. It's sort of *All the President's Men* turned inside out. Rated PG because of minor violence. 116m. **DIR:** Sydney Pollack. **CAST:** Paul Newman, Sally Field, Bob Balaban, Melinda Dillon, Wilford Brimley. **1982 DVD**

ABSENT-MINDED PROFESSOR, THE ★★★★ One of Disney's best live-action comedies, this stars Fred MacMurray in the title role of a scientist who discovers "flubber" (flying rubber). Only trouble is, no one will believe him—except Keenan Wynn, who tries to steal his invention. B&W; 104m. **DIR:** Robert Stevenson. **CAST:** Fred MacMurray, Nancy Olson, Tommy Kirk, Ed Wynn, Keenan Wynn. **1961**

ABSOLUTE BEGINNERS ★★★★ Based on the cult novel by Colin MacInnes, who chronicled the musical and social scene in London during the pivotal summer of 1958. Occasionally the accents are too thick and the references too obscure for Americans, but the overall effect is an unequivocal high. Rated PG-13 for stylized, but rather intense, violence and some profanity. 107m. **DIR:** Julien Temple. **CAST:** Eddie O'Connell, Patsy Kensit, David Bowie, James Fox, Ray Davies, Anita Morris, Sade Adu, Mandy Rice-Davies. **1986**

ABSOLUTE POWER ★★★★ A gripping thriller in the tradition of *Tightrope*, this is Clint Eastwood at his most cynical. He is a professional thief in the middle of plying his trade when a middle-aged man brings a young woman into the bedroom. Hidden in a vault behind a one-way mirror, Eastwood witnesses the woman's rape and murder. He also gets a clear look at the killer: the president of the United States (Gene Hackman). Now the question is what to do about what he's seen, and how to stay alive long enough to do it. Rated R for violence, rape, profanity, and simulated sex. 121m. **DIR:** Clint Eastwood. **CAST:** Clint Eastwood, Gene Hackman, Ed Harris, Laura Linney, Judy Davis, Scott Glenn, E. G. Marshall. **1997 DVD**

ABSOLUTELY FABULOUS ★★★★★ This is not your parents' sitcom. Two middle-aged English tarts smoke, swallow, and bed everything in their paranoid paths, and are all the more fun for being unedited and abashedly vulgar. Jennifer Saunders is the queen of excess and Joanna Lumley her promiscuous best friend in this ground-breaking, sidesplitting satire. Available on video are all eighteen 30-minute episodes, a 30-minute special, and a 90-minute made-for-television movie. Not rated; contains profanity and adult themes. 660m. **DIR:** Bob Spiers. **CAST:** Jennifer Saunders, Joanna Lumley, Julia Sawalha, Jane Horrocks, June Whitfield. **1993–1996**

ABSOLUTION ★★1/2 Slow-moving but interesting tale of a priest's emotional and physical battle with one of his students at an English school for boys. As the priest, Richard Burton gives his usual compelling performance. Nice plot twist at the end. Not rated; contains violence. 91m. **DIR:** Anthony Page. **CAST:** Richard Burton, Dominic Guard, Andrew Keir, Billy Connolly. **1977**

ABYSS, THE ★★★★ After suffering the deep-sea disappointments in *Leviathan* and *Deepstar Six*, viewers are likely to be a little cautious of getting back into the water with this thriller–adventure–fantasy film. They shouldn't be. The third time's the charm with the underwater plot, thanks to the inventiveness of director James Cameron (*The Terminator, Aliens*). Rated PG-13. 145m. **DIR:** James Cameron. **CAST:** Ed Harris, Mary Elizabeth Mastrantonio, Michael Biehn. **1989 DVD**

ACCATTONE ★★1/2 Director Pier Paolo Pasolini's first feature film adapted from his own novel follows the desperate existence of a pimp living in the slums of southern Italy. Lacks emotional depth and raw power. In Italian with (virtually unreadable) English subtitles. B&W; 116m. **DIR:** Pier Paolo Pasolini. **CAST:** Franco Citti. **1961**

•ACCEPTABLE RISK ★★★ Decent adaptation of Robin Cook's science-fiction thriller. Chad Lowe stars as the overly ambitious researcher determined to find a shortcut to medical fame. Living in a home belonging to a woman accused of witchcraft, he discovers a powerful mold that brings out the beastly side of the researchers during the trials. Lowe flexes his dramatic muscle to pull off his horrific transformation in this TBS Superstation original. Not rated; contains violence, gore, and profanity. 94m. **DIR:** William A. Graham. **CAST:** Chad Lowe, Kelly Rutherford, Sean Patrick Flanery. **2001 DVD**

ACCEPTABLE RISKS ★★★ Heavy-handed message film about the risks a chemical plant poses to the inhabitants of a new housing development. Unbelievable amount of carelessness by plant workers and blind greed by owners reduce this TV movie to near sci-fi rather than gritty docudrama. 97m. **DIR:** Rick Wallace. **CAST:** Brian Dennehy, Kenneth McMillan, Christine Ebersole, Cicely Tyson. **1986**

ACCESS CODE 🦃 Dreadful action film about an Orwellian Big Brother surveillance system that takes over the country's national security complex. Not rated, has profanity. 90m. **DIR:** Mark Sobel. **CAST:** Martin Landau, Michael Ansara, Macdonald Carey. **1984**

ACCIDENT ★★★★ Harold Pinter's complicated play retains its subtleties in this sometimes baffling British film. Dirk Bogarde is excellent as a married professor pursuing an attractive student. There are enough twists and turns in the characters' actual desires to maintain your complete attention. 105m. **DIR:** Joseph Losey. **CAST:** Dirk Bogarde, Stanley Baker, Jacqueline Sassard, Michael York. **1967**

ACCIDENTAL MEETING ★★ In this made-for-cable movie, two women joke about having each other murder someone they don't like. However, one of the women takes it seriously. For a better version of this plot, rent Hitchcock's *Strangers on a Train*. Not rated; contains violence and sexual situations. 95m. **DIR:** Michael Zinberg. **CAST:** Linda Gray, Linda Purl, Leigh McCloskey, Ernie Lively, David Hayward, Kent McCord. **1993**

ACCIDENTAL TOURIST, THE ★★★★ William Hurt and Kathleen Turner team again for this compelling adaptation of Anne Tyler's novel. Hurt's the writer of travel guides who distances himself from everybody—including wife Turner—after the death of their young son; Geena Davis is the earthy, colorful free spirit who tries to break through his wall of self-imposed isolation. Filled with strong emotional highs and lows. Rated PG. 120m. **DIR:** Lawrence Kasdan. **CAST:** William Hurt, Kathleen Turner, Geena Davis, Bill Pullman, Amy Wright, David Ogden Stiers, Ed Begley Jr. **1988**

ACCOMPANIST, THE ★★1/2 In Nazi-occupied Paris, a young pianist works for, and later flees to London with, a famous concert singer and her manager/husband. Lovely pastel photography and wonderful music but it's a bit too measured and deliberate. In French with English subtitles. Rated PG. 111m. **DIR:** Claude Miller. **CAST:** Richard Bohringer, Elena Safonova, Romane Bohringer, Samuel Labarthe, Julien Rassam. **1993**

ACCUSED, THE ★★★★ Superb, emotionally intense retelling of the precedent-setting New Bedford, Massachusetts, gang-rape case, with Jodie Foster as an innocent but definitely not saintly victim, and Kelly McGillis as a tough DA. An excellent and wrenching film. Rated R for adult themes, language, nudity, and sexual violence. 105m. **DIR:** Jonathan Kaplan. **CAST:** Jodie Foster, Kelly McGillis, Bernie Coulson, Steve Antin, Leo Rossi, Woody Brown. **1988 DVD**

ACE DRUMMOND ★★1/2 An arch villain known as The Dragon has thwarted every effort by an international group attempting to establish a round-the-world airline service. Aviation whiz Ace Drummond jumps from the Sunday funnies to the silver screen. Laughable in many respects, this is still a pretty good serial and the only filming of this character's adventures. B&W; 250m. **DIR:** Ford Beebe, Cliff Smith. **CAST:** John King, Jean Rogers, Noah Beery Jr., Lon Chaney Jr. **1936**

ACE HIGH ★★ In this violent spaghetti Western written and directed by Giuseppe Colizzi, a condemned outlaw is offered a chance to save himself from the hangman's noose. Having just completed the entertaining *The Good, The Bad, and The Ugly*, Eli Wallach is wasted. There is some humor, but the dialogue and dubbing are simply terrible. 123m. **DIR:** Giuseppe Colizzi. **CAST:** Eli Wallach, Brock Peters, Terence Hill, Kevin McCarthy, Bud Spencer. **1969**

ACE OF ACES ★★★1/2 Aviation drama set in World War I. Richard Dix, as the hero, raises this tough film above literally dozens of flying ace movies made in the early 1930s. B&W; 70m. **DIR:** J. Walter Ruben. **CAST:** Richard Dix, Elizabeth Allan, Ralph Bellamy. **1933**

ACE OF HEARTS ★★1/2 Unlikely love triangle between a girl and two ardent anarchists. Lon Chaney Sr. plays the weepy suitor who loses the girl but redeems himself when he saves the loving couple. Chaney plays it low-key throughout the film, but there's a great segment featuring his character and an attentive dog and the finale is one of his finest moments. B&W; 62m. **DIR:** Wallace Worsley. **CAST:** Lon Chaney Sr., Leatrice Joy, John Bowers, Raymond Hatton. **1921**

ACE VENTURA: PET DETECTIVE ★★1/2 Gangly Jim Carrey of TV's *In Living Color* proves that comedy doesn't have to be pretty to be a scream. Carrey hams it up as a goofy Florida gumshoe who cracks missing-animal cases. This giddy, crude comedy doesn't really have a personality of its own—it's an extension of Carrey's own hyper-nuttiness. Ace must locate the Miami Dolphins' mascot and star quarterback just before the Super Bowl. Rated PG-13 for violence, profanity, and suggested sex. 85m. **DIR:** Tom Shadyac. **CAST:** Jim Carrey, Sean Young, Courteney Cox, Tone Loc, Dan Marino. **1994 DVD**

ACE VENTURA: WHEN NATURE CALLS ★★ Diminishing returns hit this series pretty quickly, with Jim Carrey's patented gross-out humor employed to shore up a thin script. This time out our hero must retrieve a sacred animal abducted from an African tribe, before war is declared. Although only small children are likely to enjoy the infantile slapstick, they're hardly the right audience for some of Carrey's tasteless sexual gags. Rated PG-13 for profanity, violence, and blue sexual material. 91m. **DIR:** Steve Oedekerk. **CAST:** Jim Carrey, Ian McNeice, Simon Callow, Maynard Eziashi, Bob Gunton. **1995 DVD**

ACES AND EIGHTS ★★1/2 Although lacking in action, this Tim McCoy Western nevertheless has its moments. McCoy comes to the aid of a young Mexican unfairly accused of murder. B&W; 62m. **DIR:** Sam Newfield. **CAST:** Tim McCoy, Luana Walters. **1936**

ACES: IRON EAGLE III ★★★1/2 Surprising—effective and entertaining—reworking of *The Magnificent Seven/Seven Samurai* formula bears no resemblance to the other two films in the *Iron Eagle* series. It features Lou Gossett Jr. as the character of Chappy. This time, he must lead a group of World War II veterans on a mission to save a village from drug dealers. Rated R for violence and profanity. 98m. **DIR:** John Glen. **CAST:** Louis Gossett Jr., Rachel McLish, Paul Freeman, Horst Buchholz, Christopher Cazenove, Sonny Chiba, Fred Dalton Thompson, Mitchell Ryan. **1992**

ACROSS 110TH STREET ★★★1/2 This one is a real sleeper! An action-packed, extremely violent film concerning gang warfare between the Mafia and their black counterparts. Entire cast is very good, as are the action scenes. Rated R for violence and language. 102m. **DIR:** Barry Shear. **CAST:** Anthony Quinn, Yaphet Kotto, Anthony Franciosa, Richard Ward. **1972 DVD**

ACROSS THE GREAT DIVIDE ★★ Family entertainment at its most unchallenging. Two kids (Heather Rattray and Mark Hall) meet up with a shifty gambler (Robert Logan), and the three eventually unite for safety on their monotonous trek through valleys, mountains, and rivers. Rated G. 89m. **DIR:** Stewart Raffill. **CAST:** Robert Logan, George "Buck" Flower, Heather Rattray, Mark Edward Hall. **1976**

ACROSS THE MOON ★★★ Personable romantic comedy about two very different women and the circumstances that bring them together: their hoodlum boyfriends botch a robbery and are sent to prison. Elizabeth Peña and Christina Applegate are winning as the sisters-in-arms. Rated R for strong language and adult situations. 88m. **DIR:** Lisa Gottlieb. **CAST:** Christina Applegate, Elizabeth Peña, James Remar, Michael McKean, Tony Fields, Peter Berg, Michael Aniel Mundra. **1993 DVD**

ACROSS THE PACIFIC ★★★★ Prior to going off to war himself, director John Huston reassembled three of the stars from *The Maltese Falcon* for this high-spirited World War II propaganda piece. Humphrey Bogart woos Mary Astor while battling spy Sydney Greenstreet. Hugely enjoyable action film. B&W; 97m. **DIR:** John Huston. **CAST:** Humphrey Bogart, Mary Astor, Sydney Greenstreet, Victor Sen Yung, Keye Luke, Richard Loo. **1942**

ACROSS THE RIO GRANDE ★★★1/2 Jimmy Wakely straightens out a young lawyer involved with border silver-ore smugglers and captures the killer of the lawyer's father. Noteworthy as the first film appearance of Polly Bergen. B&W; 55m. **DIR:** Oliver Drake. **CAST:** Jimmy Wakely, Dub Taylor, Polly Bergen. **1949**

ACROSS THE TRACKS ★★★★ Two brothers compete for a scholarship in a county track championship. The soundtrack is excellent, the acting is convincing, and the screenplay deals with believable, real-life situations. Rated PG. 101m. **DIR:** Sandy Tung. **CAST:** Rick Schroder, Brad Pitt, Carrie Snodgress. **1990**

ACROSS THE WIDE MISSOURI ★★1/2 Scenery is the big and only plus in this plotless pedestrian tale of fortune seekers led by a Kentucky trapper seeking wealth in Indian-held virgin beaver territory. 78m. **DIR:** William Wellman. **CAST:** Clark Gable, Ricardo Montalban, Adolphe Menjou, John Hodiak, J. Carrol Naish, Alan Napier, Jack Holt. **1951**

ACT, THE ★★★ A comedy-drama with a convoluted plot of political chicanery, double cross, and robbery. The overall quality is erratic and yet this ends up being a good effort from a veteran cast. Trivia fans may note John Sebastian's involvement in the musical score. Rated R for sexual situations and language. 90m. **DIR:** Sig Shore. **CAST:** Robert Ginty, Sarah Langenfeld, Jill St. John, Eddie Albert, Pat Hingle. **1982**

ACT OF AGGRESSION ★★1/2 After his wife and daughter are raped and murdered, Jean-Louis Trintignant takes the law into his own hands in this unpleasant Gallic contribution to the *Death Wish* genre. In French with English subtitles. Not rated; contains brief nudity and violence. 94m. **DIR:** Gilbert Pires. **CAST:** Jean-Louis Trintignant, Catherine Deneuve, Claude Brasseur. **1975**

ACT OF PASSION ★★ In this made-for-television movie, Marlo Thomas plays a single woman who picks up a stranger (Kris Kristofferson) at a party. She is subsequently subjected to harassment by the police and the press when the man turns out to be a suspected terrorist. Harsh and blatantly exaggerated. 95m. **DIR:** Simon Langton. **CAST:** Marlo Thomas, Kris Kristofferson, Jon De Vries, David Rasche, Linda Thorson, Edward Winter, George Dzundza. **1984**

ACT OF PIRACY ★★1/2 When modern-day pirate Ray Sharkey and his gang rip off Gary Busey's state-of-the-art yacht, accidentally kidnapping his children at the same time, our hero embarks on a no-holds-barred mission to get his property back. Ho-hum action movie. Not rated, the film has profanity, violence, nudity, and simulated sex. 101m. **DIR:** John "Bud" Cardos. **CAST:** Gary Busey, Belinda Bauer, Ray Sharkey, Nancy Mulford, Ken Gampu. **1990**

ACT OF VENGEANCE ★★★★ In this first-rate drama, a suprisingly effective Charles Bronson plays Jock Yablonski, an honest man who wants to turn his coal-miners union around. When he runs for union president against the thoroughly corrupt incumbent (played brilliantly by Wilford Brimley), the threatened leader resorts to strong-arm tactics. Not rated; contains violence and profanity. 97m. **DIR:** John Mackenzie. **CAST:** Charles Bronson, Ellen Burstyn, Wilford Brimley, Hoyt Axton, Ellen Barkin. **1985**

ACTING ON IMPULSE ★★ A rather muddled thriller concerning needlessly warped horror-film star Linda Fiorentino, a conservative young salesman (C. Thomas Howell), and the obligatory assassin. The leads give better than the script deserves, and director Sam Irvin elicits stunningly awful performances from a host of cameo players. Rated R for profanity, violence, drug use, and kinky sexuality. 94m. **DIR:** Sam Irvin. **CAST:** C. Thomas Howell, Linda Fiorentino, Nancy Allen, Paul Bartel, Isaac Hayes, Adam Ant. **1993**

ACTION IN ARABIA ★★1/2 George Sanders fights against time and Nazi agents as he attempts to inform the Allied authorities about German plans for a pact with the Arabs in this wartime romance-adventure. The love of a woman helps to turn the tide for the western powers in this sandy adventure. B&W; 75m. **DIR:** Leonide Moguy. **CAST:** George Sanders, Virginia Bruce, Gene Lockhart, Robert Armstrong, Michael Ansara. **1944**

ACTION IN THE NORTH ATLANTIC ★★★1/2 Somewhat stodgy, flag-waving morale-booster features a fine cast in World War II-era tribute to the merchant marine. Officers Humphrey Bogart and Raymond Massey must rally their courage and crew when their convoy is attacked by a German U-boat. B&W; 127m. **DIR:** Lloyd Bacon. **CAST:** Humphrey Bogart, Raymond Massey, Alan Hale Sr., Julie Bishop, Ruth Gordon, Sam Levene, Dane Clark. **1943**

ACTION JACKSON ★★ A maverick cop (Carl Weathers) is on the trail of a corrupt auto tycoon (Craig T. Nelson). Unfortunately, *Action Jackson* is a gabfest punctuated by not-so-hot sex scenes. There are a couple of good stunt scenes, though. Rated R for violence, drug use, simulated sex, nudity, and profanity. 95m. **DIR:** Craig R. Baxley. **CAST:** Carl Weathers, Craig T. Nelson, Vanity, Sharon Stone, Thomas F. Wilson, Bill Duke. **1988 DVD**

•ACTIVE STEALTH 🦃 Captain Murphy (Daniel Baldwin) returns to South America long after a previous assault/rescue mission went awry only to find that a friend that he had left for dead is now a ruthless despot with his own armed militia. Despite its packaging, this poorly made movie contains few flying scenes. Rated R for violence. 99m. **DIR:** Fred Olen Ray. **CAST:** Daniel Baldwin, Paul Michael Robinson, Joe Lala. **1999 DVD**

ACTORS AND SIN ★★1/2 Two short films: *Actor's Blood* is a drama starring Edward G. Robinson as the devoted father of a successful Broadway actress (Marsha Hunt). *Woman's Sin* is a comedy starring Eddie Albert as an irrepressible Hollywood agent who finds a winning screenplay but loses its author. B&W; 86m. **DIR:** Ben Hecht, Lee Garmes. **CAST:** Edward G. Robinson, Eddie Albert, Marsha Hunt, Alan Reed, Dan O'Herlihy. **1952**

ACTOR'S REVENGE, AN ★★★1/2 Stylized drama set in the 1800s about a female impersonator in a Kabuki theater who seeks revenge on the killers of his parents. There's a little bit of everything in this somewhat confusing but intriguing import. In Japanese with English subtitles. 113m. **DIR:** Kon Ichikawa. **CAST:** Kazuo Hasegawa. **1963**

ACTS OF BETRAYAL 🦃 Movies this bad are usually relegated to cable at 3 A.M. Unfortunately this tale of a woman on the run from the mob is available to rent twenty-four hours a day. Not rated; contains violence. 112m. **DIR:** Joakim Ersgard. **CAST:** Maria Conchita Alonso, Matt McColm, Muse Watson, David Groh, Joe Estevez. **1997**

A.D. POLICE FILES, VOLS. 1–3 ★★★ Animated spinoff from the *Bubblegum Crisis* series that chronicles the cases of Mega Tokyo's special A.D. Police, who handle ultraviolent crimes. Dark and graphic, this series is not for younger audiences, but animation buffs will enjoy the fine artwork, music, and gritty stories. In Japanese with English subtitles. Not rated; contains violence and nudity. 40m. **DIR:** Ikegami Takamasa. **1993**

ADAM ★★★★ Daniel J. Travanti and JoBeth Williams deliver fine performances in this chillingly real account of John and Reve Walsh's search for their missing 6-year-old son, Adam. A quite believable picture, detailing the months of uncertainty and anguish that surrounded the child's disappearance from a department store. This ordeal resulted in the formation of the Missing Children's Bureau. Made for television. 97m. **DIR:** Michael Tuchner. **CAST:** Daniel J. Travanti, JoBeth Williams, Richard Masur. **1983**

ADAM AND EVALYN ★★★ An uneven mixture of comedy and drama that parallels the history of man's passion for woman. A middle-aged gambler adopts a homeless young woman and lavishes her with gifts and fatherly attention. His attitude toward her changes when his own brother starts courting her. The storyline is dated, but the performances are refreshingly personable. B&W; 80m. **DIR:** Harold French. **CAST:** Jean Simmons, Stewart Granger, Wilfrid Hyde-White, Helen Cherry, Edwin Styles. **1949**

ADAM AT 6 A.M. ★★★ In his second film, Michael Douglas—in a coming-of-age role—leaves his California professorship to find his roots in rural Missouri. There he falls in love with a small-town girl (Lee Purcell) while working as a road laborer. Ending is a gem! Rated PG for violence. 100m. **DIR:** Robert Scheerer. **CAST:** Michael Douglas, Lee Purcell, Joe Don Baker, Grayson Hall. **1970**

ADAM HAD FOUR SONS ★★★★ This classic has it all: good acting, romance, seduction, betrayal, tears, and laughter. Ingrid Bergman plays the good governess, and Susan Hayward plays the seductive hussy who tries to turn brother against brother. Warner Baxter offers a fine performance as Adam, the father. B&W; 81m. **DIR:** Gregory Ratoff. **CAST:** Ingrid Bergman, Warner Baxter, Susan Hayward. **1941**

ADAM'S RIB (1949) ★★★★1/2 The screen team of Spencer Tracy and Katharine Hepburn was always watchable, but never more so than in this comedy. As husband-and-wife lawyers on opposing sides of the same case, they remind us of what movie magic is really all about. The supporting performances by Judy Holliday, Tom Ewell, David Wayne, and Jean Hagen greatly add to the fun. B&W; 101m. **DIR:** George Cukor. **CAST:** Spencer Tracy, Katharine Hepburn, Judy Holliday, Tom Ewell, David Wayne. **1949 DVD**

ADAM'S RIB (1993) ★★★1/2 Four single women representing three generations try to live together in a small flat in a large Russian city. Gentle humor can be found in the forced intimacy and bittersweet relationships of these women as they try to maintain their independence while stepping on top of one another. In Russian with English subtitles. Not rated; contains adult themes and brief nudity. 77m. **DIR:** Vyacheslav Krishtofovich. **CAST:** Inna Churikova, Svetlana Ryabova, Maria Golubkina, Elena Bogdanova. **1993**

ADDAMS FAMILY, THE ★★★1/2 It's murder and mayhem at the Addams mansion when two sleazy promoters try to force a fake Uncle Fester (Christopher Lloyd) on the unassuming Morticia (Anjelica Huston) and Gomez (Raul Julia). Perfectly cast and filled with touches of macabre humor. This movie actually improves upon the cult television series. Rated PG-13 for brief profanity and goofy violence. 101m. **DIR:** Barry Sonnenfeld. **CAST:** Anjelica Huston, Raul Julia, Christopher Lloyd, Christina Ricci, Jimmy Workman, Judith Malina, Elizabeth Wilson, Dan Hedaya. **1991 DVD**

ADDAMS FAMILY, THE (TV SERIES) ★★★ Mid-Sixties television viewers never knew quite what to make of the deliciously bent humor in *The Addams Family*, which stretched Charles Addams' *New Yorker* cartoons into offbeat T.V. entertainment. John Astin played Gomez with maniacal intensity, while his lady-love, Morticia, was brought to somber life by Carolyn Jones. Fans of the 1991 big-screen rendition are encouraged to investigate these delightful origins. Each tape contains two half-hour episodes. 52m. **DIR:** Arthur Hiller, Jerry Hopper, Sidney Lanfield. **CAST:** Carolyn Jones, John Astin, Jackie Coogan, Ted Cassidy. **1964–1966**

ADDAMS FAMILY REUNION ★★★1/2 This third entry in the *Addams Family* franchise is a different but nonetheless engaging beast. Tim Curry and Daryl Hannah are Gomez and Morticia, who pack up the family for a little vacation when they accidentally receive an invitation for another Addams family reunion. Familiar faces, witty humor, and outrageous sight gags work splendidly on this direct-to-video. Rated PG. 90m. **DIR:** David Payne. **CAST:** Tim Curry, Daryl Hannah, Estelle Harris, Ed Begley Jr., Kevin McCarthy, Alice Ghostley. **1998**

ADDAMS FAMILY VALUES ★★★★ Fine performances mark this second big-screen romp of the Addams family. The zany plot involves the birth of a new family member and the seduction of Uncle Fester by a femme fatale. Forget sense and enjoy the nonsense. Rated PG-13 for ghoulish goings-on. 88m. **DIR:** Barry Sonnenfeld. **CAST:** Anjelica Huston, Raul Julia, Christopher Lloyd, Joan Cusack, Carol Kane, Christina Ricci, Jimmy Workman, Carel Struycken, David Krumholtz, Christopher Hart, Dana Ivey, Peter MacNicol, Sam McMurray, Nathan Lane, Peter Graves. **1993 DVD**

ADDICTED TO LOVE ★★★1/2 Robert Gordon's script is a wonderfully wacky ode to love gone sour. Nice guy Matthew Broderick unwisely allows childhood sweetheart Kelly Preston to accept a "temporary" job in New York; when she doesn't return, he follows and finds her in the arms—and bed—of an amorous Frenchman. Our hero sets up housekeeping across the street and watches, hoping to be present when his ex comes to her senses . . . and then things get truly bent when the Frenchman's ex-fiancée (Meg Ryan) shows up. Although things get a bit nasty toward the end, true love emerges in this mostly delightful, *truly* screwball comedy. Rated R for profanity, nudity, and strong sexual content. 100m. **DIR:** Griffin Dunne. **CAST:** Meg Ryan, Matthew Broderick, Kelly Preston, Tcheky Karyo, Maureen Stapleton. **1997 DVD**

ADDICTION, THE ★★★ Director Abel Ferrara once again walks on the dark side with this fatalistic, beautifully photographed tale of the supernatural. Lili Taylor is a naïve New York City philosophy student who learns a painful afterlife lesson from master vampire Christopher Walken. Allegorical and atmospheric, this is intriguing but too internalized and slow moving. Letterboxed. Not rated; contains profanity, violence, and sexual situations. B&W; 82m. **DIR:** Abel Ferrara. **CAST:** Christopher Walken, Annabella Sciorra, Lili Taylor. **1995**

ADDRESS UNKNOWN ★★★1/2 A teen discovers that his father's accidental death may not have been an accident after all when he uncovers a letter written years before. Though intended primarily for younger viewers, this mystery will entertain parents as well. Rated PG. 92m. **DIR:** Shawn Levy. **CAST:** Kyle Howard, Johna Stewart, Corbin Allred, Patrick Renna. **1997**

ADIOS AMIGO ★★★ Writer-director-actor-producer Fred Williamson's whimsical parody of the Hollywood Western is about the misadventures of a cowboy (Williamson) and his sly, con-man partner (hilariously performed by Richard Pryor). Rated PG for profanity, but not much violence. 87m. **DIR:** Fred Williamson. **CAST:** Fred Williamson, Richard Pryor, Thalmus Rasulala, James Brown, Mike Henry. **1975**

ADIOS, HOMBRE ★★ Tiny, a sleazy outlaw, and his gang try to rob a bank but find it empty, so they decide to take the town hostage until the next gold shipment arrives. Enter a falsely accused escaped convict, Will Flagherty, out to prove his innocence and a one-man war is unleashed against the outlaw gang. Good action and an over-the-top performance by Eduardo Fajardo as Tiny. Not rated; contains violence. 90m. **DIR:** Mario Caiano. **CAST:** Craig Hill, Giulia Rubini, Piero Lulli, Eduardo Fajardo, Nazzareno Zemperla, Jacques Herlin, Nello Pazzafini, Roberto Camardiel. **1966**

ADJUSTER, THE ★★ Elias Koteas stars as an insurance adjuster. His wife is obsessed with the pornography and violence she views every day as a film censor. Another couple enter their lives—a wealthy duo who spend all their money and time on elaborate sex games. If you're looking for clarity and plot, abandon faith, all ye who enter here. 102m. **DIR:** Atom Egoyan. **CAST:** Elias Koteas, Arsinée Khanjian, Maury Chaykin, Gabrielle Rose. **1992 DVD**

ADMIRABLE CRICHTON, THE ★★★ A super-efficient butler takes command when he and his aristocratic employers are shipwrecked and marooned on a desert island. Love blossoms between the social classes, but all reverts to pre-wreck status following rescue. Love does not conquer all. Somewhat dated, but entertaining anyway. 93m. **DIR:** Lewis Gilbert. **CAST:** Sally Ann Howes, Martita Hunt, Kenneth More, Cecil Parker, Diane Cilento. **1957**

ADMIRAL WAS A LADY, THE ★★1/2 Romantic comedy about a group of ex-GI's asked to watch over a young woman until she can be reunited with her fiancé. Clichéd and somewhat bland, it's not without a certain amount of charm. B&W; 87m. **DIR:** Albert S. Rogell. **CAST:** Edmond O'Brien, Wanda Hendrix, Rudy Vallee, Johnny Sands. **1948**

ADORABLE JULIA ★★1/2 Somerset Maugham tale of a middle-aged stage actress who has an affair with a younger man while her husband waits in the wings. About as original as it sounds, though the cast lends it a bit of charm. Dubbed. Not rated. B&W; 97m. **DIR:** Alfred Weidenmann. **CAST:** Lilli Palmer, Charles Boyer, Jean Sorel. **1962**

ADRENALIN: FEAR THE RUSH ★★★ Creepy, effective thriller that's sure to appeal to fans of *The X-Files.*

Set in the not-too-distant future, the film stars Christopher Lambert and Natasha Henstridge as police officers trying to capture an elusive killer. What they don't know is that their prey is a government experiment gone awry: a crazed, killing machine carrying a virus that could wipe out the rest of mankind. Director Albert Pyun has created an intense thriller. Rated R for profanity and violence. 76m. **DIR:** Albert Pyun. **CAST:** Christopher Lambert, Natasha Henstridge, Norbert Weisser, Elizabeth Barondes, Nicholas Guest. **1995**

ADRIFT ★★ Derivative made-for-TV thriller proves those behind it saw *Dead Calm*. Kate Jackson and Kenneth Welsh are the good couple whose voyage is interrupted when they pick up bad couple Bruce Greenwood and Kelly Rowan. Predictable high-seas terror. Not rated. 92m. **DIR:** Christian Duguay. **CAST:** Kate Jackson, Kenneth Welsh, Bruce Greenwood, Kelly Rowan. **1993**

ADVENTURE ★★1/2 Flat and slow-moving romantic drama has a rough merchant sailor involved with a staid librarian. Neither Joan Blondell nor Thomas Mitchell (in his patented drunk Irishman role) can save this one. B&W; 125m. **DIR:** Victor Fleming. **CAST:** Clark Gable, Greer Garson, Joan Blondell, Thomas Mitchell, Tom Tully, John Qualen, Lina Romay, Harry Davenport. **1946**

ADVENTURE OF SHERLOCK HOLMES' SMARTER BROTHER, THE ★★1/2 Even discounting the effrontery of writer-director-star Gene Wilder's creating a smarter sibling, Sigerson Holmes (Gene Wilder), one is still left with a highly uneven romp. Though the principals—who also include Marty Feldman and Dom DeLuise—try hard, the film's soggy structure (and Wilder's poor research into the canon) plunge the whole thing into mediocrity. Rated PG. 91m. **DIR:** Gene Wilder. **CAST:** Gene Wilder, Madeline Kahn, Marty Feldman, Dom DeLuise. **1975**

ADVENTURES BEYOND BELIEF 🦃 In this incoherent excuse for madcap comedy, an Elvis Presley fan helps a mobster's daughter escape from an all-girls' school. Not rated. 95m. **DIR:** Marcus Tompson. **CAST:** Skyler Cole, Jill Whitlow, Elke Sommer, Stella Stevens, Edie Adams, John Astin, Larry Storch. **1987**

ADVENTURES IN BABYSITTING ★★★1/2 A sort of *After Hours* for the teen crowd, this is a surprisingly entertaining film about what happens when 17 year old Chris Parker (Elisabeth Shue) accepts a baby-sitting assignment. There are a number of hilarious moments—our favorite being a sequence in a blues club presided over by superguitarist Albert Collins. Rated PG-13 for profanity and violence. 100m. **DIR:** Chris Columbus. **CAST:** Elisabeth Shue, Keith Coogan, Anthony Rapp, Maia Brewton, Penelope Ann Miller, Vincent D'Onofrio. **1987 DVD**

ADVENTURES IN DINOSAUR CITY ★★ Three teens enter a dimension in which cartoon characters—dinosaurs—become real. Muppet-like creatures are very well done but can't make up for the flimsy plot and silly dialogue. Rated PG for comical violence. 88m. **DIR:** Brett Thompson. **CAST:** Omri Katz, Shawn Hoffman. **1991**

ADVENTURES IN SPYING ★★1/2 In this harmless romp, bored Bernie Coulson and Jill Schoelen learn that a recent acquaintance is actually a hired killer presumed dead. Now that he knows that they know his secret, they have to outrun numerous bad guys, ranging from crooked cops to evil chemists. G. Gordon Liddy makes a great villain. Rated PG-13 for violence. 91m. **DIR:** Hil Covington. **CAST:** Bernie Coulson, Jill Schoelen, Seymour Cassel, Michael Emil, G. Gordon Liddy. **1991**

ADVENTURES OF A GNOME NAMED GNORM, THE 🦃 A buffoonish young cop and a hairy, stubby creature from a mystic underworld team up to nab a jewel thief in this overly violent fantasy-caper. Rated PG for language and violence. 86m. **DIR:** Stan Winston. **CAST:** Anthony Michael Hall, Claudia Christian, Jerry Orbach. **1993**

ADVENTURES OF A PRIVATE EYE ★★ Boring British comedy about a detective's assistant who tries his hand at investigating a blackmail case while his boss is on vacation. The film has plenty of nudity and some scenes of rather explicit sex. Not rated. 96m. **DIR:** Stanley Long. **CAST:** Christopher Neil, Suzy Kendall, Harry H. Corbett, Diana Dors, Fred Emney, Liz Fraser, Irene Handl, Ian Lavender, Jon Pertwee, Adrienne Posta. **1987**

ADVENTURES OF AN AMERICAN RABBIT, THE ★★★ In this enjoyable-for-kids feature-length cartoon, mild-mannered and sweet-natured Rob Rabbit becomes the heir to the Legacy, which magically transforms him into the star-spangled protector of all animalkind, the American Rabbit. Rated G. 85m. **DIR:** Steward Moskowitz. **1986**

ADVENTURES OF BARON MÜNCHAUSEN, THE ★★★★ Terry Gilliam, that inspired madman of the movies, completes the fantasy trilogy—which began with *Time Bandits* and *Brazil*—with this one about the celebrated eighteenth-century liar. In the Age of Reason a small theatrical troupe attempts to put on a play about Münchausen, only to have an old soldier turn up claiming to be the real thing. He goes on to prove his identity with a series of wild tales. Rated PG for violence. 126m. **DIR:** Terry Gilliam. **CAST:** John Neville, Robin Williams, Eric Idle, Oliver Reed, Uma Thurman, Sarah Polley. **1989 DVD**

ADVENTURES OF BUCKAROO BANZAI, THE ★★★★ Peter Weller plays Buckaroo Banzai, a skilled neurosurgeon and physicist who becomes bored with his scientific and medical work and embarks on a career as a rock star and two-fisted defender of justice. This offbeat genre film is a silly movie for smart people. Rated PG. 103m. **DIR:** W. D. Richter. **CAST:** Peter Weller, John Lithgow, Ellen Barkin, Jeff Goldblum. **1984**

ADVENTURES OF BULLWHIP GRIFFIN, THE ★★ Typical, flyweight Disney comedy fails to offer anything original. Roddy McDowall plays a proper English butler who finds himself smack-dab in the wilds of California during the Gold Rush. Okay for the kids but not much to recommend for a discriminating audience. 110m. **DIR:** James Neilson. **CAST:** Roddy McDowall, Suzanne Pleshette, Karl Malden, Harry Guardino, Richard Haydn, Hermione Baddeley, Cecil Kellaway, Bryan Russell. **1966**

ADVENTURES OF CAPTAIN MARVEL, THE ★★★★ Fawcett Comics' Captain Marvel is splendidly brought to life by Republic Studios in what is generally regarded as the best serial of all time, certainly the best superhero chapterplay ever produced. Sincerely acted by all involved, this serial set the standards for flying stunts for years to come. B&W; 12 chapters. **DIR:** William Witney, John English. **CAST:** Tom Tyler, Frank Coghlan Jr., William Benedict, Louise Currie. **1941**

ADVENTURES OF DON JUAN, THE ★★★★ Despite the obvious use of footage from *The Adventures of Robin Hood* and *The Private Lives of Elizabeth and Essex*, this is a solid swashbuckler. Errol Flynn plays the great lover and swordsman of the title with tongue planted firmly in cheek. The years of drinking were beginning to show on his once boyishly handsome face. Yet this is quite appropriate to his portrayal of the famous libertine. 110m. **DIR:** Vincent Sherman. **CAST:** Errol Flynn, Viveca Lindfors, Robert Douglas, Alan Hale Sr., Romney Brent, Ann Rutherford, Robert Warwick, Jerry Austin, Douglas Kennedy, Una O'Connor. **1949**

ADVENTURES OF ELMO IN GROUCHLAND, THE ★★★ Little woolly red creature Elmo from TV's *Sesame Street* dives into Oscar the Grouch's garbage can to retrieve his beloved blanket. He gets sucked down a tunnel into a yucky universe where a selfish tyrant takes whatever he wants from his disgruntled subjects. This crisply paced adventure includes messages about sharing and cooperation, and encourages interaction from the audience. Rated G. 73m. **DIR:** Gary Halvorson. **CAST:** Mandy Patinkin, Vanessa L. Williams. **1999 DVD**

ADVENTURES OF FORD FAIRLANE, THE ★★ Foul-mouthed shock comic Andrew Clay stars as rock 'n' roll private dick Ford Fairlane. There's something here to offend everybody, especially women. Rated R for profanity and violence. 101m. **DIR:** Renny Harlin. **CAST:** Andrew Clay, Priscilla Presley, Wayne Newton, Robert Englund, Ed O'Neill. **1990**

ADVENTURES OF GALLANT BESS ★★ Minor melodrama about a man who seems to be more in love with his horse than he is with the woman in his life. The photography is quite good and the performances are passable, but it is still only fair. 73m. **DIR:** Lew Landers. **CAST:** Cameron Mitchell, Audrey Long, Fuzzy Knight. **1948**

ADVENTURES OF HERCULES, THE 🦃 This is the sequel to *Hercules*, the 1983 bomb with Lou "the Hulk" Ferrigno. The first Ferrigno folly was a laughfest. This tiresome piece of junk would only benefit insomniacs. Rated PG for violence (yes, even *that* can be boring). 89m. **DIR:** Lewis Coates. **CAST:** Lou Ferrigno, Milly Carlucci. **1984 DVD**

ADVENTURES OF HUCK FINN, THE (1993) ★★★★ In this high-gloss family film from Walt Disney Pictures that recalls Hollywood's golden age, adaptor-director Stephen Sommers lovingly captures Mark Twain's witty, wink-of-the-eye style. Elijah Wood is delightful as the barefoot boy who learns some important life lessons while traveling. Rated PG for brief violence. 108m. **DIR:** Stephen Sommers. **CAST:** Elijah Wood, Courtney B. Vance, Robbie Coltrane, Jason Robards Jr., Ron Perlman, Dana Ivey, Anne Heche, James Gammon, Curtis Armstrong. **1993**

ADVENTURES OF HUCKLEBERRY FINN, THE (1939) ★★★★ Fun-filled telling of the misadventures of Mark Twain's "other hero," as he outdoes the evil thieves, "King" and "Duke," becomes smitten over Mary Jane, and develops a conscience concerning the treatment of blacks. Mickey Rooney is fine in a subdued performance, and Rex Ingram is impressive as the slave, Jim. Originally released as *Huckleberry Finn*. B&W; 90m. **DIR:** Richard Thorpe. **CAST:** Mickey Rooney, Walter Connolly, William Frawley, Rex Ingram, Minor Watson, Lynne Carver. **1939**

ADVENTURES OF HUCKLEBERRY FINN, THE (1960) ★★★★ A delightful version of the Mark Twain classic produced to commemorate the seventy-fifth anniversary of its publication. A host of colorful players bring the famous characters to life. 107m. **DIR:** Michael Curtiz. **CAST:** Eddie Hodges, Archie Moore, Buster Keaton, Tony Randall, Andy Devine, Patty McCormack, Judy Canova, John Carradine, Mickey Shaughnessy, Sterling Holloway, Neville Brand. **1960**

ADVENTURES OF HUCKLEBERRY FINN, THE (1978) ★★ This drawn-out version of Mark Twain's classic has its moments but lacks continuous action. In it, young Huck fakes his own drowning to avoid attendance at a proper eastern school for boys. When his friend, Jim (Brock Peters), is accused of his murder, he must devise a plan to free him. 97m. **DIR:** Jack B. Hively. **CAST:** Forrest Tucker, Larry Storch, Brock Peters. **1978**

ADVENTURES OF MARCO POLO, THE ★★★ Disappointing tale of the travels of the thirteenth-century Italian merchant and his "discovery" in China of spaghetti, coal, and gunpowder for civilized Europe. Should have been a rousing epic. Screenplay by Robert E. Sherwood. Look for Lana Turner as an attendant in the court of Kublai Khan. B&W; 100m. **DIR:** Archie Mayo. **CAST:** Gary Cooper, Sigrid Gurie, Basil Rathbone, George Barbier, Ernest Truex, Binnie Barnes, Alan Hale Sr., H. B. Warner, Lana Turner. **1938**

ADVENTURES OF MARK TWAIN, THE (1944) ★★★1/2 This very episodic tale follows Samuel Clemens (Fredric March) from boyhood and young manhood on his beloved Mississippi River to recognition as a writer and lecturer. A nice bit of license is taken when he is involved in a frog-jump contest with Bret Harte (John Carradine). B&W; 130m. **DIR:** Irving Rapper. **CAST:** Fredric March, Alexis Smith, Donald Crisp, Alan Hale Sr., C. Aubrey Smith, John Carradine, Walter Hampden, Joyce Reynolds, Percy Kilbride. **1944**

ADVENTURES OF MARK TWAIN, THE (1985) ★★★★ A superior work of Claymation provides insights into the creative genius of Samuel Clemens. Includes vignettes of Twain's "The Diary of Adam and Eve" and "The Mysterious Stranger" in which the character of Satan spouts an existential perspective on life and death. 86m. **DIR:** Will Vinton. **1985**

ADVENTURES OF MILO AND OTIS, THE ★★★★ Japanese director Masanori Hata spent four years making this splendid family film, in which a dog named Otis sets out to rescue his lifelong friend, a kitten named Milo, when the feline is carried away by a rushing river. Adults will enjoy this one as much as their children. Rated G. 76m. **DIR:** Masanori Hata. **CAST:** Dudley Moore. **1989 DVD**

ADVENTURES OF MILO IN THE PHANTOM TOLLBOOTH, THE ★★★ An assortment of cartoon talents, including director Chuck Jones and voice greats like Mel Blanc, Hans Conried, Daws Butler, and June Foray, make this unusual but entertaining film coalesce. Live-action footage combines with animation to tell the story of a young boy who enters a booth that takes him into the Land of Wisdom. Rated G. 89m. **DIR:** Chuck Jones, Abe Levitow, Dave Monahan. **CAST:** Butch Patrick. **1969**

ADVENTURES OF MOLE, THE ★★★ Engaging animated tale based on Kenneth Grahame's beloved children's stories. This outing, Mole and his friends journey down the river in search of excitement and adventure. They find plenty of both in this tune-filled excursion that features colorful animation and kid-friendly lessons in life. Not rated. 60m. **DIR:** Martin Gates. **1995**

ADVENTURES OF NELLIE BLY, THE ★★ In this made-for-television film, Linda Purl shines as a reporter who uncovers serious problems in factories and insane asylums. The script unfortunately is weak and the direction is uninspired. 100m. **DIR:** Henning Schellerup. **CAST:** Linda Purl, Gene Barry, John Randolph, Raymond Buktenica, J. D. Cannon. **1981**

ADVENTURES OF OZZIE AND HARRIET, THE (TV SERIES) ★★★★ This prototypical family sitcom, primarily remembered for its all-American wholesomeness, was genuinely funny. That remarkable accomplishment must be largely credited to Ozzie Nelson, who produced, directed, and co-wrote, as well as starred as the earnest father who could create chaos out of the simplest situations. Real-life wife Harriet and sons Ricky and David added warmth and naturalness. B&W; 60m. **DIR:** Ozzie Nelson. **CAST:** Ozzie Nelson, Harriet Nelson, Ricky Nelson, David Nelson, Kris Nelson, June Nelson, Don DeFore, Lyle Talbot. **1952–1966**

ADVENTURES OF PICASSO, THE ★★★ Witty, off-the-wall Swedish comedy about the life of Picasso. The rubber-faced Gosta Eckman looks like Buster Keaton playing Picasso, and Bernard Cribbins is a scream in drag as Gertrude Stein. Some truly funny moments make this semislapstick film shine. In overly simplistic Spanish, French, and English, so no subtitles are needed. Not rated; contains some ribald humor. 94m. **DIR:** Tage Danielsson. **CAST:** Gosta Ekman, Hans Alfredson, Margaretha Krook, Bernard Cribbins, Wilfred Brambell. **1988**

ADVENTURES OF PINOCCHIO, THE ★★★1/2 Martin Landau is impressive as the lonely puppet maker, Geppetto, whose latest creation takes on a life of its own. Jonathan Taylor Thomas, the voice for the wooden Pinocchio and eventually the real little boy, maintains an irresistible sense of awe and wonderment. This film, based on Carlo Collodi's fable, is a veritable special-effects bonanza combining Jim Henson's Creature Shop wizardry, animatronics, miniatures, and computer-generated images to perfection. Rated G. 88m. **DIR:** Steve Barron. **CAST:** Martin Landau, Jonathan Taylor Thomas, Genevieve Bujold, Udo Kier, Bebe Neuwirth, Rob Schneider. **1996 DVD**

ADVENTURES OF PRISCILLA, QUEEN OF THE DESERT, THE ★★★★ Those who enjoyed the exuberant energy of *Strictly Ballroom* will be equally delighted by this spirited Australian import that follows three cross-dressing entertainers through small-town stops en route to a big-city gig. Not rated; contains mild profanity and frank sexual situations. 102m. **DIR:** Stephan Elliott. **CAST:** Terence Stamp, Hugo Weaving, Guy Pearce, Bill Hunter, Sarah Chadwick. **1994 DVD**

ADVENTURES OF RED RYDER ★★★★1/2 Action-packed serial as Red Ryder thwarts at every turn a banker's attempts to defraud ranchers whose land is wanted for a coming railroad. B&W; 12 chapters. **DIR:** William Witney, John English. **CAST:** Don Barry, Tommy Cook, Noah Beery Sr. **1940 DVD**

ADVENTURES OF REX AND RINTY ★★★1/2 A trio of unscrupulous Americans steal the God-Horse, Rex, from the island of Sujan and sell it to a greedy United States ranch owner. Rex escapes, meets Rinty, and the animals team up to avoid capture by the thieves. B&W; 12 chapters. **DIR:** Ford Beebe, B. Reeves "Breezy" Eason. **CAST:** Rin Tin Tin Jr., Kane Richmond, Norma Taylor, Smiley Burnette, Harry Woods. **1935**

ADVENTURES OF ROBIN HOOD, THE ★★★★★ This classic presents Errol Flynn at his swashbuckling best. He is backed up in this color spectacular by a perfect cast of supporting actors. Lavish sets and a stirring musical score help place *Robin Hood* among the very best adventure films. 106m. **DIR:** Michael Curtiz, William Keighley. **CAST:** Errol Flynn, Basil Rathbone, Ian Hunter, Olivia de Havilland, Claude Rains, Alan Hale Sr., Eugene Pallette. **1938**

ADVENTURES OF ROCKY AND BULLWINKLE, THE 🦃 When will they learn? Not every baby-boomer cartoon property lends itself to big-screen treatment, as is the case with this ill-conceived effort involving the flying squirrel, his moose sidekick, and several live-action actors who look like they'd rather be *anywhere* else. This is a bigger bomb than anything ever hurled by Boris Badenov. Rated PG for mild profanity. 88m. **DIR:** Des McAnuff. **CAST:** René Russo, Jason Alexander, Piper Perabo, Randy Quaid, Robert De Niro, Janeane Garofalo, Carl Reiner, Jonathan Winters, John Goodman, Whoopi Goldberg. **2000 DVD**

ADVENTURES OF SADIE ★★ Three men and a very young Joan Collins shipwrecked on a desert island; you can guess the rest. 88m. **DIR:** Noel Langley. **CAST:** George Cole, Kenneth More, Joan Collins, Hattie Jacques, Hermione Gingold. **1953**

ADVENTURES OF SEBASTIAN COLE, THE ★★★★ Insightful film about a high-school boy and the eclectic characters who, in some way, influence his life and his future. Well-written, brilliantly acted and directed. Rated R for profanity. 112m. **DIR:** Tod Williams. **CAST:** Adrian Grenier, Clark Gregg, Aleksa Pallodino, Margaret Colin, John Shea, Rory Cochrane. **1998 DVD**

ADVENTURES OF SHERLOCK HOLMES, THE ★★★★1/2 The best of all the Basil Rathbone–Nigel Bruce Sherlock Holmes movies, this pits the great detective against his arch-nemesis, Dr. Moriarty (played by George Zucco). The period setting, atmospheric photography, and the spirited performances of the cast (which includes a young Ida Lupino as Holmes's client) make this a must-see for mystery fans. B&W; 85m. **DIR:** Alfred Werker. **CAST:** Basil Rathbone, Nigel Bruce, Ida Lupino, George Zucco. **1939**

ADVENTURES OF SHERLOCK HOLMES, THE (TV SERIES) ★★★ Originally created as a television series for the European market, these 36 episodes hold up reasonably well. The original scripts are much lighter than Conan Doyle's stories, resulting in a finished tone that suggests the cast had a good time. Suitable for family viewing. B&W; 52m. **DIR:** Steve Previn, Sheldon

Reynolds. **CAST:** Ronald Howard, H. Marion Crawford, Archie Duncan. **1955**

ADVENTURES OF SHERLOCK HOLMES, THE (SERIES) ★★★★★ Jeremy Brett portrays Holmes as twitchy, arrogant, wan, humorless, and often downright rude—in short, everything Conan Doyle's hero was described to be. David Burke brings youthful dash and intelligent charm to Dr. Watson. Each episode is impeccably scripted and superbly acted. Not rated; contains frank discussions of violence and drug abuse. 52m. **DIR:** Paul Annett, John Bruce, David Carson, Ken Grieve, Alan Grint, Derek Marlowe. **CAST:** Jeremy Brett, David Burke. **1986 DVD**

ADVENTURES OF TARTU ★★1/2 Robert Donat steals the show as a British spy entrusted with the crippling of a poison gas factory behind enemy lines. He is joined in this blend of comedy and suspense by lovely Valerie Hobson and perky Glynis Johns. Nothing really special about this one, but it's fun. B&W; 103m. **DIR:** Harold S. Bucquet. **CAST:** Robert Donat, Valerie Hobson, Glynis Johns, Walter Rilla, Phyllis Morris. **1943**

ADVENTURES OF TARZAN, THE ★★1/2 Early action star Elmo Lincoln dons a wig for the third time to portray the Lord of the Jungle in this ambitious chapterplay. Lincoln finds himself fighting unscrupulous Bolsheviks, wild animals, a claimant to his family name, and the hordes of the lost city of Opar. Loosely adapted from two Tarzan novels. Silent. B&W; 15 chapters. **DIR:** Robert Hill. **CAST:** Elmo Lincoln, Louise Lorraine, Percy Pembroke. **1921**

ADVENTURES OF THE KUNG FU RASCALS, THE ★★ Wacky spoof of the kung fu genre is helped by decent special effects and creature makeup. Three Stooges–like heroes—Lao Ze, Reepo, and Chen Chow Mein—fight to free their land from an evil ruler. Toilet humor is unnecessarily offensive. Rated PG-13 for comic-book violence. 90m. **DIR:** Steve Wang. **CAST:** Steve Wang, Troy Fromin, Johnnie Saiko Espiritu, Les Claypool, Ted Smith, Aaron Sims. **1991 DVD**

ADVENTURES OF THE WILDERNESS FAMILY ★★★1/2 This is a variation on the Swiss Family Robinson story. A family (oddly enough named Robinson) moves to the Rocky Mountains to escape the frustrations and congestion of life in Los Angeles. They're sick of smog, hassles, and crime. They build a cabin and brave the dangers of the wild. Rated G. 100m. **DIR:** Stewart Raffill. **CAST:** Robert Logan, Susan D. Shaw, Ham Larsen, Heather Rattray, George "Buck" Flower, Hollye Holmes. **1975 DVD**

ADVENTURES OF TOM SAWYER, THE ★★★★ One of the better screen adaptations of Mark Twain's works. Tommy Kelly is a perfect Tom Sawyer, but it's Victor Jory as the villainous Indian Joe who steals the show. Good sets and beautiful cinematography make this one work. Fine family entertainment for young and old. B&W; 93m. **DIR:** Norman Taurog. **CAST:** Tommy Kelly, Jackie Moran, Victor Jory, May Robson, Walter Brennan, Ann Gillis. **1938**

ADVENTURES OF TOPPER, THE ★★★ This television comedy consistently earned chuckles, if not an abundance of belly laughs as this video compilation attests. Leo G. Carroll is delightful as Cosmo Topper, the henpecked bank vice president who is the only one who can see a trio of ghosts—Marion Kirby (Anne Jeffreys), her husband George (Robert Sterling), "that most sporting spirit," and their booze-swilling Saint Bernard, Neil. 93m. **DIR:** Philip Rapp. **CAST:** Anne Jeffreys, Robert Sterling, Leo G. Carroll, Lee Patrick, Thurston Hall, Kathleen Freeman. **1953–1956**

ADVENTURES OF YOUNG BRAVE, THE ★★ Fanciful family adventure that will appeal more to kids than adults. Two children are helped by the spirit of an Indian in their quest for gold, and then must help the ghost complete an act of bravery in order to return to the spirit world. A little silly and not very demanding, the film still exudes some charm. Also released as *Waking Up Horton*. Rated PG. 88m. **DIR:** Harry Bromley Davenport. **CAST:** Dirk Benedict, Barbara Carrera, Kenneth Hughes, Billy Maddox. **1998 DVD**

ADVERSARY, THE ★★★ Vivid and disturbing account of a college graduate who has been out of work for months. Satyajit Ray's neorealist sense of tragedy is unforgettably dramatized in this heartfelt film. In Bengali with English subtitles. B&W; 110m. **DIR:** Satyajit Ray. **CAST:** Dhritiman Chatterjee. **1971**

•ADVERTISING RULES ★★ Occasionally entertaining German comedy about a young man named Viktor (Alexander Scheer) who stumbles into a high-powered advertising-agency job and is immediately assigned to assist on a major campaign. Things get even better for Viktor when he meets beautiful artist Rosa, and then take a turn for the worst when he uses his ad campaign to help Rosa launch her new exhibit. Viktor's moral dilemma isn't nearly as funny or insightful as the filmmakers want us to believe. Rated R for language. 109m. **DIR:** Lars Kraume. **CAST:** Alexander Scheer, Gotz George, Chulpan Khamatova. **2001 DVD**

ADVISE AND CONSENT ★★★1/2 An engrossing adaptation of Allen Drury's bestseller about behind-the-scenes Washington. Fine performances abound as the U.S. Senate is called upon to confirm a controversial nominee for Secretary of State (Henry Fonda). Easily the most riveting is Charles Laughton, at his scene-stealing best, as a smiling old crocodile of a southern senator. B&W; 140m. **DIR:** Otto Preminger. **CAST:** Henry Fonda, Don Murray, Charles Laughton, Franchot Tone, Lew Ayres, Walter Pidgeon, Peter Lawford, Paul Ford, Burgess Meredith, Gene Tierney. **1962**

ADVOCATE, THE ★★1/2 In medieval France, a country lawyer defends a pig accused of murder. It may sound like a Monty Python skit, but the film is really a serious examination of social, religious, and legal attitudes during the fifteenth century. It gets high marks for daring and originality, and for its fine cast, but the script is unnecessarily confusing and the pacing is cumbersome. Rated R for nudity and sexual scenes. 101m. **DIR:** Leslie Megahey. **CAST:** Colin Firth, Amina Annabi, Donald Pleasence, Nicol Williamson, Michael Gough. **1993**

AELITA: QUEEN OF MARS ★★★ Deeply esoteric entertainment here. A silent Russian movie concerning a disenchanted man who takes a spaceship to Mars to meet the woman of his dreams. He encounters a proletariat uprising on the planet and realizes daydreams are not all they seem. Silent. B&W; 113m. **DIR:** Yakov Protázanov. **CAST:** Yulia Solntseva. **1924 DVD**

AFFAIR, THE (1973) ★★★ Touching, honest story of a crippled songwriter (Natalie Wood) tentatively entering into her first love affair—with an attorney (Robert

Wagner). This is an unusually well-acted, sensitively told TV movie. 74m. **DIR:** Gilbert Cates. **CAST:** Natalie Wood, Robert Wagner, Bruce Davison, Kent Smith, Pat Harrington. **1973 DVD**

AFFAIR, THE (1995) ★★★★ Actual events suggested this compelling WWII drama, which concerns the forbidden romance between an unhappily married British woman and a black American soldier. Although treated decently by their English hosts, black soldiers found the color barrier just as insurmountable. A pall of impending doom hangs over this story from its first moments, but the resolution is no less tragic for its foreshadowing. Rated R for profanity, violence, nudity, and simulated sex. 105m. **DIR:** Paul Seed. **CAST:** Courtney B. Vance, Kerry Fox, Leland Gantt, Bill Nunn, Ned Beatty. **1995**

AFFAIR IN TRINIDAD ★★★ Sultry, enticing café singer Rita Hayworth teams with brother-in-law Glenn Ford to trap her husband's murderer. The two fall in love en route. 98m. **DIR:** Vincent Sherman. **CAST:** Glenn Ford, Rita Hayworth, Alexander Scourby, Torin Thatcher. **1952**

AFFAIR OF LOVE, AN ★★★★ A fortysomething woman wants to act out a sexual fantasy with a male stranger. This unconventional French romance interweaves pseudodocumentary interviews of these nameless lovers with flashbacks of their affair, as it explores rudderless middle age, first impressions, instinctive decision making, and the fear of commitment. In French with English subtitles. Rated R for nudity and sex. 80m. **DIR:** Frédéric Fonteyne. **CAST:** Nathalie Baye, Sergi Lopez. **2000 DVD**

AFFAIR TO REMEMBER, AN ★★★★ Leo McCarey's gorgeous, haunting remake of his Oscar-nominated *Love Affair*. Cary Grant and Deborah Kerr have a shipboard romance, then part for six months. They agree to meet atop the Empire State Building in six months, but an accident prevents it. 115m. **DIR:** Leo McCarey. **CAST:** Cary Grant, Deborah Kerr, Richard Denning, Cathleen Nesbitt, Robert Q. Lewis. **1957 DVD**

AFFAIRS OF ANNABEL, THE ★★★★ The pre–*I Love Lucy* Lucille Ball is very funny in this fast-paced comedy as a none-too-bright movie star whose manager (Jack Oakie) is continually dreaming up outrageous publicity stunts for her. The supporting cast of familiar Thirties faces also provides plenty of laughs, especially Fritz Feld as a supercilious foreign director. 73m. **DIR:** Ben Stoloff. **CAST:** Jack Oakie, Lucille Ball, Ruth Donnelly, Fritz Feld, Thurston Hall. **1937**

AFFAIRS OF DOBIE GILLIS, THE ★★★★ This delightful college comedy that is sexy but not obvious about it focuses on an overamorous undergrad who dates girls in spite of their parents' objections. Good songs and lively dances by solid pros lift this one above the ordinary. B&W; 74m. **DIR:** Don Weis. **CAST:** Debbie Reynolds, Bobby Van, Bob Fosse, Hans Conried, Lurene Tuttle. **1953**

AFFLICTION ★★★1/2 Small-town New Hampshire constable Nick Nolte investigates an accidental shooting that he suspects was murder; meanwhile, his personal life disintegrates as he is haunted by memories of a childhood terrorized by his drunken, abusive father (Oscar-winner James Coburn). Acting is excellent, though the story is bleak, melodramatic, and depressing. Rated R for profanity. 114m. **DIR:** Paul Schrader. **CAST:** Nick Nolte, Sissy Spacek, James Coburn, Willem Dafoe, Jim True, Mary Beth Hurt. **1998 DVD**

AFRAID OF THE DARK ★★ A young boy losing his eyesight seeks out a slasher who targets the blind. Scary in places, but the thrills are few and too far between. Rated R for nudity and violence. 91m. **DIR:** Mark Peploe. **CAST:** James Fox, Fanny Ardant, Paul McGann. **1992**

AFRICA SCREAMS ★★ Bud and Lou are joined by circus great Clyde Beatty and Frank (*Bring 'Em Back Alive*) Buck in this thin but enjoyable comedy, one of their last feature films. Most of the jungle and safari clichés are evident in this fast-paced, oddball film but they work acceptably. Fun for the kids as well as the adults. B&W; 79m. **DIR:** Charles Barton. **CAST:** Bud Abbott, Lou Costello, Hillary Brooke, Shemp Howard, Max Baer, Clyde Beatty, Frank Buck. **1949 DVD**

AFRICA—TEXAS STYLE! ★★ The idea of a movie about cowboys rounding up animals in Africa must have sounded good in theory. But in practice, it's pretty dull going. Even the location photography doesn't help. Give us *Hatari!* any day. 106m. **DIR:** Andrew Marton. **CAST:** Hugh O'Brian, John Mills, Tom Nardini. **1966**

AFRICAN DREAM, AN ★★★★ Powerful film about a British-educated black man (John Kani) who returns to Africa as a teacher. Enter Kitty Aldridge as a joyful young woman who has just become a part of the nearby British colony, circa 1906. Inspirational portrayal of two people who dare to dream of a better world. Rated PG for violence. 94m. **DIR:** John Smallcombe. **CAST:** Kitty Aldridge, John Kani. **1990**

AFRICAN QUEEN, THE ★★★★★ Humphrey Bogart and Katharine Hepburn star in this exciting World War I adventure film. Bogart's a drunkard, and Hepburn's the spinster sister of a murdered missionary. Together they take on the Germans and, in doing so, are surprised to find themselves falling in love. 106m. **DIR:** John Huston. **CAST:** Humphrey Bogart, Katharine Hepburn, Peter Bull, Robert Morley, Theodore Bikel. **1951**

AFRICAN RAGE ★★★1/2 Anthony Quinn is a nurse in an African hospital where a tribal leader is admitted amid heavy security. Quinn's kidnapping of the leader, played with great dignity and warmth by Simon Sabela, takes some very unusual and interesting turns. A surprisingly moving film. Not rated. 105m. **DIR:** Peter Collinson. **CAST:** Anthony Quinn, John Phillip Law, Marius Weyers, Sandra Prinsloo, Ken Gampu, Simon Sabela. **1985**

AFTER DARK, MY SWEET ★★★1/2 Jason Patric gives a spellbinding performance as a moody, wandering ex-boxer who may or may not be as punch drunk as he seems. He meets a beguiling widow (Rachel Ward) and an ex-detective con man (Bruce Dern) and gets mixed up in a kidnap-ransom scheme that soon turns sour. Style and atmosphere dominate this gritty adaptation of Jim Thompson's hardboiled novel. Rated R for language. 114m. **DIR:** James Foley. **CAST:** Jason Patric, Rachel Ward, Bruce Dern. **1990 DVD**

AFTER DARKNESS An odd thriller about twin brothers who share visions of their parents' deaths. 105m. **DIR:** Dominique Othenin-Girard. **CAST:** John Hurt, Julian Sands, Victoria Abril. **1985**

AFTER HOURS ★★★★ The most brutal and bizarre black comedy we are ever likely to see. Griffin Dunne stars as a computer operator who unwillingly spends a night in downtown Manhattan. A trio of strange women mystify, seduce, and horrify our hapless hero, and his life soon becomes a total nightmare. Rated R for profanity, nudity, violence, and general weirdness. 94m. **DIR:** Martin Scorsese. **CAST:** Griffin Dunne, Rosanna Arquette, Teri Garr, John Heard, Linda Fiorentino, Richard "Cheech" Marin, Tommy Chong, Catherine O'Hara, Verna Bloom. **1985**

AFTER LIFE ★★★★ Every Monday a group of dead people walks into a postmortem screening area where they are asked by staff counselors to pick a single memory to take into eternity. The memory is reenacted and captured on film at the end of the week. The deceased then segue into the Great Beyond with a celluloid slice of their past and the process begins anew. This delicate, magnetic fable about how and what we remember (and making movies) escorts us into provocative speculation as emotions and relationships evolve between staff and clients. In Japanese with English subtitles. Not rated. 118m. **DIR:** Hirokazu Kore-eda. **CAST:** Arata, Erika Oda, Taketoshi Naito, Susumu Terajima, Takashi Naito. **1999 DVD**

AFTER MIDNIGHT ★★ University students taking a course on fear form a study group to tell each other scary stories. The film has a few thrills and chills, but it suffers from its lack of originality. Rated PG-13 for violence and profanity. 98m. **DIR:** Ken Wheat, Jim Wheat. **CAST:** Pamela Segall, Marc McClure, Marg Helgenberger. **1989**

AFTER PILKINGTON ★★★ A strange tale about an Oxford professor who meets up with his childhood sweetheart. He will do anything for her, even bury a dead body. Good acting, but the plot is weird. Not rated; contains violence and nudity. 100m. **DIR:** Christopher Morahan. **CAST:** Bob Peck, Miranda Richardson, Barry Foster, Gary Waldhorn, Mary Miller. **1988**

AFTER THE FOX 🦃 Peter Sellers is at his worst, playing an Italian movie director in this flat farce. 103m. **DIR:** Vittorio De Sica. **CAST:** Peter Sellers, Victor Mature, Britt Ekland, Martin Balsam. **1966 DVD**

AFTER THE PROMISE ★★ An uneducated laborer (Mark Harmon) loses custody of his sons following the death of his ailing wife. His efforts to get them back lead him down a road of red tape. Shamelessly maudlin and predictable TV movie. 93m. **DIR:** David Greene. **CAST:** Mark Harmon, Diana Scarwid, Donnelly Rhodes. **1987**

AFTER THE REHEARSAL ★★★1/2 This Ingmar Bergman movie made for Swedish television is about a director (Erland Josephson) who is approached by a young actress with a proposition: she wants to have an affair with him. In Swedish with English subtitles. 72m. **DIR:** Ingmar Bergman. **CAST:** Erland Josephson. **1984**

AFTER THE SHOCK ★★ A telemovie depicting the heroics of a group of Bay Area residents after the October 17, 1989 earthquake. Gary Sherman shot the movie with a home-movie, you-are-there feel. 92m. **DIR:** Gary A. Sherman. **CAST:** Scott Valentine, Jack Scalia, Yaphet Kotto. **1990**

•AFTER THE STORM ★★★ Greed and lust are the themes of this made-for-cable film based on an Ernest Hemingway story. When a boat full of riches goes down in the Bahamas, two scavengers and their girlfriends must find an uneasy truce to recover the treasure. The acting is decent, but the plot (while interesting) doesn't quite stretch into a full-length movie. Rated R for brief nudity. 99m. **DIR:** Guy Ferland. **CAST:** Benjamin Bratt, Armand Assante, Mili Avital, Simone Elise Girard, Stephen Lang, Nestor Serrano. **2001 DVD**

AFTER THE THIN MAN ★★★★1/2 Second of the six wonderful *Thin Man* films made with William Powell and Myrna Loy. Powell, Loy, and Asta, the incorrigible terrier, trade quips and drinks in this decent murder mystery. The dialogue is fast-paced and quite droll, and Powell and Loy demonstrate a chemistry that explains the dozen hits they had together. Not to be missed. B&W; 113m. **DIR:** W. S. Van Dyke. **CAST:** William Powell, Myrna Loy, James Stewart, Elissa Landi, Joseph Calleia, Sam Levene. **1936**

AFTERBURN ★★★★★ Made-for-cable drama doesn't get much better than this scathing indictment of government air force contracts, and the lengths to which life-threatening mistakes will be buried beneath red tape. Laura Dern superbly handles her role as fiery Janet Harduvel, who single-handedly forced General Dynamics to acknowledge that the F-16 fighter plane that killed her husband went down due to faulty design, rather than "pilot error." 103m. **DIR:** Robert Markowitz. **CAST:** Laura Dern, Robert Loggia, Michael Rooker, Vincent Spano. **1992**

AFTERGLOW ★★1/2 Writer-director Alan Rudolph's contrived round-robin of adultery flounders uncertainly from melodrama to farce without developing any conviction, and the arch double entendres of the dialogue become coy and labored. The acting is better than the script deserves—especially by Julie Christie, who seems to grow more radiant and complex with each passing year. Rated R for profanity, nudity, and sexual situations. 113m. **DIR:** Alan Rudolph. **CAST:** Julie Christie, Nick Nolte, Lara Flynn Boyle, Jonny Lee Miller. **1997**

AGAINST A CROOKED SKY ★★ Nothing new in this familiar tale of a boy searching for his sister, who has been kidnapped by Indians. Another inferior reworking of John Ford's classic Western *The Searchers*. For fans who watch anything with a horse and a saddle. Rated PG for violence. 89m. **DIR:** Earl Bellamy. **CAST:** Richard Boone, Clint Ritchie, Henry Wilcoxon, Stewart Peterson. **1975**

AGAINST ALL FLAGS ★★★ Though Errol Flynn's energy and attractiveness had seriously ebbed by this time, he still possessed the panache to make this simple swashbuckler fun to watch. He portrays a dashing British soldier who infiltrates a pirate stronghold, pausing only to romance the fiery Maureen O'Hara. 83m. **DIR:** George Sherman. **CAST:** Errol Flynn, Maureen O'Hara, Anthony Quinn, Mildred Natwick. **1952**

AGAINST ALL ODDS (1968) (KISS AND KILL, BLOOD OF FU MANCHU) 🦃 The evil Fu Manchu hatches another dastardly plan for world domination. A complete bore. Rated PG. 93m. **DIR:** Jess (Jesus) Franco. **CAST:** Christopher Lee, Richard Greene, Shirley Eaton. **1968**

AGAINST ALL ODDS ★★★1/2 A respectable remake of *Out of the Past*, a 1947 *film noir* classic, this release stars Jeff Bridges as a man hired by a wealthy gangster (James Woods) to track down his girlfriend (Rachel Ward), who allegedly tried to kill him. Bridges finds her, they fall in love, and that's when the plot's twists really begin. Rated R for nudity, suggested sex, violence, and profanity. 128m. **DIR:** Taylor Hackford. **CAST:** Jeff Bridges, Rachel Ward, Alex Karras, James Woods. **1984 DVD**

AGAINST THE WALL ★★★★ This crackling thriller dramatizes the events leading to 1971's Attica Prison riots, which ultimately resulted in forty-three deaths, as seen through the eyes of impressionable new guard Kyle MacLachlan. It's hard to tear your eyes from the screen. Rated R for violence, profanity, and nudity. 111m. **DIR:** John Frankenheimer. **CAST:** Kyle MacLachlan, Samuel L. Jackson, Clarence Williams, III, Frederic Forrest, Harry Dean Stanton. **1994**

AGATHA ★★1/2 Supposedly based on a true event in the life of mystery author Agatha Christie (during which she disappeared for eleven days in 1926), this is a moderately effective thriller. Vanessa Redgrave is excellent in the title role, but costar Dustin Hoffman is miscast as the American detective on her trail. Rated PG. 98m. **DIR:** Michael Apted. **CAST:** Dustin Hoffman, Vanessa Redgrave, Celia Gregory. **1979**

AGE ISN'T EVERYTHING 🦃 Age-reversal comedy with a twist: young Jonathan Silverman has his body taken over by an old man in a comedy that's as old as the hills and just as dusty. Rated R for language. 91m. **DIR:** Douglas Katz. **CAST:** Jonathan Silverman, Robert Prosky, Rita Moreno, Paul Sorvino. **1991**

AGE OF GOLD ★★★ Filmmaker Luis Buñuel's surrealist masterpiece is a savage assault on organized religion, the bourgeoisie, and social ethics. Salvador Dalí contributed a few ideas to the production. In French with English subtitles. B&W; 62m. **DIR:** Luis Buñuel. **CAST:** Pierre Prevert, Gaston Modot, Lya Lys, Max Ernst. **1930**

AGE OF INNOCENCE, THE ★★★★ Daniel Day-Lewis and Michelle Pfeiffer are star-crossed lovers in this romance that also examines the mores and morals of New York in the 1870s. The film belongs to the luminous Winona Ryder, who plays Lewis's patient and formidable fiancée. Narrated by Joanne Woodward. Rated PG for suggestion of impropriety. 133m. **DIR:** Martin Scorsese. **CAST:** Daniel Day-Lewis, Michelle Pfeiffer, Winona Ryder, Geraldine Chaplin, Alec McCowen, Richard E. Grant, Mary Beth Hurt, Stuart Gordon, Robert Sean Leonard, Sian Phillips, Carolyn Farina, Michael Gough, Miriam Margolyes, Alexis Smith, Jonathan Pryce, Norman Lloyd. **1993 DVD**

AGE-OLD FRIENDS ★★★★1/2 This poignant study of aging, adapted by Bob Larbey from his Broadway play *A Month of Sundays*, makes a superb vehicle for star Hume Cronyn. While enthusiastically flirting with his kind young nurse or testily enduring his monthly Inspection Day—a visit from his estranged daughter—Cronyn's crusty codger puts his effort and concern into the well-being of best friend Vincent Gardenia. 90m. **DIR:** Allan Kroeker. **CAST:** Hume Cronyn, Vincent Gardenia, Tandy Cronyn, Esther Rolle. **1989**

AGENCY ★★ Despite the presence of Robert Mitchum, this Canadian feature about a power struggle in the world of advertising doesn't convince. Rated PG. 94m. **DIR:** George Kaczender. **CAST:** Robert Mitchum, Lee Majors, Saul Rubinek, Valerie Perrine. **1981**

AGENT OF DEATH ★★ This formulaic thriller about a staged kidnapping that turns into the real thing has a twist: The victim is the president of the United States. The payoff is that the only man who can save him is a CIA agent still bitter over the death of his wife and daughter, who were murdered during a presidential-ordered assassination. Rated R for adult situations, language, and violence. 105m. **DIR:** Sam Firstenberg. **CAST:** Eric Roberts, Michael Madsen, Ice T, Bryan Genesse. **1999**

AGENT ON ICE ★★★1/2 This exciting action film features Tom Ormeny as John Pope, a former CIA agent who has become a target for both the CIA and the Mafia. Clifford David plays the corrupt CIA official who has been laundering money for Mafia leader Frank Matera (Louis Pastore). Rated R for violence and obscenities. 96m. **DIR:** Clark Worswick. **CAST:** Tom Ormeny, Clifford David, Louis Pastore, Matt Craven. **1985**

AGENT RED 🦃 Low-budget mess stars Dolph Lundgren as a navy special operations commander trying to keep a deadly virus out of the hands of terrorists. This subpar effort sinks to the bottom of the ocean in a tidal wave of clichés and poor acting. Rated R for adult situations, language, nudity, and violence. 95m. **DIR:** Damian Lee. **CAST:** Dolph Lundgren, Randolph Mantooth, Natalie Radford. **2000 DVD**

AGGIE APPLEBY, MAKER OF MEN ★★ The heroine teaches a wimp to act like a tough guy so he can impersonate her tough boyfriend. A mixed bag that's watchable in spite of itself. But only up to a point. B&W; 73m. **DIR:** Mark Sandrich. **CAST:** Wynne Gibson, William Gargan, Charles Farrell, ZaSu Pitts, Jane Darwell, Betty Furness. **1933**

AGNES BROWNE ★★★★ Anjelica Huston shines as director and star of this warmhearted and distinctively full-bodied story of a widowed mother and her struggles to survive financially and romantically. Based on the novel *The Mammy* by Brendan O'Carroll. Rated R for profanity. 92m. **DIR:** Anjelica Huston. **CAST:** Anjelica Huston, Marion O'Dwyer, Niall O'Shea, Ciaran Owens, Ray Winstone, Tom Jones. **1999 DVD**

AGNES OF GOD ★★★ This fascinating drama features tour-de-force performances by Jane Fonda, Anne Bancroft, and Meg Tilly. Tilly's character, the childlike novice of an extremely sheltered convent, is discovered one night with the bloodied body of a baby. Psychiatrist Fonda is sent to determine Tilly's sanity in anticipation of a court hearing; Bancroft, as the Mother Superior, struggles to prevent the young girl's loss of innocence. Rated PG-13 for subject matter. 101m. **DIR:** Norman Jewison. **CAST:** Jane Fonda, Anne Bancroft, Meg Tilly, Anne Pitoniak, Winston Rekert. **1985**

AGONY AND THE ECSTASY, THE ★★★ Handsomely mounted but plodding historical drama based on Irving Stone's bestselling novel about Pope Julius II (Rex Harrison) engaging Michelangelo (Charlton Heston) to paint the ceiling of the Sistine Chapel. Heston overacts and the direction is heavy-handed. 140m. **DIR:** Carol Reed. **CAST:** Charlton Heston, Rex Harrison, Diane Cilento, Harry Andrews. **1965**

AGUIRRE: WRATH OF GOD ★★★★ Klaus Kinski gives one of his finest screen performances as the mad, traitorous Spanish conquistador who leads an expedition through the South American wilds in a quest for the lost city of El Dorado. It's a spectacular adventure story. In German with English subtitles. Not rated, the film has violence. 94m. **DIR:** Werner Herzog. **CAST:** Klaus Kinski, Ruy Guerra, Del Negro, Helena Rojo. **1972**

AH, WILDERNESS ★★★★ An American classic, this story of a family in 1910 mid-America is one of the most tasteful coming-of-age stories ever written. Playwright Eugene O'Neill based his stage play on memories of his youth at the turn of the century. B&W; 101m. **DIR:** Clarence Brown. **CAST:** Wallace Beery, Lionel Barrymore, Aline MacMahon, Cecilia Parker, Mickey Rooney, Eric Linden, Bonita Granville, Frank Albertson. **1935**

•AI: ARTIFICIAL INTELLIGENCE ★★★1/2 In the not-so-far future, the greenhouse effect causes the polar ice caps to melt and further polarizes American society. The "haves" rely on "mechas," androids capable of doing just about anything. The genius behind their creation decides to experiment with a robot capable of feeling love; in particular, a boy given to a bereaved family whose son is being kept in frozen stasis until a cure is found for his disease. When this medical miracle transpires, the loving little robot is cast aside in an unfriendly world he doesn't understand. *2001 Meets E.T.* is a bit simplistic but somehow apt for this Steven Spielberg realization of a film planned by Stanley Kubrick before his death. Based on a short story by Brian Aldiss, it contains the strengths and weaknesses of both celebrated filmmakers, yet remains a thought-provoking, unforgettable, and touching cinematic work. Rated PG-13 for violence and sex. 145m. **DIR:** Steven Spielberg. **CAST:** Haley Joel Osment, Jude Law, Frances O'Connor, Sam Robards, Jake Thomas, William Hurt. **2001 DVD**

AILEEN WUORNOS: SELLING OF A SERIAL KILLER ★★★ Chilling, disturbing, and maddening, this documentary examines the postarrest life of America's first female serial killer and those around her, including her attorney and a born-again Christian—who are either doing everything in their power to help her or attempting to cash in on the tragedy. The audience is left to decide. Not rated; contains harsh language and adult themes. 87m. **DIR:** Nick Broomfield. **CAST:** Aileen Wuornos, Arlene Pralle, Steven Glazer, Tyria Moore. **1992**

AIMEE & JAGUAR ★★★ In WWII Berlin, a Jewish resistance fighter working for a Nazi newspaper falls in love with a promiscuous housewife who has never really loved before. The fascinating subject matter and good performances make up for the deliberate pacing in this true story. In German with English subtitles. Not rated; contains mature themes and frankly sexual scenes. 126m. **DIR:** Max Färberböck. **CAST:** Maria Schrader, Juliane Kohler, Johana Wokalek. **1999 DVD**

AIR AMERICA ★★★★ The cop/buddy formula takes to the air when veteran pilot Mel Gibson teams up with rookie Robert Downey Jr. to fly top-secret U.S. missions behind enemy lines in the early Vietnam War–era jungles of Laos. Plenty of action and comedy bits make this a fun romp for the action crowd. Rated R for profanity and violence. 100m. **DIR:** Roger Spottiswoode. **CAST:** Mel Gibson, Robert Downey Jr. **1990 DVD**

AIR BUD ★★★ In true Disney form, this family film successfully combines laughter with tears. A custody battle erupts over a talented pooch when the dog's abusive clown owner takes him from the lonely boy who really loves him. Beyond this heartwarming angle is the unbelievable transition the dog makes from mascot to basketball team player. The kids will love it, and adults will be moved by the dog's plight. Rated PG for suggested animal and child abuse. 96m. **DIR:** Charles Martin Smith. **CAST:** Michael Jeter, Kevin Zegers, Wendy Makkena, Eric Christmas, Bill Cobbs. **1997 DVD**

AIR BUD: GOLDEN RECEIVER ★★1/2 Corny but cute Disney film features a talented Golden Retriever able to turn a losing football team into champs. Circus villains dognap the lovable pooch right before the big game (of course!). Heartwarming and amusing moments make for good family fun. Rated G. 90m. **DIR:** Richard Martin. **CAST:** Kevin Zegers, Gregory Harrison, Cynthia Stevenson, Nora Dunn. **1999**

•AIR BUD: WORLD PUP ★★ Doggone. Now that Golden Retriever Buddy has mastered the sports of basketball and football, he and his owner join a soccer team. Little imagination in this tired direct-to-video sequel that just rehashes plot points from the first two films. How much puppy love can one dog take? Rated G. 83m. **DIR:** Bill Bannerman. **CAST:** Kevin Zegers, Dale Midkiff, David Glyn-Jones, Caitlin Wachs. **2000 DVD**

AIR FORCE ★★★★ This is essentially wartime propaganda about a flying fortress and its crew taking on the enemy at Pearl Harbor, Manila, and the Coral Sea. However, the direction by Howard Hawks puts the film head and shoulders above similar motion pictures. B&W; 124m. **DIR:** Howard Hawks. **CAST:** John Garfield, John Ridgely, Gig Young, Charles Drake, Harry Carey, Arthur Kennedy, George Tobias. **1943**

AIR FORCE ONE ★★★★ Russian terrorists hijack the United States' most valuable aircraft and promise to kill a hostage every half hour until an imprisoned tyrant is released. But the bad guys don't know that this particular chief of state is Harrison Ford. Wolfgang Petersen's crisp thriller unfolds smoothly and intelligently, and this is far better than most genre entries. Rated R for violence and profanity. 118m. **DIR:** Wolfgang Petersen. **CAST:** Harrison Ford, Gary Oldman, Glenn Close, Wendy Crewson, Paul Guilfoyle, William H. Macy, Liesel Matthews, Dean Stockwell, Xander Berkeley. **1997 DVD**

•AIR RAGE ★★1/2 A dishonored Marine takes a passenger jet hostage in this surprisingly entertaining, although admittedly downright silly, action thriller. Rated R for violence and language. 100m. **DIR:** Fred Olen Ray. **CAST:** Ice T, Cyril O'Reilly, Kimberly Oja. **2001 DVD**

AIR RAID WARDENS ★★ The title tells all in this lesser effort from Stan Laurel and Oliver Hardy, which has them messing up on the home front until they capture a nest of saboteurs. Dated and disappointing. B&W; 67m. **DIR:** Edward Sedgwick. **CAST:** Stan Laurel, Oliver Hardy, Edgar Kennedy, Stephen McNally, Donald Meek. **1943**

AIR UP THERE, THE ★★ Aggressive college-basketball coach Kevin Bacon tries to recruit a Kenyan tribesman in a predictable, *Rocky*-type comedy-adventure about global sports imperialism. The white, alleged hero—who has a terminal me-first attitude—ends up leading the Winabi tribe in a hoops game against a rival clan for ancestral lands. Shot on location in South Africa and Kenya. Rated PG. 107m. **DIR:** Paul Michael

Glaser. **CAST:** Kevin Bacon, Charles Gitonga Maina. **1994**

AIRBORNE ★★★ California-surf teen moves in with nerdy Cincinnati relatives and becomes a target of local toughs in this pubescent comedy. The landlocked hot-dogger embraces a Gandhiesque pacifism when confronted by toughs, dates one bully's sister and—when the Midwest frost thaws—struts some amazing stuff on roller blades in a scorching downhill race finale. The rock-charged soundtrack includes original music by former Police drummer Stewart Copeland. Rated PG. 89m. **DIR:** Rob Bowman. **CAST:** Shane McDermott, Seth Green, Brittney Powell, Chris Conrad, Patrick O'Brien. **1993 DVD**

AIRHEADS 🦃 A metal band takes a radio station hostage until it plays a demo tape. Poor performances, gimmicky direction, and shallow characters make this movie a dud. Rated PG-13 for language. 115m. **DIR:** Michael Lehmann. **CAST:** Brendan Fraser, Steve Buscemi, Adam Sandler, Joe Mantegna. **1994 DVD**

AIRPLANE! ★★★★ This is a hilarious spoof of the *Airport* series—and movies in general. While the jokes don't always work, there are so many of them that this comedy ends up with enough laughs for three movies. Rated PG. 88m. **DIR:** Jim Abrahams, David Zucker, Jerry Zucker. **CAST:** Robert Hays, Julie Hagerty, Leslie Nielsen, Kareem Abdul-Jabbar, Lloyd Bridges, Peter Graves, Robert Stack. **1980**

AIRPLANE II: THE SEQUEL ★★★1/2 Viewers who laughed uncontrollably through *Airplane!* will find much to like about this sequel. The stars of the original are back, with silly jokes and sight gags galore. However, those who thought the original was more stupid than funny undoubtedly will mutter the same about the sequel. Rated PG for occasional adult content. 85m. **DIR:** Ken Finkleman. **CAST:** Robert Hays, Julie Hagerty, Peter Graves, William Shatner. **1982 DVD**

AIRPORT ★★★★ The daddy of them all, this *Grand Hotel* in the air is slick, enjoyable entertainment. Taking place on a fateful winter night, it miraculously rises above some stiff performances and an often hackneyed plot. Rated G. 137m. **DIR:** George Seaton. **CAST:** Burt Lancaster, Dean Martin, Helen Hayes, Jacqueline Bisset, Van Heflin, Jean Seberg, George Kennedy. **1970 DVD**

AIRPORT 1975 🦃 Poor sequel. Rated PG. 106m. **DIR:** Jack Smight. **CAST:** Charlton Heston, George Kennedy, Karen Black, Sid Caesar, Helen Reddy. **1974 DVD**

AIRPORT '77 🦃 If you've seen one *Airport*, you've seen them all. Rated PG for violence. 113m. **DIR:** Jerry Jameson. **CAST:** Jack Lemmon, Lee Grant, George Kennedy, Christopher Lee. **1977 DVD**

AIRPORT '79: THE CONCORDE 🦃 Bring your own air-sickness bag. Rated PG. 113m. **DIR:** David Lowell Rich. **CAST:** Alain Delon, Robert Wagner, Susan Blakely, George Kennedy, Eddie Albert, Cicely Tyson. **1979**

AKIRA ★★★★ Based by writer-director Katsuhiro Otomo on his popular comic book, this is a spectacular film set in twenty-first-century post–World War III Japan, where a member of a motorcycle gang becomes an unwilling guinea pig in a scientific experiment that backfires. Not rated, the film has oodles of violence. 124m. **DIR:** Katsuhiro Otomo. **1990 DVD**

AKIRA KUROSAWA'S DREAMS ★★★★ Celebrated Japanese director Akira Kurosawa delves into his dreams for this episodic motion picture. Like real dreams, Kurosawa's *Dreams* are snippets of situations and ideas. As such, they are often anti-climactic and even frustrating. Yet the images are breathtakingly beautiful. In Japanese with English subtitles. Rated PG. 120m. **DIR:** Akira Kurosawa. **CAST:** Akira Terao, Martin Scorsese. **1990**

AL CAPONE ★★★1/2 Rod Steiger is mesmerizing as Al Capone in this perceptive portrait of the legendary Chicago gangster. The film covers Capone's life from his first job for $75 a week to his ultimate fate behind prison walls. Filmed in black and white with a documentary-style narrative, which heightens the quality of this film. The supporting cast—Fay Spain in particular—is just right. B&W; 104m. **DIR:** Richard Wilson. **CAST:** Rod Steiger, Fay Spain, James Gregory, Martin Balsam, Nehemiah Persoff. **1959**

ALADDIN ★★★★★ The over-the-edge, manic voice work of an unleashed Robin Williams, as the genie of the lamp, supplies the laughs in this exquisite magic-carpet ride from Walt Disney Pictures. A worthy successor to *The Little Mermaid* and *Beauty and the Beast*, *Aladdin* is a classic feature-length cartoon blessed with excellent songs and a story that will fascinate all ages. The crowning touch is the deft illustration by Disney's animators. Rated G. 83m. **DIR:** John Musker, Ron Clements. **1992**

ALADDIN ★★ Update of the Aladdin tale, with Bud Spencer as the genie from the lamp, discovered this time by a boy in a junk shop in a modern city. A little too cute at times, and the humor is forced. Not rated; contains some violence. 95m. **DIR:** Bruno Corbucci. **CAST:** Bud Spencer, Luca Venantini, Janet Agren. **1987**

ALADDIN & THE KING OF THIEVES ★★★★ Robin Williams returns as the voice of the genie in this lively sequel. While the genie helps prepare for Aladdin and Jasmine's royal wedding, Aladdin discovers that his father is still alive, and is the leader of the infamous Forty Thieves. Clever animation, exciting adventures, and Williams's irrepressible humor make this second sequel much better than the first. Rated G. 80m. **DIR:** Tad Stones. **CAST:** Robin Williams, Gilbert Gottfried, Jerry Orbach, John Rhys-Davies (voices). **1996**

ALAKAZAM THE GREAT ★★1/2 Musical morality play for kids about the evils of pride and the abuse of power. When naïve little Alakazam the monkey is made king of the animals, he quickly develops an abusive personality that can only be set to rights through an arduous pilgrimage. Somewhat muddled, but watchable. 84m. **DIR:** James H. Nicholson, Samuel Z. Arkoff. **1961**

ALAMO, THE ★★★1/2 This Western, directed by and starring John Wayne, may have seemed overlong when originally released. But today it's the answer to a Duke-deprived fan's dream. Of course, there's the expected mushy flag-waving here and there. However, once Davy Crockett (Wayne), Jim Bowie (Richard Widmark), Will Travis (Laurence Harvey), and their respective followers team up to take on Santa Ana's forces, it's a humdinger of a period war movie. 161m. **DIR:** John Wayne. **CAST:** John Wayne, Richard Widmark, Laurence Harvey, Frankie Avalon, Richard Boone, Chill Wills. **1960**

ALAMO, THE: THIRTEEN DAYS TO GLORY 🦃 Jim Bowie, Davy Crockett, Col. William Travis and their men defend the Texas fort to the death, in this made-for-TV movie. The two-part film suffers from inaccuracies, and the significance of the siege is trivialized by focusing on bickering between Travis and Bowie. 168m. **DIR:** Burt Kennedy. **CAST:** James Arness, Brian Keith, Alec Baldwin, David Ogden Stiers, Raul Julia, Lorne Greene. **1987**

ALAMO BAY ★★★★ French director Louis Malle once again looks at the underbelly of the American dream. This time, he takes us to the Gulf Coast of Texas in the late 1970s where Vietnamese refugees arrived, expecting the land of opportunity, and came face-to-face, instead, with the Ku Klux Klan. Rated R for nudity, violence, and profanity. 105m. **DIR:** Louis Malle. **CAST:** Ed Harris, Amy Madigan, Ho Nquyen, Donald Moffat. **1985**

ALAN AND NAOMI ★★ Well-intentioned but muddled story about a high school student in the Forties and his attempts to help a victim of Nazi terrorism. The performances add a level of quality, but they are thwarted by the funereal tone and an inexcusably abrupt conclusion. Rated PG for mature themes. 98m. **DIR:** Sterling Vanwagenen. **CAST:** Lukas Haas, Vanessa Zaoui, Michael Gross, Amy Aquino, Kevin Connolly, Zohra Lampert. **1992**

ALAN SMITHEE FILM, AN—BURN HOLLYWOOD BURN 🦃 Director Alan Smithee steals the negative to his latest movie so producer can't ruin it in editing. Writer Joe Eszterhas vents his spleen on the incompetence of Hollywood in this witless comedy; it's a clear case of the pot calling the kettle black. (The joke is that "Alan Smithee" is the pseudonym used when a director orders his name taken off a film—which, ironically, is exactly what Arthur Hiller wisely did with this one.) Rated R for profanity. 83m. **CAST:** Ryan O'Neal, Coolio, Chuck D, Richard Jeni, Eric Idle, Sylvester Stallone, Whoopi Goldberg, Jackie Chan. **1997**

ALARMIST, THE ★★★ Honest home-security system salesman has an affair with his first client and learns that his reptilian boss and business associate are staging residential break-ins to bolster company sales. Engaging black comedy about greed, office politics, crime, paranoia, and sex is based on Keith Reddin's off-Broadway play, *Life During Wartime.* Rated R for simulated sex, language, and violence. 95m. **DIR:** Evan Dunsky. **CAST:** David Arquette, Stanley Tucci, Kate Capshaw, Mary McCormack, Ryan Reynolds. **1998 DVD**

ALASKA ★★★ Under his son's direction, Charlton Heston has the art of acting ruthless down to a science. While poaching polar bear, he meets a brother and sister on a mission to find their missing dad. Since the kids are being followed by the orphaned cub Heston wants, he keeps track of the kids. Coming-of-age element, physical dangers, and gorgeous panoramic shots of glaciers and forests are all a plus. Rated PG for mild profanity and simulated cruelty to animals. 109m. **DIR:** Fraser Heston. **CAST:** Charlton Heston, Vincent Kartheiser, Thora Birch, Dirk Benedict. **1996**

ALBERTO EXPRESS ★★★1/2 When a young man leaves home, his father demands that he repay the costs of his upbringing before he starts his own family. Fifteen years later, with his wife pregnant, the son frantically struggles to find the money before she gives birth. Fast-paced comedy will have you laughing out loud. In Italian with English subtitles. 98m. **DIR:** Arthur Joffe. **CAST:** Sergio Castellitto, Nino Manfredi, Jeanne Moreau. **1990**

ALBINO 🦃 African terrorists, led by an albino chief, frighten natives. Not rated. 96m. **DIR:** Jurgen Goslar. **CAST:** Christopher Lee, Trevor Howard, James Faulkner, Sybil Danning. **1976**

ALBINO ALLIGATOR ★★1/2 Three robbers and five hostages are cornered by the police and media in a subterranean New Orleans bar in this familiar hostage drama. This claustrophobic story (written by Christian Forte, son of 1950s pop star Fabian) is about inner struggles between good and evil, and the moral ambiguity that can arise in the name of survival. It's a character study that is imaginatively directed but often feels more like an actors'-workshop exercise than a real movie. Rated R for language and violence. 97m. **DIR:** Kevin Spacey. **CAST:** Matt Dillon, Faye Dunaway, Gary Sinise, William Fichtner, Viggo Mortensen, John Spencer, Skeet Ulrich, M. Emmet Walsh, Joe Mantegna. **1996 DVD**

ALDRICH AMES: TRAITOR WITHIN ★★★1/2 Timothy Hutton plays Ames, a browbeaten husband who just wanted to pad his paycheck a bit. Elizabeth Peña is more convincing as his materialistic wife, a shrew who doesn't care where the money comes from. The film really belongs to Joan Plowright, as the resourceful agency investigator who carefully closes the net that eventually traps Ames. Rated PG for profanity and dramatic content. 98m. **DIR:** John Mackenzie. **CAST:** Timothy Hutton, Joan Plowright, Elizabeth Peña, C. David Johnson, Eugene Lipinski. **1998**

ALEX ★★★ Courageous story of a young Australian woman who fought against the odds to compete in the 1960 Rome Olympics. Lauren Jackson is strong as the freestyle swimmer who balanced a full college workload and dealt with the death of her boyfriend while training for the Games. Not rated. 93m. **DIR:** Megan Simpson. **CAST:** Lauren Jackson, Chris Haywood, Josh Picker, Cathy Gobold, Elizabeth Hawthorne. **1993**

ALEX IN WONDERLAND ★★ A self-conscious look at the film world that misses its mark in spite of good performances and some sharp jabs at the greed that controls Hollywood. Donald Sutherland is appropriately humble as a movie director trying to follow his first film with an even better one. Rated R. 110m. **DIR:** Paul Mazursky. **CAST:** Donald Sutherland, Ellen Burstyn, Paul Mazursky, Jeanne Moreau, Federico Fellini. **1970**

ALEXANDER NEVSKY ★★★★ Another classic from the inimitable Russian director Sergei Eisenstein *(Ivan the Terrible; Battleship Potemkin)*, this film is a Soviet attempt to prepare Russia for the coming conflict with Hitlerian Germany via portrayal of Alexander Nevsky, a thirteenth-century Russian prince, and his victories over the Teutonic knights of that era. As with all state-commissioned art, the situations can be corny, but the direction is superb. In Russian with English subtitles. B&W; 105m. **DIR:** Sergei Eisenstein. **CAST:** Nikolai Cherkassov, Dmitri Orlov. **1938 DVD**

ALEXANDER THE GREAT ★★★1/2 The strange, enigmatic, self-possessed Macedonian conqueror of Greece and most of the civilized world of his time rides again. Richard Burton, with his enthralling voice and uniquely hypnotic eyes, dominates an outstanding cast in this lavish epic. 141m. **DIR:** Robert Rossen. **CAST:** Richard Burton, Fredric March, Claire Bloom, Danielle Darrieux. **1956**

ALEXANDER'S RAGTIME BAND ★★★★★ The first all-star epic musical to feature classic Irving Berlin tunes. The story of a Nob Hill elitist who starts a ragtime band on the Barbary Coast is a suitable setting for over two dozen Berlin songs composed between World War I and the early days of World War II. Tyrone Power glamorizes the setting, while the music and the nostalgia element still have the magic to involve an audience emotionally. B&W; 105m. **DIR:** Henry King. **CAST:** Alice Faye, Tyrone Power, Don Ameche, Ethel Merman, Jack Haley, Dixie Dunbar. **1938**

ALEXINA ★★1/2 Confusing erotic tale about a young woman who discovers she's not really a girl, after indulging in a relationship with another woman in this strange concoction of metamorphosis and identity crisis. Pretty baffling. Not rated; contains nudity. In French with English subtitles. 98m. **DIR:** René Feret. **CAST:** Valerie Stroh, Bernard Freyd. **1991**

ALEX'S APARTMENT 🦃 When a young woman starts a new life in a coastal town, she's confronted by a maniac who kills women as "gifts" to her. Poor script. Not rated, contains violence. 79m. **DIR:** W. Mel Martins. **CAST:** Miki Welling. **1992**

ALFIE ★★★★ Wild and ribald comedy about a Cockney playboy (Michael Caine) who finds "birds" irresistible. Full of sex and delightful charm, this quick-moving film also tells the poignant tragedy of a man uncertain about his lifestyle. Nominated for five Oscars, including best picture and best actor. 113m. **DIR:** Lewis Gilbert. **CAST:** Michael Caine, Shelley Winters, Millicent Martin, Julia Foster, Shirley Ann Field. **1966 DVD**

ALFRED HITCHCOCK PRESENTS (TV SERIES) ★★★★ This classic anthology series features a broad range of mystery and suspense. First-rate casts add to the fun. During breaks, Alfred Hitchcock himself drolly comments on the action. One of the four episodes on the initial video release, "Lamb to the Slaughter," stars Barbara Bel Geddes in a deliciously ironic tale of murder. Black humor and surprise endings are trademarks of the show. Hitchcock directed the episodes featured on Volume 1. 120m. **DIR:** Alfred Hitchcock. **CAST:** Barbara Bel Geddes, Tom Ewell, John Williams. **1962 DVD**

ALFRED HITCHCOCK'S BON VOYAGE AND AVENTURE MALGACHE ★★★ Alfred Hitchcock made these two intriguing propaganda films for the war effort and, strangely, they were never released to American audiences. *Bon Voyage* follows a downed RAF flyer and a Polish POW as they are passed from hand to hand by the French Resistance. *Aventure Malgache* chronicles the tensions in the French colony of Madagascar after the fall of France. In French with English subtitles. B&W; 57m. **DIR:** Alfred Hitchcock. **CAST:** John Blythe, The Molière Players. **1944 DVD**

ALFREDO ALFREDO ★★ At the height of his popularity in the early 1970s, Dustin Hoffman ventured over to Italy to make this marriage farce for director Pietro Germi (*Divorce—Italian Style*). Hoffman plays a man married to a woman he doesn't love in pursuit of one he does. Complications arise when Alfredo tries to get around Italy's tough divorce laws. Broad at best, this farce doesn't hold up well by today's standards. It's odd to see Hoffman dubbed into Italian by another actor. In Italian with English subtitles. Rated R for adult situations. 97m. **DIR:** Pietro Germi. **CAST:** Dustin Hoffman, Stefania Sandrelli, Carla Gravina. **1972**

•ALI ★★1/2 Boxer Muhammad Ali was once the most famous motormouthed, magnetic, vain, provocative, beloved, and reviled man in sports history. This impressionistic biopic covers his life and career from 1964 to 1974 against a backdrop of American sociopolitical unrest. It feels both lengthy and oddly underdeveloped as Ali becomes involved with the Nation of Islam, is married twice, has affairs, refuses induction into the army, and reclaims his boxing title. Rated R for profanity, violence, and sexual content. 157m. **DIR:** Michael Mann. **CAST:** Will Smith, Jamie Foxx, Jon Voight, Mario Van Peebles, Ron Silver, Jeffrey Wright, Mykelti Williamson, Jada Pinkett Smith, Giancarlo Esposito. **2001 DVD**

ALI BABA AND THE FORTY THIEVES ★★★ Youthful Ali Baba flees from an evil vizier and is protected and raised by forty thieves, the only hope of his downtrodden people. Sit back and enjoy this lighthearted sword-and-turban adventure. Now what are we to do with the forty jars if the thieves are the good guys? 87m. **DIR:** Arthur Lubin. **CAST:** Jon Hall, Maria Montez, Turhan Bey, Andy Devine, Fortunio Bonanova, Crispin Martin, Kurt Katch, Frank Puglia, Scotty Beckett. **1944**

ALI: FEAR EATS THE SOUL ★★★1/2 Outrageous albeit touching story about a love affair between an old German floor washer and an inarticulate young Arab mechanic. Rainer Warner Fassbinder delicately explores this troubled relationship with deeply-felt humanism and cool irony. Winner of the International Critics' Prize at the Cannes Film Festival. In German with English subtitles. Not rated; contains profanity and nudity. 94m. **DIR:** Rainer Werner Fassbinder. **CAST:** Brigitte Mira, El Hedi Ben Salem, Rainer Werner Fassbinder. **1974**

ALICE (1981) 🦃 In this bizarre adaptation of *Alice in Wonderland*, Alice falls for a jogger called Rabbit. Not rated. 80m. **DIR:** Jerzy Gruza, Jacek Bromski. **CAST:** Sophie Barjac, Jean-Pierre Cassel, Susannah York, Paul Nicholas. **1981**

ALICE (1988) ★★★★ Outstanding adaptation of Lewis Carroll's story by Jan Svankmajer, one of the world's leading figures in animation. The film brilliantly captures the surreal world of little Alice with bizarre erotic overtones. Not rated. 85m. **DIR:** Jan Svankmajer. **CAST:** Kristyna Kohoutova. **1988 DVD**

ALICE (1990) ★★★1/2 In this takeoff on *Alice in Wonderland*, Mia Farrow plays a wealthy New Yorker whose inner self is no longer fulfilled by an immense shopping habit. So she turns to a Chinese doctor whose magical herbs bring romance, spirituality, and even invisibility into her life. Rated PG-13 for profanity and sexual frankness. 100m. **DIR:** Woody Allen. **CAST:** Mia Farrow, Alec Baldwin, Blythe Danner, Judy Davis, William Hurt, Julie Kavner, Keye Luke, Joe Mantegna, Bernadette Peters, Cybill Shepherd. **1990 DVD**

ALICE ADAMS ★★★★ Life and love in a typical mid-American small town when there were still such things as concerts in the park and ice-cream socials. Hepburn is a social-climbing girl wistfully seeking love while trying to overcome the stigma of her father's lack of money and ambition. High point of the film is the dinner scene, at once a comic gem and painful insight into character. B&W; 99m. **DIR:** George Stevens. **CAST:** Katharine Hepburn, Fred MacMurray, Evelyn Venable, Fred Stone, Frank Albertson, Hattie McDaniel, Charley Grapewin, Hedda Hopper. **1935**

ALICE & MARTIN ★★★★ Absorbing, thoughtful tale of a young man trying desperately to escape his dark past features Alexis Loret as Martin, who flees the grip of his domineering father for a better life in Paris. Juliette Binoche is luminous as Alice, a violinist content with her life with Martin's half brother. When Martin finally wins over Alice, they are forced to unpack his emotional baggage. Powerful and compelling filmmaking. In French with English subtitles. Rated R for adult situations. 124m. **DIR:** André Téchiné. **CAST:** Juliette Binoche, Alexis Loret, Mathieu Amalric, Carmen Maura. **1998**

ALICE DOESN'T LIVE HERE ANYMORE ★★★★1/2 The feature film that spawned the television series *Alice* is a memorable character study about a woman (Ellen Burstyn, who won an Oscar for her performance) attempting to survive after her husband's death has left her penniless and with a young son to support. Rated PG for profanity and violence. 113m. **DIR:** Martin Scorsese. **CAST:** Ellen Burstyn, Kris Kristofferson, Harvey Keitel, Billy Green Bush, Alfred Lutter, Jodie Foster, Vic Tayback, Diane Ladd. **1975**

ALICE IN THE CITY ★★★ Another road movie from Wim Wenders. While touring the US, a German journalist stumbles upon a precocious 9-year-old girl who has been abandoned by her mother. Excellent eccentric tragicomedy. In German with English subtitles. B&W; 110m. **DIR:** Wim Wenders. **CAST:** Rudiger Vogler, Yella Rottlander, Lisa Kreuzer. **1974**

ALICE IN WONDERLAND (1951) ★★★1/2 The magic of the Walt Disney Studio animators is applied to Lewis Carroll's classic in this feature-length cartoon with mostly entertaining results. As with the book, the film is episodic and lacking the customary Disney warmth. But a few wonderful sequences—like the Mad Hatter's tea party and the appearances of the Cheshire cat—make it worth seeing. Rated G. 75m. **DIR:** Clyde Geronimi, Hamilton Luske, Wilfred Jackson. **1951 DVD**

ALICE IN WONDERLAND (1985) ★★★1/2 Charming live-action TV adaptation of the Lewis Carroll classic. Adults will enjoy some of their favorite stars as zany characters; Steve Allen wrote the witty original songs. Followed by a continuation, 1985's *Alice through the Looking Glass*. 94m. **DIR:** Harry Harris. **CAST:** Natalie Gregory, Sheila Allen, Scott Baio, Red Buttons, Sid Caesar, Imogene Coca, Sammy Davis Jr., Sherman Hemsley, Arte Johnson, Roddy McDowall, Jayne Meadows, Robert Morley, Anthony Newley, Donald O'Connor, Martha Raye, Telly Savalas, Ringo Starr, Shelley Winters. **1985**

ALICE IN WONDERLAND (1999) ★★1/2 The fabulous sets and marvelous critters from Jim Henson's Creature Shop notwithstanding, this is little more than an excuse for its stars to parade about in strange costumes. The focus is very odd, with certain familiar scenes extended, shortened, or changed until they no longer make sense or seem relevant, even in this wacky universe. Absent the insightful political commentary that made Carroll's originals so enchanting to readers of *all* ages, this unsatisfying Peter Barnes adaptation merely lurches from one scene to the next. Rated G. 128m. **DIR:** Nick Willing. **CAST:** Tina Majorino, Robbie Coltrane, Whoopi Goldberg, Ben Kingsley, Christopher Lloyd, Pete Postlethwaite, Miranda Richardson, Martin Short, Peter Ustinov, George Wendt, Gene Wilder. **1999 DVD**

ALICE, SWEET ALICE (COMMUNION, HOLY TERROR) ★★ A 12 year old girl goes on a chopping spree. Brooke Shields only has a small role in this, her first film. But after the success of *Pretty Baby*, the distributor changed the title, gave Brooke top billing, and rereleased this uninteresting thriller. Rated R for violence. 96m. **DIR:** Alfred Sole. **CAST:** Brooke Shields, Tom Signorelli, Paula E. Sheppard, Lillian Roth. **1977 DVD**

ALICE THROUGH THE LOOKING GLASS (1966) ★★★1/2 Another version of Lewis Carroll's immortal classic? Why not? When you've got such a talented cast working with a great story, you've got a winner. In this made-for-TV version, Alice makes an attempt to become the Queen of Wonderland by visiting the Royal Castle. 72m. **DIR:** Alan Handley. **CAST:** Ricardo Montalban, Judy Rolin, Nanette Fabray, Robert Coote, Agnes Moorehead, Jack Palance, Jimmy Durante, Tom Smothers, Dick Smothers, Roy Castle, Richard Denning. **1966**

ALICE THROUGH THE LOOKING GLASS (1985) ★★★1/2 A continuation of 1985's *Alice in Wonderland* with Natalie Gregory returning to the mystical land in search of her missing parents. The chase scenes with the monster Jabberwocky may be too scary for very young viewers. Made for TV. 93m. **DIR:** Harry Harris. **CAST:** Natalie Gregory, Sheila Allen, Steve Allen, Ernest Borgnine, Beau Bridges, Lloyd Bridges, Red Buttons, Carol Channing, Patrick Duffy, George Gobel, Eydie Gorme, Merv Griffin, Ann Jillian, Arte Johnson, Harvey Korman, Steve Lawrence, Karl Malden, Roddy McDowall, Jayne Meadows, Donna Mills, Noriyuki "Pat" Morita, Robert Morley, Anthony Newley, Louis Nye, John Stamos, Sally Struthers, Jack Warden, Jonathan Winters. **1985**

ALICE TO NOWHERE ★★★★ A bungled jewel heist sets in motion this fast-paced adventure. A nurse assigned to a job in central Australia is unknowingly carrying the stolen jewels. The action never lets up as she is pursued by the robbers to the outback. Made for Australian television and shown on independent stations in the United States. 210m. **DIR:** John Power. **CAST:** John Waters, Steve Jacobs, Rosie Jones, Ruth Cracknell. **1986**

ALICE'S ADVENTURES IN WONDERLAND ★★ This British live-action version of Lewis Carroll's classic tale is too long and boring. It is a musical that employs an endless array of silly songs, dances, and riddles. Although it sticks closely to the book, it's not as entertaining as Disney's fast-paced animated version of 1951. Rated G. 97m. **DIR:** William Sterling. **CAST:** Fiona Fullerton, Dudley Moore, Peter Sellers, Ralph Richardson, Spike Milligan. **1973**

ALICE'S RESTAURANT ★★★1/2 This film was based on Arlo Guthrie's hit record of the same name. Some insights into the 1960s counterculture can be found in the story of Guthrie's attempt to stay out of the draft. Some fine acting by a basically unknown cast. Rated PG for language and some nudity. 111m. **DIR:** Arthur Penn. **CAST:** Arlo Guthrie, Pat Quinn, James Broderick, Michael McClanathan, Geoff Outlaw, Tina Chen. **1969 DVD**

ALIEN ★★★★1/2 A superb cinematic combination of science fiction and horror, this is a heart-pounding, visually astounding shocker. The players are all excellent as the crew of a futuristic cargo ship that picks up an unwanted passenger: an alien that lives on human flesh and continually changes form. Rated R. 116m. **DIR:** Ridley Scott. **CAST:** Tom Skerritt, Sigourney Weaver, John Hurt, Ian Holm, Harry Dean Stanton, Yaphet Kotto, Veronica Cartwright. **1979 DVD**

ALIEN 3 ★★★ Ripley (Sigourney Weaver) crash-lands on an all-but-deserted penal colony for madmen and rapists. The acid-spitting, flesh-eating space creature has, unfortunately for them all, hitched a ride with our heroine, and the battle rages once again. More like *Alien* than *Aliens*, this visually stunning atmospheric thriller by first-time filmmaker David Fincher disintegrates into an outer space version of Agatha Christie's *And Then There Were None*. Rated R for profanity and violence. 115m. **DIR:** David Fincher. **CAST:** Sigourney Weaver, Charles Dutton, Charles Dance, Paul McGann, Brian Glover. **1992 DVD**

ALIEN AGENDA, THE (TV SERIES) ★★ Made for the cost of several *Star Wars* models, this ambitious trilogy attempts to tell the epic story of a war between extraterrestrials for control of Earth. Each director follows a different set of people and how they are affected; as can be expected, the results are highly varied. Titles are *Out of the Darkness, Endangered Species,* and *Under the Skin.* Not rated; contains violence, profanity, and gore. 80102. **DIR:** Kevin J. Lindenmuth, Mick McCleery, Tim Ritter, Gabriel Campisi, Ron Ford, Tom Vollman, Michael Legge. **CAST:** Sasha Graham, Debbie Rochon, Joel Wynkoop, Joseph Zaso. **1996–1997**

ALIEN ARSENAL ★★1/2 Producer Charles Band remakes his earlier films *Laserblast* and *Deadly Weapon* with only so-so results in this sci-fi thriller. Two teen misfits discover a cache of weapons in their high-school basement; can the alien owners be far behind? Good production values, but a weak script hurts the film. Rated PG-13 for violence and profanity. 90m. **DIR:** Julian Breen. **CAST:** Josh Hammond, Danielle Hoover. **1999**

ALIEN CHASER ★★ After being trapped on Earth for five thousand years, an alien is awakened from hibernation by archaeologists in search of a powerful artifact in his possession. A promising premise is soon abandoned in favor of endless chases in this made-for-video release. Rated R for strong violence and profanity. 95m. **DIR:** Mark Roper. **CAST:** Frank Zagarino, Todd Jensen, Jennifer MacDonald. **1996 DVD**

ALIEN DEAD Low-grade, alien-loose-on-Earth drivel. Rated R. 87m. **DIR:** Fred Olen Ray. **CAST:** Buster Crabbe, Linda Lewis. **1980**

ALIEN FACTOR, THE ★★★ As an amateur film, this is pretty decent. The cast and production crew are one and the same. There are four aliens on the planet Earth. Only one alien is good, and the Earthlings have a hard time figuring out which one is on their side. Rated PG. 82m. **DIR:** Don Dohler. **CAST:** Don Leifert, Tom Griffith. **1977 DVD**

ALIEN FORCE Alien warrior races to destroy a meteor bearing the souls of a billion monsters in this cheapo clone of *Starman* and *The Hidden*. Not rated; contains sexual situations and violence. 85m. **DIR:** Ron Ford. **CAST:** Tyrone Wade, Roxanne Coyne, Burt Ward. **1997**

ALIEN FROM L.A. ★★1/2 When a nerdy valley girl goes in search of her archaeologist father, she embarks on the adventure of her life. Although this is a low-budget film, it has enough action and humor to be appropriate for most family members. Rated PG for light violence. 88m. **DIR:** Albert Pyun. **CAST:** Kathy Ireland, Linda Kerridge, William R. Moses. **1983**

ALIEN INTRUDER ★★1/2 An alien virus disguises itself as a femme fatale to lure space warriors to their doom. This low-budgeter rips off so many sci-fi hits that it sustains interest. Rated R for violence and profanity. 94m. **DIR:** Ricardo Jacques Gale. **CAST:** Billy Dee Williams, Maxwell Caulfield, Tracy Scoggins, Jeff Conaway. **1992**

ALIEN NATION ★★★ There are some slow moments, but just sit back and enjoy the ride through familiar territory in this cop-buddy movie with a sci-fi slant. James Caan plays a detective in Los Angeles of the future. Mandy Patinkin is the "newcomer," as the aliens are called, who is teamed with Caan to ferret out the perpetrators of a series of mysterious murders among the aliens. Rated R for profanity, violence, and nudity. 96m. **DIR:** Graham Baker. **CAST:** James Caan, Mandy Patinkin, Terence Stamp. **1988 DVD**

ALIEN NATION, DARK HORIZON ★★★1/2 Made-for-TV film that picks up where the canceled series' cliffhanger left off. After five years of assimilation into Los Angeles life, the Tenctonese aliens are targeted for extermination by humans. To add to their woes, the slavers from whom they escaped want them back. Compelling viewing with a parallel message about tolerance. Not rated; contains violence. 93m. **DIR:** Kenneth Johnson. **CAST:** Michele Scarabelli, Terri Treas, Scott Patterson, Jeff Marcus, Gary Graham, Eric Pierpoint. **1994**

ALIEN P.I. ★★ A new twist to the old private eye theme. This time the private investigator is from the planet Styx. He's just vacationing on our planet when he stumbles onto an intergalactic crime involving an ancient Egyptian disc. Rated R for violence and nudity. 90m. **DIR:** Viktor. **CAST:** Nikki Fastinetti, John Alexander. **1987**

ALIEN PREDATORS Three young American adventurers stumble into an alien invasion. Rated R for violence and gore. 92m. **DIR:** Deran Sarafian. **CAST:** Dennis Christopher, Martin Hewitt, Lynn-Holly Johnson. **1986**

ALIEN PREY This savage alien is on a protein mission. This film contains sexual and cannibalistic scenes, making it unsuitable for the squeamish. 85m. **DIR:** Norman J. Warren. **CAST:** Barry Stokes, Sally Faulkner. **1984**

ALIEN RESURRECTION ★★★★ Following the disappointment delivered by *Alien 3*, it seemed likely we'd never see another adventure of the two-fisted alien fighter, Ripley (Sigourney Weaver), who, of course, died at the end of the initial trilogy. But she's back—through the miracle of cloning—some two hundred years later, dealing once again with the stupidity of corporate greed and the mother of all man-eaters. It's an edge-of-your-seat sci-fi knockout. Rated R for violence, profanity, and nudity. 108m. **DIR:** Jean-Pierre Jeunet. **CAST:** Sigourney Weaver, Winona Ryder, Ron Pearlman, Dominique Pinon, Michael Wincott, Dan Hedaya, J. E. Freeman, Brad Dourif, Raymond Cruz, Kim Flowers. **1997 DVD**

ALIEN SPACE AVENGER Low-budget reworking of *The Hidden*, detailing the plight of four alien convicts being stalked by an alien bounty hunter through the streets of New York. In true sci-fi fashion, they get around by hiding inside poor New Yorkers. All this time we thought they were just rude. Not rated; contains violence. 88m. **DIR:** Richard W. Haines. **CAST:** Robert Prichard. **1991**

ALIEN TERMINATOR ★★ Giant, mutant rat goes on a killing rampage in this cheesy effort. Five miles underground, scientists messing with DNA create a killer rat that likes the taste of flesh and stupid scientists who dabble with DNA. Fun on a campy level, with all the prerequisite shock effects and bare ladies. Rated R for nudity, violence, and adult language. 95m. **DIR:** David Payne. **CAST:** Maria Ford, Roger Halston, Emile Levisetti, Cassandra Leigh. **1995**

•**ALIEN VISITOR** ★★ A naked alien woman (in human form) appears to a man in the Australian outback and proceeds to educate him as to what humans are doing wrong with the world. This nobly intentioned eco-friendly movie quickly gets bogged down by its own rhetoric and agonizingly slow pace. Rated PG-13 for brief graphic nudity. 92m. **DIR:** Rolf De Heer. **CAST:** Ullie Birve, Syd Brisbane. **1995 DVD**

ALIEN WARRIOR In this unwatchable film, a father on another planet sends his son to Earth to confront the ultimate evil—a pimp. Rated R for nudity, violence, and profanity. 100m. **DIR:** Edward Hunt. **CAST:** Brett Clark, Pamela Saunders. **1985**

ALIEN WITHIN, THE Relentlessly stupid, bargain-basement retread of *Alien* from producer Roger Corman, with vapid characters who barely become interesting when they are taken over by the tentacled beastie. Rated R for violence, drug use, and nudity. 79m. **DIR:** Scott Levy. **CAST:** Roddy McDowall, Alex Hyde-White, Melanie Shatner, Don Stroud. **1995**

ALIENATOR Lame *Terminator* clone. Rated R for violence. 93m. **DIR:** Fred Olen Ray. **CAST:** Jan-Michael Vincent, John Phillip Law, P. J. Soles. **1989**

ALIENS ★★★★1/2 Fifty-seven years have passed during Warrant Officer Ripley's (Sigourney Weaver) deep-space sleep; when she wakes, the planet LV-426—where the crew of the ill-fated *Nostromo* first encountered the nasty extraterrestrial—has been colonized. Then, to everybody's surprise except Ripley's, contact is lost with the colonists. Equal to, although different from, the original. Rated R for considerable violence and profanity. 137m. **DIR:** James Cameron. **CAST:** Sigourney Weaver, Carrie Henn, Michael Biehn, Paul Reiser, Lance Henriksen, Jenette Goldstein. **1986 DVD**

ALIENS AMONG US Much ado about nothing as the family from *Welcome to Planet Earth* takes on the duties of sheriff of a western town. Low-budget mush. Also released as *Alien Avengers II*. Rated R for adult situations, language, nudity, and violence. 89m. **DIR:** David Payne. **CAST:** George Wendt, Julie Brown, Anastasia Sakelaris, Christopher M. Brown. **1997**

ALISON'S BIRTHDAY ★★1/2 A slow but interesting Australian horror story. A young girl is told by her father's ghost to leave home before her nineteenth birthday, but as you may guess, she's summoned back days before the big day, and things get nasty. 99m. **DIR:** Ian Coughlan. **CAST:** Joanne Samuel, Lou Brown. **1984**

ALIVE ★★★1/2 This gripping adaptation of Piers Paul Read's bestseller benefits from Frank Marshall's crackling direction and a reasonably unflinching script from John Patrick Shanley (*Moonstruck*). After a horrifyingly realistic plane crash in the Andes, the surviving members of a South American rugby team eventually steel themselves to the requirements of staying alive. Rated R for language. 123m. **DIR:** Frank Marshall. **CAST:** Ethan Hawke, Vincent Spano, Josh Hamilton, Bruce Ramsay. **1993**

ALIVE & KICKING ★★★ Engaging tale of a dancer and a therapist who find true love despite the odds. Jason Flemyng and Antony Sher are wonderful as the couple who try to make their relationship work in the new swinging London. Screenwriter Martin Sherman explores a gay relationship without resorting to the usual clichés, while director Nancy Meckler does a splendid job of making all this matter with a tender, human touch. Rated R for adult situations. 100m. **DIR:** Nancy Meckler. **CAST:** Jason Flemyng, Antony Sher, Dorothy Tutin, Anthony Higgins. **1996 DVD**

ALL ABOUT EVE ★★★★★ The behind-the-scenes world of the New York theater is the subject of this classic. The picture won several Academy Awards, including best picture, but it is Bette Davis as Margo Channing whom most remember. The dialogue sparkles, and the performances are of high caliber. B&W; 138m. **DIR:** Joseph L. Mankiewicz. **CAST:** Bette Davis, Anne Baxter, Marilyn Monroe, George Sanders, Celeste Holm, Gary Merrill. **1950 DVD**

ALL ABOUT MY MOTHER ★★1/2 A Madrid nurse travels to Barcelona in search of her dead son's father and becomes part of an extended family that includes a pregnant nun, a transsexual whore, a transvestite, and lesbian actresses. This brightly colored, self-conscious, campy tale of sisterhood, motherhood, and stormy relationships is patterned after, and references, Hollywood's melodramas of yesteryear. Rated R for profanity, nudity, sex, and drug use. 105m. **DIR:** Pedro Almodóvar. **CAST:** Celia Roth, Eloy Azorín, Marisa Paredes, Penelope Cruz, Candela Peña, Antonia San Juan, Rosa Maria Sardà, Toni Cantó. **1999 DVD**

•**ALL ABOUT THE BENJAMINS** ★★ Miami bounty hunter Ice Cube and small-time hood Mike Epps become odd-couple partners in a search for stolen diamonds and Epps's missing lottery ticket. The amusing banter of the two leads is scant compensation for the mess of the movie as a whole—clumsy plotting, poor pacing, sloppy editing. Rated R for profanity and violence. 94m. **DIR:** Kevin Bray. **CAST:** Ice Cube, Mike

Epps, Tommy Flanagan, Eva Mendes, Valarie Rae Miller, Carmen Chaplin. **2002**

ALL-AMERICAN MURDER ★★★ This murder mystery holds a lot of surprises. Charlie Schlatter is an ex-con who is implicated in the death of a beautiful coed. Christopher Walken is the cop who has a hunch and lets him off to prove his innocence. Unfortunately for Schlatter, dead bodies keep turning up wherever he goes. Rated R for violence, profanity, and nudity. 94m. **DIR:** Anson Williams. **CAST:** Christopher Walken, Charlie Schlatter, Josie Bissett, Amy Davis, Richard Kind, Joanna Cassidy. **1991**

ALL CREATURES GREAT AND SMALL ★★★1/2 This feature-length film picks up where the popular British television series left off, with veterinarian James Herriot (Christopher Timothy) returning to his home and practice after having served in World War II. Although he has been away for years, things quickly settle into a comfortable routine. The animal stories are lifted from Dr. Herriot's poignant, bittersweet books, with a few moments likely to require a hanky or two. 94m. **DIR:** Terence Dudley. **CAST:** Christopher Timothy, Robert Hardy, Peter Davison. **1986 DVD**

ALL DOGS GO TO HEAVEN ★★1/2 Somewhat disappointing feature-length cartoon from Disney defector Don Bluth. The convoluted story, about a con-artist dog who gets a glimpse of the afterlife, is more crude than charming. Burt Reynolds, Dom DeLuise, Loni Anderson, and Vic Tayback are among those who supply the voices. Rated G. 80m. **DIR:** Don Bluth. **1989 DVD**

ALL DOGS GO TO HEAVEN 2 ★★ This dreary, animated musical begins in heaven where a nasty bulldog plans to steal Gabriel's horn, which allows entry through heaven's pearly gates. When the horn falls to Earth, hero hound Charlie, who is tired of heaven's sedate environment, and his reluctant pal Itchy, return to Earth to prevent the evil Red from turning Alcatraz into a dank, eternal dog pound. Featuring the voices of Charlie Sheen, Ernest Borgnine, Sheena Easton, and Dom DeLuise. Rated G. 75m. **DIR:** Paul Sabella, Larry Leker. **1996 DVD**

ALL FALL DOWN ★★1/2 Sporadically powerful William Inge soap opera about the love affair of a young man (Warren Beatty) and an older woman (Eva Marie Saint), with a subplot about the man's adoring younger brother (Brandon de Wilde). Slightly overlong and handicapped by the puritanical Hollywood production code of the time. B&W; 110m. **DIR:** John Frankenheimer. **CAST:** Warren Beatty, Eva Marie Saint, Karl Malden, Angela Lansbury, Brandon de Wilde. **1962**

ALL GOD'S CHILDREN ★★ Forced busing to achieve educational integration is the crux of this story of two families, one white and one black. The cast is excellent, but a wandering script makes comprehension difficult. Rated PG for violence. 107m. **DIR:** Jerry Thorpe. **CAST:** Richard Widmark, Ned Beatty, Ossie Davis, Ruby Dee. **1980**

ALL I DESIRE ★★1/2 Serious sudser in which aging vaudevillian Barbara Stanwyck returns to her small-town roots and the family she abandoned. Stanwyck is the bright spot in this morality lesson as a tough cookie tired of being so worldly. Not rated. B&W; 80m. **DIR:** Douglas Sirk. **CAST:** Barbara Stanwyck, Richard Carlson, Lyle Bettger, Maureen O'Sullivan, Marcia Henderson, Lori Nelson. **1953**

ALL I WANT FOR CHRISTMAS ★★★ All 7 year old Thora Birch wants for Christmas is to see her divorced mother and father get back together, so she enlists the aid of a department-store Santa. It's a charming little movie, but be forewarned: children of divorced parents could get the wrong idea and be quite disturbed by the story. Rated G. 89m. **DIR:** Robert Lieberman. **CAST:** Harley Jane Kozak, Jamey Sheridan, Lauren Bacall, Leslie Nielsen, Kevin Nealon, Thora Birch. **1991**

ALL IN A NIGHT'S WORK ★★★ The heir to a publishing empire falls in love with a girl he believes has, at one time, been the mistress of his own uncle. This comedy starts well but lags before the finale. Harmless fun. 94m. **DIR:** Joseph Anthony. **CAST:** Shirley MacLaine, Dean Martin, Charlie Ruggles, Cliff Robertson, Gale Gordon, Jack Weston. **1961**

ALL MINE TO GIVE ★★★ Reaching for the heartstrings, this melodrama follows the lives of a Scottish family in 1850s Wisconsin. The backwoods life is brutal and by the film's midpoint both the mother and father have died and left the oldest child the task of parceling out his little brothers and sisters to the far-flung neighbors. A fairly decent weeper. 102m. **DIR:** Allen Reisner. **CAST:** Glynis Johns, Cameron Mitchell, Patty McCormack, Hope Emerson. **1957**

ALL MY SONS (1948) ★★★ A man recently returned from combat discovers that his father profited by selling the government inferior material that may have cost lives. Edward G. Robinson as the all-too-human monster lacking a sense of responsibility for his actions is fine, but Arthur Miller's powerful play comes across as heavy-handed and preachy on film. B&W; 94m. **DIR:** Irving Reis. **CAST:** Edward G. Robinson, Burt Lancaster, Mady Christians, Howard Duff, Lloyd Gough, Arlene Francis, Harry Morgan. **1948**

ALL MY SONS (1986) ★★★1/2 An excellent adaptation of the Arthur Miller play. A family must deal with the death of one son in World War II and the father's profit made by selling plane parts during the war. James Whitmore is the guilt-ridden father, Michael Learned his distraught wife. Made for TV. 122m. **DIR:** Jack O'Brien. **CAST:** James Whitmore, Aidan Quinn, Michael Learned, Joan Allen. **1986**

ALL NIGHT LONG ★★★ Praised by some for its offbeat style and story, this comedy, starring the odd couple of Gene Hackman and Barbra Streisand, is only occasionally convincing. Hackman stars as an executive demoted to the position of managing a twenty-four-hour grocery store. There, he meets a daffy housewife (played by a miscast Streisand) and love blooms. 95m. **DIR:** Jean-Claude Tramont. **CAST:** Gene Hackman, Barbra Streisand. **1981**

ALL OF ME ★★★★1/2 Steve Martin finds himself haunted from within by the soul of a recently deceased Lily Tomlin when an attempt to put her spirit in another woman's body backfires. This delightful comedy gives its two stars the best showcase for their talents to date. Rated PG for suggested sex, violence, and profanity. 93m. **DIR:** Carl Reiner. **CAST:** Steve Martin, Lily Tomlin, Victoria Tennant, Richard Libertini. **1984 DVD**

ALL OVER ME ★★★1/2 Urban Manhattan makes a suitably gritty backdrop for this story of two teenage girls whose lifelong friendship may be on the verge of coming apart as their lives change. While Ellen (Tara Subkoff) starts dating a drug dealer, Claude (Alison Folland) reacts to her absence with more warmth than either of them expected. Low-budget film wears its independent attitude on its sleeve, but has some affecting moments along with its heavy-duty attitude. Rated R for sexuality, drug use, and profanity. 90m. **DIR:** Alex Sichel. **CAST:** Alison Folland, Tara Subkoff, Cole Hauser, Wilson Cruz, Leisha Hailey. **1996**

•ALL OVER THE GUY ★★1/2 The on-again-off-again romance of two gay men is rendered uninteresting by the fact that both of them are unpleasant company—one a selfish jerk, the other a whining bore. Adam Goldberg and Sasha Alexander, as a secondary couple, are much more interesting, but they keep getting shoved aside in favor of their annoying neighbors. Rated R for profanity and mature themes. 92m. **DIR:** Julie Davis. **CAST:** Dan Bucatinsky, Richard Ruccolo, Adam Goldberg, Sasha Alexander, Doris Roberts, Christina Ricci, Lisa Kudrow. **2001 DVD**

ALL OVER TOWN ★★1/2 Stage favorites of the 1920s and 1930s, Olsen and Johnson display their zany patter and antics as they try to produce a show in a theater on which a hex has been put. Some funny moments, but most of this low-budget comedy is antiquated. B&W; 62m. **DIR:** James W. Horne. **CAST:** Chic Johnson, Ole Olsen, Franklin Pangborn, Mary Howard, James Finlayson. **1937**

ALL QUIET ON THE WESTERN FRONT (1930) ★★★★★ Despite some dated moments and an "old movie" look, this film still stands as a powerful statement against war and man's inhumanity to man. Lew Ayres and Louis Wolheim star in this story, set during World War I, which follows several young men into battle, examining their disillusionment and eventual deaths. B&W; 130m. **DIR:** Lewis Milestone. **CAST:** Lew Ayres, Louis Wolheim. **1930 DVD**

ALL QUIET ON THE WESTERN FRONT (1979) ★★★1/2 This is a television remake of the 1930 film, which was taken from Erich Maria Remarque's classic antiwar novel. It attempts to recall all the horrors of World War I, but even the great detail issued to this film can't hide its TV mentality and melodramatic characters. Despite this major flaw, the film is watchable for its rich look and compelling story. 126m. **DIR:** Delbert Mann. **CAST:** Richard Thomas, Ernest Borgnine, Donald Pleasence, Ian Holm, Patricia Neal, Keith Carradine. **1979 DVD**

ALL SCREWED UP ★★★1/2 Minor but entertaining Lina Wertmuller comedy-drama about farmers confronted with the noise and chaos of life in the big city. Lacks subtlety. Rated PG. Dubbed in English. 105m. **DIR:** Lina Wertmuller. **CAST:** Luigi Diberti, Nino Bignamini. **1976**

ALL THAT HEAVEN ALLOWS ★★★1/2 Douglas Sirk was Hollywood's master of the classy soap opera, and this is one of his best. Jane Wyman plays a suburban widow who is scorned by her neighbors when she is courted by a young gardener (Rock Hudson). 89m. **DIR:** Douglas Sirk. **CAST:** Jane Wyman, Rock Hudson, Agnes Moorehead, Conrad Nagel. **1955 DVD**

ALL THAT JAZZ ★★★★ While it may not be what viewers expect from a musical, this story of a gifted choreographer, Joe Gideon (Roy Scheider, in his finest performance), who relentlessly drives himself to exhaustion is daring, imaginative, shocking, and visually stunning. Rated R. 123m. **DIR:** Bob Fosse. **CAST:** Roy Scheider, Ann Reinking, Jessica Lange. **1979**

ALL THE BROTHERS WERE VALIANT ★★★ Whaling captain Robert Taylor proves his brother (Stewart Granger) innocent of desertion but is betrayed by the latter in a quest for pearls. Some good action scenes. The last movie for the gifted Lewis Stone. 96m. **DIR:** Richard Thorpe. **CAST:** Robert Taylor, Stewart Granger, Ann Blyth, Betta St. John, Keenan Wynn, James Whitmore, Kurt Kasznar, Lewis Stone. **1953**

ALL THE KIND STRANGERS ★★ This made-for-TV thriller lacks overt terror. A family of orphans lures kind strangers to their isolated home and then forces them to act as their parents. If the strangers don't measure up, they're murdered. Interesting in an eerie way. 74m. **DIR:** Burt Kennedy. **CAST:** Stacy Keach, Samantha Eggar, John Savage, Robby Benson, Arlene Farber. **1974**

ALL THE KING'S MEN ★★★★ Broderick Crawford and Mercedes McCambridge won Academy Awards for their work in this adaptation of Robert Penn Warren's Pulitzer Prize–winning novel about a corrupt politician's ascension to power. The film retains its relevance and potency. B&W; 109m. **DIR:** Robert Rossen. **CAST:** Broderick Crawford, Joanne Dru, John Ireland, Mercedes McCambridge, John Derek. **1949 DVD**

ALL THE MARBLES 🦃 Peter Falk stars as the unscrupulous manager of two female wrestlers. Rated R because of nudity, violence, and profanity. 113m. **DIR:** Robert Aldrich. **CAST:** Peter Falk, Vicki Frederick, Laurene Landon, Burt Young, Tracy Reed. **1981**

ALL THE PRESIDENT'S MEN ★★★★★ Robert Redford, who also produced, and Dustin Hoffman star in this gripping reenactment of the exposure of the Watergate conspiracy by reporters Bob Woodward and Carl Bernstein. What's so remarkable about this docudrama is, although we know how it eventually comes out, we're on the edge of our seats from beginning to end. That's inspired moviemaking. Rated PG. 136m. **DIR:** Alan J. Pakula. **CAST:** Dustin Hoffman, Robert Redford, Jason Robards Jr., Jane Alexander, Jack Warden, Martin Balsam. **1976 DVD**

ALL THE PRETTY HORSES ★★★1/2 This visually intoxicating rite of passage blends gnawing tension with languid pacing. Two young cowboys in 1949 Texas venture south of the border in search of work. Their relationships with a young misfit and a land baron and his daughter precipitate a harsh encounter with Mexican law enforcement. Several gaps in the story mar this otherwise intriguing tale of loyalty, love, purity of spirit, and death. Rated PG-13 for sexual content and violence. 112m. **DIR:** Billy Bob Thornton. **CAST:** Matt Damon, Henry Thomas, Lucas Black, Penelope Cruz, Rubén Blades. **2000 DVD**

ALL THE RIGHT MOVES ★★★1/2 Tom Cruise stars in this entertaining coming-of-age picture as a blue-collar high school senior trying to get out of a Pennsylvania mill town by way of a football scholarship. Rated R for profanity, sex, and nudity. 91m. **DIR:** Michael Chapman. **CAST:** Tom Cruise, Craig T. Nelson, Christopher Penn, Lea Thompson. **1983 DVD**

ALL THE VERMEERS IN NEW YORK ★★1/2 A stockbroker and a young Frenchwoman who meet at an art gallery in front of a Vermeer painting seem to be headed for a relationship. Whether they get there is a subject for speculation. Not rated; contains mild sexual situations. 86m. **DIR:** Jon Jost. **CAST:** Emmanuelle Chaulet, Katherine Bean, Grace Phillips. **1990 DVD**

ALL THESE WOMEN ★★ A comedy by Ingmar Bergman that is a not-so-subtle attack upon the legions of biographers who were pursuing him. The story is about a deceased cellist, Felix, who (we learn in a series of flashbacks) had been hounded by an erstwhile biographer. Bergman's first exercise in color, the movie suffers from a contrived, episodic structure. In Swedish with English subtitles. 80m. **DIR:** Ingmar Bergman. **CAST:** Bibi Andersson. **1964**

ALL THIS AND HEAVEN TOO ★★★★ Based on a true murder case, this film, set in Paris in 1840, casts Bette Davis as the governess who wins Charles Boyer's heart. Barbara O'Neil is the uncaring mother and obsessed wife who becomes jealous. When she is found murdered, Davis and Boyer become prime suspects. A classic. B&W; 121m. **DIR:** Anatole Litvak. **CAST:** Bette Davis, Charles Boyer, Jeffrey Lynn, Barbara O'Neil, Virginia Weidler, Henry Daniell, Ann Todd, June Lockhart, Harry Davenport. **1940**

ALL THROUGH THE NIGHT ★★★1/2 Humphrey Bogart and his gang take on Nazi spies in this star-studded romp. The plot is typical World War II flag-waving. But the dialogue and the cast—oh, my! This one's worth a look if only to see Jackie Gleason and Phil Silvers clowning it up a full decade before they'd become icons of the small screen. B&W; 107m. **DIR:** Vincent Sherman. **CAST:** Humphrey Bogart, Conrad Veidt, Kaaren Verne, Jane Darwell, Frank McHugh, Peter Lorre, Judith Anderson, William Demarest, Jackie Gleason, Phil Silvers, Wallace Ford, Barton MacLane, Edward Brophy, Martin Kosleck. **1942**

ALL TIED UP ★★ Zach Galligan promises to give up his wild bachelor days for Teri Hatcher, but her roommates don't believe him. When he wavers, they kidnap him to teach him a lesson. Bondage has never been so mundane. Rated R for language and adult situations. 90m. **DIR:** John Mark Robinson. **CAST:** Zach Galligan, Teri Hatcher, Lara Harris, Tracy Griffith, Abel Folk. **1992**

ALLAN QUARTERMAIN AND THE LOST CITY OF GOLD 🦃 As if they weren't bad enough in the original, Richard Chamberlain and Sharon Stone reprise their roles from the tongue-in-beak turkey, *King Solomon's Mines*. Rated PG. 95m. **DIR:** Gary Nelson. **CAST:** Richard Chamberlain, Sharon Stone, James Earl Jones, Henry Silva, Robert Donner, Cassandra Peterson. **1987**

ALLEGHENY UPRISING ★★★ John Wayne and Claire Trevor were reteamed the same year of their costarring triumph in 1939's *Stagecoach* for this potboiler set in the pre-Revolutionary American colonies, but the results were hardly as auspicious. Still, it's a decent time passer and features Brian Donlevy in one of his better villain roles. B&W; 81m. **DIR:** William A. Seiter. **CAST:** John Wayne, Claire Trevor, George Sanders, Chill Wills, Brian Donlevy. **1939**

ALLEGRO NON TROPPO ★★★★ An animated spoof of Disney's *Fantasia* by Italian filmmaker Bruno Bozzetto, this release entertainingly weds stylish slapstick with the music of Debussy, Ravel, Vivaldi, Stravinsky, Dvorak, and Sibelius. Rated PG. 75m. **DIR:** Bruno Bozzetto. **1976**

ALLEY CATS, THE ★★★ Director Radley Metzger set the screen on fire in the mid-1960s with this daring tale of a European socialite who becomes bored with her husband and decides to take a lover. Her quest eventually leads her to another woman, who unlocks her lesbian desires. Racy stuff for the period. Not rated; contains adult situations and nudity. B&W; 83m. **DIR:** Radley Metzger. **CAST:** Anna Arthur, Sabrina Koch, Karin Field, Chaz Holman. **1965 DVD**

ALLIGATOR ★★★1/2 The wild imagination of screenwriter John Sayles invests this comedy-horror film with wit and style. It features Robert Forster as a cop tracking down a giant alligator. It's good, unpretentious fun, but you have to be on your toes to catch all the gags (be sure to read the hilarious graffiti). Rated R. 94m. **DIR:** Lewis Teague. **CAST:** Robert Forster, Michael Gazzo, Robin Riker, Perry Lang, Jack Carter, Bart Braverman, Henry Silva, Dean Jagger. **1980**

ALLIGATOR PEOPLE, THE ★★ At his laboratory in a Florida swamp, a scientist experiments with using alligator tissue to regenerate human flesh. Standard 1950s science fiction, obviously inspired (to put it kindly) by *The Fly.* B&W; 74m. **DIR:** Roy Del Ruth. **CAST:** Beverly Garland, George Macready, Lon Chaney Jr., Richard Crane, Bruce Bennett. **1959**

ALLIGATOR SHOES ★★ This is pretty much a home movie by two brothers, Gary and Clay Borris. Although their characters here are grownup, they still live at home. When their mentally disturbed aunt moves in, trouble arises. This drama becomes strained before its fatal conclusion. Not rated. 98m. **DIR:** Clay Borris. **CAST:** Gary Borris, Clay Borris, Ronalda Jones, Rose Mallais-Borris. **1982**

ALLIGATOR II ★★1/2 An evil land developer prevents cops from stopping the groundbreaking ceremonies of his lakefront project, despite the fact that a mutant alligator is making lunch of anyone near the lake. Doesn't have the bite of the original John Sayles script, but manages to dig its teeth into you nonetheless. Rated PG-13. 94m. **DIR:** Brandon Clark. **CAST:** Joseph Bologna, Dee Wallace, Richard Lynch, Steve Railsback. **1990**

ALLNIGHTER, THE 🦃 Terminally dumb 1980s beach movie. Rated PG-13. 90m. **DIR:** Tamar Simon Hoffs. **CAST:** Susanna Hoffs, John Terlesky, Joan Cusack, Dedee Pfeiffer, James Anthony Shanta, Janelle Brady. **1987 DVD**

ALLONSONFAN ★★★ Marcello Mastroianni stars as a disillusioned nineteenth-century Italian nobleman in this handsomely filmed but impenetrable political drama. Imprisoned for revolutionary activities, he is released and cooperates in a plot to capture the leader of his group. In Italian with English subtitles. 100m. **DIR:** Paolo Taviani, Vittorio Taviani. **CAST:** Marcello Mastroianni, Lea Massari, Mimsy Farmer. **1974**

ALL'S FAIR ★★ Male corporate executives battle their wives and female coworkers in a weekend war game. Good cast and a promising premise are both wasted in a lot of second-rate slapstick. Rated PG-13 for double entendre humor. 89m. **DIR:** Rocky Lane. **CAST:** George

Segal, Sally Kellerman, Robert Carradine, Jennifer Edwards, Jane Kaczmarek, Lou Ferrigno. **1989**

ALMOS' A MAN ★★1/2 You'll have trouble finding firm moral ground in this adaptation of Richard Wright's short story about a boy (LeVar Burton) impatient to achieve adulthood. The conclusion leaves an unpleasant taste. Introduced by Henry Fonda; unrated and suitable for family viewing. 51m. **DIR:** Stan Lathan. **CAST:** LeVar Burton, Madge Sinclair, Robert DoQui, Christopher Brooks, Garry Goodrow. **1976**

. . . ALMOST ★★★ This Australian comedy is almost—but not quite—hilarious. Uneven timing takes the punch out of many of the sight gags as Rosanna Arquette re-creates her bored wife ready-for-adventure role from *Desperately Seeking Susan*. Rated PG. 87m. **DIR:** Michael Pattinson. **CAST:** Rosanna Arquette, Bruce Spence. **1990**

ALMOST AN ANGEL ★★1/2 Paul Hogan gets his first non–"Crocodile" Dundee role as a professional thief in Los Angeles who becomes a probational angel in heaven. The film falls from there, as Hogan's comedy turns decidedly downbeat. Rated PG for mild profanity. 96m. **DIR:** John Cornell. **CAST:** Paul Hogan, Elias Koteas, Linda Kozlowski. **1990**

ALMOST ANGELS ★★1/2 Schmaltzy film focusing on the Vienna Boys' Choir and the problems one boy encounters when his voice changes and he can no longer sing in the choir. Rated G. 93m. **DIR:** Steve Previn. **CAST:** Peter Weck, Hans Holt, Fritz Eckhardt, Bruni Lobel, Sean Scully. **1962**

ALMOST BLUE ★★1/2 Jazz saxophonist Michael Madsen is overwhelmed with grief after his wife dies. He attempts to soothe his troubled soul by immersing himself in his music and new girlfriend Lynette Walden, but they only remind him of his loss. Moody and atmospheric, the film is rather downbeat, but that's the blues. Rated R for language and adult situations. 98m. **DIR:** Keoni Waxman. **CAST:** Michael Madsen, Lynette Walden. **1992**

ALMOST FAMOUS ★★★★★ Writer-director Cameron Crowe's autobiographical account of his early years as a reporter for *Rolling Stone* magazine is a masterpiece. Details are perfect in this film about a precocious teenager whose love of rock music propels him into the world of his idols and the inevitable collision of fantasy with reality. While there are no big-bang special effects or car chases, you'll want to watch this one again. Terrific cast, great soundtrack. Rated R for profanity, drug use, and suggested sex. 122m. **DIR:** Cameron Crowe. **CAST:** Billy Crudup, Frances McDormand, Kate Hudson, Jason Lee, Patrick Fugit, Zooey Deschanel, Michael Angarano, Noah Taylor, John Fedevich, Mark Kozelek, Fairuza Balk, Anna Paquin. **2000 DVD**

ALMOST HEROES 🦃 Alcoholic frontier guide is hired in 1804 by a prissy aristocrat to chart a path to the Pacific Ocean before Lewis and Clark can complete the same task in this loud, crude spoof. Rated PG-13 for language, partial nudity, and violence. 87m. **DIR:** Christopher Guest. **CAST:** Chris Farley, Matthew Perry, Eugene Levy, Kevin Dunn. **1998**

ALMOST PERFECT AFFAIR, AN ★★★1/2 A very human love triangle evolves amidst the frenzy of film politics that surrounds the Cannes Film Festival. This romantic comedy about a young American filmmaker and the worldly but lovable wife of a powerful Italian film mogul is slow to start, but leaves you with a warm feeling. Rated PG with suggested sex and partial nudity. 92m. **DIR:** Michael Ritchie. **CAST:** Keith Carradine, Monica Vitti, Raf Vallone. **1979**

ALMOST PREGNANT ★★1/2 Bedroom farce features Tanya Roberts as Jeff Conaway's desperate-to-be-pregnant wife. She recruits both a neighbor and an in-law as donors while her husband finds his own diversions. In both an R and an unrated version, each containing nudity and profanity. 93m. **DIR:** Michael DeLuise. **CAST:** Tanya Roberts, Jeff Conaway, Joan Severance, Dom DeLuise. **1991**

ALMOST YOU ★★★★ Brooke Adams and Griffin Dunne give excellent performances as a restless husband and his down-to-earth wife. Dunne perfectly emulates the frustrated over-30 businessman and husband with comic results. Adams plays his wife, who is recovering from a car accident that gives her a new perspective on life. Rated R for language, sex, and nudity. 91m. **DIR:** Adam Brooks. **CAST:** Brooke Adams, Griffin Dunne, Karen Young, Marty Watt. **1985**

ALOHA, BOBBY AND ROSE ★★ B-movie treatment of two kids on the lam for a murder they didn't mean to commit. Paul LeMat's first starring role after *American Graffiti*. He is interesting, but the film is downbeat and uninspired. Rated R. 88m. **DIR:** Floyd Mutrux. **CAST:** Paul LeMat, Dianne Hull, Tim McIntire. **1975 DVD**

ALOHA SUMMER ★★★1/2 Chris Makepeace stars as a middle-class, Italian-American teenager who goes to the Hawaiian islands with his family in 1959. Once there, he learns important lessons about life and love. Instead of being just another empty-headed teen exploitation flick, *Aloha Summer* is blessed with sensitivity and insight. Rated PG for violence. 97m. **DIR:** Tommy Lee Wallace. **CAST:** Chris Makepeace, Don Michael Paul, Tia Carrere. **1988**

ALONE IN THE DARK 🦃 The inmates of a New Jersey mental institution break out to terrorize a doctor and his family. Rated R. 92m. **DIR:** Jack Sholder. **CAST:** Jack Palance, Donald Pleasence, Martin Landau, Dwight Schultz, Deborah Hedwall, Erland Van Lidth. **1982**

ALONE IN THE NEON JUNGLE ★★★★ Suzanne Pleshette is top-notch in this superior made-for-TV crime-drama about a woman police captain, heading up the tough Los Angeles Southeast Precinct, called "the sewer." Excellent writing pits Pleshette and her force against drugs and gangs, and a cop killer still on the loose. 90m. **DIR:** Georg Stanford Brown. **CAST:** Suzanne Pleshette, Danny Aiello, Joe Morton. **1991**

ALONE IN THE WOODS ★★1/2 Preteens will best appreciate this action-comedy about a wayward 10 year old who accidentally wanders into the wrong van during a pit stop. It isn't until later that young Justin realizes he's in the company of two bumbling crooks who have kidnapped a toy magnate's young daughter. Now it's up to Justin to save the day. Rated PG for violence. 81m. **DIR:** John Putch. **CAST:** Laraine Newman, Chick Vennera, Matthias Hues, Daniel McVicar, Brady Bluhm. **1997**

ALONG CAME A SPIDER ★★ Forensic psychologist Alex Cross (Morgan Freeman, who played the same role in 1997's *Kiss the Girls*) investigates the kidnapping of a senator's daughter. The story is ridiculous, with a detective hero who figures things out like magic and plot twists that are surprising only because they don't make sense. Although directed with dogged ferocity, this film's only asset is Freeman's solemn dignity. Rated R for violence and profanity. 105m. **DIR:** Lee Tamahori. **CAST:** Morgan Freeman, Monica Potter, Michael Wincott, Penelope Ann Miller, Michael Moriarty. **2001 DVD**

ALONG CAME JONES ★★★★ Highly watchable comic Western with Gary Cooper as an innocent cowboy who's mistaken for an infamous outlaw. Both lawmen and the real outlaw (Dan Duryea) pursue him. B&W; 90m. **DIR:** Stuart Heisler. **CAST:** Gary Cooper, Loretta Young, Dan Duryea. **1945 DVD**

•ALONG FOR THE RIDE ★★★ Star power fuels this winsome comedy about television writer Ben Clifton (Patrick Swayze) who learns from his old college girlfriend (Melanie Griffith) that he is the father of a 16-year-old son. Clifton accompanies Lulu on a road trip to meet their son, much to the displeasure of Clifton's psychiatrist wife Claire (Penelope Ann Miller). Decent production values, a willing cast, and an earnest sense of whimsy make this made-for-cable road trip worth the journey. Rated R for adult situations, language, and nudity. 100m. **DIR:** John Kaye. **CAST:** Patrick Swayze, Melanie Griffith, Penelope Ann Miller, Joseph Gordon-Levitt, Steven Bauer. **2000 DVD**

ALONG THE GREAT DIVIDE ★★1/2 With his usual determination and grit, lawman Kirk Douglas fights a sandstorm to capture an escaped criminal. The pace is slow, but the scenery is grand. B&W; 88m. **DIR:** Raoul Walsh. **CAST:** Kirk Douglas, John Agar, Walter Brennan, Virginia Mayo. **1951**

ALONG THE NAVAJO TRAIL ★★★ Deputy Marshal Roy Rogers investigates the disappearance of another government agent on Dale Evans's ranch and discovers land grabbers. Standard fare, exciting climax. B&W; 70m. **DIR:** Frank McDonald. **CAST:** Roy Rogers, George "Gabby" Hayes, Dale Evans, Douglas Fowley, Estelita Rodriguez. **1945**

ALPHA INCIDENT, THE ★★ A deadly organism from Mars, an attempted government cover-up, a radiation leak, panic, and havoc. Okay, if you like this sort of now-tired thing. Rated PG. 84m. **DIR:** Bill Rebane. **CAST:** Ralph Meeker. **1977**

ALPHABET CITY 🦃 Pretentious movie set in Manhattan's Lower East Side. Rated R for profanity, nudity, and violence. 98m. **DIR:** Amos Poe. **CAST:** Vincent Spano, Kate Vernon, Michael Winslow, Zohra Lampert, Raymond Serra. **1984**

ALPHABET MURDERS, THE ★★★ A semicomic Agatha Christie mystery with Tony Randall as Hercule Poirot and Margaret Rutherford in a cameo bit as Miss Marple. Poirot goes after a serial killer who polishes off his victims in alphabetical order. Christie fans might regard the movie as blasphemous, but Randall's fans should love it. B&W; 90m. **DIR:** Frank Tashlin. **CAST:** Tony Randall, Robert Morley, Anita Ekberg, Margaret Rutherford, James Villiers, Guy Rolfe. **1966**

ALPHAVILLE ★★★ Eddie Constantine portrays Lemmy Caution, French private eye extraordinaire, who is sent into the future to rescue a trapped scientist. It's a Dick Tracy–type of story with sci-fi leanings. In French with English subtitles. 98m. **DIR:** Jean-Luc Godard. **CAST:** Eddie Constantine, Anna Karina, Akim Tamiroff. **1965 DVD**

ALSINO AND THE CONDOR ★★ This is an earnest attempt to dramatize the conflict between the Central American governments and the Sandinista rebels in Nicaragua. The film revolves around the story of one young boy caught in the turmoil. Alan Esquivel is Alsino, the boy who escapes into a fantasy world of flight. 90m. **DIR:** Miguel Littin. **CAST:** Alan Esquivel, Dean Stockwell, Carmen Bunster. **1983**

ALTERED STATES ★★★1/2 At times you can't help but be swept along . . . and almost overwhelmed. William Hurt, Blair Brown, Bob Balaban, and Charles Haid star in this suspenseful film as scientists involved in the potentially dangerous exploration of the mind. Rated R for nudity, profanity, and violence. 102m. **DIR:** Ken Russell. **CAST:** William Hurt, Blair Brown, Bob Balaban, Charles Haid, Drew Barrymore. **1980 DVD**

ALVAREZ KELLY ★★ Edward Dymtryk unimaginatively directed this plodding Western starring William Holden as a cattle driver supplying beef to the Yankees. Confederate officer Richard Widmark wants him to steal that much-needed food for the South. Dull. 116m. **DIR:** Edward Dmytryk. **CAST:** William Holden, Richard Widmark, Janice Rule, Patrick O'Neal, Victoria Shaw. **1966 DVD**

ALWAYS (1984) ★★★ Largely autobiographical, *Always* follows Henry Jaglom and Patrice Townsend through their breakup and their reckoning of the relationship. This movie has a bittersweet feeling that is reminiscent of some of Woody Allen's films dealing with romance. Unfortunately, the movie doesn't have the laughs that Allen provides. Rated R for profanity and nudity. 105m. **DIR:** Henry Jaglom. **CAST:** Henry Jaglom, Patrice Townsend, Joanna Frank, Alan Rachins, Melissa Leo. **1984**

ALWAYS (1989) ★★★★ Steven Spielberg's transcendent remake of *A Guy Named Joe* is touching, funny, life-affirming, and lightweight. Richard Dreyfuss is in top form as a daredevil pilot who dies after saving the life of his buddy (John Goodman). Holly Hunter is the girl Dreyfuss leaves behind—until, that is, he comes back as a guardian angel to a fledgling pilot. Rated PG for brief profanity. 106m. **DIR:** Steven Spielberg. **CAST:** Richard Dreyfuss, Holly Hunter, John Goodman, Audrey Hepburn, Brad Johnson. **1989 DVD**

ALWAYS OUTNUMBERED ★★★★★ Sensational adaptation by author Walter Mosley of *Always Outnumbered, Always Outgunned*. Laurence Fishburne tears up the screen as an inner-city ex-con with a violent temper who tries to gain respect in all the wrong places. The film is episodic, reflecting its roots in a series of short stories, but all are superbly integrated. Mostly, though, it's Fishburne's show; you won't be able to take your eyes off him. Rated R for violence, profanity, nudity, and simulated sex. 105m. **DIR:** Michael Apted. **CAST:** Laurence Fishburne, Bill Cobbs, Natalie Cole, Bill Duke, Laurie Metcalf, Bill Nunn, Isaiah Washington, Cicely Tyson. **1998**

AMADEUS ★★★★★ F. Murray Abraham, who won an Oscar for his performance, gives a haunting portrayal of Antonio Salieri, the court composer for Hapsburg Emperor Joseph II. A second-rate musician, Salieri felt jealousy and admiration for the young musical genius Wolfgang Amadeus Mozart (Tom Hulce), who died at the age of thirty-five—perhaps by Salieri's hand. It's a stunning film full of great music, drama, and wit. Rated PG for mild violence. 158m. **DIR:** Milos Forman. **CAST:** Tom Hulce, F. Murray Abraham, Elizabeth Berridge. **1984 DVD**

AMANDA AND THE ALIEN ★★ Science-fiction giant Robert Silverberg's original story is ill-served by this comic spin on *Starman*, which stars Nicole Eggert as an oh-so-hip Valley Girl who rescues a cannibalistic alien being pursued by nasty government agents. The humor is pretty strained, and the one-joke premise quickly wears thin. Rated R for profanity, nudity, violence, and simulated sex. 94m. **DIR:** Jon Kroll. **CAST:** Nicole Eggert, Michael Dorn, Michael Bendetti, Stacy Keach, John Diehl. **1995**

AMARCORD ★★★★★ This landmark film is based on director Federico Fellini's reflections of his youth in a small town in prewar Italy. While celebrating the kinship that exists in the town, Fellini examines the serious shortcomings that would pave the route for fascism. Brilliantly photographed by Giuseppe Rotunno. Italian dubbed in English. 127m. **DIR:** Federico Fellini. **CAST:** Magali Noel, Bruno Zanin, Pupella Maggio. **1974 DVD**

AMATEUR, THE (1982) ★★★1/2 A CIA computer technologist (John Savage) blackmails The Company into helping him avenge the terrorist murder of his girlfriend, only to find himself abandoned—and hunted—by the CIA. Rated R for violence. 111m. **DIR:** Charles Jarrott. **CAST:** John Savage, Christopher Plummer, Marthe Keller, John Marley. **1982**

AMATEUR (1995) ★★★★ An amnesiac teams up with a nymphomaniac/virgin ex-nun to try to discover his true identity. Meanwhile, his porn star ex-wife tries to get away from him and the international crime cartel that's after them both. Great dialogue and eccentric plotting mark this deadpan comic *film noir* that is nowhere near as smutty as it sounds. Rated R for violence, language, and some sexual situations. 105m. **DIR:** Hal Hartley. **CAST:** Isabelle Huppert, Martin Donovan, Elina Lowensohn, Damian Young. **1995**

AMATI GIRLS, THE ★★ Four Italian-American sisters deal with various domestic crises, including their own sibling rivalry and an increasingly eccentric mother. A good cast is swamped by a raging flood of kitchen-sink clichés, as facile and shallow as a low-rent TV movie. Writer-director Anne DeSalvo even has a character complain about Italian stereotypes in movies—but she should talk. Rated PG. 91m. **DIR:** Anne DeSalvo. **CAST:** Mercedes Ruehl, Cloris Leachman, Sean Young, Dinah Manoff, Paul Sorvino, Lily Knight, Lee Grant. **2000 DVD**

AMAZING ADVENTURE ★★★ Feeling guilty after inheriting a fortune, Cary Grant sets out to earn his living in this comedy of stout hearts among the poor-but-honest in England during the Depression. B&W; 70m. **DIR:** Alfred Zeisler. **CAST:** Cary Grant, Mary Brian, Peter Gawthorne, Henry Kendall, Leon M. Lion. **1936**

AMAZING COLOSSAL MAN, THE ★★ Exposed to a nuclear blast, an army colonel grows as big as a house . . . and keeps on growing, as scientists and his understandably worried fiancée search for a cure. Basically a C-budget rip-off of one of Jack Arnold's stylish Universal International chillers of the Fifties. Best scene: the struggle with a king-size syringe. B&W; 80m. **DIR:** Bert I. Gordon. **CAST:** Glenn Langan, Cathy Downs, William Hudson, James Seay, Larry Thor. **1957**

AMAZING DOBERMANS ★★ Third in a series of films about do-gooder dogs pits a treasury agent (James Franciscus) against inept crooks who can't compete with the dogged determination of the Dobermans. Harmless, but hardly inspired. Rated G. 94m. **DIR:** David Chudnow, Byron Chudnow. **CAST:** James Franciscus, Barbara Eden, Fred Astaire, Jack Carter. **1976**

AMAZING DR. CLITTERHOUSE, THE ★★1/2 Psychiatrist attempting to tap into the criminal mind involves himself with a gang and ends up directing their capers. Melodrama with a comic touch has a good cast but its play-bound roots tangle it up and the finished product is lightweight. B&W; 87m. **DIR:** Anatole Litvak. **CAST:** Edward G. Robinson, Claire Trevor, Humphrey Bogart, Gale Page, Donald Crisp, Allen Jenkins, Thurston Hall. **1938**

AMAZING GRACE AND CHUCK 🦃 Paranoid fantasy about what happens when a 12 year old Little Leaguer (Joshua Zuehlke) decides to give up baseball in protest of nuclear arms. Rated PG. 115m. **DIR:** Mike Newell. **CAST:** Jamie Lee Curtis, Alex English, Gregory Peck, William L. Petersen, Dennis Lipscomb, Lee Richardson. **1987**

AMAZING HOWARD HUGHES, THE ★★ Howard Hughes was amazing, but little in this account of his life and career would so indicate. Best portrayal is Ed Flanders as longtime, finally turned-upon associate Noah Dietrich. An ambitious TV production that falls short of the mark. 215m. **DIR:** William A. Graham. **CAST:** Tommy Lee Jones, Ed Flanders, Tovah Feldshuh, Sorrell Booke, Lee Purcell, Arthur Franz. **1977**

AMAZING MR. BLUNDEN, THE ★★★ Neat little ghost story about children from the twentieth century (Lynne Frederick, Garry Miller) helping right a wrong done 100 years previously. Laurence Naismith is the mysterious (and amazing) Mr. Blunden, a nineteenth-century lawyer who is at home in the twentieth century. The children seem a little old, but on the whole the story is delightful. Rated PG. 100m. **DIR:** Lionel Jeffries. **CAST:** Laurence Naismith, Lynne Frederick, Garry Miller, Dorothy Alison, Diana Dors. **1972**

AMAZING MR. X ★★★ This drama about a bogus medium and the woman he plans to hoodwink is leisurely paced but well written and acted by a solid cast. A pleasant surprise. B&W; 78m. **DIR:** Bernard Vorhaus. **CAST:** Turhan Bey, Cathy O'Donnell, Lynn Bari. **1948**

AMAZING PANDA ADVENTURE, THE ★★★ Annoying, self-involved 12 year old evolves after spending his vacation on a panda reserve and saving a cub that poachers hope to sell to a zoo. Rick Baker of Cinovation Studios creates the animatronic pandas that are used intermittently with actual animals. Chinese highland forestry shots are absolutely breathtaking. Rated PG for violence. 85m. **DIR:** Christopher Cain. **CAST:** Ryan Slater, Ding Yi, Fei Wang, Stephen Lang. **1995**

AMAZING SPIDERMAN, THE ★★ Marvel Comics' popular character makes his live-action debut in this made-for-TV adaptation that involves Spidey's origin. Although fairly well-acted, it's missing many of the wise-cracking elements that made the comic-book character popular. The production values and special effects are decent, though, especially the wall-crawling scenes. Not rated, but appropriate for all ages. 93m. **DIR:** E. W. Swackhamer. **CAST:** Nicholas Hammond, David White, Michael Pataki, Hilly Hicks, Lisa Eilbacher. **1977**

AMAZING STORIES (TV SERIES) ★★★1/2 The best of Steven Spielberg's *Amazing Stories* have been paired up for video release. "Book Two" is by far the strongest, highlighted by director Robert Zemeckis's "Go to the Head of the Class," and Tim Burton's manic "Family Dog," an animated short that beat *The Simpsons* by several years. "Book One" includes Spielberg's overlong segment, "The Mission," in which a World War II bomber takes enemy fire and seems doomed, until rescue arrives from a most unlikely source. Danny DeVito rounds out that tape by directing and starring in the occasionally uproarious "The Wedding Ring." 70–71. **DIR:** Steven Spielberg, Robert Zemeckis, Danny DeVito, Brad Bird. **CAST:** Kevin Costner, Kiefer Sutherland, Christopher Lloyd, Mary Stuart Masterson, Casey Siemaszko, Danny DeVito, Rhea Perlman, Scott Coffey. **1985–1986**

AMAZING TRANSPARENT MAN, THE ★★ This zero-budget thriller from cult director Edgar Ulmer has gotten a bad rap over the years, while the talky sci-fi film shot back-to-back with it, *Beyond the Time Barrier*, has been overpraised. The admittedly lame premise has a refugee scientist blackmailed into turning an escaped convict invisible so he can commit bank robberies—but Ulmer provides some thrills, including an exciting, sadistic climax. B&W; 58m. **DIR:** Edgar G. Ulmer. **CAST:** Douglas Kennedy, Marguerite Chapman, James Griffith. **1960 DVD**

AMAZON ★★1/2 On the lam, Kari Vaananen hightails it into the jungles of the Amazon, where he's befriended by pilot Robert Davi. Politically correct film is only so-so. Rated R for violence and language. 88m. **DIR:** Mika Kaurismaki. **CAST:** Robert Davi, Kari Vaananen, Rae Dawn Chong. **1992**

AMAZON WOMEN ON THE MOON ★★★ This silly scrapbook send-up of Saturday-morning, sci-fi, and sitcom-TV schlock stitches together star-strewn skits, but many of the plots are threadbare. When on the mark the chuckles come easily. More often, it's like the Not Ready for Prime Time Players on a not-so-prime night. Rated R for nudity. 85m. **DIR:** John Landis, Joe Dante, Carl Gottlieb, Peter Horton, Robert K. Weiss. **CAST:** Rosanna Arquette, Ralph Bellamy, Carrie Fisher, Sybil Danning, Steve Allen, Griffin Dunne, Steve Guttenberg, Ed Begley Jr., Arsenio Hall, Howard Hesseman, Russ Meyer, B. B. King, Henny Youngman. **1987 DVD**

AMAZONS 🦃 The ridiculousness of the fight scenes in this film rivals that of the worst kung fu flick. This silly film is rated R for nudity, violence, and sex. 76m. **DIR:** Alex Sessa. **CAST:** Windsor Taylor Randolph, Penelope Reed, Joseph Whipp, Danitza Kingsley, Willie Nelson. **1986**

•AMAZONS AND GLADIATORS 🦃 The inevitable fallout from Ridley Scott's *Gladiator* continues with this bargain-basement sword and sandal drama about a young woman who is ripped from her family by an evil emperor at the age of twelve, only to escape, grow up, and join an army of Amazons in their quest to overthrow the corrupt empire. So cheesy and hammy it would make a better sandwich than film. Rated R for adult situations and violence. 89m. **DIR:** Zachary Weintraub. **CAST:** Patrick Bergin, Jennifer Rubin. **2000 DVD**

AMBASSADOR, THE ★★★1/2 *The Ambassador* confronts the Arab-Israeli conflict with a clear head and an optimistic viewpoint. Robert Mitchum plays the controversial U.S. ambassador to Israel, who tries to solve the Palestinian question while being criticized by all factions. Rock Hudson (in his last big-screen role) is the security officer who saves the ambassador's life. Rated R for violence, profanity, sex, and nudity. 97m. **DIR:** J. Lee Thompson. **CAST:** Robert Mitchum, Rock Hudson, Ellen Burstyn, Fabio Testi, Donald Pleasence. **1984**

AMBASSADOR BILL ★★★ This contrived comedy of pompous protocol versus common sense has amiable inexperienced cowpoke Will Rogers appointed ambassador to a revolution-wracked monarchy somewhere in Europe. Funny dialogue and absurd situations give the star plenty of laugh opportunities. B&W; 68m. **DIR:** Sam Taylor. **CAST:** Will Rogers, Marguerite Churchill, Gustav von Seyffertitz, Ray Milland. **1931**

AMBASSADOR MAGMA ★★ Dull artistry and an average story make this Japanese animated series rather tedious as Ambassador Magma, a giant golden robot, battles the evil would-be ruler of the universe and his army of weird demons. Dubbed in English. Not rated; contains violence. 70m. **DIR:** Yutaka Maseba. **1993**

AMBASSADOR'S DAUGHTER, THE ★★★ A beautiful Olivia de Havilland and a handsome John Forsythe star in this sophisticated romantic comedy about a congressman (Edward Arnold) attempting to curtail the amorous adventures of GIs in Paris. Winningly performed by all. 102m. **DIR:** Norman Krasna. **CAST:** Olivia de Havilland, John Forsythe, Myrna Loy, Adolphe Menjou, Tommy Noonan, Edward Arnold. **1956**

AMBITION 🦃 An unpublished author is so obsessed with a paroled slasher that he befriends the reformed psycho. Rated R for violence, language, and nudity. 100m. **DIR:** Scott Goldstein. **CAST:** Lou Diamond Phillips, Clancy Brown, Cecilia Peck, Richard Bradford, Willard E. Pugh, Grace Zabriskie. **1991**

AMBULANCE, THE ★★★★ Cartoonist Eric Roberts stumbles onto what may be a weird abduction conspiracy when dream gal Janine Turner is whisked away by a mysterious ambulance and never shows up at any of the local hospitals. Campy, strange, infused with black humor and several exciting chase scenes, this is an intriguing flick. Adding to its oddball patina is James Earl Jones as a cop on the edge. Rated R for profanity and violence. 95m. **DIR:** Larry Cohen. **CAST:** Eric Roberts, Janine Turner, James Earl Jones, Eric Braeden. **1993**

AMBUSH MURDERS, THE ★★★ Formulaic TV adaptation of a true story. The title refers to the killing of two California policemen in a black neighborhood. A black activist is framed and it's up to hardworking lawyer James Brolin to get him acquitted. Intermittently engrossing. 98m. **DIR:** Steven H. Stern. **CAST:** James Brolin, Dorian Harewood, Amy Madigan, Antonio Fargas. **1982**

AMBUSHERS, THE 🦃 Only hard-core Dean Martin fans will want to bother with this one, the third movie in the Matt Helm secret agent series. 102m. **DIR:** Henry Levin. **CAST:** Dean Martin, Senta Berger, Janice Rule, James Gregory, Albert Salmi, Kurt Kasznar, Beverly Adams. **1968**

AMELIA EARHART: THE FINAL FLIGHT ★★1/2 Diane Keaton portrays Amelia Earhart as a tantrum-throwing, whining know-it-all in this disappointing Turner Pictures production. Earhart's fabled heroism is strangely lacking in this rendition of her final flight. Only Rutger Hauer, as her drunken navigator, seems to believe in his character. Not rated; contains mild profanity. 93m. **DIR:** Yves Simoneau. **CAST:** Diane Keaton, Bruce Dern, Rutger Hauer, Paul Guilfoyle, Denis Arndt. **1994**

•AMÉLIE ★★★★ This wonderful charmer is a tribute to a Paris that we know only from late-night movies: an impressionistic, fairy-tale Paris, laden with steep stairways, postcard-perfect views of Notre Dame and the Pont des Arts, and quaint little shops on streets that we know must be cobblestoned. It's the perfect setting for a modern-day fable about a young woman who discovers that the gentlest of acts can make a large difference to the people whose lives are touched by the incident, and she therefore appoints herself as a behind-the-scenes guardian angel (or devil) to friends and neighbors. Rated R for sexual candor and brief nudity. 115m. **DIR:** Jean-Pierre Jeunet. **CAST:** Audrey Tautou, Mathieu Kassovitz, Rufus, Yolande Moreau, Artus de Penguern, Urbain Cancelier. **2001 DVD**

AMERICA This mess has a down-and-out cable station trying to get financial support from New York's latest $10 million lottery winner. Rated R. 90m. **DIR:** Robert Downey. **CAST:** Zack Norman, Tammy Grimes, Michael J. Pollard, Richard Belzer, Laura Ashton, Liz Torres. **1986**

AMERICAN ANTHEM Starring 1984 Olympic gold medal gymnast Mitch Gaylord, this film features superb gymnastics. Rated PG. 100m. **DIR:** Albert Magnoli. **CAST:** Mitch Gaylord, Janet Jones, Michelle Phillips. **1986**

AMERICAN ARISTOCRACY, AN ★★★★ One of those early Douglas Fairbanks gems when he was more interested in strenuous acrobatics and satiric commentary than ponderous costume adventures. This one deflates the pretensions of Rhode Island society. Silent. B&W; 52m. **DIR:** Lloyd Ingraham. **CAST:** Douglas Fairbanks Sr., Jewel Carmen. **1916**

•AMERICAN ASTRONAUT, THE ★★★ This black-and-white, microbudget science-fiction musical adventure is a shameless candidate for immediate Midnight Movie canonization. Galactic cowboy traveler-trader–bar hopper Sam Curtis transports such oddball cargo as the Boy Who Has Seen a Woman's Breast and a house cat from planet to planet in a celebration of cinematic corn and cheese. This slice of low-rent lunacy includes the most bizarre, exhilarating rockabilly song-and-dance numbers ever committed to celluloid. Not rated. 93m. **DIR:** Cory McAbee. **CAST:** Cory McAbee, Rocco Sisto, Greg Russell Cook, Annie Golden, James Ransone, Joshua Taylor. **2001 DVD**

AMERICAN BEAUTY ★★★★1/2 This savagely dark, frequently funny, and uncomfortably accurate indictment of the roles we play while trying to persuade the world at large that Everything Is Cool, is a hip blend of *The Graduate* and *Catcher in the Rye*. The film, zestfully directed by big-screen newcomer Sam Mendes, is galvanized by Oscar winner Kevin Spacey's amazing lead performance. The acerbic script comes from debut screenwriter Alan Ball, a playwright with a gift for slightly exaggerated truth that amplifies his various issues but never strays so far from reality that we cease to recognize ourselves in these characters. Rated R for profanity, nudity, drug use, and violence. 121m. **DIR:** Sam Mendes. **CAST:** Kevin Spacey, Annette Bening, Thora Birch, Wes Bentley, Mena Suvari, Peter Gallagher, Allison Janney, Chris Cooper. **1999 DVD**

AMERICAN BLUE NOTE ★★★ Offbeat nostalgic tale about struggling jazz musicians, circa 1960. Peter MacNicol, in an engaging performance, plays the ever-hopeful but constantly thwarted bandleader who desperately tries to keep his quintet together. Rated PG-13 for profanity. 96m. **DIR:** Ralph Toporoff. **CAST:** Peter MacNicol, Charlotte d'Amboise, Trini Alvarado. **1989**

AMERICAN BOYFRIENDS ★★★1/2 Precocious Canadian Sandy Wilcox, last seen as the gawky 12 year old of *My American Cousin*, has matured in this sequel from writer-director Sandy Wilson. This time Sandy attends the wedding of her cousin Butch (John Wildman) in Portland, Oregon. Margaret Langrick, as Sandy, has added drop-dead cuteness to her spunky personality; but Wilson's story has a decidedly bittersweet tone. Rated PG-13 for sexual connotations. 90m. **DIR:** Sandy Wilson. **CAST:** Margaret Langrick, John Wildman. **1989**

AMERICAN BUFFALO ★★1/2 David Mamet's slight stage play becomes an equally unsatisfying film: a claustrophobic and needlessly talky exercise between two men with nothing much to say. Junk-shop owner Dennis Franz allows himself to be persuaded into sharing a potential burglary with twitchy Dustin Hoffman, but the caper never moves past the planning stage. Hoffman's nervous tics are laughably overplayed and are no substitute for credible characterization. Rated R for profanity and violence. 88m. **DIR:** Michael Corrente. **CAST:** Dustin Hoffman, Dennis Franz, Sean Nelson. **1996 DVD**

AMERICAN CHRISTMAS CAROL, AN ★★ Lackluster made-for-television rendering of Charles Dickens's Christmas favorite, set in 1930s New England. Scrooge is played by Henry Winkler with some panache. 100m. **DIR:** Eric Till. **CAST:** Henry Winkler, David Wayne, Dorian Harewood, Chris Wiggins. **1979 DVD**

AMERICAN CINEMA ★★★★ Directors Martin Scorsese, Steven Spielberg, Billy Wilder, and Joseph Mankiewicz top the who's who of more than 150 filmmakers sharing their insights in this revealing examination of the $20-billion-per-year American movie industry. All aspects of Hollywood-style creation and production are discussed in detail. B&W/color; 10 hours on 5 cassetes. **DIR:** Lawrence Pitkethly. **1995 DVD**

AMERICAN CLOCK, THE ★★★★ Telling and thought-provoking look at the stock-market crash of 1929 and the great depression that followed. Engrossing story line, vivid characterizations, and wonderful performances make this a winner based on the Arthur Miller stage play. Made for cable television. 95m. **DIR:** Bob Clark. **CAST:** Kelly Preston, John Randolph, David Strathairn, Joanna Miles, Darren McGavin, Mary McDonnell, Estelle Parsons, Yaphet Kotto, Eddie Bracken,

Jim Dale, Tony Roberts, Roberts Blossom, Loren Dean. **1993**

AMERICAN CYBORG: STEEL WARRIOR ★★ Futuristic kick-boxing thriller is marred by laughable performances and a derivative storyline stolen from *The Terminator*. Rated R for violence and profanity. 95m. **DIR:** Boaz Davidson. **CAST:** Joe Lara, Nicole Hansen, John P. Ryan. **1994**

AMERICAN DREAM ★★★★ Oscar-winning documentary about the Local P-9 (meat packers) union in Austin, Minnesota, and their struggle to renegotiate wages with the Hormel Corporation. The local union bypasses its international chapter and hires a corporate image consultant. A good mix of interviews between the strikers, Hormel executives, and the international chapter. This documentary lets the viewers decide for themselves which side they should take. Rated PG-13 for profanity. 98m. **DIR:** Barbara Kopple. **1990**

AMERICAN DREAMER ★★★ JoBeth Williams plays Cathy Palmer, a would-be novelist who, in a short story contest, successfully captures the style of adventure stories that feature a superspy named Rebecca Ryan and wins a trip to Paris. But once there, Palmer is hit by a car and wakes up believing she is the fictional character. The picture never quite shines as brightly as one expects. Rated PG for violence. 105m. **DIR:** Rick Rosenthal. **CAST:** JoBeth Williams, Tom Conti, Giancarlo Giannini. **1984**

AMERICAN EAGLE 🦃 Rehashed garbage about a CIA hit man who wants out of the game. Rated R for violence and profanity. 92m. **DIR:** Robert J. Smawley. **CAST:** Asher Brauner, Robert F. Lyons. **1989**

AMERICAN EMPIRE ★★★ A formula film featuring the now-standard grand opening, dramatic problem-posing center, and slam-bang breathtaking climax, but a good, entertaining Western nonetheless. Richard Dix and Preston Foster team to found a cattle empire in Texas. Villain Leo Carrillo makes most of the trouble the pair encounters. Fans of the genre will love it. B&W; 82m. **DIR:** William McGann. **CAST:** Richard Dix, Frances Gifford, Preston Foster, Leo Carrillo, Guinn Williams. **1942**

AMERICAN FLATULATORS 🦃 This spoof of television's *American Gladiators* stinks to high heaven, and then some. Totally tasteless. Not rated; contains adult situations. 54m. **DIR:** Nolan T. Michaels. **1996**

AMERICAN FLYERS ★★★1/2 Another bicycle-racing tale from writer Steve Tesich (*Breaking Away*), who correctly decided he could milk that theme at least one more time. Kevin Costner and David Marshall Grant star as estranged brothers who get to know and like each other again during a grueling three-day overland race. Rated PG-13 for brief nudity and language. 113m. **DIR:** John Badham. **CAST:** Kevin Costner, David Marshall Grant, Rae Dawn Chong, Alexandra Paul, Janice Rule, John Amos. **1985 DVD**

AMERICAN FRIEND, THE ★★★★1/2 Tense story of an American criminal (Dennis Hopper) in Germany talking a picture framer into murdering a gangster. Extremely well-done, with lots of surprises. Cameo appearances by American film directors Sam Fuller and Nicholas Ray. Rated R for language, violence. 127m. **DIR:** Wim Wenders. **CAST:** Dennis Hopper, Bruno Ganz, Lisa Kreuzer, Gerard Blain. **1977**

AMERICAN FRIENDS ★★★★1/2 Michael Palin is an uptight Oxford instructor who learns to loosen up after meeting two American women while hiking in Switzerland. Co-writer Palin based this leisurely, elegant period piece, set in 1861, on one of his upstart ancestors. Witty and wonderful, it is a true romance in every sense of the word. Rated PG for adult themes. 95m. **DIR:** Tristram Powell. **CAST:** Michael Palin, Trini Alvarado, Connie Booth, Alfred Molina. **1993**

AMERICAN GIGOLO ★★ This story of a male hooker, Julian Kay (Richard Gere), who attends to the physical needs of bored, rich, middle-aged women in Beverly Hills, may be something different. But who needs it? This is sensationalism in the guise of social comment, though it has some incidental humor and impressive performances by Gere and Lauren Hutton. Rated R for explicit depictions of a low lifestyle. 117m. **DIR:** Paul Schrader. **CAST:** Richard Gere, Lauren Hutton, Hector Elizondo, Nina Van Pallandt. **1980 DVD**

AMERICAN GOTHIC ★★★1/2 Inventive, chilling, and atmospheric horror film pits a group of vacationers on a remote island against a grotesque, creepy family headed by Ma and Pa (Rod Steiger and Yvonne De Carlo). The latter's children, middle-aged adults who act and dress like kids, delight in killing off the newcomers one by one. An absence of gore and an emphasis on characterization make this an uncommonly satisfying film for horror buffs. Rated R for violence and profanity. 90m. **DIR:** John Hough. **CAST:** Rod Steiger, Yvonne De Carlo, Michael J. Pollard. **1988**

AMERICAN GRAFFITI ★★★★1/2 *Star Wars* creator George Lucas discovered his talent for creating lighthearted, likable entertainment with this film about the coming-of-age of a group of high school students in northern California. Blessed with a superb rock 'n' roll score and fine performances, it's the best of its kind and inspired the long-running television series *Happy Days*. Rated PG. 110m. **DIR:** George Lucas. **CAST:** Richard Dreyfuss, Ron Howard, Paul LeMat, Cindy Williams, Candy Clark, Mackenzie Phillips, Harrison Ford, Bo Hopkins, Charles Martin Smith. **1973 DVD**

AMERICAN HEART ★★★1/2 Tough, realistic film follows the volatile relationship of a recently released convict and his 15 year old son. As the father and son attempt reconciliation, they are drawn into life on the streets. Movie benefits greatly from gritty location filming and memorable performances, especially Jeff Bridges and Edward Furlong. Rated R for violence and language. 117m. **DIR:** Martin Bell. **CAST:** Jeff Bridges, Edward Furlong, Lucinda Jenney, Don Harvey. **1991**

AMERICAN HISTORY X ★★★★ Racism ravages an American middle-class family in this incendiary drama about breaking a daisy chain of hatred. A neo-Nazi skinhead returns from prison to his Venice Beach home. His evolution from young bright jock to thug to enlightened parolee and his relationship with a younger brother who is following in his toxic footsteps are captured in gripping flashbacks. The acting is excellent. Rated R for language, sex, and violence. 118m. **DIR:** Tony Kaye. **CAST:** Edward Norton, Edward Furlong, Fairuza Balk, Beverly D'Angelo, Stacy Keach, Jennifer Lien, Elliott Gould. **1998 DVD**

AMERICAN HOT WAX ★★★1/2 Though facts may be in short supply in this bio-pic of pioneer rock disc jockey Alan Freed, abundant energy and spirit make this movie a winner. Tim McIntire gives a remarkable performance as Freed. Rated PG. 91m. **DIR:** Floyd Mutrux. **CAST:** Tim McIntire, Fran Drescher, Jay Leno, John Lehne, Laraine Newman, Jeff Altman, Chuck Berry, Jerry Lee Lewis. **1978**

AMERICAN IN PARIS, AN ★★★★★ One of Gene Kelly's classic musicals, this Oscar-winning best picture features the hoofer as the free-spirited author of the title. The picture is a heady mixture of light entertainment and the music of George Gershwin. 115m. **DIR:** Vincente Minnelli. **CAST:** Gene Kelly, Leslie Caron, Nina Foch, Oscar Levant. **1951 DVD**

AMERICAN JUSTICE ★★1/2 Small-town cops near the Mexican border become involved in an illegal alien/slavery ring. It's brutal and violent and probably truer than you'd think. A fair attempt by TV's *Simon and Simon* to work together in different roles. Rated R for violence, sex, and language. 79m. **DIR:** Gary Grillo. **CAST:** Gerald McRaney, Jameson Parker, Wilford Brimley. **1986**

AMERICAN KICKBOXER ★★ A former world-champion kickboxer must fight his way back to the top following a jail term for manslaughter. Rated R for profanity. 93m. **DIR:** Frans Nel. **CAST:** John Barrett. **1991**

AMERICAN ME ★★★★★ Brilliant directorial debut by Edward James Olmos has him adopting the storytelling style of his mentor, director Robert M. Young, in depicting thirty years in the life of an East Los Angeles Latino family. Olmos stars as the pivotal character, a hardened criminal who finds his soul too late. A cinema milestone. Rated R for violence, nudity, and profanity. 126m. **DIR:** Edward James Olmos. **CAST:** Edward James Olmos, William Forsythe, Pepe Serna, Danny De La Paz, Evelina Fernandez. **1992**

AMERICAN MOVIE ★★★★ This documentary portrait of amateur Wisconsin filmmaker Mark Borchardt is a deadpan scream. It chronicles his two-year obsession with making a cheesy horror flick that will hopefully help finance another pet project. Borchardt plows through numerous personal, economic, and artistic snags, and his talent is suspect. But he and his relatives and friends (which include a grizzled, octogenarian uncle and permanently stoned musician pal) are certainly a colorful brood. Rated R for language and suggested violence. 104m. **DIR:** Chris Smith. **1999 DVD**

AMERICAN NINJA An American soldier (Michael Dudikoff) single-handedly takes on an army of martial arts mercenaries in the Philippines. Rated R for profanity and violence. 95m. **DIR:** Sam Firstenberg. **CAST:** Michael Dudikoff, Guich Koock, Judie Aronson, Steve James. **1985 DVD**

AMERICAN NINJA II ★★ Michael Dudikoff continues to set new standards for nonacting in this mindless but enjoyable-for-fans martial arts movie. Dudikoff and Steve James, who is as watchable as ever, play army rangers who come to the aid of the Marines and wipe out a passel of heroin dealers. Rated R. 96m. **DIR:** Sam Firstenberg. **CAST:** Michael Dudikoff, Steve James, Larry Poindexter, Gary Conway. **1987**

AMERICAN NINJA III Comic-book movie filled with cartoon characters. Rated R for violence and profanity. 89m. **DIR:** Cedric Sundstrom. **CAST:** Steve James, David Bradley, Marjoe Gortner. **1989**

AMERICAN NINJA IV: THE ANNIHILATION This paint-by-numbers action flick has martial arts experts trying to rescue a group of Americans held captive by a mad Arab. Rated R for violence and profanity; 96m. **DIR:** Cedric Sundstrom. **CAST:** Michael Dudikoff, David Bradley, James Booth, Robin Stille, Ken Gampu. **1991**

•AMERICAN OUTLAWS History and any semblance of movie magic get stuffed deep into the saddlebags of this lame Western as young Hollywood beefcakes resurrect the legend of the Missouri-based James Younger gang and their pursuit by mythic security guard Allan Pinkerton. Rated PG-13 for violence and language. 95m. **DIR:** Les Mayfield. **CAST:** Colin Ferrell, Will McCormack, Ali Larter, Gabriel Macht, Scott Caan, Nathaniel Arcand, Timothy Dalton, Kathy Bates. **2001 DVD**

AMERICAN PIE ★★ Four high-school chums vow to lose their virginity by the time they graduate. Crude, rampantly sexist, amateurish, and cheap-looking, this adolescent sex comedy was nevertheless a big box-office hit; think of it as *Porky's* for the 1990s. Rated R for profanity and sexual scenes. 95m. **DIR:** Paul Weitz. **CAST:** Jason Biggs, Chris Klein, Mena Suvari, Alyson Hannigan, Eugene Levy. **1999 DVD**

•AMERICAN PIE 2 ★★ After a year of college, five buddies rent a beach house with the resolve of scoring with the ladies and throwing an end-of-summer party that will make them living legends. The original cast returns as sexual misadventures veer from the pastry penetration that gave this raunchy comedy franchise instant notoriety to encounters with superglue and a strategically placed trumpet. Rated R for sex, language, nudity, and vulgarity. 104m. **DIR:** James B. Rogers. **CAST:** Jason Biggs, Alyson Hannigan, Shannon Elizabeth, Eugene Levy, Chris Klein, Thomas Ian Nicholas, Tara Reid, Seann William Scott, Mena Suvari, Eddie Kaye Thomas. **2001 DVD**

AMERICAN PRESIDENT, THE ★★★★★ Ah, if only American politics were blessed with so much nobility! Michael Douglas is just right as a chief of state who enjoys unprecedented popularity until venturing back into the "dating scene." American citizens admire a man who grieves for his wife's untimely death, but they're not so sure what to make of his growing passion for a perky environmental lobbyist (Annette Bening). Aaron Sorkin's script is clearly a populist fantasy, but so what? Rated PG-13 for profanity and adult themes. 120m. **DIR:** Rob Reiner. **CAST:** Michael Douglas, Annette Bening, Martin Sheen, Michael J. Fox, David Paymer, Anna Deavere Smith, Samantha Mathis. **1995 DVD**

AMERICAN PSYCHO ★★★1/2 The notorious Bret Easton Ellis novel about a yuppie serial killer (Christian Bale) makes a comparatively restrained and surprisingly effective film. The script by Guinevere Turner and director Mary Harron mercifully avoids most of the stomach-churning excesses of the book, although the last half hour becomes increasingly disconnected and leaves too many loose ends. Still, Harron's wry satire of 1980s materialism and Bale's fine performance in the title role make it worthwhile. Rated R for violence, sex, and profanity. 104m. **DIR:** Mary Harron. **CAST:** Christian Bale, Willem Dafoe, Jared Leto, Reese Witherspoon, Samantha Mathis, Chloe Sevigny. **2000 DVD**

•**AMERICAN RHAPSODY, AN** ★★ Woman is left behind as an infant when her parents fled the harsh Communist rule of Hungary. She spends her first six years behind the Iron Curtain before reuniting with her biological kin in California. As we witness fifteen years of volcanic events and relationships, this autobiographical, episodic film about culture shock, guilt, oppression, self-discovery, freedom, and family dynamics never firmly wraps its arms around its characters or core mother-daughter conflicts. Rated PG-13 for mature themes, language, and violence. 106m. **DIR:** Éva Gárdos. **CAST:** Nastassja Kinski, Tony Goldwyn, Kelly Endresz-Banlaki, Scarlett Johansson. **2001 DVD**

AMERICAN ROULETTE ★★ Political thriller about a deposed president (Andy Garcia) of a South American nation living in exile in London. The ex-president's life is constantly in jeopardy from Latin death squads—and the CIA and KGB play a tug of war with his loyalities. Robert Stephens gives a fine performance as a sleazy British agent. Light on action, long on talk, with a sappy ending. Rated R. 102m. **DIR:** Maurice Hatton. **CAST:** Andy Garcia, Kitty Aldridge, Robert Stephens. **1988**

AMERICAN SHAOLIN: KING OF THE KICKBOXERS II ★★★1/2 A kick boxer is humiliated during a tournament and decides he will travel to China to become a Shaolin monk. By the end you'll be rooting for him. Rated PG-13 for violence. 103m. **DIR:** Lucas Lowe. **CAST:** Reese Madigan, Daniel Dae Kim, Billy Chang, Cliff Lenderman, Zhang Zhi Yen, Trent Bushey, Kim Chan. **1991**

AMERICAN SOLDIER, THE ★★★ A German-American Vietnam veteran is hired by the Munich police to murder local criminals. Slight but significant early film by Rainer Werner Fassbinder is at once an homage to and a critique of American crime-dramas, particularly as seen by German viewers. In German with English subtitles. Not rated. B&W; 80m. **DIR:** Rainer Werner Fassbinder. **CAST:** Karl Scheydt, Elga Sorbas, Margarethe von Trotta, Rainer Werner Fassbinder. **1970**

AMERICAN STORY, AN ★★★1/2 Powerful *Hallmark Hall of Fame* television special focuses on six WWII vets who return to their hometown only to find that it has been taken over by a corrupt mayor and brutal sheriff. Challenging the diabolical duo in the election, they're forced to arm themselves in order to free their community from its home-grown tyranny. Rated PG for violence and adult themes. 97m. **DIR:** John Gray. **CAST:** Brad Johnson, Kathleen Quinlan, Tom Sizemore, Josef Sommer, David Labiosa. **1992**

AMERICAN STRAYS ★★★1/2 Episodic film featuring various losers on the road in Texas. A surprisingly good showcase for a solid group of actors who seldom fare so well with feature-length scripts. Particularly good is Eric Roberts as a family man whose family is making his life a living hell. Rated R for violence, profanity, and sexual situations. 93m. **DIR:** Michael Covert. **CAST:** Eric Roberts, Jennifer Tilly, John Savage, Carol Kane, Luke Perry, Sam Jones. **1996 DVD**

AMERICAN SUMMER, AN A teenage boy is shipped off to live with his aunt, only to become embroiled in sex, drugs, and murder. Rated R for profanity, violence, and nudity. 100m. **DIR:** James Slocum. **CAST:** Michael Landes, Amber Susa, Brian Austin Green, Joanna Kerns. **1991**

AMERICAN TAIL, AN ★★★ An immigrant mouse becomes separated from his family while voyaging to the United States. The execution and lavish animation make up for the trite and predictable story. Film picks up steam with the introduction of Dom DeLuise, as a vegetarian cat. Rated G. 82m. **DIR:** Don Bluth. **CAST:** Dom DeLuise, Phillip Glasser, Madeline Kahn, Nehemiah Persoff, Christopher Plummer (voices). **1986**

AMERICAN TAIL, AN: FIEVEL GOES WEST ★★★1/2 Fievel Mousekewitz and his family leave behind the crowded city at the urgings of a conniving cat, Cat R. Waul (voiced by John Cleese). An improvement on the first film, this sequel is a straight-ahead, comedy-propelled ode to the Old West. James Stewart is wonderful as the voice of an over-the-hill law dog, and Dom DeLuise returns for more laughs as the wild and crazy Tiger. Rated G. 85m. **DIR:** Phil Nibbelink, Simon Wells. **1991**

AMERICAN TIGER ★★ A sexy and insipid tale of the return of a stolen statue to a Chinese princess who is scorned by her suitor. Set in Miami. Rated R for hot sex scenes and violence. 93m. **DIR:** Martin Dolman. **CAST:** Donald Pleasence, Mitch Gaylord, Daniel Greene. **1989**

AMERICAN VIRGIN ★★ A pair of porn peddlers go to war when one wants to use the other's daughter for an on-line porno show. Grating "comedy" with few laughs, despite the fine cast. Rated R for nudity, profanity, and sexual situations. 87m. **DIR:** Jean-Pierre Marois. **CAST:** Bob Hoskins, Robert Loggia, Mena Suvari, Gabriel Mann, Sally Kellerman. **2000 DVD**

AMERICAN WEREWOLF IN LONDON, AN ★★★1/2 Director John Landis weaves humor, violence, and the classic horror elements of suspense in the tale of the two American travelers who find more than they bargained for on the English moors. Rated R for violence, nudity, and gore. 97m. **DIR:** John Landis. **CAST:** David Naughton, Jenny Agutter, Griffin Dunne. **1981 DVD**

AMERICAN WEREWOLF IN PARIS, AN ★★ An American tourist becomes involved with a mysterious young French woman with a secret. No relation to John Landis's *An American Werewolf in London* and none of the earlier film's wit, suspense, or thrills. The trumped-up ending is especially contrived. Rated R for violence, nudity, and profanity. 97m. **DIR:** Anthony Waller. **CAST:** Tom Everett Scott, Julie Delpy, Vince Vieluf, Phil Buckman, Julie Bowen, Thierry Lhermitte. **1997 DVD**

AMERICAN YAKUZA ★★1/2 Variation on the theme features Viggo Mortensen as an FBI agent who infiltrates the American branch of the *yakuza*, only to have his loyalties waver as he rises through their ranks. Explosive finale pits the reluctant agent against former friends and new enemies. Rated R for violence, language, and adult situations. 96m. **DIR:** Frank Cappello. **CAST:** Viggo Mortensen, Michael Nouri, Franklin Ajaye, Robert Forster. **1993 DVD**

AMERICANA ★★1/2 Strange, offbeat film about a Vietnam veteran (director David Carradine) who attempts to rebuild a merry-go-round in a rural Kansas town and meets with hostility from the locals. Carradine attempts to make a statement about rebuilding America, but this gets lost in the impressionistic haze of his film. Rated PG for violence and profanity. 90m. **DIR:** David Carradine. **CAST:** David Carradine, Barbara Hershey, Michael Greene, Bruce Carradine, John Blythe Barrymore. **1981 DVD**

AMERICANIZATION OF EMILY, THE ★★★1/2 Who would think of turning the Normandy invasion into a massive publicity event? According to screenwriter Paddy Chayefsky, the American military brass would drool over the possibilities. James Garner winningly plays the naval officer designated to be the first casualty on the beach. The script, intelligently handled by director Arthur Hiller, bristles with hard-edged humor. B&W; 117m. **DIR:** Arthur Hiller. **CAST:** James Garner, Julie Andrews, Melvyn Douglas, James Coburn, Joyce Grenfell, Keenan Wynn, Judy Carne. **1964**

AMERICANO, THE ★★1/2 Texas cowboy Glenn Ford gets embroiled with a bunch of Brazilian bad guys in this way-south-of-the-border Western. A change of scenery is commendable, but a familiar plot makes this film all but pedestrian. 85m. **DIR:** William Castle. **CAST:** Glenn Ford, Cesar Romero, Frank Lovejoy, Abbe Lane. **1954**

AMERICA'S DEADLIEST HOME VIDEO ★★★ Shot on video in a cinema verité style, this is a scathing remark on the society that has embraced reality shows like *Cops*. Here, Danny Bonaduce (?!) plays a man who inadvertently videotapes a robbery. The criminals kidnap him and then decide to have him chronicle their exploits. While the visual style becomes annoying after a half hour or so, the film still keeps a visceral punch that will leave you fascinated until the end. Not rated; contains graphic violence and profanity. 87m. **DIR:** Jack Perez. **CAST:** Danny Bonaduce. **1992**

AMERICA'S DREAM ★★★★ This compilation of three tales about the African American experience benefits from its strong cast and direction. In *Long Black Song,* Danny Glover plays a farmer whose love for his wife is tested when she falls for a traveling salesman. *The Reunion* features Lorraine Toussaint as a jazz piano player who confronts prejudices. The highlight of the trilogy, *The Boy Who Painted Christ,* stars Wesley Snipes as a small-town principal who must defend a student's painting of a black Christ. Made for cable. Rated PG-13 for profanity and adult situations. 86m. **DIR:** Bill Duke, Kevin Rodney Sullivan, Paris Barclay. **CAST:** Wesley Snipes, Danny Glover, Jasmine Guy, Lorraine Toussaint. **1995**

•AMERICA'S SWEETHEARTS ★★★1/2 Cowriter and producer Billy Crystal's pungent satire about media fascination with the Hollywood film community owes much of its sparkle to the radiant Julia Roberts, cast here as the plain sister who forever handles damage control for famous (and narcissistic) sibling Catherine Zeta-Jones. The love quadrangle that centers around Roberts, John Cusack, Zeta-Jones, and Hank Azaria is much more entertaining than the script's jabs at two-faced reporters, film junkets, and image-making, all of which have been skewered far better in projects such as, say, Robert Altman's *The Player.* Even so, Roberts and Cusack generate considerable good will, and the result goes down smoothly. Rated PG-13 for profanity and mild sexual content. 102m. **DIR:** Joe Roth. **CAST:** Julia Roberts, Billy Crystal, Catherine Zeta-Jones, John Cusack, Hank Azaria, Christopher Walken, Alan Arkin, Seth Green. **2001 DVD**

AMERICATHON 🦃 Abysmal comedy about a bankrupt American government staging a telethon to save itself. Rated R for profanity and sleaze. 86m. **DIR:** Neal Israel. **CAST:** John Ritter, Harvey Korman, Nancy Morgan, Peter Riegert, Zane Buzby, Fred Willard, Chief Dan George. **1979**

AMIN: THE RISE AND FALL 🦃 Idi Amin during his reign of terror in Uganda. Rated R for violence, nudity, and profanity. 101m. **DIR:** Richard Fleischer. **CAST:** Joseph Olita. **1981**

AMISTAD ★★★ An uprising aboard the Spanish slave ship *La Amistad* in 1839 boldly sets the stage to explore this real-life bloodbath and the exposure of the slaves to the American judicial system. Often riveting but runs out of intense drama well before it runs out of dry, windy speeches. Rated R for violence and nudity. 152m. **DIR:** Steven Spielberg. **CAST:** Djimon Hounsou, Anthony Hopkins, Morgan Freeman, Nigel Hawthorne, Stellan Skarsgard, Matthew McConaughey, Anna Paquin, David Paymer, Pete Postlethwaite. **1997 DVD**

AMITYVILLE II: THE POSSESSION ★★ Okay, so it's not a horror classic. But thanks to tight pacing, skillful special effects, and fine acting, it is a fairly suspenseful flick. Rated R for violence, implied sex, light profanity, and adult themes. 104m. **DIR:** Damiano Damiani. **CAST:** Burt Young, Rutanya Alda, James Olson, Moses Gunn. **1982**

AMITYVILLE III: THE DEMON 🦃 In this soggy second sequel to *The Amityville Horror*, Tony Roberts plays a reporter who investigates the infamous house. Rated PG for violence and gore. 105m. **DIR:** Richard Fleischer. **CAST:** Tony Roberts, Candy Clark, Robert Joy, Tess Harper, Lori Loughlin, Meg Ryan. **1983**

AMITYVILLE 4: THE EVIL ESCAPES ★★ Rest easy: the most famous haunted house on Long Island and the subject of three earlier films is now demon-free. Unfortunately, the evil has relocated to Jane Wyatt's California homestead. Ridiculous TV movie. 95m. **DIR:** Sandor Stern. **CAST:** Patty Duke, Jane Wyatt, Norman Lloyd. **1989**

AMITYVILLE: A NEW GENERATION 🦃 Low-budget and none-too-creative. The ancient Amityville evil is now lurking behind a strange-looking mirror in the possession of a young artist. Rated R for profanity, nudity, and violence. 92m. **DIR:** John Murlowski. **CAST:** Ross Partridge, Julia Nickson, David Naughton, Richard Roundtree, Terry O'Quinn. **1993**

AMITYVILLE CURSE, THE ★★1/2 The famous house of hell shakes its walls and rattles its floors for the fifth time. In this chapter, three young couples have purchased the dreadful dwelling. Naturally, things aren't what they should be. Rated R. 92m. **DIR:** Tom Berry. **CAST:** Kim Coates. **1989**

AMITYVILLE DOLLHOUSE ★★★ *The Amityville Horror* series continues with this direct-to-video effort about a possessed dollhouse. When a family moves into the notorious Amityville house, their young daughter is attracted to a replica dollhouse. Little does she know that the dollhouse is possessed by demons who immediately take over her entire family. Decent special effects and a constant feeling of doom keep the story moving.

Rated R for language, violence, and sexuality. 97m. **DIR:** Steve White. **CAST:** Robin Thomas, Starr Andreeff. **1996**

AMITYVILLE HORROR, THE 🦃 A better title for this turgid mishmash would be *The Amityville Bore*. Avoid it. Rated R. 117m. **DIR:** Stuart Rosenberg. **CAST:** James Brolin, Margot Kidder, Rod Steiger. **1979 DVD**

AMITYVILLE 1992: IT'S ABOUT TIME 🦃 A possessed mantel clock takes its toll on an unsuspecting suburban family. This sixth installment of *The Amityville Horror* series has fair effects, but it hasn't any real suspense. Rated R for nudity, violence, and profanity. 95m. **DIR:** Tony Randel. **CAST:** Stephen Macht, Shawn Weatherly, Megan Ward, Damon Martin, Nita Talbot. **1992**

AMNESIA ★★★ While plotting to fake his death so he can run away with his mistress, a small-town minister loses his memory after a bump on the head. This leads to complications as the plan he had been putting into effect catches up with him. A tongue-in-cheek erotic thriller that plays like a housebroken David Lynch film. Rated R for nudity, sexuality, profanity, and violence. 88m. **DIR:** Kurt Voss. **CAST:** Nicholas Walker, Dara Tomanovich, Sally Kirkland, Vincent Berry, Ally Sheedy, Marthe Keller, John Savage. **1997**

AMONG THE CINDERS ★★1/2 A teenager (Paul O'Shea) holds himself responsible for the accidental death of a friend, and it takes a trip to the wilds with his grandfather (Derek Hardwick) to pull him out of it. This coming-of-age drama from New Zealand has its good moments, but these are outnumbered by the unremarkable ones. Rated R for nudity, profanity, suggested sex, and brief gore. 105m. **DIR:** Rolf Haedrick. **CAST:** Paul O'Shea, Derek Hardwick. **1985**

AMONG THE LIVING ★★★1/2 Unbalanced man thought long dead kills his keeper and joins the local populace, putting his twin brother in jeopardy. Strange psychological drama is a study in small-town life and mob mentality. Its earthy dialogue, frenzied action, and outstanding camera shots and composition belie its B-movie status, putting it on a par with the best productions of the day. Albert Dekker as the twin brothers and young Susan Hayward as a gutsy tart shine. B&W; 68m. **DIR:** Stuart Heisler. **CAST:** Albert Dekker, Harry Carey, Susan Hayward, Frances Farmer, Gordon Jones, Jean Phillips, Maude Eburne, Ernest Whitman. **1941**

AMONGST FRIENDS ★★★★ Writer-director Rob Weiss's compelling little study of youth led astray makes excellent use of its cast of newcomers. Steve Parlavecchio shines as one of three Long Island teenagers seduced by the easy money of organized crime. Given its humble origins, this is a far more palatable modern gangster drama than *Goodfellas*. Rated R for profanity, violence, and nudity. 88m. **DIR:** Rob Weiss. **CAST:** Steve Parlavecchio, Joseph Lindsey, Patrick McGaw, Mira Sorvino. **1993**

AMORE (1948) ★★★★ Director Roberto Rossellini's homage to actress Anna Magnani features her in two short films that showcase her brilliant talent. In "The Human Voice," based on a one-act play by Jean Cocteau, she is alone on-screen, engaged in a telephone conversation with an unseen lover. "The Miracle," inspired by a story by Federico Fellini, is a small masterpiece about a peasant woman who must defend her belief that she has given birth to the new Messiah. It was condemned by the U.S. Catholic church, which resulted in a landmark U.S. Supreme Court decision that films are protected by the First Amendment. In Italian with English subtitles. B&W; 78m. **DIR:** Roberto Rossellini. **CAST:** Anna Magnani. **1948**

AMORE! (1993) ★★★ *Cinderella* in reverse, this features a billionaire (Jack Scalia) heading for Hollywood to make it without using his wealth or connections. Succeeding only when he pretends to be an Italian stud, he must get his new girlfriend (Kathy Ireland) to love him for himself. Silly but likable time passer. Rated PG-13 for sexual situations. 93m. **DIR:** Lorenzo Doumani. **CAST:** Jack Scalia, Kathy Ireland, George Hamilton, Brenda Epperson. **1993**

•AMORES PERROS ★★★★ *Love's a Bitch* is the English title of this Latino Tarantino mix of crime, mayhem, passion, and lost souls. Autos and a trio of stories collide at a Mexico City traffic intersection in this unsettling Oscar-nominated drama. The film exposes an underworld of urban dog fighting as we watch a young man plan to steal his brother's wife, the life of a supermodel at the height of her career, and the decaying existence of a revolutionary turned homeless hit man. This lurid dance of imagery is not for the squeamish. In Spanish with English subtitles. Rated R for gore, violence, language, and sex. 154m. **DIR:** Alejandro Gonzalez Iñárritu. **CAST:** Emilio Echevarria, Gael Garcia Bernal, Vanessa Bauche, Marco Pérez, Álvaro Guerro, Goya Toledo. **2000 DVD**

AMOROUS ADVENTURES OF MOLL FLANDERS, THE ★★ Silly sex romp features a naughty Kim Novak sampling Englishmen's wares circa 1700. Howls rather than laughs result from her many sexual escapades. Not rated, this would be equivalent to a PG-13 for endless sexual situations and innuendo. 126m. **DIR:** Terence Young. **CAST:** Kim Novak, Angela Lansbury, Richard Johnson, George Sanders. **1965**

AMOS & ANDREW ★★1/2 Samuel L. Jackson is a famous African-American playwright and activist who is mistaken for a burglar the first night in his new home on an exclusive New England resort island. Local sheriff Dabney Coleman forces jailed misfit Nicolas Cage to pretend to be a criminal who has taken Jackson hostage. Dumb but sometimes funny comedy full of goofy misunderstandings. Rated PG-13 for profanity and violence. 95m. **DIR:** E. Max Frye. **CAST:** Nicolas Cage, Samuel L. Jackson, Dabney Coleman, Michael Lerner, Margaret Colin, Brad Dourif, Chelcie Ross, Giancarlo Esposito. **1993 DVD**

AMOS AND ANDY (TV SERIES) ★★★ The first major television show with an all-black cast, *Amos and Andy* features sharp writing, energetic humor, and witty, memorable performances. CBS pulled the show in 1966 amid charges of racism, and rightfully so in that era. Now these surprisingly timeless comedies have been released on video, and they can be enjoyed if taken in the proper context. B&W; 30m. **DIR:** Charles Barton. **CAST:** Tim Moore, Spencer Williams Jr., Alvin Childress, Ernestine Wade, Amanda Randolph. **1951–1953**

AMSTERDAM KILL, THE 🦃 Robert Mitchum stars in this dud about an international drug conspiracy. Rated R. 90m. **DIR:** Robert Clouse. **CAST:** Robert Mitchum,

Bradford Dillman, Richard Egan, Leslie Nielsen, Keye Luke. **1977**

AMSTERDAMNED 🦃 When a psycho killer comes up from the depths of the Amsterdam canals seeking prey, a Dutch cop and his buddy, a scuba-diving expert, try to reel him in. Rated R for violence. 114m. **DIR:** Dick Maas. **CAST:** Huub Stapel, Monique van de Ven. **1988**

AMY ★★★1/2 Disney warmth runs though this sensitive story. Jenny Agutter is Amy, a young woman who leaves her domineering husband after the death of their deaf son. She decides to teach at a school for the deaf. A film for the whole family. Rated G. 100m. **DIR:** Vincent McEveety. **CAST:** Jenny Agutter, Barry Newman, Kathleen Nolan, Chris Robinson, Margaret O'Brien, Nanette Fabray. **1981**

AMY FISHER STORY, THE ★★1/2 The best of the made-for-television movies about the Long Island Lolita, whose affair with auto mechanic Joey Buttafuoco led her to shoot Buttafuoco's wife, Mary Jo. Drew Barrymore effectively captures the spirit of the tempting teen, but steamy footage added for video features a body double. Not rated; contains adult situations. 96m. **DIR:** Andy Tennant. **CAST:** Drew Barrymore, Anthony Denison, Harley Jane Kozak. **1993 DVD**

ANACONDA 🦃 A documentary-film crew, searching up the Amazon for a tribe of legendary Indians, finds instead a forty-foot killer snake. Asinine hodgepodge of monster movie clichés proves that money can't buy quality and even digital special effects can be cheesy. The wasted cast halfheartedly tries playing it for laughs. Rated PG-13 for profanity and unconvincing violence. 90m. **DIR:** Luis Llosa. **CAST:** Jennifer Lopez, Ice Cube, Jon Voight, Eric Stoltz, Jonathan Hyde, Owen Wilson, Kari Wuhrer. **1997 DVD**

ANALYZE THIS ★★★1/2 This very funny film, which borrows more than a little from James Coburn's 1967 counterculture hit, *The President's Analyst*, concerns what might happen if New York's toughest gangster suddenly found himself in need of therapy. When the mob boss is Robert De Niro, and the shrink is Billy Crystal, the results are quite entertaining. The supporting cast is laced with familiar character actors, none better than Joe Viterelli, simply priceless as De Niro's bodyguard. You'll be tempted into repeat viewings to catch the dialogue overshadowed the first time by the continuous laughter. Rated R for relentless profanity and considerable—albeit rather bloodless—gunfire. 106m. **DIR:** Harold Ramis. **CAST:** Robert De Niro, Billy Crystal, Lisa Kudrow, Joe Viterelli, Chazz Palminteri. **1999 DVD**

ANASTASIA (1956) ★★★1/2 Ingrid Bergman earned her second Oscar for the title role of the young woman who looks amazingly like Anastasia, Czar Nicholas's daughter. (The entire royal family was supposedly assassinated.) Is she or isn't she Anastasia? A compelling drama. 105m. **DIR:** Anatole Litvak. **CAST:** Ingrid Bergman, Yul Brynner, Helen Hayes, Akim Tamiroff. **1956**

ANASTASIA (1997) ★★★1/2 Twentieth Century Fox's first animated feature uses the Russian Revolution as a starting point for a lavish musical fairy-tale romance. This gorgeously rendered story begins in 1916 as evil sorcerer Rasputin puts a curse on the reigning Romanov family. Only the czar's daughter, Anastasia, and her grandmother survive. Ten years later the orphaned teen is struggling with amnesia when she crosses paths with her exiled grandmother in Paris. Rated G. 94m. **DIR:** Don Bluth, Gary Goldman. **CAST:** Meg Ryan, John Cusack, Angela Lansbury, Christopher Lloyd, Kelsey Grammer, Kirsten Dunst. **1997 DVD**

ANASTASIA: THE MYSTERY OF ANNA ★★1/2 Star-studded cast can't compensate for the uninspired performance by Amy Irving in the title role of this TV miniseries. She plays the mysterious woman who appeared six years after the Romanov Royalty of Russia were annihilated, claiming to have survived. Rex Harrison plays her staunchest adversary as the current head of the Romanov family. Costuming and music are superior. 208m. **DIR:** Marvin J. Chomsky. **CAST:** Amy Irving, Rex Harrison, Edward Fox, Olivia de Havilland, Omar Sharif, Susan Lucci. **1986**

ANATOMY ★★★★ Honestly chilling thriller stars Franka Potente as a promising medical student who is thrilled to land a spot in a prestigious anatomy class. Her excitement turns to fear when several of her classmates wind up in the morgue, leading her to suspect that something more sinister than murder is going on. Great, gruesome fun with lots of spine-tingling suspense. In German with English subtitles. Rated R for adult situations, language, and extreme violence. 100m. **DIR:** Stefan Ruzowitzky. **CAST:** Franka Potente, Benno Fürmann, Anna Loos, Holger Speckhahn. **2000 DVD**

ANATOMY OF A MURDER ★★★★ A clever plot, realistic atmosphere, smooth direction, and sterling performances from a topflight cast make this frank and exciting small-town courtroom drama first-rate fare. Honest realism saturates throughout. B&W; 160m. **DIR:** Otto Preminger. **CAST:** James Stewart, Arthur O'Connell, Lee Remick, Ben Gazzara, Eve Arden, Kathryn Grant, George C. Scott, Joseph Welch, Orson Bean, Murray Hamilton. **1959 DVD**

ANCHORS AWEIGH ★★★ A somewhat tedious and overlong dance film that is perked up by a few truly impressive numbers, none finer than Gene Kelly's duet with an animated Jerry the mouse (of Tom and Jerry fame). Not rated; suitable for family viewing. 140m. **DIR:** George Sidney. **CAST:** Gene Kelly, Frank Sinatra, Kathryn Grayson, Dean Stockwell. **1945 DVD**

AND BABY MAKES SIX ★★★ Colleen Dewhurst is a middle-aged mother who becomes pregnant. It's too much for her loving husband (Warren Oates), who just doesn't want the responsibility of another child. A wonderful cast proved this made-for-TV movie good enough to produce a sequel, *Baby Comes Home*. 104m. **DIR:** Waris Hussein. **CAST:** Colleen Dewhurst, Warren Oates, Mildred Dunnock, Maggie Cooper, Timothy Hutton. **1979**

AND GOD CREATED WOMAN (1957) ★★1/2 Brigitte Bardot rose to international fame as the loose-moraled coquette who finds it hard to say no to an attractive male, especially a well-heeled one. Shot with as much of Bardot exposed as the law then allowed, this rather slight story works well. In French with English subtitles. 92m. **DIR:** Roger Vadim. **CAST:** Brigitte Bardot, Curt Jurgens, Jean-Louis Trintignant, Christian Marquand. **1957 DVD**

AND GOD CREATED WOMAN (1987) 🦃 Rebecca DeMornay is unbelievable as a convict who tries to go straight. Rated R for language, nudity, and simulated sex. 97m. **DIR:** Roger Vadim. **CAST:** Rebecca DeMornay, Vincent Spano, Frank Langella, Donovan Leitch. **1987 DVD**

. . . AND GOD SPOKE ★★★1/2 Frequently hilarious mock-u-mentary about the efforts to film a large-scale religious epic. Michael Riley and Stephen Rappaport are believable as the director and producer who watch as their big-budget effort is whittled down to a renegade, zero-budget production. Industry in-jokes may fly over the heads of some viewers, but you can't help but laugh at Soupy Sales playing Moses, carrying two tablets and a six-pack of soda as part of a product-placement deal. Rated R for language and nudity. 82m. **DIR:** Arthur Borman. **CAST:** Michael Riley, Stephen Rappaport, Soupy Sales, Eve Plumb. **1994**

AND HOPE TO DIE ★★★1/2 A Frenchman who is on the run from thugs hides out with an old gangster who enlists him in a kidnap scheme. Complex, well-acted crime-drama. Rated R for nudity and violence. 95m. **DIR:** René Clement. **CAST:** Robert Ryan, Tisa Farrow, Jean-Louis Trintignant, Lea Massari, Aldo Ray. **1972**

AND I ALONE SURVIVED ★★1/2 In this TV movie Blair Brown stars as Lauren Elder, the only survivor of a plane crash in California's Sierra Nevada mountains. Based on a true event, the film tends toward the overdramatic and begs for better characterizations. Still, Brown does give a fine performance. 100m. **DIR:** William A. Graham. **CAST:** Blair Brown, David Ackroyd, Vera Miles, G. D. Spradlin. **1978**

. . . AND JUSTICE FOR ALL ★★★1/2 This is a bristling black comedy starring Al Pacino as a lawyer who becomes fed up with the red tape of our country's legal system. It's both heartrending and darkly hilarious—but not for all tastes. Rated R. 117m. **DIR:** Norman Jewison. **CAST:** Al Pacino, Jack Warden, John Forsythe, Craig T. Nelson. **1979 DVD**

AND NOTHING BUT THE TRUTH ★★★ A British film about a TV news magazine—an Anglo *A Current Affair*. Glenda Jackson stars as a documentary filmmaker who must confront a sometimes exploitative reporter (well played by Jon Finch). Superficial but interesting. 90m. **DIR:** Karl Francis. **CAST:** Glenda Jackson, Jon Finch, Kenneth Colley. **1982**

AND NOW FOR SOMETHING COMPLETELY DIFFERENT ★★★1/2 Fitfully funny but still a treat for their fans, this was the first screen outing of the Monty Python comedy troupe. It's a collection of the best bits from the team's television series. With delightful ditties, such as "The Lumberjack Song," how can you go wrong? Rated PG. 89m. **DIR:** Ian McNaughton. **CAST:** John Cleese, Eric Idle, Terry Jones, Michael Palin, Graham Chapman, Terry Gilliam. **1972 DVD**

AND NOW, MY LOVE ★★★1/2 In biography-documentary style, director Claude Lelouch juxtaposes three generations of a family while depicting the moral, political, and artistic events that shaped the members' lives. All this is wonderfully designed to show how inevitable it is for two young people (played by André Dussolier and Marthe Keller) from different backgrounds to fall in love. French, dubbed in English. 121m. **DIR:** Claude Lelouch. **CAST:** Marthe Keller, André Dussolier, Charles Denner. **1974**

AND NOW THE SCREAMING STARTS ★★★ Frightening British horror film about a young newlywed couple moving into a house haunted by a centuries-old curse on the husband's family. Well-done, with a great cast, but occasionally a bit too bloody. Rated R. 87m. **DIR:** Roy Ward Baker. **CAST:** Peter Cushing, Stephanie Beacham, Herbert Lom, Patrick Magee, Ian Ogilvy. **1973 DVD**

AND SOON THE DARKNESS ★★1/2 Two young English college girls decide to go bicycle touring through the French countryside. But when the more vivacious of the two suddenly disappears in the same spot where a young girl was killed the year before, the foundation is laid for a tale of suspense. Rated PG. 94m. **DIR:** Robert Fuest. **CAST:** Pamela Franklin, Michele Dotrice, Sandor Eles. **1970**

AND THE BAND PLAYED ON ★★★★1/2 A gripping adaptation of journalist Randy Shilts's book about the early days of the AIDS epidemic. Matthew Modine leads an all-star cast as a scientist with the Centers for Disease Control who must battle bureaucracy and ignorance to show that AIDS is everyone's problem. Part detective thriller, part tearjerker, this film drives home its message. Rated PG-13 for adult themes. 140m. **DIR:** Roger Spottiswoode. **CAST:** Matthew Modine, Alan Alda, Phil Collins, Richard Gere, Anjelica Huston, Steve Martin, Ian McKellen, Lily Tomlin. **1993 DVD**

AND THE SHIP SAILS ON ★★ Federico Fellini's heavily symbolic parable about a luxury liner sailing the Adriatic on the eve of World War I was called by one critic "a spellbinding, often magical tribute to the illusions and delusions of art." That's one way of looking at it. We found it boring. However, Fellini fans may find it rewarding. In Italian with English subtitles. 138m. **DIR:** Federico Fellini. **CAST:** Freddie Jones, Barbara Jefford, Victor Poletti. **1984 DVD**

AND THEN THERE WERE NONE ★★★★★ One of the best screen adaptations of an Agatha Christie mystery. A select group of people is invited to a lonely island and murdered one by one. René Clair's inspired visual style gives this release just the right atmosphere and tension. B&W; 98m. **DIR:** René Clair. **CAST:** Barry Fitzgerald, Walter Huston, Richard Haydn, Roland Young, Judith Anderson, Louis Hayward, June Duprez, C. Aubrey Smith. **1945 DVD**

AND THEN YOU DIE ★★★★ Canadian version of *The Long Good Friday*. Kenneth Welsh is Eddie Griffin, drug czar for Canada's coke freaks. His kingdom starts unraveling around him after the Mafia don in his area is murdered. Eddie gets caught in a squeeze play between the don's successor, an up-and-coming coke dealer, and the police. The film grabs you right from the opening frame and keeps you guessing right up to the final scene. 115m. **DIR:** Francis Mankiewicz. **CAST:** Kenneth Welsh, R. H. Thomson, Wayne Robson, Tom Harvey, George Bloomfield, Graeme Campbell. **1987**

AND YOU THOUGHT YOUR PARENTS WERE WEIRD ★★ After the death of their inventor father, two brothers devote their time and energy to following in his footsteps. Celestial intervention instills the spirit of their dad into their latest invention: a robot. Thin family fare. Rated PG. 92m. **DIR:** Tony Goodson. **CAST:** Marcia Strassman, Joshua Miller, Edan Gross, Alan Thicke. **1991**

ANDERSON TAPES, THE ★★★★ Sean Connery is perfectly cast in this exciting film about an ex-con under surveillance who wants to pull off the Big Heist. Slickly done, with tight editing and direction to keep the viewer totally involved, it holds up extremely well on video. Rated PG. 98m. **DIR:** Sidney Lumet. **CAST:** Sean Connery, Dyan Cannon, Martin Balsam, Ralph Meeker, Margaret Hamilton. **1972**

ANDERSONVILLE ★★★★ Harrowing Civil War drama focuses on the inhumane conditions suffered by prisoners of war at the Confederate Andersonville compound. As told through the eyes of a young Union corporal, director John Frankenheimer's film is a testament to the human soul and spirit. Powerful, hard-hitting performances and a tough, literate script by David W. Rintels combine to make this made-for-cable film an experience that's hard to forget. Not rated; contains profanity and violence. 168m. **DIR:** John Frankenheimer. **CAST:** Jarrod Emrick, Frederic Forrest, William H. Macy, Jan Triska, Ted Marcoux. **1996**

ANDERSONVILLE TRIAL, THE ★★★★1/2 Based on MacKinley Kantor's Pulitzer Prize novel, this made-for-TV play tells the story of Andersonville, the notorious Georgia prison where 50,000 northern soldiers suffered and close to 14,000 died. This is one of the great accounts of the Civil War. 150m. **DIR:** George C. Scott. **CAST:** Martin Sheen, William Shatner, Buddy Ebsen, Richard Basehart, Cameron Mitchell, Jack Cassidy. **1970**

ANDRE ★★★★ First-class family entertainment features a bright-eyed youngster who becomes best friends with a seal, played with remarkable versatility and skill by Tory, the sea lion. Based on a true story, *Andre* details the conflict that arises when local fishermen in Rockport, Maine, and an animal-protection agency threaten to tear the twosome apart. Kids will love it, and so will their parents. Rated PG for a very brief fistfight. 94m. **DIR:** George Miller. **CAST:** Keith Carradine, Tina Majorino, Chelsea Field, Aidan Pendleton, Shane Meier, Keith Szarabajka. **1994 DVD**

ANDREI RUBLEV ★★★★★ Considered by many to be the most important Russian film of the past thirty years, this epic is based on the life of Andrei Rublev, a monk and icon painter who wanders through a gruesome landscape, clinging to religious faith in the face of barbarism and pagan rituals in fifteenth-century Russia, then under the reign of Tartar invaders. Mesmerizing! In Russian with English subtitles. B&W; 185m. **DIR:** Andrei Tarkovsky. **CAST:** Andrej Mikhalkov, Andrei Tarkovsky. **1966 DVD**

ANDROCLES AND THE LION ★★1/2 An incredible cast still can't save this plodding story of a mild-mannered tailor (Alan Young) whose act of kindness toward a lion helps to save a group of Christians. George Bernard Shaw's pointed retelling of an old fable loses its bite in this rambling production. B&W; 105m. **DIR:** Chester Erskine. **CAST:** Alan Young, Jean Simmons, Victor Mature, Robert Newton, Maurice Evans, Elsa Lanchester, Reginald Gardiner, Gene Lockhart, Alan Mowbray, John Hoyt, Jim Backus. **1952**

ANDROID ★★★★ A highly enjoyable tongue-in-cheek sci-fi adventure takes place on a space station where a mad scientist, Dr. Daniel (played by a surprisingly subdued and effective Klaus Kinski), is trying to create the perfect android. As a group of criminal castaways arrives at the station, the doctor's current robot assistant, Max 404 (Don Opper), decides it is time to rebel. Rated PG for nudity, violence, and profanity. 80m. **DIR:** Aaron Lipstadt. **CAST:** Klaus Kinski, Don Opper, Brie Howard, Norbert Weisser. **1982**

ANDROID AFFAIR, THE ★★1/2 In this made-for-cable original, a doctor falls in love with her android patient while on the run from the people who make the androids. Interesting characters, but a slow, dull plot. Not rated; contains violence. 95m. **DIR:** Richard Kletter. **CAST:** Harley Jane Kozak, Ossie Davis, Saul Rubinek, Griffin Dunne. **1995**

ANDROMEDA STRAIN, THE ★★★★ A tense science-fiction thriller, this film focuses on a team of scientists attempting to isolate a deadly virus while racing against time and the possibility of nuclear war. Though not as flashy as other entries in the genre, it's highly effective. Rated G. 130m. **DIR:** Robert Wise. **CAST:** Arthur Hill, David Wayne, James Olson, Kate Reid, Paula Kelly. **1971 DVD**

ANDY GRIFFITH SHOW, THE (TV SERIES) ★★★★ Six volumes of one of television's most fondly remembered situation comedies. This series takes place in fictitious Mayberry, North Carolina, a sleepy little town looked after by laid-back sheriff Andy Taylor and his manic deputy, Barney Fife (Don Knotts, winner of numerous Emmy Awards for his portrayal). Each volume contains four episodes spotlighting a particular character's most memorable moments. B&W; 100m. **DIR:** Various. **CAST:** Andy Griffith, Don Knotts, Ron Howard, Jim Nabors, Frances Bavier, Howard McNear, George Lindsey, Hal Smith, Howard Morris. **1960–1965 DVD**

ANDY HARDY GETS SPRING FEVER ★★★ Another in the long-running series about all-American life in a small town. This installment finds Andy Hardy (Mickey Rooney) saddled with the trials and tribulations of producing his high-school play. B&W; 85m. **DIR:** W. S. Van Dyke. **CAST:** Mickey Rooney, Lewis Stone, Fay Holden, Cecilia Parker, Ann Rutherford. **1939**

ANDY HARDY MEETS A DEBUTANTE ★★★ Mickey Rooney again portrays the all-American teenager who dominated the long-running series. Good, wholesome family-film fare. B&W; 86m. **DIR:** George B. Seitz. **CAST:** Mickey Rooney, Lewis Stone, Cecilia Parker, Fay Holden, Judy Garland. **1940**

ANDY HARDY'S DOUBLE LIFE ★★★ Fresh from championship swimming, Esther Williams got her studio start in this warm and sentimental addition to the hit series. B&W; 92m. **DIR:** George B. Seitz. **CAST:** Mickey Rooney, Lewis Stone, Cecilia Parker, Fay Holden, Ann Rutherford, Esther Williams, William Lundigan. **1942**

ANDY HARDY'S PRIVATE SECRETARY ★★★ Kathryn Grayson is the focus in this slice of wholesome Americana from the innocent days just before World War II. Fun for the whole family. B&W; 101m. **DIR:** George B. Seitz. **CAST:** Mickey Rooney, Lewis Stone, Fay Holden, Ian Hunter, Kathryn Grayson, Gene Reynolds, Ann Rutherford. **1940**

ANDY WARHOL: SUPERSTAR ★★★★ Thoroughly fascinating exploration of the pop icon's life and times, featuring a bevy of celebrities stepping forward with their recollections. Director Chuck Workman's film is like a time capsule filled with precious memories. 87m. **DIR:** Chuck Workman. **1991**

ANDY WARHOL'S BAD ★★★1/2 Carroll Baker stars in this nasty and very sick outing from producer Andy Warhol. She plays a tough mama who runs a squad of female hit men out of her cheery suburban home. Into this strange company comes Perry King as a mysterious stranger who boards there until he completes his "mission." The film has gore, violence, and nudity. 107m. **DIR:** Jed Johnson. **CAST:** Carroll Baker, Perry King, Susan Tyrrell. **1977**

ANDY WARHOL'S DRACULA 🦃 Companion piece to Andy Warhol's equally revolting version of *Frankenstein*. Rated X for excessive violence and kinky sex. 93m. **DIR:** Paul Morrissey. **CAST:** Udo Kier, Joe Dallesandro, Vittorio De Sica, Roman Polanski. **1974**

ANDY WARHOL'S FRANKENSTEIN 🦃 Blood and gore gush at every opportunity. Rated R for obvious reasons. 94m. **DIR:** Paul Morrissey. **CAST:** Joe Dallesandro, Monique Van Vooren, Udo Kier. **1974**

ANGEL 🦃 Bad, low-budget flick about a 15 year old who moonlights as a Hollywood Boulevard hooker and is menaced by a psychotic killer. Rated R for nudity, violence, suggested sex, and profanity. 94m. **DIR:** Robert Vincent O'Neil. **CAST:** Cliff Gorman, Susan Tyrrell, Dick Shawn, Donna Wilkes. **1983 DVD**

ANGEL AND THE BADMAN ★★★★ A fine low-budget Western with John Wayne as a gunman who sees the light through the love of Quaker girl Gail Russell. Harry Carey and Bruce Cabot also are memorable in this thoughtful action film directed by longtime Wayne screenwriter James Edward Grant. B&W; 100m. **DIR:** James Edward Grant. **CAST:** John Wayne, Gail Russell, Harry Carey, Irene Rich, Bruce Cabot. **1947 DVD**

ANGEL AT MY TABLE, AN ★★★★★ New Zealand filmmaker Jane Campion's brilliant, affecting, and perceptive portrait of writer Janet Frame, detailing her emotional journey through a quirky childhood, a misdiagnosis of mental illness, and a severe, lifelong shyness. If you liked *My Left Foot*, you should love this story of an exceptional artist. Rated R for profanity and sexual frankness. 145m. **DIR:** Jane Campion. **CAST:** Kerry Fox, Alexia Keogh, Karen Fergusson. **1991**

ANGEL BABY ★★★ Psychotic patients Harry and Kate meet at a walk-in treatment center and fall in love in this gritty Australian drama. The odds against their romance and independence skyrocket when Kate becomes pregnant and they flush their medications down the toilet to protect the health of their unborn child. This offbeat film about the power of love and inner demons has several storyline cracks but the acting is excellent. Not rated; contains graphic sex and frontal nudity. 105m. **DIR:** Michael Rymer. **CAST:** John Lynch, Jacqueline McKenzie, Colin Friels, Deborra-Lee Furness. **1995**

ANGEL CITY ★★★ A family is forced to leave their West Virgina farm and travel to Florida in search of work. Exploited by a corrupt labor-camp boss, the family members open the gates for all the immigrant workers to escape and start their lives again. Made for television. 100m. **DIR:** Philip Leacock. **CAST:** Jennifer Warren, Jennifer Jason Leigh, Mitchell Ryan. **1980**

ANGEL EYES ★★★1/2 When a Chicago cop (Jennifer Lopez) and a mysterious stranger (Jim Caviezel) meet under unusual circumstances, their growing attraction draws painful secrets out of both of them. Thematically similar to director Luis Mandoki's previous film, *Message in a Bottle*, this well-acted, sensitive character study and suspenseful romantic thriller is a considerable improvement. Rated R for profanity, violence, and sexual scenes. 110m. **DIR:** Luis Mandoki. **CAST:** Jennifer Lopez, James Caviezel, Sonia Braga, Terrence Howard, Shirley Knight. **2001**

ANGEL FIST ★★ This Roger Corman production combines high kicks with hot babes. In it, a beautiful policewoman goes to Manila to avenge her sister's death. Watchable, but not twice! Rated R for nudity, sex, profanity, and violence. 76m. **DIR:** Cirio H. Santiago. **CAST:** Cat Sassoon, Melissa Moore, Michael Shaner, Denise Buick, Jessica Roberts. **1993**

ANGEL 4: UNDERCOVER ★★ Darlene Vogel inherits the role of ex-hooker turned police photographer. This outing, Angel goes undercover to find out who killed one of her friends from her hooking days and gets involved with a hard-rocking band and its charismatic leader, played by Shane Fraser. Roddy McDowall chews more than scenery as the band's slimy producer who's not above blackmail. Rated R for nudity, language, and violence. 94m. **DIR:** George Axmith. **CAST:** Darlene Vogel, Shane Fraser, Mark DeCarlo, Kerrie Clark, Roddy McDowall. **1994**

ANGEL HEART ★★★1/2 Mickey Rourke stars as a down-and-out private investigator. The elegant, dapper, and more than slightly sinister Louis Cyphre (Robert De Niro) wants a missing singer found in order to settle a vague "debt." Absolutely not for the squeamish or for children; rated R for violence, sex, and language. 113m. **DIR:** Alan Parker. **CAST:** Mickey Rourke, Lisa Bonet, Robert De Niro, Charlotte Rampling. **1987 DVD**

ANGEL IN TRAINING ★★ Low-rent family fare about a 12 year old girl who recruits her guardian angels to help save her dad's business from an untrustworthy business partner. The film wants to be another *Angels in the Outfield* but lacks the imagination. Rated G. 90m. **DIR:** Gary Graver, Chick Vennera. **CAST:** Laila Dagher, Gary Imhoff, Alexis O'Keefe. **1997 DVD**

ANGEL OF DEATH 🦃 Even among the lowly subgenre of Nazi revival movies, this rates near the bottom of the list. Rated R for violence and profanity. 90m. **DIR:** Jess (Jesus) Franco. **CAST:** Susan Andrews, Howard Vernon. **1986**

ANGEL OF DESTRUCTION ★★ When it comes to female martial arts stars, Maria Ford has a leg up on her competition. Not that she's more talented, but Ford realizes her assets and uses them accordingly. She's tracking down the serial killer who iced her sister, an undercover cop hot on the killer's trail. Plot seems overly familiar, but the presence of Ford makes the action easier to watch. Rated R for nudity, violence, and adult situations. 80m. **DIR:** Charles Philip Moore. **CAST:** Maria Ford, Charlie Spradling, Jimmy Broome, Chanda. **1994**

ANGEL OF FURY 🦃 Bottom-end martial arts trash, with security expert Cynthia Rothrock trying to keep a valuable computer out of enemy hands. If she could act ten times as well as she kicks . . . she'd *still* be terrible. Rated R for violence, torture, and profanity. 76m. **DIR:**

Ackyl Anwarv. **CAST:** Cynthia Rothrock, Christopher Daniel Barnes, Peter O'Brian. **1993**

ANGEL OF H.E.A.T. Not enough sex and skin for the hard-core crowd, and not enough plot, good acting, or production values for the spy flick lovers. Rated R. 93m. **DIR:** Myrl A. Schreibman. **CAST:** Marilyn Chambers, Dan Jesse, Mary Woronov, Stephen Johnson. **1982**

ANGEL ON MY SHOULDER (1946) ★★★★ In a break from his big-budget prestige screen biographies of the period, Paul Muni stars in this entertaining fantasy as a murdered gangster who makes a deal with the devil. He wants to return to his human form. He gets his wish and spends his time on Earth—as a judge—trying to outwit Satan. B&W; 101m. **DIR:** Archie Mayo. **CAST:** Paul Muni, Anne Baxter, Claude Rains, George Cleveland, Onslow Stevens. **1946 DVD**

ANGEL ON MY SHOULDER (1980) ★★★ Remade-for-television update of the 1946 Paul Muni fantasy about a wrongly murdered gangster returned to Earth on a Satanic errand. Genial comedy-drama. 100m. **DIR:** John Berry. **CAST:** Peter Strauss, Richard Kiley, Barbara Hershey, Janis Paige. **1980**

ANGEL TOWN An olympic kick-boxing trainer goes feet to head with street toughs. This anti–Mexican-American, anti-woman film is wimpy and stupid. Rated R for nudity, profanity, and violence. 102m. **DIR:** Eric Karson. **CAST:** Olivier Gruner, Theresa Saldana, Frank Aragon. **1990 DVD**

ANGELA ★★ Sophia Loren's 5-month-old son is kidnapped by feisty mob king John Huston. Twenty years pass, and she falls in love with a much younger man. Could the bond be more than originally thought? Turgid. 90m. **DIR:** Boris Sagal. **CAST:** Sophia Loren, Steve Railsback, John Huston, John Vernon. **1977**

ANGELA'S ASHES ★★★★ Frank McCourt's evocative memoir is realized with impressive verisimilitude in this handsome drama, which re-creates every detail of the bone-grinding, heartbreaking poverty the author endured during his childhood in Ireland. Director Alan Parker and coadaptor Laura Jones retain the pragmatic, cheerful optimism that defines McCourt's book: a child's forgiving willingness to see things in their best possible light. Various compelling young actors play McCourt during his childhood years; good as they are, they're overshadowed by Emily Watson's sterling portrayal of the boy's mother. Despite humiliation and debasement most of us would find inconceivable, this woman never loses sight of her primary goal: to protect and provide for her children. This film will, in time, take its place alongside other rich period dramas and memoirs such as *Doctor Zhivago*, *Hope and Glory*, and *Remains of the Day* . . . all films with the power to make us part of a historic setting and time that we never personally experienced. Rated R for profanity, nudity, and earthy dramatic content. 146m. **DIR:** Alan Parker. **CAST:** Emily Watson, Robert Carlyle, Michael Legge, Ciaran Owens, Joe Breen. **1999 DVD**

ANGELE ★★★1/2 Absorbing character study that blends comedy with drama in a story about a young French girl who becomes bored with life in the country and is lured into a sleazy existence in Paris with an older street hustler. A poignant drama in the tradition of Jean Renoir. In French with English subtitles. B&W; 132m. **DIR:** Marcel Pagnol. **CAST:** Orane Demazis, Fernandel, Jean Servais. **1934**

ANGELIC CONVERSATION ★★ Eclectic filmmaker and painter Derek Jarman delves into a very personal perspective of his world. A mythic figure summons his inner self to join him on a spiritual quest. Boring, heavy-handed self-indulgence saturated with personal passions and vivid visual fantasies. Liberally laced with narrations of Shakespearean sonnets by Judi Dench. 80m. **DIR:** Derek Jarman. **CAST:** Paul Reynolds, Phillip Williamson. **1985**

ANGELO, MY LOVE ★★★★ Robert Duvall wrote and directed this loosely scripted, wonderfully different movie about a streetwise 11 year old gypsy boy. Duvall reportedly conceived the project when he spotted the fast-talking, charismatic Angelo Evans on a New York street and decided he ought to be in pictures. Rated R for profanity. 115m. **DIR:** Robert Duvall. **CAST:** Angelo Evans, Michael Evans. **1983**

ANGELS AND INSECTS ★★★★ A mild-mannered naturalist in Victorian England lives with an aristocratic family, finding ironic similarities between his hosts and the bugs he studies. The film is low-key and leisurely paced, but subtly perceptive, probing under the surface of Victorian society. Excellent performances, especially by Kristin Scott Thomas as a poor relation dependent on the generosity of her intellectual inferiors. Not rated; contains graphic simulated sex and frontal nudity. 117m. **DIR:** Philip Haas. **CAST:** Mark Rylance, Patsy Kensit, Kristin Scott Thomas, Jeremy Kemp, Annette Badland, Douglas Henshall, Anna Massey. **1996 DVD**

ANGEL'S DANCE ★★★1/2 James Belushi plays a skilled hit man who is hired to train a naïve would-be assassin. For the final test, a name is chosen at random from the phone book, and it's up to the novice to terminate this person as efficiently and as quickly as possible. The hit is botched, leaving Angel Chaste wondering why someone wants her dead. She in turn does a little training of her own, all the while evading the frustrated killer on her trail. The final showdown is quite satisfying and not completely predictable. Rated R primarily for violence and language. 90m. **DIR:** David L. Corley. **CAST:** James Belushi, Kyle Chandler, Sheryl Lee, Mac Davis, Jon Polito. **1999 DVD**

ANGELS DIE HARD ★★ The bikers turn out to help a community during a mining disaster. Less ridiculous than most of its predecessors and contemporaries. Look for Dan Haggerty in an early role. Violence; adult situations. Rated R. 86m. **DIR:** Richard Compton. **CAST:** William Smith, Tom Baker, R. G. Armstrong, Dan Haggerty. **1970**

ANGELS HARD AS THEY COME ★★1/2 An above-average biker gang movie. Distinguished mainly by its reasonably authentic look and feel, due largely to the contribution of Jonathan Demme, who cowrote and produced. Rated R for violence and nudity. 86m. **DIR:** Joe Viola. **CAST:** Scott Glenn, Charles Dierkop, Gary Busey. **1972**

ANGELS IN THE OUTFIELD (1951) ★★★1/2 A gruff manager of a losing baseball team is approached by an angel who beseeches him to give up his swearing and his angry attitude. In exchange, angels will help the team earn the pennant. Charming little fantasy. Not rated, but acceptable for family viewing. B&W; 102m. **DIR:** Clarence Brown. **CAST:** Paul Douglas, Janet Leigh, Keenan Wynn, Donna Corcoran, Lewis Stone, Ellen Corby. **1951**

ANGELS IN THE OUTFIELD (1994) ★★★1/2 Youngsters should fully enjoy this tale of a boy who gets some special, spiritual help in supporting his favorite baseball team, the Angels. Fans of the 1951 original may pooh-pooh, but there's certainly nothing offensive about this bit of wish fulfillment. Danny Glover, as the disbelieving-at-first coach, Christopher Lloyd, as the head angel, and the venerable Ben Johnson, as the team's Gene Autry–like owner, add class to the proceedings. Rated PG. 102m. **DIR:** William Dear. **CAST:** Danny Glover, Tony Danza, Brenda Fricker, Christopher Lloyd, Jay O. Sanders, Joseph Gordon-Levitt, Milton Davis Jr., Taylor Negron. **1994**

ANGELS OVER BROADWAY ★★★ Codirected by legendary newsmen and playwrights Ben Hecht and Lee Garmes, this tale of streetwise Douglas Fairbanks's efforts to save would-be suicide John Qualen is full of great dialogue and pithy comments on life. But it lacks the charm that would mark it as a true classic. Recommended for its dialogue, as well as its odd tone. B&W; 80m. **DIR:** Ben Hecht, Lee Garmes. **CAST:** Douglas Fairbanks Jr., Rita Hayworth, Thomas Mitchell, John Qualen. **1940**

ANGELS WITH DIRTY FACES ★★★★1/2 This is thoroughly enjoyable entertainment. The plot is that old Hollywood standby about two childhood friends, the one who goes bad (James Cagney) and the other who follows the right path (Pat O'Brien, as the priest), and the conflict between them. Yet, as directed by Warner Bros. stalwart Michael Curtiz, it often seems surprisingly fresh. B&W; 97m. **DIR:** Michael Curtiz. **CAST:** James Cagney, Pat O'Brien, Humphrey Bogart, Ann Sheridan, George Bancroft, Bobby Jordan. **1938**

ANGIE ★★★★ Emotionally involved tale of a Bensonhurst, NY, woman who becomes pregnant and begins questioning everything about her life—especially when she meets a witty, romantic Englishman (Stephen Rea) who's everything her working-class boyfriend (James Gandolfini) isn't. Geena Davis is excellent as the Italian-American heroine, who isn't always sympathetic but will touch something deep in viewers' hearts. There are some very funny moments as well. Rated R for adult subject matter. 108m. **DIR:** Martha Coolidge. **CAST:** Geena Davis, Stephen Rea, James Gandolfini, Aida Turturro, Philip Bosco, Jenny O'Hara. **1994**

ANGKOR: CAMBODIA EXPRESS 🦃 In this subpar variation on *The Killing Fields*, Robert Walker plays an American journalist who left his girlfriend (Nancy Kwan) behind in Cambodia and returns to bring her out. 86m. **DIR:** Alex King. **CAST:** Robert Walker Jr., Christopher George, Woody Strode, Nancy Kwan. **1985**

ANGRY HARVEST ★★★★ This drama from director Agnieszka Holland features Fassbinder veterans Armin Mueller-Stahl and Elisabeth Trissenaar in a mesmerizing thriller about a Jewish woman who escapes from a train bound for the Nazi death camps. The film features brilliant performances. In German with English subtitles. Not rated; contains nudity and violence. 102m. **DIR:** Agnieszka Holland. **CAST:** Armin Mueller-Stahl, Elisabeth Trissenaar. **1986**

ANGRY RED PLANET, THE ★★1/2 Entertaining (if unoriginal) science-fiction tale of an expedition to Mars running into all sorts of alien terrors, most notable of which is a terrifying kind of giant mouse/spider hybrid. A fun film, though it takes forever to get to the action. 83m. **DIR:** Ib Melchior. **CAST:** Gerald Mohr, Nora Hayden, Les Tremayne, Jack Kruschen. **1959 DVD**

ANGUISH ★★★★ This horror-thriller is actually a movie within a movie. The first portion deals with a mother and son's odd relationship that has him murdering people for their eyes, while the second portion is actually about an audience watching the film and being terrorized by an unknown killer. *Not* recommended for those with weak stomachs. Rated R. 85m. **DIR:** Bigas Luna. **CAST:** Zelda Rubinstein, Michael Lerner. **1988 DVD**

ANGUS ★★★ Throughout his formative years Angus has been the butt of mean-spirited "fat boy" jokes. In his sophomore year, he gets blindsided by a lifelong enemy's prank when he is elected winter-ball king and must dance with a cheerleader whom he has forever adored from afar. This gentle rite of passage is predictable, but full of genuine warmth. Rated PG-13 for language. 87m. **DIR:** Patrick Read Johnson. **CAST:** Charlie Talbert, Ariana Richards, Chris Owen, George C. Scott, Kathy Bates, James van der Beek. **1995**

•ANIMAL, THE 🦃 In this flat, one-note comedy, Marvin Mange is a police evidence-room clerk who is critically injured in a car wreck and begins acting strangely after a wacko doctor saves his life with organ transplants from animals. Rated PG-13 for general vulgarity. 89m. **DIR:** Luke Grenfield. **CAST:** Rob Schneider, Colleen Haskell, Ed Asner, John C. McGinley, Michael Caton, Guy Torry. **2001 DVD**

ANIMAL BEHAVIOR ★★★ This comedy features Karen Allen as a behaviorist testing a chimp named Michael. Armand Assante, as the university's new music professor, falls for Allen. Plenty of misunderstandings add to the fun. Rated PG for no apparent reason. 79m. **DIR:** H. Anne Riley. **CAST:** Armand Assante, Karen Allen, Holly Hunter, Josh Mostel. **1989**

ANIMAL CALLED MAN, AN 🦃 Based on a *They Call Me Trinity*–type character, this comic spaghetti Western fails on all counts. A rogue enters a sharp-shooting contest and beats the local gunman. The next thing he knows, the gunman is after him. Surprise, surprise! Not rated, contains some violence. 83m. **DIR:** Roberto Mauri. **CAST:** Vassilli Karis, Craig Hill, Omero Capanna, Gillian Bray. **1973**

ANIMAL CRACKERS ★★★★ *Animal Crackers* is pure Marx Brothers, a total farce loosely based on a hit play by George S. Kaufman. Highlights include Groucho's African lecture—"One morning I shot an elephant in my pajamas. How he got into my pajamas, I'll never know"—and the card game with Harpo, Chico, and the ever-put-upon Margaret Dumont. B&W; 98m. **DIR:** Victor Heerman. **CAST:** The Marx Brothers, Margaret Dumont, Lillian Roth. **1930 DVD**

ANIMAL FACTORY ★★★★ A provocative script, compelling performances, and gripping direction fuel this sobering prison drama, which explores the harsh realities behind bars. Willem Dafoe is extraordinary as the respected convict who takes young, first-timer Edward Furlong under his wing, while Mickey Rourke stands out as a drag queen with a few tricks up her sleeve. Rated R for adult situations, language, nudity, and violence. 94m. **DIR:** Steve Buscemi. **CAST:** Willem Dafoe, Edward Furlong, Danny Trejo, John Heard, Mickey Rourke, Tom Arnold, Seymour Cassel. **2000 DVD**

ANIMAL FARM (1954) ★★1/2 Serious, sincere animated adaptation of George Orwell's ingenious satire concerning the follies of government. The treatment would have benefited from greater intensity. The attempt at creating an optimistic ending was ill-advised. Keep in mind the film isn't children's fare. 72m. **DIR:** John Halas, Joy Batchelor. **1954**

ANIMAL FARM (1999) ★★★ George Orwell's attack on totalitarian government comes to life via the genius of Jim Henson's Creature Shop. True to the 1945 novel, this Hallmark Home Entertainment film features the rebellion of farm animals against their drunken farmer followed by their oppression by pig leaders. Several celebrities, including Kelsey Grammer and Julia Louis-Dreyfus, give voice to the menagerie of animals. A word of caution to parents: this is not *Babe* and is not suitable for young children. Not rated; contains sexual innuendo, alcohol abuse, and animal cruelty. 91m. **DIR:** John Stephenson. **CAST:** Pete Postlethwaite, Alan Stanford. **1999 DVD**

ANIMAL HOUSE ★★★★1/2 Although it has spawned a seemingly relentless onslaught of inferior carbon copies, this comedy is still one of the funniest movies ever made. If you're into rock 'n' roll, partying, and general craziness, this picture is for you. We gave it a 95, because it has a good beat and you can dance to it. Rated R. 109m. **DIR:** John Landis. **CAST:** John Belushi, Tim Matheson, Karen Allen, Peter Riegert, John Vernon, Tom Hulce. **1978 DVD**

ANIMAL INSTINCTS ★★★ Maxwell Caulfield is a cop who renews his stalled relationship with his wife when he discovers that videotaping her in bed with a parade of men and women is a real turn on. Rated R for nudity, simulated sex, and language; unrated version offers much more of the same. 94m. **DIR:** Alexander Gregory Hippolyte. **CAST:** Shannon Whirry, Maxwell Caulfield, Mitch Gaylord, Delia Sheppard, David Carradine. **1992 DVD**

ANIMAL INSTINCTS 2 🦃 Somebody needs to get director Alexander Gregory Hippolyte and star Shannon Whirry out of the soft-core thriller genre; his films unfold with all the snap of drying paint, and she couldn't effectively convey sexual pleasure if her life depended on it. Rated R for nudity, simulated sex, and profanity. 92m. **DIR:** Alexander Gregory Hippolyte. **CAST:** Shannon Whirry, Woody Brown, Elizabeth Sandifer. **1994**

ANIMAL INSTINCTS: THE SEDUCTRESS 🦃 Third in the series is also the weakest. Wendy Schumacher takes over the lead role, playing a woman who finds sexual excitement in the arms of a blind musician. Lots of kinky sex and not much more. Rated R for nudity and adult situations. Unrated version also available. 90m. **DIR:** Alexander Gregory Hippolyte. **CAST:** Wendy Schumacher, James Matthew, John Bates. **1995 DVD**

ANIMAL KINGDOM, THE ★★★1/2 This filming of a Philip Barry play paved the way for his later *Holiday* and *Philadelphia Story* analyses of marriages, manners, and morals. Leslie Howard lets his hair down with bohemian girlfriend Ann Harding, but he marries snobbish Myrna Loy for appearance's sake, and it backfires. B&W; 85m. **DIR:** Edward H. Griffith. **CAST:** Leslie Howard, Myrna Loy, Ann Harding, William Gargan, Neil Hamilton, Ilka Chase, Henry Stephenson. **1932**

ANIMALYMPICS ★★★ Featuring the voices of Billy Crystal, Gilda Radner, and Harry Shearer, this feature brings the Olympics to life with animals from around the world. Though the production seems somewhat overlong, there are bright spots: a news commentator called Ba Ba Wawa and a pole-vaulting hippo. 78m. **DIR:** Steven Lisberger. **1980**

ANN VICKERS ★★★★ Rebuffed by Bruce Cabot, noble and self-sacrificing Irene Dunne scorns all men and turns to social service. Against all odds she seeks penal reform. A somewhat unique women's prison film in that the heroine is not a victimized inmate. B&W; 72m. **DIR:** John Cromwell. **CAST:** Irene Dunne, Bruce Cabot, Walter Huston, Conrad Nagel, Edna May Oliver, J. Carrol Naish. **1933**

ANNA ★★★★ In this wonderfully offbeat turn on *All About Eve*, Sally Kirkland plays a former Czech film star struggling to find work in New York. Model Paulina Porizkova is fine as the refugee who remembers Kirkland's former glories and insinuates herself into the older woman's life only to surpass her successes in America. In English and Czech with subtitles. Rated PG-13 for nudity and profanity. 100m. **DIR:** Yurek Bogayevicz. **CAST:** Sally Kirkland, Paulina Porizkova, Robert Fields, Stefan Schnabel. **1987**

ANNA AND THE KING ★★★1/2 Pageantry and exquisite costuming reign supreme in this nonmusical version of *The King and I*. Based on Anna Leonowens's diary, this features Jodie Foster as the prim schoolteacher to the King of Siam's many children. Action star Chow Yun-Fat makes a smooth transition into his majestic role, but Foster seems to slip a bit off a tightrope between Victorian repression and attraction to the captivating king. Rated PG-13 for violence and gore. 147m. **DIR:** Andy Tennant. **CAST:** Jodie Foster, Chow Yun-Fat, Tom Felton. **1999 DVD**

ANNA AND THE KING OF SIAM ★★★★ This original *King and I* boasts poignant performances that give the characters of Anna Leonowens and King Mongkut a different perspective. It's based on Margaret Landon's memoirs as a governess in the Siamese court during the last century. The story parallels the musical version, but with more details about individual family members. 128m. **DIR:** John Cromwell. **CAST:** Irene Dunne, Rex Harrison, Linda Darnell, Lee J. Cobb, Gale Sondergaard. **1946**

ANNA CHRISTIE (1922) ★★ Anna (Blanche Sweet) is a former prostitute whose struggle for a new life runs her afoul of two men—her father (George F. Marion) and a sailor (Matt Burke). Don't expect any of the edgy, sordid aspects of the Eugene O'Neill original. But Henry Sharp's solid camerawork nicely conveys the dockside scenes. Silent. B&W; 75m. **DIR:** John Griffith Wray. **CAST:** Blanche Sweet, George F. Marion, Matt Burke. **1922**

ANNA CHRISTIE (1930) ★★★★ Greta Garbo is mesmerizing and Marie Dressler hilariously memorable in this early sound classic adapted from Eugene O'Neill's play. The tag line for it in 1930 was "Garbo speaks!" And speak she does, uttering the famous line, "Gif me a viskey, ginger ale on the side, and don't be stingy, baby," while portraying a woman with a shady past. B&W; 90m. **DIR:** Clarence Brown. **CAST:** Greta Garbo, Charles Bickford, Marie Dressler. **1930**

ANNA KARENINA (1935) ★★★★ The forever fascinating, peerless Greta Garbo, a superb supporting cast headed by Fredric March, and the masterful direction of Clarence Brown make this film one of the actress's greatest, a true film classic. B&W; 95m. **DIR:** Clarence Brown. **CAST:** Greta Garbo, Fredric March, Basil Rathbone, Freddie Bartholomew, Maureen O'Sullivan, Reginald Denny, May Robson, Reginald Owen. **1935**

ANNA KARENINA (1947) ★★1/2 In this version of Tolstoy's classic story of a married woman madly in love with a military officer, Vivien Leigh is miscast as the heroine. Though she tries valiantly, she is overwhelmed by the role. An overly sentimental script doesn't help. B&W; 139m. **DIR:** Julien Duvivier. **CAST:** Vivien Leigh, Kieron Moore, Ralph Richardson, Sally Ann Howes, Michael Gough. **1947 DVD**

ANNA KARENINA (1974) ★★★1/2 Based on Tolstoy's novel, this ballet was choreographed by and stars Maya Plisetskaya, the Bolshoi's great prima ballerina. Her husband, Rodion Shchedrin, composed the music. This is an imaginative and visually interesting film, as the camera and direction are creative rather than just filming a staged ballet performance. 81m. **DIR:** Margarita Pilichino. **CAST:** Bolshoi Ballet. **1974**

ANNA KARENINA (1985) ★★ Tolstoy's classic suffers in this tedious remake for television. Garbo did it best in 1935. Paul Scofield as Anna's husband, however, is worth the watch. 150m. **DIR:** Simon Langton. **CAST:** Jacqueline Bisset, Paul Scofield, Christopher Reeve, Ian Ogilvy. **1985**

ANNA TO THE INFINITE POWER ★★★★ Is individuality determined purely by genetic code, or by some other factor beyond the control of science? This film explores the dimensions of that question via the struggles of a brilliant, troubled child—who is also the unwitting subject of a scientific experiment to establish her own identity. Brilliant. 107m. **DIR:** Robert Wiemer. **CAST:** Martha Byrne, Dina Merrill, Mark Patton, Loretta Devine, Jack Gilford. **1982**

ANNABEL TAKES A TOUR ★★1/2 A dizzy movie star and her fast-talking press agent concoct a publicity scheme. Harmless and mildly amusing, this brief programmer was the second in a series Lucille Ball and Jack Oakie did for RKO. B&W; 66m. **DIR:** Lew Landers. **CAST:** Lucille Ball, Jack Oakie, Ruth Donnelly, Frances Mercer, Donald MacBride. **1938**

ANNAPOLIS STORY, AN ★★ John Derek and Kevin McCarthy vie for the hand of Diana Lynn in this formula service academy yarn of rigid training, lights out, bed check, and romance. 81m. **DIR:** Don Siegel. **CAST:** John Derek, Diana Lynn, Kevin McCarthy. **1955**

ANNE FRANK REMEMBERED ★★★★ Moving, Oscar-winning documentary retells the sad story of the girl whom narrator Kenneth Branagh calls "probably Hitler's most famous victim." Using the testimony of Anne Frank's friends and relatives who survived the Holocaust, director Jon Blair goes beyond the famous diary (selections from which are read by Glenn Close) to give human dimension to Anne's tragically short life. Rated PG. B&W/color; 122m. **DIR:** Jon Blair. **1995**

ANNE OF AVONLEA ★★★★ Anne Shirley matures and falls in love in this sequel to *Anne of Green Gables*, which scripter-director Kevin Sullivan has helmed with the same devotion to period authenticity. 224m. **DIR:** Kevin Sullivan. **CAST:** Megan Follows, Colleen Dewhurst, Wendy Hiller. **1987**

ANNE OF GREEN GABLES (1934) ★★★ L. M. Montgomery's popular juvenile book about a spunky young orphan's influence on a conservative household receives its first sound treatment in this sentimental but entertaining picture. A good version of the classic and fine family entertainment. B&W; 80m. **DIR:** George Nicholls Jr. **CAST:** Anne Shirley, Tom Brown, O. P. Heggie, Helen Westley, Sara Haden, Charley Grapewin. **1934**

ANNE OF GREEN GABLES (1985) ★★★★ This delightful film, based on L. M. Montgomery's classic novel, is set in 1908 on Canada's Prince Edward Island. Anne (Megan Follows) is a foster child taken in by Matthew (Richard Farnsworth) and Marilla Cuthbert (Colleen Dewhurst), who mistakenly expect her to be a farmhand. Not rated; suitable for family viewing. 240m. **DIR:** Kevin Sullivan. **CAST:** Megan Follows, Richard Farnsworth, Colleen Dewhurst. **1985**

ANNE OF THE THOUSAND DAYS ★★★ The story of Anne Boleyn, Henry VIII's second wife and mother of Queen Elizabeth I, is given the big-budget treatment. Luckily, the tragic tale of a woman who is at first pressured into an unwanted union with England's lusty king, only to fall in love with him and eventually lose her head to court intrigue, is not lost beneath the spectacle. Genevieve Bujold's well-balanced performance of Anne carries the entire production. 146m. **DIR:** Charles Jarrott. **CAST:** Genevieve Bujold, Richard Burton, Anthony Quayle. **1969**

ANNIE ★★★★ A sparkling $40 million movie musical based on the Broadway production of the long-running comic strip *Little Orphan Annie.* Ten year old Aileen Quinn is just fine in the title role. Rated PG for brief profanity. 128m. **DIR:** John Huston. **CAST:** Albert Finney, Carol Burnett, Bernadette Peters, Edward Herrmann, Aileen Quinn, Tim Curry. **1982 DVD**

ANNIE, A ROYAL ADVENTURE! ★★ Disappointing, nonmusical TV sequel to the 1982 smash musical *Annie.* This time "Daddy" Warbucks heads to England to be knighted and Annie and her pal go along for the ride. They meet up with scheming Lady Edwina Hogbottom (Joan Collins) who plans to blow up Buckingham Palace and become queen. Too melodramatic and unbelievable to be enjoyed. Rated G. 92m. **DIR:** Ian Toynton. **CAST:** Ashley Johnson, George Hearn, Joan Collins. **1995**

ANNIE GET YOUR GUN ★★★1/2 Lavish, fast-moving transfer of Irving Berlin's stage hit to film with Annie Oakley (Betty Hutton), Frank Butler (Howard Keel), Buffalo Bill Cody (Louis Calhern) and Sitting Bull (J. Carrol Naish) singing and shooting up a storm. "Anything You Can Do" and "There's No Business Like Show Business" are two of the musical highlights. Oscar for the score of Adolph Deutsch and Roger Edens. 107m. **DIR:** George Sidney. **CAST:** Betty Hutton, Howard

Keel, Louis Calhern, Keenan Wynn, Edward Arnold, J. Carrol Naish. **1950 DVD**

ANNIE HALL ★★★★★ Woody Allen's exquisite romantic comedy won the 1977 Academy Awards for best picture, actress (Diane Keaton), director (Allen), and screenplay (Allen and Marshall Brickman)—and deserved every one of them. This delightful semiautobiographical romp features Allen as Alvy Singer, a more assured version of Alan Felix, from *Play It Again, Sam*, who falls in love (again) with Keaton (in the title role). Rated PG for profanity and bedroom scenes. 94m. **DIR:** Woody Allen. **CAST:** Woody Allen, Diane Keaton, Tony Roberts, Paul Simon, Shelley Duvall, Carol Kane. **1977 DVD**

ANNIE O ★★★ Hotshot hoopster Coco Yares has the bad luck to attend a school lacking a girls' basketball program, so she tries out for—and wins a spot on—the *boys'* varsity team. The predictable story treads no new ground, but Yares is a likable lead (her bland voiceovers notwithstanding), and the result is pleasant enough for family viewing. Suitable for all ages. 93m. **DIR:** J. Michael McClary. **CAST:** Coco Yares, Robert Stewart, Chad Willett. **1995**

ANNIE OAKLEY (TV SERIES) ★★★ Annie Oakley, woman rancher and expert sharpshooter, helps Sheriff Lofty Craig maintain law and order in the 1860s town of Diablo. Two nostalgia-packed episodes on one cassette: "Trouble Shooters" and "Twisted Trails." B&W; 50m. **CAST:** Gail Davis, Brad Johnson, Jimmy Hawkins. **1953**

ANNIHILATORS, THE 🦃 Another film in which Vietnam veterans reunite, organize a vigilante group, annihilate the sadistic gangs, and return to their normal lives. Rated R for grotesque violence and language. 87m. **DIR:** Charles E. Sellier Jr. **CAST:** Christopher Stone, Andy Wood, Lawrence Hilton-Jacobs, Jim Antonio, Gerrit Graham. **1985**

•ANNIVERSARY PARTY, THE ★★ A filmmaker and his actress wife celebrate their sixth anniversary and recent reconciliation with a gathering of friends, relatives, business associates, and even the neighbors they despise. The partygoers play charades, give testimonials, and make confessions as ecstasy replaces alcohol as the evening's drug of choice. The capable cast of this digital video drama is soon mired in mundane mini-encounter sessions and egos. Rated R for language, drug use, nudity, and sexual situations. 115m. **DIR:** Alan Cumming, Jennifer Jason Leigh. **CAST:** Alan Cumming, Jennifer Jason Leigh, Kevin Kline, Phoebe Cates, Jane Adams, John C. Reilly, Jennifer Beals, Denis O'Hare, Mina Badie, Gwyneth Paltrow, Michael Panes, Parker Posey. **2001 DVD**

ANOTHER COUNTRY ★★★1/2 For this film, Julian Mitchell adapted his stage play about Guy Burgess, an Englishman who became a spy for Russia in the 1930s. Little in this story reportedly was based on fact. Still, Mitchell's postulations provide interesting viewing, and Rupert Everett's lead performance—as Guy "Bennett"—is stunning. Rated PG for suggested sex and profanity. 90m. **DIR:** Marek Kanievska. **CAST:** Rupert Everett, Colin Firth, Cary Elwes. **1984**

ANOTHER DAY IN PARADISE ★★ Junkie teen lovers take a road trip with a veteran outlaw couple in this bleak crime story adapted from ex-convict Eddie Little's book. The film unflinchingly exposes the daily details of survival along the underbelly of America, but it mistakenly assumes that drug addicts are inherently intriguing. The gutsy R&B score is complemented with a Clarence Carter cameo. Rated R for drug use, language, sexuality, and violence. 99m. **DIR:** Larry Clark. **CAST:** James Woods, Melanie Griffith, Vincent Kartheiser, Natasha Gregson Wagner. **1999 DVD**

ANOTHER 48 HRS. ★★★★ Solid sequel to the 1982 box-office smash finds director Walter Hill in top form as Eddie Murphy and Nick Nolte take on a mysterious figure known only as the Iceman. While not quite as good as the first film, *Another 48 Hrs.* nevertheless proves that the original cop/buddy team is still the best. Rated R for violence, profanity, and nudity. 95m. **DIR:** Walter Hill. **CAST:** Eddie Murphy, Nick Nolte, Brian James, Kevin Tighe, Ed O'Ross. **1990 DVD**

ANOTHER MAN, ANOTHER CHANCE ★★ In 1977, director Claude Lelouch, inexplicably, decided to remake his charming film *A Man and a Woman* and set it in the American West of the late 1800s. Widow Genevieve Bujold and widower James Caan fall in love. It's light on romance and heavy on tedium. 128m. **DIR:** Claude Lelouch. **CAST:** James Caan, Genevieve Bujold, Francis Huster, Jennifer Warren, Susan Tyrrell. **1977**

ANOTHER 9 1/2 WEEKS ★★ Mickey Rourke engages in more tame sadomasochistic shenanigans in this unwarranted sequel that tries but fails to deliver the visual sheen that was the only saving grace of the original *9 1/2 Weeks*. Rated R for nudity, sexual situations, and profanity. 104m. **DIR:** Anne Goursand. **CAST:** Mickey Rourke, Angie Everhart, Steven Berkoff. **1997 DVD**

ANOTHER PAIR OF ACES ★★★1/2 Texas Ranger Rip Metcalf (Kris Kristofferson) enlists the aid of streetwise gambler Billy Roy Barker (Willie Nelson) in tracking down the vigilante killer of a crime lord. Engaging performances help elevate this modern-day Western/detective story, which was made for TV. 93m. **DIR:** Bill Bixby. **CAST:** Willie Nelson, Kris Kristofferson, Joan Severance, Rip Torn. **1991**

ANOTHER STAKEOUT ★★★1/2 Richard Dreyfuss and Emilio Estevez are back as Seattle detectives assigned to track down an escaped federal witness. Their job is complicated by a bumbling but well-meaning assistant district attorney (played with panache by Rosie O'Donnell). Rated PG-13 for profanity and violence. 109m. **DIR:** John Badham. **CAST:** Richard Dreyfuss, Emilio Estevez, Rosie O'Donnell, Madeleine Stowe, Cathy Moriarty, Dennis Farina, Marcia Strassman, John Rubinstein, Miguel Ferrer. **1993**

ANOTHER THIN MAN ★★★★ Nick and Nora Charles (William Powell and Myrna Loy) contend with a gentleman who dreams about catastrophes before they take place. As usual, the plot is secondary. Follows *After the Thin Man* (1936) and precedes *Shadow of the Thin Man* (1941). Suitable for family viewing. B&W; 105m. **DIR:** W. S. Van Dyke. **CAST:** William Powell, Myrna Loy, Virginia Grey, Otto Kruger, C. Aubrey Smith, Ruth Hussey, Nat Pendleton, Tom Neal. **1939**

ANOTHER TIME, ANOTHER PLACE (1984) ★★★ In this British import set in 1944, a woman named Janie (Phyllis Logan) lives on a small farm in Scotland with her husband, Dongal (Paul Young), fifteen years her senior. As part of a war rehabilitation program, the couple welcomes three Italian POW's onto their place, and Janie falls in love. Rated PG. 118m. **DIR:** Michael Radford. **CAST:** Phyllis Logan, Paul Young. **1984**

ANOTHER TIME, ANOTHER PLACE (1958) ★★ Ho-hum melodrama about an American newspaperwoman whose brief affair with a British journalist ends in tragedy when he dies during World War II. B&W; 98m. **DIR:** Lewis Allen. **CAST:** Lana Turner, Barry Sullivan, Glynis Johns, Sean Connery, Sidney James. **1958**

ANOTHER WOMAN ★★★★ A subtle, purposely enigmatic yet engrossing portrait of a woman reassessing her own identity and purpose. Gena Rowlands is superb as a college professor whose life is not as solid as she assumes. When she overhears another woman (Mia Farrow) in a session with her psychoanalyst, Rowlands begins to have doubts. Rated PG. 81m. **DIR:** Woody Allen. **CAST:** Gena Rowlands, Gene Hackman, Ian Holm, Mia Farrow, John Houseman, Blythe Danner, Sandy Dennis. **1988 DVD**

ANOTHER YOU ★★ In their fourth film together, Gene Wilder and Richard Pryor star in a disappointing comedy involving mistaken identities. Wilder is a pathological liar just released from a mental institution, and Pryor is a con man doing community service as his caretaker. Rated R for profanity. 100m. **DIR:** Maurice Phillips. **CAST:** Gene Wilder, Richard Pryor, Mercedes Ruehl, Stephen Lang, Vanessa L. Williams. **1991**

ANTARCTICA ★★ *Antarctica* is the true story of a 1958 expedition. While in Antarctica, Japanese scientists encounter complications and are forced to return home, leaving their team of dogs behind to fend for themselves. The dogs are pretty good naturalistic actors, but you're not drawn to them as you are to the wolves of Carroll Ballard's *Never Cry Wolf*. Dubbed in English. 112m. **DIR:** Koreyoshi Kurahara. **CAST:** Ken Takakura, Tsunehiko Watase. **1984**

ANTHONY ADVERSE ★★★1/2 Fredric March, in the title role, wanders around early nineteenth-century America and Mexico, sowing oats, and buckling swash, in this all-stops-out romantic blockbuster. B&W; 136m. **DIR:** Mervyn LeRoy. **CAST:** Fredric March, Olivia de Havilland, Anita Louise, Donald Woods, Edmund Gwenn, Claude Rains, Louis Hayward, Gale Sondergaard, Henry O'Neill. **1936**

ANTITRUST ★★ Software writer Milo leaves his buddies at a start-up company to work for a computer wizard who runs his multimillion-dollar home and business complex in Portland like a posh cybergeek campus. Milo soon discovers the success of his Bill Gates–like boss and mentor may be based more on treachery than talent. This tale unfortunately degenerates from topical drama to ludicrous thriller. Rated R for profanity and violence. 110m. **DIR:** Peter Howitt. **CAST:** Ryan Phillippe, Tim Robbins, Rachael Leigh Cook, Claire Forlani, Tygh Runyan, Ned Bellamy, Douglas McFerran. **2001 DVD**

ANTONIA & JANE ★★★★ A perceptive British comedy about an unlikely friendship between two wildly different women. Antonia and Jane are the yin and yang of personalities, and neither has ever appreciated the turmoil in the other's life. Imagine a female and British twist on Woody Allen's comedic style. Not rated; the film contains nudity, sex, and profanity. 77m. **DIR:** Beeban Kidron. **CAST:** Imelda Staunton, Saskia Reeves. **1991**

ANTONIA'S LINE ★★★ An unmarried mother returns with her teenage daughter to her Dutch village after World War II, where she establishes a happy home—not only for her own family but for all the outcasts, misfits, and free spirits who flock to her over the next fifty years. Writer-director Marleen Gorris's sentimental feminist fairy tale is short on dramatic conflict but long on warmth—a "family values" story with 1990s attitudes. In Dutch with English subtitles. Not rated; contains nudity and simulated sex. 93m. **DIR:** Marleen Gorris. **CAST:** Willeke Van Ammelrooy, Els Dottermans, Jan Decleir, Mil Seghers, Marina de Graaf. **1995 DVD**

ANTONY AND CLEOPATRA (1973) ★★ Marginal film interpretation of Shakespeare's play. Obviously a tremendous amount of work on Charlton Heston's part, casting himself as Antony, but the film is lacking in energy. Rated PG. 160m. **DIR:** Charlton Heston. **CAST:** Charlton Heston, Hildegard Neil, Eric Porter, Fernando Rey, John Castle. **1973**

ANTONY AND CLEOPATRA (1981) ★★★1/2 Timothy Dalton and Lynn Redgrave are fine as Marc Antony and Cleopatra in Shakespeare's tale of passion, war, and betrayal in Egypt and Rome. John Carradine is outstanding as the soothsayer. A Bard Productions Ltd. release. 183m. **DIR:** Lawrence Carra. **CAST:** Timothy Dalton, Lynn Redgrave, Nichelle Nichols, John Carradine, Anthony Geary, Barrie Ingham, Walter Koenig, Brian Kerwin, Kim Miyori. **1981**

ANTS! 🦃 Just another haunting remnant of boring filmmaking from the *Movie of the Week* closet. 88m. **DIR:** Robert Sheerer. **CAST:** Robert Foxworth, Lynda Day George, Suzanne Somers, Myrna Loy, Brian Dennehy. **1977**

ANTZ ★★★1/2 In this animated feature, geared more toward adults than the kiddies, computer-generated imagery creates surprisingly real scenes such as the picnic fiasco in which worker ant Z (Woody Allen's voice) and the ants' princess (voiced by Sharon Stone) find themselves stuck in the gum on a boy's shoe. This is an animated version of *Play It Again, Sam* with Allen recreating his role of the neurotic looking for love. Z also gets to flex his muscles and lead a revolt against a corrupt general (Gene Hackman). Rated PG for violence and profanity. 83m. **DIR:** Eric Darnell, Tim Johnson. **1998 DVD**

ANY FRIEND OF NICHOLAS NICKLEBY IS A FRIEND OF MINE ★★★1/2 A charming period piece by author Ray Bradbury. Fred Gwynne shines as a mysterious stranger who comes to a small Illinois town where he takes an imaginative schoolboy under his wing. This is a poignant and humorous drama comparable to PBS's award-winning *Anne of Green Gables*. 55m. **DIR:** Ralph Rosenblum. **CAST:** Fred Gwynne. **1981**

ANY GIVEN SUNDAY ★★1/2 Pro-football coach has sacrificed wife and family for a career and a team that are now in a slump. A third-string quarterback snaps his team's losing streak and becomes the media's flavor of the month, leaving the coach to reevaluate his loyalties and choices. This flawed drama oozes passion, machismo, and spectacle as it leers at team dynamics and the inner circles of big business. Rated R for language and nudity. 160m. **DIR:** Oliver Stone. **CAST:** Al Pacino, Jamie Foxx, Cameron Diaz, Dennis Quaid, Ann-Margret, Lawrence Taylor. **1999 DVD**

ANY MAN'S DEATH ★★1/2 John Savage plays a traumatized Vietnam-vet-turned-journalist sent to Africa. He discovers a strange scientist (William Hickey) whose human experiments have killed thousands. Confusing kaleidoscope of events leaves more questions than answers. Rated R for profanity and violence. 105m. **DIR:** Tom Clegg. **CAST:** John Savage, William Hickey, Mia Sara, Ernest Borgnine. **1989**

ANY NUMBER CAN PLAY ★★★1/2 Wonderful cast in an absorbing drama revolving around the personal and professional problems of honest gambling-house owner Clark Gable. Marjorie Rambeau is a standout. Screenplay by Richard Brooks. B&W; 112m. **DIR:** Mervyn LeRoy. **CAST:** Clark Gable, Alexis Smith, Wendell Corey, Audrey Totter, Darryl Hickman, Frank Morgan, Lewis Stone, Barry Sullivan, Mary Astor, Marjorie Rambeau, Leon Ames, Edgar Buchanan, William Conrad. **1949**

ANY PLACE BUT HOME ★★★ A husband and wife wind up with a boy whom their relatives had kidnapped. Problem is, the boy has been abused, and he doesn't want to go home. No spectacular performances, and no stupendous plot twists, but this made-for-cable original is watchable. Not rated; contains violence. 95m. **DIR:** Rob Hedden. **CAST:** Joe Lando, Dale Midkiff, Mary Page Keller, Cristi Conaway, Richard Roundtree, Alan Thicke. **1997**

ANY WEDNESDAY ★★ The spiciness of the original Broadway script gets lost in this film adaptation. Jason Robards Jr. plays the New York businessman who deducts his paramour's (Jane Fonda) apartment as a business expense. A poor man's *The Apartment*. 109m. **DIR:** Robert Ellis Miller. **CAST:** Jane Fonda, Jason Robards Jr., Dean Jones, Rosemary Murphy, Ann Prentiss. **1966**

ANY WHICH WAY YOU CAN 🦃 Another comedy clinker from Clint Eastwood and company. Rated PG. 116m. **DIR:** Buddy Van Horn. **CAST:** Clint Eastwood, Sondra Locke, Geoffrey Lewis, William Smith, Ruth Gordon. **1980 DVD**

ANYTHING FOR LOVE ★★★1/2 This anthology film, composed of three entries from Showtime's *Directed By* series, allows actors to make a short film from behind the camera. In Christine Lahti's *Lieberman in Love*, which won 1995's Academy Award for live-action short film, Danny Aiello stars as a mournful widower looking for love in all the wrong places, and Lahti herself offers excellent support as an avaricious hooker. Anne Archer and William L. Petersen learn that long-dormant affairs are best left alone in Richard Dreyfuss's *Present Tense, Past Perfect*. Sadly, Christian Slater's *Museum of Love* is a complete waste of time. Rated R for profanity and simulated sex. 105m. **DIR:** Richard Dreyfuss, Christine Lahti, Christian Slater. **CAST:** Danny Aiello, Christine Lahti, Nancy Travis, Paul Mercurio, Sandra Bernhard, Samantha Mathis, Anne Archer, William L. Petersen. **1996**

ANYWHERE BUT HERE ★★★ Sloppy editing and a weak script mar this predictable mother/daughter melodrama, albeit one blessed by two commanding actresses. It's yet another story about a teenage girl (Natalie Portman) alternately amused and humiliated by her free-spirited single mother (Susan Sarandon), and their attempts to find happiness in sunny California. We're left with the impression that we're watching only the high points of a much denser story. Rated PG-13 for mild profanity and sexual candor. 114m. **DIR:** Wayne Wang. **CAST:** Susan Sarandon, Natalie Portman, Eileen Ryan, Ray Baker, John Diehl, Shawn Hatosy. **1999 DVD**

ANZACS ★★★★ The ANZACS (Australian/New Zealand Army Corps) join the British in World War I to stir up a few stuffed shirts among the very stiff English. Emphasis is upon the friendship and loyalty among the Australians. Paul Hogan provides a few moments of comic relief. A powerful war film that dwells on the people involved, not the machinery. Made for television, this is not rated but deals with mature subject matter. 165m. **DIR:** George Miller. **CAST:** Andrew Clark, Paul Hogan, Megan Williams. **1985**

ANZIO ★★ Would-be blockbuster about the Allied invasion of Italy during World War II doesn't make the grade as either history or spectacle and ultimately wastes the talents of a great cast and an often inspired director. 117m. **DIR:** Edward Dmytryk. **CAST:** Robert Mitchum, Peter Falk, Robert Ryan, Earl Holliman, Arthur Kennedy, Patrick Magee, Mark Damon, Reni Santoni. **1968 DVD**

APACHE ★★ Moralistic message Western features a hammy Burt Lancaster as an idealistic warrior who resents yet understands the encroachment of the whites and refuses to live on government reservations. Strangely typical of early-to-mid-1950s Hollywood Westerns, this entry is long on conscience and short on action. 91m. **DIR:** Robert Aldrich. **CAST:** Burt Lancaster, Jean Peters, Charles Bronson, John Dehner, Monte Blue. **1954**

APACHE ROSE ★★1/2 Roy's an oil-well engineer, Dale's the skipper of a tugboat, and the fellow that's causing all the trouble runs a gambling ship. But it's still a Western because Trigger and the Sons of the Pioneers are close at hand. This is the first of the popular series to be shot in color. 75m. **DIR:** William Witney. **CAST:** Roy Rogers, Dale Evans, Bob Nolan and the Sons of the Pioneers, George Meeker, Minerva Urecal, LeRoy Mason. **1947**

APACHE WOMAN 🦃 Dull, awkwardly acted and directed story of an Indian affairs agent, Lloyd Bridges, investigating stagecoach holdups blamed on reservation Apaches. Released theatrically in color. B&W; 83m. **DIR:** Roger Corman. **CAST:** Lloyd Bridges, Joan Taylor, Lance Fuller, Paul Birch, Dick Miller, Chester Conklin. **1955**

APARAJITO ★★★ In the second part of the chronicle of a Bengali family in the Apu trilogy, Apu's father brings the family to the holy city of Benares where his son begins his education and training. Fine ensemble acting. In Bengali with English subtitles. B&W; 108m. **DIR:** Satyajit Ray. **CAST:** Pinaki Sen Gupta, Smaran Ghosal. **1957**

APART FROM HUGH ★★1/2 Two men face the difficulties of committing to a life together in this quiet, tender drama. Stylish for a debut, this low-budget effort is well written but unevenly acted. The dialogue is realistic enough to hook the viewer, but if no one hears of these actors again it will come as no surprise. Not rated; contains profanity and sexual situations. B&W; 87m. **DIR:**

Jon FitzGerald. **CAST:** David Merwin, Jennifer A. Reed, Steve Arnold. **1994**

APARTMENT, THE ★★★★★ Rarely have comedy and drama been satisfyingly blended into a cohesive whole. Director Billy Wilder does it masterfully in this film. With career advancement in mind, Jack Lemmon permits his boss to use his apartment for illicit love affairs. Then he gets involved with the boss's emotionally distraught girlfriend B&W; 125m. **DIR:** Billy Wilder. **CAST:** Jack Lemmon, Shirley MacLaine, Fred MacMurray, Ray Walston, Jack Kruschen, Edie Adams. **1960 DVD**

APARTMENT COMPLEX, THE ★★★ Impoverished grad student Chad Lowe takes a job as manager of a seedy apartment building. The residents offer endless psychological quirks for his studies, while the building harbors deadly supernatural secrets. Made for cable TV, this weak effort wavers uncertainly between straight horror and parody. Rated R for nudity, profanity, and sexual situations. 99m. **DIR:** Tobe Hooper. **CAST:** Chad Lowe, Fay Masterson, Amanda Plummer, Tyra Banks, Charles Martin Smith. **1999**

APARTMENT ZERO ★★★★ A movie buff's delight, this is a whodunit, a twisted character study, and a creepy suspense-thriller. The lead character, Adrian LeDuc, is the ultimate escapist; an Argentinian who pretends to be British, he revels in movie lore and owns a run-down movie revival house. When the cinema's failure puts Adrian in a financial crunch, he decides to take in a roommate, a good-looking American who knows nothing about movies and just may be a serial killer. Rated R for violence and profanity. 124m. **DIR:** Martin Donovan. **CAST:** Hart Bochner, Colin Firth. **1989**

APE, THE ★★ Boris Karloff finished out his contract with Monogram Studios with this story about a doctor who discovers a cure for polio that requires spinal fluid from a human being. Not too many thrills, but Karloff is always worth watching. B&W; 61m. **DIR:** William Nigh. **CAST:** Boris Karloff, Gertrude Hoffman. **1940 DVD**

APE MAN, THE ★★ Bela Lugosi was one of the great horror film stars. However, the monster-movie boom stopped short in 1935, leaving the Hungarian actor out of work. When shockers came back in vogue four years later, Lugosi took any and every role he was offered. The result was grade-Z pictures such as this one, about a scientist (Lugosi) attempting to harness the physical power of apes for humankind. Too bad. B&W; 64m. **DIR:** William Beaudine. **CAST:** Bela Lugosi, Louise Currie, Wallace Ford, Minerva Urecal. **1943 DVD**

APEX ★★★1/2 Time paradoxes have always been great sci-fi fodder, and this film is full of them. In the year 2073, a probe is sent back in time, but its interference causes a paradox that changes the future into a dying wasteland. When scientist Mitchell Cox returns from the past in an attempt to fix the future, he finds himself at war with robots bent on destroying the rest of humanity. Great special effects and a tricky screenplay. Rated R for violence. 103m. **DIR:** Phillip Roth. **CAST:** Mitchell Cox, Lisa Ann Russell, Marcus Aurelius, Adam Lawson. **1993**

APHRODITE ★★ In 1914, a group of jaded aristocrats meet on a Mediterranean island to reenact a mythological tale involving Aphrodite, the goddess of beauty. Pretty but pretentious soft-core erotica. Dubbed. Not rated; contains nudity. 96m. **DIR:** Robert Fuest. **CAST:** Horst Buchholz, Valerie Kaprisky, Capucine. **1982**

APOCALYPSE, THE Incomprehensible sci-fi with Sandra Bernhard ridiculously miscast as an outer-space salvage-ship pilot on a ship set to collide with Earth. Not rated; contains violence and profanity. 96m. **DIR:** Hubert de la Bouillerie. **CAST:** Sandra Bernhard, Cameron Dye, Frank Zagarino, Laura San Giacomo. **1996 DVD**

APOCALYPSE NOW ★★★★ An exceptional war film in every sense, this work pulsates with artistic ambition. It reaches for truth, struggles for greatness—and almost succeeds. The central character, Captain Willard (Martin Sheen), tells the story of his danger-filled journey toward a fateful meeting with a man named Kurtz, a highly decorated officer who the army contends has gone mad. Rated R. 153m. **DIR:** Francis Ford Coppola. **CAST:** Marlon Brando, Martin Sheen, Robert Duvall, Harrison Ford, Laurence Fishburne, Dennis Hopper. **1979 DVD**

APOLLO 13 ★★★★ Director Ron Howard does the next to impossible with this first-rate motion picture: he turns a piece of recent history into edge-of-your-seat entertainment. Based entirely on the real-life adventures of the Apollo 13 astronauts, who came perilously close to death during their mission, this film features a topflight cast and an insightful screenplay. Rated PG. 140m. **DIR:** Ron Howard. **CAST:** Tom Hanks, Bill Paxton, Kevin Bacon, Gary Sinise, Ed Harris, Kathleen Quinlan, David Andrews, Clint Howard, Joe Spano. **1995 DVD**

APOLOGY ★★★ This psycho-suspense film features Lesley Ann Warren as a bizarre artist who starts an anonymous phone service to get ideas. People call the recording and confess a sin they've committed. All goes well until a caller begins killing people in order to have something to be sorry for. Made for cable TV, this is unrated but it contains obscenities, gore, and simulated sex. 98m. **DIR:** Robert Bierman. **CAST:** Lesley Ann Warren, Peter Weller, George Loros, John Glover, Christopher Noth. **1986**

•**APOSTATE, THE** ★★1/2 A Jesuit priest at odds with God is summoned by the San Juan, Puerto Rico, police to help solve a series of brutal murders, one of which involves the priest's brother as a victim. The priest's faith is put to the ultimate test as he closes in on the killer, who uses his victim's blood to paint the crime scenes. Occasionally creepy but overly familiar thriller. Rated R for adult language, nudity, and violence. 94m. **DIR:** William Gove. **CAST:** Richard Grieco, Dennis Hopper, Jesus M. Alvarez, Jaime Bello. **1998 DVD**

APOSTLE, THE ★★★1/2 Texas Pentecostal preacher Sonny Dewey catches his wife in bed with a local youth director, beans the younger man with a baseball bat and flees to Louisiana. There he reopens a neglected country chapel and gathers a new flock. This meandering drama about a flawed, flamboyant servant of God is full of emotional and religious truth. Rated PG-13 for one scene of violence. 148m. **DIR:** Robert Duvall. **CAST:** Robert Duvall, Miranda Richardson, Farrah Fawcett, Todd Allen, John Beasley, Billy Bob Thornton, June Carter Cash. **1997 DVD**

APPALOOSA, THE ★★ Slight, often boring Western follows Marlon Brando's attempts to recover an Appaloosa horse stolen by a Mexican bandit. Brando's brooding, method-acting approach to the character only makes things worse in an already slow-moving film.

98m. **DIR:** Sidney J. Furie. **CAST:** Marlon Brando, John Saxon, Anjanette Comer, Frank Silvera. **1966**

APPLAUSE ★★★★1/2 This is a remarkable early sound-era movie. Filmed at actual New York locations, it tells the story of a fading vaudeville star (Helen Morgan) who loses the love of her daughter and is jilted by her lowly boyfriend. A smashing success. B&W; 78m. **DIR:** Rouben Mamoulian. **CAST:** Helen Morgan, Joan Peers. **1929**

APPLE, THE ★★1/2 In a poor section of Tehran, a devout man and his blind wife have sheltered their 12 year old twin daughters from the outside world. Based on a true story, the film is half documentary, half fiction, with the family, and others involved in their story, all playing themselves. The situation is interesting, but the film is clumsy and plodding, and the "actors" are uncomfortable in front of the camera—all except the two sisters themselves. In Farsi with English subtitles. Not rated; suitable for general audiences. 85m. **DIR:** Samirah Makhmalbaf. **CAST:** Zahra Naderi, Massoumeh Naderi, Qorban Ali Naderi, Azize Mohammadi, Soghra Behrozi. **1998 DVD**

APPLE DUMPLING GANG, THE ★★ A gambler (Bill Bixby) inherits three children who find a huge gold nugget in 1870. Tim Conway and Don Knotts trip and foul up as left-footed bad guys. Good, clean, unoriginal, predictable fare from Disney. The kids will love it. Rated G. 100m. **DIR:** Norman Tokar. **CAST:** Bill Bixby, Tim Conway, Don Knotts, Susan Clark, David Wayne, Slim Pickens, Harry Morgan. **1975**

APPLE DUMPLING GANG RIDES AGAIN, THE ★★ In this sequel to the 1975 original, Tim Conway and Don Knotts again play bumbling, inept outlaws in the Old West. Rated G. 88m. **DIR:** Vincent McEveety. **CAST:** Tim Conway, Don Knotts, Harry Morgan, Jack Elam, Kenneth Mars, Ruth Buzzi, Robert Pine. **1979**

APPLESEED ★★★1/2 Japanese animation. Two SWAT team officers pursue a terrorist through the experimental city of Olympus in this satisfying tale. More emphasis on story makes this fast-paced, absorbing feature a real gem. In Japanese with English subtitles. Not rated; the film has violence. 70m. **DIR:** Kazuyashi Katayama. **1988 DVD**

APPOINTMENT, THE 🦃 Story of a father cursed by his evil daughter. Not rated, the film has some violence. 90m. **DIR:** Lindsey C. Vickers. **CAST:** Edward Woodward, Jane Merrow. **1982**

APPOINTMENT IN HONDURAS ★★1/2 Good cast helps this farfetched story of an idealistic American (Glenn Ford) helping local misfits free their country from political tyranny. The actors do their best, but rather silly material gets in their way. Plot and dialogue are somewhat laughable. Ann Sheridan is highly watchable, as usual. 79m. **DIR:** Jacques Tourneur. **CAST:** Glenn Ford, Ann Sheridan, Zachary Scott, Jack Elam. **1953**

APPOINTMENT WITH DEATH ★★ Standard Agatha Christie mystery made boring by poor editing and pedestrian direction. Peter Ustinov is Hercule Poirot again (bringing competency if not vivaciousness to the part), trying to unravel a murder at an archaeological dig. Rated PG for adult situations. 102m. **DIR:** Michael Winner. **CAST:** Peter Ustinov, Lauren Bacall, Carrie Fisher, John Gielgud, Piper Laurie, Hayley Mills, Jenny Seagrove, David Soul, Amber Bezer. **1988**

APPOINTMENT WITH FEAR 🦃 Cancel this appointment! Not rated; contains sex, nudity, and profanity. 96m. **DIR:** Alan Smithee. **CAST:** Michelle Little, Michael Wyle, Kerry Remsen, Douglas Rowe, Garrick Dowhen. **1987**

APPRENTICE TO MURDER ★★1/2 This film of the occult was inspired by a true story in Pennsylvania in 1927. Donald Sutherland appears as a religious leader with healing and mystical powers. Chad Lowe, in his desperation to get help for his alcoholic father, falls prey to Sutherland's powers. Rated PG-13 for language and violence. 97m. **DIR:** Ralph L. Thomas. **CAST:** Donald Sutherland, Chad Lowe, Mia Sara, Rutanya Alda, Eddie Jones, Mark Burton. **1987**

APPRENTICESHIP OF DUDDY KRAVITZ, THE ★★★ Richard Dreyfuss, in an early starring role, is the main attraction in this quirky little comedy about a poor Jewish lad from a Montreal ghetto. The story is full of cruel and smart-assed humor, a trait that haunts Dreyfuss to this day. Ultimately, the film is too long and too shrill. Rated PG for sexual content. 121m. **DIR:** Ted Kotcheff. **CAST:** Richard Dreyfuss, Jack Warden, Micheline Lanctot, Denholm Elliott, Randy Quaid. **1974**

APRIL FOOLS, THE 🦃 A failed attempt at a serious romantic comedy that veers too often into awkward slapstick. Rated PG for adult situations. 95m. **DIR:** Stuart Rosenberg. **CAST:** Jack Lemmon, Catherine Deneuve, Peter Lawford, Sally Kellerman, Myrna Loy, Charles Boyer. **1969**

APRIL FOOL'S DAY ★★★ A group of college kids are invited to a mansion on a desolate island by a rich girl named Muffy St. John. They read Milton, quote Boswell, play practical jokes, and get killed off in a nice, orderly fashion. Not really a horror film; more of a mystery à la *Ten Little Indians*. Rated R for violence and profanity. 90m. **DIR:** Fred Walton. **CAST:** Jay Baker, Deborah Foreman, Griffin O'Neal, Amy Steel. **1986**

APRIL IN PARIS ★★1/2 State department employee Ray Bolger mistakenly asks a chorus girl (Doris Day) to represent America at a festival of the arts in Paris, and the obvious complications arise. The often (usually) misused Bolger gets to shine in one good number, "We're Going To Ring the Bell Tonight." 101m. **DIR:** David Butler. **CAST:** Doris Day, Ray Bolger, Claude Dauphin. **1952**

APT PUPIL ★★1/2 High-school student obsessed with the Holocaust recognizes a former Nazi officer and blackmails him into sharing the details of his death-camp atrocities. This disappointing adaptation of the Stephen King novella wants to explore the contagious potential of evil but trips over contrived plot points. Rated R for violence, language, and adult themes. 112m. **DIR:** Bryan Singer. **CAST:** Ian McKellen, Brad Renfro, Bruce Davison, David Schwimmer. **1998 DVD**

ARABESQUE ★★★1/2 Fast-paced espionage-adventure about college professor Gregory Peck and his nightmarish involvement with death-dealing secret agents is an entertaining chase film and a conscious effort to capture the 1960s. Beautiful Sophia Loren keeps Peck company. 118m. **DIR:** Stanley Donen. **CAST:** Gregory Peck, Sophia Loren, Kieron Moore, Alan Badel, Carl Duering, George Coulouris. **1966**

ARABIAN KNIGHT ★★ A most voluptuous princess sings a few songs before falling for a colorless, nondescript cobbler. The two set out to save her dad's kingdom when the evil Zig Zag (one of horror legend Vincent

Price's final roles) turns the kingdom over to an army of one-eyed soldiers. Director Richard Williams overwhelms the senses with nontraditional animation styles that contrast and tend to detract from the simple tale. Wee viewers will be confused. Rated G. 74m. **DIR:** Richard Williams. **1993**

ARABIAN NIGHTS (1942) ★★★ Scheherazade (Maria Montez) spends 86 minutes, not a thousand-and-one nights, as the prisoner of an evil caliph until rescued by dashing Jon Hall. No magic carpets or flying horses—but John Qualen as Aladdin and Shemp Howard as Sinbad? 86m. **DIR:** John Rawlins. **CAST:** Jon Hall, Maria Montez, Sabu, Leif Erickson, Billy Gilbert, Edgar Barrier, Richard Lane, Turhan Bey, John Qualen, Shemp Howard. **1942**

ARABIAN NIGHTS (1974) ★★1/2 Pier Paolo Pasolini re-creates some of Scheherazade's original tales in this uneven but breathtaking film. Nudity is plentiful; violence is heavy-handed. In Italian with English subtitles. Rated X. 128m. **DIR:** Pier Paolo Pasolini. **CAST:** Franco Citti. **1974 DVD**

•ARACHNID ★★1/2 Direct-to-video horror thriller resurrects an old B-movie formula. While searching for the source of a deadly virus in the South Pacific, a group of scientists crash-land on an island that turns out to be the breeding ground for giant alien spiders. Fortunately, the spiders are more deadly than the script and acting, which is adequate for this sort of offering. Rated R for language and violence. 95m. **DIR:** Jack Sholder. **CAST:** Chris Potter, Neus Asensi, José Sancho, Alex Reid. **2001 DVD**

ARACHNOPHOBIA ★★★★ Steven Spielberg protégé and longtime producer Frank Marshall does a splendid job with the *Jaws* formula in this crackerjack thriller about a small-town doctor (Jeff Daniels) and a Rambo-style exterminator (John Goodman) attempting to find and kill a huge South American spider, which has been producing a passel of deadly offspring. It's both funny and scary; a delightful roller-coaster ride of guffaws and gasps. Rated PG-13 for mild violence. 103m. **DIR:** Frank Marshall. **CAST:** Jeff Daniels, John Goodman, Harley Jane Kozak. **1990 DVD**

ARCADE ★★★ Computer animation enhances this tale of a virtual-reality arcade game that actually makes players engage in mortal combat. The local teens just can't stop playing, and when they start disappearing, Megan Ward must enter the game and pull its plug. Interesting update on the *Tron* theme. Rated R for violence. 85m. **DIR:** Albert Pyun. **CAST:** Megan Ward, Peter Billingsley, John de Lancie, Sharon Farrell, Norbert Weisser. **1994**

ARCADIA OF MY YOUTH 🦃 Captain Harlock and his avengers strike back against alien invaders in this maudlin, epic-length example of Japanese animation—twice the length, twice the incoherence, and more than twice the heroic/tragic death scenes. In Japanese with English subtitles. Not rated; contains violence. 130m. **DIR:** Tomoharu Katsumata. **1982**

ARCH OF TRIUMPH ★★★ In Paris before the Nazis arrive, a refugee doctor meets and falls in love with a woman with a past in this long, slow-paced, emotionless drama. It's sad, frustrating, tedious, and sometimes murky, but fans of the principal players will forgive and enjoy. B&W; 120m. **DIR:** Lewis Milestone. **CAST:** Ingrid Bergman, Charles Boyer, Charles Laughton, Louis Calhern. **1948 DVD**

ARCHER'S ADVENTURE ★★★ The two-hour running time may be a bit long for young children, but otherwise this adventure makes for good family viewing. In nineteenth-century Australia, a young man crosses the country with an untried horse that he wants to enter in a race. Plenty of engaging characters and incidents. Not rated. 120m. **DIR:** Denny Lawrence. **CAST:** Brett Climo, Robert Coleby, Tony Barry. **1985**

ARCTIC BLUE ★★ Although British Columbia makes a handsome substitute for the rugged Alaskan wilderness of this snowbound, kill-or-be-killed thriller, Ross LaManna's relentlessly stupid script destroys any possible suspense. Ecologists Dylan Walsh and Rya Kihlstedt pussyfoot with amoral murderer Rutger Hauer, allowing him and his big, bad buddies to wreak all sorts of mayhem. Dumb. Rated R for violence, profanity, and brief nudity. 95m. **DIR:** Peter Masterson. **CAST:** Rutger Hauer, Dylan Walsh, Rya Kihlstedt, Richard Bradford, Kevin Cooney. **1993 DVD**

ARE PARENTS PEOPLE? ★★★★ Lita (Betty Bronson) realizes she can get her estranged parents back together by indulging in some scandalous behavior. Nifty satire of 1920s social mores. Silent. B&W; 63m. **DIR:** Malcolm St. Clair. **CAST:** Betty Bronson, Florence Vidor, Adolphe Menjou. **1925**

ARE YOU IN THE HOUSE ALONE? ★★1/2 In this substandard made-for-television treatment of Richard Peck's Edgar Award–winning mystery novel, a beautiful high school student becomes the target of a campaign of terror that eventually leads to a sexual attack and mental torture. It's been done better before, but Kathleen Beller is exceptional as the heroine. 96m. **DIR:** Walter Grauman. **CAST:** Kathleen Beller, Blythe Danner, Tony Bill, Robin Mattson, Dennis Quaid, Ellen Travolta, Tricia O'Neil. **1978**

ARE YOU LONESOME TONIGHT ★★★ A frustrated housewife (Jane Seymour) discovers her husband is tape-recording his phone-sex conversations. Her husband disappears but leaves a clue on one of the tapes. She hires a private investigator (Parker Stevenson) and together they attempt to solve the mystery. Above-average made-for-cable thriller. Rated PG-13. 91m. **DIR:** E. W. Swackhamer. **CAST:** Jane Seymour, Parker Stevenson, Beth Broderick, Joel Brooks, Robert Pine. **1991**

ARENA ★★ Dopey sci-fi version of *Rocky* features a human who must take on extraterrestrials from around the galaxy in the famed Arena. Rated PG-13 for violence. 97m. **DIR:** Peter Manoogian. **CAST:** Claudia Christian, Hamilton Camp, Marc Alaimo. **1989**

ARIA ★★ High expectations are dashed in this unexpectedly boring collection of vignettes made by different directors using opera segments as a creative springboard. A few good moments, but the overall impression is about as memorable as a few hours of MTV. Rated R for nudity. 90m. **DIR:** Robert Altman, Bruce Beresford, Bill Bryden, Jean-Luc Godard, Derek Jarman, Franc Roddam, Nicolas Roeg. **CAST:** Buck Henry, John Hurt, Anita Morris, Bridget Fonda, Theresa Russell. **1988 DVD**

ARIEL ★★★★ An out-of-work miner goes on a cross-country trip and encounters a mugging, false arrest, and an unexpected love affair that hints of domestic happiness. This black comedy won the National Society of Film Critics Best Foreign Film award. In Finnish with English subtitles. Not rated; the film has simulated sex. 74m. **DIR:** Aki Kaurismaki. **CAST:** Turo Pajala, Matti Pelloupaa. **1990**

ARISTOCATS, THE ★★★ With Disney's twentieth animated feature film, the first to be produced in its entirety following Uncle Walt's death in 1966, the formula began to wear a bit. The original story concerns an eccentric millionairess who bequeaths her entire estate to her four cats, little realizing that the once-faithful butler (as eventual heir) will become so consumed by greed that he will attempt to orchestrate an early demise for the felines. Although the voices are wonderful—notably Phil Harris and Sterling Holloway—the songs are rather weak. Rated G. 79m. **DIR:** Wolfgang Reitherman. **1970 DVD**

ARIZONA ★★★1/2 The cowgirl reigns supreme in a Western that was ahead of its time. Jean Arthur stars as an independent woman coping with male bullies and barely taking time for romance with William Holden. The black-and-white scenery is gorgeous, and the verbal battles and fistfights are spiced up with Indian attacks. B&W; 125m. **DIR:** Wesley Ruggles. **CAST:** Jean Arthur, William Holden, Warren William, Edgar Buchanan, Porter Hall, Regis Toomey, George Chandler, Byron Foulger. **1940**

ARIZONA BOUND ★★★ The first of the Rough Riders movies, this entry keeps secret the fact that Buck Roberts (Buck Jones), Tim McCall (Tim McCoy), and Sandy Hopkins (Raymond Hatton) are Texas Rangers who work together—but fans of classic Westerns will be familiar with the best cowboy-trio series of them all. In this case, they're called upon to save a stagecoach line from crooks operating in Mesa City. B&W; 57m. **DIR:** Spencer Gordon Bennet. **CAST:** Buck Jones, Tim McCoy, Raymond Hatton, Dennis Moore, Luana Walters, Slim Whitaker. **1941**

ARIZONA BUSHWHACKERS Howard Keel, looking as if he might break into a chorus of "Old Man River" at any moment, leads a weary cast through this dreary, formulaic Western. 86m. **DIR:** Lesley Selander. **CAST:** Howard Keel, Yvonne De Carlo, John Ireland, Marilyn Maxwell, Scott Brady, Brian Donlevy, Roy Rogers Jr. **1968**

ARIZONA COWBOY ★★1/2 Rex Allen's first in a series of nineteen Westerns, giving him the distinction of being the last of the singing cowboys. Ex-GI turned rodeo star, Rex is framed for a robbery by bad guys. B&W; 67m. **DIR:** R. G. Springsteen. **CAST:** Rex Allen, Gordon Jones, Roy Barcroft. **1950**

ARIZONA DAYS ★★ Entertaining shoot-'em-up as somber-voiced Tex Ritter exposes the villain while shyly wooing the girl of his dreams. Ritter's films usually contained a tune or three and healthy doses of knock-down, drag-out fighting and this early entry is no exception. B&W; 57m. **DIR:** John English. **CAST:** Tex Ritter, Eleanor Stewart, Syd Saylor, William Faversham, Snub Pollard, Forrest Taylor, Glenn Strange, William Desmond, Earl Dwire, Budd Buster. **1937**

ARIZONA DREAMS ★★1/2 Too-eccentric-for-its-own-good dark comedy has the right cast to pull it off, but ultimately fails as it is left to wander aimlessly by director Emir Kusturica. Johnny Depp is right at home as a New York hotshot who is tricked into running his uncle's Cadillac dealership in Douglas, Arizona. There, he is enchanted by an eccentric woman played by Faye Dunaway. The only fun comes in watching this May-December romance simmer in the hot Arizona sun. Rated R for adult situations and language. 119m. **DIR:** Emir Kusturica. **CAST:** Johnny Depp, Faye Dunaway, Jerry Lewis, Lili Taylor, Paulina Porizkova. **1994**

ARIZONA GUNFIGHTER ★★★1/2 Fast-draw Bob Steele takes the law into his own hands to avenge the killing of his father. To do so he becomes part of an outlaw gang. An unusual spin on the typical Bob Steele revenge motif. B&W; 57m. **DIR:** Sam Newfield. **CAST:** Bob Steele, Jean Carmen, Ted Adams, Ernie Adams. **1937**

ARIZONA HEAT Run-of-the-mill cop story about a tough but good policeman (Michael Parks) inheriting a female partner (Denise Crosby) and tracking down a crazed cop killer. Rated R for language, violence, and sex. 91m. **DIR:** John G. Thomas. **CAST:** Michael Parks, Denise Crosby, Hugh Farrington. **1988**

ARIZONA KID ★★★1/2 Roy Rogers tracks down an outlaw guerrilla bandleader in the halcyon days before the outbreak of the Civil War. B&W; 54m. **DIR:** Joseph Kane. **CAST:** Roy Rogers, George "Gabby" Hayes. **1939**

ARIZONA LEGION ★★★★ In this energetic entry in his superior Western series for RKO Pictures, George O'Brien is a Texas Ranger who goes undercover to bring a bunch of baddies to bay. Chill Wills, as his sidekick, provides comic relief that is honestly funny. Fresh and enjoyable. B&W; 58m. **DIR:** David Howard. **CAST:** George O'Brien, Laraine Day, Chill Wills. **1939**

ARIZONA RAIDERS ★★★1/2 Two reformed Quantrill Raiders help Buster Crabbe's Arizona Rangers track down former comrades turned outlaws. Historical accuracies aside—The Arizona Rangers weren't formed until 1902—plenty of action keeps this one moving. 88m. **DIR:** William Witney. **CAST:** Audie Murphy, Ben Cooper, Buster Crabbe, Gloria Talbott. **1950**

ARIZONA RANGER ★★★1/2 The only Tim Holt Western to costar his father, onetime Western star Jack Holt, is one of Tim's best. Discharged from the Rough Riders, Tim joins the Arizona Rangers and tracks down a wife-beating outlaw. B&W; 63m. **DIR:** John Rawlins. **CAST:** Tim Holt, Jack Holt, Richard Martin, Nan Leslie, Steve Brodie. **1948**

ARIZONA STAGECOACH ★★★ A girl whose brother has been taken in by highwaymen is helped by the Range Busters when they pose as heavies themselves. Last film with the original Range Busters trio. B&W; 58m. **DIR:** S. Roy Luby. **CAST:** Ray "Crash" Corrigan, John King, Max Terhune, Nell O'Day, Charles King. **1942**

ARLINGTON ROAD ★★★ Domestic terrorism rears its ugly head in this slick, cautionary thriller. A widowed Washington, D.C., professor with a young son and a girlfriend has clean-cut neighbors who may or may not be serial bombers. The film provides plenty of nooks and crannies for conspiracy junkies to explore and gives a new deep chill to the saying "there goes the neighborhood." It pushes several social and political hot buttons on its way to a rather messy, incredulous ending. Rated R for language and violence. 117m. **DIR:** Mark Pellington. **CAST:** Jeff Bridges, Tim Robbins, Hope Davis, Joan Cusack, Spencer Treat Clark. **1999 DVD**

ARMAGEDDON ★★★1/2 The second of 1998s "destroy the world" scenarios—following *Deep Impact*—actually is better and a lot of fun, given its over-the-top performances and ultracharged macho trappings. When a rogue asteroid threatens to end Life as We Know It and conventional means fail to destroy it, deep-core driller Bruce Willis and his ragtag workers are sent through a crash course of astronaut basic training and then blasted into space to take care of things. The script is steeped with patriotic fervor, and events are anchored by the Girl Left Behind. Corny beyond words, but undeniably exciting. Rated PG-13 for violence, mild profanity, and dramatic intensity. 144m. **DIR:** Michael Bay. **CAST:** Bruce Willis, Billy Bob Thornton, Liv Tyler, Ben Affleck, Will Patton, Peter Stormare, Keith David, Steve Buscemi. **1998 DVD**

ARMED AND DANGEROUS 🦃 Fired cop Frank Dooley (John Candy) and former lawyer Norman Kane (Eugene Levy), become private security guards. Rated PG-13 for language. 89m. **DIR:** Mark L. Lester. **CAST:** John Candy, Eugene Levy, Robert Loggia, Kenneth McMillan, Meg Ryan, Jonathan Banks, Brian James. **1986**

ARMED AND DEADLY ★★1/2 This mindless *Terminator* rip-off finds gutsy scientist Beth Toussaint and her young son trapped in a nuclear weapons facility, battling a cyborg in name only (just an excuse for the villain to bare his chest and still repel bullets). Only the fast pace saves it from turkeydom. Rated R for violence and profanity. 100m. **DIR:** John Eyres. **CAST:** Frank Zagarino, Bryan Genesse, Beth Toussaint. **1994**

ARMED RESPONSE ★★ In Los Angeles's Chinatown, a Vietnam vet and his family fight a Japanese mob for possession of a jade statue. *Armed Response* starts out parodying the action-adventure genre, but loses its sense of humor in the middle and bogs down for too long, becoming boring and jingoistic. Rated R. 86m. **DIR:** Fred Olen Ray. **CAST:** David Carradine, Lee Van Cleef, Mako, Lois Hamilton, Ross Hagen, Brent Huff, Laurene Landon. **1986**

ARMITAGE III: ELECTRO BLOOD ★★ A staid police detective and his sexy, loose-cannon partner, Armitage, pursue a serial killer whose victims are robots on the colonized and teeming world of Mars. This animated tale is nearly made interesting by glimpses of possible future technology. Not rated; contains violence, nudity, and profanity. 48m. **DIR:** Ochi Hiroyuki. **1994**

ARMORED COMMAND ★★ It's World War II, and the U.S. Tank Corps is fighting its way through the German lines. Sound familiar? Predictable programmer. 99m. **DIR:** Byron Haskin. **CAST:** Howard Keel, Tina Louise, Burt Reynolds, Warner Anderson. **1961**

ARMOUR OF GOD ★★★★1/2 In this big-budget, Indiana Jones–style adventure, archaeologist Jackie Chan agrees to secure the mystical "armour of God" for baddies who have kidnapped his ex-girlfriend. The stunt work and action scenes are phenomenal, even by Chan's high standards. In Cantonese with English subtitles. Not rated; contains comic violence. 98m. **DIR:** Jackie Chan. **CAST:** Jackie Chan, Alan Tam, Rosamund Kwan. **1987**

ARMY OF DARKNESS ★★★1/2 This third film in writer-director Sam Raimi's *Evil Dead* series is by far the most polished. That's not to say it's the best, but the mixture of comedy and mayhem make it a good old time. Film fanatics will cherish some of Raimi's nods to famous fantastic films. Rated R for violence. 83m. **DIR:** Sam Raimi. **CAST:** Bruce Campbell, Embeth Davidtz, Marcus Gilbert, Ian Abercrombie, Richard Grove. **1993 DVD**

ARMY OF ONE ★★★ Dolph Lundgren stars as a wrongly accused man who escapes from prison to exact revenge on the man who put him there. Proving his innocence is secondary, but this action-packed film entertains. Available in R-rated and unrated versions; both contain violence, profanity, and sexual situations. 106m. **DIR:** Vic Armstrong. **CAST:** Dolph Lundgren, George Segal, Kristian Alfonso. **1993 DVD**

ARNOLD ★★ A delightful cast cannot save this rather muddled mess of murder and mirth. Stella Stevens, married to a corpse, suddenly discovers her costars meeting their maker in a variety of strange ways reminiscent of *The Abominable Dr. Phibes*. Rated PG for violence. 100m. **DIR:** Georg Fenady. **CAST:** Roddy McDowall, Elsa Lanchester, Stella Stevens, Farley Granger, Victor Buono, John McGiver, Shani Wallis. **1973**

AROUND THE WORLD ★★1/2 Bandleader Kay Kyser entertains the troops during World War II by hamming it up with an endless number of corny puns and gags. The offstage antics of the performers are highlighted by an electrifying duel between Mischa Auer and an offended nobleman. B&W; 80m. **DIR:** Allan Dwan. **CAST:** Kay Kyser, Mischa Auer, Joan Davis. **1943**

AROUND THE WORLD IN 80 DAYS (1956) ★★★★ Producer Mike Todd's opulent adaptation of Jules Verne's classic tale has dated a bit, but remains a treat for those who bask in the glow of gorgeous cinematography, lavish production values, and a whimsical script that retains the novel's essential elements. This film also features cameos by more than forty cinema legends. David Niven and Cantinflas accept the challenge to circumnavigate the globe within the prescribed time; their journey unfolds against Victor Young's stirring soundtrack and Lionel Lindon's glowing camerawork . . . most of which will be lost on a conventional television set. Hold out for a letterboxed version and find a friend with a wall-size TV screen; the results will more than justify the trouble. 167m. **DIR:** Michael Anderson. **CAST:** David Niven, Cantinflas, Shirley MacLaine, Robert Newton. **1956**

AROUND THE WORLD IN 80 DAYS (1974) ★★★ A turn-of-the-century English gentleman, Phileas Fogg, undertakes a wager to go around the globe in eighty days despite endless obstacles. This is well paced for youngsters, but includes dialogue that even adults will find amusing. Made for television. 60m. **DIR:** Arthur Rankin Jr., Jules Bass. **1974**

AROUND THE WORLD IN 80 DAYS (1989) ★★★1/2 Entertaining remake of Jules Verne's classic novel features Pierce Brosnan as the rigidly punctual Phileas Fogg. Having wagered that he would circle the globe in just eighty days, Fogg sets off with his French servant who provides the comic relief. They are followed by Peter Ustinov playing a detective who believes Fogg is a notorious bank robber. Fogg finds time to rescue and fall in love with an Indian princess. Period and ethnic costuming is impressive. Made for TV, this is not rated but contains sexual situations. 267m. **DIR:** Buzz Kulik. **CAST:** Pierce Brosnan, Eric Idle, Peter Ustinov, Julia Nickson. **1989**

AROUND THE WORLD IN 80 WAYS ★★ Despite a wonderfully goofy premise, this comedy from Down Under is just not very funny. Philip Quast is a young tour guide who must take his decrepit father on a world tour, but lacks the money so he fakes it, never leaving his neighborhood. Rated R for language and crudity. 90m. **DIR:** Stephen MacLean. **CAST:** Philip Quast. **1988**

AROUND THE WORLD UNDER THE SEA ★★ Volcanoes, a giant eel, a submarine, scuba gear, and a quarrel over who's in charge make this lackluster, harmless viewing. Shirley Eaton was in *Goldfinger*, in case you're a James Bond fan. 117m. **DIR:** Andrew Marton. **CAST:** Lloyd Bridges, Shirley Eaton, David McCallum, Brian Kelly, Keenan Wynn, Marshall Thompson. **1966**

AROUSERS, THE ★★1/2 Tab Hunter gives a genuinely creepy performance in this sleazy thriller about a necrophiliac gym teacher with a mother complex. Not rated; features adult themes and violence. 90m. **DIR:** Curtis Hanson. **CAST:** Tab Hunter, Roberta Collins. **1970**

ARRANGEMENT, THE 🦃 The cast is the only real reason for watching this tedious talkfest. Rated R for language. 127m. **DIR:** Elia Kazan. **CAST:** Kirk Douglas, Deborah Kerr, Faye Dunaway, Richard Boone. **1969 DVD**

ARREST BULLDOG DRUMMOND ★★1/2 Bulldog Drummond and his cronies pursue a murderer to a tropical island where he has taken refuge. Fifth in the popular series featuring John Howard. Available on a double-bill video with *Bulldog Drummond in Africa*. B&W; 57m. **DIR:** James Hogan. **CAST:** John Howard, Heather Angel, George Zucco, H. B. Warner, E. E. Clive, Reginald Denny, John Sutton. **1938**

ARRIVAL, THE (1990) ★★★ Even though we learn very little about the alien and its purpose, this film manages to involve the viewer. An old man is infected with an alien and finds he is growing younger but needs to kill women for their estrogen to stay young. Rated R for profanity and violence. 107m. **DIR:** David Schmoeller. **CAST:** Joseph Culp, Robin Frates, John Saxon, Robert Sampson, Michael J. Pollard. **1990**

ARRIVAL, THE (1996) ★★★ Sophisticated and engaging sci-fi thriller stars Charlie Sheen as an astronomer listening to the heavens for intelligent life. When he inadvertently intercepts a seemingly alien signal, his investigation gets him fired from his job. Refusing to give up, he stumbles into an alien conspiracy involving global warming and colonization. Rated PG-13. 119m. **DIR:** David N. Twohy. **CAST:** Charlie Sheen, Lindsay Crouse, Teri Polo, Ron Silver. **1996 DVD**

ARRIVAL II, THE ★★★ Sequel to the thought-provoking sci-fi flick has Zane's half brother on the run from the aliens and trying to expose their hidden agenda. While not as well acted or intellectual as the first film, this still has a lot going for it: a complex plot, solid action, and nifty gizmos. Rated PG-13 for mild violence, profanity, and brief nudity. 101m. **DIR:** Kevin S. Tenney. **CAST:** Patrick Muldoon, Jane Sibbett. **1998 DVD**

ARROGANT, THE 🦃 A waitress and a philosophy-spouting motorcyclist. There's enough profanity, violence, and nudity to earn an R rating. 86m. **DIR:** Phillippe Blot. **CAST:** Gary Graham, Sylvia Kristel. **1987**

ARROWHEAD ★★★ Charlton Heston is pitted against Jack Palance in this one-sided view of the Apache conflicts. Intense, action-packed Western. Weak script is overcome by powerful acting. B&W; 105m. **DIR:** Charles Marquis Warren. **CAST:** Charlton Heston, Jack Palance, Brian Keith. **1953**

ARROWSMITH ★★★★ Mellifluous-voiced Ronald Colman is a young, career-dedicated research doctor tempted by the profits of commercialism in this faithful rendering of Sinclair Lewis's noted novel of medicine. Helen Hayes is his first wife—doomed to die before he sees the light. This is the first film to center seriously on a doctor's career and raise the question of professional integrity and morality versus quick money and social status. B&W; 101m. **DIR:** John Ford. **CAST:** Ronald Colman, Helen Hayes, Richard Bennett, DeWitt Jennings, Beulah Bondi, Myrna Loy. **1931**

ARSENAL ★★ This imaginative, symbolic denouncement of war is rich in visual images, but takes too long to make its point. A collection of episodes that take place during the last part of World War I, this Russian offering lacks fire. B&W; 70m. **DIR:** Alexander Dovzhenko. **CAST:** Semyon Svashenko. **1929**

ARSENIC AND OLD LACE ★★★★1/2 Two sweet old ladies have found a solution for the loneliness of elderly men with no family or friends—they poison them! Then they give them a proper Christian burial in their basement. Their nephew, Mortimer (Cary Grant), an obvious party pooper, finds out and wants them to stop. This delightful comedy is crammed with sparkling performances. B&W; 118m. **DIR:** Frank Capra. **CAST:** Cary Grant, Priscilla Lane, Jack Carson, James Gleason, Peter Lorre, Raymond Massey, Jean Adair, Josephine Hull. **1944 DVD**

ARSON INC. ★★ Robert Lowery is an arson-squad investigator and Anne Gwynne is his romantic interest. They perform capably, but the script is at best predictable, and stock footage of fires is quite evident. B&W; 64m. **DIR:** William Berke. **CAST:** Robert Lowery, Anne Gwynne. **1950**

ART OF BUSTER KEATON, THE ★★★★★ The genius of silent film's unique, deadpan comic shines anew in this three-volume (ten-tape) collection of the cream of his features and short comedies, a number of which have not previously been available on cassette. 120m. **DIR:** Buster Keaton, Roscoe Arbuckle, Eddie Cline, Charles F. Reisner. **CAST:** Buster Keaton, Roscoe "Fatty" Arbuckle, Wallace Beery, Natalie Talmadge, Kathryn McGuire. **1919–1927**

ART OF DYING, THE ★★★ The *film noir* detective meets the mad slasher in this atmospheric film about a filmmaker who steals scenes from famous slasher flicks to make his own private snuff films. Director-star Wings Hauser has created a moody film with a wonderful plot. Rated R for violence, profanity, and nudity. 96m. **DIR:** Wings Hauser. **CAST:** Wings Hauser, Kathleen Kinmont, Sarah Douglas, Michael J. Pollard. **1991**

ART OF WAR, THE ★★★1/2 Wesley Snipes, an undercover operative for the United Nations, becomes a pawn in a power struggle when he is framed for the murder of the Chinese ambassador. Efficiently made and well-acted, this film will please viewers looking for high-octane escapism—that is, if you can ignore the plot holes. Rated R for violence, sex, profanity, and drug use. 117m. **DIR:** Christian Duguay. **CAST:** Wesley Snipes, Donald Sutherland, Maury Chaykin, Anne Archer, Marie Matiko, Michael Biehn, Cary-Hiroyuki Tagawa, James Hong. **2000 DVD**

ARTEMISIA ★★★ This controversial account of the artistic blossoming and sexual deflowering of the seventeenth-century female Italian painter is intriguing. Submerging us in the world of art, this film explores the moral, social, and political implications of the talented teen's desire to include the nude human body in her paintings. The story loses steam when her dual role as feminist warrior and amused voyeur is publicly scandalized by her father. In French with English subtitles. Rated R for nudity and sexuality. 102m. **DIR:** Agnes Merlet. **CAST:** Valentina Cervi, Miki Manojlovic, Michel Serrault. **1998 DVD**

ARTHUR ★★★★ Dudley Moore is Arthur, the world's richest (and obviously happiest) alcoholic. But all is not well in his pickled paradise. Arthur will lose access to the family's great wealth if he doesn't marry the uptight debutante picked out for him by his parents. He doesn't love her . . . in fact, he's in love with a wacky shoplifter (Liza Minnelli). Most of the time, it's hilarious, with John Gielgud as a sharp-tongued butler providing the majority of the laughs. Rated PG because of profanity. 97m. **DIR:** Steve Gordon. **CAST:** Dudley Moore, Liza Minnelli, Stephen Elliott, John Gielgud. **1981 DVD**

ARTHUR 2: ON THE ROCKS ★★ Some sequels simply don't take characters in the directions imagined by those who loved the original film, and *Arthur 2* is a case in point. Morose, uncomfortable, and marred by its badly contrived conclusion, call this one a good try. Rated PG for mild profanity. 99m. **DIR:** Bud Yorkin. **CAST:** Dudley Moore, Liza Minnelli, John Gielgud, Cynthia Sikes, Stephen Elliott, Paul Benedict, Geraldine Fitzgerald, Barney Martin. **1988**

ARTHUR'S HALLOWED GROUND ★★ An elderly British gent stands his ground against the system in order to protect his beloved land. A good premise, until one realizes the bit of turf in question is a field on which to play cricket! 88m. **DIR:** Freddie Young. **CAST:** Michael Elphick, Jimmy Jewel, David Swift. **1973**

ARTHUR'S QUEST ★★★ In this modern twist of the classic Mark Twain story (*A Connecticut Yankee in King Arthur's Court*), a young Prince Arthur is sent to the twentieth century by the wizard Merlin in order to hide and train the future king of Camelot. Years pass and Arthur is now a modern teenager who has completely forgotten about his medieval lineage. When Merlin returns to reclaim the adolescent king, he must convince Arthur of who he truly is, while contending with the bad guys. This is an entertaining romp that is suitable for all ages, and will certainly appeal the most to children and young teens. Rated PG for mild violence. 92m. **DIR:** Neil Mandt. **CAST:** Catherine Oxenberg, Clint Howard, Arye Gross, Eric Christian Olsen, Brian James. **1999 DVD**

ARTICLE 99 ★★★1/2 VA hospitals take it on the chin in scripter Ron Cutler's acerbic blend of *M*A*S*H* and *Catch-22*, which concerns a governmental regulation denying treatment to veterans who cannot prove their injuries are war-related. Cutler's stinging satire eventually yields to a dubiously happy ending, but getting there is a lot of fun. Rated R for profanity and graphic medical procedures. 98m. **DIR:** Howard Deutch. **CAST:** Ray Liotta, Kiefer Sutherland, Forest Whitaker, John C. McGinley, Lea Thompson, John Mahoney, Kathy Baker, Eli Wallach. **1992**

ARTISTS AND MODELS ★★★ One of the better Martin and Lewis films features Dino as a cartoonist who gets his ideas from Jerry's dreams. Cowriter and director Frank Tashlin was a former cartoonist, and brought that preposterous visual style to this movie. 109m. **DIR:** Frank Tashlin. **CAST:** Dean Martin, Jerry Lewis, Shirley MacLaine, Eva Gabor, Anita Ekberg, Eddie Mayehoff. **1955**

AS GOOD AS DEAD 🦃 Try to keep from yawning while watching this made-for-cable original about a wholesome woman who helps out a new friend, only to be mixed up in a murder. Not rated; contains violence. 95m. **DIR:** Larry Cohen. **CAST:** Judge Reinhold, Crystal Bernard, Traci Lords. **1995**

AS GOOD AS IT GETS ★★★★★ This impeccably written and performed misfit love story garnered Oscars for stars Jack Nicholson and Helen Hunt. Nicholson's a nasty, obsessive-compulsive lacking any positive redeeming values until he meets a compassionate waitress/single mom trying to raise her ailing child, and a gay artist neighbor with the most adorably ugly dog ever seen. The dialogue is tart and funny; the players couldn't be better. Rated PG-13 for profanity, violence, nudity, and sexual candor. 138m. **DIR:** James L. Brooks. **CAST:** Jack Nicholson, Helen Hunt, Greg Kinnear, Cuba Gooding Jr., Skeet Ulrich, Shirley Knight. **1997 DVD**

AS IS ★★1/2 How AIDS affects family and loved ones is dealt with in a thoughtful manner as Robert Carradine portrays a homosexual who contracts the disease. Jonathan Hadary is the lover who stands by him. Although not preachy, the film does suffer from staginess. Not rated, but the whole concept is adult in nature, and some coarse language is used. 86m. **DIR:** Michael Lindsay-Hogg. **CAST:** Robert Carradine, Jonathan Hadary, Joanna Miles, Alan Scarfe, Colleen Dewhurst. **1986**

AS SUMMERS DIE ★★★1/2 A very leisurely story set in Georgia, 1959, concerns a southern aristocratic family's attempt to wrest control of land given to a black woman years earlier, because oil deposits have been found on it. Plot line is nothing new but the performances by a veteran cast carry this HBO film. Bette Davis has some touching moments as a woman whose mental competency is challenged. 87m. **DIR:** Jean-Claude Tramont. **CAST:** Scott Glenn, Jamie Lee Curtis, Bette Davis, John Randolph, Ron O'Neal, Bruce McGill, John McIntire, Beah Richards. **1987**

AS YOU DESIRE ME ★★ Greta Garbo plays an amnesiac, and her attempt to be sexy means putting on a blond wig. It works only up to a point. Based on a play by Pirandello, the film remains resolutely stage bound. B&W; 71m. **DIR:** George Fitzmaurice. **CAST:** Greta Garbo, Erich Von Stroheim, Melvyn Douglas, Owen Moore, Hedda Hopper. **1932**

AS YOU LIKE IT ★★★ Laurence Olivier is commanding as Orlando to beautiful Elisabeth Bergner's stylized Rosalind in this early filming of Shakespeare's delightful comedy. Lovers of the Bard will be pleased. B&W; 96m. **DIR:** Paul Czinner. **CAST:** Elisabeth Bergner, Laurence Olivier, Felix Aylmer, Leon Quartermaine. **1936 DVD**

AS YOUNG AS YOU FEEL ★★1/2 Marilyn Monroe's presence in a bit part, and the fact that Paddy Chayefsky provided the original story, are the main drawing cards today in this broad spoof of big business. B&W; 77m. **DIR:** Harmon Jones. **CAST:** Monty Woolley, Thelma Ritter, David Wayne, Jean Peters, Marilyn Monroe. **1951**

ASCENT, THE ★★★ Cross between *The Great Escape* and *The Bridge on the River Kwai* minus the spellbinding acting of the two classics. Focus is on proud Italian POWs in a British concentration camp in East Africa. The men plan to leave their flag at the top of Mount Kenya in a magnificent, nose-thumbing gesture to their captors. The actual climb is death-defying with some edge-of-the-seat, hand-in-mouth moments of terror. Rated PG for violence and sexual innuendo. 96m. **DIR:** Donald Shebib. **CAST:** Vincent Spano, Ben Cross, Tony Lo Bianco, Rachel Ward. **1994**

ASCENT TO HEAVEN (MEXICAN BUS RIDE) ★★★ A young man's wedding ceremony is interrupted so he can make a two-day bus journey to get his dying mother's will ratified. On the way, he encounters a variety of hilarious adventures and delays. A good light comedy, punctuated with Luis Buñuel's great surreal touches. In Spanish with English subtitles. B&W; 85m. **DIR:** Luis Buñuel. **CAST:** Lilia Prado, Esteban Marquez. **1951**

ASH WEDNESDAY ★★1/2 Elizabeth Taylor plays an aging woman who undergoes a painful cosmetic makeover in order to make herself more appealing to husband Henry Fonda. This disjointed morality play has some good moments, but offensive close-ups of the facial operation and the melodramatic predictability of the story eventually work against it. Rated R. 99m. **DIR:** Larry Peerce. **CAST:** Elizabeth Taylor, Henry Fonda, Helmut Berger, Keith Baxter, Margaret Blye, Monique Van Vooren. **1973**

ASHANTI ★★1/2 A shopping trip turns into a tale of horror when the black wife (Beverly Johnson) of a white doctor (Michael Caine) in Africa is kidnapped and turned over to a slave trader (Peter Ustinov). Thus begins a fairly exciting chase across various exotic locales. Rated R. 118m. **DIR:** Richard Fleischer. **CAST:** Michael Caine, Peter Ustinov, Beverly Johnson, William Holden, Omar Sharif, Rex Harrison. **1979**

ASHES AND DIAMONDS ★★★★ The conflict between idealism and instinct is explored with great intensity in this story of a Polish resistance fighter who assassinates the wrong man at the end of World War II. Director Andrzej Wajda captures all the bitterness and disillusionment of political fanaticism in this powerful testament of the Polish people during the struggle that followed the war's end. In Polish with English subtitles. B&W; 102m. **DIR:** Andrzej Wajda. **CAST:** Zbigniew Cybulski. **1958**

ASK ANY GIRL ★★★ A motivation researcher tries out his theories by helping a husband hunter to snag his playboy brother. The third male lead, lecherous Rod Taylor, steals the movie. 101m. **DIR:** Charles Walters. **CAST:** David Niven, Shirley MacLaine, Gig Young, Rod Taylor, Jim Backus. **1959**

ASPEN EXTREME ★★★1/2 Paul Gross and Peter Berg leave dead-end jobs in Detroit to hire on as Aspen ski instructors, where the former's California-style good looks make an immediate impression with predatory rich lady Finola Hughes. Rated PG-13 for profanity and suggested sex. 117m. **DIR:** Patrick Hasburgh. **CAST:** Paul Gross, Peter Berg, Finola Hughes, Teri Polo, William Russ. **1993**

ASPHALT JUNGLE, THE ★★★★1/2 One of the greatest crime films of all time. This realistic study of a jewel robbery that sours reveals early on what the outcome will be while building tension for any surprises that might pop up. Sterling Hayden and a near-perfect cast charge the film with an electric current that only increases in power as they scheme their way closer to their fate. John Huston broke new ground with this landmark drama. B&W; 112m. **DIR:** John Huston. **CAST:** Sterling Hayden, Sam Jaffe, Louis Calhern, Marilyn Monroe, Jean Hagen, James Whitmore, Marc Lawrence, Anthony Caruso. **1950**

ASSASSIN ★★1/2 Now-familiar tale of a killer cyborg running loose and out of control. Robert Conrad, retired from the Agency, is brought in from the cold to hunt and destroy the robot with the symbolic name of Golem. Originally a television movie, but released on cassette with an R rating for violence. 94m. **DIR:** Sandor Stern. **CAST:** Robert Conrad, Karen Austin, Richard Young, Robert Webber. **1986 DVD**

ASSASSIN OF YOUTH (MARIJUANA) ★★ This silly, low-budget exploitation film tells the story of a courageous young reporter who goes undercover to infiltrate the marijuana cult that has been wreaking havoc with a local town. Cornball humor gives this an extra edge on most films of this nature. B&W; 67m. **DIR:** Elmer Clifton. **CAST:** Luana Walters, Arthur Gardner, Earl Dwire. **1936**

ASSASSINATION 🦃 In this predictable, poorly written action flick, Charles Bronson plays a seasoned secret service agent who is called upon to guard the first lady (Jill Ireland). Rated PG-13 for profanity and violence. 105m. **DIR:** Peter R. Hunt. **CAST:** Charles Bronson, Jill Ireland, Stephen Elliott, Jan Gan Boyd, Randy Brooks, Michael Ansara. **1987**

ASSASSINATION FILE, THE ★★★ A Secret Service agent—who resigned due to an assassination on her watch—begins an investigation into the killing. Rated R for violence, profanity, and nudity. 106m. **DIR:** John Harrison. **CAST:** Sherilyn Fenn, Paul Winfield. **1996**

ASSASSINATION GAME, THE 🦃 Dismal espionage film about a rookie CIA agent teaming up with a retired KGB agent. Rated R for violence, nudity, and profanity. 83m. **DIR:** Jonathan Winfrey. **CAST:** Robert Rusler, Theodore Bikel, Denise Bixler, Doug Wert. **1992**

ASSASSINATION OF TROTSKY, THE 🦃 Richard Burton as the exiled Soviet leader. A chaotic yawner. Rated R. 102m. **DIR:** Joseph Losey. **CAST:** Richard Burton, Alain Delon, Romy Schneider. **1972**

ASSASSINS ★★1/2 Professional hit man Sylvester Stallone finds himself the hunted rather than the hunter when up-and-coming shooter Antonio Banderas targets him as an unwanted rival, in this tedious, overlong action film. Only Julianne Moore, as a high-tech con woman, adds any spark to what plays like a clone of *The Gunfighter* and *The Mechanic*. Rated R for violence and profanity. 132m. **DIR:** John Badham. **CAST:**

Sylvester Stallone, Antonio Banderas, Julianne Moore. **1995 DVD**

ASSASSINS DE L'ORDRE, LES (LAW BREAKERS) ★★ Marcel Carné, who directed the 1944 classic *Children of Paradise*, slips into innocuousness with this less than riveting tale. Jacques Brel plays a judge who is trying to get to the bottom of corrupt police practices. 107m. **DIR:** Marcel Carné. **CAST:** Jacques Brel, Catherine Rouvel, Michel Lonsdale, Charles Denner, Didier Haudepin. **1971**

ASSAULT, THE ★★★★1/2 This Academy Award winner for best foreign language film deserves its praise. It is a tale of war and its inevitable impact. In Holland in 1945, a Nazi collaborator is murdered and the lives of the witnesses, a small boy in particular, are changed forever. Dubbed. 126m. **DIR:** Fons Rademakers. **CAST:** Derek de Lint, Marc van Uchelen, Monique van de Ven. **1986 DVD**

ASSAULT & MATRIMONY ★★★ Likable made-for-television comedy pitting real-life husband-and-wife team Jill Eikenberry and Michael Tucker against each other as warring spouses trying to kill each other. 100m. **DIR:** James Frawley. **CAST:** Jill Eikenberry, Michael Tucker, John Hillerman, Michelle Phillips. **1987**

ASSAULT AT WEST POINT ★★★ Although based on a reprehensible actual event at West Point, the story never connects. Seth Gilliam remains too detached as Johnson Whittaker, the first black cadet accepted at West Point, whose military career was derailed after he was assaulted . . . and "proved" to have beaten himself unconscious. The usually excellent Sam Waterston is uncomfortably stiff as Whittaker's defense attorney. Rated PG-13 for mild profanity and brief violence. 98m. **DIR:** Harry Moses. **CAST:** Samuel L. Jackson, Sam Waterston, Seth Gilliam, John Glover, Josef Sommer, Mason Adams. **1994**

ASSAULT OF THE KILLER BIMBOS ★★ Goofy excuse for a movie has three go-go dancers running afoul of the mob and then getting mixed up with surfers. Not to be taken seriously. Rated R for nudity, violence, and profanity. 85m. **DIR:** Anita Rosenberg. **CAST:** Christina Whitaker, Elizabeth Kaitan, Nick Cassavetes, Griffin O'Neal. **1988 DVD**

ASSAULT OF THE REBEL GIRLS (CUBAN REBEL GIRLS) 🦃 Errol Flynn's last film is a cheaply made bargain-basement production. B&W; 68m. **DIR:** Barry Mahon. **CAST:** Errol Flynn, Beverly Aadland, John McKay. **1959**

ASSAULT ON A QUEEN ★★★ Implausible, improbable, but sometimes fun story by Rod Serling, has Frank Sinatra and pals bluffing their way onto the *Queen Mary* for a million-dollar haul. Originally released at an overlong 146 minutes. Cuts help to move the story along. Okay family viewing. 105m. **DIR:** Jack Donohue. **CAST:** Frank Sinatra, Virna Lisi, Anthony Franciosa, Richard Conte. **1968**

ASSAULT ON AGATHON 🦃 While investigating a series of robberies of Greek banks, a British and an American Interpol agent uncover a plot by a World War II underground leader to start a new revolution. 96m. **DIR:** Laslo Benedek. **CAST:** Nico Minardos, Nina Van Pallandt, John Woodvine, Marianne Faithfull. **1976**

ASSAULT ON PRECINCT 13 ★★★★1/2 Here's director John Carpenter's riveting movie about a nearly deserted L.A. police station that finds itself under siege by a youth gang. It's a modern-day version of Howard Hawks's *Rio Bravo*, with exceptional performances by its entire cast. Rated R. 90m. **DIR:** John Carpenter. **CAST:** Austin Stoker, Laurie Zimmer, Tony Burton, Nancy Loomis, Darwin Joston. **1976 DVD**

ASSIGNMENT, THE ★★★★ In this superior espionage thriller, Aidan Quinn is emotionally riveting as an American naval officer who bears an uncanny resemblance to international terrorist Carlos "The Jackal" Sanchez. When he is recruited by Israeli intelligence and the CIA to impersonate the terrorist and draw him into the open, his life becomes embroiled in international intrigue and deadly consequences. Rated R for adult situations, language, nudity, and violence. 119m. **DIR:** Christian Duguay. **CAST:** Aidan Quinn, Donald Sutherland, Ben Kingsley. **1997 DVD**

ASSISI UNDERGROUND, THE ★★ Melodrama tracing the activities of a Franciscan monastery as part of the Jewish liberation network in World War II Italy. Ben Cross struggles valiantly to bring some life to this dreary fact-based tale; hard work considering the poor dialogue and unrealistic behavior of the Jews he is trying to help escape from Europe. Rated PG. 115m. **DIR:** Alexander Ramati. **CAST:** Ben Cross, James Mason, Irene Papas, Maximilian Schell, Karl Heinz Hackl, Delia Boccardo, Edmund Purdom. **1985**

ASSOCIATE, THE (1982) ★★ Disappointing comedy about an unemployed bank clerk who schemes to murder his wealthy business partner. Michel Serrault is the only bright spot in this otherwise muddled comedy. In French with English subtitles. Not rated; contains nudity and profanity. 94m. **DIR:** René Gainville. **CAST:** Michel Serrault, Claudine Auger, Catherine Alric. **1982**

ASSOCIATE, THE (1996) ★★★ Wall Street analyst Whoopi Goldberg can't catch a break in a field dominated by men, so she sets up her own partnership with a wholly fictitious male partner. Nick Thiel's script for the most part scores with well-timed jokes about gender confusion, but things become less successful when Goldberg has to actually *become* her male counterpart. Rated PG-13 for profanity and considerable blue humor. 113m. **DIR:** Donald Petrie. **CAST:** Whoopi Goldberg, Dianne Wiest, Eli Wallach, Timothy Daly, Bebe Neuwirth, Austin Pendleton, Lainie Kazan. **1996 DVD**

ASTRO-ZOMBIES 🦃 John Carradine as a mad scientist killing to obtain body parts for his new creation. 83m. **DIR:** Ted V. Mikels. **CAST:** Wendell Corey, John Carradine, Rafael Campos. **1967 DVD**

ASTRONAUT'S WIFE, THE ★★1/2 Two American astronauts begin acting very strangely after a near-fatal deep-space accident. The wife of one of the NASA space cowboys becomes pregnant with twins and either evidence or her paranoia begins to suggest she may be an incubator for alien embryos. This sensual, extraterrestrial riff on *Rosemary's Baby* lacks gnawing suspense. Rated R for language, violence, and sexuality. 110m. **DIR:** Rand Ravich. **CAST:** Johnny Depp, Charlize Theron, Joe Morton, Nick Cassavetes. **1999 DVD**

ASYLUM (1972) ★★★★ A first-rate horror anthology from England featuring fine performances. Four seemingly unrelated stories of madness by Robert Bloch are interwoven, leading to a nail-biting climax. Rated PG. 92m. **DIR:** Roy Ward Baker. **CAST:** Barbara Parkins,

Sylvia Syms, Peter Cushing, Barry Morse, Richard Todd, Herbert Lom, Patrick Magee. **1972 DVD**

ASYLUM (1996) Tired tale of a P.I. who goes undercover in a mental hospital to find out who killed his friend. Not rated; contains violence, language, and adult situations. 90m. **DIR:** James Seale. **CAST:** Robert Patrick, Malcolm McDowell, Sarah Douglas, Henry Gibson, Peter Brown, Irwin Keyes. **1996**

ASYLUM OF SATAN Girdler's first feature contains mucho sadism. Rated R. 82m. **DIR:** William Girdler. **CAST:** Charles Kissinger, Carla Borelli. **1972**

AT BERTRAM'S HOTEL ★★★★1/2 Miss Marple (Joan Hickson) takes a London vacation, courtesy of her nephew Raymond, in this superior installment of the Agatha Christie series. Miss Marple encounters some old friends during her stay at Bertram's Hotel, where she discovers that surface appearances are just a little too good to be true. Costumes and set design are luxurious. Not rated; suitable for family viewing. 102m. **DIR:** Mary McMurray. **CAST:** Joan Hickson, Caroline Blakiston, Helena Michell, George Baker, James Cossins, Preston Lockwood, Joan Greenwood. **1986**

AT CLOSE RANGE ★★★★ A powerful thriller based on true events that occurred in Pennsylvania during the summer of 1978. A rural gang leader returns to the family he abandoned years ago. His two sons try to prove themselves worthy of joining the gang. Events beyond their control lead to a brutal showdown between father and sons. Rated R for violence and profanity. 115m. **DIR:** James Foley. **CAST:** Christopher Walken, Sean Penn, Christopher Penn. **1986**

AT FIRST SIGHT (1995) ★★1/2 Jonathan Silverman's knack for physical comedy and some funny dialogue help keep this slight romantic comedy afloat. He finds the woman of his dreams in Allison Smith, but allows his meddlesome, skirt-chasing best friend to knock her out of the picture. A lack of focus is a problem, as this can't decide if it's a romantic comedy, a buddy flick, or a coming-of-age story. Rated R for profanity and sexual situations. 90m. **DIR:** Steven Pearl. **CAST:** Jonathan Silverman, Dan Cortese, Allison Smith. **1995**

AT FIRST SIGHT (1999) ★★ A blind masseur, at the urging of his new girlfriend, undergoes an operation to restore his vision. The theme of Oliver Sacks's original article—the dilemma of a man trying to adjust to his sense of sight after a lifetime without it—is fascinating. Unfortunately, the film concentrates on the strain that grows between the two lovers and becomes a tedious soap opera. Rated PG-13 for brief sexual scenes. 128m. **DIR:** Irwin Winkler. **CAST:** Mira Sorvino, Val Kilmer, Kelly McGillis, Steven Weber, Bruce Davison, Nathan Lane. **1999 DVD**

AT GUNPOINT ★★★ Fred MacMurray plays a mild-mannered storekeeper who accidentally foils a bank robbery. The grateful town makes him sheriff, then turns to him when the outlaws return. The story is a clever reworking of *High Noon* to match MacMurray's unique screen personality, and the supporting cast is uniformly fine. Not rated, but may be too violent for young children. 81m. **DIR:** Alfred Werker. **CAST:** Fred MacMurray, Dorothy Malone, Walter Brennan, Tommy Rettig, John Qualen, Skip Homeier. **1955**

AT PLAY IN THE FIELDS OF THE LORD A boring movie without redeeming social value in spite of its high-powered cast tells a dramatic story, but Babenco's overbearing style makes it unbearable to watch. Rated R for nudity and profanity. 186m. **DIR:** Hector Babenco. **CAST:** Kathy Bates, John Lithgow, Aidan Quinn, Tom Berenger, Daryl Hannah, Tom Waits. **1991**

AT SWORD'S POINT ★★1/2 The sons (and a daughter) of the fabled Three Musketeers come to the aid of the queen of France, and thwart the ambitions of a throne-hungry duke. Lighthearted adventure yarn. 81m. **DIR:** Lewis Allen. **CAST:** Cornel Wilde, Maureen O'Hara, Dan O'Herlihy, Alan Hale Jr., Robert Douglas, Blanche Yurka, Gladys Cooper. **1952**

AT THE CIRCUS ★★★1/2 The Marx Brothers were running out of steam as a comedy team by this time. Still, any film with Groucho, Harpo, and Chico is worth watching, although you'll probably feel like punching the comedy's "hero" (or is that a zero?), Kenny Baker, when he sings that highly forgettable ditty "Step Up, Take a Bow." B&W; 87m. **DIR:** Edward Buzzell. **CAST:** The Marx Brothers, Margaret Dumont, Kenny Baker, Eve Arden. **1939**

AT THE EARTH'S CORE ★★1/2 An Edgar Rice Burroughs adaptation benefits enormously from an inspired performance by Peter Cushing. He even manages to make Doug McClure look good occasionally. It's mostly for the kiddies, but we found ourselves clutching the arm of the chair a couple of times at the height of suspense. Rated PG. 90m. **DIR:** Kevin Connor. **CAST:** Doug McClure, Peter Cushing, Caroline Munro, Godfrey James. **1976 DVD**

AT WAR WITH THE ARMY ★★★★ Dean Martin and Jerry Lewis were still fresh and funny at the time of this comedy release, but a classic it isn't (though some scenes are gems). B&W; 93m. **DIR:** Hal Walker. **CAST:** Dean Martin, Jerry Lewis, Polly Bergen, Angela Greene, Mike Kellin. **1950 DVD**

ATHENA ★★ A minor musical about an eccentric family who believe regular exercise and eating all your vegetables will make your vocal chords strong. The plot is weak, but the personalities are impressive. 96m. **DIR:** Richard Thorpe. **CAST:** Jane Powell, Debbie Reynolds, Vic Damone, Edmund Purdom, Steve Reeves, Virginia Gibson, Louis Calhern, Linda Christian, Carl Benton Reid, Evelyn Varden. **1954**

ATLANTIC CITY ★★★★★ This superb motion picture has all of the elements that made the films of Hollywood's golden age great—with a few appropriately modern twists tossed in. The screenplay, by John Guare—about a struggling casino worker (Susan Sarandon) who becomes involved in a drug deal—gives us powerful drama, wonderful characters, memorable dialogue, and delightfully funny situations. And the performances by Burt Lancaster, Sarandon, and Kate Reid, in particular, are top-notch. Rated R because of brief nudity and violence. 104m. **DIR:** Louis Malle. **CAST:** Burt Lancaster, Susan Sarandon, Kate Reid. **1981**

•ATLANTIS: THE LOST EMPIRE ★★★ Although Disney deserves credit for releasing an animated fantasy without a song score, the studio could have done much better than this pallid reworking of Jules Verne. Michael J. Fox lends his voice to an enthusiastic but naïve cartographer who's determined to find the fabled lost civilization, and gets the chance to do so when an eccentric billionaire funds an expedition. But the subsequent adventures are flat and uninvolving, and you're unlikely to care about what our heroes (and villains) finally locate. Rated PG-13 for action and violence. 95m. **DIR:** Kirk Wise, Gary Trousdale. **2001 DVD**

ATLAS ★★ Roger Corman's obligatory entry in the sword-and-sandal genre (shot in Greece) is underpopulated (and, as Atlas, Michael Forest is a tad underfed), but it contains enough in-jokes and gore to keep Corman aficionados mildly amused. 80m. **DIR:** Roger Corman. **CAST:** Michael Forest, Barboura Morris, Frank Wolff. **1961**

ATOLL K (UTOPIA) 🦃 The final screen outing of the great comedy team of Stan Laurel and Oliver Hardy is a keen disappointment. B&W; 80m. **DIR:** Léo Joannon. **CAST:** Stan Laurel, Oliver Hardy. **1950 DVD**

ATOM AGE VAMPIRE 🦃 Badly dubbed Italian timewaster with cheese-ball special effects and a tired premise. B&W; 71m. **DIR:** Anton Giulio Masano. **CAST:** Alberto Lupo, Susanne Loret. **1960 DVD**

ATOM MAN VS. SUPERMAN ★★ The second and final serial based on the adventures of Superman reunites most of the principal cast from the first chapterplay and throws in the Man of Steel's nemesis, Lex Luthor. Competently played by the talented and often-seen Lyle Talbot, Luthor is out to blackmail Metropolis by threatening the city with destruction. B&W; 15 chapters. **DIR:** Spencer Gordon Bennet. **CAST:** Kirk Alyn, Noel Neill, Lyle Talbot, Tommy Bond, Pierre Watkin, Jack Ingram, Don Harvey, Terry Frost. **1950**

ATOMIC CAFE, THE ★★ Beyond being an interesting cultural document, this feature-length compilation of post–World War II propaganda, documentary, and newsreel footage on American attitudes toward the atomic bomb has little to offer. No MPAA rating. The film has no objectionable material, though some of the footage featuring casualties of atomic bomb explosions is quite graphic. B&W; 88m. **DIR:** Kevin Rafferty, Jayne Loader, Pierce Rafferty. **1982 DVD**

ATOMIC DOG 🦃 Don't get burned watching this made-for-cable original about a mutant mutt bent on radioactive revenge against the family who raised his pups—the plot makes little sense, and every dog's a Lassie wannabe. Not rated; contains violence. 95m. **DIR:** Brian Trenchard-Smith. **CAST:** Daniel Hugh Kelly, Isabella Hofmann, Cindy Pickett. **1997**

ATOMIC KID, THE 🦃 Stupid story about prospector Mickey Rooney surviving an atomic bomb blast and attracting spies. B&W; 86m. **DIR:** Leslie Martinson. **CAST:** Mickey Rooney, Robert Strauss, Whit Bissell, Hal March. **1954**

ATOMIC SUBMARINE, THE ★★★ Solid little thriller about U.S. atomic submarine and its encounter with an alien flying saucer in the Arctic suffers from budgetary limitations but benefits from a decent script, good direction, and an effective and thoroughly believable cast of fine character actors. B&W; 72m. **DIR:** Spencer Gordon Bennet. **CAST:** Arthur Franz, Dick Foran, Brett Halsey, Tom Conway, Bob Steele, Joi Lansing. **1959 DVD**

ATOR: THE FIGHTING EAGLE 🦃 A low-budget stupid sword-and-sorcery flick. Rated PG for violence and nudity. 98m. **DIR:** David Hills. **CAST:** Miles O'Keeffe, Sabrina Siani, Warren Hillman. **1983**

ATTACK! ★★★★ Jack Palance leads a strong cast as the leader of a platoon sent into an impossible situation by an officer who then refuses to admit his mistake by sending reinforcements to help them out. Terrific, gritty antiwar movie. B&W; 107m. **DIR:** Robert Aldrich. **CAST:** Jack Palance, Eddie Albert, Lee Marvin, Robert Strauss, Richard Jaeckel, Buddy Ebsen, Strother Martin. **1956**

ATTACK FORCE Z ★★ Okay Australian film concerning a group of commandos on a secret mission against the Japanese in World War II. Most notable is a young Mel Gibson as the leader of the commandos. Not rated. 84m. **DIR:** Tim Burstall. **CAST:** John Phillip Law, Sam Neill, Mel Gibson, Chris Haywood, John Waters. **1981**

ATTACK OF THE CRAB MONSTERS ★★★ Neat Roger Corman low-budget movie, seemed scarier when you were a kid, but it's still a lot of fun. A remote Pacific atoll is besieged by a horde of giant land crabs that, upon devouring members of a scientific expedition, absorb their brains and acquire the ability to speak in their voices. B&W; 64m. **DIR:** Roger Corman. **CAST:** Richard Garland, Pamela Duncan, Mel Welles, Russell Johnson, Ed Nelson. **1957**

ATTACK OF THE 50-FOOT WOMAN (1958) ★★★ One of the best "schlock" films from the 1950s. Allison Hayes stars as a woman who is kidnapped by a tremendous bald alien and transformed into a giant herself. Duddy special effects only serve to heighten the enjoyment of this kitsch classic. B&W; 66m. **DIR:** Nathan Juran. **CAST:** Allison Hayes, William Hudson, Yvette Vickers. **1958**

ATTACK OF THE 50-FOOT WOMAN (1993) ★★1/2 The effects look good, but everything else is pretty ho-hum in this arch remake of one of cinema's all-time turkeys. Scripter Joseph Dougherty's attempt to inject politically correct feminism is simply laughable, and it's hard to decide whether title character Daryl Hannah is less interesting before or after her transformation. Rated PG-13 for profanity and brief nudity. 90m. **DIR:** Christopher Guest. **CAST:** Daryl Hannah, Daniel Baldwin, William Windom, Cristi Conaway, Frances Fisher. **1993 DVD**

ATTACK OF THE GIANT LEECHES ★★ Engagingly bad, lurid programmer—originally double-billed with *A Bucket of Blood*—about an Everglades town plagued by the title monsters. Cheesy fun from an imaginative B-movie director. B&W; 62m. **DIR:** Bernard Kowalski. **CAST:** Ken Clark, Yvette Vickers, Bruno Ve Sota. **1959 DVD**

ATTACK OF THE KILLER TOMATOES 🦃 In this campy cult film, the tomatoes are funnier than the actors, most of whom are rank amateurs. Rated PG. 87m. **DIR:** John DeBello. **CAST:** David Miller, Sharon Taylor, Georges Wilson, Jack Riley. **1980**

ATTACK OF THE PUPPET PEOPLE 🦃 Cheapo special effects doom this tale of a puppeteer who makes his dolls the easy way: by shrinking humans. B&W; 78m. **DIR:** Bert I. Gordon. **CAST:** John Agar, John Hoyt, June Kenney, Laurie Mitchell. **1958**

ATTACK OF THE 60-FT. CENTERFOLD 🦃 A model ingests a formula that causes her to grow to huge proportions in this lame comedy that mixes *Attack of the 50-Ft. Woman* with T&A. Rated R for nudity and profanity. 83m. **DIR:** Fred Olen Ray. **CAST:** J. J. North, Raelyn

Saalman, Tammy Parks, Michelle Bauer, Russ Tamblyn, Ross Hagen. **1995**

ATTACK OF THE SWAMP CREATURE In one of Elvira's "Thriller Video" movies, we're subjected to the story of a mad scientist who turns himself into a giant, man-eating, walking catfish. 96m. **DIR:** Arnold Stevens. **CAST:** Frank Crowell, Patricia Robertson. **1985**

ATTENTION SHOPPERS ★★1/2 An up-and-coming sitcom star makes an appearance at a local Kmart only to find that it's nothing like he expected. This entertaining and often amusing tale is based on a true story. Rated R. 87m. **DIR:** Philip Charles MacKenzie. **CAST:** Nestor Carbonell, Michael Lerner, Martin Mull, Kathy Najimy, Luke Perry, Cara Buono, Lin Shaye, Casey Affleck. **1999 DVD**

ATTIC, THE ★★ Rather slow-moving and routine story concerning a young woman (Carrie Snodgress) fighting to free herself from the clutches of her crippled, almost insane, father. Tries to be deep and psychological and falls flat on its face. Rated PG. 97m. **DIR:** George Edwards. **CAST:** Carrie Snodgress, Ray Milland. **1979**

ATTIC: THE HIDING OF ANNE FRANK ★★★★ The true story of Anne Frank seen from the viewpoint of Miep Gies, the woman who risked everything to hide the Jewish families during World War II. William Hanley's teleplay wonderfully depicts the events outside the attic and the harsh realities of the German occupation. Great performances all around, especially from Mary Steenburgen, who portrays Gies. 95m. **DIR:** John Erman. **CAST:** Mary Steenburgen, Paul Scofield, Huub Stapel, Eleanor Bron, Frances Cuka. **1988**

ATTICA ★★★★ This made-for-TV account of the horrifying Attica prison riots of 1971 is a very detailed translation of Tom Wicker's bestselling book *A Time to Die*. Screenwriter James Henerson deserves kudos for this adaptation. The performances are uniformly excellent. 100m. **DIR:** Marvin J. Chomsky. **CAST:** Charles Durning, George Grizzard, Anthony Zerbe, Glynn Turman, Henry Darrow. **1980**

ATTILA ★★★★ With this miniseries, USA Films advanced in the quality department from run-of-the-mill made-for-TV fare to classy entertainment. Gerard Butler delivers a strong, believable performance as Attila the Hun, who finds himself becoming the world conqueror foretold in his people's legends. Powers Boothe is the crafty general, Flavius Aetius, who cunningly outwits his enemies in the Roman Empire only to face defeat at the hands of his one-time protégé. The battle scenes are spectacular—an impressive achievement given the film's relatively modest budget. Made for TV. 177m. **DIR:** Dick Lowry. **CAST:** Gerard Butler, Powers Boothe, Simmone Mackinnon, Tim Curry, Reg Rogers, Alice Krige, Steven Berkoff, Tommy Flanagan, Pauline Lynch, Liam Cunningham, Sian Phillips, Kirsty Mitchell. **2001 DVD**

AU REVOIR, LES ENFANTS ★★★★★ Louis Malle may have created his masterpiece with this autobiographical account of a traumatic incident in his youth that occurred in World War II France. Certainly this heartfelt and heartbreaking work about man's inhumanity to man is likely to remain his most unforgettable creation. Rated PG for strong themes. In French with English subtitles. 104m. **DIR:** Louis Malle. **CAST:** Gaspard Manesse, Raphael Fejto, Philippe Morier-Genoud, Francine Racette. **1987**

AUDREY ROSE Plodding melodrama about a man who annoys a couple by claiming that his dead daughter has been reincarnated as their live one. Rated PG. 113m. **DIR:** Robert Wise. **CAST:** Marsha Mason, Anthony Hopkins, John Beck. **1977 DVD**

AUGUST ★★★★ Anthony Hopkins directs and stars in this lovely Victorian romance-drama. Hopkins plays Ieuan, who lives the life of Riley in his huge country estate. Ieuan loves to drink and flirt, but all that is about to come to an end when his ex-brother-in-law comes to visit with his beautiful wife, Helen, in tow. It doesn't take long before Ieuan becomes infatuated with Helen, which leads to major complications for all involved. Gorgeous production design and an excellent cast bring this little gem to life. Rated PG for language. 99m. **DIR:** Anthony Hopkins. **CAST:** Anthony Hopkins, Leslie Phillips, Kate Burton, Rhian Morgan. **1995**

AUNTIE LEE'S MEAT PIES ★★1/2 Good for Auntie Lee, played by Karen Black. Business is booming, and she sends out her four adorable nieces (former *Playboy* Playmates) to fetch fresh ingredients, including motorists, highway patrolmen, hitchhikers. Tongue-in-cheek black comedy is mildly entertaining. Rated R for nudity, violence, and language. 100m. **DIR:** Joseph F. Robertson. **CAST:** Karen Black, Noriyuki "Pat" Morita, Huntz Hall, Michael Berryman. **1992**

AUNTIE MAME ★★★1/2 Rosalind Russell, in the title role, plays a free-thinking eccentric woman whose young nephew is placed in her care. Russell created the role on the stage; it was a once-in-a-lifetime showcase that she made uniquely her own. 143m. **DIR:** Morton Da Costa. **CAST:** Rosalind Russell, Forrest Tucker, Coral Browne, Fred Clark. **1958**

AURORA ENCOUNTER ★★★1/2 Here's one that can be enjoyed by the whole family. Jack Elam is outstanding in a story about a small Texas town visited by aliens in the late 1800s. Rated PG. 90m. **DIR:** Jim McCullough. **CAST:** Jack Elam, Peter Brown, Carol Bagdasarian, Dottie West. **1985**

AUSTIN POWERS: INTERNATIONAL MAN OF MYSTERY ★★ This tepid spoof of the 1960s and its many spy movies drools all over itself while trying to be "groovy, baby." Powers is a Carnaby Street swinger and secret agent whose wily nemesis, Dr. Evil, is a throwback to James Bond villains of yesteryear. The two have been cryogenically frozen since 1967 and thaw out in a lame battle of (nit)wits that never comically warms up to the material it wants to skewer. Rated PG-13 for language and sexually suggestive subject matter. 88m. **DIR:** Jay Roach. **CAST:** Mike Myers, Michael York, Mimi Rogers, Elizabeth Hurley, Fabiana Udenio, Robert Wagner. **1997 DVD**

AUSTIN POWERS: THE SPY WHO SHAGGED ME ★★ This limp sequel isn't really the pop-art 1960s spy spoof that its advertising campaign suggested. True, it does poke fun at the cinematic Bond, Flint, Helm, and their ilk, but only incidentally; the film really exists as a vehicle for Mike Myers's brand of slow-motion, quadruple-take humor, and an endless stream of sniggering sex and excretory jokes. If it emanates from a bodily orifice, sooner or later it's in this film. Generously rated PG-13 for coy nudity, British profanity, raunchy sexual content, and repugnant toilet humor. 93m. **DIR:** Jay Roach. **CAST:** Mike Myers, Heather Graham, Michael York, Robert Wagner, Seth Green, Mindy Sterling, Rob Lowe. **1999 DVD**

AUTHOR! AUTHOR! ★★★ Al Pacino stars as a playwright whose wife (Tuesday Weld) leaves him with five kids (not all his) to raise in this nicely done bittersweet comedy. Dyan Cannon plays the actress with whom he falls in love. Rated PG for brief profanity. 110m. **DIR:** Arthur Hiller. **CAST:** Al Pacino, Dyan Cannon, Alan King, Tuesday Weld. **1982**

AUTOBIOGRAPHY OF A PRINCESS ★★1/2 A captivating performance by Indian actress Madhur Jaffrey dominates this mundane, British teledrama about an exiled Indian princess and her father's ex-tutor (James Mason) sharing memories of colonial India. Unusual for a Merchant-Ivory production, this too-short film suffers from a lack of character development, uninspired dialogue, and an absence of lavish production quality. 59m. **DIR:** James Ivory. **CAST:** James Mason, Madhur Jaffrey. **1975**

AUTOBIOGRAPHY OF MISS JANE PITTMAN, THE ★★★★★ This terrific television movie traces black history in America from the Civil War years to the turbulent civil rights movement of the 1960s. All this is seen through the eyes of 110 year old ex-slave Jane Pittman (Cicely Tyson). The entire cast is superb, but Tyson still manages to tower above the others in the title role. There is no rating, but it should be noted that there are some violent scenes. 110m. **DIR:** John Korty. **CAST:** Cicely Tyson, Richard Dysart, Odetta, Michael Murphy, Thalmus Rasulala. **1974 DVD**

AUTOMATIC ★★★1/2 This fast-paced riff on *The Terminator* is a bit more clever than the usual knockoffs. Olivier Gruner plays a compassionate android—well-versed in Asimov's Three Laws of Robotics—that accidentally kills a human superior caught raping a coworker. Fearing the bad publicity that might result, corporate exec John Glover (wonderfully slimy) orders both android and woman exterminated . . . a fate they're not about to accept quietly. Rated R for violence, rape, nudity, and profanity. 90m. **DIR:** John Murlowski. **CAST:** Olivier Gruner, Daphne Ashbrook, John Glover, Jeff Kober. **1994**

AUTOPSY 🦃 The story involves a young medical student doing graduate study in a morgue. Rated R for nudity and graphic violence. 90m. **DIR:** Armando Crispino. **CAST:** Mimsy Farmer, Raymond Lovelock, Barry Primus. **1976 DVD**

AUTUMN AFTERNOON, AN ★★★ Aging buddies discuss the fate of one of the men's daughters in this slow-moving drama. The group decides that an arranged marriage would be best for her. Although the film is dated, it is an often penetrating, insightful look into Japanese society and the era in which it is set. In Japanese with English subtitles. 112m. **DIR:** Yasujiro Ozu. **CAST:** Chishu Ryu, Shima Iwashita. **1962**

AUTUMN IN NEW YORK ★★★1/2 Playboy restaurateur Richard Gere, master of the no-commitment seduction, finally meets his match in free-spirited Winona Ryder, whose deeply felt emotions puncture the poor guy's self-involved barrier. Allison Burnett's script approaches this familiar material as if it were fresh, and Ryder's radiant performance sells a plot that bears more than an echo of *Sweet November*. Changwei Gu's cinematography makes New York luxurious and as impersonal as the man's man we first encounter. But Gere's the surprise: He projects genuine warmth and emotional complexity, and you'll wind up caring about both these characters. Rated PG-13 for sensuality, dramatic intensity, and mild profanity. 105m. **DIR:** Joan Chen. **CAST:** Richard Gere, Winona Ryder, Anthony LaPaglia, Elaine Stritch, Vera Farmiga, Sherry Stringfield. **2000 DVD**

AUTUMN LEAVES ★★1/2 Troubled middle-aged typist Joan Crawford is further anguished after marrying a younger man (Cliff Robertson) who proves to be mentally disturbed and already married. Run-of-the-mill Crawford fare. B&W; 108m. **DIR:** Robert Aldrich. **CAST:** Joan Crawford, Cliff Robertson, Vera Miles, Lorne Greene. **1956**

AUTUMN SONATA ★★★★★ Ingmar Bergman directed this superb Swedish release about the first meeting in seven years of a daughter (Liv Ullmann) with her difficult concert pianist mother (Ingrid Bergman). A great film. In Swedish and English. Rated PG. 97m. **DIR:** Ingmar Bergman. **CAST:** Ingrid Bergman, Liv Ullmann, Lena Nyman. **1978 DVD**

AUTUMN TALE ★★★★★ A lonely winegrower is fixed up with two different men by her best friend and her son's girlfriend. French master Eric Rohmer gives us another bracing, fascinating work of art, filled with enjoyable characters and lively, intelligent conversation. It's also quite cleverly and intricately plotted, although it never feels forced or contrived. In French with English subtitles. Rated PG. 112m. **DIR:** Eric Rohmer. **CAST:** Marie Riviere, Beatrice Romand, Alain Libolt, Didier Sandre, Alexia Portal. **1998 DVD**

AVALANCHE 🦃 It's movies like this bomb that gave disaster pictures a bad name. Rated PG. 91m. **DIR:** Corey Allen. **CAST:** Rock Hudson, Mia Farrow, Robert Forster, Jeanette Nolan. **1978 DVD**

AVALON ★★★★1/2 For the third film in his Baltimore trilogy, which also includes *Tin Men* and *Diner*, writer-director Barry Levinson covers fifty years in the lives of three generations of Russian-Jewish immigrants in a heart-tugging story. Armin Mueller-Stahl gives an unforgettable performance as the ultimate grandfather, whose honest values and love of family are slowly pushed out of fashion by progress. Rated PG for brief profanity. 126m. **DIR:** Barry Levinson. **CAST:** Armin Mueller-Stahl, Aidan Quinn, Elizabeth Perkins, Joan Plowright, Elijah Wood, Lou Jacobi. **1990 DVD**

AVANT GARDE PROGRAM #2 ★★★ Fascinating collection of early silent experimental films by French and German surrealists. This program features René Clair's brilliant short, "Entr'acte," with music by Erik Satie, and Eggeling's "Symphonie Diagonale." Also on this program: Man Ray's "L'Étoile de Mer." B&W; 42m. **DIR:** René Clair, Man Ray, Eggeling. **CAST:** Erik Satie, Marcel Duchamp, Man Ray. **1924–1926**

AVANTI! ★★★★ A cynical comedy in true Billy Wilder fashion with the antics of Jack Lemmon to make the ridiculous look sublime. Lemmon plays a man who goes to Europe to claim the body of his father and learns that Dad had a mistress, and the mistress had a voluptuous daughter. 144m. **DIR:** Billy Wilder. **CAST:** Jack Lemmon, Juliet Mills, Clive Revill, Edward Andrews. **1972**

AVA'S MAGICAL ADVENTURE ★★ A 10 year old girl runs away with a two-ton friend—a circus elephant. Loads of "family fun" ensues as she is pursued by everyone from the sheriff to the bearded lady. Rated PG. 97m. **DIR:** Patrick Dempsey. **CAST:** Timothy Bottoms, Georg Stanford Brown, Patrick Dempsey. **1994**

AVENGERS, THE ★★ Only Stuart Craig's opulent production design and a token appearance by Laurie Johnson's classic television theme save this bombastic failure from total turkeydom. It's not just that stars Ralph Fiennes (Steed) and Uma Thurman (Emma Peel) display zero chemistry and atrociously overplay the deadpan humor; the film itself doesn't seem finished. Terribly disappointing. Rated PG-13 for sexual innuendo, brief nudity, and cartoonish violence. 90m. **DIR:** Jeremiah S. Chechik. **CAST:** Ralph Fiennes, Uma Thurman, Sean Connery, Jim Broadbent, Patrick Macnee. **1998 DVD**

AVENGERS, THE (TV SERIES) ★★★1/2 Patrick Macnee stars in the finest British secret agent series ever as quintessential agent John Steed. Diana Rigg as the rugged, leather-garbed Emma Peel was followed by Linda Thorson's Tara King for the program's final year. Charming, witty, and absolutely ageless, this program will remain loved for generations to come. Suitable for family viewing. 52m. **DIR:** Don Leaver, Robert Day. **CAST:** Patrick Macnee, Diana Rigg, Linda Thorson. **1965–1969 DVD**

AVENGING, THE ★★ Michael Horse's half-Native American ancestry alienates him from his two brothers when he returns from college to take over the family ranch. Slow-moving tale of betrayal and revenge. Rated PG for violence. 100m. **DIR:** Lyman Dayton. **CAST:** Michael Horse, Efrem Zimbalist Jr., Sherry Hursey, Taylor Larcher, Joseph Running Fox. **1992**

AVENGING ANGEL (1985) 🦃 Remember *Angel*, the high school student who doubled as a Hollywood hooker? Well, she's back. Rated R for nudity, profanity, and violence. 96m. **DIR:** Robert Vincent O'Neil. **CAST:** Betsy Russell, Rory Calhoun, Susan Tyrrell, Ossie Davis. **1985**

AVENGING ANGEL, THE (1995) ★★★1/2 Tom Berenger stars as a member of a militia established by the Mormon Church to protect the members of its congregation. As one of the last of his kind, he finds himself almost an outcast among his own people—until a conspiracy to murder Brigham Young makes him both a suspect and a savior. This seldom-portrayed era in American history features strong performances and plenty of action for fans of the Western. Made for TV. 96m. **DIR:** Peter Markle. **CAST:** Tom Berenger, James Coburn, Charlton Heston, Fay Masterson, Kevin Tighe, Jeffrey Jones, Tom Bower, Leslie Hope, Daniel Quinn. **1995**

AVENGING CONSCIENCE, THE ★★1/2 Edgar Allan Poe's short stories provide the inspiration for this tale of a young writer (Henry B. Walthall) obsessed with Poe. Faced with the choice of continued patronage from his strict uncle or marriage with the "Annabel Lee" (Blanche Sweet) of his dreams, our tortured hero subjects his uncle to the tortures suggested by Poe's stories. Interesting historically, this silent feature is most effective in atmospheric chills. B&W; 78m. **DIR:** D. W. Griffith. **CAST:** Henry B. Walthall, Blanche Sweet, Mae Marsh, Robert Harron, Ralph Lewis. **1914**

AVENGING FORCE ★★★ A better-than-average action-adventure flick about a former secret service agent forced out of retirement when his best friend, a black southern politician, is involved in an assassination attempt in which his son is killed. The acting is admittedly dry, but the action is top-notch, with plenty of opportunity to cheer for the hero. Rated R for violence and profanity. 104m. **DIR:** Sam Firstenberg. **CAST:** Michael Dudikoff, Steve James, James Booth, Bill Wallace, John P. Ryan, Marc Alaimo. **1986**

AVIATOR, THE ★★ This film, about a grumpy flyer (Christopher Reeve) during the 1920s who is forced to take a feisty passenger (Rosanna Arquette) on his mail route, is too similar to *High Road to China*. It has neither the high adventure nor the humor of the latter. Rated PG. 102m. **DIR:** George Miller. **CAST:** Christopher Reeve, Rosanna Arquette, Jack Warden, Scott Wilson, Tyne Daly, Sam Wanamaker. **1984 DVD**

AVIATOR'S WIFE, THE ★★★1/2 Not much happens in a film by French director Eric Rohmer, at least not in the traditional sense. In this typically Rohmer character study, a young law student (Philippe Marlaud) is crushed when he discovers his lover, Anne (Marie Riviere), in the company of another man and decides to spy on them. In French with English subtitles. Not rated; the film has no objectionable material. 104m. **DIR:** Eric Rohmer. **CAST:** Philippe Marlaud, Marie Riviere, Anne-Laure Meury. **1981 DVD**

AWAKENING, THE ★★1/2 In this mediocre horror flick, Charlton Heston plays an Egyptologist who discovers the tomb of a wicked queen. The evil spirit escapes the tomb and is reincarnated in Heston's newborn daughter. A bit hard to follow. Rated R for gore. 102m. **DIR:** Mike Newell. **CAST:** Charlton Heston, Susannah York, Jill Townsend, Stephanie Zimbalist. **1980**

AWAKENINGS ★★★★1/2 *Awakenings* is a masterpiece of characterization. In this fact-based story, a subdued Robin Williams plays a doctor who fights to use an experimental drug on a group of catatonic patients, who he believes are "alive inside." Robert De Niro is the first recipient of this medication, and his transformation is miraculous. Rated PG-13 for profanity and light violence. 121m. **DIR:** Penny Marshall. **CAST:** Robert De Niro, Robin Williams, Julie Kavner, Ruth Nelson, John Heard, Penelope Ann Miller, Max von Sydow. **1990 DVD**

AWAY ALL BOATS ★★ In this lackluster war drama, Jeff Chandler plays Captain Hanks, commander of an attack transport unit in the South Pacific during World War II. We follow Chandler and his men as they train for combat. 114m. **DIR:** Joseph Pevney. **CAST:** Jeff Chandler, George Nader, Julie Adams, Lex Barker, Keith Andes, Richard Boone, Jock Mahoney, William Reynolds, Charles McGraw, John McIntire. **1956 DVD**

AWFUL DR. ORLOFF, THE ★★★1/2 Horror classic about a demented surgeon seeking young women as unwilling skin-graft donors for his disfigured daughter. Atmospheric and creepy. Not rated, this is too strong for young viewers. 86m. **DIR:** Jess (Jesus) Franco. **CAST:** Howard Vernon, Perla Cristal. **1961**

AWFUL TRUTH, THE ★★★★ Irene Dunne and Cary Grant divorce so that they can marry others. Then they do their best to spoil one another's plans. Leo McCarey won an Oscar for directing this prime example of the screwball comedies that made viewing such a delight in the 1930s. Grant—a master of timing—is in top form, as is costar Dunne. It's hilarious all the way. B&W; 92m. **DIR:** Leo McCarey. **CAST:** Irene Dunne, Cary Grant, Ralph Bellamy, Molly Lamont. **1937 DVD**

AWFULLY BIG ADVENTURE, AN ★★★★ Hugh Grant, cast against type in one of his best performances, is the ruthlessly nasty director of a small British theater company just after World War II. Newcomer Georgina Cates is a doll as the naïve young assistant who learns a few crushing life lessons. Alan Rickman is resplendent as a leading man who knows better but still dabbles where he shouldn't. Great writing. Rated R for profanity, sexual situations, and nudity. 113m. **DIR:** Mike Newell. **CAST:** Hugh Grant, Alan Rickman, Georgina Cates, Alun Armstrong, Peter Firth, Prunella Scales, Rita Tushingham. **1994**

AY, CARMELA! ★★1/2 One of Spain's most electrifying stars, Carmen Maura, joins forces with one of her nation's most invigorating directors, Carlos Saura, in this drama about the Spanish Civil War. The film offers insight and entertainment, but it's a mystery why all that electricity generates few sparks. In Spanish with English subtitles. Not rated. 103m. **DIR:** Carlos Saura. **CAST:** Carmen Maura. **1991**

B

B. MONKEY ★★1/2 British crime-drama is filled with some of the best actors on the independent scene. Deliberately paced and filled with some fine exteriors, it seems like the filmmakers were not sure what they wanted to accomplish: tell a boy-meets-girl love story or an exposé of the underworld. While it does not commit itself, the film is engaging and full of good performances. Rated R for profanity, nudity, violence, and simulated sex. 92m. **DIR:** Michael Radford. **CAST:** Asia Argento, Jared Harris, Rupert Everett. **1998 DVD**

BABAR: THE MOVIE ★★ This adaptation of the beloved *Babar* books by Jean and Laurent de Brunhoff is hampered by a formulaic story and uninspired animation. Produced by Nelvana Studios, which also makes the Care Bears movies, it is passable kiddie fare. Rated G. 75m. **DIR:** Alan Bunce. **1989**

BABE (1982) *Baywatch*'s Yasmine Bleeth would doubtless love to forget that she made her debut here as a 12 year old orphan and Broadway wannabe who learns the tricks of the trade from homeless ex-vaudevillian Buddy Hackett. Not rated; contains mild profanity. 90m. **DIR:** Rafal Zielinski. **CAST:** Buddy Hackett, Yasmine Bleeth. **1982**

BABE, THE (1992) ★★★★ In this old-fashioned, Hollywood-style bio-pic, John Goodman hits a home run as Babe Ruth. We like it better than *The Babe Ruth Story* because of its grit and seeming no-holds-barred honesty. The legend makes for a memorable motion picture. Rated PG for profanity. 115m. **DIR:** Arthur Hiller. **CAST:** John Goodman, Kelly McGillis, Trini Alvarado, Bruce Boxleitner, Peter Donat, J. C. Quinn. **1992**

BABE (1995) ★★★★★ This amazing, live-action barnyard fable from Australia pushes the envelope on both animatronic effects and family storytelling. The animal stars—piglet Babe, a collie family, a nervous duck, and an elderly ewe—not only convincingly talk but what they talk about is so very fascinating! This story is about social tolerance. It's also wildly funny. Rated G. 91m. **DIR:** Chris Noonan. **CAST:** James Cromwell, Magda Szubanski. **1995 DVD**

BABE: PIG IN THE CITY ★★1/2 Everything that was sweet and whimsical about 1995's *Babe* has become overblown and crass in this disappointing sequel. *Pig in the City* is forced, stupid, and littered with the slapstick nonsense that frequently hallmarks sequels. This film is scary at times, thanks to unpleasant scenes of animal cruelty, and it might well give nightmares to its target small-fry audience. The story concerns Babe's trip to a mythical metropolis (superb production design by Roger Ford) in the company of Farmer Hoggett's wife, who desperately needs money to prevent their farm from being repossessed by the bank. Everything builds to a particularly messy climax in a posh restaurant. Rated G, but be wary of exposing very young children to it. 97m. **DIR:** George Miller. **CAST:** James Cromwell, Magda Szubanski, Mary Stein, Mickey Rooney. **1998 DVD**

BABE RUTH STORY, THE ★★ Bio-pic about baseball's most famous hero is long on sap and short on facts as it milks every situation for maximum sentimental value. The supporting cast is good, but William Bendix just doesn't make the grade as the immortal Bambino. B&W; 106m. **DIR:** Roy Del Ruth. **CAST:** William Bendix, Claire Trevor, Charles Bickford, Sam Levene, William Frawley, Stanley Clements. **1948**

BABES IN ARMS ★★★ Richard Rodgers and Lorenz Hart wrote the musical from which this film was taken—although most of the songs they wrote are absent. But never mind; Mickey and Judy sing, dance, and prance up a storm! B&W; 96m. **DIR:** Busby Berkeley. **CAST:** Mickey Rooney, Judy Garland, June Preisser, Guy Kibbee, Charles Winninger, Henry Hull, Margaret Hamilton. **1939**

BABES IN TOYLAND (1961) ★★ A disappointing Disney version of the Victor Herbert operetta. In Mother Goose Land, Barnaby (Ray Bolger) kidnaps Tom the Piper's Son (Tommy Sands) in order to marry Mary (Annette Funicello). The Toymaker (Ed Wynn) and his assistant (Tommy Kirk) eventually provide the means for Tom to save the day. Despite a good Disney cast, this film never gels. Rated G. 105m. **DIR:** Jack Donohue. **CAST:** Ray Bolger, Tommy Sands, Ed Wynn, Annette Funicello, Tommy Kirk. **1961**

BABES IN TOYLAND (1986) ★★ Disappointing film about an adultlike child who must save the mythical town of Toyland by believing in the magic of toys. Richard Mulligan creates a wonderful evil Barnaby Barnacle. Rated G. 96m. **DIR:** Clive Donner. **CAST:** Drew Barrymore, Noriyuki "Pat" Morita, Richard Mulligan, Eileen Brennan, Keanu Reeves, Jill Schoelen. **1986**

BABES ON BROADWAY ★★1/2 Raising funds for underprivileged children is the excuse for this musical extravaganza showcasing Mickey Rooney and Judy Garland, both of whom shine despite a trite plot. See it for the songs. B&W; 118m. **DIR:** Busby Berkeley. **CAST:** Mickey Rooney, Judy Garland, Fay Bainter, Virginia Weidler, Richard Quine, Donna Reed. **1941**

BABETTE'S FEAST ★★★★ Writer-director Gabriel Axel's Oscar-winning adaptation of Isak Dinesen's short story has the kind of wistful warmth that makes it seem like a tale told by a wise old storyteller. It also has a pixilated quality that makes it good fun. The finale is a sumptuous dinner prepared by an expatriate French chef (Stéphane Audran) for a group of devout Danish Lutherans. It may be the funniest meal ever put on screen. In French and Danish with English subtitles. Rated G. 102m. **DIR:** Gabriel Axel. **CAST:** Stéphane Audran, Jean-Philippe Lafont, Jarl Kulle, Bibi Andersson. **1987 DVD**

BABY, THE ★★★ Extremely odd film by veteran director Ted Post about a teenager who has remained an infant all his life (yes, he still lives in his crib) and with his insane, overprotective mother. Eerily effective chiller is entertaining, though many will undoubtedly find it repulsive and ridiculous. Rated PG. 80m. **DIR:** Ted Post. **CAST:** Ruth Roman, Marianna Hill, Anjanette Comer. **1974 DVD**

BABY BOOM ★★★1/2 Yuppie fairy tale about a career woman (Diane Keaton) who finds her eighty-hour-per-week corporate job interrupted by the untimely arrival of a babe-in-arms. The laughs are frequent, but the film doesn't find any warmth until Keaton flees to the country and meets local veterinarian Sam Shepard. Rated PG for language. 103m. **DIR:** Charles Shyer. **CAST:** Diane Keaton, Harold Ramis, Sam Wanamaker, Pat Hingle, Sam Shepard. **1987 DVD**

•BABY BOY ★★ This gritty but overly sensationalized South Central Los Angeles drama is about the delayed maturing of African American males (as reflected in their language and general lack of responsibility) and its effect on families and communities. Jody is a man-child who lives with his mom, sells stolen clothes, and has illegitimate children by two different women. The overall acting is uneven and a recurring theme involving Jody's dead brother feels half-baked. Rated R for language, violence, sex, nudity, and drug use. 128m. **DIR:** John Singleton. **CAST:** Tyrese Gibson, Omar Gooding, Taraji P. Henson, Snoop Dogg, Ving Rhames, Tamara Bass, Adrienne-Joi Johnson. **2001 DVD**

BABY CAKES ★★★★ Ricki Lake is adorable as the plump girl who sets her sights on gorgeous Craig Sheffer, even though her friends and family tell her that someone of his caliber wouldn't be interested in her. This delightful film proves that beauty is more than skin-deep. Playful and inspiring, with both stars especially likable. 93m. **DIR:** Paul Schneider. **CAST:** Ricki Lake, Craig Sheffer, Betty Buckley, John Karlen. **1989**

BABY DANCE, THE ★★★★1/2 Jane Anderson's searing stage play becomes an equally compelling film, which the playwright adapted and directed herself (with a little help from producer Jodie Foster). Laura Dern and Richard Lineback are a dirt-poor southern couple who cannot afford to keep the baby currently in her womb; they contact a wealthy childless couple desperate to adopt, and already-fragile emotions quickly reach the breaking point. Both women project a level of raw desperation, while both men recognize their helpless inability to honor their "covenant" in the coldly clinical fashion of attorneys and paper-laden contracts. This tough-edged, uncompromising drama is very hard to watch. Rated R for profanity, brief nudity, and strong content. 91m. **DIR:** Jane Anderson. **CAST:** Stockard Channing, Laura Dern, Richard Lineback, Peter Riegert, Sandra Seacat. **1997**

BABY DOLL ★★★★ Set in hot, humid, sleazy Mississippi, this is the story of a child bride (Carroll Baker) who sleeps in a crib, her lusting, short-on-brains husband (Karl Malden), and a scheming business rival (Eli Wallach) determined to use and abuse them both. What else but a Tennessee Williams story? When first released, the film was condemned by the Legion of Decency. Baker's skimpy pajamas became fashionable. B&W; 114m. **DIR:** Elia Kazan. **CAST:** Carroll Baker, Eli Wallach, Karl Malden, Mildred Dunnock, Lonny Chapman, Rip Torn. **1956**

BABY FACE ★★★ Ambitious Barbara Stanwyck uses her looks and her charms to work her way from a saloon to a fancy salon in this mildly scandalous but eventually moralistic study. Stanwyck does a standout job, and her aggressive sexuality is pretty much implied despite the furor it raised with the censors of the day. B&W; 70m. **DIR:** Alfred E. Green. **CAST:** Barbara Stanwyck, George Brent, Donald Cook, Douglass Dumbrille, Margaret Lindsay, John Wayne. **1933**

BABY FACE NELSON ★★1/2 C. Thomas Howell musters up all the menace he can as the notorious gangster who terrorized the streets of Chicago and kept company with allies like John Dillinger. His reign of terror and intimidation lands him on the FBI's most-wanted list and brings down the wrath of J. Edgar Hoover. Budget-minded period piece suffers by comparison. Rated R for adult situations, language, nudity, and violence. 87m. **DIR:** Scott Levy. **CAST:** C. Thomas Howell, Lisa Zane, Doug Wert, Martin Kove, F. Murray Abraham. **1996**

BABY GENIUSES 🦃 Ruthless tycoon Kathleen Turner exploits a group of adorable toddlers—and this incoherent, irresponsible "comedy" does the same thing by turning them into a bunch of miniature potty-mouthed adults. Some scenes are disturbingly suggestive. Rated PG. 94m. **DIR:** Bob Clark. **CAST:** Kathleen Turner, Christopher Lloyd, Peter MacNicol, Kim Cattrall, Dom DeLuise, Ruby Dee. **1999 DVD**

BABY GIRL SCOTT ★★★1/2 Emotional and tragic story of older parents forced to deal with a dangerously small premature baby and doctors who overstep their boundaries. Well acted and quite gripping, though a bit melodramatic. Not rated. 97m. **DIR:** John Korty. **CAST:** Mary Beth Hurt, John Lithgow. **1987**

BABY, IT'S YOU ★★★★ Writer-director John Sayles has such an unerring sense of what's right in a scene and such a superb ear for dialogue that his movies often seem more like intimate documentaries than simple fiction. So it is with this enjoyable movie about the trials and tribulations of high school kids in Trenton, New Jersey, circa 1966. *Baby, It's You* is not only funny and touching, but also very sexy. Rated R for violence, profanity, and nudity. 105m. **DIR:** John Sayles. **CAST:** Rosanna Arquette, Vincent Spano. **1983**

BABY MAKER, THE ★★ Still timely if overwrought drama of a couple who hire Barbara Hershey to have a baby when it is discovered the wife is barren. Mediocre dialogue, too many beach scenes, and some not-so-interesting subsidiary characters drag this potentially exciting drama to a halt. One of Hershey's first roles. 109m. **DIR:** James Bridges. **CAST:** Barbara Hershey, Colin Wilcox-Horne, Scott Glenn, Sam Groom, Jeannie Berlin. **1970**

BABY MONITOR: SOUND OF FEAR ★★1/2 In this made-for-cable remake, a baby-sitter overhears (via the baby monitor) two men planning her murder. Now she must somehow save the children and escape from the locked condo before the bad guys find her. This could have been a thrilling suspense film, but the characters are stupid and unlikable, and the plot is chock-full of clichés. Not rated; contains violence. 95m. **DIR:** Walter Klenhard. **CAST:** Josie Bissett, Jason Beghe, Barbara Tyson, Jeffrey Noah. **1997**

BABY OF THE BRIDE 🦃 Fifty three year old bride Rue McClanahan finds herself pregnant at the same time as daughter Kristy McNichol, an unmarried former nun. Just too, too wacky. 93m. **DIR:** Bill Bixby. **CAST:** Rue McClanahan, Ted Shackelford, Kristy McNichol. **1991**

BABY ON BOARD 🦃 Only if you absolutely love chase scenes could you enjoy this extended chase between a taxi driver, the mob, a mother, and her baby. Not rated; contains violence. 95m. **DIR:** Franky Schaeffer. **CAST:** Judge Reinhold, Carol Kane, Geza Kovacs. **1991**

BABY—SECRET OF THE LOST LEGEND ★★1/2 Set on the Ivory Coast of West Africa, this Disney story offers more than a cute fable about the discovery of a family of brontosauri. Violence and a hint of sex represent Disney's attempt to appeal to a wider audience. The special effects of the ancient critters make the show worth watching. Rated PG. 90m. **DIR:** B.W.L. Norton. **CAST:** William Katt, Sean Young, Patrick McGoohan. **1985**

BABY-SITTERS CLUB, THE ★★ Only a 10 year old girl could love this simple film based on the characters who fill Ann M. Martin's preteen novels. Seven wealthy girls expand their baby-sitting service to include a day camp. Overshadowing their interactions with the little charges are the romances of three of the girls and one's dealings with her irresponsible father. Rated PG for mild profanity. 92m. **DIR:** Melanie Mayron. **CAST:** Glenda Jackson, Bruce Davison, Schuyler Fisk, Rachael Leigh Cook, Bre Blair. **1995**

BABY TAKE A BOW ★★1/2 In Shirley Temple's first starring vehicle, she helps her dad, who's accused of stealing a valuable necklace. Shirley must outthink the investigators in order to clear Dad's name. She pouts a lot but makes up for it with her charming rendition of "On Accounta' I Love You." B&W; 76m. **DIR:** Harry Lachman. **CAST:** Shirley Temple, James Dunn, Claire Trevor. **1934**

BABY THE RAIN MUST FALL ★★1/2 This confusing character study of a convict who is paroled and reunited with his family raises a lot of questions but answers none of them. B&W; 100m. **DIR:** Robert Mulligan. **CAST:** Steve McQueen, Lee Remick, Don Murray. **1965**

BABY (2000) ★★ Disappointing TNT Original features Farrah Fawcett as a woman who can't get over the death of her second child. As her husband, Keith Carradine plays a toe-tapping drunk. The two bright spots are Alison Pill as a child raising her parents and Jean Stapleton as the grandma who sees what's wrong but feels powerless to change things. A hodgepodge. Not rated; contains mature themes. 92m. **DIR:** Robert Allen Ackerman. **CAST:** Farrah Fawcett, Keith Carradine, Alison Pill, Jean Stapleton. **2000**

BABYFEVER ★★★ Director Henry Jaglom's real-life wife and cowriter, Victoria Foyt, frets over a possible pregnancy with a man she's not sure she loves. The setting is a baby shower, where a roomful of women anguish over their biological clocks and the terrors and delights of mommyhood. Jaglom's trademark humor is less apparent than usual and Foyt's performance borders on shrill. Rated R for profanity and adult themes. 110m. **DIR:** Henry Jaglom. **CAST:** Victoria Foyt, Frances Fisher, Elaine Kagan, Dinah Lenney, Matt Salinger, Zack Norman, Eric Roberts. **1994**

BABYLON 5 (TV SERIES) ★★★★ A landmark in TV history, this creation of J. Michael "Joe" Straczynski focuses on the last of the Babylon space stations, a meeting place and peacekeeping forum for dozens of alien races. From its shaky inception through the Shadow War and a withdrawal of allegiance to Earth, Babylon 5 is the centerpiece of a science-fiction miniseries on a par with such literary milestones as Isaac Asimov's *Foundation* trilogy, Frank Herbert's *Dune*, Robert Heinlein's *Stranger in a Strange Land*, and Ray Bradbury's *The Martian Chronicles*. Made for TV. 96m. **DIR:** Various. **CAST:** Bruce Boxleitner, Michael O'Hare, Claudia Christian, Jerry Doyle, Mira Furlan, Tracy Scoggins, Caitlin Brown. **1993–1998**

BABY'S DAY OUT ★★★ Writer-producer John Hughes steals from himself, cloning the *Home Alone* formula and downsizing its youthful hero. The scion of a wealthy Chicago family, 9-month-old Baby Bink, foils his own kidnapping by gleefully crawling out a window to face the hazards of the big city. It's fast-paced and often clever, causing viewers to laugh in spite of its lack of originality. Rated PG for comic violence. 98m. **DIR:** Patrick Read Johnson. **CAST:** Joe Mantegna, Lara Flynn Boyle, Joe Pantoliano, Brian Haley, Cynthia Nixon, Fred Dalton Thompson, John Neville, Eddie Bracken. **1994 DVD**

BABYSITTER, THE (1980) ★★★1/2 Outside of some glaring plot flaws, this is an effectively eerie film. Stephanie Zimbalist is Joanna, a woman hired as a housekeeper (not a baby-sitter). But Joanna is no Mary Poppins. Not rated, has violence. 96m. **DIR:** Peter Medak. **CAST:** Patty Duke, William Shatner, Quinn Cummings, David Wallace, Stephanie Zimbalist, John Houseman. **1980**

BABYSITTER, THE (1995) 🦃 A baby-sitter is the fantasy object of everyone in the film. A stunningly pointless parade of erotic fantasies leads to a violent finale. Not even fans of Alicia Silverstone will get through this one. Rated R for profanity and sexuality. 90m. **DIR:** Guy Ferland. **CAST:** Alicia Silverstone, Jeremy London, J. T. Walsh, Lee Garlington, Nicky Katt, Lois Chiles, George Segal. **1995**

BACH AND BROCCOLI ★★ Slow-moving family-fare film made in Quebec. A 12 year old girl is forced to live with her bachelor uncle. The two establish an uneasy relationship. Not rated, but equivalent to G. 96m. **DIR:** André Melançon. **CAST:** Andrée Pelletier. **1986**

BACHELOR, THE (1993) ★★★ This exquisite period piece finds turn-of-the-century doctor Keith Carradine reexamining his life after his sister, upon whom he was very dependent, dies. He eventually finds friendship and then love with a widow, wonderfully played by Miranda Richardson. Set in England, with picture-postcard scenery and dignified performances throughout. Rated PG-13 for adult situations. 105m. **DIR:** Roberto Faenza. **CAST:** Keith Carradine, Miranda Richardson, Max von Sydow, Kristin Scott Thomas. **1993**

BACHELOR, THE (1999) ★★★1/2 Charming leads and clever gags sell this romantic comedy, a remake of Buster Keaton's 1925 silent classic, *Seven Chances*. This update breathes fresh life into a tired and creaky old premise: In order to retain a whopping inheritance, a confirmed bachelor must marry a woman—*any* woman—in just slightly over a day. The fellow is Chris O'Donnell, the gal he *really* loves is Renee Zellweger, and the story goes down easily when sold by such infectiously charming performers. Everything climaxes with a uniquely riotous chase in the oft-filmed streets of San Francisco, which must have posed a particularly unusual challenge for costume designer Terry Dresbach. Rated PG-13 for profanity and mild sensuality. 101m. **DIR:** Gary Sinyor. **CAST:** Chris O'Donnell, Renee Zellweger, Hal Holbrook, James Cromwell, Edward Asner, Brooke Shields, Artie Lange. **1999 DVD**

BACHELOR AND THE BOBBY-SOXER, THE ★★1/2 Lady judge Myrna Loy cleverly sentences playboy Cary Grant to baby-sit Shirley Temple, a panting nubile teenager. Some hilarious moments, but the comedy gets thin as Loy's lesson begins to cloy. Best bit is the play on words about the Man with the Power, Voodoo and Youdo. B&W; 95m. **DIR:** Irving Reis. **CAST:** Cary Grant, Myrna Loy, Shirley Temple, Rudy Vallee. **1947**

BACHELOR APARTMENT ★★1/2 Loose-living, wisecracking Lothario meets an unyielding stenographer. Oft-used plot gets special treatment from actor-director Lowell Sherman, who sacrifices anything for a great one-liner and makes this pre-Code corker remarkably fresh and fun. B&W; 74m. **DIR:** Lowell Sherman. **CAST:** Lowell Sherman, Irene Dunne, Mae Murray, Norman Kerry. **1931**

BACHELOR IN PARADISE ★★1/2 Author Bob Hope rents a home to do research on suburban mores and becomes confidant and adviser to the housewives in his neighborhood. Janis Paige and Paula Prentiss steal the movie. 109m. **DIR:** Jack Arnold. **CAST:** Bob Hope, Lana Turner, Janis Paige, Paula Prentiss, Jim Hutton, Agnes Moorehead, Don Porter. **1961**

BACHELOR MOTHER ★★★ The old story about a single woman who finds a baby on a doorstep and is mistaken for its mother has never been funnier than in this witty film by writer-director Garson Kanin. Ginger Rogers as the shop girl who finds her whole life upside down as a result of the confusion shows her considerable skill for comedy. David Niven, in an early starring role, is just great as the store owner's son who attempts to "rehabilitate" the fallen Rogers. B&W; 82m. **DIR:** Garson Kanin. **CAST:** Ginger Rogers, David Niven, Charles Coburn, Frank Albertson, Ernest Truex. **1939**

BACHELOR PARTY ★★ Even Tom Hanks can't save this "wild" escapade into degradation when a carefree bus driver who has decided to get married is given an all-out bachelor party by his friends. Rated R for profanity and nudity. 106m. **DIR:** Neal Israel. **CAST:** Tom Hanks, Tawny Kitaen, Adrian Zmed, George Grizzard, Robert Prescott. **1984 DVD**

BACK FROM ETERNITY ★★ No surprises in this rehash of similar films about a handful of people who survive a calamity (in this case, an airplane crash) and have to learn to cope with their predicament as well as with each other. Basically a potboiler that depends on stock footage and phony studio sets, this tired story limps along and gives Anita Ekberg plenty of opportunity to show off her torn blouse. B&W; 97m. **DIR:** John Farrow. **CAST:** Robert Ryan, Anita Ekberg, Rod Steiger, Phyllis Kirk. **1956**

BACK HOME ★★★1/2 After spending the war years in the safety of the United States, an English girl returns to her family in 1945. Unfortunately, she has become too Americanized and can't fit in. Hayley Mills plays her mother, a woman too preoccupied with her husband's homecoming to notice her daughter's heartache. A Disney Channel film, this has high production values. Not rated; contains mature themes. 103m. **DIR:** Piers Haggard. **CAST:** Hayley Mills, Hayley Carr, Jean Anderson, Rupert Frazer, Brenda Bruce. **1989**

BACK IN ACTION ★★1/2 Rogue cop Roddy Piper teams up with vengeful vigilante Billy Blanks, and the results look grim for the baddies. Karl Schiffman's wafer-thin plot barely interferes with the incessant action scenes; if Blanks and Piper were paid by the kick, they walked off with a fortune. Rated R for violence and profanity. 93m. **DIR:** Steve DiMarco, Paul Ziller. **CAST:** Billy Blanks, Roddy Piper, Bobbie Phillips, Matt Birman, Kai Soremekun. **1994**

BACK IN BUSINESS ★★ It's business as usual for former-football-player-turned-action-star Brian Bosworth, who tries desperately not to fumble this pedestrian outing. Bosworth plays a former cop lured into a sting operation that is guaranteed to pit him against the crooked cops who got him kicked off the force. Rated R for language, nudity, and violence. 93m. **DIR:** Philippe Mora. **CAST:** Brian Bosworth, Joe Torry, Dara Tomanovich, Brian James, Alan Scarfe. **1996**

BACK IN THE U.S.S.R. ★★★ Young American Frank Whaley is on a two-week tour of Moscow when he gets embroiled in the theft of a rare book stolen from the Church. First American film shot entirely in Moscow is lovely to look at, engaging in its premise. Rated PG-13 for violence. 88m. **DIR:** Deran Sarafian. **CAST:** Frank Whaley, Natalya Negoda, Andrew Divoff, Dey Young, Roman Polanski. **1992**

BACK OF BEYOND ★★★1/2 This Aussie import may be disguised as a typical B action flick but is actually a surreal surprise. A smoldering Paul Mercurio, of *Strictly Ballroom* fame, returns to the remote truck stop he abandoned twelve years earlier, hoping to atone for past sins. Colin Friels is the diamond smuggler whose female friend unearths a few eerie secrets. The transitions are clunky, but the ending is both original and unexpected. Rated R for profanity, violence, and nudity. 85m. **DIR:** Michael Robertson. **CAST:** Paul Mercurio, Colin Friels, John Polson, Rebekah Elmaloglou, Dee Smart. **1995**

BACK ROADS ★★★ Pug (Tommy Lee Jones) and prostitute (Sally Field) hitch and brawl down the back roads of the South in this sometimes raunchy, often hilarious romance-fantasy. Though it drags a bit, the performances by the two stars and an earthy, down-home charm make it worthwhile. Rated R. 94m. **DIR:** Martin Ritt. **CAST:** Sally Field, Tommy Lee Jones, David Keith. **1981**

BACK STREET ★★★ Third version of novelist Fannie Hurst's romantic tearjerker about clandestine love, with Susan Hayward as the noble mistress who stands by her lover even when he stupidly marries another woman. 107m. **DIR:** David Miller. **CAST:** Susan Hayward, John Gavin, Vera Miles. **1961**

BACK TO BACK ★★★ Two brothers clear their father, accused of an armored car robbery that happened years earlier. Good performances, action, and some unforeseen twists. Rated R for violence and language. 95m. **DIR:** John Kincade. **CAST:** Bill Paxton, Ben Johnson, Susan Anspach, Apollonia Kotero. **1990 DVD**

BACK TO BATAAN ★★★ A fun World War II action film with John Wayne at his two-fisted best. Good script, photography, acting, and battle action. Video quality is quite good. B&W; 95m. **DIR:** Edward Dmytryk. **CAST:** John Wayne, Anthony Quinn, Richard Loo, Beulah Bondi. **1945**

BACK TO HANNIBAL: THE RETURN OF TOM SAWYER AND HUCKLEBERRY FINN ★★★ Decent guess at what Mark Twain's lovable scamps might have grown up to be. Tom, a Chicago lawyer, and Huck, a St. Louis reporter, return to their hometown when their friend, Jim, the former slave, is falsely accused of murder. Lacks the wit and ingenuity of Twain but remains reasonably entertaining. Made for the Disney channel, this is family fare. 95m. **DIR:** Paul Krasny. **CAST:** Raphael Sbarge, Paul Winfield, Mitchell Anderson, Megan Follows, William Windom, Ned Beatty. **1990**

BACK TO SCHOOL ★★★1/2 A true surprise from the usually acerbic Rodney Dangerfield, who sheds his lewd 'n' crude image in favor of one more sympathetic and controlled. He stars as the self-made owner of a chain of "Tall and Fat" stores who decides to return to college. He selects his son's college in order to spend more time with the boy. Rated PG-13 for occasionally vulgar humor. 96m. **DIR:** Alan Metter. **CAST:** Rodney Dangerfield, Sally Kellerman, Burt Young, Keith Gordon, Robert Downey Jr., Ned Beatty, M. Emmet Walsh, Adrienne Barbeau, William Zabka, Severn Darden. **1986 DVD**

BACK TO THE BEACH 🦃 Annette and Frankie are married, in their 40s, live in Ohio, and have two children with behavioral problems. Rated PG for language. 88m. **DIR:** Lyndall Hobbs. **CAST:** Frankie Avalon, Annette Funicello, Connie Stevens, Lori Loughlin. **1987**

BACK TO THE FUTURE ★★★★1/2 Michael J. Fox as a teenager who is zapped back in time by mad scientist Christopher Lloyd. Once there, Fox meets his parents as teenagers, an act that could result in disaster. The first fifteen minutes of this film are pretty bad, but once Fox gets back to where he doesn't belong, it's terrific entertainment. Rated PG. 116m. **DIR:** Robert Zemeckis. **CAST:** Michael J. Fox, Christopher Lloyd, Lea Thompson, Crispin Glover, Thomas F. Wilson. **1985**

BACK TO THE FUTURE II ★★★ Futuristic sequel is so fast-paced and gimmick-laden that one only realizes after seeing it how essentially empty it is. The story jumps from 1985 to 2015 to 1985 to 1955, as Marty McFly attempts to save the future from the consequences of his tampering with the past. Convoluted, but it's an agreeable enough time passer. Rated PG for light violence and profanity. 105m. **DIR:** Robert Zemeckis. **CAST:** Michael J. Fox, Christopher Lloyd, Lea Thompson, Thomas F. Wilson, Elisabeth Shue, Charles Fleischer. **1989**

BACK TO THE FUTURE III ★★★★1/2 Director Robert Zemeckis and screenwriter Bob Gale make up for the excesses and inadequacies of *Back to the Future II* with this rip-roaring conclusion, which has Marty McFly in the Old West attempting to get back to 1985. Rated PG for light violence. 118m. **DIR:** Robert Zemeckis. **CAST:** Michael J. Fox, Christopher Lloyd, Mary Steenburgen, Lea Thompson, Thomas F. Wilson, Elisabeth Shue, Matt Clark, Richard Dysart. **1990**

BACKBEAT ★★★★ Before they became the Fab Four, the Beatles were a quintet—guitarists John Lennon, Paul McCartney, and George Harrison, backed by painter-turned-bass-player Stuart Sutcliffe and drummer Pete Best. This is an involving dramatization of the close friendship between Lennon and Sutcliffe, and how it is tested during the band's apprenticeship in seamy Hamburg, Germany. Rated R for profanity, nudity, simulated sex, and brief violence. 100m. **DIR:** Iain Softley. **CAST:** Stephen Dorff, Sheryl Lee, Ian Hart, Kai Wiesinger, Jennifer Ehle, Gary Bakewell, Chris O'Neill, Scot Williams. **1994**

BACKDOOR TO HEAVEN ★★★1/2 With superb performances from a talented cast, this strong social drama is somewhat dated but still compelling. A poor young man must make a choice: a lifetime of toil and repression or a career of crime. B&W; 86m. **DIR:** William K. Howard. **CAST:** Aline MacMahon, Wallace Ford, Stu Erwin, Van Heflin. **1939**

BACKDRAFT ★★★1/2 Spectacular special effects highlight this melodramatic movie about feuding firemen brothers (well acted by Kurt Russell and William Baldwin) whose lives are endangered by the activities of a clever arsonist. Robert De Niro is typically strong as the chief investigator. Rated R for profanity, violence, and nudity. 136m. **DIR:** Ron Howard. **CAST:** Kurt Russell, William Baldwin, Robert De Niro, Donald Sutherland, Scott Glenn, Jennifer Jason Leigh, Rebecca DeMornay. **1991 DVD**

BACKFIELD IN MOTION ★★★ Plenty to cheer about in this congenial comedy that makes it easy to rally behind Roseanne as the new mom-on-the-block, who organizes the local women into a football team to compete against their kids. Made-for-TV comedy, just wants to entertain, which it does. 95m. **DIR:** Richard Michaels. **CAST:** Roseanne, Tom Arnold, Colleen Camp, Conchata Ferrell. **1991**

BACKFIRE (1987) ★★★★ Twisting thriller involves the carefully orchestrated psychological destruction of a rich, shell-shocked Vietnam vet. Who's the culprit? Excellent combination of whodunit and whydunit. Leads Karen Allen and Keith Carradine are oblique enough to keep the real truth neatly suspended. Rated R for nudity and violence. 90m. **DIR:** Gilbert Cates. **CAST:** Karen Allen, Keith Carradine, Jeff Fahey, Bernie Casey, Dean Paul Martin. **1987**

BACKFIRE (1994) 🦃 Badly acted and written farce about a man who wants to join an all-female fire-fighting force. Rated PG-13 for sexual situations. 93m. **DIR:**

A. Dean Bell. **CAST:** Kathy Ireland, Robert Mitchum, Telly Savalas, Shelley Winters, John Mosby, Mary McCormack. **1994**

BACKGROUND TO DANGER ★★★★ Lots of action makes this one a WWII classic, with a no-nonsense cynic battling spies and attracting beautiful women right and left. Set in the neutral country of Turkey. B&W; 80m. **DIR:** Raoul Walsh. **CAST:** George Raft, Brenda Marshall, Sydney Greenstreet, Peter Lorre, Turhan Bey, Osa Massen. **1943**

BACKLASH (1988) ★★★ Subtle story of two cops (David Argue, Lydia Miller) escorting an accused murderess (Gia Carides) across the Australian desert. Argue turns in a fine performance as an embittered, abrasive policeman. Rated R for language and nudity. 85m. **DIR:** Bill Bennett. **CAST:** David Argue, Gia Carides, Lydia Miller, Brian Syron. **1988**

BACKLASH (1998) ★★ Familiar tale of a federal prosecutor, Gina Gallagher, whose case against the Colombia drug cartel becomes deadly. Forced into protective custody, she uncovers a government conspiracy and her only hope for survival is a convicted criminal. Trite setups and lousy payoffs do little to distinguish this made-for-cable mess. Rated R for adult situations, language, and violence. 103m. **DIR:** Jack Ersgard. **CAST:** Charles Durning, Tracey Needham, JoBeth Williams, Tony Plana, James Belushi. **1998**

BACKSTAB An architect who becomes embroiled in a passionate affair that leads to murder. *Fatal Attraction* wannabe. Rated R for nudity. 91m. **DIR:** James Kaufman. **CAST:** James Brolin, Meg Foster. **1990**

BACKSTAIRS ★★★★ Superb example of the German Expressionist cinema. Its twisted sets and harsh extremes in lighting surround a grim tale of the violence that interrupts the love affair between a chambermaid and her lover. Silent. B&W; 44m. **DIR:** Leopold Jessner. **CAST:** William Dieterle. **1921**

BACKSTREET DREAMS Airheaded mush about a small-time mob enforcer. Rated R for violence and profanity. 104m. **DIR:** Rupert Hitzig. **CAST:** Brooke Shields, Jason O'Malley, Anthony Franciosa, Burt Young, Sherilyn Fenn, Nick Cassavetes, Elias Koteas. **1990**

BACKSTREET JUSTICE ★★★1/2 Writer-director Chris McIntyre must have been reading a lot of Sue Grafton and Sara Paretsky, because this tough-gal–private-eye thriller borrows liberally from both authors. Linda Kozlowski is the hardened investigator trying to live down her father's reputation as a crooked cop while investigating a series of murders frightening tenants out of her inner-city apartment building. Rated R for violence, nudity, profanity, and simulated sex. 91m. **DIR:** Chris McIntyre. **CAST:** Linda Kozlowski, Hector Elizondo, John Shea, Paul Sorvino. **1993**

BACKTRACK ★★★ An impressive ensemble cast, which includes uncredited cameos by Joe Pesci and Charlie Sheen, turns this quixotic, made-for-cable thriller into an intriguing curiosity. Electronic artist Jodie Foster witnesses a mob slaying, and then flees for her life from torpedo Dennis Hopper . . . who abandons the contract after falling in love with her. A bit overlong, but interesting. Contains profanity, violence, nudity, and kinky sexual overtones. 102m. **DIR:** Dennis Hopper. **CAST:** Dennis Hopper, Jodie Foster, Dean Stockwell, Vincent Price, John Turturro, Fred Ward, Bob Dylan. **1990 DVD**

BAD AND THE BEAUTIFUL, THE ★★★★1/2 Dynamite story of a Hollywood producer (Kirk Douglas) and his turbulent relations with a studio actress (Lana Turner). Along the way there are fine performances by all of the cast. It's old Hollywood gloss, and very good, indeed. Five Oscars for this gem. B&W; 118m. **DIR:** Vincente Minnelli. **CAST:** Lana Turner, Kirk Douglas, Gloria Grahame, Dick Powell, Barry Sullivan, Walter Pidgeon, Gilbert Roland. **1952 DVD**

BAD ATTITUDE ★★ Suspended after his partner is gunned down, a cop joins forces with a prostitute who turns out to be a former assassin. Together they hunt down the guys responsible for the partner's murder. Ultra-low-budget action-thriller offers nothing new but will satisfy undemanding fans of the genre. Rated R for profanity, violence, and nudity. 87m. **DIR:** Bill Cummings. **CAST:** Nathaniel de Veaux, Susan Finque, Leon, Gina Lim. **1993**

BAD BEHAVIOUR ★★★1/2 There's not much plot in this slice-of-life film about the intertwining lives of several middle-class Londoners. What it lacks in story, though, it makes up for with warmth, humor, and nicely turned character touches. Improvised by the talented cast, the film takes a while to get rolling, but patience will be rewarded. Rated R for language and mature themes. 103m. **DIR:** Les Blair. **CAST:** Stephen Rea, Sinead Cusack, Philip Jackson, Phil Daniels, Saira Todd. **1993**

BAD BLOOD (1988) ★★★ Absolutely terrifying thriller, thanks to Ruth Raymond's performance as the psychotic mother who lusts after her long-lost son. Linda Blair has the unfortunate role of her much-abused daughter-in-law. Rated R for nudity and violence. 103m. **DIR:** Chuck Vincent. **CAST:** Ruth Raymond, Gregory Patrick, Linda Blair. **1988**

BAD BLOOD (1994) This grotesquely violent Lorenzo Lamas slugfest, which finds our hero trying to save his younger brother from the usual goons, is offensively stupid and gory. Don't watch it on a full stomach. Rated R for violence, torture, nudity, simulated sex, and profanity. 90m. **DIR:** Tibor Takacs. **CAST:** Lorenzo Lamas, Hank Cheyne, Kimberley Kates, John P. Ryan. **1994**

BAD BOYS (1983) ★★★★1/2 A grimly riveting vision of troubled youth. Sean Penn and Esai Morales are Chicago street hoods sworn to kill each other in prison. It's exciting, thought-provoking, and violent, but the violence, for once, is justified and not merely exploitative. Rated R for language, violence, and nudity. 123m. **DIR:** Rick Rosenthal. **CAST:** Sean Penn, Esai Morales, Reni Santoni, Ally Sheedy, Jim Moody, Eric Gurry. **1983 DVD**

BAD BOYS (1995) ★★★1/2 Fast-paced cop/buddy movie stars a well-matched Martin Lawrence and Will Smith as detectives assigned to investigate the theft of a large quantity of drugs from a police-evidence room. Rated R for violence, profanity, and sexual references. 118m. **DIR:** Michael Bay. **CAST:** Martin Lawrence, Will Smith, Téa Leoni, Tcheky Karyo, Theresa Randle, Joe Pantoliano. **1995 DVD**

BAD CHANNELS ★★1/2 At KDUL Radio, the music, is, well, *dull!* That is, until a new DJ enters the scene. Unfortunately, he happens to be an alien, who has come to Earth to pick up chicks, shrink them, and imprison them in small bottles for the trip back home. There's plenty of off-the-wall fun when the townsfolk, including ex-MTV veejay Martha Quinn, decide to pull this guy's plug. Rated R for violence. 88m. **DIR:** Ted Nicolaou. **CAST:** Paul Hipp, Martha Quinn, Aaron Lustig, Ian Patrick Williams. **1992**

BAD COMPANY (1972) ★★★★ This is a much underrated Civil War–era Western. The cultured Barry Brown and the streetwise Jeff Bridges team up as robbers. Charming performances by the leads and an intriguing, intelligent script by Robert Benton and David Newman make this well worth watching. Rated R. 94m. **DIR:** Robert Benton. **CAST:** Jeff Bridges, Barry Brown, Jim Davis, David Huddleston, John Savage, Jerry Houser, Geoffrey Lewis. **1972**

BAD COMPANY (1995) ★★★ Ellen Barkin brings Laurence Fishburne into the fold of an ultrasecret corporate spy agency. She's slinky and cool, he's all self-contained swagger, and this is eye candy and attitude from beginning to end. Rated R for profanity, sexual situations, violence, and brief nudity. 118m. **DIR:** Damian Harris. **CAST:** Ellen Barkin, Laurence Fishburne, Frank Langella, Michael Beach, David Ogden Stiers, Gia Carides, Spalding Gray, Daniel Hugh Kelly. **1995**

BAD DAY AT BLACK ROCK ★★★★ Spencer Tracy gives one of his greatest performances in this suspenseful, action-packed drama as a one-armed man who stirs up trouble when he arrives at a western town whose citizens have a guilty secret. Robert Ryan is superb as the main villain. Lee Marvin and Ernest Borgnine ooze menace as brutal, sadistic henchmen. 81m. **DIR:** John Sturges. **CAST:** Spencer Tracy, Robert Ryan, Anne Francis, Walter Brennan, Lee Marvin, Ernest Borgnine. **1955**

BAD DREAMS 🦃 Tale of a young woman awakened from a thirteen-year coma only to be haunted and hunted by the ghost of a maniacal leader of a hippie cult. Rated R for violence, gore, and profanity. 90m. **DIR:** Andrew Fleming. **CAST:** Jennifer Rubin, Bruce Abbott, Richard Lynch, Harris Yulin. **1988**

BAD GIRLS (1969) ★★1/2 Weak erotic drama from Claude Chabrol about a love affair between a petty bourgeois woman and a beautiful young street artist. Poor chemistry among the characters, not one of Chabrol's better films. Lacks passion. French, dubbed in English. Rated R for mild nudity. 97m. **DIR:** Claude Chabrol. **CAST:** Stéphane Audran, Jacqueline Sassard, Jean-Louis Trintignant. **1969**

BAD GIRLS (1994) ★★★1/2 Action-packed tale of four saloon gals who must elude Pinkerton bounty hunters and sadistic outlaws after one of them kills a prominent citizen in self-defense. First-rate performances by the quartet of top-billed stars and fast-paced direction by Jonathan Kaplan make this a winner. Rated R for violence and suggested sex. 81m. **DIR:** Jonathan Kaplan. **CAST:** Madeleine Stowe, Andie MacDowell, Mary Stuart Masterson, Drew Barrymore, Dermot Mulroney, James Russo, Robert Loggia, James LeGros. **1994**

BAD GIRLS FROM MARS ★★1/2 Another campy exercise from no-budget auteur Fred Olen Ray, with starlet Edy Williams as the new star of a sci-fi movie whose previous stars have all been murdered. Rated R for nudity. 86m. **DIR:** Fred Olen Ray. **CAST:** Edy Williams, Oliver Darrow, Brinke Stevens. **1990**

BAD GIRLS GO TO HELL ★★ Sleaze-film addict Joe Bob Briggs introduces another of Doris Wishman's Sixties drive-in weirdies. A dim-witted sexpot housewife is repeatedly ravaged by gross hairy men and lesbians amid tacky fifties living-room decor. Minuscule plot line features early doses of sadism and masochism with all the bawdiness of a suburban home movie. 98m. **DIR:** Doris Wishman. **CAST:** Gigi Darlene. **1965 DVD**

BAD GUYS ★★ A somewhat contrived story about two police officers who are suspended indefinitely, without pay. They decide to become professional wrestlers. Rated PG. 87m. **DIR:** Joel Silberg. **CAST:** Adam Baldwin, Mike Jolly, Michelle Nicastro, Ruth Buzzi, Sgt. Slaughter. **1985**

BAD INFLUENCE ★★ Rob Lowe stars as a demonic character who leads frustrated yuppie James Spader down the sleazy path to corruption. Disturbing amorality tale. Rated R for nudity, simulated sex, and violence. 100m. **DIR:** Curtis Hanson. **CAST:** Rob Lowe, James Spader, Lisa Zane. **1990**

BAD JIM 🦃 When an innocent man buys Billy the Kid's horse, the man, the horse, and this never-theatrically released movie all turn bad. 90m. **DIR:** Clyde Ware. **CAST:** James Brolin, Richard Roundtree, John Clark Gable, Rory Calhoun, Ty Hardin. **1989**

BAD LANDS (1939) ★★1/2 A posse chasing rapist-killer Apache Jack finds more trouble than they bargained for when their quarry reaches his friends and shifts the balance of power. Western version of RKO's own *Lost Patrol* is a somber, downbeat adventure. B&W; 70m. **DIR:** Lew Landers. **CAST:** Robert Barrat, Noah Beery Jr., Robert Coote, Guinn Williams, Andy Clyde, Francis Ford, Addison Richards, Francis McDonald. **1939**

BAD LIEUTENANT ★★★1/2 Tough, raw, uncompromising police drama follows the last days of a corrupt New York police lieutenant as he works on a rape case involving a nun. Film pulls no punches in showing the physical as well as the moral corruption of the title character. Be forewarned, some scenes are extremely tough to watch. Rated NC-17 for nudity, drug use, language, violence, and moral deprivation. 96m. **DIR:** Abel Ferrara. **CAST:** Harvey Keitel, Victor Argo, Paul Calderon. **1992 DVD**

BAD LOVE ★★ Eloise has a dead-end job. Lenny is a drifter. When they meet, they ignite a passion in each other, a passion that turns to violence when they decide to rob an aging actress. Rated R for nudity, violence, adult situations, and language. 93m. **DIR:** Jill Goldman. **CAST:** Tom Sizemore, Pamela Gidley, Jennifer O'Neill, Seymour Cassel, Debi Mazar, Margaux Hemingway, Joe Dallesandro. **1992 DVD**

BAD MAN OF DEADWOOD ★★★★ One of the best Roy Rogers films of this era. Trying to get away from an unlawful past, sharpshooter Roy Rogers joins a medicine show and becomes allied with a citizens group opposing a crooked conglomeration of businessmen. B&W; 54m. **DIR:** Joseph Kane. **CAST:** Roy Rogers, George "Gabby" Hayes, Sally Payne, Carol Adams, Henry Brandon. **1941**

BAD MANNERS ★★ Wickedly selfish Martin Mull and Karen Black adopt a ratty little boy in the hopes of bringing some normalcy into their strange family. The idea probably looked funny on paper, but quickly turns into a sophomoric take on life. Rated R. 85m. **DIR:** Bobby Houston. **CAST:** Martin Mull, Karen Black, Anne De Salvo, Murphy Dunne. **1984 DVD**

BAD MAN'S RIVER ★★ A humorous Western about the "dreaded" King gang, which robs banks along the Texas and Mexican borders. A Mexican revolutionary offers them a million dollars to blow up the arsenal used by the Mexican army, which the gang does, only to find that they have been double-crossed. 96m. **DIR:** Gene Martin. **CAST:** Lee Van Cleef, Gina Lollobrigida, James Mason. **1959 DVD**

BAD MEDICINE ★★★1/2 Steve Guttenburg and Julie Hagerty play students attending a "Mickey Mouse" med school in Central America. When they find the health conditions in a nearby village unacceptable, they set up a medical clinic. The all-star cast does not disappoint. Rated PG-13 for profanity, sex, and adult situations. 97m. **DIR:** Harvey Miller. **CAST:** Steve Guttenberg, Julie Hagerty, Alan Arkin, Bill Macy, Curtis Armstrong, Julie Kavner, Joe Grifasi, Robert Romanus, Taylor Negron. **1985**

BAD MOON ★★1/2 Single mom Mariel Hemingway doesn't suspect that her footloose brother is a werewolf—until he parks his trailer in her backyard. Foolish horror effort has many silly moments and phony special effects, but profits from pretty good acting and nice cinematography. Rated R for gore. 83m. **DIR:** Eric Red. **CAST:** Mariel Hemingway, Michael Paré. **1996 DVD**

BAD NEWS BEARS, THE ★★★★★ An utterly hilarious comedy directed by Michael Ritchie, this film focuses on the antics of some foul-mouthed Little Leaguers, their beer-guzzling coach (Walter Matthau), and girl pitcher (Tatum O'Neal). But be forewarned, the sequels, *Breaking Training* and *The Bad News Bears Go to Japan*, are strictly no-hitters. Rated PG. 102m. **DIR:** Michael Ritchie. **CAST:** Walter Matthau, Tatum O'Neal, Vic Morrow, Alfred Lutter, Jackie Earle Haley. **1976 DVD**

BAD NEWS BEARS GO TO JAPAN, THE 🦃 Worst of the *Bad News Bears* trio of films, this features Tony Curtis as a small-time promoter with big ideas. Rated PG. 91m. **DIR:** John Berry. **CAST:** Tony Curtis, Jackie Earle Haley, Tomisaburo Wakayama, George Wyner, Lonny Chapman. **1978 DVD**

BAD NEWS BEARS IN BREAKING TRAINING, THE ★★ Without Walter Matthau, Tatum O'Neal, and director Michael Ritchie, this sequel to *The Bad News Bears* truly is bad news... and rather idiotic. Jackie Earle Haley returns as the team star, and William Devane has a reasonable part as Haley's footloose father. Don't expect much. Rated PG for mild profanity. 100m. **DIR:** Michael Pressman. **CAST:** William Devane, Jackie Earle Haley, Clifton James. **1977 DVD**

BAD RONALD ★★ Scott Jacoby lives secretly in a hidden room his mother builds for him after he kills a taunting peer. When Mama passes on, a new family moves into the place. Intriguing but tedious made-for-TV movie. 72m. **DIR:** Buzz Kulik. **CAST:** Scott Jacoby, Kim Hunter, Pippa Scott, Dabney Coleman. **1978**

BAD SEED, THE ★★1/2 Despite the contrived ending and pathetically cutesy "curtain call," this story of a perfectly wicked child protected by her image is still capable of generating chills. Nancy Kelly may be more than a bit melodramatic as the concerned mother on a constant crying jag, but young Patty McCormack has that special cold beauty that makes her crimes all the more hideous. B&W; 129m. **DIR:** Mervyn LeRoy. **CAST:** Patty McCormack, Nancy Kelly, Henry Jones, Eileen Heckart, William Hopper. **1956**

BAD SLEEP WELL, THE ★★★★ A man seeks revenge for the murder of his father in this suspenseful tale of corruption. Akira Kurosawa remarkably captures the spirit of Forties crime-dramas in this engrossing film, based on an Ed McBain story. In Japanese with English subtitles. B&W; 152m. **DIR:** Akira Kurosawa. **CAST:** Toshiro Mifune, Masayuki Mori, Takashi Shimura. **1960**

BAD TASTE ★★★★ One of the grossest, yet most hysterically funny movies ever made. Aliens have come to Earth to harvest the new fast-food sensation of the universe—human flesh! It's up to the highly trained, if not totally adept, Alien Invasion Defense Service to save the world. Not rated; contains profanity and gore. 90m. **DIR:** Peter Jackson. **CAST:** Pete O'Herne. **1987 DVD**

BADGE OF THE ASSASSIN ★★★1/2 Fine reenactment of the pursuit, capture, and trial of three radical black men who killed two policemen in Harlem in 1971. James Woods and Yaphet Kotto are intense as the assistant DA and detective who must make their case stick against the three ruthless killers. Rated R for violence and profanity. 96m. **DIR:** Mel Damski. **CAST:** James Woods, Yaphet Kotto, Alex Rocco, David Harris. **1985**

BADGE 373 ★★ This police drama casts Robert Duvall as a cop out to nab his partner's killer. Pretty routine stuff is thrown together in an even more routine fashion. Rated R. 116m. **DIR:** Howard W. Koch. **CAST:** Robert Duvall, Verna Bloom, Eddie Egan, Henry Darrow. **1973**

BADLANDERS, THE ★★★ Alan Ladd is a geologist, Ernest Borgnine a rancher. Both are robbed of a gold mine, so they join forces to recover their loss from an evil businessman. Mild suspense and action, but sincere performances. 83m. **DIR:** Delmer Daves. **CAST:** Alan Ladd, Ernest Borgnine, Katy Jurado, Kent Smith, Nehemiah Persoff. **1958**

BADLANDS (1973) ★★★★ Featuring fine performances by Sissy Spacek, Martin Sheen, and Warren Oates, this is a disturbing re-creation of the Starkweather-Fugate killing spree of the 1950s. It is undeniably a work of intelligence and fine craftsmanship. However, as with Martin Scorsese's *Taxi Driver* and Bob Fosse's *Star 80*, *Badlands* is not an easy film to watch. Rated PG. 95m. **DIR:** Terence Malick. **CAST:** Martin Sheen, Sissy Spacek, Warren Oates, Ramon Bieri, Alan Vint. **1973**

BADLANDS DRIFTER (CHALLENGE OF MCKENNA) ★★ An ex-priest gets caught in a range war and tries to make things right. He ends up in a battle of power, revenge, greed, and love. Exceptional performances by the entire cast make this a better-than-average spaghetti Western, with a good story to match the action and violence. Rated R for violence. 90m. **DIR:** Leon Klimovsky. **CAST:** John Ireland, Robert Woods, Daniela Giordana, Annabella Incontrera, Roberto Camardiel. **1969**

BADMAN'S TERRITORY ★★★ Staunch and true marshal combats saddle scum when they flee across the border into territory beyond the government's reach.

Good watching. B&W; 97m. **DIR:** Tim Whelan. **CAST:** Randolph Scott, Ann Richards, George "Gabby" Hayes, Ray Collins, Chief Thundercloud. **1946**

BADMEN OF THE HILLS ★★★ A crooked sheriff tries to stop Charles Starrett's investigation into the murder of a U.S. marshal. Action-packed. B&W; 58m. **DIR:** William Berke. **CAST:** Charles Starrett, Russell Hayden, Cliff Edwards, Alan Bridge, Luana Walters. **1942**

BAGDAD CAFÉ ★★★★ This delightfully offbeat comedy-drama concerns a German businesswoman who appears in the minuscule desert town in California called Bagdad. She and the highly strung owner of the town's only diner-hotel have a major culture and personality clash. Jack Palance as a bandanna-wearing artist is so perfectly weird he practically walks off with the film. Rated PG. 91m. **DIR:** Percy Adlon. **CAST:** Marianne Sagebrecht, C.C.H. Pounder, Jack Palance. **1988 DVD**

BAIL JUMPER ★★★ A small-town thug and his ex-con girlfriend flee Missouri in search of the good life in New York City in this surreal love-on-the-run road movie. Bizarre romp through the American landscape that is reminiscent of David Lynch's *Wild at Heart* and Jim Jarmusch's *Mystery Train*. Not rated. 96m. **DIR:** Christian Faber. **CAST:** Eszter Balint, B. J. Spalding. **1989**

BAIL OUT ★★★ A funny, and often outright silly, action comedy about three bounty hunters who must bring the daughter of a millionaire to trial on drug charges. Lots of action and some great one-liners. Rated R. 88m. **DIR:** Max Kleven. **CAST:** Linda Blair, David Hasselhoff, John Vernon. **1988 DVD**

BAIT ★★ Goodness, what a mess. Only Jamie Foxx's staunchest fans will find anything to admire in this labored, interminable comedy-thriller about a petty thief who accidentally learns of a big gold heist. Hoping to flush out the deranged criminal mastermind behind that caper, federal agents put Foxx back on the streets, intending to shadow him. Naturally, nothing works out as planned, not that you'll care; Foxx's goofy, immature, and useless character doesn't *deserve* saving. Rated R for profanity, sexuality, and surprisingly nasty violence. 119m. **DIR:** Antoine Fuqua. **CAST:** Jamie Foxx, David Morse, Doug Hutchison, Nestor Serrano, Robert Pastorelli, David Paymer, Mike Epps. **2000 DVD**

BAJA ★★★★ Nothing is what it seems in this nifty little thriller. Molly Ringwald and Donal Logue star as Bebe and Alex, a couple on the run after a drug deal goes sour. They end up in a trailer in Baja, where they wait for Bebe's father to send them money. Instead, he sends Bebe's husband, who then attracts the attention of a hit man sent to kill Alex. How this whole horrible mess is resolved makes for a genuinely surprising finale. Not rated; contains violence and adult language. 92m. **DIR:** Kurt Voss. **CAST:** Molly Ringwald, Lance Henriksen, Donal Logue, M. A. Nickles, Corbin Bernsen. **1995**

BAJA OKLAHOMA ★★ Lesley Ann Warren plays a tired bartender who dreams of success as a country-and-western songwriter. Willie Nelson and Emmylou Harris make cameo appearances as themselves. Made for HBO, this contains profanity, violence, and partial nudity. 100m. **DIR:** Bobby Roth. **CAST:** Lesley Ann Warren, Peter Coyote, Swoosie Kurtz, Billy Vera. **1988**

BAKER'S HAWK ★★★★ No-nonsense Westerner Clint Walker helps the local law get a group of vigilantes under control, while his son embarks on an adventure of his own involving a hawk and a mysterious hermit. An exceptional family film. Rated G. 98m. **DIR:** Lyman Dayton. **CAST:** Clint Walker, Burl Ives, Diane Baker, Lee Montgomery, Alan Young. **1976 DVD**

BAKER'S WIFE, THE ★★★★ The new baker is coming to a town that has been without fresh-baked goods for too long. With great fanfare, the baker and his new wife arrive, but she has a roving eye. This comedy is a gem. In French with English subtitles. B&W; 124m. **DIR:** Marcel Pagnol. **CAST:** Raimu, Ginette Leclerc, Charles Moulin. **1938**

BALALAIKA ★★★ Cabaret singer Ilona Massey wins the heart of cossack Nelson Eddy. The plot is just a tool to introduce some wonderful musical numbers, but Massey is impressive in her American debut. B&W; 102m. **DIR:** Reinhold Schunzel. **CAST:** Nelson Eddy, Ilona Massey, Charlie Ruggles, Frank Morgan, Lionel Atwill, C. Aubrey Smith, Philip Terry, George Tobias, Joyce Compton. **1939**

BALANCE OF POWER ★★ Another in the arena-fighting genre. Here, a *sensei* must enter the underground ring to defend the world against an evil promoter of death matches. Billy Blanks puts his heart into it, which helps, but too many foul mouths and extreme violence steer this film away from the crowd at whom it would best be targeted—early teens. Rated R for profanity and violence. 92m. **DIR:** Rick Bennett. **CAST:** Billy Blanks, Mako, James Lew. **1996**

BALBOA 🦃 Tacky soap about a ruthless millionaire. Not rated; this film contains nudity. 92m. **DIR:** James Polakof. **CAST:** Tony Curtis, Carol Lynley, Steve Kanaly, Chuck Connors. **1982**

BALCONY, THE ★★★★ Jean Genet's hard-hitting surreal political fable is set in a brothel of illusion, where the customers take over real power during a revolution. Peter Falk sizzles in the role of a police chief who uses the whorehouse as a rallying point from which to suppress the revolution. Outrageous, poignant satire on the church and state, brilliantly performed by a top-notch cast. B&W; 87m. **DIR:** Joseph Strick. **CAST:** Shelley Winters, Peter Falk, Leonard Nimoy, Lee Grant. **1963 DVD**

BALL OF FIRE ★★★1/2 Stuffy linguistics professor Gary Cooper meets hotcha-cha dancer Barbara Stanwyck. He and seven lovable colleagues are putting together an encyclopedia. She's recruited to fill them in on slanguage. She does this, and more! Gangster Dana Andrews and motor-mouthed garbage man Allen Jenkins add to the madcap antics in what has been dubbed the last of the prewar screwball comedies. Good show! B&W; 111m. **DIR:** Howard Hawks. **CAST:** Gary Cooper, Barbara Stanwyck, Dana Andrews, Oscar Homolka, S. Z. Sakall, Richard Haydn, Henry Travers, Tully Marshall, Allen Jenkins. **1941 DVD**

BALLAD OF A GUNFIGHTER ★★ Marty Robbins is a rough-and-ready rebel who robs stages and gives to the poor. He ends up battling guys even worse than himself. Stilted dialogue and acting interlaced with a couple of good old songs. Not rated and inoffensive. 84m. **DIR:** Bill Ward. **CAST:** Marty Robbins, Joyce Redd, Bob Barron, Nestor Paiva, Laurette Luez. **1964**

BALLAD OF A SOLDIER ★★★1/2 A soldier finds love and adventure on a ten-day pass to see his mother. This import features excellent cinematography and acting, and despite the always obvious Soviet propaganda, some piercing insights into the Russian soul. In Russian with English subtitles. B&W; 89m. **DIR:** Grigori Chukhrai. **CAST:** Vladimir Ivashov, Shanna Prokhorenko. **1959 DVD**

BALLAD OF CABLE HOGUE, THE ★★★★1/2 Jason Robards has one of his finest roles as Hogue, a loner who discovers water in the desert and becomes a successful entrepreneur by opening a stagecoach stopover. Director Sam Peckinpah's deft eye for period detail and outstanding acting by all involved make this one a winner. Rated R. 121m. **DIR:** Sam Peckinpah. **CAST:** Jason Robards Jr., Stella Stevens, Strother Martin, L. Q. Jones, David Warner. **1970**

BALLAD OF GREGORIO CORTEZ, THE ★★★★1/2 This superb independent production tells the powerful story of one man's courage, pain, tragedy, and heartbreak—all of which come as the result of a simple misunderstanding. Edward James Olmos gives a haunting portrayal of the title character, who becomes a fugitive through no fault of his own. Rated PG for violence. 99m. **DIR:** Robert M. Young. **CAST:** Edward James Olmos, James Gammon, Tom Bower, Alan Vint, Timothy Scott, Barry Corbin. **1982**

BALLAD OF LITTLE JO, THE ★★★1/2 Revisionist Western stars Suzy Amis as a woman who feels trapped in a man's world, so she disguises herself as a man to get a fair shake. Amis delivers a stunning performance as she attempts to fit into a world designed for men. The usual complications arise, but Amis and a terrific supporting cast make them new and invigorating. Rated R for violence, language, and nudity. 124m. **DIR:** Maggie Greenwald. **CAST:** Suzy Amis, Bo Hopkins, David Chung, René Auberjonois, Carrie Snodgress, Ian McKellen. **1993**

BALLAD OF NARAYAMA, THE ★★★★★ Based on one of the most unusual Japanese legends: a century ago in a remote mountain village in northern Japan, a local custom dictated that when a person reached 70 years old they were taken to Mount Narayama to die. A true masterpiece of Japanese cinema and a Grand Prize winner at the 1983 Cannes Film Festival. In Japanese with English subtitles. Not rated; contains nudity and violence. 129m. **DIR:** Shohei Imamura. **CAST:** Ken Ogata. **1983**

BALLAD OF THE SAD CAFE, THE ★★★ Strangeness abounds in this visually appealing tale of a masochist's love for a hard, angular spinster. For its sparse content, the film has a deliberate slow-as-molasses pace, and in that time it takes many Southern stereotypes and turns them upside down. Based on the story by Carson McCullers. Rated PG-13 for violence. 100m. **DIR:** Simon Callow. **CAST:** Vanessa Redgrave, Keith Carradine, Rod Steiger. **1992**

BALLISTIC ★★1/2 After a government witness is murdered while under her protection, an LAPD cop (Marjean Holden) and her father (Richard Roundtree) set out after the killers. Rated R for profanity, brief nudity, and violence. 86m. **DIR:** Kim Bass. **CAST:** Marjean Holden, Joel Beeson, Sam Jones, Richard Roundtree. **1995**

BALLOON FARM ★★★ When a stranger appears in a town parched by drought and begins to plant a mysterious crop, the townsfolk think he must be insane, for nothing has been able to grow under these painfully dry conditions. The very next morning, people are flabbergasted to discover that an unusual crop of corn has risen overnight: the ears of corn have been replaced by colorful balloons with strange magical powers. Good for kids, but sleep-inducing for adults. Not rated. 92m. **DIR:** William Dear. **CAST:** Rip Torn, Mara Wilson, Laurie Metcalf. **1997**

BALLOT MEASURE 9 ★★★★★ This revealing documentary takes a frightening look at a persistent and growing lack of tolerance in this country. During a detailed examination of a campaign by the Oregon Citizens' Alliance, we learn of efforts to revoke "special rights" (aka equal rights) from homosexuals in 1992. Director Heather MacDonald creates a sense of urgency and tension while covering all sides of this issue, leaving us to call up pictures of Germany in the early 1930s. Not rated; contains profanity. 72m. **DIR:** Heather MacDonald. **1995**

BALTIMORE BULLET, THE ★★1/2 In this tale of big-league pool hustling, clever cuesters James Coburn and Bruce Boxleitner carefully build up to scoring big in a nail-biting shoot-out with suave Omar Sharif. Rated PG. 103m. **DIR:** Robert Ellis Miller. **CAST:** James Coburn, Bruce Boxleitner, Omar Sharif, Ronee Blakley. **1980**

BALTO ★★★★ This exciting animated adventure tells how wolf-dog Balto, an outcast in his Alaskan hometown, risks his life to retrieve child-saving antitoxins amid a severe epidemic and blizzard. His courage, speed, and physical strength are challenged by an avalanche, a grizzly, the icy depths of a frozen lake, and a mean sled dog. Balto's pals include a goofy snow goose and a female husky who doesn't give a hair ball whether her new friend is a half-breed or not. Rated G. 77m. **DIR:** Simon Wells. **CAST:** Kevin Bacon, Bridget Fonda, Phil Collins, Bob Hoskins, Jim Cummings (voices). **1995 DVD**

BAMBI ★★★★★ This lush adaptation of Felix Salten's beloved story represents the crowning achievement of Walt Disney's animation studio. Never again would backgrounds be delineated with such realistic detail; with animation so precise that it resembled live photography. The screenplay, too, has a bit more bite than the average Disney yarn, with equal helpings of comedy and tragedy fueling a confrontation between forest animals and that most horrific of two-legged interlopers: man. 69m. **DIR:** David Hand. **1942**

BAMBOO SAUCER (COLLISION COURSE) ★★1/2 America and the USSR compete with each other as they investigate reports of a UFO crash in the People's Republic of China. More concerned with plot and substance than special effects, this low-budget effort is thought-provoking and succeeds where a more gimmicky, less suspenseful approach would have failed. 100m. **DIR:** Frank Telford. **CAST:** Dan Duryea, John Ericson, Lois Nettleton, Nan Leslie. **1968**

BAMBOOZLED ★★★ A television writer tries to get fired from his network contract by creating a racist variety show. He becomes a sort of pop-culture Dr. Frankenstein when his *Mantan the New Millennium Minstrel Show*, featuring African Americans performing in black face, becomes a hit. This audacious, scathing, frustrating look at race relations and the blurring of image and identity is a brilliant rant that digresses into sermonizing. Rated R for language and violence. 135m. **DIR:** Spike Lee. **CAST:** Damon Wayans, Savion Glover, Tommy Davidson, Jada Pinkett, Michael Rapaport. **2000 DVD**

BANANA COP ★★★ Engaging comedy about an Anglo-Chinese Scotland Yard inspector assigned to investigate a Chinatown murder. His wisecracking partner is played by Teddy Robin Kwan, the Eddie Murphy of Hong Kong. In Cantonese with English subtitles. Not rated; contains violence. 96m. **DIR:** Po-Chih Leong. **CAST:** George Lam, Teddy Robin Kwan. **1984**

BANANAS ★★★★ Before he started making classic comedies, such as *Annie Hall*, *Zelig*, and *Broadway Danny Rose*, writer-director-star Woody Allen made some pretty wild—though generally uneven—wacky movies. This 1971 comedy, with Woody's hapless hero becoming involved in a South American revolution, does have its share of hilarious moments. Rated PG. 82m. **DIR:** Woody Allen. **CAST:** Woody Allen, Louise Lasser, Carlos Montalban, Howard Cosell. **1971 DVD**

BAND OF ANGELS ★★★★ Clark Gable delivers in a lavish adaptation of Robert Penn Warren's novel. He has a fiery involvement with a beautiful Southern belle and saves her from a fate worse than death when it's revealed she is really a mulatto. 127m. **DIR:** Raoul Walsh. **CAST:** Clark Gable, Yvonne De Carlo, Sidney Poitier, Efrem Zimbalist Jr. **1957**

BAND OF OUTSIDERS ★★1/2 Disappointing *film noir* from director Jean-Luc Godard about a robbery that ends in the accidental death of a woman at the hands of her beautiful niece. This existential crime-drama suffers from an incoherent script. In French with English subtitles. Not rated. B&W; 97m. **DIR:** Jean-Luc Godard. **CAST:** Anna Karina, Sami Frey, Claude Brasseur. **1964**

BAND OF THE HAND ★★1/2 A Vietnam vet (Stephen Lang) takes a group of incorrigible Florida teens and turns them into an anti-drug squad. That's right, it's *Mod Squad* for the 1980s and just as silly as it sounds. Rated R for profanity, brief nudity, cocaine use, and violence. 109m. **DIR:** Paul Michael Glaser. **CAST:** Stephen Lang, Michael Carmine, Lauren Holly, John Cameron Mitchell, Daniel Quinn, Leon Robinson, James Remar. **1986**

BAND WAGON, THE ★★★★ One of Vincente Minnelli's best grand-scale musicals and one of Fred Astaire's most endearing roles. He plays a Hollywood has-been who decides to try his luck onstage. This is the film that gave us "That's Entertainment." Not rated—family fare. 112m. **DIR:** Vincente Minnelli. **CAST:** Fred Astaire, Cyd Charisse, Jack Buchanan, Nanette Fabray, Oscar Levant. **1953**

BANDIT QUEEN ★★★★ True story of a child bride who fought against the system and sexual abuse to become the leader of a group of bandits. Set in India, film recounts how 11 year old Phoolan Devi, sold into marriage by her family for a cow, escapes her abusive husband. Eventually, she is captured and sexually abused by a band of outlaws. Through strength and determination, Phoolan finally becomes their leader and hero. Riveting performance by Seema Biswas as Phoolan. In Hindi with English subtitles. Not rated; contains strong sexual violence. 119m. **DIR:** Shekhar Kapur. **CAST:** Seema Biswas, Nirmal Pandey, Maoj Bajpai. **1994 DVD**

BANDITS (1967) 🦃 A boring horse opera about three outlaws rescued from the hangman's noose. Not rated, but equivalent to PG-13 for violence. 89m. **DIR:** Robert Conrad, Alfredo Zacharias. **CAST:** Robert Conrad, Jan-Michael Vincent, Roy Jensen, Pedro Armendariz Jr. **1967**

BANDITS (1987) ★★★★ An imprisoned jewel thief sends his daughter to a Swiss boarding school while plotting to avenge his wife's murder. Once free, father and daughter reunite. The romance that develops between the charming daughter and a young thief is surprisingly moving. Superior acting and a plot that twists enough to keep viewers guessing. In French with English subtitles. Not rated; contains brief nudity and violence. 98m. **DIR:** Claude Lelouch. **CAST:** Jean Yanne, Marie-Sophie Lelouch, Patrick Bruel, Charles Gerard. **1987**

BANDITS (1997) ★★★1/2 Four female-convict rock musicians become folk heroines and chart-toppers, when they escape from prison and go on the run. The film is a high-spirited crowd-pleaser, at once hardboiled and sentimental, and the songs (most of them sung in English) are catchy in a retro-ABBA sort of way. In German with English subtitles. Rated R for language (in subtitles), sexuality, and drug use. 110m. **DIR:** Katja von Garnier. **CAST:** Katja Riemann, Jasmin Tabatabai, Nicolette Krebitz, Jutta Hoffmann. **1997 DVD**

•BANDITS (2001) ★★★1/2 When two convicts escape from prison, they hit on the idea of becoming the "sleep-over bandits"; moving in with a bank manager the night before a heist and having an amazing run of successes. That is, until they encounter a bored, neglected housewife who insists on accompanying them on their career of crime and seducing both of them. If you don't mind cringing once in a while at the inept antics and take-it-to-the-edge performances of the three top-billed stars, the caper comedy is a rare example of adult entertainment that substitutes intelligence for exploitation. Rated PG-13 for profanity, violence, and sexual encounters. 122m. **DIR:** Barry Levinson. **CAST:** Bruce Willis, Billy Bob Thornton, Cate Blanchett, Troy Garity, Brian F. O'Byrne, Stacey Travis, Bobby Slayton. **2001 DVD**

BANDITS OF DARK CANYON ★★★1/2 Texas Ranger Rocky Lane helps escaped convict Bob Steele clear his name on a phony murder charge. The apparent victim is alive and working with Steele's best friend to cheat him out of his fortune. Above-average Lane Western—and they were all good. B&W; 59m. **DIR:** Philip Ford. **CAST:** Allan "Rocky" Lane, Bob Steele, Eddy Waller, Roy Barcroft, Linda Johnson. **1947**

BANDOLERO! ★★★ Escape south of the border with outlaw brothers James Stewart and Dean Martin (if you can buy this), who ride just a few furlongs ahead of the law (George Kennedy), taking Raquel Welch along as hostage. 106m. **DIR:** Andrew V. McLaglen. **CAST:** James Stewart, Dean Martin, Raquel Welch, Will Geer, George Kennedy, Andrew Prine. **1968**

BANG BANG KID, THE ★★1/2 Goofy comedy-Western with Tom Bosley as Merriweather Newberry, the inventor of a robot gunfighter (dubbed The Bang Bang Kid). The residents of a mining community hope that they can use it to defeat Bear Bullock (Guy Madison), the town boss. Good for kids; passable for grownups in a silly mood. 90m. **DIR:** Stanley Prager. **CAST:** Guy Madison, Sandra Milo, Tom Bosley, Riccardo Garrone. **1968**

BANG THE DRUM SLOWLY ★★★★ Robert De Niro and Michael Moriarty are given a perfect showcase for their acting talents in this poignant film, and they don't disappoint. The friendship of two baseball players comes alive as the team's star pitcher (Moriarty) tries to assist journeyman catcher (De Niro) in completing one last season before succumbing to Hodgkin's disease. The story may lead to death, but it is filled with life, hope, and compassion. Rated PG. 98m. **DIR:** John Hancock. **CAST:** Robert De Niro, Michael Moriarty, Vincent Gardenia. **1973**

•BANGKOK DANGEROUS ★★ Ultrastylish but excessively violent film about a mute hit man, numb to his horrible work, who meets a woman who could open his eyes to the warmth of life. Rated R for violence. 105m. **DIR:** Oxide Pang Chun, Danny Pang. **CAST:** Pawalit Mongkolpisit, Premsinee Ratanasopha, Patharawarin Timkul, Pisek Intrakanchit. **2000**

BANK DICK, THE ★★★★★ W. C. Fields is at his best in this laugh-filled comedy. In it, Fields plays a drunkard who becomes a hero. But the story is just an excuse for the moments of hilarity—of which there are many. B&W; 74m. **DIR:** Eddie Cline. **CAST:** W. C. Fields, Cora Witherspoon, Una Merkel, Shemp Howard. **1940 DVD**

BANK ROBBER 🦃 Shallow, bungling thief sticks up a downtown bank and spends the rest of the movie hiding out in a seedy, nearby hotel in this offbeat but dumb comedy caper. Rated NC-17 for sex, violence, and language. 95m. **DIR:** Nick Mead. **CAST:** Patrick Dempsey, Lisa Bonet, Olivia D'Abo, Forest Whitaker, Judge Reinhold, Michael Jeter. **1993**

BANK SHOT 🦃 George C. Scott as a lisping mastermind who plots to steal a bank by putting it on wheels. PG for language. 100m. **DIR:** Gower Champion. **CAST:** George C. Scott, Joanna Cassidy, Don Calfa. **1974**

B.A.P.S ★★ The title stands for "Black American Princesses," two of whom (Halle Berry and Natalie Desselle) are hired to pose as the granddaughters of dying millionaire Martin Landau's long-lost love. Brainless, witless, and demeaning on every level, with nary a chuckle in the whole sad, disheveled mess. A huge disappointment from usually reliable director Robert Townsend. Landau looks plainly (and understandably) embarrassed; only Ian Richardson, as the butler, escapes with his dignity more or less intact. Rated PG-13 for mild profanity. 93m. **DIR:** Robert Townsend. **CAST:** Halle Berry, Natalie Desselle, Martin Landau, Ian Richardson. **1997**

BAR GIRLS ★★ Lesbians cross paths at a Los Angeles watering hole in this sporadically funny dating game that plays like a cross between a lipsticked *Cheers* and a soap opera. Rated R for language, nudity, and simulated sex. 95m. **DIR:** Marita Giovanni. **CAST:** Nancy Allison Wolfe, Liza D'Agostino, Michael Harris, Camilla Griggs, Justine Slater. **1995 DVD**

BAR-20 RIDES AGAIN ★★★ Hopalong Cassidy and Red Connors are called to Wyoming to help an old friend deal with cattle rustlers, and the Bar-20 boys and their allies wage a terrific battle. George Hayes appears as "Windy" for the first time and starts his long career as cantankerous sidekick supreme. B&W; 65m. **DIR:** Howard Bretherton. **CAST:** William Boyd, James Ellison, Jean Rouverol, George "Gabby" Hayes, Harry Worth, Paul Fix. **1935**

BARABBAS ★★1/2 Early Dino De Laurentis opus is long on production, short on credibility. Standard gory religious spectacle follows the life of the thief Barabbas, whom Pilate freed when Jesus was condemned to die. Good cast of veteran character actors attempts to move this epic along, but fails. 144m. **DIR:** Richard Fleischer. **CAST:** Anthony Quinn, Jack Palance, Ernest Borgnine, Katy Jurado. **1962 DVD**

BARB WIRE ★★ America's second civil war has left the nation in chaos and black-leather biker Barb—in a punk/metal nod to *Casablanca*—takes on Fascist army pigs after crossing paths with an ex-lover and his freedom-fighter wife. Rated R for nudity, language, suggested sex, and violence. 98m. **DIR:** David Hogan. **CAST:** Pamela Anderson Lee, Temuera Morrison, Victoria Rowell, Steve Railsback, Jack Noseworthy. **1996 DVD**

BARBARELLA ★★1/2 Futuristic fantasy has Jane Fonda in the title role of a space beauty being drooled over by various male creatures on a strange planet. Drags at times, but Jane's fans won't want to miss it. Rated PG for partial nudity-sexual content. 98m. **DIR:** Roger Vadim. **CAST:** Jane Fonda, John Phillip Law, Anita Pallenberg, Milo O'Shea. **1968 DVD**

BARBARIAN AND THE GEISHA, THE 🦃 American ambassador to Japan during the nineteenth century finds romance with geisha. 105m. **DIR:** John Huston. **CAST:** John Wayne, Sam Jaffe, Eiko Ando. **1958**

BARBARIAN QUEEN 🦃 Another one of those lame fantasy flicks à la *Yor*, the *Conan* films, and Lou Ferrigno's *Hercules* films. Although not rated, *Barbarian Queen* has lots of nudity and violence. 75m. **DIR:** Hector Olivera. **CAST:** Lana Clarkson, Katt Shea, Frank Zagarino, Dawn Dunlap. **1985 DVD**

BARBARIAN QUEEN II: EMPRESS STRIKES BACK 🦃 More sword and sorcery from buxom babe Lana Clarkson, whom you might remember from the first *Barbarian Queen*, but then again: maybe not. Rated R. 87m. **DIR:** Joe Finley. **CAST:** Lana Clarkson, Greg Wrangler. **1989 DVD**

BARBARIANS, THE 🦃 Unconvincing fantasy film casts David and Peter Paul (wrestling's Barbarian Brothers) as twins trying to save the queen of their people. Not rated. 88m. **DIR:** Ruggero Deodato. **CAST:** Peter Paul, David Paul, Richard Lynch, Michael Berryman. **1987**

BARBARIANS AT THE GATE ★★★★ The legacy of the 1980s—corporate greed—is brilliantly indicted in Larry Gelbart's adaptation of Bryan Borrough and John Helyar's mesmerizing account of the Nabisco takeover. James Garner stars as "good ol' boy" F. Ross Johnson, the Nabisco CEO who battled the circling sharks to control the company he professed to love so dearly. Rated R for profanity. 107m. **DIR:** Glenn Jordan. **CAST:** James Garner, Jonathan Pryce, Peter Riegert, Joanna Cassidy, Fred Dalton Thompson, Mark Harelik. **1993 DVD**

BARBAROSA ★★★★ Action-packed Western stars Willie Nelson and Gary Busey as a pair of outcasts on the run. Australian director Fred Schepisi has created an exciting, funny movie that combines the scenic majesty of the great John Ford Westerns with the light touch of George Roy Hill's *Butch Cassidy and the Sundance Kid*. Rated PG for violence. 90m. **DIR:** Fred Schepisi.

CAST: Willie Nelson, Gary Busey, Isela Vega, Gilbert Roland, Danny De La Paz, George Voskovec. **1982**

BARBARY COAST, THE ★★★1/2 Inspired by Herbert Asbury's colorful history of early San Francisco, this film is tailored to fit the unique talents of its great cast. This story of femme fatale Miriam Hopkins and the men in her life is fun for the whole family and a treat for film buffs who like the look of the past as created on studio back lots. B&W; 90m. **DIR:** Howard Hawks. **CAST:** Edward G. Robinson, Miriam Hopkins, Joel McCrea, Walter Brennan, Brian Donlevy, Frank Craven. **1935**

BARCELONA ★★★1/2 An American sales rep in Spain and his naval-officer cousin engage in a round-robin of romantic complications while discussing sex and politics in their exquisitely civilized monotone voices. Rated PG-13 for mature themes. 101m. **DIR:** Whit Stillman. **CAST:** Taylor Nichols, Christopher Eigeman, Tushka Bergen, Mira Sorvino, Hellena Schmied, Nuria Badia. **1994 DVD**

BARE ESSENTIALS ★★ A yuppie guy and gal find themselves reevaluating their relationship after being shipwrecked on a tiny atoll. Plodding. 94m. **DIR:** Martha Coolidge. **CAST:** Mark Linn-Baker, Lisa Hartman, Gregory Harrison, Charlotte Lewis. **1990**

BARE KNUCKLES ★★★ A fun martial arts thriller about a modern-day bounty hunter on the trail of a vicious killer stalking women on the streets of the city. Rated R for brief nudity, violence, and adult language. 90m. **DIR:** Don Edmunds. **CAST:** Robert Viharo, Sherry Jackson, Michael Heit, Gloria Hendry, John Daniels. **1984**

BAREFOOT CONTESSA, THE ★★★ A gaggle of Hollywood vultures headed by director Humphrey Bogart picks naïve dancer Ava Gardner out of a Madrid nightclub and proceeds to mold her into a film star. A simple unpretentious soul, she marries an impotent Italian nobleman (Rossano Brazzi), dies, and is buried by her chief mentor who tells her tragic story in flashback. A cynical, bizarre tale that never delivers what it promises. 128m. **DIR:** Joseph L. Mankiewicz. **CAST:** Humphrey Bogart, Ava Gardner, Edmond O'Brien, Marius Goring, Rossano Brazzi. **1954 DVD**

BAREFOOT IN THE PARK ★★★★1/2 A young Robert Redford and Jane Fonda team up as newlyweds in this adaptation of Neil Simon's Broadway play. The comedy focuses on the adjustments of married life. Mildred Natwick plays the mother-in-law, and Charles Boyer is a daffy, unconventional neighbor. 105m. **DIR:** Gene Saks. **CAST:** Robert Redford, Jane Fonda, Charles Boyer, Mildred Natwick, Herb Edelman. **1967 DVD**

BARFLY ★★★★ Superb performances by Mickey Rourke and Faye Dunaway, as well as a dynamite jazz and R&B score, highlight this hip, flip, and often gruesomely funny semiautobiographical film written by Charles Bukowski. Rourke and Dunaway drink their way from one sodden, sleazy misadventure to another, and director Barbet Schroeder makes it all seem to truly take place on the street—or is that the gutter? Rated R for profanity, suggested sex, and violence. 97m. **DIR:** Barbet Schroeder. **CAST:** Mickey Rourke, Faye Dunaway, Alice Krige, J. C. Quinn, Frank Stallone. **1987**

BARITONE ★★★1/2 In 1933, a world-famous singer returns to Poland for the first time in twenty-five years. The infighting and scheming among his entourage, as well as the local officials, are meant as a parable of fascism, though this well-produced film is more enjoyable as a straightforward soap opera. In Polish with English subtitles. Not rated. 100m. **DIR:** Janusz Zaorski. **CAST:** Zbigniew Zapasiewicz. **1985**

BARJO ★★★ An oddball writer who obsessively catalogs everyday activities moves in with his sister and her husband and drives their emotional difficulties to the breaking point. Barjo's humorous investigations aren't well integrated with the black comedy of an impossible marriage between a man who wants order and a woman who wants "everything and its opposite," but both are amusing. In French with English subtitles. Rated R for sexual implications and discussions. 83m. **DIR:** Jerome Boivan. **CAST:** Hippolyte Girardot, Richard Bohringer, Anne Brochet. **1993**

BARKLEYS OF BROADWAY, THE ★★★ As a film team, Ginger Rogers and Fred Astaire parted in 1939. This final pairing, the result of Judy Garland's inability to make the picture, does not favorably compare with earlier efforts. Harry Warren's score, while augmented by a great George Gershwin number, is not up to snuff. Nevertheless, the film was a critical and commercial hit. 109m. **DIR:** Charles Walters. **CAST:** Fred Astaire, Ginger Rogers, Oscar Levant. **1949**

BARN BURNING ★★★★ A sterling adaptation of William Faulkner's short story. Oscar-winning scripter Horton Foote is responsible for this teleplay. Tommy Lee Jones is grand in a role that oozes menace. Introduced by Henry Fonda; unrated and suitable for family viewing. 40m. **DIR:** Peter Werner. **CAST:** Tommy Lee Jones, Diane Kagan, Shawn Whittington. **1980**

BARNABY AND ME ★★★ Sid Caesar's considerable comic talents aren't exactly strained in this Australian feature. Still, this lightweight story of a con man who mends his ways when he meets a young girl and her pet koala is good family viewing—a few laughs, and who can resist a koala bear? Rated G. 90m. **DIR:** Norman Panama. **CAST:** Sid Caesar, Juliet Mills. **1977**

BARNEY'S GREAT ADVENTURE ★★★ Public TV's pudgy purple dinosaur helps three children discover the joys and importance of nurturing their imagination. The wishes of Abby and her friend Marcella turn a small stuffed-toy Barney into a six-foot mentor and playmate during a visit to the farm of Abby's grandparents. Older brother Cody is skeptical of Barney's existence but then joins the fantasy. This musical romp is a rarity: an adventure for kids without bad guys. Rated G. 75m. **DIR:** Steve Gomer. **CAST:** Trevor Morgan, Kyla Pratt, Diana Rice, George Hearn, Shirley Douglas. **1998 DVD**

BARNUM (1986) ★★★ Made-for-television adaptation of Cy Coleman–Michael Stewart Broadway hit. Michael Crawford as flamboyant promoter Phineas T. Barnum is mesmerizing, tracing Barnum's life, from his humble beginnings to creating the Barnum and Bailey Circus. 113m. **DIR:** Terry Hughes. **CAST:** Michael Crawford. **1986 DVD**

BARNUM (1987) ★★★ Above-average TV film looks at the greatest showman on Earth, P. T. Barnum, played to the hilt by Burt Lancaster. Nice atmosphere and sets lend to the overall effect, but this is Lancaster's show all the way. 94m. **DIR:** Lee Philips. **CAST:** Burt Lancaster, Hanna Schygulla. **1987**

BARON MÜNCHHAUSEN (1943) ★★★ This lavish epic was intended to be a cinematic jewel in the crown of Hitler's Third Reich, a big-budget masterpiece designed to prove that Germany could compete with Hollywood. While the outlandish adventures of Baron Hieronymus Münchhausen are at times amusing and quite clever, the incredible visual spectacle—huge and chaotic sets, overly ornate costumes—often overwhelms the story. Very brief nudity; otherwise suitable for family viewing. 110m. **DIR:** Josef von Baky. **CAST:** Hans Albers, Brigitte Horney, Leo Slezak. **1943**

BARON MUNCHAUSEN (1961) ★★★ The adventures of the German folk hero, noted for the tallest tales ever told, are recounted here in a blend of live-action and inventive animation. Unfortunately, the story itself is rather boring, so kids are likely to get antsy. Also known as *The Fabulous Baron Munchausen.* In German with English subtitles. 110m. **DIR:** Karel Zeman. **CAST:** Milos Kopecky, Hana Brejchova. **1961**

BARON OF ARIZONA, THE ★★1/2 Vincent Price hams it up as a smooth con man who nearly succeeds in claiming most of the Arizona Territory as his own. This early directorial effort by Samuel Fuller lacks the edge he gave his best films, but it's well played by a good cast. Based on a real incident. B&W; 90m. **DIR:** Samuel Fuller. **CAST:** Vincent Price, Ellen Drew, Beulah Bondi, Vladimir Sokoloff, Reed Hadley, Robert Barrat. **1950**

BARRETTS OF WIMPOLE STREET, THE ★★★ Stagy but well-acted version of the romance between Robert Browning and Elizabeth Barrett under the watchful, jealous eye of her domineering father. First-rate cast triumphs over a slightly dated script. B&W; 110m. **DIR:** Sidney Franklin. **CAST:** Norma Shearer, Fredric March, Charles Laughton, Maureen O'Sullivan. **1934**

BARRY LYNDON ★★★ Although exquisitely photographed and meticulously designed, this three-hour motion picture adaptation of William Makepeace Thackeray's novel about an eighteenth-century rogue is a flawed masterpiece at best and is far too drawn out. However, it is worth watching for the lush cinematography by John Alcott. Rated PG for brief nudity and violence. 183m. **DIR:** Stanley Kubrick. **CAST:** Ryan O'Neal, Marisa Berenson, Patrick Magee, Hardy Kruger, Steven Berkoff, Gay Hamilton. **1975 DVD**

BARRY MCKENZIE HOLDS HIS OWN ★★1/2 Extremely vulgar comedy based on a popular Australian comic strip about the adventures of beer-swilling Aussie Barry Crocker trying to rescue his auntie (Barry Humphries in drag as "Dame Edna Everage") from vampire Count Plasma (Donald Pleasence). You'll either be appalled or laugh yourself sick, though the impenetrable slang may make you wish the movie was subtitled. Not rated. 93m. **DIR:** Bruce Beresford. **CAST:** Barry Crocker, Barry Humphries, Donald Pleasence. **1974**

BARTLEBY ★★★1/2 Herman Melville's tale of a man who "would prefer not to" seems especially timely now. Paul Scofield is the unfortunate boss who, stuck with the inert Bartleby, is forced to fire him. Superior acting makes this thought-provoking tale both moving and believable. 79m. **DIR:** Anthony Friedman. **CAST:** Paul Scofield, John McEnery. **1970**

BARTON FINK ★★★★ More inspired madness from the Coen Brothers, Joel and Ethan. John Turturro stars as a New York playwright whose success on the stage, with a play celebrating the common man, leads to a lucrative screenwriting assignment. Funny but surreal. Rated R for profanity. 112m. **DIR:** Joel Coen. **CAST:** John Turturro, John Goodman, John Mahoney, Judy Davis, Jon Polito, Michael Lerner, Tony Shalhoub. **1991**

BASE, THE ★★ There's some action in this old war horse about an undercover military operative trying to get the goods on some bad soldiers dealing in drugs. The plot is all over the place, yet things move swiftly enough to keep logic at bay most of the time. Rated R for language, nudity, and violence. 110m. **DIR:** Mark L. Lester. **CAST:** Mark Dacascos, Tim Abell, Paula Trickey, Noah Blake. **1999 DVD**

BASEBALL: A FILM BY KEN BURNS ★★★★★ The national pastime's rich and varied history, good and bad, white and black, is explored from the 1840s to the present with respect, affection, and wit. Written by Geoffrey C. Ward and Ken Burns. Narrated by John Chancellor. B&W/color. 1110m. **DIR:** Ken Burns. **1994 DVD**

BASED ON AN UNTRUE STORY ★★ This made-for-TV movie—about a perfume maker who must find her long-lost siblings in order to save her damaged olfactory nerves—is short on laughs and long on tedium. The only funny bits involve a child trapped in a trash Dumpster in Beverly Hills, but that has nothing to do with the rest of the film. Not rated; contains suggested sex. 91m. **DIR:** Jim Drake. **CAST:** Morgan Fairchild, Dan Hedaya, Victoria Jackson, Harvey Korman, Robert Goulet, David Byron, Ricki Lake, Dyan Cannon. **1993**

BASEKETBALL 🦃 In their big-screen debut, Trey Parker and Matt Stone (creators of the animated hit *South Park*) play two dimwits who become overnight sports stars when they invent a game combining baseball and basketball. The game is dull and pointless, and so is the film. Rated R for profanity and mild nudity. 98m. **DIR:** David Zucker. **CAST:** Trey Parker, Matt Stone, Yasmine Bleeth, Jenny McCarthy, Robert Vaughn, Ernest Borgnine. **1998 DVD**

BASIC INSTINCT ★★ Cop Michael Douglas finds himself seduced (repeatedly) by bisexual heiress Sharon Stone, even though she's suspected of having committed a brutal ice-pick murder. Director Paul Verhoeven takes sex and violence to extremes, perhaps in an effort to cover up the TV-movie-of-the-week weakness of Joe Eszterhas's sleazy screenplay. Rated R for nudity, simulated sex, violence, and profanity. 130m. **DIR:** Paul Verhoeven. **CAST:** Michael Douglas, Sharon Stone, George Dzundza, Jeanne Tripplehorn, Stephen Tobolowsky. **1992 DVD**

BASIL ★★★ Handsome period production design and a high-rent cast add little to this tale based on the classic novel by Wilkie Collins. Jared Leto is the wide-eyed innocent Basil, whose strict father is grooming him to take over the family estate. Basil goes against his father's wishes and his naïveté gets the best of him when he learns too late that his new bride is in cahoots with his best friend to bring him down. Claire Forlani shines as the love of Basil's heart. Rated R for violence and adult situations. 95m. **DIR:** Radha Bharadwaj. **CAST:** Jared Leto, Christian Slater, Claire Forlani, Derek Jacobi. **1997**

BASILEUS QUARTET ★★★★★ When their leader dies, the remaining members of a renowned string quartet hire a young violinist to replace him. The presence of this aggressive, virile young man forces the three older men to confront what they have made of their own lives. An intelligent, literary film, flawlessly acted. Dubbed in English. Not rated, contains nudity and sexual situations. 105m. **DIR:** Fabio Carpi. **CAST:** Hector Alterio, Omero Antonutti, Pierre Malet, François Simon. **1982**

BASKET, THE ★★1/2 During World War I, a new schoolmaster arrives in a small Washington town at the same time as two German war orphans. Together they teach the local yokels something about basketball, opera, and tolerance—in roughly that order. Earnest and well-meaning, the film suffers from a farfetched script and amateurish performances. Rated PG. 104m. **DIR:** Rich Cowan. **CAST:** Peter Coyote, Karen Allen, Robert Karl Burke, Amber Willenborg, Ellen Travolta, Joey Travolta. **2000 DVD**

BASKET CASE ★★★ Comedy and horror are mixed beautifully in this weird tale of a young man and his deformed Siamese twin out for revenge against the doctors who separated them. Gruesomely entertaining and highly recommended for shock buffs. Rated R. 91m. **DIR:** Frank Henenlotter. **CAST:** Kevin Van Hentenryck, Terri Susan Smith. **1982 DVD**

BASKET CASE 2 🦃 Shameless sequel. Rated R for violence and nudity. 90m. **DIR:** Frank Henenlotter. **CAST:** Kevin Van Hentenryck, Heather Rattray. **1990**

BASKET CASE 3: THE PROGENY ★★★ Bad is a relative term. And with this second sequel featuring the "Times Square Freak Twins" Duane and Belial Bradley, bad means good—in a sickening sort of way. The brothers head south for the delivery of Belial's mutant offspring. Along for the ride is the weirdest bunch of creatures this side of the Cantina scene in *Star Wars*. Rated R for violence, profanity, gore, and simulated mutant sex. 90m. **DIR:** Frank Henenlotter. **CAST:** Annie Ross, Kevin Van Hentenryck. **1992**

BASKETBALL DIARIES, THE ★★★ This bio-pic unveils the gritty early life of poet and author Jim Carroll, a Catholic-school basketball player who quickly descends into the nightmarish world of drug addiction. Pay attention to Mark (Marky Mark) Wahlberg, whose down-and-dirty performance is all street-smart bravura. Rated R for profanity, violence, nudity, and drug use. 102m. **DIR:** Scott Kalvert. **CAST:** Leonardo DiCaprio, Lorraine Bracco, Bruno Kirby, Ernie Hudson, Patrick McGaw, James Madio. **1995 DVD**

BASQUIAT ★★★ Artist Julian Schnabel turns filmmaker with this adoring biography of Jean-Michel Basquiat, the meteoric 1980s art sensation who died of a heroin overdose at twenty-seven. Interesting and well-acted, but those unfamiliar with Basquiat's art will get little idea of it. Rated R for profanity and simulated sex. 108m. **DIR:** Julian Schnabel. **CAST:** Jeffrey Wright, Michael Wincott, Benicio Del Toro, David Bowie, Gary Oldman, Dennis Hopper. **1996**

BASTARD, THE ★★★ TV miniseries ably adapts part one of John Jakes's American Revolution saga. Numerous well-known stars pop in for cameo appearances, while Andrew Stevens takes the lead as the illegitimate son of a British nobleman. His hopes of sharing the man's wealth dashed, he heads for America. 189m. **DIR:** Lee H. Katzin. **CAST:** Andrew Stevens, Tom Bosley, Kim Cattrall, Patricia Neal, Olivia Hussey. **1978**

BASTARD OUT OF CAROLINA ★★★★ Dorothy Allison's harrowing novel becomes an equally gut-churning study of the casual cruelties tolerated by people in dead-end lives. Poor but proud Jennifer Jason Leigh tries to improve things for herself and her two daughters, but unwisely marries white-trash Ron Eldard, whose hair-trigger temper is matched by an unhealthy attraction to elder daughter Jena Malone. A difficult subject, well told. Rated R for child abuse, rape, profanity, and violence. 98m. **DIR:** Anjelica Huston. **CAST:** Jennifer Jason Leigh, Ron Eldard, Jena Malone, Diana Scarwid, Michael Rooker, Glenne Headly, Lyle Lovett, Dermot Mulroney, Christina Ricci. **1996 DVD**

BAT, THE ★★ A mystery writer and her housemates in a creepy old mansion fall under the ominous shadow of a murderer known as "The Bat." Third filming of this creaky old play was only a moderately successful attempt to cash in on William Castle's box-office bonanzas with Vincent Price. Originally published in 1915, the 1930 film version is cited as one of Bob Kane's inspirations for *Batman*. 88m. **DIR:** Crane Wilbur. **CAST:** Agnes Moorehead, Vincent Price, Gavin Gordon, John Sutton, Darla Hood, Lenita Lane. **1959 DVD**

BAT PEOPLE 🦃 A young biologist on his honeymoon is bitten by a bat and is slowly transformed into a flying, blood-hungry rodent. Originally titled *It Lives by Night*. It sucks under any name. Rated R. 95m. **DIR:** Jerry Jameson. **CAST:** Stewart Moss, Marianne McAndrew, Michael Pataki. **1974**

BAT 21 ★★★★ In a typically effective performance, Gene Hackman is a military mastermind who is shot down during a reconnaissance mission in Vietnam, where he is trapped behind enemy lines. It's up to pilot Danny Glover to keep Hackman safe and sane until he can be rescued. Fine telling of a heroic, true-life story guarantees to keep you on the edge of your seat. Rated R for violence and profanity. 105m. **DIR:** Peter Markle. **CAST:** Gene Hackman, Danny Glover, Jerry Reed, David Marshall Grant. **1988 DVD**

BAT WHISPERS, THE ★★1/2 Mary Roberts Rinehart's venerable stage success featuring a caped killer, clutching hands, a spooky mansion, and plenty of scared females. Chester Morris made his screen debut in this slow-moving but stylish creaker about the mysterious "Bat" who informs his victims of the hour of their death and never fails to deliver. B&W; 82m. **DIR:** Roland West. **CAST:** Spencer Charters, Una Merkel, Chester Morris. **1931 DVD**

BATAAN ★★★★1/2 One of the best films about World War II chronicles the exploits of an army patrol attempting to stall the Japanese onslaught in the Philippines. B&W; 114m. **DIR:** Tay Garnett. **CAST:** Robert Taylor, George Murphy, Thomas Mitchell, Lloyd Nolan, Robert Walker, Desi Arnaz Sr., Barry Nelson. **1943 DVD**

BATHING BEAUTY ★★1/2 One of MGM's best-remembered musicals emerges dripping wet from the mists of time as a series of waterlogged vignettes flaunt new discovery Esther Williams. She plays a college girl who's crazy about songwriter Red Skelton, and jumps into a swimsuit as frequently as he dresses in drag in order to further the intrigue. 101m. **DIR:** George Sidney. **CAST:**

Esther Williams, Red Skelton, Basil Rathbone, Margaret Dumont, Bill Goodwin, Jean Porter, Nana Bryant, Donald Meek, Harry James. **1944**

BATMAN (1966) ★★★ Holy success story! The caped crusader and his youthful sidekick jump from their popular mid-1960s television series into a full-length feature film. Adam West and Burt Ward keep quip in cheek as they battle the Fearsome Foursome: the Riddler (Frank Gorshin), the Penguin (Burgess Meredith), Catwoman (Lee Meriwether), and the Joker (Cesar Romero). A lot of fun. 105m. **DIR:** Leslie Martinson. **CAST:** Adam West, Burt Ward, Frank Gorshin, Burgess Meredith, Lee Meriwether, Cesar Romero. **1966 DVD**

BATMAN (1989) ★★★1/2 So much of *Batman* is awe-inspiring that one is disappointed when this ambitious production all but collapses under its own weight in the last half hour. Still, there's much to enjoy in Jack Nicholson's bizarre, over-the-top performance as the villainous Joker, Michael Keaton's underplayed but effective dual role as millionaire-playboy Bruce Wayne and Batman, and the spectacular, *Blade Runner*–like sets. Rated PG-13 for profanity and violence. 130m. **DIR:** Tim Burton. **CAST:** Jack Nicholson, Michael Keaton, Kim Basinger, Pat Hingle, Billy Dee Williams, Jack Palance, Robert Wuhl, Michael Gough. **1989 DVD**

BATMAN & ROBIN ★★★ In this fourth outing, Batman and Robin deal with rivalry in the realms of superhero status and female companionship, the probable death of Alfred the butler, and the possibility that Mr. Freeze might turn Gotham City into a giant, flavorless frozen treat. The determined effort to make this entry less dark than the previous films for the most part succeeds, thanks to George Clooney's attitude as Batman, and Uma Thurman's sexually charged portrayal of Poison Ivy. But Alicia Silverstone seems lost as Batgirl, and there are too many scene-ending tag lines that fall flat. Yet each installment in this series visually reinvents itself and enriches the characters. Rated PG-13 for cartoonish violence. 126m. **DIR:** Joel Schumacher. **CAST:** Arnold Schwarzenegger, George Clooney, Chris O'Donnell, Uma Thurman, Alicia Silverstone, Michael Gough, Pat Hingle. **1997 DVD**

BATMAN AND ROBIN (ADVENTURES OF BATMAN AND ROBIN) ★★1/2 The Caped Crusader and Boy Wonder swoop onto celluloid for the second time as they answer Police Commissioner Gordon's plea for help and run up against "The Wizard." Not really a great serial, but fun—and it avoids the unfortunate racism that makes the 1943 serial unpleasant. B&W; 15 chapters. **DIR:** Spencer Gordon Bennet. **CAST:** Robert Lowery, John Duncan, Lyle Talbot, Jane Adams, Ralph Graves, Don Harvey, Michael Whalen. **1949**

BATMAN FOREVER ★★★1/2 A new director and a new star result in a livelier, brighter, less-brooding entry in the series. Supervillains Two-Face and the Riddler team up to unleash a reign of terror over Gotham City. Batman teams up with new sidekick, Robin, to stop them. Worth seeing for the striking visuals and playful tone, but it won't knock your socks off. Rated PG-13 for comic-book violence. 120m. **DIR:** Joel Schumacher. **CAST:** Val Kilmer, Tommy Lee Jones, Jim Carrey, Nicole Kidman, Chris O'Donnell. **1995 DVD**

BATMAN: MASK OF THE PHANTASM ★★★1/2 The caped crusader's slick animated series made an engaging feature-length debut with all of its *film noir* sensibilities intact. Definitely too story heavy for youngsters, this moody thriller—based strongly on Frank Miller's Dark Knight comics—finds Batman forced to defend a reputation tarnished by both the Joker (wonderfully voiced by Mark Hamill) and the title villain. Rated PG. 76m. **DIR:** Eric Radomski, Bruce W. Timm. **1993 DVD**

BATMAN RETURNS ★★★1/2 Director Tim Burton turns Danny DeVito into a villainous Penguin guaranteed to produce nightmares; Michelle Pfeiffer is a seductively sensational Catwoman. Set designer Bo Welch creates a gloomy, "Machine-Age Teutonic" Gotham City. Although bound to please fans, this sequel is marred by a goofy, fright-wigged Christopher Walken—and too few appearances by its star. Rated PG-13 for violence. 130m. **DIR:** Tim Burton. **CAST:** Michael Keaton, Danny DeVito, Michelle Pfeiffer, Christopher Walken, Pat Hingle, Michael Gough. **1992 DVD**

BATON ROUGE ★★★1/2 A gigolo and a psychiatrist team up to murder a rich man and blame his neurotic wife for the crime. One of a number of Spanish films that were released in the United States to cash in on the success of Antonio Banderas, this is one of the best, a sexy thriller filled with double and triple crosses and featuring an all-star Spanish cast. Not rated; contains adult situations. In Spanish with English subtitles. 105m. **DIR:** Rafael Moleon. **CAST:** Antonio Banderas, Victoria Abril, Carmen Maura. **1988**

BATS 🦃 Throwback to the swarm films, this barely watchable, low-budget flick is a time waster for both Lou Diamond Phillips and potential viewers. Phillips plays a small-town Texas sheriff investigating murders in which the "perps" are mutant bats. Strictly second-rate. Rated PG-13 for profanity and gore. 91m. **DIR:** Louis Morneau. **CAST:** Lou Diamond Phillips, Dina Meyer. **1999 DVD**

BATTERED ★★1/2 This TV docudrama will have you believing there are wife beaters lurking around every corner. The script is somewhat stiff and uninventive at times, but does offer a fairly accurate picture of the few alternatives open to the women in this desperate situation. 95m. **DIR:** Peter Werner. **CAST:** Mike Farrell, LeVar Burton, Karen Grassle, Joan Blondell, Howard Duff, Diana Scarwid. **1978**

BATTERIES NOT INCLUDED ★★★ Pleasant fantasy feature about tenement dwellers who are terrorized by thugs hired by a land developer. All seems lost until a group of tiny aliens comes to their aid. Often the movie is simply too derivative and predictable. That said, the younger set will love it. Rated PG. 106m. **DIR:** Matthew Robbins. **CAST:** Hume Cronyn, Jessica Tandy, Frank McRae, Elizabeth Peña. **1987 DVD**

BATTLE ANGEL ★★★★ A young cybernetic girl becomes a successful bounty hunter in this animated tale. Outstanding artwork and bizarre characters give life to this cyberpunk adaptation of Kishiro Yukito's wildly successful comic. In Japanese with English subtitles. Not rated; contains nudity and violence. 70m. **DIR:** Hiroshi Fukutomi. **1993 DVD**

BATTLE BENEATH THE EARTH ★★1/2 Stalwart Kerwin Mathews leads the fight against the Chinese hordes who intend to invade the United States via underground tunnels. Pretty good adventure-fantasy in the comic-book/pulp magazine tradition. 91m. **DIR:** Montgomery

Tully. **CAST:** Kerwin Mathews, Robert Ayres, Martin Benson, Viviane Ventura, Bessie Love. **1967**

BATTLE BEYOND THE STARS ★★★★ Here's something different: a space fantasy-comedy. Richard Thomas stars in this funny and often exciting movie as an emissary from a peaceful planet desperately searching for champions to save it from an evil warlord. It's *Star Wars* meets *The Magnificent Seven*, with fine tongue-in-cheek performances. Rated PG. 104m. **DIR:** Jimmy T. Murakami. **CAST:** Richard Thomas, John Saxon, Robert Vaughn, George Peppard. **1980 DVD**

BATTLE CIRCUS ★★ Humphrey Bogart and June Allyson are mismatched in this nonaction war picture. It's a soap opera about a military doctor arguing with and finally falling for a nurse on the Korean battlefield. Soggy. B&W; 90m. **DIR:** Richard Brooks. **CAST:** Humphrey Bogart, June Allyson, Keenan Wynn, Robert Keith, Steve Forrest, Philip Ahn, William Campbell. **1953**

BATTLE CRY ★★★ A platoon of Marines is followed into battle during World War II. The conflicts they face on the islands of the Pacific are contrasted to the emotional conflicts faced by their girlfriends at home. All in all, it is a successful piece of wartime fluff. 149m. **DIR:** Raoul Walsh. **CAST:** Van Heflin, Tab Hunter, Dorothy Malone, Anne Francis. **1955**

BATTLE FOR THE PLANET OF THE APES ★★ Events come full circle in this final *Apes* film, with simian Roddy McDowall attempting peaceful coexistence with conquered humanity. Naturally, not everybody plays along with such a plan, and an impending nuclear threat adds little tension to a story whose outcome is known. Rated G. 92m. **DIR:** J. Lee Thompson. **CAST:** Roddy McDowall, Severn Darden, John Huston, Claude Akins, Paul Williams. **1973**

BATTLE FORCE ★★ The effect of war on the lives of two families, one American, the other German. Passable World War II adventure. 92m. **DIR:** Humphrey Longon. **CAST:** Henry Fonda, John Huston, Stacy Keach, Helmut Berger, Samantha Eggar. **1976**

BATTLE HELL ★★ More British stiff upper lip in this tale of the H.M.S. *Amethyst* battling the communist Chinese on the Yangtze River. Pretty standard war flick, overly long, but with some good battle footage. Not rated: some violence. 112m. **DIR:** Michael Anderson. **CAST:** Richard Todd, Akim Tamiroff, Keye Luke, William Hartnell, Donald Houston, Robert Urquhart, James Kenney. **1956**

BATTLE HYMN ★★★ Fact-based story of a World War II pilot who went on to become a minister and to found an orphan's home in Korea. The script asks a bit more of star Rock Hudson than he's able to give; all in all, a decent if slightly hokey Hollywood drama. 108m. **DIR:** Douglas Sirk. **CAST:** Rock Hudson, Anna Kashfi, Dan Duryea, Don DeFore, Martha Hyer, Jock Mahoney, Alan Hale Jr. **1957**

BATTLE OF ALGIERS ★★★★ This gut-wrenching Italian-Algerian pseudo-documentary about the war between Algerian citizens and their French "protectors" was released when America's involvement in Vietnam was still to reach its peak, but the parallels between the two stories are obvious. Covering the years from 1954 to 1962, this film is an emotional experience—it is not recommended for the casual viewer and is too strong for children. B&W; 123m. **DIR:** Gillo Pontecorvo. **CAST:** Yacef Saadi, Jean Martin, Brahim Haggiag. **1965**

BATTLE OF AUSTERLITZ, THE This attempt to re-create the epic battle of the Napoleonic wars is slow, dull, abysmally dubbed, and generally uninspired. 123m. **DIR:** Abel Gance. **CAST:** Claudia Cardinale, Leslie Caron, Vittorio De Sica, Orson Welles. **1960**

BATTLE OF BRITAIN ★★1/2 It's a shame that a film that has a $12 million budget, a cast of characters straight from the British Who's Who of film and stage, great aerial photography, and a subject matter that deals with a vital period of British history could not have been better than this semi-epic. 132m. **DIR:** Guy Hamilton. **CAST:** Michael Caine, Ralph Richardson, Robert Shaw, Trevor Howard, Susannah York, Curt Jurgens, Edward Fox, Kenneth More, Christopher Plummer, Laurence Olivier, Harry Andrews, Nigel Patrick. **1969**

BATTLE OF EL ALAMEIN, THE ★★★ A re-creation of the famous twelve-day 1942 turning point clash between the artillery, tanks, and infantry of the British Eighth Army under General Montgomery and the German army's fabled Afrika Korps commanded by Field Marshal Rommel in the windswept Libyan Desert southwest of Alexandria. We know the outcome, but getting there makes for exciting watching. Rated PG. 96m. **DIR:** Calvin Jackson Padget. **CAST:** Michael Rennie, Robert Hossein, Frederick Stafford, Ettore Manni, George Hilton. **1968**

BATTLE OF THE BULGE ★★ This is a fairly decent war film. It has solid acting and exciting battle sequences but suffers on video for two reasons: the small screen hurts the epic scale and 23 minutes are cut from the original print, with some important footage missing. 140m. **DIR:** Ken Annakin. **CAST:** Henry Fonda, Robert Shaw, Robert Ryan, Dana Andrews, Charles Bronson, Telly Savalas. **1965**

BATTLE OF THE COMMANDOS Lots of phony battle scenes, bad acting, and a poor script all add up to a big bomb. 94m. **DIR:** Umberto Lenzi. **CAST:** Jack Palance, Curt Jurgens, Thomas Hunter, Diana Largo, Wolfgang Preiss. **1969**

BATTLE OF THE SEXES, THE ★★★1/2 Peter Sellers is wonderful as an elderly Scottish Highlander bent on murder. Robert Morley, always a favorite, is simply delightful and helps keep this British comedy on a fast and funny track. B&W; 88m. **DIR:** Charles Crichton. **CAST:** Peter Sellers, Robert Morley, Constance Cummings, Jameson Clark. **1960 DVD**

BATTLE SHOCK ★★ Ralph Meeker portrays an artist who becomes involved in a murder while working in Mexico. Janice Rule is his doting wife. An uneven suspenser also known under the title of *A Woman's Devotion*. 88m. **DIR:** Paul Henreid. **CAST:** Ralph Meeker, Janice Rule, Rosenda Monteros, Paul Henreid. **1956**

BATTLEFIELD EARTH This atrocious adaptation of L. Ron Hubbard's equally vapid book was a vanity project for star-producer John Travolta, who wanted to "honor" the Scientology founder. No chance of that; this unintentionally hilarious melee between conquering extraterrestrials and their enslaved human captives, set in the year 3000, is absolute swill. Rated PG-13 for violence. 117m. **DIR:** Roger Christian. **CAST:** John Travolta, Barry Pepper, Forest Whitaker, Kim Coates,

Sabine Karsenti, Michael Byrne, Richard Tyson. **2000 DVD**

BATTLEGROUND ★★★1/2 Made over the protests of MGM czar Louis B. Mayer, this rugged look at World War II's famous Battle of the Bulge was a resounding hit. Everything looks and sounds real. Oscars went to script and photography. B&W; 118m. **DIR:** William Wellman. **CAST:** Van Johnson, John Hodiak, Denise Darcel, Ricardo Montalban, George Murphy, James Whitmore. **1949**

BATTLESHIP POTEMKIN, THE ★★★★★ One of a handful of landmark motion pictures. This silent classic, directed by the legendary Sergei Eisenstein, depicts the mutiny of the crew of a Russian battleship and its aftermath. The directorial technique expanded the threshold of what was then standard cinema storytelling. The massacre of civilians on the Odessa Steps remains one of the most powerful scenes in film history. Silent. B&W; 65m. **DIR:** Sergei Eisenstein. **CAST:** Alexander Antonov, Vladimir Barsky. **1925 DVD**

BATTLESTAR GALACTICA 🦃 Adapted from the television series, this is a seventh-rate *Star Wars*. Rated PG. 125m. **DIR:** Richard A. Colla. **CAST:** Lorne Greene, Richard Hatch, Dirk Benedict, Lew Ayres, Jane Seymour. **1978 DVD**

BATTLING ORIOLES, THE ★★ Baseball player's son rejuvenates his father's team and rescues his sweetheart from a fate worse than death. Of interest mainly for its re-creation of a nineteenth-century baseball game and an unbilled performance by four *Our Gang* members in a charming segment. B&W; 56m. **DIR:** Ted Wilde, Fred L. Guiol. **CAST:** Glenn Tryon, Blanche Mehaffey, John T. Prince, Noah Young. **1924**

BAWDY ADVENTURES OF TOM JONES, THE 🦃 This ridiculous romp features Trevor Howard as the lecherous Squire Western. Young Tom Jones (played by an innocent-looking Nick Henson) is in love with Western's daughter and spends the entire film hoping to win her hand. Rated R for nudity. 89m. **DIR:** Cliff Owen. **CAST:** Nicky Henson, Trevor Howard, Joan Collins, Arthur Lowe, Georgia Brown, Madeleine Smith, Jeremy Lloyd. **1976**

BAXTER (1973) ★★1/2 Troubled schoolboy Scott Jacoby is treated by speech therapist Patricia Neal in this earnest British drama. Well-done for its type. Rated PG. 100m. **DIR:** Lionel Jeffries. **CAST:** Patricia Neal, Scott Jacoby, Jean-Pierre Cassel, Lynn Carlin, Britt Ekland. **1973**

BAXTER (1988) ★★★★ In spite of the cute bull terrier on the box cover, Baxter the dog is anything but cuddly. Listening in on his thoughts as he reacts to the humans around him, we discover a creature of simple but rigid moral standards. And when he meets a young boy who worships Hitler, we learn a chilling lesson in human nature as well. In French with English subtitles. Not rated; contains adult themes and situations. 82m. **DIR:** Jerome Boivan. **CAST:** Lise Delamare, Jean Mercure, Jacques Spiesser. **1988**

BAY BOY, THE ★★★★1/2 The story of a brief period in an adolescent boy's life while growing up in a small mining town on the Nova Scotia coast during the mid-1930s. This film develops the character, including the sexual awakening, guilt, and terror, of Donald Campbell (Kiefer Sutherland). Liv Ullmann is well cast as Donald's mother. 104m. **DIR:** Daniel Petrie. **CAST:** Liv Ullmann, Kiefer Sutherland, Joe MacPherson. **1985**

BAYWATCH: THE MOVIE ★★ Fans of the popular syndicated television series will find this expanded episode to their liking. Unfortunately, Pamela Anderson disappears before the first act is over, leaving her small-screen costars to fill in the blanks. Plenty of sand, surf, and hot bodies as the characters head off to Hawaii for training and mystery. 90m. **DIR:** Douglas Schwartz. **CAST:** David Hasselhoff, Pamela Anderson, Alexandra Paul, David Charvet, Yasmine Bleeth. **1994**

BE YOURSELF ★★1/2 Singer loves simple-minded prizefighter but loses him temporarily to a flashy blonde. A flop when it came out, this likable movie captures '"funny lady"' Fanny Brice's personality and performance at their best and is her earliest surviving feature. B&W; 77m. **DIR:** Thornton Freeland. **CAST:** Fanny Brice, Robert Armstrong, Gertrude Astor, Harry Green. **1930**

BEACH, THE ★★ This obviously wishes to be an adult-oriented blend of *Lord of the Flies* and *The Blue Lagoon*, but the metaphor about the ephemeral nature of paradise quickly turns silly and downright stupid. Characters in possession of a "great treasure" abandon all sense of humanity and basic decency, become paranoid to a degree that is unintentionally hilarious, and literally lose their minds. Matters are not helped by having to identify with the spoiled, petulant, arrogant WASP bratpacker played with no conviction whatsoever by Leonardo DiCaprio. This is lazy filmmaking: incoherent directing, irrational scripting, and ineffectual acting, particularly by the leading man. Rated R for profanity, drug use, nudity, and violence. 119m. **DIR:** Danny Boyle. **CAST:** Leonardo DiCaprio, Tilda Swinton, Virginie Ledoyen, Guillaume Canet, Robert Carlyle. **2000 DVD**

BEACH BABES FROM BEYOND 🦃 The title says it all. Not worth watching even to see celebrity relatives embarrass their families. Rated R for profanity and nudity. 78m. **DIR:** Ellen Cabot. **CAST:** Joe Estevez, Don Swayze, Joey Travolta, Burt Ward, Jacqueline Stallone, Linnea Quigley, Sarah Bellomo, Tamara Landry, Nicole Posey. **1993**

BEACH BABES 2: CAVE GIRL ISLAND ★★ The sequel to the bimbofest of 1993, *Beach Babes from Beyond*, is slightly better but not too much. Only Sarah Bellomo reprises her role from the original with new actresses stepping into the roles, and out of the clothes, of the other two leads. Filmed in 1995, but not released until three years later. Rated R for nudity and simulated sex. 82m. **DIR:** Ellen Cabot. **CAST:** Sarah Bellomo, Tina Holliman, Stephanie Hudson, Lenny Rose. **1998**

BEACH BLANKET BINGO ★★1/2 The fifth in the series, and the last true "Beach Party" film. Basically, it's the same old stuff: stars on their way up (Linda Evans) or on their way down (Buster Keaton) or at their peak (Frankie and Annette), spouting silly dialogue and singing through echo chambers. But it's one of the best of the series, whether you're laughing with it or at it. 98m. **DIR:** William Asher. **CAST:** Frankie Avalon, Annette Funicello, Paul Lynde, Harvey Lembeck, Don Rickles, Linda Evans, Jody McCrea, Marta Kristen, John Ashley, Deborah Walley, Buster Keaton. **1965 DVD**

BEACH GIRLS, THE 🦃 Teenage girls throw a big party at their uncle's Malibu beach house. Rated R for nudity.

91m. **DIR:** Pat Townsend. **CAST:** Debra Blee, Val Kline, Jeana Tomasina. **1982 DVD**

BEACH PARTY ★★1/2 Bob Cummings, a bearded, sheltered anthropologist, studies the wild dating and mating habits of beach-bound teens. He ends up courting Annette Funicello to make Frankie Avalon jealous. Cummings has his moments, as does Harvey Lembeck, as the biker Eric Von Zipper. 101m. **DIR:** William Asher. **CAST:** Robert Cummings, Dorothy Malone, Frankie Avalon, Annette Funicello, Harvey Lembeck, Jody McCrea, John Ashley, Morey Amsterdam. **1963 DVD**

BEACHCOMBER, THE ★★★ This Somerset Maugham story of a dissolute South Seas beachcomber and the lady missionary who reforms him is sculptor's clay in the expert hands of Charles Laughton and Elsa Lanchester. He is delightful as the shiftless, conniving bum; she is clever and captivating as his Bible-toting nemesis. A scene at a bar is Laughton at his wily, eye-rolling, blustering best. B&W; 80m. **DIR:** Erich Pommer. **CAST:** Charles Laughton, Elsa Lanchester, Tyrone Guthrie, Robert Newton. **1938**

BEACHES ★★★★ Here's a terrific tearjerker that casts Bette Midler and Barbara Hershey as two unlikely friends who enjoy a thirty-year relationship that's full of ups and downs. Fans of five-handkerchief films will love it. Midler is often hilarious as the show-biz-crazy Jewish gal who both loves and competes with WASPish heiress Hershey. See it if only for the mind-boggling performance of look-alike Mayim Bialik as the 11-year-old Midler, but be prepared to suspend your disbelief. Rated PG-13 for profanity and suggested sex. 120m. **DIR:** Garry Marshall. **CAST:** Bette Midler, Barbara Hershey, John Heard, Spalding Gray. **1988**

BEAKS: THE MOVIE 🦃 Hitchcock made birds menacing. *Beaks* makes them at times unintentionally funny and at other times too gruesome to watch. 86m. **DIR:** René Cardona Jr. **CAST:** Christopher Atkins, Michelle Johnson. **1987**

BEAN ★★ The charm, manic inventiveness, and cruel hilarity of Rowan Atkinson's delightful *Mr. Bean* shorts are completely absent in this lumbering mess, which wastes the star's time and talent in a witless script (from Bean team scribes Richard Curtis and Robin Driscoll, who should know better) that sends the near-silent doofus to the United States as an "art expert" accompanying a rare painting. Rated PG-13 for vulgar gestures and blue humor. 90m. **DIR:** Mel Smith. **CAST:** Rowan Atkinson, Peter MacNicol, Pamela Reed, John Mills. **1997 DVD**

BEANSTALK ★★ There's just a bit too much "fe-fi-fo-fum" to director Michael Paul Davis's script as young J. D. Daniels tosses some seeds out the window and, surprise, up sprouts a beanstalk. This updating of the old "Jack and the Beanstalk" fairy tale is aimed at kids, but even they will groan at the bad humor and lousy makeup effects. Rated PG for mild violence. 80m. **DIR:** Michael Paul Davis. **CAST:** J. D. Daniels, Richard Moll, Margot Kidder, Patrick Renna, David Naughton, Stuart Pankin. **1994**

BEAR, THE ★★★★★ *The Bear* is a wildlife adventure film that transcends its genre. It's the *Gone with the Wind* of animal movies. Some scenes might be a little frightening for the younger set. Rated PG for violence. 93m. **DIR:** Jean-Jacques Annaud. **CAST:** Jack Wallace, Tcheky Karyo. **1989 DVD**

BEAR ISLAND 🦃 Pointlessly melodramatic tale mixing gold fever, murder, and other incidental intrigue. Rated PG for mild violence. 118m. **DIR:** Don Sharp. **CAST:** Donald Sutherland, Richard Widmark, Vanessa Redgrave, Christopher Lee, Lloyd Bridges. **1980**

BEAST, THE ★★★ This abbreviated version of the made-for-television miniseries actually works better. Much of the clutter has been trimmed, making for a tighter, more suspenseful tale of a tentacled killer preying on the inhabitants of a small coastal town. More underwater thrills from Peter Benchley, writer of *Jaws*. Rated PG-13 for violence. 116m. **DIR:** Jeff Bleckner. **CAST:** William L. Petersen, Karen Sillas, Charles Martin Smith, Missy Crider, Larry Drake. **1996**

BEAST, THE ★★ A clichéd war film, unique only for its adversaries: Soviet soldiers and Afghan rebels in the deserts of Afghanistan. Though the Afghans speak subtitled native language, the Soviets speak in slang-laced Americanized English. They sound more like California surfers than Russian soldiers. Rated R, with profanity and violence. 109m. **DIR:** Kevin Reynolds. **CAST:** Steven Bauer, George Dzundza. **1988 DVD**

BEAST FROM 20,000 FATHOMS, THE ★★★ An experimental atom bomb blast in the Arctic thaws a million year old giant rhedosaurus that seeks its home in the Atlantic depths off the New York coast. Based on Ray Bradbury's *Saturday Evening Post* story. B&W; 80m. **DIR:** Eugene Lourie. **CAST:** Paul Christian, Paula Raymond, Cecil Kellaway, Donald Woods, Kenneth Tobey, Lee Van Cleef. **1953**

BEAST IN THE CELLAR, THE ★★ Boring story about a pair of aging sisters (well played by veterans Beryl Reid and Flora Robson) with something to hide. Their deranged, deformed brother is down there, and he wants out! Weak. Rated R. 87m. **DIR:** James Kelly. **CAST:** Beryl Reid, Flora Robson, T. P. McKenna, John Hamill. **1971**

BEAST MUST DIE, THE ★★ A millionaire hunter invites a group of guests to an isolated mansion. One of them is a werewolf he intends to destroy. A tame, talky reworking of Agatha Christie's *Ten Little Indians*. Rated PG. 98m. **DIR:** Paul Annett. **CAST:** Calvin Lockhart, Peter Cushing, Charles Gray, Anton Diffring. **1974 DVD**

BEAST OF THE YELLOW NIGHT ★★ Having played the hero in several Filipino Blood Island, mad-scientist movies, John Ashley here takes on the mantle of the villain. This Jekyll-and-Hyde effort is as cheesy as his earlier tropical thrillers, but the sporadic mayhem may keep you amused. Rated R. 87m. **DIR:** Eddie Romero. **CAST:** John Ashley, Mary Wilcox, Eddie Garcia. **1970 DVD**

BEAST WITH FIVE FINGERS, THE ★★★ Some eerie moments with the severed hand of a deceased pianist running loose in a mansion, choking people left and right. Another high-camp, wide-eyed performance by Peter Lorre. Fine special effects. B&W; 89m. **DIR:** Robert Florey. **CAST:** Robert Alda, Peter Lorre, Andrea King, J. Carrol Naish. **1947**

BEAST WITHIN, THE 🦃 This unbelievably gory movie consists mainly of one grisly murder after another. Rated R. 90m. **DIR:** Philippe Mora. **CAST:** Ronny Cox, Bibi Besch, Paul Clemens, Don Gordon. **1982 DVD**

BEASTMASTER, THE ★★★1/2 A young medieval warrior (Marc Singer) who possesses the ability to communicate psychically with animals takes revenge—with the help of a slave (Tanya Roberts) and a master warrior (John Amos)—on the evil sorcerer (Rip Torn). It's fun for kids of all ages. Rated PG for violence and brief nudity. 118m. **DIR:** Don Coscarelli. **CAST:** Marc Singer, Tanya Roberts, Rip Torn, John Amos, Rod Loomis. **1982 DVD**

BEASTMASTER 2: THROUGH THE PORTAL OF TIME ★★★1/2 The Beastmaster (Marc Singer) travels through a hole in time to present-day Los Angeles in order to chase down his evil nemesis. More than just another stranger-in-a-strange-land tale, this film will please fans of the genre as well as those who just like a good laugh. Rated PG-13 for violence. 107m. **DIR:** Sylvio Tabet. **CAST:** Marc Singer, Wings Hauser, Kari Wuhrer, Sarah Douglas. **1991**

BEASTMASTER III: THE EYE OF BRAXUS ★★1/2 Lamely choreographed fight scenes weaken an already marginal film, but Marc Singer, as the Beastmaster, wins us over with his ease around the animals and his wry wit. This time he must save his brother from an evil lord who has ghastly ambitions. Decent special effects and above-par soundtrack by Jan Hammer (of *Miami Vice* fame). Rated PG for violence. 92m. **DIR:** Gabrielle Beaumont. **CAST:** Marc Singer, David Warner, Tony Todd, Sandra Hess, Casper Van Dien, Lesley-Anne Down, Keith Coulouris. **1995**

BEAT GIRL ★★★ While American exploitation movies of previous generations are trotted out for camp value, this British "adults only" drama is actually quite well made. Gillian Hills plays a teen girl who is determined to do whatever it takes to end her father's marriage to a young Frenchwoman. Not rated; contains brief nudity. 83m. **DIR:** Edmond T. Grenville. **CAST:** Gillian Hills, David Farrar, Christopher Lee, Adam Faith, Shirley Ann Field, Oliver Reed. **1959**

BEAT STREET 🦃 A hackneyed plot, about kids breaking into show biz. Rated PG for profanity and violence. 106m. **DIR:** Stan Lathan. **CAST:** Rae Dawn Chong, Guy Davis. **1984**

BEAT THE DEVIL ★★★★ Because it's all played straight, critics and audiences alike didn't know what to make of this delightful though at times baffling satire of films in the vein of *The Maltese Falcon* and *Key Largo* when it first hit screens. Sadly, some still do not. Nonetheless, this droll comedy, cobbled on location in Italy by John Huston and Truman Capote, is a twenty-four-carat gem. B&W; 93m. **DIR:** John Huston. **CAST:** Humphrey Bogart, Robert Morley, Peter Lorre, Jennifer Jones, Gina Lollobrigida. **1954 DVD**

BEATRICE ★★ In creating *Beatrice*, writer-director Bertrand Tavernier set out to demythologize the Middle Ages. He succeeds all too well with this repulsive, nightmarish movie in which the angelic title character (Julie Delpy) is raped and tortured by the demented father (Bernard Pierre Donnadieu) she once idolized. In French with English subtitles. Not rated, the film has nudity, violence, and simulated sex. 128m. **DIR:** Bertrand Tavernier. **CAST:** Bernard Pierre Donnadieu, Julie Delpy, Nils Tavernier. **1987**

BEAU BRUMMELL (1924) ★★★★ John Barrymore scores a great success as the handsome dandy who works his way into the good graces of the Prince of Wales. Mary Astor is wonderful as Lady Alvanley. This is a must-see film for admirers of the silent film nearing its peak of perfection. Silent. B&W; 92m. **DIR:** Harry Beaumont. **CAST:** John Barrymore, Mary Astor, Irene Rich, Carmel Myers. **1924**

BEAU BRUMMELL (1954) ★★★1/2 Good telling of the on-again, off-again friendship and patronage between the Prince of Wales (later George IV) and court rogue and dandy Beau Brummell. Stewart Granger is fine in the title role, and Elizabeth Taylor is beautiful, but the movie belongs to Peter Ustinov as the prince, and in a small role, Robert Morley as George III. 113m. **DIR:** Curtis Bernhardt. **CAST:** Stewart Granger, Elizabeth Taylor, Peter Ustinov, Robert Morley, James Donald, Rosemary Harris, Peter Bull. **1954**

BEAU GESTE ★★★★1/2 Gary Cooper fulfilled every idealistic boy's dream of honor, sacrifice, and brotherly love in this splendid adaptation of P. C. Wren's adventure classic. Director William Wellman painstakingly recreated the arid setting of the world's most famous Foreign Legion adventure. The action is brisk and the characters are unforgettable. B&W; 114m. **DIR:** William Wellman. **CAST:** Gary Cooper, Robert Preston, Ray Milland, Brian Donlevy, J. Carrol Naish, Susan Hayward, Broderick Crawford, Albert Dekker, Donald O'Connor, James Stephenson. **1939**

BEAU PERE ★★★★ Patrick Dewaere stars again for French director Betrand Blier (*Get Out Your Handkerchiefs*) in this film, about a stepfather who falls in love with his adopted pubescent daughter. It could have been shocking—or just plain perverse. But *Beau Pere* is a bittersweet, thoroughly charming motion picture. In French with English subtitles. Not rated; the film has nudity, profanity, and adult themes. 120m. **DIR:** Bertrand Blier. **CAST:** Patrick Dewaere, Ariel Besse, Maurice Ronet, Nicole Garcia. **1982 DVD**

BEAUMARCHAIS THE SCOUNDREL ★★★1/2 An unproduced play by Sacha Guitry was the basis for this lavish and lively biography of the eighteenth-century playwright who dabbled in espionage and international politics between writing popular plays and pursuing the ladies. A first-rate cast is headed by the sly Fabrice Luchini in a film whose only drawback is that it packs too much into too little time. In French with English subtitles. Not rated; contains nudity and violence. 100m. **DIR:** Edouard Molinaro. **CAST:** Fabrice Luchini, Sandrine Kiberlain, Manuel Blanc, Michel Piccoli, Michel Serrault. **1996**

BEAUTICIAN AND THE BEAST, THE ★★★1/2 Giggle-producing combination of *The Sound of Music* and every fairy tale cliché pairs a tyrant (Timothy Dalton) with a New Yorker (Fran Drescher), and he doesn't stand a chance. When a beauty-college instructor is hired to teach the children of an Eastern European despot, she quickly turns the tiny kingdom on its ear. The two are in each other's face so often that romance inevitably blooms. Royal pageantry is a visual bonus. Rated PG for sexual innuendo. 107m. **DIR:** Ken Kwapis. **CAST:** Fran Drescher, Timothy Dalton, Ian McNeice, Patrick Malahide, Lisa Jakub. **1997**

BEAUTIES OF THE NIGHT ★★★★ A young music teacher in an industrial town escapes his boring life with fantasies in which the women around him become figures from history. Music and images mesh wonderfully in this lightweight concoction. Original title: *Les Belles de Nuit.* In French with English subtitles. B&W; 89m. **DIR:** René Clair. **CAST:** Gérard Philipe, Martine Carol, Gina Lollobrigida, Magali Vendeuil. **1952**

BEAUTIFUL ★★ Clichés fly freely in this lifeless and improbable comedy about a woman obsessed with beauty pageants. Minnie Driver is the scandal-plagued beauty queen who juggles her comical life without much success. The jokes are flat, the characters larger than life, and the situations as believable as magic beans. Rated PG-13 for language. 112m. **DIR:** Sally Field. **CAST:** Minnie Driver, Joey Lauren Adams, Hallie Kate Eisenberg, Leslie Stefanson, Kathleen Turner. **2000 DVD**

BEAUTIFUL BLONDE FROM BASHFUL BEND, THE ★★1/2 Sharpshooter-schoolmarm Betty Grable has boyfriend trouble and must deal with a kidnapping and a philandering Cesar Romero in this wacky Western farce. Tolerable family fun, but not a highlight in director Preston Sturges's career. 77m. **DIR:** Preston Sturges. **CAST:** Betty Grable, Cesar Romero, Rudy Vallee, Olga San Juan, Sterling Holloway, Hugh Herbert, Porter Hall, Margaret Hamilton. **1949**

BEAUTIFUL DREAMERS ★★★1/2 Rip Torn delivers a wonderful performance as poet Walt Whitman, who accompanies a young doctor back to his small town, where the outspoken Whitman's beliefs set the local townsfolk aback. While the rest of the cast is in tune with the vision, it's Torn who paints the brightest images in this intelligent film. Rated PG-13 for language. 108m. **DIR:** John Kent Harrison. **CAST:** Rip Torn, Colm Feore, Sheila McCarthy. **1991**

BEAUTIFUL GIRLS ★★★ Another rueful comedy about commitment-shy twentysomething men and the women who are too good for them. Scott Rosenberg's script takes a condescending view of its own characters, and his dialogue is often pretentious and literary; some lines are almost literally unspeakable. Fortunately, the cast is packed with first-rate talent, and the film is much better acted than written. Rated R for profanity. 113m. **DIR:** Ted Demme. **CAST:** Timothy Hutton, Matt Dillon, Mira Sorvino, Uma Thurman, Rosie O'Donnell, Michael Rapaport, Annabeth Gish, Martha Plimpton, Natalie Portman. **1996 DVD**

•BEAUTIFUL MIND, A ★★★★★ Russell Crowe is nothing short of astonishing in director Ron Howard's sensitive account of mathematician John Forbes Nash Jr., whose post-WWII study of game theory—the mathematics of competition—challenged established economic models that had been in place for more than a century. Sadly, Nash's meteoric career was derailed by his horrifying slide into schizophrenia, but he fought its effects with the same tenacity that he tackled the intricacies of number theory. Howard's handling of Akiva Goldsman's screenplay is masterful; rarely has the process of abstract thought been presented so successfully on screen. Jennifer Connelly holds her own as Nash's devoted wife, but you won't be able to take your eyes off Crowe; he's simply amazing. Rated PG-13 for dramatic intensity, brief violence, and mild sensuality. 134m. **DIR:** Ron Howard. **CAST:** Russell Crowe, Ed Harris, Jennifer Connelly, Paul Bettany, Adam Goldberg, Judd Hirsch, Christopher Plummer. **2001 DVD**

BEAUTIFUL PEOPLE ★★★★ Chance encounters and chaos are the basic drivers of this darkly comic, cathartic story in which fallout from the ethnic cleansing in former Yugoslavia slops over to 1993 London. A Croat and a Serb share neighboring hospital beds; a junkie soccer hooligan literally becomes a human United Nations Care Package; a well-heeled woman falls in love with a destitute immigrant. These stormy stories are as emotionally messy as life itself—and brilliantly portrayed. Rated R for language, drug use, and violence. 107m. **DIR:** Jasmin Dizdar. **CAST:** Danny Nussbaum, Nicolas Farrell, Edin Dzandzanovic, Charlotte Coleman, Charles Kay, Rosalind Ayres. **2000 DVD**

BEAUTIFUL THING ★★★ It's love in bloom between two teenage boys in working-class London. Originally produced for British TV and adapted from Jonathan Harvey's play, the film is modest, likable, and competently acted. A neighbor girl's obsession with Mama Cass seems to come out of nowhere and serves mainly as an excuse for the nostalgic tunes on the soundtrack. Rated R for profanity and mature themes. 89m. **DIR:** Hettie Macdonald. **CAST:** Glen Barry, Linda Henry, Scott Neal, Tameka Empson, Ben Daniels. **1996**

BEAUTY AND THE BEAST (1946) ★★★★★ This French classic goes far beyond mere retelling of the well-known fairy tale. Its eerie visual beauty and surrealistic atmosphere mark it as a genuine original. The tragic love story between Beauty (Josette Day) and the all-too-human Beast (Jean Marais) resembles a moving painting. In French with English subtitles. B&W; 90m. **DIR:** Jean Cocteau. **CAST:** Josette Day, Jean Marais. **1946 DVD**

BEAUTY AND THE BEAST (1991) ★★★★★ A classic feature-length cartoon from Walt Disney Pictures, this adaptation of the classic fairy tale is the animated equivalent of the stage production of *Les Misérables*; a spectacular piece of musical theater complete with heartwarming moments, uproarious comedy, even suspense. Oscars went to Alan Menken for his score and to Menken and Howard Ashman for the title song. Rated G. 85m. **DIR:** Gary Trousdale, Kirk Wise. **1991**

BEAUTY AND THE BEAST (TV SERIES) ★★★1/2 Based on the classic legend, this popular cult television series teamed Linda Hamilton's crusading district attorney with Ron Perlman's underworld dweller. Some admire the Renaissance surroundings and unusually literate scripts; others yearn for the deep, platonic love shared by the two central characters. This much is certain: You'll either roll with the poetic dialogue or find it outrageously melodramatic. Not rated; suitable for family viewing. 100m. **DIR:** Richard Franklin, Victor Lobl. **CAST:** Ron Perlman, Linda Hamilton, Roy Dotrice, Jay Acovone. **1987**

BEAUTY FOR THE ASKING 🦃 Beautician Lucille Ball creates a skin cream that sells millions. B&W; 68m. **DIR:** Glenn Tryon. **CAST:** Lucille Ball, Patric Knowles, Frieda Inescort, Donald Woods. **1939**

BEAUTY SCHOOL 🦃 *Emmanuelle* star Sylvia Kristel seriously needs a career makeover as the owner of a beauty school who's in a desperate race to win a lucrative advertising contract. Just another lame excuse to get women naked. Rated R for nudity and adult situations. 95m. **DIR:** Ernest G. Sauer. **CAST:** Sylvia Kristel, Kevin Bernhardt, Kimberly Taylor, Jane Hamilton. **1992**

BEAVIS AND BUTT-HEAD DO AMERICA ★★★ The notorious cartoon nitwits from MTV set out to replace their stolen television set, then find themselves involved with the FBI and a stolen killer virus. Never do they understand the situation. The script neatly expands the one-gag premise to feature length, with many laughs and clever complications. The deliberately sloppy animation matches the scribbled-in-a-notebook-during-study-hall style of the humor. Rated PG-13 for mild sexual humor; not appropriate for young children. 80m. **DIR:** Mike Judge. **CAST:** Mike Judge, Robert Stack (voices). **1996 DVD**

BEAVIS AND BUTT-HEAD (TV SERIES) ★★★★ Creator Mike Judge skewers almost every facet of contemporary American society with this animated, made-for-cable series about two really dumb high-school kids with an unmatched talent for dissipation. While many consider this series to be dangerously moronic, our two "heroes" provide a slick vehicle for satire that is deceptively smart. Releases for home video, unfortunately, do not include the duo's commentary on various outrageous music videos. Not rated; contains profanity. 45m. **DIR:** Mike Judge. **1992–1996 DVD**

BEBE'S KIDS ★★1/2 The comedy routines of the late, great black comedian Robin Harris were adapted to create this animated comedy. Harris's first date with a beautiful woman becomes a nightmare when he reluctantly agrees to take along her neighbor's troublemaking kids. Part *The Simpsons*, part *Alvin and the Chipmunks*, and part Harris, this was obviously a heartfelt project for all concerned. It just isn't that good. Rated PG-13 for profanity and violence. 93m. **DIR:** Bruce Smith. **1992**

BECAUSE YOU'RE MINE ★★1/2 When an opera star is drafted into the army, his training sergeant turns out to be a fan who has (surprise!) a sister with operatic ambitions. Forget the plot, just enjoy Mario Lanza's gifted voice. 101m. **DIR:** Alexander Hall. **CAST:** Mario Lanza, James Whitmore, Doretta Morrow, Jeff Donnell, Dean Miller, Paula Corday. **1952**

BECKET ★★★★ Magnificently acted spectacle of the stormy relationship between England's King Henry II (Peter O'Toole) and his friend and nemesis Archbishop Thomas Becket (Richard Burton). This visually stimulating historical pageant, set in twelfth-century England, garnered Oscar nominations for both its protagonists. 148m. **DIR:** Peter Glenville. **CAST:** Richard Burton, Peter O'Toole, Martita Hunt, Pamela Brown. **1964**

BECKY SHARP ★★1/2 Well-mounted historical drama of a callous young woman who lives for social success is lovely to look at in its original three-strip Technicolor. Fine performances by a veteran cast bolster this first sound screen adaptation of Thackeray's *Vanity Fair*. 83m. **DIR:** Rouben Mamoulian. **CAST:** Miriam Hopkins, Frances Dee, Cedric Hardwicke, Billie Burke, Alison Skipworth, Nigel Bruce. **1935**

BECOMING COLETTE ★★★ Beautifully photographed story chronicling the life of Colette, and the events that made her a world-famous author. From marriage to an older publisher to her introduction to decadent turn-of-the-century Paris, this film conveys a sumptuous eye for detail. Excellent performances from Mathilda May as the alluring Colette, Klaus Maria Brandauer as her husband, and Virginia Madsen as French actress Polaire. Rated R for nudity and adult situations. 97m. **DIR:** Danny Huston. **CAST:** Mathilda May, Klaus Maria Brandauer, Virginia Madsen, Paul Rhys. **1992**

BED AND BREAKFAST ★★★ After a man is washed up on the beach area in front of a house in Maine inhabited by a widow and her mother-in-law, the women's lives take some unexpected turns. The film examines the tender side of human relationships in a decidedly feminine fashion, while using just enough mystery and suspense to add an edge to their tale. Rated PG-13 for brief violence, suggested sex, and profanity. 96m. **DIR:** Robert Ellis Miller. **CAST:** Roger Moore, Talia Shire, Colleen Dewhurst, Ford Rainey. **1992**

BED AND SOFA ★★★★ During a housing shortage in Moscow a construction worker takes in an old friend. In the ensuing ménage à trois the worker's wife, now pregnant, turns her back on both the men in her life and leaves to make a new life for herself. A startling achievement, without precedent in the Soviet cinema. Silent. B&W; 73m. **DIR:** Abram Room. **CAST:** Nikolai Batalov, Vladimir Fogel. **1927**

BED OF ROSES ★★★1/2 Writer-director Michael Goldenberg's sweet little love story plays well in the hands of Christian Slater and Mary Stuart Masterson, cast as two emotionally damaged characters stumbling their way into a relationship. She's a workaholic investment banker without a past; he's a widower who delivers flowers because he enjoys bringing pleasure into strangers' lives. Rated PG for mild sexual content. 90m. **DIR:** Michael Goldenberg. **CAST:** Christian Slater, Mary Stuart Masterson, Pamela Segall, Josh Brolin. **1996 DVD**

BEDAZZLED (1967) ★★★★ A cult favorite, this British comedy stars Dudley Moore as a fry cook tempted by the devil (played by his onetime comedy partner, Peter Cook). Costarring Raquel Welch, it's an often hilarious updating of the Faust legend. 107m. **DIR:** Stanley Donen. **CAST:** Peter Cook, Dudley Moore, Raquel Welch, Eleanor Bron. **1967**

BEDAZZLED (2000) ★★★1/2 This update of the classic Dudley Moore/Peter Cook vehicle is almost as fun as the original. Brendan Fraser is pleasantly woebegone as an irritating nebbish who tries to attract the interest of the woman he worships from afar, but it's Elizabeth Hurley who brings the film to life; she's hilarious as the gleefully seductive and playfully villainous devil who keeps "cheating" our hero out of his right to happiness. Rated PG-13 for mild profanity, sensuality, and drug references. 93m. **DIR:** Harold Ramis. **CAST:** Brendan Fraser, Elizabeth Hurley, Frances O'Connor, Miriam Shor, Orlando Jones, Paul Adelstein. **2000 DVD**

BEDFORD INCIDENT, THE ★★★ A battle of wits aboard a U.S. destroyer tracking Soviet submarines off Greenland during the Cold War. Richard Widmark is a skipper with an obsession to hunt and hound a particular sub. A conflict develops between the captain and Sidney Poitier, a cocky magazine reporter along for the ride. B&W; 102m. **DIR:** James B. Harris. **CAST:** Richard Widmark, Sidney Poitier, Martin Balsam, Wally Cox, Eric Portman. **1965**

BEDKNOBS AND BROOMSTICKS ★★★1/2 Angela Lansbury is a witch who uses her powers to aid the Allies against the Nazis during World War II. She transports two children to faraway and strange locales during which they meet and play soccer with talking animals, among other things. This Disney film is an effective combination of special effects, animation, and live action. Rated G. 117m. **DIR:** Robert Stevenson. **CAST:** Angela Lansbury, David Tomlinson, Roddy McDowall. **1971 DVD**

BEDLAM ★★★ One of the lesser entries in the Val Lewton–produced horror film series at RKO, this release still has its moments as the courageous Anna Lee tries to expose the cruelties and inadequacies of an insane asylum run by Boris Karloff, who is first-rate, as usual. B&W; 79m. **DIR:** Mark Robson. **CAST:** Boris Karloff, Anna Lee, Ian Wolfe, Richard Fraser, Jason Robards Sr. **1946**

BEDROOM EYES ★★★ A young stockbroker peers into a window one evening and sees a woman so tantalizing he feels compelled to return every night. When the object of his voyeurism is murdered, the man must try to prove his innocence. A silly but undeniably erotic mystery. 90m. **DIR:** William Fruet. **CAST:** Kenneth Gilman, Dayle Haddon, Barbara Law, Christine Cattel. **1986**

BEDROOM EYES II 🦃 Tawdry whodunit. Rated R for nudity, profanity, and violence. 87m. **DIR:** Chuck Vincent. **CAST:** Linda Blair, Wings Hauser. **1989**

BEDROOM WINDOW, THE ★★★ Upwardly mobile architect Steve Guttenberg has it made until his boss's wife (Isabelle Huppert) sees a murder being committed—from his bedroom window. When Guttenberg goes to the police in her place, he becomes the prime suspect. This is a tense thriller that manages to stay interesting despite some wildly unbelievable plot twists. Rated R for profanity, nudity, and violence. 112m. **DIR:** Curtis Hanson. **CAST:** Steve Guttenberg, Elizabeth McGovern, Isabelle Huppert, Paul Shenar. **1987 DVD**

BEDROOMS AND HALLWAYS ★★ Gay Londoner Leo is prodded by a heterosexual buddy to join a straight men's sensitivity group in this screwball comedy of manners. Leo's revelation that he is attracted to an Irishman in the group kicks off a domino effect of sexual exploration and exploits that includes Jane Austen dream fantasies and the skewering of New Age gurus. The film begins with comic promise but runs out of juice well before its final couplings. Not rated; contains profanity, nudity, and simulated sex. 96m. **DIR:** Rose Troche. **CAST:** Kevin McKidd, James Purefoy, Jennifer Ehle, Tom Hollander, Simon Callow, Hugo Weaving. **1999 DVD**

BEDTIME FOR BONZO ★★★ This sweet-natured film is worth watching. Ronald Reagan plays a young college professor who uses a chimpanzee to prove that environment, not heredity, determines a person's moral fiber. He hires a young woman (Diana Lynn) to pose as the chimp's mom while he plays father to it. Not surprisingly, Mom and Dad fall in love. B&W; 83m. **DIR:** Frederick de Cordova. **CAST:** Ronald Reagan, Diana Lynn, Walter Slezak, Jesse White. **1951**

BEDTIME STORY ★★★ A European playboy (David Niven) and a wolfish American GI (Marlon Brando, somewhat miscast), propose to settle their differences with a bet: the first to seduce naive contest winner Shirley Jones becomes King of the Cosmopolitan Hill, and the other must quietly fade away. Although often quite sexist, the result is much funnier than the shallow concept would suggest. Remade as *Dirty Rotten Scoundrels*. Suggestive themes. 99m. **DIR:** Ralph Levy. **CAST:** David Niven, Marlon Brando, Shirley Jones. **1964**

BEER ★★★★ Hilarious comedy that examines the seamy side of the advertising industry. Loretta Swit plays a cold-blooded advertising agent who tries to turn three ordinary guys (David Alan Grier, William Russ, and Saul Stein) into beer-drinking American heroes. Dick Shawn's impression of Phil Donahue must be seen to be believed. Rated R for profanity, sex, and adult subject matter. 83m. **DIR:** Patrick Kelly. **CAST:** Loretta Swit, Rip Torn, Kenneth Mars, David Alan Grier, William Russ, Peter Michael Goetz, Dick Shawn, Saul Stein. **1985**

BEES, THE 🦃 Despite all temptation to label this a honey of a picture, it's a drone that will probably give viewers the hives. Rated PG. 83m. **DIR:** Alfredo Zacharias. **CAST:** John Saxon, John Carradine. **1978**

BEETHOVEN ★★★ When an adopted puppy grows up to be a 185-pound Saint Bernard, businessman Charles Grodin wishes he'd never allowed his family to take the dog in. Good family fun. Rated PG for doggy messes. 87m. **DIR:** Brian Levant. **CAST:** Charles Grodin, Bonnie Hunt, Dean Jones, Stanley Tucci, David Duchovny. **1992 DVD**

BEETHOVEN'S 2ND ★★★ Beethoven—a massive Saint Bernard—starts a family of his own in this lightweight sequel with more charm and less slobber than the original. Beethoven's mate is owned by a modern Cruella de Vil who is holding the canine as a trump card in her divorce case—and do she and her new boyfriend ever hate dogs! Charles Grodin also returns as an air-freshener marketer who is up to his armpits in financial and domestic problems. Rated PG. 86m. **DIR:** Rod Daniel. **CAST:** Charles Grodin, Bonnie Hunt, Nicholle Tom, Christopher Castille, Sarah Rose Karr, Debi Mazar, Christopher Penn, Kevin Dunn. **1993 DVD**

BEETHOVEN'S 3RD ★★ The third in the series starring the popular Saint Bernard is the last of the bunch, but will be appreciated by fans who have enjoyed his earlier exploits. This time, Beethoven and his "new" family go on a road trip. Rated PG. 99m. **DIR:** David Mickey Evans. **CAST:** Judge Reinhold, Julia Sweeney, Jamie Marsh, Greg Pitts. **2000 DVD**

BEETHOVEN'S NEPHEW ★★1/2 This surreal drama by Paul Morrissey takes an incisive look at the dark side of Beethoven's genius. It's a convoluted period piece that follows the bizarre exploits of Beethoven's young nephew, Karl. Interesting performances, beautiful settings, and great costumes carry this film over the slow spots. Rated R. 103m. **DIR:** Paul Morrissey. **CAST:** Wolfgang Reichmann, Dietmar Prinz, Jane Birkin, Nathalie Baye, Mathieu Carriere. **1985**

BEETLEJUICE ★★★ Like a cinematic trip through the Haunted Mansion, this film may require two viewings just to catch all the complex action and visual jokes. Alec Baldwin and Geena Davis play a young couple who accidentally drown and return as novice ghosts. The family that moves into their pretty little Connecticut farmhouse seems intent on destroying it aesthetically, and the ghostly couple are forced to call on the evil Betelgeuse (Michael Keaton). Rated PG for shock action and language. 93m. **DIR:** Tim Burton. **CAST:** Alec Baldwin, Geena Davis, Michael Keaton, Jeffrey Jones, Catherine O'Hara, Winona Ryder. **1988 DVD**

BEFORE AND AFTER ★★★1/2 A compelling study of family dynamics, the American judicial system, and personal responsibility that is undermined by a softening of the Rosellen Brown novel. Still, this meaty drama is enhanced by Edward Furlong's sadly believable portrayal of a teenager accused of murdering his girlfriend in a small New England town. Rated PG-13 for profanity and violence. 121m. **DIR:** Barbet Schroeder. **CAST:** Meryl Streep, Liam Neeson, Edward Furlong, Alfred Molina, Ann Magnuson. **1995**

BEFORE I HANG ★★★ Neat little thriller has Boris Karloff as a goodhearted doctor who creates an age-retardant serum. Trouble begins when he tests it on himself, with horrible side effects. Nicely done, the film benefits from a good supporting performance by horror veteran Edward Van Sloan. B&W; 71m. **DIR:** Nick Grindé. **CAST:** Boris Karloff, Evelyn Keyes, Bruce Bennett, Pedro De Cordoba, Edward Van Sloan. **1940**

BEFORE NIGHT FALLS ★★★★1/2 The brief and passionate life of Cuban writer Reinaldo Arenas springs vividly to life as we follow Arenas from his revolutionary younger years in Cuba to his last days in Florida where he died of complications from AIDS. Javier Bardem fills the homosexual writer with strength, warmth, and dignity in a film that is the perfect marriage of material, performance, and direction. Rated R for adult situations, language, nudity, and violence. 125m. **DIR:** Julian Schnabel. **CAST:** Javier Bardem, Johnny Depp, Olivier Martinez, Andrea di Stefano, Sean Penn, Michael Wincott. **2000 DVD**

BEFORE SUNRISE ★★★★ American tourist Ethan Hawke and French student Julie Delpy meet on a Eurail train and, on the spur of the moment, hop off in Vienna to spend the day (and the night) exploring the city and getting acquainted with each other. That's all there is to it, two young people walking and talking, but the film is a lighthearted delight. The stars are immensely charming and their dialogue, as they gradually fall in love, is credible and interesting. Rated R for profanity. 101m. **DIR:** Richard Linklater. **CAST:** Ethan Hawke, Julie Delpy. **1994 DVD**

BEFORE THE RAIN ★★★1/2 Macedonian filmmaker Milcho Manchevski tells a three-part story about the tragic, far-reaching effects of ancient blood feuds and modern-day civil strife in the remnants of Yugoslavia. Riveting and compellingly told. Not rated; contains violence, nudity, and mild profanity. 110m. **DIR:** Milcho Manchevski. **CAST:** Katrin Cartlidge, Rade Serbedzija, Gregoire Colin, Labina Mitevska. **1994**

BEFORE THE REVOLUTION ★★★1/2 Bernardo Bertolucci made this political drama at the age of twenty-two. The plot evolves around a young man who flirts with communism, while engaging in an incestuous relationship with his aunt. Great cinematography. In Italian with English subtitles. B&W; 110m. **DIR:** Bernardo Bertolucci. **CAST:** Adriana Asti, Francesco Barilli. **1962**

BEGGARS OF LIFE ★★★ Girl who kills abusive adoptive father goes on the lam with a gentle tramp and finds herself pursued by the law as well as lusting hoboes eager for her and the reward she will bring. The rest of the film doesn't quite measure up to the startling opening sequence, but it's quite a train ride as Louise Brooks tries to put some distance between herself and Wallace Beery as the head hobo who does the right thing in the last reel. B&W; 100m. **DIR:** William Wellman. **CAST:** Louise Brooks, Richard Arlen, Wallace Beery, Edgar Washington Blue, H. A. Moran. **1928**

BEGINNING OF THE END 🦃 Scientist Peter Graves tries to save Chicago from the mutant grasshoppers accidentally produced in his giant vegetable experiment. Low-budget special effects. Not rated; contains comic book–type violence and destruction. 75m. **DIR:** Bert I. Gordon. **CAST:** Peter Graves, Peggie Castle, Morris Ankrum, Thomas Browne Henry. **1957**

BEGOTTEN ★★★★ The entire film consists of two extended sequences, in which a godlike creature gives birth (literally) to mankind, and a solitary man is tortured by masked figures in a pit. Love it or hate it, it is utterly unique. Not rated, but not for the squeamish. B&W; 78m. **DIR:** Edmund Elias Merhige. **CAST:** Brian Salzberg, Donna Dempsey. **1991 DVD**

BEGUILED, THE ★★★★ An atmospheric, daring change of pace for director Don Siegel and star Clint Eastwood, this production features the squinty-eyed actor as a wounded Yankee soldier taken in by the head (Geraldine Page) of a girls' school. He becomes the catalyst for incidents of jealousy and hatred among its inhabitants, and this leads to a startling, unpredictable conclusion. Rated R. 109m. **DIR:** Don Siegel. **CAST:** Clint Eastwood, Geraldine Page, Jo Ann Harris, Elizabeth Hartman. **1971 DVD**

BEHAVE YOURSELF! ★★ A comedy written expressly for Farley Granger and Shelley Winters when they were the most popular married couple in Hollywood. They play a couple who get crossways with two different mobs, and it's all because of their pet dog—a trained smuggler who can operate between both gangs. B&W; 81m. **DIR:** George Beck. **CAST:** Shelley Winters, Farley Granger, Hans Conried, Sheldon Leonard, Lon Chaney Jr., William Demarest. **1951**

•BEHIND ENEMY LINES ★★★ This cunningly manipulative popcorn fantasy, set during the waning days of the Bosnian-Serb civil war, arrived in U.S. theaters when viewers most desperately hungered for heroic fare. As a result, Owen Wilson is perfectly cast as an apple-cheeked and towheaded naval aviator who, having tired of the NATO-brokered attempt at a treaty, zooms off course during a routine recon mission and winds up on the ground being hunted by enemy forces. Sadly, the drama is undercut by gimmicky camera angles, MTV-styled smash cuts and unexpected freeze-frames, not to mention the obnoxious, pop-flavored soundtrack, which brings the picture to a grinding halt every time some screaming rock anthem overrides the already noisy combat sound effects. Rated PG-13 for profanity and war violence. 105m. **DIR:** John Moore. **CAST:** Owen Wilson, Gene Hackman, Gabriel Macht, Charles Malik Whitfield, David Keith. **2001 DVD**

BEHIND LOCKED DOORS 🦃 Sleazy, near-plotless thriller about a nutcase who kidnaps young women for sexual "research." Not rated, but an R equivalent for nudity and rape. 79m. **DIR:** Charles Romine. **CAST:** Joyce Denner, Eve Reeves, Daniel Garth, Ivan Hagar. **1974 DVD**

BEHIND THE LINES ★★★★ Powerful WWI drama features graphic images of carnage, but the real drama is in a Scottish hospital where three men and their doctor try to make sense of it all. James Wilby is excellent as a war hero who questions his motives, while Jonny Lee Miller plays a shell-shocked officer trying to work through a memory blockage. The war images are okay, but it's the interior battles that keep this import alive. Also released as *Regeneration*. Rated R for language and violence. 100m. **DIR:** Gillies MacKinnon. **CAST:** Jonathan Pryce, James Wilby, Jonny Lee Miller, Stuart Bunce, David Hayman, Tanya Allen, John Neville. **1997**

BEHIND THE MASK ★★★ Secret-service agent infiltrates a dope-smuggling ring run by a mysterious maniac who murders his enemies with grisly abandon. Square-jawed lawmen, cold-blooded drug dealers, a beautiful heroine, and hardboiled action make this precode programmer a pulp magazine on film. B&W; 68m. **DIR:** John Francis Dillon. **CAST:** Jack Holt, Constance Cummings, Boris Karloff, Claude King, Edward Van Sloan. **1932**

BEHIND THE RISING SUN ★★1/2 The versatile J. Carrol Naish plays a Japanese publisher whose political views bring him into conflict with his son, educated in the United States. It all takes place when Japan was fighting China, not long before World War II. B&W; 89m. **DIR:** Edward Dmytryk. **CAST:** Margo, Tom Neal, J. Carrol Naish, Robert Ryan. **1943**

BEHOLD A PALE HORSE ★★ Gregory Peck is miscast in this slow, talky, vague drama of a Loyalist holdout in post–Civil War Spain who continues to harass the Franco regime. 118m. **DIR:** Fred Zinnemann. **CAST:** Gregory Peck, Anthony Quinn, Omar Sharif. **1963**

BEING, THE 🦃 Water contaminated with nuclear waste spawned a beast that likes to shove itself *through* people. Rated R for gore and nudity. 82m. **DIR:** Jackie Kong. **CAST:** Martin Landau, José Ferrer, Dorothy Malone, Ruth Buzzi. **1984**

BEING AT HOME WITH CLAUDE ★★★ Complex, provocative study of the human psyche examines the murder of a young student, and the enigmatic male prostitute who confesses to the crime. During an intense interrogation, the truth about the shocking crime comes out, but not before we're subjected to a harrowing barrage of verbal abuse. In French with English subtitles. Not rated; contains adult situations and language. 86m. **DIR:** Jean Beaudin. **CAST:** Roy Dupuis, Jacques Godin, Jean-François Pinchette, Gaston Lepage. **1992**

BEING HUMAN ★★1/2 Writer-director Bill Forsyth's big-screen meditation on the plight of unexceptional men is neither funny nor dramatic. In his best sad-eyed fashion, Robin Williams plays five roles in five historical settings, ranging from the Stone Age to modern times. A brief, humorous turn by John Turturro and a touching wrap-around story make this worth watching. Rated PG-13 for light profanity, brief violence, and suggested sex. 119m. **DIR:** Bill Forsyth. **CAST:** Robin Williams, Anna Galiena, Vincent D'Onofrio, Hector Elizondo, John Turturro, Lorraine Bracco, Lindsay Crouse, Helen Miller, Charles Miller, William H. Macy. **1994**

BEING JOHN MALKOVICH ★★★★ In this surreal, original film—which explores love, identity, alternate reality, and sex—John Cusack takes a job as a filing clerk and discovers a portal that leads him into the body of actor John Malkovich. Cameron Diaz, Cusack's mousy wife, gets drawn into his bizarre discovery and finds that she, like her husband, is sexually attracted to his avaricious "partner" (Catherine Keener), who turns the portal experience into a money-making scheme. Rated R for profanity, nudity, and simulated sex. 112m. **DIR:** Spike Jonze. **CAST:** John Cusack, Cameron Diaz, Catherine Keener, Orson Bean, Mary Kay Place, John Malkovich, Charlie Sheen, Sean Penn. **1999 DVD**

BEING THERE ★★★★1/2 This sublimely funny and bitingly satiric comedy features Peter Sellers's last great screen performance. His portrayal of a simple-minded gardener—who knows only what he sees on television yet rises to great political heights—is a classic. Shirley MacLaine and Melvyn Douglas are also excellent in this memorable film, directed by Hal Ashby. Rated PG. 130m. **DIR:** Hal Ashby. **CAST:** Peter Sellers, Shirley MacLaine, Melvyn Douglas, Jack Warden. **1979 DVD**

BELARUS FILE, THE ★★1/2 Telly Savalas returns as the lollipop-sucking police detective Kojak in this made-for-television movie about a maniac murdering Russian survivors of a Nazi concentration camp. For fans of the series only. 95m. **DIR:** Robert Markowitz. **CAST:** Telly Savalas, Suzanne Pleshette, Max von Sydow, Herbert Berghof, George Savalas. **1986**

BELFAST ASSASSIN ★★1/2 This film, about an IRA hit man and a British antiterrorist who is ordered to track down the Irish assassin on his own turf, could have used a clipper-happy editor. The film takes a pro-IRA stand, yet is open-minded enough to see the other side of the story. Not rated, but the equivalent of a PG for sex, violence, and profanity. 130m. **DIR:** Lawrence Gordon Clark. **CAST:** Derek Thompson, Ray Lonnen, Benjamin Whitrow. **1982**

BELIEVE ★★ Ben and Katherine, two young thrill seekers, are always intrigued by a good supernatural mystery. They decide that they should put their sleuthing to the test and investigate the haunted Wickwire House. Their brave quest turns fruitful when they encounter an actual ghost, and find themselves in the midst of a bigger mystery. The slow pace and droll plot of this movie will leave most older viewers yawning. Rated PG-13 for scariness. 95m. **DIR:** Robert Tinnell. **CAST:** Jan Rubes, Ricky Mabe, Elisha Cuthbert, Andrea Martin, Ben Gazzara. **1999 DVD**

BELIEVERS, THE ★★★1/2 Martin Sheen portrays a recently widowed father whose son is chosen as a sacrifice to a voodoo cult running rampant in New York. John Schlesinger is not the best director for a thriller of this type, but in this case the quality of the acting, the snap of the writing, and the strength of the story build the suspense nicely and provide a striking climax. Rated R for language, nudity, and nightmarism. 110m. **DIR:** John Schlesinger. **CAST:** Martin Sheen, Helen Shaver, Robert Loggia, Richard Masur, Elizabeth Wilson, Lee Richardson, Harris Yulin, Jimmy Smits. **1987**

BELIZAIRE THE CAJUN ★★★★ The Louisiana bayou of the 1850s is richly re-created in deep, dark swampland colors, along with the rhythms of Cajun accents and full-bodied folk music (score by Michael Doucet). Armand Assante is Belizaire, an herbal doctor who finds himself in trouble because of his affection for his childhood sweetheart and his efforts to save a friend from persecution. 114m. **DIR:** Glen Pitre. **CAST:** Armand Assante, Gail Youngs, Michael Schoeffling, Stephen McHattie, Will Patton. **1986**

BELL, BOOK AND CANDLE ★★★1/2 A modestly entertaining bit of whimsy about a beautiful witch (Kim Novak) who works her magic on an unsuspecting publisher (James Stewart). Although the performances (including those in support by Jack Lemmon, Ernie Kovacs, and Hermione Gingold) are fine, this comedy is only mildly diverting. 103m. **DIR:** Richard Quine. **CAST:** James Stewart, Kim Novak, Jack Lemmon, Ernie Kovacs. **1958 DVD**

BELL JAR, THE ★★★ Based on the novel by Sylvia Plath about the mental breakdown of an overachiever in the world of big business in the 1950s, this film has a strong lead performance by Marilyn Hassett and thoughtful direction by her husband, Larry Peerce. But the overriding melancholy of the subject matter makes it difficult to watch. Barbara Barrie is also memorable in a key supporting role. Rated R. 107m. **DIR:** Larry Peerce. **CAST:** Marilyn Hassett, Julie Harris, Anne Jackson, Barbara Barrie, Robert Klein. **1979**

BELLA MAFIA ★★★ Grand soap opera adds a female twist to the *Last Don* series. Vanessa Redgrave stars as the matriarch of a large Italian family, who watches her sons grow up and get married. When a Mafia rival kills her husband and sons, she and the women gather to exact revenge. Decent cast and direction keep this made-for-television miniseries from slipping into camp. Rated R for adult situations and violence. 117m. **DIR:** David Greene. **CAST:** Vanessa Redgrave, Dennis Farina, Nastassja Kinski, Jennifer Tilly. **1997**

BELLBOY, THE ★★ A typical hour-plus of Jerry Lewis mugging and antics so dear to those who find him funny. This time around, Jerry is a bellboy at a swank hotel. Years ago, "Fatty" Arbuckle made a film of the same name that was funny. This, unfortunately, is plotless drivel seasoned with guest appearances by Milton Berle and Walter Winchell. Rated G when rereleased in 1972. B&W; 72m. **DIR:** Jerry Lewis. **CAST:** Jerry Lewis, Alex Gerry, Sonny Sands. **1960**

BELLBOY AND THE PLAYGIRLS, THE ★★ Innocuous sex comedy about a bellboy who practices to be a private eye. This would be long forgotten but for the fact that it's Francis Ford Coppola's first screen credit. He added some color sequences for the U.S. release of this 1958 German movie. Not rated, the film has nudity. 94m. **DIR:** Fritz Umgelter, Francis Ford Coppola. **CAST:** June Wilkinson. **1962**

BELLE DE JOUR ★★★★1/2 A repressed French housewife takes a day job in a bordello, where her fantasy life spins quickly out of control. This erotic classic is less scandalous now than when it was first released. Still, this witty film has aged gracefully, and some scenes retain their power to shock and perplex (a hint: italicized subtitles signify when we are watching the woman's fantasies). Deneuve has never been better. In French with English subtitles. Rated R for mature themes. 100m. **DIR:** Luis Buñuel. **CAST:** Catherine Deneuve, Jean Sorel, Michel Piccoli, Genevieve Page, Pierre Clementi. **1967 DVD**

BELLE EPOQUE ★★★★ An army deserter hiding out in the Spanish countryside of the 1930s becomes infatuated, one by one, with the four beautiful daughters of a crusty old artist. This eccentric, beautifully photographed movie won the 1993 Oscar for best foreign film. Delightfully ribald, strongly recommended for mature audiences only. In Spanish with English subtitles. Rated R for sexual scenes. 108m. **DIR:** Fernando Trueba. **CAST:** Jorge Sanz, Fernando Fernán Gómez, Ariadna Gil, Penelope Cruz. **1992**

BELLE OF NEW YORK, THE ★★ A fantasy set at the turn of the century, this frothy film was a box-office failure about which, in his autobiography, Fred Astaire snaps: "The less said about it the better." Harry Warren's score—assembled from earlier hits—is terrific, though none of the songs have survived as standards. 82m. **DIR:** Charles Walters. **CAST:** Fred Astaire, Vera-Ellen, Marjorie Main, Keenan Wynn. **1952**

BELLE OF THE NINETIES ★★★1/2 A stereotypical Mae West vehicle, but the censors' scissors are obvious. She sings, talks back, and tangles with a boxer who wants to tame her. Some of her most famous witticisms and her better songs are in this film. Like other Mae West films, this one is a series of one-liners between clinches that spoof the battle of the sexes. B&W; 73m. **DIR:** Leo McCarey. **CAST:** Mae West, Johnny Mack Brown, Roger Pryor, John Miljan, Duke Ellington. **1934 DVD**

BELLES OF ST. TRINIAN'S, THE ★★★1/2 Alastair Sim doubles as the dotty headmistress of a bonkers school for girls and her crafty bookie brother, who wants to use the place as a cover for his nefarious operations. Joyce Grenfell adds to the hilarity in this British comedy based on English cartoonist Ronald Searle's schoolgirls with a genius for mischief. B&W; 90m. **DIR:** Frank Launder. **CAST:** Alastair Sim, Joyce Grenfell, Hermione Baddeley, George Cole. **1955**

BELLISSIMA ★★★ Luchino Visconti is known for such pioneering works as *Rocco and His Brothers*, *The Damned*, and *Death in Venice*. As for *Bellissima*, if you are programming an Anna Magnani festival, you might be interested in this oddly and determinedly lightweight comedy. The story is set in the Cinecitta Studios, where a search is on for the prettiest child in Rome. In Italian with English subtitles. B&W; 95m. **DIR:** Luchino Visconti. **CAST:** Anna Magnani, Walter Chiari, Tina Apicella. **1951**

BELLMAN AND TRUE ★★★★ This gripping crime-drama centers around a British computer genius who is forced to aid thugs in a bank heist after his son is kidnapped. Fascinating characters and suspenseful plot twists give this film depth and realism. Rated R. 114m. **DIR:** Richard Loncraine. **CAST:** Bernard Hill, Derek Newark, Richard Hope, Ken Bones, Frances Tomelty. **1988**

BELLS ARE RINGING ★★ This filmed version of the Broadway musical pits answering-service operator Judy Holliday against Dean Martin in an on-again, off-again love circle. Nothing new or exciting story-wise here, but Fred Clark and Eddie Foy ham it up enough to hold your interest. 127m. **DIR:** Vincente Minnelli. **CAST:** Judy Holliday, Dean Martin, Fred Clark, Eddie Foy Jr. **1960**

BELLS OF CORONADO ★★1/2 Grant Withers heads an evil gang of foreign agents out to smuggle uranium to unfriendly powers. Roy Rogers plays a modern-day heroic insurance agent who is able to thwart the heavies. Comic-book story is full of fast riding and action. 67m. **DIR:** William Witney. **CAST:** Roy Rogers, Dale Evans, Pat Brady, Grant Withers. **1950**

BELLS OF ROSARITA ★★1/2 Movie cowboy Roy Rogers enlists the aid of Republic Studios' top Western stars in order to save Gabby Hayes's and Dale Evans's circus. A fun Western. B&W; 54m. **DIR:** Frank McDonald. **CAST:** Roy Rogers, Dale Evans, George "Gabby" Hayes, Bob Nolan and the Sons of the Pioneers, Don Barry, Allan "Rocky" Lane, Sunset Carson, William Elliott, Robert Livingston. **1945**

BELLS OF ST. MARY'S, THE ★★★★1/2 An effective sequel to *Going My Way*, also directed by Leo McCarey, this film has Bing Crosby returning as the modern-minded priest once again up against a headstrong opponent, Mother Superior (played by Ingrid Bergman). While not as memorable as his encounter with hard-headed older priest Barry Fitzgerald in the first film, this relationship—and the movie as a whole—does have its viewing rewards. B&W; 126m. **DIR:** Leo McCarey. **CAST:** Bing Crosby, Ingrid Bergman, Ruth Donnelly. **1945 DVD**

BELLS OF SAN ANGELO ★★★1/2 This is a sharp and unusually violent Roy Rogers film. Roy portrays a lawman who attempts to capture a bunch of smugglers. With the help of Dale Evans and Andy Devine, he succeeds. B&W; 78m. **DIR:** William Witney. **CAST:** Roy Rogers, Dale Evans, Andy Devine, John McGuire. **1947**

BELLY ★★ This low-budget, disjointed drama about two "gangsta" buddies who rob, murder, and sell drugs emphasizes gritty style over substance. By the time the two friends realize the error of their ways, it's too late to save the film from its own raunchy sensationalism. Rated R for profanity, simulated sex, nudity, violence, and drug use. 95m. **DIR:** Hype Williams. **CAST:** Nas, DMX, Taral Hicks, Lavita Raynor, Tionne T-Boz Watkins. **1998 DVD**

BELLY OF AN ARCHITECT, THE ★★ Dreamlike, symbolism-laced story of an American architect (Brian Dennehy) trying to deal with hypocrisy in his art and in his life while working on a project in Italy. His efforts take on an urgency when he begins to suspect that he's dying of cancer. Alternately artful and pretentious, the film is most interesting as a showcase for Dennehy. 108m. **DIR:** Peter Greenaway. **CAST:** Brian Dennehy, Chloe Webb, Lambert Wilson. **1987**

BELOVED ★★★1/2 Oprah Winfrey produced and stars in this dignified, reverent adaptation of Toni Morrison's Pulitzer Prize–winning novel about the scars of slavery on an African-American family in post–Civil War Ohio. Viewers unfamiliar with Morrison's evocative prose and emotionally dense story may find the film too obscure. Thandie Newton, as the mysterious title character, is oddly mannered, but the rest of the cast is excellent. Rated R for mature themes and graphic depiction of slavery. 171m. **DIR:** Jonathan Demme. **CAST:** Oprah Winfrey, Danny Glover, Thandie Newton, Kimberly Elise, Beah Richards. **1998 DVD**

BELOVED ENEMY ★★★1/2 This stylish film concerns a beautiful woman (Merle Oberon) in love with a young leader in the Irish revolution (Brian Aherne). Great supporting cast adds panache to this crackerjack Samuel Goldwyn production. B&W; 86m. **DIR:** H. C. Potter. **CAST:** Merle Oberon, Brian Aherne, Karen Morley, David Niven. **1936**

BELOVED ROGUE ★★★★★ Superb example of the heights in set design, camera work, and special effects achieved in the late American silent cinema. John Barrymore is poet Francois Villon—here more of a Robin Hood than a brooding aesthete. Unreservedly recommended. Silent. B&W; 100m. **DIR:** Alan Crosland. **CAST:** John Barrymore, Conrad Veidt. **1927**

BELOW THE BELT ★★★1/2 This agreeable low-budget feature is short on technical polish but long on heart. It's a semidocumentary about a waitress (Regina Baff) who tries to become a professional wrestler, taking advice from ex-champ Mildred Burke (playing herself). There's even a *Rocky*ish finale. Made in 1974, but not released until 1980. Rated R. 91m. **DIR:** Robert Fowler. **CAST:** Regina Baff, Mildred Burke, John C. Becher, Shirley Stoler, Dolph Sweet, Ric Mancini. **1980**

BELOW THE BORDER ★★★ Energetic Rough Riders adventure has Buck Roberts (Buck Jones) going underground as a bandit while Tim McCall (Tim McCoy) poses as a cattle buyer. It's all to trap evil Roy Barcroft and put an end to his cattle rustling. B&W; 57m. **DIR:** Howard Bretherton. **CAST:** Buck Jones, Tim McCoy, Raymond Hatton, Linda Brent, Roy Barcroft, Charles King. **1942**

BELSTONE FOX, THE ★★ An orphaned fox cub is raised in captivity and cleverly eludes both hounds and hunters. The film is worth watching for the animal photography. Not rated; contains some violence to animals. 103m. **DIR:** James Hill. **CAST:** Eric Porter, Jeremy Kemp, Bill Travers, Rachel Roberts. **1973**

BEN The only thing going for this silly sequel to *Willard* is an awkwardly charming title song performed by a young Michael Jackson (a love song for a rat, no less). Rated PG for violence. 95m. **DIR:** Phil Karlson. **CAST:** Arthur O'Connell, Lee Montgomery, Rosemary Murphy. **1972**

BEN-HUR (1926) ★★★★ Colossal in every sense of the word, this greatest of silent film spectacles is still a winner today. Years in production, it cost a staggering $4 million and was two years being edited. The chariot-race and sea-battle scenes are unsurpassed. Ramon Novarro as Ben-Hur and Francis X. Bushman as Messala gave the performances of their careers. B&W; 116m. **DIR:** Fred Niblo. **CAST:** Ramon Novarro, Francis X. Bushman, May McAvoy, Betty Bronson, Carmel Myers. **1926**

BEN-HUR (1959) ★★★★★ In this film, which won eleven Oscars, a wealthy Jewish nobleman during the time of Christ incurs the hostility of the Roman military governor, who was his childhood friend. He is reduced to manning an oar on a slave galley, and his family is sent to prison. Years later he returns to seek vengeance upon his Roman tormentor. This culminates in a spectacular chariot race. Charlton Heston won an Oscar for his first-rate performance in the title role. 211m. **DIR:** William Wyler. **CAST:** Charlton Heston, Jack Hawkins, Sam Jaffe, Stephen Boyd. **1959 DVD**

BEND OF THE RIVER ★★★★ James Stewart and director Anthony Mann teamed up during the early 1950s to make a series of exceptional Westerns that helped the genre return to popularity. This one deals with Stewart leading a wagon train across the country and his dealings with ex-friend Arthur Kennedy, who hijacks their supplies. Superior Western fare in every sense. 91m. **DIR:** Anthony Mann. **CAST:** James Stewart, Arthur Kennedy, Rock Hudson, Julie Adams. **1952**

BENEATH THE BERMUDA TRIANGLE An American submarine is transported to the future in this cheap-looking rip-off of *The Philadelphia Experiment*. Rated R for profanity, violence, brief nudity, and sexual situations. 84m. **DIR:** Scott Levy. **CAST:** Jeff Fahey, Richard Tyson, Jack Coleman, Chick Vennera. **1996**

BENEATH THE PLANET OF THE APES ★★1/2 Charlton Heston let himself get sucked into this sequel to *Planet of the Apes*. Astronaut James Franciscus—sent to find out what happened to the first team sent to the planet—has more than simians to contend with; he also discovers a race of u-g-l-y mutants that worships an atomic bomb, since it made them what they are. . . . Some of the original's energy remains. Rated G. 95m. **DIR:** Ted Post. **CAST:** Charlton Heston, James Franciscus, Maurice Evans, Kim Hunter, Linda Harrison, James Gregory. **1970**

BENEATH THE 12-MILE REEF ★★★ Here is some good old-fashioned Hollywood entertainment. Film deals with sponge divers off the Florida coast. Light, enjoyable fluff. 102m. **DIR:** Robert D. Webb. **CAST:** Robert Wagner, Gilbert Roland, Terry Moore, Richard Boone. **1953 DVD**

BENEFICIARY, THE ★★ Suzy Amis is the cream that rises to the top of this sour exercise in stock characters and formulaic plotting. While the rest of the characters spend most of the film trying to get a clue, Amis squares off with a vengeance against a widow (Stacy Haiduk, beautiful and deadly) who plotted her tycoon husband's murder. Otherwise, the film has little to offer that hasn't been done to death. Made-for-cable. Rated R for violence, language, nudity, and adult situations. 90m. **DIR:** Marc Beinstock. **CAST:** Suzy Amis, Stacy Haiduk, Linden Ashby, Ron Silver, Robert Davi. **1997**

BENEFIT OF THE DOUBT ★★★ Donald Sutherland delivers a chilling performance as a man accused of murdering his wife and sent to prison for twenty years by the testimony of his daughter. Now Dad's out of prison, and Amy Irving believes that she and her son are due for a rather unpleasant visit. Good performances and crisp direction help maintain the suspense. Rated R for violence, language, and adult situations. 92m. **DIR:** Jonathan Heap. **CAST:** Donald Sutherland, Amy Irving, Graham Greene, Christopher McDonald. **1992**

BENIKER GANG, THE ★★1/2 Pleasant family film has Andrew McCarthy as Arthur Beniker, 18 year old orphanage inmate who leads an "orphanage break" of four other incorrigibles. Not too cutesy, and the story even makes some sense. Rated G; suitable for the entire family. 87m. **DIR:** Ken Kwapis. **CAST:** Andrew McCarthy, Jennie Dundas, Charles Fields, Jeff Alan-Lee, Danny Pintauro. **1985**

BENJAMIN SMOKE ★★★1/2 Music documentaries are usually so self-serving they miss the point. *Benjamin Smoke* not only hits the nail on the head, it hammers it home. Filmmakers Jem Cohen and Peter Sillen have pieced together a bewildering yet occasionally hopeful account of Atlanta lyricist-singer Robert Dickerson, who changed his name to Benjamin and started a band called Smoke. The effects of rock and roll on Benjamin and those around him begin to take their toll, creating an honest portrait of real life in the fast lane. Not rated. 73m. **DIR:** Jem Cohen, Peter Sillen. **2000**

BENJI ★★★★ *Benji* parallels *Lassie* and *Rin Tin Tin* by intuitively doing the right thing at the right time. In this film, a dog saves two children who get kidnapped. Unlike Lassie or Rin Tin Tin, Benji is a small, unassuming mutt, which makes him all the more endearing. Rated G. 86m. **DIR:** Joe Camp. **CAST:** Benji, Peter Breck, Deborah Walley, Edgar Buchanan, Frances Bavier, Patsy Garrett. **1974 DVD**

BENJI THE HUNTED ★★★ Most kids will love this adventure featuring everyone's favorite sweet-faced mutt slogging his poor little lost way through the wilderness of the Pacific Northwest to civilization. Rated G. 90m. **DIR:** Joe Camp. **CAST:** Benji. **1987**

BENNY & JOON ★★★1/2 Most viewers will enjoy this bittersweet comedy about a mentally ill artist who finds love with a quirky outsider, much to her older brother-guardian's chagrin. Folks coping with mental illness in real life will be offended by yet another film in which the problem is sanitized and trivialized. Rated PG for suggested sex and brief violence. 100m. **DIR:** Jeremiah S. Chechik. **CAST:** Johnny Depp, Mary Stuart Masterson, Aidan Quinn, Julianne Moore, Oliver Platt, C.C.H. Pounder, Dan Hedaya, Joe Grifasi, William H. Macy. **1993 DVD**

BENNY GOODMAN STORY, THE ★★★ If you enjoy good big-band music and don't mind a few errors in biographical fact, then this big brassy picture is a must for you. Steve Allen as Benny Goodman does a fine job. Watch for some other great performers in cameos. 116m. **DIR:** Valentine Davies. **CAST:** Steve Allen, Donna Reed, Teddy Wilson, Herbert Anderson, Gene Krupa, Robert F. Simon. **1955**

BENT ★★ Martin Sherman's provocative stage drama about the persecution of homosexuals by the Nazis during World War II loses much of its edge onscreen. The impact is further diluted on video, where the NC-17 film has been trimmed down to an R rating. The cast is fine, including Mick Jagger as a transvestite singer, but after all is said and done this is much ado about nothing. Rated R for language, violence, nudity, and adult situations. 104m. **DIR:** Sean Mathias. **CAST:** Lothaire Bluteau, Clive Owen, Brian Webber, Ian McKellen, Mick Jagger. **1996**

•BEOWULF Christopher Lambert stars as the title character in this futuristic retelling of the ancient epic tale of Beowulf, who quests to slay the vile man-eating Grendel and its vengeful mother. This movie squanders what was a wonderfully rich and artful story with utterly poor acting, directing, and production values. Rated R for violence and sexuality. 93m. **DIR:** Graham Baker. **CAST:** Christopher Lambert, Rhona Mitra, Oliver Cotton, Patricia Velazquez. **1999 DVD**

BERETTA'S ISLAND Former Mr. Universe Franco Columbu gets weighted down in this clumsy, low-budget action effort, playing a former Interpol agent out for revenge. Not rated; contains violence. 97m. **DIR:** Michael Preece. **CAST:** Franco Columbu, Ken Kercheval, Jo Campa, Arnold Schwarzenegger. **1992**

BERLIN AFFAIR, THE ★★ Uneven erotic psychodrama about a Japanese art student in prewar 1938 Germany who becomes involved in a bizarre love triangle with the wife of a politically affluent German diplomat and her husband. Though heavy on eroticism, the film is lean on story and character motivation. Rated R for nudity and profanity. 97m. **DIR:** Lilliana Cavani. **CAST:** Gudrun Landgrebe, Kevin McNally, Mio Takaki. **1985**

BERLIN ALEXANDERPLATZ ★★★1/2 Remember the scene in *A Clockwork Orange* in which Malcolm McDowell's eyes are wired open and he is forced to watch movies? That's how we often felt when wading through the fifteen-and-a-half hours of Rainer Werner Fassbinder's magnum opus. It has its moments of interest, and yes, even genius, but as with all of Fassbinder's films, also its excesses and false notes. In German with English subtitles. Not rated. 930m. **DIR:** Rainer Werner Fassbinder. **CAST:** Gunter Lamprecht, Hanna Schygulla, Barbara Sukowa. **1983**

BERLIN CONSPIRACY, THE Separate American and East German investigations into germ warfare and Middle East terrorism are hindered by the fall of the Berlin Wall. Bland performances and bad German accents diminish this low-budget thriller. Rated R for violence and profanity. 83m. **DIR:** Terence H. Winkless. **CAST:** Marc Singer, Mary Crosby, Stephen Davies. **1991**

BERLIN EXPRESS ★★★1/2 A taut, crisply edited espionage thriller from the director of the original *Cat People*. Filmed in semidocumentary style, *Berlin Express* takes full advantage of post–World War II Germany, incorporating actual footage of bombed-out Frankfurt and Berlin. Thrown together on a train to Berlin, Robert Ryan as an American nutrition expert, Paul Lukas as a marked German statesman trying to reunite his war-torn country, and Merle Oberon as Lukas's aide all give standout performances. B&W; 86m. **DIR:** Jacques Tourneur. **CAST:** Merle Oberon, Robert Ryan, Charles Korvin, Paul Lukas, Robert Coote. **1948**

BERLIN TUNNEL 21 ★★ Richard Thomas stars as an American soldier in Berlin in 1961. His girlfriend cannot leave the eastern section of Berlin to join him. The solution: sneak her out. Predictable. 141m. **DIR:** Richard Michaels. **CAST:** Richard Thomas, Horst Buchholz, José Ferrer, Jacques Breuer, Nicolas Farrell, Ute Christensen. **1981**

BERNADETTE ★★ This long, slow-moving French film features an almost too glamorous Sydney Penny as the impoverished young girl chosen to be the messenger at Lourdes. Rated PG for profanity. 120m. **DIR:** Jean Delannoy. **CAST:** Sydney Penny, Michelle Simonnett. **1987**

BERNARD AND THE GENIE ★★★ Pleasantly amusing Christmas movie from BBC-TV stars British comedian Lenny Henry as the genie in the lamp, released by a mild-mannered London art dealer who's having a really bad day. Once the genie is freed, the fun begins. 70m. **DIR:** Paul Welland. **CAST:** Lenny Henry, Rowan Atkinson. **1991**

BERNICE BOBS HER HAIR ★★★★ The perceptions of self-worth and personal integrity form the core of this droll adaptation of F. Scott Fitzgerald's ode to a shy young girl. Bernice (Shelley Duvall) sacrifices her luxuriously long hair for a shot at the inner circle of popularity jealously guarded by her hedonistic Jazz Era friends. Veronica Cartwright is wonderfully malignant as the fickle society girl who plays Pygmalion with her shy, unassuming cousin. Introduced by Henry Fonda. 49m. **DIR:** Joan Micklin Silver. **CAST:** Shelley Duvall, Veronica Cartwright, Bud Cort, Dennis Christopher, Gary Springer, Lane Binkley, Polly Holliday. **1976**

BERSERK ★★★1/2 Effectively staged thriller stars Joan Crawford as the owner of a once-great circus now on its last legs—until a number of accidental deaths of the performers starts packing 'em in. Joan comes under suspicion immediately when the cops begin counting the box-office receipts. Could she be guilty? 96m. **DIR:** Jim O'Connolly. **CAST:** Joan Crawford, Ty Hardin, Michael Gough, Diana Dors, Judy Geeson. **1967**

BERSERKER Silly slasher in which a Viking demon is reincarnated in his descendants. Rated R for nudity, violence, gore, and simulated sex. 85m. **DIR:** Jeff Richard. **CAST:** Joseph Alan Johnson. **1987**

BERT RIGBY, YOU'RE A FOOL ★★★ Musical-comedy star Robert Lindsay, who won a Tony for *Me and My Girl*, plays an English coal miner obsessed with the great musicals of Fred Astaire and Gene Kelly. When a strike is called at the mine, he decides to take a shot at making it as a song-and-dance man. Director Carl Reiner also scripted. There is some profanity, but the R rating seems excessive. 94m. **DIR:** Carl Reiner. **CAST:** Robert Lindsay, Cathryn Bradshaw, Robbie Coltrane, Jackie Gayle, Anne Bancroft, Corbin Bernsen. **1989**

BESHKEMPIR, THE ADOPTED SON ★★★1/2 Have you ever wished that they made more Kyrgyzstani movies? Well, here's one! Beshkempir is a young Kyrgyz boy who is just beginning to deal with his blossoming sexuality and raging hormones. His uncontrollable emotions lead the young man to learn that he was adopted—now making poor Beshkempir a subject of scorn and ridicule amongst his peers. This movie is beautifully shot, and gives an insight to a culture that is unfamiliar to many people. In Kyrgyzstani with English subtitles. Not rated; contains some language, violence, and nudity. B&W/color; 81m. **DIR:** Aktan Abdykalykov. **CAST:** Mirlan Abdykalykov, Albina Imasheva, Adir Abilkassimov, Bakit Dzhylkychiev, Mirlan Cinkozoev, Talai Mederov. **1998 DVD**

BESIEGED ★★★ English pianist in Rome is infatuated with an African medical student who lives downstairs and cleans his flat. He throws himself into her arms only to be rebuffed and told he can win her love by getting her husband released from jail. This intimate drama about love, desire, military repression, and unconditional sacrifice has uneven acting, an ambiguous ending, and relies on images for its emotional impact. But the film is saturated with sensuality. Rated R for brief nudity and sexual situations. 92m. **DIR:** Bernardo Bertolucci. **CAST:** David Thewlis, Thandie Newton, Claudio Santamaria. **1999 DVD**

BEST CHRISTMAS PAGEANT EVER, THE ★★★ An engaging television movie about a group of grade-school misfits who come of age during preparation for a school Christmas play. Well-acted but already dated. 80m. **DIR:** George Schaefer. **CAST:** Dennis Weaver, Loretta Swit, Karen Grassle. **1986**

BEST DEFENSE ★★★ Any movie that features the talents of Dudley Moore and Eddie Murphy has to be funny. Sometimes, however, laughs aren't enough. It's very easy to get confused in this film featuring Moore as the inept inventor of a malfunctioning piece of defense equipment, and Murphy as the hapless soldier forced to cope with it. The liberal use of profanity and several sex scenes make this R-rated romp unfit for youngsters. 94m. **DIR:** Willard Huyck. **CAST:** Dudley Moore, Eddie Murphy, Kate Capshaw, George Dzundza, Helen Shaver. **1984**

BEST FOOT FORWARD ★★★1/2 Film star Lucille Ball accepts military cadet Tommy Dix's invitation to his school's annual dance. The film introduced June Allyson and Nancy Walker and gave numerous high schools a fight song by adapting its biggest hit, "Buckle Down, Winsocki." Wholesome family fun. 95m. **DIR:** Edward Buzzell. **CAST:** Lucille Ball, William Gaxton, Virginia Weidler, Tommy Dix, June Allyson, Nancy Walker, Gloria De Haven. **1943**

BEST FRIENDS ★★ Burt Reynolds and Goldie Hawn star in this disappointingly tepid romantic comedy as a pair of successful screenwriters who decide to marry—thus destroying their profitable working relationship. A mess. Rated PG for profanity and adult situations. 116m. **DIR:** Norman Jewison. **CAST:** Burt Reynolds, Goldie Hawn, Ron Silver, Jessica Tandy. **1982**

BEST IN SHOW ★★★1/2 Christopher Guest's latest "mockumentary" is a hilarious indictment of devoted doggie owners who prowl the professional-show circuit, and the lengths to which they indulge their pampered pooches. Some characters are brilliantly conceived: John Michael Higgins and Michael McKean as an upscale gay couple, and Guest himself as a plain-talkin' fella who jes' loves his huntin' dog. But the shrill yuppies played by Parker Posey and Michael Hitchcock quickly grow tiresome. Animal lovers will recognize bits of themselves in this whimsical farce, which hits more often than it misses. Rated PG-13 for profanity and sexual content. 89m. **DIR:** Christopher Guest. **CAST:** Christopher Guest, Parker Posey, Michael Hitchcock, Eugene Levy, Catherine O'Hara, John Michael Higgins, Michael McKean, Jennifer Coolidge, Jane Lynch, Bob Balaban, Jim Piddock, Fred Willard. **2000 DVD**

BEST INTENTIONS, THE ★★★★ Originally a six-hour miniseries for television, this Swedish import was cut almost in half for international theatrical distribution. However, Ingmar Bergman's story, set in 1909 and concerning the courtship and early years of his parents' marriage, remains intact, with the characterizations and situations fully explored. In Swedish with English subtitles. 186m. **DIR:** Bille August. **CAST:** Samuel Froler, Pernilla August, Max von Sydow. **1992**

BEST KEPT SECRETS ★★★1/2 When a police officer is not promoted to the Special Information Unit, his wife (Patty Duke) decides to find out why. She discovers a secret file that the police department has been using for blacklisting purposes. This TV movie is guaranteed to keep your interest. 94m. **DIR:** Jerrold Freedman. **CAST:** Patty Duke, Frederic Forrest, Peter Coyote, Meg Foster. **1989**

BEST LEGS IN THE 8TH GRADE, THE ★★★ Bittersweet made-for-TV comedy focusing on the complexities of modern romance. Tim Matheson is a yuppie lawyer who gets some much-needed advice on the affairs of the heart. Annette O'Toole plays his girlfriend. 48m. **DIR:** Tom Patchett. **CAST:** Tim Matheson, Annette O'Toole, James Belushi, Kathryn Harrold. **1984**

BEST LITTLE GIRL IN THE WORLD, THE ★★★★1/2 This gut-wrenching teleplay about a girl, portrayed by Jennifer Jason Leigh who suffers from anorexia nervosa pulls no punches; some of the drama is hard to take, but if you can make it through the film's end, you'll feel rewarded. This was originally an after-school special. The entire cast turns in great performances. The equivalent of a PG for intense drama. 90m. **DIR:** Sam O'Steen. **CAST:** Jennifer Jason Leigh, Charles Durning, Eva Marie Saint, Jason Miller. **1986**

BEST LITTLE WHOREHOUSE IN TEXAS, THE ★★1/2 Dolly Parton and Burt Reynolds in a so-so version of the Broadway play, whose title explains all. Rated R for nudity, profanity, and sexual situations. 114m. **DIR:** Colin Higgins. **CAST:** Burt Reynolds, Dolly Parton, Dom DeLuise, Charles Durning. **1982**

BEST MAN, THE (1964) ★★★★ Sharp characterizations bring to life this drama of disparate political types jockeying for position and endorsement at a presidential convention. Thoroughly engrossing. B&W; 102m. **DIR:** Franklin J. Schaffner. **CAST:** Henry Fonda, Cliff Robertson, Edie Adams, Margaret Leighton, Shelley Berman, Lee Tracy, Ann Sothern. **1964**

BEST MAN, THE (1997) ★★★★1/2 *Il Testimone Dello Sposo* is a wonderfully engaging tale set during the last day of 1899 in a small Italian town. Ines Sastre is breathtaking as Francesca Babini, whose marriage to the town's wealthiest bachelor has the locals all abuzz. Unfortunately, Francesca is marrying for money, not love, but all of that changes when she sets her eyes on the best man, a world traveler named Angelo. There are laughs, hope, and lush period settings in this charming and intelligent film. In Italian with English subtitles. Rated PG. 101m. **DIR:** Pupi Avati. **CAST:** Ines Sastre, Diego Abatantuono, Dario Cantarelli. **1997**

BEST MAN, THE (1999) ★★★1/2 Dubbed a romantic comedy, this reunion flick has more than its share of serious moments. When a novelist (Taye Diggs) joins his former college chums for his best friend's wedding, he finds that his fictionalized account of their friendships has hit too close to home. He also must choose between his current flame and the friend he failed to romance in his youth. Multiple subplots and intrigues make this very watchable. Rated R for sex, nudity, profanity, and violence. 122m. **DIR:** Malcolm Lee. **CAST:** Taye Diggs, Nia Long, Morris Chestnut, Monica Calhoun. **1999 DVD**

BEST MEN ★★★1/2 As if her wedding day weren't stressful enough, bride-to-be Hope must contend with her intended being an ex-con who can't pass up the opportunity to rob a bank. Unbeknownst to Hope and his friends, Jesse is "Hamlet," a Robin Hood–like robber who picks the day of his wedding for his latest heist. Quirky character comedy succeeds, thanks to a winning cast, spirited direction, and a script that never plays dumb. Rated R for language and violence. 89m. **DIR:** Tamra Davis. **CAST:** Dean Cain, Sean Patrick Flanery, Luke Wilson, Drew Barrymore, Andy Dick, Mitchell Whitfield. **1997 DVD**

BEST OF DARK SHADOWS, THE ★★1/2 Lack of narration will leave viewers confused as this compilation jumps from one teaser to another. We meet vampires, a werewolf, a witch, ghosts, and a Jekyll and Hyde character without benefit of the background leading to these shocking developments. B&W/color; 30m. **DIR:** Lela Swift, Henry Kapland, John Sedwick. **CAST:** Jonathan

Frid, David Selby, Joan Bennett, Kate Jackson, Lara Parker, Kathryn Leigh Scott. **1965–1971**

BEST OF EVERYTHING, THE ★★1/2 Soapy but interesting movie about women in business and how their work affects their private lives. 121m. **DIR:** Jean Negulesco. **CAST:** Hope Lange, Joan Crawford, Louis Jourdan, Martha Hyer, Stephen Boyd, Robert Evans, Diane Baker. **1959**

BEST OF THE BADMEN ★★★1/2 Another of those all-star outlaw roundups with the James Boys, Younger Brothers, Sundance Kid, and Ringo Kid—all being forced into outlawry by crooked banking and railroad interests. 84m. **DIR:** William D. Russell. **CAST:** Robert Ryan, Claire Trevor, Jack Buetel, Robert Preston, Walter Brennan, Bruce Cabot. **1951**

BEST OF THE BEST ★★ An underdog U.S. national karate team battles for the world title in this martial arts *Rocky*. The numerous training montages, slow-motion fight scenes, and lessons in sportsmanship and courage all lead to a predictable, uplifting ending. Rated PG-13 for violence and language. 95m. **DIR:** Robert Radler. **CAST:** Eric Roberts, Phillip Rhee, Christopher Penn, James Earl Jones, Sally Kirkland, John P. Ryan. **1989 DVD**

BEST OF THE BEST 2 Three martial fu buddies from the original *Best* battle a Schwarzeneggeresque brute in an underworld Las Vegas gladiatorial arena that caters to decadent high rollers. Rated R for violence and language. 110m. **DIR:** Robert Radler. **CAST:** Eric Roberts, Phillip Rhee, Christopher Penn, Wayne Newton, Ralph Moeller, Meg Foster. **1993 DVD**

BEST OF TIMES, THE ★★★ Although this comedy starts off well, but then loses momentum right up to the ending, it benefits from likable performances by its lead players. Robin Williams and Kurt Russell star as two former football players who dropped the ball when their moment for glory came. But they get a second chance to win one for Taft (formerly Moron), California. Rated PG-13 for profanity and suggested sex. 100m. **DIR:** Roger Spottiswoode. **CAST:** Robin Williams, Kurt Russell, Pamela Reed, Holly Palance, Donald Moffat, Margaret Whitton, M. Emmet Walsh, R. G. Armstrong, Dub Taylor. **1986 DVD**

BEST REVENGE ★★1/2 Granger (John Heard), has come to Spain to team up with Bo (Levon Helm), who has promised him the contacts for a $4 million hashish deal. This fast-moving action-adventure has some good acting, but fails to rise above its pedestrian plot. 92m. **DIR:** John Trent. **CAST:** John Heard, Levon Helm, Alberta Watson, John Rhys-Davies. **1984 DVD**

BEST SELLER ★★★★ James Woods and Brian Dennehy give superb performances in this gripping character study about a ruthless hit man (Woods) who convinces a Joseph Wambaugh–type cop-turned-author (Dennehy) to help him write a book. Because the book threatens to expose the illegal empire of a wealthy industrialist, the authors soon find their lives in danger. The story by Larry Cohen is outrageous at times, but the electricity generated by the stars is undeniable. Rated R for profanity and violence. 110m. **DIR:** John Flynn. **CAST:** James Woods, Brian Dennehy, Victoria Tennant, Paul Shenar. **1987**

BEST YEARS OF OUR LIVES, THE ★★★★★ What happens when the fighting ends and warriors return home is the basis of this eloquent, compassionate film. William Wyler takes his time and guides a superb group of players through a tangle of postwar emotional conflicts. Harold Russell's first scene has lost none of its impact. Keep in mind World War II had just ended when this film debuted. B&W; 170m. **DIR:** William Wyler. **CAST:** Myrna Loy, Fredric March, Teresa Wright, Dana Andrews, Virginia Mayo, Harold Russell, Cathy O'Donnell. **1946 DVD**

BETHUNE ★★★1/2 This biographical teleplay gets off to a slow start, but delivers an absorbing story and masterful acting. It's the biography of Norman Bethune, the Canadian hero who served as a doctor in the combat between China and Japan. 88m. **DIR:** Eric Till. **CAST:** Donald Sutherland, Kate Nelligan, David Gardner, James Hong. **1984**

BETRAYAL (1978) ★★1/2 Based on a true incident, this soapy TV movie concerns a young woman who has an affair with her psychiatrist. What could have been revealing and vital breaks down into conventional melodrama. 100m. **DIR:** Paul Wendkos. **CAST:** Lesley Ann Warren, Rip Torn, Richard Masur, Peggy Ann Garner, Ron Silver, Bibi Besch. **1978**

BETRAYAL (1983) ★★★★★ Harold Pinter's play about the slow death of a marriage has been turned into an intelligent and innovative film that begins with the affair breaking apart and follows it backward to the beginning. Jeremy Irons and Patricia Hodge are superb. Rated R for profanity. 95m. **DIR:** David Jones. **CAST:** Jeremy Irons, Ben Kingsley, Patricia Hodge. **1983**

BETRAYAL FROM THE EAST ★★ Fast-talking, wisecracking Lee Tracy takes on imperial Japan in this biased World War II espionage programmer. Peppered with the racial slurs and stereotypes so popular during this period. B&W; 82m. **DIR:** William Berke. **CAST:** Lee Tracy, Nancy Kelly, Regis Toomey, Richard Loo, Abner Biberman, Philip Ahn. **1945**

BETRAYAL OF THE DOVE ★★★ A woman and her daughter are being spooked by someone and it looks like it is her soon-to-be ex-husband. She starts to fall in love with a doctor who used to date her best friend (Kelly LeBrock), but someone is trying to kill her. The story is interesting, but LeBrock just can't act. Not rated; contains nudity, profanity, violence, and implied sex. 94m. **DIR:** Strathford Hamilton. **CAST:** Helen Slater, Billy Zane, Kelly LeBrock, Alan Thicke, Harvey Korman, Stuart Pankin, Heather Lind. **1992**

BETRAYED (1954) ★★1/2 In German-occupied Holland a secret agent called "The Scarf" terrorizes underground attempts to overthrow the Nazis. A dated movie and an obviously much older Clark Gable don't add up in spite of a good supporting cast and authentic European settings. 108m. **DIR:** Gottfried Reinhardt. **CAST:** Clark Gable, Lana Turner, Victor Mature, O. E. Hasse, Louis Calhern, Wilfrid Hyde-White, Ian Carmichael, Nora Swinburne, Roland Culver, Niall MacGinnis. **1954**

BETRAYED (1988) ★★★1/2 A searing performance from Debra Winger surmounts baffling inconsistencies in Joe Eszterhas's script. She's sent by mentor John Heard to infiltrate a comfortably homespun rural American community that might conceal a nest of white supremacists. Its gut-wrenching impact is repeatedly dampened by the naïve and foolish actions taken by Winger. Focus on the message and forget the story.

Rated R for violence and language. 127m. **DIR:** Constantin Costa-Gavras. **CAST:** Debra Winger, Tom Berenger, John Heard, Betsy Blair, Ted Levine. **1988 DVD**

BETSY, THE ★★ A classic example of how to waste loads of talent and money. The Harold Robbins novel about a wealthy family in the auto manufacturing business was trashy to start with, but after Hollywood gets done with it, not even Laurence Olivier can save this debacle. Rated R. 125m. **DIR:** Daniel Petrie. **CAST:** Laurence Olivier, Tommy Lee Jones, Robert Duvall, Katharine Ross, Lesley-Anne Down, Jane Alexander. **1978 DVD**

BETSY'S WEDDING ★★★★ In this warm hearted and often uproarious comedy-drama, writer-director Alan Alda plays a down-on-his-luck dad who tries to raise money to give his daughter (Molly Ringwald) a big wedding. Ally Sheedy and newcomer Anthony LaPaglia are the standouts in a uniformly fine ensemble cast. Rated R for profanity. 106m. **DIR:** Alan Alda. **CAST:** Alan Alda, Molly Ringwald, Madeline Kahn, Joe Pesci, Ally Sheedy, Burt Young, Joey Bishop, Catherine O'Hara, Anthony LaPaglia. **1990**

BETTE MIDLER—ART OR BUST ★★★★ Bette Midler exudes more talent in this hour-and-a-half special than most entertainers do in a lifetime. Included are clips from her last bathhouse show and her later concert performances. Not rated; contains adult language. 82m. **DIR:** Thomas Schlamme. **CAST:** Bette Midler. **1984**

BETTER LATE THAN NEVER ★★1/2 Average made-for-television comedy about nursing home inhabitants who revolt against house rules. The premise is good, the execution so-so. Theft of a train is a nice touch. Rated PG. 100m. **DIR:** Richard Crenna. **CAST:** Harold Gould, Larry Storch, Strother Martin, Tyne Daly, Harry Morgan, Victor Buono, George Gobel, Donald Pleasence, Lou Jacobi. **1979**

BETTER OFF DEAD (1985) ★★ A mixture of clever ideas and awfully silly ones, this comedy focuses on the plight of teenage Everyman, Lane Meyer (John Cusack), who finds his world shattered when the love of his life, Beth (Amanda Wyss), takes up with a conceited jock. Lance figures he is "better off dead" than Beth-less. The film is at its best when writer-director Savage Steve Holland throws in little sketches that stand out from the familiar plot. Rated PG for profanity. 97m. **DIR:** Savage Steve Holland. **CAST:** John Cusack, David Ogden Stiers, Diane Franklin, Kim Darby, Amanda Wyss. **1985**

BETTER OFF DEAD (1993) ★★★ Very strong performances from Mare Winningham and Tyra Ferrell help save this familiar tale of an attorney fighting to save a death-row prisoner. The attorney who prosecuted the case now has second thoughts about the small-time thief and prostitute who killed a policeman. Not rated. 91m. **DIR:** M. Neema Bernette. **CAST:** Mare Winningham, Tyra Ferrell, Kevin Tighe, Don Harvey. **1993**

BETTER THAN CHOCOLATE ★★1/2 A young college dropout gets yanked out of her lesbian closet when her uptight mother comes to visit. The film is earnest and right-minded, but it's also preachy and rather trite. Rated R for profanity and mature themes. 101m. **DIR:** Anne Wheeler. **CAST:** Wendy Crewson, Karyn Dwyer, Christina Cox, Kevin Mundy, Peter Outerbridge. **1999 DVD**

BETTER TOMORROW, A ★★★1/2 Director John Woo reinvented the Hong Kong action film and began to attract world attention with this forceful melodrama that combines the action of classic Warner Brothers gangster films with the cynical sentimentality of spaghetti Westerns. In a supporting role, future star Chow Yun-Fat steals the movie. In Cantonese with English subtitles. Not rated; contains strong violence. 104m. **DIR:** John Woo. **CAST:** Leslie Cheung, Ti Lung, Chow Yun-Fat. **1986 DVD**

BETTER TOMORROW 2, A ★★★★1/2 The plot's tough to follow, and the subtitles are atrocious, but the high humor, unabashed melodrama, and roaring finale make this an action classic. Chow Yun-Fat duking it out with mafiosi in a Manhattan Chinese restaurant is a true delight. In Cantonese with English subtitles. Not rated; contains very strong violence. 100m. **DIR:** John Woo. **CAST:** Chow Yun-Fat, Leslie Cheung, Ti Lung. **1987 DVD**

BETTER TOMORROW 3, A: LOVE AND DEATH IN SAIGON ★★★1/2 This prequel set during the fall of Saigon has little to do with the two previous *Better Tomorrows*. Producer-director Tsui Hark is known for his incredible visual flamboyance and his interest in recent Asian history. This film features more of the latter, but action fans won't be displeased. In Cantonese with English subtitles. Not rated; contains strong violence. 113m. **DIR:** Tsui Hark. **CAST:** Chow Yun-Fat, Anita Mui, Tony Leung Chiu Wai. **1989 DVD**

BETTER WAY TO DIE, A ★★ Director Scott Wiper has an eye for action, but the rest of this derivative mistaken-identity thriller is blinded by stilted acting, clunky plotting, and insidious dialogue. This bad trip down memory lane is about an ex-cop whose retirement is interrupted when he's mistaken for someone else. Now all he has to do is stay alive long enough to clear things up. Wake us when it's over. Rated R for adult situations, language, and violence. 101m. **DIR:** Scott Wiper. **CAST:** Andre Braugher, Joe Pantoliano, Natasha Henstridge, Lou Diamond Phillips. **2000 DVD**

BETTY BLUE ★★ Betty is radically spontaneous and a bit wacko (we don't know why), Zorg is the man she inspires to continue writing. The trick is not to think too much but instead to bask in Jean-Jacques Beineix's sensuous visual flair. In French with English subtitles. Rated R. 117m. **DIR:** Jean-Jacques Beineix. **CAST:** Jean-Hugues Anglade, Beatrice Dalle. **1986**

BETWEEN FRIENDS ★★1/2 Two middle-aged divorcées meet and gradually form a life-sustaining friendship. This made-for-cable feature occasionally gets mired in melodramatic tendencies, but its two charismatic stars make it well worth watching. Not rated. 100m. **DIR:** Lou Antonio. **CAST:** Elizabeth Taylor, Carol Burnett, Barbara Rush, Stephen Young, Henry Ramer. **1983**

BETWEEN GOD, THE DEVIL AND A WINCHESTER 🦃 A treasure is stolen from a church in Texas and a band of outlaws and a holy man go on the trail to find it. 98m. **DIR:** Dario Silvester. **CAST:** Richard Harrison, Gilbert Roland. **1972**

BETWEEN HEAVEN AND HELL 🦃 This one is closer to Hell, mainly because it's all talk and no action. Broderick Crawford plays a sadistic drill sergeant who browbeats spoiled recruit Robert Wagner. It's all been done before and better. 94m. **DIR:** Richard Fleischer. **CAST:** Robert Wagner, Terry Moore, Broderick Crawford, Brad Dexter, Buddy Ebsen, Scatman Crothers, Skip Homeier. **1956**

BETWEEN MEN ★★★ Johnny Mack Brown heads west to find the rejected granddaughter of the man who raised him after his own father (William Farnum) fled, mistakenly thinking he was responsible for his son's death. Complicated plot line, good performances, and competent production. Above the norm. B&W; 59m. **DIR:** Robert N. Bradbury. **CAST:** Johnny Mack Brown, William Farnum, Beth Marion. **1935**

BETWEEN THE LINES ★★★★ Very good post-sixties film in the tradition of *Return of the Secaucus 7* and *The Big Chill*. Staff of a once-underground newspaper has to come to terms with the paper's purchase by a large publisher. Superb ensemble acting. Rated R for profanity and nudity. 101m. **DIR:** Joan Micklin Silver. **CAST:** John Heard, Jeff Goldblum, Lindsay Crouse, Stephen Collins, Jill Eikenberry, Bruno Kirby, Gwen Welles, Lewis J. Stadlen, Jon Korkes, Michael J. Pollard, Lane Smith, Joe Morton, Richard Cox, Marilu Henner. **1977**

BETWEEN TWO WOMEN ★★★★ For this TV movie Colleen Dewhurst won an Emmy as the mother-in-law from Hell. After her severe stroke, she is cared for by her much-maligned daughter-in-law (Farrah Fawcett). Remarkably moving and believable. 95m. **DIR:** Jon Avnet. **CAST:** Colleen Dewhurst, Farrah Fawcett, Michael Nouri, Steven Hill. **1986**

BETWEEN WARS Australian offering about an idealistic doctor. 97m. **DIR:** Michael Thornhill. **CAST:** Corin Redgrave, Arthur Dingham, Judy Morris. **1985**

BEULAH LAND ★★★1/2 A generational look at the life of a southern plantation family. The saga carries you through the Civil War and its aftermath. A polished TV production with a strong cast, all of whom turn in fine performances. 267m. **DIR:** Virgil Vogel, Harry Falk. **CAST:** Lesley Ann Warren, Michael Sarrazin, Eddie Albert, Hope Lange, Don Johnson, Meredith Baxter-Birney. **1980**

BEVERLY HILLS BODYSNATCHERS Dark comedy about a mortician and his mad-scientist assistant. R for nudity, profanity, and violence. 85m. **DIR:** Jonathan Mostow. **CAST:** Vic Tayback, Frank Gorshin, Art Metrano. **1989**

BEVERLY HILLS BRATS ★★ The son of a wealthy plastic surgeon convinces a would-be robber to kidnap him. Zany and outrageous situations make this watchable. PG-13 for nudity and profanity. 90m. **DIR:** Dimitri Sotirakis. **CAST:** Peter Billingsley, Burt Young, Martin Sheen, Terry Moore. **1989**

BEVERLY HILLS COP ★★★★ In this highly entertaining cops-and-comedy caper, Eddie Murphy plays a streetwise policeman from Detroit who takes a leave of absence to track down the men who killed his best friend. This quest takes him to the unfamiliar hills of ritzy southern California, where he's greeted as anything but a hero. Rated R for violence and profanity. 105m. **DIR:** Martin Brest. **CAST:** Eddie Murphy, Lisa Eilbacher, Judge Reinhold, John Ashton. **1984 DVD**

BEVERLY HILLS COP II ★★1/2 This sequel lacks most of the charm and freshness of the first film, choosing instead to unwind as a thunderous, pounding assault on the senses. Eddie Murphy needs all his considerable talent to enliven this confusing mess, and he just manages to pull it off. Rated R for profanity and brief nudity. 102m. **DIR:** Tony Scott. **CAST:** Eddie Murphy, Judge Reinhold, Jurgen Prochnow, Ronny Cox, John Ashton, Brigitte Nielsen, Allen Garfield, Dean Stockwell. **1987 DVD**

BEVERLY HILLS COP 3 ★★★1/2 Detroit cop Axel Foley is back in Los Angeles fighting off thugs the LAPD can't handle. Eddie Murphy is in his element as the wisecracking cop and knows how to milk one-liners for laughs. Set in a California theme park with most of the characters from the first two films back on board. Rated R for language. 100m. **DIR:** John Landis. **CAST:** Eddie Murphy, Theresa Randle, Judge Reinhold, Hector Elizondo, Bronson Pinchot, Timothy Carhart, John Saxon, Alan Young, Stephen McHattie. **1994 DVD**

BEVERLY HILLS MADAM In this TV movie, Faye Dunaway is madam Lil Hutton, whose carefully cultivated reputation is being threatened by her own call girls. 97m. **DIR:** Harvey Hart. **CAST:** Faye Dunaway, Louis Jourdan, Donna Dixon, Robin Givens, Terry Farrell, Marshall Colt. **1986**

BEVERLY HILLS 90210 ★★ Pilot movie for the Fox TV series introduces America to a whole new generation of teen idols. The film explores the problems faced by the Walsh family from Minnesota when they relocate to America's city of glamour. About as socially relevant as a Clearasil commercial. 90m. **DIR:** Tim Hunter. **CAST:** Jason Priestley, Shannen Doherty, Jennie Garth, Ian Ziering, Gabrielle Carteris, Maxwell Caulfield, Josh Mostel, Richard Cummings Jr. **1990**

BEVERLY HILLS NINJA Klutzy orphan with a soft heart is raised by a Ninja clan and tangles with murderers and counterfeiters in this mirthless comedy. Rated PG-13 for language and violence. 90m. **DIR:** Dennis Dugan. **CAST:** Chris Farley, Nicollette Sheridan, Robin Sou, Chris Rock, Nathaniel Parker. **1997 DVD**

BEVERLY HILLS VAMP Writer-director Fred Olen Ray labors in vain, trying to make this vampire movie funny. Rated R for nudity, profanity, and simulated sex. 88m. **DIR:** Fred Olen Ray. **CAST:** Eddie Deezen, Tim Conway Jr., Britt Ekland. **1989**

BEVERLY HILLBILLIES, THE (TV SERIES) ★★★ Selected episodes from the long-running TV series. Corny but effective. The immensely popular series was finally canceled not because of sagging ratings but because CBS decided to upgrade its network image. 30m. **DIR:** Ralph Levy. **CAST:** Buddy Ebsen, Irene Ryan, Donna Douglas, Max Baer, Raymond Bailey, Nancy Kulp. **1962–1971**

BEVERLY HILLBILLIES GO HOLLYWOOD, THE ★★★ Enjoyable compilation of four episodes of the popular television series finds the Clampett clan with a controlling interest in Mammoth Pictures. The studio is turned head-over-heels when the Clampetts decide to take an active interest in making movies. Plenty of the corn-fed humor that made the series so popular. 104m. **DIR:** Joseph DePew. **CAST:**- Buddy Ebsen, Irene Ryan, Donna Douglas, Max Baer, Nancy Culp, Raymond Bailey. **1964**

BEVERLY HILLBILLIES, THE (1993) ★★★ It's scary how much Cloris Leachman looks and sounds like Irene Ryan's Granny in this big-screen version of the backwoods Clampett family's invasion of Beverly Hills. Featuring good work from Jim Varney, Lily Tomlin, and Dabney Coleman, it's fun for adults who fondly remember the series and kids looking for a silly laugh. Rated PG for brief profanity. 93m. **DIR:** Penelope Spheeris. **CAST:** Jim Varney, Cloris Leachman, Lily Tomlin, Dabney Coleman, Lea Thompson, Diedrich Bader, Erika Eleniak, Rob Schneider, Dolly Parton, Buddy Ebsen, Zsa Zsa Gabor. **1993**

BEWARE! CHILDREN AT PLAY 🦃 Monster moppets make mincemeat of the adults in a small town, setting the scene for a series of gory retaliations that look more like someone broke a ketchup bottle. Not rated; contains violence. 94m. **DIR:** Mik Cribben. **CAST:** Michael Robinson, Rich Hamilton, Robin Lilly. **1989 DVD**

BEWARE, MY LOVELY ★★★★ Robert Ryan is terrifyingly right as an amnesiac psycho who can fly into a strangling rage one minute, then return to his simple-minded handyman guise the next. Ida Lupino is also superb as the widow who hires Ryan to clean her floors, an action she soon regrets. Dark suspense remains taut right up to the ending. B&W; 77m. **DIR:** Harry Horner. **CAST:** Ida Lupino, Robert Ryan, Taylor Holmes, Barbara Whiting. **1952**

BEWARE OF A HOLY WHORE ★★★★ Rainer Werner Fassbinder's wickedly funny comedy about a movie cast and crew trying to make the best of a worsening situation. Being stranded at a seaside resort would be a dream come true for most, but turns into a nightmare here. If it can go wrong, it will. Offscreen antics will appeal to those fascinated by the movie-making process. In German with English subtitles. Not rated. 103m. **DIR:** Rainer Werner Fassbinder. **CAST:** Lou Castel, Eddie Constantine, Hanna Schygulla, Margarethe von Trotta. **1971**

BEWARE OF SPOOKS ★★★ Joe E. Brown is hilarious as a cop afraid of his own shadow. He gets mixed up with a pretty girl and some thugs in a haunted house. B&W; 76m. **DIR:** Edward Sedgwick. **CAST:** Joe E. Brown, Mary Carlisle, Clarence Kolb. **1939**

BEYOND A REASONABLE DOUBT (1956) ★★★ To reveal the faults of the justice system, novelist Dana Andrews allows himself to be incriminated in a murder. The plan is to reveal his innocence at the last minute. But the one man who can exonerate him is killed. Don't expect surprise, but shock! B&W; 80m. **DIR:** Fritz Lang. **CAST:** Dana Andrews, Joan Fontaine, Sidney Blackmer, Shepperd Strudwick. **1956**

BEYOND ATLANTIS ★★ Unexciting movie about a motley bunch of adventurers looking for a fabulous treasure on an uncharted isle. Rated PG for mild violence. 89m. **DIR:** Eddie Romero. **CAST:** Patrick Wayne, John Ashley, Leigh Christian, Sid Haig. **1973**

BEYOND EVIL 🦃 A luxurious mansion happens to be haunted. Rated R. 94m. **DIR:** Herb Freed. **CAST:** John Saxon, Lynda Day George, Michael Dante. **1980**

BEYOND FEAR ★★★ A man's wife and child are taken hostage by a band of outlaws, and he must work with the police to ensure the safety of his family in this compelling film. Rated R by mid-1970s standards due to violence and profanity (very little of both, actually). 92m. **DIR:** Yannick Andrei. **CAST:** Michel Bouquet, Michael Constantine, Marilu Tolo. **1975**

BEYOND JUSTICE ★★1/2 A wealthy American hires mercenaries to rescue her son. Her Arab ex-husband has taken the spoiled brat to Morocco to become the next prince of the desert. Lots of guns, explosions, and bad acting. Rated R for profanity and violence. 113m. **DIR:** Duccio Tessari. **CAST:** Rutger Hauer, Carol Alt, Omar Sharif, Elliott Gould, Kabir Bedi. **1990 DVD**

BEYOND OBSESSION ★★ Marcello Mastroianni and Eleonora Giorgi are strange bedfellows for American Tom Berenger in this confusing Italian film about hustling, obsession, and seduction. Dubbed. Not rated; has profanity and nudity. 116m. **DIR:** Lilliana Cavani. **CAST:** Tom Berenger, Marcello Mastroianni, Eleonora Giorgi, Michel Piccoli. **1982**

BEYOND RANGOON ★★★ It takes time to warm up to Patricia Arquette, who plays a tourist trying unsuccessfully to get on with her life despite haunting personal tragedy. It is the superior performance of U Aung Ko, as her guide turned adviser, that commands our undivided attention. The two are caught up in the 1988 massacre of Burmese students and monks when the military dictatorship decides to squelch the Democracy Movement. Satisfying conclusion makes up for shaky start. Rated R for violence and profanity. 96m. **DIR:** John Boorman. **CAST:** Patricia Arquette, U Aung Ko, Frances McDormand, Spalding Gray, Adelle Lutz. **1995**

BEYOND REASON ★★★ Telly Savalas shows his stuff in this sensitve film, which he wrote and directed. He plays an iconoclastic psychologist who slowly loses touch with reality. Though thought-provoking and touching throughout, the story gets a little muddy from time to time and finishes unsatisfyingly. 88m. **DIR:** Telly Savalas. **CAST:** Telly Savalas, Diana Muldaur, Marvin Laird. **1985**

BEYOND REASONABLE DOUBT ★★★ Well-crafted mystery based on the real-life conviction for double murder of an innocent New Zealand farmer. David Hemmings turns in a polished performance as a ruthless cop who engineers Thomas's conviction. 117m. **DIR:** John Laing. **CAST:** David Hemmings, John Hargreaves. **1983**

BEYOND REDEMPTION ★★1/2 A series of gruesome murders plagues the city, and it is up to Andrew McCarthy as the lead investigator to head the quest to find the serial killer. Each murder has a biblical theme, causing McCarthy to wonder what connection the killer has with the Church. Rated R primarily for gory murder scenes. 97m. **DIR:** Chris Angel. **CAST:** Andrew McCarthy, Michael Ironside, Jayne Heitmeyer. **1999 DVD**

BEYOND SILENCE ★★★1/2 When a young girl becomes interested in music, her deaf father fears that he's losing her to a world where he can't follow. Director Caroline Link uses deafness as a metaphor for the inevitable alienation of growing children from their parents, and the film shows an uncanny insight into the undercurrents of affection and resentment that often exist side by side in families. In German with English subtitles. Rated PG-13 for mature themes. 100m. **DIR:** Caroline Link. **CAST:** Sylvie Testud, Tatjana Trieb, Howie Seago, Emmanuelle Laborit. **1996**

•BEYOND SUSPICION ★★★★ An auspicious debut for director Matthew Tabak, who has created a fascinating character study disguised as *film noir*. Jeff Goldblum is excellent as John Nolan, a semisuccessful life insurance salesman whose complacent life is interrupted by an act of violence. When a liquor store–deli clerk named Auggie Rose is killed in front of him, Nolan feels responsible and takes it upon himself to learn more about Rose. His quest for redemption begins to take its toll, not only on him but the people in his life. Tabak fills every frame with interesting characters and situations, and shows a real talent for creating mood and atmosphere. Also released as *Auggie Rose*. Rated R for adult situations, language, and violence. 109m. **DIR:** Matthew Tabak. **CAST:** Jeff Goldblum, Anne Heche, Nancy Travis, Kim Coates, Timothy Olyphant. **2000 DVD**

BEYOND THE CALL ★★★ Happily married Sissy Spacek learns that a former high-school sweetheart is about to be executed for killing a police officer, and—much to her husband's discomfort—she agrees to visit the man on death row. What follows is a series of intense conversations, during which Spacek attempts to understand what became of the gentle boy she once knew. Doug Magee's script starts well but stalls, and the conclusion is particularly dissatisfying. Rated R for violence, profanity, and dramatic intensity. 101m. **DIR:** Tony Bill. **CAST:** Sissy Spacek, David Strathairn, Arliss Howard, Janet Wright. **1996**

BEYOND THE CALL OF DUTY ★★ Another mindless adventure film, this one set on the Mekong River Delta in Vietnam. In the middle of the war, soldier Jan-Michael Vincent finds himself risking his life to save a female journalist. Pedestrian and implausible, and just a tad too late to make an impact. Rated R for violence and language. 93m. **DIR:** Cirio H. Santiago. **CAST:** Jan-Michael Vincent, Jillian McWhirter. **1992**

BEYOND THE DOOR ♥ Sick rip-off of *The Exorcist* has Juliet Mills as a woman possessed by guess what. Rated R. 94m. **DIR:** Ovidio Assonitis (Oliver Hellman). **CAST:** Juliet Mills, Richard Johnson, David Colin Jr. **1975**

BEYOND THE DOOR 2 ★★ Why, why, why? Actually, this semisequel is much better than the original mainly because its director was the famed Mario Bava. This time a young boy becomes possessed by the unseen power of hell, and many die. Alternate title: *Shock*. Rated R. 92m. **DIR:** Mario Bava. **CAST:** Daria Nicolodi, John Steiner, David Colin Jr. **1979**

BEYOND THE DOOR 3 ♥ A college student falls victim to the prince of darkness in this unscary horror yarn with laughable special effects. Rated R for profanity, nudity, and violence. 94m. **DIR:** Jeff Kwitny. **CAST:** Mary Kohnert. **1991**

BEYOND THE DOORS ♥ Jimi Hendrix, Janis Joplin, and Jim Morrison are atrociously impersonated in this docudrama that suggests they were killed by the CIA. Rated R for drug use and nudity. 117m. **DIR:** Larry Buchanan. **CAST:** Gregory Allen Chatman, Riba Meryl, Bryan Wolf. **1980**

BEYOND THE FOREST ★★ Too much Bette Davis spoils this mix of greed, adultery, abortion, and murder, even if she does utter the classic line, "What a dump!" Snarling and whining, Davis gives a performance that turns the murky-plotted film into a melodramatic mess even her most devoted fans reject. B&W; 96m. **DIR:** King Vidor. **CAST:** Bette Davis, Joseph Cotten, David Brian, Ruth Roman, Minor Watson, Regis Toomey. **1949**

BEYOND THE LAW (1962) ♥ A spaghetti Western with Lee Van Cleef as a bad guy turned good. Not rated; contains adult language and some gratuitous, badly staged violence. 90m. **DIR:** Giorgio Stegani. **CAST:** Lee Van Cleef, Antonio Sabato, Lionel Stander, Bud Spencer. **1968 DVD**

BEYOND THE LAW (1992) ★★ In one of those been-there-done-that roles, Charlie Sheen plays a cop who goes undercover to bust a motorcycle gang and prove to gang leader Michael Madsen that he's the stuff of which nightmares are made. Usual conflicts include Sheen's losing sight of reality as he slips into his new persona. Ho hum. Rated R for violence, language, and adult situations. 101m. **DIR:** Larry Ferguson. **CAST:** Charlie Sheen, Michael Madsen, Linda Fiorentino. **1992 DVD**

BEYOND THE LIMIT ★★ Dull, unconvincing adaptation of *The Honorary Consul*, Graham Greene's novel about love and betrayal in an Argentinian town stars Michael Caine as a kidnapped diplomat and Richard Gere as the doctor in love with his wife. It'll take you beyond your limit. Rated R. 103m. **DIR:** John Mackenzie. **CAST:** Michael Caine, Richard Gere, Bob Hoskins, Elpidia Carrillo. **1983**

BEYOND THE MAT ★★★ Professional wrestling is the subject of this candid documentary that dives into the bloody spectacle of the World Wrestling Federation and Extreme Championship Wrestling. The film also goes backstage to examine the tryouts of two wannabe pros, the career and personal life of family man Mick "Mankind" Foley, the twilight ring years of Terry Funk, and the inner demons and rock-bottom slide of Jake "The Snake" Roberts. Rated R for language and violence. 92m. **DIR:** Berry Blaustein. **2000 DVD**

BEYOND THE POSEIDON ADVENTURE ♥ Michael Caine heads one of two salvage crews that race each other and time to probe the upside-down wreck of the *Poseidon*. Rated PG for mild violence and language. 114m. **DIR:** Irwin Allen. **CAST:** Michael Caine, Sally Field, Telly Savalas, Jack Warden, Peter Boyle. **1979**

BEYOND THE PURPLE HILLS ★★★ Sheriff Gene Autry finds an old lawman friend murdered and arrests the victim's son, soon to be TV's Wyatt Earp, Hugh O'Brian, in his film debut. Autry realizes he can't be guilty and sets out to bring in the real killer. This film treats us to not only Autry's horse, Champion, but Little Champ as well, strutting his stuff. B&W; 70m. **DIR:** John English. **CAST:** Gene Autry, Pat Buttram, Hugh O'Brian, James Millican, Don Beddoe. **1950**

BEYOND THE RISING MOON (STAR QUEST) ★★ In the twenty-first century, a genetically created troubleshooter rebels. The same theme was handled much better in *Blade Runner*, though here the plot is secondary to the mediocre special effects and outer-space shoot-outs. 93m. **DIR:** Philip Cook. **CAST:** Tracy Davis, Hans Bachmann. **1988**

BEYOND THE STARS ★★★ Troubled teen Christian Slater, spending the summer with divorced father Robert Foxworth, runs into reclusive ex-astronaut Martin Sheen, who opens up and takes the kid under his wing. They eventually form a trust that allows Sheen to introduce Slater to a secret he discovered on the moon. Rated PG. 94m. **DIR:** David Saperstein. **CAST:** Martin Sheen, Christian Slater, Robert Foxworth, Sharon Stone, Olivia D'Abo, F. Murray Abraham. **1989**

BEYOND THE VALLEY OF THE DOLLS ♥ This was rated X when it came out, but by today's standards it's an R for gratuitous nudity and profanity. 109m. **DIR:**

Russ Meyer. **CAST:** Dolly Read, Cynthia Myers, Marcia McBroom. **1970**

BEYOND THE WALLS ★★1/2 This Israeli film pits Jewish and Arab convicts against each other with explosive consequences. A standard prison drama. Nominated for a best foreign film Oscar, it lost to *Dangerous Moves*. 103m. **DIR:** Uri Barbash. **CAST:** Arnon Zadok, Muhamad Bakri. **1984**

BEYOND THERAPY ★★ Robert Altman is a hit-and-miss director and his *Beyond Therapy* (adapted from Christopher Durang's play) qualifies as a miss. The movie, which pokes fun at psychiatrists and their patients, really is a mess filled with unconnected episodes. Most of the performances and much of the dialogue are salvageable and hilarious, however. Most notable are Tom Conti and, as a bizarre psychiatrist, Glenda Jackson. Rated R. 93m. **DIR:** Robert Altman. **CAST:** Julie Hagerty, Jeff Goldblum, Glenda Jackson, Tom Conti, Christopher Guest, Cris Campion. **1987**

BEYOND TOMORROW ★★1/2 Sudden success goes to singer Richard Carlson's head. He switches his affections from fiancée Jean Parker to captivating stage star Helen Vinson. To see that right is done, three ghosts return from the grave and change his troubled mind. An interesting premise on paper, the film fails to live up to its possibilities. B&W; 84m. **DIR:** A. Edward Sutherland. **CAST:** Jean Parker, Richard Carlson, Helen Vinson, Charles Winninger, Harry Carey, C. Aubrey Smith, Maria Ouspenskaya, Rod La Rocque. **1940 DVD**

BHAJI ON THE BEACH ★★★★ An assortment of women, all ethnic Indians living in England, take a day trip to the seaside resort at Blackpool, where their different stories mix and play themselves out. The film takes some getting used to, with its riotous, colorful images and thick British and Indian accents, but it's worth the effort—a charming, distinctive taste of an exotic subculture. Not rated; suitable for mature audiences. 99m. **DIR:** Gurinder Chadha. **CAST:** Kim Vithana, Lalita Ahmed, Shaheen Khan, Sarita Khajuria, Jimmi Harkishin, Zohra Seghal, Peter Cellier. **1993**

BHOWANI JUNCTION ★★★1/2 An exciting, often stirring drama, of the movement of passive resistance started by Mahatma Gandhi in post-World War II India. Ava Gardner stars as an Anglo-Indian being stirred by her ties to the Sikhs and their cause. Not rated, but recommended for family viewing. 110m. **DIR:** George Cukor. **CAST:** Ava Gardner, Stewart Granger, Lionel Jeffries, Bill Travers. **1956**

BIBLE, THE ★★★ An overblown all-star treatment of five of the early stories in the Old Testament. Director John Huston gives this movie the feel of a Cecil B. De Mille spectacle, but there is little human touch to any of the stories. This expensively mounted production forgets that in the Bible, individual accomplishments are equally relevant to grandeur. 174m. **DIR:** John Huston. **CAST:** Michael Parks, Ulla Bergryd, Richard Harris, John Huston, Ava Gardner. **1966 DVD**

BICENTENNIAL MAN ★★★1/2 Isaac Asimov's classic science-fiction story gets opulent treatment in this expanded adaptation, which gives star Robin Williams another of his signature "sensitive" roles, in this case a new NDR-114 robot initially purchased as a family companion and servant. But Andrew, as he comes to be called, proves unusually creative and able to reason for himself, which over the course of several generations leads the android to remake himself in his masters' image. It's a popular sci-fi conceit: the notion that human passion, senses, and even mortality are so cherished that an android who never ages would willingly sacrifice immortality for a chance to obtain these prized abilities. The problem is that Nicholas Kazan's script has no conflict whatsoever, merely comic relief to offset the story's increasingly melancholy atmosphere. Rated PG for mild profanity and sexual candor. 132m. **DIR:** Chris Columbus. **CAST:** Robin Williams, Embeth Davidtz, Sam Neill, Oliver Platt, Kiersten Warren, Wendy Crewson, Hallie Kate Eisenberg. **1999 DVD**

BICYCLE THIEF, THE ★★★★ Considered by critics an all-time classic, this touching, honest, beautifully human film speaks realistically to the heart with simple cinematic eloquence. A bill-poster's bicycle, on which his job depends, is stolen. Ignored by the police, who see nothing special in the loss, the anguished worker and his young son search Rome for the thief. In Italian with English subtitles. B&W; 90m. **DIR:** Vittorio De Sica. **CAST:** Lamberto Maggiorani, Lianella Carell, Enzo Staiola. **1949 DVD**

BIG ★★★★ In this intelligent script from Gary Ross and Anne Spielberg, Tom Hanks stars as the "big person" embodiment of young David Moscow, who wishes for a creaky amusement-park fortune-telling machine to make him "big." Hanks, as the result, performs brilliantly as the 13 year old in a 35 year old body; he's ably assisted by spunky Elizabeth Perkins as an associate at the children's toy company where he's able to land a job. Rated PG for mild sexual themes. 102m. **DIR:** Penny Marshall. **CAST:** Tom Hanks, Elizabeth Perkins, Robert Loggia, John Heard, Jared Rushton, David Moscow. **1988 DVD**

BIG BAD JOHN ★★ Bayou bad boys take leave of the swamps, setting out on a trail of violence to settle an old score. This macho masher offers a heavyweight country-and-western soundtrack. Filmed in Colorado, Texas, and New Mexico. Rated R for violence. 86m. **DIR:** Burt Kennedy. **CAST:** Jimmy Dean, Jack Elam, Ned Beatty, Romy Windsor, Jeff Osterhage, Bo Hopkins. **1990**

BIG BAD MAMA ★★ Here's an okay film concerning a mother (Angie Dickinson), sort of a second-rate Ma Barker, leading her daughters on a robbery spree during the Depression. It's not a classic by any means, but the action keeps things moving along. Rated R for violence, nudity, and sex. 83m. **DIR:** Steve Carver. **CAST:** Angie Dickinson, Tom Skerritt, William Shatner, Joan Prather. **1974 DVD**

BIG BAD MAMA II 🦃 A shabby sequel to a so-so movie. Rated R for violence and nudity. 85m. **DIR:** Jim Wynorski. **CAST:** Angie Dickinson, Robert Culp, Danielle Brisebois, Julie McCullough, Bruce Glover. **1987**

BIG BANG THEORY, THE ★★1/2 When an aspiring actress is attacked by a sleazy producer and then sexually abused by a motorcycle cop, she finds herself in the role of a lifetime. Darling Narita stars as the actress who loses her apartment, job, and dignity in one afternoon, but gains newfound power when she dons the cop's outfit and hits the streets on his motorcycle. Rated R for violence, language, and adult situations. 98m. **DIR:** Ash.

CAST: Darling Narita, Peter Greene, Michael Newland, Eric Shrody. **1997**

BIG BIRD CAGE, THE ★★ Some of the women-in-prison movies that producer Roger Corman cranked out in the Seventies were worth seeing because some talented filmmakers brought a high level of ability and excitement to them. This, however, is one of the boring ones. Rated R for nudity and violence. 88m. **DIR:** Jack Hill. **CAST:** Pam Grier, Anitra Ford, Sid Haig. **1972**

BIG BLUE, THE 🦃 This underwater adventure drowns largely because Rosanna Arquette attempts to re-create her ditzy *Desperately Seeking Susan* persona. Underwater shots are the only plus. Rated PG for mature themes. 118m. **DIR:** Luc Besson. **CAST:** Rosanna Arquette, Jean-Marc Barr, Jean Reno, Griffin Dunne. **1988 DVD**

BIG BLUFF, THE 🦃 A young woman with a terminal disease marries a gigolo who plots to murder her. B&W; 70m. **DIR:** W. Lee Wilder. **CAST:** John Bromfield, Martha Vickers, Robert Hutton, Rosemarie Bowe. **1955**

BIG BRASS RING, THE ★★★ This film exists thanks to an unproduced script by Orson Welles, which is further "sweetened" by Oja Kodar and F. X. Feeney; the result is yet another predictable study of corrupt politicians and their slimy secrets. William Hurt is more deadpan than usual as a candidate for governor of Missouri, a bid threatened by an old mentor (Nigel Hawthorne) with some compromising photographs and rather aberrant sexual tastes of his own. These carnal antics are displayed in a blatant manner that seems intended to shock and titillate; while such things may have been hot stuff when Welles first concocted them, they all seem trite and familiar these days. Miranda Richardson scores some points as Hurt's alcoholic and ambitious wife. Rated R for nudity, profanity, violence, and simulated sex. 104m. **DIR:** George Hickenlooper. **CAST:** William Hurt, Nigel Hawthorne, Miranda Richardson, Irène Jacob. **1999 DVD**

BIG BRAWL, THE ★★★ Director Robert Clouse again fails to reach the heights attained with his *Enter the Dragon*. Nevertheless, this kung fu comedy has its moments—most provided by star Jackie Chan. 95m. **DIR:** Robert Clouse. **CAST:** Jackie Chan, José Ferrer, Kristine DeBell, Mako. **1980**

BIG BROADCAST OF 1938, THE ★★★★ A delightful musical with a talented cast of performers who were just starting their careers. Part of the fun is watching them develop confidence and proficiency. The slight plot about ocean liners involved in a senseless race on the high seas is just an excuse for the cast members to entertain the passengers. B&W; 91m. **DIR:** Mitchell Leisen. **CAST:** W. C. Fields, Bob Hope, Martha Raye, Dorothy Lamour, Kirsten Flagstad, Shirley Ross, Ben Blue, Leif Erickson. **1938**

BIG BULLY ★★1/2 Concept and a meandering script overcome common sense in this misfired satire, which features Rick Moranis as a meek writer who returns to his small-town school to teach, only to renew ties with a much-feared childhood bully (now grown up into Tom Arnold). Older viewers are unlikely to appreciate the picture's ill-advised morals. Rated PG for slapstick violence. 93m. **DIR:** Steve Miner. **CAST:** Rick Moranis, Tom Arnold, Julianne Phillips, Carol Kane, Jeffrey Tambor, Don Knotts. **1996 DVD**

BIG BUS, THE ★★★ A superluxurious nuclear-powered bus runs into trouble while carrying a group of misfits from New York to Denver. This spoof appeared four years before *Airplane!* It's not as funny, but it does have a silly and sarcastic playfulness. One of those few films that work better on the small screen. Rated PG. 88m. **DIR:** James Frawley. **CAST:** Joseph Bologna, Stockard Channing, John Beck, Lynn Redgrave, José Ferrer, Ruth Gordon, Richard B. Shull, Sally Kellerman, Ned Beatty, Richard Mulligan, Larry Hagman, Howard Hesseman, Harold Gould. **1976**

BIG BUSINESS ★★★1/2 Bette Midler and Lily Tomlin play two sets of mismatched twins, one raised in a West Virginia country setting and another accustomed to wealth and power in New York City. Despite the unoriginal, one-joke plot, the stars manage some genuinely funny moments. Rated PG for light profanity. 95m. **DIR:** Jim Abrahams. **CAST:** Bette Midler, Lily Tomlin, Fred Ward, Edward Herrmann, Michele Placido, Daniel Gerroll, Barry Primus, Michael Gross, Deborah Rush, Nicolas Coster. **1988**

BIG BUSINESS GIRL ★★★ One of Hollywood's first career-girl movies and a star vehicle for Loretta Young and Joan Blondell. The comedy-drama mixes career problems with romantic dilemmas and is aimed primarily at a female audience with elements Hollywood still uses to appeal to women today. B&W; 75m. **DIR:** William A. Seiter. **CAST:** Loretta Young, Joan Blondell, Ricardo Cortez, Jack Albertson, Dorothy Christy, Bobby Gordon. **1931**

BIG BUST OUT, THE 🦃 Four female convicts escape from a prison somewhere in the Middle East when they are sent to do janitorial work at a convent. Idiotic. 75m. **DIR:** Richard Jackson. **CAST:** Vonetta McGee, Karen Carter, Linda Fox, Monica Taylor. **1973**

BIG CAT, THE ★★★ A marauding mountain lion complicates feuding between high country ranchers in this enjoyable adventure film. 75m. **DIR:** Phil Karlson. **CAST:** Lon McCallister, Preston Foster, Forrest Tucker. **1949**

BIG CHILL, THE ★★★★1/2 As with John Sayles's superb *Return of the Secaucus 7*, this equally impressive and thoroughly enjoyable film by writer-director Lawrence Kasdan concerns a weekend reunion of old friends, all of whom have gone on to varied lifestyles after once being united in the hip, committed 1960s. It features a who's who of the day's hot young stars as the friends. Rated R for nudity and profanity. 103m. **DIR:** Lawrence Kasdan. **CAST:** Tom Berenger, William Hurt, Glenn Close, Jeff Goldblum, JoBeth Williams, Kevin Kline, Mary Kay Place, Meg Tilly. **1983 DVD**

BIG COMBO, THE ★★★ A classic American gangster film done in the *film noir* style. Cornel Wilde has the starring role as a half-crazed policeman who is after gangsters and will do whatever is necessary to get them. Quite violent for its time and very well photographed, with an exciting climax. B&W; 89m. **DIR:** Joseph H. Lewis. **CAST:** Cornel Wilde, Jean Wallace, Richard Conte. **1955 DVD**

BIG COUNTRY, THE ★★★ Big-budget Western pits Gregory Peck and Charlton Heston as adversaries in an ongoing feud between rival cowmen Burl Ives and

Charles Bickford. This would-be epic looks good but lacks the punch and plot of the best and most famous Westerns. 163m. **DIR:** William Wyler. **CAST:** Gregory Peck, Jean Simmons, Charlton Heston, Carroll Baker, Burl Ives, Charles Bickford. **1958**

BIG DADDY ★★ This attempt to blend star Adam Sandler's two audiences—the fans of his big-screen moron comedy and the romantics pleasantly surprised by the (comparative) sensitivity of his character in *The Wedding Singer*—is uncomfortable at best, particularly because a small child is part of the package. Sandler's character, an aging adolescent who refuses to accept adult responsibility, decides to adopt a 5-year-old as a means of showing a former girlfriend that he's ready for "responsibility." Sandler's efforts to impress us as a natural father figure are clumsy at best. The boy is played by twins who certainly know how to milk pity; despite the inept direction, you can't help but adore the little guy. Too bad the same cannot be said about the film itself. Rated PG-13 for incessant vulgarity, sexual candor, and mild profanity. 95m. **DIR:** Dennis Dugan. **CAST:** Adam Sandler, Joey Lauren Adams, Jon Stewart, Allen Covert, Rob Schneider, Cole Sprouse, Dylan Sprouse. **1999 DVD**

BIG DEAL ON MADONNA STREET ★★★★ Mario Monicelli directed this tale as a classic spoof of the perfect-crime film that depicts in great detail the elaborate planning and split-second timing involved in huge thefts. Monicelli's characters—who are attempting to burglarize a safe—also formulate intricate plans and employ precise timing, but everything they do results in humiliating disaster—providing a hilarious comedy of errors. In Italian with English subtitles. B&W; 91m. **DIR:** Mario Monicelli. **CAST:** Marcello Mastroianni, Vittorio Gassman, Toto, Renato Salvatori, Claudia Cardinale. **1960 DVD**

BIG EASY, THE ★★★★ Everything is easy in the Big Easy (aka New Orleans) for slick and only slightly sleazy police lieutenant Remy McSwain (Dennis Quaid). That is, until Anne Osbourne (Ellen Barkin), an upright and uptight assistant district attorney, comes along. *The Big Easy* is a wild, southern-style variation on the old-fashioned cop films of the thirties and forties. Rated R for violence, profanity, and sensuality. 100m. **DIR:** Jim McBride. **CAST:** Dennis Quaid, Ellen Barkin, Ned Beatty, John Goodman, Lisa Jane Persky, Ebbe Roe Smith, Tom O'Brien, Charles Ludlam. **1987 DVD**

BIG FALL, THE ★★ When a femme fatale hires an L.A. detective to find her missing brother, he is surprised that the case turns out to be something quite different. Not so for viewers, who have seen this kind of Raymond Chandler parody/homage done many other times, and usually much better. Rated R for strong violence, sexual situations, and strong profanity. 94m. **DIR:** C. Thomas Howell. **CAST:** C. Thomas Howell, Sophie Ward, Jeff Kober. **1997**

•**BIG FAT LIAR** ★★1/2 Mildly amusing "get even" flick pits an eighth grader against the movie producer who stole his essay. The sleazy producer doesn't stand a chance when Frankie Muniz goes to extreme measures to prove his story has been pirated. The inane antics quickly wear thin and will only prove riveting to the preteen crowd. Rated PG for language. 89m. **DIR:** Shawn Levy. **CAST:** Frankie Muniz, Paul Giamatti, Amanda Bynes, Amanda Detmer. **2002 DVD**

BIG FELLA ★★1/2 Singing dockworker in Marseilles works secretly with the police to find a rich British runaway boy. A gentle tale of missed opportunities and unrequited love. B&W; 70m. **DIR:** J. Elder Wills. **CAST:** Paul Robeson, Elisabeth Welch, Roy Emerton, James Hayter, Lawrence Brown, Eldon Grant. **1937 DVD**

BIG FIX, THE ★★★1/2 Novelist Roger Simon's laid-back detective, Moses Wine, comes to the screen in this flawed thriller. The setting—which harkens back to the revolutionary 1960s—has become dated, but a murder mystery of any stripe is still suspenseful. Rated PG. 108m. **DIR:** Jeremy Paul Kagan. **CAST:** Richard Dreyfuss, Susan Anspach, Bonnie Bedelia. **1978**

BIG FOOT 🦃 Legendary monster comes down from the hills and beats the hell out of everybody. 94m. **DIR:** Robert F. Slatzer. **CAST:** John Carradine, Joi Lansing, John Mitchum, Chris Mitchum. **1971**

BIG GIRLS DON'T CRY—THEY GET EVEN ★★★1/2 Don't let the awful title (it was originally called *Stepkids*) keep you away from this low-key but charming comedy about a young teen who revolts against the revolving-door marriages of her parents that has left her part of a bizarrely extended family. Rated PG-13 for profanity. 96m. **DIR:** Joan Micklin Silver. **CAST:** Hilary Wolf, David Strathairn, Margaret Whitton, Griffin Dunne, Adrienne Shelly. **1992**

BIG GREEN, THE ★★ This drab, inert comedy recycles the story from *Little Giants* and *The Mighty Ducks*. This time the sport is soccer, but nothing else has changed. Rated PG. 97m. **DIR:** Holly Goldberg Sloan. **CAST:** Steve Guttenberg, Olivia D'Abo, Jay O. Sanders, John Terry, Chauncey Leopardi. **1995**

BIG HAND FOR THE LITTLE LADY, A ★★★1/2 A compulsive gambler (Henry Fonda) talks his way into a high-stakes poker game, bets everything he owns, then promptly keels over, leaving his wife (Joanne Woodward) to play out his hand. Nifty Western-comedy is a bit too padded (it was originally a one-hour TV play, *Big Deal in Laredo*), but the expert cast puts it over. 95m. **DIR:** Fielder Cook. **CAST:** Henry Fonda, Joanne Woodward, Jason Robards Jr., Charles Bickford, Burgess Meredith, Paul Ford, John Qualen, Robert Middleton. **1966**

BIG HANGOVER, THE ★★1/2 One-joke movie, with Van Johnson as a veteran who almost drowned in a bombed-out wine cellar, becoming drunk at the slightest odor of alcohol. Becomes preachy when he, as a junior lawyer, turns against his employer for racial discrimination. B&W; 82m. **DIR:** Norman Krasna. **CAST:** Van Johnson, Elizabeth Taylor, Fay Holden, Leon Ames, Edgar Buchanan, Selena Royle, Gene Lockhart, Rosemary DeCamp. **1950**

BIG HEAT, THE ★★★★ A crackerjack classic of crime *film noir*. Homicide detective Dave Bannion (Glenn Ford) is bent on solving the puzzle of an unexpected suicide of a fellow police officer, even though he is told by his superiors to leave bad enough alone. Exceptional acting, especially by Lee Marvin and Gloria Grahame. B&W; 90m. **DIR:** Fritz Lang. **CAST:** Glenn Ford, Gloria Grahame, Jocelyn Brando, Alexander Scourby, Lee Marvin, Jeanette Nolan, Carolyn Jones. **1953 DVD**

BIG HIT, THE ★★1/2 Sweet-natured hit man wants to be liked by everyone in this outrageous action-comedy. Things fall apart when he and two assassins kidnap an Asian girl who turns out to be their boss's goddaughter. Some high energy and offbeat, dark humor, but this Hollywood–Hong Kong hybrid sometimes trips over a forced hipness. Rated R for language, violence, and nudity. 93m. **DIR:** Che-Kirk Wong. **CAST:** Mark Wahlberg, Lou Diamond Phillips, Bokeem Woodbine, China Chow, Avery Brooks, Christina Applegate, Elliott Gould, Lainie Kazan, Lela Rochon. **1998 DVD**

BIG HOUSE, THE ★★★★ The granddaddy of all hard-hitting prison movies, with tough cons, abusive guards, and the inevitable doomed "bust-out." Every cliché is here, from the dim-witted gang leader and his cautious friend to the weakling snitch. But it was fresh then and still holds up. Oscar nominations for best picture and Wallace Beery's performance. B&W; 87m. **DIR:** George Hill. **CAST:** Chester Morris, Wallace Beery, Lewis Stone, Robert Montgomery, Leila Hyams. **1930**

BIG JAKE ★★★ Big John Wayne takes up the trail of a gang of no-goods who kidnapped his grandson and shot up Maureen O'Hara's homestead and hired hands. One wishes there had been more scenes with Wayne and O'Hara together in this film, their last together. 110m. **DIR:** George Sherman. **CAST:** John Wayne, Richard Boone, Maureen O'Hara, Patrick Wayne, Chris Mitchum, Bobby Vinton, Bruce Cabot. **1971**

BIG JIM MCLAIN ★★ This relic of the McCarthy era has John Wayne and James Arness as two-fisted investigators for the House Un-American Activities Committee. Clumsy and dull. B&W; 90m. **DIR:** Edward Ludwig. **CAST:** John Wayne, James Arness, Nancy Olson, Veda Ann Borg, Hans Conried. **1952**

BIG KAHUNA, THE ★★★ Three corporate hustlers—cynical Kevin Spacey, burnt-out Danny DeVito, and idealistic Peter Facinelli—nervously prowl their convention hotel suite, hoping for the big sale that will save their careers. Roger Rueff's script, adapted from his play, is a shallow retread of better plays such as *Death of a Salesman*, but the actors relish sinking their teeth into the ripe, stagy dialogue. DeVito shines in a restrained, sensitive performance. Rated R for profanity. 90m. **DIR:** John Swanbeck. **CAST:** Kevin Spacey, Danny DeVito, Peter Facinelli. **1999 DVD**

BIG LEBOWSKI, THE ★★ You won't care a jot for any of the characters in this deranged *film noir*, which separates this misfire from other Joel and Ethan Coen productions. Jeff Bridges, a fortysomething loser, gets mistaken for a Pasadena millionaire who shares his name; what follows involves a hoochy-coochy trophy wife, an artist who paints in the nude, a trio of mock-Nazi nihilists, a Stetson-garbed stranger, and Saddam Hussein. Rated R for nudity, drug use, violence, and profanity. 117m. **DIR:** Joel Coen. **CAST:** Jeff Bridges, John Goodman, Julianne Moore, Steve Buscemi, David Huddleston, Philip Seymour Hoffman, Tara Reid. **1998 DVD**

BIG LIFT, THE ★★1/2 Montgomery Clift gives an emotionally charged performance as an air force pilot who becomes romantically involved with a young German girl in post–World War II Berlin. Excellent location photography gives a lift to this uneven melodrama. B&W; 120m. **DIR:** George Seaton. **CAST:** Montgomery Clift, Paul Douglas, Cornell Borchers, O. E. Hasse. **1950 DVD**

BIG MAN ★★★ An unemployed coal miner (Liam Neeson) gets involved with illegal bare-knuckle boxing and hoodlums in this Scottish drama. The brawling is gritty and glamourless in an intriguing story that ends with a surprising turn of events. Rated R for violence. 94m. **DIR:** David Leland. **CAST:** Liam Neeson, Joanne Whalley, Ian Bannen, Billy Connolly, Hugh Grant. **1991**

BIG MAN ON CAMPUS ★★★ This spoofy retelling of *The Hunchback of Notre Dame* story is a surprising bit of good-natured fun. Sincere comic touches by Allan Katz and Corey Parker help make this teen-marketed sexual-oriented fluff seem a little more substantial. Above average. Rated PG-13 for mild profanity. 102m. **DIR:** Jeremy Paul Kagan. **CAST:** Allan Katz, Corey Parker, Tom Skerritt, Cindy Williams. **1989**

BIG MOMMA'S HOUSE ★★ Two FBI agents are out to nab a vicious bank robber in this hokey cross-dressing comedy. They follow a female teller, who dated the dangerous fugitive, to a small southern town where one agent tries to break the case by masquerading as the teller's 300-pound grandmother. The film is fun when the phony Big Momma delivers a baby, takes karate lessons, and plays basketball, but is dull and lame for the most part. Rated PG-13 for sexual references, violence, and language. 95m. **DIR:** Raja Gosnell. **CAST:** Martin Lawrence, Nia Long, Paul Giamatti, Ella Mitchell, Terrence Howard. **2000 DVD**

BIG MOUTH, THE ★★ The bloom was off the rose by this point in Jerry Lewis's solo career, and this standard gangster comedy is a profound disappointment. Title character Jerry (an apt description in a film where everybody shouts all the time) gets involved in a witless search for stolen diamonds. Lewis's character bits and attempts at disguise are pretty flimsy. For true fans only. 107m. **DIR:** Jerry Lewis. **CAST:** Jerry Lewis, Harold J. Stone. **1967**

BIG NEWS ★★★ Robert Armstrong plays a boozing newspaper reporter who gets framed for the murder of his editor. Armstrong's wife, Carole Lombard, writes a women's column for a rival paper and puts in some time trying to sober up her hubby and clear him of the crime. Snappy comedy-mystery. B&W; 75m. **DIR:** Gregory La Cava. **CAST:** Robert Armstrong, Carole Lombard. **1929**

BIG NIGHT ★★★★ What a delight! Immigrant brothers Tony Shalhoub and Stanley Tucci open an authentic Italian restaurant on the New Jersey shore in the late 1950s, hoping to impress customers with their exquisite cuisine. Alas, boorish Americans prefer the cheap wine and checkered tablecloths at a competitive joint just across the street. Granted the opportunity to prepare a meal for entertainer Louis Prima, the brothers empty their bank account and hope to achieve fame by serving a truly magnificent feast. This poignant character study demonstrates that art and commerce rarely mix. Rated R for profanity and sexual content. 107m. **DIR:** Campbell Scott, Stanley Tucci. **CAST:** Stanley Tucci, Tony Shalhoub, Minnie Driver, Isabella Rossellini, Ian Holm. **1995 DVD**

BIG ONE, THE ★★★★ Grass-roots activist and media junkie Michael Moore films the cross-country marketing tour for his book *Downsize This! Random Threats* *from an Unarmed American* to further prove that big business is running amok. He tries to figure out why Fortune 500 companies are downsizing while posting record-breaking profits. The mischievous documentarian is in top form—like when he grills Nike CEO Phil Knight about exploiting Pacific Rim children—but his inner comedian at times overwhelms his blue-collar advocacy and investigative reporting. Rated PG-13 for language. 96m. **DIR:** Michael Moore. **1998**

BIG PARADE, THE ★★★★★ A compelling depiction of World War I, this silent film has long been recognized as King Vidor's masterpiece. As the saying goes, it has everything: romance, humor, love, tragedy, and suspense. B&W; 126m. **DIR:** King Vidor. **CAST:** John Gilbert, Renée Adorée, Hobart Bosworth. **1925**

BIG PICTURE, THE ★★★★ Christopher Guest and Michael McKean spoof the film industry in this engaging, hip, and sometimes uneven story of a promising young filmmaker who finds himself thoroughly corrupted by the temptations of Hollywood. Guest and McKean hit most of their targets with skilled assistance from Martin Short as a wacked-out agent. Rated PG-13 for brief profanity and brief nudity. 100m. **DIR:** Christopher Guest. **CAST:** Kevin Bacon, Michael McKean, Martin Short, Jennifer Jason Leigh. **1989**

BIG RED ★★★ This pleasant family film drawn from the beloved children's book of the same title features Walter Pidgeon as the owner of a sleek Irish setter named Big Red, which spends its formative years with young Gilles Payant. 89m. **DIR:** Norman Tokar. **CAST:** Walter Pidgeon, Gilles Payant, Emile Genest, Janette Bertrand. **1962 DVD**

BIG RED ONE, THE ★★★★1/2 This release gave Lee Marvin his best role in years. As a grizzled sergeant leading a platoon of "wetnoses" into the dangers of battle, he's excellent. Based on writer-director Sam Fuller's personal reminiscences of World War II. It's a terrific war movie. Rated PG. 113m. **DIR:** Samuel Fuller. **CAST:** Lee Marvin, Mark Hamill, Robert Carradine, Bobby DiCicco. **1980 DVD**

BIG RIP-OFF, THE 🦃 In the closing days of the Civil War, an outlaw stumbles across a dying Confederate soldier who tells him of hidden gold in the home of his blind father. Unbelievably, the outlaw passes himself off to the blind father as his son. Before he can find the gold, the blind man is killed by a gang of outlaws and our hero(?) goes after the gang. Rated R for violence. 90m. **DIR:** Francesco Rosi. **CAST:** Chip Corman, Rosemarie Dexter, Piero Lulli, Dana Ghia, Aldo Berti. **1967**

BIG SCORE, THE ★★1/2 Fred Williamson breaks all the rules in going after drug king Joe Spinell. Williamson, the director, doesn't make the story move fast enough. Rated R for violence and profanity. 85m. **DIR:** Fred Williamson. **CAST:** Fred Williamson, John Saxon, Richard Roundtree, Nancy Wilson, Ed Lauter, Joe Spinell, Michael Dante. **1983**

BIG SHOTS ★★★1/2 A funny and exciting film about kids, but not just for kids. After the death of his father, an 11 year old boy from the suburbs strikes up a friendship with a young black boy who teaches him the ways of the street. Rated PG-13. 91m. **DIR:** Robert Mandel. **CAST:** Ricky Busker, Darius McCrary, Robert Joy, Robert Prosky, Paul Winfield, Jerzy Skolimowski. **1988**

BIG SKY, THE ★★ Even the normally reliable director Howard Hawks can't enliven this average tale of early-day fur trappers on an expedition up the Missouri River. Action was Hawks's forte, and there just isn't enough to sustain the viewer's interest. Plenty of beautiful scenery, but that's about it. B&W; 122m. **DIR:** Howard Hawks. **CAST:** Kirk Douglas, Arthur Hunnicutt, Dewey Martin. **1952**

BIG SLEEP, THE (1946) ★★★★1/2 Raymond Chandler's fans couldn't complain about this moody, atmospheric rendition of Philip Marlowe's most bizarre case. Bogart's gritty interpretation of the tough-talking P.I. is a high point in his glorious career, and sultry Lauren Bacall throws in enough spark to ignite several city blocks. Not rated, contains adult themes and violence. B&W; 114m. **DIR:** Howard Hawks. **CAST:** Humphrey Bogart, Lauren Bacall, Martha Vickers, Bob Steele, Elisha Cook Jr., Dorothy Malone. **1946 DVD**

BIG SLEEP, THE (1978) 🦃 Remake of the classic screen detective yarn. Rated R for violence, profanity, and nudity. 100m. **DIR:** Michael Winner. **CAST:** Robert Mitchum, James Stewart, Sarah Miles, Oliver Reed, Candy Clark, Edward Fox. **1978 DVD**

BIG SLICE, THE ★★ Two writers decide to make their lives exciting. Between phone sex and police raids, the plot expands into one big mess. Rated R for violence and suggested sex. 86m. **DIR:** John Bradshaw. **CAST:** Heather Locklear, Casey Siemaszko, Leslie Hope, Justin Louis, Kenneth Welsh, Nicholas Campbell, Henry Ramer. **1990**

BIG SOMBRERO, THE ★★1/2 An impoverished Gene Autry comes to the aid of Elena Verdugo and saves her from land swindlers as well as a money-grubbing fiancé in this south-of-the-border tale. This is more of a musical than a horse opera. 77m. **DIR:** Frank McDonald. **CAST:** Gene Autry, Elena Verdugo, Stephen Dunne, George J. Lewis, Martin Garralaga, Gene Roth. **1949**

BIG SQUEEZE, THE ★★1/2 When she discovers her shiftless husband has secretly collected a $130,000 accident settlement, a barmaid enlists the aid of a con artist to help her get the half to which she feels entitled. Mild caper film in the *Last Seduction* mold is neither clever nor quirky enough to reach that level. Rated R for nudity, sexual situations, and profanity. 107m. **DIR:** Marcus De Leon. **CAST:** Lara Flynn Boyle, Peter Dobson, Danny Nucci. **1995 DVD**

BIG STAMPEDE, THE ★★★1/2 In one of John Wayne's best B Westerns for Warner Bros., our hero is a deputy sheriff who goes undercover to bring a corrupt cattle baron to justice. Noah Beery Sr. is in fine form as the bad guy (black hat and all), who builds up his stock by rustling steers and killing anyone who stands in his way. Good action and suspense for the genre, with Wayne (allowed more than one take per scene) more convincing than he would be in the series of low-budget Westerns that followed. B&W; 54m. **DIR:** Tenny Wright. **CAST:** John Wayne, Noah Beery Sr., Paul Hurst, Mae Madison, Luis Alberni, Berton Churchill, Lafe McKee. **1932**

BIG STEAL, THE ★★★1/2 Four sets of desperate and disparate characters chase each other over bumpy roads in the Southwest and Mexico following a robbery. An intriguing film, somewhat difficult to follow but great fun to watch. B&W; 71m. **DIR:** Don Siegel. **CAST:**

Robert Mitchum, Jane Greer, William Bendix, Ramon Novarro, Patric Knowles. **1949**

BIG STORE, THE ★★ Singer (and nonactor) Tony Martin inherits a department store and calls on the Marx Brothers to save him. The last and weakest of the Marx Brothers' movies for MGM, this misfire is woefully understocked in laughs. Even so, Groucho manages some good bits, often in scenes with his classic foil, Margaret Dumont, and Chico and Harpo team for a delightful piano duet. 103m. **DIR:** Charles F. Riesner. **CAST:** The Marx Brothers, Tony Martin, Virginia Grey, Margaret Dumont, Douglass Dumbrille. **1941**

BIG STREET, THE ★★1/2 Though somewhat too sentimental at times, this Damon Runyon story of a busboy's (Henry Fonda) sincere devotion to a couldn't-care-less-for-him nightclub singer (Lucille Ball) is often touching and lively. Lucille Ball gives her best big-screen performance and you couldn't ask for a better gangster than Barton MacLane. B&W; 88m. **DIR:** Irving Reis. **CAST:** Henry Fonda, Lucille Ball, Hans Conried, Barton MacLane, Agnes Moorehead, Ray Collins, Sam Levene, Louise Beavers. **1942**

BIG SWEAT, THE 🦃 A born loser finds himself running from the law soon after his prison release. Not rated; contains profanity and violence. 85m. **DIR:** Ulli Lommel. **CAST:** Steve Molone, Robert Z'Dar. **1990**

BIG TEASE, THE ★★★1/2 A Scottish hairdresser goes to Hollywood to compete in the World Freestyle Hairdressing Championship, only to learn that he's been invited merely to sit in the audience. Undaunted, he sets out to crash the competition, accompanied by a BBC film crew. Cheerful and waspishly funny, this comedy feels almost thrown together; in fact, it's quite well written and carefully crafted by people who are clearly having a wonderful time. Rated R for profanity. 86m. **DIR:** Kevin Allen. **CAST:** Craig Ferguson, Frances Fisher, Chris Langham, Mary McCormack, David Rasche, Larry Miller, Charles Napier. **1999 DVD**

BIG TOP PEE-WEE ★★ Pee-wee Herman plays a country bumpkin whose greatest pleasure in life is his pet hog. The circus comes to town, and Pee-wee invites them to pitch the Big Top on his land. Film contains the longest kiss in screen history. Rated PG for hog and human love rites. 86m. **DIR:** Randal Kleiser. **CAST:** Pee-Wee Herman, Kris Kristofferson, Susan Tyrrell, Valeria Golino. **1988**

BIG TOWN, THE ★★ Chicago, circa 1957. A talented small-town boy (Matt Dillon) with a penchant for crapshooting goes off to the big city. But the production loses focus and drive. Rated R for language, nudity, and sex. 110m. **DIR:** Ben Bolt. **CAST:** Matt Dillon, Diane Lane, Tommy Lee Jones, Bruce Dern, Tom Skerritt, Lee Grant, Suzy Amis. **1987**

BIG TRAIL, THE ★★★1/2 John Wayne made his starring debut in this exciting, although somewhat dated epic. Contrary to Hollywood legend, the Duke acquits himself well enough as a revenge-minded scout leading a wagon train across the wilderness. His allegedly stiff acting was long thought to be the reason for the film's box-office failure. In truth, the film was shot in widescreen 55mm and cinema owners were unwilling to invest in the projection equipment needed to show the film in Fox Grandeur, as it was called. B&W; 110m. **DIR:** Raoul Walsh. **CAST:** John Wayne, Marguerite Churchill, El Brendel, Ian Keith, Tyrone Power Sr. **1930**

BIG TREES, THE ★★1/2 Lumberman Kirk Douglas wants the redwoods on homesteaders' land in this colorful adventure set in northwest California in 1900. A remake of 1938's *Valley of the Giants*. 89m. **DIR:** Felix Feist. **CAST:** Kirk Douglas, Eve Miller, Patrice Wymore, Edgar Buchanan, John Archer, Alan Hale Jr. **1952 DVD**

BIG TROUBLE (1985) ★★ *Big Trouble* has its moments, but alas, they are few and far between. Alan Arkin meets up with a rich married woman (Beverly D'Angelo), and the two plot against her husband (Peter Falk). Crazy plot twists abound, but none of them are all that funny. Rated R for profanity and adult subject matter. 93m. **DIR:** John Cassavetes. **CAST:** Peter Falk, Alan Arkin, Beverly D'Angelo, Charles Durning, Robert Stack, Paul Dooley, Valerie Curtin, Richard Libertini. **1985**

•BIG TROUBLE (2002) ★★ This messy, sometimes funny, sometimes incredibly dull comedy involves a bomb in a suitcase that unites and changes the lives of numerous people. A high-school squirt gun game of "Killer" and a Mafia hit on a businessman set off a chain of events involving Russian arms smugglers, a toad that sprays hallucinogenic fluid, nitwit ex-convicts, a loser adman, goats, and a man who lives in a tree. The script is based on Dave Barry's wacky novel. Rated PG-13 for profanity, violence, and sexual content. 85m. **DIR:** Barry Sonnenfeld. **CAST:** Tim Allen, Zooey Deschanel, René Russo, Dennis Farina, Janeane Garofalo, Heavy D, Tom Sizemore, Stanley Tucci, Jason Lee, Omar Epps, Ben Foster, Johnny Knoxville, Sofia Vergara, Patrick Warburton. **2002 DVD**

BIG TROUBLE IN LITTLE CHINA ★★★1/2 An adventure-fantasy with Kurt Russell as a pig trucker unwittingly swept into a mystical world underneath San Francisco's Chinatown ruled by a sinister 2,000 year old ghost. The movie is a lighthearted special-effects showcase designed to look a bit silly, in the style of old serials. Rated PG-13. 99m. **DIR:** John Carpenter. **CAST:** Kurt Russell, Kim Cattrall, Dennis Dun, James Hong, Victor Wong, Kate Burton. **1986 DVD**

BIG VALLEY, THE (TV SERIES) ★★★ Set in Stockton, California, circa 1878, this is the TV-born saga of the Barkleys, a family of cattle ranchers. Victoria is the iron-willed widow who heads the clan. Jarrod, her oldest son, is a suave attorney. His brother Nick is a rugged cowpoke. Their half brother is Heath, whose illegitimacy has bred a rebellious streak. All three are protective of Audra, their gorgeous, haughty sister. A pair of two-part episodes are available on tape: "Legend of a General" and "Explosion." 90m. **DIR:** Virgil Vogel. **CAST:** Barbara Stanwyck, Richard Long, Peter Breck, Lee Majors, Linda Evans. **1965–1969**

BIG WEDNESDAY ★★ Only nostalgic surfers with more than a little patience will enjoy this ode to the beach by writer-director John Milius. Rated PG. 120m. **DIR:** John Milius. **CAST:** Jan-Michael Vincent, Gary Busey, William Katt, Lee Purcell, Patti D'Arbanville. **1978**

BIG WHEEL, THE ★★1/2 Smart-mouthed Mickey Rooney rises from garage mechanic to champion racing-car driver in this well-worn story worn thinner by a poor script and poorer direction. More than 20 of the film's 92 minutes are given over to earsplitting scenes of high-speed racing. B&W; 92m. **DIR:** Edward Ludwig. **CAST:** Mickey Rooney, Thomas Mitchell, Spring Byington, Allen Jenkins, Michael O'Shea. **1949 DVD**

BIGAMIST, THE ★★★ Ida Lupino stepped behind the camera to direct several underrated *film noir* excursions in the early Fifties, of which this is among the best. Title character Edmond O'Brien is neurotic, not conventionally villainous. Lupino's only acting role in one of her directing efforts. B&W; 80m. **DIR:** Ida Lupino. **CAST:** Edmond O'Brien, Joan Fontaine, Ida Lupino, Edmund Gwenn, Jane Darwell, Kenneth Tobey. **1953**

BIGFOOT: THE UNFORGETTABLE ENCOUNTER ★★1/2 Attempt at wholesome family entertainment delivers the basics, but does nothing special with them. When a young boy meets the legendary Bigfoot creature, his encounter makes him a media star and the creature the target of some ruthless bounty hunters. Kids will enjoy this outdoor adventure that introduces such life lessons as friendship and courage into the mix. Rated PG for language. 86m. **DIR:** Corey Michael Eubanks. **CAST:** Zachery Ty Bryan, Matt McCoy, Crystal Chappell, Clint Howard, Rance Howard. **1995**

BIGGLES—ADVENTURES IN TIME ★★★★ Delightful fantasy film focuses on the adventures of a New York frozen-food merchandiser, Jim Ferguson (Alex Hyde-White), who discovers he has a time twin—a World War I British fighter ace named Biggles (Neil Dickson). Every time Biggles is in danger, Ferguson finds himself bouncing back through time to come to his twin's rescue. Rated PG for profanity and violence. 100m. **DIR:** John Hough. **CAST:** Neil Dickson, Alex Hyde-White, Peter Cushing, Fiona Hutchison, William Hootkins. **1985**

BIKINI BEACH ★★ This silly film captures Frankie Avalon and Annette Funicello in their best swim attire. A group of kids who always hang out at the beach try to prevent a man from closing it. Ho-hum. 100m. **DIR:** William Asher. **CAST:** Frankie Avalon, Annette Funicello, Keenan Wynn, Don Rickles. **1964 DVD**

BIKINI BISTRO 🦃 Videotaped rubbish starring porn queen Marilyn Chambers as herself. Rated R for nudity and profanity. 84m. **DIR:** Ernest G. Sauer. **CAST:** Marilyn Chambers, Amy Lynn Baxter, Isabelle Fortea, Joan Gerardi. **1995 DVD**

BIKINI CARWASH COMPANY, THE 🦃 When naive Midwesterner Joe Dusic agrees to take over his uncle's California car wash, he revives the failing business by employing some of the beach's best babes. Tedious male fantasy. Two versions available: R-rated for nudity and an unrated version featuring even more of the same. 87m. **DIR:** Ed Hansen. **CAST:** Joe Dusic. **1990 DVD**

BIKINI CARWASH COMPANY 2 🦃 After being tricked into selling their beloved car-wash chain to a crooked developer, the beautiful entrepreneurs launch a new business: a 24-hour lingerie shopping network. Need we say more? Available in two versions, R-rated and unrated, both with nudity and sexual situations. 94m. **DIR:** Gary Orona. **CAST:** Kristi Ducati, Suzanne Browne, Neriah Napaul, Rikki Brando. **1993**

BIKINI ISLAND 🦃 Inane, low-budget T&A flick focuses on five swimsuit models stalked on an exotic location shoot. A number of likely suspects emerge but, of course, are red herrings. Rated R for nudity, violence, and profanity. 90m. **DIR:** Anthony Markes. **CAST:** Holly Floria, Jackson Robinson. **1991**

BILITIS ★★★★ A surprisingly tasteful and sensitive soft-core sex film, this details the sexual awakening of the title character, a 16-year-old French girl, while she spends the summer with a family friend. Rated R for nudity and simulated sex. 93m. **DIR:** David Hamilton. **CAST:** Patti D'Arbanville, Bernard Giraudeau, Mathieu Carriere. **1982**

BILL ★★★★1/2 Extremely moving drama based on the real-life experiences of Bill Sackter, a retarded adult forced to leave the mental institution that has been his home for the past forty-five years. Mickey Rooney won an Emmy for his excellent portrayal of Bill. Dennis Quaid plays a filmmaker who offers kindness to Bill as he tries to cope with life on the "outside." Not rated. 100m. **DIR:** Anthony Page. **CAST:** Mickey Rooney, Dennis Quaid, Largo Woodruff. **1981**

BILL AND TED'S BOGUS JOURNEY ★★★★ This sequel, which finds our heroes traveling through Heaven and Hell rather than through time, is better than its predecessor. The special effects are first rate, and the comedy has moved up a notch. Rated PG. 90m. **DIR:** Peter Hewitt. **CAST:** Keanu Reeves, Alex Winter, Bill Sadler, Joss Ackland, Pam Grier, George Carlin. **1991 DVD**

BILL AND TED'S EXCELLENT ADVENTURE ★★★ A wild romp through time with two total idiots who must find a way to pass history class. Using a time-traveling telephone booth, these two go through history enlisting the help of famous people such as Napoleon and Socrates. A good, clean, excellent way to waste an hour and a half, dude. Rated PG. 90m. **DIR:** Stephen Herek. **CAST:** Keanu Reeves, Alex Winter, George Carlin. **1989 DVD**

BILL OF DIVORCEMENT, A ★★★1/2 Melodramatic weeper about a man's return to his family after confinement in a mental hospital rises above the material due to a stunning cast and deft direction by Hollywood master George Cukor. Katharine Hepburn in her first film really carries this somewhat overwrought soap opera. B&W; 70m. **DIR:** George Cukor. **CAST:** John Barrymore, Billie Burke, Katharine Hepburn, David Manners, Bramwell Fletcher, Henry Stephenson, Paul Cavanagh, Elizabeth Patterson. **1932**

BILL: ON HIS OWN ★★★1/2 This is the sequel to the 1981 drama *Bill*. Mickey Rooney continues his role as Bill Sackter, a mentally retarded adult forced to live on his own after spending forty-five years in an institution. Helen Hunt costars as the college student who tutors him. It doesn't have quite the emotional impact that *Bill* carried, but it's still good. 104m. **DIR:** Anthony Page. **CAST:** Mickey Rooney, Helen Hunt, Teresa Wright, Dennis Quaid, Largo Woodruff. **1983**

BILLBOARD DAD ★★ While not nearly as cloying as their current television series, this direct-to-video comedy starring the Olsen twins will most likely appeal to preteen girls who will have no problem getting past the fact that they've seen this all before. Mary-Kate and Ashley play the daughters of a single father. They take out an advertisement on a local billboard to find a new mom for Dad. Whimsical in a childish sort of way, the film should entertain its target audience. Rated G. 90m.

DIR: Alan Metter. **CAST:** Mary-Kate Olsen, Ashley Olsen, Carl Banks. **1998**

BILLIE ★★1/2 Tomboyish Patty Duke upsets everyone when she joins a boys' track team. Lightweight story with a good turn by Billy DeWolfe as the town mayor. Not rated. 87m. **DIR:** Don Weis. **CAST:** Patty Duke, Jim Backus, Warren Berlinger, Jane Greer, Billy DeWolfe, Dick Sargent, Ted Bessell. **1965**

BILLION DOLLAR HOBO, THE ★★ This film has Tim Conway playing his familiar down-and-out bumpkin role, but the rest of the cast is wasted. The slow pace is a further drawback. Rated G for family viewing. 96m. **DIR:** Stuart E. McGowan. **CAST:** Tim Conway, Will Geer. **1978**

BILLION FOR BORIS, A 🦃 Boris discovers that his TV set can view the future. He uses this knowledge to win big at the racetrack. Not rated; contains some foul language. 94m. **DIR:** Alex Grasshoff. **CAST:** Tim Kazurinsky, Lee Grant. **1990**

BILLIONAIRE BOYS CLUB ★★1/2 Severely edited version of the miniseries starring Judd Nelson as Joe Hunt, a notorious commodities broker-cum-murderer. Nelson conveys Hunt's hypnotic personality and greed, though the production is saddled with unimaginative editing and tinny music. Based on an actual Los Angeles murder case. Made for TV. 94m. **DIR:** Marvin J. Chomsky. **CAST:** Judd Nelson, Ron Silver. **1987**

BILLY BATHGATE ★★★★1/2 A compelling gangster movie with superb performances, this work, based by screenwriter Tom Stoppard on the novel by E. L. Doctorow, concerns the odyssey of young Billy Bathgate (Loren Dean) who goes from being a poor street kid in 1935 to a coveted position in the crime organization of crazy, big-time hood Dutch Schultz (Dustin Hoffman). Rated R for violence, nudity, and profanity. 106m. **DIR:** Robert Benton. **CAST:** Dustin Hoffman, Nicole Kidman, Bruce Willis, Steven Hill, Loren Dean, Steve Buscemi, Stanley Tucci. **1991**

BILLY BUDD ★★★1/2 Herman Melville's brooding, allegorical novel of the overpowering of the innocent is set against a backdrop of life on an eighteenth-century British warship. The plight of a young sailor subjected to the treacherous whims of his ship's tyrannical first mate is well acted throughout. It is powerful filmmaking and succeeds in leaving its audience unsettled and questioning. B&W; 112m. **DIR:** Peter Ustinov. **CAST:** Terence Stamp, Robert Ryan, Peter Ustinov. **1962**

BILLY ELLIOT ★★★★ This charming British entry, set in a coal-mining community in 1984 northern England, concerns a young lad who embarrasses his gruff father and older brother by abandoning boxing lessons for . . . ballet. Julie Walters shines as the chain-smoking dance instructor who sees potential in the boy, and scripter Lee Hall shades this familiar material with such fresh enthusiasm that you cannot help being captivated. Rated R for profanity and earthy dialogue. 110m. **DIR:** Stephen Daldry. **CAST:** Julie Walters, Gary Lewis, Jamie Bell, Jamie Draven, Adam Cooper. **2000 DVD**

BILLY GALVIN ★★★1/2 Surprisingly good slice-of-life drama about steelworkers in Boston. Karl Malden is excellent as Jack Galvin, a hard-bitten steelworker who doesn't want his son, Billy (Lenny Von Dohlen, also excellent), to follow in his footsteps. Rated PG for language. 99m. **DIR:** John Gray. **CAST:** Karl Malden, Lenny von Dohlen, Toni Kalem, Keith Szarabajka, Alan North, Barton Heyman, Joyce Van Patten. **1986**

BILLY JACK ★★1/2 This film that seems to suggest that a good kick in the groin will bring "peace and love" was a box-office sensation. The star, Tom Laughlin, produced and directed. Rated PG. 114m. **DIR:** Tom Laughlin. **CAST:** Tom Laughlin, Delores Taylor, Clark Howat, Bert Freed, Julie Webb. **1971 DVD**

BILLY LIAR ★★★★ Poignant slices of English middle-class life are served expertly in this finely played story of a lazy young man who escapes dulling routine by retreating into fantasy. The eleven minutes Julie Christie is on screen are electric and worth the whole picture. B&W; 96m. **DIR:** John Schlesinger. **CAST:** Tom Courtenay, Julie Christie, Finlay Currie, Ethel Griffies, Mona Washbourne. **1963 DVD**

BILLY MADISON 🦃 *Saturday Night Live*'s Adam Sandler plays a rich nitwit going back to school. The filmmakers (including cowriter Sandler) still need several years of comedy school. Rated PG-13 for mild profanity and cartoon violence. 90m. **DIR:** Tamra Davis. **CAST:** Adam Sandler, Bradley Whitford, Josh Mostel, Bridgette Wilson, Darren McGavin. **1995 DVD**

BILLY THE KID ★★★1/2 The legendary outlaw is romanticized, but the highlights of his life and death are straight from the history books. Predictable but fascinating, chiefly because the studio used top stars and photographed lush surroundings. Pat Garrett is missing, though. The sheriff who tangles with the Kid is completely fictional. 95m. **DIR:** David Miller. **CAST:** Robert Taylor, Brian Donlevy, Chill Wills, Ethel Griffies, Mary Howard, Gene Lockhart, Ian Hunter, Guinn Williams. **1941**

BILLY THE KID MEETS THE VAMPIRES 🦃 Billy the Kid takes a vacation and meets up with some of the lousiest actors and actresses this side of Mars. Not rated. 118m. **DIR:** Steve Postal. **CAST:** Michael K. Saunders, Debra Orth, Angela Shepard. **1991**

BILLY THE KID RETURNS ★★1/2 Roy Rogers plays a look-alike to the dead Billy the Kid and restores the tranquillity of Lincoln County after subduing the criminal element. Fun for fans. B&W; 58m. **DIR:** Joseph Kane. **CAST:** Roy Rogers, Smiley Burnette, Lynne Roberts, Morgan Wallace, Fred Kohler Sr., Trigger. **1938 DVD**

BILLY THE KID VS. DRACULA 🦃 Hokey horror film casts John Carradine as the famous vampire, on the loose in a small western town. 95m. **DIR:** William Beaudine. **CAST:** John Carradine, Chuck Courtney, Melinda Plowman, Virginia Christine, Harry Carey Jr. **1966**

BILLY ZE KICK ★★1/2 Uneven comedy-mystery about a bumbling cop who discovers that the fictitious tales he's been delivering to his daughter about a serial killer are beginning to spread throughout his own neighborhood as a reality. Stupid cartoon-like characters quickly become annoying and redundant. In French with English subtitles. Rated R for violence. 87m. **DIR:** Gérard Mordillat. **CAST:** Francis Perrin. **1985**

BILLY'S HOLLYWOOD SCREEN KISS ★★★ A gay photographer obsesses over one of his models, a handsome young waiter who hasn't yet decided whether he likes girls or boys. Garnished with coy in-jokes, flamboyant drag queens, and campy fantasy sequences, the film is really an updated version of the soulful, soft-focus date movies of the 1960s and 1970s. Rated R for profanity and mature themes. 92m. **DIR:** Tommy O'Haver. **CAST:** Sean P. Hayes, Brad Rowe, Richard Ganoung, Meredith Scott Lynn, Paul Bartel, Holly Woodlawn. **1998 DVD**

BILOXI BLUES ★★★★ As second in Neil Simon's loosely autobiographical trilogy (after *Brighton Beach Memoirs*), this witty glimpse of growing up in a Deep South World War II boot camp stars Matthew Broderick. When not clashing with the sly drill sergeant or learning about the birds and bees from an amused wartime prostitute, Broderick makes perceptive comments about life, the war, and his army buddies. Rated PG-13 for language and sexual themes. 106m. **DIR:** Mike Nichols. **CAST:** Matthew Broderick, Christopher Walken, Matt Mulhern, Casey Siemaszko. **1988 DVD**

BIMBO MOVIE BASH 🦃 Directors David Parker and Mike Mendez string together a series of cheap exploitation films in order to come up with a silly plot about female aliens invading Earth. Totally worthless. Rated R for adult situations, language, nudity, and violence. 90m. **DIR:** David Parker, Mike Mendez. **CAST:** Adrienne Barbeau, Shannon Tweed, Morgan Fairchild, Julie Strain, Linnea Quigley. **1996**

BINGO 🦃 This mishmash attempt at comedy follows a dog who chases his master cross-country. The cute dog of the title can't save this film from the fleas. Rated PG for brief violence and brief profanity. 87m. **DIR:** Matthew Robbins. **CAST:** Cindy Williams, David Rasche. **1991**

BINGO LONG TRAVELING ALL-STARS AND MOTOR KINGS, THE ★★★ This is a comedy-adventure of a barnstorming group of black baseball players as they tour rural America in the late 1930s. Billy Dee Williams, Richard Pryor, and James Earl Jones are three of the team's players. Only the lack of a cohesive script keeps this from receiving more stars. Rated PG. 110m. **DIR:** John Badham. **CAST:** Billy Dee Williams, James Earl Jones, Richard Pryor, Ted Ross. **1976**

BIO-DOME 🦃 Two idiots (Pauly Shore, Stephen Baldwin) mistake a sealed-environment scientific experiment for a shopping mall. Cheap, stupid, and unfunny; Shore can't keep from laughing at his own antics, but you'll have no such trouble. Rated PG-13 for mild profanity. 95m. **DIR:** Jason Bloom. **CAST:** Pauly Shore, Stephen Baldwin, William Atherton, Henry Gibson, Taylor Negron, Patty Hearst. **1995 DVD**

BIOHAZARD 🦃 Aliens are contacted by a beautiful psychic in this low-budget *Alien* rip-off. Rated R for violence. 84m. **DIR:** Fred Olen Ray. **CAST:** Angelique Pettyjohn, Aldo Ray. **1984**

BIOHAZARD: THE ALIEN FORCE ★★ Another cheesy *Alien* rip-off with slimy beasts from space bursting out of human chests. Not bad if you don't mind ultra-low-budget schlock. Rated R for violence. 88m. **DIR:** Steve Latshaw. **CAST:** Steve Zurk, Susan Fronsoe, Tom Ferguson, Patrick Moran, Katheryn Culliver, Chris Mitchum. **1994**

BIONIC WOMAN, THE ★★ What we have here is the female equivalent of TV's *The Six Million Dollar Man*. Lindsay Wagner is the superwoman who annihilates the bad guys. 96m. **DIR:** Richard Moder. **CAST:** Lindsay Wagner, Lee Majors, Richard Anderson. **1975**

BIRCH INTERVAL, THE ★★★ Engaging, poignant 11 year old Susan McClung learns lessons of life and love while living with relatives in Amish Pennsylvania. An excellent cast makes this sadly neglected film a memorable viewing experience. 104m. **DIR:** Delbert Mann. **CAST:** Eddie Albert, Rip Torn, Susan McClung, Ann Wedgeworth, Anne Revere. **1976**

BIRCH WOOD ★★★★ A tubercular young pianist goes to rest at the forest home of his brother. The brother cannot accept the recent death of his wife, but the pianist sees his impending death as a natural part of life. A moving story, beautifully photographed in rural Poland. In Polish with English subtitles. 99m. **DIR:** Andrzej Wajda. **CAST:** Daniel Olbrychski. **1970**

BIRD ★★★★1/2 Clint Eastwood's *Bird* soars with a majesty all its own. About the life of legendary saxophonist Charlie "Bird" Parker, it is the ultimate jazz movie. It features Parker's inspired improvised solos in abundance, while telling the story of the brilliant but troubled and drug-addicted artist. Parker is solidly played by Forest Whitaker. Rated R for profanity and drug use. 140m. **DIR:** Clint Eastwood. **CAST:** Forest Whitaker, Diane Venora, Samuel E. Wright, Keith David. **1988 DVD**

BIRD MAN OF ALCATRAZ ★★★★ In one of his best screen performances, Burt Lancaster plays Robert Stroud, the prisoner who became a world-renowned authority on birds. B&W; 143m. **DIR:** John Frankenheimer. **CAST:** Burt Lancaster, Karl Malden, Thelma Ritter, Telly Savalas. **1962**

BIRD OF PARADISE ★★1/2 Even the reliable Joel McCrea can't save this bit of South Sea island silliness. The seafaring McCrea attempts to woo native princess Dolores Del Rio. This kind of thing looks awfully dumb today. B&W; 80m. **DIR:** King Vidor. **CAST:** Joel McCrea, Dolores Del Rio, John Halliday, Skeets Gallagher, Lon Chaney Jr. **1932 DVD**

BIRD OF PREY 🦃 A good cast embarrasses itself in this awful drama about a freedom fighter out to avenge the death of his father in postcommunist Bulgaria. Rated R for sexual situations, violence, and profanity. 101m. **DIR:** Temistocles Lopez. **CAST:** Boyan Milushev, Jennifer Tilly, Richard Chamberlain, Lenny von Dohlen, Robert Carradine, Lesley Ann Warren. **1995**

BIRD ON A WIRE ★★1/2 Formulaic action-comedy casts Goldie Hawn as a hotshot corporate lawyer and Mel Gibson as a mystery man from her past. A promising plot is eschewed in favor of madcap chases. Rated PG-13 for profanity, violence, and nudity. 106m. **DIR:** John Badham. **CAST:** Mel Gibson, Goldie Hawn, David Carradine, Bill Duke, Joan Severance. **1990 DVD**

BIRD WITH THE CRYSTAL PLUMAGE, THE ★★★ Stylish thriller weaves a complex adventure of an American writer who witnesses a murder and is drawn into the web of mystery and violence. Minor cult favorite, well photographed and nicely acted by resilient Tony Musante and fashion plate Suzy Kendall. Rated PG. 98m. **DIR:** Dario Argento. **CAST:** Tony Musante, Suzy Kendall, Eva Renzi, Enrico Maria Salerno. **1969 DVD**

BIRDCAGE, THE ★★★1/2 American version of *La Cage aux Folles* lacks some of the poignance and hilarity of the original; however, this remake has a number of high points, particularly in the performances of Robin Williams, Nathan Lane, and Gene Hackman. Williams and Lane are a gay couple who must "go straight" to fool Hackman, a conservative politician whose daughter is engaged to Williams's son. Rated R for profanity and adult content. 118m. **DIR:** Mike Nichols. **CAST:** Robin Williams, Gene Hackman, Nathan Lane, Dianne Wiest, Christine Baranski, Hank Azaria, Dan Futterman, Calista Flockhart. **1996 DVD**

BIRDS, THE ★★★★ Alfred Hitchcock's *The Birds* is an eerie, disturbing stunner, highlighted by Evan Hunter's literate adaptation of Daphne du Maurier's ominous short story. Rod Taylor and Tippi Hedren are thrown into an uneasy relationship while our avian friends develop an appetite for something more substantial than bugs and berries. Hitchcock's unswerving attention to character lends credibility to the premise. Not rated, but may be too intense for younger viewers. 120m. **DIR:** Alfred Hitchcock. **CAST:** Rod Taylor, Tippi Hedren, Jessica Tandy, Suzanne Pleshette, Veronica Cartwright, Ethel Griffies. **1963 DVD**

BIRDS II, THE: LAND'S END 🦃 This idiotic sequel to Hitchcock's classic is a complete mess, with inane plotting, overwrought acting, and a climax that feels like the camera just ran out of film. Director Rick Rosenthal was disgusted enough to hide behind the alias Alan Smithee. Rated R for violence and profanity. 87m. **DIR:** Rick Rosenthal. **CAST:** Brad Johnson, Chelsea Field, James Naughton, Jan Rubes, Tippi Hedren. **1994**

BIRDS AND THE BEES, THE ★★ This poor remake of the 1941 Barbara Stanwyck–Henry Fonda comedy hit, *The Lady Eve*, has military cardsharper David Niven setting daughter Mitzi Gaynor on playboy millionaire George Gobel in hopes of getting rich from the marriage. "Lonesome George" wiggles free, but falls for her anyway. Don't settle for imitations. Insist on the original. 94m. **DIR:** Norman Taurog. **CAST:** George Gobel, Mitzi Gaynor, David Niven. **1956**

BIRDS OF PREY ★★★★ Ex–World War II fighter pilot turned peacetime Salt Lake City traffic helicopter jockey (David Janssen) hears the siren song of war anew when he witnesses a bank heist in progress and chases the robbers, who make their getaway in their own 'copter. An aerial battle of wits follows. Terrific flying sequences. 81m. **DIR:** William A. Graham. **CAST:** David Janssen, Ralph Meeker, Elayne Heilveil. **1973**

BIRDY ★★★★1/2 Matthew Modine and Nicolas Cage give unforgettable performances in this dark, disturbing, yet somehow uplifting study of an odd young man named Birdy (Modine) from South Philadelphia who wants to be a bird. That way he can fly away from all his troubles—which worsen manifold after a traumatic tour of duty in Vietnam. Rated R for violence, nudity, and profanity. 120m. **DIR:** Alan Parker. **CAST:** Matthew Modine, Nicolas Cage, John Harkins, Sandy Baron, Karen Young, Bruno Kirby. **1985 DVD**

BIRGIT HAAS MUST BE KILLED ★★★★★ It is hard to imagine a more perfect film than this spellbinding, French thriller-drama. Though its plot revolves around the assassination of a German terrorist (Birgit Haas) by a French counterspy organization, this film says as much about human relationships as it does espionage. In French with English subtitles. Not rated; the film contains well-handled violence and nudity. 105m. **DIR:** Laurent Heynemann. **CAST:** Philippe Noiret, Jean Rochefort, Lisa Kreuzer. **1981**

BIRTH OF A NATION, THE ★★★★ Videotape will probably be the only medium in which you will ever see this landmark silent classic. D. W. Griffith's epic saga of the American Civil War and its aftermath is today considered too racist in its glorification of the Ku Klux Klan ever to be touched by television or revival theaters. This is filmdom's most important milestone (the first to tell a cohesive story) but should only be seen by those emotionally prepared for its disturbing point of view. B&W; 158m. **DIR:** D. W. Griffith. **CAST:** Lillian Gish, Mae Marsh, Henry B. Walthall, Miriam Cooper. **1915 DVD**

BIRTH OF THE BLUES ★★★★1/2 Although highly fictionalized, this Bing Crosby musical has the feel of New Orleans and the unmistakable beat of the bands from New Orleans's jazz age. B&W; 85m. **DIR:** Victor Schertzinger. **CAST:** Bing Crosby, Mary Martin, Brian Donlevy, Eddie "Rochester" Anderson. **1941**

BIRTHDAY BOY, THE ★★ A Cinemax Comedy Experiment that proves once again how difficult it is to produce an even moderately funny film. James Belushi (who also wrote the script) is a sporting-goods salesman who journeys cross-country on his birthday in an attempt to sell his old gym coach a load of basketballs. Not rated; contains adult language. 30m. **DIR:** Claude Conrad. **CAST:** James Belushi, Michelle Riga, Dennis Farina, Ron Dean, Jim Johnson, Ed Blatchford, Fred Kaz. **1986**

•BIRTHDAY GIRL ★★★ Mild-mannered British bank clerk John attempts to upgrade his loner lifestyle by purchasing a Russian mail-order bride. He gets much more woman than he may be able to handle when his brooding fiancée arrives with no apparent knowledge of English and is soon joined by two fellow male Soviets of suspect character. The film transforms from black romantic comedy to oddball crime story with both sly and hard-to-swallow twists as John's life plunges from honeymoon into nightmare. Partially in Russian with English subtitles. Rated R for language, violence, and sexuality. 93m. **DIR:** Jez Butterworth. **CAST:** Nicole Kidman, Ben Chaplin, Mathieu Kassovitz, Vincent Cassel. **2002 DVD**

BISHOP'S WIFE, THE ★★★ Harmless story of debonair angel (Cary Grant) sent to Earth to aid a bishop (David Niven) in his quest for a new church. The kind of film they just don't make anymore. No rating, but okay for the whole family. B&W; 108m. **DIR:** Henry Koster. **CAST:** Cary Grant, Loretta Young, David Niven, James Gleason. **1947 DVD**

BITCH, THE 🦃 Joan Collins has the title role in this fiasco, an adaptation of sister Jackie Collins's book. Rated R. 93m. **DIR:** Gerry O'Hara. **CAST:** Joan Collins, Kenneth Haigh, Michael Coby. **1979**

BITE THE BULLET ★★★★1/2 A six-hundred-mile horse race is the subject of this magnificent adventure, an epic in every sense of the word. A real sleeper, hardly noticed during its theatrical release. Rated PG. 131m. **DIR:** Richard Brooks. **CAST:** Gene Hackman, James Coburn, Candice Bergen, Ben Johnson, Jan-Michael Vincent, Dabney Coleman, Ian Bannen. **1975 DVD**

BITTER HARVEST (1981) ★★★★ In this made-for-television film based on a true incident, Ron Howard gives an excellent performance as an at-first panicky and then take-charge farmer whose dairy farm herd becomes sick and begins dying. His battle to find out the cause of the illness (chemicals in the feed), provides for scary, close-to-home drama. Good supporting cast. 104m. **DIR:** Roger Young. **CAST:** Ron Howard, Art Carney, Richard Dysart. **1981**

BITTER HARVEST (1993) ★★ Strange tale about a farm boy (Stephen Baldwin) corrupted by two beautiful strangers (Patsy Kensit and Jennifer Rubin). Baldwin is good, but excessive subplots lessen the film's impact. Rated R for nudity, sex, violence, and profanity. 98m. **DIR:** Duane Clark. **CAST:** Stephen Baldwin, Patsy Kensit, Jennifer Rubin, Adam Baldwin, M. Emmet Walsh. **1993**

BITTER MOON ★★ Roman Polanski again assaults audience sensibilities with this lurid psychodrama about self-destructive obsession and sexual terrorism. On a Mediterranean cruise, an unsuccessful American novelist in a wheelchair shocks and seduces a starchy Englishman with perverse details of his relationship with his French wife. This ludicrous portrait is visually seductive but not as darkly funny as intended. Rated R for simulated sex and language. 139m. **DIR:** Roman Polanski. **CAST:** Peter Coyote, Hugh Grant, Emmanuelle Seigner, Kristin Scott Thomas. **1994**

BITTER RICE ★★★ A steamy temperature-raiser in its day, this Italian neorealist drama of exploited rice workers—spiced up with some sex scenes—is tame and obvious today. Well directed, though, and as a curio, worth a look. B&W; 108m. **DIR:** Giuseppe De Santis. **CAST:** Silvana Mangano, Vittorio Gassman, Raf Vallone, Doris Dowling. **1948**

BITTER SUGAR ★★★ An idealistic young Cuban Communist learns that real life is quite different from the political theory on which he has been raised. Director Leon Ichaso uses trendy black-and-white photography and New Wave techniques to polish what is essentially anti-Castro propaganda. Not rated; contains sexual situations. In Spanish with English subtitles. B&W; 104m. **DIR:** Leon Ichaso. **CAST:** Rene Lavan, Mayte Vilan, Miguel Gutierrez. **1997 DVD**

BITTER SWEET (1940) ★★ Redeemed only by the lilting songs of Noel Coward, this tragic story of a violinist's romance with a dancer was the MacDonald-Eddy team's first financial failure, and it augered the end of their long reign. 92m. **DIR:** W. S. Van Dyke. **CAST:** Jeanette MacDonald, Nelson Eddy, George Sanders, Herman Bing, Felix Bressart, Ian Hunter, Sig Ruman, Veda Ann Borg. **1940**

BITTER TEA OF GENERAL YEN, THE ★★★★ An American joins her missionary fiancé in China and finds herself drawn to a Chinese warlord who takes her prisoner. When released this movie was panned by reviewers upset by the interracial theme. A historical note: This film was chosen to open New York's Radio City Music Hall. B&W; 89m. **DIR:** Frank Capra. **CAST:** Barbara Stanwyck, Nils Asther, Gavin Gordon, Lucien Littlefield, Toshia Mori, Richard Loo, Walter Connolly. **1933**

BITTER TEARS OF PETRA VON KANT, THE ★★★ A lesbian fashion designer falls in love with another woman and is met with betrayal when her lover has an affair with an American serviceman. Overlong drama gets a lift from solid performances and great cinematography by Michael Ballhaus (*Raging Bull*, *The Last Temptation of Christ*). In German with English subtitles. Not rated; contains nudity and profanity. 124m. **DIR:** Rainer Werner Fassbinder. **CAST:** Margit Carstensen, Hanna Schygulla. **1972**

BITTER VENGEANCE ★★1/2 A husband sets his wife up to look like his killer in this made-for-cable original. Weak story and sappy characters. Not rated; contains nudity, violence, and suggested sex. 90m. **DIR:** Stuart Cooper. **CAST:** Virginia Madsen, Bruce Greenwood, Kristen Hocking, Eddie Velez, Gordon Jump. **1994**

BITTERSWEET (1999) 🦃 Angie Everhart is a model for bad behavior as the barrel-blasting babe looking for revenge against her former boyfriend, now a member of the mob. This direct-to-video effort doesn't deliver the bang for the buck. Rated R for adult situations, language, and violence. 92m. **DIR:** Luca Bercovici. **CAST:** Angie Everhart, James Russo, Eric Roberts, Brian Wimmer, Joe Penny. **1999 DVD**

BITTERSWEET LOVE 🦃 Young married couple discover that they are a half brother and sister. Rated PG. 92m. **DIR:** David Miller. **CAST:** Lana Turner, Robert Lansing, Celeste Holm, Robert Alda, Meredith Baxter-Birney. **1976**

BIZARRE, BIZARRE ★★★1/2 Frenetic farce set in Victorian England at the home of a writer of mystery novels. In French with English subtitles. 90m. **DIR:** Marcel Carné. **CAST:** Louis Jouvet, Françoise Rosay, Michel Simon, Jean-Pierre Aumont. **1937**

BIZET'S CARMEN ★★★★★ Julia Migenes-Johnson and Placido Domingo excel in this film adaptation of the opera by Georges Bizet. It is about a gypsy whose fierce independence maddens the men who become obsessed with her. In French with English subtitles. Rated PG for mild violence. 152m. **DIR:** Francesco Rosi. **CAST:** Placido Domingo, Julia Migenes-Johnson. **1985 DVD**

BLACK ADDER III (TV SERIES) ★★★★ Third in a trilogy of the *Black Adder* series, this is one of the most wicked, delightfully sardonic send-ups of British costume drama ever made. Rat-faced Rowan Atkinson is a sly former aristocrat and butler to the Prince of Wales, son of mad King George III. He's kept perpetually on his toes by the unpredictable idiocy of his twit of a prince, played with exquisite vacuousness by Hugh Laurie. 60m. **DIR:** Mandie Fletcher. **CAST:** Rowan Atkinson, Hugh Laurie. **1989 DVD**

BLACK & WHITE (1998) ★★★ Thriller about a cop suspected of being a serial killer manages to entertain while never really growing out of its B-movie genre. Rated R for violence, nudity, sexual situations, and profanity. 97m. **DIR:** Yuri Zeltser. **CAST:** Gina Gershon, Ron Silver, Alison Eastwood, Barry Primus. **1998 DVD**

BLACK AND WHITE (2000) ★★ Race, class, and sexual boundaries blur in this voyeuristic tour of modern Manhattan in which privileged white kids reinvent themselves as gangstas, and African American thugs morph into recording artists. The film alternates between improvised and structured scenes as a documentary filmmaker, her bisexual husband, and a rogue cop stir up trouble in a wannabe hip-hop version of *Nashville*. Rated R for language, drug use, nudity, sex, and violence. 100m. **DIR:** James Toback. **CAST:** Alan Houston, Ben Stiller, Robert Downey Jr., Brooke Shields, Mike Tyson, Claudia Schiffer, Ollie "Power" Grant, Method Man, Elijah Wood, Bijou Phillips. **2000 DVD**

BLACK AND WHITE IN COLOR ★★★★ A group of self-satisfied Frenchmen at a remote African trading post become stung by patriotism at the outbreak of World War I, and they organize a surprise assault on a nearby German fort. This sleeper won an Oscar for best foreign film. In French with English subtitles. Not rated; contains nudity, profanity, and violence. 90m. **DIR:** Jean-Jacques Annaud. **CAST:** Jean Carmet, Jacques Dufilho, Catherine Rouvel, Jacques Spiesser, Dora Doll. **1977**

BLACK ARROW, THE (1948) ★★★1/2 Hero Louis Hayward is in fine form as he fights the evil George Macready in this highly enjoyable entry into the swashbuckler genre. Some fine action scenes, with a slam-bang finale. B&W; 76m. **DIR:** Gordon Douglas. **CAST:** Louis Hayward, George Macready, Janet Blair, Edgar Buchanan. **1948**

BLACK ARROW (1984) ★★★1/2 In this enjoyable Disney adventure film, Sir Daniel Brackley (Oliver Reed), a corrupt and wealthy landowner, is robbed by the Black Arrow, an outlaw. He then conceives of a plan to marry his ward, Joanna (Georgia Slowe), and send his nephew (Benedict Taylor) to his death. The tide turns when his nephew and the Black Arrow combine forces to rescue Joanna. 93m. **DIR:** John Hough. **CAST:** Oliver Reed, Georgia Slowe, Benedict Taylor, Fernando Rey, Donald Pleasence. **1984**

BLACK BEAUTY (1946) ★★★ Based on Anna Sewell's novel that is about a little girl's determined effort to find her missing black colt. Though pedestrian at times, the treatment is still effective enough to hold interest and bring a tear or two. B&W; 74m. **DIR:** Max Nosseck. **CAST:** Mona Freeman, Richard Denning, Evelyn Ankers, J. M. Kerrigan, Terry Kilburn. **1946**

BLACK BEAUTY (1971) ★★ One of the world's most-loved children's books, *Black Beauty* has never been translated adequately to the screen. This version is passable at best. Kids who've read the book may want to see the movie, though this movie won't make anyone want to read the book. Great Britain/Germany/Spain. 106m. **DIR:** James Hill. **CAST:** Mark Lester, Walter Slezak, Patrick Mower. **1971**

BLACK BEAUTY (1994) ★★★★ The Humane Society should use this fine film to counter cruelty to horses. Told from the horse's point of view, every injustice is magnified tenfold. Anna Sewell would have been proud of Caroline Thompson's sensitive screen adaptation of her timeless novel. The horse carries the show, only utilizing humans to move the plot along. Rated G for family viewing. 88m. **DIR:** Caroline Thompson. **CAST:** Sean Bean, Andrew Knott, David Thewlis. **1994 DVD**

BLACK BELT JONES ★★★ A likable kung fu action film about a self-defense school in Watts combating a "Mafioso"-type group. Not a classic film, but an easy pace and good humor make this a fun action movie. Rated PG for violence. 87m. **DIR:** Robert Clouse. **CAST:** Jim Kelly, Scatman Crothers, Gloria Hendry. **1974**

BLACK BIRD, THE ★★★ Surprisingly enjoyable comedy produced by and starring George Segal as Sam Spade Jr. The visual gags abound, and an air of authenticity is added by the performances of 1940s detective film regulars Lionel Stander, Elisha Cook, and Lee Patrick. The latter two costarred with Humphrey Bogart in *The Maltese Falcon*, on which the film is based. It's funny, with a strong performance from Segal. Rated PG. 98m. **DIR:** David Giler. **CAST:** George Segal, Stéphane Audran, Lionel Stander, Lee Patrick. **1975**

BLACK CAESAR ★★ In this passable gangster flick, Fred Williamson stars as Tommy Gibbs, bloodthirsty, gun-wielding Godfather of Harlem. The soundtrack by the Godfather of Soul, James Brown, doesn't hurt. Rated R. 92m. **DIR:** Larry Cohen. **CAST:** Fred Williamson, Art Lund, Val Avery, Julius W. Harris, William Wellman Jr., D'Urville Martin, Gloria Hendry. **1973 DVD**

BLACK CAMEL, THE ★★1/2 Chan investigates murder on the set of a movie being shot in Hawaii. Because it takes place on his home turf, this early entry in the series includes scenes of the wily detective at home with his ten (!) kids. B&W; 71m. **DIR:** Hamilton MacFadden. **CAST:** Warner Oland, Sally Eilers, Bela Lugosi, Dwight Frye. **1931**

BLACK CASTLE, THE ★★★ Lightweight costume drama with gothic overtones benefits from typically strong performances by horror veterans Boris Karloff and Lon Chaney Jr. in supporting roles. The bulk of the story revolves around the efforts of an English adventurer to wrest a beautiful woman from the evil clutches of her murderous husband. B&W; 81m. **DIR:** Nathan Juran. **CAST:** Richard Greene, Boris Karloff, Stephen McNally, Paula Corday, Lon Chaney Jr., John Hoyt, Michael Pate. **1952**

BLACK CAT, THE (1934) ★★★★ A surrealistic, strikingly designed horror-thriller that has become a cult favorite thanks to its pairing of Boris Karloff and Bela Lugosi. Lugosi has one of his very few good-guy roles as a concerned citizen who gets drawn into a web of evil that surrounds Karloff's black magic. Available on a videocassette double feature with *The Raven*. B&W; 70m. **DIR:** Edgar G. Ulmer. **CAST:** Boris Karloff, Bela Lugosi, Jacqueline Wells. **1934**

BLACK CAT, THE (1981) ★★ Feline gore from Lucio Fulci, made when he was the most prolific of the low-budget Italian exploitation-horror directors. A very loose Poe adaptation. Rated R for violence. 92m. **DIR:** Lucio Fulci. **CAST:** Patrick Magee, Mimsy Farmer, David Warbeck. **1981 DVD**

BLACK CAT RUN ★★ The chase is on for Patrick Muldoon, who plays a gas station attendant suspected of murder and on the run. Can he rescue his kidnapped girlfriend from escaped convicts before the law catches up with him? Rated R for language and violence. 90m. **DIR:** D. J. Caruso. **CAST:** Patrick Muldoon, Amelia Heinle, Jake Busey, Peter Greene. **1998 DVD**

BLACK CAULDRON, THE ★★★ At the time, this was the most expensive animated film ever made and, for Disney, its first real failure in that field—largely due to the fact that the writers jammed all five of the *Chronicles of Prydain* into one film. Parents may also want to steer younger kids clear since the Horned King and his zombies seem more suited to *Lord of the Rings* than to family fare. Still, the animation is dazzling. Rated PG for scary scenes and mild violence. 80m. **DIR:** Ted Berman, Richard Rich. **1985 DVD**

BLACK CHRISTMAS ★★★ During the holiday season, members of a sorority house fall victim to the homicidal obscene phone-caller living in their attic. Margot Kidder is quite convincing as a vulgar, alcoholic college kid with asthma. Atmospheric and frightening. Try to remember that it came before *Halloween* and *When A Stranger Calls*. Rated R. 99m. **DIR:** Bob Clark. **CAST:** Olivia Hussey, Keir Dullea, Margot Kidder, John Saxon. **1975 DVD**

BLACK CIRCLE BOYS ★★ The writers leave no cliché unturned in this lifeless thriller of a good boy who falls in with a bad crowd. Scott Bairstow stands out as the good kid who is drawn to the wrong side of the tracks, but all of his goodwill is wasted when the film becomes unexpectedly cruel. Rated R for adult situations, language, and violence. 101m. **DIR:** Matthew Carnahan. **CAST:** Scott Bairstow, Eric Mabius, Tara Subkoff, Donnie Wahlberg. **1997 DVD**

BLACK COBRA 3 🦃 The CIA has been sending military aid to insurgent forces in a Third World country ripped by war. Rated R for violence. 89m. **DIR:** Dan Edwards. **CAST:** Fred Williamson, Forry Smith, Debra Ward. **1990**

BLACK DAY BLUE NIGHT ★★1/2 Atmospheric stab at *film noir* stars Michelle Forbes and Mia Sara as two women on the run from life, whose encounter with a handsome stranger in the middle of the Arizona desert changes their lives forever. Rated R for nudity, profanity, violence, and adult situations. 99m. **DIR:** J. S. Cardone. **CAST:** Gil Bellows, Michelle Forbes, Mia Sara, J. T. Walsh. **1995**

BLACK DEVIL DOLL FROM HELL ★★ Direct-to-video melodrama in which a miniature voodoo doll goes on a gruesome rampage. Most of the time, sluggish and predictable. Not rated. 70m. **DIR:** Chester T. Turner. **CAST:** Rickey Roach. **1984**

BLACK DOG ★★ Trucker, parolee, and stalwart family man Jack Crews has served time for vehicular manslaughter and now feels forced to drive a semi loaded with suspect cargo from Georgia to New Jersey to save his home from foreclosure. Road carnage piles up at a furious clip as the story's moral implications grind in all gears. Rated PG-13 for language and violence. 88m. **DIR:** Kevin Hooks. **CAST:** Patrick Swayze, Randy Travis, Meat Loaf, Gabriel Casseus, Brian Vincent, Brenda Strong, Charles Dutton, Stephen Tobolowsky. **1998 DVD**

BLACK DRAGONS 🦃 A silly film about Japanese agents who are surgically altered to resemble American businessmen and chiefs of industry. B&W; 62m. **DIR:** William Nigh. **CAST:** Bela Lugosi, Joan Barclay, Clayton Moore. **1949**

BLACK EAGLE ★★1/2 A decent martial arts flick about a CIA agent (Sho Kosugi) sent to recover a top-secret laser-tracking device from a U.S. fighter downed in the Mediterranean. The KGB has also sent a man (Jean-Claude Van Damme), and the two agents do the international tango. Rated R for violence. 93m. **DIR:** Eric Karson. **CAST:** Sho Kosugi, Jean-Claude Van Damme, Vladimir Skomarovsky, Doran Clark. **1988 DVD**

BLACK FOX ★★ The first installment of the *Black Fox* trilogy. Christopher Reeve and the slave he freed, Tony Todd, are Texan pioneers in 1861 who consider themselves to be blood brothers. American Indians come across as rather savage, and Reeve is especially wooden. However, both the interracial friendship and Todd's performance are refreshing. Not rated; contains violence. 92m. **DIR:** Steven H. Stern. **CAST:** Christopher Reeve, Tony Todd, Raul Trujillo. **1993**

BLACK FRIDAY ★★★1/2 College professor Stanley Ridges is mortally wounded when he is caught in a gun battle between rival gangsters. To save his life, surgeon Boris Karloff transplants the brain of one of the wounded gangsters into Ridges's body, thus setting in motion a tragic chain of events. Karloff and Bela Lugosi are superb, but this is Ridges's showcase all the way. B&W; 70m. **DIR:** Arthur Lubin. **CAST:** Boris Karloff, Bela Lugosi, Stanley Ridges, Anne Nagel, Anne Gwynne, Paul Fix. **1940 DVD**

BLACK FURY ★★★★ Paul Muni is excellent as Joe Radek, an apolitical eastern European immigrant coal miner who unwittingly falls into the middle of a labor dispute. The acting is good, but the film doesn't reach its happy ending in a logical manner, so things just seem to fall into place without any reason. B&W; 95m. **DIR:** Michael Curtiz. **CAST:** Paul Muni, Karen Morley, William Gargan, Barton MacLane. **1935**

BLACK GOD (WHITE DEVIL) ★★ Uneventful tale set in the impoverished northern Brazil, about a poor peasant who changes from a fanatical preacher into an honorable bandit. Poor film-to-video transfer and hard-to-read subtitles. In Portuguese with English subtitles. Not rated; contains violence. 102m. **DIR:** Glauber Rocha. **CAST:** Yona Magalhaeds. **1964**

BLACK GODFATHER, THE ★★★ Public spirited black gangsters take time out from their more nefarious activities to keep the Mafia from selling heroin in their neighborhood. Unpretentious exploitation drama with plenty of action. Rated R for sexual situations and violence. 96m. **DIR:** John Evans. **CAST:** Rod Perry. **1974 DVD**

BLACK HAND, THE ★★ Gene Kelly offers a fine dramatic performance as a young man who must avenge the murder of his father. He becomes embroiled in the machinations of the Black Hand, (a.k.a. the Mafia) at the turn of the century. 93m. **DIR:** Richard Thorpe. **CAST:** Gene Kelly, J. Carrol Naish, Teresa Celli. **1950**

•BLACK HAWK DOWN ★★★★1/2 If *Saving Private Ryan* raised the bar on war films, this film knocks the bar off its posts. This is a brutal picture, both in terms of on-screen carnage, and the emotional wallop it packs along the way. Granted the luxury of hindsight, the American mission undertaken during the 1993 U.N. peacekeeping mission in Somalia seems every bit as ill-advised and catastrophic as the lunatic events depicted in 1981's *Gallipoli*... and yet American soldiers rose valiantly to the occasion. Talk about the few and the proud; clearly, this historic event was begging to be commemorated and this film meets that challenge, and then some. Rated R for profanity and continuous war violence. 143m. **DIR:** Ridley Scott. **CAST:** Josh Hartnett, Ewan McGregor, Tom Sizemore, Eric Bana, William Fichtner, Ewen Bremner, Sam Shepard. **2001 DVD**

BLACK HOLE, THE 🦃 Space movie clichés. Rated PG. 97m. **DIR:** Gary Nelson. **CAST:** Maximilian Schell, Anthony Perkins, Robert Forster, Joseph Bottoms, Yvette Mimieux, Ernest Borgnine. **1979 DVD**

BLACK ICE ★★ When mystery woman Joanna Pacula drops by for her usual rendezvous with a married politician, things get out of hand and he dies. Low-impact thriller. Rated R for nudity, violence, and language. Unrated version contains more of the same. 90m. **DIR:** Neill L. Fearnley. **CAST:** Michael Ironside, Michael Nouri, Joanna Pacula. **1992**

BLACK JACK ★★★ George Sanders is soldier of fortune Michael Alexander who has a drug-smuggling scheme in Tangiers aboard his yacht, the *Black Jack*. Despite the initial feeling that this is a dated film, the twists in plot will hold viewers' attentions. B&W; 103m. **DIR:** Julien Duvivier. **CAST:** George Sanders, Herbert Marshall, Agnes Moorehead, Patricia Roc, Marcel Dalio. **1949 DVD**

BLACK KLANSMAN, THE 🦃 This exploitative melodrama follows the efforts of a light-skinned black musician to avenge the death of his daughter, killed when the Ku Klux Klan bombed a church. Not rated, but includes violence and sexual situations. B&W; 88m. **DIR:** Ted V. Mikels. **CAST:** Richard Gilden, Rima Kutner. **1966**

•**BLACK KNIGHT** ★★ Amusement park employee Martin Lawrence finds himself magically transported to medieval England in this raunchy, cheap-looking variation on *A Connecticut Yankee in King Arthur's Court.* Any resemblance to Mark Twain ends there; this is for Lawrence's fans only. Rated PG-13 for profanity and crude sexual humor. 95m. **DIR:** Gil Junger. **CAST:** Martin Lawrence, Marsha Thomason, Tom Wilkinson, Vincent Regan, Daryl Mitchell. **2001 DVD**

BLACK LEGION ★★★1/2 Factory worker joins a terrorist group after losing a promotion to a foreigner. Grim study of bigotry and hatred based on headlines of the day was Humphrey Bogart's first solo starring role, and both he and the film received critical acclaim. Good example of the social consciousness that pervaded Warner Bros. films and set them apart from other studios during the 1930s. B&W; 83m. **DIR:** Archie Mayo. **CAST:** Humphrey Bogart, Erin O'Brien-Moore, Dick Foran, Ann Sheridan, Joe Sawyer, Helen Flint, Henry Brandon. **1937**

BLACK LIKE ME ★★★ Based on the book by John Griffin, this film poses the question: What happens when a white journalist takes a drug that turns his skin black? James Whitmore plays the reporter, who wishes to experience racism firsthand. Somewhat provocative at its initial release, but by today's standards, a lot of the punch is missing. B&W; 107m. **DIR:** Carl Lerner. **CAST:** James Whitmore, Roscoe Lee Browne, Will Geer, Sorrell Booke. **1964 DVD**

BLACK LIZARD ★★★ Strange tale in which a transvestite kidnaps a jeweler's daughter to ransom her for a rare jewel and to have her become one of his living dolls on his secret island. If you like the bizarre, you will enjoy this film. In Japanese with English subtitles. Not rated; contains violence. 90m. **DIR:** Kinji Fukasaku. **CAST:** Akihiro Maru Yama, Yukio Mishima. **1968**

BLACK MAGIC (1949) ★★1/2 Orson Welles revels in the role of famous eighteenth-century charlatan Count Cagliostro—born Joseph Balsamo, a peasant with imagination and a flair for magic, hypnosis, and the power of superstition. The story is of Cagliostro's attempt to gain influence and clout in Italy using his strange and sinister talents. The star codirected (without credit). B&W; 105m. **DIR:** Gregory Ratoff. **CAST:** Orson Welles, Akim Tamiroff, Nancy Guild, Raymond Burr, Frank Latimore. **1949**

BLACK MAGIC (1992) ★★1/2 Writer-director Daniel Taplitz's overly satirical tone finally mars this quirky made-for-cable tale, which turns on whether southern seductress Rachel Ward is a witch. Although the premise and performances are engaging, the story eventually spirals out of control. Rated PG-13. 94m. **DIR:** Daniel Taplitz. **CAST:** Rachel Ward, Judge Reinhold, Brian James, Anthony LaPaglia. **1992**

BLACK MAGIC WOMAN 🦃 A dreadfully boring overworking of *Fatal Attraction*. Rated R for rubbish and erotic scenes. 91m. **DIR:** Deryn Warren. **CAST:** Mark Hamill, Amanda Wyss. **1990**

BLACK MALE ★★ Two con men, to pay off loan sharks, attempt to blackmail a doctor, but their plan backfires when the doctor turns out to be more ruthless than the mobsters. Bokeem Woodbine and Justin Pierce star as the con men on the run from the mob, the police, and the good doctor. Rated R for adult situations, language, nudity, and violence. 90m. **DIR:** George Baluzy, Mike Baluzy. **CAST:** Bokeem Woodbine, Roger Rees, Justin Pierce, Sascha Knopf. **1999 DVD**

BLACK MARBLE, THE ★★★ A Los Angeles cop (Robert Foxworth) and his new partner (Paula Prentiss) attempt to capture a dog snatcher (Harry Dean Stanton) who is demanding a high ransom from a wealthy dog lover. Along the way, they fall in love. Based on Joseph Wambaugh's novel. Rated PG—language and some violence. 110m. **DIR:** Harold Becker. **CAST:** Paula Prentiss, Harry Dean Stanton, Robert Foxworth. **1980**

BLACK MARKET RUSTLERS ★★1/2 The Range Busters break up a gang of rustlers that are supplying beef for the World War II black market. B&W; 54m. **DIR:** S. Roy Luby. **CAST:** Ray "Crash" Corrigan, Dennis Moore, Max Terhune, Glenn Strange. **1946**

BLACK MASK ★★1/2 Elite, biologically engineered combat squad takes over the Hong Kong drug trade when the government targets them for termination. A former squad member living quietly as a librarian is forced to stop the manic activities of his past associates. The action scenes are feverish, the humor is corny, and this English-dubbed version of the 1996 original has a hip-hop soundtrack. Rated R for violence, gore, sexual content, and language. 96m. **DIR:** Daniel Lee. **CAST:** Jet Li, Karen Mok, Francoise Yip, Lau Ching-wan, Patrick Lung Kang. **1999 DVD**

BLACK MOON RISING ★★ The only redeeming point of this little car theft number is its occasional accent on humor. The cast is top-notch, but the material is mostly pedestrian. Rated R for language, nudity, sex, and some rather gruesome violence. 93m. **DIR:** Harley Cokliss. **CAST:** Tommy Lee Jones, Linda Hamilton, Robert Vaughn, Richard Jaeckel, Lee Ving, Bubba Smith. **1986 DVD**

BLACK NARCISSUS ★★★1/2 Worldly temptations, including those of the flesh, create many difficulties for a group of nuns starting a mission in the Himalayas. Superb photography makes this early postwar British effort a visual delight. Unfortunately, key plot elements were cut from the American prints by censors. 99m. **DIR:** Michael Powell. **CAST:** Deborah Kerr, Jean Simmons, David Farrar, Flora Robson, Sabu. **1947 DVD**

BLACK ORCHID, THE ★★1/2 Sophia Loren plays the widow of a criminal and Anthony Quinn is the businessman who is romancing her in this patchy weeper. B&W;

96m. **DIR:** Martin Ritt. **CAST:** Sophia Loren, Anthony Quinn, Ina Balin, Peter Mark Richman. **1959**

BLACK ORPHEUS ★★★★★ The Greek myth of Orpheus, the unrivaled musician, and his ill-fated love for Eurydice has been updated and set in Rio de Janeiro during carnival for this superb film. A Portuguese-French coproduction, it has all the qualities of a genuine classic. Its stunning photography captures both the magical spirit of the original legend and the tawdry yet effervescent spirit of Brazil. 98m. **DIR:** Marcel Camus. **CAST:** Breno Mello, Marpessa Dawn, Lea Garcia, Lourdes de Oliveira. **1959 DVD**

BLACK PANTHER, THE ★★1/2 In 1974 Donald Neilson (Donald Sumpter), known as the Black Panther, robbed a series of post offices and killed their employees. Neilson also plotted the kidnapping of a wealthy teenage heiress that went awry. *The Black Panther* portrays Neilson's actions in such a matter-of-fact fashion that it removes all the horror. Still, some good action and a few intense scenes. Not rated, has violence and nudity. 90m. **DIR:** Ian Merrick. **CAST:** Donald Sumpter, Debbie Farrington, Marjorie Yates, David Swift. **1977**

BLACK PIRATE, THE ★★★1/2 One of superstar Douglas Fairbanks's most popular films, this early color production packs enough thrills for a dozen pictures. Written by Fairbanks, *Pirate* contains a duel to the death with cutlasses on the beach, a daring underwater raid on a pirate ship, and one of the most famous of all movie stunts: Fairbanks's ride down the ship's sail on a knife, cleverly achieved with an apparatus hidden from the camera. Silent. B&W; 122m. **DIR:** Albert Parker. **CAST:** Douglas Fairbanks Sr., Donald Crisp, Billie Dove, Anders Randolph. **1926 DVD**

BLACK RAIN (1988) ★★★★ This winner at the Cannes Film Festival and best picture in Japan is a vivid portrait of the Hiroshima atomic bombing. It recounts the horror of the event and centers on the lives of one family five years later as they cope with radiation sickness. In Japanese with English subtitles. Not rated; too strong for youngsters. B&W; 123m. **DIR:** Shohei Imamura. **CAST:** Yoshiko Tanaka. **1988 DVD**

BLACK RAIN (1989) ★★★★ Michael Douglas gives a solid performance in this nonstop action film as a maverick New York cop who is assigned to deliver a Yakuza gangster to the Japanese authorities, only to allow him to escape upon arrival at the airport. Despite protests from the Japanese police, Douglas insists on staying on to help recapture the escaped criminal, and it is up to Ken Takakura to baby-sit the hot-tempered American detective. Rated R for violence and profanity. 110m. **DIR:** Ridley Scott. **CAST:** Michael Douglas, Andy Garcia, Ken Takakura, Kate Capshaw. **1989 DVD**

BLACK RAINBOW ★★★1/2 A father-daughter evangelical scam takes a twist when the girl (Rosanna Arquette) actually *does* develop precognitive talents. She then claims to have pinpointed a murderer. Old-world southern decadence permeates this nifty little thriller. Rated R for nudity, violence, and profanity. 103m. **DIR:** Mike Hodges. **CAST:** Rosanna Arquette, Jason Robards Jr., Tom Hulce. **1991**

BLACK RAVEN, THE ★★ Fogbound, poverty-row, old dark house cheapie about a murder-filled night at a country inn. Interesting mainly for its cast. B&W; 64m. **DIR:** Sam Newfield. **CAST:** George Zucco, Wanda McKay, Robert Livingston, Glenn Strange. **1943**

BLACK ROBE ★★★★ Thought-provoking drama follows the struggle of Jesuit priest Father LaForgue (Lothaire Bluteau) as he journeys through the frozen Canadian wilderness in 1634 with the help of Algonquian Indians who become increasingly distrustful of the strange man they call "Blackrobe." This impressive motion picture manages to examine Christianity and tribal beliefs without trivializing either. Rated R for violence, nudity, and simulated sex. 105m. **DIR:** Bruce Beresford. **CAST:** Lothaire Bluteau, Aden Young, Sandrine Holt, August Schellengberg. **1991 DVD**

BLACK ROOM, THE ★★★ Boris Karloff is excellent as twin brothers with an age-old family curse hanging over their heads. Well-handled thriller never stops moving. B&W; 67m. **DIR:** Roy William Neill. **CAST:** Boris Karloff, Marian Marsh, Robert Allen, Katherine DeMille, Thurston Hall. **1935**

BLACK ROSE OF HARLEM ★★ Gangland romance, set in 1931, about a mobster's henchman who falls for a nightclub singer. Atmospheric but unoriginal, this period piece only comes to life when its hoodlum heroes are rubbing each other out. Rated R for violence, adult situations, and profanity. 81m. **DIR:** Fred Gallo. **CAST:** Cynda Williams, Nick Cassavetes, Joe Viterelli, Lawrence Monoson, Richard Brooks, Garrett Morris, Richard T. Jones, Maria Ford. **1995**

BLACK ROSES ★★1/2 Black Roses is the name of a hard-rock group that comes to sleepy Mill Basin for a concert. Soon, the concert hall becomes a hell on Earth. Want to see a guy get sucked into a wall-mounted speaker? It's here. Rated R for violence, nudity, and language. 90m. **DIR:** John Fasano. **CAST:** John Martin, Ken Swofford. **1988**

BLACK SABBATH ★★★1/2 Above-average trio of horror tales given wonderful atmosphere by director Mario Bava. Boris Karloff plays host and stars in the third story, a vampire opus entitled "The Wurdalak." One of the others, "A Drop of Water," is based on a story by Chekhov; the third, "The Telephone," involves disconnected calls of the worst sort. 99m. **DIR:** Mario Bava. **CAST:** Boris Karloff, Mark Damon, Suzy Andersen. **1964 DVD**

BLACK SCORPION ★★★ Writer Craig J. Nevius's good-natured superhero saga stars sultry Joan Severance as a former cop turned black-garbed avenger of the night, whose appearance owes a lot to Michelle Pfeiffer's nasty leathers in *Batman Returns*. Joan's considerably more blatant about her sexual hunger, but the modern *noir* setting—in this case the City of Angels—is every bit as deliciously seamy. Rated R for profanity, violence, nudity, and simulated sex. 90m. **DIR:** Jonathan Winfrey. **CAST:** Joan Severance, Bruce Abbott, Stephen Lee, Rick Rossovich. **1995 DVD**

BLACK SCORPION II: AFTERSHOCK Star Joan Severance turns coproducer for this sequel to her modestly successful superhero spoof, and the result is absolutely atrocious: hammy overacting, unfinished effects shots, and a "plot" that defies description. Rated R for profanity, violence, and nudity. 85m. **DIR:** Jonathan Winfrey. **CAST:** Joan Severance, Whip Hubley, Stoney Jackson, Sherrie Rose, Stephen Lee, Garrett Morris. **1996 DVD**

BLACK SHEEP ★★ Bungling brother of a gubernatorial candidate is full of good intentions as he nearly destroys his sibling's well-oiled campaign. A low-level aide is assigned to keep the likable klutz out of trouble. The film pushes family values with schmaltzy determination and tries to camouflage its lack of fresh humor with crude comedy. Rated PG-13 for language, drug use, and violence. 87m. **DIR:** Penelope Spheeris. **CAST:** Chris Farley, David Spade, Tim Matheson, Gary Busey. **1996**

BLACK SISTER'S REVENGE ★★1/2 Shamefully, a new title and cover art imply that the movie is a blaxploitation action-adventure. In reality, it's a serious drama, originally titled *Emma Mae,* about a black girl from Georgia struggling to fit in with other kids in an L.A. ghetto. It's a low-budget movie lacking technical flair, but it deserves more attention than the misleading advertising is going to bring it. Not rated. 100m. **DIR:** Jamaa Fanaka. **CAST:** Jerri Hayes, Ernest Williams, II. **1976**

BLACK STALLION, THE ★★★★★ Before taking our breath away with the superb *Never Cry Wolf*, director Carroll Ballard made an impressive directorial debut with this gorgeous screen version of the well-known children's story. Kelly Reno plays the young boy stranded on a deserted island with "The Black," a wild, but very intelligent, horse who comes to be his best friend. It's a treat the whole family can enjoy. Rated G. 118m. **DIR:** Carroll Ballard. **CAST:** Kelly Reno, Mickey Rooney, Teri Garr, Hoyt Axton, Clarence Muse. **1979 DVD**

BLACK STALLION RETURNS, THE ★★★★ A sequel to the 1979 film *The Black Stallion*, this is first-rate fare for the young and the young at heart. The story, based on the novel by Walter Farley, picks up where the first film left off. Alec Ramsey (Kelly Reno) is a little older and a little taller, but he still loves his horse, "The Black." And this time, Alec must journey halfway around the world to find the stallion, which has been stolen by an Arab chieftain. Rated PG for slight violence. 93m. **DIR:** Robert Dalva. **CAST:** Kelly Reno, Vincent Spano, Teri Garr, Allen Garfield, Woody Strode. **1983**

BLACK SUNDAY (1961) ★★★★ Italian horror classic about the one day each century when Satan roams the Earth. Brilliant cinematography and art direction help establish a chilling, surreal atmosphere in this tale of a witch who swears vengeance on the offspring of those who brutally killed her centuries ago. B&W; 83m. **DIR:** Mario Bava. **CAST:** Barbara Steele, John Richardson, Ivo Garrani, Andrea Checci. **1961 DVD**

BLACK SUNDAY (1977) ★★★ An Arab terrorist group attempts to blow up the president at a Super Bowl in Miami's Orange Bowl. Tension is maintained throughout. Rated R. 143m. **DIR:** John Frankenheimer. **CAST:** Robert Shaw, Bruce Dern, Marthe Keller, Fritz Weaver. **1977**

BLACK SWAN, THE ★★★1/2 A pirate movie that benefits most from colorful performances by its big-name cast. 85m. **DIR:** Henry King. **CAST:** Tyrone Power, Maureen O'Hara, George Sanders, Laird Cregar, Anthony Quinn, Thomas Mitchell. **1942**

BLACK TIGHTS ★★★1/2 There are several attractive performers in this British film that aficionados of dance should not miss: Cyd Charisse, Zizi Jeanmaire, and in her last film before retirement, Moira Shearer. It's a good film that even those who are not dance groupies might enjoy. The film is also known under the French title *Un, Deux, Trois, Quatre!* 140m. **DIR:** Terence Young. **CAST:** Cyd Charisse, Zizi Jeanmaire, Moira Shearer, Roland Petit Dance Company. **1960 DVD**

BLACK VEIL FOR LISA, A ★★ Serviceable gangster melodrama with John Mills as the token Anglo star imported to Rome to make the movie marketable outside Italy. Tolerable action flick, if a trifle talky. Not rated. 88m. **DIR:** Massimo Dallamano. **CAST:** John Mills, Luciana Paluzzi, Robert Hoffman. **1968**

BLACK VENUS 🦃 Lavish nineteenth-century Parisian costumes and settings can't salvage this endless sex romp. Poorly dubbed. Rated R. 80m. **DIR:** Claude Mulot. **CAST:** Josephine Jacqueline Jones, Emiliano Redondo. **1983**

BLACK WATER 🦃 Extremely slow, boring movie about an English lawyer who only wants to go fishing in Tennessee, but ends up on the run. Not rated; contains profanity and nudity. 105m. **DIR:** Nicolas Gessner. **CAST:** Julian Sands, Stacey Dash, Ned Beatty, Ed Lauter, Denise Crosby, Brian McNamara, Johnny Cash, Rod Steiger. **1989**

BLACK WIDOW ★★★★ A superb thriller from director Bob Rafelson that recalls the best of the Bette Davis–Joan Crawford "bad girl" films of earlier decades. Debra Winger stars as an inquisitive federal agent who stumbles upon an odd pattern of deaths by apparently natural causes: the victims are quite wealthy, reclusive, and leave behind a young—and very rich—widow. Rated R for nudity and adult situations. 103m. **DIR:** Bob Rafelson. **CAST:** Debra Winger, Theresa Russell, Sami Frey, Dennis Hopper, Nicol Williamson, Terry O'Quinn. **1987**

BLACK WINDMILL, THE ★★★1/2 Straightforward story is enhanced by Don Siegel's razor-sharp direction and Michael Caine's engrossing performance as an intelligence agent whose son has been kidnapped. The suspense builds carefully to a satisfying climax. Rated R. 106m. **DIR:** Don Siegel. **CAST:** Michael Caine, Joseph O'Conor, Donald Pleasence, John Vernon, Janet Suzman, Delphine Seyrig. **1974**

BLACKBEARD THE PIRATE ★★★ Entertaining pirate yarn with some good action and fine characterizations. Gorgeous Linda Darnell is the charming damsel in distress. In the title role, Robert Newton is a bit overzealous at times, but puts in a fine performance. Go for it. 99m. **DIR:** Raoul Walsh. **CAST:** Robert Newton, Linda Darnell, William Bendix, Keith Andes. **1952**

BLACKBEARD'S GHOST ★★★ This fun Disney comedy has Peter Ustinov playing a ghost who must prevent his ancestors' home from becoming a gambling casino. 107m. **DIR:** Robert Stevenson. **CAST:** Peter Ustinov, Dean Jones, Suzanne Pleshette, Elsa Lanchester. **1968**

BLACKBELT ★★ A martial arts instructor protects a rising pop star from a psychopathic fan. Some good action sequences make this film stand out a little from other fight flicks. Rated R for nudity, profanity, and graphic violence. 90m. **DIR:** Charles Philip Moore. **CAST:** Don "The Dragon" Wilson, Matthias Hues, Richard Beymer. **1992**

BLACKBELT 2: FATAL FORCE ★★ A wanna-be epic martial arts action film. It has Vietnam vets, heroin junkies, heavily armed elite missions forces, gunrunners, karate cops—one black, one white—and a strip club for good measure. Rated R for violence, profanity, and nudity. 83m. **DIR:** José Mari Avellana. **CAST:** Blake Bahner, Ronald William Lawrence, Roxanne Baird, Michael Vlastas. **1993**

BLACKBIRD, THE ★★★1/2 A murderous criminal, who masquerades as a crippled mission keeper suffers the fate promised by mothers to children who make faces. Silent. B&W; 70m. **DIR:** Tod Browning. **CAST:** Lon Chaney Sr., Renée Adorée, Owen Moore. **1925**

BLACKBOARD JUNGLE, THE ★★★★ Glenn Ford plays a high school instructor who desperately tries to reach some emotionally turbulent youths in the New York school system. Hard-hitting, gritty drama. Excellent adaptation of Evan Hunter's powerful novel. B&W; 101m. **DIR:** Richard Brooks. **CAST:** Glenn Ford, Anne Francis, Vic Morrow, Sidney Poitier. **1955**

BLACKENSTEIN Tasteless and grotesque entry in the subgenre of blaxploitation horror films. Rated R for violence and nudity. 92m. **DIR:** William A. Levey. **CAST:** John Hart, Joe DiSue. **1973**

•BLACKHEART ★★1/2 A con team thinks they've discovered the big score in a woman who recently inherited a huge sum of money. Greed and jealousy, however, turn everyone against each other. Dark thriller with an impressive cast. Rated R for violence, profanity, and nudity. 95m. **DIR:** Dominic Shiach. **CAST:** Richard Grieco, Christopher Plummer, Fiona Loewi, Maria Conchita Alonso. **1998 DVD**

BLACKJACK ★★1/2 Dull, lightweight, made-for-TV action fare starring Dolph Lundgren as a mercenary suffering from a debilitating phobia acquired during a firefight who is trying to save a supermodel from the hands of a serial killer. Especially disappointing considering the combined talents of Lundgren and director John Woo. Rated R for violence and profanity. 112m. **DIR:** John Woo. **CAST:** Dolph Lundgren, Kate Vernon, Phillip Mackenzie, Kam Heskin, Fred Williamson, Saul Rubinek. **1998 DVD**

BLACKMAIL (1929) ★★★ Many bits of film business that were to become Alfred Hitchcock trademarks are evident in this film, including the first of his cameo appearances. Story of a woman who faces the legal system as well as a blackmailer for murdering an attacker in self-defense was originally shot as a silent film but partially reshot and converted into England's first sound release. B&W; 86m. **DIR:** Alfred Hitchcock. **CAST:** Anny Ondra, Sara Allgood, John Longden, Charles Paton, Donald Calthrop, Cyril Ritchard. **1929 DVD**

BLACKMAIL (1991) ★★★ Made-for-cable thriller will keep you guessing. Miguel Tejada-Flores spins a complicated yarn of greed and betrayal—adapted from a short story by Bill Crenshaw—concerning two blackmailers who set up a rich wife. Farfetched, but entertaining. 96m. **DIR:** Reuben Preuss. **CAST:** Susan Blakely, Dale Midkiff, Beth Toussaint, Mac Davis, John Saxon. **1991**

BLACKOUT (1978) ★★★ At times, this movie, about a New York City apartment building attacked by a gang of escaped criminals during a blackout, reeks of a disaster film. Still, there are good action scenes and enough drama to make you almost forget the shortcomings. Rated R for violence. 86m. **DIR:** Eddy Matalon. **CAST:** Jim Mitchum, Robert Carradine, Belinda Montgomery, June Allyson, Jean-Pierre Aumont, Ray Milland. **1978**

BLACKOUT (1985) ★★★1/2 A police detective (Richard Widmark) becomes obsessed with an unsolved murder. Six years after the incident he begins to find valuable clues. This superior made-for-HBO movie has violence and profanity. 99m. **DIR:** Douglas Hickox. **CAST:** Richard Widmark, Keith Carradine, Kathleen Quinlan, Michael Beck. **1985**

BLACKOUT (1990) A disturbed woman returns to her childhood home after receiving a letter from her missing father. Rated R for nudity and violence. 90m. **DIR:** Doug Adams. **CAST:** Carol Lynley, Gail O'Grady, Michael Keys-Hall, Joanna Miles. **1990**

BLACKOUT (1995) ★★★ Conservative banker Brian Bosworth suffers a concussion during a street accident, and suddenly dreams of a vastly different—and far more violent—life. Attempts to investigate this other existence unleash all sorts of goons, every one trying to kill our hero. Bosworth sells the concept and is occasionally amusing as an "ordinary" guy repeatedly astonished by his skills as a trained killer. Rated R for violence, profanity, nudity, and simulated sex. 98m. **DIR:** Allan A. Goldstein. **CAST:** Brian Bosworth, Brad Dourif, Claire Yarlett, Marta DuBois. **1995**

BLACKWATER TRAIL ★★★1/2 Riveting Australian thriller stars Judd Nelson as a writer who returns to his small hometown for the funeral of a close friend. When the dead man's sister suggests her brother was killed, the writer's investigation puts him on the trail of a serial killer. Creepy and effective. Not rated; contains adult situations, language, nudity, and violence. 97m. **DIR:** Ian Barry. **CAST:** Judd Nelson, Brett Climo, Gabrielle Fitzpatrick, Mark Lee, Peter Phelps, Rowena Wallace. **1995**

BLACULA ★★★1/2 An old victim (William Marshall) of Dracula's bite is loose in modern L.A. Surprisingly well-done shocker. Fierce and energetic, with a solid cast. Rated R for violence. 92m. **DIR:** William Crain. **CAST:** William Marshall, Denise Nicholas, Vonetta McGee, Thalmus Rasulala. **1972**

BLADE (1973) ★★★ Middle-aged New York detective Blade (John Marley) stalks the psycho who murdered the daughter of a powerful right-wing congressman. Along the way he uncovers a lot of other goings-on in the naked city. The story's not much, but TV addicts can count the faces that later went on hit shows (*Barney Miller*'s Steve Landesberg, *The Love Boat*'s Ted Lange, *McMillan and Wife*'s John Schuck). Rated R for violence. 90m. **DIR:** Ernest Pintoff. **CAST:** John Marley, Jon Cypher, Kathryn Walker, William Prince, Michael McGuire, Joe Santos, John Schuck, Keene Curtis, Ted Lange, Marshall Efron, Steve Landesberg. **1973**

BLADE (1998) ★★★ This gore-laden vampire flick is trashy, flashy, and outrageously violent. Wesley Snipes, starring as the character first introduced in a Marvel comic book, makes an ultracool hero with a twist: He's half vampire, a "day-walker" with superhuman strength and silver-laced weapons, who's determined to exterminate his nastier brethren. The film runs a bit long, but moves at a brisk clip. Rated R for profanity, violence, and gobs o' gore. 115m. **DIR:** Stephen Norrington. **CAST:** Wesley Snipes, Stephen Dorff, Kris Kristofferson, N'Bushe Wright, Donal Logue, Udo Kier, Traci Lords. **1998 DVD**

•BLADE II ★★★ Garden variety vampires lose their prominence at the top of the food chain when a DNA experiment gone bad unleashes a race of super Nosferatus that suck and munch on humans and the Undead alike with gruesome abandon. Half-man, half-vampire Marvel Comics hero Blade agrees to help an elite termination squad of neck nibblers to bring down this greater evil, and initiates an action-packed bloodbath. Rated R for profanity, violence, gore, drug use, and sexual content. 108m. **DIR:** Guillermo del Toro. **CAST:** Wesley Snipes, Kris Kristofferson, Norman Reedus, Leonor Varela, Danny John-Jules, Ron Perlman. **2002**

BLADE IN THE DARK, A ★★1/2 Fair thriller from Italian director Lamberto Bava (*Demons*) is full of psychobabble, and even though the advanced viewer will probably have the killer figured out way before the end of the movie, the film moves along nicely and keeps you interested. Rated R for violence and language. 96m. **DIR:** Lamberto Bava. **CAST:** Andrea Occhipinti, Anny Papa. **1983 DVD**

BLADE MASTER, THE Muscleman Miles O'Keeffe chops his way across the countryside battling nasty sorcerers and spirits in a quest to conquer evil. Rated PG. 92m. **DIR:** David Hills. **CAST:** Miles O'Keeffe, Lisa Foster. **1984**

BLADE RIDER ★★ Several *Branded* TV episodes with cavalry and Indian themes loosely patched together to make up a video feature. Released to TV under the title *Ride to Glory*. Sadly, even the famous *Branded* opening theme is edited out. 102m. **DIR:** Various!. **CAST:** Chuck Connors, Burt Reynolds, Lee Van Cleef, Robert Lansing, David Brian. **1966 DVD**

BLADE RUNNER ★★★★1/2 This Ridley Scott (*Alien*) production is thought-provoking and visually impressive. Harrison Ford stars as a futuristic Philip Marlowe trying to find and kill the world's remaining rebel androids in 2019 Los Angeles. The film may not be for everyone, but those who appreciate something of substance will find it worthwhile. Rated R for brief nudity and violence. 118m. **DIR:** Ridley Scott. **CAST:** Harrison Ford, Rutger Hauer, Sean Young, Daryl Hannah, Joanna Cassidy, Edward James Olmos, M. Emmet Walsh. **1982 DVD**

BLADES OF COURAGE ★★★1/2 Christianne Hirt is a Canadian ice skater with a promising future in the Olympics. Unfortunately she is assigned a coach who employs ruthless methods to achieve what he desires. Aside from the stereotyped pushy mother, this is a realistic film that reveals the effort involved in developing a champion. It is well acted with some choice figure-skating numbers. Not rated. 98m. **DIR:** Randy Bradshaw. **CAST:** Christianne Hirt, Colm Feore, Stuart Hughes, Rosemary Dunsmore. **1988**

BLAIR WITCH PROJECT, THE A fiendishly clever publicity campaign fueled the release of this ultra-low-budget quickie, which turned out to be one of the biggest swindles ever perpetrated on unsuspecting movie audiences. This "faux documentary" about three young filmmakers who meet an uncertain fate while investigating an old legend in the Maryland woods fails to deliver on all counts. Rated R for profanity. 82m. **DIR:** Daniel Myrick, Eduardo Sanchez. **CAST:** Heather Donahue, Michael C. Williams, Joshua Leonard. **1999 DVD**

BLAKE'S 7 (TV SERIES) ★★★ In a postnuclear future, Earth and other populated planets are strictly controlled by "the Federation." Blake's 7, a group of escaped criminals and rebels, wanders the galaxy seeking to undercut the Federation's omnipotence. This British TV series, a cult favorite in the United States, is less campy than *Dr. Who* but not as intellectual as *The Prisoner*. Each tape includes two episodes. 105m. **DIR:** Various. **CAST:** Gareth Thomas, Sally Knyvette, Paul Darrow. **1978–1981**

BLAME IT ON RIO ★★1/2 A middle-aged male sex fantasy directed by Stanley Donen (*Lucky Lady; Charade*), features Michael Caine as a befuddled fellow who finds himself involved in an affair with the teenage daughter (Michelle Johnson) of his best friend (Joseph Bologna). Although essentially in bad taste, *Blame It on Rio* does have a number of very funny moments. Rated R for nudity, profanity, and suggested sex. 110m. **DIR:** Stanley Donen. **CAST:** Michael Caine, Joseph Bologna, Valerie Harper, Michelle Johnson. **1984 DVD**

BLAME IT ON THE BELLBOY ★★★★ An English-mangling Italian bellboy (Bronson Pinchot) manages to mix up the identities of a real estate salesman (Dudley Moore), a hit man (Bryan Brown), and a philandering husband (Richard Griffiths). What could have been hopelessly moronic is deliciously giddy and frequently funny. Rated PG-13 for profanity, brief violence, and silly simulated sex. 78m. **DIR:** Mark Herman. **CAST:** Dudley Moore, Bryan Brown, Richard Griffiths, Andreas Katsulas, Patsy Kensit, Alison Steadman, Penelope Wilton, Bronson Pinchot. **1992**

BLAME IT ON THE NIGHT Mick Jagger cowrote the original story for this movie but wisely chose not to appear in it. It's a trite tale of a rock singer who discovers he has a 13 year old son. Rated PG-13. 85m. **DIR:** Gene Taft. **CAST:** Nick Mancuso, Byron Thames, Leslie Ackerman, Dick Bakalyan. **1984**

BLANK CHECK ★★★1/2 When 11 year old Brian Bonsall's bike is run over by mobster Miguel Ferrer, the boy ends up with a blank check. Our young hero uses it for $1 million worth of fun, only to find that money can't buy happiness. Kids will definitely enjoy Bonsall's adventures and the state-of-the-art toys. Rated PG for light violence. 93m. **DIR:** Rupert Wainwright. **CAST:** Brian Bonsall, Karen Duffy, James Rebhorn, Jayne Atkinson, Michael Faustino, Chris Demetral, Miguel Ferrer, Rick Ducommun, Tone Loc, Michael Lerner, Debbie Allen, Lu Leonard. **1994**

BLANKMAN ★★★ Not-bad superhero spoof suffers from too much profanity for the kids and not enough laughs for adults. Rated PG-13. 92m. **DIR:** Mike Binder. **CAST:** Damon Wayans, David Alan Grier, Robin Givens, Christopher Lawford. **1994 DVD**

BLAST ★★★ When terrorists take over an international sports event and hold the women's swimming team hostage, it's up to a trapped janitor, working with the FBI, to save the day. Familiar elements find new life in this *Die Hard* repeat. Rated R for language and violence. 98m. **DIR:** Albert Pyun. **CAST:** Linden Ashby, Andrew Divoff, Kimberly Warren, Rutger Hauer, Tina Cote. **1996 DVD**

BLAST FROM THE PAST ★★★★ Delightful spoof on Sixties life unfolds when a paranoid genius insists that his wife stay underground with him until the Cuban Missile Crisis passes . . . for 35 years! At that point, their son (Brendan Fraser), born and raised in their bomb shelter, must go above ground for some supplies. His innocence and good manners create hilarious situations as he deals with big city life in the Nineties. Rated PG-13 for sexual innuendo and language. 110m. **DIR:** Hugh Wilson. **CAST:** Brendan Fraser, Alicia Silverstone, Christopher Walken, Sissy Spacek, David Foley. **1999 DVD**

BLASTFIGHTER ♥ Michael Sopkiw is a dull ex-convict trying to clean up an immoral populace. Not rated; contains violence. 93m. **DIR:** John Old Jr. **CAST:** Michael Sopkiw, Valerie Blake, George Eastman, Mike Miller. **1984**

BLAZE ★★ Paul Newman stars as progressive Louisiana governor Earl Long in this late 1950s story of back-room politics and Long's affair with Bourbon Street stripper Blaze Starr. The look behind the scandalous headlines of yesteryear never really ignites. Rated R. 108m. **DIR:** Ron Shelton. **CAST:** Paul Newman, Lolita Davidovich. **1989**

BLAZE STARR: THE ORIGINAL ★★ The famous stripper plays an actress who finds relief from the stresses of making movies by joining a Florida nudist camp. Campy in the extreme. Original title: *Blaze Starr Goes Nudist*. Not rated, no sexual content, but lotsa nude volleyball games (and nude checkers, too!) 79m. **DIR:** Doris Wishman. **CAST:** Blaze Starr. **1962**

BLAZING SADDLES ★★★1/2 Mel Brooks directed this sometimes hilarious, mostly crude spoof of Westerns. The jokes come with machine-gun rapidity, and the stars race around like maniacs. If it weren't in such bad taste, it would be perfect for the kiddies. Rated R. 93m. **DIR:** Mel Brooks. **CAST:** Cleavon Little, Gene Wilder, Harvey Korman, Madeline Kahn, Mel Brooks, Slim Pickens. **1974 DVD**

BLEAK HOUSE ★★★★ First-rate adaptation of Charles Dickens's novel was made for the BBC as a miniseries. The skilled cast is headed by Diana Rigg and Denholm Elliott. Superb sets, costumes, and photography add to the period flavor. A must-see for Dickens aficionados. Made for TV. 391m. **DIR:** Ross Devenish. **CAST:** Diana Rigg, Denholm Elliott, Peter Vaughan, T. P. McKenna. **1985**

BLEEDERS ♥ Not surprisingly, the best thing about this moronic monster movie is the fake blood gel pack that adorns the box art. Rated R for violence, language, and adult situations. 92m. **DIR:** Peter Svatek. **CAST:** Rutger Hauer, Roy Dupuis, Jackie Burroughs, Kristine Lehman. **1997 DVD**

BLESS THE BEASTS AND CHILDREN ♥ A group of misfit teenagers at a ranch resort rebel against their counselors to save a nearby herd of buffalo. Rated R for explicit violence. 109m. **DIR:** Stanley Kramer. **CAST:** Billy Mumy, Barry Robins, Miles Chapin, Ken Swofford, Jesse White, Vanessa Brown. **1972**

BLESS THE CHILD ★★1/2 Yawn . . . another child desired by Satan? Devoted nurse Kim Basinger becomes the reluctant foster parent of her wayward younger sister's autistic little girl, but it turns out that the child attracts the "Forces of Darkness." Basinger loses the kid, regains the kid, loses the kid again, and generally behaves like such a boob that you'll be cheering on the Satanists. Rated R for violence, drug content, and profanity. 107m. **DIR:** Chuck Russell. **CAST:** Kim Basinger, Jimmy Smits, Rufus Sewell, Ian Holm, Angela Bettis, Christina Ricci. **2000 DVD**

BLESSED EVENT ★★★★ Lee Tracy plays a tabloid columnist whose specialty is uncovering celebrity marriages caused by pre-nuptial pregnancies. It's always fun to watch fast-talking Tracy, and here he's perfectly complemented by the delightfully grumpy Ned Sparks. B&W; 84m. **DIR:** Roy Del Ruth. **CAST:** Lee Tracy, Ned Sparks, Mary Brian, Dick Powell. **1932**

BLIND DATE (1984) ★★ Not to be confused with the comedies of the same name, this *Blind Date* is about a man who gets a reprieve from his sightless existence through the miraculous effects of an experimental machine. He uses his newfound perceptions to stalk a psychotic killer through some extremely visual Greek locations. Beyond the sights and decent acting, however, the story tends to plod. Rated R for violence. 100m. **DIR:** Nico Mastorakis. **CAST:** Joseph Bottoms, Keir Dullea, Kirstie Alley, James Daughton. **1984**

BLIND DATE (1987) ♥ A tasteless exercise in slapstick that sends Bruce Willis on a last-minute blind date with Kim Basinger. Rated PG-13 for adult situations. 93m. **DIR:** Blake Edwards. **CAST:** Bruce Willis, Kim Basinger, John Larroquette, William Daniels, George Coe, Mark Blum, Phil Hartman. **1987 DVD**

BLIND FAITH ★★1/2 Courtney B. Vance is a resourceful attorney suddenly faced with the need to represent his nephew in a murder trial. Nothing is quite what it seems, however, and it becomes clear that the boy's father would rather see his son go to jail than acknowledge the truth. The script becomes particularly preachy in the third act, by which point the film has worn out its welcome. Rated R for profanity, violence, nudity, and dramatic intensity. 120m. **DIR:** Ernest R. Dickerson. **CAST:** Courtney B. Vance, Charles Dutton, Lonette McKee, Garland Whitt, Birdie M. Hale, Kadeem Hardison. **1998**

BLIND FURY ★★★ In this outrageously violent, tongue-in-cheek martial arts movie, Rutger Hauer stars as a blind swordsman who comes to the aid of an army buddy (Terry O'Quinn) when the latter is kidnapped by gangsters and forced to make designer drugs. Directed in a completely over-the-top fashion by Phillip Noyce, *Blind Fury* is a real hoot. Rated R for violence and profanity. 86m. **DIR:** Phillip Noyce. **CAST:** Rutger Hauer, Terry O'Quinn, Brandon Call, Lisa Blount, Randall "Tex" Cobb. **1990 DVD**

BLIND HUSBANDS ★★★ A doctor and his wife are in an Alpine village so that he can do some mountain climbing. His wife falls prey to the attentions of a suave Austrian army officer who seduces her. In addition to directing and starring, Erich Von Stroheim adapted the screenplay from his own story and designed the sets. A shocker when first released. Silent. B&W; 98m. **DIR:** Erich Von Stroheim. **CAST:** Sam de Grasse, Francis Billington, Erich Von Stroheim, Gibson Gowland. **1919**

BLIND JUSTICE ★★★ Writer Daniel Knauf's so-called original Western is a blatant reworking of two enduring Japanese series: the blind samurai films and the *Lone Wolf and Cub* comics. Armand Assante plays a phlegmatic, blind ex-Union soldier who briefly abandons his quest to find an infant's father . . . long enough to blow away some baddies terrorizing a small town. The cast gives a lot more than the derivative script deserves. Rated R for violence, profanity, and brief nudity. 85m. **DIR:** Richard Spence. **CAST:** Armand Assante, Elisabeth Shue, Robert Davi, Adam Baldwin. **1994 DVD**

BLIND RAGE 🦃 If you really believe that four blind men could rob a bank during business hours, you deserve this film. Rated R for violence and profanity. 81m. **DIR:** Efren C. Pinion. **CAST:** D'Urville Martin, Leo Fong, Tony Ferrer, Dick Adair, Darnell Garcia, Charlie Davao, Leila Hermosa, Fred Williamson, Jessie Crowder. **1978**

BLIND SIDE ★★★1/2 Just-plain-folks Ron Silver and Rebecca DeMornay accidentally hit and kill a Mexican cop on a deserted, fog-enshrouded highway. After panic propels them to flee the scene, their attempts to resume normal lives are sabotaged by the arrival of smooth-talking Rutger Hauer . . . who seems to know far more than he openly admits. Made-for-cable psychological thriller. Rated R for profanity, violence, nudity, and simulated sex. 98m. **DIR:** Geoff Murphy. **CAST:** Rutger Hauer, Rebecca DeMornay, Ron Silver, Jonathan Banks. **1993 DVD**

BLIND SPOT ★★★★ In this *Hallmark Hall of Fame* presentation, Joanne Woodward does an outstanding job of portraying a strong-headed congresswoman who must cope with the death of her drug-addicted top aide who is also her son-in-law. Laura Linney is superb as Phoebe, Woodward's drug-addicted and pregnant daughter who wants to lead her own life. The story line is quite moving and shows the viewer how each character feels. Rated PG-13 for drug use. 99m. **DIR:** Michael Toshiyuki Uno. **CAST:** Joanne Woodward, Laura Linney, Reed Edward Diamond, Fritz Weaver. **1993**

BLIND TRUST (POUVOIR INTIME) ★★★★ Four misfit robbers drive away with an armored car only to find a guard locked in the back with the money. Intense and fascinating. In French with English subtitles. Rated PG-13 for profanity and violence. 86m. **DIR:** Yves Simoneau. **CAST:** Marie Tifo, Pierre Curzi, Jacques Robert Gravel. **1987**

BLIND VENGEANCE ★★★1/2 Gerald McRaney plays the father of a grown son killed by small-town white supremacist Lane Smith and two goons. Rather than blindly orchestrate a bloodbath, McRaney simply shadows his prey . . . always watching, masked behind dark sunglasses, and waiting for them to panic. Intelligent made-for-cable melodrama. Rated R for violence and profanity. 93m. **DIR:** Lee Philips. **CAST:** Gerald McRaney, Lane Smith, Marg Helgenberger. **1990**

BLIND VISION ★★1/2 Mail clerk Lenny Von Dohlen watches the voluptuous Deborah Shelton through a telescope, admiring her from afar. Little does Von Dohlen realize that he's not alone, and when one of Shelton's boyfriends ends up dead, he becomes one of the main suspects in this intriguing made-for-cable thriller. 92m. **DIR:** Shuki Levy. **CAST:** Louise Fletcher, Lenny von Dohlen, Ned Beatty, Deborah Shelton, Robert Vaughn. **1991**

BLINDFOLD: ACTS OF OBSESSION ★★1/2 Only voyeurs anxious to see television star Shannen Doherty nude will enjoy this humdrum thriller. She tries to hold on to her new husband by initiating a series of progressively kinkier sexual games, while a serial killer uses the same methods on other women. Based on this evidence, Doherty won't have much of a film career. Available in R-rated and unrated versions. 93m. **DIR:** Lawrence L. Simeone. **CAST:** Judd Nelson, Shannen Doherty, Kristian Alfonso, Drew Snyder, Michael Woods. **1994**

BLINDMAN'S BLUFF ★★★ Robert Urich successfully portrays a recently blind man whose former girlfriend is about to marry his best friend. A neighbor is murdered and Urich is the main suspect. Enjoyable made-for-cable whodunit. Rated PG-13. 86m. **DIR:** James Quinn. **CAST:** Robert Urich, Lisa Eilbacher, Patricia Clarkson, Ken Pogue, Ron Perlman. **1991**

BLINDSIDE ★★ Only the acting talent of Harvey Keitel distinguishes this would-be suspense film yawner. Keitel stars as a former surveillance expert who discovers a murder plot. Rated R for violence and profanity. 102m. **DIR:** Paul Lynch. **CAST:** Harvey Keitel, Lori Hallier, Allen Fawcett. **1988**

BLINDSIDED ★★1/2 An ex-cop turned burglar becomes blind after being shot during a setup. He goes to the ocean to recuperate and falls in love with a mysterious woman. The plot is a bit farfetched and a little hard to follow at times. Not rated, made for cable, but contains violence and suggested sex. 95m. **DIR:** Tom Donnelly. **CAST:** Jeff Fahey, Mia Sara, Rudy Ramos, Jack Kehler, Brad Hunt, Ben Gazzara. **1992**

BLINK ★★★★ Superior suspense film benefits from director Michael Apted's flair for characterization and Madeleine Stowe's powerhouse performance as a musician whose sight is restored after years of blindness. Stowe witnesses a murder, but her brain is having trouble processing visual information, and this leads to sudden flashbacks of things she's seen hours and even days before. So the police think she's a crackpot. Rated R for profanity, violence, nudity, and simulated sex. 106m. **DIR:** Michael Apted. **CAST:** Madeleine Stowe, Aidan Quinn, James Remar, Peter Friedman, Bruce A. Young, Paul Dillon, Matt Roth, Laurie Metcalf. **1994**

BLINK OF AN EYE ★★ Psychic soldier Michael Paré is called into action to rescue the daughter of a rich American from the grasp of Third World terrorists. Interesting premise gets so-so attention from cast and writer. Rated R for violence and language. 90m. **DIR:** Bob Misiorowski. **CAST:** Michael Paré, Janis Lee. **1992**

BLISS (1986) ★★★★ In this biting black comedy from Australia, a business executive (Barry Otto) nearly dies from a heart attack. He finds himself in a hellish version of the life he once had. Not everyone will appreciate this nightmarish vision of modern life, but it is one of the most original motion pictures of recent years. Rated R. 93m. **DIR:** Ray Lawrence. **CAST:** Barry Otto, Lynette Curran, Helen Jones, Jeff Truman. **1986**

BLISS (1997) ★★★★ A young married couple endures emotional problems that are both alleviated and exacerbated when she, then he, takes instruction from the same tantric sex therapist. Amusingly aware of its own occasional ridiculousness until things take a melodramatic turn into repressed memories of child abuse. Serious about eroticism, as opposed to exploitative; you might even learn a few useful tricks here. Rated R for nudity and strong sexual content. 98m. **DIR:** Lance

Young. **CAST:** Craig Sheffer, Sheryl Lee, Terence Stamp. **1997**

BLISS OF MRS. BLOSSOM, THE ★★★1/2 Good farce, as only the British can produce it, with Shirley MacLaine as the discontented wife of brassiere manufacturer Richard Attenborough. Witty, adult story, with fine plot twists. Rated PG. 93m. **DIR:** Joseph McGrath. **CAST:** Shirley MacLaine, Richard Attenborough, James Booth. **1968**

BLITHE SPIRIT ★★★★ Rex Harrison arranges a séance and recalls the spirit of his mischievous first wife. She decides to stick around and sabotage his second marriage. Wonderfully witty adaptation of Noel Coward's play with Margaret Rutherford hilarious as an off-base medium. 96m. **DIR:** David Lean. **CAST:** Rex Harrison, Constance Cummings, Kay Hammond, Margaret Rutherford. **1945 DVD**

BLOB, THE (1958) ★★★ This was Steve McQueen's first starring role. He plays a teenager battling parents and a voracious hunk of protoplasm from outer space. Long surpassed by more sophisticated sci-fi, it's still fun to watch. 86m. **DIR:** Irvin S. Yeaworth Jr. **CAST:** Steve McQueen, Aneta Corseaut, Olin Howlin. **1958 DVD**

BLOB, THE (1988) ★★★★ Frightening and occasionally comedic remake of the 1958 cult classic. This time around, Kevin Dillon and Shawnee Smith battle the gelatinous ooze as it devours the inhabitants of a small ski resort. The best horror remake since *The Fly*. A thrill ride for those with the stomach to take it. Rated R for profanity and state-of-the-art gruesomeness. 95m. **DIR:** Charles Russell. **CAST:** Kevin Dillon, Shawnee Smith, Donovan Leitch, Jeffrey DeMunn, Candy Clark, Joe Seneca. **1988 DVD**

BLOCK-HEADS ★★★★ Twenty years after the end of World War I, Stan Laurel is discovered still guarding a bunker. He returns to a veterans' home, where Oliver Hardy comes to visit and take him to dinner. A well-crafted script provides the perfect setting for the boys' escapades. Their characters have seldom been used as well in feature films. B&W; 55m. **DIR:** John G. Blystone. **CAST:** Stan Laurel, Oliver Hardy, Patricia Ellis, Minna Gombell, Billy Gilbert, James Finlayson. **1938**

BLOCKHOUSE, THE 🦃 Set during World War II, this hideous drama follows the exploits of a group of workers who become trapped in a German army bunker. 90m. **DIR:** Clive Rees. **CAST:** Peter Sellers, Charles Aznavour, Peter Vaughan, Jeremy Kemp. **1973**

BLONDE CRAZY ★★★ An early version of *The Sting*, where small-time con artists James Cagney and Joan Blondell are tricked out of five grand and plot to get it back—with interest. B&W; 79m. **DIR:** Roy Del Ruth. **CAST:** James Cagney, Joan Blondell, Louis Calhern, Guy Kibbee, Ray Milland. **1931**

BLONDE HEAVEN ★★ Young girl comes to the big city with dreams of becoming an immortal star, and she may just get her wish when she is drawn into a vampire coven. It's likely the erotic nature of the film will appeal to viewers most. Rated R for nudity, violence, and simulated sex. 80m. **DIR:** Ellen Cabot. **CAST:** Julie Strain, Raelyn Saalman, Joe Estevez, Michelle Bauer. **1995**

BLONDE ICE ★★ Odd, obscure melodrama about an unbalanced woman who makes a career of killing her husbands and boyfriends because she likes the attention she gets. (Not to mention the money.) Another long-forgotten curiosity revived for video. 73m. **DIR:** Jack Bernhard. **CAST:** Leslie Brooks, Robert Paige, Walter Sands, John Holland, James Griffith. **1949**

BLONDE VENUS 🦃 This is a rambling, incomprehensible piece of glitzy fluff. B&W; 90m. **DIR:** Josef von Sternberg. **CAST:** Marlene Dietrich, Cary Grant, Herbert Marshall. **1932**

BLONDES HAVE MORE GUNS ★★1/2 Wild and wacky send-up of such thrillers as *Basic Instinct* and *Seven.* Comedian Michael McGaharin is right on the money as Detective Harry Bates, quick with the one-liners and hot on the trail of a serial killer. In true B-movie fashion, Harry falls for the prime suspect, a mysterious woman named Montana (Elizabeth Key, blonde and then some). The best part is that none of this is taken with a grain of salt. Rated R for nudity, violence, profanity, and adult situations. 84m. **DIR:** George Merriweather. **CAST:** Michael McGaharin, Elizabeth Key. **1995**

BLONDIE ★★★1/2 The first and one of the best in the long-running series, this film establishes the characters by putting them in a stressful situation and letting them get some laughs out of it. Dagwood loses his job on the eve of his fifth wedding anniversary and doesn't want it to spoil the family celebration. B&W; 75m. **DIR:** Frank Strayer. **CAST:** Penny Singleton, Arthur Lake, Larry Simms, Jonathan Hale, Gene Lockhart, Ann Doran, Gordon Oliver, Kathleen Lockhart. **1938 DVD**

BLONDIE HAS SERVANT TROUBLE ★★★ A funny blend of comic-strip characters and haunted-house shenanigans even though the setup is more contrived than usual. Mr. Dithers wants the Bumsteads to move into a haunted house for business reasons. The outcome is predictable but still funny. B&W; 75m. **DIR:** Frank Strayer. **CAST:** Penny Singleton, Arthur Lake, Jonathan Hale, Esther Dale, Larry Simms, Irving Bacon, Fay Helm. **1940**

BLONDIE HITS THE JACKPOT ★★ This weak series entry was the next-to-last feature made in a 12-year period and boredom was setting in. Dagwood loses his job (again) and has to go to work on a construction crew. Blondie helps the family budget by entering a radio quiz show with predictable results. B&W; 75m. **DIR:** Edward L. Bernds. **CAST:** Penny Singleton, Arthur Lake, Larry Simms, Marjorie Kent, Jerome Cowan, Lloyd Corrigan. **1949**

BLONDIE IN SOCIETY ★★★1/2 A doggone cute comedy, this feature has the Bumsteads competing with a Great Dane for laughs. Dagwood brings the dog home and Blondie promptly enters the animal in a dog show. Then a very important client decides he wants the dog and causes complications. B&W; 75m. **DIR:** Frank Strayer. **CAST:** Penny Singleton, Arthur Lake, Larry Simms, Jonathan Hale, William Frawley, Garry Owen, Robert Mitchell Boys Choir. **1941**

BLONDIE KNOWS BEST ★★★1/2 One of the funnier entries, chiefly due to Shemp Howard's comedic timing. Dagwood impersonates his boss, Mr. Dithers, and winds up in the care of a couple of psychologists and a half-dozen dogs. B&W; 75m. **DIR:** Abby Berlin. **CAST:** Penny Singleton, Arthur Lake, Larry Simms, Marjorie Kent, Jonathan Hale, Shemp Howard, Jerome Cowan. **1946**

BLONDIE TAKES A VACATION ★★★1/2 Scene-stealing character players almost take the spotlight away from the Bumstead family. Everybody takes more pratfalls than usual in a clever episode as the Bumsteads try to save a mountain lodge from bankruptcy. B&W; 75m. **DIR:** Frank Strayer. **CAST:** Penny Singleton, Arthur Lake, Donald Meek, Donald MacBride, Elizabeth Dunne, Irving Bacon. **1939**

BLONDIE'S BLESSED EVENT ★★★ Blondie's daughter, Cookie, makes her first appearance in the series, making the film one of the most anxiously awaited episodes in the series. Because of Cookie, the film has more heart and personality. It also shifts the focus from Blondie and Dagwood to Cookie and Alexander. B&W; 75m. **DIR:** Frank Strayer. **CAST:** Penny Singleton, Arthur Lake, Hans Conried, Mary Wickes, Arthur O'Connell, Norma Jean Wayne. **1942**

BLOOD ALLEY ★★ Humphrey Bogart was originally set to star opposite wife Lauren Bacall in this story of a merchant marine captain helping Chinese refugees make it to Hong Kong, but he dropped out. For diehard Duke Wayne fans only. 115m. **DIR:** William Wellman. **CAST:** John Wayne, Lauren Bacall, Paul Fix, Mike Mazurki. **1955**

BLOOD AND BLACK LACE ★★1/2 This sometimes frightening Italian horror film features a psychotic killer eliminating members of the modeling industry with gusto. Decent entry in the genre from specialist Mario Bava. 88m. **DIR:** Mario Bava. **CAST:** Cameron Mitchell, Eva Bartok. **1964 DVD**

BLOOD AND CONCRETE, A LOVE STORY ★★ A down-and-out con man gets tangled up in the dirty dealings of an idiotic drug lord. Limp attempt to be an avant-garde film. Rated R for violence and profanity. 97m. **DIR:** Jeffrey Reiner. **CAST:** Billy Zane, Jennifer Beals, Darren McGavin, Harry Shearer. **1990**

BLOOD & DONUTS ★★ Tongue-in-cheek horror film in which a vampire comes back to life and falls in love with a clerk at a donut shop. A little wild, a little funny, and a lot weird. Brief cameo by director David Cronenberg. Rated R for vampire violence and nudity. 89m. **DIR:** Holly Dale. **CAST:** Gordon Currie, Justin Lewis, Helene Clarkson, David Cronenberg. **1995**

BLOOD AND GUNS (TEPEPA) 🦃 Orson Welles's screen presence is at a loss in this dull action yarn about three men whose lives intertwine after the Mexican revolution. Rated R for profanity and violence. 90m. **DIR:** Giulio Petroni. **CAST:** Orson Welles, Tomas Milian, John Steiner. **1968**

BLOOD AND ROSES 🦃 The ghost of a centuries dead vampire possesses a young woman in an attempt to fulfill an ancient curse. Although artistically filmed, the script shuns almost all vampire lore. 74m. **DIR:** Roger Vadim. **CAST:** Mel Ferrer, Elsa Martinelli, Annette Vadim. **1960**

BLOOD AND SAND (1922) ★★★1/2 One of Rudolph Valentino's most successful vehicles, although it lacks the action and pacing of his best pictures, *Son of the Sheik* and *The Eagle*. Silent. B&W; 80m. **DIR:** Fred Niblo. **CAST:** Rudolph Valentino, Nita Naldi, Lila Lee. **1922 DVD**

BLOOD AND SAND (1941) ★★★ The "Moment of Truth" is not always just before the matador places his sword, as Tyrone Power learns in this classic story of a poor boy who rises to fame in the bullring. Linda Darnell loves him, Rita Hayworth leads him on, in this colorful remake of a 1922 Valentino starrer. 123m. **DIR:** Rouben Mamoulian. **CAST:** Tyrone Power, Rita Hayworth, Anthony Quinn, Linda Darnell, Anna Nazimova, John Carradine. **1941**

BLOOD AND WINE ★★★ A Miami wine merchant (Jack Nicholson) and a small-time crook (Michael Caine) plan a jewel heist at the expense of one of the merchant's wealthy clients. Director Bob Rafelson really lays on the humid *film noir* atmosphere (Miami seems to have become one of Hollywood's favorite hotbeds of corruption). The plot, however, is never as clever or complicated as we are led to expect. Acting by the powerhouse cast is first-rate. Rated R for profanity and violence. 115m. **DIR:** Bob Rafelson. **CAST:** Jack Nicholson, Stephen Dorff, Jennifer Lopez, Judy Davis, Michael Caine. **1997**

BLOOD BEACH 🦃 Poor horror story of mysterious forces sucking people down into the sand. Rated R. 89m. **DIR:** Jeffrey Bloom. **CAST:** John Saxon, Marianna Hill, Otis Young. **1981**

BLOOD BEAST TERROR, THE ★★ The performances of genre stalwarts Peter Cushing and Robert Flemyng—as a scientist investigating hideous murders and the doctor whose moth-woman daughter is committing them—help elevate this tepid British horror. The monster is laughable. 88m. **DIR:** Vernon Sewell. **CAST:** Peter Cushing, Robert Flemyng. **1967 DVD**

BLOOD BROTHERS ★★ A boy who witnesses the gang murder of a local Asian grocer wants to go to the police but is reluctant because his older brother is one of the gang members. Unfortunately, this is a low-budget film that has nothing going for it except good intentions. Not rated; contains profanity and violence. 91m. **DIR:** Bruce Pittman. **CAST:** Mia Korf, Clark Johnson, Bill Nunn. **1996**

BLOOD CASTLE (1970) 🦃 Original title: *Scream of the Demon Lover.* Lamebrain hack-'em-up set against pseudogothic backdrop. Rated R. 97m. **DIR:** J. L. Merino. **CAST:** Erna Schurer, Agostina Belli. **1970**

BLOOD CASTLE (1972) ★★ Adaptation of the real-life saga of Elisabeth Bathory, a seventeenth-century Hungarian countess who bathed in virgin blood in the belief it kept her young and beautiful. This Spanish-Italian coproduction inserts enough exploitable elements to ensure an R rating. Also known as *The Legend of Blood Castle*. 87m. **DIR:** Jorge Grau. **CAST:** Lucia Bose, Ewa Aulin. **1972**

BLOOD DINER 🦃 Two brothers kill women to obtain body parts for a demonic ceremony. Not rated, but filled with violence, nudity, and gore. 88m. **DIR:** Jackie Kong. **CAST:** Rick Burks, Carl Crew. **1987**

BLOOD DOLLS ★★★ You want odd? You got it. Computer guru Virgil is eccentric. He wears a mask to conceal his misshapen head, keeps an all-girl rock band caged in his study, and has three living dolls that kill for him. Producer Charles Band directs with tongue firmly in cheek and delivers one of the best films of his career. Particularly fun is the inclusion of two different endings to the film. Rated R for violence, profanity, and adult situations. 90m. **DIR:** Charles Band. **CAST:** Jack Maturin, Debra Mayer, Nicholas Worth, Phil Fondacaro. **1999 DVD**

BLOOD FEAST 🦃 First and most infamous of the drive-in gore movies bolsters practically nonexistent plot of crazed murderer with gallons of director Herschell Gordon Lewis's patented stage blood. 75m. **DIR:** Herschell

Gordon Lewis. **CAST:** Connie Mason, Thomas Wood. **1963 DVD**

BLOOD FEUD ★★1/2 Marcello Mastroianni, a lawyer, and Giancarlo Giannini, a sleazy hood, compete for the romantic attentions of a beautiful Sicilian widow (Sophia Loren) in this abrasive, overblown potboiler in 1920s Italy. Dubbed in English. Not rated; contains profanity and violence. B&W; 112m. **DIR:** Lina Wertmuller. **CAST:** Sophia Loren, Marcello Mastroianni, Giancarlo Giannini. **1979**

BLOOD FRENZY ★★ In this made-for-video horror-thriller, a psychotherapist takes a group of her patients into the desert for a retreat. Predictably, someone starts killing them off one by one. Who is the killer? Who cares? Not rated, the movie contains violence. 90m. **DIR:** Hal Freeman. **CAST:** Wendy MacDonald, Hank Garrett, Lisa Loring. **1987**

BLOOD GAMES 🦃 Dopey, misogynistic movie about an all-female traveling softball team. Rated R for violence and nudity. 90m. **DIR:** Tanya Rosenberg. **CAST:** Gregory Cummins, Laura Albert. **1990**

BLOOD, GUTS, BULLETS & OCTANE ★★ Two sleazy used-car dealers go along with a shady smuggling deal to remedy their financial problems. This low-budget blend of *Pulp Fiction* and *Glengarry Glen Ross* is derivative, overdone, and ultimately pointless. Writer-director-costar Joe Carnahan shows talent, but he's a bit too much in love with the sound of his own dialogue. Rated R for violence and profanity. 86m. **DIR:** Joe Carnahan. **CAST:** Dan Leis, Joe Carnahan, Dan Harlan, Ken Rudulph, Hugh McCord. **1998 DVD**

BLOOD HARVEST 🦃 Tiny Tim in a slasher movie—it just doesn't get any worse than this. Not rated; contains nudity and gore. 90m. **DIR:** Bill Rebane. **CAST:** Tiny Tim, Itonia, Dean West. **1987**

BLOOD HORSE ★★ In this second installment of the *Black Fox* trilogy, Christopher Reeve and the slave he freed, Tony Todd, plot to save hostages from "savage" Indians. American Indians actually get fairer treatment in this episode, as the settlers are shown to be bloody and brutal. Set in Texas in the 1860s, this has an uninspired made-for-TV look, but puts a fresh twist on the racial problems of the last century. Not rated; contains violence. 92m. **DIR:** Steven H. Stern. **CAST:** Christopher Reeve, Tony Todd, Raul Trujillo. **1993**

BLOOD IN THE STREETS ★★ In this French-Italian film, a prison warden (Oliver Reed) is forced to release a prisoner as ransom for his kidnapped wife. There are some exciting chase scenes in this overall so-so film. Rated R for sex, nudity, language, and violence. 111m. **DIR:** Sergio Sollima. **CAST:** Oliver Reed, Fabio Testi, Agostina Belli. **1974**

BLOOD LINK 🦃 All his life, a prominent physician has had strange hallucinations about older women being brutally murdered. He discovers that he is seeing through the eyes of his Siamese twin. Rated R for nudity and violence. 98m. **DIR:** Alberto De Martino. **CAST:** Michael Moriarty, Penelope Milford, Cameron Mitchell. **1983**

BLOOD MONEY (1993) ★★★ This highly engaging film features an excellent cast in a story about an underworld bail-bondsman who falls for a thrill-seeking socialite. His life becomes complicated by another female cohort. B&W; 65m. **DIR:** Rowland Brown. **CAST:** George Bancroft, Frances Dee, Judith Anderson, Chick Chandler, Blossom Seeley. **1933**

•BLOOD MONEY (1999) ★★ Dull mob story about a Wall Street mogul who returns to his mob roots when his brother is murdered. Well-made but fatally slow-moving. Any episode of *The Sopranos* is preferable to this. Rated R for violence, language, and sexual content. 95m. **DIR:** Aaron Lipstadt. **CAST:** Brian Bloom, Alan Arkin, Alicia Coppola, Jennifer Gatti, Bruce Kirby. **1999**

BLOOD MOON (WEREWOLF VERSUS THE VAMPIRE WOMAN, THE) ★★ Video retitling of *The Werewolf versus the Vampire Woman*, with Paul Naschy as his recurring character from Spanish horror movies, the tortured lycanthrope Waldemar. Naschy's cheapjack efforts merge Universal-style nostalgic monster ingredients with the sexploitation demands of the Seventies. Idiotic but watchable. Rated R. 86m. **DIR:** Leon Klimovsky. **CAST:** Paul Naschy, Patty Shepard. **1970**

BLOOD OF A POET ★★1/2 This pretentious and self-centered first film by France's multitalented Jean Cocteau is also intriguing, provoking, and inventive. Enrique Rivero stars in and narrates this highly personal excursion into a poet's inner life: his fears and obsessions, his relation to the world about him, and the classic poetic preoccupation with death. In French with English subtitles. B&W; 55m. **DIR:** Jean Cocteau. **CAST:** Enrique Rivero. **1930 DVD**

BLOOD OF DRACULA ★★ Okay American-international teen horror about a troubled girl who comes under the vampiric (and vaguely lesbian) influence of a sinister teacher. Occasionally atmospheric, but never scary. B&W; 68m. **DIR:** Herbert L. Strock. **CAST:** Sandra Harrison. **1957**

BLOOD OF DRACULA'S CASTLE 🦃 Quite possibly the worst Dracula movie ever made. The film has a werewolf, a hunchback, women in chains, human sacrifices, a laughable script, and a ten-dollar budget. Rated PG. 84m. **DIR:** Al Adamson, Jean Hewitt. **CAST:** John Carradine, Paula Raymond, Alex D'Arcy, Robert Dix. **1967**

BLOOD OF HEROES ★★1/2 Fairly decent hybrid of *Rollerball* and *Road Warrior* about bush-league team of wannabes playing a brutal no-holds-barred combination of hockey, squash, and football. Rutger Hauer stars as a former star of the game who takes the team to the majors. Rated R for violence, nudity, profanity, and simulated sex. 91m. **DIR:** David Peoples. **CAST:** Rutger Hauer, Joan Chen. **1989**

BLOOD OF OTHERS, THE ★★ A disappointment, considering the talent involved (in front of *and* behind the camera), this made-for-cable miniseries is a generally unconvincing adaptation of a Simone de Beauvoir novel about a doomed love affair in the occupied Paris of World War II. 176m. **DIR:** Claude Chabrol. **CAST:** Jodie Foster, Michael Ontkean, Sam Neill, Stéphane Audran, Jean-Pierre Aumont, Lambert Wilson, Micheline Presle. **1984**

BLOOD OF THE HUNTER ★★★ Location photography and decent performances heat up this Canadian thriller. Gabriel Arcand plays a trapper who is framed for murder, then must rise to the occasion when the real killer takes his wife hostage. Michael Biehn is seductively evil as the mysterious stranger. Rated R for violence. 92m. **DIR:** Gilles Carle. **CAST:** Michael Biehn,

Gabriel Arcand, Alexandra Vandernoot, Edward Meeks, François-Eric Gendron. **1994**

BLOOD OF THE INNOCENT ★★★1/2 Strong supporting performances and a clever script lift this action-thriller above its brethren, although star Thomas Ian Griffith still needs to work on his line readings. He heads to Warsaw, bent on avenging the murder of his younger brother, and uncovers a corrupt scheme involving missing Russian peasants and illegal organ harvesting. Rated R for violence and profanity. 95m. **DIR:** Bob Misiorowski. **CAST:** Thomas Ian Griffith, Joanna Trzepiecinska, Rutger Hauer, John Rhys-Davies. **1994**

BLOOD OF THE VAMPIRE ★★1/2 Pretty good imitation Hammer horror flick (from the vintage period of British gothic shockers), with Donald Wolfit as the title fiend. Semicampy fun, with some genuine thrills, but the direction is too flat for the film to be taken seriously. Even worse, all source prints for its video release are faded almost to sepia, robbing the film of its once gorgeous color. 87m. **DIR:** Henry Cass. **CAST:** Barbara Shelley, Donald Wolfit, Vincent Ball. **1958**

BLOOD ON THE BADGE 🦃 When a cop's partner is killed by terrorists, he goes on an unbelievable one-man campaign of revenge. A truly poor film. Not rated; contains profanity and violence. 92m. **DIR:** Bret McCormick. **CAST:** Joe Estevez, David Harrod. **1992**

BLOOD ON THE MOON ★★★1/2 Robert Mitchum is in top form in this atmospheric Western concerning cattle ranchers trying to terminate homesteaders. B&W; 88m. **DIR:** Robert Wise. **CAST:** Robert Mitchum, Barbara Bel Geddes, Robert Preston. **1948**

BLOOD ON THE SUN ★★★1/2 This hard-hitting action-drama finds James Cagney fighting Japanese military and government men in Japan just before World War II. An unusual plot and good pace make this worth watching. B&W; 98m. **DIR:** Frank Lloyd. **CAST:** James Cagney, Robert Armstrong, Wallace Ford, Sylvia Sidney. **1945 DVD**

BLOOD ORGY OF THE SHE DEVILS 🦃 Ritualistic murders. Rated PG. 73m. **DIR:** Ted V. Mikels. **CAST:** Lila Zaborin, Tom Pace. **1972**

BLOOD RAGE 🦃 When a 10 year old boy kills a stranger at a drive-in movie, he escapes punishment by blaming his twin brother. It played movie houses and cable TV as *Nightmare at Shadow Woods*. Rated R. 83m. **DIR:** John Grissmer. **CAST:** Louise Lasser, Mark Soper. **1983**

BLOOD RED 🦃 Sicilian grape farmers feud with a tycoon over land in 1850 California. Rated R for violence and nudity. 102m. **DIR:** Peter Masterson. **CAST:** Eric Roberts, Giancarlo Giannini, Dennis Hopper, Burt Young. **1989**

BLOOD RELATIONS 🦃 Repugnant gorefest features three generations of a wealthy family lusting after a beautiful gold digger. Rated R for nudity, violence, and gore. 88m. **DIR:** Graeme Campbell. **CAST:** Jan Rubes, Kevin Hicks, Lynne Adams, Ray Walston. **1987**

BLOOD RELATIVES ★★★1/2 Quebec inspector Donald Sutherland, investigating the murder of a teenage girl, uncovers a conspiracy involving members of the girl's family. Not one of Claude Chabrol's best, but even a lesser effort by the French Hitchcock is better than most anything else on the mystery rack. 100m. **DIR:** Claude Chabrol. **CAST:** Donald Sutherland, Aude Landry, Lisa Langlois, Stéphane Audran, Donald Pleasence, David Hemmings. **1978**

BLOOD ROSE 🦃 Murky, grade-C horror from France was billed as "the first sex-horror film" for its U.S. release. Rated R. 87m. **DIR:** Claude Mulot. **CAST:** Philippe Lemaire, Anny Duperey, Howard Vernon. **1969**

BLOOD SALVAGE 🦃 Psychotic family preys on distressed motorists, abducting them and then selling their vital organs to a demented doctor. Too bad the folks behind this mess couldn't give it a brain. Rated R for violence and profanity. 90m. **DIR:** Tucker Johnstone. **CAST:** Danny Nelson, Lori Birdsong, Ray Walston, John Saxon, Evander Holyfield. **1989**

BLOOD SCREAMS ★★1/2 Atmospheric thriller about a sleepy Mexican village that harbors a deep, dark secret that surfaces to torment two Americans. Rated R for nudity and violence. 75m. **DIR:** Glenn Gebhard. **CAST:** Russ Tamblyn, Stacey Shaffer. **1988**

BLOOD SIMPLE ★★★★1/2 A slyly suspenseful, exciting (and sometimes agonizing) edge-of-your-seat story of how a bar owner (Dan Hedaya) hires a private eye (M. Emmet Walsh) to follow his wife (Frances McDormand) to find out if she's cheating on him. *Blood Simple* is defined as a "state of confusion that follows the commission of a murder, e.g., 'He's gone blood simple.'" Rated R for suggested sex, violence, and profanity. 96m. **DIR:** Joel Coen. **CAST:** John Getz, Frances McDormand, Dan Hedaya, M. Emmet Walsh. **1984 DVD**

BLOOD SISTERS 🦃 A group of sorority girls must spend the night in a haunted house with a maniac. Rated R for nudity. 85m. **DIR:** Roberta Findlay. **CAST:** Amy Brentano, Shannon McMahon. **1987**

BLOOD SONG (HAUNTED SYMPHONY) ★★ Ben Cross stars as a classical composer haunted by what appear to be spirits of the dead. Visually stunning film features fine performances but has a self-destructive sense of importance. 85m. **DIR:** David Tausik. **CAST:** Ben Cross, Beverly Garland, Jennifer Burns. **1994**

BLOOD SPATTERED BRIDE, THE ★★ Sheridan Le Fanu's *Carmilla* gets another reworking in this intermittently stylish exploitation movie from Spain. Although the climax was heavily censored by U.S. distributors, it's still R-rated. 95m. **DIR:** Vicente Aranda. **CAST:** Simon Andreu, Maribel Martin, Alexandra Bastedo. **1974 DVD**

BLOOD SPELL 🦃 A modern-day evil sorcerer possesses his son in an attempt to gain immortality. Rated R for graphic violence. 87m. **DIR:** Deryn Warren. **CAST:** Anthony Jenkins. **1987**

BLOOD SUCKERS FROM OUTER SPACE ★★ Low-budget horror spoof about an alien virus that causes people to vomit up their guts, turning them into sneaky zombies out to suck the innards from hapless victims. Although sometimes funny, the film is uneven. Not rated; contains profanity and partial nudity. 79m. **DIR:** Glenn Coburn. **CAST:** Thom Meyer, Pat Paulsen. **1984**

•BLOOD SURF 🦃 Leapin' lizards! A reality-television film crew down in Australia to film the latest extreme sport, blood surfing, finds itself being stalked and hunted by a legendary saltwater crocodile. No one is safe on land, in the water, or watching the film on video. Rated R for adult situations, language, and violence. 88m. **DIR:** James D. R. Hickox. **CAST:** Matt Borlenghi, Joel West, Taryn Reif. **2000 DVD**

BLOOD THIRSTY ★★ Misleadingly promoted as a lesbian vampire movie, this is actually a more serious-minded film about a woman who becomes addicted to self-mutilation. Too poorly made to have much effect. Rated R for nudity, sex, violence, and profanity. 88m. **DIR:** Jeff Frey. **CAST:** Monique Parent, Leslie Danon, Matt Baily, Julie Strain. **1998 DVD**

BLOOD TIES (1987) ★★ Brad Davis is an innocent American engineer blackmailed into assassinating his cousin, an anticrime justice in Sicily. Not rated; contains strong language, violence, and nudity. 98m. **DIR:** Giacomo Battiato. **CAST:** Brad Davis, Tony Lo Bianco, Vincent Spano, Barbara de Rossi, Ricky Tognazzi, Michael Gazzo. **1987**

BLOOD TIES (1993) ★★1/2 This interesting bite on the vampire legend finds a group of former blood suckers trying to fit into society. Into their Los Angeles lair comes a teenager whose parents were murdered by vampire killers, now hot on his trail. The group must decide whether to fight back or flee, great fodder for moral arguments and exciting close calls. Rated R for sexuality, violence, and strong language. 93m. **DIR:** Jim McBride. **CAST:** Harley Venton, Patrick Bauchau, Bo Hopkins, Michelle Johnson, Jason London. **1993**

BLOOD VOWS: THE STORY OF A MAFIA WIFE ★★★1/2 A fairy-tale romance between a beautiful orphan (Melissa Gilbert) and a dashing lawyer (Joe Penny) results in a nightmarish prison for her after they marry. It seems his clan needs him back home for a war between Mafia families and she can't deal with the violence or the restrictions put on mob women. Some chilling moments. Originally shown as a TV movie. 104m. **DIR:** Paul Wendkos. **CAST:** Melissa Gilbert, Joe Penny, Talia Shire, Eileen Brennan. **1987**

BLOOD WARRIORS ★★ Ho-hum action epic with ex-Marine David Bradley forced to wage war against his former best friend, now a drug runner so vile and despicable that he'd molest his own sister and hold orphans hostage. Rated R for profanity, violence, and suggested sex. 96m. **DIR:** Sam Firstenberg. **CAST:** David Bradley, Frank Zagarino, Jennifer Campbell. **1993**

BLOOD WEDDING ★★★ Excellent ballet adaptation of Federico Garcia Lorca's classic tragedy is impeccably performed by a great, lavishly costumed cast in an empty rehearsal hall. Carlos Saura's direction gives this production a great sense of power and beauty. In Spanish with English subtitles. 72m. **DIR:** Carlos Saura. **CAST:** Antonio Gades, Cristina Hoyos. **1981**

BLOODBATH AT THE HOUSE OF DEATH ★★ Although advertised as one, this British movie is not all that much of a spoof on horror films. In the story, a team of paranormal specialists investigates a house that was the scene of a mysterious massacre. Vincent Price plays a nutty devil worshiper. Not rated, but equivalent to an R for violence, gore, sex, nudity, and profanity. 92m. **DIR:** Ray Cameron. **CAST:** Vincent Price, Kenny Everett, Pamela Stephenson, Gareth Hunt, Don Warrington, John Fortune, Sheila Steafel. **1985**

BLOODBEAT 🦃 This cheap supernatural flick tries to pass off the idea that a samurai ghost is haunting the backwoods of an American wilderness. 84m. **DIR:** Fabrice A. Zaphiratos. **CAST:** Helen Benton, Terry Brown. **1985**

BLOODBROTHERS ★★★1/2 Richard Gere and Marilu Henner take top honors in this drama. Plot revolves around a family of construction workers and the son (Gere) who wants to do something else with his life. Rated R. 116m. **DIR:** Robert Mulligan. **CAST:** Richard Gere, Paul Sorvino, Tony Lo Bianco, Marilu Henner. **1978**

BLOODFIST ★★ Typical martial arts chop-out, peopled by actual World Kickboxing Association champs, karate kings, and a wealth of other unsightly folks who just can't act. Forgettable. Rated R for ketchup. 86m. **DIR:** Terence H. Winkless. **CAST:** Don "The Dragon" Wilson, Bob Kaman. **1989 DVD**

BLOODFIST 2 ★★ In this martial arts flick, lightweight kick-boxing champ Don Wilson goes to the Philippines and falls into a trap set by the ruler of an island fortress. A rip-off of the genre-classic *Enter the Dragon.* Rated R for nudity, violence, and profanity. 85m. **DIR:** Andy Blumenthal. **CAST:** Don "The Dragon" Wilson. **1989 DVD**

BLOODFIST III: FORCED TO FIGHT ★★ This sequel finds star Don "The Dragon" Wilson as a new convict forced into being a target for various prison gangs. Rated R for violence and profanity. 90m. **DIR:** Oley Sassone. **CAST:** Don "The Dragon" Wilson, Richard Roundtree, Richard Paul. **1991 DVD**

BLOODFIST IV—DIE TRYING ★★ Repo man Don "The Dragon" Wilson finds himself up against the CIA, FBI, and international terrorists. Plenty of martial arts action. Rated R for violence and profanity. 86m. **DIR:** Paul Ziller. **CAST:** Don "The Dragon" Wilson, Cat Sassoon, Amanda Wyss, Katie Brown, Liz Torres, James Tolkan. **1992 DVD**

BLOODFIST V: HUMAN TARGET ★★ Serviceable martial arts entry features Don "The Dragon" Wilson as an undercover FBI agent who, while suffering amnesia is pegged as a double agent. He must fight for his life while fighting to regain his memory. Rated R for violence and adult language. 84m. **DIR:** Jeff Yonis. **CAST:** Don "The Dragon" Wilson, Denice Duff, Danny Lopez, Steve James. **1994 DVD**

BLOODFIST VI: GROUND ZERO ★★1/2 Either Don "The Dragon" Wilson finally is learning to act, or we're simply getting used to him. This time out, he's a compassionate military courier (kind to rabbits) who gets trapped in a nuclear-missile silo with terrorists bent on targeting major North American cities. Rated R for violence, profanity, and laughably gratuitous nudity. 90m. **DIR:** Rick Jacobson. **CAST:** Don "The Dragon" Wilson, Cat Sassoon, Robin Curtis, Jonathan Fuller, Steve Garvey. **1994 DVD**

BLOODHOUNDS ★★1/2 A writer (Corbin Bernsen) and a police detective (Christine Harnos) team up to track down an escaped killer. Plenty of opportunity here for witty dialogue, but it just doesn't happen, which makes this made-for-cable original nothing more than a second-rate action movie. Not rated; contains violence. 95m. **DIR:** Michael Katleman. **CAST:** Corbin Bernsen, Christine Harnos. **1996**

BLOODHOUNDS II ★★★ A man is killing off rapists who escaped justice in the courts, and now he wants a famous author to help him write a manifesto about how vigilantes can solve America's problems. This made-for-cable original is a solid little thriller, sprinkled with enough wit and terror to be fun. Not rated; contains violence. 95m. **DIR:** Stuart Cooper. **CAST:** Corbin Bernsen, Nia Peeples, Ian Tracey, Suki Kaiser, Jim Byrnes, Amy Yasbeck. **1996**

BLOODHOUNDS OF BROADWAY ★★★ This featherweight period comedy was stitched together by writer-director Howard Brookner from four stories by Damon Runyan. While not as hilarious as one might hope, this story has its moments, the best of which are provided by Randy Quaid as a lovesick loser and Madonna as the object of his affections. Rated PG for brief profanity and stylized violence. 90m. **DIR:** Howard Brookner. **CAST:** Matt Dillon, Jennifer Grey, Julie Hagerty, Rutger Hauer, Madonna, Esai Morales, Anita Morris, Randy Quaid. **1989**

BLOODKNOT ★★★ Seductress Kate Vernon impersonates a dead man's girlfriend in order to ingratiate herself with his family, in this intriguing erotic thriller. Randy Kornfield's script remains pretty clever until the final act. Still, getting there will keep you guessing. Rated R for nudity, simulated sex, profanity, and violence. 98m. **DIR:** Jorge Montesi. **CAST:** Patrick Dempsey, Kate Vernon, Margot Kidder, Krista Bridges, Craig Sheffer. **1995**

BLOODLETTING ★★★ This direct-to-video film is *Natural Born Killers* done right. Young Ariauna Albright blackmails serial killer James L. Edwards into teaching her the art of murder and soon the two are on the road, killing as they go. Performances are well done, and there is a sense of style to this tale that could easily have become exploitation. Not rated; contains violence, gore, and profanity. 96m. **DIR:** Matthew Jason Walsh. **CAST:** Ariauna Albright, James L. Edwards, Joseph Daw, Sasha Graham, Tina Krause. **1996**

BLOODLINE 🦃 Audrey Hepburn falls heir to a pharmaceutical fortune in this inexcusably repulsive montage of bad taste and incoherence. Rated R for sex scenes. 116m. **DIR:** Terence Young. **CAST:** Audrey Hepburn, Ben Gazzara, James Mason, Omar Sharif. **1979**

BLOODLUST: SUBSPECIES III ★★ This better-than-expected continuation of the vampire series features impressive, gory special effects. Anders Hove returns as vampire Radu, pitting two sisters against each other in a battle over their souls. Rated R for language, nudity, and violence. 81m. **DIR:** Ted Nicolaou. **CAST:** Anders Hove, Melanie Shatner, Denice Duff, Kevin Blair. **1993**

BLOODMATCH 🦃 Senseless vengefest as a man seeks the five people who fixed a kick-boxing contest five years earlier. Not rated; contains excessive violence and profanity as well as a sprinkling of nudity. 87m. **DIR:** Albert Pyun. **CAST:** Benny Urquidez, Thom Mathews. **1991**

BLOODMOON (1989) ★★ Okay Australian slasher features a deranged private school teacher who kills couples at the nearby lovers' lane. It seems he transfers his anger at his unfaithful wife onto his promiscuous female students. Rated R for nudity, violence, and gore. 104m. **DIR:** Alec Mills. **CAST:** Loon Lissek. **1989**

BLOODMOON (1997) ★★1/2 Vehicle for Australian kick boxer Gary Daniels, cast as a cop on the trail of a serial killer who specializes in martial artists. The plot is tired, but at least the action scenes are lively. Rated R for strong violence and profanity. 104m. **DIR:** Tony Leung. **CAST:** Gary Daniels, Chuck Jeffreys, Frank Gorshin. **1997 DVD**

BLOODSPORT ★★ Jean-Claude Van Damme plays a martial arts master who arrives in Hong Kong to compete in the *kumite*, a violent championship contest. The fighting sequences are tremendous, but the framing story offers only clichés. Rated R for violence and language. 100m. **DIR:** Newt Arnold. **CAST:** Jean-Claude Van Damme, Donald Gibb, Leah Ayres, Normann Burton, Forest Whitaker, Bolo Yeung. **1987**

BLOODSPORT II ★★ Less a sequel than a remake of the Jean-Claude Van Damme movie, with only the slightest glimmer of a plot to space out the fight scenes between contestants at an international free-form martial arts competition. Rated R for violence and profanity. 86m. **DIR:** Alan Mehrez. **CAST:** Daniel Bernhardt, Noriyuki "Pat" Morita, Donald Gibb, James Hong, Lori Lynn Dickerson, Philip Tan, Lisa McCullough, Ong Soo Han. **1996 DVD**

BLOODSPORT III 🦃 Less fighting means less of what fans of this series want to see as Daniel Bernhardt is forced to compete in another *kumite* competition. Not rated; contains violence, sexual situations, and profanity. 92m. **DIR:** Alan Mehrez. **CAST:** Daniel Bernhardt, John Rhys-Davies, Amber Van Lent, James Hong, Noriyuki "Pat" Morita. **1997 DVD**

BLOODSPORT IV: THE DARK KUMITE ★★ This in-name-only sequel to the previous *Bloodsports* stars Daniel Bernhardt as an undercover cop investigating mysterious deaths at a prison. While there, he is forced to join an illegal martial arts competition. For die-hard martial arts fans only. Rated R for violence, profanity, and sex. 100m. **DIR:** Elvis Restaino. **CAST:** Daniel Bernhardt, Ivan Ivanov, Lisa Stothard, Stefanos Miltsakakis, Derek McGrath. **1998 DVD**

BLOODSTONE ★★ An adventure film in the tradition of *Raiders of the Lost Ark*, this falls short of the mark. The story involves newlyweds who become involved in a jewel heist in the Middle East. Loaded with humor and lots of action, but marred by poor performances. Rated PG-13 for violence. 90m. **DIR:** Dwight H. Little. **CAST:** Brett Stimely. **1988 DVD**

BLOODSTONE: SUBSPECIES II ★★★1/2 A lovely college student is bitten by a vampire and spends most of the movie cringing from her shiveringly ugly master. Enjoy the comic-book sensibilities, imaginative direction, and the dark sense of humor permeating this low-budget howler. Rated R for violence and profanity. 107m. **DIR:** Ted Nicolaou. **CAST:** Anders Hove, Denice Duff. **1993**

BLOODSUCKERS, THE ★★1/2 Lots of blood, gory special effects, and some good humor. Not bad for this type of film. Also known as *Return from the Past* and *Dr. Terror's Gallery of Horrors*. Not for the squeamish. 84m. **DIR:** David L. Hewitt. **CAST:** Lon Chaney Jr., John Carradine. **1967**

BLOODSUCKING FREAKS (THE INCREDIBLE TORTURE SHOW) 🦃 This putrid film is an endurance test for even the most hard-core horror buffs. The scene where one of the maniacs sucks a woman's brains out with a straw has to be one of the most repulsive moments ever put on film. Rated R for nudity and violence. 89m. **DIR:** Joel M. Reed. **CAST:** Seamus O'Brian, Niles McMaster. **1978 DVD**

BLOODSUCKING PHARAOHS IN PITTSBURGH ★★ Campy horror farce comparable to *Night of the Living Dead* meets *Rocky Horror Picture Show*. This time a cult killer sleazes about the city, slicing up victims with a chain saw. 89m. **DIR:** Alan Smithee. **CAST:** Jake Dengel. **1991 DVD**

BLOODTHIRSTY BUTCHERS 🦃 As the title suggests, an extremely violent series of murders is committed in very gruesome fashion. Rated R. 80m. **DIR:** Andy Milligan. **CAST:** John Miranda, Annabella Wood. **1970**

BLOODTIDE 🦃 Cheap horror film about bizarre rituals on a Greek isle. Rated R. 82m. **DIR:** Richard Jeffries. **CAST:** James Earl Jones, José Ferrer, Lila Kedrova. **1984**

BLOODY BIRTHDAY 🦃 Three children, born during an eclipse of the moon, run amok, killing everyone in sight. Rated R. 85m. **DIR:** Edward Hunt. **CAST:** Susan Strasberg, José Ferrer, Lori Lethin, Joe Penny. **1986**

BLOODY MAMA ★★1/2 Shelley Winters plays Ma Barker in this gangster flick. Her four sons share her notoriety as Depression-era bandits. Rated R. 90m. **DIR:** Roger Corman. **CAST:** Shelley Winters, Don Stroud, Pat Hingle, Robert Walden, Bruce Dern, Robert De Niro. **1970**

BLOODY MOON ★★ A high-body-count exploitation horror film, this is one of the more perfunctory outings by Jess (Jesus) Franco, and thus one of his least revolting. Women are stabbed, choked, and in one memorable instance, buzz-sawed to death. A gory clip was used in Pedro Almodóvar's *Matador*. Rated R. 83m. **DIR:** Jess (Jesus) Franco. **CAST:** Olivia Pascal, Christoph Moosbrugger. **1981**

BLOODY MURDER 🦃 Teens battle a masked killer at a summer camp in the kind of tired slasher movie that *Scream* parodied. Rated R for violence (mild by the genre's standards) and profanity. 88m. **DIR:** Ralph Portillo. **CAST:** Jessica Morris, Peter Guillemette, Michael Stone. **2000 DVD**

BLOODY NEW YEAR ★★1/2 Five teenagers become stranded on an abandoned island resort that's caught in a time warp. Zombie ghosts begin to pop up, first taunting the kids, then terrorizing, and finally killing them. Fairly well produced and boasting some decent special effects. Rated R for violence and nudity. 90m. **DIR:** Norman J. Warren. **CAST:** Suzy Aitchison, Colin Heywood, Cathrine Roman. **1987**

BLOODY PIT OF HORROR ★★ Nudie photographers and their comely models run afoul of a psycho who thinks he's the reincarnated Crimson Executioner when they visit a supposedly abandoned castle for a photo session. A laugh riot, if you've got a sick sense of humor—otherwise, steer clear. 74m. **DIR:** Max Hunter (Massimo Pupillo). **CAST:** Mickey Hargitay. **1965 DVD**

BLOODY WEDNESDAY ★★1/2 A peculiar psychological horror story whose prime attraction is that it never gets predictable. After a man suffers a nervous breakdown, his brother sets him up as the caretaker of a vacant hotel. Unfortunately, the story is never satisfactorily resolved. Not rated. 97m. **DIR:** Mark G. Gilhuis. **CAST:** Raymond Elmendorf, Pamela Baker. **1985**

BLOW ★★★ Johnny Depp plays George Jung, a real-life drug dealer now doing time on a long string of offenses. Following Jung from his early pot-selling days in 1960s L.A. through the cocaine boom of the 1970s and 1980s, the story is familiar but well-acted. The presence of Ray Liotta as Jung's affectionate father emphasizes the film's similarity (and inferiority) to Martin Scorsese's *GoodFellas*. Rated R for profanity, violence, and drug use. 124m. **DIR:** Ted Demme. **CAST:** Johnny Depp, Ray Liotta, Rachel Griffiths, Penélope Cruz, Paul Reubens. **2001 DVD**

BLOW DRY ★★1/2 The British National Hairdressing Championship brings about a wary reconciliation between a barber, his ex-wife, and her female lover. Writer Simon Beaufoy reportedly tried to distance himself from this uneasy mix of soap opera and low-camp farce. The talented actors do their best, but they might have preferred to follow Beaufoy's example. Rated R for profanity. 90m. **DIR:** Paddy Breathnach. **CAST:** Alan Rickman, Natasha Richardson, Rachel Griffiths, Rachael Leigh Cook, Josh Hartnett. **2001 DVD**

BLOW OUT ★★★★ John Travolta and Nancy Allen are terrific in this thriller by director Brian De Palma. The story concerns a motion picture sound man (Travolta) who becomes involved in murder when he rescues a young woman (Allen) from a car that crashes into a river. It's suspenseful, thrill-packed, adult entertainment. Rated R because of sex, nudity, profanity, and violence. 107m. **DIR:** Brian De Palma. **CAST:** John Travolta, Nancy Allen, John Lithgow, Dennis Franz. **1981 DVD**

BLOW-UP ★★★★★ Director Michelangelo Antonioni's first English-language film was this stimulating examination into what is or is not reality. On its surface, a photographer (David Hemmings) believes he has taken a snapshot of a murder taking place. Vanessa Redgrave arrives at his studio and tries to seduce him out of the photo. 108m. **DIR:** Michelangelo Antonioni. **CAST:** Vanessa Redgrave, David Hemmings, Sarah Miles. **1966**

BLOWBACK ★★ A serial killer thought to be executed shows up again to exact revenge on the jury that convicted him. Ludicrous thriller tries to be stylish but is really only dull. Rated R for violence, nudity, profanity, and sexual situations. 93m. **DIR:** Mark L. Lester. **CAST:** Mario Van Peebles, James Remar, Stephen Caffrey. **1999 DVD**

•BLOWIN' SMOKE ★★1/2 Steve Zahn stars as Freak, a comical stoner who has everything to say about work, relationships, food, sex, and pot (especially sex and pot). This movie is all about his influence on people while under the influence himself. Not bad and often funny, this movie suffers only from a lack of originality. Rated R for drug use, language, and sexual situations. 88m. **DIR:** Paul Todisco. **CAST:** Steve Zahn, Josh Hamilton. **1999 DVD**

BLOWING WILD 🦃 Wildcat Barbara Stanwyck lusts almost in vain for Gary Cooper in this foul tale of bandits in the Mexican oil fields. 90m. **DIR:** Hugo Fregonese. **CAST:** Gary Cooper, Barbara Stanwyck, Anthony Quinn, Ruth Roman, Ward Bond. **1953**

BLOWN AWAY (1992) ★★ Pedestrian thriller has Corey Haim getting involved with young and dangerous Nicole Eggert, despite the warnings of older brother Corey Feldman. It's not until Eggert goes out of control that Haim sees her true colors. Haim spends half the film out of his clothes trying to prove that he's a big boy now. Rated R for nudity, language, and violence; unrated version contains more sex. 91/93. **DIR:** Brenton Spencer. **CAST:** Corey Haim, Corey Feldman, Nicole Eggert, Gary Farmer, Jean Leclerc. **1992**

BLOWN AWAY (1994) ★★★1/2 A grudge fight turns into an explosive situation as a bomb-squad expert must deal with a mad bomber he once put away. Tommy Lee Jones holds this good, but not great film together with another strong villainous performance. Rated R for language and violence. 120m. **DIR:** Stephen Hopkins. **CAST:** Jeff Bridges, Tommy Lee Jones, Lloyd Bridges, Suzy Amis, Forest Whitaker. **1994 DVD**

BLUE God-awful, pretentious Western with Terence Stamp as a monosyllabic gunman. 113m. **DIR:** Silvio Narizzano. **CAST:** Terence Stamp, Joanna Pettet, Karl Malden, Ricardo Montalban, Sally Kirkland. **1968**

BLUE ★★★1/2 A grieving French widow tries to sink into anonymity after her famous composer husband and child are killed in a car wreck. She becomes haunted by the unfinished personal and professional business of her dead spouse. Intoxicating imagery, classical music, and sensuality all induce a trancelike euphoria. For her frosty, somber performance, Juliette Binoche won the Venice Film Festival Best Actress award. In French with English subtitles. Rated R for nudity, sex, and language. 97m. **DIR:** Krzysztof Kieslowski. **CAST:** Juliette Binoche, Benoit Regent, Florence Pernel. **1993**

BLUE AND THE GRAY, THE ★★★1/2 Star-studded saga dramatizes many viewpoints of the only war in history pitting American against American. Seen mostly through the eyes of an artist-correspondent, this TV miniseries is a polished, if occasionally sanitized, version of the bloodiest conflict in U.S. history. 295m. **DIR:** Andrew V. McLaglen. **CAST:** Stacy Keach, John Hammond, Lloyd Bridges, Rory Calhoun, Colleen Dewhurst, Warren Oates, Geraldine Page, Rip Torn, Robert Vaughn, Sterling Hayden, Paul Winfield, Gregory Peck. **1982 DVD**

BLUE ANGEL, THE ★★★★★ This stunning tale about a straitlaced schoolteacher's obsession with a striptease dancer in Germany is the subject of many film classes. The photography, set design, and script are all top-notch, and there are spectacular performances by all. In German with English subtitles. B&W; 98m. **DIR:** Josef von Sternberg. **CAST:** Emil Jannings, Marlene Dietrich, Kurt Gerron. **1930**

BLUE BIRD, THE ★★1/2 Following on the success of *The Wizard of Oz*, this extravagant fantasy features Shirley Temple as a spoiled brat who seeks true happiness by leaving her loving parents' home. Film is remarkable for the star's characterization of a spiteful little crab, which contrasts markedly with her usual sunny roles. 88m. **DIR:** Walter Lang. **CAST:** Shirley Temple, Spring Byington, Nigel Bruce. **1940**

BLUE CHIPS ★★★ University-basketball coach is tempted to flush his squeaky-clean recruitment ethics down the toilet after suffering through his first losing season in a long career. Writer Ron Shelton shows a collegiate system filled with money-laundering alumni with deep pockets and blue-chip players who brazenly solicit under-the-table perks. The movie plunges deep into the aesthetics of the game and is packed with familiar NBA faces. Rated PG-13 for language. 108m. **DIR:** William Friedkin. **CAST:** Nick Nolte, Shaquille O'Neal, J. T. Walsh, Anfernee Hardaway, Alfre Woodard, Matt Nover, Mary McDonnell. **1994**

BLUE CITY Estranged son Judd Nelson returns to his hometown and learns that his father, previously the mayor, has been killed. Rated R for language and violence. 83m. **DIR:** Michelle Manning. **CAST:** Judd Nelson, Ally Sheedy, David Caruso, Paul Winfield, Scott Wilson, Anita Morris. **1986**

BLUE COLLAR ★★★★1/2 This film delves into the underbelly of the auto industry by focusing on the fears, frustrations, and suppressed anger of three factory workers, superbly played by Richard Pryor, Harvey Keitel, and Yaphet Kotto. It is the social comment and intense drama that make this a highly effective and memorable film. Good music, too. Rated R for violence, sex, nudity, and profanity. 114m. **DIR:** Paul Schrader. **CAST:** Richard Pryor, Harvey Keitel, Yaphet Kotto. **1978 DVD**

BLUE COUNTRY ★★★1/2 A lighthearted comedy involving a nurse who leaves the city to enjoy a free and independent life in the country. She meets up with a bachelor who equally enjoys his freedom. Their encounters with the local townspeople provide amusing glimpses of French folk life. In French with English subtitles. 90m. **DIR:** Jean-Charles Tacchella. **CAST:** Brigitte Fossey, Jacques Serres, Ginette Garcin, Armand Meffre, Ginett Mathieu. **1977**

BLUE DAHLIA, THE ★★★★ In this sexy and stylish *film noir,* recently returned WWII veteran Alan Ladd is blamed for the murder of his unscrupulous wife. Mysterious and gorgeous Veronica Lake offers to help, but can he trust her? Tightly scripted by Raymond Chandler and vibrantly acted, this is a memorable effort. Not rated; contains violence. B&W; 100m. **DIR:** George Marshall. **CAST:** Alan Ladd, Veronica Lake, William Bendix, Howard DaSilva, Doris Dowling, Hugh Beaumont. **1946**

BLUE DE VILLE ★★★ Engaging cross-country odyssey in which three diverse types travel together in a classic, mint blue 1959 Cadillac. Interesting characters, outrageous situations, and gorgeous scenery. 100m. **DIR:** Jim Johnston. **CAST:** Jennifer Runyon, Kimberly Pistone, Mark Thomas Miller. **1986**

BLUE DESERT ★★★ Two men, one a policeman and the other a drifter, court a woman who is being terrorized in a small desert town. Solid three-person thriller that keeps the viewer intrigued with plot twists galore and solid acting. Rated R for violence. 98m. **DIR:** Bradley Battersby. **CAST:** D. B. Sweeney, Courteney Cox, Craig Sheffer. **1991**

BLUE FIN ★★ The son of a commercial fisherman finds that growing up is hard to do, especially when he has to do so before he's ready. On a fishing trip with his father, the boy is caught in a storm, and must act responsibly for the first time in his life. 93m. **DIR:** Carl Schultz. **CAST:** Hardy Kruger, Greg Rowe, Liddy Clark, Hugh Keays-Byrne. **1977**

BLUE FIRE LADY ★★1/2 The story of racetracks and horse racing, the trust and love between an animal and a person are well handled in this family film. It chronicles the story of Jenny (Cathryn Harrison) and her love for horses, which endures despite her father's disapproval. 96m. **DIR:** Ross Dimsey. **CAST:** Catherine Harrison, Mark Holden, Peter Cummins. **1983**

BLUE FLAME ★★ Intriguing premise wears out its welcome long before the film is over. It starts off promisingly enough, with two aliens hiding out in the mind of a cop. Inside, they force the cop to face his darkest fears and desires. Brian Wimmer is OK as the cop, but the rest of the cast isn't very arresting. Rated R for violence and sexuality. 88m. **DIR:** Cassian Elwes. **CAST:** Brian Wimmer, Jad Mager, Kerri Green, Ian Buchanan, Cecilia Peck. **1993**

BLUE GARDENIA, THE ★★1/2 Woman on the lam for a murder she can't remember is befriended by the reporter sworn to bring her to justice. Standard crime film boasts a good cast and title song by Nat "King" Cole but never manages to rise above the competition. B&W; 90m. **DIR:** Fritz Lang. **CAST:** Anne Baxter, Richard Conte, Ann Sothern, Raymond Burr, Jeff Donnell, George Reeves, Ruth Storey, Richard Erdman. **1953 DVD**

BLUE HAWAII ★★★1/2 In this enjoyable Elvis Presley flick, the star plays a returning soldier who works with tourists against his mom's (Angela Lansbury) wishes. 101m. **DIR:** Norman Taurog. **CAST:** Elvis Presley, Joan Blackman, Angela Lansbury, Iris Adrian. **1962 DVD**

BLUE HOTEL ★★ Unsatisfying interpretation of Stephen Crane's short story. David Warner chews the scenery as a stranger in town who fears his life will be taken by the other guests of the hotel he occupies. The entire silly affair, which flirts with the notion of predestination, revolves around a card game. Introduced by Henry Fonda; unrated and suitable for family viewing. 55m. **DIR:** Ján Kadár. **CAST:** David Warner, James Keach, John Bottoms, Rex Everhart. **1984**

BLUE HOUR, THE ★★★1/2 Bittersweet German love story about a male prostitute who falls for his female neighbor after her bullish boyfriend walks out. Excellent performances highlight this improbable love story that looks at love from both sides. In German with English subtitles. Not rated; contains nudity, sex, and frank language. 87m. **DIR:** Marcel Gisler. **CAST:** Andreas Herder, Dina Leipzig, Cristof Krix. **1991 DVD**

BLUE ICE ★★★1/2 Michael Caine's engaging lead performance as retired-spy-turned-nightclub-owner Harry Anders (he's hoping to make a franchise of this character) rises smoothly above a derivative Ron Hutchinson script that borrows quite heavily from Len Deighton's *The Ipcress File*... which also starred Caine, as another Harry (Palmer). This particular Harry, jazz lover and chef extraordinaire, gets mixed up with Sean Young, who may be more than a consul's wife. Rated R for violence, nudity, profanity, and simulated sex. 96m. **DIR:** Russell Mulcahy. **CAST:** Michael Caine, Sean Young, Ian Holm, Bob Hoskins, Bobby Short. **1993**

BLUE IGUANA ★★ For his first film, writer-director John Lafia attempted a *Raising Arizona*–style spoof of the hard boiled detective story—and failed. The story concerns a "recovery specialist" (Dylan McDermott) who is coerced by IRS agents Tovah Feldshuh and Dean Stockwell into going after $40 million in contraband money. The supporting actors are allowed to overact to bizarre proportions. Rated R for violence. 90m. **DIR:** John Lafia. **CAST:** Dylan McDermott, Jessica Harper, James Russo, Tovah Feldshuh, Dean Stockwell. **1988**

BLUE IN THE FACE ★★★1/2 With standing sets and numerous players left over after making *Smoke*, director Wayne Wang and scripter Paul Auster quickly put together this companion film, which once again stars Harvey Keitel as Brooklyn cigar-shop manager Auggie Wren. The free-form result is highly improvisational, with cute bits from numerous celebrity guest stars. The quirky soundtrack comes from John Lurie and the Lounge Lizards, who also appear on camera. Although not as compelling as *Smoke*, this is oddly appealing. Rated R for profanity and nudity. 98m. **DIR:** Wayne Wang. **CAST:** Harvey Keitel, Jim Jarmusch, Mel Gorham, Giancarlo Esposito, Lou Reed, Jared Harris, Lily Tomlin, Michael J. Fox, Madonna, Roseanne, Mira Sorvino. **1995**

BLUE JEANS ★★ A group of French school-boys takes a trip to England to try to lose their virginity. This dull film's only redemption is that one innocent boy learns a few of life's lessons. In French with English subtitles. Not rated; contains profanity. 80m. **DIR:** Hughes des Rozier. **CAST:** Gilles Budin, Michel Gibet, Gabriel Cattand, Gerard Croce, Pierre Borizans. **1978**

BLUE JUICE ★★1/2 Here's an odd little film, a British surf comedy-drama that features very little surf or comedy. The emphasis is on the drama, which follows a group of young people looking for the perfect wave, love, and the meaning of life. While the characters and situations are as flat as the water, the film manages to sling to the surface thanks to early appearances from Catherine Zeta-Jones and Ewan McGregor. Rated R for adult situations. 90m. **DIR:** Carl Prechezer. **CAST:** Sean Pertwee, Catherine Zeta-Jones, Ewan McGregor, Steven Mackintosh, Peter Gunn. **1995 DVD**

BLUE KITE, THE ★★★★ Once again, we have a first-rate Chinese film that has been banned in its homeland. This one tells the story of a young schoolteacher, from her first marriage in 1953 to the Cultural Revolution in 1967. Along the way she loses three husbands—and, eventually, her own freedom—to the persecutions of the communist regime. Strong, engrossing drama, balancing political tragedy with small flashes of humor and irony. In Mandarin with English subtitles. Not rated; contains mature themes and mild violence. 138m. **DIR:** Tian Zhuangzhuang. **CAST:** Tian Yi. **1994**

BLUE KNIGHT, THE (1973) ★★★1/2 William Holden gives an excellent, Emmy-winning performance as the hero of Joseph Wambaugh's bestselling novel. *The Blue Knight* chronicles the last four days in the life of an aging L.A. street cop. Lee Remick is superb as Holden's girlfriend. Originally made for television and cut down from a four-part, 200-minute presentation. Not rated. 103m. **DIR:** Robert Butler. **CAST:** William Holden, Lee Remick, Joe Santos, Sam Elliott, David Moody, Jamie Farr. **1973**

BLUE KNIGHT, THE (1975) ★★ This is the second made-for-TV production based on Joseph Wambaugh's bestselling book. In this rendering, George Kennedy assumes the role of tough L.A. cop Bumper Morgan, who is searching frantically for a cop killer. The story is average, but Kennedy gives a typically strong portrayal. 78m. **DIR:** J. Lee Thompson. **CAST:** George Kennedy, Alex Rocco, Verna Bloom, Glynn Turman. **1975**

BLUE LAGOON, THE ★★1/2 Two things save *The Blue Lagoon* from being a complete waste: Nestor Almendros's beautiful cinematography and the hilarious dialogue. Unfortunately, the laughs are unintentional. The screenplay is a combination of *Swiss Family Robinson* and the story of Adam and Eve, focusing on the growing love and sexuality of two children stranded on a South Sea island. Rated R for nudity and suggested sex. 101m. **DIR:** Randal Kleiser. **CAST:** Brooke Shields, Christopher Atkins, Leo McKern, William Daniels. **1980 DVD**

BLUE LIGHT, THE ★★★1/2 After starring in a series of mountain films, a peculiarly German genre that served to celebrate nature, former dancer Leni Riefenstahl made her directorial debut with this, another in the series. The plot is little more than a folk tale about an artist who pursues a beautiful girl who is the only one who can reach the top of a local mountain. Beautifully filmed, with a rich command of film language. In German with English subtitles. B&W; 77m. **DIR:** Leni Riefenstahl. **CAST:** Leni Riefenstahl, Max Holzboer. **1932**

BLUE LIGHTING, THE ★★ Lightweight action movie starring Sam Elliott as a hired gun sent to Australia to retrieve a precious gem from IRA renegade Robert Culp. Culp knows Elliott's coming and sets a series of traps for him. A passable time waster. Rated PG. 95m. **DIR:** Lee Philips. **CAST:** Sam Elliott, Robert Culp, Rebecca Gilling. **1986**

BLUE MAX, THE ★★★ For those with a yen for excellent aerial-combat gymnastics, superb photography, and a fine Jerry Goldsmith music score, this is the film. The story line is quite a different matter. Seen from the eyes of Kaiser Wilhelm II, air aces, and their superior officers, the plot is very standard material. The cast is fine but somewhat restrained. See it for the marvelous dogfights. You can tolerate the story. 156m. **DIR:** John Guillermin. **CAST:** George Peppard, James Mason, Ursula Andress, Jeremy Kemp. **1966**

BLUE MONEY ★★★ Larry Gormley (Tim Curry) discovers a suitcase with half a million dollars in his cab. The money turns out to belong to the mob, and they want it back. Not a very original idea, but well written, acted, and directed, this comedy provides plenty of fast-moving fun. Made for British television. 82m. **DIR:** Colin Bucksey. **CAST:** Tim Curry, Debby Bishop, Billy Connolly, Frances Tomelty. **1984**

BLUE MONKEY ★★★ A small-city hospital becomes contaminated by a patient infected by an unknown insect that causes terminal gangrene as it gestates eggs. One of these insects becomes mutated and grows to huge proportions. A low-budget film, this movie sometimes has the charm, humor, and suspense of classics like *The Thing* and *Them*. Rated R for violence and language. 98m. **DIR:** William Fruet. **CAST:** Steve Railsback, Susan Anspach, Gwynyth Walsh, John Vernon, Joe Flaherty, Robin Duke. **1987**

BLUE MONTANA SKIES ★★★1/2 The fur flies when Gene Autry and Smiley "Frog" Burnette discover the murder of their partner, which leads them on the trail of Canadian border pelt smugglers. Unusual snow-country Western action. B&W; 54m. **DIR:** B. Reeves "Breezy" Eason. **CAST:** Gene Autry, Smiley Burnette, June Storey, Harry Woods, Dorothy Granger. **1939**

•**BLUE MOON** ★★★1/2 Sweet, romantic fantasy stars Ben Gazzara and Rita Moreno as a happily married couple of forty years who receive a magical opportunity to revisit their past in order to put their present in order. Soon after Gazzara's Frank Cavallo retires, Maggie (Moreno) drags him off to their vacation home in the Catskills where, during a rare blue moon, they are awakened by a young couple who claim they have rented the cabin. Who the couple are and what they are doing there allow Frank and Maggie to take a long look at their life. Warm, sincere performances, and a thoughtful screenplay. Rated PG-13 for language. 89m. **DIR:** John Gallagher. **CAST:** Ben Gazzara, Rita Moreno, Alanna Ubach, Brian Vincent. **2000 DVD**

BLUE MURDER AT ST. TRINIAN'S ★★★1/2 A cast of comedy veterans puts new life into a routine plot in this delightful romp. St. Trinian's is an all-girl school where the teenage students do mischief from morning to night. They have a field day when they find their new headmistress is a diamond smuggler. B&W; 87m. **DIR:** Frank Launder. **CAST:** Alastair Sim, Terry-Thomas, Lionel Jeffries, Joyce Grenfell, George Cole, Ferdinand Mayne, Eric Barker. **1955**

BLUE RIVER ★★★ Sam Elliott is the angry but highly principled man whose repressive authority is challenged by even angrier teen Jerry O'Connell. O'Connell is quite convincing as the brilliant but troubled teen in this intimate and above-average look at the emotional glue holding a family together. Rated PG-13 for violence. 90m. **DIR:** Larry Elikann. **CAST:** Jerry O'Connell, Susan Dey, Sam Elliott, Nick Stahl, Neal McDonough, Jean Marie Barnwell, Patrick Renna. **1995 DVD**

BLUE SKIES ★★★1/2 Bing Crosby and Fred Astaire are a couple of song-and-dance men whose friendship is threatened when both fall for chorine Joan Caulfield. Plus thirty wonderful Irving Berlin songs. The newly introduced "You Keep Coming Back Like a Song" was Oscar nominated. B&W; 104m. **DIR:** Stuart Heisler. **CAST:** Bing Crosby, Fred Astaire, Joan Caulfield, Billy De-Wolfe, Olga San Juan. **1946**

BLUE SKIES AGAIN ★★ A sure-fielding, solid-hitting prospect tries to break into the lineup of a minor league team. There's just one problem: The determined ball player is a female. Nothing more than a routine grounder. Rated PG. 96m. **DIR:** Richard Michaels. **CAST:** Harry Hamlin, Robyn Barto, Mimi Rogers, Kenneth McMillan, Dana Elcar. **1983**

BLUE SKY ★★★ Director Tony Richardson's last film before his AIDS-related death in 1991. This gutsy unforgettable film is about the pain and power of love as well as the questionable atomic-testing policies of our government during the early 1960s. A military nuclear engineer who witnesses a Nevada test-site cover-up also faces domestic problems when the scandalous behavior of his emotionally shredded wife threatens to end both their marriage and his career. Rated PG-13 for language and suggested sex. 101m. **DIR:** Tony Richardson. **CAST:** Jessica Lange, Tommy Lee Jones, Amy Locane, Powers Boothe, Anna Klemp, Chris O'Donnell. **1994 DVD**

BLUE STEEL (1934) ★★★ Fun but undistinguished B Western with a very young John Wayne as a cowpoke who saves a town from extinction when he reveals there's gold in them thar hills. B&W; 60m. **DIR:** Robert N. Bradbury. **CAST:** John Wayne, Eleanor Hunt, George "Gabby" Hayes, Ed Peil, Yakima Canutt, George Cleveland. **1934**

BLUE STEEL (1990) ★★ Female rookie cop gets involved with a Wall Street broker who turns out to be a serial killer in this lurid, visually stunning thriller. The film's high-gloss photography, however, doesn't fully compensate for the often ridiculous story line. Rated R. 102m. **DIR:** Kathryn Bigelow. **CAST:** Jamie Lee Curtis, Ron Silver, Clancy Brown, Elizabeth Peña, Louise Fletcher. **1990**

BLUE STREAK ★★ After two years behind bars, the mastermind of a bungled Los Angeles jewel heist returns to the scene of his crime to retrieve a $17 million diamond that he hid in an air duct. The building has been converted into a police station so he impersonates a cop to gain access to a secured upper floor. He is mistaken for a new department transferee, assigned a partner, and gets involved in dull misadventures, shoot-outs, and chases in this progressively noisy and dumb action-comedy. Rated R for language and violence. 93m. **DIR:** Les Mayfield. **CAST:** Martin Lawrence, Luke Wilson, Peter Greene, William Forsythe. **1999 DVD**

BLUE SUNSHINE ★★1/2 Oddball mystery-thriller dealing with a series of random killings. Low-budget film is both ridiculous and terrifying at the same time. Rated PG for mild language and violence. 97m. **DIR:** Jeff Lieberman. **CAST:** Zalman King, Deborah Winters, Mark Goddard, Robert Walden, Charles Siebert. **1976**

BLUE THUNDER ★★★★1/2 A state-of-the-art helicopter is the centerpiece of this action-paced police melodrama. Piloted by Roy Scheider, the craft—a.k.a. "Blue Thunder"—battles a second rogue helicopter commanded by villain Malcolm McDowell high above the crowded streets of downtown Los Angeles. The result is a gripping and immensely entertaining—if somewhat implausible—adventure-thriller. Rated R for violence, nudity, and profanity. 109m. **DIR:** John Badham. **CAST:** Roy Scheider, Malcolm McDowell, Candy Clark, Warren Oates. **1983 DVD**

BLUE TIGER ★★★ Vengeance clashes with Japanese mysticism in this thoughtful thriller that begins as single mother Virginia Madsen helplessly watches her young son die in gunfire between warring crime factions (a *very* grim scene). She adopts a most unusual ploy to locate the killer, and soon gets more than she anticipated. Madsen brings intelligence and credibility to what might otherwise have been a ho-hum revenge saga. Rated R for violence, profanity, and simulated sex. 88m. **DIR:** Norberto Barba. **CAST:** Virginia Madsen, Toru Nakamura, Dean Hallo, Ryo Ishibashi, Harry Dean Stanton. **1994 DVD**

BLUE TORNADO ★★ Starts out wanting to be *Top Gun* and ends trying to be *E.T.—The Extra-Terrestrial*. It fails on both levels. Some impressive aerial shots save the film. Rated PG-13. 96m. **DIR:** Tony Dobb. **CAST:** Dirk Benedict, Ted McGinley, Patsy Kensit. **1990**

BLUE VELVET ★★★★1/2 In this brilliant but disturbing film, Kyle MacLachlan and Laura Dern play youngsters who become involved in the mystery surrounding nightclub singer Isabella Rossellini. It seldom lets the viewer off easy, yet it is nevertheless a stunning cinematic work. Rated R for violence, nudity, and profanity. 120m. **DIR:** David Lynch. **CAST:** Kyle MacLachlan, Isabella Rossellini, Dennis Hopper, Laura Dern, Dean Stockwell. **1986 DVD**

BLUE YONDER, THE ★★★1/2 Heartfelt tale of a boy (Huckleberry Fox) who goes back in time via a time machine to warn his late grandfather (Peter Coyote) of his unsuccessful attempt at a nonstop transatlantic flight. Good performances keep the creaky plot airborne. 89m. **DIR:** Mark Rosman. **CAST:** Peter Coyote, Huckleberry Fox, Art Carney, Dennis Lipscomb, Joe Flood, Mittie Smith, Frank Simons. **1985**

BLUEBEARD (1944) ★★★ Atmospheric low-budget thriller by resourceful German director Edgar G. Ulmer gives great character actor John Carradine one of his finest leading roles as a strangler who preys on women. B&W; 73m. **DIR:** Edgar G. Ulmer. **CAST:** John Carradine, Jean Parker, Nils Asther, Ludwig Stossel, Iris Adrian. **1944 DVD**

BLUEBEARD (1963) ★★★1/2 Claude Chabrol, justifiably known as the Gallic Hitchcock, tells the story of the Frenchman who married and murdered eleven women in order to support his real family. Chabrol approaches the material in the same manner that Chaplin did in *Monsieur Verdoux*—as a satirical parable of capitalism. Not for all tastes, obviously, but well worth a look. Screenplay by Françoise Sagan. Original title *Landru*. Dubbed in English. 114m. **DIR:** Claude Chabrol. **CAST:** Charles Denner, Michèle Morgan, Danielle Darrieux, Hildegarde Neff. **1963**

BLUEBEARD (1972) ★★1/2 Richard Burton stars in this film, which has its tongue planted firmly in cheek. The legend of the multiple murderer is intermingled with Nazi lore to come out as a reasonably convincing foray into a combination of black comedy and classic horror films. Rated R. 125m. **DIR:** Edward Dmytryk. **CAST:** Richard Burton, Raquel Welch, Karin Schubert, Joey Heatherton. **1972 DVD**

BLUEBEARD'S EIGHTH WIFE ★★1/2 The first script written by Charles Brackett and Billy Wilder together, this sophisticated comedy is guilty of trying too hard. The slight story is about a seven-times-divorced millionaire who thinks he knows all about women. But he's buffaloed when he meets a nobleman's daughter. The personalities are stronger than the plot. B&W; 80m. **DIR:** Ernst Lubitsch. **CAST:** Gary Cooper, Claudette Colbert, David Niven, Edward Everett Horton, Tyler Brooke, Elizabeth Patterson, Herman Bing. **1938**

BLUEBERRY HILL ★★ Carrie Snodgress plays a neurotic mother in 1956. Her daughter finds out the truth about her deceased father and also discovers, that she has inherited his piano skills. Zzzzz. Rated R for nudity and language. 93m. **DIR:** Strathford Hamilton. **CAST:** Carrie Snodgress, Margaret Avery, Matt Lattanzi. **1987**

BLUES BROTHERS, THE ★★★1/2 Director John Landis attempted to film an epic comedy and came pretty darn close. In it, the musicians of the title, John Belushi and Dan Aykroyd, attempt to save an orphanage. The movie's excesses—too many car crashes and chases—are offset by Belushi and Aykroyd as the Laurel and Hardy of backbeat; the musical turns of Aretha Franklin, James Brown, and Ray Charles; and Landis's flair for comic timing. Rated R. 132m. **DIR:** John Landis. **CAST:** John Belushi, Dan Aykroyd, John Candy, Carrie Fisher. **1980 DVD**

BLUES BROTHERS 2000 ★★★1/2 In this follow-up to the 1980 comedy, the accent this time is on the music. Featuring a mind-boggling assemblage of blues and R&B greats, it serves not only as homage to the late Junior Wells but also as an ear-pleasing celebration of one of America's few original art forms. From Aretha Franklin's reprise of her classic "Respect" to an eye-popping all-star finale jam featuring practically every notable performer in the blues and R&B fields, it's a real treat for fans of the music. Rated PG-13 for profanity and partial nudity. 123m. **DIR:** John Landis. **CAST:** Dan Aykroyd, John Goodman, Joe Morton, Nia Peeples, Kathleen Freeman, Frank Oz, Steve Lawrence. **1998 DVD**

BLUME IN LOVE ★★★★ Sort of the male version of *An Unmarried Woman*, this Paul Mazursky film is the heartrending, sometimes shocking tale of a lawyer (George Segal) who can't believe his wife (Susan Anspach) doesn't love him anymore. He tries everything to win her back (including rape), and the result is a drama the viewer won't soon forget. Superb performances by Segal, Anspach, and Kris Kristofferson (as the wife's new beau) help immensely. Rated R for suggested sex, profanity, and violence. 117m. **DIR:** Paul Mazursky. **CAST:** George Segal, Susan Anspach, Kris Kristofferson, Marsha Mason, Shelley Winters. **1973**

BMX BANDITS ★★★ An exciting story of young Australian kids and their BMX bikes. Features great stunts, funny East End of London villains, and a satisfying ending. Not Rated. 92m. **DIR:** Brian Trenchard-Smith. **CAST:** David Argue, John Ley, Nicole Kidman. **1983**

BOARDING SCHOOL ★★★1/2 A European boarding school for girls, located next to an all-boys' boarding school, creates the setting for sexual high jinks and young love in this sexy comedy. The 1956 theme is enhanced by some Bill Haley music. Rated R for nudity. 100m. **DIR:** André Farwagi. **CAST:** Nastassja Kinski, Gerry Sundquist, Kurt Raab. **1978 DVD**

BOAT IS FULL, THE ★★★ Markus Imhoof's film about refugees from the Nazis trying to obtain refuge in Switzerland is tragic and extraordinarily effective. It could have been a better movie, but it could hardly have been more heartbreaking. No MPAA rating. 100m. **DIR:** Markus Imhoof. **CAST:** Tina Engel, Marin Walz. **1983**

BOATNIKS, THE ★★1/2 Disney comedy in which Robert Morse plays a heroic Coast Guard officer who manages a romantic relationship with Stephanie Powers while pursuing bumbling thieves (Phil Silvers, Norman Fell, and Mickey Shaughnessy). Rated G. 99m. **DIR:** Norman Tokar. **CAST:** Stephanie Powers, Phil Silvers, Norman Fell, Robert Morse, Mickey Shaughnessy. **1970**

BOB & CAROL & TED & ALICE ★★★★1/2 In this comedy, Natalie Wood and Robert Culp (Carol and Bob) play a modern couple who believe in open marriage, pot smoking, etc. Their friends, conservative Elliott Gould and Dyan Cannon (Ted and Alice), are shocked by Bob and Carol's behavior. Meanwhile, Bob and Carol try to liven up Ted and Alice's marriage by introducing them to their way of life. Lots of funny moments. Rated R. 104m. **DIR:** Paul Mazursky. **CAST:** Natalie Wood, Robert Culp, Elliott Gould, Dyan Cannon. **1969**

BOB LE FLAMBEUR ★★★★★ This is an exquisite example of early French *film noir*. In it are all the trappings of the classic gangster movie. The most fascinating element of this import is the title character, Bob Montagne (Roger Duchesne), who plans to rob a casino of $800 million. In French with English subtitles. B&W; 102m. **DIR:** Jean-Pierre Melville. **CAST:** Roger Duchesne, Isabel Corey, Daniel Cauchy, Howard Vernon. **1955 DVD**

BOB ROBERTS ★★★★ The writing-directing debut of star Tim Robbins is a fake documentary about a folk-singing, millionaire crypto-fascist's campaign for a seat in the Senate. Robbins's occasionally pedantic but most often clever satire features numerous cameos and his own hilarious, hate-filled compositions. (Robbins, by the way, refused to release a soundtrack album—lest real right-wing politicians appropriate the songs for their own anthems.) Rated R for profanity and sexual themes. 105m. **DIR:** Tim Robbins. **CAST:** Tim Robbins, Alan Rickman, Giancarlo Esposito, Gore Vidal. **1992 DVD**

BOBBIE JO AND THE OUTLAW ★1/2 Lynda Carter, hungry for excitement, tags along with Marjoe Gortner and his gang. An orgy of murders and robberies ensues. Lots of violence, little credibility. Rated R for nudity, violence, and profanity. 89m. **DIR:** Mark L. Lester. **CAST:** Marjoe Gortner, Lynda Carter, Jesse Vint, Merrie Lynn Ross, Belinda Balaski, Gerrit Graham. **1976**

BOBBY DEERFIELD ★★★1/2 A racing driver (Al Pacino) becomes obsessed with the cause of how a competitor was seriously injured in an accident on the track. In a visit to the hospitalized driver, he meets a strange lady (Marthe Keller) and has an affair. Rated PG. 124m. **DIR:** Sydney Pollack. **CAST:** Al Pacino, Marthe Keller, Romolo Valli. **1977**

BOBO, THE 🦃 A bumbling matador (Peter Sellers) has to seduce a high-priced courtesan (Britt Ekland) in order to get employment as a singer. 105m. **DIR:** Robert Parrish. **CAST:** Peter Sellers, Britt Ekland, Rossano Brazzi. **1967**

BOCA ★★★ Dedicated journalist Rae Dawn Chong's quest—to prove that renegade Rio de Janeiro police officers are murdering street children—is mere window dressing for another of Zalman King's arty, erotic escapades. Our heroine is equally formidable in or out of her clothing. Ed Silverstein's story touches on political intrigue during Martin Sheen's brief appearances as a CIA spook. Rated R for rape, simulated sex, nudity, violence, and profanity. 91m. **DIR:** Zalman King. **CAST:** Rae Dawn Chong, Martin Kemp, Tarcisio Meira, Martin Sheen. **1994**

BOCCACCIO 70 ★★★★ As with its Renaissance namesake, this film tells stories—three of them, in fact, by three of Italy's greatest directors. Federico Fellini's entry, "The Temptation of Dr. Antonio," showcases Anita Ekberg. The second playlet, by Luchino Visconti, is "The Bet," which features Romy Schneider as a not-so-typical housewife. "The Raffle," by Vittorio De Sica, is reminiscent of a dirty joke told badly, and it tends to cheapen the panache of the first two. In Italian with English subtitles. 165m. **DIR:** Federico Fellini, Luchino Visconti, Vittorio De Sica. **CAST:** Anita Ekberg, Sophia Loren, Romy Schneider, Tomas Milian. **1962**

BODIES, REST & MOTION ★★1/2 Set in a Southwest desert city, this ponderous comedy-drama looks at the dreams and disillusionment of twentysomethings. Phoebe Cates, Bridget Fonda, and Eric Stoltz contribute a consistent charm. Rated R for adult situations and language. 93m. **DIR:** Michael Steinberg. **CAST:** Phoebe Cates, Bridget Fonda, Tim Roth, Eric Stoltz. **1993**

BODILY HARM ★★ A wife tries to clear her husband's name when he's sued for malpractice. Though his career has been ruined, her help is unappreciated. This dull-edged television movie does little justice to its

Hitchcockian pretensions. 100m. **DIR:** Thomas Wright. **CAST:** Joe Penny, Lisa Hartman, Kathleen Quinlan. **1992**

•**BODY, THE** ★★★ An Israeli archaeologist uncovers a stunning find: an ancient body that may be the remains of Jesus Christ. When a Jesuit priest arrives to investigate the possibility—and to confirm his own faith—the world around them explodes into chaos and danger. Exciting thriller is a nice balance of action and intrigue. Rated PG-13 for violence. 108m. **DIR:** Jonas McCord. **CAST:** Antonio Banderas, Olivia Williams, John Shrapnel, John Wood, Jason Flemyng. **2000 DVD**

BODY AND SOUL (1924) ★★1/2 Escaped convict assumes the role of a minister in a small town in the South, rapes the daughter of a loyal supporter, and steals her money. Downbeat story has a happy ending (it's all been a dream caused by a newspaper story). Paul Robeson in his first feature film is full of the devil as the brutish, drunken minister, and literally sets the congregation rolling in one of the liveliest church services on film. B&W; 79m. **DIR:** Oscar Micheaux. **CAST:** Paul Robeson, Marshall Rodgers, Lawrence Chenault, Lillian Johnson. **1924**

BODY AND SOUL (1947) ★★★★★ The best boxing film ever, this is an allegorical work that covers everything from the importance of personal honor to corruption in politics. It details the story of a fighter (John Garfield) who'll do anything to get to the top—and does, with tragic results. Great performances, gripping drama, and stark realism make this a must-see. B&W; 104m. **DIR:** Robert Rossen. **CAST:** John Garfield, Lilli Palmer, Hazel Brooks, Anne Revere, William Conrad. **1947 DVD**

BODY AND SOUL (1981) ★★★ Okay remake of the 1947 boxing classic. It's not original, deep, or profound, but entertaining. However, the original, with John Garfield, is better. Rated R for violence and profanity. 100m. **DIR:** George Bowers. **CAST:** Leon Isaac Kennedy, Jayne Kennedy, Perry Lang. **1981**

BODY ARMOR ★★★ Above-average made-for-video thriller pits hero-for-hire Ken Conway (Matt McColm) against evil Dr. Ramsey Krago (Ron Perlman), who develops deadly viruses just so he can sell the cures to the world's governments. Director Jack Gill was formerly a top stunt director and knows how to keep the bodies flying. Rated R for violence, sexual situations, nudity, and profanity. 95m. **DIR:** Jack Gill. **CAST:** Matt McColm, Annabel Schofield, Ron Perlman, Carol Alt, Morgan Brittany, Clint Howard, John Rhys-Davies. **1996 DVD**

BODY COUNT ★★★1/2 Tough, gripping crime-drama stars Forest Whitaker as the mastermind behind an art museum robbery. When an alarm is accidentally tripped, the police arrive and Whitaker is killed in the crossfire. His four accomplices manage to get away, but their trip is fraught with tension and further complicated when they pick up a stranded motorist. Good cast has fun being bad. Rated R for adult situations, language, and violence. 84m. **DIR:** Robert Patton-Spruill. **CAST:** David Caruso, Linda Fiorentino, John Leguizamo, Ving Rhames, Forest Whitaker, Donnie Wahlberg. **1997 DVD**

BODY COUNT (1997) (DIRECT TO VIDEO) ★★1/2 *Who's the Boss?* star Alyssa Milano continues her leap into adult roles in this formulaic thriller. As Milano and her rich boyfriend make out in his parents' basement, art thieves kill the parents upstairs. When the couple is discovered, they are forced to engage in a deadly game of cat and mouse. Some menacing moments give their direct-to-video effort an edge. Rated R for adult situations, language, and violence. 88m. **DIR:** Kurt Voss. **CAST:** Alyssa Milano, Justin Theroux, Ice T. **1997 DVD**

BODY DOUBLE ★★★1/2 This Brian De Palma thriller is often gruesome, disgusting, and exploitative. But you can't take your eyes off the screen. Craig Wasson is first-rate as a young actor who witnesses a brutal murder, and Melanie Griffith is often hilarious as the porno star who holds the key to the crime. Rated R for nudity, suggested sex, profanity, and violence. 110m. **DIR:** Brian De Palma. **CAST:** Craig Wasson, Melanie Griffith, Gregg Henry, Deborah Shelton. **1984 DVD**

BODY HEAT ★★★★1/2 This is a classic piece of *film noir*; full of suspense, characterization, atmosphere, and sexuality. Lawrence Kasdan makes his directorial debut with this topflight 1940s-style entertainment about a lustful romance between an attorney (William Hurt) and a married woman (Kathleen Turner) that leads to murder. Rated R because of nudity, sex, and murder. 113m. **DIR:** Lawrence Kasdan. **CAST:** William Hurt, Kathleen Turner, Richard Crenna, Mickey Rourke, Ted Danson. **1981 DVD**

BODY IN THE LIBRARY, THE ★★★1/2 Agatha Christie's Miss Marple (Joan Hickson) stays close to home in this mystery when she is summoned by a good friend with the misfortune to have found a body in her library at Gossington Hall, St. Mary Mead. Careful armchair sleuths will find this one solvable, but red herrings abound. Not rated; suitable for family viewing. 153m. **DIR:** Silvio Narizzano. **CAST:** Joan Hickson, Gwen Watford, Andrew Cruickshank, Moray Watson, Valentine Dyall. **1984**

BODY LANGUAGE (1992) ★★★ Heather Locklear doesn't quite fit the role of the first woman executive at a major corporation, but Linda Purl does a great job portraying the psychotic new secretary. Above-average made-for-cable thriller. 91m. **DIR:** Arthur Allan Seidelman. **CAST:** Heather Locklear, Linda Purl, Edward Albert. **1992**

BODY LANGUAGE (1995) ★★1/2 When, oh when, will movie attorneys stop thinking with their glands? Tom Berenger is wholly unbelievable as a supposedly intelligent lawyer who gets talked by sultry Heidi Schanz into killing her husband. Naturally, things aren't quite what they seem. Costar Nancy Travis, as Berenger's perceptive partner, is much better than the rest; she makes the film watchable. Rated R for nudity, simulated sex, profanity, and violence. 100m. **DIR:** George Case. **CAST:** Tom Berenger, Nancy Travis, Robert Patrick, Eddie Jones, Dana Gladstone, Heidi Schanz. **1995**

BODY MOVES 🦃 This dance flick is about as formulaic as you can get. Two dance troupes suffer through infighting on their way to a final showdown in the local dance contest. Rated PG-13 for profanity. 98m. **DIR:** Gerry Lively. **CAST:** Kirk Rivera. **1990**

BODY OF EVIDENCE ★★1/2 Madonna's slut-in-distress is reasonably credible in Brad Mirman's flimsy erotic thriller, which finds our heroine (?) accused of murdering her elderly lover with a most unusual weapon: herself. Rated R for profanity and nudity. 99m.

DIR: Uli Edel. **CAST:** Madonna, Willem Dafoe, Joe Mantegna, Anne Archer, Jurgen Prochnow. **1993**

BODY OF INFLUENCE 🦃 A Beverly Hills psychiatrist falls in love with one of his sexy patients, who then tries to murder him. Rated R for simulated sex, nudity, profanity, and violence. 96m. **DIR:** Alexander Gregory Hippolyte. **CAST:** Nick Cassavetes, Shannon Whirry, Sandahl Bergman, Don Swayze, Richard Roundtree. **1993**

BODY OF INFLUENCE 2 ★★ There's plenty of flesh on display in this familiar tale of a psychologist who falls for a new patient with some dark secrets in her past. R-rated and unrated versions; both contain nudity, adult situations, and profanity. 88/94. **DIR:** Brian J. Smith. **CAST:** Jodie Fisher, Daniel Anderson. **1996 DVD**

BODY PARTS ★★ Maurice Renard's classic short story, "The Hands of Orlac," gets hauled out one more time for this ludicrous update from gore-hound Eric Red. Criminal psychologist Jeff Fahey loses his right arm and then receives another—from a serial killer—thanks to the miracles of modern science. Rated R for profanity and outrageous gruesomeness. 88m. **DIR:** Eric Red. **CAST:** Jeff Fahey, Kim Delaney, Brad Dourif, Lindsay Duncan. **1991**

BODY PUZZLE ★★ Pretty ho-hum. A serial killer collects pieces of his victims and puts them together like a puzzle. Joanna Pacula may be next on the list, or the inspiration behind the gruesome crimes. Rated R for violence, nudity, and language. 90m. **DIR:** Larry Louis. **CAST:** Joanna Pacula, Tom Aaron, Frank Quinn. **1993 DVD**

BODY ROCK 🦃 A youngster from the South Bronx sees break dancing as his ticket to the big time. Rated PG-13. 93m. **DIR:** Marcelo Epstein. **CAST:** Lorenzo Lamas, Vicki Frederick, Cameron Dye, Ray Sharkey. **1984**

BODY SHOT ★★ Underexposed thriller finds obsessed paparazzo Robert Patrick accused of murdering a reclusive rock star he previously harassed. Halfhearted attempt at *film noir*. Rated R for nudity, language, and violence. 98m. **DIR:** Dimitri Logothetis. **CAST:** Robert Patrick, Michelle Johnson, Ray Wise. **1993 DVD**

BODY SHOTS ★★ Four males and four females meet at a Los Angeles nightclub with sex predominant on the agenda. This lurid, cautionary tale then dissects date rape in *Rashomon*-like fashion while the real cancer of the film—alcoholism—feels like an afterthought. Characters talk into the camera about libido and meaningful human contact but seem more hung up on their own self-importance. Rated R for language, violence, and sexual content. 102m. **DIR:** Michael Cristofer. **CAST:** Sean Patrick Flanery, Jerry O'Connell, Tara Reid, Amanda Peet, Ron Livingston, Emily Procter, Brad Rowe, Sybil Temchen. **1999 DVD**

BODY SLAM ★★ A down-and-out rock 'n' roll promotional manager signs up a couple of renegade professional wrestlers to go on a barnstorming tour. Although this film is silly, it has a lot of heart. Rated PG for mild violence. 92m. **DIR:** Hal Needham. **CAST:** Dirk Benedict, Tanya Roberts, Roddy Piper, Lou Albano, Barry Gordon. **1987**

BODY SNATCHER, THE ★★★★ Boris Karloff gives one of his finest performances in the title role of this Val Lewton production, adapted from the novel by Robert Louis Stevenson. Karloff is a sinister grave robber who provides dead bodies for illegal medical research and then uses his activities as blackmail to form a bond of "friendship" with the doctor he services, Henry Daniell (in an equally impressive turn). B&W; 77m. **DIR:** Robert Wise. **CAST:** Henry Daniell, Boris Karloff, Bela Lugosi. **1945**

BODY SNATCHERS, THE ★★★1/2 Third screen version of Jack Finney's science-fiction tale is distinctive in its own way, although we still prefer Don Siegel's 1956 version. This time the invasion takes place on a military base, with director Abel Ferrara's stark storytelling enhanced by the atmospheric cinematography of Bojan Bazelli. Rated R for violence, nudity, and profanity. 87m. **DIR:** Abel Ferrara. **CAST:** Gabrielle Anwar, Terry Kinney, Meg Tilly, Forest Whitaker, Christine Elise, R. Lee Ermey, Reilly Murphy. **1993 DVD**

BODY STROKES (SIREN'S CALL) ★★ Well, dip me in turpentine! Here's a flesh feast that doesn't involve cops turned strippers, or sex radio-talk-show hosts involved with psychos. This one's about an artist who turns to two women for inspiration—and what inspiration they provide. Not rated; contains nudity, adult situations, and language. 99m. **DIR:** Edward Holzman. **CAST:** Dixie Beck, Kristen Knittle, Catherine Weber, Bobby Johnston. **1995 DVD**

BODYGUARD, THE ★★★ Lawrence Kasdan originally wrote *The Bodyguard* in 1972 with Steve McQueen in mind, and Kevin Costner attempts a homage to the charismatic action star as the protector to singer-actress Whitney Houston. The result proved extremely popular with filmgoers, so who are we to argue? While Houston is just fine in her big-screen debut, Costner's impersonation of McQueen seems cold rather than cool. So, if you're so inclined, enjoy. Rated R for profanity, suggested sex, and violence. 129m. **DIR:** Mick Jackson. **CAST:** Kevin Costner, Whitney Houston, Gary Kemp, Bill Cobbs, Ralph Waite. **1992 DVD**

BOEING, BOEING ★★★ An obviously bored Jerry Lewis plays straight man to Tony Curtis's oversexed American news hound, who keeps a Parisian apartment for dalliances with stewardesses. Although it tries for the manic intensity of a 1940s screwball comedy, this mildly amusing sex farce never rises above kitsch . . . and is rather dated. 102m. **DIR:** John Rich. **CAST:** Jerry Lewis, Tony Curtis, Dany Saval, Thelma Ritter. **1965**

BOG 🦃 Unlucky group of people on an excursion into the wilderness run into the recently defrosted monster Bog. Rated PG. 87m. **DIR:** Don Keeslar. **CAST:** Gloria De Haven, Aldo Ray, Marshall Thompson. **1983**

BOGGY CREEK II ★★ Pseudo-documentary schlockmaster Charles B. Pierce is at it again in this basic retelling of the search for a legendary swamp monster in southern Alabama. Cut-rate production values abound. Rated PG. 93m. **DIR:** Charles B. Pierce. **CAST:** Cindy Butler, Chuck Pierce. **1983**

BOGIE ★★1/2 Boring biography of Humphrey Bogart unconvincingly enacted by Bogie and Bacall look-alikes. Too much time is spent on the drinking and temper problems of Bogie's third wife, Mayo Methot, and not enough time is spent on Lauren Bacall. Kathryn Harrold as Bacall is so bad, however, that it's probably a blessing her part is small. 100m. **DIR:** Vincent Sherman. **CAST:** Kevin O'Connor, Kathryn Harrold, Ann Wedgeworth, Patricia Barry. **1980**

BOGUS ★★★ Young Haley Joel Osment delivers a surprisingly even performance as a lonely orphan forced to live with a stressed-out, career-minded Whoopi Goldberg. His imaginary friend (Gérard Depardieu) helps him deal with the recent upheaval in his young life. Remarkably, Osment is never overshadowed by the two big-name stars. Humor and tenderness play equal parts in this pleasant diversion. Rated PG. 112m. **DIR:** Norman Jewison. **CAST:** Whoopi Goldberg, Gérard Depardieu, Haley Joel Osment, Nancy Travis. **1996**

•**BOGUS WITCH PROJECT, THE** 🦃 Hosted by Pauly Shore, this collection of bad parodies of *The Blair Witch Project* spoofs the same scenes, the same dialogue, the same camera work, etc. Truly despicable. Rated R for language. 85m. **DIR:** Various. **CAST:** Pauly Shore. **2000 DVD**

BOHEMIAN GIRL, THE ★★★ Laurel and Hardy portray gypsies in this typical tale of the gypsy band versus the country officials. A variety of misadventures occur, and the film is entertaining, especially with the hilarious scene of Stan attempting to fill wine bottles and becoming more and more inebriated. B&W; 70m. **DIR:** James W. Horne, Charles R. Rogers. **CAST:** Stan Laurel, Oliver Hardy, Thelma Todd, Antonio Moreno. **1936**

BOILER ROOM ★★★ Promises of million-dollar incomes lure twentysomething males into a Long Island company that pushes junk stocks through high-pressure phone sales in this modern morality play. The film is fleshed out with an office romance and a tense father-son relationship in which a judge's son takes a job in the "chop shop" brokerage firm. Rated R for language and violence. 92m. **DIR:** Ben Younger. **CAST:** Giovanni Ribisi, Tom Everett Scott, Ben Affleck, Ron Rifkin, Nia Long. **2000 DVD**

BOILING POINT (1990) ★★★★ Riveting tale of revenge from director Takeshi Kitano, who mixes breakneck action with meaningful character development to create an exciting montage of violence and humanity. Takeshi also stars as a former Japanese gangster who teams up with a gas station attendant to take on the local *yakuza*. In Japanese with English subtitles. Not rated; contains adult situations and language. 98m. **DIR:** Takeshi Kitano. **CAST:** Masahiko Ono, Yuriko Ishida, Takahito Igughi, Takeshi Kitano. **1990 DVD**

BOILING POINT (1993) ★★★ Cop Wesley Snipes attempts to snare the crook (Dennis Hopper) who masterminded the drug-rip-off-related killing of another officer. Action buffs will be pleased by the high-octane storytelling style of filmmaker James B. Harris, who relies a bit too much on contrivance. Rated R for profanity, violence, and suggested sex. 92m. **DIR:** James B. Harris. **CAST:** Wesley Snipes, Dennis Hopper, Lolita Davidovich, Dan Hedaya, Viggo Mortensen, Seymour Cassel, Jonathan Banks, Christine Elise, Tony Lo Bianco, Valerie Perrine, James Tolkan. **1993 DVD**

•**BOJANGLES** ★★1/2 This made-for-cable original gives us a slice in the life of Bill "Bojangles" Robinson, tap dancer extraordinaire. On stage, he projected a refined image of a black gentleman, but offstage his gambling and extramarital affairs eventually left him divorced and broke at his death. The dancing is good, with Gregory Hines doing a fantastic job mimicking Bojangles, but the rest of the story is light on conflict and plot. Not rated; contains profanity. 101m. **DIR:** Joseph Sargent. **CAST:** Gregory Hines, Peter Riegert, Kimberly Elise, Maria Ricossa, Savion Glover. **2001 DVD**

BOLD CABALLERO, THE ★★1/2 This little-known color film is the first sound Zorro movie and an early effort from Republic Studios, better known for their action-filled serials. Robert Livingston plays the masked avenger who sweeps tyranny out of his part of California, while clearing himself of a murder charge. 69m. **DIR:** Wells Root. **CAST:** Robert Livingston, Heather Angel, Sig Ruman, Robert Warwick, Charles Stevens, Slim Whitaker. **1936**

BOLDEST JOB IN THE WEST, THE ★★ A bloodless bank robbery leads to the slaughter of a small western town and one of the gang members escaping with all the loot. Is this a comedy, a parody, or a serious action film? Veteran Spanish character-actor Fernando Sancho saves this clichéd Western from the trash can. Rated PG for violence. 100m. **DIR:** Joseph Loman (Jose Antonio De La Loma). **CAST:** Mark Edwards, Fernando Sancho, Carmen Seville. **1969**

BOLERO (1982) ★★ Like American Alan Rudolph, French director Claude Lelouch is an obsessive romantic whose admirers (a small cult in this country) seem to appreciate his fervent style more than his plots. In this case, even though *Bolero* is almost three hours long, there's little plot to speak of. The film spans fifty years in the lives of a number of characters who live for music. To confuse matters, most of the cast plays multiple roles. You'll either be mesmerized or bored stiff. 173m. **DIR:** Claude Lelouch. **CAST:** James Caan, Geraldine Chaplin, Robert Hossein, Nicole Garcia, Daniel Olbrychski, Richard Bohringer. **1982**

BOLERO (1984) 🦃 American heiress in the 1920s trying to lose her virginity. 106m. **DIR:** John Derek. **CAST:** Bo Derek, George Kennedy, Andrea Occhipinti, Ana Obregon, Olivia D'Abo. **1984**

BOMBARDIER ★★★1/2 This is a solid action film dealing with the training of flyers during World War II. There is nothing new in the familiar formula of this film, but a good cast and fast pace make it enjoyable. B&W; 99m. **DIR:** Richard Wallace. **CAST:** Pat O'Brien, Randolph Scott, Eddie Albert, Robert Ryan, Anne Shirley, Barton MacLane. **1943**

BOMBAY TALKIE ★★ An early effort from the team of producer Ismail Merchant, writer Ruth Prawer Jhabvala, and director James Ivory. (They finally hit it big in 1986 with *A Room With a View*.) In this drama, a British novelist (Jennifer Kendal) travels to India in search of romance, which she finds in the person of an Indian movie star (Shashi Kapoor). Pretty dull; the most fascinating parts have to do with the Indian film industry. 112m. **DIR:** James Ivory. **CAST:** Shashi Kapoor, Jennifer Kendal, Zia Mohyeddin. **1970**

BOMBSHELL (1933) ★★★★ A fast-moving satire on Hollywood types that hasn't lost its bite or its hilarity. One reason is Jean Harlow, as she essentially plays herself in this story of a sex symbol who is used and abused. B&W; 97m. **DIR:** Victor Fleming. **CAST:** Jean Harlow, Lee Tracy, Pat O'Brien, Frank Morgan, Franchot Tone, Una Merkel, C. Aubrey Smith. **1933**

BOMBSHELL (1997) ★★1/2 Young scientist Henry Thomas tries to stop his superiors from releasing a cancer-killing drug that contains a flaw that could wipe out the world. His only allies are his assistant and fiancée, who combat corporate greed and the government to stop the release. Rated R for language and violence. 95m. **DIR:** Paul Wynne. **CAST:** Henry Thomas, Frank Whaley, Madchen Amick, Pamela Gidley, Brian James. **1997**

BON VOYAGE! ★★★1/2 One of Walt Disney's few adult-oriented comedies, this film combines elements of sophisticated comedy with dialogue and props from old-fashioned slapstick yarns. All the problems that could possibly befall this family on an overseas vacation are captured in pie-in-the-face detail. 130m. **DIR:** James Neilson. **CAST:** Fred MacMurray, Jane Wyman, Michael Callan, Tommy Kirk, Kevin Corcoran, Deborah Walley. **1962**

BON VOYAGE, CHARLIE BROWN ★★★ An animated film starring the "Peanuts" gang, this is well suited for viewing by the younger generation. It's basically a "Peanuts" guide to world travel. Rated G. 75m. **DIR:** Bill Melendez. **1980**

BONANZA (TV SERIES) ★★★ Western series tells the story of patriarch Ben Cartwright and his three sons, all from different mothers. Adam is suave and mature. Hoss is a big man with a bigger heart. Little Joe is earnest and hot-tempered. Together they make the Ponderosa the most prosperous ranch in the Comstock Lode country. The Cartwrights used their position, their money, their fists, and their guns to help those in distress. Volume I includes the pilot episode, "A Rose for Lotta," as well as "The Underdog," guest-starring Charles Bronson. Volume II features James Coburn in "The Dark Gate" and DeForest Kelley in "Honor of Cochise." 120m. **DIR:** Edward Ludwig, William F. Claxton, Robert Gordon, Don McDougall. **CAST:** Lorne Greene, Pernell Roberts, Dan Blocker, Michael Landon, Victor Sen Yung. **1959–1973 DVD**

BONE COLLECTOR, THE ★★★ Quadriplegic forensic expert with a death wish comes out of medical retirement to solve a series of abduction-murders. He enlists the aid of a female street cop to do his field work as his bedroom becomes a high-tech command post and he is fed clues to the crimes by the killer. This familiar but compelling cat-and-mouse thriller was adapted from Jeffery Deaver's 1997 novel. Rated R for grisly violence and language. 118m. **DIR:** Phillip Noyce. **CAST:** Denzel Washington, Angelina Jolie, Queen Latifah, Michael Rooker, Luis Guzman, Ed O'Neill. **1999 DVD**

BONE DADDY ★★1/2 Grisly made-for-cable thriller stars Rutger Hauer as a medical examiner turned best-selling novelist. Unfortunately, his book and success have upset a killer from his past, who begins a new killing spree based on the doctor's book. The prerequisite shocks (the killer likes to remove the bones from his victims while they are still alive) are not nearly enough back story to make much of this or the characters matter. Rated R for violence, language, and adult situations. 90m. **DIR:** Mario Azzopardi. **CAST:** Rutger Hauer, Barbara Williams, R. H. Thomson. **1998**

•BONES Four kids move into an abandoned building haunted by the remains of a murdered legendary hoodlum and turn it into a dance club in this unimaginative supernatural gorefest. Rated R for language, drug use, violence, gore, and sexuality. 92m. **DIR:** Ernest R. Dickerson. **CAST:** Snoop Dogg, Pam Grier, Michael T. Weiss, Khalil Kain, Bianca Lawson, Clifton Powell. **2001 DVD**

BONEYARD, THE ★★ An aging detective and lady psychic team up to solve some grisly goings-on at the local mortuary. Their investigation leads them to the city morgue, where three possessed corpses plague them. Bizarre. 98m. **DIR:** James Cummins. **CAST:** Ed Nelson, Norman Fell, Phyllis Diller. **1990**

BONFIRE OF THE VANITIES ★★ Tom Wolfe's novel has been shaped into a trivial, cartoon-style movie by director Brian De Palma. This savage comedy about the very rich bumping heads with the very poor in New York City boasts great photography by Vilmos Zsigmond, but the characters aren't very interesting, especially if you liked the book. Rated R for some nudity and violence. 126m. **DIR:** Brian De Palma. **CAST:** Bruce Willis, Tom Hanks, Melanie Griffith, Saul Rubinek, Morgan Freeman. **1990 DVD**

•BONGWATER ★★ A casual pot dealer finds his life turned on its ear when a charismatic waitress enters his life. So-called raucous comedy is only occasionally funny and more often unbearable because of its unlikable characters. Especially disappointing due to the stellar cast. Rated R for drug content, profanity, and sexuality/nudity. 96m. **DIR:** Richard Sears. **CAST:** Luke Wilson, Alicia Witt, Amy Locane, Brittany Murphy, Jack Black, Andy Dick, Jamie Kennedy, Scott Caan, Patricia Wettig. **1998 DVD**

BONJOUR TRISTESSE ★★★ Jean Seberg is a spoiled teenager who tries to ruin the affair between her widowed father (David Niven) and his mistress (Deborah Kerr) in this dated soap opera. Kerr gives a fine performance and Niven is just right as the suave playboy, but Otto Preminger failed again to make a star of Seberg. Not rated. 94m. **DIR:** Otto Preminger. **CAST:** Deborah Kerr, David Niven, Jean Seberg, Mylene Demongeot. **1958**

BONNIE AND CLYDE ★★★★★ This still fresh and innovative gangster film was one of the first to depict graphic violence, turning the genre inside out, combining comedy, bloodshed, pathos, and social commentary with fascinating results. 111m. **DIR:** Arthur Penn. **CAST:** Warren Beatty, Faye Dunaway, Gene Hackman, Estelle Parsons, Michael J. Pollard, Gene Wilder. **1967 DVD**

BONNIE PRINCE CHARLIE ★★★★ A rousing adventure about Scotland's fight to rid itself of English rule with David Niven in one of his few appearances as an adventurer. Not as flamboyant or as violent as recent films with the same theme, but rich in pageantry and spectacle as well as talk. B&W; 118m. **DIR:** Anthony Kimmins. **CAST:** David Niven, Finlay Currie, Margaret Leighton, Jack Hawkins. **1948**

BONNIE SCOTLAND ★★★ Stan Laurel and Oliver Hardy venture to Scotland so that Stan can reap a "major" inheritance—which turns out to be merely bagpipes and a snuffbox. By mistake, they join the army and are sent to India, where they help to quell a native uprising. The thin plot offers the boys an opportunity to play off each other's strengths: Ollie's reactions and Stan's fantasy world that keeps becoming reality. B&W; 80m. **DIR:** James W. Horne. **CAST:** Stan Laurel, Oliver Hardy, James Finlayson, June (Vlasek) Lang, William Janney. **1935**

BONNIE'S KIDS ★★1/2 Two amoral girls molested by their stepfather kill him and move in with their criminal uncle. Lots of action, but all rather pointless. Rated R for simulated sex, nudity, adult themes, and violence. 105m. **DIR:** Arthur Marks. **CAST:** Tiffany Bolling, Steve Sandor, Robin Mattson, Scott Brady. **1982**

BOOGENS, THE ★★★ Effective little chiller about miners discovering something nasty down in the darkness. The lighting and atmosphere create a feeling of dread, and creatures are wisely kept out of sight for the bulk of the film. Rated R for violence and nudity. 95m. **DIR:** James L. Conway. **CAST:** Rebecca Balding, Fred McCarren, Anne-Marie Martin. **1981**

BOOGEYMAN, THE ★★★1/2 Despite the lame title, this is an inventive, atmospheric fright flick about pieces of a broken mirror causing horrifying deaths. Good special effects add to the creepiness. Rated R for violence and gore. 86m. **DIR:** Ulli Lommel. **CAST:** Suzanna Love, Michael Love, John Carradine. **1980 DVD**

BOOGEYMAN 2, THE 🦃 Cheapo sequel. Rated R for violence and gore. 79m. **DIR:** Bruce Star. **CAST:** Suzanna Love, Shana Hall, Ulli Lommel. **1983**

BOOGIE BOY ★★ A recent prison parolee takes on one more job and in predictable fashion the deal goes sour. If we hadn't seen this one hundred times before, this might seem like a good idea for a film. As it stands, this plot has become a genre all its own and this film isn't one of the better entries. Rated R for language, violence, and excessive drug use. 98m. **DIR:** Craig Hamann. **CAST:** Mark Dacascos, Jaimz Woolvett, Emily Lloyd, Frederic Forrest, Traci Lords, Joan Jett. **1997 DVD**

BOOGIE NIGHTS ★★★1/2 Writer-director Paul Thomas Anderson's study of the adult film industry tries for a definitive analysis of the 1970s, as experienced by those working at a decidedly fringe occupation. But Anderson's players often are stronger than the words and actions he has given them. Mark Wahlberg is excellent as a young stud delighted with the opportunity to exploit his one natural gift who subsequently becomes intoxicated by success, drugs, and grandiose ambitions. Julianne Moore is equally fine as the "veteran actress" in this porn stable, and Burt Reynolds delivers his best work in years as the father-figure director-producer. Rated R for nudity, simulated sex, profanity, drug use, and violence. 152m. **DIR:** Paul Thomas Anderson. **CAST:** Mark Wahlberg, Julianne Moore, Burt Reynolds, Heather Graham, Don Cheadle, John C. Reilly, William H. Macy, Ricky Jay. **1997 DVD**

BOOK OF LOVE ★★ *Porky's*-like humor doesn't help the story of a new-kid-in-town who falls for the girlfriend of the guy who plays the front four on the high school football team. Familiar. Rated PG-13 for brief profanity and teenage high jinks. 85m. **DIR:** Robert Shaye. **CAST:** Chris Young, Keith Coogan, Michael McKean. **1991**

BOOK OF SHADOWS: BLAIR WITCH 2 ★★ The sequel to the freak hit of 1999 follows the misadventures of five tourists who search the woods for evidence showing that the first film was factual. Less inept than the original, this one raises the would-be franchise to the level of any other hackneyed slasher flick. Traces of amateurism remain, however, especially in Lanny Flaherty's crude performance as the local sheriff. Rated R for profanity, nudity, violence, and drug use. 90m. **DIR:** Joe Berlinger. **CAST:** Kim Director, Jeffrey Donovan, Erica Leerhsen, Tristene Skyler, Stephen Barker Turner, Lanny Flaherty. **2000 DVD**

BOOM IN THE MOON 🦃 Buster Keaton's worst film. It involves his being conned by villains into flying a rocket to the moon. 83m. **DIR:** Jaime Salvador. **CAST:** Buster Keaton. **1946**

BOOM TOWN ★★★★ Big-budget MGM star vehicle has buddies Clark Gable and Spencer Tracy striking it rich, going broke, and striking it rich again in the oil fields of the Southwest. Great fun. B&W; 116m. **DIR:** Jack Conway. **CAST:** Clark Gable, Spencer Tracy, Hedy Lamarr, Chill Wills, Frank Morgan, Lionel Atwill, Claudette Colbert. **1940**

BOOMERANG (1947) ★★★★ Still-riveting drama, based on a true story about a prosecuting attorney who believes the man he is supposed to try for the murder of a minister is innocent. A terrific cast, expertly directed by Elia Kazan. Not rated. B&W; 88m. **DIR:** Elia Kazan. **CAST:** Dana Andrews, Jane Wyatt, Lee J. Cobb, Sam Levene, Ed Begley Sr., Karl Malden. **1947**

BOOMERANG (1992) ★★1/2 Dapper advertising executive Eddie Murphy is a real ladies' man who likes to love 'em and lead 'em on—until his sexy, new boss Robin Givens gives him a taste of his own medicine. A few laughs (mostly supplied by Martin Lawrence) and a little bit of heart (courtesy of the gorgeous Halle Berry) help this predictable romantic comedy. Rated R for nudity and profanity. 118m. **DIR:** Reginald Hudlin. **CAST:** Eddie Murphy, Robin Givens, Halle Berry, David Alan Grier, Martin Lawrence, Grace Jones, Geoffrey Holder, Eartha Kitt. **1992**

BOOST, THE ★★ The controversy surrounding the off-screen, *Fatal Attraction*-style relationship between James Woods and Sean Young is certainly more interesting than the movie itself. Woods gives a typically high-powered performance in this uncomfortably intense drama as a Beverly Hills investment broker who begins to use cocaine and loses control. The story lacks coherence. Rated R for nudity, profanity and drug use. 96m. **DIR:** Harold Becker. **CAST:** James Woods, Sean Young, Steven Hill. **1989**

BOOT HILL ★★ Once again, Terence Hill and Bud Spencer are teamed in a spaghetti Western. This one pits them against bad guy Victor Buono. It's violent, bloody, and far from good. Rated PG. 87m. **DIR:** Giuseppe Colizzi. **CAST:** Terence Hill, Bud Spencer, Woody Strode, Lionel Stander, Victor Buono. **1969 DVD**

BOOTHILL BANDITS ★★★ Top-notch Range Busters Western, as they rout Wells Fargo bandits. Glenn Strange is a standout as a lumbering, moronic killer. B&W; 58m. **DIR:** S. Roy Luby. **CAST:** Ray "Crash" Corrigan, John King, Max Terhune, Glenn Strange, John Merton, Jean Brooks. **1942**

BOOTMEN ★★1/2 A young Australian steelworker with a talent for tap dancing decides to put on a show to benefit laid-off factory workers. The attempt to revive the let's-put-on-a-show musical has some working-class energy, but it suffers from disjointed editing and too many backstage and blue-collar clichés. Rated R for profanity and brief violence. 92m. **DIR:** Dein Perry. **CAST:** Adam Garcia, Sophie Lee, Sam Worthington, William Zappa. **2000**

BOOTS MALONE ★★1/2 Workmanlike Western, nothing special, but with a typically solid William Holden performance in the title role of a tough guy who trains a boy to be a jockey. B&W; 103m. **DIR:** William Dieterle. **CAST:** William Holden, Johnny Stewart, Ed Begley Sr., Harry Morgan, Whit Bissell. **1952**

BOOTY CALL ★★1/2 In this condom comedy, a young man who has been dating a woman for nearly two months without consummating their romance is way behind the power curve according to his street-wise buddy. The two lady hounds then double date in an evening interrupted by several late-night expeditions in search of "safe sex" protection. Rated R for nonstop sexual references, simulated sex, and language. 80m. **DIR:** Jeff Pollack. **CAST:** Tommy Davidson, Jamie Foxx, Tamala Jones, Vivica A. Fox. **1997 DVD**

BOPHA! ★★★1/2 Percy Mtwa's play, set during South Africa's final days under apartheid, concerns a dedicated black police officer (Danny Glover) increasingly doubtful of his servitude to white superiors. Matters come to a head with the arrival of a sadistic Special Branch liaison (Malcolm McDowell), but concluding events suggest a rather unpleasant moral: there is no atonement for past mistakes. It's a particularly unfortunate message, in light of the film's subject. Rated PG-13 for profanity, violence, and brief nudity. 120m. **DIR:** Morgan Freeman. **CAST:** Danny Glover, Malcolm McDowell, Alfre Woodard, Marius Weyers, Maynard Eziashi. **1994**

BORDER, THE ★★★1/2 Jack Nicholson is first-rate in this often effective drama about a border patrol officer who rebels against the corruption in his department and the rampant greed of his wife, Valerie Perrine. Rated R. 107m. **DIR:** Tony Richardson. **CAST:** Jack Nicholson, Harvey Keitel, Valerie Perrine, Warren Oates, Elpidia Carrillo, Bill McLaughlin. **1982**

BORDER HEAT 🦃 This action flick, set in Texas, has all the excitement of a siesta. Rated R for violence. 93m. **DIR:** Tony Gaudioz. **CAST:** Darlanne Fluegel, John Vernon. **1988**

BORDER PATROL ★★★ In this Hopalong Cassidy entry, Hoppy must put a stop to the criminal atrocities committed by the owner of a silver mine who is using Mexicans as virtual slaves. Robert Mitchum makes his film debut as one of the bad guys. Not the best of the series, but still good, with plenty of action. B&W; 66m. **DIR:** Lesley Selander. **CAST:** William Boyd, Andy Clyde, Russell Simpson, Duncan Renaldo, Robert Mitchum. **1943**

BORDER PHANTOM ★★1/2 Like all B Westerns, this looks pretty creaky today, but it's entertaining, thanks to Bob Steele's energetic performance and an intriguing premise, which involves mysterious murders and slavery. B&W; 59m. **DIR:** S. Roy Luby. **CAST:** Bob Steele, Harley Wood, Don Barclay, Karl Hackett. **1937**

BORDER RADIO 🦃 A disillusioned rock star steals a large sum of performance money owed to him by a sleazy club owner. Not rated; contains profanity and violence. B&W; 89m. **DIR:** Allison Anders, Dean Lent, Kurt Voss. **CAST:** Chris D., Luana Anders. **1988**

BORDER SHOOTOUT ★★★1/2 Fine actioner from an Elmore Leonard story features an honest farmer (Cody Glenn) who is suddenly appointed deputy in a corrupt town that is at the mercy of a spoiled, violent brat (Jeff Kaake). Glenn Ford portrays his usual tough-but-cool character as the sheriff out transporting a prisoner when all hell breaks loose back home. 110m. **DIR:** C. J. McIntyre. **CAST:** Cody Glenn, Glenn Ford, Jeff Kaake, Charlene Tilton, Michael Ansara. **1989**

BORDER STREET ★★★★ This hard-hitting Polish film is set in the ghettos into which Nazis forced Jews during the Third Reich and where many of them died for lack of food and medicine. There are a few lapses into low-grade melodrama, but mostly this is a gripping story that retains its power. 75m. **DIR:** Alexander Ford. **CAST:** M. Cwiklinska. **1950**

BORDER VIGILANTES ★★1/2 A rich silver strike pits the unscrupulous element against the honest miners and bankers in a frontier settlement, and Hopalong Cassidy and his cronies brazenly defy the crooks and start a small war. One of the most satisfying entries in the long-running series. B&W; 55m. **DIR:** Derwin Abrahams. **CAST:** William Boyd, Russell Hayden, Andy Clyde, Frances Gifford, Victor Jory, Ethel Wales, Morris Ankrum, Tom Tyler, Hank Worden. **1941**

BORDERLAND ★★★1/2 Hopalong Cassidy, an outlaw! Well, sort of. In this B oater, Hoppy must pretend to be a bad guy to save the day. The characterizations are strong. The script is literate, and Morris Ankrum is great as the main outlaw. Good fun for all. B&W; 82m. **DIR:** Nate Watt. **CAST:** William Boyd, James Ellison, George "Gabby" Hayes. **1937**

BORDERLINE ★★★1/2 Charles Bronson gives one of his better portrayals in this release, which got the jump on the similar *The Border*, with Jack Nicholson, by nearly two years. As in the later film, the central character—a border guard—becomes involved with the problems of an illegal alien and her child. The result is a watchable action film. Rated R. 105m. **DIR:** Jerrold Freedman. **CAST:** Charles Bronson, Bruno Kirby, Bert Remsen, Ed Harris, Wilford Brimley. **1980 DVD**

BORIS AND NATASHA ★★★ Reasonably amusing live-action rendition of animator Jay Ward's most famous no-goodniks, the cold war klutzes from Pottsylvania who bedeviled Rocky and Bullwinkle. Our "heroes" are sent to the United States . . . little knowing their beloved "Fearless Leader" has merely set them up as bait. Unbilled appearances are made by John Candy, John Travolta, and June Foray (Rocky's original cartoon voice). Originally shown on cable. 88m. **DIR:** Charles Martin Smith. **CAST:** Sally Kellerman, Dave Thomas, Paxton Whitehead, Andrea Martin, Alex Rocco, Anthony Newley. **1992**

B.O.R.N. ★★ *B.O.R.N.* (Body Organ Replacement Network) involves the same concept as *Coma*. The body organ black marketeers are at it again, only this time they're kidnapping healthy, unsuspecting people right off the street. Rated R for profanity, nudity, gore. 98m. **DIR:** Ross Hagen. **CAST:** Ross Hagen, Hoke Howell, P. J. Soles, William Smith. **1988**

BORN AGAIN 🦃 President Nixon's special counsel Charles Colson. Rated PG. 110m. **DIR:** Irving Rapper. **CAST:** Dean Jones, Anne Francis, Jay Robinson, Dana Andrews. **1978**

BORN AMERICAN 🦃 Three high school buddies cross the Russian border while on summer vacation in Lapland. Rated R for sex and violence. 103m. **DIR:** Renny

Harlin. **CAST:** Mike Norris, Steve Durham, David Coburn, Albert Salmi, Thalmus Rasulala. **1986 DVD**

BORN BAD ★★1/2 Six teens try to rob a bank but end up trapped inside with hostages and surrounded by police. It's no *Dog Day Afternoon*, but as a made-for-video thriller it's not bad. Rated R for profanity, violence, and brief nudity. 84m. **DIR:** Jeff Yonis. **CAST:** James Remar, Justin Walker, Corey Feldman. **1997 DVD**

BORN FREE ★★★★★ An established family classic, this is the tale of Elsa the lioness and her relationship with an African game warden and his wife. 96m. **DIR:** James Hill. **CAST:** Virginia McKenna, Bill Travers, Geoffrey Keen, Peter Lukoye. **1966**

BORN IN EAST L.A. ★★★1/2 Cheech, minus Chong, had a surprise box-office hit with this comedy, which started off as a video takeoff of Bruce Springsteen's "Born in the U.S.A." While not a comedy classic, this low-budget film has a number of funny moments. Rated R for profanity. 85m. **DIR:** Richard "Cheech" Marin. **CAST:** Richard "Cheech" Marin, Daniel Stern, Paul Rodriguez, Jan-Michael Vincent. **1987 DVD**

BORN INNOCENT ★★★ Rape with a broomstick marked this made-for-television film a shocker when first aired. The scene has been toned down, but the picture still penetrates with its searing story of cruelty in a juvenile detention home. Linda Blair does well as the runaway teenager. Joanna Miles is excellent as a compassionate teacher whose heart lies with her charges. It's strong stuff. 100m. **DIR:** Donald Wrye. **CAST:** Linda Blair, Kim Hunter, Joanna Miles. **1974**

BORN KILLER Teenagers on an outing cross paths with two vicious convicts who torture them and leave them for dead. They're the lucky ones: they don't have to sit through this mess. 90m. **DIR:** Kimberley Casey. **CAST:** Ted Prior, Ty Hardin. **1990**

BORN LOSERS ★★★ This biker exploitation movie is better than the celebrated *Billy Jack*, which also starred Tom Laughlin. Granted, we still have to sit through scenes with terrible amateur actors, but at least there is no girl singing off-key about her brother being dead. 112m. **DIR:** T. C. Frank. **CAST:** Tom Laughlin, Elizabeth James, Jeremy Slate, William Wellman Jr., Robert Tessier. **1967 DVD**

BORN OF FIRE ★★ A classical concert flutist (Peter Firth) journeys to the Middle East in hopes of finding the reason for his father's death. The flutist only becomes embroiled in the same drama that befell his father. A boring, confusing story. Contains sex, nudity, and violence. 84m. **DIR:** Jamil Dehlaui. **CAST:** Peter Firth, Suzan Crowley, Stefan Kalipha. **1987**

BORN ON THE FOURTH OF JULY ★★★1/2 Tom Cruise's superb performance is the reason to watch this overblown screen biography of Vietnam veteran and antiwar activist Ron Kovic. Characters suddenly appear and disappear. Despite all this, Kovic's tale is a powerful one, and Cruise's breakthrough performance makes it memorable. Rated R for profanity, nudity, simulated sex, and violence. 135m. **DIR:** Oliver Stone. **CAST:** Tom Cruise, Kyra Sedgwick, Willem Dafoe, Raymond J. Barry, Tom Berenger. **1989 DVD**

BORN TO BE BAD ★★★ Conniving opportunist Joan Fontaine scrambles for a secure foothold in life while stepping on anything or anyone in her way. Although more than a bit melodramatic, Nicholas Ray's adult look at sexual relationships was ahead of its time and still has impact today. B&W; 94m. **DIR:** Nicholas Ray. **CAST:** Joan Fontaine, Robert Ryan, Joan Leslie, Zachary Scott, Mel Ferrer. **1950**

BORN TO BE WILD Replace *Free Willy*'s orca with a man in a gorilla suit and you've got the idea. Rated PG for the boy's defiance. 98m. **DIR:** John Gray. **CAST:** Wil Horneff, Helen Shaver, John C. McGinley, Peter Boyle. **1995**

BORN TO DANCE ★★★ A curiosity piece because Jimmy Stewart croons "Easy to Love" without the help of a ghost singer on the soundtrack. The real star is Cole Porter, who wrote some of his most enduring melodies for the film. Eleanor Powell proves she has no peers when it comes to tap dancing. 105m. **DIR:** Roy Del Ruth. **CAST:** Eleanor Powell, James Stewart, Una Merkel, Buddy Ebsen, Virginia Bruce, Frances Langford, Reginald Gardiner. **1936**

BORN TO KILL ★★★1/2 Tough film about two bad apples whose star-crossed love brings them both nothing but grief is one of the best examples of American *film noir*. Lawrence Tierney's aggressive pursuit of his wife's sister (Claire Trevor) defies description. This hard-boiled crime melodrama is an early surprise from director Robert Wise. B&W; 97m. **DIR:** Robert Wise. **CAST:** Lawrence Tierney, Claire Trevor, Walter Slezak, Elisha Cook Jr., Audrey Long, Philip Terry. **1947**

BORN TO RIDE ★★★1/2 A smirking, rebellious, yet likable John Stamos stars as a 1930s motorcycle pioneer with this choice: a year behind bars or an army assignment training the cavalry for a motorcycle mission in Spain. Rated PG for violence and profanity. 90m. **DIR:** Graham Baker. **CAST:** John Stamos, John Stockwell, Teri Polo, Sandy McPeak. **1991**

BORN TO RUN ★★ Acceptable made-for-TV take on teen angst is a good showcase for star Richard Grieco but little else. He's a street racer who must put everything on the line when his brother gets involved with the mob. Pretty predictable. 97m. **DIR:** Albert Magnoli. **CAST:** Richard Grieco, Joe Cortese, Jay Acovone, Shelli Lether. **1993**

BORN TO WIN ★★★1/2 In one of his best performances, George Segal plays a New York junkie with a $100-a-day habit. Ivan Passer's direction is more inventive than successful, and the film often seems to be going in several directions. But the acting makes up, including a brief appearance by a young Robert De Niro. Also known as *Addict*. Rated R for profanity. 90m. **DIR:** Ivan Passer. **CAST:** George Segal, Karen Black, Hector Elizondo, Paula Prentiss, Jay Fletcher, Robert De Niro. **1971 DVD**

BORN WILD ★★★★ Spectacular scenery and wildlife footage enhance this wonderful tale of one man's efforts to save two leopard cubs, and a fledgling photographer's efforts to bring his story to the world. Real-life conservationist John Varty portrays himself, while Brooke Shields shines as the novice photographer who finds herself drawn to Varty's cause. Rated PG for some minor violence. 98m. **DIR:** Duncan McLachlan. **CAST:** Brooke Shields, John Varty, David Keith, Martin Sheen. **1995 DVD**

BORN YESTERDAY (1950) ★★★★1/2 Judy Holliday is simply delightful as a dizzy dame who isn't as dizzy as everyone thinks she is, in this comedy directed by George

Cukor. William Holden is the professor hired by a junk-dealer-made-good (Broderick Crawford) to give Holliday lessons in how to be "high-toned." The results are highly entertaining—and very funny. B&W; 103m. **DIR:** George Cukor. **CAST:** Judy Holliday, William Holden, Broderick Crawford, Howard St. John. **1950 DVD**

BORN YESTERDAY (1993) ★★★★ Updated remake of the classic 1950 George Cukor comedy works well because of the chemistry among stars Melanie Griffith, Don Johnson, and John Goodman. Married in real life, Griffith and Johnson send off almost visible sparks. Goodman adds a deceptive likability to a crooked wheeler-dealer. Rated PG for profanity. 100m. **DIR:** Luis Mandoki. **CAST:** Melanie Griffith, John Goodman, Don Johnson, Edward Herrmann, Max Perlich, Fred Dalton Thompson, Nora Dunn. **1993**

BORROWER, THE ★★ The director of *Henry: Portrait of a Serial Killer* brings us this gory tale of an alien killer sentenced to life without parole on planet Earth. Better-than-average effects help to ease us through the film's weak plot. Rated R for profanity and violence. 97m. **DIR:** John McNaughton. **CAST:** Rae Dawn Chong, Don Gordon, Antonio Fargas. **1991**

BORROWERS, THE (1993) ★★★ Quaint BBC miniseries sticks to Mary Norton's books, but lacks the visual flair necessary to suspend disbelief. The title characters are a little family who live under the floorboards of an English home and borrow items to make their living space more comfortable. When they're discovered, they flee outdoors where every step is a new adventure. The cast rises to the occasion, but poor special effects help expose the illusion. Not rated. 199m. **DIR:** John Henderson. **CAST:** Ian Holm, Penelope Wilton, Rebecca Callard, Sian Phillips. **1993**

BORROWERS, THE (1997) ★★★★ Inventively directed, imaginatively designed, and cleverly scripted, this sterling adaptation of Mary Norton's novels has excitement to spare. The Borrowers are Norton's fabricated explanation for misplaced socks and missing jewelry; the "culprits" are mouse-sized little people who "borrow" these items for their own purposes. It's great fun for all ages. Rated PG for comic violence. 83m. **DIR:** Peter Hewitt. **CAST:** John Goodman, Jim Broadbent, Mark Williams, Hugh Laurie, Bradley Pierce, Flora Newbigin, Tom Felton. **1997 DVD**

BORSALINO ★★★1/2 Style over substance—and when the result is *this* stylish, that's a major triumph. Jean-Paul Belmondo and Alain Delon are friendly rival gangsters in 1930s Marseilles. Everything is geared to make this an eye-filling, fast-paced romp. The only liability: English dubbing of the French dialogue. Rated PG. 125m. **DIR:** Jacques Deray. **CAST:** Jean-Paul Belmondo, Alain Delon, Michel Bouquet, Catherine Rouvel. **1970**

BOSOM BUDDIES (TV SERIES) ★★★ Before achieving Oscar-winning acclaim for his acting, Tom Hanks played a cross-dressing ad man in this predictable sitcom. Peter Scolari costars as the two take on a double life. By day, they're girl-crazy stud muffins; by night they're Hildegard and Buffy living in a women-only apartment building. Gags run a bit thin but the duo is likable enough to make viewers overlook its flaws. Four volumes, each containing two episodes and lasting approximately 50m. **DIR:** Joel Zwick, Chris Thompson, Don Van Atta. **CAST:** Tom Hanks, Peter Scolari, Wendie Jo Sperber, Donna Dixon, Holland Taylor, Telma Hopkins. **1980–1984**

BOSS ★★1/2 In the Old West, bounty hunter Fred Williamson and his sidekick D'Urville Martin ride into a town and set themselves up as the law. It's part of their plan to capture a bad guy with a hefty price on his head. Familiar but entertaining oater. Original title: *Boss Nigger*. Not rated. 87m. **DIR:** Jack Arnold. **CAST:** Fred Williamson, D'Urville Martin, R. G. Armstrong, William Smith, Barbara Leigh. **1975**

•BOSS OF BOSSES ★★★★ Based on the book by the two FBI agents who followed Gambino crime-family godfather Paul Castellano until his violent death, this film portrays Castellano as a thinker who wanted the Mafia to focus on legitimate enterprises. Chazz Palminteri brilliantly creates a man torn between the crime and violence he grew up with and his desire to become a respectable businessman. Riveting. Not rated; contains violence and language. 92m. **DIR:** Dwight H. Little. **CAST:** Chazz Palminteri, Richard Foronjy, Dayton Callie, Mark Margolis. **2001 DVD**

BOSS' SON, THE ★★★ Enjoyable drama about a young man's passage to adulthood. Our hero jumps at the chance to run the family factory. But when Dad decides his son must earn his way to the top, the boy learns what it truly means to earn a living. A little slow but rewarding. Not rated. 102m. **DIR:** Bobby Roth. **CAST:** Asher Brauner, Rita Moreno, Rudy Solari, Henry G. Sanders, James Darren, Piper Laurie. **1978**

BOSS' WIFE, THE ★★★1/2 After the first twenty minutes, this comedy starts rolling. Daniel Stern and Melanie Mayron play Joel and Janet, a two-career couple trying to make time for a baby. When Joel's boss (Christopher Plummer) finally notices him, he expects Joel to spend the weekend at the company resort. Laughs abound when Joel is pursued by the boss's nymphomaniac wife (beautiful Arielle Dombasle). Rated R for nudity, obscenities and sexual situations. 83m. **DIR:** Ziggy Steinberg. **CAST:** Daniel Stern, Christopher Plummer, Arielle Dombasle, Fisher Stevens, Melanie Mayron, Martin Mull. **1986**

BOSSA NOVA ★★★1/2 Amy Irving plays a lonely American in Rio de Janeiro who teaches English to the locals. Her students include a lawyer with a crush on her, an arrogant soccer star, and a woman who is carrying on an Internet romance with (she thinks) a sexy New York artist. Although the romantic round-robin is plot heavy in the second half, the film is relaxed and charming overall, with a sunny atmosphere and an appealing cast. In English and Portuguese with subtitles where needed. Rated R for profanity and mild sexual scenes. 95m. **DIR:** Bruno Barreto. **CAST:** Amy Irving, Antonio Fagundes, Alexandre Borges, Debora Bloch, Drica Moraes, Stephen Tobolowsky. **1999 DVD**

BOSTON KICKOUT ★★1/2 One of the few films ever made with the word *kick* in the title that doesn't deal with kick boxing. John Simm rises above weak material as one of four high-school buddies who discovers reality after graduation. Simm sees the light at the end of the tunnel, and with the help of a special woman, he attempts to reach it. Rated R for adult situations, language, and violence. 107m. **DIR:** Paul Hills. **CAST:** John

Simm, Emer McCourt, Marc Warren, Andrew Lincoln. **1995 DVD**

BOSTON STRANGLER, THE ★★★ True account, told in semidocumentary style, of Beantown's notorious deranged murderer, plumber Albert De Salvo. Tony Curtis gives a first-class performance as the woman killer. 120m. **DIR:** Richard Fleischer. **CAST:** Tony Curtis, Henry Fonda, Mike Kellin, Murray Hamilton, Sally Kellerman, Hurd Hatfield, George Kennedy, Jeff Corey. **1968**

BOSTONIANS, THE ★★★ A visually striking but dry production from Merchant Ivory Productions. Most of the sparks of conflict come not from the tortured love affair between Christopher Reeve and Madeleine Potter or the main theme of women's fight for equality, but from the few scenes of direct confrontation between Reeve and Vanessa Redgrave. The setting is Boston during the Centennial. 120m. **DIR:** James Ivory. **CAST:** Christopher Reeve, Vanessa Redgrave, Jessica Tandy, Madeleine Potter, Nancy Marchand, Wesley Addy, Linda Hunt, Nancy New, Jon Van Ness, Wallace Shawn. **1984 DVD**

BOTANY BAY ★★1/2 Alan Ladd stars as an unjustly accused criminal aboard a ship about to establish a penal colony in British-occupied Australia. He finds himself confronting a cruel captain (James Mason) and romancing a beautiful young actress (Patricia Medina). Atmospheric costume drama. 94m. **DIR:** John Farrow. **CAST:** Alan Ladd, James Mason, Patricia Medina. **1953**

BOTTLE ROCKET ★★★★ Fresh out of a mental institution, twentysomething Anthony joins a misfit mastermind and a rich wimp for a robbery. While on the lam the trio bungle their way into a big heist set up by a smooth-talking con man. Rated R for language, violence, suggested sex, and nudity. 98m. **DIR:** Wes Anderson. **CAST:** Luke Wilson, Owen Wilson, Robert Musgrave, Lumi Cavazos, James Caan. **1996 DVD**

BOUDU SAVED FROM DROWNING ★★★★★ This is the original *Down and Out in Beverly Hills*, except that the tramp (the beloved Michel Simon) is saved by an antiquarian bookseller after a suicide attempt in the Seine. Unlike the play on which it was based and unlike the Hollywood version—both of which have the bum accept his responsibilities— *Boudu* is a celebration of joyful anarchy. A masterpiece. In French with English subtitles. B&W; 88m. **DIR:** Jean Renoir. **CAST:** Michel Simon, Charles Granval, Max Dalban, Jean Dasté. **1932**

BOULEVARD ★★★ The dark side of Toronto's red-light district is brought to light in this gritty drama. Rae Dawn Chong is fine as a tough-as-nails hooker who takes in a young runaway and teaches her the ropes. They team up to bring down a vicious pimp, well played by Lou Diamond Phillips. Lance Henriksen costars as a vice cop with a mean streak. Rated R for violence, language, and nudity. 96m. **DIR:** Penelope Buitenhuis. **CAST:** Rae Dawn Chong, Lou Diamond Phillips, Lance Henriksen, Kari Wuhrer. **1994**

BOULEVARD NIGHTS ★★ Well-intentioned but dramatically dull account of a Chicano youth's desire to break out of East Los Angeles. Richard Yniguez is sincere in the lead role and Danny De La Paz is sympathetic as his brother, but the whole thing comes across like a preachy soap opera. Rated R for violence and profanity. 102m. **DIR:** Michael Pressman. **CAST:** Richard Yniguez, Marta DuBois, Danny De La Paz, Carmen Zapata, Victor Millan. **1979**

BOULEVARD OF BROKEN DREAMS ★★★1/2 A famous Hollywood screenwriter returns home to Australia to win back his wife and daughter. Good acting, a wonderful plot, interesting side plots, and superb supporting characters make this a very enjoyable film, except for several unnecessary musical interludes. Rated PG-13 for profanity and frontal nudity. 95m. **DIR:** Pino Amenta. **CAST:** John Waters, Penelope Stewart, Kim Gyngell, Nicki Paull, Andrew McFarlane, Kevin Miles. **1988**

BOUNCE ★★★★ This lean, low-key story about love, fate, commitment, guilt, and spin control is a terrific date movie. A hotshot Los Angeles ad agency partner gives his boarding pass to a writer stranded at O'Hare Airport. He later learns that the plane crashed with no survivors and seeks out the scribe's widow. Soulful performances, mushrooming compassion, and gemlike pockets of dialogue give credibility to the film's occasionally farfetched plot points. Rated PG-13 for language and sensuality. 102m. **DIR:** Don Roos. **CAST:** Gwyneth Paltrow, Ben Affleck, Tony Goldwyn, Natasha Henstridge, Johnny Galecki. **2000 DVD**

BOUND ★★★ Ex-con Gina Gershon falls in love with gangster's moll Jennifer Tilly, and the two concoct a risky scheme to steal $2 million from the mob. First-time writers-directors Larry and Andy Wachowski mimic the *Pulp Fiction* brand of outrageous excess, but there's no denying the raw talent on hand. This may be trash, but it's trash with style. Rated R for violence, torture, profanity, nudity, and simulated sex. 108m. **DIR:** Andy Wachowski, Larry Wachowski. **CAST:** Jennifer Tilly, Gina Gershon, Joe Pantoliano, John P. Ryan, Christopher Meloni, Richard Sarafian. **1996 DVD**

BOUND AND GAGGED: A LOVE STORY ★★1/2 Ginger Lynn Allen is kidnapped by her friends, Elizabeth Saltarrelli and Chris Denton, and taken on a wild ride through backwoods Minnesota, terrorizing locals and gangsters alike. Complications really set in when Saltarrelli declares her love for Allen. Fun road trip has some potholes, but steers the course. Rated R for language, adult situations, and violence. 96m. **DIR:** Daniel Appleby. **CAST:** Ginger Lynn Allen, Elizabeth Saltarrelli, Chris Mulkey, Karen Black, Chris Denton. **1993 DVD**

BOUND BY HONOR ★★★ Taylor Hackford's often exciting and emotional drama, portraying aspects of modern Chicano immigrant life through the stories of three young East Los Angeles men, in the late 1970s and 1980s. Unfortunately, at nearly three hours, the film seems at least 30 minutes too long. The film may also remind viewers of Edward James Olmos's superior *American Me*. Jesse Borrego is memorable as a Chicano artist who finds salvation with the paintbrush. Rated R, with strong violence and profanity. 172m. **DIR:** Taylor Hackford. **CAST:** Damian Chapa, Jesse Borrego, Benjamin Bratt. **1993**

BOUND FOR GLORY ★★★★ David Carradine had one of the best roles of his career as singer-composer Woody Guthrie. Film focuses on the depression years when Guthrie rode the rails across America. Director Hal Ashby explores the lives of those hit hardest during those times. Haskell Wexler won the Oscar for his beautiful cinematography. Rated PG. 147m. **DIR:** Hal Ashby. **CAST:** David Carradine, Ronny Cox, Melinda Dillon, Randy Quaid, Gail Strickland, Ji-Tu Cumbuka, John Lehne. **1976 DVD**

BOUNTY, THE ★★★★ Mel Gibson is Fletcher Christian, and Anthony Hopkins is Captain William Bligh in this, the fourth and most satisfying screen version of *The Mutiny on the Bounty*. This sweeping seafaring epic from the director of *Smash Palace* is the first movie to present the historic events accurately—and to do so fascinatingly. Rated PG for nudity and violence. 132m. **DIR:** Roger Donaldson. **CAST:** Mel Gibson, Anthony Hopkins, Laurence Olivier, Edward Fox, Daniel Day-Lewis, Liam Neeson. **1984 DVD**

BOUNTY HUNTER ★★ Star-director Robert Ginty plays a federal bounty hunter investigating the murder of an Indian buddy. This pits him against a corrupt sheriff (Bo Hopkins). Not rated, the film has violence and profanity. 91m. **DIR:** Robert Ginty. **CAST:** Robert Ginty, Bo Hopkins. **1989**

BOUNTY HUNTERS Michael Dudikoff and Lisa Howard play competing bounty hunters hot on the trail of a high-priced fugitive. Lots of car chases and flying bullets do little to make this pedestrian effort worth a look. Rated R for language, nudity, and violence. 98m. **DIR:** George Erschbamer. **CAST:** Michael Dudikoff, Lisa Howard, Benjamin Ratner. **1997 DVD**

BOUNTY MAN, THE ★★★1/2 Made-for-television Western is dark, complex, and quite good. Bounty hunter Clint Walker follows a murderer into a town but is set upon by a group of outlaws. Richard Basehart is particularly good as the outlaw leader. 73m. **DIR:** John Llewellyn Moxey. **CAST:** Clint Walker, Richard Basehart, Margot Kidder, John Ericson, Arthur Hunnicutt, Gene Evans. **1972**

BOUNTY TRACKER ★★1/2 A by-the-numbers kill-or-be-killed saga, with Lorenzo Lamas reasonably adept as a licensed bounty hunter who swears vengeance on the scum who killed his brother. Good for viewers with minimal expectations. Rated R for profanity and violence. 92m. **DIR:** Kurt Anderson. **CAST:** Lorenzo Lamas, Matthias Hues, Cyndi Pass, Paul Regina. **1993**

BOURNE IDENTITY, THE ★★★1/2 Robert Ludlum's white-knuckle bestseller makes a thrilling TV miniseries starring Richard Chamberlain as an amnesiac U.S. spy dodging assassins' bullets in Europe while trying to make sense of his situation. Jaclyn Smith complicates matters as the woman he kidnaps as protection and then falls in love with. Some slow moments, but it rallies toward the end when the truth finally begins to surface. Not rated. 185m. **DIR:** Roger Young. **CAST:** Richard Chamberlain, Jaclyn Smith, Anthony Quayle, Donald Moffat, Yorgo Voyagis, Denholm Elliott. **1988**

BOWERY AT MIDNIGHT *Very* cheaply made story about a maniac on a killing spree in the Bowery. B&W; 63m. **DIR:** Wallace Fox. **CAST:** Bela Lugosi, John Archer, Wanda McKay, Tom Neal. **1942 DVD**

BOWERY BOYS, THE (SERIES) ★★1/2 When William Wyler brought Sidney Kingsley's play, *Dead End*, to the big screen in 1937, he unknowingly created a phenomenon known over the years as The Dead End Kids, The Little Tough Guys, The East Side Kids and, finally, The Bowery Boys. While the Dead End Kids enlivened a number of terrific Warner Bros. gangster films, the Bowery Boys were the low-camp clowns of their day. Leo Gorcey and Huntz Hall led a group of (by then) middle-aged men playing teenagers hatching knuckleheaded schemes in a sweet shop run by Gorcey's father, Bernard, whom he cast, along with brother David, in the series after seizing creative control in 1946. When Bernard Gorcey died in 1956, Leo left the series, and seven films were made with Stanley Clements teaming up with Hall to lead the "boys" in their final and least interesting adventures. B&W; 60m. **DIR:** William Beaudine, Edward L. Bernds. **CAST:** Leo Gorcey, Huntz Hall, Bobby Jordan, William Benedict, David Gorcey, Gabriel Dell, Bernard Gorcey, Stanley Clements. **1946–1958**

BOWFINGER ★★★1/2 A poverty-row filmmaker (Steve Martin) is just about to give up his dream of big-screen success when he hits upon the idea of using clandestinely shot footage of a major movie star (Eddie Murphy) unknowingly interacting with his cast members. These include a delivery boy (Murphy) who is a dead ringer for the "star" and finds himself performing a number of death-defying stunts. There are some genuinely hilarious moments in this somewhat uneven movie written and directed by Martin, with Murphy terrific in his dual role and Heather Graham hilarious as a starlet who will do anything to get her big break. Perfect for a night of relaxed, at-home viewing. Rated PG-13 for profanity and suggested sex. 98m. **DIR:** Steve Martin. **CAST:** Steve Martin, Eddie Murphy, Heather Graham, Christine Baranski, Jamie Kennedy, Robert Downey Jr., Adam Alexi-Malle, Kohl Suddoth, Barry Newman, Terence Stamp. **1999 DVD**

BOX OF MOONLIGHT ★★★★ Smart, slightly surrealistic tale of an uptight engineer's encounter with a semipathetic free spirit. Both men learn from each other's imperfect approaches to life, and writer-director Tom DiCillo (*Living in Oblivion*) is too sympathetic to both characters to presume that one knows better than the other. Sumptuously filmed in the Tennessee countryside. Rated R for profanity, nudity, and violence. 111m. **DIR:** Tom DiCillo. **CAST:** John Turturro, Sam Rockwell, Catherine Keener, Lisa Blount. **1997 DVD**

BOXCAR BERTHA ★★1/2 Small-town girl (Barbara Hershey) hooks up with a gang of train robbers (led by David Carradine) in this *Bonnie and Clyde* coattailer. Martin Scorsese buffs will be disappointed. Rated R. 97m. **DIR:** Martin Scorsese. **CAST:** David Carradine, Barbara Hershey, Barry Primus, Bernie Casey, John Carradine. **1972 DVD**

BOXER, THE ★★★1/2 This introspective, lean drama is set amid the seesawing sectarian violence and peace negotiations of Belfast. Danny Boy Flynn is a promising pugilist who served a fourteen-year prison sentence for his ties with the IRA. He returns to his old neighborhood, reopens a gym for Catholic and Protestant youths, and rekindles his relationship with a former girlfriend. Rated R for language and violence. 107m. **DIR:** Jim Sheridan. **CAST:** Daniel Day-Lewis, Emily Watson, Brian Cox, Ken Stott, Gerard McSorley. **1997 DVD**

BOXING HELENA ★★ In this voyeuristic story of obsession, domination, and sexual inadequacy, a surgeon amputates the arms and legs of a bitchy temptress and imprisons her in his mansion. Writer-director Jennifer

Chambers Lynch shoots for the same hypererotic feel that mark the films of her father, David Lynch. Rated R for nudity, sex, and profanity. 105m. **DIR:** Jennifer Chambers Lynch. **CAST:** Julian Sands, Sherilyn Fenn, Bill Paxton, Kurtwood Smith, Art Garfunkel. **1993 DVD**

BOXOFFICE 🦃 From lousy nightclubs to the big time. Not rated; contains language and nudity. 92m. **DIR:** Josef Bogdanovich. **CAST:** Robin Clark, Monica Lewis, Carole Cortne, Eddie Constantine, Aldo Ray, Edie Adams, Peter Hurkos. **1981**

BOY AND HIS DOG, A ★★★★1/2 Looking for intelligence and biting humor in a science-fiction satire? Try this Hugo Award–winning screen adaptation of Harlan Ellison's novel, which focuses on the adventures of a young scavenger (Don Johnson) and his telepathic dog as they roam the Earth circa 2024 after a nuclear holocaust. Rated R for violence, sexual references, and nudity. 87m. **DIR:** L. Q. Jones. **CAST:** Don Johnson, Suzanne Benton, Jason Robards Jr. **1976 DVD**

BOY CALLED HATE, A ★★ Scott Caan debuted in this violent tale of a misunderstood troublemaker and the abused young woman he rescues from a rape and then takes on a mini-crime-spree. Production values could be better, as the soundtrack sometimes drowns out the dialogue. Rated R for profanity, violence, and sexual situations. 98m. **DIR:** Mitch Marcus. **CAST:** Scott Caan, Missy Crider, James Caan, Elliott Gould, Adam Beach. **1995**

BOY, DID I GET A WRONG NUMBER! 🦃 When you get a wrong number, hang up and dial again. Too bad the cast and director didn't. 99m. **DIR:** George Marshall. **CAST:** Bob Hope, Elke Sommer, Phyllis Diller. **1966**

BOY FRIEND, THE ★★★ Ken Russell, at his least self-indulgent and most affectionate, provides a plucky parody of twenties musicals. The inventiveness and opulence call to mind the work of Busby Berkeley. Twiggy's performance is engaging. Rated G. 110m. **DIR:** Ken Russell. **CAST:** Twiggy, Christopher Gable, Max Adrian, Tommy Tune, Glenda Jackson. **1971**

BOY IN BLUE, THE ★★★ Nice little screen biography of Ned Hanlan (Nicolas Cage), the famed Canadian lad who owned the sport of international sculling (rowing) for ten years during the end of the nineteenth century. Although the picture plays like a thin retread of *Rocky*—particularly with respect to its music—the result is no less inspirational. Inexplicably rated R for very brief nudity and coarse language. 97m. **DIR:** Charles Jarrott. **CAST:** Nicolas Cage, Christopher Plummer, Cynthia Dale, David Naughton. **1986**

BOY IN THE PLASTIC BUBBLE, THE ★★ John Travolta has his hands full in this significantly altered television adaptation of the boy who, because of an immunity deficiency, must spend every breathing moment in a sealed environment. Vapid stuff needlessly mired with sci-fi jargon. Not rated. 100m. **DIR:** Randal Kleiser. **CAST:** John Travolta, Glynnis O'Connor, Ralph Bellamy, Robert Reed, Diana Hyland, Buzz Aldrin. **1976 DVD**

BOY MEETS GIRL ★★★ An early spoof of Hollywood with James Cagney and Pat O'Brien as wisecracking, irreverent studio contract writers. On the side they help a young widow with her romantic problems. B&W; 86m. **DIR:** Lloyd Bacon. **CAST:** James Cagney, Pat O'Brien, Marie Wilson, Ralph Bellamy, Frank McHugh, Dick Foran, Ronald Reagan, Penny Singleton. **1938 DVD**

BOY NAMED CHARLIE BROWN, A ★★★★ Charles Schulz's "Peanuts" gang jumps to the big screen in this delightful, wistful tale of Charlie Brown's shot at fame in a national spelling bee. Rated G. 85m. **DIR:** Bill Melendez. **1969**

BOY TAKES GIRL ★★ A young girl learns to adapt when her parents leave her at a farming cooperative one summer. Some adult themes and more romance than may be acceptable for younger viewers, but this comedy-drama is passable for older kids. 93m. **DIR:** Michal Bat-Adam. **CAST:** Gabi Eldor, Hillel Neeman, Dina Limon. **1983**

BOY WHO COULD FLY, THE ★★★★ Writer-director Nick Castle has created a marvelous motion picture which speaks to the dreamer in all of us. His heroine, Milly (Lucy Deakins), is a newcomer to a small town where her neighbor, Eric (Jay Underwood), neither speaks nor responds to other people. All he does is sit on his roof and pretend to fly. Rated PG for dramatic intensity. 114m. **DIR:** Nick Castle. **CAST:** Lucy Deakins, Jay Underwood, Bonnie Bedelia, Fred Savage, Colleen Dewhurst, Fred Gwynne, Mindy Cohn. **1986**

BOY WITH GREEN HAIR, THE ★★★ A young war orphan's hair changes color, makes him a social outcast, and brings a variety of bigots and narrow minds out of the woodwork in this food-for-thought fable. The medium is the message in this one. 82m. **DIR:** Joseph Losey. **CAST:** Dean Stockwell, Robert Ryan, Barbara Hale, Pat O'Brien. **1948**

•BOYCOTT ★★★★ Engrossing, enlightening, and stylish telling of the Montgomery, Alabama, bus boycott started with Rosa Parks's refusal to give up her seat and continued by Martin Luther King Jr. Jeffrey Wright, as King, is astounding. Rated PG for language and violence. 113m. **DIR:** Clark Johnson. **CAST:** Jeffrey Wright, Terrence Howard, C.C.H. Pounder, Carmen Ejogo. **2001 DVD**

BOYFRIENDS AND GIRLFRIENDS ★★★★ Another of French director Eric Rohmer's delightful "Comedies and Proverbs," this import deals with two beautiful young women who become friends and have romantic adventures with various lovers. As usual, not much happens in a dramatic sense, but no one can capture the moment like Rohmer, who has us fall in love with his characters as they fall in and out of love with each other. In French with English subtitles. 102m. **DIR:** Eric Rohmer. **CAST:** Emmanuelle Chaulet, Sophie Renoir, Anne-Laure Meury, Eric Viellard, François-Eric Gendron. **1987 DVD**

BOYS (1996) ★★★ A young man brings an unconscious beautiful woman back to his boardinghouse. There, he begins to fall in love with her even as her mysterious and perhaps deadly story comes to light. Unlikely but intriguing film is buoyed by its stars—Lukas Haas and Winona Ryder—who are both excellent. Based on the short story "Twenty Minutes" by James Salter. Rated PG-13 for profanity. 86m. **DIR:** Stacy Cochran. **CAST:** Winona Ryder, Lukas Haas, John C. Reilly, James LeGros, Skeet Ulrich. **1996**

BOYS, THE (1997) ★★★1/2 Teamwork saves the day in this likable tale of a group of drinking buddies who play hockey. When their coach and bar owner finds himself in debt to the mob, it's up to this ragtag group of friends to play some real hockey. Released in Canada as *Les Boys*, the film has spawned two sequels and is one of Canada's highest grossing films. Not rated; contains violence. 110m. **DIR:** Louis Saia. **CAST:** Marc Messier, Remy Girard, Patrick Huard, Serge Theriault, Michelle Barrette. **1997 DVD**

BOYS AND GIRLS ★★★ Freddie Prinze Jr. and Claire Forlani play college students whose blossoming friendship nurses them through a series of romantic disappointments. Will they ever see that they're made for each other? Three guesses. The overfamiliar script is redeemed by sprightly direction and appealing performances—especially by Forlani, who glows with intelligence, warmth, and vulnerability. Rated PG-13 for mature themes and a brief sexual scene. 97m. **DIR:** Robert Iscove. **CAST:** Freddie Prinze Jr., Claire Forlani, Jason Biggs, Amanda Detmer, Heather Donahue. **2000 DVD**

BOYS CLUB, THE ★★★ Satisfying thriller features Chris Penn in a harrowing performance as a psychotic stranger who takes three teenage boys hostage when he hides out in their clubhouse. As the situation becomes more intense, the boys are forced to become men in order to escape their tormentor. Atmospheric and moody. Rated R for violence and language. 92m. **DIR:** John Fawcett. **CAST:** Christopher Penn, Dominic Zamprogna, Devon Sawa, Stuart Stone. **1996 DVD**

BOYS DON'T CRY ★★★★ Definitely not for the faint of heart or closed of mind, this truth-is-stranger-than-fiction re-creation of actual events is a remarkably self-assured debut from director/coscripter Kimberly Pierce, who wrote the screenplay with Andy Bienen as a graduate thesis. It blossomed into a feature-length film that is fascinating, compelling, and ultimately horrifying: the study of a remarkably brave and self-destructively foolish individual determined to construct and enjoy her own special life, no matter what the consequences. The neo-documentary, cinema verité style is amplified by its largely unrecognized cast, led by Oscar-winner Hilary Swank as a young woman determined to "pass" as a boy among the white-trash dregs of rural Nebraska. Swank's positively stunning lead performance, as captivating and mesmerizing a job of acting as you're likely to see, is a ferociously self-assured interpretation of a modern tragic heroine . . . or hero, depending on one's point of view. Powerful stuff. Rated R for profanity, violence, nudity, drug use, and strong sexual content. 114m. **DIR:** Kimberly Pierce. **CAST:** Hilary Swank, Chloe Sevigny, Peter Sarsgaard, Brendan Sexton III, Alison Folland, Alicia Goranson. **1999 DVD**

BOYS FROM BRAZIL, THE ★★1/2 In this thriller, Gregory Peck plays an evil Nazi war criminal with far-fetched plans to resurrect the Third Reich. Laurence Olivier as a Jewish Nazi-hunter pursues him. Rated R. 123m. **DIR:** Franklin J. Schaffner. **CAST:** Gregory Peck, Laurence Olivier, James Mason, Lilli Palmer. **1978 DVD**

BOYS FROM BROOKLYN, THE 🦃 Absolutely hilarious bomb with Bela Lugosi as a mad scientist turning people into apes on a forgotten island. Better known as *Bela Lugosi Meets a Brooklyn Gorilla*, a much more appropriate title. B&W; 72m. **DIR:** William Beaudine. **CAST:** Bela Lugosi, Duke Mitchell, Sammy Petrillo. **1952 DVD**

BOYS IN COMPANY C, THE ★★★ The film opens with the arrival of various draftees in the Marine Corps induction center and comes close, at times, to being the powerful film the subject of the Vietnam war suggests. The combat scenes are particularly effective, and the deaths of soldiers are gory without being overdone. Rated R for violence. 127m. **DIR:** Sidney J. Furie. **CAST:** Stan Shaw, Andrew Stevens, James Canning, James Whitmore Jr. **1978**

BOYS IN THE BAND, THE ★★★ Widely acclaimed film about nine men who attend a birthday party and end up exposing their lives and feelings to one another in the course of the night. Eight of the men are gay; one is straight. One of the first American films to deal honestly with the subject of homosexuality. Sort of a large-scale *My Dinner with André* with the whole film shot on one set. Rated R. 119m. **DIR:** William Friedkin. **CAST:** Kenneth Nelson, Peter White, Leonard Frey, Cliff Gorman. **1970**

BOYS NEXT DOOR, THE (1985) ★★★ This story of two alienated teenage youths, Charlie Sheen and Maxwell Caulfield, going on a killing spree in Los Angeles, makes for some tense viewing. Sheen and Caulfield decide to go to L.A. Once in the city, one violent encounter spawns another. Beware: This one is extremely graphic in its depiction of violence. Rated R. 88m. **DIR:** Penelope Spheeris. **CAST:** Charlie Sheen, Maxwell Caulfield, Hank Garrett, Patti D'Arbanville, Christopher McDonald, Moon Zappa. **1985**

BOYS NEXT DOOR, THE (1996) ★★★★ Powerful *Hallmark Hall of Fame* production uses humor to deliver its message about the plight of mentally ill adults. Tony Goldwyn plays the social worker to four men who are sharing a house and making a go at independent living. Their needs are endless, and Goldwyn must choose between them and keeping his marriage together. Not rated; contains mature themes. 99m. **DIR:** John Erman. **CAST:** Tony Goldwyn, Nathan Lane, Courtney B. Vance, Michael Jeter, Robert Sean Leonard, Mare Winningham. **1996**

BOYS' NIGHT OUT ★★★1/2 Three otherwise staid married men finance an apartment and set out to share a live-in girl on the one night a week they are "allowed" out. They pick Kim Novak unaware she is a sociology student studying the sexual fantasies of suburban males. Good farce, and not the least bit smutty. Well ahead of its time with a wonderful cast. 115m. **DIR:** Michael Gordon. **CAST:** Kim Novak, James Garner, Tony Randall, Howard Duff, Janet Blair, Patti Page, Jessie Royce Landis, Oscar Homolka, Howard Morris, Anne Jeffreys, Zsa Zsa Gabor, Fred Clark, William Bendix. **1962**

BOYS OF ST. VINCENT ★★★★★ This Dickensian tale of abuse and retribution, stars a mesmerizing Henry Czerny in a cold-blooded performance as a handsome, intelligent brother with a sick desire for his young charges. This is especially heart-wrenching because neither the accused nor the abused ever asks for pity. Not rated; contains profanity, violence, sexual situations, nudity, and adult themes. 186m. **DIR:** John N. Smith. **CAST:** Henry Czerny, Johnny Morina, Brian

Dooley, Brian Dodd, Lise Roy, Sebastian Spence, David Hewlett. **1992**

BOYS OF THE CITY ★★ Somewhere between their incarnations as the Dead End Kids and the Bowery Boys, the forties version of the Brat Pack turned up as the East Side Kids in low-budget movies. In this one, the gang takes a trip to the mountains, where they solve the murder of a judge by gangsters. B&W; 68m. **DIR:** Joseph H. Lewis. **CAST:** Bobby Jordan, Leo Gorcey, Dave O'Brien, Donald Haines. **1940**

BOYS ON THE SIDE ★★★1/2 To try her luck in Los Angeles, New York nightclub singer Whoopi Goldberg answers a newspaper ad and ends up as a companion to strait-laced Mary-Louise Parker on a cross-country drive. A stop in Pittsburgh adds Drew Barrymore. This road/buddy movie explores the special relationships that can develop among women. Rated R for violence, nudity, and profanity. 117m. **DIR:** Herbert Ross. **CAST:** Whoopi Goldberg, Mary-Louise Parker, Drew Barrymore, Matthew McConaughey, James Remar, Billy Wirth, Anita Gillette. **1995 DVD**

BOYS' TOWN ★★★★ Spencer Tracy gives one of his most memorable performances in this MGM classic about Father Flanagan and his struggle to give orphans and juvenile delinquents a chance at life. Overtly manipulative, but rewarding. B&W; 93m. **DIR:** Norman Taurog. **CAST:** Spencer Tracy, Mickey Rooney, Henry Hull. **1938**

BOYS WILL BE BOYS ★★★ *Home Alone* meets *Rambo* in this tale of two brothers left alone for the first time while their parents attend a company function. The brothers rise to the occasion when their father's business rival arrives to create chaos. It's up to the miniwarriors to salvage their dad's job and the house before the folks get home. Enjoyable romp benefits from large cast of recognizable faces. Rated PG for violence. 90m. **DIR:** Dom DeLuise. **CAST:** Randy Travis, Julie Hagerty, Michael DeLuise, Jon Voight, Mickey Rooney, Ruth Buzzi. **1997 DVD**

BOYZ N THE HOOD ★★★★1/2 Although *Boyz N the Hood* may appear to be an exploitation flick about gang violence, it is far from being so. This powerful drama, which marks the directing debut of 23 year old John Singleton, is a responsible, heart-tugging tale of a modern tragedy, focusing on a group of young men and women caught in the war zone of south central Los Angeles. Rated R for profanity, violence, and nudity. 111m. **DIR:** John Singleton. **CAST:** Ice Cube, Cuba Gooding Jr., Morris Chestnut, Laurence Fishburne, Nia Long, Tyra Ferrell. **1991 DVD**

BRADDOCK: MISSING IN ACTION III ★★ After the war has ended, Colonel Braddock (Chuck Norris) returns to Vietnam to rescue a group of Amerasian children in a POW camp. A dark, grainy, low-budget film cowritten by Norris. If you liked the first two films, you'll probably enjoy this one, too. Rated R for violence. 90m. **DIR:** Aaron Norris. **CAST:** Chuck Norris, Aki Aleong. **1987**

BRADY BUNCH MOVIE, THE ★★★1/2 The big-screen version of the 1970s sitcom is actually a disarming parody of the old show's relentless wholesomeness, with the simple plot (the Bradys need $20,000 to save their home) serving as a framework for bits from a number of episodes. Rated PG-13 for mild profanity. 90m. **DIR:** Betty Thomas. **CAST:** Shelley Long, Gary Cole, Michael McKean, Henriette Mantel, Christine Taylor, Jennifer Elise Cox. **1995**

BRADY BUNCH, THE (TV SERIES) ★★ The 1970s sitcom overdoses on bell-bottoms, polyester, and saccharine sweetness. Four-volume series features two episodes on each. The first volume features the two families merging on the honeymoon. Other highlights include a stint by Davy Jones of the Monkees, Marcia's fat nose, and Jan's identity crisis. Not hilarious in its heyday, the series has not improved with time. 50m. **DIR:** Russ Mayberry, Jack Arnold, Peter Baldwin, John Rich, Hal Cooper, Oscar Rudolph. **CAST:** Florence Henderson, Robert Reed, Ann B. Davis. **1971–1973**

BRADY'S ESCAPE ★★★ A minor HBO-produced film concerning an American attempting to escape the Nazis in Europe during World War II. Nothing original is added to the familiar plot. 96m. **DIR:** Pal Gabor. **CAST:** John Savage, Kelly Reno. **1984**

BRAIN, THE (1965) ★★ Adequate remake of the oft-filmed *Donovan's Brain*, a little short on thrills and originality, but atmospheric fun nevertheless. A German-British coproduction. B&W; 85m. **DIR:** Freddie Francis. **CAST:** Peter Van Eyck, Anne Heywood, Bernard Lee, Jack MacGowran. **1965**

BRAIN, THE (1988) ★★1/2 Hokey special effects take away from this shocker about a TV psychologist (David Gale) and his alien brain. The brain (eyes, nose, and long, sharp teeth added) starts munching anyone who gets in the way. Occasionally entertaining, this is one film that never reaches its potential. Rated R for violence and mild gore. 94m. **DIR:** Edward Hunt. **CAST:** Tom Breznahan, Cyndy Preston, David Gale. **1988**

BRAIN DAMAGE ★★1/2 A wisecracking giant worm escapes from its elderly keepers and forces a teenager to kill people. Although the low budget hampers the special effects, the offbeat execution makes this worth a look for horror fans. Rated R for sexual situations and graphic violence. 90m. **DIR:** Frank Henenlotter. **CAST:** Rich Herbst, Gordon MacDonald. **1988 DVD**

BRAIN DEAD ★★★ A research doctor (Bill Pullman) is pressured by his corporate sponsor to use his research on brain patterns to open a chain of attitude adjustment centers. Something snaps, and the mild-mannered doctor soon becomes the apparent victim of severe paranoia. Rated R for profanity, violence, and nudity. 85m. **DIR:** Adam Simon. **CAST:** Bill Pullman, Bud Cort, George Kennedy, Bill Paxton. **1989**

BRAIN DONORS ★★★1/2 Three bumbling misfits—a shyster lawyer, a quick-witted taxi driver, and a dim-witted houseboy—join together to form a ballet company in this often hilarious take on the Marx Brothers. John Turturro steals the show as he spews out an endless stream of lightning-fast jokes à la Groucho. Rated PG for sexual innuendo and nudity. 79m. **DIR:** Dennis Dugan. **CAST:** John Turturro, Bob Nelson, Mel Smith, Nancy Marchand, John Savident, George de la Pena, Spike Alexander. **1992**

BRAIN EATERS, THE ★★ Robert Heinlein's *The Puppet Masters* is the unacknowledged source for this grade-C sci-fi melodrama in the *Invasion of the Body Snatchers* tradition. It's too brief to overstay its welcome, and has earned a cult following. B&W; 60m. **DIR:**

Bruno VeSota. **CAST:** Joanna Lee, Jody Fair, Ed Nelson, Leonard Nimoy. **1958**

BRAIN FROM PLANET AROUS, THE ★★★ Great little film is much better than the plot or title would suggest. Giant brain from outer space takes over John Agar's body in an attempt to conquer the world. Not far behind is another brain that inhabits the body of Agar's dog and tries to prevent it. Good stuff. B&W; 70m. **DIR:** Nathan Juran. **CAST:** John Agar, Joyce Meadows, Robert Fuller. **1958 DVD**

BRAIN OF BLOOD A mad doctor performs brain transplants and creates a hulking monster. 83m. **DIR:** Al Adamson. **CAST:** Kent Taylor, John Bloom, Regina Carroll, Grant Williams. **1971**

BRAIN SMASHER . . . A LOVE STORY ★★★ Andrew Clay is the brain smasher, a notorious professional bouncer who takes pride in his work. Teri Hatcher is an international model who recruits Clay to protect her and her sister from killer Chinese monks. Honest! Veteran character actors help levitate this one above mediocrity. Rated PG-13 for violence and profanity. 88m. **DIR:** Albert Pyun. **CAST:** Andrew Clay, Teri Hatcher, Brian James, Tim Thomerson, Charles Rocket, Nicholas Guest, Deborah Van Valkenburgh. **1993**

BRAIN THAT WOULDN'T DIE, THE A doctor experiments with human limbs. B&W; 81m. **DIR:** Joseph Green. **CAST:** Jason "Herb" Evers, Virginia Leith, Adele Lamont. **1963 DVD**

BRAINIAC, THE ★★★ Mexi-monster stuff about a nobleman, executed as a warlock in 1661, who comes back to life to seek revenge on the descendants of those who killed him. Every so often he transforms himself into a monster with a long, snaky tongue to suck out people's brains. With their low production values and indifferent dubbing, most Mexican horror films are good only for camp value. This one has those same flaws, but you'll also find it has some eerily effective moments. 77m. **DIR:** Chano Urveta. **CAST:** Abel Salazar. **1961**

BRAINSCAN ★★ After a teenager plays a video game in which he commits murder, real killings exactly like the ones in his "game" begin to occur. This none-too-original rehash of the Freddy Krueger films is doggedly predictable, with cheap special effects and a double cop-out ending. Rated R for gore. 96m. **DIR:** John Flynn. **CAST:** Edward Furlong, Frank Langella, T. Ryder Smith, Amy Hargreaves. **1994**

BRAINSTORM ★★★1/2 Christopher Walken and Natalie Wood star in this sci-fi thriller about an invention that can read and record physical, emotional, and intellectual sensations as they are experienced by an individual and allow them to be reexperienced by another human being. But what happens if it's used for evil? Rated PG for nudity and profanity. 106m. **DIR:** Douglas Trumbull. **CAST:** Christopher Walken, Natalie Wood, Louise Fletcher. **1983 DVD**

BRAINWASHED ★★1/2 Disquieting psychological thriller about a man who is imprisoned by Nazis during World War II. Story documents his struggle to remain rational while being brainwashed by his captors. 102m. **DIR:** Gerd Oswald. **CAST:** Curt Jurgens, Claire Bloom, Hansjor Felmy, Albert Lieven. **1961**

BRAINWAVES ★★★ A young San Francisco wife and mother undergoes brain surgery as a result of an accident. An experimental brain wave transfer is performed in an attempt to restore her to a normal life, producing startling results since the brain waves came from a murder victim. Rated R for some nudity and mild violence. 83m. **DIR:** Ulli Lommel. **CAST:** Keir Dullea, Suzanna Love, Vera Miles, Percy Rodrigues, Paul Wilson, Tony Curtis. **1982**

BRAM STOKER'S BURIAL OF THE RATS Horror films just don't get worse than this cheeseball dreck, which exploits Bram Stoker's good name merely as cachet for a lot of nude women and soft-core coupling. Rated R for nudity, simulated sex, violence, and gore. 85m. **DIR:** Dan Golden. **CAST:** Adrienne Barbeau, Maria Ford, Kevin Alber. **1995**

BRAM STOKER'S DRACULA ★★1/2 Vlad the Impaler, a.k.a. Dracula, becomes a tragic figure in Francis Ford Coppola's visually opulent but overwrought version of the famous vampire tale. Some offbeat casting and an overemphasis on sex and nudity. Rated R for nudity, gore, and violence. 130m. **DIR:** Francis Ford Coppola. **CAST:** Gary Oldman, Winona Ryder, Anthony Hopkins, Keanu Reeves, Richard E. Grant, Cary Elwes, Bill Campell, Tom Waits, Sadie Frost. **1992 DVD**

BRAM STOKER'S SHADOWBUILDER ★★ Modern-day adaptation of Bram Stoker's story about a demon summoned from the pits of hell and the determined priest assigned to protect a 12 year old boy who may be the savior. The decent special effects aren't enough to hide the rudimentary acting, plotting, and direction. Rated R for violence. 101m. **DIR:** Jamie Dixon. **CAST:** Michael Rooker, Kevin Zegers, Shawn Thompson, Steven Blum, Tony Todd. **1997 DVD**

BRAM STOKER'S THE MUMMY ★★ Late entry into the classic movie monster marathon suffers from familiar plot and low budget. Lou Gossett Jr. is the Egyptologist who learns that an ancient mummy is waiting to be reincarnated. The rehash of *The Awakening* is as musty and dusty as its leading lady. Rated R for adult situations, nudity, and violence. 99m. **DIR:** Jeffrey Obrow. **CAST:** Louis Gossett Jr., Amy Locane, Eric Lutes. **1997 DVD**

BRAMBLE BUSH, THE ★★ Soap opera about a doctor who pulls the plug on his terminally ill best friend while having an affair with the sick buddy's wife. There are enough subplots for an afternoon full of daytime dramas in this mildly diverting movie. 93m. **DIR:** Daniel Petrie. **CAST:** Richard Burton, Angie Dickinson, Barbara Rush, Tom Drake, James Dunn, Henry Jones. **1960**

BRANDED ★★1/2 Farfetched sagebrush melodrama finds Alan Ladd and his shady sidekick hatching a plot to fleece an old rancher and his wife—as Ladd impersonates their long-missing son. Pretty creaky, but a good cast, some exciting chase scenes, and fine outdoor Technicolor photography make this worth watching. 103m. **DIR:** Rudolph Maté. **CAST:** Alan Ladd, Mona Freeman, Charles Bickford, Robert Keith, Joseph Calleia, Peter Hanson, Tom Tully, Milburn Stone. **1951**

BRANNIGAN ★★★1/2 John Wayne travels to London to bring back a fugitive in this enjoyable cops-and-robbers chase film. It's fun to see the Duke in jolly old England and the cast is outstanding. Rated PG. 111m. **DIR:** Douglas Hickox. **CAST:** John Wayne, Richard Attenborough, Judy Geeson, Mel Ferrer, Ralph Meeker, John Vernon. **1975 DVD**

BRASS ★★ Routine made-for-TV cop thriller starring Carroll O'Connor as a top New York City police officer and a politically sensitive kidnap-murder case. The pilot for a proposed series. 94m. **DIR:** Corey Allen. **CAST:** Carroll O'Connor, Lois Nettleton, Jimmy Baio, Paul Shenar. **1985**

BRASS MONKEY, THE ★★ In this British thriller we get a not-very-effective story based on a radio program. Carole Landis is a radio singer who prevents the theft of a Buddhist religious icon. The script is weak, and Landis and the other players seem bored. B&W; 84m. **DIR:** Thornton Freeland. **CAST:** Carole Landis, Carroll Levis, Herbert Lom, Avril Angers, Ernest Thesiger. **1948**

BRASS TARGET ★★ Pure Hollywood hokum at its most ridiculous would ask us to believe that Gen. George Patton (George Kennedy) was murdered after World War II because of a large gold robbery committed by his staff. Not much to recommend this boring film. Rated PG for moderate language and violence. 111m. **DIR:** John Hough. **CAST:** Sophia Loren, George Kennedy, John Cassavetes, Robert Vaughn, Max von Sydow, Bruce Davison. **1978**

BRASSED OFF ★★★1/2 Odd but appealing mixture of romance, comedy, class-war polemic, and marching-band musical. A coal-mining town in the north of England faces ruin when the government tries to close down its colliery. At the same time, the local miners' brass band has a shot at winning a national competition. Rated R for profanity. 107m. **DIR:** Mark Herman. **CAST:** Pete Postlethwaite, Tara Fitzgerald, Ewan McGregor, Stephen Tompkinson. **1996 DVD**

BRAVADOS, THE ★★★1/2 In this revenge Western, Gregory Peck tracks down the four men who raped and killed his wife. Directors Budd Boetticher and Anthony Mann handled this theme more involvingly in their films with Randolph Scott and James Stewart, respectively, but this is nonetheless a serviceable Western. 98m. **DIR:** Henry King. **CAST:** Gregory Peck, Joan Collins, Stephen Boyd, Henry Silva, Lee Van Cleef. **1958**

BRAVE LITTLE TOASTER, THE ★★★★ This delightful animated feature, based on a charming children's story by sci-fi author Thomas M. Disch, concerns a quintet of electrical appliances that journey to the big city in the hopes of finding the human master who abandoned them in a country summer cottage. Suitable for family viewing. 92m. **DIR:** Jerry Rees. **1987**

BRAVE LITTLE TOASTER GOES TO MARS, THE ★★1/2 This tale—which concerns the efforts of our intrepid appliances—is buried beneath humdrum animation and atrocious songs. The script includes a few humorous digs at adolescence, and there's one brilliant bit of voice casting. Rated G. 73m. **DIR:** Robert Ramirez. **1997**

BRAVE ONE, THE ★★★★ Above-average family film about a Mexican boy whose pet bull is sold. Knowing that its fate is to die in the bullfighting ring, the boy tracks his pet to Mexico City, where he does everything he can to save it. Winner of an Academy Award for best original story, which went unclaimed for almost twenty years because screenwriter "Robert Rich" was really the blacklisted Dalton Trumbo. 102m. **DIR:** Irving Rapper. **CAST:** Michel Ray, Rodolfo Hoyos, Elsa Cardenas, Joi Lansing. **1956 DVD**

BRAVEHEART ★★★★★ Superb historical epic, directed by and starring Mel Gibson, has both rousing action and a strong dramatic storyline. *Braveheart* is a cinematic event. Its themes of love, honor, betrayal, remorse, and self-sacrifice are carefully sculptured into an unforgettable motion picture. Rated R for violence and nudity. 177m. **DIR:** Mel Gibson. **CAST:** Mel Gibson, Sophie Marceau, Patrick McGoohan, Brendan Gleeson, James Cosmo, David O'Hara, Angus MacFadyen. **1995 DVD**

BRAZIL ★★★★ A savage blend of *1984* and *The Time Bandits* from Monty Python director Terry Gilliam. Jonathan Pryce stars as a bemused paper shuffler in a red tape–choked future society at the brink of collapsing under its own bureaucracy. Definitely not for all tastes, but a treat for those with an appreciation for social satire. Were it not for a chaotic conclusion and slightly overlong running time, this would be a perfect picture. Rated R for language and adult situations. 131m. **DIR:** Terry Gilliam. **CAST:** Jonathan Pryce, Robert De Niro, Katherine Helmond, Ian Holm, Bob Hoskins, Michael Palin, Ian Richardson. **1985 DVD**

BREACH OF CONDUCT ★★ A major's wife is sexually harassed by the deranged army-base commander. Rated PG-13 for violence. 93m. **DIR:** Tim Matheson. **CAST:** Peter Coyote, Courtney Thorne-Smith, Keith Amos, Beth Toussaint. **1994**

BREACH OF TRUST ★★1/2 So-so shoot-'em-up is elevated by decent stunt work and chase scenes. A high-tech drug-money laundering scheme connects a beautiful undercover cop and a small-time hood. Mobsters follow close at their heels. Rated R for sex, nudity, profanity, and violence. 96m. **DIR:** Charles Wilkinson. **CAST:** Michael Biehn, Leilani Sarelle, Miguel Sandoval, Kim Coates, Ed Lauter. **1995**

BREAD AND CHOCOLATE ★★★★ An uneducated Italian man (Nino Manfredi in a wonderfully Chaplinesque performance) tries to provide for his family by seeking work in Switzerland, a country not kind to illegal immigrants. This bittersweet comedy was a popular favorite at art houses in the 1970s. In Italian with English subtitles. Not rated; contains no objectionable material. 109m. **DIR:** Franco Brusati. **CAST:** Nino Manfredi, Anna Karina, Johnny Dorelli. **1974 DVD**

•BREAD AND ROSES ★★ Universal social, political, and economical issues are laced with realism, left-wing principles, and personal intimacy in this bittersweet drama. The Justice for Janitors cause in Los Angeles struggles to unionize custodians, forcing minority workers to choose between security and solidarity or the status quo. The intermittent petals of truth ("Uniforms make us invisible," says one disgruntled custodian) remind us that *Norma Rae*, *Matewan*, and *El Norte* have been here before—with more passion. Rated R for language and adult themes. 106m. **DIR:** Kenneth Loach. **CAST:** Pilar Padilla, Adrien Brody, Elpidia Carrillo, George Lopez, Alonso Chavez, Monica Rivas. **2000 DVD**

BREAD AND SALT ★★★1/2 Having left Moscow in 1985 when Russia was firmly entrenched in Communism, vivacious Irina Muravyova returns, along with a scholar of Russian studies, Richard Lourie. The two investigate the influence of capitalism on the average person in this fine documentary. On the one hand there are high prices and unemployment, and on the other hand there are choices, new freedoms, and the opportunity for some to become millionaires. Not rated; contains profanity. 95m. **DIR:** Jeanne Collachia. **1992**

•BREAD AND TULIPS ★★★ Earthy, sensual Rosalba is accidentally left behind at a roadside rest stop while vacationing by bus with her large extended family. She decides to hitchhike home and makes a liberating stopover in Venice where a suicidal Icelandic waiter takes her underwing, an anarchist florist gives her a job, and she takes up the accordion. Her husband then hires an out-of-work plumber turned private eye to track her down in this whimsical tale of self-discovery and eccentricity. In Italian with English subtitles. Rated PG-13 for profanity. 115m. **DIR:** Silvio Soldini. **CAST:** Licia Maglietta, Bruno Ganz, Giuseppe Battiston. **2001 DVD**

BREAK, THE ★★★ Vincent Van Patten is the most convincing thing in this *Rocky*esque tale of a geeky teenager hoping to become a tennis star. There are some decent moments, including a fun appearance by Martin Sheen as a bookie betting against his own son. However, we have seen too much of this before, and Ben Jorgensen is a bit too wide-eyed as the aspiring pro. Rated PG-13 for profanity and brief nudity. 104m. **DIR:** Lee H. Katzin. **CAST:** Vincent Van Patten, Ben Jorgensen, Martin Sheen, Rae Dawn Chong, Valerie Perrine, Gerrit Graham. **1994**

BREAK OF DAWN ★★★1/2 Based on a true story, this chronicles Pedro J. Gonzalez's entry to the United States in 1928 and his rapid rise to popularity as the first Mexican radio show host. When his influence over the East L.A. population threatens the racist DA, he's framed for rape. Low-budget, yet convincing. In English and Spanish with English subtitles when needed. Not rated, contains mature themes. 100m. **DIR:** Isaac Artenstein. **CAST:** Oscar Chavez, Tony Plana, Maria Rojo, Pepe Serna. **1988 DVD**

BREAK OF HEARTS ★★1/2 Mediocre drama about a struggling composer and her troubled marriage to a highly acclaimed symphony conductor. Some good acting makes up for the predictable script. B&W; 80m. **DIR:** Phillip Moeller. **CAST:** Katharine Hepburn, Charles Boyer, John Beal. **1935**

BREAK UP ★★★ Direct-to-video suspense thriller gets a major boost from a top-notch cast and sharp direction. A battered wife is suspected of killing her womanizing husband and a good cop/bad cop duo is assigned to protect her, then track her down when she's accused of the murder. Director Paul Marcus gets plenty of mileage out of the formulaic script, while the cast more than rises to the challenge. Rated R for adult situations, language, nudity, and violence. 101m. **DIR:** Paul Marcus. **CAST:** Bridget Fonda, Kiefer Sutherland, Steven Weber, Penelope Ann Miller, Hart Bochner. **1998 DVD**

BREAKAWAY ★★ A mob messenger tries to stay one step ahead of a professional killer long enough to enjoy the money she stole from her former boss. Aside from the casting of scandal-ridden ice skater Tonya Harding in a supporting role, there's nothing memorable here. Rated R for violence, nudity, sexual situations, and profanity. 95m. **DIR:** Sean Dash. **CAST:** Teri Thompson, Joe Estevez, Tonya Harding, Tony Noakes. **1996**

BREAKDOWN ★★★★ This creepy thriller turns a stranded-motorist scenario into a seamless blend of panic, anguish, and crackerjack action scenes. Jeff and Amy Taylor, who have car trouble while taking a scenic route through the Southwest, are relieved when a polite trucker stops to help. Their relief is short-lived when Amy accepts a ride to a nearby diner and then apparently melts into the desolate landscape. Rated R for language, violence, and terror. 96m. **DIR:** Jonathan Mostow. **CAST:** Kurt Russell, Kathleen Quinlan, J. T. Walsh, M. C. Gainey, Jack Noseworthy, Rex Linn. **1997 DVD**

BREAKER! BREAKER! 🦃 A quickie thrown together to cash in on the CB craze. Rated PG. 86m. **DIR:** Don Hulette. **CAST:** Chuck Norris, George Murdock, Terry O'Connor, Don Gentry. **1977 DVD**

BREAKER MORANT ★★★★★ This is one Australian import you won't want to miss. Imagine the high adventure of the original *Gunga Din*, the wisecracking humor of *To Have and Have Not*, and the character drama of *The Caine Mutiny* all rolled into one supermovie. Rated PG. 107m. **DIR:** Bruce Beresford. **CAST:** Edward Woodward, Jack Thompson, John Waters, Bryan Brown, Charles Tingwell. **1979 DVD**

BREAKFAST AT TIFFANY'S ★★★★ An offbeat yet tender love story of a New York writer and a fey party girl. Strong performances are turned in by George Peppard and Audrey Hepburn. Hepburn's Holly Golightly is a masterful creation that blends the sophistication of a Manhattan "escort" with the childish country girl of her roots. Henry Mancini's score is justly famous, as it creates much of the mood for this wistful story. 115m. **DIR:** Blake Edwards. **CAST:** Audrey Hepburn, George Peppard, Patricia Neal, Buddy Ebsen, Mickey Rooney, Martin Balsam. **1961 DVD**

BREAKFAST CLUB, THE ★★★★ A group of assorted high school misfits gets to be friends while serving weekend detention in this terrific comedy, directed by John Hughes, the king of watchable teen films. Rated R. 100m. **DIR:** John Hughes. **CAST:** Emilio Estevez, Molly Ringwald, Paul Gleason, Judd Nelson, Anthony Michael Hall, Ally Sheedy. **1985 DVD**

BREAKFAST IN HOLLYWOOD ★★ This is a romantic comedy based on the radio series of the same name. The plot is thin, but there are some nice musical moments from Nat King Cole and Spike Jones. B&W; 91m. **DIR:** Harold Schuster. **CAST:** Bonita Granville, Beulah Bondi, Tom Breneman. **1946**

BREAKFAST OF CHAMPIONS ★★ In this badly miscalculated adaptation of Kurt Vonnegut's novel, Bruce Willis seems lost as the car salesman who wants to kill himself, while Nick Nolte is wasted as his assistant, who likes to dress up in women's clothes. Unlike the novel, which was sharp and witty, this film is dull and unfunny. Rated R for adult situations and language. 110m. **DIR:** Alan Rudolph. **CAST:** Bruce Willis, Nick Nolte, Albert Finney, Barbara Hershey, Glenne Headly, Omar Epps. **1999 DVD**

BREAKHEART PASS ★★★ Charles Bronson is a government agent on the trail of gunrunners in the Old West. Most of the action of this modest Western takes place aboard a train, so the excited pitch needed to fully sustain viewers' interest is never reached. Rated PG—some violence and rough language. 95m. **DIR:** Tom Gries. **CAST:** Charles Bronson, Ben Johnson, Ed

Lauter, Richard Crenna, Charles Durning, Jill Ireland, John Mitchum. **1976**

BREAKIN' ★★ The dancing scenes are wonderful but as a whole, this is pretty lame. The film would have us believe that jazz dancer Kelly (Lucinda Dickey) could hook up with street dancers Ozone ("Shabba-Doo") and Turbo ("Boogaloo Shrimp") to win dance contests and finally break (no pun intended) into big-time show biz. Rated PG for profanity and violence. 90m. **DIR:** Joel Silberg. **CAST:** Lucinda Dickey, Adolfo Quinones, Michael Chambers, Ben Lokey. **1984**

BREAKIN' 2 ELECTRIC BOOGALOO ★★1/2 This sometimes exhilarating break-dancing movie is better than the original. This time, Kelly (Lucinda Dickey), Ozone (Adolfo "Shabba-Doo" Quinones), and Turbo (Michael "Boogaloo Shrimp" Chambers) put on a show to save a local arts center for children. Rated PG for brief violence and suggested sex. 90m. **DIR:** Sam Firstenberg. **CAST:** Lucinda Dickey, Adolfo Quinones, Michael Chambers. **1984**

BREAKING ALL THE RULES 🦃 Teenagers look for love (translation: lust) and adventure on the last day of summer vacation. 91m. **DIR:** James Orr. **CAST:** Carl Marotte, Thor Bishopric, Carolyn Dunn. **1984**

BREAKING AWAY ★★★★★ There comes a time in every young man's life when he must loose the ties of home, family, and friends and test his mettle. Dennis Christopher is the young man who retains an innocence we too often mistake for naïveté; Paul Dooley and Barbara Barrie are the often humorously confused parents who offer subtle, sure guidance. This is a warm portrayal of family life and love, of friendships, of growing up and growing away. Rated PG for brief profanity. 100m. **DIR:** Peter Yates. **CAST:** Dennis Christopher, Dennis Quaid, Daniel Stern, Jackie Earle Haley, Paul Dooley, Barbara Barrie. **1979 DVD**

BREAKING FREE ★★1/2 A fledgling juvenile delinquent finds the right path when he is put to work at a summer camp for blind children. Made for the Disney Channel, this is an earnest drama whose honest characters are more compelling than the predictable story. Rated PG. 100m. **DIR:** David Mackay. **CAST:** Christine Taylor, Jeremy London, Gina Phillips, Nicolas Surovy. **1995**

BREAKING GLASS ★★1/2 British film about a new wave singer's rise to the top, at the expense of personal relationships. Hazel O'Connor's heavy music isn't for all tastes, and the plot line is as old as film itself, but the actors are sincere. 104m. **DIR:** Brian Gibson. **CAST:** Phil Daniels, Hazel O'Connor, Jon Finch, Jonathan Pryce. **1980**

BREAKING HOME TIES ★★★ Texas farm family drama, set in the 1950s, in which the proud father sends his only son off to college in the big city. Well-written TV drama with believable characters and good acting. 95m. **DIR:** John Wilder. **CAST:** Jason Robards Jr., Eva Marie Saint, Doug McKeon, Erin Gray, Claire Trevor. **1987**

BREAKING IN ★★★★ This low-key character comedy comes from director Bill Forsyth and screenwriter John Sayles. Burt Reynolds, in one of his finest screen performances, is a professional thief who becomes the mentor for a crazy housebreaker (Casey Siemaszko). A fascinating slice of life. Rated R for profanity. 95m. **DIR:** Bill Forsyth. **CAST:** Burt Reynolds, Casey Siemaszko, Albert Salmi, Harry Carey Jr. **1989 DVD**

BREAKING POINT (1989) ★★★1/2 Decent World War II espionage thriller, this remake of *36 Hours* features Corbin Bernsen as a top U.S. intelligence officer who becomes the victim of an elaborate Nazi plot. Made for cable, this is unrated but contains mature themes. 90m. **DIR:** Peter Markle. **CAST:** Corbin Bernsen, Joanna Pacula, John Glover, David Marshall Grant. **1989**

BREAKING POINT (1993) ★★★ Solid performances and British Columbia locales highlight this slick little thriller, with Gary Busey well cast as a former cop who reluctantly rejoins the force after the return of a nasty serial killer dubbed "the surgeon." Since we quickly learn the maniac's identity, it's more a *Columbo*-style procedural than a mystery, but Busey makes it work. Rated R for violence, profanity, and suggested sex. 95m. **DIR:** Paul Ziller. **CAST:** Gary Busey, Kim Cattrall, Darlanne Fluegel. **1993**

BREAKING THE ICE ★★ In this improbable meld of music and ice skating, Bobby Breen gets a job singing at a Philadelphia rink, and meets skating moppet Irene Dare. B&W; 79m. **DIR:** Eddie Cline. **CAST:** Bobby Breen, Charlie Ruggles, Dolores Costello, Billy Gilbert, Margaret Hamilton. **1938**

BREAKING THE RULES ★★★1/2 Three friends reunite and learn that one of them is dying of cancer. They take a cross-country trip to California and meet an unusual woman along the way. Annie Potts is brilliant as Mary, the wacky artist who wants to beautify the country. Rated PG-13 for profanity and suggested sex. 100m. **DIR:** Neal Israel. **CAST:** Jason Bateman, C. Thomas Howell, Jonathan Silverman, Annie Potts, Krista Tesreau. **1991**

BREAKING THE SURFACE: THE GREG LOUGANIS STORY ★★ Unlike diving, a movie is meant to make a big splash. But this made-for-cable original about diver Greg Louganis barely makes a ripple. Uninspired acting and scarce plot are just a few of the problems here. Not rated; contains violence. 95m. **DIR:** Steven H. Stern. **CAST:** Mario Lopez, Michael Murphy, Rosemary Dunsmore, Bruce Weitz. **1996**

BREAKING THE WAVES ★★★★1/2 Exquisite, thought-provoking tale of a young woman whose marriage to a strong and handsome oil-rig worker is jeopardized when he's paralyzed due to an accident. Encouraged by her husband to seek out other lovers, Bess's quest to heal her husband opens a world of emotions inside her. Rated R for adult situations, language, and nudity. 159m. **DIR:** Lars von Trier. **CAST:** Emily Watson, Stellan Skarsgard, Katrin Cartlidge, Jean-Marc Barr, Udo Kier. **1996 DVD**

BREAKING UP ★★★ Russell Crowe and Salma Hayek star as a couple struggling to end a once-good relationship now held together by nothing more than sex and force of habit. Adapted from Michael Cristofer's two-character play, this never escapes its theatrical origins but provides a good showcase for its two talented stars. Rated R for sexual situations, profanity, and nudity. 89m. **DIR:** Robert Greenwald. **CAST:** Russell Crowe, Salma Hayek. **1995**

BREAKING UP IS HARD TO DO ★★ Superficial made-for-TV movie about six men, all recently divorced, going through the usual trials and tribulations as they try to heal the wounds. 96m. **DIR:** Lou Antonio. **CAST:** Ted Bessell, Jeff Conaway, Robert Conrad, Billy Crystal, Tony Musante, David Ogden Stiers. **1979**

BREAKOUT (1975) ★★★ While not exactly Charles Bronson at his best, this action-adventure film does have its moments as the star, playing a devil-may-care helicopter pilot, rescues Robert Duvall, an American businessman framed for murder and held captive in a Mexican jail. Rated PG. 96m. **DIR:** Tom Gries. **CAST:** Charles Bronson, Robert Duvall, Jill Ireland, John Huston, Sheree North, Randy Quaid. **1975 DVD**

BREAKOUT (1998) Totally inept family comedy about an inventor whose son and his friends are kidnapped to force him to abandon his invention. The film turns into a low-rent *Home Alone* clone of the worst order. Not rated. 86m. **DIR:** John Bradshaw. **CAST:** Robert Carradine, Evan Bonifant, James Hong. **1998**

BREAKS, THE ★★★ Hip-hop comedy about an Irish boy raised by an African American family in the hood. Mitch Mullany, who wrote the script and stars as Derrick, is a fish out of water as his attempts to fit in create one hysterical moment after another. Rated R for adult situations and language. 86m. **DIR:** Eric Meza. **CAST:** Mitch Mullany, Carl Anthony Payne, III, Paula Jai Parker, Clifton Powell, Loretta Devine. **1999 DVD**

BREAKTHROUGH Richard Burton as a heroic German officer who saves the life of an American colonel (Robert Mitchum) after the Nazis thwart an attempt on Hitler's life. Rated PG. 115m. **DIR:** Andrew V. McLaglen. **CAST:** Richard Burton, Robert Mitchum, Rod Steiger, Curt Jurgens. **1978**

BREATH OF SCANDAL, A ★★ This intended high-style romantic comedy set in Austria in the gossip-rife court of Franz Joseph has little going for it. The script, taken from the Molnar play that poor John Gilbert adapted for his disastrous first talkie, is uninspired. The casting is uninspired. The directing is uninspired. But the scenery and costumes are nice. 98m. **DIR:** Michael Curtiz. **CAST:** Sophia Loren, John Gavin, Maurice Chevalier, Angela Lansbury. **1960**

BREATHING FIRE ★★1/2 Better-than-average kickboxing effort teams brothers Jonathan Ke Quan and Jerry Trimble against their father, the mastermind behind a bank robbery. Good action and decent performances. Rated R for violence. 92m. **DIR:** Lou Kennedy. **CAST:** Jonathan Ke Quan, Jerry Trimble. **1991 DVD**

BREATHING LESSONS ★★★★ Joanne Woodward steals the show in this, the 180th *Hallmark Hall of Fame*. Woodward plays a whimsical, meddling woman who tries to make things right but usually makes matters worse. James Garner, excellent as her long-suffering husband, resigns himself to their unpredictable but lasting relationship. Based on Anne Tyler's novel, this film focuses on relationships rather than actions and events and has a surprisingly powerful effect on viewers. 93m. **DIR:** John Erman. **CAST:** James Garner, Joanne Woodward, Paul Winfield, Joyce Van Patten. **1994**

BREATHING ROOM ★★ The usual complications plague a couple in this look at a relationship in jeopardy. The writing and direction are flaccid as the film examines a one-month period in the couple's lives as they attempt to find common ground in their relationship. Not very exciting or original. Rated R for adult situations and language. 90m. **DIR:** Jon Sherman. **CAST:** Susan Lloyd, Dan Futterman, Nadia Dajani, Stryker Hardwicke, David Thornton. **1996**

BREATHLESS (1959) ★★★★★ Richard Gere or Jean-Paul Belmondo? The choice should be easy after you see the Godard version of this story of a carefree crook and his "along for the ride" girlfriend. See it for Belmondo's performance as the continent's most charming crook, but while you're along for the ride, note just how well made a film can be. B&W; 89m. **DIR:** Jean-Luc Godard. **CAST:** Jean-Paul Belmondo, Jean Seberg. **1959 DVD**

BREATHLESS (1983) Richard Gere plays a car thief hunted by police. Rated R for nudity, profanity, and violence. 100m. **DIR:** Jim McBride. **CAST:** Richard Gere, Valerie Kaprisky, Art Metrano, John P. Ryan. **1983 DVD**

BREED APART, A ★★★1/2 When a billionaire collector hires an adventurous mountain climber to steal the eggs of an endangered pair of nesting eagles, the result is a nicely paced film that manages to combine drama, suspense, romance, and even a touch of post-Vietnam commentary. Rutger Hauer plays the strange recluse who lives in a tent-palace in the loneliest reaches of the Blue Ridge Mountains. Rated R for sex, nudity, and violence. 95m. **DIR:** Philippe Mora. **CAST:** Rutger Hauer, Kathleen Turner, Powers Boothe, Donald Pleasence. **1984**

BREEDERS (1986) Aliens come to Earth yet again to mate with women in this lurid sci-fi chiller. Not rated; contains nudity, violence, rape, gore, and profanity. 77m. **DIR:** Tim Kincaid. **CAST:** Teresa Farley, Lance Lewman, Frances Raines, Jennifer Delora, Ed French. **1986 DVD**

BREEDERS (1996) Aliens from a dying planet battle college students in this tired made-for-video feature. Rated R for violence, nudity, and sexual situations. 93m. **DIR:** Paul Matthews. **CAST:** Todd Jensen, Samantha Janus, Oliver Tobias. **1996 DVD**

BRENDA STARR Spoof of long-running comic-strip character features an unconvincing Brooke Shields. This was completed in 1987 but not released until 1992. Rated PG for profanity. 94m. **DIR:** Robert Ellis Miller. **CAST:** Brooke Shields, Timothy Dalton, Tony Peck, Diana Scarwid. **1992 DVD**

BREWSTER MCCLOUD ★★★ If you liked Robert Altman's *M*A*S*H* (the movie) and *Harold and Maude*, and your humor lies a few degrees off-center, you'll enjoy this "flight of fantasy" about a boy (Bud Cort) who wants to make like a bird. Rated R. 104m. **DIR:** Robert Altman. **CAST:** Bud Cort, Sally Kellerman. **1970**

BREWSTER'S MILLIONS (1945) ★★1/2 This is the fifth of seven film versions of the 1902 novel and stage success about a young man who will inherit millions if he is able to spend $1 million quickly and quietly within a set period of time. Dennis O'Keefe and company perform this Tinsel Town stalwart in fine fashion, making for a bright, entertaining comic romp. B&W; 79m. **DIR:** Allan Dwan. **CAST:** Dennis O'Keefe, Helen Walker, June Havoc, Mischa Auer, Eddie "Rochester" Anderson, Gail Patrick. **1945**

BREWSTER'S MILLIONS (1985) ★★★ It took director Walter Hill to bring Richard Pryor out of his movie slump with this unspectacular, but still entertaining, comedy about a minor-league baseball player who stands to inherit $300 million if he can fulfill the provisions of a rather daffy will. It's no classic, but still much, much better than *The Toy* or *Superman III*. Rated PG for profanity. 97m. **DIR:** Walter Hill. **CAST:** Richard Pryor, John Candy, Lonette McKee, Stephen Collins, Pat Hingle, Tovah Feldshuh, Hume Cronyn. **1985 DVD**

BRIAN'S SONG ★★★★★ This is one of the best movies ever made originally for television. James Caan is Brian Piccolo, a running back for football's Chicago Bears. His friendship with superstar Gale Sayers (Billy Dee Williams) becomes a mutually stimulating rivalry on the field and inspirational strength when Brian is felled by cancer. As with any quality film that deals with death, this movie is buoyant with life and warmth. Rated G. 73m. **DIR:** Buzz Kulik. **CAST:** James Caan, Billy Dee Williams, Jack Warden, Judy Pace, Shelley Fabares. **1970 DVD**

BRIDE, THE ★1/2 This remake of James Whale's classic 1935 horror-comedy of the macabre, *Bride of Frankenstein*, has some laughs. But these, unlike in the original, are unintentional. Rock singer Sting makes a rather stuffy, unsavory Dr. Charles (?!) Frankenstein, and Jennifer Beals is terribly miscast as his second creation. Rated PG-13 for violence, suggested sex, and nudity. 119m. **DIR:** Franc Roddam. **CAST:** Sting, Jennifer Beals, Geraldine Page, Clancy Brown, Anthony Higgins, David Rappaport. **1985 DVD**

BRIDE AND THE BEAST, THE Stock jungle footage is used to pad out this tale of the new bride of a big-game hunter who, under hypnosis, discovers that she lived a past life as a gorilla. 78m. **DIR:** Adrian Weiss. **CAST:** Charlotte Austin, Lance Fuller, Johnny Roth, Steve Calvert, William Justine. **1958**

BRIDE CAME C.O.D., THE ★★★ Bette Davis plays a runaway bride, and James Cagney goes after her on behalf of her rich father. A fun comedy in spite of an overused plot line. B&W; 92m. **DIR:** William Keighley. **CAST:** Bette Davis, James Cagney, Jack Carson, Eugene Pallette, George Tobias. **1941**

BRIDE OF CHUCKY ★★ Playing Chucky's old flame, Jennifer Tilly uses witchcraft to bring him back to life. Instead, she winds up inside a bride doll. Using teen lovebirds, the odd couple head back to Chucky's grave to make the transformation complete. Excessive gore and senseless violence is sprinkled with moments of comic relief. Facial expressions on both dolls are disturbing and oddly impressive. Brad Dourif voices the devilish Chucky. Rated R for gore, profanity, violence, and sexual situations. 89m. **DIR:** Ronny Yu. **CAST:** Jennifer Tilly, Nick Stabile, Katherine Heigl. **1999 DVD**

BRIDE OF FRANKENSTEIN ★★★★★ This is a first-rate sequel to *Frankenstein*. This time, Henry Frankenstein (Colin Clive) is coerced by the evil Dr. Praetorius (Ernest Thesiger in a delightfully weird and sinister performance) into creating a mate for the monster. B&W; 75m. **DIR:** James Whale. **CAST:** Boris Karloff, Colin Clive, Valerie Hobson, Dwight Frye, Ernest Thesiger, Elsa Lanchester. **1935 DVD**

BRIDE OF RE-ANIMATOR ★★★ Not as effective but just as bloodily wacked-out, this sequel brings back most of the cast and crew behind the first film to wreak more havoc at Miskatonic University. Fans of the first *Re-Animator* won't want to miss it. Not rated; contains profanity, nudity, and gore. 99m. **DIR:** Brian Yuzna. **CAST:** Bruce Abbott, Jeffrey Combs, David Gale, Claude Earl Jones. **1989 DVD**

BRIDE OF THE GORILLA ★★ Love and marriage on a jungle plantation give Raymond Burr more than he bargained for as he falls victim to an evil curse. Intermittently engrossing. B&W; 65m. **DIR:** Curt Siodmak. **CAST:** Raymond Burr, Barbara Payton, Lon Chaney Jr., Tom Conway, Paul Cavanagh, Woody Strode. **1951**

BRIDE OF THE MONSTER ★★ Another incredibly inept but hilarious film from Ed Wood Jr., this stinker uses most of the mad scientist clichés and uses them poorly as a cadaverous-looking Bela Lugosi tries to do fiendish things to an unconscious (even while alert) Loretta King. This bottom-of-the-barrel independent monstrosity boasts possibly the worst special-effects monster of all time, a rubber octopus that any novelty store would be ashamed to stock. B&W; 69m. **DIR:** Edward D. Wood Jr. **CAST:** Bela Lugosi, Tor Johnson, Tony McCoy, Loretta King. **1955 DVD**

•BRIDE OF THE WIND ★★ This biography of Alma Schindler, who married three giants of twentieth-century art (composer Gustav Mahler, architect Walter Gropius, writer Franz Werfel) and carried on with many others, is drab and uninvolving. The film is hampered by a disjointed script, a meager budget, and a dull performance by Sarah Wynter that makes one wonder why Schindler's men found her so fascinating. Rated R for nudity and sexual scenes. 99m. **DIR:** Bruce Beresford. **CAST:** Sarah Wynter, Jonathan Pryce, Vincent Perez, Simon Verhoeven. **2001 DVD**

BRIDE WALKS OUT, THE ★★★ This fast-paced comedy relies more on the dialogue and personalities of the supporting cast than on the stars or the story. Newlyweds Barbara Stanwyck and Gene Raymond can't get along on the amount of money he makes, and her spending estranges them. Lots of fun. B&W; 75m. **DIR:** Leigh Jason. **CAST:** Barbara Stanwyck, Gene Raymond, Robert Young, Ned Sparks, Helen Broderick, Billy Gilbert, Ward Bond, Hattie McDaniel. **1936**

BRIDE WITH WHITE HAIR, THE ★★★★ A swordsman and a witch join forces during China's Mo Dynasty to battle the evil supernatural powers of a pair of bisexual Siamese twins. Like many of the astonishing fantasy-adventures coming out of Hong Kong, this one can be hard to follow. But when it's this gorgeous, fast, and furious, you don't mind watching it a few times. Not rated; contains violence and sexual situations. In Chinese with English subtitles; dubbed version also available. 92m. **DIR:** Ronny Yu. **CAST:** Brigitte Lin, Leslie Cheung, Elaine Lui. **1993 DVD**

BRIDE WORE BLACK, THE ★★★★ François Truffaut pays homage to Alfred Hitchcock in this suspenseful drama about a woman who tracks down and kills a group of men who killed her husband on their wedding day. Fine Bernard Herrmann score. 95m. **DIR:** François Truffaut. **CAST:** Jeanne Moreau, Claude Rich, Jean-Claude Brialy, Michel Bouquet, Michel Lonsdale, Charles Denner. **1968 DVD**

BRIDE WORE RED, THE ★★ A trampy club singer pretends to be a society debutante, and all the rich guys fall in love with her. Joan Crawford played so many street girls who posed as classy ladies, her movies became a cliché. This is probably the definitive one. B&W; 103m. **DIR:** Dorothy Arzner. **CAST:** Joan Crawford, Franchot

Tone, Robert Young, Billie Burke, Reginald Owen, Dickie Moore, George Zucco. **1937**

BRIDES OF CHRIST ★★★★★ Set during the 1960s, this Australian miniseries centers on a group of Catholic women—nuns, novices, and schoolgirls—and their life choices. The high quality of this production draws you into their insular world, as well as a time of immense social change. Made for Australian TV. Not rated. 100m. **DIR:** Ken Cameron. **CAST:** Brenda Fricker, Josephine Byrnes, Sandy Gore, Kym Wilson, Naomi Watts. **1991**

BRIDES OF DRACULA ★★★1/2 The depraved son of a debauched noblewoman is held prisoner by her to spare the countryside his blood lust. When a pretty young teacher sets him free, his mother is the first victim of his reign of terror. David Peel is the blond vampire and Peter Cushing reprises his role as Dr. Van Helsing in this nicely acted Hammer Films horror entry. 85m. **DIR:** Terence Fisher. **CAST:** Peter Cushing, David Peel, Martita Hunt, Yvonne Monlaur, Freda Jackson, Miles Malleson, Mona Washbourne. **1960**

BRIDES OF THE BEAST 🦃 First entry in a dreadful trio of Filipino Blood Island, mad-scientist potboilers. Original title: *Brides of Blood.* 85m. **DIR:** Eddie Romero, Gerardo de Leon. **CAST:** John Ashley, Kent Taylor, Beverly Hills. **1968**

BRIDESHEAD REVISITED ★★★★ Evelyn Waugh's novel of British upper-class decadence gets royal treatment in this adaptation from John Mortimer. Jeremy Irons stars as the impressionable Oxford youth bedazzled by Sebastian Flyte (Anthony Andrews), youngest of the ill-fated Marchmain family. Not rated; includes frank sexual themes and brief nudity. 388m. **DIR:** Charles Sturridge, Michael Lindsay-Hogg. **CAST:** Jeremy Irons, Anthony Andrews, Diana Quick, Laurence Olivier, Claire Bloom, John Gielgud, Stéphane Audran, Mona Washbourne, John Le Mesurier, Simon Jones. **1981**

BRIDGE, THE ★★★★1/2 Just before the end of World War II, a small group of schoolboys are drafted by the German army and assigned to defend a worthless bridge against the approaching Americans. Nominated for an Academy Award as Best Foreign Language Film, this is one of the great antiwar movies. B&W; 106m. **DIR:** Bernhard Wicki. **CAST:** Foiker Bohnet, Fritz Wepper, Michael Hinz. **1959 DVD**

BRIDGE AT REMAGEN, THE ★★★ Solid World War II drama concerns the German attempt to hold or blow up one of the last remaining bridges leading into the fatherland. Well-done action sequences keep things moving along at a good pace. Not a great film, but it should fill the bill for fans of the genre. 115m. **DIR:** John Guillermin. **CAST:** George Segal, Ben Gazzara, Robert Vaughn, E. G. Marshall, Bradford Dillman, Peter Van Eyck. **1969 DVD**

BRIDGE OF DRAGONS ★★★ Dolph Lundgren stars as a warrior who must decide between loyalty to his increasingly evil leader and the life of a young princess who is being forced into becoming the leader's bride. Lundgren fans should eat up the action and ignore the other outright silliness. Rated R for violence. 95m. **DIR:** Isaac Florentine. **CAST:** Dolph Lundgren, Cary-Hiroyuki Tagawa, Rachel Shane. **1999 DVD**

BRIDGE OF SAN LUIS REY, THE ★★1/2 Five people meet death when an old Peruvian rope bridge collapses. This snail's-pace, moody version of Thornton Wilder's fatalistic 1920s novel traces their lives. Not too hot, and neither was the 1929 version. B&W; 85m. **DIR:** Rowland V. Lee. **CAST:** Lynn Bari, Anna Nazimova, Louis Calhern, Akim Tamiroff, Francis Lederer, Blanche Yurka, Donald Woods. **1944 DVD**

BRIDGE ON THE RIVER KWAI, THE ★★★★★ This powerful, dramatic story centers around the construction of a bridge by British and American prisoners of war under the command of Japanese colonel Sessue Hayakawa. Alec Guinness is the stiff-upper-lipped British commander who uses the task as a way of proving British superiority. 161m. **DIR:** David Lean. **CAST:** William Holden, Alec Guinness, Jack Hawkins, Sessue Hayakawa, James Donald. **1957 DVD**

BRIDGE TO HELL ★1/2 After a group of World War II POWs escape, a bridge is their last obstacle and they decide to take it out after crossing. (Sound familiar?) Lots of shooting and explosions. Unfortunately, not much of a plot. Not rated; contains violence and profanity. 94m. **DIR:** Umberto Lenzi. **CAST:** Andy J. Forest. **1989**

BRIDGE TO NOWHERE ★★1/2 Five streetwise city kids head to the rough-and-rugged country for a fun-filled weekend. Once they trespass on the land of an extremely vicious and violent man (Bruno Lawrence), they are forced to fight for survival. Parental discretion advised. 87m. **DIR:** Ian Mune. **CAST:** Bruno Lawrence, Alison Routledge, Margaret Umbers, Philip Gordon. **1986**

BRIDGE TO SILENCE ★★1/2 Sincere performances by a talented cast, including Marlee Matlin in her first speaking role, cannot quite overcome a melodramatic story in which a deaf woman (Matlin) nearly loses custody of her daughter to the mother (Lee Remick) who never understood her. Made for television. 95m. **DIR:** Karen Arthur. **CAST:** Marlee Matlin, Lee Remick, Josef Sommer, Michael O'Keefe. **1989**

BRIDGE TOO FAR, A ★★★1/2 Here's another story of a famous battle with the traditional all-star cast. In this case it's World War II's "Operation Market Garden," a disastrous Allied push to get troops behind German lines and capture an early bridgehead on the Rhine. Rated PG. 175m. **DIR:** Richard Attenborough. **CAST:** Dirk Bogarde, James Caan, Michael Caine, Sean Connery, Laurence Olivier, Robert Redford. **1977 DVD**

BRIDGES AT TOKO-RI, THE ★★★★1/2 With this picture, screenwriter Valentine Davies and director Mark Robson created one of the cinema's most authentic depictions of war. It is certainly the best motion picture about the Korean War. James Michener's novel, as adapted here, centers on a bomber pilot and his crew, part of an aircraft-carrier force assigned to destroy vital North Korean bridges. 103m. **DIR:** Mark Robson. **CAST:** William Holden, Fredric March, Grace Kelly, Mickey Rooney, Earl Holliman, Charles McGraw, Robert Strauss, Willis Bouchey, Gene Reynolds. **1954 DVD**

BRIDGES OF MADISON COUNTY, THE ★★★★ Touching story of a brief romantic encounter between a free-spirited photographer for *National Geographic* magazine and an emotionally neglected wife of an Iowa farmer. Clint Eastwood and Meryl Streep are superb as the two kindred spirits who find themselves thrown together for four unforgettable hot summer days in 1965. Rated PG-13 for suggested sex and profanity. 135m. **DIR:** Clint Eastwood. **CAST:** Clint Eastwood, Meryl Streep, Annie Corley, Victor Slezak, Jim Haynie. **1995 DVD**

BRIDGET JONES'S DIARY ★★1/2 Single British career woman keeps a diary as she sorts Mr. Right from Mr. Wrong and tries to bolster her sagging self-esteem. She dates her lecher boss and a starchy human-rights attorney in a rather mundane romantic comedy that trips over several unconvincing plot points. The film provides a few laughs but fails to ignite any urgent interest on which loves-me, loves-me-not petal it ends. The script is based on journalist Helen Fielding's popular 1996 British novel that began—like TV's *Sex and the City*—as a newspaper column. Rated R for profanity, sex, and violence. 95m. **DIR:** Sharon Maguire. **CAST:** Renee Zellweger, Hugh Grant, Colin Firth, Jim Broadbent, Gemma Jones. **2001**

BRIEF ENCOUNTER ★★1/2 This is a remake of the 1945 classic film that was based on Noel Coward's play *Still Life*. It tells the story of two married strangers who meet in a British train terminal and fall into a short-lived but intense romance. This made-for-television production suffers in comparison. 103m. **DIR:** Alan Bridges. **CAST:** Richard Burton, Sophia Loren. **1974**

BRIEF ENCOUNTER ★★★★1/2 In this evergreen classic, a chance meeting in a railroad station results in a doomed, poignant love affair between two lonely people married to others. Celia Johnson is the woman, Trevor Howard the man. A compassionate look at the innocence of sudden, unforeseen romance. David Lean's direction results in a moving, memorable film for all time. B&W; 85m. **DIR:** David Lean. **CAST:** Celia Johnson, Trevor Howard, Stanley Holloway, Joyce Carey, Cyril Raymond. **1945 DVD**

BRIG, THE ★★1/2 One of the more self-conscious efforts of the American New Cinema of the 1960s, adapted from a stage play set in a Marine Corps prison. With almost no dialogue, the film conveys the dehumanizing aspects of life as a prisoner. But even at this abbreviated length (it was originally 120m.), it's hard to watch. B&W; 57m. **DIR:** Jonas Mekas, Adolfas Mekas. **CAST:** Warren Finnerty. **1965**

BRIGADOON ★★★★ Enchanting musical stars Van Johnson and Gene Kelly as two Americans who discover Brigadoon, a Scottish village with a life span of only one day for every hundred years. In the village, Kelly meets Cyd Charisse, and they naturally dance up a storm. 108m. **DIR:** Vincente Minnelli. **CAST:** Gene Kelly, Van Johnson, Cyd Charisse, Elaine Stewart, Barry Jones. **1954 DVD**

•BRIGHAM CITY ★★1/2 A small-town sheriff in Utah suffers a crisis of faith when a serial killer surfaces in his picture-perfect community. The film has sincerity and good intentions, but the characters are more interesting than the story, and the pacing flags as the climax approaches. Rated PG-13 for brief violence. 119m. **DIR:** Richard Dutcher. **CAST:** Richard Dutcher, Matthew A. Brown, Wilford Brimley, Carrie Morgan. **2001 DVD**

BRIGHT ANGEL ★★★1/2 Thoroughly engrossing film follows a young woman's attempt to free her brother from jail. A real sleeper that grabs hold and refuses to let go right up to its uncompromising conclusion. Rated R for language, nudity, and violence. 94m. **DIR:** Michael Fields. **CAST:** Dermot Mulroney, Lili Taylor, Mary Kay Place, Bill Pullman, Burt Young, Valerie Perrine, Sam Shepard. **1991**

BRIGHT EYES ★★★1/2 Delicious melodrama finds Shirley Temple living in a fine mansion as the maid's daughter. After her mom's untimely death, three people vie for her adoption rights. Curly Shirley is irresistible as the ever-cheerful little Bright Eyes. 83m. **DIR:** David Butler. **CAST:** Shirley Temple, James Dunn, Jane Withers, Judith Allen. **1934 DVD**

BRIGHT LIGHTS, BIG CITY ★★ Films grappling with the evils of substance abuse run the risk of glamorizing the subject they intend to criticize, and that is precisely the problem with this adaptation of Jay McInerney's novel (even though he wrote his own screenplay). Rated R for language and graphic drug emphasis. 110m. **DIR:** James Bridges. **CAST:** Michael J. Fox, Kiefer Sutherland, Phoebe Cates, Swoosie Kurtz, Frances Sternhagen, John Houseman, Jason Robards Jr., Dianne Wiest, William Hickey. **1988**

BRIGHT SHINING LIE, A ★★★1/2 In this controversial exposé of the Vietnam War, Bill Paxton dominates the screen as John Paul Vann, a shrewd strategist and career soldier sent into Vietnam in 1962 as one of the American "advisors." His subsequent candor about the corrupt South Vietnamese torpedoes his military career; he later returns and continues to lock horns with higher-ups over the "right" way to fight the war. Terry George's film paints a grim picture of a war America clearly didn't understand. Rated R for profanity, violence, and nudity. 120m. **DIR:** Terry George. **CAST:** Bill Paxton, Amy Madigan, Vivian Wu, Donal Logue, James Rebhorn, Kurtwood Smith, Eric Bogosian. **1998 DVD**

BRIGHTON BEACH MEMOIRS ★★★1/2 Neil Simon's reminiscences of his adolescence make for genuinely enjoyable viewing. Refreshingly free of Simon's often too-clever dialogue, it aims for the heart and, more often than not, hits its mark. Rated PG-13 for sexual references. 110m. **DIR:** Gene Saks. **CAST:** Jonathan Silverman, Blythe Danner, Bob Dishy, Brian Drillinger, Stacey Glick, Judith Ivey, Lisa Waltz. **1986 DVD**

BRIGHTON STRANGLER, THE ★★1/2 John Loder runs amok after a Nazi bomb destroys the London theater where he has been playing a murderer in a drama. Stunned in the explosion, he confuses his true identity with the character he has been playing. A chance remark by a stranger sends him off to the seaside resort of Brighton, where he performs his stage role for real! B&W; 67m. **DIR:** Max Nosseck. **CAST:** John Loder, June Duprez, Miles Mander, Rose Hobart, Ian Wolfe. **1945**

BRIGHTY OF THE GRAND CANYON ★★ Acceptable little film for the family. Brighty is a desert mule who teams up with Dick Foran, a prospector who has discovered a large vein of gold in the Grand Canyon. The photography is quite good. 89m. **DIR:** Norman Foster. **CAST:** Joseph Cotten, Dick Foran, Karl Swenson, Pat Conway. **1967 DVD**

BRILLIANT DISGUISE, A ★★ Anthony Denison plays sportswriter Andy Manola, who falls for Michelle, a woman with seemingly multiple personalities. According to psychiatrist Corbin Bernsen, she's dangerous and it doesn't surprise him when Manola's friends and colleagues start dropping like flies. Or is someone setting her up? The search for the truth provides plenty of steamy opportunity for Lysette Anthony to take off her clothes. Rated R for nudity, violence, and strong language. 97m. **DIR:** Nick Vallelonga. **CAST:** Lysette Anthony, Anthony Denison, Corbin Bernsen, Gregory McKinney. **1993**

BRILLIANT LIES ★★1/2 Adapted from a play by David Williamson, this Australian drama starts out as a he-said, she-said tale of sexual harassment in which a secretary suing for wrongful dismissal and her macho ex-boss both appear to be unscrupulous liars. But the script abuses the audience by withholding important story points until the finale, rendering the whole thing dishonest. Not rated; contains strong profanity. 88m. **DIR:** Richard Franklin. **CAST:** Anthony LaPaglia, Gia Carides, Zoe Carides, Ray Barrett. **1996**

BRIMSTONE ★★★★ Undercover lawman Rod Cameron breaks up a cattle-rustling family headed by Walter Brennan. Solid performances and direction make this one of Cameron's best Westerns. 90m. **DIR:** Joseph Kane. **CAST:** Rod Cameron, Walter Brennan, Forrest Tucker, Jack Holt, Adrian Booth, Jim Davis. **1949**

BRIMSTONE AND TREACLE ★★★ Sting plays an angelic-diabolic young drifter who insinuates himself into the home lives of respectable Denholm Elliott and Joan Plowright in this British-made shocker. Rated R. 85m. **DIR:** Richard Loncraine. **CAST:** Denholm Elliott, Joan Plowright, Suzanna Hamilton, Sting. **1982**

BRING IT ON ★★★1/2 "They're sexy . . . and cute . . . and popular to boot!" This predictable saga of rival cheerleading squads earns high marks for energy and earnest performances. White-bread San Diego gal (Kirsten Dunst), upon taking command of her high-school cheerleading squad, learns to her horror that the former captain has for years stolen hip-hop routines from an East Compton group. Now, with both squads heading for the championships, our heroine faces a crisis. File this one under good, dumb—and occasionally sexy—fun. Rated PG-13 for profanity and sensuality. 98m. **DIR:** Peyton Reed. **CAST:** Kirsten Dunst, Eliza Dushku, Jesse Bradford, Gabrielle Union, Clare Kramer, Nicole Bilderback. **2000 DVD**

BRING ME THE HEAD OF ALFREDO GARCIA ★★1/2 Warren Oates gives an outstanding performance as a piano player in Mexico who becomes mixed-up with vicious bounty hunters. Hard-core Sam Peckinpah fans will appreciate this one more than the casual viewer. Rated R. 112m. **DIR:** Sam Peckinpah. **CAST:** Warren Oates, Isela Vega, Gig Young, Robert Webber, Emilio Fernandez, Kris Kristofferson, Helmut Dantine. **1974**

BRINGING OUT THE DEAD ★★1/2 If the point of a story is a character's redemption, but redemption occurs in a doomed environment, then what have we gained? That's the problem facing this dreary, unsettling, and ultimately overwhelming indictment of big-city emergency medicine. Plainly reminiscent of *Taxi Driver*, this reunion by director Martin Scorsese and scripter Paul Schrader (adapting Joe Connelly's novel) starts off in what seems like a realistic universe, but ultimately drifts into the heightened realm of exaggerated, *film noir* farce. Nicolas Cage stars as a battered and burned-out EMS paramedic lately plagued by the ghost of a young woman he failed to save. True, the horror is presented with Scorsese's characteristically energized, often balletic grace, but eventually the trick camerawork and throbbing pop soundtrack become tiresome. Rated R for profanity, violence, medical gore, and drug use. 118m. **DIR:** Martin Scorsese. **CAST:** Nicolas Cage, Patricia Arquette, John Goodman, Ving Rhames, Tom Sizemore. **1999 DVD**

BRINGING UP BABY ★★★★★ A classic screwball comedy, this Howard Hawks picture has lost none of its punch even after fifty years. Katharine Hepburn plays a daffy rich girl who gets an absentminded professor (Cary Grant) into all sorts of trouble. *Bringing Up Baby* is guaranteed to have you falling out of your seat with helpless laughter. B&W; 102m. **DIR:** Howard Hawks. **CAST:** Cary Grant, Katharine Hepburn, Charlie Ruggles, May Robson. **1938**

BRINK OF LIFE ★★★ Early Ingmar Bergman film set entirely in a hospital maternity ward, where three women ponder their pregnancies and the relationships that preceded them. Rather bleak and naturalistic, this is an actors' piece, though Bergman still controls the film emotionally in subtle ways. In Swedish with English subtitles. B&W; 82m. **DIR:** Ingmar Bergman. **CAST:** Eva Dahlbeck, Ingrid Thulin, Bibi Andersson, Max von Sydow, Erland Josephson. **1957**

BRINKS JOB, THE ★★★1/2 Peter Falk stars in this enjoyable release in which a gang of klutzy crooks pulls off "the crime of the century." It's a breezy caper film reminiscent of George Roy Hill's *Butch Cassidy and the Sundance Kid* and *The Sting*. Rated PG. 103m. **DIR:** William Friedkin. **CAST:** Peter Falk, Peter Boyle, Allen Garfield, Warren Oates, Paul Sorvino, Gena Rowlands. **1978**

BRITANNIA HOSPITAL ★★★ A wildly inadequate hospital serves as a metaphor for a sick society in this okay black comedy by British director Lindsay Anderson (*If; O Lucky Man*). Rated R. 115m. **DIR:** Lindsay Anderson. **CAST:** Leonard Rossiter, Graham Crowden, Malcolm McDowell, Joan Plowright. **1982 DVD**

BROADCAST NEWS ★★★★★ Writer-director-producer James L. Brooks tackles the flashy emptiness of contemporary television journalism. William Hurt stars as the coming trend in news anchors—all enthusiasm and no education—who clashes amiably with Albert Brooks as the reporter's reporter: blessed with insight and a clever turn of phrase, but no camera presence. Both are attracted to dedicated superproducer Holly Hunter, an overachiever who schedules brief nervous breakdowns into her workday. Rated R for profanity. 131m. **DIR:** James L. Brooks. **CAST:** William Hurt, Albert Brooks, Holly Hunter, Jack Nicholson, Robert Prosky, Joan Cusack. **1987 DVD**

BROADWAY BILL ★★★ One of Frank Capra's favorite films and one of the few he remade in later years. Warner Baxter stars as a horse owner who cares more about animals than his superficial family. He shirks family responsibility and his inheritance to train his favorite horse, Broadway Bill. Capra's remake was called *Riding High* and starred Bing Crosby. B&W; 90m. **DIR:** Frank Capra. **CAST:** Warner Baxter, Myrna Loy, Helen Vinson, Walter Connolly, Frankie Darro, Jason Robards Sr., Lucille Ball, Ward Bond, Dennis O'Keefe, Margaret Hamilton, Alan Hale Sr., Lynne Overman, Douglass Dumbrille. **1934**

BROADWAY DANNY ROSE ★★★★1/2 The legendary talent agent Broadway Danny Rose (Woody Allen) takes on an alcoholic crooner (Nick Apollo Forte) and carefully nurtures him to the brink of stardom in this hilarious comedy, also written and directed by Allen. Mia Farrow is delightful as a gangster's moll who inadvertently gets Rose in big trouble. Rated PG for brief violence. B&W; 86m. **DIR:** Woody Allen. **CAST:** Woody Allen, Mia Farrow, Milton Berle, Sandy Baron. **1984 DVD**

BROADWAY MELODY, THE ★★ Prototype of all the backstage musical romances. Two sisters (Anita Page and Bessie Love) run afoul of big-city corruption when they leave the sticks to pursue their destinies in New York. Stolid acting and awkward sound-recording techniques are mostly unrelieved, although the "Singin' in the Rain" number (the first of many times the song will be heard in MGM musicals) still packs a rough kind of charm. Somehow it won an Oscar as the year's best picture. B&W; 104m. **DIR:** Harry Beaumont. **CAST:** Anita Page, Bessie Love, Charles King. **1929**

BROADWAY MELODY OF 1940 ★★★ Fine performances redeem this otherwise tired tale of friendship and rivalry between dancing partners. The dancing of course, is flawless; the Cole Porter songs are outstanding. B&W; 102m. **DIR:** Norman Taurog. **CAST:** Fred Astaire, Eleanor Powell, George Murphy, Frank Morgan, Ian Hunter. **1940**

BROADWAY MELODY OF 1938 ★★1/2 Fifteen year old Judy Garland stops the show in this tuneful musical anthology when she sings the now legendary "Dear Mr. Gable" version of "You Made Me Love You." The finale stretches credibility until it snaps as Eleanor Powell, in top hat and tails, dances with a division of chorus boys before a neon skyline. B&W; 110m. **DIR:** Roy Del Ruth. **CAST:** Robert Taylor, Eleanor Powell, George Murphy, Binnie Barnes, Sophie Tucker, Judy Garland, Buddy Ebsen, Willie Howard, Billy Gilbert. **1937**

BROADWAY MELODY OF 1936 ★★★ Backstage musical comedy. Obnoxious gossip columnist Jack Benny tries to use dancer Eleanor Powell to harass producer Robert Taylor. Forget the plot and enjoy the singing and dancing—including Taylor's rendition of "I've Got a Feelin' You're Foolin'," the only time he sang on-screen in his own voice. B&W; 110m. **DIR:** Roy Del Ruth. **CAST:** Jack Benny, Eleanor Powell, Robert Taylor, Una Merkel, Buddy Ebsen. **1935**

BROADWAY RHYTHM ★★1/2 A reworking of Jerome Kern's last Broadway musical, *Very Warm for May*, with one of the finest songs Kern ever wrote, "All the Things You Are." The routine plot pits ex-vaudevillian performers against the new breed of singers. B&W; 114m. **DIR:** Roy Del Ruth. **CAST:** George Murphy, Ginny Simms, Gloria De Haven, Lena Horne, Hazel Scott, Tommy Dorsey, Charles Winninger, Ben Blue. **1943**

BROADWAY SERENADE ★★★ A musical aimed strictly at Jeanette MacDonald fans. She does all the singing as a woman at odds with her husband and her career. The splashy finale was directed by Busby Berkeley. B&W; 113m. **DIR:** Robert Z. Leonard. **CAST:** Jeanette MacDonald, Lew Ayres, Ian Hunter, Frank Morgan, Virginia Grey, Rita Johnson, William Gargan. **1929**

BROADWAY TO CHEYENNE ★★1/2 A New York mob moves west to set up a cattlemen's protection association, but a New York cop on vacation breaks up their racket. This was Rex Bell's first Western, and it set the formula for many of his pictures. B&W; 60m. **DIR:** Harry Fraser. **CAST:** Rex Bell, George "Gabby" Hayes, Marceline Day. **1932**

BROKEDOWN PALACE ★★★ Two female midwestern high-school graduates take a trip to Bangkok where they meet a seductive Australian who offers them a free flight to Hong Kong. At the airport, they are arrested for drug trafficking; an expatriate Yankee lawyer and his Thai wife come to their rescue. Similar material has been covered with much more tension, but the acting is excellent and the photography is stunning. Rated PG-13 for language, violence, and drug use. 100m. **DIR:** Jonathan Kaplan. **CAST:** Claire Danes, Kate Beckinsale, Bill Pullman, Jacqueline Kim. **1999 DVD**

BROKEN ANGEL ★★ Distraught parents find their world turned upside down when their daughter disappears after a gang fight during her senior prom. Made for TV movie that superficially skims the surface of parental trust and love. 94m. **DIR:** Richard T. Heffron. **CAST:** William Shatner, Susan Blakely, Roxann Biggs, Brock Peters. **1992**

BROKEN ARROW (1950) ★★★ Jeff Chandler is the Apache chief Cochise and James Stewart is a cavalry scout in this sympathetic look at Indians and white settlers struggling to coexist on the Western frontier in the 1870s. The film was the first to treat the Indian with respect and understanding. 93m. **DIR:** Delmer Daves. **CAST:** James Stewart, Jeff Chandler, Debra Paget, Will Geer, Arthur Hunnicutt, Basil Ruysdael, Jay Silverheels. **1950**

BROKEN ARROW (1996) ★★★★ In this thrill-packed film, Christian Slater, a copilot on top-secret B-3 Stealth bombers, is shocked when his mentor, John Travolta, uses a practice mission as a way to steal nuclear weapons. Angered over being passed up for promotions, Travolta plans to use the threat of widespread destruction to blackmail the U.S. government. Rated R for violence and profanity. 108m. **DIR:** John Woo. **CAST:** John Travolta, Christian Slater, Samantha Mathis, Delroy Lindo, Frank Whaley, Bob Gunton, Howie Long, Jack Thompson. **1996 DVD**

BROKEN BLOSSOMS ★★★1/2 The tragic story of a young Chinese boy's unselfish love for a cruelly mistreated white girl. Lillian Gish is heart-twisting as the girl; Richard Barthelmess's portrayal of the Chinese boy made him an overnight star. Donald Crisp, later famous in warm and sympathetic roles, is the unfortunate girl's evil tormentor. Silent. B&W; 68m. **DIR:** D. W. Griffith. **CAST:** Lillian Gish, Richard Barthelmess, Donald Crisp. **1919 DVD**

BROKEN CHAIN, THE ★★★ Solid action film looks at the quandary the Indian Nations faced during the American Revolution. With all sides vying for their help, the Nation is placed in a no-win situation eventually pitting tribe against tribe. Made for TV. 94m. **DIR:** Lamont Johnson. **CAST:** Eric Schweig, Wes Studi, Buffy Sainte-Marie, Pierce Brosnan, J. C. White Shirt, Graham Greene. **1993**

BROKEN ENGLISH ★★★1/2 The Romeo and Juliet theme is played out amidst racial tension among ethnic groups immigrating to modern New Zealand. Aleksandra Vujcic plays a young Croatian waitress who falls in love with a Maori coworker, in defiance of her volatile, possessive father. Rated NC-17 for profanity, nudity, and graphic simulated sex. 91m. **DIR:** Gregor Nicholas. **CAST:** Aleksandra Vujcic, Julian Arahanga, Rade Serbedzija. **1996**

BROKEN HARVEST ★★★★ A sad family drama set in 1950s rural Ireland, this is played out against a larger theme of a country and its people in turmoil. Warm family love and simmering rivalries are intensified by parochial values, an oppressive church, and bitterness reaching back to the Irish Civil War. This effective-looking period piece is extremely atmospheric and evocative, but sometimes too slow and overly dramatized. Still, it is the natural follow-up to *Michael Collins*. Not rated; contains violence. 106m. **DIR:** Maurice O'Callaghan. **CAST:** Colin Lane, Marian Quinn, Niall O'Brien, Darren McHugh. **1995 DVD**

BROKEN HEARTS CLUB, THE ★★★1/2 Following the romantic ups and downs of a small circle of gay friends, this film surpasses the standard gay-themed indie film by virtue of its clever, playful dialogue and sincere performances from a strong ensemble cast. A slide into facile pathos toward the end fails to dampen the film's easygoing charm. Rated R for mature themes and profanity. 94m. **DIR:** Greg Berlanti. **CAST:** Timothy Olyphant, Zach Braff, Dean Cain, Andrew Keegan, Nia Long, John Mahoney. **2000 DVD**

BROKEN LANCE ★★★★ Spencer Tracy's superb performance as a cattle baron at odds with his Indian wife and bickering sons is but one of the pleasures in this first-rate adult Western. The screenplay, based on 1949's *House of Strangers*, won an Oscar, and Katy Jurado was nominated for best supporting actress. 97m. **DIR:** Edward Dmytryk. **CAST:** Spencer Tracy, Richard Widmark, Jean Peters, Robert Wagner, Katy Jurado, Earl Holliman, Hugh O'Brian. **1954**

BROKEN TRUST (1992) 🦃 Only fans of daytime television may be able to find something to salvage in this laughable story of a woman terrorized by her sister and business rivals. Rated R for nudity. 84m. **DIR:** Ralph Portillo. **CAST:** Kimberly Foster, Kathryn Harris, Nick Cassavetes, Don Swayze, Edward Arnold. **1992**

BROKEN TRUST (1995) ★★★ Tom Selleck is a judge dedicated to upholding judicial standards. What weakens the film is the unbelievable plot that has him setting up a corruption sting that lays waste to both family and friends before he questions his strictly right-or-wrong world. Not rated; contains violence. 90m. **DIR:** Geoffrey Sax. **CAST:** Tom Selleck, William Atherton, Marsha Mason, Elizabeth McGovern. **1995**

BROKEN VESSELS ★★★1/2 Powerful tale of two ambulance drivers who find common ground on the mean streets. Unlike Martin Scorsese's *Bringing Out the Dead*, director Scott Ziehl's film is filled with memorable characters, explosive situations, and a reality that benefits the performers. Jason London and Todd Field are excellent as the new paramedic and the veteran who rely on each other even though the odds are against them. Rated R for adult situations, language, violence, and nudity. 91m. **DIR:** Scott Ziehl. **CAST:** Jason London, Todd Field, Roxana Zal, Susan Traylor, James Hong, Patricia Cranshaw. **1998 DVD**

BROKEN VOWS ★★★1/2 Effective made-for-television melodrama stars Tommy Lee Jones as a priest caught between his vows and the love of a woman. Delicately handles the moral dilemma of the priest, who must decide to give up a job he does extremely well or give up the woman who brings solace to his life. Not rated. 95m. **DIR:** Jud Taylor. **CAST:** Tommy Lee Jones, Annette O'Toole, Milo O'Shea, David Groh, Madeleine Sherwood. **1986**

BRONCO (TV SERIES) ★★★1/2 Originally tapped to take over the role of *Cheyenne* when Clint Walker walked out during a salary dispute, Ty Hardin became *Bronco* in a series that drew many of its stories from historic events. In "Shadow of Jesse James," Bronco must arrest the famed outlaw (James Coburn). In "Death of an Outlaw," Bronco Layne finds himself involved in the Lincoln County Wars alongside Billy the Kid and Pat Garrett. 49m. **DIR:** Leslie Goodwins, Robert L. Strock. **CAST:** Ty Hardin, James Coburn, Allan "Rocky" Lane, Rhodes Reason. **1958–1962**

BRONCO BILLY ★★★ This warmhearted character study centers around Clint Eastwood as Bronco Billy, the owner of a run-down Wild West show. Sondra Locke is deserted on her honeymoon by her husband (Geoffrey Lewis). Desperate, she agrees to join the show as Eastwood's assistant and that's when the lightweight tale takes a romantic turn. Rated PG. 119m. **DIR:** Clint Eastwood. **CAST:** Clint Eastwood, Sondra Locke, Geoffrey Lewis, Scatman Crothers, Sam Bottoms, Bill McKinney, Dan Vadis. **1980 DVD**

BRONX EXECUTIONER, THE 🦃 A group of humans battle for their lives against cyborgs bent on their destruction. Not rated; contains violence. 88m. **DIR:** Bob Collins. **CAST:** Margie Newton, Chuck Valenti, Woody Strode. **1989**

BRONX TALE, A ★★★★ Robert De Niro makes an impressive directorial debut with this atmospheric, exquisitely detailed character study of a youngster torn between his hardworking, bus-driver dad (De Niro) and the flashy mobster (played superbly by screenwriter Chazz Palminteri) who rules their Bronx neighborhood. It's hard-edged at times—disturbingly so in segments on racial hatred—but ultimately rewarding. Rated R for violence and profanity. 122m. **DIR:** Robert De Niro. **CAST:** Robert De Niro, Chazz Palminteri, Joe Pesci, Lillo Brancato, Francis Capra, Taral Hicks. **1993 DVD**

BRONX WAR, THE ★★★ Two drug-dealing factions—one black, one Hispanic—declare war and a nonstop bloodfest ensues. A capable actor (who is credited only as Joseph) leads the Hispanics. Not rated, but equivalent to an R for violence, profanity, and nudity. 91m. **DIR:** Joseph B. Vasquez. **CAST:** Fabio Urena, Charmain Cruz, Andre Brown. **1989**

BRONZE BUCKAROO ★★1/2 Singing cowboy Bob Blake and his harmonizing henchmen ride to the rescue of a brother and sister victimized by a crooked neighbor. Plenty of music and humor fill out this "all-colored cast" shoot-'em-up. B&W; 58m. **DIR:** Richard C. Kahn. **CAST:** Herbert Jeffrey, Spencer Williams Jr., Clarence Brooks, Lucius Brooks, Artie Young. **1938**

BROOD, THE ★★ Fans of director David Cronenberg will no doubt enjoy this offbeat, grisly horror tale about genetic experiments. Others need not apply. Rated R. 90m. **DIR:** David Cronenberg. **CAST:** Oliver Reed, Samantha Eggar, Art Hindle. **1979**

BROOKLYN STATE OF MIND, A ★★ Paint-by-numbers portrait of an Italian-American neighborhood in New York and the denizens who live there. Director Frank Rainone paints a superficial picture of life on the streets, allowing clichés rather than characters to inhabit his frame. There isn't one honest moment in this tale of a young man who falls under the intimidation of the local mob boss. Rated PG-13 for language and violence. 92m. **DIR:** Frank Rainone. **CAST:** Danny Aiello, Vincent Spano, Rick Aiello, Tony Danza, Jennifer Esposito. **1997**

•**BROTHER** ★★★ After a Japanese gang war, yakuza tough guy Yamamoto is forced to leave Tokyo and search Los Angeles for his half brother Ken. The two crime soldiers then join forces with a local hood and battle rival gangs for control of the L.A. drug trade. The coalition's success leads to a confrontation with the Italian Mafia that tests Yamamoto's code of brotherhood, honor, and discipline. The film is overly violent and sometimes confusing, but its offbeat story of hardened killers awaiting their own inevitable demise is intriguing. Rated R for violence, language, and nudity. 113m. **DIR:** Takeshi Kitano. **CAST:** Beat Takeshi, Omar Epps, Claude Maki. **2000 DVD**

BROTHER FROM ANOTHER PLANET, THE ★★★★ In this thoughtful comic fantasy, a dark-skinned extraterrestrial (Joe Morton) on the lam from alien cops crash-lands his spaceship in New York harbor, staggers ashore on Ellis Island, then makes his way to Harlem. Not rated, the film has profanity and violence. 110m. **DIR:** John Sayles. **CAST:** Joe Morton, Darryl Edwards, Steve James. **1984 DVD**

BROTHER JOHN ★★ In this not-so-heavenly melodrama, Sidney Poitier stars as an angel who returns to his Alabama hometown to see how things are going. He steps into bigotry and labor troubles. Not one of Poitier's best. Rated PG. 94m. **DIR:** James Goldstone. **CAST:** Sidney Poitier, Paul Winfield, Will Geer, Beverly Todd, Bradford Dillman. **1971**

BROTHER OF SLEEP ★★ In a remote village in nineteenth-century Austria, a self-taught musical genius is an outcast among his brutish, stupid neighbors. Overwrought and Wagnerian, the film is often ludicrous and outlandish. As the supposed artistic genius, Andre Eiserman's performance is unconvincing. In German with English subtitles. Rated R for nudity. 127m. **DIR:** Joseph Vilsmaier. **CAST:** Andre Eisermann, Dana Vavrova, Ben Becker. **1996**

BROTHER ORCHID ★★★ Comedy, action, sentimentality, and social comment are intertwined in this generally enjoyable gangster movie about a good-natured hood (Edward G. Robinson) who goes broke in Europe trying to get a little class. Old-fashioned fun. B&W; 91m. **DIR:** Lloyd Bacon. **CAST:** Edward G. Robinson, Humphrey Bogart, Ann Sothern, Donald Crisp, Ralph Bellamy, Allen Jenkins, Cecil Kellaway, Morgan Conway, Paul Guilfoyle, Tom Tyler. **1940**

BROTHER SUN, SISTER MOON ★★★★ Alec Guinness stars as the Pope in this movie about religious reformation. The film shows a young Francis of Assisi starting his own church. He confronts the Pope and rejects the extravagant and pompous ceremonies of the Catholic Church, preferring simple religious practices. Rated PG. 121m. **DIR:** Franco Zeffirelli. **CAST:** Graham Faulkner, Judi Bowker, Alec Guinness. **1973**

BROTHERHOOD, THE ★★ A *Godfather* predecessor, *The Brotherhood* stars Kirk Douglas and Alex Cord as Italian brothers who inherit their father's criminal empire. Douglas doesn't make a convincing Italian, but the story is good and overcomes the poor casting and cinematography. Not rated, contains violence and mild profanity. 96m. **DIR:** Martin Ritt. **CAST:** Kirk Douglas, Alex Cord, Irene Papas, Luther Adler, Susan Strasberg, Murray Hamilton. **1968 DVD**

BROTHERHOOD OF DEATH Satanic Ku Klux Klansmen battle gun-toting black Vietnam veterans in the pre–civil rights movement South. Rated R for violence and language. 85m. **DIR:** Bill Berry. **CAST:** Roy Jefferson, Le Tari, Haskell V. Anderson. **1976**

BROTHERHOOD OF JUSTICE ★★ Rich teenagers decide to band together after their high school is vandalized. Yuppie *Death Wish*. Ninety minutes of bad dialogue, but the message is worth something. Rated PG for violence. 97m. **DIR:** Charles Braverman. **CAST:** Keanu Reeves, Kiefer Sutherland, Lori Loughlin, Billy Zane. **1986**

BROTHERHOOD OF SATAN Ridiculous thriller about a small town taken over by witches and devil worshipers. Rated PG. 92m. **DIR:** Bernard McEveety. **CAST:** Strother Martin, L. Q. Jones, Charles Bateman, Ahna Capri. **1971**

BROTHERHOOD OF THE ROSE ★★1/2 Lifelong friends Peter Strauss and David Morse become CIA operatives, with Morse betraying his friend. Originally a made-for-television miniseries, this film works better in its abbreviated version. Rated PG-13. 103m. **DIR:** Marvin J. Chomsky. **CAST:** Robert Mitchum, Peter Strauss, Connie Sellecca, David Morse. **1989**

•**BROTHERHOOD OF THE WOLF** ★★★1/2 An eighteenth-century royal-court scientist and his Native American Indian blood brother star in this genre-bending French import that is part costume drama, martial arts adventure, monster movie, romance, and thriller. The two heroes, charted to catch a ferocious beast, encounter hand-to-hand combat, black magic, an elite brothel, and political and religious intrigue. The film is overly long but never predictable. In French with English subtitles. Rated R for violence, gore, nudity, and sex. 146m. **DIR:** Christophe Gans. **CAST:** Samuel Le Bihan, Mark Dacascos, Vincent Cassel, Emilie Dequenne, Monica Bellucci. **2002 DVD**

BROTHERLY LOVE ★★★1/2 A revenge melodrama. Judd Hirsch plays twin brothers, one a respectable businessman, the other a sociopath. When the latter is released from a mental ward, he vows to ruin his brother. This TV movie is not rated, but contains some violence. 94m. **DIR:** Jeff Bleckner. **CAST:** Judd Hirsch, Karen Carlson, George Dzundza, Barry Primus, Lori Lethin, Josef Sommer. **1985**

BROTHERS, THE ★★★1/2 Four African American pals have an assortment of romantic ups and downs. Honest laughs and strong, intelligent performances from the ensemble cast compensate for the familiar storyline. Morris Chestnut and Gabrielle Union are appealing as the central couple, while D. L. Hughley handles most of the comic relief. Rated R for profanity and sexual scenes. 103m. **DIR:** Gary Hardwick. **CAST:** Morris Chestnut, D. L. Hughley, Bill Bellamy, Shemar Moore, Gabrielle Union. **2001 DVD**

BROTHERS IN ARMS ★★ Adequate slasher features backwoods crazies hunting humans as part of their religious rituals. A terrifying, suspense-filled chase with plenty of bloodshed. Rated R for extreme violence. 95m. **DIR:** George Jay Bloom III. **CAST:** Todd Allen, Jack Starrett. **1988 DVD**

BROTHERS IN LAW ★★★★ Callow young lawyer Ian Carmichael learns how the British courts really work when an elder barrister takes him under his wing. A most enjoyable British satire, with Terry-Thomas particularly funny as a perennial defendant. 94m. **DIR:** Roy Boulting. **CAST:** Ian Carmichael, Richard Attenborough, Terry-Thomas, Jill Adams, John Le Mesurier. **1957**

BROTHERS IN THE SADDLE ★★★ Steve Brodie is the ne'er-do-well brother of straight shooter Tim Holt in this above-average Western. Uncommonly hard-edged for a series Western of the late 1940s, when interest in the genre was flagging and most cowboy movies were lifeless remakes. B&W; 60m. **DIR:** Lesley Selander. **CAST:** Tim Holt, Richard Martin, Steve Brodie. **1949**

BROTHERS IN TROUBLE ★★★ The tribulations of a loose family of Pakistani emigrants living in England are explored with honesty in this often compelling drama, produced for the BBC. Not rated; contains nudity, violence, sexual situations, and profanity. 102m. **DIR:** Udayan Prasad. **CAST:** Om Puri, Angeline Ball, Pavan Malhotra. **1995**

BROTHERS KARAMAZOV, THE ★★★ Director Richard Brooks, who also scripted, and a fine cast work hard to give life to Russian novelist Fyodor Dostoyevsky's turgid account of the effect of the death of a domineering father on his disparate sons: a fun-lover, a scholar, a religious zealot, and an epileptic. Studio promotion called it absorbing and exciting. It is, but only in flashes. 146m. **DIR:** Richard Brooks. **CAST:** Yul Brynner, Claire Bloom, Lee J. Cobb, Maria Schell, Richard Basehart, William Shatner, Albert Salmi. **1957**

BROTHER'S KEEPER ★★★★ The strange case of upstate New York's Ward brothers makes for an intriguing documentary. The four aged brothers lived and worked together on a small dairy farm. When one of the brothers is found dead in bed, and one of the remaining three is charged with murder, their lives change forever. Joe Berlinger and Bruce Sinofsky make their feature-film debut with this impressively detailed examination of the case, and of the brothers' incredible lifestyle. 116m. **DIR:** Joe Berlinger, Bruce Sinofsky. **1992**

BROTHERS LIONHEART, THE ★★1/2 This slow-moving children's fantasy filmed in Sweden, Denmark, and Finland features two brothers who are reunited after death in a medieval world where they fight dragons and villains in an attempt to free their war leader, Ulva, who will rid the country of tyrants. If you don't fall asleep within the first forty-five minutes, you will be rewarded with a fine fairy tale. Rated G. 108m. **DIR:** Olle Hellbron. **CAST:** Staffan Gotestam, Lars Soderdahl, Allan Edwall. **1977**

BROTHERS MCMULLEN, THE ★★★ Writer-director-star Edward Burns's low-budget comedy about the romantic entanglements of three Irish-American brothers—one happily married, one unhappily engaged, one footloose and commitment shy—was the surprise hit of the 1995 Sundance Film Festival. The film was somewhat overpraised; the female characters are shallow, and the male bonding is a bit hackneyed. Still, it's a promising debut; Burns may yet prove to be a major talent. Rated R for profanity and mature themes. 98m. **DIR:** Edward Burns. **CAST:** Edward Burns, Jack Mulcahy, Mike McGlone, Connie Britton, Maxine Bahns. **1995 DVD**

BROTHERS OF THE WEST ★★1/2 Standard plot in which the hero (Tom Tyler) must clear his framed brother. B&W; 58m. **DIR:** Sam Katzman. **CAST:** Tom Tyler, Lois Wilde. **1937**

BROWNING VERSION, THE (1951) ★★★★ Michael Redgrave, in perhaps his greatest performance, is an aging teacher betrayed by his wife and disliked by his students, forced into early retirement by illness. He feels his whole life has been a failure. Fine adaptation by Terence Rattigan of his play. B&W; 90m. **DIR:** Anthony Asquith. **CAST:** Michael Redgrave, Jean Kent, Nigel Patrick, Wilfrid Hyde-White, Ronald Howard, Bill Travers. **1951**

BROWNING VERSION, THE (1994) ★★★ This updated remake of the 1951 Michael Redgrave classic is a nice try, but it loses something by moving the action into the 1990s. Albert Finney is fine as usual, although he's better at portraying the old teacher's gruffness than his sensitivity, and his final I'm-a-failure speech doesn't quite ring true. Good supporting cast. Rated R for profanity. 97m. **DIR:** Mike Figgis. **CAST:** Albert Finney, Greta Scacchi, Matthew Modine, Julian Sands, Michael Gambon, Ben Silverston. **1994**

BROWN'S REQUIEM ★★★ Hardboiled story about a private investigator, hired by a suspiciously wealthy golf caddie to watch over his younger sister, who uncovers a perverse conspiracy. Adequate telling of the James Ellroy novel. Rated R for profanity, violence, and nudity. 97m. **DIR:** Jason Freeland. **CAST:** Michael Rooker, Kevin Corrigan, Selma Blair, Tobin Bell, Brad Dourif, Jack Conley, Brian James, Valerie Perrine, Harold Gould, Barry Newman. **1998 DVD**

BRUBAKER ★★★ Robert Redford stars as Henry Brubaker, a reform-minded penologist who takes over a decrepit Ohio prison only to discover the state prison system is even more rotten than its facilities. The film begins dramatically enough, with Redford masquerading as one of the convicts. After that, its dramatic impact lessens. Rated R. 132m. **DIR:** Stuart Rosenberg. **CAST:** Robert Redford, Yaphet Kotto, Jane Alexander, Murray Hamilton. **1980**

BRUCE LEE: CURSE OF THE DRAGON ★★★ Rare footage and a slick style will appeal to Lee fans. The focus is on his work and his athletic prowess, although his childhood and untimely death are probed. Addendum about Lee's deceased son, Brandon, seems slightly tacky. Narrated by George Takei. Not rated. 90m. **DIR:** Fred Weintraub, Tom Khun. **CAST:** Bruce Lee, James Coburn, Linda Emery Lee, Brandon Lee, Chuck Norris. **1993**

•**BRUISER** ★★ My, how the mighty have fallen. Extremely disappointing return to horror for writer-director George Romero, whose latest film feels like death warmed over, which would normally be a good thing. Here a mild-mannered guy named Henry puts on a life mask and becomes capable of all the nasty things Henry would never do. If it weren't so funny in a bad way this film would truly be a sad feather in Romero's cap. Rated R for adult situations, language, nudity, and violence. 99m. **DIR:** George A. Romero. **CAST:** Jason Flemyng, Peter Stormare, Nina Garbiras, Leslie Hope. **2000 DVD**

BRUTAL TRUTH, THE ★★★ Friends who haven't seen each other in a long time gather at a secluded mountain cabin to celebrate their ten year high-school reunion. Everything seems to be just dandy until one of them turns up dead, and everyone else must figure out if the death was the result of a suicide or a homicide. Dark secrets that had been suppressed for a decade come to light, and the finger of guilt revolves to point at each person in turn. Basically, this movie is *The Big Chill* for a twenty-something crowd. The acting is decent, but the story tends to drag at times. Rated R for violence, language, and sexual situations. 89m. **DIR:** Cameron Thor. **CAST:** Christina Applegate, Molly Ringwald, Johnathon Schaech, Justin Lazard, Moon Zappa, Paul Gleason. **1999 DVD**

BRUTE FORCE ★★★ Hardened convict and sadistic correctional officer bring down a prison when they collide. An insider's look at the lives of cellmates via dialogue and flashbacks humanizes them but they all take part in an almost cartoonishly gruesome murder. Not rated, but suggested for mature audiences. B&W; 98m. **DIR:** Jules Dassin. **CAST:** Burt Lancaster, Hume Cronyn, Charles Bickford, Howard Duff, Whit Bissell, Sam Levene, John Hoyt. **1947 DVD**

BRUTE MAN, THE ★★ A homicidal maniac escapes from an asylum. Unmemorable, standard B-movie stuff, notable mainly as a showcase for actor Rondo Hatton. This was Hatton's last film. He died in the year of its release, at the age of 42. B&W; 60m. **DIR:** Jean Yarbrough. **CAST:** Tom Neal, Rondo Hatton, Jane Adams. **1946 DVD**

BRYLCREEM BOYS, THE ★★★1/2 Handsome love story set in Ireland during World War II. Bill Campbell plays a downed Canadian pilot who finds himself interned in a POW camp with German pilot Angus MacFayden. When the men are allowed to go to the local town, they both fall in love with the same woman. Gorgeous scenery and an interesting take on the war. Rated PG-13 for language and violence. 106m. **DIR:** Terence Ryan. **CAST:** Bill Campbell, William McNamara, Angus MacFadyen, Jean Butler. **1996 DVD**

•**BUBBLE BOY** ★★ Sweet and goofy Jimmy who was born without immunities, lives in a germ-free environment under the junkyard dog vigilance of his mother. When the girl next door announces that she is going to Niagara Falls to marry her high-school prom date, Jimmy builds a mobile protective bubble suit and races from his California home to confess his love to her before she ties the knot. During the journey, he encounters a parade of stereotypical characters that includes a knife-wielding biker, circus freaks, and a religious cult. Rated PG-13 for language and sexual references. 84m. **DIR:** Blair Hayes. **CAST:** Jake Gyllenhaal, Marley Shelton, Swoosie Kurtz, Danny Trejo, John Carroll Lynch. **2001 DVD**

BUBBLEGUM CRASH, VOLS. 1–3 ★★★ Japanese animation. The Knight Sabers, unofficial superhero protectors of Mega Tokyo, are back in continuing new adventures based on the popular *Bubblegum Crisis* series. Though they have gotten on with their lives, the resourceful women reunite to meet the evil Voice and his nefarious minions. In Japanese with English subtitles. Not rated; contains violence and nudity. 45m. **DIR:** Noda Yasuyuki, Kiyotsumu Toshifumi, Fukushima Hiroyuki, Ishiodori Hiroshi. **1991**

BUBBLEGUM CRISIS, VOLS. 1–8 ★★★ Eight-part Japanese animated epic. Compelling stories with some visually stunning (albeit graphically violent) sequences involving the Knight Sabers and archenemies, the Boomers, genetically altered, Terminator-like mutants. This stylish series owes more than a passing nod to Ridley Scott's *Blade Runner*. In Japanese with English subtitles. Not rated with profanity and violence. 3053. **DIR:** Akiyama Katsuhito, Hayashi Hiroki, Oobari Masami, Takayama Fumihiko, Gooda Hiroaki. **1987–90**

BUCCANEER, THE (1958) ★★ Studio-bound remake of C. B. De Mille's 1938 romance of pirate Jean Lafitte. A cast capable of hamming *and* acting, but that's not enough to make this stiff color creaker come alive. 121m. **DIR:** Anthony Quinn. **CAST:** Yul Brynner, Charlton Heston, Claire Bloom, Charles Boyer, Douglass Dumbrille, Lorne Greene, Ted de Corsia. **1958**

BUCCANEERS, THE (1995) ★★★★ An exquisite adaptation of Edith Wharton's final novel, this atmospheric drama conveys the high fashion and simmering emotions of the nineteenth-century aristocracy. Best of all, it costars Mira Sorvino as one of four New World teenagers who conquer Old World London with their high spirits. Packaged with *A Lady Does Not Write*, an uninspired but informative sixty-minute documentary about Wharton. Not rated; contains sexual situations. 288m. **DIR:** Philip Saville. **CAST:** Carla Gugino, Mira Sorvino, Alison Elliott, Rya Kihlstedt, Cherie Lunghi. **1995**

BUCK AND THE PREACHER ★★1/2 Harry Belafonte and director Sidney Poitier play two escaped slaves heading west. On the way, they meet up with "bad guy" Cameron Mitchell and lovely Ruby Dee. So-so Western. Rated PG. 102m. **DIR:** Sidney Poitier. **CAST:** Sidney Poitier, Harry Belafonte, Ruby Dee, Cameron Mitchell. **1972 DVD**

BUCK BENNY RIDES AGAIN ★★★ A Western spoof made to capitalize on Jack Benny's popular radio program. Most of his radio colleagues join him as he tries to impersonate a wild and woolly cowboy. Benny's humor hasn't dated nearly as much as some of his contemporaries. B&W; 82m. **DIR:** Mark Sandrich. **CAST:** Jack Benny, Eddie "Rochester" Anderson, Ellen Drew, Phil Harris, Dennis Day, Andy Devine, Virginia Dale. **1940**

BUCK PRIVATES ★★★ Abbott and Costello are at their best in their first starring film, but it's still no classic. On the lam, the two are forced to enlist during World War II. B&W; 82m. **DIR:** Arthur Lubin. **CAST:** Bud Abbott, Lou Costello, Lee Bowman, Alan Curtis, Jane Frazee. **1941 DVD**

BUCK PRIVATES COME HOME ★★ Bud Abbott and Lou Costello reprise their roles from their first big hit, this time mustering out of the service and bringing an orphan with them. B&W; 77m. **DIR:** Charles Barton. **CAST:** Bud Abbott, Lou Costello, Beverly Simmons,

Nat Pendleton, Tom Brown, Don Beddoe, Donald MacBride. **1947 DVD**

BUCK ROGERS: DESTINATION SATURN (PLANET OUTLAWS) ★★1/2 Edited-down version of the popular serial loses much of the continuity of the twelve-episode chapterplay, but still proves to be great fun as ideal hero Buster Crabbe enthusiastically goes after the vile Killer Kan. B&W; 91m. **DIR:** Ford Beebe, Saul Goodkind. **CAST:** Buster Crabbe, Constance Moore, Jackie Moran, Jack Mulhall, Anthony Warde, C. Montague Shaw, Philip Ahn. **1939**

BUCK ROGERS IN THE 25TH CENTURY ★★ Updating of the Buck Rogers legend finds Buck (Gil Gerard), after years of suspended animation, awakened in a future society under attack by the power-mad Princess Ardala (Pamela Hensley). Substandard space fare was originally made as a TV pilot. Rated PG. 89m. **DIR:** Daniel Haller. **CAST:** Gil Gerard, Erin Gray, Pamela Hensley, Tim O'Connor, Henry Silva. **1979**

BUCKET OF BLOOD, A ★★★ A funny beatnik spoof—and horror-movie lampoon—in the style of the original *Little Shop of Horrors*, put together by the same creative team. Dick Miller is a nerdy sculptor whose secret is pouring wet clay over the bodies of murder victims; the resulting, contorted sculptures make him a superstar among the cognoscenti. B&W; 66m. **DIR:** Roger Corman. **CAST:** Dick Miller, Barboura Morris, Ed Nelson, Anthony Carbone. **1959**

BUCKEYE AND BLUE ★★ Disappointing *Bonnie and Clyde*–style Western featuring Robin Lively and Jeff Osterhage as a couple of desperadoes who engage in a crime spree after the Civil War. No new twists on this tired theme. Rated PG. 94m. **DIR:** J. C. Compton. **CAST:** Robyn Lively, Jeff Osterhage, Rick Gibbs, Will Hannah. **1988**

BUCKSKIN ★★1/2 Trite, overwritten, A. C. Lyles-produced Western featuring a score of familiar-face, long-in-the-tooth actors—which is the best feature of this film about a heroic marshal battling a domineering cattle baron. 97m. **DIR:** Michael Moore. **CAST:** Barry Sullivan, Wendell Corey, Joan Caulfield, Bill Williams, John Russell, Barbara Hale, Lon Chaney Jr., Barton MacLane. **1968**

BUCKSKIN FRONTIER ★★★ Railroad representative Richard Dix and freight-line owner Lee J. Cobb fight over business and a crucial mountain pass in this big-budget, fast-action Western. B&W; 82m. **DIR:** Lesley Selander. **CAST:** Richard Dix, Jane Wyatt, Lee J. Cobb, Albert Dekker, Joe Sawyer, Victor Jory, Lola Lane. **1943**

BUCKTOWN 🦃 This mindless blaxploitation flick finds Fred Williamson journeying to a southern town to bury his brother, who has been killed by corrupt cops. Rated R. 95m. **DIR:** Arthur Marks. **CAST:** Fred Williamson, Pam Grier, Thalmus Rasulala, Tony King, Bernie Hamilton, Art Lund. **1975 DVD**

BUD AND LOU ★★★ Made-for-TV movie explores the tensions between comedians Bud Abbott (Harvey Korman) and Lou Costello (Buddy Hackett). Based, we assume, on the excellent book of the same name by Bob Thomas, this film is at its best when examining the poignant offscreen relationship between the two funnymen. Its greatest flaw is that the stars are unable to make the duo's most celebrated routines even amusing. 99m. **DIR:** Robert C. Thompson. **CAST:** Harvey Korman, Buddy Hackett, Michele Lee, Arte Johnson, Robert Reed. **1978**

•BUDDHA OF SUBURBIA, THE ★★★★ In the 1970s, a half-British, half-Indian teenager struggles to adjust to a strange new life when his father becomes a celebrity guru and moves him from the comfortable suburbs to swinging London. Hanif Kureishi *(My Beautiful Laundrette)* scripted this adaptation of his seriocomic novel, and fills it with amusing, well-drawn characters. David Bowie provides an excellent score. Not rated; contains nudity and sexual situations. 220m. **DIR:** Roger Michell. **CAST:** Roshan Seth, Naveen Andrews, Susan Fleetwood, Brenda Blethyn. **1993**

BUDDY ★★1/2 Based on the true story of an animal-loving 1920s socialite who tried to raise a baby gorilla as if he were her own, this film is an awkward mix of cute and creepy. Youngsters will be enthralled by the first section, featuring dozens of cuddly animals, but they may be shocked when Buddy rebels against his forced humanization. Adults may admire the sociological quandaries of the climax, yet find the setup much too cloying. Rated PG for gorilla-related fits. 84m. **DIR:** Caroline Thompson. **CAST:** René Russo, Robbie Coltrane, Alan Cumming, Irma P. Hall, Paul Reubens. **1997 DVD**

BUDDY, BUDDY ★★ Jack Lemmon is a clumsy would-be suicide who decides to end it all in a hotel. Walter Matthau is a hit man who rents the room next door and finds the filling of his contract difficult. The results are less than hilarious but do provoke a few smiles. Rated R because of profanity and brief nudity. 96m. **DIR:** Billy Wilder. **CAST:** Jack Lemmon, Walter Matthau, Paula Prentiss, Klaus Kinski. **1981**

BUDDY HOLLY STORY, THE ★★★★1/2 Gary Busey's outstanding performance as Buddy Holly makes this one of the few great rock 'n' roll movies. Not only does he convincingly embody the legend from Lubbock, Texas, he also sings Holly's songs—including "That'll Be the Day," "Not Fade Away," and "It's So Easy"—with style and conviction. Backed by Don Stroud and Charles Martin Smith, who also play and sing impressively. Rated PG. 114m. **DIR:** Steve Rash. **CAST:** Gary Busey, Don Stroud, Charles Martin Smith, Dick O'Neill. **1978 DVD**

BUDDY SYSTEM, THE ★★ In the middle of this movie, the would-be novelist (Richard Dreyfuss) takes his unbound manuscripts to the edge of the sea and lets the wind blow the pages away. He should have done the same thing with the screenplay for this mediocre romantic comedy. The plot is that old chestnut about a fatherless little kid (Wil Wheaton) who helps his mom (Susan Sarandon) and an eligible man (Dreyfuss) get together. Rated PG for profanity. 110m. **DIR:** Glenn Jordan. **CAST:** Richard Dreyfuss, Susan Sarandon, Nancy Allen, Wil Wheaton. **1984**

BUDDY'S SONG ★★★1/2 Roger Daltrey delivers a surprisingly strong performance as a loser who takes hope in his son's singing career. Very watchable albeit painfully so at times. Rated R for nudity, profanity, and violence. 107m. **DIR:** Claude Whatham. **CAST:** Roger Daltrey, Chesney Hawkes, Sharon Duce, Michael Elphick. **1991**

BUENA VISTA SOCIAL CLUB, THE ★★★★1/2 German director Wim Wenders films the efforts of American guitarist Ry Cooder to reunite a group of long-forgotten Cuban musicians who flourished during Havana's tourist heyday in the 1940s and 1950s. Though their ages range from sixty-five to over ninety, they've lost little of their talent for music and none of their joy in making it, and the film is a wonderful record of both. In Spanish with English subtitles. Rated G. 102m. **DIR:** Wim Wenders. **CAST:** Ry Cooder, Joachim Cooder, Rubén González, Ibrahim Ferrer, Compay Segundo, Omara Portuondo, Eliades Ochoa. **1999 DVD**

BUFFALO BILL ★★★1/2 The famed frontiersman William Cody gets the Hollywood biography treatment in this slick, but sometimes bland motion picture. Joel McCrea brings his usual dignity to the role. 90m. **DIR:** William Wellman. **CAST:** Joel McCrea, Maureen O'Hara, Linda Darnell, Thomas Mitchell, Anthony Quinn, Edgar Buchanan. **1944**

BUFFALO BILL AND THE INDIANS ★★1/2 In this offbeat Western, Paul Newman, Burt Lancaster, Harvey Keitel, Geraldine Chaplin, Joel Grey, Kevin McCarthy, and Will Sampson are fun to watch as they interact like jazz musicians jamming on the theme of distorted history and the delusion of celebrity. Rated PG. 120m. **DIR:** Robert Altman. **CAST:** Paul Newman, Joel Grey, Kevin McCarthy, Burt Lancaster, Harvey Keitel, Geraldine Chaplin, Will Sampson. **1976**

BUFFALO GIRLS ★★★1/2 As the hard-fightin', hard-drinkin', and hard-lovin' Calamity Jane, Anjelica Huston rides herd over a sprawling, enjoyable tale of the last days of the West. Obviously a labor of love by all concerned. Made for TV; contains profanity and violence. 192m. **DIR:** Rod Hardy. **CAST:** Anjelica Huston, Melanie Griffith, Sam Elliott, Gabriel Byrne, Peter Coyote, Jack Palance, Reba McEntire, Tracey Walter, Floyd Red Crow Esterman, Charlayne Woodard, John Diehl, Andrew Bicknell, Paul Lazar, Russell Means. **1995**

BUFFALO JUMP ★★★1/2 Enjoyable, family-oriented Canadian drama stars Wendy Crewson as a young woman who inherits a ranch in the middle of nowhere. She rises to the challenge and learns some very valuable lessons about growing up. Pleasant affair. Not rated. 97m. **DIR:** Eric Till. **CAST:** Wendy Crewson, Paul Gross. **1989**

BUFFALO '66 ★★★★ Teen tap dancer Layla is kidnapped by freshly paroled Billy in this gritty, moody drama. The greasy sociopath vaguely apologizes to his victim, then bullies her into posing as his wife during a visit to the home of his creepy parents in Buffalo. When the charade ends, Billy plans to kill a former Bills placekicker, but finds Layla harder to shake than the emotional demons from his past. Rated R for profanity, nudity, sexual situations, and violence. 110m. **DIR:** Vincent Gallo. **CAST:** Vincent Gallo, Christina Ricci, Anjelica Huston, Ben Gazzara. **1998 DVD**

BUFFALO SOLDIERS ★★★ Danny Glover rides tall in the saddle in this semifactual tale of the legendary African American Calvary Corp. and their mission to track down Apache warrior Victorio. Even though the script plays loose with the facts, a decent cast and strong direction helps this action-adventure achieve full gallop. Not rated; contains violence. 94m. **DIR:** Charles Haid. **CAST:** Danny Glover, Bob Gunton, Carl Lumbly, Glynn Turman, Mykelti Williamson. **1997**

BUFFALO STAMPEDE ★★★ Zane Grey story has buffalo hunter Randolph Scott in love with the daughter of an outlaw stirring up Indian trouble. B&W; 59m. **DIR:** Henry Hathaway. **CAST:** Randolph Scott, Harry Carey, Buster Crabbe, Noah Beery Sr. **1933**

BUFFET FROID (COLD CUTS) ★★★★ Outrageously funny surreal black comedy about three hapless murderers. This whimsical study in madness is laced with brilliant performances and great direction by Bertrand Blier. Highly engaging. In French with English subtitles. Not rated; contains nudity, profanity, and violence. 95m. **DIR:** Bertrand Blier. **CAST:** Gérard Depardieu, Bernard Blier, Jean Carmet. **1979 DVD**

BUFFY, THE VAMPIRE SLAYER ★★★1/2 A high school cheerleader has to put down her pom-poms and forgo hanging out at the mall when she discovers that she's the latest in a long line of women whose job it is to kill vampires. It's better than it sounds. Rated PG-13 for violence and profanity. 100m. **DIR:** Fran Rubel Kuzui. **CAST:** Kristy Swanson, Donald Sutherland, Rutger Hauer, Luke Perry. **1992 DVD**

BUFORD'S BEACH BUNNIES ★★ Harry Buford, owner of the Bunny Hole, offers a large reward to whichever Bunny employee can make his son Cheeter lose his virginity. Extremely bad acting and dialogue. The background action is funnier than the plot. Rated R for nudity, profanity, and graphic sex. 94m. **DIR:** Mark Pirro. **CAST:** Jim Hanks, Rikki Brando, Monique Parent, Amy Page, Barrett Cooper, Ina Rogers, Charley Rossman, David Robinson. **1992**

BUG ★★1/2 Weird horror film with the world, led by Bradford Dillman, staving off masses of giant mutant beetles with the ability to commit arson, setting fire to every living thing they can find. Rated PG for violence. 100m. **DIR:** Jeannot Szwarc. **CAST:** Bradford Dillman, Joanna Miles, Richard Gilliland. **1975**

BUG BUSTER ★★ Time how long it takes you to be reminded of *Arachnophobia*. This time instead of spiders it's cockroaches terrorizing people, but nothing else has changed plot-wise. A nasty-spirited film that lacks any likable characters. Rated R for violence, gore, and simulated sex. 93m. **DIR:** Lorenzo Doumani. **CAST:** Randy Quaid, Katherine Heigl, Meredith Salenger, James Doohan, George Takei. **1998 DVD**

BUGGED! ★★★ Delightfully refreshing and goofy, this big bug flick is probably the best film to ever come out of Troma. Director Ronald K. Armstrong plays a clueless exterminator out to save the world from an invasion of—wait for it—giant grasshoppers. So sit back and enjoy this quirky spoof. Rated PG-13 for gore, violence, and profanity. 90m. **DIR:** Ronald K. Armstrong. **CAST:** Priscilla K. Basque, Ronald K. Armstrong. **1996**

BUGLES IN THE AFTERNOON ★★1/2 In this modest Western a young army officer is made a victim by a jealous rival. Set in the time of Custer's last stand, it has fairly good scenery and cinematography. 85m. **DIR:** Roy Rowland. **CAST:** Ray Milland, Hugh Marlowe, Helena Carter, Forrest Tucker, Barton MacLane, George Reeves. **1952**

BUGS BUNNY/ROAD RUNNER MOVIE, THE ★★★★ Classic cartoons made by Chuck Jones for Warner Bros. are interwoven into this laughfest; the first and best of the 1970s and '80s feature-length compilations. Includes such winners as "Duck Amuck" and "What's Opera, Doc?" Rated G. 92m. **DIR:** Chuck Jones, Phil Monroe. **1979**

BUGS BUNNY, SUPERSTAR ★★★★ A delightful collection of nine classic Warner Bros. cartoons from the Thirties and Forties. Produced mainly as a tribute to director Bob Clampett, this tape is a must-see if only for the hilarious *Fantasia* parody "Corny Concerto." Rated G. 90m. **DIR:** Larry Jackson. **1975**

BUG'S LIFE, A ★★★★★ The story features an industrious worker ant whose inventive talents place his colony in peril from a band of marauding grasshoppers. Determined to compensate for the trouble he has caused, the little fellow undertakes a dangerous journey to "the city," where he hopes to find some resourceful "warrior bugs" for a final reckoning with the grasshoppers. This film is witty, luxuriously animated, and lots of fun. Rated G; suitable for all ages. 94m. **DIR:** John Lasseter. **1998 DVD**

BUGSY ★★★★1/2 Charming, shrewd, and given to fits of uncontrollable temper and violence, gangster Benjamin "Bugsy" Siegel becomes obsessed with the creation of Las Vegas, an expensive project that puts him dangerously at odds with his partners. Rated R for violence, brief profanity, and nudity. 135m. **DIR:** Barry Levinson. **CAST:** Warren Beatty, Annette Bening, Harvey Keitel, Ben Kingsley, Elliott Gould, Joe Mantegna, Bebe Neuwirth, Wendy Phillips, Richard Sarafian, Bill Graham. **1991 DVD**

BUGSY MALONE ★★★1/2 The 1920s gangsters weren't really as cute as these children, who run around shooting whipping cream out of their pistols. But if you can forget that, this British musical provides light diversion. Rated G. 93m. **DIR:** Alan Parker. **CAST:** Scott Baio, Florrie Augger, Jodie Foster, John Cassisi, Martin Lev. **1976**

BULL DURHAM ★★★★ Tim Robbins plays a rookie pitcher for a minor league baseball team. He has a lightning-fast throw, but he's apt to hit the team mascot as often as the strike zone. Kevin Costner is a dispirited catcher brought in to "mature" Robbins. A quirky, intelligent comedy with plenty of surprises, the film contains some of the sharpest jabs at sports since *Slap Shot*. Rated R for profanity and sexual content. 104m. **DIR:** Ron Shelton. **CAST:** Kevin Costner, Susan Sarandon, Tim Robbins, Trey Wilson, Robert Wuhl. **1988 DVD**

BULLDOG COURAGE ★★1/2 Tim McCoy is excellent in the dual role of father and son in this slow-paced series Western. When Slim Braddock is killed, it's up to his son, Tim, to avenge his death after a period of several years. This was one of McCoy's last starring films. B&W; 66m. **DIR:** Sam Newfield. **CAST:** Tim McCoy, Joan Woodbury, Paul Fix, Eddie Buzzard. **1935**

BULLDOG DRUMMOND ★★★ Ronald Colman smoothly segued from silent to sound films playing the title's ex–British army officer adventurer in this exciting, witty, definitive first stanza of what became a popular series. B&W; 89m. **DIR:** F. Richard Jones. **CAST:** Ronald Colman, Joan Bennett, Lilyan Tashman. **1929**

BULLDOG DRUMMOND COMES BACK ★★★ The first of seven films starring John Howard as the adventurer-sleuth is an atmospheric tale of revenge. The crazed widow of one of Bulldog Drummond's former enemies makes off with our hero's girl, Phyllis. A gem available on tape with *Bulldog Drummond Escapes*. B&W; 59m. **DIR:** Louis King. **CAST:** John Howard, John Barrymore, Louise Campbell, E. E. Clive, Reginald Denny, J. Carrol Naish. **1937**

BULLDOG DRUMMOND ESCAPES ★★ Famed ex–British army officer Bulldog Drummond comes to the aid of his ladylove when she becomes embroiled in an international espionage ring. Young Ray Milland stars in his only outing as the World War I hero in this okay series entry. Paired on tape with *Bulldog Drummond Comes Back*. B&W; 65m. **DIR:** James Hogan. **CAST:** Ray Milland, Guy Standing, Heather Angel, Porter Hall, Reginald Denny, E. E. Clive, Fay Holden. **1937 DVD**

BULLDOG DRUMMOND IN AFRICA ★★1/2 An international spy ring has struck again. This time they've kidnapped Colonel Neilson and hidden him somewhere in North Africa, and Hugh "Bulldog" Drummond isn't going to stand for it. Good fun. Double-billed with *Arrest Bulldog Drummond* on tape. B&W; 58m. **DIR:** Louis King. **CAST:** John Howard, Heather Angel, J. Carrol Naish, H. B. Warner, Anthony Quinn. **1938**

BULLDOG DRUMMOND'S BRIDE ★★1/2 The last of Paramount's Bulldog Drummond series. A crack bank robber uses Drummond's honeymoon flat as a hideout for himself and his explosives. Not the best of the series, but it's still a rousing adventure. On tape with *Bulldog Drummond's Secret Police*. B&W; 56m. **DIR:** James Hogan. **CAST:** John Howard, Heather Angel, Reginald Denny, H. B. Warner, Eduardo Ciannelli. **1939**

BULLDOG DRUMMOND'S PERIL ★★★ Bulldog Drummond has a personal stake in a chase that takes him from London to Switzerland—the synthetic diamond that was stolen is a wedding gift intended for our hero and his patient fiancée, Phyllis. Full of close calls, witty dialogue, and an injection of controlled lunacy by the great John Barrymore. On tape with *Bulldog Drummond's Revenge*. B&W; 66m. **DIR:** James Hogan. **CAST:** John Howard, John Barrymore, Louise Campbell, H. B. Warner, Reginald Denny. **1938**

BULLDOG DRUMMOND'S REVENGE ★★★ The second film in Paramount's Drummond series featuring John Howard, this entry focuses on the hero's attempts to recover a powerful explosive. Aided by the colorful Colonel Neilson (John Barrymore at his most enjoyable), Drummond fights evildoers at every turn. Released on a double bill with *Bulldog Drummond's Peril*. B&W; 55m. **DIR:** Louis King. **CAST:** John Howard, John Barrymore, Louise Campbell, Reginald Denny, E. E. Clive. **1937**

BULLDOG DRUMMOND'S SECRET POLICE ★★1/2 Stylish entry in the long-running series finds gentleman adventurer Bulldog Drummond searching a forbidding castle for hidden treasure while matching wits with a crazed murderer. Double billed with *Bulldog Drummond's Bride* on videotape. B&W; 54m. **DIR:** James Hogan. **CAST:** John Howard, Heather Angel, Reginald Denny, Leo G. Carroll, H. B. Warner. **1939 DVD**

BULLET ★★1/2 Flashy but empty crime-drama pits an ex-con (Mickey Rourke) against the drug lord (Tupac Shakur) who framed him. Ted Levine steals the show as Rourke's uncontrollable brother. Quite a step down for the director, former music-video whiz Julien Temple. Rated R for violence and profanity. 96m. **DIR:** Julien Temple. **CAST:** Mickey Rourke, Tupac Shakur, Ted Levine. **1996**

BULLET FOR SANDOVAL, A ★★1/2 A gritty story of Warner, a rebel soldier who deserts to be with his fiancée at childbirth. When he arrives at the Sandoval hacienda he finds her dead and her father blames him for his daughter's death. Warner is given his baby son and thrown out. He assembles a band of renegades to seek vengeance on Sandoval. Good acting from Ernest Borgnine and George Hilton. Rated PG. 96m. **DIR:** Julio Buchs. **CAST:** Ernest Borgnine, George Hilton, Annabella Incontrera, Alberto De Mendoza, Leo Anchoriz. **1969**

BULLET FOR THE GENERAL, A ★★★ A spaghetti Western with a social conscience. Gian Maria Volonté hams it up as a Mexican revolutionary explaining his cause to Lou Castel, who unbeknownst to him is really an American mercenary hired to assassinate him. Dubbed in English. 95m. **DIR:** Damiano Damiani. **CAST:** Gian Maria Volonté, Lou Castel, Martine Beswick, Klaus Kinski. **1967 DVD**

BULLET IN THE HEAD ★★★★ In 1967, three childhood friends are forced to leave Hong Kong and head for Vietnam, where they believe they can make enough money to buy their way out of their troubles. Instead, they find a land operating under the rules of insanity. John Woo considers this to be his best film, a sprawling epic of loyalty and betrayal in wartime, even though it is not a conventional war film (i.e., none of the characters are soldiers). Not rated; contains strong violence. 136m. **DIR:** John Woo. **CAST:** Tony Leung Chiu Wai, Jacky Cheung, Waise Lee, Simon Yam. **1990 DVD**

BULLET TO BEIJING ★★★ Michael Caine revives British agent Harry Palmer in this involving made-for-cable espionage thriller. A victim of government downsizing, Palmer ends up helping a Russian tycoon and his assistant keep a dangerous weapon from falling into the hands of the North Koreans. Rated R for language, nudity, and violence. 105m. **DIR:** George Mihalka. **CAST:** Michael Caine, Jason Connery, Mia Sara, Michael Gambon, Michael Sarrazin. **1995**

BULLETPROOF (1988) ★★1/2 Gary Busey plays a one-man army named Frank "Bulletproof" McBain, an ex-CIA agent who single-handedly takes on a band of multinational terrorists. It's silly, but fun—thanks to Busey and a strong cast of character actors. Rated R for profanity, nudity, and violence. 95m. **DIR:** Steve Carver. **CAST:** Gary Busey, Darlanne Fluegel, Henry Silva, Thalmus Rasulala, L. Q. Jones, Rene Enriquez, R. G. Armstrong, Luke Askew. **1988**

BULLETPROOF (1996) ★★ This action-comedy buddy picture is a less-than-satisfying mix of raunchy humor and pedestrian shoot-outs. A small-time crook is hired to finalize a big drug deal, but his best friend and partner in crime turns out to be a cop. The two squabble and survive with only a few bright comic moments in this generally mean-spirited mess. Rated R for violence, nudity, and language. 84m. **DIR:** Ernest R. Dickerson. **CAST:** Damon Wayans, Adam Sandler, James Caan, Kristen Wilson, James Farentino. **1996 DVD**

BULLETPROOF HEART ★★★ A hardened, emotionless hit man is contracted to kill a female socialite and takes along a buddy. The men find themselves transformed by an eerie brush with the doomed woman who is expecting them. This provocative *film noir* leer into the face of impending death is given a compelling edge by its excellent cast. Rated R for language, sex, and violence. 98m. **DIR:** Mark Malone. **CAST:** Anthony LaPaglia, Mimi Rogers, Peter Boyle, Matt Craven. **1995**

BULLETS OR BALLOTS ★★★1/2 A hard-nosed cop (Edward G. Robinson), after being unceremoniously fired from the police force, joins up with the big-time crime boss (Barton MacLane) who has long been his friendly enemy. William Keighley's high-spirited direction helps put over this action-packed but melodramatic gangster movie. B&W; 81m. **DIR:** William Keighley. **CAST:** Edward G. Robinson, Joan Blondell, Barton MacLane, Humphrey Bogart, Frank McHugh. **1936**

BULLETS OVER BROADWAY ★★★★ During the Roaring Twenties, a playwright-turned-director finds his artistic vision compromised when much-needed backing for his latest production is secured from a big-time gangster, who insists that his no-talent mistress be featured in an important role. Rated PG. 99m. **DIR:** Woody Allen. **CAST:** John Cusack, Chazz Palminteri, Dianne Wiest, Mary-Louise Parker, Jennifer Tilly, Jim Broadbent, Tracey Ullman, Jack Warden, Joe Viterelli, Harvey Fierstein, Rob Reiner. **1994 DVD**

BULLFIGHTER AND THE LADY, THE ★★★★ Many of the themes explored in the superb series of low-budget Westerns director Budd Boetticher later made with Randolph Scott *(Decision at Sundown; The Tall T)* are evident in this first-rate drama. A skeet-shooting champ (Robert Stack) decides to become a bullfighter. B&W; 123m. **DIR:** Budd Boetticher. **CAST:** Robert Stack, Joy Page, Gilbert Roland, Katy Jurado. **1951**

BULLFIGHTERS, THE ★★★ While not a classic, this latter-day Laurel and Hardy film is surprisingly good—especially when you consider that the boys had lost all control over the making of their pictures by this time. The story has Laurel resembling a famous bullfighter, and, of course, this leads to chaos in the ring. B&W; 61m. **DIR:** Malcolm St. Clair. **CAST:** Stan Laurel, Oliver Hardy, Margo Woode, Richard Lane, Carol Andrews. **1945**

BULLIES 🦃 A family moves to a small town that happens to be run by a murderous family of moonshiners. Rated R for graphic violence and profanity. 96m. **DIR:** Paul Lynch. **CAST:** Jonathan Crombie, Janet Laine Green, Olivia D'Abo. **1985**

BULLITT ★★★★ Although a bit dated now, this police drama directed by Peter Yates still features one of star Steve McQueen's best screen performances. The San Francisco car-chase sequence is still a corker. 113m. **DIR:** Peter Yates. **CAST:** Steve McQueen, Robert Vaughn, Jacqueline Bisset, Norman Fell, Don Gordon, Suzanne Somers. **1968 DVD**

BULLSEYE ★★★ In this surprisingly entertaining—albeit featherweight—caper comedy from director Michael Winner, Michael Caine and Roger Moore essay dual roles as two identical pairs of con men. Sally Kirkland costars as the brains (and body) of the organization. Rated PG-13 for profanity. 95m. **DIR:** Michael Winner. **CAST:** Michael Caine, Roger Moore, Sally Kirkland. **1990**

BULLSHOT (BULLSHOT CRUMMOND) ★★1/2 A movie can be fun for a while, then overstay its welcome. Such is the case with this spoof of Herman Cyril "Scapper" McNiele's *Bulldog Drummond* mystery-spy adventures. Everything is played to the hilt, and the characters become caricatures. Although this is occasionally irritating, the star-screenwriters do create some funny moments. Rated PG for profanity, sex, and violence. 95m. **DIR:** Dick Clement. **CAST:** Alan Shearman, Diz White, Ron House, Frances Tomelty, Michael Aldridge. **1985**

BULLWHIP ★★1/2 In this agreeable movie, Guy Madison avoids the hangin' tree by agreeing to marry a fiery half-breed (Rhonda Fleming). If the plot sounds familiar, it should. Jack Nicholson used a similar one in *Goin' South*. 80m. **DIR:** Harmon Jones. **CAST:** Rhonda Fleming, Guy Madison, James Griffith, Don Beddoe. **1958**

•BULLY ★★ Loosely based on the 1993 events that led a group of South Florida teens to kill one of their own, this fact-based drama is as tawdry and exploitatively sleazy as the tragedy itself. Director Larry Clark never met a crotch or breast shot he couldn't fall in love with, and the debased characters are not interesting. The film finally comes alive and turns darkly humorous in the last act, when the kids go to pieces after having committed the vile deed, but by then you're unlikely to care. Not rated; contains violence, drug use, nonstop profanity and nudity, and simulated sex. 106m. **DIR:** Larry Clark. **CAST:** Brad Renfro, Rachel Miner, Nick Stahl, Bijou Phillips, Michael Pitt, Kelli Garner, Daniel Franzese, Leo Fitzpatrick. **2001 DVD**

BULWORTH ★★★1/2 Warren Beatty is a disillusioned senator who jump-starts his moribund reelection campaign by biting the hand that feeds him. It's pretty damn funny to watch ol' Warren outfit himself in gang-banger togs while delivering his eye-opening political messages . . . in rap, no less. Rated R for profanity and drug use. 107m. **DIR:** Warren Beatty. **CAST:** Warren Beatty, Halle Berry, Oliver Platt, Paul Sorvino, Jack Warden, Don Cheadle, Sean Astin. **1998 DVD**

BUMBLEBEE FLIES ANYWAY, THE ★★★ Touching tale of a young man suffering from amnesia, who befriends the other children in a hospital for the terminally ill. Elijah Wood, as Barney Snow, slowly tries to reconstruct his memories after an accident. Snow finds time to make friends with cancer patient Mazzo, played with dignity by Joseph Perrino, and fall in love with Mazzo's sister Cassie, played by Rachael Leigh Cooke. Janeane Garofalo shines as the only doctor who sees Snow as a person and not a patient. Rated PG-13 for language. 95m. **DIR:** Martin Duffy. **CAST:** Elijah Wood, Janeane Garofalo, Rachael Leigh Cook, Joseph Perrino, Roger Rees. **2000**

BUNCO ★★1/2 Passable made-for-television crime thriller has Robert Urich and Tom Selleck as a pair of police detectives out to bust a confidence ring. Typical TV fare. 90m. **DIR:** Alexander Singer. **CAST:** Robert Urich, Tom Selleck, Donna Mills, Michael Sacks, Will Geer, Arte Johnson, James Hampton, Bobby Van. **1976**

BUNDLE OF JOY ★★★ In this breezy remake of Ginger Rogers's *Bachelor Mother*, Debbie Reynolds portrays a department-store salesgirl who takes custody of an infant. (Eddie Fisher is suspected of being the father.) A scandal ensues. 98m. **DIR:** Norman Taurog. **CAST:** Debbie Reynolds, Eddie Fisher, Adolphe Menjou, Tommy Noonan. **1956**

BUNKER, THE ★★★★ Based on *Newsweek* reporter James P. O'Donnell's book about the fall of Hitler's regime, this HBO movie reveals a confused, unsteady leader (Anthony Hopkins at his Emmy-winning best) surrounded by his top men. Aware of his mental demise, some of his men dare to defy his orders. Glory-days flashbacks make a stark contrast to his final days. Susan Blakely's Eva Braun comes across as a complete airhead. Piper Laurie's chilling performance as Goebbels's wife will inspire a few nightmares. Not rated; contains mature themes, profanity, and animal cruelty. 151m. **DIR:** George Schaefer. **CAST:** Anthony Hopkins, Richard Jordan, Piper Laurie, Susan Blakely. **1980**

BUNNY'S TALE, A ★★★ Engaging comedy-drama stars Kirstie Alley as feminist author Gloria Steinem, who became a Bunny at a Playboy Club in order to get the real story behind the Hugh Hefner empire. Her experiences make for major entertainment, and this made-for-TV film never slips into the peekaboo trap it easily could have. 97m. **DIR:** Karen Arthur. **CAST:** Kirstie Alley, Cotter Smith, Deborah Van Valkenburgh, Joanna Kerns, Delta Burke. **1985**

BUONA SERA, MRS. CAMPBELL ★★★1/2 Great farce, with Gina Lollobrigida having convinced three World War II soldiers that they fathered her child, collecting support payments from each. Then she learns the ex-GIs are returning to Italy for a twenty-year reunion. 113m. **DIR:** Melvin Frank. **CAST:** Gina Lollobrigida, Peter Lawford, Phil Silvers, Telly Savalas, Shelley Winters, Lee Grant. **1968**

'BURBS, THE ★★ In this weird and ultimately unsatisfying comedy, Tom Hanks plays a suburbanite who becomes more and more concerned about the bizarre family who has moved in next door. Essentially it's *Neighbors* all over again, with Hanks, Carrie Fisher, Rick Ducommun, and Bruce Dern turning in strong performances. Despite some inspired touches from director Joe Dante, it falls flat in the final third. Rated PG for violence and profanity. 102m. **DIR:** Joe Dante. **CAST:** Tom Hanks, Bruce Dern, Carrie Fisher, Rick Ducommun, Corey Feldman, Wendy Schaal, Henry Gibson. **1989**

BURDEN OF DREAMS ★★★★★ Documentary specialist Les Blank unearthed a rare treasure in Ecuador, where Werner Herzog labored for years to make *Fitzcarraldo*, a lavish film depicting a man's obsessive quest to bring opera to the jungle. Shooting on location, among fighting tribes, Herzog's task becomes a parallel quest of compulsion. Blank makes the metaphors meaningful, more powerful even than Herzog did. Not rated. 94m. **DIR:** Les Blank. **CAST:** Werner Herzog, Klaus Kinski, Mick Jagger, Jason Robards Jr., Claudia Cardinale. **1982**

BUREAU OF MISSING PERSONS ★★★ Pat O'Brien is the whole show as a rough, wisecracking police detective, helping fugitive Bette Davis prove she is innocent of murder. Fast-paced. B&W; 73m. **DIR:** Roy Del Ruth. **CAST:** Bette Davis, Pat O'Brien, Lewis Stone, Glenda Farrell, Allen Jenkins, Hugh Herbert. **1933**

BURGLAR (RUSSIAN) ★★★ Two unemployed brothers, beset by family problems, find an outlet in Leningrad's punk-rock scene. Nothing special, but worth seeing for a look at an underground musical culture that's not dominated by commercial interests. In Russian with English subtitles. Not rated. 101m. **DIR:**

Valery Ogorodnikov. **CAST:** Konstantin Kinchev, Oleg Yelykomov. **1987**

BURGLAR (U.S.) ★★★ Whoopi Goldberg stars in this amiable but unspectacular caper comedy as a retired cat burglar forced back into a life of crime by a crooked cop (G. W. Bailey). She ends up the prime suspect in a rather messy murder case. Goldberg does well in a role originally written for Bruce Willis. Rated R for profanity and violence. 91m. **DIR:** Hugh Wilson. **CAST:** Whoopi Goldberg, Bob Goldthwait, G. W. Bailey, Lesley Ann Warren. **1987 DVD**

BURGLAR FROM HELL 🦃 This low-budget independent film lacks decent acting, dialogue, cinematography, and sound, but it does have something of a plot, sort of—a burglar killed and buried comes back to life when a group of young adults rents a house for the weekend. Not rated; contains profanity, violence, nudity, and gore. 100m. **DIR:** Chip Herman. **CAST:** Matt O'Connor, Ben Stanski, Barry Gaines. **1999**

BURIED ALIVE (1979) ★★ If *Psycho*'s Norman Bates wasn't loony enough for you, here's another demented taxidermist who takes necrophilia to extremes that are gross even for Italian gore films. This is probably the slickest, most compulsively watchable effort by bad-taste auteur Joe D'Amato. Rated R. 90m. **DIR:** Joe D'Amato (Aristide Massaccesi). **CAST:** Sam Modesto, Ann Cardin. **1979**

BURIED ALIVE (1990) ★★★★ Nice guy Tim Matheson is poisoned by his greedy wife (Jennifer Jason Leigh, at her nastiest) and her lover; believed dead, Matheson is buried in a cheap casket (having fortunately bypassed technicalities such as embalming). Excellent contemporary take on Poe's "Premature Burial." Made for cable. Rated R for mild violence. 93m. **DIR:** Frank Darabont. **CAST:** Tim Matheson, Jennifer Jason Leigh, William Atherton, Hoyt Axton. **1990**

BURIED ALIVE II ★★1/2 An unfaithful husband poisons his wife and buries her so he can run off with his mistress. But the poison only puts his wife in a deep coma, and when she wakes up, she's not very happy. The plot in this made-for-cable original is full of holes, and the acting is buried under bad lines. Rated PG-13; contains violence. 95m. **DIR:** Tim Matheson. **CAST:** Ally Sheedy, Stephen Caffrey, Tracey Needham, Tim Matheson. **1997**

BURKE AND WILLS ★★ Like most Australian period movies, this historical drama about a failed attempt to travel through the uncharted interior of nineteenth-century Australia is meticulously produced, but ends up being more exhausting than entertaining. It's also about 45 minutes too long. It's rated PG-13 for language and brief nudity. 140m. **DIR:** Graeme Clifford. **CAST:** Jack Thompson, Nigel Havers, Greta Scacchi. **1987**

BURMESE HARP, THE ★★★★ A haunting Japanese antiwar film about a soldier who, at the end of World War II, disguises himself as a monk and embarks on a soul-searching journey back to a mountain fortress where his comrades met their death. In Japanese with English subtitles. B&W; 116m. **DIR:** Kon Ichikawa. **CAST:** Shoji Yasui, Rentaro Mikuni. **1956**

BURN! ★★★★ Marlon Brando's performance alone makes *Burn!* worth watching. Seldom has a star so vividly and memorably lived up to his promise as acting great, and that's what makes this film a must-see. Brando plays Sir William Walker, an egotistical mercenary sent by the British to instigate a slave revolt on a Portuguese-controlled sugar-producing island. He succeeds all too well by turning José Dolores (Evaristo Marquez) into a powerful leader and soon finds himself back on the island, plotting the downfall of his Frankenstein monster. Rated PG. 112m. **DIR:** Gillo Pontecorvo. **CAST:** Marlon Brando, Evaristo Marquez, Renato Salvatori. **1969**

BURN UP! ★★ Nothing overly original about this Japanese animated story. Three female police officers get embroiled in the investigation of a notorious white slaver, but obvious plotting undermines fair animation. Not rated; contains nudity and violence. 50m. **DIR:** Yasunori Ide. **1991**

BURN, WITCH, BURN ★★★★ A college psychology professor sets out to debunk the occult only to find himself under attack by a practitioner of the supernatural. A superb screenplay by Charles Beaumont and Richard Matheson helps make this British film one of the best on the subject of witchcraft. 90m. **DIR:** Sidney Hayers. **CAST:** Peter Wyngarde, Janet Blair, Margaret Johnson, Anthony Nicholls. **1962**

BURNDOWN ★★★ This is a murder mystery with the killer the victim of radioactivity. Peter Firth is the police chief trying to solve the murders, and Cathy Moriarty is a news reporter trying to find the far more complex problem of a nuclear leak and cover-up that could be deadly to the entire town. Rated R for violence. 87m. **DIR:** James Allen. **CAST:** Peter Firth, Cathy Moriarty. **1989**

BURNING, THE 🦃 Similar to many other blood feasts, it's the story of a summer camp custodian who, savagely burned as a result of a teenage prank, comes back years later for revenge. Rated R. 90m. **DIR:** Tony Maylam. **CAST:** Brian Matthews, Leah Ayres, Brian Backer. **1981**

BURNING BED, THE ★★★★ Farrah Fawcett is remarkably good in this made-for-TV film based on a true story. She plays a woman reaching the breaking point with her abusive and brutish husband, well played by Paul LeMat. Fawcett not only proves she can act, but that she has the capacity to pull off a multilayered role. Believable from start to finish, this is a superior television film. 105m. **DIR:** Robert Greenwald. **CAST:** Farrah Fawcett, Paul LeMat, Richard Masur, Grace Zabriskie. **1984**

BURNING COURT, THE ★★★ Variation on the haunted-house theme, with a family gathered at their cursed estate by a dying uncle. More stylized than scary. French, dubbed in English. Not rated. B&W; 102m. **DIR:** Julien Duvivier. **CAST:** Jean-Claude Brialy, Nadja Tiller, Perrette Pradier. **1962**

BURNING HILLS, THE ★★1/2 Average revenge tale of wounded homesteader Tab Hunter pursued by a cattleman's posse. Natalie Wood, terribly miscast as a Mexican half-breed, comes to his side. Screenplay by Irving Wallace from a Louis L'Amour novel. 94m. **DIR:** Stuart Heisler. **CAST:** Tab Hunter, Natalie Wood, Skip Homeier, Eduard Franz, Earl Holliman, Claude Akins, Ray Teal. **1956**

BURNING SEASON, THE ★★★★ This absorbing docudrama traces the meteoric rise of Brazil's Chico Mendes, played with quiet dignity by Raul Julia.

Mendes's story is of a small-town rubber tapper who reluctantly opposes rapacious businessmen determined to raze the Amazon forest and create cattle-grazing country. Rated R for profanity, violence, torture, and brief nudity. 125m. **DIR:** John Frankenheimer. **CAST:** Raul Julia, Carmen Argenziano, Esai Morales, Edward James Olmos, Sonia Braga, Nigel Havers. **1994**

BURNING SECRET ★★ A cool, overly restrained mystery-romance, set in an Austrian health spa in the years between the world wars. Faye Dunaway and Klaus Maria Brandauer star as emotionally crippled strangers who meet when Brandauer befriends her young son. Remarkably short on passion. Rated PG. 110m. **DIR:** Andrew Birkin. **CAST:** Faye Dunaway, Klaus Maria Brandauer. **1988**

BURNT BY THE SUN ★★★★★ Deserving Best Foreign Language Film Academy Award winner about a Russian revolutionary hero (director Nikita Mikhalkov) whose quiet country holiday is upset by the arrival of his young wife's former lover and, more alarmingly, Stalin's purges of the 1930s. In Russian with English subtitles. Rated R for nudity, sex, and violence. 134m. **DIR:** Nikita Mikhalkov. **CAST:** Nikita Mikhalkov, Oleg Menchikov, Ingeborga Dapkounaite, Nadia Mikhalkov. **1994**

BURNT OFFERINGS ★★ Good acting cannot save this predictable horror film concerning a haunted house. Rated PG. 115m. **DIR:** Dan Curtis. **CAST:** Oliver Reed, Karen Black, Burgess Meredith, Bette Davis, Lee Montgomery, Eileen Heckart. **1976**

BUS IS COMING, THE ★★★ The message of this production is: racism (both black and white) is wrong. In this film, Billy Mitchell (Mike Sims) is a young black soldier who returns to his hometown after his brother is murdered. Billy's white friend encourages him to investigate the death of his brother, while his black friends want to tear the town down. The acting is not the greatest, but the film does succeed in making its point. Rated PG for violence. 102m. **DIR:** Wendell J. Franklin. **CAST:** Mike Simms, Stephanie Faulkner, Burl Bullock. **1971**

BUS STOP ★★★★1/2 Marilyn Monroe plays a show girl who is endlessly pursued by an oaf of a cowboy named Bo (Don Murray). He even kidnaps her when she refuses to marry him. Lots of laughs as Bo mistreats his newly found "angel." Arthur O'Connell is excellent as Verg, Bo's older and wiser friend who advises Bo on the way to treat women. 96m. **DIR:** Joshua Logan. **CAST:** Marilyn Monroe, Don Murray, Arthur O'Connell, Betty Field, Casey Adams. **1956 DVD**

BUSHIDO BLADE 🦃 Richard Boone gives an outrageously hammy performance as Commander Matthew Perry, whose mission is to find a valuable sword. Rated R for violence. 104m. **DIR:** Tom Kotani. **CAST:** Richard Boone, Frank Converse, James Earl Jones, Toshiro Mifune, Mako. **1979**

BUSHWHACKED 🦃 Incompetent delivery man is framed for murder and poses as a Ranger Scout leader to six woodland tenderfoots (one of them a girl) while trying to clear himself. Rated PG-13 for language. 96m. **DIR:** Greg Beeman. **CAST:** Daniel Stern, Jon Polito, Brad Sullivan. **1995**

BUSHWHACKERS ★★★ Ex-Confederate John Ireland tries to hang up his guns, but a ruthless land baron forces him to buckle 'em on again. Routine range-war tale saved by a better-than-competent cast. B&W; 70m. **DIR:** Rod Amateau. **CAST:** John Ireland, Dorothy Malone, Wayne Morris, Lawrence Tierney, Lon Chaney Jr. **1951**

BUSINESS AFFAIR, A ★★★ A flawed, if enjoyable, reversal on the old *Taming of the Shrew* theme. The focus grows a little blurry around the halfway mark, but there are some fine performances and strong characters in this romantic European comedy. A gorgeous model irritates her famous, badly behaved novelist husband when she writes a bestseller. Christopher Walken, in one of his more controlled performances, is the publisher who woos her professionally and personally. Rated R for profanity and nudity. 105m. **DIR:** Charlotte Brandstrom. **CAST:** Jonathan Pryce, Carole Bouquet, Christopher Walken, Sheila Hancock. **1993**

BUSINESS AS USUAL ★★ Glenda Jackson plays a dress-shop manager fired after going to bat for an employee who's been sexually harrassed by a higher-up. Writer-director Lezli-An Barrett's script covers a wide range of issues but never develops any dramatic tension or strong characters. Rated PG. 89m. **DIR:** Lezli-An Barrett. **CAST:** Glenda Jackson, John Thaw, Cathy Tyson, Mark McGann, James Hazeldine. **1987**

BUSINESS FOR PLEASURE ★★ Kinky but unsatisfactory erotic drama about a businessman who likes to watch. That's the plot of writer Zalman King's sexual cavalcade that finds a businesswoman so desperate to save her company that she's willing to procure sexual entertainment for an investor. Like all King escapades, there is enough soft-core to heat up a chilly night, but not nearly enough plot to make it matter. Not rated; contains adult situations, language, and nudity. 97m. **DIR:** Rafael Eisenman. **CAST:** Caron Bernstein, Gary Stretch, Jeroen Krabbé, Joanna Pacula. **1996**

•BUSINESS OF STRANGERS, THE ★★★ Career woman Julie is making city-to-city management presentations when she fires her assistant Paula for being late to a meeting. She then receives word that her company's CEO is flying out to see her, thinks that she also will be fired, and meets with headhunter Nick to strategize her professional recovery. Flights are canceled, futures are rearranged, and Julie and Paula reunite for a night of drinking in which Nick becomes the target of a revenge plot. The drama loses its footing but conjures up the bleakness, insecurities, and cannibalism of corporate ladder climbing. Rated R for profanity and sexual content. 84m. **DIR:** Patrick Stettner. **CAST:** Stockard Channing, Julia Stiles, Frederick Weller. **2001**

BUSTED UP ★★1/2 A story about a local-circuit barefisted fighter and a nightclub singer. Typical plot, average acting, but professionally produced and technically polished. Rated R for violence and language. 93m. **DIR:** Conrad E. Palmisano. **CAST:** Irene Cara, Paul Coufos, Tony Rosato, Stan Shaw. **1986**

BUSTER ★★★ Pop star Phil Collins makes his film debut in this enjoyable story about the British Great Train Robbery of 1963. Collins is Buster Edwards, who became a folk hero after he and his cronies pulled off the greatest robbery in the history of England. It's enjoyable fare and an interesting character study. Rated R for language and brief nudity. 93m. **DIR:** David Greene. **CAST:** Phil Collins, Julie Walters, Sheila Hancock. **1988**

BUSTER AND BILLIE ★★ A handsome high school boy falls in love with a homely but loving girl in the rural South. Set in the 1940s, the film has an innocent, sweet quality until it abruptly shifts tone and turns into a mean-spirited revenge picture. Rated R for violence and nudity. 100m. **DIR:** Daniel Petrie. **CAST:** Jan-Michael Vincent, Joan Goodfellow, Pamela Sue Martin, Clifton James. **1974**

BUSTER AND FATTY ★★★ Two of silent film's greatest comedy stars, Buster Keaton and Roscoe "Fatty" Arbuckle, cavort in five hilarious examples of the art of slapstick: *Coney Island*, *The Butcher Boy* (Keaton's film debut), *Good Night Nurse*, *Out West*, and the long-thought-lost *Back Stage*. B&W; 94m. **DIR:** Roscoe Arbuckle. **CAST:** Roscoe "Fatty" Arbuckle, Buster Keaton, Al St. John, Alice Lake, Agnes Neilson, Joe Bordeaux. **1917–19**

BUSTER KEATON: A HARD ACT TO FOLLOW ★★★★★ Offered in three parts, this is a truly superb narrative study of Buster Keaton's matchless stone-faced comic genius. The episodes, titled "From Vaudeville to Movies," "Star without a Studio," and "A Genius Recognized," chronicle Buster Keaton's amazing and mercurial career from near start to close with compassion, insight, and captivating accuracy. A unique opportunity to see one of the greats of the silent screen at work. B&W/color; 52m. **DIR:** Kevin Brownlow, David Gill. **1987**

BUSTER KEATON FESTIVAL VOL. 1–3 ★★★★ Hilarious collection of silent shorts from the legendary comic genius. Includes such priceless gems as: *The Paleface*, *The Boat*, *Daydreams*, *The Balloonatic*, and *The Blacksmith*. Silent. B&W; 55m. **DIR:** Buster Keaton, Eddie Cline, Malcolm St. Clair. **CAST:** Buster Keaton, Virginia Fox, Joe Roberts, Eddie Cline, Sybil Seely, Bonnie Hill, Freeman Wood, Joseph Keaton, Myra Keaton, Louise Keaton, Phyllis Haver, Renée Adorée. **1921–1922**

BUSTIN' LOOSE ★★1/2 Take superbad ex-con Richard Pryor, stick him on a school bus with goody-two-shoes teacher Cicely Tyson and eight ornery schoolchildren, and what have you got? A cross-country, comic odyssey as long as Pryor is up to his madcap antics. But *Bustin' Loose* bogs down in its last half hour. Rated R for profanity and violence. 94m. **DIR:** Oz Scott. **CAST:** Richard Pryor, Cicely Tyson, Robert Christian, Alphonso Alexander, Janet Wong. **1981 DVD**

BUT I'M A CHEERLEADER 🦃 A high-school cheerleader who is attracted to girls is sent to a deprogramming camp to get "straightened out." A competent cast and a promising idea are wrecked on a clumsy script and the kind of inept production that would give home movies a bad name. Rated R for profanity and mature themes. 85m. **DIR:** Jamie Babbit. **CAST:** Natasha Lyonne, Cathy Moriarty, Bud Cort, Mink Stole, RuPaul. **1999 DVD**

BUT NOT FOR ME ★★1/2 Clark Gable does a credible job as an aging Broadway producer who feels the ravages of time in both his professional career and private life. Predictable comedy-drama but the leading players (especially Lilli Palmer) and a title song by Ella Fitzgerald help. B&W; 105m. **DIR:** Walter Lang. **CAST:** Clark Gable, Carroll Baker, Lilli Palmer, Lee J. Cobb, Barry Coe, Thomas Gomez, Charles Lane. **1959**

BUTCH AND SUNDANCE: THE EARLY DAYS ★★ Director Richard Lester has made better films (see *A Hard Day's Night* and *Superman II*), and because his usual film is a comedy, this outing is especially disappointing. Nearly all of the jokes fall flat despite a screenplay that hints at the original film with Paul Newman and Robert Redford. Rated PG for some mildly crude language and (very little) violence. 111m. **DIR:** Richard Lester. **CAST:** William Katt, Tom Berenger, Brian Dennehy, John Schuck, Jeff Corey. **1979**

BUTCH CAMP 🦃 Embarrassing tale of a meek gay office worker who enrolls in Commandant Samantha Rottweiler's "Butch Camp" and finds the whole experience humiliating. He's not the only one. Poor production values and an eat-all-of-the-scenery performance by comedian Judy Tenuta seal the film's fate. Not rated; contains nudity, language, and adult situations. 85m. **DIR:** Alessandro de Gaetano. **CAST:** Paul Denniston, Judy Tenuta, Jordan Roberts, Bill Ingraham. **1998**

BUTCH CASSIDY AND THE SUNDANCE KID ★★★★1/2 George Roy Hill directed this gentle Western spoof featuring personal-best performances by Paul Newman, Robert Redford, and Katharine Ross. A spectacular box-office success, and deservedly so, the release deftly combines action with comedy. Rated PG. 112m. **DIR:** George Roy Hill. **CAST:** Paul Newman, Robert Redford, Katharine Ross. **1969 DVD**

BUTCHER BOY, THE ★★ Imagine *Tom Sawyer* transplanted to Ireland and set in the early 1960s, then mixed with the walking-nightmare hallucinations of Roman Polanski's *Repulsion*. Toss in thick Irish accents, blend with a shrieking directorial style, and you've got this savage, blackly comic study of a feisty kid losing his mind. Rated R for profanity, violence, and just about every perversion you could imagine. 105m. **DIR:** Neil Jordan. **CAST:** Stephen Rea, Fiona Shaw, Eamonn Owens, Alan Boyle, Milo O'Shea, Sinead O'Connor. **1998**

BUTCHER'S WIFE, THE ★★ You don't have to be clairvoyant to know what's going to happen in this comedy about a North Carolina psychic who weds a New York City butcher because she thinks he's the man of her dreams. Apart from isolated moments of inspiration, *The Butcher's Wife* is comparable with a so-so episode of *Bewitched*. Rated PG-13 for profanity. 105m. **DIR:** Terry Hughes. **CAST:** Demi Moore, Jeff Daniels, George Dzundza, Mary Steenburgen, Frances McDormand, Margaret Colin. **1991 DVD**

BUTTERFIELD 8 ★★★ Severe illness helped sway votes her way when Elizabeth Taylor copped an Oscar for her by-the-numbers portrayal of a big-ticket call girl who wants to go straight after finding someone she thinks is Mr. Right. Adapted from the John O'Hara novel. 109m. **DIR:** Daniel Mann. **CAST:** Elizabeth Taylor, Laurence Harvey, Eddie Fisher, Dina Merrill, Mildred Dunnock, Betty Field. **1960 DVD**

BUTTERFLIES ARE FREE ★★★★ Edward Albert is a blind youth determined to be self-sufficient in spite of his overbearing mother and the distraction of his will-o'-the-wisp next-door neighbor (Goldie Hawn). This fast-paced comedy benefits from some outstanding performances, none better than that by Eileen Heckart. Her concerned, protective, and sometimes overloving mother is a treasure to behold. Rated PG. 109m. **DIR:**

Milton Katselas. **CAST:** Goldie Hawn, Edward Albert, Eileen Heckart, Mike Warren. **1972 DVD**

BUTTERFLY (1982) ★★ Sex symbol Pia Zadora starts an incestuous relationship with her father (Stacy Keach). Orson Welles, as a judge, is the best thing about this film. Rated R. 107m. **DIR:** Matt Cimber. **CAST:** Pia Zadora, Stacy Keach, Orson Welles, Lois Nettleton. **1982**

BUTTERFLY (2000) ★★★★ In this compassionate drama, a young, asthmatic village boy lives with his parents and brother in 1930s Spain. His schoolteacher, a liberal who blends arts and science into his daily curriculum, befriends the lad on the eve of civil war, arming him with a copy of *Treasure Island* and a butterfly net. Family scandal, the oft-neglected wonders of the world, and the seeds of fear, cowardice, and betrayal earmark the film's themes. In Spanish with English subtitles. Rated R for sex, nudity, and adult themes. 97m. **DIR:** Jose Luis Cuerda. **CAST:** Manuel Lozano, Fernando Fernán Gómez, Uxia Blanco. **2000 DVD**

BUTTERFLY KISS ★★ Amanda Plummer frantically hams it up as a crazed lesbian serial killer, with Saskia Reeves as her simpering, stupid girlfriend. The actresses do good work, but their characters are unconvincingly written, and the film is extremely unpleasant. There's no real suspense, just grisly tension while waiting for the next victim to be clubbed to death. Rated R for profanity, violence, and simulated sex. 88m. **DIR:** Michael Winterbottom. **CAST:** Amanda Plummer, Saskia Reeves, Kathy Jamieson, Desmond McAteer, Lisa Jane Riley. **1994**

BUY AND CELL 🦃 A Wall Street broker takes the rap for his boss's insider trading. Rated R. 91m. **DIR:** Robert Boris. **CAST:** Robert Carradine, Michael Winslow, Randall "Tex" Cobb, Fred Travalena, Ben Vereen, Malcolm McDowell. **1989**

BUYING TIME ★★1/2 A young man goes undercover to procure evidence that will convict a drug-dealing killer, but he finds his own life in jeopardy. Rated R for nudity, profanity, violence, and animal abuse. 97m. **DIR:** Mitchell Gabourie. **CAST:** Jeff Schultz, Laura Cruickshank, Page Fletcher, Dean Stockwell. **1989**

BY DAWN'S EARLY LIGHT ★★★ This slick adaptation of William Prochnau's *Trinity's Child*, unfolds like an updated *Fail-Safe*. Nuclear terrorists trick the Soviet Union into believing the U.S. has struck first, and the reprisal is launched before the mistake is detected. Not rated made-for-cable film; contains profanity. 104m. **DIR:** Jack Sholder. **CAST:** Powers Boothe, Rebecca DeMornay, James Earl Jones, Martin Landau, Darren McGavin, Jeffrey DeMunn, Peter MacNicol, Rip Torn. **1990**

BY DESIGN ★★1/2 Patty Duke plays a lesbian fashion designer who decides she'd like to have a baby. She attempts to get pregnant by a heterosexual man. Interesting subject matter gets an uneven result. Rated R. 88m. **DIR:** Claude Jutra. **CAST:** Patty Duke, Sara Botsford, Saul Rubinek. **1981**

BY LOVE POSSESSED ★★1/2 Problems among the upper crust of a small New England town include alcoholism, impotence, and rape charges. It all adds up to dull soap opera with so-so performances. Very loosely based on the novel by James Gould Cozzens. 115m. **DIR:** John Sturges. **CAST:** Lana Turner, Efrem Zimbalist Jr., Jason Robards Jr., Barbara Bel Geddes, George Hamilton, Susan Kohner, Thomas Mitchell, Everett Sloane, Carroll O'Connor. **1961**

BY THE BLOOD OF OTHERS ★★★ The town fathers of a small village search for a plan to rescue two women held hostage by a mentally disturbed young man. Like his father, novelist Georges Simenon, director Marc Simenon brings psychological depth to this suspense drama. In French with English subtitles. 95m. **DIR:** Marc Simenon. **CAST:** Mariangela Melato, Yves Beneyton, Bernard Blier. **1973**

BY THE LAW ★★★★ Adapted from Jack London's short story, "The Unexpected," this is a grim story of three trappers isolated by Alaskan storms and floods. Silent. Russian. B&W; 90m. **DIR:** Lev Kuleshov. **CAST:** Alexandra Khokhlova, Sergei Komarov, Vladimir Fogel. **1926**

BY THE LIGHT OF THE SILVERY MOON ★★★ More trouble for the Winfield family in this sequel to *On Moonlight Bay*, with innocent Leon Ames suspected by his family of being involved with a French actress. Post–WWI setting, with many familiar songs from that period. 102m. **DIR:** David Butler. **CAST:** Doris Day, Gordon MacRae, Leon Ames, Rosemary DeCamp, Billy Gray, Mary Wickes, Russell Arms. **1953**

BY THE SWORD ★★1/2 Plenty of swordplay fails to sharpen this standard tale of revenge set in the professional world of sword fighting. F.Murray Abraham is the old pro, Eric Roberts the Olympic star and son of the man killed by Abraham years earlier in the heat of passion. Abraham plays a dangerous cat-and-mouse game with Roberts as he insinuates himself into his life, and then must face off against him when the truth is revealed. Rated R for language and violence. 91m. **DIR:** Jeremy Paul Kagan. **CAST:** F. Murray Abraham, Eric Roberts, Mia Sara, Christopher Rydell. **1991**

BY WAY OF THE STARS ★★★1/2 Breathtaking outdoor adventure stars Zachary Bennett as young Lucas Bienman, a nineteenth-century Prussian teen who heads to the New World to find his father. When Luke arrives in the untamed Canadian West, his trek is filled with adventure and close calls, not to mention Indians, and a killer hot on his trail. Gorgeous scenery and decent cast make this *Hallmark Hall of Fame* presentation an adventure for the entire family. Rated PG. 150m. **DIR:** Allan Winton King. **CAST:** Zachary Bennett, Tantoo Cardinal, Gema Zamprogna, Jan Rubes. **1992**

BYE-BYE ★★★ Two French-Arab brothers move from Paris to Marseilles to live with their uncle, where they experience hostility toward "foreigners" and the hardships of the street. Writer-director Karim Dridi's film has persuasive acting and quiet, slice-of-life realism. In translation, unfortunately, it is marred by clumsy English subtitles. In French and Arabic with English subtitles. Not rated; contains mature themes, mild profanity (in subtitles), and one sexual episode. 102m. **DIR:** Karim Dridi. **CAST:** Sami Bouajila, Nozha Khouadra, Philippe Ambrosini, Ouassini Embarek. **1995**

BYE BYE, BABY 🦃 Bizarre twist on Noel Coward's *Private Lives*. The film was clearly shot simultaneously in English and Italian, with dialogue that sounds like badly translated Esperanto. Rated R for nudity. 90m. **DIR:** Enrico Oldoini. **CAST:** Carol Alt, Luca Barbareschi, Brigitte Nielsen, Jason Connery. **1989 DVD**

BYE BYE BIRDIE ★★★ A rock star's approaching appearance in a small town turns several lives upside down in this pleasant musical-comedy. Based on the successful Broadway play, this is pretty lightweight stuff, but a likable cast and good production numbers make it worthwhile. No rating; okay for the whole family. 112m. **DIR:** George Sidney. **CAST:** Dick Van Dyke, Ann-Margret, Janet Leigh, Paul Lynde, Bobby Rydell. **1963 DVD**

BYE BYE BRAZIL ★★★1/2 This is a bawdy, bizarre, satiric, and sometimes even touching film that follows a ramshackle traveling tent show—the Caravana Rolidei—through the cities, jungle, and villages of Brazil. In Portuguese with English subtitles. Rated R. 110m. **DIR:** Carlos Diegues. **CAST:** José Wilker, Betty Faria. **1980**

BYE BYE, LOVE ★★ Three divorced male buddies—all child-custody weekend warriors—get a forty-eight-hour crash course in single parenting and dating. Rated PG-13 for language. 105m. **DIR:** Sam Weisman. **CAST:** Matthew Modine, Randy Quaid, Paul Reiser, Janeane Garofalo, Rob Reiner. **1995**

CABARET ★★★★★ This classic musical-drama takes place in Germany in 1931. The Nazi party has not yet assumed complete control, and the local cabaret unfolds the story of two young lovers, the ensuing mood of the country, and the universal touch of humanity. Everything is handled with taste—bisexual encounters, the horrors of the Nazi regime, and the bawdy entertainment of the nightclub. "Host" Joel Grey is brilliant. Michael York and Liza Minnelli are first-rate. So is the movie. Rated PG. 128m. **DIR:** Bob Fosse. **CAST:** Liza Minnelli, Michael York, Helmut Griem, Joel Grey. **1972 DVD**

CABARET BALKAN ★★★★1/2 During one night in Belgrade, the lives of a number of characters intertwine in a series of chance encounters. The film paints a harrowing picture of a society about to self-destruct, suffused with rage and despair, yet lit by flashes of bitter humor that underscore the characters' humanity. It's an unforgettable descent into something very much like Dante's *Inferno* right here on earth. In Serbo-Croatian with English subtitles. Rated R for violence and profanity (in subtitles). 100m. **DIR:** Goran Paskaljevic. **CAST:** Lazar Ristovski, Miki Manojlovic, Nikola Ristanovski, Nebojsa Glogovac. **1998**

CABEZA DE VACA ★★★★ Director Nicolas Echevarria draws on his experience as a documentary filmmaker for this engrossing study of Spanish explorer Alvar Nunez Cabeza de Vaca, who landed in Florida in 1528 and rose from an Indian slave to a respected shaman with another tribe. In Spanish with English subtitles. Rated R for violence and profanity. 112m. **DIR:** Nicolas Echevarria. **CAST:** Juan Diego. **1992 DVD**

CABIN BOY Pathetic, filthy-rich geek mistakes a grungy fishing trawler for a cruise ship in this lame fantasy-comedy version of *Captains Courageous*. Rated PG-13 for language. 80m. **DIR:** Adam Resnick. **CAST:** Chris Elliott, Ritch Brinkley, Brian Doyle-Murray, James Gammon, Brian James, Melora Walters, Andy Richter. **1994**

CABIN BY THE LAKE ★★ Judd Nelson plays a screenwriter working on a movie about a serial killer who drowns his victims and tends to their submerged bodies every day. Although he says he's just researching his next film, Nelson *is* the serial killer. This made-for-cable original tries to be a black comedy, but suffers from extreme seriousness at times, and extreme silliness at others. Not rated; contains violence. 95m. **DIR:** Po-Chih Leong. **CAST:** Judd Nelson, Hedy Burress, Michael Weatherly, Susan Gibney. **2000**

CABIN IN THE COTTON ★★★ An ambitious young sharecropper is educated by, and then works for, a rich landowner. His loyalties are challenged when he learns of widespread theft by tenant farmers. Worth the price of rental to hear vixen Bette Davis utter the immortal, and often misquoted line: "Ah'd *like* ta' kiss ya, but ah jus' washed mah hair." B&W; 78m. **DIR:** Michael Curtiz. **CAST:** Richard Barthelmess, Bette Davis, Dorothy Jordan, Russell Simpson. **1932**

CABIN IN THE SKY ★★★ One of Hollywood's first general-release black films and Vincente Minnelli's first feature. Eddie Anderson shows acting skill that was sadly and too long diluted by his playing foil for Jack Benny. Ethel Waters, as always, is superb. The film is a shade racist, but bear in mind that it was made in 1943, when Tinsel Town still thought blacks did nothing but sing, dance, and love watermelon. B&W; 100m. **DIR:** Vincente Minnelli. **CAST:** Eddie "Rochester" Anderson, Lena Horne, Ethel Waters, Rex Ingram, Louis Armstrong. **1943**

CABINET OF DOCTOR CALIGARI, THE ★★★1/2 A nightmarish story and surrealistic settings are the main ingredients of this early German classic of horror and fantasy. Cesare, a hollow-eyed sleepwalker (Conrad Veidt), commits murder while under the spell of the evil hypnotist Dr. Caligari (Werner Krauss). Ordered to kill Jane, a beautiful girl (Lil Dagover), Cesare defies Caligari, and instead abducts her. Silent. B&W; 51m. **DIR:** Robert Wiene. **CAST:** Werner Krauss, Conrad Veidt, Lil Dagover. **1919 DVD**

CABIRIA ★★ This feature purportedly had a decisive influence on D. W. Griffith's epic ambitions. It made an international star out of Bartolomeo Pagano, whose role of strongman Maciste predated Schwarzenegger by many decades. Italian playwright Gabriele D'Annunzio lent his name—and some subtitles—to the picture. Silent. Italian. B&W; 95m. **DIR:** Giovanni Pastrone. **CAST:** Bartolomeo Pagano. **1914 DVD**

CABLE GUY, THE ★★★ Jim Carrey's first attempt to project "serious" isn't exactly dramatic; it's like his usual antic slapstick in a more irritating vein. The basic idea is frightening: What if Ace Ventura wanted to be your friend and wouldn't take no for an answer? Director Ben Stiller tries to turn this tale of an obsessive pay-TV installer into a satire of both stalker movies and television culture in general, but it's still too much of a silly Carrey vehicle to work out its more intelligent ideas. Rated PG-13. 91m. **DIR:** Ben Stiller. **CAST:**

Jim Carrey, Matthew Broderick, Leslie Mann. **1996 DVD**

CABO BLANCO ♥ A miserable suspense-thriller remake of *Casablanca*. As good as he can be when he wants to, Charles Bronson is no Humphrey Bogart. Rated R. 87m. **DIR:** J. Lee Thompson. **CAST:** Charles Bronson, Dominique Sanda, Jason Robards Jr. **1982 DVD**

CACTUS ★★★1/2 Have patience with this warm and witty tale of a French lady (Isabelle Huppert) injured in an auto accident while visiting Australia. A young blind man helps her adjust to her diminishing eyesight. The supporting cast and Australian locale add to this story of growth and awareness. Rated PG. 96m. **DIR:** Paul Cox. **CAST:** Isabelle Huppert, Robert Menzies, Norman Kaye. **1986 DVD**

CACTUS FLOWER ★★★ Watch this one for Goldie Hawn's performance that earned her an Academy Award as best supporting actress. She's the slightly wonky girlfriend of dentist Walter Matthau, who actually loves his nurse (Ingrid Bergman). Although adapted from a hit Broadway play by Abe Burrows, this film version is pretty short on laughs. Ingrid Bergman is far too serious in her role, and Matthau simply doesn't make a credible dentist. Rated PG for adult situations. 103m. **DIR:** Gene Saks. **CAST:** Walter Matthau, Ingrid Bergman, Goldie Hawn. **1969 DVD**

CADDIE ★★★★ This is an absorbing character study of a woman who struggles to support herself and her children in Australia in the 1920s. Thanks greatly to the star's performance, it is yet another winner from down under. MPAA unrated, but contains mild sexual situations. 107m. **DIR:** Donald Crombie. **CAST:** Helen Morse, Takis Emmanuel, Jack Thompson, Jacki Weaver. **1976**

CADDY, THE ★★★ In this lesser comedy from the Martin and Lewis team, the fellas enter the world of golf. Jerry plays a would-be golf pro. Strictly formulaic, but highlighted by several entertaining clashes between the two stars. 95m. **DIR:** Norman Taurog. **CAST:** Dean Martin, Jerry Lewis, Donna Reed, Fred Clark. **1953**

CADDYSHACK ★★ Only Rodney Dangerfield, as an obnoxious refugee from a leisure-suit collectors' convention, offers anything of value in this rip-off of the *Animal House* formula. Chevy Chase and Bill Murray sleepwalk through their poorly written roles, and Ted Knight looks a little weary. Rated R for nudity and sex. 99m. **DIR:** Harold Ramis. **CAST:** Chevy Chase, Rodney Dangerfield, Ted Knight, Michael O'Keefe, Bill Murray. **1980 DVD**

CADDYSHACK II ♥ Deciding to pass on this abysmal sequel may be the smartest career move Rodney Dangerfield ever made. Rated PG for profanity. 103m. **DIR:** Allan Arkush. **CAST:** Jackie Mason, Chevy Chase, Dan Aykroyd, Robert Stack, Dyan Cannon, Randy Quaid, Jonathan Silverman. **1988 DVD**

CADENCE ★★1/2 Well-meant film about the evils of racism is skewed by director Martin Sheen's overly sympathetic portrait of a prejudiced stockade commander who attempts to use newcomer Charlie Sheen to spy on his cell mates, all of whom are black. More notable for good intentions than dramatic power. Rated PG-13 for profanity and violence. 97m. **DIR:** Martin Sheen. **CAST:** Charlie Sheen, Martin Sheen, Laurence Fishburne, Michael Beach, Ramon Estevez. **1991 DVD**

CADILLAC MAN ★★★★ Philandering car salesman Robin Williams embarks on the worst few days of his life when his wife (Pamela Reed) demands more alimony, a gangster wants payment on a $20,000 gambling debt, and his boss demands that he sell a month's worth of cars in one day—then distraught husband Tim Robbins comes roaring into the dealership with an automatic weapon looking for the man who has been bedding his wife. Well acted and often hilarious. Rated R for violence, profanity, and nudity. 95m. **DIR:** Roger Donaldson. **CAST:** Robin Williams, Tim Robbins, Pamela Reed, Fran Drescher, Zack Norman. **1990 DVD**

CADILLAC RANCH ★★★1/2 Three estranged sisters reunite to search for their father's hidden legacy in this offbeat action-comedy. Suzy Amis, Renee Humphrey, and Caroleen Feeney have little in common except a desire to find what's buried at the famous Cadillac Ranch in Texas. Rated R for language, violence, and sexuality. 95m. **DIR:** Lisa Gottlieb. **CAST:** Suzy Amis, Renee Humphrey, Caroleen Feeney, Christopher Lloyd, Linden Ashby. **1996 DVD**

CAESAR AND CLEOPATRA ★★1/2 George Bernard Shaw's wordy play about Rome's titanic leader and Egypt's young queen. Claude Rains and Vivien Leigh are brilliant. 127m. **DIR:** Gabriel Pascal. **CAST:** Claude Rains, Vivien Leigh, Stewart Granger, Francis L. Sullivan, Flora Robson. **1946 DVD**

CAFÉ AU LAIT ★★ Visually lively but shallow look at racial relations in Paris, where a pregnant young woman refuses to tell her two boyfriends—one Jewish, one black—which is the prospective father. Not rated; contains some nudity. 94m. **DIR:** Mathieu Kassovitz. **CAST:** Mathieu Kassovitz, Julie Mauduech, Hubert Kounde. **1994**

CAFE EXPRESS ★★★1/2 Chaplinesque comedy starring Nino Manfredi, best known in this country for *Bread and Chocolate*. He plays a similar character here, a vendor selling coffee on a commuter train. Because such sales are illegal, he is hounded by conductors and other petty types. A bit lightweight, but Manfredi is always fun to watch. 105m. **DIR:** Nanni Loy. **CAST:** Nino Manfredi, Adolfo Celi, Vittorio Mezzogiorno. **1980**

CAFE ROMEO ★★★ Raised with old-world traditions that no longer apply to them, six lifelong friends seek out a niche in the world as they venture from their neighborhood coffeehouse. Second-generation Italian-Americans are the focus of this somewhat uneven romantic comedy. Rated R for profanity. 93m. **DIR:** Rex Bromfield. **CAST:** Catherine Mary Stewart, Jonathan Crombie. **1991**

CAFE SOCIETY ★★★ New York's 1950s nightclub scene was laced with sin and wealthy ne'er-do-wells having more cash than common sense, and this nasty little melodrama follows the very public scandal that destroyed one young man, brought temporary fame to a naïve party girl, and forever changed the salacious environment. Deeper characterization would have been nice. Rated R for profanity, nudity, simulated sex, and drug use. 108m. **DIR:** Raymond DeFelitta. **CAST:** Frank Whaley, Peter Gallagher, Lara Flynn Boyle, John Spencer, Anna Thomson, David Patrick Kelly. **1995**

CAGE ★★★ Fine actioner features Lou Ferrigno as a brain-damaged Vietnam vet drawn into an underworld gambling arena. Although the dialogue is uninspired, Ferrigno shines. Rated R for violence and profanity. 101m. **DIR:** Lang Elliott. **CAST:** Lou Ferrigno, Reb Brown, Michael Dante. **1988 DVD**

CAGE II: ARENA OF DEATH, THE 🦃 Absolutely ludicrous tale of a muscle man (Lou Ferrigno) who is kidnapped and made to fight in the infamous "cage" battles to the death. When his partner comes looking for him, you know it won't be long until they're in the ring facing each other. No-budget doldrums with only Ferrigno's undeniable but wasted screen presence to give it any life. Rated R for violence and profanity. 94m. **DIR:** Lang Elliott. **CAST:** Lou Ferrigno, Reb Brown, James Shigeta, Shannon Lee. **1994**

CAGED FEAR 🦃 Innocent woman gets thrown behind bars. Not even good trash. Rated R for nudity, violence, language. 93m. **DIR:** Bobby Houston. **CAST:** David Keith, Ray Sharkey, Deborah May, Karen Black. **1991**

CAGED HEART, THE (L'ADDITION) ★★★ This absorbing French film has Bruno Winkler (Richard Berry) arrested for shoplifting when he tries to help a beautiful young woman (Victoria Abril). Once behind bars, he's accused of aiding a crime lord in his escape and shooting a guard. One can't help but get caught up in the story. Rated R for violence and profanity. 85m. **DIR:** Denis Amar. **CAST:** Richard Berry, Richard Bohringer, Victoria Abril. **1985**

CAGED HEAT ★★ A typical R-rated women's prison-break picture from Roger Corman's New World Pictures. For a change, this one is set in the United States. Otherwise its distinctions are marginal, despite direction by Jonathan Demme. 84m. **DIR:** Jonathan Demme. **CAST:** Juanita Brown, Erica Gavin, Barbara Steele. **1974 DVD**

CAGED HEAT 2: STRIPPED OF FREEDOM 🦃 It's hard to believe they still make these women-behind-bars movies, but what's even harder to believe is that nothing has changed. Same script, same lecherous inmates and guards, same young innocent thrown in with the wolves. Rated R for nudity, adult situations, violence, and language. 84m. **DIR:** Cirio H. Santiago. **CAST:** Jewel Shepard, Pamela D'Pella, Chanel Akiko Hirai. **1994**

CAGED HEAT 3000 🦃 The makers of this film take the women-in-prison genre into the future with the same results: an excuse to get women naked. Not rated; contains nudity, violence, and adult language. 85m. **DIR:** Aaron Osborne. **CAST:** Cassandra Leigh, Kena Land, Bob Ferrelli. **1995**

CAHILL—US MARSHAL ★★1/2 John Wayne was still making B Westerns in the 1970s—to the disappointment of those who (rightly) expected better. Although still enjoyable, this film about a lawman (Wayne) whose son (Gary Grimes) becomes a bank robber is routine at best. Still, the performances by the Duke and George Kennedy (as the chief baddie) do bring pleasure. Rated PG. 103m. **DIR:** Andrew V. McLaglen. **CAST:** John Wayne, George Kennedy, Gary Grimes, Neville Brand. **1973**

CAINE MUTINY, THE ★★★★ Superb performances by Humphrey Bogart, Van Johnson, José Ferrer, and Fred MacMurray, among others, make this adaptation of Herman Wouk's classic novel an absolute must-see. This brilliant film concerns the hard-nosed Captain Queeg (Bogart), who may or may not be slightly unhinged, and the subsequent mutiny by his first officer and crew, who are certain he is. Beautifully done, a terrific movie. 125m. **DIR:** Edward Dmytryk. **CAST:** Humphrey Bogart, José Ferrer, Van Johnson, Robert Francis, Fred MacMurray. **1954 DVD**

CAINE MUTINY COURT MARTIAL, THE ★★★★ Splendid adaptation of Herman Wouk's brilliant Pulitzer Prize–winning novel. Brad Davis comes aboard in the Humphrey Bogart role as Queeg, whose unorthodox actions aboard the U.S.S. *Caine* forced his crew to mutiny. Director Robert Altman keeps everything shipshape, and evokes outstanding performances from the enlisted men. Rated PG. 100m. **DIR:** Robert Altman. **CAST:** Brad Davis, Eric Bogosian, Jeff Daniels, Peter Gallagher, Michael Murphy. **1988**

CAIRO ★★★1/2 One of Jeanette MacDonald's last films, and she gets to warble with a woman singer instead of her leading man. Ethel Waters costars in this spoof of wartime spy melodramas. Robert Young provides the obligatory romantic interest, but the chief highlight is the music. B&W; 101m. **DIR:** W. S. Van Dyke. **CAST:** Jeanette MacDonald, Ethel Waters, Robert Young, Dooley Wilson, Reginald Owen. **1942**

CAL ★★★★ Superb Irish film, which focuses on "the troubles" in Northern Ireland, stars John Lynch as Cal, a teenage boy who wants to sever his ties with the IRA. This turns out to be anything but easy, as the leader tells him, if he isn't for them, he's against them. Cal hides out at the home of Marcella (Helen Mirren, in a knockout of a performance). She's the widow of a policeman he helped murder. Nevertheless, they fall in love. Rated R for sex, nudity, profanity, and violence. 102m. **DIR:** Pat O'Connor. **CAST:** Helen Mirren, John Lynch, Donal McCann. **1984**

CALAMITY JANE (1953) ★★★ A legend of the Old West set to music for Doris Day, who mends her rootin', tootin' ways in order to lasso Howard Keel. The song "Secret Love" copped an Oscar. Cute 'n' perky. 101m. **DIR:** David Butler. **CAST:** Doris Day, Howard Keel, Allyn Ann McLerie, Philip Carey. **1953 DVD**

CALAMITY JANE (1984) ★★★★ Director James Goldstone provides more than just the story of Calamity Jane, which is fascinating in itself as a tale of one of America's early feminists. His unglamorous production and straightforward storytelling give a true feeling of the Old West. Jane Alexander, in an Emmy-nominated performance, shows the many sides of this spirited lady. A made-for-TV movie. 100m. **DIR:** James Goldstone. **CAST:** Jane Alexander, Frederic Forrest, David Hemmings, Ken Kercheval, Talia Balsam. **1984**

CALENDAR GIRL ★★ Three teenage Nevada boys head for Hollywood to meet Marilyn Monroe. Clearly intended as both a tribute to Monroe and a warm memoir of adolescence, the film fails on both counts as it swings between dumb slapstick and even dumber sentimentality. Anyone old enough to remember Monroe is too old to fall for this. Rated PG-13 for mild profanity. 90m. **DIR:** John Whitesell. **CAST:** Jason Priestley, Gabriel Olds, Jerry O'Connell. **1993**

CALIFORNIA CASANOVA ★★★ Tyrone Power Jr. is delightful as a bumbling nerd who is transformed by a charming count. Best scenes: when Power receives advice from a number of sources on how to be irresistible. Rated R for nudity and profanity. 94m. **DIR:** Nathaniel Christian. **CAST:** Jerry Orbach, Audrey Landers, Tyrone Power. **1991**

CALIFORNIA DREAMING ★★ Wimpy film about a dork from Chicago trying to fit into the California lifestyle. The cast is good, but the story is maudlin and slow-moving. Rated R for partial nudity. 93m. **DIR:** John Hancock. **CAST:** Glynnis O'Connor, Seymour Cassel, Dennis Christopher, Tanya Roberts. **1979**

CALIFORNIA GOLD RUSH ★★ The writer Bret Harte (Robert Hays) is in the right place at the right time to chronicle the gold rush days of California from Sutter's Fort. Rated PG. 100m. **DIR:** Jack B. Hively. **CAST:** Robert Hays, John Dehner, Ken Curtis, Henry Jones, Dan Haggerty. **1985**

CALIFORNIA SUITE ★★★1/2 This enjoyable adaptation of the Neil Simon play features multiple stars. The action revolves around the various inhabitants of a Beverly Hills hotel room. We are allowed to enter and observe the private lives of the various guests in the room during the four watchable short stories within this film. Rated PG. 103m. **DIR:** Herbert Ross. **CAST:** Jane Fonda, Alan Alda, Maggie Smith, Richard Pryor, Bill Cosby. **1978 DVD**

CALIGULA 🦃 A $15 million porno flick with big stars. Rated X for every excess imaginable. 156m. **DIR:** Tinto Brass. **CAST:** Malcolm McDowell, Peter O'Toole, Teresa Ann Savoy, Helen Mirren. **1980 DVD**

CALL HER SAVAGE ★★ Clara Bow no longer had "it" by the time she attempted to make a comeback in this ludicrous melodrama. She plays a half-white, half-native girl who tries to fit into proper society. B&W; 80m. **DIR:** John Francis Dillon. **CAST:** Clara Bow, Monroe Owsley, Gilbert Roland, Thelma Todd. **1932**

CALL ME ★★ In this silly suspense-thriller, a New York newspaper columnist (Patricia Charbonneau) mistakenly believes an obscene phone caller to be her boyfriend and soon finds herself involved with murder and mobsters. Rated R for violence, profanity, nudity, and simulated sex. 96m. **DIR:** Sollace Mitchell. **CAST:** Patricia Charbonneau, Patti D'Arbanville, Sam Freed, Boyd Gaines, Stephen McHattie, Steve Buscemi. **1988**

CALL ME BWANA ★★1/2 A bogus writer of safari books sent to Africa to locate a downed space capsule encounters Russian agents. Too few one-liners by the past master. 103m. **DIR:** Gordon Douglas. **CAST:** Bob Hope, Anita Ekberg, Edie Adams, Lionel Jeffries. **1963**

•**CALL ME CLAUS** ★★★ Cute Christmas film borrows from several seasonal standards but still manages to stand on its own. Whoopi Goldberg stars as the cynical shopping-network executive chosen to replace Santa Claus. Nigel Hawthorne, excellent as the current Santa, must convince her to accept her destiny. Simple story amuses and touches the heart, while music by Garth Brooks energizes at all the right moments. Not rated; aimed to entertain the whole family. 91m. **DIR:** Peter Werner. **CAST:** Whoopi Goldberg, Nigel Hawthorne, Taylor Negron. **2001 DVD**

CALL NORTHSIDE 777 ★★★★ A Chicago reporter digs into the 11-year-old murder of a policeman and the life sentence of a possibly innocent man. Based on fact. Outstanding on-location filming. Also released as *Calling Northside 777*. B&W; 111m. **DIR:** Henry Hathaway. **CAST:** James Stewart, Richard Conte, Lee J. Cobb, Helen Walker, Betty Garde, Howard Smith, John McIntire, Paul Harvey. **1948**

CALL OF THE PRAIRIE ★★1/2 The Bar-20's Johnny Nelson has gotten too chummy with the wrong crowd. Hoppy, away selling cattle, returns to clean out the vermin. B&W. 63m. **DIR:** Howard Bretherton. **CAST:** William Boyd, James Ellison, George "Gabby" Hayes, Muriel Evans, Chester Conklin, Hank Mann, Al Bridges. **1936**

CALL OF THE WILD (1972) ★★★1/2 Charlton Heston stars in this adaptation of Jack London's famous novel. A domesticated dog is stolen and forced to pull a snow sled in Alaska as John (Charlton Heston) searches for gold. Some profanity and violence. Rated PG. 100m. **DIR:** Ken Annakin. **CAST:** Charlton Heston, Michele Mercier, Maria Rohm, Rik Battaglia. **1972 DVD**

CALL OF THE WILD (1992) ★★★ Fairly loyal to Jack London's best-selling novel, this drama focuses on the many changes a domesticated dog must undergo after being stolen for arctic sledding. Rick Schroder is the only human to show him genuine kindness after his ordeal begins. High production values and authentic location shots are a plus. Not rated; contains simulated animal abuse. 97m. **DIR:** Alan Smithee. **CAST:** Rick Schroder, Gordon Tootoosis, Duncan Fraser, Mia Sara. **1992**

CALL OF THE WILD: THE DOG OF THE YUKON ★★★★ Rousing *Hallmark Hall of Fame* adaptation of Jack London's wilderness adventure stars Rutger Hauer as the miner who inherits Buck, a wild dog who becomes his best friend. The bond is sealed when they save each other, but Buck is forced to decide whether to stay with Thornton or return to the wild. Outstanding production values and stirring narration by Richard Dreyfuss complement this handsome production. Rated PG. 91m. **DIR:** Peter Svatek. **CAST:** Rutger Hauer, Bronwen Booth, Charles Powell, John Novak. **1996**

CALL OUT THE MARINES ★★1/2 The prime attraction here is the team of Victor McLaglen and Edmund Lowe in their last comedy together. As always, they play a pair of battling marine buddies, this time engaged in a rivalry over saloon singer Binnie Barnes. Several songs (by Mort Greene and Harry Revel) are no great shakes. 66m. **DIR:** Frank Ryan. **CAST:** Victor McLaglen, Edmund Lowe, Binnie Barnes, Paul Kelly, Robert Smith, Franklin Pangborn. **1942**

CALL TO GLORY ★★★1/2 Engrossing pilot episode for a short-lived TV series. Set in the early 1960s, it follows an air force officer's family through the events of the Kennedy presidency. The taut script ably balances the story of their struggle to deal with military life and still retains the flavor of a historical chronicle of the times. This uniformly well-acted and -directed opening show promised much quality that was unfortunately unfulfilled in later episodes. 97m. **DIR:** Thomas Carter. **CAST:** Craig T. Nelson, Cindy Pickett, Keenan Wynn, Elisabeth Shue, David Hollander. **1984**

CALL TO REMEMBER, A ★★★★ Poignant drama about a Holocaust survivor who receives a call that one of her children—who she thought was killed in Nazi Germany—may be alive. The complexity of her family's past and present lives threatens to overwhelm them all.

Rated R for profanity. 111m. **DIR:** Jack Bender. **CAST:** Blythe Danner, Joe Mantegna, David Lascher. **1997**

•CALLE 54 ★★★★★ This exhilarating, intimate musical homage to the many contours and heroes of Latin jazz features a dozen impassioned, uninterrupted performances captured live in the Sony recording studio on Manhattan's 54th Street. Single-color backgrounds (dusk orange, sky blue, deep red) complement the varied musical moods and the sound has a purity and balance that borders on the sacred. There is no live audience on which to feed. The musicians just brilliantly stew in their own creative juices. Rated G. 100m. **DIR:** Fernando Trueba. **CAST:** Tito Puente, Gato Barbieri, Elaine Elias, Michel Camilo, Jerry Gonzales, Chano Dominguez, Chico O'Farill, Carlos "Patato" Valdes, Bebo Valdes, Cucho Valdez, Israel Lopez, Orlando Rios, Pacquito D'Rivera. **2000 DVD**

CALLER, THE 🦃 Sci-fi thriller about a man and a woman playing a cat-and-mouse game of mind trips. Rated R for violence and profanity. 97m. **DIR:** Arthur Allan Seidelman. **CAST:** Malcolm McDowell, Madolyn Smith. **1987**

CALLIE AND SON ★★1/2 Syrupy drama about a poor waitress who becomes the queen of a Texas publishing empire. On the way, she is reunited with her long-lost son. Sometimes halfway engrossing; sometimes really disturbing. Rated PG. 150m. **DIR:** Waris Hussein. **CAST:** Lindsay Wagner, Jameson Parker, Dabney Coleman, Andrew Prine, Michelle Pfeiffer, James Sloyan. **1981 DVD**

•CALLING, THE 🦃 A mother learns that her son has been handpicked by her husband to help a satanic cult kick start the apocalypse. Gee, most fathers don't even have the time to play catch. Only rent it if your video store has a liberal refund policy. Rated R for adult situations, language, and violence. 89m. **DIR:** Richard Caesar. **CAST:** Laura Harris, Nick Brimble, Alice Krige. **2000 DVD**

CALLING DR. DEATH ★★1/2 The first in a series of six B features inspired by the then-popular *Inner Sanctum* radio series, each featuring Lon Chaney Jr. as a man who may or may not be guilty of a crime. Here he's a neurologist suspected of murdering his cheating wife. B&W; 62m. **DIR:** Reginald LeBorg. **CAST:** Lon Chaney Jr., Patricia Morison, J. Carrol Naish, David Bruce. **1943**

CALLING WILD BILL ELLIOTT ★★1/2 In his first assignment in an A picture for Republic Studios, Wild Bill Elliott pals up with Gabby Hayes to fight off evil robbers harassing the lovely Anne Jeffreys. Gabby Hayes is supposed to be a funny sidekick, but here he is more of an anvil around the neck. Average. B&W; 78m. **DIR:** Spencer Gordon Bennet. **CAST:** William Elliott, Anne Jeffreys, George "Gabby" Hayes. **1943**

CALM AT SUNSET ★★★★ Powerful study of a father-son relationship stars Michael Moriarty as the father who makes every attempt to steer his son away from the fishing business. When the son disregards and signs up on another boat, he sets the stage for a confrontation that eventually brings the family together. Excellent performances and an intelligent script make this *Hallmark Hall of Fame* production a winner. Rated PG. 98m. **DIR:** Daniel Petrie. **CAST:** Michael Moriarty, Peter Facinelli, Kevin Conway, Melvin Van Peebles, Christopher Orr, Kate Nelligan. **1996**

CALTIKI, THE IMMORTAL MONSTER ★★1/2 Explorers find an ancient bloblike monster living under a Mayan temple. They kill it but bring a sample back to the city, where it starts to regenerate and grow. Although cut for United States release and atrociously dubbed, this Italian monster movie isn't half bad thanks to atmospheric photography by future horror director Mario Bava (who also directed some of the film). B&W; 76m. **DIR:** Robert Hampton (Riccardo Freda). **CAST:** John Merivale, Didi Sullivan, Gerard Herter. **1959**

CAME A HOT FRIDAY ★★ Mildly amusing film set in 1949 New Zealand, where two con men make their fortune cheating bookmakers all across the country. Rated PG for language and adult situations. 101m. **DIR:** Ian Mune. **CAST:** Peter Bland, Philip Gordon, Billy T. James, Michael Lawrence. **1985**

CAMELOT ★★★ The legend of King Arthur and the Round Table—from the first meeting of Arthur (Richard Harris) and Guinevere (Vanessa Redgrave) to the affair between Guinevere and Lancelot (Franco Nero), and finally the fall of Camelot—is brought to life in this enjoyable musical. Rated G. 178m. **DIR:** Joshua Logan. **CAST:** Richard Harris, Vanessa Redgrave, Franco Nero, David Hemmings, Lionel Jeffries. **1967 DVD**

CAMERAMAN, THE ★★★★ This silent casts Buster Keaton as a freelance news cameraman trying desperately to impress a girl and earn his spurs with a scoop. He finally gets in the thick of a Chinese tong war, filming his way to success in a hail of bullets. A superb example of Keaton comedy genius. Silent. B&W; 70m. **DIR:** Edward Sedgwick. **CAST:** Buster Keaton, Marceline Day, Edward Brophy. **1928**

CAMERON'S CLOSET ★★★ A young boy with psychic powers unwittingly unleashes a demon in his closet. The above-par special effects, by Oscar winner Carlo Rambaldi (*E.T.* and *Alien*), and an ever-growing tension makes this a neat little supernatural thriller. Not rated; contains violence. 90m. **DIR:** Armand Mastroianni. **CAST:** Cotter Smith, Mel Harris, Tab Hunter, Chuck McCann, Leigh McCloskey. **1989**

CAMILA (1984) ★★★1/2 A romantic and true story of forbidden love in the classic tradition. Susu Pecoraro is Camila O'Gorman, the daughter of a wealthy aristocrat in Buenos Aires in the mid-1800s. Imanol Arias plays Ladislao Gutierrez, a Jesuit priest. In Spanish with English subtitles. Not rated, but with sex, nudity, and violence. 105m. **DIR:** Maria Luisa Bemberg. **CAST:** Susu Pecoraro, Imanol Arias, Hector Alterio, Mona Maris. **1984**

CAMILLA (1994) ★★1/2 A female bonding/road picture. Jessica Tandy is an eccentric retired violinist who heads for Toronto with her tenant, composer Bridget Fonda. The characters are fun, but their situation is implausible and the script too cutesy. Rated PG-13 for profanity and brief nudity. 101m. **DIR:** Deepa Mehta. **CAST:** Jessica Tandy, Bridget Fonda, Elias Koteas, Maury Chaykin, Hume Cronyn. **1994 DVD**

CAMILLE ★★★★ Metro-Goldwyn-Mayer's lavish production of the Dumas classic provided screen goddess Greta Garbo with one of her last unqualified successes and remains the consummate adaptation of this popular weeper. The combined magic of the studio and Garbo's presence legitimized this archaic creaker about a dying woman and her love affair with a younger man (Robert Taylor, soon to be one of MGM's biggest stars). B&W; 108m. **DIR:** George Cukor. **CAST:** Greta Garbo, Robert Taylor, Lionel Barrymore, Henry Daniell, Laura Hope Crews, Elizabeth Allan, Lenore Ulric, Jessie Ralph. **1936**

CAMILLE CLAUDEL ★★★★ Poignant, romantic tragedy based on the life of sculptor Camille Claudel. Isabelle Adjani gives an emotion-charged performance as the 21-year-old artist who becomes romantically involved with the great French sculptor Auguste Rodin in Paris during the late 1800s. In French with English subtitles. Not rated; contains nudity and is recommended for adults. 149m. **DIR:** Bruno Nuytten. **CAST:** Isabelle Adjani, Gérard Depardieu, Laurent Grevill, Alain Cuny. **1990 DVD**

CAMORRA ★★ Lina Wertmuller lacks her usual bite in this well-intentioned but conventional crime story. The movie details the efforts of an ex-prostitute to band the women of Naples together against the mobsters. Rated R for violence and sexual situations. 115m. **DIR:** Lina Wertmuller. **CAST:** Angela Molina, Francisco Rabal, Harvey Keitel. **1986**

CAMOUFLAGE (1977) ★★★★ Biting satire of Polish intellectuals focuses on a middle-aged professor and his callow young colleague. While much of the sting will be lost on non-Polish-speaking audiences, the humor comes across well. In Polish with English subtitles. Not rated. B&W; 106m. **DIR:** Krzysztof Zanussi. **CAST:** Zbigniew Zapasiewicz, Piotr Garlicki. **1977**

CAMOUFLAGE (1999) ★★1/2 Familiar faces flesh out this occasionally amusing slapstick comedy starring Leslie Nielsen as a private investigator ready to call it quits. He's stopped dead in his tracks when he agrees to show actor Marty Mackenzie (Lochlyn Munro) the ropes. Their first case involves the plot to kill an Oregon gravel-pit owner. Director James Keach keeps things light enough never to be taken seriously. Rated R for adult situations, language, and violence. 98m. **DIR:** James Keach. **CAST:** Leslie Nielsen, Lochlyn Munro, Vanessa Angel, William Forsythe, Patrick Warburton. **1999 DVD**

CAMP NOWHERE ★★1/2 Affluent teens rent their own summer hideaway to get away from the nightmarish theme camps (such as Camp Broadway and Camp Micro Chippewa) offered by their parents in this mild, disposable romp. There are no adults, no counselors, and no rules. But the folks at home push for a Parents' Day that nearly drags the kids' secret out of the woods. Rated PG. 94m. **DIR:** Jonathan Price. **CAST:** Jonathan Jackson, Christopher Lloyd, M. Emmet Walsh, Wendy Makkena. **1994**

CAMPUS MAN ★★ In this well-intended and generally watchable movie, a college student (John Dye) produces an all-male pinup calendar and strikes it rich. Rated PG. 95m. **DIR:** Ron Casden. **CAST:** John Dye, Kim Delaney, Kathleen Wilhoite, Steve Lyon, Morgan Fairchild, Miles O'Keeffe. **1987**

CAN-CAN ★★★ Frank Sinatra plays an 1890s French attorney defending Shirley MacLaine's right to perform the risqué cancan in a Parisian nightclub. The stars appear, at times, to be walking through their roles. Cole Porter songs include "I Love Paris," "C'est Magnifique," and the wonderful "Just One of Those Things." 131m. **DIR:** Walter Lang. **CAST:** Shirley MacLaine, Frank Sinatra, Maurice Chevalier, Juliet Prowse, Louis Jourdan. **1960**

CAN IT BE LOVE 🦃 Run-of-the-mill teen sex comedy about two horny guys looking to do something about it. Dreadful. Rated R for nudity and language. 90m. **DIR:** Peter Maris. **CAST:** Charles Klausmeyer, Richard Beaumont. **1992**

CAN SHE BAKE A CHERRY PIE? ★★★ Karen Black plays a woman whose husband leaves her before she has fully awakened one morning. She meets Eli, played by Michael Emil, a balding character actor whose body is slowly sliding into his knees. This is a small film, and its appeal is quiet. It also is an example of what can be right with American movie-making, even when the money isn't there. No rating, but considerable vulgar language, sexual situations. 90m. **DIR:** Henry Jaglom. **CAST:** Karen Black, Michael Emil. **1984**

CAN YOU HEAR THE LAUGHTER? THE STORY OF FREDDIE PRINZE ★★1/2 Freddie Prinze was a Puerto Rican comedian who rose from the barrio to television stardom in a relatively brief time. His premier achievement was a starring role in *Chico and the Man,* with Jack Albertson. Sympathetic, but no punches are pulled on the facts surrounding his death. 106m. **DIR:** Burt Brinckerhoff. **CAST:** Ira Angustain, Kevin Hooks, Randee Heller, Julie Carmen. **1979**

CANADIAN BACON ★★ What begins as a funny and savvy political comedy quickly dissolves into the kind of sophomoric drivel writer-director Michael Moore would normally lampoon. Neither Moore's script nor his direction keeps up the pace as America tries to improve the national economy by waging war on Canada. Unfortunately, there is nothing special about John Candy's final performance. Rated PG for profanity. 95m. **DIR:** Michael Moore. **CAST:** John Candy, Rhea Perlman, Kevin Pollak, Bill Nunn, Rip Torn, Alan Alda, Dan Aykroyd. **1995 DVD**

CANCEL MY RESERVATION ★★ Tired reworking of a Bob Hope formula comedy is slow going despite a pretty good cast and a plot lifted from a Louis L'Amour novel. Hope plays a popular TV show host who heads to Arizona for a rest and gets mixed up with crooks. Highlight of the film is a nightmare sequence with cameos of celebrities including John Wayne and Bing Crosby. Rated G. 99m. **DIR:** Paul Bogart. **CAST:** Bob Hope, Eva Marie Saint, Ralph Bellamy, Forrest Tucker, Anne Archer, Keenan Wynn, Chief Dan George. **1972**

CANDIDATE, THE ★★★1/2 Michael Ritchie expertly directed this incisive look at a political hopeful (Robert Redford) and the obstacles and truths he must confront on the campaign trail. Rated PG. 109m. **DIR:** Michael Ritchie. **CAST:** Robert Redford, Peter Boyle, Don Porter, Allen Garfield. **1972 DVD**

CANDIDE ★★★ Voltaire's classic tale of the wanderer trying to see the best in everything is updated to the World War II era with mixed results. Clever, but more talky than funny despite a top-flight French cast. Dubbed in English. B&W; 93m. **DIR:** Norbert Carbonnaux. **CAST:** Jean-Pierre Cassel, Daliah Lavi, Pierre Brasseur, Michel Simon, Jean Richard, Louis de Funes. **1960**

CANDLES AT NINE ★★ Old-dark-house mystery about a young woman who inherits a fortune from a great-uncle she hardly knew, with the stipulation that she has to spend a month living in his gloomy mansion. Musical star Jessie Matthews was the draw for this British film that is competently made but unexceptional. B&W; 84m. **DIR:** John Harlow. **CAST:** Jessie Matthews, John Stuart, Beatrix Lehmann. **1944**

CANDLESHOE ★★1/2 Confused Disney comedy about a street kid (Jodie Foster) duped by shady Leo McKern into posing as an heir to Helen Hayes. Marred by typically excessive Disney physical "humor" (read: slapstick). Rated G. 101m. **DIR:** Norman Tokar. **CAST:** David Niven, Helen Hayes, Jodie Foster, Leo McKern, Vivian Pickles. **1977 DVD**

CANDY MOUNTAIN ★★★★ Mediocre musician (Kevin J. O'Connor) takes to the highway in search of legendary guitar craftsman Elmore Silk. Celebrated photographer and underground filmmaker Robert Frank joins screenwriter Rudy Wurlitzer to create an engaging, offbeat, visually beautiful film. Rated R for nudity and profanity. 90m. **DIR:** Robert Frank, Rudy Wurlitzer. **CAST:** Kevin J. O'Connor, Harris Yulin, Tom Waits, Bulle Ogier, David Johansen, Leon Redbone, Joe Strummer, Dr. John. **1987**

CANDYMAN, THE (1968) 🦃 English drug peddler in Mexico City plots to kidnap the child of an American movie star. 98m. **DIR:** Herbert J. Leder. **CAST:** George Sanders, Leslie Parrish. **1968**

CANDYMAN (1992) ★★★★ A very scary flick set in the slums of Chicago, it concerns a mythical hook-handed killer who can be called forth by looking in a mirror and chanting his name five times. Virginia Madsen researches the Candyman's story and finds out he is all too real. Rated R for violence, profanity and nudity. 101m. **DIR:** Bernard Rose. **CAST:** Virginia Madsen, Tony Todd, Xander Berkeley, Kasi Lemmons, Vanessa L. Williams, Michael Culkin. **1992 DVD**

CANDYMAN: FAREWELL TO THE FLESH ★★ Murdered slave turned artist returns from the dead to prey upon the denizens of modern New Orleans. This gruesome sequel flashes back to the slave's alleged "crime" against a plantation owner and his horrific dispatch by a frenzied mob. Rated R for violence, gore, and language. 94m. **DIR:** Bill Condon. **CAST:** Tony Todd, Kelly Rowan, Veronica Cartwright, Timothy Carhart. **1995**

CANDYMAN 3: DAY OF THE DEAD ★★ In this, the obligatory third installment of the series, the Candyman returns from the grave to wreak vengeance upon those who have uttered his name five times while gazing into a reflective surface. Donna D'Errico of *Baywatch* fame plays the femme fatale and descendant of the original Candyman. It is up to her to send the Candyman back to hell for him to wait until Candyman 4 comes along. This film has an occasionally entertaining murder scene but mostly it's just a waste of time. Rated R for grisly murders and tidbits of other questionable material. 93m. **DIR:** Turi Meyer. **CAST:** Tony Todd, Donna D'Errico, Nick Corri, Alexia Robinson, Lupe Ontiveros. **1999 DVD**

CANNERY ROW ★★★ It's hard to dislike this film, starring Nick Nolte and Debra Winger. Despite its artificiality, halting pace, and general unevenness, there are so many marvelous moments—most provided by Frank McRae as the lovable simpleton Hazel—that you don't regret having seen it. Rated PG for slight nudity, profanity, and violence. 120m. **DIR:** David S. Ward. **CAST:** Nick Nolte, Debra Winger, Audra Lindley, M. Emmet Walsh, Frank McRae. **1982**

CANNIBAL HOLOCAUST ★★ An expedition follows a previous safari of filmmakers into the Amazon. They find some film cans near a village and view the horrific contents in New York. The farthest reaches of exploitation are explored in this most extreme—and disturbing—entry in the late-Seventies cannibal movie subgenre, directed by the field's pioneer auteur. Not rated, but with graphic violence. 95m. **DIR:** Ruggero Deodato. **CAST:** Francesca Ciardi, Luca Barbareschi, Robert Kerman. **1979**

CANNIBAL WOMEN IN THE AVOCADO JUNGLE OF DEATH ★★1/2 *Playboy* playmate Shannon Tweed stars in this comedic adventure about a feminist anthropologist in search of the infamous cannibal women, a group of ultraleft feminists who eat their mates. Some great sight gags, with most of the funny bits belonging to semimacho guide Bill Maher. Rated PG-13 for nudity. 90m. **DIR:** J. D. Athens. **CAST:** Shannon Tweed, Adrienne Barbeau, Bill Maher, Barry Primus. **1988 DVD**

CANNONBALL ★★ David Carradine plays an unpleasant antihero out to beat the rest of the cast in an exotic race. Rated R for violence. 93m. **DIR:** Paul Bartel. **CAST:** David Carradine, Veronica Hamel, Gerrit Graham, Sylvester Stallone, Robert Carradine, Carl Gottlieb, Belinda Balaski. **1976**

CANNONBALL RUN 🦃 This star-studded bore is the story of an unsanctioned, totally illegal cross-country car race in which there are no rules and few survivors. Rated PG for profanity. 95m. **DIR:** Hal Needham. **CAST:** Burt Reynolds, Roger Moore, Farrah Fawcett, Dom DeLuise, Dean Martin, Sammy Davis Jr. **1981 DVD**

CANNONBALL RUN II 🦃 Awful rehash of *Cannonball Run*. Rated PG. 108m. **DIR:** Hal Needham. **CAST:** Burt Reynolds, Dom DeLuise, Shirley MacLaine, Marilu Henner, Telly Savalas, Dean Martin, Sammy Davis Jr., Frank Sinatra. **1984 DVD**

CAN'T BUY ME LOVE ★★ The title song is the Beatles' classic tune. Unfortunately, this film is all downhill from there. Patrick Dempsey plays a nerd who learns that popularity isn't all it's cracked up to be. The message is delivered in heavy-handed style. Still, teens will love it. Rated PG-13 for profanity. 94m. **DIR:** Steve Rash. **CAST:** Amanda Peterson, Patrick Dempsey, Courtney Gains, Tina Caspary, Seth Green, Sharon Farrell, Dennis Dugan, Ami Dolenz, Steve Franken. **1987**

CAN'T HARDLY WAIT ★★★ Well-crafted teen party movie that has amusingly torn away the facades of typical characters and replaced them with more natural personas over the course of one really bitchin' graduation party. The film has an appropriate woozy look, fine pacing, and a good sense of humor. Rated PG-13 for substance abuse, sex, and language. 96m. **DIR:** Deborah Kaplan, Harry Elfont. **CAST:** Jennifer Love Hewitt, Ethan Embry, Seth Green, Lauren Ambrose, Peter Facinelli, Charlie Korsmo, Jenna Elfman. **1998**

CAN'T HELP SINGING ★★★★1/2 A spirited Western with music by Jerome Kern, this is the only Technicolor film Deanna Durbin made. Songs include the title number, "Californi-yay," "More and More," and "Swing Your Sweetheart." All told, a delight. 89m. **DIR:** Frank Ryan. **CAST:** Deanna Durbin, Robert Paige, Akim Tamiroff,

David Bruce, June Vincent, Clara Blandick, Ray Collins, Leonid Kinskey. **1944**

CAN'T STOP THE MUSIC Despite the title, the music of the Village People was stopped cold by this basically awful musical about show biz. Rated PG. 118m. **DIR:** Nancy Walker. **CAST:** The Village People, Valerie Perrine, Bruce Jenner, Steve Guttenberg, Paul Sand, Tammy Grimes, June Havoc, Jack Weston, Barbara Rush, Leigh Taylor-Young. **1980 DVD**

CANTERBURY TALES, THE ★★★1/2 Four of Chaucer's stories are adapted by Pier Paolo Pasolini in his inimitable style—gleefully offensive satire, with the Church the first of many targets. Not for the genteel. Rated X for nudity and simulated sex. 109m. **DIR:** Pier Paolo Pasolini. **CAST:** Hugh Griffith, Laura Betti, Tom Baker, Josephine Chaplin, Pier Paolo Pasolini. **1971 DVD**

CANTERVILLE GHOST, THE ★★★ It's a battle of two of filmdom's most notorious scene stealers: Charles Laughton as a 300-year-old ghost and oh-so-cute pigtailed little Margaret O'Brien. The fantasy tale of American soldiers in a haunted English castle during World War II takes second place to these two scenery munchers. B&W; 92m. **DIR:** Jules Dassin. **CAST:** Charles Laughton, Robert Young, Margaret O'Brien, William Gargan, Reginald Owen. **1944**

CANTERVILLE GHOST, THE ★★★ Modern retelling of the classic Oscar Wilde short story, with John Gielgud as the blowhard ghost who tries to terrorize a spunky American family. Gielgud is excellent as the ghost, but Ted Wass is highly unsatisfactory as the father, and the ghostly shenanigans have a dangerous quality about them that was not present in the original. Not rated; suitable for older children. 96m. **DIR:** Paul Bogart. **CAST:** John Gielgud, Ted Wass, Andrea Marcovicci, Alyssa Milano, Harold Innocent, Lila Kaye. **1986**

CANVAS ★★1/2 Artist turns to a life of crime to make good on a deal his brother had with the mob. Pedestrian but watchable. Rated R for language and violence. 94m. **DIR:** Alain Zaloum. **CAST:** Gary Busey, John Rhys-Davies, Cary Lawrence. **1992**

CAPE FEAR (1962) ★★★★ Great cast in a riveting tale of a lawyer (Gregory Peck) and his family menaced by a vengeful ex-con (Robert Mitchum), who Peck helped to send up the river eight years earlier. Now he's out, with big plans for Peck's wife and especially his daughter. B&W; 106m. **DIR:** J. Lee Thompson. **CAST:** Gregory Peck, Polly Bergen, Robert Mitchum, Lori Martin, Martin Balsam, Telly Savalas, Jack Kruschen. **1962 DVD**

CAPE FEAR (1991) ★★ A profound disappointment from Martin Scorsese, this remake of J. Lee Thompson's suspense classic seems to have everything going for it: a great cast, a story by John D. MacDonald, and even cameos by stars of the original. But somehow it all boils down to Robert De Niro doing an impression of Freddy Krueger from *A Nightmare on Elm Street*. Rated R for violence and profanity. 130m. **DIR:** Martin Scorsese. **CAST:** Robert De Niro, Nick Nolte, Jessica Lange, Joe Don Baker, Robert Mitchum, Gregory Peck, Juliette Lewis, Martin Balsam, Fred Dalton Thompson, Illeana Douglas. **1991 DVD**

CAPER OF THE GOLDEN BULLS, THE Stephen Boyd plays a wealthy American who is blackmailed into robbing the Royal Bank of Spain. Not rated, has some violence. 106m. **DIR:** Russell Rouse. **CAST:** Stephen Boyd, Yvette Mimieux, Giovanna Ralli, Vito Scotti, J. G. Devlin, Arnold Moss, Walter Slezak. **1966**

CAPITAL PUNISHMENT David Carradine pops up briefly in this inane action-thriller starring Gary Daniels as a DEA agent trying to end the reign of a drug lord. Characters and situations are as thin as paper. Rated R for language and violence. 88m. **DIR:** David Huey. **CAST:** Gary Daniels, David Carradine, Tadashi Yamashita, Mel Novak. **1991**

CAPITOL CONSPIRACY, THE ★★1/2 Don "The Dragon" Wilson stars as a government agent who, as a child, was part of a program to instill clairvoyant abilities. Now someone is trying to kill everyone associated with that program. Silly plot made bearable by Wilson's martial artistry and a rare appearance by horror icon Barbara Steele. Also known as *The Prophet*. Rated R for violence and nudity. 83m. **DIR:** Fred Olen Ray. **CAST:** Don "The Dragon" Wilson, Barbara Steele, Wendy Schumacher, Paul Michael Robinson. **1999 DVD**

CAPONE ★★ Made-for-TV gangster effort brings nothing new to the formula. Behind bars for tax evasion, notorious mobster Al Capone still manages to run Chicago. It's up to FBI agent Keith Carradine to put an end to Capone's reign of terror. Additional footage added for video. Rated R for violence and nudity. 97m. **DIR:** Michael Pressman. **CAST:** Keith Carradine, Ray Sharkey, Debrah Farentino, Charles Haid. **1989 DVD**

CAPRICORN ONE ★★★★ In this suspenseful release, the government stages a mock flight to Mars in a television studio, with astronauts James Brolin, Sam Waterston, and O. J. Simpson pretending to be in outer space and landing on the planet. Then the news is released by the Pentagon that the ship crashed upon reentry and all aboard were killed, which puts the lives of the astronauts in danger. Rated PG. 124m. **DIR:** Peter Hyams. **CAST:** Elliott Gould, James Brolin, Hal Holbrook, Sam Waterston, Karen Black, O. J. Simpson, Telly Savalas. **1978 DVD**

CAPTAIN AMERICA (1944) ★★★ Joe Simon and Jack Kirby's comic-book character is brought to movie life to tangle with the fiendishly refined Lionel Atwill, who has not only a destructive ray machine but a machine capable of bringing dead animals back to life! Two-fisted District Attorney Dick Purcell manfully pursues Atwill. B&W; 15 chapters. **DIR:** John English, Elmer Clifton. **CAST:** Dick Purcell, Lorna Gray, Lionel Atwill, Charles Trowbridge, Russell Hicks, John Davidson, Frank Reicher, Hugh Sothern. **1944**

CAPTAIN AMERICA (1979) ★★ A criminal genius plots to extort millions from the government with a stolen nuclear device. Of course the only man who can stop him is the star-spangled avenger. This is average TV fare with a disappointingly simple plot. Not rated, but suitable for all viewers. 90m. **DIR:** Rod Holcomb. **CAST:** Reb Brown, Len Birman, Heather Menzies, Steve Forrest. **1979**

CAPTAIN AMERICA (1990) The golden-age comic-book character tries to make the leap to the big screen with disastrous results. In 1941, America's supersoldier is defeated by the Red Skull, and accidentally thrown into suspended animation. Fifty years later, he awakens in time to foil a scheme by his old enemy. Rated PG-13 for violence and profanity. 104m. **DIR:** Albert Pyun.

CAST: Matt Salinger, Ronny Cox, Ned Beatty, Darren McGavin, Melinda Dillon, Scott Paulin. **1990**

CAPTAIN AMERICA II: DEATH TOO SOON 🦃 Ridiculous made-for-television adventure of the comic-book hero. Plodding. 100m. **DIR:** Ivan Nagy. **CAST:** Reb Brown, Christopher Lee, Connie Sellecca, Len Birman. **1979**

CAPTAIN APACHE ★★ Muddled Western has Lee Van Cleef in title role gunning down dozens of one-dimensional characters who cross his path or appear likely to. Rated PG for violence. 94m. **DIR:** Alexander Singer. **CAST:** Lee Van Cleef, Stuart Whitman, Carroll Baker, Percy Herbert. **1971**

CAPTAIN BLOOD ★★★★1/2 Errol Flynn's youthful enthusiasm, great character actors, realistic miniature work, and Erich Wolfgang Korngold's score all meld together under Michael Curtiz's direction and provide audiences with perhaps the best pirate film of all time. B&W; 95m. **DIR:** Michael Curtiz. **CAST:** Errol Flynn, Olivia de Havilland, Basil Rathbone, Lionel Atwill, Ross Alexander, Guy Kibbee, Henry Stephenson. **1935**

CAPTAIN CAUTION ★★1/2 In command of a ship during the War of 1812 with England, Victor Mature, in the title role, is taken for a coward when he urges prudence. Richard Wallace's fast-paced, cannon-bellowing direction quells all restlessness, however. B&W; 85m. **DIR:** Richard Wallace. **CAST:** Victor Mature, Louise Platt, Bruce Cabot, Leo Carrillo, Vivienne Osborne, El Brendel, Robert Barrat, Miles Mander, Roscoe Ates. **1940**

•CAPTAIN CORELLI'S MANDOLIN ★★1/2 For ninety minutes, this gorgeous-looking love story meanders on a Greek island during World War II as the daughter of the island's doctor falls out of love with a fisherman and into the arms of an Italian soldier. The story focus then shifts from romantic triangle to the brutality of war. It's *Mediterraneo* (Italian soldiers living la dolce vita in 1941 on a Greek isle) crossed with *The English Patient* (love and combat wounds festering circa World War II) without the bittersweet magnetism and emotional tension. Rated R for language, nudity, sexuality, and violence. 127m. **DIR:** John Madden. **CAST:** Nicolas Cage, Penelope Cruz, John Hurt, Christian Bale, David Morrissey, Irene Papas. **2001 DVD**

CAPTAIN HORATIO HORNBLOWER ★★★★ An enjoyable adventure film that is faithful to the C. S. Forester novels and to the reputation of the rugged British seacoast where it was filmed. Gregory Peck's wooden acting style serves the character well, and he warms up when Virginia Mayo's Lady Wellesley becomes an unwanted passenger aboard his ship. 117m. **DIR:** Raoul Walsh. **CAST:** Gregory Peck, Virginia Mayo, Dennis O'Dea, James Robertson Justice, Robert Beatty. **1951**

CAPTAIN JANUARY ★★★ Orphan Shirley Temple is taken in by a lonely lighthouse keeper (Guy Kibbee). The incredible dance number featuring Shirley and a local fisherman (Buddy Ebsen) is worth the price of the rental. B&W; 75m. **DIR:** David Butler. **CAST:** Shirley Temple, Guy Kibbee, Buddy Ebsen, Jane Darwell. **1936**

CAPTAIN KIDD ★★ Not even Charles Laughton's mugging and posturing can redeem this swashbuckling yarn about the pirate whose treasure is still being sought. 89m. **DIR:** Rowland V. Lee. **CAST:** Charles Laughton, Randolph Scott, Reginald Owen, John Carradine, Sheldon Leonard, Barbara Britton, Gilbert Roland. **1945 DVD**

CAPTAIN KRONOS: VAMPIRE HUNTER ★★★1/2 British film directed by the producer of *The Avengers* television show. It's an unconventional horror tale about a sword-wielding vampire killer. An interesting mix of genres. Good adventure, with high production values. Rated PG for violence. 91m. **DIR:** Brian Clemens. **CAST:** Horst Janson, John David Carson, Caroline Munro, Shane Briant. **1974**

CAPTAIN NEWMAN, M.D. ★★★ The movie fluctuates between meaningful laughter and heavy drama. An excellent ensemble neatly maintains the balance. Gregory Peck is at his noble best as a sympathetic army psychiatrist. The film's most gripping performance comes from Bobby Darin, who plays a psychotic. 126m. **DIR:** David Miller. **CAST:** Gregory Peck, Angie Dickinson, Tony Curtis, Eddie Albert, Jane Withers, Bobby Darin, Larry Storch. **1963**

CAPTAIN NUKE AND THE BOMBER BOYS ★★★ Junior-high fantasy about three youths who ditch school in order to avoid punishment. They hide out in a burnt-out pizza parlor, where they discover what looks like a nuclear bomb. When they send a picture of the device to the FBI for confirmation, they are pegged as terrorists, and the chase begins. Rated PG-13 for language. 90m. **DIR:** Charles Gale. **CAST:** Joe Mantegna, Joanna Pacula, Joe Piscopo, Martin Sheen, Rod Steiger, Ryan Thomas Johnson. **1995**

CAPTAIN RON ★★★ A lighthearted comedy about a Chicago businessman (Martin Short) who inherits his uncle's yacht and drags his family to the Caribbean. In search of someone to pilot the boat—actually a broken-down hulk—the group finds Captain Ron (Kurt Russell), a less-than-skilled skipper. Some hilarious bits. Rated PG-13 for profanity. 100m. **DIR:** Thom Eberhardt. **CAST:** Kurt Russell, Martin Short, Mary Kay Place, Paul Anka. **1992**

CAPTAIN SCARLETT ★★1/2 A dashing hero thought to be dead returns to France after the Napoleonic Wars to discover his estate has been confiscated by a nasty nobleman. Saving ladies in distress and righting wrongs becomes his life. Simple, predictable, and good clean fun. 75m. **DIR:** Thomas Carr. **CAST:** Richard Greené, Leonora Amar, Nedrick Young. **1953 DVD**

CAPTAIN SINBAD ★★1/2 This whimsical fantasy pits Sinbad against the evil El Kerim. There's plenty of color and magic to enthrall younger audiences. 85m. **DIR:** Byron Haskin. **CAST:** Guy Williams, Heidi Bruhl, Pedro Armendariz, Abraham Sofaer, Henry Brandon, Geoffrey Toone. **1963**

CAPTAINS COURAGEOUS (1937) ★★★★★ This is an exquisite adaptation of Rudyard Kipling's story about a spoiled rich kid who falls from an ocean liner and is rescued by fishermen. Through them, the lad learns about the rewards of hard work and genuine friendship. Spencer Tracy won a well-deserved best-actor Oscar for his performance as the fatherly fisherman. B&W; 116m. **DIR:** Victor Fleming. **CAST:** Spencer Tracy, Freddie Bartholomew, Lionel Barrymore, Melvyn Douglas, Mickey Rooney. **1937**

CAPTAINS COURAGEOUS (1995) ★★★ Made-for-cable movie is a watchable if inaccurate version of Rudyard Kipling's classic. Setting has been changed from the late 1800s to 1934 and it is the captain's son who seems to have the greatest impact on the demanding young heir who spends three months at sea on a no-frills fishing boat learning about hard work and friendship. 95m. **DIR:** Michael Anderson. **CAST:** Robert Urich, Kenny Vadas, Kaj-Erik Eriksen, Eric Sneider, Duncan Fraser, Robert Wisden. **1995**

CAPTAINS OF THE CLOUDS ★★★ Set in Canada in 1940, this enjoyable film stars a typically robust James Cagney as a bush pilot who joins the Royal Canadian Air Force. Lots of romance and humor add to the fun. Good color photography, too, but not much action. 113m. **DIR:** Michael Curtiz. **CAST:** James Cagney, Dennis Morgan, Alan Hale Sr., Brenda Marshall, George Tobias. **1942**

CAPTAIN'S PARADISE, THE ★★★★ From the opening shot, in which he is "shot," Alec Guinness displays the seemingly artless comedy form that marked him for stardom. He plays the bigamist skipper of a ferry, a wife in each port, flirting with delicious danger. Timing is all, and close shaves—including a chance meeting of the wives—yields edge-of-seat entertainment. Lotsa fun. B&W; 77m. **DIR:** Anthony Kimmins. **CAST:** Alec Guinness, Celia Johnson, Yvonne De Carlo, Bill Fraser. **1953**

CAPTAIN'S TABLE ★★1/2 This is a delightful comedy about a skipper of a cargo vessel who is given trial command of a luxury liner. Has some wildly funny moments. Not rated. B&W; 90m. **DIR:** Jack Lee. **CAST:** John Gregson, Peggy Cummins, Donald Sinden, Nadia Gray. **1960**

CAPTIVE ★★1/2 A rich man's daughter is kidnapped by a trio of young European anarchists whose only purpose is to convert her to their way of thinking. Arty but obscure. Not rated; contains nudity, suggested sex, and violence. 95m. **DIR:** Paul Mayersberg. **CAST:** Irina Brook, Oliver Reed. **1986 DVD**

CAPTIVE HEART ★★★★1/2 Exciting, well-written, marvelously performed story that examines the plight of British POWs and their Nazi captors. A superior job by all involved. B&W; 108m. **DIR:** Basil Dearden. **CAST:** Michael Redgrave, Rachel Kempson, Basil Radford, Jack Warner. **1948**

CAPTIVE HEARTS ★★1/2 Quiet little drama about two bomber crewmen (Chris Makepeace and Michael Sarrazin) shot down over a small Japanese town in the waning days of World War II. Makepeace is in over his head with this role, but Pat Morita, as the village elder, and Sarrazin carry the picture. Rated PG for language and violence. 102m. **DIR:** Paul Almond. **CAST:** Noriyuki "Pat" Morita, Chris Makepeace, Michael Sarrazin. **1988**

CAPTIVE IN THE LAND, A ★★★ The first U.S.-Soviet production in thirteen years, this drama gives new meaning to the term Cold War. Sam Waterston is an American meteorologist leaving the Arctic when he parachutes down to a marooned Alexander Potapov. An intense psychological drama ensues when a storm leaves both men trapped in the icy desolation of an endless winter. Though the acting is emotionally charged and their dueling philosophies are intriguing, the film feels claustrophobic. Rated PG for profanity. 98m. **DIR:** John Berry. **CAST:** Sam Waterston, Alexander Potapov. **1991**

CAPTIVE RAGE A plane carrying American citizens is hijacked. Rated R for violence, profanity, and nudity. 99m. **DIR:** Cedric Sundstrom. **CAST:** Oliver Reed, Robert Vaughn. **1988**

CAPTIVE WILD WOMAN ★★ John Carradine uses "glandular treatments" to transform an ape into the curvy Acquanetta (!!), who sleepwalks instead of acts. So bad it translates into good grade-B fun. Spawned sequels *Jungle Woman* and *Jungle Captive*. Not rated. B&W; 61m. **DIR:** Edward Dmytryk. **CAST:** John Carradine, Acquanetta, Evelyn Ankers, Milburn Stone, Martha Vickers. **1943**

CAPTIVES ★★★ Julia Ormond plays a dentist who rebounds from a painful divorce by falling in love with a patient (Tim Roth)—one of the inmates she treats at a high-security prison. Low-key drama made for the BBC resembles a cross between *Brief Encounter* and *The Crying Game,* though not quite as good. Still, worthwhile for fans of the two stars. Rated R for violence and adult situations. 100m. **DIR:** Angela Pope. **CAST:** Tim Roth, Julia Ormond, Richard Hawley, Peter Capaldi. **1994 DVD**

CAPTURE OF GRIZZLY ADAMS, THE ★★1/2 Like an 1850s version of *The Fugitive*'s Richard Kimble, Grizzly Adams hides in the woods with his animal friends to avoid punishment for a murder he didn't commit. In this TV movie, a sequel to the popular series, he risks capture to visit his orphanage-bound daughter. Not rated; contains no objectionable material. 96m. **DIR:** Don Keeslar. **CAST:** Dan Haggerty, Kim Darby, Noah Beery Jr., Keenan Wynn, June Lockhart, Chuck Connors, G. W. Bailey. **1982**

CAPTURED ALIVE Really amateurish film has a plane crashing and a bunch of hillbillies subsequently kidnapping the survivors to help them transport toxic waste. Rated R for violence, profanity, and nudity. 90m. **DIR:** Chris McIntyre. **CAST:** Dan Pinto. **1995**

CAR, THE ★★ A black luxury sedan terrorizes a small New Mexico town in this none-too-scary film. The car is supposedly possessed by the devil, but you'll be possessed by the urge to go to sleep. Rated PG for mild violence. 95m. **DIR:** Elliot Silverstein. **CAST:** James Brolin, Kathleen Lloyd, John Marley, John Rubinstein. **1977 DVD**

CAR 54, WHERE ARE YOU? (1991) David Johansen, as Officer Toody, is hilarious, but this goofy comedy can't hold it together. Lingering too long on numerous sight gags costs them their punch and several musical scenes seem very out of place. The fragile plot about catching a gangster is overshadowed by numerous unimportant subplots. Original TV-series cast members make cameo appearances. Rated PG-13 for comic-book violence. 85m. **DIR:** Bill Fishman. **CAST:** David Johansen, John C. McGinley, Fran Drescher, Nipsey Russell, Al Lewis, Rosie O'Donnell, Daniel Baldwin. **1991**

CAR 54 WHERE ARE YOU? (TV SERIES) ★★★1/2 Early-'60s television series about the comic misadventures of Bronx policemen Gunther Toody and Francis Muldoon. The laugh track is annoyingly loud but the shows are quite funny, with outrageous situations and memorable characters. Each cassette contains two episodes; there were sixty in all. B&W; 50m. **DIR:** Nat Hiken, Stanley Prager. **CAST:** Joe E. Ross, Fred Gwynne, Paul Reed, Al Lewis, Charlotte Rae. **1961–1963**

CAR WASH ★★★1/2 This is an ensemble film that features memorable bits from Richard Pryor, George Carlin, Franklin Ajaye, Ivan Dixon, and the Pointer Sisters. There are plenty of laughs, music, and even a moral in this fine low-budget production. Rated PG. 97m. **DIR:** Michael Schultz. **CAST:** Richard Pryor, Franklin Ajaye, Sully Boyar, Ivan Dixon. **1976 DVD**

CARACARA ★★ A woman becomes embroiled in a convoluted assassination plot against Nelson Mandela. The cast tries but just can't rise above subpar material. Rated R for violence, profanity, and nudity. 93m. **DIR:** Graeme Clifford. **CAST:** Natasha Henstridge, Lauren Hutton, Johnathon Schaech. **1999 DVD**

CARAVAGGIO ★★★★ Derek Jarman's extraordinary and revealing film is based on the life and art of Caravaggio, perhaps the greatest of Italian post-Renaissance painters. This controversial biography explores the artist's life, which was troubled by extremes of passion and artistic radicalism. Not rated; contains nudity, profanity, and violence. 97m. **DIR:** Derek Jarman. **CAST:** Nigel Terry, Sean Bean, Tilda Swinton, Spencer Leigh, Michael Gough. **1986**

CARAVAN TO VACCARES 🦃 If this cliché-ridden film had followed the plot of Alistair MacLean's novel, it might have been exciting. Read the book instead. Rated PG. 98m. **DIR:** Geoffrey Reeve. **CAST:** David Birney, Charlotte Rampling, Michel Lonsdale, Marcel Bozzuffi. **1974**

CARAVAN TRAIL ★★★★ The leader (Eddie Dean) of a wagon train of settlers takes the job of marshal to restore homesteaders' land being stolen by outlaws. He enlists the aid of some not-so-bad outlaws to stop the land grabbers. Lash LaRue (in his second supporting role to Dean) steals the picture. LaRue went on to star in his own series of well-received Bs. 57m. **DIR:** Robert Emmett Tansey. **CAST:** Eddie Dean, Lash LaRue, Charles King. **1946**

CARAVANS 🦃 An American diplomat is sent to the Middle East to bring back the daughter of an American politician. Rated PG. 123m. **DIR:** James Fargo. **CAST:** Anthony Quinn, Michael Sarrazin, Jennifer O'Neill, Christopher Lee, Joseph Cotten, Barry Sullivan, Jeremy Kemp. **1978**

CARBON COPY ★★★1/2 This amiable lightweight comedy of racial manners stars George Segal as a white corporate executive who suddenly discovers he has a teenage black son just itching to be adopted in lily-white San Marino, California. Rated PG. 92m. **DIR:** Michael Schultz. **CAST:** George Segal, Susan Saint James, Denzel Washington, Jack Warden, Dick Martin. **1981**

CARDIAC ARREST ★★ Garry Goodrow, maverick detective, investigates a series of grisly murders that has the cops puzzled and the citizens of San Francisco living in fear. Rated R for violence and adult situations. 90m. **DIR:** Murphy Mintz. **CAST:** Garry Goodrow, Mike Chan, Max Gail. **1980 DVD**

CARDINAL, THE ★★★ Director Otto Preminger's epic view of a vital and caring young Catholic priest's rise from a backwoods clergyman to cardinal. Alternately compelling and shallow. Watch for the late Maggie McNamara in her last role. 175m. **DIR:** Otto Preminger. **CAST:** Tom Tryon, Romy Schneider, Carol Lynley, John Huston. **1963**

CARE BEARS MOVIE, THE ★★★ Poor animation mars this children's movie about bears who cheer up a pair of kids. Rated G, no objectionable material. 80m. **DIR:** Aran Selznick. **CAST:** Mickey Rooney, Georgia Engel. **1985**

CAREER ★★★★ Anthony Franciosa delivers a surprisingly powerful performance as an actor for whom success is always just beyond reach. In his pursuit for the one big part, he sacrifices his personal happiness and youth. Exemplary supporting performances by Dean Martin and Carolyn Jones. B&W; 105m. **DIR:** Joseph Anthony. **CAST:** Anthony Franciosa, Dean Martin, Shirley MacLaine, Carolyn Jones, Joan Blackman. **1959**

CAREER GIRLS ★★1/2 Two former roommates, now successful businesswomen, get together for a weekend reunion and have flashbacks to their hungry college days. Writer-director Mike Leigh's noted style of semi-improvisational scripting comes up empty this time. In the course of two days, the women run into far too many of their old friends and lovers, greeting each contrivance with cries of "What a coincidence!" Rated R for profanity and some sexuality. 87m. **DIR:** Mike Leigh. **CAST:** Katrin Cartlidge, Lynda Steadman, Kate Byers, Mark Benton. **1997**

CAREER OPPORTUNITIES ★★ The town liar is locked in a department store overnight with the town beauty and two bumbling burglars in this just passable film written and coproduced by John Hughes. Rated PG-13 for brief profanity and violence. 83m. **DIR:** Bryan Gordon. **CAST:** Frank Whaley, Jennifer Connelly, Barry Corbin, Noble Willingham, William Forsythe, Dermot Mulroney, Kieran Mulroney, John Candy. **1991 DVD**

CAREFREE ★★★ In this blend of music, slapstick situations, and romantic byplay, Ginger Rogers is a crazy, mixed-up girl-child who goes to psychiatrist Fred Astaire for counsel. His treatment results in her falling in love with him. While trying to stop this, he falls in love with her. Of course they dance! It's more screwball comedy than musical. B&W; 80m. **DIR:** Mark Sandrich. **CAST:** Fred Astaire, Ginger Rogers, Ralph Bellamy, Jack Carson. **1938**

CAREFUL ★★★★ *Careful* is set in a candy-colored mountain village where avalanches are so common that no one speaks above a whisper. This makes for a psychological tension that drives its inhabitants to extremes that are equally bizarre and amusing. Not rated; contains brief nudity. 96m. **DIR:** Guy Maddin. **CAST:** Kyle McCulloch, Gosia Dobrowolska, Paul Cox. **1992 DVD**

CAREFUL HE MIGHT HEAR YOU ★★★★1/2 A child's-eye view of the harsh realities of life, this Australian import is a poignant, heartwarming, sad, and sometimes frightening motion picture. A young boy named P. S. (played by 7-year-old Nicholas Gledhill) gets caught up in a bitter custody fight between his two aunts. While the movie does tend to become a tearjerker on occasion, it does so without putting off the viewer. Rated PG for suggested sex and violence. 116m. **DIR:** Carl Schultz. **CAST:** Robyn Nevin, Nicholas Gledhill, Wendy Hughes, John Hargreaves. **1983**

CARIBBEAN MYSTERY, A ★★★1/2 In this BBC-produced Agatha Christie mystery, the quiet atmosphere of a tropical-island resort is shattered by intrigue and murder, and Miss Marple is soon on the scene. Although quite elderly, she shows awareness and vitality with a turn of her head and the sparkle in her eyes. The theme music, characterizations, and cinematography make this story enjoyable. Not rated; suitable for family viewing. 100m. **DIR:** Christopher Petit. **CAST:** Joan Hickson, Donald Pleasence, T. P. McKenna, Michael Feast, Sheila Ruskin. **1989**

CARIBE ★★ In this bland spy thriller, CIA agent Kara Glover and her partner arrange a weapons sale for their own personal gain. But the contact, Stephen McHattie, has no intention of fulfilling his part of the bargain. He kills Glover's partner and confiscates the weapons. Beautiful photography of the Belize jungles and mountains rescues this tired spy thriller. Rated R. 90m. **DIR:** Michael Kennedy. **CAST:** John Savage, Kara Glover, Stephen McHattie. **1987**

CARIBOO TRAIL ★★★★ Cattleman Randolph Scott finds gold in Canada but has to fight off Victor Jory's claim jumpers. Gorgeous Colorado scenery stands in for the Canadian wilderness. 81m. **DIR:** Edwin L. Marin. **CAST:** Randolph Scott, George "Gabby" Hayes, Bill Williams, Victor Jory, Douglas Kennedy, Dale Robertson, Jim Davis. **1950**

CARLA'S SONG ★★★1/2 Glasgow bus driver experiences a political awakening in this angry, melancholy look at the Nicaraguan war between right-wing U.S.-backed Contras and the leftist Sandanista government. In 1987, he befriends a female Nicaraguan refugee and they travel to her homeland where they cross paths with a blunt, outspoken former CIA operative. In English and Spanish with English subtitles. Not rated; contains adult themes and language. 127m. **DIR:** Kenneth Loach. **CAST:** Robert Carlyle, Oyanka Cabezas, Scott Glenn. **1998 DVD**

CARLITO'S WAY ★★★★ Al Pacino, a former drug dealer trying to go straight, finds himself being pulled back into the criminal underworld when his best friend and attorney asks for his help. It's trash, but great trash. Rated R for nudity, profanity, violence, simulated sex, and drug use. 141m. **DIR:** Brian De Palma. **CAST:** Al Pacino, Sean Penn, Penelope Ann Miller, John Leguizamo, Ingrid Rogers, Luis Guzman, James Rebhorn, Viggo Mortensen, Richard Foronjy, Adrian Pasdar. **1993 DVD**

CARLTON-BROWNE OF THE F.O. ★★1/2 A British foreign-office secretary is assigned to a small island nation, formerly of the empire. For serious buffs this is an interesting, but not classic, bit of movie history. Not rated and only mildly ribald. B&W; 88m. **DIR:** Jeffrey Dell. **CAST:** Terry-Thomas, Peter Sellers, Luciana Paluzzi. **1958**

CARMEN JONES ★★★★ An exceptionally well-staged adaptation of Oscar Hammerstein's updating of the famous opera with Georges Bizet's music intact. As in the opera, a flirt causes a soldier to go off the deep end because of his passion for her, but the main event is the music. The cast includes celebrity singers, but their voices were dubbed to suit the operatic range of the music. 105m. **DIR:** Otto Preminger. **CAST:** Dorothy Dandridge, Harry Belafonte, Pearl Bailey, Diahann Carroll, Brock Peters, Roy Glenn, Olga James. **1954 DVD**

CARMEN MIRANDA: BANANAS IS MY BUSINESS ★★★1/2 To Yanks she was the lady with the fruit on her head, but in Brazil, Carmen Miranda was huge. Brazilian filmmaker Helena Solberg nearly explains the cult of personality surrounding a woman who tried to use the Hollywood system, but found it ate her up. This merely whets the appetite since Solberg's mistake was to interject a personal but mostly inane narrative that never moves past broad generalizations. U.S.-Brazilian production. Not rated. B&W/color; 91m. **DIR:** Helena Solberg. **1994 DVD**

CARMILLA ★★★★ This tale from the cable TV series *Nightmare Classics* features a lonely southern girl (Ione Skye) befriending a stranger (Meg Tilly) who just happens to be a vampire. Some positively chilling scenes!! Not rated, contains gore and violence. 52m. **DIR:** Gabrielle Beaumont. **CAST:** Ione Skye, Meg Tilly, Roddy McDowall, Roy Dotrice. **1989**

CARNAL KNOWLEDGE ★★★★ The sexual dilemmas of the modern American are analyzed and come up short in this thoughtful film. Jack Nicholson and singer Art Garfunkel are college roommates whose lives are followed through varied relationships with the opposite sex. Nicholson is somewhat of a stinker, and one finds oneself more in sympathy with the women in the cast. Rated R. 96m. **DIR:** Mike Nichols. **CAST:** Jack Nicholson, Candice Bergen, Art Garfunkel, Ann-Margret. **1971 DVD**

CARNIVAL IN FLANDERS ★★★★ This sly drama is about a village that postpones its destruction by collaborating with its conquerors. A clever, subtle work, this classic tries to re-create the great paintings of the masters depicting village life during carnival time. In French with English subtitles. B&W; 92m. **DIR:** Jacques Feyder. **CAST:** Françoise Rosay, Andre Alerme, Jean Murat, Louis Jouvet, Micheline Cheirel. **1936**

CARNIVAL OF BLOOD 🦃 Boring horror mystery about a series of murders committed at New York's Coney Island. 87m. **DIR:** Leonard Kirman. **CAST:** Earle Edgerton, Judith Resnick, Burt Young. **1976**

CARNIVAL OF SOULS ★★★1/2 Creepy film made on a shoestring budget in Lawrence, Kansas, concerns a girl who, after a near-fatal car crash, is haunted by a ghoulish, zombielike character. Extremely eerie, with nightmarish photography, this little-known gem has a way of getting to you. Better keep the lights on. B&W; 80m. **DIR:** Herk Harvey. **CAST:** Candace Hilligoss, Sidney Berger. **1962 DVD**

CARNIVAL ROCK 🦃 This tedious tale about a nightclub offers little enjoyment. Great music, though, by the Platters and David Houston. 80m. **DIR:** Roger Corman. **CAST:** Susan Cabot, Dick Miller, Brian Hutton. **1958**

CARNIVAL STORY ★★ Familiar story of rivalry between circus performers over the affections of the girl they both love. No real surprises. Filmed in Germany. 95m. **DIR:** Kurt Neumann. **CAST:** Anne Baxter, Steve Cochran, Jay C. Flippen, George Nader. **1954 DVD**

CARNOSAUR ★★1/2 Writer-director Adam Simon's unpleasantly bleak, end-of-the-world chiller winds up as nothing more than a laughably crude *Jurassic Park* rip-off. Mad scientist Diane Ladd genetically alters chicken eggs so that human females will give birth to dinosaurs, effectively terminating our reign on Earth. Has Colonel Sanders heard about this one? Rated R for gore and profanity. 83m. **DIR:** Adam Simon. **CAST:** Diane

Ladd, Raphael Sbarge, Jennifer Runyon, Clint Howard. **1993 DVD**

CARNOSAUR 2 ★★★1/2 Superior sequel dredges up several familiar formulas and uses them to good advantage. You'll recognize which films are being ripped off in good, gory fashion in this exciting tale of a group of technicians who find more than they bargained for when they attempt to restore power to a top-secret mining facility. Confined setting, honest suspense, and decent special effects keep the chills coming. Rated R for gore. 83m. **DIR:** Louis Morneau. **CAST:** John Savage, Cliff De Young, Rick Dean, Ryan Thomas Johnson, Don Stroud. **1994 DVD**

CARNOSAUR 3: PRIMAL SPECIES ★★1/2 Roger Corman's dinosaur franchise continues with this predictable sequel about a team of antiterrorist special forces whose latest assignment is to eliminate some escaped man-eating carnosaurs. Scott Valentine plays the team leader who discovers that the carnosaurs are practically indestructible. Fans of the first two films will find plenty to like, while those looking for something different will be disappointed. Rated R for violence and language. 85m. **DIR:** Jonathan Winfrey. **CAST:** Scott Valentine, Janet Gunn, Morgan Englund, Rick Dean. **1995 DVD**

CARNY ★★★★ This film takes us behind the bright lights into the netherworld of the "carnies," people who spend their lives cheating, lying, and stealing from others yet consider themselves superior to their victims. Gary Busey, Jodie Foster, Robbie Robertson are all outstanding. The accent in *Carny* is on realism with disenchanted losers who live only from day to day. Rated R. 107m. **DIR:** Robert Kaylor. **CAST:** Gary Busey, Jodie Foster, Robbie Robertson, Meg Foster, Bert Remsen. **1980**

CARO DIARIO ★★1/2 Three stories related by and starring Nanni Moretti, who has been called Italy's Woody Allen. The third story, where Moretti's mysterious skin disorder baffles a series of doctors, is the funniest. The others—Moretti tooling around Rome on his motor scooter and cruising the islands off the Italian coast—are self-indulgent, and laughs are rare. Not rated; suitable for general audiences. 128m. **DIR:** Nanni Moretti. **CAST:** Nanni Moretti, Jennifer Beals. **1993**

CAROLINA SKELETONS ★★★ Lou Gossett Jr., adept as usual, stars in this fact-based story about a war hero's return to a southern town in search of the truth behind his brother's execution years earlier. Quality performances from Gossett and Bruce Dern. Made for cable. Rated R for profanity and violence. 94m. **DIR:** John Erman. **CAST:** Louis Gossett Jr., Bruce Dern. **1992 DVD**

CAROLINE? ★★★★ *Hallmark Hall of Fame* presentation is an excellent exercise in sustained suspense. Stephanie Zimbalist is the question mark in question, the long-lost daughter who has been presumed dead for the past fifteen years. When Caroline suddenly shows up to claim the family inheritance, her very presence raises suspicions and doubts. Pamela Reed is especially effective as the newest family member who begins to realize that things are not exactly what they seem. 100m. **DIR:** Joseph Sargent. **CAST:** Stephanie Zimbalist, Pamela Reed, George Grizzard, Patricia Neal. **1989**

CAROLINE AT MIDNIGHT ★★★★ Here's an erotic thriller with a surprising finish. A journalist receives a phone call from a deceased girlfriend and finds himself involved with the frightened wife of a dirty cop who may have been responsible for the girlfriend's death. Rated R for nudity, rape, simulated sex, profanity, and violence. 89m. **DIR:** Scott McGinnis. **CAST:** Timothy Daly, Mia Sara, Paul LeMat, Clayton Rohner, Zach Galligan, Virginia Madsen, Judd Nelson. **1993**

CAROUSEL ★★★★★ A unique blend of drama and music with the eloquent Rodgers and Hammerstein score performed by the best of both Hollywood and opera. Molnar's famous story of *Liliom*, the carnival barker who gets one day to prove he's worthy of Heaven, is transferred to Maine, where majestic backdrops add emotional emphasis. Exceptional. 128m. **DIR:** Henry King. **CAST:** Gordon MacRae, Shirley Jones, Gene Lockhart, Cameron Mitchell, Barbara Ruick, Claramae Turner, Robert Rounseville, Jacques d'Amboise. **1956 DVD**

CARPATHIAN EAGLE ★★ Murdered men begin popping up with their hearts cut out. A police detective scours the town and racks his brain looking for the killer, not realizing how close he is. What all this has to do with the title is never resolved in this addition to Elvira's "Thriller Video." 60m. **DIR:** Francis Megahy. **CAST:** Anthony Valentine, Suzanne Danielle, Sian Phillips. **1982**

CARPENTER, THE ★★★ Once you realize writer Doug Taylor and director David Wellington had their tongues planted firmly in cheek, you will enjoy this tale of a neglected wife, after a mental breakdown, moving into an unfinished country home where a mysterious night carpenter becomes her protector. Not a spoof, just handled with style and wit. Not rated, but has gore, profanity, and nudity. 87m. **DIR:** David Wellington. **CAST:** Wings Hauser, Lynne Adams. **1989**

CARPETBAGGERS, THE ★★★ Howard Hughes–like millionaire George Peppard makes movies, love, and enemies in the Hollywood of the 1920s and 1930s. Alan Ladd, as a Tom Mix clone, helps in this, his last picture. Carroll Baker is steamy. Very tame compared with the porno-edged Harold Robbins novel. 150m. **DIR:** Edward Dmytryk. **CAST:** George Peppard, Alan Ladd, Audrey Totter, Carroll Baker, Robert Cummings, Lew Ayres, Martin Balsam, Archie Moore. **1964**

CARPOOL ★★ A workaholic father (David Paymer) and his children are kidnapped on their way to school by would-be robber Tom Arnold. Arnold and Paymer might make a good team (one blusters, the other cringes), but they're stuck with a script mixing corny jokes and even cornier family values sermons. The kids are all straight from a Hollywood casting office, and Arthur Hiller's arthritic direction doesn't help. Rated PG-13 for mild profanity and cartoon violence. 105m. **DIR:** Arthur Hiller. **CAST:** Tom Arnold, David Paymer, Rhea Perlman, Rachael Leigh Cook, Rod Steiger. **1996**

CARRIE (1952) ★★★★ Theodore Dreiser's *Sister Carrie*: Jennifer Jones in the title role and Laurence Olivier as her morally blinded married lover make this tale a classic. Basil Ruysdael is perfect in a bit as Olivier's unyielding employer. B&W; 118m. **DIR:** William Wyler. **CAST:** Jennifer Jones, Laurence Olivier, Eddie Albert, Basil Ruysdael, Miriam Hopkins. **1952**

CARRIE (1976) ★★★★1/2 The ultimate revenge tale for anyone who remembers high school as a time of rejection and ridicule. The story follows the strange life of Carrie White (Sissy Spacek), a student severely humiliated by her classmates and stifled by the Puritan beliefs of her mother (Piper Laurie), a religious fanatic. Rated R for nudity, violence, and profanity. 97m. **DIR:** Brian De Palma. **CAST:** Sissy Spacek, Piper Laurie, John Travolta, Nancy Allen, Amy Irving. **1976 DVD**

CARRIED AWAY ★★★★ Dennis Hopper is superb as a middle-aged man whose comfortable life is coming to an end. His mother is dying, his teaching career is nearly over, and his longtime girlfriend Rosealee wants a lifelong commitment. Joseph is at a crossroads, and the crossing guard turns out to be new 17-year-old student Catherine, who sets her sights on the vulnerable Joseph. Rated R for nudity, adult situations, and profanity. 108m. **DIR:** Bruno Barreto. **CAST:** Dennis Hopper, Amy Irving, Amy Locane, Julie Harris, Gary Busey, Hal Holbrook. **1996**

CARRINGTON ★★★1/2 The unorthodox relationship between painter Dora Carrington and homosexual writer Lytton Strachey, from their meeting in 1915 to his death (and her suicide) in 1932. Jonathan Pryce makes the eccentric Strachey a genuinely magnetic figure. Rated R for profanity, nudity, and simulated sex. 122m. **DIR:** Christopher Hampton. **CAST:** Emma Thompson, Jonathan Pryce, Steven Waddington, Rufus Sewell, Samuel West, Penelope Wilton. **1995 DVD**

CARRINGTON, V. C. ★★★ Everybody's Englishman David Niven gives one of the finest performances of his career. A stalwart British army officer, accused of stealing military funds, undertakes to conduct his own defense. This is a solid, engrossing drama. Filmed in England and released heavily cut in the United States under the title *Court Martial*. B&W; 105m. **DIR:** Anthony Asquith. **CAST:** David Niven, Margaret Leighton, Noelle Middleton, Laurence Naismith, Victor Maddern, Maurice Denham. **1955**

CARRY ON ADMIRAL ★★ His Majesty's navy suffers semi-hilariously at the hands of a madcap crew tangled in ribald high jinks, double identity, and comic cuts. Originally titled *The Ship Was Loaded*. 81m. **DIR:** Val Guest. **CAST:** David Tomlinson, Peggy Cummins, Alfie Bass, Ronald Shiner. **1957**

CARRY ON AT YOUR CONVENIENCE ★★ The British *Carry On* comedy players were still carrying on in 1971, but they were starting to run out of breath. Not rated, but full of innuendoes. 86m. **DIR:** Gerald Thomas. **CAST:** Sidney James, Kenneth Williams, Charles Hawtrey, Joan Sims. **1971**

CARRY ON BEHIND 🦃 Archaeologists and holiday campers stumble over each other while trying to share the same location. Not rated. 90m. **DIR:** Gerald Thomas. **CAST:** Elke Sommer, Kenneth Williams, Sidney James, Joan Sims. **1975**

CARRY ON CLEO ★★★1/2 It's a matter of personal taste, but we find this to be the funniest of the *Carry On* series. (Of course, you might not find any of them funny.) It's designed as a spoof of the then-current Burton-Taylor *Cleopatra*. *Dr. Who* fans will spot Jon Pertwee in a small role. 92m. **DIR:** Gerald Thomas. **CAST:** Amanda Barrie, Sidney James, Kenneth Williams, Kenneth Connor, Joan Sims, Charles Hawtrey, Jim Dale, Jon Pertwee. **1965**

CARRY ON COWBOY ★★1/2 Another in a very long, and weakening, line of British farces, many of them spoofs of highly popular films. Replete with the usual double-entendre jokes and sight gags, this one sends up *High Noon*. 91m. **DIR:** Gerald Thomas. **CAST:** Sidney James, Kenneth Williams, Joan Sims, Angela Douglas, Jim Dale. **1966**

CARRY ON CRUISING ★★★ One of the earlier, and therefore better, entries in the long-lived British series. The jokes are more energetic, less forced. In this one, the players try desperately to fill in for the regular crew of a Mediterranean cruise ship. Not rated. B&W; 99m. **DIR:** Gerald Thomas. **CAST:** Sidney James, Kenneth Williams, Kenneth Connor, Liz Fraser. **1962**

CARRY ON DOCTOR ★★★ Adding veteran British comic Frankie Howerd to the cast helped perk up this *Carry On* entry a bit. The usual gang plays the bumbling staff of a hospital, caught up in a battle over a secret weight-loss formula. Not rated. 95m. **DIR:** Gerald Thomas. **CAST:** Frankie Howerd, Sidney James, Kenneth Williams, Charles Hawtrey, Jim Dale, Hattie Jacques, Joan Sims, Peter Butterworth. **1968**

CARRY ON EMMANUELLE 🦃 The last of the *Carry On* series, and not a moment too soon. Not rated. 88m. **DIR:** Gerald Thomas. **CAST:** Suzanne Danielle, Kenneth Williams, Kenneth Connor, Joan Sims, Peter Butterworth, Beryl Reid. **1978**

CARRY ON NURSE ★★★ Daffy struggle between patients and hospital staff. It's one of the most consistently amusing entries in this British comedy series. 90m. **DIR:** Gerald Thomas. **CAST:** Kenneth Connor, Kenneth Williams, Charles Hawtrey, Terence Longden. **1960**

CARS THAT EAT PEOPLE (THE CARS THAT ATE PARIS) ★★★ Peter Weir began with this weird black comedy-horror film about an outback Australian town where motorists and their cars are trapped each night. Rated PG. 90m. **DIR:** Peter Weir. **CAST:** John Meillon, Terry Camilleri, Kevin Miles. **1975**

CARSON CITY CYCLONE ★★★★ Donald "Red" Barry plays a cocky young defense attorney framed for the murder of his father (a judge and banker). Intricate plot that proves how good B Westerns can be. B&W; 55m. **DIR:** Howard Bretherton. **CAST:** Don Barry, Noah Beery Sr., Roy Barcroft. **1943**

CARSON CITY KID ★★★★ Top-notch Roy Rogers period Western dominated by Bob Steele in an offbeat villainous role. Roy Rogers, in the title role, pursues a cunning gambler who murdered his brother. B&W; 54m. **DIR:** Joseph Kane. **CAST:** Roy Rogers, George "Gabby" Hayes, Bob Steele, Noah Beery Jr., Pauline Moore. **1940**

CARTIER AFFAIR, THE 🦃 Less than funny comic romance that involves a male secretary falling in love with his soap-opera-legend boss. 96m. **DIR:** Rod Holcomb. **CAST:** Joan Collins, David Hasselhoff, Telly Savalas, Jay Gerber, Hilly Hicks. **1985 DVD**

CARTOONS GO TO WAR ★★★★ An extremely tight an[illegible]made look at the use of cartoons during World War [illegible]ay to lift morale among civilians and train soldiers without preaching. Though brief, this A&E documentary clearly puts the war effort into a new context while entertaining us. Rare footage is blended with sharp revelations by historians and several well-spoken animators such as Chuck Jones. Not rated. B&W/color; 50m. **DIR:** Sharon R. Baker. **1995**

CARTOUCHE ★★★★ Great stuff: an eighteenth-century swashbuckler done with wit, incredible style, and an intoxicating passion for action and romance. Jean-Paul Belmondo and Claudia Cardinale head a band of brigands. In French with English subtitles. 115m. **DIR:** Philippe de Broca. **CAST:** Jean-Paul Belmondo, Claudia Cardinale, Odile Versois, Marcel Dalio, Philippe Lemaire. **1964**

CASABLANCA ★★★★★ A kiss may be just a kiss and a sigh just a sigh, but there is only one *Casablanca*. This feast of romance and World War II intrigue is an all-time classic. Rated PG. B&W; 102m. **DIR:** Michael Curtiz. **CAST:** Humphrey Bogart, Ingrid Bergman, Claude Rains, Paul Henreid, Peter Lorre, Sydney Greenstreet. **1942 DVD**

CASANOVA (1976) ★★★1/2 Federico Fellini's account of the sexually bogus Venetian nobleman is a surreal journey into self-obsession and deviance. Casanova is depicted as a tedious braggart. In English and Italian with subtitles. Not rated; contains nudity and profanity and is recommended for adult viewing. 139m. **DIR:** Federico Fellini. **CAST:** Donald Sutherland. **1976**

CASANOVA (1987) ★★ After infamous eighteenth century ladies' man Richard Chamberlain is arrested as an undesirable, the viewer—unfortunately—suffers through his entire life story. A drag. Not rated; contains nudity and sexual situations. 122m. **DIR:** Simon Langton. **CAST:** Richard Chamberlain, Faye Dunaway, Sylvia Kristel, Ornella Muti, Hanna Schygulla, Sophie Ward. **1987**

CASANOVA BROWN ★★★ Gary Cooper's plans to remarry are complicated when he learns his recently divorced ex-wife (Teresa Wright) is about to have a baby. Mild laughs but good performances. Frank Morgan steals the show. B&W; 94m. **DIR:** Sam Wood. **CAST:** Gary Cooper, Teresa Wright, Frank Morgan, Anita Louise, Jill Esmond. **1944**

CASANOVA'S BIG NIGHT ★★1/2 The evergreen Bob Hope is a lowly tailor's assistant masquerading as the great lover Casanova in this costume comedy set in plot-and-intrigue-ridden Venice. Old Ski Nose is irrepressible, sets are sumptuous, and costumes lavish, but the script and direction don't measure up. Funny, but not *that* funny. 86m. **DIR:** Norman Z. McLeod. **CAST:** Bob Hope, Joan Fontaine, Basil Rathbone, Audrey Dalton, Frieda Inescort, Hope Emerson, Hugh Marlowe, John Carradine, John Hoyt, Robert Hutton, Raymond Burr, Lon Chaney Jr. **1954**

CASBAH ★★1/2 Oft-filmed story of a charismatic thief who loses himself in the underworld gets the musical treatment this time. The tunes are good, but it's difficult to erase the image of Charles Boyer as the tragic romantic who followed his heart rather than his instincts. B&W; 93m. **DIR:** John Berry. **CAST:** Tony Martin, Yvonne De Carlo, Peter Lorre, Marta Toren, Hugo Haas, Thomas Gomez, Douglas Dick, Virginia Gregg. **1948**

CASE FOR MURDER, A ★★1/2 From the beginning, it's easy to spot the murderer in this plotless suspense thriller. A lawyer in a prestigious firm is murdered, and all the evidence points to his wife, who can't remember where she was that evening. The acting is decent, but the story is boring. Rated R for violence and suggested sex. 94m. **DIR:** Duncan Gibbins. **CAST:** Jennifer Grey, Peter Berg, Belinda Bauer, Eugene Roche, Robert Do Qui. **1993**

CASE OF DEADLY FORCE, A ★★★★ Richard Crenna plays a determined attorney who helps a victim's family win the first-ever "wrongful death" suit against the Boston Police Department after an innocent black man is shot to death. Based on a true story of police corruption and violence, this drama is surprisingly taut and packs an emotional punch. Made for TV. 95m. **DIR:** Michael Miller. **CAST:** Richard Crenna, John Shea, Tate Donovan. **1986**

CASE OF LIBEL, A ★★★★★ Slick, superb made-for-cable adaptation of Henry Denker's famed Broadway play. The story closely follows the legendary Westbrook Pegler–Quentin Reynolds libel suit, wherein columnist Pegler had attempted to smear Reynolds's reputation with a series of vicious lies. Ranks with the finest courtroom dramas on film. Not rated. 92m. **DIR:** Eric Till. **CAST:** Edward Asner, Daniel J. Travanti, Gordon Pinsent, Lawrence Dane. **1984**

CASE OF THE BLACK CAT, THE ★★1/2 In his only film as Perry Mason, Ricardo Cortez takes over from Warren William to investigate the death of a man who was killed after changing his will. One of the better entries in the series. B&W; 66m. **DIR:** William McGann. **CAST:** Ricardo Cortez, June Travis, Jane Bryan. **1936**

CASE OF THE CURIOUS BRIDE, THE ★★ Perry Mason is dragged away from his new hobby—gourmet cooking—to investigate the case of a woman being blackmailed by her "dead" husband. Look fast for Errol Flynn as a corpse. B&W; 74m. **DIR:** Michael Curtiz. **CAST:** Warren William, Margaret Lindsay, Claire Dodd, Allen Jenkins, Warren Hymer, Errol Flynn, Mayo Methot. **1935**

CASE OF THE HOWLING DOG, THE ★★ Suave Warren William is a far cry from Raymond Burr in this, the first of a half-dozen Perry Mason movies made shortly after Erle Stanley Gardner created the character. Mary Astor is a suspect in a murder case that begins when two men claim to be married to her. B&W; 75m. **DIR:** Alan Crosland. **CAST:** Warren William, Mary Astor, Helen Trenholme, Allen Jenkins. **1934**

CASE OF THE LUCKY LEGS, THE ★★★★ Best entry in the Warner Bros. series of Perry Mason pictures, this has the wisecracking lawyer (Warren William) battling a perennial hangover, doctor's orders, and pesky police officers as he tries to find the murderer of a con man. B&W; 61m. **DIR:** Archie Mayo. **CAST:** Warren William, Genevieve Tobin, Patricia Ellis, Lyle Talbot, Allen Jenkins, Barton MacLane, Porter Hall, Henry O'Neill. **1935**

CASE OF THE STUTTERING BISHOP, THE ★★ Donald Woods is Perry Mason number three in the last film of the series. His job: ascertain whether a woman who claims to be the heiress to a dead man's fortune is an impostor. B&W; 70m. **DIR:** William Clemens. **CAST:** Donald Woods, Ann Dvorak, Anne Nagel. **1937**

CASE OF THE VELVET CLAWS, THE ★★1/2 Perry Mason's honeymoon with new wife Della Street(!) is interrupted by one of those pesky murders, this one involving the publisher of a sleazy tabloid. One of the better entries, though it was Warren William's last time as Mason. B&W; 60m. **DIR:** William Clemens. **CAST:** Warren William, Claire Dodd, Winifred Shaw. **1936**

CASEY'S SHADOW ★★1/2 Only the droll playing of star Walter Matthau makes this family film watchable. Matthau is a horse trainer deserted by his wife and left to raise three sons. Only the star's fans will want to ride it out. Rated PG. 116m. **DIR:** Martin Ritt. **CAST:** Walter Matthau, Alexis Smith, Robert Webber, Murray Hamilton. **1978**

•CASH CROP ★★1/2 Andy Yates finds that his parents have been covertly growing marijuana to supplement their meager farm earnings. The local law enforcement, along with a snoopy DEA Agent, halfheartedly conducts raids on the suspected farmers, while Andy and a few friends figure out how to handle the situation. Inspired by actual events, the movie is nowhere near as gripping as it should be. Rated R for language and drug content. 96m. **DIR:** Stuart Burkin. **CAST:** Wil Horneff, Jeffrey DeMunn, Mary McCormack, James van der Beek, John Slattery. **1999 DVD**

CASH MCCALL ★★★ James Garner is great as a fast-moving financial wizard who must slow down his plan to take over a plastic factory when he pauses to woo the owner's daughter. Lightweight—but the stars shine. 102m. **DIR:** Joseph Pevney. **CAST:** James Garner, Natalie Wood, Dean Jagger, Nina Foch, Henry Jones, E. G. Marshall. **1959**

CASINO (1980) ★★ This pedestrian telemovie features former *Mannix* star Mike Connors as the action-oriented owner of a plush hotel and casino. 100m. **DIR:** Don Chaffey. **CAST:** Mike Connors, Gene Evans, Barry Van Dyke, Gary Burghoff, Joseph Cotten, Lynda Day George, Robert Reed, Barry Sullivan. **1980**

CASINO (1995) ★★★★ Teaming with scripter Nicholas Pileggi, Martin Scorsese gives us a record of the events that transformed Las Vegas from sin-laden mecca to family-oriented Disneyland, as experienced by casino owner Robert De Niro and best friend Joe Pesci, a hair-trigger mob assassin. The only sour note comes from Sharon Stone, who simply doesn't have the acting chops required by her role. Rated R for violence, profanity, drug use, and nudity. 182m. **DIR:** Martin Scorsese. **CAST:** Robert De Niro, Joe Pesci, Sharon Stone, Kevin Pollak, James Woods, John Bloom. **1995 DVD**

CASINO ROYALE (1954) ★★★★ 007 fans who believe Sean Connery to have been the first screen incarnation of their favorite secret agent will be surprised and thrilled by this Bonded treasure, originally aired live on an American television anthology series. Barry Nelson stars as an Americanized "Jimmy" Bond who faces the menacing Le Chiffre (Peter Lorre, in a deliciously evil role) across a gambling table. From the Ian Fleming novel, this remains a surprisingly faithful adaptation of its source material. B&W; 55m. **DIR:** William H. Brown. **CAST:** Barry Nelson, Peter Lorre, Linda Christian. **1954**

CASINO ROYALE (1967) ★★ This is the black sheep of the James Bond family of films. Not wanting to compete with the Sean Connery vehicles, this film was intended to be a stylish spoof. For the most part, it's an overblown bore. 130m. **DIR:** John Huston, Ken Hughes, Robert Parrish, Joseph McGrath, Val Guest. **CAST:** Peter Sellers, Ursula Andress, David Niven, Orson Welles, Joanna Pettet, Woody Allen, Deborah Kerr, William Holden, Charles Boyer, John Huston, George Raft, Jean-Paul Belmondo. **1967**

CASPER ★★★ Casper the friendly ghost redefines "friendly" as the adolescent spirit develops a crush on the young daughter of a ghost therapist. Mainly for kids, but parents should take note: A twist in the story may lead impressionable children to believe it's possible to bring dead parents back to life. Rated PG. 96m. **DIR:** Brad Silberling. **CAST:** Christina Ricci, Bill Pullman, Cathy Moriarty, Eric Idle. **1995**

CASPER: A SPIRITED BEGINNING ★★★ Family-friendly, direct-to-video prequel to the theatrical *Casper,* this film tells the story of Casper's arrival in the world of ghosts and of one teacher's fight to prevent a historic landmark from being demolished. Voices of James Earl Jones, Jeremy Foley, Pauly Shore. Rated PG. 90m. **DIR:** Sean McNamara. **CAST:** Steve Guttenberg, Lori Loughlin, Rodney Dangerfield, Michael McKean, Brendon Ryan Barrett. **1997**

CASS TIMBERLANE ★★ Sinclair Lewis's story of a prominent judge married to a voluptuous younger woman turns into a silly, superficial soap opera. Spencer Tracy and Lana Turner are mismatched as the judge and his wife. B&W; 119m. **DIR:** George Sidney. **CAST:** Spencer Tracy, Lana Turner, Zachary Scott, Mary Astor, Tom Drake, Albert Dekker. **1947**

CASSANDRA CROSSING, THE 🦃 A plague-infested train heads for a weakened bridge. Rated PG. 127m. **DIR:** George Pan Cosmatos. **CAST:** Richard Harris, Sophia Loren, Burt Lancaster, Ava Gardner, Martin Sheen. **1977 DVD**

CAST A DEADLY SPELL ★★★1/2 Scriptwriter Joseph Dougherty's premise is hard to resist: that, in a slightly altered Los Angeles of 1948, *everybody* would use magic as a means to get ahead . . . except one lone private detective named H. Phillip Lovecraft (Fred Ward), last of the truly honest men. This made-for-cable *noir* fantasy is often wry and always entertaining. Rated R for violence and profanity. 93m. **DIR:** Martin Campbell. **CAST:** Fred Ward, David Warner, Julianne Moore, Clancy Brown. **1991**

CAST A GIANT SHADOW ★★ The early history of Israel is told through the fictionalized biography of American Col. Mickie Marcus (Kirk Douglas). Marcus, an expatriate army officer, is cajoled into aiding Israel in its impending war to wrest independence from its hostile Arab neighbors. Highly romanticized piece of historical fluff. 142m. **DIR:** Melville Shavelson. **CAST:** Kirk Douglas, Senta Berger, Angie Dickinson. **1966 DVD**

CAST AWAY ★★★★ Workaholics take it on the chin in this compelling drama, which hurls FedEx systems engineer Tom Hanks onto the favorite nightmare of "what if?" fiction: the deserted island. When a plane crash (a gripping, horrifying sequence) strands our hero on a tiny remote island, he finally appreciates what he took most for granted back home: contact with other people. Although what follows is something of a Boys' Adventure Story, Hanks and director Robert Zemeckis hold our interest for an impressive length of time, no small feat considering that roughly half this film features only Hanks and contains minimal dialogue. Rated PG-13 for dramatic intensity. 143m. **DIR:** Robert Zemeckis.

CAST: Tom Hanks, Helen Hunt, Nick Searcy, Christopher Noth, Lari White. **2000 DVD**

CAST THE FIRST STONE ★★★ When schoolteacher Jill Eikenberry is raped and becomes pregnant, she decides to keep the baby despite public protest. When school officials doubt her version of the story, they dismiss her. Eikenberry fights back by hiring lawyer Richard Masur, who not only helps her win the case, but helps restore her dignity as well. Riveting made-for-television movie. 94m. **DIR:** John Korty. **CAST:** Jill Eikenberry, Lew Ayres, Richard Masur, Elizabeth Ruscio, Joe Spano. **1990**

CASTAWAY ★★ Nicolas Roeg adds some surreal touches to this otherwise mediocre film about a wealthy publisher (Oliver Reed) who advertises for a woman to live with him for a year on a deserted tropical island. His dreams of animal passion turn into domestic doldrums when his companion (Amanda Donohoe) opts for celibacy. Rated R for profanity, nudity, and simulated sex. 118m. **DIR:** Nicolas Roeg. **CAST:** Oliver Reed, Amanda Donohoe. **1987**

CASTAWAY COWBOY, THE ★★★1/2 James Garner plays a Texas cowboy in Hawaii during the 1850s. There he helps a lovely widow (Vera Miles) start a cattle ranch despite problems created by a land-grabbing enemy (Robert Culp). Good family entertainment. Rated G. 91m. **DIR:** Vincent McEveety. **CAST:** James Garner, Vera Miles, Robert Culp, Eric Shea. **1974 DVD**

CASTLE, THE (1983) ★★★1/2 This highly metaphorical story from Franz Kafka's incomplete novel is translated literally here and makes for a very strange and humorous affair. Maximilian Schell is a land surveyor who is employed by the mysterious inhabitants of a castle, only to be denied access to the place once he arrives there. Not rated, has sex and nudity. 89m. **DIR:** Rudolf Noelte. **CAST:** Maximilian Schell, Cordula Trantow, Trudik Daniel. **1983**

CASTLE, THE (1997) ★★★ The head of a cheerful, lowbrow Australian family decides to put up a fight when the airport next door wants to expand by demolishing his ramshackle home. An unexpected smash hit in Australia, this goofy, eccentric, low-budget comedy is hard to resist. Performances are appealing, and the writing has some of the droll spirit of a well-made Monty Python skit. Rated R for profanity. 82m. **DIR:** Rob Sitch. **CAST:** Michael Caton, Anne Tenney, Stephen Curry, Anthony Simcoe, Charles Tingwell. **1997 DVD**

CASTLE FREAK ★★ Disappointing bogeyman movie from Stuart Gordon, who should know better. When a couple (genre favorites Jeffrey Combs and Barbara Crampton) inherit a castle in Italy, they pack up everything and move. The castle comes with all the modern conveniences, including a bloodthirsty creature who preys on the locals. Gory special effects are no substitution for suspense. Rated R for gore, nudity, and adult language. 93m. **DIR:** Stuart Gordon. **CAST:** Jeffrey Combs, Barbara Crampton, Jonathan Fuller, Jessica Dollarhide. **1995 DVD**

CASTLE IN THE DESERT ★★★ Charlie Chan travels to the Mojave Desert as the guest of a millionaire whose wife is descended from the infamous Borgias. By some odd coincidence, people begin to die by poison. Full of secret panels, mysterious shadows, and close-ups of gloved hands, this is one of the most satisfying of the later Chans. B&W; 61m. **DIR:** Harry Lachman. **CAST:** Sidney Toler, Arleen Whelan, Richard Derr, Douglass Dumbrille, Henry Daniell. **1942**

CASTLE OF BLOOD (CASTLE OF TERROR) ★★★ Grand fun: the best of the black-and-white Italian horrors ground out in the Sixties following Mario Bava's wild *Black Sunday*. A stranger (George Riviere) meets Edgar Allan Poe in a tavern, and the author bets him he can't spend the night alone in a haunted mansion. Who could resist? U.S. TV title: *Castle of Terror*. B&W; 84m. **DIR:** Anthony M. Dawson. **CAST:** Barbara Steele, George Riviere. **1964**

CASTLE OF CAGLIOSTRO, THE ★★★★ Japanese animation with wider appeal than most Japanese animated features. International thief Wolf and his partners in crime attempt to rescue a young princess from a marriage to the wicked Count Cagliostro. Memorable animation, story, and characters. 100m. **DIR:** Hayao Miyazaki. **1980 DVD**

CASTLE OF EVIL 🦃 Take an electronic humanoid, a dead scientist, some faulty wiring, what appears to be a good cast, and throw them together with a budget that must have run into the tens of dollars and you get this pathetic suspense movie. 81m. **DIR:** Francis D. Lyon. **CAST:** Virginia Mayo, Scott Brady, David Brian, Hugh Marlowe. **1966**

CASTLE OF FU MANCHU 🦃 The worst Fu Manchu film ever made. 92m. **DIR:** Jess (Jesus) Franco. **CAST:** Christopher Lee, Richard Greene, Maria Perschy. **1968**

CASTLE OF THE CREEPING FLESH 🦃 Knee-slapper of a bad Eurotrash horror opus, witlessly enlivened by open-heart surgery footage. Once (incorrectly) credited to director Jess Franco, rather than the actual culprit—leading man Adrian Hoven. Not rated. 90m. **DIR:** Percy G. Parker. **CAST:** Adrian Hoven, Janine Reynaud, Howard Vernon. **1968**

CASTLE OF THE LIVING DEAD ★★1/2 What makes this otherwise run-of-the-mill horror yarn worth watching are some impressive scenes toward the end. They were added by Michael Reeves, a young Englishman who directed several powerful horror films before his suicide. Christopher Lee plays a count who preserves people with an embalming formula. Donald Sutherland, in his film debut, plays two parts, including an old witch woman! B&W; 90m. **DIR:** Herbert Wise. **CAST:** Christopher Lee, Philippe Leroy, Donald Sutherland. **1964**

CASUAL SEX? ★★★ Oddball, likable comedy about two single girls (Lea Thompson and Victoria Jackson) who go hunting for men at a health resort. Although not providing roll-in-the-aisles laughter, *Casual Sex?* is a real attempt at making some sense of the safe-sex question. Rated R for sexual frankness, language and nudity. 90m. **DIR:** Genevieve Robert. **CAST:** Lea Thompson, Victoria Jackson, Stephen Shellen, Mary Gross, Andrew Clay. **1988 DVD**

CASUALTIES ★★★ Better-than-average revenge thriller stars Caroline Goodall as a woman trapped in a violent marriage to a vicious cop who won't let her leave. Mark Harmon plays the stranger who convinces her to turn the tables on her spouse. Intense situations and thoughtful characters create a heightened level of suspense. Rated R for adult situations, language, and violence. 85m. **DIR:** Alex Graves. **CAST:** Mark Harmon,

Caroline Goodall, Jonathan Gries, Michael Beach. **1997**

CASUALTIES OF LOVE: THE LONG ISLAND LOLITA STORY ★★ One of a trio of made-for-TV movies that exploited the alleged affair between teenager Amy Fisher and auto mechanic Joey Buttafuoco. The acting by the two leads is surprisingly good. 94m. **DIR:** John Herzfeld. **CAST:** Jack Scalia, Alyssa Milano, Leo Rossi, Phyllis Lyons. **1993**

CASUALTIES OF WAR ★★★★ Michael J. Fox turns in an exceptional performance in this thought-provoking Vietnam War drama as the lone dissenter during his squad's rape and murder of a Vietnamese girl. Director Brian De Palma graphically brings home the horror of a war without purpose and heroes without valor. Rated R for violence, simulated sex, and profanity. 106m. **DIR:** Brian De Palma. **CAST:** Michael J. Fox, Sean Penn, Don Harvey, John C. Reilly. **1989 DVD**

CAT, THE (1966) [turkey] Poor story of a lost boy who is rescued by a wildcat. 87m. **DIR:** Ellis Kadison. **CAST:** Peggy Ann Garner, Barry Coe, Roger Perry, Dwayne Rekin. **1966**

CAT, THE (1971) (LE CHAT) ★★★ Adaptation of the Georges Simenon novel about a long-married couple. Somewhere along the line their love turned to mutual loathing, and the husband transferred his affections to their pet cat. Not much happens, but watching Jean Gabin and Simone Signoret convey their feelings with almost no dialogue can be fascinating. In French with English subtitles. 88m. **DIR:** Pierre Granier-Deferre. **CAST:** Jean Gabin, Simone Signoret. **1971**

CAT AND MOUSE ★★★★1/2 Written, produced, and directed by Claude Lelouch, *Cat and Mouse* is a deliciously urbane and witty whodunit guaranteed to charm and deceive while keeping you marvelously entertained. The plot has more twists and turns than a country road, and the characters are . . . well . . . just slightly corrupt and totally fascinating. In French with English subtitles. Rated PG. 107m. **DIR:** Claude Lelouch. **CAST:** Michèle Morgan, Jean-Pierre Aumont, Serge Reggiani, Valerie Lagrange. **1975**

CAT AND THE CANARY, THE (1927) ★★★1/2 An exceptional silent version of a mystery that has been subsequently remade several times. The entire cast is wonderful as a spooky group that spends the night in a mysterious old house. Laura LaPlante is in top form. B&W; 75m. **DIR:** Paul Leni. **CAST:** Laura LaPlante, Tully Marshall, Flora Finch, Creighton Hale. **1927 DVD**

CAT AND THE CANARY, THE (1939) ★★★ A group of relatives gather at a creepy old mansion to read the will of a rich man ten years after his death. Sliding panels, portraits with eyes that move, and a knife-wielding maniac in a fright mask make this comedy-chiller a real winner. Bob Hope, in this third version of a silent classic, initiates his successful teaming with Paulette Goddard. Brash, fun, and genuinely spooky. B&W; 74m. **DIR:** Elliott Nugent. **CAST:** Bob Hope, Paulette Goddard, Douglass Montgomery, Gale Sondergaard, George Zucco, John Beal. **1939**

CAT AND THE CANARY, THE (1978) ★★★1/2 A surprisingly entertaining remake of the 1927 period thriller about a group of people trapped in a British mansion and murdered one by one. Rated PG. 90m. **DIR:** Radley Metzger. **CAST:** Honor Blackman, Michael Callan, Edward Fox, Wendy Hiller, Carol Lynley, Olivia Hussey. **1978 DVD**

CAT AND THE FIDDLE, THE ★★★★ Jeanette MacDonald sings "The Night Was Made for Love," and the screen comes alive with romance. Ramon Novarro costars in a tuneful rendition of a Jerome Kern operetta about a struggling composer who gets upset because MacDonald sings "She Didn't Say Yes" in response to his romantic overtures. B&W; 90m. **DIR:** William K. Howard. **CAST:** Jeanette MacDonald, Ramon Novarro, Frank Morgan, Jean Hersholt, Charles Butterworth. **1934**

CAT BALLOU ★★★ In this offbeat, uneven but fun comedy-Western, Jane Fonda plays Cat, a former schoolteacher out to avenge her father's death. Michael Callan is her main romantic interest. Lee Marvin outshines all with his Oscar-winning performance in the dual roles of the drunken hired gun and his evil lookalike. 96m. **DIR:** Elliot Silverstein. **CAST:** Jane Fonda, Lee Marvin, Michael Callan, Jay C. Flippen. **1965 DVD**

CAT CHASER ★★ Peter Weller gives a stiff performance as an ex-Marine who gets mixed up in love, revenge, and murder. Rated R for violence, language, nudity, simulated sex, and rape. 97m. **DIR:** Abel Ferrara. **CAST:** Peter Weller, Kelly McGillis, Charles Durning, Frederic Forrest, Tomas Milian. **1988**

CAT FROM OUTER SPACE, THE ★★1/2 Disney comedy–sci-fi about a cat from outer space with a magical collar. The cat needs the United States to help it return to its planet. Rated G. 103m. **DIR:** Norman Tokar. **CAST:** Ken Berry, Sandy Duncan, Harry Morgan, Roddy McDowall. **1978 DVD**

CAT GIRL ★★ Dreary British B movie recommended only to fans of Barbara Shelley, who plays a young girl linked by a family curse to the spirit of a murderous panther. B&W; 70m. **DIR:** Alfred Shaughnessy. **CAST:** Barbara Shelley. **1957**

CAT IN THE BRAIN, A [turkey] No real plot to tell of in this tepid entry from Italian gore master Lucio Fulci in which he plays himself, a horror film director growing sick of it all. Rated R for violence, gore, nudity, and simulated sex. 87m. **DIR:** Lucio Fulci. **CAST:** Lucio Fulci, David L. Thompson, Brett Halsey. **1990 DVD**

CAT ON A HOT TIN ROOF (1958) ★★★★ This heavy drama stars Elizabeth Taylor as the frustrated Maggie and Paul Newman as her alcoholic, ex-athlete husband. They've returned to his father's (Big Daddy, played by Burl Ives) home upon hearing he's dying. They are joined by Newman's brother, Gooper, and his wife, May, and their many obnoxious children. 108m. **DIR:** Richard Brooks. **CAST:** Elizabeth Taylor, Paul Newman, Burl Ives, Jack Carson. **1958 DVD**

CAT ON A HOT TIN ROOF (1985) ★★★1/2 Updated rendition of the famed Tennessee Williams play strikes to the core in most scenes but remains oddly distanced in others. The story itself is just as powerful as it must have been in 1955, with its acute examination of a family under stress. Jessica Lange is far too melodramatic as Maggie the Cat. Things really come alive, though, when Big Daddy (Rip Torn) and Brick (Tommy Lee Jones) square off. A near miss. Unrated, has sexual situations. 140m. **DIR:** Jack Hofsiss. **CAST:** Jessica Lange, Tommy Lee Jones, Rip Torn, Kim Stanley, David Dukes, Penny Fuller. **1985 DVD**

CAT O'NINE TAILS ★★1/2 One of Italian horror maestro Dario Argento's least memorable films gets bogged down in tedious plotting. Blind Karl Malden and newspaperman James Franciscus team up to find a murderer. Dubbed in English. Rated PG. 112m. **DIR:** Dario Argento. **CAST:** Karl Malden, James Franciscus, Catherine Spaak, Carlo Alighiero. **1971 DVD**

CAT PEOPLE (1942) ★★★★ Simone Simon, Kent Smith, and Tom Conway are excellent in this movie about a shy woman (Simon) who believes she carries the curse of the panther. Jacques Tourneur knew the imagination was stronger and more impressive than anything filmmakers could show visually and played on it with impressive results. B&W; 73m. **DIR:** Jacques Tourneur. **CAST:** Simone Simon, Kent Smith, Tom Conway. **1942**

CAT PEOPLE (1982) ★★ While technically a well-made film, *Cat People* spares the viewer nothing—incest, bondage, bestiality. It makes one yearn for the films of yesteryear, which achieved horror through implication. Rated R for nudity, profanity, and gore. 118m. **DIR:** Paul Schrader. **CAST:** Nastassja Kinski, Malcolm McDowell, John Heard, Annette O'Toole, Ed Begley Jr., Ruby Dee, Scott Paulin. **1982 DVD**

CAT WOMEN OF THE MOON Another ludicrous entry in the travel-to-a-planet-of-barely-dressed-women subgenre. 64m. **DIR:** Arthur Hilton. **CAST:** Sonny Tufts, Marie Windsor, Victor Jory. **1954 DVD**

CATAMOUNT KILLING, THE Choppy and clichéd film about the perfect crime gone sour. Rated PG. 82m. **DIR:** Krzysztof Zanussi. **CAST:** Horst Buchholz, Ann Wedgeworth, Polly Holliday. **1985**

CATCH AS CATCH CAN ★★ Vittorio Gassman plays a television-commercial actor who finds the animal kingdom out to get him. The dubbed English makes it worse. Not rated, has sex and nudity. 92m. **DIR:** Franco Indovina. **CAST:** Vittorio Gassman, Martha Hyer, Gila Golan, Claudio Gora, Massimo Serato. **1968**

CATCH ME A SPY ★★★ This is a good suspense-thriller with, surprisingly, a few laughs. The story is built around an East-West espionage theme in which both sides trade for their captured spies. Rated PG. 93m. **DIR:** Dick Clement. **CAST:** Kirk Douglas, Marlene Jobert, Trevor Howard. **1971**

CATCH ME IF YOU CAN ★★★ When financially troubled Cathedral High is threatened with closure, the student council resorts to gambling on illegal car races. Above average teen action flick. Rated PG. 105m. **DIR:** Stephen Sommers. **CAST:** Matt Lattanzi, M. Emmet Walsh, Geoffrey Lewis. **1989**

CATCH THE HEAT ★★ Tiana Alexander is a narcotics cop in San Francisco sent undercover to South America to bust Rod Steiger. Even Alexander's kung fu prowess is routine with these cardboard characters. Rated R. 88m. **DIR:** Joel Silberg. **CAST:** David Dukes, Tiana Alexander, Rod Steiger, Brian Thompson, Jorge Martinez, John Hancock. **1987**

CATCH-22 ★★★ This release stars Alan Arkin as a soldier in World War II most interested in avoiding the insanity of combat. Its sarcasm alone is enough to sustain interest. Rated R. 121m. **DIR:** Mike Nichols. **CAST:** Alan Arkin, Martin Balsam, Richard Benjamin, Anthony Perkins, Art Garfunkel. **1970 DVD**

CATERED AFFAIR, THE ★★★1/2 Bette Davis portrays a woman from the Bronx who is determined to give her daughter a big wedding. This Paddy Chayefsky drama, which he and Gore Vidal adapted from Chayefsky's teleplay, has much of the realistic flavor of his classic *Marty*. B&W; 93m. **DIR:** Richard Brooks. **CAST:** Bette Davis, Ernest Borgnine, Debbie Reynolds, Barry Fitzgerald, Rod Taylor. **1956**

CATHERINE & CO. ★★1/2 British-born Jane Birkin is one of France's most popular actresses, though this, one of her typical soft-core sex comedies, hardly shows why. She plays a young woman who, having drifted into an innocent sort of prostitution, decides to incorporate herself with four regular "stockholders." Rated R. 99m. **DIR:** Michel Boisrone. **CAST:** Jane Birkin, Patrick Dewaere, Jean-Claude Brialy, Jean-Pierre Aumont. **1975**

CATHERINE THE GREAT ★★ Stodgy spectacle from Great Britain is sumptuously mounted but takes its own time in telling the story of the famed czarina of Russia and her (toned-down) love life. Elisabeth Bergner in the title role lacks a real star personality, and dashing Douglas Fairbanks Jr. and sage Flora Robson provide the only screen charisma evident. Fair for a historical romance, but it won't keep you on the edge of your seat. B&W; 92m. **DIR:** Paul Czinner. **CAST:** Elisabeth Bergner, Douglas Fairbanks Jr., Flora Robson, Joan Gardner, Gerald Du Maurier. **1934 DVD**

CATHOLICS ★★★★1/2 This film has Martin Sheen playing the representative of the Father General (the Pope). He comes to Ireland to persuade the Catholic priests there to conform to the "new" teachings of the Catholic Church. The Irish priests and monks refuse to discard traditional ways and beliefs. Trevor Howard is excellent as the rebellious Irish abbot. 78m. **DIR:** Jack Gold. **CAST:** Trevor Howard, Martin Sheen, Raf Vallone, Andrew Keir. **1973**

CATLOW ★★ A Louis L'Amour yarn is the basis for this minor Western about a gold robbery. Typical effort by formerly blacklisted Sam Wanamaker. Rated PG. 103m. **DIR:** Sam Wanamaker. **CAST:** Yul Brynner, Richard Crenna, Leonard Nimoy, Daliah Lavi, Jeff Corey, Jo Ann Pflug. **1971**

CATS ★★★1/2 While not as personal or as exciting as seeing it live, this videotaped performance of Andrew Lloyd Webber's musical is still enjoyable. Restaged and cast for this special performance, *Cats* comes alive with colorful characters, memorable tunes (one specially written for this performance), and a sense of awe. Even though it has been playing for more than ten years onstage, this is the perfect opportunity for fans in small towns to appreciate the myth and the magic. Not rated. 115m. **DIR:** David Mallet. **CAST:** Elaine Paige, John Mills, Ken Page. **1998 DVD**

•CATS & DOGS ★★ War erupts between those of the canine and feline persuasions when a nutty professor (Jeff Goldblum) creates a vaccine against dog allergies. Making the cats fiendish cheats compared to the tried-and-true dogs gives the film a horror-flick aura. The humor, largely relying on Roadrunner-ish pain, isn't really funny when applied to the family pet. Disappointing. Rated PG for comic-book violence. 86m. **DIR:** Lawrence Guterman. **CAST:** Jeff Goldblum, Elizabeth Perkins, Alexander Pollock. **2001 DVD**

CATS DON'T DANCE ★★★ Song-and-dance cat Danny ventures from Kokomo, Indiana, to 1939 Hollywood in search of stardom in this animated musical. Danny, a relentless optimist, can't understand why animals are cast only as animals—and never in leading roles. His career dreams are threatened by a ruthless child actress. Rated G. 76m. **DIR:** Mark Dindal. **1997**

CAT'S EYE ★★★1/2 Writer Stephen King and director Lewis Teague, who brought us *Cujo*, reteam for this even better horror release: a trilogy of terror in the much-missed *Night Gallery* anthology style. It's good, old-fashioned, tell-me-a-scary-story fun. Rated PG-13 for violence and gruesome scenes. 98m. **DIR:** Lewis Teague. **CAST:** James Woods, Robert Hays, Kenneth McMillan, Drew Barrymore, Candy Clark, Alan King. **1985**

•CAT'S MEOW, THE ★★★ The mysterious death in 1924 of film producer Thomas Ince (Cary Elwes), after a cruise on William Randolph Hearst's yacht, is the subject of this modest, well-acted little film, which recounts scandalous, persistent rumors involving Hearst (Edward Herrmann), his mistress Marion Davies (Kirsten Dunst), and Charlie Chaplin (Eddie Izzard). Herrmann (perfectly cast) and Dunst are especially good. Rated PG-13 for mild profanity and mature themes. 110m. **DIR:** Peter Bogdanovich. **CAST:** Kirsten Dunst, Cary Elwes, Edward Herrmann, Eddie Izzard, Meg Tilly, Joanna Lumley. **2001 DVD**

CAT'S PLAY ★★★★ A chaste friendship between a widow and a retired music teacher runs into trouble when one of her friends makes romantic gestures toward the man. A deliberately paced but lovely film. In Hungarian with English subtitles. 115m. **DIR:** Karoly Maak. **CAST:** Margit Dayka, Samu Balasz. **1974**

CATTLE QUEEN OF MONTANA ★★ Barbara Stanwyck gives a strong performance in this otherwise routine Western. Plot revolves around Stanwyck trying to protect her farm from land grabbers, who also murdered her father. Meanwhile, the Indians are out to wipe out everybody. 88m. **DIR:** Allan Dwan. **CAST:** Barbara Stanwyck, Ronald Reagan, Gene Evans, Jack Elam. **1954 DVD**

CAUGHT (1949) ★★★ Starry-eyed model Barbara Bel Geddes marries neurotic millionaire Robert Ryan, who proceeds to make her life miserable. His treatment drives her away and into the arms of young doctor James Mason. B&W; 88m. **DIR:** Max Ophüls. **CAST:** Robert Ryan, Barbara Bel Geddes, James Mason, Natalie Schafer, Ruth Brady, Curt Bois, Frank Ferguson. **1949**

CAUGHT (1996) ★★★1/2 A young drifter, after being "adopted" by a New Jersey fish merchant and his wife, begins a torrid affair with the woman. When the couple's weasel-like son moves back home unexpectedly, the unstable atmosphere spins toward an appalling climax. Not rated; contains profanity, simulated sex, and brief but intense violence. 109m. **DIR:** Robert M. Young. **CAST:** Edward James Olmos, Maria Conchita Alonso, Arie Verveen, Steven Schub. **1996**

CAUGHT IN THE ACT ★★1/2 Gregory Harrison stars as a drama teacher in this made-for-cable original. He finds an extra $10 million in his bank account and then is arrested for murder. Unfortunately, the viewer can figure out the entire plot in the first ten minutes. Rated PG-13 for violence and suggested sex. 93m. **DIR:** Deborah Reinisch. **CAST:** Gregory Harrison, Leslie Hope, Patricia Clarkson, Kimberly Scott, Kevin Tighe. **1993**

CAUGHT IN THE DRAFT ★★★1/2 A gun-shy movie idol attempts to avoid the draft and mistakenly enlists in the army. Some very good gags; even the (then) topical ones stand up. B&W; 82m. **DIR:** David Butler. **CAST:** Bob Hope, Dorothy Lamour, Eddie Bracken, Lynne Overman, Irving Bacon. **1941**

CAULDRON OF BLOOD 🦃 Boris Karloff plays a blind sculptor who uses the skeletons of women his wife has murdered as the foundations for his projects. 95m. **DIR:** Edward Mann (Santos Alocer). **CAST:** Boris Karloff, Viveca Lindfors, Jean-Pierre Aumont. **1968**

CAUSE OF DEATH ★★ A college student and his girlfriend become entangled in a drug lord's attempt to retrieve an illicit fortune. A cut-rate remake (rip-off?) of *Marathon Man*. Rated R for violence and nudity. 86m. **DIR:** Philip J. Jones. **CAST:** Michael Barak, Sydney Coale Phillips, Daniel Martine. **1991 DVD**

CAVALCADE ★★★★1/2 A richly detailed pageant of life in London between 1900 and 1930, this film is as innovative as it was when it was declared best picture of 1933. The drama of relationships focuses on the way World War I affected their lives. A truly remarkable film. B&W; 111m. **DIR:** Frank Lloyd. **CAST:** Clive Brook, Diana Wynyard, Ursula Jeans, Margaret Lindsay, Bonita Granville, Billy Bevan, Una O'Connor, Beryl Mercer, Frank Lawton. **1933**

CAVE GIRL 🦃 A high school student gets lost in a cave during a field trip and pops up in prehistoric times. Rated R for nudity and profanity. 85m. **DIR:** David Oliver. **CAST:** Daniel Roebuck, Cindy Ann Thompson. **1985**

CAVE OF THE LIVING DEAD 🦃 An Interpol inspector and a witch join forces to locate some missing girls. 89m. **DIR:** Akos von Ratony. **CAST:** Adrian Hoven, Karin Field, Erika Remberg, Wolfgang Preiss, John Kitzmiller. **1964 DVD**

CAVEMAN ★★ Ex-Beatle Ringo Starr plays the prehistoric hero in this spoof of *One Million Years B.C.* Because of the amount of sexual innuendo, it is definitely not recommended for kids. Rated PG. 92m. **DIR:** Carl Gottlieb. **CAST:** Ringo Starr, Barbara Bach, John Matuszak, Shelley Long, Dennis Quaid. **1981**

•CAVEMAN'S VALENTINE, THE ★★★★1/2 A homeless urban psychotic (Samuel L. Jackson) investigates the death of a frozen corpse found near his Central Park cave. A unique and compelling combination of a cleverly plotted murder mystery and an examination of schizophrenia from inside and out, with a tour-de-force performance by Jackson. Rated R for profanity, sexual scenes, and brief violence. 105m. **DIR:** Kasi Lemmons. **CAST:** Samuel L. Jackson, Colm Feore, Ann Magnuson, Damir Andrei, Aunjanue Ellis. **2001 DVD**

CB4 ★★ This attempt to parody the rap music industry has some very funny moments, but overall it fails as a satire and becomes a silly sex comedy full of profanity and misogyny. Rated R for violence, profanity, and nudity. 88m. **DIR:** Tamra Davis. **CAST:** Chris Rock, Allen Payne, Deezer D, Phil Hartman, Art Evans, Theresa Randle, Willard E. Pugh, Richard Gant, Charlie Murphy, Chris Elliott. **1993**

C.C. & COMPANY ★★1/2 Basically idiotic action film has Broadway Joe Namath (in his first feature) cast as C.C. Ryder, misfit member of a rowdy biker gang, attempting to "split" when he falls for top fashion photographer Ann-Margret. Rated R for mild language and nudity. 90m. **DIR:** Seymour Robbie. **CAST:** Joe Namath, Ann-Margret, William Smith, Sid Haig, Jennifer Billingsley, Greg Mullavey. **1970**

CEASE FIRE ★★★1/2 An answer to the comic book–style heroism of *Rambo* and the *Missing in Action* movies, *Cease Fire* is a heartfelt, well-acted, and touching drama about the aftereffects of Vietnam and the battle still being fought by some veterans. Don Johnson stars as Tim Murphy, a veteran whose life begins to crumble after fifteen years of valiant effort at fitting back into society. Rated R for profanity and violence. 97m. **DIR:** David Nutter. **CAST:** Don Johnson, Lisa Blount, Robert F. Lyons, Richard Chaves, Chris Noel. **1985**

CECIL B. DEMENTED 🦃 Guerilla filmmaker Cecil and his renegade rainbow-coalition cronies kidnap a bitchy, foul-mouthed starlet at gunpoint from a movie premiere and force her to participate in a cinematic rant against All Things Hollywood. The funniest element of this crude satire is its title. Rated R for profanity, violence, and sexual situations. 87m. **DIR:** John Waters. **CAST:** Stephen Dorff, Melanie Griffith, Alicia Witt, Adrian Grenier, Maggie Gyllenhaal, Eric M. Barry. **2000 DVD**

CEILING ZERO ★★★★ Once again, director Howard Hawks focuses on a group of professionals: pilots battling thick fog and crude ground-to-air communications to get the mail through. Cocky flier James Cagney joins old friend Pat O'Brien's crew only to neglect his duties in favor of seducing a fellow flier June Travis. Fast-paced and riveting; one of the finest of the Cagney-O'Brien teamings. B&W; 95m. **DIR:** Howard Hawks. **CAST:** James Cagney, Pat O'Brien, June Travis, Stu Erwin, Barton MacLane, Isabel Jewell. **1935**

CELEBRATING BIRD: THE TRIUMPH OF CHARLIE PARKER ★★★★ Fascinating documentary that chronicles jazz legend Charlie Parker's career through interviews and live performances. Parker, nicknamed Bird, created a new style of jazz before his untimely death at 34. Other jazz greats—Dizzy Gillespie, Charles Mingus, and Thelonius Monk—add to the pleasure. 58m. **DIR:** Gary Giddins, Kendrick Simmons. **CAST:** Charlie Parker. **1987 DVD**

CELEBRATION, THE ★★1/2 A Danish clan gathers for the patriarch's sixtieth birthday party—and if you can't guess what "shocking" secrets will come out, then you probably haven't seen many dysfunctional-family-reunion pictures lately. The film has the novelty of its documentary style (shot on video with available light) to compensate for trite characters and monotonous predictability. In Danish with English subtitles. Rated R for profanity and sexual scenes. 101m. **DIR:** Thomas Vinterberg. **CAST:** Ulrich Thomsen, Henning Moritzen, Thomas Bo Larsen, Paprika Steen. **1998 DVD**

CELEBRITY (1984) ★★★1/2 Three high school buddies go too far on a drunken binge, with one of them raping a country girl. This crime binds the three as they go on with their lives. Each gains fame in a different medium (writing, acting, and preaching). Twenty-five years later, they're reunited in a highly publicized trial. This sudsy TV miniseries will have you glued to your set. 313m. **DIR:** Paul Wendkos. **CAST:** Michael Beck, Joseph Bottoms, Ben Masters. **1984**

CELEBRITY (1998) ★★1/2 In trendy Manhattan, a journalist (Kenneth Branagh) skids down the ladder of fame while his neurotic ex-wife (Judy Davis) climbs up. The black-and-white photography is the tip-off that writer-director Woody Allen is on his high horse again, making sour jokes about the shallowness of celebrity worship. Many stars do cute little two-scene bits, like guests at a show-biz party taking turns entertaining. Rated R for profanity. B&W; 114m. **DIR:** Woody Allen. **CAST:** Kenneth Branagh, Judy Davis, Charlize Theron, Leonardo DiCaprio, Famke Janssen, Winona Ryder. **1998 DVD**

CELESTE ★★ Ponderously pedestrian, spasmodically amusing and touching, this tale concerns the blooming fondness between the author Marcel Proust and his maid, who says of him, "At times I feel like his mother, and at times his child." This movie is historically interesting, but ultimately bleak and lackluster. In German with English subtitles. Not rated. 107m. **DIR:** Percy Adlon. **CAST:** Eva Mattes, Jurgen Arndt. **1981**

CELESTIAL CLOCKWORK ★★1/2 This comic Cinderella story about a Venezuelan opera singer who moves to France to become a movie musical star is alternately charming and dull. In a mix of old-fashioned storytelling, performance art, and fantasy, immigrant Ana is tricked by a jealous roommate and prevented from meeting an opera producer. Ana's teacher, a clairvoyant gay waiter, and a lesbian psychoanalyst conspire to secure her an audition. In French and Spanish with English subtitles. Not rated, but appropriate for adults. 86m. **DIR:** Fina Torres. **CAST:** Ariadna Gil, Arielle Dombasle, Evelyne Didi, Frederic Longbois, Lluis Homar. **1996**

CELIA, CHILD OF TERROR ★★★ Misleadingly promoted on video as a horror movie (the original title was simply *Celia*), this Australian import is about a 9 year old girl having trouble adjusting to life in a conservative suburb after her beloved grandmother dies. Not rated, but not suitable for young children. 110m. **DIR:** Ann Turner. **CAST:** Rebecca Smart. **1989**

CELINE AND JULIE GO BOATING ★★★★★ Described by one critic as "the most important film since *Citizen Kane*," this entertaining movie succeeds both as an intellectual inquiry (into the nature of fiction) and as sheer cinematic fun. Two women—a librarian and a magician—visit a mysterious house only to forget what they observed every time they leave. As they gradually reconstruct the story, they realize that a little girl is in danger within. In French with English subtitles. 192m. **DIR:** Jacques Rivette. **CAST:** Dominique Labourier, Juliet Berto, Bulle Ogier, Marie-France Pisier, Barbet Schroeder. **1974**

CELL, THE ★★★1/2 A child psychologist uses experimental technology to probe the mind of a comatose serial killer in the hopes of saving his final victim. An introductory set piece orients the viewer for the surreal scenes to come by creating the dream/inner-mind landscape of a young boy in a coma, then plunging us into the bizarre, threatening world of the twisted villian. Well-crafted suspense and strong acting also help sustain our suspension of disbelief. Rated R for violence, profanity, nudity, and sexual images. 107m. **DIR:** Tarsem Singh. **CAST:** Jennifer Lopez, Vince Vaughn, Vincent D'Onofrio, Marianne Jean-Baptiste, Dylan

Baker, Jake Weber, James Gammon, Pruitt Taylor Vince. **2000 DVD**

CELLAR, THE ★★★ An ancient Indian demon, called upon to rid the world of the white man, resides in the basement of a rural farmhouse. When a young boy comes to visit his divorced father, no one believes his story about the hideous creature. A relatively scary monster movie directed by the man who brought us the wonderful *Night of the Demons.* Rated PG-13 for violence. 90m. **DIR:** Kevin S. Tenney. **CAST:** Patrick Kilpatrick, Suzanne Savoy, Ford Rainey. **1990**

CELLAR DWELLER 🦃 Typical junk about a hideous, satanic monster. Not rated; contains violence. 78m. **DIR:** John Carl Buechler. **CAST:** Deborah Mullowney, Vince Edwards, Yvonne De Carlo. **1987**

CELLULOID CLOSET, THE ★★★★ Oscar-nominated documentary about the portrayal of homosexuals and lesbians in film history is charming and informative on any level. It's a feast of clips for film buffs, with thoughtful narration (written by Armistead Maupin, read by Lily Tomlin) and illuminating commentary by a variety of writers, actors, and filmmakers (Harvey Fierstein, Paul Rudnick, Susan Sarandon, Tom Hanks, Arthur Laurents, etc). Rated R for mature themes. B&W/color; 102m. **DIR:** Robert Epstein, Jeffrey Friedman. **1995**

CELTIC PRIDE ★★★ During the NBA play-offs, two fanatical followers of the Boston Celtics, Daniel Stern and Dan Aykroyd, accidentally kidnap Damon Wayans, the star player from the opposing Utah Jazz team. While never laugh-out-loud funny, this comedy does have its moments, thanks to fine character turns from the stars. Rated PG-13 for humorous violence and profanity. 90m. **DIR:** Tom DeCerchio. **CAST:** Daniel Stern, Damon Wayans, Dan Aykroyd, Gail O'Grady, Adam Hendershott, Paul Guilfoyle. **1996**

CEMENT GARDEN, THE ★★ This oddball little film is definitely not for everyone. Four children in working-class England find themselves suddenly orphaned and, to avoid being separated, the kids bury Mama's corpse in concrete in the basement. Sixteen year old Jack (Andrew Robertson) has decidedly unbrotherly feelings about his nubile older sister (Charlotte Gainsbourg). It's dreary, spiritless, and extremely ugly to look at. Not rated; contains profanity, incest, and other sexual activity. 101m. **DIR:** Andrew Birkin. **CAST:** Andrew Robertson, Charlotte Gainsbourg, Sinead Cusack, Alice Coulthard, Ned Birkin. **1993 DVD**

CEMETERY CLUB, THE ★★★1/2 Ellen Burstyn, Olympia Dukakis, and Diane Ladd are excellent as three widows who have trouble adjusting to life without their husbands. Screenwriter Ivan Menehell, who penned the original play, is not entirely successful in translating his snappy bits of stage repartee into screen action. Rated PG-13 for profanity. 107m. **DIR:** Bill Duke. **CAST:** Ellen Burstyn, Olympia Dukakis, Diane Ladd, Danny Aiello, Lainie Kazan, Jeff Howell, Christina Ricci, Bernie Casey, Wallace Shawn. **1993**

CEMETERY HIGH 🦃 This is one high school you won't want to attend. Not rated; contains violence, nudity, gore, and simulated sex. 80m. **DIR:** Gorman Bechard. **CAST:** Debi Thibeault. **1987**

CENTER OF THE WEB 🦃 Threadbare plot about an undercover agent for the Justice Department who's framed for the assassination of a state governor. Rated R for violence, nudity, and profanity. 90m. **DIR:** David A. Prior. **CAST:** Ted Prior, Tony Curtis, Charlene Tilton, Robert Davi, Bo Hopkins, Charles Napier. **1992**

•CENTER OF THE WORLD, THE 🦃 Stripper Florence takes her show on the road when an infatuated dot-com millionaire offers her ten grand to spend three days with him in Las Vegas in a drama that pretentiously explores laptop culture, self-deception, erotic fantasy, and muted human emotions. Not rated; contains profanity, nudity, and graphic sexual content. 86m. **DIR:** Wayne Wang. **CAST:** Molly Parker, Peter Sarsgaard, Carla Gugino. **2001 DVD**

CENTER STAGE ★★1/2 This film, which spotlights the ballet world, is something of a mess, from the stereotypic characters to the mix of classical scores with bubblegum pop tunes. Although the picture deserves credit for casting actual dancers and showcasing their athletic grace, the script lacks pizzazz. Rated PG-13 for profanity and sexual candor. 113m. **DIR:** Nicholas Hytner. **CAST:** Amanda Schull, Zoe Saldana, Susan May Pratt, Peter Gallagher, Donna Murphy, Debra Monk, Ethan Stiefel. **2000 DVD**

CENTERFOLD GIRLS 🦃 Insane brute spends his time killing beautiful, exotic models. Rated R. 93m. **DIR:** John Peyser. **CAST:** Andrew Prine, Tiffany Bolling, Aldo Ray, Ray Danton, Jeremy Slate. **1974**

CENTRAL STATION ★★★1/2 A crusty old woman in Rio de Janeiro finds herself saddled with an orphan boy. When she reluctantly agrees to escort him cross-country to find his father, her maternal instincts come unbidden to the surface. This foreign-language variation on John Cassavetes's *Gloria* is predictable but well acted by the two principals, with a fascinating look at parts of Brazil tourists seldom see. In Portuguese with English subtitles. Rated R for profanity (in subtitles). 115m. **DIR:** Walter Salles Jr. **CAST:** Fernanda Montenegro, Vincius de Oliveira, Marilia Pera, Soia Lira. **1998 DVD**

CENTURY ★★★★ Luscious turn-of-the-century drama set in London. Clive Owen is excellent as an idealistic doctor on the verge of a major breakthrough concerning diabetes. Robert Stephens is his mentor, a seasoned doctor who is threatened. Miranda Richardson shines as the lab assistant who stands by the young doctor's side. Gorgeous scenery and excellent production values take us back to a time and place that no longer exists. Not rated. 115m. **DIR:** Stephen Poliakoff. **CAST:** Miranda Richardson, Charles Dance, Clive Owen, Robert Stephens. **1993**

•CEREMONY 🦃 College students are trapped in a mansion with a demon from hell in this amateurish horror movie that will have you rooting for the demon to kill them just so the movie will end sooner. Not rated; contains horror violence. 74m. **DIR:** Joe Castro. **CAST:** Steven R. Diebold, Amy Rohren, Emilie Talbot, Forrest J. Ackerman. **1994**

CERTAIN FURY 🦃 Tatum O'Neal is Scarlet ("Scar")—a dumb white street woman; Irene Cara is Tracy—a dumb pampered black woman. They're thrown together and run for their lives from police and drug dealers. Rated R for violence. 87m. **DIR:** Stephen Gyllenhaal. **CAST:** Tatum O'Neal, Irene Cara, Nicholas Campbell, George Murdock, Moses Gunn, Peter Fonda. **1985**

CÉSAR ★★★★1/2 The final and best part of the Marseilles trilogy that includes *Marius* and *Fanny*. You can watch it on its own, but you won't enjoy it nearly as much unless you see all three parts: the cumulative effect is resoundingly emotional. In French with English subtitles. B&W; 117m. **DIR:** Marcel Pagnol. **CAST:** Raimu, Orane Demazis, Pierre Fresnay. **1933**

CÉSAR AND ROSALIE ★★★1/2 Beautifully orchestrated story of human passion about a woman (Romy Schneider) and her relationship with two lovers over a period of years. Excellent cast and a subtle screenplay and direction give strength to this comedy-drama. In French with English subtitles. Not rated. 104m. **DIR:** Claude Sautet. **CAST:** Yves Montand, Romy Schneider, Sami Frey, Umberto Orsini, Eva Marie Meineke. **1972**

CHAIN, THE ★★★ Obsessed American cop Gary Busey loses his job while pursuing gunrunner Victor Rivers, who leads our hero on a merry chase in the wilds of Central America. Alas, both men are captured by brutish soldiers, and the film turns into a modern echo of *The Defiant Ones*. Better than average for this sort of stuff. Rated R for profanity and violence. 96m. **DIR:** Luca Bercovici. **CAST:** Gary Busey, Victor Rivers, Rez Cortez, Joonee Gamboa, Craig Judd, James Rose. **1996**

CHAIN LIGHTNING ★★ A slow-moving story about a World War II veteran who volunteers to test-fly a new jet during peacetime. But Bogart isn't the type to play a wimp, so the movie is not very credible. B&W; 94m. **DIR:** Stuart Heisler. **CAST:** Humphrey Bogart, Eleanor Parker, Raymond Massey, Richard Whorf, James Brown, Fay Baker, Morris Ankrum. **1950**

CHAIN OF COMMAND (1993) 🦃 Mindless violence as an ex–Green Beret witnesses a war crime and is then forced to take on his superiors when they try to quiet him. Rated R for violence, nudity, and adult language. 98m. **DIR:** David Worth. **CAST:** Michael Dudikoff, Todd Curtis, Keren Tishman, R. Lee Ermey. **1993**

CHAIN OF COMMAND (2000) ★★ Tiresome low-budget rehash of a dozen other presidential thrillers we've seen in the past. Patrick Muldoon wanders aimlessly as a Secret Service agent assigned to protect the attaché case that contains the president's nuclear-attack button. The action escalates when other factions display an interest in the case. Good actors trapped in a bad idea. Rated R for language and violence. 96m. **DIR:** John Terlesky. **CAST:** Roy Scheider, Patrick Muldoon, Michael Biehn, Maria Conchita Alonso. **2000 DVD**

CHAIN OF DESIRE 🦃 Intended as a message film about AIDS, this fails to engage or involve the viewer on any level. The film consists of just one sexual encounter after another. Not rated; contains profanity, sex, and drug use. 107m. **DIR:** Temistocles Lopez. **CAST:** Linda Fiorentino, Elias Koteas, Malcolm McDowell, Tim Guinee, Grace Zabriskie. **1993**

CHAIN REACTION (1980) ★★★ Engrossing drama following a nuclear power plant employee (Ross Thompson) accidentally exposed to a lethal dose of radiation during a near meltdown. Rated R for some explicit sex, nudity, and violence. 87m. **DIR:** Ian Barry, George Miller. **CAST:** Steve Bisley, Anna-Maria Winchester. **1980**

CHAIN REACTION (1996) ★★★ When water is proven to be a clean source of energy via some inventive technology, the dark forces of the capitalistic status quo move in, leaving the scientists working on the project either dead or on the run from the authorities. Star Keanu Reeves doesn't bring this one quite up to *Speed*, but it's diverting enough as an evening's viewing. Rated PG-13 for profanity and violence. 106m. **DIR:** Andrew Davis. **CAST:** Keanu Reeves, Morgan Freeman, Rachel Weisz, Fred Ward, Kevin Dunn, Brian Cox, Joanna Cassidy, Chelcie Ross. **1996 DVD**

CHAINED ★★★ A typical potboiler from the 1930s that still radiates the vibes between Clark Gable and Joan Crawford. In this one he plays a macho South American rancher. The swimming scene with Gable and Crawford has as much sex appeal as an R-rated movie without nudity, just knowing looks. B&W; 75m. **DIR:** Clarence Brown. **CAST:** Clark Gable, Joan Crawford, Otto Kruger, Stu Erwin, Mickey Rooney, Akim Tamiroff, Una O'Connor. **1934**

CHAINED FOR LIFE 🦃 This murder drama featuring Siamese twins Daisy and Violet Hilton is certainly one of the saddest and most exploitative feature films of all. Cheap and embarrassing, this tawdry attempt to cash in on a physical deformity is long, boring, and in terrible taste. B&W; 81m. **DIR:** Harry Fraser. **CAST:** Daisy Hilton, Violet Hilton. **1951**

CHAINED HEAT 🦃 The story of women in prison, this cheapo offers few surprises. Rated R. 95m. **DIR:** Paul Nicholas. **CAST:** Linda Blair, John Vernon, Nita Talbot, Stella Stevens, Sybil Danning, Tamara Dobson. **1983 DVD**

CHAINS 🦃 Schmaltzy clone of the cult favorite *The Warriors*. Violence and seminudity. 93m. **DIR:** Roger J. Barski. **CAST:** Jimi Jourdan. **1990**

CHAINS OF GOLD ★★★1/2 A crusading social worker combs Los Angeles to find a young friend kidnapped by a particularly nasty drug-running street gang. The somewhat chaotic script comes from four hands (including John Travolta's), but director Rod Holcomb maintains a snappy pace that circumvents a few glaring inconsistencies. Made for cable; rated R for language and violence. 95m. **DIR:** Rod Holcomb. **CAST:** John Travolta, Marilu Henner, Bernie Casey, Hector Elizondo, Joey Lawrence. **1991 DVD**

CHAIR, THE ★★1/2 Atmospheric movie about a psychologist (James Coco) who sets up shop in an abandoned prison and runs tests on a select group of inmates. More spooky than scary. Rated R for profanity, violence, and gore. 94m. **DIR:** Waldemar Korzenioswsky. **CAST:** James Coco, Trini Alvarado, Paul Benedict, John Bentley, Stephen Geoffreys. **1989**

CHAIRMAN OF THE BOARD 🦃 Wacky prop comedian Carrot Top tries to weave his high-energy live act into a lame comedy about a surf geek and inventor who inherits a corporation. Rated PG-13 for language and sex-related humor. 95m. **DIR:** Alex Zamm. **CAST:** Carrot Top (Scott Thompson), Jack Warden, Raquel Welch, Larry Miller, Courtney Thorne-Smith, Estelle Harris, Mystro Clark, Jack Plotnick, M. Emmet Walsh. **1998 DVD**

CHALK GARDEN, THE ★★★ Adapted from the play of the same name by Enid Bagnold. The plot centers around a spoiled brat (Hayley Mills) who is the bane of her grandmother's (Edith Evans) life until she is made to see the light of day by the new governess (Deborah Kerr). Sensational acting all around. 106m. **DIR:**

Ronald Neame. **CAST:** Deborah Kerr, Edith Evans, Hayley Mills, John Mills, Elizabeth Sellars. **1964**

CHALLENGE, THE ★★★1/2 An American (Scott Glenn) gets caught in the middle of a decades-old private war between two brothers in modern-day Japan. This movie has ample rewards for both samurai film aficionados and regular moviegoers. Rated R for profanity and violence. 112m. **DIR:** John Frankenheimer. **CAST:** Scott Glenn, Toshiro Mifune, Calvin Young. **1982**

CHALLENGE OF A LIFETIME ★★★ A depressed middle-aged woman decides to pick herself up by training for the Hawaiian Ironman competition. Worth seeing for the always-fun Penny Marshall and underground star Mary Woronov in a rare TV appearance. Not rated; contains no objectionable material. 95m. **DIR:** Russ Mayberry. **CAST:** Penny Marshall, Richard Gilliland, Mary Woronov, Jonathan Silverman, Paul Gleason, Cathy Rigby, Mark Spitz. **1985**

CHALLENGE TO BE FREE ★★ This forgettable film features a fur trapper being chased across one thousand miles of frozen Arctic wasteland by twelve men and one hundred dogs. Rated G. 88m. **DIR:** Tay Garnett, Ford Beebe. **CAST:** Mike Mazurki, Vic Christy, Jimmy Kane. **1974**

CHALLENGE TO LASSIE ★★ A Disney-type fable rewritten to suit Lassie at the height of her fame. The Disney remake (*Greyfriar's Bobby*) is more believable and better suited to family tastes. This one is strictly for Lassie buffs. 76m. **DIR:** Richard Thorpe. **CAST:** Edmund Gwenn, Donald Crisp, Alan Webb, Alan Napier, Henry Stephenson, Sara Allgood, Geraldine Brooks, Reginald Owen. **1949**

CHALLENGE TO WHITE FANG 🦃 White Fang is a German shepherd running loose in the Yukon trying to stop crooks from cheating an old man out of his gold mine. Not rated. 89m. **DIR:** Lucio Fulci. **CAST:** Franco Nero, Virna Lisi, Harry Carey Jr. **1986**

CHALLENGERS, THE ★★★1/2 Strong coming-of-age drama about a young girl, terrifically played by Gema Zamprogna, addresses important issues about growing up without seeming preachy. After her father dies, and she's forced to move to a small town, Mackie (Zamprogna) decides that the only way to fit into a local group of boys is to become one of them. Her masquerade works, but provides complications that force her to realize her own self-worth. Girls and boys alike will enjoy Mackie's adventures and realizations. Rated PG. 97m. **DIR:** Eric Till. **CAST:** Gema Zamprogna, Eric Christmas, Gwynyth Walsh. **1993**

•CHAMBER, THE ★★★1/2 Overly lengthy books sometimes play better on the big screen, where a taut script can pare down the excess wordage and cut to the chase. That's certainly the case with this adaptation of John Grisham's book, which turns on the unlikely notion that a newly minted young lawyer would be assigned to get his unapologetically racist uncle off death row. The drama comes from the character interplay; the actual "surprise" in the narrative really doesn't amount to much . . . nor is it terribly surprising. Rated R for profanity and violent images. 113m. **DIR:** James Foley. **CAST:** Chris O'Donnell, Gene Hackman, Faye Dunaway, Robert Prosky, Raymond J. Barry, David Marshall Grant. **1996 DVD**

CHAMBER OF FEAR 🦃 Another of the Mexican films featuring footage of Boris Karloff shot in Los Angeles just before his death (see *Sinister Invasion*). 87m. **DIR:** Juan Ibanez, Jack Hill. **CAST:** Boris Karloff. **1968**

CHAMBER OF HORRORS (1940) ★★1/2 Breezy British thriller about a mysterious crypt and the search for the keys to unlock its secrets. Popular melodrama penned by Edgar Wallace boasts a torture chamber as well as a spooky mansion complete with creepy servants and all the trimmings. Fun but familiar fare. B&W; 80m. **DIR:** Norman Lee. **CAST:** Lilli Palmer, Leslie Banks, Romilly Lange, Gina Malo. **1940 DVD**

CHAMBER OF HORRORS (1966) ★★1/2 A mad killer stalks 1880s Baltimore. Two wax-museum owners attempt to bring him to justice. Originally produced as a television pilot titled *House of Wax*, but it was considered too violent. Tame and silly. 99m. **DIR:** Hy Averback. **CAST:** Patrick O'Neal, Cesare Danova, Wilfrid Hyde-White, Suzy Parker, Tony Curtis, Jeanette Nolan. **1966**

CHAMBERMAID ON THE TITANIC, THE ★★1/2 To get even with the wife he thinks has been unfaithful, a French coal miner invents a one-night stand with a maid from the *Titanic* the night before its ill-fated voyage. The tale grows in the telling, making him a sort of celebrity—until the chambermaid turns up alive. In French with English subtitles. Not rated; contains mature themes and sexual situations. 96m. **DIR:** Bigas Luna. **CAST:** Olivier Martinez, Romane Bohringer, Aitana Sanchez-Gijon. **1997**

CHAMELEON (1995) ★★1/2 Latter-day "super cop" outing involving a revenge-obsessed DEA agent (Anthony LaPaglia) who's a master of disguise. His superiors unwittingly help him out when they assign him to bust a drug cartel—whose head just happens to be responsible for the murder of the lawman's wife and child. LaPaglia has a field day in the central role, but the film's plot is just a bit too derivative. Rated R for violence. 108m. **DIR:** Michael Pavone. **CAST:** Anthony LaPaglia, Kevin Pollak, Wayne Knight, Melora Hardin, Derek McGrath, Andy Romano, Robin Thomas, Richard Brooks. **1995**

CHAMELEON (1998) ★★1/2 Cheesy sci-fi actioner about an androidlike warrior battling the evil corporations. Entertaining if not outstanding. Rated R for nudity, sexual situations, violence, and profanity. 90m. **DIR:** Stuart Cooper. **CAST:** Bobbie Phillips, Eric Lloyd, John Adam. **1998**

CHAMELEON III: DARK ANGEL ★★ This third entry in UPN's science-fiction series once again stars Bobbie Phillips as the superhero Kam, who uses her special powers to save a young genius from the dark forces. Phillips shows more depth this outing, but the production values and script are meager and unforgiving. Rated R. 87m. **DIR:** John Lafia. **CAST:** Bobbie Phillips, Doug Penty, Suzi Dougherty. **2000**

CHAMELEON STREET ★★★★ *Chameleon Street* is not an address; he's a man: a real-life Detroit imposter named William Douglas Street. And this quirky, entertaining film tells his story. A fascinating, offbeat screen portrait by writer-director-star Wendell B. Harris Jr., it details how Street successively poses as a *Time* magazine reporter, a physician who actually performs surgery, an attorney who befriends Detroit Mayor Coleman Young, a foreign-exchange college student from France, and other purely bogus individuals. Rated R. 98m. **DIR:** Wendell B. Harris Jr. **CAST:** Wendell B. Harris Jr. **1989**

CHAMP, THE (1931) ★★★★ Wallace Beery is at his absolute best in the Oscar-winning title role of this tearjerker, about a washed-up fighter and his adoring son (Jackie Cooper) who are separated against their will. King Vidor manages to make even the hokiest bits of hokum work in this four-hankie feast of sentimentality. B&W; 87m. **DIR:** King Vidor. **CAST:** Wallace Beery, Jackie Cooper, Irene Rich. **1931**

CHAMP, THE (1979) ★★★1/2 This remake is a first-class tearjerker. Billy Flynn (Voight), a former boxing champion, works in the backstretch at Hialeah when not drinking or gambling away his money. His son, T.J. (Schroder), calls him "Champ" and tells all his friends about his father's comeback, which never seems to happen. Rated PG. 121m. **DIR:** Franco Zeffirelli. **CAST:** Jon Voight, Faye Dunaway, Rick Schroder, Jack Warden. **1979**

CHAMPAGNE 🦃 Alfred Hitchcock regarded this silent feature as one of his worst films, and who are we to disagree? B&W; 69m. **DIR:** Alfred Hitchcock. **CAST:** Betty Balfour, Gordon Harker. **1928**

CHAMPAGNE FOR CAESAR ★★★★ Satire of early television and the concept of game shows is funnier now than when it was originally released. A treasure trove of trivia and great one-liners, this intelligent spoof features actor Ronald Colman as Beauregarde Bottomley, self-proclaimed genius and scholar who exacts his revenge on soap tycoon Vincent Price by appearing on his quiz show and attempting to bankrupt his company by winning all their assets. B&W; 99m. **DIR:** Richard Whorf. **CAST:** Ronald Colman, Celeste Holm, Vincent Price, Barbara Britton, Art Linkletter. **1950**

CHAMPAGNE SAFARI, THE ★★★1/2 Fascinating documentary about Charles Bedaux, one of the world's richest men in the 1930s. This film is built around the footage of a lavish "safari" he took through the Canadian Rockies in a fleet of Citroëns bearing all the luxuries he and his party could want. (He even hired Oscar-winning cinematographer Floyd Crosby to film it.) B&W/color; 100m. **DIR:** George Ungar. **1995**

CHAMPION ★★★★ One of Hollywood's better efforts about the fight game. Kirk Douglas is a young boxer whose climb to the top is accomplished while forsaking his friends and family. He gives one of his best performances in an unsympathetic role. B&W; 100m. **DIR:** Mark Robson. **CAST:** Kirk Douglas, Arthur Kennedy, Ruth Roman. **1949 DVD**

CHAMPIONS ★★★★ The touching true story of English steeplechase jockey Bob Champion (John Hurt), who fought a desperate battle against cancer to win the 1981 Grand National. Rated PG. 113m. **DIR:** John Irvin. **CAST:** John Hurt, Edward Woodward, Jan Francis, Ben Johnson. **1984 DVD**

CHAN IS MISSING ★★★★ In this delightful independent production, filmed in San Francisco's Chinatown, two cab drivers attempt to track down a friend who disappeared after they gave him $5,000 to purchase a taxi license. Although in form a mystery, this comedy is also a gentle jab at racial stereotypes and a revealing study of problems faced by members of the Asian-American community. Not rated, the film has some profanity. 81m. **DIR:** Wayne Wang. **CAST:** Wood Moy, Marc Hayashi. **1982**

CHANCES ARE ★★★1/2 In this derivative but generally charming romantic comedy, a surprisingly effective Robert Downey Jr. plays the reincarnated soul of Cybill Shepherd's husband (Christopher McDonald). Downey has retained a dormant memory of his past life. It returns during a visit to Shepherd's home just as he is about to seduce "their" daughter (Mary Stuart Masterson). It's good silly fun from then on—even if you've seen *Here Comes Mr. Jordan* or *Heaven Can Wait*. Rated PG for mild profanity. 108m. **DIR:** Emile Ardolino. **CAST:** Cybill Shepherd, Robert Downey Jr., Ryan O'Neal, Mary Stuart Masterson, Christopher McDonald, Josef Sommer. **1989 DVD**

CHANDU THE MAGICIAN ★★1/2 Stylishly produced and full of exotic sets, sleight of hand, and special effects, this imaginative fantasy suffers from a stolid performance by Edmund Lowe. Bela Lugosi, however, is in rare form as the gleefully maniacal Roxor, master of the black arts. An enjoyable curiosity. B&W; 70m. **DIR:** William Cameron Menzies, Marcel Varnel. **CAST:** Edmund Lowe, Bela Lugosi, Irene Ware, Henry B. Walthall. **1932**

CHANEL SOLITAIRE ★★ This halfhearted rendering of the rise to prominence of French designer Coco Chanel (played by fragile Marie-France Pisier) is long on sap and short on plot. For the terminally romantic only. Rated R. 120m. **DIR:** George Kaczender. **CAST:** Marie-France Pisier, Timothy Dalton, Rutger Hauer, Karen Black, Brigitte Fossey. **1981**

CHANG ★★★★ "Chang" means elephant, and in this remarkable pseudo-documentary by the explorers-filmmakers who later teamed to make *King Kong*, the threat of a rampaging herd of the beasts looms over daily life among villagers in primitive Thailand. This is a restored version, from first-rate source prints, of one of the most vivid location adventures of its day. B&W; 67m. **DIR:** Merian C. Cooper, Ernest B. Schoedsack. **1927 DVD**

CHANGE OF HABIT ★★ In direct contrast to the many comedy-musicals that Elvis Presley starred in, this drama offers a more substantial plot. Elvis plays a doctor helping the poor in his clinic. Mary Tyler Moore plays a nun who is tempted to leave the order to be with Elvis. Rated G. 93m. **DIR:** William A. Graham. **CAST:** Elvis Presley, Mary Tyler Moore, Barbara McNair, Jane Elliot, Edward Asner. **1970**

CHANGE OF SEASONS, A 🦃 Poor Shirley MacLaine. The only difference between this and *Loving Couples*, which closely followed it into release, is that Anthony Hopkins and Bo Derek costar as the ultramodern mate swappers. Rated R. 102m. **DIR:** Richard Lang. **CAST:** Shirley MacLaine, Anthony Hopkins, Bo Derek, Michael Brandon. **1980**

CHANGELING, THE ★★★★ This ghost story is blessed with everything a good thriller needs: a suspenseful story, excellent performances by a top-name cast, and well-paced solid direction by Peter Medak. The story centers around a composer whose wife and daughter are killed in a tragic auto accident. Rated R. 109m. **DIR:** Peter Medak. **CAST:** George C. Scott, Trish Van Devere, Melvyn Douglas, Jean Marsh, Barry Morse. **1979 DVD**

CHANGING HABITS ★★1/2 Estranged from her father, an aspiring young artist supports herself by shoplifting art supplies and working at a nunnery in exchange for room and board. That this character is more appealing than obnoxious is due to the charms of star Moira Kelly. Rated R for profanity and sexual situations. 92m. **DIR:** Lynn Roth. **CAST:** Moira Kelly, Christopher Lloyd, Dylan Walsh, Eileen Brennan, Teri Garr, Shelley Duvall, Frances Bay, Anne Haney, Taylor Negron, Annabelle Gurwitch. **1997 DVD**

•CHANGING LANES ★★1/2 Recovering alcoholic New York businessman scrapes car fenders with an arrogant upscale Manhattan attorney during rush hour and begins a feud that threatens to ruin the personal, financial, and professional lives of both men. This spotty Wall Street thriller fails to launch into white-knuckle orbit as it explores themes about corporate ethics, greed, corruption, and our vulnerability to determined evil. The film's *Falling Down* projectile is weakened by unconvincing character arcs. Rated R for language. 100m. **DIR:** Roger Michell. **CAST:** Ben Affleck, Samuel L. Jackson, Toni Collette, William Hurt, Sydney Pollack, Amanda Peet, Dylan Baker. **2002 DVD**

CHANTILLY LACE ★★★1/2 This modern spin on Clare Boothe's *The Women* gets considerable mileage from its high-octane ensemble cast but ultimately disappoints because of its improvisational nature. Director-coplotter Linda Yellen encouraged her seven stars to develop their own dialogue but failed to provide enough structure. It's entertaining to watch these ladies discuss men, relationships, and jobs, but the third act is self-indulgently maudlin. Rated R for profanity, brief nudity, simulated sex. 105m. **DIR:** Linda Yellen. **CAST:** Lindsay Crouse, Jill Eikenberry, Martha Plimpton, Ally Sheedy, Talia Shire, Helen Slater, JoBeth Williams. **1993**

CHAPAYEV ★★★ Although this was obviously designed as propaganda for the Bolshevik revolution, it is still well-made and entertaining, with a minimum of proselytizing. The film follows the overthrow of the czar from the point of view of Chapayev, a Russian general. In Russian with English subtitles. B&W; 95m. **DIR:** Sergei Vasiliev, Georgi Vasiliev. **CAST:** Boris Bobochkin. **1934**

CHAPLIN ★★★1/2 Richard Attenborough takes almost a scandal-sheet approach in this bio-pic of Charlie Chaplin, forgetting what made Chaplin so important was the movies he made. Worth seeing for Robert Downey Jr.'s impersonation of Chaplin. Rated PG-13 for profanity and nudity. 145m. **DIR:** Richard Attenborough. **CAST:** Robert Downey Jr., Dan Aykroyd, Geraldine Chaplin, Kevin Dunn, Anthony Hopkins, Milla Jovovich, Moira Kelly, Kevin Kline, Diane Lane, Penelope Ann Miller, Paul Rhys, John Thaw, Marisa Tomei, Nancy Travis, James Woods. **1992 DVD**

CHAPLIN REVUE, THE ★★★★ Assembled and scored by Charlie Chaplin for release in 1959, this revue is composed of three of his longer, more complex and polished films: *A Dog's Life*, which established Chaplin's reputation as a satirist; *Shoulder Arms*, a model for *The Great Dictator*; and *The Pilgrim*, in which escaped convict Chaplin assumes the garb of a minister. B&W; 121m. **DIR:** Charles Chaplin. **CAST:** Charlie Chaplin, Edna Purviance, Tom Wilson, Sydney Chaplin. **1959**

CHAPTER TWO ★★★1/2 Writer Neil Simon examines the problems that arise when a recently widowed author courts and marries a recently divorced actress. George Schneider (James Caan) is recovering from the death of his wife when he strikes up a whirlwind courtship with actress Jennie MacLaine (Marsha Mason). They get married, but George is tormented by the memory of his first, beloved wife. Rated PG. 124m. **DIR:** Robert Moore. **CAST:** James Caan, Marsha Mason, Valerie Harper, Joseph Bologna. **1979**

CHARACTER (KARAKTER) ★★★ In 1920s Rotterdam, a young man struggles to succeed against both the stigma of his illegitimate birth and the machinations of his biological father, a heartless, petty government official. This 1997 Oscar winner for best foreign film has relentless pacing, attractive actors, and handsome cinematography to recommend it, but the melodrama is rather bombastic and overwrought. In Dutch with English subtitles. Rated R for mature themes. 114m. **DIR:** Mike van Diem. **CAST:** Fedja van Huet, Jan Decleir, Betty Schuurman, Victor Low. **1997**

CHARADE ★★★★1/2 A comedy-mystery directed in the Alfred Hitchcock suspense style featuring the ever-suave Cary Grant helping widow Audrey Hepburn find the fortune stashed by her late husband. Walter Matthau, George Kennedy, and James Coburn are first-rate in support. 114m. **DIR:** Stanley Donen. **CAST:** Cary Grant, Audrey Hepburn, Walter Matthau, James Coburn, George Kennedy. **1963 DVD**

CHARGE OF THE LIGHT BRIGADE, THE (1936) ★★★★ October 25, 1854: Balaclava, the Crimea; military minds blunder, and six hundred gallant Britishers, sabers flashing, ride to their deaths. The film, which climaxes with one of the most dramatic cavalry charges in history, is based on Tennyson's famous poem. B&W; 116m. **DIR:** Michael Curtiz. **CAST:** Errol Flynn, Olivia de Havilland, Patric Knowles, Donald Crisp, David Niven, Henry Stephenson. **1936**

CHARGE OF THE LIGHT BRIGADE, THE (1968) ★★★1/2 Good depiction of the events leading up to the ill-fated 1854 Crimea engagement of the famed British unit that was controlled and directed by a glory-seeking and incompetent gentry. The climactic charge is moviemaking at its best. Rated PG-13 for violence. 128m. **DIR:** Tony Richardson. **CAST:** Trevor Howard, John Gielgud, Vanessa Redgrave, Harry Andrews, Jill Bennett, David Hemmings. **1968**

CHARIOTS OF FIRE ★★★★★ Made in England, this is the beautifully told and inspiring story of two runners who competed for England in the 1924 Olympics. Rated PG, the film has no objectionable content. 123m. **DIR:** Hugh Hudson. **CAST:** Ben Cross, Ian Charleson, Nigel Havers, Nicolas Farrell, Alice Krige, Cheryl Campbell, Ian Holm, John Gielgud, Dennis Christopher, Brad Davis, Nigel Davenport. **1981 DVD**

CHARIOTS OF THE GODS ★★ Based on Erich Von Daniken's bestselling book, this German production presents the theory that centuries ago Earth was visited by highly advanced space folks. The film is a nice travelogue, but its theories are never proved. Of minor interest only. Rated G. 98m. **DIR:** Harald Reinl. **1974 DVD**

CHARLEY AND THE ANGEL ★★ Time-worn plot about a guardian angel who teaches an exacting man (Fred MacMurray) a few lessons in kindness and humility. The kids won't mind, but chances are you've seen a better version already. Rated G. 93m. **DIR:** Vincent McEveety. **CAST:** Fred MacMurray, Cloris Leachman, Harry Morgan, Kurt Russell, Vincent Van Patten. **1973**

CHARLEY VARRICK ★★★★ A bank robber (Walter Matthau) accidentally steals money from the mob (he hits a bank where its ill-gotten gains are laundered). Matthau is superb as Varrick, the "last of the independents," and Joe Don Baker sends chills up the spine as the hit man relentlessly pursuing him. Rated PG. 111m. **DIR:** Don Siegel. **CAST:** Walter Matthau, Joe Don Baker, Felicia Farr, Andrew Robinson, John Vernon. **1973**

CHARLIE CHAN AND THE CURSE OF THE DRAGON QUEEN ★★ Although there are moments in this tongue-in-cheek send-up of the 1930s Charlie Chan mystery series that recapture the fun of yesteryear, overall it's just not a very good movie. Rated PG. 97m. **DIR:** Clive Donner. **CAST:** Peter Ustinov, Lee Grant, Angie Dickinson, Richard Hatch. **1981**

CHARLIE CHAN AT MONTE CARLO ★★ Warner Oland's last apperance as the Asian detective was this below-average entry. Charlie and son investigate the murder of a messenger and the theft of a million dollars' worth of bonds. B&W; 71m. **DIR:** Eugene Ford. **CAST:** Warner Oland, Keye Luke, Virginia Field, Sidney Blackmer. **1937**

CHARLIE CHAN AT THE OLYMPICS ★★★ In one of the better series entries, Charlie helps track a stolen device that can fly a plane by remote control. The film features footage from the Berlin Olympics and of the *Hindenburg*, which exploded before this was released. B&W; 71m. **DIR:** H. Bruce Humberstone. **CAST:** Warner Oland, Katherine DeMille, Allan "Rocky" Lane, Keye Luke. **1937**

CHARLIE CHAN AT THE OPERA ★★★1/2 Charlie Chan is called in to help solve the mysterious disappearance of a mental patient. Crazed baritone Boris Karloff chews up the scenery magnificently as the odds-on killer, but sly Warner Oland as Chan and Keye Luke as his number-one son hold their own in this often confusing mystery. The thirteenth film in the Fox series, this is one of the best. B&W; 68m. **DIR:** H. Bruce Humberstone. **CAST:** Warner Oland, Boris Karloff, Charlotte Henry, Keye Luke, Thomas Beck, William Demarest. **1936**

CHARLIE CHAN AT THE RACETRACK ★★1/2 On a ship from Honolulu to Los Angeles, Charlie investigates the death of an old friend who was about to expose a racetrack-swindling operation. One of three Chan mysteries made in 1936. B&W; 70m. **DIR:** H. Bruce Humberstone. **CAST:** Warner Oland, Keye Luke, Helen Wood, Thomas Beck. **1936**

CHARLIE CHAN AT THE WAX MUSEUM ★★★ A radio broadcast from a wax museum means murder—as Charlie Chan weaves his way through false clues, false faces, and poison darts to unravel the eerie goings-on. Spooky settings and top character actors like Marc Lawrence make this one of the best of the Sidney Toler Chans made for 20th Century Fox. This one is compact and tantalizing. B&W; 64m. **DIR:** Lynn Shores. **CAST:** Sidney Toler, C. Henry Gordon, Marc Lawrence, Marguerite Chapman. **1949**

CHARLIE CHAN AT TREASURE ISLAND ★★1/2 San Francisco's 1939 World's Fair is the setting for this Chan entry, as Charlie (Sidney Toler) is aided by sideshow magician Cesar Romero in finding out who killed a mystery novelist. B&W; 72m. **DIR:** Norman Foster. **CAST:** Sidney Toler, Cesar Romero, Victor Sen Yung, Pauline Moore. **1939**

CHARLIE CHAN IN CITY IN DARKNESS ★★ None of the younger Chans are on hand as Charlie, at a reunion with his war buddies in Paris, looks into the murder of an arms dealer who was selling to the Germans. Average entry with a touch of war propaganda. B&W; 75m. **DIR:** Herbert Leeds. **CAST:** Sidney Toler, Lynn Bari, Richard Clarke, Leo G. Carroll, Lon Chaney Jr. **1939**

CHARLIE CHAN IN EGYPT ★★★ In one of the better Charlie Chan films, the Oriental detective investigates when the body of an archaeologist is found inside a pharaoh's tomb. Worth seeing for some effective chills and an early appearance by Rita Hayworth (still billed as "Rita Casino"). B&W; 65m. **DIR:** Louis King. **CAST:** Warner Oland, Pat Paterson, Thomas Beck, Rita Hayworth, Stepin Fetchit. **1935**

CHARLIE CHAN IN HONOLULU ★★1/2 Sidney Toler and Victor Sen Yung make their debut as Charlie Chan and son Jimmy, here trying to keep anyone from leaving a ship docked at Honolulu while they investigate an onboard murder. B&W; 67m. **DIR:** H. Bruce Humberstone. **CAST:** Sidney Toler, Phyllis Brooks, Victor Sen Yung, George Zucco. **1939**

CHARLIE CHAN IN LONDON ★★★ Chan visits an English country estate in order to prove that a man about to be executed for murder is innocent. A superior series entry, written by detective novelist Philip MacDonald. B&W; 79m. **DIR:** Eugene Forde. **CAST:** Warner Oland, Drue Leyton, Douglas Walton, Alan Mowbray, Ray Milland, E. E. Clive. **1934**

CHARLIE CHAN IN PANAMA ★★1/2 Charlie Chan races to expose an enemy agent who plans to blow up the Panama Canal in order to keep U.S. Navy ships from passing through. Still pretty good, despite the once-topical war references. B&W; 67m. **DIR:** Norman Foster. **CAST:** Sidney Toler, Jean Rogers, Lionel Atwill, Victor Sen Yung. **1940**

CHARLIE CHAN IN PARIS ★★1/2 Former Fu Manchu Warner Oland drew on almost twenty years of cinematic experience playing Oriental menaces to make the character of Charlie Chan uniquely his own. This seventh entry in the series shows why he succeeded so well. The Honolulu sleuth seeks the knife-wielding killer who murdered one of his agents. Chan's oldest son Lee (Keye Luke) makes his initial appearance and aids his father. B&W; 72m. **DIR:** Lewis Seiler. **CAST:** Warner Oland, Mary Brian, Erik Rhodes, John Miljan, Thomas Beck, Keye Luke. **1935**

CHARLIE CHAN IN RENO ★★1/2 While staying at a Reno hotel for women seeking divorces, a Honolulu woman is accused of murder. This gives Charlie another excuse to travel, although the emphasis in this series entry is on good, old-fashioned mystery instead of location. B&W; 70m. **DIR:** Norman Foster. **CAST:** Sidney Toler, Ricardo Cortez, Phyllis Brooks, Victor Sen Yung, Slim Summerville. **1939**

CHARLIE CHAN IN RIO ★★1/2 The last of the better-budgeted Charlie Chans was an improvement over the previous efforts. Chan (Sidney Toler) arrives in Rio de Janeiro to bring back a murderess, only to discover that she has been killed. Chan brings the killer to bay with the aid of a psychic. B&W; 60m. **DIR:** Harry Lachman. **CAST:** Sidney Toler, Mary Beth Hughes, Cobina

Wright Jr., Victor Jory, Harold Huber, Richard Derr. **1941**

CHARLIE CHAN IN SHANGHAI ★★1/2 On what is supposed to be a vacation in his homeland of China, Charlie is drawn into a murder involving a ring of drug smugglers. Costar Charles Locher later changed his name to Jon Hall. B&W; 70m. **DIR:** James Tinling. **CAST:** Warner Oland, Irene Hervey, Keye Luke, Jon Hall. **1935**

CHARLIE CHAN IN THE SECRET SERVICE ★★ First of Monogram Pictures's *Charlie Chan* programmers, as the poverty-row studio picked up the series from 20th Century Fox. A scientist working on a new explosive is murdered, and the secret service calls upon Charlie to find his killer. For die-hard fans only. B&W; 65m. **DIR:** Phil Rosen. **CAST:** Sidney Toler, Mantan Moreland, Gwen Kenyon, Benson Fong. **1944**

CHARLIE CHAN ON BROADWAY ★★★ A nightclub singer plans to publish her diary, revealing all she knows about some of New York's shadiest characters. When she is murdered, it's Charlie Chan to the rescue. One of the better Chan films, with a good use of Manhattan nightlife setting. B&W; 68m. **DIR:** Eugene Ford. **CAST:** Warner Oland, Keye Luke, Joan Marsh, J. Edward Bromberg, Lon Chaney Jr. **1937**

CHARLIE CHAN'S MURDER CRUISE ★★ Unmemorable mystery has the Oriental sleuth investigating the murder of a Scotland Yard detective on a cruise ship. Not the worst of the series, but for Chan completists only. B&W; 75m. **DIR:** Eugene Forde. **CAST:** Sidney Toler, Marjorie Weaver, Lionel Atwill, Victor Sen Yung, Leo G. Carroll. **1940**

CHARLIE CHAN'S SECRET ★★1/2 Charlie Chan travels from Honolulu to San Francisco in search of a missing heir. When the heir is murdered and then mysteriously appears during a séance, Chan nabs the culprit. Sliding panels, supernatural overtones, and plenty of red herrings highlight this tenth entry in the long-running series. B&W; 72m. **DIR:** Gordon Wiles. **CAST:** Warner Oland, Rosina Lawrence, Charles Quigley, Astrid Allwyn, Jonathan Hale. **1936**

CHARLIE CHAPLIN . . . OUR HERO ★★★ Another trio of slapstick comedies starring Charlie Chaplin, who also scripted and directed the first two: *A Night at the Show* and *In the Park.* The third, *Hot Finish,* was originally titled *Mabel At the Wheel.* B&W; 58m. **DIR:** Charles Chaplin, Mabel Normand, Mack Sennett. **CAST:** Charlie Chaplin, Edna Purviance, Lloyd Bacon, Mabel Normand, Chester Conklin, Al St. John. **1914–15**

CHARLIE CHAPLIN CARNIVAL ★★★ One of a number of anthologies made up of two-reel Chaplin films, this one is composed of *The Vagabond*, *The Count*, *Behind the Screen*, and *The Fireman*. Charlie Chaplin, Edna Purviance (forever his leading lady), and the giant Eric Campbell provide most of the hilarious, romantic, touching moments. Bedrock fans will find *The Vagabond* a study for the longer films that followed in the 1920s— *The Kid*, in particular. B&W; 80m. **DIR:** Charles Chaplin. **CAST:** Charlie Chaplin, Edna Purviance, Eric Campbell, Lloyd Bacon. **1916**

CHARLIE CHAPLIN CAVALCADE ★★★ Another in a series of anthologies spliced up out of two- and three-reel Chaplin comedies. This features four of his best: *One A.M.*, *The Pawn-shop*, *The Floorwalker*, *The Rink*. As in most of Chaplin's short comedies, the sidesplitting action results mainly from underdog Chaplin clashing with the short-fused giant Eric Campbell. B&W; 81m. **DIR:** Charles Chaplin. **CAST:** Charlie Chaplin, Henry Bergman, Edna Purviance, John Rand, Wesley Ruggles, Frank J. Coleman, Albert Austin, Eric Campbell, Lloyd Bacon, Leo White. **1916**

CHARLIE CHAPLIN FESTIVAL ★★★ The third in a number of Chaplin film anthologies. Featuring *Easy Street*, one of his best-known hits, this group contains *The Cure*, *The Adventurer*, and *The Immigrant*, and gives viewers the full gamut of famous Chaplin emotional expressions. The coin sequence in the latter is sight-gag ingenuity at its best. B&W; 80m. **DIR:** Charles Chaplin. **CAST:** Charlie Chaplin, Eric Campbell, Edna Purviance, Albert Austin, Henry Bergman. **1917**

CHARLIE CHAPLIN—THE EARLY YEARS VOL. 1–4 ★★★★ Outstanding series of silent shorts features classic masterpieces: *The Immigrant*, *Easy Street*, *The Count*, *The Pawnbroker*, *The Floorwalker*, *The Vagabond*, *Behind the Screen*, and *The Ring*. Silent. B&W. **DIR:** Charles Chaplin. **CAST:** Charlie Chaplin, Edna Purviance, Eric Campbell, Albert Austin, Henry Bergman, Lloyd Bacon, Charlotte Mineau, James T. Kelly, Leo White. **1915–1917**

CHARLIE, THE LONESOME COUGAR ★★★ A misunderstood cougar comes into a lumber camp in search of food and companionship. After adopting the animal, the men are not certain whether it will adapt back to its wild habitat, or even if they want it to. More believable than the story line would suggest. Rated G. 75m. **DIR:** Not credited!. **CAST:** Ron Brown, Bryan Russell, Linda Wallace, Jim Wilson, Rex Allen. **1968 DVD**

CHARLIE'S ANGELS ★★1/2 You'll hate yourself in the morning, but there's no denying the pizzazz and playful fun of this big-screen adaptation of the notorious TV series. Cameron Diaz and Drew Barrymore are properly voluptuous, while Lucy Liu sports her usual sour-lemon grimace as the more serious member of the butt-kicking trio of sexy undercover operatives. The script-by-committee is all over the map, but director McQ keeps up the pace. Say what you will: This isn't boring. Rated PG-13 for violence, profanity, sensuality, brief nudity, and suggested sex. 92m. **DIR:** McQ. **CAST:** Cameron Diaz, Drew Barrymore, Lucy Liu, Bill Murray, Sam Rockwell, Tim Curry, Kelly Lynch, Crispin Glover. **2000 DVD**

CHARLIE'S GHOST ★★★★ Engaging comedy, based on a story by Mark Twain, stars young Trenton Knight as the much-put-upon Charlie. His archaeologist father unearths the legendary Coronado's grave, thus unleashing his spirit. Lots of fun delivered by a strong cast. Rated PG for some minor violence. 92m. **DIR:** Anthony Edwards. **CAST:** Richard "Cheech" Marin, Anthony Edwards, Trent Knight, Charles Rocket, Linda Fiorentino, Daphne Zuniga. **1994**

•CHARLOTTE GRAY ★★1/2 A woman in World War II parachutes into occupied France to work with the Resistance and look for her lover, a downed RAF pilot. Attractive locations and fine acting are the chief virtues of this farfetched and weakly motivated melodrama. Rated PG-13 for violence. 121m. **DIR:** Gillian Armstrong. **CAST:** Cate Blanchett, Billy Crudup, Michael Gambon, Rupert Penry-Jones. **2001 DVD**

CHARLOTTE'S WEB ★★ Disappointing adaptation of E. B. White's beloved children's book. Charlotte the spider, Wilbur the pig, and Templeton the rat lose all their charm and turn into simpering participants in a vacuous musical. For kids only. Rated G. 85m. **DIR:** Charles A. Nichols, Iwao Takamoto. **1973 DVD**

CHARLY ★★★★ Cliff Robertson won the best-actor Oscar for his role in this excellent science-fiction film as a retarded man turned into a genius through scientific experiments. Claire Bloom is also excellent as the caseworker who becomes his friend. Rated PG. 103m. **DIR:** Ralph Nelson. **CAST:** Cliff Robertson, Claire Bloom, Lilia Skala, Dick Van Patten. **1968**

CHARRO! ★★ Nonmusical Western was intended to introduce Elvis Presley, serious actor. However, the only thing this misfire proved was that its star could go without shaving. Try Don Siegel's *Flaming Star* instead. 98m. **DIR:** Charles Marquis Warren. **CAST:** Elvis Presley, Ina Balin, Victor French. **1969**

CHASE, THE (1946) ★★ If the tempo were faster and the writing tighter, this film might have been interesting. As it is, it staggers along. The plot is quite predictable as Michele Morgan runs away from her husband. B&W; 86m. **DIR:** Arthur Ripley. **CAST:** Robert Cummings, Michèle Morgan, Peter Lorre, Steve Cochran. **1946**

CHASE, THE (1966) ★★1/2 Convoluted tale of prison escapee (Robert Redford) who returns to the turmoil of his Texas hometown. The exceptional cast provides flashes of brilliance, but overall, the film is rather dull. Redford definitely showed signs of his superstar potential here. 135m. **DIR:** Arthur Penn. **CAST:** Robert Redford, Jane Fonda, Marlon Brando, Angie Dickinson, Janice Rule, James Fox, Robert Duvall, E. G. Marshall, Miriam Hopkins, Martha Hyer. **1966**

CHASE, THE (1994) ★★ Avoid this frivolous action-comedy unless you want to spend nearly 90 minutes in the front seat of a red BMW. Charlie Sheen plays a wrongly convicted prison escapee who takes the daughter of California's richest man hostage. They feud for several miles and then fall in love with the cops in hot pursuit. Wild action scenes include front-seat sex and cadavers bouncing down the freeway. A predictable yarn. Rated PG-13 for nudity, sex, and language. 88m. **DIR:** Adam Rifkin. **CAST:** Charlie Sheen, Kristy Swanson, Ray Wise, Cary Elwes, Henry Rollins. **1994**

CHASERS ★★1/2 The misadventures of two Navy Shore Patrol lawmen (Tom Berenger, William McNamara) escorting a female prisoner (Erika Eleniak) to Charleston, SC. The premise is borrowed from *The Last Detail*, but the drawn out story never really gets rolling. Still, the stars are attractive, and the supporting cast is good; it might be worth a look on a slow night. Rated R for profanity, nudity, and sexual scenes. 103m. **DIR:** Dennis Hopper. **CAST:** Tom Berenger, William McNamara, Erika Eleniak, Gary Busey, Crispin Glover, Dean Stockwell, Marilu Henner, Dennis Hopper. **1994 DVD**

CHASING AMY ★★★ Love blossoms between two young comic-book artists, even though she's a lesbian. The real obstacle to their happiness is the hero's sulky immaturity and his business partner, who seems jealous and possessive for more than platonic reasons. Rated R for profanity and nudity. 105m. **DIR:** Kevin Smith. **CAST:** Ben Affleck, Joey Lauren Adams, Jason Lee, Dwight Ewell, Jason Mewes. **1997 DVD**

CHASING DREAMS ★★★ Here's another film made before a current top-billed player's stardom. In this case Kevin Costner is in and out of the story within the first five minutes. We're left with a low-budget, but very appealing, tearjerker. While Costner's away at college, his slightly younger brother must work on the farm, care for their ill youngest brother, and somehow sneak in baseball practice. Rated PG for profanity. 96m. **DIR:** Sean Roche, Therese Conte. **CAST:** David Brown, Jim Shane, Kevin Costner. **1981**

CHATO'S LAND ★★1/2 Unjustly accused of murdering a lawman, a half-breed Apache (the top-billed, but seldom seen Charles Bronson) must fight off a posse bent on killing him. Overly violent Western substitutes types for characters and bloodshed for story structure. Rated PG. 110m. **DIR:** Michael Winner. **CAST:** Charles Bronson, Jack Palance, Jill Ireland, Richard Basehart, James Whitmore, Simon Oakland, Richard Jordan. **1972 DVD**

CHATTAHOOCHEE ★★★★ British actor Gary Oldman gives a brilliant performance as an American war hero who attempts a bizarre suicide and ends up in the nightmarish Chattahoochee State Mental Hospital. Once inside, he devotes himself to exposing the horrific treatment of the patients. Rated R for brutality, nudity, and profanity. 98m. **DIR:** Mick Jackson. **CAST:** Gary Oldman, Dennis Hopper, Frances McDormand, Pamela Reed, Ned Beatty, M. Emmet Walsh. **1990**

CHATTANOOGA CHOO CHOO ★★ The story deals with a bet to make a New York-to-Chattanooga train trip within a deadline. George Kennedy plays the comedy villain and owner of a football team of which Joe Namath is the coach. Rated PG for mild profanity. 102m. **DIR:** Bruce Bilson. **CAST:** George Kennedy, Barbara Eden, Joe Namath, Melissa Sue Anderson. **1984**

CHEAP DETECTIVE, THE ★★★ Follow-up to *Murder By Death* from director Robert Moore and writer Neil Simon is an affectionate parody of the Humphrey Bogart classics. Generally enjoyable. Rated PG. 92m. **DIR:** Robert Moore. **CAST:** Peter Falk, Ann-Margret, Eileen Brennan, Sid Caesar, Stockard Channing, James Coco, Dom DeLuise, Louise Fletcher, John Houseman, Madeline Kahn, Fernando Lamas, Marsha Mason, Phil Silvers, Vic Tayback, Abe Vigoda, Paul Williams, Nicol Williamson. **1978 DVD**

CHEAP SHOTS ★★ An aging Greek proprietor tries to save his motel from ruin. Urged by a full-time boarder, he makes blue films of a couple staying in one of his cabins. Not rated. The film includes some profanity and nudity. 92m. **DIR:** Jeff Ureles, Jerry Stoeffhaas. **CAST:** Louis Zorich, David Patrick Kelly, Mary Louise Wilson, Patience Moore. **1991**

CHEAPER TO KEEP HER 🦃 A sexist private detective tracks down ex-husbands who haven't paid their alimony. Rated R. 92m. **DIR:** Ken Annakin. **CAST:** Mac Davis, Tovah Feldshuh, Art Metrano, Ian McShane. **1980**

CHEAT, THE ★★★★ A socialite gambles heavily on Wall Street, loses, and borrows money from a rich Oriental. Sensational melodrama in its time, and it holds up well today. Silent. B&W; 60m. **DIR:** Cecil B. DeMille. **CAST:** Sessue Hayakawa, Fannie Ward. **1915 DVD**

CHEATERS ★★★1/2 A team of high-school students from an underfunded public school in a bad part of town, takes on the challenge of the Academic Decathalon. Things get interesting when they get a copy of the exam before the competition begins. Decent acting and an interesting take on the morality of cheating give the film (based on a true story) an edge over most run-of-the-mill made-for-cable movies. Not rated; contains profanity. 105m. **DIR:** John Stockwell. **CAST:** Jeff Daniels, Jena Malone, Luke Edwards, Blake Heron, Paul Sorvino. **2000 DVD**

CHEATIN' HEARTS ★★★★ Gorgeously photographed, multilayered story of three strong women and the men in their lives, in the "new" West. Sally Kirkland must come to terms with her philandering husband (James Brolin) and a new life as her two daughters make their own way in the world. Intriguing look, if a bit slow, at adult choices and the resulting consequences. Rated R for profanity and nudity. 88m. **DIR:** Rod McCall. **CAST:** Sally Kirkland, James Brolin, Kris Kristofferson, Pamela Gidley. **1993**

CHECK AND DOUBLE CHECK 🦃 This sad comedy starring radio's Amos 'n' Andy in blackface was RKO's biggest hit for the 1930 season and made Freeman Gosden and Charles Correll the top stars for that year—but they never made another film. B&W; 80m. **DIR:** Melville Brown. **CAST:** Freeman Gosden, Charles Correll, Sue Carol, Charles Norton. **1930**

CHECK IS IN THE MAIL, THE 🦃 Story of a man who is tired of the capitalist system. Rated R for profanity. 83m. **DIR:** Joan Darling. **CAST:** Brian Dennehy, Anne Archer, Hallie Todd, Chris Herbert, Michael Bowen, Dick Shawn, Beau Starr. **1986**

CHECKERED FLAG ★★1/2 A race car driver must face his ex-friend after stealing his girlfriend. An overdose of macho get-even feats serve as annoying distractions until the two learn to work together on a winning team. Not rated, contains nudity, profanity, and violence. 100m. **DIR:** John Glen, Michael Levine. **CAST:** Bill Campbell, Rob Estes, Amanda Wyss, Carrie Hamilton, Pernell Roberts. **1990**

CHECKING OUT 🦃 A nervous fellow believes his own fatal heart attack is mere hours away. Rated R for language. 95m. **DIR:** David Leland. **CAST:** Jeff Daniels, Melanie Mayron, Michael Tucker, Ann Magnuson. **1989**

CHEECH AND CHONG'S NEXT MOVIE ★★ This is Cheech and Chong's (Richard Marin and Thomas Chong) in-between movie—in between *Up in Smoke*, their first, and *Nice Dreams*, number three. If you liked either of the other two, you'll like *Next Movie*. But if you didn't care for the duo's brand of humor there, you won't in this one either. Rated R for nudity and profanity. 99m. **DIR:** Thomas Chong. **CAST:** Cheech and Chong, Evelyn Guerrero, Betty Kennedy. **1980**

CHEERS FOR MISS BISHOP ★★★ Nostalgic, poignant story of a schoolteacher in a midwestern town who devotes her life to teaching. A warm reassuring film in the tradition of *Miss Dove* and *Mr. Chips*. B&W; 95m. **DIR:** Tay Garnett. **CAST:** Martha Scott, William Gargan, Edmund Gwenn, Sterling Holloway, Sidney Blackmer. **1941**

CHEETAH ★★★ Two L.A. teens journey to Kenya to spend six months with their parents. A chance encounter with a cheetah cub sets the stage for a well-handled version of the old-fashioned Disney adventure movies for kids. Rated G. 83m. **DIR:** Jeff Blyth. **CAST:** Keith Coogan, Lucy Deakins. **1989**

CHEF IN LOVE, A ★★★ Gourmet French chef Pascal searches the Soviet Union in the 1920s for gastronomic delights. He then opens a restaurant, which is invaded by the Red Army. The chef faces abuse and even the loss of his princess lover to a sourpuss army officer, but will not abandon his eatery. In French with English subtitles. Rated PG-13 for nudity and sexual situations. 98m. **DIR:** Nan Dzhordzhadze. **CAST:** Pierre Richard, Micheline Presle, Nino Kirtadze, Teimour Kahmhadze, Jean-Yves Gautier, Ramaz Tchkhikvadze. **1996**

CHERNOBYL: THE FINAL WARNING ★★★ Well-intended look at the Chernobyl nuclear power plant disaster in Russia. This telefilm takes a close look at one family affected by the accident, as well as the broad impact it had and continues to have on the entire world. 94m. **DIR:** Anthony Page. **CAST:** Jon Voight, Jason Robards Jr., Sammi Davis, Annette Crosbie, Ian McDiarmid. **1991**

CHEROKEE FLASH ★★★ Old-time outlaw Roy Barcroft tries to go straight, but his old henchmen don't intend to allow him to do so. Barcroft's foster son, Sunset Carson, comes to his rescue. B&W; 58m. **DIR:** Thomas Carr. **CAST:** Sunset Carson, Roy Barcroft, Linda Stirling, Tom London, John Merton. **1945**

CHEROKEE KID, THE ★★★1/2 Sinbad makes an engaging gunslinger in this amiable, made-for-HBO Western spoof, which sends him through numerous low-key adventures that help him develop the skill to challenge heartless railroad tycoon James Coburn. A Martinez is quite funny as the loquacious companion who tells the Kid's story during a somber funeral, and Burt Reynolds is a hoot as a tale-spinning mountain man. Rated PG-13 for violence and profanity. 91m. **DIR:** Paris Barclay. **CAST:** Sinbad, James Coburn, Gregory Hines, A Martinez, Ernie Hudson, Mark Pellegrino, Burt Reynolds. **1996**

CHERRY FALLS ★★★ This goof on slasher films takes an unusual turn. The killer isn't after sex-starved teenagers but their virginal counterparts. That puts the local authorities between a rock and a hard place when they must struggle with whether or not to force their children to go all the way. Amusing premise and campy performances redeem this familiar fare. Rated R for adult situations, language, and violence. 92m. **DIR:** Geoffrey Wright. **CAST:** Brittany Murphy, Jay Mohr, Michael Biehn, Gabriel Mann, Candy Clark. **2000 DVD**

CHERRY 2000 ★★1/2 Made before she graduated to better roles in *Stormy Monday* and *Working Girl*, Melanie Griffith starred in this barely released movie as a sort of female Mad Max. Set in the year 2017, the semi-parody casts Griffith as a mercenary who guides yuppie David Andrews through the deserts of the Southwest, now the domain of psychotic terrorists, in search of a robot warehouse. Rated PG-13. 93m. **DIR:** Steve DeJarnett. **CAST:** Melanie Griffith, David Andrews, Ben Johnson, Tim Thomerson, Brian James, Harry Carey Jr., Michael C. Gwynne. **1988 DVD**

CHEYENNE (TV SERIES) ★★★★ This Western series ranks with *Gunsmoke*, *Rawhide*, and *Maverick* as one of the best of its kind. Clint Walker plays Cheyenne

Bodie, who roams the West in episodes that explore every possible theme in the genre. In "White Warrior," one of two shows released so far on video, Michael Landon plays a white man raised by Indians who causes problems for wagon master Cheyenne. In "The Iron Trail," Cheyenne must stop outlaw Dennis Hopper, who is out to kidnap President Ulysses S. Grant. B&W; 49m. **DIR:** Leslie Martinson, Lee Sholem. **CAST:** Clint Walker, Michael Landon, Dennis Hopper. **1955–1962**

CHEYENNE AUTUMN ★★★1/2 John Ford brings us this story of the mistreatment of the American Indian. His standard heroes, the U.S. cavalry, play the role of the villains as they try to stop a group of Cheyenne Indians from migrating back to their Wyoming homeland from a barren reservation in Oklahoma. 160m. **DIR:** John Ford. **CAST:** Richard Widmark, Karl Malden, Carroll Baker, James Stewart, Edward G. Robinson, Ricardo Montalban, Sal Mineo. **1964**

CHEYENNE SOCIAL CLUB, THE ★★★ This Western-comedy has a number of pleasing moments. James Stewart, an itinerant cowhand, and his low-key cohort Henry Fonda inherit some property in Cheyenne—which turns out to be a bordello. The premise is good, but at times director Gene Kelly doesn't have a firm grip on the script or on these hugely talented actors. Rated PG. 103m. **DIR:** Gene Kelly. **CAST:** James Stewart, Henry Fonda, Shirley Jones, Sue Ane Langdon. **1970**

CHEYENNE TAKES OVER ★★★ Lash LaRue's long-needed vacation at the Lobos ranch is anything but restful as he discovers it's been taken over by an impersonator who claims birthright to the land. B&W; 58m. **DIR:** Ray Taylor. **CAST:** Lash LaRue, Al St. John, Nancy Gates. **1947**

CHEYENNE WARRIOR ★★★ Against the backdrop of the Civil War, expectant mother Rebecca Carver and her husband are making the long trek west when a gang of vicious marauders kill her husband and leave her stranded in a remote trading post. There she teams with a Cheyenne warrior who also encountered the marauders, and was left for dead. Message of tolerance is well presented without seeming preachy. Rated PG-13 for violence. 86m. **DIR:** Mark Griffiths. **CAST:** Kelly Preston, Pato Hoffman, Bo Hopkins, Dan Haggerty, Rick Dean. **1994 DVD**

CHICAGO JOE AND THE SHOWGIRL ★★ Based on the real-life Cleft Chin Murder Case in 1944 London, this disappointing thriller stars Kiefer Sutherland as a U.S. serviceman who teams up with an English dancer (Emily Lloyd) for a crime spree that ends in one murder and another attempted murder. Rated R for violence and profanity. 103m. **DIR:** Bernard Rose. **CAST:** Kiefer Sutherland, Emily Lloyd, Patsy Kensit, Liz Fraser, Alexandra Pigg. **1990**

CHICKEN CHRONICLES, THE 🦃 The carnal pursuits of a high school senior. Rated PG. 95m. **DIR:** Francis Simon. **CAST:** Steve Guttenberg, Ed Lauter, Lisa Reeves, Meredith Baer, Phil Silvers. **1977**

CHICKEN RANCH ★★★ This documentary about the brothel that was the setting for the musical *The Best Little Whorehouse in Texas* presents a different picture of prostitution. Although shot in a cinema verité style—the workers and customers speak for themselves, with no passing of judgment by the filmmakers—the movie paints a relentlessly grim picture of the oldest profession. Not rated. 84m. **DIR:** Nick Broomfield, Sandi Sissel. **1983**

CHICKEN RUN ★★★★1/2 This wry, wacky, egg-farm version of *The Great Escape* is a clever claymation adventure set on a 1950s English poultry ranch. Stern, greedy Mrs. Tweedy and her hen-pecked husband run the farm like a prisoner-of-war camp. Ginger is a scrappy, determined hen that asks a cocky rooster to help all her feathered friends escape before the Tweedys process them into pot pies. The film includes many of the mood swings that made Babe so richly rewarding, and an exciting rescue inside a pot pie factory (think *Modern Times* crossed with Indiana Jones heroics). Rated G. 85m. **DIR:** Nick Park, Peter Lord. **2000 DVD**

CHIEFS ★★★★ A string of unsolved murders in 1920 in a small southern town is at the base of this engrossing suspense-drama. The story follows the various police chiefs from the time of the murders to 1962 when the town's first black police chief is intrigued by the case and the spell it casts over the town and its political boss (Charlton Heston). 200m. **DIR:** Jerry London. **CAST:** Charlton Heston, Wayne Rogers, Billy Dee Williams, Brad Davis, Keith Carradine, Stephen Collins, Tess Harper, Paul Sorvino, Victoria Tennant. **1985**

CHIKAMATSU MONOGATARI ★★★★★ Because of a misunderstanding, a clerk and the wife of his employer are forced to flee their homes. One of Kenji Mizoguchi's masterpieces, a tragedy of ill-fated love in seventeenth-century Japan. In Japanese with English subtitles. Not rated. 110m. **DIR:** Kenji Mizoguchi. **CAST:** Kazuo Hasegawa, Kyoko Kagawa. **1954**

CHILD BRIDE OF SHORT CREEK ★★ Based on a true account, this is the story of a polygamist community in Arizona disbanded by the police. Made for TV. 100m. **DIR:** Robert Michael Lewis. **CAST:** Christopher Atkins, Diane Lane, Conrad Bain, Dee Wallace. **1981**

CHILD IN THE NIGHT ★★1/2 With all the devices of a murder mystery in place, the new twist to the theme in this TV movie involves *Peter Pan*'s Captain Hook. A boy swears that the pirate villain had a hand in killing his father. 93m. **DIR:** Mike Robe. **CAST:** JoBeth Williams, Tom Skerritt, Elijah Wood, Darren McGavin, Season Hubley. **1990**

CHILD IS WAITING, A ★★★ Difficult to watch but emotionally satisfying. Judy Garland, in a brilliant performance, is a worker at a hospital treating mentally retarded children. 102m. **DIR:** John Cassavetes. **CAST:** Burt Lancaster, Judy Garland, Gena Rowlands, Steven Hill, Paul Stewart. **1963**

CHILD OF DARKNESS, CHILD OF LIGHT ★★ Two American teenage girls become pregnant while remaining virgins; according to Church prophecy, one will bear the child of God and the other will spawn the son of Satan . . . but which is which? What hath *The Omen* wrought? Dedicated performances save this produced-for-TV Catholic chiller from complete turkeydom. Rated PG-13. 85m. **DIR:** Marina Sargenti. **CAST:** Anthony Denison, Brad Davis, Paxton Whitehead, Sydney Penny, Sela Ward. **1991**

CHILD OF GLASS ★★ When a boy's parents buy an old New Orleans mansion, he discovers that it is haunted. Inoffensive Disney made-for-TV movie with a hammy performance by Olivia Barash as the ghost. 93m. **DIR:**

John Erman. **CAST:** Steve Shaw, Katy Kurtzman, Barbara Barrie, Biff McGuire, Nina Foch, Anthony Zerbe, Olivia Barash. **1978**

CHILDREN OF A LESSER GOD ★★★★★ Based on the Tony Award–winning play by Mark Medoff, this superb film concerns the love that grows between a teacher (William Hurt) for the hearing-impaired and a deaf woman (Oscar-winner Marlee Matlin). The performances are impeccable, the direction inspired, and the story unforgettable. Considering the problems inherent in telling its tale, this represents a phenomenal achievement for first-time film director Randa Haines. Rated R for suggested sex, profanity, and adult themes. 118m. **DIR:** Randa Haines. **CAST:** William Hurt, Marlee Matlin, Piper Laurie, Philip Bosco. **1986 DVD**

CHILDREN OF AN LAC, THE ★★★★ Just before the fall of Saigon in 1975, three women did the next to impossible: They managed the escape of hundreds (perhaps thousands) of Vietnamese children. One of these women was actress Ina Balin, who plays herself here. The performances and production values of this made-for-television film are very good. 100m. **DIR:** John Llewellyn Moxey. **CAST:** Ina Balin, Shirley Jones, Beulah Quo, Alan Fudge, Ben Piazza. **1980**

CHILDREN OF FURY ★★1/2 FBI agents try to capture a group of religious fanatics without harming the children in their care. Based on the true story of one of the longest standoffs in FBI history, this made-for-TV movie is pretty familiar stuff, with heroic good guys and cardboard villains. Not rated; contains violence. 85m. **DIR:** Charles Haid. **CAST:** Dennis Franz, Tess Harper, Kyle Secor, Paul LeMat, Ed Begley Jr. **1995**

CHILDREN OF HEAVEN ★★★★ Young boy in Tehran picks up his sister's pink shoes from the cobbler and loses them while running errands in this gentle, languid drama. The siblings devise a plan to keep their money-strapped parents from discovering the loss by sharing a lone pair of sneakers that they each must wear to school. This simple story of sibling unity and resourcefulness quietly becomes a poetic, emotionally rich fable as modern Iran is filtered through children's eyes. In Farsi with English subtitles. Rated PG. 88m. **DIR:** Majid Madjidi. **CAST:** Amir Naji, Mir Farrokh Hashemian, Bahare Seddiqi. **1998**

CHILDREN OF NATURE ★★★★ This enthralling look at old age was the first film from Iceland to receive an Oscar nomination for best foreign-language movie. It details the story of an elderly couple, abandoned by families into a nursing home. They escape one night, and head for the woman's homeland in Northern Iceland. In Icelandic with English subtitles. Not rated. 85m. **DIR:** Fridrik Thor Fridriksson. **CAST:** Gisli Halldorsson, Sigridur Hagalin, Bruno Ganz. **1991**

CHILDREN OF NOISY VILLAGE, THE ★★★★ *My Life as a Dog* director Lasse Hallstrom adapted stories by Swedish writer Astrid Lindgren (best known for her *Pippi Longstocking* series). The stories are linked as tales created by the children of a small, happy town for the amusement of themselves and their neighbors. Children may need a little encouragement to sit through this the first time, but as a family film it can be pleasantly habit-forming. Not rated. Dubbed in English. 88m. **DIR:** Lasse Hallstrom. **CAST:** Linda Bergstrom, Anna Sahlin, Ellem Demercus. **1986**

CHILDREN OF PARADISE, THE ★★★★★ Long beloved by connoisseurs the world over is this rich and rare film of infatuation, jealousy, deception, grief, murder, and true love lost forever—set in pre-1840 Paris. Brilliant performances carefully controlled by superb direction make this fascinating account of the timeless foibles of men and women a true cinema classic. As Baptiste, the mime, in love with an unattainable beautiful woman, Jean-Louis Barrault is matchless. In French with English subtitles. B&W; 188m. **DIR:** Marcel Carné. **CAST:** Jean-Louis Barrault, Arletty, Maria Casares, Pierre Brasseur, Albert Remay, Leon Larive. **1944**

CHILDREN OF RAGE ★★1/2 This little-seen film deserves credit for doing something that few were willing to do at the time it was made: look beyond the actions of Palestinian terrorists to try to understand their motives. Unfortunately, good intentions don't compensate for lack of drama in this talky story about an Israeli doctor who attempts to open lines of communications with terrorists. Not rated; contains violence. 106m. **DIR:** Arthur Allan Seidelman. **CAST:** Helmut Griem, Olga Georges-Picot, Cyril Cusack, Simon Ward. **1975**

CHILDREN OF SANCHEZ, THE ★★★ Anthony Quinn stars as a poor Mexican worker who tries to keep his large family together. This well-intentioned film is slightly boring. Rated PG. 126m. **DIR:** Hall Bartlett. **CAST:** Anthony Quinn, Dolores Del Rio. **1978**

CHILDREN OF THE CORN Yet another adaptation of a Stephen King horror story. A young couple come to a midwestern farming town where a young preacher with mesmerizing powers has instructed all the children to slaughter adults. Rated R for violence and profanity. 93m. **DIR:** Fritz Kiersch. **CAST:** Peter Horton, Linda Hamilton, R. G. Armstrong, John Franklin. **1984 DVD**

CHILDREN OF THE CORN II: THE FINAL SACRIFICE A sour-pussed teen cult leader instigates more violence in this follow-up to Stephen King's original short story. Rated R for violence, simulated sex, and the world's most gruesome nosebleed. 94m. **DIR:** David F. Price. **CAST:** Terence Knox, Paul Scherrer, Rosalind Allen, Ned Romero. **1993**

CHILDREN OF THE CORN III: URBAN HARVEST ★★★1/2 After their father is killed by a deadly force in the cornfield, brothers Eli and Joshua are adopted by a young couple in Chicago. Eli brings along some corn from home, and while Joshua attempts to fit in, Eli summons the evil spirit to do his bidding. Rated R for gore and language. 91m. **DIR:** James D. R. Hickox. **CAST:** Daniel Cerny, Ron Melendez, Michael Ensign. **1995 DVD**

CHILDREN OF THE CORN IV: THE GATHERING ★★ Those nasty children from the cornfield return in this fourth chapter. This time the return of the corn beastie causes the children of a small town to develop horrendous fevers and zombielike personas while the adults just die, die, die. More of the same for people who liked the first three. Rated R for violence. 85m. **DIR:** Greg Spence. **CAST:** Naomi Watts, Brent Jennings, Samaria Graham, William Windom, Karen Black. **1996 DVD**

•**CHILDREN OF THE CORN: REVELATION** ★★ The corn stalks in *Field of Dreams* must be in cahoots with this nonending direct-to-video film franchise: If you make it, they will come. How else can you explain this familiar dose of corn about a woman who learns that her grandmother's condominium complex has been built on top of the cursed corn field from the first film? Only for those with short-term memory. Rated R for adult situations, drug use, language, nudity, and violence. 82m. **DIR:** Guy Magar. **CAST:** Claudette Mink, Kyle Cassie, Michael Ironside. **2001 DVD**

CHILDREN OF THE CORN V: FIELDS OF TERROR ★★ A group of college kids passes through the town where the title children live and kill for a satanic beastie who lives in the corn rows. Not one of the best of the series. Rated R for violence and horror. 83m. **DIR:** Ethan Wiley. **CAST:** Stacy Galina, Alexis Arquette, Adam Wylie, Greg Vaughan, Eva Mendez, Ahmet Zappa, Fred Williamson, David Carradine. **1998 DVD**

CHILDREN OF THE CORN 666: ISAAC'S RETURN ★★ More of the same from the continuing direct-to-video franchise that has nothing to do with Stephen King's original story. This outing, a young woman returns to Nebraska in search of her birth mother and discovers her family has ties to the devil. Hokum from beginning to end. Rated R for adult situations, language, and violence. 78m. **DIR:** Kari Skogland. **CAST:** Natalie Ramsey, John Franklin, Stacy Keach, Nancy Allen, Alix Koromzay. **1999 DVD**

CHILDREN OF THE DAMNED ★★1/2 Inevitable, but disappointing, sequel to the 1960 sleeper, *Village of the Damned*. Worldwide, only six of the alien children have survived, so the children band together. B&W; 90m. **DIR:** Tony Leader. **CAST:** Ian Hendry, Alan Badel, Barbara Ferris, Alfred Burke. **1963**

CHILDREN OF THE DUST ★★★★ Superior miniseries is based on actual events and people of the nineteenth-century American West. Former gunfighter Gypsy Smith (Sidney Poitier) is all guts and compassion and hero to both Indians and African Americans. Not rated; contains violence and sexual situations. 180m. **DIR:** David Green. **CAST:** Sidney Poitier, Michael Moriarty, Regina Taylor, Billy Wirth, Joanna Going, Farrah Fawcett. **1995**

CHILDREN OF THE FULL MOON 🦃 Even the curvaceous horror hostess Elvira and her off brand of humor can't salvage this cross between *Rosemary's Baby* and *The Wolfman*. 60m. **DIR:** Tom Clegg. **CAST:** Christopher Cazenove, Celia Gregory, Diana Dors. **1982**

CHILDREN OF THE NIGHT ★★★ Stylish horror-thriller goes right for the jugular in grand fashion. Peter DeLuise stars as a teacher who's summoned to the small town of Allburg when one of his friends claims that he has two female vampires locked up in a bedroom. Plenty of great, gory effects, and some splendid, campy acting. Rated R for violence and language. 92m. **DIR:** Tony Randel. **CAST:** Peter DeLuise, Karen Black, Maya McLaughlin, Ami Dolenz. **1992**

CHILDREN OF THE REVOLUTION ★★★ A fanatical Australian Communist has a one-night stand in 1949 Russia with Joseph Stalin and a double agent. She returns Down Under pregnant, marries a sweet-natured party associate, and raises a son who parlays an infatuation with prison into a lucrative position as a police-rights activist. Rated R for sexuality and language. 101m. **DIR:** Peter Duncan. **CAST:** Judy Davis, Sam Neill, Richard Roxburgh, F. Murray Abraham, Rachel Griffiths, Geoffrey Rush. **1996**

CHILDREN OF TIMES SQUARE, THE ★★★ A baby-faced teenage runaway is suddenly confronted with the pimps and drug dealers who prey on the desperate newcomers to New York City. Violent, powerful, made-for-TV message film. 95m. **DIR:** Curtis Hanson. **CAST:** Howard Rollins Jr., Joanna Cassidy, David Ackroyd, Larry B. Scott. **1986**

CHILDREN SHOULDN'T PLAY WITH DEAD THINGS 🦃 Typical "evil dead" entry; amateur filmmakers work in a spooky graveyard and make enough noise to, well, wake the dead. Rated PG. 85m. **DIR:** Bob Clark. **CAST:** Alan Ormsby, Anya Ormsby, Jeffrey Gillen. **1972 DVD**

CHILDREN'S HOUR, THE ★★★1/2 Originally this was a moderately well-received play by Lillian Hellman, which director William Wyler filmed in 1937 (as *These Three*). Not satisfied with his first attempt, Wyler directed this remake about rumored lesbianism in a school for girls. Good performances from a veteran cast. B&W; 107m. **DIR:** William Wyler. **CAST:** Audrey Hepburn, Shirley MacLaine, James Garner, Miriam Hopkins, Veronica Cartwright, Fay Bainter. **1962**

•CHILD'S CHRISTMAS IN WALES, A (1986) ★★★★★ This marvelous made-for-TV production is a little slice of seasonal heaven. Denholm Elliott brings the proper gravity and gentle good humor to his off-camera narration of Dylan Thomas's poetic short story, which follows a young lad's snow-bound Christmas Day adventures in the company of fussy aunts, mischievous uncles, and a town filled with nervous cats attempting to cross frozen fences without becoming target practice for snowball-hurling ragamuffins. As the final poignant scene fades to black, it's easy to believe that long-ago holiday celebrations had a special magic all their own . . . one that's sadly missing these days. Suitable for all ages. Not rated. 50m. **DIR:** Don McBrearty. **CAST:** Denholm Elliott, Mathonway Reeves, Michael Fawkes, Glynis Davies, Jo Paige. **1986**

CHILD'S CHRISTMAS IN WALES, A (1987) ★★ Dylan Thomas's holiday classic gets a tasteful but disappointingly clumsy treatment in this made-for-public-television special. Director Don McBrearty's images do not complement Thomas's brilliantly evocative words, and often actually contradict them. More like Walton Mountain than Thomas's mythical Welsh town of Llareggub. Not rated. 55m. **DIR:** Don McBrearty. **CAST:** Denholm Elliott, Mathonway Reeves. **1987**

CHILD'S PLAY ★★1/2 Hokey, violent horror film finds a dying criminal putting his soul into a doll. When a mother buys the doll for her son's birthday, predictable mayhem occurs. Good special effects and some humorous dialogue keep this one from becoming routine. Rated R. 87m. **DIR:** Tom Holland. **CAST:** Catharine Hicks, Chris Sarandon, Brad Dourif. **1988 DVD**

CHILD'S PLAY 2 ★★★ Chucky, the psychopathic doll from the 1988 original, returns to wreak more havoc as he attempts to transfer his demented soul into the body of a little boy. Effects wizard Kevin Yagher's new Chucky puppet adds to the terror. Rated R for violence and profanity. 88m. **DIR:** John Lafia. **CAST:** Alex Vincent, Jenny Agutter, Gerrit Graham, Christine Elise, Grace Zabriskie, Brad Dourif. **1990 DVD**

CHILD'S PLAY 3 ★★ A mess of molten plastic at the end of *Child's Play 2*, Chucky the killer doll is resurrected eight years later when the new CEO of the toy company that manufactured the Good Guys dolls resumes production. Chucky once again sets out to trade souls with Andy, now a teenaged cadet at a state-run military school. Rated R for violence and profanity. 89m. **DIR:** Jack Bender. **CAST:** Justin Whalin, Brad Dourif. **1991**

CHILL FACTOR ★★ A short-order cook (Skeet Ulrich) and an ice-cream truck driver (Cuba Gooding Jr.) go on the lam with a deadly biological weapon to keep it out of the hands of a demented arms dealer. They need the ice-cream truck because the weapon will detonate if the temperature rises above fifty degrees. Stitched together from pieces of better movies (*Speed*, *Raiders of the Lost Ark*, *The Wages of Fear*) and hammered across with clumsy enthusiasm, the film quickly becomes noisy and overbearing. Rated R for profanity and violence. 105m. **DIR:** Hugh Johnson. **CAST:** Cuba Gooding Jr., Skeet Ulrich, Peter Firth, David Paymer, Daniel Hugh Kelly. **1999 DVD**

CHILLER ★★★ A wealthy corporate widow's heir prematurely thaws out at a cryogenics facility. This made-for-TV sci-fi-horror film sketchily explores the possibility of life after death. Fright-master Wes Craven does a fair job of building suspense. 100m. **DIR:** Wes Craven. **CAST:** Michael Beck, Paul Sorvino, Jill Schoelen, Beatrice Straight, Laura Johnson. **1985 DVD**

CHILLERS ★★ Bored travelers at a bus depot exchange scary stories while waiting for a bus that never seems to come. Not that scary. Not rated; contains violence. 90m. **DIR:** Daniel Boyd. **CAST:** Jesse Emery, Marjorie Fitzsimmons, Jim Wolfe. **1988**

CHILLING, THE 🦃 Frozen bodies in a cryogenics facility are charged back to life during a lightning storm. A truly horrible experience. Rated R for profanity. 91m. **DIR:** Jack A. Sunseri, Deland Nuse. **CAST:** Linda Blair, Dan Haggerty, Troy Donahue. **1991**

CHILLY SCENES OF WINTER ★★★★ You'll probably find this excellent little film in the comedy section of your local video store, but don't be fooled; it's funny all right, but it has some scenes that evoke the true pain of love. John Heard plays a man in love with a married woman (Mary Beth Hurt). She also loves him, but is still attached to her husband. Rated PG for language and sex. 96m. **DIR:** Joan Micklin Silver. **CAST:** John Heard, Mary Beth Hurt, Peter Riegert, Kenneth McMillan, Gloria Grahame. **1979**

CHIMES AT MIDNIGHT (FALSTAFF) ★★★1/2 This arresting film combines parts of five of the Bard's plays in which the popular, indelible Sir John Falstaff appears. Orson Welles as the famous roly-poly tosspot is superb, but the film is hampered by its anemic budget. Ralph Richardson narrates. B&W; 115m. **DIR:** Orson Welles. **CAST:** Orson Welles, Jeanne Moreau, Margaret Rutherford, John Gielgud, Keith Baxter, Alan Webb, Walter Chiari. **1967**

CHINA BEACH (TV SERIES) ★★★1/2 Television pilot film for Emmy Award–winning dramatic series. Set at a medical base in Vietnam, this is basically *M*A*S*H* without the laughs. Dana Delaney shines as a nurse who has seen so much that she's becoming numb. Sixties songs are a plus. 97m. **DIR:** Rod Holcomb. **CAST:** Dana Delany, Nan Woods, Michael Patrick Boatman, Tim Ryan, Chloe Webb. **1988**

CHINA CRY ★★★★ Based on the autobiography by Nora Lamm, this gripping drama is the story of one woman's struggle for justice in 1950s Communist China. Julia Nickson gives an outstanding performance as the adult version of the lead character, whose idyllic, privileged life as the daughter of a doctor (James Shigeta) is all but destroyed after the Japanese invade Shanghai in 1941. Rated PG-13. 103m. **DIR:** James F. Collier. **CAST:** Julia Nickson, Russell Wong, James Shigeta, France Nuyen. **1991**

CHINA GATE ★★1/2 A romantic triangle develops in North Vietnam in the late Fifties. Not bad, but Angie Dickinson and Lee Van Cleef as Asians just don't cut it. B&W; 95m. **DIR:** Samuel Fuller. **CAST:** Angie Dickinson, Gene Barry, Nat King Cole, Lee Van Cleef. **1957**

CHINA GIRL 🦃 Romeo and Juliet on Friday the 13th. Rated R for violence and profanity. 90m. **DIR:** Abel Ferrara. **CAST:** James Russo, David Caruso, Richard Panebianco, Sari Chang, Russell Wong, Joey Chin, James Hong. **1987**

CHINA IS NEAR ★★★1/2 Marco Bellocchio, infamous for the tiresome *Devil in the Flesh*, displays a talent for both sardonic humor and political satire in this early film. The main characters plot against each other to gain political office, sexual satisfaction, and financial security. Their various connivings eventually bring them together as a sort of large, squabbling family. In Italian with English subtitles. B&W; 110m. **DIR:** Marco Bellocchio. **CAST:** Glauco Mauri, Elda Tattoli. **1968**

CHINA LAKE MURDERS, THE ★★★ Made-for-cable TV movie centers around the killings committed by a man masquerading as a California highway patrolman. Michael Parks is the killer who befriends tormented sheriff Tom Skerritt. 89m. **DIR:** Alan Metzger. **CAST:** Tom Skerritt, Michael Parks, Lauren Tewes, Nancy Everhard. **1990**

CHINA MOON ★★★★ Hotshot Florida detective Ed Harris falls in love with femme fatale Madeleine Stowe, and finds himself a suspect when her brutal husband is murdered. It's hard-boiled detective fiction in the classic vein with terrific performances and atmospheric direction. Rated R for profanity, nudity, simulated sex, and violence. 99m. **DIR:** John Bailey. **CAST:** Ed Harris, Madeleine Stowe, Benicio Del Toro, Pruitt Taylor Vince, Roger Aaron Brown, Charles Dance. **1994 DVD**

CHINA, MY SORROW ★★★ In communist China, a mischievous boy is sent to a wilderness reeducation camp where he struggles with hardship and the penalties for nonconformity. A satisfying blend of tension and unexpected humor. In Mandarin with English subtitles. 86m. **DIR:** Dai Sijie. **CAST:** Guo Liang-Yi, Tieu Quan Nghieu, Vuong Han Lai, Sam Chi-Vy. **1989**

CHINA O'BRIEN ★★ A former cop returns home to avenge her father's murder, using kung fu on the drug-dealing perpetrators. Rated R for violence and profanity. 90m. **DIR:** Robert Clouse. **CAST:** Cynthia Rothrock. **1990 DVD**

CHINA O'BRIEN 2 ★★ When a vengeful kingpin is sprung from jail, the streets aren't safe in a lady sheriff's town. Rated R for profanity. 85m. **DIR:** Robert Clouse. **CAST:** Cynthia Rothrock, Richard Norton. **1985**

CHINA SEAS ★★★1/2 Clark Gable is the captain of a Chinese river steamer in pirate-infested waters. Jean Harlow is once again the lady with a spotted past, who we all know is the perfect mate for Gable if he'd only realize it himself. An enjoyable screen romp. B&W; 90m. **DIR:** Tay Garnett. **CAST:** Clark Gable, Jean Harlow, Wallace Beery, Lewis Stone. **1935**

CHINA SKY ★★ Heroic doctor Randolph Scott puts down his stethoscope long enough to pick up a carbine and help Chinese guerrillas knock off hundreds of Japanese soldiers in this potboiler based on a Pearl Buck story. B&W; 78m. **DIR:** Ray Enright. **CAST:** Randolph Scott, Ruth Warrick, Anthony Quinn, Ellen Drew, Richard Loo. **1945**

CHINA SYNDROME, THE ★★★★★ This taut thriller, about an accident at a nuclear power plant, features strong performance and solid direction. It's superb entertainment with a timely message. Rated PG. 123m. **DIR:** James Bridges. **CAST:** Jane Fonda, Jack Lemmon, Michael Douglas, Scott Brady. **1979 DVD**

CHINA WHITE ★★ Shoot-'em-up takes place in Amsterdam's Chinatown when two Chinese drug lords threaten the Italian Mafia's profit margin. Add a romantic liaison and you have a just-watchable actioner. Rated R for violence and profanity. 99m. **DIR:** Ronny Yu. **CAST:** Russell Wong, Steven Vincent Leigh, Lisa Schrage, Billy Drago. **1990**

CHINATOWN ★★★★★ Robert Towne's fascinating, Oscar-winning script fuels this complicated thriller. Jack Nicholson is a seedy private investigator hired for what seems a simple case of spousal infidelity, but rapidly escalates into a complex affair of mistaken identity and investment schemes. Faye Dunaway is the mysterious woman who may—or may not—know more than she admits. Rated R for language, violence, and brief nudity. 131m. **DIR:** Roman Polanski. **CAST:** Jack Nicholson, Faye Dunaway, John Huston, Perry Lopez, Diane Ladd, John Hillerman, Burt Young. **1974 DVD**

CHINATOWN MURDERS, THE: MAN AGAINST THE MOB ★★★ L.A. cop George Peppard and his partners battle a prostitution ring operating out of Chinatown. Made-for-TV movie is most effective at re-creating the sights and sounds of the 1940s, though the story is average TV fodder. 102m. **DIR:** Michael Pressman. **CAST:** George Peppard, Richard Bradford, Charles Haid, Julia Nickson, Ursula Andress. **1989**

CHINESE BOX ★★1/2 A dying journalist and author moons over his unconsummated love for a former prostitute and in between cocktail parties becomes fascinated by a scarred street hustler. This tepid, metaphoric meditation on affairs of the heart and the return of Hong Kong to Chinese rule is only partially satisfying. Rated R for language and mature themes. In English and Mandarin with English subtitles. 109m. **DIR:** Wayne Wang. **CAST:** Jeremy Irons, Gong Li, Maggie Cheung, Rubén Blades, Michael Hui. **1998 DVD**

CHINESE BOXES ★★★ Arty thriller about an innocent American caught up in murderous intrigue in West Berlin. The plot is as puzzling as the game of the title. Thoughtful, patient viewers may enjoy it. Not rated; the film has violence and profanity. 87m. **DIR:** Christopher Petit. **CAST:** Will Patton, Gottfried John, Robbie Coltrane. **1984**

CHINESE CAT, THE ★★ Second entry in the Monogram run of *Charlie Chan* mystery B features. Made just as the series was running out of energy. The red herrings drop like flies as rivals battle for possession of a statuette bearing a rare diamond. B&W; 65m. **DIR:** Phil Rosen. **CAST:** Sidney Toler, Benson Fong, Joan Woodbury, Mantan Moreland, Ian Keith. **1944**

CHINESE CONNECTION, THE ★★★ This action-packed import, in which Bruce Lee plays a martial arts expert out to avenge the death of his mentor, is good, watchable fare. But be forewarned: It's dubbed, and not all that expertly. Rated R. 107m. **DIR:** Lo Wei. **CAST:** Bruce Lee, Miao Ker Hsio. **1979 DVD**

CHINESE GHOST STORY, A ★★★1/2 Atmospheric supernatural love story in ancient China where a young student takes shelter from a storm in a haunted temple where he falls for a beautiful ghost. Impressive special effects are laced with comical situations. In Cantonese with English subtitles. 93m. **DIR:** Ching Siu Tung. **CAST:** Leslie Cheung, Wong Tsu Tsien, Wu Ma. **1987 DVD**

CHINESE ROULETTE ★★★ A businessman, his wife, and their lovers are forced into an intense psychological game of truth telling by the couples' paraplegic daughter in this fascinating social satire. In German with English subtitles. Not rated; contains nudity and profanity. 96m. **DIR:** Rainer Werner Fassbinder. **CAST:** Anna Karina, Margit Carstensen, Ulli Lommel, Brigitte Mira. **1976**

CHINESE WEB, THE 🦃 Peter Parker (alias Spider-man) wards off a corrupt businessman. 95m. **DIR:** Don McDougall. **CAST:** Nicholas Hammond, Robert F. Simon, Benson Fong, John Milford, Ted Danson. **1978**

CHINO ★★ A surprisingly low-key Charles Bronson Western about a horse breeder who attempts to live a peaceful life. An above-average performance by Bronson and an adequate one by his wife, Jill Ireland, as Chino's love interest. Rated PG. 98m. **DIR:** John Sturges. **CAST:** Charles Bronson, Jill Ireland, Vincent Van Patten. **1973 DVD**

CHIPMUNK ADVENTURE, THE ★★ Alvin, Simon, and Theodore go on a round-the-world adventure in this uninspired feature-length cartoon. What made the original, scruffy chipmunks so appealing is missing here, replaced by a sort of ersatz Disney plot about jewel-smuggling villains. The kids may get a kick out of this, but anyone over the age of nine is advised to find something else to do. Rated G. 76m. **DIR:** Janice Karman. **1987**

•CHIPPENDALES MURDER, THE ★★ Based on a true story, this made-for-cable drama chronicles the rise of the Chippendales dancers and the strife between the owner and the choreographer of the group. Mild entertainment at best, this film doesn't have enough substance to really hold the viewer's interest. Not rated. 95m. **DIR:** Eric Bross. **CAST:** Naveen Andrews, Paul Hipp, Alex DeBoe, Dan Horton, James Moriarty, Natalie Radford. **2000**

CHIPS, THE WAR DOG ★★★1/2 This heart-wrenching account of the Dogs for Defense program formed during World War II focuses on the incredible bond formed between a lonely private and a heroic German shepherd. William Devane plays the military leader determined to train donated family pets to accompany soldiers on dangerous missions. Made for the Disney Channel, the only objectionable scenes take place on the battlefield. 95m. **DIR:** Ed Kaplan. **CAST:** Brandon Douglas, William Devane, Ned Vaughn, Paxton Whitehead, Ellie Cornell, Robert Miranda. **1989**

CHISHOLMS, THE ★★★ This made-for-TV oater is a vast saga of a family's trek west from Virginia to California. A bit talky, but worth a viewing. 300m. **DIR:** Mel Stuart. **CAST:** Robert Preston, Rosemary Harris, Ben Murphy, Brian Kerwin. **1979**

CHISUM ★★★1/2 The best of the John Wayne Westerns directed by Andrew V. McLaglen, this sprawling epic centers around the revenge sought by Billy the Kid (Geoffrey Duel) after his mentor (Patric Knowles) is murdered by the corrupt, land-grabbing bad guys. Rated G. 111m. **DIR:** Andrew V. McLaglen. **CAST:** John Wayne, Forrest Tucker, Christopher George, Ben Johnson, Patric Knowles, Bruce Cabot, Glenn Corbett. **1970**

CHITTY CHITTY BANG BANG ★★1/2 This musical extravaganza, based on a book by Ian Fleming, is aimed at a children's audience. In it, a car flies, but the flat jokes and songs leave adult viewers a bit seasick as they hope for a quick finale. However, the kiddies will like it. Rated G. 142m. **DIR:** Ken Hughes. **CAST:** Dick Van Dyke, Sally Ann Howes, Anna Quayle, Lionel Jeffries, Benny Hill. **1968 DVD**

CHLOE IN THE AFTERNOON ★★★★ This film concludes director Eric Rohmer's series of "moral fables." It is a trifle featherweight and utterly charming. Will the faithful hero have an affair with bohemian Chloe (played deftly by singer-actress Zouzou)? In French with English subtitles. No rating. 97m. **DIR:** Eric Rohmer. **CAST:** Bernard Verley, Zouzou, Françoise Verley, Françoise Fabian, Beatrice Romand. **1972 DVD**

CHLOE: LOVE IS CALLING YOU ★★1/2 Strange little bayou romance about a vengeful voodoo woman and the child she stole from a white family fifteen years before. Young Chloe is raised to believe herself the daughter of spell-casting Mandy, so when she falls in love with a wealthy white man she's warned off. Mandy breaks up the engagement party and kidnaps Chloe to be used as a human sacrifice in a voodoo ritual. Lots of atmospheric location footage and local players lend this curio its reality and heighten the frenzied finale. B&W; 54m. **DIR:** Marshall Neilan. **CAST:** Olive Borden, Reed Howes, Mollie O'Day, Frank Joyner, Georgette Harvey, Philip Ober. **1934**

CHOCOLAT (1989) ★★★★ A subtle, sophisticated, remarkably restrained French look at the colonial life of the past in Africa, as viewed from the innocent perspective of an 8 year old girl. Cecile Ducasse is memorable as the girl, whose story of growing racial awareness is told in flashback. In French with English subtitles. Rated PG-13 for profanity. 105m. **DIR:** Claire Dennis. **CAST:** Cecile Ducasse. **1989 DVD**

CHOCOLAT (2000) ★★★★★ A new chocolate shop in a small French village becomes a battleground between the free-spirited shopkeeper (Juliette Binoche) and the town's uptight mayor (Alfred Molina). The script takes some liberties with Joanne Harris's novel, but the result is a heartwarming, great-spirited parable of love and tolerance—a luscious candy box in its own right made all the sweeter by its topflight cast. Rated PG-13 for mature themes. 121m. **DIR:** Lasse Hallstrom. **CAST:** Juliette Binoche, Alfred Molina, Judi Dench, Johnny Depp, Lena Olin. **2000 DVD**

CHOCOLATE SOLDIER, THE ★★ Nelson Eddy and Rise Stevens play husband and wife opera stars whose marriage is skidding in this clever, winning remake of the Lunt-Fontanne hit, *The Guardsman.* Delightful. B&W; 102m. **DIR:** Roy Del Ruth. **CAST:** Nelson Eddy, Rise Stevens, Florence Bates, Nigel Bruce. **1941**

CHOCOLATE WAR, THE ★★★1/2 Actor Keith Gordon makes an impressive directorial debut with this comedy-drama about a bereaved student (Ilan Mitchell-Smith) facing the horrors of a sadistic teacher (John Glover) and a secret society of students at his Catholic high school. Some excellent performances and a story that keeps you fascinated. Rated R for profanity and violence. 103m. **DIR:** Keith Gordon. **CAST:** John Glover, Ilan Mitchell-Smith, Wally Ward, Adam Baldwin, Bud Cort. **1989**

CHOICE, THE ★★ Abortion is the controversy in this made-for-television film. Susan Clark stars as a mother who must help her daughter make the critical decision on whether to have an abortion or not. Too sentimental, but the performances are commendable. 100m. **DIR:** David Greene. **CAST:** Susan Clark, Mitchell Ryan, Jennifer Warren. **1981**

CHOICE OF ARMS, A ★★★ Yves Montand is a retired gangster who has chosen a peaceful life raising stud horses and giving his beautiful wife, Catherine Deneuve, all she could hope for. Gérard Depardieu is the convict who arrives seeking asylum. In French with subtitles; this film is unrated. 114m. **DIR:** Alain Corneau. **CAST:** Yves Montand, Gérard Depardieu, Catherine Deneuve, Michel Galabru, Gerard Lanvin. **1983**

CHOIRBOYS, THE 🦃 Despite its stellar ensemble cast, this remains one of the worst police dramas ever lensed. Rated R for profanity and raunch. 119m. **DIR:** Robert Aldrich. **CAST:** Charles Durning, Louis Gossett Jr., Perry King, Randy Quaid, Burt Young, James Woods, Blair Brown. **1977**

CHOKE CANYON 🦃 A two-fisted physicist takes on an evil industrialist in this absurd action-adventure movie. Rated PG. 96m. **DIR:** Chuck Bail. **CAST:** Stephen Collins, Janet Julian, Lance Henriksen, Bo Svenson. **1986**

C.H.O.M.P.S. ★★ A small-town enterprise is saved from bankruptcy when a young engineer (Wesley Eure) designs a computer-controlled watchdog. *C.H.O.M.P.S.* has a lot of the absurdity of a cartoon. Kids under twelve may enjoy it, but the profanity thrown in for the PG rating is purely gratuitous. 90m. **DIR:** Don Chaffey. **CAST:** Wesley Eure, Valerie Bertinelli, Conrad Bain, Chuck McCann, Red Buttons, Jim Backus. **1979**

CHOOSE ME ★★★★ A feast of fine acting and deliciously different situations, this stylish independent film works on every level and proves that inventive, nonmainstream entertainment is still a viable form. Written and directed by Alan Rudolph, the film is a funny, quirky, suspenseful, and surprising essay on love, sex, and the wacky state of male-female relationships in the 1980s. Rated R for violence and profanity. 110m. **DIR:** Alan Rudolph. **CAST:** Lesley Ann Warren, Keith Carradine, Genevieve Bujold. **1984 DVD**

•CHOPPER ★★ Real-life Mark "Chopper" Read became a cult figure and bestselling author after littering Australia with multiple murders and other assorted crimes. Here he commits a bloody prison assault, has an inmate slice off the top of his ears so he can get transferred to safer quarters, and is released into society where he terrorizes his old haunts. The acting is excellent but the film burrows deep into sensationalism rather than a revelatory character study. Not rated; contains profanity, nudity, extreme violence, and drug use. 94m. **DIR:** Andrew Dominik. **CAST:** Eric Bana, Simon Lyndon, Vince Colosimo, Dan Wyllie, David Field, Kate Beaham. **2000 DVD**

CHOPPER CHICKS IN ZOMBIETOWN ★★1/2 A mad mortician is killing people and reanimating their bodies to work in a mine. A parody of both biker movies and zombie flicks from the crazies at Troma Inc. Rated R for profanity and violence. 84m. **DIR:** Dan Hoskins. **CAST:** Jamie Rose, Vicki Frederick, Ed Gale, Don Calfa, Martha Quinn. **1991**

CHOPPING MALL ★★1/2 A group of teenagers hold the ultimate office party at the local shopping mall. At midnight it is impenetrably sealed and security droids, armed with high-tech weaponry, go on patrol, incapacitating any unauthorized personnel. This film has a good sense of humor and good visual effects. Rated R for nudity, profanity, and violence. 77m. **DIR:** Jim Wynorski. **CAST:** Kelli Maroney, Tony O'Dell, John Terlesky, Russell Todd. **1986**

CHORUS LINE, A ★★★★ The screen version of Michael Bennett's hit Broadway musical allows the viewer to experience the anxiety, struggle, and triumph of a group of dancers auditioning for a stage production. Director Richard Attenborough gracefully blends big production numbers with intimate moments. Rated PG for profanity and sexual descriptions. 120m. **DIR:** Richard Attenborough. **CAST:** Michael Douglas, Alyson Reed, Terrence Mann, Audrey Landers, Jan Gan Boyd. **1985**

CHORUS OF DISAPPROVAL, A ★★★ Film version of the hilarious Alan Ayckbourn play. Jeremy Irons is fun to watch as the protagonist, who stirs up intrigue in a small town when he joins its little theatre company, and Anthony Hopkins is truly bizarre as its domineering director. Rated PG for profanity and suggested sex. 92m. **DIR:** Michael Winner. **CAST:** Jeremy Irons, Anthony Hopkins, Jenny Seagrove. **1989**

CHOSEN, THE ★★★★★ A flawless, arresting drama illustrating the conflict between friendship and family loyalty experienced by two young men. Based on the novel of the same name by Chaim Potok, the story, centering on Jewish issues, transcends its setting to attain universal impact. Rated G. 105m. **DIR:** Jeremy Paul Kagan. **CAST:** Robby Benson, Rod Steiger, Maximilian Schell. **1978**

CHRIST STOPPED AT EBOLI ★★ Based on a renowned Italian novel about Carlo Levi, a political exile who was punished in 1935 for his antifascist writings and exiled to a village in southern Italy. Irene Papas livens things up with her resounding laugh, but ultimately this quiet tale is forgettable. In Italian with English subtitles. 118m. **DIR:** Francesco Rosi. **CAST:** Gian Maria Volonté, Irene Papas, Alain Cuny, Lea Massari, François Simon. **1983**

CHRISTIAN THE LION ★★1/2 A lion born in a London zoo is returned to the wilds in Kenya. This pleasant film is also interesting for the real-life drama. Bill Travers portrayed George Adamson, the wildlife expert, in *Born Free.* Now, Adamson is seen helping Christian adapt to his natural habitat. Rated G for family viewing. 89m. **DIR:** Bill Travers, James Hill. **CAST:** Bill Travers, Virginia McKenna, George Adamson. **1976**

CHRISTIANE F. ★★ Although quite interesting in places, this West German film dealing with young heroin addicts ultimately becomes a bore. In German with English subtitles. 124m. **DIR:** Uli Edel. **CAST:** Natja Brunkhorst, Thomas Haustein. **1981 DVD**

CHRISTINA ★★ Contrived mystery film about a wealthy foreigner (Barbara Parkins) who pays an unemployed aircraft engineer (Peter Haskell) twenty-five thousand dollars to marry her so she can acquire a U.S. passport . . . or so we think. 95m. **DIR:** Paul Krasny. **CAST:** Barbara Parkins, Peter Haskell, James McEachin, Marlyn Mason. **1974**

CHRISTINE ★★★1/2 Novelist Stephen King and director John Carpenter team up for topflight, tasteful terror with this movie about a 1958 Plymouth Fury with spooky powers. It's scary without being gory; a triumph of suspense and atmosphere. Rated R for profanity and violence. 111m. **DIR:** John Carpenter. **CAST:** Keith Gordon, John Stockwell, Alexandra Paul, Harry Dean Stanton, Robert Prosky, Christine Belford, Roberts Blossom. **1983 DVD**

CHRISTMAS CAROL, A (1938) ★★★1/2 This film version of Charles Dickens's Christmas classic is a better-than-average retelling of Ebenezer Scrooge's transformation from a greedy malcontent to a generous, compassionate businessman. Reginald Owen is fine as Scrooge, and so is the rest of the cast. B&W; 69m. **DIR:** Edwin L. Marin. **CAST:** Reginald Owen, Gene Lockhart, Kathleen Lockhart, Leo G. Carroll, Terry Kilburn. **1938**

CHRISTMAS CAROL, A (1951) ★★★★★ Starring Alastair Sim as Ebenezer Scrooge, the meanest miser in all of London, this is a wondrously uplifting story—as only Charles Dickens could craft one. Recommended for the whole family, *A Christmas Carol* is sure to bring a tear to your eye and joy to your heart. B&W; 86m. **DIR:** Brian Desmond Hurst. **CAST:** Alastair Sim, Kathleen Harrison, Jack Warner, Michael Hordern. **1951 DVD**

CHRISTMAS CAROL, A (1984) ★★★★ This solid rendition of Dickens's classic follows the text and style of the original story more closely than previous versions. Only George C. Scott's performance keeps this from being the best realization of Dickens's story; he makes an excellent, crotchety Scrooge, but as the reformed Scrooge he is simply gruff, not at all like Alastair Sim's dramatic transformation in the earlier version. Good cinematography and grand settings. Rated PG. 100m. **DIR:** Clive Donner. **CAST:** George C. Scott, Frank Finlay, Angela Pleasence, David Warner, Edward Woodward, Susannah York. **1984**

CHRISTMAS CAROL, A (1999) ★★★★ Dickens's much redone classic is infused with new life in this TNT/Hallmark Entertainment collaboration. Naturally, the special effects have improved over earlier efforts but more impressive than that is what Patrick Stewart brings to the part of Ebenezer Scrooge. Having performed dramatic readings from Dickens's masterpiece for a decade, he seems to embody the author's anti-greed theme and his transformation from ogre to benefactor is nothing short of miraculous. Not rated; suitable for family viewing. 89m. **DIR:** David Jones. **CAST:** Patrick Stewart, Richard E. Grant, Joel Grey. **1999**

CHRISTMAS COAL MINE MIRACLE, THE ★★★ In this made-for-television film a crew of striking coal miners, threatened by their union-busting bosses, enter a mine and are trapped by an explosion. The action is good, but the tone is too sweet. Also known as *Christmas Miracle in Caulfield, U.S.A.* 100m. **DIR:** Jud Taylor. **CAST:** Mitchell Ryan, Kurt Russell, Andrew Prine, John Carradine, Barbara Babcock, Melissa Gilbert, Don Porter, Shelby Leverington. **1977**

CHRISTMAS EVIL A toy factory employee goes slowly insane. Not rated, but the equivalent of an R rating for sex and violence. 91m. **DIR:** Lewis Jackson. **CAST:** Brandon Maggart, Jeffrey DeMunn. **1983 DVD**

CHRISTMAS IN CONNECTICUT ★★ A New York cooking show host, Dyan Cannon, actually knows nothing about the culinary arts and a national park ranger, Kris Kristofferson, hailed a hero for his rescue of a little boy during a snowstorm, are brought together and fall in love. This lightweight, syrupy romance farce is strictly by the numbers. Cannon tries hard but Kristofferson is as wooden as ever. Directorial debut of Arnold Schwarzenegger. No rating. 93m. **DIR:** Arnold Schwarzenegger. **CAST:** Dyan Cannon, Kris Kristofferson, Tony Curtis, Richard Roundtree, Kelly Cinnante. **1992**

CHRISTMAS IN CONNECTICUT ★★★1/2 In this spirited comedy, a successful newspaper family-advice columnist (Barbara Stanwyck) arranges a phony family for herself—all for the sake of publicity. The acting is good and the pace is quick, but the script needs polishing. Nonetheless, it's a Christmas favorite. B&W; 101m. **DIR:** Peter Godfrey. **CAST:** Barbara Stanwyck, Dennis Morgan, Sydney Greenstreet, S. Z. Sakall, Reginald Gardiner, Una O'Connor. **1945**

CHRISTMAS IN JULY ★★★1/2 Touching, insightful comedy-drama about a young couple's dreams and aspirations. Dick Powell is fine as the young man who mistakenly believes that he has won a contest and finds all doors opening to him—until the error is discovered. This one is a treat for all audiences. Once you've seen it, you'll want to see all of Preston Sturges's films. B&W; 67m. **DIR:** Preston Sturges. **CAST:** Dick Powell, Ellen Drew, Raymond Walburn, William Demarest, Ernest Truex, Franklin Pangborn. **1940**

CHRISTMAS KID, THE ★★ A woman dies on Christmas Eve while giving birth to a son who is christened "The Christmas Kid" and raised by the town. He becomes a gunman and is hired by the town boss but switches sides when his girlfriend is killed. He becomes the sheriff and cleans up the lawlessness. A good story and acting. Filmed in Spain. Rated G. 87m. **DIR:** Sidney Pink. **CAST:** Jeffrey Hunter, Louis Hayward, Gustavo Rojo, Perla Cristal, Luis Prendes, Jack Taylor. **1966**

CHRISTMAS LILIES OF THE FIELD ★★★ A handyman (Billy Dee Williams) returns to help nuns and orphans once again, in this sequel to the award-winning 1963 film. A solid, well-intentioned movie, yet not quite achieving the charm of the original. Not rated, but suitable for all ages. 98m. **DIR:** Ralph Nelson. **CAST:** Billy Dee Williams, Maria Schell, Fay Hauser. **1979**

CHRISTMAS REUNION, A ★★★★ A good tearjerker in which a boy, unwanted by his grandfather, hears a story told by a man who looks like Santa Claus about a grandson and grandfather who must learn to accept each other. Good acting and writing. Not rated, but suitable for all audiences. 92m. **DIR:** David Hemmings. **CAST:** Edward Woodward, Meredith Edwards, James Coburn, Gweirydd Gwyndaf. **1993**

CHRISTMAS STORY, A ★★★★ Both heartwarming and hilarious, this is humorist Jean Shepherd's recollections of being a kid in the 1940s and the monumental Christmas that brought the ultimate longing—for a regulation Red Ryder air rifle. Problem is, his parents don't think it's such a good idea. Peter Billingsley is marvelous as the kid. Melinda Dillon and Darren McGavin also shine as the put-upon parents. A delight for young and old. Rated PG. 98m. **DIR:** Bob Clark. **CAST:** Peter Billingsley, Darren McGavin, Melinda Dillon, Ian Petrella. **1983 DVD**

CHRISTMAS TO REMEMBER, A ★★★★ Grandpa Larson (Jason Robards), who never got over his son's death, resents his grandson's visit. His unkind manner toward the boy convinces the youngster that he must run away. Eva Marie Saint plays Grandma Larson, who rebukes her husband for his cruelty. Joanne Woodward makes a cameo appearance. Not rated, this provides fine family entertainment comparable with a G rating. 96m. **DIR:** George Englund. **CAST:** Jason Robards Jr., Eva Marie Saint, Joanne Woodward. **1979**

CHRISTMAS WIFE, THE ★★★1/2 Jason Robards delivers his usual superior performance as a newly widowed man who goes to a lonely hearts agency. Julie Harris, as his arranged date, has quite a little secret to hide. Fine seasonal heart-warmer created for HBO. 73m. **DIR:** David Jones. **CAST:** Jason Robards Jr., Julie Harris, Don Francks. **1988 DVD**

CHRISTMAS WITHOUT SNOW, A ★★★★ John Houseman and the entire cast shine in this beautiful made-for-TV story about a dictatorial choirmaster, a newly divorced woman, a church choir, and their combined problems while rehearsing for a performance of Handel's *Messiah* oratorio. Definitely worth viewing. 100m. **DIR:** John Korty. **CAST:** John Houseman, Ramon Bieri, James Cromwell, Valerie Curtin. **1980**

CHRISTOPHER COLUMBUS (1985) Stinkeroo travelogue-as-history, edited down from a lethally boring and misbegotten miniseries. 128m. **DIR:** Alberto Lattuada. **CAST:** Gabriel Byrne, Faye Dunaway, Oliver Reed, Max von Sydow, Eli Wallach, Nicol Williamson, José Ferrer, Virna Lisi, Raf Vallone. **1985**

CHRISTOPHER COLUMBUS: THE DISCOVERY (1992) For all we care, this lamebrained movie about the famous Italian explorer can remain undiscovered. Tom Selleck as King Ferdinand is the worst casting since John Wayne as Genghis Khan. Rated PG-13 for violence and nudity. 120m. **DIR:** John Glen. **CAST:** Marlon Brando, Tom Selleck, Georges Corraface, Rachel Ward, Robert Davi. **1992**

CHRISTOPHER STRONG ★★1/2 Katharine Hepburn's second film, this one gave her her first starring role. She is a record-breaking flyer who falls passionately in love with a married man she cannot have. High-plane soap opera. Kate's legions of fans will love it, however. B&W; 77m. **DIR:** Dorothy Arzner. **CAST:** Katharine Hepburn, Colin Clive, Billie Burke, Helen Chandler, Jack LaRue. **1933**

CHROME SOLDIERS ★★★ Gary Busey returns home from Desert Storm to find his brother dead. Busey and four other Vietnam veterans take on a corrupt sheriff in this surprisingly good made-for-cable movie. 91m. **DIR:** Thomas Wright. **CAST:** Gary Busey, Ray Sharkey, William Atherton, Nicholas Guest, Yaphet Kotto. **1992**

CHRONOPOLIS ★★★★ Highly original and imaginative science-fiction animation feature about a city lost in space where strange pharaoh-like immortals put an end to their deathless state by fabricating time, represented by metamorphosing white balls. Filmmaker Piotr Kamler took five years to complete this project. Not rated. In French with English subtitles. 70m. **DIR:** Piotr Kamler. **1982**

CHU CHU AND THE PHILLY FLASH ★★ This is another bittersweet comedy about a couple of losers. It's supposed to be funny. It isn't. The stars, Alan Arkin and Carol Burnett, do manage to invest it with a certain wacky charm, but that isn't enough to make up for its shortcomings. Rated PG. 100m. **DIR:** David Lowell Rich. **CAST:** Alan Arkin, Carol Burnett, Jack Warden, Ruth Buzzi. **1981**

CHUCK AMUCK: THE MOVIE ★★★★ Released in tandem with Warner Bros. animator Chuck Jones's lighthearted autobiography, this equally compelling documentary provides ample evidence of the artist's impressive work on shorts such as "What's Opera, Doc?" and "Duck Dodgers in the 24th Century." Richly informative anecdotes unfold while Jones, pencil in hand, effortlessly demonstrates the conceptual origins of beloved characters such as Bugs Bunny, the Road Runner, and Pepe Le Pew. Jones is quite witty and charming in his own right. Not rated. 52m. **DIR:** John Needham. **1989**

CHUCK & BUCK ★★ Sexual experimentation provides gnarled, long-term ramifications for two preteen buddies in this low-budget, deadpan story. Chuck has become a Los Angeles music producer with a fiancée, swank Hollywood Hills home, and cool car. Buck is a case of arrested development who moves to L.A. and stalks his former playmate. The ambiguity of the film intrigues, but the characters' actions fail to convince. Rated R for language and sex. 96m. **DIR:** Miguel Arteta. **CAST:** Chris Weitz, Mike White, Beth Colt, Lupe Ontiveros, Paul Weitz. **2000 DVD**

CHUCK BERRY HAIL! HAIL! ROCK 'N' ROLL ★★★★★ Put simply, this is the greatest rock 'n' roll concert movie ever made. Keith Richards, Eric Clapton, Julian Lennon, and Linda Ronstadt are just some of the singers and players who back Berry during his sixtieth-birthday-tribute concert at St. Louis's Fox Theatre. Rated PG. 120m. **DIR:** Taylor Hackford. **CAST:** Chuck Berry, Keith Richards, Bo Diddley, Little Richard, Eric Clapton, Linda Ronstadt, Johnnie Johnson. **1987**

C.H.U.D. ★★ The performances by John Heard and Daniel Stern make this cheapo horror film watchable. C.H.U.D. (Cannibalistic Humanoid Underground Dwellers) are New York City bag people who have been exposed to radiation and start treating the other inhabitants of the city as lunch. Rated R for violence, profanity, and gore. 88m. **DIR:** Douglas Cheek. **CAST:** John Heard, Daniel Stern, Christopher Curry. **1984 DVD**

C.H.U.D. II (BUD THE C.H.U.D.) 🦃 This is not a sequel at all, but a thinly disguised *Return of the Living Dead III.* Rated R for violence. 84m. **DIR:** David Irving. **CAST:** Brian Robbins, Gerrit Graham, Robert Vaughn, Bianca Jagger, June Lockhart, Norman Fell. **1989**

CHUKA ★★ A hard-bitten gunfighter and a disgraced cavalry officer try to keep marauding Indians from getting to the voluptuous Italian beauty who happened to end up in the Southwest in full makeup. Ho hum. 105m. **DIR:** Gordon Douglas. **CAST:** Rod Taylor, John Mills, Ernest Borgnine, Luciana Paluzzi, James Whitmore, Louis Hayward. **1967**

CHUMP AT OXFORD, A ★★★ Stan Laurel receives a scholarship to Oxford, and Oliver Hardy accompanies him. They are the butt of pranks and jokes until Stan receives a blow on the head and becomes a reincarnation of a college hero. A fair script, but the Stan and Ollie characters never seem to fit well into it. B&W; 63m. **DIR:** Alf Goulding. **CAST:** Stan Laurel, Oliver Hardy, Wilfred Lucas, Forrester Harvey, James Finlayson, Anita Garvin. **1940**

CHUNGKING EXPRESS ★★★ This mildly intoxicating slice of Hong Kong romance *noir* is split into two faintly connected stories. A cop gets dumped by his girlfriend and tries to fall in love with the next woman he encounters. Next, a cop gets dumped by a stewardess and is harmlessly stalked by a daffy food-counter clerk. In Mandarin and Cantonese with English subtitles. Rated PG-13 for language and violence. 103m. **DIR:** Wong Kar-Wai. **CAST:** Tony Leung Chiu Wai, Faye Wang, Brigitte Lin, Takeshi Kaneshiro, Valerie Chow. **1995**

•CHUNHYANG ★★★1/2 In medieval Korea, two young lovers are separated by class and by the machinations of a lecherous provincial governor. The film moves smoothly between this story and a modern *tansori* singer (a venerable Korean art form) who performs the tale before a present-day audience. The novel structure, good acting, and beautiful photography make this a winner. In Korean with English subtitles. Rated R for sexual themes. 120m. **DIR:** Kwon-taek Im. **CAST:** Hyo-jeong Lee, Seung-woo Cho, Sung-nyu Kim. **2001 DVD**

CHURCH, THE ★★1/2 Horror impresario Dario Argento wrote this tale of demons entombed under a Gothic cathedral who are let loose during a renovation project. Not rated; contains violence, profanity, and gore. 110m. **DIR:** Michele Soavi. **CAST:** Hugh Quarshie, Tomas Arana, Feodor Chaliapin. **1991 DVD**

CIA CODENAME ALEXA 🦃 An intelligence agent and a gung-ho cop reprogram a terrorist to turn against her boss. Ridiculous. Rated R for violence and profanity. 90m. **DIR:** Joseph Merhi. **CAST:** Lorenzo Lamas, O. J. Simpson, Kathleen Kinmont, Alex Cord. **1992**

CIA II: TARGET: ALEXA 🦃 The CIA tries to recover a stolen microchip in this very violent, plotless film. Rated R for violence. 90m. **DIR:** Lorenzo Lamas. **CAST:** Lorenzo Lamas, Kathleen Kinmont, Pamela Dixon, John Savage. **1993**

CIAO FEDERICO! ★★★ A revealing portrait of Federico Fellini at work, directing the actors who populate the unreal world of *Satyricon.* Immersed in the creative process, Fellini is captured by documentary filmmaker Gideon Bachmann. In English and Italian with English subtitles. Not rated. 55m. **DIR:** Gideon Bachmann. **CAST:** Federico Fellini, Martin Potter, Hiram Keller, Roman Polanski, Sharon Tate. **1971**

CIAO! MANHATTAN 🦃 Far more pornographic than any skin flick, this sleazy, low-budget release features

Edie Sedgwick, a onetime Andy Warhol "superstar," in a grotesque parody of her life. 84m. **DIR:** John Palmer, David Weisman. **CAST:** Edie Sedgwick, Isabel Jewell, Baby Jane Holzer, Roger Vadim, Viva, Paul America. **1983**

CIAO PROFESSORE ★★1/2 *To Sir with Love* goes Italian when a pompous, uptight teacher is accidentally assigned to a poor school in a tough neighborhood. The setting is unusual and the kids are cute, but all the clichés are trotted out with dull predictability. In Italian with English subtitles. Rated R for profanity. 91m. **DIR:** Lina Wertmuller. **CAST:** Paolo Villaggio, Isa Danieli, Gigio Morra, Ester Carloni, Sergio Solli. **1993**

CIDER HOUSE RULES, THE ★★★★ A young man (Tobey Maguire) leaves the orphanage where he grew up, working in an apple orchard, and falling for his best friend's girl while the friend is off fighting World War II. John Irving's novel becomes a sincere, sagacious film about lessons taught and learned among the forests and orchards of Maine. Irving won a well-deserved Oscar for his smooth, intelligent script, as did Michael Caine, equally deserving for his performance as the compassionate doctor who runs the orphanage. Rated PG-13 for mature themes of abortion and incest. 131m. **DIR:** Lasse Hallstrom. **CAST:** Tobey Maguire, Michael Caine, Charlize Theron, Delroy Lindo, Paul Rudd, Kate Nelligan. **1999 DVD**

CIGARETTE GIRL FROM MOSSELPROM, THE ★★1/2 A man falls in love with a cigarette girl who unwittingly becomes a movie star, and in turn falls for the cameraman. Charming, quirky tale of unrequited love and unattained dreams. A clever ending makes this silent movie worth a look if your tastes are eclectic enough. Silent. B&W; 78m. **DIR:** Yuri Zhelyabuzhsky. **CAST:** Yulia Solntseva. **1924**

CIMARRON (1931) ★★★ One of the panoramic, expensive early sound films, this Western based on Edna Ferber's novel presents the story of a pioneer family bent on building an empire out of the primitiveness of early Oklahoma. It won the Academy Award for best picture, but some scenes now seem dated. B&W; 124m. **DIR:** Wesley Ruggles. **CAST:** Richard Dix, Irene Dunne, Estelle Taylor, William Collier Jr., Roscoe Ates. **1931**

CIMARRON (1960) ★★★ Overlong Western opens with a spectacular re-creation of the 1889 Oklahoma land rush, but bogs down into a familiar building-of-the-West tale. Tries for epic status but misses the mark. 147m. **DIR:** Anthony Mann. **CAST:** Glenn Ford, Maria Schell, Anne Baxter, Arthur O'Connell, Mercedes McCambridge, Russ Tamblyn, Vic Morrow, Robert Keith, Aline MacMahon, Harry Morgan, Charles McGraw, Royal Dano, Edgar Buchanan. **1960**

CINCINNATI KID, THE ★★★★ Steve McQueen had one of his earliest acting challenges in this study of a determined young poker player on his way to the big time. He lets nothing stand in his way, especially not the reigning king of the card tables, Edward G. Robinson. 113m. **DIR:** Norman Jewison. **CAST:** Steve McQueen, Ann-Margret, Edward G. Robinson, Karl Malden, Tuesday Weld. **1965**

CINDERELLA (1950) ★★★★ In this underappreciated Disney delight, a pretty youngster, who is continually berated and abused by her stepmother and stepsisters, is given one night to fulfill her dreams by a fairy godmother. The mice characters are among the studio's best, and the story moves along at a good clip. Almost in the league of *Snow White and the Seven Dwarfs* and *Pinocchio*, this animated triumph is sure to please the young and the young-at-heart. Rated G. 75m. **DIR:** Wilfred Jackson, Hamilton Luske, Clyde Geronimi. **1950**

CINDERELLA (1964) ★★★ This film is a reworking of the live 1957 CBS broadcast of the Rodgers and Hammerstein musical that featured the young Julie Andrews. The score is unchanged with the exception of an additional "Loneliness of Evening," which had been cut from *South Pacific*. A charming show for the entire family. 100m. **DIR:** Charles S. Dubin. **CAST:** Lesley Ann Warren, Stuart Damon, Ginger Rogers, Walter Pidgeon, Celeste Holm. **1964**

CINDERELLA (1976) ★★ Imagine the classic fairy tale retold by way of sex comedy and you have this generally harmless piece of fluff, tame by modern standards. The film was a hit and followed shortly thereafter by the sequel *Fairy Tales*. Not rated; contains nudity and suggested sex. 94m. **DIR:** Michael Pataki. **CAST:** Cheryl Smith, Kirk Scott, Sy Richardson. **1976**

CINDERELLA (1985) ★★★★ This is one of the most entertaining of producer Shelley Duvall's *Faerie Tale Theatre* entries. Jennifer Beals is a shy, considerate, and absolutely gorgeous Cinderella; Matthew Broderick does his aw-shucks best as the smitten Prince Henry. Sweetly romantic, a treat for all. Not rated—family fare. 60m. **DIR:** Mark Cullingham. **CAST:** Jennifer Beals, Matthew Broderick, Jean Stapleton, Eve Arden, Edie McClurg. **1985**

CINDERELLA (1987) ★★★★ The immortal fairy tale is set to music by Sergei Prokofiev and performed by the world-acclaimed Berlin Comic Opera Ballet. The beautiful Hannelore Bey and Roland Gawlick as the principals provide a balance to the comedy of the rest of the ballet corps. 75m. **DIR:** Tom Schilling. **CAST:** Berlin Comic Opera Ballet. **1987**

CINDERELLA LIBERTY ★★★1/2 Marsha Mason earned an Oscar nomination as a feisty Seattle hooker with a worldly-wise 11 year old son in this quirky little romance, which also stars James Caan as a sailor who learns to love them both. The plot is predictable, but the performances are genuinely touching. Rated R for profanity and sexual themes. 117m. **DIR:** Mark Rydell. **CAST:** James Caan, Marsha Mason, Eli Wallach. **1973**

CINDERFELLA ★★ Musical version of the oft-told fairy tale has little to recommend it. Adapted for the talents of star Jerry Lewis, it will only appeal to his fans. 91m. **DIR:** Frank Tashlin. **CAST:** Jerry Lewis, Anna Maria Alberghetti, Ed Wynn. **1960**

CINEMA PARADISO ★★★★ A pleasant sense of nostalgia pervades this Oscar winner for best foreign language film. Giuseppe Tornatore's story focuses on the love of a young boy—and indeed the entire Sicilian village where he lives—for movies. In Italian with English subtitles. Not rated, the film has profanity and suggested sex. 123m. **DIR:** Giuseppe Tornatore. **CAST:** Philippe Noiret, Jacques Perrin, Salvatore Cascio, Marco Leonardi. **1989 DVD**

CIRCLE OF DANGER ★★★ An American in England investigates his brother's death during a commando raid. Survivors of the raid offer clues in this murky, moody, talky mystery. B&W; 86m. **DIR:** Jacques Tourneur. **CAST:** Ray Milland, Patricia Roc, Marius Goring, Hugh Sinclair. **1951**

CIRCLE OF DECEIT ★★★ A reporter troubled by his failing marriage accepts an assignment in war-torn Lebanon, where he hopes to find some meaning to the questions of life that trouble him. If that description sounds pretentious, it's because this film more than occasionally is. Still, location shooting in Lebanon and strong performances make this better than it deserves to be. In German with English subtitles. Not rated; contains violence and sexuality. 108m. **DIR:** Volker Schlöndorff. **CAST:** Bruno Ganz, Hanna Schygulla, Jean Carmet, Jerzy Skolimowski. **1981**

CIRCLE OF FEAR ★★1/2 Disgruntled Vietnam vet personally biffs almost every Filipino in Manila, searching for the nasties who kidnapped his daughter and sold her into sex slavery. Passable macho-actioner. Patrick Dollaghan does a shameless Michael Douglas impression. Rated R. 87m. **DIR:** Clark Henderson. **CAST:** Patrick Dollaghan, Wesley Penning, Joey Aresco, Vernon Wells. **1989**

CIRCLE OF FRIENDS ★★★★ Minnie Driver contributes a career-making lead performance as a college-age Irish woman—circa 1957—coming to grips with earthly love and Catholic fidelity in this charming adaptation of Maeve Binchy's bestseller. Rated PG-13 for candid sexuality. 96m. **DIR:** Pat O'Connor. **CAST:** Minnie Driver, Chris O'Donnell, Geraldine O'Rawe, Saffron Burrows, Alan Cumming, Colin Firth. **1995 DVD**

CIRCLE OF IRON ★★★ Bruce Lee was preparing the screenplay for this martial arts fantasy shortly before he died. Ironically, the lead role fell to David Carradine, who had also been chosen over Lee for the lead in the television series *Kung Fu*. Fans of the genre will love it. Rated R for violence. 102m. **DIR:** Richard Moore. **CAST:** David Carradine, Jeff Cooper, Christopher Lee, Roddy McDowall, Eli Wallach, Erica Creer. **1979**

CIRCLE OF LOVE 🦃 This is a terrible rehash of Max Ophuls's *La Ronde*. 105m. **DIR:** Roger Vadim. **CAST:** Jane Fonda, Jean-Claude Brialy, Maurice Ronet, Jean Sorel, Anna Karina. **1964**

CIRCLE OF PASSION ★★★ French-Canadian production features director Charles Finch as a banker trapped in a loveless marriage. Passion returns to his life when he takes a business trip to Paris and romances hat maker Sandrine Bonnaire. When he falls in love with her, he must confront the reality of his marriage. Jane March is wonderful as the emotionally deprived wife. In English and French. Rated R for adult situations and language. 94m. **DIR:** Charles Finch. **CAST:** Charles Finch, Jane March, Sandrine Bonnaire, Julian Sands, James Fox. **1996**

CIRCLE OF TWO 🦃 Eccentric artist develops a romantic—but somehow platonic—relationship with a teenage girl. Rated PG for nudity. 105m. **DIR:** Jules Dassin. **CAST:** Richard Burton, Tatum O'Neal, Kate Reid, Robin Gammell. **1980**

CIRCONSTANCES ATTENUANTES ★★★ A hard-nosed, retired judge and his wife are stranded in an auberge filled with criminals. The ending is a bit far-fetched, but the film is enjoyable. In French with English subtitles. B&W; 90m. **DIR:** Jean Boyer. **CAST:** Michel Simon, Arletty, Dorville, Andrex, Robert Ozanne, Georges Lannes. **1955**

CIRCUITRY MAN ★★★ Kinky tale of a futuristic world where computer chips simulate drugs and sex. A beautiful bodyguard must smuggle the chips across the country through an elaborate underground maze. Dennis Christopher steals the show as a scummy subterranean dweller who helps her get there. Rated R for violence and profanity. 85m. **DIR:** Steven Lovy. **CAST:** Dana Wheeler-Nicholson, Jim Metzler, Lu Leonard, Dennis Christopher, Vernon Wells. **1989**

CIRCUITRY MAN II: PLUGHEAD REWIRED ★★ Sequel misses the mark with the belief that more is better. Vernon Wells returns as the notorious Plughead, a villain who loves to tap into people's minds and then give them a dose of his twisted sense of pain. It's up to hero Circuitry Man (Jim Metzler) and a beautiful agent played by Deborah Shelton to put an end to Plughead's reign of terror. Rated R for violence, language, and adult situations. 97m. **DIR:** Steven Lovy, Robert Lovy. **CAST:** Jim Metzler, Deborah Shelton, Vernon Wells, Traci Lords, Dennis Christopher. **1993**

CIRCUMSTANCES UNKNOWN ★★★ Suspenseful made-for-cable original about a deranged jeweler who likes to kill happily married couples. Judd Nelson is very good at portraying the psycho killer. Not rated; contains violence. 95m. **DIR:** Robert Lewis. **CAST:** Judd Nelson, Isabel Glasser, William R. Moses. **1995**

•CIRCUS ★★1/2 This convoluted tale of con men and bad guys stars John Hannah and Famke Janssen as a married team of confidence artists who get swept into a violent world of lies and betrayal by a mob boss anxious to find a patsy to take a tax fall for him. The more the con artists play the game, the worse their chances become of making it through alive. Colorful hit men, loan sharks, and enforcers aren't enough to make this any more than a one-ring affair. Rated R for adult language, sex, and violence. 95m. **DIR:** Rob Walker. **CAST:** John Hannah, Famke Janssen, Fred Ward, Peter Stormare, Eddie Izzard. **2000 DVD**

CIRCUS OF FEAR 🦃 For its U.S. theatrical release, this tired Edgar Wallace mystery was shorn of half an hour, retitled *Psycho Circus*, and issued in black and white—but don't expect its video restoration to do anything but make its flaws more obvious. B&W; 90m. **DIR:** John Llewellyn Moxey. **CAST:** Christopher Lee, Suzy Kendall, Klaus Kinski. **1967**

CIRCUS OF HORRORS ★★★ British thriller about a renegade plastic surgeon using a circus as a front. After making female criminals gorgeous, he enslaves them in his Temple of Beauty. When they want out, he colorfully offs them. Well made with good performances. This is the more violent European version. 87m. **DIR:** Sidney Hayers. **CAST:** Anton Diffring, Erika Remberg, Yvonne Romain, Donald Pleasence. **1960 DVD**

CIRCUS, THE/A DAY'S PLEASURE ★★★ This double feature admirably showcases Charlie Chaplin's world-famous gifts for comedy and pathos. In the first, vagabond Charlie hooks up with a traveling circus and falls for the bareback rider, who loves a muscle-bound trapeze artist. In the second feature, Charlie and his family try in vain to have Sunday fun. Silent. B&W; 105m. **DIR:** Charles Chaplin. **CAST:** Charlie Chaplin, Al-

Ian Garcia, Merna Kennedy, Harry Crocker, Betty Morrisey, George Davis, Henry Bergman. **1928 DVD**

CIRCUS WORLD 🦃 Even John Wayne can't help this sappy soap opera set under the big top. 135m. **DIR:** Henry Hathaway. **CAST:** John Wayne, Rita Hayworth, Claudia Cardinale, John Smith, Lloyd Nolan, Richard Conte. **1964**

CISCO KID, THE ★★★ The Cisco Kid and his faithful companion, Pancho, battle the French Occupation Army and American gunners in Mexico. Enjoyable, lighthearted Western is spiced with humor and enthusiastic performances by Jimmy Smits and Richard "Cheech" Marin. Made for TV. 95m. **DIR:** Luis Valdez. **CAST:** Jimmy Smits, Richard "Cheech" Marin, Sadie Frost, Ron Perlman, Bruce Payne. **1994**

CISCO KID (TV SERIES) ★★★ The Cisco Kid, O'Henry's Robin Hood of the Old West, and his English language mangling sidekick Pancho, rode the TV range for 176 episodes. The only series of its type filmed entirely in color. Volume one features two of the best episodes: "Quarter Horse" and "Postmaster." 50m. **DIR:** Eddie Davis. **CAST:** Duncan Renaldo, Leo Carrillo. **1951**

CISCO PIKE ★★★ Time has taken its toll on this weekend-in-the-life-of tale of a former drug dealer, well played by Kris Kristofferson, and his efforts to unload one last deal. Gene Hackman shows up as the crooked cop who agrees to clear the dealer's record in exchange for a favor. The dealer's weekend journey introduces him to era icons such as Viva, Karen Black, Harry Dean Stanton, and Antonio Fargas—and Bill L. Norton does a splendid job of making it all matter. Rated R for adult situations, language, and nudity. 94m. **DIR:** Bill L. Norton. **CAST:** Kris Kristofferson, Karen Black, Gene Hackman, Harry Dean Stanton, Viva, Roscoe Lee Browne, Antonio Fargas. **1972**

CITADEL, THE ★★★1/2 Superb acting by a fine cast marks this adaptation of novelist A. J. Cronin's story of an impoverished doctor who temporarily forsakes his ideals. B&W; 112m. **DIR:** King Vidor. **CAST:** Robert Donat, Rosalind Russell, Ralph Richardson, Rex Harrison, Emlyn Williams, Francis L. Sullivan, Felix Aylmer, Mary Clare, Cecil Parker. **1938**

CITIZEN COHN ★★★★★ James Woods is the ultimate unstoppable force in this mesmerizing made-for-cable account of attorney Roy Cohn's meteoric rise to power. Blessed with a viciously prideful mother (Lee Grant), the anti-Semitic and blatantly homophobic Cohn (who was both Jewish and gay) quickly learned how to dominate by intimidation. David Franzoni's fascinating script unfolds in flashback, as Cohn lies dying of AIDS in a hospital bed. 110m. **DIR:** Frank Pierson. **CAST:** James Woods, Joe Don Baker, Joseph Bologna, Ed Flanders, Frederic Forrest, Lee Grant, Pat Hingle. **1992 DVD**

CITIZEN KANE ★★★★★ The story of a reporter's quest to find the "truth" about the life of a dead newspaper tycoon closely parallels the life of William Randolph Hearst. This picture is an enjoyable experience for first-time viewers, as well as for those who have seen it ten times. B&W; 119m. **DIR:** Orson Welles. **CAST:** Orson Welles, Joseph Cotten, Everett Sloane, Agnes Moorehead, Ray Collins, George Coulouris, Ruth Warrick, Dorothy Comingore. **1941 DVD**

CITIZEN RUTH ★★★1/2 This stinging social satire, about the battle over abortion rights, wisely balances its skewering of both pro-life and pro-choice camps. Ruth Stoops is a derelict who has abandoned her children and is arrested for criminal endangerment of a fetus. She then becomes a media pawn for opposing camps of moral crusaders. Rated R for language, simulated sex, and mature subject matter. 104m. **DIR:** Alexander Payne. **CAST:** Laura Dern, Swoosie Kurtz, Kurtwood Smith, Mary Kay Place, Kelly Preston, Burt Reynolds, M. C. Gainey. **1996**

CITIZEN X ★★★★★ In this brilliant thriller, based on the actual events surrounding a Soviet serial killer who operated for most of a decade before finally being caught, Stephen Rea stars as the forensic-analyst-turned-detective assigned to the case in 1982. With party official Donald Sutherland as his clandestine ally, Rea doggedly builds a case against the unknown specter responsible for scores of murders. Rated R for violence, profanity, and brief nudity. 102m. **DIR:** Chris Gerolmo. **CAST:** Stephen Rea, Donald Sutherland, Jeffrey DeMunn, Joss Ackland, John Wood, Max von Sydow. **1995 DVD**

CITIZEN'S BAND ★★★★ Delightful character study centers around a group of people who use citizens band radios. Screenwriter Paul Brickman and director Jonathan Demme turn this slight premise into a humorous and heartwarming collection of vignettes with Paul LeMat appealing as the central character and Charles Napier screamingly funny as a philandering truck driver. Rated PG. 98m. **DIR:** Jonathan Demme. **CAST:** Paul LeMat, Candy Clark, Ann Wedgeworth, Marcia Rodd, Charles Napier, Alix Elias, Roberts Blossom, Bruce McGill, Ed Begley Jr. **1977**

CITY FOR CONQUEST ★★★1/2 James Cagney gives another outstanding performance as a self-sacrificing man who gives his all in the boxing ring to advance the career of his musician brother. Everyone shines in this curious blend of beautiful music and crime melodrama. B&W; 101m. **DIR:** Anatole Litvak. **CAST:** James Cagney, Ann Sheridan, Arthur Kennedy, Frank Craven, Donald Crisp, Frank McHugh, George Tobias, Jerome Cowan, Anthony Quinn, Lee Patrick, Blanche Yurka, Elia Kazan. **1940**

CITY GIRL ★★★ A Minnesota wheat farmer marries a waitress during a visit to Chicago and brings her back to his farm. A fragmentary, tantalizing glimpse at what was almost a Murnau masterpiece. Before the film's completion Murnau was pulled from the project, and the continuity, accordingly, is choppy. Silent. B&W; 89m. **DIR:** F. W. Murnau. **CAST:** Charles Farrell, Mary Duncan, David Torrence. **1930**

CITY HALL ★★★★ A memorable performance by Al Pacino as the world-weary mayor of New York City is but one of the highlights of this involving drama. When a 6 year old child is killed after being caught in the crossfire between a police detective and a gangster, it's up to deputy mayor John Cusack to supervise damage control. However, his investigation uncovers a trail of corruption that could bring down the entire power structure of the city. First-rate work by all involved. Rated R for violence and profanity. 117m. **DIR:** Harold Becker. **CAST:** Al Pacino, John Cusack, Bridget Fonda, Danny

Aiello, Martin Landau, David Paymer, Anthony Franciosa. **1996 DVD**

CITY HEAT ★★★ Clint Eastwood and Burt Reynolds portray a cop and a private eye, respectively, in this enjoyable action-comedy, directed by Richard Benjamin. It's fun for fans of the stars. Rated PG for violence. 94m. **DIR:** Richard Benjamin. **CAST:** Clint Eastwood, Burt Reynolds, Jane Alexander, Madeline Kahn, Irene Cara, Richard Roundtree, Rip Torn, Tony Lo Bianco. **1984**

CITY IN FEAR ★★★ David Janssen is excellent in his last role, a burned-out writer goaded by a ruthless publisher (Robert Vaughn). The plot concerns a mad killer on the loose in a big city. High-quality made-for-TV feature. 150m. **DIR:** Jud Taylor. **CAST:** David Janssen, Robert Vaughn, Susan Sullivan, William Prince, Perry King, William Daniels. **1980**

CITY IN PANIC 🦃 A brutal killer stalks the city streets, murdering homosexuals. Not rated; contains nudity and graphic violence. 85m. **DIR:** Robert Bouvier. **CAST:** Dave Adamson. **1987**

CITY LIGHTS ★★★★★ In his finest film, Charlie Chaplin's little tramp befriends a blind flower seller, providing her with every kindness he can afford. Charlie develops a friendship with a drunken millionaire and takes advantage of it to help the girl even more. Taking money from the millionaire so the girl can have an eye operation, he is arrested and sent to jail. His release from jail and the subsequent reunion with the girl may well be the most poignant ending of all his films. B&W; 81m. **DIR:** Charles Chaplin. **CAST:** Charlie Chaplin, Virginia Cherrill, Harry Myers, Hank Mann. **1931 DVD**

CITY LIMITS 🦃 Another in the endless parade of life-after-the-apocalypse, *Mad Max* rip-off films. Rated PG-13 for brief nudity, violence, and language. 85m. **DIR:** Aaron Lipstadt. **CAST:** Darrell Larson, John Stockwell, Kim Cattrall, Rae Dawn Chong, Robby Benson, James Earl Jones. **1984**

CITY OF ANGELS ★★★★ Nicolas Cage is a heavenly messenger who falls in love with Earth-bound surgeon Meg Ryan in this melodramatic fairy tale; their hesitant, sensuous relationship unfolds against the actual West Coast "city of angels"—teeming with dark-cloaked apparitions perched on billboards and tall buildings. Rated PG-13 for profanity, operating room intensity, and sensuality. 114m. **DIR:** Brad Silberling. **CAST:** Nicolas Cage, Meg Ryan, Dennis Franz, Andre Braugher. **1998 DVD**

CITY OF HOPE ★★★★1/2 Divided into two main stories, writer-director-star John Sayles's brilliant screenplay is about modern-day city life and the corruption found therein. There are no good guys or bad guys, just folks who are trying to survive. With a superb cast enlivening even the smallest parts, the result is a motion picture with uncommon resonance. Rated R for profanity and violence. 129m. **DIR:** John Sayles. **CAST:** Vincent Spano, Tony Lo Bianco, Joe Morton, John Sayles, Angela Bassett, David Strathairn, Maggie Renzi, Anthony Denison, Kevin Tighe, Barbara Williams. **1991**

CITY OF INDUSTRY ★★★ Scripter Ken Solarz and director John Irvin spin a moody, modern *film noir* around a robbery that turns sour only after its perfect execution. When the twitchy, psychopathic driver decides to keep everything himself, he kills all but one of his partners. That one survivor becomes almost superhuman in his quest for vengeance. Rated R for violence, profanity, and nudity. 97m. **DIR:** John Irvin. **CAST:** Harvey Keitel, Stephen Dorff, Famke Janssen, Timothy Hutton, Wade Dominguez. **1997 DVD**

CITY OF JOY ★★★★ A disillusioned American surgeon (Patrick Swayze) goes to India and discovers purpose in life in poverty-stricken Calcutta. Swayze's character and story are a bit contrived, but the film is saved by Om Puri's superb performance as a fearful farmer who becomes a hero. Rated PG-13 for profanity and violence. 134m. **DIR:** Roland Joffe. **CAST:** Patrick Swayze, Pauline Collins, Om Puri, Art Malik. **1992**

CITY OF LOST CHILDREN, THE ★★★ A mad scientist, unable to have dreams of his own, kidnaps children in order to steal their dreams. This oddball fairy tale never really becomes as compelling as it intends to be; it's more a collection of visual and dramatic effects than a unified, forceful story. Many of those effects, however, are striking and make the film fascinating. In French with English subtitles. Rated R for mild violence and general nightmarish atmosphere. 112m. **DIR:** Marc Caro, Jean-Pierre Jeunet. **CAST:** Ron Perlman, Daniel Emilfork, Judith Vittet, Dominique Pinon. **1995 DVD**

CITY OF SHADOWS ★★ It's the old story of Cain and Abel, set in the not-so-distant future. The first brother is a cop who lives by his own rules and deals out justice in like fashion, and the other is a maniac outlaw who kidnaps little boys and kills them. Some good action sequences along with satisfactory acting make this a passable film. 92m. **DIR:** David Mitchell. **CAST:** John P. Ryan, Paul Coufos, Tony Rosato. **1986**

CITY OF THE VAMPIRES 🦃 Sort of a *Night of the Living Dead* with vampires instead, this film fails to live up to the promise of its premise. Not rated; contains violence and gore. 83m. **DIR:** Ron Bonk. **CAST:** Matthew Jason Walsh, Anne-Marie O'Keefe. **1995**

CITY OF WOMEN ★★1/2 Marcello Mastroianni plays a middle-aged womanizer who follows a beautiful woman to a mansion, where he is held hostage. Federico Fellini's controversial film has been criticized as antifeminist, although it is really anti-everything. MPAA not rated, but contains profanity and nudity. 139m. **DIR:** Federico Fellini. **CAST:** Marcello Mastroianni, Ettore Manni. **1981 DVD**

CITY ON FIRE ★★★ Violent crime-drama about an undercover cop out to bust a syndicate of jewel thieves in Hong Kong. Pretty impressive screen action with an explosive climactic shoot-out. In Cantonese with English subtitles. Not rated; contains violence and nudity. 98m. **DIR:** Ringo Lam. **CAST:** Chow Yun-Fat. **1989 DVD**

CITY SLICKERS ★★★★ Three buddies experiencing individual midlife crises decide that going on a cattle drive will be just the thing to cure their collective depression. The result is a comedy guaranteed to cheer anyone up, with great one-liners and hilarious physical comedy. Jack Palance is outstanding as the leathery trail boss who terrifies his city-bred drovers. Rated PG-13 for profanity. 109m. **DIR:** Ron Underwood. **CAST:** Billy Crystal, Bruno Kirby, Daniel Stern, Patricia Wettig, Helen Slater, Jack Palance, Tracey Walter, Josh Mostel. **1991 DVD**

CITY SLICKERS II ★★★★ The city slickers look for a lost treasure and trip all over themselves. The often funny screenplay has the same flavor as the first film with a different slant on the personalities—Jon Lovitz replaces Bruno Kirby, but the rest of the cast is the same, with Jack Palance playing his original character's twin brother. Rated PG-13 for language. 110m. **DIR:** Paul Weiland. **CAST:** Billy Crystal, Jack Palance, Daniel Stern, Jon Lovitz, Patricia Wettig, Bill McKinney, Noble Willingham, Josh Mostel, Bob Balaban. **1994**

CITY THAT NEVER SLEEPS ★★★1/2 Dated but delectable film about a Chicago policeman (Gig Young) who decides to leave his wife and the force to run away with a cheap show girl. In a corny device, the city talks to us—via an offscreen narrator—to introduce its citizens and explain its purpose in society. Not rated, it contains violence. B&W; 90m. **DIR:** John H. Auer. **CAST:** Gig Young, Mala Powers, Edward Arnold, William Talman. **1953**

CITY WAR ★★★ The stars of John Woo's *A Better Tomorrow* are reteamed as a pair of cops stalked by a vengeful gangster. Neither the script nor the direction are up to Woo's standards, but the actors make this a satisfying thriller. In Cantonese with English subtitles. Not rated; contains strong violence. 100m. **DIR:** Sun Chung. **CAST:** Chow Yun-Fat, Danny Lee. **1988 DVD**

CITY WITHOUT MEN ★★ Wan drama of women who live in a boardinghouse near the prison where their husbands are serving time. Good cast, but otherwise forgettable. B&W; 75m. **DIR:** Sidney Salkow. **CAST:** Linda Darnell, Michael Duane, Sara Allgood, Glenda Farrell, Margaret Hamilton. **1943**

CIVIL ACTION, A ★★★★ This legal drama boasts an intelligent script and a dynamite supporting performance from Robert Duvall, superbly cast as a seasoned attorney, wholly unmindful of the moral bankruptcy of the side he represents. This is a true story about personal-injury attorney Jan Schlichtmann, who went to bat against Beatrice Foods and W. R. Grace & Co. in the hopes of proving that corporate negligence was responsible when an unnaturally high number of children in tiny Woburn, Massachusetts, died of leukemia in the 1970s. A small band of local parents suspected poisoned drinking water due to industrial dumping. The film demonstrates our current legal system's inability to extract truth or justice from demons with deep pockets. Rated PG for profanity. 118m. **DIR:** Steven Zaillian. **CAST:** John Travolta, Robert Duvall, Tony Shalhoub, William H. Macy, John Lithgow, Kathleen Quinlan. **1998 DVD**

CIVIL WAR, THE ★★★★★ Weaving an eloquent tapestry of letters, diaries, war dispatches, and contemporary newspaper reports, with academic opinion, award-winning director-producer Ken Burns brings the Civil War of 1861–1865 vividly to life in epic proportion. A brilliant tour de force. Unforgettable. B&W/color; 660m. **DIR:** Ken Burns. **1990**

CIVIL WAR DIARY ★★★1/2 This low-budget family film is a fairly realistic account of a Civil War-era clan, as told by its youngest member. The story centers on the home front at a time when the older males are choosing sides and leaving the farm. Not rated, but with violence. 82m. **DIR:** Kevin Meyer. **CAST:** Todd Duffey, Miriam Byrd-Nethery, Holis McCarthy. **1990**

CIVILIZATION ★★★ Though little-known today, Thomas Ince was one of the first great American film producers and *Civilization* was his crowning effort. Seeing the overwhelming response to D. W. Griffith's epic *Birth of a Nation*, Ince abandoned the short Westerns and dramas that made him wealthy and he put all his efforts into this moralistic antiwar blockbuster. But America entered World War I and *Civilization* died at the box office. Silent with intertitles. B&W; 102m. **DIR:** Thomas Ince. **CAST:** Howard Hickman, Enid Markey, Lola May. **1916**

•CLAIM, THE ★★★ Greed, regret, love, and a grim reach for redemption are transplanted from Thomas Hardy's novel *The Mayor of Casterbridge* into the 1867 Sierra Nevada gold-mining settlement of Kingdom Come in this engrossing drama. The past of a prospector-turned-businessman catches up to him just as a railroad surveying party determines his town's future. The film's snowy landscapes and dense tone bring to mind *McCabe and Mrs. Miller* but this unfocused Western doesn't conjure up its predecessor's haunting spirit. Rated R for language, violence, and sexuality. 120m. **DIR:** Michael Winterbottom. **CAST:** Peter Mullan, Wes Bentley, Nastassja Kinski, Sarah Polley, Milla Jovovich. **2000 DVD**

•CLAIRE DOLAN ★★★ An Irish woman (Katrin Cartlidge) working as a high-priced call girl in Manhattan is prompted to reexamine her life when her mother dies and she falls in love with a cabdriver (Vincent D'Onofrio). The film's icy design reflects the emotionlessness with which Claire conducts her professional life, and the mood of urban isolation is reminiscent of European art films of the 1960s. It's an easy film to admire but a hard one to enjoy. Not rated; an R equivalent for sex. 95m. **DIR:** Lodge H. Kerrigan. **CAST:** Katrin Cartlidge, Vincent D'Onofrio, Colm Meaney, Patrick Husted. **1998**

CLAIRE OF THE MOON ★★1/2 Two women with conflicting points of view are roommates at a writers' retreat. They get on each other's nerves until a seminar conducted by a congenial, openly gay lecturer launches them into a sexual relationship. Controversial film is well acted and directed, but not for all tastes. Not rated; contains nudity, simulated sex, and profanity. 92m. **DIR:** Nicole Conn. **CAST:** Trisha Todd, Karen Trumbo, Daimon Craig, Faith DeVitt. **1992 DVD**

CLAIRE'S KNEE ★★★★★ There is no substitute for class, and director Eric Rohmer exhibits a great deal of it in this fifth film in a series entitled *Six Moral Tales.* The plot is simplicity itself. Jerome (Jean-Claude Brialy) renews his friendship with a writer (Aurora Cornu) whose roommate has two daughters; one is Claire. Jerome is intrigued by Claire but is obsessed with her knee—her right knee, to be specific. In French with English subtitles. PG rating. 103m. **DIR:** Eric Rohmer. **CAST:** Jean-Claude Brialy, Aurora Cornu, Beatrice Romand. **1971 DVD**

CLAMBAKE ★★★ Typical Elvis Presley musical-romance has a *Prince and the Pauper* scenario. Elvis, an oil baron's son, trades places with Will Hutchins, a penniless water-ski instructor, in order to find a girl who'll love him for himself and not his money. When Elvis falls for a gold-digging Shelley Fabares, he must compete with Bill Bixby, the playboy speedboat racer. 100m. **DIR:** Arthur H. Nadel. **CAST:** Elvis Presley, Shelley Fabares,

Will Hutchins, Bill Bixby, Gary Merrill, James Gregory. **1967 DVD**

CLAN OF THE CAVE BEAR 🦃 In this dreadfully dumb adaptation of Jean M. Auel's bestselling fantasy novel, a Cro-Magnon child is grudgingly adopted by a tribe of Neanderthals. Rated R. 100m. **DIR:** Michael Chapman. **CAST:** Daryl Hannah, Pamela Reed, Thomas Waites. **1986 DVD**

CLARA'S HEART ★★1/2 Despite a wonderful performance by Whoopi Goldberg, this is a strangely unaffecting drama about a Jamaican maid who helps a youngster (Neil Patrick Harris) come to terms with life. The characters are so unsympathetic, though, that the viewer cannot help but lose interest. PG-13 for profanity. 107m. **DIR:** Robert Mulligan. **CAST:** Whoopi Goldberg, Michael Ontkean, Kathleen Quinlan, Spalding Gray, Beverly Todd, Neil Patrick Harris. **1988**

CLARENCE ★★★ Clarence, the angel who guided Jimmy Stewart through *It's A Wonderful Life*, is back for more fun in this charming (made-for-TV) sequel that finds the guardian angel assisting a young mother headed for tragedy. Not a classic, but filled with the best of intentions. Rated G. 92m. **DIR:** Eric Till. **CAST:** Robert Carradine, Kate Trotter. **1990**

CLARENCE DARROW ★★★★ This television adaptation of the stage play is a tour de force for Henry Fonda. Highlights from the career of one of the most gifted legal minds ever to pace the courtrooms of America. 81m. **DIR:** John Rich. **CAST:** Henry Fonda. **1978**

CLARENCE, THE CROSS-EYED LION ★★ A family comedy that plays like a TV sitcom because that's basically what it is. Writer-star Marshall Thompson wrote this story about an adult lion with a focus problem and an American family in Africa with soft hearts. The story and characters were immortalized on TV in *Daktari*. 98m. **DIR:** Andrew Marton. **CAST:** Marshall Thompson, Betsy Drake, Richard Haydn, Cheryl Miller. **1965**

CLASH BY NIGHT ★★★1/2 Intense, adult story is a dramatist's dream but not entertainment for the masses. Barbara Stanwyck gives another of her strong characterizations as a woman with a past who marries amiable Paul Douglas only to find herself gravitating toward tough but sensual Robert Ryan. Gritty realism and outstanding performances make this a slice-of-life tragedy that lingers in the memory. B&W; 105m. **DIR:** Fritz Lang. **CAST:** Barbara Stanwyck, Paul Douglas, Robert Ryan, Marilyn Monroe, Keith Andes, J. Carrol Naish. **1952**

CLASH OF THE TITANS ★★1/2 Perseus (Harry Hamlin), the son of Zeus (Laurence Olivier), mounts his flying horse, Pegasus, and fights for the hand of Andromeda (Judi Bowker). Plagued by corny situations and stilted dialogue, only the visual wonders by special-effects wizard Ray Harryhausen make this movie worth seeing. Rated PG for violence and gore. 118m. **DIR:** Desmond Davis. **CAST:** Laurence Olivier, Harry Hamlin, Judi Bowker, Burgess Meredith, Maggie Smith. **1981**

CLASS 🦃 Unfunny comedy about two preppies, one of whom falls in love with the other's alcoholic mother. Rated R for nudity, profanity, sex, and violence. 98m. **DIR:** Lewis John Carlino. **CAST:** Rob Lowe, Jacqueline Bisset, Andrew McCarthy, Stuart Margolin. **1983 DVD**

CLASS ACT ★★★ Rap singers Kid 'N Play follow up their *House Party* successes with this ingratiating, lightweight teen comedy. Kid (Christopher Reid, the one with the mile-high hair) plays a brilliant, straight-A student who moves to a new school. Unfortunately, his official record gets switched with those belonging to a nonachieving, streetwise troublemaker (played by Christopher Martin). Rated PG-13, with profanity and sexual references. 98m. **DIR:** Randall Miller. **CAST:** Christopher Reid, Christopher Martin, Lamont Jackson, Doug E. Doug. **1992**

CLASS ACTION ★★★1/2 When a crusading lawyer agrees to represent a group of people whose cars had the habit of exploding on impact, he discovers his daughter is handling the defense. Rated R for profanity and violence. 106m. **DIR:** Michael Apted. **CAST:** Gene Hackman, Mary Elizabeth Mastrantonio, Colin Friels, Joanna Merlin, Laurence Fishburne, Jonathan Silverman, Jan Rubes, Matt Clark, Fred Dalton Thompson. **1991**

CLASS OF '44 ★★★ Sequel to the very popular *Summer of '42* proves once again it's tough to top the original. Gary Grimes and Jerry Houser are back again. This time we follow the two through college romances. No new ground broken, but Grimes is very watchable. Rated PG. 95m. **DIR:** Paul Bogart. **CAST:** Gary Grimes, Jerry Houser, William Atherton, Deborah Winters. **1973**

CLASS OF MISS MACMICHAEL, THE ★★ British film about obnoxious students battling obnoxious teachers. Mixes *The Blackboard Jungle*, *To Sir with Love*, and *Teachers* without expanding on them. Loud and angry, but doesn't say much. Rated R for profanity. 91m. **DIR:** Silvio Narizzano. **CAST:** Glenda Jackson, Oliver Reed, Michael Murphy. **1978**

CLASS OF 1984 ★★1/2 Violent punkers run a school. A new teacher arrives and tries to change things, but his pregnant wife is raped. He takes revenge by killing all the punkers. Rated R for violence. 93m. **DIR:** Mark L. Lester. **CAST:** Perry King, Merrie Lynn Ross, Roddy McDowall, Timothy Van Patten. **1982**

CLASS OF 1999 ★★1/2 Exciting sequel to *Class of 1984*. High school has become a battleground in 1999, forcing the administration to rely on android faculty to teach the kids. When the new teachers malfunction, they initiate a killer curriculum. Rated R for violence. 96m. **DIR:** Mark L. Lester. **CAST:** Bradley Gregg, Traci Lin, John P. Ryan, Pam Grier, Stacy Keach, Malcolm McDowell. **1989**

CLASS OF 1999 II: THE SUBSTITUTE ★★1/2 Agreeable sequel finds rogue android soldier Sasha Mitchell posing as a high-school teacher to rid the school of human vermin. He's programmed to kill and finds plenty of prey among the thugs and gangs that rule the halls, but a mysterious stranger is out to force Mitchell to do his dirty work. Rated R for violence, language, and nudity. 90m. **DIR:** Spiro Razatos. **CAST:** Sasha Mitchell, Nick Cassavetes, Caitlin Dulany, Jack Knight. **1993**

CLASS OF NUKE 'EM HIGH 🦃 The makers of *The Toxic Avenger* strike again in this poor black comedy-monster movie. Rated R for nudity, profanity, and graphic violence. 84m. **DIR:** Richard W. Haines, Samuel Weil. **CAST:** Janelle Brady, Gilbert Brenton. **1987 DVD**

CLASS OF NUKE 'EM HIGH 2: SUBHUMANOID MELTDOWN ★★ Bad acting, scantily clad women, gross special effects, and a totally off-the-wall plot are all parts of this tongue-in-cheek flick from the wackos at Troma Inc. Remember, it's *supposed* to be this bad. Rated R for violence, profanity, and nudity. 96m. **DIR:** Eric Louzil. **CAST:** Brick Bronsky, Lisa Gaye. **1991**

CLASS OF NUKE 'EM HIGH III 🦃 These students flunk out in reading, writing, and radiation. More of the same, but worse. Rated R for violence and language. 97m. **DIR:** Eric Louzil. **CAST:** Lisa Gaye, Brick Bronsky, Leesa Rowland. **1995**

CLASS OF '61 ★★★ When the Civil War erupted, friendly West Point cadets found themselves donning opposing uniforms. This made-for-TV production is effectively poignant and surprisingly stylish. Oscar-winning cinematographer Janusz Kaminski (*Schindler's List*) uses strong visuals and montages to explain the chaos and confusion of the war, and it generally works on an emotional level. However, it ends too abruptly. Not rated; contains mild profanity and violence. 95m. **DIR:** Gregory Hoblit. **CAST:** Dan Futterman, Joshua Lucas, Clive Owen, Sophie Ward, Niall O'Brien, Christien Anholt, Andre Braugher. **1992**

CLASSIC FOREIGN SHORTS: VOLUME 2 ★★★1/2 Excellent collection of foreign-film shorts by Europe's hottest movie directors. Featured in this collection is François Truffaut's early "Les Mistons," Jean-Luc Godard's first short, "All the Boys Named Patrick," Roman Polanski's "The Fat and the Lean," and "Two Men and a Wardrobe." Also: early featurettes by Michelangelo Antonioni ("U.N.") and Orson Welles ("Hearts of Age"). B&W; 100m. **DIR:** Jean-Luc Godard, Roman Polanski, Michelangelo Antonioni, François Truffaut, Orson Welles. **1989**

CLAUDIA ★★ Tame British soaper concerning the traumatized wife of a wealthy control-freak who escapes her husband's dominance. She starts a new life and falls in love with a young musician, but hubby tracks her down. Not rated, but equivalent to PG-13. 88m. **DIR:** Anwar Kawadri. **CAST:** Deborah Raffin, Nicholas Ball. **1985**

CLAY PIGEON, THE ★★★ It is just after World War II. Sailor Bill Williams comes out of a coma to find he is going to be court-martialed for treason. When he is also accused of murder, he gets on the trail of the real killer. Tight plot and taut direction make this a seat-edge thriller. B&W; 63m. **DIR:** Richard Fleischer. **CAST:** Bill Williams, Barbara Hale, Richard Quine, Richard Loo, Frank Fenton, Frank Wilcox, Martha Hyer. **1949**

CLAY PIGEONS ★★1/2 An auto mechanic in a small Montana town gets tangled in a murderous web spun by a seemingly amiable truck driver, played with reptilian charm by Vince Vaughn. Scott Wilson as a folksy sheriff and the delightful Janeane Garofalo as a sarcastic FBI agent add class to the film, but director David Dobkin keeps tripping over the holes in the needlessly complicated script. Rated R for profanity, nudity, violence, and sexual scenes. 104m. **DIR:** David Dobkin. **CAST:** Joaquin Phoenix, Janeane Garofalo, Vince Vaughn, Georgina Cates, Scott Wilson. **1998 DVD**

CLEAN AND SOBER ★★★★ Michael Keaton gives a brilliant performance in this highly effective drama as a hotshot executive who wakes up one morning to find that his life is totally out of control. He checks into a drug rehabilitation center to dry out and discovers the shocking truth about himself. An impressive filmmaking debut for Glenn Gordon Caron, creator of television's *Moonlighting*. Rated R for violence and profanity. 124m. **DIR:** Glenn Gordon Caron. **CAST:** Michael Keaton, Morgan Freeman, M. Emmet Walsh, Kathy Baker. **1988 DVD**

CLEAN SHAVEN ★★★ To call a film schizophrenic is not usually a compliment, but it best describes this stylish concoction that bucks conventionality. Writer-director Lodge Kerrigan pushes us inside the head of a recently released mental patient searching for his young daughter. This minimalist and creepy flick loses points for being just a little too different. Letter-boxed. Not rated; contains violence, profanity, and sexual situations. 80m. **DIR:** Lodge H. Kerrigan. **CAST:** Peter Greene, Robert Albert, Jennifer McDonald, Megan Owen, Molly Castelloe. **1993 DVD**

CLEAN SLATE (COUP DE TORCHON) (1981) ★★★★ Set during 1938 in a French West African colonial town, this savage and sardonic black comedy is a study of the circumstances under which racism and fascism flourish. Philippe Noiret stars as a simple-minded sheriff who decides to wipe out corruption. In French with English subtitles. Not rated; the film has nudity, implied sex, violence, profanity, and racial epithets. 128m. **DIR:** Bertrand Tavernier. **CAST:** Philippe Noiret, Isabelle Huppert, Stéphane Audran. **1981**

CLEAN SLATE (1994) ★★★1/2 Private eye Dana Carvey starts each day fresh—with no idea of who he is. This strange form of amnesia means trouble, since he's supposed to testify against a powerful crime boss who commited a murder our hero doesn't remember. Carvey is fun to watch in a movie that is only occasionally funny. The best scenes involve Carvey's comic canine co-star, Barkley. Rated PG-13 for violence and profanity. 107m. **DIR:** Mick Jackson. **CAST:** Dana Carvey, Valeria Golino, James Earl Jones, Kevin Pollak, Michael Murphy, Michael Gambon. **1994**

CLEAR AND PRESENT DANGER ★★★★1/2 Tom Clancy's principled, thoughtful hero, Jack Ryan, is forced to take on the president of the United States when he steps in for his ailing boss to lead the fight against the Colombian drug cartels and corruption in the ranks. The result is a first-rate spy thriller. Rated PG-13 for violence, profanity, and nudity. 141m. **DIR:** Phillip Noyce. **CAST:** Harrison Ford, Willem Dafoe, Anne Archer, James Earl Jones, Joaquim de Almeida, Henry Czerny, Harris Yulin, Donald Moffat, Dean Jones, Hope Lange. **1994 DVD**

CLEARCUT ★★★ Native American Graham Greene finds the destruction of Indian land by a Canadian paper mill an injustice, and to make his point, kidnaps the mill manager. Interesting message complemented by above-average acting and some gorgeous photography. Rated R for language and violence. 98m. **DIR:** Richard Bugajski. **CAST:** Graham Greene, Floyd Red Crow Westerman, Raul Trujillo, Michael Hogan. **1992**

CLEO FROM 5 TO 7 ★★★1/2 Filmed in real time, this new wave film follows 90 minutes in the life of a nightclub singer awaiting the results of a critical medical test. Sharp-eyed viewers can look for Jean-Luc Godard, Anna Karina, Sami Frey, Jean-Claude Brialy, and others as performers in a comedy film viewed by the protagonist. In French with English subtitles. Not rated. 90m. **DIR:** Agnes Varda. **CAST:** Corinne Marchand, Antoine Bourseiller, Michel Legrand. **1962 DVD**

CLEOPATRA (1934) ★★★★ One of the most opulent and intelligent films Cecil B. De Mille ever directed. Its success arises in large part from historical accuracy and the superb peformances by all the principals. B&W; 95m. **DIR:** Cecil B. DeMille. **CAST:** Claudette Colbert, Warren William, Henry Wilcoxon, C. Aubrey Smith. **1934**

CLEOPATRA (1963) ★★★★ This multimillion-dollar, four-hour-long extravaganza created quite a sensation when released. Its all-star cast includes Elizabeth Taylor (as Cleopatra) and Richard Burton (as Marc Antony). The story begins when Caesar meets Cleopatra in her native Egypt and she has his son. Later she comes to Rome to join Caesar when he becomes the lifetime dictator of Rome. Marc Antony gets into the act as Cleopatra's Roman lover. 243m. **DIR:** Joseph L. Mankiewicz. **CAST:** Elizabeth Taylor, Richard Burton, Rex Harrison, Roddy McDowall, Pamela Brown. **1963 DVD**

CLEOPATRA JONES 🦃 Secret agent Cleopatra Jones returns from an overseas assignment to save her old neighborhood. Rated PG for violence. 80m. **DIR:** Jack Starrett. **CAST:** Tamara Dobson, Shelley Winters, Bernie Casey, Brenda Sikes. **1973 DVD**

CLEOPATRA JONES AND THE CASINO OF GOLD ★★ Tamara Dobson stars as a U.S. agent out to shut down a drug empire run by the Dragon Lady (Stella Stevens). A big budget saves this yawner from turkeydom. Rated R for violence, profanity, and nudity. 96m. **DIR:** Chuck Bail. **CAST:** Tamara Dobson, Stella Stevens, Norman Fell. **1975**

CLERKS ★★★ Convenience-store clerk Dante Hicks spends a day in Quick Stop purgatory when he reluctantly opens shop for a no-show coworker. He develops shell shock from sexual revelations by his girlfriend, mopes over the marriage of a high-school flame, plays street hockey on the store rooftop, trades psychobabble with a cynical video-store clerk, and deals with a parade of weird customers. Rated R due to language. B&W; 99m. **DIR:** Kevin Smith. **CAST:** Brian O'Halloran, Jeff Anderson, Marilyn Ghigliotti, Lisa Spoonauer. **1994 DVD**

CLIENT, THE ★★★★ Outstanding thriller, based on a John Grisham novel, stars a highly effective Susan Sarandon as a no-nonsense New Orleans lawyer who becomes the only person to stand between a young murder witness and a politically ambitious district attorney. Rated PG-13 for violence and profanity. 120m. **DIR:** Joel Schumacher. **CAST:** Susan Sarandon, Tommy Lee Jones, Mary-Louise Parker, Anthony LaPaglia, Anthony Edwards, Ossie Davis, Brad Renfro, David Speck, J. T. Walsh, Will Patton, William H. Macy, Kimberly Scott, William Sanderson. **1994 DVD**

CLIFFHANGER ★★ Expert mountain climber Sylvester Stallone attempts to rescue his girlfriend from the clutches of criminal John Lithgow, who is holding her hostage in the Rockies. Action fans may enjoy this one, but its preponderance of clichés will turn off more discriminating viewers. Rated R for violence and profanity. 115m. **DIR:** Renny Harlin. **CAST:** Sylvester Stallone, John Lithgow, Michael Rooker, Janine Turner. **1993 DVD**

CLIFFORD 🦃 The novelty of seeing the full-grown Martin Short playing a malevolent 10 year old wears off *very* quickly. Rated PG, but not suitable for small children. 90m. **DIR:** Paul Flaherty. **CAST:** Martin Short, Charles Grodin, Dabney Coleman, Mary Steenburgen. **1994**

CLIMATE FOR KILLING, A ★★★1/2 Effective murder mystery about a headless and handless corpse that may be linked to a murder-suicide from sixteen years before. John Beck is the dedicated sheriff's captain and Steven Bauer is the big-city detective sent to evaluate him. Rated R for violence, profanity, and nudity. 104m. **DIR:** J. S. Cardone. **CAST:** John Beck, Steven Bauer, Mia Sara, John Diehl, Katharine Ross. **1991**

CLIMAX, THE ★★★ Boris Karloff plays the house physician of Vienna's Royal Theater with an obsessive crush on opera star June Vincent. When she has no time for the good doctor, he kills her. Years later, when a new star appears on the scene, the madness continues in this eerie and atmospheric thriller. Not rated. 86m. **DIR:** George Waggner. **CAST:** Boris Karloff, Susanna Foster, Turhan Bey, Gale Sondergaard, June Vincent. **1944**

CLIMB, THE ★★★ Straightforward account of the 1953 German assault on Nanga Parbat, the world's fifth highest peak. Bruce Greenwood is Herman Buhl, the arrogant climber who reached the summit alone. Rated PG, but suitable for the whole family. 86m. **DIR:** Donald Shebib. **CAST:** Bruce Greenwood, James Hurdle, Kenneth Walsh, Ken Pogue, Thomas Hauff. **1988 DVD**

CLINTON AND NADINE ★★★ Andy Garcia and Ellen Barkin enliven this otherwise routine cable-TV revenge thriller. He's determined to learn who killed his brother, and she's a sympathetic call girl in the right place at the right time. Violence and brief nudity. 108m. **DIR:** Jerry Schatzberg. **CAST:** Andy Garcia, Ellen Barkin, Morgan Freeman, Michael Lombard. **1987**

CLIVE BARKER'S SALOME AND THE FORBIDDEN ★★★ The famous horror scribe presents two short films based on classic tales made early in his career. The first tells the tale of the famous dancer, while the second re-creates *Faust*. Of the two, *The Forbidden* is the more entertaining segment with its negative-image photography. While far from the best work in Barker's oeuvre, this anthology serves as a fine example of some of the themes that would later dominate his work. Made between 1972 and 1978, these were not released until 1995. Not rated; contains violent images. B&W; 70m. **DIR:** Clive Barker. **CAST:** Doug Bradley, Clive Barker, Julie Blake, Peter Atkins. **1995 DVD**

CLOAK AND DAGGER (1946) ★★1/2 Director Fritz Lang wanted to make this as a warning about the dangers of the atomic age. But Warner Bros. reedited the film into a standard spy melodrama. The story has American scientist Gary Cooper, working for the OSS, sneaking into Nazi Germany to grab an Italian scientist who is helping the Nazis build the atom bomb. B&W; 106m. **DIR:** Fritz Lang. **CAST:** Gary Cooper, Lilli Palmer, Robert Alda, James Flavin, J. Edward Bromberg, Marc Lawrence. **1946**

CLOAK AND DAGGER (1984) ★★★ A highly imaginative boy (Henry Thomas, of *E.T.*) who often plays pretend games of espionage with his fantasy friend, Jack

Flack (Dabney Coleman), finds himself involved in a real life-and-death situation when he stumbles on to the evil doings of a group of spies (led by Michael Murphy). It's suspenseful and fast-paced but not so scary and violent as to upset the kiddies. Rated PG. 101m. **DIR:** Richard Franklin. **CAST:** Henry Thomas, Dabney Coleman, Michael Murphy, John McIntire, Shelby Leverington. **1984**

CLOCK, THE ★★★ Dated but still entertaining film directed by Judy Garland's then-husband, Vincente Minnelli. Judy stars as a working girl who meets and falls in love with soldier Robert Walker. He's on a forty-eight-hour leave, so they decide to make the most of the time they have together. 90m. **DIR:** Vincente Minnelli. **CAST:** Judy Garland, Robert Walker, James Gleason, Keenan Wynn. **1945**

CLOCKERS ★★★★ Novelist Richard Price's gritty, thought-provoking examination of the modern world of drug dealing gets first-class treatment from coscripter-director Spike Lee. Occasional moralizing is offset by some riveting performances, especially that of Delroy Lindo as a remorseless drug kingpin. Apart from the grisly opening scenes—centering on the examination of a street-killing victim—there is surprisingly little violence or exploitation. Rated R for profanity and violence. 128m. **DIR:** Spike Lee. **CAST:** Harvey Keitel, John Turturro, Delroy Lindo, Mekhi Phifer, Keith David, Mike Starr. **1995 DVD**

CLOCKMAKER (1998) ★★ Imaginative low-budget time-travel fantasy about three kids sneaking into a clockmaker's home and messing with a machine, resulting in the computer age coming almost a hundred years too soon. The efforts of the filmmakers are hampered, however, by the poor acting of the young lead. Rated PG for mild violence. 90m. **DIR:** Christopher Rémy. **CAST:** Anthony Medwetz, Katie Johnston, Pierrino Mascarino. **1998**

CLOCKMAKER, THE (1973) ★★★★ A small-town clock maker is stunned to learn that his son, whom he raised after the death of his wife, has committed a murder and is on the run from the police. Examining his life, he realizes how little he actually knows the boy. This strong, confident first film from Bertrand Tavernier, based on a Georges Simenon novel, features one of Philippe Noiret's finest performances. In French with English subtitles. Not rated. 105m. **DIR:** Bertrand Tavernier. **CAST:** Philippe Noiret, Jean Rochefort, Christine Pascal. **1973 DVD**

•**CLOCKSTOPPERS** ★★ Nickelodeon's readily disposable sci-fi adventure action comedy is not about stopping time but rather speeding up characters into a "hypertime" in which everyone around them appears to be frozen or barely moving. Physicist George Gibbs implants this imperfect "molecular acceleration" in a watch that his son Zak pilfers from the family laundry room. Zak learns that his dad has been kidnapped into hyperspace by an evil millionaire and uses the timepiece to retrieve him before he irrevocably ages. Rated PG. 94m. **DIR:** Jonathan Frakes. **CAST:** Jesse Bradford, French Stewart, Michael Biehn, Paula Garcés, Robin Thomas. **2002 DVD**

CLOCKWATCHERS ★★ First-time director Jill Sprecher's corrosive little picture wants to be an indictment of a sterile, small-minded office environment, but it's difficult to appreciate this tedious little drama, even as an object lesson. Basically, this is a one-act theater exercise stretched to interminable lengths. Rated PG-13 for profanity. 96m. **DIR:** Jill Sprecher. **CAST:** Toni Collette, Parker Posey, Lisa Kudrow, Alanna Ubach. **1998 DVD**

CLOCKWISE ★★★1/2 No one plays a pillar of pomposity better than John Cleese. In *Clockwise*, he gets a perfect role for his patented persona. Brian Stimpson, a headmaster, runs everything by the clock—in the extreme. However, his complete control is soon shattered by a misunderstanding—and hilarity is the result. Rated PG. 96m. **DIR:** Christopher Morahan. **CAST:** John Cleese, Penelope Wilton, Alison Steadman, Stephen Moore, Sharon Maiden, Joan Hickson. **1987 DVD**

CLOCKWORK ORANGE, A ★★★★ Not for every taste, this is a stylized, "ultraviolent" black comedy. Malcolm McDowell stars as the number-one "malchick," Alex, who leads his "droogs" through "a bit of the old ultraviolence" for a real "horror show." Rated R. 137m. **DIR:** Stanley Kubrick. **CAST:** Malcolm McDowell, Patrick Magee, Adrienne Corri. **1971 DVD**

CLONES, THE ★★1/2 In a sinister plot to control the weather, several government scientists are duplicated and placed in strategic meteorological stations. Basically silly film is made watchable by the believable performances of Michael Greene and Gregory Sierra, and there's a terrific roller coaster–chase finale. Rated PG for language and violence. 86m. **DIR:** Paul Hunt, Lamar Card. **CAST:** Michael Greene, Bruce Bennett, Gregory Sierra, John Drew Barrymore. **1973**

CLONUS HORROR, THE ★★1/2 Government scientists are hard at work creating a master race of superhumans in a laboratory. One of them breaks free to warn the world. Not a bad time waster for science-fiction fans. Also known as *Parts: The Clonus Horror*. Rated R. 90m. **DIR:** Robert S. Fiveson. **CAST:** Tim Donnelly, Dick Sargent, Peter Graves, Keenan Wynn, Lurene Tuttle. **1979**

CLOSE ENCOUNTERS OF THE THIRD KIND ★★★★ This is director Steven Spielberg's enchanting, pre-*E.T.* vision of an extraterrestrial visit to Earth. The movie goes against many long-nurtured conceptions about space aliens. The humans, such as Richard Dreyfuss, act more bizarre than the nonthreatening childlike visitors. Spielberg never surrenders his role as storyteller to the distractions of special effects. Rated PG. 132m. **DIR:** Steven Spielberg. **CAST:** Richard Dreyfuss, François Truffaut, Teri Garr, Melinda Dillon. **1977 DVD**

CLOSE MY EYES ★★1/2 Love triangles don't get much more startling than this alternately cold, bitchy, sensitive, and beguiling British drama about incest between a brother and his older, married sister. The acting is superb, with Alan Rickman stealing scenes as the filthy rich husband who suspects his wife is having an affair. Rated R for nudity, profanity, and sexual themes. 109m. **DIR:** Stephen Poliakoff. **CAST:** Alan Rickman, Saskia Reeves, Clive Owen. **1991**

CLOSE TO EDEN ★★★★ A visiting Russian's encounter with a family of farmers, descended from Genghis Khan, is the device director Nikita Mikhalkov uses to study the effects of modernization on Inner Mongolia. As this slow-moving film goes on, the events become increasingly surreal. In Mongol, Chinese, and Russian with English subtitles. Not rated, the film has violence and profanity. 106m. **DIR:** Nikita Mikhalkov. **CAST:** Badema, Bayaertu, Vladimir Gostukhin. **1991**

CLOSE TO HOME ★★1/2 Canadian docudrama focuses on the link from child abuse and neglect to teen runaways and prostitution. A bit heavy-handed but still an effective message to parents. 93m. **DIR:** Rick Beairsto. **CAST:** Daniel Allman. **1985**

CLOSELY WATCHED TRAINS ★★★★1/2 A bittersweet coming-of-age comedy-drama against a backdrop of the Nazi occupation of Czechoslovakia. A naïve young train dispatcher is forced to grow up quickly when asked to help the Czech underground. This gentle film is one of the more artistic efforts to come from behind the Iron Curtain. B&W; 91m. **DIR:** Jiri Menzel. **CAST:** Vaclav Neckar, Jitka Bendova. **1966 DVD**

CLOSER, THE ★★1/2 Danny Aiello reprises his stage role as a businessman whose pending retirement sets into motion an evening of high stakes for those anxious to succeed him. Aiello is the one to watch here. Rated R for profanity. 86m. **DIR:** Dimitri Logothetis. **CAST:** Danny Aiello, Michael Paré, Justine Bateman, Diane Baker, Joe Cortese. **1990**

CLOSER YOU GET, THE ★★★1/2 The battle of the sexes takes an eccentric turn in this gentle Irish comedy, in which a group of men in a rugged village on the Donegal coast decide to improve their romantic prospects by "fooling" some gorgeous American gals into thinking their town is a tourist destination. ("Ideal age range between twenty and twenty-one," their *Miami Herald* ad reads. "Must be fit and sporty.") This little community doesn't exactly lack for good female companionship, however, and the village ladies are justifiably annoyed. The ensuing gender sparring plays out whimsically with fresh and unmannered characters. Rated PG-13 for fleeting profanity and sexual candor. 92m. **DIR:** Aileen Ritchie. **CAST:** Niamh Cusack, Sean McGinley, Ian Hart, Ewan Stewart, Sean McDonagh, Cathleen Bradley, Pat Shortt. **2000**

•CLOSET, THE ★★★★ This French comedy about personal biases, changing social mores, sexual politics, and latent revenge provides some huge laughs. Francois Pignon is a boorish accountant who has been abandoned by his wife and teen son. After overhearing that he is to be fired from his job at a condom factory, he sends to the office fake pictures of his bare buttocks being fondled at a gay club. Rumors of Francois's apparent lifestyle spread rapidly, and the reactions from his coworkers (including a macho homophobic) and estranged family produce several surprises as the masquerade rejuvenates Francois's life. In French with English subtitles. Rated R for language and sexuality. 85m. **DIR:** Francis Veber. **CAST:** Daniel Auteuil, Gérard Depardieu, Thierry Lhermitte, Michel Aumont. **2001 DVD**

CLOSET LAND ★★ A writer of innocuous children's books is taken from her bed and tortured by a government representative. This bizarre suspense tale is, unfortunately, message-laden. Rated R for profanity and violence. 93m. **DIR:** Radha Bharadwaj. **CAST:** Madeleine Stowe, Alan Rickman. **1991**

CLOUD DANCER ★★★1/2 This film features one of David Carradine's best performances. As the king of daredevil pilots, he struggles to keep ahead of his ambitious protégé (Joseph Bottoms) as well as fighting his love for Jennifer O'Neill. Rated PG. 108m. **DIR:** Barry Brown. **CAST:** David Carradine, Jennifer O'Neill, Joseph Bottoms, Colleen Camp. **1980**

CLOUD WALTZING ★★★ Beautiful photography and a respectable performance by Kathleen Beller are the highlights of this telefilm. The story is only marginal. Beller stars as an American journalist who is sent to France to do an exclusive interview with a hard-nosed French wine maker. She uses many ploys, including a hot-air balloon ride, to get her interview and finally her man. 103m. **DIR:** Gordon Flemyng. **CAST:** Kathleen Beller, François-Eric Gendron. **1987**

CLOUDED YELLOW, THE ★★★1/2 Near misses and a suspenseful chase across the English countryside are made all the more enjoyable by a superior cast. Accused murderer Jean Simmons goes on the lam with retired spy Trevor Howard. Nothing, of course, is as it seems. Not rated; contains implied violence. B&W; 96m. **DIR:** Ralph Thomas. **CAST:** Jean Simmons, Trevor Howard, Sonia Dresdel, Barry Jones. **1951**

CLOUDS OVER EUROPE ★★1/2 Handsome test pilot Laurence Olivier teams up with a man from Scotland Yard to discover why new bombers are disappearing in this on-the-verge-of-war thriller. B&W; 82m. **DIR:** Tim Whelan. **CAST:** Laurence Olivier, Valerie Hobson, Ralph Richardson. **1939**

CLOVER ★★★ On their wedding night, a couple are in a car accident, and the husband dies. His wife must deal not only with her grief but with a daughter from her husband's previous union, and with his family, who were not too thrilled about the interracial marriage. Add to this the ghost of the husband, who keeps popping up to open old wounds. This made-for-cable original is a good little drama. Not rated. 95m. **DIR:** Jud Taylor. **CAST:** Elizabeth McGovern, Ernie Hudson, Loretta Devine, Zelda Harris. **1997**

CLOWN, THE ★★★ Red Skelton in a dramatic role? Yes, it's true. In this film, a reworking of *The Champ*, he portrays a comedian who wins the love of his estranged son. Skelton is commendable and Tim Considine is excellent as the son. This film has an average story line but is well performed. B&W; 91m. **DIR:** Robert Z. Leonard. **CAST:** Red Skelton, Jane Greer, Tim Considine, Loring Smith. **1953**

CLOWN AT MIDNIGHT, THE ★★ A group of teenagers helping restore an old Canadian opera house finds itself the target of a demented killer dressed like the clown from Pagliacci's opera. Some atmosphere and costarring roles by Margot Kidder and Christopher Plummer do little to make this more than a routine exercise. Rated R for violence, language, nudity, and adult situations. 92m. **DIR:** Jean Pellerin. **CAST:** James Duval, Sarah Lassez, Tatyana Ali, Margot Kidder, Christopher Plummer. **1998**

CLOWNHOUSE ★★1/2 Novices willing to try a relatively bloodless horror flick might give this little programmer a try. Writer-director Victor Salva's script is strictly by the numbers as it sets the stage for three brothers to fight for their lives against three clowns (actually lunatics from a local asylum). Rated R for profanity and mild violence. 81m. **DIR:** Victor Salva. **CAST:** Nathan Forrest Winters. **1989**

CLOWNS, THE ★★★★1/2 Federico Fellini's television documentary is a three-ring spectacle of fun and silliness, too. Here, style is substance, and the only substance worth noting is the water thrown onto the journalist who asks the cast of circus crazies, "What does it all mean?" In Italian with English subtitles. 90m. **DIR:** Federico Fellini. **CAST:** Mayo Morin, Lima Alberti. **1971**

CLUB, THE (1985) ★★★ A highly paid rookie joins an Australian football team whose last championship was twenty years ago. A powerful story of winning and losing, of business and loyalty, and of determination. Intense and polished. Rated PG for profanity and violence. 93m. **DIR:** Bruce Beresford. **CAST:** Jack Thompson, Harold Hopkins, Graham Kennedy, John Howard. **1985**

CLUB, THE (1993) ★★ At their high-school prom six teens' deepest, darkest fears become reality. They'll have the devil to pay as they are initiated into a deadly club. Nifty special effects help save this routine shocker. Rated R for violence, language, and adult situations. 88m. **DIR:** Brenton Spencer. **CAST:** Joel Wyner, Kim Coates, Andrea Roth, Rino Romano, Kelli Taylor. **1993**

CLUB DES FEMMES ★★★ The romantic adventures of three young women who live in a plush mansion where no men are allowed were fairly shocking by 1930s American standards, but this lightweight import is just a diverting curio today. In French with English subtitles. B&W; 88m. **DIR:** Jacques Deval. **CAST:** Danielle Darrieux, Valentine Tessier. **1936**

CLUB EXTINCTION 🦃 A grim, depressing movie—ostensibly set in twenty-first-century Berlin—that fails on all levels. The plot revolves around apparent suicides that one cop believes are murders. Rated R for violence and gore. 112m. **DIR:** Claude Chabrol. **CAST:** Alan Bates, Jennifer Beals, Andrew McCarthy, Jan Niklas. **1990**

CLUB FED ★★ Gangster's moll Judy Landers, framed on a murder charge, is sent to a minimum security prison run by a corrupt warden. There are more "guest stars" than laughs in this too-familiar comedy. Rated PG-13 for double entendre humor. 91m. **DIR:** Nathaniel Christian. **CAST:** Judy Landers, Burt Young, Lance Kinsey, Karen Black, Sherman Hemsley, Allen Garfield, Joseph Campanella, Lyle Alzado, Mary Woronov. **1991**

CLUB LIFE ★★ Neon lovers! May we have your attention please. This is just the film for you. The neon used in the disco surpasses anything you've ever seen. Rated R. 93m. **DIR:** Norman Thaddeus Vane. **CAST:** Tony Curtis, Dee Wallace, Michael Parks, Yana Nirvana. **1987**

CLUB MED ★1/2 Another tired retread of the *Fantasy Island/Love Boat/Hotel* scenario. 104m. **DIR:** Bob Giraldi. **CAST:** Jack Scalia, Linda Hamilton, Patrick Macnee, Bill Maher. **1986**

CLUB PARADISE ★★ Robin Williams and Jimmy Cliff start their own little Club Med–style resort. PG-13 for language and drug humor. 104m. **DIR:** Harold Ramis. **CAST:** Robin Williams, Peter O'Toole, Jimmy Cliff, Twiggy, Rick Moranis, Adolph Caesar, Eugene Levy, Joanna Cassidy. **1986**

CLUB VAMPIRE 🦃 Sleazy, would-be vampire chiller from the Corman factory is not a film, but a thin excuse to wallow in depravity. Rated R for violence, gore, profanity, and nudity. 76m. **DIR:** Andy Ruben. **CAST:** John Savage, Starr Andreeff. **1997**

CLUBHOUSE DETECTIVES ★★ When a boy believes he has witnessed a murder, he turns to his clubhouse buddies for help in solving the crime. Definitely geared for the *Hardy Boys* crowd. Rated PG for violence. 85m. **DIR:** Eric Henoershot. **CAST:** Michael Ballam, Michael Galeota, Jimmy Galeota, Suzanne Barnes. **1995**

CLUBLAND ★★ The hopes and heartbreaks of the music business are showcased in this occasionally engaging tale of one band's quest for stardom. The script sounds authentic when it's not dishing out tired clichés and characters, but the L.A. music scene deserves better. Rated R for adult situations, language, and nudity. 93m. **DIR:** Mary Lambert. **CAST:** Alexis Arquette, Jimmy Tuckett, Brad Hunt, Heather Stephens, Lori Petty. **1999 DVD**

CLUE ★★1/2 Inspired by the popular board game, the movie is a pleasant spoof of whodunits. The delightful ensemble establishes a suitably breezy style. Silliness eventually overwhelms the proceedings. As a gimmick, the film was originally shown in theatres with three different endings. All versions are included on the videocassette. Rated PG. 100m. **DIR:** Jonathan Lynn. **CAST:** Eileen Brennan, Tim Curry, Madeline Kahn, Christopher Lloyd, Michael McKean, Martin Mull, Lesley Ann Warren. **1985 DVD**

CLUELESS ★★★1/2 Delightful spoof of spoiled Beverly Hills brats features adorably petulant Alicia Silverstone as the leader of the pack. In her efforts to manipulate the romances of her peers, she puts her own love life on hold . . . temporarily. What's great about this film is the hilarious spin on teen fads and slang. Unlike most teen flicks, this can be enjoyed by adults as well. Rated PG-13 for profanity and drug use. 92m. **DIR:** Amy Heckerling. **CAST:** Alicia Silverstone, Paul Rudd, Stacey Dash, Brittany Murphy, Dan Hedaya. **1995 DVD**

COAL MINER'S DAUGHTER ★★★★1/2 Sissy Spacek gives a superb, totally believable performance in this film biography of country singer Loretta Lynn. The title role takes Spacek from Lynn's impoverished Appalachian childhood through marriage at thirteen up to her mid-thirties and reign as the "First Lady of Country Music." Rated PG. 125m. **DIR:** Michael Apted. **CAST:** Sissy Spacek, Tommy Lee Jones, Beverly D'Angelo, Levon Helm. **1980**

COAST PATROL, THE ★★ Set on the Maine coast and shot on the Pacific off Long Beach, this lively melodrama of smugglers and speedboat chases is Fay Wray's first film of record. If you're a fan, enjoy. Silent with musical score. B&W; 76m. **DIR:** Bud Barsky. **CAST:** Fay Wray, Kenneth McDonald. **1925**

COAST TO COAST ★★ Dyan Cannon stars as a wacko blonde who's been railroaded into a mental hospital by her husband. Cannon escapes by bopping her psychiatrist over the head with a bust of Freud, and the chase is on. A trucker (Robert Blake) gives Cannon a lift, and they romp from Pennsylvania to California. Rated PG for profanity. 95m. **DIR:** Joseph Sargent. **CAST:** Dyan Cannon, Robert Blake, Quinn Redeker, Michael Lerner, Maxine Stuart, Bill Lucking. **1980**

COBB ★★★★ Ty Cobb, the most despised and possibly greatest player in the history of baseball, is seen as a belligerent bigot and beater of women as he slides into the final throes of cancer, heart disease, diabetes, and alcoholism. Rated R for language, sex, and violence. 128m. **DIR:** Ron Shelton. **CAST:** Tommy Lee Jones, Robert Wuhl, Lolita Davidovich. **1994**

COBRA, THE (1967) 🦃 Dana Andrews battles communist drug smugglers in this stultifying spy stinker. Not rated. 97m. **DIR:** Mario Sequi. **CAST:** Dana Andrews, Anita Ekberg, Peter Martell. **1967**

COBRA (1986) ★★ Sylvester Stallone comes back for more *Rambo*-like action as a tough city cop on the trail of a serial killer in this unrelentingly grim and gruesome thriller. It is packed with action and violence. Rated R for violence, gore, and profanity. 95m. **DIR:** George Pan Cosmatos. **CAST:** Sylvester Stallone, Brigitte Nielsen, Reni Santoni, Andrew Robinson. **1986 DVD**

COBRA WOMAN ★★★★1/2 A cult classic. Maria Montez is so bad she's good as twin sisters, one evil and one good. 70m. **DIR:** Robert Siodmak. **CAST:** Maria Montez, Jon Hall, Sabu, Mary Nash, Lon Chaney Jr., Moroni Olsen, Edgar Barrier. **1944**

COCA COLA KID, THE ★★★ A nude scene between Eric Roberts and Greta Scacchi in a bed covered with feathers is enough to make anyone's temperature rise, but as a whole this little film doesn't have enough bite to it. Roberts plays a gung-ho troubleshooter from the popular beverage company who comes to Australia to sell the drink to a hard-nosed businessman (Bill Kerr) who has a monopoly on a stretch of land with his own soft drink. Worth a look. Rated R for nudity. 90m. **DIR:** Dusan Makavejev. **CAST:** Eric Roberts, Greta Scacchi, Bill Kerr. **1985 DVD**

COCAINE COWBOYS 🦃 This inept thriller concerns a struggling rock band whose members resort to drug smuggling in order to finance their music career. Rated R for nudity and graphic violence. 86m. **DIR:** Ulli Lommel. **CAST:** Jack Palance, Tom Sullivan, Andy Warhol, Suzanna Love. **1979**

COCAINE: ONE MAN'S SEDUCTION ★★★1/2 Though this is not another *Reefer Madness*, the subject could have been handled a little more subtly. Still, the melodrama is not obtrusive enough to take away from Dennis Weaver's brilliant performance as a real estate salesman who gets hooked. Not rated, but the equivalent of a PG for adult subject matter. 97m. **DIR:** Paul Wendkos. **CAST:** Dennis Weaver, Karen Grassle, Pamela Bellwood, James Spader, David Ackroyd, Jeffrey Tambor. **1983**

COCAINE WARS 🦃 John Schneider plays an undercover agent in a South American country who takes on a drug lord's empire. Rated R for violence, profanity, and nudity. 82m. **DIR:** Hector Olivera. **CAST:** John Schneider, Kathryn Witt, Federico Luppi, Royal Dano. **1986**

COCKEYED CAVALIERS ★★★ One of the better Wheeler and Woolsey vehicles, a costume comedy set in sixteenth-century Britain with the wacky duo posing as the king's physicians. Funniest bit is a parody of Garbo's *Queen Christina*. B&W; 72m. **DIR:** Mark Sandrich. **CAST:** Bert Wheeler, Robert Woolsey, Thelma Todd, Noah Beery Sr. **1934**

COCKFIGHTER ★★ Title says it all. Warren Oates and Harry Dean Stanton can't breathe life into this simplistic look at the illegal sport of cockfighting. For Oates fans only. Rated R. 83m. **DIR:** Monte Hellman. **CAST:** Warren Oates, Harry Dean Stanton, Richard B. Shull, Troy Donahue, Millie Perkins. **1974 DVD**

COCKTAIL 🦃 Tom Cruise, as the fast-rising newcomer of the glass-and-bottle set. Rated R for language and brief nudity. 104m. **DIR:** Roger Donaldson. **CAST:** Tom Cruise, Bryan Brown, Elisabeth Shue, Laurence Luckinbill. **1988**

COCOANUTS ★★★1/2 The Marx Brothers' first movie was one of the earliest sound films and suffers as a result. Notice how all the maps and newspapers are sopping wet (so they wouldn't crackle into the supersensitive, primitive microphones). The romantic leads are laughably stiff, and even the songs by Irving Berlin are forgettable. However, the Marxes—all four of them, Groucho, Harpo, Chico, and Zeppo—supply some classic moments, making the picture well worth watching. B&W; 96m. **DIR:** Joseph Santley, Robert Florey. **CAST:** The Marx Brothers, Kay Francis, Margaret Dumont. **1929 DVD**

COCOON ★★★★★ *Cocoon* is a splendid entertainment about a group of people in a retirement home who find what they believe is the fountain of youth. Only trouble is the magic place belongs to a group of extraterrestrials, who may or may not be friendly. Rated PG-13 for suggested sex, brief nudity, and light profanity. 118m. **DIR:** Ron Howard. **CAST:** Don Ameche, Wilford Brimley, Hume Cronyn, Brian Dennehy, Jack Gilford, Steve Guttenberg, Barret Oliver, Maureen Stapleton, Jessica Tandy, Gwen Verdon, Tahnee Welch. **1985**

COCOON: THE RETURN ★★★1/2 Daniel Petrie pulls off something of a minor miracle in this sequel, which has the elderly Earthlings returning home to help their alien friends rescue some cocoons that have been endangered by an earthquake. Petrie keeps our interest by concentrating on the characters and getting uniformly splendid performances. Rated PG for slight profanity. 112m. **DIR:** Daniel Petrie. **CAST:** Don Ameche, Wilford Brimley, Courteney Cox, Hume Cronyn, Brian Dennehy, Jack Gilford, Steve Guttenberg, Maureen Stapleton, Jessica Tandy, Gwen Verdon, Tahnee Welch, Barret Oliver. **1988**

CODE NAME: CHAOS ★★ Stellar cast works desperately to save this misguided comedy about former CIA spooks gathering their resources on a tropical island in order to send the rest of the world into chaos. Rated R for profanity. 96m. **DIR:** Antony Thomas. **CAST:** Diane Ladd, Robert Loggia, David Warner, Alice Krige, Brian Kerwin. **1989**

CODE NAME: DANCER ★★★ Kate Capshaw plays a former CIA agent living a quiet married life in L.A., when she's called back to Cuba to settle an old score. TV movie originally titled *Her Secret Life*. 93m. **DIR:** Buzz Kulik. **CAST:** Kate Capshaw, Jeroen Krabbé, Gregory Sierra, Cliff De Young. **1987**

CODE NAME: EMERALD ★★★1/2 Better-than-average World War II espionage film about a double agent (Ed Harris) who attempts to rescue a U.S. Army officer (Eric Stoltz) held for interrogation in a French prison. The plot moves along at a good clip despite the lack of action. Rated PG for violence and sex. 95m. **DIR:** Jonathan Sanger. **CAST:** Ed Harris, Max von Sydow, Horst Buchholz, Helmut Berger, Cyrielle Claire, Eric Stoltz. **1985**

CODE NAME JAGUAR ★★1/2 Despite familiar trappings and the occasional stumbling block, this political thriller does just fine thanks to Danny Nucci's engaging performance. He plays the naïve Stuart Dempsey, who has just moved to New York and is immediately mistaken for an international assassin. The script asks us to believe way too much, but the cast is likable enough to win us over. Victoria Sanchez shines as his new girlfriend who isn't what she seems. Rated R for language and violence. 93m. **DIR:** John Hamilton. **CAST:** Danny Nucci, Victoria Sanchez, Jack Langedijk, David Carradine. **2000 DVD**

CODE NAME: WILD GEESE ★★ Marginal action-adventure is set in the Golden Triangle of Asia. A group of mercenaries hire out as a task force to destroy the opium trade for the Drug Enforcement Administration. Rated R. 101m. **DIR:** Anthony M. Dawson. **CAST:** Lewis Collins, Lee Van Cleef, Ernest Borgnine, Mimsy Farmer, Klaus Kinski. **1984**

CODE OF SILENCE ★★★★ With this film, Chuck Norris proved himself the heir to Charles Bronson as the king of the no-nonsense action movie. In *Code of Silence*, the star gives a right-on-target performance as tough cop Sgt. Eddie Cusack, who takes on warring mob families and corrupt police officers. Rated R for violence and profanity. 102m. **DIR:** Andrew Davis. **CAST:** Chuck Norris, Henry Silva, Bert Remsen, Dennis Farina, Mike Genovese, Ralph Foody, Nathan Davis. **1985 DVD**

CODENAME: KYRIL ★★★1/2 When the Kremlin discovers that someone has been leaking secrets to British intelligence, an assassin (Ian Charleson) is dispatched to England to discover the traitor's identity. Edward Woodward is the laconic agent on his trail in this splendidly acted, tautly directed spy film. Made for cable. Rated R for violence. 115m. **DIR:** Ian Sharp. **CAST:** Edward Woodward, Ian Charleson, Denholm Elliott, Joss Ackland, Richard E. Grant. **1988**

COFFY 🦃 Pam Grier is wasted in this feeble blaxploitation action flick. Rated R. 91m. **DIR:** Jack Hill. **CAST:** Pam Grier, Booker Bradshaw, Sid Haig, Allan Arbus, Robert DoQui. **1973 DVD**

COHEN AND TATE ★★ Roy Scheider stars as a burned-out Mafia hit man. He contracts for one last job: the kidnapping of a 9 year old boy (Harley Cross) who has witnessed the murder of his informant parents by the mob. Rated R for violence and profanity. 86m. **DIR:** Eric Red. **CAST:** Roy Scheider, Adam Baldwin, Harley Cross. **1989**

COLD AROUND THE HEART ★★★ Writer John Ridley takes a stab at directing with this "neo-noir" tale of double-crossing lovers on the run from the law and each other. David Caruso and Kelly Lynch are fine as the untrustworthy lovers who turn on each other when they heist some stolen diamonds. Rated R for adult situations, language, nudity, and violence. 96m. **DIR:** John Ridley. **CAST:** David Caruso, Kelly Lynch, Stacey Dash, Christopher Noth, John Spencer. **1996**

COLD-BLOODED ★★★1/2 Unusual comedy starring Jason Priestley as a slightly simpleminded bookie promoted to hit man. Tutored under the exacting and sometimes doting eyes of Peter Riegert, Priestley learns he is finally good at something. The twist comes in the form of Kimberly Williams, turning this into a humorously weird, if overwrought, love story. Rated R for profanity and violence. 93m. **DIR:** M. Wallace Wolodarsky. **CAST:** Jason Priestley, Peter Riegert, Robert Loggia, Janeane Garofalo, Michael J. Fox, Kimberly Williams. **1994 DVD**

COLD COMFORT ★★ A traveling salesman is rescued from certain death only to be kept prisoner by a madman as a gift to his eighteen year old daughter. Rated R for profanity and nudity. 88m. **DIR:** Vic Sarin. **CAST:** Maury Chaykin, Margaret Langrick. **1988**

COLD COMFORT FARM ★★★★ Triumphant, droll film adaptation of Stella Gibbons's 1932 English literary satire. A sophisticated young Londoner goes to live with her grim, rustic relatives. Rather than being terrified or intimidated, she self-confidently sets about arranging fulfilling lives for one and all. A small masterpiece of amused British mockery with a delightful generosity at its heart. Rated PG. 105m. **DIR:** John Schlesinger. **CAST:** Kate Beckinsale, Eileen Atkins, Rufus Sewell, Ian McKellen, Sheila Burrell, Joanna Lumley. **1995**

COLD FEET (1984) ★★★1/2 This enjoyable low-key romance features a film writer (Griffin Dunne) who has just left his complaining, childlike wife (Blanche Baker) and vowed to go it alone. Enter an attractive scientist (Marissa Chibas) who has just dumped her overbearing boyfriend. Rated PG for slight profanity. 91m. **DIR:** Bruce Van Dusen. **CAST:** Griffin Dunne, Marissa Chibas, Blanche Baker. **1984**

COLD FEET (1989) ★★★1/2 The scheme is to smuggle emeralds from Mexico into the United States inside a horse that is being imported for stud purposes. Offbeat fun. Rated R for nudity and language. 94m. **DIR:** Robert Dornhelm. **CAST:** Keith Carradine, Sally Kirkland, Tom Waits, Rip Torn. **1989**

COLD FEVER ★★★1/2 Viewers with a taste for the offbeat should hunt for this gentle comedy about a Japanese businessman who unwillingly journeys to Iceland to perform a memorial ceremony for his deceased parents. The odd locations and odder characters are reminiscent of the films of Jim Jarmusch. In Japanese and Icelandic with English subtitles. Not rated; contains profanity. 85m. **DIR:** Fridrik Thor Fridriksson. **CAST:** Masatoshi Nagase, Lili Taylor, Fisher Stevens, Seijun Suzuki. **1995**

COLD FRONT ★★★1/2 Martin Sheen is an L.A. cop on assignment in Vancouver who is teamed up with Michael Ontkean to solve a murder that involves a hit man who has gone berserk. Fast-paced thriller. Not rated, with violence and strong language. 94m. **DIR:** Paul Bnarbic. **CAST:** Martin Sheen, Beverly D'Angelo, Michael Ontkean, Kim Coates. **1989**

COLD HEAVEN ★★1/2 In this moody, murky melodrama, the unfaithful wife of a physician watches in horror as her mate is run over by a speedboat near Acapulco. His body then disappears from a hospital autopsy slab! Rated R for profanity and nudity. 105m. **DIR:** Nicolas Roeg. **CAST:** Theresa Russell, Mark Harmon, James Russo, Talia Shire, Will Patton, Richard Bradford. **1992**

COLD JUSTICE ★★1/2 There's plenty of bare-fisted action in this tale of a priest who is actually a con man with an unsaintly agenda. Rated R for violence. 106m. **DIR:** Terry Green. **CAST:** Dennis Waterman, Roger Daltrey, Ron Dean, Penelope Milford. **1989**

COLD LIGHT OF DAY, THE ★★★★ Chilling crime-drama stars Richard E. Grant as a hard-nosed detective on the trail of a serial killer of little girls. When all of his avenues run out, the detective decides to use a little girl as live bait with disastrous results. Atmospheric, hard-hitting thriller works on many levels. Not rated; contains profanity and violence. 101m. **DIR:** Rudolf Van Den Berg. **CAST:** Richard E. Grant, Lynsey Baxter, Simon Cadell, James Laurenson. **1995**

COLD RIVER ★★★★ In the autumn of 1932, an experienced guide takes his 14 year old daughter and his 12 year old stepson on an extended camping trip. Far out in the wilderness, the father dies of a heart attack, and the children must survive a blizzard, starvation, and an encounter with a wild mountain man. A fine family movie. Rated PG. 94m. **DIR:** Fred G. Sullivan. **CAST:** Suzanna Weber, Pete Teterson, Richard Jaeckel. **1981**

COLD ROOM, THE This made-for-television movie is a waste of good material. Amanda Pays accompanies father George Segal to East Germany only to find she has fallen into a time-warp and now faces Gestapo agents and mysteries about her own life. 95m. **DIR:** James Dearden. **CAST:** George Segal, Amanda Pays, Warren Clarke, Anthony Higgins. **1984**

COLD SASSY TREE ★★★ Small-town drama reflects on the lives of residents of Cold Sassy Tree—a rural community built on the site of a former sassafras grove, and still isolated with a post–Civil War mentality in the early 1900s. Good performances and well-meaning sentimentality abound. This cable TV-movie is not rated. 97m. **DIR:** Joan Tewkesbury. **CAST:** Faye Dunaway, Richard Widmark, Frances Fisher, Neil Patrick Harris. **1989**

COLD STEEL Brainless rehash about a cop out for revenge for the murder of his father. Rated R for violence, nudity, and profanity. 91m. **DIR:** Dorothy Ann Puzo. **CAST:** Brad Davis, Adam Ant, Sharon Stone, Jonathan Banks. **1988**

COLD SWEAT (1970) Dated, offensively sexist piece of machismo. Rated R. 94m. **DIR:** Terence Young. **CAST:** Charles Bronson, Liv Ullmann, Jill Ireland, James Mason, Gabriele Ferzetti, Michael Constantine. **1970 DVD**

COLD SWEAT (1993) ★★ A hit man (Ben Cross) decides to quit the business after he kills an innocent bystander. Persuaded to do one more job, he goes after the ambitious, double-crossing partner of a ruthless businessman, whose wife is cheating on him with his partner and Cross's contact. A good idea overcome by the film's sexual content. Rated R for simulated sex, nudity, violence, and profanity. 93m. **DIR:** Gail Harvey. **CAST:** Ben Cross, Adam Baldwin, Shannon Tweed, Dave Thomas. **1993**

COLD TURKEY ★★ This comedy, about a small town in Iowa where the whole populace tries to give up smoking at once, sat on the shelf for two years, and understandably—despite the knockout cast and a few funny scenes, the humor is mean-spirited and decidedly unpleasant. Rated PG. 99m. **DIR:** Norman Lear. **CAST:** Dick Van Dyke, Pippa Scott, Tom Poston, Bob Newhart, Edward Everett Horton, Vincent Gardenia, Barnard Hughes. **1971**

COLDFIRE Lots of action and violence and zero personality in this tale of a dedicated cop trying to stop the flow of a deadly designer drug. Not rated; contains violence and adult situations. 90m. **DIR:** Wings Hauser. **CAST:** Wings Hauser, Michael Easton. **1992**

COLDITZ STORY, THE ★★★1/2 Tight direction, an intelligent script, and a terrific cast make this one of the most compelling British dramas of the 1950s and one of the best prison films of all time. John Mills is outstanding as the glue that keeps the escape plans together, but the entire crew works well together. B&W; 97m. **DIR:** Guy Hamilton. **CAST:** John Mills, Eric Portman, Lionel Jeffries, Bryan Forbes, Ian Carmichael, Theodore Bikel, Anton Diffring, Richard Wattis. **1957**

•COLLATERAL DAMAGE ★★1/2 Los Angeles firefighter Arnold Schwarzenegger goes after the Colombian terrorist whose bomb killed his wife and son. Despite some uncanny resonances with the September 11 attacks (which prompted a five-month delay in the film's release), this one's a disappointment. Schwarzenegger is earnest, and there are good cameos from John Turturro and John Leguizamo, but the script's ridiculous contrivances, including a groan-inducing climactic surprise, can't be overcome. Rated R for violence and profanity. 108m. **DIR:** Andrew Davis. **CAST:** Arnold Schwarzenegger, Elias Koteas, Francesca Neri, Clifford Curtis, John Turturro, John Leguizamo. **2002 DVD**

COLLECTION, THE ★★★★ A superb cast shines in this British television adaptation of the Harold Pinter play about the consequences of an unusual romantic triangle. The stars bring a professional elegance and extra viewer interest to the downbeat story. Made for TV. 64m. **DIR:** Michael Apted. **CAST:** Alan Bates, Malcolm McDowell, Helen Mirren, Laurence Olivier. **1975**

COLLECTOR, THE ★★★★1/2 In this chiller, Terence Stamp plays a disturbed young man who, having no friends, collects things. Unfortunately, one of the things he collects is beautiful Samantha Eggar. He keeps her as his prisoner and waits for her to fall in love with him. Extremely interesting profile of a madman. 119m. **DIR:** William Wyler. **CAST:** Terence Stamp, Samantha Eggar, Maurice Dallimore, Mona Washbourne. **1965**

COLLECTOR'S ITEM ★★★1/2 This erotic suspense-drama is a surprise sleeper. Tony Musante meets up with gorgeous Laura Antonelli whom he had seduced sixteen years earlier. The actors give intense performances and Antonelli just may have found a role model in Glenn Close of *Fatal Attraction* fame. Not rated, but strictly adult fare with nudity and profanity. 99m. **DIR:** Giuseppe Patroni Griffi. **CAST:** Tony Musante, Laura Antonelli, Florinda Bolkan. **1988**

COLLEGE ★★★1/2 An anti-athletics bookworm, Buster Keaton, goes to college on a scholarship. His girl falls for a jock, and Keaton decides to succeed in athletics to win her back. He fails hilariously in every attempt, but finally rescues her by unwittingly using every athletic skill. B&W; 65m. **DIR:** James W. Horne. **CAST:** Buster Keaton, Anne Cornwall, Flora Bramley, Grant Winters. **1927 DVD**

COLLEGE SWING ★★★1/2 One of Betty Grable's first major musicals, this film kids collegiates and intellectual attitudes by showing what happens when Gracie Allen inherits a small-town college and staffs it with vaudeville performers. Some hummable tunes by Frank Loesser, a witty Preston Sturges script. B&W; 86m. **DIR:** Raoul Walsh. **CAST:** Bob Hope, Betty Grable, George

Burns, Gracie Allen, Martha Raye, Ben Blue, Robert Cummings, John Payne, Jerry Colonna. **1938**

COLLISION COURSE ★★ A tough Detroit cop gets mixed up with a Japanese police officer as they track the smugglers of an experimental car part. Some nice bits of comedy can't save this mishmash of action and Japan bashing. Rated PG for violence and profanity. 99m. **DIR:** Lewis Teague. **CAST:** Noriyuki "Pat" Morita, Jay Leno, Chris Sarandon, Ernie Hudson, John Hancock, Al Waxman, Randall "Tex" Cobb, Tom Noonan. **1989**

COLONEL EFFINGHAM'S RAID ★★1/2 Slight small-town story about Charles Coburn's efforts to preserve a local monument is pleasant enough and has marvelous characters. Not a great film, but harmless fun and at times thought-provoking. B&W; 70m. **DIR:** Irving Pichel. **CAST:** Charles Coburn, Joan Bennett, William Eythe, Allyn Joslyn, Elizabeth Patterson, Donald Meek. **1945**

COLONEL REDL ★★1/2 The ponderous and deliberate nature of this film, which tells the story of a pawn in a struggle for power in the Austro-Hungarian Empire just prior to World War I, keeps it from becoming fully satisfying. In German with English subtitles. Rated R for profanity, nudity, simulated sex, and violence. 144m. **DIR:** István Szabó. **CAST:** Klaus Maria Brandauer, Armin Mueller-Stahl. **1985 DVD**

COLONY, THE (1995) ★★ John Ritter moves his family into an idyllic, high-tech neighborhood, only to blanch at the price they must pay for security. Sad to see Ritter in such poorly written, made-for-TV tripe. Rated PG-13 for violence and profanity. 93m. **DIR:** Rob Hedden. **CAST:** John Ritter, Hal Linden, Mary Page Keller, Marshall Teague, Todd Jeffries, Alexandra Picatto, Cody Dorkin, June Lockhart. **1995**

COLONY (1996) ★★★ Effective chiller about the body in rebellion picks up some of the themes from the works of David Cronenberg (the new flesh being the most prevalent) and becomes a triumph of originality over budget. While the film stumbles here and there, the overall picture shines in telling its tale of body parts taking on a mind of their own. Some versions list the title on the box as *Colony Mutation*. Rated R for violence, profanity, gore, and simulated sex. 83m. **DIR:** Thomas Berna. **CAST:** Dave Rommel, Susan Cane. **1996**

COLOR ME BARBRA ★★ Streisand's second TV special doesn't hold a candle to her first, *My Name Is Barbra*. 60m. **DIR:** Dwight Hemion. **CAST:** Barbra Streisand. **1966**

COLOR ME BLOOD RED 🦃 An artist discovers the perfect shade of red for his paintings. Not rated; the film has violence. 70m. **DIR:** Herschell Gordon Lewis. **CAST:** Don Joseph. **1965 DVD**

COLOR ME DEAD ★★1/2 An innocent accountant (Tom Tryon) gets caught in the middle of an illegal uranium robbery and is poisoned with a deadly slow-working drug. He tries to find out why he was murdered. Carolyn Jones is effective as Tryon's girlfriend-secretary and gives the story poignancy; but the screenplay is wanting. Not rated; contains violence. 91m. **DIR:** Eddie Davis. **CAST:** Tom Tryon, Carolyn Jones, Rick Jason. **1969**

COLOR OF COURAGE, THE ★★★1/2 The Supreme Court case from the 1940s, *Sipes v. McGhee*, comes alive in this made-for-cable movie, where a black family moves into a neighborhood with a restrictive covenant in place. While the McGhee family fights the restriction, Mrs. McGhee befriends Mrs. Sipes in spite of their differences. With only a glimpse of the real violence and hate generated by this case, the film focuses on the improbable friendship of the two women. Rated PG. 91m. **DIR:** Lee Rose. **CAST:** Linda Hamilton, Lynn Whitfield, Bruce Greenwood, Roger Guenveur Smith. **1998**

•COLOR OF FRIENDSHIP, THE ★★★ Respectable attempt by Disney to address important racial issues in a family forum. Lindsey Haun is good as Mahree, a South African student who gets to stay in America as part of an exchange program. Imagine the black host family's surprise when they learn that Mahree is white, and vice versa. Even though the film is more about entertainment than education, the message comes across loud and clear. Both sides have a lot to learn, and the film presents issues without preaching. Not rated. 87m. **DIR:** Kevin Hooks. **CAST:** Lindsey Haun, Shadia Simmons, Carl Lumbly, Penny Johnson, Anthony Burnett. **2000**

COLOR OF JUSTICE ★★ Writer-director Lionel Chetwynd's strident drama, intended to reflect our legal system's unfair treatment of black suspects, quickly deteriorates into an insulting, moronic indictment of liberals, Christians, feminists, opportunistic politicians, and the media. The acting—by performers capable of much better—is laughably over-the-top. Rated R for profanity and violence. 93m. **DIR:** Lionel Chetwynd. **CAST:** F. Murray Abraham, Bruce Davison, Gregory Hines, Judd Hirsch, Saul Rubinek. **1997**

COLOR OF MONEY, THE ★★★★ A sequel to *The Hustler*, this film features outstanding performances by Paul Newman as the now-aging pool champion and Tom Cruise as his protégé. The story may be predictable, even clichéd, but the actors make it worth watching. Rated R for nudity, profanity, and violence. 117m. **DIR:** Martin Scorsese. **CAST:** Paul Newman, Tom Cruise, Mary Elizabeth Mastrantonio, Helen Shaver, John Turturro. **1986 DVD**

COLOR OF NIGHT 🦃 Anguished psychiatrist Bruce Willis takes over a murdered colleague's therapy group, only to encounter death threats and the sultry advances of pouty Jane March, whose image as an erotic seductress vanishes with every poorly delivered line of vapid dialogue. This mess comes from the director who gave us *The Stunt Man*? Rated R for profanity, nudity, simulated sex, and violence. 121m. **DIR:** Richard Rush. **CAST:** Bruce Willis, Jane March, Rubén Blades, Lesley Ann Warren, Scott Bakula, Brad Dourif, Lance Henriksen. **1994 DVD**

COLOR OF PARADISE, THE ★★★ When a blind boy goes home from his city school to his mountain village, he finds that his widowed father is about to remarry and doesn't want him around. This pastoral Iranian character study is slow-moving and low-key. Even so, director Majid Majidi weaves a subtle spell, like a sinister fairy tale, and the exquisite photography captures the unearthly beauty of the setting and characters. In Farsi with English subtitles. Rated PG. 90m. **DIR:** Majid Majidi. **CAST:** Mohsen Ramezani, Hossein Mahjoub, Salime Feizi, Elham Sharifi, Farahnaz Safari. **1999 DVD**

COLOR OF POMEGRANATES, THE ★★★★ Visually rich but difficult film is best viewed as a mosaic epic of the spiritual history of Armenia, a nation long persecuted by its neighbors for its Christianity. The film, which went unseen for years while its creator was in a Soviet jail, is structured around incidents in the life of the eighteenth-century poet Sayat Nova. In Armenian with English subtitles. 73m. **DIR:** Sergi Parajanov. **CAST:** Sofico Chiaureli. **1969 DVD**

COLOR PURPLE, THE ★★★★★ Steven Spielberg's adaptation of Alice Walker's Pulitzer Prize–winning novel about the growth to maturity and independence of a mistreated black woman is one of those rare brings a tear to the eye and joy to the heart. Walker's story, set between 1909 and 1947 in a small town in Georgia, celebrates the qualities of kindness, compassion, and love. Rated PG-13 for violence, profanity, and suggested sex. 130m. **DIR:** Steven Spielberg. **CAST:** Whoopi Goldberg, Danny Glover, Adolph Caesar, Margaret Avery, Oprah Winfrey, Rae Dawn Chong, Akosua Busia. **1985 DVD**

COLORADO SERENADE ★★★ Eddie Dean and stuntman extraordinaire Dave Sharpe help a crusading judge clean out a nest of outlaws. More trouble arises when the judge learns his long lost son is the leader of the gang. 68m. **DIR:** Robert Emmett Tansey. **CAST:** Eddie Dean, Roscoe Ates, David Sharpe, Forrest Taylor, Dennis Moore. **1946**

COLORADO SUNSET ★★★ A phony protective association causes a milk war among ranchers until they vote Gene Autry in as sheriff. B&W; 61m. **DIR:** George Sherman. **CAST:** Gene Autry, Smiley Burnette, June Storey, Buster Crabbe. **1939**

COLORS ★★★★ Robert Duvall gives a powerhouse performance in this hard-hitting police drama. He's a cool, experienced cop who attempts to teach his young, hotheaded partner (Sean Penn) how to survive in East Los Angeles. Penn manages to match Duvall and director Hopper holds it all together, although he does go overboard in the sex and violence department. Rated R for language, profanity, suggested sex, and nudity. 119m. **DIR:** Dennis Hopper. **CAST:** Sean Penn, Robert Duvall, Maria Conchita Alonso, Randy Brooks, Don Cheadle. **1988 DVD**

COLOSSUS OF NEW YORK, THE ★★1/2 When a brilliant scientist is killed in a car crash, his father transplants his brain into a giant robot, with predictably dire results. Unlike most cheapo 1950s horror films, this studio production at least takes itself seriously, but genre fans will find it drab. B&W; 70m. **DIR:** Eugene Lourie. **CAST:** John Baragrey, Otto Kruger, Charles Herbert, Mala Powers, Ross Martin. **1958**

COLOSSUS: THE FORBIN PROJECT ★★★1/2 Low-key thriller about a supercomputer designed for defense that becomes too big for its bytes. Colossus launches its own plan for world domination. This intelligent production is disturbing and very well made. Lack of stars and a downbeat story kept it from becoming the box-office hit it deserved. Rated PG. 100m. **DIR:** Joseph Sargent. **CAST:** Eric Braeden, Susan Clark, William Schallert. **1969**

COLUMBO: MURDER BY THE BOOK ★★★1/2 Steven Spielberg steers a winning cast through a provoking "perfect crime" script by writer Steven Bochco (*Hill Street Blues*, *L.A. Law*). As homicide detective Columbo, Peter Falk is hard-pressed to trip up smug murderer Jack Cassidy. One of the best episodes of the long-running television series. 79m. **DIR:** Steven Spielberg. **CAST:** Peter Falk, Jack Cassidy, Martin Milner, Rosemary Forsyth. **1971**

COMA ★★★1/2 A doctor (Genevieve Bujold) becomes curious about several deaths at a hospital where patients have all lapsed into comas. Very original melodrama keeps the audience guessing. One of Michael Crichton's better film efforts. Rated PG for brief nudity and violence. 113m. **DIR:** Michael Crichton. **CAST:** Genevieve Bujold, Michael Douglas, Richard Widmark, Rip Torn, Elizabeth Ashley. **1978 DVD**

COMANCHE TERRITORY ★★★ An old-fashioned Western that tampers with history to cover loopholes in the plot, this cowboy tale shows Jim Bowie helping Indians cope with the greed of settlers who should have known better. Good action and colorful sets make the movie work. 76m. **DIR:** George Sherman. **CAST:** Maureen O'Hara, Macdonald Carey, Charles Drake, James Best, Will Geer. **1950**

COMANCHEROS, THE ★★★★ Big John Wayne is the laconic Texas Ranger assigned to bring in dandy gambler Stuart Whitman for murder. Along the way, Wayne bests bad guy Lee Marvin, and Whitman proves himself a hero by helping the big guy take on the ruthless gun- and liquor-running villains of the title, led by Nehemiah Persoff. It's a fine Western with lots of nice moments. 107m. **DIR:** Michael Curtiz. **CAST:** John Wayne, Stuart Whitman, Lee Marvin, Ina Balin, Bruce Cabot, Nehemiah Persoff, Bob Steele. **1961**

COMBAT KILLERS ★★ The captain of an American platoon in the Philippines during the closing days of World War II puts his men through unnecessary dangers in fighting Japanese forces. Straightforward adventure will please war fans, though others may find it routine. The movie is unrated and contains some violence and profanity. 96m. **DIR:** Ken Loring. **CAST:** Paul Edwards, Marlene Dauden. **1980**

COMBINATION PLATTER ★★★ Delightfully engaging film about the mostly illegal immigrant employees of a Chinese restaurant in New York and their bid to stay in the United States. Explored herein are their bouts with love, money, racism, and honor. Winner of the best screenplay award at the 1993 Sundance Festival. Not rated; contains some profanity (mostly in Chinese). 85m. **DIR:** Tony Chan. **CAST:** Jeff Lau, Colleen O'Brien, Colin Mitchell, Kenneth Lu. **1993**

COME ALONG WITH ME ★★★ Rather high-brow amusement is provided by this adaptation of Shirley Jackson's unfinished novel. Estelle Parsons portrays an eccentric widow who sells everything before moving on to a new town. With a new name she begins her career as a dabbler in the supernatural. Not rated, but suitable for all ages. 60m. **DIR:** Joanne Woodward. **CAST:** Estelle Parsons, Barbara Baxley, Sylvia Sidney. **1981**

COME AND GET IT ★★★1/2 Based on Edna Ferber's novel, this involving film depicts life in Wisconsin's lumber country. It captures the robust, resilient nature of the denizens. Edward Arnold is perfectly cast as the grasping capitalist who needs to have his eyes opened. Walter Brennan's performance earned an Oscar for best supporting actor. B&W; 105m. **DIR:** Howard Hawks, William Wyler. **CAST:** Edward Arnold, Joel McCrea, Frances Farmer, Walter Brennan. **1936 DVD**

COME AND SEE ★★★★ During World War II, a provincial teenager experiences the horrors of war as the Nazis ravage Byelorussia. In Russian with English subtitles. Not rated, but far too upsetting for children. 146m. **DIR:** Elem Klimov. **CAST:** Alexei Kravchenko, Olga Mironova. **1985 DVD**

COME BACK AFRICA ★★★1/2 Lionel Rogosin, director of the extraordinary *On the Bowery*, has created another overwhelming portrait of human tragedy in this drama about a black South African who loses a series of jobs while trying to keep his residency in Johannesburg. Exploited by a racist bureaucracy, the central character is forced to endure the horrible conditions of the hazardous coal mines. Not rated, but recommended to adult viewers. B&W; 83m. **DIR:** Lionel Rogosin. **1959**

COME BACK, LITTLE SHEBA ★★★★ A maudlin, emotionally anguished housewife dreams of long past, happier days while her small world and drunken husband are upset by a younger woman. Shirley Booth made her screen debut and won an Oscar for her work here. Cast against type, Burt Lancaster as the husband matches her all the way. B&W; 99m. **DIR:** Daniel Mann. **CAST:** Shirley Booth, Burt Lancaster, Terry Moore, Richard Jaeckel. **1952**

COME BACK TO THE FIVE AND DIME, JIMMY DEAN, JIMMY DEAN ★★★1/2 This film concerns the twenty-year reunion of the Disciples of James Dean, a group formed by high school friends from a small Texas town after *Giant* was filmed on location nearby. Their get-together forces the members to confront the lies they have been living since those innocent days. Not rated; contains profanity and mature subject matter. 110m. **DIR:** Robert Altman. **CAST:** Sandy Dennis, Cher, Karen Black, Sudie Bond, Kathy Bates, Marta Heflin. **1982**

COME BLOW YOUR HORN ★★★1/2 Frank Sinatra looks very much at home as a bachelor playboy, teaching his younger brother how to live the good life. Based on Neil Simon's hit play, coproduced by director Bud Yorkin and screenwriter Norman Lear. Not rated, with (now) innocent sexual innuendo. 112m. **DIR:** Bud Yorkin. **CAST:** Frank Sinatra, Lee J. Cobb, Molly Picon, Barbara Rush, Jill St. John, Tony Bill, Dan Blocker. **1963**

COME ON TARZAN ★★★★ Wild horses are being sold for dog food. Ken Maynard and steed Tarzan must stop it. Top-notch. B&W; 61m. **DIR:** Alan James. **CAST:** Ken Maynard, Kate Campbell, Roy Stewart. **1932**

COME SEE THE PARADISE ★★★ One of the great tragedies of World War II was the internment of American citizens who were of Japanese descent. British writer-director Alan Parker attempts to put a human face on this regrettable piece of U.S. history, but he isn't wholly successful. Rated R for violence, nudity, and profanity. 133m. **DIR:** Alan Parker. **CAST:** Dennis Quaid, Tamlyn Tomita, Sab Shimono. **1990**

COME SEPTEMBER ★★★ A generational war between "elderly" Rock Hudson and young Bobby Darin, with Gina Lollobrigida and Sandra Dee as the love interests. Pretty Italian settings and bouncy energy make for a fun, if dated, light comedy. Not rated. 114m. **DIR:** Robert Mulligan. **CAST:** Rock Hudson, Gina Lollobrigida, Sandra Dee, Bobby Darin, Joel Grey, Walter Slezak. **1961**

•COME UNDONE ★★ This labored coming-of-age and out-of-the-closet drama jumps wildly back and forth in time as a university-bound boy experiences his first gay encounter, falls in love, and recovers from a suicide attempt. Mathieu is vacationing at a French seaside village with his sister and clinically depressed mother when he meets a former teen hustler who dreams of attending computer school. Their bittersweet bonding and squabbling enhances and disrupts Mathieu's budding independence and inner peace. In French with English subtitles. Not rated; contains graphic sex. 100m. **DIR:** Sébastien Lifshitz. **CAST:** Jérémie Elkaïm, Stéphane Rideau, Dominique Reymond, Laetitia Legrix, Marie Matheron. **2001 DVD**

COMEBACK ★★★1/2 Real-life rock singer Eric Burdon (lead singer of the Animals) stars in this rock 'n' roll drama. Burdon plays a white blues singer trying to get back on top. 96m. **DIR:** Christel Buschmann. **CAST:** Eric Burdon. **1982**

COMEBACK KID, THE ★★ John Ritter plays a down-and-out major leaguer who ends up coaching a group of street kids. Mediocre made-for-TV movie. 97m. **DIR:** Peter Levin. **CAST:** John Ritter, Doug McKeon, Susan Dey, Jeremy Licht, James Gregory. **1980**

COMEDIAN, THE ★★★★★ Originally aired live as a *Playhouse 90* drama, this film features Mickey Rooney as Sammy Hogarth, a ruthless, egomaniacal comedy star. His insatiable desire for unconditional adoration and obedience from those closest to him makes life a nightmare for his humiliated brother Lester (Mel Torme) and gag writer (Edmond O'Brien). Rod Serling's tight screenplay and the outstanding performances combine to make this an undated classic. B&W; 90m. **DIR:** John Frankenheimer. **CAST:** Mickey Rooney, Mel Torme, Edmond O'Brien, Kim Hunter. **1957**

COMEDIANS, THE ★★ In this drama, Elizabeth Taylor and Richard Burton inadvertently become involved in the political violence and unrest of Haiti under Papa Doc Duvalier. The all-star cast does little to improve an average script—based on Graham Greene's novel. 160m. **DIR:** Peter Glenville. **CAST:** Elizabeth Taylor, Richard Burton, Alec Guinness, Peter Ustinov, Paul Ford, Lillian Gish, James Earl Jones, Cicely Tyson. **1967**

COMEDY OF TERRORS ★★★ Screenwriter Richard Matheson's horror-comedy follow-up to his big-screen riff on Poe's *The Raven* lacks its predecessor's punch. However, there's much to be said for any film featuring the combined talents of Vincent Price, Peter Lorre, Boris Karloff, and Basil Rathbone. The plot has Price hamming it up as a funeral director who aggressively pursues customers to bolster his business—the fact that they haven't died yet doesn't seem to dissuade him. 88m. **DIR:** Jacques Tourneur. **CAST:** Vincent Price, Peter Lorre, Boris Karloff, Basil Rathbone, Joe E. Brown, Joyce Jameson. **1963**

COMES A HORSEMAN ★★★★ Dark, somber, but haunting Western set in the 1940s about the efforts of a would-be land baron (Jason Robards Jr.) to cheat his long-suffering neighbor (Jane Fonda) out of her land. She fights back with the help of a World War II veteran (James Caan) and a crusty old-timer (Richard Farnsworth). Rated PG for violence. 118m. **DIR:** Alan J. Pakula. **CAST:** Jane Fonda, James Caan, Jason Robards Jr., George Grizzard, Richard Farnsworth, Jim Davis. **1978 DVD**

COMFORT AND JOY ★★★★1/2 Scottish filmmaker Bill Forsyth scores again with this delightful tale of a disc jockey (Bill Paterson) whose life is falling apart. His girlfriend walks out on him, taking nearly everything he owns. Birds seem to like decorating his pride and joy: a red BMW. And what's worse, he gets involved in a gangland war over—are you ready for this?—the control of ice-cream manufacturing and sales. It's one you'll want to see. Rated PG. 90m. **DIR:** Bill Forsyth. **CAST:** Bill Paterson, Eleanor David, C. P. Grogan, Alex Norton. **1984**

COMFORT OF STRANGERS, THE ★★★ Disturbing thriller follows a British couple on vacation in Venice. Film takes its time about getting to the heart of matters, but Christopher Walken's performance is especially delicious as a crazed stranger. Rated R for nudity and violence. 117m. **DIR:** Paul Schrader. **CAST:** Christopher Walken, Natasha Richardson, Rupert Everett, Helen Mirren. **1991**

COMIC, THE 🦃 Set in a police state of the near future, an aspiring comic kills a popular entertainer in order to get a chance to perform in his stead. Not rated; brief nudity. 90m. **DIR:** Richard Driscoll. **CAST:** Steve Munroe. **1985**

COMIN' ROUND THE MOUNTAIN ★★★1/2 One of Abbott and Costello's best offerings, this one has the sexy Dorothy Shay and a cute plot about a shy country gal from the Ozarks trying to have a romantic liaison with Lou Costello to unite two feuding families. B&W; 77m. **DIR:** Charles Lamont. **CAST:** Bud Abbott, Lou Costello, Dorothy Shay, Kirby Grant, Robert Easton, Joe Sawyer. **1951**

COMING HOME ★★★★1/2 Jane Fonda, Jon Voight, and Bruce Dern give superb performances in this thought-provoking drama about the effect the Vietnam War has on three people. Directed by Hal Ashby, it features a romantic triangle with a twist: Fonda, the wife of a gung-ho officer, Dern, finds real love when she becomes an aide at a veteran's hospital and meets a bitter but sensitive paraplegic, Voight. Rated R. 127m. **DIR:** Hal Ashby. **CAST:** Jane Fonda, Jon Voight, Bruce Dern, Robert Carradine, Robert Ginty, Penelope Milford. **1978 DVD**

COMING OUT ALIVE ★★★ Enjoyable suspense chiller involving one mother's search for her child after he's abducted by her estranged husband. Scott Hylands is wonderful in his role as a soldier-for-hire who helps her out. 77m. **DIR:** Don McBrearty. **CAST:** Helen Shaver, Scott Hylands, Michael Ironside, Anne Ditchburn, Monica Parker. **1984**

COMING OUT OF THE ICE ★★★1/2 An engrossing made-for-television movie based on a true story. An American spends thirty-eight years in a Soviet prison camp for not renouncing his American citizenship. 97m. **DIR:** Waris Hussein. **CAST:** John Savage, Willie Nelson, Ben Cross, Francesca Annis. **1987**

COMING OUT UNDER FIRE ★★★★ Arthur Dong's compelling and award-winning documentary examines the lives of nine homosexuals and lesbians during World War II. Utilizing archive film, photographs, and present-day interviews, this amazing documentary exposes the hypocrisy of the armed forces "don't ask, don't tell" policy as it pertained to the soldiers and sailors who chose recruitment over branding as sexual deviates. Come face-to-face with the men and women who served their country in silence. Not rated; contains nudity. B&W; 71m. **DIR:** Arthur Dong. **1994**

COMING TO AMERICA ★★★1/2 Eddie Murphy deserves credit for trying to do something different in *Coming to America*. Murphy, who also wrote the story, stars as a pampered African prince who refuses to marry the pretty and pliable queen his father (James Earl Jones) has picked for him, opting instead to journey to New York City to find an intelligent, independent woman to be his lifelong mate. The film is a little slow at times, but the laughs are frequent enough to hold one's interest. Rated R for profanity, nudity, and suggested sex. 116m. **DIR:** John Landis. **CAST:** Eddie Murphy, Arsenio Hall, James Earl Jones, John Amos, Madge Sinclair. **1988 DVD**

COMING UNGLUED ★★1/2 Kids try to interfere with the plans of their father to get a promotion that would require the whole family to move to a different city. Despite the "Daddy knows least" stereotype, this is inoffensive family entertainment. Not rated. 93m. **DIR:** Fred Gerber. **CAST:** Judge Reinhold, Joely Fisher. **1999**

COMING UP ROSES ★★1/2 This offbeat comedy is about the efforts of a projectionist in a small mining village in south Wales to keep a local movie theatre open. Endearing characters performed with zest by an all-Welsh-speaking cast but the movie never rises above the poor film direction. In Welsh with English subtitles. Not rated. 90m. **DIR:** Stephen Bayly. **CAST:** Dafydd Hywel, Lola Gregory, Bill Paterson. **1986**

COMMAND DECISION ★★★1/2 Tense, gripping look at the psychology and politics of waging war under pressure. Confrontation and anguish color this engrossing drama, based on the stage hit. B&W; 112m. **DIR:** Sam Wood. **CAST:** Clark Gable, Walter Pidgeon, Van Johnson, Brian Donlevy, Charles Bickford, John Hodiak, Edward Arnold, John McIntire. **1948**

COMMANDMENTS ★★★ Aidan Quinn stars as a man who thinks God is out to get him. To get even, he decides to break all ten commandments. In the midst of his sinning, he finds love. Rated R for language and nudity. 92m. **DIR:** Daniel Taplitz. **CAST:** Aidan Quinn, Courteney Cox, Anthony LaPaglia. **1996**

COMMANDO ★★★1/2 "Commando" John Matrix makes Rambo look like a wimp. As played by big, beefy Arnold Schwarzenegger, he "eats Green Berets for breakfast." He soon goes on the warpath when his 11-year-old daughter is kidnapped by a South American dictator (Dan Hedaya) he once helped depose. Rated R for violence and profanity. 90m. **DIR:** Mark L. Lester. **CAST:** Arnold Schwarzenegger, Rae Dawn Chong, Dan Hedaya, James Olson, Alyssa Milano. **1986 DVD**

COMMANDO SQUAD ★★ Lots of action but no substance in this standard tale of American drug agents operating undercover in Mexico. Kathy Shower is a tough female agent who tries to rescue her lover/coagent (Brian Thompson). Rated R for strong language and violence. 90m. **DIR:** Fred Olen Ray. **CAST:** Brian Thompson, Kathy Shower, William Smith, Sid Haig, Robert Quarry, Ross Hagen, Mel Welles. **1987**

COMMANDOS 🦃 Italian World War II film with dubbed English and not enough action. Rated PG for violence.

89m. **DIR:** Armando Crispino. **CAST:** Lee Van Cleef, Jack Kelly, Marino Masé. **1968 DVD**

COMMANDOS STRIKE AT DAWN ★★1/2 Okay WWII tale of underground fighter Paul Muni, who goes up against the Nazis after they invade his Norwegian homeland. The great cast deserved a better script than this, though it is nice to watch Muni and Lillian Gish practice their art. Some good action sequences keep things moving. B&W; 96m. **DIR:** John Farrow. **CAST:** Paul Muni, Lillian Gish, Cedric Hardwicke, Anna Lee, Alexander Knox, Ray Collins. **1942**

COMMISSAR, THE ★★★★ A cinematic gift from Glasnost, it's a long-repressed Soviet film about a female Soviet officer and her relationship with a family of Jewish villagers. Challenging and innovative, it's a pro-Semitic film from the mid-Sixties that languished on a shelf for two decades before being freed by changing times. It surfaced in the U.S. in 1988. In Russian with English subtitles. 115m. **DIR:** Aleksandr Askoldov. **CAST:** Nonna Mordyukova. **1988**

COMMITMENTS, THE ★★★★ The music is wonderful in this R&B musical about a Dublin promoter (Robert Arkins) who decides to put together the ultimate Irish soul band. Andrew Strong is particularly amazing as the soulful lead vocalist. Rated R for profanity. 125m. **DIR:** Alan Parker. **CAST:** Robert Arkins, Michael Aherne, Angeline Ball, Maria Doyle, Dave Finnegan, Bronagh Gallagher, Felim Gormley, Glen Hansard, Dick Massey, Johnny Murphy, Kenneth McCluskey, Andrew Strong. **1991 DVD**

COMMITTED ★★★ Jennifer O'Neill stars as a nurse who is tricked into committing herself into a mental institution. O'Neill is reasonably convincing as the single sane person in a sea of insanity. Rated R for violence. 101m. **DIR:** William A. Levey. **CAST:** Jennifer O'Neill, Robert Forster, Ron Palillo. **1990**

COMMON BONDS ★★ The prison system helps rehabilitate a born loser by chaining him to a handicapped man's wheelchair. Airheaded message drama. Not rated, but with profanity and violence. 109m. **DIR:** Allan A. Goldstein. **CAST:** Rae Dawn Chong, Michael Ironside, Brad Dourif. **1991**

•**COMMON GROUND** ★★★★ Made-for-cable trilogy of stories about trials and tribulations faced by gays and lesbians. Presented with honest emotion and just enough humor and melodrama, the stories span three decades, and each makes an important statement without standing on a soapbox. Brittany Murphy is excellent as a woman discharged from the navy in the 1950s for being a lesbian, while Jonathan Taylor Thomas and Steven Weber play a high-school student and his teacher in the 1970s grappling with their sexuality. Modern segment finds a gay couple ready to tie the knot despite the protests of father Edward Asner. Rated R for adult situations, language, and violence. 105m. **DIR:** Donna Deitch. **CAST:** Eric Stoltz, Brittany Murphy, Jason Priestley, Margot Kidder, Jonathan Taylor Thomas, Steven Weber, James LeGros, Edward Asner, Andrew Airlie. **2000**

COMMON LAW, THE ★★1/2 Constance Bennett has a field day as a kept woman who dumps her older lover and becomes painter Joel McCrea's model. True love wins out in the end, naturally. Predictable melodrama. B&W; 72m. **DIR:** Paul Stein. **CAST:** Constance Bennett, Joel McCrea, Hedda Hopper, Marion Shilling. **1931**

COMMON THREADS: STORIES FROM THE QUILT ★★★★ In *Common Threads: Stories from the Quilt*, AIDS becomes a shared ground for survivors of loved ones. They fashion a giant quilt with the names of the deceased stitched into each design. This stirring documentary is not only a tribute to the dead and dying, it is a study of how parents, lovers, and friends of victims have learned to deal constructively with loss—and to bring the impact of AIDS to the public. Not rated. 80m. **DIR:** Robert Epstein, Jeffrey Friedman. **1990**

COMMUNION ★★★1/2 Science-fiction author Whitley Strieber based this remarkable movie on his alleged real-life close encounters of the third kind. Unlike Steven Spielberg's fantasy-like film about the first mass-human contact with aliens, Strieber's story, directed by his longtime friend Phillippe Mora, is an often terrifying movie. And it's all the more powerful because of Strieber's insistence that the events depicted are true. Rated R for profanity. 100m. **DIR:** Philippe Mora. **CAST:** Christopher Walken, Lindsay Crouse, Frances Sternhagen, Andreas Katsulas. **1989 DVD**

COMPANION, THE ★★ Made-for-cable movie, about a woman writer who buys a perfect male android, starts out interestingly enough, but you'll soon tire of the empty plot. Rated R for violence and suggested sex. 94m. **DIR:** Gary Fleder. **CAST:** Kathryn Harrold, Bruce Greenwood, Talia Balsam, Joely Fisher, Brian James. **1994**

COMPANY BUSINESS ★★★ In what may be the first post-Cold War spy thriller, Gene Hackman plays an ex-CIA agent who is enlisted to escort an imprisoned KGB agent (Mikhail Baryshnikov) back to Russia. The two spies must band together to escape double-crossers on both sides of the parting Iron Curtain. Rated PG-13 for violence and profanity. 96m. **DIR:** Nicholas Meyer. **CAST:** Gene Hackman, Mikhail Baryshnikov, Kurtwood Smith, Terry O'Quinn. **1991**

COMPANY MAN ★★1/2 A nerdy Connecticut schoolteacher bumbles his way into the CIA, where his ineptitude brings about the Bay of Pigs invasion in 1961. The film is clumsy and cheap-looking, but its amiable, anything-for-a-laugh wackiness pays off in several funny moments. Woody Allen (uncredited) is especially good as the CIA's head man in Havana. Rated PG-13 for sexual humor. 81m. **DIR:** Douglas McGrath, Peter Askin. **CAST:** Douglas McGrath, Sigourney Weaver, John Turturro, Woody Allen, Alan Cumming. **2001 DVD**

COMPANY OF WOLVES, THE ★★★1/2 Neither a horror film nor a fantasy for the kiddies, this dark, psychologically oriented rendering of the "Little Red Riding Hood" story is for thinking viewers only. Angela Lansbury stars as Grandmother, who turns the dreams of her granddaughter (Sarah Patterson) into tales of spooky terror. Rated R for violence and gore. 95m. **DIR:** Neil Jordan. **CAST:** Angela Lansbury, David Warner, Sarah Patterson. **1985**

COMPETITION, THE ★★★1/2 Richard Dreyfuss and Amy Irving star in this exquisitely crafted and completely enjoyable romance about two classical pianists who, while competing for top honors in a recital program, fall in love. Lee Remick and Sam Wanamaker add excellent support. Watch it with someone you love.

Rated PG. 129m. **DIR:** Joel Oliansky. **CAST:** Richard Dreyfuss, Amy Irving, Lee Remick, Sam Wanamaker. **1980**

COMPLEAT BEATLES, THE ★★★★ Even experts on the life and times of the Fab Four are likely to find something new and enlightening. Furthermore, while not a consistent work, this film provides something of interest for fans and nonfans. 119m. **DIR:** Patrick Montgomery. **CAST:** Malcolm McDowell, The Beatles. **1982**

COMPROMISING POSITIONS ★★ In the first half hour, this is a hilarious and innovative takeoff on murder mysteries and a devastatingly witty send-up of suburban life. However, it soon descends into the clichés of the mystery genre. That's too bad, because the plot, about an overly amorous dentist who is murdered, has great possibilities. Rated R for nudity, profanity, and violence. 98m. **DIR:** Frank Perry. **CAST:** Susan Sarandon, Raul Julia, Edward Herrmann, Judith Ivey, Mary Beth Hurt, Anne De Salvo, Josh Mostel. **1985**

COMPULSION ★★★1/2 Superb characterizations add up to first-rate melodrama in this retelling of the infamous 1924 Leopold-Loeb murder case. Orson Welles is brilliant as the brooding defense attorney. B&W; 103m. **DIR:** Richard Fleischer. **CAST:** Orson Welles, Bradford Dillman, Dean Stockwell, Diane Varsi, Martin Milner, E. G. Marshall. **1959**

COMPUTER WORE TENNIS SHOES, THE ★★ A student becomes a genius after being short-circuited with a computer. The movie is weak, with the "excitement" provided by mobsters and gamblers. 87m. **DIR:** Robert Butler. **CAST:** Kurt Russell, Cesar Romero, Joe Flynn, William Schallert. **1969**

COMRADE X ★★★ American reporter Clark Gable pursues Russian streetcar conductor Hedy Lamarr in this fair reworking of the *Ninotchka* theme. Eve Arden is a standout. B&W; 90m. **DIR:** King Vidor. **CAST:** Clark Gable, Hedy Lamarr, Oscar Homolka, Felix Bressart, Eve Arden, Sig Ruman. **1940**

COMRADES IN ARMS 🦃 Extremely bad dialogue kills this film in which a Russian and an American join forces to combat an international drug cartel. Rated R for violence and profanity. 91m. **DIR:** J. Christian Ingvordsen. **CAST:** Lyle Alzado, Lance Henriksen, Rick Washburne. **1991**

COMRADES OF SUMMER, THE ★★★1/2 Sports fans will get a kick out of this amiable made-for-cable fairy tale that finds washed-up player Joe Mantegna sent to help the Russians field a baseball team for the 1992 Olympics. Although patterned after a slew of similar underdog fantasies, this one works thanks to Mantegna's enthusiasm and Robert Rodat's script. Rated R for profanity and suggested sex. 90m. **DIR:** Tommy Lee Wallace. **CAST:** Joe Mantegna, Natalya Negoda, Mark Rolston, Michael Lerner. **1992**

CON, THE ★★1/2 To pay off a large debt, a con artist pretends to fall in love with a very nerdy—but soon to be rich—guy in this made-for-cable original. Unconvincing characters and a predictable plot make the viewer lose interest. Rated PG-13 for violence. 95m. **DIR:** Steven Schachter. **CAST:** Rebecca DeMornay, William H. Macy, Frances Sternhagen, Mike Nussbaum, Don Harvey, Angela Paton. **1997**

CON AIR ★★★★ Although improbable and predictable, this thriller from British director Simon West is an impressive big-screen debut. Nicolas Cage is a decent guy who winds up in prison on a bad rap and dutifully serves eight years. Cage finally catches a flight home on a rather special C-123K transport. Rated R for violence and profanity. 115m. **DIR:** Simon West. **CAST:** Nicolas Cage, John Cusack, John Malkovich, Steve Buscemi, Ving Rhames, Colm Meaney, Mykelti Williamson, Rachel Ticotin. **1997 DVD**

CON ARTISTS, THE 🦃 What could have been a lark turns into a ho-hum caper. 87m. **DIR:** Sergio Corbucci. **CAST:** Anthony Quinn, Capucine. **1977 DVD**

CONAGHER ★★★1/2 Katharine Ross is a lonely widow with two children running a stagecoach way station and Sam Elliott is a cowhand she's attracted to, in this made-for-cable Western. Elliott seems to have been born to play cowboys. A welcome addition to a fading genre. 118m. **DIR:** Reynaldo Villalobos. **CAST:** Sam Elliott, Katharine Ross, Barry Corbin, Billy Green Bush, Ken Curtis, Paul Koslo, Gavan O'Herlihy, Pepe Serna, Dub Taylor. **1991**

CONAN THE BARBARIAN ★★★1/2 Featuring Arnold Schwarzenegger in the title role, this sword-and-sorcery epic is just as corny, raunchy, sexist, and unbelievably brutal as the original tales by Robert E. Howard. Therefore, it seems likely Conan fans will be delighted. Rated R for nudity, profanity, and violence. 129m. **DIR:** John Milius. **CAST:** Arnold Schwarzenegger, Sandahl Bergman, James Earl Jones, Mako. **1982 DVD**

CONAN THE DESTROYER ★★★ In this lightweight, violent sequel, Conan (Arnold Schwarzenegger) bests beasts and bloodthirsty battlers at every turn with the help of his sidekick (Tracey Walter), a wizard (Mako), a staff-wielding thief (androgynous Grace Jones), and a giant warrior (Wilt Chamberlain) as they go on a perilous mission to find a sacred stone. Rated PG for violence. 103m. **DIR:** Richard Fleischer. **CAST:** Arnold Schwarzenegger, Grace Jones, Wilt Chamberlain, Tracey Walter. **1984 DVD**

CONCEALED WEAPON 🦃 Cheap thriller about an actor who lands the role of a lifetime, then finds the script coming to life. Rated R for nudity, violence, and adult language. 85m. **DIR:** David Payne, Milas Zivkovich. **CAST:** Daryl Haney, Suzanne Wouk, Monica Simpson, Mark Driscoll. **1994**

CONCEIVING ADA ★★ A computer genius develops a software program that enables her to establish contact with Ada Lovelace, the daughter of Lord Byron, who was herself an early experimenter in the mathematical principles that would one day lead to computer science. The film has a tantalizing premise, but the execution is haphazard. Not rated; contains brief nudity and sexual scenes. 85m. **DIR:** Lynn Hershman Leeson. **CAST:** Tilda Swinton, Franchesca Faridany, Karen Black, Timothy Leary, John O'Keefe. **1997 DVD**

CONCRETE ANGELS ★★ Set in 1964 Toronto, this downbeat teen drama revolves around several friends trying to put together a band to enter in a competition. Separate stories of the boys are spun off, told with more realism than most teen films about the early Sixties. Not rated, but an R equivalent. 97m. **DIR:** Carlo Liconti. **CAST:** Joseph Dimambro, Luke McKeehan. **1987**

CONCRETE JUNGLE, (1962) THE (CRIMINAL, THE) ★★★ Grim, claustrophobic prison drama is tightly directed and well acted (especially by the underrated

Stanley Baker), and remains one of the best films of its kind as well as one of director Joseph Losey's most satisfying works. Often referred to in filmographies as *The Criminal*, this uncompromising look at life "inside" boasts gutsy, believable performances. B&W; 86m. **DIR:** Joseph Losey. **CAST:** Stanley Baker, Margit Saad, Sam Wanamaker, Gregoire Aslan, Jill Bennett, Laurence Naismith, Edward Judd. **1962**

CONCRETE JUNGLE, THE (1982) ★★ This women's-prison melodrama has it all: an innocent girl who learns the ropes the hard way, an evil matron in collusion with the head bad girl, gratuitous shower and mud-wrestling scenes, and plentiful overacting. In short, a trash classic. Rated R for violence, nudity, and profanity. 99m. **DIR:** Tom DeSimone. **CAST:** Tracy Bregman, Jill St. John, Barbara Luna, Peter Brown, Nita Talbot. **1982**

CONDITION RED ★★ James Russo stands out in an otherwise unbelievable piece of jailhouse drivel. Playing a guard who is sick of his job, he becomes involved with a female inmate and helps her escape. Plot, dialogue, and other actors are not credible. Rated R for nudity, sex, violence, gore, and profanity. 85m. **DIR:** Mika Kaurismaki. **CAST:** James Russo, Cynda Williams, Paul Calderon, Victor Argo. **1995**

CONDORMAN ★★ This Disney film has everything you've ever seen in a spy film—but it was better the first time. A comic-book writer (Michael Crawford) gets his chance to become a spy when he goes after a beautiful Russian defector (Barbara Carrera). Rated PG. 90m. **DIR:** Charles Jarrott. **CAST:** Michael Crawford, Oliver Reed, James Hampton, Barbara Carrera. **1981 DVD**

CONDUCT UNBECOMING ★★★ When the wife of a Bengal Lancer is raped, a secret trial of the accused man is conducted by the officers at an outpost in India. Good performances from a star cast are the main reason to see this stagy drama with a disappointing ending. Rated PG. 107m. **DIR:** Michael Anderson. **CAST:** Michael York, Richard Attenborough, Trevor Howard, Stacy Keach, Christopher Plummer, Susannah York. **1975**

CONEHEADS ★★★ Critically lambasted comedy based on the old *Saturday Night Live* sketch is bound to be a hit with preteens. Dan Aykroyd and Jane Curtin reprise their roles as Beldar and Prymaat, aliens from the planet Remulac who are forced to masquerade as humans after being stranded on Earth. Rated PG for brief profanity and some gross comedy bits. 87m. **DIR:** Steve Barron. **CAST:** Dan Aykroyd, Jane Curtin, Michelle Burke, Michael McKean, Jason Alexander, Lisa Jane Persky, Laraine Newman, Chris Farley, Dave Thomas, Sinbad, Jan Hooks, Phil Hartman, Jon Lovitz, David Spade, Michael Richards. **1993 DVD**

CONFESSION, THE ★★1/2 A high-profile cast is wasted in this meandering courtroom drama. Ben Kingsley overcomes the hysterics, playing a man on trial for killing the doctors responsible for letting his son die. Unfortunately, Alec Baldwin has little to work with as the attorney defending him. More melodrama than drama, the film tackles important issues, but drops the ball halfway to the goal. Rated R for violence and language. 114m. **DIR:** David Hugh Jones. **CAST:** Ben Kingsley, Alec Baldwin, Amy Irving, Jay O. Sanders. **1999 DVD**

CONFESSIONAL, THE ★★1/2 An insane priest blackmails young women who have confessed to "impure" actions, and resorts to murder when his activities are threatened to be exposed. This British thriller is distasteful but also luridly inventive, if you're not easily offended. Rated R for gruesome violence and nudity. 104m. **DIR:** Pete Walker. **CAST:** Anthony Sharp, Susan Penhaligon, Stephanie Beacham. **1977**

CONFESSIONS OF A POLICE CAPTAIN 🦃 Heavy-handed melodrama wastes a fine performance by Martin Balsam as a good cop amid an avalanche of corruption. This Italian-made film is given to excess. Rated PG. 102m. **DIR:** Damiano Damiani. **CAST:** Martin Balsam, Franco Nero, Marilu Tolo. **1971**

CONFESSIONS OF A SERIAL KILLER ★★1/2 Based on the exploits of serial killer Henry Lee Lucas, this shocker shot in semidocumentary form is realistically gritty and hard to watch, but compelling nonetheless. The film manages to repulse with every murder. Robert A. Burns is appropriately creepy as the person confessing. Not rated; contains violence, nudity, and strong language. 85m. **DIR:** Mark Blair. **CAST:** Robert A. Burns, Dennis Hill. **1987**

CONFESSIONS OF A SORORITY GIRL ★★1/2 This made-for-cable remake of the 1957 American-International drive-in classic *Sorority Girl* is appropriately low budget, featuring scandalous storylines and shocking behavior by so-called sorority girls. It's all done tongue-in-cheek, with knowing nods to the era, including tacky production design and campy performances. You can't help but smile as Sabrina, the new girl on campus, stops at nothing to steal the sorority presidency away from goody-two-shoes Rita. Rated R for adult situations and language. 82m. **DIR:** Uli Edel. **CAST:** Brian Bloom, Jamie Luner, Sadie Kratzig, Alyssa Milano. **1993 DVD**

CONFIDENTIAL ★★ A film that starts off well but quickly strangles on its own *film noir* style. A newspaper reporter investigating an old murder in 1949 Los Angeles is slain, and a hard-bitten detective tries to find the reasons why. Rated R for nudity, language, and violence. 95m. **DIR:** Bruce Pittman. **CAST:** August Schellenberg, Chapelle Jaffe, Neil Munro. **1988**

CONFIDENTIALLY YOURS ★★1/2 François Truffaut's last film is a stylized murder mystery in the tradition of Hitchcock, but it's only a lighthearted soufflé. Jean-Louis Trintignant plays a real estate agent framed for murder. Rated PG. In French with English subtitles. B&W; 110m. **DIR:** François Truffaut. **CAST:** Fanny Ardant, Jean-Louis Trintignant, Jean-Pierre Kalfon. **1983 DVD**

CONFLICT ★★ Humphrey Bogart wants to get rid of his wife so he can marry his mistress in this reverse rip-off of *The Postman Always Rings Twice*. A suspense film that should have been better considering the talent involved. B&W; 86m. **DIR:** Curtis Bernhardt. **CAST:** Humphrey Bogart, Alexis Smith, Rose Hobart, Sydney Greenstreet, Charles Drake, Grant Mitchell. **1945 DVD**

CONFLICT OF INTEREST 🦃 Gratuitously sleazy cop thriller. Noteworthy only to watch Judd Nelson put another nail in the coffin of his once-promising career. Rated R for violence, nudity, and profanity. 87m. **DIR:** Gary Davis. **CAST:** Christopher McDonald, Alyssa Milano, Dey Young, Judd Nelson. **1993**

CONFORMIST, THE ★★★★ Fascinating character study of Marcello Clerici (Jean-Louis Trintignant), a follower of Mussolini. He becomes increasingly obsessed with conformity as he tries to suppress a traumatic homosexual experience suffered as a youth. He is forced to prove his loyalty to the fascist state by murdering a former professor who lives in exile. In French with English subtitles. Rated R for language and subject matter. 107m. **DIR:** Bernardo Bertolucci. **CAST:** Jean-Louis Trintignant, Stefania Sandrelli, Dominique Sanda, Pierre Clementi. **1971**

CONGO ★★★ A field expedition to an uncharted jungle locale, featuring characters with diverse ulterior motives, runs into a pack of vicious gray-haired gorillas protecting a legendary diamond mine. Rated PG-13 for violence. 102m. **DIR:** Frank Marshall. **CAST:** Dylan Walsh, Laura Linney, Ernie Hudson, Joe Don Baker, Tim Curry. **1995 DVD**

CONNECTICUT YANKEE, A ★★★1/2 Based on Mark Twain's famous 1889 fantasy of a "modern man" thrust back to King Arthur's Court in a dream caused by a blow to the head. In the title role, Will Rogers happily helps young love in both the story and the story within the story. B&W; 96m. **DIR:** David Butler. **CAST:** Will Rogers, William Farnum, Frank Albertson, Maureen O'Sullivan, Myrna Loy. **1931**

CONNECTION, THE (1961) ★★★★ A group of junkies await the arrival of their heroin dealer while a documentary filmmaker records their withdrawal symptoms. A classic of the American avant-garde cinema, filmed in real time and featuring a topflight jazz score. B&W; 103m. **DIR:** Shirley Clarke. **CAST:** William Redfield, Warren Finnerty, Garry Goodrow, Roscoe Lee Browne. **1961**

CONNECTION (1973) ★★★1/2 Charles Durning steals the show in this made-for-television movie. As an out-of-work newspaperman desperately in need of money, he becomes the intermediary between an insurance company and a high-priced jewel thief. Taut direction and a literate script help. 73m. **DIR:** Tom Gries. **CAST:** Charles Durning, Ronny Cox, Zohra Lampert, Dennis Cole, Dana Wynter. **1973**

CONQUEROR, THE 🦃 John Wayne plays Genghis Khan, and the results are unintentionally hilarious. 111m. **DIR:** Dick Powell. **CAST:** John Wayne, Susan Hayward, Pedro Armendariz, Agnes Moorehead. **1956 DVD**

CONQUEROR WORM, THE ★★★ In this graphic delineation of witch-hunting in England during the Cromwell period, Vincent Price gives a sterling performance as Matthew Hopkins, a self-possessed and totally convincing witch finder. The production values are very good considering the small budget. A must-see for thriller fans. 88m. **DIR:** Michael Reeves. **CAST:** Vincent Price, Ian Ogilvy, Hilary Dwyer. **1968**

CONQUEST ★★★ A better-than-average Greta Garbo picture because she isn't the whole show. Charles Boyer plays Napoleon—and Garbo is Marie Walewska, his Polish mistress. This is the story of how they met and why he deserted Josephine for her. B&W; 112m. **DIR:** Clarence Brown. **CAST:** Greta Garbo, Charles Boyer, May Whitty, Reginald Owen, Alan Marshal, Henry Stephenson, Leif Erickson. **1937**

CONQUEST OF THE PLANET OF THE APES ★★ Having been rescued by Ricardo Montalban at the end of his previous film adventure, simian Roddy McDowall matures and leads his fellow apes—now domesticated—in a freedom revolt that sets the stage for the events in the very first film. Very melodramatic and formulaic, with few clichés left unused. Rated PG for violence. 87m. **DIR:** J. Lee Thompson. **CAST:** Roddy McDowall, Ricardo Montalban, Don Murray, Severn Darden. **1972**

CONRACK ★★★★ In this sleeper, based on a true story, Jon Voight plays a dedicated white teacher determined to bring the joys of education to deprived blacks inhabiting an island off the coast of South Carolina. Rated PG. 107m. **DIR:** Martin Ritt. **CAST:** Jon Voight, Paul Winfield, Hume Cronyn, Madge Sinclair. **1974**

CONSENTING ADULTS (1985) ★★★1/2 Based on a bestselling novel by Laura Z. Hobson, this made-for-TV film tells the story of an all-American family when their son proclaims his homosexuality. It is told with taste and style. 100m. **DIR:** Gilbert Cates. **CAST:** Marlo Thomas, Martin Sheen, Talia Balsam, Barry Tubb, Ben Piazza. **1985**

CONSENTING ADULTS (1992) 🦃 Almost every scene in this film is telegraphed, leaving little suspense. A name cast is wasted. Rated R for profanity, nudity, and violence. 99m. **DIR:** Alan J. Pakula. **CAST:** Kevin Kline, Mary Elizabeth Mastrantonio, Kevin Spacey, Rebecca Miller, E. G. Marshall, Forest Whitaker. **1992**

CONSOLATION MARRIAGE ★★★ Slow-moving but well-made (for early talkie) soap opera about two jilted sweethearts (Irene Dunne and Pat O'Brien) who marry each other on the rebound, then their old lovers come back. Stilted dialogue is a drawback, but the film remains interesting for the early performances of the stars. Not rated, but suitable for all audiences. B&W; 81m. **DIR:** Paul Sloane. **CAST:** Irene Dunne, Pat O'Brien, John Halliday, Myrna Loy. **1931**

CONSPIRACY OF FEAR, THE ★★★ After the death of his father, a young man tries to figure out why everyone is so interested in a mysterious package his father was supposed to have. This made-for-cable thriller might have been a better film, but the cinematography and editing, which give us something of a cross between a music video and a home movie, distract the viewer from the action. Not rated; contains profanity and violence. 110m. **DIR:** John Eyres. **CAST:** Geraint Wyn Davies, Leslie Hope, Andrew Lowery, Christopher Plummer. **1996**

CONSPIRACY: THE TRIAL OF THE CHICAGO 8 ★★★ Docudrama-style made-for-cable-TV movie about the notorious court proceedings that followed the riots of the 1968 Democratic convention. Solid performances by a top-notch cast. 118m. **DIR:** Jeremy Paul Kagan. **CAST:** Robert Carradine, Elliott Gould, Martin Sheen, Robert Loggia. **1987 DVD**

CONSPIRACY THEORY ★★★★ Being paranoid doesn't mean that they *aren't* out to get you, Mel Gibson is a terrified little man with fuzzy memories of something related to the "them" he blames for everything from fluoridated water to NASA's plans to assassinate the U.S. president. Gibson's role turns serious quickly; Julia Roberts supports him well as a sympathetic Justice Department attorney who gradually realizes he isn't just imagining things. Rated R for violence and profanity. 140m. **DIR:** Richard Donner. **CAST:** Mel Gibson, Julia Roberts, Patrick Stewart, Cylk Cozart. **1997 DVD**

CONSPIRATOR ★★1/2 A bride, who comes to realize her British army officer husband is a Soviet spy, is torn between love and loyalty. Wooden performances by the stars. B&W; 85m. **DIR:** Victor Saville. **CAST:** Robert Taylor, Elizabeth Taylor, Robert Flemyng, Honor Blackman, Wilfrid Hyde-White. **1949**

CONSUMING PASSIONS ★★ Morbid, gross, and sometimes amusing movie about a nerdish junior executive who discovers a "secret ingredient"—human beings—that saves a sagging candy company. Adapted from a play written by Michael Palin and Terry Jones of *Monty Python's Flying Circus* fame, the film suffers from the one-joke premise. Rated R for language, sexual situations, and overall grossness. 95m. **DIR:** Giles Foster. **CAST:** Tyler Butterworth, Jonathan Pryce, Freddie Jones, Sammi Davis, Prunella Scales, Vanessa Redgrave, Thora Hird. **1988**

CONTACT ★★★★ In this adaptation of Carl Sagan's sole novel, Jodie Foster is self-absorbed astronomer Ellie Arroway, who rejects blind faith and spiritualism while believing strongly in the possibility of life in other galaxies and that such beings would communicate with Earth. Indeed such contact is established. Naturally, government officials interfere, and there's considerable political intrigue prior to a heady final act reminiscent of the "stargate" sequel in *2001: A Space Odyssey*. We need more thoughtful science fiction like this. Rated PG. 150m. **DIR:** Robert Zemeckis. **CAST:** Jodie Foster, Matthew McConaughey, James Woods, John Hurt, Tom Skerritt, Angela Bassett, William Fichtner, David Morse. **1997 DVD**

CONTAGIOUS ★★1/2 This insipid little made-for-cable thriller features an epidemic of cholera sweeping across parts of the United States. Lindsay Wagner plays a doctor who tries to find the source, save her family, and deal with hundreds of patients. All very predictable. Not rated. 95m. **DIR:** Joe Napolitano. **CAST:** Lindsay Wagner, Elizabeth Peña, Tom Wopat, Ken Pogue. **1997**

CONTEMPT ★★★1/2 A cult film to be, if it isn't already, this one takes a tongue-in-cheek, raised-eyebrow look at European moviemaking. Jack Palance is a vulgar producer; Fritz Lang, playing himself, is his director; Jean-Luc Godard plays Lang's assistant, and in directing this film turned it into an inside joke—in real (not reel) life, he held the film's producer Joseph E. Levine in contempt. 103m. **DIR:** Jean-Luc Godard. **CAST:** Brigitte Bardot, Jack Palance, Fritz Lang, Jean-Luc Godard, Michel Piccoli. **1963**

CONTENDER, THE ★★★★ Joan Allen was nominated as best actress for her portrayal of a vice presidential nominee who finds her appointment threatened by the disclosure of an alleged sexual indiscretion from her youth. Writer-director Rod Lurie does an excellent job of presenting the title character's ethical standards (she will not address the charge) and of surrounding her with memorable characters. Rated R for nudity, simulated sex, and profanity. 126m. **DIR:** Rod Lurie. **CAST:** Gary Oldman, Joan Allen, Jeff Bridges, Christian Slater, Sam Elliott, William L. Petersen, Saul Rubinek, Philip Baker Hall, Mike Binder, Robin Thomas, Mariel Hemingway. **2000 DVD**

CONTINENTAL DIVIDE ★★★1/2 As lighthearted romantic comedies go, this one is tops. John Belushi stars as Ernie Souchak, a Chicago newspaper columnist unexpectedly sent into the Rockies to write a story about an ornithologist (Blair Brown). Just as unexpectedly, they fall in love. Rated PG because of slight amounts of nudity. 103m. **DIR:** Michael Apted. **CAST:** John Belushi, Blair Brown, Allen Garfield, Carlin Glynn. **1981**

CONTRABAND ★★ A mediocre Italian gangster movie, dubbed into English. This time the main vice is contraband goods rather than hard drugs or prostitution. But the story is the same. 87m. **DIR:** Lucio Fulci. **CAST:** Fabio Testi, Ivana Monti. **1980 DVD**

CONTRACT ★★★★ Enjoyable and provocative satire takes place at the wedding party of the son of a well-to-do doctor. The arranged marriage is already off to a bad start, and things get steadily worse. In Polish with English subtitles. Not rated, the film features nudity. 111m. **DIR:** Krzysztof Zanussi. **CAST:** Leslie Caron, Maja Komorowska, Tadeusz Lomnicki. **1980**

CONTRACT FOR LIFE: THE S.A.D.D. STORY ★★★1/2 Based on the work of real-life hockey coach Bob Anastas, this chronicles the creation of Students Against Drunk Driving. After two of his all-stars are killed while driving drunk, Anastas (beautifully played by Stephen Macht) inspires his students to band together to prevent similar tragedies. Well done! 46m. **DIR:** Joseph Pevney. **CAST:** Stephen Macht. **1984**

CONUNDRUM ★★★1/2 Writer-director Douglas Barr's twisty little thriller should keep you guessing, while cops Michael Biehn and Marg Helgenberger pursue the baddies who brutally killed the former's wife. The supporting characters are unusually well developed for this genre, and the plot remains credible to the very end. Rated R for violence, profanity, nudity, and simulated sex. 98m. **DIR:** Douglas Barr. **CAST:** Marg Helgenberger, Michael Biehn, Ron White, Peter MacNeill, Dan Lett. **1995**

CONVENT, THE ★★★★ Sweltering tale of an American professor and his French wife, whose visit to the ancient convent Arrabida sparks a classic tale of seduction and betrayal. While Michael works on his thesis, Helene is swept away by Baltar, the guardian of the archives. In English, French, and Portuguese with English subtitles. Not rated. 90m. **DIR:** Manoel de Oliveria. **CAST:** John Malkovich, Catherine Deneuve, Lenor Silveira, Luis Miguel Cintra. **1995 DVD**

CONVERSATION, THE ★★★★★ Following his box-office and artistic triumph with *The Godfather*, director Francis Ford Coppola made this absorbing character study about a bugging-device expert (Gene Hackman) who lives only for his work but finds himself developing a conscience. Although not a box-office hit when originally released, this is a fine little film. Rated PG. 113m. **DIR:** Francis Ford Coppola. **CAST:** Gene Hackman, John Cazale, Allen Garfield, Cindy Williams, Harrison Ford. **1974 DVD**

CONVERSATION PIECE ★★ Burt Lancaster portrays a bewildered, reclusive professor whose life changes direction when he encounters a countess and her children. In Italian with English subtitles. 122m. **DIR:**

Luchino Visconti. **CAST:** Burt Lancaster, Silvana Mangano, Helmut Berger, Claudia Cardinale. **1974**

CONVICT COWBOY ★★★★ An honorable lifer finds fame and inner peace on the prison rodeo circuit. The entire cast is excellent, including cameo player Ben Gazzara as the warden who believes in "rehabilitation through ranching." Rick Way and Jim Lindsay's script suggests that some men might better their lives through honest repentance. Rated R for profanity and violence. 106m. **DIR:** Rod Holcomb. **CAST:** Jon Voight, Kyle Chandler, Marcia Gay Harden, Stephen McHattie, Ben Gazzara. **1995**

CONVICTED ★★★ Fact-based drama focuses on inadequacies in the judicial system when family man John Larroquette is accused of being a rapist and sentenced to five years in prison. Wife Lindsay Wagner spends five years searching for the truth in this inspiring made-for-TV tale of truth and justice. 94m. **DIR:** David Lowell Rich. **CAST:** John Larroquette, Lindsay Wagner, Carroll O'Connor, Burton Gilliam. **1990**

CONVOY (1940) ★★★1/2 Excellent documentary-style, stiff-upper-lip British film about the daily danger faced by the officers and crew of cargo convoys and the warships that protect them. Producer Michael Balcon gave this movie his customary stamp of authenticity and humanity. B&W; 95m. **DIR:** Pen Tennyson. **CAST:** Clive Brook, John Clements, Judy Campbell, Edward Chapman, Michael Wilding, Charles Farrell, Albert Lieven. **1940**

CONVOY (1978) ★★ Truckers, led by Kris Kristofferson, go on a tri-state protest over police brutality, high gas prices, and other complaints. An uneven script and just fair acting mar this picture. Rated PG. 110m. **DIR:** Sam Peckinpah. **CAST:** Kris Kristofferson, Ali MacGraw, Ernest Borgnine, Madge Sinclair, Burt Young. **1978**

COOGAN'S BLUFF ★★★★ Clint Eastwood and director Don Siegel in their first collaboration. The squinty-eyed star hunts down a murderous fugitive (Don Stroud) in the asphalt jungle. Rated PG. 100m. **DIR:** Don Siegel. **CAST:** Clint Eastwood, Lee J. Cobb, Susan Clark, Tisha Sterling, Don Stroud, Betty Field, Tom Tully. **1968**

COOK, THE THIEF, HIS WIFE & HER LOVER, THE ★★★★ British film about a long-suffering wife who carries on an affair in a restaurant owned by her sadistic, obnoxious husband. Gorgeously crafted yet explicit and sometimes distressingly brutal. A dark, haunting comedy with few bodily functions ignored, but the story is about excessive behavior—so nothing seems gratuitous. Rated NC-17 for nudity, violence, profanity, and simulated sex... you name it. 123m. **DIR:** Peter Greenaway. **CAST:** Michael Gambon, Helen Mirren, Richard Bohringer, Alan Howard. **1990**

COOKIE ★★★1/2 In this frothy piece of fluff, Emily Lloyd stars as the rebellious daughter of a gangster (Peter Falk) who cannot figure out how to keep his offspring in line. It's entertaining but forgettable. Rated R for profanity and violence. 93m. **DIR:** Susan Seidelman. **CAST:** Emily Lloyd, Peter Falk, Dianne Wiest, Jerry Lewis, Michael Gazzo, Brenda Vaccaro, Adrian Pasdar. **1989**

COOKIE'S FORTUNE ★★★★ Southern eccentrics are alive and well in this quirky character comedy from director Robert Altman and scripter Anne Rapp. The story, laced with Gothic overtones and a small-town Mississippi setting, concerns the aftermath of a suicide by one of the community's leading citizens. Tempers flare, libidos soar into hyperdrive, and some rather unexpected family secrets are revealed. Events are dominated by Glenn Close's Camille Dixon, a fussy, bossy, and unapologetically nasty shrike who believes that rules were made solely for the common herd. Rated PG-13 for profanity, sexual candor, and brief violence. 118m. **DIR:** Robert Altman. **CAST:** Glenn Close, Julianne Moore, Liv Tyler, Chris O'Donnell, Charles Dutton, Patricia Neal, Ned Beatty, Courtney B. Vance, Donald Moffat, Lyle Lovett. **1999 DVD**

COOL AS ICE 🦃 Vanilla Ice's first starring role as a motorcycle rider who woos a small-town girl proves he is an even worse actor than he is a rap singer. If that's possible. Rated PG for profanity. 91m. **DIR:** David Kellogg. **CAST:** Vanilla Ice, Kristin Minter, Michael Gross, Sidney Lassick, Dody Goodman, Candy Clark. **1991**

COOL BLUE ★★ Bumbling artist meets mysterious siren in urban bohemia. Miscast, labored, and pitifully unbelievable, *Cheers* star Woody Harrelson looks as if he needs a few belts. Rated R. 90m. **DIR:** Mark Mullen, Richard Shepard. **CAST:** Woody Harrelson. **1988**

COOL, DRY PLACE, A ★★★ After his wife leaves him, a small-town lawyer is forced to spend more time with his five-year-old son in this engaging but somewhat meandering comedy-drama. Young Bobby Moat, who plays the son, is a real scene-stealer. Rated PG-13 for sexual situations and mild profanity. 97m. **DIR:** John N. Smith. **CAST:** Vince Vaughn, Monica Potter, Joey Lauren Adams, Bobby Moat. **1998**

COOL HAND LUKE ★★★★★ One of Paul Newman's greatest creations is the irrepressible Luke. Luke is a prisoner on a southern chain gang and not even the deprivations of these subhuman conditions will break his spirit. George Kennedy's performance is equally memorable and won him a supporting Oscar. 126m. **DIR:** Stuart Rosenberg. **CAST:** Paul Newman, George Kennedy, J. D. Cannon, Lou Antonio, Robert Drivas, Strother Martin. **1967 DVD**

COOL RUNNINGS ★★★★ Inspired by the phenomenal popularity of the 1988 Olympics' Jamaican bobsled team, this is a wildly fictionalized *Rocky*-type comedy. Four black tropical sportsmen (a soapbox-derby racer and three sprinters) take the Calgary Winter Olympics by storm while overcoming physical, social, and personal adversity. Their misadventures produce an avalanche of infectious belly laughs. One of John Candy's last films. Rated PG. 95m. **DIR:** Jon Turteltaub. **CAST:** Doug E. Doug, Leon, Malik Yoba, Rawle D. Lewis, John Candy. **1993 DVD**

COOL SURFACE, THE ★★★ In this quirky thriller, aspiring screenwriter Robert Patrick bases his new screenplay on a neighbor, an actress played by Teri Hatcher. Things really start snowballing when Hatcher attempts to land the lead in Patrick's movie and life. Change-of-pace role for Patrick, who plays a mouse ready to roar. Rated R for nudity, violence, and language. 88m. **DIR:** Erik Anjou. **CAST:** Robert Patrick, Teri Hatcher, Matt McCoy, Ian Buchanan, Cyril O'Reilly. **1993**

COOL WORLD ★★ Cartoonist Gabriel Byrne is lured by his sexy creation Kim Basinger into a bizarre animated world that came from his imagination. Brad Pitt is the detective who attempts to bring Byrne back. Like no feature-length cartoon you've ever seen before. Rated PG-13 for sexual content. 98m. **DIR:** Ralph Bakshi. **CAST:** Kim Basinger, Gabriel Byrne, Brad Pitt. **1992**

COOLER CLIMATE, A ★★★1/2 Scripter Marsha Norman delivers a respectable adaptation of Zena Collier's novel about two lonely, dissimilar women eventually becoming allies and friends. Sally Field is a naïve wife who, out of humiliation, foolishly abandons her former life after learning that her husband is having an affair; Judy Davis is a brittle, wealthy socialite suffering through her own loveless marriage. Field, determined to turn herself around, accepts a job as the condescending Davis's housekeeper . . . a position that everybody in the local community warns is likely to be brief. But the resolute Field—always best playing plucky characters—digs in her heels, and the eventual thaw and bonding is no less entertaining for its predictability. Rated PG-13 for profanity, brief nudity, and simulated sex. 99m. **DIR:** Susan Seidelman. **CAST:** Sally Field, Judy Davis, Winston Rekert, Jerry Wasserman, Carly Pope. **1999**

COOLEY HIGH ★★★★ Highly enjoyable comedy-drama set in an inner-city Chicago high school in the early 1960s. This is probably the only *American Graffiti* clone that doesn't suffer by comparison. Featuring a first-rate soundtrack of vintage Motown tunes. Rated PG for mild profanity and sexual concerns. 107m. **DIR:** Michael Schultz. **CAST:** Glynn Turman, Lawrence Hilton-Jacobs, Garrett Morris, Cynthia Davis. **1975 DVD**

COOPERSTOWN ★★★★ Superior baseball fantasy focuses on a bitter ex-ball player, who is unhappy because he hasn't been inducted into the hall of fame. He is visited by the ghost of a friend who died on the eve of his own induction. Film captures the essence of baseball. 108m. **DIR:** Charles Haid. **CAST:** Alan Arkin, Hope Lange, Graham Greene, Ed Begley Jr., Josh Charles, Ann Wedgeworth. **1992**

COP ★★ This crime thriller quickly goes from being a fascinating character study to just another sleazy and mindless slasher flick. Rated R for violence, gore, simulated sex, nudity, and profanity. 110m. **DIR:** James B. Harris. **CAST:** James Woods, Lesley Ann Warren, Charles Durning, Charles Haid, Raymond J. Barry, Randi Brooks. **1988**

COP AND A HALF ★★★1/2 When youngster Norman D. Golden witnesses a gang-style murder, he uses his knowledge to coerce the authorities into making him a police officer. Burt Reynolds is in his element as the gruff detective assigned to take care of the boy. A predictable but fun romp. Rated PG for brief profanity and violence. 93m. **DIR:** Henry Winkler. **CAST:** Burt Reynolds, Ray Sharkey, Ruby Dee, Holland Taylor, Frank Sivero, Norman D. Golden, II. **1993 DVD**

COP FOR THE KILLING, A ★★ Typical crime-drama fails to present a credible case. James Farentino plays a Los Angeles police lieutenant out to avenge the murder of his partner by a vicious drug lord. Nothing new in this made-for-television effort. Rated R for intense situations. 87m. **DIR:** Dick Lowry. **CAST:** James Farentino, Steven Weber, Susan Walters, Charles Haid, Harold Sylvester. **1994**

COP IN BLUE JEANS, THE 🦃 An undercover cop (Thomas Milian) tries to take out an underworld boss (Jack Palance). Not rated; contains violence. 92m. **DIR:** Bruno Corbucci. **CAST:** Tomas Milian, Jack Palance, Maria Rosaria Omaggio, Guido Mannari. **1978**

COP-OUT ★★ In this ambitious but shoestring-budgeted murder mystery, a detective tries to get his incarcerated brother off the hook. The resolution of this whodunit comes as no real surprise. Not rated, though there is partial nudity, violence, and considerable profanity. 102m. **DIR:** Lawrence L. Simeone. **CAST:** David D. Buff. **1991**

COPACABANA 🦃 Not even Groucho Marx can save this slight comedy about the problems caused by a woman applying for two jobs at the same nightclub. B&W; 92m. **DIR:** Alfred E. Green. **CAST:** Groucho Marx, Carmen Miranda, Andy Russell, Steve Cochran, Abel Green. **1947**

COPLAND ★★★1/2 Sylvester Stallone's the power in name only for sleepy Garrison, N.J.—a "bedroom community" for New York City cops hoping to leave behind the danger of their jobs. But Garrison's bucolic streets conceal a cesspool of corruption. James Mangold's moody direction is better than his plot, but this remains a noteworthy stretch for an actor trying to leave *Rocky* and *Rambo* behind. Rated R for violence and profanity. 100m. **DIR:** James Mangold. **CAST:** Sylvester Stallone, Harvey Keitel, Ray Liotta, Robert De Niro, Peter Berg, Janeane Garofalo, Robert Patrick, Michael Rapaport, Annabella Sciorra. **1997 DVD**

COPPER CANYON ★★ A gunslinger helps homesteaders stake their claims after the Civil War. This would have been a more believable picture with a different cast. Milland's British accent and Lamarr's Austrian one are completely out of place in the American Southwest. 83m. **DIR:** John Farrow. **CAST:** Ray Milland, Hedy Lamarr, Macdonald Carey, Mona Freeman, Harry Carey Jr., Frank Faylen, Hope Emerson, Ian Wolfe, Peggy Knudsen. **1950**

COPS AND ROBBERS ★★ This mediocre cops-on-the-take caper features two burned-out New York cops who decide to use all they've learned to pull off the perfect crime. Rated PG for violence. 89m. **DIR:** Aram Avakian. **CAST:** Joseph Bologna, Cliff Gorman. **1973**

COPS AND ROBBERSONS ★★1/2 Mild-mannered suburban dad Chevy Chase is a wannabe detective who gets a taste of the real thing. Hardboiled cop Jack Palance moves in to set up surveillance on Chase's new neighbor (Robert Davi), a counterfeiter with the nasty habit of murdering his customers. The few chuckles almost make it worthwhile. Rated PG for violence. 95m. **DIR:** Michael Ritchie. **CAST:** Chevy Chase, Jack Palance, Dianne Wiest, Robert Davi, David Barry Gray, Jason James Richter, Fay Masterson, Miko Hughes, M. Emmet Walsh. **1994 DVD**

COPYCAT ★★★★ Impressive suspense-thriller about a criminal psychologist who develops agoraphobia after a serial killer makes an attempt on her life. She is forced out of her hiding place when a detective seeks her help in solving a recent series of murders, not knowing that the psychologist may be next on the killer's list. Rated R for violence, nudity, and profanity. 123m. **DIR:** Jon Amiel. **CAST:** Sigourney Weaver, Holly Hunter, Dermot Mulroney, Will Patton, John Rothman, J. E. Freeman, Harry Connick Jr., William McNamara. **1996 DVD**

COQUETTE ★★★ A sticky soap opera that looks hokey today, but it wowed audiences in 1929. Mary Pickford won an Oscar for the role of a college girl who lies in court to get her father off. He was charged with murder, and the film itself is a Flapper Age melodrama that set a pattern for so-called women's movies. B&W; 81m. **DIR:** Sam Taylor. **CAST:** Mary Pickford, Matt Moore, Johnny Mack Brown, Louise Beavers. **1929**

•**CORKY ROMANO** 🦃 Mafia offspring Chris Kattan goes undercover in the FBI to destroy the evidence against his gangster father (Peter Falk) in this wretchedly unfunny fiasco, one of the worst movies ever from a *Saturday Night Live* alumnus—and that's saying something. Rated PG-13 for profanity, drug use, and crude sexual humor. 85m. **DIR:** Rob Pritts. **CAST:** Chris Kattan, Vinessa Shaw, Peter Falk, Peter Berg, Christopher Penn, Fred Ward, Richard Roundtree. **2001 DVD**

CORLEONE ★★ Dull Italian drama about two childhood friends in Sicily who decide to fight the powerful landowners who control their homeland. Aside from the title, which is the name of the Sicilian town where they live, this has no connection to the *Godfather* movies. Rated R for profanity, violence. 115m. **DIR:** Pasquale Squiteri. **CAST:** Giuliano Gemma, Claudia Cardinale, Francisco Rabal. **1985**

CORN IS GREEN, THE (1945) ★★★★ Bette Davis leads a winning cast in this well-mounted film of British playwright-actor Emlyn Williams's drama of education vs. coal in a rough-edged Welsh mining village. John Dall is the young miner whom schoolteacher Davis grooms to win a university scholarship. B&W; 114m. **DIR:** Irving Rapper. **CAST:** Bette Davis, John Dall, Joan Lorring, Nigel Bruce, Rhys Williams, Mildred Dunnock. **1945**

CORN IS GREEN, THE (1979) ★★★1/2 Based on Emlyn Williams's play and directed by George Cukor, this telefilm stars Katharine Hepburn. She gives a tour-de-force performance as the eccentric spinster-teacher who helps a gifted young man discover the joys of learning. 100m. **DIR:** George Cukor. **CAST:** Katharine Hepburn, Ian Saynor, Bill Fraser, Patricia Hayes, Anna Massey. **1979**

CORNBREAD, EARL AND ME ★★1/2 A fine cast of black performers is ill served by this overdone drama about racism. A gifted basketball player is mistakenly killed by the police. It's a familiar plot directed with little inspiration by Joseph Manduke. Rated R. 95m. **DIR:** Joseph Manduke. **CAST:** Moses Gunn, Bernie Casey, Rosalind Cash, Madge Sinclair. **1975 DVD**

CORNERED ★★★ Fresh from his success as hard-boiled sleuth Philip Marlowe in *Murder, My Sweet*, former song-and-dance man Dick Powell continued to score as a dramatic actor in this thriller about a discharged Canadian airman on the trail of Nazi collaborators who murdered his French wife. The hunt takes him from France to Switzerland to Argentina. B&W; 102m. **DIR:** Edward Dmytryk. **CAST:** Dick Powell, Walter Slezak, Micheline Cheirel, Luther Adler, Morris Carnovsky. **1946**

CORONER, THE 🦃 The city coroner, rather than waiting for folks to die, likes to kidnap people and drag them down to his basement to conduct vicious experiments on them. Either that, or he bores them to death. The acting and effects are downright abysmal. Rated R primarily for violence. 79m. **DIR:** Juan A. Mas. **CAST:** Jane Longenecker, Dean St. Louis. **1999 DVD**

CORONER CREEK ★★★★ Solid Western marks the first film in the series produced by the company set up by Randolph Scott and Harry Brown. Their collaboration culminated in the superb series directed by Budd Boetticher *(Ride Lonesome, The Tall T)*. Even so, this film is no slouch, with Scott attempting to track down the man responsible for the murder of his fiancée. 90m. **DIR:** Ray Enright. **CAST:** Randolph Scott, Marguerite Chapman, George Macready, Forrest Tucker, Edgar Buchanan. **1948**

CORPORATE AFFAIRS ★★ Short on laughs, sex comedy focuses on the sexcapades of corporate executives, each clawing his or her way to the top. Rated R for nudity, profanity, and violence. 82m. **DIR:** Terence H. Winkless. **CAST:** Peter Scolari, Mary Crosby, Chris Lemmon, Ken Kercheval. **1990**

CORPORATE LADDER ★★ Tired tale of backstabbing vixen who is willing to do anything in her attempt to reach the top. Kathleen Kinmont is appropriately menacing, but she's constantly fighting an uphill battle thanks to trite writing and uninspired direction. Rated R for language, nudity, and violence. 112m. **DIR:** Nick Vallelonga. **CAST:** Kathleen Kinmont, Anthony John Denison, Talisa Soto, Jennifer O'Neill, Ben Cross. **1996**

CORPSE GRINDERS, THE 🦃 This silly horror comedy about two cat-food makers who use human corpses in their secret recipe has a cult reputation as one of those so-bad-it's-good movies. 72m. **DIR:** Ted V. Mikels. **CAST:** Sean Kenney, Monika Kelly. **1972**

CORPSE VANISHES, THE 🦃 Hokey pseudoscientific thriller about crazed scientist Bela Lugosi and his efforts to keep his elderly wife young through transfusions from young girls. B&W; 64m. **DIR:** Wallace Fox. **CAST:** Bela Lugosi, Luana Walters, Tristram Coffin, Minerva Urecal, Elizabeth Russell. **1942 DVD**

CORREGIDOR 🦃 An early World War II movie made on the cheap, and it shows. Elissa Landi is the girl in a romantic triangle. There isn't any action whatever. B&W; 73m. **DIR:** William Nigh. **CAST:** Elissa Landi, Donald Woods, Otto Kruger, Frank Jenks, Ian Keith, Wanda McKay. **1943**

CORRIDOR OF MIRRORS ★★★★1/2 A nail-biter about an artist obsessed with the painting of a Renaissance-era woman. He convinces himself that he is the reincarnation of her lover and seeks her modern counterpart. Lushly photographed and suspensefully produced to make every goose pimple count. Directed by England's foremost action-film specialist who later went on to direct James Bond movies. B&W; 94m. **DIR:** Terence Young. **CAST:** Christopher Lee, Eric Portman, Lois Maxwell, Edana Romney, Barbara Mullen, Hugh Sinclair. **1948**

CORRIDORS OF BLOOD ★★★ Kindly surgeon (Boris Karloff) in nineteeth-century London tries to perfect anesthesia and becomes addicted to narcotics. In a mental fog, he is blackmailed by grave robbers. A suprisingly effective thriller originally withheld from release in the United States for five years. 86m. **DIR:** Robert Day. **CAST:** Boris Karloff, Francis Matthews, Adrienne Corri, Betta St. John, Nigel Green, Christopher Lee. **1957 DVD**

CORRINA, CORRINA ★★★★1/2 Set in the 1950s, Whoopi Goldberg goes to work as a maid for jingle writer Ray Liotta, who has recently lost his wife to cancer and all but lost his little daughter to her self-imposed world of silence. Writer-producer-director Jessie Nelson imbues spirit-lifting entertainment with deft insights into the human condition. Rated PG. 114m. **DIR:** Jessie Nelson. **CAST:** Whoopi Goldberg, Ray Liotta, Tina Majorino, Wendy Crewson, Larry Miller, Erica Yohn, Jenifer Lewis, Joan Cusack, Harold Sylvester, Steven Williams, Don Ameche. **1994 DVD**

CORRUPT ★★ Turtle-paced psychological thriller featuring Harvey Keitel as a corrupt narcotics officer. Not rated, but equivalent to an R for violence and profanity. 99m. **DIR:** Roberto Faenza. **CAST:** Harvey Keitel, John Lydon, Sylvia Sidney, Nicole Garcia. **1984 DVD**

CORRUPT ONES, THE ★★★ Robert Stack plays a photographer who receives the key to a Chinese treasure. Not surprisingly, he soon finds that he's not alone in his search for the goodies. This is a good—but not great—adventure film. 92m. **DIR:** James Hill. **CAST:** Robert Stack, Nancy Kwan, Elke Sommer, Werner Peters. **1966**

CORRUPTOR, THE ★★★1/2 Chow Yun-Fat is the primary attraction in this 1990s *noir* tale of a Chinatown cop who believes he can mix with forces on the Dark Side without becoming tainted. The story concerns our hero's ethical awakening, when it becomes clear that the underworld Tongs are determined to corrupt his naïve and likable younger partner. The result is a slick and suspenseful B film. Rated R for violence, profanity, nudity, sexual content, and drug use. 111m. **DIR:** James Foley. **CAST:** Chow Yun-Fat, Mark Wahlberg, Ric Young, Paul Ben-Victor, Andrew Pang, Brian Cox. **1999 DVD**

CORSICAN BROTHERS, THE (1941) ★★★1/2 Alexandre Dumas's classic story of twins who remain spiritually tied, though separated, crackles in this lavish old Hollywood production. Intrigue and swordplay abound. Douglas Fairbanks Jr. is fine, backed by two of the best supporting players ever: J. Carrol Naish and Akim Tamiroff. B&W; 112m. **DIR:** Gregory Ratoff. **CAST:** Douglas Fairbanks Jr., Ruth Warrick, J. Carrol Naish, Akim Tamiroff, H. B. Warner, Henry Wilcoxon. **1941**

CORSICAN BROTHERS, THE (1984) 🦃 Loosely based on the book by Alexandre Dumas, this forgettable film features Tommy Chong and Richard "Cheech" Marin as twins. Rated R. 90m. **DIR:** Thomas Chong. **CAST:** Cheech and Chong, Roy Dotrice. **1984**

CORVETTE SUMMER 🦃 This mindless car-chase film finds Mark Hamill in Las Vegas hunting car thieves who have ripped off his Corvette. Rated PG. 105m. **DIR:** Matthew Robbins. **CAST:** Mark Hamill, Kim Melford, Annie Potts. **1978**

COSI ★★★★ An amateur stage director's first real assignment is to stage a version of Mozart's *Cosi Fan Tutte* with the occupants of an Australian mental home. His job is complicated because the patients can't sing, read Italian, or memorize lines and the head of the institute is dead set against the idea. When he falls for his troubled leading lady, the stage is set for a wild evening of fun. Bright, cheery Australian import. Rated R for adult situations and language. 100m. **DIR:** Mark Joffe. **CAST:** Ben Mendelsohn, Barry Otto, Toni Collette, Rachel Griffiths, Aden Young, Colin Friels. **1996**

COSMIC MAN, THE 🦃 An invisible alien comes to this planet in a giant levitating Ping-Pong ball. B&W; 72m. **DIR:** Herbert Greene. **CAST:** John Carradine, Bruce Bennett, Angela Greene. **1959 DVD**

COSMIC MONSTERS, THE ★★ Low-budget horror from Great Britain. Giant carnivorous insects invade our planet. An alien in a flying saucer arrives to save the day. The effects are cheap. B&W; 75m. **DIR:** Gilbert Gunn. **CAST:** Forrest Tucker, Gaby André. **1958**

COSMIC SLOP ★★1/2 You could almost agree with the blurb on the box that this is a "multicultural *Twilight Zone*," except it is too preachy and the special effects are pathetic. However, the first episode in this three-story, sci-fi anthology, executive produced by directors Reginald and Warrington Hudlin (*House Party*), has the kind of mind-numbing impact that will stay with you for days. Made for HBO. Rated R for violence and profanity. 87m. **DIR:** Reginald Hudlin, Warrington Hudlin, Kevin Sullivan. **CAST:** Robert Guillaume, Nicholas Turturro, George Clinton, Paula Jai Parker, Chi McBride. **1994**

COTTON CLUB, THE ★★★★ The story about two pairs of brothers, one black and one white, is set at Harlem's most famous nightclub. Cornet player Gere and moll Diane Lane make love while Gregory Hines dances his way into the heart of songbird Lonette McKee. Rated R for violence, nudity, profanity, and suggested sex. 128m. **DIR:** Francis Ford Coppola. **CAST:** Richard Gere, Diane Lane, James Remar, Gregory Hines, Lonette McKee. **1984 DVD**

COTTON COMES TO HARLEM ★★★★ The comedy-drama based on Chester Himes's book introduces Coffin Ed and Gravedigger Jones, two cops who accuse a local clergyman of swindling the citizens. The movie was filmed in Harlem and started a trend of serio-comic films with all-black casts that exploited stereotypical characters but still pleased audiences. Excellent cast and fine production values. Rated R. 97m. **DIR:** Ossie Davis. **CAST:** Godfrey Cambridge, Raymond St. Jacques, Calvin Lockhart, Redd Foxx, Cleavon Little, Emily Yancy, Judy Pace. **1970 DVD**

COTTON MARY ★★★★1/2 Madhur Jeffrey excels as Cotton Mary, an Anglo-Indian military nurse in 1954 postcolonial India. Afraid of being forced to return to her common roots when anticolonial sentiment sweeps her village, Cotton Mary endears herself to privileged Lily Macintosh, who invites the nurse into her estate to care for her newborn baby. Once there, Cotton Mary begins a campaign to take over the household. A wonderful film, filled with exquisite period detail and beautiful performances. Rated R for adult situations and language. 124m. **DIR:** Ismail Merchant. **CAST:** Greta Scacchi, Madhur Jeffrey, James Wilby, Neena Gupta, Sarah Badel, Gemma Jones. **1999 DVD**

COUCH IN NEW YORK, A 🦃 Could a film be more boring? Sophisticated Manhattan shrink William Hurt decides on a change of scenery, and—sight unseen—swaps apartments with Parisian Juliette Binoche. She proves more successful than he at "treating" his clients (who seem not to care about switching "therapists" in midtreatment); he grows curious, returns to New York, and poses as a new "patient." Utterly ludicrous, and a total yawn. Rated PG-13 for profanity. 105m. **DIR:** Chantal Akerman. **CAST:** William Hurt, Juliette Binoche, Stephanie Buttle, Paul Guilfoyle, Richard Jenkins. **1996 DVD**

COUCH TRIP, THE ★★1/2 Dan Aykroyd and Walter Matthau offer a few moments of mirth in this middling comedy about a computer hacker (Aykroyd) who escapes from a mental institution and becomes a hugely successful media shrink. Charles Grodin is exceptional as the neurotic radio doctor Aykroyd replaces, and Mary Gross has some terrific scenes as Grodin's wacky wife. Rated R for profanity and suggested sex. 95m. **DIR:** Michael Ritchie. **CAST:** Dan Aykroyd, Walter Matthau, Charles Grodin, Donna Dixon, Richard Romanus, Mary Gross, David Clennon, Arye Gross. **1988**

COUNT DRACULA ★★1/2 Christopher Lee dons the cape once again in this mediocre version of the famous tale about the undead fiend terrorizing the countryside. Rated R. 98m. **DIR:** Jess (Jesus) Franco. **CAST:** Christopher Lee, Herbert Lom, Klaus Kinski. **1970**

COUNT OF MONTE CRISTO, THE (1912) ★★★ The famous Irish actor James O'Neill, father of playwright Eugene, is captured for posterity in his popular interpretation of the Alexandre Dumas story. An unmoving camera is focused onstage, and O'Neill is supremely hammy, but this is an invaluable record of a bygone time. Silent. B&W; 90m. **DIR:** Edwin S. Porter. **CAST:** James O'Neill. **1912**

COUNT OF MONTE CRISTO, THE (1934) ★★★★ In the title role, Robert Donat heads a superb, fine-tuned cast in this now-classic film of Dumas's great story. Innocent sailor Edmond Dantes, falsely accused of aiding the exiled Napoleon and infamously imprisoned for fifteen years, escapes to levy revenge on those who framed him. A secret cache of treasure makes it all very sweet. B&W; 119m. **DIR:** Rowland V. Lee. **CAST:** Robert Donat, Elissa Landi, Irene Hervey, Louis Calhern, Sidney Blackmer, Raymond Walburn, O. P. Heggie. **1934**

COUNT OF MONTE CRISTO, THE (1975) ★★★1/2 Solid TV adaptation of the Alexandre Dumas classic. Richard Chamberlain cuts a dashing figure as the persecuted Edmond Dantes. The casting of Tony Curtis as the evil Mondego works surprisingly well. 100m. **DIR:** David Greene. **CAST:** Richard Chamberlain, Tony Curtis, Louis Jourdan, Donald Pleasence, Taryn Power. **1975**

•COUNT OF MONTE CRISTO, THE (2002) ★★★ The oft-filmed Dumas tale of a man's revenge gets a handsome production here. Compensating for a weak, jokey script and a vapid performance by leading lady Dagmara Dominczyk are handsome photography and good performances by Jim Caviezel in the title role and Guy Pearce as the chief villain—plus, of course, the story itself, which is always hard to mess up. Rated PG-13 for swashbuckling action. 118m. **DIR:** Kevin Reynolds. **CAST:** Jim Caviezel, Guy Pearce, Dagmara Dominczyk, Richard Harris, Luis Guzman. **2002 DVD**

COUNT YORGA, VAMPIRE ★★★ Contemporary vampire terrorizes Los Angeles. Somewhat dated, but a sharp and powerful thriller. Stars Robert Quarry, an intense, dignified actor who appeared in several horror films in the early 1970s, then abruptly left the genre. Rated R for violence. 91m. **DIR:** Bob Kelljan. **CAST:** Robert Quarry, Roger Perry, Donna Anders, Michael Murphy. **1970 DVD**

COUNTDOWN ★★★ This lesser-known Robert Altman film finds James Caan and Robert Duvall as American astronauts preparing for a moon shot. Realistic scenes and great acting—well worth watching. Not rated. 101m. **DIR:** Robert Altman. **CAST:** James Caan, Robert Duvall, Charles Aidman. **1968**

COUNTERFEIT TRAITOR, THE ★★★★ A spy story based on a real-life character. William Holden is exceptionally good as the Swedish-American businessman who poses as a Nazi sympathizer. Authentic location work and good production values give this one an edge. 141m. **DIR:** George Seaton. **CAST:** William Holden, Lilli Palmer, Klaus Kinski, Hugh Griffith, Eva Dahlbeck. **1962**

COUNTERFORCE 🦃 An elite special missions force is hired to protect an exiled Middle East democratic leader. A bore. Rated R. 98m. **DIR:** J. Anthony Loma. **CAST:** George Kennedy, Jorge Rivero, Andrew Stevens, Isaac Hayes, Louis Jourdan, Robert Forster. **1987**

COUNTESS FROM HONG KONG, A 🦃 Charlie Chaplin's final and most disappointing effort, this pits stowaway Sophia Loren against extremely dull Marlon Brando in a shipboard love story that lacks laughs, coherence, and romance. Rated G. 108m. **DIR:** Charles Chaplin. **CAST:** Marlon Brando, Sophia Loren, Sydney Chaplin, Tippi Hedren, Patrick Cargill, Bill Nagy, Geraldine Chaplin, Margaret Rutherford, Charlie Chaplin. **1967**

COUNTRY ★★★★ A quietly powerful movie about the plight of farmers struggling to hold on while the government and financial institutions seem intent on fostering their failure. *Country* teams Jessica Lange and Sam Shepard on-screen, for the first time since the Oscar-nominated *Frances*, in a film as topical as today's headlines. Rated PG. 109m. **DIR:** Richard Pearce. **CAST:** Jessica Lange, Sam Shepard, Wilford Brimley, Matt Clark. **1984**

COUNTRY GENTLEMEN ★★ Fast-talking confidence men Ole Olsen and Chic Johnson sell shares in a worthless oil field to a group of World War I veterans, then learn thar's oil in them thar hills! Humorous, but what a weary plot! This flick did little for the comic duo, who always fared better on the stage. B&W; 54m. **DIR:** Ralph Staub. **CAST:** Ole Olsen, Chic Johnson, Joyce Compton, Lila Lee. **1936**

COUNTRY GIRL, THE (1954) ★★★★1/2 Bing Crosby and Grace Kelly give terrific performances in this little-seen production. Crosby plays an alcoholic singer who wallows in self-pity until he seizes a chance to make a comeback. Kelly won an Oscar for her sensitive portrayal of his wife. B&W; 104m. **DIR:** George Seaton. **CAST:** Bing Crosby, Grace Kelly, William Holden, Anthony Ross. **1954**

COUNTRY GIRL, THE (1982) ★★★1/2 Cable TV remake of Clifford Odets's tragic play pales somewhat compared to the Bing Crosby–Grace Kelly rendition. In this filmed stage-play version Dick Van Dyke is the alcoholic actor who has one last chance at a comeback. Ken Howard is the brash young director who blames Van Dyke's wife (Faye Dunaway) for the actor's decline. 137m. **DIR:** Gary Halvorson. **CAST:** Faye Dunaway, Dick Van Dyke, Ken Howard. **1982**

COUNTRY LIFE ★★★★ Chekhov's play *Uncle Vanya*, about family squabbles on a Russian country estate, is transplanted to an Australian sheep ranch shortly after World War I. This film is almost as faithful as *Vanya on 42nd Street*, and considerably funnier, with a boisterous and hearty spirit of which Chekhov would approve. As the dissolute country doctor, Sam Neill is in top form. Rated PG-13 for mild profanity and adult situations. 103m. **DIR:** Michael Blakemore. **CAST:** Sam Neill, Greta Scacchi, John Hargreaves, Kerry Fox, Patricia Kennedy, Maurie Fields, Googie Withers, Michael Blakemore. **1994**

COUNTRYMAN ★★★1/2 A strange and fun film following the adventures of a young marijuana-smuggling woman (Kristian Sinclair) whose airplane crash-lands in Jamaica. She is rescued by Countryman and led to safety. Lots of Rasta humor and supernatural happenings keep the viewer entertained. *Countryman* also has a great reggae music soundtrack. Rated R for nudity and adult themes. 103m. **DIR:** Dickie Jobson. **CAST:** Hiram Keller, Kristian Sinclair. **1984**

COUP DE GRACE ★★ In 1920, the daughter of a once-wealthy family falls in love with the militaristic leader of a group of soldiers. Mostly impenetrable pontificating on sex and politics, poorly adapted from a novel by Marguerite Yourcenar. In German with English subtitles. Not rated. 95m. **DIR:** Volker Schlöndorff. **CAST:** Margarethe von Trotta, Matthias Habich, Mathieu Carriere. **1976**

COUPE DE VILLE ★★★★1/2 It's 1963, the last glorious months before the fall of Kennedy's Camelot, and three estranged brothers are recruited to bring a 1954 Cadillac from Michigan to Florida as a surprise gift for their mother's fiftieth birthday. Delightful comedy. Rated PG-13 for profanity and brief violence. 110m. **DIR:** Joe Roth. **CAST:** Daniel Stern, Patrick Dempsey, Arye Gross, Alan Arkin. **1990**

COURAGE MOUNTAIN ★★★★ Ignore all those highfalutin critics who gave this well-made family film a thumbs-down. Director Christopher Leitch has done a marvelous job in turning this quasi-sequel to *Heidi* into compelling entertainment. Plenty of suspense, strong characterizations, and an edge-of-your-seat ending. Rated PG for brief violence. 120m. **DIR:** Christopher Leitch. **CAST:** Juliette Caton, Charlie Sheen, Leslie Caron. **1990**

COURAGE OF LASSIE ★★1/2 Everybody's favorite collie is called Bill and suffers postwar trauma in this unusual entry into the popular series. Bill leaves his wilderness home to become Elizabeth Taylor's dog, but is injured and somehow ends up in the canine corps. 92m. **DIR:** Fred M. Wilcox. **CAST:** Elizabeth Taylor, Frank Morgan, Tom Drake, Selena Royle, Harry Davenport, George Cleveland. **1946**

COURAGE UNDER FIRE ★★★★ Decorated Gulf War hero Denzel Washington investigates the background of a medevac pilot scheduled to receive a Medal of Honor. Unfortunately, the award is posthumous, and Washington is battling his own demons, having given the order that killed his best friend during "friendly fire." Rated R for violence and profanity. 116m. **DIR:** Edward Zwick. **CAST:** Denzel Washington, Meg Ryan, Lou Diamond Phillips, Michael Moriarty, Matt Damon, Seth Gilliam, Bronson Pinchot, Scott Glenn. **1996 DVD**

COURAGEOUS DR. CHRISTIAN, THE ★★1/2 In this episode in the Dr. Christian series, Jean Hersholt again plays the saintlike physician. Predictable but pleasing. B&W; 67m. **DIR:** Bernard Vorhaus. **CAST:** Jean Hersholt, Dorothy Lovett, Robert Baldwin, Tom Neal. **1940**

COURAGEOUS MR. PENN ★★ Stilted title of this bloodless biography of religious leader William Penn is indicative of the mediocrity of the entire production. B&W; 79m. **DIR:** Lance Comfort. **CAST:** Clifford Evans, Deborah Kerr. **1943**

COURT JESTER, THE ★★★ Romance, court intrigue, a joust, and in the middle of it all the one and only Danny Kaye as a phony court jester full of double-takes and double-talk. This is one funny film of clever and complicated comic situations superbly brought off. 101m. **DIR:** Norman Panama, Melvin Frank. **CAST:** Danny Kaye, Glynis Johns, Basil Rathbone, Angela Lansbury, Mildred Natwick, Robert Middleton. **1956 DVD**

COURT-MARTIAL OF BILLY MITCHELL, THE ★★★ In 1925, Army General Billy Mitchell was court-martialed for calling the army and the navy almost treasonous for their neglect of military air power after World War I. Gary Cooper is marvelous as Mitchell, but the show is almost stolen by prosecuting attorney Rod Steiger. 100m. **DIR:** Otto Preminger. **CAST:** Gary Cooper, Rod Steiger, Charles Bickford, Ralph Bellamy, Elizabeth Montgomery, Jack Lord, Peter Graves, Darren McGavin. **1955**

COURT-MARTIAL OF JACKIE ROBINSON, THE ★★★1/2 Well-made television drama examines baseball great Jackie Robinson's battles against racism in the army from 1942 to 1944. Andre Braugher is very good as the young Robinson, with veterans Ruby Dee and Bruce Dern lending stellar support in small but important roles. 94m. **DIR:** Larry Peerce. **CAST:** Andre Braugher, Daniel Stern, Ruby Dee, Stan Shaw, Paul Dooley, Bruce Dern. **1990**

COURTESANS OF BOMBAY ★★★★ Fascinating mix of documentary and fiction explores the lives of impoverished Indian women who support themselves through a combination of performing and prostitution. Made for British television, the film is chiefly concerned with the social context of a society that encourages such lifestyles. Not rated; the subject matter is discreetly handled but too frank for young children. 73m. **DIR:** Ismail Merchant, James Ivory, Ruth Prawer Jhabvala. **CAST:** Saeed Jaffrey. **1983**

COURTNEY AFFAIR, THE ★★★ British family saga stretching across four and a half decades: 1900–1945. Classy soap opera in which a housemaid marries money and trades the backstairs for the drawing room. B&W; 112m. **DIR:** Herbert Wilcox. **CAST:** Anna Neagle, Michael Wilding, Coral Browne. **1947**

COURTSHIP ★★★★ A touching and engrossing period play (set in 1915) from the pen of Horton Foote, whose superb dialogue makes this tale of a young woman's coming-of-age easy to believe. A wonderful transport back to the more chivalrous days of yesteryear. No rating. 85m. **DIR:** Howard Cummings. **CAST:** Hallie Foote, Amanda Plummer, Rochelle Oliver, Michael Higgins, William Converse-Roberts. **1987**

COURTSHIP OF EDDIE'S FATHER, THE ★★★ A delightful blend of sophisticated romance and family idealism that inspired a successful TV series in the 1960s. Little Ronny Howard is exceptional as the motherless son who gives Dad, Glenn Ford, advice on his love life. 117m. **DIR:** Vincente Minnelli. **CAST:** Glenn Ford, Ron Howard, Stella Stevens, Dina Merrill, Shirley Jones, Jerry Van Dyke, Roberta Sherwood. **1963**

COURTYARD, THE ★★★1/2 An architect moves into an apartment complex in Los Angeles, and within a week finds himself embroiled in a murder investigation. Between repeated attempts to find the murderer, he falls in love with the dead man's sister. Credible performances from Andrew McCarthy and Madchen Amick shore up the complex plot in this made-for-cable original. Rated R for profanity, violence, and nudity. 105m. **DIR:** Fred Walton. **CAST:** Andrew McCarthy, Madchen Amick, David Packer, Bonnie Bartlett, Vincent Schiavelli, Richard "Cheech" Marin. **1995**

COUSIN BETTE ★★★★ Set in France during the nineteenth century, director Des McAnuff's film is filled with juicy performances and a wicked screenplay based on Balzac's novel. Jessica Lange, as Bette, gets even with her extended family through a plan involving greed, sexual temptation, and loyalty. Elisabeth Shue is the saucy temptress who sets Bette's plan into motion. Rated R for language, adult situations, and nudity. 110m. **DIR:** Des McAnuff. **CAST:** Jessica Lange, Elisabeth Shue, Bob Hoskins, Hugh Laurie, Aden Young, Kelly Macdonald. **1997 DVD**

COUSIN BOBBY ★★★★ Filmmaker Jonathan Demme hadn't seen his second cousin, the Reverend Robert Castle, for thirty years until a family reunion inspired him to make this film. A socially conscious minister, Castle believes that one man can make a difference: in modern footage, we see him leading a congregation in Harlem and fighting institutionalized racism. A small gem. Not rated; no objectionable material. 70m. **DIR:** Jonathan Demme. **1992**

COUSIN, COUSINE ★★★1/2 Marie-Christine Barrault and Victor Lanoux star in this beloved French comedy in the U.S., remade as *Cousins*. Married to others, they become cousins. Once the kissing starts, their relationship expands beyond the boundaries of convention. In French with English subtitles. 95m. **DIR:** Jean-Charles Tacchella. **CAST:** Marie-Christine Barrault, Victor Lanoux, Marie-France Pisier, Guy Marchand. **1975**

COUSINS ★★★★1/2 *Cousins* is an utter delight; a marvelously acted, written, and directed romance. Ted Danson, Isabella Rossellini, Sean Young, and William Petersen star as star-crossed spouses, cousins, and lovers in this Americanized takeoff on the 1975 French comedy hit, *Cousin, Cousine*. *Cousins* is about love rather than sex, making it a rare modern movie with heart. Rated PG-13 for profanity and suggested sex. 109m. **DIR:** Joel Schumacher. **CAST:** Ted Danson, Isabella Rossellini, Sean Young, William L. Petersen, Lloyd Bridges, Norma Aleandro, Keith Coogan. **1989 DVD**

COVER GIRL ★★★ Beautiful Rita Hayworth, a performer in Gene Kelly's nightclub act, must choose between a fabulous gig as a *Vanity* magazine cover girl—which may lead to a future with a millionaire producer—or life with an extremely petulant, chauvinistic Kelly. Let's-put-on-a-show scenario works well. 107m. **DIR:** Charles Vidor. **CAST:** Rita Hayworth, Gene Kelly, Phil Silvers, Eve Arden. **1944**

COVER GIRL MURDERS, THE ★★1/2 If you like to see beautiful women in skimpy bathing suits, you'll love this made-for-cable original—just don't expect much of a plot or great acting. During a remote-island photo shoot, the cover girls are murdered one by one. Rated PG-13 for violence and an attempted rape. 87m. **DIR:** James A. Contner. **CAST:** Lee Majors, Jennifer O'Neill, Adrian Paul, Beverly Johnson, Vanessa Angel, Arthur Taxier, Bobbie Phillips, Fawna MacLaren, Mowava Pryor. **1993**

COVER ME ★★ When a female cop is fired for shooting a bad guy, she has one chance to get her job back—take off her clothes and go undercover as a centerfold model. Silly thriller is helped by performers who give it the old college try despite the fact the material is ridiculous. Rated R for sexuality, language, and violence. 94m. **DIR:** Michael Schroeder. **CAST:** Rick Rossovich, Elliott Gould, Corbin Bernsen, Courtney Taylor, Paul Sorvino. **1995**

COVER-UP ★★ Reporters flock to Israel after an American military base is bombed. Violence begets violence in this confusing espionage thriller. Not rated; contains violence, profanity, and nudity. 89m. **DIR:** Manny Coto. **CAST:** Dolph Lundgren, Louis Gossett Jr., John Finn. **1990**

COVERED WAGON, THE ★★★1/2 Touted as "the biggest thing the screen has had since *The Birth of A Nation*," this epic pioneer saga broke audience attendance records all over the world and remained in circulation for many years. Love, adventure, humor, danger, and despair overlap each other in this somewhat dated but still exciting blockbuster. A landmark Western. Silent. B&W; 83m. **DIR:** James Cruze. **CAST:** J. Warren Kerrigan, Lois Wilson, Alan Hale Sr., Ernest Torrence, Tully Marshall. **1923**

COVERED WAGON DAYS ★★1/2 The Three Mesquiteers have until sunset to prove a friend innocent of a murder actually committed by silver smugglers. B&W; 54m. **DIR:** George Sherman. **CAST:** Robert Livingston, Duncan Renaldo, Raymond Hatton. **1940**

COVERT ASSASSIN ★★★ Roy Scheider is in fine form in this action-thriller that features him as ex-NATO antiterrorist task-force commander Peter Stride. After he's asked to resign, Stride accepts an offer from a beautiful baroness to track down the terrorists who killed her husband. Exotic locations, exciting action sequences, and sympathetic characters work in this low-budget film's favor. Rated R for violence and adult language. 114m. **DIR:** Tony Wharmby. **CAST:** Roy Scheider, Sam Wanamaker, Ted McGinley, Patricia Millardet, Christopher Buchholz. **1993**

COW TOWN ★★1/2 Action and stunts as well as a good crew of familiar faces make this, Gene Autry's seventy-second film as himself, better than many of his earlier efforts. Grazing rights, stampedes, gunplay, and a song or two (or three) are packed into the film. B&W; 70m. **DIR:** John English. **CAST:** Gene Autry, Gail Davis, Harry Shannon, Jock Mahoney. **1950**

COWARD OF THE COUNTY ★★★ This made-for-TV film is based on Kenny Rogers's hit song. He plays a World War II Georgia preacher with a pacifist nephew.

When the nephew's girlfriend is raped, he's put to the ultimate test of his nonviolent beliefs. The acting and setting are believable, making this a film worth viewing. 110m. **DIR:** Dick Lowry. **CAST:** Kenny Rogers, Fredric Lehne, Largo Woodruff, Mariclare Costello, Ana Alicia. **1981**

COWBOY AND THE BALLERINA, THE ★★ This telemovie is romance at its most basic. Lee Majors plays a former world-champion rodeo rider who meets a Russian ballerina (Leslie Wing) who is attempting to defect. Corny but adequate time passer. 100m. **DIR:** Jerry Jameson. **CAST:** Lee Majors, Leslie Wing, Christopher Lloyd, Anjelica Huston. **1984**

COWBOY AND THE LADY, THE ★★ Offbeat casting did not help in this slow comedy about a city girl who falls for a rodeo star. The Oscar-nominated title song is by Lionel Newman and Arthur Quenzer. B&W; 91m. **DIR:** H. C. Potter. **CAST:** Gary Cooper, Merle Oberon, Walter Brennan, Patsy Kelly, Harry Davenport. **1938**

COWBOY MILLIONAIRE ★★★ The accent is on humor in this series Western, which has two-fisted George O'Brien and sidekick Edgar Kennedy acting as "colorful cowboy types" at a hotel out west. It's just a way to raise money to finance their mining operation. B&W; 65m. **DIR:** Eddie Cline. **CAST:** George O'Brien, Edgar Kennedy. **1935**

COWBOY WAY, THE ★★★ Two New Mexico rodeo ropers—one a keeper of near civility, the other part crude clown and part prairie Peter Pan—put their personal feud aside while rescuing a friend's Cuban daughter from New York City immigrant smugglers. This comic if unenlightened fish-out-of-water story about squabbling saddle rats who kiss and make up and help someone out along the way has a rousing finale. Rated PG-13 for language and violence. 102m. **DIR:** Gregg Champion. **CAST:** Kiefer Sutherland, Woody Harrelson, Cara Buono, Dylan McDermott, Ernie Hudson. **1994 DVD**

COWBOYS, THE ★★★★1/2 Along with Don Siegel's *The Shootist*, this is the best of John Wayne's latter-day Westerns. The Duke plays a rancher whose wranglers get gold fever. He's forced to recruit a bunch of green kids in order to take his cattle to market. Bruce Dern is on hand as the outlaw leader who fights our hero in one of the genre's most memorable (and violent) scenes. Rated PG. 128m. **DIR:** Mark Rydell. **CAST:** John Wayne, Roscoe Lee Browne, Bruce Dern, Colleen Dewhurst, Slim Pickens. **1972 DVD**

COYOTE UGLY ★★★ Surprisingly decent melodrama about a small-town girl (Piper Perabo) who hits the Big Apple with her dream of becoming a successful songwriter. Finding romance with Adam Garcia, she is reduced to working in a sleazy bar. Although the hype for this flick focused on the outrageous antics of the sexy female bartenders, it, fortunately for viewers, was misleading. Rated PG-13 for language, sexual innuendo, and erotic dancing. 100m. **DIR:** David McNally. **CAST:** Piper Perabo, Adam Garcia, John Goodman, Maria Bello. **2000 DVD**

CRACK HOUSE ★★ Okay exploitation film about the tragic world of crack cocaine. Two young lovers from the barrio are swept into the nightmare when the boyfriend avenges the murder of his cousin by a rival gang. Rated R for nudity, violence, and profanity. 97m. **DIR:** Michael Fischa. **CAST:** Richard Roundtree, Jim Brown, Anthony Geary. **1990**

CRACK-UP ★★1/2 Cast against type, Pat O'Brien does a commendable job portraying an art critic investigating a forgery ring in this taut low-budget suspense-thriller. B&W; 93m. **DIR:** Irving Reis. **CAST:** Pat O'Brien, Claire Trevor, Herbert Marshall. **1946**

CRACKER (TV SERIES) ★★★★★ In this British crime series, Robbie Coltrane is dazzling as Fitz, a forensic psychologist blessed with shrewd insight and the ability to think just like the sickos in these grim stories. Fitz is far from admirable; he smokes, drinks, and gambles too much, pays scant attention to his wife and children, and lacks the diplomacy to suffer fools gladly. But his talent is impossible to ignore. Not rated, but equivalent to PG-13 for violence, explicit dialogue, and strong sexual content. 135m. **DIR:** Roy Battersby. **CAST:** Robbie Coltrane, Barbara Flynn, Geraldine Somerville. **1993–95**

CRACKER FACTORY ★★★★ This made-for-TV drama features Natalie Wood as Cassie Barrett, an alcoholic housewife who loses her grip on reality. Her long-suffering husband, Charlie (Peter Haskell), silently offers support while she spends her rehabilitation in the Cracker Factory, a mental institution. Not rated, but the mature topic warrants parental discretion. 95m. **DIR:** Burt Brinckerhoff. **CAST:** Natalie Wood, Peter Haskell, Shelley Long, Vivian Blaine, Perry King. **1979**

CRACKERJACK ★★★ This *Die Hard*-in-a-mountain-chalet would be even better if star Thomas Ian Griffith were a better actor; his reactions of surprised horror cannot be distinguished from his lady-killing smiles. He's a suicidal cop still grieving over the loss of his family, who gets a chance at atonement when deranged neo-Nazi Christopher Plummer attacks an ice-bound resort filled with guests . . . including our hero's brother. Rated R for violence, profanity, and nudity. 96m. **DIR:** Michael Mazo. **CAST:** Thomas Ian Griffith, George Touliatos, Lisa Bunting, Nastassja Kinski, Christopher Plummer. **1994**

CRACKERS A bunch of down-and-out San Franciscans decide to turn to crime in order to survive. Rated PG. 92m. **DIR:** Louis Malle. **CAST:** Donald Sutherland, Jack Warden, Sean Penn, Wallace Shawn. **1984**

CRACKING UP No laughs here. Rated R. 83m. **DIR:** Jerry Lewis. **CAST:** Jerry Lewis, Herb Edelman, Zane Buzby, Dick Butkus, Milton Berle. **1983**

CRADLE WILL FALL, THE ★★ This made-for-television suspense movie falls flat. Lauren Hutton is an attorney who gets entangled with a doctor (Ben Murphy). Along comes another doctor—straight out of Dachau, one would think—who turns things upside down. The story is silly and the direction uninspired. 100m. **DIR:** John Llewellyn Moxey. **CAST:** Lauren Hutton, Ben Murphy, James Farentino, Charlita Bauer, Carolyn Ann Clark. **1983**

CRADLE WILL ROCK ★★★★ This ambitious, fact-based ensemble drama is set during the Depression, when a rather unique blend of desperation and innovation prompted yet another clash between art and politics. The U.S. government's Federal Theatre Project, designed to lift national spirits by bringing low-cost theater to millions of Americans, is "co-opted" by composer-playwright Marc Blitzstein and the flamboyant

Orson Welles, who hope to produce a play revolving around the rise of unions in response to onerous working conditions. Much of writer-director Tim Robbins's film, a captivating brew of fact and fancy, is advocacy filmmaking in the same manner that the original *Cradle Will Rock* was advocacy theater. The result is energetic, important, and fun to watch. Rated R for profanity, nudity, and sexual content. 132m. **DIR:** Tim Robbins. **CAST:** Hank Azaria, Rubén Blades, Joan Cusack, John Cusack, Cary Elwes, Cherry Jones, Angus MacFadyen, Bill Murray, Vanessa Redgrave, Susan Sarandon, John Turturro, Emily Watson. **1999 DVD**

CRAFT, THE ★★ Four high-school misfits form a coven of witches and cast black-magic spells on their tormenting peers. A promisingly mischievous idea and good leading performances are frittered away in a standard special-effects marathon. There are a few good, creepy moments, but the story doesn't hold together from scene to scene. Rated R for profanity and violence. 100m. **DIR:** Andrew Fleming. **CAST:** Robin Tunney, Fairuza Balk, Neve Campbell, Rachel True, Skeet Ulrich. **1996 DVD**

CRAIG'S WIFE ★★★ In her first film success, Rosalind Russell is brilliant as Harriet Craig, the wife of the title, a heartless domestic tyrant whose neurotic preference for material concerns over human feelings alienates all around her. John Boles is her long-suffering, slow-to-see-the-light husband. B&W; 75m. **DIR:** Dorothy Arzner. **CAST:** Rosalind Russell, John Boles, Billie Burke, Jane Darwell, Thomas Mitchell, Alma Kruger. **1936**

CRANES ARE FLYING, THE ★★★★ During World War II, a young woman is so shattered at the news of her lover's death that she agrees to marry a man she doesn't care for. Sublime, moving, and beautifully filmed, this little gem was named Best Film at Cannes. In Russian with English subtitles. B&W; 94m. **DIR:** Mikhail K. Kalatozov. **CAST:** Tatyana Samoilova, Alexei Batalov. **1957 DVD**

CRASH! (1977) 🦃 Made quickly to cash in on the big-budget *The Car*, released the same year, this low-budget film will leave the viewer dozing. Rated PG for violence. 85m. **DIR:** Charles Band. **CAST:** José Ferrer, Sue Lyons, John Carradine. **1977**

CRASH (1996) ★★1/2 After a near-fatal auto accident, a film producer is drawn into a shadowy cult of people who are turned on by vehicular mayhem. Based on J. G. Ballard's 1973 novel, the film is neither credible nor involving, as no link exists between sex and car crashes, and the characters' emotionally sterile lives are tiresome to watch. Rated NC-17 for profanity, nudity, and graphic simulated sex. 98m. **DIR:** David Cronenberg. **CAST:** James Spader, Holly Hunter, Deborah Unger, Elias Koteas, Rosanna Arquette. **1996 DVD**

CRASH AND BURN ★★1/2 Futuristic tale of a rebel television station infiltrated by an android from the corporation that now runs the world. Fast-paced, with above-par special effects, this film is directed with uncommon grace by B-movie king Charles Band. Rated R for violence and profanity. 85m. **DIR:** Charles Band. **CAST:** Paul Ganus, Megan Ward, Ralph Waite. **1990 DVD**

CRASH DIVE ★★ An American nuclear submarine becomes the staging ground for suspense when terrorists invade, holding the crew hostage and threatening to blow up Washington, D.C. Standard action fare held back by low budget and lackluster direction. Rated R for language and violence. 90m. **DIR:** Andrew Stevens. **CAST:** Michael Dudikoff, Frederic Forrest, Jay Acovone. **1996**

CRASH OF FLIGHT 401 ★★ Based on fact, this made-for-television movie tells the story of the disastrous airliner crash in the Florida Everglades in December of 1972 and the eventful rescue of seventy-three survivors. Routine. 100m. **DIR:** Barry Shear. **CAST:** William Shatner, Eddie Albert, Adrienne Barbeau. **1978**

CRASHOUT ★★1/2 Okay story about the odyssey of six convicts who crash out of prison. Unfortunately, the fine character development is hurt by a sometimes static plot and disappointing climax. William Bendix, however, is wonderfully unsympathetic as the self-serving ringleader. B&W; 82m. **DIR:** Lewis R. Foster. **CAST:** William Bendix, Arthur Kennedy, Luther Adler, William Talman, Marshall Thompson. **1955**

CRATER LAKE MONSTER, THE 🦃 Inexpensive, unimpressive film about a prehistoric creature emerging from the usually quiet lake of the title and raising hell. Rated PG. 89m. **DIR:** William R. Stromberg. **CAST:** Richard Cardella, Glenn Roberts. **1977 DVD**

CRAVING, THE 🦃 A witch burned at the stake hundreds of years ago comes back to life and resurrects her werewolf henchman to do her dirty work. Rated R for violence and nudity. 93m. **DIR:** Jack Molina. **CAST:** Paul Naschy. **1980**

CRAWLERS 🦃 Dreadful, low-budget effort. Tree roots exposed to toxic chemicals change into vicious vines. Rated R for sex, violence, and language. 94m. **DIR:** Martin Newlin. **CAST:** Jason Saucier, Mary Sellers. **1993**

CRAWLING EYE, THE ★★★ Acceptable horror-thriller about an unseen menace hiding within the dense fog surrounding a mountaintop. A nice sense of doom builds throughout, and the monster remains unseen (always the best way) until the very end. B&W; 85m. **DIR:** Quentin Lawrence. **CAST:** Forrest Tucker, Janet Munro. **1958 DVD**

CRAWLING HAND, THE 🦃 Low-budget tale of a dismembered hand at large in a small town. B&W; 89m. **DIR:** Herbert L. Strock. **CAST:** Peter Breck, Rod Lauren, Kent Taylor. **1963 DVD**

CRAWLSPACE 🦃 Terrible imitation of the classic *Peeping Tom*, with Klaus Kinski as a sadistic landlord who engages in murder and voyeurism. Rated R. 82m. **DIR:** David Schmoeller. **CAST:** Klaus Kinski, Talia Balsam. **1986**

CRAZED 🦃 A demented man living in a boardinghouse becomes obsessed with a young woman. Not rated; contains violence and profanity. 88m. **DIR:** Richard Cassidy. **CAST:** Laslo Papas, Belle Mitchell, Beverly Ross. **1984**

CRAZIES, THE ★★ A military plane carrying an experimental germ warfare virus crashes near a small midwestern town, releasing a plague of murderous madness. George Romero attempts to make a statement about martial law while trying to capitalize on the success of his cult classic, *Night of the Living Dead*. Rated R. 103m. **DIR:** George A. Romero. **CAST:** Lane Carroll, W. G. McMillan, Lynn Lowry, Richard Liberty. **1975**

•**CRAZY/BEAUTIFUL** ★★★1/2 Well-constructed and credibly played characters fuel this high-school romance, which involves a scholastically dedicated Latino guy (Jay Hernandez) who loses his academic focus after falling in love with the deeply troubled WASP daughter (Kirsten Dunst) of a wealthy congressman. What begins as a lark quickly turns serious, as both characters discover how difficult it is to inhabit each other's worlds. The fairy tale conclusion is a bit too pat, but the two leads generate a lot of goodwill along the way. Rated PG-13 for profanity, drug and alcohol use, and sexual content. 95m. **DIR:** John Stockwell. **CAST:** Kirsten Dunst, Jay Hernandez, Bruce Davison, Taryn Manning, Lucinda Jenney. **2001 DVD**

CRAZY FOR LOVE ★★1/2 Village-idiot Bourvil will come into an inheritance, but only if he can finish his grade-school education. Naturally, other family members try to ensure that he will fail. Innocuous slapstick comedy with Brigitte Bardot, in her first film, giving no indication of being a star in the making. In French with English subtitles. B&W; 80m. **DIR:** Jean Boyer. **CAST:** Bourvil, Jane Marken, Brigitte Bardot. **1953**

CRAZY FROM THE HEART ★★★ Made-for-cable comedy-drama looks at the relationship between a Texas high school principal and a Mexican janitor. As they become more fond of each other, the pressures of an interracial affair come to bear. A little sugary at times, but still manages to keep focused on the main issues. 96m. **DIR:** Thomas Schlamme. **CAST:** Christine Lahti, Rubén Blades, William Russ, Louise Latham, Mary Kay Place, Tommy Muniz. **1991**

CRAZY HORSE ★★★1/2 Fine Turner Network production chronicles the rise and fall of the Lakota warrior renowned for taking down Custer. Among the Indians, he had a humble start, and his greatest battles would be waged within his tribe in the name of love and loyalty. Throughout the film there are dreamlike sequences in which Crazy Horse is channeled advice from a murdered chief. Michael Greyeyes is very believable as the legendary hero. Not rated; contains nudity and violence. 90m. **DIR:** John Irvin. **CAST:** Michael Greyeyes, Irene Bedard, Lorne Cardinal, John Finn. **1996**

CRAZY IN ALABAMA ★★★1/2 Small-town southern housewife kills her husband, leaves her seven kids with relatives and lugs her husband's head to Hollywood in a hatbox in this bizarre, comic tale about racism, freedom, spousal abuse, and personal growth. The lady becomes an actress while back home her 13-year-old nephew is engulfed by a civil rights storm stirred up by the local sheriff. The film's infectious passion offsets a muddled start and several plot spasms. Rated PG-13 for violence, language, and sensuality. 104m. **DIR:** Antonio Banderas. **CAST:** Melanie Griffith, Lucas Black, Meat Loaf Aday, David Morse, Cathy Moriarty. **1999 DVD**

CRAZY IN LOVE ★★★ Holly Hunter shares an island home with her mother and grandmother, whose bitter experiences with men may be a bad influence on Hunter's marriage. Minor but enjoyable romantic drama. Not rated; contains no objectionable material. 93m. **DIR:** Martha Coolidge. **CAST:** Holly Hunter, Gena Rowlands, Bill Pullman, Julian Sands, Herta Ware, Frances McDormand. **1992**

CRAZY MAMA ★★★ Vibrant film blends crime, comedy, and finely drawn characterizations in this story of three women on a crime spree from California to Arkansas and their experiences with the various men they pick up along the way. Successful mixture of music and atmosphere of the 1950s, coupled with a 1970s attitude, makes this an enjoyable film. Rated PG. 82m. **DIR:** Jonathan Demme. **CAST:** Stuart Whitman, Cloris Leachman, Ann Sothern, Jim Backus. **1975**

CRAZY MOON ★★ This is another entry in the *Harold and Maude* genre: neurotic, alienated young man gets his act together when he falls in love with a spunky disabled woman who is managing to cope with real problems. Rated PG-13. 89m. **DIR:** Allan Eastman. **CAST:** Kiefer Sutherland, Vanessa Vaughan. **1986**

CRAZY PEOPLE ★★★1/2 Dudley Moore is an ad writer who grows weary of lying to people. His "honest" ad campaigns get him confined to a mental institution. Pure formula, but the ads are often hilarious. Rated R for profanity and scatological humor. 91m. **DIR:** Tony Bill. **CAST:** Dudley Moore, Daryl Hannah, Paul Reiser, J. T. Walsh. **1990**

CRAZY RAY, THE ★★★1/2 René Clair's classic fantasy about a scientist's paralyzing ray is basically an experimental film. A handful of people who have not been affected by the ray take advantage of the situation and help themselves to whatever they want but eventually begin to fight among themselves. B&W; 60m. **DIR:** René Clair. **CAST:** Henri Rollan, Madeline Rodrigue, Albert Préjean. **1923**

CRAZYSITTER, THE ★★ Very dark premise, of an ex-con turned nanny (Beverly D'Angelo) who tries to sell her spoiled charges, is a comic hard sell. The obnoxious children choose the broken-down D'Angelo when their self-centered parents finally decide to hire a disciplinarian. Few light moments. Whimsical musical intro by David and Eric Wurst promises more than the film delivers. Rated PG-13 for profanity and criminal activity. 92m. **DIR:** Michael James McDonald. **CAST:** Beverly D'Angelo, Brady Bluhm, Rachel Duncan, Ed Begley Jr., Carol Kane. **1994 DVD**

CREATION OF THE HUMANOIDS ★★ In this futuristic parable, Don Megowan plays a cop who is paranoid about the development of near-perfect androids. This low-budget vision of the future is long on talk, short on action, and hard to take seriously. 75m. **DIR:** Wesley E. Barry. **CAST:** Don Megowan. **1962**

CREATOR ★★ This film, about a scientist (Peter O'Toole) who is attempting to bring back to life the wife who died thirty years before, during childbirth, is, at first, a very witty and occasionally heart-tugging comedy. However, in its last third, it turns into a sort of second-rate tearjerker. Rated R for nudity, profanity, and simulated sex. 108m. **DIR:** Ivan Passer. **CAST:** Peter O'Toole, Mariel Hemingway, Vincent Spano, Virginia Madsen, David Ogden Stiers, John Dehner. **1985 DVD**

CREATURE FROM BLACK LAKE ★★ This is another forgettable, cliché-ridden horror film. Dennis Fimple and John David Carson play two college students who go to the swamps of Louisiana in search of the missing link. Through the reluctant help of the locals, they come face-to-face with a man in an ape suit. Rated PG. 97m. **DIR:** Joy N. Houck Jr. **CAST:** Jack Elam, Dub Taylor, Dennis Fimple, John David Carson. **1979**

CREATURE FROM THE BLACK LAGOON ★★★1/2 In the remote backwaters of the Amazon, members of a scientific expedition run afoul of a vicious prehistoric man-fish inhabiting the area and are forced to fight for their lives. Excellent film (first in a trilogy) features true-to-life performances, a bone-chilling score by Joseph Gershenson, and beautiful, lush photography that unfortunately turns to mud in the murky 3-D video print. 79m. **DIR:** Jack Arnold. **CAST:** Richard Carlson, Julie Adams, Richard Denning, Nestor Paiva, Antonio Moreno, Whit Bissell. **1954 DVD**

CREATURE FROM THE HAUNTED SEA, THE 🦃 A muddled horror-comedy about a Bogart-type crook planning to steal a treasure with the help of a mythical sea monster. B&W; 60m. **DIR:** Roger Corman. **CAST:** Anthony Carbone, Betsy Jones-Moreland. **1960**

CREATURE WALKS AMONG US, THE ★★1/2 Surprisingly imaginative, intermittently scary second sequel to *Creature from the Black Lagoon* shows what would happen if the Amazon gill man were surgically altered to enable him to breathe on land. For once, the lengthy passages between monster attacks aren't boring. B&W; 78m. **DIR:** John Sherwood. **CAST:** Jeff Morrow, Rex Reason, Leigh Snowden. **1956**

CREATURES THE WORLD FORGOT 🦃 Migrating cavemen battle for superiority of the tribe. Rated PG, but contains some nudity. 95m. **DIR:** Don Chaffey. **CAST:** Julie Ege, Tony Bonner. **1970**

CREEPER, THE ★★ A feline phobia almost sends the daughter of a research scientist clawing up the walls. Dad's conducting experiments on cats—that's right, cats—for a mysterious miracle serum. Silly. 64m. **DIR:** Jean Yarbrough. **CAST:** Onslow Stevens, Eduardo Ciannelli. **1948**

CREEPERS ★★ Plodding Italian production casts Jennifer Connelly as a young girl with the ability to communicate with, and control, insects. She must use her little friends to track down the maniac who's been murdering students at the Swiss girls' school she's attending. Rated R for gore. 82m. **DIR:** Dario Argento. **CAST:** Jennifer Connelly, Donald Pleasence, Daria Nicolodi, Dalila Di Lazzaro. **1985**

CREEPING FLESH, THE ★★★ Peter Cushing and Christopher Lee are top-notch in this creepy tale about an evil entity accidentally brought back to life by an unsuspecting scientist. While not as good as the stars' Hammer Films collaborations this will still prove pleasing to their fans. Rated PG. 91m. **DIR:** Freddie Francis. **CAST:** Peter Cushing, Christopher Lee, Lorna Heilbron. **1972**

CREEPING TERROR, THE ★★ A so-bad-it's-good classic. Lake Tahoe is terrorized by a pair of outer-space monsters, played by extras dressed in old carpets. One of the cheapest movies you'd ever want to see. B&W; 75m. **DIR:** Art J. Nelson. **CAST:** Vic Savage, Shannon O'Neill. **1964**

CREEPOZOIDS 🦃 A post-apocalyptic sci-fi–horror yarn about military deserters who find an abandoned science lab that has a bloodthirsty monster wandering in the halls. Rated R for violence, nudity, and profanity. 72m. **DIR:** David DeCoteau. **CAST:** Linnea Quigley, Ken Abraham. **1987**

CREEPS, THE ★★★ A mad scientist finds a way to bring back to life the fictional creatures Dracula, Frankenstein's monster, the wolfman, and the mummy. Trouble is, his process didn't work properly, and they're all only three feet tall. That ridiculous premise actually makes for a fairly amusing horror spoof, although non-horror buffs probably will miss the in-jokes that fuel this made-for-video flick. Rated R for violence and nudity. 80m. **DIR:** Charles Band. **CAST:** Rhonda Griffin, Justin Lauer, Phil Fondacaro, Bill Moynihan. **1997 DVD**

CREEPSHOW ★★★★ Stephen King, the modern master of printed terror, and George Romero, the director who frightened unsuspecting moviegoers out of their wits with *Night of the Living Dead*, teamed for this funny and scary tribute to the E.C. horror comics of the 1950s. Like *Vault of Horror* and *Tales from the Crypt*, two titles from that period, it's an anthology of ghoulish bedtime stories. Rated R for profanity and gore. 120m. **DIR:** George A. Romero. **CAST:** Hal Holbrook, Adrienne Barbeau, Fritz Weaver, Leslie Nielsen, Stephen King. **1982 DVD**

CREEPSHOW 2 ★★ Three tales of horror and terror based on short stories by Stephen King and a screenplay by George Romero should have turned out a lot better than this. "Ol' Chief Wooden Head" stars George Kennedy and Dorothy Lamour as senior citizens in a slowly dying desert town. "The Raft" concerns four friends whose vacation at a secluded lake turns into a nightmare. "The Hitchhiker" features Lois Chiles as a hit-and-run driver. Rated R for nudity, violence, and profanity. 92m. **DIR:** Michael Gornick. **CAST:** Lois Chiles, George Kennedy, Dorothy Lamour. **1987**

CREMATORS, THE 🦃 Semipro effort by the coscenarist for *It Came from Outer Space*, with a nearly identical premise. Not rated. 90m. **DIR:** Harry Essex. **CAST:** Maria Di Aragon, Marvin Howard. **1972 DVD**

CREW, THE (1994) ★★★★ Five people on a weekend cruise stop to rescue a couple on a burning boat, only to find themselves tossed into a sexual soup peppered with cattiness and pop psychology. Not the *Dead Calm* rip-off you'd expect. In fact, surprises float from all directions in this outrageous little flick. Unfortunately, you have to close your eyes to a major plot hole that keeps this bunch together—but it's a forgivable sin. Rated R for profanity and violence. 99m. **DIR:** Carl Colpaert. **CAST:** Viggo Mortensen, Donal Logue, Jeremy Sisto, Pamela Gidley, Laura Del Sol, John Philbin, Sam Jenkins. **1994**

CREW, THE (2000) ★★★1/2 Although it's cleverly written and well-acted, this is the kind of movie that critics don't seem to like. A quartet of over-the-hill gangsters revert to their old ways in order to save their Florida retirement home from developers. A kind of melding of *The Godfather* and *Grumpy Old Men*. Just sit back and enjoy. Rated PG-13 for suggested sex, violence, and profanity. 87m. **DIR:** Michael Dinner. **CAST:** Richard Dreyfuss, Burt Reynolds, Dan Hedaya, Seymour Cassel, Carrie-Anne Moss, Jennifer Tilly, Lainie Kazan, Miguel Sandoval, Jeremy Piven, Casey Siemaszko. **2000 DVD**

¡CRIA! ★★★★ In this haunting and sometimes surreal film, a 9 year old girl is obsessed with her mother's death. She blames her father, and then feels responsible when he dies as well. Psychological depth and a mesmerizing performance from young Ana Torrent save the melodramatic story. In Spanish with English subtitles. 115m. **DIR:** Carlos Saura. **CAST:** Ana Torrent, Geraldine Chaplin. **1975**

CRICKET, THE ★★★1/2 A roadside café is the setting for this James M. Cain–like triangle involving an older woman, her new husband, and the woman's grown daughter. Although marketed as a steamy sex drama, it's considerably better than that, thanks to fine performances and probing direction by Alberto Lattuada. In Italian with English subtitles. Not rated; contains nudity and violence. 130m. **DIR:** Alberto Lattuada. **CAST:** Anthony Franciosa, Clio Goldsmith. **1982**

CRIER, THE ★★1/2 There's a bit of *The Evil Dead* in this film based on the Mexican legend of La Lloroña, a woman who cries over the loss of her children. First-time director Glynn Beard focuses on the chills and puts makeup effects to good use at key moments. Rated R for violence and profanity. 82m. **DIR:** Glynn Beard. **CAST:** Glynn Beard, Margaret Erin-Easley, Lorena Gutierrez. **1995**

CRIES AND WHISPERS ★★★★★ Directed and written by Ingmar Bergman and hauntingly photographed by Sven Nykvist, this Swedish-language film tells a story of a dying woman, her two sisters, and a servant girl. Faultless performances make this an unforgettable film experience. Rated R. 106m. **DIR:** Ingmar Bergman. **CAST:** Harriet Andersson, Liv Ullmann, Ingrid Thulin, Kari Sylwan. **1972 DVD**

CRIES OF SILENCE ★★ Somber tale of a 15 year old girl who is discovered in the marshes of Mississippi after a devastating hurricane in 1969. It's up to a kindly doctor to break the girl's silence and discover her dark secret. This tale of child abuse is too heavy-handed to be effective. Not rated. 109m. **DIR:** Avery Crounse. **CAST:** Kathleen York, Karen Black, Ed Nelson, Erin Buchanan. **1996**

CRIME & PASSION ★★ A weak comedy of sex and money that gives us Omar Sharif as a rich businessman who becomes sexually aroused when bad things happen to him. Karen Black provides some moments of zing with her particular brand of oddness. Her seduction of Joseph Bottoms is a classic. Weird and wild. Rated R. 92m. **DIR:** Ivan Passer. **CAST:** Omar Sharif, Karen Black, Joseph Bottoms, Bernhard Wicki. **1975 DVD**

CRIME AND PUNISHMENT (1935) ★★★★ The most faithful film version of the Dostoyevski novel, this film makes good use of atmospheric lighting, dramatic shadows, and eerie mood music. Peter Lorre stars as Raskolnikov, a mild-mannered man who unwittingly becomes a murderer. He successfully escapes the police, but his conscience takes over. Thought-provoking as well as entertaining. B&W; 88m. **DIR:** Josef von Sternberg. **CAST:** Peter Lorre, Edward Arnold, Marian Marsh, Elisabeth Risdon, Mrs. Patrick Campbell. **1935**

CRIME AND PUNISHMENT (1935) ★★★★ Excellent screen adaptation of Dostoyevski's complex, brooding novel. Director Pierre Chenal's poetic, surreal touch adds to the climate of dark realism in this tragedy about a murderer who struggles with his conscience after commiting a brutal, senseless crime. In French with English subtitles. B&W; 110m. **DIR:** Pierre Chenal. **CAST:** Harry Baur, Pierre Blanchar. **1935**

CRIME AND PUNISHMENT (1970) ★★★★ Another fine adaptation of Dostoyevski's story about an impoverished student living in squalor in a rooming house and murdering an old pawnbroker. Solid performances and a fine script. In Russian with English subtitles. B&W; 220m. **DIR:** Lev Kulijanov. **CAST:** Georgi Taratorkin. **1970**

CRIME AND PUNISHMENT (1998) ★★★★ Smashing adaptation of Dostoyevski's classic novel, featuring Patrick Dempsey as intellectual Rodya Raskolnikov, whose decision to kill a pawnbroker in order to save his sister from prostitution leads him down a dark path of guilt and torment. Ben Kingsley costars as the police chief who knows the truth, but must rely on Raskolnikov's guilt to bring it to the surface. The film, shot in Poland, looks authentic and beautiful. The honest and faithful script depicts the harsh realities of a class system. Made for television. Rated PG-13. 120m. **DIR:** Joseph Sargent. **CAST:** Patrick Dempsey, Ben Kingsley, Julie Delpy, Eddie Marsan. **1998**

CRIME & PUNISHMENT IN SUBURBIA ★★★1/2 Interesting take on the Dostoyevski tale about murder and guilt, played out on a youth-friendly battlefield. Rosanne is a popular high-school cheerleader who dates the quarterback and is the envy of her classmates, but her home life is another story. Her mother is having an affair, and her stepfather is a drunk. Rosanne's attempt to kill her abusive stepfather goes awry when her mother is arrested for the murder. Three people know the truth, but are any of them adult enough to come forward? There's lots of emotional ping-pong in the script, while the actors keep things real. Rated R for adult situations, language, and violence. 93m. **DIR:** Rob Schmidt. **CAST:** Monica Keena, Vincent Kartheiser, Jeffrey Wright, Michael Ironside, Ellen Barkin. **2000 DVD**

CRIME KILLER, THE A confusing plot has a no-nonsense cop getting suspended, teaming up with two of his ex–Vietnam buddies, and smashing a guns-and-airplane deal with an Arab connection. Insipid. Not rated. 90m. **DIR:** George Pan-Andreas. **CAST:** George Pan-Andreas, Leo Morrell, Athan Karras. **1985**

CRIME LORDS ★★ Wayne Crawford directs and stars in this cop-buddy drama that originates in Los Angeles and ends on the streets of Hong Kong. Both story and stars are predictable. Rated R for violence. 96m. **DIR:** Wayne Crawford. **CAST:** Wayne Crawford, Martin Hewitt. **1990**

CRIME OF DR. CRESPI, THE ★★ Moody poverty-row item whose main distinction is its casting, principally Erich Von Stroheim as a vengeful surgeon. B&W; 63m. **DIR:** John H. Auer. **CAST:** Erich Von Stroheim, Dwight Frye, Paul Guilfoyle. **1935**

CRIME OF MONSIEUR LANGE, THE ★★★★ Jean Renoir's compelling masterpiece sprang from the director's belief that the common man, by united action, could overcome tyranny. When the head of a printing press disappears with all of the firm's funds, the employees band together and raise enough money to go into business as a publisher of popular novelettes. In French with English subtitles. B&W; 90m. **DIR:** Jean Renoir. **CAST:** René Lefévre, Jules Berry. **1935**

CRIME OF PASSION ★★1/2 The story of a tough newspaperwoman who will do anything to hold onto her man is a good showcase for Barbara Stanwyck. But it's a contrived and predictable movie, the type she made many times during her long career. The film has more suggestive scenes than usual for its era. B&W; 85m. **DIR:** Gerd

Oswald. **CAST:** Barbara Stanwyck, Sterling Hayden, Raymond Burr, Fay Wray, Royal Dano, Stuart Whitman. **1957**

CRIME OF THE CENTURY ★★★★ This HBO original explores the 1932 Lindbergh baby kidnapping and murder. Stephen Rea stars as Bruno Richard Hauptmann, the illegal immigrant scapegoated for the heinous crime that shocked the entire nation. Scripter William Nicholson makes it clear that Hauptmann had some peripheral involvement to the case . . . but was nowhere near the mastermind painted by impatient police officers pressured for results. Rated PG for dramatic intensity. 120m. **DIR:** Mark Rydell. **CAST:** Stephen Rea, Isabella Rossellini, J. T. Walsh, Michael Moriarty, Allen Garfield, John Harkins, Barry Primus, David Paymer. **1996**

CRIME STORY ★★★ Something more serious from action star Jackie Chan, who this time plays a detective investigating a kidnapping while wrestling with police corruption. While Chan gets to display his trademark stunt work, this film is darker and more complicated than his other outings. Rated R for violence. 104m. **DIR:** Che-Kirk Wong. **CAST:** Jackie Chan, Kent Chang, Law Kang, Ken Lo, Christine Ng. **1993 DVD**

CRIME ZONE 🦃 A young couple struggles to escape a futuristic society turned police state. Rated R for nudity and profanity. 96m. **DIR:** Luis Llosa. **CAST:** David Carradine, Peter Nelson, Sherilyn Fenn. **1988**

CRIMEBROKER ★★1/2 Jacqueline Bisset stars as a judge by day—bank robber by night—in this entertaining but absurd thriller. Rated R for nudity and violence. 93m. **DIR:** Ian Barry. **CAST:** Jacqueline Bisset, Masaya Kato, Gary Day, John Bach. **1993**

CRIMES AND MISDEMEANORS ★★★★★ Martin Landau plays a successful doctor who attempts to end a foolish affair. However, his emotionally unstable mistress refuses to let him go. On the periphery are Woody Allen's antics as a documentary filmmaker hired by his egotistical brother-in-law to make a movie about the latter's career as a TV sitcom king. Rated PG-13 for adult themes. 104m. **DIR:** Woody Allen. **CAST:** Martin Landau, Woody Allen, Alan Alda, Mia Farrow, Anjelica Huston, Jerry Orbach, Sam Waterston. **1989 DVD**

CRIMES AT THE DARK HOUSE ★★ Wilkie Collins's *The Woman in White* served as the source material for this typically florid, over-the-top outing for Britain's Tod Slaughter, the king of eye-rolling camp. B&W; 61m. **DIR:** George King. **CAST:** Tod Slaughter. **1940**

CRIMES OF PASSION 🦃 By day she's a highly paid fashion designer; by night, she's a kinky high-priced hooker. Rated R for nudity, suggested sex, profanity, and violence. 107m. **DIR:** Ken Russell. **CAST:** Kathleen Turner, Anthony Perkins, John Laughlin. **1984 DVD**

CRIMES OF STEPHEN HAWKE, THE ★★ The cast is a bit better than usual for this, one of Tod Slaughter's early outings, in which a serial killer and a charitable moneylender share a deadly secret. But Slaughter's grandiosely overdone style is, as ever, an acquired taste. B&W; 65m. **DIR:** George King. **CAST:** Tod Slaughter, Marjorie Taylor, Eric Portman. **1936**

CRIMES OF THE HEART ★★★★1/2 In this superb screen adaptation of Beth Henley's Pulitzer Prize–winning play, Diane Keaton, Jessica Lange, and Sissy Spacek star as three eccentric sisters who stick together despite an onslaught of extraordinary problems. It is a film of many joys. Not the least of which are the performances of the stars, fine bits by Sam Shepard and Tess Harper in support, the biting humor, and the overall intelligence. Rated PG-13 for subject matter. 105m. **DIR:** Bruce Beresford. **CAST:** Diane Keaton, Jessica Lange, Sissy Spacek, Sam Shepard, Tess Harper, David Carpenter, Hurd Hatfield. **1986**

CRIMETIME ★★★ The fine line between reality and fantasy begins to blur for Bobby, an actor who portrays a serial killer on a television show that re-creates true crimes. As the bodies add up, so do the ratings. When the killer stops, Bobby is out of a job. The two meet and produce a solution that guarantees them both work. Rated R for adult situations, language, nudity, and violence. 95m. **DIR:** George Sluizer. **CAST:** Stephen Baldwin, Pete Postlethwaite, Geraldine Chaplin, Karen Black, Sadie Frost. **1997**

CRIMEWAVE ★★★ Hired assassins try to silence a housewife in this hyperkinetic slapstick comedy. Too scattered to be satisfying (and too low-budget for its ambition), it nevertheless has many inventive and hilarious moments. Cowritten by Sam Raimi and Joel and Ethan Coen. Rated PG-13 for violence. 83m. **DIR:** Sam Raimi. **CAST:** Louise Lasser, Brian James, Bruce Campbell. **1985**

CRIMINAL CODE, THE ★★★★ A powerful performance by Boris Karloff as a revenge-minded convict, elevates this Howard Hawks release from interesting to memorable. It's a lost classic that deserves its release on video. The story involves a district attorney (impressively played by Walter Huston) who overzealously pursues his job, with the result that an innocent man (Phillips Holmes) is sent to prison. B&W; 83m. **DIR:** Howard Hawks. **CAST:** Boris Karloff, Walter Huston, Phillips Holmes. **1931**

CRIMINAL HEARTS ★★ Low-rent road movie features Amy Locane as the jilted lover out to teach her ex-boyfriend a lesson when she picks up hitchhiker Kevin Dillon. It doesn't take long before these two are on the run from the cops and their pasts. Rated R for adult situations, language, and violence. 92m. **DIR:** David Payne. **CAST:** Kevin Dillon, Amy Locane, Morgan Fairchild, M. Emmet Walsh, Don Stroud. **1995**

CRIMINAL JUSTICE ★★ Writer-director Andy Wolk's disagreeably vague and stridently preachy telescript is partly salvaged by Forest Whitaker's masterful lead performance as a felon accused of robbing and knifing a young woman, whose veracity (as the only witness) is never sufficiently questioned. Not rated, but with considerable profanity. 90m. **DIR:** Andy Wolk. **CAST:** Forest Whitaker, Anthony LaPaglia, Rosie Perez, Jennifer Grey. **1990**

CRIMINAL LAW ★★1/2 Gary Oldman gives a strong performance in this suspense-thriller as an attorney who successfully defends accused killer Kevin Bacon. It is only after proving his client's innocence by discrediting eyewitnesses, that Oldman discovers Bacon is guilty—and intends to kill again. At first, the film bristles with tension and intelligence, yet it goes on to become predictable and ludicrous. Rated R for violence, simulated sex, and profanity. 112m. **DIR:** Martin Campbell. **CAST:** Gary Oldman, Kevin Bacon, Karen Young, Tess Harper, Joe Don Baker. **1989**

CRIMINAL LIFE OF ARCHIBALDO DE LA CRUZ, THE ★★★★ Luis Buñuel's violently erotic satire about a perverted young aristocrat who believes a music box he owned as a child has the power to kill. This surreal black comedy is an uncompromising attack on the social, religious, and political ramifications of contemporary society. A must-see! In Spanish with English subtitles. Not rated. B&W; 91m. **DIR:** Luis Buñuel. **CAST:** Ernesto Alonso, Miroslava Stern. **1955**

CRIMINAL MIND, THE ★★1/2 A decent cast saves this tired thriller about two brothers who wind up on opposite sides of the law—one becomes a district attorney, the other a mob member. When his brother is killed, the district attorney gets it from all sides, including the mob and the FBI. Rated R for violence, language, and sexuality. 93m. **DIR:** Joseph Vittorie. **CAST:** Ben Cross, Frank Rossi, Tahnee Welch, Lance Henriksen, Mark Davenport. **1993**

CRIMINAL PASSION ★★1/2 A homicide detective teams with her ex-lover to nab a senator's son suspected of being a serial killer. When privilege distances the suspect from the cops, she decides the only way to get her man is to go undercover and insinuate herself into his life. R-rated and unrated versions available; both contain nudity, adult situations, violence, and strong language. 96m. **DIR:** Donna Deitch. **CAST:** Joan Severance, Anthony Denison, Wolfgang Bodison, Henry Darrow, John Allen Nelson. **1994**

CRIMINALLY INSANE ★★ This debut outing for Priscilla Alden's obese psychopath, Crazy Fat Ethel, should cure any compulsive overeaters in the audience. A sequel followed thirteen years later (*Crazy Fat Ethel II*). Not rated. 61m. **DIR:** Nick Phillips. **CAST:** Priscilla Alden. **1974**

CRIMSON CODE ★★★ Effective vigilante thriller stars Patrick Muldoon as an FBI agent who is a member of the Serial Killer Apprehension team. When numerous suspects on his list start dying and disappearing, he suspects foul play. His search for the truth puts him at odds with his superiors, who might be in on the conspiracy. This made-for-cable thriller punches all the right buttons. Also released as *The Red Team*. Rated R for adult situations, language, and violence. 90m. **DIR:** Jeremy Haft. **CAST:** Patrick Muldoon, Cathy Moriarty, C. Thomas Howell, Tim Thomerson, Fred Ward. **1999 DVD**

CRIMSON PIRATE, THE ★★★★1/2 One of the all-time great swashbucklers, this follow-up to *The Flame and the Arrow* features the incredibly agile Burt Lancaster besting villains and winning fair maids in high style. Lancaster's partner from his circus days, Nick Cravat, joins in for some rousing action scenes. It's part adventure story, part spoof, and always entertaining. 104m. **DIR:** Robert Siodmak. **CAST:** Burt Lancaster, Nick Cravat, Eva Bartok, Torin Thatcher, Christopher Lee. **1952**

•CRIMSON RIVERS, THE ★★★★ The French Alps provide the eerie background for this chilling thriller about a serial killer tormenting a remote university town and its inhabitants. France's leading serial killer investigator teams up with a police detective to canvass the university and the surrounding towns, hoping to catch the killer before he strikes again. Each icy step reveals hidden secrets and unspeakable acts of torture and murder, all clues to a dark past that has returned to haunt the small village. Every frame is filled with suspense and beauty. Dubbed in English. Rated R for language and extreme violence. 105m. **DIR:** Mathieu Kassovitz. **CAST:** Jean Reno, Vincent Cassel, Nadia Farès, Jean-Pierre Cassel. **2000 DVD**

CRIMSON TIDE ★★★★1/2 Top-notch undersea adventure explodes with star power, as by-the-book captain Gene Hackman finds himself at odds with new executive officer Denzel Washington. An American submarine carrying nuclear weapons is galvanized into action when Russian rebels steal a similarly armed vessel. Director Tony Scott's best film by far. Rated R for violence and profanity. 115m. **DIR:** Tony Scott. **CAST:** Denzel Washington, Gene Hackman, George Dzundza, Viggo Mortensen, James Gandolfini, Matt Craven, Lillo Brancato, Rick Schroder. **1995 DVD**

CRINOLINE HEAD ★★ Made in the wake of the superior *Scream*, this indie film attempts to give viewers more of the same but falls shy of the mark. The plot has a kook wearing a crinoline on his head and butchering the local teens in some decidedly gross ways. Not rated; contains gore, violence, and profanity. 90m. **DIR:** Tommy Faircloth. **CAST:** Brian Kelly, Tracy Powlas. **1997**

CRIPPLED MASTERS, THE ★★★ Standard martial arts–revenge film with one difference: the heroes are an armless man and a legless man, who combine to form an unbeatable fighting machine. Despite the exploitative nature of the film, the two fighters are worthy of this showcase. Rated R for violence. 90m. **DIR:** Joe Law. **CAST:** Frankie Shum, Jack Conn. **1982**

CRISIS AT CENTRAL HIGH ★★★★1/2 In the late Fifties Little Rock, Arkansas, was rocked by the integration of the school system. This television film is a retelling of those events as seen through the eyes of teacher Elizabeth Huckaby, one of the principal characters involved. Joanne Woodward is simply wonderful as the caught-in-the-middle instructor. 125m. **DIR:** Lamont Johnson. **CAST:** Joanne Woodward, Charles Durning, Henderson Forsythe, William Russ. **1981**

CRISS CROSS (1948) ★★★ A less than riveting plot mars this otherwise gritty *film noir*. Burt Lancaster plays an armored-car guard who, along with his less than trustworthy wife, gets involved with a bunch of underworld thugs. B&W; 87m. **DIR:** Robert Siodmak. **CAST:** Burt Lancaster, Yvonne De Carlo, Dan Duryea, Stephen McNally, Richard Long. **1948**

CRISSCROSS (1992) ★★★ Some fine performances highlight this slice-of-life character study about a 12-year-old boy who discovers the shocking truth about his mother's nighttime job. Screenwriter Scott Sommer adds some interesting touches to this tale set in the Sixties, but director Chris Menges directs in too laid-back a fashion.Rated R for profanity, nudity, and violence. 100m. **DIR:** Chris Menges. **CAST:** Goldie Hawn, Arliss Howard, James Gammon, Keith Carradine, David Arnott, J. C. Quinn, Steve Buscemi. **1992**

CRITICAL CARE ★★★ Although there's plenty to attack in the world of managed care and insurance industry meddling, *Critical Care* tiptoes around this lofty subject and instead becomes the tale of a young doctor seeking an epiphany, an understanding of what all those years of study and hospital rotation really meant. Rated

R for profanity and mild sexual content. 105m. **DIR:** Sidney Lumet. **CAST:** James Spader, Kyra Sedgwick, Helen Mirren, Margo Martindale, Albert Brooks, Wallace Shawn, Anne Bancroft. **1997 DVD**

CRITICAL CHOICES ★★1/2 This made-for-cable original focuses on both sides (pro-life and pro-choice) of the protest at an abortion clinic. Unfortunately, the movie straddles the fence so much, and ends so abruptly, we hardly know what to make of it. Uninspired acting and minimal plot only muddy the waters further. Not rated; contains profanity and violence. 88m. **DIR:** Claudia Weill. **CAST:** Betty Buckley, Pamela Reed, Diana Scarwid, Liisa Repo-Martell, Brian Kerwin. **1996**

CRITICAL CONDITION ★★1/2 Mishmash of a comedy has some funny moments but ultimately tests the viewer's patience. Richard Pryor stars as a hustler who must feign insanity to stay out of prison. While under observation in a psychiatric ward of a big hospital, Pryor surprisingly finds himself in charge of the institution. Rated R for profanity, violence, and scatological humor. 105m. **DIR:** Michael Apted. **CAST:** Richard Pryor, Rachel Ticotin, Rubén Blades, Joe Mantegna, Bob Dishy, Joe Dallesandro, Garrett Morris, Randall "Tex" Cobb. **1987**

CRITIC'S CHOICE ★★ A disappointment in spite of its cast, the film is a superficial version of Ira Levin's successful Broadway play. The contrivances begin when a theater critic has to review his wife's new play, then goes to his first wife for advice. Good cast tries to make the best of poor script and uninspired direction. 100m. **DIR:** Don Weis. **CAST:** Bob Hope, Lucille Ball, Rip Torn, Marilyn Maxwell, Jim Backus, Marie Windsor, Jerome Cowan. **1963**

CRITTERS ★★★1/2 This mild horror film with its hilarious spots could become a cult classic. In it, eight ravenous critters escape from a distant planet and head for Earth. Two futuristic bounty hunters pursue them, and the fun begins. Rated PG-13 for gore and profanity. 90m. **DIR:** Stephen Herek. **CAST:** Dee Wallace, M. Emmet Walsh, Scott Grimes, Don Opper, Terrence Mann. **1986**

CRITTERS 2: THE MAIN COURSE ★★ *Critters 2* takes off where the first one ended, but dwells too much on a dopey subplot. Rated PG-13 for violence and profanity. 87m. **DIR:** Mick Garris. **CAST:** Scott Grimes, Liane Curtis, Don Opper, Barry Corbin, Terrence Mann. **1987**

CRITTERS 3 Those ferocious fur balls from outer space are back for more, this time inhabiting an apartment building. Low rent all the way. Rated PG-13 for violence. 86m. **DIR:** Kristine Peterson. **CAST:** Christopher Cousins, Joseph Cousins, Don Opper. **1991**

CRITTERS 4 ★★ Ferocious fur balls are back for a bigger bite of the pie. Go figure! Rated PG-13 for violence. 94m. **DIR:** Rupert Harvey. **CAST:** Don Opper, Paul Whitthorne, Angela Bassett, Brad Dourif. **1991**

CROCODILE (1981) An island paradise is turned into a hellhole by a giant crocodile. Not rated; contains profanity and violence. 95m. **DIR:** Sompote Sands. **CAST:** Nat Puvanai. **1981**

CROCODILE (2000) Computer-generated mammoth crocodile feasts on college students vacationing in a houseboat. They're the lucky ones. Rated R for violence. 94m. **DIR:** Tobe Hooper. **CAST:** Mark McLaughlin, Caitlin Martin, Chris Solari. **2000 DVD**

"CROCODILE" DUNDEE ★★★★1/2 In this hilarious Australian import, Paul Hogan plays the title character, a hunter who allegedly crawled several miles for help after a king-size crocodile gnawed off a leg. This slight exaggeration persuades an American newspaper reporter to seek him out and persuade him to join her on a trip to New York, where the naive outbacker faces a new set of perils. Rated PG-13 for profanity and violence. 98m. **DIR:** Peter Faiman. **CAST:** Paul Hogan, Linda Kozlowski, John Meillon, Mark Blum, David Gulpilil, Michael Lombard. **1986 DVD**

"CROCODILE" DUNDEE II ★★★1/2 This follow-up to the wildly successful release from Down Under adds action to the winning formula of laughs, surprises, romance, and adventure. Mick Dundee (Paul Hogan) and Sue Charlton (Linda Kozlowski) are living a relatively quiet life in New York City until some Colombian drug dealers step in. The results should please fans of the first film. Rated PG for violence and light profanity. 110m. **DIR:** John Cornell. **CAST:** Paul Hogan, Linda Kozlowski, John Meillon, Charles Dutton, Hector Ubarry, Juan Fernandez. **1988 DVD**

•CROCODILE DUNDEE IN LOS ANGELES ★★ Disappointing entry in the *Crocodile Dundee* series wastes too much footage setting up jokes and not enough executing them. Plodding story has Linda Kozlowski investigating a film studio with Paul Hogan along for the ride. Relegating Hogan to third wheel for the film's first half is a big mistake. On the plus side, Serge Cockburn, as the couple's son, is a delight. Rated PG for language and violence. 96m. **DIR:** Simon Wincer. **CAST:** Paul Hogan, Linda Kozlowski, Serge Cockburn. **2001 DVD**

CROMWELL ★★ Richard Harris hams it up again in this overblown historical melodrama. A fine cast founders amid tradition-soaked locations and beautiful backgrounds. The accoutrements and design are splendid, but the story is lacking and Harris's performance is inept. 145m. **DIR:** Ken Hughes. **CAST:** Richard Harris, Alec Guinness, Robert Morley, Frank Finlay, Dorothy Tutin, Timothy Dalton, Patrick Magee. **1970**

CRONOS ★★★★ In this atmospheric Mexican vampire movie, a kindly old antique dealer discovers an alchemist's ancient, eternal-life device—and the thirst for blood that comes from using it. Rife with clever religious symbolism, satiric wit, and some tender family values, this subtle, intelligent chiller harks back to the Hammer horrors of the 1960s and Roger Corman's best Edgar Allan Poe pictures. In English and Spanish with English subtitles. Not rated, with limited graphic effects and gore. 92m. **DIR:** Guillermo del Toro. **CAST:** Federico Luppi, Ron Perlman, Claudio Brook, Tamara Shanath. **1993**

CROOKED HEARTS ★★ The talents of an ensemble cast are showcased in this slow-paced story of a family's struggle to give each other room to grow. The film resembles movies adapted from John Irving novels, only here, the surreal humor and irony are missing. Rated R for profanity and partial nudity. 113m. **DIR:** Michael Bortman. **CAST:** Vincent D'Onofrio, Jennifer Jason Leigh, Peter Berg, Cindy Pickett, Juliette Lewis, Marg Helgenberger, Peter Coyote. **1991**

CROOKLYN ★★★1/2 As low key as Spike Lee gets, this episodic movie focuses on an African-American family in 1970s Brooklyn. It's filled with shouting matches, but it's also a warm and well-observed character comedy, featuring a tough, natural performance by young Zelda Harris as the only girl in a brood full of rambunctious boys. Rated PG-13. 132m. **DIR:** Spike Lee. **CAST:** Zelda Harris, Alfre Woodard, Delroy Lindo, David Patrick Kelly, Carlton Williams. **1994 DVD**

CROOKS AND CORONETS (SOPHIE'S PLACE) ★★ This picture had only a limited release in the United States and for good reason. It wasn't cunning and bold enough for a good crime picture, and certainly not funny enough for a quality comedy. Dame Edith Evans owns a large estate and the other characters are villains trying to steal the valuable property from her. Not rated. 102m. **DIR:** Jim O'Connolly. **CAST:** Edith Evans, Telly Savalas, Cesar Romero, Warren Oates, Harry H. Corbett. **1970**

CROSS COUNTRY ★★ Michael Ironside plays Detective Ed Roersch, who pursues Richard Beymer following the murder of an expensive call girl. Although this movie involves prostitution, blackmail, murder, and deceit, it still manages to bore. Rated R for nudity, sex, profanity, and violence. 95m. **DIR:** Paul Lynch. **CAST:** Richard Beymer, Nina Axelrod, Michael Ironside, Brent Carver. **1983**

CROSS CREEK ★★★1/2 About the life of 1930s author Marjorie Kinnan Rawlings (Mary Steenburgen), this watchable release illustrates how Rawlings's relationships with backwoods folks inspired her novels, particularly *The Yearling* and *Jacob's Ladder*. Rated PG for brief violence. 122m. **DIR:** Martin Ritt. **CAST:** Mary Steenburgen, Rip Torn, Peter Coyote, Dana Hill. **1983 DVD**

CROSS MISSION ★★ There's lots of shooting, some martial arts, even a little voodoo in this predictable tale about a pretty photographer and a handsome soldier of fortune in a banana republic. They are taken prisoner by the rebels, then converted to the cause. Rated R. 90m. **DIR:** Al Bradley. **CAST:** Richard Randall. **1989**

CROSS MY HEART (1987) ★★ Interminable comedy about the disastrous third date of two vulnerable people trying to keep silly secrets from each other. Martin Short and Annette O'Toole are unmemorable as the couple. Rated R for nudity and language. 88m. **DIR:** Armyan Bernstein. **CAST:** Martin Short, Annette O'Toole, Paul Reiser, Joanna Kerns. **1987**

CROSS MY HEART (1991) ★★★★★ Jacques Fansten's bittersweet film spotlights the innocence, the pain, the insecurities, and the resilience of children. With surprising humor and rare sensitivity, the film examines the efforts of a group of children to comfort one of their own. In French with English subtitles. Not rated. 105m. **DIR:** Jacques Fansten. **1991**

CROSS OF IRON ★★★1/2 With this action-packed war film, director Sam Peckinpah proved that he hadn't lost the touch that made *Ride the High Country* and *The Wild Bunch* such memorable movies. Still, *Cross of Iron* did not receive much acclaim when released. Perhaps it was the theme: the heroics of weary German soldiers in World War II. A precursor of *Das Boot*, this film is an interesting work by one of Hollywood's more original directors. Rated R. 119m. **DIR:** Sam Peckinpah. **CAST:** James Coburn, Maximilian Schell, James Mason, David Warner. **1977 DVD**

CROSSCUT ★★1/2 Hard-edged action and gorgeous Pacific Northwest scenery enhance this gritty crime-thriller about a New York mobster who has made a fatal mistake: he killed a rival's son. The mobster hightails it to logging country, where his cover is jeopardized by the local loggers, who play just as rough as the mob. Rated R for violence, profanity, and adult situations. 90m. **DIR:** Paul Raimondi. **CAST:** Costas Mandylor, Megan Gallagher, Casey Sander, Jay Acovone. **1995**

CROSSFIRE (1947) ★★★1/2 While on leave from the army, psychopathic bigot Robert Ryan meets Sam Levene in a nightclub and later murders him during an argument. An army buddy is blamed; another is also murdered. Often billed as a *film noir*, this interesting film is more of a message indicting anti-Semitism, and it was the first major Hollywood picture to explore racial bigotry. B&W; 86m. **DIR:** Edward Dmytryk. **CAST:** Robert Ryan, Robert Mitchum, Robert Young, Sam Levene, Gloria Grahame, Paul Kelly, Steve Brodie. **1947**

CROSSFIRE (1986) Outlaws are saved from execution by a gang of Mexican freedom fighters. 82m. **DIR:** Robert Conrad, Alfredo Zacharias. **CAST:** Robert Conrad, Jan-Michael Vincent, Manuel Ochoa Lopez. **1986**

CROSSING, THE ★★ Australian melodrama about a young woman in a romantic triangle forced into choosing between life in a small town with her current boyfriend or with his best friend who left town to pursue a career in the art world. Clichéd. Rated R for nudity and profanity. 92m. **DIR:** George Ogilvie. **CAST:** Russell Crowe, Robert Mammone, Danielle Spencer. **1992**

CROSSING DELANCEY ★★★★1/2 Amy Irving has the role of her career as the independent New Yorker scrutinized by Susan Sandler's deft and poignant screenplay. Irving has a bookstore job that brings her into close contact with the Big Apple's literary scene; she fulfills deeper needs with visits to her feisty grandmother (Reizl Bozyk). Grandmother has matchmaking plans, involving street vendor Peter Riegert, whose flawless timing is one of the many highlights here. Rated PG for language and mild sexual themes. 97m. **DIR:** Joan Micklin Silver. **CAST:** Amy Irving, Peter Riegert, Reizl Bozyk, Jeroen Krabbé, Sylvia Miles. **1988**

CROSSING GUARD, THE ★★★ A jeweler is shredded by grief after his young daughter is killed by a drunk driver. He resolutely tells his estranged wife that he plans to shoot the culprit now that he has been released from prison. It's an unpleasant but riveting story about strained moral responsibility, the licking of emotional wounds, the contradictions of masculinity, and the tragic cracks into which whole families can tumble. Rated R for violence, nudity, and language. 114m. **DIR:** Sean Penn. **CAST:** Jack Nicholson, David Morse, Anjelica Huston, Robin Wright, Piper Laurie. **1995 DVD**

CROSSING THE BRIDGE ★★★ Gutsy, credible performances give this 1970s coming-of-age story a raw edge as three Detroit buddies get jolted into adulthood when a plan to smuggle hash across the Canadian border goes sour. Written and directed with apparent autobiographical clarity by Mike Binder. Rated R for language and violence. 103m. **DIR:** Mike Binder. **CAST:** Josh Charles, Jason Gedrick, Stephen Baldwin, Cheryl Pollak, Richard Edson. **1992**

CROSSING THE LINE (1990) ★★1/2 When a motorcycle accident puts his best friend in a coma, rich kid Rick

Hearst takes the heat. Exciting race footage sets the pace for this domestic drama about sibling rivalry. Rated R for strong language. 94m. **DIR:** Gary Graver. **CAST:** John Saxon, Rick Hearst, Jon Stafford, Cameron Mitchell. **1990**

CROSSOVER DREAMS ★★★★ Rubén Blades plays a popular Latino musician who tries his talents at the big time. The price he pays for his efforts is high. And while this may all sound like one big movie cliché, it's now time to add that the cast put in performances that redefine the story, giving this trite tale a bite that will surprise the viewer. 85m. **DIR:** Leon Ichaso. **CAST:** Rubén Blades, Shawn Elliot, Elizabeth Peña, Tom Signorelli, Frank Robles. **1985**

CROSSROADS (1986) ★★★1/2 A superb blues score by guitarist Ry Cooder highlights this enjoyable fantasy about an ambitious young bluesman (Ralph Macchio) who "goes down to the crossroads," in the words of Robert Johnson, to make a deal with the devil for fame and fortune. Most viewers will enjoy the performances, the story, and the music in this all-too-rare big-screen celebration of the blues and its mythology. Rated R for profanity, suggested sex, and violence. 105m. **DIR:** Walter Hill. **CAST:** Ralph Macchio, Joe Seneca, Jami Gertz, Joe Morton, Dennis Lipscomb, Harry Carey Jr. **1986**

•CROSSROADS (2002) ★★ Three preteen Georgia girls bury a box of memorabilia and swear to meet on their high-school grad night to reopen it. The girls are no longer friends by grad time but meet anyway at the prodding of a now-pregnant trio member. They then hitch a ride to L.A. so one girl can meet her mom for the first time, another can visit her boyfriend, and the third can compete in a karaoke contest. This silly, predictable story substitutes virgin-slut melodrama for substance. Rated PG-13 for mild profanity, alcohol use, suggested sex, and sexual situations. 94m. **DIR:** Tamra Davis. **CAST:** Britney Spears, Anson Mount, Taryn Manning, Zoe Saldana, Justin Long, Kim Cattrall, Dan Aykroyd. **2002 DVD**

CROSSWORLDS ★★★1/2 Good and evil collide in this imaginative science-fiction adventure. Josh Charles stars as Joe Talbot, a young man whose peaceful existence is disrupted when he's swept into the mystical valley of "Crossworld," a place where all dimensions of the universe converge. When Talbot's bedroom is invaded by aliens looking for a magic crystal, he escapes with the crystal. Talbot is joined by a mercenary and a beautiful woman from another galaxy in his attempt to keep the crystal from the forces of evil. Interesting premise and likable cast distinguish this made-for-cable effort from the rest of the pack. Rated PG-13 for violence. 91m. **DIR:** Krishna Rao. **CAST:** Josh Charles, Rutger Hauer, Stuart Wilson, Andrea Roth. **1996 DVD**

CROUCHING TIGER, HIDDEN DRAGON ★★★★ In ancient China, two Wudan warriors try to retrieve a stolen legendary sword and befriend a young female martial arts practitioner who becomes wedged between forces of good and evil. Social codes and restraints clash with personal loyalty and desire, and combatants literally fly lithely on their feet across rooftops and water in an eighteenth century fantasy of exotic swordplay, duplicitous identities and agendas, historic melodrama, and comic relief. In Mandarin with English subtitles. Rated PG-13 for violence and sex. 119m. **DIR:** Ang Lee. **CAST:** Chow Yun-Fat, Michelle Yeoh, Zhang Ziyi, Chang Chen. **2000 DVD**

CROUPIER ★★★★ Gaming-table attendant and wannabe author Jack Manfred mentally insulates himself from his clientele at a posh London casino as well as from his own personal relationships. He then begins living life through his literary alter ego Jake. But when he gets involved in a casino heist, deception and violence soon shatter his one-way-mirror window on the world. Rated R for language, violence, nudity, and sex. 91m. **DIR:** Mike Hodges. **CAST:** Clive Owen, Gina McKee, Kate Hardie, Alex Kingston. **1998**

CROW, THE ★★★★ The accidental death of Brandon Lee during production did not prevent director Alex Proyas from making a genuinely gripping, comic-book horror–thriller. Lee plays a musician who comes back from the dead to wreak vengeance on the urban criminals who killed him and his fiancée. Looking like the Joker and distributing bloody justice, our hero stalks a darkly lit hellscape of decaying tenements, maddening noise, and sadistic sociopathy. Rated R for violence, language, brief nudity, and drug use. 97m. **DIR:** Alex Proyas. **CAST:** Brandon Lee, Ernie Hudson, Michael Wincott, David Patrick Kelly, Jon Polito. **1994 DVD**

CROW: CITY OF ANGELS, THE ★★ Not a sequel but a virtual remake of the 1994 film, with French actor Vincent Perez (struggling with English) as a motorcycle mechanic back from the dead to avenge his own murder. This time, the urban-hell atmosphere is even darker and dirtier—even the cocaine is black. The chic despair and morbid obsession with death is overwrought, and at times unintentionally comic. Rated R for violence, profanity, and drug use. 80m. **DIR:** Tim Pope. **CAST:** Vincent Perez, Mia Kirshner, Richard Brooks, Iggy Pop. **1996 DVD**

CROWD, THE ★★★★1/2 Director King Vidor's pioneering slice-of-life story of a working-class family in a big city during the Jazz Age still holds up beautifully after sixty years. James Murray, in his only major movie, gives an extraordinary performance as a hardworking clerk who never seems to get ahead. Not rated; suitable for all but the youngest children. B&W; 90m. **DIR:** King Vidor. **CAST:** James Murray, Eleanor Boardman. **1928**

CRUCIBLE, THE ★★★★★ In 1692 Massachusetts, nineteen Salem Puritans were hanged by their peers after a clique of young girls accused them of witchcraft. Arthur Miller turned the incident into a 1953 stage play that was—among other interpretations—an indictment of McCarthy-era communist hunts. Miller has now turned his play into a crisp, volcanic film about repressed sexuality, collective evil, and mass hysteria. Rated PG-13 for brief nudity, intense adult situations, and brief violence. 115m. **DIR:** Nicholas Hytner. **CAST:** Winona Ryder, Daniel Day-Lewis, Joan Allen, Paul Scofield, Bruce Davison. **1996**

CRUCIBLE OF HORROR ★★★1/2 Intense story of a violent, domineering man (Michael Gough in one of his better roles) who drives his passive wife and nubile daughter to murder. The suspense and terror build unrelentingly. Keep the lights on! Rated R. 91m. **DIR:** Viktors Ritelis. **CAST:** Michael Gough, Yvonne Mitchell. **1971**

CRUCIFER OF BLOOD ★★1/2 Charlton Heston is far from believable as Sherlock Holmes in this melodramatic, yet atmospheric cable movie about a thirty year old curse involving a stolen treasure. Written and directed by Heston's son, Fraser. Richard Johnson fares a bit better as Dr. Watson, while Susannah Harker steals the film as their client. Rated PG. 105m. **DIR:** Fraser Heston. **CAST:** Charlton Heston, Richard Johnson, Susannah Harker, John Castle, Clive Wood, Simon Callow, Edward Fox. **1991**

CRUDE OASIS, THE ★★1/2 A bored young housewife escapes her small-town blues through her dreams. When she discovers her husband is having an affair, she finds solace in the arms of a stranger. Rated R for profanity and adult situations. 82m. **DIR:** Alex Graves. **CAST:** Jennifer Taylor, Aaron Shields, Robert Peterson. **1995**

CRUEL INTENTIONS 🦃 This hilarious update of Choderlos de Laclos's *Les Liaisons Dangereuses* is a travesty from start to finish: a lackluster comedy-drama, which must have resulted from a wager among cast members to see who could deliver the most inept performance. They all win. Rated R for profanity, base sexual behavior, drug use, and brief nudity. 97m. **DIR:** Roger Kumble. **CAST:** Ryan Philippe, Sarah Michelle Gellar, Reese Witherspoon, Selma Blair, Louise Fletcher, Joshua Jackson. **1999 DVD**

CRUEL INTENTIONS 2 ★★1/2 Originally shot as a pilot for television, this direct-to-video drama fails to capture the sexual chemistry and treachery that made *Dangerous Liaisons* so much fun. When Sebastian and his sexy stepsister, Kathryn, transfer to the elite Manchester Prep, he decides to stop his womanizing and settle down with the headmaster's daughter. His days of happiness are numbered as Kathryn attempts to derail their affair. Rated R for adult situations and language. 87m. **DIR:** Roger Kumble. **CAST:** Robin Dunne, Sarah Thompson, Keri Lynn Pratt, Amy Adams. **2000 DVD**

CRUEL SEA, THE ★★★1/2 The ever-changing and unpredictable wind-lashed sea is the star of this gripping documentary-style adventure about a stalwart British warship during World War II. B&W; 121m. **DIR:** Charles Frend. **CAST:** Jack Hawkins, Virginia McKenna, Stanley Baker, Donald Sinden. **1953**

CRUEL STORY OF YOUTH ★★★ Two bored middle-class teenagers set up a scheme to extort money from businessmen. Nagisa Oshima is clearly more interested in exploring Godardian techniques than in his emotionally bereft characters (though the approach is suited to them). An interesting but chilly film. In Japanese with English subtitles. B&W; 97m. **DIR:** Nagisa Oshima. **CAST:** Yusuke Kawazu, Miyuji Kuwano. **1960**

CRUISE, THE ★★★ Real-life double-decker bus guide Timothy "Speed" Levitch bares his love/hate relationship with all things Manhattan and eloquently chats about the chaos of the universe in this grainy black-and-white documentary. The film is a sort of "My Tour with Andre," with the passionate Levitch providing a running commentary on New York City's colorful history and inhabitants, always in quest of a fascinating story or enlightenment. Not rated. B&W; 76m. **DIR:** Bennett Miller. **1998**

CRUISE INTO TERROR 🦃 Dreadful suspense flick made for the tube. 100m. **DIR:** Bruce Kessler. **CAST:** Dirk Benedict, John Forsythe, Lynda Day George, Christopher George, Stella Stevens, Ray Milland, Frank Converse, Lee Meriwether, Hugh O'Brian. **1977**

CRUISING 🦃 A horror in the real sense of the word. Rated R. 106m. **DIR:** William Friedkin. **CAST:** Al Pacino, Paul Sorvino, Karen Allen, Richard Cox, Don Scardino. **1980**

CRUMB ★★★★1/2 If you think your family is strange, wait until you get a glimpse into the tortured, dysfunctional Crumb clan. Director Terry Zwigoff cleverly uses others to reveal the sexual and psychological demons of Robert Crumb, the creator of Fritz the Cat. Psychically damaged family members, candid ex-lovers, and Crumb himself reveal humorous, creepy, and startling secrets about this talented, offbeat artist. Rated R for profanity and nudity. 119m. **DIR:** Terry Zwigoff. **CAST:** Robert Crumb. **1994 DVD**

CRUSADES, THE (1935) ★★1/2 A Cecil B. DeMille epic that improves with time, this sword-sandal-and-shmaltz dramatization of the Third Crusade takes too many liberties with history to ring completely true. Loretta Young stars as Berengaria of Navarre, the hapless lady in love with Richard the Lion-Hearted. The movie is more about their touch-and-go romance than the pursuit of the Holy Grail. But it has moments of excitement. B&W; 123m. **DIR:** Cecil B. DeMille. **CAST:** Loretta Young, Henry Wilcoxon, Ian Keith, Joseph Schildkraut, Mischa Auer, Montagu Love. **1935**

CRUSADES, THE (1995) ★★★★★ Monty Pythoner and medieval expert Terry Jones has found a new way to educate—by making us laugh. This four-tape set presents a complete history of the Crusades and breaks new ground as a documentary with a style that blends paintings, location footage, reenactments, and computer imagery. Always amusing, host Jones springs to life in the midst of a mural, or pokes his head into the edge of the screen to make humorous asides or biting bon mots. Made for A&E. Not rated. 200m. **DIR:** Alan Ereira, David Wallace. **CAST:** Terry Jones. **1995 DVD**

CRUSH, THE (1993) 🦃 Trash from the very start, a teen tart from hell becomes obsessed with the hunkish, nice-guy journalist who rents her parents' guest house. Rated R for language, sexual themes, and violence. 90m. **DIR:** Alan Shapiro. **CAST:** Alicia Silverstone, Cary Elwes, Jennifer Rubin. **1993 DVD**

CRUSH (1994) ★★★ When Marcia Gay Harden flees the car accident that leaves her best friend in a coma, she heads straight for the writer her pal was to have interviewed. Harden's character seduces the writer and befriends his teenage daughter. This Australian tale of obsession is told with a weirdness that almost excuses its predictability. Not rated; contains profanity, nudity, and sexual situations. 97m. **DIR:** Alison Maclean. **CAST:** Marcia Gay Harden, William Zappa, Donough Rees, Caitlin Bossley. **1993**

CRUSH (2001) ★★1/2 An affair between the headmistress at an English school (Andie MacDowell) and a much younger church organist (Kenny Doughty) arouses the disapproval (and envy) of her so-called best friends. Acting is decent (though MacDowell, miscast, looks uncomfortable) but the contrived story, unpleasant characters, and veiled sexism drag everything down. Rated R for profanity and sexual scenes. 105m. **DIR:** John McKay. **CAST:** Andie MacDowell, Imelda

Staunton, Anna Chancellor, Kenny Doughty, Bill Paterson. **2001 DVD**

CRUSOE ★★1/2 This film by noted cinematographer-turned-director Caleb Deschanel is an attractive but incomplete examination of *Robinson Crusoe* updated to the early nineteenth century. Crusoe is now a young slave trader in Virginia. Aidan Quinn makes an appealing title character. Rated PG-13. 97m. **DIR:** Caleb Deschanel. **CAST:** Aidan Quinn, Ade Sapara. **1989**

CRY-BABY 🦃 John Waters's flimsy remake of *Hairspray* features Johnny Depp as a *drape* from the bad side of town. Rated PG-13 for violence and profanity. 89m. **DIR:** John Waters. **CAST:** Johnny Depp, Amy Locane, Polly Bergen, Susan Tyrrell, Iggy Pop, Ricki Lake, Traci Lords, Troy Donahue, Joey Heatherton, David Nelson, Patty Hearst, Joe Dallesandro, Willem Dafoe. **1990**

CRY BLOOD, APACHE ★★1/2 Joel McCrea, in a cameo appearance as a favor to his son, tells in flashback how he and a bunch of prospectors slaughtered a band of Indians. A girl, the lone survivor of the massacre, promises to lead them to a secret gold mine. Rated R. 85m. **DIR:** Jack Starrett. **CAST:** Jody McCrea, Dan Kemp, Jack Starrett, Joel McCrea. **1970 DVD**

CRY DANGER ★★★ Dick Powell plays a wisecracking ex-con who has been framed for a robbery. Upon his release, he sets out to take revenge on the people who set him up. Rhonda Fleming is the woman he loves. Not bad! Not rated, this contains violence. B&W; 80m. **DIR:** Robert Parrish. **CAST:** Dick Powell, Rhonda Fleming, William Conrad, Richard Erdman. **1950**

CRY FOR LOVE, A ★★★1/2 Taut teledrama about two people—one an alcoholic, the other addicted to uppers—who, through some very real difficulties, fall in love. Their attempts to help each other over the crises of substance abuse draw them closer together. 100m. **DIR:** Paul Wendkos. **CAST:** Susan Blakely, Powers Boothe, Gene Barry, Edie Adams, Lainie Kazan, Charles Siebert. **1980**

CRY FREEDOM ★★★★1/2 Director Richard Attenborough and screenwriter John Briley's superb film about South African apartheid begins by chronicling the growing friendship between nonviolent black leader Steve Biko (Denzel Washington) and white newspaperman Donal Woods (Kevin Kline). When Biko is brutally murdered, Woods must fight to tell the truth to the rest of the world. Rated PG for violence. 130m. **DIR:** Richard Attenborough. **CAST:** Kevin Kline, Penelope Wilton, Denzel Washington, Ian Richardson. **1987 DVD**

CRY FROM THE MOUNTAIN ★★1/2 A man takes his preteen son on a camping trip, during which he plans to reveal that he and the boy's mother are getting divorced. Created by the Billy Graham Ministry, this film features attractive Alaskan scenery but is extremely preachy. Rated PG; no objectionable material. 88m. **DIR:** James F. Collier. **CAST:** Chris Kidd, Wes Parker, Rita Walter. **1985**

CRY IN THE DARK, A ★★★★1/2 A chilling, superbly acted true-life drama set in 1980 Australia, this film features Meryl Streep and Sam Neill as the parents of an infant who is stolen by a wild dog while they are camping out—or so they say. The authorities begin to doubt their story and the Australian people begin spreading rumors that the baby was killed in a sacrificial rite. Thus begins this harrowing motion picture. Rated PG-13 for mature themes. 120m. **DIR:** Fred Schepisi. **CAST:** Meryl Streep, Sam Neill, Charles Tingwell. **1988 DVD**

CRY IN THE NIGHT, A ★★ Based on the Mary Higgins Clark bestseller, this begins as a decent mystery-thriller and soon descends into campy melodrama. Perry King is a wealthy Canadian who falls for Carol Higgins Clark, a dead ringer for his dead mama. Apt to leave you giggling. Rated PG-13 for violence. 99m. **DIR:** Robin Spry. **CAST:** Perry King, Carol Higgins Clark. **1992**

CRY IN THE WILD, A ★★★1/2 En route to visit his father, an embittered teenager must crash-land a small plane over the Canadian forest when the pilot suddenly dies. Poignant boy-against-nature film. Rated PG for profanity and violence. 81m. **DIR:** Mark Griffiths. **CAST:** Jared Rushton, Ned Beatty, Pamela Sue Martin. **1990 DVD**

CRY IN THE WIND ★★★ David Morse is a bitterly lonely mountain man who kidnaps shy and pretty schoolgirl Megan Follows. Though effectively harsh, the flick only touches the surface of what was the largest manhunt in Pennsylvania history. 95m. **DIR:** Charles Correll. **CAST:** David Morse, Megan Follows, David Soul. **1991**

CRY OF BATTLE ★★ The son (James MacArthur) of a wealthy businessman gets caught in the Philippines during the Japanese occupation and has to resort to guerrilla warfare. Poorly directed, but does address the ethical questions of racism and the conduct of war. Not rated; with violence. B&W; 99m. **DIR:** Irving Lerner. **CAST:** James MacArthur, Van Heflin, Rita Moreno, Leopoldo Salcedo, Sidney Clute. **1957**

CRY OF THE BANSHEE ★★ Uninspired film casts Vincent Price as a witch-hunting magistrate whose family is threatened when a curse is placed upon his house by practitioners of the old religion. Price fared much better in the similar *The Conqueror Worm.* Rated R for violence and nudity. 87m. **DIR:** Gordon Hessler. **CAST:** Vincent Price, Elisabeth Bergner, Hugh Griffith. **1970**

CRY OF THE INNOCENT ★★★1/2 Exciting made-for-TV suspense-thriller has Rod Taylor playing the grieving husband and father who loses his wife and children when a plane crashes into their summer home in Ireland. When a Dublin detective tells Taylor the crash was no accident, Taylor is determined to find out who planted the bomb in the plane. 93m. **DIR:** Michael O'Herlihy. **CAST:** Rod Taylor, Joanna Pettet, Nigel Davenport, Cyril Cusack, Jim Norton, Alexander Knox. **1980**

CRY TERROR ★★ Disappointingly slow, but well-acted BBC teleplay about a recently paroled ex-con being hounded by a vicious gang. The gang holds his brother and the patrons of a roadside garage hostage until they get the loot from a bank job the ex-con pulled. 71m. **DIR:** Robert Tronson. **CAST:** Bob Hoskins, Susan Hampshire. **1974**

CRY, THE BELOVED COUNTRY (1952) ★★★★ A touching film about the problems of apartheid in South Africa with Sidney Poitier and Canada Lee exceptionally good as preachers fighting prejudice in their homeland. Based on Alan Paton's controversial novel of the same name and the inspiration for the Kurt Weill musical drama, *Lost in the Stars.* B&W; 105m. **DIR:** Zoltán

Korda. **CAST:** Sidney Poitier, Canada Lee, Joyce Carey, Charles Carson, Geoffrey Keen. **1952**

CRY, THE BELOVED COUNTRY (1995) ★★★1/2 In 1940s South Africa, a black minister (James Earl Jones) and a bigoted white farmer (Richard Harris) are forced by a shared tragedy to search for some common ground. This third film version of Alan Paton's modern classic novel is solemn and rather plodding, but deeply and sincerely felt, with towering, heartrending performances by Jones and Harris. Rated PG-13 for mature themes. 108m. **DIR:** Darrell Roodt. **CAST:** James Earl Jones, Richard Harris. **1995**

CRY UNCLE! ★★ This is a sometimes very funny spoof of private eye yarns. Allen Garfield is good as a detective who gets involved in all sorts of trouble, but the script is next to tasteless. 87m. **DIR:** John G. Avildsen. **CAST:** Allen Garfield. **1971 DVD**

CRY WOLF ★★ A muddled murder mystery that wastes the talents of its stars. But their personalities still glow. The idea of a feisty woman like Barbara Stanwyck fighting her brother-in-law for her late husband's estate is a good premise, especially with suave, self-confident Errol Flynn as the brother-in-law. Unfortunately, the script lets them both down before the finish. B&W; 83m. **DIR:** Peter Godfrey. **CAST:** Errol Flynn, Barbara Stanwyck, Geraldine Brooks, Richard Basehart, Jerome Cowan. **1947**

CRYING CHILD, THE ★★★ This fascinating supernatural thriller is about a woman who loses a child, but still hears a baby crying in the night. Several chilling scenes and good performances all around in this made-for-cable original. Not rated. 95m. **DIR:** Robert Lewis. **CAST:** Mariel Hemingway, Finola Hughes, George Del Hoyo, Kin Shriner. **1996**

CRYING FREEMAN, VOLS. 1–3 ★★★★ Very faithful adaptation of the Japanese comic book about a young artist forced into a life of violence as chief assassin and eventual leader of a secret criminal society. Fine animation captures the original (and much admired) artwork of creators Koike and Ikegami. Dubbed in English. Not rated; contains violence and nudity. 50m. **DIR:** Johei Matsuura. **1991–1992**

CRYING GAME, THE ★★★★★ Brilliant, adult-oriented motion picture by writer-director Neil Jordan casts sad-eyed Stephen Rea as an IRA volunteer assigned to guard British soldier Forest Whitaker, and that's when the plot's ingenious twists and turns begin. Newcomer Jaye Davidson makes a startling film debut. This evocative exploration of the human condition should be on every serious film buff's must-see list. Rated R for violence, profanity, and nudity. 113m. **DIR:** Neil Jordan. **CAST:** Stephen Rea, Miranda Richardson, Forest Whitaker, Jaye Davidson, Jim Broadbent, Ralph Brown, Adrian Dunbar. **1992 DVD**

CRYPT OF THE LIVING DEAD 🦃 Arguably the worst of a trilogy of horror films directed by Ray Danton, this modern vampire opus—originally titled *Hannah, Queen of Vampires*—is cheap and predictable. Rated R. 83m. **DIR:** Ray Danton. **CAST:** Andrew Prine, Mark Damon, Patty Sheppard. **1972**

CRYSTAL TRIANGLE 🦃 Animated tale of an archaeologist who becomes involved in the search for "the message of God" while battling demons and Soviet and American spies. Truly inane. In Japanese with English subtitles. Not rated; contains violence and nudity. 86m. **DIR:** Seiji Okuda. **1987**

CRYSTALSTONE ★★1/2 Although it has a magical undercurrent, *Crystalstone* is more about the very down-to-earth adventures of two children escaping from a wicked guardian than about the fantastical Crystalstone. A good film for older children, with just enough action and ghoulishness to amuse them. Rated PG. 103m. **DIR:** Antonio Pelaez. **CAST:** Frank Grimes, Kamlesh Gupia. **1987**

CTHULHU MANSION 🦃 A magician unleashes the devil's foot soldiers on a group of thugs hiding out at his home. Probably the world's worst adaptation of an H. P. Lovecraft concept. Rated R for profanity and violence. 92m. **DIR:** Juan Piquer Simon. **CAST:** Frank Finlay, Marcia Layton, Brad Fisher. **1990**

CUBA ★★★ A thinly veiled remake of *Casablanca*, this Richard Lester film is nonetheless far superior to J. Lee Thompson's similar *Cabo Blanco* (which starred Charles Bronson). Sean Connery and Brooke Adams play one-time lovers renewing their passion during the fall of Batista in 1959. As usual, Lester invests his tale with memorable bits. Rated R. 121m. **DIR:** Richard Lester. **CAST:** Sean Connery, Brooke Adams, Jack Weston, Hector Elizondo, Denholm Elliott, Chris Sarandon, Lonette McKee. **1979 DVD**

CUBE ★★★1/2 Suspenseful tale of six strangers who wake up and find themselves trapped in a prison made out of rotating, booby-trapped cubes. After a rather gruesome vivisection, you never know what to expect as the strangers try to make sense of their environment and escape. Rated R for violence and language. 90m. **DIR:** Vincenzo Natali. **CAST:** Maurice Dean Wint, Nikki De Boer, Nicky Guadagni, David Hewlett, Andrew Miller, Wayne Robson, Julian Richings. **1997 DVD**

CUJO ★★★1/2 Stephen King's story of a mother and son terrorized by a rabid Saint Bernard results in a movie that keeps viewers on the edge of their seats. Rated R for violence and language. 91m. **DIR:** Lewis Teague. **CAST:** Dee Wallace, Danny Pintauro, Daniel Hugh-Kelly, Christopher Stone. **1983 DVD**

CUL-DE-SAC ★★★ Early Roman Polanski black comedy, about hoods on the lam who briefly victimize a man and his luscious young wife. Early Polanski is just like later Polanski . . . an acquired taste. One of the director's first films in English. B&W; 111m. **DIR:** Roman Polanski. **CAST:** Donald Pleasence, Françoise Dorleac, Lionel Stander, Jack MacGowran, Jacqueline Bisset. **1966**

CULPEPPER CATTLE CO., THE ★★★1/2 A strong supporting cast makes this coming-of-age story set in the Old West into a real treat for fans of shoot-'em-ups. Gary Grimes is a 16 year old farm boy who dreams of becoming a cowboy. Rated R for violence. 92m. **DIR:** Dick Richards. **CAST:** Gary Grimes, Billy Green Bush, Luke Askew, Bo Hopkins, Geoffrey Lewis, Royal Dano. **1972**

CULT OF THE COBRA ★★ An Asian high priestess goes to Manhattan to seek vengeance on the American soldiers who defiled her temple. Don't confuse this drab thriller with the camp favorite *Cobra Woman*. B&W; 80m. **DIR:** Francis D. Lyon. **CAST:** Faith Domergue, Richard Long, Marshall Thompson, Kathleen Hughes, Jack Kelly. **1955**

CUP, THE ★★★1/2 In an Indian monastery of exiled Tibetan monks, a group of the younger monks search for a TV set so they can watch the World Cup soccer finals. This gentle little slice-of-monastic-life drama has a great deal of simple charm, showing that these exotic characters are not as foreign or strange as they may seem at first glance. In Hindi and Tibetan with English subtitles. Rated G. 94m. **DIR:** Khyentse Norbu. **CAST:** Orgyen Tobgyal, Neten Chokling, Jamyang Lodro, Lama Chonjor, Godu Lama, Thinley Nudi. **1999**

CUP FINAL ★★★★ This drama caused a stir in its native Israel, thanks to its refreshingly evenhanded examination of the relationship between an Israeli prisoner and a squad of PLO soldiers in 1982. The Israeli is taken prisoner, and then is shuttled across war-torn Lebanon with the PLO. In Hebrew with English subtitles. 107m. **DIR:** Eran Riklis. **CAST:** Moshe Ivgi. **1992**

CUPID 🦃 While waiting for Cupid to bring him true love, a young psycho murders all the women who fail to make the grade. Rated R for violence and profanity. 95m. **DIR:** Doug Campbell. **CAST:** Zach Galligan, Ashley Laurence, Mary Crosby. **1997**

CUPID AND CATE ★★★1/2 Mary-Louise Parker plays the oddball in what seems to be a normal family. Her engagement to a bore is threatened by her attraction to a hunk and she is forced to confront her own self-centered and childish perceptions of the world. Comic moments are outweighed by high drama in this intriguing coming-of-age film. Not rated; contains mature themes. 95m. **DIR:** Brent Shields. **CAST:** Mary-Louise Parker, Peter Gallagher, Philip Bosco. **2000**

CURDLED ★★1/2 Gore hound Angela Jones decides her life calling is to become a postforensic maid and mop up after gruesome crimes. William Baldwin is the blue-blood killer who fascinates her with his serial decapitations. Lacking enough reason behind the rhyme, this is too strange to embrace, either as black comedy or thriller. Rated R for profanity, gore, and implied violence. 94m. **DIR:** Reb Braddock. **CAST:** William Baldwin, Angela Jones, Mel Gorham, Daisy Fuentes, Barry Corbin. **1995**

CURE, THE ★★★ An 11 year old boy who contracted AIDS from a blood transfusion is rescued from peer isolation by a young neighbor. The ravaging physical effects of AIDS are too slickly packaged, but the story is filled with credible compassion. Rated PG-13 for language. 95m. **DIR:** Peter Horton. **CAST:** Joseph Mazzello, Brad Renfro, Diana Scarwid, Annabella Sciorra, Bruce Davison. **1995**

CURIOSITY KILLS ★★★ C. Thomas Howell and Rae Dawn Chong help make an improbable story fascinating. He's a photographer paying the rent by working as handyman in his inner-city warehouse-turned-apartment complex; she's a neighbor who joins him to learn why a new tenant showed up so quickly after the apparent suicide of another neighbor. Rated R for violence and gore. Made for cable. 86m. **DIR:** Colin Bucksey. **CAST:** C. Thomas Howell, Rae Dawn Chong, Courteney Cox, Paul Guilfoyle. **1990**

CURLY SUE ★★ Writer-director John Hughes pours on the syrupy sweetness again with this tale of a homeless father-daughter duo who con their way into the life of a beautiful attorney. A diabetic's nightmare. Rated PG for brief profanity. 98m. **DIR:** John Hughes. **CAST:** James Belushi, Kelly Lynch, Alisan Porter, John Getz, Fred Dalton Thompson. **1991**

CURLY TOP ★★★ Millionaire songwriter John Boles adopts moppet Shirley Temple who plays matchmaker when he falls in love with her sister Rochelle Hudson. Almost too-cute Shirley sings "Animal Crackers in My Soup." Arthur Treacher provides his usual droll humor. B&W; 74m. **DIR:** Irving Cummings. **CAST:** Shirley Temple, John Boles, Rochelle Hudson, Jane Darwell, Arthur Treacher. **1935**

CURSE, THE 🦃 A meteor crashes and infects the water of a small town with alien parasites. Rated R for violence. 92m. **DIR:** David Keith. **CAST:** Wil Wheaton, John Schneider, Claude Akins. **1987**

CURSE II—THE BITE 🦃 Not even closely related to the first movie. Not rated; contains violence and gore. 97m. **DIR:** Fred Goodwin. **CAST:** Jill Schoelen, J. Eddie Peck, Jamie Farr, Bo Svenson. **1988**

CURSE III: BLOOD SACRIFICE ★★ After her sister interrupts the ritual killing of a goat by a group of African natives, a farmer's wife (Jenilee Harrison) must face a curse placed on her by the village's witch doctor. Christopher Lee portrays a local doctor who may or may not have something to do with it. Too bad. Rated R for profanity, nudity, and violence. 91m. **DIR:** Sean Burton. **CAST:** Christopher Lee, Jenilee Harrison. **1990**

CURSE IV: THE ULTIMATE SACRIFICE ★★★ This pseudosequel, originally called *Catacombs*, is a surprisingly stylish low-budget thriller. The memorable Feodor Chaliapin has a supporting role here. He's an aging patriarch who befriends his aide, a young priest troubled by a premature mid-life crisis. To make matters worse, a beautiful schoolteacher has invaded the brotherly order, and there's an ancient evil lurking below in the catacombs. Rated R, but fairly tame except for some blood, violence, and subject matter. 84m. **DIR:** David Schmoeller. **CAST:** Timothy Van Patten, Laura Schaefer, Jeremy West, Ian Abercrombie, Feodor Chaliapin. **1993**

CURSE OF FRANKENSTEIN, THE ★★★1/2 Hammer Films' version of the Frankenstein story about a scientist who creates a living man from the limbs and organs of corpses. Peter Cushing gives a strong performance as the doctor, with Christopher Lee his equal as the sympathetic creature. Some inspired moments are peppered throughout this well-handled tale. 83m. **DIR:** Terence Fisher. **CAST:** Peter Cushing, Christopher Lee, Robert Urquhart. **1957**

CURSE OF INFERNO, THE ★★ A pair of bumbling bankrobbers match wits with a rich and very crooked businessman. The presence of Janine Turner is the film's only saving grace. Rated R for profanity. 87m. **DIR:** John Warren. **CAST:** Pauly Shore, Janine Turner, Ned Beatty. **1997**

CURSE OF KING TUT'S TOMB, THE 🦃 Made-for-TV misfire concerning the mysterious events surrounding the opening of King Tut's tomb. 100m. **DIR:** Philip Leacock. **CAST:** Eva Marie Saint, Robin Ellis, Raymond Burr, Harry Andrews, Tom Baker. **1980**

CURSE OF THE BLACK WIDOW ★★ Made-for-TV movie with a recycled script and a cast that seems to have been plucked from an unshot *Love Boat* installment. Who's the killer that's leaving victims draped in gooey webbing? Only director Dan Curtis's familiarity with the genre gives this telefilm some bounce. 100m. **DIR:** Dan Curtis. **CAST:** Anthony Franciosa, Donna Mills, Patty Duke, June Allyson. **1977**

CURSE OF THE BLUE LIGHTS 🦃 Teenagers must find a way to escape from an underground world populated by demons. Not rated, but gory enough for an R rating. 96m. **DIR:** John H. Johnson. **CAST:** Brent Ritter. **1989**

CURSE OF THE CAT PEOPLE, THE ★★★ When Val Lewton was ordered by the studio to make a sequel to the successful *Cat People*, he came up with this gentle fantasy about a child who is haunted by spirits. Not to be confused with the 1980s version of *Cat People*. B&W; 70m. **DIR:** Gunther Von Fristch, Robert Wise. **CAST:** Simone Simon, Kent Smith, Jane Randolph, Elizabeth Russell. **1944**

CURSE OF THE CRIMSON ALTAR 🦃 Supposedly based on H. P. Lovecraft's "Dreams in the Witch-House," this film bears no resemblance to that classic. Rated PG for violence. 87m. **DIR:** Vernon Sewell. **CAST:** Boris Karloff, Christopher Lee, Michael Gough, Barbara Steele. **1970**

CURSE OF THE CRYING WOMAN, THE ★★1/2 One of the better Mexican monster movies released straight to TV by American International Pictures in the 1960s. The film's visual style appears to have been influenced by *Nosferatu* and *Black Sunday*. B&W; 74m. **DIR:** Rafael Baledon. **CAST:** Rosita Arenas, Abel Salazar. **1961**

CURSE OF THE CRYSTAL EYE ★★★1/2 Better-than-average update of the Saturday-morning serial obviously owes a debt to *Raiders of the Lost Ark*. Jameson Parker and Cynthia Rhodes attempt to retrieve the infamous Crystal Eye from a hidden desert fortress while fighting off friends and foes alike. Impressive action sequences and a rousing sense of adventure elevate this one above the many low-budget affairs that followed *Raiders*. Rated R for violence. 82m. **DIR:** Joe Tornatore. **CAST:** Jameson Parker, Cynthia Rhodes, Mike Lane, David Sherwood, André Jacobs. **1993**

CURSE OF THE DEMON ★★★★1/2 Horrifying tale of an American occult expert, Dr. Holden (Dana Andrews), traveling to London to expose a supposed devil cult led by sinister Professor Karswell (Niall MacGinnis). Unfortunately for Holden, Karswell's cult proves to be all too real as a demon from hell is dispatched by the professor to put an end to the annoying investigation. Riveting production is a true classic of the genre. B&W; 96m. **DIR:** Jacques Tourneur. **CAST:** Dana Andrews, Peggy Cummins, Niall MacGinnis, Maurice Denham. **1958**

CURSE OF THE FLY ★★1/2 British-made film has only the slightest connection to the original *The Fly* and *The Return of the Fly*, as scientist Brian Donlevy tries to perfect his matter-teleportation machine that mutates living tissue. B&W; 86m. **DIR:** Don Sharp. **CAST:** Brian Donlevy, George Baker, Carole Gray, Burt Kwouk. **1965**

•**CURSE OF THE JADE SCORPION, THE** ★★★ A crack insurance investigator (Woody Allen) is hypnotized into pulling a series of jewel heists, then unwittingly investigates his own crimes. Allen goes featherlight in an affectionate, quaintly charming re-creation of the screwball crime comedies of the 1940s. There are a few big laughs, but several good chuckles and many warm smiles. Rated PG-13 for some sexual content. 103m. **DIR:** Woody Allen. **CAST:** Woody Allen, Helen Hunt, Dan Aykroyd, David Ogden Stiers, Wallace Shawn, Charlize Theron, Elizabeth Berkley. **2001 DVD**

CURSE OF THE LIVING DEAD (KILL, BABY, KILL) ★★★ More commonly available on video as *Kill, Baby, Kill*. It's the great Mario Bava's closing essay in gothic horror, a tremendously atmospheric supernatural mystery about a Transylvanian village and the doctor who tries to free it from a hideous curse in which murder victims are found with gold coins imbedded in their hearts. Slow-paced, but stay with it. 75m. **DIR:** Mario Bava. **CAST:** Giacomo Rossi-Stuart. **1966**

CURSE OF THE MUMMY'S TOMB, THE 🦃 Wholly unmemorable flapping-bandage horror. An atypically dull effort from England's Hammer Studios. 80m. **DIR:** Michael Carreras. **CAST:** Terence Morgan, Fred Clark, Ronald Howard, Jeanne Roland, Michael Ripper. **1964**

CURSE OF THE PINK PANTHER, THE ★★★ No, this isn't another trashy compilation of outtakes featuring the late Peter Sellers. Instead, series producer-writer-director Blake Edwards has hired Ted Wass to play a bumbling American detective searching for the still-missing Jacques Clouseau, and he's a delight. When Wass is featured, *Curse* is fresh and diverting—and, on a couple of memorable occasions, it's hilarious. Rated PG for nudity, profanity, violence, and scatological humor. 109m. **DIR:** Blake Edwards. **CAST:** Ted Wass, David Niven, Robert Wagner, Harvey Korman, Herbert Lom. **1983**

CURSE OF THE PUPPET MASTER ★★ The durable direct-to-video franchise is showing its age with this sixth entry. This one deals with another mad scientist trying to create a perfect race of puppet people. Obviously the filmmakers have never seen Congress in action. Time to cut the strings on this franchise. Rated R for violence and language. 90m. **DIR:** David DeCoteau. **CAST:** George Peck, Emily Harrison, Josh Green, Michael Guerin, Marc Newburger. **1998 DVD**

CURSE OF THE QUEERWOLF ★★1/2 Once you get past the juvenile humor of this film, there are some genuine laughs to be found in this horror-comedy. Here, a man is bitten on the tush by a transsexual lycanthrope (a queerwolf) and finds himself becoming one as well. The only thing that seems to help slow his transformation is a photo of John Wayne. Go figure. Not rated; contains sexual humor and profanity. 90m. **DIR:** Mark Pirro. **CAST:** Michael Palazzolo, Kent Butler, Forrest J. Ackerman, Conrad Brooks. **1987**

CURSE OF THE STARVING CLASS ★★1/2 Sam Shepard's play-turned-film has his customarily dreary tone and is far too symbolic for its own good. Stars James Woods and Kathy Bates never fully realize their roles as destitute farmers about to lose their property (poetic license aside, just-plain-folks don't *talk* like this). Rated R for profanity and brief nudity. 102m. **DIR:** J. Michael McClary. **CAST:** James Woods, Kathy Bates, Randy Quaid, Henry Thomas, Kristin Fiorella, Louis Gossett Jr. **1994**

CURSE OF THE UNDEAD ★★★ Horror-Western starring Michael Pate as a mysterious gunslinger who's immune to bullets. John Hoyt plays the town doctor, baffled when several young girls end up dead, all with puncture wounds in their necks, and Eric Fleming is the preacher who suspects there's evil in town. Not rated.

B&W; 89m. **DIR:** Edward Dein. **CAST:** Eric Fleming, Michael Pate, Kathleen Crowley, John Hoyt, Bruce Gordon. **1959**

CURSE OF THE WEREWOLF, THE ★★★1/2 After being brutally raped in a castle dungeon by an imprisoned street beggar, a young woman gives birth to a son with a strange appetite for blood. His heritage remains a mystery until adulthood, whereupon he begins transforming into a wolf as the full moon rises. Oliver Reed is fine in the role of the werewolf, one of his earliest screen performances. 91m. **DIR:** Terence Fisher. **CAST:** Oliver Reed, Clifford Evans, Yvonne Romain, Anthony Dawson. **1961**

CURSE OF THE YELLOW SNAKE, THE ★★ An Oriental death cult is on the rampage in this lively comic-strip fantasy from the pen of the incredibly prolific pulp author Edgar Wallace, whose hundreds of yarns were the foundation for a cottage industry in West German exploitation movies from the Fifties through the Seventies. B&W; 98m. **DIR:** Franz Gottlieb. **CAST:** Joachim Fuchsberger. **1963**

CURTAIN CALL ★★★ Whimsical if familiar story about a New York brownstone haunted by the spirits of two Broadway stars. Of course the only person who can see them is a book publisher whose ghostly encounters bring to question his sanity. Anyone who has seen *Heart and Souls* or *Topper* will recognize the premise, yet the engaging cast does wonders in making all of this less than transparent. Rated PG-13. 94m. **DIR:** Peter Yates. **CAST:** James Spader, Michael Caine, Polly Walker, Maggie Smith, Buck Henry, Sam Shepard, Marcia Gay Harden. **1997 DVD**

CURTAINS 🦃 A movie actress gets herself committed to a mental institution as preparation for an upcoming film. Rated R. 89m. **DIR:** Jonathan Stryker. **CAST:** John Vernon, Samantha Eggar, Linda Thorson, Anne Ditchburn. **1983**

CUSTODIAN, THE ★★★1/2 An Australian cop decides he's had it with corruption in the police force, so he tackles the problem in a very unconventional way. He's also dealing with his own problems, including being thrown out of his house by his alcoholic wife. Very well-acted, with an intriguing plot. Not rated; contains nudity, violence, and profanity. 96m. **DIR:** John Dingwall. **CAST:** Anthony LaPaglia, Hugo Weaving, Barry Otto, Kelly Dingwall, Bill Hunter, Gosia Dobrowolska. **1993**

CUT AND RUN 🦃 A television journalist in South America covering a bloody cocaine war. Rated R for violence, profanity, and nudity. 87m. **DIR:** Ruggero Deodato. **CAST:** Lisa Blount, Leonard Mann, Willie Aames, Richard Lynch, Richard Bright, Michael Berryman, John Steiner, Karen Black. **1985 DVD**

CUTAWAY ★★ Stephen Baldwin plays a U.S. Customs agent named Vic Cooper, who goes undercover as a sky diver in order to catch smugglers. It's not long before Vic is seduced by the high-risk thrill of the sport as well as by fellow sky diver Maxine Bahns, who distracts him from his mission. The skydiving footage is exciting, but the plot is more familiar than fun. Rated R for violence. 104m. **DIR:** Guy Manos. **CAST:** Stephen Baldwin, Tom Berenger, Casper Van Dien, Dennis Rodman, Ron Silver. **2000 DVD**

CUTTER'S WAY ★★★★ This comes very close to being a masterpiece. The screenplay, by Jeffrey Alan Fiskin, adapted from the novel *Cutter and Bone* by Newton Thornburg, is a murder mystery. The three lead performances are first-rate. Rated R because of violence, nudity, and profanity. 105m. **DIR:** Ivan Passer. **CAST:** Jeff Bridges, John Heard, Lisa Eichhorn, Ann Dusenberry. **1981 DVD**

CUTTHROAT ISLAND ★★★ A pirate's scrappy daughter scalps her father to honor his dying request and finds part of a treasure map tattooed on his skull. She then must wrest other pieces of the map from a scam artist and a notorious sea villain to locate a fabulous isle booty. The film's slow-motion effects are overdone and its humor is often too cute, but this sprawling swashbuckler develops a sportive seediness and rich, atmospheric funk. Rated PG-13 for language and violence. 123m. **DIR:** Renny Harlin. **CAST:** Geena Davis, Matthew Modine, Frank Langella, Maury Chaykin, Harris Yulin, Stan Shaw. **1995 DVD**

CUTTING CLASS ★★ A mass murderer is on the loose at a local high school. Sound familiar? Well . . . it is. Rated R for violence and profanity. 91m. **DIR:** Raspo Pallenberg. **CAST:** Donovan Leitch, Jill Schoelen, Brad Pitt, Roddy McDowall, Martin Mull. **1989**

CUTTING EDGE, THE ★★★1/2 Ice-hockey player D.B. Sweeney reluctantly becomes the figure-skating partner of ice queen Moira Kelly. Few surprises, but those who thaw at the idea of a love story will find it entertaining. Rated PG for profanity. 101m. **DIR:** Paul Michael Glaser. **CAST:** D. B. Sweeney, Moira Kelly, Roy Dotrice, Dwier Brown, Terry O'Quinn. **1992 DVD**

CUTTING MOMENTS ★★★ Fueled by pure imagination and a hard-core attitude, this highly enjoyable anthology film hits the mark far more often than it misses. The best is the title segment, although wise viewers will fast-forward past *Don't Nag Me*. The special effects of gore guru Tom Savini are also on hand in the film, a special treat for fans. Not rated; contains gore, violence, profanity, and nudity. 76m. **DIR:** Douglas Buck, Casey Kehoe, Timothy Healy, Gino Panaro, Craig Wallace. **CAST:** Nica Ray, Gary Betsworth, Jared Barsky. **1998**

CYBER BANDITS ★★ Secret plans for a virtual-reality weapon are tattooed onto a heroic sailor's back in order to prevent world domination by a megalomaniac millionaire. Farfetched action outing that uses high technology as camouflage for its own lack of invention. Rated R for violence and adult situations. 86m. **DIR:** Erik Fleming. **CAST:** Martin Kemp, Alexandra Paul, Robert Hays, Adam Ant, Grace Jones, Henry Gibson, James Hong. **1995**

CYBER CITY OEDO 808 ★★1/2 Three convicts are offered early release in exchange for service as "Cyber Police"—investigators charged with solving crimes of a technological nature. Above-average animation makes this one more watchable than some, but the lack of character detail leaves much to be desired. In Japanese with English subtitles. Not rated; contains profanity. 46m. **DIR:** Yoshiaki Kawajiri. **1990**

CYBER NINJA ★★★1/2 Eye-popping special effects and elaborate set design highlight this Japanese space opera reminiscent of *Star Wars*. Saki, a warrior/princess, has been abducted and taken to the Dark Overlord, who plans to use her as a sacrifice to unleash a powerful evil that will sweep the land. It's up to Cyber Ninja and a small band of rebels to battle the Overlord and save the princess. Dubbed. Not rated; contains fantasy-type violence. 80m. **DIR:** Keita Amamiya. **CAST:** Hanbei Kawai, Hiroki Ida, Eri Morishita, Makoto Yokoyama. **1988**

CYBER TRACKER ★★ Don "The Dragon" Wilson stars as a government agent who suddenly finds himself framed for murder and targeted for elimination by lethal androids called cyber trackers. These androids are commissioned by the government to execute violent criminals on the spot. Rated R for violence, nudity, and profanity. 91m. **DIR:** Richard Pepin. **CAST:** Don "The Dragon" Wilson, Richard Norton, Stacie Foster, Steve Burton, Abby Dalton, Jim Maniaci. **1994 DVD**

CYBER TRACKER 2 ★★1/2 A secret-service agent and his TV-news-anchor wife are forced to prove their innocence when cyborgs created to resemble them go on a killing spree. Some high-energy shoot-outs and explosion scenes galore distinguish this routine but competent high-tech testosterone-fest. Rated R for violence and strong language. 97m. **DIR:** Richard Pepin. **CAST:** Don "The Dragon" Wilson, Stacie Foster, Tony Burton, Jim Maniaci, Anthony DeLongis, John Kessir, Stephen Rowe, Steve Burton. **1995**

CYBERZONE ★★1/2 Sporadically effective *Blade Runner* rip-off about a twenty-first-century bounty hunter searching for four female "pleasure "droids" hijacked by a corporate mogul. The movie's offbeat combination of titillation and low-rent sci-fi is undeniably cheesy but nonetheless entertaining. Rated R for sexual situations and violence. 80m. **DIR:** Fred Olen Ray. **CAST:** Marc Singer, Matthias Hues, Rochelle Swanson, Robin Clark, Kin Shriner, Cal Bartlett, Robert Quarry, Ross Hagen, Brinke Stevens. **1995**

CYBORG 🦃 A study in bad. Bad script. Bad acting. Bad directing. Bad special effects. A soldier of the future (Jean-Claude Van Damme) seeks vengeance against the savage gang that killed his family. Rated R for violence. 90m. **DIR:** Albert Pyun. **CAST:** Jean-Claude Van Damme, Deborah Richter, Dayle Haddon. **1989 DVD**

CYBORG 2 🦃 This turgid sequel-in-name-only steals profusely from *Blade Runner* and *Max Headroom.* A martial-arts instructor (Elias Koteas) does the unthinkable by falling in love with a pouting cyborg (Angelina Jolie). Rated R for violence, profanity, nudity, and simulated sex. 99m. **DIR:** Michael Schroeder. **CAST:** Elias Koteas, Angelina Jolie, Allen Garfield, Billy Drago, Jack Palance. **1993 DVD**

CYBORG 3: THE RECYCLER ★★ Outrageous situations and campy performances save the day for this tired sequel about a cyborg who discovers she is pregnant. It's actually quite fun to watch Malcolm McDowell chew the scenery as the bad guy. Rated R for violence. 90m. **DIR:** Michael Schroeder. **CAST:** Zach Galligan, Khrystyne Haje, Richard Lynch, Malcolm McDowell. **1994**

CYBORG COP ★★ Convoluted concoction borrows from several different genres, but can't come to grips with its own identity. A former DEA agent locates his brother on a Caribbean island, but learns that his sibling has become a cyborg in a cruel experiment. John Rhys-Davies is cheerfully villainous, while the rest of the cast must grin and bear tiresome clichés. Rated R for violence and language. 94m. **DIR:** Sam Firstenberg. **CAST:** David Bradley, Todd Jensen, Alonna Shaw, John Rhys-Davies. **1993**

CYBORG SOLDIER ★★ A renegade cop is assigned the duty of wiping out a series of berserk cyborg slaves. Plenty of action and just enough storyline. Rated R for violence. 97m. **DIR:** Sam Firstenberg. **CAST:** David Bradley, Morgan Hunter, Jill Pierce, Dale Cutts, Victor Mellaney. **1993**

CYBORG: THE SIX MILLION DOLLAR MAN ★★★ Pilot for the long-running ABC series is more serious and subdued than the episodes to follow. Col. Steve Austin (Lee Majors), after flying an experimental jet that crashes, is turned into a superman with powerful robotic limbs. Very good. 73m. **DIR:** Richard Irving. **CAST:** Lee Majors, Darren McGavin, Martin Balsam. **1973**

CYCLO ★★★1/2 Innocence, evil, poverty, and wealth all rub shoulders amid Ho Chi Minh City's teeming downtown streets soon after the Vietnam War in this hallucinogenic drama about the fragility of life and family. A teen bicycle-taxi driver is intoxicated with a false sense of power when he and his older sister are sucked into the city's cruel criminal underworld. In Vietnamese and French with English subtitles. Not rated; contains sexual content, adult themes, and violence. 124m. **DIR:** Tran Anh Hung. **CAST:** Le Van Loc, Tony Leung Chiu Wai, Tran Nu Yen-Khe, Nguyen Nhu Quynh. **1996**

CYCLONE 🦃 Stupid action flick about a top-secret military experiment. Rated R for violence and profanity. 89m. **DIR:** Fred Olen Ray. **CAST:** Heather Thomas, Martin Landau, Jeffrey Combs, Troy Donahue, Martine Beswick, Robert Quarry, Huntz Hall. **1986**

CYCLONE IN THE SADDLE 🦃 Absolute bottom-of-the-barrel wagon train oater. B&W; 52m. **DIR:** Elmer Clifton. **CAST:** Rex Lease, Bobby Nelson, William Desmond, Yakima Canutt. **1935**

CYCLOPS, THE ★★1/2 Low-budget whiz Bert I. Gordon does it again with this cheaply made but effective film about a woman (Gloria Talbott) whose brother is transformed into a big, crazy monster by—what else?—radiation. Neat little movie. B&W; 75m. **DIR:** Bert I. Gordon. **CAST:** James Craig, Lon Chaney Jr., Gloria Talbott. **1957**

CYRANO DE BERGERAC (1925) ★★★★ This silent French version of the classic drama may seem stagy to modern viewers, especially in comparison to the 1990 version starring Gérard Depardieu. But the story is still gripping, and new English intertitles and the original hand tinting make this restored version a pleasure to watch for viewers who have suffered through hard-to-view silent films. 114m. **DIR:** Augusto Genina. **CAST:** Pierre Magnier, Linda Mogila, Angelo Ferrari. **1925 DVD**

CYRANO DE BERGERAC (1950) ★★★★ Charming, touching story of steadfast devotion and unrequited love done with brilliance and panache. As the fearless soldier of the large nose, José Ferrer superbly dominates this fine film. Mala Powers is beautiful as his beloved Roxanne. William Prince, who now often plays heavies, makes Christian a proper, handsome, unimaginative nerd. B&W; 112m. **DIR:** Michael Gordon. **CAST:** José Ferrer, Mala Powers, William Prince. **1950 DVD**

CYRANO DE BERGERAC (1990) ★★★★★ This lavish French production is both ethereal and earthy, poetic and robust, a quintessential, cinematic new version of the classic play about an unattractive cavalier with the soul of perfect romance. The most charismatic and fascinating Gallic actor of the day—Gérard Depardieu—creates the definitive Cyrano. Rated PG. 135m. **DIR:** Jean-Paul Rappeneau. **CAST:** Gérard Depardieu, Anne Brochet, Vincent Perez, Jacques Weber. **1990**

D

D-DAY THE SIXTH OF JUNE ★★ Slow-moving account of the Normandy invasion in World War II. Story concentrates on Allied officers Robert Taylor's and Richard Todd's romantic and professional problems. 106m. **DIR:** Henry Koster. **CAST:** Robert Taylor, Richard Todd, Dana Wynter, Edmond O'Brien. **1956**

D.I., THE ★★★ Jack Webb embodies the tough, nononsense drill instructor so commonly associated with the Marine Corps in this straightforward story of basic training and the men that it makes (or breaks). Don Dubbins plays the troublesome recruit who makes life miserable for Webb; many other roles are played by real-life members of the armed services. B&W; 106m. **DIR:** Jack Webb. **CAST:** Jack Webb, Don Dubbins, Lin McCarthy, Monica Lewis, Jackie Loughery, Virginia Gregg. **1957**

D. W. GRIFFITH TRIPLE FEATURE ★★★ Kentucky dreamer and failed playwright David Wark Griffith was the American film industry's first great mover and shaker. Three fine examples of his early short films make up this feature: *The Battle of Elderbush Gulch*, *Iola's Promise*, and *The Goddess of Sagebrush Gulch*. Silent. B&W; 50m. **DIR:** D. W. Griffith. **CAST:** Mae Marsh, Lillian Gish, Charles West, Blanche Sweet, Mary Pickford. **1922**

DA ★★★★ New York City playwright Martin Sheen returns to his Irish home when his adoptive father (Barnard Hughes) dies. While in the house in which he was raised, Sheen relives his less-than-idyllic youth with the help of his father's cantankerous ghost. Both sentimental and uncompromising, this special film benefits from a performance of a lifetime by Hughes and one of nearly equal merit by Sheen. Rated PG for profanity. 96m. **DIR:** Matt Clark. **CAST:** Barnard Hughes, Martin Sheen, William Hickey, Doreen Hepburn. **1988**

DAD ★★★★ In this wonderful weeper, Ted Danson is a successful businessman who attempts to make an emotional connection with his 75 year old father (Jack Lemmon) before it is too late. Writer-director Gary David Goldberg, who adapted the novel by William Wharton, doesn't let us off easy. Rated PG. 116m. **DIR:** Gary David Goldberg. **CAST:** Jack Lemmon, Ted Danson, Olympia Dukakis, Kathy Baker, Kevin Spacey, Ethan Hawke. **1989**

DADDY LONG LEGS ★★★1/2 The oft-told tale of the wealthy playboy secretly arranging the education of a poor orphaned waif, is, as expected, secondary to the song and dance. Leslie Caron has a natural grace not seen in many of Fred Astaire's partners; their dances seem to flow. A highlight is Fred's drumstick solo in "History of the Beat." Academy Award nominations for Johnny Mercer's "Something's Got to Give" and the scoring by Alfred Newman. 126m. **DIR:** Jean Negulesco. **CAST:** Fred Astaire, Leslie Caron, Terry Moore, Thelma Ritter. **1955 DVD**

DADDY NOSTALGIA ★★★ Enjoyable exploration of the relationship between a daughter and her dying father. Dirk Bogarde and Jane Birkin are magical as they try to work out their differences and come to understand and respect each other. Director Bertrand Tavernier scores again. In French with English subtitles. Rated PG. 105m. **DIR:** Bertrand Tavernier. **CAST:** Dirk Bogarde, Jane Birkin, Odette Laure. **1990**

DADDY'S BOYS ★★ Depression-era crime-drama about an ex-farmer turned bank robber. Typical Roger Corman production has a few surprises but is basically familiar stuff. Rated R for violence and sexual situations. 84m. **DIR:** Joe Minion. **CAST:** Daryl Haney, Laura Burkett. **1988**

DADDY'S DYIN' AND WHO'S GOT THE WILL ★★★1/2 Mildly enjoyable comedy about a group of southern eccentrics who just may be rich—if they can find the last will and testament of their nearly dearly departed dad. Entertaining, although the feudin' and fussin' does get to be a bit much. Rated PG-13 for profanity. 117m. **DIR:** Jack Fisk. **CAST:** Beau Bridges, Beverly D'Angelo, Tess Harper, Judge Reinhold, Amy Wright, Keith Carradine, Bert Remsen. **1990**

DADDY'S GIRL ★★ Gabrille Boni is effective as Jody, a psychotic 11-year-old who will do anything to stop anyone who comes between her and her father. Don Mitchell (William Katt) adores his adopted daughter Jody so much that he is blind to her deceptive ways. When Karen, the girl's older cousin, moves in with the family, she uncovers Jody's dark side. Paint-by-the-numbers plotting and lackluster direction do little to make this exercise in horror more than it is. Rated R for violence and language. 95m. **DIR:** Martin Kitrosser. **CAST:** William Katt, Michele Greene, Roxana Zal, Gabrille Boni. **1996**

DADDY'S GONE A-HUNTING ★★★ Veteran director Mark Robson knows how to get the best out of the material he has to work with. And this is an exciting, neatly crafted psychological drama—in which Carol White gets involved with a psychotic photographer (Scott Hylands). If you get a chance to go a-hunting for this one at your local video store, you won't go unrewarded. Not rated, but with some violent content. 108m. **DIR:** Mark Robson. **CAST:** Carol White, Paul Burke, Scott Hylands, Mala Powers. **1969**

DAENS ★★★★ Powerful, moving tribute to the human will. Jan DeCleir delivers a stunning performance as Father Daens, a man of the cloth who puts everything on the line in order to improve the wretched working conditions in the local factories. Pitting himself against church officials, local government, and big business, Father Daens discovers the difference between what's right and what's popular. Nominated for Best Foreign Language Film. In Flemish and French with English subtitles. Not rated; contains strong images. 134m. **DIR:** Syijn Coninx. **CAST:** Jan Decleir, Gerard Desarthe, Antje De Boeck, Michael Pas. **1992**

DAFFY DUCK'S MOVIE: FANTASTIC ISLAND ★★ This pedestrian compilation is for Warner Bros. cartoon fanatics and toddlers only. Chunks of fairly funny shorts are strung together with a weak, dated parody of TV's *Fantasy Island*. Daffy deserved better. Rated G. 78m. **DIR:** Friz Freleng. **1983**

DAFFY DUCK'S QUACKBUSTERS ★★★★★ The best feature-length compilation of Warner Bros. cartoons since Chuck Jones's *The Bugs Bunny/Road Runner Movie*, this release features two new cartoons—"Quackbusters" and "Night of the Living Duck"—as well as classics from Jones ("Claws for Alarm," "Transylvania 6-5000," and "The Abominable Snow Rabbit") and Friz Freleng ("Hyde and Go Tweet"). The wraparound story is animated with as much care as the original cartoons, and the result is a delight for young and old. 80m. **DIR:** Greg Ford, Terry Lennon. **1988**

DAGGER OF KAMUI, THE ★★★ The beautifully animated film from veteran director Rin Taro is wounded by a somewhat overlong (and sometimes terribly corny) story. Jiro, a young Ninja, is bent on discovering the secret that caused the death of his parents and threatens the destruction of the Tokugawa shogunate. In Japanese with English subtitles. Not rated; contains violence. 132m. **DIR:** Rin Taro. **1985**

DAGORA, THE SPACE MONSTER 🦃 A cache of gems stolen by Japanese gangsters is ripped off by a giant, flying, diamond-eating jellyfish. Probably a true story. 80m. **DIR:** Inoshiro Honda. **CAST:** Yosuke Natsuki. **1964**

DAIN CURSE, THE 🦃 A poor, two-hour version of a just passable TV miniseries based on the Dashiell Hammett classic. 123m. **DIR:** E. W. Swackhamer. **CAST:** James Coburn, Hector Elizondo, Jason Miller, Jean Simmons. **1978**

DAISIES IN DECEMBER ★★★★ Joss Ackland and Jean Simmons shine as a pair of senior citizens who tentatively grope their way into a relationship, in this charming story from scripter Jenny Paschall. Ackland initially resents being dumped at a seaside enclave for seniors while the rest of his family enjoys a skiing vacation, but he's eventually won over by longtime resident Simmons's obvious joy in every little delight that each morning provides. Watch for Ian Crowe, charming in a small role as a solicitous taxi driver. Rated PG for mild profanity. 97m. **DIR:** Mark Haber. **CAST:** Joss Ackland, Jean Simmons, Pippa Guard, Judith Barker, Barbara Lott, Ian Crowe. **1995**

DAISY MILLER ★★ This limp screen adaptation of a story by the great novelist Henry James is more a study on rambling dialogue than on the clashing of two cultures. Rated G. 93m. **DIR:** Peter Bogdanovich. **CAST:** Cybill Shepherd, Barry Brown, Cloris Leachman, Mildred Natwick, Eileen Brennan. **1974**

DAKOTA (1945) ★★1/2 Any Western with John Wayne, Walter Brennan, and Ward Bond has to be a winner, right? Wrong. This substandard film may be interesting to see for their performances, but you also have to put up with the incredibly untalented Vera Ralston (she was the wife of Republic Studio head Herbert Yates). It's almost worth it. B&W; 82m. **DIR:** Joseph Kane. **CAST:** John Wayne, Vera Hruba Ralston, Walter Brennan, Ward Bond. **1945**

DAKOTA (1988) ★★★ Outstanding cinematography highlights this run-of-the-mill story of a troubled teen on the run. Lou Diamond Phillips is the teen who works off a debt by training horses on a Texas farm. In the process he learns he must also face his past. Rated PG-13. 90m. **DIR:** Fred Holmes. **CAST:** Lou Diamond Phillips, Dee Dee Morton. **1988 DVD**

DAKOTA INCIDENT ★★1/2 It's a fight to the finish in this fairly good Western as the Indians attack a stagecoach rolling through Dakota Territory in those thrilling days of yesteryear. 88m. **DIR:** Lewis R. Foster. **CAST:** Dale Robertson, Linda Darnell, John Lund. **1956**

DALEKS—INVASION EARTH 2150 A.D. ★★★ The always watchable Peter Cushing revives his distinctive interpretation of the ever-popular Dr. Who in this honorable sequel to *Dr. Who and the Daleks*. This time, the title creatures are attempting to take over Earth. 84m. **DIR:** Gordon Flemyng. **CAST:** Peter Cushing, Bernard Cribbins, Andrew Keir, Ray Brooks. **1966**

DALEY: THE LAST BOSS ★★★ Hal Holbrook narrates this PBS documentary about Richard J. Daley, mayor of Chicago for more than twenty years. While he is best remembered as a proponent of law and order at any cost (demonstrated by his reaction to antiwar protests at the 1968 Democratic Convention), this documentary presents him as one of the last of the old-style "machine" politicians who built Chicago into the major urban center it is today. B&W/color; 112m. **DIR:** Barak Goodman. **1995**

DAM BUSTERS, THE ★★★★1/2 Richard Todd and Michael Redgrave star in this British film about the development and use of a specially designed bomb to destroy a dam in Germany during World War II. An outstanding cast and great script. 205m. **DIR:** Michael Anderson. **CAST:** Richard Todd, Michael Redgrave, Ursula Jeans, Basil Sydney. **1954**

DAMAGE ★★ When Stephen Fleming—a respected British Parliament member—meets his son's new girlfriend, he's overcome by a sexual obsession that sends his entire world into a tragic tailspin. A high-gloss soap that is as cold and detached as the enigmatic woman at its lurid core. Rated R for language, nudity, and violence. 100m. **DIR:** Louis Malle. **CAST:** Jeremy Irons, Juliette Binoche, Miranda Richardson, Rupert Graves, Leslie Caron, Ian Bannen. **1993 DVD**

DAMES ★★★ Music, songs, dancing, great Busby Berkeley numbers. Plot? Know the one about backing a Broadway musical? But, gee, it's fun to see and hear Joan Blondell, Dick Powell, Ruby Keeler, ZaSu Pitts, Guy Kibbee, and Hugh "Woo-woo" Herbert again. B&W; 90m. **DIR:** Ray Enright. **CAST:** Joan Blondell, Dick Powell, Ruby Keeler, ZaSu Pitts, Guy Kibbee, Hugh Herbert. **1934**

DAMIEN: OMEN II ★★★1/2 In this first sequel to *The Omen*, William Holden plays the world's richest man, Richard Thorn. In the previous picture, Richard's brother is shot by police while attempting to kill his son, who he believed to be the Antichrist, son of Satan. *Damien: Omen II* picks up seven years later. Rated R. 107m. **DIR:** Don Taylor. **CAST:** William Holden, Lee Grant, Lew Ayres, Sylvia Sidney. **1978**

DAMN THE DEFIANT! ★★★★ Authenticity is the hallmark of this sea saga of the Napoleonic period. This British production pits the commanding officer of a British warship against a hated second officer. The performances are superb. 101m. **DIR:** Lewis Gilbert. **CAST:** Alec Guinness, Dirk Bogarde, Maurice Denham, Anthony Quayle. **1962 DVD**

DAMN YANKEES ★★★1/2 A torrid, wiggling vamp teams with a sly, hissing devil to frame the Yankees by turning a middle-aged baseball fan into a wunderkind and planting him on the opposing team, the Washington Senators. Gwen Verdon is sensational as the temptress Lola, who gets whatever she wants. Hollywood called on her to reprise her role in the original Broadway musical hit. Lots of pep and zing in this one. 110m. **DIR:** George Abbott, Stanley Donen. **CAST:** Gwen Verdon, Ray Walston, Tab Hunter. **1958**

DAMNATION ALLEY (SURVIVAL RUN) ★★ The nuclear holocaust movie, which disappeared after its heyday in the 1950s, is revived, complete with giant mutations and roaming survivors. While it's not a bad movie, it's not particularly good, either. The laser effects are awful. Rated PG. 91m. **DIR:** Jack Smight. **CAST:** Jan-Michael Vincent, George Peppard, Dominique Sanda, Jackie Earle Haley, Paul Winfield. **1977**

DAMNED, THE ★★★1/2 Deep, heavy drama about a German industrialist family that is destroyed under Nazi power. This film is difficult to watch, as the images are as bleak as the story itself. In German with English subtitles. Rated R for sex. 155m. **DIR:** Luchino Visconti. **CAST:** Dirk Bogarde, Ingrid Thulin, Helmut Griem, Helmut Berger. **1969**

DAMNED RIVER ★★★ Four Americans take a rafting adventure vacation down the Zambezi River in Zimbabwe. Things get out of hand when their guide turns out to be a pyschopath and a *Deliverance* game of survival is played out. Rated R for violence. 96m. **DIR:** Michael Schroeder. **CAST:** Stephen Shellen, John Terlesky. **1989**

DAMSEL IN DISTRESS, A ★★★ By choice, Fred Astaire made this one without Ginger, who complemented him, but with Joan Fontaine—then a beginner—who could not dance. Fred's an American popular composer in stuffy London. He mistakenly thinks heiress Joan is a chorus girl. B&W; 98m. **DIR:** George Stevens. **CAST:** Fred Astaire, Joan Fontaine, Gracie Allen, George Burns, Constance Collier, Reginald Gardiner. **1937**

DAN CANDY'S LAW (ALIEN THUNDER) ★★ The Royal Canadian Mounted Police always get their man. So where's the suspense? Not in this movie, that's for sure. The most appealing element is the glorious Canadian scenery. Rated PG. 90m. **DIR:** Claude Fournier. **CAST:** Donald Sutherland, Kevin McCarthy, Chief Dan George, Francine Racette. **1973**

DANCE ★★ Mediocre story of a group of dancers, working with a high-pressure new choreographer, who are polishing their toe shoes for the National New York Ballet auditions. An interesting soundtrack, with IAM IAM, but the only star is black dancer, Carlton Wilborn. Not rated. 92m. **DIR:** Robin Murray. **CAST:** Johan Renvall, Ellen Troy, Carlton Wilborn. **1988**

DANCE, FOOLS, DANCE ★★1/2 Joan Crawford plays a determined young woman who becomes a crime reporter and tries to make her reputation by bringing gangster Clark Gable to justice. The sparks fly—and their torrid teaming and some risqué bits of business rescue this precode melodrama from the stale plot line. B&W; 81m. **DIR:** Harry Beaumont. **CAST:** Joan Crawford, Clark Gable, Cliff Edwards, Natalie Moorhead. **1931**

DANCE, GIRL, DANCE ★★★1/2 Lucille Ball doing a striptease! That's just one of the highlights of this RKO comedy-drama about a couple of ambitious chorus girls who struggle to make it big on Broadway. B&W; 89m. **DIR:** Dorothy Arzner. **CAST:** Maureen O'Hara, Louis Hayward, Lucille Ball. **1940**

DANCE HALL ★★ This is a minor musical about a nightclub owner (Cesar Romero) who falls in love with one of his employees (Carole Landis). Not great. The cast saves this film from being a dud. B&W; 74m. **DIR:** Irving Pichel. **CAST:** Carole Landis, Cesar Romero, William Henry, June Storey. **1941**

DANCE HALL RACKET Lenny Bruce plays creepy killer Vincent, bodyguard to a vice lord. B&W; 60m. **DIR:** Phil Tucker. **CAST:** Lenny Bruce. **1953**

DANCE ME OUTSIDE ★★★★ Original and provocative, this film strips away preconceptions to show us that life on the reservation is not what you'd expect. Based on W. P. Kinsella's book, it's a surprisingly dense coming-of-age story peppered with savvy humor. A small Canadian production, it features four teenagers trying to deal with the murder of a friend, as well as their own growing pains, all the while addressing racial tensions from the native perspective. Rated R for profanity and violence. 87m. **DIR:** Bruce McDonald. **CAST:** Ryan Black, Adam Beach, Lisa LaCroix, Michael Greyeyes, Jennifer Podemski, Kevin Hicks, Sandrine Holt. **1994**

DANCE OF DEATH Don't waste your time. Not rated. 75m. **DIR:** Juan Ibanez. **CAST:** Boris Karloff, Andres Garcia. **1971 DVD**

DANCE OF THE DAMNED ★★ Well-made but ultimately boring tale about a suicidal stripper and her chance meeting with a vampire. They spend the night discussing life, death, and the feel of the sun, but that's about it. Producer Roger Corman remade this as the much better *To Sleep with a Vampire*. Rated R for profanity, nudity, and violence. 83m. **DIR:** Katt Shea Ruben. **CAST:** Cyril O'Reilly, Starr Andreeff, Maria Ford. **1989**

DANCE OR DIE ★★ Another listless made-for-video thriller. This one pits a drug-addicted Las Vegas choreographer against mob drug dealers and federal drug agents. 81m. **DIR:** Richard W. Munchkin. **CAST:** Ray Kieffer, Rebecca Barrington. **1988**

DANCE 'TIL DAWN Typical teen tripe traps vapid rich kids in the same room as geeky teens with their chaperoning, shallow parents. Blech. Rated PG for sexual innuendo. 96m. **DIR:** Paul Schneider. **CAST:** Christina Applegate, Tempestt Bledsoe, Tracey Gold, Kelsey Grammer, Edie McClurg, Alyssa Milano, Alan Thicke. **1988 DVD**

DANCE WITH A STRANGER ★★★★1/2 A superbly acted, solidly directed import, this British drama is a completely convincing tale of tragic love. Miranda Richardson makes a stunning film debut as the platinum-blonde hostess in a working-class nightclub who falls in love with a self-indulgent, upper-class snob (Rupert Everett). The screenplay was based on the true story of Ruth Ellis, who, on July 13, 1955, was hanged at London's Holloway prison for shooting her lover outside a pub. Rated R for profanity, nudity, sex, and violence. 102m. **DIR:** Mike Newell. **CAST:** Miranda Richardson, Rupert Everett, Ian Holm, Matthew Carroll. **1985 DVD**

DANCE WITH DEATH ★★1/2 Sordid thriller with Barbara Alyn Woods as a cop who goes undercover as a stripper to flush out a killer. Getting naked was obviously a prerequisite to getting a role. Rated R for nudity, violence, and strong language. 90m. **DIR:** Charles Philip Moore. **CAST:** Maxwell Caulfield, Martin Mull, Barbara Alyn Woods, Drew Snyder. **1991**

DANCE WITH ME ★★★ This conventional love story makes an agreeable showcase for Latin superstar Chayanne, whose smile could light an auditorium. That's good, because scripter Daryl Matthews's tale is formulaic: A jaded dance pro is reawakened to life's possibilities after meeting a kind, attractive stranger. Ironically, the two stars spend little time dancing with each other. Rated PG for mild sensual content. 126m. **DIR:** Randa Haines. **CAST:** Vanessa L. Williams, Chayanne, Kris Kristofferson, Jane Krakowski, Beth Grant, Joan Plowright. **1998 DVD**

DANCER IN THE DARK ★★ An immigrant factory worker (Icelandic pop singer Björk), going slowly blind, retreats into fantasies of Hollywood musicals. Some wags dubbed this one *Blair Witch—The Musical* thanks to the out-of-focus photography and boring, seemingly improvised dialogue. The songs, written by Björk, are tuneless but surprisingly hypnotic and rather well danced. Winner—inexplicably—of best actress and the Palme d'Or awards at Cannes. Rated R for brief violence. 140m. **DIR:** Lars von Trier. **CAST:** Björk, Catherine Deneuve, David Morse, Peter Stormare, Udo Kier, Joel Grey. **2000 DVD**

DANCER, TEXAS: POP. 81 ★★★★ A group of friends—who promised themselves that they would leave their small town when they graduated from high school—wrestles with that promise as the time finally arrives. Excellent performances, writing, and direction. Rated PG. 97m. **DIR:** Tim McCanlies. **CAST:** Breckin Meyer, Peter Facinelli, Ethan Embry, Eddie Mills. **1998 DVD**

DANCERS ★★1/2 Only lovers of ballet will enjoy this wafer-thin drama, since its latter half is devoted solely to an American Ballet Theatre production of *Giselle*. The minimal attempt at parallel storytelling concerns the conceited company star-director and the dancer who falls under his spell. Rated PG for sexual themes. 99m. **DIR:** Herbert Ross. **CAST:** Mikhail Baryshnikov, Leslie Browne. **1987**

DANCES WITH WOLVES ★★★★★ Heartfelt, thoroughly involving saga of a disillusioned Union soldier's flight from the Civil War, and his eventual finding of inner peace in harmony with nature and the Lakota Sioux. A brilliant filmmaking debut from director-star Kevin Costner, this epic reestablished the Western's viability at the box office. In English and Lakota Sioux with subtitles. Rated PG-13 for violence and brief nudity. 185m. **DIR:** Kevin Costner. **CAST:** Kevin Costner, Mary McDonnell, Graham Greene, Rodney A. Grant. **1990 DVD**

DANCING AT LUGHNASA ★★1/2 Five sisters and the out-of-wedlock son of one of them eke out a hardscrabble existence in rural Ireland of the 1930s. Brian Friel's play won numerous awards and has a devoted following, but on film it plays like a self-conscious rehash of *The Glass Menagerie*, gloomy, predictable, and a little dreary. However, acting by the strong cast is first-rate. Rated PG. 92m. **DIR:** Pat O'Connor. **CAST:** Meryl Streep, Michael Gambon, Kathy Burke, Catherine McCormack, Sophie Thompson. **1998 DVD**

•DANCING IN SEPTEMBER ★★★★ This insightful look inside the world of network TV shows how ratings matter more than truth. A jaded staff writer breaks away from an established show to start her own sitcom, only to fall victim to the same sellouts. This made-for-cable film is both funny and tragic, and features some excellent acting. Rated R for profanity and violence. 107m. **DIR:** Reggie Rock Bythewood. **CAST:** Nicole Ari Parker, Isaiah Washington, Vicellous Reon Shannon, Malinda Williams. **2000 DVD**

DANCING IN THE DARK ★★1/2 Interesting drama about Edna Cormick (Martha Henry) who—after twenty years of being the ideal housewife, finds her life torn apart in a few short hours. From her hospital bed, Edna reconstructs the events that led up to her act of vengeance. Although this film is extremely slow-moving, feminists are likely to appreciate it. Rated PG-13. 93m. **DIR:** Leon Marr. **CAST:** Martha Henry, Neil Munro, Rosemary Dunsmore. **1986 DVD**

DANCING LADY ★★★ Joan Crawford goes from burlesque dancer to Broadway star in this backstage drama set to music. A good film, this was also one of her early money-makers. Fred Astaire made his screen debut in one dance number. B&W; 94m. **DIR:** Robert Z. Leonard. **CAST:** Joan Crawford, Clark Gable, Fred Astaire, Franchot Tone, May Robson, Grant Mitchell, Sterling Holloway, Ted Healy, The Three Stooges. **1933**

DANCING MOTHERS ★★★ Bee-sting-lipped Jazz Age flapper Clara Bow romps through this verge-of-sound silent about flaming youth. Enthusiastic performances offset the simple plot. B&W; 60m. **DIR:** Herbert Brenon. **CAST:** Clara Bow, Alice Joyce, Dorothy Cumming, Norman Trevor. **1926**

DANCING WITH DANGER 🦃 A scissor-wielding maniac is on the loose in this poorly acted and directed, made-for-cable, so-called mystery movie. Rated PG-13 for violence. 90m. **DIR:** Stuart Cooper. **CAST:** Cheryl Ladd, Ed Marinaro, Miguel Sandoval, Pat Skipper, Stanley Kamel. **1994**

DANDELIONS 🦃 This German-made soft-porn film stars Rutger Hauer as a cold, sadistic leather boy. Made in 1974. Dubbed in English. 92m. **DIR:** Adrian Hoven. **CAST:** Rutger Hauer, Dagmar Lassander. **1987**

DANDY IN ASPIC, A ★★ Who's on whose side? That's the question that pops up most often in this confusing, rather flat spy thriller. Laurence Harvey plays a double agent based in Berlin who is ordered to kill himself. This was director Anthony Mann's last film; he died during production and Harvey completed the direction. 107m. **DIR:** Anthony Mann. **CAST:** Laurence Harvey, Tom Courtenay, Mia Farrow, Lionel Stander, Harry Andrews. **1968**

DANGAIO ★★★1/2 Japanese animation. Four psionically enhanced warriors learn to work together against an evil space pirate and his minions. Strong characterization and visuals add much to this above-average story. In Japanese with English subtitles. Not rated; violence. 45m. **DIR:** Toshihiro Hirano. **1990**

DANGER ★★★ Three *film noir* episodes created for television: "The Lady on the Rock," "The System," and "Death Among the Relics." Sophisticated Alfred Hitchcock–like suspense chillers. Turn down the lights. B&W; 77m. **DIR:** Sidney Lumet. **CAST:** Don Hammer, Olive Deering, Kim Stanley, Eli Wallach. **1952**

DANGER LIGHTS ★★★ Louis Wolheim plays a tough-as-nails rail-yard boss who befriends hobo Robert Armstrong and jeopardizes his chances with a young Jean Arthur, who is "almost" a fiancée. This story, done many times before and since, works well against the backdrop of a railroad world that is now largely gone. B&W; 73m. **DIR:** George B. Seitz. **CAST:** Louis Wolheim, Jean Arthur, Robert Armstrong, Hugh Herbert. **1930**

DANGER MAN (TV SERIES) ★★★1/2 CBS-TV imported this British-produced thriller, the first of three spy-flavored dramas to star Patrick McGoohan (see additional entries under *Secret Agent* and *The Prisoner*). The series debuted in May, 1961, and quietly went off the air after an undistinguished run of 24 episodes. McGoohan starred as the "Danger Man," a freelancer named John Drake, who worked as a security investigator in affiliation with NATO. A bit violent, but suitable for family viewing. B&W; 55m. **DIR:** Various. **CAST:** Patrick McGoohan. **1961**

DANGER OF LOVE ★★ Truth is duller than fiction in this made-for-TV *Fatal Attraction* clone based on the true story of a suburban New York woman who murders her lover's wife. Rated R for violence and sexual situations. 97m. **DIR:** Joyce Chopra. **CAST:** Joe Penny, Jenny Robertson, Deborah Benson, Joseph Bologna, Fairuza Balk. **1992**

DANGER ZONE, THE (1986) 🦃 Contrived low-budget flick about a psychopathic murderer on the loose. Rated R for language, nudity, and violence. 90m. **DIR:** Henry Vernon. **CAST:** Michael Wayne, Jason Williams, Suzanne Tara, Robert Canada, Juanita Ranney. **1986**

DANGER ZONE (1995) ★★★ Billy Zane, our charming hero, gets mixed up with mercenaries trying to recover stolen plutonium, which is disguised as toxic waste and hidden somewhere within the jungles of South Africa. The stunts are a lot of fun. Rated R for profanity, violence, and nudity. 92m. **DIR:** Allan Eastman. **CAST:** Billy Zane, Ron Silver, Cary-Hiroyuki Tagawa, Robert Downey Jr., Lisa Collins. **1995**

DANGER: DIABOLIK ★★★ Director Mario Bava departed from the horror genre he normally specialized in, and staged this pop-art fantasy, based on an Italian comic strip of the time. Master criminal Diabolik outwits the police and government agents assigned to catch him in a garishly colored, playful spoof that sometimes is worthy of silent serial master Louis Feuillade. 105m. **DIR:** Mario Bava. **CAST:** John Phillip Law, Marisa Mell, Michel Piccoli, Terry-Thomas, Adolfo Celi. **1967**

DANGEROUS (1935) ★★ One of the weakest movies to earn its star an Oscar. Bette Davis plays a former stage-star-turned-alcoholic rescued by an idealistic architect (Franchot Tone). B&W; 78m. **DIR:** Alfred E. Green. **CAST:** Bette Davis, Franchot Tone, Alison Skipworth, Margaret Lindsay, John Eldredge, Dick Foran. **1935**

DANGEROUS, THE (1984) ★★★ Rod Hewitt's overly complicated plot concerns a bad guy turned good, a good cop turned rogue, the usual seedy drug barons, two knife-wielding psychopaths, Ninja assassins bent on revenge, and a couple of Hollywood veterans slumming as colorful snitches. The squalid New Orleans setting is appropriate for the tough-guy heroics, and the script achieves brief moments of poetic grace. Rated R for profanity, violence, nudity, and simulated sex. 92m. **DIR:** Rod Hewitt. **CAST:** Robert Davi, Michael Paré, Cary-Hiroyuki Tagawa, Elliott Gould, John Savage, Joel Grey. **1994**

DANGEROUS BEAUTY ★★★★1/2 Catherine McCormack shines as sixteenth-century Venice courtesan Veronica Franco, who becomes legendary with her verbal and sexual skills, and ability to sway the heads of foreign diplomats. Her pursuit of a married man, the oncoming plague, and persecution by the Church threaten her existence. *Dangerous Beauty* is filled with visual and verbal splendor. Rated R for nudity, adult situations, and language. 112m. **DIR:** Marshall Herskovitz. **CAST:** Catherine McCormack, Rufus Sewell, Oliver Platt, Jacqueline Bisset, Fred Ward, Moira Kelly. **1998 DVD**

DANGEROUS CHARTER 🦃 Three fishermen find an abandoned yacht with a corpse on board. B&W; 74m. **DIR:** Robert Gottschalk. **CAST:** Chris Warfield, Sally Fraser, Chick Chandler. **1962**

DANGEROUS COMPANY ★★ The true story of convict Ray Johnson, who lived in and out of prison for years until his reform. Excellent acting saves what would otherwise be a tedious biography. 100m. **DIR:** Lamont Johnson. **CAST:** Beau Bridges, Carlos Brown, Karen Carlson, Kene Holiday, Ralph Macchio. **1982**

DANGEROUS CURVES ★★★1/2 A college senior gets a chance to earn a position with a corporation if he can deliver a birthday present to the boss's daughter. The present is a bright red Porsche. This zany comedy, aimed at the younger set, actually has a wider appeal. The young leads are appealing, and the support of Robert Klein and Robert Stack add to the enjoyment. Rated PG. 93m. **DIR:** David Lewis. **CAST:** Tate Donovan, Danielle von Zerneck, Robert Stack, Robert Klein, Robert Romanus. **1988 DVD**

DANGEROUS GAME (1990) ★★1/2 Group of adventurous kids break into a large department store, but a vengeful cop enters the picture and decides to teach the rowdy youths a lesson in blue light specials. Rated R for violence. 102m. **DIR:** Stephen Hopkins. **CAST:** Steven Grives, Marcus Graham, Miles Buchanan, Kathryn Walker. **1990**

DANGEROUS GAME, A (1993) ★★★1/2 Manipulation is the name of this game when a director (Harvey Keitel) plays mind games with the cast in the movie he's making. Keitel's life is out of control as he crosses all boundaries between real life and reel life on his volatile set. The movie seems to be going nowhere for an hour and then explodes with passion and violence. Madonna is in top form as an actress playing an actress. Rated R for violence, profanity, sexual situations, nudity, and drug use. Not rated director's cut also available. 107m. **DIR:** Abel Ferrara. **CAST:** Harvey Keitel, Madonna, James Russo. **1993**

DANGEROUS GROUND ★★1/2 South African exile Vusi travels home to bury his father after thirteen years in America. His younger brother is a malcontent soldier and another brother is missing. Vusi teams up with a stripper to save his brother and dent South Africa's new urban drug problems. Rated R for violence, drug use, and brief nudity. 92m. **DIR:** Darrell Roodt. **CAST:** Ice Cube, Elizabeth Hurley, Ving Rhames, Sechaba Morajele, Eric Miyeni. **1997 DVD**

DANGEROUS HEART ♥ In this made-for-cable original, the widow of a cop unwittingly starts dating the drug dealer who killed her husband. He only wants the money her husband stole from him. Boring, unbelievable, badly acted, and poorly written. Not rated; contains violence and sexual situations. 95m. **DIR:** Michael Scott. **CAST:** Timothy Daly, Lauren Holly, Jeffrey Nordling, Alice Carter, Bill Nunn. **1993**

DANGEROUS INDISCRETION ★★★ Entertaining B-movie thriller stars C. Thomas Howell as an advertising executive who beds the beautiful Joan Severance. When her husband discovers the indiscretion, however, he sets out to make Howell's life a living hell. Engrossing, sexy, and well made. Howell's performance here can be counted among his best. Rated R for nudity, sexual situations, and profanity. 81m. **DIR:** Richard Kletter. **CAST:** C. Thomas Howell, Malcolm McDowell, Sue Mathew, Joan Severance. **1994**

DANGEROUS LIAISONS ★★★★ Based on the classic French novel *Les Liaisons Dangereuses,* this exquisitely filmed story of competitive sexual gamesmanship between two ex-lovers is charged with sensual energy. The cast, led by a marvelously brittle Glenn Close and John Malkovich, is first-rate. There's a sumptuous rhythm to the language and a lush setting that beautifully captures upper-class, eighteenth-century France. Rated R. 120m. **DIR:** Stephen Frears. **CAST:** Glenn Close, John Malkovich, Michelle Pfeiffer, Mildred Natwick, Swoosie Kurtz, Uma Thurman. **1989 DVD**

DANGEROUS LIFE, A ★★1/2 Interesting made-for-cable portrayal of the Philippine uprising against Ferdinand and Imelda Marcos during the mid-Eighties. Gary Busey plays a reporter stationed in Manila when all hell breaks loose. Not rated, but some violence. 163m. **DIR:** Robert Markowitz. **CAST:** Gary Busey, Rebecca Gilling, James Handy. **1988**

DANGEROUS LOVE ♥ A maniac killer with a camera begins murdering his dates and taping their deaths. Rated R for nudity, profanity, and violence. 96m. **DIR:** Marty Ollstein. **CAST:** Elliott Gould, Lawrence Monoson, Anthony Geary. **1988**

DANGEROUS MINDS ★★1/2 High-school instructor LouAnne Johnson's inner-city memoirs are transformed into a dissatisfying film, with Michelle Pfeiffer miscast as an ex-Marine who demonstrates the true value of education to a bunch of "bad kids." The characters lack depth, the tone is inconsistent, and the story is all over the map. If you want motivation, stick with *Stand and Deliver*. Rated R for profanity and violence. 99m. **DIR:** John N. Smith. **CAST:** Michelle Pfeiffer, George Dzundza, Courtney B. Vance, Robin Bartlett, Bruklin Harris. **1995 DVD**

DANGEROUS MISSION ★★ In this below-average movie, Piper Laurie witnesses a mob killing in New York City and has to flee the city because the killers are after her. The chase ends at Glacier National Park. A good cast but an overdone plot. 75m. **DIR:** Louis King. **CAST:** Victor Mature, Piper Laurie, Vincent Price, William Bendix. **1954**

DANGEROUS MOONLIGHT (SUICIDE SQUADRON) ★★★ Polish pianist Anton Walbrook stops tickling the ivories and starts squeezing the trigger as he climbs into the cockpit as a bomber pilot for the RAF during World War II. Excellent aerial sequences. B&W; 83m. **DIR:** Brian Desmond Hurst. **CAST:** Anton Walbrook, Sally Gray, Derrek de Marney. **1941**

DANGEROUS MOVES ★★★★1/2 Worthy of its Oscar for best foreign film of 1984, this French film about a chess match between two grand masters in Geneva is not just for fans of the game. Indeed, the real intensity that is created here comes from the sidelines: the two masters' camps, the psych-out attempts, the political stakes, and the personal dramas. Rated PG for adult situations and language. 95m. **DIR:** Richard Dembo. **CAST:** Michel Piccoli, Leslie Caron, Alexandre Arbatt, Liv Ullmann. **1984**

DANGEROUS OBSESSION ♥ As his illness plagued him in real life, so too did it plague director Lucio Fulci's later work as evidenced by this boring film about a woman kidnapping the doctor whose mistake during surgery killed her boyfriend. Not rated; contains violence. 81m. **DIR:** Lucio Fulci. **CAST:** Corinne Clery. **1988**

DANGEROUS PASSAGE ★★ Routine adventure-drama finds Robert Lowery in Central America, where he discovers that an inheritance awaits him back in the States. Phyllis Brooks provides the love interest. Mysterious shadows and attempts on Lowery's life provide the tension. B&W; 61m. **DIR:** William Burke. **CAST:** Robert Lowery, Phyllis Brooks, Jack LaRue, Victor Kilian. **1944**

DANGEROUS PASSION ★★ Good cast brings life to this pedestrian crime-drama. Carl Weathers wins the respect of mob boss Billy Dee Williams when he takes the rap for a murder. Then he beats the rap, is recruited into the family, and soon falls for his boss's sultry wife. Lonette McKee is quite good as the femme fatale in this made-for-television film. Not rated; contains adult situations. 94m. **DIR:** Michael Miller. **CAST:** Carl Weathers, Billy Dee Williams, Lonette McKee. **1989**

DANGEROUS PLACE, A ★★1/2 The *Karate Kid* formula still has some juice, particularly in the hands of young martial arts star Ted Jan Roberts. This time out, he infiltrates a gang of kids believed responsible for the death of his older brother. Sean Dash's story is strictly a fairy tale, but the result should be reasonably appealing to younger fans. Rated R for violence and profanity. 97m. **DIR:** Jerry P. Jacobs. **CAST:** Ted Jan Roberts, Corey Feldman, Erin Gray, Marshall Teague, Mako, Dick Van Patten. **1994**

DANGEROUS PREY ★★ An outlandish premise helps keep this otherwise unremarkable outing afloat. As a result of getting romantically involved with a Russian gunrunner, a stuntwoman (Shannon Whirry) is abducted and sent to an institute where a troop of seductive hit women are trained. Whirry makes a wooden *macha* heroine, but fans of fast-paced shoot-outs and explosions won't be disappointed. Rated R. 92m. **DIR:** Lloyd A. Simandl. **CAST:** Shannon Whirry, Ciara Hunter, Joseph Laufer, Beatrice De Borg, Carlo Cartier, Michael Rogers. **1995**

DANGEROUS PURSUIT ★★ A nightclub waitress sleeps with a stranger for money and then realizes he is a contract killer. Three years later, after running to the other side of the United States and getting married to a cop, she discovers the stranger in her new town and that he is going to kill again. Mediocre made-for-cable thriller. 96m. **DIR:** Sandor Stern. **CAST:** Gregory Harrison, Alexandra Powers, Brian Wimmer, Scott Valentine, Robert Prosky. **1989**

DANGEROUS RELATIONS ★★★1/2 This apparently lurid prison drama is actually a thoughtful tale about an estranged father and son attempting to make peace while forced to serve their parole under the same roof. Made for TV. 93m. **DIR:** Georg Stanford Brown. **CAST:** Louis Gossett Jr., Blair Underwood, Rae Dawn Chong, David Harris, Clarence Williams, III. **1993**

DANGEROUS SUMMER, A 🦃 Set in Australia, this film deals with a posh resort damaged by fire and the subsequent investigation. Not rated; the film has violence and profanity. 100m. **DIR:** Quentin Masters. **CAST:** James Mason, Tom Skerritt, Ian Gilmour, Wendy Hughes. **1984**

DANGEROUS TOUCH ★★ Kate Vernon stars as a radio sex therapist who finds herself falling in lust with mysterious stranger Lou Diamond Phillips. Before long, she realizes there's something amiss and finds herself knee-deep in a quagmire of blackmail, revenge, and murder. Loaded with action and steamy sex but could have used a more cohesive plot. Not rated, but the equivalent of an R for nudity and sexual situations. 99m. **DIR:** Lou Diamond Phillips. **CAST:** Lou Diamond Phillips, Kate Vernon, Max Gail. **1993 DVD**

DANGEROUS VENTURE ★★1/2 Better-than-average Hopalong Cassidy adventure finds our heroes searching for Aztec ruins in the Southwest. B&W; 55m. **DIR:** George Archainbaud. **CAST:** William Boyd, Andy Clyde, Rand Brooks. **1947**

DANGEROUS WHEN WET ★★ Fame and fortune await she who swims the English Channel. Esther Williams plays a corn-fed wholesome who goes for it; Fernando Lamas cheers her on. Semisour Jack Carson and high-kicking Charlotte Greenwood clown. Good music and a novel underwater Tom and Jerry cartoon sequence. 95m. **DIR:** Charles Walters. **CAST:** Esther Williams, Fernando Lamas, Jack Carson, Charlotte Greenwood, Denise Darcel. **1953**

DANGEROUS WOMAN, A ★★1/2 Debra Winger stars as a mentally impaired but well-meaning woman whose life begins falling apart. An affair with a new handyman brings romance, while an unjust accusation of stealing calls up more volatile emotions. The film lacks a cohesive dramatic structure and distinct point of view. Rated R for profanity, violence, and simulated sex. 99m. **DIR:** Stephen Gyllenhaal. **CAST:** Debra Winger, Barbara Hershey, Gabriel Byrne, David Strathairn, Laurie Metcalf, Chloe Webb, John Terry, Jan Hooks, Paul Dooley, Viveka Davis, Richard Riehle. **1993**

DANGEROUSLY CLOSE ★★ In this disappointing modern-day vigilante film, a group of students, led by a Vietnam veteran teacher, tries to purge their school of "undesirable elements" by any means necessary—including murder. Film starts out promising enough but soon loses focus with its rambling script and stereotypical situations. Rated R for profanity, violence, and brief nudity. 95m. **DIR:** Albert Pyun. **CAST:** John Stockwell, Carey Lowell, Bradford Bancroft, Madison Mason. **1986**

DANGERS OF THE CANADIAN MOUNTED ★★ A rumored horde of Genghis Khan's treasure trove inspires the mysterious "Chief" into a frenzy of territorial railway sabotage along the Alaskan-Canadian boundary. The battle for the security of the border escalates until the ringleaders and the treasure are plucked from a sunken Chinese junk and placed in the hands of authorities. B&W; 12 Chapters. **DIR:** Fred Brannon, Yakima Canutt. **CAST:** Jim Bannon, Virginia Belmond, Anthony Warde, Dorothy Granger, Tom Steele, Dale Van Sickel, I. Stanford Jolley. **1948**

DANIEL ★★1/2 Sidney Lumet directed this disappointing and ultimately depressing screen version of E. L. Doctorow's thinly veiled account of the Rosenberg case of thirty years ago, in which the parents of two young children were electrocuted as spies. If it weren't for Timothy Hutton's superb performance in the title role (as one of the children), *Daniel* would be much less effective. Rated R for profanity and violence. 130m. **DIR:** Sidney Lumet. **CAST:** Timothy Hutton, Mandy Patinkin, Lindsay Crouse, Edward Asner, Amanda Plummer. **1983**

DANIEL BOONE ★★★★ Action-packed story of the early American frontier features rugged outdoor star George O'Brien in the title role and evil John Carradine as a renegade who aids the Indians. This rousing film is great schoolboy adventure stuff. B&W; 77m. **DIR:** David Howard. **CAST:** George O'Brien, Heather Angel, John Carradine. **1936**

DANIEL BOONE, TRAIL BLAZER ★★1/2 This is a slightly better-than-average Western that has Daniel Boone (Bruce Bennett) not only pathfinding for settlers but fighting off what seems to be the entire population of Native Americans. Good performances and lots of action save it from being mundane. 76m. **DIR:** Albert C. Gannaway. **CAST:** Bruce Bennett, Lon Chaney Jr., Faron Young. **1956**

DANIELLA BY NIGHT ★★1/2 A relic from the days when "art film" was a code term for extra "ooh-la-la," this murder mystery was a hit in 1962 because it offered Elke Sommer (in her last pre-Hollywood film) in a brief nude scene. In French with English subtitles. Not rated; contains sexual situations. 83m. **DIR:** Max Pecas, Radley Metzger. **CAST:** Elke Sommer, Ivan Desny. **1962 DVD**

DANIELLE STEEL'S DADDY ★★1/2 Made-for-television movie based on Danielle Steel's best-selling book. Patrick Duffy plays Oliver Watson, whose seemingly perfect life takes a tailspin when his wife takes a powder on him and their three children. Forced to juggle single parenthood with a burgeoning career as an advertising executive, Watson moves to L.A. and falls for an actress. 95m. **DIR:** Michael Miller. **CAST:** Patrick Duffy, Lynda Carter, Kate Mulgrew. **1990**

DANIELLE STEEL'S FINE THINGS ★★ Condensed television miniseries based on bestseller by author Danielle Steel. Too much soap and not enough opera in this tale of newlyweds, D. W. Moffett and Tracy Pollan, who discover she suffers from the most incurable of miniseries diseases. Ho-hum, but costar Cloris Leachman has some nice moments. 145m. **DIR:** Tom Moore.

CAST: D. W. Moffett, Tracy Pollan, Noley Thornton, Cloris Leachman, Darrell Larson. **1990**

DANIELLE STEEL'S KALEIDOSCOPE ★★★ Tearjerker about three sisters who were separated at a young age and eventually reunited. If you like Danielle Steel's work, you'll like this movie. Not rated, but suitable for all audiences. 96m. **DIR:** Jud Taylor. **CAST:** Jaclyn Smith, Perry King, Colleen Dewhurst, Patricia Kalember, Claudia Christian. **1992**

DANIELLE STEEL'S ONCE IN A LIFETIME ★★★ After being struck by a car, an unconscious writer (Lindsay Wagner) replays her losses and mistakes. Having lost her husband and daughter in a fire, she has failed to recognize her second chance for happiness. Perhaps more compelling than her love life are her attempts to help her deaf son. Passable melodramatic fare. Not rated, contains sexual situations. 90m. **DIR:** Michael Miller. **CAST:** Lindsay Wagner, Barry Bostwick, Rex Smith, Amy Aquino, Darrell Thomas Utley. **1994**

DANNY ★★★ A warm, touching, predictable story of an unhappy little girl who obtains a horse that has been injured and then sold off by the spoiled daughter of the wealthy stable owners. A fine family film. Rated G. 90m. **DIR:** Gene Feldman. **CAST:** Rebecca Page, Janet Zarish. **1977**

DANNY BOY (1941) ★★ Estranged from her husband and small son, a singer searches for them, only to find that they have become street musicians. Overly sentimental, but the music is nice enough. B&W; 80m. **DIR:** Oswald Mitchell. **CAST:** Ann Todd, Wilfrid Lawson. **1941**

DANNY BOY (1982) ★★★★ A young saxophone player witnesses the brutal murder of two people and becomes obsessed with understanding the act. Set in Ireland, this movie is enhanced by haunting musical interludes that highlight the drama of the people caught up in the Irish "troubles." There are flaws, most notably in some of the coincidences, but the overall effect is mesmerizing. Rated R. 92m. **DIR:** Neil Jordan. **CAST:** Stephen Rea, Marie Kean, Ray McAnally, Donal McCann. **1982**

DANNY, THE CHAMPION OF THE WORLD ★★★★★ This smashing adaptation of Roald Dahl's children's story benefits from the inspired casting of Jeremy Irons and his precocious son, Samuel, as the only two people standing up to would-be land baron Robbie Coltrane. The elder Irons won't allow his property to become part of a local tycoon's ever-expanding haven for big-city bird hunters. Young Samuel Irons fiercely loves and believes in his father and helps to win the day while fighting his own battles. Suitable for all ages. 99m. **DIR:** Gavin Millar. **CAST:** Jeremy Irons, Robbie Coltrane, Samuel Irons, Cyril Cusack, Lionel Jeffries, Ronald Pickup, Jean Marsh, Michael Hordern. **1989**

DANNY THOMAS SHOW, THE (TV SERIES) ★★★★ Also known as *Make Room for Daddy*. These early episodes featured Jean Hagen as Danny's wife. Thomas, a nightclub entertainer, spends a lot of time away from his family—but even when he's home, the family goes on without him. Hilarious bits arise as he tries to reclaim his place as head of the household. Rusty Hamer steals every scene he appears in as Thomas's precocious son. 110m. **DIR:** Sheldon Leonard. **CAST:** Danny Thomas, Jean Hagen, Rusty Hamer, Sherry Jackson. **1953–56**

DANSE MACABRE ★★ Filmed on location in the Soviet Union, this horror film features Robert Englund as an American choreographer working at a world-renowned ballet college. When girls from around the world are allowed to enroll, trouble begins. One by one they are murdered. Rated R for nudity, violence, and profanity. 97m. **DIR:** Greydon Clark. **CAST:** Robert Englund. **1991**

DANTE'S INFERNO ★★1/2 This early film by director Ken Russell exhibits great cinematic style but falls short in dramatic execution. The movie focuses on the morose and brilliant poet and painter Dante Gabriel Roth, played by Oliver Reed with comic pathos. Not very engaging. Not rated, but recommended for adult viewers. B&W; 90m. **DIR:** Ken Russell. **CAST:** Oliver Reed. **1968**

DANTE'S PEAK ★★★1/2 Pierce Brosnan is an intuitive volcanologist who believes that the Pacific Northwest community of Dante's Peak is endangered by a local volcano. Naturally, nobody believes him; yet he's eventually proven correct. In fairness, Brosnan and his colleagues seem like authentic scientists. Some of the hair's-breadth escapes are preposterous, but the film definitely knows how to keep your adrenaline running. Rated PG-13 for profanity and violence. 108m. **DIR:** Roger Donaldson. **CAST:** Pierce Brosnan, Linda Hamilton, Charles Hallahan, Grant Heslov, Elizabeth Hoffman, Jamie Renée Smith, Jeremy Foley. **1997 DVD**

DANTON ★★★1/2 Polish director Andrzej Wajda takes the French revolutionary figure (well played by Gérard Depardieu) and the events surrounding his execution by onetime comrades and turns it into a parable of modern life. It may not be good history, but the film does provide food for thought. In French. Rated PG. 136m. **DIR:** Andrzej Wajda. **CAST:** Gérard Depardieu, Wojiech Pszoniak, Patrice Chereau. **1982**

DANZON ★★★★ Completely agreeable romantic drama about a thirty-something telephone operator who lives a shielded life with her teenage daughter in Mexico City. Her only foray into the world comes every Wednesday night when she dances the seductive *Danzon* with Carmello, her dance partner of six years. When he fails to appear one evening, she embarks on a journey of self-discovery and awakening in search of him. In Spanish with English subtitles. Rated PG. 103m. **DIR:** Maria Novaro. **CAST:** Maria Rojo, Blanca Guerra, Tito Vasconcelos, Carmen Salinas. **1992**

DARBY O'GILL AND THE LITTLE PEOPLE ★★★1/2 Darby O'Gill is an Irish storyteller who becomes involved with some of the very things he talks about, namely leprechauns, the banshee, and other Irish folk characters. This wonderful tale is one of Disney's best films and a delightful fantasy film in its own right. It features a young and relatively unknown Sean Connery as Darby's future son-in-law. 93m. **DIR:** Robert Stevenson. **CAST:** Albert Sharpe, Janet Munro, Sean Connery, Jimmy O'Dea. **1959**

DARING DOBERMANS, THE ★★1/2 Fun sequel to *The Doberman Gang* is a little more kiddy-oriented, but it's still okay, featuring another well-planned caper for the canine stars. Rated PG for very light violence and language. 90m. **DIR:** Byron Chudnow. **CAST:** Charles Knox

Robinson, Tim Considine, David Moses, Joan Caulfield. **1973**

DARING GAME ★★1/2 Ivan Tors, producer of TV's *Sea Hunt* and *Flipper*, heads back into the water for this unsuccessful series pilot. It's about a team of commandos nicknamed The Flying Fish who are proficient on land, air, and sea. No better or worse than a lot of stuff that *did* make it to TV. 101m. **DIR:** Laslo Benedek, Ricou Browning. **CAST:** Lloyd Bridges, Nico Minardos, Michael Ansara, Joan Blackman, Shepperd Strudwick. **1968**

DARING YOUNG MAN, THE ★★★ Above-average comedy featuring Joe E. Brown as a bumbling serviceman who becomes mixed up with foreign spies and a radio-controlled bowling ball. B&W; 73m. **DIR:** Frank Strayer. **CAST:** Joe E. Brown, Marguerite Chapman, William Wright. **1942**

DARK, THE (1979) ★★ A deadly alien. Rated R. 92m. **DIR:** John "Bud" Cardos. **CAST:** William Devane, Cathy Lee Crosby, Richard Jaeckel, Keenan Wynn, Vivian Blaine. **1979**

DARK, THE (1994) 🦃 Beneath a graveyard lives a subterranean creature with the power to destroy or heal. It is pursued by a vindictive cop out to destroy it and a scientist who wants to save it. Rated R for violence, nudity, and profanity. 87m. **DIR:** Craig Pryce. **CAST:** Stephen McHattie, Cynthia Belliveau, Jaimz Woolvett, Brian James. **1994**

DARK ADAPTED EYE, A ★★★★ Secrets and skulduggery abound in this BBC mystery based on a Ruth Rendell novel written under her nom de plume, Barbara Vine. The past constantly overlaps the present in this fictional account of one of the last female murderers to be hanged in Great Britain. Not rated; contains mild profanity, violence, sexual situations, and adult themes. 152m. **DIR:** Tim Fywell. **CAST:** Helena Bonham Carter, Sophie Ward, Celia Imrie. **1994**

DARK AGE ★★1/2 What begins as a blatant *Jaws* rip-off becomes an entertaining thriller about a giant killer crocodile. A bit tough to follow due to Australian accents, but this flick offers a tolerable way to kill an hour and a half. Rated R for violence. 90m. **DIR:** Arch Nicholson. **CAST:** John Jarratt, Nikki Coghill, Max Phipps. **1987**

DARK ANGEL, THE ★★★1/2 This episode of the PBS series *Mystery!* is eerie, edgy, and atmospheric. Based on an 1864 Sheridan Le Fanu novel which is said to have influenced Bram Stoker, this Gothic piece explores the darker side of familial ties, focusing on vices, decay, and misplaced trust. The melodrama is made memorable by the deliciously creepy performance of Peter O'Toole. 150m. **DIR:** Peter Hammond. **CAST:** Peter O'Toole, Jane Lapotaire, Alan MacNaughton, Tim Woodward. **1992**

DARK ANGEL: THE ASCENT ★★1/2 All hell breaks loose when a particularly nasty she-devil gets bored torturing the eternally damned and decides to take her skills to the surface. Angela Featherstone triumphs as the bewitching demon who finds plenty to punish. Gory special effects and lots of tongue-out-of-cheek humor make this low-budget exercise worth a look. Rated R for gore and adult situations. 80m. **DIR:** Linda Hassani. **CAST:** Angela Featherstone, Daniel Markel, Mike Genovese, Nicholas Worth, Milton James. **1994**

•DARK ASYLUM ★★ An abandoned high-security insane asylum is the setting for this wannabe suspense shocker that pits a female psychiatrist against a psychotic maniac. Despite the commitment of several familiar faces, it's difficult to go crazy over this atmospheric made-for-cable thriller that is short on chills. Rated R for language and violence. 96m. **DIR:** Gregory Gieras. **CAST:** Paulina Porizkova, Jurgen Prochnow, Judd Nelson, Larry Drake. **2001 DVD**

DARK BACKWARD, THE ★★ A self-professed comedian can't get a laugh from his audience. Eventually, he is given a hand—a third one, growing from an arm in the middle of his back. Likely to become a cult film. Rated R for profanity. 100m. **DIR:** Adam Rifkin. **CAST:** Judd Nelson, Bill Paxton, Wayne Newton, James Caan, Lara Flynn Boyle. **1991**

•DARK BLUE WORLD ★★1/2 Two Czech pilots flee the Nazis to fight with the RAF, where both become involved with an English war widow. The hackneyed story and confusing structure (flashing back and forth from the war to 1950 Czechoslovakia) work against the film, though there are some good aerial combat scenes. Rated R for nudity and sexual scenes. 114m. **DIR:** Jan Sverák. **CAST:** Ondrej Vetchy, Krystof Hádek, Tara Fitzgerald, Charles Dance. **2001**

DARK BREED ★★★ A space mission returns to Earth bearing some uninvited guests, monstrous parasites bent on taking over our planet. It's up to Agent Nick Saxon (Jack Scalia) to save us. About what one would expect from a sci-fi thriller where the hero's name is Nick Saxon, though it's lively enough. Rated R for strong violence. 104m. **DIR:** Richard Pepin. **CAST:** Jack Scalia, Jonathan Banks, Robin Curtis. **1996**

DARK CITY ★★★ This hypnotic nightmare blends gothic comic-book fantasy with science-fiction *noir*. John Murdoch awakens in a hotel room bathtub and discovers he is wanted for murders he can't remember committing. While pursued by police, he learns that bald extraterrestrials called the Strangers are controlling the minds of the city's entire populace as they study the human soul and try to avert their own extinction. The story is muddled but the visuals are absolutely stunning. Rated R for language, nudity, and violence. 103m. **DIR:** Alex Proyas. **CAST:** Rufus Sewell, Kiefer Sutherland, Jennifer Connelly, William Hurt, Richard O'Brien. **1998 DVD**

DARK COMMAND ★★★★1/2 Raoul Walsh, who directed John Wayne's first big Western, *The Big Trail*, was reunited with the star after the latter's triumph in *Stagecoach* for this dynamic shoot-'em-up. Walter Pidgeon is Quantrill, a once-honest man who goes renegade and forms Quantrill's Raiders. It's up to the Duke, with help from his *Stagecoach* costar Claire Trevor, Roy Rogers, and Gabby Hayes, to set things right. B&W; 94m. **DIR:** Raoul Walsh. **CAST:** John Wayne, Claire Trevor, Walter Pidgeon, Roy Rogers, George "Gabby" Hayes. **1940 DVD**

DARK CORNER, THE ★★★1/2 Released from prison after being framed by his partner, private eye Mark Stevens finds he is being dogged by a man in a white suit. Before he can fathom why, he finds his ex-partner's body under his bed, and the police once again closing in. His secretary, Lucille Ball, helps unravel the sinister murder scheme. Above-average *film noir*. B&W; 99m.

DIR: Henry Hathaway. **CAST:** Mark Stevens, Clifton Webb, Lucille Ball, William Bendix, Kurt Kreuger. **1946**

DARK CRYSTAL, THE ★★★★ Jim Henson of "The Muppets" fame created this lavish fantasy tale in the style of J .R .R. Tolkien (*The Lord of the Rings*), using the movie magic that brought E.T. and Yoda (*The Empire Strikes Back*) to life. It's a delight for children of all ages. Rated PG. 93m. **DIR:** Jim Henson, Frank Oz. **1983 DVD**

DARK EYES ★★★1/2 Based on several short stories by Anton Chekhov, this film takes its title from a Russian ballad that fills the soundtrack. Marcello Mastroianni is wonderfully endearing as a dapper, love-struck Italian who meets a young Russian woman at a spa and later in her village. The Russian scenery, replete with rolling hills at dawn and singing Gypsies, is a tourist's dream. In Italian with English subtitles. 118m. **DIR:** Nikita Mikhalkov. **CAST:** Marcello Mastroianni, Marthe Keller, Silvana Mangano. **1987**

DARK FORCES ★★★ Robert Powell plays a modern-day conjurer who gains the confidence of a family by curing their terminally ill son; or does he? The evidence stacks up against Powell as we find he may be a foreign spy and stage magician extraordinaire. While uneven, this film is decent entertainment. Rated PG for brief nudity and some violence. 96m. **DIR:** Simon Wincer. **CAST:** Robert Powell, Broderick Crawford, David Hemmings, Carmen Duncan, Alyson Best. **1984**

DARK HABITS ★★ This surreal comedy features Carmen Maura as a nightclub singer. Director Pedro Almodóvar has a touch of Luis Buñuel without the depth or intelligence. This is fitfully funny, self-indulgent, and overlong. In Spanish with English subtitles. Not rated, but recommended for adults. 116m. **DIR:** Pedro Almodóvar. **CAST:** Carmen Maura. **1984**

DARK HALF, THE ★★★1/2 Based on Stephen King's tale of a writer and his homicidal pseudonym. When threatened with the exposure of his literary alter ego, writer Timothy Hutton sees his chance to rid himself and his family of that dark side. But his alter ego manifests itself as a nasty killer bent on revenge. Rated R for violence and profanity. 115m. **DIR:** George A. Romero. **CAST:** Timothy Hutton, Amy Madigan, Michael Rooker, Julie Harris, Robert Joy, Kent Broadhurst, Beth Grant, Rutanya Alda, Tom Mardirosian. **1993 DVD**

DARK HARBOR ★★ In this complex but unfulfilling thriller, a couple, disillusioned with each other, find a wounded man on the side of the road. The brief encounter leads to an emotional showdown when the stranger shows up at their secluded Maine house. The film attempts to be a sexually charged thriller, but lacks conviction and stamina. Rated R for adult situations, language, nudity, and violence. 89m. **DIR:** Adam Coleman Howard. **CAST:** Alan Rickman, Polly Walker, Norman Reedus. **1999 DVD**

DARK HORSE ★★★1/2 Inspirational tale of a lonely teenage girl who gets into trouble and is sentenced to ten weekends of community service at a horse ranch. Great family entertainment, played out in heart-tugging, sentimental fashion. Not rated. 98m. **DIR:** David Hemmings. **CAST:** Ed Begley Jr., Mimi Rogers, Ari Meyers, Donovan Leitch, Samantha Eggar, Tab Hunter. **1992**

DARK JOURNEY ★★★ Espionage with a twist. A British and a German spy fall in love in Stockholm during World War I. B&W; 82m. **DIR:** Victor Saville. **CAST:** Vivien Leigh, Conrad Veidt, Joan Gardner, Anthony Bushell. **1937**

DARK MIRROR, THE ★★★1/2 Olivia de Havilland, who did this sort of thing extremely well, plays twin sisters—one good, one evil—enmeshed in murder. Lew Ayres is the shrink who must divine who is who. Good suspense. B&W; 85m. **DIR:** Robert Siodmak. **CAST:** Olivia de Havilland, Lew Ayres, Thomas Mitchell, Richard Long. **1946**

DARK NIGHT OF THE SCARECROW ★★★ Despite its hasty beginning that fails to set up a strong premise for the pivotal scene of the movie, this is a chilling film that mixes the supernatural with a moral message. Borrows some ideas from such films as *To Kill a Mockingbird* and *Of Mice and Men*. Not rated. 100m. **DIR:** Frank De-Felitta. **CAST:** Charles Durning, Tonya Crowe, Jocelyn Brando. **1981**

DARK OBSESSION ★★ Painful to watch and ultimately pointless, this focuses on a sadistic husband's obsession with controlling his wife. Released with two ratings; NC-17 and R, this contains nudity, profanity, and violence. 97m. **DIR:** Nick Broomfield. **CAST:** Amanda Donohoe, Gabriel Byrne, Douglas Hodge, Ian Carmichael, Michael Hordern. **1990 DVD**

DARK OF THE SUN (MERCENARIES) (1968) ★★★★ Tough-as-nails mercenary Rod Taylor and his friend Jim Brown lead troops-for-hire deep into hostile guerrilla territory to retrieve a fortune in diamonds, and to rescue (if possible) the inhabitants of a remote European settlement in the Congo. Not rated, but violent and unsettling. 101m. **DIR:** Jack Cardiff. **CAST:** Rod Taylor, Yvette Mimieux, Jim Brown, Peter Carsten, Kenneth More, Andre Morell, Calvin Lockhart. **1968**

DARK PASSAGE ★★★ This is an okay Humphrey Bogart vehicle in which the star plays an escaped convict who hides out at Lauren Bacall's apartment while undergoing a face change. The stars are watchable, but the uninspired direction (including some disconcerting subjective camera scenes) and the outlandish plot keep the movie from being a real winner. B&W; 106m. **DIR:** Delmer Daves. **CAST:** Humphrey Bogart, Lauren Bacall, Bruce Bennett, Agnes Moorehead. **1947**

DARK PAST, THE ★★ A psychotic killer escapes from prison and a psychologist attempts to convince the hood to give himself up. Lee J. Cobb is marvelous as the psychiatrist and William Holden is wonderful as the bad guy. Nina Foch is top-notch as Holden's moll. A remake of *Blind Alley*. 75m. **DIR:** Rudolph Maté. **CAST:** William Holden, Lee J. Cobb, Nina Foch, Adele Jergens. **1948**

DARK PLACES ★★★1/2 Christopher Lee and Joan Collins play two fortune hunters trying to scare away the caretaker (Robert Hardy) of a dead man's mansion so they can get to the bundle of cash stashed in the old house. The film has a sophisticated psychological twist to it that is missing in most horror films, but the cardboard bats on clearly visible wires have got to go! Rated PG for gore and profanity. 91m. **DIR:** Don Sharp. **CAST:** Christopher Lee, Joan Collins, Herbert Lom, Robert Hardy, Jane Birkin, Jean Marsh. **1973**

DARK PLANET 🦃 Cheap, poorly written sci-fi featuring a cast that presumably wasn't aware what it was getting into. Rated R for violence. 96m. **DIR:** Albert Magnoli.

CAST: Paul Mercurio, Michael York, Harley Jane Kozak, Maria Ford. **1996 DVD**

DARK PRINCE: THE INTIMATE TALES OF MARQUIS DE SADE ★★ Nick Mancuso atrociously overacts as the infamous marquis, whose life and writings have been so loosely treated over the years that there's no point even comparing them to the real person. This Roger Corman production is recommended only to die-hard trash addicts. Rated R for nudity, sexual situations, and violence. 88m. **DIR:** Gwyneth Gibby. **CAST:** Nick Mancuso, Janet Gunn, John Rhys-Davies, Charlotte Nielsen. **1996**

DARK RIDER A corny chase film about a guy on a bike who saves a desert town from small-time gangsters. Not rated; contains violence and profanity. 94m. **DIR:** Bob Ivy. **CAST:** Joe Estevez, Doug Shanklin. **1991**

DARK RIVER: A FATHER'S REVENGE ★★★ When his daughter dies, a man stands alone to prove the town's leading industry is to blame. This better-than-average TV film covers some familar territory, but contains some exceptional performances. 95m. **DIR:** Michael Pressman. **CAST:** Mike Farrell, Tess Harper, Helen Hunt. **1989**

DARK SECRET OF HARVEST HOME, THE ★★1/2 Novelist-actor Tom Tryon's bewitching story of creeping horror gets fair treatment in this dark and foreboding film of Janus personalities and incantations in picturesque New England. 118m. **DIR:** Leo Penn. **CAST:** Bette Davis, Rosanna Arquette, David Ackroyd, Michael O'Keefe. **1978**

DARK SECRETS A reporter researching an exposé of a Hugh Hefner–like figure is seduced by his hedonistic world. Heavy-breathing trash. Rated R for nudity, sexual situations, violence, and profanity. 90m. **DIR:** John Bowen. **CAST:** Monique Parent, Justin Carroll, Julie Strain, Joe Estevez. **1996 DVD**

DARK SHADOWS (TV SERIES) ★★★ A truly different soap opera, this includes a bona fide vampire—one Barnabas Collins (convincingly portrayed by Jonathan Frid). Volumes 1 to 4, for example, begin with a greedy grave robber who gives the vampire new life, and culminate with the vampire's choosing a local girl for his bride. Mysterious, frightening, and atmospheric. B&W; 105—120. **DIR:** John Sedwick, Lela Swift. **CAST:** Jonathan Frid, Joan Bennett, Kathryn Leigh Scott, John Karlen, Alexandra Moltke. **1966–1967**

DARK SIDE, THE ★★★ Extremely seedy street thriller in which a naïve New York cabbie falls for a pretty girl on the run from a pair of ruthless porn-film merchants who specialize in snuff movies. Rated R for brutality and language. 95m. **DIR:** Constantino Magnatta. **CAST:** Tony Galati, Cyndy Preston. **1987**

DARK SIDE OF GENIUS ★★1/2 The L.A. art scene is the backdrop of this erotic thriller about a paroled murderer whose recent nude paintings have made him the toast of the town. Finola Hughes stars as an art reporter who senses something more diabolical, delves deeper into the art world, and unleashes a desire within her that might end up costing her life. Rated R for nudity, violence, and adult language. 86m. **DIR:** Phedon Papamichael. **CAST:** Finola Hughes, Glenn Shadix, Patrick Richwood, Moon Zappa. **1994**

DARK SIDE OF THE MOON, THE A lunar mission crew sheds some light on the moon's shaded half and its relationship to the Bermuda Triangle. Rated R. 96m. **DIR:** D. J. Webster. **CAST:** Will Bledsoe, Alan Blumenfeld, John Diehl, Robert Sampson. **1989**

DARK STAR ★★★1/2 This is one of the strangest sci-fi films you are likely to run across. Four astronauts have been in space entirely too long as they seek and destroy unstable planets. Director John Carpenter's first film is very funny in spurts and always crazy. Rated PG because of language. 83m. **DIR:** John Carpenter. **CAST:** Dan O'Bannon, Brian Narelle. **1974 DVD**

DARK TIDE ★★1/2 Brigitte Bako's atrocious acting mars what might have been a reasonably taut erotic thriller containing—for once—a nice balance between dramatic tension and soft-core groping. She's the catalyst who turns island thugs against researcher Chris Sarandon, who ignores imminent danger while collecting venom from incredibly malicious sea snakes. Rated R for profanity, nudity, violence, rape, and simulated sex. 94m. **DIR:** Luca Bercovici. **CAST:** Brigitte Bako, Richard Tyson, Chris Sarandon. **1993**

DARK TOWER A supernatural entity starts killing people. Rated R for violence and profanity. 91m. **DIR:** Ken Barnett. **CAST:** Michael Moriarty, Jenny Agutter, Theodore Bikel, Carol Lynley, Anne Lockhart, Kevin McCarthy. **1987**

DARK UNIVERSE, THE Just another *Alien* rip-off as a group of scientists prevent some nasty creatures from turning Earth into their very own intergalactic fast-food franchise. Not rated; contains nudity, violence, and profanity. 83m. **DIR:** Steve Latshaw. **CAST:** Blake Pickett, Cherie Scott, Bently Tittle, John Maynard, Paul Austin Sanders. **1993 DVD**

DARK VICTORY ★★★★ This Warner Bros. release gave Bette Davis one of her best roles, as a headstrong heiress who discovers she has a brain tumor. A successful operation leads to a love affair with her doctor (George Brent). In the midst of all this bliss, Davis learns the tragic truth: surgery was only a halfway measure, and she will die in a year. Sure it's corny. But director Edmund Goulding, Davis, and her costars make it work. B&W; 106m. **DIR:** Edmund Goulding. **CAST:** Bette Davis, George Brent, Humphrey Bogart, Ronald Reagan, Geraldine Fitzgerald. **1939 DVD**

DARK WATERS ★★1/2 Muddled story of orphaned girl(?), Merle Oberon, and her strange and terrifying experiences in the bayou backwaters of Louisiana is atmospheric, but fails to deliver enough of a story to justify its moody buildup. But the supporting players (along with the misty bogs) really carry the ball in this film. B&W; 90m. **DIR:** André de Toth. **CAST:** Merle Oberon, Franchot Tone, Thomas Mitchell, Fay Bainter, Rex Ingram, John Qualen, Elisha Cook Jr. **1944 DVD**

DARK WIND ★★★ Investigating a murder on his reservation, Navajo cop Lou Diamond Phillips finds a mystery involving rival tribes, drug smugglers, and government agents. Documentary filmmaker Errol Morris approaches his material matter-of-factly, but a capable cast maintains the suspense and intrigue. Rated R for language and violence. 111m. **DIR:** Errol Morris. **CAST:** Lou Diamond Phillips, Gary Farmer, Fred Ward, Guy Boyd. **1991**

DARKMAN ★★★★ Sam Raimi's *Darkman* borrows elements from *The Invisible Man*, *The Phantom of the*

Opera, and the Marvel Comics line of brooding superheroes. Liam Neeson is just right as the horribly disfigured scientist who becomes a crime fighter. Some of the sequences in this ultraviolent but inventive movie are so outrageous, they'll make your jaw drop. Rated R for violence and profanity. 96m. **DIR:** Sam Raimi. **CAST:** Liam Neeson, Frances McDormand, Colin Friels, Larry Drake. **1990 DVD**

DARKMAN II: THE RETURN OF DURANT ★★ He's back, only without Liam Neeson or a credible plot. Though decidedly brutal and occasionally nonsensical, this has a certain comic-book stylishness that keeps it from completely sinking. Arnold Vosloo steps into the role of the disfigured scientist matching wits against Larry Drake as Durant, the man who messed him up. Released directly to video. Rated R for profanity and violence. 93m. **DIR:** Bradford May. **CAST:** Larry Drake, Arnold Vosloo, Kim Delaney, Renee O'Connor. **1995 DVD**

DARKMAN III: DIE, DARKMAN, DIE ★★1/2 Any ongoing series potential has been eradicated by this quickie entry, which turns Sam Raimi's tragic superhero into just another wisecracking killer-for-vengeance. Without the outrageous stunts and hyperkinetic visuals that made the first film so memorable, viewers are far more likely to cheer for villain Jeff Fahey. At least he has the talent to properly deliver his florid dialogue! Rated R for violence, profanity, and gore. 87m. **DIR:** Bradford May. **CAST:** Jeff Fahey, Darlanne Fluegel, Roxann Biggs, Arnold Vosloo. **1995**

DARKNESS ★★ Poor lighting and sound bring down this amateurish film in which vampires overrun a small town. Famed genre director John Carpenter edited the film under a pseudonym. Not rated; contains violence and gore. 90m. **DIR:** Leif Jonker. **CAST:** Gary Miller, Michael Gisick. **1994**

DARKSIDE, THE ★★ A rookie cab driver picks up a porn star who is being pursued by thugs. There's some good suspense here, but melodramatic acting holds it back. Rated R for nudity, violence, and profanity. 95m. **DIR:** Constantino Magnatta. **CAST:** Tony Galati, Cyndy Preston. **1987**

DARLING ★★★★ John Schlesinger's direction is first-rate, and Julie Christie gives an Oscar-winning portrayal of a ruthless model who bullies, bluffs, and claws her way to social success, only to find life at the top meaningless. B&W; 122m. **DIR:** John Schlesinger. **CAST:** Julie Christie, Dirk Bogarde, Laurence Harvey, Jose Luis de Villalonga. **1965**

DARLING LILI ★★★ Dismissed out of hand on original release, and a box office flop to boot, this actually is a charming WWI romance with a Mata Hari–style narrative. Johnny Mercer and Henry Mancini provide the bouncy score. The planes later turned up in Roger Corman's *Von Richthofen and Brown*. Rated G. 136m. **DIR:** Blake Edwards. **CAST:** Julie Andrews, Rock Hudson, Jeremy Kemp, Lance Percival. **1970**

DARWIN CONSPIRACY, THE ★★ Yet another campy sci-fi outing in which an experiment to increase the intelligence of man is tested on an unwilling human guinea pig. More of the same. Rated PG. 90m. **DIR:** Winrich Kolbe. **CAST:** Jason Brooks, Robert Floyd, Stacy Haiduk, Kevin Tighe. **1998**

D.A.R.Y.L. ★★★★ In this delightful science-fiction film, Barret Oliver stars as a boy adopted by Mary Beth Hurt and Michael McKean. He turns out to be a perfect little fellow . . . maybe a little too perfect. *D.A.R.Y.L.* is a film the whole family can enjoy. Rated PG for violence and light profanity. 99m. **DIR:** Simon Wincer. **CAST:** Barret Oliver, Mary Beth Hurt, Michael McKean, Josef Sommer. **1985**

DAS BOOT (THE BOAT) ★★★★★ During World War II, forty thousand young Germans served aboard Nazi submarines. Only ten thousand survived. This West German film masterpiece re-creates the tension and claustrophobic conditions of forty-three men assigned to a U-boat in 1941. This is the English-dubbed version. 150m. **DIR:** Wolfgang Petersen. **CAST:** Jurgen Prochnow, Herbert Gronemeyer. **1981 DVD**

DATE WITH AN ANGEL 🦃 A beautiful angel loses control of her wings and lands in the arms of a mortal. Rated PG for profanity. 105m. **DIR:** Tom McLoughlin. **CAST:** Michael E. Knight, Phoebe Cates, Emmanuelle Beart, David Dukes. **1987**

DATE WITH JUDY, A ★★1/2 Ho-hum musical comedy about rival teenagers Jane Powell and Elizabeth Taylor fighting for the affections of Robert Stack. High point is Carmen Miranda teaching Wallace Beery to dance. 113m. **DIR:** Richard Thorpe. **CAST:** Jane Powell, Wallace Beery, Elizabeth Taylor, Carmen Miranda, Robert Stack, Xavier Cugat, Scotty Beckett, Leon Ames. **1948**

DAUGHTER OF DARKNESS ★★★1/2 Lovely Mia Sara follows her bad dreams back to her hometown of Budapest, where she learns that her relatives actually hang from the family tree. They're vampires. Rated R for horror and violence. 93m. **DIR:** Stuart Gordon. **CAST:** Mia Sara, Anthony Perkins, Jack Coleman, Robert Reynolds. **1987 DVD**

DAUGHTER OF DR. JEKYLL ★★ Okay horror film about a girl (Gloria Talbott) who thinks she's inherited the famous dual personality. B&W; 71m. **DIR:** Edgar G. Ulmer. **CAST:** Gloria Talbott, John Agar, Arthur Shields, John Dierkes. **1957 DVD**

DAUGHTER OF HORROR 🦃 The longest sixty minutes of your life. B&W; 60m. **DIR:** John Parker. **CAST:** Adrienne Barrett, Bruno Ve Sota. **1955 DVD**

DAUGHTER OF THE DRAGON ★★1/2 Dr. Fu Manchu returns yet again to wreak vengeance on his enemies, but this time he forces his daughter Ling Moy to assist him. After the evil mastermind's death Ling Moy embraces her father's hate-driven ways and continues in his murderous footsteps until permanently stopped by a lover. Sliding panels, torture, sacrifice, and hairbreadth escapes plus touching performances by Anna May Wong and Sessue Hayakawa highlight this last Paramount entry into the saga of Sax Rohmer's twisted genius. B&W; 70m. **DIR:** Lloyd Corrigan. **CAST:** Anna May Wong, Warner Oland, Bramwell Fletcher, Sessue Hayakawa, Frances Dade. **1931**

DAUGHTERS OF DARKNESS ★★★ Slick, handsomely mounted, and often genuinely eerie updating of the Elisabeth Bathory legend. Amid kinky trappings and soft-focus camera work, a wealthy woman vampire seduces a young couple at a European spa. Dated, but still striking and original. Rated R. Available in 87- and 96-m. versions of varying explicitness. **DIR:** Harry

Kumel. **CAST:** Delphine Seyrig, Daniele Ouimet, John Karlen, Fons Rademakers. **1971 DVD**

DAUGHTERS OF SATAN 🦃 Modern-day witches. Rated R for nudity and violence. 96m. **DIR:** Hollingsworth Morse. **CAST:** Tom Selleck, Barra Grant. **1972**

DAUGHTERS OF THE DUST ★★★★ Writer-director Julie Dash's absolutely gorgeous motion picture is set in 1902 on one of the sea islands off Georgia and North Carolina. It plays like a series of vintage photographs set to music combined with dramatic sequences. The story centers around a final ceremony being held prior to an African-American family's journey North. Fascinating. Not rated, the film has no objectionable material. 113m. **DIR:** Julie Dash. **CAST:** Adisa Anderson, Cheryl Lynn Bruce, Cora Lee Day. **1992 DVD**

DAVE ★★★★ Moments of sheer hilarity elevate this Capra-esque fantasy, in which an actor is hired to impersonate the president. When the chief executive has a heart attack, our hero is coerced into continuing the masquerade—and this allows him to start turning the country around. Kevin Kline is superb in a dual role. This one will tickle your funny bone and warm your heart. Rated PG for profanity and suggested sex. 100m. **DIR:** Ivan Reitman. **CAST:** Kevin Kline, Sigourney Weaver, Frank Langella, Kevin Dunn, Ving Rhames, Ben Kingsley, Charles Grodin, Arnold Schwarzenegger, Jay Leno, Oliver Stone. **1993 DVD**

DAVID AND BATHSHEBA ★★ Mediocre biblical epic with a polished cast nearly defeated by mundane script. Normally reliable director Henry King can't breathe life into this soporific soap opera. 116m. **DIR:** Henry King. **CAST:** Gregory Peck, Susan Hayward, Raymond Massey, Kieron Moore. **1951**

DAVID AND LISA ★★★1/2 Mentally disturbed teenagers (Keir Dullea and Janet Margolin) meet and develop a sensitive emotional attachment while institutionalized. Abetted by Howard DaSilva as their understanding doctor, Dullea and Margolin make this study highly watchable. Independently produced, this one was a sleeper. B&W; 94m. **DIR:** Frank Perry. **CAST:** Keir Dullea, Janet Margolin, Howard DaSilva, Neva Patterson, Clifton James. **1962 DVD**

DAVID COPPERFIELD (1935) ★★★★1/2 A first-rate production of Charles Dickens's rambling novel about a young man's adventures in nineteenth-century England. W. C. Fields and Edna May Oliver are standouts in an all-star cast. B&W; 100m. **DIR:** George Cukor. **CAST:** Freddie Bartholomew, Frank Lawton, Lionel Barrymore, W. C. Fields, Edna May Oliver, Basil Rathbone. **1935**

DAVID COPPERFIELD (2000) ★★★★ A TNT/Hallmark Entertainment production, this enjoyable miniseries resurrects Charles Dickens's classic, coming-of-age tale. The title character, portrayed by adorable Max Dolbey as a boy and later by heartthrob Hugh Dancy, faces many trials—but none greater than his demonic stepfather. Sally Field as Copperfield's cranky aunt and Michael Richards as young Copperfield's friend infuse the film with humor. 187m. **DIR:** Peter Medak. **CAST:** Hugh Dancy, Max Dolbey, Michael Richards, Sally Field, Anthony Andrews. **2000**

DAVID HOLZMAN'S DIARY ★★★★ Viewers who think that indie films were invented in the 1990s should run, not walk, to see this little gem. In a parody of cinema verité, a young filmmaker in New York decides to put his entire life on camera in the hope that it will become clearer to him. Instead, he only infuriates everyone around him. It's so well done that you may find yourself thinking it's real, but it's all scripted and acted. Not rated; contains no objectionable material. B&W; 74m. **DIR:** Jim McBride. **CAST:** L. M. "Kit" Carson, Eileen Dietz, Louise Levine. **1968**

DAVINCI'S WAR ★★ Ex–Special Services agent recruits a hit man to help rout the CIA-sponsored drug smuggling ring responsible for the death of his sister. Standard shoot-'em-up with a bit of a message. Rated R for violence, sex, and profanity. 94m. **DIR:** Raymond Martino. **CAST:** Joey Travolta, Michael Nouri, Vanity, James Russo, Sam Jones. **1993 DVD**

DAVY CROCKETT AND THE RIVER PIRATES ★★★ Fess Parker, as idealized Davy Crockett, takes on Big Mike Fink (Jeff York) in a keelboat race and tangles with Indians in the second Walt Disney–produced Davy Crockett feature composed of two television episodes. Thoroughly enjoyable and full of the kind of boyhood images that Disney productions evoked so successfully in the late 1940s and '50s. Fun for the whole family. 81m. **DIR:** Norman Foster. **CAST:** Fess Parker, Buddy Ebsen, Kenneth Tobey, Jeff York. **1956**

DAVY CROCKETT, KING OF THE WILD FRONTIER ★★★1/2 Finely played by all involved, this is actually a compilation of three episodes that appeared originally on television and were then released theatrically. 88m. **DIR:** Norman Foster. **CAST:** Fess Parker, Buddy Ebsen, Hans Conried, Kenneth Tobey. **1955**

DAWN OF THE DEAD ★★★★ This film is the sequel to *Night of the Living Dead.* The central characters are three men and one woman who try to escape from man-eating corpses. As a horror movie, it's a masterpiece, but if you have a weak stomach, avoid this one. Rated R. 126m. **DIR:** George A. Romero. **CAST:** David Emge, Ken Foree, Scott Reiniger, Tom Savini. **1978 DVD**

DAWN ON THE GREAT DIVIDE ★★★ With a bigger budget than usual and a story with more plot twists than the average B Western, the result is a good shoot-'em-up in the series vein. Buck Jones, of course, dominates as the two-fisted leader of a wagon train who takes on Indians, bad guys, and corrupt officials with equal aplomb. It was the last movie made by Jones, who died heroically trying to save lives during a fire at Boston's Coconut Grove on November 28, 1942. B&W; 63m. **DIR:** Howard Bretherton. **CAST:** Buck Jones, Raymond Hatton, Rex Bell, Mona Barrie. **1942**

DAWN PATROL, THE ★★★★ Basil Rathbone is excellent as a commanding officer of a frontline British squadron during World War I who has no choice but to order raw replacements into the air against veteran Germans. Errol Flynn and David Niven shine as gentlemen at war. A fine film. B&W; 103m. **DIR:** Edmund Goulding. **CAST:** Errol Flynn, Basil Rathbone, David Niven, Melville Cooper, Barry Fitzgerald, Donald Crisp. **1938**

DAWN RIDER ★★ John Wayne is out for revenge in this formula B Western. His loving father is killed during a robbery, and it's up to a gangly, slightly stilted Wayne to get the bad guys. B&W; 56m. **DIR:** Robert N. Bradbury. **CAST:** John Wayne, Marion Burns, Yakima Canutt, Reed Howes. **1935 DVD**

DAWNING, THE ★★★1/2 Leisurely paced coming-of-age film focuses on a naïve Irish girl whose life changes when she meets a renegade IRA leader. Seaside shots are spectacular as well as haunting. Equivalent to a PG for violence. 97m. **DIR:** Robert Knights. **CAST:** Anthony Hopkins, Rebecca Pidgeon, Trevor Howard, Jean Simmons. **1988**

DAY AFTER, THE ★★★★ Excellent made-for-TV movie special received much advance publicity because of its timely topic: the effects of a nuclear war. Jason Robards Jr. plays a hospital doctor who treats many of the victims after the nuclear attack. 126m. **DIR:** Nicholas Meyer. **CAST:** Jason Robards Jr., JoBeth Williams, Steve Guttenberg, John Cullum, John Lithgow. **1983**

DAY AND THE HOUR ★★ Drab war drama, set in Nazi-occupied France, has widow Simone Signoret involved with American paratrooper Stuart Whitman. B&W; 115m. **DIR:** René Clement. **CAST:** Simone Signoret, Stuart Whitman, Genevieve Page, Michel Piccoli, Reggie Nalder. **1963**

DAY AT THE BEACH ★★★ A group of friends travels to an empty beach house and breaks in, helping themselves to its luxurious accommodations. The resident returns and is held hostage. The group finds out that their tied-up host is a member of the mob, and they have a lot more on their hands than they expected. Darkly humorous at times, this movie is only hindered by low production values, and the occasionally dragging plot. Not rated; may be inappropriate for children. 93m. **DIR:** Nick Veronis. **CAST:** Jane Adams, Patrick Fitzgerald, Neal Jones, Catherine Kellner, Joe Ragno, Paul Gleason, Nick Veronis. **1998**

DAY AT THE RACES, A ★★★1/2 The Marx Brothers—Groucho, Harpo, and Chico, that is—were still at the peak of their fame in this MGM musical-comedy. Though not as unrelentingly hilarious and outrageous as the films they made at Paramount with Zeppo, it is nonetheless enjoyable. B&W; 111m. **DIR:** Sam Wood. **CAST:** The Marx Brothers, Allan Jones, Maureen O'Sullivan, Margaret Dumont. **1937**

DAY FOR NIGHT ★★★★★ One of the best of the film-within-a-film movies ever made, this work by the late François Truffaut captures the poetry and energy of the creative artist at his peak. In French with English subtitles. Beware of the badly dubbed English version. Rated PG. 120m. **DIR:** François Truffaut. **CAST:** Jacqueline Bisset, Jean-Pierre Léaud, François Truffaut. **1973**

DAY IN OCTOBER, A ★★1/2 WWII drama set in Nazi-occupied Denmark, about efforts to evacuate Danish Jews into neutral Sweden. Competently made film seems overly familiar, despite the efforts of a strong cast. Rated PG. 97m. **DIR:** Kenneth Madsen. **CAST:** D. B. Sweeney, Kelly Wolf, Tovah Feldshuh. **1992**

DAY IN THE COUNTRY, A ★★★★ A young girl seduced on an afternoon outing returns to the scene fourteen years later, an unhappily married woman. Jean Renoir's lyrical impressionistic tragedy is based on a story by Guy de Maupassant. Mesmerizing cinematography by Claude Renoir and Henri Cartier-Bresson. In French with English subtitles. 40m. **DIR:** Jean Renoir. **CAST:** Sylvia Bataille, George Darnoux. **1935**

DAY IN THE DEATH OF JOE EGG, A ★★★ This competent British production features the wonderful Alan Bates and Janet Suzman as a married couple whose small son, physically and mentally disabled since birth, causes them to consider euthanasia. Doesn't sound too funny, but in a strange way it is. 106m. **DIR:** Peter Medak. **CAST:** Alan Bates, Janet Suzman, Peter Bowles. **1972**

DAY MY PARENTS RAN AWAY, THE ★★★ Bobby Jacoby plays a teen who has been abandoned by parents in search of a better life. Left to his own devices and their credit cards, he indulges in his wildest fantasies, throwing parties, letting the laundry pile up, and feasting on TV dinners. Then reality hits, and he decides that he wants his folks back, but they don't want to come home. Rated PG for some adult situations. 95m. **DIR:** Martin Nicholson. **CAST:** Matt Frewer, Bobby Jacoby, Brigid Conley Walsh, Blair Brown, Martin Mull. **1993**

DAY OF ATONEMENT ★★ A complicated plot, derivative situations, and cardboard characters do little to distinguish this weak mobster effort about warring factions in Miami. Even the high-caliber cast can't save it, despite a noble effort from Christopher Walken as a vicious drug lord. Rated R for violence and language. 119m. **DIR:** Alexandre Arcady. **CAST:** Christopher Walken, Jennifer Beals, Jill Clayburgh, Richard Berry, Roger Hanin. **1993**

DAY OF JUDGMENT, A ★★1/2 After the local preacher leaves for lack of a congregation (maybe because none of them can act), the nasties of a small town are taught their lesson by the grim reaper. Not rated; contains violence. 101m. **DIR:** C.D.H. Reynolds. **CAST:** William T. Hicks. **1981**

DAY OF THE ANIMALS 🦃 Nature goes nuts after the Earth's ozone layer is destroyed. Rated R for violence, profanity, and gore. 98m. **DIR:** William Girdler. **CAST:** Christopher George, Lynda Day George, Richard Jaeckel, Leslie Nielsen, Michael Ansara, Ruth Roman. **1977 DVD**

DAY OF THE ASSASSIN 🦃 Chuck Connors plays a James Bond–type hero in this dull action film. Not rated; contains violence and profanity. 94m. **DIR:** Brian Trenchard-Smith, Carlos Vasallo. **CAST:** Chuck Connors, Glenn Ford, Richard Roundtree, Jorge Rivero, Henry Silva, Andres Garcia. **1979**

DAY OF THE DEAD ★★ The third film in George A. Romero's *Dead* series doesn't hold up to its predecessors. Like earlier films in the series, *Day of the Dead* portrays graphic scenes of cannibalism, dismemberment, and other gory carnage. Unlike the other films, this one has no truly likable characters to root for. Not rated; contains scenes of violence. 100m. **DIR:** George A. Romero. **CAST:** Lori Cardille, Terry Alexander, Richard Liberty, Joseph Pilato. **1985 DVD**

DAY OF THE DOLPHIN, THE ★★★ Fine film centering on a research scientist (George C. Scott) who teaches a pair of dolphins to speak, and how they're kidnapped and used in an assassination attempt. Rated PG for language. 104m. **DIR:** Mike Nichols. **CAST:** George C. Scott, Trish Van Devere, Paul Sorvino, Fritz Weaver. **1973**

DAY OF THE JACKAL, THE ★★★★ Edward Fox is a cunning assassin roaming Europe in hopes of a crack at General Charles de Gaulle. High suspense and a marvelous performance by Fox underscore a strong story line. Rated PG. 141m. **DIR:** Fred Zinnemann. **CAST:** Edward Fox, Alan Badel, Tony Britton, Cyril Cusack. **1973 DVD**

DAY OF THE LOCUST, THE ★★★★1/2 This drama is both extremely depressing and spellbinding. It shows the unglamorous side of Hollywood in the 1930s. The people who don't succeed in the entertainment capital are the focus of the film. Rated R. 144m. **DIR:** John Schlesinger. **CAST:** Donald Sutherland, Karen Black, Burgess Meredith, Bo Hopkins, William Atherton. **1975**

DAY OF THE TRIFFIDS, THE ★★★1/2 This British film has triffids—alien plants—arriving on Earth during a meteor shower. The shower blinds most of the Earth's people. Then the plants grow, begin walking, and eat humans. This one will grow on you. 95m. **DIR:** Steve Sekely. **CAST:** Howard Keel, Nicole Maurey, Janette Scott, Kieron Moore, Mervyn Johns. **1963**

DAY OF WRATH ★★★1/2 Slow-moving, intriguing story of a young woman who marries an elderly preacher but falls in love with his son. Visually effective and well acted by all the principals, this film relies too much on symbolism but is still worthy as a study of hysteria and the motivations behind fear. B&W; 98m. **DIR:** Carl Dreyer. **CAST:** Lisbeth Movin, Thorkild Roose. **1944**

DAY ONE ★★★ Television tackles the creation of the nuclear bomb as American scientists work on the Manhattan Project. Stellar cast helps this true story, which is rich in production values and benefits from a riveting screenplay. Not rated. 141m. **DIR:** Joseph Sargent. **CAST:** Brian Dennehy, David Strathairn, Michael Tucker, Richard Dysart, David Ogden Stiers. **1989**

DAY THAT SHOOK THE WORLD, THE ★★★ A slow start can't reduce one's fascination with the shocking incident—the assassination of Austria's Archduke Ferdinand and his wife—that resulted in World War I. Rated R for violence, including disturbing hunting scenes and graphic torture footage. 111m. **DIR:** Veljko Bulajic. **CAST:** Christopher Plummer, Maximilian Schell, Florinda Bolkan. **1978**

DAY THE EARTH CAUGHT FIRE, THE ★★★★ Veteran director Val Guest helmed this near-classic film concerning the fate of the Earth following simultaneous nuclear explosions at both poles, sending the planet on a collision course with the sun. Incredibly realistic production is unsettling, with Edward Judd perfectly cast as an Everyman caught up in the mass panic and hysteria. B&W; 99m. **DIR:** Val Guest. **CAST:** Edward Judd, Janet Munro, Leo McKern. **1962**

DAY THE EARTH STOOD STILL, THE ★★★★ *The Day the Earth Stood Still* is one of the better science-fiction films. Even though some of the space gimmicks are campy and not up to today's standards of special effects, the film holds up well because of a good adult script and credible performances by Michael Rennie and Patricia Neal. B&W; 92m. **DIR:** Robert Wise. **CAST:** Michael Rennie, Patricia Neal, Hugh Marlowe, Sam Jaffe, Billy Gray. **1951**

DAY THE SUN TURNED COLD, THE ★★★1/2 Intriguing mystery-drama about the police captain in a bleak town in northern China trying to investigate a 10 year old case when a young man accuses his mother of having murdered his father. Well-filmed tale may be too somber for casual viewers, but rewarding for the patient. Not rated. In Chinese with English subtitles. 99m. **DIR:** Yim Ho. **CAST:** Siqin Gowa, Tuo Zhong Hua, Li Hu. **1994**

DAY THE WORLD ENDED, THE ★★ After a nuclear holocaust, a handful of survivors battle each other and the local mutant monster. Minor melodrama featuring one of Roger Corman's cheaper monster suits. B&W; 82m. **DIR:** Roger Corman. **CAST:** Richard Denning, Lori Nelson, Mike Connors. **1956**

DAY TIME ENDED, THE 🦃 Grade-Z sci-fi clunker, about nature gone wild. 79m. **DIR:** John "Bud" Cardos. **CAST:** Jim Davis, Dorothy Malone, Chris Mitchum. **1980**

DAYBREAK (1993) ★★★★ Writer-director Stephen Tolkin's cautionary drama, based on Alan Bowne's play *Beirut*, takes place in a decrepit New York City of the near future, controlled by a fascistic government that has made social outcasts of those stricken with an AIDS-like plague. One young woman (Moira Kelly), dismayed by the Orwellian youth patrols, contacts underground rebels who spirit diseased victims to safer quarters. Rated R for nudity, simulated sex, profanity, and violence. 91m. **DIR:** Stephen Tolkin. **CAST:** Cuba Gooding Jr., Moira Kelly, Omar Epps, Alice Drummond, Martha Plimpton, John Savage. **1993**

•DAYBREAK (2000) ★★ Uninspired made-for-cable remake of the made-for-television movie *A Short Walk to Daylight*, in which occupants of an L.A. subway train find themselves trapped under the city after a strong earthquake. The survivors face the usual roadblocks as they try to reach the surface and safety, including a cliché-ridden script and by-the-numbers direction that fails to make efficient use of the budget limitations. What's the great Roy Scheider doing in this mess? Rated R for language. 93m. **DIR:** Jean Pellerin. **CAST:** Ted McGinley, Ursula Brooks, Adam Wylie, Jaime Bergman, Roy Scheider. **2000 DVD**

DAYDREAMER, THE (1966) ★★★ This *Children's Treasures* presentation combines live action with puppetry to bring a young Hans Christian Andersen and his tales to life. 80m. **DIR:** Jules Bass. **CAST:** Paul O'Keefe, Burl Ives, Tallulah Bankhead, Terry-Thomas, Victor Borge, Ed Wynn, Patty Duke, Boris Karloff, Ray Bolger, Hayley Mills, Jack Gilford, Margaret Hamilton. **1966**

DAYDREAMER, THE (1970) (LE DISTRAIT) ★★★ This early vehicle for popular French comedian Pierre Richard, who also wrote and directed, is a hodgepodge of gags in varying comic styles. He plays a bumbler who lands a job at an ad agency and nearly destroys the place. In French with English subtitles. 80m. **DIR:** Pierre Richard. **CAST:** Pierre Richard, Bernard Blier, Maria Pacome, Marie-Christine Barrault. **1970**

DAYLIGHT ★★★ Working-class Sylvester Stallone, once an emergency-medical-services chief, happens to be on hand when a spectacular accident traps people inside New York's Holland Tunnel. The survivors overcome numerous obstacles while trying to find a way out before the tunnel collapses. Rated PG-13 for violence, profanity, and dramatic intensity. 115m. **DIR:** Rob Cohen. **CAST:** Sylvester Stallone, Amy Brenneman, Viggo Mortensen, Dan Hedaya, Jay O. Sanders, Karen Young, Claire Bloom. **1996 DVD**

DAYS AND NIGHTS IN THE FOREST ★★★★ In one of his best films, Satyajit Ray presents a deceptively simple tale of four city men vacationing in the country, where they meet a variety of women who draw out their personalities. Delicately woven, this is a rewarding film for those up to its deliberate pace. In Hindi with English subtitles. B&W; 115m. **DIR:** Satyajit Ray. **CAST:** Soumitra Chatterjee, Sharmila Tagore. **1969**

DAYS OF GLORY ★★ A young Gregory Peck (in his first film) and a cast of practically unknown European actors try their darndest to make this story of guerrilla warfare on the Russian front work, but the end result is limp and unconvincing. B&W; 86m. **DIR:** Jacques Tourneur. **CAST:** Gregory Peck, Tamara Toumanova, Alan Reed, Maria Palmer. **1944**

DAYS OF HEAVEN ★★★★1/2 Each frame looks like a page torn from an exquisitely beautiful picture book. The film begins in the slums of Chicago, where Bill (Richard Gere) works in a steel mill. He decides to take Abby (Brooke Adams), his girl, and Linda (Linda Manz), his young sister, to the Texas Panhandle to work in the wheat fields at harvest time. That's the beginning of an idyllic year that ends in tragedy. Rated PG. 95m. **DIR:** Terence Malick. **CAST:** Richard Gere, Brooke Adams, Sam Shepard, Linda Manz. **1978 DVD**

DAYS OF OLD CHEYENNE ★★★★ Don Barry accepts the job of town marshal from Big Bill Harmon (William Haade) in the belief Harmon is interested in maintaining law and order. Above-average oater. B&W; 56m. **DIR:** Elmer Clifton. **CAST:** Don Barry, Emmet Lynn, Lynn Merrick, William Haade. **1943**

DAYS OF THRILLS AND LAUGHTER ★★★1/2 An homage to classic silent-film comedians and daredevils, this collection of clips includes, among other winners, Charlie Chaplin's dinner-roll dance from *Gold Rush*. A worthwhile nostalgia film. B&W; 93m. **DIR:** Robert Youngson. **CAST:** Buster Keaton, Stan Laurel, Oliver Hardy, Charlie Chaplin, Harold Lloyd, Douglas Fairbanks Sr., The Keystone Kops. **1961**

DAYS OF THUNDER ★★★★ Star Tom Cruise and director Tony Scott take their *Top Gun* tactics to the racetrack in this fast-car fantasy set during the Daytona 500, and the result is remarkably satisfying. Screenwriter Robert Towne takes the standard story and infuses it with a richness that recalls the golden age of Hollywood. Rated PG-13 for profanity and violence. 108m. **DIR:** Tony Scott. **CAST:** Tom Cruise, Robert Duvall, Nicole Kidman, Randy Quaid, Michael Rooker, Cary Elwes. **1990 DVD**

DAYS OF WINE AND ROSES, THE (1958) ★★★1/2 Unpolished but still excellent television original from which the 1962 film was adapted. Cliff Robertson is the up-and-coming executive and Piper Laurie, his pretty wife, whose lives are shattered by alcoholism. Written for the *Playhouse 90* series, it is introduced by Julie Harris and framed with interviews with the featured players. B&W; 90m. **DIR:** John Frankenheimer. **CAST:** Cliff Robertson, Piper Laurie. **1958**

DAYS OF WINE AND ROSES (1962) ★★★1/2 In this saddening film, Jack Lemmon and Lee Remick shatter the misconceptions about middle-class alcoholism. B&W; 117m. **DIR:** Blake Edwards. **CAST:** Jack Lemmon, Lee Remick, Charles Bickford, Jack Klugman. **1962**

DAYS OF WRATH ★★★ One of the best non-Leone spaghetti Westerns. A veteran gunfighter teaches the town bastard how to use a gun. He gains his self-respect and the fear of the townspeople. All goes well until the gunfighter kills his student's only friend, the town sheriff. The student turns on the teacher, putting to use all that he's been taught. A strong performance by veteran Hollywood heavy Lee Van Cleef. Rated PG. 97m. **DIR:** Tonino Valerii. **CAST:** Lee Van Cleef, Giuliano Gemma, Walter Rilla, Crista Linder, Piero Lulli, Andrea Bosic. **1967**

DAYTON'S DEVILS ★★ Leslie Nielsen leads a group of has-beens and ex-cons—or, as the video box says, "a melting pot of losers"—in a robbery of an air force base bank. 107m. **DIR:** Jack Shea. **CAST:** Leslie Nielsen, Rory Calhoun, Lainie Kazan, Barry Sadler, Georg Stanford Brown. **1968**

DAYTRIPPERS, THE ★★★1/2 After a Long Island housewife finds an apparent love note to her husband, she wedges herself into the family station wagon with her mother, father, sister, and sister's boyfriend to search Manhattan for the suspect spouse. Their misadventures provide plenty of comic relief. The closer they get to solving their mystery, the more they learn the truth about themselves. Rated R for language and mature themes. 87m. **DIR:** Greg Mottola. **CAST:** Hope Davis, Anne Meara, Parker Posey, Pat McNamara, Liev Schreiber, Stanley Tucci. **1996 DVD**

DAZED AND CONFUSED ★★★1/2 Writer-director Richard Linklater shows how the final day of high school in 1976 affects the outgoing seniors and incoming freshmen. Contains occasional truths and a lot of heart. Rated R for profanity and drug use. 103m. **DIR:** Richard Linklater. **CAST:** Jason London, Rory Cochrane, Adam Goldberg, Anthony Rapp, Sasha Jenson, Milla Jovovich, Michelle Burke. **1993 DVD**

D.C. CAB 🦃 Take the bus. Rated R. 99m. **DIR:** Joel Schumacher. **CAST:** Gary Busey, Mr. T, Adam Baldwin, Max Gail. **1983**

DEAD, THE ★★★★★ John Huston's final bow is an elegant adaptation of James Joyce's short story about a party given by three women for a group of their dearest friends. During the evening, conversation drifts to those people, now dead, who have had a great influence on the lives of the guests and hostesses at the party. Huston, who died before the film was released, seems to be speaking to us from beyond the grave. This is one of his best. Rated PG. 81m. **DIR:** John Huston. **CAST:** Anjelica Huston, Donal McCann, Ingrid Craigie, Dan O'Herlihy, Marie Kean, Donal Donnelly, Sean McClory. **1987**

DEAD AGAIN ★★★★★ A highly stylized suspense thriller in which a Los Angeles detective is hired to uncover the identity of a woman who has lost her memory. He enlists the aid of a hypnotist, who discovers that the woman may have led a previous life that may have involved the detective. Either way, someone is out to kill them both. Rated R for violence. 107m. **DIR:** Kenneth Branagh. **CAST:** Kenneth Branagh, Emma Thompson, Andy Garcia, Derek Jacobi, Hanna Schygulla, Robin Williams, Campbell Scott. **1991 DVD**

DEAD AHEAD ★★★ In this made-for-cable original, a woman's son is taken hostage, and she stalks the band of criminals through the wilderness. Good action and plot, but the acting is a little stiff. Not rated; contains violence. 95m. **DIR:** Stuart Cooper. **CAST:** Stephanie Zimbalist, Peter Onorati, Sarah Chalke. **1996**

DEAD AHEAD: THE EXXON VALDEZ DISASTER ★★★★ First-rate advocacy cinema from scripter Michael Baker, who documents the ecological disaster that resulted when the Exxon Valdez dumped 11 million gallons of oil into Alaska's Prince William Sound. John Heard, as the site's leading environmental champion, is appropriately outraged; Christopher Lloyd has the tougher role as the Exxon bureaucrat sacrificed as the incident's scapegoat. 88m. **DIR:** Paul Seed. **CAST:** John Heard, Christopher Lloyd, Ron Frazier, Michael Murphy, Rip Torn. **1992**

DEAD AIR ★★★1/2 A disc jockey receives harassing phone calls, then several female acquaintances turn up dead, and he is the prime suspect. A well-scripted mystery that will keep you guessing until the end. Not rated; contains violence and suggested sex. 93m. **DIR:** Fred Walton. **CAST:** Gregory Hines, Debrah Farentino, Beau Starr, Gloria Reuben, Laura Harrington, Michael Harris. **1994**

DEAD ALIVE ★★★1/2 Over-the-top New Zealand gorefest is so disgusting, it's hilarious. When shy and introverted Timothy Balme's doting mother is bitten by a Sumatran rat monkey, she begins to exhibit zombielike traits, including eating the flesh of the undead. Before you know it, the house is zombie central, and the lengths Balme must go through to alleviate the problem are extreme, to say the least. Rated R for violence, gore, and language; unrated version contains buckets more gore. 85m. **DIR:** Peter Jackson. **CAST:** Timothy Balme, Diana Penalver, Elizabeth Moody. **1992 DVD**

DEAD AND BURIED ★★ This muddled venture by the creators of *Alien* (Ronald Shusett and Dan O'Bannon) involves a series of gory murders, and the weird part is that the victims seem to be coming back to life. The puzzle is resolved during the suspenseful, eerie ending—definitely the high point of the movie. Rated R for violence. 92m. **DIR:** Gary A. Sherman. **CAST:** James Farentino, Melody Anderson, Jack Albertson, Dennis Redfield. **1981**

•DEAD AWAKE ★★★ Bizarre but surprisingly satisfying mystery about an insomniac blamed for a murder he didn't commit. Weird music score almost ruins everything but twisted tale holds viewers' attention. Rated R for language, sexual content, and violence. 98m. **DIR:** Marc S. Grenier. **CAST:** Stephen Baldwin, Macha Grenon, Michael Ironside. **2001 DVD**

DEAD BADGE ★★★ Intense made-for-cable thriller about a rookie cop who is assigned a dead cop's badge. It's supposed to be an honor, but rookie Dan Sampson (Brian Wimmer) finds it a curse. When he begins to look into the circumstances behind the cop's death, Sampson's investigation is cut short by some crooked cops who suggest that he leave things alone. Good cast pumps life into this good cop–bad cop scenario. Rated R for violence. 95m. **DIR:** Douglas Barr. **CAST:** Brian Wimmer, M. Emmet Walsh, James B. Sikking, Yaphet Kotto, Olympia Dukakis. **1994**

DEAD-BANG ★★★1/2 Don Johnson stars as real-life L.A. detective Jerry Buck, whose investigation into the murder of a police officer leads to the discovery of a chilling conspiracy. Johnson's strong performance is supported by an excellent cast. John Frankenheimer directs with authority and adds texture to the familiar plot. Rated R for violence, profanity, nudity, and simulated sex. 109m. **DIR:** John Frankenheimer. **CAST:** Don Johnson, Penelope Ann Miller, William Forsythe, Bob Balaban, Tim Reid. **1988 DVD**

DEAD BEAT ★★★ Dead girls tell no tales—at least that is what local heartthrob Kit and his former girlfriend are hoping. When a female high-school student disappears, Kit knows what happened to her. Keeping it a secret from Kit's new girlfriend is going to be murder. Sara Gilbert and Natasha Gregson Wagner shine as the two women in Kit's life, while Bruce Ramsay shows a flair for dark comedy as Kit. Rated R for language. 94m. **DIR:** Adam Dubov. **CAST:** Bruce Ramsay, Natasha Gregson Wagner, Sara Gilbert, Balthazar Getty. **1994**

DEAD CALM ★★★1/2 A married couple (Sam Neill and Nicole Kidman) are terrorized at sea by a maniac (Billy Zane) in this intelligent, stylish thriller from Australian director Phillip Noyce. Although impressive overall, the movie has some unnecessarily explicit scenes. A near classic. Rated R for violence, profanity, nudity, and simulated sex. 95m. **DIR:** Phillip Noyce. **CAST:** Sam Neill, Nicole Kidman, Billy Zane. **1989 DVD**

DEAD CENTER ★★ Derivative thriller finds punk Justin Lazard caught between some rock and a hard place when a drug deal turns sour. He agrees to be trained by the government as a professional assassin. The only twist here is that Lazard is being set up for a fall. Rated R for violence, language, and nudity. 90m. **DIR:** Steve Carver. **CAST:** Justin Lazard, Rachel York, Eb Lottimer. **1994**

DEAD CERTAIN ★★ A psycho killer (Brad Dourif yet again) is tracked by an equally seedy cop. Better made than average, but that doesn't help the tired plot. Not rated, but an R equivalent for violence and sexuality. 93m. **DIR:** Anders Palm. **CAST:** Francesco Quinn, Brad Dourif, Karen Russell. **1990**

DEAD COLD ★★ When a couple travels to a snowy wilderness to celebrate their second honeymoon, they are surprised by a mysterious traveler who arrives at their door. Ludicrous suspense film is low on surprises and high on camp. Rated R for violence, profanity, and nudity. 91m. **DIR:** Kurt Anderson. **CAST:** Lysette Anthony, Chris Mulkey, Peter Dobson. **1995**

DEAD CONNECTION ★★1/2 Pedestrian thriller fails to live up to its pedigree. Instead, this is just another shaggy-dog story about a phone-sex killer and the hard-as-nails detective (Michael Madsen) intent on catching him. Lisa Bonet is the reporter who knows a hot story when she sees one. Madsen's moody performance is a treat. Rated R for violence, nudity, and language. 93m. **DIR:** Nigel Dick. **CAST:** Michael Madsen, Lisa Bonet, Gary Stretch. **1993**

DEAD DON'T DIE, THE 🦃 George Hamilton must take on the Zombie Master in order to clear his dead brother's name. Made for TV. 76m. **DIR:** Curtis Harrington. **CAST:** George Hamilton, Ray Milland, Joan Blondell, Linda Cristal, Ralph Meeker. **1975**

DEAD EASY ★★★1/2 George, Alexa, and Armstrong are three friends who anger a crime boss whose overreaction sets off a chain of events that results in every small-time hood and paid killer chasing them. Well-done contemporary crime-thriller. Rated R for nudity, violence, language. 90m. **DIR:** Bert Diling. **CAST:** Scott Burgess, Rosemary Paul, Tim McKenzie. **1978**

DEAD END (1937) ★★★ Many famous names combined to film this story of people trying to escape their oppressive slum environment. Humphrey Bogart is cast in one of his many gangster roles from the 1930s. Joel McCrea conforms to his Hollywood stereotype by playing the "nice guy" architect, who dreams of rebuilding New York's waterfront. B&W; 93m. **DIR:** William Wyler. **CAST:** Humphrey Bogart, Sylvia Sidney, Joel McCrea, Claire Trevor. **1937**

DEAD END (1997) ★★ Overly familiar tale of a police sergeant who is framed for his ex-wife's murder. Forced to flee with his son, the cop finds he has to befriend the criminals he once busted in order to survive the streets. Nothing new. Rated R for violence, language, nudity, and adult situations. 93m. **DIR:** Douglas Jackson. **CAST:** Eric Roberts, Jacob Tierney, Eliza Roberts, Jayne Heitmeyer. **1997 DVD**

DEAD-END DRIVE-IN ★★ It's the year 1990. After widespread economic collapse, the world is in chaos. The Dead-End Drive-In is a relocation camp for the undesirable element. Rated R for language, violence, and nudity. 92m. **DIR:** Brian Trenchard-Smith. **CAST:** Ned Manning, Natalie McCurry. **1986**

DEAD EYES OF LONDON ★★1/2 A German remake of the Bela Lugosi chiller *The Human Monster.* Once again the director of a home for the blind uses the place as a front for criminal activities. Interesting vehicle for Klaus Kinski, who gives a great maniacal performance. Even so, the film lacks the eerie atmosphere of the original. B&W; 104m. **DIR:** Alfred Vohrer. **CAST:** Klaus Kinski, Karin Baal. **1961**

DEAD FOR A DOLLAR ★★ Three double-crossing gunmen try to hunt down a $200,000 bank-robbery cache, but a woman outsmarts them all. A good performance by John Ireland is all that holds the film together. Not rated; contains violence. 92m. **DIR:** Osvaldo Civirani. **CAST:** George Hilton, John Ireland, Sandra Milo, Piero Vida. **1968**

DEAD FUNNY ★★★ Offbeat black comedy about two women deciding what to do with the body of one of their boyfriends when he's found dead in the kitchen. Andrew McCarthy plays the obnoxious boyfriend who likes practical jokes, Elizabeth Peña and Paige Turco the women who use the moment to reminisce about the events leading up to the discovery. Good performances and a twisted sense of humor help the proceedings along. Rated R for language and violence. 91m. **DIR:** John Feldman. **CAST:** Elizabeth Peña, Paige Turco, Andrew McCarthy. **1995**

DEAD HATE THE LIVING, THE ★★★1/2 Highly amusing horror film filled to the brim with nods to genre films past and present. Director David Parker has concocted a tale of indie filmmakers making their own no-budget zombie film in an abandoned hospital. While there, they accidentally unleash real zombies and their master Eibon. The film manages to be a horror fan's kind of film without sinking into the aren't-we-smug kind of mugging so prevalent in many of today's horror teen films. Highly recommended for horror buffs. Rated R for gore, violence, and profanity. 90m. **DIR:** David Parker. **CAST:** Eric Clawson, Matt Stephens. **2000 DVD**

DEAD HEART ★★ Bryan Brown stars in this Australian film as a rural lawman faced with the duty of imposing government justice on aboriginal elders who, he believes, have committed murder to avenge the desecration of their sacred grounds. While the film may have deeper impact in its native land, to American eyes it seems merely grim and nasty. Not rated; contains violence, nudity, sexual situations, and profanity. 107m. **DIR:** Nicholas Parsons. **CAST:** Bryan Brown, Ernie Dingo, Angie Milliken, Gnarnay Yarrahe Waitaire. **1996 DVD**

DEAD HEAT ★★ In this so-so but gory spoof of the living-dead genre, Treat Williams and Joe Piscopo star as a pair of L.A. police detectives who find the mastermind behind a group of robberies that are being committed by criminals brought back from the dead. The special effects are pretty good, but 60 percent of the jokes fall flat. Rated R for violence and profanity. 86m. **DIR:** Mark Goldblatt. **CAST:** Treat Williams, Joe Piscopo, Lindsay Frost, Darren McGavin, Vincent Price, Keye Luke. **1988**

DEAD HEAT ON A MERRY-GO-ROUND ★★★1/2 Thoroughly engrossing film depicts the heist of an airport bank. Not a breezy caper flick, it unfolds a complex plot in a darkly intelligent manner. The cast is impeccable. James Coburn delivers one of his most effective performances. 104m. **DIR:** Bernard Girard. **CAST:** James Coburn, Camilla Sparv, Aldo Ray, Ross Martin, Severn Darden, Robert Webber. **1966**

DEAD HUSBANDS ★★1/2 This black comedy takes inspiration from the ubiquitous chain letter, but the difference is, the wife at the bottom of the list must kill the husband at the top. One woman has to work doubly hard to get her husband added to the list. The film would have worked, if the plot weren't too silly (even for a farce), and if they hadn't cast bumbling John Ritter as the troublesome husband. At least the music in this made-for-cable original is a real kick. Rated PG-13 for violence. 95m. **DIR:** Paul Shapiro. **CAST:** John Ritter, Nicollette Sheridan, Sonja Smits, Amy Yasbeck. **1998**

•DEAD IN A HEARTBEAT ★★★1/2 Suspenseful race against the clock unfolds when a distraught father (Timothy Busfield) blames the heart surgeon for his son's death. After ingeniously planting bombs in her patients' pacemakers, he taunts her by withholding the names of his next victims. Judge Reinhold is surprisingly believable as a police bomb expert. Tense life-or-death situations are riveting. Not rated; contains violence and mature themes. 93m. **DIR:** Paul Antier. **CAST:** Penelope Ann Miller, Judge Reinhold, Timothy Busfield, Fulvio Cecere. **2002**

DEAD IN THE WATER ★★★1/2 Bryan Brown energizes this droll little made-for-cable thriller, as an amoral womanizer determined to plot the perfect murder—of his wife—so he can retire in comfort with his sexy secretary. Things naturally go awry, and our poor antihero finds himself suspected in a murder he *didn't* commit. Rated PG-13. Mild violence and sexual themes. 90m. **DIR:** Bill Condon. **CAST:** Bryan Brown, Teri Hatcher, Anne De Salvo, Veronica Cartwright. **1991 DVD**

DEAD MAN ★★★1/2 A strange but poetic art-house Western, strictly for fans of enigmatic metaphors, literary allusions, and dream-state storytelling. Johnny Depp stars as a wanderer in the old West. He may be a misplaced eastern dude or the ghost of English poet William Blake, and his guide through the badlands is a philosophical Indian named Nobody. Meanwhile, a disgruntled industrialist has hired three gunfighters to hunt him down. B&W; 120m. **DIR:** Jim Jarmusch. **CAST:** Johnny Depp, Gary Farmer, Robert Mitchum, Lance Henriksen, Michael Wincott, John Hurt, Alfred Molina, Gabriel Byrne. **1996 DVD**

DEAD MAN ON CAMPUS ★★ MTV production about college roommates facing failure who turn to an old school code that awards a 4.0 GPA to the surviving roommates of a suicide victim. They set out on a search for the most likely candidate. Bad taste abounds yet some incidents are hilarious. Rated R for drug use, language, and sexual situations. 94m. **DIR:** Alan Cohn. **CAST:** Tom Everett Scott, Mark Paul Gosselaar, Corey Page, Lochlyn Munro. **1998 DVD**

DEAD MAN OUT ★★★ Awaiting execution, an inmate on Death Row (Rubén Blades) goes mad. This creates a problem for the state, since an insane man cannot be executed. The state-appointed psychiatrist (Danny Glover) contemplates whether or not he should declare Ben sane again in time for him to die. Ron Hutchinson's teleplay is riveting, and Glover and Blades deliver fine performances. Not rated. 87m. **DIR:** Richard Pearce. **CAST:** Danny Glover, Rubén Blades, Larry Block, Samuel L. Jackson, Sam Stone, Maria Ricossa, Ali Giron, Val Ford. **1988**

DEAD MAN WALKING (1987) ★★★ Surprisingly well-done low-budget science fiction in which a disease has divided the world's population into the haves and the have-nots. A young man (Jeffrey Combs) hires a daredevil mercenary (Wings Hauser) to rescue his girlfriend (Pamela Ludwig) from the plague zone. Rated R for violence. 90m. **DIR:** Gregory Brown. **CAST:** Wings Hauser, Brian James, Jeffrey Combs, Pamela Ludwig. **1987**

DEAD MAN WALKING (1995) ★★★★ Sister Helen Prejean's 1993 bestseller is the basis for this compelling account of her life's work: as spiritual adviser for condemned killers awaiting execution on death row in New Orleans's Angola Prison. Susan Sarandon contributes a superb performance as the dedicated but often overwhelmed Sister Prejean, while Sean Penn is memorable as her first "client." The film wishes to demonstrate the evils of capital punishment. Rated R for profanity, violence, rape, and nudity. 120m. **DIR:** Tim Robbins. **CAST:** Susan Sarandon, Sean Penn, Robert Prosky, Raymond J. Barry, R. Lee Ermey. **1995 DVD**

DEAD MAN'S CURVE ★★ Based on the urban myth that if your college roommate commits suicide you get a 4.0 for that semester, this made-for-cable original examines what happens when two roommates decide to improve their grades by killing their other roommate and making it look like suicide. While the movie starts out okay, it ultimately fails because it's filled with scenes too strange to be credible, plot twists that only seem to confuse, and odd camera shots. Rated R for profanity and violence. 95m. **DIR:** Dan Rosen. **CAST:** Matthew Lillard, Michael Vartan, Randall Batinkoff, Keri Russell, Dana Delany. **1997**

DEAD MAN'S EYES ★★1/2 Blinded by jealous model Acquanetta, artist Lon Chaney Jr. is suspected of murdering the man who provides eye tissue to restore his sight. Average entry in the *Inner Sanctum* mystery series. B&W; 64m. **DIR:** Reginald LeBorg. **CAST:** Lon Chaney Jr., Acquanetta, Jean Parker, Paul Kelly. **1944**

DEAD MAN'S GULCH ★★★ Story of two former pony express riders. One becomes an outlaw, the other a lawman. B&W; 56m. **DIR:** John English. **CAST:** Don Barry, Lynn Merrick. **1943**

DEAD MAN'S WALK ★★★★1/2 The high caliber of Western drama that began with the adaptation of Larry McMurtry's *Lonesome Dove* continues with this prequel, in which a young Gus McCrae and Woodrow Call have their first encounter with adventure and the Texas Rangers. Like the other films in the series, it's a dusty and perilous vision of the Old West made all the more poignant by the naïveté of its protagonists. Made for TV. 271m. **DIR:** Yves Simoneau. **CAST:** F. Murray Abraham, Keith Carradine, Patricia Childress, Brian Dennehy, Edward James Olmos, Harry Dean Stanton, David Arquette, Jonny Lee Miller. **1997 DVD**

DEAD MEN CAN'T DANCE ★★ Interesting premise can't rise above the exploitation roots of this gender-bender war film featuring Kathleen York as a CIA agent in South Korea training as a combat army ranger. York and her female comrades are called into action when York's boyfriend tries to steal nuclear warheads from the enemy. This gung-ho effort suffers from poor execution. Rated R for adult situations, language, and violence. 97m. **DIR:** Stephen Anderson. **CAST:** Michael Biehn, Kathleen York, Adrian Paul, R. Lee Ermey. **1997**

DEAD MEN DON'T DIE ★★1/2 Nosy television newscaster Elliott Gould stumbles across a story most reporters would die for. Unfortunately, Gould does, but is resurrected through a voodoo spell. Now a zombie, he sets out to solve his own murder. Somewhat funny, proves that for television anchors there is life after death. Rated R for violence and language. 94m. **DIR:** Malcolm Marmorstein. **CAST:** Elliott Gould, Melissa Sue Anderson, Mark Moses, Mabel King. **1991**

DEAD MEN DON'T WEAR PLAID ★★★★ In this often hilarious and always entertaining comedy, Steve Martin plays a private eye who confronts the suspicious likes of Humphrey Bogart, Burt Lancaster, Alan Ladd, Bette Davis, and other stars of Hollywood's Golden Age, with the help of tricky editing and writer-director Carl Reiner. Rachel Ward co-stars as Martin's sexy client. Rated PG for adult themes. B&W; 89m. **DIR:** Carl Reiner. **CAST:** Steve Martin, Rachel Ward, Reni Santoni, Carl Reiner, George Gaynes. **1982 DVD**

DEAD MEN TELL ★★1/2 When an old lady is killed just before setting sail to find a rumored pirate treasure worth $60 million, Charlie Chan investigates. A spooky atmosphere helps cover up the obvious low budget. B&W; 61m. **DIR:** Harry Lachman. **CAST:** Sidney Toler, Sheila Ryan, Victor Sen Yung. **1941**

DEAD MEN WALK ★★ Master character actor George Zucco makes the most of one of his few leading roles, a dual one at that, in this grade-Z cheapie about vampires and zombies. B&W; 67m. **DIR:** Sam Newfield. **CAST:** George Zucco, Mary Carlisle, Nedrick Young, Dwight Frye. **1943 DVD**

DEAD NEXT DOOR, THE ★★★ Though he receives no credit, Sam Raimi produced and financed this low-budget zombie film that marked the debut of cult director J. R. Bookwalter. As a virus sweeps the world and turns people into zombies, the government creates a zombie squad to take care of the problem. Not rated; contains violence, gore, and profanity. 84m. **DIR:** J. R. Bookwalter. **CAST:** Peter Ferry, Bogdan Pecic, Scott Spiegel. **1989**

DEAD OF NIGHT (1945) ★★★★1/2 The granddaddy of the British horror anthologies still chills today, with the final sequence—in which ventriloquist Michael Redgrave fights a losing battle with his demonic dummy—rating as an all-time horror classic. The other stories are told almost as effectively. B&W; 104m. **DIR:** Alberto Cavalcanti, Basil Dearden, Robert Hamer, Charles Crichton. **CAST:** Mervyn Johns, Michael Redgrave, Sally Ann Howes, Miles Malleson, Googie Withers, Basil Radford. **1945**

DEAD OF NIGHT (1977) ★★ This trilogy of shockers written by Richard Matheson has some interesting twists, but is far inferior to his other achievements. Elvira is host on this, another in her "Thriller Video" series. 76m. **DIR:** Dan Curtis. **CAST:** Ed Begley Jr., John Hackett, Patrick Macnee. **1977**

DEAD OF WINTER ★★★ When aspiring actress Mary Steenburgen steps in at the last minute to replace a performer who has walked off the set of a film in production, she is certain it is the chance of a lifetime. But once trapped in a remote mansion with the creepy filmmakers, she begins to believe it may be the last act of her lifetime. The story is a bit contrived, but one only realizes it after the film is over. Rated R for profanity and violence. 98m. **DIR:** Arthur Penn. **CAST:** Mary Steenburgen, Roddy McDowall, Jan Rubes, William Russ, Ken Pogue. **1987**

DEAD ON ★★ A woman has an affair with a man and then suggests that they kill each other's spouses. If you like all sex and no plot, you'll love this. Available in R and unrated versions, both with nudity, graphic sex, violence, and profanity. 90m. **DIR:** Ralph Hemecker. **CAST:** Matt McCoy, Tracy Scoggins, Shari Shattuck, David Ackroyd, Thomas Wagner. **1993**

DEAD ON SIGHT ★★1/2 Jennifer Beals stars as a woman who is seeing visions of horrible violence in her sleep. Then she awakens and discovers the vicious dream murders have actually occurred. Joined by an unbelieving detective (Daniel Baldwin), Beals decides she must stop the murderer herself—or become his next victim. So-so mystery-thriller works more often than not, but borrows heavily from other films and you're never quite sure you haven't seen it before. Rated R for violence and profanity. 96m. **DIR:** Reuben Pruess. **CAST:** Jennifer Beals, Daniel Baldwin, Kurtwood Smith. **1994**

DEAD ON THE MONEY ★★1/2 Clever made-for-cable thriller has debonair Corbin Bernsen and John Glover vying for the affections of Amanda Pays, who always wanted a man who would love her to death. Too bad one of her suitors is willing to accommodate that request. 92m. **DIR:** Mark Cullingham. **CAST:** Corbin Bernsen, Amanda Pays, John Glover, Kevin McCarthy, Eleanor Parker. **1990**

DEAD PIT, THE ★★1/2 A woman at a mental asylum accidentally unleashes the spirit of a crazed surgeon and the hordes of lobotomized zombies on whom he experimented. The film treads on familiar ground but has a sense of stylishness. Rated R for violence and profanity. 95m. **DIR:** Brett Leonard. **CAST:** Jeremy Slate, Cheryl Lawson. **1989**

DEAD POETS SOCIETY ★★★1/2 Robin Williams offers an impressive change-of-pace as an unorthodox English teacher. He inspires a love of poetry and intellectual freedom in his students at a strict, upscale New England prep school. Though not entirely satisfying in its resolution, the film offers much of the heart and mood of *Goodbye, Mr. Chips* and *The Prime of Miss Jean Brodie*. Richly textured by Australian filmmaker Peter Weir. Rated PG. 124m. **DIR:** Peter Weir. **CAST:** Robin Williams, Robert Sean Leonard, Norman Lloyd, Ethan Hawke. **1989 DVD**

DEAD POOL, THE ★★★★ Clint Eastwood's fifth Dirty Harry adventure is a surprisingly strong entry in the long-running series. Action and chuckles are in abundance as our hero tracks down a weirdo who is murdering celebrities on a list that also carries Harry's name. It's good fun for fans. Rated R for violence and profanity. 92m. **DIR:** Buddy Van Horn. **CAST:** Clint Eastwood, Patricia Clarkson, Liam Neeson, Evan Kim. **1988 DVD**

DEAD PRESIDENTS ★★★★ Three New York kids—two African Americans and a Puerto Rican—grow up to be Marines in the late 1960s and return from Vietnam to a decaying neighborhood short on jobs and teeming with drugs and criminal temptations. The film crackles with all the adrenal temperament of a soul-music opera. Rated R for violence, nudity, and language. 125m. **DIR:** Allen Hughes, Albert Hughes. **CAST:** Larenz Tate, Bokeem Woodbine, Chris Tucker, Keith David, N'Bushe Wright, Freddy Rodriguez. **1995 DVD**

DEAD RECKONING (1947) ★★★ World War II veteran Humphrey Bogart is caught in a web of circumstance when he seeks the solution to an old army buddy's disappearance. Lizabeth Scott and Morris Carnovsky tell too many lies trying to cover it all up. A brutal yet sensitive example of *film noir*. Bogart is excellent. B&W; 100m. **DIR:** John Cromwell. **CAST:** Humphrey Bogart, Lizabeth Scott, Morris Carnovsky, Charles Cane, Marvin Miller, Wallace Ford, George Chandler. **1947**

DEAD RECKONING (1990) ★★★ Cliff Robertson enlivens this cat-and-mouse thriller, as the doting husband of a younger wife (Susan Blakely) who may—or may not—be conspiring with her ex-lover (Rick Springfield) to kill him. At times faintly reminiscent of Roman Polanski's *Knife in the Water* (though nowhere as subtle), this made-for-cable tale kicks into gear once our uneasy trio is stranded in an abandoned lighthouse. Rated R for considerable violence. 95m. **DIR:** Robert Lewis. **CAST:** Cliff Robertson, Susan Blakely, Rick Springfield. **1990**

DEAD RINGER ★★★ Proof positive that nobody's as good as Bette Davis when she's bad. She plays twins—one good, one bad. The bad one gets the upper hand. Bette chews the scenery with so much relish that the movie is fun to watch in spite of its ghoulish plot. B&W; 116m. **DIR:** Paul Henreid. **CAST:** Bette Davis, Peter Lawford, Karl Malden, Jean Hagen, Estelle Winwood, George Macready, Bert Remsen. **1964**

DEAD RINGERS ★★1/2 Director and coscripter David Cronenberg toys intriguingly with the connective link between identical twins until the film sinks into a depressing spiral of depravity and gratuitous gore. Jeremy Irons is superb as both halves of twin gynecologists specializing in fertility. Rated R for graphic medical procedures, sexual themes, and unsettling violence. 115m. **DIR:** David Cronenberg. **CAST:** Jeremy Irons, Genevieve Bujold, Heidi Von Palleske, Stephen Lack. **1988 DVD**

DEAD SILENCE (1989) When a financially strapped film director is sponsored by a mob leader, he must use the mobster's no-talent son in the lead. What could have been hilarious and clever falls short. Rated R for profanity and violence. 90m. **DIR:** Harrison Ellenshaw. **CAST:** Clete Keith, Doris Anne Soyka, Joseph Scott, Craig Fleming. **1989**

DEAD SILENCE (1996) ★★★1/2 This gripping thriller turns on a clever premise: a trio of violent psychopaths hold a busload of deaf-mute girls hostage in a standoff with the police. James Garner the hostage negotiator who takes charge of the case, and Marlee Matlin, as the girls' teacher, is a plucky young woman with more courage than common sense. Donald Stewart's script has a few surprises, and is guaranteed to keep viewers at the edges of their seats. Rated R for violence, profanity, and strong sexual content. 100m. **DIR:** Daniel Petrie Jr. **CAST:** James Garner, Marlee Matlin, Kim Coates, Charles Martin Smith, Kenneth Welsh, James Villemaire, Mimi Kuzyk, Lolita Davidovich. **1996 DVD**

•DEAD SIMPLE ★★★1/2 Daniel Stern is excellent as Frank, a henpecked hotel owner who dreams of becoming a country western singer and songwriter. His dreams are constantly questioned by his wife Helen (Patricia Richardson), who believes more in the Bible than her husband. When Frank gets the opportunity to sing one of his songs at a local amateur hour, he runs into semicelebrities Roy Baker (James Caan) and his girlfriend Julie Mitchell (Lacey Kohl). The chance meeting turns into something more sinister and nothing is what it seems in this fun-house ride. A winning cast and enough twists and turns to keep even the most jaded viewer glued to the screen. Also released as *Viva Las Nowhere*. Rated R for adult situations and language. 98m. **DIR:** Jason Bloom. **CAST:** James Caan, Daniel Stern, Patricia Richardson, Sherry Stringfield, Lacey Kohl. **2000 DVD**

DEAD SLEEP ★★★ Australian thriller features Linda Blair as a nurse in a rather peculiar psychiatric hospital. It seems that the head doctor (Tony Bonner) keeps patients comatose to "cure" them of their day-to-day anxieties. If this weren't bad enough, he resorts to murder on the rebellious ones. Rated R for nudity, profanity, and violence. 92m. **DIR:** Alec Mills. **CAST:** Linda Blair, Tony Bonner, Andrew Booth. **1990**

DEAD SOLID PERFECT ★★★★ Dan Jenkins's witty golf fable becomes an equally engaging made-for-cable film, with Randy Quaid starring as a second-stringer desperate to have his shot at success. Jenkins and co-scripter-director Bobby Roth deftly capture the boring routine of cross-country tours. 97m. **DIR:** Bobby Roth. **CAST:** Randy Quaid, Kathryn Harrold, Larry Riley, Corinne Bohrer, Jack Warden. **1988**

DEAD SPACE A galactic lawman answers a distress signal from a space lab. Everyone associated with this film exhibits dead space from the shoulders up. Rated R for violence and nudity. 72m. **DIR:** Fred Gallo. **CAST:** Marc Singer, Laura Tate, Bryan Cranston, Judith Chapman. **1990**

DEAD TIDES ★★ Murky action-adventure pits boat captain Roddy Piper against a drug dealer, the Coast Guard, and the DEA. Has its moments, but not enough of them. Rated R for violence, language, and nudity. 100m. **DIR:** Serge Rodnunsky. **CAST:** Roddy Piper, Tawny Kitaen, Trevor Goddard, Miles O'Keeffe. **1996**

DEAD TIRED (GROSSE FATIGUE) ★★★ Michel Blanc, France's answer to Woody Allen, plays himself and his dead ringer in this strange parody on success. Bored with making personal appearances, he trades places with his look-alike for a temporary reprieve. Unfortunately, his double refuses to step aside. Cameo appearances by Philippe Noiret and Roman Polanski at the end of the film are worth waiting for. In French with English subtitles. Rated R for nudity, profanity, and violence. 85m. **DIR:** Michel Blanc. **CAST:** Michel Blanc, Carole Bouquet, Philippe Noiret, Roman Polanski. **1994**

DEAD TO RIGHTS ★★1/2 Charles Bronson and Dana Delany make for an unlikely father-daughter team of police officers tracking the killer of another family member. It's better as a thriller than as a drama, with the domestic arguments simply getting in the way of the plot. Made for television. Rated R for violence and profanity. 93m. **DIR:** Rod Holcomb. **CAST:** Charles Bronson, Dana Delany, Xander Berkeley, Louis Giambalvo, Jenette Goldstein. **1993**

DEAD WEEKEND This infantile, $1.98 quickie about a shape-shifting alien visitor is merely a thin excuse for star Stephen Baldwin to have his way with five different women. Rated R for nudity, simulated sex, profanity, and violence. 82m. **DIR:** Amos Poe. **CAST:** Stephen Baldwin, David Rasche, Alexis Arquette, Nicholas Worth. **1995**

DEAD ZONE, THE ★★★★ This is an exciting adaptation of the Stephen King suspense novel about a man who uses his psychic powers to solve multiple murders and perhaps prevent the end of the world. Rated R for violence and profanity. 103m. **DIR:** David Cronenberg. **CAST:** Christopher Walken, Brooke Adams, Tom Skerritt, Herbert Lom, Martin Sheen. **1983 DVD**

DEADBOLT ★★★ Effective thriller finds student Justine Bateman looking for a roommate to help share expenses. Enter Adam Baldwin, who seems perfect. Then his true colors start shining through, and Bateman finds herself a captive in her own apartment. Baldwin is appropriately creepy. Not rated; contains adult language and violence. 95m. **DIR:** Douglas Jackson. **CAST:** Justine Bateman, Adam Baldwin, Chris Mulkey, Michele Scarabelli. **1992 DVD**

DEADFALL ★★★ Gimmicky tale of con artists has plenty going for it, most notably director Christopher Coppola's over-the-top approach to the material. Young con artist Michael Biehn mistakenly kills his father during a sting, then teams up with his uncle and gets involved in a series of double crosses. High-rent cast keeps this one interesting. Rated R for nudity, violence, and language. 99m. **DIR:** Christopher Coppola. **CAST:** Michael Biehn, Sarah Trigger, Nicolas Cage, James Coburn, Charlie Sheen, Peter Fonda, Talia Shire. **1993**

DEADLINE (1987) ★★★ Christopher Walken is good as a reporter covering the conflict in Beirut, finding himself becoming personally involved when he falls for a German nurse working for the rebels. This film is very much in the vein of *Salvador* and *Under Fire*, but cannot duplicate their tension. Rated R. 100m. **DIR:** Nathaniel Gutman. **CAST:** Christopher Walken, Hywel Bennett. **1987**

DEADLINE (1988) ★★★ John Hurt gives a moving performance as an alcoholic British journalist who becomes involved in a doomed love affair with a beautiful noblewoman (Imogen Stubbs). Together they weather a revolution on an island estate in the Persian Gulf. Rated R for nudity, profanity, and graphic violence. 110m. **DIR:** Richard Stroud. **CAST:** John Hurt, Imogen Stubbs, Robert McBain, Greg Hicks. **1988**

DEADLINE (1999) ★★ Stop the presses! Former newspaper editor implicated in the murder of new publisher who fired him. Former editor claims he was framed, vows to clear his name. This isn't news. It's more of the same old direct-to-video stuff, with a bored Patrick Bergin playing the framed editor. Read the back of the video box and skip the movie. Also released as *Press Run*. Rated R for language and violence. 94m. **DIR:** Robbie Ditchburn. **CAST:** Patrick Bergin, Annie Dufresne, Terry Simpson, Richard Zeman. **1999 DVD**

DEADLINE AT DAWN ★★ Penned by Clifford Odets, this film is predictable and anticlimactic. While on liberty, sailor Bill Williams is slipped a mickey by Lola Lane and, upon awakening, he finds her dead. With the help of a dancer (Susan Hayward) and a cabbie (played flatly by Paul Lukas), he sets out to clear himself. B&W; 83m. **DIR:** Harold Clurman. **CAST:** Susan Hayward, Paul Lukas, Lola Lane, Bill Williams, Jerome Cowan. **1946**

DEADLINE USA ★★★★ In this hard-hitting newspaper drama, Humphrey Bogart plays an editor who has to fight the city's underworld while keeping the publisher (superbly portrayed by Ethel Barrymore) from giving in to pressure and closing the paper down. While Kim Hunter is wasted in the small role as Bogart's ex-wife, the picture has much to recommend it. B&W; 87m. **DIR:** Richard Brooks. **CAST:** Humphrey Bogart, Kim Hunter, Ethel Barrymore. **1952**

DEADLOCK ★★★★ High marks to this high-tech update of *The Defiant Ones*, which pairs Rutger Hauer and Mimi Rogers (both superb) as convicts linked by futuristic collars necessitating their remaining in close proximity . . . at the risk of impromptu decapitations. Broderick Miler's clever script blends perfectly with Lewis Teague's wry direction. Rated R for violence and sexual content. 95m. **DIR:** Lewis Teague. **CAST:** Rutger Hauer, Mimi Rogers, Joan Chen, James Remar. **1991 DVD**

DEADLOCK 2 ★★ Another sequel in which none of the originals appears. To keep their exploding collars from detonating, Esai Morales and Nia Peeples must stick together while breaking out of the "Playland" prison. There is a spark between these two, but Morales is too good an actor for such cheesy entertainments. Made for TV. Not rated; contains violence and profanity. 120m. **DIR:** Graeme Campbell. **CAST:** Esai Morales, Nia Peeples. **1995**

DEADLOCKED ★★★1/2 Charles S. Dutton is spellbinding as a distraught father determined to free a son convicted of rape and murder. Taking the jury hostage, he commands the prosecutor (David Caruso) to find out what really happened. Tense moments and a generous sprinkling of surprises will keep viewers enthralled in this TNT Original. Not rated; contains sex, violence, and profanity. 89m. **DIR:** Michael Watkins. **CAST:** Charles Dutton, David Caruso, Jo D. Jonz. **2000**

DEADLY ADVICE ★★★1/2 A Greek chorus of dead British murderers dish up advice and a skewed morality to Jane Horrocks, who has found a decisive way of dealing with her oppressive, sharp-tongued mother. There aren't as many surprises as there should be, but the dialogue is humorously understated and Horrocks is a gleeful comedian. Rated R for violence, profanity, brief nudity, and sexual situations. 91m. **DIR:** Mandie Fletcher. **CAST:** Jane Horrocks, Brenda Fricker, Imelda Staunton, Jonathan Pryce. **1993**

DEADLY ALLIANCE Two shoestring filmmakers get caught up in the dealings of a secret cartel composed of the world's seven largest oil companies. 90m. **DIR:** Paul Salvatore Parco. **CAST:** Mike Lloyd Gentry. **1975**

DEADLY BET ★★1/2 A compulsive gambler and alcoholic almost loses everything, including his girlfriend, to a ruthless kick boxer. Watchable if unmemorable little film. Rated R for profanity and seemingly endless violence. 93m. **DIR:** Richard W. Munchkin. **CAST:** Jeff Wincott, Charlene Tilton, Steven Vincent Leigh. **1992**

DEADLY BLESSING A strange religious sect. Rated R because of nudity and bloody scenes. 102m. **DIR:** Wes Craven. **CAST:** Maren Jensen, Susan Buckner, Sharon Stone, Lois Nettleton, Ernest Borgnine, Jeff East. **1981**

DEADLY COMPANION Slow-moving, confusing film has Michael Sarrazin trying to find his wife's killer. Not rated; contains violence and nudity. 90m. **DIR:** George Bloomfield. **CAST:** Anthony Perkins, Michael Sarrazin, Susan Clark, Howard Duff. **1986**

DEADLY COMPANIONS, THE ★★1/2 When gunfighter Brian Keith accidentally kills the son of dance-hall hostess Maureen O'Hara, he attempts to make amends by escorting her through hostile Indian Territory. A less than grade-A Western made notable because it was director Sam Peckinpah's first feature. 90m. **DIR:** Sam Peckinpah. **CAST:** Brian Keith, Maureen O'Hara, Chill Wills, Steve Cochran. **1961 DVD**

DEADLY CURRENTS ★★★ Exiled CIA agent William L. Petersen finds himself in a political hotbed when he befriends stranger George C. Scott on the small island of Curaçao. Things heat up when several factions arrive on the island to settle an old score with Scott. Exotic locales and double and triple crosses add color and suspense to this thriller, made for cable under the title *Curaçao*. Rated R for language and violence. 93m. **DIR:** Carl Schultz. **CAST:** William L. Petersen, George C. Scott, Julie Carmen, Trish Van Devere, Philip Anglim. **1993**

DEADLY DAPHNE'S REVENGE Troma, masters of the no-budget cheapie, have taken a standard rape drama and tacked on scenes of a mental patient to create an utterly confusing film. Rated R for violence. 98m. **DIR:** Richard Harding Gardner. **CAST:** Laurie Tait Partridge, Anthony Holt, Richard Harding Gardner. **1993**

DEADLY DESIRE ★★★ Greed and lust rear their ugly heads in this made-for-cable thriller, about a cop-turned-private investigator (Jack Scalia) lured into a web woven by sexpot Kathryn Harrold. Nothing new here, but the performances are strong. Rated R for violence and sex. 93m. **DIR:** Charles Correll. **CAST:** Jack Scalia, Kathryn Harrold, Will Patton, Joe Santos. **1991**

DEADLY DREAMS ★★ Run-of-the-mill suspenser about a writer who dreams that the psychotic murderer who slew his parents is coming after him. Soon his dreams spill over into reality. Rated R for violence, nudity, and language. 79m. **DIR:** Kristine Peterson. **CAST:** Mitchell Anderson. **1988**

DEADLY EMBRACE Sexual decadence ends in murder. Soft-core porn dud. 82m. **DIR:** Ellen Cabot. **CAST:** Jan-Michael Vincent, Jack Carter, Ken Abraham. **1988**

DEADLY ENCOUNTER (1972) ★★★1/2 Hounded by mobsters, Susan Anspach enlists the aid of her old lover Larry Hagman, an ex–combat helicopter pilot. Great aerial stunts are a treat and help keep the action moving right along. Pretty good for television. 100m. **DIR:** William A. Graham. **CAST:** Larry Hagman, Susan Anspach, James Gammon, Michael C. Gwynne. **1972 DVD**

DEADLY ENCOUNTER (1975) A rich woman schemer. Rated R for sexual talk. 90m. **DIR:** R. John Hugh. **CAST:** Dina Merrill, Carl Betz, Leon Ames. **1975**

DEADLY EYES Grain full of steroids creates rats the size of small dogs. Rated R for gore, nudity, and simulated sex. 87m. **DIR:** Robert Clouse. **CAST:** Sam Groom, Sara Botsford, Scatman Crothers. **1982**

DEADLY FORCE ★★★ Wings Hauser (*Vice Squad*) plays "Stony" Jackson Cooper, an ex-cop who returns to his old Los Angeles stomping grounds to stomp people until he finds the maniac who stomped a buddy's daughter to death. Rated R for violence, nudity, and profanity. 95m. **DIR:** Paul Aaron. **CAST:** Wings Hauser, Joyce Ingalls, Paul Shenar. **1983**

DEADLY FRIEND ★★ A teenage whiz revives his murdered girlfriend by inserting a computer chip into her brain. The girl becomes a robot-zombie and kills people. This would-be thriller has much in common with its title character. It's cold, mechanical, and brain-dead. Rated R for violence. 99m. **DIR:** Wes Craven. **CAST:** Matthew Laborteaux, Michael Sharrett, Kristy Swanson. **1986**

DEADLY GAME ★★1/2 What hath Richard Connell wrought? Scripter Wes Claridge is merely the latest to borrow liberally from "The Most Dangerous Game," this time pitting seven virtual strangers against a masked (and well-armed) maniac. Made for cable TV. Rated R for profanity and violence. 93m. **DIR:** Thomas Wright. **CAST:** Michael Beck, Jenny Seagrove, Roddy McDowall, Mitchell Ryan, Marc Singer. **1991 DVD**

DEADLY GAMES ★★ The central motif of this goofy slasher drama is a board game. Sam Groom is excellent as the small-town cop-protagonist. R rating. 95m. **DIR:** Scott Mansfield. **CAST:** Sam Groom, Steve Railsback, Alexandra Morgan, Colleen Camp, June Lockhart, Jo Ann Harris, Dick Butkus. **1982**

DEADLY HARVEST Mankind's unrelenting industrialization of arable land and subsequent cold winters (and summers!) wreak havoc with America's ecological system. Rated PG. 86m. **DIR:** Timothy Bond. **CAST:** Clint Walker, Nehemiah Persoff, Kim Cattrall, David Brown. **1976**

DEADLY HERO ★★★1/2 Strange yet engaging bad-cop film with Don Murray as a New York police officer struggling to stay on the force after an incident's repercussions threaten his upcoming pension. The film is dated by the trendy mid-Seventies fashions and popular art, yet that is ironically one of its more interesting qualities. Rated PG for violence and profanity. 102m. **DIR:** Ivan Nagy. **CAST:** Don Murray, Diahn Williams, Lilia Skala, George S. Irving, Conchata Ferrell, Ron Weyand, James Earl Jones, Treat Williams. **1975**

DEADLY HEROES Ludicrous action-thriller about a pair of American agents who must hunt down a team of terrorists who kidnapped one of their wives. Virtually unwatchable except for the occasional line of dialogue that's so bad it's good. Rated R for profanity, violence, and brief nudity. 104m. **DIR:** Menahem Golan. **CAST:** Michael Paré, Jan-Michael Vincent, Billy Drago, Claudette Mink. **1993**

DEADLY IMPACT ★★ Fred Williamson and Bo Svenson work well together in this otherwise contrived, Italian-made action film about an attempt to rip off Las Vegas gambling houses. Rated R. 90m. **DIR:** Larry Ludman. **CAST:** Fred Williamson, Bo Svenson. **1985**

DEADLY INTENT ★★ A murderous archaeologist returns from an expedition with a priceless jewel and blood on his hands. He's soon murdered and everybody who knew him is after the jewel. Although the cast is talented, the film is flawed by poor pacing and bad logic. Rated R for violence and language. 83m. **DIR:** Nigel Dick. **CAST:** Lisa Eilbacher, Steve Railsback, Maud Adams, Lance Henriksen, Fred Williamson. **1988**

DEADLY MANTIS, THE ★★1/2 Can heroic scientists head off a mammoth praying mantis winging its way from the North Pole to New York City? Okay special effects, though even at 78 minutes it seems too long. B&W; 78m. **DIR:** Nathan Juran. **CAST:** Craig Stevens, William Hopper. **1957**

DEADLY OBSESSION ★★ This contrived, uneven thriller is about a disfigured psychopath who dwells in the tunnels and caves beneath a wealthy private college. He terrorizes the campus inhabitants in an effort to extort large sums of money. Rated R, contains nudity and violence. 93m. **DIR:** Jeno Hodi. **CAST:** Jeffrey R. Iorio. **1988**

DEADLY OUTBREAK ★★★ Action star Jeff Speakman stands between terrorists and a deadly chemical in this moderately suspenseful action film. Speakman stars as a U.S. Embassy first sergeant assigned to a chemical facility outside Tel Aviv where a visiting team of scientists turns out to be terrorists. Some spectacular stunts and decent acting make this direct-to-video effort better than the norm. Rated R for violence and profanity. 94m. **DIR:** Rick Avery. **CAST:** Jeff Speakman, Ron Silver, Rochelle Swanson. **1995**

DEADLY PAST ★★ A paroled man is drawn into a murder conspiracy when his ex-girlfriend first seduces, then recruits him to help her. Good performance by Dedee Pfeiffer in this otherwise turgid thriller. Rated R for nudity, profanity, and violence. 90m. **DIR:** Tibor Takacs. **CAST:** Carol Alt, Dedee Pfeiffer, Ron Marquette, Mark Dacascos. **1994**

DEADLY POSSESSION ★★ Aussie thriller presents two college students on the trail of a masked slasher plaguing downtown Adelaide. Low-budget chiller picks up pace halfway through, and then leaves several burning questions. Not rated. 99m. **DIR:** Craig Lahiff. **CAST:** Penny Cook, Anna-Maria Winchester, Olivia Hamnett. **1987**

DEADLY PREY Absolutely wretched piece of celluloid about a secret mercenary boot camp. Rated R for violence and profanity. 87m. **DIR:** David A. Prior. **CAST:** Cameron Mitchell, Troy Donahue. **1987**

DEADLY RIVALS Emerald smuggling and corporate espionage in this confusing thriller. Rated R for nudity, profanity, and violence. 93m. **DIR:** James Dodson. **CAST:** Andrew Stevens, Cela Wise, Margaux Hemingway, Joseph Bologna, Richard Roundtree. **1992**

DEADLY SANCTUARY Two newly orphaned sisters fall prey to prison, prostitution, murder, and a torturous hellfire club. 93m. **DIR:** Jess (Jesus) Franco. **CAST:** Sylva Koscina, Mercedes McCambridge, Jack Palance, Klaus Kinski, Akim Tamiroff. **1970**

DEADLY SPYGAMES ★★1/2 A government agent and his ex-lover are sent to destroy a Cuban radar station and prevent World War III. James Bond fans may enjoy this spy spoof, but it could be too silly for others. Not rated; contains mild sexual situations. 86m. **DIR:** Jack M. Sell. **CAST:** Jack M. Sell, Adrianne Richmond, Troy Donahue, Tippi Hedren. **1989**

DEADLY STRANGER ★1/2 A drifter (Michael J. Moore) takes a job on a plantation where the owner and a local union leader are conspiring to exploit migrant workers. Clichéd movie wastes the talents of Darlanne Fluegel and the time of the viewer. Not rated; nudity. 93m. **DIR:** Max Kleven. **CAST:** Darlanne Fluegel, Michael J. Moore, John Vernon. **1988**

DEADLY SURVEILLANCE ★★★★ An unexpected treat. What could have been another tired and gory struggle between good cops and nasty drug lords emerges as fresh, witty, and engaging, thanks to a deft script from Hal Salwen and director Paul Ziller. Michael Ironside plays against type as a dedicated cop. Rated R for nudity, violence, and profanity. 92m. **DIR:** Paul Ziller. **CAST:** Michael Ironside, Christopher Bondy, Susan Almgren, David Carradine. **1991**

DEADLY TARGET ★★ After being captured in Los Angeles, a Chinese gangster gets away with the help of a Chinese triad. Hong Kong detective Gary Daniels enlists the aid of a maverick cop and a Chinese card dealer to zero in on his prey. This one misses the mark. Rated R for violence, nudity, and profanity. 92m. **DIR:** Charla Driver. **CAST:** Gary Daniels, Ken McLeod, Max Gail, Byron Mann. **1994**

DEADLY TRACKERS, THE ★★1/2 Extremely violent Western follows sheriff Richard Harris's attempt to track down the outlaw gang responsible for killing his family during a bank robbery. Film starts out well, but quickly becomes a standard revenge tale and is far too long. Be warned: There are some truly brutal scenes throughout. Rated R. 110m. **DIR:** Barry Shear. **CAST:** Richard Harris, Rod Taylor, Neville Brand, William Smith, Al Lettieri, Isela Vega. **1973**

DEADLY TWINS A typical revenge flick about twin sisters who are gang raped. Not rated; contains adult themes. 87m. **DIR:** Joe Oaks. **CAST:** Judy Landers, Audrey Landers. **1985**

DEADLY VENGEANCE The poor acting, editing, and lighting in this insipid film make one wonder if it was planned by a couple of beginning film students over a keg of beer. Contains obscenities, simulated sex scenes, and violence. 84m. **DIR:** A. C. Qamar. **CAST:** Arthur Roberts, Alan Marlowe, Bob Holden. **1985**

DEADLY VOYAGE ★★★★ This gripping, fact-based drama concerns events that took place in 1992, when a Russian container ship left Ghana, West Africa, with a handful of stowaways on board. This very ship had recently been fined for the same infraction. The first mate takes charge when the new stowaways are discovered; the result is brutal and incredibly compelling . . . because one man gets away. But how long can he elude capture on a ship at sea? Rated R for profanity, nudity, and violence. 90m. **DIR:** John Mackenzie. **CAST:** Omar Epps, Joss Ackland, Sean Pertwee, David Suchet, Andrew Divoff. **1996**

DEADLY WEAPON ★★★ Producer Charles Band remakes his own *Laserblast* with this improved version. Writer-director Michael Miner gives the film a sense of comic bookishness that allows the viewer to sit back and enjoy the silliness of a boy finding a laser gun and using it to his own ends. Rated PG-13 for violence and profanity. 89m. **DIR:** Michael Miner. **CAST:** Rodney Easton, Kim Walker, Joe Regalbuto, William Sanderson. **1988**

DEADMAN'S CURVE ★★★ This made-for-TV bio-pic recounts the true story of Fifties rock stars Jan and Dean. An endearing sense of humor and their engaging surf sound propels them to the top. Then a near-fatal auto accident brings their career to a screeching halt. Richard Hatch and Bruce Davison deliver strong performances as Jan Berry and Dean Torrence. The use of Jan and Dean's original hits adds spark to the film. 100m. **DIR:** Richard Compton. **CAST:** Richard Hatch, Bruce Davison, Pamela Bellwood, Susan Sullivan, Dick Clark, Wolfman Jack. **1978**

DEADMAN'S REVENGE ★★★1/2 Suspenseful and humorous tale about an evil railroad man who steals people's property and has them arrested for crimes they did not commit. One innocent man is after the crook to collect what is rightfully his, and along the way meets his long-lost son. Well acted and fun to watch. Rated PG-13 for mild violence. 92m. **DIR:** Alan J. Levi. **CAST:** Bruce Dern, Michael Ironside, Vondie Curtis-Hall, Keith Coulouris, Daphne Ashbrook, Tobin Bell, John M. Jackson, Doug McClure, Randy Travis. **1994**

DEADMATE ★★1/2 Writer-director Straw Weisman concocts a spooky and bizarre tale about a woman who marries a mortician unaware that he, and most of the town, like to do strange things to dead bodies. Not rated; contains violence and nudity. 93m. **DIR:** Straw Weisman. **CAST:** Elizabeth Manning, David Gregory, Lawrence Brockius, Adam Wahl, Judith Mayes, Kelvin Keraga. **1988**

DEADTIME STORIES Bizarre, ghoulish versions of fairy tales. 89m. **DIR:** Jeffrey S. Delman. **CAST:** Scott Valentine. **1987**

DEAL OF THE CENTURY ★★ A two-bit arms hustler (Chevy Chase) peddles an ultrasophisticated superweapon to a Central American dictator. This black comedy ends up in that nether world of the near misses. Rated PG for violence and profanity. 99m. **DIR:** William Friedkin. **CAST:** Chevy Chase, Sigourney Weaver, Gregory Hines, Vince Edwards. **1983**

DEALERS Boring British rip-off of *Wall Street*. Rated R for violence and profanity. 92m. **DIR:** Colin Bucksey. **CAST:** Rebecca DeMornay, Paul McGann, Derrick O'Connor. **1989**

DEAR AMERICA: LETTERS HOME FROM VIETNAM ★★★★ This docudrama traces the Vietnam conflict from 1964 to 1973 through the eyes of American soldiers writing to their loved ones at home. The live footage has been so carefully selected that you forget that the letter you are hearing is being read by an actor instead of the person on the screen. Offscreen narration by a *Who's Who* of actors, including Robert De Niro, Ellen Burstyn, Tom Berenger, Michael J. Fox, Sean Penn, Martin Sheen, and Robin Williams. Rated PG. 86m. **DIR:** Bill Couturie. **1988**

DEAR BRIGITTE ★★1/2 A clever premise gone wrong. Boy genius who handicaps horses won't play unless he gets to go to meet Brigitte Bardot. What could have been charming comes across as contrived pap. 100m. **DIR:** Henry Koster. **CAST:** James Stewart, Fabian, Glynis Johns, Billy Mumy, Cindy Carol, Jesse White, Ed Wynn, Brigitte Bardot. **1965**

DEAR DEAD DELILAH 🦃 Delilah (Agnes Moorehead) is about to die, but there's a fortune buried somewhere on her property that her loony relatives will do anything to get ahold of. Rated R for blood. 90m. **DIR:** John Farris. **CAST:** Agnes Moorehead, Will Geer, Michael Ansara, Dennis Patrick. **1972**

DEAR DETECTIVE ★★1/2 A lighthearted film with moments of quality about a female homicide detective involved in a series of murdered local government officials, counterpointed by an amusing love interest with a mild-mannered university professor. Not rated with mild violence. Made for TV. 92m. **DIR:** Dean Hargrove. **CAST:** Brenda Vaccaro, Arlen Dean Snyder, Ron Silver, Michael MacRae, Jack Ging, M. Emmet Walsh. **1979**

DEAR GOD ★★★ This inoffensive comedy serves as a starring debut for Greg Kinnear, cast as an amiable con artist forced into honest labor as a means of cleaning his criminal record. He winds up in the post office's dead dead-letter section, where he takes an interest in the pleas of citizens desperate enough to write—and mail—letters to God. Rated PG for mild profanity. 112m. **DIR:** Garry Marshall. **CAST:** Greg Kinnear, Laurie Metcalf, Maria Pitillo, Tim Conway, Hector Elizondo, Roscoe Lee Browne, Jon Seda. **1996**

DEAR HEART ★★★1/2 Very likable comedy about a romance between two middle-aged people. She's a small-town postmistress in Manhattan for a convention, he's a salesman already engaged to another woman. B&W; 114m. **DIR:** Delbert Mann. **CAST:** Glenn Ford, Geraldine Page, Michael Anderson Jr., Angela Lansbury. **1964**

DEAR WIFE ★★1/2 The second of three amusing films involving the same cast of characters, and mostly the same players. This sequel to *Dear Ruth* has fresh-faced younger sister (to Joan Caulfield) Mona Freeman conniving to elect heartthrob William Holden to the state senate seat sought by her politician father Edward Arnold. Billy DeWolfe fills it all out with his peculiar brand of haughty humor. B&W; 88m. **DIR:** Richard Haydn. **CAST:** Joan Caulfield, William Holden, Mona Freeman, Edward Arnold, Billy DeWolfe. **1949**

DEATH AND THE MAIDEN ★★★1/2 In an unnamed South American country, a woman (Sigourney Weaver) terrorizes the man (Ben Kingsley) who she says raped and tortured her under the former fascist regime. Chilean writer Ariel Dorfman's play examines the fine line between justice and vengeance. A taut and fascinating film, very well acted and tensely directed by suspense veteran Roman Polanski. Rated R for profanity and violence. 103m. **DIR:** Roman Polanski. **CAST:** Sigourney Weaver, Ben Kingsley, Stuart Wilson. **1994**

DEATH ARTIST 🦃 If you don't believe executive producer Roger Corman could do a word-for-word remake of his classic black comedy *A Bucket of Blood* without a single laugh, see this. But that's the only reason to see it. Rated R for violence, nudity, sexual situations, substance abuse, and profanity. 79m. **DIR:** Michael James McDonald. **CAST:** Anthony Michael Hall, Justine Bateman, Shadoe Stevens, Sam Lloyd. **1996**

DEATH AT LOVE HOUSE ★★ Much tamer than the lurid title would suggest. Robert Wagner plays a writer who becomes obsessed with a movie queen who died years earlier. This mildly suspenseful hokum is made palatable by the engaging cast. Made for TV. 78m. **DIR:** E. W. Swackhamer. **CAST:** Robert Wagner, Kate Jackson, Sylvia Sidney, Joan Blondell, Dorothy Lamour, John Carradine, Bill Macy, Marianna Hill. **1976**

DEATH BECOMES HER ★★★1/2 Meryl Streep and Goldie Hawn seem to have a ball clowning around in this marvelously entertaining, special-effects-laden fantasy about the secret of eternal life and the war between two women. There are scenes in this very, very twisted comedy guaranteed to make your jaw drop, and it is most definitely not for children. That said, open-minded adults and older teenagers will get a real kick out of it. Rated PG-13 for profanity, nudity, and violence. 104m. **DIR:** Robert Zemeckis. **CAST:** Meryl Streep, Goldie Hawn, Bruce Willis, Isabella Rossellini, Ian Ogilvy. **1992 DVD**

DEATH BEFORE DISHONOR 🦃 Grade Z war film. Rated R for violence and profanity. 112m. **DIR:** Terry Leonard. **CAST:** Fred Dryer, Brian Keith, Joanna Pacula, Paul Winfield. **1986 DVD**

DEATH BENEFIT ★★★ A young woman falls off a cliff, but was it an accident, or was she murdered to collect on her life insurance? This made-for-cable original, based on a true story, follows an attorney's investigation into the mysterious death. Rated PG-13 for suggested sex. 89m. **DIR:** Mark Piznarski. **CAST:** Peter Horton, Carrie Snodgress, Wendy Makkena, Elizabeth Ruscio, Penny Johnson. **1996**

DEATH CHASE ★★ An innocent jogger is caught up in a shoot-out, given a gun by a dying man, and suddenly finds himself in the midst of an elaborate chase. The premise is intriguing, but the execution is uninspired in this shoddily made thriller. 88m. **DIR:** David A. Prior. **CAST:** William Zipp, Paul Smith, Jack Starrett, Bainbridge Scott. **1988**

DEATH DREAMS ★★★ The ghost of a little girl tries to communicate the identity of her killer to her grieving mother. No one believes her. A well-acted, made-for-TV mystery. 94m. **DIR:** Martin Donovan. **CAST:** Christopher Reeve, Fionnula Flanagan, Marg Helgenberger. **1992**

DEATH DRUG ★★ A truthful yet cliché-filled movie about a promising young musician who starts using angel dust. Although the drug PCP deserves any bad rap it gets, this movie is a mediocre effort. Not rated, but fairly inoffensive. 73m. **DIR:** Oscar Williams. **CAST:** Philip

Michael Thomas, Vernee Watson, Rosalind Cash. 1986

DEATH HOUSE 🦃 Framed for murder by the mob, Dennis Cole discovers that prisoners are being used for dangerous scientific experiments with nasty side effects. Give this one life without parole. Not rated; contains nudity, violence, and profanity. 92m. **DIR:** John Saxon. **CAST:** Dennis Cole, John Saxon, Anthony Franciosa. 1992

DEATH HUNT ★★★1/2 Based on the true story of a hazardous manhunt in the Canadian Rockies, *Death Hunt* pits trapper Charles Bronson against Mountie Lee Marvin. This gritty adventure film, directed by Peter Hunt, also features vicious dogfights and bloody shootouts set against the spectacular scenery of the Yukon Territory. Rated R. 97m. **DIR:** Peter R. Hunt. **CAST:** Charles Bronson, Lee Marvin, Andrew Stevens, Angie Dickinson, Carl Weathers, Ed Lauter. 1981

DEATH IN BRUNSWICK ★★1/2 Short-order cook and all-around loser Sam Neill (in an endearing performance) falls for a much younger Greek barmaid who already has a fiancé. Rowdy and fast-moving, but the plot is ludicrous. Rated R for profanity, violence, nudity, and sexual situations. 106m. **DIR:** John Ruane. **CAST:** Sam Neill, Zoe Carides, John Clarke, Yvonne Lawley. 1990

DEATH IN THE GARDEN ★★★1/2 A disparate group of refugees flees a Central American riot by escaping into the jungle. One of cinema master Luis Buñuel's most obscure films, this strikingly photographed adventure contains little of his usual satirical edge, though it offers a fairly gripping story. Also known as *Evil Eden.* In Spanish with English subtitles. Not rated. 90m. **DIR:** Luis Buñuel. **CAST:** Georges Marchal, Simone Signoret, Michel Piccoli, Charles Vanel. 1956

DEATH IN VENICE ★★ Slow, studied film based on Thomas Mann's classic novel about an artist's quest for beauty and perfection. The good cast seems to move through this movie without communicating with one another or the audience. Visually absorbing, but lifeless. Adult language, adult situations throughout. Rated PG. 130m. **DIR:** Luchino Visconti. **CAST:** Dirk Bogarde, Marisa Berenson, Mark Burns, Silvana Mangano. 1971

DEATH KISS, THE ★★★ Entertaining movie-within-a-movie whodunit is a treat for fans of early 1930s films and a pretty well-paced mystery to boot as Bela Lugosi (in fine, hammy form) is embroiled in the investigation of a murder that took place during filming. B&W; 75m. **DIR:** Edwin L. Marin. **CAST:** Bela Lugosi, David Manners, Adrienne Ames, John Wray, Vince Barnett, Edward Van Sloan. 1933

DEATH MACHINE ★★ Claustrophobic thriller about a psychotic genius who unleashes his killing machine on the female boss that axed his project and fired him. Some futuristic thrills evolve as the prey is joined by two friends in a desperate attempt to terminate the "Death Machine." Rated R for violence and language. 99m. **DIR:** Stephen Norrington. **CAST:** Brad Dourif, Ely Pouget, William Hootkins. 1994 DVD

DEATH OF A BUREAUCRAT ★★★ An entertaining black comedy about a man's struggle with the red tape of bureaucracy. He attempts to replace his dead relative in a graveyard after having to have him illegally exhumed. Delightful farce. In Spanish with English subtitles. Not rated. B&W; 87m. **DIR:** Tomas Gutierrez Alea. **CAST:** Salvador Wood. 1966

DEATH OF A CENTERFOLD ★★ This made-for-TV film chronicles the brutal murder of Playboy playmate Dorothy Stratten. Bob Fosse's *Star 80* does a much better job. Not rated. 100m. **DIR:** Gabrielle Beaumont. **CAST:** Jamie Lee Curtis, Robert Reed, Bruce Weitz. 1981

DEATH OF A GUNFIGHTER ★★★ Any time you see the name Alan Smithee in the directorial slot, that means the real director had his name taken off the credits. In this case, Don Siegel and Robert Totten were alternately at the helm of what still emerges as a sturdy Western. Richard Widmark is very good as the sheriff who has outlived his usefulness to the town but refuses to change, thus setting the stage for tragic results. Rated PG. 100m. **DIR:** Alan Smithee. **CAST:** Richard Widmark, Lena Horne, Carroll O'Connor, John Saxon, Kent Smith. 1969

DEATH OF A PROPHET ★★1/2 Docudrama combines live footage of Sixties civil rights movement among black Americans as well as interviews with people who were close to Malcolm X. Morgan Freeman reenacts Malcolm X during the twenty-four hours prior to his assassination. Freeman portrays Malcolm X as a patient, religious man who believed there was an African connection with the quality of life black Americans could enjoy. Not rated, contains violence. 60m. **DIR:** Woodie King Jr. **CAST:** Morgan Freeman, Yolanda King, Mansoor Najee-ullah, Sam Singleton. 1991 DVD

DEATH OF A SALESMAN ★★★★ Impressive TV version of the Arthur Miller play. Dustin Hoffman is excellent as the aging, embittered Willy Loman, who realizes he has wasted his life and the lives of his family. Kate Reid is his long-suffering wife and Charles Durning is the neighbor. Thoughtful and well produced. 135m. **DIR:** Volker Schlöndorff. **CAST:** Dustin Hoffman, Kate Reid, John Malkovich, Stephen Lang, Charles Durning. 1985

DEATH OF A SCOUNDREL ★★★ If anyone could portray a suave, debonair, conniving, ruthlessly charming, amoral, despicable, notorious, manipulating cad, it was George Sanders. He does so to a *tee* in this portrait of the ultimate rake—based on the life of financier Serge Rubenstein. 119m. **DIR:** Charles Martin. **CAST:** George Sanders, Zsa Zsa Gabor, Tom Conway, Yvonne De Carlo, Nancy Gates, Coleen Gray, Victor Jory, John Hoyt. 1956

DEATH OF A SOLDIER ★★1/2 Based on a true story. In 1942 an American GI stationed in Australia murdered three Melbourne women. The incident aggravated U.S.-Australian relations, and General MacArthur ordered the execution of the serviceman to firm up Allied unity. James Coburn plays a major who believes the GI isn't sane enough to stand trial. Rated R for profanity, violence, and nudity. 93m. **DIR:** Philippe Mora. **CAST:** James Coburn, Bill Hunter, Reb Brown, Maurie Fields. 1985

DEATH OF ADOLF HITLER, THE ★★★ Made-for-British-television dramatization of the last ten days of the dictator's life, all spent in the underground bunker where he received the news of Germany's defeat. Frank Finlay is excellent as Hitler, avoiding the usual stereotypes. The low-key nature of the production renders it eerie, but strangely unmoving. Not rated. 107m. **DIR:** Rex Firkin. **CAST:** Frank Finlay, Caroline Mortimer, Ray McAnally. **1972**

DEATH OF THE INCREDIBLE HULK, THE ★★★ Supposedly dead David Banner (Bill Bixby) works as a janitor at a laboratory where a world-renowned scientist is creating a formula that could free Banner from the monster within him. Unfortunately, an international spy ring also wants the formula. Made for TV. 96m. **DIR:** Bill Bixby. **CAST:** Bill Bixby, Lou Ferrigno, Philip Sterling, Andreas Katsulas. **1990**

DEATH ON THE NILE ★★★1/2 The second in the series of films based on the Hercule Poirot mysteries, written by Agatha Christie, is good, but nothing special. Peter Ustinov stars as the fussy Belgian detective adrift in Africa with a set of murder suspects. Despite a better-than-average Christie plot, this film, directed by John Guillermin, tends to sag here and there. Rated PG. 140m. **DIR:** John Guillermin. **CAST:** Peter Ustinov, Bette Davis, David Niven, Mia Farrow, Angela Lansbury, George Kennedy, Jack Warden. **1978 DVD**

DEATH RACE 2000 ★★★ Futuristic look at what has become our national sport: road racing where points are accumulated for killing people with the race cars. David Carradine and Sylvester Stallone star in this tongue-in-cheek sci-fi action film. Stallone is a howl as one of the competitors. Rated R—violence, nudity, and language. 78m. **DIR:** Paul Bartel. **CAST:** David Carradine, Sylvester Stallone, Louisa Moritz, Mary Woronov, Joyce Jameson, Fred Grandy. **1975 DVD**

DEATH RIDES A HORSE 🦃 Needlessly tedious spaghetti Western about a young boy who witnesses the butchery of his family and then grows up to take his revenge. Rated PG for violence. 114m. **DIR:** Giulio Petroni. **CAST:** Lee Van Cleef, John Phillip Law, Mario Brega, Anthony Dawson. **1969 DVD**

DEATH RIDES THE PLAINS ★★★ The Lone Rider must stop a rancher who sells his land and then kills the multiple buyers. Offbeat land-grab plot. A class act. B&W; 56m. **DIR:** Sam Newfield. **CAST:** Robert Livingston, Al St. John, I. Stanford Jolley. **1943**

DEATH SPA ★★1/2 A disturbing gore flick about the dead wife of a health-spa owner who makes things unbearable for him and the patrons of his state-of-the-art spa. Not rated; contains violence, nudity, profanity, and gore. 89m. **DIR:** Michael Fischa. **CAST:** William Bumiller, Brenda Bakke, Merritt Butrick, Robert Lipton, Alexa Hamilton, Rosalind Cash, Shari Shattuck. **1990**

DEATH SQUAD, THE ★★ A self-appointed coterie of cops is rubbing out criminals beating the rap on legal technicalities. A former officer is given the job of finding out who's doing it and cleaning house. Clint Eastwood did it all infinitely better in *Magnum Force*. Made for television. 78m. **DIR:** Harry Falk. **CAST:** Robert Forster, Michelle Phillips, Claude Akins, Melvyn Douglas. **1974**

DEATH TAKES A HOLIDAY ★★★ Strange story of Death forsaking its duty for three days wrapped up in a love story. Intriguing concept gets "the works" from matinee idol Fredric March and ethereal beauty Evelyn Venable, and some eerie scenes make this one worth a watch. B&W; 80m. **DIR:** Mitchell Leisen. **CAST:** Fredric March, Evelyn Venable, Henry Travers, Kent Taylor, Guy Standing, Gail Patrick. **1934**

DEATH TARGET ★★ Three soldiers for hire reunite in one last bid for fortune. But when one of the guys falls for a drug-addict hooker, her loony pimp gets into the act, putting a wrench in the works for everyone. Macho. No rating. 72m. **DIR:** Peter Hyams. **CAST:** Jorge Montesi, Elaine Lakeman. **1983**

•DEATH TO SMOOCHY ★★ As is typical when Danny DeVito gets behind a camera, this tiresome and relentlessly tawdry little comedy suffers from an excessive attack of "The Shrills": Most characters scream at each other, rather than holding conversations. The story concerns a nasty and corrupt TV children's show host (Robin Williams) who vows revenge after being replaced by a mild-mannered folksinger (Edward Norton) in a puffy purple rhino suit. And yes, what follows is every bit as bad as you'd expect, from that description. Rated R for profanity and sexual candor. 109m. **DIR:** Danny DeVito. **CAST:** Robin Williams, Edward Norton, Catherine Keener, Danny DeVito, Jon Stewart. **2002 DVD**

DEATH TRAIN ★★★★ An excellent adaptation of an Alistair MacLean story about a renegade Soviet general who terrorizes the world with two nuclear bombs. One bomb is aboard a hijacked train traveling through Europe. A blend of fine acting, editing, and suspense makes for a top-notch film. Not rated, made for cable, but contains violence. 95m. **DIR:** David S. Jackson. **CAST:** Pierce Brosnan, Patrick Stewart, Alexandra Paul, Ted Levine, Christopher Lee. **1992**

DEATH VALLEY ★★ Paul LeMat and Catharine Hicks star in this okay horror film about a vacation that turns into a nightmare. Rated R for violence and gore. 87m. **DIR:** Dick Richards. **CAST:** Paul LeMat, Catharine Hicks, Stephen McHattie, Wilford Brimley. **1982 DVD**

DEATH VALLEY MANHUNT ★★★ Wild Bill Elliott routs the efforts of swindlers to take over Gabby Hayes and the homesteaders' oil well. Ingenue Anne Jeffreys later gained fame on TV's *Topper*. B&W; 55m. **DIR:** John English. **CAST:** William Elliott, George "Gabby" Hayes, Anne Jeffreys. **1943**

DEATH WARMED UP ★★ In this winner of the 1984 Grand Prix International Festival of Fantasy and Science Fiction Films, a psycho doctor is transforming patients into mutant killers, until a former patient comes after revenge. Rated R for violence, nudity, and profanity. 83m. **DIR:** David Blyth. **CAST:** Michael Hurst, Margaret Umbers, David Leitch. **1983**

DEATH WARRANT ★★ Action-fu star Jean-Claude Van Damme has plenty to kick about as he plays an undercover cop sent into the slammer to investigate a series of inmate deaths. Before the final showdown, there are beatings and big-house clichés galore. Rated R for language and violence. 89m. **DIR:** Deran Sarafian. **CAST:** Jean-Claude Van Damme, Robert Guillaume, Cynthia Gibb, George Dickerson. **1990 DVD**

DEATH WATCH ★★★★ A thought-provoking look at the power and the misuse of the media in a future society. Harvey Keitel has a camera implanted in his brain. A television producer (Harry Dean Stanton) uses Keitel to film a documentary of a terminally ill woman (Romy Schneider) without her knowledge. Suspenseful science-fiction drama. Rated R for profanity and suggested sex. 117m. **DIR:** Bertrand Tavernier. **CAST:** Romy

Schneider, Harvey Keitel, Harry Dean Stanton, Max von Sydow. **1980**

DEATH WEEKEND ★★ Don Stroud is chillingly convincing as a vicious sadist who, with the help of two demented pals, terrorizes lovers Brenda Vaccaro and Chuck Shamata at their *House by the Lake*, which was the film's theatrical title. Director William Fruet dwells too much on the cruelty. As a result, the film is uncomfortable to watch. Rated R for violence and profanity. 89m. **DIR:** William Fruet. **CAST:** Brenda Vaccaro, Don Stroud, Chuck Shamata. **1977**

DEATH WISH ★★★★ Charles Bronson gives an excellent performance as Paul Kersey, a mild-mannered New Yorker moved to violence when his daughter is raped and his wife killed by sleazy muggers. It's a gripping story of one man's revenge. Rated R because of nudity and violence (includes a graphic rape scene). 93m. **DIR:** Michael Winner. **CAST:** Charles Bronson, Hope Lange, Vincent Gardenia, Jeff Goldblum. **1974 DVD**

DEATH WISH II This carbon-copy sequel to the successful *Death Wish* is a revolting, violent crime chiller. Rated R because of nudity and violence. 93m. **DIR:** Michael Winner. **CAST:** Charles Bronson, Jill Ireland, Vincent Gardenia, J. D. Cannon, Anthony Franciosa. **1982**

DEATH WISH III Paul Kersey (Charles Bronson) loses a loved one and then goes on another rampage. Rated R for violence, profanity, drug use, nudity, and sex. 99m. **DIR:** Michael Winner. **CAST:** Charles Bronson, Deborah Raffin, Ed Lauter, Martin Balsam. **1985**

DEATH WISH IV: THE CRACKDOWN Charles Bronson is back as the vigilante, but this time he's hired to destroy two drug families operating in Los Angeles. Rated R for violence and language. 98m. **DIR:** J. Lee Thompson. **CAST:** Charles Bronson, Kay Lenz, John P. Ryan, Perry Lopez, Soon-Tek Oh, George Dickerson, Dana Barron. **1987**

DEATH WISH V: THE FACE OF DEATH ★★★1/2 Vigilante Charles Bronson returns to hunt a ruthless mobster who just happens to be his fiancée's ex-husband. The story is quite captivating, and the film doesn't contain too much gore or violence. Rated R for nudity, profanity, and violence. 95m. **DIR:** Allan A. Goldstein. **CAST:** Charles Bronson, Lesley-Anne Down, Robert Joy, Michael Parks, Chuck Shamata, Kenneth Welsh. **1993 DVD**

DEATHDREAM ★★★1/2 The underrated director Bob Clark made some interesting low-budget movies in his native Canada before gaining commercial success (and critical scorn) with the *Porky's* series. This unsettling horror tale, an update of "The Monkey's Paw" as a comment on the Vietnam War and modern family life, is one of his best. It's a creepy mood piece, also known as *Dead of Night*. Rated R. 88m. **DIR:** Bob Clark. **CAST:** John Marley, Richard Backus, Lynn Carlin, Anya Ormsby. **1972**

DEATHFIGHT ★★ Brother battles brother in this decent martial arts flick that features the art of shoot boxing. When the patriarch of the family selects his adopted son to run the family smuggling business, the natural son frames his brother for murder. Rated R for nudity, violence, and profanity. 92m. **DIR:** Anthony Maharaj. **CAST:** Richard Norton, Karen Moncrieff, Chuck Jeffreys, Ron Vreeken, Franco Guerrero, José Mari Avellana, Tetchie Agbayani. **1992**

DEATHGAME ★★ Timothy Bottoms wastes his time and talent in this rip-off of *Escape from L.A.*, as a weary police investigator who searches for a missing young woman and winds up as prey in an enclosed arena. The cheap sets and gratuitous nudity brand it as yet another quickie from producer Roger Corman. Rated R for violence, profanity, nudity, and simulated sex. 80m. **DIR:** Randolph Cheveldave. **CAST:** Timothy Bottoms, Alfonso Quijada, Vince Murdocco, Nicholas Hill, David McCallum, Jody Thompson. **1996**

DEATHMASK ★★ This talky, confusing screenplay is interesting in concept but is never sure where it's going. The plot involves a medical investigator who, after his daughter drowns, pours all his energy into investigating the death of a young boy. Not rated. 103m. **DIR:** Richard Friedman. **CAST:** Farley Granger, Lee Bryant, Arch Johnson. **1984**

DEATHMOON A simple-minded telefilm about a businessman who is cursed by an old crone and turns into a werewolf. Not rated. 90m. **DIR:** Bruce Kessler. **CAST:** Robert Foxworth, Charles Haid, France Nuyen. **1985**

DEATHSHIP ★★ This story of a modern-day lost *Flying Dutchman* involves a World War II battleship—haunted by those who died on it. The ship destroys any seagoing vessels it can find because it needs blood. There are a few chills along the way, but not enough. Rated R for violence and brief nudity. 91m. **DIR:** Alvin Rakoff. **CAST:** George Kennedy, Richard Crenna, Nick Mancuso, Sally Ann Howes, Kate Reid, Saul Rubinek. **1980**

DEATHSHOT Two Illinois detectives will stop at nothing to break up a drug ring. 90m. **DIR:** Mitch Brown. **CAST:** Richard C. Watt, Frank Himes. **1973**

DEATHSPORT ★★ Not really a sequel to *Death Race 2000*, but cut from the same cloth. Both are low-budget action films centered around futuristic no-holds-barred road races. The first film, though, was a lot more fun. Rated R for violence and nudity. 82m. **DIR:** Henry Suso, Allan Arkush. **CAST:** David Carradine, Claudia Jennings, Richard Lynch. **1978 DVD**

DEATHSTALKER This film has a muscle-bound warrior attempting to save a beautiful princess (Barbi Benton) from an evil wizard. Rated R for nudity, profanity, simulated rape, and violence. 80m. **DIR:** John Watson. **CAST:** Richard Hill, Barbi Benton, Lana Clarkson. **1984 DVD**

DEATHSTALKER II: DUEL OF THE TITANS ★★1/2 Deathstalker and a feisty deposed princess battle the evil magician who has taken over her kingdom. Lowbrow fun is too busy making fun of itself to be taken seriously. The R rating is for nudity and violence. 85m. **DIR:** Jim Wynorski. **CAST:** John Terlesky, Monique Gabrielle. **1987 DVD**

DEATHSTALKER III—THE WARRIORS FROM HELL ★★1/2 Tongue-in-cheek sword-and-sorcery tale about the search for three magical stones that will lead to the riches of the world. You have so much fun with this one, you forget how hokey it really is. Rated R for nudity and violence. 85m. **DIR:** Alfonso Corona. **CAST:** John Allen Nelson, Carla Herd, Thom Christopher, Terri Treas. **1988**

DEATHSTALKER IV: MATCH OF THE TITANS Unbelievably bad sword-and-sorcery flick finds all the greatest warriors gathered for a tournament. Acting is nonexistent and fight scenes are poorly staged. Rated R for nudity and violence. 85m. **DIR:** Howard R. Cohen. **CAST:** Richard Hill, Maria Ford, Michelle Moffett, Brett Clark. **1992**

DEATHTRAP ★★★ An enjoyable mystery-comedy based on the Broadway play, this Sidney Lumet film stars Michael Caine, Christopher Reeve, and Dyan Cannon. Caine plays a once-successful playwright who decides to steal a brilliant murder mystery just written by one of his students (Reeve), murder the student, and collect the royalties. Rated PG for violence and adult themes. 116m. **DIR:** Sidney Lumet. **CAST:** Michael Caine, Christopher Reeve, Dyan Cannon, Irene Worth, Henry Jones. **1982 DVD**

DEBAJO DEL MUNDO (UNDER EARTH) ★★★★ A Polish family's prosperous life is shattered when the German army invades their small farming community. This Spanish film captures the spirit of a family torn apart by war. A great cast gives compelling performances in this poignant drama. Dubbed in English. Rated R for profanity and graphic violence. 100m. **DIR:** Beda Docampo Feijoo, Juan Bautista Stagnaro. **CAST:** Sergio Renan. **1988**

•DEBT, THE ★★★ In a change of pace from his usual action roles, Lorenzo Lamas stars as a mild-mannered guy forced by gambling debts to participate in a mob theft. Michael Paré makes the most of a well-written part as the bookie who forces him into a situation that is dangerous for both of them. Also released as *Back to Even*. Rated R for violence, profanity, and sexual situations. 92m. **DIR:** Rod Hewitt. **CAST:** Lorenzo Lamas, Heidi Thomas, Angela Jones, Herb Mitchell, Michael Paré. **1998 DVD**

DEBUT, THE ★★★ Filipino Americans in Los Angeles face challenges as conflicts between ethnic tradition and assimilation affect family and friends in this compelling, somewhat oversimplified drama. Most of the film orbits a birthday party thrown for 18-year-old Rose. The presence of a gangsta son of a guest and rifts between fathers and sons threaten to dampen the celebration as the film addresses parental sacrifice, the pursuit of one's dreams, bigotry, teen delinquency, and interracial relationships. Partially in Tagalog with English subtitles. Not rated; contains profanity and violence. 88m. **DIR:** Gene Cajayon. **CAST:** Dante Basco, Eddie Garcia, Bernadette Balagtas, Tirso Cruz III, Darion Basco, Gina Alajar, Joy Bisco. **2000**

DECAMERON, THE ★★★★ Earthy, vibrant adaptation of eight stories from the fourteenth-century work by Boccaccio. Probably Pier Paolo Pasolini's most purely enjoyable film. Dubbed in English. 111m. **DIR:** Pier Paolo Pasolini. **CAST:** Franco Citti. **1971**

DECAMERON NIGHTS ★★★ Louis Jourdan is Boccaccio, the poet, storyteller, and humanist best known for *The Decameron*. Three of his tales are told within the overall frame of his trying to win the love of a recent widow (Joan Fontaine). Each story features the cast members as various characters. The sets and costumes add greatly to this period comedy. 75m. **DIR:** Hugo Fregonese. **CAST:** Joan Fontaine, Louis Jourdan, Joan Collins, Binnie Barnes, Marjorie Rhodes, Godfrey Tearle. **1953**

DECEIT ★★★ Alien sex fiends sent to destroy Earth find a little time to sample its women. When one of them chooses a street-smart prostitute she proves to be more than a match for them. Original, offbeat story is amusing as well as thought-provoking, if somewhat erratic. Rated R for nudity, profanity, and violence. 92m. **DIR:** Albert Pyun. **CAST:** Norbert Weisser, Samantha Phillips, Diane DeFoe, Christian Andrews, Scott Paulin. **1993**

DECEIVED ★★★1/2 In this suspense thriller, Goldie Hawn finds out what happens when Mr. Right (John Heard) turns out to be the bogeyman. Director Damian Harris keeps the screws turned tight. Rated PG-13 for violence and profanity. 104m. **DIR:** Damian Harris. **CAST:** Goldie Hawn, John Heard, Robin Bartlett, Amy Wright, Jan Rubes, Kate Reid. **1991 DVD**

DECEIVER ★★★ An unemployed, alcoholic, epileptic textile heir takes several polygraph tests after his phone number is found in the pocket of a murdered hooker. Cops grill him until he turns the tables and makes several seamy accusations about their personal lives and taunts them to tell the truth. This lurid mind game about displaced hostility and personal demons is a triumph of style over substance. Rated R for language, violence, and sexual content. 102m. **DIR:** Jonas Pate, Josh Pate. **CAST:** Tim Roth, Michael Rooker, Renee Zellweger, Christopher Penn, Ellen Burstyn, Michael Parks. **1998 DVD**

DECEIVERS, THE ★★1/2 Melodramatic yarn set in 1820s India and based on the true story of the murderous Thuggee cult. Pierce Brosnan goes undercover and joins the cult. This slow-going film has its moments. Rated PG-13. 103m. **DIR:** Nicholas Meyer. **CAST:** Pierce Brosnan, Shashi Kapoor, Saeed Jaffrey. **1988**

DECEMBER ★★★ Intelligent, thoughtful drama unfolds on the day after Pearl Harbor has been bombed by the Japanese. Five New England prep school friends gather to discuss the implications of the event, and how it will affect them. Compelling. Rated PG. 92m. **DIR:** Gabe Torres. **CAST:** Wil Wheaton, Brian Krause, Balthazar Getty, Chris Young. **1991**

DECEMBER BRIDE ★★★★1/2 Suppressed desire flies in the face of a shocked society in this oddly beautiful love story. Strong-willed Saskia Reeves is a servant who takes up with two brothers, defying all convention in their rural Irish village at the turn of the century. Director Thaddeus O'Sullivan uncovers the tremulous eroticism beneath a stony emotional landscape. It takes true talent to reveal such passion when everyone keeps his clothes on. Not rated; contains adult themes. 90m. **DIR:** Thaddeus O'Sullivan. **CAST:** Saskia Reeves, Donal McCann, Ciarán Hinds. **1994**

DECEMBER 7TH: THE MOVIE ★★★ Cinematographer Gregg Toland, commissioned by the Navy Department to prepare a documentary on the Pearl Harbor attack, instead made this feature-length film where the military, in the form of Walter Huston as Uncle Sam, was criticized for being unprepared in the Pacific. The navy suppressed the film, editing it to a 34-minute short, which, on its own, won an Oscar as best documentary. A curiosity and, as such, recommended. B&W; 82m. **DIR:** John Ford, Gregg Toland. **CAST:** Walter Huston, Harry Davenport. **1943**

DECEPTION (1946) ★★★1/2 A better-than-average Bette Davis melodrama, with Claude Rains as a domineering orchestra conductor who imposes his will on musician Davis. The leads make this detergent drama work with their intensity and apparent desire to one-up each other in front of the camera. 110m. **DIR:** Irving Rapper. **CAST:** Bette Davis, Paul Henreid, Claude Rains. **1946**

DECEPTION (1993) ★★1/2 Postcard gorgeous but empty-headed exotic pseudothriller is amazingly fun because it makes so little sense. When an aviation-supply vendor is burned beyond recognition in a plane crash, his wife tries to keep their business afloat. While settling bills, she finds a packet of coded baseball cards that leads to clandestine bank accounts around the world. Rated PG-13 for profanity. 95m. **DIR:** Graeme Clifford. **CAST:** Andie MacDowell, Liam Neeson, Viggo Mortensen. **1993**

DECISION AT SUNDOWN ★★★★ Full of hate, Randolph Scott arrives in town to avenge himself and kill the man responsible for his wife's death. Many surprises in the brooding script. A class act. 77m. **DIR:** Budd Boetticher. **CAST:** Randolph Scott, John Carroll, Karen Steele, Noah Beery Jr., Bob Steele. **1957**

DECLINE OF THE AMERICAN EMPIRE, THE ★★★★ Writer-director Denys Arcand focuses on two groups, one male and one female. Both reveal secrets about their lives. Rated R for profanity, nudity, and simulated sex. In French with English subtitles. 101m. **DIR:** Denys Arcand. **CAST:** Dominique Michel, Dorothee Berryman, Louise Portal. **1986**

DECLINE OF WESTERN CIVILIZATION, THE ★★★★ The L.A. punk scene captured at its 1979 peak, before MTV and the music industry sanitized it into oblivion (and made the stinging title seem sarcastic). Director Penelope Spheeris is both a fan of the music and an objective observer of the scene, which she depicts in engrossing detail. Not rated; the film contains profanity. 100m. **DIR:** Penelope Spheeris. **1981**

DECONSTRUCTING HARRY ★★★ Woody Allen strays into Ingmar Bergman territory with a familiar writer's conceit—the notion of fictional characters "coming to life" and confronting their creator. The result is a film in which it's occasionally difficult to determine whether we're watching this story's central character, his fictional alter egos, or an amalgam of both. Allen stars as Harry Block, an aptly named writer suffering from the ultimate writer's block: an inability to survive in the real world. Harry has put himself, and all the people he knows, into his fiction. His latest novel is so thinly disguised that it has egregiously insulted, alienated, and infuriated nearly everybody he knows. Rated R for nudity, sexual content, and profanity. 95m. **DIR:** Woody Allen. **CAST:** Woody Allen, Kirstie Alley, Bob Balaban, Billy Crystal, Judy Davis, Amy Irving, Elisabeth Shue, Robin Williams. **1997 DVD**

DECORATION DAY ★★★★★ This superior adaptation of John William Corrington's novel finds retired judge James Garner investigating a mystery when an old friend (Bill Cobbs) refuses to accept a long overdue Medal of Honor. Originally produced as a television *Hallmark Hall of Fame* special, this stirring character study benefits from superb performances—particularly by Garner—and first-rate production values. 91m. **DIR:** Robert Markowitz. **CAST:** James Garner, Bill Cobbs, Judith Ivey, Ruby Dee, Laurence Fishburne. **1991**

DECOY ★★★ This otherwise average kill-or-be-killed saga is highlighted by its unusual characters, notably Peter Weller as a bald disciple of Cree mysticism. He and his best friend agree to shelter flighty Darlene Vogel from baddies intending to kidnap her as a means of pressuring dear ol' Dad. Naturally, things get a little complicated. Rated R for violence, torture, and profanity. 97m. **DIR:** Vittorio Rambaldi. **CAST:** Peter Weller, Robert Patrick, Charlotte Lewis, Darlene Vogel. **1995**

DEDEE D'ANVERS ★★1/2 Simone Signoret's first starring role was as a prostitute in this melodrama. She works the docks but tries to get out of the life with the help of a kindly sailor. Pretty gloomy. In French with English subtitles. B&W; 95m. **DIR:** Yves Allegret. **CAST:** Simone Signoret, Marcel Pagliero, Bernard Blier. **1949**

DEDICATED MAN, A ★★ Haunting British romance about a workaholic who asks a lonely spinster to pose as his wife. All goes well until she starts asking questions about his past. The *Romance Theatre* presentation will disappoint viewers hoping for high passions. 50m. **DIR:** Robert Knights. **CAST:** Alec McCowen, Joan Plowright, Christopher Irving. **1982**

DEE SNIDER'S STRANGELAND Exercise in futility as former Twisted Sister lead singer Dee Snider writes and costars in this sleazy thriller about a psychopath who lures young people to his lair over the Internet and then subjects them to all kinds of horrible torture. Amateurishly acted and directed. Rated R for violence, language, nudity, and adult situations. 91m. **DIR:** John Pipelow. **CAST:** Dee Snider, Michael Gage, Brett Harrelson, Elizabeth Peña, Linda Cardellini. **1998**

DEEP, THE ★★ The success of *Jaws* prompted this screen adaptation of another Benchley novel, but the results weren't nearly as satisfying. A good cast founders in this waterlogged tale of treasure hunting. Rated PG. 123m. **DIR:** Peter Yates. **CAST:** Robert Shaw, Jacqueline Bisset, Nick Nolte, Louis Gossett Jr., Eli Wallach, Robert Tessier. **1977 DVD**

DEEP BLUE SEA ★★ At a midocean research station where scientists are experimenting on sharks, the creatures develop superhuman intelligence and turn on their captors. The script is almost idiotic, with one cornball line after another, as if the writers never even expected us to believe it. The special effects, like the story, are flashy but unconvincing, and the actors are a mixed bag—generally, the better they are the sooner they get munched. Rated R for violence and profanity. 106m. **DIR:** Renny Harlin. **CAST:** Saffron Burrows, Samuel L. Jackson, Thomas Jane, LL Cool J, Jacqueline McKenzie, Michael Rapaport, Stellan Skarsgard, Aida Turturro. **1999 DVD**

•DEEP CORE ★★ A powerful deep-mining machine not only gets at the Earth's most deeply hidden treasures, but also causes earthquakes, tsunamis, and volcanic eruptions around the globe. Only a group of scientists can prevent disaster, if they aren't stopped by greedy industrialists. Cheesy, sci-fi action. Rated PG-13 for violence, profanity, and brief sexuality. 90m. **DIR:** Rodney McDonald. **CAST:** Craig Sheffer, James Russo, Terry Farrell, Wil Wheaton. **2000 DVD**

DEEP COVER (1980) A Soviet spy poses as a Cambridge professor. Rated R for nudity, violence, and profanity. 81m. **DIR:** Richard Loncraine. **CAST:** Tom Conti, Donald Pleasence, Denholm Elliott. **1980**

DEEP COVER (1992) ★★★★ With this no-nonsense action film about a straitlaced cop (brilliantly played by Laurence Fishburne) who goes undercover for the DEA, Bill Duke hits his stride as a director. Duke tells his story of Fishburne's descent into decadence, danger, and disillusionment in a compelling, in-your-face fashion. Rated R for violence, profanity, and nudity. 112m. **DIR:** Bill Duke. **CAST:** Laurence Fishburne, Jeff Goldblum, Victoria Dillard, Charles Martin Smith, Sidney Lassick, Clarence Williams, III, Gregory Sierra. **1992 DVD**

DEEP CRIMSON ★★★ Middle-aged, toupee-obsessed Raymond hustles money from Mexican widows and spinsters after answering their lonely hearts ads. He dates an overweight nurse with two children who sympathizes with his scam. She then abandons her two children and accompanies him on a multiple-murder spree. This lushly photographed crime-thriller is both grisly and perversely fascinating. In Spanish with English subtitles. Not rated; contains violence, profanity, and sexual themes. 109m. **DIR:** Arturo Ripstein. **CAST:** Regina Orozco, Daniel Giminez-Cacho, Marisa Paredes, Veronica Merchant. **1996**

DEEP END ★★★1/2 A young man working in a London bathhouse becomes obsessed with a beautiful female coworker. Offbeat drama with realistic performances by the cast. Rated R. 88m. **DIR:** Jerzy Skolimowski. **CAST:** John Moulder-Brown, Jane Asher, Diana Dors. **1970 DVD**

•DEEP END, THE ★★★ A school carpool mom barely blinks before plunging into the moral and statutory minefield of finding and then hiding a corpse. She wears a mask of stoic maternal resolve while dumping the body of her teen son's older gay lover into Lake Tahoe. Escalating confrontations with sleazy blackmailers soon test her mettle in a lurid melodrama that strains our suspension of disbelief at times. Rated R for language, violence, and sexual content. 99m. **DIR:** Scott McGehee, David Siegel. **CAST:** Tilda Swinton, Jonathan Tucker, Goran Visnjic, Raymond J. Barry, Joshua Lucas, Peter Donat. **2001 DVD**

DEEP END OF THE OCEAN, THE ★★★1/2 Based on Jacqueline Mitchard's weepy bestseller about family catastrophe, this melodrama begins when the family's youngest child disappears, with the parents not knowing whether he was kidnapped or simply wandered off, and an older brother who feels responsible for having "failed" to properly watch after the little guy. Flash-forward nine years, to the moment when a kid shows up to mow the lawn . . . and is immediately recognized as the long-missing boy. The inevitable questions and answers cut to the core of human relationships, and the desperate need for healing among these players: husband and wife, parent and child, brother and brother. Rated PG-13 for profanity. 148m. **DIR:** Ulu Grosbard. **CAST:** Michelle Pfeiffer, Treat Williams, Jonathan Jackson, John Kapelos, Ryan Merriman, Whoopi Goldberg. **1999 DVD**

DEEP IMPACT ★★★ This standard-issue sci-fi melodrama dilutes its cataclysmic premise with too much talk and too little action, and when the climactic "money shots" finally *do* arrive, they're over before viewers can adjust to the results. The film only really comes alive during its exciting outer-space sequences, when veteran astronaut Robert Duvall leads a crew in an effort to destroy the rogue comet that threatens to annihilate all life on Earth. Rated PG-13 for dramatic intensity and brief profanity. 115m. **DIR:** Mimi Leder. **CAST:** Robert Duvall, Téa Leoni, Elijah Wood, Vanessa Redgrave, Maximilian Schell, Morgan Freeman. **1998 DVD**

DEEP IN MY HEART ★★ Most of the films presenting the lives of great composers have been tepid and silly. This biography of Sigmund Romberg is no exception. The songs are wonderful, but the rest is pure drivel. Along the way, Gene Kelly, Tony Martin, and Ann Miller drop by for brief musical visits, and that's it. Only fair. 132m. **DIR:** Stanley Donen. **CAST:** José Ferrer, Merle Oberon, Paul Henreid, Walter Pidgeon, Helen Traubel. **1954**

DEEP IN THE HEART OF TEXAS ★★★1/2 This is a well-directed, finely photographed film about post–Civil War land snatching. It's the first in a series of seven films to co-star the two great Western stars, Johnny Mack Brown and Tex Ritter. This one has lots of black hats, a few white hats, and plenty of action. B&W; 74m. **DIR:** Elmer Clifton. **CAST:** Johnny Mack Brown, Tex Ritter. **1942 DVD**

•DEEP IN THE WOODS ★★1/2 Who's afraid of the big bad wolf? How about the five-member drama troupe that has been hired to perform a stylized take on *Little Red Riding Hood* for an eccentric father and his equally creepy mute son. When the curtain comes down, the actors find themselves being stalked and killed by someone in a wolf suit. Leave it to the French to turn a fairy tale into a teen slasher film. Despite the English dubbing, the film manages to maintain its own sense of style and rhythm. Rated R for adult situations, language, nudity, and violence. 90m. **DIR:** Lionel Delplanque. **CAST:** Clotilde Courau, Clément Sibony, Vincent Lecouer, Alexia Stresi, Maud Buquet. **2000 DVD**

DEEP RED (1975) ★★★ Another stylish and brutal horror-mystery from Italian director Dario Argento. His other works include *The Bird with the Crystal Plumage* and *Suspiria*. Like those, this film is slim on plot and a bit too talky, but Argento builds tension beautifully with rich atmosphere and driving electronic music. Rated R for violence. 98m. **DIR:** Dario Argento. **CAST:** David Hemmings, Daria Nicolodi, Gabriele Lavia. **1975 DVD**

DEEP RED (1994) ★★★★ This well-made thriller casts Michael Biehn as a private investigator in the near future who agrees to track down a missing husband. When the man, a scientist working on a top-secret project called "Deep Red," is killed just as Biehn finds him, our hero realizes he's being used. Flashback style is disconcerting at first, but the acting and premise hold the viewer's interest. Made for cable. 86m. **DIR:** Craig R. Baxley. **CAST:** Michael Biehn, Joanna Pacula, Lisa Collins, John de Lancie, Tobin Bell, John Kapelos, Steven Williams, Michael Des Barres. **1994**

DEEP RISING ★★ A gang of modern-day pirates intercepts a cruise ship in midocean to plunder the super-rich passengers—but a swarm of sea serpents has beaten them to it, devouring everyone on board. Writer-director Stephen Sommers throws everything he can think of into this waterlogged thriller, but the special effects and sets aren't credible, the action isn't exciting, and the comic relief isn't funny. Rated R for profanity and gore. 106m. **DIR:** Stephen Sommers. **CAST:** Treat Williams, Famke Janssen, Kevin J. O'Connor, Anthony Heald, Wes Studi. **1997 DVD**

DEEP SIX, THE ★★★1/2 Good action and the magnetism of popular Alan Ladd as a WWI naval officer who doesn't know the meaning of the word *fear*. 105m. **DIR:** Rudolph Maté. **CAST:** Alan Ladd, William Bendix, Efrem Zimbalist Jr., Dianne Foster, Joey Bishop. **1958**

DEEP TROUBLE ★★ In this made-for-cable original, Robert Wagner plays a deep-sea diver who happens upon an armored car, filled with diamonds, under the waves. Now he must hide the jewels, save a beautiful woman, and avenge the death of his partner. Too unbelievable to be enjoyed. Not rated; contains violence. 95m. **DIR:** Armand Mastroianni. **CAST:** Robert Wagner, Isabelle Pasco, Jean-Yves Berteloot, Frederic Darie, Jean-François Pages, Ben Cross. **1993 DVD**

DEEPSTAR SIX 🦃 A secret navy underwater colonization project goes awry. Rated R for violence and profanity. 105m. **DIR:** Sean S. Cunningham. **CAST:** Taurean Blacque, Nancy Everhard, Greg Evigan, Miguel Ferrer, Nia Peeples, Matt McCoy, Cindy Pickett. **1989 DVD**

DEER HUNTER, THE ★★★★★ Five friends work at the dangerous blast furnace in a steel mill in the dingy town of Clairton, Pennsylvania, in 1968. At quitting time, they make their way to their favorite local bar to drink away the pressures of the day. For three of the friends, it is the last gathering before they leave for Vietnam, where they find horror and death. A gripping study of heroism and the meaning of friendship. Rated R for profanity and violence. 183m. **DIR:** Michael Cimino. **CAST:** Robert De Niro, John Cazale, John Savage, Meryl Streep, Christopher Walken. **1978 DVD**

DEERSLAYER (1920) ★★1/2 Silent German version of Fenimore Cooper's frontier stories was trimmed by more than half for American release in 1923, but what's left is pretty good. Bela Lugosi is an impressive Chingachgook and is able to maintain his dignity despite the hoary plot machinations. Idyllic settings, realistic costuming, and a charming framework of scouts being read this story around a campfire engage a viewer and make one hope for the eventual discovery of the whole film. B&W; 60m. **DIR:** Arthur Wellin. **CAST:** Emil Mamelok, Bela Lugosi, Herten Heden, Gottfried Krause. **1920**

DEERSLAYER, THE (1978) ★★1/2 Made-for-TV movie, based on James Fenimore Cooper's classic, is a film of adventure in early America. The heroes, Hawkeye (Steve Forrest) and Chingachgook (Ned Romero), attempt to save a Mohican princess and avenge the death of Chingachgook's son. 98m. **DIR:** Richard Friedenberg. **CAST:** Steve Forrest, John Anderson, Ned Romero, Joan Prather. **1978**

DEF BY TEMPTATION ★★★ A divinity student is tempted by a seductive succubus who wants his soul. This independently produced horror-comedy is entertaining and well-acted by its all-black cast. Rated R for profanity and violence. 95m. **DIR:** James Bond, III. **CAST:** James Bond, III, Kadeem Hardison, Melba Moore. **1990 DVD**

DEF-CON 4 ★★1/2 The first half of this film contains special effects the equal of any in modern science fiction, an intelligent script, and excellent acting. The second half is one postholocaust yawn. The overall impression is that perhaps the filmmakers ran out of time or money or both. Rated R for language and violence. 85m. **DIR:** Paul Donovan. **CAST:** Maury Chaykin, Kate Lynch, Tim Choate, Lenore Zann. **1985 DVD**

DEFENDERS, THE ★★★ Reginald Rose's 1961–1965 television show gets an update in this made-for-cable original series, but one of the faces remains the same: E. G. Marshall as patriarch Lawrence Preston, head of the legal firm that bears his name. Unfortunately, time and countless subsequent film and TV lawyers have blunted what once had a dramatic edge. Rated R for profanity and violence. 100m. **DIR:** Andy Wolk. **CAST:** Beau Bridges, E. G. Marshall, Martha Plimpton, Roma Maffia, Mark Blum, John Larroquette. **1997**

DEFENDERS, THE: TAKING THE FIRST ★★1/2 A lot of interesting ideas get lost in this made-for-cable movie based on the television series of the same name. It's easy to admire where the writers were going, but we never warm up to the protagonists, an uncle-niece lawyer team, and the plot doesn't make much sense. Rated PG. 96m. **DIR:** Andy Wolk, Peter Wolk. **CAST:** Beau Bridges, Martha Plimpton, Philip Casnoff, Jeremy London. **1998**

DEFENDING YOUR LIFE ★★★★1/2 Once again, star-writer-director Albert Brooks has come up with that increasing rarity: an intelligent comedy. Brooks plays an advertising executive who dies in a car accident and finds himself in Judgment City, where he must defend the cowardly, self-involved life he led on Earth. Fine support from Meryl Streep, Rip Torn, Lee Grant and Buck Henry. Rated PG for brief profanity. 100m. **DIR:** Albert Brooks. **CAST:** Albert Brooks, Meryl Streep, Rip Torn, Lee Grant, Buck Henry. **1991 DVD**

DEFENSE OF THE REALM ★★★★ In London, two reporters (Gabriel Byrne and Denholm Elliott) become convinced that a scandal involving a government official (Ian Bannen) may be a sinister cover-up. Acting on this belief puts both their lives in danger. A tough-minded British thriller that asks some thought-provoking questions. Rated PG for suspense. 96m. **DIR:** David Drury. **CAST:** Gabriel Byrne, Greta Scacchi, Denholm Elliott, Ian Bannen, Bill Paterson, Fulton MacKay. **1986**

DEFENSELESS ★★★ A successful attorney (Barbara Hershey) becomes involved with a sleazy landlord (J. T. Walsh) who is a child pornographer. Suspenseful whodunit, with Sam Shepard as a detective who investigates the landlord's mysterious murder. Rated R for violence, profanity, and murder. 104m. **DIR:** Martin Campbell. **CAST:** Barbara Hershey, Sam Shepard, Mary Beth Hurt, J. T. Walsh. **1991**

DEFIANCE ★★★ Potent story depicts savage New York street gang terrorizing helpless neighborhood. Outsider Jan-Michael Vincent reluctantly gets involved. This well-directed film packs quite a wallop. Rated R for violence and profanity. 102m. **DIR:** John Flynn. **CAST:** Jan-Michael Vincent, Art Carney, Theresa Saldana, Danny Aiello, Fernando Lopez. **1980**

DEFIANT ONES, THE ★★★★ Director Stanley Kramer scored one of his few artistic successes with this compelling story about two escaped convicts (Tony Curtis and Sidney Poitier) shackled together—and coping with mutual hatred—as they run from the authorities in the South. B&W; 97m. **DIR:** Stanley Kramer.

CAST: Tony Curtis, Sidney Poitier, Theodore Bikel, Charles McGraw, Lon Chaney Jr. **1958 DVD**

DÉJÀ VU (1984) 🦃 Stupid story about reincarnation. Rated R. 91m. **DIR:** Anthony Richmond. **CAST:** Jaclyn Smith, Shelley Winters, Claire Bloom, Nigel Terry. **1984**

DÉJÀ VU (1998) ★★1/2 A young woman about to be married finds herself inexplicably attracted to another man—almost as if they had met somewhere before. The familiar plot has a clever O. Henry–style twist at the end, but the jabbering talkiness of the script is a drawback. Noel Harrison (son of Rex) and Anna Massey (daughter of Raymond) easily steal the show as the couple's staid British hosts. Rated PG-13 for mature themes. 116m. **DIR:** Henry Jaglom. **CAST:** Victoria Foyt, Stephen Dillane, Vanessa Redgrave, Glynis Barber, Noel Harrison, Anna Massey, Rachel Kempson. **1998**

DELI, THE ★★★1/2 la *Clerks* and *Smoke*, this film set in a Brooklyn deli is less interested in plot than in displaying a gallery of neighborhood characters. Plenty of familiar faces and some snappy dialogue makes this a winning if slight independent comedy. Not rated; contains profanity. 98m. **DIR:** John Gallagher. **CAST:** Mike Starr, Matt Kesslar, Frank Vincent, Burt Young, Heather Matarazzo, Judith Malina. **1997**

DELIBERATE STRANGER, THE ★★★ Mark Harmon is impressive in his first major role as serial killer Ted Bundy in this better-than-average TV movie. The script for all the time it spends depicting Bundy's crimes doesn't provide enough insight into what made Bundy tick. 192m. **DIR:** Marvin J. Chomsky. **CAST:** Mark Harmon, Frederic Forrest, George Grizzard, Ben Masters, Glynnis O'Connor, M. Emmet Walsh, John Ashton. **1986**

DELICATE DELINQUENT, THE ★★★ Jerry Lewis stars on his own for the first time in this surprisingly agreeable story about a goofball delinquent who ends up as a policeman. B&W; 100m. **DIR:** Don McGuire. **CAST:** Jerry Lewis, Darren McGavin, Horace McMahon, Martha Hyer. **1957**

DELICATESSEN ★★★1/2 In a post-apocalyptic world, a former circus clown comes to a town that has advertised for a butcher's assistant. What our hero doesn't know is that it's a short-term job, during which he'll be well fed until it's time for the boss to stock his shelves. Inventive black comedy will appeal enormously to some and offend others. In French with English subtitles. Not rated; the film has violence and nudity. 95m. **DIR:** Jean-Pierre Jeunet, Marc Caro. **CAST:** Marie-Laure Dougnac, Dominique Pinon, Karen Viard, Jean Claude Dreyfus. **1991**

DELINQUENT DAUGHTERS ★1/2 A reporter and a cop decide to find out just what's going on with today's kids after a high school girl commits suicide. Slow-moving cheapie that is merely a hyped-up dud. B&W; 71m. **DIR:** Albert Herman. **CAST:** June Carlson, Fifi D'Orsay, Teala Loring. **1944**

DELIRIOUS ★★★1/2 In this frequently funny, albeit outrageous, fantasy, soap-opera writer John Candy has a car accident and wakes up to find himself in the fictional town of his television show. *Delirious* was not a critical or box-office success, but we found it clever, surprising, and amiably goofy. Rated PG. 94m. **DIR:** Tom Mankiewicz. **CAST:** John Candy, Mariel Hemingway, Raymond Burr, David Rasche, Charles Rocket, Dylan Baker, Jerry Orbach, Renee Baker. **1991 DVD**

DELIVERANCE ★★★★★ Jon Voight, Burt Reynolds, and Ned Beatty are superb in this first-rate film about a canoe trip down a dangerous river that begins as a holiday but soon turns into a weekend of sheer horror. Based on the novel by James Dickey. Rated R for profanity, sex, and violence. 109m. **DIR:** John Boorman. **CAST:** Jon Voight, Burt Reynolds, Ned Beatty, Ronny Cox, James Dickey. **1972 DVD**

DELIVERY BOYS ★★1/2 This average teen comedy features pizza delivery boys who break dance during their time off. They plan to compete in a break dance contest that offers a $10,000 prize but encounter problems in getting there on time. Rated R. 94m. **DIR:** Ken Handler. **CAST:** Jody Olivery, Joss Marcano, Mario Van Peebles. **1984**

DELLAMORTE, DELLAMORE ★★★1/2 Former Dario Argento acolyte Michele Soavi comes into his own with this strange horror-comedy whose plot keeps making abrupt shifts every reel or so. Rupert Evert is the groundskeeper of a cemetery where the dead just won't stay put. Highly recommended for horror buffs. Rated R for considerable gruesome behavior. 105m. **DIR:** Michele Soavi. **CAST:** Rupert Everett, François Hadji-Lazaro, Mickey Knox. **1994**

DELTA FORCE, THE ★★ In this disappointing action film, which is perhaps best described as "The Dirty Dozen at the Airport," Chuck Norris and Lee Marvin are leaders of an antiterrorist group charged with saving the passengers on a hijacked airliner. Rated R for profanity and violence. 126m. **DIR:** Menahem Golan. **CAST:** Chuck Norris, Lee Marvin, Martin Balsam, Joey Bishop, Robert Forster, Lainie Kazan, George Kennedy, Hanna Schygulla, Susan Strasberg, Bo Svenson, Robert Vaughn, Shelley Winters. **1986 DVD**

DELTA FORCE 2 ★★ An outrageously exciting skydiving sequence highlights this otherwise routine and overly cold-blooded action-adventure about a commando leader (Chuck Norris) who goes after a Colombian drug lord (Billy Drago). Rated R for language and violence. 115m. **DIR:** Aaron Norris. **CAST:** Chuck Norris, Billy Drago, John P. Ryan, Richard Jaeckel. **1990 DVD**

DELTA FORCE 3 ★★1/2 Platoon of second-generation stars fill in for Chuck Norris in this adequate third entry for the action-seeking Delta Force. Rated R for violence and profanity. 97m. **DIR:** Sam Firstenberg. **CAST:** Nick Cassavetes, Eric Douglas, Mike Norris, Matthew Penn, John P. Ryan. **1990**

DELTA FORCE, COMMANDO TWO 🦃 An enemy government tricks a military official in order to steal nuclear weapons, and impending global disaster has to be halted by the Delta Force. A complete mess throughout. Rated R for violence. 100m. **DIR:** Frank Valenti. **CAST:** Richard Hatch, Fred Williamson, Van Johnson. **1991**

DELTA FOX 🦃 A hired assassin finds that he himself has been set up to be killed. Rated R. 92m. **DIR:** Ferd Sebastian, Beverly Sebastian. **CAST:** Priscilla Barnes, Richard Lynch, Stuart Whitman, John Ireland, Richard Jaeckel. **1977**

DELTA HEAT ★★★ An LAPD police officer teams up with a New Orleans ex-cop-turned-swamp-rat to track down a killer drug dealer. At first this looks like a boring movie, but keep watching; it actually gets better. Rated R for violence and profanity. 91m. **DIR:** Michael Fischa.

CAST: Anthony Edwards, Lance Henriksen, Betsy Russell, Linda Dona, Rod Masterson. **1992**

DELTA OF VENUS ★★1/2 Arty smutmeister Zalman King's take on Anaïs Nin's carnal classic is about as exciting as watching paint dry. Pouty Marek Vasut plays an American writer caught in France during the early years of World War II who proceeds to live out the erotic tales she pens for an unknown benefactor. As usual, King's camera work is far too deliberately self-conscious. Rated R for considerable nudity, simulated sex, profanity, and drug use. 102m. **DIR:** Zalman King. **CAST:** Costas Mandylor, Eric Da Silva, Marek Vasut, Zette, Audie England. **1995**

DELUGE (1933) ★★ The destruction of much of New York by earthquakes and a tidal wave. B&W; 70m. **DIR:** Felix Feist. **CAST:** Peggy Shannon, Sidney Blackmer, Lois Wilson, Matt Moore, Edward Van Sloan, Fred Kohler Sr., Samuel S. Hinds. **1933**

DELUGE, THE (POTOP) (1973) ★★★ Overlong period piece set in the seventeenth century during the turbulent Polish-Swedish war. The story evolves around the stormy relationship between a barbaric soldier and a young gentlewoman. Based on the novel by Nobel Prize–winning author Henryk Sienkiewicz. In Polish with English subtitles. Not rated; contains violence. 185m. **DIR:** Jerzy Hoffman. **CAST:** Daniel Olbrychski. **1973**

DELUSION (1980) 🦃 A nurse relates a series of murders that occurred while she cared for an elderly invalid. Rated R for violence and gore. 83m. **DIR:** Alan Beattie. **CAST:** Patricia Pearcy, David Hayward, John Dukakis, Joseph Cotten. **1980**

DELUSION (1991) ★★★ A computer whiz, having just embezzled $480 thousand, heads for Reno, picks up a Las Vegas show girl and her boyfriend (who is a hit man for the mob). Very odd little movie, but some will find this a real gem. Rated R for profanity, nudity, and violence. 99m. **DIR:** Carl Colpaert. **CAST:** Jim Metzler, Jennifer Rubin, Kyle Secor, Robert Costanzo, Jerry Orbach, Tracey Walter. **1991**

DELUSIONS OF GRANDEUR ★★★ In seventeenth-century Spain, a valet is given the job of royal tax collector and uses his position to boost taxes on the rich and give the money to the poor. Likable slapstick farce. In French with English subtitles. Not rated; contains no objectionable material. 85m. **DIR:** Gerard Oury. **CAST:** Yves Montand, Louis de Funes. **1971**

DEMENTIA 13 ★★★ Early Francis Coppola film is a low-budget shocker centering on a family plagued by violent ax murders that are somehow connected with the death of the youngest daughter many years before. Acting is standard, but the photography, creepy locations, and weird music are what make this movie click. Produced by Roger Corman. B&W; 75m. **DIR:** Francis Ford Coppola. **CAST:** William Campbell, Luana Anders, Patrick Magee. **1963 DVD**

DEMETRIUS AND THE GLADIATORS 🦃 Film centers on the search for the robe that Christ wore before he was crucified. Overblown. 101m. **DIR:** Delmer Daves. **CAST:** Victor Mature, Susan Hayward, Debra Paget, Michael Rennie, Anne Bancroft, Ernest Borgnine, Richard Egan, Jay Robinson. **1954 DVD**

DEMOLITION MAN ★★1/2 High-concept action-thrillers just don't get much dumber than this, which attempts to argue that society is much better with heapin' helpings of exaggerated violence. Renegade cop Sylvester Stallone goes into the deep freeze for several decades, and then wakes in an insipid future civilization which cannot handle the mayhem of crazed psychotic Wesley Snipes. Stallone has said it himself—he just can't play comedy. Rated R for profanity and violence. 114m. **DIR:** Marco Brambilla. **CAST:** Sylvester Stallone, Wesley Snipes, Sandra Bullock, Nigel Hawthorne. **1993 DVD**

DEMOLITIONIST, THE ★★1/2 Nicole Eggert plays "Robo-Babe" in this cheesy yet satisfying futuristic action-thriller set in the near future. When an undercover cop is killed by a vicious mobster, her body is reconstructed into a one-woman fighting machine with superhuman strength. Rated R for violence, profanity, and nudity. 100m. **DIR:** Robert Kurtzman. **CAST:** Nicole Eggert, Richard Grieco, Bruce Abbott, Susan Tyrrell. **1995 DVD**

DEMON (GOD TOLD ME TO) ★★★1/2 A minor masterpiece, this movie opens with several mass murders. The only thing that connects these incidents is they are committed by pleasant, smiling people who explain their acts by saying, "God told me to." Rated R for nudity, profanity, and violence. 95m. **DIR:** Larry Cohen. **CAST:** Tony Lo Bianco, Sandy Dennis, Sylvia Sidney, Deborah Raffin, Sam Levene, Mike Kellin. **1977**

DEMON BARBER OF FLEET STREET, THE ★★1/2 Long before Vincent Price was the embodiment of evil, there was Tod Slaughter, master of the Grand Guignol school of lip-smacking villainy and star of many bloody thrillers. Partially based on a true occurrence, this popular folktale tells the story of Sweeney Todd, an amoral barber who cuts the throats of his clients. Seldom seen in America since World War II, this influential film was a great success for the flamboyant Slaughter and provides the basis for the musical theater hit. B&W; 76m. **DIR:** George King. **CAST:** Tod Slaughter, Bruce Seton. **1936**

DEMON CITY SHINJUKU ★★★ Evil threatens to overrun the Earth in this sometimes-scary tale that unfortunately has all the usual elements of animation cliché: the beautiful heroine, the mystic guy with a sword, and demons, demons, demons. Yet surprisingly good. In Japanese with English subtitles. Not rated; contains violence, nudity, and profanity. 81m. **DIR:** Yoshiaki Kawajiri. **1993 DVD**

DEMON IN MY VIEW, A ★★★ One of Anthony Perkins' last roles was a psycho. But this time his reign of terror takes place in Europe, where he is a mild apartment dweller who is hiding a murderous past. A fine, edgy performance by Perkins highlights this intelligent thriller. Rated R for violence. 98m. **DIR:** Petra Hafter. **CAST:** Anthony Perkins. **1992**

DEMON KEEPER ★★ Creaky, haunted-house thriller. Fake medium Edward Albert summons up a real spirit and unleashes a demon. The special effects are better than usual, but the dialogue is frightfully unfunny. Rated R for horror, violence and language. 90m. **DIR:** Joe Tornatore. **CAST:** Dirk Benedict, Edward Albert, Katrina Maltby, Mike Lane. **1994**

DEMON SEED ★★★ Good, but not great, science-fiction film about a superintelligent computer designed by scientist Fritz Weaver to solve problems beyond the scope of man. The computer, however, has other ideas. Weaver's wife (Julie Christie) becomes its unwilling guinea pig and, eventually, mate. Rated R. 94m. **DIR:** Donald Cammell. **CAST:** Julie Christie, Fritz Weaver, Gerrit Graham. **1977**

DEMON WIND ★★★ After one of the dumbest reasons ever to go to a spooky house, a group of young people are systematically dispatched. Some great one-liners and slimy special effects. Rated R for violence, nudity, and gore. 97m. **DIR:** Charles Philip Moore. **CAST:** Eric Larson, Francine Lapensee, Bobby Johnson. **1990**

DEMONIAC 🦃 Director Jess Franco plays the lead himself in this dreary affair (originally titled *Ripper of Notre Dame* and, in a hard-core-porn version, *Exorcism & Black Masses*). Rated R. 87m. **DIR:** Jess (Jesus) Franco. **CAST:** Jess Franco, Lina Romay, Oliver Mathot. **1979**

DEMONIC TOYS 🦃 An army of toys is brought to life by a demon. A plastic baby doll's wisecracks are the only highlight of this film. Not rated, but has profanity and violence. 86m. **DIR:** Peter Manoogian. **CAST:** Tracy Scoggins, Bentley Mitchum. **1991**

DEMONOID 🦃 A couple unearth a severed hand while working in a Mexican mine. Rated R for graphic violence. 78m. **DIR:** Alfredo Zacharias. **CAST:** Samantha Eggar, Stuart Whitman. **1981**

DEMONS ★★★ Selected at random, people on the street are invited to an advance screening of a new horror film. When the members of the audience try to escape, they find themselves trapped. Although much of the acting is poor and some story elements are plain stupid, this actually is a very frightening movie. Not rated, but features graphic violence and adult language. 89m. **DIR:** Lamberto Bava. **CAST:** Urbano Barberini. **1986 DVD**

DEMONS 2 🦃 Cross between George Romero's zombies and *The Evil Dead* attacking the inhabitants of a high-rise apartment building. Not rated, but an R equivalent for violence and gore. 88m. **DIR:** Lamberto Bava. **CAST:** David Knight, Nancy Brilli. **1987 DVD**

DEMONS IN THE GARDEN ★★★★ Fascinating portrait of a family damaged by fratricidal rivalries and morally wasted by corruption, as seen through the eyes of a young boy during post–Civil War Spain. Breathtaking cinematography by José Luis Alcaine. In Spanish with English subtitles. Not rated; contains adult themes. 100m. **DIR:** Manuel Gutiérrez Aragón. **CAST:** Angela Molina, Imanol Arias. **1982**

DEMONS OF THE MIND ★★1/2 One of the last significant Hammer films before the British horror factory's demise in 1976. A Bavarian nobleman, fearing his children are possessed, keeps them locked away. Gillian Hills, in a role intended for Marianne Faithfull, is especially effective. Rated R. 89m. **DIR:** Peter Sykes. **CAST:** Paul Jones, Yvonne Mitchell, Gillian Hills. **1972**

DEMONSTONE ★★ In Manila a beautiful woman is possessed by an evil spirit bent on frying assorted gang members. Throw in Jan-Michael Vincent as an ex-Marine and all hell breaks loose. Rated R for adult language, violence, and nudity. 90m. **DIR:** Andrew Prowse. **CAST:** R. Lee Ermey, Jan-Michael Vincent, Nancy Everhard. **1989**

DEMPSEY ★★★ Treat Williams plays Jack Dempsey, World Heavyweight Champion boxer from 1919 to 1926. Stylish and with riveting plot twists. As Dempsey's first wife, Sally Kellerman is particularly effective. Not rated, contains violence and profanity. 110m. **DIR:** Gus Trikonis. **CAST:** Treat Williams, Sam Waterston, Sally Kellerman, Victoria Tennant, Peter Mark Richman, Jesse Vint. **1983**

DENIAL ★★★ Erotic tale of free-spirited young woman Robin Wright whose chance encounter with hunky artist Jason Patric turns her life upside down. Wright leaves to regain her identity, only to be consumed by Patric's memory. Rated R for nudity. 103m. **DIR:** Erin Dignam. **CAST:** Jason Patric, Robin Wright, Barry Primus, Rae Dawn Chong. **1991**

DENISE CALLS UP ★★★1/2 A circle of New York friends and acquaintances carry on their complicated relationships by phone, fax, and modem, unable or unwilling to meet face-to-face. Director Hal Salwen's script is witty and complicated, and the acting is first-rate—especially considering that virtually the entire film is composed of close-ups of people talking on the phone, with no two of them ever on screen at the same time. Rated PG-13 for mature themes and mild profanity. 80m. **DIR:** Hal Salwen. **CAST:** Timothy Daly, Dana Wheeler-Nicholson, Caroleen Feeney, Liev Schreiber, Alanna Ubach, Sylvia Miles. **1996**

DENNIS POTTER: THE LAST INTERVIEW ★★★★ Talking heads are rarely as compelling as this chatfest filmed by the BBC in June of 1994, a few weeks before Potter died of cancer. Swigging champagne and morphine, freed from the constraints of consequence, Potter is revealed as the intelligent wag he was. Not only does Potter discuss his work, such as *The Singing Detective* and *Pennies from Heaven*, but he opens up about his life. Rarely are such bare-bones, low-budget films this fascinating. Not rated; contains profanity. 70m. **DIR:** Tom Poolew. **CAST:** Dennis Potter, Melvyn Bragg. **1994**

DENNIS THE MENACE ★★★★ The first movie to be made from the famous comic strip has the advantage of a John Hughes script to give it wit and style. The story centers on the relationship between 6 year old Dennis Mitchell and his grouchy neighbor, Mr. Wilson. An affable mixture of talents in a classy family-oriented movie. Rated PG. 101m. **DIR:** Nick Castle. **CAST:** Walter Matthau, Christopher Lloyd, Joan Plowright, Lea Thompson, Mason Gamble, Robert Stanton. **1993**

DENNIS THE MENACE: DINOSAUR HUNTER ★★1/2 Dennis unearths a dinosaur bone in the front yard. A friend of his father's, who majored in paleontology, comes to live with the family and causes chaos for the entire neighborhood. The story is predictable and viewers will wish the father would just get a backbone. Rated G. 95m. **DIR:** Doug Rogers. **CAST:** William Windom, James W. Jansen, Patricia Estrinn, Patsy Garrett, Victor DiMattia, Barton Tinapp. **1987**

DENTIST, THE ★★ This tedious horror film cuts to the nerve only because of the relentless soundtrack of dentist-office noises and endless close-ups of dental equipment. Otherwise, this made-for-cable original about an obsessive and violent dentist is as dull as an overused drill. Rated R for profanity, violence, nudity, and suggested sex. 89m. **DIR:** Brian Yuzna. **CAST:** Corbin Bernsen, Linda Hoffman, Earl Boen. **1996 DVD**

DENTIST 2, THE: BRACE YOURSELF ★★ It's the same old drill for psychopath dentist Dr. Allan Feinstone, once again played by Corbin Bernsen. Having escaped from prison, Feinstone finds himself in a small town where he kills the local dentist and sets up shop in this made-for-cable sequel. Rated R for violence, language, and adult situations. 99m. **DIR:** Richard Dana Smith. **CAST:** Corbin Bernsen, Clint Howard, Jillian McWhirter. **1998 DVD**

DENVER AND RIO GRANDE, THE ★★1/2 A fairly routine Western about railroad men and their rivalries. Enlivened by a spectacular train crash staged by outdoor specialist Byron Haskin. 89m. **DIR:** Byron Haskin. **CAST:** Edmond O'Brien, Sterling Hayden, Dean Jagger, ZaSu Pitts, J. Carrol Naish. **1952**

DENVER KID ★★★ Border patrolman Rocky Lane joins an outlaw gang to solve a brutal massacre. B&W; 60m. **DIR:** Philip Ford. **CAST:** Allan "Rocky" Lane, Eddy Waller, William Henry, Douglas Fowley. **1948**

DERANGED ★★★1/2 Based on the life of serial killer Ed Gein, this little-seen but much-adored film is a true gem. The film's cutting-edge use (at the time) of intrusion into the narrative by a reporter gives it a documentary feel. Generally well acted, this is a chilling look at one man's depraved lifestyle. Rated R for violence and profanity. 82m. **DIR:** Alan Ormsby, Jeff Gillen. **CAST:** Roberts Blossom, Cosette Lee, Leslie Carlson. **1974**

DERSU UZALA ★★★★1/2 This epic about the charting of the Siberian wilderness (circa 1900) is surprisingly as intimate in relationships and details as it is grand in vistas and scope. A Japanese-Russian coproduction, the second half of this Oscar winner is much better than the first. In Russian and Japanese with English subtitles. 140m. **DIR:** Akira Kurosawa. **CAST:** Maxim Munzuk, Yuri Solomin. **1974 DVD**

DESCENDING ANGEL ★★★★ First-rate made-for-cable thriller about a resourceful fellow (Eric Roberts) who begins to suspect his fiancée's Romanian father (George C. Scott) might have allied himself with Hitler's Nazis during World War II. The theme may be a bit shopworn, but the execution is superb. Not rated, but with violence, profanity, and brief nudity. 98m. **DIR:** Jeremy Paul Kagan. **CAST:** George C. Scott, Eric Roberts, Diane Lane, Jan Rubes. **1990**

•DESECRATION ★★1/2 After the accidental death of a nun, a series of supernatural events are unleashed on a small community. Intriguing religious-themed film marks the debut of a promising talent. While the film has its problems, it manages to get in a few good scares. Not rated; contains violence. 88m. **DIR:** Dante Tomaselli. **CAST:** Irma St. Paule, Danny Lopes. **1999 DVD**

DESERT BLOOM ★★★ This poignant study of awakening adolescence and family turmoil is effectively set against a backdrop of 1950 Las Vegas, as the atomic age dawns. The story unfolds slowly but sensitively. Thirteen year old Annabeth Gish gives a remarkably complex performance as a brilliant girl who must cope with an abusive stepfather, an ineffectual mother, and a sexpot aunt. Rated PG. 106m. **DIR:** Eugene Corr. **CAST:** Jon Voight, JoBeth Williams, Ellen Barkin, Allen Garfield, Annabeth Gish. **1986**

DESERT FOX, THE ★★★★ A tour-de-force performance by James Mason marks this film biography of German Field Marshal Rommel. His military exploits are glossed over in favor of the human story of the disillusionment and eventual involvement in the plot to assassinate Hitler. B&W; 88m. **DIR:** Henry Hathaway. **CAST:** James Mason, Jessica Tandy, Cedric Hardwicke, Luther Adler, Desmond Young. **1951**

DESERT HEARTS ★★★1/2 A sensitive portrayal of the evolving relationship between a young, openly lesbian woman and a quiet university professor ten years her senior in 1959. Patricia Charbonneau and Helen Shaver superbly set off the development of their individual and joint characters. Some may find the explicit love scenes upsetting, but the humor and characterization entirely overrule any objection, and the bonus of 1950s props and sets is a treat. Rated R for profanity and sex. 90m. **DIR:** Donna Deitch. **CAST:** Helen Shaver, Patricia Charbonneau, Audra Lindley, Gwen Welles, Dean Butler. **1986 DVD**

DESERT HEAT ★★ The kind of heat that usually causes an uncomfortable rash. Totally predictable revenge fantasy stars Jean-Claude Van Damme as a loner willing to call it a day when he is attacked by a biker gang. He finds a new reason for living when he vows to get even. This direct-to-video effort is tired and full of clichés. Rated R for violence and language. 95m. **DIR:** John G. Avildsen. **CAST:** Jean-Claude Van Damme, Noriyuki "Pat" Morita, Danny Trejo, Larry Drake. **1999 DVD**

DESERT KICKBOXER ★★ More kick-boxing action, with John Haymes Newton as a border guard who takes on a ruthless drug dealer and his drug empire. You've seen it all before. Rated R for violence. 86m. **DIR:** Isaac Florentine. **CAST:** John Haymes Newton, Paul Smith, Judie Aronson. **1992**

DESERT PHANTOM ★★★ Tenderfoot sharpshooter drumming up business for an ammunition firm turns out to be a tough hombre looking for the man who murdered his sister and her husband. In between throwing lead and punches he helps a girl save her ranch and unmasks the "phantom" who's been murdering cowhands to keep them off the trail of a rich mine. Rich characterizations, lots of action, and good pacing make this independent oater a winner. B&W; 65m. **DIR:** S. Roy Luby. **CAST:** Johnny Mack Brown, Sheila Manners, Ted Adams, Karl Hackett, Hal Price, Charles King. **1936**

DESERT RATS, THE ★★★★ Very good World War II drama focuses on the British North African campaign against the German forces, led by Field Marshal Rommel. Richard Burton heads a small, outnumbered unit charged with holding a strategic hill while facing the enemy onslaught. Tough, realistic. B&W; 88m. **DIR:** Robert Wise. **CAST:** Richard Burton, Robert Newton, James Mason, Chips Rafferty. **1953**

DESERT SONG, THE ★★★★ This version of Sigmund Romberg's popular romance has colorful settings in the desert and the charming voices of Kathryn Grayson and Gordon MacRae. It's also highly enjoyable with glorious music. 110m. **DIR:** H. Bruce Humberstone. **CAST:** Kathryn Grayson, Gordon MacRae, William Conrad, Raymond Massey. **1953**

DESERTER, THE 🦃 Arid, interminable spaghetti Western (a U.S.-Italian-Yugoslavian coproduction) with an absolute stiff for a leading man, and a bewildered supporting cast. Rated PG. 99m. **DIR:** Burt Kennedy. **CAST:** Bekim Fehmiu, John Huston, Richard Crenna, Chuck

Connors, Ricardo Montalban, Woody Strode, Slim Pickens, Ian Bannen, Brandon de Wilde, Patrick Wayne. **1971**

DESIGNATED MOURNER, THE ★★★★ Despite its static setting, Wallace Shawn's exquisite play comes alive in director David Hare's hands. Mike Nichols gives a rare, impressive performance as a man who testifies against an unnamed country's totalitarian regime. His ex-wife and her father have been detained there because their intellect frightens their suppressors. Although the action is limited, this gripping film works because the talent involved delivers the goods with total conviction. Rated R for language. 95m. **DIR:** David Hare. **CAST:** Mike Nichols, Miranda Richardson, David de Keyser. **1997 DVD**

DESIGNING WOMAN ★★★1/2 Diverting comedy with sportswriter Gregory Peck and successful dress designer Lauren Bacall marrying after a whirlwind romance. Mickey Shaughnessy, as Peck's bodyguard, steals the show. 118m. **DIR:** Vincente Minnelli. **CAST:** Gregory Peck, Lauren Bacall, Sam Levene, Dolores Gray, Mickey Shaughnessy, Chuck Connors. **1957 DVD**

DESIRE ★★ Dull story about a common Scottish fisherman and a globe-trotting feminist. They fell in love when they were young, and whenever they meet again, their love is always rekindled. Not rated; contains profanity and simulated sex. 108m. **DIR:** Andrew Birkin. **CAST:** Greta Scacchi, Vincent D'Onofrio, Anais Jeanneret, Hanns Zischler, Barbara Jones. **1993**

DESIRE AND HELL AT SUNSET MOTEL ★★★ When hot and sultry Sherilyn Fenn checks into the Sunset Motel with her husband, Whip Hubley, they get more room service than they bargained for. She wants her husband, who thinks she's fooling around, dead, and her lover, David Johansen, is willing to oblige. Director Alien Castle's film debut is a handsome, lush stab at *film noir*. Rated PG-13 for profanity and violence. 87m. **DIR:** Allen Castle. **CAST:** Sherilyn Fenn, Whip Hubley, David Hewlett, David Johansen, Paul Bartel. **1990**

DESIRE UNDER THE ELMS ★★ A hard-hearted New England farmer (Burl Ives) brings home an immigrant bride (Sophia Loren), who promptly falls into the arms of his weakling son (Anthony Perkins). Eugene O'Neill's play was already ponderously dated by the time it was filmed, and Loren (whose command of English was still shaky) is miscast. B&W; 114m. **DIR:** Delbert Mann. **CAST:** Burl Ives, Sophia Loren, Anthony Perkins, Frank Overton, Pernell Roberts, Anne Seymour. **1958**

DESIRÉE ★★ A romantic tale of Napoleon's love for 17 year old seamstress Desirée Clary. Marlon Brando bumbles about as Napoleon in this tepid travesty of history. 110m. **DIR:** Henry Koster. **CAST:** Marlon Brando, Jean Simmons, Merle Oberon, Michael Rennie, Cameron Mitchell, Isobel Elsom, John Hoyt, Cathleen Nesbitt. **1954**

DESK SET ★★★1/2 Robert Fryer and Lawrence Carr's Broadway play benefits from the chemistry between Tracy and Hepburn. This isn't their best movie, but it's still fun to watch. Hepburn bucks Tracy's attempts to rework the research department of a TV network. Joan Blondell steals her every scene as a wisecracking coworker. 103m. **DIR:** Walter Lang. **CAST:** Spencer Tracy, Katharine Hepburn, Joan Blondell, Dina Merrill, Neva Patterson. **1957**

DESOLATION ANGELS ★★1/2 Male egos take it on the chin in this low-budget, partly improvised film whose credits include thanks to "the makers of Prozac." Writer-director Tim McCann is good with both his actors and his camera, but the characters in this story of sexual violence are too clichéd to have any real impact. Rated R for violence, profanity, and sexual situations. 94m. **DIR:** Tim McCann. **CAST:** Michael Rodrick, Jennifer Thomas, Peter Bassett. **1995 DVD**

DESPAIR ★★★★ Karlovich (Dirk Bogarde), a Russian living in Germany in 1930, runs an unsuccessful chocolate factory. The stock market crash in America pushes his business into even deeper trouble, and he begins to lose touch with himself in a major way. Black comedy at its blackest. Rated R. 119m. **DIR:** Rainer Werner Fassbinder. **CAST:** Dirk Bogarde, Klaus Lowitsch. **1979**

DESPERADO ★★ A traveling Mexican musician uses an arsenal of weapons stashed in his guitar case to avenge the death of his lover. This sequel to *El Mariachi* is bigger, bolder, bloodier, steamier, and more cartoonish than the original, but its endless waves of balletic shoot-outs soon become tiring. Rated R for violence, nudity, sex, and language. 106m. **DIR:** Robert Rodriguez. **CAST:** Antonio Banderas, Steve Buscemi, Salma Hayek, Richard "Cheech" Marin, Joaquim de Almeida, Quentin Tarantino. **1995 DVD**

DESPERADOS, THE ★★ After the Civil War, a paranoid parson heads a gang of cutthroats and outlaws, including his three sons, in a violent crime spree. Roughly made (in Spain) and quite savage. Rated PG. 90m. **DIR:** Henry Levin. **CAST:** Vince Edwards, Jack Palance, Neville Brand, George Maharis, Sylvia Syms, Christian Roberts. **1969**

DESPERATE ★★★ Tidy little chase film finds Steve Brodie and his wife Audrey Long on the lam from the law and a gang of thieves after he witnesses a warehouse robbery that results in the death of a police officer. The story is anything but new, yet director Anthony Mann breathes some life into it and keeps the level of suspense up. B&W; 73m. **DIR:** Anthony Mann. **CAST:** Steve Brodie, Audrey Long, Raymond Burr, Douglas Fowley. **1947**

DESPERATE HOURS, THE (1955) ★★★★ Three escaped convicts terrorize a suburban Indiana family; based on Joseph Hayes's novel and play. Humphrey Bogart is too old for the part that made a star of Paul Newman on Broadway, but the similarity to the *The Petrified Forest* must have been too good to pass up. Fredric March takes top acting honors. Not rated. B&W; 112m. **DIR:** William Wyler. **CAST:** Humphrey Bogart, Fredric March, Arthur Kennedy, Martha Scott, Gig Young. **1955**

DESPERATE HOURS (1990) ★★1/2 Desperate remake of William Wyler's 1955 suspense classic, with Mickey Rourke taking over the Humphrey Bogart role. Rourke's pointless posturing and director Michael Cimino's tendency toward overkill make it more campy than chilling. Rated R for violence and profanity. 106m. **DIR:** Michael Cimino. **CAST:** Mickey Rourke, Anthony Hopkins, Mimi Rogers, Lindsay Crouse, Kelly Lynch, Elias Koteas, David Morse, Shawnee Smith. **1990 DVD**

DESPERATE JOURNEY ★★1/2 Average WWII propaganda film follows the exploits of an RAF bomber crew that is shot down while on a special mission over Poland. They escape and begin a treacherous and sometimes humorous journey across Germany, trying to return to England. B&W; 106m. **DIR:** Raoul Walsh. **CAST:** Errol Flynn, Ronald Reagan, Alan Hale Sr., Arthur Kennedy, Raymond Massey. **1942**

DESPERATE LIVING ★★ A "monstrous fairy tale," director John Waters calls it. This story is about a murderess (played by Mink Stole) and her escapades through a village of criminals who are ruled by a demented queen (Edith Massey). But various scenes provide enough humor and wit for anyone with a taste for the perverse and a yen for some good old-fashioned misanthropy. Not rated, but the equivalent of an X, due to violence, nudity, and unbridled gore. 95m. **DIR:** John Waters. **CAST:** Mink Stole, Edith Massey, Jean Hill, Liz Renay, Susan Lowe. **1977**

DESPERATE MEASURES ★★ This so-called thriller concerns a cop, trying to save his son's life, who must deal with a homicidal sociopath who happens to be the only suitable bone-marrow donor in the entire civilized world. Yeah, right. Rated R for profanity and violence. 100m. **DIR:** Barbet Schroeder. **CAST:** Andy Garcia, Michael Keaton, Brian Cox, Marcia Gay Harden, Erik King. **1998 DVD**

DESPERATE MOTIVE ★★★1/2 Creepy David Keith moves into his long-lost cousin's home with hopes of moving into his life. Chilling because it seems so plausible, although successful adman William Katt is a little too trusting. Keith's economic and intent performance foils Marg Helgenberger's edgy destructiveness. Rated R for violence and profanity. 92m. **DIR:** Andrew Lane. **CAST:** David Keith, Marg Helgenberger, Mel Harris, William Katt. **1991**

DESPERATE MOVES ★★★ Steve Tracy plays a young nerd from a small Oregon town traveling to California to pursue his dreams. Touching and amusing, if occasionally silly. Good effort by supporting cast. Not rated, but would probably fall near the PG-13 category. 106m. **DIR:** Oliver Hellman. **CAST:** Steve Tracy, Eddie Deezen, Isabel Sanford, Paul Benedict, Christopher Lee. **1986**

DESPERATE PREY ★★★ After accidentally capturing the murder of a prominent lawyer on videotape, a woman becomes the target of a brutal killer. Rated R for violence and nudity. 102m. **DIR:** Danny Vendramini. **CAST:** Claudia Karvan, Catherine McClements, Alexannder Petersons. **1992**

DESPERATE REMEDIES ★★ Utterly bizarre film loaded with outrageous costumes, lush imagery, surreal sets, and twisted performances. A pair of women work together to save the crumbling life of a third—at any cost. Rated R for nudity and sexuality. 92m. **DIR:** Stewart Main, Peter Wells. **CAST:** Jennifer Ward-Lealand, Kevin Smith, Lisa Chappell, Clifford Curtis, Michael Hurst, Kiri Mills. **1994**

DESPERATE TRAIL ★★★1/2 In this offbeat, intense Western, revenge-minded marshal Sam Elliott relentlessly tracks down daughter-in-law Linda Fiorentino, whom he blames for the death of his son. She falls in with a con man, which leads to some comic misadventures and even love, but this Old West Bonnie and Clyde are forced to continually look over their shoulders, often seeing what they fear most. Made for TV. 96m. **DIR:** P. J. Pesce. **CAST:** Sam Elliott, Craig Sheffer, Linda Fiorentino, Frank Whaley. **1995**

DESPERATE WOMEN ★★ Three convicted women crossing a desert on their way to prison meet up with an ol' softy (Dan Haggerty) who takes them under his wing. 98m. **DIR:** Earl Bellamy. **CAST:** Dan Haggerty, Susan Saint James, Ronee Blakley, Ann Dusenberry. **1978**

DESPERATELY SEEKING SUSAN ★★★★1/2 A delightfully daffy, smart, and intriguing comedy made from a feminine perspective. Rosanna Arquette stars as a bored housewife who adds spice to her life by following the personal column love adventures of the mysterious Susan (Madonna). One day, our heroine decides to catch a glimpse of her idol and, through a set of unlikely but easy-to-take plot convolutions, ends up switching places with her. Rated PG-13 for violence. 104m. **DIR:** Susan Seidelman. **CAST:** Rosanna Arquette, Madonna, Robert Joy, Mark Blum, Laurie Metcalf, Aidan Quinn. **1985 DVD**

DESTINATION MOON ★★★1/2 Story involves the first American spaceship to land on the moon. Even though the sets are dated today, they were what scientists expected to find when people did land on the moon. This film boasts the classic pointed spaceship and bubble helmets on the space travelers, but it is still great fun for fans of the genre. Rated PG-13. 99m. **DIR:** Irving Pichel. **CAST:** Warner Anderson, John Archer, Tom Powers, Dick Wesson. **1950 DVD**

DESTINATION TOKYO ★★★★ Superior World War II adventure focuses on a submarine crew as they attempt to penetrate Tokyo Bay and destroy Japanese vessels. Cary Grant's fine performance as the commander is complemented by a crackling script and assured direction by Delmer Daves. B&W; 135m. **DIR:** Delmer Daves. **CAST:** Cary Grant, John Garfield, Alan Hale Sr., Dane Clark, Warner Anderson. **1943**

DESTINY ★★★1/2 Fritz Lang's first important success is a triumph of style that delves into the nature of love. Consisting of interlocking stories, dream sequences, and nightmarish associations, Lang's fable tells the story of a young woman who challenges Death for the life of her lover but cannot bring herself to offer the sacrifices the grim one demands. Silent. B&W; 114m. **DIR:** Fritz Lang. **CAST:** Lil Dagover, Walter Janssen, Bernhard Goetzke, Rudolf Klein-Rogge. **1921 DVD**

DESTINY TO ORDER ★★1/2 A writer's creations come to life to haunt him in this strange love story. A bit disjointed, this is nonetheless a fun film. Not rated; contains violence and profanity. 93m. **DIR:** Jim Purdy. **CAST:** Stephen Quimette, Alberta Watson, Michael Ironside. **1990**

DESTINY TURNS ON THE RADIO ★★1/2 Quentin Tarantino portrays a godlike creature playing with the fates of Las Vegas losers in this arch, rather precious comedy. Rated R for profanity. 102m. **DIR:** Jack Baran. **CAST:** James LeGros, Dylan McDermott, Nancy Travis, Quentin Tarantino, James Belushi. **1995**

DESTRUCTORS, THE ★★ Anthony Quinn plays a narcotics agent who just can't seem to get the goods on a major drug dealer (James Mason). Dated. Not rated. 89m. **DIR:** Robert Parrish. **CAST:** Michael Caine, Anthony Quinn, James Mason. **1974**

DESTRY RIDES AGAIN ★★★★ *Destry*'s plot may seem a trifle clichéd, but it is the classic Western that copycats imitate. The story of a mild-mannered citizen who finds himself grudgingly forced to stand up against the bad guys may seem familiar, especially with Jimmy Stewart in the lead. But this is the original. B&W; 95m. **DIR:** George Marshall. **CAST:** James Stewart, Marlene Dietrich, Brian Donlevy, Mischa Auer, Una Merkel. **1939**

DETECTIVE, THE (1954) ★★★1/2 The versatile Alec Guinness is sublime in this deft film presentation of G. K. Chesterton's priest-detective in action. Here Father Brown seeks out purloined art treasures and the culprits responsible. Joan Greenwood, of the ultrathroaty voice, and the rest of the cast fit like Savile Row tailoring. Intelligent, highly entertaining fare from Britain. B&W; 91m. **DIR:** Robert Hamer. **CAST:** Alec Guinness, Joan Greenwood, Peter Finch, Bernard Lee, Sidney James. **1954**

DETECTIVE, THE (1968) ★★★ A disgusted NYPD detective (Frank Sinatra), railroads the wrong man into the electric chair while seeking a homosexual's killer. He loses his job and leaves his nympho wife (Lee Remick). Filmed on location in New York, this is one of the first hard-look-at-a-cop's-life films. 114m. **DIR:** Gordon Douglas. **CAST:** Frank Sinatra, Lee Remick, Al Freeman Jr., Jacqueline Bisset, Ralph Meeker, Jack Klugman, Robert Duvall, William Windom. **1968**

DETECTIVE SADIE AND SON ★★★ Debbie Reynolds plays a rough-and-ready street cop forced into early retirement by her yuppie boss. She becomes a neighborhood vigilante, and her heroic deeds land her back on the force—training her less-than-dedicated son. A few funny moments are found among the encounters with numerous assailants and muggers. Made for TV, this contains considerable violence. 94m. **DIR:** John Llewellyn Moxey. **CAST:** Debbie Reynolds, Brian McNamara, Sam Wanamaker. **1988**

DETECTIVE SCHOOL DROPOUTS ★★★★ David Landsberg and Lorin Dreyfuss co-star in this hilarious comedy. (The two wrote the screenplay as well.) Landsberg plays Wilson, whose obsession with detective stories loses him a string of jobs. Finally, he goes to P.I. Miller (Dreyfuss) for lessons in investigation. The two accidentally become involved in an intrigue with star-crossed lovers. Rated PG for obscenities. 92m. **DIR:** Filippo Ottoni. **CAST:** David Landsberg, Lorin Dreyfuss, Christian De Sica, Valeria Golino, George Eastman. **1985**

DETERRENCE ★★★★ In the near future, the president and a handful of his advisers try to avert a nuclear confrontation with Iraq while stranded at a diner in the Colorado mountains. The claustrophobic setting works to the advantage of this tense, well-acted nuclear thriller, reminiscent of such cold war thrillers as *Fail-Safe*. Rated R for profanity and violence. 101m. **DIR:** Rod Lurie. **CAST:** Kevin Pollak, Timothy Hutton, Sean Astin, Sheryl Lee Ralph, Badja Djola. **1999 DVD**

DETONATOR II: NIGHT WATCH ★★ Pierce Brosnan reprises his international action hero in this, his last role before becoming James Bond. A team of experts goes toe-to-toe with international terrorists. Passable entertainment with Brosnan playing a much grittier hero. Rated R for violence and profanity. 99m. **DIR:** David S. Jackson. **CAST:** Pierce Brosnan, Alexandra Paul, William Devane. **1995**

DETOUR (1945) ★★★ Routine story about a drifter enticed into crime is skillfully constructed, economically produced, and competently acted; it has long been considered one of the best (if not *the* best) low-budget films ever made. Ann Savage as the beguiling, destructive enchantress playing off Tom Neal's infatuation rings just as true in this bargain-basement production as it does in the highly acclaimed adult crime-dramas produced by the major studios. B&W; 69m. **DIR:** Edgar G. Ulmer. **CAST:** Tom Neal, Ann Savage, Claudia Drake, Tim Ryan. **1945 DVD**

DETOUR (1999) ★★★ After a failed attempt to rip off a fortune in mob drug money, Jeff Fahey hopes to lay low in his boyhood small-town home—until the vengeful gangsters track him down. Made to order for action fans, this is a bit livelier than the usual made-for-video product. Rated R for profanity, violence, and nudity. 93m. **DIR:** Joey Travolta. **CAST:** Jeff Fahey, Gary Busey, Michael Madsen, James Russo, Tim Thomerson. **1999**

DETROIT 9000 (DETROIT HEAT) ★★1/2 Two Detroit cops, one black and one white, look for the vicious hoods who robbed a political rally. Tamer than usual blaxploitation thriller. Rated R for violence, profanity, and brief nudity. 106m. **DIR:** Arthur Marks. **CAST:** Alex Rocco, Hari Rhodes, Vonetta McGee, Scatman Crothers. **1973 DVD**

DETROIT ROCK CITY ★★ Four Cleveland "stoners" set out on an odyssey to see the heavy metal band Kiss in Detroit. Everything that can go wrong does, but between fights and muggings the guys manage to find romance. Focusing on sex, drugs, and rock 'n' roll, this R-rated film is meant to exclude viewers under 17. Unfortunately, few over 17 would want to see it. Rated R for drug use, sex, violence, and profanity. 98m. **DIR:** Adam Rifkin. **CAST:** Edward Furlong, Giuseppe Andrews, James DeBello, Sam Huntington. **1999 DVD**

DEUCE BIGALOW: MALE GIGOLO ★★★ Wacky career-change flick features Rob Schneider as a scruffy fish-tank cleaner who falls into a gig as a gigolo. Each of his "dates" turns out to be bizarre and offbeat and he finds himself boosting their self-esteems rather than their libidos. One-liners play second fiddle to Schneider's hilarious facial reactions throughout the film. Rated R for sexual innuendo, profanity, and violence. 90m. **DIR:** Mike Mitchell. **CAST:** Rob Schneider, Arija Bareikis, William Forsythe, Eddie Griffin, Oded Fehr. **1999 DVD**

DEVI (THE GODDESS) ★★★★ Excellent social satire from India's gifted Satyajit Ray. A deeply religious landowner becomes convinced that his beautiful daughter-in-law is the incarnation of the Hindu goddess Kali, to whom he becomes fanatically devoted. In Bengali with English subtitles. B&W; 96m. **DIR:** Satyajit Ray. **CAST:** Chhabi Biswas, Soumitra Chatterjee. **1960**

DEVIL AND DANIEL WEBSTER, THE ★★★★ This wickedly witty tale, based on a Stephen Vincent Benét story, delivers some potent messages. Edward Arnold, so often cast as a despicable villain, is riveting as the noble Webster. This eloquent hero must defend ingenuous James Craig in a bizarre courtroom. Both of their immortal souls are at stake. Opposing Webster is Mr.

Scratch, also known as the Devil. Walter Huston gives a dazzling performance in the role. B&W; 85m. **DIR:** William Dieterle. **CAST:** Edward Arnold, Walter Huston, James Craig, Anne Shirley, Jane Darwell, Simone Simon, Gene Lockhart. **1941**

DEVIL AND MAX DEVLIN, THE ★★ This is visible proof that it takes more than just a few talented people to create quality entertainment. Despite Elliott Gould, Bill Cosby, and Susan Anspach, this Disney production—another takeoff on the Faustian theme of a pact made with the devil—offers little more than mediocre fare. It's basically a waste of fine talent. Rated PG. 96m. **DIR:** Steven H. Stern. **CAST:** Elliott Gould, Bill Cosby, Susan Anspach, Adam Rich. **1981 DVD**

DEVIL AND MISS JONES, THE ★★★★ One of those wonderful comedies Hollywood used to make. Witty, sophisticated, poignant, and breezy, this one has millionaire Charles Coburn going undercover as a clerk in his own department store in order to probe employee complaints and unrest. Delightful doings. B&W; 92m. **DIR:** Sam Wood. **CAST:** Jean Arthur, Robert Cummings, Charles Coburn, Spring Byington, S. Z. Sakall, William Demarest. **1941**

DEVIL AT 4 O'CLOCK, THE ★★★ This script may be weak and predictable, but the acting of Spencer Tracy and Frank Sinatra make this a watchable motion picture. Tracy is a priest who is in charge of an orphanage. When their island home is endangered by an impending volcanic eruption, he seeks the aid of a group of convicts headed by Sinatra. 126m. **DIR:** Mervyn LeRoy. **CAST:** Spencer Tracy, Frank Sinatra, Kerwin Mathews, Jean-Pierre Aumont. **1961**

DEVIL BAT, THE ★★ Pretty fair thriller from PRC gives us Bela Lugosi as yet another bloodthirsty mad scientist who trains oversize rubber bats to suck blood from selected victims by use of a scent. B&W; 69m. **DIR:** Jean Yarbrough. **CAST:** Bela Lugosi, Suzanne Kaaren, Dave O'Brien, Guy Usher. **1941 DVD**

DEVIL BAT'S DAUGHTER ★★ Unimaginative sequel to *Devil Bat* finds heroine Rosemary La Planche fearing for her sanity as her father spends more and more of his time experimenting with those darn bats.... Low-budget bore. B&W; 66m. **DIR:** Frank Wisbar. **CAST:** Rosemary La Planche, Michael Hale, Molly Lamont. **1946 DVD**

DEVIL COMMANDS, THE ★★★ Good entry in Boris Karloff's mad-doctor series for Columbia Pictures has the star attempting to communicate with his dead wife by using brain waves and corpses. Karloff's performance is the main asset here, although director Edward Dmytryk deserves credit for creating a strong atmosphere of forboding and moving the story along at a good clip. B&W; 65m. **DIR:** Edward Dmytryk. **CAST:** Boris Karloff, Amanda Duff, Richard Fiske, Anne Revere, Ralph Penny. **1941**

DEVIL DOG: THE HOUND OF HELL 🦃 Made-for-television movie is even more ridiculous than the title implies. 95m. **DIR:** Curtis Harrington. **CAST:** Richard Crenna, Yvette Mimieux, Victor Jory, Ken Kercheval, Nick Esposito. **1976**

DEVIL DOGS OF THE AIR ★★★ James Cagney is a hotshot barnstormer who joins the Marine Air Corps and refuses to conform to tradition and the authority of Pat O'Brien. Familiar roles for the stars but they play them so well. Great aerial stunt work is a plus. B&W; 86m. **DIR:** Lloyd Bacon. **CAST:** James Cagney, Pat O'Brien, Margaret Lindsay, Frank McHugh, Russell Hicks, Ward Bond. **1935**

DEVIL DOLL, THE (1936) ★★★1/2 Imaginative fantasy-thriller pits crazed Lionel Barrymore and his tiny "devil dolls" against those who have done him wrong. Although not as original an idea now as it was then, the acting, special effects, and director Tod Browning's odd sense of humor make this worth seeing. B&W; 79m. **DIR:** Tod Browning. **CAST:** Lionel Barrymore, Maureen O'Sullivan, Frank Lawton, Henry B. Walthall. **1936**

DEVIL DOLL (1964) ★★ Isn't it amazing how many horror movies have been made with the same story of a ventriloquist's dummy occupied by a human soul? This low-key British version has some creepy moments as Hugo the dummy stalks his victims with a knife, but lackadaisical direction holds the movie back. B&W; 80m. **DIR:** Lindsay Shonteff. **CAST:** Bryant Halliday, William Sylvester, Yvonne Romain. **1964 DVD**

DEVIL GIRL FROM MARS 🦃 Messenger (the Devil Girl) sent from her native planet to kidnap Earth men for reproductive purposes. B&W; 76m. **DIR:** David MacDonald. **CAST:** Patricia Laffan, Hazel Court, Hugh McDermott. **1955 DVD**

DEVIL HORSE, THE ★★★ One of the best Mascot serials and a real audience favorite, this top-notch adventure features Harry Carey as a man tracking his brother's killer, evil Noah Beery. Codirector Richard Talmadge was one of the most famous and popular of silent stuntmen, and his apt hand as well as a fine cast, good photography, and exciting stunts make this a memorable serial. B&W; 12 chapters. **DIR:** Otto Brower, Richard Talmadge. **CAST:** Harry Carey, Noah Beery Sr., Frankie Darro, Greta Granstedt, Barrie O'Daniels, Yakima Canutt, Lane Chandler. **1932**

DEVIL HUNTER YOHKO ★★ Japanese animation. Imagine schoolgirl Yohko's surprise when she finds out that she is the next in a long line of Devil Hunters. This one is definitely not for children. In Japanese with English subtitles. Not rated; contains violence and nudity. 45m. **DIR:** Tetsuro Aoki. **1990**

DEVIL IN A BLUE DRESS ★★★★ This old-fashioned murder mystery is about an ex-G.I., Easy Rawlins, who finds himself forced out of a job in the aircraft industry in post-WWII Los Angeles. In order to make his house payments, Easy agrees to find the missing mistress of a mayoral candidate, thus embarking on his first case as a private eye. Based on the popular detective series by Walter Mosley, this film gives a rare glimpse of the African American culture of the time against a superb, jump-blues soundtrack. Rated R for violence, profanity, nudity, and simulated sex. 102m. **DIR:** Carl Franklin. **CAST:** Denzel Washington, Tom Sizemore, Jennifer Beals, Don Cheadle, Maury Chaykin, Terry Kinney. **1995 DVD**

DEVIL IN THE FLESH (1946) ★★★1/2 Story of an adulterous love affair between a young man and the wife of a soldier during World War I is moving and tragic. The mutual attraction of the two turns to passion after the girl's husband leaves for the front, and the growing guilt that they feel turns their love into torment. French with English subtitles. B&W; 110m. **DIR:** Claude Autant-Lara. **CAST:** Micheline Presle, Gérard Philipe, Denise Grey. **1946**

DEVIL IN THE FLESH (1998) ★★ You can always count on video to keep the sex thriller genre alive. This one stars Rose McGowan as the new girl in school who makes the life of a caring male teacher a living nightmare. Rated R for language, violence, nudity, and adult situations. 92m. **DIR:** Steve Cohen. **CAST:** Rose McGowan, Alex McArthur, Sherrie Rose. **1998**

DEVIL IN THE HOUSE OF EXORCISM, THE ★★ Originally titled *House of Exorcism*. Not as crummy as everybody says it is, but no Oscar candidate, either. Producer Alfred Leone took some footage from *Lisa and the Devil* and footage shot by Mario Bava, added some scenes shot by himself, and cobbled together this noisy *Exorcist* rip-off. Bava hides behind the pseudonym Mickey Lion. Rated R. 93m. **DIR:** Mario Bava. **CAST:** Elke Sommer, Robert Alda, Telly Savalas. **1975**

DEVIL, PROBABLY, THE ★★★ If you've never seen a film by French director Robert Bresson, this isn't the one to start with. A young Frenchman is unable to find any meaning in life, and his friends try to persuade him that life is worth living. Bresson's stark staging and unblinking camera enhance the gloom in a film that will seem merely pessimistic to those not on his wavelength. Not rated; contains nudity and adult situations. In French with English subtitles. 95m. **DIR:** Robert Bresson. **CAST:** Antoine Monnier, Tina Irissari. **1977**

DEVIL RIDES OUT, THE ★★★1/2 Adapted from Dennis Wheatley's witchcraft novel, this is one of the finest films to come out of Britain's Hammer Films. The direction by Terence Fisher is top-notch and the scenes of mounting terror are still effective today. 95m. **DIR:** Terence Fisher. **CAST:** Christopher Lee, Charles Gray. **1967 DVD**

DEVIL THUMBS A RIDE, THE ★★★1/2 After murdering an innocent citizen during a robbery, a cold-blooded killer hitches a ride with a tipsy, unsuspecting salesman, picks up two female riders, and continues his murderous path. Nifty *noir*. B&W; 62m. **DIR:** Felix Feist. **CAST:** Lawrence Tierney, Ted North, Nan Leslie. **1947**

DEVIL WITHIN HER, THE 🦃 Hilariously bad at times, plodding the rest. Rated R for violence, nudity, and profanity. 90m. **DIR:** Peter Sasdy. **CAST:** Joan Collins, Donald Pleasence, Eileen Atkins, Ralph Bates, Caroline Munro, John Steiner. **1975**

DEVILFISH ★★1/2 That's actually Lamberto Bava hiding behind the director credit and what we have here is actually a *Jaws* rip-off hiding in plain sight. The film concerns a government-created monster shark terrorizing Florida. The script has many layers to it, but poor acting and a woefully bad creature sink this film. Not rated; contains violence, gore, simulated sex, and profanity. 92m. **DIR:** John Old Jr. **CAST:** Michael Sopkiw, Valentine Monnier. **1984**

DEVILMAN VOL. 1–2 ★★ Vaguely reminiscent of the works of H. P. Lovecraft, this animated film has only a few points of interest. In order to defend the world from an impending demon invasion, two young men gain supernatural powers by becoming demons themselves. In Japanese with English subtitles. Not rated; contains violence and nudity. 55m. **DIR:** Tstutomu Iida. **1987–1990 DVD**

DEVILS, THE ★★★★ Next to *Women in Love*, this is director Ken Russell's best film. Exploring witchcraft and politics in France during the seventeenth century, it's a mad mixture of drama, horror, camp, and comedy. Ugly for the most part (with several truly unsettling scenes), it is still fascinating. Rated R. 109m. **DIR:** Ken Russell. **CAST:** Oliver Reed, Vanessa Redgrave, Dudley Sutton, Max Adrian, Gemma Jones. **1971**

DEVIL'S ADVOCATE ★★★1/2 Al Pacino dominates this intriguing fantasy, as the charismatic head of a New York City law firm that woos cocky Florida defense attorney Keanu Reeves and his sexpot wife. Our young hero has never lost a case, a talent not lost on his new mentor, whose hypnotic appeal speaks of greater-than-average powers . . . and, indeed, as the title suggests, this particular firm is controlled by Satan himself. Although the script plays somewhat fast and loose with actual biblical content, Pacino's portrayal of Pure Evil is a thrill ride unto itself. Rated R for violence, profanity, nudity, simulated sex, and perverse sexual content. 138m. **DIR:** Taylor Hackford. **CAST:** Keanu Reeves, Al Pacino, Charlize Theron, Jeffrey Jones, Judith Ivey, Craig T. Nelson. **1997 DVD**

DEVIL'S ARITHMETIC, THE ★★★1/2 Self-absorbed modern teen Kirsten Dunst gets a painful lesson in her own Jewish heritage, when she opens the door for Elijah during a Passover celebration and finds herself inexplicably catapulted back in time, into the body of a relative who survived incarceration in a WWII Nazi death camp. Robert J. Avrech's script, adapted from Jane Yolen's novel, is honorable, even though this film clearly is intended as a family experience, and thus mutes the story's worst atrocities. Although tough going at times, this one should be watched by all; the lessons here must never be forgotten . . . as Dunst's character learns. Rated PG-13 for violence, brief nudity, and dramatic intensity. 95m. **DIR:** Donna Deitch. **CAST:** Kirsten Dunst, Brittany Murphy, Paul Freeman, Mimi Rogers, Louise Fletcher. **1999**

•DEVIL'S BACKBONE, THE ★★★1/2 At a remote, all-but-abandoned orphanage during the Spanish Civil War, a boy encounters strange happenings and runs afoul of a sullen caretaker. The eerie, moody ghost story begins slowly but grows more involving as it goes along, and the atmosphere of foreboding and dread is hard to shake. In Spanish with English subtitles. Rated R for violence. 106m. **DIR:** Guillermo del Toro. **CAST:** Eduardo Noriega, Marisa Paredes, Federico Luppi, Iñigo Garcés. **2001**

DEVIL'S BRIGADE, THE ★★1/2 During World War II, a disciplined Canadian troop is sent to Utah to train with a ragtag gang of American army misfits for a planned joint operation. Not rated, but has graphic battle scenes. 130m. **DIR:** Andrew V. McLaglen. **CAST:** William Holden, Cliff Robertson, Vince Edwards, Michael Rennie, Dana Andrews, Claude Akins, Carroll O'Connor, Richard Jaeckel. **1968 DVD**

DEVIL'S BROTHER, THE ★★★1/2 Opera star Dennis King makes a formidable lead, and Laurel and Hardy make hearty helpers with his romantic problems with Thelma Todd. Auber's operetta gets glowing treatment with its musical numbers produced with big budgets and lots of pizazz. The original title was *Fra Diavolo*, and it confused audiences on first release, so it was anglicized for a reissue and became an instant hit. B&W; 88m. **DIR:** Charles R. Rogers. **CAST:** Stan Laurel, Oliver Hardy, Dennis King, Thelma Todd, James Finlayson, Henry Armetta. **1933**

DEVIL'S CANYON ★★ Essentially a prison-break movie dressed up in cowboy clothes. Lawman Dale Robertson is railroaded into the Arizona State Pen at the turn of the century after killing two men in self-defense. Static, claustrophobic, set-bound—originally made in 3-D. 92m. **DIR:** Alfred Werker. **CAST:** Dale Robertson, Virginia Mayo, Stephen McNally, Arthur Hunnicutt. **1953**

DEVIL'S COMMANDMENT, THE ★★★ Serious horror fans should make an effort to find this movie, which marked the beginning of the revival of the gothic horror film in Europe. Another version of the story of Countess Bathory, who tried to salvage her youth with the blood of young women, the film was sliced up by both its Italian and American distributors. The distinctive visual sense of director Riccardo Freda (assisted by cinematographer Mario Bava) is still compelling. Dubbed in English. B&W; 71m. **DIR:** Riccardo Freda. **CAST:** Gianna Maria Canale, Antoine Balpetre, Paul Muller. **1956**

DEVIL'S DISCIPLE, THE ★★★1/2 An amusing romp through the American Revolution, by way of George Bernard Shaw. The movie follows a straitlaced pastor (Burt Lancaster) and an engaging rogue (Kirk Douglas), who suspend their differences long enough to outwit a British garrison. B&W; 82m. **DIR:** Guy Hamilton. **CAST:** Burt Lancaster, Kirk Douglas, Laurence Olivier, Janette Scott, Eva LeGallienne, Harry Andrews, George Rose. **1959**

DEVIL'S EYE, THE ★★ Disappointing comedy. In order to cure the sty in his eye, the devil sends Don Juan (Jarl Kulle) from hell to breach a woman's chastity. Bibi Andersson plays Britt-Marie, the pastor's virgin daughter. 90m. **DIR:** Ingmar Bergman. **CAST:** Jarl Kulle, Bibi Andersson, Gunnar Björnstrand. **1960**

DEVIL'S MESSENGER, THE ★★ A film of note for its curio value only. Lon Chaney plays the devil (in a dark, short-sleeved sport shirt!), who takes pity on a young suicide victim and sends her back to Earth to lure sinners to their doom. An uncredited Curt Siodmak (*Donovan's Brain*) worked on the script. B&W; 72m. **DIR:** Herbert L. Strock. **CAST:** Lon Chaney Jr., Karen Kadler, John Crawford. **1961**

DEVIL'S OWN, THE ★★★1/2 Undercover IRA soldier Brad Pitt comes to the United States on a mission to secure missiles for the lads back home, and as part of his "deep cover" moves in with salt-of-the-earth Irish cop Harrison Ford and his family . . . who know nothing of their visitor's background. The secret leaks when events go predictably awry. The complex script does a good job of humanizing a character we'd normally dismiss as a monster, and the central metaphor is laced with irony: "Don't look for a happy ending; it's not an American story, it's an Irish one." Rated R for violence and profanity. 110m. **DIR:** Alan J. Pakula. **CAST:** Harrison Ford, Brad Pitt, Margaret Colin, Rubén Blades, Treat Williams. **1997 DVD**

•DEVIL'S PREY ★★ Timely but tiresome thriller about a group of friends who find out too late that the rave party they're so anxious to attend is actually a trap set by a cult leader seeking out new victims for their satanic sacrifices. Patrick Bergin makes an appropriately creepy cult leader, but the film doesn't have a prayer when you factor in the overly familiar screenplay that pits one woman against the entire cult, less than convincing action, and pedestrian direction. Horror fans won't find any ecstasy at this rave. Rated R for adult situations, drugs, language, and violence. 91m. **DIR:** Bradford May. **CAST:** Patrick Bergin, Bryan Kirkwood, Charlie O'Connell, Ashley Jones. **2001 DVD**

DEVIL'S RAIN, THE ★★1/2 Great cast in a fair shocker about a band of devil worshipers at large in a small town. Terrific makeup, especially Ernest Borgnine's! Rated PG for language and violence. 85m. **DIR:** Robert Fuest. **CAST:** Ernest Borgnine, Ida Lupino, William Shatner, Eddie Albert, Tom Skerritt, Keenan Wynn, John Travolta. **1975 DVD**

DEVIL'S UNDEAD, THE ★★★1/2 A surprisingly entertaining and suspenseful release starring the two kings of British horror, Christopher Lee and Peter Cushing, as a sort of modern-day Holmes and Watson in a tale of demonic possession. Rated PG. 91m. **DIR:** Peter Sasdy. **CAST:** Christopher Lee, Peter Cushing, Georgia Brown, Diana Dors. **1979**

DEVIL'S WEDDING NIGHT, THE ★★ Say this for the Italians: even when their movies stink, they pack them with exploitable ingredients. Here, it's vampire queen Sara Bay (Rosalba Neri before she Anglicized her name), disrobing at every opportunity just as she did in *Lady Frankenstein*, and seducing knuckleheaded twin brothers, both played by Mark Damon. Rated R. 85m. **DIR:** Paul Solvay. **CAST:** Sara Bay, Mark Damon, Frances Davis. **1973**

DEVLIN ★★★ Dedicated cop Bryan Brown takes quite a pounding in scripter David Taylor's twisty adaptation of Roderick Thorp's book, which finds our hero set up as the prime suspect in a highly visible political slaying. Devlin gradually works his way into a complex scheme involving departmental corruption. Totally preposterous made-for-cable mystery, but entertaining. 110m. **DIR:** Rick Rosenthal. **CAST:** Bryan Brown, Roma Downey, Lloyd Bridges, Lisa Eichhorn, Jan Rubes. **1992**

DEVLIN CONNECTION III, THE ★★ One of the *Devlin Connection* TV episodes entitled "Love, Sex, Sin and Death at Point Dume" features Rock Hudson and Jack Scalia as a father-son duo who try to find a murderer before he kills their friend (Leigh Taylor-Young). Nothing special here, folks. 50m. **DIR:** Christian I. Nyby, II. **CAST:** Rock Hudson, Jack Scalia, Leigh Taylor-Young, Tina Chen. **1982**

DEVONSVILLE TERROR, THE ★★★ Three witches are killed in Devonsville in 1683, and one of them places a curse on the townspeople. Flash forward to the present. This film has good performances, high production values, and a scary script that is not based on special effects. Rated R for nudity, violence, mild gore. 97m. **DIR:** Ulli Lommel. **CAST:** Paul Wilson, Suzanna Love, Donald Pleasence. **1983 DVD**

DEVOTION ★★1/2 Watchable but farfetched tale about a rich young woman who poses as a dowdy nanny in order to get close to the man of her dreams. All goes well until his wife comes between them. B&W; 81m. **DIR:** Robert Milton. **CAST:** Ann Harding, Leslie Howard, O. P. Heggie. **1931 DVD**

DIABOLICALLY YOURS ★★★ How would you like to wake up after an accident to find a beautiful wife and a luxurious mansion that you have no recollection of? Sound great? Unfortunately, it's the start of a nightmare. This French film is unrated, but contains violence. 94m. **DIR:** Julien Duvivier. **CAST:** Alain Delon, Senta Berger. **1967**

DIABOLIQUE (1955) ★★★★ Classic thriller builds slowly but rapidly gathers momentum along the way. Both wife and mistress of a headmaster conspire to kill him. The twisted plot of murder has since been copied many times. In French with English subtitles. B&W; 107m. **DIR:** Henri-Georges Clouzot. **CAST:** Simone Signoret, Vera Clouzot, Charles Vanel, Paul Meurisse. **1955 DVD**

DIABOLIQUE (1996) ★★1/2 Deliver us from remakes that attempt to "improve" on the original! Sharon Stone's delightfully slinky outfits are the only genuine attraction in this updated so-called thriller, which pairs her with Isabelle Adjani as the mistress and wife who decide to murder abusive school headmaster Chazz Palminteri. What was fresh and genuinely frightening in French director Henri-Georges Clouzot's original is old hat here. Rated R for violence, nudity, profanity, and simulated sex. 108m. **DIR:** Jeremiah S. Chechik. **CAST:** Sharon Stone, Isabelle Adjani, Chazz Palminteri, Kathy Bates, Spalding Gray, Allen Garfield. **1996 DVD**

DIAL: HELP ★★1/2 While at times a bit contrived, this film has an ease about it as a young woman gets hooked up with a dead operator and begins to see her friends dying. Rated R for violence and profanity. 96m. **DIR:** Ruggero Deodato. **CAST:** Charlotte Lewis, William Berger. **1989**

DIAL M FOR MURDER (1954) ★★★★ Alfred Hitchcock imbues this classic thriller with his well-known touches of sustained suspense. Ray Milland is a rather sympathetic villain whose desire to inherit his wife's fortune leads him to one conclusion: murder. His plan for pulling off the perfect crime is foiled temporarily. Undaunted, he quickly switches to Plan B, with even more entertaining results. 105m. **DIR:** Alfred Hitchcock. **CAST:** Grace Kelly, Robert Cummings, Ray Milland, John Williams. **1954**

DIAL M FOR MURDER (1981) ★★1/2 This made-for-TV remake of the Alfred Hitchcock film isn't truly awful—if nothing else, it has a good cast going through the familiar paces. But you'd want to see it only if you can't get the original. 100m. **DIR:** Boris Sagal. **CAST:** Christopher Plummer, Angie Dickinson, Anthony Quayle, Ron Moody, Michael Parks. **1981**

DIAMOND FLEECE, THE ★★1/2 An ex-convict who is a master at security systems is hired to protect a $5 million diamond. All the actors, especially Brian Dennehy, do a wonderful job, but the plot lacks depth. Made for cable. 91m. **DIR:** Al Waxman. **CAST:** Ben Cross, Kate Nelligan, Brian Dennehy, Tony Rosato. **1992**

DIAMOND HEAD ★★ Domineering Hawaiian plantation boss Charlton Heston comes close to ruining his family with his dictatorial ways. The lush scenery is the only credible thing in this pineapple opera. 107m. **DIR:** Guy Green. **CAST:** Charlton Heston, Yvette Mimieux, George Chakiris, France Nuyen, James Darren. **1963**

•DIAMOND MEN ★★★★ Veteran Pennsylvania diamond salesman Eddie has a heart attack and introduces brash, younger replacement Bobby to his small-town route in this comic, low-key drama. Bobby may have a genuine heart under all his swagger and leopard-skin undershorts, so Eddie gives him a crash course in sensitivity training as well as salesmanship. In return, Bobby enlists the aid of a brothel madam to get Eddie laid. The reciprocal mentoring bumps up against quiet romance and glamourless crime in an intimate gem about generation gaps, affection versus sex, and the art of persuasion. Not rated. 100m. **DIR:** Daniel Cohen. **CAST:** Robert Forster, Donnie Wahlberg, Bess Armstrong, Jasmine Guy. **2000**

•DIAMOND OF JERU, THE ★★★ A troubled couple journey to Borneo to reignite their love with a search for a rare diamond. There, they find themselves betrayed by nefarious locals and rescued by an American guide. Entertaining, if not rousing, adventure based on the short story by Louis L'Amour. Not rated; contains mild violence. 89m. **DIR:** Dick Lowry, Ian Barry. **CAST:** Billy Zane, Paris Jefferson, Keith Carradine. **2001**

DIAMOND TRAP, THE ★★1/2 A stubborn New York detective follows the trail of a femme fatale. Touches of lighthearted comedy liven this droll made-for-TV film about a $12-million diamond heist. Otherwise, this mystery has little in the way of genuine plot twists. 93m. **DIR:** Don Taylor. **CAST:** Howard Hesseman, Brooke Shields, Ed Marinaro, Darren McGavin. **1992**

DIAMONDBACKS ★★ A lone engineer at a remote NASA outpost battles the members of a right-wing militia. Plot takes a backseat to stunts and pyrotechnics, which are average but plentiful. Not rated; contains violence and profanity. 91m. **DIR:** Barnard Salzman. **CAST:** Miles O'Keeffe, Eb Lottimer, Timothy Bottoms, Chris Mitchum. **1999 DVD**

DIAMONDS ★★★ Well-planned plot and good chemistry between Robert Shaw and Richard Roundtree make this an enjoyable film of action and intrigue. When a British entrepreneur hires an ex-con and his girlfriend to assist him in a $100 million diamond heist the stage is set for an amazing number of plot twists. 108m. **DIR:** Menahem Golan. **CAST:** Robert Shaw, Richard Roundtree, Barbara Hershey, Shelley Winters. **1975 DVD**

DIAMONDS ARE FOREVER ★★★★ This release was supposed to be Sean Connery's last appearance as James Bond before he decided to *Never Say Never Again*. It's good fun for 007 fans and far superior to most of the Roger Moore films that followed it. Rated PG. 119m. **DIR:** Guy Hamilton. **CAST:** Sean Connery, Jill St. John, Charles Gray, Bruce Cabot. **1971 DVD**

DIAMOND'S EDGE ★★★1/2 When his detective older brother is thrown in jail, a young teen takes over his current case. Though it was made for younger viewers, adults will enjoy this private eye spoof's clever homages to classic mystery films. Rated PG. 83m. **DIR:** Stephen Bayly. **CAST:** Dursley McLinden, Colin Dale, Susannah York, Patricia Hodge, Roy Kinnear, Bill Paterson, Jimmy Nail, Saeed Jaffrey. **1988**

DIAMONDS ON WHEELS ★★ Subpar Disney adventure pits a group of teenage auto-racing enthusiasts against a mob of jewel thieves. Strictly formula; even toddlers will realize they've seen it before. Rated G. 87m. **DIR:** Jerome Courtland. **CAST:** Peter Firth, Patrick Allen. **1973**

DIANE ★★ Lana Turner's swan song at MGM, the studio that developed her star power, and Roger Moore's Hollywood debut. She plays the mistress of a sixteenth-century French king, and he plays the king. Lots of court intrigue, pageantry, and aimless talk. 110m. **DIR:** David Miller. **CAST:** Lana Turner, Roger Moore, Marisa Pavan, Henry Daniell, Taina Elg, Cedric Hardwicke, Torin Thatcher, Ian Wolfe, Gene Reynolds. **1956**

DIARY OF A CHAMBERMAID (1946) ★★ Octave Mirbeau's once daring novel had most of its quirky and sensational elements watered down for this Hollywood version directed by Jean Renoir during his American sojourn in the 1940s. Not one of his better American films. B&W; 86m. **DIR:** Jean Renoir. **CAST:** Burgess Meredith, Paulette Goddard. **1946**

DIARY OF A CHAMBERMAID (1964) ★★★★ Excellent remake of Jean Renoir's 1946 film concerns the personal dilemma of a maid (Jeanne Moreau) caught in the grip of fascism in 1939 France. Director Luis Buñuel paints a cynical portrait of the bourgeoisie—a stunning character study. French dialogue with English subtitles. B&W; 95m. **DIR:** Luis Buñuel. **CAST:** Jeanne Moreau, Michel Piccoli, Georges Geret, Daniel Ivernel. **1964 DVD**

DIARY OF A COUNTRY PRIEST ★★★★1/2 The slow pace at the beginning of this tale about a priest trying to minister to his parish might tend to put some viewers off. However, with Bresson's poetic style and camera work, the wait is well worth it. In French with English subtitles. B&W; 120m. **DIR:** Robert Bresson. **CAST:** Claude Laydu, Nicole Ladmiral, Nicole Maurey. **1950**

DIARY OF A HITMAN 🦃 A hired killer struggles with his conscience when asked to perform his last hit on a young wife and her baby. Laughable dialogue, Forest Whitaker's Italian accent, and Sherilyn Fenn's awful acting are just three contributing factors to this mess. Rated R for violence, profanity, and nudity. 90m. **DIR:** Roy London. **CAST:** Forest Whitaker, Sherilyn Fenn, James Belushi, Lois Chiles, Sharon Stone. **1991**

DIARY OF A LOST GIRL ★★★★ In this silent classic, Louise Brooks plays a young girl who is raped by her father's business partner (Fritz Rasp). Banished to a girls' reformatory, she eventually escapes, falling prey to the false sanctuary provided by a whorehouse madame. Those who maintain there is a docility to silent films may be surprised by the relatively mature subject matter in this film. B&W; 99m. **DIR:** G. W. Pabst. **CAST:** Louise Brooks, Joseph Rovensky, Fritz Rasp, André Roanne, Valeska Gert. **1929 DVD**

DIARY OF A MAD HOUSEWIFE ★★★ Most women will detest Jonathan (Richard Benjamin), the self-centered, social climber husband of Tina (Carrie Snodgress). He has had an affair and also lost all their savings in a bad investment. Tina, a college graduate, has been unhappily stuck at home for years with their two children. She finally finds happiness in an affair with George (Frank Langella). Rated R for profanity, sex, and nudity. 94m. **DIR:** Frank Perry. **CAST:** Richard Benjamin, Carrie Snodgress, Frank Langella. **1970**

DIARY OF A MAD OLD MAN ★★★1/2 An old man in failing health is rejuvenated by his growing obsession with his beautiful daughter-in-law. Delicate, tastefully handled film adapted from a Japanese novel. Rated PG-13 for brief nudity. In English. 93m. **DIR:** Lili Rademakers. **CAST:** Ralph Michael, Beatie Edney, Derek de Lint. **1987**

DIARY OF A MADMAN 🦃 Unatmospheric adaptation of Guy de Maupassant's *The Horla*—with Vincent Price as a murderous sculptor. 96m. **DIR:** Reginald LeBorg. **CAST:** Vincent Price, Nancy Kovack, Ian Wolfe. **1963**

DIARY OF A SEDUCER ★★★1/2 Darkly comic tale of a young French female student whose mundane life is brightened when a fellow student lends her a copy of a rare book that has a strange sexual hold over its readers. How the written word drives readers to extremes to fulfill their romantic wishes makes for a funny, offbeat film. In French with English subtitles. Not rated; contains adult situations. 95m. **DIR:** Daniele Dubroux. **CAST:** Chiara Mastroianni, Melvin Poupaud, Jean-Pierre Léaud. **1996**

DIARY OF A SERIAL KILLER ★★★ Gary Busey and Arnold Vosloo dish up delicious performances as a reporter and the serial killer who grants him an exclusive. At first, reporter Busey is enthralled with the offer, but when the body count begins to climb, he decides to cancel the killer. Good take on an interesting premise misses the mark due to clumsy plotting and silly dialogue. Rated R for adult situations, language, and violence. 92m. **DIR:** Joshua Wallace. **CAST:** Gary Busey, Arnold Vosloo, Michael Madsen, Julia Campbell. **1997 DVD**

DIARY OF A TEENAGE HITCHHIKER ★★ Trite dialogue and an inappropriate score lessen the impact of this made-for-TV drama documenting the dangers of hitchhiking for young women. Inferior. 96m. **DIR:** Ted Post. **CAST:** Charlene Tilton, Dick Van Patten, Katherine Helmond, James Carroll Jordan, Katy Kurtzman, Dominique Dunne, Craig T. Nelson. **1979**

DIARY OF ANNE FRANK, THE ★★★★1/2 Excellent adaptation of the Broadway play dealing with the terror Jews felt during the Nazi raids of World War II. Two families are forced to hide in a Jewish sympathizer's attic to avoid capture by the Nazis. Anne (Millie Perkins) is the teenage girl who doesn't stop dreaming of a better future. Shelley Winters won an Oscar for her role as the hysterical Mrs. Van Daan, who shares sparse food and space with the Frank family. B&W; 170m. **DIR:** George Stevens. **CAST:** Millie Perkins, Joseph Schildkraut, Shelley Winters. **1959**

DIARY OF FORBIDDEN DREAMS ★★1/2 A bizarre variation on the classic fantasy *Alice In Wonderland*, this concerns a beautiful young woman (Sydne Rome) who becomes lost in a remote area of the Italian Riviera. The film suffers from too many diversions that create a complete mess. Rated R for nudity and language. 94m. **DIR:** Roman Polanski. **CAST:** Hugh Griffith, Marcello Mastroianni, Sydne Rome. **1981**

DICK ★★★ Spoof of the Watergate break-in features two unlikely teens as the leak to the press. A delightful start, with the girls exuding a charming combination of innocence and joy as Nixon's Secret Youth Advisors and dog walkers, takes rather a nasty turn in the latter half. The dramatic change in the duo hits a low in the final cheesy scene that is unforgettably bad. Rated PG-13 for language, obscene gestures, and drug use. 94m. **DIR:** Andrew Fleming. **CAST:** Kirsten Dunst, Michelle Williams, Dan Hedaya, Will Ferrell. **1999 DVD**

DICK TRACY (1937) ★★★ Chester Gould's comic-strip detective Dick Tracy (Ralph Byrd) chases a mysterious criminal known as *The Spider* who has kidnapped his brother and turned him into a slave. Great stunts and plenty of action in this one. B&W; 15 chapters. **DIR:** Ray Taylor, Alan James. **CAST:** Ralph Byrd, Kay Hughes, Smiley Burnette, Lee Van Atta, Francis X. Bushman. **1937 DVD**

DICK TRACY (1990) ★★★★ Chester Gould's comic-strip detective (Warren Beatty) takes on a bevy of baddies while fending off the affections of the sultry Breathless (Madonna) in this stylish, old-fashioned piece of screen entertainment. Al Pacino has a field day as the main heavy, Big Boy Caprice, while other big-name stars and character actors do cameo bits. Rated PG for violence. 120m. **DIR:** Warren Beatty. **CAST:** Warren Beatty, Madonna, Glenne Headly, Al Pacino, Dustin Hoffman, James Caan, Mandy Patinkin, Paul Sorvino, Charles Durning, Dick Van Dyke, R. G. Armstrong, William Forsythe. **1990 DVD**

DICK TRACY MEETS GRUESOME ★★1/2 Everybody's favorite Dick Tracy, Ralph Byrd, returns to the role he originated in serials for Republic Studios just in time to do battle with Gruesome, played with style by the great Boris Karloff. B&W; 65m. **DIR:** John Rawlins. **CAST:** Ralph Byrd, Boris Karloff, Anne Gwynne, Edward Ashley, June Clayworth. **1947 DVD**

DICK TRACY RETURNS ★★★ Ralph Byrd's second outing as comic-strip detective Dick Tracy finds the unbeatable G-man hot on the trail of the murderous Stark gang, an evil family that has killed one of Tracy's men. B&W; 15 chapters. **DIR:** William Witney, John English. **CAST:** Ralph Byrd, Lynne Roberts, Charles Middleton, David Sharpe, Jerry Tucker, Ned Glass. **1938**

DICK TRACY VS. CRIME INC. ★★★ Dick Tracy is called in to help stop the mysterious "Ghost," a ruthless member of the Council of Eight, a group of influential citizens attempting to rid the city of crime. B&W; 15 chapters. **DIR:** William Witney, John English. **CAST:** Ralph Byrd, Michael Owen, Jan Wiley, John Davidson, Ralph Morgan. **1941**

DICK TRACY VERSUS CUEBALL ★★ Dick Tracy chases a bald strangler who made off with a fortune in jewelry in this low-budget feature film. Morgan Conway's anemic Dick Tracy holds this one back, but Dick Wessel as Cueball peps up this modest programmer. B&W; 62m. **DIR:** Gordon Douglas. **CAST:** Morgan Conway, Anne Jeffreys, Lyle Latell, Rita Corday, Dick Wessel. **1946 DVD**

DICK TRACY'S DILEMMA ★★1/2 Two-fisted detective Dick Tracy (Ralph Byrd) finds himself up against a maniacal killer with an iron hook. B&W; 60m. **DIR:** John Rawlins. **CAST:** Ralph Byrd, Lyle Latell, Kay Christopher, Jack Lambert, Ian Keith. **1947 DVD**

DICK TRACY'S G-MEN ★★★ FBI agent Dick Tracy is forced to pursue the evil Zarnoff, the head of an international spy ring, after already capturing him and witnessing his execution. The ruthless spy lord is revived by drugs and redoubles his efforts at sabotage, putting Tracy and his men in one tight spot after another. B&W; 15 chapters. **DIR:** William Witney, John English. **CAST:** Ralph Byrd, Irving Pichel, Ted Pearson, Jennifer Jones, Walter Miller. **1939**

DICK TURPIN ★★ Tom Mix exchanges chaps and six-guns for cape and sword in this rather stolid portrayal of the legendary English highwayman. Good production values and crisp photography, but this one's no match for Mix's more traditional Western adventures. Silent. B&W; 70m. **DIR:** John G. Blystone. **CAST:** Tom Mix, Kathleen Myers. **1925**

DICK VAN DYKE SHOW, THE (TV SERIES) ★★★★ Comedy writer Dick Van Dyke spends his days devising jokes with quipsters Morey Amsterdam and Rose Marie for "The Alan Brady Show" and his nights in suburbia with well-meaning wife Mary Tyler Moore and their son, Larry Matthews. Inevitably, some complication comes along to upset the delicate balance, but matters are soon resolved. Hilarious in its day, this sitcom still works. B&W; 58m. **DIR:** Carl Reiner. **CAST:** Dick Van Dyke, Mary Tyler Moore, Rose Marie, Morey Amsterdam, Larry Matthews, Richard Deacon, Jerry Paris, Ann Morgan Guilbert, Carl Reiner. **1961–1966**

DIE! DIE! MY DARLING! ★★1/2 This British thriller was Tallulah Bankhead's last movie. She plays a crazed woman who kidnaps her late son's fiancée for punishment and salvation. Grisly fun for Bankhead fans, but may be too heavy-handed for others. Not rated, the film has violence. 97m. **DIR:** Silvio Narizzano. **CAST:** Tallulah Bankhead, Stefanie Powers, Peter Vaughan, Donald Sutherland. **1965**

DIE HARD ★★★★1/2 If this rip-roaring action picture doesn't recharge your batteries, you're probably dead. Alan Rickman and Alexander Godunov play terrorists who invade an L.A. high-rise. The direction of John McTiernan packs a wallop. Bruce Willis is more human, not to mention chattier, than most action heroes. Rated R for violence, nudity, profanity, and drug use. 131m. **DIR:** John McTiernan. **CAST:** Bruce Willis, Alan Rickman, Bonnie Bedelia, Alexander Godunov, Paul Gleason, William Atherton, Hart Bochner, James Shigeta, Reginald Vel Johnson. **1988 DVD**

DIE HARD 2: DIE HARDER ★★★★ In this solid sequel, maverick cop Bruce Willis takes on terrorists in a Washington D.C. airport, while his wife (Bonnie Bedelia) circles overhead in a plane which is running out of fuel. Willis does a fine job of reprising his wisecracking hero. Rated R for violence and profanity. 124m. **DIR:** Renny Harlin. **CAST:** Bruce Willis, Bonnie Bedelia, William Atherton, Reginald Vel Johnson, Franco Nero, John Amos, Dennis Franz, Art Evans, Fred Dalton Thompson. **1990 DVD**

DIE HARD WITH A VENGEANCE ★★★1/2 In this third entry in the series, it's Bruce Willis versus a mad bomber who terrorizes New York City to divert attention from a massive break-in at the federal reserve bank. It's a nonstop chase with spectacular stunts, but if you need a bit of logic with your thrills you had better pass it by. Rated R for violence and profanity. 130m. **DIR:** John McTiernan. **CAST:** Bruce Willis, Jeremy Irons, Samuel L. Jackson, Graham Greene, Colleen Camp. **1995 DVD**

DIE LAUGHING 🦃 Robby Benson stars as Pinsky, a young cabbie with aspirations of becoming a rock recording star. Rated PG. 108m. **DIR:** Jeff Werner. **CAST:** Robby Benson, Linda Grovenor, Charles Durning, Bud Cort. **1980**

DIE, MONSTER, DIE! 🦃 A slow-moving H. P. Lovecraft adaptation about a young man (Nick Adams) visiting his fiancée's family estate. 80m. **DIR:** Daniel Haller. **CAST:** Boris Karloff, Nick Adams, Suzan Farmer. **1965 DVD**

DIE SCREAMING, MARIANNE 🦃 Graphic horror film concerns a young girl (Susan George) who is pursued by numerous crazies. Rated R. 99m. **DIR:** Pete Walker. **CAST:** Susan George, Barry Evans. **1972 DVD**

DIFFERENT FOR GIRLS ★★★1/2 Overgrown adolescent Paul Prentice (Rupert Graves) meets the shy youth he protected from bullies when they were both in school—but Karl has had a sex change and is now Kim (Steven Mackintosh). Still as repressed as Paul is pugnacious, Kim lets herself be drawn out of her shell by his well-meaning but troublesome attempts at understanding. Two excellent performances and a sharply observed script make this British comedy-drama worth seeing. Rated R for nudity, sexual situations, and profanity. 96m. **DIR:** Richard Spence. **CAST:** Steven Mackintosh, Rupert Graves, Miriam Margolyes, Saskia Reeves, Neil Dudgeon, Ian Dury. **1996 DVD**

DIFFERENT STORY, A ★★★1/2 Perry King and Meg Foster play homosexuals who realize their romances are just not clicking. They fall in love with each other, marry, grow rich, and, eventually, dissatisfied. King and Foster are genuinely funny and appealing. Rated PG. 107m. **DIR:** Paul Aaron. **CAST:** Perry King, Meg Foster, Valerie Curtin, Peter Donat. **1979**

DIGGER ★★★★ Wonderful coming-of-age tale about a 12 year old boy named Digger, well played by Adam Hann-Byrd, who goes to stay with his grandmother on an island in the Pacific Northwest while his parents work out problems back home. At first a stranger in a strange land, Digger eventually warms up to his surroundings and the people of the island. Leslie Nielsen is a delight as the man trying to woo Digger's grandmother, played by Olympia Dukakis. Rated PG. 92m. **DIR:** Robert Turner. **CAST:** Adam Hann-Byrd, Joshua Jackson, Barbara Williams, Timothy Bottoms, Olympia Dukakis, Leslie Nielsen. **1994**

DIGGING TO CHINA ★★★1/2 Timothy Hutton makes his director's debut with this winning drama about a mentally challenged man (Kevin Bacon) who befriends a young girl. Both dream of escaping from their dreary existence, and together they form a bond that makes their families suspicious. How the two overcome prejudice and find happiness makes for engaging viewing. The screenplay by Karen Janszen is filled with emotional heart tugs and whimsy. Rated PG for language. 103m. **DIR:** Timothy Hutton. **CAST:** Kevin Bacon, Mary Stuart Masterson, Cathy Moriarty, Evan Rachel Wood. **1997 DVD**

DIGGSTOWN ★★★★1/2 Imagine the best parts of *The Sting* and *Rocky* combined in one terrific movie, and you get a good idea how supremely entertaining *Diggstown* is. James Woods and Lou Gossett work wonderfully together as a pair of con men who attempt to scam crook Bruce Dern, at his slimy best. Rated R for profanity and violence. 97m. **DIR:** Michael Ritchie. **CAST:** James Woods, Louis Gossett Jr., Bruce Dern, Oliver Platt, Heather Graham, Randall "Tex" Cobb. **1992 DVD**

DIGIMON: THE MOVIE ★★ A popular cartoon series expands for this mildly entertaining feature-length film in which a group of kids and their digital-monster pals battle an Internet disaster that threatens worldwide communications. Does this sound like kid stuff? Nonfans of the TV series may experience some confusion about who's who. And the uneven animation lacks depth which the disjointed plot cannot redeem. Rated PG for violence. 84m. **DIR:** Takaaki Yamashita, Hisashi Nakayama, Masahiro Aizawa. **2000 DVD**

DIGITAL MAN ★★ Special effects are the only saving grace of this low-budget effort about a high-tech killing machine and the team of commandos sent to destroy it. Rated R for violence and language. 95m. **DIR:** Phillip Roth. **CAST:** Ken Olandt, Kristen Dalton, Adam Baldwin, Ed Lauter, Matthias Hues. **1994**

DILLINGER (1945) ★★★ This look at the life and style of archetypal American gangster-antihero John Dillinger bids fair to be rated a *film noir*. Tough guy offscreen Lawrence Tierney is perfect in the title role. B&W; 89m. **DIR:** Max Nosseck. **CAST:** Edmund Lowe, Anne Jeffreys, Lawrence Tierney, Eduardo Ciannelli, Marc Lawrence, Elisha Cook Jr. **1945**

DILLINGER (1973) ★★★★ John Milius made an explosive directorial debut with this rip-roaring gangster film featuring Warren Oates in his best starring role. As a jaunty John Dillinger, he has all the charisma of a Cagney or a Bogart. Rated R for profanity and violence. 96m. **DIR:** John Milius. **CAST:** Warren Oates, Ben Johnson, Cloris Leachman, Michelle Phillips, Richard Dreyfuss, Harry Dean Stanton, Geoffrey Lewis, Steve Kanaly, Frank McRae. **1973 DVD**

DILLINGER (1990) ★★★ Shallow but often stylish look at the famous gangster's life. Mark Harmon makes for a suave, cool John Dillinger but an acid jazz background score and a superficial screenplay detract from the film's overall effect. Not rated; contains mild profanity and violence. 95m. **DIR:** Rupert Wainwright. **CAST:** Mark Harmon, Sherilyn Fenn, Will Patton, Bruce Abbott, Tom Bower, Patricia Arquette, Vince Edwards, Lawrence Tierney. **1990**

DILLINGER & CAPONE ★★ Martin Sheen and F. Murray Abraham are wasted in this crime-drama about an unholy alliance forged between the famous gangsters. Five years after being presumed dead, John Dillinger reemerges and is recruited by Al Capone to pull off a bank heist. Low budget and hokey dialogue keep this one from reaching for more. Rated R for violence and language. 95m. **DIR:** Jon Purdy. **CAST:** Martin Sheen, F. Murray Abraham, Sasha Jenson, Don Stroud. **1995**

DIM SUM: A LITTLE BIT OF HEART ★★★★ An independently made American movie about the tension and affection between a Chinese mother and daughter living in San Francisco's Chinatown. The film moves quietly, but contains many moments of humor. The restraint of the mother, who wants her daughter to marry, and the frustration of the daughter, who wants to live her life as she chooses, are beautifully conveyed by real-life mother and daughter Laureen and Kim Chew. Victor Wong, as a rambunctious uncle, is a gas. Rated PG. 88m. **DIR:** Wayne Wang. **CAST:** Laureen Chew, Kim Chew, Victor Wong. **1985**

DIMPLES ★★★ Dimpled darling Shirley Temple tries to care for her lovable rogue grandfather Frank Morgan, a street pickpocket who works the crowds she gathers with her singing and dancing. A rich patron takes her in hand, gets her off the street, and on the stage. B&W; 79m. **DIR:** William A. Seiter. **CAST:** Shirley Temple,

Frank Morgan, Helen Westley, Stepin Fetchit, John Carradine. **1936 DVD**

DINER ★★★★1/2 Writer-director Barry Levinson's much-acclaimed bittersweet tale of growing up in the late 1950s, unlike *American Graffiti*, is never cute or idealized. Instead, it combines insight, sensitive drama, and low-key humor. Rated R for profanity and adult themes. 110m. **DIR:** Barry Levinson. **CAST:** Steve Guttenberg, Daniel Stern, Mickey Rourke, Kevin Bacon, Ellen Barkin. **1982 DVD**

DINGAKA ★★★1/2 Cultures collide in this South African film as Masai warrior Ken Gampu tracks his daughter's killer to a metropolis and comes face-to-face with civilized justice. Spectacularly filmed by writer-producer Jamie Uys, this impressive movie features knockout performances by African film star Gampu as the accused and Stanley Baker as his attorney. 98m. **DIR:** Jamie Uys. **CAST:** Stanley Baker, Juliet Prowse, Ken Gampu, Bob Courtney. **1965**

DINGO ★★★1/2 Jazz legend Miles Davis has his only acting role in this winning tale of an Australian man whose life's ambition is to play the trumpet like his idol. Colin Friels costars as John "Dingo" Anderson, a family man who is willing to throw it all away in order to pursue his dreams. A trip to Paris and to the great jazz clubs helps Dingo make up his mind. Offbeat and original, director Rolf de Heer's film is a celebration of music and life. Not rated. 108m. **DIR:** Rolf De Heer. **CAST:** Colin Friels, Miles Davis, Helen Buday. **1992 DVD**

DINNER AT EIGHT (1933) ★★★★★ A sparkling, sophisticated, and witty comedy of character written by George S. Kaufman and Edna Ferber for the Broadway stage, this motion picture has a terrific all-star cast and lots of laughs. It's an all-time movie classic. B&W; 113m. **DIR:** George Cukor. **CAST:** John Barrymore, Jean Harlow, Marie Dressler, Billie Burke, Wallace Beery. **1933**

DINNER AT EIGHT (1990) ★★★ Commendable television remake of MGM's classic comedy. Socialite Marsha Mason has nothing but problems while planning a dinner party for visiting English dignitaries. The lives of those on her guest list are equally explored as the night of the party arrives. 92m. **DIR:** Ron Lagomarsino. **CAST:** John Mahoney, Marsha Mason, Stacy Edwards, Joel Brooks, Tim Kazurinsky, Harry Hamlin, Ellen Greene, Lauren Bacall, Charles Durning. **1990**

DINNER AT THE RITZ ★★1/2 Good cast makes British whodunit about Annabella seeking her father's murderer an enjoyable diversion. Well-produced, with just a light enough touch to balance out all the familiar elements of crime melodrama. Early David Niven effort displays his unique qualities at comedy and light drama. B&W; 77m. **DIR:** Harold Schuster. **CAST:** David Niven, Paul Lukas, Annabella, Romney Brent. **1937**

DINNER GAME, THE ★★★★ A boorish cad gets his just desserts in this delightful French romp, which efficiently sets up a provocative underdog scenario and then turns richly comical as the tables are turned most efficiently. A condescending publisher and his equally obnoxious friends regularly meet for a dinner party where each is responsible for bringing an "idiot" as a guest. The victims have no idea that they're on hand merely to be humiliated, and their boorish yuppie "sponsors" compare notes later in the evening and award points to whoever brought the "best idiot." Our boorish publisher learns of a lowly—and lonely—accountant who reproduces famous monuments with matchsticks, and will discuss the topic with the zeal of a soccer fanatic. Fortunately for us, things don't work out quite as expected, and the resulting farce—punctuated by some truly inspired telephone humor—becomes increasingly hilarious. Unfairly rated PG-13 for minor profanity and sexual content. 82m. **DIR:** Francis Verber. **CAST:** Thierry Lhermitte, Jacques Villeret, Francis Huster, Daniel Prevost, Alexandra Vandernoot, Catherine Frot. **1998 DVD**

•DINNER WITH FRIENDS ★★★★ This engaging drama centers on two couples who began their lives together twelve years ago. One couple is thriving, and the other is floundering, but the issues these friends bring up question the nature of all relationships, good and bad. Superb acting by the four principals adds the finishing spice to an excellent and thought-provoking character study. Rated R for profanity. 94m. **DIR:** Norman Jewison. **CAST:** Dennis Quaid, Andie MacDowell, Greg Kinnear, Toni Collette. **2001 DVD**

DINO ★★ Sal Mineo plays a troubled teen. Brian Keith is the savvy psychologist who helps him understand his emotions in this utterly predictable film. The street jargon is strained. B&W; 96m. **DIR:** Thomas Carr. **CAST:** Sal Mineo, Brian Keith, Susan Kohner, Frank Lovejoy, Joe De Santis. **1957**

DINOSAUR ★★★★ Although very small fry may be frightened by the story's grimmer elements, this magnificent achievement will play superbly for all remaining ages: an exciting, animated epic with equal measures of character detail and survival-at-all-costs thrills. The visual experience is enchanting: a mix of digitally enhanced, live-action backgrounds on which the computer-animated characters frolic and fight. The protagonist, a peaceful Iguanodon, is "adopted" by a family of lemurs; these unlikely heroes prove their value after joining a massive herd of similarly herbivorous dinosaurs, all being led across a scarred desert wasteland to find a lush nesting ground that may no longer exist. Directors Ralph Zondag and Eric Leighton orchestrate the various adventures with breathtaking ferocity. James Newton Howard's dynamic symphonic score amplifies the excitement. Rated PG for violent and dramatic story content. 84m. **DIR:** Ralph Zondag, Eric Leighton. **DVD**

DINOSAUR BABES ★★ They don't get much campier than this hilariously bad dinosaur movie in which some of the highlights include Amazons hunting for male sacrifices, and a man on a UFO using a laser to kill a T-Rex. Not rated; contains nudity and violence. 90m. **DIR:** Brett Piper. **CAST:** Jeff Corniello, Mike Whitehead, Melissa Ann, Kelly Lynn. **1991**

DINOSAUR VALLEY GIRLS 🦃 Take a look at the title and you'll get the idea of what's in store from this dull T&A fantasy. Not rated; contains nudity. 94m. **DIR:** Donald F. Glut. **CAST:** William Marshall, Griffin Drew, Karen Black. **1996 DVD**

DINOSAURUS! ★★1/2 Workers at a remote construction site accidentally stumble upon a prehistoric brontosaurus, tyrannosaurus rex, and a caveman (all quite alive) while excavating the area. Sure, the monsters look fake, and most of the humor is unintentional, but this film is entertaining nonetheless. 85m. **DIR:** Irvin S.

Yeaworth Jr. **CAST:** Ward Ramsey, Paul Lukather. **1960**

DIPLOMANIACS ★★1/2 In this preposterous romp, Bert Wheeler and Robert Woolsey play Indian-reservation barbers sent to a peace convention in Switzerland. This is a musical comedy, so don't expect too much plot. Hugh Herbert is a delight. Woo-woo! B&W; 63m. **DIR:** William A. Seiter. **CAST:** Bert Wheeler, Robert Woolsey, Marjorie White, Hugh Herbert, Louis Calhern, Edgar Kennedy. **1933**

DIPLOMATIC IMMUNITY ★★ A slipshod actioner about a marine (Bruce Boxleitner) who pursues his daughter's killer to Paraguay. Rated R for violence, profanity, and nudity. 95m. **DIR:** Peter Maris. **CAST:** Bruce Boxleitner, Billy Drago, Tom Breznahan, Christopher Neame, Robert Forster, Meg Foster. **1991**

DIPLOMATIC SIEGE ★★ This totally preposterous political thriller features Peter Weller and Daryl Hannah as bomb experts sent to disarm a nuclear warhead hidden inside the U.S. embassy in Bucharest. When terrorists take over the embassy, the two find themselves racing against time to save the day. The filmmaker's attempt to juggle too many balls creates chaos rather than suspense. Rated R for language and violence. 94m. **DIR:** Gustavo Graef-Marino. **CAST:** Peter Weller, Daryl Hannah, Tom Berenger. **1999 DVD**

DIRECT HIT ★★ The assassin with a heart of gold has become a genre unto itself, and this entry brings nothing new to the party. William Forsythe plays a CIA hit man who wants out of the business but agrees to one last hit. When he finds out that the woman is an innocent victim, he turns the tables and becomes her bodyguard. The usual chaos ensues. Rated R for violence, language, and adult situations. 91m. **DIR:** Joseph Merhi. **CAST:** William Forsythe, Jo Champa, Richard Norton, George Segal. **1993**

DIRT BIKE KID, THE A boy buys an old dirt bike that turns out to have a life of its own. Rated PG for vulgarity. 91m. **DIR:** Hoite C. Caston. **CAST:** Peter Billingsley, Stuart Pankin, Anne Bloom, Patrick Collins. **1985**

DIRTY DANCING ★★★★ A surprise hit. Jennifer Grey stars as a teenager poised at the verge of adulthood in the early Sixties. She accompanies her family on a Catskills vacation and meets up with rhythm-and-blues in the form of dancers Patrick Swayze and Cynthia Rhodes. Nothing new, but the players present the material with exuberant energy. Rated PG-13 for language and sexual themes. 97m. **DIR:** Emile Ardolino. **CAST:** Jennifer Grey, Patrick Swayze, Cynthia Rhodes, Jerry Orbach, Jack Weston. **1987 DVD**

DIRTY DISHES ★★ The American-born daughter-in-law of Luis Buñuel makes her directorial debut with this mediocre comedy. A beautiful French housewife finds herself trapped in an uneventful marriage. This leads to an explosive encounter with a lecherous neighbor. Takes its theme from the superior *Diary of a Mad Housewife*. In French with English subtitles. Not rated. 99m. **DIR:** Joyce Buñuel. **CAST:** Pierre Santini, Liliane Roveryre, Liza Braconnier. **1982**

DIRTY DOZEN, THE ★★★★1/2 Lee Marvin is assigned to take a group of military prisoners behind German lines and strike a blow for the Allies. It's a terrific entertainment—funny, star-studded, suspenseful, and even touching. 145m. **DIR:** Robert Aldrich. **CAST:** Lee Marvin, Ernest Borgnine, Charles Bronson, Jim Brown, John Cassavetes, Donald Sutherland, Clint Walker. **1967 DVD**

DIRTY DOZEN, THE: THE DEADLY MISSION ★★ Second TV sequel to the 1967 classic has none of the style or suspense of the original, although some situations were lifted directly from it. The battle scenes are well staged. Telly Savalas, whose character died in the original, is now the commander of twelve new misfits. 100m. **DIR:** Lee H. Katzin. **CAST:** Telly Savalas, Ernest Borgnine, Randall "Tex" Cobb, Vince Edwards, Gary Graham, Wolf Kahler. **1987**

DIRTY DOZEN, THE: THE FATAL MISSION ★★ Telly Savalas again leads a reluctant ragtag gang in this third TV sequel to the 1967 hit. Welcome plot twists include both a Nazi agent and a woman officer among the Dozen. Okay battle scenes. 100m. **DIR:** Lee H. Katzin. **CAST:** Telly Savalas, Ernest Borgnine, Jeff Conaway, Alex Cord, Erik Estrada, Ernie Hudson, James Carroll Jordan, Ray "Boom Boom" Mancini, John Matuszak, Natalija Nogulich, Heather Thomas, Anthony Valentine, Richard Yniguez. **1988**

DIRTY DOZEN, THE: THE NEXT MISSION ★★ This disappointing made-for-TV sequel brings back Lee Marvin as the hard-as-nails Major Reisman; Ernest Borgnine and Richard Jaeckel also reprise their roles. This time the Dozen are sent to assassinate a German general who is plotting to kill Hitler. Not rated. 99m. **DIR:** Andrew V. McLaglen. **CAST:** Lee Marvin, Ernest Borgnine, Richard Jaeckel, Ken Wahl, Larry Wilcox. **1985**

DIRTY GAMES The daughter of a murdered scientist tries to prevent terrorists from blowing up a nuclear dump site. Not rated; contains violence. 97m. **DIR:** Gary Hofmeyr. **CAST:** Jan-Michael Vincent, Valentina Vargas, Ronald France, Michael McGovern. **1993**

DIRTY HARRY ★★★★1/2 This is the original and still the best screen adventure of Clint Eastwood's maverick San Francisco detective. Outfoxed by a maniacal killer (Andy Robinson), "Dirty Harry" Callahan finally decides to deal out justice in his own inimitable and controversial fashion for an exciting, edge-of-your-seat climax. Rated R. 102m. **DIR:** Don Siegel. **CAST:** Clint Eastwood, Harry Guardino, John Mitchum, Reni Santoni, Andrew Robinson, John Vernon. **1971 DVD**

DIRTY LAUNDRY Stupid chase film involving a young man and a group of drug-dealing thugs. Rated PG-13 for profanity. 81m. **DIR:** William Webb. **CAST:** Leigh McCloskey, Jeanne O'Brien, Frankie Valli, Sonny Bono. **1987**

DIRTY LITTLE SECRET ★★1/2 A woman and three other criminals kidnap a young boy, who is really the woman's son. She wants him back, but the others just want the money. A few plot surprises spice up this made-for-cable original, but flat acting and uninspired lines dull the overall flavor. Rated R for violence. 95m. **DIR:** Rob Fresco. **CAST:** Tracey Gold, Jack Wagner, Mary Page Keller, Ian Tracey, Michal Suchanek. **1998**

DIRTY MARY, CRAZY LARRY ★★★ Race-car driver Peter Fonda and his two accomplices lead Vic Morrow and a small army of law enforcement officers on a frantic, nonstop chase in this satisfying low-budget action film. Rated R for language and violence. 93m. **DIR:** John

Hough. **CAST:** Peter Fonda, Susan George, Vic Morrow, Adam Roarke, Roddy McDowall. **1974**

DIRTY PAIR: AFFAIR ON NOLANDIA 🦃 A ridiculously contrived and poorly animated story has two scantily clad female intergalactic troubleshooters investigating cases with very little brain power. Japanese, dubbed in English. Not rated; contains nudity, profanity, and violence. 57m. **DIR:** Masahara Okuwaki. **1985**

DIRTY PICTURES ★★★★ When the controversial Robert Mapplethorpe exhibit "The Perfect Moment" comes to Cincinnati, the community reacts belligerently—in staunch support and in rapid opposition. The director of the Cincinnati Arts Center is put on trial, and the whole issue of "what is art?" is debated in court. This award-winning, fact-based, made-for-cable film features an outstanding performance by James Woods. Rated R for profanity, nudity, and sexual images. 104m. **DIR:** Frank Pierson. **CAST:** James Woods, Craig T. Nelson, Diana Scarwid. **2000 DVD**

DIRTY ROTTEN SCOUNDRELS ★★★★1/2 This remake of *Bedtime Story* is a genuine laugh riot. Michael Caine plays a sophisticated con man whose successful bilking of wealthy female tourists is endangered by upstart Steve Martin. Their battle of wits reaches comic highs when they duel over the fortune and affections of American heiress Glenne Headly. Rated PG for profanity. 110m. **DIR:** Frank Oz. **CAST:** Steve Martin, Michael Caine, Glenne Headly, Barbara Harris. **1988 DVD**

DIRTY TRICKS 🦃 This Canadian-made movie brings the comedy-thriller genre to an all-time low. Rated PG. 91m. **DIR:** Alvin Rakoff. **CAST:** Elliott Gould, Kate Jackson, Rich Little, Arthur Hill, Nicholas Campbell. **1980**

DIRTY WORK (1992) ★★1/2 A gambling, crooked bail bondsman murders a drug dealer and steals his money. He doesn't realize the money is marked by a crime boss. Rated R for violence and profanity. 88m. **DIR:** John McPherson. **CAST:** Kevin Dobson, John Ashton, Donnelly Rhodes, Jim Byrnes, Mitchell Ryan. **1992**

DIRTY WORK (1998) ★★ Mouthy loser and his chubby lifelong buddy are tired of "taking crap" and become so good at revenge that they begin charging people to do their dirty work. This outrageous, mean-spirited comedy is occasionally hilarious but generally trashy. Rated PG-13 for crude sexual humor and language. 81m. **DIR:** Bob Saget. **CAST:** Norm MacDonald, Artie Lange, Jack Warden, Christopher McDonald. **1998 DVD**

DISAPPEARANCE, THE (1977) ★★★★ This exciting film has Donald Sutherland portraying a professional hit man who can't do his job properly after his wife disappears. He pursues a top man in the organization (Christopher Plummer) because he believes that he is responsible for his wife's disappearance. Rated R for sex and violence. 80m. **DIR:** Stuart Cooper. **CAST:** Donald Sutherland, Francine Racette, David Hemmings, John Hurt, Christopher Plummer. **1977**

•DISAPPEARANCE (2002) ★★1/2 Harry Hamlin and Susan Dey reunite fourteen years after their romantic pairing on *L.A. Law*. Unfortunately, the sparks don't fly. The family's visit to a ghost town is filled with spooky sounds and elusive glimpses but lacks graphic evidence of their pursuers. This won't play well with modern audiences who will demand answers to the many questions raised by the eery film. Not rated; contains hints of violence and gore. 92m. **DIR:** Walter Klenhard. **CAST:** Harry Hamlin, Susan Dey. **2002**

DISAPPEARANCE OF AIMEE, THE ★★★1/2 Strong performers and taut direction made this one made-for-television movie that is way above average. Faye Dunaway plays preacher Aimee Semple McPherson, whose mysterious disappearance in 1926 gave rise to all sorts of speculation. A literate script, solid supporting performances by Bette Davis and James Woods, and plenty of period flavor make this one a winner. 110m. **DIR:** Anthony Harvey. **CAST:** Faye Dunaway, Bette Davis, James Woods, Severn Darden. **1976**

DISAPPEARANCE OF CHRISTINA, THE ★★★ In this made-for-cable original, an unhappy, wealthy wife disappears during a boating trip. The police think her husband killed her, while he is sure that she's still alive and is trying to drive him crazy. Interesting plot with an unexpected ending. Rated PG-13 for violence. 92m. **DIR:** Karen Arthur. **CAST:** John Stamos, Kim Delaney, C.C.H. Pounder, Robert Carradine. **1993**

DISAPPEARANCE OF GARCIA LORCA, THE ★★1/2 A Spanish youth meets the famous poet and playwright Federico Garcia Lorca; years later he braves the terrors of Francoís fascist regime to investigate Lorca's death during the Spanish Civil War. The mystery is so drawn out and the solution so wholly fictitious that it gives us no insight into Lorca's fate. Rated R for violence and some sexual content. 142m. **DIR:** Marcos Zurinaga. **CAST:** Esai Morales, Andy Garcia, Jeroen Krabbé, Giancarlo Giannini, Miguel Ferrer, Edward James Olmos, Marcela Walerstein. **1997**

DISASTER AT SILO 7 ★★★ An actual incident suggested the events in this occasionally absorbing drama that follows the aftermath of a disastrous fuel leak in an eastern Texas nuclear-missile silo. The script's reach is bigger than its grasp; an abrupt conclusion leaves numerous plot points and character antagonisms unresolved. The made-for-television restrictions just don't permit the story to be properly gritty. Rated PG for mild profanity. 94m. **DIR:** Larry Elikann. **CAST:** Michael O'Keefe, Joe Spano, Patricia Charbonneau, Ray Baker, Perry King, Peter Boyle, Dennis Weaver. **1988**

DISCLOSURE ★★★★ Intelligent and gripping drama about a male business executive who files sexual harassment charges against his female superior, a former flame. Once Paul Attanasio's screenplay—based on the novel by Michael Crichton—gets past this role-reversal plot twist, the film really hits its stride, keeping the viewer guessing until the end. Although it appears to be another sex thriller à la Douglas's previous hits, *Basic Instinct* and *Fatal Attraction*, *Disclosure* is closer to a clever corporate-intrigue variation on *All the President's Men*. Rated R for simulated sex and profanity. 120m. **DIR:** Barry Levinson. **CAST:** Michael Douglas, Demi Moore, Donald Sutherland, Caroline Goodall, Dennis Miller, Roma Maffia, Dylan Baker, Rosemary Forsyth. **1994 DVD**

DISCOVERY PROGRAM ★★★★ Marvelous collection of four short stories including the 1987 Oscar winner for best short film, "Ray's Male Heterosexual Dance Hall," which spoofs networking executives. "The Open Window" is also a comedy featuring a would-be actor who goes off the deep end when he can't get a good night's sleep. Not rated, contains profanity, violence, and nudity. 106m. **DIR:** Bryan Gordon, Damian Harris, Rupert Wainwright, Stephen Anderson. **CAST:** Eric Stoltz, James Spader. **1987**

DISCREET CHARM OF THE BOURGEOISIE, THE ★★★★ Dinner is being served in this Luis Buñuel masterpiece, but the food never gets a chance to arrive at the table. Every time the hosts and guests try to begin the meal, some outside problem rises. Typically French, typically Buñuel, typically hilarious. Winner of the best foreign film Oscar for 1972. 100m. **DIR:** Luis Buñuel. **CAST:** Fernando Rey, Delphine Seyrig, Stéphane Audran, Bulle Ogier, Jean-Pierre Cassel, Michel Piccoli. **1972**

DISEMBODIED, THE ★★ Ridiculous jungle horror worth seeing for Allison (*Attack of the 50-Foot Woman*) Hayes as Tonda, a bored doctor's wife who moonlights as a voodoo priestess. B&W; 66m. **DIR:** Walter Grauman. **CAST:** Paul Burke, Allison Hayes, Eugenia Paul, John E. Weingraf. **1957**

•DISH, THE ★★★ Australia's involvement with the 1969 Apollo 11 moon mission arrived with an expected wallop when its radio telescope in rural Parkes was elevated from the Southern Hemisphere's backup broadcaster to primary broadcaster of Neil Armstrong's "one giant leap for mankind." It is a modern wonder that the ten-year-old, multibillion-dollar program became solely reliant on an untested crew based in a sheep paddock to capture this priceless moment in history. Rated PG-13 for language. 97m. **DIR:** Rob Sitch. **CAST:** Sam Neill, Patrick Warburton, Kevin Harrington, Tom Long, Genevieve Mooy, Eliza Szonert, Taylor Kane. **2000 DVD**

DISH DOGS ★★★1/2 A pair of philosophical slacker surfers have the perfect lifestyle, working their way around California as dishwashers. But their scorn for commitment is tested when a sexy stripper comes into their lives. A genial youth comedy that's refreshingly less raunchy than most of this ilk. Rated R for profanity and nudity. 95m. **DIR:** Robert Kubilos. **CAST:** Sean Astin, Matthew Lillard, Shannon Elizabeth, Brian Dennehy. **1998 DVD**

DISHONORED ★★★1/2 Sin and sex are the real stars of this Marlene Dietrich movie. She plays a World War I Austrian spy who tangles with an overly amorous Russian agent. Dietrich's second Hollywood vehicle was the first to make good use of her mystique. B&W; 91m. **DIR:** Josef von Sternberg. **CAST:** Marlene Dietrich, Victor McLaglen, Lew Cody, Gustav von Seyffertitz, Warner Oland. **1931**

DISHONORED LADY 🦃 Beautiful magazine executive is accused of killing her former boyfriend. Ponderous adaptation of a successful Broadway drama. B&W; 85m. **DIR:** Robert Stevenson. **CAST:** Hedy Lamarr, Dennis O'Keefe, John Loder, William Lundigan. **1947**

DISORDERLIES 🦃 Ralph Bellamy and a few rap songs by The Fat Boys are all there are to recommend this embarrassingly bad film. Rated PG. 87m. **DIR:** Michael Schultz. **CAST:** The Fat Boys, Tony Plana, Ralph Bellamy, Anthony Geary. **1987**

DISORDERLY ORDERLY, THE ★★★ Jerry Lewis is out of control at a nursing home in a good solo effort directed by comedy veteran Frank Tashlin, who reached his peak here. Comic gems abound in this film, which isn't just for fans. In fact, if you've never been one of Jerry's faithful, give this one a try to see if you can't be swayed. You just might be surprised. 90m. **DIR:** Frank Tashlin. **CAST:** Jerry Lewis, Glenda Farrell, Susan Oliver, Everett Sloane, Jack E. Leonard, Kathleen Freeman. **1964**

DISORGANIZED CRIME ★★ Misadventures of five ex-cons trying to pull a bank heist in a small Montana town. Some fine performances are wasted in this disorganized mess that can't decide whether it's a comedy or an action-drama. Rated R for violence and profanity. 98m. **DIR:** Jim Kouf. **CAST:** Hoyt Axton, Corbin Bernsen, Rubén Blades, Fred Gwynne, Ed O'Neill, Lou Diamond Phillips, Daniel Roebuck, William Russ. **1989**

DISPLACED PERSON, THE ★★★★ Man's cruel, ugly side is exposed in this adaptation of Flannery O'Connor's brutal short story. Irene Worth is a struggling Georgia farm widow who allows a Polish World War II refugee and his family to live and work on her land. The woman's initially sympathetic feelings gradually mirror those of her other worthless laborers, who fear that their lives of relative laziness are jeopardized by this "unwanted foreigner." Introduced by Henry Fonda; unrated and suitable for family viewing. 58m. **DIR:** Glenn Jordan. **CAST:** Irene Worth, John Houseman, Shirley Stoler, Lane Smith, Robert Earl Jones. **1976**

DISRAELI ★★★1/2 Worth seeing solely for George Arliss's Oscar-winning performance, *Disraeli* shows how pretentious movies became when the talkies arrived. He plays the wily English prime minister who outwits the Russians in a fight over the Suez Canal. B&W; 89m. **DIR:** Alfred E. Green. **CAST:** George Arliss, Florence Arliss, Joan Bennett, Anthony Bushell. **1929**

DISTANT DRUMS ★★ Good old laconic Gary Cooper tracks down gun smugglers who are selling fire sticks to renegade Seminole Indians in the Everglades. A tired story and screenplay manage to get by on Cooper, good photography, and music. 101m. **DIR:** Raoul Walsh. **CAST:** Gary Cooper, Mari Aldon, Richard Webb, Ray Teal, Arthur Hunnicutt, Robert Barrat, Clancy Cooper. **1951**

DISTANT JUSTICE ★★ George Kennedy rises above the material in this tale of a dedicated police chief who takes the law into his own hands and helps a friend find out who killed his wife and kidnapped his daughter. Rated R for violence and adult language. 91m. **DIR:** Toru Murakawa. **CAST:** George Kennedy, David Carradine, Bunta Sugawara, Eric Lutes. **1992**

DISTANT THUNDER (1974) ★★★★ Outstanding drama by Satyajit Ray about the effects of a famine on the lives of various family members in World War II India. Beautiful cinematography sweeps the viewer through the desert landscapes of India. In Bengali with English subtitles. 92m. **DIR:** Satyajit Ray. **CAST:** Soumitra Chatterjee. **1974**

DISTANT THUNDER (1988) ★★1/2 After roaming the wilds of the Pacific Northwest with his Vietnam-vet buddies for several years, ex-soldier John Lithgow decides to return to civilization and find the son (Ralph Macchio) he hasn't seen in over a decade. Lithgow struggles valiantly with the downbeat material, but Macchio is miscast and no help at all. Rated R for violence and profanity. 114m. **DIR:** Rick Rosenthal. **CAST:** John Lithgow, Ralph Macchio. **1988**

DISTANT VOICES/STILL LIVES ★★★★★ An impressionistic memory film, based on the director's family memories and history. Set in England in the late 1940s, it explores the relationships and emotions of a middle-class family as they undergo domestic brutality, failed marriages, and the pains of life. The film's rich humanity and its unique use of a robust musical score overcome its cynicism. Offbeat and original. 85m. **DIR:** Terence Davies. **CAST:** Freda Dowie, Pete Postlethwaite, Angela Walsh, Dean Williams. **1988**

DISTINGUISHED GENTLEMAN, THE ★★★1/2 Con man–style takeoff on *Mr. Smith Goes to Washington*. Eddie Murphy is a street hustler who hustles a seat in the House of Representatives. The first two-thirds of the movie, with an accent on comedy, are the best. Rated R for profanity, suggested sex, and nudity. 100m. **DIR:** Jonathan Lynn. **CAST:** Eddie Murphy, James Garner, Sheryl Lee Ralph, Lane Smith, Joe Don Baker, Grant Shaud, Kevin McCarthy, Charles Dutton. **1992 DVD**

DISTORTIONS ★★1/2 The crazy plot developments in the final fifteen minutes of the film—about a widow (Olivia Hussey) being held captive by her wicked aunt (Piper Laurie)—make this rather contrived film interesting. Rated PG for violence. 98m. **DIR:** Armand Mastroianni. **CAST:** Steve Railsback, Olivia Hussey, Piper Laurie, Rita Gam, Edward Albert, Terence Knox, June Chadwick. **1987**

DISTURBANCE, THE 🦃 Perfectly dreadful tale of a psychotic trying to come to grips with himself while slaughtering the requisite nubile young women. Not rated, the film has violence and profanity. 81m. **DIR:** Cliff Guest. **CAST:** Timothy Greeson. **1989**

DISTURBED ★★1/2 At first glance this film looks quite hokey, but soon the viewer starts to wonder if sex-obsessed Sandy Ramirez (Pamela Gidley) really *is* dead, or if Dr. Russell (Malcolm McDowall) is actually just going crazy. Rated R for nudity, profanity, and violence. 96m. **DIR:** Charles Winkler. **CAST:** Malcolm McDowell, Geoffrey Lewis, Priscilla Pointer, Clint Howard, Pamela Gidley. **1990**

DISTURBING BEHAVIOR ★★ High-school rebels and misfits are turning one by one into squeaky-clean overachievers in Stepford wives fashion. These model citizens wear letter sweaters, get great grades, hold bake sales—and fly into homicidal rages. It is up to a new student, a punkish sexpot and a stoner, to put an end to all this hellish conformity. This indictment of adults as grim reapers of free thinking is neither chilling nor suspenseful. Rated R for drug use, violence, and nudity. 83m. **DIR:** David Nutter. **CAST:** James Marsden, Katie Holmes, Nick Stahl, Bruce Greenwood, Bill Sadler. **1998 DVD**

DIVA ★★★★ In this stunningly stylish suspense film by first-time director Jean-Jacques Beineix, a young opera lover unknowingly becomes involved with the underworld. Unbeknownst to him, he's in possession of some very valuable tapes—and the delightful chase is on. In French with English subtitles. Rated R for profanity, nudity, and violence. 123m. **DIR:** Jean-Jacques Beineix. **CAST:** Frederic Andrei, Wilhemenia Wiggins Fernandez. **1982 DVD**

DIVE, THE ★★★★ This Norwegian-British production tells of two veteran divers who are asked to return for an emergency dive to fix a broken oil pipeline. Outstanding performances and photography. Not rated but suitable for family viewing. 97m. **DIR:** Tristan DeVere Cole. **CAST:** Bjorn Sundquist, Frank Grimes. **1990**

DIVE BOMBER ★★★ The planes and acting styles date this one pretty badly, but the story line, about a military doctor working on ways to prevent blackouts while flying, is still intriguing. 133m. **DIR:** Michael Curtiz. **CAST:** Errol Flynn, Fred MacMurray, Ralph Bellamy, Alexis Smith, Craig Stevens, Robert Armstrong, Regis Toomey. **1941**

DIVIDED BY HATE ★★1/2 A deluded preacher lures a woman and her children into a white-supremacist hate group. Her husband tries everything to get his family back, with little success. This made-for-cable drama, based on a true story, is a chilling examination of hate groups, but the acting is lackluster and the film is more message than entertainment. Not rated; contains violence. 95m. **DIR:** Tom Skerritt. **CAST:** Dylan Walsh, Andrea Roth, Jim Beaver, Tom Skerritt. **1997**

•DIVIDED WE FALL ★★★★★ Czech couple in a small town occupied by the Germans during the last years of World War II hides a "fugitive" Jew in their pantry and makes a desperate sacrifice to avoid detection. This provocative Holocaust drama is saturated with tension and streaked with dark comedy. Refusing to wallow in obvious sentiment, this seriocomic tribute to the human spirit illustrates how abnormal times invade and change the lives of normal people. In Czech and German with English subtitles. Rated PG-13 for language, sexual content, and violence. 122m. **DIR:** Jan Hrebejk. **CAST:** Boleslav Polivka, Anna Siskova, Csonger Kissai, Jaroslav Dusek. **2000 DVD**

DIVINE 🦃 Filmmaker John Waters's special tribute to the famous transvestite comic features Divine in a rare, early short "The Diane Linkletter Story" and the only existing performance of the famous "The Neon Woman" show. Unless you're a die-hard fan of John Waters or Divine, this exercise in cinema of the absurd could be torture. Not rated; contains profanity and nudity. 110m. **DIR:** John Waters. **CAST:** Divine. **1990**

DIVINE MADNESS ★★★1/2 Here's the sassy, unpredictable Bette Midler as captured in concert by director Michael Ritchie. Some of it is great; some of it is not. It helps if you're a Midler fan. Rated R for profanity. 95m. **DIR:** Michael Ritchie. **CAST:** Bette Midler. **1980 DVD**

DIVINE NYMPH, THE ★★1/2 This story of love and passion resembles an Italian soap opera at best. Laura Antonelli is the young beauty who is unfaithful to her fiancé. In Italian with English subtitles. Rated R for nudity. 89m. **DIR:** Giuseppe Patroni Griffi. **CAST:** Laura Antonelli, Terence Stamp, Marcello Mastroianni. **1977**

DIVING IN ★★ A feel-good movie about a teenager's ambition to make his high school diving team and overcome a fear of heights. Predictable. Rated PG-13. 92m. **DIR:** Strathford Hamilton. **CAST:** Burt Young, Matt Lattanzi, Matt Adler, Kristy Swanson. **1990**

DIVORCE AMERICAN STYLE ★★★1/2 Delightfully daffy comedy about a couple going through divorce. What would normally be fertile ground for melodrama is actually a breeding ground for lively insights about the human condition. Dick Van Dyke and Debbie Reynolds are wonderful as the couple who realize that the only thing left in their marriage is their routine. How they go about rectifying this makes for engaging viewing. Not rated. 109m. **DIR:** Bud Yorkin. **CAST:** Dick Van Dyke, Debbie Reynolds, Jason Robards Jr., Jean Simmons, Van Johnson, Joe Flynn, Tom Bosley. **1967**

DIVORCE HIS: DIVORCE HERS ★★1/2 This less-than-exceptional TV movie follows the breakup of a marriage in which both partners explain what they think led to the failure of their marriage. The talents of Elizabeth Taylor and Richard Burton are barely tapped. 144m. **DIR:** Waris Hussein. **CAST:** Richard Burton, Elizabeth Taylor, Carrie Nye, Barry Foster, Gabriele Ferzetti. **1972 DVD**

DIVORCE—ITALIAN STYLE ★★★1/2 Considered naughty in its day, now this Italian black comedy about a philandering husband's plans to rid himself of his wife simply plays as the fast, racy romp it is. Endlessly imitated in later, lesser rip-offs. Oscar for original screenplay. B&W; 104m. **DIR:** Pietro Germi. **CAST:** Marcello Mastroianni, Daniela Rocca, Stefania Sandrelli. **1962 DVD**

DIVORCE OF LADY X, THE ★★★★ In this British comedy, Laurence Olivier plays a lawyer who allows Merle Oberon to spend the night at his place. Although nothing actually happened that night, Olivier finds himself branded "the other man" in her divorce. A series of hilarious misunderstandings are the result. 90m. **DIR:** Tim Whelan. **CAST:** Merle Oberon, Laurence Olivier, Binnie Barnes, Ralph Richardson. **1938**

DIVORCEE, THE ★★ Dated melodrama about a woman with loose morals. Silly by today's standards, this was racy when made and earned Norma Shearer a best-actress Oscar. A curiosity piece with a good cast. B&W; 83m. **DIR:** Robert Z. Leonard. **CAST:** Norma Shearer, Robert Montgomery, Chester Morris, Conrad Nagel, Florence Eldridge. **1930**

DIXIANA ★★ Slow-moving musical about a pretty young performer and her affairs of the heart just meanders about with tepid numbers and heavy-handed humor. Bill "Bojangles" Robinson does a cameo tap routine, but the rest of the entertainment is uninspired. B&W; 100m. **DIR:** Luther Reed. **CAST:** Bebe Daniels, Everett Marshall, Bert Wheeler, Robert Woolsey, Joseph Cawthorn. **1930 DVD**

DIXIE CHANGING HABITS ★★★1/2 Suzanne Pleshette plays Dixie, who runs a highly successful prostitution ring. When she's busted, she must spend time in a convent directed by Cloris Leachman as the Mother Superior. All in all, this made-for-TV comedy is highly entertaining. 96m. **DIR:** George Englund. **CAST:** Suzanne Pleshette, Cloris Leachman, Kenneth McMillan, John Considine. **1982**

DIXIE DYNAMITE 🦃 Imagine one of those cheesy Burt Reynolds good-ol'-boys movies, where he and some buddies raise heck in revenge for mistreatment from the local deputy. Now imagine it without Burt Reynolds. The ever-watchable Warren Oates isn't enough. Rated PG. 89m. **DIR:** Lee Frost. **CAST:** Warren Oates, Christopher George, Jane Anne Johnstone, R. G. Armstrong. **1976 DVD**

DIXIE JAMBOREE ★★ Another B movie from lowly PRC Studios. The action takes place on the showboat *Ellabella* and the characters range from con men to various musicians and roustabouts. B&W; 80m. **DIR:** Christy Cabanne. **CAST:** Guy Kibbee, Lyle Talbot, Eddie Quillan, Frances Langford, Fifi D'Orsay, Charles Butterworth. **1945**

DIXIE LANES 🦃 Chaotic comedy revolving around the bad luck of a family named Laid Law. Not rated, but equivalent to a PG-13. 90m. **DIR:** Don Cato. **CAST:** Hoyt Axton, Karen Black, Art Hindle, Tina Louise, Ruth Buzzi, Moses Gunn, John Vernon. **1988**

DJANGO ★★ Spaghetti Western lacks convincing performances. A border town is about to explode, and the stranger, Django (Franco Nero), lights the fuse. 90m. **DIR:** Sergio Corbucci. **CAST:** Franco Nero. **1965 DVD**

DJANGO SHOOTS FIRST ★★★ One of the better comic spaghetti Westerns. Django's son inherits half a town. The only problem is he must share it with his old man's crooked partner. Good performances by Glenn Saxon and veteran European character actor Fernando Sancho highlight this funny, entertaining film. Not rated. 96m. **DIR:** Alberto De Martino. **CAST:** Glenn Saxon, Fernando Sancho, Evelyn Stewart, Erica Blanc, Alberto Lupo. **1966**

DNA ★★1/2 A young scientist and a CIA agent battle a monster created with DNA stolen from the scientist's jungle lab. Decent special effects somewhat compensate for a confusing plot in this made-for-video monster movie that borrows equally from *Alien* and *Predator*. Rated R for profanity and violence. 94m. **DIR:** William Mesa. **CAST:** Mark Dacascos, Jurgen Prochnow, Robin McKee. **1997**

DO THE RIGHT THING ★★★★1/2 Writer-director-star Spike Lee's controversial study of the deep-rooted racism in America starts off as a hilarious multicharacter comedy and evolves into a disturbing, thought-provoking, and timely drama. The events take place during the hottest day of the year in a one-block area of the Brooklyn neighborhood of Bedford-Stuyvesant, where tensions exist among the blacks, Italians, and Koreans who live and work there. Rated R for violence, profanity, and nudity. 120m. **DIR:** Spike Lee. **CAST:** Danny Aiello, Ossie Davis, Ruby Dee, Richard Edson, Giancarlo Esposito, Spike Lee, Bill Nunn, John Savage, John Turturro. **1989 DVD**

DO YOU REMEMBER DOLLY BELL? ★★★1/2 Delightful coming-of-age story set in 1960s Sarajevo, when stable political circumstances brought a flood of Western culture to Yugoslavia. In Serbo-Croatian with English subtitles. Not rated; mild sexual content. B&W; 106m. **DIR:** Emir Kusturica. **CAST:** Slavko Stimac, Mira Banjac. **1981**

D.O.A. (1949) ★★★1/2 CPA Edmond O'Brien, slowly dying from radiation poisoning, seeks those responsible in this fast-paced, stylized *film noir* thriller. Most unusual is the device of having the victim play detective and hunt his killers as time runs out. Neville Brand takes honors as a psychopath who tries to turn the tables on the victim before he can inform the police. B&W; 83m. **DIR:** Rudolph Maté. **CAST:** Edmond O'Brien, Pamela Britton, Luther Adler, Lynne Baggett, Neville Brand. **1949 DVD**

D.O.A. (1988) ★★ This failed update of the 1949 *film noir* classic makes the crippling mistake of hauling its Chandleresque story line into the 1980s. Dennis Quaid is the hard-drinking college professor who wakes to find he's been fatally poisoned; with mere hours to live, he drags love-struck college student Meg Ryan along on the hunt for his killer. Rated R for language and violence. 96m. **DIR:** Rocky Morton, Annabel Jankel. **CAST:** Dennis Quaid, Meg Ryan, Charlotte Rampling, Daniel Stern, Jane Kaczmarek. **1988**

DOBERMAN GANG, THE ★★1/2 A vicious pack of Doberman pinschers are trained as bank robbers in this implausible but well-made action tale. Rated PG for language, mild violence. 87m. **DIR:** Byron Chudnow. **CAST:** Byron Mabe, Julie Parrish, Simmy Bow, Hal Reed. **1972**

DOC HOLLYWOOD ★★★ En route to Beverly Hills, Dr. Benjamin Stone (Michael J. Fox) has a car accident in South Carolina, where the local residents are in need of an M.D. Doc Stone persists in his hopes for fame and fortune until he meets the pretty Lou (Julie Warner) and falls in love. Good formula fun. Rated PG-13 for nudity and profanity. 110m. **DIR:** Michael Caton-Jones. **CAST:** Michael J. Fox, Julie Warner, Bridget Fonda, Woody Harrelson, George Hamilton. **1991 DVD**

DOC SAVAGE . . . , THE MAN OF BRONZE ★★★ Perfectly acceptable—although campy—first appearance by the famed hero of pulp novels, Doc Savage. Ron Ely makes a suitable Savage, complete with torn shirt and deadpan delivery. Special effects and set design are minimal, a true shame since this is the last film produced by science-fiction pioneer George Pal. Rated PG—some violence. 100m. **DIR:** Michael Anderson. **CAST:** Ron Ely, Pamela Hensley, Darrell Zwerling, Michael Miller, Paul Gleason. **1975**

DOCKS OF NEW YORK, THE ★★★★ A solid drama of love and death on a big-city waterfront. Rough-edged George Bancroft rescues would-be suicide Betty Compson, marries her, clears her of a murder charge, and goes to jail for her. The direction is masterful, the camera work and lighting superb in this, one of the last silent films to be released. B&W; 60m. **DIR:** Josef von Sternberg. **CAST:** George Bancroft, Betty Compson, Olga Baclanova, Mitchell Lewis. **1928**

DOCTOR, THE ★★★★ A doctor discovers the sore throat that's been bothering him is actually cancer, and, in becoming a patient, experiences the dehumanizing effects of the medical establishment. An effective drama with a superlative star performance by William Hurt. Rated PG-13 for profanity and scenes of surgery. 128m. **DIR:** Randa Haines. **CAST:** William Hurt, Christine Lahti, Elizabeth Perkins, Mandy Patinkin, Adam Arkin, Charlie Korsmo, Wendy Crewson, Bill Macy. **1991**

DR. AKAGI ★★★★ This sort of Japanese Damon Runyon story is filled with erotic undertows, raw vitality, and oddball, multishaded characterizations. The title physician is obsessed with battling a hepatitis epidemic in Japan just before World War II. He is supported by his village's most in-demand whore, a drug-addicted surgeon, and other outcasts when his activities land him in trouble with military authorities. A compelling blend of drama, melodrama, comedy, and carnality intermingles the outrageous with the restrained. In Japanese with English subtitles. Not rated. 128m. **DIR:** Shobei Inamura. **CAST:** Akira Emoto, Kumiko Aso, Jacques Gamblin. **1999**

DOCTOR AND THE DEVILS, THE ★★★ This film, based on a true story, with an original screenplay by Dylan Thomas, is set in England in the 1800s. Dr. Cook (Timothy Dalton) is a professor of anatomy, who doesn't have enough corpses to use in class demonstrations. Not for the squeamish. Rated R for language, simulated sex, and violence. 93m. **DIR:** Freddie Francis. **CAST:** Timothy Dalton, Jonathan Pryce, Twiggy, Julian Sands, Stephen Rea, Phyllis Logan, Beryl Reid, Sian Phillips. **1985**

DOCTOR AT LARGE ★★★ Young Dr. Simon Sparrow wants to join the hospital staff, but the grumpy superintendent isn't buying. Comic conniving ensues as Sparrow seeks a place. Third in a series of seven films featuring Dr. Sparrow. 98m. **DIR:** Ralph Thomas. **CAST:** Dirk Bogarde, James Robertson Justice, Shirley Eaton. **1957**

DOCTOR AT SEA ★★★ Fed up with the myriad complications of London life and romance, young, handsome Dr. Simon Sparrow seeks a rugged man's world by signing up on a passenger-carrying freighter as ship's doctor. He goes from the frying pan into the fire when he meets Brigitte Bardot on the high seas! Second in the highly successful British comedy series. 92m. **DIR:** Ralph Thomas. **CAST:** Dirk Bogarde, Brigitte Bardot, Brenda de Banzie, James Robertson Justice. **1955**

DR. BETHUNE ★★★★ Big-budget story of the Canadian doctor who is revered in China for the many lives he saved when that country fought Japan. Donald Sutherland played the same character in the TV-movie *Bethune* (also on video), and he emphasizes the man's larger-than-life qualities, both positive and negative, in this unusually absorbing biography. Not rated; contains adult themes. 115m. **DIR:** Phillip Borsos. **CAST:** Donald Sutherland, Helen Mirren, Helen Shaver, Colm Feore, Anouk Aimée. **1990**

DR. BLACK AND MR. HYDE 🦃 Dr. Black develops a serum to cure his kidney ailment that turns him into a monster with white skin. Rated R. 88m. **DIR:** William Crain. **CAST:** Bernie Casey, Rosalind Cash. **1976**

DR. BUTCHER, M.D. (MEDICAL DEVIATE) 🦃 Italian cannibal-zombie movie, and you know what that means—gore galore. Rated R. Dubbed in English. 80m. **DIR:** Francesco Martino. **CAST:** Ian McCulloch, Alexandra Cole. **1979**

DR. CALIGARI 🦃 Purportedly an update-parody of the German classic, this self-consciously bizarre movie is all gaudy art design and no plot. Rated R for sexual obsessions. 80m. **DIR:** Stephen Sayadian. **CAST:** Madeleine Reynal. **1989 DVD**

DR. CHRISTIAN MEETS THE WOMEN 🦃 Kindly old Dr. Christian takes on a diet charlatan in this stanza of the film series. B&W; 60m. **DIR:** William McGann. **CAST:** Jean Hersholt, Dorothy Lovett, Edgar Kennedy, Frank Albertson, Veda Ann Borg, Rod La Rocque. **1940**

DR. CYCLOPS ★★★ Oscar-nominated special effects dominate this tale of a brilliant physicist (Albert Dekker) in the remote jungles of Peru. He shrinks a group of his colleagues to miniature size in order to protect his valuable radium discovery. Entertaining film is best remembered as one of the earliest Technicolor horror movies, with lush photography and an effective performance by Dekker. 75m. **DIR:** Ernest B. Schoedsack. **CAST:** Albert Dekker, Janice Logan, Charles Halton, Thomas Coley, Victor Kilian. **1940**

DR. DEATH: SEEKER OF SOULS ★★1/2 Dr. Death discovered how to cheat death one thousand years ago by periodically transferring his soul into another body. He's willing to share his talents with others, too. The makers of this low-rent terror tale had a tongue-in-cheek sense of humor, and it shows. Look for a cameo by head Stooge Moe Howard. Rated R, though pretty tame by current standards. 87m. **DIR:** Eddie Saeta. **CAST:** John Considine, Barry Coe, Cheryl Miller, Florence Marly, Jo Morrow. **1973**

DOCTOR DETROIT ★★1/2 Dan Aykroyd stars in this comedy as a soft-spoken English professor who becomes a comic book–style pimp. Aykroyd has some genuinely funny moments, but the movie is uneven overall. Rated R for profanity, nudity, and violence. 89m. **DIR:** Michael Pressman. **CAST:** Dan Aykroyd, Howard Hesseman, Nan Martin, T. K. Carter. **1983**

DOCTOR DOLITTLE (1967) ★★1/2 Rex Harrison plays the title role in this children's tale, about a man who finds more satisfaction being around animals than people. Children may find this film amusing, but for the most part, the acting is weak, and any real script is nonexistent. 152m. **DIR:** Richard Fleischer. **CAST:** Rex Harrison, Samantha Eggar, Anthony Newley, Richard Attenborough. **1967 DVD**

DR. DOLITTLE (1998) ★★★★1/2 An MD discovers he can talk to the animals, but he would rather not. Eddie Murphy's restrained performance only adds to this funny film. Not as noble or feel-good as *Babe* but on its own level just as amazing that the filmmakers could pull this off as well as they do. This film is truly for the entire family. Rated PG-13 for language. 110m. **DIR:** Betty Thomas. **CAST:** Eddie Murphy, Ossie Davis, Oliver Platt, Peter Boyle, Norm MacDonald, Albert Brooks, Chris Rock, Reni Santoni, John Leguizamo, Julie Kavner, Garry Shandling, Ellen DeGeneres, Brian Doyle-Murray, Philip Proctor. **1998 DVD**

•**DR. DOLITTLE 2** ★★ The good doctor once again talks to the animals in this crude, lightweight mix of social commentary and juvenile entertainment. A beaver asks Dolittle to help save a forest from being strip harvested by an evil lumber mogul and his attorney. His challenge is to get a wild Pacific West bear to mate with a circus bear and give birth to cubs, which in turn will require the forest to be placed under federal protection. A dog narrates the story as a boring subplot evolves involving the doctor's self-focused teen daughter. Rated PG. 82m. **DIR:** Steve Carr. **CAST:** Eddie Murphy, Kevin Pollak, Jeffrey Jones, Kristen Wilson, Raven-Symone, Kyla Pratt, Lil' Zane. **2001 DVD**

DR. FAUSTUS ★★ Richard Burton is the man who sells his soul and Elizabeth Taylor is Helen of Troy in this weird adaptation of Christopher Marlowe's retelling of the ancient legend. Strictly for Taylor and Burton fans. 93m. **DIR:** Richard Burton. **CAST:** Richard Burton, Elizabeth Taylor. **1968**

DR. FRANKENSTEIN'S CASTLE OF FREAKS Italian exploitation film with Rossano Brazzi, Michael Dunn, and Edmond Purdom at the nadir of their careers. Rated R. 89m. **DIR:** Robert H. Oliver. **CAST:** Rossano Brazzi, Michael Dunn, Edmund Purdom. **1973**

DR. GIGGLES An escaped lunatic with a medical fixation employs stainless-steel technology to dispatch the usual libidinous teenagers. Tiresome low-rent shocker. Malpractice all the way. Rated R for violence and gore. 95m. **DIR:** Manny Coto. **CAST:** Larry Drake, Holly Marie Combs, Glenn Quinn, Cliff De Young, Richard Bradford. **1992 DVD**

DR. GOLDFOOT AND THE BIKINI MACHINE ★★ Camp appeal saves this low-budget drive-in fare, as mad scientist Vincent Price creates an army of seductive female robots in an attempt to gain power and wealth. Silliness ensues. 88m. **DIR:** Norman Taurog. **CAST:** Vincent Price, Frankie Avalon, Susan Hart, Dwayne Hickman, Fred Clark. **1965 DVD**

DR. GOLDFOOT AND THE GIRL BOMBS Vincent Price returns as the notorious mad scientist Dr. Goldfoot, this time turning his female robots into bombs. 85m. **DIR:** Mario Bava. **CAST:** Vincent Price, Fabian, Laura Antonelli, Franco Franchi. **1966**

DR. HECKYL AND MR. HYPE ★★★1/2 Oh, no, not another *Dr. Jekyll and Mr. Hyde* parody! But this is quite funny, right up there with Jerry Lewis's *The Nutty Professor.* Oliver Reed is hilarious as both an ugly podiatrist and his alter ego, a handsome stud. Writer-director Charles B. Griffith, who wrote the original *Little Shop of Horrors,* has a field day here. Rated R for nudity. 99m. **DIR:** Charles B. Griffith. **CAST:** Oliver Reed, Sunny Johnson, Mel Welles, Jackie Coogan, Corinne Calvet, Dick Miller. **1980**

DOCTOR IN DISTRESS ★★★ In this high jinks–jammed British comedy of medical student and young physician trials and tribulations, head of hospital Sir Lancelot Spratt reveals he is human when he falls in love. Hero Dr. Simon Sparrow has trouble romancing a beautiful model. It's all fast-pace and very funny. Fourth in a series of seven that began with *Doctor in the House*. B&W; 103m. **DIR:** Ralph Thomas. **CAST:** Dirk Bogarde, Samantha Eggar, James Robertson Justice. **1963**

DOCTOR IN THE HOUSE ★★★1/2 This well-paced farce features a superb British cast. It's about the exploits of a group of medical students intent on studying beautiful women and how to become wealthy physicians. This low-key comedy of manners inspired six other *Doctor* movies and eventually led to a TV series. Not rated. 92m. **DIR:** Ralph Thomas. **CAST:** Dirk Bogarde, Muriel Pavlow, Kenneth More, Donald Sinden, Kay Kendall, James Robertson Justice, Donald Houston. **1954**

DR. JEKYLL AND MR. HYDE (1920) ★★★1/2 Still considered one of the finest film versions of Robert Louis Stevenson's story, this features John Barrymore in a bravura performance as the infamous doctor who becomes a raging beast. Barrymore always prided himself on changing into the dreadful Hyde by contorting his body rather than relying on heavy makeup. Silent. B&W; 63m. **DIR:** John S. Robertson. **CAST:** John Barrymore, Martha Mansfield, Nita Naldi, Louis Wolheim, Charles Lane. **1920 DVD**

DR. JEKYLL AND MR. HYDE (1932) ★★★★1/2 Fredric March's Oscar-winning performance is the highlight of this terrific horror film, which is also the best of the many versions of Robert Louis Stevenson's classic tale of good and evil. The direction by Rouben Mamoulian is exquisite. B&W; 98m. **DIR:** Rouben Mamoulian. **CAST:** Fredric March, Miriam Hopkins, Rose Hobart. **1932**

DR. JEKYLL AND MR. HYDE (1941) ★★★ A well-done version of Robert Louis Stevenson's classic story about a good doctor who dares to venture into the unknown. The horror of his transformation is played down in favor of the emotional and psychological consequences. Spencer Tracy and Ingrid Bergman are excellent, the production lush. B&W; 114m. **DIR:** Victor Fleming. **CAST:** Spencer Tracy, Ingrid Bergman, Lana Turner, Donald Crisp, C. Aubrey Smith, Sara Allgood. **1941**

DR. JEKYLL AND MR. HYDE (1973) 🦃 Kirk Douglas stars in this major misfire, a made-for-television musical based on Robert Louis Stevenson's classic tale. 90m. **DIR:** David Winters. **CAST:** Kirk Douglas, Susan George, Stanley Holloway, Michael Redgrave, Donald Pleasence. **1973**

DR. JEKYLL AND MS. HYDE ★★ Disappointing spoof on the well-known horror story features Tim Daly as the obsessed scientist. Adding estrogen to his life-altering formula, he creates a beautiful but evil alter ego (Sean Young). Humor is coarse, relying heavily on the anatomy and eliciting groans and guffaws rather than genuine belly laughs. Rated PG-13 for nudity, profanity, and sexual situations. 90m. **DIR:** David F. Price. **CAST:** Timothy Daly, Sean Young, Lysette Anthony, Stephen Tobolowsky, Harvey Fierstein. **1995**

DR. JEKYLL AND SISTER HYDE ★★ One of many variations on a Jack the Ripper theme, this one has a mad scientist driven to terrible deeds with slightly different results. Contains far too many midnight scenes in foggy old London Town. No rating, but contains violence and nudity. 94m. **DIR:** Roy Ward Baker. **CAST:** Ralph Bates, Martine Beswick, Gerald Sim. **1971 DVD**

DR. KILDARE'S STRANGE CASE ★★★ Friendly old Dr. Gillespie and his medical whiz junior, Dr. Kildare, are featured in this tale of the deranged. Lew Ayres deals with a cuckoo. Nurse Laraine Day provides love interest; Lionel Barrymore is at the ready to counsel as Dr. Gillespie. This is one of the best of the Kildare series. B&W; 76m. **DIR:** Harold S. Bucquet. **CAST:** Lew Ayres, Lionel Barrymore, Laraine Day, Nat Pendleton, Samuel S. Hinds, Emma Dunn. **1940**

DR. MABUSE, THE GAMBLER (PARTS I AND II) ★★★★ This is it—the granddaddy of all criminal mastermind films. The pacing, though slow and deliberate, pays off in a spectacular climax, with the evil and elusive Mabuse gone mad in a counterfeiter's cellar. Silent. B&W; **DIR:** Fritz Lang. **CAST:** Rudolf Klein-Rogge. **1922–1923 DVD**

DOCTOR MORDRID ★★★1/2 Jeffrey Combs is Doctor Mordrid, a sorcerer biding his time in a New York brownstone. He keeps watch over the portal to another dimension, a dimension that is reigned over by his mortal enemy. Fanciful special effects. Rated R for violence and nudity. 102m. **DIR:** Albert Band, Charles Band. **CAST:** Jeffrey Combs, Yvette Nipar, Brian Thompson, Jay Acovone. **1992**

DR. NO ★★★★ The first of the James Bond movie sensations, it was in this film that Sean Connery began his ascent to stardom as the indomitable British secret agent 007. Bond is sent to Jamaica to confront the evil Dr. No, a villain bent on world domination. Ursula Andress was the first of the (now traditional) sensual Bond heroines. As with most of the series' films, there is a blend of nonstop action and tongue-in-cheek humor. 111m. **DIR:** Terence Young. **CAST:** Sean Connery, Ursula Andress, Jack Lord, Bernard Lee, Joseph Wiseman. **1962 DVD**

DR. OTTO AND THE RIDDLE OF THE GLOOM BEAM ★★★ A fun and wacky journey into the mind of Jim Varney. Dr. Otto has a deranged plan and Lance Sterling is the only person who can stop him in this refreshingly strange comedy. A must for Varney fans. Rated PG. 97m. **DIR:** John R. Cherry, III. **CAST:** Jim Varney. **1986**

DR. PETIOT ★★★1/2 Michel Serrault delivers a chilling performance as the monstrous French doctor who murdered the desperate Jews he was paid to protect. After receiving all their valuables, he never gave them the promised safe passage to Argentina. Based on fact, this WWII horror story is all the more haunting as we witness the fiendish glee he takes with each new victim. Not rated, but definitely not for family viewing. In French with English subtitles. 102m. **DIR:** Christian de Chalonge. **CAST:** Michel Serrault, Pierre Romans, Zbigniew Horoks, Berangere Bonvoisin. **1990**

DR. PHIBES RISES AGAIN ★★★1/2 Good-natured terror abounds in this fun sequel to *The Abominable Dr. Phibes*, with Vincent Price reprising his role as a disfigured doctor desperately searching for a way to restore his dead wife to life. Entertaining. Rated PG for mild violence. 89m. **DIR:** Robert Fuest. **CAST:** Vincent Price, Robert Quarry, Peter Jeffrey, Fiona Lewis, Peter Cushing, Hugh Griffith, Terry-Thomas, Beryl Reid. **1972 DVD**

DOCTOR QUINN MEDICINE WOMAN ★★★ This pilot film for Jane Seymour's TV series is surprisingly riveting. Seymour convincingly plays a Boston doctor who goes west to start her practice. Scorned by the rugged pioneers she encounters, she must seek ways to prove her talents to them. Not rated; contains violence. 94m. **DIR:** Jeremy Paul Kagan. **CAST:** Jane Seymour, Joe Lando, Diane Ladd, Guy Boyd, Colm Meaney. **1992**

DR. STRANGE ★★ Another Marvel Comics superhero comes to life. Dr. Strange is chosen by the guardian of the spirit world to protect Earth from the evil villainess who is set on invading. The adventures of our hero are high on magic and sorcery for a fair rendition of the comic-book hero. 94m. **DIR:** Philip DeGuere. **CAST:** Peter Hooten, Clyde Kusatsu, Jessica Walter, Eddie Benton, John Mills. **1978**

DR. STRANGELOVE OR HOW I LEARNED TO STOP WORRYING AND LOVE THE BOMB ★★★★★ Stanley Kubrick's black comedy masterpiece about the dropping of the "bomb." Great performances from an all-star cast, including Peter Sellers in three hilarious roles. Don't miss it. B&W; 93m. **DIR:** Stanley Kubrick. **CAST:** Peter Sellers, Sterling Hayden, George C. Scott, Slim Pickens, Keenan Wynn, James Earl Jones. **1964 DVD**

DR. SYN ★★1/2 Master character actor George Arliss's final film has him playing a traditional English vicar who blossoms into a pirate when the sun goes down. Nothing earthshaking here, but direction and rich atmosphere make it all palatable. B&W; 80m. **DIR:** Roy William Neill. **CAST:** George Arliss, Margaret Lockwood, John Loder, Roy Emerton, Graham Moffatt. **1937**

DR. SYN, ALIAS THE SCARECROW ★★1/2 Showcased in America as a three-part television program in 1964, colorful tale of a man who poses as a minister by day and a champion of the oppressed by night. Patrick

McGoohan brings style and substance to the legendary Dr. Syn. 129m. **DIR:** James Neilson. **CAST:** Patrick McGoohan, George Cole, Tony Britton, Geoffrey Keen, Kay Walsh. **1962**

DR. T AND THE WOMEN ★★★1/2 A gynecologist finds himself involved in an affair when his wife loses touch with reality. Given that this is a Robert Altman film, there is, of course, much more going on than just that: this is a multicharacter ensemble piece in which the large cast has been encouraged to improvise. The result is a rich, flavorful character study that will appeal to the director's fans and possibly make a few converts to his unorthodox style of storytelling. Rated R for nudity and sex. 121m. **DIR:** Robert Altman. **CAST:** Richard Gere, Helen Hunt, Farrah Fawcett, Laura Dern, Shelley Long, Tara Reid, Kate Hudson, Liv Tyler, Robert Hays, Matt Malloy, Andy Richter, Lee Grant. **2000 DVD**

DOCTOR TAKES A WIFE, THE ★★★1/2 This delightful comedy employs an oft-used plot. Through a series of misadventures, Ray Milland is incorrectly identified as Loretta Young's handsome husband. So he takes advantage of the misunderstanding. All ends happily. B&W; 89m. **DIR:** Alexander Hall. **CAST:** Ray Milland, Loretta Young, Reginald Gardiner, Edmund Gwenn, Gail Patrick. **1940**

DR. TARR'S TORTURE DUNGEON ★★1/2 A reporter investigating an insane asylum in nineteenth-century France discovers that the director, whose therapy includes having patients act out their obsessions, is really one of the inmates. Much better than the usual Mexican schlock. Rated R for sex and violence. 88m. **DIR:** Juan Lopez Moctezuma. **CAST:** Claudio Brook, Ellen Sherman. **1972**

DR. TERROR'S HOUSE OF HORRORS ★★★ Good anthology horror entertainment about a fortune teller (Peter Cushing) who has some frightening revelations for his clients. A top-flight example of British genre moviemaking. 98m. **DIR:** Freddie Francis. **CAST:** Peter Cushing, Christopher Lee, Roy Castle, Donald Sutherland. **1965**

DR. WHO AND THE DALEKS ★★★ In this feature film derived from the BBC television series, an eccentric old scientist takes his friends to a planet that has been devastated by nuclear war, where they help a peace-loving people fight a race of war-mongering mutants who have encased their fragile bodies in robot shells. This juvenile science-fiction adventure should please youngsters. Rated G. 83m. **DIR:** Gordon Flemyng. **CAST:** Peter Cushing, Roy Castle, Jennie Linden, Barrie Ingham. **1965**

DR. WHO: REVENGE OF THE CYBERMEN ★★★ This is the first video from the popular British TV series and stars the fourth Dr. Who, Tom Baker. In this film, the evil Cybermen attempt to destroy the planet Voga, which is made of solid gold, the only item that can kill them. A good introduction to *Dr. Who*, the longest-running science-fiction TV series. 92m. **DIR:** Michael E. Briant. **CAST:** Tom Baker, Elizabeth Sladen. **1986**

DR. WHO (TV SERIES) ★★★★ Created in Britain in the early Sixties, *Dr. Who* is the longest-running science-fiction television series ever. Although marketed as a kids' show, *Dr. Who* appealed mostly to adults who understood the humor and the references. The first year left the viewers in the dark as to who the doctor and his niece really were, but gradually revealed the secret of their past (the good doctor and his niece were time lords of alien ancestry). Not rated, but suitable for kids. 95m. **DIR:** Various. **CAST:** William Hartnell, Patrick Troughton, Jon Pertwee, Tom Baker, Peter Davison, Colin Baker, Sylvester McCoy, William Russell, Jacqueline Hill, Carol Ann Ford. **1963–1989**

DOCTOR X ★★★1/2 From mayhem to murder, from cannibalism to rape—this picture offers it all. Dr. X is played with panache by Lionel Atwill. Lee Tracy is the reporter who tries valiantly to uncover and expose the mysterious doctor. This piece of vintage horror is a sure bet. 80m. **DIR:** Michael Curtiz. **CAST:** Lionel Atwill, Preston Foster, Fay Wray, Lee Tracy. **1932**

DR. ZHIVAGO ★★★★ In this epic film, Omar Sharif is Zhivago, a Russian doctor and poet whose personal life is ripped apart by the upheaval of the Russian Revolution. The choppy and lengthy screenplay is often sacrificed to the spectacle of vast panoramas, detailed sets, and impressive costumes, but these artistic elements, along with a beautiful musical score, make for cinema on a grand scale. Rated PG-13. 176m. **DIR:** David Lean. **CAST:** Omar Sharif, Julie Christie, Geraldine Chaplin, Rod Steiger, Alec Guinness, Tom Courtenay. **1965**

DOCTORS' WIVES 🦃 Trashy film that focuses on the seedy side of being a doctor's wife. Rated PG. 100m. **DIR:** George Schaefer. **CAST:** Gene Hackman, Richard Crenna, Carroll O'Connor, Janice Rule, Dyan Cannon, Cara Williams. **1971**

DODES 'KA-DEN ★★★★ Akira Kurosawa's first color film is a spellbinding blend of fantasy and reality. The film chronicles the lives of a group of Tokyo slum dwellers that includes children, alcoholics, and the disabled. Illusion and imagination are their weapons as they fight for survival. In Japanese with English subtitles. 140m. **DIR:** Akira Kurosawa. **CAST:** Yoshitaka Zushi. **1970**

DODGE CITY ★★★★ Swashbuckler Errol Flynn sets aside his sword for a pair of six-guns to clean up the wild, untamed frontier city of the title. The best of Flynn's Westerns, this release is beautifully photographed in color with an all-star supporting cast. 105m. **DIR:** Michael Curtiz. **CAST:** Errol Flynn, Olivia de Havilland, Ann Sheridan, Bruce Cabot, Alan Hale Sr., Ward Bond. **1939**

DODSWORTH ★★★★ Walter Huston, in the title role, heads an all-star cast in this outstanding adaptation of the Sinclair Lewis novel. Auto tycoon Samuel Dodsworth is the epitome of the classic American self-made man. His wife is an appearance-conscious nouveau riche snob. An intelligent, mature script, excellent characterizations, and sensitive cinematography make this film a modern classic. B&W; 101m. **DIR:** William Wyler. **CAST:** Walter Huston, Ruth Chatterton, Mary Astor, David Niven, Spring Byington, Paul Lukas, John Payne, Maria Ouspenskaya. **1936 DVD**

DOES THIS MEAN WE'RE MARRIED? ★★1/2 Romantic comedy contains a sprinkling of bittersweet moments as an American comedienne earns her French green card by marrying an irresponsible playboy. Rated PG-13 for profanity, nudity, and violence. 93m. **DIR:** Carol Wiseman. **CAST:** Patsy Kensit, Stephane Freiss. **1990**

DOG DAY 🦃 Lee Marvin is an American fugitive on the run in this maudlin and often offensive tale of intrigue set in France. Sex, profanity, and violence. 101m. **DIR:** Yves Boisset. **CAST:** Lee Marvin, Jean Carmet, Victor Lanoux, Miou-Miou, Tina Louise. **1985 DVD**

DOG DAY AFTERNOON ★★★★1/2 A masterpiece of contemporary commentary. Al Pacino once again proves himself to be in the front rank of America's finest actors. Director Sidney Lumet scores high with masterful pacing and real suspense. This is an offbeat drama about a gay man who's involved in bank robbing. Highly recommended. Rated R. 130m. **DIR:** Sidney Lumet. **CAST:** Al Pacino, John Cazale, Charles Durning, Carol Kane, Chris Sarandon. **1975 DVD**

DOG EAT DOG ★★ Moll Jayne Mansfield and sundry gangsters, hiding out on a Greek island, fight over $1 million in cash. It's a dog all right, though the dialogue is good for some cheap laughs. B&W; 86m. **DIR:** Ray Nazarro. **CAST:** Cameron Mitchell, Jayne Mansfield, Isa Miranda. **1963**

DOG OF FLANDERS, A (1960) ★★★★ Ouida's world-famous 1872 tear jerking novel about a boy and his dog and their devotion to each other tastefully filmed in its European locale. Nello (David Ladd) delivers milk from a cart pulled by the dog Patrasche. Donald Crisp and Theodore Bikel shine in character roles, but the picture belongs to Ladd and the scene-stealing mutt fans will recall from *Old Yeller*. Have Kleenex handy. 96m. **DIR:** James B. Clark. **CAST:** David Ladd, Donald Crisp, Theodore Bikel. **1960**

DOG OF FLANDERS, A (1999) ★★1/2 The venerable children's classic about a poor boy and his dog gets a well-intentioned but lackluster retelling. The dog takes a backseat to the puppy-love romance between the boy and a neighbor girl, and the film's authentic look clashes badly with the too-modern dialogue; still, the strong supporting cast helps. An interesting sidelight: the 1960 version starred David Ladd, whose ex-wife Cheryl Ladd plays the girl's mother here. Rated PG. 100m. **DIR:** Kevin Brodie. **CAST:** Jeremy James Kissner, Jack Warden, Jesse James, Madylin Sweeten, Jon Voight, Cheryl Ladd. **1999**

DOG PARK ★★★ A dog park serves as the breeding ground for love and romance in this engaging comedy about a classified-ad writer who's afraid to commit to anyone but his dog. When he finally meets the woman who makes him sit up and beg, he discovers that she also has commitment issues. How their respective dogs manage to bring them together makes for enjoyable viewing. Rated R for adult situations and language. 91m. **DIR:** Bruce McCulloch. **CAST:** Luke Wilson, Natasha Henstridge, Kathleen Robertson, Janeane Garofalo, Bruce McCulloch, Harland Williams. **1998**

DOG SOLDIER: SHADOWS OF THE PAST ★★ Japanese animation. A troubled ex-Green Beret and his buddy are enlisted by the government to take on a supervillain who has stolen a virus with a potential for biological warfare. Only for die-hard animation fans. In Japanese with English subtitles. Not rated; contains violence. 45m. **DIR:** Hiroyuki Ebata. **1989**

DOG STAR MAN ★★★★ An abstract vision of the creation of the universe—an epic work consisting of a prelude and four parts, making brilliant use of superimpositions, painting on film, distorting lenses, and rhythmic montage. This feature makes for hypnotic experimenting in silent filmmaking. 78m. **DIR:** Stan Brakhage. **1964**

DOG TROUBLE ★★1/2 This television fantasy, based on T. Ernesto Bethancourt's *The Dog Days of Arthur Cane*, borrows heavily from the Disney *Shaggy Dog* series. Here, selfish behavior causes young Arthur to be cursed by a very unusual spell. Now an Australian sheepdog (adeptly played by the expressive Bandit), Arthur must somehow redeem himself to become a boy again. The lack of originality and a cliché-ridden plot override the moral: children should be generous and giving. Rated G. 40m. **DIR:** Robert C. Thompson. **CAST:** Ross Harris, John Scott Clough, Linda Henning, Alex Henteloff. **1984**

DOGFIGHT ★★1/2 River Phoenix is one of a group of Marines who stage an "ugly date" contest on the eve of their departure to Vietnam. Even though the premise is incredibly mean-spirited, this is actually a fairly entertaining flick. Rated R for profanity and brief violence. 95m. **DIR:** Nancy Savoca. **CAST:** River Phoenix, Lili Taylor, Richard Panebianco, Anthony Clark, Mitchell Whitfield, Holly Near. **1991**

DOGFIGHTERS, THE ★★ These "Top Guns" are stuck in a bottom-feeder movie that lacks originality and a budget to make a difference. Robert Davi is totally miscast as a fighter pilot sent to destroy a plutonium plant in Eastern Europe. Unspectacular special effects and ho-hum aerial sequences do little to pick things up. Rated R for profanity and violence. 96m. **DIR:** Barry Zetlin. **CAST:** Robert Davi, Alexander Godunov, Ben Gazzara, Lara Harris. **1995**

DOGMA ★★1/2 Two fallen angels (Matt Damon, Ben Affleck) may trigger the Apocalypse if they succeed in reentering Heaven, so a lapsed Catholic (Linda Fiorentino) is recruited to stop them. Writer-director Kevin Smith's doomsday comedy sparked protests for its supposed blasphemy, but it is more irreverent (and certainly profane) than sacrilegious. It also has a high percentage of misfired gags and a poor performance by Fiorentino weighing it down. Rated R for profanity. 125m. **DIR:** Kevin Smith. **CAST:** Ben Affleck, Matt Damon, Linda Fiorentino, Salma Hayek, Jason Lee, Alan Rickman, Chris Rock. **1999 DVD**

DOGPOUND SHUFFLE Ron Moody and David Soul as two drifters who rescue a dog from the pound. Rated PG for language. 98m. **DIR:** Jeffrey Bloom. **CAST:** Ron Moody, David Soul, Raymond Sutton, Pamela McMyler, Ray Stricklyn. **1974**

DOGS IN SPACE ★★ Michael Hutchence, the lead singer of the Australian rock group INXS, stars in this film about the pop culture in Melbourne in 1978. This is a trip through the sexually permissive commune that merely serves as a setting for the singing performances of Hutchence. This is really only for the enjoyment of his fans and not the general public. Rated R for profanity, nudity, and suggested sex. 109m. **DIR:** Richard Lowenstein. **CAST:** Michael Hutchence, Saskia Post, Chris Haywood. **1988**

DOGS OF HELL Low-budget thriller about a rural sheriff and a pack of rottweilers. Originally filmed in 3-D, the movie is rated R for profanity and graphic violence. 90m. **DIR:** Worth Keeter. **CAST:** Earl Owensby. **1982**

DOGS OF WAR, THE ★★ A graphic account of the coup d'etat of a West African dictatorship (starring Christopher Walken as the leader of a band of mercenaries). Unfortunately, this movie doesn't quite hold together. Rated R for violence. 102m. **DIR:** John Irvin. **CAST:** Christopher Walken, Tom Berenger, Colin Blakely, Hugh Millais. **1980 DVD**

DOIN' TIME 🦃 *Doin' Time* is a bum rap. Rated R for profanity and sex. 84m. **DIR:** George Mendeluk. **CAST:** Jeff Altman, Dey Young, Richard Mulligan, John Vernon, Judy Landers, Colleen Camp, Melanie Chartoff, Graham Jarvis, Pat McCormick, Eddie Velez, Jimmie Walker. **1984**

DOIN' TIME ON PLANET EARTH ★★1/2 A teenage nerd living in Sunnydale, Arizona ("Prune Capital of the World"), feels so out of place that he wonders if he isn't really from another planet. His unique "adoption fantasy" is fed by the arrival of two weirdos (Adam West and Candace Azzara). First-time director Charles Matthau (son of Walter) makes the most of a meager budget and an uneven cast. Rated PG. 83m. **DIR:** Charles Matthau. **CAST:** Nicholas Strouse, Adam West, Candy Azzara, Martha Scott, Matt Alden, Andrea Thompson. **1988**

DOLEMITE ★★ Nightclub owner tracks down the drug dealers who framed him. Supposedly a parody of blaxploitation movies, you'll be laughing at this rather than with it. Rated R for nudity, sexual situations, violence, and profanity. 89m. **DIR:** D'Urville Martin. **CAST:** Rudy Ray Moore, D'Urville Martin, Jerry Jones. **1975 DVD**

DOLL ★★★★ Per Oscarsson gives a remarkable performance as a lonely, depraved night watchman who steals a mannequin from a department store and engages in bizarre fantasies with it. Psychologically unsettling film. In Swedish with English subtitles. B&W; 94m. **DIR:** Arne Mattson. **CAST:** Per Oscarsson. **1962**

DOLL FACE ★★★ "Hubba Hubba Hubba." That's the song that launched Perry Como, and it was in this movie that it was first sung. Vivian Blaine is fine as a burlesque dancer who shoots to the top with the help of her boyfriend. It's one of those nice, often overlooked movies. B&W; 80m. **DIR:** Lewis Seiler. **CAST:** Vivian Blaine, Dennis O'Keefe, Perry Como, Carmen Miranda. **1945**

DOLL IN THE DARK, A 🦃 A Japanese tourist is kidnapped by a florist who is obsessed with Asian women in this weak rip-off of *The Collector*. Not rated; contains profanity, sexual situations, and violence. 94m. **DIR:** Philip Scarpaci. **CAST:** Billy Drago, Naomi Kawashima, Josh Brauer. **1998**

DOLLAR ★★ Three married couples bicker, flirt, separate, and unite all in one overblown weekend at a ski lodge. Noteworthy only for the radiant presence of a young Ingrid Bergman. In Swedish with English subtitles. B&W; 74m. **DIR:** Gustav Molander. **CAST:** Ingrid Bergman. **1938**

$ (DOLLARS) ★★★★★ Simply one of the best heist capers ever filmed. Warren Beatty, bank employee, teams with Goldie Hawn, hooker, to duplicate critical safe deposit keys for a cool $1.5 million. Intriguing concept, deftly directed in a fashion that reveals continuous unexpected plot twists. Rated R for violence and sexual situations. 119m. **DIR:** Richard Brooks. **CAST:** Warren Beatty, Goldie Hawn, Gert Fröbe, Robert Webber. **1972**

DOLLMAKER, THE ★★★★ Jane Fonda won an Emmy for her intensely quiet portrayal of a mother of five in 1940s Kentucky. As a devoted mother, her only personal happiness is sculpting dolls out of wood. When her husband is forced to take work in Detroit, their relocation causes many personal hardships and setbacks. The story is beautifully told. This made-for-TV movie is unrated, but it provides excellent family entertainment. 140m. **DIR:** Daniel Petrie. **CAST:** Jane Fonda, Levon Helm, Amanda Plummer, Susan Kingsley, Ann Hearn, Geraldine Page. **1984**

DOLLMAN ★★1/2 Futuristic cop chases a suspect through a time warp, crash landing on present-day Earth, where the bigger-than-life hero finds himself only thirteen inches tall—but with an attitude. The carnage that permeates this film is vicious. Rated R for violence. 87m. **DIR:** Albert Pyun. **CAST:** Tim Thomerson, Jackie Earle Haley, Nicholas Guest. **1991**

DOLLMAN VS. DEMONIC TOYS ★★ In this high-concept, low-budget jumble, several drive-in regulars meet for one final, lackluster showdown. Dollman (Tim Thomerson) teams up with Tracy Scoggins and shrunken nurse Melissa Behr (so reduced in *Bad Channels*) to fight possessed toys. Rated R for violence, language, and brief nudity. 84m. **DIR:** Charles Band. **CAST:** Tim Thomerson, Tracy Scoggins, Melissa Behr, Phil Brock, Phil Fondacaro. **1993**

DOLLS ★★1/2 During a fierce storm, six people are stranded at the home of a kindly old doll maker and his wife. One by one, they are attacked by malevolent little creatures in funny outfits. (No, not Campfire Girls.) From the same people who made *Re-Animator* and *From Beyond*. Rated R for violence. 77m. **DIR:** Stuart Gordon. **CAST:** Stephen Lee, Guy Rolfe, Hilary Mason. **1987**

DOLL'S HOUSE, A (1973) ★★★ Jane Fonda is quite good in this screen version of Henrik Ibsen's play about a liberated woman in the nineteenth century, and her struggles to maintain her freedom. Pacing is a problem at times, but first-class acting and beautiful sets keep the viewer interested. 103m. **DIR:** Joseph Losey. **CAST:** Jane Fonda, David Warner, Trevor Howard. **1973**

DOLL'S HOUSE, A (1989) ★★★★ A spoiled housewife (Claire Bloom), confident that her husband adores her, is in for a rude awakening when a past transgression resurfaces and threatens her carefree existence. Fine rendition of Ibsen's masterpiece. Rated G. 96m. **DIR:** Patrick Garland. **CAST:** Claire Bloom, Anthony Hopkins, Ralph Richardson, Denholm Elliott. **1989**

DOLLY DEAREST ★★1/2 When an American family takes ownership of a run-down Mexican doll factory, they find that their new lease in life is no *Child's Play*. As luck would have it, the factory sits next to an ancient burial ground. Rated R for violence. 94m. **DIR:** Maria Lease. **CAST:** Rip Torn, Sam Bottoms, Denise Crosby. **1991**

DOLLY SISTERS, THE ★★★★ A rare case of a fictionalized movie biography that offers style and truth. 114m. **DIR:** Irving Cummings. **CAST:** Betty Grable, June Haver, John Payne, Reginald Gardiner, Frank Latimore, S. Z. Sakall. **1945**

DOLORES CLAIBORNE ★★★★ This thoughtful Stephen King adaptation is drawn from another of the terror master's straight dramas and benefits from Kathy

Bates's performance as a Maine housekeeper accused of murdering her employer and now reluctantly reunited with her estranged daughter. Rated R for profanity, violence, and deviant sexual behavior. 131m. **DIR:** Taylor Hackford. **CAST:** Kathy Bates, Jennifer Jason Leigh, Judy Parfitt, Christopher Plummer, David Strathairn, Eric Bogosian, John C. Reilly. **1995 DVD**

•DOMESTIC DISTURBANCE ★★★ In many ways, this tidy little thriller is reasonably shrewd and sensible, which makes the logical lapses in its script particularly unforgivable. John Travolta plays a devoted father and ex-husband whose only son has a habit of lying, and thus isn't believed when he insists that his new stepfather killed a guy. Although the film sets a good mood and amplifies suspense nicely, as we move into the final act we're annoyed and no longer cooperative, having been dragged through several glaring plot holes that easily could've been avoided. Rated PG-13 for violence and profanity. 89m. **DIR:** Harold Becker. **CAST:** John Travolta, Vince Vaughn, Teri Polo, Matthew O'Leary, Steve Buscemi. **2001 DVD**

DOMINICK AND EUGENE ★★★★1/2 Fraternal twin brothers Dominick and Eugene Luciano have big plans for the future. Eugene (Ray Liotta), an ambitious medical student, plans to take care of Dominick (Tom Hulce), who is considered "slow" but nonetheless has been supporting them by working as a trash collector. All "Nicky" wants is to live in a house by a lake where he and his brother can be together. This is a deeply touching film; superbly directed and acted. Rated PG-13. 103m. **DIR:** Robert M. Young. **CAST:** Tom Hulce, Ray Liotta, Jamie Lee Curtis, Todd Graff, Robert Levine. **1988 DVD**

DOMINION 🦃 Kids are a pain in the neck in this horror flick about pint-sized vampires. Not rated; contains violence and profanity. 70m. **DIR:** Todd Sheets. **CAST:** Carol Barta, Frank Dunlay, Auggi Alvarez, Tonia Monahan, Jenny Admire. **1994**

DOMINIQUE IS DEAD ★★1/2 Weird film from England about a greedy man attempting to rid himself of his wife in order to get his hands on her money. Of course, things don't quite work out as planned. Mildly interesting movie, also known as *Dominique*. Rated PG. 98m. **DIR:** Michael Anderson. **CAST:** Cliff Robertson, Jean Simmons, Jenny Agutter, Flora Robson, Judy Geeson. **1978**

DOMINO ★★ Artsy Italian film delves into the surreal as it follows Brigitte Nielsen in her quest for love. She's been looking in all the wrong places and now thinks she's found it in the voice of an obscene caller. Rated R for nudity and countless sexual situations. 96m. **DIR:** Ivana Massetti. **CAST:** Brigitte Nielsen. **1989**

DOMINO PRINCIPLE, THE 🦃 Assassination/double-cross/conspiracy thriller. R for violence. 100m. **DIR:** Stanley Kramer. **CAST:** Gene Hackman, Richard Widmark, Candice Bergen, Eli Wallach, Mickey Rooney. **1977**

DON IS DEAD, THE ★★★1/2 Director Richard Fleischer gives us yet another story of a Mafia family struggling for control of Las Vegas interests (à la *The Godfather*). Well-acted performances make for better-than-average viewing. Rated R for violence. 115m. **DIR:** Richard Fleischer. **CAST:** Anthony Quinn, Frederic Forrest, Robert Forster, Al Lettieri, Angel Tompkins, Charles Cioffi. **1973**

DON JUAN ★★★ The now-legendary Great Profile John Barrymore is at the top of his hand-kissing, cavalier womanizing form in this entertaining romantic adventure. The first silent released with canned music and sound effects. Silent. B&W; 111m. **DIR:** Alan Crosland. **CAST:** John Barrymore, Mary Astor, Estelle Taylor, Myrna Loy. **1926**

DON JUAN DEMARCO ★★★ Johnny Depp plays a mental patient who imagines himself the descendant of the famous lover; Marlon Brando is his aging psychiatrist, envying "Don Juan's" romantic outlook. Depp's personal charm keeps the soggy nonsense afloat. Rated PG-13 for mildly sexual situations. 90m. **DIR:** Jeremy Leven. **CAST:** Johnny Depp, Marlon Brando, Faye Dunaway, Rachel Ticotin, Bob Dishy, Talisa Soto, Richard Sarafian, Franc Luz, Geraldine Pailhas. **1995 DVD**

DON KING: ONLY IN AMERICA ★★★★ Boxing promoter and entrepreneur Don King uses his flamboyant style and questionable business practices to rise to the top of the boxing game only to encounter numerous pitfalls along the way. Outstanding biography benefits immensely from Ving Rhames, who virtually becomes this man. Made for cable. Rated R for adult situations, language, nudity, and violence. 112m. **DIR:** John Herzfeld. **CAST:** Ving Rhames, Vondie Curtis-Hall, Jeremy Piven, Loretta Devine. **1997**

DON Q, SON OF ZORRO ★★★1/2 Derring-do in old California as the inimitable Douglas Fairbanks fights evildoers and greedy oppressors while saving ladylove Mary Astor from a fate worse than death. Well-mounted, inventive, and fast-paced. Silent. B&W; 111m. **DIR:** Donald Crisp. **CAST:** Douglas Fairbanks Sr., Mary Astor, Jack McDonald, Donald Crisp. **1925**

DON QUIXOTE (1933) ★★★ A strange amalgam of Cervantes' novel and a quasi-operatic treatment by composer Jacques Ibert. Of interest primarily to opera purists and G. W. Pabst buffs, it is a splendid document of the great opera basso, Feodor Chaliapin. Pabst's moody visuals nicely complement the singing. In French with English subtitles. B&W; 82m. **DIR:** G. W. Pabst. **CAST:** Feodor Chaliapin. **1933**

DON QUIXOTE (1988) ★★★★★ A thrilling and gorgeous production of the tale of the old knight who dreams of chivalry and fighting windmills. Critics hailed this performance as one of the greatest large-cast ballets ever recorded. A must for a grand night at the ballet. 120m. **DIR:** Marius Petipa, Alexander Gorsky. **CAST:** Kirov Ballet. **1988 DVD**

DON QUIXOTE (2000) ★★★1/2 This TNT/Hallmark Entertainment collaboration allows John Lithgow to brilliantly adapt Miguel de Cervantes's aging Everyman into a noble knight. The most mundane scene takes on an exciting aura as he sets out to right imagined wrongs. As his devoted sidekick, Bob Hoskins provides first-rate comic relief. Not rated; contains comic-book violence. 120m. **DIR:** Peter Yates. **CAST:** John Lithgow, Bob Hoskins, Isabella Rossellini, Vanessa L. Williams. **2000**

DONA FLOR AND HER TWO HUSBANDS ★★★★ A ribald Brazilian comedy about a woman (Sonia Braga) haunted by the sexy ghost of her first husband (José

Wilker), who's anything but happy about her impending remarriage, this film inspired the Sally Field vehicle *Kiss Me Goodbye*. The original is better all around. In Portuguese with English subtitles. Not rated; the film has nudity. 106m. **DIR:** Bruno Barreto. **CAST:** Sonia Braga, José Wilker, Mauro Mendonca. **1978**

DONKEY SKIN (PEAU D'ÂNE) ★★★★ Looking for a fairy tale for an adult audience? A princess, about to be forced to marry her own father, hides out as a scullery maid. Before long, the local Prince Charming sees through her drab disguise. A delightful combination of the real and the dreamlike that could have been unbearably cute in less skilled hands. Okay for kids, but not really intended for them. In French with English subtitles. 90m. **DIR:** Jacques Demy. **CAST:** Catherine Deneuve, Jean Marais, Jacques Perrin, Delphine Seyrig. **1970**

DONNA HERLINDA AND HER SON ★★★ This highly enjoyable, raunchy comedy explores the bizarre relationship a mother has with her sexually liberated homosexual son. It's a delightful comedy of manners featuring a memorable cast and a director with a great touch for deadpan humor. In Spanish with English subtitles. 90m. **DIR:** Jaime Humberto Hermosillo. **CAST:** Guadalupe Del Toro, Marco Antonio Trevino. **1986**

DONNER PASS: THE ROAD TO SURVIVAL ★★ This fair made-for-TV retelling of the true story of the Donner party is based on historical accounts and tells of the snowstorm that traps the party and the physical hardship and starvation that lead to the infamous conclusion. Made for TV. 98m. **DIR:** James L. Conway. **CAST:** Robert Fuller, Diane McBain, Andrew Prine, John Anderson, Michael Callan. **1978**

DONNIE BRASCO ★★★★1/2 In this crime-drama, the title character, an FBI agent has burrowed so deep into the Mafia that he becomes "a made guy." It's a seductive life, one based on loyalty and trust. Brasco is particularly fond of Lefty Ruggiero, his mentor. Still, the question remains, is he a hood called Brasco or an agent named Joe Pistone? Based on a true story, this film is enthralling throughout. Rated R for profanity and violence. 121m. **DIR:** Mike Newell. **CAST:** Al Pacino, Johnny Depp, Michael Madsen, Bruno Kirby, James Russo, Anne Heche. **1997 DVD**

•DONNIE DARKO ★★★★ A constant current of apprehension and doom runs through this offbeat psychological thriller about a disturbed teenage boy and his unnatural relationship with a human-sized rabbit that frequents his dreams and tells him to do bad things. Jake Gyllenhaal is perfect in the title role. Unpredictable, thought-provoking, and creepy, *Donnie Darko* challenges you with its abstract reasoning and dreamlike states. Rated R for adult situations, drugs, language, and violence. 122m. **DIR:** Richard Kelly. **CAST:** Jake Gyllenhaal, Mary McDonnell, Jena Malone, Drew Barrymore, Noah Wyle, Patrick Swayze, Katharine Ross. **2001 DVD**

DONOR, THE ★★ Action star Jeff Wincott plays Billy Castle, a professional stuntman who is a specimen of perfect health. That's good for his job, but bad for his private life, as Billy becomes an unwitting donor for an illegal organ bank. Rated R for violence, language, and nudity. 94m. **DIR:** Damien Lee. **CAST:** Jeff Wincott, Michelle Johnson, Gordon Thompson. **1994**

DONOR UNKNOWN ★★1/2 A wealthy man suffers a heart attack and wakes up to find he's had a heart transplant. As he attempts to learn about the donor, he uncovers a sinister conspiracy in this slow-moving but sometimes interesting made-for-cable original. Not rated; contains violence and suggested sex. 93m. **DIR:** John Harrison. **CAST:** Peter Onorati, Alice Krige, Clancy Brown, Richard Portnow, Sam Robards. **1995**

DONOVAN'S BRAIN ★★★ After his death in a plane crash, a powerful business magnate has his brain removed by a research scientist (Lew Ayres) who hopes to communicate with the organ by feeding it electricity. Before you know it, the brain is in control, forcing the doctor to obey its ever-increasing demands. Credible acting and tight pacing. B&W; 83m. **DIR:** Felix Feist. **CAST:** Lew Ayres, Nancy Davis, Gene Evans, Steve Brodie. **1953 DVD**

DONOVAN'S REEF ★★★ Director John Ford's low, knock-about style of comedy prevails in this tale of two old drinking, seafaring buddies—John Wayne and Lee Marvin—forced to aid another pal, Jack Warden, in putting on an air of respectability to impress the latter's visiting daughter (Elizabeth Allen). 109m. **DIR:** John Ford. **CAST:** John Wayne, Lee Marvin, Elizabeth Allen, Jack Warden, Dorothy Lamour. **1963 DVD**

DON'S ANALYST, THE ★★1/2 A therapist gives a Mafia don a new look at life in this mildy entertaining comedy. Great cast gives it a shot, though. Rated R for language and nudity. 103m. **DIR:** David Jablin. **CAST:** Kevin Pollak, Robert Loggia, Joseph Bologna, Angie Dickinson, Sherilyn Fenn. **1997**

DON'S PARTY ★★★1/2 *Don's Party* is a hilarious, and at times vulgar, adult comedy. Like the characters in *Who's Afraid of Virginia Woolf?*, the eleven revelers at Don's party lose all control, and the evening climaxes in bitter hostilities and humiliating confessions. With no MPAA rating, the film has nudity and profanity. 91m. **DIR:** Bruce Beresford. **CAST:** John Hargreaves, Pat Bishop, Graham Kennedy. **1976 DVD**

DON'T ANSWER THE PHONE ★★ Also known as *The Hollywood Strangler*, this unpleasantly brutal exploitation quickie might have been better in more competent hands. Rated R for violence and nudity. 94m. **DIR:** Robert Hammer. **CAST:** James Westmoreland. **1981 DVD**

DON'T BE A MENACE TO SOUTH CENTRAL WHILE DRINKING YOUR JUICE IN THE 'HOOD 🦃 Unfunny, stereotypical, stupid, and crass. The Wayans family should have known better. Rated R for profanity and mock violence. 89m. **DIR:** Paris Barclay. **CAST:** Shawn Wayans, Marlon Wayans, Suli McCullough, Chris Spencer, Darrell Heath. **1996 DVD**

DON'T BE AFRAID OF THE DARK ★★★ Scary TV movie as newlyweds Kim Darby and Jim Hutton move into a weird old house inhabited by eerie little monsters who want Kim for one of their own. The human actors are okay, but the creatures steal the show. 74m. **DIR:** John Newland. **CAST:** Kim Darby, Jim Hutton, Pedro Armendariz Jr., William Demarest. **1973**

DON'T BOTHER TO KNOCK ★★★ An early and very effective performance by Marilyn Monroe as a neurotic baby-sitter who goes over the edge. Will hold your interest. Anne Bancroft's film debut. B&W; 76m. **DIR:** Roy

Ward Baker. **CAST:** Richard Widmark, Marilyn Monroe, Anne Bancroft, Elisha Cook Jr. **1952**

DON'T CRY, IT'S ONLY THUNDER ★★★★ Here is one of those "little" movies that slipped by without much notice yet is so satisfying when discovered by adventurous video renters. A black market wheeler-dealer (Dennis Christopher), lining his pockets behind the lines during the Vietnam War is forced to aid some Asian nuns and their ever-increasing group of Saigon street orphans. The results are predictably heartwarming and occasionally heartbreaking, but the film never drifts off into sentimental melodrama. Rated PG. 108m. **DIR:** Peter Werner. **CAST:** Dennis Christopher, Susan Saint James. **1982**

DON'T DO IT ★★ This supposed comedy takes a cold look at love among the Generation X crowd as three couples right out of central casting change their moods as often as their partners. Rated R for profanity, adult themes, and sexual situations. 90m. **DIR:** Eugene Hess. **CAST:** Alexis Arquette, Balthazar Getty, Heather Graham, James LeGros, Sheryl Lee, James Marshall, Esai Morales. **1995 DVD**

DON'T DRINK THE WATER ★★★★1/2 Jackie Gleason plays a caterer on a vacation with his wife and daughter. When the plane taking them to Greece is hijacked behind the Iron Curtain, Gleason is accused of spying and finds asylum in the U.S. embassy. Based on Woody Allen's wacky play. Rated G. 100m. **DIR:** Howard Morris. **CAST:** Jackie Gleason, Estelle Parsons, Ted Bessell, Joan Delaney, Michael Constantine, Howard St. John, Danny Meehan, Richard Libertini. **1969**

DON'T FENCE ME IN ★★★★1/2 Outstanding Roy Rogers film. Fans rate it one of his five best. Reporter Dale Evans comes west seeking legendary gunslinger Wildcat Kelly, who turns out to be Gabby Hayes. Hayes steals the film, which includes the Sons of the Pioneers' classic "Tumbling Tumbleweeds" as well as the Cole Porter title song. B&W; 71m. **DIR:** John English. **CAST:** Roy Rogers, George "Gabby" Hayes, Dale Evans, Robert Livingston, Marc Lawrence, Bob Nolan and the Sons of the Pioneers. **1945**

DON'T GO IN THE HOUSE A mom-obsessed killer grows up wanting to set pretty young women on fire. Rated R. 82m. **DIR:** James Ellison. **CAST:** Dan Grimaldi. **1980 DVD**

DON'T GO NEAR THE WATER ★★★ World War II navy public-relations personnel try to grab the glory away from the other services. Mickey Shaughnessy's role as a foul-mouthed enlisted man is one of the greatest jokes ever played on movie censors. Turn up the sound and pay attention—they apparently didn't. 107m. **DIR:** Charles Walters. **CAST:** Glenn Ford, Gia Scala, Earl Holliman, Anne Francis, Keenan Wynn, Fred Clark, Eva Gabor, Russ Tamblyn, Mickey Shaughnessy, Mary Wickes, Jack Albertson. **1957**

DON'T GO TO SLEEP ★★1/2 Supernatural thriller goes the distance but comes up short as the deceased daughter of a couple returns from the grave in order to reunite her family—on the other side. Made-for-television suspense works because of above-average cast. 100m. **DIR:** Richard Lang. **CAST:** Dennis Weaver, Valerie Harper, Ruth Gordon, Robert Webber. **1982**

DON'T HANG UP ★★★1/2 Wonderful transcontinental romance features Rosanna Arquette and David Suchet as two lonely people on opposite continents who discover friendship and then love via a series of long-distance phone calls. Arquette plays a handicapped New York actress who is embarrassed by her crutches. Suchet plays a man who suffers from agoraphobia, and finds solace in his London apartment through his conversations with the actress. It's a sentimental, poignant tale of blind love and faith. Not rated. 84m. **DIR:** Barry Davis. **CAST:** Rosanna Arquette, David Suchet. **1990**

DON'T LET YOUR MEAT LOAF ★★ Three Brooklyn friends who want to be professional comics try to raise money to open their own comedy club. Filmmaker Leander Sales deserves credit for making a movie on an apparently nonexistent budget, but the amateurish result hardly seems worth the effort. Not rated; contains mild violence, brief nudity, sexual situations, substance abuse, and profanity. 81m. **DIR:** Leander Sales. **CAST:** Leander Sales, Dana S. Hubbard, Brad Albright, Khadijah Karriem. **1995**

DON'T LOOK BACK (1967) ★★★ A documentary account directed by D. A. Pennebaker of folksinger/poet ("guitarist," he calls himself) Bob Dylan on a 1965 tour of England. The tedium of travel and pressures of performing are eased by relaxing moments with fellow travelers Joan Baez, Alan Price, and (briefly) Donovan. Shot in striking black and white, with excellent sound quality. Not rated, it contains some vulgarity. B&W; 96m. **DIR:** D. A. Pennebaker. **CAST:** Bob Dylan, Joan Baez, Donovan, Alan Price. **1967**

DON'T LOOK BACK (1996) ★★★ It's awfully hard to like this story's protagonist, a drunk and drug user who steals money from the mob, then involves childhood friends by leading the bad guys to his small hometown. Although star Eric Stoltz doesn't do anything to make this guy endearing, there's plenty of suspense while worrying about his completely innocent buddies. Rated R for profanity, violence, and drug use. 90m. **DIR:** Geoff Murphy. **CAST:** Eric Stoltz, John Corbett, Josh Hamilton, Billy Bob Thornton, Annabeth Gish, Dwight Yoakam, Amanda Plummer, Peter Fonda. **1996**

DON'T LOOK BACK: THE STORY OF LEROY "SATCHEL" PAIGE ★★ Made-for-television docudrama about legendary baseball player Leroy "Satchel" Paige and his crusade to get black ball players out of the Negro leagues and into the majors. Despite a good cast and inspiring subject matter, film comes up short. 89m. **DIR:** Richard A. Colla. **CAST:** Louis Gossett Jr., Cleavon Little, Clifton Davis, Jim Davis, Hal Williams, Beverly Todd, Ernie Barnes, Ossie Davis. **1981**

DON'T LOOK IN THE BASEMENT ★★1/2 When the director of an insane asylum is murdered by one of the inmates, his assistant takes over. But that doesn't put an end to the murders. This is one horror movie in which the low budget actually helps; the lack of professionalism in the production gives it a disturbingly eerie aura. Rated R for violence. 95m. **DIR:** S. F. Brownrigg. **CAST:** William McGee. **1973 DVD**

DON'T LOOK NOW ★★★★ Excellent psychic thriller about a married couple who, just after the accidental drowning of their young daughter, start having strange occurrences in their lives. Beautifully photographed by director Nicolas Roeg. Strong performances by Julie Christie and Donald Sutherland make this film a must-see. Rated R. 110m. **DIR:** Nicolas Roeg. **CAST:** Julie Christie, Donald Sutherland. **1973**

DON'T MESS WITH MY SISTER A young man trapped in a forced marriage. Not rated; contains profanity, violence, and sexual situations. 85m. **DIR:** Meir Zarchi. **CAST:** Joe Perce, Jeannine Lemay. **1985 DVD**

DON'T OPEN TILL CHRISTMAS ★★1/2 A crazed maniac mutilates and kills bell-ringing Santas, and no one has a clue to the killer's identity, not even the filmmakers. But even with this problem, there is still a good bit of suspense. Not rated; contains graphic violence and profanity. 86m. **DIR:** Edmund Purdom. **CAST:** Edmund Purdom, Caroline Munro, Gerry Sundquist. **1985**

DON'T RAISE THE BRIDGE, LOWER THE RIVER Weak vehicle for Jerry Lewis concerns his efforts to keep his marriage alive. Rated G. 99m. **DIR:** Jerry Paris. **CAST:** Jerry Lewis, Terry-Thomas, Jacqueline Pearce, Bernard Cribbins. **1968**

•DON'T SAY A WORD ★★★ Andrew Klavan's Edgar Award–winning novel is a helluva thriller, but you'd never know it from this ham-fisted adaptation, which retains only the central storyline while utterly ignoring critical details and character issues. Michael Douglas does a fine job as a psychiatrist trapped into prying a secret from a young woman's mind; if he doesn't retrieve the information quickly, his kidnapped daughter will be killed. The film moves briskly, though not fast enough to obscure the glaring plot holes and unlikely leaps of logic. Rated R for profanity, violence, brief nudity, and children in peril. 113m. **DIR:** Gary Fleder. **CAST:** Michael Douglas, Sean Bean, Brittany Murphy, Guy Torry, Jennifer Esposito, Famke Janssen, Oliver Platt. **2001 DVD**

DON'T SLEEP ALONE Sleazy thriller about a pretty young woman who may be killing her lovers. Rated R for adult situations, language, nudity, and violence. 81m. **DIR:** Tim Andrew. **CAST:** Lisa Welti, Doug Jeffry, Robert Donovan. **1997**

DON'T TALK TO STRANGERS ★★★ In this made-for-cable original, a woman remarries and, on her way to California, her son is kidnapped. Her ex-husband is suspected, but people are not always what they appear to be. Suspenseful and enjoyable. Rated R for violence. 94m. **DIR:** Robert Lewis. **CAST:** Pierce Brosnan, Shanna Reed, Terry O'Quinn, Keegan MacIntosh, Michael MacRae. **1994**

DON'T TELL HER IT'S ME ★★★ A syrupy-sweet romantic comedy about a cancer patient (Steve Guttenberg) who can't get back into dating after his recovery has left him with no hair and a bloated face. His sister (Shelley Long) comes to his aid and turns him into the type of man the girl of his dreams (Jami Gertz) would want. Rated PG-13 for mild violence and brief profanity. 103m. **DIR:** Malcolm Mowbray. **CAST:** Steve Guttenberg, Jami Gertz, Shelley Long, Kyle MacLachlan, Madchen Amick. **1991**

DON'T TELL MOM THE BABYSITTER'S DEAD ★★ After their baby-sitter drops dead, four rowdy kids rely on their 17 year old sister to put food on the table. Unfortunately, the funniest line in this adolescent comedy is the film's title. Rated PG-13 for language. 142m. **DIR:** Stephen Herek. **CAST:** Christina Applegate, Joanna Cassidy, John Getz, Keith Coogan, Josh Charles. **1991 DVD**

DOOLINS OF OKLAHOMA ★★★★1/2 Oklahoma outlaw Bill Doolin attempts to go straight when he meets the right girl, only to be hounded by his own gang and an unrelenting marshal. Historically inaccurate, but well staged and action packed. B&W; 90m. **DIR:** Gordon Douglas. **CAST:** Randolph Scott, Louise Allbritton, George Macready, John Ireland, Noah Beery Jr. **1949**

DOOM ASYLUM A man responsible for his wife's accidental death inhabits an old abandoned asylum. Not rated; contains nudity and graphic violence. 77m. **DIR:** Richard Friedman. **CAST:** Patty Mullen, Ruth Collins. **1987**

DOOM GENERATION, THE ★★ Three teen slackers go on a cross-country sex-and-violence spree, meeting various bizarre characters and gaining a reputation as dangerous outlaws. Writer-director Gregg Araki's low-rent knockoff of *Natural Born Killers* has energy and anarchic spirit, but the jokes are lame and the shocks are sophomoric. Rated R for profanity, violence, nudity, and simulated sex. 85m. **DIR:** Gregg Araki. **CAST:** James Duval, Rose McGowan, Johnathon Schaech, Cress Williams, Parker Posey, Heidi Fleiss. **1995 DVD**

DOOMED CARAVAN ★★1/2 A crook with dreams of empire tries to take over a tough widow's freighting business and Hopalong Cassidy and his pals come to her rescue. B&W; 61m. **DIR:** Lesley Selander. **CAST:** William Boyd, Russell Hayden, Andy Clyde, Minna Gombell, Morris Ankrum, Georgia Hawkins. **1941**

DOOMED MEGALOPOLIS, PARTS 1–4 ★★★ The evil, adept Kato wars with the forces of good as he seeks to unleash the slumbering spirit that guards Tokyo in this nicely executed animated horror story with strong, original visuals and a suspenseful plot. Fine animation. Dubbed in English. Not rated; contains violence and nudity. 50m. **DIR:** Rin Taro. **1992**

DOOMED TO DIE ★★ Monogram's popular series about the aged Chinese detective, Mr. Wong, was running out of steam by the time this film, the fourth in the series, was released. Wong (Boris Karloff) is called in by hardboiled homicide captain Grant Withers after a millionaire is murdered and his ship is sunk. B&W; 68m. **DIR:** William Nigh. **CAST:** Boris Karloff, Grant Withers, Marjorie Reynolds, Melvin Lang, Guy Usher. **1940 DVD**

DOOMSDAY FLIGHT, THE ★★★ Rod Serling wrote the script for this made-for-television movie, the first to depict the hijacking of an airliner. A distraught Edmond O'Brien blackmails an airline company by planting a bomb aboard a passenger plane. May not be as provocative today. Still, good acting is on hand as the search for the bomb is carried out. 100m. **DIR:** William A. Graham. **CAST:** Jack Lord, Edmond O'Brien, Van Johnson, John Saxon, Michael Sarrazin. **1966**

DOOMSDAY GUN ★★★★ Slick drama with Frank Langella cast as genius inventor Gerald Bull, the wholly amoral scientist determined to develop the world's biggest gun. And that's just what he did—for Saddam Hussein, with the tacit approval of U.S. and British intelligence agencies. Rated PG-13 for profanity. 106m. **DIR:** Robert Young. **CAST:** Frank Langella, Alan Arkin, Kevin Spacey, Michael Kitchen, Francesca Annis, Tony Goldwyn, James Fox. **1994**

DOOMWATCH ★★1/2 Sci-fi for the *Masterpiece Theatre* crowd, with plenty of British reserve. A scientist aids the army in investigating an island where pollution has turned the population into mutants. Thoughtful, though not very scary. Based on a BBC miniseries. Not rated. 92m. **DIR:** Peter Sasdy. **CAST:** George Sanders, Ian Bannen, Judy Geeson. **1972 DVD**

DOOR TO DOOR ★★★1/2 An aspiring salesman learns the ropes from a veteran who has a variety of other ways of augmenting his income (very few of them legal). A gentle, offbeat comedy. Rated PG. 85m. **DIR:** Patrick Bailey. **CAST:** Ron Leibman, Arliss Howard, Jane Kaczmarek. **1984**

DOORS, THE ★★★1/2 Writer-director Oliver Stone's screen biography of rock group The Doors is a lot like the band it portrays: outrageous, exciting, boring, insightful, silly, and awfully pretentious. Nevertheless, Val Kilmer gives an inspired, spookily accurate performance as Jim Morrison. Rated R for simulated sex, profanity, and violence. 135m. **DIR:** Oliver Stone. **CAST:** Val Kilmer, Meg Ryan, Frank Whaley, Kevin Dillon, Kyle MacLachlan, Billy Idol, Dennis Burkley, Josh Evans, Kathleen Quinlan. **1991 DVD**

DOORS, THE SOFT PARADE ★★ For diehard Doors fans this tape is sheer heaven. Directed by Doors member Ray Manzarek, it's a collection of backstage clips and performances by the band, including the infamous Miami concert. Songs include "The Changeling," "Wishful Sinner," "Wild Child," "Build Me a Woman," "The Unknown Soldier," "The Soft Parade," and "Hello I Love You." Not rated. 50m. **DIR:** Ray Manzarek. **1969**

•DOORWAY, THE 🦃 Run-of-the-mill no-budget shocker about a nasty demon and its victims takes place in a haunted house and provides only the same old clichés. Rated R for violence, profanity, nudity, and simulated sex. 90m. **DIR:** Michael B. Druxman. **CAST:** Roy Scheider, Lauren Woodland, Christian Harmony. **2000 DVD**

DOPPELGANGER: THE EVIL WITHIN ★★ Drew Barrymore is either a schizoid murderer or actually has the evil counterpart she claims. A few chills before it deteriorates into drive-in hell. Rated R for profanity, violence, and nudity. 105m. **DIR:** Avi Nesher. **CAST:** Drew Barrymore, George Newbern. **1992**

DORIAN GRAY 🦃 Horrid updating of the Oscar Wilde classic novel. Fascinating story has never been more boring, with some good actors wasted. Alternate title: *The Secret of Dorian Gray*. Rated R. 93m. **DIR:** Massimo Dallamano. **CAST:** Helmut Berger, Richard Todd, Herbert Lom. **1970**

DORM THAT DRIPPED BLOOD, THE (PRANKS) 🦃 The only good thing about this film is the title. Rated R for violence. 84m. **DIR:** Jeffrey Obrow, Stephen Carpenter. **CAST:** Pamela Holland, Stephen Sachs. **1981**

DOT AND THE BUNNY ★★★ A little girl falls asleep, dreaming of her adventures with a lop-eared rabbit as they search for a missing baby kangaroo. Real-life backgrounds make this a unique production that involves animated characters parading about the Australian jungle. 79m. **DIR:** Yoram Gross. **1982**

DOUBLE AGENTS ★★★ A German agent tries to smuggle war secrets from England to France, while British intelligence tries to discover her identity and stop her. Intricate World War II suspense-drama. Dubbed. B&W; 81m. **DIR:** Robert Hossein. **CAST:** Marina Vlady, Robert Hossein. **1959**

DOUBLE BLAST ★★1/2 Action-packed kick-boxing film finds 10 year old Lorne Berfield and his 13 year old sister (Crystal Summer) tracking down the kidnappers of a noted scientist (Linda Blair). Kung-fu action mixed with *Indiana Jones*–like adventure makes this a pleasant diversion. Things really kick in when their father, kick-boxing champion Dale "Apollo" Cook, gets involved. Rated PG for violence. 89m. **DIR:** Tim Spring. **CAST:** Linda Blair, Dale "Apollo" Cook, Joe Estevez, Lorne Berfield, Crystal Summer. **1993**

DOUBLE CROSS ★★1/2 A small fender bender, a seductive blonde, and a simple little white lie prove disastrous for new stranger-in-town Patrick Bergin. When he locks fenders with ravishing Kelly Preston, Bergin is all too happy to forget about his car when he gets the chance to race Preston's engine. His life is in need of a tune-up when his sexual tryst implicates him in a small-town murder. Rated R for violence, adult situations, and language. 96m. **DIR:** Michael Keusch. **CAST:** Patrick Bergin, Kelly Preston, Jennifer Tilly, Kevin Tighe. **1994**

DOUBLE DEAL 🦃 Casual direction and a poor adaptation of a story that wasn't very good in the first place resulted in this dull programmer from RKO. B&W; 83m. **DIR:** Abby Berlin. **CAST:** Richard Denning, Marie Windsor, Carleton Young, Fay Baker, Taylor Holmes, Paul E. Burns, James Griffith. **1950**

DOUBLE DRAGON 🦃 Cheesy clash of good and evil based on the wildly popular video game in which a crime lord tries to snatch the second half of a magical medallion from three teens and rule the world. Rated PG-13 for language and violence. 95m. **DIR:** Jim Yukich. **CAST:** Robert Patrick, Mark Dacascos, Scott Wolf, Kristina Malandro Wagner, Julia Nickson. **1994 DVD**

DOUBLE DYNAMITE ★★1/2 Disappointing comedy about a bank teller (Frank Sinatra) who receives a generous reward for saving a gangster's life completely by accident. Sinatra and Groucho Marx can't rise above the weak script and direction. B&W; 80m. **DIR:** Irving Cummings. **CAST:** Frank Sinatra, Jane Russell, Groucho Marx. **1951**

DOUBLE EDGE ★★ Faye Dunaway plays an aggressive New York reporter on assignment in Jerusalem. She realizes that there are no clear-cut answers. Dunaway is believable as she struggles with both her toughness and vulnerability. Not rated; contains sex and violence. 96m. **DIR:** Amos Kollek. **CAST:** Faye Dunaway, Amos Kollek, Shmuel Shiloh, Muhamad Bakri. **1992**

DOUBLE EXPOSURE (1982) ★★★1/2 This psychological thriller about a photographer (Michael Callan) who has nightmares of murders that come true has some pretty ghoulish scenes. The cast puts in solid performances. Not rated; contains violence, profanity, nudity, and adult subject matter. 95m. **DIR:** Wiliam Byron Hillman. **CAST:** Michael Callan, Joanna Pettet, James Stacy, Pamela Hensley, Cleavon Little, Seymour Cassel, Robert Tessier. **1982**

DOUBLE EXPOSURE (1987) ★★★ Two aspiring Venice Beach photographers divide their time between trying to impress the local bathing beauties and solving a murder that they accidentally photographed (shades of *Blow-up!*). Standard comedy thriller done with a little panache. Rated R for nudity. 100m. **DIR:** Nico Mastorakis. **CAST:** Mark Hennessy, Scott King, John Vernon. **1987**

DOUBLE EXPOSURE (1989) ★★★ This biographical film about Depression-era photographer Margaret Bourke-White has a familiar plot: strong woman fights for equality in a man's profession. Exceptional performances save this telefilm from mediocrity. 94m. **DIR:** Lawrence Schiller. **CAST:** Farrah Fawcett, Frederic Forrest, David Huddleston, Jay Patterson. **1989**

DOUBLE EXPOSURE (1993) ★★ Abusive, obsessive husband Ian Buchanan believes his lovely wife (Jennifer Gatti) is having an affair, and hires private detective Ron Perlman to investigate. When the news comes back positive, Buchanan plots to do away with his wife. When Gatti turns up dead, the plot blows up in Buchanan's face. But did he really do it? Rated R for nudity, violence, and language. 93m. **DIR:** Claudia Hoover. **CAST:** Ron Perlman, Ian Buchanan, Jennifer Gatti, Dedee Pfeiffer, James McEachin, William R. Moses. **1993**

DOUBLE HAPPINESS ★★★ A 22 year old aspiring actress struggles to balance her life while living in Canada with her overprotective parents who are immigrants from Hong Kong. She has trouble negotiating her ethnicity with the world: her thespian goals do not meet the Old World expectations of her folks, and—even more horrific—she is secretly dating a white man. Partly in Chinese with English subtitles. Rated PG-13 for language, nudity, and suggested sex. 87m. **DIR:** Mina Shum. **CAST:** Sandra Oh, Alannah Ong, Stephen Chang, Frances You. **1995**

DOUBLE IMPACT ★★★ Jean-Claude Van Damme gets a chance to strut his acting stuff in the dual role of twin brothers—one a Beverly Hills aerobic instructor, the other a Hong Kong smuggler—who join forces to avenge their parents' murder. Enough action for Van Damme fans, coupled with a surprising amount of comedy. Rated R for violence, profanity, and simulated sex. 118m. **DIR:** Sheldon Lettich. **CAST:** Jean-Claude Van Damme, Geoffrey Lewis, Alan Scarfe. **1991 DVD**

DOUBLE INDEMNITY ★★★★★ This is one of the finest suspense films ever made. Fred MacMurray is an insurance salesman who, with Barbara Stanwyck, concocts a scheme to murder her husband and collect the benefits. The husband's policy, however, contains a rider that states that if the husband's death is caused by a moving train the policy pays double face value. Edward G. Robinson is superb as MacMurray's suspicious boss. B&W; 106m. **DIR:** Billy Wilder. **CAST:** Fred MacMurray, Barbara Stanwyck, Edward G. Robinson, Porter Hall. **1944 DVD**

DOUBLE JEOPARDY (1992) ★★ Romantic thrillers don't come much dumber than this mess, which finds Salt Lake City schoolmaster Bruce Boxleitner the sole witness to ex-girlfriend Rachel Ward's justifiable (?) murder of her violent boyfriend. Made for cable. 100m. **DIR:** Lawrence Schiller. **CAST:** Rachel Ward, Bruce Boxleitner, Sela Ward, Sally Kirkland, Jay Patterson. **1992**

DOUBLE JEOPARDY (1999) ★★★ Framed for a murder she didn't commit, Ashley Judd eludes her determined parole officer (Tommy Lee Jones) as she hunts down her rotten husband. To really enjoy this film, reality must be suspended and the improbable accepted as possible. The worst thing a viewer can do, in terms of enjoying this flick, is to wage a debate over the double jeopardy statute. Some tense moments lead to a satisfying confrontation. Rated R for sex, violence, and language. 93m. **DIR:** Bruce Beresford. **CAST:** Tommy Lee Jones, Ashley Judd, Benjamin Weir, Jay Brazeau, Bruce Greenwood. **1999 DVD**

DOUBLE LIFE, A ★★★★ Ronald Colman gives an Oscar-winning performance as a famous actor whose stage life begins to take over his personality and private life, forcing him to revert to stage characters, including Othello, to cope with everyday situations. Brilliantly written by Garson Kanin and Ruth Gordon, and impressively acted by a standout cast. Top treatment of a fine story. B&W; 104m. **DIR:** George Cukor. **CAST:** Ronald Colman, Edmond O'Brien, Shelley Winters, Ray Collins. **1947**

DOUBLE LIFE OF VERONIQUE, THE ★★★★ In this exquisite adult fairy tale, the luminous Irène Jacob plays the dual role of two identical women, one Polish and one French, who live parallel lives. It is an enigmatic but gorgeous film; one that often seems like a series of paintings come to life on-screen. In French and Polish with English subtitles. Not rated; the film has nudity and suggested sex. 105m. **DIR:** Krzysztof Kieslowski. **CAST:** Irène Jacob, Halina Gryglaszewska, Kalina Jedrusik. **1991**

DOUBLE MCGUFFIN, THE ★★★1/2 Here's another family (as opposed to children's) movie. It's full of Hitchcock references in a story about some smart kids who uncover a plot to kill the leader of a Middle Eastern country. The three nominal stars only have supporting parts; they get top billing just for marquee value. From Joe Camp, the one-man movie factory who created the *Benji* films. Rated PG. 101m. **DIR:** Joe Camp. **CAST:** Ernest Borgnine, George Kennedy, Elke Sommer, Rod Browning, Lisa Whelchel, Vincent Spano, Lyle Alzado. **1979**

DOUBLE-O KID, THE ★★ During a summer internship for the CIA, an obnoxious teenager stumbles across a terrorist who plans to make a plane full of scientists disappear into the Bermuda Triangle. Too many chase scenes and unbelievable getaways ruin this film. Rated PG-13 for violence and profanity. 95m. **DIR:** Duncan McLachlan. **CAST:** Corey Haim, Brigitte Nielsen, Wallace Shawn, Nicole Eggert, Basil Hoffman, John Rhys-Davies, Karen Black, Anne Francis. **1992**

DOUBLE OBSESSION ★★ *Fatal Attraction* meets *Single White Female* as college coed Margaux Hemingway falls for roommate Maryam d'Abo. When d'Abo falls in love with someone else, the fun begins. Vindictive roommates have become a genre all their own, and this entry tries to punch the right buttons, but to no avail. Over-the-top acting erases any hope. Rated R for violence, language, and nudity. 88m. **DIR:** Eduardo Montes. **CAST:** Margaux Hemingway, Maryam D'Abo, Frederic Forrest, Scott Valentine. **1992**

DOUBLE REVENGE ★★1/2 Tough Guy Joe Dallesandro bungles a small-town robbery, resulting in the death of a local businessman's wife. You guessed it—everybody wants revenge. Rated R. 96m. **DIR:** Armand Mastroianni. **CAST:** Leigh McCloskey, Joe Dallesandro, Nancy Everhard, Theresa Saldana, Richard Rust. **1988**

DOUBLE STANDARD 🦃 A prolific circuit-court justice gets caught leading a double family life. Made for TV. 95m. **DIR:** Louis Rudolph. **CAST:** Robert Foxworth, Pamela Bellwood, Michele Greene. **1988**

DOUBLE SUICIDE ★★★★ Stunning portrait of erotic obsession and passion in turn-of-century Japan. Director Masahiro Shinoda explores sexual taboos in his story of a merchant and a geisha whose ill-fated love affair is orchestrated entirely by outside forces. This poignant drama is presented in the style of a Bunraku puppet play. In Japanese with English subtitles. Not rated. B&W; 105m. **DIR:** Masahiro Shinoda. **CAST:** Kichiemon Nakamura, Shima Iwashita. **1969 DVD**

DOUBLE TAKE (1997) ★★★ A struggling writer witnesses a murder and testifies, sending the accused to jail. But when he sees the real murderer running around free, he realizes he's made a terrible mistake. Or has he? Predictable but entertaining. Rated R for profanity, violence, and nudity. 86m. **DIR:** Mark L. Lester. **CAST:** Craig Sheffer, Brigitte Bako, Costas Mandylor. **1997**

DOUBLE TAKE (2001) ★★ It's the old mismatched-characters-become-buddies-in-a-crisis formula in this irritating tale of a slick Wall Street banker (Orlando Jones) and a loudmouthed street hustler (Eddie Griffin). Jones and Griffin have good screen rapport and a few amusing moments, but they are undone by an obnoxious script with too many off-the-wall plot twists. Rated PG-13 for violence and profanity. 88m. **DIR:** George Gallo. **CAST:** Orlando Jones, Eddie Griffin, Edward Herrmann, Vivica A. Fox. **2001 DVD**

DOUBLE TAP ★★1/2 An undercover FBI agent falls in love with a hit man and they find themselves the target of an evil drug lord. Entertaining but nothing spectacular. Rated R for profanity and violence. 87m. **DIR:** Greg Yaitanes. **CAST:** Stephen Rea, Heather Locklear, Peter Greene, Kevin Gage, A Martinez. **1997 DVD**

DOUBLE TEAM ★★1/2 CIA operative balks at gunning down an international terrorist in front of a child and is exiled to a swank island. He later escapes and teams up with a weapons specialist to hunt down his missed target. The film's exhilarating showdown in a Rome coliseum involves a prowling tiger, land mines, martial arts combat, and a newborn baby tucked into a handbasket. The action is impressively choreographed, but the script stinks. Rated R for violence. 91m. **DIR:** Tsui Hark. **CAST:** Jean-Claude Van Damme, Dennis Rodman, Mickey Rourke, Natacha Lindinger. **1997 DVD**

DOUBLE THREAT ★★ An aging screen queen (Sally Kirkland) becomes concerned when her gigolo/costar gets interested in her young body double. Tricky behind-the-scenes thriller boasts a few unexpected twists. Available in R and unrated versions; both feature profanity, nudity, and sexual situations. 94/96. **DIR:** David A. Prior. **CAST:** Sally Kirkland, Andrew Stevens, Sherrie Rose, Chick Vennera, Richard Lynch, Anthony Franciosa. **1992**

DOUBLE TROUBLE (1967) ★★ Typical Elvis Presley musical. This time he plays a rock 'n' roll singer touring England. When a teenage heiress (whose life is constantly threatened) falls for him, he gets caught up in the action. 92m. **DIR:** Norman Taurog. **CAST:** Elvis Presley, Annette Day. **1967**

DOUBLE TROUBLE (1991) ★★ Inane actioner features muscle-bound twins (wrestling duo Peter Paul and David Paul) on either side of the law. They team up to pursue a deadly diamond thief. Rated R for violence and profanity. 87m. **DIR:** John Paragon. **CAST:** Peter Paul, David Paul, Roddy McDowall, Steve Kanaly. **1991**

DOUBLE VISION 🦃 A prudish identical twin steps into her naughty sister's shoes to retrace the last days before her death. Despite a fine supporting cast, sexy Kim Cattrall can't wade through this murky murder mystery. Not rated; contains profanity. 92m. **DIR:** Robert Knights. **CAST:** Kim Cattrall, Gale Hansen, Christopher Lee, Macha Meril. **1992**

DOUBLE WEDDING ★★★★ William Powell as a painter and Myrna Loy as a dress designer play Cupid in an effort to get Florence Rice married to John Beal. But the plan backfires. A delightful slapstick comedy. Lots of fun. B&W; 87m. **DIR:** Richard Thorpe. **CAST:** William Powell, Myrna Loy, Florence Rice, Edgar Kennedy, Sidney Toler, Jessie Ralph, Mary Gordon, John Beal. **1937**

DOUBLECROSSED ★★★1/2 Dennis Hopper is a casting agent's dream come true as a drug smuggler-turned-DEA informant in this fascinating fact-based study. Hopper's beguiling con artist is impossible to dislike. Rated R for violence and relentlessly foul language. 111m. **DIR:** Roger Young. **CAST:** Dennis Hopper, Robert Carradine, Richard Jenkins, Adrienne Barbeau, G. W. Bailey. **1991**

DOUBTING THOMAS ★★★ Wealthy manufacturer Will Rogers foils his stagestruck wife's acting ambition in this moderately amusing but outdated comedy. B&W; 78m. **DIR:** David Butler. **CAST:** Will Rogers, Billie Burke, Alison Skipworth, Sterling Holloway, Frank Albertson, John Qualen. **1935**

DOUGH AND DYNAMITE/KNOCKOUT, THE ★★★ Two of the best slapstick two-reelers Mack Sennett's famous Keystone Studios churned out during the heyday of fast-and-furious, rough-and-tumble comedies. *The Knockout*, actually a Fatty Arbuckle film, has Charlie Chaplin playing the referee, the third man in the ring, in a fight sequence between behemoths (to him) Edgar Kennedy and Arbuckle. *Dough and Dynamite* is set in a French restaurant. B&W; 54m. **DIR:** Mack Sennett, Charles Chaplin. **CAST:** The Keystone Kops. **1914**

DOUGHBOYS ★★ Buster Keaton mistakenly enlists in the army and in spite of himself becomes a hero. His second sound film, and a letdown from start to finish. B&W; 79m. **DIR:** Edward Sedgwick. **CAST:** Buster Keaton, Sally Ellers, Cliff Edwards, Edward Brophy. **1930**

DOUGHGIRLS, THE ★★ The setting is crowded Washington D.C. during World War II when a hotel room could hardly be had. Not even for honeymooners who find they have to share their suite with an assortment of military men and women. A comedy that relies on the wartime era for its laughs, and the personalities take a backseat to the dated dialogue. B&W; 102m. **DIR:** James V. Kern. **CAST:** Ann Sheridan, Jane Wyman, Eve Arden, Alexis Smith, Jack Carson, Craig Stevens, Charlie Ruggles, Alan Mowbray, Regis Toomey. **1944**

DOUG'S 1ST MOVIE ★★ This artlessly animated version of the cartoon show is a bland riff on *E.T.* Doug Funny is a middle schooler in a town populated with green-, blue-, and purple-faced kids with either monotone or whiny voices. He is harassed by a bully, competes for the attention of a girl, and discovers that a prominent citizen is covering up pollution problems. Rated G. 77m. **DIR:** Maurice Joyce. **1999**

DOWN AMONG THE "Z" MEN 🦃 Before there was a Monty Python there were the Goons, a British comedy team that featured Peter Sellers, among others (see cast). B&W; 82m. **DIR:** Maclean Rogers. **CAST:** Peter Sellers, Harry Secombe, Michael Bentine, Spike Milligan, Carol Carr. **1961**

DOWN AND DIRTY ★★★★ Brutal but brilliant black comedy about a slumlord of a shantytown in Rome. Nino Manfredi is excellent as a money-hoarding patriarch whose obsession with his stash leads to a plot by his wife and delinquent sons to kill him. In Italian with English subtitles. Not rated; contains violence, profanity, and nudity. 115m. **DIR:** Ettore Scola. **CAST:** Nino Manfredi, Francesco Anniballi. **1976**

DOWN AND OUT IN AMERICA ★★★★ Oscar-winning documentary about the "new poor," working-class people who have been caught on the downward spiral into poverty. Actress-turned-director Lee Grant makes it clear that these people are not isolated cases, but victims of conditions that affect more and more American families every year. Not rated. 60m. **DIR:** Lee Grant. **1985**

DOWN AND OUT IN BEVERLY HILLS ★★★1/2 When a Los Angeles bum (Nick Nolte) loses his dog to a happy home, he decides to commit suicide in a Beverly Hills swimming pool. The pool's owner (Richard Dreyfuss) saves the seedy-looking character's life and thereby sets in motion a chain of events that threatens to destroy his family's rarefied existence. Rated R. 102m. **DIR:** Paul Mazursky. **CAST:** Nick Nolte, Bette Midler, Richard Dreyfuss, Little Richard, Tracy Nelson, Elizabeth Peña, Evan Richards. **1986**

DOWN ARGENTINE WAY ★★★ Tuneful Technicolor extravaganza is the granddaddy of all the fruit-filled South American musical–comedy–romances cranked out in the 1940s. The incredible production numbers feature the rubber-jointed Nicholas Brothers and the incredible Carmen Miranda. 92m. **DIR:** Irving Cummings. **CAST:** Don Ameche, Betty Grable, Carmen Miranda, Charlotte Greenwood, J. Carrol Naish, Henry Stephenson. **1940**

DOWN BY LAW ★★★★1/2 *Stranger Than Paradise* director Jim Jarmusch improves on his static deadpan style by allowing his *Down by Law* characters a bit more life. In fact, he appears to be leaning more optimistically toward activity. He gives the film an energetic Italian comedian (Roberto Benigni), who looks like a dark-haired Kewpie doll. This lively imp inspires his lethargic companions (John Lurie, Tom Waits) to speak, sing, and generally loosen up a little. Rated R for nudity and profanity. 90m. **DIR:** Jim Jarmusch. **CAST:** John Lurie, Tom Waits, Roberto Benigni, Ellen Barkin. **1986**

DOWN CAME A BLACKBIRD ★★★★ Journalist Laura Dern, a pill-popping alcoholic forever scarred by her experiences in a war-torn country, profiles the saintly counselor who runs a clinic for torture survivors. Before long, the writer is less an observer and more a patient. Kevin Droney's sensitive script concludes with a real surprise. Rated R for nudity, torture, violence, rape, and profanity. 112m. **DIR:** Jonathan Sanger. **CAST:** Raul Julia, Laura Dern, Vanessa Redgrave, Cliff Gorman, Sarita Choudhury, Jay O. Sanders. **1995**

DOWN DAKOTA WAY ★★1/2 Roy Rogers takes a harder line with the bad guys in this exciting B Western, tracking down the no-goods responsible for the death of his friend, a veterinarian who could finger the man responsible for flooding the market with diseased meat. 67m. **DIR:** William Witney. **CAST:** Roy Rogers, Dale Evans, Pat Brady, Monte Montana, Roy Barcroft. **1949**

•DOWN FROM THE MOUNTAIN ★★★1/2 This film chronicles a live concert by the musicians who performed the songs in the Coen brothers' *O Brother, Where Art Thou?* The first half hour or so is frustrating because the filmmakers neglect to identify the people on-screen or even to explain what the film is about. But then the concert begins and the great music takes over; from then on it's wonderful. Not rated; suitable for general audiences. 98m. **DIR:** Nick Doob, Chris Hegedus, D. A. Pennebaker. **CAST:** John Hartford, Alison Krauss, Gillian Welch, Emmylou Harris, Ralph Stanley. **2000 DVD**

DOWN IN THE DELTA ★★★★ A Chicago grandmother, desperate to save her daughter and grandchildren from the dangers of the streets, bundles them off to live with her brother-in-law in rural Mississippi. Poet Maya Angelou, directing her first film, lacks the finesse to smooth out the rough edges in Myron Goble's episodic script, but she's sensitive enough to emphasize its family-values message, and smart enough not to interfere with her first-rate cast. Rated PG-13 for mild profanity. 107m. **DIR:** Maya Angelou. **CAST:** Alfre Woodard, Al Freeman Jr., Loretta Devine, Wesley Snipes, Esther Rolle, Mary Alice. **1998 DVD**

DOWN, OUT & DANGEROUS ★★1/2 Mildly suspenseful made-for-cable original about a successful businessman who makes the mistake of helping a homeless psychotic killer. Rated R for violence and profanity. 90m. **DIR:** Noel Nosseck. **CAST:** Richard Thomas, Bruce Davison, Cynthia Ettinger. **1995**

DOWN PERISCOPE ★★★ Kelsey Grammer stars as a maverick submarine commander whose unorthodox behavior lands him a sad diesel-powered sub and a crew of navy misfits. Their mission: outmaneuver the cream of the U.S. Navy's nuclear fleet. Standard-issue military screwball comedy made palatable by a strong ensemble cast. Rated PG for mild profanity. 92m. **DIR:** David S. Ward. **CAST:** Kelsey Grammer, Lauren Holly, Rob Schneider, Harry Dean Stanton, Bruce Dern, William H. Macy, Rip Torn, Harland Williams. **1995**

DOWN TEXAS WAY ★★1/2 An agreeable if undistinguished entry in the Rough Riders series, this feature has Rangers Buck Jones and Tim McCoy coming to the aid of their pal, Raymond Hatton, when he is accused of murder. B&W; 57m. **DIR:** Howard Bretherton. **CAST:** Buck Jones, Tim McCoy, Raymond Hatton, Luana Walters, Harry Woods, Glenn Strange. **1942**

DOWN THE DRAIN ★★ A criminal lawyer sets up a big heist. Standard cross, no-honor-among-thieves story. Rated R for nudity, language, and violence. 105m. **DIR:** Robert C. Hughes. **CAST:** Andrew Stevens, Teri Copley, John Matuszak, Joseph Campanella, Don Stroud. **1990**

DOWN TO EARTH (1917) ★★★★ One of the brightest of the early Douglas Fairbanks social comedies. All the "big guns" are here—scenarist Anita Loos; her husband, director John Emerson; and some sparkling camerawork by Victor Fleming (before he turned full-time director). Silent. B&W; 52m. **DIR:** John Emerson. **CAST:** Douglas Fairbanks Sr., Eileen Percy, Gustav von Seyffertitz. **1917**

DOWN TO EARTH (2001) ★★ When a stand-up comic (Chris Rock) is pulled from his body ahead of time, the Heavenly Host finds him one that belonged to a recently murdered rich man. If the plot rings a bell, it's the third go-round after *Here Comes Mr. Jordan* (1941) and *Heaven Can Wait* (1978). This one is by far the least of the three; stretching the story to fit Rock leaves it all but shapeless. Rated PG-13 for mild profanity and sexual humor. 87m. **DIR:** Chris Weitz, Paul Weitz. **CAST:** Chris Rock, Regina King, Chazz Palminteri, Eugene Levy, Jennifer Coolidge, Greg Germann, Frankie Faison. **2001 DVD**

DOWN TO THE SEA IN SHIPS ★★★ The plot involving a family of whalers has appeal, but vivid scenes filmed at sea aboard real New England whalers out of Bedford make it worthwhile. B&W; 83m. **DIR:** Elmer Clifton. **CAST:** William Walcott, Marguerite Courtot, Clara Bow. **1922**

DOWN TO YOU ★★ Two New York City college students discover that falling in love is much easier than maintaining a long-term relationship. Although this tepid romantic comedy plays like a teen sweetheart fantasy with its stars often talking directly to the audience, its characters include two porn actors and a nymphomaniac. Go figure. Rated PG-13 for sexual content and profanity. 90m. **DIR:** Kris Isacsson. **CAST:** Freddie Prinze Jr., Julia Stiles, Selma Blair, Shawn Hatosy, Zak Orth, Rosario Dawson. **2000**

DOWN TWISTED ★★ Stylish *Romancing the Stone*–type thriller about an innocent waitress who agrees to help her roommate out of a jam. Before she knows it, she's stuck in Central America with a disreputable soldier of fortune and people shooting at her. The convoluted plot gets better as it goes along, though you may not find it worth the effort. Rated PG-13. 88m. **DIR:** Albert Pyun. **CAST:** Carey Lowell, Charles Rocket, Thom Mathews, Linda Kerridge. **1987**

DOWN UNDER 🦃 Patrick Macnee narrates this crudely shot tale of two southern California surfers in Australia. Stale and pointless. 90m. **DIR:** Not credited!. **CAST:** Don Atkinson, Donn Dunlop, Patrick Macnee. **1984**

DOWNDRAFT ★★1/2 There's absolutely no logic to this action thriller, but it certainly moves. Vincent Spano leads a military-assault team into an impregnable mountain bunker, which has been commandeered by a mad scientist and his bloodthirsty cyborg surrogate. The dialogue is ludicrous, but the stunts are pretty slick. Rated R for violence and profanity. 92m. **DIR:** Michael Mazo. **CAST:** Vincent Spano, Kate Vernon, Paul Koslo, John Novak, William Taylor, John Pyper-Ferguson. **1996**

DOWNHILL RACER ★★★1/2 Robert Redford struggles with an unappealing character, in this study of an Olympic skier. But Gene Hackman is excellent as the coach, and the exciting scenes of this snow sport hold the film together. Rated PG. 101m. **DIR:** Michael Ritchie. **CAST:** Robert Redford, Gene Hackman, Camilla Sparv. **1969**

DOWNHILL WILLIE ★★★ Amiable comedy about a clueless guy who may be short on brain cells but is a pro on skis. When Willie decides to enter the notorious "Kamikaze Run," he's pitted against a slew of hot-shot skiers, including an egotistical ski instructor and an alcoholic ex-Olympian. Typical teen-comedy high jinks ensue in this fun but tame underdog story filled with exciting skiing sequences and beautiful ski bunnies. Rated PG for language and sexual innuendo. 90m. **DIR:** David Mitchell. **CAST:** Keith Coogan, Lochlan Monroe, Staci Keanan, Estelle Harris, Fred Stoller. **1996 DVD**

DOWNTOWN ★★ Anthony Edwards plays a rookie cop who is transferred to a hard-core inner-city neighborhood. An uneven attempt to balance comedy and violent action. The excellent cast outstrips the project. Rated R. 96m. **DIR:** Richard Benjamin. **CAST:** Anthony Edwards, Forest Whitaker, Penelope Ann Miller, Joe Pantoliano. **1990**

D.P. ★★★★ The shattering loss of innocence by war's true victims—children—is examined in this Emmy-winning adaptation of Kurt Vonnegut's poignant story. Julius Gordon is one of many orphans cared for by nuns in post–World War II Germany, a truly "displaced person" because he is the only boy with black skin. Not rated; suitable for family viewing. 60m. **DIR:** Alan Bridges. **CAST:** Stan Shaw, Rosemary Leach, Julius Gordon. **1985**

DRACULA (1931) ★★★★ Bela Lugosi found himself forever typecast after brilliantly bringing to life the bloodthirsty Transylvanian vampire of the title in this 1931 genre classic, directed by Tod Browning. His performance and that of Dwight Frye as the spider-eating Renfield still impress even though this early talkie seems somewhat dated today. B&W; 75m. **DIR:** Tod Browning. **CAST:** Bela Lugosi, Dwight Frye, David Manners, Helen Chandler, Edward Van Sloan. **1931 DVD**

DRACULA (1931) ★★★ The familiar tale of the bloodthirsty Count Dracula is enacted by a Spanish-speaking cast in this sister production to the famous 1931 American counterpart. The count actually rises from his coffin on camera, and the women (especially the unholy brides) are erotic and enticing. Bela Lugosi is still the consummate Dracula, but this overlong production has some memorable moments. In Spanish with English subtitles. B&W; 104m. **DIR:** George Melford. **CAST:** Carlos Villarias, Lupita Tovar, Pablo Alvarez Rubio.

DRACULA (1973) ★★★★ Surprisingly effective made-for-television version of Bram Stoker's classic tale has Jack Palance as a sympathetic count trapped by his vampirism. Director Dan Curtis and scripter Richard Matheson had previously collaborated on the excellent *The Night Stalker* telefilm and work together equally well here. 99m. **DIR:** Dan Curtis. **CAST:** Jack Palance, Simon Ward, Nigel Davenport, Pamela Brown, Fiona Lewis. **1973**

1931DRACULA (1979) ★★1/2 This *Dracula* is a film of missed opportunities. Frank Langella makes an excellent Count Dracula. It's a pity he has so little screen time. The story, for the uninitiated, revolves around the activities of a bloodthirsty vampire who leaves his castle in Transylvania for fresh hunting in London. Rated R. 109m. **DIR:** John Badham. **CAST:** Frank Langella, Laurence Olivier, Donald Pleasence, Jan Francis. **1979 DVD**

DRACULA A.D. 1972 ★★★ A spectacular opening sequence featuring Dr. Van Helsing (Peter Cushing) and Count Dracula (Christopher Lee) fighting atop a runaway coach is the high point in this Hammer film that jumps from a period setting to modern-day London. Things go a bit downhill from there as a wannabe vampire leads a band of hippies into the clutches of the ageless count. The San Francisco band, Stoneground, plays two songs in a party scene. Rated PG. 100m. **DIR:** Alan Gibson. **CAST:** Peter Cushing, Christopher Lee, Stephanie Beacham, Michael Coles, Christopher Neame. **1972**

DRACULA AND SON ★★ French vampire spoof was probably much funnier before the inane English dubbing was added. The Dracula family looks for a new home after the Communists run them out of their Transylvanian home. Rated PG. 88m. **DIR:** Edouard Molinaro. **CAST:** Christopher Lee, Bernard Ménez. **1976**

DRACULA: DEAD AND LOVING IT ★★★ Perhaps we're too generous toward this silly send-up by director Mel Brooks; however, it does make a fine viewing companion to the filmmaker's superior *Young Frankenstein*. While Brooks pokes fun at Coppola's pompous *Bram Stoker's Dracula*, he also pays homage to Lugosi's interpretation of the title character and the innovations brought to the familiar story by Hammer Films in *Horror of Dracula*. Rated PG-13 for comic gore and scatological humor. 90m. **DIR:** Mel Brooks. **CAST:** Leslie Nielsen, Peter MacNicol, Steven Weber, Amy Yasbeck, Lysette Anthony, Harvey Korman, Mel Brooks, Mark Blankfield, Chuck McCann, Anne Bancroft, Avery Schreiber. **1996**

DRACULA HAS RISEN FROM THE GRAVE ★★1/2 Freddie Francis took over the directorial reins from Terence Fisher for Hammer Films's third Dracula–Christopher Lee vehicle, and the result, while visually striking (Francis is an Oscar-winning cinematographer), is a major step down dramatically. A tepid revenge plot has the Count going after the niece of a monsignor. Rated G. 92m. **DIR:** Freddie Francis. **CAST:** Christopher Lee, Veronica Carlson, Rupert Davies, Barry Andrews. **1968**

DRACULA—PRINCE OF DARKNESS ★★★ Christopher Lee returns in his most famous role with mixed results. This first sequel to *Horror of Dracula* lacks the vigor and tension of its predecessor as the revived count stalks a group of travelers. 90m. **DIR:** Terence Fisher. **CAST:** Christopher Lee, Barbara Shelley, Andrew Keir, Suzan Farmer. **1966 DVD**

DRACULA RISING After 500 years, a reincarnated woman is saved from an evil vampire by the wonderful vampire who loved her before; a good idea sucked dry by poor acting. Rated R for violence and nudity. 85m. **DIR:** Fred Gallo. **CAST:** Christopher Atkins, Stacey Travis, Doug Wert, Tara McCann. **1992**

•DRACULA: THE DARK PRINCE ★★1/2 This movie is based on the true story of Vlad Dracula, also known as Vlad the Impaler, the fifteenth-century Romanian prince whose ruthlessness and eating habits inspired Bram Stoker to write his famous vampire novel. Rudolf Martin plays the title role of a man destined to raise an army and drive the invading Turks out of Romania. More *Braveheart* than stake-in-the-heart, *Dracula* suffers from an underprivileged budget which makes an otherwise epic tale fall flat from its own limitations. Rated R for violence. 89m. **DIR:** Joe Chappelle. **CAST:** Rudolf Martin, Jane March, Roger Daltrey, Peter Weller. **2000 DVD**

DRACULA 2000 Thirsty Prince of Darkness seeks out a female New Orleans Virgin Megastore clerk who is having terrible nightmares and hallucinations—and has the transfused blood of the Goth neck nibbler flowing through her veins. Rated R for violence, gore, sexual content, and nudity. 97m. **DIR:** Patrick Lussier. **CAST:** Justine Waddell, Christopher Plummer, Gerard Butler, Jonny Lee Miller, Colleen (Vitamin C) Fitzpatrick. **2000 DVD**

DRACULA VS. FRANKENSTEIN Dracula's eternal search for blood. Pretty bad. Rated R. 90m. **DIR:** Al Adamson. **CAST:** J. Carrol Naish, Lon Chaney Jr., Jim Davis. **1971**

DRACULA'S DAUGHTER ★★★1/2 The lady in the title tries to break her addiction to human blood after she exorcises and burns the remains of her dead sire—but the cure doesn't take. This brooding film is stylish and creates its own strange mood through imaginative sets, art design, music, and compelling performances by Gloria Holden as the unhappy undead and Irving Pichel as her dour but dedicated servant. B&W; 69m. **DIR:** Lambert Hillyer. **CAST:** Gloria Holden, Otto Kruger, Marguerite Churchill, Edward Van Sloan, Irving Pichel. **1936**

DRACULA'S GREAT LOVE ★★ Anyone who isn't familiar with the cinematic exploits of Spanish horror film star Paul Naschy (Jacinto Molina to all you bilingual fans) may not want to begin here. Barrel-chested, hirsute Pablo is better suited to werewolves—in such romps as *Fury of the Wolfman*—than Transylvania's seducer. Some of this film's extensive nudity was cut, but it's still R-rated. 83m. **DIR:** Javier Aguirre. **CAST:** Paul Naschy, Haydee Politoff. **1972**

DRACULA'S LAST RITES (1980) The vampires here (none named Dracula) are the mortician, police chief, and doctor in a small town. Originally called *Last Rites*. Rated R. 88m. **DIR:** Domonic Paris. **CAST:** Patricia Lee Hammond, Gerald Fielding. **1980**

DRACULA'S WIDOW ★★ The bloodsucking lord of Transylvania is dead, but his estranged wife doesn't believe it. She tracks down the last remaining descendant of Jonathan Harker, who assures her of her spouse's demise. She then goes on a rampage, slaughtering a satanic vampire cult in hopes of finding Dracula's remains. Rated R for violence and nudity. 86m. **DIR:** Christopher Coppola. **CAST:** Josef Sommer, Sylvia Kristel, Lenny von Dohlen, Stefan Schnabel. **1988**

DRAGNET (1947) ★★1/2 This low-budget feature focuses on international jewelry thievery, with Henry Wilcoxon of Scotland Yard tracking crooks from London to New York, aided by airline hostess Mary Brian. Chock-full of action and skulduggery. B&W; 71m. **DIR:** Leslie Goodwins. **CAST:** Henry Wilcoxon, Mary Brian, Douglass Dumbrille, Virginia Dale. **1947**

DRAGNET (1954) ★★★★ The feature-length (color!) version of the popular detective series with director-star Jack Webb as the no-nonsense Sgt. Joe Friday, and Ben Alexander as his original partner, Frank Smith. In the story, based as always on a true case, Friday and Smith are assigned to solve the murder of a mobster. All clues seem to lead to his former associates. 89m. **DIR:** Jack Webb. **CAST:** Jack Webb, Ben Alexander, Richard Boone, Ann Robinson, Dennis Weaver. **1954**

DRAGNET (1987) ★★1/2 Dan Aykroyd's deliriously funny impersonation of Jack Webb can only carry this comedy so far. While Tom Hanks adds some moments of his own, the screenplay about political double-dealing tends to bog down. Rated PG-13 for profanity and violence. 107m. **DIR:** Tom Mankiewicz. **CAST:** Dan Aykroyd, Tom Hanks, Alexandra Paul, Harry Morgan, Christopher Plummer, Dabney Coleman, Elizabeth Ashley, Jack O'Halloran, Kathleen Freeman. **1987 DVD**

DRAGON CHOW ★★★ Humorous and touching film about a Pakistani man living in West Germany. He lands a job in a mediocre Chinese restaurant where he strikes up a friendship with an Oriental waiter. Good slice-of-life character study. In German, Urdu, and Mandarin with English subtitles. Not rated. B&W; 75m. **DIR:** Jan Schuttes. **CAST:** Bhaskar, Ric Young. **1987**

DRAGON KNIGHT ★★ Based on a popular Japanese video game, the film doesn't achieve much beyond the usual titillation. The animation is fair, but the story of a mischievous swordsman rescuing a castleful of helpless women is doomed from the start. In Japanese with English subtitles. Not rated; contains nudity, sexual situations and violence. 40m. **DIR:** Jun Fukuda. **1991**

DRAGON SEED ★★1/2 This study of a Chinese town torn asunder by Japanese occupation is taken from the novel by Nobel Prize winner Pearl S. Buck. It's occasionally gripping but in general too long. B&W; 145m. **DIR:** Jack Conway, Harold S. Bucquet. **CAST:** Katharine Hepburn, Walter Huston, Turhan Bey, Hurd Hatfield. **1944**

DRAGON: THE BRUCE LEE STORY ★★★★ The life of martial arts superstar Bruce Lee is given first-class treatment, in this mixture of fact and fantasy. The fight scenes are spectacular, and the acting of Jason Scott Lee and Lauren Holly is excellent. Look for Van Williams, Lee's costar in the *Green Hornet* series, in a brief bit as the director of that TV show. Rated PG-13 for violence, profanity, nudity, and simulated sex. 120m. **DIR:** Rob Cohen. **CAST:** Jason Scott Lee, Lauren Holly, Michael Learned, Nancy Kwan, Robert Wagner. **1993 DVD**

•DRAGONFLY ★★1/2 A recently widowed doctor (Kevin Costner) believes that his dead wife is trying to communicate with him, but his friends and coworkers think he's simply going mad with grief. Odds are you won't care much either way; the ghost-movie clichés are thicker than the dragonflies in the movie's preview trailer (which never appear in the film itself). Rated PG-13 for mature themes. 104m. **DIR:** Tom Shadyac. **CAST:** Kevin Costner, Joe Morton, Ron Rifkin, Linda Hunt, Kathy Bates. **2002 DVD**

DRAGONHEART ★★★★ In tenth-century England, swordsman Dennis Quaid vows to slay all dragons when his young charge, a prince and future king, turns to evil after his life is saved by dragon magic. A marvelously entertaining film filled with surprises, this is one sword-and-sorcery epic that won't disappoint fans of the genre or casual viewers. Sean Connery supplies the voice of Draco, "the last of the dragons." Rated PG-13 for violence. 106m. **DIR:** Rob Cohen. **CAST:** Dennis Quaid, Sean Connery, Dina Meyer, Julie Christie, David Thewlis, Pete Postlethwaite. **1996 DVD**

DRAGONS FOREVER ★★★1/2 A lawyer is persuaded to work against chemical plant owners who want to take over a site used by local fishermen. Amazing martial arts highlight this exciting comedy featuring Hong Kong's talented director-actor Jackie Chan. In Cantonese with English subtitles. Not rated; contains violence. 88m. **DIR:** Sammo Hung. **CAST:** Jackie Chan. **1986 DVD**

DRAGONSLAYER ★★1/2 Peter MacNicol plays a sorcerer's apprentice who, to save a damsel in distress, must face a fearsome fire-breathing dragon. While the special effects are spectacular, the rest of the film doesn't quite live up to them. It's slow, and often too corny for older viewers. Rated PG for violence. 110m. **DIR:** Matthew Robbins. **CAST:** Peter MacNicol, Caitlin Clarke, Ralph Richardson. **1981**

DRAGONWORLD ★★1/2 A touch of whimsy and a sense of fun make this modern-day fairy tale excellent for children. The target audience will forgive the cheesy special effects and poor production values, and instead concentrate on the tale of a young man who stumbles across a real dragon in Scotland. When finances become scarce, he's forced to sell the dragon to an evil promoter. It's a fairy tale, so you know it has a happy ending. Rated PG. 84m. **DIR:** Ted Nicolaou. **CAST:** Sam MacKenzie, Brittney Powell, John Calvin, Lila Kaye, Courtland Mead, Andrew Keir. **1994**

•DRAGSTRIP GIRL ★★ Remake of the 1957 drive-in, teen rebel classic fails to capture the spirit of the original. Director Mary Lambert doesn't have a clue that this star-crossed tale of a rich white girl and a hoodlum Hispanic boy from opposite sides of the track is supposed to be camp. Even though Lambert insists, it's hard to take any of this seriously. Made-for-cable. Rated R for adult situations and language. 83m. **DIR:** Mary Lambert. **CAST:** Mark Dacascos, Natasha Gregson Wagner, Raymond Cruz, Traci Lords. **1994 DVD**

DRAUGHTMAN'S CONTRACT, THE ★★★1/2 Set in 1964 in the English countryside, this stylish British production is about a rich lady (Janet Suzman) who hires an artist to make detailed drawings of her house. Then strange things begin to happen—a murder not being the least. Rated R for nudity, profanity, and violence. 103m. **DIR:** Peter Greenaway. **CAST:** Anthony Higgins, Janet Suzman. **1982 DVD**

DRAW ★★1/2 Kirk Douglas and James Coburn play outlaw and lawman respectively. Both appear on a collision course for a gunfight but, alas, what we are treated to is a trick ending. Lots of missed chances in this one. Made for HBO cable television. 98m. **DIR:** Steven H. Stern. **CAST:** James Coburn, Kirk Douglas. **1984**

DREAM A LITTLE DREAM ★★ An obnoxious teen has the hots for Miss Unattainable (Meredith Salenger). When the two get caught up in Jason Robards Jr.'s dream, he gets his chance to be with her. Mediocre. Rated PG-13 for language. 115m. **DIR:** Marc Rocco. **CAST:** Jason Robards Jr., Corey Feldman, Corey Haim, Meredith Salenger, Piper Laurie. **1989**

DREAM A LITTLE DREAM 2 🦃 Like the first one really deserved a sequel? This one involves spies, special glasses, and the two Coreys! Rated PG-13 for language and adult situations. 91m. **DIR:** James Lemmo. **CAST:**

Corey Haim, Corey Feldman, Robyn Lively, Stacie Randall. **1994**

DREAM DATE ★★1/2 Single father Clifton Davis remembers what he was like when he started dating, and doesn't like it when his daughter is ready for her first date. Made-for-TV farce enlivened by an effective cast. Not rated. 96m. **DIR:** Anson Williams. **CAST:** Clifton Davis, Tempestt Bledsoe, Kadeem Hardison, Anne-Marie Johnson, Richard Moll, Pauly Shore. **1989**

DREAM FOR CHRISTMAS, A ★★ Overwhelmed by a soundtrack far too dramatic for its simple settings, this tale of a black pastor and his family who move to California to start a congregation is full-fledged Americana. A very basic production that parallels the television hit, *The Waltons.* And it came from the very same creator: Earl Hamner. 100m. **DIR:** Ralph Senensky. **CAST:** George Spell, Hari Rhodes, Beah Richards. **1973**

DREAM HOUSE ★★1/2 Silly sci-fi story in which a futuristic, computerized house decides that its occupants are detrimental to its safety requirements. Rated R for profanity. 90m. **DIR:** Graeme Campbell. **CAST:** Timothy Busfield, Lisa Jakub, Jennifer Dale, Cameron Graham. **1998**

DREAM LOVER (1986) 🦃 A struggling musician suffers bloodcurdling nightmares. Rated R for violence. 104m. **DIR:** Alan J. Pakula. **CAST:** Kristy McNichol, Ben Masters, Paul Shenar, Justin Deas, John McMartin, Gayle Hunnicutt. **1986**

DREAM LOVER (1994) ★★1/2 Rebounding from a divorce, Ray (James Spader) marries Lena (Madchen Amick), who seems to be the woman of his dreams. Then he finds out that her name isn't really Lena—and that's just the beginning. This psychological thriller is rather coldly calculated, but slickly made and unpredictable—it will certainly hold your interest, though you may hate yourself in the morning. Rated R for profanity and nudity. 103m. **DIR:** Nicholas Kazan. **CAST:** James Spader, Madchen Amick, Bess Armstrong, Fredric Lehne, Larry Miller, Clyde Kusatsu. **1994 DVD**

DREAM MACHINE 🦃 Macho male teen fantasy has Corey Haim securing the automobile of his dreams by being in the right place at the right time. This comedy starts to run on empty long before it reaches the finishing line. Rated PG. 85m. **DIR:** Lyman Dayton. **CAST:** Corey Haim, Evan Richards, Susan Seaforth Hayes, Jeremy Slate. **1990**

DREAM MAN 🦃 Patsy Kensit plays a cop with psychic powers who can't tell if the man she loves killed his wife. Go figure. Rated R for nudity, violence, and language. 94m. **DIR:** René Bonniere. **CAST:** Patsy Kensit, Bruce Greenwood, Andrew McCarthy, Jim Byrnes, Denise Crosby. **1994**

DREAM OF KINGS, A ★★★★ Anthony Quinn turns in an unforgettable performance in this powerful and touching drama set in Chicago's Greek community. He plays an earthy, proud father determined to raise enough money to flee from America to Greece with his ailing young son. A moving character study. Not rated. 111m. **DIR:** Daniel Mann. **CAST:** Anthony Quinn, Irene Papas, Inger Stevens, Sam Levene, Val Avery. **1969**

DREAM OF PASSION, A ★★★1/2 Melina Mercouri plays a Greek actress who is preparing to play Medea. As a publicity stunt, she goes to a prison to meet a real-life Medea. Ellen Burstyn is brilliant as the American prisoner who has killed her three children in order to take revenge on her husband. Rated R. 106m. **DIR:** Jules Dassin. **CAST:** Melina Mercouri, Ellen Burstyn, Andreas Voutsinas, Despo Diamantidou. **1978**

DREAM STREET ★★ Good struggles with evil in this sentimental morality tale of London's infamous Limehouse slum. Two brothers, in love with the same girl, vie for her attentions. Good eventually wins. Silent. B&W; 138m. **DIR:** D. W. Griffith. **CAST:** Carol Dempster, Charles Emmett Mack, Ralph Graves, Tyrone Power Sr., Morgan Wallace. **1921**

DREAM TEAM, THE ★★★★1/2 When a psychiatrist (Dennis Boutsikaris) takes four mental patients on a field trip to Yankee Stadium, he is unexpectedly waylaid and his quartet of lovable loonies is let loose in the Big Apple. This gem of a comedy features terrific ensemble performances. It'll steal your heart—guaranteed. Rated PG for profanity and violence. 113m. **DIR:** Howard Zieff. **CAST:** Michael Keaton, Christopher Lloyd, Peter Boyle, Stephen Furst, Lorraine Bracco, Dennis Boutsikaris. **1989**

DREAM TO BELIEVE ★★★ If you like *Flashdance*, *Rocky*, and the *World Gymnastics Competition*, you'll love this Cinderella story. It's the soap drama of a teenage girl who, against physical odds, turns herself into an accomplished gymnast. No rating. 96m. **DIR:** Paul Lynch. **CAST:** Olivia D'Abo, Rita Tushingham, Keanu Reeves. **1985**

DREAM WITH THE FISHES ★★★1/2 An odd, rocky friendship develops between a suicidal voyeur (David Arquette) and the dying neighbor he's been spying on (Brad Hunt); each is intrigued by the other, and they agree to spend their last few days together. Offbeat and appealing, this eccentric comedy keeps surprising you just as you think you've got it all figured out. Not rated; contains profanity and mature themes. 97m. **DIR:** Finn Taylor. **CAST:** David Arquette, Brad Hunt, Kathryn Erbe, Cathy Moriarty. **1997**

DREAMANIAC 🦃 A heavy-metal composer teams up with a succubus to kill teens in this tired picture that doesn't break any new ground. Not rated; contains gore, violence, profanity, and nudity. 82m. **DIR:** David DeCoteau. **CAST:** Thomas Bern, Kim McKamy, Sylvia Summers. **1986**

DREAMCHILD ★★★★ Some of those familiar with *Alice's Adventures in Wonderland* may be surprised to learn that there was a real Alice. Lewis Carroll first told his fanciful stories to 10 year old Alice Liddel on a summer boat ride on July 1, 1862. In 1932, Alice went to New York City to participate in a Columbia University tribute to Carroll. These facts provide the basis for this rich and thought-provoking film. Rated PG. 94m. **DIR:** Gavin Millar. **CAST:** Coral Browne, Peter Gallagher, Ian Holm, Jane Asher, Nicola Cowper. **1986**

DREAMER ★★ Small-towner Tim Matheson pursues his dream: to become a champion bowler. As exciting as a film about bowling can be. (Which is to say, not very.) Rated PG. 86m. **DIR:** Noel Nosseck. **CAST:** Tim Matheson, Susan Blakely, Jack Warden. **1979**

DREAMING OF JOSEPH LEES ★★1/2 Eva, a young woman in Somerset, England, falls in love with her second cousin, Joseph Lees. Afraid to commit to him, Eva marries another and tries to wipe Lees from her memory. When Lees and Eva are reunited at a family wedding, Eva finds herself trapped in a loveless marriage to a man who will do anything to keep her. The film fails to explore the depth of the love triangle that threatens Eva's happiness. Nice 1950s period detail and handsome performances, but not much else. Rated R for adult situations, language, and nudity. 92m. **DIR:** Eric Styles. **CAST:** Samantha Morton, Lee Ross, Rupert Graves. **1999**

DREAMING OUT LOUD ★★1/2 Chester Lauck and Norris Goff, better known as radio's Lum and Abner, fare well in this first of a film series based on their misadventures at the Jot-em Down Store in Pine Ridge, Arkansas. The cracker-barrel philosophers quietly, and with humor, exert a variety of influences on their fellow citizens. It's corn, but clean corn. B&W; 65m. **DIR:** Harold Young. **CAST:** Chester Lauck, Norris Goff, Frances Langford, Robert Wilcox, Irving Bacon, Frank Craven, Phil Harris. **1940**

DREAMLIFE OF ANGELS, THE ★★★1/2 Director Erick Zonca examines the unconventional friendship that develops between two young women: a friendly, cheerful drifter and a beautiful blonde with hidden depths of anger and self-loathing. The film is low-key but fascinating, revealing subtle psychological impulses that first draw the two women together, then drive them apart in anger and confusion. In French with English subtitles. Rated R for nudity and sexual scenes. 113m. **DIR:** Erick Zonca. **CAST:** Elodie Bouchez, Natacha Regnier, Gregoire Colin, Jo Prestia, Patrick Mercado. **1998 DVD**

DREAMS ★★1/2 Fascinating but confusing drama about a photo agency head and her top model. In Swedish with English subtitles. B&W; 86m. **DIR:** Ingmar Bergman. **CAST:** Eva Dahlbeck, Harriet Andersson, Gunnar Björnstrand, Ulf Palme. **1955**

DREAMS COME TRUE 🦃 A restless young factory worker meets a young woman with whom he shares an unusual power, the ability to control and live in their dreams. Rated R. 95m. **DIR:** Max Kalmanowicz. **CAST:** Michael Sanville, Stephanie Shuford. **1984**

DREAMS LOST, DREAMS FOUND ★★1/2 Decent Harlequin Romance movie takes place in scenic Scotland. Kathleen Quinlan stars as a widow who buys a cursed castle. She meets a handsome lord but can't decide if he's worthy of her love. Soap opera-ish but location shots are a plus. Not rated; contains sexual situations. 102m. **DIR:** Willi Patterson. **CAST:** Kathleen Quinlan, David Robb, Colette O'Neil, Charles Gray, Betsy Brantley. **1987**

DREAMSCAPE ★★★★ If you can go along with its intriguing but farfetched premise—that trained psychics can enter other people's nightmares and put an end to them—this film will reward you with topflight special effects, thrills, chills, and surprises. Rated PG-13 for suggested sex, violence, and profanity. 99m. **DIR:** Joseph Ruben. **CAST:** Dennis Quaid, Max von Sydow, Christopher Plummer, Eddie Albert, Kate Capshaw. **1984 DVD**

DRESS GRAY ★★★★★ Extremely well-made TV miniseries about the closing of ranks at a military academy after an unpopular plebe is murdered. Alec Baldwin is the beleaguered cadet who refuses to be the scapegoat or let the investigation die. Compelling Gore Vidal script is enhanced by a stellar cast. Not rated; contains mild profanity. 192m. **DIR:** Glenn Jordan. **CAST:** Alec Baldwin, Hal Holbrook, Eddie Albert, Lloyd Bridges, Susan Hess. **1986**

DRESSED TO KILL (1941) ★★1/2 Private eye Michael Shayne attempts to solve a confusing multiple murder that centers around an acting troupe and a very old grudge. Fun, tongue-in-cheek mystery involves a subplot about Shayne's doomed efforts to marry a burlesque queen and boasts a very clever murder plot and device. B&W; 75m. **DIR:** Eugene Forde. **CAST:** Lloyd Nolan, Mary Beth Hughes, Sheila Ryan, William Demarest, Ben Carter, Erwin Kaiser, Henry Daniell, Mantan Moreland. **1941**

DRESSED TO KILL (1946) ★★★ Final entry in Universal's popular Rathbone/Bruce Sherlock Holmes series. This one involves counterfeiting, specifically a Bank of England plate hidden in one of three music boxes. After filming was completed, Rathbone—fearing typecasting—had had enough; his concerns clearly were genuine, as he did not work again for nearly nine years. Not rated—suitable for family viewing. B&W; 72m. **DIR:** Roy William Neill. **CAST:** Basil Rathbone, Nigel Bruce, Patricia Morison, Edmund Breon, Frederic Worlock, Harry Cording. **1946 DVD**

DRESSED TO KILL (1980) ★★★1/2 Director Brian De Palma again borrows heavily from Alfred Hitchcock in this story of sexual frustration, madness, and murder set in New York City. Angie Dickinson plays a sexually active housewife whose affairs lead to an unexpected conclusion. Rated R for violence, strong language, nudity, and simulated sex. 105m. **DIR:** Brian De Palma. **CAST:** Michael Caine, Angie Dickinson, Nancy Allen, Keith Gordon. **1980 DVD**

DRESSER, THE ★★★★★ Peter Yates directed this superb screen treatment of Ronald Harwood's play about an eccentric stage actor (Albert Finney) in wartime England and the loyal valet (Tom Courtenay) who cares for him, sharing his triumphs and tragedies. Rated PG for language. 118m. **DIR:** Peter Yates. **CAST:** Albert Finney, Tom Courtenay, Edward Fox, Zena Walker. **1983**

DRESSMAKER, THE ★★★1/2 In London during World War II, a teenage girl lives with two maiden aunts, one who tries to insulate her and one who encourages her to enjoy herself. Worth seeing for the performances of three superb actresses (including Jane Horrocks in her debut), though the ending is a bit perfunctory. Not rated, with sexual discussions that put this above the heads of young children. 90m. **DIR:** Jim O'Brien. **CAST:** Joan Plowright, Billie Whitelaw, Jane Horrocks, Tim Ransom. **1988**

DRIFTER, THE ★★ A successful businesswoman picks up a hitchhiker and they have a one-night stand. Afterward he refuses to leave her alone and her life is in jeopardy. Perhaps with a better script this could have been a reverse *Fatal Attraction*. Rated R for violence, nudity, and profanity. 89m. **DIR:** Larry Brand. **CAST:** Kim Delaney, Timothy Bottoms, Miles O'Keeffe. **1988 DVD**

DRIFTIN' KID ★★1/2 It seems every B-Western star was required to make at least one oater wherein he played a dual role. Tom Keene does it here—but it's all been done better elsewhere. Outlaws after government grazing contracts. B&W; 57m. **DIR:** Robert Emmett Tansey. **CAST:** Tom Keene, Betty Miles, Frank Yaconelli, Stanley Price. **1941**

DRIFTING WEEDS ★★★★★ The leader of a troupe of traveling actors visits an old lover and his illegitimate son when the actors pass through a distant village. An exquisitely simple but moving drama from the master Japanese director Yasujiro Ozu. Also known as *Floating Weeds*. In Japanese with English subtitles. 119m. **DIR:** Yasujiro Ozu. **CAST:** Ganjiro Nakamura, Machiko Kyo. **1959**

DRILLER KILLER, THE 🦃 A maniac named Reno falls for his roommate. When rejected by her, he goes crazy. Not rated; contains violence, gore, and profanity. 84m. **DIR:** Abel Ferrara. **CAST:** Carolyn Mare, Jimmy Laine. **1979 DVD**

•DRIVE BY ★★1/2 Impressive debut by cowriter-director Juan Frausto, who takes us deep into the mean streets of Chicago where gangs are a way of life. Even though the film suffers from a low budget, the director manages to create a faux cinema verité where his story about an older brother trying to keep his younger brother out of gangs feels right, and the actors give natural, occasionally chilling performances. Another example of independent filmmaking that would have been diluted by the studios. Rated R for drugs, language, and violence. 97m. **DIR:** Juan Frausto. **CAST:** Felipe Comacho, Lou Meza, Raul Salinas. **2000 DVD**

DRIVE-IN ★★★ Enjoyable film about a day in the life of a small Texas town. At dusk all the citizens head off for the local drive-in theater. With as many as three plots developing, *Drive-In* is like a Southern *American Graffiti*. Rated PG. 96m. **DIR:** Rod Amateau. **CAST:** Lisa Lemole, Glen Morshower, Gary Cavagnaro, Trey Wilson. **1976 DVD**

DRIVE-IN MASSACRE ★★1/2 If you're in the mood for a slasher movie, you could do worse than this ultralow-budget gorefest. The title says it all: Psycho killer bumps off patrons at a drive-in movie, but there are some bits that will please anyone who has ever spent summer nights at an outdoor cinema. Rated R for gore and nudity. 78m. **DIR:** Stuart Segall. **CAST:** Jake Barnes, Adam Lawrence. **1976**

DRIVE LIKE LIGHTNING ★★★ A guilt-ridden ex-daredevil is hired to drive a stunt car to Los Angeles. At first this looks like just another bad cross-country truck driving movie, but don't let first impressions fool you. A nice surprise. Not rated; made for cable. 96m. **DIR:** Bradford May. **CAST:** Steven Bauer, Cynthia Gibb, William Russ, Paul Koslo. **1991**

DRIVE ME CRAZY ★★★1/2 This teen Pygmalion is a cut above most high-school caste comedies. A girl social climber gets dumped by a popular jock just before the big dance. She then dates and initiates the makeover of a grungy boy neighbor who has been dumped by his punkette girlfriend. Romance and several surprises blossom in a solidly written film that develops characters rather than just caricatures. Rated PG-13 for language and teen drug and alcohol use. 94m. **DIR:** John Schultz. **CAST:** Melissa Joan Hart, Adrian Grenier, Ali Larter, Gabriel Carpenter. **1999 DVD**

DRIVEN ★★ Car owner Carl grooms rookie racer Jimmy to win the world championship in this messy melodrama and swaggering homage to 200-plus mph open-wheel competition. The track footage and digital effects are breathless orgies of sound, speed, color, cataclysm, and flying debris. The knotted personal relationships between siblings, pals, teammates, and lovers are contrived. Rated PG-13 for language and car crashes. 117m. **DIR:** Renny Harlin. **CAST:** Sylvester Stallone, Kip Pardue, Estella Warren, Burt Reynolds, Robert Sean Leonard, Til Schweiger, Gina Gershon, Cristiàn de la Fuente, Stacy Edwards. **2001 DVD**

DRIVER, THE ★★★★ High-energy crime drama focuses on a professional getaway driver (Ryan O'Neal) and his police pursuer (Bruce Dern). Walter Hill's breakneck pacing and spectacular chase scenes make up for the lack of plot or character development. It's an action movie pure and simple. Rated PG for violence and profanity. 90m. **DIR:** Walter Hill. **CAST:** Ryan O'Neal, Bruce Dern, Isabelle Adjani, Ronee Blakley, Matt Clark. **1978**

DRIVER'S SEAT, THE ★★ Tedious Italian-made drama featuring Elizabeth Taylor in one of her less memorable performances as a psychotic woman with a death wish. Rated PG. 101m. **DIR:** Giuseppe Patroni Griffi. **CAST:** Elizabeth Taylor, Ian Bannen, Mona Washbourne, Andy Warhol. **1973**

DRIVING ME CRAZY ★★★1/2 Charming comedy stars German actor Thomas Gottschalk as the inventor of a car that runs on turnips. He discovers capitalism and Los Angeles with the help of Billy Dee Williams. Predictable, but fun in a low-key way. Rated PG-13. 88m. **DIR:** Jon Turteltaub. **CAST:** Billy Dee Williams, Thomas Gottschalk, Dom DeLuise, Michelle Johnson, George Kennedy. **1991**

DRIVING MISS DAISY ★★★★★ Alfred Uhry's stage play is brought to stunning, emotionally satisfying life by director Bruce Beresford and his superb cast. The story concerns the twenty-five-year relationship of the feisty Miss Daisy (Jessica Tandy) and a wise, wily chauffeur, Hoke (Morgan Freeman). Dan Aykroyd is remarkably effective as Daisy's doting son. Rated PG for profanity. 99m. **DIR:** Bruce Beresford. **CAST:** Morgan Freeman, Jessica Tandy, Dan Aykroyd, Patti LuPone, Esther Rolle. **1989 DVD**

DROP DEAD FRED ★★1/2 A young woman has a childhood imaginary friend who reappears to help her through a crisis. A wild romp with stunning visual effects that some viewers may find offensive. Rated PG-13 for profanity and brief nudity. 98m. **DIR:** Ate De Jong. **CAST:** Phoebe Cates, Rik Mayall, Marsha Mason, Tim Matheson, Carrie Fisher, Ron Eldard. **1991**

DROP DEAD GORGEOUS (1991) 🦃 Sally Kellerman's career remains in the toilet with this disaster. Made for cable. 88m. **DIR:** Paul Lynch. **CAST:** Jennifer Rubin, Peter Outerbridge, Stephen Shellen, Sally Kellerman, Michael Ironside. **1991**

DROP DEAD GORGEOUS (1999) ★★1/2 Spoofed documentary of a teen pageant in "small minded-ville" Minnesota pits sweet, economically challenged Kirsten Dunst against spoiled brat Denise Richards. The "documentary" crew captures innumerable "let's offend everybody" comments before expanding its scope to include the mysterious accidents of some of the contestants. Only the very thick-skinned will find this amusing. Rated PG-13 for religious and ethnic jokes and profanity. 95m. **DIR:** Michael Patrick. **CAST:** Kirsten Dunst, Denise Richards, Kirstie Alley, Ellen Barkin. **1999 DVD**

DROP SQUAD, THE ★★★ Intriguing idea that needed a more sophisticated execution. DROP is an acronym for Deprogramming and Restoration of Pride. Eriq La Salle, an African-American advertising exec selling questionable products to a black market, finds himself kidnapped and brutally reprogrammed. Too many characters and a subplot involving dissension within the squad blur the lines and divert the dramatic tension. Rated R for profanity and violence. 88m. **DIR:** David C. Johnson. **CAST:** Eriq La Salle, Vondie Curtis-Hall, Ving Rhames, Vanessa L. Williams, Spike Lee, Michael Ralph. **1994 DVD**

DROP ZONE ★★★1/2 When two brothers are assigned by their superiors at U.S. marshal headquarters to guard an important witness, they are caught off guard by a midair kidnapping of their charge—with deadly consequences. The government writes the witness off as dead and blame the brothers. Plenty of action and stunts, and a commanding performance by Wesley Snipes make this one a winner. Rated R for violence and profanity. 101m. **DIR:** John Badham. **CAST:** Wesley Snipes, Gary Busey, Yancy Butler, Michael Jeter, Malcolm Jamal-Warner, Corin Nemec, Kyle Secor, Luca Bercovici. **1994 DVD**

DROWNING BY NUMBERS ★★ Director Peter Greenaway brings us another exercise in excess and esoteric glibness. Three women, all friends and all three with the same first name, exact revenge on their sadistic husbands by drowning them. Rated R for violence, profanity, and nudity. 121m. **DIR:** Peter Greenaway. **CAST:** Joan Plowright, Juliet Stevenson, Joely Richardson. **1988**

DROWNING MONA ★★★1/2 This dark, tasteless, and cynical comedy is funny as hell, although the suggestively violent segments may repel mainstream viewers. It's a warped murder mystery involving a roster of nitwit suspects so hilariously feeble-minded that they can't *help* but look guilty . . . particularly since everybody in the entire hamlet of Verplanck, New York, loathed the victim. Peter Steinfeld aptly calls his script a "white-trash *Murder on the Orient Express*." Rated PG-13 for crude humor, violence, and a bit of eccentric sexual behavior. 95m. **DIR:** Nick Gomez. **CAST:** Danny DeVito, Bette Midler, Neve Campbell, Jamie Lee Curtis, Casey Affleck, William Fichtner, Marcus Thomas, Peter Dobson. **2000 DVD**

DROWNING POOL, THE ★★1/2 Disappointing follow-up to *Harper*, with Paul Newman re-creating the title role. Director Stuart Rosenberg doesn't come up with anything fresh in this stale entry into the detective genre. Rated PG—violence. 108m. **DIR:** Stuart Rosenberg. **CAST:** Paul Newman, Joanne Woodward, Anthony Franciosa, Richard Jaeckel, Murray Hamilton, Melanie Griffith, Gail Strickland, Linda Haynes. **1976**

DRUGSTORE COWBOY ★★★★1/2 A gritty, often shocking examination of life on the edge, this superb character study features Matt Dillon in a terrific performance as the leader of a gang of drug users in the 1960s. Dillon and his cohorts keep their habits fed by robbing drugstores until their luck runs out. Rated R for profanity and violence. 100m. **DIR:** Gus Van Sant. **CAST:** Matt Dillon, Kelly Lynch, James Remar, William S. Burroughs, James LeGros, Heather Graham. **1989 DVD**

DRUM 🦃 Sweaty, sexed-up continuation of *Mandingo*, Kyle Onstott's lurid tale of plantation life in the pre–Civil War South. 110m. **DIR:** Steve Carver. **CAST:** Ken Norton, Warren Oates, Pam Grier, John Colicos, Yaphet Kotto. **1976**

DRUM BEAT ★★1/2 Indian fighter Alan Ladd is detailed to ensure peace with marauding Modocs on the California-Oregon border in 1869. His chief adversary, in beads and buckskins, is Charles Bronson. As usual, white man speaks with forked tongue, but everything ends well. 111m. **DIR:** Delmer Daves. **CAST:** Alan Ladd, Audrey Dalton, Marisa Pavan, Robert Keith, Anthony Caruso, Warner Anderson, Elisha Cook Jr., Charles Bronson. **1954**

DRUM TAPS ★★★ Ken Maynard and the Boy Scouts drive land grabbers from the range. Only time Kermit Maynard (who had his own Western series) ever appears in one of his brother's Westerns. B&W; 61m. **DIR:** J. P. McGowan. **CAST:** Ken Maynard, Frank Coghlan Jr., Kermit Maynard. **1933**

DRUMS ★★★1/2 Stiff-upper-lip British Empire epic starts slow but builds to an exciting climax as soldiers of the queen aid young Prince Sabu in his struggle against usurping uncle Raymond Massey. 99m. **DIR:** Zoltán Korda. **CAST:** Sabu, Raymond Massey, Valerie Hobson, Roger Livesey, David Tree. **1938**

DRUMS ALONG THE MOHAWK ★★★★ Claudette Colbert and Henry Fonda are among a group of sturdy settlers of upstate New York during the Revolutionary War. Despite the episodic nature of its story, this emerges as another richly detailed film from director John Ford. Beautifully photographed in color, the work benefits from vibrant supporting performances by Edna May Oliver, Jessie Ralph, John Carradine, and Ward Bond. 103m. **DIR:** John Ford. **CAST:** Claudette Colbert, Henry Fonda, Edna May Oliver, John Carradine, Jessie Ralph, Robert Lowery, Ward Bond. **1939**

DRUMS IN THE DEEP SOUTH ★★1/2 Two friends, both in love with the same girl, find themselves on opposite sides in the Civil War. 87m. **DIR:** William Cameron Menzies. **CAST:** James Craig, Guy Madison, Barbara Payton, Craig Stevens. **1951**

DRUMS OF FU MANCHU ★★★1/2 This exciting serial presents the definitive Fu Manchu with smooth, sinister Henry Brandon splendidly cast as the greatest of all Far Eastern menaces. Sir Dennis Nayland Smith and his associates tackle the deadly doctor to keep him from finding the scepter of the great Genghis Khan. B&W; 15 chapters. **DIR:** William Witney, John English. **CAST:** Henry Brandon, Robert Kellard, Gloria Franklin, Olaf Hytten, Tom Chatterton, Luana Walters, George Cleveland, Dwight Frye. **1940**

DRUMS OF JEOPARDY ★★1/2 Russian scientist Dr. Karlov blames his daughter's death on the royal family and vows revenge. Each of Karlov's intended victims receives a piece of the jewels known as the Drums of Jeopardy before dying. There are plenty of chases and wild fights, good laboratory scenes, and a carpet-chewing performance by Warner Oland as a Bolshevik Dr. Fu Manchu. B&W; 105m. **DIR:** George B. Seitz. **CAST:** Warner Oland, June Collyer, Lloyd Hughes, Mischa Auer, Clara Blandick. **1931**

DRUNKEN ANGEL ★★★★ Master director Akira Kurosawa here displays an early interest in good guys and bad guys. Toshiro Mifune is a petty gangster who learns from an idealistic slum doctor (Takashi

Shimura) that he is dying of tuberculosis. In Japanese with English subtitles. B&W; 102m. **DIR:** Akira Kurosawa. **CAST:** Toshiro Mifune, Takashi Shimura. **1949**

DRUNKS ★★★ Gary Lennon's stageplay makes an uneasy transition to film, mostly because director Peter Cohn does little beyond pointing his camera and shooting. Members of Alcoholics Anonymous tell their individual stories; some are interesting, but most go nowhere. Richard Lewis holds our attention as the one fully fleshed character. Interesting idea, fitful execution. Rated R for profanity and nudity. 90m. **DIR:** Peter Cohn. **CAST:** Richard Lewis, Faye Dunaway, Spalding Gray, Lisa Gay Hamilton, George Martin, Amanda Plummer, Parker Posey, Howard Rollins Jr., Dianne Wiest. **1997 DVD**

DRY CLEANING ★★★ A middle-class married couple takes in a young bisexual drifter who disrupts their blandly comfortable existence. Director Anne Fontaine keeps the domestic drama low-key and convincing, avoiding melodrama and soap-opera excess. Character relationships are ambiguous and puzzling, with dangerous undercurrents, and the resolution is both unexpected and inevitable. In French with English subtitles. Not rated; contains mature themes and sexual scenes. 97m. **DIR:** Anne Fontaine. **CAST:** Miou-Miou, Charles Berling, Stanislas Merhar, Mathilde Seigner. **1997 DVD**

DRY WHITE SEASON, A ★★★★ A white schoolteacher in South Africa slowly becomes aware of what apartheid means to black people. Based on the novel by André Brink, this adaptation occasionally becomes melodramatic. Overall, however, this powerful story riveting. Rated R for violence and profanity. 106m. **DIR:** Euzhan Palcy. **CAST:** Donald Sutherland, Janet Suzman, Jurgen Prochnow, Zakes Mokae, Susan Sarandon, Marlon Brando. **1989**

DRYING UP THE STREETS 🦃 Canadian exposé of drugs and prostitution. Not rated. 90m. **DIR:** Robin Spry. **CAST:** Sarah Torgov, Don Francks, Len Cariou, Calvin Butler. **1984**

D3: THE MIGHTY DUCKS ★★ If you saw either of the first two Ducks movies, here we go again. This time the gang takes on the stuck-up snobs at a high-class prep school and has to prove itself against the school's cutthroat varsity hockey team. Guess who wins. Both the kids and the formula are getting too old to retain the series' original charm. Rated PG. 104m. **DIR:** Robert Lieberman. **CAST:** Emilio Estevez, Jeffrey Nordling, Heidi Kling, Joss Ackland. **1996**

D2: THE MIGHTY DUCKS ★★★ Just a notch below the original. Coach Emilio Estevez and his youthful team of hockey players and misfits represent America in an international competition. Sure it's contrived, but kids won't care. Rated PG. 107m. **DIR:** Sam Weisman. **CAST:** Emilio Estevez, Michael Tucker, Jan Rubes, Kathryn Erbe, Cartsen Norgaard. **1994**

DU BARRY WAS A LADY ★★ A slow-moving adaptation of a popular stage hit minus most of the music that made it popular. Set in the court of Louis XIV, this musical romp gives Red Skelton a chance to mug and Gene Kelly a chance to dance. 101m. **DIR:** Roy Del Ruth. **CAST:** Red Skelton, Lucille Ball, Gene Kelly, Zero Mostel, Virginia O'Brien, Donald Meek, Louise Beavers, Tommy Dorsey. **1943**

DU-BEAT-E-O ★★ More of a pastiche than a feature movie, *du-BEAT-e-o* has the air of something thrown together by a bunch of guys goofing around in a film-editing room. The skeleton plot has underground L.A. filmmaker Dubeateo (Ray Sharkey) and his editor (Derf Scratch of the punk band Fear) trying to turn some scattered footage of rocker Joan Jett into a movie. Not rated, there is nudity and profanity. 84m. **DIR:** Alan Sacks. **CAST:** Ray Sharkey, Derf Scratch. **1984**

DUCHESS AND THE DIRTWATER FOX, THE 🦃 This Western-comedy romp never clicks. Rated PG. 103m. **DIR:** Melvin Frank. **CAST:** George Segal, Goldie Hawn, Conrad Janis, Thayer David, Bill McLaughlin. **1976**

DUCHESS OF IDAHO ★★1/2 Esther Williams attempts to have businessman John Lund become interested in her friend, lovesick Paula Raymond, only leading to Esther being pursued by him and a bandleader, Van Johnson. A badly arranged appearance by 40 year old Eleanor Powell—her swan song. 99m. **DIR:** Robert Z. Leonard. **CAST:** Esther Williams, Van Johnson, John Lund, Paula Raymond, Lena Horne, Eleanor Powell. **1950**

DUCK SOUP ★★★★★ Groucho, Harpo, Chico, and Zeppo in their best film: an antiestablishment comedy that failed miserably at the box office at the time of its release. Today, this Leo McCarey–directed romp has achieved its proper reputation as the quintessential Marx Brothers classic. B&W; 70m. **DIR:** Leo McCarey. **CAST:** The Marx Brothers, Margaret Dumont, Louis Calhern, Raquel Torres, Edgar Kennedy. **1933 DVD**

DUCKTALES: THE MOVIE—TREASURE OF THE LOST LAMP ★★★ Adapted from a Disney cartoon series for television, this is a *Raiders of the Lost Ark*–style animated adventure in which Uncle Scrooge McDuck and his three great-nephews set out after lost treasure. In the style of the classic Donald Duck comic books by Carl Barks.Rated G. 106m. **DIR:** Bob Hathcock. **1990**

DUDE RANGER ★★★★ In this sturdy, well-played, and skillfully directed adaptation of the Zane Grey story, George O'Brien is a city boy who heads west to claim his inheritance: a ranch he fully intends to sell the first chance he gets. As it turns out, rustlers have been depleting his stock, and O'Brien stays on to find the culprits. B&W; 65m. **DIR:** Eddie Cline. **CAST:** George O'Brien, Irene Hervey. **1934**

DUDE, WHERE'S MY CAR? ★★ After a night of heavy partying, two stoners—contending with lapsed memories, a lost auto, irate girlfriends, and a missing suitcase of stolen money—are pursued by a transvestite stripper and a UFO cult. This juvenile comedy includes such male teen fantasies as "hot alien chicks" who can suck an entire Popsicle off its stick in one gulp. Rated PG-13 for violence, nudity, and sexual content. 84m. **DIR:** Danny Leiner. **CAST:** Ashton Kutcher, Seann William Scott, Kristy Swanson, Jennifer Garner, Marla Sokoloff. **2000 DVD**

DUDES ★★ Billed as the first punk-rock Western, this film starts off well as a comedy about three New York City rockers (Jon Cryer, Daniel Roebuck and Flea) who decide to go to California in hopes of finding a better life. After the first goofy 20 minutes, *Dudes* abruptly turns violent. Rated R for violence and profanity. 90m. **DIR:** Penelope Spheeris. **CAST:** Jon Cryer, Catherine Mary Stewart, Daniel Roebuck, Flea, Lee Ving. **1988**

DUDLEY DO-RIGHT ★★★ This film is silly and unrelentingly corny, but it's also rather fun. It will resonate best with older viewers who fondly remember the Jay Ward cartoon series on which it's based; writer-director Hugh Wilson has retained all the key elements, from the raised-eyebrow double takes to the melodramatically deadpan announcer (Corey Burton) who provides ironic commentary about all on-screen events. Brendan Fraser is properly stalwart and virtuous as the square-shouldered Canadian Mountie who genuinely deserves to wear a medal that reads "pretty good conduct," and Alfred Molina is ideal as the black-garbed, black-mustached Snidely Whiplash, the very epitome of comic villainy. The two spar over Sarah Jessica Parker's fair and true Nell Fenwick, in an amusing story line that elevates Canadian values at the expense of boorish American behavior. Rated PG for comic violence and slightly suggestive sensuality. 76m. **DIR:** Hugh Wilson. **CAST:** Brendan Fraser, Sarah Jessica Parker, Alfred Molina, Eric Idle, Robert Prosky, Alex Rocco. **1999 DVD**

DUEL ★★★★★ Early Spielberg film was originally a 73-minute ABC made-for-TV movie, but this full-length version was released theatrically overseas. The story is a simple one: a mild-mannered businessman (Dennis Weaver) alone on a desolate stretch of highway suddenly finds himself the unwitting prey of the maniacal driver of a big, greasy oil tanker. 91m. **DIR:** Steven Spielberg. **CAST:** Dennis Weaver, Eddie Firestone. **1971 DVD**

DUEL AT DIABLO ★★1/2 Overly complicated Western stars James Garner as a revenge-minded scout helping a cavalry troop transport guns and ammunition through Indian Territory. Subplots abound in this well-meant but unnecessarily dreary indictment of racism. The performances are good, however. 103m. **DIR:** Ralph Nelson. **CAST:** James Garner, Sidney Poitier, Bibi Andersson, Dennis Weaver, Bill Travers, John Hoyt. **1966**

DUEL IN THE SUN ★★★ Sprawling, brawling Western has land baron Lionel Barrymore's sons, unbroken, short-fused Gregory Peck, and solid-citizen Joseph Cotten vying for the hand of hot-blooded, half-breed Jennifer Jones. Peck and Jones take a lusty love-hate relationship to the max in the steaming desert. A near epic with a great musical score. 130m. **DIR:** King Vidor. **CAST:** Jennifer Jones, Gregory Peck, Joseph Cotten, Lionel Barrymore, Walter Huston, Lillian Gish, Harry Carey. **1946 DVD**

DUEL OF CHAMPIONS Alan Ladd is a weary centurion leader in ancient Rome fighting for the glory that once was. Forgettable. 105m. **DIR:** Ferdinando Baldi. **CAST:** Alan Ladd, Robert Keith, Franco Fabrizi. **1961**

DUEL OF HEARTS ★★ Lush TV adaptation of Barbara Cartland's bestseller. A free-spirited woman falls for a handsome lord and takes a position as his mother's companion. Dim romantic adventure, but the cast rises to the occasion. 95m. **DIR:** John Hough. **CAST:** Alison Doody, Michael York, Geraldine Chaplin, Benedict Taylor, Richard Johnson. **1990**

DUELLISTS, THE ★★★★ *The Duellists* traces a long and seemingly meaningless feud between two soldiers in the Napoleonic Wars. This fascinating study of honor among men is full of irony and heroism. Rated R. 101m. **DIR:** Ridley Scott. **CAST:** Keith Carradine, Harvey Keitel, Albert Finney, Edward Fox, Cristina Raines, Robert Stephens, Tom Conti. **1977**

DUET FOR ONE ★★★ As an English virtuoso violinist with multiple sclerosis, Julie Andrews gives an outstanding performance in this high-class tearjerker. Alan Bates is her sympathetic but philandering husband. Max von Sydow is the psychiatrist who attempts to help her. And Rupert Everett plays her protégé who shuns the classical world for big-time show biz. Rated R. 110m. **DIR:** Andrei Konchalovsky. **CAST:** Julie Andrews, Alan Bates, Max von Sydow, Rupert Everett. **1987**

DUETS ★★★★ Enchanting, wistful, and sometimes hard-edged character study about a disillusioned cabdriver and five singers who are caught up in the karaoke subculture, their various stories coming together during a contest for a $5,000 prize. Andre Braugher stands out dramatically, while Gwyneth Paltrow not only entrances with her understated performance but also surprises with a fine singing voice. Rated R for profanity, some violence, nudity, and simulated sex. 112m. **DIR:** Bruce Paltrow. **CAST:** Maria Bello, Andre Braugher, Paul Giamatti, Huey Lewis, Gwyneth Paltrow, Scott Speedman, Angie Dickinson. **2000 DVD**

DUMB AND DUMBER ★★★★ Jim Carrey and Jeff Daniels work extremely well together in this hilarious story of two dim bulbs who unwittingly become involved in a high-stakes kidnapping scheme. It's all low humor—with plenty of time for the toilet—yet you laugh in spite of yourself. Rated PG-13 for humorous violence, scatological humor, and nudity. 106m. **DIR:** Peter Farrelly. **CAST:** Jim Carrey, Jeff Daniels, Lauren Holly, Teri Garr, Karen Duffy, Mike Starr, Charles Rocket, Victoria Rowell, Cam Neely, Felton Perry. **1994 DVD**

DUMB WAITER, THE ★★ This TV adaptation of Harold Pinter's absurdist drama will probably not appeal to general audiences. Two hit men (John Travolta and Tom Conti) await their latest assignment in a deserted restaurant's basement. 60m. **DIR:** Robert Altman. **CAST:** John Travolta, Tom Conti. **1987**

DUMBO ★★★★ Disney's cartoon favorite about the outcast circus elephant with the big ears is a family classic. It has everything: personable animals, a poignant story, and a happy ending. It is good fun and can still invoke a tear or two in the right places. 64m. **DIR:** Ben Sharpstein. **1941 DVD**

DUNE (1984) The only good thing about the movie version of *Dune* is it makes one want to read (or reread) the book. Otherwise, it's a $47 million mess. Rated PG-13 for gore, suggested sex, and violence. 145m. **DIR:** David Lynch. **CAST:** Sting, Kyle MacLachlan, Max von Sydow, Jurgen Prochnow, Sean Young, Kenneth McMillan, Richard Jordan, Dean Stockwell, Patrick Stewart, José Ferrer, Brad Dourif, Francesca Annis. **1984 DVD**

DUNE (2000) ★★★1/2 Although a vast improvement on the big-screen version, this opulent Sci-Fi Channel original still reduces some characters to one-dimensional status—particularly the villainous Harkonnen family—and makes short shrift of the novel's most interesting characters. That said, it does a much better job of making all of author Frank Herbert's story points clear as young Paul Atreides goes through his rite of passage to become the savior of the desert world. Made for TV. 285m. **DIR:** John Harrison. **CAST:** William Hurt,

Alec Newman, Saskia Reeves, Ian McNeice, P. H. Moriarty, Julie Cox, Giancarlo Giannini, Matt Keeslar, Barbora Kodetova. **2000 DVD**

DUNE WARRIORS ★★ Rip-off of *The Magnificent Seven* set in an apocalyptic future stars David Carradine as the head honcho of a band of mercenaries. Plenty of action to cover up the familiar plot. Rated R for violence, profanity, and nudity. 77m. **DIR:** Cirio H. Santiago. **CAST:** David Carradine, Richard Hill, Luke Askew, Jillian McWhirter. **1991**

DUNERA BOYS, THE ★★★★ Bob Hoskins is sensational in this harrowing war drama about a group of Jewish refugees who are ironically suspected of being German informants by the British army. They are shipped to a prison camp in Australia on the HMT *Dunera*. A film of great intelligence and humanity. Rated R for violence and profanity. 150m. **DIR:** Greg Snedon. **CAST:** Joe Spano, Bob Hoskins, Warren Mitchell. **1987**

DUNGEONMASTER, THE 🦃 It's corny, it's bad, it's simplistic. Rated PG-13 for mild violence. 73m. **DIR:** Rosemarie Turko, John Carl Buechler, Charles Band, David Allen, Steve Ford, Peter Manoogian, Ted Nic. **CAST:** Jeffrey Byron, Richard Moll. **1985**

DUNGEONS & DRAGONS ★★ Even fans of the popular role-playing game will find it difficult to admire anything about this ill-fated adaptation, which starts with a terrible script and then suffers further from inept direction and eleventh-hour editing that may have shortened the pain, but renders the finished film incomprehensible. On top of that, it's racist; poor Marlon does little but fetch and carry for the hunky white hero. Rated PG-13 for violence and profanity. 107m. **DIR:** Courtney Solomon. **CAST:** Jeremy Irons, Justin Whalin, Marlon Wayans, Zoe McLellan, Thora Birch, Kristen Wilson, Richard O'Brien. **2000 DVD**

DUNSTON CHECKS IN ★★★ Dunston is a small orangutan who has been trained to steal jewels from swank hotel rooms. The hairy bandit tires of his mean master, befriends a mischievous teen at the four-star hotel they are plundering, and turns a huge formal ball into chaos. This dose of energetic silliness is given a big boost from its impressive cast. Rated PG. 90m. **DIR:** Ken Kwapis. **CAST:** Jason Alexander, Faye Dunaway, Eric Lloyd, Rupert Everett, Glenn Shadix, Paul Reubens. **1995**

DUNWICH HORROR, THE 🦃 Torpid horror-thriller made when folks didn't know that it's impossible to adapt H. P. Lovecraft. Dean Stockwell foreshadowed his hammy role in *Dune* with this laughable portrayal of a warlock. Rated PG for violence. 90m. **DIR:** Daniel Haller. **CAST:** Sandra Dee, Dean Stockwell, Sam Jaffe, Ed Begley Sr., Talia Shire. **1970 DVD**

DUPLICATES ★★★1/2 Surprisingly good made-for-cable movie. A hospital in upstate New York is really a government research facility for altering criminal minds. Good acting by all—and a well-written script. 91m. **DIR:** Sandor Stern. **CAST:** Gregory Harrison, Kim Greist, Cicely Tyson, Lane Smith, Bill Lucking, Kevin McCarthy. **1992**

DURANGO ★★★★ Based on Irish author John B. Keane's autobiographical novel, this delightful Hallmark Hall of Fame features Matt Keeslar as a headstrong cattle man who defies the local buyers. In order to get a fair price, he attempts a cattle drive. Along the way, he grows up, takes on the thugs sent to thwart him, and matures in his feelings for a lovely lass. Unrated, contains violence. 92m. **DIR:** Brent Shields. **CAST:** Matt Keeslar, Patrick Bergin, George Hearn, Nancy St. Alban, Brenda Fricker. **1999**

DUST ★★ A Bergmanesque tale of a lonely South African farmer's daughter and her descent into madness after she kills her abusive father. Jane Birkin does a commendable job as the bitter farm maid, but the film is very moody, with lots of mumbled lines and long still shots. Not rated; contains violence and suggested sex. 87m. **DIR:** Marion Hansel. **CAST:** Jane Birkin, Trevor Howard. **1985**

DUST DEVIL ★★★ A South African devil arises from the desert to stalk hapless (and hopeless) victims. Moody and gory, this great-looking horror flick is too slow and artsy for its own good, and disjointed editing undermines creepy ritualism and eye-catching settings. Rated R for strong violence, sexuality, and language. 87m. **DIR:** Richard Stanley. **CAST:** Robert Burke, Chelsea Field, Zakes Mokae, Rufus Swart. **1992**

DUSTY ★★★ An emotional story of a retired, lonely shepherd in Australia who is adopted by Dusty, a stray sheepdog. 89m. **DIR:** John Richardson. **CAST:** Bill Kerr, Noel Trevarthen, Carol Burns, Nicholas Holland, John Stanton. **1985**

DUTCH ★★★ Dutch Dooley (Ed O'Neill) agrees to what seems like a simple task: picking up his girlfriend's son from an Atlanta boarding school and driving him home to Chicago. Written by John Hughes, isn't quite *Planes, Trains and Automobiles.* Rated PG-13 for profanity. 95m. **DIR:** Peter Faiman. **CAST:** Ed O'Neill, JoBeth Williams, Ethan Randall. **1991**

DYBBUK, THE ★★★1/2 Eerie film version of a popular folktale set in nineteenth-century Poland. A student kills himself when the father of the girl to whom he has been pledged in marriage breaks the promise in order to marry her into a rich family. The girl is then possessed by the spirit of the dead boy. A well-made film for its time and place. In Yiddish with English subtitles. 122m. **DIR:** Michael Wasynski. **CAST:** Abraham Morevski. **1938**

DYING TO GET RICH ★★★ Susan has a plan: To kill her husband and get all his money. Helping her are her lover, two stoners, a female friend, and a biker. Since this is a comedy, the plan naturally goes awry with the murder ending up as only a flesh wound. Rob Schneider and Michael Biehn as the two would-be assassins steal the show. Rated R for violence, profanity, and simulated sex. 90m. **DIR:** John Landis. **CAST:** Nastassja Kinski, Billy Zane, Dan Aykroyd, Lara Flynn Boyle, Michael Biehn, Rob Schneider, Adrian Paul. **1999 DVD**

DYING TO REMEMBER ★★★ A fashion designer dreams about a former life in which she was murdered. She goes to San Francisco looking for answers and finds the man who may have killed her. The movie has a good suspenseful plot and is also well-acted. Rated PG-13 for violence. 87m. **DIR:** Arthur Allan Seidelman. **CAST:** Melissa Gilbert, Ted Shackelford, Scott Plank, Christopher Stone, Jay Robinson. **1993**

DYING YOUNG ★★1/2 A free-spirited, working-class woman finds herself falling in love with the scion of a wealthy San Francisco family after she's hired to help him recover from the side effects of chemotherapy treatments. Julia Roberts and Campbell Scott elevate this uninspired *Love Story* clone. Rated R for profanity. 110m. **DIR:** Joel Schumacher. **CAST:** Julia Roberts, Campbell Scott, Vincent D'Onofrio, Colleen Dewhurst, David Selby, Ellen Burstyn. **1991**

DYNAMITE AND GOLD ★★1/2 Passable made-for-television effort teams Willie Nelson and Delta Burke as two fortune seekers looking for buried cache of gold. Also known as *Where the Hell's That Gold?* 91m. **DIR:** Burt Kennedy. **CAST:** Willie Nelson, Delta Burke, Jack Elam, Gerald McRaney. **1990**

DYNAMITE CANYON ★★1/2 Tom Keene infiltrates an outlaw gang that is attempting to grab Evelyn Finley's ranch for its copper deposits. It's a bit slower than other Keene oaters. B&W; 58m. **DIR:** Robert Emmett Tansey. **CAST:** Tom Keene, Evelyn Finley, Kenne Duncan. **1941**

DYNAMITE PASS ★★1/2 Unconventional shoot-'em-up has cowpoke Tim Holt and sidekick Richard Martin helping a construction engineer battle a tyrannical toll-road operator and his hired guns. All of the principals and supporting players give it their best shot, and this modest little oater has a nice edge to it. B&W; 61m. **DIR:** Lew Landers. **CAST:** Tim Holt, Richard Martin, Regis Toomey, Lynne Roberts, John Dehner, Robert Shayne, Cleo Moore, Denver Pyle, Ross Elliott. **1950**

DYNAMO Miserable rip-off of the Bruce Lee legend. Rated R for violence, nudity, and simulated sex. 93m. **DIR:** Hwa I. Hong. **CAST:** Bruce Li, Mary Han, James Griffith, Steve Sandor. **1978**

E

EACH DAWN I DIE ★★★★ Energetic Warner Bros. film occasionally slips the bounds of believability but never fails to be entertaining. James Cagney is terrific as the youthful reporter who is framed for murder after exposing a crooked district attorney. B&W; 92m. **DIR:** William Keighley. **CAST:** James Cagney, George Raft, George Bancroft, Jane Bryan, Maxie Rosenbloom. **1939**

EAGLE, THE ★★★ Produced to boost the legendary Rudolph Valentino's then-sagging popularity, this satirical romance of a Russian Cossack lieutenant who masquerades as a do-gooder bandit to avenge his father's death proved a box-office winner for the star. Valentino is at his romantic, swoon-inducing, self-mocking best in the title role. Silent. B&W; 72m. **DIR:** Clarence Brown. **CAST:** Rudolph Valentino, Vilma Banky, Louise Dresser, Clark Ward, Spottiswoode Aitken. **1925**

EAGLE HAS LANDED, THE ★★★ Michael Caine is a Nazi agent who is given orders to plan and carry out the kidnapping or murder of Prime Minister Churchill. This movie gets started on a promising note, but it is sabotaged by a weak, contrived ending. Rated PG. 123m. **DIR:** John Sturges. **CAST:** Michael Caine, Donald Sutherland, Robert Duvall. **1977 DVD**

EAGLE'S BROOD ★★★ Hopalong Cassidy and Johnny Nelson aid an old Mexican outlaw whose son has been killed and grandson kidnapped. Second in the long-running series, this fine entry has a maturity and edge to it that would be rounded off within the next few years as the target audience changed. B&W; 59m. **DIR:** Howard Bretherton. **CAST:** William Boyd, James Ellison, William Farnum, George "Gabby" Hayes, Joan Woodbury, Paul Fix. **1935**

EAGLE'S WING ★★ When an Indian brave steals a magnificent white stallion from a fur trapper, a struggle of wits, courage, and endurance begins for the horse. Magnificent scenery highlights this British production. Rated PG. 100m. **DIR:** Anthony Harvey. **CAST:** Martin Sheen, Sam Waterston, Harvey Keitel, Stéphane Audran, Caroline Langrishe. **1980**

EARLY FROST, AN ★★★★1/2 This timely, extremely effective drama focuses on a family's attempt to come to grips with the fact that their son is not only gay but has AIDS as well. Gena Rowlands, one of Hollywood's most neglected actresses, and Aidan Quinn take the acting honors as mother and son. One of those rare television movies that works on all levels, it is highly recommended. 100m. **DIR:** John Erman. **CAST:** Gena Rowlands, Ben Gazzara, Aidan Quinn, Sylvia Sidney, John Glover. **1985**

EARLY RUSSIAN CINEMA: BEFORE THE REVOLUTIONS (VOL. 1–10) ★★★★★ Soviet cinema didn't emerge fully formed from the heads of Eisenstein, Vertov, and Dovzhenko. Russia enjoyed a booming film industry prior to the revolution, but the Soviets found many of these films too cosmopolitan and removed them from circulation. This collection of twenty-eight works unearthed by Glasnost provides a fascinating look at a wide spectrum of pre-Soviet society. Silent. B&W; 695m. **DIR:** Evgenii Bauer, Ladislaw Starewicz, Yakov Protázanov. **1908–1918**

EARLY SUMMER ★★★1/2 Involved and involving story about a young woman rebelling against an arranged marriage in post–World War II Tokyo. Yasujiro Ozu, one of Japan's most respected directors, deftly presents this tale of culture clash, which won the Japanese Film of the Year Award in 1951. In Japanese with English subtitles. B&W; 135m. **DIR:** Yasujiro Ozu. **CAST:** Setsuko Hara. **1951**

EARRINGS OF MADAME DE . . . , THE ★★★★ A giddily romantic roundelay sparked by a pair of diamond earrings. They keep changing hands but always come back to haunt the fickle countess who owned them first. The style is a bit too lighthearted for what is ultimately a tragic story, but Max Ophüls imbues it with wit and technical flash. In French with English subtitles. 105m. **DIR:** Max Ophüls. **CAST:** Charles Boyer, Danielle Darrieux, Vittorio De Sica. **1953**

EARTH ★★★★ One of the last classic silent films, this short homage to the spirit of the collective farmer and his intangible ties to the land employs stunning camera shots. Certain scenes from the original print no longer exist, but what remains of this film tells a beautiful, moving story. Russian, silent. B&W; 56m. **DIR:** Alexander Dovzhenko. **CAST:** Semyon Svashenko. **1930 DVD**

EARTH ★★★★ As India nears independence from Great Britain in 1947, long-simmering ethnic hatred among Hindus, Moslems, and Sikhs begins to boil to the surface. Writer-director Deepa Mehta tells her story from the viewpoint of an eight-year-old girl whose governess has admirers of all persuasions, and the romantic dilemma symbolizes the conflicts in the country as a whole. The film is melancholy, elegiac, and quite moving. In Hindi with English subtitles. Not rated; deals with mature themes and contains brief scenes of violence and sexuality. 104m. **DIR:** Deepa Mehta. **CAST:** Aamir Khan, Nandita Das, Rahul Khanna, Kitu Gidwani, Maia Sethna. **1998**

EARTH GIRLS ARE EASY ★★★ A wacky but consistently funny musical comedy is based on the bizarre premise of some extraterrestrial visitors crash-landing in the swimming pool behind Valley girl Geena Davis's house. Davis and friend Julie Brown decide to shave the hairy intruders, discover they are hunks, and acquaint the visitors with the L.A. lifestyle. Rated PG for mild profanity. 100m. **DIR:** Julien Temple. **CAST:** Geena Davis, Jeff Goldblum, Julie Brown, Jim Carrey, Damon Wayans, Michael McKean, Charles Rocket. **1989 DVD**

EARTH VS. THE FLYING SAUCERS ★★★★ Stunning special effects by Ray Harryhausen enhance this familiar 1950s plot about an invasion from outer space. After misinterpreting a message for peace from the initially easygoing aliens, the military opens fire—and then all hell breaks loose! B&W; 83m. **DIR:** Fred F. Sears. **CAST:** Hugh Marlowe, Joan Taylor, Donald Curtis, Morris Ankrum. **1956**

EARTH VS. THE SPIDER ★★ A giant spider invades a mountain community in this American-International rip-off of Jack Arnold's *Tarantula*. Special effects are so-so; one of Bert I. Gordon's more tolerable time wasters. B&W; 72m. **DIR:** Bert I. Gordon. **CAST:** Ed Kemmer, June Kenney, Gene Roth. **1958**

EARTHLING, THE ★★★1/2 A dying man (William Holden) and an orphaned boy (Rick Schroder) meet in the Australian wilderness in this surprisingly absorbing family film. A warning to parents: There is a minor amount of profanity, and a scene in which the boy's mother and father are killed may be too shocking for small children. Rated PG. 102m. **DIR:** Peter Collinson. **CAST:** William Holden, Rick Schroder, Jack Thompson, Olivia Hamnett, Alwyn Kurts. **1980**

EARTHLY POSSESSIONS ★★★1/2 Novelist Anne Tyler's always loopy characters strike again in this odd little tale, which concerns a mildly repressed housewife whose desire to "see more of the world" comes true in a wholly unexpected manner: She is taken hostage by a rather inept bank robber. Scripter Steven Roberts isn't able to get the necessary depth in this adaptation and your willingness to accept these unlikely events therefore rests solely with the two stars. While both do their best, you're likely to remain somewhat dissatisfied. Rated PG-13 for profanity and gunplay. 103m. **DIR:** James Lapine. **CAST:** Susan Sarandon, Stephen Dorff, Elisabeth Moss, Jay O. Sanders. **1999 DVD**

EARTHQUAKE ★★ Once you get past the special-effects mastery of seeing Los Angeles destroyed, you've got a pretty weak film on your hands. The classic *San Francisco* did it better. Rated PG. 129m. **DIR:** Mark Robson. **CAST:** Charlton Heston, Genevieve Bujold, Lorne Greene, Ava Gardner, Walter Matthau, George Kennedy. **1974 DVD**

EARTHWORM TRACTORS ★★★ Big mouth Joe E. Brown plays braggart salesman Alexander Botts for all the comedy he can squeeze out of tractor jokes. Based on the noted *Saturday Evening Post* stories of the 1930s, this is one of Brown's better efforts. Fun stuff. B&W; 63m. **DIR:** Ray Enright. **CAST:** Joe E. Brown, Gene Lockhart, Guy Kibbee, Dick Foran. **1936**

EASIER SAID ★★★1/2 Bo Clancey delivers a winning performance as a Manhattan book editor who chucks it all to write the great American novel, but finds too many distractions to hit the keys. Leaving his miserable job, boss, and unfaithful girlfriend, Clancey heads for the Colorado Rockies, where he agrees to manage his uncle's lodge in exchange for some peace and quiet. He gets anything but as a wild and wacky troupe of locals parades through his life, providing Clancey with plenty of opportunity to strut his stuff. The script is filled with humorous insights and interesting characters. Rated R for language. 94m. **DIR:** H. Todd von Mende. **CAST:** Bo Clancey, Tricia Gregory, Alex McLeod. **1999**

EAST IS EAST ★★1/2 Though he's been living thirty years in England, a Pakistani father tries to impose the old-country ways on his seven children, who consider themselves English. Intended as a comedy of clashing cultures, the film suffers from two different styles: Om Puri plays the father as if he were doing *King Lear*, while his kids seem to have wandered in from some BBC sitcom. Rated R for profanity. 101m. **DIR:** Iain Softley. **CAST:** Om Puri, Linda Bassett, Jordan Routledge, Archie Panjabi, Emil Marwa. **1999 DVD**

EAST OF BORNEO ★★★ Intrepid and tenacious Rose Hobart searches the teeming Borneo jungle for her supposedly lost doctor husband Charles Bickford, who isn't lost at all but living it up as personal physician to native prince Georges Renavent. Filled with wildlife, this jungle adventure is lots of fun and ends with a bang. B&W; 77m. **DIR:** George Melford. **CAST:** Rose Hobart, Charles Bickford, Georges Renavent, Noble Johnson. **1931**

EAST OF EDEN ★★★1/2 This above-average television miniseries maintains the integrity of the source material by John Steinbeck without dipping too far into pathos. One major change: the focus shifts from the two sons who crave Papa's affection, to the deliciously evil woman—Jane Seymour—who twists them all around her little finger. Stick with the 1955 original. Not rated. 240m. **DIR:** Harvey Hart. **CAST:** Jane Seymour, Timothy Bottoms, Bruce Boxleitner, Warren Oates, Anne Baxter, Lloyd Bridges, Howard Duff, Karen Allen. **1982**

EAST OF EDEN ★★★★★ The final portion of John Steinbeck's renowned novel of miscommunication and conflict between a father and son was transformed into a powerful, emotional movie. James Dean burst onto the screen as the rebellious son in his first starring role. Jo Van Fleet received an Oscar for her role as Kate, a bordello madam and Dean's long-forgotten mother. 115m. **DIR:** Elia Kazan. **CAST:** James Dean, Jo Van Fleet, Julie Harris, Raymond Massey, Burl Ives. **1955**

EAST OF ELEPHANT ROCK ★★ This story of the 1948 British struggle to maintain a Far Eastern colony focuses on a new governor general's takeover after his predecessor is murdered by terrorists. The film is slow-paced and burdened with soap-opera overtones. Rated R. 93m. **DIR:** Don Boyd. **CAST:** John Hurt, Jeremy Kemp, Judi Bowker. **1981**

EAST OF KILIMANJARO ★★ A deadly virus has affected the cattle of the area in Africa east of Kilimanjaro. A daring photographer throws his weight into the fight against the microbe. Routine adventure. 75m. **DIR:** Arnold Belgard. **CAST:** Marshall Thompson, Gaby André. **1957**

EAST SIDE, WEST SIDE ★★1/2 A middling adaptation of Marcia Davenport's bestseller, with Barbara Stanwyck married to James Mason who is fooling around with Ava Gardner, but Stanwyck hangs in there trying to win back his love. This is a rare chance to see Nancy Davis (Reagan) in action. B&W; 108m. **DIR:** Mervyn LeRoy. **CAST:** Barbara Stanwyck, James Mason, Van Heflin, Ava Gardner, Cyd Charisse, Nancy Davis, Gale Sondergaard. **1949**

EAST-WEST ★★★1/2 At the end of World War II, refugees from the Russian Revolution are invited back to help rebuild their homeland, but it's all a sham—most of them are immediately killed or imprisoned. The film follows one of the few families allowed to live in relative peace, and shows how their humanity suffers as the oppressive life under Stalin wears them down. The solemn and drab film is disjointed in its last half hour, but the story remains engrossing. In French and Russian with English subtitles. Rated R for sexual scenes. 121m. **DIR:** Regis Wargnier. **CAST:** Sandrine Bonnaire, Oleg Menchikov, Sergei Bodrov Jr., Catherine Deneuve. **1999**

EASTER PARADE ★★★★ Judy Garland and Fred Astaire team up for this thoroughly enjoyable musical. Irving Berlin provided the songs for the story about Astaire trying to forget ex–dance partner Ann Miller as he rises to the top with Garland. The result is an always watchable—and repeatable—treat. 104m. **DIR:** Charles Walters. **CAST:** Judy Garland, Fred Astaire, Peter Lawford, Jules Munshin, Ann Miller. **1948**

EASTERN CONDORS ★★★★ À la *The Dirty Dozen*, a group of hardened criminals are sent to Vietnam on a suicide mission. Star-director Sammo Hung, who usually plays comical parts, may be built like a cannonball, but he can move like one, too! In Cantonese with English subtitles. Not rated; contains strong violence. 100m. **DIR:** Sammo Hung. **CAST:** Sammo Hung, Yuen Biao, Haing S. Ngor. **1986 DVD**

EASTSIDE ★★ Mario Lopez takes a walk on the wild side as an ex-con who becomes involved with a local mob boss. Each new job complicates his attempts to go straight. Not much new here. Rated R for language and violence. 94m. **DIR:** Lorena David. **CAST:** Mario Lopez, Elizabeth Bogush, Mark Espinoza, Richard Lynch. **1999**

EASY COME, EASY GO ★★ For Elvis Presley fans only. Elvis sings some snappy songs, but the plot is not going to be filed under great scripts—our star is a frogman searching for treasure on behalf of the United States Navy. 95m. **DIR:** John Rich. **CAST:** Elvis Presley, Elsa Lanchester, Dodie Marshal, Pat Priest. **1967**

EASY LIVING ★★★1/2 Shorn of the clichés one usually expects from movies about over-the-hill athletes, this picture offers a realistic account of an aging professional football player (Victor Mature) coming to terms with the end of a long career and a stormy home life. Lucille Ball and Lizabeth Scott are wonderful as the understanding secretary and shrewish wife, respectively. B&W; 77m. **DIR:** Jacques Tourneur. **CAST:** Victor Mature, Lucille Ball, Lizabeth Scott, Sonny Tufts. **1949**

EASY MONEY ★★ In this fitfully funny comedy, slob Rodney Dangerfield attempts to clean up his act, with the help of pal Joe Pesci, to qualify for a large inheritance. Rated R for profanity and suggested sex. 95m. **DIR:** James Signorelli. **CAST:** Rodney Dangerfield, Joe Pesci, Geraldine Fitzgerald, Candy Azzara. **1983 DVD**

EASY RIDER ★★★1/2 Time has not been kind to this 1969 release about two drifters (Peter Fonda and Dennis Hopper) motorcycling their way across the country only to be confronted with violence and bigotry. Jack Nicholson's keystone performance, however, still makes it worth watching. Rated R. 94m. **DIR:** Dennis Hopper. **CAST:** Peter Fonda, Dennis Hopper, Jack Nicholson, Karen Black, Luana Anders. **1969 DVD**

EASY TO LOVE ★★1/2 Tony Martin and Van Johnson vie for the love of mermaid Esther Williams in this most lavish of her numerous water spectacles. A toe-curling, high-speed sequence performed on water skis tops the Busby Berkeley numbers staged in lush Cypress Gardens at Winter Haven, Florida. 96m. **DIR:** Charles Walters. **CAST:** Esther Williams, Tony Martin, Van Johnson, Carroll Baker, John Bromfield. **1953**

EASY VIRTUE ★★ In this melodrama, based loosely on a Noel Coward play, the wife of an alcoholic falls in love with a younger man who commits suicide. Her past life prevents her from leading a normal life. Considering the directorial credit, this is close to dull. A British production. B&W; 73m. **DIR:** Alfred Hitchcock. **CAST:** Isabel Jeans, Franklyn Dyall, Ian Hunter. **1927 DVD**

EASY WHEELS ★★★ Life, love, and the pursuit of a better draft beer with the leather-bound unshaven. Dumb fun. Rated R. 94m. **DIR:** David O'Malley. **CAST:** Paul LeMat, Eileen Davidson, Barry Livingston, George Plimpton. **1989**

EAT A BOWL OF TEA ★★★★ This little domestic charmer, set in New York's post–World War II Chinatown, concerns the trouble that brews between a young Chinese-American veteran (Russell Wong) and the girl (Cora Miao) he meets and marries during a brief visit to China. Scripter Judith Rascoe has faithfully adapted Louis Chu's novel. Rated PG-13 for sexual themes. 114m. **DIR:** Wayne Wang. **CAST:** Cora Miao, Russell Wong, Victor Wong, Lau Siu Ming. **1989**

EAT AND RUN 🦃 Science-fiction spoof is about a four-hundred-pound alien named Murry Creature. Rated R for nudity. 85m. **DIR:** Christopher Hunt. **CAST:** Ron Silver, R. L. Ryan. **1986**

EAT DRINK MAN WOMAN ★★★★ This comic feast about food, fatherhood, and frayed family ties focuses on the delicate balancing acts required to make the most of both great meals and life itself. While a widowed master Taipei chef is losing his sense of taste, his three modern, unmarried daughters wind their way through the mine fields of independence and man-woman relationships. Their ritual Sunday dinners become stormy buffets of battered feelings and surprise announcements. In Mandarin with English subtitles. No MPAA rating. 123m. **DIR:** Ang Lee. **CAST:** Sihung Lung, Kuei-Mei Yang, Chien-Lien Wu, Yu-Wen Wang. **1994 DVD**

EAT MY DUST ★★ A low-budget 1976 race yarn notable only for the fact that it gave Ron Howard the power to direct his next starring vehicle, *Grand Theft Auto*, which, in turn, led to such treats as *Night Shift* and *Splash*. Rated PG. 90m. **DIR:** Charles B. Griffith.

CAST: Ron Howard, Christopher Norris, Dave Madden, Warren Kemmerling. **1976 DVD**

EAT OR BE EATEN ★★★ This spoof centers around newscasters Haryll Hee and Sharyll Shee as they cover the crisis in Labyrinth County. Between news coverage we see clever commercials that poke fun at those we normally see, as well as takeoffs on TV evangelists and sitcoms. This one has lots of laughs. Not rated, it deals with adult topics and is comparable to a PG. 30m. **DIR:** Phil Austin. **CAST:** Firesign Theatre Players. **1985**

EAT THE PEACH ★★ *Eat the Peach* takes place in an Irish village and tells the story of Vinnie and Arthur, two friends who see the Elvis Presley film *Roustabout* in which a cyclist rides the carnival Wall of Death, and decide to create their own. A slight and subtle movie. You want to like it, but it just never kicks in. Rated PG. 90m. **DIR:** Peter Ormrod. **CAST:** Stephen Brennan, Eamon Morrissey, Catherine Byrne, Niall Toibin. **1987**

EAT THE RICH 🦃 This ludicrous exercise in bad taste uses profanity, violence, and toilet jokes to elicit laughs. Rated R. 92m. **DIR:** Peter Richardson. **CAST:** Lanah Pellay, Ronald Allen, Sandra Dorne. **1987**

EATEN ALIVE ★★ Director Tobe Hooper's follow-up to *The Texas Chainsaw Massacre* has a similar theme but is less successful. The owner of a run-down Louisiana motel kills whoever wanders into his corner of the swamp, with the aid of a large, hungry alligator. This horror flick is often sloppy, but buffs will want to see it, anyway, for its cast. Rated R for strong violence. 97m. **DIR:** Tobe Hooper. **CAST:** Neville Brand, Mel Ferrer, Carolyn Jones, Marilyn Burns, William Finley, Stuart Whitman, Robert Englund. **1976 DVD**

EATING ★★★★ A group of women talk about food, sex, and self-esteem. A highly entertaining social drama evocative of some of Woody Allen's more serious work. 110m. **DIR:** Henry Jaglom. **CAST:** Nelly Alard, Lisa Richards, Frances Bergen, Mary Crosby, Gwen Welles. **1991**

EATING PATTERN ★★ This film traces the further adventures of the *Lexx*, a living, breathing, feeding spaceship, and her crew. Bizarre, sometimes silly sci-fi flick is like a story from the pages of *Heavy Metal*. Rated R for some sci-fi gore and violence. 93m. **DIR:** Rainer Matsutani. **CAST:** Brian Downey, Eva Habermann, Michael McManus, Doreen Jacobi, Rutger Hauer. **1996**

EATING RAOUL ★★★★ A hilarious black comedy cowritten and directed by Paul Bartel, this low-budget film presents an inventive but rather bizarre solution to the recession. When Mary Bland (Mary Woronov) is saved by her frying-pan-wielding husband, Paul (Bartel), from a would-be rapist, the happily married couple happily discover that the now-deceased attacker was rolling in dough—so they roll him and hit on a way to end their economic woes. Rated R for nudity, profanity, sexual situations, and violence. 83m. **DIR:** Paul Bartel. **CAST:** Paul Bartel, Mary Woronov, Robert Beltran, Susan Saiger. **1982**

EBBTIDE ★★ Harry Hamlin, who has become a familiar face in this genre, plays an attorney who becomes involved with his main suspect's wife. Their liaison drags him into a web of clichés and through a maze of stock sex-thriller characters, all who do their thing and then make a hasty exit. There's very little suspense and the usual dose of direct-to-video sex. Not rated; contains nudity, adult situations, violence, and strong language. 94m. **DIR:** Craig Lahiff. **CAST:** Harry Hamlin, Judy McIntosh, John Waters, Susan Lyons. **1994**

EBENEZER ★★★1/2 This Wild West version of Charles Dickens's *A Christmas Carol* rides tall in the saddle thanks to Jack Palance's Scrooge. When saloon owner Scrooge cheats a young man out of his land and lays off his bartender on Christmas Eve, he sets the stage for the traditional visit from three Christmas ghosts. While this made-for-television movie is slow going at the beginning, it does pick up in the second act and even delivers a shoot-out for the third. Rated PG for mild violence. 94m. **DIR:** Ken Jubenvill. **CAST:** Jack Palance, Rick Schroder, Amy Locane, Albert Schultz, Joshua Silberg. **1997**

EBONY TOWER, THE ★★★ Sir Laurence Olivier is well cast as an aging artist who shields himself from the world outside his estate in this fine screen adaptation of the John Fowles novel. This absorbing British TV drama is not rated, but it contains some partial nudity. 80m. **DIR:** Robert Knights. **CAST:** Laurence Olivier, Greta Scacchi. **1986**

ECHO OF THUNDER, THE ★★★★ Filmed in Australia, this moving *Hallmark Hall of Fame* reveals a "bare bones" family struggling against the elements of the outback as well as financial disaster. When her husband's oldest daughter comes to live with them, a woman must learn to accept her or destroy the whole family. Not rated; contains adult themes. 90m. **DIR:** Simon Wincer. **CAST:** Judy Davis, Jamey Sheridan, Lauren Hewett, Emily Jane Browning. **1998**

ECHO PARK ★★★ Tom Hulce, Susan Dey, and Michael Bowen star as three young show-biz hopefuls living in one of Los Angeles's seedier neighborhoods. Director Robert Dornhelm and screenwriter Michael Ventura have some interesting things to say about the quest for fame, and the stars provide some memorable moments. Rated R for nudity, profanity, and violence. 93m. **DIR:** Robert Dornhelm. **CAST:** Susan Dey, Tom Hulce, Michael Bowen, Christopher Walker, Shirley Jo Finney, John Paragon, Richard "Cheech" Marin, Cassandra Peterson. **1986 DVD**

ECHOES IN THE DARKNESS ★★★1/2 This Joseph Wambaugh crime-drama is based on the 1979 true-life murder of schoolteacher Susan Reinert (Stockard Channing). It's a toned-down TV movie devoid of most of the usual Wambaugh grit. At just under four hours, it takes quite a commitment for one night's viewing. Not rated. 234m. **DIR:** Glenn Jordan. **CAST:** Peter Coyote, Robert Loggia, Stockard Channing, Peter Boyle, Gary Cole, Treat Williams, Cindy Pickett. **1987**

ECLIPSE, THE ★★★1/2 A woman dissolves an affair with an older man, only to become involved with a self-centered young stockbroker in Rome's frenzied Borsa. Michelangelo Antonioni's meditation on doomed love has some good moments. Winner of the Grand Prize at Cannes. In Italian with English subtitles. B&W; 123m. **DIR:** Michelangelo Antonioni. **CAST:** Alain Delon, Monica Vitti, Francisco Rabal. **1962**

ECSTASY ★★1/2 Completely overshadowed since its release by the notoriety of Hedy Lamarr's nude scenes, this new packaging in video should shift the emphasis back to the film itself, which is basically a romance of illicit love. Filmed in pre-Hitler Czechoslovakia, this version is subtitled in English. B&W; 88m. **DIR:** Gustav Machaty. **CAST:** Hedy Lamarr, Aribert Mog. **1933**

ED ★★1/2 This disposable but entertaining comedy features a baseball-playing chimp. Ed is a smart-aleck primate who becomes the mascot for the demoralized minor league Santa Rosa Rockets. He not only wears the pants on the team (and uses toilets, too), but also snaps the losing streak—both on the field and off—of a demoralized fastball pitcher. The familiar ballpark story is written by David Mickey Evans (*The Sandlot*). Rated PG. 97m. **DIR:** Bill Couturie. **CAST:** Matt LeBlanc, Jayne Brook, Bill Cobbs, Jack Warden. **1996**

ED & HIS DEAD MOTHER ★★★1/2 Goofy fun finds mama's boy Steve Buscemi so desperate to get dear old Mom back that he pays shyster salesman John Glover to bring her back from the dead. Well, *Guess Who's Coming to Dinner*? One problem: Mom now eats bugs and has other undead habits as well. Traditional havoc ensues. Rated PG-13 for language, adult situations, and horror violence. 93m. **DIR:** Jonathan Wacks. **CAST:** Steve Buscemi, Ned Beatty, Miriam Margolyes, John Glover, Sam Jenkins. **1992**

•ED GEIN ★★★1/2 Steve Railsback stars as the tormented title character—a man still under the influence of his domineering mother long after her death. The unending voices in his head lead this mild-mannered man to murder, dismemberment, and worse. The true 1950s events that this movie was based on also inspired other films like *Psycho*, *Texas Chainsaw Massacre*, and *Silence of the Lambs*. Steve Railsback is fantastic as Ed Gein, adding an air of reality unseen in most horror films. Rated R for graphic violence and gore. 88m. **DIR:** Chuck Parello. **CAST:** Steve Railsback, Carrie Snodgress. **2000 DVD**

ED WOOD ★★★★1/2 Director Tim Burton's brilliant black-and-white study of "the worst filmmaker in Hollywood history" features unforgettable performances by Johnny Depp, in the title role, and Martin Landau, as Bela Lugosi. Although not for all tastes, this loving tribute to grade-Z movies and the campy pleasures they provide is a film buff's delight. Rated R for profanity, drug use, and men in women's clothing. B&W; 124m. **DIR:** Tim Burton. **CAST:** Johnny Depp, Martin Landau, Sarah Jessica Parker, Bill Murray, Patricia Arquette, Jeffrey Jones, G. D. Spradlin, Vincent D'Onofrio, Mike Starr. **1994**

EDDIE ★★1/2 Vocal female basketball fan Eddie Franklin enters a free-throw contest and winds up coaching a fictitious New York Knicks team. The Knicks are languishing at the hoop and turnstile, so it's up to Eddie to improve their court performance, smooth out their personal affairs, and stand up to the team's flamboyant billionaire owner. The film's fan-appreciation messages are a nice touch, but the real NBA—with its eccentric superstars and tabloid melodrama—is a much bigger scream. Rated PG-13 for language. 88m. **DIR:** Steve Rash. **CAST:** Whoopi Goldberg, Frank Langella, Dennis Farina, Lisa Ann Walter. **1996 DVD**

EDDIE AND THE CRUISERS ★★★1/2 Long after his death, rock 'n' roll singer Eddie Wilson's (Michael Paré) songs become popular all over again. This revives interest in a long-shelved concept album. The tape for it has been stolen, and it's up to Wilson's onetime collaborator (Tom Berenger) to find them. Only other people want the tapes, too, and they may be willing to kill to get them. The songs are great! Rated PG. 92m. **DIR:** Martin Davidson. **CAST:** Tom Berenger, Michael Paré, Ellen Barkin. **1983 DVD**

EDDIE AND THE CRUISERS II: EDDIE LIVES! ★★★ Solid sequel to *Eddie and the Cruisers* finds Eddie (Michael Paré) hiding out in Montreal while his songs enjoy new popularity. This prompts him to try music again and, of course, puts him on the inevitable road back to stardom. Thoughtful, well-intentioned film. Rated PG-13 for profanity and suggested sex. 100m. **DIR:** Jean-Claude Lord. **CAST:** Michael Paré, Marini Orsini, Bernie Coulson. **1989**

EDDIE MACON'S RUN ★★1/2 John Schneider is a prison escapee who manages to stay one step ahead of the law. Kirk Douglas costars as the hard-nosed policeman on his trail. It's a predictable, lightweight movie. Rated PG for vulgar language and violence. 95m. **DIR:** Jeff Kanew. **CAST:** John Schneider, Kirk Douglas, Lee Purcell, Leah Ayres. **1983**

EDDY DUCHIN STORY, THE ★★1/2 Overly sentimental telling of the troubled professional and family life of pianist-bandleader Eddy Duchin. Many fine piano renditions of the standards of the era ("Body and Soul," "Sweet Sue"), and Duchin's theme song, "Chopin Nocturne in E Flat," all dubbed by Carmen Cavallaro. 123m. **DIR:** George Sidney. **CAST:** Tyrone Power, Kim Novak, Victoria Shaw, James Whitmore, Rex Thompson. **1956**

EDEN ★★★★ Joanna Going is exceptional in writer-director Howard Goldberg's touching tale of a 1960s housewife named Helen, who is quickly tiring of the constraints placed on her by a domineering husband and a degenerating illness. When the couple takes in a student, Helen finds a soul mate who understands her desire to be free. With the student's encouragement, Helen begins to have out-of-body experiences that leave her physically weak but provide the freedom she seeks. Both heartfelt and haunting, *Eden* is a film of hope and desire. Rated R for language and adult situations. 106m. **DIR:** Howard Goldberg. **CAST:** Joanna Going, Dylan Walsh, Sean Patrick Flanery. **1996 DVD**

EDEN (TV SERIES) ★★ This erotic soap opera is brought to you by the folks at *Playboy* and features one of the best-looking casts on the small screen. The story (such as it is) centers on Eden, a beach resort where guests, staff, and hormones run wild. Not rated, contains nudity and sexual situations. 98m. **DIR:** Victor Lobl. **CAST:** Barbara Alyn Woods, Steve Chase, Darcy DeMoss. **1993**

EDGAR ALLAN POE'S MADHOUSE 🦃 The film has nothing to do with Poe and only manages to degrade his name. Not rated; contains violence, profanity, and nudity. 75m. **DIR:** Todd Sheets. **CAST:** Tonia Monahan, Jenny Admire, Kim Adler, Matt Lewis, Mike Hellman. **1992**

EDGE, THE ★★★1/2 Writer David Mamet and director Lee Tamahori have combined forces to produce a genuinely muscular thriller and contest of wills between a reclusive billionaire and the hotshot fashion photographer who may have designs on the other man's wife. Both become stranded in the Alaskan wilderness and subsequently are forced to cooperate in order to survive. Rated R for profanity, violence, and gore. 121m.

DIR: Lee Tamahori. **CAST:** Anthony Hopkins, Alec Baldwin, Elle Macpherson, Harold Perrineau Jr., L. Q. Jones. **1997 DVD**

EDGE OF DARKNESS ★★★★1/2 A complex mystery produced as a miniseries for British television. The story revolves around a nuclear processing plant and its covert government relations. Bob Peck offers an intense portrayal of a British police detective who, step-by-step, uncovers the truth as he investigates the murder of his daughter. 307m. **DIR:** Martin Campbell. **CAST:** Bob Peck, Joe Don Baker, Jack Woodson, John Woodvine, Joanne Whalley. **1986**

EDGE OF DARKNESS ★★★★1/2 Powerful acting by a stage-trained cast make this a better-than-average war picture. The plot focuses on efforts of the Norwegian underground to run off the Nazis during World War II. B&W; 120m. **DIR:** Lewis Milestone. **CAST:** Errol Flynn, Ann Sheridan, Walter Huston, Judith Anderson, Helmut Dantine, Nancy Coleman, Morris Carnovsky, John Beal. **1943**

EDGE OF HONOR ★★★ Group of Explorer Scouts on an expedition come across a cache of high-tech weapons belonging to a group of smugglers. This one gets a merit badge for exciting action and ingenuity. Rated R for language and violence. 92m. **DIR:** Michael Spence. **CAST:** Corey Feldman, Meredith Salenger, Scott Reeves, Ken Jenkins, Don Swayze, Christopher Neame. **1991**

EDGE OF SANITY ★★ Anthony Perkins is retooling his psychopathic screen persona again in this handsome-looking but mediocre British production of *Dr. Jekyll and Mr. Hyde.* No new twists on this old theme, but plenty of sexy girls and sordid violence. Rather forgettable. Not rated, this uncensored version is recommended for adults only. 86m. **DIR:** Gerard Kikoine. **CAST:** Anthony Perkins, Glynis Barber, David Lodge. **1989**

EDGE OF SEVENTEEN ★★ This candid coming-out story of a gay teen in 1984 Sandusky, Ohio, is an uneven mix of poignant drama, heartbreaks, comic pop-culture nostalgia, soap-opera schlock, and unsavory sex. Gangly, dewy-eyed Eric is attracted to a fellow amusement-park buffet server. He wrestles with self-identity, enters a predatory gay bar scene, and is befriended by a lesbian nightclub manager. Not rated; contains simulated sex, profanity, and violence. 100m. **DIR:** David Moreton. **CAST:** Chris Stafford, Gabrych Anderson, Tina Holmes, Stephanie McVay, Lea DeLaria. **1999 DVD**

EDIE & PEN ★★★1/2 Victoria Tennant's engaging script explores the relationship between two dissimilar women who meet in Reno while getting quickie divorces, then become fast friends. Conservative Stockard Channing has been humiliated by a cheating husband who dumped her, while party-hardy Jennifer Tilly is all set to become a bride again . . . the very next day! Skirt-chasing Scott Glenn saves the film from non-stop girl talk. Rated PG-13 for profanity and simulated sex. 98m. **DIR:** Matthew Irmas. **CAST:** Stockard Channing, Jennifer Tilly, Scott Glenn, Stuart Wilson, Michael McKean, Martin Mull, Michael O'Keefe, Joanna Gleason. **1996**

EDISON, THE MAN ★★★1/2 The second half of MGM's planned two-part tribute to Thomas Alva Edison (following by months the release of *Young Tom Edison*). Spencer Tracy is perfect as the great inventor from young manhood through age 82. Great family viewing. B&W; 107m. **DIR:** Clarence Brown. **CAST:** Spencer Tracy, Rita Johnson, Lynne Overman, Charles Coburn, Gene Lockhart, Henry Travers. **1940**

EDITH AND MARCEL ★★★★ Based on the real life of famous torch singer Edith Piaf (Evelyn Bouix), this powerful musical-drama follows the passionate affair she had with champion boxer Marcel Cerdan (Marcel Cerdan Jr.). Director Claude Lelouch brings to life the stormy romance that captured the attention of the world. In French with English subtitles. 170m. **DIR:** Claude Lelouch. **CAST:** Evelyne Bouix, Marcel Cerdan Jr., Jacques Villeret, Francis Huster. **1983**

ED'S NEXT MOVE ★★★ A naïve young geneticist moves from the Midwest to Manhattan and strikes up a tentative courtship with a struggling musician. Writer-director John Walsh crams in every idea he can think of for his first film, and not all of them work. Still, the performances are likable and the film is briskly paced. Rated R for profanity. 88m. **DIR:** John Walsh. **CAST:** Matt Ross, Callie Thorne, Kevin Carroll. **1996**

EDTV ★★★1/2 Perhaps the spookiest thing about this film is that it *doesn't* seem all that far-fetched. The notion of turning one ordinary fellow's life into an ongoing TV show makes this film more prophet than parody. And no, scripters Lowell Ganz and Babaloo Mandel aren't guilty of blatant theft; where Andrew Niccol's *The Truman Show* was elegant and ferociously clever, this effort is down 'n' dirty, like the macabre spontaneity of homegrown local-access cable programming. The programmer of a struggling cable channel, who at first is pleased by the success of her idea, realizes that she has contributed to the destruction of a really nice guy: a goofy San Francisco video-store clerk with no immediate concept of his pending loss of dignity. It all works because the unwitting celebrity is understated, deceptively unaffected, and wholly endearing. Rated PG-13 for profanity and sexual candor. 122m. **DIR:** Ron Howard. **CAST:** Matthew McConaughey, Jenna Elfman, Woody Harrelson, Sally Kirkland, Martin Landau, Ellen DeGeneres, Rob Reiner, Dennis Hopper, Elizabeth Hurley. **1999**

EDUCATING RITA ★★★★1/2 A boozing, depressed English professor (Michael Caine) takes on a sharp-witted, eager-to-learn hairdresser (Julie Walters) for Open University tutorials and each educates the other, in this delightful romantic comedy based on a London hit play. Rated PG for profanity. 110m. **DIR:** Lewis Gilbert. **CAST:** Michael Caine, Julie Walters, Michael Williams. **1983**

EDUCATION OF LITTLE TREE, THE ★★★★ Orphaned 8-year-old boy is nurtured by his grandparents in backwoods East Tennessee. His white grandfather and Cherokee grandmother teach him what they call the "Indian way" of relating to nature, moonshining, church, neighbors, and the encroachment of a hypocritical civilization. This adaptation of Forrest Carter's 1986 novel has a cleansing sense of decency and dignity. Rated PG. 117m. **DIR:** Richard Friedenberg. **CAST:** Joseph Ashton, James Cromwell, Tantoo Cardinal, Graham Greene, Mika Boorem. **1998 DVD**

EDUCATION OF SONNY CARSON, THE ★★★ This grim but realistic movie is based on the autobiography of Sonny Carson, a ghetto-raised black youth whose life was bounded by gangs, drugs, and crime. There's no upbeat happy ending and no attempt to preach, either; the film simply shows ghetto life for the frightening hell it is. Rated R. 104m. **DIR:** Michael Campus. **CAST:** Rony Clanton, Don Gordon, Joyce Walker, Paul Benjamin. **1974**

EDWARD AND MRS. SIMPSON ★★★ This miniseries does a commendable, if overlong, job of capturing the romance between a manipulative American divorcée and a rather simpleminded king. Talky in that inimitable *Masterpiece Theatre* style, but by the end we are quite convinced Mrs. Simpson saved the future of the English monarchy by keeping Edward VIII off the throne. Originally aired as seven episodes on PBS, it has been released in a truncated version on video. Not rated. 270m. **DIR:** Waris Hussein. **CAST:** Edward Fox, Cynthia Harris. **1980**

EDWARD SCISSORHANDS ★★★ A mean-spirited, violent ending irrevocably mars what might have been a charming fantasy. Through the character of Edward Scissorhands (Johnny Depp), a sweet-natured android whose exposure to civilization is anything but pleasant, cowriter-director Tim Burton seems to be exorcising the pain of his own adolescence. Rated PG-13 for violence and profanity. 89m. **DIR:** Tim Burton. **CAST:** Johnny Depp, Winona Ryder, Dianne Wiest, Anthony Michael Hall, Alan Arkin, Vincent Price, Kathy Baker, Conchata Ferrell. **1990 DVD**

EDWARD II ★★★ This bizarre, medieval costume drama—the characters speak in rich Elizabethan prose while wearing mostly modern attire—grabs Christopher Marlowe's sixteenth-century play *(The Troublesome Reign of Edward II)* by the throat and heaves it into the 1990s. The story about the downfall of England's openly gay king skewers sexual obsessions, repression, and politics with an intriguing sense of timelessness and moral decay. Rated R for profanity, nudity, and violence. 90m. **DIR:** Derek Jarman. **CAST:** Steven Waddington, Andrew Tiernan, Tilda Swinton, Nigel Terry. **1992**

EEGAH! 🦃 Teenage caveman gets the hots for brain-dead babe. 90m. **DIR:** Nicholas Merriwether (Arch Hall Sr.). **CAST:** Arch Hall Jr., Richard Kiel, Marilyn Manning, William Watters. **1962**

EEL, THE ★★★1/2 An office worker spends eight years in prison for killing his wife and her lover. After he is released, he tries to begin life anew as a barber in a small fishing village. Winner of the grand prize at the Cannes Film Festival, this meandering character study may try the patience of viewers unaccustomed to Japanese films. In Japanese with English subtitles. Not rated; contains strong violence, nudity, and sexual situations. 117m. **DIR:** Shohei Imamura. **CAST:** Koji Yakusho, Misa Shimizu, Fujio Tsuneta. **1997 DVD**

EFFECT OF GAMMA RAYS ON MAN-IN-THE-MOON MARIGOLDS, THE ★★★ Toxic drama based on Paul Zindel's Pulitzer Prize–winning play about an eccentric, widowed mother and her two daughters. Joanne Woodward is excellent as Beatrice, whose dreams of a better life have taken a toll on her reality. Her youngest daughter, Matilda, escapes her dreary existence through her animals and school, where her science project (the title of the film) serves as a metaphor for her mother's relationship with her and her sister. Rated PG. 100m. **DIR:** Paul Newman. **CAST:** Joanne Woodward, Nell Potts, Roberta Wallach, Judith Lowry, David Spielberg. **1972**

EFFI BRIEST ★★★ In the late 1800s, a young girl seeks to escape her stifling marriage to a much older man by having an affair with a soldier. Rainer Werner Fassbinder faithfully adapted this film from a novel that is Germany's equivalent of *Madame Bovary* or *Anna Karenina*. His intention is to evoke the stifling domesticity of German society of the time, a goal that may not entertain all viewers. In German with English subtitles. B&W; 140m. **DIR:** Rainer Werner Fassbinder. **CAST:** Hanna Schygulla, Wolfgang Schenck, Ulli Lommel. **1974**

EFFICIENCY EXPERT, THE (SPOTSWOOD) ★★★ Echoes of *Local Hero* are present in this offbeat film about British efficiency expert Anthony Hopkins plying his trade in 1960s Australia and beginning to question his own efficacy. While this film doesn't have the charm and truly off-the-wall humor of director Bill Forsyth's cult comedy, it is generally enjoyable. Rated PG for violence. 96m. **DIR:** Mark Joffe. **CAST:** Anthony Hopkins, Ben Mendelsohn, Toni Collette, Bruno Lawrence, Rebecca Rigg. **1992**

EGG ★★★ Delightful, bittersweet comedy from Holland about a quiet, illiterate baker who romances an awkward and lonely schoolteacher. In Dutch with English subtitles. 58m. **DIR:** Danniel Danniel. **CAST:** Johan Leysen, Marijke Veugelers. **1988**

EGG AND I, THE ★★★ Hayseed Fred MacMurray spirits his finishing-school bride Claudette Colbert away from Boston to cope with chicken farming in the rural Pacific Northwest. Everything goes wrong. Marjorie Main and Percy Kilbride as Ma and Pa Kettle made comic marks bright enough to earn them their own film series. Not a laugh riot, but above-average funny. B&W; 108m. **DIR:** Chester Erskine. **CAST:** Claudette Colbert, Fred MacMurray, Louise Allbritton, Marjorie Main, Percy Kilbride, Donald MacBride, Samuel S. Hinds, Fuzzy Knight. **1947**

EGYPTIAN, THE ★★1/2 With the exception of Edmund Purdom, most of the cast is ill-used in this highly atmospheric, bumpy biblical spectacle centering on a physician. 140m. **DIR:** Michael Curtiz. **CAST:** Jean Simmons, Edmund Purdom, Victor Mature, Gene Tierney, Peter Ustinov, Michael Wilding. **1954**

EIGER SANCTION, THE ★★1/2 Laughable but entertaining adaptation of Trevanian's equally laughable but entertaining novel. Clint Eastwood is a college professor by day and supersecret agent by night. Outrageously overblown characters and plenty of opportunities for Eastwood to strut his macho stuff. Rated R for violence and sex. 128m. **DIR:** Clint Eastwood. **CAST:** Clint Eastwood, George Kennedy, Jack Cassidy, Thayer David, Vonetta McGee. **1975 DVD**

EIGHT DAYS A WEEK ★★1/2 Likable but not very significant romantic comedy about a young man so in love with his next-door neighbor that he camps out under her balcony until she becomes his. Writer-director Michael Davis's attempt at a lighthearted *Romeo and Juliet* has some funny, almost human moments dealing with teenage dating, but ultimately slips into situation comedy territory. Rated R for language. 92m. **DIR:**

Michael Davis. **CAST:** Joshua Schaffer, Keri Russell, R. D. Robb, Mark L. Taylor, Catharine Hicks. **1999**

8MAN 🦃 After a Tokyo detective is murdered, his body is turned into a cyborg cop in this extremely slow, boring film. Not rated; contains violence. 91m. **DIR:** Yasuhiro Horiuchi. **CAST:** Kai Shishido, Etsushi Takahashi, Sachiko Ayashi, Osamu Ohtomo, Joe Shishido. **1992**

EIGHT MEN OUT ★★★★1/2 Writer-director John Sayles scores a home run with this baseball drama about the 1919 Black Sox scandal—when members of the Chicago White Sox conspired to throw the World Series. A superb ensemble cast, which includes Sayles as Ring Lardner, shines in this true-life shocker, with David Strathairn and John Cusack giving standout performances. Rated PG for profanity. 120m. **DIR:** John Sayles. **CAST:** Charlie Sheen, John Cusack, Christopher Lloyd, D. B. Sweeney, David Strathairn, Michael Lerner, Clifton James, John Sayles, Studs Terkel. **1988 DVD**

8MM ★★1/2 Ostensibly a murder mystery but actually a deliberate attempt to test the tolerance of mainstream viewers who hope they don't know anyone this depraved. The desultory pacing fails to involve us in the mystery that sends surveillance expert Nicolas Cage in search of a missing young woman who may have participated (as victim) in an authentic snuff film. Our hero's subsequent descent into human slime, however, remains as detached as Cage's often somnambulant performance. Rated R for violence, profanity, nudity, and sexual deviancy. 123m. **DIR:** Joel Schumacher. **CAST:** Nicolas Cage, Joaquin Phoenix, James Gandolfini, Peter Stormare, Anthony Heald, Chris Bauer, Catherine Keener. **1999 DVD**

8 SECONDS ★★1/2 This sanitized story of real-life bull rider Lane Frost—the youngest cowboy ever inducted into the Rodeo Hall of Fame—needs more grit. Lane's meteoric rise to superstardom, his showdown with the notorious bull, Red Rock, and the toll of the circuit on his marriage to a championship barrel racer is promising material, but the story—in rodeo lingo—doesn't quite cowboy up. Rated PG-13 for language. 97m. **DIR:** John G. Avildsen. **CAST:** Luke Perry, Cynthia Geary, Stephen Baldwin, Red Mitchell, Carrie Snodgress. **1994 DVD**

8 1/2 ★★★★★ Perhaps one of Federico Fellini's strongest cinematic achievements. *8 1/2* is the loose portrayal of a film director making a personal movie and finding himself trapped in his fears, dreams, and irresolutions. This brilliant exercise features outstanding performances, especially by Marcello Mastroianni. Dubbed into English. Not rated. B&W; 135m. **DIR:** Federico Fellini. **CAST:** Marcello Mastroianni, Anouk Aimée, Claudia Cardinale, Barbara Steele, Sandra Milo. **1963 DVD**

8 1/2 WOMEN ★★ A financier and his son console themselves over the death of their wife/mother by establishing a private harem and stocking it with sexual slaves. Beautifully photographed and self-consciously "shocking," the film is utterly removed from anything resembling real life. Rated R for mature themes, profanity, nudity, and sexual scenes. 121m. **DIR:** Peter Greenaway. **CAST:** John Standing, Matthew Delamere, Vivian Wu, Shizuka Inoh, Toni Collette. **1999 DVD**

8 HEADS IN A DUFFEL BAG ★★ Mafia courier Joe Pesci is transporting the title package (proof that the victims of a mob hit are dead) when an airport switcheroo sends the grisly stash on a Mexican vacation with a college student. The premise is ghoulish but not very original, and the frantic, hammy performances elicit only a few scattered laughs. Rated R for profanity and grisly humor. 93m. **DIR:** Tom Schulman. **CAST:** Joe Pesci, Andy Comeau, Kristy Swanson, George Hamilton, Dyan Cannon, David Spade, Todd Louiso. **1997**

800 LEAGUES DOWN THE AMAZON ★★ Exotic locations and capable stars can't save this Jules Verne story from sinking twenty thousand leagues under the sea. Barry Bostwick floats through this tiresome yawner about a falsely accused man who risks capture and execution when he attempts to return home for his daughter's wedding. Adventuresome trip down the Amazon is the only high point. Rated PG-13 for violence. 85m. **DIR:** Luis Llosa. **CAST:** Barry Bostwick, Adam Baldwin, Daphne Zuniga, Tom Verica, E. E. Bell. **1993 DVD**

18 AGAIN 🦃 Yet another unsuccessful attempt to portray the older man magically switching into a young man's body. Rated PG for language and sexual suggestion. 100m. **DIR:** Paul Flaherty. **CAST:** George Burns, Charlie Schlatter, Tony Roberts, Anita Morris, Miriam Flynn, Jennifer Runyon, Red Buttons. **1988 DVD**

EIGHTEENTH ANGEL, THE ★★★ In this chiller from the writer of *The Omen*, a teacher and his daughter move to Rome where they become mixed up with the Etruscan order, a monastery that believes Satan will return to Earth in the form of an innocent child. Cloning, Satanism, and the death of a child are all thrown into the mix and the film moves along with a momentum all its own. Similarities to the older film, however, are undeniable. Rated R for gore, profanity, and violence. 90m. **DIR:** William Bindley. **CAST:** Christopher McDonald, Rachael Leigh Cook, Maximilian Schell. **1997**

8 MILLION WAYS TO DIE ★★ An alcoholic ex-cop, Jeff Bridges, attempts to help a high-priced L.A. prostitute get away from her crazed Colombian coke-dealer boyfriend, Andy Garcia. Considering the talent involved, this one should have been a real killer, but there are holes in the script and dead spots throughout. Rated R for violence, nudity, and language. 115m. **DIR:** Hal Ashby. **CAST:** Jeff Bridges, Rosanna Arquette, Alexandra Paul, Andy Garcia. **1986**

EIGHTH DAY, THE ★★★1/2 A corporate workaholic is taught to enjoy life by a man with Down's syndrome (Pascal Duquenne). When writer-director Jaco Van Dormael borrows shamelessly from *Rain Man, Forrest Gump, King of Hearts*, and *One Flew over the Cuckoo's Nest*, his film is trite and superficial. When he uses his own imagination, though, the film soars. Duquenne, who has Down's syndrome in real life, gives a performance of amazing range and variety. In French with English subtitles. Not rated; contains mature themes and mild profanity. 114m. **DIR:** Jaco Van Dormael. **CAST:** Daniel Auteuil, Pascal Duquenne, Miou-Miou, Isabelle Sadoyan, Henri Garcin, Michele Maes. **1996**

84 CHARING CROSS ROAD ★★1/2 Anne Bancroft manages to act manic even while reading books in this true story based on the life of Helene Hanff, a writer and reader who begins a twenty-year correspondence with a London bookseller (Anthony Hopkins). Along with her orders for first editions, Hanff sends witty letters and care packages to the employees during the hard postwar times. Hanff and the bookseller begin to rely on the correspondence, yet never get to meet. Rated PG for language. 99m. **DIR:** David Jones. **CAST:** Anne Bancroft, Anthony Hopkins, Judi Dench, Maurice Denham. **1986**

84 CHARLIE MOPIC ★★★1/2 Powerfully realistic tour of Vietnam, circa 1969. A reconnaissance patrol sets out "in country" with an army motion picture (MOPIC) cameraman recording everything he can. What begins as a routine mission soon turns into a nightmare of terror and survival. A compelling and engrossing experience. Rated R for violence and profanity. 95m. **DIR:** Patrick Duncan. **CAST:** Richard Brooks, Christopher Borgard. **1989**

EIJANAIKA (WHY NOT?) ★★★★ Set in the 1860s when Japan opened up to world trade after a military dictatorship, in power more than 700 years, was toppled, putting the emperor back in power and causing a rebellion by his subjects. Fascinating. In Japanese with English subtitles. Not rated, the film has nudity, profanity, and violence. 151m. **DIR:** Shohei Imamura. **CAST:** Shigeru Izumiya, Kaori Momoi, Ken Ogata, Mitsuko Baisho. **1981**

EL (THIS STRANGE PASSION) ★★★★ Surreal portrait of a wealthy and devout middle-aged man, who is driven to madness by his pathological jealousy and obsession with religious ritual. Director Luis Buñuel has created an ironic dramatization of the destructive effect obsession can have on marriage and sexuality. In Spanish with English subtitles. B&W; 82m. **DIR:** Luis Buñuel. **CAST:** Arturo De Cordova. **1952**

EL AMOR BRUJO ★★ This occasionally brilliant big-screen production of Manuel de Falla's ballet will appeal primarily to flamenco fans. The cast is excellent but overall the movie fails to fascinate. In Spanish with English subtitles. Rated PG for brief, stylized violence and references to sex in lyrics. 100m. **DIR:** Carlos Saura. **CAST:** Antonio Gades, Cristina Hoyos, Laura Del Sol. **1986**

EL BRUTO (THE BRUTE) ★★★1/2 Exceptional surreal drama from Luis Buñuel about a tough slaughterhouse laborer who is exploited by a tyrannical landowner. Some strange melodramatic twists laced with moments of irony make this Mexican film one of Buñuel's stronger efforts. Spanish dialogue with English subtitles. Not rated. B&W; 83m. **DIR:** Luis Buñuel. **CAST:** Pedro Armendariz, Katy Jurado, Andres Soler. **1952**

EL CID ★★★ Some of the best battle action scenes ever filmed are included in this 1961 spectacle about the medieval Spanish hero El Cid. Unfortunately, on smaller home screens much of the splendor will be lost. You will be left with the wooden Charlton Heston and the beautiful Sophia Loren in a love story that was underdeveloped due to the movie's emphasis on spectacle. 184m. **DIR:** Anthony Mann. **CAST:** Charlton Heston, Sophia Loren, Raf Vallone, Hurd Hatfield. **1961**

EL CONDOR ★★ A disappointing Western, this features cardboard performances by Jim Brown and Lee Van Cleef as two adventurers determined to take a fortress of gold called El Condor. Not rated, but equivalent to an R for nudity and violence. 102m. **DIR:** John Guillermin. **CAST:** Jim Brown, Lee Van Cleef, Patrick O'Neal. **1970**

EL DIABLO ★★★1/2 When one of his students is kidnapped by outlaws, schoolteacher Anthony Edwards joins forces with gunfighter Lou Gossett to bring her back. This cable-produced Western adds offbeat plot twists and oddball bits of comedy to the shoot-'em-up formula. It's entertaining, if not particularly believable. 115m. **DIR:** Peter Markle. **CAST:** Anthony Edwards, Louis Gossett Jr., John Glover, M. C. Gainey, Sarah Trigger, Robert Beltran, Joe Pantoliano. **1990 DVD**

EL DORADO ★★★★1/2 Few stars could match John Wayne's ability to dominate a scene—and one of those few, Robert Mitchum, costars in this tale of a land war between Edward Asner and R. G. Armstrong. Mitchum plays the drunk, and Wayne is the gunfighter with whom he forms an uneasy alliance. It's an upscale B Western with some of the best scenes ever in a cowboy movie. 126m. **DIR:** Howard Hawks. **CAST:** John Wayne, Robert Mitchum, James Caan, Arthur Hunnicutt, Edward Asner, Michele Carey, Christopher George, Charlene Holt, Jim Davis, Paul Fix, R. G. Armstrong, Johnny Crawford. **1967 DVD**

EL MARIACHI ★★★ This contemporary shoot-'em-up semi-spoofs spaghetti Westerns and Mexican action flicks. It's a visually choppy, grungy gem—shot on a fourteen-day, $7,000 schedule and cleaned up somewhat by Columbia Pictures before release—about a wandering Mexican musician who is pursued by thugs when he's mistaken for a rival hit man. In Spanish with English subtitles. Rated R for violence. 80m. **DIR:** Robert Rodriguez. **CAST:** Carlos Gallardo, Consuelo Gomez, Jaime de Hoyos, Peter Marquardt, Reinol Martinez. **1993 DVD**

EL NORTE ★★★★★ A rewarding story about two Guatemalans, a young brother and sister, whose American dream takes them on a long trek to El Norte—the United States. This American-made movie is funny, frightening, poignant, and sobering—a movie that stays with you. In Spanish with subtitles. Rated R for profanity and violence. 139m. **DIR:** Gregory Nava. **CAST:** Zaide Silvia Gutierrez, David Villalpando. **1983**

EL PASO KID ★★★ Ex-outlaw Sunset Carson becomes a lawman through a series of coincidences, eventually redeeming himself for his past. B&W; 54m. **DIR:** Thomas Carr. **CAST:** Sunset Carson, Hank Patterson. **1946**

EL PROFESSOR HIPPIE ★★1/2 Veteran comedian Luis Sandrini plays a college professor who, because of his freethinking attitudes and concerns for moral questions over matters of business, has more in common with his students than his colleagues. This gentle comedy is a real audience pleaser. In Spanish. 91m. **DIR:** Fernando Ayala. **CAST:** Luis Sandrini. **1969**

EL SUPER ★★★★ A funny and touching view of Cuban exiles living in a basement apartment during a cold winter in New York City. Raymundo Hidalgo-Gato turns in a strong performance as the superintendent who dreams of his homeland while struggling with the conditions of his new culture. In Spanish with English subtitles. Not rated. 80m. **DIR:** Leon Ichaso. **CAST:** Raymundo Hidalgo-Gato, Elizabeth Peña. **1979**

ELEANOR: FIRST LADY OF THE WORLD ★★★ Jean Stapleton's Eleanor Roosevelt will either charm you or grate on your nerves in this made-for-TV movie. But either way, you'll be inspired by the story of Mrs. Roosevelt's determination. 102m. **DIR:** John Erman. **CAST:** Jean Stapleton, E. G. Marshall, Coral Browne, Joyce Van Patten. **1982**

ELEANOR ROOSEVELT STORY, THE ★★★★ Hillary Rodham Clinton provides a special introduction to the video of this film that won the Oscar for best documentary. Using newsreel footage and photographs, it focuses on the years following the death of Eleanor's husband, Franklin, as she overcame personal tragedy to devote her life to public service. An inspirational film. Narrated by Achibald MacLeish. B&W; 90m. **DIR:** Richard Kaplan. **1965**

ELECTION ★★★★1/2 Tracy (Reese Witherspoon) is guaranteed to win the school election for class president until her teacher, Mr. McAllister (Matthew Broderick), finds her some worthy opposition. Little does he know how badly Tracy wants to win, and the high school soon turns into a war zone with Mr. McAllister getting himself in deeper than he ever expected. The excellent cast, witty script, and insightful direction make this dark comedy an absolute delight. Rated R for language, light violence, and adult situations. 103m. **DIR:** Alexander Payne. **CAST:** Matthew Broderick, Reese Witherspoon, Chris Klein. **1999 DVD**

ELECTRA GLIDE IN BLUE ★★★★ Robert Blake plays an Arizona cop with aspirations of being a detective. This extremely violent melodrama features good performances by the entire cast with several twists and turns to keep the viewer guessing. Rated R. 106m. **DIR:** James William Guercio. **CAST:** Robert Blake, Billy Green Bush, Mitchell Ryan, Elisha Cook Jr., Jeannine Riley, Royal Dano. **1973**

ELECTRIC DREAMS ★★★ An ingenious blending of the motion picture with the rock music video, this release deals with the complications that arise when an absent-minded architect, Miles (Lenny Von Dohlen), buys his first home computer. It isn't long before the computer (the voice is Bud Cort, of *Harold and Maude* fame) begins to develop a rather feisty personality. Rated PG for profanity. 96m. **DIR:** Steve Barron. **CAST:** Lenny von Dohlen, Virginia Madsen, Bud Cort (voice). **1984**

ELECTRIC HORSEMAN, THE ★★★ Directed by Sydney Pollack, this film brought the third teaming of Jane Fonda and Robert Redford on the screen. The result is a winsome piece of light entertainment. Redford plays Sonny Steele, a former rodeo star who has become the unhappy spokesman for Ranch Breakfast, a brand of cereal. He's always in trouble and in danger of blowing the job—until he decides to rebel. Rated PG. 120m. **DIR:** Sydney Pollack. **CAST:** Robert Redford, Jane Fonda, Valerie Perrine, Willie Nelson, John Saxon, Nicolas Coster, Wilford Brimley. **1979 DVD**

ELEGANT CRIMINAL, THE ★★★★ Handsomely produced true story of a nineteenth-century intellectual who rebelled against his loveless upbringing by embarking on a life of crime, one designed to lead to his execution. In the title role, Daniel Auteuil is both charming and brutal, seductive and cold. Not rated, the film has violence and sexual situations. In French with English subtitles. 120m. **DIR:** Francis Girod. **CAST:** Daniel Auteuil, Jean Poiret, Marie-Armelle Deguy. **1990**

ELEKTRA ★★★ This *Live from the Met* production is the Greek legend of Elektra and her obsession with revenge. Overly dramatic performances and operatic theatrics. Only opera buffs and Birgit Nilsson fans need to view this one. In German with English subtitles. 112m. **DIR:** Brian Large. **CAST:** Birgit Nilsson. **1980**

ELEMENT OF CRIME, THE ★★★ Uneven attempt at *film noir*, about an ex-cop who returns to a postnuclear Europe to uncover the mystery of a serial killer who preys on young girls. Brilliant camera work shot entirely in sepia tone is not enough to sustain interest. Not rated; contains nudity and violence. 105m. **DIR:** Lars von Trier. **CAST:** Michael Elphick, Esmond Knight. **1988 DVD**

ELEMENTARY SCHOOL, THE ★★★★ In post-WWII Prague, a pair of mischievous schoolboys are fascinated by their new schoolteacher, a former soldier who brings military discipline to his new job. This Oscar-nominated film from the director of *Kolya* is a comical but knowing portrait of small-town life that is in a class with the work of such Czech masters as Jiri Menzel and Milos Forman. In Czech with English subtitles. Not rated; contains sexual situations. 100m. **DIR:** Jan Sverák. **CAST:** Vaclav Jakoubek, Jan Triska, Zdenek Sverak, Radoslav Budac. **1990**

ELENA AND HER MEN ★★★ One of Jean Renoir's personal favorites, this musical fantasy is about the power of love, and the evil of dictators. Ingrid Bergman is supported by a fine cast in this enjoyable comedy-drama. Originally released in America as *Paris Does Strange Things*. In French with English subtitles. 98m. **DIR:** Jean Renoir. **CAST:** Ingrid Bergman, Jean Marais, Mel Ferrer, Juliette Greco. **1956**

ELENI ★★★ Interesting film adaptation of Nicholas Gage's factual book *Eleni*. In 1948, during the civil war in Greece, a small mountain village is terrorized by a group of Communist guerrillas. Eleni Gatzoyiannis (Kate Nelligan) defies the Communists and their attempts to abduct her children and is subsequently tortured and executed in cold blood. Eleni's son Nicholas Gage (John Malkovich) returns to Greece after many years as a reporter for the *New York Times*, devoting his life there to unmasking her killers. Rated PG for language and violence. 116m. **DIR:** Peter Yates. **CAST:** Kate Nelligan, John Malkovich, Linda Hunt. **1985**

ELEPHANT BOY ★★★ Sabu made his film debut and became a star in this drama about a boy who claims to know where elephants go to die. Robert Flaherty's codirection gives the film a travelogue quality, but it interests and delights just the same. B&W; 80m. **DIR:** Robert Flaherty, Zoltán Korda. **CAST:** Sabu, W. E. Holloway, Walter Hudd, Bruce Gordon. **1937**

ELEPHANT MAN, THE ★★★★ Unlike the David Lynch film, this is a straight adaptation (made for television) of the Broadway play about the hideously deformed Victorian John Merrick. Philip Anglim plays Merrick without makeup, using only pantomime to suggest his appearance, and his performance is tremendously moving. 112m. **DIR:** Jack Hofsiss. **CAST:** Philip Anglim, Kevin Conway, Penny Fuller. **1982**

ELEPHANT MAN, THE ★★★★ Though it has its flaws, this film is a fascinating and heartbreaking study of the life of John Merrick, a hopelessly deformed but kind and intelligent man who struggles for dignity. John Hurt is magnificent in the title role. Rated PG. B&W; 125m. **DIR:** David Lynch. **CAST:** Anthony Hopkins, John Hurt, Anne Bancroft, Wendy Hiller, Freddie Jones. **1980**

ELEPHANT WALK ★★ Elizabeth Taylor plays the bride of a Ceylon tea planter (Peter Finch) bewildered by her new home and carrying on with the hired hand (Dana Andrews). Dull, unconvincing drama; the climactic elephant stampede is too little, too late. 103m. **DIR:** William Dieterle. **CAST:** Elizabeth Taylor, Peter Finch, Dana Andrews, Abraham Sofaer. **1954**

ELEVATOR TO THE GALLOWS ★★★★ Marvelously twisted tale of murder and deceit features Jeanne Moreau as a wealthy woman plotting to have her husband killed by her lover. Her lover's getaway car is stolen by two teenagers who fit murder into their joyride, leaving the lover to take the rap. Jazz score by Miles Davis is perfect backdrop to nonstop decadence. (Also known as *Frantic*.) Not rated, in French with English subtitles. B&W; 87m. **DIR:** Louis Malle. **CAST:** Jeanne Moreau, Maurice Ronet, Georges Poujouly. **1957**

11 HARROWHOUSE ★★1/2 Confused heist caper vacillates wildly between straight drama and dark comedy. Diamond salesman Charles Grodin is talked into stealing valuable gems. Too farfetched to be taken seriously. An excellent cast goes to waste. Rated PG—mild sexual overtones. 95m. **DIR:** Aram Avakian. **CAST:** Charles Grodin, Candice Bergen, James Mason, John Gielgud. **1974**

ELFEGO BACA: SIX GUN LAW ★★1/2 Two-fisted lawyer Elfego Baca is charismatically portrayed by top actor Robert Loggia in this compilation of episodes from *Walt Disney Presents* originally aired from 1958 to 1962. Defending justice in Tombstone, Arizona, Elfego Baca fights for the lives of an Englishman framed for murder and a rancher charged with bank robbery. 77m. **DIR:** Christian Nyby. **CAST:** Robert Loggia, James Dunn, Lynn Bari, James Drury, Jay C. Flippen, Kenneth Tobey, Annette Funicello, Patric Knowles, Audrey Dalton. **1962**

ELIMINATORS, THE 🦃 A mad scientist creates the perfect weapon, the "Mandroid." Rated PG. 95m. **DIR:** Peter Manoogian. **CAST:** Andrew Prine, Denise Crosby, Patrick Reynolds, Roy Dotrice. **1986**

ELIZABETH ★★★★1/2 England's sixteenth-century royal highness is given a modern blast of bravado as she is jerked from dungeon to throne amidst bloody Catholic and Protestant feuding. Elizabeth becomes both pawn and power broker in a series of scandals and conspiracies before crowning herself England's Virgin Queen. This visually lush, revisionist lesson in survival and self-empowerment excellently captures physical details of the past as well as the fire of the queen's soul. Rated R for violence and sexuality. 124m. **DIR:** Shekhar Kapur. **CAST:** Cate Blanchett, Joseph Fiennes, Geoffrey Rush, Chris Eccleston. **1998 DVD**

ELIZABETH R ★★★★★ Double oscar winner Glenda Jackson won an Emmy Award for her brilliant, multihued portrayal of England's queen Elizabeth I in this six-part BBC *Masterpiece Theater* dramatic chronicle of the forty-six-year reign of history's most heralded monarch. Engrossing and superb in every aspect, this ranks as one of public television's most outstanding miniseries. 540m. **DIR:** Claude Whatham, Herbert Wise, Richard Martin, Donald McWhinnie. **CAST:** Glenda Jackson, Ronald Hines, Vivian Pickles, Nicholas Selby, Robin Ellis. **1972 DVD**

ELLA CINDERS ★★★ Solid vehicle for comedienne Colleen Moore (then approaching the peak of her screen fame). It's an update on the Cinderella story, locating the fairy tale's events in contemporary Hollywood. The best scenes satirize moviemaking and the big studios of the day. Silent. B&W; 60m. **DIR:** Alfred E. Green. **CAST:** Colleen Moore, Lloyd Hughes. **1926**

ELLEN FOSTER ★★★1/2 This *Hallmark Hall of Fame* production questions the wisdom of keeping biological families together when neglect and abuse are present. Jena Malone is superb as a 10 year old forced to run the household while Mom dies and Dad drinks. Things get even worse when her steely-hearted grandmother (chillingly portrayed by Julie Harris) forces her to live in her mansion. Not rated; contains adult themes. 90m. **DIR:** John Erman. **CAST:** Jena Malone, Julie Harris, Ted Levine, Glynnis O'Connor, Debra Monk, Kate Burton, Barbara Garrick. **1997**

ELLIS ISLAND ★★★ This TV miniseries, of the soap-opera variety, follows the lives of three immigrants who come to the United States at the turn of the century. All struggle to find acceptance, happiness, and success in the promised land. 310m. **DIR:** Jerry London. **CAST:** Richard Burton, Faye Dunaway, Ben Vereen, Melba Moore, Ann Jillian, Greg Martyn, Peter Riegert. **1984**

ELMER GANTRY ★★★★ Burt Lancaster gives one of his most memorable performances in this release as a phony evangelist who, along with Jean Simmons, exploits the faithful with his fire-and-brimstone sermons. Arthur Kennedy is the reporter out to expose their operation in this screen version of Sinclair Lewis's story set in the midwest of the 1920s. 145m. **DIR:** Richard Brooks. **CAST:** Burt Lancaster, Jean Simmons, Dean Jagger, Arthur Kennedy, Shirley Jones. **1960 DVD**

ELUSIVE CORPORAL, THE ★★★★1/2 Twenty-five years after he made his greatest masterpiece, *La Grande Illusion*, Renoir reexamines men in war with almost equally satisfying results. This time the soldiers are Frenchmen in a World War II prison camp. This is a delicate drama infused with considerable wit. In French with English subtitles. 108m. **DIR:** Jean Renoir. **CAST:** Jean-Pierre Cassel, Claude Brasseur, Claude Rich. **1962**

ELUSIVE PIMPERNEL, THE ★★1/2 Lesser remake of the 1934 swashbuckling adventure, *The Scarlet Pimpernel*. David Niven pales in comparison to Leslie Howard's portrayal of the death-defying savior. Not enough action to sustain viewer interest. 107m. **DIR:** Michael Powell. **CAST:** David Niven, Margaret Leighton, Cyril Cusack, Jack Hawkins. **1950**

ELVES 🦃 Santa's little helpers are genetically mutated by former Nazi scientists. Not rated; the film has violence, nudity, and profanity. 89m. **DIR:** Jeff Mandel. **CAST:** Dan Haggerty, Deanna Lund. **1989**

ELVIRA MADIGAN ★★★★ A simple and tragic story of a young Swedish officer who falls in love with a beautiful circus performer. Outstanding photography makes this film. Try to see the subtitled version. 89m. **DIR:** Bo Widerberg. **CAST:** Pia Degermark, Thommy Berggren. **1967 DVD**

ELVIRA, MISTRESS OF THE DARK ★★★1/2 The late-night TV scream queen of B-film horror makes her debut as a movie star. It was well worth the wait! Elvira descends upon a midwestern town to sell her late aunt's estate. What ensues is a laugh riot, albeit with more breast jokes than you can count. You'll scream when you see Elvira as a baby. Rated PG-13 for profanity. 90m. **DIR:** James Signorelli. **CAST:** Elvira, Morgan Shepherd, Daniel Greene, Jeff Conaway, Susan Kellerman. **1988 DVD**

ELVIS AND ME 🦃 Originally a TV miniseries, this film version of Priscilla Presley's biography is disturbingly one-sided. 192m. **DIR:** Larry Peerce. **CAST:** Dale Midkiff, Susan Walters, Billy Green Bush. **1988**

ELVIS '56 ★★★★ Impressive documentary traces the evolution of Elvis Presley from naïve teenage rocker to jaded superstar—all in the space of one year. Narrated by Levon Helm (of The Band), the film uses television appearances, newsreel footage, publicity stills, and recordings to re-create the pivotal year in Elvis's career and life. 60m. **DIR:** Alan Raymond, Susan Raymond. **CAST:** Documentary. **1987 DVD**

ELVIS MEETS NIXON ★★1/2 Alan Rosen's satiric script takes an actual event and uses it to outrageously parody both individuals in this made-for-cable production. While the meeting itself did occur (Presley wanted to become an undercover agent in the war against drugs), this overly broad dramatization gets most of its mileage from pithy commentary by Dick Cavett and other amused spectators. Rated R for profanity and mild violence. 95m. **DIR:** Allan Arkush. **CAST:** Rick Peters, Curtis Armstrong, Richard Beymer, Bob Gunton. **1997**

ELVIS—THAT'S THE WAY IT IS ★★★★1/2 Col. Tom Parker insisted that Elvis make this documentary about his concert at the International Hotel in Las Vegas. It was one of Col. Parker's wisest decisions because it showcased Elvis's personality better than any of his thirty-one feature-length films. 107m. **DIR:** Denis Sanders. **1970**

ELVIS: THE LOST PERFORMANCES ★★★ Only if you like Elvis would you enjoy these outtakes from two of his live-concert movies, *Elvis—That's the Way It Is* (1970) and *Elvis on Tour* (1972). Also included is footage of Elvis rehearsing at a sound studio in 1970. 60m. **DIR:** Patrick Michael Murphy. **CAST:** Elvis Presley. **1992**

ELVIS—THE MOVIE ★★★★ A fictional account of Elvis Presley's rise to stardom, it probes deeply into the family life of rock 'n' roll's king. This TV movie should rate highly with fans of Elvis, as well as those just interested in a good story. Excellent voice re-creation by Ronnie McDowell. 117m. **DIR:** John Carpenter. **CAST:** Kurt Russell, Shelley Winters, Pat Hingle, Melody Anderson, Season Hubley, Charlie Hodge, Ellen Travolta, Ed Begley Jr. **1979**

EMANON 🦃 The Messiah comes to New York City. Rated PG-13 for minor obscenities. 98m. **DIR:** Stuart Paul. **CAST:** Stuart Paul, Cheryl M. Lynn, Jeremy Miller. **1986**

EMBRACE OF THE VAMPIRE ★★ Alyssa Milano has it hot and heavy for vampire hunk Martin Kemp, the man of her dreams. Problems arise when she's forced to choose between her human boyfriend and her dreamy bloodsucker. The film plods along with steamy but predictable results. Not rated; contains nudity, violence, and profanity. 93m. **DIR:** Anne Goursand. **CAST:** Martin Kemp, Alyssa Milano, Harrison Puett, Charlotte Lewis, Jennifer Tilly. **1994 DVD**

EMBRYO ★★1/2 Rock Hudson plays a scientist who succeeds in developing a fetus into a full-grown woman in record time. But something isn't quite right. Adequate thriller with a good ending. Rated PG. 104m. **DIR:** Ralph Nelson. **CAST:** Rock Hudson, Barbara Carrera, Diane Ladd. **1976**

EMERALD FOREST, THE ★★★★ In this riveting adventure film based on a true story, Powers Boothe stars as Bill Markham, an American engineer who, with his family, goes to the Amazon jungle to build a dam. There, his 5-year-old son is stolen by a native tribe known as the Invisible People. Markham spends the next ten years trying to find his son. Rated R for nudity, suggested sex, profanity, and violence. 110m. **DIR:** John Boorman. **CAST:** Powers Boothe, Meg Foster, Charley Boorman. **1985 DVD**

EMERALD JUNGLE ★★ Originally titled *Eaten Alive by Cannibals*, this fitfully entertaining entry in the Italian cannibal parade was given its video moniker in the hope it would steal some of the thunder from John Boorman's unrelated *The Emerald Forest*. Heavily cut for U.S. release, but still plenty gross. Rated R. 90m. **DIR:** Umberto Lenzi. **CAST:** Robert Kerman, Janet Agren, Mel Ferrer. **1980**

EMIGRANTS, THE ★★★★1/2 Completely absorbing but at times disturbingly sad saga of a group of impoverished farmers leaving mid-1800s Sweden to search for instant riches in America. The hardships and the resulting doubts suffered en route are graphically told and spellbinding. When this English-dubbed version was released in the United States in 1972, it garnered many Oscar nominations including best picture, director, and actress (Liv Ullmann). Rated PG for adult language and content. 151m. **DIR:** Jan Troell. **CAST:** Max von Sydow, Liv Ullmann, Allan Edwall. **1971**

EMIL AND THE DETECTIVES ★★★1/2 One of the better live-action adventures made by the Disney Studios in the early 1960s, this grand little tale follows the escapades of a young boy who hires a gang of young, amateur sleuths after he's been robbed. Wholly improbable, but neatly constructed from the classic children's novel by Erich Kastner. 99m. **DIR:** Peter Tewksbury. **CAST:** Roger Mobley, Walter Slezak, Bryan Russell, Heinz Schubert. **1964**

EMILY ★★ This British film was Koo Stark's premiere in soft-core porn. She plays a teenager returning home from boarding school who finds out that her mother is a well-paid prostitute. This bit of news upsets Emily momentarily, but she manages to create her own sexual world with a female painter, the painter's husband, and her boyfriend, James. Lots of nudity and sex. Rated R. 87m. **DIR:** Henry Herbert. **CAST:** Koo Stark. **1982**

EMILY BRONTË'S WUTHERING HEIGHTS ★★★1/2 Based on the 1847 book, this features gorgeous Juliette Binoche as the somewhat schizophrenic Cathy. Physically and emotionally she's bound to Heathcliff (Ralph Fiennes), yet she longs to belong to her neighbor's upper-crust society. Fiennes adopts a devilish persona as he wreaks his revenge on all who have hurt him. A notch above a soap but equally compelling. Not rated; contains violence. 104m. **DIR:** Peter Kosminsky. **CAST:** Juliette Binoche, Ralph Fiennes, Janet McTeer, Sophie Ward. **1992**

EMINENT DOMAIN ★★1/2 Unsettling political thriller with Donald Sutherland as a high-ranking official in Poland who is stripped of his power, only to get stonewalled when he attempts to find out the reason. Plenty of suspense. Rated PG-13 for profanity. 102m. **DIR:** John Irvin. **CAST:** Donald Sutherland, Anne Archer, Jodhi May, Paul Freeman. **1991**

EMMA (1932) ★★★★ The legendary Marie Dressler was Oscar nominated for this comedy-drama about an aging, dowdy housekeeper who falls in love with and marries the rich widower who hired her. B&W; 73m. **DIR:** Clarence Brown. **CAST:** Marie Dressler, Myrna Loy, Jean Hersholt, John Miljan, Richard Cromwell, Leila Bennett. **1932**

EMMA (1996) ★★★★ Jane Austen's novel of a charming young meddler (Gwyneth Paltrow) arranging everyone's romantic lives while neglecting her own makes a charming, well-acted film. Director Douglas McGrath makes it all look a little too candied and idealized, and Jeremy Northam is a bit too young and handsome for his role as Emma's older friend, but those are only minor drawbacks in a breezy and engaging entertainment. Rated PG. 111m. **DIR:** Douglas McGrath. **CAST:** Gwyneth Paltrow, Jeremy Northam, Toni Collette, Greta Scacchi, Juliet Stevenson, Sophie Thompson. **1996 DVD**

EMMA (1996) ★★★★ The A&E team behind *Pride and Prejudice* created a lavish and wry comedy with a markedly different flavor than Gwyneth Paltrow's frothy theatrical version. A crisp, fast pace is enhanced by Kate Beckinsale's precise delivery, though she's occasionally too brittle in the title role. Especially intriguing are the amusing enactments of Emma's meddlesome daydreams and flights of fancy. Not rated. 107m. **DIR:** Diarmuid Lawrence. **CAST:** Kate Beckinsale, Mark Strong, Prunella Scales, Bernard Hepton, Raymond Coulthard, Samantha Morton, Olivia Williams, Dominic Rowan, Lucy Robinson. **1996 DVD**

EMMANUELLE ★★★ Sylvia Kristel became an international star as a result of this French screen adaptation of Emmanuelle Argan's controversial book about the initiation of a diplomat's young wife into the world of sensuality. In the soft-core sex film genre, this stands out as one of the best. Rated R for nudity. 92m. **DIR:** Just Jaeckin. **CAST:** Sylvia Kristel, Marika Green, Daniel Sarky, Alain Cuny. **1974 DVD**

EMMA'S SHADOW ★★★★ Enchanting story of an 11-year-old girl from wealthy parents who fakes her own kidnapping in the 1930s. Winner of the Danish best film award. In Danish with English subtitles. Not rated. 93m. **DIR:** Soeren Kragh-Jacobsen. **CAST:** Line Kruse, Borje Ahlstedt. **1988**

EMPEROR AND THE ASSASSIN, THE ★★★1/2 In third century B.C., a warlord obsessed with becoming China's first emperor discovers that his bloodline is tainted; an assassin vows never to kill again only to seek redemption through his sword. A court concubine becomes the link between both men, and an ancestral mandate to unify the seven dominant kingdoms of China brings massive human suffering to a country scarred by 550 years of bloodshed. The narrative of this lavish, bloody epic about royal egos, lust, and revenge drags at times, but its visual sweep is staggering. In Mandarin with English subtitles. Rated R for violence and language. 161m. **DIR:** Chen Kaige. **CAST:** Gong Li, Zhang Fengyi, Li Xuejian. **2000 DVD**

EMPEROR JONES, THE ★★★1/2 This liberal version of Eugene O'Neill's prize-winning play invents entire sections that were written to capitalize on star Paul Robeson's fame as a singer as well as an introductory piece that provides a background for Robeson's character, the doomed Jones. This is still an interesting and sometimes strong film despite the drastic changes. Surviving prints that have been transferred to tape are not always in the best of condition, so quality will vary on this title. B&W; 72m. **DIR:** Dudley Murphy. **CAST:** Paul Robeson, Dudley Digges, Frank Wilson. **1933**

EMPEROR WALTZ, THE ★★★1/2 Bing Crosby is a traveling phonograph salesman who attempts to make a sale and obtain an endorsement from Austria's Emperor Franz Josef. Continuously witty and at times hilarious screenplay by producer Charles Brackett and director Billy Wilder. Not many songs but lots of fun. 116m. **DIR:** Billy Wilder. **CAST:** Bing Crosby, Joan Fontaine, Roland Culver, Lucile Watson, Richard Haydn, Sig Ruman. **1948**

EMPEROR'S NEW GROOVE, THE ★★★★ This lightning-swift animated feature is every bit as fast, furious, and funny as a classic Warner Bros. cartoon . . . at many, many times the length. David Spade voices the spoiled-brat emperor of a mythical kingdom who, after being changed into a llama by his power-hungry adviser, must learn humility while relying on the assistance of a good-natured peasant (John Goodman). Patrick Warburton steals the show as the adviser's muscle-bound but surprisingly genteel assistant. Rated G. 78m. **DIR:** Mark Dindal. **2000 DVD**

EMPEROR'S SHADOW, THE ★★★★1/2 In the third century B.C., the first emperor of China tries to unite his squabbling realm in the face of opposition from a childhood friend, now a revered musician. This lavish historical epic has something for everyone: cast-of-thousands spectacle, political intrigue, sexual scheming, and psychological insight, all superbly acted and beautifully photographed against stunning scenery. In Mandarin with English subtitles. Not rated; contains violence and brief sexual scenes. 123m. **DIR:** Zhou Xiaowen. **CAST:** Jiang Wen, Ge You, Xu Qing. **1996 DVD**

EMPIRE CITY ★★ Standard fare features Michael Paré as a hard-as-nails detective who is paired with a female cop to help solve a murder in this attempt at *film noir*. Not rated; contains violence, adult situations, and language. 71m. **DIR:** Mark Rosner. **CAST:** Michael Paré, Mary Mara, Beau Starr, Peter Frechette. **1991**

EMPIRE OF THE ANTS 🦃 H. G. Wells must somersault in his grave every time somebody watches this insulting adaptation of one of his more intriguing sci-fi stories. Rated PG for violence. 90m. **DIR:** Bert I. Gordon. **CAST:** Joan Collins, Robert Lansing, Albert Salmi, Robert Pine. **1977 DVD**

EMPIRE OF THE DARK ★★ Run-of-the-mill devil flick concerning a Los Angeles police officer (writer-director-star Steve Barkett) who saves his baby son from a demonic cult. Twenty years later he and the now grown-up son must battle the cult again. Not rated; contains violence and profanity. 93m. **DIR:** Steve Barkett. **CAST:** Steve Barkett, Richard Harrison. **1991**

EMPIRE OF THE SUN ★★★1/2 J. G. Ballard's harrowing autobiographical examination of life in a World War II Japanese prison camp has been given the Hollywood treatment by director Steven Spielberg, who filmed on location in Shanghai. Christian Bale, as Young Ballard, winds up in a concentration camp for four years. Too much surface gloss prevents this from being a classic, but it nonetheless contains scenes of surprising power and poignancy. Rated PG for language and intensity. 145m. **DIR:** Steven Spielberg. **CAST:** Christian Bale, John Malkovich, Miranda Richardson, Nigel Havers. **1987 DVD**

EMPIRE RECORDS ★★ A day in the life of a group of record-store employees. Filled with eccentric characters and hard-driving music, this film is annoying but funny often enough. Features songs by the Gin Blossoms, the Cranberries, Toad the Wet Sprocket, and Evan Dando. Rated PG-13 for sexual situations, profanity, and drugs. 89m. **DIR:** Alan Moyle. **CAST:** Anthony LaPaglia,

Maxwell Caulfield, Debi Mazar, Rory Cochrane, Johnny Whitworth, Robin Tunney. **1995 DVD**

EMPIRE STATE 🦃 Powerful real-estate magnate becomes involved with some shady dealings in London. Rated R for nudity and violence. 104m. **DIR:** Ron Peck. **CAST:** Martin Landau, Ray McAnally, Catherine Harrison. **1987**

EMPIRE STRIKES BACK, THE ★★★★★ In George Lucas's follow-up to *Star Wars*, Billy Dee Williams joins Mark Hamill (Luke Skywalker), Harrison Ford (Han Solo), Carrie Fisher (Princess Leia), and the gang in their fight against the forces of the Empire led by Darth Vader. It's more action-packed fun in that faraway galaxy a long time ago. Rated PG. 124m. **DIR:** Irvin Kershner. **CAST:** Billy Dee Williams, Harrison Ford, Carrie Fisher, Mark Hamill, Anthony Daniels, Dave Prowse, James Earl Jones (voice). **1980**

EMPLOYEES' ENTRANCE ★★★1/2 Warren William is especially sleazy as the manager of a department store who takes advantage of the fact that jobs are scarce due to the Depression. Surprisingly frank comedy-drama made before the Hays Office started to clamp down. B&W; 75m. **DIR:** Roy Del Ruth. **CAST:** Warren William, Loretta Young, Wallace Ford, Allen Jenkins. **1933**

EMPTY CANVAS, THE ★★ Would-be painter Horst Buchholz falls for gold-digging model Catherine Spaak. Maudlin pap. B&W; 118m. **DIR:** Damiano Damiani. **CAST:** Bette Davis, Horst Buchholz, Catherine Spaak, Daniela Rocca, Georges Wilson. **1964**

EMPTY HOLSTERS ★★★ Cowboy crooner Dick Foran is framed for murder and sent up the river. Once out of prison, Foran is forced to prove his innocence and defend the townsfolk without the aid of his six-shooters. Veteran heavy Glenn Strange, in a nice twist, is a good-guy sidekick. B&W; 58m. **DIR:** B. Reeves "Breezy" Eason. **CAST:** Dick Foran, Glenn Strange. **1937**

ENCHANTED APRIL ★★★★1/2 In order to escape their boring lives and demanding husbands, two female friends hatch a plot, with the help of two women they've never met, to rent a luxurious mansion on the Italian Riviera. For all four of them, their little getaway turns out to be full of surprises, delights, and life-changing realizations. A warm-hearted romp that is as magical as its setting. Rated PG. 97m. **DIR:** Mike Newell. **CAST:** Miranda Richardson, Joan Plowright, Josie Lawrence, Polly Walker, Alfred Molina, Michael Kitchen, Jim Broadbent. **1992**

ENCHANTED COTTAGE, THE ★★★1/2 An engrossing blend of romance, fantasy, and melodrama. Robert Young gives one of his best big-screen performances as a battle-scarred World War II veteran. Dorothy McGuire offers a beautifully realized portrayal of a young woman whose inner loveliness is hidden beneath a painfully plain exterior. As the blind friend who sees so much more than everyone else, Herbert Marshall is as suave as ever. B&W; 91m. **DIR:** John Cromwell. **CAST:** Dorothy McGuire, Robert Young, Herbert Marshall, Spring Byington, Hillary Brooke. **1945**

ENCHANTED FOREST, THE ★★★ Pleasant fantasy about an old hermit who teaches a young boy to love the forest and its creatures lacks a big-studio budget but is fine family fare. 77m. **DIR:** Lew Landers. **CAST:** Edmund Lowe, Harry Davenport, Brenda Joyce, Billy Severn, John Litel. **1945 DVD**

ENCHANTED ISLAND 🦃 Dull adaptation of Herman Melville's *Typee*. 95m. **DIR:** Allan Dwan. **CAST:** Dana Andrews, Jane Powell, Arthur Shields, Don Dubbins. **1958**

ENCHANTMENT ★★★1/2 An enchanting fantasy that bubbles over with romantic intentions. An old man watches his grandniece make some of the same mistakes he made in his romantic life and finds a way for her to benefit from those mistakes. Light entertainment made enjoyable by a strong cast. B&W; 101m. **DIR:** Irving Reis. **CAST:** David Niven, Teresa Wright, Evelyn Keyes, Farley Granger, Jayne Meadows, Leo G. Carroll, Shepperd Strudwick. **1948**

ENCINO MAN ★★★ This teen comedy—about a couple of misfits who find a caveman frozen in their backyard—is surprisingly funny. Sean Astin and Pauly Shore are best friends who defrost the prehistoric man. Rated PG for mild sexual innuendos. 88m. **DIR:** Les Mayfield. **CAST:** Sean Astin, Brendan Fraser, Pauly Shore, Megan Ward, Michael DeLuise, Mariette Hartley, Richard Masur. **1992 DVD**

ENCORE ★★★ Somerset Maugham introduces three of his short stories in this sequel to *Trio*. The best of the three is "Gigolo and Gigolette" in which trapeze artist Glynis Johns begins to feel used by her husband as he promotes her death-defying act. The other two ("The Ant and the Grasshopper" and "Winter Cruise") are more humorous. B&W; 85m. **DIR:** Harold French, Pat Jackson, Anthony Pelissier. **CAST:** Glynis Johns, Nigel Patrick, Kay Walsh, Roland Culver, Ronald Squire, Peter Graves. **1952**

ENCOUNTER AT RAVEN'S GATE ★★★1/2 A small Australian town is stricken by unusual occurrences: electrical faults, violent and psychotic human behavior. Solid acting, vivid characterizations, a refreshing atmosphere of alternative cinema, and a sedately haunting soundtrack make this one worth a watch. Rated R for violence. 85m. **DIR:** Rolf De Heer. **CAST:** Ritchie Singer, Steven Vidler, Vincent Gil, Saturday Rosenberg. **1988**

ENCOUNTER WITH THE UNKNOWN ★★★1/2 Rod Serling narrates a series of true events in psychic phenomena. The episodes are based on studies made by Dr. Jonathan Rankin between 1949 and 1970. Each deals with a person's encounter with the unknown or supernatural. Rated PG. 90m. **DIR:** Harry Thomason. **CAST:** Rod Serling, Rosie Holotik, Gene Ross. **1973**

END, THE ★★★1/2 The blackest of black comedies, this stars Burt Reynolds (who also directed) as an unfortunate fellow who is informed he's dying of a rare disease. Poor Burt can hardly believe it. So he decides to end it all. In the process, he meets a maniac (Dom DeLuise) who is more than willing to lend a hand. It's surprisingly funny. Rated R. 100m. **DIR:** Burt Reynolds. **CAST:** Burt Reynolds, Sally Field, Dom DeLuise, Joanne Woodward, David Steinberg, Pat O'Brien, Myrna Loy, Kristy McNichol, Robby Benson. **1978 DVD**

END OF DAYS ★★1/2 When Satan comes to New York City to mate and gain control of the world for the next millenium, he takes over the body of a financial executive to prey on a young woman that the Vatican is protecting. But the priests fail to stop ol' Scratch, so it's up to one-man-army Arnold Schwarzenegger to take him on. Terrific opening scenes slide into a where-do-we-go-from-here dilemma for director Peter Hyams, who is forced to top himself once too often. The result is an overreliance on special effects at the expense of strong storytelling. Rated R for violence, profanity, nudity, and simulated sex. 120m. **DIR:** Peter Hyams. **CAST:** Arnold Schwarzenegger, Gabriel Byrne, Kevin Pollak, Robin Tunney, C.C.H. Pounder, Rod Steiger, Derrick O'Connor, Miriam Margolyes, Udo Kier, Mark Margolis. **1999 DVD**

END OF INNOCENCE, THE ★★ Seriocomic story of a woman driven over the edge who "finds herself" only after a drug overdose. All that saves the film are occasional flashes of style and self-mockery from first-time feature director Dyan Cannon (who also wrote). Rated R for profanity and sexual situations. 92m. **DIR:** Dyan Cannon. **CAST:** Dyan Cannon, John Heard, George Coe, Rebecca Schaeffer, Billie Bird, Viveka Davis. **1990**

END OF ST. PETERSBURG, THE ★★★1/2 The story of a worker who gradually becomes aware of his duty to his class. He becomes a part of the 1917 Revolution. Although pure propaganda, this powerful indictment of czarist Russia has a fervor and sweep that transcends its message. Silent, with English intertitles. B&W; 75m. **DIR:** V. I. Pudovkin. **CAST:** Ivan Chuvelov. **1927**

END OF SUMMER 🦃 Positively laughable exercise in turn-of-the-century bodice ripping, with artist Jacqueline Bisset unable to pledge her love to randy Peter Weller; it's the sort of oh-so-melodramatic treacle that gives romance novels a bad name. Rated R for nudity, simulated sex, and drug use. 95m. **DIR:** Linda Yellen. **CAST:** Jacqueline Bisset, Peter Weller, Julian Sands, Amy Locane. **1995**

END OF THE AFFAIR, THE ★★1/2 From production designer Anthony Pratt's impeccable re-creation of WWII London, to the convincing yet unassuming manner with which director Neil Jordan populates every scene, *The End of the Affair* looks and feels like a product of the era it simulates. But the story—adapted from one of Graham Greene's most tortured novels of guilt and Catholic angst—is a sluggish, ponderous, three-character melodrama so much a product of its very British origins that it becomes a parody of the clipped, unemotional atmosphere that we always associate with our cousins across the pond. In a word, it's boring, and you won't care a whit about the adulterous affair that ultimately destroys all three of these self-absorbed boors. Rated R for nudity and strong sexual content. 105m. **DIR:** Neil Jordan. **CAST:** Ralph Fiennes, Julianne Moore, Stephen Rea, Ian Hart, Jason Isaacs, James Bolam, Sam Bould. **1999 DVD**

END OF THE LINE ★★★ Financed as a labor of love by executive producer and costar Mary Steenburgen, this first film by director Jay Russell features Wilford Brimley as a railroad worker who, with buddy Levon Helm, steals a train engine to protest the closing of the freight depot where he has worked for thirty-eight years. The skilled peformances will keep you interested right to the end of the line. Rated PG for profanity. 105m. **DIR:** Jay Russell. **CAST:** Wilford Brimley, Levon Helm, Kevin Bacon, Bob Balaban, Barbara Barrie, Mary Steenburgen, Holly Hunter, Bruce McGill, Howard Morris. **1988**

END OF THE ROAD ★★ Stacy Keach plays a college graduate who falls out of society, receives help from an unorthodox psychotherapist named Doctor D (James Earl Jones), then becomes intimately involved with a married couple. The imagery can be compelling, but the finale is too graphic. Rated X (by 1960s standards) but more like a hard R for sex, nudity, and adult themes. 110m. **DIR:** Aram Avakian. **CAST:** Stacy Keach, Harris Yulin, Dorothy Tristan, James Earl Jones. **1969**

END OF THE TRAIL ★★★★ The great Western star Colonel Tim McCoy was a lifelong champion of the American Indian. This is his magnum opus, a movie sympathetic to Native Americans made nearly twenty years before *Broken Arrow.* It's an ambitious, somewhat dated story of a cavalry officer (McCoy) falsely accused of treason and forced to prove his innocence by uncovering the true villain. B&W; 62m. **DIR:** D. Ross Lederman. **CAST:** Tim McCoy, Luana Walters, Wheeler Oakman. **1932**

END OF THE WORLD 🦃 Aliens plot to destroy the Earth while disguised as religious figures. Rated PG. 87m. **DIR:** John Hayes. **CAST:** Christopher Lee, Sue Lyons, Lew Ayres, Dean Jagger, Macdonald Carey. **1977**

END OF VIOLENCE, THE ★★★ Director Wim Wenders attempts to address the state of life in Los Angeles through the eyes of numerous spy cameras situated throughout the city, and the kidnapping of a popular Hollywood producer. It's a melting pot of ideas that never comes to a full boil, and by tackling so much in so little time, Wenders hasn't delivered more than an interesting idea. Rated R for language. 122m. **DIR:** Wim Wenders. **CAST:** Andie MacDowell, Bill Pullman, Gabriel Byrne, Traci Lind, Loren Dean. **1997 DVD**

ENDANGERED SPECIES ★★★1/2 Everything about this nifty science-fiction suspense-thriller is well-done. The story deals with bizarre incidents involving cattle mutilation and is based on fact. In it, a country sheriff (JoBeth Williams) and a hard-boiled New York detective (Robert Urich) join forces to find out who or what is responsible. Rated R for discreetly handled nudity, violence, and profanity. 97m. **DIR:** Alan Rudolph. **CAST:** Robert Urich, JoBeth Williams, Paul Dooley, Hoyt Axton. **1982**

ENDLESS DESCENT 🦃 A group of otherworldly genetic mutants in a subaquarian chamber. Not rated; contains violence, profanity, and gore. 79m. **DIR:** Juan Piquer Simon. **CAST:** Jack Scalia, R. Lee Ermey, Ray Wise, Deborah Adair. **1989**

ENDLESS GAME, THE ★★ With a creakily indifferent tone, writer-director Bryan Forbes's cold war–styled spy thriller overdoses on the residual cynicism of a once-vibrant genre. Albert Finney stars as a retired agent summoned back to learn why aged members of a disbanded European operation are being killed. Not rated; explicit dialogue, brief nudity, and violence. 120m. **DIR:** Bryan Forbes. **CAST:** Albert Finney, George Segal, Anthony Quayle, Nanette Newman. **1990**

ENDLESS LOVE ★★ Though this story of a teenage love affair has all the elements of a great romance, it is marred by implausibility and inconsistency. The film improves as it progresses and even offers some compelling moments, but not enough to compensate for its flaws. Rated R because of sex and nudity. 115m. **DIR:** Franco Zeffirelli. **CAST:** Brooke Shields, Martin Hewitt, Shirley Knight, Don Murray. **1981**

ENDLESS NIGHT 🦃 Routine suspense from the pen of Agatha Christie. Not rated; contains slight nudity and some violence. 95m. **DIR:** Sidney Gilliat. **CAST:** Hayley

Mills, Hywel Bennett, Britt Ekland, George Sanders. **1972 DVD**

ENDLESS SUMMER, THE (1966) ★★★★ The only surfing documentary ever to gain an audience outside the Beach Boys set, this is an imaginatively photographed travelogue that captures the joy, danger, and humor of searching for the perfect wave. Much of the success is attributable to the whimsical narration. 95m. **DIR:** Bruce Brown. **CAST:** Mike Hynson, Robert August. **1966 DVD**

ENDLESS SUMMER II (1994) ★★★ Bruce Brown's long-delayed sequel to his 1966 cult hit about surfing around the world is basically more of the same. This time, superior 1990s technology makes much of the footage truly spectacular. Brown again narrates with hokey charm. A must-see for surfing fans, a pleasant diversion for others. Rated PG for brief glimpses of some topless beaches. 107m. **DIR:** Bruce Brown. **CAST:** Patrick O'Connell, Robert "Wingnut" Weaver. **1994**

ENDURANCE ★★1/2 This film about Ethiopian runner Haile Gebrsellasie, a gold medalist at the 1996 Atlanta Olympics, is an uneasy mix of documentary race footage (directed by Bud Greenspan) and awkward reenactments of events from Gebrsellasie's life, with the runner and family playing themselves. Director Leslie Woodhead concentrates more on atmosphere than events, and the result is often tedious, with important facts tossed off in the closing credits rather than dramatized during the film itself. Rated PG. 83m. **DIR:** Leslie Woodhead. **CAST:** Haile Gebrsellasie, Yonas Zergaw, Shawananness Gebrsellasie, Tedesse Haile. **1998**

ENEMIES—A LOVE STORY ★★★★ Director Paul Mazursky achieves a delicate mixture of drama and comedy in his adaptation of the novel by Isaac Bashevis Singer. Set in New York in 1949, the film focuses on the hectic life of Holocaust survivor and womanizer Herman Broder (Ron Silver). Rated R for profanity, nudity, and simulated sex. 120m. **DIR:** Paul Mazursky. **CAST:** Ron Silver, Anjelica Huston, Lena Olin, Margaret Sophie Stein, Alan King, Paul Mazursky. **1989**

ENEMY ACTION ★★1/2 Low-budget Roger Corman production about officers trying to stop a terrorist plan to detonate stolen bombs in Washington, DC. Standard thriller fare enlivened by Randolph Mantooth as a scene-stealing villain. Rated R for violence and profanity. 84m. **DIR:** Brian Katkin. **CAST:** C. Thomas Howell, Lisa Thornhill, Randolph Mantooth, Richard Lynch. **1999**

ENEMY AT THE GATES ★★★1/2 This serious-minded WWII thriller, something of a Russian-front response to *Saving Private Ryan*, will captivate viewers during its grim battle scenes and the fascinating battle of wits between a Nazi marksman and the celebrated Russian sniper Vassili Zaitsev (an actual historical figure). Unfortunately, everybody's dialogue is lamentably corny, and a secondary plot—a romantic triangle—is simply silly. Rated R for profanity, simulated sex, and grim war violence. 128m. **DIR:** Jean-Jacques Annaud. **CAST:** Jude Law, Joseph Fiennes, Rachel Weisz, Ed Harris, Bob Hoskins. **2001 DVD**

ENEMY BELOW, THE ★★★1/2 Robert Mitchum as the captain of a U.S. Navy destroyer and Curt Jurgens as the commander of a German submarine play a deadly game of chess as they pursue each other across the South Atlantic during World War II. This little-seen aquatic duel is well worth viewing. 98m. **DIR:** Dick Powell. **CAST:** Robert Mitchum, Curt Jurgens, David Hedison, Theodore Bikel, Russell Collins, Kurt Kreuger, Frank Albertson, Doug McClure. **1957**

ENEMY FROM SPACE ★★★★ Brian Donlevy makes his second appearance as Professor Quatermass, a scientist hero who discovers that aliens are slowly taking over the governments of Earth—starting with Britain. It's an uncommonly powerful film. The first entry in the theatrical trilogy was *The Creeping Unknown* and the last was *Five Million Years to Earth*. B&W; 85m. **DIR:** Val Guest. **CAST:** Brian Donlevy, William Franklyn. **1957 DVD**

ENEMY MINE ★★ A would-be outer-space epic. Two futuristic foes, an Earthman (Dennis Quaid) and a reptilian alien (Louis Gossett Jr.), are stranded on a hostile planet and forced to rely on each other for survival. Rated PG-13 for violence and profanity. 108m. **DIR:** Wolfgang Petersen. **CAST:** Dennis Quaid, Louis Gossett Jr., Brian James, Richard Marcus, Lance Kerwin. **1985 DVD**

ENEMY OF THE LAW ★★★★ The Texas Rangers track down an outlaw gang who, years before, robbed a safe and hid the money. There are some hilarious escapades in this well-above-average oater. Tex Ritter's songs are always good. B&W; 59m. **DIR:** Harry Fraser. **CAST:** Tex Ritter, Dave O'Brien, Guy Wilferson, Charles King. **1945**

ENEMY OF THE STATE ★★★ If it's possible for a film to be too visually dynamic, then this is it. Director Tony Scott, obsessed with unbridled technology and rapid-fire style-for-its-own-sake, nearly overwhelms the intriguing story at the heart of this disturbing commentary on the fragility of personal privacy. Will Smith stars as a lawyer who gets sucked into a conspiracy case involving a rogue NSA dirty-trickster who killed a U.S. congressman. Our hero's life is turned upside down until he meets up with a former agent with lots of answers. When all is said and done, credibility isn't so much stretched as mangled beyond recognition. But it does succeed on a "kick-ass" level. Rated R for violence and profanity. 127m. **DIR:** Tony Scott. **CAST:** Will Smith, Gene Hackman, Jon Voight, Regina King, Loren Dean, Jake Busey, Barry Pepper. **1998 DVD**

ENEMY TERRITORY ★★ This film features a good premise but suffers from poor acting, writing, and production values. Gary Frank is an insurance salesman trapped inside a ghetto apartment building and battling a vicious gang. Rated R for language, extreme violence, and brief nudity. 89m. **DIR:** Peter Manoogian. **CAST:** Gary Frank, Ray Parker Jr., Jan-Michael Vincent, Frances Foster. **1987**

ENEMY UNSEEN ★★1/2 Mercenary tracks down the kidnapped daughter of a wealthy industrialist through the darkest regions of Africa, where she is about to be sacrificed in a ritual to the crocodile spirits. Rated R for violence. 90m. **DIR:** Elmo De Witt. **CAST:** Vernon Wells, Stack Pierce. **1991**

ENEMY WITHIN, THE ★★★1/2 This remake of *Seven Days in May* lacks the earlier film's urgency—and Rod Serling's taut script—but it's still a riveting idea. When an unpopular U.S. president decides to severely trim the military budget, a retaliatory coup is initiated by the vice president, the secretary of defense and a hawkish general. Only one honorable soldier stands in their way. This low-budget film still turns on a terrifying (and all too credible) concept. Rated PG-13 for profanity and violence. 86m. **DIR:** Jonathan Darby. **CAST:** Forest Whitaker, Sam Waterston, Dana Delany, Josef Sommer, George Dzundza, Jason Robards Jr. **1994**

ENFORCER, THE (1951) ★★★1/2 A big-city district attorney, Humphrey Bogart, attempts to break up the mob in this effective crime drama. At under 90 minutes, it moves like lightning and is refreshingly devoid of most of the clichés of the genre. B&W; 87m. **DIR:** Bretaigne Windust. **CAST:** Humphrey Bogart, Zero Mostel, Everett Sloane, Ted de Corsia, Roy Roberts. **1951**

ENFORCER, THE (1976) ★★★★ A step up from the muddled *Magnum Force* and a nice companion piece to *Dirty Harry*, this third entry in the popular series has detective Harry Callahan grudgingly team with a female cop (Tyne Daly) during his pursuit of a band of terrorists. John Mitchum gives a standout performance in his final series bow as tough cop Frank DiGeorgio. It'll make your day. Rated R. 96m. **DIR:** James Fargo. **CAST:** Clint Eastwood, Tyne Daly, Harry Guardino, Bradford Dillman, John Mitchum. **1976 DVD**

ENGLISH PATIENT, THE ★★★★ Even before the ceremonies were held, this old-style, David Lean–esque epic had Oscar written all over it. Set during World War II, the film begins with a spectacular, fiery plane crash in which there is one survivor, known to his caretaker only as "the English patient." Ralph Fiennes, as the mysterious title character, carries us through flashbacks, conspiracies, and the properly slower pace of the character-driven storytelling. All involved are to be commended for this modern, high class fare. Rated R for sex and violence. 160m. **DIR:** Anthony Minghella. **CAST:** Ralph Fiennes, Juliette Binoche, Willem Dafoe, Kristin Scott Thomas, Naveen Andrews, Colin Firth, Jurgen Prochnow, Kevin Whately. **1996 DVD**

ENGLISHMAN ABROAD, AN ★★★★ Much acclaimed BBC production dramatizing actress Coral Browne's actual Moscow encounter with an exiled British diplomat accused of spying for the Russians. Alan Bates is witty, sarcastic, and ultimately tragic as the infamous Guy Burgess—longing for some taste of the England now so unattainable to him. A superb script by Alan Bennett. 63m. **DIR:** John Schlesinger. **CAST:** Alan Bates, Coral Browne, Charles Gray. **1988**

ENGLISHMAN WHO WENT UP A HILL BUT CAME DOWN A MOUNTAIN, THE ★★★★ Charming British fluff, set during World War I, about a cartographer who, after declaring "the first mountain in Wales" to be sixteen feet short of official British mountain height, is delayed by eccentric locals until they can build it up from lowly hill status. Rated PG for language and some sexual innuendo. 99m. **DIR:** Christopher Monger. **CAST:** Hugh Grant, Tara Fitzgerald, Colm Meaney, Kenneth Griffith. **1995 DVD**

ENIGMA ★★ Espionage yarn succumbs to lethargy. The KGB sics an elite group of assassins on five Soviet dissidents. A CIA agent (Martin Sheen) attempts to thwart the insidious scheme by entangling his former lover with the top Russian agent. Rated PG. 101m. **DIR:** Jeannot Szwarc. **CAST:** Martin Sheen, Brigitte Fossey, Sam Neill, Derek Jacobi, Michel Lonsdale, Frank Finlay. **1982**

ENJO ★★★★ Like many of the best Japanese films, this is a simple story told with unerring precision. Adapted from a novel by Yukio Mishima, it is the story of a religious young man who decides to destroy a sacred temple in Kyoto in order to keep it from being defiled by tourists. The black-and-white photography is breathtaking. In Japanese with English subtitles. B&W; 96m. **DIR:** Kon Ichikawa. **CAST:** Raizo Ichikawa. **1958**

•ENLIGHTENMENT GUARANTEED ★★1/2 Two German brothers spend time in a Buddhist monastery in Japan and walk away with new outlooks on life in this lightweight midlife-crisis comedy shot on digital video. Gustav is a feng shui consultant who learns that the search for perfection is its own reward. Uwe is a kitchen countertop salesman abandoned by his wife, who learns to put hate behind him and move forward. They reassess their relationship in a film that is as spare and sometimes lulling as monastery life itself. In German with English subtitles. Not rated. 105m. **DIR:** Doris Dörrie. **CAST:** Gustav Peter Wöhler, Uwe Ochsenknecht. **2001**

ENOLA GAY: THE MEN, THE MISSION, THE ATOMIC BOMB ★★★ In this made-for-TV drama, Patrick Duffy plays Paul Tibbets, the man in charge of the plane that dropped the atomic bomb over Hiroshima. The film delves into the lives and reactions of the crew members in a fairly effective manner. 150m. **DIR:** David Lowell Rich. **CAST:** Billy Crystal, Kim Darby, Patrick Duffy, Gary Frank, Gregory Harrison. **1980**

ENSIGN PULVER ★★★ This sequel to *Mr. Roberts* doesn't quite measure up. The comedy, which takes place aboard a World War II cargo ship, can't stay afloat despite the large and impressive cast. Robert Walker Jr. is no match for Jack Lemmon, who played the original Ensign Pulver in 1955. 104m. **DIR:** Joshua Logan. **CAST:** Robert Walker Jr., Burl Ives, Walter Matthau, Tommy Sands, Millie Perkins, Kay Medford, Larry Hagman, Jack Nicholson. **1964**

ENTANGLED ★★ Judd Nelson overacts his way through this thriller about a jealous American novelist involved in a romantic triangle and murder. Pierce Brosnan's charismatic performance deserves better than this amazingly transparent plot. Rated R for profanity, nudity, and violence. 98m. **DIR:** Max Fischer. **CAST:** Judd Nelson, Pierce Brosnan, Laurence Treil. **1992**

ENTER LAUGHING ★★1/2 Carl Reiner's semiautobiographical comedy, about a young man who shucks his training and ambitions as a pharmacist to become a comedian, is studded with familiar faces and peopled by engaging personalities—but doesn't really leave a lasting memory. 112m. **DIR:** Carl Reiner. **CAST:** Reni Santoni, José Ferrer, Shelley Winters, Elaine May, Jack Gilford, Janet Margolin, Michael J. Pollard, Don Rickles, Rob Reiner, Nancy Kovack. **1967**

ENTER THE DRAGON ★★★★ Bruce Lee soared to international superstardom with this fast-paced, tongue-in-cheek kung fu film. A big-budget American version of the popular Chinese genre, it has a good plot and strong performances—from Lee, John Saxon, and Jim Kelly. Rated R due to violence. 97m. **DIR:** Robert Clouse.

CAST: Bruce Lee, John Saxon, Jim Kelly, Ahna Capri, Yang Tse, Angela Mao. **1973 DVD**

ENTER THE NINJA ★★ A passable martial arts adventure about practitioners of an ancient Oriental art of killing. Rated R. 94m. **DIR:** Menahem Golan. **CAST:** Franco Nero, Susan George, Sho Kosugi, Alex Courtney. **1981**

ENTERTAINER, THE ★★★★ Laurence Olivier is brilliant as Archie Rice, a self-deceiving, low-moraled, small-talent vaudeville song-and-dance man in this slice-of-life drama based on the play written especially for him by John Osborne. Constantly nagged about his failures, insulted by audiences, and careless of all who love him, Archie is finally brought down by a raging ego that demands undeserved admiration. Olivier reveled in the role, declaring, "It's what I really am. I am not Hamlet." 97m. **DIR:** Tony Richardson. **CAST:** Laurence Olivier, Brenda de Banzie, Joan Plowright, Roger Livesey, Alan Bates, Albert Finney. **1960 DVD**

ENTERTAINING ANGELS ★★★★ This biography of Dorothy Day, who devoted her life to helping the poor and homeless beginning in the Great Depression, is inspirational in the best sense of the word. Although produced by a religious group, this film shows how one person truly can make a difference. This is an excellent family film. Rated PG-13 for adult situations and a little profanity. 111m. **DIR:** Michael Ray Rhodes. **CAST:** Moira Kelly, Martin Sheen, Heather Graham, Lenny von Dohlen, Melinda Dillon, Paul Lieber, Brian Keith, Tracey Walter, Allyce Beasley. **1996**

ENTERTAINING MR. SLOANE ★★ Joe Orton, the young British playwright whose short life formed the basis of *Prick Up Your Ears*, wrote the play from which this film was made. Neither play nor film has aged well. An amoral young man is taken in at a house where both a grotesque middle-aged woman and her brother, a latent homosexual, have romantic designs on him. Well performed, but no longer shocking enough to be effective. Not rated. 94m. **DIR:** Douglas Hickox. **CAST:** Beryl Reid, Peter McEnery, Harry Andrews, Alan Webb. **1970**

ENTITY, THE 🦃 Barbara Hershey stars as a woman who is sexually molested by an invisible, sex-crazed demon. Rated R for nudity, profanity, violence, and rape. 115m. **DIR:** Sidney J. Furie. **CAST:** Barbara Hershey, Ron Silver, Jacqueline Brooks. **1983**

ENTRAPMENT ★★ Disappointing thriller wastes the talents of Sean Connery, a world-class thief who appears to be ensnared in the web of a sexy insurance investigator (Catherine Zeta-Jones). Slow start and preposterous ending can't be salvaged by decent special effects. Rated PG-13 for violence, language, and partial nudity. 112m. **DIR:** Jon Amiel. **CAST:** Sean Connery, Catherine Zeta-Jones, Ving Rhames, Maury Chaykin, Will Patton. **1999 DVD**

ENTRE NOUS (BETWEEN US) ★★★★★ This down-to-earth, highly human story by director Diane Kurys concentrates on the friendship between two women, Madeline (Miou-Miou) and Lena (Isabelle Huppert), who find they have more in common with each other than with their husbands. It is an affecting tale the viewer won't soon forget. Rated PG for nudity, suggested sex, and violence. 110m. **DIR:** Diane Kurys. **CAST:** Miou-Miou, Isabelle Huppert, Guy Marchand. **1983 DVD**

ENTROPY ★★1/2 Stephen Dorff plays a very demanding new director who keeps having problems with the production, cast, and crew of his inaugural film. While bringing his movie together, Dorff's social life begins to fall apart, too. This movie is full of fine performances, but suffers from a plot and pace that quickly atrophy. Rated R. 110m. **DIR:** Phil Joanou. **CAST:** Stephen Dorff, Judith Godreche, Kelly Macdonald, Lauren Holly, Hector Elizondo. **1999**

•EPICENTER ★★1/2 A U.S. agent, assigned to escort a criminal to an interrogation, finds her job much more difficult when a huge quake hits L.A., raining debris and chaos everywhere. So-so action film with average special effects and a determined, tough performance by Traci Lords. Rated R for violence, sexuality, and profanity. 89m. **DIR:** Richard Pepin. **CAST:** Traci Lords, Gary Daniels, Jeff Fahey. **2000**

EQUALIZER, THE: "MEMORIES OF MANON" ★★★ Edward Woodward's commanding performance as *The Equalizer* gives weight to this made-for-TV release about a New York avenger and his discovery of danger stalking the daughter (Melissa Anderson) he didn't know he had. Fans of Woodward will enjoy a second look. 96m. **DIR:** Tony Wharmby. **CAST:** Edward Woodward, Melissa Sue Anderson, Anthony Zerbe, Robert Lansing, Jon Polito, Keith Szarabajka. **1988**

EQUINOX (1993) ★★1/2 Oodles of glossy style and a fine Matthew Modine performance aren't quite enough to maintain intense interest in this enigmatic, surreal tale of twin brothers—timid, shy writer, Henry, and mean-spirited criminal, Freddy. Lara Flynn Boyle costars as a woman who draws the brothers together. Though writer-director Rudolph offers intriguing ideas, he's never quite clear or passionate enough to bring the ideas home. Rated R, with profanity. 100m. **DIR:** Alan Rudolph. **CAST:** Matthew Modine, Lara Flynn Boyle, Fred Ward. **1993**

EQUINOX (THE BEAST) (1971) ★★ Good special effects save this unprofessional movie about college students searching for their archaeology professor. On their search, they must face monsters and the occult. Rated PG. 82m. **DIR:** Jack Woods. **CAST:** Edward Connell, Barbara Hewitt. **1971**

EQUINOX FLOWER ★★★★ An interesting look at the Japanese custom of arranged marriages. Setsuko's parents had an arranged marriage and want the same for her; she, having found her own true love, rebels. In Japanese with English subtitles. Not rated, but suitable for all audiences. 115m. **DIR:** Yasujiro Ozu. **CAST:** Shin Saburi. **1958**

EQUUS ★★★★ Peter Firth plays a stable boy whose mysterious fascination with horses results in an act of meaningless cruelty and violence. Richard Burton plays the psychiatrist brought in to uncover Firth's hidden hostilities. The expanding of Peter Shaffer's play leaves the film somewhat unfocused but the scenes between Burton and Firth are intense, riveting, and beautifully acted. This was Burton's last quality film role; he was nominated for best actor. Rated R for profanity and nudity. 137m. **DIR:** Sidney Lumet. **CAST:** Richard Burton, Peter Firth, Colin Blakely, Joan Plowright, Harry Andrews, Eileen Atkins, Jenny Agutter. **1977**

ER: THE SERIES PREMIERE ★★★★★ The pilot for the high-rated television series created by Michael Crichton features the adventures, both inspiring and tragic, of the employees of an emergency room. Brilliantly acted, tautly directed, and expertly written, this is network television at its best. Not rated. 90m. **DIR:** Rod Holcomb. **CAST:** Anthony Edwards, George Clooney, Sherry Stringfield, Noah Wyle, Eriq La Salle, Miguel Ferrer. **1995**

ERASABLE YOU ★★★ Black comedy about a divorced man who lives in poverty with his new wife because the first one claims his entire salary in alimony. They hire a hit man to kill her, unleashing a flood of unforeseeable complications. A sleeper with funny twists. Not rated; contains profanity and violence. 85m. **DIR:** Harry Bromley-Davenport. **CAST:** Timothy Busfield, M. Emmet Walsh, Melora Hardin. **1998**

ERASER ★★★ Arnold Schwarzenegger plays a federal marshal working for the Witness Protection Program. To protect his witness—a defense-contractor employee who discovers illegal sales of superweapons to foreign buyers—and maintain world peace, Schwarzenegger wipes out half the planet. Lots of shoot-outs and explosions, but only two or three scenes display the grand-scale fun and inventiveness we have come to expect from an Arnold actioner. Rated R for violence and profanity. 107m. **DIR:** Charles Russell. **CAST:** Arnold Schwarzenegger, James Caan, Vanessa L. Williams, James Coburn, Robert Pastorelli. **1996 DVD**

ERASERHEAD ★★★ Weird, weird movie . . . Director David Lynch created this nightmarish film about Henry Spencer (Jack Nance), who, we assume, lives in the far (possibly post-apocalyptic) future when everyone is given a free lobotomy at birth. Nothing else could explain the bizarre behavior of its characters. B&W; 90m. **DIR:** David Lynch. **CAST:** Jack Nance, Charlotte Stewart, Jeanne Bates. **1978 DVD**

ERENDIRA ★★1/2 In this disturbing and distasteful black comedy, Irene Papas stars as a wealthy old woman who loses everything in a fire accidentally set by her sleepwalking granddaughter, Erendira (Claudia Ohana). The grandmother turns her charge into a prostitute and insists that she earn back over $1 million. In Spanish with English subtitles. Not rated, the film has nudity, profanity, simulated sex, and violence. 103m. **DIR:** Ruy Guerra. **CAST:** Irene Papas, Claudia Ohana, Michel Lonsdale. **1983**

ERIC ★★★★ This made-for-TV movie is the true story of Eric Lund, a teenager with a promising athletic future who becomes terminally ill. John Savage, in the title role, gives a meaningful portrayal of a young man who refuses to give up. Patricia Neal, as the mother, gives the kind of warm, sensitive performance she is noted for, and there is a fine supporting cast. 100m. **DIR:** James Goldstone. **CAST:** Patricia Neal, John Savage, Claude Akins, Sian Barbara Allen, Mark Hamill, Nehemiah Persoff. **1975**

ERIK THE VIKING ★★★ The first half hour of this account of the exploits of Erik the Red is so awful, one is tempted to hit the reject button. However, perseverance pays off in this movie from ex-Monty Python crazy Terry Jones. It actually gets to be fun. Rated PG-13 for profanity and suggested sex. 106m. **DIR:** Terry Jones. **CAST:** Tim Robbins, Mickey Rooney, Eartha Kitt, Terry Jones, Imogen Stubbs, John Cleese, Antony Sher. **1989**

ERIN BROCKOVICH ★★★★1/2 Part legal drama and part advocacy cinema, and fueled throughout by Julia Roberts's most personal performance to date, this engaging film is smart, sassy, and quietly chilling, the latter because it's based on frankly horrifying events that occurred in an isolated California desert community early in the 1990s. Susannah Grant's deft script turns Roberts into an unlikely heroine: a single mother, with three young children, who we meet as she's trying to obtain yet another job. Circumstances finally bring her to the offices of an independent attorney (Albert Finney, also excellent), where Erin's natural curiosity and intelligence flame after coming across a "routine" real estate transaction laced with medical records. Watch for the actual Erin Brockovich early on, in a brief appearance as a waitress. Rated R for profanity. 130m. **DIR:** Steven Soderbergh. **CAST:** Julia Roberts, Albert Finney, Aaron Eckhart, Marg Helgenberger, Cherry Jones. **2000 DVD**

ERMO ★★1/2 A provincial Chinese noodle seller envies her neighbor's color TV—not to mention the neighbor's virile young husband. This domestic comedy has appealing players, but a leaden pace and far too many shots of noodles being squeezed out of an ancient pasta maker. In Mandarin with English subtitles (which are often unintentionally amusing). Not rated; suitable for general audiences. 93m. **DIR:** Zhou Xiaowen. **CAST:** Alia, Liu Pei Qi, Ge Zhijun, Zhang Haiyan. **1994**

ERNEST GOES TO AFRICA ★★ The lovable oaf heads to Africa, where he finds adventure and romance. Even though this outing was filmed entirely on that continent, it's strictly for die-hard fans who haven't grown tired of his mugging. Rated PG. 90m. **DIR:** John R. Cherry, III. **CAST:** Jim Varney, Linda Kash, Jamie Bartlett. **1997**

ERNEST GOES TO CAMP 🦃 Could have been called *Meatballs XI* for all the originality it contains. Rated PG for profanity and scatological humor. 95m. **DIR:** John R. Cherry, III. **CAST:** Jim Varney, Victoria Racimo, John Vernon, Iron Eyes Cody, Lyle Alzado. **1987**

ERNEST GOES TO JAIL ★★★★ Comic gem in which the indisputably talented Jim Varney plays not only the well-meaning and dim-witted Ernest P. Worrell but also the crafty villain of the piece. Rated PG for brief violence. 82m. **DIR:** John R. Cherry, III. **CAST:** Jim Varney, Gailard Sartain, Randall "Tex" Cobb, Charles Napier. **1990**

ERNEST GREEN STORY, THE ★★★★1/2 This true story of the first black graduate of Little Rock, Arkansas's Central High School in 1958 shows racism at its ugliest and determination at its most magnificent. Ernest Green, along with eight other brave black students, withstood taunts, threats, and attacks to enforce the 1954 Supreme Court decision opposing segregated schools. Superb acting and an outstanding musical score. Not rated; contains violence and racial slurs. 101m. **DIR:** Eric Laneuville. **CAST:** Morris Chestnut, C.C.H. Pounder, Gary Grubbs, Tina Lifford, Avery Brooks, Ruby Dee. **1992**

ERNEST IN THE ARMY ★★ In order to fulfill his dream of driving tanks, Ernest P. Worrell joins the Army Reserves, where he creates havoc for his superiors and a disgruntled Middle East dictator who is no match for the goofy grunt. Pretty much what you would expect from this franchise. Rated PG. 85m. **DIR:** John R. Cherry, III. **CAST:** Jim Varney, Hayley Tyson, David Miller. **1997**

ERNEST RIDES AGAIN ★★ *Ernest Rides Again*, and again, and again. The series has almost run out of steam in this weak entry, as Ernest discovers a long-lost Revolutionary War cannon, rumored to hold the real Crown Jewels of England. It's a race to see who can get to the cannon first, but no one crosses the finish line in terms of evoking laughs. Tape contains featurette, *Mr. Bill Goes to Washington*. Rated PG for mild innuendo. 100m. **DIR:** John R. Cherry, III. **CAST:** Jim Varney, Ron K. James, Duke Ernsberger, Linda Kash, Jeffrey Pillars. **1993**

ERNEST SAVES CHRISTMAS ★★★ In this family movie, a vast improvement over *Ernest Goes to Camp*, TV pitchman Jim Varney returns as Ernest P. Worrell. This time the obnoxious but well-meaning Ernest attempts to help Santa Claus (Douglas Seale) find a successor. The script is funny without being moronic, and sentimental without being maudlin. Rated PG. 95m. **DIR:** John R. Cherry, III. **CAST:** Jim Varney, Douglas Seale, Oliver Clark, Billie Bird. **1988**

ERNEST SCARED STUPID ★★★1/2 Ernest P. Worrell accidentally reawakens a troll from its 200 year old tomb and puts the town's children in danger. While those with an aversion to slapstick may not enjoy it, this horror spoof is old-fashioned movie fun. Rated PG for scary stuff. 91m. **DIR:** John R. Cherry, III. **CAST:** Jim Varney, Eartha Kitt. **1991**

ERNIE KOVACS: TELEVISION'S ORIGINAL GENIUS ★★★★ This tribute to the late Ernie Kovacs, produced for cable television, is a series of clips from Kovacs's television career along with comments from friends and family. Those familiar with Kovacs's work will fondly remember his innovative creations: Percy Dovetonsils, Eugene, and the Nairobi Trio. For others, this serves as an introduction to Kovacs's comic genius. 86m. **DIR:** Keith Burns. **CAST:** Ernie Kovacs, Edie Adams, Jack Lemmon, Steve Allen, Chevy Chase, John Barbour. **1982**

EROTIKILL ★★ The indefatigable Spanish director Jess Franco—who's made so many cheap exploitation pictures, even *he* can't remember them all—is at the helm, and, briefly, in the cast of this raunchy opus about a female bloodsucker (Lina Romay) prowling the decadent Riviera. Definitely not for the kiddies, or the easily offended. You can find an even more explicit U.S. video edition under the title *Loves of Irina*. Rated R. 90m. **DIR:** Jess (Jesus) Franco. **CAST:** Lina Romay, Jack Taylor, Alice Arno. **1981**

EROTIQUE ★★★ Four internationally known female directors contribute a segment each to this collection of short films. Best is Taiwanese Clara Law's story of young lovers restrained by cultural barriers, but all of the stories are intriguing, despite the obvious low budgets. Not rated; contains nudity, profanity, and sexual situations. 120m. **DIR:** Lizzie Borden, Monika Treut, Ana Maria Magalhaes, Clara Law. **CAST:** Priscilla Barnes, Camilla Soeberg, Claudia Ohana. **1995 DVD**

ERRAND BOY, THE ★★★ One of Jerry Lewis's better solo efforts, as he proceeds (in his own inimitable style) to make a shambles of the Hollywood movie studio where he is employed as the local gofer. Very funny. B&W; 92m. **DIR:** Jerry Lewis. **CAST:** Jerry Lewis, Brian Donlevy, Sig Ruman. **1961**

ERUPTION ★★ An American photojournalist in a South American country is endangered by both rebel attempts to unseat the country's dictator and a volcano that's about to blow. Typical slapdash Roger Corman production that seems to exist mostly as an excuse to use some volcano footage. Rated R for profanity and violence. 106m. **DIR:** Gwyneth Gibby. **CAST:** F. Murray Abraham, Cyril O'Reilly, Patricia Velazquez. **1998**

ESCAPADE IN FLORENCE Uninspired story about two young men and their misadventures in picturesque Italy. 80m. **DIR:** Steve Previn. **CAST:** Ivan Desny, Tommy Kirk, Annette Funicello, Nino Castelnuovo. **1962**

ESCAPADE IN JAPAN ★★★1/2 Little Jon Provost, his friend Roger Nakagawa, and Japan itself are the stars of this charming film about a young boy who survives an airplane crash in Japan and is taken in by a family of isolated fishers. This is one of the all-time best kids-on-the-run films. 93m. **DIR:** Arthur Lubin. **CAST:** Jon Provost, Roger Nakagawa, Cameron Mitchell, Teresa Wright. **1957**

ESCAPE, THE ★★ A convict escapes from prison and falls in love with a young woman. Then the authorities catch up with him. Not rated, but contains nudity, violence, and profanity. 91m. **DIR:** Stuart Gillard. **CAST:** Patrick Dempsey, Brigitte Bako, Colm Feore, Vincent Gale, W. Morgan Sheppard. **1995**

ESCAPE ARTIST, THE ★★ Confusing, rambling account of a boy (Griffin O'Neal, who might be appealing with better material) who uses a love of magic and escape artistry to frame the city politicos responsible for killing his father. Rated PG—mild violence and profanity. 96m. **DIR:** Caleb Deschanel. **CAST:** Griffin O'Neal, Raul Julia, Teri Garr, Joan Hackett, Desi Arnaz Sr. **1982**

ESCAPE CLAUSE ★★★ Insurance actuary Andrew McCarthy is stunned to learn he's the target of a killer, supposedly hired by his wife . . . and then his wife turns up dead! Scripter Danilo Bach's clever little thriller rises above the usual genre melodrama and should keep you guessing until the very end. Rated R for violence, nudity, profanity, and simulated sex. 95m. **DIR:** Brian Trenchard-Smith. **CAST:** Andrew McCarthy, Paul Sorvino, Connie Britton, Kate McNeil, Kenneth Welsh. **1996**

ESCAPE FROM ALCATRAZ ★★★★ Any movie that combines the talents of star Clint Eastwood and director Don Siegel is more than watchable. This is a gripping and believable film about the 1962 breakout from the supposedly perfect prison. Patrick McGoohan is also excellent as the neurotic warden. Rated PG. 112m. **DIR:** Don Siegel. **CAST:** Clint Eastwood, Patrick McGoohan, Roberts Blossom, Jack Thibeau. **1979 DVD**

ESCAPE FROM ATLANTIS ★★★ Escapist family adventure stars Jeff Speakman as a father who treats his family to a cruise in the Bahamas. When they enter the Bermuda Triangle, they are transported to the mythical land of Atlantis. The ooh-and-aah factor wears off when his daughter is mistaken for the long-lost queen and an evil king refuses to let her leave the island. Lots of fun and imagination in this made-for-cable effort. Rated PG-13 for violence. 93m. **DIR:** Strathford Hamilton. **CAST:** Jeff Speakman, Tim Thomerson, Justin Burnette, Mercedes McNab, Breck Wilson, Brian Bloom. **1997**

ESCAPE FROM FORT BRAVO ★★★1/2 Union officer William Holden is in charge of a wilderness outpost holding Confederate prisoners. He must keep them in while trying to keep out marauding Indians. Good suspense and action scenes. B&W; 98m. **DIR:** John Sturges. **CAST:** William Holden, Eleanor Parker, John Forsythe, William Demarest, William Campbell, John Lupton, Richard Anderson, Polly Bergen. **1953**

ESCAPE FROM MARS ★★ Plodding sci-fi flick about the first manned trip to Mars. Rated PG. 88m. **DIR:** Neill L. Fearnley. **CAST:** Christine Elise, Peter Outerbridge, Allison Hossack, Michael Shanks. **1999**

ESCAPE FROM NEW YORK ★★★1/2 The year is 1997. *Air Force One*—with the president (Donald Pleasence) on board—is hijacked by a group of revolutionaries and sent crashing into the middle of Manhattan, which has been turned into a top-security prison. It's up to Snake Plissken (Kurt Russell), a former war hero gone renegade, to get him out in twenty-four hours. It's fun, surprise-filled entertainment. Rated R. 99m. **DIR:** John Carpenter. **CAST:** Kurt Russell, Lee Van Cleef, Ernest Borgnine, Donald Pleasence, Adrienne Barbeau. **1981 DVD**

ESCAPE FROM SOBIBOR ★★★★ Inspiring true-life tale of the largest prisoner escape from a Nazi death camp, with a superior cast led by Alan Arkin. Harrowing prison camp scenes elevate the suspense as the prisoners plan and then execute their daring escape. Edited for video, this made-for-television entry rises to the occasion with a tight script by Reginald Rose. 120m. **DIR:** Jack Gold. **CAST:** Rutger Hauer, Alan Arkin, Joanna Pacula. **1987 DVD**

ESCAPE FROM SURVIVAL ZONE ★★ On the eve of World War III, a trio of television journalists take a course in survival training, only to face a whacked-out former Marine commander. Predictable melodrama. Not rated; contains violence and profanity. 85m. **DIR:** Chris Jones. **CAST:** Terrence Ford, Paris Jefferson, Raymond Johnson. **1991**

ESCAPE FROM THE KGB 🦃 A jet-setting CIA agent is sent to infiltrate a Siberian spaceport. Insipid. Not rated. 99m. **DIR:** Harald Phillipe. **CAST:** Thomas Hunter, Marie Versini, Ivan Desny, Walter Barnes. **1987**

ESCAPE FROM THE PLANET OF THE APES ★★★ Escaping the nuclear destruction of their own world and time, intelligent simians Roddy McDowall and Kim Hunter arrive on ours. This third *Apes* entry makes wonderful use of the *Strangers in a Strange Land* theme, which turns ugly all too quickly as humanity decides to destroy the apes. Rated G. 98m. **DIR:** Don Taylor. **CAST:** Roddy McDowall, Kim Hunter, Eric Braeden, Bradford Dillman, William Windom, Ricardo Montalban. **1971**

ESCAPE: HUMAN CARGO ★★★1/2 This fact-based thriller concerns the frustrating series of events that began in 1977, when Texan John McDonald (Treat Williams) contracted to build prefab housing in Saudi Arabia. Williams is credible as the headstrong American unwilling to tolerate dishonesty or abuse, who only gradually realizes that he's in over his head and must outwit his "hosts" if he is to survive. Rated R for nudity, profanity, and violence. 110m. **DIR:** Simon Wincer. **CAST:** Treat Williams, Stephen Lang, Sasson Gabay, Zeev Revach. **1997**

ESCAPE ME NEVER ★★★ A blend of colorful personalities keeps this one afloat. Since it isn't typical of any of the major stars involved, it's interesting to see how a sophisticated composer handles his loveless marriage and his passionate love of music. B&W; 105m. **DIR:** Peter Godfrey. **CAST:** Errol Flynn, Ida Lupino, Eleanor Parker, Gig Young, Reginald Denny, Isobel Elsom, Albert Basserman, Ludwig Stossel. **1947**

ESCAPE TO ATHENA ★★★ Roger Moore as a Nazi officer? Sonny Bono as a member of the Italian Resistance? Elliott Gould as a hippie in a World War II concentration camp? Sound ridiculous? It is. It's a *Hogan's Heroes* for the big screen but, in a dumb sort of way, entertaining. Rated PG. 101m. **DIR:** George Pan Cosmatos. **CAST:** Roger Moore, Telly Savalas, David Niven, Claudia Cardinale, Stefanie Powers, Richard Roundtree, Elliott Gould, Sonny Bono. **1979**

ESCAPE TO BURMA 🦃 A tea plantation, wild animals, and a hunted man seeking refuge. B&W; 87m. **DIR:** Allan Dwan. **CAST:** Barbara Stanwyck, Robert Ryan, David Farrar, Murvyn Vye. **1955**

ESCAPE TO LOVE ★★★ This adventurous romance pits a beautiful American student (Clara Perryman) and her lover against the Polish KGB as they speed on a train toward Paris. Their passion increases to a point where they must both reach a life-changing decision. 105m. **DIR:** Herb Stein. **CAST:** Clara Perryman. **1982**

ESCAPE TO THE SUN ★★★ Two young university students try to escape from the oppressive Soviet Union under the watchful eyes of the KGB. They try first for an exit visa; only one visa is issued, and one of the students is taken into custody. The two are forced to make a heroic escape to the West. Rated PG for violence. 94m. **DIR:** Menahem Golan. **CAST:** Laurence Harvey, Josephine Chaplin, John Ireland, Jack Hawkins. **1972**

ESCAPE TO WHITE MOUNTAIN ★★ Hard-to-like teenager runs away from his father and their junkyard. When a kindly Apache man gives him a lift, he introduces the teen to Apache beliefs, which is the only highlight to an otherwise poorly acted, low-budget film. When the Apaches speak among themselves, English subtitles are used. Not rated; contains profanity and violence. 80m. **DIR:** Rob Sabal. **CAST:** Caleb Smith, Ethelbah Midnite, Caesar Del Trecco, Mike Minjarez. **1994**

ESCAPE TO WITCH MOUNTAIN ★★★1/2 In this engaging Disney mystery-fantasy, two children with strange powers are pursued by men who want to use them for evil purposes. It's good! Rated G. 97m. **DIR:** John Hough. **CAST:** Eddie Albert, Ray Milland, Kim Richards, Ike Eisenmann. **1975**

ESCAPE 2000 🦃 A nauseating science-fiction film from Britain, this consists of a series of close-ups of people in the throes of death. Rated R. 92m. **DIR:** Brian Trenchard-Smith. **CAST:** Steve Railsback, Olivia Hussey, Michael Craig, Carmen Duncan, Roger Ward. **1981**

ESCAPE UNDER PRESSURE ★★ An archaeologist and her husband battle against antiquities smugglers to save a pair of rare idols from falling into the wrong hands. Low-budget action-adventure that never seems to take off. Rated R. 91m. **DIR:** Jean Pellerin. **CAST:** Rob Lowe, Larissa Miller, Harry Van Gorkum, Craig Wasson. **1999 DVD**

ESCAPES ★★★ Low-budget anthology in the *Twilight Zone* vein, featuring six stories of the bizarre and done with great style by director David Steensland. Top honors go to "A Little Fishy," a grimly funny tale, and "Who's There?" a neat yarn about an escaped laboratory experiment and a Sunday jogger. 71m. **DIR:** David Steensland. **CAST:** Vincent Price, Michael Patton-Hall, John Mitchum, Todd Fulton, Jerry Grisham, Ken Thorley. **1985**

•ESSEX BOYS ★★ The cast, including Sean Bean *(Ronin)* and Tom Wilkinson *(Shakespeare in Love)*, decently approaches this British Tarantino clone about an ex-gangster just released from prison attempting to regain control of the streets he left behind, but their efforts are in vain. The story is pedestrian and familiar, while the conflicts lack the intensity of real life. Rated R for adult situations, drug use, language, and violence. 103m. **DIR:** Terry Winsor. **CAST:** Sean Bean, Alex Kingston, Charlie Creed-Miles, Tom Wilkinson, Larry Lamb. **2000 DVD**

E.T.—THE EXTRA-TERRESTRIAL ★★★★★ The most entertaining science-fiction film of all time, this is Steven Spielberg's gentle fairy tale about what happens when a young boy meets up with a very special fellow from outer space. Sheer wonder is joined with warmth and humor in this movie classic. Rated PG. 115m. **DIR:** Steven Spielberg. **CAST:** Dee Wallace, Henry Thomas, Peter Coyote, Robert MacNaughton, Drew Barrymore. **1982**

ETERNAL, THE ★★ Murky supernatural thriller about an American woman haunted by memories of her ancestral home in Ireland. When her hallucinations start controlling her life she packs up her husband and son to return home. Instead of a warm welcome from her creepy uncle, she gets chills from what he has stored down in the basement. Despite its eerie look, the film fails to generate anything more than an occasional jump moment. Rated R for adult situations, language, and violence. 95m. **DIR:** Michael Almereyda. **CAST:** Alison Elliott, Jared Harris, Lois Smith, Rachel O'Rourke, Christopher Walken, Jason Miller. **1998 DVD**

ETERNAL EVIL ★★★ This mystical thriller has a filmmaker experimenting with astral projection and running afoul of souls who jump from one body to another when one is used up. Intriguing film with slick production values. Rated R for violence. 86m. **DIR:** George Mihalka. **CAST:** Winston Rekert, Karen Black. **1986 DVD**

ETERNAL RETURN, THE ★★★ Interesting modern adaptation of the Tristan and Isolde legend from a script by Jean Cocteau. In French with English subtitles. B&W; 110m. **DIR:** Jean Delannoy. **CAST:** Jean Marais, Madeleine Sologne, Jean Murat. **1943**

ETERNALLY YOURS ★★★ A stellar cast of accomplished scene stealers deftly brings off this iffy story of a magician (David Niven) and his wife (Loretta Young), who thinks his tricks are overshadowing their marital happiness. B&W; 95m. **DIR:** Tay Garnett. **CAST:** Loretta Young, David Niven, C. Aubrey Smith, ZaSu Pitts, Billie Burke, Eve Arden, Hugh Herbert, Broderick Crawford. **1939**

ETERNITY A reincarnated goodie-two-shoes battling his greedy brother. Rated R for nudity and simulated sex. 122m. **DIR:** Steven Paul. **CAST:** Jon Voight, Armand Assante, Wilford Brimley, Eileen Davidson. **1990**

ETHAN FROME ★★★★ Edith Wharton's austere novel about nineteenth-century Puritan values and doomed love is given an equally austere film treatment in this longish but well-acted drama. Liam Neeson is memorable as the title character, a deformed recluse. Joan Allen plays Frome's bitter wife while Patricia Arquette steals his heart and seals his fate. A bit severe, chilly, and static for some viewers—others will love its literary purity. Rated PG. 147m. **DIR:** John Madden. **CAST:** Liam Neeson, Patricia Arquette, Joan Allen, Katharine Houghton. **1993**

EUBIE! ★★★★ Originally a Broadway tribute to legendary composer Eubie Blake, this is nonstop song, dance, and vaudeville entertainment. Gregory Hines and Maurice Hines are outstanding with their toe-stomping tap routines. About twenty of Blake's tunes are performed on this tape—including "I'm Just Wild About Harry," "I've Got the Low Down Blues," and "In Honeysuckle Time." Not rated. 85m. **DIR:** Julianne Boyd. **CAST:** Gregory Hines, Terri Burrell, Maurice Hines, Leslie Dockery. **1981**

EUREKA ★★★★1/2 Another stunner from Nicolas Roeg is about an ambitious gold miner (Gene Hackman) who makes his fortune in the snowbound Canadian wilderness, then retires to his very own Caribbean island. Rated R for sex, nudity, violence, and profanity. 130m. **DIR:** Nicolas Roeg. **CAST:** Gene Hackman, Theresa Russell, Rutger Hauer, Jane Lapotaire, Mickey Rourke, Ed Lauter, Joe Pesci. **1983**

EUROPA, EUROPA ★★★★ Based on the autobiography of Solomon Perel, this stunning film traces the author's real-life death-defying adventures during World War II in war-torn Europe. A Jewish teenager who first masquerades as a Communist and later is accepted into the Nazi Youth Party, Perel sees the war from all sides in this ironic, spine-tingling story. In German and Russian with English subtitles. Rated R for nudity. 115m. **DIR:** Agnieszka Holland. **CAST:** Marco Holschneider, Delphine Forest. **1990**

EUROPEANS, THE ★★★★ This intelligent, involving adaptation of the Henry James novel is another wonder from director James Ivory. Lee Remick is one of two freethinking, outspoken foreigners who descend on their Puritan relatives in nineteenth-century New England. The result is a character-rich study of a clash of cultures. Rated PG. 90m. **DIR:** James Ivory. **CAST:** Lee Remick, Robin Ellis, Wesley Addy, Tim Choate, Lisa Eichhorn, Tim Woodward, Kristin Griffith. **1979**

EVE OF DESTRUCTION Gregory Hines is a counterinsurgency expert battling a state-of-the-art female robot. Rated R for violence, nudity, and profanity. 90m. **DIR:** Duncan Gibbins. **CAST:** Gregory Hines, Renee Soutendijk, Michael Greene. **1991**

EVEL KNIEVEL ★★1/2 Autobiography of motorcycle stuntman Evel Knievel. George Hamilton is surprisingly good as Knievel. Some nice stunts. Rated PG. 90m. **DIR:**

Marvin J. Chomsky. **CAST:** George Hamilton, Sue Lyons, Rod Cameron. **1972**

EVELYN PRENTICE ★★★ Myrna Loy kills a blackmailer and her unknowing lawyer husband defends another woman accused of the crime. Strangely remote movie saved by a twist ending and the debut of Rosalind Russell. B&W; 80m. **DIR:** William K. Howard. **CAST:** William Powell, Myrna Loy, Una Merkel, Rosalind Russell, Harvey Stephens, Isabel Jewell, Edward Brophy, Jessie Ralph. **1934**

EVEN COWGIRLS GET THE BLUES ★★ Born with unusually large thumbs, Sissy Hankshaw becomes the world's greatest hitchhiker, a passion she pursues when not hanging out at a health spa with a band of nonconformist cowgirls. An incoherent, undramatic, and humorless adaptation of Tom Robbins's popular, counterculture novel. Rated R for profanity, violence, and suggested sex. 102m. **DIR:** Gus Van Sant. **CAST:** Uma Thurman, John Hurt, Rain Phoenix, Noriyuki "Pat" Morita, Keanu Reeves, Lorraine Bracco, Angie Dickinson, Sean Young, Crispin Glover, Ed Begley Jr., Carol Kane, Roseanne, Buck Henry, Grace Zabriskie, Udo Kier. **1994**

EVENING STAR, THE ★★★1/2 The central cast members of 1983's *Terms of Endearment* reunite for this sequel, adapted from the novel by Larry McMurtry. The results aren't quite as successful, if only because Shirley MacLaine's feisty Aurora isn't given a sparring partner to match Debra Winger's fiery delivery as Emma, in the first film. A few characters vie for that position: Miranda Richardson, as a divorced Houston socialite jealous because she wasn't given custody of Emma's children; and Juliette Lewis, as the most tempestuous of those kids. Marion Ross shines, as Aurora's long-devoted housekeeper, and Jack Nicholson briefly returns as astronaut Garrett Breedlove. MacLaine holds the film together as the true "evening star," who appears first, burns brightest, and lasts longest. Rated PG-13 for profanity, earthy dialogue, and brief nudity. 129m. **DIR:** Robert Harling. **CAST:** Shirley MacLaine, Jack Nicholson, Marion Ross, Miranda Richardson, Mackenzie Astin, George Newbern, Juliette Lewis, Bill Paxton, Ben Johnson, Donald Moffat. **1996 DVD**

EVENT HORIZON ★★ Dreary sci-fi flick just can't seem to gather any kind of momentum. A team of interplanetary rescuers discovers a derelict ship taken over by supernatural forces and then proceeds to die one by one. It's a regrettable waste of a fine cast and intriguing premise. Rated R for violence, profanity, nudity, and suggested sex. 95m. **DIR:** Paul Anderson. **CAST:** Laurence Fishburne, Sam Neill, Kathleen Quinlan, Joely Richardson, Richard T. Jones, Jack Noseworthy. **1997 DVD**

EVER AFTER ★★★★1/2 Exquisite retelling of the *Cinderella* story with a luminous Drew Barrymore as the young charmer who rises above her station to steal the heart of the prince. Anjelica Huston is excellent as the wicked stepmother who schemes to keep Barrymore away from her true love, the crown prince of France. Director Andy Tennant delivers a live-action fairy tale filled with heart and humor, and just the right amount of magic. Rated PG-13 for language. 100m. **DIR:** Andy Tennant. **CAST:** Drew Barrymore, Anjelica Huston, Dougray Scott, Jeanne Moreau. **1998 DVD**

EVERGREEN ★★★★ Superb showcase for the legendary Jessie Matthews spans two generations in its story of a British music-hall entertainer and her talented daughter (both roles played by Jessie Matthews). The captivating Rodgers and Hart score includes "Dancing on the Ceiling" and the rousing showstopper "Over My Shoulder." B&W; 85m. **DIR:** Victor Saville. **CAST:** Jessie Matthews. **1934**

•EVERLASTING PIECE, AN ★★★★ Director Barry Levinson and writer-star Barry McEvoy perfectly complement each other in this frequently amusing tale of two prison barbers who set out to monopolize the hairpiece trade in Belfast. McEvoy and Brian F. O'Byrne shine as the Catholic and Protestant who are willing to set aside their differences in order to take over the wig business from a prisoner who wigged out. As if selling the simple folk of Belfast hairpieces wasn't difficult enough, the two men must stay one step ahead of the competition, who will do anything to put them out of business. The filmmakers find humor in the most unexpected places, creating a film that lives and breathes on its own terms. Rated R for language. 103m. **DIR:** Barry Levinson. **CAST:** Barry McEvoy, Brian F. O'Byrne, Anna Friel, Billy Connolly. **2000 DVD**

EVERLASTING SECRET FAMILY, THE ★★1/2 Strange Australian film about a secret society of powerful men who choose teenage boys to be their possessions. Not rated; contains nudity and sexual situations. 93m. **DIR:** Michael Thornhill. **CAST:** Arthur Dignam, Mark Lee, Heather Mitchell, John Meillon. **1988**

EVERSMILE NEW JERSEY 🦃 Daniel Day-Lewis shows little of the talent he displayed in *My Left Foot*. Here he plays a traveling dentist. As exciting as getting teeth pulled. Rated PG. 103m. **DIR:** Carlos Sorin. **CAST:** Daniel Day-Lewis, Mirjana Jokovic. **1989**

EVERY BREATH ★★ Weak thriller runs out of breath well before the race is over. Judd Nelson stars as a young man who is seduced by a couple's looks, money, and kinky games. As he plays, he finds out that his hosts have some very weird ideas. What might have been decadent is merely docile. Rated R for nudity, adult situations, and language. 89m. **DIR:** Steve Bing. **CAST:** Judd Nelson, Joanna Pacula, Patrick Bauchau. **1993**

EVERY DAY'S A HOLIDAY ★★★1/2 A heavily censored script weakens the Mae West allure, but she still gives us a fascinating picture of highly suggestive sex. West is the only woman in the movie (which she wrote) about a shady lady who impersonates a French singer to get the cops off her back. Most of the movie is just an excuse for her to sing some of her trademark songs. B&W; 80m. **DIR:** A. Edward Sutherland. **CAST:** Mae West, Edmund Lowe, Charles Winninger, Lloyd Nolan, Walter Catlett, Chester Conklin, Charles Butterworth, Louis Armstrong. **1938**

EVERY GIRL SHOULD BE MARRIED ★★1/2 A bit of light comic froth balanced mostly on Cary Grant's charm and polish. He plays a baby doctor. Betsy Drake, who later got him offscreen, plays a salesgirl bent on leading him to the altar. The title is irksome, but the picture's diverting, innocent fun. B&W; 85m. **DIR:** Don Hartman. **CAST:** Cary Grant, Betsy Drake, Franchot Tone, Diana Lynn, Alan Mowbray. **1948**

EVERY MAN FOR HIMSELF AND GOD AGAINST ALL ★★★★ Based on a real incident, the story of Kasper Hauser (Bruno S.) tells of a man who had been kept in confinement since birth. Hauser's appearance in Nuremberg in the 1820s was a mystery. He tried to adjust to a new society while maintaining his own vision. Also released as *The Mystery of Kasper Hauser*. In German with English subtitles. No MPAA rating. 110m. **DIR:** Werner Herzog. **CAST:** Bruno S., Walter Ladengast, Brigitte Mira. **1975**

EVERY MOTHER'S WORST FEAR ★★★ In this made-for-cable original, a 16-year-old girl is lured from home by someone she meets on the Internet. Her mother frantically follows a tenuous thread of clues to track her down. The story is inspired by true events, but this script stretches the credibility a little too thin, despite the valiant acting efforts of Cheryl and Jordan Ladd. Rated PG-13 for violence. 91m. **DIR:** Bill L. Norton. **CAST:** Cheryl Ladd, Jordan Ladd, Robert Wisden, Ted McGinley. **1998**

EVERY OTHER WEEKEND ★★★★ Upset that both her career and her two young children are slipping away from her, a divorced actress kidnaps the children from their father (who has custody) and takes them on the road in the hope of reforging a connection with them. Worth seeing for a typically strong performance by French actress Nathalie Baye, who excels at bringing difficult characters to full life. Not rated; contains adult situations. 100m. **DIR:** Nicole Garcia. **CAST:** Nathalie Baye, Miki Manojlovic. **1990**

EVERY TIME WE SAY GOODBYE ★★★ A change-of-pace role for Tom Hanks, who stars as an American pilot in WWII Jerusalem who falls in love with a young Jewish girl. Hanks brings a certain well-rounded realism to this dramatic part, injecting the seriousness with humor, and Cristina Marsillach is very subtle as the Jewish girl. Rated PG-13 for mild profanity, brief nudity, and mature themes. 97m. **DIR:** Moshe Mizrahi. **CAST:** Tom Hanks, Cristina Marsillach, Benedict Taylor. **1987**

EVERY WHICH WAY BUT LOOSE ★★★ After *Smokey and the Bandit* cleaned up at the box office, Clint Eastwood decided to make his own modern-day cowboy movie. This 1978 release proved to be one of the squinty-eyed star's biggest money-makers. The film is far superior to its sequel, *Any Which Way You Can*. Rated R. 114m. **DIR:** James Fargo. **CAST:** Clint Eastwood, Sondra Locke, Geoffrey Lewis, Clyde (the ape), Ruth Gordon. **1978 DVD**

EVERYBODY SING ★★ Judy Garland is the focus in this let's-put-on-a-show musical. The movie offers a rare performance by Fanny Brice singing comedy songs. The best is "Quainty, Dainty Me." Judy Garland sings swing, and Allan Jones sings love songs in this minor tunefest. B&W; 80m. **DIR:** Edwin L. Marin. **CAST:** Judy Garland, Fanny Brice, Allan Jones, Billie Burke, Monty Woolley, Reginald Gardiner, Henry Armetta. **1938**

EVERYBODY WINS ★★1/2 Private eye Nick Nolte meets woman of mystery Debra Winger and finds himself drawn into her efforts to clear a man convicted of murder. The script by playwright Arthur Miller (his first since *The Misfits* in 1960) has a clever enough plot, but the dialogue is stiff, and director Karel Reisz paces the film at a reckless gallop. Rated R. 94m. **DIR:** Karel Reisz. **CAST:** Nick Nolte, Debra Winger, Will Patton, Judith Ivey, Kathleen Wilhoite, Jack Warden. **1990**

EVERYBODY'S ALL-AMERICAN ★★★1/2 Though a bit long-winded at times, this story (based on a book by *Sports Illustrated*'s Frank Deford) is a must-see for anyone who believes professional athletes have it made. Dennis Quaid is the college football hero who believes he can go on catching passes as a professional forever. He soon finds himself unable to cope. Jessica Lange (as Quaid's wife) and Timothy Hutton round out an unnecessary love triangle. Rated R for profanity and suggested sex. 122m. **DIR:** Taylor Hackford. **CAST:** Dennis Quaid, Jessica Lange, Timothy Hutton, John Goodman. **1988**

EVERYBODY'S FINE ★★★★ Giuseppe Tornatore followed up his international sensation, *Cinema Paradiso,* with this more cynical, more complex, but quite affecting work. Marcello Mastroianni corrals a fabulous late-in-his-career role as an elderly widower who decides to travel about Italy, seeing his grown children. He's under the delusion that "everybody's fine," when in reality they've all gotten into various kinds of trouble or financial difficulty. In Italian with English subtitles. Not rated. 108m. **DIR:** Giuseppe Tornatore. **CAST:** Marcello Mastroianni, Michèle Morgan. **1991**

EVERYONE SAYS I LOVE YOU ★★★ Old-fashioned musical/comedy about what we all go through when we fall in love is filtered through the romances of an extended, affluent, Upper East Side family. Love-struck people—played by usually nonsinging and nondancing actors—suddenly stop their daily routines to croon and shuffle their feet to romantic and exuberant pop chestnuts all over New York, Venice, and Paris. Rated R for language. 101m. **DIR:** Woody Allen. **CAST:** Woody Allen, Natasha Lyonne, Drew Barrymore, Edward Norton, Lukas Haas, Gaby Hoffman, Natalie Portman, Alan Alda, Goldie Hawn, Julia Roberts, Tim Roth. **1996 DVD**

EVERYTHING HAPPENS AT NIGHT ★★★ A Sonja Henie movie with a minimum of ice-skating scenes, this film is largely a vehicle for then newcomers Ray Milland and Robert Cummings. Both fall for Henie, a skater they meet in Europe while trying to uncover the mystery behind a political assassination. It's rather contrived, but it works. B&W; 76m. **DIR:** Irving Cummings. **CAST:** Sonja Henie, Ray Milland, Robert Cummings, Maurice Moscovich, Leonid Kinskey, Alan Dinehart, Fritz Feld, Victor Varconi. **1939**

EVERYTHING RELATIVE ★★★★ You won't find a better or more relevant film about lesbians than this striking independent effort that features top-notch production values, a thoughtful and witty script, plus outstanding performances. The film follows seven female college friends who reunite fifteen years later to reminisce about old times and update their lives. Available in R-rated and not-rated versions; both contain adult situations, language and nudity. 105m. **DIR:** Sharon Pollack. **CAST:** Monica Bell, Gabriella Messina, Stacey Nelkin, Ellen McLaughlin, Olivia Negron, Andrea Weber, Carol Schneider. **1996**

EVERYTHING THAT RISES ★★★★ Dennis Quaid directs and stars in this fine TNT original. His character is a macho cowboy who must confront his own fears when his son is paralyzed. Slow start gives way to riveting emotion so keep the Kleenex handy. Not rated; contains adult themes and violence. 90m. **DIR:** Dennis Quaid. **CAST:** Dennis Quaid, Ryan Merriman, Mare Winningham, Harve Presnell, Meat Loaf. **1998**

EVERYTHING YOU ALWAYS WANTED TO KNOW ABOUT SEX BUT WERE AFRAID TO ASK ★★★★ This gave Woody Allen, scriptwriter, star, and director, an opportunity to stretch out without having to supply all the talent himself. Several sequences do not feature Woody at all. The film is broken up into vignettes supposedly relating to questions asked. Rated R. 87m. **DIR:** Woody Allen. **CAST:** John Carradine, Woody Allen, Lou Jacobi, Louise Lasser, Anthony Quayle, Lynn Redgrave, Tony Randall, Burt Reynolds, Gene Wilder. **1972 DVD**

EVE'S BAYOU ★★★★ This languid, episodic Southern Gothic drama ventures into an African-American family closet and immediately begins rattling skeletons. "The summer I killed my father, I was 10 years old," begins the narration of Eve Baptiste as she nuzzles the film into early 1960s backwater Louisiana, where her affluent family is up to its eyeballs in voodoo, adultery, and emotional turmoil. Rated R for suggested sex, language, and violence. 109m. **DIR:** Kasi Lemmons. **CAST:** Jurnee Smollett, Samuel L. Jackson, Lynn Whitfield, Debbi Morgan, Diahann Carroll. **1997 DVD**

EVIDENCE OF BLOOD ★★★ This small-town mystery reunited *Passion Fish* costars Mary McDonnell and David Strathairn. Dalene Young's script (based on the book by Thomas H. Cook) is filled with genuine plot twists and turns as a Pulitzer Prize–winning author returns to his small hometown for a little rest and relaxation but finds himself drawn to a 40-year-old mystery haunting the locals. Filled with atmosphere and interesting characters, *Evidence of Blood* is a better-than-average made-for-cable thriller that delivers the goods. Rated PG-13 for language and violence. 120m. **DIR:** Andrew Mondshein. **CAST:** Mary McDonnell, David Strathairn. **1997**

EVIL, THE ★★★ Psychologist Richard Crenna, his wife, and some of his students are trapped in an old mansion where an unseen force kills them off one by one. It's your basic haunted-house story with one added twist: the devil himself makes a memorable appearance in the person of Victor Buono, a choice bit of casting. Rated R for violence and nudity. 89m. **DIR:** Gus Trikonis. **CAST:** Richard Crenna, Joanna Pettet, Andrew Prine, Cassie Yates, Victor Buono, Mary Louise Weller. **1978 DVD**

EVIL CLUTCH 🦃 She's a babe, she's a beast, she's a good time, until you get her aroused, and then the monster in her comes out. Most men wouldn't know the difference. Rated R for violence and nudity. 88m. **DIR:** Andreas Marfori. **CAST:** Caralina C. Tassoni, Diego Ribon, Luciano Crovato. **1988**

EVIL DEAD, THE ★★★★ Five college students spending the weekend at a cabin in the Tennessee woods accidentally revive demons who possess their bodies. This low-budget wonder isn't much in the plot department, but it features lots of inventive camera work and gruesome special effects. Most of the violence is committed against unfeeling demons, so it's not that hard to take, though a sequence in which a woman is molested by a tree (!) is in poor taste. Not rated, but the black-humored violence isn't for children. 86m. **DIR:** Sam Raimi. **CAST:** Bruce Campbell, Ellen Sandweiss. **1982 DVD**

EVIL DEAD 2 ★★★1/2 The original *Evil Dead* didn't have a lot of plot, and the sequel has even less. Ash, the survivor of the first film, continues to battle demons in the cabin in the woods. A few lost travelers happen by to provide additional demon fodder. It's more of a remake than a sequel, except that this time director Sam Raimi has explicitly fashioned it as a tribute to one of his greatest influences: the Three Stooges. The overt slapstick may turn off some horror fans. Not rated, it contains nonstop violence and gore. 85m. **DIR:** Sam Raimi. **CAST:** Bruce Campbell, Sarah Barry. **1987 DVD**

EVIL ED ★★★ A quiet film editor becomes a little too involved with his job when he is assigned to work on a gory horror series. This Swedish import (shot in English) may appeal to those with a taste for dry humor as well as die-hard horror buffs, but be forewarned—it is extremely gruesome. Rated R for strong violence, gore, and nudity. 90m. **DIR:** Anders Jacobsson. **CAST:** Johan Ruebeck, Olof Rhodin, Pete Lofbergh. **1995 DVD**

EVIL HAS A FACE ★★1/2 Stiff acting and a predictable plot stunt what could have been an interesting made-for-cable thriller about a police sketch artist who discovers a terrible secret about her own past when she sketches the picture of a child molester. Not rated; contains violence. 95m. **DIR:** Rob Fresco. **CAST:** Sean Young, William R. Moses, Joe Guzaldo. **1996**

EVIL LAUGH 🦃 A typical slasher film about college students spending the weekend in an abandoned house while a crazed serial killer stalks and kills them. Rated R for violence and nudity. 90m. **DIR:** Dominick Brascia. **CAST:** Steven Bad, Dominick Brascia. **1986**

EVIL LIVES ★★ Supernatural silliness about an immortal man who stalks college coeds for the life force necessary to bring his dead lover back to life. Couple of moments of clarity are blurred by flat acting and lifeless direction. Rated R for adult situations, language, nudity, and violence. 90m. **DIR:** Thunder Levin. **CAST:** Tristan Rodgers, Arabella Holzbog, Tyrone Power, Sonia Curtis, Griffin O'Neal, Paul Ben-Victor. **1997**

EVIL MIND, THE (THE CLAIRVOYANT) ★★★ Nicely mounted story of fake mentalist who realizes that his phony predictions are actually coming true. The elegant Claude Rains gives a fine performance as a man who has inexplicably acquired a strange power and finds himself frightened by it. Interesting and fun. B&W; 80m. **DIR:** Maurice Elvey. **CAST:** Claude Rains, Fay Wray, Mary Clare. **1934**

EVIL OBSESSION ★★ Homer (Corey Feldman) joins an acting class to get closer to the supermodel with whom he is obsessed. Is he the one who is brutally murdering other models? You'll have no trouble guessing the identity of the killer in this average erotic thriller. Rated R for nudity, sexual situations, violence, and profanity. 95m. **DIR:** Richard W. Munchkin. **CAST:** Corey Feldman, Kimberly Stevens, Mark Derwin, Brian James. **1995**

EVIL OF DRACULA ★★★ The new teacher at a prestigious girls' school discovers that the headmaster is a vampire. Once you get over seeing Asian actors in a Dracula story, this is a surprisingly good vampire movie. Dubbed in English. Not rated; contains mild violence.

82m. **DIR:** Michio Yamamoto. **CAST:** Toshio Kurosawa, Kunie Tanaka. **1974**

EVIL OF FRANKENSTEIN, THE ★★1/2 A weaker entry in Hammer Films's popular Frankenstein series pits Dr. Frankenstein (Peter Cushing) against an underhanded hypnotist (Peter Woodthorpe). Good production values and handsome set pieces, but the monster makeup is silly and the script convoluted. 98m. **DIR:** Freddie Francis. **CAST:** Peter Cushing, Duncan Lamont, Peter Woodthorpe. **1964**

EVIL ROY SLADE ★★★ Westerns take a beating in this entertaining spoof as bad guy supreme swaps bullets and clichés with his rival and encounters just about every stock character the genre has to offer. One of the best sagebrush satires. Made for TV as a pilot for a proposed series. 97m. **DIR:** Jerry Paris. **CAST:** John Astin, Dick Shawn, Mickey Rooney, Edie Adams, Henry Gibson, Dom DeLuise, Milton Berle. **1972**

EVIL SPAWN 🦃 An antiaging serum turns a vain actress into a giant werebug. Not rated, with nudity, violence, and sexual situations. 88m. **DIR:** Kenneth J. Hall. **CAST:** Bobbie Bresee, John Carradine. **1987 DVD**

EVIL SPIRITS 🦃 Tongue-in-cheek humor fails to save this low-budget shocker about a landlady whose backyard is overcrowded with the buried bodies of her tenants. Rated R for nudity and violence. 95m. **DIR:** Gary Graver. **CAST:** Arte Johnson, Karen Black, Robert Quarry. **1991**

EVIL THAT MEN DO, THE ★★1/2 Believe it or not, Charles Bronson has made a watchable film for a change. He plays a professional killer who comes out of retirement to avenge the brutal murder of an old friend. Rated R for violence and profanity. 90m. **DIR:** J. Lee Thompson. **CAST:** Charles Bronson, Theresa Saldana, José Ferrer, Joseph Maher. **1984 DVD**

EVIL TOONS 🦃 Silly slasher spoof features an animated beast possessing the cleaning lady's body. Rated R for nudity, profanity, and violence. 88m. **DIR:** Fred Olen Ray. **CAST:** Madison Stone, David Carradine, Arte Johnson, Dick Miller. **1990 DVD**

EVIL TOWN 🦃 In a quaint mountain town, a mad doctor is keeping the citizens from aging at the expense of young tourists. Rated R for violence, nudity, and language. 88m. **DIR:** Edward Collins. **CAST:** James Keach, Dean Jagger, Robert Walker Jr., Michele Marsh. **1987**

EVIL UNDER THE SUN ★★★★ This highly entertaining mystery, starring Peter Ustinov as Agatha Christie's Belgian detective Hercule Poirot, is set on a remote island in the Adriatic Sea where a privileged group gathers at a luxury hotel. Of course, someone is murdered and Poirot cracks the case. Rated PG because of a scene involving a dead rabbit. 102m. **DIR:** Guy Hamilton. **CAST:** Peter Ustinov, Jane Birkin, Colin Blakely, James Mason, Roddy McDowall, Diana Rigg, Maggie Smith, Nicholas Clay. **1982 DVD**

EVIL WITHIN, THE ★★★ Gory fun as a parasitic creature crawls out of the bowels of hell and into the womb of an unsuspecting woman who then slaughters every guy she can get into the sack. Rated R for gore, violence, adult situations, and language. 88m. **DIR:** Alain Robak. **CAST:** Emmanuelle Escourrou, Jean-François Gallotte, Christina Sinniger. **1994**

EVILS OF THE NIGHT 🦃 Vampires from outer space hire two idiot mechanics to kidnap teenagers for them. Rated R for nudity, simulated sex, and violence. 85m. **DIR:** Mardi Rustam. **CAST:** Neville Brand, Aldo Ray, John Carradine, Tina Louise, Julie Newmar, Karrie Emerson, Tony O'Dell. **1985**

EVILSPEAK 🦃 A devil-worshiping medieval Spanish priest is brought into modern times by a student on a computer. Rated R for nudity, violence, and gore. 89m. **DIR:** Eric Weston. **CAST:** Clint Howard, R. G. Armstrong, Joe Cortese, Claude Earl Jones. **1982**

EVITA ★★★1/2 The long-awaited film of Andrew Lloyd Webber and Tim Rice's pop opera about the legendary first lady of Argentina (who died of cancer at thirty-three) is musically impressive, well-photographed, and spectacularly staged and edited. Madonna is poised and confident (with the score modified to suit her voice), but the film really belongs to Antonio Banderas, robust and riveting (and with a surprisingly strong singing voice), as the omnipresent narrator swaggering through Evita's life. Rated PG. 134m. **DIR:** Alan Parker. **CAST:** Madonna, Antonio Banderas, Jonathan Pryce, Jimmy Nail. **1996 DVD**

•EVOLUTION ★★★1/2 When a meteor crashes to Earth, the atmosphere on our planet brings to life a host of organisms that evolve at a tremendous rate of speed. A trio of doctors and a would-be fireman are the only hope for humanity, as the military and the politicians make one stupid decision after another. Director Ivan Reitman makes every laugh and special effect count, as if he'd made the film before. Well, in fact, he did—as *Ghostbusters*. But this in no way takes away from the fun of watching this silly, inventive romp. Rated PG-13 for scatological humor. 101m. **DIR:** Ivan Reitman. **CAST:** David Duchovny, Julianne Moore, Orlando Jones, Seann William Scott, Ted Levine, Dan Aykroyd, Ethan Suplee. **2001 DVD**

EVOLUTION'S CHILD ★★★ Scientists discover a three-thousand year old man frozen in the Italian Alps, and ask a fertility doctor to extract the corpse's frozen sperm for a more complete DNA analysis. As you might expect, the sample somehow winds up in one of the doctor's patients, and a unique child is born. At times touching, at times stretching credibility too thin, this made-for-cable original entertains but doesn't seem to offer any new ideas, despite the emphasis on the science of the situation. Not rated. 95m. **DIR:** Jeffrey Reiner. **CAST:** Ken Olin, Taylor Nichols, Heidi Swedberg, Susan Gibney, Jacob Smith. **1999**

EVOLVER ★★★ Engaging high-tech thriller about a new interactive game that begins to think for itself. Teen Ethan Randall is excited when he wins the chance to try out the new "Evolver" in his home. Excitement turns to terror when the family learns the game, a robot that hunts, was actually a prototype for a government weapon. Now it has reverted back to its original program, and the game becomes real. Lots of fun and good special effects make this thriller a good bet. Rated R for violence and language. 90m. **DIR:** Mark Rosman. **CAST:** Ethan Randall, Cindy Pickett, John de Lancie, Cassidy Rae, Paul Dooley. **1994 DVD**

EWOK ADVENTURE, THE ★★ Two children use the help of the friendly Ewok people to find their kidnapped parents in this dull entry in the *Star Wars* family of films. Subpar special effects. Not rated, but would probably rank a PG for mild violence. 96m. **DIR:** John Korty.

CAST: Eric Walker, Warwick Davis, Fionnula Flanagan, Guy Boyd. **1984**

EWOKS: THE BATTLE FOR ENDOR ★★ Those almost too lovable, diminutive rascals from *Return of the Jedi* appear in their own adventure as they try to help two orphans stop an evil entity from destroying them all. Hokey and a bit cutesy. Contains some scenes that may be too intense for children. 98m. **DIR:** Jim Wheat, Ken Wheat. **CAST:** Wilford Brimley, Warwick Davis, Paul Gleason. **1986**

EX, THE ★★1/2 Yancy Butler delivers a deliciously over-the-top performance as a woman who sets out to destroy her ex-husband and his new family. Dierdre (Butler) is definitely psychotic and uses her wiles to infiltrate the family and tear it apart from within. Some genuine moments of suspense can't hide the fact we've seen it all before. Rated R for violence, language, and nudity. 87m. **DIR:** Mark L. Lester. **CAST:** Yancy Butler, Nick Mancuso, Suzy Amis. **1996**

EX-LADY ★★ Early women's lib, with Bette Davis reluctantly marrying her lover, knowing it will take the romance out of their relationship. Nothing much. B&W; 67m. **DIR:** Robert Florey. **CAST:** Bette Davis, Gene Raymond, Frank McHugh. **1933**

EX-MRS. BRADFORD, THE ★★★★ Appealing story about physician William Powell and ex-wife Jean Arthur "keeping company" again is fast and funny. Arthur has a taste for murder mysteries and wants to write them, and Powell is attempting to help the police solve a series of murders. The pace is quick and the dialogue sparkles in this vintage gem. B&W; 80m. **DIR:** Stephen Roberts. **CAST:** William Powell, Jean Arthur, James Gleason, Eric Blore, Robert Armstrong, Lila Lee, Grant Mitchell. **1936**

EXCALIBUR ★★★★ Swords cross and magic abounds in this spectacular, highly enjoyable version of the Arthurian legend. A gritty, realistic view of the rise to power of King Arthur, the forbidden love of Queen Guinevere and Sir Lancelot, and the quest of the Knights of the Round Table for the Holy Grail. Highlighted by lush photography and fine performances. Rated R. 140m. **DIR:** John Boorman. **CAST:** Nicol Williamson, Nigel Terry, Helen Mirren, Nicholas Clay, Cherie Lunghi, Corin Redgrave, Paul Geoffrey, Liam Neeson, Patrick Stewart. **1981 DVD**

EXCALIBUR KID, THE ★★ Boring tale of yet another teen being sent to the time of King Arthur in order to help out in some grand task that apparently only he can achieve. This time out the teen must help Merlin and Arthur recover Excalibur before an evil witch can take over the kingdom. You'll have a case of déjà vu. Rated PG for mild violence and profanity. 90m. **DIR:** James Head. **CAST:** Jason McSkimming, Mak Fyfe, Natalie Ester. **1998**

EXCELLENT CADAVERS ★★★1/2 Chazz Palminteri delivers an impassioned and wholly credible performance as Judge Giovanni Falcone, one of the few individuals who stood up to the increasingly violent Mafia in the 1980s, in this absorbing but inexplicably truncated adaptation of Alexander Stille's fascinating book. Falcone's assignment was tantamount to a death wish in a country where such government crusaders routinely were killed (and thus turned into "excellent cadavers"), but the judge got his big break when a career mafioso (F. Murray Abraham), appalled by his younger colleagues' lack of honor, spilled his guts in a mass trial that became a national sensation. This would have made a superb miniseries, but the film screams of compromise and considerable eleventh-hour trimming. Rated R for violence and profanity. 86m. **DIR:** Ricky Tognazzi. **CAST:** Chazz Palminteri, F. Murray Abraham, Anna Galiena, Andy Luotto, Lina Sastri. **1999 DVD**

EXCESS BAGGAGE 🦃 Neglected rich girl Alicia Silverstone fakes her own kidnapping to get Daddy's attention, then winds up missing for real when thief Benicio Del Toro hijacks her car. Sloppy, witless would-be romantic comedy suffers from moronic dialogue, lurching direction, and an ugly, disheveled look. Rated PG-13 for mild violence and profanity. 101m. **DIR:** Marco Brambilla. **CAST:** Alicia Silverstone, Benicio Del Toro, Christopher Walken, Harry Connick Jr., Nicholas Turturro, Michael Bowen, Jack Thompson. **1997 DVD**

EXCESSIVE FORCE ★★★ Good cast and an unexpected, eleventh-hour snap of the tail enliven this otherwise standard kill-or-be-killed actionfest. Van Damme wannabe Thomas Ian Griffith scripts himself a heroic role as a cop determined to nail syndicate boss Burt Young. Plenty o' kicks and licks and enough intelligent plotting to furrow a few brows. Rated R for profanity, nudity, simulated sex, and excessive violence. 87m. **DIR:** Jon Hess. **CAST:** Thomas Ian Griffith, Lance Henriksen, Tom Hodges, James Earl Jones, Charlotte Lewis, Burt Young. **1993**

EXCESSIVE FORCE II: FORCE ON FORCE ★★ Stacie Randall plays special agent Harly Cordell, who is determined to bring down her ex-boyfriend, a former Navy SEAL turned terrorist. When a series of assassinations rocks Los Angeles, Cordell suspects it's the work of Francis Lydell (Dan Gauthier), the man who left her for dead. Now it's payback time. Rated R for violence, language, and adult situations. 88m. **DIR:** Jonathan Winfrey. **CAST:** Stacie Randall, Dan Gauthier, Jay Patterson, John Mese. **1995**

EXCHANGE, THE ★★ Four brothers lead semicrooked lives in this independent film based on a story that's "mostly true." The one intriguing idea—a true moral dilemma where one brother must kill another to protect the rest of the family—comes in the last twenty minutes. The rest of the film is bogged down by details of the brothers' lives and scams. Rated R for profanity, violence, nudity, and simulated sex. 95m. **DIR:** Ed Nicoletti. **CAST:** Robert Stephenson, Athony Mangano, Robert Wahlberg, Sam Levasser, Les J. N. Mau. **1999**

EXECUTION, THE ★★ Five women survivors of the Holocaust, now living in Los Angeles, have a chance meeting with a former Nazi doctor from their camp. They plot to seduce and then kill him. There is some suspense in this made-for-TV movie, but it is too melodramatic to be believable. 100m. **DIR:** Paul Wendkos. **CAST:** Jessica Walter, Barbara Barrie, Sandy Dennis, Valerie Harper, Michael Lerner, Robert Hooks. **1985**

EXECUTION OF PRIVATE SLOVIK, THE ★★★★ Superior made-for-television film chronicles the fate of American soldier Eddie Slovik, who was executed for desertion during World War II. Intelligent teleplay, powerful performances, and sensitive direction. 120m. **DIR:** Lamont Johnson. **CAST:** Martin Sheen, Ned Beatty, Gary Busey, Charles Haid, Mariclare Costello. **1974**

EXECUTIONER, THE ★★ This British spy picture features George Peppard as an intelligence agent who believes he is being compromised by fellow spy Keith Michell. Joan Collins is the love interest. Average. Rated PG. 107m. **DIR:** Sam Wanamaker. **CAST:** George Peppard, Joan Collins, Judy Geeson, Oscar Homolka, Keith Michell, Nigel Patrick. **1970**

EXECUTIONER'S SONG, THE ★★★1/2 Pulitzer Prize novelist Norman Mailer's made-for-television adaptation of his engrossing account of convicted killer Gary Gilmore's fight to get Utah to carry out his death sentence. The performances of Tommy Lee Jones and Rosanna Arquette are electrifying. Not rated. 200m. **DIR:** Lawrence Schiller. **CAST:** Tommy Lee Jones, Rosanna Arquette, Christine Lahti, Eli Wallach. **1982**

EXECUTIVE ACTION ★★★★ This forceful film, based on Mark Lane's book *Rush to Judgment*, features a fascinating look at possible reasons for the assassination of John F. Kennedy. Rated PG. 91m. **DIR:** David Miller. **CAST:** Burt Lancaster, Robert Ryan, Will Geer, Gilbert Green, John Anderson. **1973**

EXECUTIVE DECISION ★★★★ Kurt Russell, a U.S. government expert on Middle East terrorism, finds himself out of his office and on a do-or-die mission with gung ho commando leader Steven Seagal when an American airliner is taken hostage in midair. Even though this movie runs over two hours, its suspense never flags. Excellent writing, direction, and performances. Rated R for violence and profanity. 135m. **DIR:** Stuart Baird. **CAST:** Kurt Russell, Steven Seagal, Halle Berry, John Leguizamo, Oliver Platt, Joe Morton, David Suchet, Len Cariou, B. D. Wong, Marla Maples Trump. **1996 DVD**

EXECUTIVE POWER ★★ A good cast is wasted in this tired political thriller about an ex–Secret Service agent investigating whether the death of a presidential adviser was really suicide. Rated R for violence and profanity. 97m. **DIR:** David R. Corley. **CAST:** Craig Sheffer, John Heard, Andrea Roth, Joanna Cassidy, William Atherton, Denise Crosby. **1997**

EXECUTIVE SUITE ★★★★ An all-star cast is top-notch in this film about the world of corporate life. Based on Cameron Hawley's novel, the drama examines the intense power struggles in big business with honesty and panache. B&W; 104m. **DIR:** Robert Wise. **CAST:** William Holden, June Allyson, Barbara Stanwyck, Fredric March, Louis Calhern, Walter Pidgeon, Shelley Winters, Dean Jagger, Nina Foch, Paul Douglas. **1954**

EXECUTIVE TARGET ★★★ Not much more than a ninety-five-minute car chase, but it's not a bad one. The cast is adequate with the exception of Angie Everhart, who seems hopelessly lost in the role of a killer. If car chases are your thing, this is just the movie for you. Rated R for profanity and violence. 95m. **DIR:** Joseph Merhi. **CAST:** Michael Madsen, Keith David, Angie Everhart, Dayton Callie, Kathy Christopherson, Roy Scheider. **1996**

EXILED IN AMERICA Extremely bad acting and a poor script kill this film, in which a revolutionary hero is hunted by Central American terrorists. Not rated; contains violence. 85m. **DIR:** Paul Leder. **CAST:** Maxwell Caulfield, Edward Albert, Wings Hauser, Viveca Lindfors, Stella Stevens. **1990**

EXISTENZ ★★★1/2 A designer of virtual reality computer games goes on the run, pursued by terrorists out to destroy her. David Cronenberg's science-fiction thriller takes us into a world where the line between fantasy and reality grows dangerously thin—puzzles within puzzles, games within games—right up to the very last shot. Rated R for profanity and violence. 97m. **DIR:** David Cronenberg. **CAST:** Jennifer Jason Leigh, Jude Law, Ian Holm, Willem Dafoe, Don McKellar, Sarah Polley. **1999 DVD**

EXIT ★★ Shannon Whirry plays one of a group of strippers taken hostage by a pair of criminals. She breaks loose and joins forces with bodyguard Joe Bucci. This is one preposterous, silly movie with dialogue so bad it's actually quite funny. Rated R for violence, profanity, and nudity. 90m. **DIR:** Ric Roman Waugh. **CAST:** Shannon Whirry, David Bradley, Larry Manetti, Joe Bucci. **1996**

EXIT IN RED ★★1/2 Psychiatrist Mickey Rourke finds himself framed for murder after having an affair with one of his patients. So-so little thriller is full of plot holes, but performances and style keep it afloat. Rated R for language, violence, and nudity. 96m. **DIR:** Yurek Bogayevicz. **CAST:** Mickey Rourke, Annabel Schofield, Anthony Michael Hall, Carré Otis. **1996**

EXIT TO EDEN The usually reliable Garry Marshall directs the worst film of his career, an offensive, witless mess about love and intrigue at a sex-fantasy resort. Rated R for profanity, nudity, and simulated sex. 113m. **DIR:** Garry Marshall. **CAST:** Dana Delany, Paul Mercurio, Rosie O'Donnell, Dan Aykroyd, Hector Elizondo, Iman. **1994 DVD**

EXIT WOUNDS ★★ A trigger-happy maverick cop (Steven Seagal) is banished to an inner-city precinct where almost every other officer is on the take. The incoherent plot serves as a flimsy pretext for the brutal, nonstop violence that has become Seagal's trademark, with some decent actors getting caught in the cross fire. Rated R for violence and profanity. 117m. **DIR:** Andrzej Bartkowiak. **CAST:** Steven Seagal, DMX, Tom Arnold, Isaiah Washington, Anthony Anderson. **2001 DVD**

EXODUS ★★1/2 The early days of Israel are seen through the eyes of various characters, in this epic, adapted from the novel by Leon Uris. Directed by the heavy-handed Otto Preminger, its length and plodding pace caused comic Mort Sahl to quip, "Otto, let my people go," at a preview. 213m. **DIR:** Otto Preminger. **CAST:** Paul Newman, Eva Marie Saint, Ralph Richardson, Peter Lawford, Lee J. Cobb, Sal Mineo, Jill Haworth. **1960**

EXORCIST, THE ★★★★1/2 A sensation at the time of its release, this horror film—directed by William Friedkin (*The French Connection*)—has lost some of its punch because of the numerous imitations it spawned. An awful sequel, *Exorcist II: The Heretic*, didn't help much either. Rated R. 121m. **DIR:** William Friedkin. **CAST:** Ellen Burstyn, Max von Sydow, Linda Blair, Jason Miller, Lee J. Cobb. **1973 DVD**

EXORCIST II: THE HERETIC The script is bad, the acting poor, and the direction lacking in pace or conviction. Rated R for violence and profanity. 110m. **DIR:** John Boorman. **CAST:** Richard Burton, Linda Blair, Louise Fletcher, James Earl Jones, Max von Sydow. **1977**

EXORCIST III: LEGION ★★ This time priests discover some unutterable evil and turn to detective George C. Scott for help. Rated R for all sorts of ghastly stuff. 108m. **DIR:** William Peter Blatty. **CAST:** George C. Scott, Ed Flanders, Brad Dourif. **1990 DVD**

EXOTICA ★★★ Strange characters—an emotionally shredded tax auditor, a gay pet-store owner, a young lap dancer, the pregnant owner of the title's plush strip club, and the club's sleazy emcee—wallow neck deep in fixations, mysterious pasts, tragedy, fantasies, and lust. Not rated; contains nudity, adult situations, and profanity. 103m. **DIR:** Atom Egoyan. **CAST:** Bruce Greenwood, Elias Koteas, Mia Kirshner, Don McKellar, Arsinée Khanjian. **1994 DVD**

EXPECT NO MERCY 🦃 Federal agent gets trapped inside a virtual-reality facility, where he must do battle against virtual-reality assassins. The results are virtually stupid. Rated R for violence and adult language. 91m. **DIR:** Zale Dalen. **CAST:** Billy Blanks, Jalal Merhi, Wolf Larson, Laurie Holden. **1995**

EXPERIENCE PREFERRED . . . BUT NOT ESSENTIAL ★★★★★ This delightful British import, which is somewhat reminiscent of Scottish director Bill Forsyth's *Gregory's Girl* and *Local Hero*, follows the awkward and amusing adventures of a young woman during her first summer job at a Welsh coastal resort in 1962. She comes to town insecure and frumpy and leaves at the end of the summer pretty, sexy, and confident. Rated PG for language. 80m. **DIR:** Peter Duffell. **CAST:** Elizabeth Edmonds, Sue Wallace, Geraldine Griffith, Karen Meagher, Ron Bain, Alun Lewis, Robert Blythe. **1983**

EXPERIMENT IN TERROR ★★★1/2 A sadistic killer (Ross Martin) kidnaps the teenage sister (Stefanie Powers) of a bank teller (Lee Remick). An FBI agent is hot on the trail, fighting the clock. The film crackles with suspense. The acting is uniformly excellent. Martin paints an unnerving portrait of evil. B&W; 123m. **DIR:** Blake Edwards. **CAST:** Glenn Ford, Lee Remick, Stefanie Powers, Ross Martin, Ned Glass. **1962**

EXPERT, THE ★★★ Special-forces expert Jeff Speakman decides to settle a blood feud by breaking into the prison where his nemesis waits. An otherwise routine kickfest is enlivened by a better-than-average script. Rated R for violence and profanity. 92m. **DIR:** Rick Avery. **CAST:** Jeff Speakman, James Brolin, Michael Shaner, Alex Datcher, Jim Varney. **1994**

EXPERTS, THE ★★ John Travolta and Arye Gross star as two hip nightclub entrepreneurs from New York City. Charles Martin Smith is a KGB agent who whisks the boys off to a secret American-like community in Russia. Top-notch cast. Rated PG-13 for violence and profanity. 94m. **DIR:** Dave Thomas. **CAST:** John Travolta, Arye Gross, Kelly Preston, Deborah Foreman, James Keach, Charles Martin Smith. **1988**

EXPLORERS ★★★1/2 The young and the young at heart are certain to have a grand time watching *Explorers*. It's a just-for-fun fantasy about three kids (Ethan Hawke, River Phoenix, and Jason Presson) taking off on the greatest adventure of all: a journey through outer space. Rated PG for minor violence and light profanity. 109m. **DIR:** Joe Dante. **CAST:** Ethan Hawke, River Phoenix, Jason Presson, Dick Miller, Robert Picardo. **1985**

EXPOSED ★★ Nastassja Kinski stars in this mediocre and confusing film as a high-priced fashion model whose constant exposure in magazines and on television has made her the target for the sometimes dangerous desires of two men. Former ballet star Rudolph Nureyev is also featured. Rated R. 100m. **DIR:** James Toback. **CAST:** Nastassja Kinski, Rudolf Nureyev, Harvey Keitel, Ian McShane. **1983 DVD**

EXPOSURE 🦃 Passive photojournalist (Peter Coyote) working in Brazil learns a gruesome art form of knife fighting in this exotic and senseless thriller. Rated R for profanity, nudity, and violence. 106m. **DIR:** Walter Salles Jr. **CAST:** Peter Coyote, Tcheky Karyo, Amanda Pays. **1992 DVD**

EXPRESS TO TERROR ★★ This mystery set on a supertrain will come in handy for those times when you're missing those old NBC *Wednesday Night at the Movies* flicks. 120m. **DIR:** Dan Curtis. **CAST:** George Hamilton, Steve Lawrence, Stella Stevens, Don Meredith, Fred Williamson, Don Stroud. **1979**

EXTERMINATING ANGEL, THE ★★★★★ Luis Buñuel always did love a good dinner party. In *The Discreet Charm of the Bourgeoisie,* the dinner party never could get underway, and here the elite *après-opéra* diners find they cannot escape the host's sumptuous music room. This is a very funny film—in a very black key. In Spanish with English subtitles. B&W; 95m. **DIR:** Luis Buñuel. **CAST:** Silvia Pinal, Enrique Rambal. **1962**

EXTERMINATOR, THE ★★ A vigilante who takes the law into his own hands when the law refuses to punish the gang members who made a cripple of his best friend. Rated R. 101m. **DIR:** James Glickenhaus. **CAST:** Christopher George, Samantha Eggar, Robert Ginty, Steve James, Tony DiBenedetto. **1980 DVD**

EXTERMINATOR 2, THE 🦃 In this disgusting cheapo, Robert Ginty returns as the one-man vigilante force. 104m. **DIR:** Mark Buntzman. **CAST:** Robert Ginty, Deborah Gefner, Frankie Faison, Mario Van Peebles. **1984**

EXTERMINATORS OF THE YEAR 3000 🦃 This one rips off George Miller's *The Road Warrior* almost to the letter. Rated R for violence and profanity. 101m. **DIR:** Jules Harrison. **CAST:** Robert Jannucci, Alicia Moro, Alan Collins, Fred Harris, Beryl Cunningham, Luca Venantini. **1983**

EXTRA GIRL, THE ★★★ Madcap silent comedienne Mabel Normand's last film—and a winner! Normand plays a naïve, star-struck midwestern girl who fantasizes about fame in films. She wins a beauty contest, goes to Hollywood, and winds up a no-name extra. Silent with music score. B&W; 87m. **DIR:** Dick Jones. **CAST:** Mabel Normand, Ralph Graves. **1923**

EXTRAORDINARY ADVENTURES OF MR. WEST IN THE LAND OF THE BOLSHEVIKS, THE ★★ An American tourist (Podobed) finds some of the realities beyond the stereotypes of Soviet Russia. Offbeat and uneven. Silent. B&W; 55m. **DIR:** Lev Kuleshov. **CAST:** Podobed, Vsevelod Pudovkin. **1924**

•EXTREME DAYS ★★ Seemingly patent, made for today's teen market, this hybrid of extreme sports and spiritual reflection can't make up its mind what it wants to be. Just out of college, four friends take a road trip down California to Baja, making pit stops to engage in a number of extreme sports like skateboarding, surfing, and snowboarding. When one of their grandfathers dies, the mood turns somber and reflective as they make their way to pay their respects. The film is too nice to be sincere. Rated PG for language. 93m. **DIR:** Eric Hannah. **CAST:** Dante Basco, Ryan Browning, A. J. Buckley, Derek Hamilton, Cassidy Rae. **2001 DVD**

EXTREME JUSTICE ★★★ Intelligent performances and a disturbing story line ripped from current headlines are nearly sabotaged by director Mark L. Lester's emphasis on ludicrous violence and gratuitous mayhem. Bad-boy cop Lou Diamond Phillips gets assigned to an LAPD "death squad" headed by old buddy Scott Glenn; our heroes then watch and wait while slimeballs jeopardize innocent civilians. Rated R for rape, violence, profanity, nudity, and drug use. 95m. **DIR:** Mark L. Lester. **CAST:** Lou Diamond Phillips, Scott Glenn, Chelsea Field, Yaphet Kotto, Ed Lauter. **1993 DVD**

EXTREME MEASURES ★★1/2 Farfetched thriller, which exploits the sort of medical nightmares usually found in Robin Cook novels. Hugh Grant's an emergency-room doctor puzzled by a homeless man's bizarre symptoms; the subsequent investigation eventually leads to a revered surgeon (Gene Hackman). Grant simply isn't convincing as a reluctant detective, and it's inconceivable that such a charming fellow wouldn't find somebody to believe him. Dumb, dumb, dumb. Rated R for violence, profanity, and nudity. 117m. **DIR:** Michael Apted. **CAST:** Hugh Grant, Gene Hackman, Sarah Jessica Parker, David Morse, Bill Nunn. **1996 DVD**

EXTREME PREJUDICE ★★★★ Nick Nolte is in peak form in this modern-day Western as a two-fisted Texas Ranger whose boyhood friend, Powers Boothe, has become a drug kingpin across the border in Mexico. The federal government sends six high-tech agents to nail Boothe with "extreme prejudice." Rated R for profanity, drug use, nudity, and violence. 96m. **DIR:** Walter Hill. **CAST:** Nick Nolte, Powers Boothe, Maria Conchita Alonso, Michael Ironside, Rip Torn, Clancy Brown, William Forsythe. **1987 DVD**

EXTREMITIES ★★1/2 This well-meant but difficult-to-watch thriller casts Farrah Fawcett (in a first-rate performance) as a single woman who is brutalized in her own home by a homicidal maniac (James Russo). When she manages to outwit her attacker, she must decide between bloody revenge and human compassion. Robert M. Young directs this adaptation by William Mastrosimone of his play with authority and realism. Rated R for violence. 100m. **DIR:** Robert M. Young. **CAST:** Farrah Fawcett, James Russo, Diana Scarwid, Alfre Woodard. **1986 DVD**

EYE FOR AN EYE ★★1/2 Sally Field plays a suburbanite whose daughter is raped and murdered. When the killer gets off on a technicality, Mama decides to go after him herself. The film is slickly made and suspenseful, but manipulative and unpleasant; under the lynch-mob surface there are hints of a more honest, thoughtful film about grief, loss, and anger. Rated R for profanity and two brutal rape scenes. 101m. **DIR:** John Schlesinger. **CAST:** Sally Field, Kiefer Sutherland, Ed Harris, Joe Mantegna, Alexandra Kyle. **1996 DVD**

EYE FOR AN EYE ★★1/2 This surprisingly entertaining kung fu movie features Chuck Norris as Shawn Kane, an ex-cop trying to crack a narcotics-smuggling ring. With the help of a lovely news editor (Maggie Cooper) and a martial-arts master (Mako) who doubles as a walking fortune cookie, Kane confronts a sinister Christopher Lee and, finally, a human tank called The Professor. Rated R. 106m. **DIR:** Steve Carver. **CAST:** Chuck Norris, Christopher Lee, Richard Roundtree, Mako, Maggie Cooper. **1981 DVD**

EYE OF THE BEHOLDER 🦃 Our brief critique can't do justice to this failed thriller's excessive shortcomings, starting with the unintentionally hilarious premise and directorial flourishes too heavy-handed and silly for words. Rated R for nudity, violence, and profanity. 101m. **DIR:** Stephan Elliott. **CAST:** Ewan McGregor, Ashley Judd, Jason Priestley, k. d. lang, Patrick Bergin, Genevieve Bujold. **1999 DVD**

EYE OF THE DEMON 🦃 A yuppie couple relocates to a New England island. TV movie originally titled *Bay Coven*. 92m. **DIR:** Carl Schenkel. **CAST:** Tim Matheson, Pamela Sue Martin, Barbara Billingsley, Woody Harrelson, Susan Ruttan. **1987**

EYE OF THE NEEDLE ★★★1/2 In this adaptation of Ken Follett's novel, Donald Sutherland stars as the deadly Nazi agent who discovers a ruse by the Allies during World War II. Plenty of suspense and thrills for those new to the story. Rated R because of nudity, sex, and violence. 112m. **DIR:** Richard Marquand. **CAST:** Donald Sutherland, Ian Bannen, Kate Nelligan, Christopher Cazenove. **1981 DVD**

EYE OF THE SNAKE 🦃 They don't make them any worse than this. Not rated; contains adult language and situations. 91m. **DIR:** Max Reid. **CAST:** Sydney Penny, Malcolm McDowell, Lois Chiles, Jason Cairns. **1990**

EYE OF THE STORM ★★ After witnessing his parents' brutal murder, a boy is blinded by the trauma. Raised by his older brother, the two run a Bates-type hotel. The latest unlucky boarders are an abusive drunk (Dennis Hopper) and his glitzy wife (Lara Flynn Boyle). Rated R for profanity and violence. 98m. **DIR:** Yuri Zeltser. **CAST:** Craig Sheffer, Lara Flynn Boyle, Bradley Gregg, Leon Rippy, Dennis Hopper. **1991**

EYE OF THE TIGER ★★★ Buck Mathews (Gary Busey) stands up against a motorcycle gang and the corrupt law enforcement that have plagued a small town in Texas. Busey and Yaphet Kotto give quality performances that save this formula vengeance film. Rated R for violence and language. 90m. **DIR:** Richard C. Sarafian. **CAST:** Gary Busey, Yaphet Kotto, Seymour Cassel. **1986 DVD**

EYE OF THE WOLF ★★ Jeff Fahey plays a zoologist who takes the only witness to a murder, a wild wolf, into protective custody. Forget the hokey plot and just enjoy the gorgeous Canadian scenery. Rated PG-13 for violence. 96m. **DIR:** Arnaud Selignac. **CAST:** Jeff Fahey, Sophie Duez, Lorne Brass. **1994**

EYE ON THE SPARROW ★★★ Mare Winningham and Keith Carradine star in this fact-based made-for-TV drama about a blind couple trying to buck the system and become adoptive parents. Winningham's performance is especially forceful, but both actors are amazingly convincing. 94m. **DIR:** John Korty. **CAST:** Mare Winningham, Keith Carradine, Conchata Ferrell. **1987**

EYES BEHIND THE STARS 🦃 A reporter and a UFO specialist investigate reports that extraterrestrial beings have landed on Earth. Not rated. 95m. **DIR:** Roy Garrett. **CAST:** Robert Hoffman, Nathalie Delon, Martin Balsam. **1972**

EYES OF A STRANGER ★★ *The Love Boat*'s Julie, Lauren Tewes, plays a reporter who decides to track down a psychopathic killer. Lots of blood and some sexual molestation. Rated R. 85m. **DIR:** Ken Wiederhorn. **CAST:** Lauren Tewes, Jennifer Jason Leigh. **1981**

EYES OF A WITNESS ★★1/2 Mildly engaging drama about an American businessman whose attempt to rescue his daughter from the Kenya bush lands him in deep trouble when he's accused of murdering a high-ranking official. Daniel J. Travanti and Jennifer Grey play the father and daughter whose lives are thrown into jeopardy in the made-for-television drama shot on location. Not rated; contains some violence. 90m. **DIR:** Peter R. Hunt. **CAST:** Daniel J. Travanti, Jennifer Grey, Carl Lumbly, Daniel Gerroll. **1994**

EYES OF AN ANGEL ★★★1/2 Heart-tugger about a man at the end of his rope, who finds renewed hope through his daughter and an injured Doberman. After his wife dies of a drug overdose and he's left with his 10-year-old daughter, Bobby Allen (well played by John Travolta) decides to pick up stakes and start new in another city. When he fails to realize his daughter's emotional attachment to a dog they left behind, he sets into motion a cross-country odyssey that touches the heart and soul. Rated PG-13 for language and adult themes. 91m. **DIR:** Robert Harmon. **CAST:** John Travolta, Ellie Raab. **1989**

EYES OF FIRE ★★★ Old-West settlers accused of witchcraft are surrounded by woods made from the souls of earlier settlers—and the witch who cast the spell upon them. Above-average special-effects highlight this original tale. Rated R for violence and nudity; 90m. **DIR:** Avery Crounse. **CAST:** Dennis Lipscomb, Rebecca Stanley, Guy Boyd. **1983**

EYES OF LAURA MARS, THE ★★ Laura Mars (Faye Dunaway) is a kinky commercial photographer whose photographs, which are composed of violent scenes, somehow become the blueprints for a series of actual killings. It soon becomes apparent the maniac is really after her. Although well acted and suspenseful, this is an unrelentingly cold and gruesome movie. Rated R. 103m. **DIR:** Irvin Kershner. **CAST:** Faye Dunaway, Tommy Lee Jones, Brad Dourif, René Auberjonois. **1978 DVD**

EYES OF TAMMY FAYE, THE ★★★1/2 This affectionate, almost gushy documentary takes a sympathetic and surprisingly persuasive view of the amazing career of Tammy Faye Messner (formerly Bakker), from her meteoric rise with ex-husband Jim Bakker on TV's *PTL Club* to their equally spectacular fall after Jim's affair with a church secretary. Tammy comes off as honest, spunky, and likably tacky. Narrated by famed drag performer RuPaul. Rated PG-13 for mature themes. 79m. **DIR:** Fenton Bailey, Randy Barbato. **CAST:** Tammy Faye (Bakker) Messner, Jim Bakker. **2000 DVD**

EYES OF TEXAS ★★★★1/2 Villainess Nana Bryant out to acquire valuable ranch land at any cost, including using vicious killer dogs to discourage prospective landowners. Director William Witney brought much-needed action and a harder, often brutal, edge to the Rogers films in the late 1940s after they had stagnated into overblown musicals in the mid-1940s. B&W; 70m. **DIR:** William Witney. **CAST:** Roy Rogers, Andy Devine, Nana Bryant, Lynne Roberts, Roy Barcroft, Bob Nolan and the Sons of the Pioneers. **1948**

EYES OF THE AMARYLLIS ★★1/2 A young girl goes to Nantucket to care for her grandmother, an invalid awaiting the return of her long-dead husband. This well-intended low-budget film is likely to bore kids, though it may interest adults who recall the Natalie Babbitt novel on which it was based. Not rated; contains no objectionable material. 84m. **DIR:** Frederick King Keller. **CAST:** Ruth Ford, Martha Byrne. **1982**

EYES OF THE BEHOLDER ★★ Okay thriller about a doctor who performs a new radical surgery on disturbed Lenny Von Dohlen, who escapes and wreaks havoc. Pretty pedestrian, but an interesting cast keeps things merrily rolling along. Rated R for violence. 89m. **DIR:** Lawrence L. Simeone. **CAST:** Joanna Pacula, Matt McCoy, George Lazenby, Charles Napier, Lenny von Dohlen. **1992**

EYES OF THE BIRDS ★★★★ Powerful fact-based psychological drama set in a supposedly model South American prison. A Red Cross investigation into prison conditions leads to reprisals. Unlike most prison movies, this film's effect comes from what it implies rather than what it shows. In French with English subtitles. 83m. **DIR:** Gabriel Auer. **CAST:** Roland Amastutz, Philippe Clevot. **1983**

EYES OF THE SERPENT 🦃 Long ago and far away, two sisters, one good, one evil, vie for control of a pair of magical swords. It's obvious no one in this film fought over acting lessons. Not rated; contains nudity, violence, and adult situations. 86m. **DIR:** Ricardo Jacques Gale. **CAST:** Diana Frank, Lenore Andriel, Tom Schultz, David Michael Sterling. **1994**

EYES WIDE SHUT ★★★ Kubrick enthusiasts will love this stylized descent into rampant sensual excess, which makes a striking epitaph for one of the greatest film directors of all time. Tom Cruise and Nicole Kidman heat up the screen as a happily married New York couple who come apart at the seams after she shares one of her sexual fantasies. The notion that his wife betrayed him—if only in her mind—proves more than Cruise can handle, and he spends the next forty-eight hours in a whirlwind of sexual temptation that becomes more improbable by the hour. With an adapted script heavily influenced by the Freudian content in Arthur Schnitzler's source novel, we must consider that our hero's misadventures may occur solely in his mind. Mainstream viewers are apt to find it a lot of fuss, with very little payoff. But it sure is interesting to watch. Rated R for nudity, simulated sex, strong sexual content, profanity, and drug use. 159m. **DIR:** Stanley Kubrick. **CAST:** Tom Cruise, Nicole Kidman, Sydney Pollack, Marie Richardson, Rade Serbedzija, Leelee Sobieski, Alan Cumming. **1999 DVD**

EYES WITHOUT A FACE ★★★★1/2 Georges Franju, one of the underrated heroes of French cinema, creates an austerely beautiful horror film about a plastic surgeon who, in systematic experiments, removes the faces of beautiful young women and tries to graft them onto the ruined head of his daughter. Imaginative cinematography by Eugen Shuftan with music by Maurice Jarre. Subtitled, not rated. (Originally released in America as *The Horror Chamber of Dr. Faustus*.) B&W;

102m. **DIR:** Georges Franju. **CAST:** Pierre Brasseur, Alida Valli, Edith Scob, Juliette Mayniel. **1960**

EYEWITNESS ★★★★ A humdinger of a movie. William Hurt plays a janitor who, after discovering a murder victim, meets the glamorous television reporter (Sigourney Weaver) he has admired from afar. In order to prolong their relationship, he pretends to know the killer's identity—and puts both their lives in danger. Rated R for violence and profanity. 102m. **DIR:** Peter Yates. **CAST:** William Hurt, Sigourney Weaver, Christopher Plummer, James Woods. **1981**

F

F FOR FAKE ★★ This sad and sloppy film by Orson Welles supposedly chronicles the exploits of several famous fakers. Quick cuts and a rambling narrative do nothing to enhance this vanity piece. Not rated; contains brief nudity. 98m. **DIR:** Orson Welles. **CAST:** Orson Welles, Elmyr de Hory, Clifford Irving, Oja Kodar. **1973**

FABULOUS BAKER BOYS, THE ★★★★1/2 This deliciously sultry character study concerns a pair of mildly contentious piano-playing brothers (played by offscreen brothers Jeff and Beau Bridges) who, in an effort to revitalize a lounge act mired in tired old standards, hire a feisty singer (Michelle Pfeiffer). She becomes the catalyst that prompts age-old regrets to surface. Rated R for language. 113m. **DIR:** Steve Kloves. **CAST:** Jeff Bridges, Michelle Pfeiffer, Beau Bridges, Jennifer Tilly. **1989 DVD**

FABULOUS DORSEYS, THE ★★ A mildly musical, plotless dual biography of the Dorsey brothers as they fight their way to the top while fighting with each other, trombone and clarinet at the ready. Janet Blair is cute, William Lundigan is personable, and Paul "Pops" Whiteman is along for the ride. B&W; 88m. **DIR:** Alfred E. Green. **CAST:** Tommy Dorsey, Jimmy Dorsey, Janet Blair, William Lundigan, Paul Whiteman. **1947**

FABULOUS FLEISCHER FOLIO, THE (VOLUME FIVE) ★★ The Christmas cartoons of Max and Dave Fleischer are featured in this Disney video release, which is for animation buffs and youngsters only. Included are: "Rudolph the Red-Nosed Reindeer," "The Ski's the Limit," "Peeping Penguins," "Bunny Mooning," "Snow Fooling," and "Christmas Comes But Once a Year." 43m. **DIR:** Dave Fleischer. **1937–1949**

FABULOUS TEXAN, THE ★★★ Upon returning from the Civil War, Confederate officers Wild Bill Elliott and John Carroll find their part of Texas to be under the dictatorial rule of carpetbagger Albert Dekker. While not directed with much inspiration, this benefits from earnest performances. B&W; 95m. **DIR:** Edward Ludwig. **CAST:** William Elliott, John Carroll, Albert Dekker, Catherine McLeod, Andy Devine, Jim Davis. **1947**

FABULOUS VILLAINS, THE ★★1/2 From the first filming of the Frankenstein monster in 1906 to Batman's villainous enemy The Joker, and Freddy Kruger, this mixture of silent and sound clips, publicity stills, and trailers, documents the famous and infamous villains and monsters of motion pictures. Even Popeye's Bluto is included. 58m. **DIR:** James Gordon. **1992**

FACADE 🦃 Absolutely shoddy tale about a murder and the attempt to cover it up. Also known as *Death Valley*. Rated R for profanity and sexual situations. 93m. **DIR:** Carl Colpaert. **CAST:** Daniella Elle, Brad Garrett, Angus MacFadyen, Dawn Radenburgh, Eric Roberts, Camilla Overbye Roos, Roger Guenveur Smith, Joe Viterelli. **1997**

FACE AT THE WINDOW, THE ★★1/2 Tod Slaughter produced and starred in a number of lurid gothic plays that barnstormed through the English provinces in the 1920s and eventually were made into low-budget horror films. This one, about a fiendish killer in 1880s Paris, was the most cinematic, and thus probably the best. Worth seeing as a curio, but it still drags, even at barely an hour. B&W; 65m. **DIR:** George King. **CAST:** Tod Slaughter, Marjorie Taylor, John Warwick. **1939**

FACE BEHIND THE MASK, THE ★★★★ An excellent B movie that anticipates the better-known *films noir* of the later 1940s. Peter Lorre gives one of his best performances as an immigrant watchmaker. When his face is scarred in an accident, he is unable to find work and bitterly turns to crime. B&W; 69m. **DIR:** Robert Florey. **CAST:** Peter Lorre, Evelyn Keyes, Don Beddoe. **1941**

FACE DOWN ★★★ A detective finds himself embroiled in a murder case that leads him back to the police department he was ejected from years earlier. Stylish, well-written *film noir*. Rated R for sexuality, violence, and profanity. 107m. **DIR:** Thom Eberhardt. **CAST:** Joe Mantegna, Peter Riegert, Cameron Thor, Kelli Maroney, Adam Ant. **1997**

FACE IN THE CROWD, A ★★★★ A sow's ear is turned into a silk purse in this Budd Schulberg story, scripted by the author, of a television executive who discovers gold in a winsome hobo she molds into a tube star. But all that glitters is not gold. A fine cast makes this a winning film, which brought Andy Griffith and Lee Remick to the screen for the first time. B&W; 125m. **DIR:** Elia Kazan. **CAST:** Andy Griffith, Patricia Neal, Lee Remick, Anthony Franciosa, Walter Matthau, Kay Medford. **1957**

FACE OF ANOTHER, THE ★★★★ Excellent surreal drama that explores the dehumanization and identity crisis of a man disfigured in an accident. A great parable of the Frankenstein theme, with hauntingly erotic overtones. In Japanese with English subtitles. B&W; 124m. **DIR:** Hiroshi Teshigahara. **CAST:** Tatsuya Nakadai. **1966**

FACE OF MARBLE, THE 🦃 Mad scientist John Carradine revives the dead in this typical entry from the poverty-row studio Monogram. B&W; 72m. **DIR:** William Beaudine. **CAST:** John Carradine, Claudia Drake, Robert Shayne, Willie Best. **1946**

FACE THE EVIL ★★ Former Playmate Shannon Tweed manages to keep her clothes on in this unimaginative, derivative thriller. Tweed apes Bruce Willis, playing an actress on a location shoot at a museum attempting to stop bad guy Lance Henriksen from getting his hands on some nasty nerve gas. Rated R for language and violence. 92m. **DIR:** Paul Lynch. **CAST:** Shannon Tweed, Bruce Payne, Lance Henriksen, Jayne Heitmeyer. **1996 DVD**

FACE THE MUSIC ★★1/2 Molly Ringwald and Patrick Dempsey are divorced songwriters forced to write one last ditty together. The plot is contrived and Ringwald just can't sing, but this romance is pleasant enough, if predictable. Rated PG-13 for profanity and sexual situations. 93m. **DIR:** Carol Wiseman. **CAST:** Molly Ringwald, Patrick Dempsey, Lysette Anthony. **1992**

FACE TO KILL FOR, A ★★ At times predictable, at times outrageous, this made-for-cable original just doesn't satisfy. A woman with disfiguring facial scars goes to prison for a crime she didn't commit. After she serves her time, she gets cosmetic surgery and a new identity, then seeks revenge on the man who framed her. Not rated; contains violence. 95m. **DIR:** Michael Toshiyuki Uno. **CAST:** Crystal Bernard, Doug Savant, Billy Dean, Claire Rankin, Barry Corbin. **1998**

FACE/OFF ★★★★ This outrageous thriller pits FBI agent Sean Archer against terrorist Castor Troy. The two mortal enemies surgically swap faces in a story that wallows in barbaric lunacy. The emotional connection between the two men—one a hero and the other a villain—becomes a seductive creep show as they become trapped not only in each other's body but also in each other's daily life. Rated R for language and violence. 138m. **DIR:** John Woo. **CAST:** John Travolta, Nicolas Cage, Joan Allen, Alessandro Nivola, Dominique Swain, Gina Gershon. **1997 DVD**

FACES OF WOMEN ★★★★ A novel comedy about the roles of women in contemporary African society. Despite amateurish touches, it is overall a delightful, original work. Not rated; contains nudity and sexual situations. In African tribal dialects with English subtitles. 105m. **DIR:** Desire Ecare. **CAST:** Eugenie Cisse Roland, Albertine Guessan. **1985**

FACTS OF LIFE ★★★ Dated comedy vehicle for Bob Hope and Lucille Ball as suburbanites trying to have an affair because their respective spouses take them for granted. Pretty wan as satire, but there are enough bright lines and bits of slapstick to keep fans of the stars happy. 103m. **DIR:** Melvin Frank. **CAST:** Bob Hope, Lucille Ball, Ruth Hussey, Don DeFore, Louis Nye. **1960**

FACULTY, THE ★★ This science-fiction thriller about conformity versus individualism is an *Invasion of the Body Snatchers* update with gruesome special effects and plenty of splatter. High-school misfits are stalked and butchered by teachers who are oddly preoccupied with more than just missing homework. Rated R for violence, gore, drug use, nudity, and language. 116m. **DIR:** Robert Rodriguez. **CAST:** Elijah Wood, Clea DuVall, Shawn Hatosy, Josh Harnett, Robert Patrick, Laura Harris, Piper Laurie, Bebe Neuwirth, Salma Hayek, Jon Stewart. **1998 DVD**

FADE TO BLACK ★★★ Movie buffs and horror fans will especially love this funny, suspenseful, and entertaining low-budget film that features Dennis Christopher in a tour-de-force performance. Christopher plays Eric Binford, an odd young man who spends most of his time absorbing films. His all-night videotaping sessions and movie orgies only make him out of step with other people his age, and soon Eric goes over the edge. Rated R. 100m. **DIR:** Vernon Zimmerman. **CAST:** Dennis Christopher, Linda Kerridge, Tim Thomerson, Morgan Paull, Marya Small. **1980 DVD**

FADE TO BLACK ★★ A professor of social anthropology videotapes a murder from his window, but the police won't believe him. He decides he must play detective with the help of his wheelchair-bound friend. A bad attempt at remaking Alfred Hitchcock's brilliant *Rear Window*. Not rated, made for cable, but contains violence. 95m. **DIR:** John McPherson. **CAST:** Timothy Busfield, Heather Locklear, Michael Beck, Louis Giambalvo, David Byron, Cloris Leachman. **1993**

FAHRENHEIT 451 ★★★★ Still the best adaptation of a Ray Bradbury book to hit the screen (big or small). Oskar Werner is properly troubled as a futuristic "fireman" responsible for the destruction of books, who begins to wonder about the necessity of his work. This is director François Truffaut's first English-language film, and he treats the subject of language and literature with a dignity not found in most American films. Not rated—family fare. 111m. **DIR:** François Truffaut. **CAST:** Oskar Werner, Julie Christie, Cyril Cusack, Anton Diffring. **1967 DVD**

FAIL-SAFE ★★★★ In this gripping film, a United States aircraft is mistakenly assigned to drop the big one on Russia, and the leaders of the two countries grapple for some kind of solution as time runs out. B&W; 111m. **DIR:** Sidney Lumet. **CAST:** Henry Fonda, Walter Matthau, Fritz Weaver, Larry Hagman, Dom DeLuise, Frank Overton. **1964 DVD**

FAIR GAME ★★1/2 A Miami lawyer is stalked by ex-KGB renegades after she tries to repossess their command-post freighter. She's protected by a homicide detective and the two face all sorts of danger as they go on the run and fall in lust. The action is exhilarating, but the script for supermodel Cindy Crawford's coming-out party as lead actress is amateurish. Rated R for violence, nudity, suggested sex, and language. 90m. **DIR:** Andrew Sipes. **CAST:** Cindy Crawford, William Baldwin, Steven Berkoff, Christopher McDonald. **1995 DVD**

FAIRY TALE: A TRUE STORY ★★★★ The infamous "Cottingley Fairy Hoax," perpetrated by two young girls on a credulous British public shortly after World War I, is the basis for this enchanting, family-oriented fantasy. Precocious Frances and Elise, living at the edge of a beck they know is inhabited by fairies, fabricate some photos of the camera-shy creatures in a misguided effort to "share" their discovery. These photos come to the attention of Sir Arthur Conan Doyle, whose enthusiastic acceptance of same becomes an embarrassment to best friend Harry Houdini, who routinely debunks such nonsense. Michael Howells's production design is gorgeous and impeccably true to its setting and era. Rated PG for no particular reason. 99m. **DIR:** Charles Sturridge. **CAST:** Florence Hoath, Elizabeth Earl, Paul McGann, Phoebe Nicholls, Peter O'Toole, Harvey Keitel. **1997**

FAITHFUL ★★ Depressed housewife Cher matches wits with the hit man (Chazz Palminteri) hired by husband Ryan O'Neal. The interplay between Cher and Palminteri can't overcome the basic implausibility of the entire plot, and the film's origin as a talky stage play (written by Palminteri) is all too clear. O'Neal's performance seems like an afterthought. Rated R for profanity. 88m. **DIR:** Paul Mazursky. **CAST:** Cher, Ryan O'Neal, Chazz Palminteri, Paul Mazursky, Amber Smith. **1996**

•**FAITHLESS** ★★1/2 The script by the great Ingmar Bergman tells of a destructive affair between an actress and a filmmaker, with the elderly filmmaker reflecting ruefully from lonely old age. The film's main interest is its semiautobiographical origin; otherwise, the characters are selfish and despicable, the performances monotonous, and the direction (by Bergman protégée Liv Ullmann) leaden. In Swedish with English subtitles. Rated R for profanity (in subtitles), nudity, and sexual themes. 142m. **DIR:** Liv Ullmann. **CAST:** Lena Endre, Erland Josephson, Krister Henriksson. **2000 DVD**

FAKEOUT ★★ A Las Vegas singer goes to jail instead of ratting on her boyfriend. Later, agreeing to falsely testify in exchange for her freedom, she becomes a target for death. Not rated; contains violence. 89m. **DIR:** Matt Cimber. **CAST:** Telly Savalas, Pia Zadora, Desi Arnaz Jr., Larry Storch. **1982**

FALCON AND THE SNOWMAN, THE ★★★★★ In this powerful motion picture, Timothy Hutton and Sean Penn give stunning performances as two childhood friends who decide to sell United States secrets to the Russians. Based on a true incident, this release makes no judgments. The viewer is left to decide right and wrong, and whether Boyce met with justice. Rated R for violence and profanity. 131m. **DIR:** John Schlesinger. **CAST:** Timothy Hutton, Sean Penn, Pat Hingle, Lori Singer, Richard Dysart. **1985 DVD**

FALCON IN MEXICO, THE ★★ The ninth film in the long-running series finds the suave sleuth south of the border as he tries to recover a woman's portrait. The owner of the gallery where the painting was displayed has been murdered and the artist responsible for the painting was reportedly killed fifteen years earlier, but Tom Conway as the smooth Falcon untangles the mystery. B&W; 70m. **DIR:** William Berke. **CAST:** Tom Conway, Mona Maris, Nestor Paiva, Bryant Washburn. **1944**

FALCON TAKES OVER, THE ★★★ Early entry in the popular *Falcon* mystery-film series sets star George Sanders in a search for a missing woman. He encounters a good many of Hollywood's favorite character actors and actresses as well as much of the plot from Raymond Chandler's *Farewell My Lovely*, of which this is the first filmed version. B&W; 63m. **DIR:** Irving Reis. **CAST:** George Sanders, James Gleason, Ward Bond, Hans Conried, Lynn Bari. **1942**

FALCON'S BROTHER, THE ★★★ The sophisticated Falcon (played by former Saint, George Sanders) races against time to prevent the assassination of a South American diplomat. Aided by his brother (in fact Sanders's real-life brother, Tom Conway), the Falcon realizes his goal but pays with his life at the end. Brother Tom vows to continue the work his martyred sibling has left undone. This well-made, nicely acted little detective film is a true oddity. B&W; 63m. **DIR:** Stanley Logan. **CAST:** George Sanders, Tom Conway, Don Barclay, Jane Randolph, Amanda Varela. **1942**

FALL ★★★ When a cabbie picks up a stunning supermodel, an unlikely romance blooms. Charming and sexy love story with rich, attractive characters. Not rated; contains profanity and strong sexual situations. 90m. **DIR:** Eric Schaeffer. **CAST:** Eric Schaeffer, Amanda De Cadanet, Francie Swift, Lisa Vidal, Rudolf Martin. **1996 DVD**

FALL FROM GRACE ★★★★ Enthralling espionage thriller made its debut on television, but is best served here without the annoying commercial breaks. The tension is high as military forces convene to trick Hitler and his advisors with misinformation in order to pull off the attack on D day. Filled with vibrant performances, exquisite production detail, and a taut script, the film is exciting and suspenseful. Not rated; contains some violence. 180m. **DIR:** Waris Hussein. **CAST:** James Fox, Michael York, Patsy Kensit, Tara Fitzgerald, Gary Cole. **1994**

FALL OF THE HOUSE OF USHER, THE ★★ Low-budget, semiprofessional adaptation of the famous horror tale. Produced in England, it is by turns amateurish, tedious, and genuinely scary. B&W; 74m. **DIR:** Ivan Barnett. **CAST:** Gwen Watford, Kaye Tendeter, Irving Steen. **1949**

FALL OF THE HOUSE OF USHER, THE ★★★1/2 Imagination and a chilling sense of the sinister make this low-budget Roger Corman version of Edgar Allan Poe's famous haunted house story highly effective. Vincent Price is without peer as Usher. 79m. **DIR:** Roger Corman. **CAST:** Vincent Price, Mark Damon, Myrna Fahey. **1960**

FALL OF THE HOUSE OF USHER, THE 🦃 Edgar Allan Poe tale is tacky, inept, and dull. Rated PG. 101m. **DIR:** Stephen Lord. **CAST:** Martin Landau, Robert Hays, Charlene Tilton, Ray Walston. **1979**

FALL OF THE ROMAN EMPIRE, THE ★★★★ During the early and mid-1960s, Hollywood looked to the history books for many of its films. Director Anthony Mann has fashioned an epic that is a feast for the eyes and does not insult the viewers' intelligence. *The Fall of the Roman Empire* has thrilling moments of action and characters the viewer cares about. 149m. **DIR:** Anthony Mann. **CAST:** Sophia Loren, James Mason, Stephen Boyd, Alec Guinness, Christopher Plummer, John Ireland, Mel Ferrer. **1964**

FALL TIME ★★1/2 A direct-to-video release starring Mickey Rourke as a none-too-believable criminal philosopher masterminding a bank heist in a small, 1950s Wisconsin town. Three high-school kids accidentally get in on the action when a ghoulish prank is mistaken for part of the heist. Stephen Baldwin's performance and a surprising ending are the only things going for this muddled story. Rated R for profanity and violence. 88m. **DIR:** Paul Warner. **CAST:** Mickey Rourke, Stephen Baldwin, Sheryl Lee, David Arquette, Jason London, Jonah Bleachman. **1993 DVD**

FALLEN ★★★ When homicide cop Denzel Washington finds himself framed for copycat murders by the vengeful spirit of a recently executed serial killer, it seems that our hero has no chance of defeating this malevolent entity. Washington brings considerable depth to his character, but it's not enough to wholly save a film that runs half an hour too long. Rated R for profanity and violence. 124m. **DIR:** Gregory Hoblit. **CAST:** Denzel Washington, John Goodman, Donald Sutherland, Embeth Davidtz, James Gandolfini, Elias Koteas. **1998 DVD**

FALLEN ANGEL ★★★1/2 This made-for-television drama deals with the controversial topic of child pornography. A young girl, Jennifer (played by Dana Hill), is pushed into pornography by a so-called adult friend, Howard (played by Richard Masur). Jennifer sees no hope of getting out of her predicament, because she can't communicate with her mother (played by Melinda Dillon). Very timely topic! 100m. **DIR:** Robert Michael Lewis. **CAST:** Dana Hill, Richard Masur, Melinda Dillon, Ronny Cox, David Hayward. **1981 DVD**

FALLEN ANGELS ★★★★ High marks to this two-volume anthology series that adapts some of the moodiest short fiction of the 1940s. Each tale is set in or near seamy World War II–era Los Angeles locales and involves the sort of characters made famous by Raymond Chandler and Cornell Woolrich. The private eyes talk tough, the women are hard as nails, and the cops are always on the take or on the lam. Not rated, with considerable violence and strong sexual content. 90m. **DIR:** Steven Soderbergh, Jonathan Kaplan, Phil Joanou, Tom Hanks, Tom Cruise, Alfonso Cuaron. **CAST:** Laura Dern, Gary Busey, Bonnie Bedelia, James Woods, Tom Hanks, Peter Gallagher, Gary Oldman, Joe Mantegna, Bruno Kirby, Isabella Rossellini, Alan Rickman, Diane Lane. **1993 DVD**

FALLEN IDOL, THE ★★★★ A small boy hero-worships a household servant suspected of murdering his wife in this quiet Graham Greene thriller. Largely told from the child's point of view, this one is pulse-raising. As always, the late Ralph Richardson is great. Bernard Lee later became "M" in the Bond films. B&W; 94m. **DIR:** Carol Reed. **CAST:** Ralph Richardson, Michèle Morgan, Bobby Henrey, Jack Hawkins, Bernard Lee. **1948**

FALLEN SPARROW, THE ★★★ In this sometimes confusing but generally engrossing film, John Garfield is a veteran of the Spanish Civil War whose wartime buddy is later murdered by Fascists in New York City. Many powerful scenes and strong performances make this one of Garfield's best films. 94m. **DIR:** Richard Wallace. **CAST:** John Garfield, Maureen O'Hara, Walter Slezak, Patricia Morison, Martha O'Driscoll. **1943**

FALLING DOWN ★★★★ Defense worker Michael Douglas is mad as hell, and he's not going to take it anymore. So he goes on an impromptu reign of terror in East Los Angeles. *Falling Down* has been misinterpreted as endorsing violence, but it is, above all, a thoughtful and believable character study. Rated R for violence and profanity. 112m. **DIR:** Joel Schumacher. **CAST:** Michael Douglas, Robert Duvall, Barbara Hershey, Rachel Ticotin, Frederic Forrest, Tuesday Weld, Lois Smith. **1993 DVD**

FALLING FROM GRACE ★★★★ Famous country singer finds that going home again may not be such a good idea after all. During a family visit to his rural Indiana hometown, he rekindles a relationship with an old girlfriend who not only married his brother, but also is having an affair with their dad. This opens a Pandora's box of festering regrets and emotional wounds that writer Larry McMurtry instills with a sense of truth rarely found in films today. Rated PG-13 for profanity. 101m. **DIR:** John Mellencamp. **CAST:** John Mellencamp, Mariel Hemingway, Kay Lenz, Claude Akins, Dub Taylor. **1992**

FALLING IN LOVE ★★★ Robert De Niro and Meryl Streep are fine as star-crossed lovers who risk their marriages for a moment of passion. Thanks to the uneven direction of Ulu Grosbard and an unbelievable story by Michael Cristofer, the stars' performances are the only outstanding features in this watchable love story. Rated PG for profanity and adult situations. 107m. **DIR:** Ulu Grosbard. **CAST:** Robert De Niro, Meryl Streep, Harvey Keitel. **1984 DVD**

FALLING IN LOVE AGAIN ★★1/2 Elliott Gould stars as a middle-aged dreamer who is obsessed with his younger days in the Bronx. Gould and wife (Susannah York) are on vacation and headed east to recapture the past. The film suffers from countless long flashbacks of his youthful romance with a WASP princess (Michelle Pfeiffer) and is a poor attempt at romantic comedy. Rated R. 103m. **DIR:** Steven Paul. **CAST:** Elliott Gould, Susannah York, Michelle Pfeiffer, Stuart Paul. **1980 DVD**

FALSE ARREST ★★★ Based on a 1981 Arizona case, this features Donna Mills being falsely accused of killing her husband's partner. Perjuring witnesses land her in the slammer. Her only hope is proving that even the DA lied to get her convicted. Believable and well-done with Mills at her best. Not rated; contains nudity and violence. 102m. **DIR:** Bill L. Norton. **CAST:** Donna Mills, Robert Wagner, Steven Bauer, James Handy, Lane Smith. **1991**

FALSE COLORS ★★1/2 Typical entry in the Hopalong Cassidy series places Hoppy on the side of the innocent people who are being terrorized and murdered by ace heavy Douglass Dumbrille, who wants their property and water rights. B&W; 65m. **DIR:** George Archainbaud. **CAST:** William Boyd, Andy Clyde, Jimmy Rogers, Claudia Drake, Douglass Dumbrille, Robert Mitchum. **1943**

FALSE IDENTITY ★★★ Stacy Keach returns to his home after seventeen years in prison and cannot remember many prior events. A clumsy finale is the one shortcoming of this otherwise interesting suspense drama. Rated PG-13. 97m. **DIR:** James Keach. **CAST:** Stacy Keach, Genevieve Bujold, Veronica Cartwright. **1990**

FAME ★★★1/2 Today everybody wants to be a star. *Fame* addresses that contemporary dream in a most charming and lively fashion. By focusing on the aspirations, struggles, and personal lives of a group of talented and ambitious students at New York City's High School for the Performing Arts, it manages to say something about all of us and the age we live in. Rated R. 130m. **DIR:** Alan Parker. **CAST:** Irene Cara, Lee Curreri, Eddie Barth, Laura Dean, Paul McCrane, Barry Miller, Gene Anthony Ray, Maureen Teefy. **1980**

FAMILY, THE (1970) ★★★ Charles Bronson is mad. Some creep framed him and, what's worse, stole his girl! Bronson is out for revenge. This film has plenty of action, but nothing new to offer. Rated R. 100m. **DIR:** Sergio Sollima. **CAST:** Charles Bronson, Jill Ireland, Telly Savalas, Michael Constantine, George Savalas. **1970**

FAMILY, THE (1987) ★★★ This bustling, good-natured film, thick with anecdotes, covers the life of a man growing up in Italy from the turn of the century to the present. It is a celebration of family life. In Italian with English subtitles. The film has no objectionable material. 140m. **DIR:** Ettore Scola. **CAST:** Vittorio Gassman, Fanny Ardant, Stefania Sandrelli. **1987**

FAMILY BUSINESS ★★1/2 Despite the high-powered cast of Sean Connery, Dustin Hoffman, and Matthew Broderick, this is a disappointing drama about a three generation crime family from director Sidney Lumet.

Rated R for profanity and violence. 116m. **DIR:** Sidney Lumet. **CAST:** Sean Connery, Dustin Hoffman, Matthew Broderick. **1989**

FAMILY GAME, THE ★★★★1/2 This is a very funny film about a modern Japanese family faced with the same problems as their Western counterparts. A teen with school problems, a father striving for middle-class affluence, and a new tutor who shakes things up result in what was voted best film of 1983 in Japan. With English subtitles. 107m. **DIR:** Yoshimitsu Morita. **CAST:** Yusaku Matsuda, Juzo Itami. **1983**

FAMILY JEWELS, THE ★★1/2 Jerry Lewis tries to outperform Alec Guinness (in *Kind Hearts and Coronets*) in this syrupy tale of a wealthy young heiress (Donna Butterworth) forced to select a guardian from among six uncles. Lewis plays all six, but his seventh—the family chauffeur—is the only one with any credibility. It's a long stretch for thin material. 100m. **DIR:** Jerry Lewis. **CAST:** Jerry Lewis, Donna Butterworth, Sebastian Cabot. **1965**

FAMILY LIFE ★★★1/2 A middle-class British girl strives to break free of her parents, who resort to increasingly severe measures to keep her under their control. Powerful drama filmed in a near-documentary style. Not rated. 95m. **DIR:** Kenneth Loach. **CAST:** Sandy Ratcliff, Bill Dean. **1971**

FAMILY MAN, THE ★★★★ Nicholas Cage owns this marvelous holiday fantasy, as a high-powered, high-living Wall Street bachelor who gets a most unusual gift one Christmas Eve: a chance to live the life he never had with former girlfriend Téa Leoni, complete with two kids, a slobbery dog, and a mortgage in the suburbs. Although initially horrified by this "reduction" in stature, our hero eventually learns to appreciate the finer qualities of family life, and watching Cage come to grips with the details is a hoot. Leoni is just as fine as the woman who *thought* she knew her husband, and Makenzie Vega will break your heart as the little girl suddenly worried that her father has been replaced by an alien. Rated PG-13 for profanity and sexual candor. 125m. **DIR:** Brett Ratner. **CAST:** Nicolas Cage, Téa Leoni, Jeremy Piven, Saul Rubinek, Don Cheadle, Makenzie Vega. **2000 DVD**

FAMILY MATTER, A ★★★ Handsome production values elevate this standard Mafia soap opera. Supermodel Carol Alt plays a Mafia princess bent on revenge, not realizing that the man she loves is the same one who killed her father. Syndicated television feature also known as *Vendetta*. Not rated. 112m. **DIR:** Stuart Margolin. **CAST:** Carol Alt, Eric Roberts, Burt Young, Eli Wallach, Nick Mancuso. **1990**

FAMILY OF COPS ★★1/2 Charles Bronson is okay as a police commander investigating a murder involving his daughter, but this made-for-television suspense drama lacks conviction. Instead, it's a by-the-numbers exercise for Bronson, whose character tries to balance the work and family sides of his character but never delivers the goods. Rated PG-13 for violence. 93m. **DIR:** Ted Kotcheff. **CAST:** Charles Bronson, Daniel Baldwin, Barbara Williams, Angela Featherstone, John Vernon. **1995 DVD**

FAMILY PLOT ★★★★ Alfred Hitchcock's last film proved to be a winner. He interjects this story with more humor than his other latter-day films. A seedy medium and her ne'er-do-well boyfriend (Barbara Harris and Bruce Dern) encounter a sinister couple (Karen Black and William Devane) while searching for a missing heir. They all become involved in diamond theft and attempted murder. Rated PG. 120m. **DIR:** Alfred Hitchcock. **CAST:** Karen Black, Bruce Dern, Barbara Harris, William Devane, Ed Lauter, Cathleen Nesbitt, Katherine Helmond. **1976 DVD**

FAMILY PRAYERS ★★★1/2 Poignant coming-of-age drama introduces Tzvi Ratner-Stauber as a 13 year old trying to make sense of his life. When his parents (Joe Mantegna and Anne Archer) start questioning their marriage, he must discard youth for adulthood. In the process he learns some valuable lessons, especially from his eccentric aunt, wonderfully played by Patti LuPone. Rated PG for language. 109m. **DIR:** Scott Rosenfelt. **CAST:** Joe Mantegna, Anne Archer, Paul Reiser, Allen Garfield, Patti LuPone, Tzvi Ratner-Stauber. **1991**

FAMILY THING, A ★★★★ Arkansas redneck Robert Duvall gets the shock of his life after his mother dies, and a sealed letter reveals that he's actually the result of his father having "been with" a black servant who subsequently died during childbirth. Worse yet, our hero learns of an older half brother living in urban Chicago, and curiosity leads him to a meeting with genial cop James Earl Jones. The two men interact wonderfully in this balanced script, which only stumbles during Duvall's weird exodus through downtown Chicago. Irma P. Hall steals the film as a blind, irascible aunt who emphasizes the strength and value of family ties. Rated PG-13 for profanity and mild violence. 109m. **DIR:** Richard Pearce. **CAST:** Robert Duvall, James Earl Jones, Michael Beach, Irma P. Hall, David Keith. **1996 DVD**

FAMILY UPSIDE DOWN, A ★★★ A touching, all too real drama about a previously self-sufficient couple whose age makes them dependent on their grown children. Hayes, Duke, and Zimbalist were nominated, and Astaire won an Emmy for this affecting made-for-television film. 100m. **DIR:** David Lowell Rich. **CAST:** Helen Hayes, Fred Astaire, Efrem Zimbalist Jr., Patty Duke. **1978**

FAMILY VIEWING ★★★★ Canadian filmmaker Atom Egoyan has created a brilliant surreal portrait of a dysfunctional family in this absorbing character study. The story centers around a troubled young man who attempts to piece together the events that led to the disappearance of his mother. Not rated, but recommended for adults. 86m. **DIR:** Atom Egoyan. **CAST:** David Hemblen. **1988**

FAN, THE (1981) ★★★1/2 In this fast-moving suspense yarn, a young fan is obsessed with a famous actress (Lauren Bacall). When his love letters to her are ignored, he embarks on a murder spree. *The Fan* is an absorbing thriller. The acting is first-rate and the camera work breathtaking. Rated R. 95m. **DIR:** Edward Bianchi. **CAST:** Lauren Bacall, James Garner, Maureen Stapleton, Michael Biehn. **1981**

FAN, THE (1996) ★★1/2 Traveling knife salesman Robert De Niro's devotion to baseball gets out of hand when favorite player Wesley Snipes goes into a slump. High-octane action director Tony Scott isn't comfortable with the thriller genre, and Phoef Sutton's script is just plain stupid. Legitimate concerns about celebrities stalked by psychotic fans are lost in this disorganized mess. Rated R for violence and profanity. 120m. **DIR:** Tony Scott. **CAST:** Robert De Niro, Wesley Snipes, Ellen Barkin, John Leguizamo, Benicio Del Toro, Patti D'Arbanville. **1996 DVD**

FANCY PANTS ★★★1/2 Bob Hope and Lucille Ball in their prime were an unbeatable comic team. Here they specialize in slapstick with Hope posing as a British earl to impress the locals in her New Mexican town. 92m. **DIR:** George Marshall. **CAST:** Bob Hope, Lucille Ball, Bruce Cabot. **1950**

FANDANGO ★★ This is an unfunny comedy about a group of college chums (led by Kevin Costner and Judd Nelson) going on one last romp before being inducted into the army—or running away from the draft—in 1971. *Fandango* seems as if it's going to get better any minute, but it doesn't. Rated PG for profanity. 91m. **DIR:** Kevin Reynolds. **CAST:** Kevin Costner, Judd Nelson, Sam Robards, Chuck Bush, Brian Cesak. **1984**

FANFAN THE TULIP ★★★1/2 In this affectionate parody of swashbucklers, a French soldier in Louis XV's army has more adventures than Errol Flynn had in any three movies. Not only does he defeat the enemy army virtually single-handedly, but also wins the hand of the princess while doing so. An international hit that first brought Gina Lollobrigida to world attention. In French with English subtitles. 104m. **DIR:** Christian Jaque. **CAST:** Gérard Philipe, Gina Lollobrigida, Noel Roquevert. **1951**

FANNY (1932) ★★★★ The middle part of a trilogy that began with *Marius* and ended with *César*, this can be viewed on its own. Young Marius leaves Marseilles to become a sailor, not knowing that his fiancée, Fanny, is pregnant. In his absence, she marries another man, who agrees to raise the child as his own. The film itself is static—it was conceived for the stage—but the performances are superb, particularly Raimu as Marius's father. In French with English subtitles. B&W; 120m. **DIR:** Marc Allegret. **CAST:** Raimu, Orane Demazis, Pierre Fresnay. **1932**

FANNY (1961) ★★★★ Leslie Caron is a beautiful and lively Fanny in this 1961 film. She plays a young girl seeking romance with the boy she grew up with. Unfortunately, he leaves her pregnant as he pursues a life at sea. 133m. **DIR:** Joshua Logan. **CAST:** Leslie Caron, Maurice Chevalier, Charles Boyer, Horst Buchholz, Baccaloni, Lionel Jeffries. **1961**

FANNY AND ALEXANDER ★★★★★ Set in Sweden around the turn of the century, this movie follows the adventures of two children. Some have called this Ingmar Bergman's first truly accessible work. It is undeniably his most optimistic. In Swedish with English subtitles. Rated R for profanity and violence. 197m. **DIR:** Ingmar Bergman. **CAST:** Pernilla Allwin, Bertil Guve. **1983**

FANTASIA ★★★★★ Originally intended as the first in a series of projects blending animation with classical music, *Fantasia* proved disappointing for Walt Disney (although its box-office take still made it the year's second most popular picture). Plans for a sequel were abandoned, but the original grew steadily more popular during subsequent rereleases . . . particularly with the counterculture crowd, which embraced the new 70mm prints and Dolby sound of its 1970s reissue. *Fantasia* was first conceived as a feature-length vehicle for Mickey Mouse, but his comedic segment is far from the film's most popular sequence. Fans generally cite the delicacy of various movements from Tchaikovsky's "The Nutcracker Suite," or the genuine terror inflicted by the dark figure of evil in Mussorgsky's "Night on Bald Mountain." 120m. **DIR:** Walt Disney. **1940 DVD**

FANTASIA 2000 ★★★★★ Call this another of those rare seminal moments in the history of celluloid enchantment; nothing less can describe the sheer exhilaration of watching *Fantasia 2000*, although it'll lose much of its punch when divorced from the IMAX screen on which it debuted. Fans of the original are certain to enjoy this spectacular follow-up, and even those who find the 1940 classic to be somewhat tedious will have to admire the economical pacing here. Its eight sequences—one old, seven new—move crisply to their musical selections, and the music itself is livelier than the original; highlights are the sequences set to Gershwin's "Rhapsody in Blue" and Elgar's "Pomp and Circumstance," both superbly edited and absolutely delightful. Rated G and suitable for all ages. 75m. **DIR:** Pixote Hunt, Hendel Butoy, Eric Goldberg, James Algar, Francis Glebas, Gaetan Brizzi, Paul Brizzi. **2000 DVD**

FANTASIES A female Walter Mitty. Rated R for brief nudity. 81m. **DIR:** John Derek. **CAST:** Bo Derek, Peter Hooten, Anna Alexiadis. **1984**

FANTASIST, THE A psychotic killer in Dublin sets up his victims with provocative phone calls, then kills them. Rated R for violence and nudity. 98m. **DIR:** Robin Hardy. **CAST:** Christopher Cazenove, Timothy Bottoms. **1986**

FANTASTIC PLANET ★★★ This French-Czechoslovakian production is an animated metaphor concerning the class struggles—and, eventually, war—between two races on an alien planet. Lovely animation and a non-preachy approach to the story combine to produce a fine little film that makes its points and sticks in the memory. Short, but sincere and effective. Voices of Barry Bostwick, Nora Heflin. Rated PG—intense subject matter and some violence. 71m. **DIR:** René Laloux. **1973 DVD**

FANTASTIC VOYAGE ★★★ Scientists journey into inner space—the human body—by being shrunk to microscopic size. They then are threatened by the system's natural defenses. This Richard Fleischer film still packs an unusually potent punch. 100m. **DIR:** Richard Fleischer. **CAST:** Stephen Boyd, Raquel Welch, Edmond O'Brien, Donald Pleasence, Arthur O'Connell, William Redfield, Arthur Kennedy. **1966 DVD**

FANTASTICKS, THE ★★★1/2 Two young lovers meet behind the backs of their feuding fathers, not knowing that the feud is only a ruse to bring the lovers together. Sweet, touching, and well-sung, with many lovely moments. Reminiscent of the young Judy Garland, Jean Louisa Kelly is especially fine. Rated PG. 86m. **DIR:** Michael Ritchie. **CAST:** Joel Grey, Jean Louisa Kelly, Joseph McIntyre, Jonathon Morris, Brad Sullivan, Barnard Hughes, Teller. **2000 DVD**

FANTASY ISLAND ★★1/2 Dreams and fantasies come true and then some on a mysterious millionaire's island paradise in this sub-average TV-er that spawned the hit series. Yawn. 100m. **DIR:** Richard Lang. **CAST:** Ricardo Montalban, Bill Bixby, Sandra Dee, Peter Lawford, Carol Lynley, Hugh O'Brian. **1977**

FAR AND AWAY ★★★★ Director Ron Howard's sweeping tale of Irish immigrants who come to America in search of land in the late 1800s is truly an entertaining saga. Tom Cruise and his real-life wife Nicole Kidman play a bickering couple from different social classes who find themselves adrift in the New World. Look for the letter-boxed edition to more fully enjoy Howard's grand vision. Rated PG-13 for violence and profanity. 140m. **DIR:** Ron Howard. **CAST:** Tom Cruise, Nicole Kidman, Thomas Gibson, Robert Prosky, Barbara Babcock, Colm Meaney, Eileen Pollock, Michelle Johnson. **1992 DVD**

FAR COUNTRY, THE ★★★1/2 James Stewart is a tough-minded cattleman intent on establishing himself in Alaska during the Klondike gold rush of 1896. The result is fine Western fare. 97m. **DIR:** Anthony Mann. **CAST:** James Stewart, Ruth Roman, Walter Brennan, Corinne Calvet, John McIntire, Jay C. Flippen, Steve Brodie, Harry Morgan. **1955 DVD**

FAR FROM HOME ★★★ On vacation, pubescent Drew Barrymore and divorced dad Matt Frewer make the mistake of stopping at a trailer camp where a mad killer is at work. Off-kilter thriller with some interesting twists. Rated R for violence and nudity. 86m. **DIR:** Meiert Avis. **CAST:** Matt Frewer, Drew Barrymore, Richard Masur, Karen Austin, Susan Tyrrell, Jennifer Tilly, Dick Miller. **1988 DVD**

FAR FROM HOME: THE ADVENTURES OF YELLOW-DOG ★★★ Heartwarming film shortchanges viewers by depriving us of more of Yellow Dog's adventures with his young master (Jesse Bradford) and on his own. The boy and his faithful companion make a treacherous journey through gorgeous but uncivilized Canadian forests after their boat capsizes. Bruce Davison and Mimi Rogers are fine as the boy's distraught parents who refuse to give up the search. Rated PG for some gross bug-eating and hunting scenes. 81m. **DIR:** Phillip Borsos. **CAST:** Bruce Davison, Mimi Rogers, Jesse Bradford, Tom Bower. **1994**

FAR FROM THE MADDING CROWD ★★★★ The combination of the world-class director and a stellar British cast makes this Thomas Hardy adaptation a lovely, intelligent epic. Julie Christie plays a country girl who becomes entangled in the lives of three diverse men. Cinematographer-now-director Nicolas Roeg beautifully captured the rustic countryside. 169m. **DIR:** John Schlesinger. **CAST:** Julie Christie, Terence Stamp, Alan Bates, Peter Finch. **1967**

FAR FRONTIER ★★★★ Top-of-the-line, hard-edged, later Roy Rogers oater as desperadoes smuggle deported owl hoots back into the U.S. in oil drums. Border patrolman Rogers makes the vicious scheme a losing venture. Action-packed. B&W; 67m. **DIR:** William Witney. **CAST:** Roy Rogers, Gail Davis, Andy Devine, Roy Barcroft, Clayton Moore, Riders of the Purple Sage. **1948**

FAR NORTH ★★★ Actor-playwright Sam Shepard's first film as a director is a surprisingly funny comedy-drama about three generations of a farming family. Yet underlying the humor is a typically Shepardian sense of tragedy as wayward daughter Jessica Lange comes home after her father is hurt in a farming accident. Rated PG-13 for profanity and sexy scenes. 87m. **DIR:** Sam Shepard. **CAST:** Jessica Lange, Charles Durning, Tess Harper, Donald Moffat, Ann Wedgeworth, Patricia Arquette. **1988**

FAR OFF PLACE, A ★★★1/2 Disney adventure film is an awkward blend of *The Gods Must Be Crazy* and *The Rescuers Down Under*. In order to escape the ivory poachers who killed their parents, two teenagers must cross the treacherous Kalahari Desert with the aid of a young Bushman. Two scenes of extreme violence make this film a bit too strong for children under 10. Rated PG for violence and brief profanity. 107m. **DIR:** Mikael Salomon. **CAST:** Reese Witherspoon, Ethan Randall, Jack Thompson, Sarel Bok, Maximilian Schell. **1993**

FAR OUT MAN 🦃 A bad script, worse acting, frequent play on gastric distress. Rated R. 85m. **DIR:** Thomas Chong. **CAST:** Tommy Chong, Martin Mull, Rae Dawn Chong, C. Thomas Howell, Judd Nelson, Richard "Cheech" Marin. **1990**

FAR PAVILIONS, THE ★★★ In this romantic adventure, Ben Cross plays Ash, a young British officer in imperial India. Oddly enough, he had been raised as an Indian until he was eleven. As an adult, he is reunited with his childhood friend the Princess Anjuli (Amy Irving). Despite her impending marriage to the elderly Rajaha (Rossano Brazzi), Ash and Anjuli fall in love. Rated PG for sex and violence. 108m. **DIR:** Peter Duffell. **CAST:** Ben Cross, Amy Irving, Omar Sharif, Christopher Lee, Benedict Taylor, Rossano Brazzi. **1983 DVD**

FARAWAY, SO CLOSE ★★★★ Sequel to *Wings of Desire* focuses on the seriocomic adventures of the second angel as he follows Bruno Ganz into the corporeal realm and falls prey to earthly temptation. Offbeat but heartwarming and thought-provoking. In English and German with English subtitles. Rated PG-13 for violence and profanity. 140m. **DIR:** Wim Wenders. **CAST:** Otto Sanders, Peter Falk, Horst Buchholz, Willem Dafoe, Nastassja Kinski, Heinz Ruhmann, Bruno Ganz, Solveig Dommartin, Rudiger Volger, Lou Reed. **1993 DVD**

FAREWELL MY CONCUBINE ★★★1/2 This emotionally engorged, visually staggering epic is about a pair of male Peking opera stars whose commitment to art and each other is challenged throughout fifty years of civil war, foreign invasion, social revolution, political convulsions, and private squabbling. One performer, forced to forsake his true sexual identity, becomes the odd player out in a volatile love triangle when his mentor marries a courtesan. This exotic backstage pass to the theatrical and political growing pains of China loses momentum but should not be missed. In Mandarin with English subtitles. Rated R. 154m. **DIR:** Chen Kaige. **CAST:** Leslie Cheung, Zhang Fengyi, Gong Li. **1993 DVD**

FAREWELL MY LOVELY ★★★★1/2 This superb film adaptation of Raymond Chandler's celebrated mystery novel stands as a tribute to the talents of actor Robert Mitchum who makes a perfect, world-weary Philip Marlowe, private eye. The detective's search for the long-lost love of a gangster takes us into the netherworld of pre–World War II Los Angeles for a fast-paced period piece. Rated R. 97m. **DIR:** Dick Richards. **CAST:** Robert Mitchum, Charlotte Rampling, John Ireland, Sylvia Miles, Harry Dean Stanton. **1975 DVD**

FAREWELL TO ARMS, A ★★★★ Ernest Hemingway's well-crafted story of doomed love between a wounded ambulance driver and a nurse in Italy during World War I. Adolphe Menjou is peerless, Helen Hayes dies touchingly, and Gary Cooper strides away in the rain. B&W; 78m. **DIR:** Frank Borzage. **CAST:** Helen Hayes, Gary Cooper, Adolphe Menjou, Mary Philips, Jack LaRue. **1932 DVD**

FAREWELL TO THE KING ★★★1/2 In this old-fashioned, boy's-eye-view adventure epic from writer-director John Milius, Nick Nolte plays a World War II soldier who deserts following Gen. Douglas MacArthur's retreat from Corregidor. Nolte ends up in the jungles of Borneo, where he becomes a king. Nigel Havers is excellent as the British officer who incites the natives to battle. Rated PG-13 for profanity and violence. 114m. **DIR:** John Milius. **CAST:** Nick Nolte, Nigel Havers, Frank McRae, James Fox. **1989**

FARGO ★★★★1/2 In this remarkable *film noir*, a soft-spoken car salesman arranges for his wife to be kidnapped with the idea of keeping most of the ransom provided by her wealthy father. Unfortunately, nothing goes quite as he plans. It's hilarious, twisted, and sometimes shocking—in other words, a must-see. Rated R for violence, gore, and profanity. 97m. **DIR:** Joel Coen. **CAST:** Frances McDormand, William H. Macy, Steve Buscemi, Peter Stormare, Harve Presnell, Jose Feliciano. **1996 DVD**

FARINELLI IL CASTRATO ★★ The life of eighteenth-century castrato singer Farinelli becomes a low-camp melodrama, sumptously mounted but dramatically unbelievable and funny in the wrong places. Farinelli's "voice" is electronically synthesized from a tenor and soprano; the effect is interesting, but the lip-synching is so unconvincing that it destroys the credibility of the music scenes. In Italian and French with English subtitles. Rated R for nudity and simulated sex. 110m. **DIR:** Gerard Corbiau. **CAST:** Stefano Dionisi, Enrico Lo Verso, Elsa Zylberstein, Javier Bardem, Jeroen Krabbé. **1994**

FARMER AND CHASE ★★★ Aging bank robber Ben Gazzara reluctantly agrees to let his callow son accompany him on what he intends to be his last job. But the job goes bad, leaving the pair with a bank full of hostages and no way out. Credit first-time writer-director Michael Seitzman with keeping his focus sharp and picking a first-rate cast. Rated R for strong profanity, violence, and sexual situations. 97m. **DIR:** Michael Seitzman. **CAST:** Ben Gazzara, Lara Flynn Boyle, Todd Field. **1997**

FARMER TAKES A WIFE, THE ★★ Tiresome musical remake of a 1935 Janet Gaynor–Henry Fonda drama (filmed under the same title). This depiction of life along the Erie Canal in the early nineteenth century is a mistake from word one. 81m. **DIR:** Henry Levin. **CAST:** Betty Grable, Dale Robertson, Thelma Ritter, John Carroll, Eddie Foy Jr., Merry Anders. **1953**

FARMER'S DAUGHTER, THE ★★★ Loretta Young won the best actress Oscar for her delightful performance in this charming comedy about a Swedish woman who clashes with the man she loves over a congressional election. B&W; 97m. **DIR:** H. C. Potter. **CAST:** Loretta Young, Joseph Cotten, Ethel Barrymore, Charles Bickford, Lex Barker, Keith Andes, James Arness. **1947**

FARMER'S WIFE, THE ★★★ Alfred Hitchcock toyed with slapstick comedy in this early silent feature about a farmer who seeks high and low for a new bride after his wife dies. Naturally, he overlooks his housekeeper, who has loved him from afar for years. Unusual point-of-view shots feature characters talking to other people by looking directly into the camera. B&W; 97m. **DIR:** Alfred Hitchcock. **CAST:** Jameson Thomas, Lillian Hall-Davies, Gordon Harker, Gibb McLaughlin, Maud Gill, Louise Pounds. **1928 DVD**

FARSCAPE (TV SERIES) ★★★ Astronaut John Crichton attempts an experimental voyage only to find himself catapulted into a wormhole, which leads him to a far-flung place in the galaxy where he is caught up in a struggle between escaped prisoners and a militaristic government. *Farscape* takes a bit of getting used to, but it's worth it for the fine performances and excellent touches by Jim Henson's Creature Shop. The series improved as it added more unusual characters and intensified the plight of its protagonists. Made for TV. 60m. **DIR:** Various. **CAST:** Ben Browder, Claudia Black, Virginia Hey, Anthony Simcoe. **1999 DVD**

•FAST AND THE FURIOUS, THE ★★★1/2 This high-octane saga of late-night, inner-city street racing is a marvelous guilty pleasure. Undercover cop Paul Walker, initially assigned to infiltrate this illegal activity, bonds with tough-talkin', high-struttin' Vin Diesel (a career-making performance) and then discovers that he likes his new friends too much to betray them. The car chases are staged for maximum excitement, and the film moves along rapidly enough to zip past the plot's few but glaring twists. This is what *Gone in 60 Seconds should* have been. Rated PG-13 for profanity, violence, and sexual content. 106m. **DIR:** Rob Cohen. **CAST:** Paul Walker, Vin Diesel, Michelle Rodriguez, Jordana Brewster, Rick Yune, Chad Lindberg. **2001 DVD**

FAST BREAK ★★1/2 As a basketball coach, Gabe Kaplan resurrects some of the laughs he got with his sweathogs on *Welcome Back, Kotter*. Kaplan plays a New York deli worker who quits to coach a college basketball team in Nevada. Kaplan must beat a tough rival team in order to get a contract at the university, so he whips the unpromising team into shape. Rated PG. 107m. **DIR:** Jack Smight. **CAST:** Gabe Kaplan, Harold Sylvester, Mike Warren, Bernard King, Reb Brown. **1979**

FAST, CHEAP AND OUT OF CONTROL ★★★ Documentary filmmaker Errol Morris profiles a wild-animal tamer, a topiary gardener, a robot builder, and a man who studies the naked mole rat of Africa. At first the men appear to have nothing in common but enthusiasm for their work—then Morris begins to draw odd little connections between them that keep catching the viewer off guard. On the down side, though, he also seems at times be poking mean-spirited fun at them; a little less condescension might have made this interesting film far more compelling. 80m. **DIR:** Errol Morris. **CAST:** Dave Hoover, George Mendonca, Ray Mendez, Rodney Brooks. **1997**

FAST FOOD 🦃 Typical inane college sex comedy. Rated PG-13 for sexual situations. 91m. **DIR:** Michael A. Simpson. **CAST:** Jim Varney, Traci Lords. **1989**

FAST FORWARD ★★ An undisguised variation on the cliché of "let's put on a show so we can make it in show biz." In it, eight high school kids from Sandusky, Ohio, journey to New York for a promised audition. A bubbly bit of fluff that relies on sheer energy to patch up its plot and make up for the lack of an inspired score. Sometimes, it works. Rated PG. 100m. **DIR:** Sidney Poitier. **CAST:** John Scott Clough, Don Franklin. **1985**

FAST GETAWAY Spectaular stunts aren't enough to save this mindless tale of a 16-year-old kid who robs banks with his dad. There's not enough here to make a withdrawal. Rated PG-13 for violence. 85m. **DIR:** Spiro Razatos. **CAST:** Corey Haim, Cynthia Rothrock, Leo Rossi, Marcia Strassman. **1990**

FAST GETAWAY II ★★ Direct-to-video trash stars Corey Haim as a former bank-robber-turned-security-adviser who discovers that all of the banks he's supposed to be protecting are being robbed—and that someone is trying to set him up to take the fall. Ludicrous storyline, sloppy direction, and a particularly annoying performance by Haim make this one to avoid. Rated PG-13 for profanity. 94m. **DIR:** Oley Sassone. **CAST:** Corey Haim, Cynthia Rothrock, Leo Rossi. **1993**

FAST LANE FEVER ★★1/2 A street gang with souped-up streetcars bullies others into racing for money. An underdog good guy loses to the bad guys, then comes back against all odds. Interesting cars and a fascinating look at Australia through the camera lens. Rated R for profanity, sex, and violence. 94m. **DIR:** John Clark. **CAST:** Terry Serio, Deborah Conway, Max Cullen, Graham Bond. **1982**

FAST MONEY ★★ Yancy Butler and Matt McCoy play star-crossed lovers on the run from the law and the mob when they find themselves in possession of a suitcase full of mob money. Familiar. Rated R for violence, profanity, and nudity. 93m. **DIR:** Alexander Wright. **CAST:** Yancy Butler, Matt McCoy, John Ashton, Trevor Goddard, Patrika Darbo. **1996**

•FAST SOFA ★★ Even though it's based on a best-selling novel, *Fast Sofa* is not a page-turner. Jake Busey plays the aimless Rick, who ditches his girlfriend and hits the road in search of himself and his favorite porn star, the delectable Ginger Quail. In keeping with all road trips, Rick encounters numerous eccentric and colorful characters and situations, but they're not nearly as eccentric or colorful as cowriter-director Salome Breziner believes they are. Rated R for adult situations, drugs, and language. 110m. **DIR:** Salome Breziner. **CAST:** Jake Busey, Jennifer Tilly, Adam Goldberg, Natasha Lyonne, Bijou Phillips, Crispin Glover, Seymour Cassel. **2001 DVD**

FAST TALKING ★★ This Australian comedy stars Rod Zuanic as a little punk that you'd love to shake and put on the straight and narrow. The fact that he has a miserable home life that doesn't hold much of a future for him doesn't make this fast talker any more endearing. 93m. **DIR:** Ken Cameron. **CAST:** Rod Zuanic, Steve Bisley, Tracy Mann, Dennis Moore, Toni Allaylis, Chris Truswell. **1986**

FAST TIMES AT RIDGEMONT HIGH ★★1/2 In 1979, Cameron Crowe went back to high school to discover what today's teens are up to and wrote about his experiences. Youngsters will love it, but adults will probably want to skip the movie and read the book. Rated R for nudity, profanity, and simulated sex. 92m. **DIR:** Amy Heckerling. **CAST:** Sean Penn, Jennifer Jason Leigh, Judge Reinhold, Brian Backer, Phoebe Cates, Ray Walston, Forest Whitaker, Eric Stoltz, Nicolas Cage. **1982 DVD**

FAST-WALKING ★★★1/2 This one is definitely not for everyone, but if you are adventurous, it may surprise you. James Woods plays a prison guard whose yearning for the good life leads him into a jailbreak scheme. Film plays for black comedy and generally succeeds. Rated R for violence, language, nudity. 116m. **DIR:** James B. Harris. **CAST:** James Woods, Kay Lenz, Tim McIntire, Robert Hooks, Susan Tyrrell. **1983**

FASTEST GUITAR ALIVE, THE ★★ Weak action yarn about Confederate spies who steal a fortune. Worth a viewing, mainly for Roy Orbison's appearance. 87m. **DIR:** Michael Moore. **CAST:** Roy Orbison, Sammy Jackson, Maggie Pierce, Joan Freeman. **1968**

FASTEST GUN ALIVE, THE ★★★ Serviceable Western casts Glenn Ford as a mild-mannered storekeeper who gets unwanted fame as a fast draw. After beating a string of cowpokes seeking a reputation, Ford must face a miscast Broderick Crawford, a badman who doesn't relish the idea of being thought of as second best. 92m. **DIR:** Russell Rouse. **CAST:** Glenn Ford, Broderick Crawford, Jeanne Crain, Leif Erickson, Russ Tamblyn, Rhys Williams, Noah Beery Jr., Chubby Johnson, J. M. Kerrigan, Allyn Joslyn. **1956**

FAT CITY ★★★★1/2 This neglected treasure is perhaps the best film ever made about boxing. Tank-town matches between hopefuls and has-beens along California's Central Valley keep Stacy Keach and Jeff Bridges in hamburger and white port. A classic piece of Americana and one of John Huston's greatest achievements. Rated PG. 96m. **DIR:** John Huston. **CAST:** Stacy Keach, Jeff Bridges, Susan Tyrrell, Nicholas Colasanto, Candy Clark. **1972**

•FAT GIRL ★★ A homely French teenager both loves and resents her older, prettier sister. French filmmaker Catherine Breillat continues the drive she began with *Romance* (1999) to stretch the bounds of mainstream film sex. The result is more of the same Eurotrash, with Breillat's trademarks: graphic sex and violence coupled with hilariously pretentious dialogue. In French with English subtitles. Not rated; contains profanity (in subtitles), nudity, sexual scenes, and brief climactic violence. 83m. **DIR:** Catherine Breillat. **CAST:** Anaïs Reboux, Roxane Mesquida, Libero De Rienzo, Arsinée Khanjian. **2001**

FAT MAN AND LITTLE BOY ★★1/2 In spite of its historically significant story line—the World War II development of the atomic bomb—this film remains curiously flat and distanced. The clash between military chief General Leslie R. Groves (Paul Newman) and scientific genius J. Robert Oppenheimer (Dwight Schultz) seems mannered and forced. Rated PG-13 for intensity. 126m. **DIR:** Roland Joffe. **CAST:** Paul Newman, Dwight Schultz, Bonnie Bedelia, John Cusack, Laura Dern, Natasha Richardson. **1989**

FATAL ATTRACTION (1985) ★★★1/2 In this suspenseful film, two people get caught up in sexual fantasy games so intense that they begin to act them out—in public. *Fatal Attraction* would receive a higher rating if it had a smoother transition from the innocent flirting to the heavy-duty sexual activity that leads to the film's thrilling and ironic close. Rated R for nudity, violence, and profanity. 90m. **DIR:** Michael Grant. **CAST:** Sally Kellerman, Stephen Lack, Lawrence Dane, John Huston. **1985**

FATAL ATTRACTION (1987) ★★★★ This adult shocker works beautifully as a nail-biting update of *Play Misty for Me*. It's the married man's ultimate nightmare. Glenn Close chews up the screen as Michael Douglas's one-night stand; when he (very married, to Anne Archer, an underappreciated talent) backs away and tries to resume his ordinary routine, Close becomes progressively more dangerous. Rated R for nudity and language. 119m. **DIR:** Adrian Lyne. **CAST:** Glenn Close, Michael Douglas, Anne Archer. **1987 DVD**

FATAL BEAUTY 🦃 Whoopi Goldberg stars as an improbably resourceful cop pursuing several smarmy drug pushers. Rated R for language and excessive violence. 104m. **DIR:** Tom Holland. **CAST:** Whoopi Goldberg, Sam Elliott, Rubén Blades, Harris Yulin, John P. Ryan, Jennifer Warren, Brad Dourif. **1987 DVD**

FATAL BOND 🦃 Linda Blair doesn't turn any heads in this fatally flawed thriller about a woman who suspects her lover is a serial killer. Rated R for nudity, violence, and language. 89m. **DIR:** Phil Avalon. **CAST:** Linda Blair, Jerome Elhers, Stephen Leeder, Joe Bugner, Donal Gibson. **1991**

FATAL CHARM ★★1/2 Teenager Amanda Peterson initiates a relationship by mail with beguiling Christopher Atkins, sentenced and jailed for the brutal murders of numerous young women. Although Nicolas Niciphor's script tosses in a few clever twists, the ho-hum execution (director Fritz Kiersch, hiding behind a pseudonym) turns this made-for-cable production into a standard thriller. Rated R for violence, nudity, and profanity. 90m. **DIR:** Alan Smithee. **CAST:** Christopher Atkins, Amanda Peterson, Mary Frann, James Remar, Andrew Robinson, Peggy Lipton. **1992**

FATAL COMBAT ★★1/2 Stop me if you've heard this one before: A billionaire broadcaster holds death matches between top athletes. His audience: wealthy aristocrats bored with the dullness of everyday life. But when a top martial artist is kidnapped and forced to fight for that audience, the billionaire may have bitten off more than he can chew. Ultimately tedious *Mortal Kombat/ Street Fighter* rip-off is buoyed somewhat by the undeniable video presence of star Jeff Wincott. Rated R for profanity and violence. 93m. **DIR:** Damien Lee. **CAST:** Jeff Wincott, Phillip Jarrett, Richard Fitzpatrick, Guylaine St. Onge, Joseph Dimambro, Sven-Ole Thorsen. **1995**

FATAL EXPOSURE ★★1/2 Mare Winningham partially salvages this routine made-for-cable thriller—as a resourceful single parent whose photo order gets mixed up by the processing lab . . . which sends her home with pictures originally intended for a hired killer. Nick Mancuso is engaging as a neighbor with a mysterious past. Rated PG-13. 89m. **DIR:** Alan Metzger. **CAST:** Mare Winningham, Nick Mancuso, Christopher McDonald, Geoffrey Blake. **1991**

FATAL GAMES 🦃 In a school for young athletes, a murderer begins eliminating the students, using a javelin. Not rated; contains explicit nudity and violence. 88m. **DIR:** Michael Elliot. **CAST:** Sally Kirkland, Lynn Banashek, Teal Roberts. **1984**

FATAL HOUR, THE ★★1/2 Boris Karloff is cast as homicide detective Mr. Wong in this suspenseful thriller about murder and jewel smuggling. Grant Withers is solid as Police Captain Street. B&W; 68m. **DIR:** William Nigh. **CAST:** Boris Karloff, Grant Withers, Marjorie Reynolds, Charles Trowbridge. **1940 DVD**

FATAL IMAGE, THE ★★★ Watchable made-for-TV film features a Philadelphia mother-daughter team (Michele Lee and Justine Bateman) as they find romance, murder, and each other on a Parisian vacation. Bateman's obsession with her camcorder enables her to inadvertently film a murder. Now the murderer and her henchman want the videotape and are willing to kill the American tourists to get it. 96m. **DIR:** Thomas Wright. **CAST:** Michele Lee, Justine Bateman, François Dunoyer. **1990 DVD**

FATAL INSTINCT ★★1/2 Sexy thriller is ready-made for video, throwing sex and violence into a sordid tale of a private detective who jeopardizes everything in his life to prove the woman he loves isn't guilty. Rated R for nudity, language, and violence; unrated version contains more sexual content. 95m. **DIR:** John Dirlam. **CAST:** Michael Madsen, Laura Johnson, Tony Hamilton. **1992**

FATAL INSTINCT ★★★ Carl Reiner sends up a bevy of thrillers in this hit-and-miss spoof. Armand Assante is a dumb-as-dirt detective who gets mixed up with a femme fatale. This goofy movie has its share of laughs. Rated PG-13 for light profanity, silly violence, and wacky sex. 89m. **DIR:** Carl Reiner. **CAST:** Armand Assante, Sean Young, Sherilyn Fenn, Kate Nelligan, Christopher McDonald, James Remar, Tony Randall, Clarence Clemmons, Eartha Kitt, Ronnie Schell, Carl Reiner. **1993**

FATAL INVERSION, A ★★★★★ The most impressive of the psychological thrillers adapted by the BBC from a Ruth Rendell novel written under her nom de plume, Barbara Vine. An eerie script and exciting direction befits her strange tale of a bacchanalian summer shared by five young adults who later learn that a corrosive past can ooze into the present. This has an ending you won't be able to shake. Not rated; contains nudity, drug use, and sexual situations. 150m. **DIR:** Tim Fywell. **CAST:** Jeremy Northam, Douglas Hodge, Gordon Warnecke, Saira Todd, Julia Ford. **1991**

FATAL MISSION ★★ It took five screenwriters, including Peter Fonda, to bring this formulaic jungle-action film to the screen. Fonda portrays a Special Forces agent during the Vietnam War. Rated R for violence. 84m. **DIR:** George Rowe. **CAST:** Peter Fonda, Mako, Jim Mitchum, Tia Carrere. **1990**

FATAL PAST ★★ Hokum about a gangster's mistress and bodyguard, reincarnated tragic figures from ancient Japan, doomed to live out their fate once again in modern-day Los Angeles. Unbeknownst to them, they are about to play out a dangerous re-creation of their previous lives, and only one woman, a snoopy newspaper reporter, can bring the events full circle. Too confusing for its own good. Rated R for nudity, violence, and adult language. 85m. **DIR:** Clive Fleury. **CAST:** Costas Mandylor, Kasia Figura, Terence Cooper, Steven Grimes. **1993**

FATAL VISION ★★★★1/2 This excellent TV miniseries is based on the actual case of convicted murderer, Dr. Jeffrey MacDonald. In 1970, MacDonald (Gary Cole) murdered his pregnant wife and two daughters. Although he denies the charges, his father-in-law (Karl Malden) becomes suspicious and helps to convict him. 198m. **DIR:** David Greene. **CAST:** Karl Malden, Gary Cole, Eva Marie Saint, Gary Grubbs, Mitchell Ryan, Andy Griffith. **1984**

FATALLY YOURS ★★ Bad acting and editing erase the entertainment value of this tired reincarnation tale. When a writer is drawn to a vacant and crumbling house, he immediately fashions a novel mirroring past events that, surprisingly, connect him to the house. Rated EM for violence, profanity, nudity, and sexual situations. 90m. **DIR:** Tim Everitt. **CAST:** Rick Rossovich, George Lazenby, Roddy McDowall, Sage Stallone, John Capodice, Sarah MacDonell, Robert Gentile. **1995**

FATHER (1966) ★★★ Istvan Szabo, best known for the Oscar-winning *Mephisto*, directed this drama. A boy creates an elaborate fantasy about the heroism of his father, who was killed in World War II. As an adult, he is led to abandon his fantasies and examine the reality of his heritage. Slow-moving but provocative. In Hungarian with English subtitles. B&W; 89m. **DIR:** István Szabó. **CAST:** Andras Balint, Miklos Gabor. **1966**

FATHER (1990) ★★★★ A small, intense Australian drama starring Max Von Sydow as a popular pub owner and doting granddad who may have been a vicious Nazi officer. This is propelled by riveting performances from Sydow and Carol Drinkwater as the daughter who absolutely does not want to think the worst, even when reality begins to tear away her defenses. Rated PG-13 for profanity and implied violence. 106m. **DIR:** John Power. **CAST:** Max von Sydow, Carol Drinkwater, Julia Blake, Steve Jacobs. **1990**

FATHER & SCOUT ★★1/2 Somewhat amusing made-for-television comedy about a nerdy dad who is forced to take his Eagle Scout son on a camping trip. Of course Dad knows nothing about the great outdoors, but before the trip is done, both father and son will have bonded. Rated PG. 92m. **DIR:** Richard Michaels. **CAST:** Bob Saget, Brian Bonsall, Heidi Swedberg, Stuart Pankin. **1994**

FATHER GOOSE ★★★ A bedraggled, unshaven, and unsophisticated Cary Grant is worth watching even in a mediocre comedy. Grant plays a hard-drinking Australian coast watcher during the height of World War II. His reclusive life-style on a remote Pacific island is interrupted when he is forced to play nursemaid to a group of adolescent schoolgirls and their prudish teacher (Leslie Caron). 115m. **DIR:** Ralph Nelson. **CAST:** Cary Grant, Leslie Caron. **1964 DVD**

FATHER HOOD ★★1/2 A con man finds his latest big score sabotaged by the unexpected arrival of his runaway daughter, who wants him to save his son from the same institution that brutalized her. Not all of the movie works, but Patrick Swayze is funny and believable in a role that seems to have been fashioned out of cardboard. Rated PG-13 for brief profanity and violence. 95m. **DIR:** Darrell Roodt. **CAST:** Patrick Swayze, Halle Berry, Sabrina Lloyd, Brian Bonsall, Michael Ironside, Diane Ladd, Bob Gunton, Adrienne Barbeau. **1993**

FATHER OF THE BRIDE (1950) ★★★1/2 Spencer Tracy's proud and frantic papa is the chief attraction in this droll examination of last-minute preparations prior to daughter Elizabeth Taylor's wedding. Writers Frances Goodrich and Albert Hackett include a few too many scenes of near-slapstick hysteria, but the quieter moments between father and daughter are wonderful (if a bit dated). 93m. **DIR:** Vincente Minnelli. **CAST:** Spencer Tracy, Elizabeth Taylor, Joan Bennett, Leo G. Carroll, Don Taylor, Billie Burke. **1950**

FATHER OF THE BRIDE (1991) ★★★1/2 Steve Martin is the father who becomes increasingly aghast at the costs and craziness involved in his daughter's marriage. With this remake of the 1950 Spencer Tracy film, director Charles Shyer and the star create a heartwarming comedy the whole family can enjoy. Rated PG for brief profanity. 105m. **DIR:** Charles Shyer. **CAST:** Steve Martin, Diane Keaton, Martin Short, Kimberly Williams, George Newbern, B. D. Wong. **1991 DVD**

FATHER OF THE BRIDE PART II ★★★★ With their spin on *Father's Little Dividend*, married moviemakers Charles Shyer and Nancy Meyers outdo their first entry in the updated series. Of course, Steve Martin's comic timing—both physical and verbal—deserves much of the credit for the effectiveness of this heartwarming and hilarious sequel that centers around the consequences of having a baby. Rated PG. 106m. **DIR:** Charles Shyer. **CAST:** Steve Martin, Diane Keaton, Martin Short, Kimberly Williams, George Newbern, B. D. Wong, Peter Michael Goetz, Jane Adams, Eugene Levy. **1995 DVD**

FATHERLAND ★★★1/2 Nazi Germany defeated Western Europe in this thoughtful adaptation of Robert Harris's book, which opens in the early 1960s, with an aging Hitler anxious to begin negotiations with U.S. President Joseph Kennedy. But a visiting American journalist uncovers evidence suggesting that Germany perpetrated a horrible atrocity during World War II. Dedicated sci-fi readers won't find anything new here, but the drama unfolds with intelligence and conviction. Rated PG-13 for violence, profanity, and brief nudity. 106m. **DIR:** Chris Menaul. **CAST:** Rutger Hauer, Miranda Richardson, Peter Vaughan, Michael Kitchen, Jean Marsh. **1994**

FATHERS & SONS ★★★1/2 Mystical overtones enhance this drama of a teenager in jeopardy (Rory Cochrane) and his widower dad (Jeff Goldblum), who tries to shield his son from life's more painful lessons as the boy becomes entangled with a local drug dealer. Slow going, but atmospheric, well-acted, and artfully directed. Rated PG for profanity, sexuality, and brief nudity. 109m. **DIR:** Paul Mones. **CAST:** Jeff Goldblum, Rory Cochrane, Rosanna Arquette, Joie Lee. **1992**

FATHER'S DAY ★★ Overly rational Los Angeles attorney Billy Crystal and insecure ex-hippy Robin Williams chase after a teenager with questionable parentage, thanks to a former girlfriend who—years earlier—dallied with both our heroes. This misfired remake of Francis Veber's *Les Compères* proves, once again, that Hollywood hasn't a clue how to match the style and humor of French sex comedies. Rated PG-13 for profanity and mild sexual content. 98m. **DIR:** Ivan Reitman. **CAST:** Robin Williams, Billy Crystal, Julia Louis-Dreyfus,

Nastassja Kinski, Charlie Hofheimer, Bruce Greenwood. **1997 DVD**

FATHER'S LITTLE DIVIDEND ★★★ In *Father of the Bride*, the marriage of daughter Elizabeth Taylor to Don Taylor made a wreck out of Spencer Tracy. Now, in the sequel, she's expecting. This play off of a winner doesn't measure up to the original, but it's entertaining fare anyway. Spencer Tracy could bluster and be flustered with the best. 82m. **DIR:** Vincente Minnelli. **CAST:** Spencer Tracy, Elizabeth Taylor, Joan Bennett, Don Taylor, Billie Burke. **1951 DVD**

FATHER'S REVENGE, A ★★★★ When his daughter, a flight assistant, is taken hostage in Germany by terrorists, a high school basketball coach (Brian Dennehy) decides to take matters into his own hands. The often-seen Dennehy is given one of his better-written roles in this TV movie, and he does a terrific job with it. 93m. **DIR:** John Herzfeld. **CAST:** Brian Dennehy, Ron Silver, Joanna Cassidy, Anthony Valentine. **1987**

FATSO ★★1/2 Too many juvenile toilet jokes mar what might have been a humorous study of a man's confrontation with his own obesity. Dom DeLuise stars as the chubby Italian-American who wrestles with a variety of diets. Messages get lost amid the shrill performances. Rated PG for language and questionable humor. 94m. **DIR:** Anne Bancroft. **CAST:** Dom DeLuise, Anne Bancroft, Candy Azzara, Ron Carey. **1980**

FAUST ★★★★★ The undisputed master of early German cinema, Friedrich W. Murnau triumphs once again with the legendary story of Faust. Gosta Ekman gives an excellent performance as Faust and Emil Jannings plays the Devil with comic pathos. Silent with English intertitles. B&W; 100m. **DIR:** F. W. Murnau. **CAST:** Emil Jannings, Gosta Ekman, Camilla Horn. **1926 DVD**

FAVOR, THE ★★★ Although this romantic comedy desperately wants to be a ribald sex farce, it's just not played with the proper tone. Harley Jane Kozak, pining for a long-unseen high-school sweetheart, emerges as an unsympathetic busybody when she persuades best friend Elizabeth McGovern to meet and sleep with the guy. Despite a rather amusing climax, we never really like any of these people. Rated R for profanity and frank sexuality. 97m. **DIR:** Donald Petrie. **CAST:** Harley Jane Kozak, Elizabeth McGovern, Bill Pullman, Brad Pitt, Ken Wahl, Larry Miller. **1994 DVD**

FAVOR, THE WATCH AND THE VERY BIG FISH, THE ★★ In this muddled madcap comedy, Bob Hoskins tries hard as a photographer who gets distracted by the mysterious Natasha Richardson while searching for the perfect model to portray Jesus Christ—whom he finally finds in Jeff Goldblum. Annoyingly frantic. Rated R for profanity, nudity, and violence. 89m. **DIR:** Ben Lewin. **CAST:** Bob Hoskins, Jeff Goldblum, Natasha Richardson, Michel Blanc, Jean-Pierre Cassel, Angela Pleasence. **1992**

FAWLTY TOWERS (TV SERIES) ★★★★ This British television series is a true comedy classic. Written by Monty Python's John Cleese and his ex-wife, Connie Booth, the show is a situation comedy about the problems of running a small seaside inn. The characters are typical and the story lines mundane, but in the hands of Cleese and company, each episode is a near-perfect ballet of escalating frustration. For sheer, double-over belly laughs, this series has never been equaled. 75m. **DIR:** John Cleese, Connie Booth. **CAST:** John Cleese, Prunella Scales, Connie Booth. **1975**

FBI MURDERS, THE ★★★★1/2 Superior made-for-TV drama focuses on the manhunt for two thrill killers, played with penetrating menace by Michael Gross and David Soul. When these two family men go on a robbing rampage, the FBI gets involved. Intelligent screenplay and inspired casting make this a must-see. 95m. **DIR:** Dick Lowry. **CAST:** Ronny Cox, Bruce Greenwood, Michael Gross, Doug Sheehan, David Soul. **1988**

FBI STORY, THE ★★★ A glowing history of the FBI from Prohibition to the cold war, through the career of a fictitious agent (James Stewart). Some good episodes reminiscent of Warner Bros.' G-Man pictures of the thirties, but with too many forays into Stewart's family life. Not rated, but with lots of gunplay. 149m. **DIR:** Mervyn LeRoy. **CAST:** James Stewart, Vera Miles, Larry Pennell, Nick Adams, Murray Hamilton, Diane Jergens. **1959**

FEAR (1955) ★★ Neither star Ingrid Bergman nor her then-husband director Roberto Rossellini are able to save this tired drama of an indiscreet wife being blackmailed by her lover's ex. As ever, Bergman scores personally. B&W; 91m. **DIR:** Roberto Rossellini. **CAST:** Ingrid Bergman, Kurt Kreuger, Mathias Wiemann. **1955**

FEAR (1988) ★★★ Vicious, brutal story of four escaped convicts who go on a rampage of murder and kidnapping. Cliff De Young and Kay Lenz star as a married couple whose vacation is terrifyingly interrupted when the cons take them hostage. A surprisingly fine performance by Frank Stallone highlights this impressive study in terror. Rated R for violence and profanity. 96m. **DIR:** Robert A. Ferretti. **CAST:** Cliff De Young, Kay Lenz, Frank Stallone. **1988**

FEAR (1990) ★★★1/2 Until a rather rushed climax, which culminates in a maze of mirrors, this made-for-cable thriller makes a slick showcase for Ally Sheedy. As a psychic who "tunes in" to the thoughts of serial killers, she assists skeptical police and then pens bestsellers based on her exploits . . . until she encounters a deranged killer who's *also* a psychic. Rated R for violence and nudity. 98m. **DIR:** Rockne S. O'Bannon. **CAST:** Ally Sheedy, Lauren Hutton, Michael O'Keefe, Stan Shaw. **1990**

FEAR, THE (1994) ★★ This by-the-numbers drive-in movie with characters right out of central casting is especially misogynist and uneventful. Rated R for violence, profanity, and sexual situations. 98m. **DIR:** Vincent Robert. **CAST:** Eddie Bowz, Ann Turkel, Leland Hayward, Darin Heames, Vince Edwards, Anna Karina, Wes Craven. **1994 DVD**

FEAR (1996) ★★1/2 A 16-year-old girl ventures into a seamy Seattle pool hall where she meets her Prince Charming. We all know he is dirt. So does her dad, who wedges himself between the two young lovers until the psychotic suitor storms the family's house with his scum buddies. Family dynamics are developed with stings of truth, but the ending is a sensationalized thrillfest. Rated R for language, gore, nudity, violence, and suggested sex. 95m. **DIR:** James Foley. **CAST:** Reese Witherspoon, Mark Wahlberg, William L. Petersen, Alyssa Milano, Amy Brenneman. **1996 DVD**

FEAR AND LOATHING IN LAS VEGAS Director-cowriter Terry Gilliam's adaptation of Hunter S. Thompson's infamous, pseudobiographical epic of gonzo-journalistic social commentary is a veritable mess from start to finish: an absolutely unwatchable jumble of surrealistic images and uncontrolled, self-indulgent performances by leads Johnny Depp (fitfully funny as Thompson surrogate Raoul Duke) and Benicio Del Toro (utterly loathsome as bestial "Dr. Gonzo"). Rated R for profanity, drug use, and incessant deviant behavior. 119m. **DIR:** Terry Gilliam. **CAST:** Johnny Depp, Benicio Del Toro, Tobey Maguire, Mark Harmon, Cameron Diaz, Gary Busey, Ellen Barkin. **1998 DVD**

FEAR, ANXIETY AND DEPRESSION ★★ Todd Solondz wrote and directed this Woody Allen-ish vehicle for himself. He plays a nerdish playwright who pursues an outrageously punk performer and his best friend's girl while being relentlessly chased by his female counterpart. Rated R for profanity and violence. 84m. **DIR:** Todd Solondz. **CAST:** Todd Solondz, Jill Wisoff. **1989**

FEAR CITY ★★ After a promising directorial debut with *Ms. 45*, Abel Ferrara backslid with this all-too-familiar tale about a psychopath killing prostitutes in New York City. Some good performances and action sequences still can't save this one. Rated R for violence, nudity, and profanity. 93m. **DIR:** Abel Ferrara. **CAST:** Tom Berenger, Billy Dee Williams, Rae Dawn Chong, Melanie Griffith, Rossano Brazzi, Jack Scalia. **1985 DVD**

FEAR, THE: HALLOWEEN NIGHT 🦃 More unsuspecting young people face off against the wooden creature named Morty, who is as stiff as the plot and direction. Rated R for violence and language. 95m. **DIR:** Chris Angel. **CAST:** Gordon Currie, Stacy Grant, Phillip Rhys, Betsy Palmer. **1999 DVD**

FEAR IN THE NIGHT (DYNASTY OF FEAR) ★★★1/2 Effective British shocker about a teacher and his off-balance bride at a desolate boys' school. Another suspensful offering from Hammer Films. Rated PG. 94m. **DIR:** Jimmy Sangster. **CAST:** Ralph Bates, Judy Geeson, Peter Cushing, Joan Collins. **1972**

FEAR INSIDE, THE ★★★ Christine Lahti's gripping performance lends credibility to this otherwise routine made-for-cable shocker. She plays a frantic agoraphobiac (fear of open spaces) unable to flee her home after it's invaded by a pair of nasty psychopaths. The cat-and-mouse games wear thin after a while, but Lahti definitely puts us in her corner. 105m. **DIR:** Leon Ichaso. **CAST:** Christine Lahti, Dylan McDermott, Jennifer Rubin. **1992**

FEAR NO EVIL 🦃 The story of the satanic high school student hell-bent on destroying a senior class. Rated R. 96m. **DIR:** Frank LaLoggia. **CAST:** Stephan Arngrim, Elizabeth Hoffman. **1981**

FEAR OF A BLACK HAT ★★★ This rap film chronicles a year on the road with the group N.W.H. (Niggaz With Hats) as they wax pseudophilosophically about their lives and songs, squabble with recording rivals, split up, and reunite. Just as rap seems to be forever coupled to drive-by shootings, misogyny, and street life, along comes a comic mockumentary reminding us that there's no business like show business. Rated R for language and nudity. 87m. **DIR:** Rusty Cundieff. **CAST:** Mark Christopher Lawrence, Larry B. Scott, Rusty Cundieff, Kasi Lemmons. **1994**

FEAR STRIKES OUT ★★1/2 Anthony Perkins stars in this compelling, if melodramatic, biography of baseball player Jim Piersall, whose dramatic mental breakdown during the season was played to a national audience. Elmer Bernstein's music is particularly effective, but a little more baseball and a bit less psychology would have helped this film. B&W; 81m. **DIR:** Robert Mulligan. **CAST:** Anthony Perkins, Karl Malden, Norma Moore, Adam Williams, Perry Wilson, Peter J. Votrian. **1957**

FEARLESS (1978) 🦃 This confusing, raunchy Italian film features Joan Collins as a rather inept striptease artist in Vienna. Not rated; it contains violence and nudity. 89m. **DIR:** Stelvio Massi. **CAST:** Joan Collins, Maurizio Merli. **1978**

FEARLESS (1993) ★★★★ This offbeat exploration of mankind's spiritual side focuses on Jeff Bridges's inability to resume his normal, day-to-day life after surviving a plane crash. This fascinating and rewarding movie may pose more questions than it answers, but it's highly satisfying. Rated R for profanity and violence. 124m. **DIR:** Peter Weir. **CAST:** Jeff Bridges, Isabella Rossellini, Rosie Perez, Tom Hulce, John Turturro, Benicio Del Toro, Deirdre O'Connell. **1993 DVD**

FEARLESS TIGER 🦃 When his brother dies from a drug overdose, a wealthy man goes to Hong Kong and learns martial arts to avenge him. Toothless nonsense. Rated R for violence and profanity. 88m. **DIR:** Ron Hulme. **CAST:** Jalal Mehri, Jamie Farr, Monika Schnarre, Bolo Yeung. **1993**

FEARLESS VAMPIRE KILLERS, OR, PARDON ME, BUT YOUR TEETH ARE IN MY NECK, THE ★★★★ Roman Polanski playfully revamps Transylvanian folklore as an elderly, nutty professor and his mousy protégé hunt down a castle-dwelling bloodsucker who has kidnapped the buxom daughter of a lecherous innkeeper. This misadventure of two of the most unlikeliest of heroes gushes with ghoulish, offbeat humor. 111m. **DIR:** Roman Polanski. **CAST:** Roman Polanski, Jack MacGowran, Alfie Bass, Sharon Tate, Ferdinand Mayne. **1966**

FEAST OF JULY ★★★1/2 Fans of Greek tragedy and doomed love affairs will have plenty to sink their teeth into, as this tale of a nineteenth-century woman betrayed by her lover is a downer of classic dimensions. Embeth Davidtz brings texture and complexity to a difficult role. Director Christopher Menaul has a couple of tricks we haven't seen before, and the attention to setting and scenery is unsurpassed. The ending, however, will surprise no one. Rated R for violence, sexual situations, and adult themes. 116m. **DIR:** Chris Menaul. **CAST:** Embeth Davidtz, Ben Chaplin, Tom Bell, James Purefoy, Greg Wise, Kenneth Anderson. **1995**

FEATHERED SERPENT, THE 🦃 Charlie Chan mystery—with Roland Winters the least convincing of the movie Chans—is unwatchable. B&W; 61m. **DIR:** William Beaudine. **CAST:** Roland Winters, Keye Luke, Victor Sen Yung. **1948**

FEDERAL HILL ★★★ Set in the Federal Hill district of Providence, R.I., this portrait of five friends and gang members explores the options open to one gang member when he decides he wants out. Strong performances help the script along, but not enough to make this an important movie. Rated R for language and violence. B&W; 100m. **DIR:** Michael Corrente. **CAST:** Nicholas

Turturro, Jason Andrews, Libby Langdon, Michael Raynor, Robert Turano. **1994**

FEDERAL OPERATOR 99 ★★★ Topflight action serial pits government agent against piano-playing villain and his henchmen (and one *mean* henchwoman) who deal in theft, death, destruction, and extortion. Great stunts, ingenious perils and escapes—plus good acting—make what passed as a routine chapterplay in its day a top entry in the genre. This stands as a perfect example of the quality Saturday-afternoon entertainment that died with the advent of television. B&W; 12 episodes. **DIR:** Spencer Gordon Bennet, Wallace Grissell, Yakima Canutt. **CAST:** Marten Lamont, George J. Lewis, Helen Talbot, Lorna Gray, LeRoy Mason, Hal Taliaferro, Bill Stevens. **1945**

FEDORA ★★★★ This marvelous ball-of-twine mystery is writer-director Billy Wilder's bookend to his 1950 classic *Sunset Boulevard*. Down-on-his-luck producer William Holden flies to a Greek isle to lure a Garbo-like actress out of retirement. This is not an old man's dismissal of Hollywood as many believe; in fact, it is Wilder's last great film. 114m. **DIR:** Billy Wilder. **CAST:** William Holden, Marthe Keller, Hildegarde Neff, José Ferrer. **1978**

FEDS ★★ A second-string comedy about two women (Mary Gross and Rebecca DeMornay) who work to beat the odds and graduate from the FBI's training academy. Some good laughs, but not enough. Rated PG-13 for mild language. 83m. **DIR:** Dan Goldberg. **CAST:** Mary Gross, Rebecca DeMornay, Ken Marshall. **1988**

FEEL MY PULSE ★★1/2 Silent screwball comedy boasts a hypochondriac heiress who inherits a sanitarium that is used by bootleggers as a front and a hideout. Bebe Daniels does a fine job as the germ-wary, sheltered young girl who encounters a life she didn't dream existed. Silent. B&W; 86m. **DIR:** Gregory La Cava. **CAST:** Bebe Daniels, Richard Arlen, William Powell. **1928**

FEELING MINNESOTA ★★ Sibling rivalry goes wild when black sheep Keanu Reeves shows up at his brother's wedding and runs off with bride Cameron Diaz. Steven Baigelman's film is coarse and oafish, arch and leaden, with a condescension toward its blue-collar characters that leaves an ugly aftertaste. Rated R for profanity and violence. 95m. **DIR:** Steven Baigelman. **CAST:** Keanu Reeves, Cameron Diaz, Vincent D'Onofrio, Delroy Lindo, Dan Aykroyd, Courtney Love, Tuesday Weld. **1996 DVD**

FELICIA'S JOURNEY ★★★1/2 Bob Hoskins shines during this sluggish psychological drama, as a malevolent nightmare concealed within a figure so benign and charming, that we're unlikely to credit the danger . . . until it's too late. This fussy, prissy catering manager crosses paths with a despondent 17-year-old girl who has left Ireland and journeyed to England's industrial midlands in search of the young man who said that he would cherish her forever. What follows is revealed with impressive narrative skill by director Atom Egoyan, who skillfully manipulates past and present, weaving current events with flashbacks and even some of the girl's dreams. But this film lacks the larger character tapestry and layered density of *The Sweet Hereafter*, which better justified the director's somber, protracted pacing. Ultimately, the payoff isn't nearly as interesting as the setup, and the final scenes are laced with too much contrivance and coincidence. Rated PG-13 for dramatic intensity. 114m. **DIR:** Atom Egoyan. **CAST:** Bob Hoskins, Elaine Cassidy, Arsinée Khanjian, Peter McDonald, Gerard McSorley. **1999 DVD**

FELLINI SATYRICON ★★★1/2 Federico Fellini's visionary account of ancient Rome before Christ is a bizarre, hallucinatory journey. Imaginative art direction, lavish costumes, and garish makeup create a feast for the eyes. Composer Nino Rota's brilliant score is another plus. Italian dialogue with English subtitles. Not rated; contains nudity and violence. 129m. **DIR:** Federico Fellini. **CAST:** Martin Potter, Hiram Keller, Gordon Mitchell, Capucine. **1969 DVD**

FELLINI'S ROMA ★★★★ Federico Fellini's odyssey through Rome is the director's impressionistic account of the city of his youth. With the help of a small film crew, Fellini explores the Italian capital with his own unique brand of visionary wit. A brilliant piece of moviemaking. In Italian with English subtitles. Not rated. 128m. **DIR:** Federico Fellini. **CAST:** Peter Gonzales, Marne Maitland, Federico Fellini. **1972 DVD**

FELLOW TRAVELER ★★1/2 What could have been a gripping drama, set amid the horror and persecution of Hollywood's McCarthyesque witch-hunts, loses its momentum when Michael Eaton's script descends into pop psychobabble. Ron Silver stars as a screenwriter who, while hiding in England (where he fled, rather than testify before the House Un-American Activities Committee), learns that his best friend has committed suicide—after some dealings with HUAC. Made for HBO. 91m. **DIR:** Philip Saville. **CAST:** Ron Silver, Hart Bochner, Imogen Stubbs, Daniel J. Travanti. **1989**

FELONY ★★1/2 Relentless action keeps this low-budget crime-thriller from hitting the skids. A renegade CIA agent sets up an ambush that leaves twelve cops dead. When the ambush is recorded by one of those television-reality shows, the agent orders that the tape be retrieved and the witnesses killed. The only one willing to stand up to him is a detective on the edge. Rated R for violence and adult language. 90m. **DIR:** David A. Prior. **CAST:** Jeffrey Combs, Lance Henriksen, Leo Rossi, Ashley Laurence, David Warner, Joe Don Baker. **1995**

FEMALE ★★★ The lady president of an automobile manufacturing company, used to having things her own way, falls in love with a man who won't bend. Amusing romantic comedy with a feminist undercurrent. B&W; 60m. **DIR:** Michael Curtiz. **CAST:** Ruth Chatterton, George Brent, Johnny Mack Brown, Ruth Donnelly, Douglass Dumbrille. **1933**

FEMALE JUNGLE ★★ A suitably sleazy, low-rent crime potboiler that was one of Jayne Mansfield's first movies. Lawrence Tierney is a police detective stalking a killer. One of the few features directed by Roger Corman stock-company actor Bruno VeSota. Alternate title: *The Hangover*. B&W; 56m. **DIR:** Bruno VeSota. **CAST:** Jayne Mansfield, Lawrence Tierney, John Carradine, Kathleen Crowley. **1956**

FEMALE PERVERSIONS ★★ A dynamic attorney (Tilda Swinton) seems on the fast track to professional success, but she's plagued by troubling romantic relationships, and tormented by unresolved feelings for her father and her kleptomaniac sister (Amy Madigan). Director Susan Streitfeld's film isn't as interesting as it sounds; it's pretentious, obscure, grating, and poorly acted all around—even by the usually reliable Madigan. Rated R for profanity, nudity, and graphic sex. 119m. **DIR:** Susan Streitfeld. **CAST:** Tilda Swinton, Amy Madigan, Karen Sillas, Frances Fisher, Laila Robins, Clancy Brown. **1997**

FEMALE TROUBLE ★★ The story of Dawn Davenport (Divine) from her days as a teenage belligerent through her rise to fame as a criminal and then to her death as a convicted murderer. As in other films by Waters, the theme here is the Jean Genet–like credo "crime equals beauty." Though it is unrated, this film is the equivalent of an X, due to sex, nudity, and violence. 90m. **DIR:** John Waters. **CAST:** Divine, Edith Massey, Cookie Mueller, David Lochary, Mink Stole, Michael Potter. **1973**

FEMME FATALE ★★ Colin Firth plays a newlywed who travels to Los Angeles to track down his runaway bride. A sordid look at L.A. nightlife is the main attraction in this otherwise routine suspense film. Rated R for nudity and violence. 96m. **DIR:** Andre Guttfreund. **CAST:** Colin Firth, Lisa Zane, Billy Zane, Scott Wilson. **1990**

FEMME FONTAINE: KILLER BABE FOR THE CIA ★★ The only thing missing from this retread of spy movies is the kitchen sink. Professional assassin Drew Fontaine's latest assignment is personal: She's out to avenge the murder of her father. She has her work cut out for her, including doing battle with a gang of lesbian "feminazis." Don't ask. Rated R for nudity, violence, and profanity. 93m. **DIR:** Margot Hope. **CAST:** Margot Hope, James Hong, Catherine Dao, Arthur Roberts. **1995**

FENCE, THE ★★1/2 Bill Wirth plays Terry Griff, a 29-year-old who has been incarcerated since the age of fifteen. Now on parole, he attempts to get his life together. His efforts are short-lived when his parole officer frames him for a crime he didn't commit. Film eventually dwindles down to predictable subplots, all nicely wrapped up by the final frame. Not rated. 90m. **DIR:** Peter Pistor. **CAST:** Billy Wirth, Marc Alaimo, Erica Gimpel, Paul Benjamin. **1994 DVD**

FER-DE-LANCE ★★ Made-for-TV suspense film is mildly entertaining as a cargo of poisonous snakes escape aboard a crippled submarine at the bottom of the sea, making life unpleasant for all concerned. 100m. **DIR:** Russ Mayberry. **CAST:** David Janssen, Hope Lange, Jason "Herb" Evers, Ivan Dixon. **1974**

FERNANDEL THE DRESSMAKER ★★ Using Fernandel as the hub, the film is a bit of whimsy about a gentleman's tailor who desires to become a world-famous couturier. Even with a lightweight plot, watching this famous comedian is certainly worth the time and effort to wade through the nonsense. In French with English subtitles. B&W; 84m. **DIR:** Jean Boyer. **CAST:** Fernandel, Suzy Delair, Françoise Fabian. **1957**

FERNGULLY—THE LAST RAINFOREST ★★★ A fairy discovers the ugly truth about the human race, which once worked alongside her magical peoples in nurturing the rainforest but is now destroying it. Robin Williams's inspired voice work (as Batty) elevates this environmental plea aimed at children. Other voices are provided by Tim Curry, Samantha Mathis, Christian Slater, Grace Zabriskie, Richard "Cheech" Marin, and Tommy Chong. Rated G. 76m. **DIR:** Bill Kroyer. **1992**

FERNGULLY 2: THE MAGICAL RESCUE ★★ Direct-to-video sequel lacks the appeal and voice talent of the first film, although younger children probably won't care. Batty Koda, Crysta, Pips, and the Beetle Boys must rise to the occasion when humans cart off three baby animals from the forest. Rated G. 75m. **DIR:** Phil Robinson. **CAST:** James Baker, Jamie Baker, Kermit Beachwood, Erik Bergmann. **1997 DVD**

FEROCIOUS FEMALE FREEDOM FIGHTERS ★★ À la Woody Allen's *What's Up Tiger Lily?*, this is a junky martial arts movie redubbed by a Los Angeles comedy troupe. The spotty results tend toward the sophomoric, though you'll probably laugh at some of it. Not rated; the film contains violence and crude humor. 74m. **DIR:** Jopi Burnama. **CAST:** Eva Arnez, Barry Prima. **1989**

FERRIS BUELLER'S DAY OFF ★★★★ Writer-director John Hughes strikes again, this time with a charming tale of a high school legend in his own time (Matthew Broderick, playing the title character) who pretends to be ill in order to have a day away from school. The expressive Broderick owns the film, although he receives heavy competition from Jeffrey Jones, whose broadly played dean of students has been trying to nail Ferris Bueller for months. Rated PG-13 for mild profanity. 104m. **DIR:** John Hughes. **CAST:** Matthew Broderick, Alan Ruck, Mia Sara, Jeffrey Jones, Jennifer Grey, Charlie Sheen, Cindy Pickett, Lyman Ward. **1986 DVD**

FEUD, THE ★★★ Two families in neighboring small towns are drawn into a feud that neither wants—but which neither will be the first to quit. This film isn't as satirical as the Thomas Berger novel on which it is based, but it's an agreeable farce nonetheless. Rated R. 96m. **DIR:** Bill D'Elia. **CAST:** René Auberjonois, Ron McLarty, Joe Grifasi. **1988**

FEVER ★★1/2 Ex-con Armand Assante wants only to go straight and reunite with former girlfriend Marcia Gay Harden, who has set up housekeeping with compassionate lawyer Sam Neill. Macho sparring between the two men is interrupted when Harden is kidnapped by one of Assante's enemies. Lurid and violent made-for-cable fodder. Rated R for violence and language. 99m. **DIR:** Larry Elikann. **CAST:** Sam Neill, Armand Assante, Marcia Gay Harden, Joe Spano. **1991 DVD**

FEVER LAKE ★★ This slickly made picture has production values equal to any big budget film, but it is unemotionally involving and never develops a sense of terror. What could have been *The Shining* for the teen set instead steers toward mediocrity. Not rated; contains violence. 95m. **DIR:** Ralph Portillo. **CAST:** Corey Haim, Mario Lopez, Bo Hopkins. **1997**

FEVER PITCH ★★ Ryan O'Neal plays a sports journalist writing about gambling. To research his story, O'Neal becomes a gambler, loses his wife, endangers his job, and becomes involved with a sleazy bookie. Rated R for profanity and violence. 95m. **DIR:** Richard Brooks. **CAST:** Ryan O'Neal, Catharine Hicks, Giancarlo Giannini, Bridgette Anderson, Chad Everett, John Saxon, William Smith. **1985 DVD**

FEW GOOD MEN, A ★★★★ Calling this film the best Perry Mason movie ever made may sound like a put-down, but it isn't. Director Rob Reiner keeps the viewer guessing throughout this courtroom-based drama, which features Tom Cruise as a wisecracking navy defense lawyer whose clients have been accused of murder. The acting is first-rate. Rated R for violence and profanity. 134m. **DIR:** Rob Reiner. **CAST:** Tom Cruise, Jack Nicholson, Demi Moore, Kevin Bacon, Kiefer Sutherland, Kevin Pollak, James Marshall, J. T. Walsh, Christopher Guest, Matt Craven, Wolfgang Bodison, Cuba Gooding Jr. **1992 DVD**

FFOLKES ★★★ Of course, no movie with Roger Moore is a classic, but this tongue-in-cheek spy thriller with the actor playing against his James Bond stereotype provides some good, campy entertainment. This film features Moore as a woman-hating, but cat-loving, gun for hire who takes on a band of terrorists. Rated PG. 99m. **DIR:** Andrew V. McLaglen. **CAST:** Roger Moore, James Mason, Anthony Perkins, Michael Parks, David Hedison. **1980**

FIANCÉ, THE ★★ Dull erotic thriller with Lysette Anthony as a wife who becomes the focus of a stranger after they have a brief but personal conversation. Rated R for profanity, violence, and sexual situations. 94m. **DIR:** Martin Kitrosser. **CAST:** William R. Moses, Lysette Anthony, Patrick Cassidy. **1997**

FIDDLER ON THE ROOF ★★★★ A lavishly mounted musical, this 1971 screen adaptation of the long-running Broadway hit, based on the stories of Sholem Aleichem, works remarkably well. This is primarily thanks to Topol's immensely likable portrayal of Tevye, the proud but put-upon father clinging desperately to the old values. Rated G. 181m. **DIR:** Norman Jewison. **CAST:** Topol, Norman Crane, Leonard Frey, Molly Picon, Paul Mann, Rosalind Harris. **1971 DVD**

FIDDLIN' BUCKAROO ★★★ Secret service agent Ken Maynard, on the trail of outlaw Fred Kohler, is mistakenly arrested for a crime Kohler's gang committed. One of several Maynard Westerns he directed himself, this one is heavy on the music end. B&W; 65m. **DIR:** Ken Maynard. **CAST:** Ken Maynard, Fred Kohler Sr., Frank Rice. **1933**

FIELD, THE ★★★★ Richard Harris gives a superb performance in this drama, which is not unlike the dark side of John Ford's *The Quiet Man*. Tom Berenger plays an American who comes to Ireland in search of his roots and with plans to modernize the country, which include buying and paving a piece of fertile land lovingly tended by Harris and his son (Sean Bean). Rated PG-13 for violence and profanity. 107m. **DIR:** Jim Sheridan. **CAST:** Richard Harris, John Hurt, Sean Bean, Tom Berenger, Brenda Fricker, Frances Tomelty. **1990 DVD**

FIELD OF DREAMS ★★★★★ A must-see motion picture, this spirit-lifting work stars Kevin Costner as an Iowa farmer who hears a voice telling him to build a baseball diamond in the middle of his cornfield. Against all common sense, he does so and sets in motion a chain of wonderful events. Costner gets strong support from Amy Madigan, Burt Lancaster, James Earl Jones, and Ray Liotta in this all-ages delight adapted from the novel, *Shoeless Joe*, by W. P. Kinsella. Rated PG for brief profanity. 106m. **DIR:** Phil Alden Robinson. **CAST:** Kevin Costner, Amy Madigan, James Earl Jones, Burt Lancaster, Ray Liotta, Timothy Busfield, Dwier Brown. **1989 DVD**

FIELD OF FIRE 🦃 Battling behind enemy lines in Cambodia, a special combat squad attempts to retrieve a downed military expert. Hokey heroics. Rated R for profanity and nudity. 100m. **DIR:** Cirio H. Santiago. **CAST:** David Carradine. **1992**

FIELD OF HONOR (1986) ★★ Tale of a Dutch infantryman in the Korean War left for dead after a surprise attack by the Chinese. Everett McGill is the survivor who hides out with two shell-shocked kids. Rated R for violence, profanity, and nudity. 93m. **DIR:** Hans Scheepmaker. **CAST:** Everett McGill, Ron Brandsteder, Hey Young Lee. **1986**

FIELD OF HONOR (1988) ★★ A nineteenth-century French saga about young men at war, with aspirations to the classic status of *The Red Badge of Courage*. Despite its aim at tragic symmetry, the film's muddled and meandering script causes it to fall short. Strangely uninvolving. In French with English subtitles. 89m. **DIR:** Jean-Pierre Denis. **CAST:** Cris Campion. **1988**

FIEND WITHOUT A FACE ★★★1/2 Surprisingly effective little horror chiller with slight overtones of the "Id" creature from *Forbidden Planet*. Scientific thought experiment goes awry and creates nasty creatures that look like brains with coiled tails. Naturally, they eat people. Story builds to a great climax. B&W; 74m. **DIR:** Arthur Crabtree. **CAST:** Marshall Thompson, Kim Parker, Terry Kilburn. **1958**

FIENDISH PLOT OF DR. FU MANCHU, THE 🦃 Peter Sellers plays a dual role of "insidious Oriental villain" Fu Manchu, who is out to rule the world, and his arch-enemy, the Holmes-like Nayland Smith of Scotland Yard. Rated PG. 108m. **DIR:** Piers Haggard. **CAST:** Peter Sellers, Helen Mirren, Sid Caesar, David Tomlinson. **1980**

FIERCE CREATURES ★★★ The cast from *A Fish Called Wanda* obviously had fun making this nonsequel, but its broader tone provides less of the deft British wit that made their first effort so entertaining. John Cleese plays a stuffy civil servant sent to increase a zoo's profit margin, a task he embraces by suggesting to relocate all cuddly animals and concentrate solely on "fierce" creatures. Jamie Lee Curtis is the corporate shark sent to help Cleese; Michael Palin is one of the flustered keepers. Kevin Kline plays two roles, neither very successfully. The plot essentially disappears midway through the disjointed film, although the rising sexual tension between Cleese and Curtis is pretty funny. Rated PG-13 for strong sexual content. 93m. **DIR:** Robert Young, Fred Schepisi. **CAST:** John Cleese, Jamie Lee Curtis, Kevin Kline, Michael Palin, Ronnie Corbett, Carey Lowell. **1997 DVD**

FIESTA ★★1/2 One of Esther Williams's lesser movies, helped by the scenery of Mexico, the excitement of bullfighting, and the dancing skills of Cyd Charisse. Esther Williams poses as her brother in the bullring so he can slip away to compose music. Only Williams swims better than she bullfights, and there's no water in the ring. A novelty that's mildly entertaining. 104m. **DIR:** Richard Thorpe. **CAST:** Esther Williams, Ricardo Montalban, Cyd Charisse, Mary Astor, Fortunio Bonanova, John Carroll. **1947**

15 MINUTES ★★ Those who expect the absolute worst in human behavior will find much to validate their fears in this trashy little thriller about a couple of Eastern European psychopaths who enter our country, kill several people, and then hope to make a fortune by getting caught and selling the story to the highest bidders. The film, which wallows in deplorable conduct by protagonist, antagonist, and everybody in between, is intended to indict our current cultural narcissism and fascination with filth, but unfortunately panders to the very qualities it criticizes. Rated R for profanity, sexual candor, and grim violence. 120m. **DIR:** John Herzfeld. **CAST:** Robert De Niro, Edward Burns, Kelsey Grammer, Avery Brooks, Melina Kanakaredes. **2001 DVD**

FIFTH AVENUE GIRL ★★ Limp social comedy features Ginger Rogers as a homeless but levelheaded young lady who is taken in by Walter Connolly, one of those unhappy movie-land millionaires who is just dying to find someone to lavish gifts on. B&W; 83m. **DIR:** Gregory La Cava. **CAST:** Ginger Rogers, Walter Connolly, Verree Teasdale, Tim Holt, James Ellison, Kathryn Adams. **1939**

FIFTH ELEMENT, THE ★★★1/2 This hyperkinetic sci-fi thriller doesn't score for logic or coherence, but it sure knows how to dazzle and excite. Twenty-third-century cabbie Bruce Willis gets involved with a gorgeous extraterrestrial who holds the key to saving the universe. The two dodge nasty aliens, befriend a befuddled priest and a manic media talk show host, all while staying one step ahead of the dangerously insane villain. You may hate yourself in the morning, but you'll have to admit this is a lot of fun. Rated PG-13 for nudity, violence, and profanity. 127m. **DIR:** Luc Besson. **CAST:** Bruce Willis, Gary Oldman, Ian Holm, Milla Jovovich, Chris Tucker, Luke Perry, Brian James. **1997 DVD**

FIFTH FLOOR, THE 🦃 College lass is mistakenly popped into an insane asylum. Rated R for violence and nudity. 90m. **DIR:** Howard Avedis. **CAST:** Bo Hopkins, Dianne Hull, Patti D'Arbanville, Mel Ferrer, Sharon Farrell. **1980**

FIFTH MONKEY, THE ★★★ Ben Kingsley is upstaged by four chimpanzees in this uplifting adventure. Kingsley plays a Brazilian peasant desperately trying to earn enough money to marry the woman he loves by selling snakeskins. Rated PG-13 for violence. 93m. **DIR:** Eric Rochat. **CAST:** Ben Kingsley. **1990**

FIFTH MUSKETEER, THE ★★ An uninspired retelling of *The Man in the Iron Mask*. Beau Bridges is watchable enough as King Louis XIV and his twin brother, Philipe, who was raised as a peasant by D'Artagnan (Cornel Wilde) and the Three Musketeers (Lloyd Bridges, José Ferrer, and Alan Hale Jr.). The film never springs to life. Rated PG. 103m. **DIR:** Ken Annakin. **CAST:** Beau Bridges, Sylvia Kristel, Ursula Andress, Cornel Wilde, Olivia de Havilland, José Ferrer, Rex Harrison, Lloyd Bridges, Alan Hale Jr. **1979**

FIFTY/FIFTY ★★★ Peter Weller and Robert Hays star as former CIA operatives, now mercenaries on opposite sides of a bloody civil war. Treachery and betrayal soon force them to trust only each other, especially when the CIA sends troubleshooter Charles Martin Smith to get them to organize a rebellion. Rated R for nudity, violence, and profanity. 101m. **DIR:** Charles Martin Smith. **CAST:** Peter Weller, Robert Hays, Charles Martin Smith. **1993**

55 DAYS AT PEKING ★★ A lackluster big-screen adventure about the Boxer Revolt in 1900. Charlton Heston, David Niven, and the rest of the large cast seem made of wood. 150m. **DIR:** Nicholas Ray. **CAST:** Charlton Heston, Ava Gardner, David Niven, John Ireland. **1963**

54 ★★ The rise and fall of Studio 54, the trendy Manhattan disco of the 1970s and 1980s, provides the background for a timid rehash of *Saturday Night Fever*. The story is trite, the characters are uninteresting, even the disco music on the soundtrack is boring. The film's only asset is Mike Myers as club owner Steve Rubell; too bad the film wasn't about him instead. Rated R for profanity, drug use, and sexual scenes. 89m. **DIR:** Mark Christopher. **CAST:** Ryan Phillippe, Salma Hayek, Neve Campbell, Mike Myers. **1998**

52 PICK-UP ★1/2 Generally unentertaining tale of money, blackmail, and pornography, as adapted from Elmore Leonard's story. Roy Scheider's secret fling with Kelly Preston leads to big-time blackmail and murder. It's more cards than Scheider could ever pick up, and a more mean and nasty movie than most people will want to watch. Rated R for nudity, profanity, simulated sex, and violence. 111m. **DIR:** John Frankenheimer. **CAST:** Roy Scheider, Ann-Margret, Vanity, John Glover, Clarence Williams III, Kelly Preston. **1986 DVD**

FIG LEAVES ★★★ The age-old problem facing a woman who has "nothing to wear" is the subject of this amusing fluff. Adam and Eve Smith start out in the Garden of Eden, and then progress to the big city in 1926, living as plumber and wife. Eve secretly gets a job as a fashion model and has the chance to wear all the new styles she wants and rekindle her romance with Adam. Lots of fun, and a visual feast. B&W; 68m. **DIR:** Howard Hawks. **CAST:** George O'Brien, Olive Borden, Phyllis Haver, Andre de Beranger, William Austin, Heinie Conklin. **1926**

FIGHT CLUB 🦃 If director David Fincher and screenwriter Jim Uhls intended to make us believe that we haven't advanced a jot from the putrescent slime that once may have spawned mankind, they succeeded brilliantly. This appalling, grotesque, and interminable endurance test is fairy-tale fiction for serial killers, imbeciles who succumb to road rage, and frustrated white guys: all the morons who seek excuses to justify their increasingly bad behavior and hair-trigger tempers. Proceed with caution. Rated R for profanity, violence, torture, nudity, and sexual content. 139m. **DIR:** David Fincher. **CAST:** Brad Pitt, Edward Norton, Helena Bonham Carter, Meat Loaf, Jared Leto. **1999 DVD**

FIGHT FOR US ★★ After the fall of the Marcos regime in the Philippines, right-wing death squads terrorize the countryside. Poor production values, amateur-night actors, and pedestrian direction take the fight out of this one. Rated R for violence, profanity, and simulated sex. 92m. **DIR:** Lino Brocka. **CAST:** Phillip Salvador. **1990**

FIGHTER ATTACK ★★ An American pilot (Sterling Hayden) shot down in Italy joins up with an Italian terrorist group to block off a Nazi supply tunnel. Familiar World War II melodrama. 80m. **DIR:** Lesley Selander. **CAST:** Sterling Hayden, Joy Page, J. Carrol Naish. **1953**

FIGHTING BACK ★★★ A deli owner decides to organize a neighborhood committee against crime after his wife and mother are victims of violence. You can't help but cheer him on. A rapid succession of violent acts, profanity, and occasional nudity make this R-rated film questionable for young audiences. 98m. **DIR:** Lewis Teague. **CAST:** Tom Skerritt, Patti LuPone, Michael Sarrazin, Yaphet Kotto, David Rasche, Ted Ross. **1982**

FIGHTING CARAVANS ★★★1/2 Despite the title, this is a Zane Grey Western—and a good one, full of intrigue, action, and, for leavening, a smattering of comedy. Lanky, taciturn Gary Cooper, wanted by the law, avoids arrest by conning a wagon-train girl to pose as his wife. Romance blooms as the train treks west, into the sights of hostile forces. B&W; 80m. **DIR:** Otto Brower, David Burton. **CAST:** Gary Cooper, Lily Damita, Ernest Torrence, Eugene Pallette, Charles Winninger. **1931 DVD**

FIGHTING CODE ★★1/2 Buck Jones impersonates a girl's dead brother in order to solve a murder and save the ranch from a scheming lawyer. A young Ward Bond shows why he later became such a star and fine actor. B&W; 65m. **DIR:** Lambert Hillyer. **CAST:** Buck Jones, Ward Bond. **1933**

FIGHTING FATHER DUNNE ★★★1/2 Inspirational, at times tearjerking, tale of one priest's effort to care for the homeless boys of St. Louis in 1905. You'll be amazed by the clever priest's ability to acquire supplies and services with goodwill instead of hard cash. B&W; 93m. **DIR:** Ted Tetzlaff. **CAST:** Pat O'Brien, Barry Fitzgerald, Darryl Hickman. **1948**

FIGHTING KENTUCKIAN, THE ★★★ Worth seeing if only for the rare and wonderful on-screen combination of John Wayne and Oliver Hardy, this period adventure casts the duo as frontiersmen who come to the aid of the homesteading Napoleonic French. If only Vera Hruba Ralston weren't the Duke's love interest, this could have been a real winner. B&W; 100m. **DIR:** George Waggner. **CAST:** John Wayne, Vera Hruba Ralston, Philip Dorn, Oliver Hardy. **1949 DVD**

FIGHTING MAD ★★★ A quiet, unassuming farmer (Peter Fonda) is driven to distraction by a ruthless businessman who wants to assume his property. Instead of a free-for-all of violence and car crashes (as in other Fonda films of the time), this ranks as an in-depth character study. Rated R for violence. 90m. **DIR:** Jonathan Demme. **CAST:** Peter Fonda, Lynn Lowry, John Doucette, Philip Carey, Scott Glenn, Kathleen Miller. **1976**

FIGHTING MARINES, THE ★★ U.S. Marines run up against a modern-day pirate. The plot's thin, the acting forced, but the special effects are remarkable. Pieced together from twelve serial chapters. B&W; 69m. **DIR:** Joseph Kane, B. Reeves "Breezy" Eason. **CAST:** Grant Withers, Adrian Morris, Ann Rutherford, Jason Robards Sr., Pat O'Malley. **1936**

FIGHTING PRINCE OF DONEGAL, THE ★★★1/2 A rousing adventure-action film set in sixteenth-century Ireland. When Peter McEnery succeeds to the title of Prince of Donegal, the Irish clans are ready to fight English troops to make Ireland free. This is a Disney British endeavor that is definitely worth watching. 110m. **DIR:** Michael O'Herlihy. **CAST:** Peter McEnery, Susan Hampshire, Tom Adams, Gordon Jackson. **1966**

FIGHTING RANGER, THE ★★★ Entertaining but predictable piece has Buck Jones and sidekick Frank Rice chasing down a killer. Good cast and production values. B&W; 60m. **DIR:** George B. Seitz. **CAST:** Buck Jones, Frank Rice, Ward Bond, Frank La Rue. **1934**

FIGHTING SEABEES, THE ★★★ John Wayne and Dennis O'Keefe are construction workers fighting the Japanese in their own way while each attempts to woo Susan Hayward away from the other. This 1944 war film, which costars William Frawley, is actually better than it sounds. B&W; 100m. **DIR:** Edward Ludwig. **CAST:** John Wayne, Dennis O'Keefe, Susan Hayward, William Frawley, Duncan Renaldo. **1944 DVD**

FIGHTING SHADOWS ★★★ Royal Canadian Mountie Tim O'Farrell (Tim McCoy) returns to his former home to find out who is terrorizing fur trappers there. Standard fare is made watchable by the stars. B&W; 57m. **DIR:** David Selman. **CAST:** Tim McCoy, Ward Bond. **1935**

FIGHTING 69TH, THE ★★★ Tough-guy James Cagney does a good job as a loner who buckles under fire and causes the death of some of his comrades in this all-male World War I story. Based partly on fact, this virile Warner Brothers blockbuster boasts good cinematography and great battle scenes. B&W; 89m. **DIR:** William Keighley. **CAST:** James Cagney, Pat O'Brien, George Brent, Jeffrey Lynn, Alan Hale Sr., Frank McHugh, Dennis Morgan, Dick Foran, William Lundigan. **1940**

FIGHTING SULLIVANS, THE (SULLIVANS, THE) ★★★★ This fact-based story of five brothers who died together when the cruiser *Juneau* was torpedoed by the Germans emotionally devastated World War II moviegoers. The early scenes of the boys growing up in Waterloo, Iowa, is fine Americana, but be forewarned: the ending has some of the saddest, most heart-wrenching moments ever filmed. B&W; 111m. **DIR:** Lloyd Bacon. **CAST:** Thomas Mitchell, Anne Baxter, Selena Royle, Ward Bond, Bobby Driscoll. **1944 DVD**

FIGHTING WESTERNER, THE ★★★ Rugged mining engineer Randolph Scott works undercover to learn who is responsible for murders at a radium mine. Tense mystery-Western. B&W; 54m. **DIR:** Charles Barton. **CAST:** Randolph Scott, Kathleen Burke, Ann Sheridan, Chic Sale. **1935**

FILTH AND THE FURY, THE ★★★1/2 Director Julien Temple's documentary about the rise and fall of the Sex Pistols is a follow-up, and in some ways a rebuttal, to his own 1980 film *The Great Rock and Roll Swindle*, where the Pistols' manager Malcolm McLaren held forth at great length about his own role in the band's meteoric success. Focusing here on the band members themselves, Temple balances present day interviews with the surviving Pistols with a long-lost interview from 1978 with the late Sid Vicious. The free-form, gonzo technique is engaging. Rated R for profanity and drug use. 107m. **DIR:** Julien Temple. **CAST:** Johnny Rotten, Paul Cook, Steve Jones, Glen Matlock, Sid Vicious. **1999 DVD**

FINAL ALLIANCE 🦃 Will Colton (David Hasselhoff) returns to a hometown that has been overrun by gangs. Rated R for violence and language. 93m. **DIR:** Mario Di Leo. **CAST:** David Hasselhoff, Bo Hopkins, John Saxon. **1990**

FINAL ANALYSIS ★★ Hitchcock meets Ken and Barbie in this silly suspense movie about a psychiatrist who becomes a murder suspect. Too serious to be funny and too campy to be believable. Rated R for violence, profanity, and nudity. 122m. **DIR:** Phil Joanou. **CAST:** Richard Gere, Kim Basinger, Uma Thurman, Eric Roberts, Paul Guilfoyle, Keith David. **1992 DVD**

FINAL APPEAL ★★★ Decent thriller stars JoBeth Williams as a wife who thinks she has it all until she walks in on her abusive husband and his mistress. When she's forced to kill him in self-defense, no one will believe her, including her attorney brother. When she's arrested for murder, it begins to look like someone is out to frame her. Likable cast makes this made-for-television thriller watchable. Rated PG-13 for violence. 94m. **DIR:** Eric Till. **CAST:** JoBeth Williams, Brian Dennehy. **1993**

FINAL APPROACH ★★ Confusing, muddled sci-fi entry has test pilot James B. Sikking trying to recall the moments before a fateful crash. Virtual reality effects are film's only saving grace, which attempts to surprise viewers with a twist ending, but one that comes too little, too late. Rated PG-13. 101m. **DIR:** Eric Steven Stahl. **CAST:** James B. Sikking, Hector Elizondo, Madolyn Smith, Kevin McCarthy. **1992**

FINAL CHAPTER—WALKING TALL 🦃 Garbage. Rated R for violence. 112m. **DIR:** Jack Starrett. **CAST:** Bo Svenson, Margaret Blye, Forrest Tucker, Lurene Tuttle, Morgan Woodward, Libby Boone. **1977**

FINAL COMBAT, THE ★★★★ In a post-apocalypse world, a lonely man makes an attempt to break away and find a kind of happiness. He soon discovers that he must fight for what he desires rather than try to run away. The good performances and the compelling story are accentuated by the fact that there is no dialogue in the movie. Rated R for violence. B&W; 93m. **DIR:** Luc Besson. **CAST:** Pierre Jolivet, Fritz Wepper, Jean Bouise, Jean Reno. **1984**

FINAL COMEDOWN, THE 🦃 Dated, heavy-handed film about a black man who becomes involved with a group of militants. Rated R for violence, profanity, and nudity. 84m. **DIR:** Oscar Williams. **CAST:** Billy Dee Williams, D'Urville Martin, Celia Kaye, Raymond St. Jacques. **1972**

FINAL CONFLICT, THE ★★ The third and last in the *Omen* trilogy, this disturbing but passionless film concerns the rise to power of the son of Satan, Damien Thorn (Sam Neill), and the second coming of the Saviour. It depends more on shocking spectacle than gripping tension for its impact. Rated R. 108m. **DIR:** Graham Baker. **CAST:** Sam Neill, Rossano Brazzi, Don Gordon, Lisa Harrow, Mason Adams. **1981**

FINAL COUNTDOWN, THE ★★1/2 Farfetched but passable story about an aircraft carrier traveling backward in time to just before the start of World War II. The crew must then decide whether or not to change the course of history. Some good special effects and performances by the leads manage to keep this one afloat. Rated PG. 104m. **DIR:** Don Taylor. **CAST:** Kirk Douglas, Martin Sheen, Katharine Ross. **1980**

FINAL CUT, THE ★★★1/2 You can't beat following a bomb-disposal squad for edge-of-the-seat suspense, and this slick little thriller keeps the screws properly tightened. Sam Elliott puts his world-weary charm to good use as a former demolition expert summoned when local cops are stymied by a serial bomber whose devices are never wired the same way twice. Rated R for profanity, violence, and simulated sex. 99m. **DIR:** Roger Christian. **CAST:** Sam Elliott, Charles Martin Smith, Anne Ramsey, Ray Baker, Matt Craven, John Hannah, Amanda Plummer. **1995**

FINAL DAYS, THE ★★★1/2 Solid made-for-television dramatization of the last days of Richard M. Nixon's presidency. Based on the bestselling novel by Bob Woodward and Carl Bernstein, the reporters who uncovered the Watergate scandal, the drama features a powerful performance by Lane Smith as Nixon. Handsome production values and a sense of time and place go a long way, but it's the fine-tuned writing, direction, and acting that bring this historical flashback to life. Rated PG. 150m. **DIR:** Richard Pearce. **CAST:** Lane Smith, Richard Kiley, David Ogden Stiers, Ed Flanders, Theodore Bikel. **1989**

FINAL DEFEAT, THE ★★ After the Civil War, Guy Madison leads a group of ex-Confederate rebels on a rampage through the West. He unknowingly takes on a government undercover agent who tricks him into believing that he knows the whereabouts of a buried treasure. A good score and the presence of Madison make this a nice film. Rated PG. 90m. **DIR:** E. G. Rowland. **CAST:** Guy Madison, Edd Byrnes, Louise Barrett, Enio Girolami, Pedro Sanchez. **1968**

FINAL DESTINATION ★★ A teenager's premonition saves him and several others from a plane crash; then, some mysterious force begins killing the survivors one by one. What starts out like *The Sixth Sense* quickly turns into an unimaginative variation on the standard teen-slasher formula, with cruel fate this time taking the place of the usual serial killer. Rated R for violence and profanity. 90m. **DIR:** James Wong. **CAST:** Devon Sawa, Ali Larter, Kerr Smith, Kristen Cloke, Daniel Roebuck, Chad E. Donella, Seann William Scott. **2000 DVD**

FINAL EMBRACE ★★1/2 Video director Oley Sassone treads on familiar turf, a seamy tale of murder in the music video business. Attractive cast, but there's more plot and energy in a music video. Rated R for nudity, violence, and adult language. 88m. **DIR:** Oley Sassone. **CAST:** Robert Rusler, Nancy Valen, Dick Van Patten, Linda Dona. **1992**

FINAL EQUINOX 🦃 Government agent tries to save the Earth's people from being turned into vegetables. Not rated; contains profanity, nudity, violence, and substance abuse. 93m. **DIR:** Serge Rodnunsky. **CAST:** Joe Lara, Tina May Simpson, Gary Kasper, Martin Kove, David Warner. **1996**

FINAL EXAM 🦃 A mad slasher hacks his way through a college campus. Rated R. 90m. **DIR:** Jimmy Huston. **CAST:** Joel S. Rice. **1981**

FINAL EXECUTIONER, THE 🦃 Following a nuclear holocaust, a small undamaged elite hunt down the contaminated human leftovers. Not rated; contains violence and sex. 95m. **DIR:** Romolo Guerrieri. **CAST:** William Mang, Marina Costa, Harrison Muller, Woody Strode. **1983**

FINAL EXTRA, THE ★★ After a star reporter is shot by an arch-criminal known as The Shadow, the case is taken over by his sister and an eager cub reporter. Obscure silent mystery will appeal only to nostalgia buffs. B&W; 75m. **DIR:** James Hogan. **CAST:** Marguerite de la Motte, Grant Withers. **1927**

•**FINAL FANTASY: THE SPIRITS WITHIN** ★★1/2 Survivors of a war-ravaged Earth battle ghostly alien invaders. This sci-fi adventure, based on a popular computer game, was highly touted as the first film completely computer-generated in a photorealistic style, and much of the animation is truly stunning. However, the story is incoherent, betraying its video-game roots, and the characters are boring; the stunning animation doesn't extend to facial expressions or lip movements. Rated PG-13 for violence. 106m. **DIR:** Hironobu Sakaguchi, Motonori Sakakibara. **2001 DVD**

FINAL IMPACT ★★ Ex-world kick-boxing champ (Lorenzo Lamas) trains an innocent kid (Mike Worth) for the finals in an effort to avenge his own defeat. Reasonably watchable. Rated R for violence and profanity. 97m. **DIR:** Joseph Merhi, Stephen Smoke. **CAST:** Lorenzo Lamas, Michael Worth, Jeff Langton, Kathleen Kinmont. **1991**

FINAL JUDGMENT 🦃 Brad Dourif stars as a Hollywood priest whose shady past catches up with him when he becomes the prime suspect in the murder of a stripper. Rated R for violence, nudity, and profanity. 90m. **DIR:** Louis Morneau. **CAST:** Brad Dourif, Isaac Hayes, Karen Black, Maria Ford, Orson Bean, David Ledingham. **1992**

FINAL JUSTICE 🦃 Repulsive revenge melodrama pitting three suburban couples against a pair of vicious backwoodsmen. Rated R for rape, strong violence, nudity, sexual situations, and profanity. 92m. **DIR:** Brent Huff. **CAST:** James Brolin, Brent Huff, Shawn Huff, Rob Roy Fitzgerald. **1994**

FINAL JUSTICE 🦃 Joe Don Baker plays a rural sheriff who travels to Italy to take on the Mafia and halt criminal activities. Rated R for nudity, violence, and language. 90m. **DIR:** Greydon Clark. **CAST:** Joe Don Baker, Venantino Venantini, Helena Abella, Bill McKinney. **1984 DVD**

FINAL MISSION ★★ OK attempt at creating a virtual-reality thriller is sabotaged by inane dialogue and tired direction. Fighter pilots are being brainwashed during flight simulations and then turn kamikaze when they get inside the real thing. Young hotshot pilot (Billy Wirth) investigates and runs up against the standard-issue plot complications and stock villains. Good idea gone awry. Rated R for language and violence. 92m. **DIR:** Lee Redmond. **CAST:** Billy Wirth, Corbin Bernsen, Elizabeth Gracen, Steve Railsback. **1994**

FINAL NOTICE 🦃 Failed TV pilot with Gil Gerard as a romantic private eye who has help from a stuffy yet sexy librarian (Melody Anderson). Boring made-for-cable fodder. 91m. **DIR:** Steven H. Stern. **CAST:** Gil Gerard, Melody Anderson, Jackie Burroughs, Kevin Hicks, Louise Fletcher, David Ogden Stiers, Steve Landesberg. **1989**

FINAL OPTION, THE ★★★★ Judy Davis stars in this first-rate British-made suspense thriller as the leader of a fanatical antinuclear group that takes a group of U.S. and British officials hostage and demands that a nuclear missile be launched at a U.S. base in Scotland. If not, the hostages will die. And it's up to Special Air Services undercover agent Peter Skellen (Lewis Collins) to save their lives. Rated R for violence and profanity. 125m. **DIR:** Ian Sharp. **CAST:** Judy Davis, Lewis Collins, Richard Widmark, Robert Webber, Edward Woodward. **1982**

FINAL ROUND ★★ Undiscriminating action fans may tolerate this low-rent translation of Richard Connell's "*The Most Dangerous Game,*" but there's little appeal for mainstream viewers. Thanks to poor lighting, Lorenzo Lamas's fight scenes are barely visible . . . no doubt to hide the $1.98 sets. Rated R for violence, profanity, and nudity. 90m. **DIR:** George Erschbamer. **CAST:** Lorenzo Lamas, Anthony DeLongis, Kathleen Kinmont. **1993**

FINAL TERROR, THE ★★ Rachel Ward and Daryl Hannah weren't big stars when they made this mediocre low-budget slasher flick for onetime B-movie king Sam Arkoff and now they probably wish they hadn't. Rated R for brief nudity and violence. 82m. **DIR:** Andrew Davis. **CAST:** Rachel Ward, Daryl Hannah, John Friedrich, Adrian Zmed. **1981**

FINAL VERDICT ★★★ Based on true events, this is a slow-paced account of one girl's adoration of her lawyer father (Treat Williams). Set in Los Angeles circa 1919, this made-for-TV film does an above-average job. 93m. **DIR:** Jack Fisk. **CAST:** Treat Williams, Glenn Ford, Olivia Burnette, Ashley Crow, Raphael Sbarge. **1991**

FINAL VOYAGE 🦃 A security guard battles jewel thieves in this awful rip-off of *Die Hard*, *Speed 2*, *Under Siege*, and any movie ever made on a boat. Rated R for violence and profanity. 94m. **DIR:** Jim Wynorski. **CAST:** Dylan Walsh, Ice T, Erika Eleniak, Claudia Christian, Rick Ducommun. **1999 DVD**

FIND THE LADY ★★★ In this slapstick rendition of a cops-and-robbers spoof, John Candy, as the cop, and Mickey Rooney, as a kidnapper, create lots of laughs on the way to a very funny finish. 90m. **DIR:** John Trent. **CAST:** John Candy, Mickey Rooney, Peter Cook, Lawrence Dane, Alexandra Bastedo. **1986**

FINDING FORRESTER ★★★★ Sean Connery fits the title role perfectly in this tale of an unlikely young genius and the gun-shy older professional who mentors him. A cranky reclusive writer, Connery becomes a tutor and father figure for Rob Brown's Jamal, an inner-city kid who has embraced basketball as a means of fitting in with his peers while concealing his greater talent for the written word. The result, though familiar and predictable, cannot fail to charm anybody with a soft spot for a favorite teacher. Rated PG-13 for profanity and dramatic intensity. 136m. **DIR:** Gus Van Sant. **CAST:** Sean Connery, Rob Brown, F. Murray Abraham, Anna Paquin, Busta Rhymes, Michael Nouri. **2000 DVD**

FINDING GRACELAND ★★ Whimsical tale of a hitchhiking Elvis and his effects on a young motorist crumbles under its own weight. At first the film shows lots of promise. Johnathon Schaech stars as a young man heading to Memphis who picks up a hitchhiker (played by Harvey Keitel) who claims to be Elvis. Both men have reasons to reach Memphis, but it is the road trip there that is most telling. Lots of plot holes force this comedy-drama off the road long before the characters reach their destination. Bridget Fonda costars as a Marilyn Monroe look-alike who tags up with the two men. Rated PG-13 for language. 97m. **DIR:** David Winkler. **CAST:** Harvey Keitel, Johnathon Schaech, Bridget Fonda. **1998 DVD**

FINE MADNESS, A ★★★ Whimsical story of a daffy, radical poet, well portrayed by Sean Connery (proving that, even in the 1960s, he could stretch further than James Bond). Many of the laughs come from his well-developed relationship with wife Joanne Woodward, although the film occasionally lapses into lurid slapstick. Not rated; adult themes. 104m. **DIR:** Irvin Kershner.

CAST: Sean Connery, Joanne Woodward, Jean Seberg. **1966**

FINE MESS, A 🦃 Supposedly inspired by the Laurel and Hardy classic, *The Music Box*. Gag after gag falls embarrassingly flat. Rated PG. 100m. **DIR:** Blake Edwards. **CAST:** Ted Danson, Howie Mandel, Richard Mulligan, Stuart Margolin, Maria Conchita Alonso, Jennifer Edwards, Paul Sorvino. **1986**

FINE ROMANCE, A ★★★ This is a lovely little romantic comedy with Julie Andrews and Marcello Mastroianni as a couple of discarded lovers whose spouses have left them. Thrust together to contemplate their options, both go through emotional withdrawal and loss, eventually finding happiness with each other. Rated PG-13 for profanity. 83m. **DIR:** Gene Saks. **CAST:** Julie Andrews, Marcello Mastroianni. **1993**

FINEST HOUR, THE ★★1/2 Two new navy SEAL recruits form an alliance after trying to outdo one another. After being separated for a couple of years, they team up again during the Persian Gulf War. Very dull plot that could have been shorter. Rated R for profanity, violence, and nudity. 105m. **DIR:** Shimon Dotan. **CAST:** Rob Lowe, Gale Hansen, Tracy Griffith, Eb Lottimer. **1991**

FINGER MAN ★★ Captured crook saves his hide by helping the Internal Revenue get the goods on crime kingpin Forrest Tucker. Frank Lovejoy as the reluctant informer does a credible job, but crazy Timothy Carey as Tucker's top enforcer steals the show. B&W; 81m. **DIR:** Harold Schuster. **CAST:** Frank Lovejoy, Forrest Tucker, Peggie Castle, Timothy Carey. **1955**

FINGER ON THE TRIGGER ★★ Ex-Union and ex-Confederate soldiers band together to defeat a party of Indians on the warpath. They must make bullets out of the only source available, a stash of golden horseshoes. This B Western filmed in Spain is Rory Calhoun's only European Western. Not rated; contains violence. 89m. **DIR:** Sidney Pink. **CAST:** Rory Calhoun, James Philbrook, Todd Martin, Leo Anchoriz, Silvia Solar. **1965**

FINGERS ★★★★ Harvey Keitel gives an electric performance as a would-be concert pianist who is also a death-dealing collector for his loan-sharking dad. Extremely violent and not for all tastes, but there is an undeniable fascination toward the Keitel character and his tortured life. Rated R. 91m. **DIR:** James Toback. **CAST:** Harvey Keitel, Jim Brown, Tisa Farrow, Michael Gazzo. **1978**

FINGERS AT THE WINDOW ★★★ An evil schemer employs a series of weak-willed men to hack to death witnesses who threaten his impersonation of a wealthy medical specialist. Entertaining and engaging, this breezy thriller from MGM's B unit takes some swipes at the psychiatric profession and features two of the oddest protagonists ever found in the ax-murder film. Offbeat and funny. B&W; 80m. **DIR:** Charles Lederer. **CAST:** Lew Ayres, Laraine Day, Basil Rathbone, Walter Kingsford, James Flavin, Miles Mander. **1942**

FINIAN'S RAINBOW ★★1/2 Those who believe Fred Astaire can do no wrong haven't seen this little oddity. Francis Coppola's heavy direction is totally inappropriate for a musical and the story's concerns about racial progress, which were outdated when the film first appeared, are positively embarrassing now. Rated G. 145m. **DIR:** Francis Ford Coppola. **CAST:** Fred Astaire, Petula Clark, Tommy Steele, Keenan Wynn, Barbara Hancock, Don Francks. **1968**

FINISH LINE ★★ Pressured by his coach father to excel, a high school athlete begins using steroids. Well-meaning drama, made for cable TV, is as predictable as most TV movies. Not rated. 96m. **DIR:** John Nicolella. **CAST:** James Brolin, Josh Brolin, Mariska Hargitay, Billy Vera. **1989**

FINISHING SCHOOL ★★★1/2 A poor little rich girl finds true love with a med student. Surprisingly progressive, this film was codirected and written by a woman—Wanda Tuchock—rare, indeed, for the 1930s. Some scenes are melodramatic and attitudes are dated, but overall the film remains engrossing. B&W; 73m. **DIR:** Wanda Tuchock, George Nicholls Jr. **CAST:** Frances Dee, Billie Burke, Ginger Rogers, Bruce Cabot, John Halliday. **1934**

FINISHING TOUCH, THE ★★1/2 Soon-to-be-divorced husband-and-wife detectives are assigned to the same case, a psychotic killer who sells the videotapes of the murders. The viewer knows exactly what will happen in the unimaginative plot. Rated R for nudity, profanity, and graphic sex. 82m. **DIR:** Fred Gallo. **CAST:** Michael Nader, Shelley Hack, Arnold Vosloo, Art Evans. **1991**

FINNEGAN BEGIN AGAIN ★★★★ In this endearing romance, Robert Preston plays Michael Finnegan, an eccentric retired advice columnist who befriends schoolteacher Elizabeth (Mary Tyler Moore) after learning of her secret affair with a married undertaker (Sam Waterston). Their eventual romance becomes a warm, funny, and tender portrayal of love blossoming in later life. Made for cable. 97m. **DIR:** Joan Micklin Silver. **CAST:** Mary Tyler Moore, Robert Preston, Sam Waterston, Sylvia Sidney. **1985**

FIRE! ★★ Another of producer Irwin Allen's suspense spectaculars involving an all-star cast caught in a major calamity. This one concerns a mountain town in the path of a forest fire set by an escaped convict. Worth watching once. 100m. **DIR:** Earl Bellamy. **CAST:** Ernest Borgnine, Vera Miles, Alex Cord, Donna Mills, Lloyd Nolan, Ty Hardin, Neville Brand, Gene Evans, Erik Estrada. **1977 DVD**

FIRE AND ICE ★★★★ Animated film is geared more to adults than children. Sword-and-sorcery fantasy keeps the action moving. The plot begins with evil sorcerer Nekron planning world domination. It thickens when he kidnaps the princess, Teegra, to force her father to turn his kingdom over to him as his daughter's ransom. Rated PG. 81m. **DIR:** Ralph Bakshi. **1983**

FIRE BIRDS 🦃 Lame revision of *Top Gun*. Rated PG-13 for violence and language. 85m. **DIR:** David Greene. **CAST:** Nicolas Cage, Sean Young, Tommy Lee Jones. **1990**

FIRE DOWN BELOW ★★★1/2 Steven Seagal goes after some nasty corporate types who are covertly dumping toxic waste in Kentucky's Appalachian hills while the locals suffer at their hands. It's the old save-the-ranch cowboy B-movie formula with extra kicks, and fun for fans of no-brainer entertainment. Rated R for violence and profanity. 105m. **DIR:** Felix Enriquez Alcala. **CAST:** Steven Seagal, Marg Helgenberger, Kris Kristofferson, Harry Dean Stanton, Stephen Lang, Levon Helm, Ed Bruce, Brad Hunt, Richard Masur, Randy Travis. **1997 DVD**

FIRE, ICE & DYNAMITE 🦃 Stunt director Willy Bogner oversees ex–James Bond star Roger Moore in this stunt-filled yet ultimately boring crime caper. Rated PG for violence. 105m. **DIR:** Willy Bogner. **CAST:** Roger Moore, Shari Belafonte. **1990**

FIRE IN THE SKY ★★ UFO buffs might get a lift out of this dramatization of the alleged abduction of Travis Walton (D. B. Sweeney) in 1975, but most viewers will be disappointed. Rated PG-13 for profanity and nudity. 110m. **DIR:** Robert Lieberman. **CAST:** D. B. Sweeney, Robert Patrick, James Garner, Craig Sheffer, Peter Berg, Henry Thomas, Noble Willingham, Kathleen Wilhoite. **1993**

FIRE NEXT TIME, THE ★★★ Preachy futuristic disaster film repeatedly delivers a heavy-handed environmental message. As a result of global warming, coastal towns are flooding while plains dry up. Amidst this, Craig T. Nelson tries to reunite his estranged family. Unbelievable plot twists and occasional lectures weaken the film's overall effectiveness. Not rated; contains profanity and suggestive comments. 180m. **DIR:** Tom McLoughlin. **CAST:** Craig T. Nelson, Bonnie Bedelia, Richard Farnsworth, Jurgen Prochnow. **1992**

FIRE OVER ENGLAND ★★★ A swashbuckling adventure of Elizabethan England's stand against the Spanish Armada. Made in the 1930s, it wasn't released in this country until 1941, in order to evoke American support and sympathy for Britain's plight against the Nazi juggernaut during its darkest days. This is only one of the three films that united husband and wife Laurence Olivier and Vivien Leigh. B&W; 92m. **DIR:** Alexander Korda. **CAST:** Laurence Olivier, Vivien Leigh, Flora Robson. **1936 DVD**

FIRE WITH FIRE ★★ What hath Shakespeare wrought? The true story of a girl's Catholic school that invited the residents of a neighboring boy's reform school to a dance. Another good girl/bad boy melodrama wherein misunderstood teens triumph against all odds. Craig Sheffer and Virginia Madsen are appealing, but the plot is laughable. Rated PG-13 for mild sex and language. 103m. **DIR:** Duncan Gibbins. **CAST:** Craig Sheffer, Virginia Madsen, Jon Polito, Kate Reid, Jean Smart. **1986**

FIRE WITHIN, THE ★★★★ After his release from a sanatorium, a suicidal alcoholic looks for reasons not to kill himself. What sounds like a terribly depressing movie becomes a sharp study of a complex character in the hands of Louis Malle (who also scripted). In French with English subtitles. B&W; 121m. **DIR:** Louis Malle. **CAST:** Maurice Ronet, Lena Skerla, Jeanne Moreau, Alexandra Stewart. **1963**

FIREBIRD 2015 AD 🦃 In the near future, gas is so scarce that the government outlaws private ownership of automobiles and sets up an agency to destroy them. Rated PG. 97m. **DIR:** David Robertson. **CAST:** Darren McGavin, Doug McClure, George Touliatos. **1981**

FIRECREEK ★★★ When an easygoing farmer accepts the job of sheriff in a small town, he finds himself forced to stand up to a gang of ruthless outlaws. Like *The Cheyenne Social Club* before it, this downbeat Western is of interest only for the interplay of its top-billed stars—for some of us this is more than enough to make it worth watching. 104m. **DIR:** Vincent McEveety. **CAST:** James Stewart, Henry Fonda, Inger Stevens, Dean Jagger, Ed Begley Sr., Gary Lockwood, Jack Elam, Jay C. Flippen, Barbara Luna, James Best, Brooke Bundy, Morgan Woodward, John Qualen. **1968**

FIREFLY, THE ★★★1/2 One of Jeanette MacDonald's most popular movies even though her perennial costar, Nelson Eddy, is not in it. This is the only film they made separately that clicked. Allan Jones gets to sing the film's best song, "Donkey Serenade." MacDonald gets to sing most of the others, including "Giannina Mia" and "Love Is Like a Firefly" from Rudolf Friml's 1912 operetta. B&W; 137m. **DIR:** Robert Z. Leonard. **CAST:** Jeanette MacDonald, Allan Jones, Warren William, Douglass Dumbrille, Billy Gilbert, George Zucco, Henry Daniell. **1937**

FIREFOX ★★★1/2 Clint Eastwood doffs his contemporary cowboy garb to direct, produce, and star in this action-adventure film about an American fighter pilot assigned to steal a sophisticated Russian aircraft. The film takes a while to take off, but when it does, it's good, action-packed fun. Rated PG for violence. 124m. **DIR:** Clint Eastwood. **CAST:** Clint Eastwood, Freddie Jones, David Huffman, Warren Clarke, Ronald Lacey, Stefan Schnabel. **1982**

FIREHAWK ★★ Walk through the park as survivors of a downed American helicopter platoon must contend with the oncoming Vietcong, plus the traitor among them with his own agenda. Plenty of action keeps this from being a total disaster. Rated R for violence and adult language. 92m. **DIR:** Cirio H. Santiago. **CAST:** Martin Kove, Vic Trevino, Matt Salinger, Terrence "T. C." Carson. **1992**

FIREHOUSE (1972) ★★ Rookie flame fighter Richard Roundtree saves face and his marriage amid the hostile big-city firehouse environment of racism. 80m. **DIR:** Alex March. **CAST:** Richard Roundtree, Andrew Duggan, Richard Jaeckel, Val Avery, Paul LeMat, Vince Edwards, Sheila Frazier. **1972**

FIREHOUSE (1987) 🦃 *Charlie's Angels* clone set in a firehouse. Rated R. 91m. **DIR:** J. Christian Ingvordsen. **CAST:** Barrett Hopkins, Shannon Murphy, Violet Brown, John Anderson, Peter Onorati. **1987 DVD**

FIRELIGHT ★★★★ This lush, haunting Victorian romance is a sort of *Baby M* meets *Jane Eyre*. It's about surrogate motherhood, parenting, and—rather bizarrely—euthanasia. In the 1830s, 22 year old Swiss governess Elizabeth makes a secret pact with a British landowner to bear him an heir. Emotional and moral dilemmas emerge as Elizabeth discovers she cannot renounce her love for her child, and pragmatic life-shaping decisions begin bouncing like bad checks. Rated R for simulated sex, nudity, and language. 104m. **DIR:** William Nicholson. **CAST:** Sophie Marceau, Stephen Dillane, Dominique Belcourt. **1998**

FIREMAN'S BALL, THE ★★1/2 Highly acclaimed comedy of a small-town firemen's gathering that turns into a sprawling, ludicrous disaster. Fairly weak considering direction by Milos Forman. In Czech with English subtitles. 73m. **DIR:** Milos Forman. **CAST:** Jan Vostricil. **1968**

FIREPOWER (1979) ★★ *Firepower* is a muddled, mindless mess. A research chemist is blown up by a letter bomb while his wife, Sophia Loren, watches helplessly. The chemist was about to prove that a company owned by the third-richest man in the world, Carl Stegner (George Touliatos), has been distributing drugs responsible for causing the cancerous deaths of many people. The widow joins Justice Department agent James Coburn in trying to bring Stegner out of seclusion. Rated R. 104m. **DIR:** Michael Winner. **CAST:** Sophia Loren, James Coburn, O. J. Simpson, Eli Wallach, Vincent Gardenia, Anthony Franciosa, George Touliatos. **1979**

FIREPOWER (1993) 🦃 Two cops infiltrate a crime-ridden section of twenty-first-century Los Angeles on the trail of a crime lord who arranges no-holds-barred death matches. Rated R for violence. 94m. **DIR:** Richard Pepin. **CAST:** Chad McQueen, Gary Daniels, Joseph Ruskin, Jim Hellwig. **1993**

FIRES ON THE PLAIN ★★★★ Kon Ichikawa's classic uses World War II and soldiers' cannibalism as symbols for the brutality of man. This film is uncomplicated and its emotion intensely focused, giving it a stark and disturbing vision. In Japanese with English subtitles. 105m. **DIR:** Kon Ichikawa. **CAST:** Eiji Funakoshi. **1959**

FIRES WITHIN ★★ Boring love triangle involving an American fisherman, a Cuban refugee, and a Cuban political prisoner. Writer Cynthia Cidre failed to create a film with either believable characters or an engaging plot. 90m. **DIR:** Gillian Armstrong. **CAST:** Jimmy Smits, Greta Scacchi, Vincent D'Onofrio, Luis Avalos. **1991 DVD**

FIRESTARTER ★★★1/2 Stephen King writhes again. This time, Drew Barrymore stars as the gifted (or is that haunted) child of the title, who has the ability—sometimes uncontrollable—to ignite objects around her. David Keith is the father who tries to protect her from the baddies. Suspenseful, poignant, and sometimes frightening entertainment that goes beyond its genre. Rated R for violence. 115m. **DIR:** Mark L. Lester. **CAST:** David Keith, Drew Barrymore, George C. Scott, Martin Sheen. **1984 DVD**

FIRESTORM ★★ This gloriously hokey disaster-action movie is an unintentional hoot. Smoke-jumper Jesse Graves parachutes into forests with an elite squad of firefighters armed with shovels, axes, and chain saws. Oozing more sap than the surrounding pines, the story begins with the rescue of a little girl and her dog from a doomed rural cabin. It lamely shifts into thriller mode as Jesse tries to save a female ornithologist from a prison escapee and a rampant forest inferno. Rated R for language and violence. 89m. **DIR:** Dean Semler. **CAST:** Howie Long, William Forsythe, Suzy Amis, Scott Glenn. **1998 DVD**

•FIRETRAP ★★ Traditional high-rise disaster film about a high-tech thief (Dean Cain) after a computer chip, who finds himself trapped by a towering office-building fire set by a corrupt employee after the same chip. Cain makes an okay hero, forced to choose between getting away with the chip or helping those trapped in the conflagration. The script never catches on fire, but some impressive special effects pump up the heat. Rated R for violence. 99m. **DIR:** Harris Done. **CAST:** Dean Cain, Lori Petty, Mel Harris, Richard Tyson. **2001 DVD**

FIREWALKER 🦃 Two soldiers of fortune search for hidden treasure and end up in a Mayan temple of doom. Rated PG. 96m. **DIR:** J. Lee Thompson. **CAST:** Chuck Norris, Louis Gossett Jr., Melody Anderson, John Rhys-Davies. **1986**

FIREWORKS ★★★★ Japanese cop Nishi splits his time between *yakuza* stakeouts and vigils at his cancer-stricken wife's hospital bed before fine-tuning his own destiny. Nishi retires from the police force after a shoot-out leaves fellow officers dead and crippled. The incident and its aftermath are revisited in flashbacks as he takes his spouse on a doctor-prescribed vacation. This combination crime-thriller and melodrama is tender, savage, explosive, languid, comic, and poetic. In Japanese with English subtitles. Not rated; contains violence and profanity. 103m. **DIR:** Takeshi Kitano. **CAST:** Takeshi Kitano, Kayoko Kishimoto, Ren Osugi, Susumu Terajima, Tetsu Watanabe. **1997 DVD**

FIRING LINE, THE ★★ Amateurish effort from writer-director John Gale about a rebel uprising in a South American country. Rated R for violence. 93m. **DIR:** John Gale. **CAST:** Reb Brown, Shannon Tweed, Carl Terry. **1991 DVD**

FIRM, THE ★★★★ Director Sydney Pollack takes the old-style Hollywood approach in this adaptation of John Grisham's bestselling suspense-thriller by surrounding star Tom Cruise with a top-flight cast of supporting actors—and it works. Cruise plays an ambitious young lawyer who joins a law firm in Memphis only to find that his high salary and impressive perks come with a price: either go along with the company's corrupt dealings or become its next victim. Gripping. Rated R for profanity, violence, and suggested sex. 154m. **DIR:** Sydney Pollack. **CAST:** Tom Cruise, Gene Hackman, Jeanne Tripplehorn, Ed Harris, Holly Hunter, Hal Holbrook, David Strathairn, Wilford Brimley, Gary Busey. **1993 DVD**

FIRST AFFAIR ★★★ Melissa Sue Anderson stars as a naïve Harvard scholarship student. She finds herself romantically inclined toward her English professor's husband. A strong entourage of actors helps make this an insightful commentary about the difficulties of keeping a marriage together, and the pain of losing one's innocence. Made for television. 100m. **DIR:** Gus Trikonis. **CAST:** Loretta Swit, Melissa Sue Anderson, Joel Higgins, Charley Lang, Kim Delaney, Amanda Bearse. **1983**

FIRST AND TEN ★★1/2 A pilot for the Home Box Office series of the same name, this football satire chronicles the hapless exploits of a West Coast team. Its locker room humor may limit it to an adult audience, but there are sufficient laughs. 97m. **DIR:** Donald Kushner. **CAST:** Fran Tarkenton, Geoffrey Scott, Reid Shelton, Ruta Lee, Delta Burke. **1985**

FIRST BLOOD ★★★1/2 Sylvester Stallone is top-notch as a former Green Beret who is forced to defend himself from a redneck cop (Brian Dennehy) in the Oregon mountains. The action never lets up. A winner for fans. Rated R for violence and profanity. 97m. **DIR:** Ted Kotcheff. **CAST:** Sylvester Stallone, Richard Crenna, Brian Dennehy, David Caruso, Jack Starrett. **1982 DVD**

FIRST DAUGHTER ★★★ TBS Superstation launched its own version of a female James Bond with Secret Service agent Alex McGregor. An athletic Mariel Hemingway plays the never-say-die heroine who must protect the president's daughter on a survivalist camping trip. Her tense style conflicts with that of the group guide (Doug Savant), until both are called to action when their teenage charge is abducted. Tense thriller boasts some riveting moments. Not rated; contains violence.

92m. **DIR:** Armand Mastroianni. **CAST:** Mariel Hemingway, Doug Savant, Gregory Harrison. **1999**

FIRST DEADLY SIN, THE ★★ Lawrence Sanders's excellent mystery is turned into a so-so cop flick with Frank Sinatra looking bored as aging Detective Edward X. Delaney, on the trail of a murdering maniac (David Dukes). Costar Faye Dunaway spends the entire picture flat on her back in a hospital bed. Rated R. 112m. **DIR:** Brian G. Hutton. **CAST:** Frank Sinatra, Faye Dunaway, James Whitmore, David Dukes, Brenda Vaccaro, Martin Gabel, Anthony Zerbe. **1980 DVD**

FIRST DEGREE ★★ Rob Lowe is actually pretty good as a charming cop who wins the affections of a gorgeous widow when he investigates her husband's murder. Questions surface about possible suspects including the mob, the not-very-grief-stricken wife, and even the investigator. The plot takes a few extra zags, leaving us merely perplexed, and the ending creates just one more puzzle. Rated R for nudity, violence, and profanity. 98m. **DIR:** Jeff Woolnough. **CAST:** Rob Lowe, Leslie Hope, Tom McCamus, Joseph Griffin. **1995**

. . . FIRST DO NO HARM ★★1/2 A Midwestern couple nearly lose everything they have when their 4-year-old son develops epilepsy. Director Jim Abrahams made this TV movie inspired by his own son's experience with epilepsy and with doctors whose reliance on debilitating drugs causes more harm than good. But too much of the story plays like a self-righteous indictment of doctors and an infomercial for the ketogenic diet. Not rated. 94m. **DIR:** Jim Abrahams. **CAST:** Meryl Streep, Fred Ward, Seth Adkins, Allison Janney. **1997**

FIRST FAMILY 🦃 Unfunny farce about an inept president, his family, and his aides. Rated R. 104m. **DIR:** Buck Henry. **CAST:** Bob Newhart, Gilda Radner, Madeline Kahn, Richard Benjamin, Harvey Korman, Bob Dishy, Rip Torn. **1980**

FIRST KID ★★ Sinbad's larger-than-life persona is wasted on this inert fluff fest. The contrast between his electric personality and the somberness of his fellow secret agents provides the film's running joke. A heartwarming relationship develops between him and his young charge as Sinbad provides the fathering the president has neglected to do. Oddly, it takes Timothy Busfield's dramatic pathos to wake up viewers, which says little for a comedy. Rated PG for violence. 97m. **DIR:** David Mickey Evans. **CAST:** Sinbad, Brock Pierce, Timothy Busfield, Robert Guillaume, Zachery Ty Bryan. **1996**

FIRST KNIGHT ★★★★ Apart from the anachronistic performance by Richard Gere as a kung-fu-fighting (!) Lancelot, this is a memorable retelling of the King Arthur legend, with its emphasis on a historical, romantic approach as opposed to fantasy. Director Jerry Zucker keeps it big and impressive, developing his characters in a believable fashion. Rated PG-13 for violence. 133m. **DIR:** Jerry Zucker. **CAST:** Sean Connery, Richard Gere, Julia Ormond, Ben Cross, John Gielgud. **1995 DVD**

FIRST LOVE ★★ A somber movie about a college student who is unlucky in love. While the film has an interesting cast, sharp dialogue, and a refreshingly honest story, it's basically muddleheaded. Rated R for nudity and language. 92m. **DIR:** Joan Darling. **CAST:** William Katt, Susan Dey, John Heard, Beverly D'Angelo, Robert Loggia. **1977**

FIRST LOVE ★★★ Cute Deanna Durbin take on a "modern" Cinderella story. She's the orphaned and unwanted niece forced to live with wealthy relatives; Robert Stack is the rich kid who steals her heart and gives Deanna her first screen kiss. Funnier than you'd expect, but some viewers may find Durbin's brand of music annoyingly dated. Not rated. B&W; 85m. **DIR:** Henry Koster. **CAST:** Deanna Durbin, Robert Stack, Eugene Pallette, Helen Parrish. **1939**

FIRST MAN INTO SPACE, THE ★★1/2 An arrogant test pilot is mutated, by cosmic rays, into a blood-hungry monster. Although it's dated and scientifically incorrect, this sci-fi chiller still has some B-film fun. Not rated, but suitable for all viewers. B&W; 78m. **DIR:** Robert Day. **CAST:** Marshall Thompson. **1958 DVD**

FIRST MEN IN THE MOON ★★★1/2 This whimsical adaptation of an H. G. Wells novel benefits greatly from the imaginative genius of Ray Harryhausen, who concocts the critters—stop-motion and otherwise—that menace some turn-of-the-century lunar explorers who arrive via a Victorian-era spaceship. Although the tone is initially tongue-in-cheek, this adventurous plot eventually develops some rather chilling teeth. Not rated, but great fun for the entire family. 103m. **DIR:** Nathan Juran. **CAST:** Edward Judd, Martha Hyer, Lionel Jeffries, Peter Finch. **1964 DVD**

FIRST MONDAY IN OCTOBER ★★★ This is a Walter Matthau picture, with all the joys that implies. As he did in *Hopscotch*, director Ronald Neame allows Matthau, who plays a crusty Supreme Court justice, to make the most of every screen moment. Jill Clayburgh plays the first woman appointed to the Supreme Court. Rated R for nudity and profanity. 98m. **DIR:** Ronald Neame. **CAST:** Walter Matthau, Jill Clayburgh, Barnard Hughes, Jan Sterling. **1981**

FIRST NAME: CARMEN ★★★ Jean-Luc Godard does a fabulous job portraying an eccentric filmmaker whose niece has hired him to direct a movie; actually, she is using him as a front for a terrorist attack. Slow-moving at times. In French with English subtitles. Not rated; contains profanity and nudity. 85m. **DIR:** Jean-Luc Godard. **CAST:** Maruschka Detmers, Jacques Bonnaffe, Myriem Roussel, Jean-Luc Godard. **1983 DVD**

FIRST 9 1/2 WEEKS, THE ★★ Prequel in name only, this is a somber tale of a New York currency trader who winds up in New Orleans to seal a deal with a billionaire. Instead, he strikes up an affair with the billionaire's wife, and is then framed for murder by the jealous husband. Ho hum. People don't rent these for the plot; the performances aren't much better. Malcolm McDowell delivers his trademark sneer as the bad guy. Rated R for adult situations, nudity, language, and violence. 104m. **DIR:** Alexander Wright. **CAST:** Malcolm McDowell, Paul Mercurio, Clara Bellar. **1998 DVD**

FIRST NUDIE MUSICAL, THE ★★★ A struggling young director saves the studio by producing the world's first pornographic movie musical à la Busby Berkeley. Pleasant but extremely crude little romp. Not as bad as it sounds, but definitely for the very open-minded, and that's being generous. Rated R for nudity. 100m. **DIR:** Mark Haggard. **CAST:** Bruce Kimmel, Stephen Nathan, Cindy Williams, Diana Canova. **1979**

FIRST POWER, THE 🦃 Repulsive thing-that-wouldn't-die trash. Rated R. 100m. **DIR:** Robert Resnikoff. **CAST:**

Lou Diamond Phillips, Tracy Griffith, Jeff Kober, Mykelti Williamson, Dennis Lipscomb. **1990 DVD**

FIRST TARGET ★★★1/2 *First Daughter* sequel replaces Mariel Hemingway with Daryl Hannah as Secret Service agent Alex McGregor. This time Agent McGregor must thwart a conspiracy to assassinate the president at a national park dedication. Lots of twists and turns and a strong inkling that no one can be trusted make for spellbinding viewing; the sexy villainess doesn't hurt, either. Not rated; contains voilence and sexual situations. 94m. **DIR:** Armand Mastroianni. **CAST:** Daryl Hannah, Doug Savant, Gregory Harrison. **2000**

FIRST TIME, THE ★★★ With parents pushing poor Charlie into a relationship with a girl—any girl!—he resists. But when he gets into filmmaking, the opposite sex goes mad for him. This campus comedy is rated PG-13 for mature situations and language. 96m. **DIR:** Charlie Loventhal. **CAST:** Tim Choate, Krista Erickson, Wallace Shawn, Wendie Jo Sperber. **1982**

FIRST TIME FELON ★★★1/2 Daniel Thierrault's script is a fact-based account of an insolent gang banger who, arrested on a minor charge and given the opportunity to avoid jail by attending a rehabilitation boot camp, learns personal integrity but then finds that the world at large still dismisses him as an ex-convict. It's tough sledding for the first fifteen minutes, during which you won't care at all for the violent thugs, but the story quickly improves. Rated R for profanity, drug use, and violence. 105m. **DIR:** Charles S. Dutton. **CAST:** Omar Epps, Delroy Lindo, Rachel Ticotin, Justin Pierce, William Forsythe. **1997 DVD**

FIRST TURN-ON, THE 🦃 This cheapie features four campers and their counselor trapped in a cave seeking amusement. Not rated; contains nudity and profanity and sexual situations. 88m. **DIR:** Michael Herz, Samuel Weil. **CAST:** Michael Sanville. **1983**

FIRST WIVES CLUB, THE ★★★★ The ladies get their revenge in this delightful adaptation of Olivia Goldsmith's bestselling novel. Well-heeled Manhattanites Bette Midler, Goldie Hawn, and Diane Keaton all have been left by husbands now squiring much younger bimbos. Refusing to roll over and play dead, the spurned women concoct elaborate schemes to regain financial control from their ex-husbands. Overall this is gender humor at its funniest, with Midler positively stealing the show. Rated PG for mild profanity. 104m. **DIR:** Hugh Wilson. **CAST:** Bette Midler, Goldie Hawn, Diane Keaton, Maggie Smith, Dan Hedaya, Bronson Pinchot, Jennie Dundas, Eileen Heckart, Stephen Collins, Elizabeth Berkeley, Marcia Gay Harden, Sarah Jessica Parker. **1996 DVD**

FIRST WORKS, VOLUMES 1 & 2 ★★1/2 Each volume contains commercial film clips, candid interviews, and the student films of top Hollywood directors. While the interviews are old, and many of the clips and photographs are faded, it's worth watching for the student films, if you can stand the bargain-basement production values. Not rated; contains profanity. B&W/color; 120m. **DIR:** Robert Kline. **CAST:** Roger Corman, Taylor Hackford, Spike Lee, Paul Mazursky, Oliver Stone, Robert Zemeckis, John Carpenter, Richard Donner, Ron Howard, John Milius, Martin Scorsese, Susan Seidelman. **1995**

FIRST YANK INTO TOKYO 🦃 Tom Neal has plastic surgery so he can pose as a Japanese soldier and help an American POW escape. B&W; 82m. **DIR:** Gordon Douglas. **CAST:** Tom Neal, Barbara Hale, Richard Loo, Keye Luke, Benson Fong. **1945**

FIRSTBORN ★★★★ An emotionally charged screen drama that deftly examines some topical, thought-provoking themes, this stars Teri Garr as a divorced woman who gets involved with the wrong man (Peter Weller) to the horror of her two sons. Rated PG for profanity and violence. 100m. **DIR:** Michael Apted. **CAST:** Teri Garr, Peter Weller. **1984**

FISH CALLED WANDA, A ★★★★1/2 Monty Python veteran John Cleese wrote and starred in this hilarious caper comedy. Jamie Lee Curtis and Kevin Kline are American crooks who plot to double-cross their British partners in crime (Michael Palin and Tom Georgeson) with the unwitting help of barrister Cleese. Be forewarned: *Wanda* has something in it to offend everyone. Rated R for profanity and violence. 108m. **DIR:** Charles Crichton. **CAST:** John Cleese, Jamie Lee Curtis, Kevin Kline, Michael Palin, Tom Georgeson, Patricia Hayes. **1988 DVD**

FISH HAWK ★★★ Excellent drama about an Indian (Will Sampson) who befriends a young farm boy in turn-of-the-century rural America. Sampson has a drinking problem, which he kicks in an effort to return to his former life. Rated G; contains very mild profanity. 95m. **DIR:** Donald Shebib. **CAST:** Will Sampson, Don Francks, Charles Fields, Chris Wiggins. **1984**

FISH THAT SAVED PITTSBURGH, THE ★★1/2 Curious mixture of disco, astrology, and comedy. A failing basketball team turns to a rather eccentric medium for help, and the resulting confusion makes for a few amusing moments. Features a veritable smorgasbord of second-rate actors, from Jonathan Winters to basketball great Julius Irving (Dr. J.). Proceed at your own risk. Rated PG for profanity. 102m. **DIR:** Gilbert Moses. **CAST:** Stockard Channing, Flip Wilson, Jonathan Winters, Julius Erving. **1979**

FISHER KING, THE ★★★★1/2 Jack Lucas is a radio talk-show host whose irreverent manner indirectly causes a tragedy; his remorse plunges him into an alcoholic haze. Enter a street person named Parry, who involves Jack in a quest for the Holy Grail in New York City. This adult-oriented fairy tale will win the hearts of those who haven't lost their sense of wonder. Rated R for profanity, nudity, and violence. 137m. **DIR:** Terry Gilliam. **CAST:** Robin Williams, Jeff Bridges, Mercedes Ruehl, Amanda Plummer, Michael Jeter. **1991 DVD**

F.I.S.T. ★★ It's too bad that *F.I.S.T.* is so predictable and cliché-ridden, because Sylvester Stallone gives a fine performance. As Johnny Kovak, leader of the Federation of Interstate Truckers, he creates an even more poignant character than Rocky Balboa. It is ironic that Stallone, after being favorably compared with Marlon Brando, should end up in a film so similar to *On the Waterfront* . . . and with Rod Steiger yet! Rated PG. 145m. **DIR:** Norman Jewison. **CAST:** Sylvester Stallone, Rod Steiger, Peter Boyle, Melinda Dillon, David Huffman, Tony Lo Bianco. **1978**

FIST FIGHTER ★★ A drifter (Jorge Rivero) heads to Central America to avenge a friend's murder. For fans of two-fisted action-oriented movies. Rated R for violence. 99m. **DIR:** Frank Zuniga. **CAST:** Jorge Rivero, Mike Connors, Edward Albert. **1988**

FIST OF IRON ★★ Strictly for the kick-boxing and martial arts set. There's enough mayhem in this tale of a fight-to-the-death match and the men who enter to satisfy fans of the genre. Rated R for extreme violence. 94m. **DIR:** Richard W. Munchkin. **CAST:** Michael Worth, Matthias Hues, Sam Jones, Marshall Teague, Jenilee Harrison. **1994**

FIST OF LEGEND ★★★1/2 Jet Li stars as the vengeful disciple of a kung fu master who was killed in a match that he never should have lost. When Jet Li discovers the possibility of foul play in a supposedly honorable fight, he tracks down those responsible and makes them pay dearly for their indiscretions. While the story may be lacking, the martial arts scenes are top-notch. Rated R for violence. 102m. **DIR:** Gordon Chan, Woo-Ping Yuen. **CAST:** Jet Li, Yasuaki Kurata. **1994 DVD**

FIST OF STEEL 🦃 A futuristic gladiator battles rivals for survival in a postapocalyptic world. Not again. Not rated; contains violence, profanity, nudity, substance abuse, and sexual situations. 97m. **DIR:** Irvin Johnson. **CAST:** Dale "Apollo" Cook, Gregg Douglass, Cynthia Khan, Don Nakaya Nielsen. **1993**

FIST OF THE NORTH STAR 🦃 Ultraviolent and incoherent live-action adaptation of the postapocalyptic Japanese animated series; if this stuff appeals to you, stick with the original. Rated R for violence, profanity, and gore. 88m. **DIR:** Tony Randel. **CAST:** Gary Daniels, Costas Mandylor, Christopher Penn, Isako Washio, Melvin Van Peebles, Malcolm McDowell. **1995 DVD**

FIST OF THE NORTH STAR ★★1/2 Japanese animation. Extreme violence is the main plot ingredient in this animated post-apocalyptic kung fu epic wherein a trio of brothers vie for the title of "Fist of the North Star." Released in some U.S. theatrical markets, probably because of the unrivaled spectacle of animated carnage. 110m. **DIR:** Toyoo Ashida. **1986 DVD**

FISTFUL OF DOLLARS, A ★★★ Clint Eastwood parlayed his multiyear stint on television's *Rawhide* into international fame with this film, a slick remake of Akira Kurosawa's *Yojimbo*. Eastwood's laconic "Man With No Name" blows into a town nearly blown apart by two feuding families; after considerable manipulation by all concerned, he moves on down the road. 96m. **DIR:** Sergio Leone. **CAST:** Clint Eastwood, Mario Brega, Gian Maria Volonté. **1964 DVD**

FISTFUL OF DYNAMITE, A ★★★ After his success with Clint Eastwood's "Man with No Name" Westerns, Sergio Leone made this sprawling, excessive film set during the Mexican revolution. A thief, played by Rod Steiger, is drawn into the revolution by Irish mercenary James Coburn. Soon both are blowing up everything in sight and single-handedly winning the war. 121m. **DIR:** Sergio Leone. **CAST:** Rod Steiger, James Coburn, Maria Monti, Romolo Valli. **1972**

FISTS OF FURY ★★★ Bruce Lee's first chop-socky movie (made in Hong Kong) is corny, action-filled, and violent. It's no *Enter the Dragon*, but his fans—who have so few films to choose from—undoubtedly will want to see it again. Rated R. 102m. **DIR:** Lo Wei. **CAST:** Bruce Lee, Maria Yi, James Tien, Nora Miao. **1972 DVD**

FIT TO KILL 🦃 Filmmaker Andy Sidaris continues his series of female spy movies, which usually serve as just an excuse to get women out of their clothes. This one has less flesh than usual, so there's nothing to watch at all. Rated R for nudity, violence, and adult situations. 94m. **DIR:** Andy Sidaris. **CAST:** Dona Speir, Roberta Vasquez, Julie Strain, Cynthia Brimhall. **1993**

FITZCARRALDO ★★★1/2 For Werner Herzog, the making of this film was reportedly quite an ordeal. Watching it may be an ordeal for some viewers as well. In order to bring Caruso, the greatest voice in the world, to the backwater town of Iquitos, the title character (Klaus Kinski) decides to haul a large boat over a mountain. Not rated; this film has profanity. In German with English subtitles. 157m. **DIR:** Werner Herzog. **CAST:** Klaus Kinski, Claudia Cardinale. **1982 DVD**

FITZWILLY ★★★1/2 Dick Van Dyke is perfectly suited to this amiable comedy, as a loyal butler who supports his employer's philanthropic generosity by leading her staff on a series of heists. It seems that the poor old dear doesn't know she's flat broke, and only Fitzwilly's quick thinking keeps her afloat . . . an arrangement threatened when a new secretary is hired. Take note of the early John Williams soundtrack. Suitable for all ages. 102m. **DIR:** Delbert Mann. **CAST:** Dick Van Dyke, Barbara Feldon, John McGiver, Edith Evans, Harry Townes, John Fiedler, Norman Fell, Cecil Kellaway. **1967**

FIVE BLOODY GRAVES ★★ Somewhat imaginative as Death narrates the tale of an odd mix of travelers pursued across the desert by a savage band of Indians. Extreme violence. Also titled: *Gun Riders* and *Lonely Man*. 81m. **DIR:** Al Adamson. **CAST:** Robert Dix, Scott Brady, Jim Davis, John Carradine. **1969 DVD**

FIVE CAME BACK ★★★ A plane carrying the usual mixed bag of passengers goes down in the jungle. Only five of the group will survive. The cast, fine character players all, makes this melodrama worthwhile, though it shows its age. B&W; 75m. **DIR:** John Farrow. **CAST:** Chester Morris, Wendy Barrie, John Carradine, Allen Jenkins, Joseph Calleia, C. Aubrey Smith, Patric Knowles, Lucille Ball. **1939**

FIVE CARD STUD ★★1/2 Muddled Western with a whodunit motif. Gambler-gunfighter Dean Martin attempts to discover who is systematically murdering the members of a lynching party. Robert Mitchum adds some memorable moments as a gun-toting preacher, but most of the performances are lifeless, with Roddy McDowall's gunslinger the most ludicrous of all. This is far from top-notch Henry Hathaway. 103m. **DIR:** Henry Hathaway. **CAST:** Dean Martin, Robert Mitchum, Inger Stevens, Roddy McDowall, Katherine Justice, Yaphet Kotto, Denver Pyle. **1968**

FIVE CORNERS ★★★1/2 Most viewers will feel a little *Moonstruck* after watching this bizarre comedy-drama written by John Patrick Shanley. Jodie Foster stars as a young woman who attempts to get help from the tough-guy-turned-pacifist (Tim Robbins) who saved her from being raped by an unhinged admirer (John Turturro) when the latter is released from prison. Moments of suspense and hard-edged realism are effectively mixed with bits of offbeat comedy. Rated R for violence and adult themes. 92m. **DIR:** Tony Bill. **CAST:** Jodie Foster, Tim Robbins, John Turturro. **1988 DVD**

5 DARK SOULS ★★1/2 Modest little chiller tells of three wannabes who are led into the woods by the high school's most popular clique, a group of five teens with plans of putting the trio in a snuff movie. This risqué film treads the line between trash and respectability, and manages to come across fairly well. Not rated; contains violence. 90m. **DIR:** Jason Paul Collum. **CAST:** Tina Ona Paukstelis, Matthew Winkler, Christopher D. Harder. **1996**

FIVE DAYS ONE SUMMER ★★★ This is an old-fashioned romance, with Sean Connery as a mountain climber caught in a triangle involving his lovely niece and a handsome young guide. Two handkerchiefs and a liking for soap operas are suggested. Rated PG for adult situations. 108m. **DIR:** Fred Zinnemann. **CAST:** Sean Connery, Anna Massey, Betsy Brantley, Lambert Wilson. **1983**

5 DEAD ON THE CRIMSON CANVAS ★★ Ambitious production tries to pay homage to the Italian *giallo* films but doesn't succeed. The pieces are all there, but nothing seems to work well together. Not rated; contains violence and profanity. 96m. **DIR:** Joseph A. Parda. **CAST:** Liz Haverty, Joseph Zaso, Mony Damevsky. **1996**

FIVE EASY PIECES ★★★★1/2 Shattering drama concerns Jack Nicholson's return to his family home after years of self-imposed exile. Playing a once promising pianist who chose to work in the oil fields, Nicholson has rarely been better; his fully shaded character with its explosions of emotion are a wonder to behold. One of the gems of the seventies. The chicken-salad scene in the diner is now a classic. Rated R. 90m. **DIR:** Bob Rafelson. **CAST:** Jack Nicholson, Karen Black, Susan Anspach, Billy Green Bush, Sally Struthers, Ralph Waite, Fannie Flagg. **1970 DVD**

FIVE FINGERS ★★★★1/2 James Mason, the trusted valet to the British ambassador in World War II Ankara, sells government secrets to the Germans. He gets rich but does no harm as the Germans mistakenly think he is a double agent and take no action on the material he gives them. It seems farfetched, but it's based on fact. Wonderful suspense. Also released as *Operation Cicero*. B&W; 108m. **DIR:** Joseph L. Mankiewicz. **CAST:** James Mason, Danielle Darrieux, Michael Rennie, Walter Hampden. **1952**

FIVE GOLDEN DRAGONS An innocent man runs into an international crime ring in Hong Kong. Boring, poorly made adventure. 93m. **DIR:** Jeremy Summers. **CAST:** Robert Cummings, Rupert Davies, Margaret Lee, Brian Donlevy, Christopher Lee, George Raft, Dan Duryea. **1967**

FIVE GOLDEN HOURS ★★★ Ernie Kovacs is hilarious as a professional mourner who lives off the generosity of grieving widows. Things become complicated when he falls for penniless Italian baroness Cyd Charisse. B&W; 89m. **DIR:** Mario Zampi. **CAST:** Ernie Kovacs, Cyd Charisse, Dennis Price, John Le Mesurier, Kay Hammond, George Sanders. **1961**

FIVE GRAVES TO CAIRO ★★★ A British officer schemes to outwit Field Marshall Rommel by posing as a waiter at a desert outpost where Rommel is visiting. The great Billy Wilder's second film as a director is a fairly standard espionage tale that seems out of place in his body of work, though traces of his usual themes can be spotted. B&W; 96m. **DIR:** Billy Wilder. **CAST:** Franchot Tone, Anne Baxter, Erich Von Stroheim. **1943**

FIVE HEARTBEATS, THE ★★★★★ Everything is just right with writer-director Robert Townsend's musical comedy–drama about the rise and fall of a 1960s soul group. Townsend gets excellent performances from his actors (especially Michael Wright) and always manages to put an unexpected twist on the often-too-familiar show biz story. Rated R for profanity and violence. 120m. **DIR:** Robert Townsend. **CAST:** Robert Townsend, Michael Wright, Leon, Harry J. Lennix, Tico Wells, Diahann Carroll, Harold Nicholas, Tressa Thomas, John Terrell. **1991 DVD**

FIVE MILLION YEARS TO EARTH ★★★★ The best of the big-screen *Quatermass* adventures has the professor and his colleagues investigating the discovery of an alien craft buried in London. While the special effects may appear somewhat quaint today, the solid writing and performances make it rewarding for open-minded viewers. This sequel to *The Creeping Unknown* and *Enemy from Space* was released as *Quatermass and the Pit* in England. The series ends with the made-for-TV *Quatermass Conclusion*. Rated PG. 98m. **DIR:** Roy Ward Baker. **CAST:** James Donald, Barbara Shelley, Andrew Keir, Julian Glover, Maurice Good. **1968**

FIVE PENNIES, THE ★★★ A lively biography of jazzman Red Nichols with his contemporaries playing themselves in the jam sessions. The story line is a little sticky as it deals with family tragedies as well as triumphs. But the music is great, and there are twenty-five musical numbers. Red Nichols dubbed the soundtrack, and that's a bonus when he and Louis Armstrong are duetting. 117m. **DIR:** Melville Shavelson. **CAST:** Danny Kaye, Barbara Bel Geddes, Tuesday Weld, Louis Armstrong, Bob Crosby, Ray Anthony, Shelley Manne, Bobby Troup, Harry Guardino. **1959**

FIVE SENSES, THE ★★1/2 The lives of several friends and strangers intersect when a little girl disappears. The theme of the senses is carried out through the characters: a masseuse (touch), an optometrist (sight), a pastry cook (taste), etc. It's well-made and earnestly acted, but a bit too solemn, formal, and self-consciously "artistic." Rated R for profanity and sexual scenes. 105m. **DIR:** Jeremy Podeswa. **CAST:** Mary-Louise Parker, Pascale Bussières, Richard Clarkin, Brendan Fletcher, Marco Leonardi. **1999 DVD**

FIVE THOUSAND FINGERS OF DR. T, THE ★★★★ A delightful fantasy about children. Tommy Rettig would rather play baseball than practice the piano. Hans Conried plays Dr. Terwilliker, the piano teacher who gives the kid nightmares. Dr. Seuss cowrote the script. 89m. **DIR:** Roy Rowland. **CAST:** Hans Conried, Mary Healy, Peter Lind Hayes, Henry Kulky, Tommy Rettig. **1952**

FIVE WEEKS IN A BALLOON ★★★ Up, up, and away on a balloon expedition to Africa, or, Kenya here we come! Author Jules Verne wrote the story. Nothing heavy here, just good, clean fun and adventure in the mold of *Around the World in Eighty Days*. 101m. **DIR:** Irwin Allen. **CAST:** Red Buttons, Barbara Eden, Fabian, Cedric Hardwicke, Peter Lorre, Herbert Marshall, Billy Gilbert, Reginald Owen, Henry Daniell, Barbara Luna, Richard Haydn. **1962**

FIXER, THE ★★1/2 Writer-director Charles Robert Carner's saga of high-level corruption and political intrigue in Chicago is nothing new and seems to exist only because star-producer Jon Voight wanted a project that would allow him to blossom from an evil man into a repentant hero. He plays a longtime "arranger" of corrupt deals who experiences an epiphany after a near-crippling accident. Rated R for profanity, violence, nudity, simulated sex, and gore. 105m. **DIR:** Charles Robert Carner. **CAST:** Jon Voight, Brenda Bakke, J. J. Johnston, Miguel Sandoval, Brent Jennings. **1997**

FLAME AND THE ARROW, THE ★★★★ Burt Lancaster is at his acrobatic, tongue-in-cheek best in this film as a Robin Hood–like hero in Italy leading his oppressed countrymen to victory. It's a rousing swashbuckler. 88m. **DIR:** Jacques Tourneur. **CAST:** Burt Lancaster, Virginia Mayo, Nick Cravat. **1950**

FLAME OF THE BARBARY COAST ★★1/2 John Wayne plays a Montana rancher who fights with a saloon owner (Joseph Schildkraut) over the affections of a dance hall girl (Ann Dvorak). It's watchable, nothing more. B&W; 91m. **DIR:** Joseph Kane. **CAST:** John Wayne, Ann Dvorak, William Frawley, Joseph Schildkraut. **1945**

FLAME OVER INDIA ★★★★1/2 Rip-snorting adventure film has British officer Kenneth More and American governess Lauren Bacall escorting a young Hindu prince to safety during a political and religious uprising. J. Lee Thompson's flawless direction, a fine script, and terrific performances make this little-known film a classic. 130m. **DIR:** J. Lee Thompson. **CAST:** Lauren Bacall, Kenneth More, Herbert Lom, Wilfrid Hyde-White, I. S. Johar, Ian Hunter. **1959**

FLAME TO THE PHOENIX, A ★★ On the eve of Hitler's invasion of Poland, British diplomats plan their strategy while the Polish underground prepares for a long, bloody struggle. This talky drama is hard to follow, with characters of various nationalities all speaking with British accents. Not rated, the movie contains brief nudity and sexual situations. 80m. **DIR:** William Brayne. **CAST:** Frederick Treves, Ann Firbank. **1983**

FLAMENCO ★★1/2 This concert performance of flamenco song and dance is superbly photographed, and there are moments when it blazes with startling, ferocious grace. Unfortunately, the singing dominates the dance and guitar playing, and the sparse subtitles give only a brief opening narration and the names of the songs being performed. As a result, the film soon grows monotonous for those who can't understand the language. In Spanish with English subtitles. Not rated; suitable for general audiences. 100m. **DIR:** Carlos Saura. **CAST:** Enrique Morente, Jose Menese, Jose Merce, Marlo Maya, Matilde Coral. **1995**

FLAMING STAR ★★★★ A solid Western directed by Don Siegel (*Dirty Harry*), this features Elvis Presley in a remarkably effective performance as a half-breed Indian who must choose sides when his mother's people go on the warpath. 92m. **DIR:** Don Siegel. **CAST:** Elvis Presley, Barbara Eden, Steve Forrest, Dolores Del Rio, John McIntire. **1960**

FLAMINGO KID, THE ★★★1/2 A teen comedy-drama with more on its mind than stale sex jokes. Matt Dillon stars as Jeffrey Willis, a Brooklyn kid who discovers how the other half lives when he takes a summer job at a beach resort. A good story that explores the things (and people) that shape our values as we reach adulthood. A genuine pleasure, and you'll be glad you tried it. Rated PG-13 for frank sexual situations. 100m. **DIR:** Garry Marshall. **CAST:** Matt Dillon, Richard Crenna, Jessica Walter, Janet Jones, Hector Elizondo. **1984 DVD**

FLAMINGO RISING, THE ★★★1/2 This *Hallmark Hall of Fame* production delightfully blends 1960s nostalgia with a dreamer's whimsy. Brian Benben stars as an outlandish showman who builds his drive-in theater across from a funeral parlor. William Hurt, as the staid mortician, battles Benben's cheesy gimmicks, while Benben's wife tries to keep his feet on the ground. Superior acting and story make this an appealing film. Not rated; contains mature themes. 96m. **DIR:** Martha Coolidge. **CAST:** William Hurt, Brian Benben, Elizabeth McGovern, Christopher Larkin. **2001**

FLAMINGO ROAD ★★★1/2 A typical Joan Crawford soap opera with her dominating the weak men in her life. In this one she plays a carnival dancer who intrigues Zachary Scott and David Brian in a small town where the carnival stops. Fast-moving melodrama. B&W; 94m. **DIR:** Michael Curtiz. **CAST:** Joan Crawford, David Brian, Sydney Greenstreet, Zachary Scott, Gladys George. **1949**

FLASH, THE (1990) ★★★1/2 DC comic book hero is accurately portrayed in this TV movie that piloted a short-lived series. Highly watchable with decent special effects and a light touch of good humor. Not rated; contains violence. 94m. **DIR:** Robert Iscove. **CAST:** John Wesley Shipp, Amanda Pays, Michael Nader, Tim Thomerson, Alex Desert. **1990**

FLASH (1998) ★★★ An above-average story about a young boy and his best friend, who just happens to be a horse. Together, they face hard times. Solid family fare. Rated G. 89m. **DIR:** Simon Wincer. **CAST:** Lucas Black, Brian Kerwin, Ellen Burstyn, Ed Corbin. **1998**

FLASH GORDON ★★★1/2 If you don't take it seriously, this campy film based on the classic Alex Raymond comic strip of the 1930s is a real hoot. Sam Jones, as Flash, and Melody Anderson, as Dale Arden, race through the intentionally hokey special effects to do battle with Max von Sydow, who makes an excellent Ming the Merciless. Rated PG. 110m. **DIR:** Mike Hodges. **CAST:** Sam Jones, Topol, Max von Sydow, Melody Anderson, Timothy Dalton. **1980 DVD**

FLASH GORDON CONQUERS THE UNIVERSE ★★★ The third and last of Universal's landmark Flash Gordon serials finds the Earth in jeopardy again as Ming the Merciless spreads an epidemic known as the Plague of the Purple Death in yet another attempt to rule the universe. This serial was a strong competitor in that great period from 1937 to 1945 when the chapterplay market was important. B&W; 12 chapters. **DIR:** Ford Beebe, Ray Taylor. **CAST:** Buster Crabbe, Carol Hughes, Charles Middleton, Frank Shannon, Lee Powell. **1940 DVD**

FLASH GORDON: ROCKETSHIP (SPACESHIP TO THE UNKNOWN; PERILS FROM PLANET MONGO) ★★★ Original feature version of the first *Flash Gordon* serial is one of the best reedited chapter plays ever released. Boyish Buster Crabbe is the perfect Flash Gordon; Jean Rogers is one of the loveliest of all serial queens; and classic character heavy Charles Middleton becomes the embodiment of malevolent villainy as the infamous Ming the Merciless. B&W; 97m. **DIR:** Frederick Stephani. **CAST:** Buster Crabbe, Jean Rogers, Frank Shannon, Charles Middleton, Priscilla Lawson. **1936**

FLASH OF GREEN, A ★★★1/2 This is a compelling adaptation of John D. MacDonald's novel about a small-town Florida reporter (Ed Harris) whose boredom, lust, and curiosity lead him into helping an ambitious, amoral county official (Richard Jordan) win approval for a controversial housing project. The acting is superb. 118m. **DIR:** Victor Nunez. **CAST:** Ed Harris, Blair Brown, Richard Jordan, George Coe, Isa Thomas, William Mooney, Joan Goodfellow, Helen Stenborg, John Glover. **1984**

FLASHBACK ★★ Straitlaced FBI agent Kiefer Sutherland is assigned to take hippie prankster Dennis Hopper to Oregon, where he is to stand trial. On the way Hopper switches places with Sutherland, and the chase is on. Clichés abound in this mushy mishmash. Rated R for profanity and violence. 106m. **DIR:** Franco Amurri. **CAST:** Dennis Hopper, Kiefer Sutherland, Carol Kane, Cliff De Young, Paul Dooley, Richard Masur, Michael McKean. **1990**

FLASHDANCE ★★★ Director Adrian Lyne explodes images on the screen with eye-popping regularity while the spare screenplay centers on the ambitions of Alex Owens (Jennifer Beals), a welder who dreams of making the big time as a dancer. Alex finds this goal difficult to attain—until contractor Nick Hurley (Michael Nouri) decides to help. Rated R for nudity, profanity, and implied sex. 96m. **DIR:** Adrian Lyne. **CAST:** Jennifer Beals, Michael Nouri, Lilia Skala. **1983**

FLASHFIRE ★★1/2 John Warren and Dan York's sloppily scripted cop thriller lurches to such an abrupt halt, you'll wonder who pulled the financial plug. Billy Zane is barely credible as a detective trying to solve his partner's murder with the help of a gregarious hooker who saw the killers. Routine stuff, handled with very little wit. Rated R for profanity, nudity, violence, and simulated sex. 89m. **DIR:** Elliot Silverstein. **CAST:** Billy Zane, Louis Gossett Jr., Kristin Minter. **1993 DVD**

FLASHPOINT ★★★1/2 Kris Kristofferson and Treat Williams star in this taut, suspenseful, and action-filled thriller as two Texas border officers who accidentally uncover an abandoned jeep containing a skeleton, a rifle, and $800,000 in cash—a discovery that puts their lives in danger. Rated PG-13 for profanity and violence. 95m. **DIR:** William Tannen. **CAST:** Kris Kristofferson, Treat Williams, Rip Torn, Kevin Conway, Tess Harper. **1984**

FLAT TOP ★★ A mediocre World War II action film following the exploits of an aircraft carrier battling the Japanese forces in the Pacific. Most of the battle scenes are taken from actual combat footage. B&W; 83m. **DIR:** Lesley Selander. **CAST:** Richard Carlson, Sterling Hayden, Keith Larsen, Bill Phillips. **1952**

FLATBED ANNIE AND SWEETIE PIE: LADY TRUCKERS ★★1/2 Annie Potts is Flatbed Annie, a veteran trucker who trains a novice named Sweetie Pie (Kim Darby). The two team up in an effort to support their costly rig. Mildly entertaining diversion. Made for TV. 104m. **DIR:** Robert Greenwald. **CAST:** Annie Potts, Kim Darby, Harry Dean Stanton, Arthur Godfrey, Rory Calhoun. **1979**

FLATLINERS ★★★ In this morbid but compelling thriller a group of medical students experiment with death. They kill each other one by one and then are brought back to life. But things don't work out as they expect. Rated R. 111m. **DIR:** Joel Schumacher. **CAST:** Kiefer Sutherland, Julia Roberts, Kevin Bacon, William Baldwin, Oliver Platt. **1990 DVD**

FLAWLESS ★★1/2 Manhattan's seedy East Village is the setting for this fractured tale about a hate-love relationship between former security guard Walt and flamboyant drag queen Rusty. The film begins as Walt tries to stop a robbery and has a stroke. He then reluctantly takes singing lessons from Rusty to improve his slurred speech. The film works when it sticks to the volatile relationship of its two main characters, but often strays to messy subplots involving drug thugs and a gay beauty contest. Rated R for language and violence. 111m. **DIR:** Joel Schumacher. **CAST:** Robert De Niro, Philip Seymour Hoffman. **1999 DVD**

FLED ★★ Two convicts—one black and one white—flee a Georgia chain-gang massacre while cuffed together at the wrist and spend the rest of the movie trying not to get killed by the Cuban mob and corrupt FBI agents. Typical, overly vicious odd couple action-comedy. Rated R for language, violence, and brief nudity. 105m. **DIR:** Kevin Hooks. **CAST:** Laurence Fishburne, Stephen Baldwin, Will Patton, Robert Hooks, David Dukes, Salma Hayek, Michael Nader, Victor Rivers, Robert Burke. **1996 DVD**

FLESH Joe Dallesandro as a street hustler who can't stay away from transvestites, sleazy women, and drugs. Not rated, contains nudity and profane language. 90m. **DIR:** Paul Morrissey. **CAST:** Joe Dallesandro, Geraldine Smith, Patti D'Arbanville, Candy Darling. **1968 DVD**

FLESH AND BLOOD (1922) ★★1/2 Prison escapee, disguised as a crippled violin player, discovers his daughter is in love with his enemy's son. True to the melodramatic sentiment of the time, Lon Chaney Sr. hobbles back to prison a cripple but throws his crutches away at the gates and enters a proud man. B&W; 73m. **DIR:** Irving Cummings. **CAST:** Lon Chaney Sr., DeWitt Jennings, Noah Beery Sr., Ralph Lewis, Jack Mulhall. **1922**

FLESH AND BLOOD (SWORD AND THE ROSE, THE (1985)) ★★★1/2 Set in medieval Europe, *Flesh and Blood* follows the lives of two men—mercenary soldier Rutger Hauer and the son of a feudal lord (Tom Burlinson)—and their love for the same woman (Jennifer Jason Leigh). The cast is stellar, the sets are lavish, and the plot turns will keep the viewer guessing, but not in the dark. Rated R for violence, sex, nudity, profanity. 126m. **DIR:** Paul Verhoeven. **CAST:** Rutger Hauer, Jennifer Jason Leigh, Tom Burlinson, Susan Tyrrell, Ronald Lacey, Jack Thompson. **1985**

FLESH AND BONE ★★★1/2 In the prologue to this suspenseful, thought-provoking film, a young boy named Arliss becomes an unwilling accomplice to murder when his father uses him in a robbery that goes awry. Years later, the adult Arliss drifts from place to place, seemingly to avoid memories of his dark past. An act of kindness toward a pretty stranger leads to a day of reckoning. The offbeat drama is not for all tastes. Rated R for violence, profanity, nudity, and simulated sex. 127m. **DIR:** Steve Kloves. **CAST:** Dennis Quaid, Meg Ryan, James Caan, Gwyneth Paltrow, Scott Wilson, Christopher Rydell. **1993 DVD**

FLESH AND THE DEVIL ★★★ Story of a woman who flouts moral conventions by pursuing a third man while married to two others. The sensual pairing of sultry Greta Garbo with suave John Gilbert electrifies this film. B&W; 103m. **DIR:** Clarence Brown. **CAST:** Greta Garbo, John Gilbert. **1927**

FLESH EATERS, THE ★★ This is the notorious cult horror epic—rarely available, even on video, in its uncut form—about a mad scientist (Martin Kosleck) who unleashes voracious organisms into the waters surrounding his tropical island laboratory. A seminal gore film, scripted by comics writer Arnold Drake, it'll have you chuckling at its amateurish performances one minute, then gagging at its surprisingly vivid special effects in the next. B&W; 87m. **DIR:** Jack Curtis. **CAST:** Martin Kosleck, Rita Morley. **1964**

FLESH EATING MOTHERS ★★ Tepid mix of gore and gags in a suburb where adulterous mothers become infected with a virus that turns them into cannibalistic zombies. Not rated, comic violence. 90m. **DIR:** James Aviles Martin. **CAST:** Robert Lee Oliver, Donatella Hecht. **1988**

FLESH FEAST 🦃 Veronica Lake was working as a waitress in Florida when she coproduced and starred in this film about a plastic surgeon who uses maggots as a unique form of dermabrasion. Rated R. 72m. **DIR:** Brad F. Grinter. **CAST:** Veronica Lake. **1970**

FLESH GORDON ★★1/2 Porno version of the famed serial *Flash Gordon*, this fitfully amusing parody's main point of interest is the often excellent miniature work and dimensional animation by Jim Danforth and other special-effects pros. The story, about a sex ray aimed at Earth by Emperor Wang of the planet Porno, is obvious and amateurish. Rated X for nudity, language, and overall content. 70m. **DIR:** Howard Ziehm, Michael Benveniste. **CAST:** Jason Williams, Suzanne Fields, John Hoyt. **1974 DVD**

FLESH GORDON 2: FLESH GORDON MEETS THE COSMIC CHEERLEADERS ★★★ A surprisingly good set design makes this tasteless sequel entertaining. Flesh is kidnapped by cosmic cheerleaders and taken to their home planet where a villain has sapped the collective libido of the male population. Filled with gratuitous nudity and bad jokes, this one is not for everybody. Available in R-rated and unrated versions, both with nudity and sexual situations. 101m. **DIR:** Howard Ziehm. **CAST:** Vince Murdocco, Robyn Kelly, Tony Travis, Morgan Fox. **1993 DVD**

FLESHBURN ★★★1/2 An Indian who left five men in the desert to die breaks out of an insane asylum to hunt down and wreak his revenge against the psychiatrists who sentenced him. This film promises to be more than exploitation, and it does not let you down. Rated R for profanity and violence. 91m. **DIR:** George Gage. **CAST:** Sonny Landham, Steve Kanaly, Karen Carlson. **1983 DVD**

FLESHTONE ★★ Eccentric artist gets involved in phone sex to ease his loneliness, only to become the main suspect when his phone date ends up dead. Is there just one script out there being remade over and over again? R-rated and unrated versions; both contain nudity, adult situations, and violence. 89/91. **DIR:** Harry Hurwitz. **CAST:** Martin Kemp, Lise Cutter, Tim Thomerson. **1994**

FLETCH ★★★★ Chevy Chase is first-rate as Gregory McDonald's wisecracking reporter, I. M. "Fletch" Fletcher, who starts out doing what seems to be a fairly simple exposé of drug dealing in Los Angeles and ends up taking on a corrupt cop (Joe Don Baker), a tough managing editor (Richard Libertini), and a powerful millionaire (Tim Matheson) who wants Fletch to kill him. The laughs are plenty and the action almost nonstop. Rated PG for violence and profanity. 96m. **DIR:** Michael Ritchie. **CAST:** Chevy Chase, Joe Don Baker, Tim Matheson, Dana Wheeler-Nicholson, Richard Libertini, M. Emmet Walsh. **1985 DVD**

FLETCH LIVES ★★★1/2 Chevy Chase returns to the role of I. M. Fletcher and scores another triumph. In this one, Fletch finds himself heir to a southern plantation and quits his newspaper job—only to become both a murder suspect and a target for unscrupulous villains. If you enjoyed the original *Fletch*, this sequel is guaranteed to satisfy. Rated PG. 98m. **DIR:** Michael Ritchie. **CAST:** Chevy Chase, Cleavon Little, Hal Holbrook, Julianne Phillips, Richard Libertini, Randall "Tex" Cobb, George Wyner. **1989**

FLIGHT FROM VIENNA ★★★ Theodore Bikel gets to demonstrate the range of his acting abilities as a Hungarian official trying to defect to the West. B&W; 54m. **DIR:** Denis Kavanagh. **CAST:** Theodore Bikel, John Bentley, Donald Gray. **1956**

FLIGHT OF BLACK ANGEL ★★1/2 This potentially intriguing made-for-cable thriller, about a renegade fighter pilot with a stolen tactical nuclear weapon, turns unsavory and relentlessly stupid at the halfway point. Training instructor Peter Strauss takes it personally when one of his former students, believing himself a self-styled "angel of the Lord," uses real missiles on trainees and then heads out on a mission to annihilate Las Vegas. Rated R for language and violence. 102m. **DIR:** Jonathan Mostow. **CAST:** Peter Strauss, William O'Leary. **1991**

FLIGHT OF DRAGONS, THE ★★★★ Stop-motion animation and the voices of John Ritter, James Earl Jones, Harry Morgan, and James Gregory bring this fantasy to life. Good wizards select a man to stop the evil reign of the Red Wizards. Grade-schoolers will be fascinated by this tale. 98m. **DIR:** Arthur Rankin Jr., Jules Bass. **1982**

FLIGHT OF RAINBIRDS, A ★★★ Fun bedroom farce features Jeroen Krabbé as both an endearing, innocent klutz and his sexy alter ego/mentor. He must analyze his stern Calvinist upbringing before he can enjoy life and find romance. In Dutch with English subtitles. Not rated; contains nudity and sexual situations. 94m. **DIR:** Ate De Jong. **CAST:** Jeroen Krabbé, Marijke Merckens, Henriette Tol, Huib Rooymans, Claire Wauthion. **1981**

FLIGHT OF THE EAGLE ★★★1/2 This Swedish production presents the true adventure of three foolhardy 1897 polar explorers (one played by Max von Sydow) who tried to conquer the Arctic in a balloon. In Swedish with English subtitles. Not rated; the film has some gore. 139m. **DIR:** Jan Troell. **CAST:** Max von Sydow. **1982**

FLIGHT OF THE INNOCENT ★★★★ When his family is murdered, a sweet-natured 10-year-old boy miraculously escapes, only to be pursued by the killers. This emotionally involving film examines a modern-day phenomenon: the kidnapping of children from well-to-do families in northern Italy by their southern neighbors, who hold their victims for ransom. In Italian with English subtitles. Rated R for violence and profanity. 115m. **DIR:** Carlo Carlei. **CAST:** Manuel Colao, Federico Pacifici, Sal Borgese, Giusi Cataldo, Lucio Zagaria, Massimo Lodolo, Francesca Neri, Jacques Perrin. **1993**

FLIGHT OF THE INTRUDER, THE ★★ Spectacular aerial-action sequences almost salvage this jingoistic, one-dimensional war film in which navy fliers Brad Johnson and Willem Dafoe ignore orders and bomb a restricted area in Hanoi. Based on the novel by Stephen Coonts. Rated PG-13 for profanity and violence. 115m. **DIR:** John Milius. **CAST:** Danny Glover, Willem Dafoe, Brad Johnson, Rosanna Arquette. **1991**

FLIGHT OF THE NAVIGATOR ★★★ This all-ages Disney delight concerns a youngster (Joey Kramer) who has the unique ability to communicate with machines and uses this to help a UFO find its way home. Kids will love its crazy creatures, special effects, and action-packed conclusion, while parents will appreciate its nice balance of sense and nonsense. Rated PG for mild cussing. 90m. **DIR:** Randal Kleiser. **CAST:** Joey Kramer, Veronica Cartwright, Cliff De Young, Sarah Jessica Parker, Howard Hesseman, Matt Adler. **1986**

FLIGHT OF THE PHOENIX, THE ★★★★ An all-star international cast shines in this gripping adventure about the desert crash of a small plane and the grueling efforts of the meager band of passengers to rebuild and repair it against impossible odds, not the least of which are starvation and heat prostration. 143m. **DIR:** Robert Aldrich. **CAST:** James Stewart, Richard Attenborough, Peter Finch, Ernest Borgnine, Hardy Kruger, Ronald Fraser, Christian Marquand, Ian Bannen, George Kennedy, Dan Duryea. **1966**

FLIGHT TO FURY ★★1/2 Jack Nicholson wrote the screenplay for this clever low-budget thriller. Nicholson plays a member of a group of conniving thieves smuggling diamonds out of the Philippines. B&W; 73m. **DIR:** Monte Hellman. **CAST:** Dewey Martin, Fay Spain, Jack Nicholson. **1964**

FLIGHT TO MARS ★★1/2 Scientists and newsmen crash on Mars during a space voyage and discover a race of humans living beneath the surface of the planet. Although slow, a fairly effective plea for international and intergalactic harmony. 72m. **DIR:** Lesley Selander. **CAST:** Cameron Mitchell, Arthur Franz, Marguerite Chapman, Morris Ankrum, John Litel, Virginia Huston. **1951 DVD**

FLIM-FLAM MAN, THE ★★★ A con man (George C. Scott) teaches an army deserter (Michael Sarrazin) the art of fleecing yokels. Scott is an altogether charming, wry, winning rascal in this improbable, clever film, which is highlighted by a spectacular car-chase scene. 104m. **DIR:** Irvin Kershner. **CAST:** George C. Scott, Michael Sarrazin, Sue Lyons, Harry Morgan, Jack Albertson. **1967**

FLINCH ★★1/2 OK thriller offers a pair of live store mannequins who witness a murder while working the window of a popular department store. Of course, the police won't believe them so it's up to them to find the killer. Live-mannequin angle is the only new trick up this film's sleeve, though it is fascinating to watch costar Nick Mancuso give the most over-the-top performance of his career. Rated R for violence and nudity. 93m. **DIR:** George Erschbamer. **CAST:** Judd Nelson, Gina Gershon, Nick Mancuso. **1994**

FLINTSTONES, THE ★★★ Yuppie nostalgia and the amazing efforts of Jim Henson's Creature Shop are this film's major attractions, but the appeal wears thin pretty quickly. In spite of—or because of—the efforts of a rumored thirty-five writers, this live-action recreation of the 1960s animated series lurches awkwardly from one scene to the next. Very small children will love it, but they won't understand the topical references or the occasionally risqué humor. Rated PG for cartoonish violence and mild sexuality. 105m. **DIR:** Brian Levant. **CAST:** John Goodman, Elizabeth Perkins, Rick Moranis, Rosie O'Donnell, Elizabeth Taylor, Kyle MacLachlan, Halle Berry. **1994 DVD**

FLINTSTONES IN VIVA ROCK VEGAS, THE ★★ Fred and Barney are bachelors seeking the perfect women. Problems arise when Wilma's mother snubs Fred and an unscrupulous suitor vies for Wilma's hand in marriage. Endless wordplays make the most of the prehistoric angle. Kids will enjoy the sights and adults can giggle over the clever lines. Rated PG for scatological humor and comic book violence. 90m. **DIR:** Brian Levant. **CAST:** Mark Addy, Stephen Baldwin, Kristen Johnston, Jane Krakowski. **2000**

FLIPPER (1963) ★★★ America's love of dolphins took root in this gentle adventure. After Luke Halpin saves a wounded dolphin, he must convince his fisherman father (Chuck Connors) that dolphins help man and should not be destroyed. Filmed in the Florida Keys. 85m. **DIR:** James B. Clark. **CAST:** Chuck Connors, Luke Halpin. **1963**

FLIPPER (1996) ★★★ Amiable Paul Hogan is the brightest spot in this ordinary update of the 1960s television series. City kid Elijah Wood learns how to become a man while spending the summer with his uncle and a mirthful dolphin, but Alan Shapiro makes a *serious* mistake with the degenerate nature of his story's villain, who more properly belongs in an Arnold Schwarzenegger thriller. Rated PG for a surprising level of violence. 96m. **DIR:** Alan Shapiro. **CAST:** Paul Hogan, Elijah Wood, Chelsea Field, Isaac Hayes, Jonathan Banks, Jason Fuchs, Jessica Wesson. **1996**

FLIPPER'S NEW ADVENTURE ★★★ One of the better sequels shows the affection and teamwork enjoyed by a young boy and his pet dolphin when they outwit blackmailers. Filmed in the Bahamas and released less than a year after, *Flipper* made a sensational movie debut. The sequel led to a TV series. 103m. **DIR:** Leon Benson. **CAST:** Luke Halpin, Brian Kelly, Pamela Franklin, Francesca Annis, Tom Helmore. **1964**

FLIPPER'S ODYSSEY ★★1/2 Rin Tin Tin with fins heroically saves a photographer, a lonely fisherman's dog, and his own young master. Flipper outacts the rest of the cast. Underwater shots are the highlight. 77m. **DIR:** Paul Landres. **CAST:** Brian Kelly, Luke Halpin, Tommy Norden. **1965**

FLIPPING ★★★ Intense crime thriller set in Hollywood stars David Amos as Mike Moore, who yearns to be a wiseguy with a lot of power. Until then, Mike works as a collector for crime boss Leo (Keith David). Mike's partners are a tight-knit group until Leo orders them to kill a rival crime boss. Their loyalties to each other and Leo are severely tested. Rated R for adult situations, language, and violence. 102m. **DIR:** Gene Mitchell. **CAST:** David Amos, David Proval, Keith David, Barry Primus, Tony Burton. **1996**

FLIRT ★★★1/2 Independent filmmaker Hal Hartley (*Trust*, *Amateur*) goes for something a bit more experimental in this film which is actually three short films, each telling the same story with a different cast, different location (Manhattan, Berlin, and Tokyo), and a different perspective. The results are both intriguing and provocative, though more so for Hartley fans than newcomers. Not rated; contains sexual themes. 85m. **DIR:** Hal Hartley. **CAST:** Bill Sage, Martin Donovan, Karen Sillas, Michael Imperioli, Hal Hartley. **1996**

FLIRTATION WALK ★★1/2 Dull story of romantic mix-ups and misunderstandings between a West Point cadet and the commanding officer's daughter. Surprisingly few songs, all forgettable. Nominated for best picture, but, in 1934, so were eleven other movies. B&W; 98m. **DIR:** Frank Borzage. **CAST:** Dick Powell, Ruby Keeler, Pat O'Brien, Guinn Williams, Ross Alexander, John Eldredge. **1934**

FLIRTING ★★★★ This Australian comedy/drama is the second film in a projected coming-of-age trilogy. In the first film, *The Year My Voice Broke*, we meet Danny in a small town in the Australian outback. In *Flirting*, Danny is at an all-boys boarding school, across a lake from an all-girls school. Amid the typical prep school studies, socials, and antics, Danny is surprised to find himself falling for a young Ugandan girl. These two Duigan films are genuine sleepers. 96m. **DIR:** John Duigan. **CAST:** Noah Taylor, Thandie Newton, Nicole Kidman. **1992**

FLIRTING WITH DISASTER ★★★★1/2 Neurotic yuppie Ben Stiller goes on a cross-country search for his biological parents (Lily Tomlin, Alan Alda), leaving adoptive parents Mary Tyler Moore and George Segal sulking back home in New York. Hilariously original and inventive comedy is reminiscent of Preston Sturges at his madcap best; the star-studded cast is in peak form. Rated R for profanity and brief nudity. 92m. **DIR:** David O. Russell. **CAST:** Ben Stiller, Patricia Arquette, Téa Leoni, Mary Tyler Moore, George Segal, Lily Tomlin, Alan Alda. **1996 DVD**

FLOATING AWAY ★★★ Rosanna Arquette tries hard to lift this saga above ordinary cliché, but she's not able to surmount Tim Sandlin's by-the-numbers script, adapted from his book *Sorrow Floats*. She plays a young mother who turns to alcohol after her beloved father's death, and who loses everything—home, child, friends—when her two-timing husband decides that he has had enough. Unfortunately, some of this story's incidental characters are just too bizarre for words. Rated R for profanity, nudity, rape, and violence. 105m. **DIR:** John Badham. **CAST:** Rosanna Arquette, Paul Hogan, Judge Reinhold, Brendan Fletcher. **1998**

FLOOD! ★★★ Bureaucratic peevishness is responsible for a small town being caught short when a dam bursts. Slick and predictable, but interesting just the same. If you like this, you'll like its sister film, *Fire!* 100m. **DIR:** Earl Bellamy. **CAST:** Robert Culp, Martin Milner, Barbara Hershey, Richard Basehart, Carol Lynley, Roddy McDowall, Cameron Mitchell, Teresa Wright. **1976**

FLOOD: A RIVER'S RAMPAGE ★★★ Torrential rains set the stage for this Hallmark production take on the disastrous floods that took their toll on the Midwest. Richard Thomas, Kate Vernon, and Jan Rubes are among those downriver from the pending natural disaster, hoping to salvage their homesteads. Predictable, but it's easy to rally around these characters. Rated PG. 92m. **DIR:** Bruce Pittman. **CAST:** Richard Thomas, Kate Vernon, Jan Rubes. **1997 DVD**

FLOR SYLVESTRE ★★★1/2 Mexican-born beauty Dolores Del Rio made many schlocky movies in America but had to return to her native country to appear in quality productions. This tale of two families torn apart by the Mexican revolution is one of the best. The story is a little corny, but beautifully photographed and directed. In Spanish with English subtitles. B&W; 94m. **DIR:** Emilio Fernandez. **CAST:** Dolores Del Rio, Pedro Armendariz, Emilio Fernandez. **1945**

FLORENTINE, THE ★★1/2 A barkeep and his regulars provide the background for this film, based on the play by Damien Gray, that deals with the impending marriage of the barkeep's sister. Interesting, but not stupendously entertaining. Rated R for profanity and violence. 104m. **DIR:** Nick Stagliano. **CAST:** Virginia Madsen, Luke Perry, Michael Madsen, Christopher Penn, Hal Holbrook, James Belushi, Tom Sizemore, Burt Young, Mary Stuart Masterson. **1999 DVD**

FLORIDA STRAITS ★★1/2 Raul Julia is a Cuban refugee who enlists the aid of charter boaters Fred Ward and Daniel Jenkins to help him get back to Cuba and rescue the woman he loves. Although a bit contrived in spots, this is watchable. An unrated HBO production that contains some violence and rough language. 98m. **DIR:** Mike Hodges. **CAST:** Raul Julia, Fred Ward, Daniel H. Jenkins, Jaime Sanchez, Victor Argo, Ilka Tanya Payan, Antonio Fargas. **1986**

FLOUNDERING ★★★ James LeGros is the hero, of sorts, in this black, and sometimes bleak, comedic look at life in Los Angeles for the less-than-privileged. LeGros's life spirals downhill until he is literally sleeping in the gutter, but a cynical outlook and sharp writing keep this off-kilter comedy on track. Rated R for profanity, adult themes, drug use, sexual situations, and profanity. 97m. **DIR:** Peter McCarthy. **CAST:** James LeGros, John Cusack, Ethan Hawke, Steve Buscemi, Kim Wayans. **1994 DVD**

FLOWER DRUM SONG ★★ Set in San Francisco's colorful Chinatown, this Rodgers and Hammerstein musical rings sour. It has its bright moments, but the score is largely second-rate. The plot is conventional: a modern son's views versus those of an old-fashioned father. Ingredients include the usual Oriental cliché of an arranged marriage. 131m. **DIR:** Henry Koster. **CAST:** Jack Soo, Nancy Kwan, Benson Fong, Miyoshi Umeki, Juanita Hall, James Shigeta. **1962**

FLOWER OF MY SECRET, THE ★★★★ Pedro Almodovar goes light on camp and deeper into emotional empathy with this tale of a middle-aged romance novelist. As her marriage crumbles, she comes to hate her work—and a big part of herself. One of the Spanish bad boy's more compelling character studies. In Spanish with English subtitles. Rated R. 108m. **DIR:** Pedro Almodóvar. **CAST:** Marisa Paredes, Juan Echanove, Imanol Arias, Rossy De Palma. **1995**

FLOWERS IN THE ATTIC ★★1/2 After the death of their father, four children are taken (by their mother) to live with their religious-zealot grandmother and dying grandfather. The kids are locked into the attic of the family mansion because of some dark family secrets. Louise Fletcher chews up the scenery as the domineering grandmother in this adaptation of V. C. Andrews's gothic horror novel. Rated PG-13. 92m. **DIR:** Jeffrey Bloom. **CAST:** Louise Fletcher, Victoria Tennant, Kristy Swanson, Jeb Adams. **1987 DVD**

FLUBBER ★★1/2 Disappointing remake of Disney's *The Absent-Minded Professor* is aptly retitled. Special-effects advancements, as well as particular innovations provided by Industrial Light & Magic, make the invention rather than the inventor the film's star. Robin Williams simply reacts to the hyperactive green goo, allowing it to steal every scene. Rated PG for comic book violence. 94m. **DIR:** Les Mayfield. **CAST:** Robin Williams, Marcia Gay Harden, Clancy Brown, Ted Levine, Wil Wheaton, Edie McClurg. **1997 DVD**

FLUKE ★★★ This odd little film about reincarnation and karma has a distinctively European flavor that is strangely appealing. Rated PG for violence and mild profanity. 105m. **DIR:** Carlo Carlei. **CAST:** Matthew Modine, Nancy Travis, Eric Stoltz, Max Pomeranc, Samuel L. Jackson. **1995**

FLUNKY, WORK HARD! ★★★ This short feature is the earliest surviving work of Japanese filmmaker Mikio Naruse. It's an odd mix about an insurance salesman struggling to provide for his wife and son. But it provides a priceless look at Japanese life before World War II. In Japanese with English subtitles. B&W; 28m. **DIR:** Mikio Naruse. **CAST:** Isamu Yamaguchi. **1931**

FLUSTERED COMEDY OF LEON ERROL, THE ★★★ When he wasn't portraying a rubber-legged drunk in features, former vaudeville and burlesque comic Leon Errol scored big in dozens of comedy shorts. This compilation—"Crime Rave," "Man I Cured," and "A Panic in the Parlor"—shows why. B&W; 56m. **DIR:** Hal Yates. **CAST:** Leon Errol, Virginia Vale, Frank Faylen. **1939–1941**

FLY, THE ★★★★ Classic horror film builds slowly but really pays off. A scientist (Al Hedison, soon to become David) experimenting with unknown forces turns himself into the hideous title character. Impressive production with top-notch acting and real neat special effects. 94m. **DIR:** Kurt Neumann. **CAST:** David Hedison, Patricia Owens, Vincent Price, Herbert Marshall. **1958**

FLY, THE ★★★1/2 A brilliant research scientist, Seth Brundle (Jeff Goldblum), has developed a way to transport matter. One night, thoroughly gassed, he decides to test the device on himself. Unfortunately, a pesky housefly finds its way into the chamber with the scientist. It must also be said that this otherwise entertaining update simply falls apart at the conclusion. Rated R for gore and slime. 100m. **DIR:** David Cronenberg. **CAST:** Jeff Goldblum, Geena Davis, John Getz. **1986**

FLY II, THE ★1/2 This sequel to David Cronenberg's masterfully crafted 1986 horror remake of *The Fly* doesn't have the right chemistry. The weak, unbelievable story centers around the birth of an heir (Eric Stoltz) to the original fly. This one doesn't fly. Rated R for violence, adult situations, and profanity. 104m. **DIR:** Chris Walas. **CAST:** Eric Stoltz, Daphne Zuniga, Lee Richardson, John Getz. **1989**

FLY AWAY HOME ★★★★ Uplifting musical score by Mark Isham enhances this heartwarming, fact-based adventure. An eccentric inventor (Jeff Daniels) is reunited with his withdrawn daughter (Anna Paquin) following her mother's death. When a flock of Canadian geese bond to the girl, father and daughter share an incredible journey to restore the natural migration patterns of the geese. Terry Kinney, as Daniels's brother, injects delightfully comic moments. Rated PG for mild profanity. 105m. **DIR:** Carroll Ballard. **CAST:** Jeff Daniels, Anna Paquin, Dana Delany, Terry Kinney. **1996 DVD**

FLY BOY ★★★ Better-than-average direct-to-video family adventure about a 10-year-old boy who finds joy and comfort spending time with his grandfather, a former WWII flying ace. James Karen is wonderful as the grandfather, a kindly man who dreams of flying one more time before his death. How his last wish comes true is at the heart of this winning, respectful film. Rated PG. 86m. **DIR:** Richard Stanley. **CAST:** Miko Hughes, James Karen, Kathleen Lloyd, Gregory Itzin. **1999**

FLY BY NIGHT ★★1/2 Two rappers join forces and achieve success when they take on the guise of gangsta rappers, but find themselves trapped by their newfound success. Little real insight and poor execution. Rated R for language and adult situations. 93m. **DIR:** Steve Gomer. **CAST:** Jeffrey Sams, Ron Brice, MC Lyte, Leo Burmester, Todd Graff. **1992**

FLYING BLIND ★★★ This is the third release of upscale B pictures from the William H. Pine–William C. Thomas production unit that operated at Paramount Pictures from 1941 through 1945. The previous films were *Power Dive* and *Forced Landing*, and all three share the same topic: aviation. The script here is by Maxwell Shane and deals with heroes versus evil foreign agents in the United States. B&W; 70m. **DIR:** Frank McDonald. **CAST:** Richard Arlen, Jean Parker. **1941**

FLYING DEUCES ★★★ Stan Laurel and Oliver Hardy join the foreign legion to help Ollie forget his troubled romantic past. Many laugh-filled situations, although the script has weak areas and the movie occasionally drags. B&W; 65m. **DIR:** A. Edward Sutherland. **CAST:** Stan Laurel, Oliver Hardy, Jean Parker. **1939 DVD**

FLYING DOWN TO RIO ★★1/2 We're sure the joy of watching Fred Astaire and Ginger Rogers dance is the only thing that has prevented the negatives of this embarrassing movie from being burned. The climactic dance number, in which chorus girls perform on airplane wings, is so corny it has now passed into the realm of camp. B&W; 89m. **DIR:** Thornton Freeland. **CAST:** Dolores Del Rio, Ginger Rogers, Fred Astaire. **1933**

FLYING FOOL, THE ★★1/2 The story about the protective older brother and his kid brother falling for the same girl was old when this vintage talkie was released, but top-notch dialogue and good aviation sequences make this breezy programmer good entertainment. B&W; 73m. **DIR:** Tay Garnett. **CAST:** William Boyd, Marie Prevost, Russell Gleason, James Gleason. **1929**

FLYING LEATHERNECKS ★★★1/2 John Wayne is the apparently heartless commander of an airborne fighting squad, and Robert Ryan is the caring officer who questions his decisions in this well-acted war film. The stars play off each other surprisingly well, and it's a shame they didn't do more films together. 102m. **DIR:** Nicholas Ray. **CAST:** John Wayne, Robert Ryan, Jay C. Flippen. **1951**

FLYING SERPENT, THE ★★ Mad doctor Zucco keeps mythological Mexican bird Quetzalcoatl (the same monster that turns up, much bigger, in Larry Cohen's *Q*) in a cage, periodically letting it out to attack his enemies. One of the all-time great, unintentional laugh riots from poverty row studio PRC, directed by Sam Newfield under one of his many pseudonyms, Sherman Scott. B&W; 59m. **DIR:** Sam Newfield. **CAST:** George Zucco, Ralph Lewis. **1946 DVD**

FLYING TIGERS, THE ★★1/2 Exciting dogfight action scenes make this low-budget John Wayne World War II vehicle watchable, but the story sags a bit. B&W; 102m. **DIR:** David Miller. **CAST:** John Wayne, John Carroll, Mae Clarke, Gordon Jones. **1942 DVD**

•FLYPAPER ★★1/2 A variety of desperate characters cross paths in this quirky action-comedy that doesn't seem to make a lot of sense, and that's a plus. Trying to make sense out of any of this would be a waste of time. Instead, sit back and enjoy the offbeat antics of actors Craig Sheffer and Robert Loggia, who play two friends trying to protect a woman from a couple of hit men, and John C. McGinley, whose fiancée sets him up with a beautiful woman to test his loyalty. Toss in a snake farmer and a student who make out in a bed of snakes to test a new antiserum and you have an idea of what to expect. Not everything in the script sticks to this *Flypaper*, but what does is worth a look. Rated R for adult situations, drug use, language, and violence. 108m. **DIR:** Klaus Hoch. **CAST:** Craig Sheffer, Robert Loggia, Sadie Frost, John C. McGinley, Illeana Douglas, Lucy Liu. **1997 DVD**

FM ★★★ Before television's *WKRP in Cincinnati* spoofed hip radio, there was this enjoyable comedy, with Martin Mull stealing scenes as a crazed disc jockey. Fans of seventies rock will enjoy the soundtrack and live appearances by the era's superstars. Rated PG for profanity. 104m. **DIR:** John A. Alonzo. **CAST:** Michael Brandon, Martin Mull, Eileen Brennan, Cleavon Little, Cassie Yates, Alex Karras, Norman Lloyd, James Keach. **1978 DVD**

FOG, THE ★★★ This is one of those *almost* movies. Director John Carpenter is on familiar ground with this story of nineteenth-century colonists back from the dead, terrorizing a modern-day fishing village. The lack of any real chills or surprises makes this one a nice try but no cigar. Rated R. 91m. **DIR:** John Carpenter. **CAST:** Adrienne Barbeau, Jamie Lee Curtis, John Houseman, Hal Holbrook, Janet Leigh. **1980**

FOG ISLAND ★★ This *Old Dark House* rip-off from poverty row's Monogram Pictures never takes off, but mystery and suspense buffs should enjoy its rare teaming of genre veterans George Zucco and Lionel Atwill. B&W; 72m. **DIR:** Terry Morse. **CAST:** George Zucco, Veda Ann Borg, Lionel Atwill, Jerome Cowan. **1945**

FOLKS ★★1/2 Comedy about a stock-exchange whiz who finds his perfect life turned upside down. Depending on your mood, this can be entertaining, or tasteless, and unfunny. Rated PG-13 for violence and profanity. 108m. **DIR:** Ted Kotcheff. **CAST:** Tom Selleck, Don Ameche, Anne Jackson, Christine Ebersole, Wendy Crewson, Michael Murphy. **1992**

FOLLOW ME, BOYS! ★★★1/2 Heartwarming Disney film in which Fred MacMurray plays the new Boy Scout leader in a small 1930s town. 131m. **DIR:** Norman Tokar. **CAST:** Vera Miles, Fred MacMurray, Lillian Gish, Kurt Russell. **1966**

FOLLOW ME QUIETLY ★★★ Low-budget thriller about a deranged killer who strangles people when it rains. Tight, fast-moving detective drama with standout performances. B&W; 60m. **DIR:** Richard Fleischer. **CAST:** William Lundigan, Dorothy Patrick, Jeff Corey. **1949**

FOLLOW THAT CAMEL ★★★1/2 This British comedy, part of the *Carry On* series, features Phil Silvers as the conniving Sgt. Knockers. Lots of laughs, mostly derived from puns and sexist jokes. Some dialogue is a bit racy for young children. Not rated. 91m. **DIR:** Gerald Thomas. **CAST:** Phil Silvers, Jim Dale, Peter Butterworth, Charles Hawtrey, Anita Harris, Joan Sims, Kenneth Williams. **1967**

FOLLOW THAT DREAM ★★★1/2 Elvis is almost too sweet as the naive hillbilly who, along with his family, moves to a Florida beach. Some laughs result from their inability to fit in. The story is based on Richard Powell's novel *Pioneer Go Home*. Not rated; contains no objectionable material. 110m. **DIR:** Gordon Douglas. **CAST:** Elvis Presley, Arthur O'Connell, Joanna Moore, Anne Helm, Jack Kruschen. **1962**

FOLLOW THE BOYS ★★★1/2 A World War II morale builder that still works as entertainment. The story is trite, but the star turns are terrific, particularly Orson Welles's magic act with Marlene Dietrich. George Raft heads the cast as a Hollywood star organizing a USO tour and putting it ahead of his private life. B&W; 110m. **DIR:** A. Edward Sutherland. **CAST:** George Raft, Vera Zorina, Marlene Dietrich, Orson Welles, Jeanette MacDonald, W. C. Fields, Sophie Tucker, The Andrews Sisters, Maria Montez, Nigel Bruce. **1944**

FOLLOW THE FLEET ★★★★ Fred Astaire and Ginger Rogers are at their best as a dance team separated by World War II. However, sailor Astaire still has time to romance Rogers while shipmate Randolph Scott gives the same treatment to her screen sister Harriet Hilliard (Mrs. Ozzie Nelson). Look for Lucille Ball in a small part. B&W; 110m. **DIR:** Mark Sandrich. **CAST:** Fred Astaire, Ginger Rogers, Randolph Scott, Harriet Nelson, Betty Grable. **1936**

•FOLLOW THE STARS HOME ★★★1/2 Fine *Hallmark Hall of Fame* presentation of Luanne Rice's romantic novel. Kimberly Williams stars as a mother determined to keep her impaired daughter though it costs her marriage. Blair Brown, as her nearly meddlesome mother, and Campbell Scott, as the child's caring uncle, form her support system. Some melodramatic twists only serve to make the ending more satisfying. Not rated; contains mature themes. 95m. **DIR:** Dick Lowry. **CAST:** Kimberly Williams, Blair Brown, Campbell Scott, Eric Close. **2001 DVD**

•FOLLOWING ★★★★ In this lean, low-budget British suspense yarn, an unemployed writer follows people on the street under the guise of gathering material for a book. The thin wall between observation and interaction crumbles when a man he is shadowing confronts him, questions his motives, and introduces him to the world of burglary. This clammy thriller time-hops with a vengeance, flashing backward and forward between tight clusters of information that require constant reprocessing in a crimescape littered with deception, violations of privacy, mind games, and violence. Not rated. B&W; 70m. **DIR:** Christopher Nolan. **CAST:** Jeremy Theobald, Alex Haw, Lucy Russell. **1998 DVD**

FOOD OF THE GODS 🦃 H. G. Wells's story is trashed in this Bert I. Gordon bomb. After ingesting an unknown substance, various animals become giants and threaten the occupants of a remote mountain cabin. Rated PG. 88m. **DIR:** Bert I. Gordon. **CAST:** Marjoe Gortner, Ida Lupino, Pamela Franklin, Ralph Meeker. **1976**

FOOD OF THE GODS PART II 🦃 Disgusting sequel. Rated R for violence, profanity, and nudity. 90m. **DIR:** Damien Lee. **CAST:** Paul Coufos. **1989**

FOOL AND HIS MONEY, A ★★★ A fool and his money may soon be parted, and that's exactly what advertising executive Morris Codman is counting on. Jonathan Penner plays Morris, who is looking for the next big thing. When God speaks to him through his television set, he's inspired to invent a new religion. Heaven help the poor flock who are about to get fleeced in this frequently funny comedy. Rated R for language. 84m. **DIR:** Daniel Adams. **CAST:** Jonathan Penner, Sandra Bullock, George Plimpton, Wendy Adams. **1988**

FOOL FOR LOVE ★★★1/2 Writer-star Sam Shepard's disturbing, thought-provoking screenplay is about people who, as one of his characters comments, "can't help themselves." Shepard plays a cowboy-stuntman who is continuing his romantic pursuit of Kim Basinger in spite of her objections. For open-minded adults who appreciate daring, original works. Rated R for profanity and violence. 107m. **DIR:** Robert Altman. **CAST:** Sam Shepard, Kim Basinger, Harry Dean Stanton, Randy Quaid. **1986**

FOOL KILLER, THE ★★ Set in the 1800s, this is a tale of a mischievous young runaway who learns about a legendary killer—who may well be his new traveling companion. A shivery variation on *Huckleberry Finn*. Not rated. B&W; 100m. **DIR:** Servando Gonzalez. **CAST:** Anthony Perkins, Edward Albert, Dana Elcar, Salome Jens, Henry Hull. **1967**

FOOLIN' AROUND ★★★ Gary Busey went from his acclaimed title performance in *The Buddy Holly Story* to starring in this amiable rip-off of *The Graduate* and *The Heartbreak Kid*. Still, Busey, as a working-class boy who falls in love with rich girl Annette O'Toole, is always watchable. He and O'Toole make the movie's lack of originality easier to take. Rated PG. 111m. **DIR:** Richard T. Heffron. **CAST:** Gary Busey, Annette O'Toole, John Calvin, Eddie Albert, Cloris Leachman, Tony Randall. **1980**

FOOLISH ★★ Stand-up comedian Foolish Waise and his hustler brother Fifty Dollah run afoul of a scary mobster while chasing their very personalized visions of the American Dream. Sidebars of this profanity-laced, muddled comic melodrama include a family death, romantic conflicts, and both domestic and street violence. Rated R for language, nudity, and sexual content. 86m. **DIR:** Dave Meyers. **CAST:** Eddie Griffin, Master P, Andrew Clay, Jonathan Banks, Amy Petersen, Marla Gibbs. **1999 DVD**

FOOLISH WIVES ★★★★ Anticipating Orson Welles by two decades, director and star Erich Von Stroheim also wrote, produced, codesigned, and cocostumed this stark and unsettling account of a sleazy rogue's depraved use of women to achieve his aims. Von Stroheim is brilliant as the oily, morally corrupt, bogus nobleman plying his confidence game against the naïve rich in post–World War I Monaco and Monte Carlo. The final scene is a masterful simile. Silent. B&W; 107m. **DIR:** Erich Von Stroheim. **CAST:** Erich Von Stroheim, Mae Busch, Rudolph Christians. **1921–1922 DVD**

FOOLS 🦃 An aging star of horror pictures falls in love with the beautiful wife of an attorney. Rated PG. 97m. **DIR:** Tom Gries. **CAST:** Jason Robards Jr., Katharine Ross, Scott Hylands. **1970**

FOOLS OF FORTUNE ★★ The troubles in Northern Ireland turn the idyllic childhood of Willie Clinton into a nightmare, and as an adult he plots his revenge. Based on the novel by William Trevor, this is a profoundly disturbing drama that features good perfomances but is of an intensity that makes it nearly unwatchable. Rated PG-13 for violence. 109m. **DIR:** Pat O'Connor. **CAST:** Mary Elizabeth Mastrantonio, Iain Glen, Julie Christie, Michael Kitchen, Sean McClory. **1990**

FOOLS RUSH IN ★★★ East meets West in this pleasant comedy about a New York builder and a Las Vegas photographer (whose roots are in central Mexico) and the rocky marriage they create out of their one-night stand. Both in-laws step in to complicate matters and to allow the culture-clash jokes to accelerate. The few serious scenes take a backseat to humor. Rated PG-13 for sexual situations and language. 105m. **DIR:** Andy Tennant. **CAST:** Matthew Perry, Salma Hayek, Jon Tenney, Carlos Gomez, Jill Clayburgh, John Bennett Perry. **1997 DVD**

FOOTLIGHT PARADE ★★★1/2 Brash and cocksure James Cagney is a hustling stage director bent upon continually topping himself with Busby Berkeley–type musical numbers, which, not surprisingly, are directed by Busby Berkeley. Another grand-scale musical from the early days of sound films. B&W; 100m. **DIR:** Lloyd Bacon. **CAST:** James Cagney, Ruby Keeler, Joan Blondell, Dick Powell, Guy Kibbee, Hugh Herbert, Frank McHugh. **1933**

FOOTLIGHT SERENADE ★★ Heavyweight boxing champion Victor Mature means trouble for Broadway entertainers John Payne and Betty Grable when he joins their stage show. So-so musical. One of a series Grable made to boost morale during World War II. B&W; 80m. **DIR:** Gregory Ratoff. **CAST:** John Payne, Betty Grable, Victor Mature, Jane Wyman, James Gleason, Phil Silvers. **1942**

FOOTLOOSE ★★★★ A highly entertaining film that combines the rock beat exuberance of *Flashdance* and *Risky Business* with an entertaining—and even touching—story. This features Kevin Bacon as a Chicago boy who finds himself transplanted to a small rural town where rock music and dancing are banned—until he decides to do something about it.. Rated PG for slight profanity and brief violence. 107m. **DIR:** Herbert Ross. **CAST:** Kevin Bacon, Lori Singer, John Lithgow, Dianne Wiest, Christopher Penn, Sarah Jessica Parker. **1984**

FOOTSTEPS IN THE DARK ★★1/2 A dated but interesting blend of comedy and crime with Errol Flynn at his self-mocking best. He is a mystery novelist who plays amateur detective and finds out he's bitten off more than he can chew. He gets out of it by laughing at it. One of Flynn's first modern-dress adventure roles. B&W; 96m. **DIR:** Lloyd Bacon. **CAST:** Errol Flynn, Brenda Marshall, Ralph Bellamy, William Frawley, Alan Hale Sr., Lucile Watson, Lee Patrick, Grant Mitchell, Allen Jenkins. **1941**

FOR A FEW DOLLARS MORE ★★1/2 Plot-heavy and overlong sequel to *A Fistful of Dollars* finds Clint Eastwood's "Man With No Name" partnered with shifty Lee Van Cleef, with both in pursuit of bad guy Gian Maria Volonté. Eastwood has his hands full, but the story contains few surprises. 130m. **DIR:** Sergio Leone. **CAST:** Clint Eastwood, Lee Van Cleef, Gian Maria Volonté, Klaus Kinski. **1965 DVD**

FOR A LOST SOLDIER ★★1/2 During World War II, a 12-year-old Dutch boy has an affair with a Canadian soldier in this film adapted from the autobiographical novel by Rudi van Dantzig. This Dutch import, one of the most professionally directed and acted of gay love stories, handles the subject matter with taste but is definitely not for everyone. In English and Dutch with subtitles. Not rated, the film has profanity, nudity, and simulated sex. 92m. **DIR:** Roeland Kerbosch. **CAST:** Jeroen Krabbé, Maarten Smit, Andrew Kelly. **1993**

FOR BETTER AND FOR WORSE ★★ A mixture of misguided "slapschtick" and unfunny lines sinks this otherwise passable comedy in which the pope is invited to a wedding—and accepts. Rated PG-13 for mild profanity. 94m. **DIR:** Paolo Barzman. **CAST:** Patrick Dempsey, Kelly Lynch, Gerard Rinaldi. **1992**

FOR BETTER OR WORSE ★★★ Jason Alexander directed and stars in this lightweight comedy about a hapless loser (his fiancée has left him; he attends twelve-step programs just for the company) whose life is turned upside down when his criminal brother shows up. Before Alexander can protest, he's on the run with his no-good brother and beautiful new sister-in-law, fleeing thugs and falling in love. Rated PG-13 for violence and profanity. 95m. **DIR:** Jason Alexander. **CAST:** Jason Alexander, James Woods, Lolita Davidovich, Joe Mantegna, Jay Mohr. **1995**

FOR HIRE ★★ An author's latest book sets into motion a tale of murder for hire. When his source is threatened by exposure, the author turns to a terminally ill cabdriver to take care of his problem. The relationship between author Joe Mantegna and cabdriver Rob Lowe shows promise, but once the setup has been established, it's all downhill. Rated R for language and violence. 93m. **DIR:** Jean Pellerin. **CAST:** Joe Mantegna, Rob Lowe. **1997 DVD**

FOR KEEPS 🦃 The serious issue of teen pregnancy is irresponsibly trivialized. Rated PG-13 for frank language. 98m. **DIR:** John G. Avildsen. **CAST:** Molly Ringwald, Randall Batinkoff, Kenneth Mars, Brenda Vaccaro, Conchata Ferrell, Miriam Flynn. **1988**

FOR LADIES ONLY ★★★ A young, good-looking farm-belt guy goes to New York to become a star. He finally turns to stripping to make more money. This stale, TV film is a predictable morality play made fresher with the role reversal. 94m. **DIR:** Mel Damski. **CAST:** Gregory Harrison, Lee Grant, Louise Lasser, Dinah Manoff. **1981**

FOR LOVE ALONE ★★★1/2 An Australian girl is frustrated by the romantic double standard of the 1930s. Helen Buday plays the lovelorn student willing to waste her life on her selfish professor (Hugo Weaving) until she meets a dashing banker (Sam Neill). Buday and Neill are excellent, but Weaving offers a very wooden performance. Rated PG for partial nudity and simulated sex. 102m. **DIR:** Stephen Wallace. **CAST:** Helen Buday, Sam Neill, Hugo Weaving. **1985**

FOR LOVE OF IVY ★★★★ Sidney Poitier delivers a terrific performance as Jack Parks, trucking company owner by day and gambling operator by night. Ivy (Abbey Lincoln) is a maid for a wealthy family. When she decides to leave their employ, the family's children (Beau Bridges and Lauri Peters) connive to get Parks to take her out and make her happy. Carroll O'Connor and Nan Martin play Ivy's employers. This is a fine comedy-drama with a wonderful ending. 101m. **DIR:** Daniel Mann. **CAST:** Sidney Poitier, Abbey Lincoln, Beau Bridges, Nan Martin, Carroll O'Connor, Lauri Peters. **1968 DVD**

FOR LOVE OF THE GAME ★★★★ While not quite up to the heroic status of 1984's *The Natural*—although it certainly *wants* to be—this is a worthy crescendo to what history undoubtedly will term the Costner Baseball Trilogy. This, from the Michael Shaara novel, finally, is *his* character's story: no mere observer of sanctified events *(Field of Dreams)* or witness to another player's rise to success *(Bull Durham)*, Costner's Billy Chapel is a well-respected and much-honored veteran pitcher who has spent his entire professional career with the Detroit Tigers . . . and now faces the tumultuous decision whether to allow himself to be traded when the team is sold, or leave the game entirely. On top of this, in a subplot that isn't quite as successful, the love of his life has decided to abandon him. Events leading up to both these catastrophes are played out in flashback between the innings of a climactic, season-ending game. Fans disenchanted by what baseball has become need look no further than the films that have portrayed it best, and this one deserves placement in their company. Rated PG-13 for mild sensuality and profanity. 137m. **DIR:** Sam Raimi. **CAST:** Kevin Costner, Kelly Preston, John C. Reilly, Jena Malone, Brian Cox. **1999 DVD**

FOR LOVE OR MONEY ★★★1/2 An ambitious, fast-talking hotel concierge is on the way to realizing his ultimate dream until romance conflicts with finance. This movie is the kind of thing Michael J. Fox does best and could have been titled *The Secret of My Success, Part II*. That's not a put-down, either; this entertaining comedy should be popular with Fox's fans. Rated PG for brief profanity and suggested sex. 95m. **DIR:** Barry Sonnenfeld. **CAST:** Michael J. Fox, Gabrielle Anwar, Anthony Higgins, Bob Balaban, Michael Tucker, Udo Kier, Dan Hedaya, Isaac Mizrahi, Patrick Breen, Simon Jones. **1993**

FOR ME AND MY GAL ★★★ A colorful tribute to the great and grand days of vaudeville before World War I, this tuneful trip down memory lane boosted Judy Garland's stock out of sight and made a star of Gene Kelly, he of the fleet-footed and beguiling smile. Flaws aside—the predictable plot needs a shave—this is a generally warm, invigorating picture rife with the nostalgia of happy times. B&W; 104m. **DIR:** Busby Berkeley. **CAST:** Judy Garland, Gene Kelly, George Murphy, Stephen McNally, Keenan Wynn. **1942**

FOR PETE'S SAKE ★★★ Lightweight comedy vehicle tailor-made to fit the talents of Barbra Streisand. In this one she plays the wife of cabdriver Michael Sarrazin, trying to raise money for him while becoming involved with underworld thugs. Strictly for Streisand fans. Rated PG. 90m. **DIR:** Peter Yates. **CAST:** Barbra Streisand, Michael Sarrazin, Estelle Parsons, Molly Picon. **1974**

FOR QUEEN AND COUNTRY ★★★1/2 A taut, tragic combination of social commentary and ghetto thriller focusing on racism in contemporary England. American actor Denzel Washington is superb as a black working-class British soldier who returns home from military service to find himself restricted to a second-class life. Rated R. 108m. **DIR:** Martin Stellman. **CAST:** Denzel Washington, Amanda Redman, George Baker. **1989**

FOR RICHER, FOR POORER ★★ Self-made millionaire Jack Lemmon despairs when son Jonathan Silverman seems content to do little beyond spending Dad's money. The solution? Give it all away, thus *forcing* the bum to pull his own weight. Lame made-for-cable comedy. Rated PG. 90m. **DIR:** Jay Sandrich. **CAST:** Jack Lemmon, Talia Shire, Jonathan Silverman, Joanna Gleason, Madeline Kahn. **1992**

FOR RICHER OR POORER ★★ A wacky businessman with a penchant for theme parks and his spoiled wife go on the lam after a ballistic IRS agent decides to take them down. Things pick up when the couple hides out in an Amish colony. The running joke is the contrast between the overly indulged city slickers and the simple world they've entered. Unfortunately, only half the gags really work. Rated PG-13 for language and sexual situations. 118m. **DIR:** Bryan Spicer. **CAST:** Tim Allen, Kirstie Alley, Jay O. Sanders, Michael Lerner, Wayne Knight, Larry Miller. **1997 DVD**

FOR ROSEANNA ★★★1/2 In a small Italian village, devoted husband Marcello (Jean Reno) is desperate to fulfill the wish of his dying wife, Roseanna (Mercedes Ruehl), to be buried next to her dead daughter. Problem is, there are only a few sites left in the graveyard, so while Roseanna is busy trying to find a new wife to take her place, Marcello desperately tries to keep everyone else in town alive. This rather dark premise masks a sweetly romantic film. Rated PG-13 for sexual situations. 95m. **DIR:** Paul Weiland. **CAST:** Jean Reno, Mercedes Ruehl, Polly Walker, Mark Frankel. **1997**

FOR THE BOYS ★★★1/2 Show-biz pseudobiography is an ambitious, larger-than-life examination of the impact on America of the last three major wars. The story is told through the experiences of two USO entertainers, the brash Dixie Leonard (Bette Midler) and the egotistical Eddie Sparks (James Caan). Not all of its ambitions are met, but this musical still succeeds as an emotional experience. Rated R for profanity and violence. 148m. **DIR:** Mark Rydell. **CAST:** Bette Midler, James Caan, George Segal, Patrick O'Neal, Christopher Rydell, Arliss Howard, Arye Gross, Norman Fell, Rosemary Murphy, Bud Yorkin. **1991 DVD**

FOR THE FIRST TIME ★★★ An opera star on tour in Europe meets and falls in love with a deaf girl. More substance than usual for a Mario Lanza movie. Sadly the last film in his short career. 97m. **DIR:** Rudolph Maté. **CAST:** Mario Lanza, Johanna Von Koszian, Kurt Kasznar, Zsa Zsa Gabor. **1959**

FOR THE LOVE OF BENJI ★★★1/2 The adorable mutt cleverly saves the day again when he takes on a spy ring in Athens. The whole family can enjoy this one together. Rated G. 85m. **DIR:** Joe Camp. **CAST:** Benji, Patsy Garrett, Cynthia Smith, Allen Fuizat, Ed Nelson. **1977 DVD**

FOR THE LOVE OF IT ★★1/2 This would-be wacky comedy is so confusing, you'll find yourself absorbed. Don Rickles wants the Russians' secret plans to take over the Middle East to create a new video game called "Doom's Day," but the CIA and FBI are also interested in them. Some of the chase scenes become so involved that the viewer forgets this is a comedy. Rated PG for violence and adult themes. 98m. **DIR:** Hal Kanter. **CAST:** Don Rickles, Deborah Raffin, Jeff Conaway, Tom Bosley, Henry Gibson, Barbi Benton, Adam West, Norman Fell, Noriyuki "Pat" Morita. **1980**

FOR THE MOMENT ★★1/2 Promoted as a nostalgic romance, this wartime drama is a fairly downbeat affair. Two airmen undergoing training in Canada early in World War II fall in love with married women whose husbands have already left for the war. Rated PG-13 for adult situations, profanity, and violence. 120m. **DIR:** Aaron Kim Johnston. **CAST:** Russell Crowe, Christianne Hirt, Wanda Cannon. **1995**

FOR US THE LIVING: THE MEDGAR EVERS STORY ★★★★ Assassinated civil-rights activist Medgar Evers is profiled in this inspirational drama. Adapted from Evers's wife's biography, this film gives a look at the total person, not just the legends surrounding him. Originally made for television, this is unrated. 90m. **DIR:** Michael Schultz. **CAST:** Howard Rollins Jr., Irene Cara, Margaret Avery, Roscoe Lee Browne. **1983**

FOR WHOM THE BELL TOLLS ★★★1/2 The film version of Ernest Hemingway's story about patriots and outsiders fighting side by side during the Spanish Civil War. The pace is slow, and the purpose of the fight is never made clear. Greek actress Katina Paxinou won a supporting Oscar and her performance is still fiery and entertaining, but Gary Cooper is listless and Ingrid Bergman self-conscious. 174m. **DIR:** Sam Wood. **CAST:** Gary Cooper, Ingrid Bergman, Katina Paxinou, Akim Tamiroff, Joseph Calleia, Arturo De Cordova, Mikhail Rasumny. **1943 DVD**

FOR YOUR EYES ONLY ★★★1/2 For the first time since Roger Moore took over the role of 007 from Sean Connery, we have a film in the style that made the best Bond films—*From Russia with Love* and *Goldfinger*—so enjoyable. *For Your Eyes Only* is genuine spy adventure, closer in spirit to the novels by Ian Fleming. Rated PG. 127m. **DIR:** John Glen. **CAST:** Roger Moore, Carole Bouquet, Lynn-Holly Johnson, Topol. **1981 DVD**

FOR YOUR LOVE ONLY ★★ European beauty Nastassja Kinski stars as a young student who has an affair with her teacher, which leads to murder and blackmail. Pretty dull soap opera made for German television and released theatrically in 1982. Not rated; contains sexual situations and violence. 97m. **DIR:** Wolfgang Petersen. **CAST:** Nastassja Kinski, Christian Quadflieg. **1976**

FORBIDDEN ★★★ Made-for-cable film about a gentile woman who falls in love with a Jewish man during World War II: a crime in Hitler's Germany. Enough suspense here to keep the viewer attentive, but not enough atmosphere to make it as intense as the melodramatic soundtrack assumes it to be. Not rated, but the equivalent of a PG for some violence and light sex. 114m. **DIR:** Anthony Page. **CAST:** Jacqueline Bisset, Jurgen Prochnow, Irene Worth, Peter Vaughan. **1984 DVD**

FORBIDDEN CHOICES ★★1/2 This superficial adaptation of Carolyn Chute's *The Beans of Egypt, Maine* misses the novel's rich texture and emerges as little more than an unsympathetic, episodic study of a young stud who can't keep his pants zipped. Martha Plimpton does nice work as the narrator, who falls for this fellow from the wrong side of the tracks, and eventually regrets this choice. Rated R for profanity, nudity, simulated sex, and rape. 109m. **DIR:** Jennifer Warren. **CAST:** Martha Plimpton, Kelly Lynch, Rutger Hauer, Patrick McGaw. **1994**

FORBIDDEN DANCE, THE 🦃 The Lambada, the sensuous Brazilian dance craze. Rated PG-13. 90m. **DIR:** Greydon Clark. **CAST:** Laura Herring, Jeff James, Richard Lynch. **1990 DVD**

FORBIDDEN FRUIT ★★★1/2 Usually known as a comedian, Fernandel plays it straight in this drama based on a novel by Georges Simenon. He's a middle-aged country doctor who tries to break out of his bourgeois life by having an affair with a young prostitute. Once-scandalous film is no longer shocking, but still a compelling story. In French with English subtitles. Not rated; contains brief nudity. B&W; 97m. **DIR:** Henri Verneuil. **CAST:** Fernandel, Françoise Arnoul, Sylvie. **1952**

FORBIDDEN GAMES (1951) ★★★★★ It has been said that *Forbidden Games* is to World War II what *Grand Illusion* is to World War I. The horror of war has never been more real than as portrayed here against the bucolic surroundings of the French countryside. At the nucleus of the plot is Paulette, played by 5-year-old Brigitte Fossey. Witnessing German troops kill her parents twists the girl, who acquires an attraction for the symbols of death. A truly tragic, must-see work. In French with English subtitles. B&W; 87m. **DIR:** René Clement. **CAST:** Brigitte Fossey, Georges Poujouly. **1951**

FORBIDDEN GAMES (1995) 🦃 Private investigator looks into the death of a modeling-agency director in a soft-core erotic thriller that should be forbidden. Not rated; contains nudity, violence, and profanity. 89m. **DIR:** Edward Holzman. **CAST:** Jeff Griggs, Lesli Kay Sterling, Gail Harris. **1995**

FORBIDDEN PLANET ★★★★1/2 This is the most highly regarded sci-fi film of the 1950s. Its special-effects breakthroughs are rather tame today, but its story remains interesting. As a space mission from Earth lands on the Planet Altair-4 in the year 2200, they encounter a doctor (Walter Pidgeon) and his daughter (Anne Francis) who are all that remain from a previous colonization attempt. It soon becomes apparent that some unseen force on the planet does not bid them welcome. 98m. **DIR:** Fred M. Wilcox. **CAST:** Walter Pidgeon, Anne Francis, Leslie Nielsen, Jack Kelly. **1956 DVD**

FORBIDDEN QUEST ★★★★ Filmmaker Peter Delpeut mixed documentary footage taken by polar explorers of the early twentieth century with a fictional story about one such failed expedition to create this fascinating piece of history. Although some viewers might prefer to see the real-life scenes by themselves, this method is much more accessible (and provides a use for those cases when only fragments of film have survived). Not rated. B&W/color; 75m. **DIR:** Peter Delpeut. **1995**

FORBIDDEN SINS ★★1/2 Shannon Tweed stars as an attorney who falls in love with the rich client she's defending on a murder case. Of course, all is not as it seems. Rated R for profanity, nudity, violence, and sexual situations. 90m. **DIR:** Robert Angelo. **CAST:** Shannon Tweed, Corbin Timbrook, Timothy Vahle, Myles O'Brien. **1998**

FORBIDDEN SUN 🦃 Lauren Hutton as an ex-Olympian who coaches a group of young female hopefuls on the isle of Crete. Rated R for violence and adult situations. 88m. **DIR:** Zelda Barron. **CAST:** Lauren Hutton, Cliff De Young, René Estevez. **1989 DVD**

FORBIDDEN TRAIL ★★★1/2 In this superior series Western, one of several Buck Jones made for Columbia Pictures in the 1930s, the star and Al Smith play a couple of happy-go-lucky cowboys who find themselves in the middle of a range war. Jones, usually the stalwart, square-jawed defender of justice, takes a comedic approach to his part, and the results are quite pleasing. B&W; 71m. **DIR:** Lambert Hillyer. **CAST:** Buck Jones, Barbara Weeks, Mary Carr, Al Smith. **1932**

FORBIDDEN TRAILS ★★ In this, the least interesting of the Rough Riders Westerns, a pair of hardened criminals (Charles King and Bud Osborne) force a youngster (Dave O'Brien) to take part in their evil schemes. Robert N. Bradbury's direction lacks the energy brought to the series by Howard Bretherton, but the stars are as watchable as ever. B&W; 55m. **DIR:** Robert N. Bradbury. **CAST:** Buck Jones, Tim McCoy, Raymond Hatton, Dave O'Brien, Tristram Coffin, Charles King. **1941**

FORBIDDEN WORLD ★★ Jesse Vint was rescued from the obscurity of his deep-space death in *Silent Running*, and his reward was a starring role in this rip-off of *Alien* in which an experimental foodstuff starts killing the inhabitants of a space colony. Rated R for violence. 77m. **DIR:** Allan Holzman. **CAST:** Jesse Vint, Dawn Dunlap, June Chadwick, Linden Chiles. **1982**

FORBIDDEN ZONE 🦃 Absurd, would-be "cult" film has Herve Villechaize as the ruler of a bizarre kingdom located in the "Sixth Dimension." A sort-of comedy, this should be avoided by all means. Rated R for nudity and adult content. B&W; 76m. **DIR:** Richard Elfman. **CAST:** Herve Villechaize, Susan Tyrrell, Marie-Pascale Elfman, Viva. **1980**

FORBIDDEN ZONE: ALIEN ABDUCTION 🦃 Science-fiction trappings do little to hide the fact that this film is just an excuse to get women out of their clothes. Three women discover they've each been abducted by an alien and used for sexual experiments. Not rated; contains nudity and adult situations. 90m. **DIR:** Lucian S. Diamonde. **CAST:** Darcy De Moss, Pia Reyes, Dmitri Bogmaz, Carmen Lacatus. **1996**

FORCE, THE ★★1/2 OK crime-drama about a rookie cop who crosses paths with a hardboiled homicide detective who winds up dead. When he begins to investigate the circumstances behind the death, he's met with resistance by everyone on the force, including his superiors, who suggest he drop the matter. No surprises here, but enough close calls to warrant a look. Rated R for violence, language, and nudity. 94m. **DIR:** Mark Rosman. **CAST:** Jason Gedrick, Kim Delaney, Gary Hudson. **1994**

FORCE FIVE ★★ In this action-packed but predictable martial-arts film, a soldier of fortune and his four buddies rescue a woman held on a remote island. Rated R for violence, nudity, and profanity. 78m. **DIR:** Robert Clouse. **CAST:** Gerald Gordon, Nick Pryor, Bradford Dillman, Tom Villard. **1981**

FORCE OF ARMS ★★ A war drama with more talk than action, this film steals some of Hemingway's *A Farewell to Arms* and adds modern wartime philosophy. A soldier feels responsible when his buddies are killed in battle but regains self-esteem when he falls in love with a WAC. B&W; 99m. **DIR:** Michael Curtiz. **CAST:** William Holden, Nancy Olson, Gene Evans, Frank Lovejoy. **1951**

FORCE OF EVIL ★★★ A lawyer (John Garfield) abandons his principles and goes to work for a racketeer in this somber, downbeat story of corruption and loss of values. Compelling story and acting compensate for some of the heavy-handedness of the approach. A good study of ambition and the different paths it leads the characters on. B&W; 78m. **DIR:** Abraham Polonsky. **CAST:** John Garfield, Thomas Gomez, Roy Roberts, Marie Windsor. **1948**

FORCE OF ONE ★★★ This is the follow-up to *Good Guys Wear Black*. In this karate film, Chuck Norris cleans up a California town that has drug problems. As always, it only takes one good guy (Norris) to kick and/or punch some sense into the bad guys. Rated PG. 90m. **DIR:** Paul Aaron. **CAST:** Chuck Norris, Jennifer O'Neill, James Whitmore, Pepe Serna. **1979**

FORCE TEN FROM NAVARONE 🦃 Poor sequel to the classic *Guns of Navarone*. 118m. **DIR:** Guy Hamilton. **CAST:** Robert Shaw, Harrison Ford, Edward Fox, Franco Nero, Barbara Bach, Carl Weathers, Richard Kiel. **1978 DVD**

FORCED MARCH ★★★ Chris Sarandon is a deteriorating American Method actor portraying Miklos Radnoti, in a movie about the Hungarian poet's ordeal at a Jewish labor camp. As a film about the making of a film it is engaging at times—especially as it relates each character's dedication to the project. Not rated. 104m. **DIR:** Rick King. **CAST:** Chris Sarandon, Renee Soutendijk, Josef Sommer, John Seitz. **1989**

FORCED VENGEANCE ★★1/2 Even pacing and a somewhat suspenseful plot are not enough to make this film a must-see—unless you're a die-hard Chuck Norris fan, that is. This time, our martial arts master plays a casino security chief living in the Far East. Rated R for violence, nudity, and profanity. 90m. **DIR:** James Fargo. **CAST:** Chuck Norris, Mary Louise Weller, Camilla Griggs, Michael Cavanaugh, David Opatoshu, Seiji Sakaguchi. **1982**

FORCES OF NATURE ★★★1/2 The path to true love gets rocky in this engaging and occasionally wild tale. Poor Ben Affleck just wants to reach Savannah in time for his own wedding, but the journey is punctuated by countless examples of marriages gone bad, not to mention the delectable distraction of free-spirited Sandra Bullock. Although rainstorms and hurricanes impede our hero's progress, the script never loses sight of the primary quandary: Ben's a nice guy, and nice guys don't dump their soon-to-be wives . . . no matter how sparkling the temptation. Rated PG-13 for profanity and mild sexual content. 102m. **DIR:** Bronwen Hughes. **CAST:** Sandra Bullock, Ben Affleck, Maura Tierney, Steve Zahn, Blythe Danner, Ronny Cox, David Strickland, Meredith Scott Lynn. **1999 DVD**

FORD: THE MAN & THE MACHINE ★★1/2 This TV biography of Henry Ford runs out of gas long before the film does. Canadian effort stars Cliff Robertson as the grandfather of the automobile, only to let senility slip in and affect the script. Episodic storytelling revs its engine for those interested in such fare, but doesn't flesh out the story enough for a full road trip. 210m. **DIR:** Allan Eastman. **CAST:** Cliff Robertson, Hope Lange, Michael Ironside, Heather Thomas, R. H. Thomson. **1987**

FOREIGN AFFAIRS ★★★ Opposites attract in this light, warm story of a college professor and a sanitation engineer who meet in England and fall in love. Stars rise above familiar story line and keep interest level up. 106m. **DIR:** Jim O'Brien. **CAST:** Joanne Woodward, Brian Dennehy, Eric Stoltz, Stephanie Beacham, Ian Richardson. **1993**

FOREIGN BODY ★★★ An Indian émigré in London, longing to make a fortune and lose his virginity, makes both wishes come true by posing as a doctor to upper-class hypochondriacs. So-so script benefits from perky performances by a superior British cast. Rated PG-13 for ribald humor. 108m. **DIR:** Ronald Neame. **CAST:** Victor Banerjee, Warren Mitchell, Amanda Donohoe, Trevor Howard. **1986**

FOREIGN CORRESPONDENT ★★★★★ Classic Alfred Hitchcock thriller still stands as one of his most complex and satisfying films. Joel McCrea stars as an American reporter in Europe during the war, caught up in all sorts of intrigue, romance, etc., in his dealings with Nazi spies, hired killers, and the like as he attempts to get the truth to the American public. B&W; 120m. **DIR:** Alfred Hitchcock. **CAST:** Joel McCrea, Laraine Day, Herbert Marshall, George Sanders, Edmund Gwenn. **1940**

FOREIGN FIELD, A ★★★★ Three Allied soldiers, determined to revisit the spot that most changed their lives, return to Normandy nearly fifty years after D day. Memories, ranging from bitter to bittersweet, flood them as they discover the past was not quite as they remembered. A spirited and weathered cast brings a touching and unexpectedly funny perspective to that bloody chapter of World War II. Made for British and American TV. Not rated; contains profanity. 90m. **DIR:** Charles Sturridge. **CAST:** Alec Guinness, Leo McKern, John Randolph, Jeanne Moreau, Lauren Bacall, Geraldine Chaplin, Edward Herrmann. **1993**

FOREIGN STUDENT ★★1/2 In 1956 at a small Virginia university, a visiting French student (Marco Hofschneider) falls in love with a young black woman (Robin Givens). This low-budget drama has sincere performances, sensitive direction, and pretty photography, but the script is trite and predictable, and the dialogue is often unintentionally funny. Rated R for nudity. 93m. **DIR:** Eva Sereny. **CAST:** Marco Hofschneider, Robin Givens, Rich Johnson, Charlotte Ross, Edward Herrmann, Jack Coleman, Charles Dutton, Hinton Battle, Anthony Herrera. **1994**

FOREST WARRIOR ★★★★ Surprisingly enjoyable family film in which Chuck Norris stars as a forest spirit who joins a group of kids to defend the forest from a greedy lumber mogul. Excellent performances make for an entertaining and inspirational adventure. Instead of *Walker, Texas Ranger* think *Walker, Power Ranger*, and you'll get the general idea. 98m. **DIR:** Aaron Norris. **CAST:** Chuck Norris, Terry Kiser, Max Gail, Roscoe Lee Browne, Trent Knight, Megan Paul, Josh Wolford, Jordan Brower, Michael Friedman, William Sanderson, Loretta Swit, Michael Beck. **1996**

FOREVER ★★ How long does this movie seem to last? The title says it all. Once the filmmakers get past the initial plot device—a music-video director moves into a haunted house and falls in love with a ghost—the film seems to fall apart. There's way too much going on for the film's own good, and the hammy performances don't lend credibility to the serious undercurrents. Rated R for sexuality. 93m. **DIR:** Thomas Palmer Jr. **CAST:** Sean Young, Keith Coogan, Diane Ladd, Sally Kirkland. **1992**

FOREVER AMBER ★★★1/2 After much tampering by censors, Kathleen Winsor's (then) lusty bestseller made it to the screen. Linda Darnell plays ambitious tavern wench Amber St. Clare, who seduces all in sight until she becomes the mistress of Charles II. First-rate production and cast. 140m. **DIR:** Otto Preminger. **CAST:** Linda Darnell, Cornel Wilde, Richard Greene, George Sanders, Glenn Langan, Richard Haydn, Jessica Tandy, Anne Revere, John Russell, Leo G. Carroll, Margaret Wycherly. **1947**

FOREVER AND A DAY ★★★★ A morale builder during World War II and worth seeing for its cast, this film is a series of episodes linked together by a regal house in war-torn London. An American with British ancestry (Kent Smith) visits the house with plans to take it over. B&W; 104m. **DIR:** René Clair, Robert Stevenson, Herbert Wilcox, Victor Saville, Cedric Hardwicke, Edmund Goulding. **CAST:** Kent Smith, Charles Laughton, Anna Neagle, Ray Milland, Claude Rains, Ida Lupino, Merle Oberon, Brian Aherne, Victor McLaglen, Robert Cummings, Buster Keaton, Elsa Lanchester. **1943 DVD**

FOREVER DARLING ★★1/2 Lucille Ball's marriage to chemist Desi Arnaz is in trouble. Her guardian angel (James Mason) tries to put things right. Mild romantic comedy with too few of the *I Love Lucy*–style antics. 96m. **DIR:** Alexander Hall. **CAST:** Lucille Ball, Desi Arnaz Sr., James Mason, Louis Calhern, Marilyn Maxwell. **1956**

FOREVER JAMES DEAN ★★★★ Anyone remotely interested in the mercurial star James Dean will want to see this documentary—tracing Deán's career from his first Pepsi commercial to the final scene in *Giant.* From Emmy-winning filmmaker Ara Chekmayan. 69m. **DIR:** Ara Chekmayan. **1988**

FOREVER LOVE ★★★ Strong performances distinguish this tearjerker about a young woman who slips into a twenty-year coma. Lizzie and Alex Brooks are the picture-perfect couple, recently married and the loving parents of a young daughter. When Lizzie has a stroke and slips into a coma, Alex plans to care for her until she comes out of it, but the presence of his wife's best friend complicates his decision to remain faithful. Reba McEntire and Tim Matheson are potent in this film that treads on familiar made-for-television territory. Not rated. 120m. **DIR:** Michael Switzer. **CAST:** Reba McEntire, Tim Matheson, Bess Armstrong, Heather Stephens, Scott Foley. **1998**

FOREVER LULU 🦃 Ridiculous rip-off of *Desperately Seeking Susan*. Rated R for nudity, profanity, and violence. 86m. **DIR:** Amos Kollek. **CAST:** Hanna Schygulla, Deborah Harry, Alec Baldwin, Paul Gleason, Annie Golden, Dr. Ruth Westheimer, Charles Ludlam. **1987**

FOREVER MARY ★★★ A teacher in between assignments accepts a position at a notorious boys' reform school. His students are tough street kids with little hope of redemption. Updated version of *To Sir With Love*, Italian style. In Italian with English subtitles. Not rated; contains violence and profanity. 100m. **DIR:** Marco Risi. **CAST:** Michele Placido, Claudio Amendola. **1989**

FOREVER TOGETHER ★★★★ A young boy who finds himself falling in love with a girl who thinks of him as a friend gets advice from an unlikely source: a dead jazz musician whose spirit won't leave Earth until he is joined by his own true love. A delightful mix of sentimentality and comedy makes this a good film for family viewing. Also released as *Can't Be Heaven*. Rated PG for some mild swearing. 88m. **DIR:** Richard Friedman. **CAST:** Bryan Burke, Jamie Williams, Michelle Trachtenberg, Diane Ladd, Ralph Macchio, Rachel Ticotin, Garry Marshall. **1999 DVD**

FOREVER YOUNG (1983) ★★ This slow-moving British soap opera features a handsome priest who is idolized by a lonely boy. Not rated, but brief nudity and mature themes would make it comparable with a PG. 85m. **DIR:** David Drury. **CAST:** James Aubrey, Nicholas Gecks, Alec McCowen. **1983**

FOREVER YOUNG (1993) ★★★ In a charming performance, Mel Gibson plays a test pilot who has himself cryogenically frozen in 1939 only to wake up in 1992—alone. Gibson and his costars give this piece of fluff a buoyancy. Rated PG for profanity. 104m. **DIR:** Steve Miner. **CAST:** Mel Gibson, Jamie Lee Curtis, Elijah Wood, Isabel Glasser, Joe Morton, David Marshall Grant. **1993 DVD**

FORGET MOZART ★★ Poorly paced, surreal whodunit revolving around Mozart. But who killed him? In German with English subtitles. Not rated, contains nudity. 93m. **DIR:** Salvo Luther. **CAST:** Armin Mueller-Stahl. **1986**

FORGET PARIS ★★★1/2 A romantic comedy with more comedy than romance focusing on what happens after the honeymoon ends and the marriage begins. Billy Crystal's sly, observant humor elicits some good belly laughs, and, as usual, Debra Winger brings a sassy intelligence to her character that adds emotional depth missing from the script. Rated PG-13. 100m. **DIR:** Billy Crystal. **CAST:** Billy Crystal, Debra Winger, Joe Mantegna, Cynthia Stevenson, Richard Masur, Julie Kavner, William Hickey. **1995 DVD**

FORGOTTEN, THE ★★★1/2 Six Vietnam Green Beret POWs are released after seventeen years only to be put through more torture by U.S. officials. A disturbing psychological thriller, this made-for-cable TV movie has violence and some strong language. 96m. **DIR:** James

Keach. **CAST:** Keith Carradine, Steve Railsback, Stacy Keach. **1989 DVD**

FORGOTTEN CITY ★★ James Wheeler follows in the footsteps of his dead brother in the search for a fabled lost city of gold. Several bad guys want the gold for themselves and end up giving Wheeler a run for his money. The acting is poor, and the city is rather unimpressive, consisting of a small cave strewn with plastic treasure. Also released as *The Vivero Letter* in 1998. Rated R for violence. 96m. **DIR:** H. Gordon Boos. **CAST:** Robert Patrick, Fred Ward, Chiara Caselli. **1998 DVD**

FORGOTTEN ONE, THE ★★1/2 Unusual romantic triangle, in which novelist Terry O'Quinn moves into a house haunted by a ghost from his past life. The ghost attempts to have O'Quinn kill himself, so that they may be together in the afterlife. Kristy McNichol contributes a fine performance. Rated R for nudity and profanity. 89m. **DIR:** Phillip Badger. **CAST:** Terry O'Quinn, Kristy McNichol. **1989**

FORGOTTEN PRISONERS ★★★ The horrors of life in a Turkish prison are vividly depicted in this gut-wrenching made-for-cable drama that focuses on human rights. Ron Silver is excellent as a lawyer hired by Amnesty International. 92m. **DIR:** Robert Greenwald. **CAST:** Ron Silver, Hector Elizondo, Roger Daltrey. **1990**

FORGOTTEN SILVER ★★★1/2 Director Peter Jackson explores the life and career of forgotten New Zealand cinema pioneer Colin McKenzie, who invented sound movies in 1908 and color film in 1914. The only catch is that the film is a hilarious hoax; McKenzie never existed. Still, the "vintage" footage and the on-camera comments by actor Sam Neill and historian Leonard Maltin were so convincing that, when it was shown without a disclaimer on New Zealand TV, 80 percent of the audience believed it. This one is an absolute must for film buffs. Not rated; suitable for all audiences. 53m. **DIR:** Peter Jackson. **CAST:** Costa Botes, Marguerite Hurst, Peter Jackson, Leonard Maltin, Sam Neill. **1996 DVD**

FORGOTTEN TUNE FOR THE FLUTE, A ★★★ This Glasnost romantic comedy is a little long and stumbles with a somewhat contrived ending, but it's a joy otherwise. It introduces to the West the vivacious and talented Tatyana Dogileva and is a perfect remedy for American movie watchers who think all Russian films are solemn enterprises at best, epic drags at worst. In Russian with English subtitles. 131m. **DIR:** Eldar Ryazanov. **CAST:** Tatyana Dogileva. **1988**

FORLORN RIVER ★★★ Exciting Zane Grey story has horse thieves trying to buy army mounts with six-guns. Good photography, literate script. B&W; 56m. **DIR:** Charles Barton. **CAST:** Buster Crabbe, June Martel, Harvey Stephens. **1937**

FORMULA, THE ★★ Take a plot to conceal a method of producing enough synthetic fuel to take care of the current oil shortage and add two superstars like George C. Scott and Marlon Brando. Sounds like the formula for a real blockbuster, doesn't it? Unfortunately, it turns out to be the formula for a major disappointment. Rated R. 117m. **DIR:** John G. Avildsen. **CAST:** George C. Scott, Marlon Brando, Marthe Keller, John Gielgud, G. D. Spradlin. **1980**

FORREST GUMP ★★★★★ Based on the novel by Winston Groom, the feel-good movie of 1994 boasts a magnificent performance by Tom Hanks and remarkable special effects. Despite his 75 I.Q., Hanks's title character finds himself a major player in events from the 1950s to the 1980s as director Robert Zemeckis's wizardry places him in context with everyone from Elvis Presley to President John F. Kennedy by using stand-ins and actual documentary footage. Somehow, this sleight of hand becomes anything but a slight piece of entertainment. Rated PG-13 for violence and profanity. 142m. **DIR:** Robert Zemeckis. **CAST:** Tom Hanks, Sally Field, Robin Wright, Gary Sinise, Mykelti Williamson, Michael Connor Humphreys. **1994 DVD**

•FORSAKEN, THE ★★ A young man driving cross-country picks up a hitchhiker who dragoons him into hunting vampires. Grimy, brutal, and awash with stage blood, the film is relentlessly unpleasant. Rated R for violence and profanity. 90m. **DIR:** J. S. Cardone. **CAST:** Kerr Smith, Brendan Fehr, Johnathon Schaech, Izabella Miko, Carrie Snodgress. **2001 DVD**

FORSAKING ALL OTHERS ★★★ Offbeat casting with Clark Gable as the nice guy, for years secretly in love with Joan Crawford, while she allows herself to be manipulated by a cad. The movie is stolen by lovely Billie Burke and droll Charles Butterworth. B&W; 84m. **DIR:** W. S. Van Dyke. **CAST:** Joan Crawford, Clark Gable, Robert Montgomery, Charles Butterworth, Billie Burke, Rosalind Russell. **1934**

FORT APACHE ★★★★1/2 The first entry in director John Ford's celebrated cavalry trilogy stars Henry Fonda as a post commandant who decides to make a name for himself by starting a war with the Apaches, against the advice of an experienced soldier (John Wayne). Great film. B&W; 127m. **DIR:** John Ford. **CAST:** John Wayne, Henry Fonda, Shirley Temple, Ward Bond, John Agar, George O'Brien. **1948**

FORT APACHE—THE BRONX ★★★1/2 Jarring violence surfaces throughout this story about New York's crime-besieged South Bronx, but absorbing dramatic elements give this routine cops-and-criminals format gutsy substance. Paul Newman, as an idealistic police veteran, proves his screen magnetism hasn't withered with time. The supporting cast is top-notch. Rated R for violence, profanity, and sexual references. 125m. **DIR:** Daniel Petrie. **CAST:** Paul Newman, Ken Wahl, Edward Asner, Kathleen Beller, Rachel Ticotin. **1981 DVD**

FORT OSAGE ★★★ Nefarious businessmen cause an Indian uprising while taking money from settlers. Compact oater is better than one would expect. B&W; 72m. **DIR:** Lesley Selander. **CAST:** Rod Cameron, Jane Nigh, Morris Ankrum, Douglas Kennedy. **1951**

FORT SAGANNE ★★★★ Gérard Depardieu stars as a young peasant who dreams of being an officer in the French Foreign Legion but is forced to join as a lowly enlisted man. Stationed at a forgotten desert outpost in Algeria, his subsequent adventures and personal tragedies make for engrossing viewing. In French with English subtitles. Not rated; contains nudity and violence. 180m. **DIR:** Alain Corneau. **CAST:** Gérard Depardieu, Catherine Deneuve, Philippe Noiret, Sophie Marceau. **1984**

FORTRESS (1985) ★★1/2 In this drawn-out story of a mass kidnapping in the Australian outback, Rachel Ward is passable as a teacher in a one-room school. She is abducted along with her students, ranging in age from about 6 to 14. The story centers around their attempts to escape. 90m. **DIR:** Arch Nicholson. **CAST:** Rachel Ward, Sean Garlick, Rebecca Rigg. **1985**

FORTRESS (1993) ★★1/2 Grim science-fiction thriller about a married couple thrown into a monstrous, underground prison for having a second child. Inmates are controlled by small explosive devices that are blasted into the digestive system via the throat. The couple must escape before their baby is delivered and turned into a "kidbot" that is half human and half gadgetry. Another cultish, ghoulish, deadpan joke from the maker of *Re-Animator*. Rated R for violence and profanity. 92m. **DIR:** Stuart Gordon. **CAST:** Christopher Lambert, Loryn Locklin, Kurtwood Smith. **1993 DVD**

FORTRESS 2: RE-ENTRY ★★ Christopher Lambert returns to reprise his role as the father that had one too many children and was incarcerated as a result. This time around, the fortress is an impenetrable coed prison orbiting Earth from which Lambert must figure out how to escape. Plagued by halfhearted performances and below-par effects, *Fortress 2* cannot escape from its own inconsistencies. Rated R for nudity, violence, and profanity. 92m. **DIR:** Geoff Murphy. **CAST:** Christopher Lambert, Pam Grier. **1999 DVD**

FORTUNE, THE ★★1/2 Two would-be criminals bungle an attempt to kidnap and murder a young heiress. The great look and sound of this film can't compensate for story problems and lack of real comedy (despite an outlandish performance by Jack Nicholson). 88m. **DIR:** Mike Nichols. **CAST:** Jack Nicholson, Warren Beatty, Stockard Channing, Florence Stanley, Richard B. Shull, Tom Newman. **1975**

FORTUNE AND MEN'S EYES ★★1/2 Well acted but unpleasant and ultimately an exploitative look at homosexuality in prison. Rated R for violence and suggested sex. 102m. **DIR:** Harvey Hart. **CAST:** Wendell Burton, Michael Greer, Zooey Hall. **1971**

FORTUNE COOKIE, THE ★★★★1/2 Jack Lemmon is accidentally injured by a player while filming a football game from the sidelines. His brother-in-law, Walter Matthau, sees this as an ideal attempt to make some lawsuit money. So starts the first of the usually delightful Lemmon-Matthau comedies. Matthau is at his scene-stealing best in this Oscar-winning role. B&W; 125m. **DIR:** Billy Wilder. **CAST:** Jack Lemmon, Walter Matthau, Ron Rich, Cliff Osmond. **1966 DVD**

FORTUNE DANE ★★1/2 Originally a pilot for a TV series, this fair action film features Carl Weathers as a cop out to find who corrupted his banker father. Rated PG for violence. 83m. **DIR:** Nicholas Sgarro, Charles Correll. **CAST:** Carl Weathers, Adolph Caesar. **1986**

FORTUNE'S FOOL ★★1/2 Best known for his dramatic roles, Emil Jannings hams it up in this German comedy about a profiteering meat-packer. Jannings displays the gifts that made him a dominating screen figure. Silent. B&W; 60m. **DIR:** Reinhold Schunzel. **CAST:** Emil Jannings, Daguey Servaes, Reinhold Schunzel. **1925**

FORTUNES OF WAR (1987) ★★★ Based on Olivia Manning's novels *Balkan Trilogy* and *Levant Trilogy*, this BBC epic focuses on the effects of World War II on a nonmilitary British couple living in Romania. The husband is attracted to rebel factions and lofty ideals, while his wife must focus on daily life and reality. Slow-moving and overlong. 335m. **DIR:** James Cellan Jones. **CAST:** Kenneth Branagh, Emma Thompson, Ronald Pickup, Rupert Graves. **1987**

FORTUNES OF WAR (1993) ★★★ When a desperate American relief worker takes a risky smuggling job, he doesn't realize how big a risk he's taking. As he makes his way to the delivery point with a shipment of drugs, he learns it's not just imprisonment that's awaiting him, but also a violent death. Rated R for violence and profanity. 107m. **DIR:** Thierry Notz. **CAST:** Matt Salinger, Michael Ironside, Haing S. Ngor, Michael Nouri. **1993**

FORTY CARATS ★★★1/2 This comedy has Liv Ullmann playing a 40-year-old divorcée being pursued by a rich 22-year-old, Edward Albert. Laughs abound as Ullmann's grown daughter (Deborah Raffin) and ex-husband (Gene Kelly) react to her latest suitor. Rated PG. 110m. **DIR:** Milton Katselas. **CAST:** Liv Ullmann, Edward Albert, Gene Kelly, Nancy Walker, Deborah Raffin. **1973**

•40 DAYS AND 40 NIGHTS ★★★ San Francisco Web-page designer Matt resists the promiscuous singles life of his roommate and coworkers in this funny sex comedy about not having sex and the myths and misconceptions of libido. After his girlfriend dumps him, Matt tries to end his obsession with her and regain control of his life by giving up carnal pleasures for Lent. He becomes the hot topic of an Internet betting site called "The Vow" that monitors his every move and undermines his courtship of a woman he meets in a laundromat. Rated R for language, sexual content, and nudity. 94m. **DIR:** Michael Lehmann. **CAST:** Josh Hartnett, Shannyn Sossamon, Vinessa Shaw, Paulo Costanzo, Adam Trese. **2002**

FORTY-NINERS ★★1/2 A frontiersman saves a group of settlers on their way to California during the great gold rush from a thieving wagonmaster and marauding Indians. Good-natured, if familiar, pioneer film. B&W; 53m. **DIR:** John P. McCarthy. **CAST:** Tom Tyler, Betty Mack, Alan Bridge, Fern Emmett, Gordon Wood. **1932**

FORTY POUNDS OF TROUBLE ★★★1/2 Thoroughly enjoyable retread of *Little Miss Marker* finds casino manager Tony Curtis saddled with adorable moppet Claire Wilcox after her father takes leave. In an effort to impress visiting songstress Suzanne Pleshette, Curtis assumes the father role, and then must decide what course to take when the girl's father dies in an accident. Wilcox is a little charmer, and the chemistry between Curtis and Pleshette is magical. 106m. **DIR:** Norman Jewison. **CAST:** Tony Curtis, Suzanne Pleshette, Claire Wilcox, Howard Morris, Phil Silvers, Larry Storch. **1963**

FORTY SEVEN RONIN ★★★1/2 A fascinating glimpse into the mentality of the Japanese during World War II, this two-volume cassette rates complete watching by completists only. The first volume is made from an old, scratchy print and is a slow-paced account of how an insult to a powerful lord's honor brings terrible and unjust punishment. The second tape, made from a pristine 35mm. print, recaps most of the events from part one as the lord's retainers plot a daring revenge. In Japanese with English subtitles. Not rated; the film has brief violence. 112m. **DIR:** Kenji Mizoguchi. **CAST:** Chojuro Kawarasaki, Knemon Nakamura. **1942 DVD**

FORTY THIEVES ★★★ An ex-convict comes to town paroled into the custody of Sheriff Hopalong Cassidy.

Unhappy about Hoppy's control, he rounds up his old gang, the Forty Thieves. B&W; 61m. **DIR:** Lesley Selander. **CAST:** William Boyd, Andy Clyde, Jimmy Rogers, Louise Currie. **1944**

FOUL PLAY ★★★ Gloria Mundy (Goldie Hawn) accidentally becomes involved in a plot to assassinate the Pope. Detective Tony Carlson (Chevy Chase) tries to protect and seduce her. Hawn is good as the damsel in distress, but Chase is hardly the Cary Grant type. Still it's fun. Rated PG. 116m. **DIR:** Colin Higgins. **CAST:** Goldie Hawn, Chevy Chase, Dudley Moore, Burgess Meredith, Marilyn Sokol. **1978**

FOUNTAINHEAD, THE ★★1/2 Gary Cooper tries his best in this Ayn Rand novel, brought to the screen without any of the book's vitality or character development. "Coop" is cast as Howard Roark, a Frank Lloyd Wright-type architect whose creations are ahead of their time and therefore go unappreciated. Patricia Neal is the love interest. B&W; 114m. **DIR:** King Vidor. **CAST:** Gary Cooper, Patricia Neal, Raymond Massey, Kent Smith, Robert Douglas. **1949**

FOUR ADVENTURES OF REINETTE AND MIRABELLE ★★★1/2 French film that is actually slices of everyday life for two different girls—one naïve and one sophisticated. Not much plot; this is more of a character study. Slow-moving but pleasant. In French with English subtitles. 95m. **DIR:** Eric Rohmer. **CAST:** Joelle Miguel, Jessica Forde. **1986**

FOUR BAGS FULL ★★★★ In Nazi-occupied Paris, two scoundrels attempt to transport a contraband slaughtered pig across town. But when word of their cargo gets out, the Nazis are the least of their worries. First-rate comic thriller with a refreshingly cynical look at Frenchmen during the war. In French with English subtitles. Not rated. B&W; 90m. **DIR:** Claude Autant-Lara. **CAST:** Jean Gabin, Bourvil, Louis de Funes. **1956**

FOUR DAUGHTERS ★★★★1/2 Widower Claude Rains helps his daughters through the ups and downs of small-town romance in this irresistible tearjerker from a Fannie Hurst novel. Great cast, with John Garfield a standout in his first film. B&W; 90m. **DIR:** Michael Curtiz. **CAST:** Claude Rains, Rosemary Lane, Lola Lane, Priscilla Lane, Gale Page, John Garfield. **1938**

•4 DAYS ★★ A teen and his father double-cross a bank robbery partner who winds up hot on the boy's trail. On his journey to reunite with his father, the boy meets several interesting characters—most notably a woman escaping from a cruel husband—all of whom are unpleasant and unsavory, much like this movie. Rated R for violence, sexuality, and language. 88m. **DIR:** Curtis Wehrfritz. **CAST:** Kevin Zegers, Lolita Davidovich, William Forsythe, Colm Meaney. **1999**

FOUR DAYS IN JULY ★★★ A stark, cold realistic view of war-torn Northern Ireland, concentrating on two couples: one Catholic, and one Protestant. Irish accents may be difficult, but the almost intrusive nature of this "fly-on-the-wall" directorial style makes it worth the effort. 99m. **DIR:** Mike Leigh. **CAST:** Brid Brennan, Desmond McAleer, Charles Lawson, Paula Hamilton. **1984**

FOUR DAYS IN SEPTEMBER ★★★★ Brazilian Marxist students kidnap the American ambassador to protest their oppressive military government, then argue among themselves about their next move as the secret police swing into action against them. Fact-based docudrama lets the narrative speak for itself and shows a satisfying grasp of the dramatic nuances of the story. In Portuguese with English subtitles. Rated R for profanity (in subtitles) and violence. 106m. **DIR:** Bruno Barreto. **CAST:** Alan Arkin, Pedro Cardoso, Claudia Abreu, Matheus Nachtergaele. **1997**

FOUR DEUCES, THE ★★ Jack Palance is a gang leader during Prohibition times in this high-camp action film about gangsters. The movie is poorly conceived, with an odd mixture of blood and spoof. *The Four Deuces* does not have an MPAA rating, but it contains sex, nudity, violence, and profanity. 87m. **DIR:** William H. Bushnell Jr. **CAST:** Jack Palance, Carol Lynley, Warren Berlinger, Adam Roarke, Gianni Russo, H. B. Haggerty, John Haymer, Martin Kove, E. J. Peaker. **1975**

FOUR EYES AND SIX GUNS ★★1/2 Fairly amusing comedy-Western about an optometrist who goes west to run a store and ends up helping Wyatt Earp clean up Tombstone. Made for TV. 92m. **DIR:** Peter Markle. **CAST:** Judge Reinhold, Patricia Clarkson, Fred Ward, Dan Hedaya, M. Emmet Walsh, Dennis Burkley, John Schuck, Jonathan Gries, Austin Pendleton. **1992**

FOUR FACES WEST ★★★ A small-scale Western that tends to be overlooked, it uses a standard formula (an outlaw is pursued by a determined sheriff). But the writing, acting, and direction find those nuances that can make a story fresh. B&W; 90m. **DIR:** Alfred E. Green. **CAST:** Joel McCrea, Frances Dee, Charles Bickford, Joseph Calleia. **1948**

FOUR FEATHERS, THE ★★★★ A young man (John Clements) from a military background is branded a coward when he forsakes military duty for a home and family during time of war. Rejected by his family, friends, and fiancée, he sets out to prove his manhood. This motion picture was one of the few English productions of its era to gain wide acceptance. It still holds up well today. 115m. **DIR:** Zoltán Korda. **CAST:** Ralph Richardson, John Clements, June Duprez, C. Aubrey Smith. **1939**

FOUR FEATHERS, THE ★★★ Solid television retelling of the A. E. W. Mason story, with plenty of action and derring-do. Beau Bridges portrays the Britisher fighting against Sudanese tribesmen in nineteenth-century Africa. Although the transition of the story from British to American ideals is shaky, the story itself is powerful. 110m. **DIR:** Don Sharp. **CAST:** Beau Bridges, Robert Powell, Simon Ward, Jane Seymour, Harry Andrews. **1978**

4:50 FROM PADDINGTON ★★★1/2 Agatha Christie's spinster detective, Miss Marple, is more challenged than usual when she must find the murderer *and* the corpse. A railway traveler witnesses a woman being strangled on a passing train, and reports the murder... but the body can't be found! Strong performances, picturesque set designs, and moody score bring this 1950s mystery to life. Not rated; suitable for family viewing. 110m. **DIR:** Martyn Friend. **CAST:** Joan Hickson, David Horovitch, David Waller, Jill Meager, Maurice Denham. **1987**

FOUR FOR TEXAS ★★ Nonsensical story about tough-guy Frank Sinatra teaming up with fast-shooting Dean Martin to operate a floating gambling casino. Long and pretty silly. 124m. **DIR:** Robert Aldrich. **CAST:** Frank

Sinatra, Dean Martin, Anita Ekberg, Ursula Andress, Victor Buono, Charles Bronson, Mike Mazurki, Richard Jaeckel. **1963 DVD**

FOUR FRIENDS ★★ Arthur Penn directed and Steve Tesich (*Breaking Away*) wrote this interesting but ultimately disappointing film about America as seen through the eyes of a young immigrant (Craig Wasson) and the love he shares with two friends for a freethinking young woman (Jodi Thelen). Rated R because of violence, nudity, and profanity. 114m. **DIR:** Arthur Penn. **CAST:** Craig Wasson, James Leo Herlihy, Jodi Thelen. **1981**

FOUR HORSEMEN OF THE APOCALYPSE ★★ The 1921 silent version of this complex antiwar tale of two brothers who fight on opposite sides during World War I is still the best. When Rudolph Valentino played Julio, you cared. This one, updated to World War II, falls flat, despite a fine cast. 153m. **DIR:** Vincente Minnelli. **CAST:** Glenn Ford, Ingrid Thulin, Charles Boyer, Lee J. Cobb, Paul Henreid, Paul Lukas. **1961**

400 BLOWS, THE ★★★★★ Poignant story of a boy and the world that seems to be at odds with him is true and touching as few films have ever been. Powerful, tender, and at times overwhelmingly sad, this great film touches all the right buttons without being exploitative. In French with English subtitles. B&W; 99m. **DIR:** François Truffaut. **CAST:** Jean-Pierre Léaud, Patrick Auffay, Claire Maurier, Albert Remy. **1959 DVD**

FOUR IN A JEEP ★★1/2 Just after World War II, Vienna was nationally divided into four zones. This picture deals with a police patrol made up of American, Soviet, British, and French troops who clash over cases with which they must deal. It's not a terribly exciting film, but it does evoke some emotion about this tragic episode in postwar history. B&W; 96m. **DIR:** Leopold Lindtberg. **CAST:** Viveca Lindfors, Ralph Meeker. **1951**

FOUR JACKS AND A JILL ★★ Four broke but big-hearted musicians take in a young singer who manages to tangle them up with gangsters and the law. Full of tunes and silly coincidences, this typical low-budget studio B film is short on story and shorter still on credibility. B&W; 68m. **DIR:** Jack B. Hively. **CAST:** Ray Bolger, Anne Shirley, June Havoc, Desi Arnaz Sr., Eddie Foy Jr., Fritz Feld, Henry Daniell. **1942**

FOUR JILLS IN A JEEP ★★★1/2 A typical morale-builder from World War II, and a curiosity. It dramatizes the real-life tour of four Hollywood actresses as they cheer the troops with song and dance. The movie includes the talents of other Hollywoodites who symbolized the best show business had to offer during the war years. B&W; 89m. **DIR:** William A. Seiter. **CAST:** Kay Francis, Carole Landis, Martha Raye, Mitzi Mayfair, Betty Grable, Alice Faye, Carmen Miranda, Phil Silvers, Dick Haymes, Jimmy Dorsey. **1944**

FOUR MUSKETEERS, THE ★★★★★ In this superb sequel to Richard Lester's *The Three Musketeers*, the all-star cast is remarkably good, and the director is at the peak of his form. The final duel between Michael York and Christopher Lee is a stunner. Rated PG. 108m. **DIR:** Richard Lester. **CAST:** Oliver Reed, Raquel Welch, Richard Chamberlain, Frank Finlay, Michael York, Christopher Lee, Faye Dunaway, Charlton Heston. **1975 DVD**

FOUR RODE OUT 🦃 U.S. marshall in pursuit of a Mexican bank robber. 90m. **DIR:** John Peyser. **CAST:** Pernell Roberts, Sue Lyons, Julian Mateos, Leslie Nielsen. **1968**

FOUR ROOMS 🦃 Four pointless, painfully unfunny black comedies are tied together at a decayed hotel on New Year's Eve. Rated R for language, nudity, drug use, and violence. 95m. **DIR:** Quentin Tarantino, Alexandre Rockwell, Allison Anders, Robert Rodriguez. **CAST:** Tim Roth, Antonio Banderas, Jennifer Beals, Valeria Golino, Madonna, Quentin Tarantino, Marisa Tomei. **1995 DVD**

FOUR SEASONS, THE ★★★1/2 Written and directed by Alan Alda, this film focuses on the pains and joys of friendship shared by three couples who are vacationing together. Despite a flawed and uneven script, the characters have been skillfully drawn and convincingly played by an excellent cast. *Four Seasons* is by no means perfect, yet it is an appealing, uplifting piece of entertainment. Rated PG. 117m. **DIR:** Alan Alda. **CAST:** Alan Alda, Carol Burnett, Len Cariou, Sandy Dennis, Rita Moreno, Jack Weston. **1981**

FOUR SKULLS OF JONATHAN DRAKE, THE ★★★ A family is haunted by a 200 year old curse in which the men are decapitated on their sixtieth birthdays. Could it involve villainous Dr. Zurich (Henry Daniell), whose hobby is head shrinking? Good-looking horror-thriller with a fun performance by Daniell. B&W; 70m. **DIR:** Edward L. Cahn. **CAST:** Eduard Franz, Henry Daniell, Valerie French, Grant Richards. **1959**

FOUR WEDDINGS AND A FUNERAL ★★★★ A reserved Englishman meets an attractive American at a wedding and falls in love with her, but his inability to express his feelings seems to forestall any possibility of a relationship—until they meet again and again. The ensemble cast give this clever film true charm. Rowan Atkinson is hilarious as a nervous novice priest. Rated R for profanity, suggested sex, and adult themes. 118m. **DIR:** Mike Newell. **CAST:** Hugh Grant, Andie MacDowell, Kristin Scott Thomas, Simon Callow, James Fleet, John Hannah, Charlotte Coleman, David Bower, Corin Redgrave, Rowan Atkinson, Anna Chancellor. **1994 DVD**

4D MAN ★★★ A scientist (Robert Lansing) learns of a method of moving through objects (walls, doors, bank vaults, etc.), without realizing the terrible consequences, which eventually lead to madness and murder. Eerie sci-fi film hampered only by often brash music. From the director of *The Blob*. 85m. **DIR:** Irvin S. Yeaworth Jr. **CAST:** Robert Lansing, Lee Meriwether, James Congdon, Robert Strauss, Patty Duke. **1959 DVD**

4TH FLOOR, THE ★★1/2 A young woman moves into a new apartment and suspects that she may have a murderous neighbor. Great cast is fun as her weirdo neighbors, but film is full of familiar clichés. Rated R for profanity and violence. 90m. **DIR:** Josh Klausner. **CAST:** Juliette Lewis, William Hurt, Shelley Duvall, Austin Pendleton. **1999 DVD**

FOURTH MAN, THE ★★★1/2 Jeroen Krabbé plays a gay alcoholic writer prone to hallucinations. Invited to lecture at a literary society, he meets a mysterious woman who he becomes convinced intends to kill him. This emerges as an atmospheric, highly original chiller. In Dutch with English subtitles. Not rated; the film has nudity, simulated sex, violence, and profanity. 128m.

DIR: Paul Verhoeven. **CAST:** Jeroen Krabbé, Renee Soutendijk. **1984 DVD**

FOURTH PROTOCOL, THE ★★★ Michael Caine is the best component of this stiff screen version of Frederick Forsyth's thriller. Caine is a British agent who suspects "something big" is being smuggled into England; his guess is accurate, and he discovers an atomic-bomb delivery is being supervised by ultracool Russian agent Pierce Brosnan. Rated R for violence, nudity, and language. 119m. **DIR:** John Mackenzie. **CAST:** Michael Caine, Pierce Brosnan, Joanna Cassidy, Ned Beatty. **1987**

FOURTH STORY ★★★ Mark Harmon's amiable private detective lands a most intriguing case when a puzzled woman (Mimi Rogers) hires him to find her husband . . . who simply vanished after breakfast one morning. Although the finale is somewhat clumsy in this made-for-cable thriller, getting there is quite fun. Rated PG-13 for brief nudity. 91m. **DIR:** Ivan Passer. **CAST:** Mark Harmon, Mimi Rogers, Paul Gleason, Michael Patrick Boatman, Cliff De Young, M. Emmet Walsh. **1991**

FOURTH WAR, THE ★★ Old war-horse Roy Scheider can't adjust to a peaceful, politicized new army—especially when he confronts a Soviet colonel (Jurgen Prochnow) of similiar persuasions. Fine performances by Scheider and Prochnow are wasted in this mediocre thriller. Rated R for violence and profanity. 95m. **DIR:** John Frankenheimer. **CAST:** Roy Scheider, Jurgen Prochnow, Harry Dean Stanton, Tim Reid. **1990**

FOURTH WISE MAN, THE ★★★1/2 A surprisingly well-done fable about a physician who sets out to join three other notables in a quest to witness the birth of the Messiah, but this fourth wise man (Martin Sheen) encounters stumbling blocks along the way. Stylishly produced TV movie. 72m. **DIR:** Michael Ray Rhodes. **CAST:** Martin Sheen, Alan Arkin, Eileen Brennan, Ralph Bellamy, Richard Libertini, Harold Gould, Lance Kerwin, Adam Arkin. **1985**

FOURTH WISH, THE ★★★★ This moving Australian tearjerker features a 12-year-old boy dying of leukemia. His father's desire to grant his final wishes gets progressively harder to arrange. Wonderful story of a father's love, but be prepared with a box of Kleenex nearby. Not rated. 120m. **DIR:** Don Chaffey. **CAST:** John Meillon, Robert Bettles, Robyn Nevin. **1976**

48 HRS. ★★★★1/2 Add *48 Hrs.* to the list of the best cops-and-robbers movies ever made. It's so action-packed, it'll keep you on the edge of your seat. There's more good news: It's funny too. In the story, a cop (Nick Nolte) goes looking for a psychotic prison escapee (James Remar) with the help of a fast-talking con man (Eddie Murphy). There's never a dull moment. Rated R for violence, profanity, and nudity. 96m. **DIR:** Walter Hill. **CAST:** Eddie Murphy, Nick Nolte, Annette O'Toole, Frank McRae, James Remar, David Patrick Kelly. **1982 DVD**

49TH PARALLEL, THE ★★★★ Rich suspense drama about a World War II German U-boat sunk off the coast of Canada whose crew makes it to shore and tries to reach safety in neutral territory. The cast is first-rate, the characterizations outstanding. Original story won an Oscar. B&W; 105m. **DIR:** Michael Powell. **CAST:** Laurence Olivier, Anton Walbrook, Eric Portman, Leslie Howard, Raymond Massey, Finlay Currie, Glynis Johns. **1941**

42ND STREET ★★★★ Every understudy's dream is to get a big chance and rise to stardom. Such is the premise of *42nd Street*. This Depression-era musical of 1933 is lifted above cliché by its vitality and sincerity. B&W; 98m. **DIR:** Lloyd Bacon. **CAST:** Dick Powell, Ruby Keeler, Ginger Rogers, Warner Baxter, Una Merkel. **1933 DVD**

FOX AND HIS FRIENDS ★★1/2 Filmmaker Rainer Werner Fassbinder has the starring role as a lower-class carnival entertainer known as Fox, the Talking Head, who strikes it rich after a hard life by winning the lottery. His wealth attracts an elegant, bourgeois homosexual lover who proceeds to take advantage of him. In German with English subtitles. Not rated; contains nudity and is recommended for adult viewers. 123m. **DIR:** Rainer Werner Fassbinder. **CAST:** Rainer Werner Fassbinder, Peter Chatel, Karlheinz Böhm, Harry Baer. **1975**

FOX AND THE HOUND ★★★1/2 Gorgeous animation in the classic Disney style elevates this not-so-classic children's film in which a little fox and a puppy become friends. Later, when they've grown up, their bond clashes with their natural instincts. The younger set will enjoy this lightweight film, but it falls squarely in the void between the studio's two great eras of feature-length cartoons. Rated G. 83m. **DIR:** Art Stevens, Ted Berman, Richard Rich. **1981 DVD**

FOXES ★★★ Adrian Lyne directed this fitfully interesting film, about four young women who share an apartment in Los Angeles. The cast is good but somehow it all falls flat. Rated R. 106m. **DIR:** Adrian Lyne. **CAST:** Jodie Foster, Sally Kellerman, Cherie Currie, Randy Quaid, Scott Baio. **1980**

FOXFIRE (1987) ★★★★1/2 Jessica Tandy is mesmerizing in this *Hallmark Hall of Fame* presentation. She plays an elderly Appalachian woman who must choose between her beloved mountaintop cabin and a new home with her son and his children. Hume Cronyn is the ghost of her late husband whom Tandy keeps very much alive, and John Denver is the singing son who wants to care for her. The Blue Ridge Mountains are as much a part of this lovely film as Tandy's thoughtful performance. Rated PG. 118m. **DIR:** Jud Taylor. **CAST:** Jessica Tandy, Hume Cronyn, John Denver. **1987 DVD**

FOXFIRE (1996) ★★ Angelina Jolie, a pouty stranger with only a nickname, drifts into the unhappy lives of four teenage girls, and naturally changes their lives forever. This adaptation of a Joyce Carol Oates novel begins on strong footing as Jolie teaches the girls to fight against sexual and social abuse. However, it suffers greatly from slipshod direction, semideveloped characters, and enough dangling plot threads to weave a sequel. Rated R for nudity, profanity, sexual situations, and violence. 102m. **DIR:** Annette Haywood-Carter. **CAST:** Angelina Jolie, Hedy Buress, Jenny Shimizu, Jenny Lewis, Sarah Rosenberg. **1996 DVD**

FOXFIRE LIGHT 🦃 A love triangle in the Ozarks. Badly written. Rated PG for adult situations. 102m. **DIR:** Allen Baron. **CAST:** Leslie Nielsen, Tippi Hedren, Lara Parker, Barry Van Dyke, Burton Gilliam. **1982**

FOXTRAP 🦃 Fred Williamson plays a bodyguard sent to Europe to find a missing heiress. Rated R for violence, drug use, and sexual situations. 88m. **DIR:** Fred Williamson. **CAST:** Fred Williamson, Christopher Connelly, Arlene Golonka. **1986**

FOXTROT ★★1/2 Peter O'Toole plays a European aristocrat who escapes World War II when he takes a yacht to a deserted island and sets up residence with his wife (Charlotte Rampling), his ship's captain (Max von Sydow), and his servant (Jorge Luke). *Foxtrot* centers on the wastes of the leisure class even in a time of war. Rated R for sex, nudity, and violence. 91m. **DIR:** Arturo Ripstein. **CAST:** Peter O'Toole, Charlotte Rampling, Max von Sydow, Jorge Luke, Helena Rojo, Claudio Brook. **1975**

FOXY BROWN ★★ Pam Grier takes on the mobsters who butchered her boyfriend. Grier and Jack Hill—the man who directed her in several Filipino sexploitation prison flicks—are reteamed for this wildly sadistic urban-crime melodrama. A richly deserved R rating. 94m. **DIR:** Jack Hill. **CAST:** Pam Grier, Peter Brown, Terry Carter. **1974**

•FRAILTY ★★★ A troubled young man (Matthew McConaughey) goes to the FBI with a strange story about a notorious serial killer, who he says is his brother. Well-acted and creepy, expertly directed by Bill Paxton (who plays McConaughey's demented father in flashbacks), the film is marred only by a far-fetched ending that's also a bit of a cop-out. Rated R for violence and profanity. 100m. **DIR:** Bill Paxton. **CAST:** Bill Paxton, Matthew McConaughey, Powers Boothe, Matthew O'Leary, Jeremy Sumpter. **2001 DVD**

FRAME BY FRAME ★★★ Michael Biehn and Marg Helgenberger stand out in this made-for-cable crime-thriller. They play undercover cops Stash and Ekberg, devoted to their jobs and each other. When Stash's wife is brutally murdered in a mob-style hit, all evidence points back to them. Now the two cops are the chief suspects in the murder, and it doesn't take long for them to suspect each other as well. Rated R for violence, profanity, and adult situations. 97m. **DIR:** Douglas Barr. **CAST:** Michael Biehn, Marg Helgenberger. **1995**

FRAME UP ★★ A watchable mishmash about a sheriff's investigation of a boy's murder. Rated R for rape scenes and language. 90m. **DIR:** Paul Leder. **CAST:** Wings Hauser, Bobby DiCicco, Frances Fisher. **1990**

FRAMED (1930) ★★★ Atmospheric melodrama that makes the most of lighting, shadows, and sexy situations. The story is your basic melodrama: girl wants revenge on the man who shot her father but falls for the killer's son instead. One of the first gangster melodramas of the 1930s. B&W; 71m. **DIR:** George Archainbaud. **CAST:** Evelyn Brent, Regis Toomey, Ralf Haralde. **1930**

FRAMED (1975) 🦃 Thoroughly nauseating and graphically violent story of a man framed for a crime he did not commit. Rated R for gory violence and language. 106m. **DIR:** Phil Karlson. **CAST:** Joe Don Baker, Conny Van Dyke, Gabriel Dell, Brock Peters, John Marley. **1975**

FRAMED (1990) ★★★ This wry little caper comedy plunges Jeff Goldblum, as a talented art forger, into the realm of bewilderment and uncertainty he occupied so well with *Into the Night*. Gary Rosen's script goes for chuckles rather than belly laughs, but the tricky finale will be enjoyed by those who appreciate the genre. Not rated, with mild profanity and sexual situations. 90m. **DIR:** Dean Parisot. **CAST:** Jeff Goldblum, Kristin Scott Thomas, Todd Graff, Michael Lerner, James Hong. **1990**

FRANCES ★★★★1/2 This chilling, poignant motion picture explains why Frances Farmer was never allowed to reign as a star in Hollywood. Jessica Lange is superb as the starlet who snubs the power structure and pays a horrifying price for it. Kim Stanley is also impressive as Frances's mother, a money- and fame-hungry hag who uses her daughter. Sam Shepard is the one person who loves Frances for who she really is. An unforgettable film. Rated R. 139m. **DIR:** Graeme Clifford. **CAST:** Jessica Lange, Kim Stanley, Sam Shepard, Jeffrey DeMunn. **1982 DVD**

FRANCESCO ★★★ Mickey Rourke may seem an odd choice to play a monk, but playing against type is what makes his performance as the real-life Francesco so believable. Set in Italy during the thirteenth century, the film chronicles the spiritual awakening of Francesco, the decadent son of a wealthy merchant who abandons his past and sets forth to help the poor and needy of his town. Shot on location, the film features an appealing supporting cast who help bring this remarkable story to life. Rated PG-13 for adult situations. 105m. **DIR:** Liliana Cavani. **CAST:** Mickey Rourke, Helena Bonham Carter, Andrea Ferreol, Hanns Zischler. **1989 DVD**

FRANCIS GARY POWERS: THE TRUE STORY OF THE U-2 SPY INCIDENT ★★★1/2 In this made-for-television movie, the infamous 1960 U-2 spy plane shot down over Russia is dramatized. The best performances in this true story are supplied by the supporting cast. Based on U-2 pilot Francis Gary Powers's book, it's worth viewing. 120m. **DIR:** Delbert Mann. **CAST:** Lee Majors, Noah Beery Jr., Nehemiah Persoff, Brooke Bundy, William Daniels, James Gregory, Lew Ayres. **1976**

FRANCIS GOES TO THE RACES ★★★ Francis the talking mule teaches another mule how to win races so he can help Donald O'Connor cope with some crooks at the track. Enjoyable in spite of a very hokey plot. B&W; 88m. **DIR:** Arthur Lubin. **CAST:** Donald O'Connor, Piper Laurie, Cecil Kellaway, Larry Keating, Jesse White. **1951**

FRANCIS IN THE HAUNTED HOUSE ★★★ Last entry in the series of seven *Francis, the Talking Mule* films. This time Mickey Rooney (replacing Donald O'Connor as the savvy mule's confidant) and Francis find themselves involved with a gang of murdering thieves in a creepy castle. When Rooney goes to the police with the mule's rendition of events, he finds himself pursued by both police and crooks. 80m. **DIR:** Charles Lamont. **CAST:** Mickey Rooney, Virginia Welles, Paul Cavanagh. **1956**

FRANCIS IN THE NAVY ★★ Sixth of the seven-picture series starring Francis, the talking mule. (Chill Wills provides his voice.) Silly, but the kids will enjoy it. B&W; 80m. **DIR:** Arthur Lubin. **CAST:** Donald O'Connor, Martha Hyer, Jim Backus, David Janssen, Clint Eastwood, Martin Milner, Paul Burke. **1955**

FRANCIS JOINS THE WACS ★★★ Chill Wills appears in person and does the voice of the talking mule. He competes with himself for laughs in a comedy that sends Francis and his human pal to the WACS by mistake. B&W; 94m. **DIR:** Arthur Lubin. **CAST:** Donald

O'Connor, Chill Wills, Mamie Van Doren, ZaSu Pitts, Lynn Bari, Julie Adams, Joan Shawlee. **1954**

FRANCIS, THE TALKING MULE ★★★1/2 First in a series from Universal, this well-known comedy tells the story of how a dimwitted student at West Point (Donald O'Connor) first met up with the famous talking mule of the title. The gags really fly as Francis proceeds to get O'Connor in all sorts of outrageous predicaments, consistently pulling him out just in the nick of time. Some screamingly funny scenes. Chill Wills (voice). Followed by six sequels. B&W; 91m. **DIR:** Arthur Lubin. **CAST:** Donald O'Connor, Patricia Medina, ZaSu Pitts, Tony Curtis, Ray Collins. **1950**

FRANCOIS TRUFFAUT: STOLEN MOMENTS ★★★ You have to have seen many of Truffaut's films to appreciate this letter-boxed homage to the late director-writer-actor. The glitterati of the French cinema came out in force to praise and dissect Truffaut, but too many assumptions were made regarding the audience's knowledge. Occasionally there is so much going on that you can barely take it all in while reading the subtitles. Interesting, but not what it could have been. Not rated; contains profanity. 93m. **DIR:** Serge Toubiana, Michel Pascal. **CAST:** Fanny Ardant, Nathalie Baye, Gérard Depardieu, Marcel Ophuls, Marie-France Pisier, Eric Rohmer, Bertrand Tavernier, Ewa Truffaut, Laura Truffaut, Madeleine Morgenstern. **1993**

FRANK & JESSE ★★★1/2 Yet another revisionist retelling of the infamous outlaws, with star-coproducer Rob Lowe turning his character (Jesse James) into a martyred hero of the Deep South. Script is outrageously politically correct, but the earnest performances will grow on you. Rated R for violence and brief nudity. 105m. **DIR:** Robert Boris. **CAST:** Rob Lowe, Bill Paxton, Randy Travis, Dana Wheeler-Nicholson, Maria Pitillo, William Atherton. **1995 DVD**

FRANK AND OLLIE ★★★★ A warmhearted documentary portrait of Frank Thomas and Ollie Johnston, two of the so-called Nine Old Men, the legendary original Disney animators. Thomas and Johnston also happen to be the best of friends and have been since they joined Disney in the 1930s. The film explores the nature of great animation and of enduring friendship. Rich humor and cartoon clips abound. Rated PG for mild profanity. 89m. **DIR:** Theodore Thomas. **CAST:** Frank Thomas, Ollie Johnston. **1995**

FRANKENSTEIN (1931) ★★★★ Despite all the padding, grease paint, and restrictive, awkward costuming, Boris Karloff gives a strong, sensitive performance in this 1931 horror classic—with only eyes and an occasional grunt to convey meaning. It still stands as one of the great screen performances. B&W; 71m. **DIR:** James Whale. **CAST:** Colin Clive, Mae Clarke, Boris Karloff, John Boles. **1931 DVD**

FRANKENSTEIN (1973) ★★1/2 Bo Svenson's sympathetic portrayal of the monster is the one saving grace of this essentially average made-for-TV retelling of Mary Wollstonecraft Shelley's horror tale. 130m. **DIR:** Glenn Jordan. **CAST:** Robert Foxworth, Susan Strasberg, Bo Svenson, Willie Aames. **1973**

FRANKENSTEIN (1984) ★★★ Solid made-for-TV adaptation of Mary Shelley's often-filmed tale. Robert Powell gives a believable performance as a young Dr. Frankenstein, whose creation (David Warner) runs amok. Fine period flavor, crisp direction, and an excellent cast headed by Warner and John Gielgud. 81m. **DIR:** James Ormerod. **CAST:** Robert Powell, David Warner, Carrie Fisher, John Gielgud, Terence Alexander, Susan Wooldridge. **1984**

FRANKENSTEIN (1992) ★★★ Taking some liberties with Mary Shelley's classic tale, this film at least portrays the creature sympathetically. Randy Quaid is the much hunted being who implores his creator (Patrick Bergin) to help him find peace in a threatening world. Lush forest footage is a plus; plot inconsistencies a minus. Made for cable; contains violence, gore, and nudity. 117m. **DIR:** David Wickes. **CAST:** Patrick Bergin, Randy Quaid, John Mills, Lambert Wilson, Fiona Gillies. **1992**

FRANKENSTEIN AND ME ★★1/2 An orphaned boy obsessed with movie monsters thinks he has found the answer to his problems when a traveling carnival comes to town, displaying what they claim is the real Frankenstein monster. Bland kiddie movie may also entertain parents who grew up with classic horror movies. Rated PG for mild violence. 91m. **DIR:** Robert Tinnell. **CAST:** Jamieson Boulanger, Burt Reynolds, Louise Fletcher. **1996**

FRANKENSTEIN AND THE MONSTER FROM HELL ★★ The release of Hammer Films veteran Terence Fisher's final directorial effort would be a major event, but for one thing: this is a censored TV print, not the R-rated original. But the out-of-print Japanese Laserdisc merits three stars. 93m. **DIR:** Terence Fisher. **CAST:** Peter Cushing, Shane Briant, Madeleine Smith, Dave Prowse, Patrick Troughton, Bernard Lee. **1974**

FRANKENSTEIN CREATED WOMAN ★★★ The doctor captures the spirit of a man through a new technique he has discovered and places it into the body of beautiful Susan Denberg. It's not long before Denberg is out and about killing people. High production values and a superb cast help an otherwise mediocre story line. 92m. **DIR:** Terence Fisher. **CAST:** Peter Cushing, Susan Denberg. **1967 DVD**

FRANKENSTEIN GENERAL HOSPITAL ★★ Horror fans will appreciate some of the in-jokes in this parody, set in a hospital where the original Dr. Frankenstein's great-great-grandson is at work on the usual monster. Mark Blankfield has some funny bits as Bob Frankenstein, but the rest is thin going. Rated R for nudity. 92m. **DIR:** Deborah Roberts. **CAST:** Mark Blankfield. **1988**

FRANKENSTEIN ISLAND A group of men stranded on a remote island stumble upon a colony of young women in leopard-skin bikinis. Rated PG. 89m. **DIR:** Jerry Warren. **CAST:** John Carradine, Robert Clarke, Steve Brodie, Cameron Mitchell, Andrew Duggan. **1981**

FRANKENSTEIN MEETS THE SPACE MONSTER The Frankenstein here is actually an android named Frank sent into outer space by NASA. Also known as *Mars Invades Puerto Rico*. B&W; 75m. **DIR:** Robert Gaffney. **CAST:** James Karen, Nancy Marshall, Robert Reilly. **1965**

FRANKENSTEIN MEETS THE WOLF MAN ★★★1/2 As the title suggests, two of Universal's most famous monsters clash in this series horror film. Very atmospheric, with beautiful photography, music, set design, and special effects. Only drawback is Bela Lugosi's overblown portrayal of the Frankenstein monster. B&W;

73m. **DIR:** Roy William Neill. **CAST:** Lon Chaney Jr., Patric Knowles, Bela Lugosi, Ilona Massey, Maria Ouspenskaya. **1943**

FRANKENSTEIN 1970 Boris Karloff as the great-grandson of the famous doctor, attempting to create a monster of his own. B&W; 83m. **DIR:** Howard W. Koch. **CAST:** Boris Karloff, Tom Duggan, Jana Lund, Don Barry. **1958**

FRANKENSTEIN REBORN! ★★1/2 Unaired pilot for a potential television series called *Filmonsters* in the *Goosebumps* tradition from producer Charles Band. The cast is game and the story stays close to its source material with decent makeup effects, but the film seems confused as to whether it is set in the 1800s or present day. Rated PG for mild violence. 70m. **DIR:** Julian Breen. **CAST:** Haven Burton, Ben Gould, Jaason Simmons. **1998**

FRANKENSTEIN SINGS ★★★ Absolutely ridiculous but somehow charming musical horror film that has more in common with the "Monster Mash" than with *The Rocky Horror Picture Show*. Based on the stage play *I'm Sorry but the Bridge Is Out, You'll Have to Spend the Night* by Sheldon Allman and Bobby "Boris" Pickett. Directors Cohen and Sokolow were also partially responsible for Disney's *Toy Story*. Rated PG. 83m. **DIR:** Joel Cohen, Alec Sokolow. **CAST:** Candace Cameron, Ian Bohen, Sarah Douglas, John Kassir, Bobby Pickett, Jimmie Walker. **1995**

FRANKENSTEIN UNBOUND ★★1/2 Director Roger Corman makes his comeback with this twisted retelling of the Frankenstein legend in which a scientist from the year 2031 is sucked back in time and meets up with author Mary Godwin (soon to be Mary Shelley), as well as the infamous Dr. Victor Frankenstein. Rated R for violence and gore. 90m. **DIR:** Roger Corman. **CAST:** John Hurt, Raul Julia, Bridget Fonda, Jason Patric. **1990**

FRANKENSTEIN'S DAUGHTER The makeup is ridiculous, the sets are cheap, and the performers need to be oiled. B&W; 85m. **DIR:** Richard Cunha. **CAST:** John Ashley, Sandra Knight, Donald Murphy, Harold Lloyd Jr. **1958 DVD**

FRANKENWEENIE ★★★★ Young Barret Oliver brings his dog Sparky back to life. Director Tim Burton's first live-action short subject, made during his tenure at Walt Disney Studios, reworks the classic Mary Shelley tale of life after death into an affectionate tribute to the style of James Whale. Exquisite! Rated PG. 28m. **DIR:** Tim Burton. **CAST:** Daniel Stern, Shelley Duvall, Joseph Maher, Barret Oliver. **1984**

FRANKIE AND JOHNNY (1934) Poorly acted costume drama inspired by the now-legendary love-triangle song. B&W; 66m. **DIR:** Chester Erskine. **CAST:** Helen Morgan, Chester Morris, Lilyan Tashman. **1934**

FRANKIE AND JOHNNY (1966) ★★★ As the song goes, Elvis, as a Mississippi riverboat singer-gambler, betrays his lady (Donna Douglas) with his roving heart. He easily captures the attention of beautiful young ladies but must suffer the consequences. Elvis fans won't be disappointed. 87m. **DIR:** Frederick de Cordova. **CAST:** Elvis Presley, Donna Douglas, Sue Ane Langdon, Harry Morgan, Nancy Kovack, Audrey Christie. **1966 DVD**

FRANKIE AND JOHNNY (1991) ★★★1/2 It's the supporting characters in this angst-ridden Terrence McNally drama who make it such a treat. Set primarily in a diner, *Frankie and Johnny* offers occasionally deft and delicious servings of one-liners; but Al Pacino and Michelle Pfeiffer are somehow not quite right in their roles as unlikely lovers. Rated R for profanity and nudity. 117m. **DIR:** Garry Marshall. **CAST:** Al Pacino, Michelle Pfeiffer, Hector Elizondo, Kate Nelligan, Nathan Lane, Jane Morris. **1991 DVD**

FRANKIE STARLIGHT ★★★★ In this gentle Irish import, Anne Parillaud is the French emigré who flees her native country after World War II, only to find she never quite fits into her new life. Corban Walker shines in the title role of an adult dwarf writing the story of his unusual mother. Rated R for profanity, brief nudity, and sexual situations. 100m. **DIR:** Michael Lindsay-Hogg. **CAST:** Anne Parillaud, Matt Dillon, Gabriel Byrne, Corban Walker, Alan Pentony, Rudi Davis, Georgina Cates. **1995**

FRANTIC ★★★1/2 Director Roman Polanski bounces back with this clever and often darkly funny Hitchcockian thriller, which makes Harrison Ford a stranger in the very strange underbelly of Paris. He's a surgeon visiting the city to lecture at a medical conference; when his wife (Betty Buckley) vanishes from their hotel room, he confronts indifference through official channels before trying to puzzle things out on his own. Inexplicably rated R for minimal violence. 120m. **DIR:** Roman Polanski. **CAST:** Harrison Ford, Emmanuelle Seigner, Betty Buckley, John Mahoney, David Huddleston. **1988 DVD**

FRANZ Leon falls in love with a woman named Leonie. He is tortured by his oppressive mother and his war memories. In French with English subtitles. 88m. **DIR:** Jacques Brel. **CAST:** Jacques Brel. **1972**

FRASIER THE LOVABLE LION (FRASIER THE SENSUOUS LION) ★★1/2 Cute film about a zoology professor who discovers he can talk with Frasier, the oversexed lion at the Lion Country Safari Theme Park in Irvine, California. It is a children's film, even though the subject matter does border on being adult. 97m. **DIR:** Pat Shields. **CAST:** Michael Callan, Katherine Justice. **1973**

FRATERNITY VACATION A teen-lust comedy with no laughs, no imagination, and no point. Rated R for profanity and nudity. 95m. **DIR:** James Frawley. **CAST:** Stephen Geoffreys, Sheree Wilson, Cameron Dye, Leigh McCloskey. **1985 DVD**

FRAUDS ★★1/2 Demented insurance-investigator Phil Collins turns a young couple's claim into a deadly game of cat and mouse. Teetering between black comedy and chills, this is an artistic jumble, though its very weirdness gives it a curious appeal. The plot slips past the realm of plausibility in the final act. Rated R for violence and profanity. 94m. **DIR:** Stephan Elliott. **CAST:** Phil Collins, Hugo Weaving, Josephine Byrnes. **1992**

FREAK CITY ★★★1/2 Natalie Cole shines in this drama, as one of several disabled or disturbed residents in a care facility that becomes a new home for a bitter young woman (Samantha Mathis) confined to a wheelchair. The parts are somewhat stereotyped—Jonathan Silverman as a blind man unwilling to stand up to his domineering mother, Marlee Matlin as a developmentally disabled woman who nonetheless remains spirited and cheerful—but the execution is warm and engaging; Jane Shepard's script carefully maintains the dignity of all these characters. But Cole owns the film, as a former singer who has retreated from reality; a scene wherein she emerges from her shell and croons one ballad is a throat-catching grabber. Rated R for profanity. 104m. **DIR:** Lynne Littman. **CAST:** Natalie Cole, Samantha Mathis, Marlee Matlin, Peter Sarsgaard, Jonathan Silverman, Estelle Parsons. **1999**

FREAKED ★★★1/2 Hilariously demented comedy about a sideshow proprietor who uses toxic waste to create custom-made freaks. Like *Gremlins* made by the *Airplane!* team with an MTV-rude attitude: loud, fast, gross, and obnoxious—and we mean that in a good way. Rated R for profanity and general tastelessness. 80m. **DIR:** Alex Winter, Tom Stern. **CAST:** Alex Winter, Randy Quaid, Bill Sadler, Megan Ward, Mr. T, Bob Goldthwait, Brooke Shields. **1993**

FREAKMAKER ★★ Retitled video version of a badly washed-out print of the British horror shocker, *Mutations.* Mad doctor Donald Pleasence botches one experiment in genetics after another. This wildly sadistic movie is buoyed by its own tastelessness, which includes exploiting some real sideshow performers in a way Tod Browning never imagined. Rated R. 92m. **DIR:** Jack Cardiff. **CAST:** Donald Pleasence, Tom Baker, Michael Dunn. **1973**

FREAKS ★★★★ This legendary "horror" movie by Tod Browning is perhaps the most unusual film ever made and certainly one of the most unsettling. Based on Tod Robbins's *Spurs*, this is the story of a circus midget who falls in love with a statuesque trapeze artist and nearly becomes her victim as she attempts to poison him for his money. Incensed by her betrayal of their little friend, the armless, legless, pinheaded "freaks" exact their revenge. B&W; 64m. **DIR:** Tod Browning. **CAST:** Wallace Ford, Leila Hyams, Olga Baclanova, Roscoe Ates. **1932 DVD**

FREAKSHOW 🦃 Z-grade anthology boasts five terror tales narrated by the "Freakmaster" (Gunnar Hansen), and the lowest production values this side of a student film. Rated R for violence, sexual situations, and strong language. 102m. **DIR:** William Cooke, Paul Talbot. **CAST:** Gunnar Hansen, Shannon Michelle Parsons, Brian D. Kelly, Jennifer Peluso, Gene Aimone, Josh Craig. **1995 DVD**

FREAKY FRIDAY ★★★1/2 One of Disney's better comedies from the 1970s, this perceptive fantasy allows mom Barbara Harris and daughter Jodie Foster to share a role-reversing out-of-body experience. Adapted with wit by Mary Rodgers from her own book. Rated G. 95m. **DIR:** Gary Nelson. **CAST:** Jodie Foster, Barbara Harris, John Astin, Ruth Buzzi, Kaye Ballard. **1977**

FREDDIE AS F.R.O.7 ★★1/2 The British fascination with secret agents and magical kingdoms has been fused somewhat awkwardly in this kiddies-only animated film. The cast supplying voices is impressive, however, with Ben Kingsley, Billie Whitelaw, Michael Hordern, and Jonathan Pryce among the participants. Rated G. 90m. **DIR:** Jon Acevski. **1992**

•FREDDY GOT FINGERED 🦃 MTV personality Tom Green (who makes Pauly Shore look like Buster Keaton) plays a would-be cartoonist in this rock-bottom stinker; his humor is coarse, tasteless, and not funny for a second. Rated R for profanity and crude sexual humor. 87m. **DIR:** Tom Green. **CAST:** Tom Green, Rip Torn, Marisa Coughlan, Julie Hagerty, Anthony Michael Hall, Drew Barrymore. **2001 DVD**

FREDDY'S DEAD: THE FINAL NIGHTMARE ★★★ In what has been promised as the last in the *Nightmare on Elm Street* series of films, the audience gets just what is expected. A new batch of teenagers is served up for slaughter, only this time they are led by an adult who just happens to be Freddy Krueger's daughter. The finale was in 3-D in the theaters and something is lost in the video transfer. Rated R for violence and profanity. 96m. **DIR:** Rachel Talalay. **CAST:** Robert Englund, Lisa Zane, Yaphet Kotto. **1991 DVD**

FREE AND EASY ★★★ Buster Keaton's first sound movie has him chaperoning a beauty pageant winner to Hollywood, and stumbling into the movies himself. A good transition from silents to talkies for this wonderful clown. B&W; 92m. **DIR:** Edward Sedgwick. **CAST:** Buster Keaton, Anita Page, Robert Montgomery, Dorothy Sebastian. **1930**

FREE ENTERPRISE ★★★ Wonderfully engaging romp about two wannabe filmmakers who literally worship the ground that William Shatner walks on. When they get a chance to meet their hero, their lives are dramatically changed. Told with its tongue definitely in cheek, director Robert Meyer Burnett's comedy is filled with enough hip commentary and references to please most fans of the genre. Eric McCormack and Rafer Weigel are hilarious as the two fans who find that there is life after *Star Trek*. Rated R for adult situations, language, and nudity. 114m. **DIR:** Robert Meyer Burnett. **CAST:** William Shatner, Eric McCormack, Audie England, Rafer Weigel, Patrick Van Horn. **1998 DVD**

FREE MONEY ★★★★ Outrageously campy and quirky comedy will leave you gasping for breath in mirth and amazement. Marlon Brando stars as the crooked sheriff, Mira Sorvino as the FBI agent who's out to put him behind bars, and Charlie Sheen and Thomas Haden Church as his two luckless sons-in-law. Rated R for profanity and sexuality. 91m. **DIR:** Yves Simoneau. **CAST:** Marlon Brando, Donald Sutherland, Thomas Haden Church, Mira Sorvino, Charlie Sheen, David Arquette. **1998 DVD**

FREE OF EDEN ★★★1/2 A young woman growing up in Brooklyn decides to get an education and rise above the poverty and dead-end fate for which she's destined. She convinces a former teacher—now a high-powered, cutthroat executive—to tutor her, and both teacher and pupil learn more than they expected. Only a few contrived scenes mar this fascinating made-for-cable original. Not rated; contains profanity and violence. 98m. **DIR:** Leon Ichaso. **CAST:** Sidney Poitier, Phylicia Rashad, Robert Hooks, Sydney Tamiia Poitier. **1998**

FREE RIDE ★★ Disjointed rip-off of *Animal House*, with Gary Herschberger playing a supercool professional student, and Reed Rudy as his bunkie. Fitfully funny. Rated R for language and nudity. 92m. **DIR:** Tom Trbovich. **CAST:** Gary Herschberger, Reed Rudy, Dawn Schneider, Peter DeLuise, Warren Berlinger, Mamie Van Doren, Frank Campanella. **1986**

FREE SOUL, A ★★1/2 Primarily a showcase for Lionel Barrymore, who won an Oscar for his role of a cantankerous attorney. The character is based on Adela Rogers St. John's father, a lawyer known for his colorful but irascible ways. Remade as *The Girl Who Had Every-*

thing. With Elizabeth Taylor. B&W; 89m. **DIR:** Clarence Brown. **CAST:** Clark Gable, Lionel Barrymore, Norma Shearer, Leslie Howard, James Gleason. **1931**

FREE, WHITE, AND 21 ★★ A southern black man is accused of raping a white woman who is working for the civil rights movement. The main attraction of this dated movie is that it is made in a pseudodocumentary style—as a trial during which the testimony is shown in the form of flashbacks. Interesting, though very overlong. B&W; 102m. **DIR:** Larry Buchanan. **CAST:** Frederick O'Neal, Annalena Lund. **1963**

FREE WILLY ★★★★ Family entertainment about a friendship between a troubled boy and an endangered killer whale has a true dramatic edge. Strong character development and a staunch avoidance of clichés make this a treat for the entire family. Rated PG for brief profanity. 112m. **DIR:** Simon Wincer. **CAST:** Jason James Richter, Lori Petty, Jayne Atkinson, August Schellengberg, Michael Madsen, Michael Ironside, Richard Riehle. **1993 DVD**

FREE WILLY 2: THE ADVENTURE HOME ★★★ Willy the whale—with a new animatronic double and stock footage replacing original star Keiko—returns for another wild, wet adventure that tests his friendship with the teen orphan Jesse. The two pals and their families meet and frolic in the Pacific Northwest before an offshore oil spill cuts short their happy reunion and leads to several tight scrapes. Rated PG. 96m. **DIR:** Dwight H. Little. **CAST:** Jason James Richter, Michael Madsen, August Schellengberg, Francis Capra, Jayne Atkinson, Mary Kate Schellhardt. **1995**

FREE WILLY 3: THE RESCUE ★★★ The majestic whale's buddy from previous Willy films returns as a research tech. His team must determine why whale populations are decreasing. Befriending the young son of an illegal whaler, the duo determines to thwart the threat to Willy's pod. Parents should be prepared to discuss the film parents' lawlessness and appropriate consequences for their actions. Great underwater photography. Rated PG for violence. 85m. **DIR:** Sam Pillsbury. **CAST:** Jason James Richter, August Schellengberg, Annie Corley, Vincent Berry, Patrick Kilpatrick. **1997**

FREEBIE AND THE BEAN ★★★ Before astounding filmgoers with the outrageous black comedy *The Stunt Man*, director Richard Rush twisted the cop genre around with this watchable (but not spectacular) release. James Caan and Alan Arkin play San Francisco detectives who wreak havoc while on the trail of gangster Jack Kruschen. Rated R. 113m. **DIR:** Richard Rush. **CAST:** Alan Arkin, James Caan, Valerie Harper, Loretta Swit. **1974**

FREEDOM SONG ★★★★ Powerfully emotional film about the civil rights movement. Told with sly humor and emotional intensity, *Freedom Song* focuses on the young (mostly teenagers) and is bolstered by a terrific cast and Phil Alden Robinson's usual meticulous direction. Not rated; contains profanity. 150m. **DIR:** Phil Alden Robinson. **CAST:** Danny Glover, Vondie Curtis-Hall, Vicellous Reon Shannon, Glynn Turman, Stan Shaw, Michael Jai White, David Strathairn. **2000**

FREEDOM STRIKE ★★ Formulaic action-adventure about a downed Air Force pilot helping his airborne buddies fight the Gulf War from behind enemy lines. The performances and action are as economical as the budget. Rated R for language and violence. 93m. **DIR:** Jerry P. Jacobs. **CAST:** Michael Dudikoff, Tone Loc, Felicity Waterman, Jay Anthony, Nicolas Coster. **1998 DVD**

FREEFALL ★★★1/2 Although this thriller eventually becomes too tricky for its own good, John Irvin's slick direction doesn't let you ponder apparent plot inconsistencies. Wildlife photographer Pamela Gidley goes to Africa to shoot a rare bird, and winds up involved with assassins and Interpol agents who seem convinced she has something they desire. Plot twists abound, and most of them work. Rated R for violence, nudity, and suggested sex. 96m. **DIR:** John Irvin. **CAST:** Eric Roberts, Pamela Gidley, Jeff Fahey. **1994**

FREEJACK ★★★ Technology in the year 2009, when the haves have more and the have-nots are destitute, has made it possible for the ultrarich to extend their lives—by finding a donor from the past. Emilio Estevez is the race-car driver who, after a spectacular crash, wakes up to find himself eighteen years in the future and runnng from those who want to erase his mind. It's not great, but not bad. Rated R for violence and profanity. 101m. **DIR:** Geoff Murphy. **CAST:** Emilio Estevez, Mick Jagger, René Russo, Anthony Hopkins, Jonathan Banks, David Johansen. **1992 DVD**

FREEWAY (1988) ★★★ A fad film mirroring the real-life series of freeway killings in the Los Angeles area. A nurse (Darlanne Fluegel), dissatisfied with the police investigation of the murder of her boyfriend by a freeway sniper, pursues the killer on her own. Good acting, exciting direction, and some great action sequences make up for the threadbare plot. Rated R for violence, profanity, and nudity. 95m. **DIR:** Francis Delia. **CAST:** Darlanne Fluegel, James Russo, Richard Belzer, Michael Callan. **1988**

FREEWAY (1996) 🦃 Bent, punk retelling of *Little Red Riding Hood*—which concerns a shrill teenager's clash with a serial killer—is gratuitously violent, numbingly profane, and utterly without redeeming value. Rated R for profanity, violence, drug use, and strong sexual content. 101m. **DIR:** Matthew Bright. **CAST:** Kiefer Sutherland, Reese Witherspoon, Wolfgang Bodison, Dan Hedaya, Amanda Plummer, Brooke Shields. **1996 DVD**

FREEWAY 2: CONFESSIONS OF A TRICKBABY ★★★1/2 This sequel to the cult hit *Freeway* (by the same writer-director) has nothing in common with its predecessor but the notion of updating a Brothers Grimm story to a modern setting. In this case, Hansel and Gretel are a pair of female career criminals on the run from prison and in search of Sister Gomez, a witch in a candy house. Bizarre and imaginative, with a perverse performance by Vincent Gallo as the wicked witch. Rated R for violence, profanity, sexual situations, and drug use. 97m. **DIR:** Matthew Bright. **CAST:** Natasha Lyonne, Maria Celedonio, Vincent Gallo. **1999 DVD**

FREEWAY MANIAC 🦃 Matricidal maniac escapes from an insane asylum, not once but twice. *Playboy* cartoonist Gahan Wilson wrote this turkey. 94m. **DIR:** Paul Winters. **CAST:** Loren Winters, James Courtney. **1988**

FREEZE—DIE—COME TO LIFE ★★★★ Vitaly Kanevski's gritty, uncomfortable look at the hard life in a part of the Soviet Union that's about as far from Moscow as one can get and still be in the USSR. It's the depressing, evocatively filmed story of two youngsters trying to overcome poverty and brutality in the bleak frozen terrain of the Soviet Orient. In Russian with English subtitles. Not rated. 105m. **DIR:** Vitaly Kanevski. **1990**

FREEZE FRAME ★★1/2 This totally unbelievable tale of how a team of would-be high school reporters expose corporate corruption is just the right confection for younger, after-school viewers. The idea comes across loud and clear: it's okay to be a smart young woman. Not rated, but with mild violence. 78m. **DIR:** William Bindley. **CAST:** Shannen Doherty, Charles Haid, Robyn Douglass, Seth Michaels. **1992**

FRENCH CAN CAN ★★★ Jean Renoir's rich cinematic style is evident in this comedy-drama starring Jean Gabin as a nightclub owner. Renoir tosses his can-can artists at the viewer, seducing us with the consuming spectacle. In French with English subtitles. 93m. **DIR:** Jean Renoir. **CAST:** Jean Gabin. **1955**

FRENCH CONNECTION, THE ★★★★★ Gene Hackman is an unorthodox New York narcotics cop in this Oscar-winning performance. He and his partner (Roy Scheider) are investigating the flow of heroin coming into the city from France. The climactic chase is the best in movie history. Rated R. 104m. **DIR:** William Friedkin. **CAST:** Gene Hackman, Fernando Rey, Roy Scheider, Eddie Egan, Sonny Grosso. **1971 DVD**

FRENCH CONNECTION II, THE ★★ Disappointing sequel to the 1971 winner for best picture has none of the thrills, chills, and action of the original. Instead, New York detective Popeye Doyle (Gene Hackman), who has journeyed to Paris to track the drug trafficker who eluded him in the States, finds himself addicted to heroin and suffering withdrawal. He isn't the only one who suffers.... There's the viewer, too. Rated R. 119m. **DIR:** John Frankenheimer. **CAST:** Gene Hackman, Fernando Rey, Bernard Fresson, Jean-Pierre Castaldi, Charles Milot. **1975**

FRENCH DETECTIVE, THE ★★★★ Suspenseful police drama featuring Lino Ventura as a tough, independent veteran cop who pursues a hood working for a corrupt politician. Solid performances by Ventura and Patrick Dewaere. In French with English subtitles. 93m. **DIR:** Pierre Granier-Deferre. **CAST:** Lino Ventura, Patrick Dewaere, Victor Lanoux, Jacques Serres. **1975**

FRENCH EXIT ★★★★ Entertaining and charismatic love story about two competing screenwriters who fall in love despite the fact they're complete opposites and are often fighting over the same job. Rated R for profanity. 88m. **DIR:** Daphina Kastner. **CAST:** Jonathan Silverman, Madchen Amick, Molly Hagan, Vince Grant, Craig Vincent. **1996**

FRENCH KISS ★★★1/2 When her fiancé falls in love during a business trip to Paris and cancels their wedding plans, jilted Meg Ryan decides to fly from Canada to France and win him back. Along the way, she meets French jewel thief Kevin Kline, who, for reasons unknown to her, can't seem to let her out of his sight. Fans of the stars will enjoy this frothy romp. Rated PG-13 for profanity and suggested sex. 111m. **DIR:** Lawrence Kasdan. **CAST:** Meg Ryan, Kevin Kline, Timothy Hutton, Jean Reno, François Cluzet, Susan Anbeh. **1995 DVD**

FRENCH LESSONS ★★★1/2 Romantic comedy about an English teenager who goes to Paris to study French for the summer. She is determined to fall in love and learns more out of the classroom than in. Rated PG. 90m. **DIR:** Brian Gilbert. **CAST:** Jane Snowden, Diana Blackburn, Françoise Brion. **1986**

FRENCH LIEUTENANT'S WOMAN, THE ★★★★★ A brilliant adaptation of John Fowles' bestseller, starring Meryl Streep as the enigmatic title heroine and Jeremy Irons as her obsessed lover. Victorian and modern attitudes on love are contrasted in this intellectually and emotionally engrossing film. Rated R because of sexual references and sex scenes. 123m. **DIR:** Karel Reisz. **CAST:** Meryl Streep, Jeremy Irons, Leo McKern, Hilton McRae, Emily Morgan. **1981 DVD**

FRENCH LINE, THE ★★ This is a dull musical with forgettable songs. Ultrarich heroine Jane Russell can't find true love. She masquerades as a fashion model during a voyage, hoping her money won't show while she snags a man. Despite presenting Miss Russell in 3-D, the film was a bust. 102m. **DIR:** Lloyd Bacon. **CAST:** Jane Russell, Gilbert Roland, Mary McCarty, Craig Stevens, Steven Geray, Arthur Hunnicutt. **1954**

FRENCH POSTCARDS ★★★1/2 This film benefits from the skillful supporting performances by two noted French film stars, Marie-France Pisier and Jean Rochefort. The younger set of characters are well played by David Marshall Grant, Miles Chapin, Valerie Quennessen, and Blanche Baker. *French Postcards* is an enjoyable way to spend a couple of hours. Rated PG. 92m. **DIR:** Willard Huyck. **CAST:** David Marshall Grant, Blanche Baker, Miles Chapin, Debra Winger, Marie-France Pisier, Valerie Quennessen, Jean Rochefort. **1979**

FRENCH QUARTER ★★1/2 Everyone in the cast plays two characters, one in modern times and one at the turn of the century, in this drama set in New Orleans. Both stories are connected by voodoo magic, as a woman discovers she is the reincarnation of a prostitute. Slow-moving but intriguing. Rated R for sexual situations. 101m. **DIR:** Dennis Kane. **CAST:** Bruce Davison, Virginia Mayo. **1977**

FRENCH SILK ★★ Cheesy world of lingerie modeling is platform for a hack made-for-television thriller about a CEO of a lingerie company (Susan Lucci) who is framed for murder. Shari Belafonte plays a supermodel who holds the key to the mystery. Rated PG-13 for adult situations. 90m. **DIR:** Noel Nosseck. **CAST:** Susan Lucci, Lee Horsley, Shari Belafonte, Jim Metzler. **1993**

FRENCH TWIST ★★1/2 A good-hearted lesbian (director Josiane Balasko) disrupts the lives of a not-so-happily-married couple in this earnest but clumsy sex farce. The three stars try hard, but their characters are selfish, unsympathetic dolts, and there's not much they can do to redeem them. In French with English subtitles. Rated R for nudity and mature content. 107m. **DIR:** Josiane Balasko. **CAST:** Josiane Balasko, Victoria Abril, Alain Chabat. **1995**

FRENCH WAY, THE ★★ Famed burlesque dancer Josephine Baker appears as a café singer in this underdressed comedy about a boy and a girl who want to marry but can't. Baker begins to do her famous feather dance, but the ending is edited out. In French with English subtitles. B&W; 73m. **DIR:** Jacques De Baroncelli. **CAST:** Josephine Baker, Micheline Presle, Georges Marshall. **1952**

FRENCH WOMAN, THE ★★ Laughable erotic thriller loosely based on the bestselling memoirs of Madame Claude, who operated a "modeling agency" of high-priced hookers. Rated R for nudity. 97m. **DIR:** Just Jaeckin. **CAST:** Françoise Fabian, Murray Head, Dayle Haddon, Klaus Kinski, Robert Webber. **1977**

FRENCHMAN'S FARM ★★1/2 A fairly tame Australian import about a female law student who has a psychic experience and witnesses a murder that took place forty years earlier. Some good suspense, but the psychic-encounter scene is overdone. Rated R for language and violence. 86m. **DIR:** Ron Way. **CAST:** Tracy Tainsh, Ray Barrett, Norman Kaye, John Meillon. **1986**

FRENZY ★★★★1/2 Marks a grand return to one of Hitchcock's favorite themes: that of a man accused of a murder he did not commit and all but trapped by the circumstantial evidence. Rated R. 116m. **DIR:** Alfred Hitchcock. **CAST:** Jon Finch, Barry Foster, Barbara Leigh-Hunt, Anna Massey, Alec McCowen. **1972 DVD**

FREQUENCY ★★★1/2 The beguiling premise behind this clever sci-fi yarn concerns a modern-day cop who would give anything to undo the past, particularly the chain of events that resulted in his father's death thirty years earlier. Thanks to a ham radio and "the mother of all sunspots," the two men are able to communicate with each other, across the barrier of time; both discover that things *can* be changed, although not always for the better. The result is a clever "What if?" tale, well worth your time. Rated PG-13 for violence and mild profanity. 118m. **DIR:** Gregory Hoblit. **CAST:** Dennis Quaid, Jim Caviezel, Andre Braugher, Elizabeth Mitchell, Noah Emmerich. **2000 DVD**

FRESH ★★★★ A 12-year-old Brooklyn dope runner named Fresh attempts to rescue his sister from the squalor of addiction and avenge a school friend's death. This harrowing urban drama about survival and redemption in inner-city America plays like a coiled spring that could snap at any moment. Rated R for language and violence. 110m. **DIR:** Boaz Yakin. **CAST:** Sean Nelson, Samuel L. Jackson, Giancarlo Esposito, N'Bushe Wright. **1994 DVD**

FRESH HORSES ★★ Adult version of *Pretty in Pink*. Molly Ringwald continues as the kid from the wrong side of the tracks, only this time there's nothing upbeat about her. Andrew McCarthy is once again typecast as a middle-class nice guy. Rated PG-13 for profanity and violence. 106m. **DIR:** David Anspaugh. **CAST:** Molly Ringwald, Andrew McCarthy, Patti D'Arbanville. **1988**

FRESHMAN, THE ★★★★ This offbeat comedy stars Matthew Broderick as a film student who gets a job with an Italian-American importer who looks suspiciously like Don Corleone. Marlon Brando gets a wonderful opportunity to parody his Oscar-winning *Godfather* performance. Brando and Broderick are superb. Rated PG. 102m. **DIR:** Andrew Bergman. **CAST:** Marlon Brando, Matthew Broderick, Bruno Kirby, Penelope Ann Miller, Maximilian Schell. **1990 DVD**

FRESHMAN, THE ★★★★ If you've never seen the great silent comedian Harold Lloyd, here's the place to start. In this entertaining film, he plays a college freshman who will do anything to become popular. B&W; 76m. **DIR:** Sam Taylor, Fred Newmeyer. **CAST:** Harold Lloyd, Jobyna Ralston. **1925**

FRIDA ★★ Tedious, disjointed account of the life of Mexican painter Frida Kahlo, considered to be the most important woman artist of the twentieth century. The film desperately fails to give any insight into the artist's life, which was laced with human tragedy and self-obsession. In Spanish with English subtitles. Not rated; contains mild nudity. 108m. **DIR:** Paul Leduc. **CAST:** Ofelia Medina. **1984**

FRIDAY ★★ This uneven comedy is about a day of stoop life in south central Los Angeles. The film has an appealing low-key tone, ends with an antigun message, and introduces some oddball neighborhood characters. Rated R for language, drug use, and violence. 101m. **DIR:** F. Gary Gray. **CAST:** Ice Cube, Chris Tucker, Nia Long, Tiny Lester, Bernie Mac, John Witherspoon, Regina King. **1995 DVD**

FRIDAY FOSTER ★★1/2 In this blaxploitation effort, Pam Grier plays the title character, a fashion photographer who doubles as a two-fisted avenger—this time taking on antiblack terrorists. A strong supporting cast helps. Rated R. 90m. **DIR:** Arthur Marks. **CAST:** Pam Grier, Julius W. Harris, Thalmus Rasulala, Carl Weathers, Eartha Kitt, Godfrey Cambridge, Yaphet Kotto. **1975**

FRIDAY THE 13TH ★★★ The original slasher flick. A group of Crystal Lake camp counselors are systematically murdered by a maniac. Not much of a plot, just the killer hacking and slashing his way through the dwindling counselor population. Fine makeup effects by master Tom Savini highlight this spatterfest that has fostered many imitations and a series of eight Jason Voorhees slice-and-dicers. Rated R for gore. 95m. **DIR:** Sean S. Cunningham. **CAST:** Betsy Palmer, Adrienne King, Harry Crosby, Kevin Bacon. **1980 DVD**

FRIDAY THE 13TH, PART II ★★ This sequel to the box-office hit of the same name is essentially the *Psycho* shower scene repeated *ad nauseam*. A group of young people are methodically sliced and diced by Jason, the masked maniac. Though the makeup effects in this rehash were reportedly toned down, there is still enough blood for gore hounds. Rated R for gruesomeness, no matter how toned-down. 87m. **DIR:** Steve Miner. **CAST:** Amy Steel, John Furey, Adrienne King, Betsy Palmer. **1981 DVD**

FRIDAY THE 13TH, PART III ★★ More gruesome ax, knife, and meat-cleaver murders occur at sunny Crystal Lake. Works the same as the first two, though for the theatrical release it had the hook of being in 3-D. The video isn't in 3-D, so Jason is just his old two-dimensional self hacking and hewing his way through another unlucky group of campers. Won't they ever learn? Rated R for obvious reasons. 96m. **DIR:** Steve Miner. **CAST:** Dana Kimmel, Paul Kratka. **1982**

FRIDAY THE 13TH, PART V—A NEW BEGINNING Well, they did it. The producers promised *Friday the 13th—The Final Chapter* would be the last of its kind. They lied. Rated R for graphic violence and simulated sex. 92m. **DIR:** Danny Steinmann. **CAST:** John Shepherd, Melanie Kinnaman, Richard Young. **1985**

FRIDAY THE 13TH, PART VI: JASON LIVES ★★★ It may be hard to believe, but this fifth sequel to the unmemorable *Friday the 13th* is actually better than all those that preceded it. Of course this thing is loaded with violence, but it is also nicely buffered by good comedy bits and one-liners. Rated R for language and violence. 85m. **DIR:** Tom McLoughlin. **CAST:** Thom Mathews, Jennifer Cooke. **1986**

FRIDAY THE 13TH, PART VII: THE NEW BLOOD ★★1/2 Jason returns, only this time someone's waiting for him: a mentally disturbed teenage girl with telekinetic powers. The result is a bloodbath as the two battle to decide who will star in Part VIII. A decent sequel with a little less gore than usual. Rated R for violence, language, and nudity. 90m. **DIR:** John Carl Buechler. **CAST:** Lar Park Lincoln, Terry Kiser. **1988**

FRIDAY THE 13TH, PART VIII: JASON TAKES MANHATTAN ★★ Fans of the series may be disappointed with the lack of blood in this seventh sequel. Jason torments a group of teenagers aboard a cruise ship and then takes to the streets of the Big Apple. Rated R for violence and profanity. 100m. **DIR:** Rob Hedden. **CAST:** Jensen Daggett, Scott Reeves, Peter Mark Richman. **1989**

FRIDAY THE 13TH—THE FINAL CHAPTER ★★★ It has been said that the only reason makeup master Tom Savini agreed to work on this film was that it gave him a chance to kill Jason, the maniacal killer whom he created in the original film. Well, Jason does die. Oh, boy! Does he ever! But not before dispatching a new group of teenagers. Savini's work is the highlight of this flick, which is really just a rehash of the first three. Rated R for extreme gruesomeness. 90m. **DIR:** Joseph Zito. **CAST:** Kimberly Beck, Corey Feldman, Peter Barton, Joan Freeman. **1984**

FRIDAY THE 13TH: THE ORPHAN 🦃 No relation to the popular slasher series, this one has a disturbed youth killing everyone around him. Rated R for violence and language. 88m. **DIR:** John Ballard. **CAST:** Mark Owens, Joanna Miles. **1979**

FRIED GREEN TOMATOES ★★★★ Adapted from Fannie Flagg's novel, *Fried Green Tomatoes at the Whistle Stop Café*, this touching motion picture is the story of friendships between two sets of women. Kathy Bates is the put-upon, overweight housewife who finds herself in the rec room of a senior citizens' home listening to Jessica Tandy's tales of the Depression-era adventures of two young women. It's wonderful. Rated PG-13 for profanity and violence. 120m. **DIR:** Jon Avnet. **CAST:** Kathy Bates, Mary Stuart Masterson, Mary-Louise Parker, Jessica Tandy, Cicely Tyson, Chris O'Donnell, Stan Shaw, Gailard Sartain, Lois Smith. **1991 DVD**

FRIEND OF THE DECEASED, A ★★★ A Ukrainian intellectual, unable to find work, hires a hitman to kill him, then changes his mind and hires another hitman to protect him from the first. Despite the low-comedy premise, this sardonic drama explores the social and emotional dislocation of life in the former Soviet Union. In Russian with English subtitles. Rated R for nudity and profanity (in subtitles). 100m. **DIR:** Vyacheslav Krishtofovich. **CAST:** Alexander Lazarev, Tatiana Krivitska, Yevgeni Pashin, Yelena Korikova, Constantin Kosyshin. **1997**

FRIENDLY FIRE ★★★★ A gripping account of an American couple who run into government indifference when they attempt to learn the truth about their son's death—by American artillery fire—in Vietnam. Based on a true story. Both Carol Burnett and Ned Beatty give smashing performances as the grieved couple. Picture won four Emmy awards. Not rated; made for TV. 180m. **DIR:** David Greene. **CAST:** Carol Burnett, Ned Beatty, Sam Waterston, Timothy Hutton. **1979**

FRIENDLY PERSUASION ★★★★ Jessamyn West's finely crafted novel of a Quaker family beset by the realities of the Civil War in southern Indiana is superbly transferred to film by an outstanding cast guided by gifted direction. 140m. **DIR:** William Wyler. **CAST:** Gary Cooper, Dorothy McGuire, Marjorie Main, Anthony Perkins, Robert Middleton, Richard Eyer. **1956 DVD**

FRIENDS ★★1/2 The friendship between three South African women is threatened when one uses terrorism against the oppressive government still ruling the country in the late 1980s. The atmosphere, chilling in the face of institutionalized racism, and strong performances nearly overcome the narrative's basic flaws. Not rated; contains profanity, violence, nudity, and sexual situations. 109m. **DIR:** Elaine Proctor. **CAST:** Kerry Fox, Dambisa Kente, Michele Burgers. **1994 DVD**

•FRIENDS AND LOVERS ★★ A group of friends goes on a weekend ski trip and spends it screaming at each other and interchanging beds. Eccentric but ultimately dull. Rated R for sexuality and profanity. 104m. **DIR:** George Haas. **CAST:** Stephen Baldwin, Claudia Schiffer, Robert Downey Jr., Danny Nucci, Alison Eastwood, Suzanne Cryer. **1999 DVD**

FRIENDS, LOVERS & LUNATICS ★★ Chaos abounds as six different relationships evolve. Everything comes to a head when the title characters all arrive at a cabin on the same weekend. Listless attempt at screwball comedy. Rated R. 87m. **DIR:** Stephen Withrow. **CAST:** Daniel Stern, Sheila McCarthy, Page Fletcher, Deborah Foreman. **1989**

FRIENDS OF EDDIE COYLE, THE ★★★★ Eddie "Fingers" Coyle (Robert Mitchum) turns to his friends for help when a prison stretch is hanging over his head, but no one in his life can really be trusted. Trying to lay aside some money for his wife while he is incarcerated, Eddie supplies guns for a gang of bank robbers and sets himself up for even more trouble. One of Mitchum's finest performances during his brief renaissance in the 1970s. Rated R for violence and profanity. 102m. **DIR:** Peter Yates. **CAST:** Robert Mitchum, Peter Boyle, Richard Jordan, Steven Keats, Alex Rocco, Joe Santos, Mitchell Ryan. **1973**

FRIENDSHIP IN VIENNA, A ★★★ So-so Disney Home Video does not do justice to its weighty subject. Two schoolgirl friends are suddenly torn apart in 1938 because one is Jewish and the other the daughter of a Hitler supporter. They vow to remain friends despite outside forces. This film lacks the sincere passion the subject demands. Not rated; contains violence. 94m. **DIR:** Arthur Allan Seidelman. **CAST:** Jenny Lewis, Kamie Harper, Edward Asner, Jane Alexander, Stephen Macht, Rosemary Forsyth. **1993**

FRIGHT NIGHT ★★★★1/2 Charley Brewster (William Ragsdale) is a fairly normal teenager save one thing: he's convinced his neighbor, Jerry Dandrige (Chris Sarandon), is a vampire—and he is! So Charley enlists the aid of former screen vampire hunter Peter Vincent (Roddy McDowall), and the result is a screamingly funny horror spoof. Rated R for nudity, profanity, and gore. 105m. **DIR:** Tom Holland. **CAST:** Chris Sarandon,

William Ragsdale, Roddy McDowall, Amanda Bearse, Stephen Geoffreys. **1985 DVD**

FRIGHT NIGHT II ★★★ Charley Brewster (William Ragsdale) is back, after undergoing some psychiatric counseling from his original *Fright Night* encounter with the vampire next door. Like its predecessor, this one takes a fang-in-cheek attitude toward horror flicks, but it isn't the certifiable spoof the original was. Rated R for profanity, violence, and brief nudity. 90m. **DIR:** Tommy Lee Wallace. **CAST:** William Ragsdale, Roddy McDowall, Traci Lynn, Julie Carmen, Jonathan Gries. **1989**

FRIGHTENERS, THE ★★★ After suffering a near-death experience, Frank Bannister finds himself caught between two worlds: the living and the dead. So, with the help of some ghostly compatriots, he sets up a scam as an exorcist and battles an evil creature haunting both worlds. Diverting. Rated R for violence and profanity. 109m. **DIR:** Peter Jackson. **CAST:** Michael J. Fox, Trini Alvarado, Peter Dobson, John Astin, Jeffrey Combs, Dee Wallace, Jake Busey, R. Lee Ermey. **1996 DVD**

FRIGHTMARE 🦃 An eccentric horror-movie star is called back from the dead. Not rated; this film contains some violence. 86m. **DIR:** Norman Thaddeus Vane. **CAST:** Luca Bercovici, Jennifer Starret, Nita Talbot. **1982**

FRINGE DWELLERS, THE ★★★★ This Australian production, which follows the domestic problems of a family of Aborigines who move from a shantytown to a proper suburban neighborhood, is an intriguing, touching, but nonsentimental look at a race of people unfamiliar to most Americans. It's rated PG for language. 98m. **DIR:** Bruce Beresford. **CAST:** Justine Saunders, Kristina Nehm, Bob Maza. **1987**

FRISCO KID, THE ★★★ Gene Wilder and Harrison Ford make a surprisingly effective and funny team as a rabbi and outlaw, respectively, making their way to San Francisco. Good fun. Rated PG. 122m. **DIR:** Robert Aldrich. **CAST:** Gene Wilder, Harrison Ford, William Smith, Ramon Bieri, Penny Peyser. **1979**

FRITZ THE CAT ★★★ This is an X-rated rendition of Robert Crumb's revolutionary feline, and it's the most outrageous cartoon ever produced. Fritz the Cat has appeared in Zap Comix and Head Comix, as well as in other underground mags. It's sometimes funny and sometimes gross, but mostly just so-so. 77m. **DIR:** Ralph Bakshi. **1972 DVD**

FROGS ★★ In this fair horror film, Ray Milland has killed frogs, so frogs come to kill his family. The whole cast dies convincingly. Rated PG. 91m. **DIR:** George McCowan. **CAST:** Ray Milland, Sam Elliott, Joan Van Ark. **1972 DVD**

FROGS FOR SNAKES ★★★ Low-echelon criminals compete for roles in a theater group run by a loan shark in a strange, seedy Manhattan neighborhood. The characters spout their favorite monologues between bouts of sex, maiming, and murder. Rated R for language, violence, nudity, and sexual content. 92m. **DIR:** Amos Poe. **CAST:** Barbara Hershey, Robbie Coltrane, Lisa Marie, Harry Hamlin, Ron Perlman, Clarence Williams, III, John Leguizamo, Debi Mazar, Ian Hart. **1999**

FROM A FAR COUNTRY ★★★ Polish biography of Pope John Paul II features a winning performance by Warren Clark and stunning location footage. Made-for-television drama spans several decades, from his days as a small boy in 1926 Poland, through the turbulent years of World War II, and finally his appointment to the Vatican. Self-serving but fascinating nonetheless. Also known as *Zdalekiego Kraju*. Not rated. 120m. **DIR:** Krzysztof Zanussi. **CAST:** Warren Clarke, Sam Neill, Robert Frazer, Lisa Harrow, Carol Gilles. **1981**

FROM BEYOND ★★★ A lecherous scientist and his assistant create a machine that stimulates a gland in the brain that allows one to see into another dimension. Then the fun begins—with better-than-average special effects, scary-looking monsters, and suspenseful horror. Made by the creators of *Re-Animator*. Rated R for graphic violence and nudity. 89m. **DIR:** Stuart Gordon. **CAST:** Jeffrey Combs, Barbara Crampton, Ken Foree. **1986**

FROM BEYOND THE GRAVE ★★★ One of the best Amicus horror anthologies, this features Peter Cushing as the owner of a curio shop, Temptations Ltd., where customers get more than they bargain for. A strong cast of character actors enlivens this fine adaptation of four R. Chetwynd-Hayes stories: "The Gate Crasher," "An Act of Kindness," "The Elemental," and "The Door." Rated PG. 97m. **DIR:** Kevin Connor. **CAST:** Peter Cushing, Margaret Leighton, Ian Bannen, David Warner, Donald Pleasence, Lesley-Anne Down, Diana Dors. **1973**

FROM DUSK TILL DAWN ★★ This vampire opus has everything—except believable characters, a coherent storyline, and a sense of style. Still, fans of the horror genre may get a kick out of what happens when a pair of bank-robbing brothers hook up with a family on vacation and end up at the nightclub from hell. Rated R for violence, gore, profanity, and nudity. 110m. **DIR:** Robert Rodriguez. **CAST:** Harvey Keitel, George Clooney, Quentin Tarantino, Juliette Lewis, Eric Liu, Fred Williamson, Richard "Cheech" Marin, Tom Savini. **1996 DVD**

FROM DUSK TILL DAWN 2: TEXAS BLOOD MONEY ★★1/2 This direct-to-video sequel lacks the bite and ferociousness of the original, and is sorely missing the on-screen presence of original stars Quentin Tarantino and George Clooney. All hell breaks loose when one of a team of bank robbers is bitten by a vampire, thus turning most of the crew into invincible blood suckers. The special effects are hit-and-miss. Rated R for violence, language, and adult situations. 88m. **DIR:** Scott Spiegel. **CAST:** Robert Patrick, Bo Hopkins, Duane Whitaker, Muse Watson, Danny Trejo, Brett Harrelson. **1999 DVD**

•FROM HELL ★★★★ This visually sumptuous horror thriller makes an excellent companion piece to *Sleepy Hollow*, with Johnny Depp starring as a tormented London police inspector whose opium habit produces (he believes) a glimpse into the depraved forces driving a serial killer dubbed Jack the Ripper, in the autumn of 1888. The fascinating, detail-laden screenplay is adapted from the equally dense Alan Moore/Eddie Campbell graphic novel, and Martin Childs's superlative production design drags the viewer through the heart of London's slums. Although frequently gruesome, this is a gorgeous example of pure cinema, and a treat for fans of razor-sharp suspense. Rated R for profanity, strong violence, sexual candor, drug use, and gore. 121m. **DIR:** Allen Hughes, Albert Hughes. **CAST:** Johnny Depp, Heather Graham, Ian Holm, Robbie Coltrane, Jason Flemyng. **2001 DVD**

FROM HELL IT CAME ★★ The murdered prince of a South Seas tribe returns as a vengeful walking tree. A so-bad-it's-good classic featuring the only monster in screen history who would lose a footrace with the Mummy. B&W; 71m. **DIR:** Dan Milner. **CAST:** Tod Andrews, Tina Carver, Linda Watkins, Gregg Palmer. **1957**

FROM HELL TO BORNEO ★★ George Montgomery owns an island. Crooks and smugglers want it. He defends it. Sweat and jungle. 96m. **DIR:** George Montgomery. **CAST:** George Montgomery, Torin Thatcher, Julie Gregg, Lisa Moreno. **1964**

FROM HELL TO VICTORY 🦃 This hokey story of a bunch of strangely allied friends during World War II has nothing to offer. Rated PG. 100m. **DIR:** Hank Milestone. **CAST:** George Peppard, George Hamilton, Capucine, Horst Buchholz, Sam Wanamaker. **1979**

FROM HERE TO ETERNITY ★★★★★ This smoldering drama, depicting the demands of military life just before America's involvement in World War II, earned the Academy Award for best picture of 1953. This riveting classic includes the historic on-the-beach love scene that turned a few heads during its time. And no wonder! Director Fred Zinnemann took chances with this realistic portrait of the U.S. military. B&W; 118m. **DIR:** Fred Zinnemann. **CAST:** Burt Lancaster, Montgomery Clift, Deborah Kerr, Frank Sinatra, Donna Reed, Ernest Borgnine. **1953 DVD**

FROM HERE TO ETERNITY ★★★ William Devane and Natalie Wood find playtime during wartime in this watchable TV remake of the 1953 movie classic. This glossy melodrama depicts army-base life and a general sense of moral chaos brought on by World War II. 110m. **DIR:** Buzz Kulik. **CAST:** Natalie Wood, William Devane, Steve Railsback, Kim Basinger. **1979**

FROM HOLLYWOOD TO DEADWOOD ★★★ Two loser detectives need to score a case or give it up. Finding a missing starlet leaving a trail of blackmail and murder may be too much for them. Offbeat mystery. Rated R for violence and language. 96m. **DIR:** Rex Pickett. **CAST:** Scott Paulin, Jim Haynie, Barbara Schock. **1989**

FROM RUSSIA WITH LOVE ★★★★1/2 The definitive James Bond movie. Sean Connery's second portrayal of Agent 007 is right on target. Lots of action, beautiful women, and great villains. Connery's fight aboard a passenger train with baddy Robert Shaw is as good as they come. 118m. **DIR:** Terence Young. **CAST:** Sean Connery, Lotte Lenya, Robert Shaw, Daniela Bianchi. **1963 DVD**

FROM THE DEAD OF NIGHT ★★1/2 After a near-death experience, Lindsay Wagner is pursued by spirits of the dead. For a made-for-TV movie, this one has some pretty scary moments—if only it didn't take so long to get to them. 190m. **DIR:** Paul Wendkos. **CAST:** Lindsay Wagner, Bruce Boxleitner, Robin Thomas, Diahann Carroll, Robert Prosky. **1989**

FROM THE EARTH TO THE MOON ★★★ Entertaining tale based on Jules Verne's story of a turn-of-the-century trip to the Moon led by Joseph Cotten and sabotaged by George Sanders. 100m. **DIR:** Byron Haskin. **CAST:** Joseph Cotten, George Sanders, Debra Paget, Don Dubbins. **1958 DVD**

FROM THE HIP ★★★ Thoroughly unrealistic but nonetheless entertaining courtroom comedy that works in spite of director Bob Clark's tendency to forget that he's no longer making *Porky's*. Judd Nelson stars as a brash young attorney. John Hurt delivers a particularly fine, high-powered performance as a ruthless egomaniac who considers himself better than the rest of humanity. Rated PG for language. 111m. **DIR:** Bob Clark. **CAST:** Judd Nelson, Elizabeth Perkins, John Hurt, Ray Walston, Darren McGavin. **1987 DVD**

FROM THE JOURNALS OF JEAN SEBERG ★★★★ Mary Beth Hurt is both sensational and heartbreaking as the celebrated actress whose immediate rise to fame and eventual downfall are chronicled in director Mark Rappaport's incisive and challenging film. Be prepared as you go behind the scenes and witness the relationship between film and those who inhabit its frames. Funny, touching, and ultimately sad. Not rated. 97m. **DIR:** Mark Rappaport. **CAST:** Mary Beth Hurt. **1995 DVD**

FROM THE LIVES OF THE MARIONETTES ★★ This Ingmar Bergman film, which details the vicious sex murder of a prostitute by an outwardly compassionate and intelligent man, is a puzzle that never really resolves itself. Nevertheless, fans will no doubt consider it another triumphant essay on the human condition. B&W; 104m. **DIR:** Ingmar Bergman. **CAST:** Robert Atzorn, Christine Buchegger, Heinz Bennent. **1980**

FROM THE MIXED-UP FILES OF MRS. BASIL E. FRANKWEILER ★★★★ Two children run away from home and hide out in the Metropolitan Museum, dodging security guards and the police. When they come across a mysterious statue, their curiosity leads them to the statue's former owner, Mrs. Basil E. Frankweiler. Now the real adventure begins in this charming and delightful film. Rated PG. 92m. **DIR:** Marcus Cole. **CAST:** Lauren Bacall, Jean Marie Barnwell, Jesse Lee. **1995 DVD**

FROM THE TERRACE ★★ Overblown denouncement of the struggle for success and the almighty dollar is just so much Technicolor trash despite the luminous presence of Paul Newman and Joanne Woodward. 144m. **DIR:** Mark Robson. **CAST:** Paul Newman, Joanne Woodward, Myrna Loy, Ina Balin, Leon Ames, Elizabeth Allen, Barbara Eden, George Grizzard, Patrick O'Neal, Felix Aylmer. **1960**

FRONT, THE ★★★★ Focusing on the horrendous blacklist of entertainers in the 1950s, this film manages to drive its point home with wit and poignance. This film is about writers who find a man to submit their scripts to after they have been blacklisted. Woody Allen plays the title role. Rated PG. 94m. **DIR:** Martin Ritt. **CAST:** Woody Allen, Zero Mostel, Andrea Marcovicci, Joshua Shelley, Georgann Johnson. **1976**

FRONT PAGE, THE ★★★1/2 Third version (of four to date) of the Ben Hecht–Charles MacArthur play is not quite as frantic as its predecessors, but retains some flavor of the era. Rated PG for profanity. 105m. **DIR:** Billy Wilder. **CAST:** Jack Lemmon, Walter Matthau, Carol Burnett, Charles Durning, Herb Edelman, Vincent Gardenia, Allen Garfield, Harold Gould, Susan Sarandon, David Wayne. **1974 DVD**

FRONT PAGE, THE ★★★★ A newspaper editor and his ace reporter do battle with civic corruption and each other in the first version of this oft-filmed hit comedy. The fast-paced, sparkling dialogue and the performances of the Warner Bros. stable of character actors have not aged after more than sixty years. This classic movie retains a great deal of charm. B&W; 99m. **DIR:** Lewis Milestone. **CAST:** Pat O'Brien, Adolphe Menjou, Mary Brian, Edward Everett Horton. **1931**

FRONTIER HORIZON ★★★ In this modern-day Western, the Three Mesquiteers ride to the rescue when a group of ranchers battle unscrupulous land grabbers. Jennifer Jones makes an early screen appearance here under the name Phyllis Isley. B&W; 56m. **DIR:** George Sherman. **CAST:** John Wayne, Ray "Crash" Corrigan, Raymond Hatton, Jennifer Jones. **1939**

FRONTIER PONY EXPRESS ★★1/2 Good action-packed Western finds Roy Rogers (in one of his early starring roles) coming to the aid of pony express riders who have been preyed on by robbers. B&W; 54m. **DIR:** Joseph Kane. **CAST:** Roy Rogers, Lynne Roberts, Raymond Hatton, Edward Keane. **1939**

FROZEN ASSETS About what you'd expect from a comedy about a sperm bank. The plot is even worse than the performances by Shelley Long and Corbin Bernsen. Rated PG-13 for profanity and sexual themes. 92m. **DIR:** George Miller. **CAST:** Corbin Bernsen, Shelley Long. **1992**

FROZEN GHOST, THE ★★ Unsurprising *Inner Sanctum* mystery in which a stage hypnotist is suspected of causing the death of a member of his audience. B&W; 61m. **DIR:** Harold Young. **CAST:** Lon Chaney Jr., Evelyn Ankers, Martin Kosleck, Milburn Stone, Elena Verdugo. **1945**

FROZEN LIMITS, THE ★★1/2 In this mediocre slapstick comedy, six British men accidently read a 40-year-old news story about a gold rush in Alaska. They pack their bags and head to the United States, only to run into trouble. Not rated, but suitable for all audiences. B&W; 82m. **DIR:** Marcel Varnel. **CAST:** Jimmy Nervo, Teddy Knox, Bud Flanagan, Chesney Allen, Charlie Naughton, Jimmy Gold, Moore Marriott. **1939**

FROZEN TERROR ★★1/2 Pretty good spaghetti horror from the son of the late horror maestro, Mario Bava. Bava *fils* unfortunately hasn't lived up to the promise displayed here. The video title (the film's original moniker was *Macabro*) refers to the unbalanced leading lady's prize possession: the head of her departed lover, stored in the refrigerator. Rated R. 91m. **DIR:** Lamberto Bava. **CAST:** Bernice Stegers. **1980**

FUGITIVE, THE (1947) ★★★ Intriguing John Ford version of Graham Greene novel is a flawed minor masterpiece. Complex story about a self-doubting priest escaping a relentless police lieutenant in Mexico where the government strives to control the Catholic church. B&W; 99m. **DIR:** John Ford. **CAST:** Henry Fonda, Dolores Del Rio, Pedro Armendariz, J. Carrol Naish, Leo Carrillo, Ward Bond, Robert Armstrong, John Qualen. **1947**

FUGITIVE, THE (TV SERIES) ★★★★ Wildly popular TV series that featured an innocent man falsely convicted of murdering his wife and sentenced to death. Escaping, he becomes both pursuer and pursued as he seeks the one-armed man he saw at the scene of the crime while evading a single-minded police lieutenant. Each episode features well-known stars. **DIR:** Richard Donner, William A. Graham, Jerry Hopper. **CAST:** David Janssen, Barry Morse, Bill Raisch, Mickey Rooney, Suzanne Pleshette, Susan Oliver, Ron Howard, Kurt Russell, John McIntire. **1963–1966**

FUGITIVE, THE: THE LAST EPISODE (TV SERIES) ★★★1/2 Dr. Richard Kimble is sentenced to death for the murder of his wife. He escapes from Indiana police lieutenant Philip Gerard and goes in search of the one-armed man he believes was the real culprit. After four outstanding seasons, the series ends in run-of-the-mill fashion when Kimble finally encounters the one-armed man. Though somewhat disappointing, this two-part episode is a must for fans. 120m. **DIR:** Don Medford. **CAST:** David Janssen, Barry Morse, Bill Raisch, Diane Brewster. **1967**

FUGITIVE, THE (1993) ★★★★★ In a riveting performance, Harrison Ford stars as Dr. Richard Kimble, an innocent man accused of murdering his wife. Tracked by the relentless U.S. Marshal Sam Girard, Kimble tries to prove his innocence by finding the one-armed man he believes committed the crime. Rated PG-13 for profanity and violence. 133m. **DIR:** Andrew Davis. **CAST:** Harrison Ford, Tommy Lee Jones, Sela Ward, Joe Pantoliano, Jeroen Krabbé, Andreas Katsulas, Daniel Roebuck. **1993 DVD**

FUGITIVE GIRLS Here's a video treasure for camp buffs—a women's prison movie written by Ed *(Plan 9 from Outer Space)* Wood! Rated R for nudity and sexual situations. 90m. **DIR:** A. C. Stephen. **CAST:** Jabee Abercrombie, Rene Bond, Edward D. Wood Jr. **1975**

FUGITIVE KIND, THE ★★ This picture takes Tennessee Williams's stage play *Orpheus Descending*, shakes it up, and lets a new story line fall out. Marlon Brando is a wanderer who woos southern belles while strumming a guitar. As one of the wooed, Joanne Woodward gives a fine performance. B&W; 135m. **DIR:** Sidney Lumet. **CAST:** Marlon Brando, Joanne Woodward, Anna Magnani, Victor Jory. **1959**

FUGITIVE RAGE ★★ Babes break out of prison to battle the mob, corrupt cops, and a secret government agency. Of course, they have time for a shower first.... Director Fred Olen Ray has done so many of these he could probably shoot them in his sleep—and this time it looks like he did. Rated R for nudity, sexual situations, violence, and profanity. 90m. **DIR:** Fred Olen Ray. **CAST:** Wendy Schumacher, Shauna O'Brien, Jay Richardson. **1996**

FUGITIVE ROAD Erich Von Stroheim as a border guard helping immigrants escape to America. 69m. **DIR:** Frank Strayer. **CAST:** Erich Von Stroheim. **1934**

FUGITIVE VALLEY ★★★ An outlaw gang led by "The Whip" terrorizes the West until the Range Busters infiltrate the outlaws and uncover several surprises, including a lady Robin Hood. B&W; 61m. **DIR:** S. Roy Luby. **CAST:** Ray "Crash" Corrigan, John King, Max Terhune, Julie Duncan, Glenn Strange. **1941**

FULFILLMENT ★★ When an impotent farmer senses his wife's attraction to his visiting brother, he suggests that she sleep with the other man to conceive the child they can't have. Self-serious made-for-TV drama, originally shown as *The Fulfillment of Mary Gray*. Not rated, the film features sexual situations. 96m. **DIR:**

Piers Haggard. **CAST:** Cheryl Ladd, Ted Levine, Lewis Smith. **1989**

FULL BODY MASSAGE ★★★ When a worldly masseuse begins working for a wealthy businesswoman, the two aren't sure their differing worlds are compatible. However, after several appointments, it becomes apparent that each has much to learn from the other. Talky yet engrossing drama is enhanced by near-perfect performances from both Rogers and Brown and taut direction by Roeg. Rated R for profanity and nudity. 93m. **DIR:** Nicolas Roeg. **CAST:** Mimi Rogers, Bryan Brown. **1995**

FULL DISCLOSURE ★★★1/2 Fred Ward delivers a hardboiled performance as newspaper reporter John McWhirter, who finds himself between a rock and a hard place. Desperate to revive his once celebrated career, McWhirter agrees to harbor a political refugee. What he doesn't know is that his guest is actually a Palestinian operative wanted by the FBI and other interested parties, including a cold and calculating hit woman. A decent, timely thriller. Rated R for language and violence. 97m. **DIR:** John Bradshaw. **CAST:** Fred Ward, Christopher Plummer, Rachel Ticotin, Kim Coates, Penelope Ann Miller, Virginia Madsen. **2000 DVD**

FULL ECLIPSE ★★★ This horror yarn never quite takes off, in spite of a clever premise. Dedicated cop Mario Van Peebles is recruited by an elite assault squad comprised of—surprise!—drug-induced werewolves, who really put the bite on bad guys. Unresolved moral conflicts and a sloppy finale ultimately sabotage what could have been a great thriller. Rated R for violence, profanity, and strong sexual content. 93m. **DIR:** Anthony Hickox. **CAST:** Mario Van Peebles, Patsy Kensit, Anthony Denison, Jason Beghe, Bruce Payne. **1993 DVD**

FULL EXPOSURE ★★ Seedy, made-for-TV crime-drama features Anthony Denison as a police detective on a case involving a murdered call girl and her missing video diary of clients. He's teamed with rookie Lisa Hartman, and things really heat up when she goes undercover as a call girl and finds herself attracted to the lifestyle. Not rated. 95m. **DIR:** Noel Nosseck. **CAST:** Lisa Hartman, Anthony Denison, Jennifer O'Neill, Vanessa L. Williams. **1989**

FULL FATHOM FIVE ★★1/2 Adequate actioner focuses on Panamanian countermeasures to an American invasion. Michael Moriarty is the captain of an American submarine ordered to destroy a Soviet nuclear sub. Rated PG for violence. 82m. **DIR:** Carl Franklin. **CAST:** Michael Moriarty, Maria Rangel, Michael Cavanaugh. **1990**

FULL HEARTS AND EMPTY POCKETS ★★ A German youth in Rome begins with nothing and, through luck and happy coincidence, rises to a position of wealth and power. Forgettable European production will appeal only to those who can't resist another look at the streets of Rome. Dubbed in English. B&W; 88m. **DIR:** Camillo Mastrocinque. **CAST:** Thomas Fritsch, Alexandra Stewart, Gino Cervi, Senta Berger, Linda Christian, Françoise Rosay. **1963**

FULL METAL JACKET ★★★★ Stanley Kubrick and Vietnam? How can that combination miss? Well, it does and it doesn't. Kubrick scores higher in smaller moments than in scenes seemingly intended to be climactic. Don't be surprised if days later, fragments are still with you. Rated R for violence and some inventive and colorful profanity. 120m. **DIR:** Stanley Kubrick. **CAST:** Matthew Modine, Adam Baldwin, Vincent D'Onofrio, R. Lee Ermey, Dorian Harewood, Arliss Howard, Ed O'Ross. **1987 DVD**

FULL MONTY, THE ★★★★ You won't soon find a better comedy than this delightful study of the extremes to which unemployment will drive desperate men. Strapped for cash and respect and inspired by a visit from the Chippendales dancers to their small town, six average fellows decide to turn themselves into lean, mean dancing machines. To secure an audience for their decidedly unbuff bodies, they declare that they'll take their act all the way to "the full monty" . . . a complete onstage strip. Life is all about respect, and this ranks as one of the most hilarious ways of achieving that goal. Rated R for profanity and nudity. 95m. **DIR:** Peter Cattaneo. **CAST:** Robert Carlyle, Mark Addy, William Snape, Steve Huison, Tom Wilkinson, Paul Barber, Hugo Speer. **1996 DVD**

FULL MOON IN BLUE WATER ★★ Gene Hackman and Teri Garr bring wonderful moments to this offbeat comedy-drama. Otherwise, the film is corny and uneven. Rated R for profanity and light violence. 94m. **DIR:** Peter Masterson. **CAST:** Gene Hackman, Teri Garr, Burgess Meredith, Elias Coteas, Kevin Cooney. **1988 DVD**

FULL MOON IN PARIS ★★ French film from Eric Rohmer does not sustain its momentum with this tale of a young girl's disillusionment with her live-in lover. Perhaps the problem is her self-absorption and lack of commitment, but you just don't seem to care about what happens. In French with English subtitles. 102m. **DIR:** Eric Rohmer. **CAST:** Pascale Ogier, Fabrice Luchini, Tcheky Karyo. **1984 DVD**

FULLER BRUSH GIRL, THE ★★★ Lucy's in typical form as a dizzy cosmetics salesgirl up to her mascara in murder and hoodlums. Wisecracking dialogue and familiar character faces help this one out. Harmless fun. B&W; 85m. **DIR:** Lloyd Bacon. **CAST:** Lucille Ball, Eddie Albert, Jerome Cowan, Lee Patrick. **1950**

FULLER BRUSH MAN, THE ★★★ Red Skelton slapsticks along his route as a door-to-door salesman and gets involved with murder. Sadly unsung master gagster Buster Keaton deserves a lot of credit for the humor he adds to many other Skelton films. B&W; 93m. **DIR:** S. Sylvan Simon. **CAST:** Red Skelton, Janet Blair, Don McGuire, Adele Jergens, Buster Keaton. **1948**

FUN ★★★ *Heavenly Creatures* meets *Natural Born Killers* in this story of two misfits who cement their unnaturally close bond with an act of murder. Products of tabloid-TV America, the two girls titillate each other with stories of the (fictional) abuses they've endured and wonder who will play them in the TV movie based on their exploits. Well-acted, but the script seems familiar and the direction is show-offishly busy. Rated R for violence and adult situations. 105m. **DIR:** Rafal Zielinski. **CAST:** Alicia Witt, Renee Humphrey, William R. Moses. **1993 DVD**

FUN AND FANCY FREE ★★★1/2 The first segment of this Disney feature is the story of Bongo, a circus bear who runs away and falls for a female bear. It's a moderately entertaining tale. When Edgar Bergen narrates the clever version of "Jack and the Beanstalk," pitting Mickey, Donald, and Goofy against Willie the Giant, things pick up considerably. 96m. **DIR:** Walt Disney. **CAST:** Edgar Bergen, Luana Patten, Dinah Shore. **1947 DVD**

FUN IN ACAPULCO ★★1/2 Beautiful Acapulco sets the stage for this sun-filled Elvis Presley musical. This time he's a lifeguard by day and a singer by night at a fancy beachfront resort. Typical of Elvis's films. 97m. **DIR:** Richard Thorpe. **CAST:** Elvis Presley, Ursula Andress, Paul Lukas, Alejandro Rey, Elsa Cardenas. **1963**

FUN WITH DICK AND JANE ★★★★ How does one maintain one's life-style after a sacking from a highly paid aerospace position? George Segal and Jane Fonda have a unique solution. They steal. This comedy caper is well named, because some quality fun is in store for the audience. Rated PG. 95m. **DIR:** Ted Kotcheff. **CAST:** Jane Fonda, George Segal, Ed McMahon. **1977**

FUNERAL, THE (1987) ★★★1/2 An old man's sudden death creates hilarious havoc for his surviving family members in this engagingly offbeat comedy directed by Juzo Itami. The Japanese burial ritual becomes the stage where the younger generation struggles with the complex rituals of the traditional Buddhist ceremony. In Japanese with English subtitles. 124m. **DIR:** Juzo Itami. **CAST:** Nobuko Miyamoto, Tsutomu Yamazaki. **1987 DVD**

FUNERAL, THE (1996) ★★1/2 Two 1930s gangsters (Christopher Walken, Chris Penn) gather to bury their kid brother, while plotting revenge on the presumed killer (Benicio Del Toro, in the film's best performance). Atmospheric and well-acted but marred by pretentious dialogue and an unconvincing, ultraviolent climax. The endless flood of profanity seems out of place in the 1930s. Rated R for violence, profanity, and simulated sex. 98m. **DIR:** Abel Ferrara. **CAST:** Christopher Walken, Christopher Penn, Vincent Gallo, Benicio Del Toro, Annabella Sciorra, Isabella Rossellini. **1996 DVD**

FUNERAL IN BERLIN ★★★1/2 Second in Michael Caine's series of three "Harry Palmer" films, following *The Ipcress File* and preceding *The Billion-Dollar Brain*. This time, working-class spy Palmer assists in the possible defection of a top Russian security chief (Oscar Homolka). As usual, Caine can do no wrong; his brittle performance and the authentic footage of the Berlin Wall add considerably to the film's bleak tone. Not rated; suitable for family viewing. 102m. **DIR:** Guy Hamilton. **CAST:** Michael Caine, Oscar Homolka, Eva Renzi, Paul Hubschmid, Guy Doleman. **1967 DVD**

FUNHOUSE, THE ★★1/2 Looking for a watchable modern horror film? Then welcome to this film about a group of teens trapped in the carnival attraction of the title proves that buckets of blood and severed limbs aren't essential elements to movie terror. Rated R. 96m. **DIR:** Tobe Hooper. **CAST:** Elizabeth Berridge, Cooper Huckabee, Miles Chapin, Largo Woodruff, Sylvia Miles. **1981 DVD**

FUNLAND ★★1/2 Schizophrenic comedy about a family amusement park taken over by the mob. Although scripted by two *Saturday Night Live* writers, this flick doesn't know whether it wants to be a comedy, a drama, or a thriller. It does offer some weird and funny bits, though. Rated PG-13. 98m. **DIR:** Michael A. Simpson. **CAST:** William Windom, David L. Lander, Bruce Mahler, Jan Hooks, Lane Davies. **1986**

FUNNY ABOUT LOVE ★★ We love Gene Wilder, but he's neither lovable nor funny in this misbegotten movie about a cartoonist who feels his "biological clock" ticking and attempts to have a baby with a caterer (Christine Lahti). Rated PG-13 for suggested sex and profanity. 92m. **DIR:** Leonard Nimoy. **CAST:** Gene Wilder, Christine Lahti, Mary Stuart Masterson, Stephen Tobolowsky, Robert Prosky, Susan Ruttan, Anne Jackson. **1990**

FUNNY DIRTY LITTLE WAR (NO HABRA MAS PENAS NI OLVIDO) ★★★ This allegorical, comedic piece begins in the small town of Colonia Vela. The comedy centers around the struggle between the Marxists and the Peronistas in 1974, shortly before the death of Juan Perón. The action quickly builds from a series of foolish misunderstandings to a very funny confrontation. Spanish with English subtitles. Not rated. 80m. **DIR:** Hector Olivera. **CAST:** Federico Luppi, Hector Bidonde. **1985 DVD**

FUNNY FACE ★★★1/2 One of the best of Fred Astaire's later pictures. This time he's a fashion photographer who discovers naïve Audrey Hepburn and turns her into a sensation. Typical fairy-tale plot, enlivened by Astaire's usual charm and a good score based on the works of George Gershwin. 103m. **DIR:** Stanley Donen. **CAST:** Fred Astaire, Audrey Hepburn, Kay Thompson, Michel Auclair, Ruta Lee. **1957 DVD**

FUNNY FARM ★★ Chevy Chase and Madolyn Smith star as Andy and Elizabeth Farmer who give up the city life for greener pastures in Vermont. Their idyllic country life goes awry with a series of predictable disasters, laboriously dramatized. Rated PG for adult language and situations. 101m. **DIR:** George Roy Hill. **CAST:** Chevy Chase, Madolyn Smith, Joseph Maher, Brad Sullivan, MacIntyre Dixon. **1988 DVD**

FUNNY GIRL ★★★★ The early years of Ziegfeld Follies star Fanny Brice were the inspiration for a superb stage musical. Barbra Streisand re-created her Broadway triumph in as stunning a movie debut in 1968 as Hollywood ever witnessed. She sings, roller-skates, cracks jokes, and tugs at your heart in a tour-de-force performance. Rated G. 155m. **DIR:** William Wyler. **CAST:** Barbra Streisand, Omar Sharif, Walter Pidgeon, Kay Medford. **1968 DVD**

FUNNY LADY ★★★ The sequel to *Funny Girl* is not the original, but still worth seeing. We follow comedienne Fanny Brice after she became a stage luminary only to continue her misfortunes in private life. James Caan plays her second husband, producer Billy Rose, and Omar Sharif returns in his role of Fanny's first love. But Streisand's performance and a few of the musical numbers carry the day. 149m. **DIR:** Herbert Ross. **CAST:** Barbra Streisand, James Caan, Omar Sharif, Ben Vereen. **1975 DVD**

FUNNY THING HAPPENED ON THE WAY TO THE FORUM, A ★★★★ Ancient Rome is the setting for this fast-paced musical comedy. Zero Mostel is a never-ending source of zany plots to gain his freedom and line his toga with loot as a cunning slave. He is ably assisted by Phil Silvers and Jack Gilford in this bawdy romp through classic times. Look for Buster Keaton in a nice cameo. 99m. **DIR:** Richard Lester. **CAST:** Zero Mostel,

Phil Silvers, Jack Gilford, Michael Crawford, Buster Keaton. **1966 DVD**

FUNNYBONES ★★★★1/2 Oliver Platt is the unfunny son of a successful comedian who travels to Blackpool, England, in search of new material and family roots. Platt brings just the right edginess and desire to the film, and Jerry Lewis does a surprisingly good dramatic turn as his dad. Watch for Lee Evans, whose physical comedy is amazing, but ignore the lame subplot involving wax eggs and Oliver Reed. Rated R for profanity and violence. 128m. **DIR:** Peter Chelsom. **CAST:** Oliver Platt, Leslie Caron, Jerry Lewis, Lee Evans, Richard Griffiths, Oliver Reed, George Carl, Freddie Davies. **1995**

FUNNYMAN Despite his star billing, Christopher Lee only has a cameo role in this impenetrable horror nonsense about visitors to an old mansion being killed in Freddie Krueger–like ways by a demon harlequin. Rated R for graphic violence, nudity, sexual situations, adult situations, substance abuse, and profanity. 89m. **DIR:** Simon Sprackling. **CAST:** Tim James, Christopher Lee, Benny Young, Ingrid Lacey, Pauline Black. **1995 DVD**

FURTHER ADVENTURES OF TENNESSEE BUCK, THE ★★ Yet another cheap imitation of Indiana Jones, with David Keith playing an incorrigible jungle adventurer hired as a guide by a young couple. Kathy Shower, a 1987 *Playboy* playmate, is the female side of the couple; she can't act worth a lick. Rated R for violence, language, nudity, and simulated sex. 90m. **DIR:** David Keith. **CAST:** David Keith, Kathy Shower, Sidney Lassick. **1988**

FURY (1936) ★★★★ A stranger in a small town (Spencer Tracy) becomes the innocent victim of a lynch mob and turns into a one-man mob himself when he luckily survives. The script gets a bit contrived toward the end, but it's still powerful stuff, brutally well directed by Fritz Lang. B&W; 94m. **DIR:** Fritz Lang. **CAST:** Sylvia Sidney, Spencer Tracy, Walter Abel, Edward Ellis, Bruce Cabot, Walter Brennan. **1936**

FURY, THE (1978) ★★★ A contemporary terror tale that utilizes the average-man-against-the-unknown approach that made Hitchcock's suspense films so effective. In the story, Kirk Douglas is forced to take on a super-powerful government agency that kidnapped his son (Andrew Stevens), who has psychic powers. It's a chiller. Rated R. 118m. **DIR:** Brian De Palma. **CAST:** Kirk Douglas, Andrew Stevens, Amy Irving, Fiona Lewis, John Cassavetes, Charles Durning. **1978 DVD**

FURY OF HERCULES, THE ★★ Some Yugoslavian exteriors and the presence of Brad Harris, one of the more formidable post-Steve Reeves sword-and-sandal stars, boost this battle-filled saga about a corrupt kingdom. And, for once, the English dubbing is decent. 97m. **DIR:** Gianfranco Parolini. **CAST:** Brad Harris, Bridgette Corey. **1962**

FURY OF THE CONGO There's no fury and precious little Congo in this dull jungle filler. B&W; 69m. **DIR:** William Berke. **CAST:** Johnny Weissmuller, Sherry Moreland, William Henry, Lyle Talbot. **1951**

FURY OF THE WOLF MAN ★★ Fifth of a popular Spanish series featuring the sympathetic werewolf Waldemar Daninsky. Badly dubbed, but high production values make it watchable. Not rated; the film has violence. 85m. **DIR:** José Maria Zabalza. **CAST:** Paul Naschy. **1971**

FURY WITHIN, THE ★★1/2 A family in the middle of a separation is also being terrorized by a poltergeist. A few deaths and other strange occurrences add to the confusion about who's behind the haunting, but overzealous acting and overblown dialogue make this made-for-cable original more silly than scary. Rated PG-13 for violence. 95m. **DIR:** Noel Nosseck. **CAST:** Ally Sheedy, Costas Mandylor, Vincent Berry. **1998**

FUTURE FEAR Producer Roger Corman cannibalizes his own library to flesh out this weak thriller about a scientist who creates an antidote to a deadly virus. So bad calling it a B movie would be an insult to B movies. Rated R for adult situations, language, and violence. 80m. **DIR:** Lewis Baumander. **CAST:** Jeff Wincott, Maria Ford, Stacy Keach, Shawn Thompson. **1997**

FUTURE HUNTERS A warrior from the future travels back to the present. Rated R for violence, profanity, and nudity. 96m. **DIR:** Cirio H. Santiago. **CAST:** Robert Patrick. **1985**

FUTURE SHOCK ★★ In this hit-or-miss episodic thriller, three patients face their worst fears when doctor Martin Kove subjects them to virtual-reality therapy. The best bit features Bill Paxton as a roommate from hell. Rated PG-13 for violence and sexual situations. 93m. **DIR:** Eric Parkinson. **CAST:** Vivian Schilling, Martin Kove, Carrot Top (Scott Thompson), Brian James, Bill Paxton. **1993**

FUTURE ZONE David Carradine stars as a modern-day cop whose son time travels into the past to rescue him from death. Rated R for violence and profanity. 90m. **DIR:** David A. Prior. **CAST:** David Carradine, Ted Prior, Charles Napier. **1990**

FUTUREKICK A kung fu kick-boxing mystery set in a bleak futuristic technocratic society. Low-budget rip-off. Rated R for nudity, profanity, and violence. 80m. **DIR:** Damian Klaus. **CAST:** Meg Foster, Christopher Penn, Eb Lottimer. **1991**

FUTURESPORT ★★ Okay, who ordered the *Rollerball* remake? Proving that there's nothing new under the sun, this made-for-television science-fiction drama stars Dean Cain as Tre, the undisputed champion of Futuresport. When assassins threaten the life of Tre and his girlfriend, they turn to the creator of the game, Orbike Fixx, who convinces the opposing side to play one final game that will decide definitively world domination. Mundane and familiar plot elements do little to make any of this exciting. The video contains additional footage not shown on television. Rated R for language and violence. 89m. **DIR:** Ernest R. Dickerson. **CAST:** Dean Cain, Vanessa L. Williams, Wesley Snipes, Rachel Shane, Bill Smitrovich. **1998 DVD**

FUTUREWORLD ★★★ An amusement park of the future caters to any adult fantasy. Lifelike androids carry out your every whim. A fun place, right? Not so, as reporter Peter Fonda finds out in this sequel to *Westworld*. This is okay escapist fare. Rated PG. 104m. **DIR:** Richard T. Heffron. **CAST:** Peter Fonda, Blythe Danner, Arthur Hill, Yul Brynner, Stuart Margolin, John P. Ryan. **1976**

FUTZ ★★ Once controversial, now merely a curiosity piece, this film adaptation of an avant-garde play by New York's famed La Mama troupe is like something

out of a time capsule. There's no real plot, but it's set in a farm community where one farmer is ostracized for falling in love with his prize pig Amanda. Not rated, contains nudity and sexual situations. 92m. **DIR:** Tom O'Horgan. **CAST:** Seth Allen, Sally Kirkland. **1969**

FUZZ ★★★ Raquel Welch and Burt Reynolds star as police in this comedy-drama. Yul Brynner plays a bomb-happy villain. It has a few good moments, but you'd have to be a member of the Burt Reynolds fan club to really love it. Rated PG. 92m. **DIR:** Richard A. Colla. **CAST:** Raquel Welch, Burt Reynolds, Yul Brynner, Tom Skerritt. **1972 DVD**

F/X ★★★1/2 In this fast-paced, well-acted suspense-thriller, Bryan Brown plays special-effects wizard Rollie Tyler, who accepts thirty thousand dollars from the Justice Department's Witness Relocation Program to stage the fake assassination of a mob figure who has agreed to name names. After he successfully fulfills his assignment, Tyler is double-crossed and must use his wits and movie magic to survive. Rated R for profanity, suggested sex, and violence. 110m. **DIR:** Robert Mandel. **CAST:** Bryan Brown, Brian Dennehy, Diane Venora, Cliff De Young, Mason Adams, Jerry Orbach. **1986 DVD**

F/X 2: THE DEADLY ART OF ILLUSION ★★★ Special-effects expert Bryan Brown gets himself into trouble again when he agrees to help a police officer catch a serial killer. With the help of ex-cop Brian Dennehy and some of his own movie magic, Brown outwits the bad guys in this fast-paced, enjoyable, and never-believable-for-a-minute sequel. Rated PG-13 for violence, nudity, and profanity. 104m. **DIR:** Richard Franklin. **CAST:** Bryan Brown, Brian Dennehy, Rachel Ticotin, Joanna Gleason, Philip Bosco, Kevin J. O'Connor, Tom Mason. **1991 DVD**

G

G-MEN VS. THE BLACK DRAGON ★★1/2 The British, Chinese, and American secret service team up to fight the deadly Black Dragon Society of Japan. The action and stunts are top-notch in this serial. B&W; 15 chapters. **DIR:** William Witney. **CAST:** Rod Cameron, Constance Worth, George J. Lewis. **1943**

GABBEH ★★★★ This magical, beautifully-colored fable begins as a woman emerges from the rug being washed in a stream by an old couple. She tells the story of her life in a tribe of desert nomads, waiting for her father to give permission for her to marry the lover who follows the tribe at a distance. An utterly delightful (if sometimes confusing) film that is a real eye-opener to viewers unfamiliar with Arab cultures. In Farsi with English subtitles. Not rated; contains no offensive material. 72m. **DIR:** Mohsen Makhmalbaf. **CAST:** Shaghayegh Jodat. **1996**

GABE KAPLAN AS GROUCHO ★★★ Even avid Grouchophiles will enjoy this one-man made-for-cable show about everyone's favorite Marx brother. Gabe Kaplan does a comfortable impersonation, and the script mixes laughs with honest (but never spiteful) biography. 89m. **DIR:** John Bowab. **CAST:** Gabe Kaplan. **1982**

GABRIEL OVER THE WHITE HOUSE ★★★ A corrupt politician becomes president and then experiences a change of heart, soul, and mind. A highly-moralistic fable intended as a tribute to FDR and a condemnation of the presidents who preceded him. Acted with sincerity and directed with a sentimental hand. B&W; 87m. **DIR:** Gregory La Cava. **CAST:** Walter Huston, Franchot Tone, Jean Parker, Karen Morley, Dickie Moore, C. Henry Gordon, Samuel S. Hinds. **1933**

GABRIELA ★★★ Sexy Sonia Braga is both cook and mistress for bar owner Marcello Mastroianni in this excellent adaptation of Brazilian novelist Jorge Amado's comic romp *Gabriela, Clove and Cinnamon*. In Portuguese with English subtitles. Rated R. 102m. **DIR:** Bruno Barreto. **CAST:** Sonia Braga, Marcello Mastroianni, Antonio Cantafora. **1983**

GABY, A TRUE STORY ★★★★ Rachel Levin gives a smashing portrayal of a brilliant young woman trapped in a body incapacitated by cerebral palsy. Based on the true-life drama of Gabriela Brimmer. Assisted by a screenplay that steers clear of maudlin situations, the cast delivers powerful performances. Rated R for profanity and sexual frankness. 120m. **DIR:** Luis Mandoki. **CAST:** Liv Ullmann, Norma Aleandro, Robert Loggia, Rachel Levin, Lawrence Monoson, Robert Beltran. **1987**

GADJO DILO ★★★★1/2 Amiable young Frenchman armed with a music recorder and bootlegged cassette searches bleak, wintry Romania for the gypsy singer adored by his deceased father. He is befriended by a gypsy elder, smitten by a foul-mouthed dancer, and eyed with contempt by villagers. Subtitled *The Crazy Stranger*, this rambling tale of pride, prejudice, passion, and reciprocated violence embraces us more like long-lost relatives than armchair tourists. In Romany and French with English subtitles. Rated R for profanity, simulated sex, nudity, and violence. 100m. **DIR:** Tony Gatlif. **CAST:** Romain Duris, Isidor Serban, Rona Hartner, Florin Moldovan. **1998**

GAL YOUNG 'UN ★★★ Set in the early 1900s, this charming low-budget film focuses on a young man who woos a lonely, elderly (and comparatively rich) widow. He cons her into marriage with his boyish charm and uses her money to set up his own moonshine still. Featuring fine performances and good use of locations. This film is not rated. 105m. **DIR:** Victor Nunez. **CAST:** Dana Peru, David Peck, J. Smith-Cameron. **1986**

GALACTIC GIGOLO ★★ Brainless, relentlessly silly movie about an alien (Carmine Capobianco) who wins a trip to Prospect, Connecticut. Rated R for language and nudity. 80m. **DIR:** Gorman Bechard. **CAST:** Carmine Capobianco, Debi Thibeault, Frank Stewart, Ruth Collins. **1987**

GALAXIES ARE COLLIDING ★★★ Some hilarious insights await a man so afraid of marriage that he walks out on his bride-to-be. Looking for the meaning of life, he and his best friend head to the desert, where they encounter all sorts of social misfits. How these strangers help him focus on his real feelings provide writer-director John Ryman numerous opportunities to explore the human condition. Rated R for adult language. 97m. **DIR:** John Ryman. **CAST:** Kelsey Grammer,

Dwier Brown, Karen Medak, Susan Walters, Rick Overton. **1992**

GALAXINA ★★ See Captain Cornelius Butt (Avery Schreiber), of the spaceship *Infinity*, consume a raw egg and regurgitate a rubbery creature that later calls him "Mommy." Visit an intergalactic saloon that serves humans (they're on the menu, not the guest list). Low-budget space spoof. Rated R. 95m. **DIR:** William Sachs. **CAST:** Avery Schreiber, Dorothy Stratten, Stephen Macht. **1980 DVD**

GALAXIS 🦃 Brigitte Nielsen is on a mission to save her planet from evil ruler Richard Moll. Who cares? Rated R for violence. 91m. **DIR:** William Mesa. **CAST:** Brigitte Nielsen, Richard Moll, John H. Brennan, Craig Fairbrass. **1995**

GALAXY OF TERROR ★★1/2 In this movie, which was also known as *Planet of Horrors*, the crew of a spaceship sent to rescue a crash survivor finds itself facing one horror after another on a barren planet. This chiller wastes no time in getting to the thrills. Rated R because of profanity, nudity, and violence. 82m. **DIR:** B. D. Clark. **CAST:** Erin Moran, Edward Albert, Ray Walston. **1981**

GALAXY QUEST ★★★★ Delightful send-up of *Star Trek* has the cast of a canceled, 20-year-old television show attending a sci-fi convention only to be beamed up by real aliens who want their help in defeating a powerful, intergalactic enemy. Screenwriters David Howard and Robert Gordon mine every possible aspect of ground-breaking TV production for humor. There's the egotistical actor (Tim Allen) idolized for his role as the ship's captain, the classically trained actor (Alan Rickman) who feels his "alien" character is beneath him, a busty blonde (Sigourney Weaver) whose only function is to repeat the computer's announcements. Highly entertaining and even heartwarming. Rated PG. 104m. **DIR:** Dean Parisot. **CAST:** Tim Allen, Sigourney Weaver, Alan Rickman, Tony Shalhoub, Sam Rockwell, Daryl Mitchell, Enrico Colantoni. **1999 DVD**

•**GALE FORCE** 🦃 You know a film is low budget when it blatantly borrows action scenes from other films and incorporates them into its plot. See if you recognize the scenes in this shallow tale of a reality television series set on a tropical island where contestants must search for a $10 million treasure. Obstacles include a violent storm and even more violent thieves intent on taking the money for their own. Rated R for language and violence. 96m. **DIR:** Jim Wynorski. **CAST:** Treat Williams, Michael Dudikoff, Tim Thomerson, Curtis Armstrong. **2001 DVD**

GALL FORCE ★★ Japanese animation. A wandering, boorish plot acts as a thin disguise for yet another "pre-pubescent-girls-get-naked-in-space" story. Occasional cleverness saves this from the turkey bin. In Japanese with English subtitles. Not rated; contains nudity. 86m. **DIR:** Katsuhito Akiyama. **1986**

GALL FORCE 2 ★★1/2 While marginally better than the original, this animated sequel still has little to recommend it other than some vivid artwork. In this one, Lufy, one of the heroines from the original, is brought back to life only to face the dilemma of continuing a bitter war or trying to save the last habitable world, Earth. In Japanese with English subtitles. Not rated; contains violence and nudity. 50m. **DIR:** Katsuhito Akiyama. **1987**

GALLAGHER'S TRAVELS ★★ An English reporter teams up with an Australian photographer to track down an animal-smuggling ring. There's not much adventure. 94m. **DIR:** Michael Caulfield. **CAST:** Ivar Kants, Joanne Samuel, Stuart Campbell, Jennifer Hagan. **1987**

GALLANT HOURS, THE ★★★1/2 This is not an action epic, but a thoughtful view of the ordeal of command, with James Cagney in a fine performance as Fleet Admiral William F. Halsey Jr. Done in semidocumentary style, following Halsey's command from 1942 through the battle of Guadalcanal. B&W; 111m. **DIR:** Robert Montgomery. **CAST:** James Cagney, Dennis Weaver, Ward Costello, Richard Jaeckel. **1960**

GALLIPOLI ★★★★1/2 Add this to the list of outstanding motion pictures from Australia and the very best films about war. Directed by Peter Weir this appealing character study, which is set during World War I, manages to say more about life on the battlefront than many of the more straightforward pictures in the genre. Rated PG because of violence. 110m. **DIR:** Peter Weir. **CAST:** Mark Lee, Mel Gibson, Robert Grubb, Tim McKenzie, David Argue. **1981 DVD**

GALLOPING GHOST, THE ★★ College football melodrama starring real-life football legend Red Grange. Antiquated. B&W; 12 chapters. **DIR:** B. Reeves "Breezy" Eason. **CAST:** Harold "Red" Grange, Dorothy Gulliver. **1931**

GALLOWGLASS ★★1/2 Not one of the better BBC adaptations of a Ruth Rendell novel written under her nom de plume, Barbara Vine. Lacking a much-needed edginess and complexity, this is merely nasty. The main characters in this mystery about damaging obsessiveness are so odious that one feels no sympathy for them, and thus no attachment to the story. Not rated; contains brief nudity and sexual situations. 150m. **DIR:** Tim Fywell. **CAST:** Arkie Whietely, John McArdle, Michael Sheen, Paul Rhys, Claire Hackett. **1992**

GAMBIT ★★★1/2 An engaging caper comedy that teams Michael Caine's inventive but unlucky thief with Shirley MacLaine's mute and mysterious woman of the world . . . or *is* she? The target is a valuable art treasure, jealously guarded by ruthless owner Herbert Lom, and Caine's plan is—to say the least—unusual. Caine and MacLaine make a grand pair; it's a shame they didn't get together for another film of this sort. Not rated; suitable for family viewing. 108m. **DIR:** Ronald Neame. **CAST:** Michael Caine, Shirley MacLaine, Herbert Lom. **1966**

GAMBLE, THE 🦃 Matthew Modine plays an impoverished nobleman who loses in a bet. Rated R for nudity and violence. 108m. **DIR:** Carlo Vanzina. **CAST:** Matthew Modine, Faye Dunaway, Jennifer Beals. **1988**

GAMBLE ON LOVE ★★ Las Vegas provides the backdrop for this slow-moving film. Liz (Beverly Garland) inherits a casino from her father and falls in love with the brash casino manager. This relationship leads to an explosive climax. 105m. **DIR:** Jim Balden. **CAST:** Beverly Garland. **1982**

GAMBLER, THE (1974) ★★★1/2 This gritty film features James Caan in one of his best screen portrayals as a compulsive, self-destructive gambler. Director Karel Reisz keeps the atmosphere thick with tension. Always thinking he's on the edge of a big score, Caan's otherwise intelligent college professor character gets him deeper and deeper into trouble. It's a downer, but still worth watching. Rated R. 111m. **DIR:** Karel Reisz. **CAST:** James Caan, Paul Sorvino, Lauren Hutton, Jacqueline Brooks, Morris Carnovsky. **1974**

GAMBLER, THE (1980) ★★★ Bringing his late 1970s hit record to life, Kenny Rogers teams with Bruce Boxleitner in this story of a drifting cardplayer, his lost son, a shady railroad magnate, and the usual bunch of black-hatted villains. This made-for-TV movie spawned two equally entertaining sequels. 95m. **DIR:** Dick Lowry. **CAST:** Kenny Rogers, Bruce Boxleitner, Christine Belford, Harold Gould, Clu Gulager. **1980**

GAMBLER, PART II—THE ADVENTURE CONTINUES, THE ★★★ Reprising his role as gambler Brady Hawks, Kenny Rogers ambles his way farther west with sidekick Bruce Boxleitner—toward the poker game to end all poker games in San Francisco. Fans loved how to fold 'em the first time around, so here it is again. Made for TV. 190m. **DIR:** Dick Lowry. **CAST:** Kenny Rogers, Bruce Boxleitner, Linda Evans, Johnny Crawford, Cameron Mitchell, Mitchell Ryan, Harold Gould, Gregory Sierra, Ken Swofford. **1983**

GAMBLER, PART III—THE LEGEND CONTINUES, THE ★★★ Again playing gambler Brady Hawks, Kenny Rogers nearly becomes a cropper on the end of a rope when he's hung by a zealous Mexican army officer. Made for TV. 185m. **DIR:** Dick Lowry. **CAST:** Kenny Rogers, Bruce Boxleitner, Melanie Chartoff, Matt Clark, George Kennedy, Charles Durning, Jeffrey Jones. **1987**

GAMBLER RETURNS, THE: LUCK OF THE DRAW ★★1/2 A high-stakes, winner-take-all poker game is held in San Francisco, but the main draw is cameo appearances by the stars of classic TV-Western series. Overlong, but fun for fans. Made for TV. 180m. **DIR:** Dick Lowry. **CAST:** Kenny Rogers, Rick Rossovich, Reba McEntire, Claude Akins, Gene Barry, Paul Brinegar, David Carradine, Chuck Connors, Johnny Crawford, James Drury, Linda Evans, Brian Keith, Jack Kelly, Patrick Macnee, Doug McClure, Hugh O'Brian, Park Overall, Mickey Rooney, Dub Taylor, Clint Walker. **1991**

GAME, THE (1988) ★★1/2 *The Game* is what the rich and powerful play once a year, a high-tech hunting party in which humans are the prey. Joseph Campanella infiltrates the group to seek revenge on the men who killed his family, while soldier of fortune Craig Alan gives them a run for their money on the battlefield. Not rated; contains violence. 96m. **DIR:** Cole McKay. **CAST:** Joseph Campanella, Craig Alan. **1988**

GAME, THE (1997) ★★★★★ Corporate executive Michael Douglas has lost focus; he's successful, but just going through the motions—both at home and at work. Then brother Sean Penn comes up with a surprise birthday present that sends Douglas on a trip straight to his own personal hell. This clever, thought-provoking film packs the kind of punch evidenced by so few of its brethren and invites second and third viewings. The cast is marvelous and the "game" unforgettable. Rated R for violence and profanity. 128m. **DIR:** David Fincher. **CAST:** Michael Douglas, Sean Penn, Deborah Unger, James Rebhorn, Peter Donat, Carroll Baker, Anna Katarina, Armin Mueller-Stahl. **1997 DVD**

GAME FOR VULTURES ★★ A long, dusty, and violent trek through the agonies of South Africa's ongoing conflict. Strong cast, strong theme, weak movie. Rated R for lots of machine-gun violence. 113m. **DIR:** James Fargo. **CAST:** Joan Collins, Richard Harris, Richard Roundtree, Ray Milland. **1986**

GAME IS OVER, THE ★★★ Emile Zola's novel *La Curée* was the basis for this adult story of a young woman who marries an older man but finds herself attracted to (and eventually sharing a bed with) his son. Well-acted, this film by Jane Fonda's then-husband Roger Vadim holds up well for today's audiences. In French. 96m. **DIR:** Roger Vadim. **CAST:** Jane Fonda, Peter McEnery, Michel Piccoli, Tina Marquand. **1966**

GAME OF DEATH 🦃 The climactic twenty minutes of Bruce Lee in action fighting Kareem Abdul-Jabbar and Danny Inosanto are thrilling. The rest of the film is not. Rated R. 102m. **DIR:** Robert Clouse. **CAST:** Bruce Lee, Kareem Abdul-Jabbar, Danny Inosanto, Gig Young, Hugh O'Brian, Colleen Camp, Dean Jagger, Chuck Norris. **1979 DVD**

GAME OF LOVE, THE ★★1/2 A group of people (young, old, single, married, and divorced) congregate at a local night spot in this routine romantic drama. Ken Olin is the bar owner who oversees the whole scene and gives out advice. Rated PG for adult themes. 94m. **DIR:** Bobby Roth. **CAST:** Ken Olin, Ed Marinaro, Max Gail, Robert Rusler, Belinda Bauer, Tracy Nelson, Jack Blessing, Gerrit Graham, Janet Margolin, Brynn Thayer. **1987**

GAME OF SEDUCTION ★★ A professional killer accepts a bet that he cannot seduce a proper married woman. Tired continental erotica with a cast that should know better. Dubbed. Not rated; contains nudity and sexual situations. 81m. **DIR:** Roger Vadim. **CAST:** Sylvia Kristel, Nathalie Delon, Jon Finch. **1985**

GAMERA: GUARDIAN OF THE UNIVERSE ★★★ Gamera helps a team of scientists battle flying monsters that are attacking Japan in this first of a new series of Gamera movies. While a bigger budget and computer effects make this far superior to the cheesy 1960s movies, at heart it remains true to the spirit of the originals (unlike many such revivals). Not rated; contains monster violence. 99m. **DIR:** Shusuke Kaneko. **CAST:** Tsuyoshi Ihara, Akira Onodera. **1995**

GAMERA THE INVINCIBLE ★★ Typical cheesy Japanese giant-monster movie starring a prehistoric fire-breathing turtle. (It flies, too.) Neither as silly nor as campy as its sequels, this features clumsily spliced-in footage of Albert Dekker and Brian Donlevy that was added for the U.S. market. B&W; 86m. **DIR:** Noriyaki Yuasa. **CAST:** Albert Dekker, Brian Donlevy. **1965**

GAMERA VERSUS BARUGON ★★ In this first sequel, the giant flying turtle becomes a good guy, as he was to remain for the rest of the series. The bad guy, Barugon, is a giant dinosaur. Of course, several Japanese cities are leveled as the two battle, but no problem—civilization was reconstructed in time for the next sequel. 101m. **DIR:** Shigeo Tanaka. **CAST:** Kojiro Hongo. **1966**

GAMERA VERSUS GAOS ★★ Ever the friend of little children, Gamera does his giant flaming Frisbee impression once again to save his little pals from Gaos, another giant monster. Opinion differs as to whether Gaos more closely resembles a bat or a fox, as if it mattered at all to the poor stuntman sweating it out inside that rubber suit. 87m. **DIR:** Noriyaki Yuasa. **CAST:** Kojiro Hongo. **1967**

GAMERA VERSUS GUIRON ★★ Flame on! The twirling turtle battles spearheaded Guiron, an evil giant (of course) monster from outer space. Does Japan have a Ministry of Giant Monsters responsible for naming all these behemoths? 82m. **DIR:** Noriyaki Yuasa. **1969**

GAMERA VERSUS ZIGRA Fans of this kind of stuff will be disappointed to note that, in the last of the Gamera movies, the titanic turtle battles a silly Transformer-style swordfish. Some film student should do a paper comparing this with *Godzilla vs. the Smog Monster.* 87m. **DIR:** Noriyaki Yuasa. **CAST:** Reiko Kasahara. **1971**

GAMES OF COUNTESS DOLINGEN OF GRATZ, THE ★★1/2 Baffling drama concerning a schizoid woman (Carol Kane). She indulges in an exercise in reality and fantasy that centers around a little girl's erotic experience. The film's uneven narrative structure only adds to the confusion. In French with English subtitles. Not rated; contains nudity. 110m. **DIR:** Catherine Binet. **CAST:** Georges Perec, Michel Lonsdale, Carol Kane. **1981**

GAMMA PEOPLE, THE Weak science-fiction tale about children being transformed into homicidal monsters or geniuses. B&W; 79m. **DIR:** John Gilling. **CAST:** Paul Douglas, Eva Bartok, Leslie Phillips, Walter Rilla. **1956**

GANDHI ★★★★★ One of the finest screen biographies ever, this film chronicles the life of the Indian leader. Running three hours, it is an old-style "big" picture, with spectacle, great drama, superb performances, and an enormous cast. Yet for all its hugeness, *Gandhi* achieves a remarkable intimacy. Viewers will feel as if they have actually known the man Indians called the "Great Soul." Rated PG for violence. 188m. **DIR:** Richard Attenborough. **CAST:** Ben Kingsley, Candice Bergen, Edward Fox, John Gielgud, Martin Sheen, John Mills, Trevor Howard, Saeed Jaffrey, Roshan Seth. **1982 DVD**

GANG BUSTERS As a film about prison life and various attempts at breakout, this picture simply doesn't measure up. B&W; 78m. **DIR:** Bill Karan. **CAST:** Myron Healey, Sam Edwards, Don Harvey, Frank Gerstle. **1955**

GANG IN BLUE ★★1/2 Dedicated cop Mario Van Peebles suffers racist taunts from a secret squad of rogue officers with a white supremacist agenda. Naturally, our hero is determined to expose every last one of the miscreants. Rick Natkin and David Fuller's script is needlessly shrill and lopsided, and paints nearly all Caucasian characters as vicious, unrepentant swine. Rated R for violence and profanity. 100m. **DIR:** Melvin Van Peebles. **CAST:** Mario Van Peebles, Josh Brolin, Melvin Van Peebles, Cynda Williams, Stephen Lang, J. T. Walsh. **1996**

GANG RELATED ★★1/2 Two corrupt New York homicide cops rob and kill drug dealers and then blame their crimes on street gangs in this unconventional, uneven police thriller. One victim turns out to be an undercover DEA agent, and two outlaw detectives dig themselves deeper into trouble when they are assigned to the murder they committed. Rated R for violence, language, and nudity. 106m. **DIR:** Jim Kouf. **CAST:** James Belushi, Tupac Shakur, Dennis Quaid, Lela Rochon, David Paymer, James Earl Jones. **1997 DVD**

GANG'S ALL HERE, THE ★★★1/2 A good example of the pizazz of wartime musicals, this is one of the most colorful. Credit goes to Carmen Miranda's dancing style, Busby Berkeley's imaginative choreography, Alice Faye's songs of love, and Benny Goodman's music. That's still entertainment! 103m. **DIR:** Busby Berkeley. **CAST:** Alice Faye, Carmen Miranda, James Ellison, Sheila Ryan, Benny Goodman, Phil Baker, Eugene Pallette, Edward Everett Horton. **1943**

GANGS, INC. (PAPER BULLETS) ★★ Low-budget crime drama about an anguished woman with an unhappy past who seeks justification in a life of crime. B&W; 72m. **DIR:** Phil Rosen. **CAST:** Joan Woodbury, Jack LaRue, Alan Ladd, John Archer, Vince Barnett. **1941**

GANGS OF SONORA ★★★ The Three Mesquiteers aid a lady newspaper editor opposing a corrupt official trying to prevent Wyoming's entrance into the Union. B&W; 56m. **DIR:** John English. **CAST:** Robert Livingston, Bob Steele, Rufe Davis, Robert Frazer. **1941**

GANGSTER, THE ★★1/2 Slow-moving film about a gang boss with an attitude just doesn't make the grade despite a great cast and realistic locales. B&W; 82m. **DIR:** Gordon Wiles. **CAST:** Barry Sullivan, Belita, Joan Lorring, Akim Tamiroff, Harry Morgan, John Ireland, Sheldon Leonard, Elisha Cook Jr., Leif Erickson, Charles McGraw. **1947**

GANGSTER STORY ★★★ Walter Matthau ventured behind the camera for the first and only time to make this B movie about a smooth operator who gets in over his head with a treacherous mobster. Just as you'd expect from Matthau, this quirky *noir* exercise has a strong vein of dry humor (beginning with the theme song, "The Itch for Scratch"). B&W; 66m. **DIR:** Walter Matthau. **CAST:** Walter Matthau, Carol Grace. **1960**

GANGSTER WARS ★★1/2 This movie traces the lives of mobsters "Lucky" Luciano, "Bugsy" Siegel, and Meyer Lansky from their childhood friendship to becoming the most powerful leaders in organized crime during the 1920s. This is an action-packed gangster movie, which at times is difficult to follow and tends to lead the viewer down some dead ends. Rated PG for violence. 121m. **DIR:** Richard C. Sarafian. **CAST:** Michael Nouri, Brian Benben, Joe Penny. **1981**

GANGSTER'S BOY ★★1/2 Jackie Cooper's first dramatic role uses every cliché possible to showcase his boyish appeal. His role of the school valedictorian ostracized by his classmates when they learn that his father was a bootlegger was intended to make him the James Dean of his day. It didn't. B&W; 79m. **DIR:** William Nigh. **CAST:** Jackie Cooper, Robert Warwick, Betty Blythe. **1938**

GANJASAURUS REX A prodrug propaganda film about a prehistoric monster that awakens when the authorities begin burning marijuana crops. Not rated. 88m. **DIR:** Ursi Reynolds. **CAST:** Paul Bassis, Dave Fresh, Rosie Jones. **1988**

GARBAGE PAIL KIDS MOVIE, THE Disgusting would-be comedy. Rated PG-13. 100m. **DIR:** Rod Amateau. **CAST:** Anthony Newley, Mackenzie Astin, Katie Barberi. **1987**

wise intelligent college professor character gets him deeper and deeper into trouble. It's a downer, but still worth watching. Rated R. 111m. **DIR:** Karel Reisz. **CAST:** James Caan, Paul Sorvino, Lauren Hutton, Jacqueline Brooks, Morris Carnovsky. **1974**

GAMBLER, THE (1980) ★★★ Bringing his late 1970s hit record to life, Kenny Rogers teams with Bruce Boxleitner in this story of a drifting cardplayer, his lost son, a shady railroad magnate, and the usual bunch of black-hatted villains. This made-for-TV movie spawned two equally entertaining sequels. 95m. **DIR:** Dick Lowry. **CAST:** Kenny Rogers, Bruce Boxleitner, Christine Belford, Harold Gould, Clu Gulager. **1980**

GAMBLER, PART II—THE ADVENTURE CONTINUES, THE ★★★ Reprising his role as gambler Brady Hawks, Kenny Rogers ambles his way farther west with sidekick Bruce Boxleitner—toward the poker game to end all poker games in San Francisco. Fans loved how to fold 'em the first time around, so here it is again. Made for TV. 190m. **DIR:** Dick Lowry. **CAST:** Kenny Rogers, Bruce Boxleitner, Linda Evans, Johnny Crawford, Cameron Mitchell, Mitchell Ryan, Harold Gould, Gregory Sierra, Ken Swofford. **1983**

GAMBLER, PART III—THE LEGEND CONTINUES, THE ★★★ Again playing gambler Brady Hawks, Kenny Rogers nearly becomes a cropper on the end of a rope when he's hung by a zealous Mexican army officer. Made for TV. 185m. **DIR:** Dick Lowry. **CAST:** Kenny Rogers, Bruce Boxleitner, Melanie Chartoff, Matt Clark, George Kennedy, Charles Durning, Jeffrey Jones. **1987**

GAMBLER RETURNS, THE: LUCK OF THE DRAW ★★1/2 A high-stakes, winner-take-all poker game is held in San Francisco, but the main draw is cameo appearances by the stars of classic TV-Western series. Overlong, but fun for fans. Made for TV. 180m. **DIR:** Dick Lowry. **CAST:** Kenny Rogers, Rick Rossovich, Reba McEntire, Claude Akins, Gene Barry, Paul Brinegar, David Carradine, Chuck Connors, Johnny Crawford, James Drury, Linda Evans, Brian Keith, Jack Kelly, Patrick Macnee, Doug McClure, Hugh O'Brian, Park Overall, Mickey Rooney, Dub Taylor, Clint Walker. **1991**

GAME, THE (1988) ★★1/2 *The Game* is what the rich and powerful play once a year, a high-tech hunting party in which humans are the prey. Joseph Campanella infiltrates the group to seek revenge on the men who killed his family, while soldier of fortune Craig Alan gives them a run for their money on the battlefield. Not rated; contains violence. 96m. **DIR:** Cole McKay. **CAST:** Joseph Campanella, Craig Alan. **1988**

GAME, THE (1997) ★★★★★ Corporate executive Michael Douglas has lost focus; he's successful, but just going through the motions—both at home and at work. Then brother Sean Penn comes up with a surprise birthday present that sends Douglas on a trip straight to his own personal hell. This clever, thought-provoking film packs the kind of punch evidenced by so few of its brethren and invites second and third viewings. The cast is marvelous and the "game" unforgettable. Rated R for violence and profanity. 128m. **DIR:** David Fincher. **CAST:** Michael Douglas, Sean Penn, Deborah Unger, James Rebhorn, Peter Donat, Carroll Baker, Anna Katarina, Armin Mueller-Stahl. **1997 DVD**

GAME FOR VULTURES ★★ A long, dusty, and violent trek through the agonies of South Africa's ongoing conflict. Strong cast, strong theme, weak movie. Rated R for lots of machine-gun violence. 113m. **DIR:** James Fargo. **CAST:** Joan Collins, Richard Harris, Richard Roundtree, Ray Milland. **1986**

GAME IS OVER, THE ★★★ Emile Zola's novel *La Curée* was the basis for this adult story of a young woman who marries an older man but finds herself attracted to (and eventually sharing a bed with) his son. Well-acted, this film by Jane Fonda's then-husband Roger Vadim holds up well for today's audiences. In French. 96m. **DIR:** Roger Vadim. **CAST:** Jane Fonda, Peter McEnery, Michel Piccoli, Tina Marquand. **1966**

GAME OF DEATH ♥ The climactic twenty minutes of Bruce Lee in action fighting Kareem Abdul-Jabbar and Danny Inosanto are thrilling. The rest of the film is not. Rated R. 102m. **DIR:** Robert Clouse. **CAST:** Bruce Lee, Kareem Abdul-Jabbar, Danny Inosanto, Gig Young, Hugh O'Brian, Colleen Camp, Dean Jagger, Chuck Norris. **1979 DVD**

GAME OF LOVE, THE ★★1/2 A group of people (young, old, single, married, and divorced) congregate at a local night spot in this routine romantic drama. Ken Olin is the bar owner who oversees the whole scene and gives out advice. Rated PG for adult themes. 94m. **DIR:** Bobby Roth. **CAST:** Ken Olin, Ed Marinaro, Max Gail, Robert Rusler, Belinda Bauer, Tracy Nelson, Jack Blessing, Gerrit Graham, Janet Margolin, Brynn Thayer. **1987**

GAME OF SEDUCTION ★★ A professional killer accepts a bet that he cannot seduce a proper married woman. Tired continental erotica with a cast that should know better. Dubbed. Not rated; contains nudity and sexual situations. 81m. **DIR:** Roger Vadim. **CAST:** Sylvia Kristel, Nathalie Delon, Jon Finch. **1985**

GAMERA: GUARDIAN OF THE UNIVERSE ★★★ Gamera helps a team of scientists battle flying monsters that are attacking Japan in this first of a new series of Gamera movies. While a bigger budget and computer effects make this far superior to the cheesy 1960s movies, at heart it remains true to the spirit of the originals (unlike many such revivals). Not rated; contains monster violence. 99m. **DIR:** Shusuke Kaneko. **CAST:** Tsuyoshi Ihara, Akira Onodera. **1995**

GAMERA THE INVINCIBLE ★★ Typical cheesy Japanese giant-monster movie starring a prehistoric fire-breathing turtle. (It flies, too.) Neither as silly nor as campy as its sequels, this features clumsily spliced-in footage of Albert Dekker and Brian Donlevy that was added for the U.S. market. B&W; 86m. **DIR:** Noriyaki Yuasa. **CAST:** Albert Dekker, Brian Donlevy. **1965**

GAMERA VERSUS BARUGON ★★ In this first sequel, the giant flying turtle becomes a good guy, as he was to remain for the rest of the series. The bad guy, Barugon, is a giant dinosaur. Of course, several Japanese cities are leveled as the two battle, but no problem—civilization was reconstructed in time for the next sequel. 101m. **DIR:** Shigeo Tanaka. **CAST:** Kojiro Hongo. **1966**

GAMERA VERSUS GAOS ★★ Ever the friend of little children, Gamera does his giant flaming Frisbee impression once again to save his little pals from Gaos, another giant monster. Opinion differs as to whether Gaos more closely resembles a bat or a fox, as if it mattered at all to the poor stuntman sweating it out inside that rubber suit. 87m. **DIR:** Noriyaki Yuasa. **CAST:** Kojiro Hongo. **1967**

GAMERA VERSUS GUIRON ★★ Flame on! The twirling turtle battles spearheaded Guiron, an evil giant (of course) monster from outer space. Does Japan have a Ministry of Giant Monsters responsible for naming all these behemoths? 82m. **DIR:** Noriyaki Yuasa. **1969**

GAMERA VERSUS ZIGRA Fans of this kind of stuff will be disappointed to note that, in the last of the Gamera movies, the titanic turtle battles a silly Transformer-style swordfish. Some film student should do a paper comparing this with *Godzilla vs. the Smog Monster.* 87m. **DIR:** Noriyaki Yuasa. **CAST:** Reiko Kasahara. **1971**

GAMES OF COUNTESS DOLINGEN OF GRATZ, THE ★★1/2 Baffling drama concerning a schizoid woman (Carol Kane). She indulges in an exercise in reality and fantasy that centers around a little girl's erotic experience. The film's uneven narrative structure only adds to the confusion. In French with English subtitles. Not rated; contains nudity. 110m. **DIR:** Catherine Binet. **CAST:** Georges Perec, Michel Lonsdale, Carol Kane. **1981**

GAMMA PEOPLE, THE Weak science-fiction tale about children being transformed into homicidal monsters or geniuses. B&W; 79m. **DIR:** John Gilling. **CAST:** Paul Douglas, Eva Bartok, Leslie Phillips, Walter Rilla. **1956**

GANDHI ★★★★★ One of the finest screen biographies ever, this film chronicles the life of the Indian leader. Running three hours, it is an old-style "big" picture, with spectacle, great drama, superb performances, and an enormous cast. Yet for all its hugeness, *Gandhi* achieves a remarkable intimacy. Viewers will feel as if they have actually known the man Indians called the "Great Soul." Rated PG for violence. 188m. **DIR:** Richard Attenborough. **CAST:** Ben Kingsley, Candice Bergen, Edward Fox, John Gielgud, Martin Sheen, John Mills, Trevor Howard, Saeed Jaffrey, Roshan Seth. **1982 DVD**

GANG BUSTERS As a film about prison life and various attempts at breakout, this picture simply doesn't measure up. B&W; 78m. **DIR:** Bill Karan. **CAST:** Myron Healey, Sam Edwards, Don Harvey, Frank Gerstle. **1955**

GANG IN BLUE ★★1/2 Dedicated cop Mario Van Peebles suffers racist taunts from a secret squad of rogue officers with a white supremacist agenda. Naturally, our hero is determined to expose every last one of the miscreants. Rick Natkin and David Fuller's script is needlessly shrill and lopsided, and paints nearly all Caucasian characters as vicious, unrepentant swine. Rated R for violence and profanity. 100m. **DIR:** Melvin Van Peebles. **CAST:** Mario Van Peebles, Josh Brolin, Melvin Van Peebles, Cynda Williams, Stephen Lang, J. T. Walsh. **1996**

GANG RELATED ★★1/2 Two corrupt New York homicide cops rob and kill drug dealers and then blame their crimes on street gangs in this unconventional, uneven police thriller. One victim turns out to be an undercover DEA agent, and two outlaw detectives dig themselves deeper into trouble when they are assigned to the murder they committed. Rated R for violence, language, and nudity. 106m. **DIR:** Jim Kouf. **CAST:** James Belushi, Tupac Shakur, Dennis Quaid, Lela Rochon, David Paymer, James Earl Jones. **1997 DVD**

GANG'S ALL HERE, THE ★★★1/2 A good example of the pizazz of wartime musicals, this is one of the most colorful. Credit goes to Carmen Miranda's dancing style, Busby Berkeley's imaginative choreography, Alice Faye's songs of love, and Benny Goodman's music. That's still entertainment! 103m. **DIR:** Busby Berkeley. **CAST:** Alice Faye, Carmen Miranda, James Ellison, Sheila Ryan, Benny Goodman, Phil Baker, Eugene Pallette, Edward Everett Horton. **1943**

GANGS, INC. (PAPER BULLETS) ★★ Low-budget crime drama about an anguished woman with an unhappy past who seeks justification in a life of crime. B&W; 72m. **DIR:** Phil Rosen. **CAST:** Joan Woodbury, Jack LaRue, Alan Ladd, John Archer, Vince Barnett. **1941**

GANGS OF SONORA ★★★ The Three Mesquiteers aid a lady newspaper editor opposing a corrupt official trying to prevent Wyoming's entrance into the Union. B&W; 56m. **DIR:** John English. **CAST:** Robert Livingston, Bob Steele, Rufe Davis, Robert Frazer. **1941**

GANGSTER, THE ★★1/2 Slow-moving film about a gang boss with an attitude just doesn't make the grade despite a great cast and realistic locales. B&W; 82m. **DIR:** Gordon Wiles. **CAST:** Barry Sullivan, Belita, Joan Lorring, Akim Tamiroff, Harry Morgan, John Ireland, Sheldon Leonard, Elisha Cook Jr., Leif Erickson, Charles McGraw. **1947**

GANGSTER STORY ★★★ Walter Matthau ventured behind the camera for the first and only time to make this B movie about a smooth operator who gets in over his head with a treacherous mobster. Just as you'd expect from Matthau, this quirky *noir* exercise has a strong vein of dry humor (beginning with the theme song, "The Itch for Scratch"). B&W; 66m. **DIR:** Walter Matthau. **CAST:** Walter Matthau, Carol Grace. **1960**

GANGSTER WARS ★★1/2 This movie traces the lives of mobsters "Lucky" Luciano, "Bugsy" Siegel, and Meyer Lansky from their childhood friendship to becoming the most powerful leaders in organized crime during the 1920s. This is an action-packed gangster movie, which at times is difficult to follow and tends to lead the viewer down some dead ends. Rated PG for violence. 121m. **DIR:** Richard C. Sarafian. **CAST:** Michael Nouri, Brian Benben, Joe Penny. **1981**

GANGSTER'S BOY ★★1/2 Jackie Cooper's first dramatic role uses every cliché possible to showcase his boyish appeal. His role of the school valedictorian ostracized by his classmates when they learn that his father was a bootlegger was intended to make him the James Dean of his day. It didn't. B&W; 79m. **DIR:** William Nigh. **CAST:** Jackie Cooper, Robert Warwick, Betty Blythe. **1938**

GANJASAURUS REX A prodrug propaganda film about a prehistoric monster that awakens when the authorities begin burning marijuana crops. Not rated. 88m. **DIR:** Ursi Reynolds. **CAST:** Paul Bassis, Dave Fresh, Rosie Jones. **1988**

GARBAGE PAIL KIDS MOVIE, THE Disgusting would-be comedy. Rated PG-13. 100m. **DIR:** Rod Amateau. **CAST:** Anthony Newley, Mackenzie Astin, Katie Barberi. **1987**

ing them—defends and becomes infatuated with a young man who murdered his psychiatrist aunt. A series of flashbacks indicate that his Freudian guardian had not really raised the lad from childhood, but rather used him as a research experiment. In French with English subtitles. Not rated. 113m. **DIR:** Raúl Ruiz. **CAST:** Catherine Deneuve, Michel Piccoli, Melvin Poupaud. **1998**

GENERAL, THE (1927) ★★★★★ *The General* is a film based on an incident in the Civil War. Buster Keaton is an engineer determined to recapture his stolen locomotive. Magnificent battle scenes are mere backdrops for Keaton's inspired acrobatics and comedy. Solid scripting, meticulous attention to detail, and ingenious stunt work make this picture excellent. B&W; 74m. **DIR:** Buster Keaton. **CAST:** Buster Keaton, Marion Mack, Glen Cavender, Jim Farley, Joseph Keaton. **1927 DVD**

GENERAL, THE (1998) ★★★★ It's impossible not to enjoy the bravura filmmaking here, even with its reprehensible central character: Martin Cahill. Although ruthless and brutally efficient when it came to his aptitude for crime—during a 20-year career, Cahill is credited with having stolen over $60 million—the notorious Dublin gangster acquired populist favor, mostly because of how he kept befuddling the police. John Boorman presents all these shenanigans, no matter how felonious, with the enthusiastic elan of a contemporary swashbuckling epic. The result is unexpectedly engaging: a celebration of often-nasty behavior that turns ugly only when Cahill finally gets too brazen even for his own reputation. Rated R for profanity and violence. 129m. **DIR:** John Boorman. **CAST:** Brendan Gleeson, Adrian Dunbar, Sean McGinley, Jon Voight, Maria Doyle Kennedy, Angeline Ball. **1998 DVD**

GENERAL DELLA ROVERE ★★★★ Vittorio De Sica gives a first-rate performance as a small-time swindler who is arrested by the occupying German army and blackmailed into impersonating an executed Italian general. Brilliantly directed by Roberto Rossellini. In Italian with English subtitles. B&W; 130m. **DIR:** Roberto Rossellini. **CAST:** Vittorio De Sica, Hannes Messemer, Sandra Milo, Giovanna Ralli. **1957**

GENERAL DIED AT DAWN, THE ★★★ Nicely turned story of adventurer Gary Cooper battling Chinese warlord Akim Tamiroff. Film is a bit short on action but draws some fine character studies. Madeleine Carroll is good as Cooper's love interest, but it is Tamiroff who steals the show. B&W; 97m. **DIR:** Lewis Milestone. **CAST:** Gary Cooper, Akim Tamiroff, Madeleine Carroll, Porter Hall, Dudley Digges. **1936**

GENERAL IDI AMIN DADA ★★★★ Barbet Schroeder often makes films about people you wouldn't want to spend much time with—*Barfly, Reversal of Fortune*—but never more so than in this documentary about murderous Ugandan dictator Idi Amin. Amin cooperated fully in the making of this film, which nevertheless shows him to be an extremely bizarre, self-inflated despot. Mesmerizingly weird. Not rated. 90m. **DIR:** Barbet Schroeder. **1975**

GENERAL SPANKY ★★ A feature-length version of the *Our Gang* series, later popular on TV as *The Little Rascals*. A good attempt to give new life to the characters, but it just proved that audiences can sit still just so long while kids get mischief out of their systems. B&W; 71m. **DIR:** Fred Newmeyer, Gordon Douglas. **CAST:** Spanky McFarland, Buckwheat Thomas, Carl "Alfalfa" Switzer, Phillips Holmes, Rosina Lawrence, Louise Beavers, Hobart Bosworth, Ralph Morgan, Irving Pichel. **1936**

GENERAL'S DAUGHTER, THE ★★★1/2 Nelson DeMille's novel serves as a good blueprint for this engaging conspiracy thriller, which gives us a fiercely capable hero in the form of Warrant Officer Paul Brenner, a CID investigator with the "special power" to interrogate and arrest any military person anywhere in the world. The story concerns the grotesque murder of Captain Elisabeth Campbell, whose naked body is found in the middle of the military base commanded by her own father, a highly decorated general. Our hero quickly discovers no shortage of suspects. Rated R for profanity, violence, rape, nudity, and deviant sexual behavior. 115m. **DIR:** Simon West. **CAST:** John Travolta, Madeleine Stowe, James Cromwell, Timothy Hutton, Clarence Williams, III, James Woods. **1999 DVD**

GENERATION, A (1954) ★★★ During World War II, two young men in occupied Warsaw join the Resistance. While Andrzej Wajda's first feature film was somewhat restrained by government involvement, it questions the difference between the official and apparent versions of Polish life. In Polish with English subtitles. Not rated. B&W; 90m. **DIR:** Andrzej Wajda. **CAST:** Tadeusz Lomnicki, Tadeusz Janezar, Roman Polanski. **1954**

GENERATION (1969) ★★★ Remember the generation gap? If not, then you're not likely to enjoy this dated but modestly amusing comedy about a businessman (David Janssen) trying to cope with his pregnant daughter and hippie son-in-law, who want to have their baby at home. Rated PG. 104m. **DIR:** George Schaefer. **CAST:** David Janssen, Kim Darby, Peter Duel, Carl Reiner, Andrew Prine, James Coco, Sam Waterston. **1969**

•GENERATION X ★★★1/2 This made-for-TV movie features the characters of the popular comic-book spin-off from *X-Men*. While at times it shows its low budget, the film has decent special effects and follows the storyline of the comics somewhat closely. The cast is all game, making the film that much more enjoyable, even though Finola Hughes looks ridiculous in her blond wig. Exciting and fast paced. Rated PG-13 for violence. 92m. **DIR:** Jack Sholder. **CAST:** Finola Hughes, Matt Frewer. **1996**

GENEVIEVE ★★★1/2 Captivating, low-key comedy about friendly rivals who engage in a race after finishing a vintage car rally in England. No pretenses or false claims in this charming film, just great performances, beautiful countryside, and a spirit of fun and camaraderie. This stylish feature gave Kenneth More one of his best roles and showcased the charm and comedy flair of Kay Kendall, one of Britain's top talents. 86m. **DIR:** Henry Cornelius. **CAST:** Kenneth More, Kay Kendall, Dinah Sheridan, John Gregson, Arthur Wontner. **1954**

GENGHIS COHN ★★★★ Extremely creative and unusual, this supernatural black comedy turns the tables on racial stereotyping. Antony Sher plays the ghost of a Jewish comedian who comes back to haunt the former SS officer who killed him at Dachau. No rattling chains here, as the dead comic has a revenge scheme that is both hysterically twisted and deadly somber. The very weirdness inherent to this flick is what makes it work.

Made for British television. Not rated; contains profanity, violence, and nudity. 100m. **DIR:** Elijah Moshinsky. **CAST:** Robert Lindsay, Diana Rigg, Antony Sher. **1993**

GENTLE GIANT ★★★ A touching, Disneyesque story of a lonely boy and an orphaned black bear cub. Mildly awkward acting and editing, but the film's heart is pure and the animal scenes are very good. Not rated, with only minimal violence. 93m. **DIR:** James Neilson. **CAST:** Dennis Weaver, Vera Miles, Clint Howard, Ralph Meeker. **1967**

GENTLE SAVAGE ★★★1/2 In this well-paced Western, William Smith portrays an American Indian framed for the rape and beating of a white girl in a small town. The girl's stepfather, who actually committed the crime, incites the townsmen to go after the innocent man. When the townsmen kill the hapless fellow's brother, the American Indian community retaliates. Rated R for violence. 85m. **DIR:** Sean MacGregor. **CAST:** William Smith, Gene Evans, Barbara Luna, Joe Flynn. **1978**

GENTLEMAN BANDIT, THE ★★★ Ralph Waite gives a convincing portrait of Father Pagano, who was accused of a series of armed robberies in 1978. This made-for-TV biography chronicles his ordeal when mistakenly identified by seven eyewitnesses. Good viewing. 96m. **DIR:** Jonathan Kaplan. **CAST:** Ralph Waite, Julie Bovasso, Jerry Zaks, Joe Grifasi, Estelle Parsons, Vincent Spano. **1981**

GENTLEMAN FROM CALIFORNIA ★★1/2 Ricardo Cortez returns from Spain to find his California homeland being robbed and plundered by unscrupulous newcomers. He soon becomes the Robin Hood of the Californians. B&W; 58m. **DIR:** Gus Meins. **CAST:** Ricardo Cortez, Marjorie Weaver, Katherine DeMille, Helen Holmes. **1937**

GENTLEMAN JIM ★★★★1/2 Errol Flynn has a field day in this beautifully filmed biography of heavyweight champion Jim Corbett. Always cocky and light on his feet, Flynn is a joy to behold and will make those who considered him a star instead of an actor think twice. Ward Bond is equally fine as John L. Sullivan. Said to have been Flynn's favorite role. B&W; 104m. **DIR:** Raoul Walsh. **CAST:** Errol Flynn, Jack Carson, Alan Hale Sr., Alexis Smith, Ward Bond. **1942**

GENTLEMEN PREFER BLONDES ★★ Howard Hawks gets surprisingly good performances from his stars, Jane Russell and Marilyn Monroe, in this 1953 musical comedy. As usual, Hawks does his best to make good scenes, but this time the silly plot—about two women searching for husbands—thwarts his estimable talents. 91m. **DIR:** Howard Hawks. **CAST:** Jane Russell, Marilyn Monroe, Charles Coburn, Tommy Noonan, Elliott Reid, George Winslow. **1953 DVD**

GENTLEMEN'S AGREEMENT ★★★1/2 A writer doing a feature on anti-Semitism passes himself off as a Jew. Along with the anticipated problems, he gets surprising reactions from friends and coworkers. With 1947's *Crossfire* this was a Hollywood pace-setter in attacking bigotry, but it has lost some bite. Oscars for the best picture, director Elia Kazan, and supporting actress Celeste Holm. B&W; 118m. **DIR:** Elia Kazan. **CAST:** Gregory Peck, Dorothy McGuire, John Garfield, Celeste Holm, Anne Revere, June Havoc, Albert Dekker, Jane Wyatt, Dean Stockwell, Sam Jaffe. **1947 DVD**

GENUINE RISK ★★★1/2 Losers caught in a love triangle tangle in this neat homage to Forties crime-boss pictures. The film is ragged, but it's also erotic and occasionally funny. Rated R for profanity, nudity, and violence. 86m. **DIR:** Kurt Voss. **CAST:** Terence Stamp, Michelle Johnson. **1990**

GEN-X COPS ★★1/2 The Gen-X Cops are almost as unpredictable and dangerous as the criminals they hunt, and it is up to them and their flashy style to capture the vile Akatura who has gotten hold of a shipment of smuggled explosives. The Gen-X Cops will either save the day or get kicked off the force trying. *Gen-X Cops* is full of martial-arts action, but nothing too impressive. Rated R for violence. 113m. **DIR:** Benny Chan. **CAST:** Nicholas Tse, Stephen Fung, Sam Lee, Grace Ip, Toru Nakamura, Eric Tsang, Daniel Wu. **1999 DVD**

GEORGE BALANCHINE'S THE NUTCRACKER ★★★ Despite the presence of Macaulay Culkin, this is a rather stage-bound filming of the New York City Ballet's annual production of Tchaikovsky's masterpiece. Not very cinematic, but luscious to look at and glorious to listen to. Plus, the dancing is often marvelous. Narrated by Kevin Kline. Rated G. 93m. **DIR:** Emile Ardolino. **CAST:** Macaulay Culkin, Darci Kistler, Kyra Nichols, Wendy Whelan. **1993**

GEORGE BURNS AND GRACIE ALLEN SHOW, THE (TV SERIES) ★★★1/2 In this classic series, George Burns plays a nearly imperturbable entertainer, married to madcap Gracie Allen. Allen turns everyday life into a nonstop adventure by innocently causing a whirlwind of confusion. She's endlessly endearing. Burns is dryly delightful, puffing on his cigar and looking into the camera, commenting on the developing plot. B&W; 120m. **DIR:** Ralph Levy. **CAST:** George Burns, Gracie Allen, Harry Von Zell, Ronnie Burns, Bea Benaderet, Hal March, Bob Sweeney, Fred Clark, Larry Keating. **1950–1958**

GEORGE CARLIN: JAMMIN' IN NEW YORK ★★★★ More irreverent humor from the master of wordplay. Comedian George Carlin disburses hilarious words of wisdom on everything from the Persian Gulf War to airline announcements. Taped at The Paramount in Madison Square Garden, New York City. Not rated, contains adult language. 60m. **DIR:** Rocco Urbishi. **CAST:** George Carlin. **1992 DVD**

GEORGE MCKENNA STORY, THE ★★★1/2 Based on a true story, a new principal tries to make a gang-ridden high school a better place to learn. He gains the respect of the students and most of the faculty, but a few teachers try to have him removed. Denzel Washington does a nice job of portraying the compassionate principal, and Lynn Whitfield is wonderful as his neglected wife. Not rated; contains violence. 93m. **DIR:** Eric Laneuville. **CAST:** Denzel Washington, Lynn Whitfield, Akosua Busia, Richard Masur. **1986**

GEORGE OF THE JUNGLE ★★★ Winning Brendan Fraser plays the lucky if unintelligent jungle boy in Disney's faithful live-action adaptation of Jay Ward's 1960s cartoon character. Off-beat humor alternately annoys and amuses as Fraser pursues romance with a daffy heiress. Jim Henson's Creature Shop does wonders with animatronics and computer-generated images. Particularly impressive stunt on the San Francisco–Oakland Bay Bridge is a must-see. Rated PG for comic-book violence. 92m. **DIR:** Sam Weisman. **CAST:** Brendan Fraser, Leslie Mann, Holland Taylor, Sinbad. **1997 DVD**

GEORGE WALLACE ★★★★ Powerful performance by Gary Sinise as Alabama's controversial governor portrays a complicated man more concerned with being elected than with preserving racial inequities. Based on Marshall Frady's book *Wallace*, this fine TNT miniseries goes beyond the inflammatory headlines into the planning stage of each incident that warranted national attention and, at times, intervention. An interesting use of black-and-white newsreels as well as new footage at key historic moments in the film is very effective. Not rated; contains sexual situations, violence, and profanity. 180m. **DIR:** John Frankenheimer. **CAST:** Gary Sinise, Mare Winningham, Clarence Williams, III, Angelina Jolie, Joe Don Baker, Terry Kinney, William Sanderson. **1997**

GEORGE WASHINGTON ★★★★ Director David Gordon Green frames this tale of tragedy and hope against beautiful, almost lyrical images that defy the reality of the situation. Set in the South, the film stars a powerful Donald Holden as George, dubbed George Washington by his 12-year-old admirer Nasia. Nasia's hero worship of George sets into motion a tragic chain of events, but not before we're exposed to the hopes and dreams of the young principals. Not rated. 89m. **DIR:** David Gordon Green. **CAST:** Candace Evanofski, Donald Holden, Curtis Cotton, III, Eddie Rouse, Paul Schneider. **2000 DVD**

GEORGE WASHINGTON ★★★1/2 Sweeping made-for-TV chronicle of George Washington as surveyor and fighter in the French and Indian Wars through his years as commander of the victorious colonial army. Some dull home scenes at Mount Vernon but there are ample battles and fascinating revelations of the infighting among the "professional" generals who surrounded him. Based on the books of James Thomas Flexner. 408m. **DIR:** Buzz Kulik. **CAST:** Barry Bostwick, Patty Duke, David Dukes, Jaclyn Smith, Lloyd Bridges, José Ferrer, Hal Holbrook, Trevor Howard, Jeremy Kemp, Richard Kiley, Stephen Macht, James Mason, Rosemary Murphy, Clive Revill, Robert Stack, Anthony Zerbe. **1984**

GEORGE WASHINGTON SLEPT HERE ★★★ Some mild laughs when Jack Benny and Ann Sheridan buy a run-down Colonial house and are frustrated at every attempt to make it habitable. Many of the situations were repeated, to better advantage, in *Mr. Blandings Builds His Dream House*. B&W; 91m. **DIR:** William Keighley. **CAST:** Jack Benny, Ann Sheridan, Charles Coburn, Percy Kilbride, Hattie McDaniel. **1942**

GEORGE WASHINGTON: THE FORGING OF A NATION ★★★1/2 A fine made-for-TV sequel to 1984's *George Washington*. The film covers Washington's two terms in office and the myriad problems he faced as the leader of a new nation. 210m. **DIR:** William A. Graham. **CAST:** Barry Bostwick, Patty Duke, Jeffrey Jones, Richard Bekins, Penny Fuller, Lise Hilboldt. **1986**

GEORGE WHITE'S SCANDALS ★★ Joan Davis saves this fairly minor musical from collapsing. B&W; 95m. **DIR:** Felix Feist. **CAST:** Joan Davis, Jack Haley, Jane Greer, Philip Terry. **1945**

GEORGE'S ISLAND ★★★1/2 Adventure looms for 10-year-old orphan George when he's taken away from his grandfather and placed in a foster home. Escaping in a boat, he comes across an island that's a virtual playground, if it weren't for the ghosts of swashbuckling pirates guarding a treasure. Rated PG for some pirate violence that might scare younger children. 89m. **DIR:** Paul Donovan. **CAST:** Ian Bannen, Sheila McCarthy, Maury Chaykin. **1991**

GEORGIA (1987) ★★★1/2 Intense psychological drama. Judy Davis stars in dual roles as a successful attorney investigating her own mother's accidental drowning and as the mother, a photographer. While attempting to find out more, she runs into some deadly roadblocks. Davis is powerfully mesmerizing as both a professional woman and a free spirit whose acquaintances are at the core of this mystery. Not rated; contains violence and adult situations. 90m. **DIR:** Ben Lewin. **CAST:** Judy Davis, John Bach, Julia Blake, Alex Menglet, Marshall Naper. **1987**

GEORGIA (1995) ★★ At the core of the film's waning narrative is the volatile relationship between Sadie, a wannabe rock singer with an anguished, grating voice, and her nightingale folk-rock older sister Georgia. Leaving muddy footprints all over the ladies' frayed domestic canvas are the tics, lures, hassles, and glamour of show business. Rated R for language, simulated sex, substance abuse, and nudity. 117m. **DIR:** Ulu Grosbard. **CAST:** Jennifer Jason Leigh, Mare Winningham, Ted Levine, John Doe, Max Perlich, John C. Reilly. **1995 DVD**

GEORGIA, GEORGIA ★★ This film, adapted by Maya Angelou from one of her stories, is a dated but fairly interesting study of racism. The story centers around the relationship between a white photographer and a black singer. If you get mildly involved with this movie, stay with it. Rated R. 91m. **DIR:** Stig Bjorknan. **CAST:** Diana Sands, Dirk Benedict, Minnie Gentry, Roger Furman. **1972**

GEORGY GIRL ★★★1/2 Generations clash as suave, patient fairy godfather James Mason works to make chubby London mod girl Lynn Redgrave his mistress in this totally engaging British comedy. Charlotte Rampling is a standout as the chubby's tough-bitch roommate. Mason, of course, gives another of his flawless characterizations. B&W; 100m. **DIR:** Silvio Narizzano. **CAST:** Lynn Redgrave, James Mason, Alan Bates, Charlotte Rampling. **1966**

GERMANY IN AUTUMN ★★★ Dense political anthology that includes contributions by a dozen filmmakers, collectively inspired by two notorious events involving terrorists that took place in Germany in 1977. Some episodes will have no resonance for non-German viewers, but two command special attention: a sly skit about TV executives by novelist Heinrich Boll; and Rainer Werner Fassbinder's painfully realistic segment in which he berates his then-lover and argues politics with his mother. In German with English subtitles. Not rated; contains adult themes and nudity. 124m. **DIR:** Heinrich Boll, Alf Brustellin, Bernhard Sinkel, Hans Peter Cloos, Katja Rupe, Rainer Werner Fassbinder, Alexander Kluge, Beate Mainka-Jellinghaus, Maximiliane Mainka, Peter Schubert, Edgar Reitz, Volker Schlöndorff. **CAST:** Hannelore Hoger, Katja Rupe, Hans Peter Cloos, Rainer Werner Fassbinder. **1978**

GERONIMO: AN AMERICAN LEGEND ★★★1/2 Strong performances and a thought-provoking screenplay add grit to this powerhouse Western about the Apache warrior. Told through the eyes of an idealistic officer, this near epic is a collection of what Howard Hawks called "good scenes" that will please fans of the genre. Rated PG-13 for profanity and violence. 110m. **DIR:** Walter Hill. **CAST:** Jason Patric, Gene Hackman, Robert Duvall, Wes Studi, Matt Damon, Rodney A. Grant, Kevin Tighe, Steve Reevis, Scott Wilson, Carlos Palomino. **1994 DVD**

GERTRUDE ★★★★1/2 A woman leaves her husband for a younger man. When her lover proves equally unsatisfying, she embarks on a series of affairs before realizing that true happiness lies within herself. Danish director Carl Dreyer's last film almost completely eliminates camera movement in order to force our attention onto what is happening between the characters. In Danish with English subtitles. 116m. **DIR:** Carl Dreyer. **CAST:** Nina Pens Rede, Bendt Rothe. **1963**

GERVAISE ★★★ Soap-opera fans will be the best audience for this adaptation of an Emile Zola novel. Set in 1850 Paris, the movie follows the sad life of a woman who is abandoned by her lover, unlucky in business, and sent into penury by her drunken husband. In French with English subtitles. B&W; 120m. **DIR:** René Clement. **CAST:** Maria Schell, François Perier, Suzy Delair. **1956**

GET CARTER (1971) ★★★★ Michael Caine is memorable as Jack Carter, a vicious London gangster whose search for his brother's killer leads him down a trail of lies, deceit, and death, and through Newcastle looking for the man who gave the order. Director Mike Hodges is Caine's best friend, allowing him the opportunity to create an unlikable character with no apologies. Brutal and tough, the film remains a classic of its kind. Rated R for adult situations, language, and violence. 111m. **DIR:** Mike Hodges. **CAST:** Michael Caine, Ian Hendry, Britt Ekland, John Osborne. **1971 DVD**

GET CARTER (2000) ★★★★ When his brother dies under suspicious circumstances, mob enforcer Jack Carter journeys from Las Vegas to Seattle only to find his efforts to uncover the truth thwarted by his estranged family as well as the local criminal underground. This action-packed remake of the 1971 cult classic brings back Michael Caine, this time in a memorable supporting role, while giving Sylvester Stallone his best role since *Copland*. Rated R for violence, profanity, sex, and drug use. 102m. **DIR:** Stephen T. Kay. **CAST:** Sylvester Stallone, Miranda Richardson, Rachael Leigh Cook, Rhona Mitra, Johnny Strong, John C. McGinley, Alan Cumming, Michael Caine, Mickey Rourke. **2000 DVD**

GET CHRISTIE LOVE! ★★ A television entry in the blaxploitation genre, this adventure centers on a female police detective (Teresa Graves) who tracks drug dealers on the streets of Los Angeles in the 1970s. Fairly tame when compared to others in its genre. 75m. **DIR:** William A. Graham. **CAST:** Teresa Graves, Harry Guardino, Louise Sorel, Paul Stevens. **1974**

GET CRAZY ★★★1/2 Here's the wildest, weirdest, and most outrageous rock 'n' roll comedy any of us is likely to see. It's a story about a rock concert on New Year's Eve. Malcolm McDowell plays a Mick Jagger–style rock singer, Allen Goorwitz is a Bill Graham–ish promoter, and Daniel Stern is his lovesick stage manager. Rated R for nudity, profanity, violence, and suggested sex. 92m. **DIR:** Allan Arkush. **CAST:** Malcolm McDowell, Allen Garfield, Daniel Stern, Ed Begley Jr., Miles Chapin, Lou Reed, Stacey Nelkin, Bill Henderson, Franklin Ajaye, Bobby Sherman, Fabian. **1983**

GET ON THE BUS ★★★1/2 A mixed bag of African American characters sets out for Washington, D.C., and the Million Man March. The script and characters are cliché-ridden, but director Spike Lee and a superb cast, all working at the top of their considerable powers, give the film its urgency of conviction and a patina of documentary realism. Things bog down in the last few minutes, when the bombastic speeches defeat even these fine actors. Rated R for profanity. 122m. **DIR:** Spike Lee. **CAST:** Charles Dutton, Andre Braugher, Ossie Davis, Richard Belzer. **1996 DVD**

GET OUT YOUR HANDKERCHIEFS ★★★1/2 Winner of the 1978 Academy Award for best foreign film, this stars Gérard Depardieu as a clumsy husband so desperate to make his melancholic wife happy and pregnant that he provides her with a lover (Patrick Dewaere). A mostly improbable existential drama. In French. Not rated, contains nudity. 108m. **DIR:** Bertrand Blier. **CAST:** Gérard Depardieu, Patrick Dewaere, Carole Laure. **1978 DVD**

GET OVER IT ★★ A popular high-school girl dumps her jock boyfriend in this shopworn and occasionally gross teen comedy. He tries to coax her back by auditioning for a school play in which she stars. His best friend's sister coaches him in the art of love and Shakespeare, and it doesn't take a rocket scientist to predict who falls in love. Rated R for language, violence, and sexual situations. 85m. **DIR:** Tommy O'Haver. **CAST:** Kirsten Dunst, Ben Foster, Melissa Sagemiller, Shane West, Sisqo, Martin Short. **2001 DVD**

GET REAL ★★★ A gay teenager falls in love with his school's most handsome athlete, who furtively returns his affections but won't speak to him in the halls. The story is familiar, even a little trite, and at times it's as solemn and moony as most teenagers in love, straight or gay. It could have used a little more humor, perhaps, but the appealing cast puts it over with conviction. Rated R for language and sexual content. 110m. **DIR:** Simon Shore. **CAST:** Ben Silverstone, Brad Gorton, Charlotte Brittain, Stacy Hart. **1998 DVD**

GET SHORTY ★★★★★ John Travolta solidified his status as the comeback king of the 1990s with his performance in this smart, often outrageous screen adaptation of the Elmore Leonard novel. Travolta plays Chili Palmer, a collector for the mob who, after being sent to Hollywood to collect some outstanding debts, decides to go into business for himself—specifically, the movie business. This is the best insider's look at the sleazy side of Tinsel Town since Robert Altman's *The Player*. Rated R for profanity and violence. 105m. **DIR:** Barry Sonnenfeld. **CAST:** John Travolta, Gene Hackman, René Russo, Danny DeVito, Bette Midler, Dennis Farina, Delroy Lindo, James Gandolfini, David Paymer, Martin Ferrero, Miguel Sandoval, Jonathan Gries, Linda Hart. **1995 DVD**

GET SMART AGAIN ★★1/2 This pleasant trip down memory lane reunites the cast of the TV sitcom for one last go at the creeps of KAOS. Breezy, pleasant, and funnier than you'd expect, in a silly way. Made for TV. 93m. **DIR:** Gary Nelson. **CAST:** Don Adams, Barbara Feldon. **1989**

GET TO KNOW YOUR RABBIT ★★★ This cute comedy won't appeal to everyone but will captivate fans of the Smothers Brothers' brand of offbeat humor. Tom Smothers wants to be a magician so he takes lessons from Orson Welles. But it's a lost cause. The satire hurts, but the laughs help. Rated R. 91m. **DIR:** Brian De Palma. **CAST:** Tom Smothers, Orson Welles, John Astin, Katharine Ross, Samantha Jones, M. Emmet Walsh. **1972**

GETAWAY, THE ★★★1/2 Surprisingly effective scene-for-scene remake of director Sam Peckinpah's flawed but sometimes brilliant action film. Alec Baldwin lacks the charisma of Steve McQueen as a convict who secures his release from prison with the help of his wife, but Kim Basinger outdoes Ali MacGraw as the other half of this modern-day outlaw couple. Rated R for violence, profanity, nudity and simulated sex. 115m. **DIR:** Roger Donaldson. **CAST:** Alec Baldwin, Kim Basinger, James Woods, Michael Madsen, David Morse, Jennifer Tilly, James Stephens, Burton Gilliam, Richard Farnsworth. **1994 DVD**

GETAWAY, THE ★★★★ Top-notch adventure and excitement occur when convict Steve McQueen has his wife seduce the Texas Parole Board chairman (Ben Johnson) in exchange for his early freedom. McQueen becomes jealous and resentful after the deal is consummated and kills the chairman, setting off a shotgun-charged chase. Rated PG. 122m. **DIR:** Sam Peckinpah. **CAST:** Steve McQueen, Ali MacGraw, Ben Johnson, Sally Struthers. **1972 DVD**

GETTING AWAY WITH MURDER ★★ A fabulous cast is wasted on this unfunny stab at black comedy. When Jack Lambert (Dan Aykroyd) suspects his neighbor is actually a Nazi war criminal, he decides to take the law into his own hands. After killing poor Max Mueller (Jack Lemmon), Lambert realizes it's a case of mistaken identity. Okay, you can laugh now. Rated R for profanity. 92m. **DIR:** Harvey Miller. **CAST:** Dan Aykroyd, Jack Lemmon, Lily Tomlin, Bonnie Hunt, Brian Kerwin. **1996**

GETTING EVEN WITH DAD ★★★1/2 enjoyable, lightweight comedy that serves mainly as a showcase for its big-name Hollywood players. An 11-year-old boy blackmails his con man father into going straight in an effort to bond with him. Rated PG. 110m. **DIR:** Howard Deutch. **CAST:** Ted Danson, Macaulay Culkin, Glenne Headly, Hector Elizondo, Gailard Sartain, Saul Rubinek. **1994 DVD**

GETTING GOTTI ★★★1/2 The high-profile crime trial of reputed mob boss John Gotti gets the made-for-television treatment in this absorbing, hard-hitting courtroom drama. Lorraine Bracco stars as the assistant U.S. attorney who grew up with Gotti, and now wants to put him behind bars. Anthony Denison is both appropriately charming and volatile as Gotti, whose Teflon alibi is about to get the acid test. Director Robert Young convincingly separates high drama from fact to deliver a film that packs quite a punch. 93m. **DIR:** Robert Young. **CAST:** Lorraine Bracco, Anthony Denison, Ellen Burstyn. **1994**

GETTING IN ★★ Medical thriller desperately in need of a transfusion. Med student Gabriel Higgs failed to make the cut to attend Johns Hopkins Medical School. Sixth on the waiting list, he attempts to bribe students ahead of him in order to improve his chances. No need: Someone is murdering the candidates, and it looks like Higgs is the guilty party. Rated R for violence, adult situations, and language. 94m. **DIR:** Doug Liman. **CAST:** Kristy Swanson, Andrew McCarthy, Stephen Mailer, Dave Chappelle. **1993**

GETTING IT RIGHT ★★★★1/2 Surrounded by a wonderful cast of endearing eccentrics, Jesse Birdsall sails through his role as a 31-year-old virgin who becomes a sensitive lover (to Lynn Redgrave's madcap neglected socialite). Something of an updated version of the British social comedies of the sixties (*Georgy Girl*, *Alfie*). Highly recommended. Rated R for nudity and sexual situations. 102m. **DIR:** Randal Kleiser. **CAST:** Jesse Birdsall, Helena Bonham Carter, Peter Cook, John Gielgud, Jane Horrocks, Lynn Redgrave. **1989**

GETTING OF WISDOM, THE ★★★★ Out of Australia, this better-than-average rite-of-passage story of an unrefined country girl (Susannah Fowle) who gets sent off to school in the city displays all the qualities of top-notch directing. The girl is easy prey for her more sophisticated, yet equally immature classmates. The story takes place in the mid-1800s and is taken from the classic Australian novel by Henry Handel Richardson. Not rated, but the equivalent of a G. 100m. **DIR:** Bruce Beresford. **CAST:** Susannah Fowle, Sheila Helpmann, Patricia Kennedy, Hilary Ryan. **1980**

GETTING OUT ★★★1/2 An intense performance from Rebecca DeMornay knocks this right out of the usual range of made-for-TV flicks. She plays a tough troubled woman trying to turn her life around, without much help from her nightmare of a mother. The script has some depth to it, but the real treasure is DeMornay. Not rated; contains violence and sexual situations. 92m. **DIR:** John Korty. **CAST:** Rebecca DeMornay, Ellen Burstyn, Robert Knipper, Carol Mitchell-Leon, Richard Jenkins. **1993**

GETTING OVER 🦃 This low-budget black exploitation flick is so poorly lit that it's hard to discern the facial expressions of the actors. Not rated; it contains profanity. 108m. **DIR:** Bernie Rollins. **CAST:** John Daniels, Gwen Brisco, Paulette Gibson. **1980**

GETTING PERSONAL ★★1/2 Michael Landes and Hedy Burress are extremely likable as a young couple trying to connect. After waking up on her porch, Landes sees Burress as the woman of his dreams, but only if he can resolve the nightmarish conflicts of his past. The story and direction are adequate, but the stars make this trip worth the time. Also released as *Lost and Found*. Rated R for language. 82m. **DIR:** Ron Burrus. **CAST:** Michael Landes, Geoffrey Blake, Hedy Burress, John Shea, Lane Smith. **1999 DVD**

GETTING PHYSICAL ★★★1/2 Alexandra Paul plays Nadine, a pudgy junk-food addict who decides to toughen up after her purse is stolen. Couch potatoes can vicariously experience the joy of Nadine's transformation from chubby wimp to lean bodybuilder. A must-see for everyone who dreams about a fitter life-style. Made for television, this is unrated and very mild. 95m. **DIR:** Steven H. Stern. **CAST:** Alexandra Paul, Sandahl Bergman, David Naughton. **1984**

GETTING STRAIGHT ★★1/2 During the campus riots of the 1960s, Hollywood jumped on the bandwagon with such forgettable films as *The Strawberry Statement* and *R.P.M.* Add *Getting Straight* to the list. Elliott Gould plays a "hip" graduate student caught up in campus unrest. It now seems like an odd curio. Rated PG. 124m. **DIR:** Richard Rush. **CAST:** Elliott Gould, Candice Bergen, Max Julien, Jeff Corey, Robert F. Lyons. **1970**

GETTYSBURG ★★ Civil War buffs will revel in the authenticity writer-director Ronald F. Maxwell brings to this epic film, while all others will find it overlong and lethargic. That said, the sections in the first half of the movie featuring Jeff Daniels and Sam Elliott are superb. Rated PG for violence. 248m. **DIR:** Ronald F. Maxwell. **CAST:** Tom Berenger, Jeff Daniels, Sam Elliott, Martin Sheen, Richard Jordan, Stephen Lang, C. Thomas Howell, Kevin Conway, Andrew Prine, John Diehl, Richard Anderson, Maxwell Caulfield, Timothy Scott, George Lazenby. **1993 DVD**

GHETTO BLASTER 🦃 Another war vet returns home to find it overrun by gangs and decides to do something about it. Rated R for violence, nudity, and profanity. 82m. **DIR:** Alan A. Stewart. **CAST:** Richard Hatch, R. G. Armstrong, Richard Jaeckel. **1988**

GHIDRAH, THE THREE-HEADED MONSTER ★★★ A giant egg from outer space crashes into Japan and hatches the colossal three-headed flying monster of the title. It takes the combined forces of Godzilla, Rodan, and Mothra to save Tokyo. Good Japanese monster movie is marred only by dumb subplot of evil agent out to kidnap a Martian princess. 85m. **DIR:** Inoshiro Honda. **CAST:** Yosuke Natsuki, Yuriko Hoshi, Hiroshi Koizumi. **1965**

GHOST, THE (1963) ★★★ Barbara Steele is a faithless wife who poisons her husband, only to have him return and exact revenge. Entertaining Italian gothic that's a sequel of sorts to the same director's *The Horrible Dr. Hitchcock*. A must for devotees of Italian chillers, with splendidly atmospheric camera work. 93m. **DIR:** Robert Hampton (Riccardo Freda). **CAST:** Barbara Steele, Peter Baldwin. **1963**

GHOST (1990) ★★★ This generally diverting romantic-fantasy-comedy-drama casts Patrick Swayze as a murder victim who tries to protect his wife (Demi Moore) from his killers with the help of a psychic (Whoopi Goldberg). The scenes between Swayze and Moore are designed to be ultraromantic, Goldberg's scenes are played for laughs, and the crimes are hard-edged. Director Jerry Zucker isn't always successful in balancing so many elements and tones. Rated PG-13 for violence, suggested sex, and profanity. 105m. **DIR:** Jerry Zucker. **CAST:** Patrick Swayze, Demi Moore, Whoopi Goldberg, Tony Goldwyn. **1990 DVD**

GHOST AND MR. CHICKEN, THE ★★★ Okay, so you can spot the stunt double and Don Knotts's twitches are a little, well, obvious. Still, fans of Knotts's familiar routine will enjoy watching their skinny underdog hero solve a ghost story while winning the prettiest girl in town. One of the better of Knotts benign, yet entertaining, comedies. Not rated. 90m. **DIR:** Alan Rafkin. **CAST:** Don Knotts, Joan Staley, Dick Sargent, Liam Redmond, Skip Homeier, Philip Ober. **1966**

GHOST AND MRS. MUIR, THE ★★★★ Romantic comedy at its best in this heartwarming tale about a young widow who decides to live in the lighthouse home of a long-dead sailor, setting the stage for a perfect love story. 104m. **DIR:** Joseph L. Mankiewicz. **CAST:** Gene Tierney, Rex Harrison, Edna Best, George Sanders, Anna Lee, Natalie Wood. **1947**

GHOST AND THE DARKNESS, THE ★★★★ A thrilling, chilling yarn about the endangerment of Great Britain's building of a railway through eastern Africa by a pair of clever, man-eating lions. Despite his success against difficult odds, army engineer Val Kilmer has never encountered such a situation. So he joins forces with a great white hunter to put an end to this almost unworldly duo. Rated R for violence and profanity. 109m. **DIR:** Stephen Hopkins. **CAST:** Michael Douglas, Val Kilmer, Tom Wilkinson, John Kani, Bernard Hill, Brian McCardle, Om Puri. **1996 DVD**

GHOST BREAKERS ★★★1/2 Amusing Bob Hope romp finds him investigating the eerie mansion inherited by Paulette Goddard. The laughs mix evenly with the thrills in this hilarious blend of gags and mayhem. Often imitated (film was inspiration for Martin-Lewis vehicle *Scared Stiff*) but never equaled. Great atmosphere. 85m. **DIR:** George Marshall. **CAST:** Bob Hope, Paulette Goddard, Richard Carlson, Anthony Quinn, Paul Lukas. **1940 DVD**

GHOST BRIGADE ★★ A band of ghost soldiers is trying to take over Earth. An interesting concept, but the story moves way too slowly. Rated R for violence and profanity. 80m. **DIR:** George Hickenlooper. **CAST:** Corbin Bernsen, Martin Sheen, Adrian Pasdar, Ray Wise, Cynda Williams. **1992**

GHOST CATCHERS, THE ★★★ Nightclub performers Ole Olsen and Chic Johnson help a southern colonel and his two daughters rid their mansion of ghosts. Typically wacky shenanigans from the *Hellzapoppin* duo. Look carefully for Mel Torme as a jazz drummer, and Morton Downey Sr., who sings "These Foolish Things." B&W; 69m. **DIR:** Eddie Cline. **CAST:** Ole Olsen, Chic Johnson, Gloria Jean, Martha O'Driscoll, Leo Carrillo, Lon Chaney Jr., Andy Devine. **1944**

GHOST CHASE ★★ Teen filmmakers are taken on by a ruthless movie mogul after one of the boys inherits some seemingly worthless trinkets from his grandfather. Decent special effects, but acting and dialogue are lifeless. Rated PG for profanity. 89m. **DIR:** Roland Emmerich. **CAST:** Jason Lively, Tim McDaniel, Jill Whitlow, Paul Gleason. **1988**

GHOST DAD ★★★1/2 This family-oriented, *Topper*-style comedy casts Bill Cosby as a daddy (what else?) who continues to provide for his family—even after he's dead. The story's serious underpinnings give resonance to this comic delight. Rated PG. 95m. **DIR:** Sidney Poitier. **CAST:** Bill Cosby, Denise Nicholas, Kimberly Russell. **1990 DVD**

GHOST DOG: THE WAY OF THE SAMURAI ★★★★ Contract killer adheres to the tenets of an 18th-century Samurai handbook in this gangster hip-hop Eastern Western. His best friend is a Haitian ice-cream vendor who does not understand a word he says. His enemies are twilight-year Italian-American hoods whose boss watches TV cartoons. This violent, often wildy funny spin on Sam Peckinpah's infatuation with men on the brink of extinction is set on a seedy Sopranos turf and fueled by music from Wu-Tang Clan's RZA, "the Thelonious Monk of hip-hop." Rated R for language and violence. 116m. **DIR:** Jim Jarmusch. **CAST:** Forest

Whitaker, Henry Silva, Trissa Vessey, John Tormey, Isaach de Bankole. **2000 DVD**

GHOST FEVER 🦃 Southern cops investigate strange happenings at Magnolia Mansion. Director Alan Smithee doesn't exist; it's a fake name applied when the real director (in this case, Lee Madden) doesn't want his name on the final product. Rated PG. 86m. **DIR:** Alan Smithee. **CAST:** Sherman Hemsley, Luis Avalos. **1985**

GHOST GOES WEST, THE ★★★★ A millionaire buys a Scottish castle and transports it stone by stone to America only to discover that it comes complete with a ghost. Robert Donat gives a memorable performance in this bit of whimsy. B&W; 100m. **DIR:** René Clair. **CAST:** Robert Donat, Jean Parker. **1935**

GHOST IN MONTE CARLO, A ★★ Weak, flimsy period piece mystery concerns revenge and intrigue among the royalty in beautiful Monte Carlo. 93m. **DIR:** John Hough. **CAST:** Sarah Miles, Oliver Reed, Christopher Plummer, Samantha Eggar, Ron Moody, Fiona Fullerton, Lysette Anthony. **1990**

GHOST IN THE MACHINE ★★1/2 Fans of the *Nightmare on Elm Street* films should enjoy this high-tech variation, where a dying serial killer infiltrates a mainframe computer. No surprises, and the special effects are a bit cheap, but the film is efficiently packaged. Rated R for violence. 95m. **DIR:** Rachel Talalay. **CAST:** Karen Allen, Chris Mulkey, Ken Thorley. **1993**

GHOST IN THE NOONDAY SUN 🦃 Too silly pirate parody. Not rated. 90m. **DIR:** Peter Medak. **CAST:** Peter Sellers, Anthony Franciosa, Peter Boyle, Spike Milligan, Clive Revill. **1974**

GHOST IN THE SHELL ★★★ In a vast Asian city of the future, a female cyborg investigates the sinister doings of a mysterious supercriminal invading the 21st century's information highways. This engrossing Japanese animated feature is definitely not for small children. The confusing plot and dull American voices are drawbacks, but the visual style is fascinating and the action often brilliantly executed. Not rated; contains some nudity and much violence. 82m. **DIR:** Oshii Mamoru. **1995 DVD**

GHOST OF FRANKENSTEIN ★★★1/2 Dr. Frankenstein's second son takes a crack at monster rehabilitation and all's well until Ygor shares his thoughts (literally). This was the fourth Frankenstein film from Universal Studios and the beginning of the series' skid to programmer status. Luckily, Bela Lugosi is back as Ygor, the supporting cast is good, the music score is first-rate, and there are enough dynamic set pieces to liven up the story. B&W; 67m. **DIR:** Erle C. Kenton. **CAST:** Lon Chaney Jr., Cedric Hardwicke, Ralph Bellamy, Lionel Atwill, Bela Lugosi. **1942**

GHOST PATROL ★★ Colonel Tim McCoy takes a commanding lead in this low-budget film about a government agent investigating the strange crashes of airplanes carrying top-secret information. An effort to cash in on the unexpected success of Gene Autry's *Phantom Empire* and Tom Mix's *Miracle Rider*. B&W; 57m. **DIR:** Sam Newfield. **CAST:** Tim McCoy, Claudia Dell, Walter Miller, Wheeler Oakman, Slim Whitaker. **1936**

GHOST SHIP ★★1/2 Creaky but occasionally spooky British tale of a couple who buy a ship only to discover it is haunted by the ghosts of some unhappy previous owners. Not rated. B&W; 69m. **DIR:** Vernon Sewell. **CAST:** Dermot Walsh, Hazel Court, Joss Ackland. **1951 DVD**

GHOST STORY 🦃 This film, based on the bestselling novel by Peter Straub, is about as frightening as an episode of *Sesame Street*. Rated R because of shock scenes involving rotting corpses and violence. 110m. **DIR:** John Irvin. **CAST:** John Houseman, Douglas Fairbanks Jr., Melvyn Douglas, Fred Astaire, Alice Krige, Craig Wasson, Patricia Neal. **1981 DVD**

GHOST TOWN ★★ A passable time waster mixing two genres, the horror film and the Western. Modern-day deputy (Franc Luz) with a penchant for the Old West stumbles into a satanic netherworld: ghost town in the middle of the Arizona desert. Rated R for nudity, violence, and profanity. 85m. **DIR:** Richard Governor. **CAST:** Franc Luz, Catherine Hickland, Bruce Glover. **1988**

GHOST TOWN LAW ★★★ Atmospheric B Western has the Rough Riders on the trail of a gang that murdered two of their colleagues. The gang, in a nice touch, hides out in a ghost town, where there might be more than just outlaws for our heroes to contend with. B&W; 62m. **DIR:** Howard Bretherton. **CAST:** Buck Jones, Tim McCoy, Raymond Hatton, Charles King. **1942**

GHOST TOWN RENEGADES ★★★ Outlaws try to take over an abandoned mining town from its rightful owners. Lash's bullwhip dispenses its usual fast justice. B&W; 57m. **DIR:** Ray Taylor. **CAST:** Lash LaRue, Jack Ingram, Terry Frost. **1947**

GHOST WALKS, THE ★★1/2 Actors rehearsing a play in a spooky old house get more than they planned on as an escaped lunatic is thrown into the mix. B&W; 65m. **DIR:** Frank Strayer. **CAST:** John Miljan, June Collyer, Richard Carle, Henry Kolker, Johnny Arthur. **1935**

GHOST WARRIOR ★★1/2 In Japan, two skiers exploring a cave find a 400-year-old samurai warrior entombed in ice. He is taken to the United States in a hush-hush operation and revived. Although slow at times, this film is an entertaining, though violent, diversion. Rated R for violence. 86m. **DIR:** Larry Carbol. **CAST:** Hiroshi Fujioka, John Calvin, Janet Julian, Andy Wood. **1984**

GHOST WORLD ★★★★ An alienated teen (Thora Birch) responds to a personal ad as a prank, but when she gets to know the lonely 35ish geek who placed it (Steve Buscemi), she finds him a kindred spirit. What starts as a sort of female *Catcher in the Rye* evolves into something surprisingly touching and bittersweet, with fine acting (especially by Buscemi). Rated R for profanity. 111m. **DIR:** Terry Zwigoff. **CAST:** Thora Birch, Steve Buscemi, Scarlett Johansson, Brad Renfro, Illeana Douglas. **2001 DVD**

GHOST WRITER ★★ Harmless piece of fluff about a writer who moves into her new home only to find it haunted by an actress who was murdered and wants to find her killer. Lightweight. Rated PG for adult situations. 94m. **DIR:** Kenneth J. Hall. **CAST:** Audrey Landers, Judy Landers, Jeff Conaway, Joey Travolta, Dick Miller. **1989**

GHOSTBUSTERS ★★★★ Bill Murray, Dan Aykroyd, Sigourney Weaver, and Harold Ramis are terrific in this very funny and often frightening comedy-horror film about a special organization that fights evil spirits. Is it *The Exorcist* meets *Saturday Night Live*? That's pretty close—but it's better. Rated PG for profanity and scary scenes. 107m. **DIR:** Ivan Reitman. **CAST:** Bill Murray, Dan Aykroyd, Sigourney Weaver, Harold Ramis, Annie Potts, Ernie Hudson, William Atherton, Rick Moranis. **1984 DVD**

GHOSTBUSTERS II ★★1/2 In this watchable sequel to the 1984 box-office blockbuster, the original cast returns to take on an explosion of evil spirits on a fateful New Year's Eve. The formula now seems fairly tired, despite some funny moments at the outset. Older kids are more likely to enjoy the shenanigans than adults. Rated PG. 110m. **DIR:** Ivan Reitman. **CAST:** Bill Murray, Dan Aykroyd, Sigourney Weaver, Harold Ramis, Rick Moranis, Ernie Hudson, Annie Potts. **1989 DVD**

GHOSTRIDERS ★★ Just before being hanged in 1886, a notorious criminal puts a curse on the preacher responsible for his execution. One hundred years later he and his gang return to wreak vengeance on the preacher's descendants. Rated R for violence and language. 85m. **DIR:** Alan L. Stewart. **CAST:** Bill Shaw. **1987**

GHOSTS CAN'T DO IT ★★ Bo knows breast exposure. Too bad hubby-director John doesn't know anything about making a coherent or even moderately funny movie. Anthony Quinn is Bo's dead husband who appears to her somewhere in the sky, which is a guess because the two only appear on the screen together at the very beginning. Poor ghost effects don't help. Rated R for nudity and profanity. 95m. **DIR:** John Derek. **CAST:** Bo Derek, Anthony Quinn, Don Murray, Julie Newmar, Leo Damian. **1990**

GHOSTS OF BERKELEY SQUARE ★★1/2 After accidentally killing themselves while plotting to murder a superior officer, two British officers are condemned to haunt an old mansion until it is visited by royalty. Routine ghost comedy made palatable by a good cast. B&W; 85m. **DIR:** Vernon Sewell. **CAST:** Robert Morley, Felix Aylmer, Ernest Thesiger, Wilfrid Hyde-White. **1947**

•GHOSTS OF MARS Those who thought John Carpenter could do no worse than *Escape from L.A.* were sadly mistaken; this moronic and unintentionally funny sci-fi thriller is a dog from start to finish. Martian cop Natasha Henstridge and notorious criminal Ice Cube become unlikely allies while fighting dangerous spirits that infect people and turn them into violent refugees from a KISS concert; we haven't seen this many heads roll since Tim Burton's *Sleepy Hollow*. Rated R for violence, profanity, and drug use. 98m. **DIR:** John Carpenter. **CAST:** Ice Cube, Natasha Henstridge, Jason Statham, Pam Grier, Clea DuVall, Joanna Cassidy. **2001 DVD**

GHOSTS OF MISSISSIPPI ★★ This rehash of the 1963 slaying of civil-rights activist Medgar Evers and the trial 30 years later that puts accused killer Byron De La Beckwith behind bars is more pat and dry than dramatic. The film is not so much about the NAACP official who was shot in the back in his own driveway, but rather the white district attorney who reopens the case just as his marriage to an old money southern belle collapses. Rated PG-13 for violence and language. 123m. **DIR:** Rob Reiner. **CAST:** Alec Baldwin, James Woods, Whoopi Goldberg, Craig T. Nelson, William H. Macy, Susann Thompson. **1996 DVD**

GHOSTS ON THE LOOSE Silly movie pits moronic East Side Kids against a bored Bela Lugosi and his German henchmen in this pallid variation on the "old haunted house" theme. B&W; 65m. **DIR:** William Beaudine. **CAST:** The East Side Kids, Bela Lugosi, Ava Gardner, Rick Vallin. **1943 DVD**

GHOUL, THE ★★1/2 Trading on the success he achieved in *Frankenstein* and *The Mummy*, Boris Karloff plays an Egyptologist seeking eternal life through a special jewel. He dies and the jewel is stolen, bringing him back from the dead to seek revenge on the thief. B&W; 73m. **DIR:** T. Hayes Hunter. **CAST:** Boris Karloff, Cedric Hardwicke, Ernest Thesiger, Ralph Richardson, Kathleen Harrison. **1933**

GHOUL, THE ★★1/2 "Stay out of the garden, dear, there's a flesh-eating monster living there." One of Peter Cushing's many horror films. No gore, but not boring, either. Rated R. 88m. **DIR:** Freddie Francis. **CAST:** Peter Cushing, John Hurt, Gwen Watford. **1975**

GHOULIES Gruesome. Rated PG-13 for violence and sexual innuendo. 87m. **DIR:** Luca Bercovici. **CAST:** Peter Liapis, Lisa Pelikan, John Nance. **1985**

GHOULIES II Dreadful sequel that dramatizes the further adventures of those mischievous little demons. Rated PG-13 for violence. 89m. **DIR:** Albert Band. **CAST:** Damon Martin, Royal Dano. **1987 DVD**

GHOULIES III Third chapter in the series finds the ghoulish slime-balls creating havoc at a local university. Like this movie, they flunk out! Rated R for violence. 94m. **DIR:** John Carl Buechler. **CAST:** Kevin McCarthy, Evan Mackenzie. **1989**

GHOULIES IV This series about pesky little creatures summoned up by black magic got real old even before the first chapter came out. Rated R for mayhem. 84m. **DIR:** Jim Wynorski. **CAST:** Peter Liapis, Barbara Alyn Woods, Stacie Randall, Bobby DiCicco. **1993**

G.I. BLUES ★★★1/2 Juliet Prowse improves this otherwise average Elvis Presley film. The action takes place in Germany, where Elvis makes a bet with his GI buddies he can date the aloof Prowse, who plays a nightclub dancer. 104m. **DIR:** Norman Taurog. **CAST:** Elvis Presley, Juliet Prowse. **1960 DVD**

G.I. JANE ★★★★ Demi Moore demonstrates true grit in this testosterone-laden tale of Lt. Jordan O'Neil, the nation's first female officer allowed to participate in Navy SEAL training. Minimizing this character's stridency or "Joan of Arc" tendencies, results in a well-balanced story about a capable and intelligent young woman fighting for the chance to demonstrate her skills. While hardly the last word on basic training, this film introduces several intriguing characters, from a poetry-quoting training chief to a foxy U.S. senator, who may not be as dedicated a sponsor as O'Neil believes. Rated R for profanity, violence, and brief nudity. 125m. **DIR:** Ridley Scott. **CAST:** Demi Moore, Viggo Mortensen, Anne Bancroft, Jason Beghe, Daniel Von Bargen, John Michael Higgins. **1997 DVD**

GIANT ★★★1/2 The third part of director George Stevens's American Trilogy, which also included *Shane* and *A Place in the Sun*, this 1956 release traces the life of a cattle rancher through two generations. Although the lead performances by Elizabeth Taylor, Rock Hudson, and James Dean are unconvincing when the stars are poorly "aged" with makeup, *Giant* is still a stylish, if overlong movie that lives up to its title. 198m. **DIR:**

George Stevens. **CAST:** James Dean, Rock Hudson, Elizabeth Taylor, Carroll Baker, Dennis Hopper. **1956**

GIANT BEHEMOTH, THE ★★1/2 A dinosaur attacks London in what is a virtual remake of the same director's *Beast from 20,000 Fathoms.* The animated monster by Willis O'Brien (the original *King Kong*) isn't bad, but he was clearly working with a low budget. B&W; 79m. **DIR:** Eugene Lourie. **CAST:** Gene Evans, Andre Morell, Jack MacGowran. **1959**

GIANT CLAW, THE A must-see for bad-movie buffs, this sci-fi thriller pitting air force jets against a prehistoric bird features a puppet monster so tacky you'll love it. 76m. **DIR:** Fred F. Sears. **CAST:** Jeff Morrow, Mara Corday, Morris Ankrum. **1957**

GIANT FROM THE UNKNOWN Legendary conquistador buried for centuries in the mountains of California comes to life and continues his cruel ways until archaeologists devise a way to end him. B&W; 77m. **DIR:** Richard Cunha. **CAST:** Ed Kemmer, Sally Fraser, Buddy Baer, Morris Ankrum, Bob Steele. **1958 DVD**

GIANT GILA MONSTER, THE Slimy, slow-moving monster lizard prowls the Texas countryside. B&W; 74m. **DIR:** Ray Kellogg. **CAST:** Don Sullivan. **1959 DVD**

GIANT OF METROPOLIS, THE ★★1/2 This above-average sword-and-sandal adventure has nothing to do with Fritz Lang's silent classic, *Metropolis*, despite title similarities. Set in 10,000 B.C., it's about a mythical strongman (Gordon Mitchell) who emerges from the desert to battle a sadistic despot. 82m. **DIR:** Umberto Scarpelli. **CAST:** Gordon Mitchell. **1962 DVD**

GIANT ROBO ★★★★ Broadly played and beautifully drawn, this Japanese animated series blends the feel of traditional Saturday matinee serials with today's best animation. Super villains and heroes (including the radio-controlled Giant Robo and his boy master) clash over the fate of the world. Absolutely stunning animation with delightful characters and action. Dubbed in English. Not rated, but suitable for most audiences. 55m. **DIR:** Yasuhiro Imagawa. **1992**

GIDEON'S TRUMPET ★★★★ Henry Fonda is the chief delight in this factual account of Clarence Earl Gideon, who was thrown into prison in the early 1960s for a minor crime—and denied a legal counsel because he could not afford to pay for one. Gideon boned up on the laws of our land and concluded that everybody was entitled to a lawyer, whether or not such was affordable. This made-for-TV movie accurately follows Anthony Lewis's source book. Not rated; suitable for family viewing. 104m. **DIR:** Robert Collins. **CAST:** Henry Fonda, John Houseman, José Ferrer. **1980**

GIDGET ★★1/2 The eternal beach bunny, Gidget (Sandra Dee), becomes involved with Cliff Robertson in order to make the man she's infatuated with (James Darren) notice her. This is the first and the best of a subpar surfer series. 95m. **DIR:** Paul Wendkos. **CAST:** Sandra Dee, James Darren, Arthur O'Connell, Cliff Robertson, Doug McClure. **1959**

GIDGET GOES HAWAIIAN ★★ Everyone's favorite "girl-midget" (played here by Deborah Walley, taking over from Sandra Dee) returns to the screen in this inoffensive, brainless sequel to the 1959 box-office hit. 102m. **DIR:** Paul Wendkos. **CAST:** Deborah Walley, James Darren, Michael Callan, Carl Reiner, Peggy Cass, Eddie Foy Jr. **1961**

GIDGET GOES TO ROME ★★ The irrepressible beach bunny presses onward, if not upward, in this below-average sequel to *Gidget*. 101m. **DIR:** Paul Wendkos. **CAST:** Cindy Carol, James Darren, Jeff Donnell, Jessie Royce Landis. **1963**

GIFT, THE ★★★ A 55-year-old bank worker (Pierre Mondy) decides to take early retirement. So his coworkers give him an unusual gift, an expensive hooker (Clio Goldsmith), who is asked to seduce him without his knowing her profession. An amiable sex comedy that most adult viewers will find diverting. In French with English subtitles. Rated R for nudity and profanity. 105m. **DIR:** Michel Lang. **CAST:** Clio Goldsmith, Pierre Mondy, Claudia Cardinale. **1982**

GIFT, THE ★★1/2 A psychic in the rural South, whose visions helped to convict a wife-beating neighbor of murder, later becomes convinced that the real killer is still at large. It doesn't take much ESP to see where things are going and who the culprit is, but the cast is better than usual for this kind of film, which handles the formula with energy and style. Rated R for profanity, nudity, and suggested violence. 111m. **DIR:** Sam Raimi. **CAST:** Cate Blanchett, Keanu Reeves, Greg Kinnear, Hilary Swank, Giovanni Ribisi. **2000 DVD**

GIFT OF LOVE, THE ★★ Inspired by, but bearing very little resemblance to, O. Henry's short-story masterpiece "The Gift of the Magi," this fluffy TV special features Marie Osmond and Timothy Bottoms as star-crossed lovers. Osmond's acting skills are minimal, but her turn-of-the-century gowns are splendid. 96m. **DIR:** Don Chaffey. **CAST:** Marie Osmond, Timothy Bottoms, James Woods, June Lockhart. **1978**

GIFT OF LOVE: THE DANIEL HUFFMAN STORY ★★★ This heartwarming tale chronicles the tough decision made by 17-year-old Daniel Huffman: to donate one of his kidneys to save his grandmother's life. Unfortunately, that also means the high-school football star will never play the game again, and may never get a scholarship to attend college. While the story is inspiring, there's not enough to make a decent movie, and so this made-for-cable effort winds up being a ninety-minute commercial for organ donation. Not rated; contains mild profanity. 93m. **DIR:** John Korty. **CAST:** Debbie Reynolds, Ed Marinaro, John Bourgeois, Dan MacDonald, Elden Henson. **2000**

GIG, THE ★★★ Very nicely done comedy-drama concerning a group of men who get together once a week to play Dixieland jazz. Film admirably avoids the clichés associated with this type of buddy film. Nice ensemble acting, with Cleavon Little and Joe Silver leading the way. Give this one a try. 92m. **DIR:** Frank D. Gilroy. **CAST:** Wayne Rogers, Cleavon Little, Joe Silver, Andrew Duncan, Daniel Nalbach. **1985**

GIGASHADOW ★★ The further adventures of the *Lexx*, a gigantic living spaceship, and its bizarre crew. For fans of the *Lexx* series only. Rated R for violence and sexuality. 93m. **DIR:** Robert Sigl. **CAST:** Malcolm McDowell, Brian Downey, Eva Habermann, Michael McManus, Michael Habeck. **1997**

GIGI ★★★★ Young Leslie Caron, being groomed as a courtesan, has more serious romance (with Louis Jourdan) on her mind. This exquisite Lerner-Loewe confection won nine Oscars and was the last nugget from the Golden Age of MGM Musicals. Maurice Chevalier and Hermione Gingold lend an unforgettable touch of class. 116m. **DIR:** Vincente Minnelli. **CAST:** Leslie Caron, Louis Jourdan, Maurice Chevalier, Hermione Gingold, Jacques Bergerac, Eva Gabor. **1958 DVD**

GILDA ★★★★ Glenn Ford plays a small-time gambler who goes to work for a South American casino owner and his beautiful wife, Gilda (Rita Hayworth). When the casino owner disappears and is presumed dead, Ford marries Hayworth and proceeds to make her life miserable. Then the husband returns, seeking revenge against them. There is some violence in this film. B&W; 110m. **DIR:** Charles Vidor. **CAST:** Glenn Ford, Rita Hayworth, George Macready, Joseph Calleia, Steven Geray. **1946 DVD**

GILDA LIVE ★★ We've always loved Gilda Radner's characters from *Saturday Night Live,* and they're all represented in *Gilda Live*. But something is missing in her live show. The result is very few laughs. Rated R. 96m. **DIR:** Mike Nichols. **CAST:** Gilda Radner, Don Novello, Paul Shaffer. **1980**

GIMME SHELTER ★★★★ This documentary chronicles the events leading up to and including the now-infamous free Rolling Stones concert in 1969 at the Altamont Speedway outside San Francisco. It's the dark side of Woodstock, with many unforgettable scenes, including the actual murder of a spectator by the Hell's Angels in front of the stage as the Stones are playing. Rated R for violence, language, and scenes of drug use. 91m. **DIR:** David Maysles, Albert Maysles, Charlotte Zwerin. **CAST:** The Rolling Stones, Melvin Belli. **1970**

GIN GAME, THE ★★★★1/2 A sensitive, insightful, and touchingly funny, award-winning Broadway play taped live in London with its two original stars. The enchanting performances are highlighted with superb simplicity in this two-character play that explores the developing relationship between two senior citizens. Not rated, but freely sprinkled with profanity. 82m. **DIR:** Mike Nichols. **CAST:** Jessica Tandy, Hume Cronyn. **1984**

GINGER 🦃 We don't want to say this is the best of the three films starring Cheri Caffaro as a socialite turned crime fighter—let's just say it's the least repulsive. Rated R for violence and nudity. 89m. **DIR:** Don Schain. **CAST:** Cheri Caffaro, Cindy Barnett. **1971**

GINGER ALE AFTERNOON 🦃 Tedious would-be comedy about a bickering couple. Rated R for profanity and brief nudity. 88m. **DIR:** Rafal Zielinski. **CAST:** Dana Andersen, John M. Jackson, Yeardley Smith. **1989**

GINGER AND FRED ★★★★ Set in the bizarre world of a modern-television supernetwork, this Fellini fantasy presents Giulietta Masina and Marcello Mastroianni as Ginger and Fred—a dance couple of the late Forties who copied the style of Fred Astaire and Ginger Rogers. The two are reunited for *Here's to You*, a television extravaganza. This is a brilliant satire of television and modern life. Rated PG-13 for profanity and adult themes. 127m. **DIR:** Federico Fellini. **CAST:** Marcello Mastroianni, Giulietta Masina, Franco Fabrizi. **1986**

GINGER IN THE MORNING ★★1/2 A lonely salesman, Monte Markham, picks up a hitchhiker, Sissy Spacek, and romance blossoms in this okay romantic comedy. No great revelations about human nature will be found in this one, just harmless fluff that will be forgotten soon after it's been viewed. 89m. **DIR:** Gordon Wiles. **CAST:** Sissy Spacek, Monte Markham, Slim Pickens, Susan Oliver, Mark Miller. **1973 DVD**

•GINGER SNAPS ★★★ Better-than-average direct-to-video Canadian thriller about the bond that develops between sisters Ginger and Brigitte when they get picked on at school. That bond is tested when Ginger is attacked by a werewolf, turning her into a vicious beast and forcing Brigitte to take drastic steps in order to save her sister and the bullies at school. Director John Fawcett has a lot of fun with the premise, substituting Ginger's animal urges with puberty to good result. Filled with smart dialogue, engaging performances and just enough gore to keep core fans happy. Not rated; contains adult situations, language, nudity, and violence. 108m. **DIR:** John Fawcett. **CAST:** Emily Perkins, Katherine Isabelle, Kris Lemche, Mimi Rogers. **2000 DVD**

GINGERBREAD MAN, THE ★★★1/2 Southern defense attorney Rick Magruder is hired by a sultry waitress to get her father committed to a mental institution. The apparently deranged elder escapes from custody and stalks Magruder's family. The acting in this atmospheric, melodramatic thriller about manipulation and lust is excellent. Rated R for language, violence, and nudity. 115m. **DIR:** Robert Altman. **CAST:** Kenneth Branagh, Embeth Davidtz, Robert Downey Jr., Robert Duvall, Daryl Hannah, Mae Whitman, Famke Janssen, Tom Berenger. **1998 DVD**

GIRL, THE (1986) ★★★ A strange and disturbing European film analyzing the seduction of a powerful attorney by a 14-year-old schoolgirl. Lust, passion, and murder become the norm. Unfortunately, what might have been a very powerful film becomes slow and plods to the finish. Though no rating is available, there is ample sex and nudity throughout the film. 104m. **DIR:** Arne Mattson. **CAST:** Franco Nero, Bernice Stegers, Clare Powney, Christopher Lee. **1986**

GIRL, THE (1999) 🦃 A lesbian romance between an art student and a nightclub singer is threatened by the singer's involvement with a sinister man. The best to be said for this dreary, leaden, excruciating *film noir* is that the actresses seem to have carefully memorized their few lines. Not rated; contains profanity, sexual scenes, and mature themes. 84m. **DIR:** Sandra Zeig. **CAST:** Claire Keim, Agathe De La Boulaye, Cyril Lecomte, Sandra Nkake. **1999**

GIRL, A GUY AND A GOB, A ★★★ A silly, predictable comedy that tends to grow on you; it focuses on a working girl, her happy-go-lucky sailor boyfriend, and an upper-crust executive. Dated, of course, but cute and polished. Movie buffs will be interested to note the producer was legendary Harold Lloyd. Not rated; contains nothing offensive. B&W; 90m. **DIR:** Richard Wallace. **CAST:** Lucille Ball, George Murphy, Edmond O'Brien, Henry Travers. **1941**

GIRL CAN'T HELP IT, THE ★★★ Tom Ewell is given the task of turning squealing Jayne Mansfield into a singer on the clear understanding that he keep his hands to himself, a tough request when faced with the would-be singer's winning ways and obvious charms. Great rock 'n' roll by some of its premier interpreters is the real reason for watching this film. 99m. **DIR:** Frank Tashlin. **CAST:** Tom Ewell, Jayne Mansfield, Edmond

O'Brien, Julie London, Henry Jones, Fats Domino, The Platters, The Treniers, Little Richard, Gene Vincent and His Blue Caps, Eddie Cochran, Barry Gordon, Ray Anthony, Nino Tempo, The Chuckles. **1957**

GIRL CRAZY ★★★ Girls are driving the ever-ebullient Mickey Rooney bonkers. His family sends him to a small southwestern college, hoping the "craze" will fade, but he meets Judy Garland, and away we go into another happy kids-give-a-show musical with glorious George and Ira Gershwin tunes. B&W; 99m. **DIR:** Busby Berkeley, Norman Taurog. **CAST:** Mickey Rooney, Judy Garland, June Allyson, Rags Ragland, Guy Kibbee, Nancy Walker, Henry O'Neill. **1943**

GIRL FROM HUNAN ★★★ At the turn of the century, a Chinese woman's arranged marriage and her place in decent society are threatened by her opposition to the accepted moral standards of her community. In Cantonese with English subtitles. Not rated. 99m. **DIR:** Xie Fei, U Lan. **CAST:** Na Renhua, Liu Qing, Deng Xiaotuang. **1988**

GIRL FROM MISSOURI, THE ★★★★1/2 A delightful comedy that shows Jean Harlow's comedic style to advantage, this is the movie that gave censors headaches because it boldly and bluntly said that some women will do anything for money. B&W; 74m. **DIR:** Jack Conway. **CAST:** Jean Harlow, Franchot Tone, Patsy Kelly, Lewis Stone, Lionel Barrymore, Alan Mowbray, Nat Pendleton, Clara Blandick. **1934**

GIRL FROM PETROVKA, THE ★★★ American journalist Hal Holbrook falls in love with Russian Goldie Hawn while on assignment in the Soviet Union. The manipulative script often becomes overly melodramatic, but the film still works as an effective tearjerker. Something about Hawn's guileless, resourceful character is impossible to resist, and the story's conclusion packs a surprising punch. Rated PG for adult situations. 104m. **DIR:** Robert Ellis Miller. **CAST:** Goldie Hawn, Hal Holbrook, Anthony Hopkins. **1974**

GIRL FROM PHANTASIA ★★★ The title character is gatekeeper of another world who mistakenly crosses into ours in hopes of finding that love has finally returned. Instead, she finds a lecherous young man and a sorceror sworn to destroy her world. A decent entry in the Japanese-animation genre. In Japanese with English subtitles. Not rated; contains violence and nudity. 40m. **DIR:** Jun Kamiya. **1993**

GIRL HAPPY ★★★ This is *Where the Boys Are* in reverse, as Elvis plays chaperon to a Chicago mobster's daughter in Fort Lauderdale, Florida. While Elvis romances vixenish Mary Ann Mobley, his nerdish charge (Shelley Fabares) constantly gets into trouble with a sexy Italian. 96m. **DIR:** Boris Sagal. **CAST:** Elvis Presley, Shelley Fabares, Mary Ann Mobley. **1964**

GIRL HUNTERS, THE ★★1/2 Mickey Spillane plays his creation Mike Hammer in this unusual detective film about a private eye who pulls himself together after a seven-year binge, when he discovers that the woman he thought he sent to her death might still be alive. Lloyd Nolan and Shirley Eaton are the only real actors in this uneven production—the rest of the cast are Spillane's cronies, and many of his favorite bars and hangouts are carefully re-created in this British-made film. 103m. **DIR:** Roy Rowland. **CAST:** Mickey Spillane, Shirley Eaton, Lloyd Nolan, Hy Gardner, Scott Peters. **1963 DVD**

GIRL IN A SWING, THE ★★★1/2 In this atmospheric and sensual suspense-thriller, a young executive travels to Amsterdam, where he falls in love with a woman who may be a murderer. Rated R for nudity, profanity, and violence. 119m. **DIR:** Gordon Hessler. **CAST:** Meg Tilly, Rupert Frazer. **1989**

GIRL IN BLACK STOCKINGS, THE ★★1/2 Who's the mad killer stalking women at a Utah resort? So-so mystery. B&W; 71m. **DIR:** Howard W. Koch. **CAST:** Anne Bancroft, Lex Barker, Mamie Van Doren, John Dehner, Marie Windsor, Stuart Whitman. **1957**

GIRL IN BLUE, THE ★★1/2 Trifling romantic drama about a man obsessed with a woman he glimpsed fleetingly years before. Filmed in Montreal. Not rated, the movie contains brief nudity and sexual situations. 105m. **DIR:** George Kaczender. **CAST:** David Selby, Maud Adams. **1973**

GIRL IN EVERY PORT, A ★★★ Tough sailor with an eye for the ladies discovers a swaggering rival has been beating his time at all ports of call. Louise Brooks has quite a decision to make but she takes it in stride and follows her heart. Breezy, adult comedy-drama is fun to watch and filled with the little touches and interesting interplay between characters that would come to distinguish director Howard Hawks's sound films. B&W; 79m. **DIR:** Howard Hawks. **CAST:** Victor McLaglen, Robert Armstrong, Louise Brooks, Leila Hyams, Francis McDonald. **1928**

GIRL IN EVERY PORT, A ★★ Silly film about sailors involved in horse-racing scheme milks the old hide-the-horse-on-the-ship gag for all that it's worth (which isn't much) and then some. B&W; 86m. **DIR:** Chester Erskine. **CAST:** Groucho Marx, William Bendix, Marie Wilson, Don DeFore, Gene Lockhart. **1952**

GIRL IN THE CADILLAC ★★ An innocent woman inadvertently becomes involved with a trio of bank robbers, falling for one of them. Tolerable if unexceptional comedy-action-romance. Rated R for profanity, violence, and brief nudity. 89m. **DIR:** Lucas Platt. **CAST:** Erika Eleniak, William McNamara, Michael Lerner, Bud Cort. **1995**

GIRL IN THE PICTURE, THE ★★★ A slight but charming movie from Scotland. John Gordon Sinclair plays a Glasgow photographer who's feeling stagnant in his relationship with his design-student girlfriend. The problems they face are never dealt with, but it doesn't seem to matter because the going with this amusing pair is so enjoyable. Rated PG. 90m. **DIR:** Cary Parker. **CAST:** Gordon John Sinclair, Irina Brook, David McKay, Gregor Fisher, Paul Young, Rikki Fulton. **1985**

GIRL, INTERRUPTED ★★★1/2 This adaptation of Susanna Kaysen's memoir aspires to be a feminine response to *One Flew Over the Cuckoo's Nest*, and to the degree that it involves stars Winona Ryder and Angelina Jolie (Oscar winner), this ambition is fulfilled. But the other residents of fictitious Claymore Institute, which stands in for the facility where Kaysen voluntarily committed herself in the 1960s, emerge as little more than stereotypes and stick figures; and some of these women are even held up for the ridicule of cheap laughs. This film should be a quiet classic along the lines of *I Never Promised You a Rose Garden*, but Mangold's superficial handling and the "girls just wanna have fun" atmosphere prove damaging. Rated R for profanity, brief nudity, and dramatic intensity. 125m. **DIR:** James Mangold. **CAST:** Winona Ryder, Angelina Jolie, Clea DuVall, Brittany Murphy, Elisabeth Moss, Jared Leto, Jeffrey Tambor. **1999 DVD**

GIRL MOST LIKELY, THE ★★★1/2 This musical, a remake of *Tom, Dick and Harry*, succeeds because it's light and breezy. The choreography is by the late Gower Champion and is wonderful to watch. This is a fine film for the entire family. 98m. **DIR:** Mitchell Leisen. **CAST:** Jane Powell, Cliff Robertson, Tommy Noonan, Una Merkel. **1957**

GIRL OF THE GOLDEN WEST, THE ★★1/2 Jeanette MacDonald is an 1850s saloon owner attracted to bold bandit Nelson Eddy in this sloppy, hitless musical version of a 1905 play (better done by Puccini). B&W; 120m. **DIR:** Robert Z. Leonard. **CAST:** Jeanette MacDonald, Nelson Eddy, Walter Pidgeon, Leo Carrillo, Buddy Ebsen, Monty Woolley, H. B. Warner, Charley Grapewin. **1938**

•GIRL ON THE BRIDGE ★★★★ Strange but engrossing film about a suicidal woman who finds the perfect life partner in a knife thrower. Dark and bizarre but nonetheless fascinating. In French with English subtitles. Rated R for some sexuality. B&W; 92m. **DIR:** Patrice Leconte. **CAST:** Daniel Auteuil, Vanessa Paradis, Frederic Pfluger, Catherine Lascault. **1999 DVD**

GIRL RUSH ★★1/2 Mildly amusing comedy about vaudeville performers who attempt to stage a show called *The Frisco Follies* for a group of miners. Their efforts are met with resistance by a menacing gambler played by Robert Mitchum. B&W; 65m. **DIR:** Gordon Douglas. **CAST:** Robert Mitchum, Frances Langford, Wally Brown. **1944**

GIRL 6 ★★ Out-of-work actress Theresa Randle takes a job as a phone-sex operator and becomes obsessed with the work and some of her unseen clients. There are good performances, with several star cameos, but the film staggers back and forth between melodrama and racy comedy, never settling on a style or clearly developing a theme. Rated R for profanity and suggested sex. 109m. **DIR:** Spike Lee. **CAST:** Theresa Randle, Isaiah Washington, Spike Lee, Debi Mazar, Peter Berg. **1996**

GIRL WHO HAD EVERYTHING, THE ★★ A dated melodrama obviously produced to capitalize on Elizabeth Taylor's beauty. She plays the daughter of a lawyer, and she falls in love with a criminal her father is slated to defend in court. Good performances; weak script. B&W; 69m. **DIR:** Richard Thorpe. **CAST:** Elizabeth Taylor, William Powell, Fernando Lamas, Gig Young, James Whitmore. **1953**

GIRL WHO SPELLED FREEDOM, THE ★★★★1/2 Disney does an excellent job of adapting the Yann family's true story, dramatizing their flight from Cambodia to find refuge with a Tennessee family. Made for TV, this fine film is unrated. 90m. **DIR:** Simon Wincer. **CAST:** Wayne Rogers, Mary Kay Place, Jade Chinn, Kathleen Sisk. **1985**

GIRL WITH A SUITCASE ★★★★ A singer quits her job to follow her lover, who eventually jilts her. She then falls in love with his teenage brother, who returns her affection even though she knows it can never work. This hackneyed plot succeeds thanks to sensitive writing and first-rate performances by Claudia Cardinale and Jacques Perrin as the young lovers. In Italian with English subtitles. B&W; 111m. **DIR:** Valerio Zurlini. **CAST:** Claudia Cardinale, Jacques Perrin, Gian Maria Volonté. **1961**

GIRL WITH THE HATBOX, THE ★★ A greedy pig-faced employer gives his employee a lottery ticket instead of wages. She wins and is then plagued with advances from her boss. Slapstick, postrevolution esoterica. Silent. B&W; 67m. **DIR:** Boris Barnet. **CAST:** Anna Sten, Vladimir Fogel. **1927**

GIRL WITH THE HUNGRY EYES, THE ★★ Annoyingly ambiguous thriller tells the story of a dead model (she committed suicide thirty years earlier) who returns to drain the blood of the living. Rated R for nudity, violence, and horror. 85m. **DIR:** Jon Jacobs. **CAST:** Christina Fulton, Isaac Turner, Leon Herbert, Bret Carr. **1993**

GIRLFIGHT ★★★1/2 Brooklyn high-school girl literally boxes her way from juvenile head case to empowered young woman. This teenage love story about confronting external obstacles and internal demons is set amid the blood, sweat, and tears of the ring; the squalor of inner-city streets; and the emotional litter of a dysfunctional home. Rated R for profanity, sex, and violence. 113m. **DIR:** Karyn Kusama. **CAST:** Michelle Rodriguez, Paul Calderon, Ray Santiago, Jaime Tirelli, Santiago Douglas. **2000 DVD**

GIRLFRIEND FROM HELL ★★★1/2 A painfully shy girl becomes the life—and death—of the party when she is possessed by the devil. Inventive low-budget comedy. Rated R for sexual situations and profanity. 92m. **DIR:** Daniel M. Paterson. **CAST:** Liane Curtis, Dana Ashbrook, James Daughton. **1989**

GIRLFRIENDS ★★★★ Realistic film about a young Jewish woman who learns to make it on her own after her best friend/roommate leaves to get married. Melanie Mayron's performance is the highlight of this touching and offbeat comedy drama. Rated PG. 88m. **DIR:** Claudia Weill. **CAST:** Melanie Mayron, Anita Skinner, Eli Wallach, Christopher Guest, Viveca Lindfors. **1978**

GIRLS ARE FOR LOVING 🦃 The last of the *Ginger* films, with stripper Ginger (Cheri Caffaro) battling international bad guys in her spare time. Rated R for nudity, violence, and simulated sex. 90m. **DIR:** Don Schain. **CAST:** Cheri Caffaro, Timothy Brown. **1973**

GIRLS! GIRLS! GIRLS! ★★ In this musical-comedy, Elvis Presley is chased by an endless array of beautiful girls. Sounds like the ideal situation? Not for poor Elvis as he tries to choose just one. 105m. **DIR:** Norman Taurog. **CAST:** Elvis Presley, Stella Stevens, Benson Fong, Laurel Goodwin, Jeremy Slate. **1962**

GIRLS IN PRISON ★★ Pointless remake of the 1956 film that has only the slithery performance of Anne Heche to recommend it. Otherwise, it's just bad camp noir. Rated R for profanity, violence, and nudity. 83m. **DIR:** John McNaughton. **CAST:** Anne Heche, Ione Skye, Missy Crider. **1994**

GIRLS JUST WANT TO HAVE FUN 🦃 Sarah Jessica Parker stars as a young woman who just *lovvves* to dance. Rated PG for profanity. 90m. **DIR:** Alan Metter. **CAST:** Sarah Jessica Parker, Lee Montgomery, Morgan Woodward, Jonathan Silverman. **1985 DVD**

GIRLS OF HUNTINGTON HOUSE ★★ With Shirley Jones as the teacher in a halfway house for unwed young mothers-to-be, this made-for-TV story explores the plight of a group of young women trying to make a most difficult decision. Simplistic dialogue and plot developments help to water down the impact of this one. 73m. **DIR:** Alf Kjellin. **CAST:** Shirley Jones, Sissy Spacek, Mercedes McCambridge, Pamela Sue Martin. **1973**

GIRLS TOWN (1956) ★★ It overstays its welcome by about 15 minutes, but this trash opus about a bad girl (Mamie Van Doren) sent to a prison farm is otherwise a laugh riot. And what a cast! The Platters supply some musical numbers. B&W; 92m. **DIR:** Charles Haas. **CAST:** Mamie Van Doren, Mel Torme, Paul Anka, Ray Anthony, Maggie Hayes, Cathy Crosby, Gigi Perreau, Gloria Talbott, Jim Mitchum, Elinor Donahue, Sheilah Graham. **1959**

GIRLS TOWN (1996) ★★1/2 Three high-school classmates react with shock and anger to the suicide of a fourth friend. Director Jim McKay and Denise Casano developed the script from improvisations with the three lead actresses, and their scenes have energy and bite. Minor characters, though, are not so well developed, and scenes involving them seem forced and lack conviction. Rated R for profanity. 90m. **DIR:** Jim McKay. **CAST:** Lili Taylor, Bruklin Harris, Anna Grace, Aunjanue Ellis. **1996**

GIT ALONG, LITTLE DOGIES ★★ Typical of Gene Autry's prewar films, this thin story of a spoiled, willful girl who is eventually tamed and socialized by the silver-voiced cowboy is heavy on the music and singing stars. B&W; 60m. **DIR:** Joseph Kane. **CAST:** Gene Autry, Smiley Burnette, Judith Allen, William Farnum. **1937**

GIVE A GIRL A BREAK ★★ This somewhat hackneyed story of three would-be's vying to replace a star when she quits a Broadway show is nice, passes the time, but lacks stature. 82m. **DIR:** Stanley Donen. **CAST:** Debbie Reynolds, Marge Champion, Gower Champion, Kurt Kasznar, Bob Fosse, Helen Wood, Lurene Tuttle. **1953**

GIVE 'EM HELL, HARRY! ★★★★ This is the film version of James Whitmore's wonderful portrayal of President Harry S Truman. Taken from the stage production, the film is a magnificent tribute and entertainment. Rated PG. 102m. **DIR:** Steve Binder. **CAST:** James Whitmore. **1975**

GIVE ME A SAILOR ★★★ Light and breezy romantic comedy starring Bob Hope and Jack Whiting as two sailors in love with the same woman. The woman's ugly-duckling sister agrees to help Hope land her, in exchange for Hope's helping the sister land Whiting. Lots of lunacy and slapstick follow as the ugly duckling becomes a swan, turning the tables on everyone. B&W; 78m. **DIR:** Elliott Nugent. **CAST:** Bob Hope, Martha Raye, Betty Grable, Jack Whiting. **1938**

GIVE MY REGARDS TO BROAD STREET ★★ Paul McCartney wrote and stars in this odd, but not really offensive, combination of great rock music and a truly insipid story as a rock singer who loses the master tapes for his album and finds his future seriously threatened. Forget the story and enjoy the songs. Rated PG for mild violence. 108m. **DIR:** Peter Webb. **CAST:** Paul McCartney, Ringo Starr, Barbara Bach, Linda McCartney. **1984**

GLADIATOR, THE (1986) (TELEVISION) ★★ Competent but attenuated TV film about a mechanic (Ken Wahl) who goes on the vengeance trail after his younger brother is killed by a deranged DUI. Some of the drama works, but often the narrative becomes repetitious. 94m. **DIR:** Abel Ferrara. **CAST:** Ken Wahl, Nancy Allen, Robert Culp, Stan Shaw, Rosemary Forsyth, Bart Braverman. **1986**

GLADIATOR (1992) ★★★ A middle-class kid moves to the tough South Side of Chicago, where he gets involved with the world of illegal underground boxing. Some down-and-dirty fight scenes and the presence of character actors Brian Dennehy, Robert Loggia, and Ossie Davis make this film more than a clone of *Rocky*. Rated R for violence, profanity, and nudity. 98m. **DIR:** Rowdy Herrington. **CAST:** James Marshall, Cuba Gooding Jr., Robert Loggia, Ossie Davis, Brian Dennehy, John Heard. **1992**

GLADIATOR (2000) ★★★★ This ambitious Roman Empire action epic recounts the tale of a virtuous and earnest fighting man, devoted to his country and its ideals, who is betrayed by those loyal only to themselves and political ambition. Russell Crowe stars as the wronged Maximus, who is made a slave after his noble emperor is murdered by the man's greedy son, who then appoints himself emperor and initiates the events that will lead to the fall of Rome. Maximus wants only to return to Rome, where he hopes to kill the vile and depraved creep. The gladitorial games are sensational, the computer-enhanced re-creation of Rome's glory breathtaking. Rated R for constant, bloody violence and strongly suggested sexual deviancy. 154m. **DIR:** Ridley Scott. **CAST:** Russell Crowe, Joaquin Phoenix, Connie Nielsen, Oliver Reed, Richard Harris, Derek Jacobi, Djimon Hounsou. **2000**

GLADIATOR COP II: THE SWORDSMAN ★★ An ex-cop and a man who believes himself to be Alexander the Great among others battle for control of a mythical sword. Passable action-fantasy is held up by decent acting and stunt work, but holds little interest in the way of story. Rated R for violence. 85m. **DIR:** Nick Rotundo. **CAST:** Lorenzo Lamas, Frank Alexander, James Hong. **1995**

GLASS BOTTOM BOAT, THE ★★★ Doris Day is hired by amorous scientist Rod Taylor as his biographer. Slapstick complications arise when she is suspected of being a Russian spy. 110m. **DIR:** Frank Tashlin. **CAST:** Doris Day, Rod Taylor, Arthur Godfrey, Paul Lynde, Dom DeLuise. **1966**

GLASS CAGE, THE ★★★ Erotic thriller is the story of a former CIA agent (Richard Tyson) who finds himself in New Orleans, searching for his ex-lover. He finds her but winds up enmeshed with nasty mob types and corrupt cops. Stylish. Rated R for violence, nudity, and sexual situations. 96m. **DIR:** Michael Schroeder. **CAST:** Charlotte Lewis, Richard Tyson, Stephen Nichols, Joseph Campanella, Richard Moll, Eric Roberts. **1996**

GLASS HOUSE, THE (1972) ★★★★ This powerful prison drama is based on a story by Truman Capote. An idealistic new prison guard (Clu Gulager) is overwhelmed by the gang violence within the prison. Alan Alda plays a new prisoner who becomes the target of a violent gang leader (Vic Morrow). R for sex and violence. 89m. **DIR:** Tom Gries. **CAST:** Vic Morrow, Clu Gulager, Billy Dee Williams, Dean Jagger, Alan Alda. **1972 DVD**

•**GLASS HOUSE, THE (2001)** ★★ When the parents of two teens are killed in a car accident, the squabbling siblings are sent to live with former neighbors who have a swank see-through home and a murky secret agenda. This guardians-from-hell thriller throws some delirious, wicked curves before wallowing through a finale so creatively bankrupt and derivative that it taints all that went before it. Rated R for language, violence, and drug use. 101m. **DIR:** Daniel Sackheim. **CAST:** Leelee Sobieski, Trevor Morgan, Stellan Skarsgard, Diane Lane, Bruce Dern. **2001 DVD**

GLASS KEY, THE ★★★★ Solid version of Dashiell Hammett's excellent novel has Alan Ladd as the bodyguard to politician Brian Donlevy, who is accused of murder. It's up to Ladd to get him off, and he has to take on vicious gangsters to get the job done. Fine work by everyone involved makes this a cinematic gem. B&W; 85m. **DIR:** Stuart Heisler. **CAST:** Brian Donlevy, Alan Ladd, Veronica Lake, William Bendix. **1942**

GLASS MENAGERIE, THE ★★★★ Director Paul Newman made this impressive screen drama to immortalize wife Joanne Woodward's excellent portrayal of faded southern belle Amanda Winfield, whose strong opinions tend to make her adventure-hungry son (John Malkovich) miserable, and drive her shy daughter (Karen Allen) deeper within herself. This is the best film version to date of Tennessee Williams semiautobiographical play. Rated PG. 134m. **DIR:** Paul Newman. **CAST:** Joanne Woodward, John Malkovich, Karen Allen, James Naughton. **1987**

GLASS SHIELD, THE ★★★ An ambitious yet overobvious and uninvolving look at corruption in a southern California sheriff's station, as seen through the conflicted, morally compromised eyes of a naïve black rookie. Rated PG-13 for violence. 107m. **DIR:** Charles Burnett. **CAST:** Michael Patrick Boatman, Lori Petty, Ice Cube, Elliott Gould, Richard Anderson, Michael Ironside, Bernie Casey. **1995 DVD**

GLASS SLIPPER, THE ★★1/2 The supporting players steal the spotlight from the leads, throwing this musical version of *Cinderella* off balance. The ballet scenes are beautifully staged to make it worth seeing for dance enthusiasts, but others may be bored. Estelle Winwood is especially good as the fairy godmother. An unusual musical, but not a memorable one. 94m. **DIR:** Charles Walters. **CAST:** Leslie Caron, Michael Wilding, Estelle Winwood, Keenan Wynn, Elsa Lanchester, Barry Jones, Lurene Tuttle, Amanda Blake, Lisa Daniels. **1955**

GLEAMING THE CUBE ★★★ Better-than-average murder-mystery aimed at the teenage crowd. Christian Slater stars as a skateboard ace who kick starts a murder investigation when his adopted Vietnamese brother is found hanged in a motel. Spectacular, exciting skateboard stunts and an appealing performance by Slater help glide over the holes in the plot. Rated PG-13. 104m. **DIR:** Graeme Clifford. **CAST:** Christian Slater, Steven Bauer, Richard Herd, Ed Lauter. **1989 DVD**

GLEN AND RANDA ★★★ As with all cult films, this will not appeal to everyone. The film, at times thought-provoking, is both depressing and satirical. Two young people, Glen (Steve Curry) and Randa (Shelley Plimpton), set out on a search for knowledge across postholocaust America. Rated R for nudity and violence. 94m. **DIR:** Jim McBride. **CAST:** Steven Curry, Shelley Plimpton, Woodrow Chambliss, Garry Goodrow. **1986**

GLEN OR GLENDA ★★ Incredible film by the incomparably *inept* Edward D. Wood Jr., tells the powerful story of a young transvestite who finally summons up the courage to come out of the closet and ask his fiancée if he can wear her sweater. B&W; 67m. **DIR:** Edward D. Wood Jr. **CAST:** Bela Lugosi, Dolores Fuller, Daniel Davis, Lyle Talbot, Timothy Farrell, George Weiss. **1953 DVD**

GLENGARRY GLEN ROSS ★★★★★ Powerhouse performances and a blistering script highlight David Mamet's adaptation of his own Pulitzer-winning stage play, set during 24 frantic hours in the lives of four rapacious real estate salesmen. Al Pacino and Jack Lemmon are the two central players, the former a relaxed "closer" able to entice anybody into anything, the latter increasingly frantic over a lengthy bad streak. Rated R for relentless profanity. 120m. **DIR:** James Foley. **CAST:** Al Pacino, Jack Lemmon, Ed Harris, Alan Arkin, Kevin Spacey, Jonathan Pryce, Alec Baldwin. **1992**

GLENN MILLER STORY, THE ★★★1/2 Follows the life story of famous trombonist and bandleader Glenn Miller, who disappeared in a plane during World War II. Jimmy Stewart delivers a convincing portrayal of the popular bandleader whose music had all of America tapping its feet. Miller's music is the highlight of the film, with guest appearances by Louis Armstrong and Gene Krupa. 113m. **DIR:** Anthony Mann. **CAST:** James Stewart, June Allyson, Charles Drake, Harry Morgan, Frances Langford, Gene Krupa, Louis Armstrong. **1954**

GLIMMER MAN, THE ★★★1/2 Steven Seagal is a student of Eastern philosophy and a top-notch detective imported from New York to Los Angeles to help catch a serial killer known as the Family Man. Keenen Ivory Wayans is the local detective assigned to the case, who resents being teamed with a mysticism-spouting know-it-all. Their chemistry makes the convoluted story work. Rated R for profanity and violence. 92m. **DIR:** John Gray. **CAST:** Steven Seagal, Keenen Ivory Wayans, Bob Gunton, Brian Cox, Michelle Johnson, John Jackson, Stephen Tobolowsky. **1996 DVD**

•**GLIMPSE OF HELL, A** ★★★★ The true-life story of a fatal explosion aboard the USS *Iowa* in 1989, in which forty-seven sailors were killed, and the cover-up that ensued. A top-notch cast, tight screenplay, and riveting direction make this one worth seeing. Rated PG-13 for violence, gore, and profanity. 85m. **DIR:** Mikael Salomon. **CAST:** James Caan, Robert Sean Leonard, Daniel Roebuck. **2001**

•**GLITTER** ★★ Though universally panned, we noted a few redeeming points in Mariah Carey's premiere film. As a hard-knocks kid with a golden voice, she's discovered by a hustling deejay. Carey's voice is dynamite and Max Beesley as her producer/love interest steals every scene. On the down side, there is a music-video feel at inappropriate times, Carey's acting range needs to be developed, and the plot could have been tightened by shaving off fifteen minutes. Rated PG-13 for language, violence, and sexual situations. 104m. **DIR:** Vondie Curtis-Hall. **CAST:** Mariah Carey, Max Beesley, Terrence Howard. **2001 DVD**

GLITTER DOME, THE ★★1/2 Made-for-HBO cable version of Joseph Wambaugh's depressingly downbeat story concerning two police detectives in Los Angeles, James Garner and John Lithgow, out to solve a murder. Both cops appear on the edge of losing control. 90m. **DIR:** Stuart Margolin. **CAST:** James Garner, Margot Kidder, John Lithgow, Colleen Dewhurst, John Marley. **1985**

GLITZ 🦃 Drearily botched TV adaptation of excellent Elmore Leonard crime novel, with Jimmy Smits ineffective as Miami Beach detective. 96m. **DIR:** Sandor Stern. **CAST:** Jimmy Smits, Markie Post, John Diehl. **1988**

GLOBAL AFFAIR, A ★★1/2 When a child is abandoned at the United Nations, all nation members put in a claim for custody. Nothing much. B&W; 84m. **DIR:** Jack Arnold. **CAST:** Bob Hope, Michele Mercier, Robert Sterling, Lilo Pulver, Elga Andersen, Yvonne De Carlo. **1964**

GLORIA (1980) ★★★1/2 After his family is executed by the Mafia, a little boy hides out with a female neighbor. Together they must flee or be killed. Gena Rowlands is very good in the title role as the streetwise Gloria, whose savvy and brains keep the two alive. Rated R—language, violence. 121m. **DIR:** John Cassavetes. **CAST:** Gena Rowlands, Buck Henry, John Adames, Julie Carmen, Lupe Guarnica. **1980**

GLORIA (1999) ★★1/2 A gangster's moll shelters a boy when his parents are murdered and both wind up running from the mob. This tolerable but unnecessary remake of John Cassavetes 1980 melodrama showcases a cheerfully hammy Sharon Stone trying to fill the shoes of the redoubtable Gena Rowlands. Rated R for profanity and violence. 108m. **DIR:** Sidney Lumet. **CAST:** Sharon Stone, Jeremy Northam, Cathy Moriarty, Jean-Luke Figueroa, Mike Starr, George C. Scott, Sarita Choudhury. **1999 DVD**

GLORIANA ★★★1/2 Written by Benjamin Britten to celebrate the coronation of Queen Elizabeth II, this opera is the love story of Elizabeth I and the Earl of Essex. A beautiful production filmed for TV. 146m. **DIR:** Derek Bailey. **CAST:** Sarah Walker, Anthony Rolfe Johnson. **1984**

GLORIFYING THE AMERICAN GIRL ★★1/2 The only film produced by legendary showman Florenz Ziegfeld, this dreary backstage rags-to-riches story reeked of mothballs even in 1929. Recognizing that, Ziegfeld padded it out with Follies production numbers that provide the only reason to watch this. Highlights are an Eddie Cantor skit, a bevy of celebrity cameos, and torch singer Helen Morgan giving her all on "What I Wouldn't Do for That Man." B&W; 95m. **DIR:** Millard Webb. **CAST:** Mary Eaton, Edward Crandall, Eddie Cantor, Helen Morgan. **1929**

GLORY ★★★★★ If nothing else, *Glory* rights a terrible wrong. It brings to light the fact that black soldiers fought valiantly on the side of the Union during the Civil War. Yet this excellent film is more than an important lesson in history; it is also a fully involving antiwar movie blessed with unforgettable scenes and scintillating actors (including Oscar recipient Denzel Washington). Rated R for violence and brief profanity. 202m. **DIR:** Edward Zwick. **CAST:** Matthew Broderick, Denzel Washington, Cary Elwes, Morgan Freeman. **1989 DVD**

GLORY AT SEA ★★ Typical British salute to those who fought in World War II—Trevor Howard, the captain of a decrepit battleship, wins the respect of his men while under fire. B&W; 90m. **DIR:** Compton Bennett. **CAST:** Trevor Howard, Richard Attenborough, Sonny Tufts, James Donald. **1952**

GLORY BOYS, THE ★★1/2 A many-sided Middle Eastern, terrorist/counterterrorist plot and counterplot. Solid production values, but the overfamiliar scenario is a waste. No rating but contains violence and profanity. 130m. **DIR:** Michael Ferguson. **CAST:** Rod Steiger, Anthony Perkins, Alfred Burke, Joanna Lumley. **1984**

GLORY! GLORY! ★★★1/2 Marvelously irreverent spoof of television evangelism features Richard Thomas as the dedicated but boring successor to his father's multi-million-dollar church. Thomas hires delightfully saucy Ellen Greene, a hard-core rock 'n' roll singer, to be Sister Ruth. Made for cable. 152m. **DIR:** Lindsay Anderson. **CAST:** Richard Thomas, Ellen Greene, James Whitmore, Winston Rekert. **1989**

GLORY STOMPERS, THE 🦃 Silly cycle movie, about rival biker clubs. Not rated, some violence. 81m. **DIR:** Anthony M. Lanza. **CAST:** Dennis Hopper, Jody McCrea, Chris Noel, Jock Mahoney, Casey Kasem. **1967**

GLORY YEARS ★★ Three old high school buddies on their twenty-year reunion use their alumni fund to gamble in Las Vegas. The whole film reeks of a bad *Big Chill* rip-off. Originally an HBO miniseries. Not rated, has profanity, sex, and nudity. 150m. **DIR:** Arthur Allan Seidelman. **CAST:** George Dzundza, Archie Hahn, Tim Thomerson, Tawny Kitaen, Michael Fairman, Sandy Simpson, Beau Starr, Donna Pescow. **1987**

GNOME-MOBILE, THE ★★1/2 This one is kid city. From Disney, of course. Walter Brennan doubles as a wealthy businessman and a gnome who must find a wife for his grandson-gnome. The Gnome-Mobile is one fancy Rolls-Royce. 104m. **DIR:** Robert Stevenson. **CAST:** Walter Brennan, Ed Wynn, Matthew Garber, Karen Dotrice. **1967**

GO ★★★★ The events of a single night are traced from the viewpoints of three interlocking sets of characters: a supermarket clerk, her friends and coworkers, and two young actors. The complicated, sometimes raunchy story is well acted by a cast of rising young stars, and moves at a lightning pace, with an audacious surprise around every corner. Rated R for profanity, nudity, drug use, and sexual scenes. 103m. **DIR:** Doug Liman. **CAST:** Sarah Polley, Katie Holmes, Desmond Askew, Jay Mohr, Scott Wolf, William Fichtner, Timothy Olyphant, Jane Krakowski, Taye Diggs. **1999 DVD**

GO-BETWEEN, THE ★★★★ In class-distinction-ruled Edwardian England, a high-society lady and an aloof, mysterious farmer use an innocent boy to carry their messages and assist their clandestine romance behind her fiancé's back. A delicate, haunting film, winner of the 1971 Cannes Grand Prix. Rated PG. 116m. **DIR:** Joseph Losey. **CAST:** Julie Christie, Alan Bates, Edward Fox, Margaret Leighton, Michael Redgrave. **1970**

GO FISH ★★1/2 A low-budget amateur film about courtship and love in Chicago's lesbian community. Shot on weekends over most of a year, the film is lighthearted and playful, but it's also rather primitive and clumsy. The acting is especially awkward and camera conscious. Not rated; contains lesbian love scenes and frank discussions of sex. B&W; 85m. **DIR:** Rose Troche. **CAST:** Guinevere Turner, V. S. Brodie. **1994 DVD**

GO FOR BROKE! ★★★1/2 This a paean to the grit and guts of the Japanese-Americans who comprised the 442nd Regiment during World War II. Their gallantry and team spirit, in the face of homefront prejudice and battlefront horror, earned them a nation's respect and presidential citation for outstanding accomplishments in combat. 90m. **DIR:** Robert Pirosh. **CAST:** Van Johnson, Warner Anderson. **1951 DVD**

GO INTO YOUR DANCE ★★★ The only film to costar husband and wife Al Jolson and Ruby Keeler is a charming curiosity piece. Besides Jolson's singing and Keeler's dancing, this backstage drama has exotic Helen Morgan singing some of the torch songs she made famous. B&W; 89m. **DIR:** Archie Mayo. **CAST:** Al Jolson, Ruby Keeler, Helen Morgan, Glenda Farrell, Benny Rubin, Phil Regan, Patsy Kelly, Barton MacLane. **1935**

GO, JOHNNY, GO! 🦃 Despite the presence of some great rock 'n' roll and R&B acts, this story of a boy plucked from anonymity to become a star is about as dull as they come. B&W; 75m. **DIR:** Paul Landres. **CAST:** Jimmy Clanton, Alan Freed, Sandy Stewart, Chuck Berry, Jo-Ann Campbell, Eddie Cochran, Ritchie Valens, The Cadillacs, Jackie Wilson, The Flamingos. **1958**

GO KILL AND COME BACK ★★ Unique opening, but routine viewing, as a bounty hunter tracks a notorious bandit hoping to locate a treasure of buried gold. Only the always-fine acting of veteran Gilbert Roland and a great musical score by Francesco De Masi make this worthwhile. Rated PG; contains violence. 98m. **DIR:** Enzo G. Castellari. **CAST:** George Hilton, Gilbert Roland, Edd Byrnes, Kareen O'Hara, Gerard Herter, Pedro Sanchez. **1968**

GO-MASTERS, THE ★★★★ An impressive coproduction from Japan and China. Set primarily during the Sino-Japanese War, it details the odyssey of a young man who becomes a champion player in the ancient art of Go at a heartrending price. A fascinating tale of obsession, heartbreak, and the tragedies of war. In Chinese and Japanese with English subtitles. Not rated, the film has violence. 123m. **DIR:** Junya Sato, Duan Ji-Shun. **CAST:** Sun Dao-Lin. **1984**

GO NOW ★★★1/2 Better than average disease-of-the-week movie that emphasizes character and relationships over "ain't that a pity" symptom voyeurism. *The Full Monty*'s Robert Carlyle is excellent as a happy-go-lucky Scottish bloke who isn't so happy once he's struck with multiple sclerosis. Juliet Aubrey has the less showy but equally challenging part of his physically active girlfriend, torn between loyalty and her own conflicting needs. Not rated; contains language, nudity, sex, drug use, and mild violence. 88m. **DIR:** Michael Winterbottom. **CAST:** Robert Carlyle, Juliet Aubrey, James Nesbitt. **1995**

GO TELL THE SPARTANS ★★★★ In one of the best Vietnam war films, Burt Lancaster is a commander who begins to wonder "what we're doing over there." It's a very honest portrayal of America's early days in Vietnam, with Lancaster giving an excellent performance. Rated R. 114m. **DIR:** Ted Post. **CAST:** Burt Lancaster, Craig Wasson, Marc Singer. **1978**

GO WEST ★★★1/2 Far from prime-screen Marx Brothers, this is still one of their best MGM movies and a treat for their fans. Good comedy bits combine with a rip-roaring climax (stolen by screenwriter Buster Keaton from *The General*) for a highly watchable star comedy. B&W; 81m. **DIR:** Edward Buzzell. **CAST:** The Marx Brothers, John Carroll, Diana Lewis, Walter Woolf King. **1940 DVD**

GO WEST, YOUNG MAN ★★ No Mae West movie is all bad, but this one comes close. West based her screenplay on someone else's story so it doesn't fit very well. The censors snipped her usual one-liners and diluted the humor. She plays a glamorous movie star who falls for a handsome stranger and decides to steal him from his girlfriend with predictable results. B&W; 80m. **DIR:** Henry Hathaway. **CAST:** Mae West, Randolph Scott, Warren William, Alice Brady, Lyle Talbot, Isabel Jewell, Jack LaRue, Margaret Perry. **1936**

GOALIE'S ANXIETY AT THE PENALTY KICK ★★★ An athlete suffering from alienation commits a senseless murder for no apparent reason in this slow-moving, existential thriller. Arthur Brauss gives a moody performance. Excellent adaptation by Wim Wenders of the Peter Handke novel. In German with English subtitles. B&W; 101m. **DIR:** Wim Wenders. **CAST:** Arthur Brauss, Erika Pluhar. **1971**

GOBLIN 🦃 Sloppily made direct-to-video chiller has a couple besieged by the title demon. Not rated; contains violence, profanity, and gore. 75m. **DIR:** Todd Sheets. **CAST:** Jenny Admire, Tonia Monahan, Bobby Westrick. **1993**

GOD BLESS THE CHILD ★★★★ Inspiring made-for-TV drama about one man's fight to insure that a homeless mother and her daughter get the help and find the dignity they deserve. Mare Winningham delivers a heartbreaking performance as the woman abandoned in a new city by her husband. Winningham struggles to raise her daughter under extreme circumstances, and social worker Dorian Harewood changes their lives in this roller coaster of emotions. Grace Johnston will steal your heart as the understanding daughter. Not rated. 93m. **DIR:** Larry Elikann. **CAST:** Mare Winningham, Dorian Harewood, Grace Johnston. **1988**

GOD IS MY WITNESS ★★★★ Although India is second only to the U.S. in the number of movies it produces every year, *God Is My Witness* is the sole mainstream Indian film that has been distributed here. But it's a doozy. Gloriously overstuffed with action, melodrama, musical numbers, and broad heroics that harken back to the heyday of John Wayne, this is like a dozen movies all rolled into one. Not rated; contains mild violence. In Hindu with English subtitles. 193m. **DIR:** Mukul S. Anand. **CAST:** Amitabh Bachchan, Sridevi, Danny Denzongpa. **1992**

GOD SAID, HA! ★★★★ Julia Sweeney brings her touching and courageous one-woman show to the screen, and the results are equally affecting. The former *Saturday Night Live* comedian explores the struggles she went through when her brother died of cancer, and her subsequent struggle when she learned she also had cancer. There's a sweet poignancy to every word she speaks, which she delivers with honesty. Frequently funny, sometimes sad, always entertaining. Rated PG-

13 for language. 86m. **DIR:** Julia Sweeney. **CAST:** Julia Sweeney. **1998**

GODDESS, THE ★★★ A lonely girl working in a Maryland five-and-dime dreams of film stardom, goes to Hollywood, clicks in a minor role, and makes the big time, only to find it all bittersweet. Stage star Kim Stanley, largely ignored by Hollywood, does well in the title role, though she was far from suited for it. Paddy Chayefsky supposedly based his screenplay on Marilyn Monroe. B&W; 105m. **DIR:** John Cromwell. **CAST:** Kim Stanley, Lloyd Bridges, Betty Lou Holland, Joyce Van Patten, Steven Hill. **1958**

GODFATHER, THE ★★★★★ Mario Puzo's popular novel comes to life in artful fashion. Filmed in foreboding tones, the movie takes us into the lurid world of the Mafia. Marlon Brando won an Oscar for his performance, but it's Al Pacino who grabs your attention with an unnerving intensity. Rated R. 175m. **DIR:** Francis Ford Coppola. **CAST:** Marlon Brando, Al Pacino, James Caan, Richard Castellano, John Cazale, Diane Keaton, Talia Shire, Robert Duvall, Sterling Hayden, John Marley, Richard Conte, Al Lettieri. **1972**

GODFATHER EPIC, THE ★★★★★ Few screen creations qualify as first-class entertainment and cinematic art. Francis Ford Coppola's *The Godfather* series unquestionably belongs in that category. Yet as good as *The Godfather* and *The Godfather, Part II* are, they are no match for *The Godfather Epic*. By editing the two films together in chronological order, for the videotape release of *The Godfather Epic*, Coppola has created a master work. See it! Rated R. 380m. **DIR:** Francis Ford Coppola. **CAST:** Marlon Brando, Talia Shire, James Caan, Robert Duvall, John Cazale, Al Pacino, Diane Keaton, Robert De Niro. **1977**

GODFATHER, PART II, THE ★★★★★ This gripping sequel equals the quality of the original, an almost unheard-of circumstance in Hollywood. Francis Ford Coppola skillfully meshes past and present, intercutting the story of young Don Corleone, an ambitious, immoral immigrant, and his son Michael, who lives up to his father's expectations, turning the family's crime organization into a sleek, cold, modern operation. Winner of seven Academy Awards. Rated R. 200m. **DIR:** Francis Ford Coppola. **CAST:** Al Pacino, Robert Duvall, Diane Keaton, Robert De Niro, John Cazale, Talia Shire, Lee Strasberg, Michael Gazzo. **1974**

GODFATHER, PART III, THE ★★★★1/2 From the first frame of this Shakespeare-influenced final chapter in the screen's finest gangster epic, we are thrust back into the world of the Corleone family. It is two decades after the "modern-day" events in *Part II*, and Michael has moved the family interests out of crime and into legitimate enterprises. But sinister forces lurking within his empire compel him to revert to the old, violent ways. Rated R for violence and profanity. 163m. **DIR:** Francis Ford Coppola. **CAST:** Al Pacino, Diane Keaton, Talia Shire, Andy Garcia, Eli Wallach, Joe Mantegna, Sofia Coppola, George Hamilton, Richard Bright, Helmut Berger, Don Novello, John Savage. **1990**

GODS AND MONSTERS ★★★★ This fact-based character drama contains a mesmerizing portrait of bleak, frustrated old age. Ian McKellen's sensational lead performance explores the final sad days of classic horror-film director James Whale, who took his own life in 1957. The retired filmmaker's empty days, highlighted only by the promise of interviews that become no more than fan-boy queries about working with Boris Karloff, change with the arrival of a strapping new gardener who becomes companion, confessor, and . . . but that would be telling. Carter Burwell's sound track is haunting and unforgettable. Rated R for nudity and sexual candor. 105m. **DIR:** Bill Condon. **CAST:** Ian McKellen, Brendan Fraser, Lynn Redgrave. **1998 DVD**

GOD'S ARMY ★★★ A young Mormon grapples with his faith while serving a mission in Los Angeles under the tutelage of an older mentor. The boy's faith is never really in danger, though; the film is a mixture of reverent Sunday school lesson and vanity production for writer-producer-director-costar Richard Dutcher (whose character literally works miracles). Non-Mormons may remain unmoved, but will appreciate the film's skilled production and sincere performances. Rated PG. 118m. **DIR:** Richard Dutcher. **CAST:** Matthew Brown, Richard Dutcher, DeSean Terry, Michael Buster. **2000 DVD**

GOD'S LITTLE ACRE ★★★★ This is a terrific little film focusing on poor Georgia farmers. Robert Ryan gives one of his best performances as an itinerant farmer. Aldo Ray, Jack Lord, and Buddy Hackett lend good support. B&W; 110m. **DIR:** Anthony Mann. **CAST:** Robert Ryan, Aldo Ray, Tina Louise, Jack Lord, Fay Spain, Buddy Hackett. **1958**

GODS MUST BE CRAZY, THE ★★★★★ This hilarious, poignant, exciting, thought-provoking, violent, slapstick concoction involves three separate stories. One is about a Bushman whose tribe selects him to get rid of an evil thing sent by the gods: a Coke bottle. The second features the awkward love affair of a teacher and a klutzy scientist. The last involves a band of terrorists fleeing for their lives. These all come together for a surprising and satisfying climax. Not rated, the film has violence. 109m. **DIR:** Jamie Uys. **CAST:** Marius Weyers, Sandra Prinsloo. **1980**

GODS MUST BE CRAZY II, THE ★★★★ Those who loved the original *Gods Must Be Crazy* will find more to enjoy in this gentle tale, which has the Bushman hero trying to find his two children after they've been carried away in a poacher's truck. Rated PG for brief profanity and light violence. 97m. **DIR:** Jamie Uys. **CAST:** N!Xau, Lena Farugia, Hans Strydom. **1990**

GODS OF THE PLAGUE ★★ Incredibly boring drama about a professional killer who eludes a police manhunt with the help of his underworld friends. Hard-to-read subtitles. In German with English subtitles. Not rated; contains graphic nudity. B&W; 92m. **DIR:** Rainer Werner Fassbinder. **CAST:** Hanna Schygulla, Margarethe von Trotta. **1970**

GODSEND, THE 🦃 Cheaply rips off *The Exorcist* and *The Omen* in its tale of a demented daughter. Rated R. 93m. **DIR:** Gabrielle Beaumont. **CAST:** Cyd Hayman, Malcolm Stoddard, Angela Pleasence. **1979**

GODSON, THE ★★ Rodney Dangerfield costars in this lame mob comedy that doesn't get any respect even as it attempts to spoof previous gangster films. Here, the number-three son of a notorious mafioso is being groomed for the family business, much to the dismay of the rest of the family. The cast doesn't have much to score with, and the humor is scattershot, with only a couple of gags hitting the bull's-eye. Rated PG-13 for language, cartoon violence, and adult situations. 89m. **DIR:** Bob Hoge. **CAST:** Kevin McDonald, Rodney Dangerfield, Dom DeLuise, Fabiana Udenio, Lou Ferrigno, Irwin Keyes. **1998 DVD**

GODZILLA ★★★★ This take on the "Big G" is an engaging update of classic 1950s monster movies, highlighted by an amazingly streamlined, lifelike huge creature as well as the trashing of New York City. The dialogue occasionally is corny, particularly that between a plucky biologist hero and his estranged girlfriend, but her weaknesses are eclipsed by the gung-ho news cameraman, and the resourceful French secret agent who knows more about the giant scaly monster than he's telling. It all builds to a manic chase sequence that never loses its momentum. Rated PG-13 for monster-scale carnage. 139m. **DIR:** Roland Emmerich. **CAST:** Matthew Broderick, Jean Reno, Maria Pitillo, Hank Azaria, Kevin Dunn, Michael Lerner, Harry Shearer. **1998 DVD**

GODZILLA, KING OF THE MONSTERS ★★★1/2 First, and by far the best, film featuring the four-hundred-foot monstrosity that was later reduced to a superhero. Here he's all death and destruction, and this movie really works, thanks to some expert photographic effects and weird music. B&W; 80m. **DIR:** Inoshiro Honda, Terry Morse. **CAST:** Raymond Burr, Takashi Shimura. **1956 DVD**

GODZILLA 1985 🦃 Once again, the giant Japanese lizard tramples cars and crushes tall buildings in his search for radioactive nutrition. Rated PG. 91m. **DIR:** Kohji Hashimoto, R. J. Kizer. **CAST:** Raymond Burr, Keiji Kobayashi. **1985**

GODZILLA 2000 ★★1/2 And people complained about the recent American remake of *Godzilla*? Toho's latest installment in the "Big G's" exploits is a pallid adventure flick, with cardboard city effects and folks in rubber suits that look quaintly tiresome. Our destructive friend abandons his latest rampage long enough to wrestle a weird outer-space whatsit, while the human characters stand around and look stupid. Our nomination for the year's worst line: one observer's insistence at the end that "We are *all* Godzilla!" Rated PG for monster stomping. 97m. **DIR:** Takao Okawara. **CAST:** Takehiro Murata, Hiroshi Abe, Naomi Nishida, Takeo Nakahara, Mayu Suzuki. **2000 DVD**

GODZILLA VERSUS BIOLLANTE ★★1/2 Resurrected after more than a decade and given an A-movie budget, Godzilla is still just a big lug in a green monster suit. This time he battles a giant slime mold. Well-made but overlong. Rated PG for (and we quote the MPAA) "traditional Godzilla violence." 104m. **DIR:** Kazuki Omori. **1989**

GODZILLA VS. GIGAN 🦃 A basic rehash of previous Godzilla movies, only this time much more boring. 89m. **DIR:** Jun Fukuda. **CAST:** Hiroshi Ishikawa. **1972**

GODZILLA VS. MECHAGODZILLA ★★ For Godzilla fans only. An enemy from space builds a metal Godzilla in an effort to take over the world. Godzilla is pressed into action to destroy the beast. Rated PG. 82m. **DIR:** Jun Fukuda. **CAST:** Masaaki Daimon. **1975**

GODZILLA VS. MONSTER ZERO ★★★ Pretty good monster movie has an alien civilization "borrowing" Godzilla and Rodan to help defeat the hometown menace Monster Zero (known previously and since as Ghidrah). 90m. **DIR:** Inoshiro Honda. **CAST:** Nick Adams, Akira Takarada. **1966 DVD**

GODZILLA VS. MOTHRA ★★★ Fine Godzilla movie pits the "king of the monsters" against archenemy Mothra for its first half, later has him taking on twin caterpillars recently hatched from the moth's giant egg. Excellent battle scenes in this one, with Godzilla's first appearance a doozy. 90m. **DIR:** Inoshiro Honda. **CAST:** Akira Takarada, Yuriko Hoshi, Hiroshi Koizumi. **1964 DVD**

GODZILLA VS. THE SEA MONSTER 🦃 Godzilla must tackle a giant, rotten-looking crab monster. 85m. **DIR:** Jun Fukuda. **CAST:** None Credited. **1966**

GODZILLA VS. THE SMOG MONSTER 🦃 In this ecology-minded disaster flick, the big guy takes on an amorphous, pollution-belching monstrosity spawned by the excesses of industrial waste. 87m. **DIR:** Yoshimitu Banno. **CAST:** Akira Yamauchi. **1972**

GODZILLA'S REVENGE ★★ In his dreams, a young boy visits Monster Island and learns about self-respect from Godzilla's son. Goofy kid's movie, assembled from scenes made for other Godzilla films. Rated G. 92m. **DIR:** Inoshiro Honda. **CAST:** Kenji Sahara. **1969 DVD**

GOIN' SOUTH ★★★ Star Jack Nicholson also directed this odd little Western tale of an outlaw (Nicholson) saved from the gallows by a spinster (Mary Steenburgen). The catch is he must marry her and work on her farm. Lots of attempts at comedy, but only a few work. Look for John Belushi in a small role as a Mexican cowboy. Rated PG, contains some violence and language. 109m. **DIR:** Jack Nicholson. **CAST:** Jack Nicholson, Mary Steenburgen, John Belushi. **1978**

GOIN' TO TOWN ★★★ A Mae West comedy that poses the idea that there are men who can resist La West. That's farfetched, even for Hollywood. She plays a cattle queen who inherits an oil field and falls hard for the British engineer who surveys her property. He rebuffs her. She does a Pygmalion twist on herself and becomes a sophisticated lady and even sings opera to impress the guy. Good one-liners and enjoyable songs, but Mae West is the only impressive player. B&W; 74m. **DIR:** Alexander Hall. **CAST:** Mae West, Paul Cavanagh, Ivan Lebedeff, Marjorie Gateson, Monroe Owsley, Grant Withers. **1935**

GOING ALL THE WAY ★★★ Nostalgic romantic drama about two soldiers returning to their small hometown after the Korean War. Athletic Gunner and shy photographer Sonny become mismatched allies as they look for purpose in their lives. Quaint slice of Americana benefits from a superb cast and excellent direction. Rated R for adult situations, language, and nudity. 103m. **DIR:** Mark Pellington. **CAST:** Ben Affleck, Jeremy Davies, Amy Locane, Rachel Weisz, Rose McGowan. **1997 DVD**

GOING APE! ★★ Tony Danza plays the heir to a million-dollar fortune-with-a-catch: he has to care for three unpredictable simians. Because the film is padded with familiar material, little fun shines through. Rated PG. 87m. **DIR:** Jeremy Joe Kronsberg. **CAST:** Tony Danza, Jessica Walter, Stacey Nelkin, Danny DeVito, Art Metrano, Joseph Maher. **1981**

GOING BANANAS 🦃 Idiotic safari film. Rated PG. 95m. **DIR:** Boaz Davidson. **CAST:** Dom DeLuise, Jimmie Walker, David Mendenhall, Herbert Lom. **1988**

GOING BERSERK 🦃 This is an unfunny comedy starring former *SCTV* regulars John Candy, Joe Flaherty, and Eugene Levy. Rated R. 85m. **DIR:** David Steinberg. **CAST:** John Candy, Joe Flaherty, Eugene Levy, Alley Mills, Pat Hingle, Richard Libertini. **1983**

GOING HOLLYWOOD ★★★1/2 The music is better than the story. Marion Davies plays a hometown girl who is determined to have both Crosby and a career in that order. The best song is "Temptation" sung by Crosby in his inimitable crooning fashion. Very brisk pace; very enjoyable staging of musical numbers. B&W; 80m. **DIR:** Raoul Walsh. **CAST:** Bing Crosby, Marion Davies, Fifi D'Orsay, Patsy Kelly, Ned Sparks, Stu Erwin. **1933**

GOING IN STYLE ★★★★ Three retirees who gather daily on a park bench need to add some spice to their empty existence. So they decide to rob a bank. This crime caper has some unexpected plot twists with a perfect sprinkling of humor. A delight throughout. Rated PG. 96m. **DIR:** Martin Brest. **CAST:** George Burns, Art Carney, Lee Strasberg, Charles Hallahan, Pamela Payton-Wright. **1979**

GOING MY WAY ★★★★1/2 Bing Crosby won the best-actor Oscar in 1944 for his delightful portrayal of the easygoing priest who finally wins over his strict superior (Barry Fitzgerald, who also won an Oscar for his supporting role). Leo McCarey wrote and directed this funny, heartwarming character study and netted two Academy Awards for his efforts, as well as crafting the year's Oscar-winning best picture. B&W; 130m. **DIR:** Leo McCarey. **CAST:** Bing Crosby, Barry Fitzgerald, Rise Stevens, Gene Lockhart, Frank McHugh. **1944**

GOING OVERBOARD 🦃 Lame comedy about a cruise-ship waiter who yearns to be a stand-up comic. The jokes are all wet. Rated PG-13. 97m. **DIR:** Valerie Breman. **CAST:** Adam Sandler, Tom Hodges, Lisa Collins, Billy Zane, Ricky Paul Goldin, Burt Young. **1989 DVD**

GOING PLACES ★★ Memorable only as one of Gérard Depardieu's first screen appearances. He and Patrick Dewaere play amiable low-lifes who dabble in petty thievery. Contains one of filmdom's most acutely uncomfortable scenes, when one of the young lads gets shot in the testicles. In French with English subtitles. Rated R for sex. 117m. **DIR:** Bertrand Blier. **CAST:** Gérard Depardieu, Patrick Dewaere, Miou-Miou, Jeanne Moreau, Isabelle Huppert, Brigitte Fossey. **1974 DVD**

GOING UNDER ★★ The wacky crew of the sub *Standard* set sail for *Airplane*-style high jinx on the open sea. The jokes are seaworthy, but the execution is all wet. Rated PG. 81m. **DIR:** Mark W. Travis. **CAST:** Bill Pullman, Wendy Schaal, Ned Beatty, Robert Vaughn, Bud Cort, Michael Winslow. **1991**

GOING UNDERCOVER 🦃 Chris Lemmon plays an air-head gumshoe hired by Jean Simmons to protect her stepdaughter. Rated PG-13 for violence. 89m. **DIR:** James Keneim Clarke. **CAST:** Jean Simmons, Lea Thompson, Chris Lemmon. **1988**

GOLD COAST ★★★ Yet another Elmore Leonard novel hits the screen, this one a mostly serious story about a crime lord's widow who discovers she can keep her inherited millions only if she remains faithful to her husband's memory... which is to say, she avoids contact with all other men. For the rest of her life. Alas, she and a small-potatoes grifter fall in love, and both explore various avenues to shake the attention of the vicious cowboy killer watching to ensure the lady's fidelity. The script doesn't really do justice to the book. Rated R for violence, profanity, nudity, and suggested sex. 111m. **DIR:** Peter Weller. **CAST:** David Caruso, Marg Helgenberger, Jeff Kober, Barry Primus, Wanda de Jesus. **1997**

GOLD DIGGERS OF 1935 ★★★ Classic Busby Berkeley musical production numbers dominate this absurd story of mercenary schemers swarming around the rich at a posh resort. Though the film sags and lags, the kitsch director's staging of "Lullaby of Broadway" is a piece of cinematic brilliance. B&W; 95m. **DIR:** Busby Berkeley. **CAST:** Dick Powell, Adolphe Menjou, Winifred Shaw, Glenda Farrell. **1935**

GOLD DIGGERS OF 1933 ★★★★ Typical 1930s song-and-dance musical revolves around a Broadway show. Notable tunes include: "We're in the Money," sung by Ginger Rogers; "Forgotten Man," sung by Joan Blondell; and "Shadow Waltz," by the chorus girls. Enjoyable fare if you like nostalgic musicals. B&W; 96m. **DIR:** Mervyn LeRoy. **CAST:** Joan Blondell, Ruby Keeler, Dick Powell, Aline MacMahon, Ginger Rogers, Sterling Holloway. **1933**

GOLD DIGGERS: THE SECRET OF BEAR MOUNTAIN ★★ Disappointing attempt to create a female version of Tom Sawyer and Huckleberry Finn's adventures. Preteens may enjoy the watery cave but David Keith's abusive character may make this inappropriate viewing for the very audience at which it's aimed. Rated PG for violence. 95m. **DIR:** Kevin James Dobson. **CAST:** Christina Ricci, Anna Chlumsky, David Keith, Brian Kerwin, Polly Draper. **1995**

GOLD OF NAPLES, THE ★★★1/2 A charming quartet of vignettes: Sophia Loren as a wife who cheats on her pizza-baker husband; demon cardplayer Vittorio De Sica being put down by a clever child; Toto as a henpecked husband; and Silvana Mangano playing a married whore whose marital arrangement is more than passing strange. B&W; 107m. **DIR:** Vittorio De Sica. **CAST:** Sophia Loren, Vittorio De Sica, Toto, Silvana Mangano. **1954**

GOLD RUSH, THE ★★★★★ Charlie Chaplin's classic comedy is immortal for the scrumptious supper of a boiled boot, the teetering Klondike cabin, and the dance of the dinner rolls. Some parts are very sentimental, but these give the viewer time to catch his or her breath after laughing so much. B&W; 100m. **DIR:** Charles Chaplin. **CAST:** Charlie Chaplin, Mack Swain, Georgia Hale. **1925 DVD**

GOLDEN AGE OF COMEDY, THE ★★★★ This compilation introduced new generations of moviegoers to the great years of silent comedy and continues to do so. Many of the shorts with Laurel and Hardy will be familiar to viewers, but the segments with Will Rogers spoofing silent-film greats Douglas Fairbanks and Tom Mix, and the footage with Harry Langdon (once considered a comedic equal to Charlie Chaplin, Buster Keaton, and Harold Lloyd) are seldom seen and well worth the wait. B&W; 78m. **DIR:** Robert Youngson. **CAST:** Stan Laurel, Oliver Hardy, Will Rogers, Harry Langdon, Ben Turpin, Carole Lombard, Snub Pollard. **1957**

•GOLDEN BOWL, THE ★★★1/2 A fortune-hunting Italian prince marries a wealthy American heiress, while his ex-lover marries the heiress's billionaire father; the expected deceptions and betrayals follow in this poised and tasteful adaptation of Henry James's final novel. Fine performances, especially by Nick Nolte as the billionaire and Uma Thurman as his brittle, neurotic wife. Rated R for one sexual scene. 134m. **DIR:** James Ivory. **CAST:** Uma Thurman, Jeremy Northam, Kate Beckinsale, Nick Nolte, Anjelica Huston, James Fox. **2000 DVD**

GOLDEN BOY ★★★★ William Holden made a strong starring debut in this screen adaptation of Clifford Odet's play about a musician who becomes a boxer. Though a bit dated today, Holden and costar Barbara Stanwyck still shine. B&W; 100m. **DIR:** Rouben Mamoulian. **CAST:** William Holden, Barbara Stanwyck, Adolphe Menjou, Lee J. Cobb. **1939**

GOLDEN CHILD, THE ★★ Eddie Murphy stars as a Los Angeles social worker who is stunned when members of a religious sect call him "The Chosen One" and expect him to save a magical child from the forces of evil. You'll be even more stunned when you watch this cheesy comedy-adventure and realize it was one of the biggest hits of its year. Rated PG-13 for violence and profanity. 96m. **DIR:** Michael Ritchie. **CAST:** Eddie Murphy, Charlotte Lewis, Charles Dance, Randall "Tex" Cobb, Victor Wong, James Hong. **1986 DVD**

GOLDEN COACH, THE ★★★★ Jean Renoir's little-known Franco-Italian masterpiece features Anna Magnani in a stunning performance as the leading lady of an eighteenth-century acting troupe touring South America. Magnani finds herself caught in a complex love triangle with a soldier, a vain bullfighter, and a viceroy who gives her a golden coach. In English. 95m. **DIR:** Jean Renoir. **CAST:** Anna Magnani. **1952**

GOLDEN DEMON ★★★ As a rule, most Japanese love stories are sad. This story of true love broken by pride, tradition, and avarice is an exception. The story of a poor young man, in love with his adopted parents' daughter, who loses her to a rich entrepreneur (an arranged marriage), is richly entertaining. In Japanese with English subtitles. 91m. **DIR:** Koji Shima. **CAST:** Jun Negami. **1953**

GOLDEN EARRINGS ★★★★ An enjoyable romantic romp that wouldn't have worked with a different cast. Marlene Dietrich plays a gypsy who becomes a spy to help British officer Ray Milland escape the Nazis in Germany's Black Forest. The story sounds silly and contrived, but Dietrich's performance makes it compelling. B&W; 95m. **DIR:** Mitchell Leisen. **CAST:** Marlene Dietrich, Ray Milland, Murvyn Vye, Quentin Reynolds, Reinhold Schunzel, Bruce Lester, Dennis Hoey, John Dehner. **1947**

GOLDEN GATE ★★★ Good cast, good idea, lousy direction. Matt Dillon is a young, cocky FBI agent who spins a case out of air against a Chinese laundry worker in 1962. Trouble is, Dillon's got a conscience and tries to make amends to the man's daughter, played by the sensuous Joan Chen. The metaphysical slant is interesting, but this is turgid going, as the plot just about ceases midway through the story. Rated R for profanity and sexual situations. 101m. **DIR:** John Madden. **CAST:** Matt Dillon, Joan Chen, Bruno Kirby. **1993**

GOLDEN HONEYMOON, THE ★★★★ Delightful adaptation of Ring Lardner's deft and biting story. James Whitmore steals the show as talkative Charley Tate, a crusty old windbag married fifty happy years to his patient wife, Lucy (Teresa Wright). While celebrating their golden anniversary in Florida, she meets up with an old flame, and Charley feels the need to prove that Lucy didn't choose the wrong fella fifty years back. Introduced by Henry Fonda; unrated and suitable for family viewing. 52m. **DIR:** Noel Black. **CAST:** James Whitmore, Teresa Wright, Stephen Elliott, Nan Martin. **1980**

GOLDEN SEAL, THE ★★★1/2 A young boy (Torquil Campbell) living with his parents (Steven Railsback and Penelope Milford) on the Aleutian Islands makes friends with a rare golden seal and her pup. It's a good story, predictably told. Rated PG. 95m. **DIR:** Frank Zuniga. **CAST:** Torquil Campbell, Steve Railsback, Penelope Milford. **1983**

GOLDEN STALLION, THE ★★1/2 Offbeat entry to the Roy Rogers series places the emphasis on Trigger and his efforts to save a cute palomino mare from a life of crime. Absolute hooey, but fun to watch, for kids and animal lovers. 67m. **DIR:** William Witney. **CAST:** Roy Rogers, Dale Evans, Estelita Rodriguez, Pat Brady. **1949**

GOLDEN VOYAGE OF SINBAD, THE ★★★★ First-rate Arabian Nights adventure pits Captain Sinbad (John Phillip Law) against the evil Prince Koura (Tom Baker) for possession of a magical amulet with amazing powers. This is a superb fantasy, with some truly incredible effects by master animator Ray Harryhausen. Rated G. 105m. **DIR:** Gordon Hessler. **CAST:** John Phillip Law, Tom Baker, Caroline Munro, Gregoire Aslan, John Garfield Jr. **1974 DVD**

GOLDENEYE ★★★★ The James Bond franchise roared back to life with the dapper Pierce Brosnan as the newest actor carrying 007's *License to Kill*. Teamed with a gorgeous computer programmer, Bond battles a renegade Soviet military officer planning to wreak worldwide havoc with a lethal orbiting satellite. Slick pacing, deliciously evil villains, and audacious stunts prove once again that Bond can more than hold his own. Rated PG-13 for violence and sexual content. 130m. **DIR:** Martin Campbell. **CAST:** Pierce Brosnan, Sean Bean, Izabella Scorupco, Famke Janssen, Joe Don Baker, Judi Dench, Robbie Coltrane. **1995 DVD**

GOLDENGIRL 🦃 This modern retread of *Frankenstein* fails on all counts. Rated PG. 104m. **DIR:** Joseph Sargent. **CAST:** Susan Anton, James Coburn, Curt Jurgens, Robert Culp, Leslie Caron, Jessica Walter. **1979**

GOLDFINGER ★★★★ So enjoyable to watch that it's easy to forget the influence of the film on the spy-adventure genre. From the precredits sequence (cut out of most TV versions) to the final spectacular fight with Goldfinger's superhuman henchman, Oddjob (Harold Sakata), the film firmly establishes characters and situations that measured not only future Bond films but all spy films to follow. Sean Connery is the ultimate 007, John Barry's music is unforgettable, and Oddjob made bowler hats fashionable for heavies. 108m. **DIR:** Guy Hamilton. **CAST:** Sean Connery, Gert Fröbe, Honor Blackman, Harold Sakata. **1964 DVD**

GOLDWYN FOLLIES, THE 🦃 Goldwyn's folly is a better title for this turkey. 120m. **DIR:** George Marshall. **CAST:** Adolphe Menjou, Andrea Leeds, Kenny Baker,

The Ritz Brothers, Vera Zorina, Edgar Bergen. **1938 DVD**

GOLDY, THE LAST OF THE GOLDEN BEARS 🦃 Low production values, inane dialogue, and inconsistent time jumps make a mess of this let's-save-a-bear programmer. 91m. **DIR:** Trevor Black. **CAST:** Jeff Richards. **1984**

GOLEM, THE (HOW HE CAME INTO THE WORLD) (DER GOLEM, WIE ER IN DIE WELT) ★★★★ Director Paul Wegener plays the lead role as the Golem, an ancient clay figure from Hebrew mythology that is brought to life by means of an amulet activated by the magic word "Aemaet" (the Hebrew word for truth). In a story similar to *Frankenstein*, the man of clay roams through medieval Prague in a mystic atmosphere created by the brilliant cameraman Karl Freund. Silent. B&W; 70m. **DIR:** Paul Wegener. **CAST:** Paul Wegener. **1920 DVD**

GOLGOTHA ★★ Early, seldom-seen depiction of the passion of Jesus Christ was reverently filmed in France, where it was a big box-office success. Adapted from the four gospels of the New Testament, using only direct quotes for the lines spoken by Jesus. In French with English subtitles. B&W; 100m. **DIR:** Julien Duvivier. **CAST:** Robert le Vigan, Jean Gabin, Harry Baur. **1935**

GOLIATH AND THE BARBARIANS ★★ Steve Reeves plays Goliath in this so-so Italian action film. In this episode, he saves Italy from invading barbaric tribes. As in many of Reeves films, the only object of interest is the flexing of his muscles. 86m. **DIR:** Carlo Campogalliani. **CAST:** Steve Reeves, Bruce Cabot, Giulia Rubini, Chelo Alonso. **1960**

GOLIATH AND THE DRAGON ★★ The original, Italian version of this film had Maciste (Italy's mythological hero, renamed Goliath by U.S. distributors) fighting a three-headed, fire-breathing dog and other horrors—but *not* a dragon. So the Americans had a life-size dragon's head built for Mark Forest to swing his sword at, and hired Jim Danforth to animate a miniature dragon thrashing about for the long shots—and spliced the whole thing, lasting a couple of minutes, into the existing film. 87m. **DIR:** Vittorio Cottafari. **CAST:** Mark Forest, Broderick Crawford, Gaby André. **1960 DVD**

GOLIATH AND THE VAMPIRES ★★ A horde of barbarians who drink blood, torture their victims, and dissolve amid puffs of blue smoke are the formidable adversaries for Goliath (actually, Maciste) in this colorful, mindlessly enjoyable sword-and-sandal fantasy. U.S. television title: *The Vampires*. 91m. **DIR:** Giacomo Gentilomo. **CAST:** Gordon Scott, Jacques Sernas, Gianna Maria Canale. **1964**

GOLIATH AWAITS ★★1/2 This undersea adventure is about the discovery of a sunken ocean liner, many of whose original passengers are still alive after years on the bottom. It was much better as a two-part (200-minute) miniseries on TV. 95m. **DIR:** Kevin Connor. **CAST:** Mark Harmon, Robert Forster, Eddie Albert, Emma Samms, Christopher Lee, John Carradine, Frank Gorshin, Jean Marsh. **1981**

GONE ARE THE DAYS ★★★ After witnessing a shooting, the Daye family is assigned to a witness relocation agent (Harvey Korman), who is creatively unsuccessful in a long-distance game of hide-and-seek. This wacky comedy is pleasantly acted and well photographed. A Disney made-for-cable production. Good fun for the family. 90m. **DIR:** Gabrielle Beaumont. **CAST:** Harvey Korman, Susan Anspach, Robert Hogan. **1984**

GONE FISHIN' 🦃 This *Ishtar* for the 1990s throws together two great actors and lets them sink under the weight of slow-moving shtick. Danny Glover and Joe Pesci are two slow thinkers who manage to wreak havoc wherever they go. Rated PG for violence. 92m. **DIR:** Christopher Cain. **CAST:** Danny Glover, Joe Pesci, Nick Brimble, Rosanna Arquette. **1997**

GONE IN 60 SECONDS 🦃 Stuntman-turned-film-auteur H. B. Halicki wrecks a bunch of cars faster than you can say Hal Needham. Rated PG for violence. 97m. **DIR:** H. B. Halicki. **CAST:** H. B. Halicki, Marion Busia, George Cole, James McIntire, Jerry Daugirda. **1974 DVD**

GONE IN 60 SECONDS ★★ Producer Jerry Bruckheimer's bombastic action epics are known to be long on visual glitz and short on plot and characterization, but this one's shabby even by his usual standards. Based loosely on H. B. Halicki's 1974 original, this remake lacks its predecessor's raw energy . . . rather crippling for a project that should exude an aura of danger and radiate sheer speed. It does neither, instead idling and stalling precisely when better filmmakers would understand how to kick it into gear. Blame director Dominic Sena, whose experience with TV commercials and music videos serves him poorly here; he thinks in short bursts and thus helms an overly edited mess that can't even deliver one decent car chase. Rated PG-13 for violence, profanity, and mild sensuality. 119m. **DIR:** Dominic Sena. **CAST:** Nicolas Cage, Giovanni Ribisi, Angelina Jolie, Will Patton, Delroy Lindo, Robert Duvall, Timothy Olyphant. **2000 DVD**

GONE TO TEXAS ★★★ Sam Elliott plays frontier hero Sam Houston in this sprawling, action-packed, but overlong biography. 144m. **DIR:** Peter Levin. **CAST:** Sam Elliott, Michael Beck, James Stephens, Devon Ericson. **1986 DVD**

GONE WITH THE WEST ★★ With this excellent cast, one would expect more, but this is a confusing and vague tale about an Old West ex-con on the vengeance trail. 92m. **DIR:** Bernard Gerard. **CAST:** James Caan, Stefanie Powers, Aldo Ray, Barbara Werle, Robert Walker Jr., Sammy Davis Jr., Michael Conrad. **1972 DVD**

GONE WITH THE WIND ★★★★★ The all-time movie classic with Clark Gable and Vivien Leigh as Margaret Mitchell's star-crossed lovers in the final days of the Old South. Need we say more? 222m. **DIR:** Victor Fleming. **CAST:** Clark Gable, Vivien Leigh, Leslie Howard, Olivia de Havilland, Thomas Mitchell, Hattie McDaniel. **1939**

GONIN ★★ Five desperate men of varied backgrounds band together to steal a huge amount of money from a Tokyo crime boss. The enraged hoodlum hires two gay assassins to hunt them down. This bloody thriller has a seductive visual pull, especially during the action scenes, but weak character development and plotting. In Japanese with English subtitles. Not rated; contains violence, profanity, rape, nudity, and torture. 109m. **DIR:** Takashi Ishii. **CAST:** Koichi Sato, Naoto Takenaka, Jimpachi Nezu, Masahiro Motoki, Kippei Shiina, Takeshi Kitano, Kazuya Kimura, Megumi Yokoyama. **1998 DVD**

GONZA THE SPEARMAN ★★★★ Powerful, classic tale of love, honor, and tragedy set in the early 1700s in Japan. Director Masahiro Shinoda's brilliant adaptation of well-known bunkaru playwright Monzaemon Chikamatsu's story features an equally impressive score by composer Toru Takemitsu. In Japanese with English subtitles. Not rated; contains nudity and violence. 126m. **DIR:** Masahiro Shinoda. **CAST:** Hiromi Go. **1986**

GOOD BURGER ★★1/2 Nickelodeon teams sweet-natured Kel Mitchell with an exasperated Kenan Thompson to create goofy Abbott-and-Costello–ish knockoffs. The two, working at a small hamburger stand, must compete with a flashy new mega-burger haven. Corny and unbelievable with endless sight gags and physical humor to break down one's natural groan response. Aimed at preteens, adults may catch themselves laughing as well. Rated PG for wreckless driving without a license and comic-book violence. 90m. **DIR:** Brian Robbins. **CAST:** Kel Mitchell, Kenan Thompson, Sinbad, Abe Vigoda, Dan Schneider, Shar Jackson. **1997**

GOOD EARTH, THE ★★★★ Nobel Prize novelist Pearl Buck's engrossing, richly detailed story of a simple Chinese farm couple whose lives are ruined by greed is impressively brought to life in this milestone film. Luise Rainer won the second of her back-to-back best-actress Oscars for her portrayal of the ever-patient wife. The photography and special effects are outstanding. B&W; 138m. **DIR:** Sidney Franklin. **CAST:** Paul Muni, Luise Rainer, Keye Luke, Walter Connolly, Jessie Ralph. **1937**

GOOD EVENING MR. WALLENBERG ★★★★ Truly harrowing account of Raoul Wallenberg, the Swedish businessman ultimately responsible for protecting thousands of Jews in Budapest during the final hours of World War II. While this film is often difficult to bear, Stellan Skarsgard's compelling portrayal of Wallenberg shines complete with all the madness, frustration, and sheer horror of the world around him. In Swedish, German, and Hungarian with English subtitles. Not rated; contains violence and nudity. 115m. **DIR:** Kjell Grede. **CAST:** Stellan Skarsgard, Katharina Thalbach, Karoly Eperjes. **1990**

GOOD FATHER, THE ★★★★1/2 In this brilliant British import, Anthony Hopkins is a walking time bomb. A separation from his wife has left him on the outside of his son's life. Hopkins's reaction is so extreme that he is haunted by nightmares. Director Mike Newell lays on the suspense artfully with this device while detailing the revenge Hopkins plots against the wife of a friend who is in similar circumstances. Rated R for profanity, suggested sex, and stylized violence. 90m. **DIR:** Mike Newell. **CAST:** Anthony Hopkins, Jim Broadbent, Harriet Walter, Simon Callow, Joanne Whalley. **1986**

GOOD FIGHT, THE ★★1/2 Christine Lahti and Terry O'Quinn elevate this courtroom drama above the clichés as divorced attorneys drawn back together after she takes on an impossible case. The chemistry between the two explodes when their love of the law clears the way for a rekindled romance. The best moments take place in the courtroom and not the bedroom. Not rated. 91m. **DIR:** John David Coles. **CAST:** Christine Lahti, Terry O'Quinn, Kenneth Welsh, Lawrence Dane. **1992**

GOOD GUYS AND THE BAD GUYS, THE ★★★ Watchable comedy-Western gets better as it gets older, primarily because "they don't make 'em like they used to." Robert Mitchum and George Kennedy play two former foes who join forces to thwart the plans of young upstart David Carradine and his gang. Rated PG. 91m. **DIR:** Burt Kennedy. **CAST:** Robert Mitchum, George Kennedy, David Carradine, John Carradine, Tina Louise, Martin Balsam, Lois Nettleton, Douglas Fowley, Marie Windsor, John Davis Chandler. **1969**

GOOD GUYS WEAR BLACK ★★ This Chuck Norris action film starts out well but quickly dissolves into a routine political action-thriller that really goes nowhere. Lightweight entertainment. Rated PG. 96m. **DIR:** Ted Post. **CAST:** Chuck Norris, Anne Archer, James Franciscus, Lloyd Haynes, Jim Backus, Dana Andrews. **1979 DVD**

GOOD IDEA ★★ Odd characters abound in this anarchic comedy. Anthony Newley tries to win his ex-wife back from her new husband, a crooked architect. John Candy is funny as a daft cop, but it's only a small role, although the video packaging makes him look like the star. Original title: *It Seemed Like a Good Idea at the Time*. Rated PG. 106m. **DIR:** John Trent. **CAST:** Anthony Newley, Stefanie Powers, Isaac Hayes, Lloyd Bochner, Yvonne De Carlo, Lawrence Dane, John Candy. **1975**

GOOD LUCK ★★1/2 Paraplegic dental technician Bernard Lemley asks blind former Seattle Seahawks receiver "Olee" Olezniak to help him change society's image of the disabled. Lem's first challenge is to break through Olee's unhealthy preoccupation with impotency, bowel movements, and self-pity while the bitter ex-jock sits in jail. The squabbling new buddies then test each other's trust and team up to enter a whitewater rafting race. Most of the movie follows their amusing, raunchy, but often awkwardly staged road trip. Rated R for profanity and suggested sex. 98m. **DIR:** Richard LaBrie. **CAST:** Gregory Hines, Vincent D'Onofrio, Max Gail. **1997 DVD**

GOOD MAN IN AFRICA, A ★★1/2 The film never achieves the right satirical tone in this story about a bumbling, boozy, British bureaucrat in a fictional African nation. Colin Friels is rendered almost invisible by the strong performances of Sean Connery, John Lithgow, and Lou Gossett Jr. As a comedy, it simply isn't very funny; as a drama, it's too irreverent. Rated R for profanity, nudity, and sex. 95m. **DIR:** Bruce Beresford. **CAST:** Colin Friels, Joanne Whalley, Sean Connery, Louis Gossett Jr., John Lithgow, Diana Rigg, Sarah Jane Fenton. **1994**

GOOD MEN AND BAD ★★ The final episode of the *Black Fox* trilogy starring Christopher Reeve and Tony Todd, set in Texas in the 1860s. An extremely stiff Reeve, crushed by the murder of his wife, threatens to cross the line from good to evil while seeking revenge. Todd is the freed slave who tries to find justice for blood brother Reeve within the boundaries of the law. As with the other episodes, the only intriguing aspects are Todd's performance and the interracial aspects of the story. Not rated; contains violence. 92m. **DIR:** Steven H. Stern. **CAST:** Christopher Reeve, Tony Todd, Raul Trujillo. **1993**

GOOD MORNING, BABYLON ★★★ This follows the misadventures of two brothers who come to America to find their fortunes as artists and find jobs on the production of D. W. Griffith's silent classic, *Intolerance*. The movie has moments of lyrical beauty and its story is sweet. But the dialogue has been translated from Italian in an occasionally awkward fashion. Rated PG-13 for nudity and profanity. 115m. **DIR:** Paolo Taviani, Vittorio Taviani. **CAST:** Vincent Spano, Joaquim de Almeida, Greta Scacchi, Charles Dance. **1987**

GOOD MORNING, VIETNAM ★★★1/2 Robin Williams stars as disc jockey Adrian Cronauer, who briefly ruled Saigon's Armed Forces Radio in 1965. Williams's improvisational monologues are the high points in a film that meanders too much, but Forest Whitaker also shines. Rated R for language and violence. 120m. **DIR:** Barry Levinson. **CAST:** Robin Williams, Forest Whitaker, Tung Thanh Tran, Chintara Sukapatana, Bruno Kirby, Robert Wuhl, J. T. Walsh. **1987 DVD**

GOOD MOTHER, THE ★★ Single mom Anna (Diane Keaton) finds romance with an irresistible Irish artist (Liam Neeson). Anna's ex-husband accuses the artist of sexually abusing his daughter. This film will make you speculate on the rightness or wrongness of Anna's sexually open child-rearing techniques. Rated R for nudity and obscenities. 104m. **DIR:** Leonard Nimoy. **CAST:** Diane Keaton, Jason Robards Jr., Ralph Bellamy, Liam Neeson, James Naughton. **1988**

GOOD NEIGHBOR SAM ★★★ This comedy is similar to many of the lightweight potboilers given to Jack Lemmon in the 1960s. It is an overlong farce about a married advertising designer who pretends marriage to his foreign neighbor next door so she can secure an inheritance. 130m. **DIR:** David Swift. **CAST:** Jack Lemmon, Romy Schneider, Dorothy Provine, Edward G. Robinson. **1964**

GOOD NEWS ★★★ Football hero Peter Lawford resists the class vamp and wins the big game and the campus cutie who loves him in this quintessential musical of college life. The dialogue is painfully trite and trying, but energy and exuberance abound. 95m. **DIR:** Charles Walters. **CAST:** June Allyson, Peter Lawford, Patricia Marshall, Joan McCracken, Mel Torme. **1948 DVD**

GOOD OLD BOYS, THE ★★★★★ Hewey Calloway is as wild as the country in which he's lived, a fact that adds tension during his visit to the west Texas homestead of his soft-spoken brother. Not only does Hewey lock horns with a pompous lawman along the trail, but he renews a long-standing feud with his strong-willed sister-in-law. An awkward romance with schoolmarm Spring Refro adds charm to this story in which the brothers must save the Calloway ranch from a scheming banker. Familiar conventions of the genre avoid cliché, and the result is extremely satisfying. Made for TV. 110m. **DIR:** Tommy Lee Jones. **CAST:** Tommy Lee Jones, Sissy Spacek, Terry Kinney, Frances McDormand, Sam Shepard, Wilford Brimley, Matt Damon, Blayne Weaver, Bruce McGill, Larry Mahan, Richard Jones. **1995**

GOOD SAM ★★ Gary Cooper plays a guy who can't say no in this barely watchable "comedy." He's Mr. Nice-Guy to everyone but his own family. He feels he has to help everyone, so he lends all his money to "friends" and the "needy." B&W; 114m. **DIR:** Leo McCarey. **CAST:** Gary Cooper, Ann Sheridan, Edmund Lowe. **1948**

GOOD SON, THE ★★★ Against-the-grain casting makes this updated *Bad Seed* a kinky hoot. Cutie-pie Macaulay Culkin stars in his first R-rated movie as a wicked, psychotic child whose cousin temporarily moves in after his mother dies. This psychological thriller delivers some creepy chills as Culkin escorts his new pal to the edge of hell. Going *Home Alone* again will never be the same. Rated R for profanity and violence. 87m. **DIR:** Joseph Ruben. **CAST:** Macaulay Culkin, Elijah Wood, Quinn Culkin, Wendy Crewson. **1993**

GOOD THE BAD AND THE UGLY, THE ★★★★ The best of Italian director Sergio Leone's spaghetti Westerns with Clint Eastwood, this release features the latter in the dubiously "good" role, with Lee Van Cleef as "the bad" and Eli Wallach as "the ugly." All three are after a cache of gold hidden in a Confederate army graveyard. For Leone fans, it's full of what made his movies so memorable. Others might find it a bit long, but no one can deny its sense of style. 161m. **DIR:** Sergio Leone. **CAST:** Clint Eastwood, Eli Wallach, Lee Van Cleef. **1966 DVD**

GOOD WIFE, THE 🦃 One woman's yearning for sexual fulfillment. Rated R. 97m. **DIR:** Ken Cameron. **CAST:** Rachel Ward, Bryan Brown, Sam Neill, Steven Vidler. **1987 DVD**

GOOD WILL HUNTING ★★★★1/2 When a janitor at MIT is discovered to be a natural mathematical genius, he and the powers-that-be turn to a troubled psychologist to sort out the boy's problems. Surprisingly straightforward direction with a few quirky touches, and superb performances result in a near masterpiece of cinema that can be enjoyed by viewers of all ages and backgrounds. Damon co-wrote the Oscar-winning screenplay with friend and co-star Ben Affleck. This is one not to miss. Rated R for profanity and violence. 126m. **DIR:** Gus Van Sant. **CAST:** Matt Damon, Robin Williams, Ben Affleck, Minnie Driver, Stellan Skarsgard, Casey Affleck, Cole Hauser. **1997 DVD**

GOODBYE AGAIN ★★1/2 Françoise Sagan melodrama starring Ingrid Bergman as a fashion designer who uses callow Tony Perkins to make noncommittal boyfriend Yves Montand jealous. The Paris settings and capable cast make it painless. Look for Diahann Carroll. 120m. **DIR:** Anatole Litvak. **CAST:** Ingrid Bergman, Anthony Perkins, Yves Montand, Jessie Royce Landis, Peter Bull, Diahann Carroll. **1961**

GOODBYE BIRD, THE ★★ A teenage boy having a difficult time coping with his parents' divorce gets in trouble at school and is assigned to a work program at the local pound. He decides to rescue the unwanted creatures therein by setting up an animal shelter in a deserted barn. Sentimental, farfetched story may still please youngsters. Rated G. 91m. **DIR:** William Clark. **CAST:** Christopher Pettiet, Cindy Pickett, Wayne Rogers. **1992**

GOODBYE COLUMBUS ★★★★ This film marked the start of Ali MacGraw's and Richard Benjamin's movie careers. Ali plays a rich, spoiled Jewish-American princess who meets a college dropout (Benjamin) at her country club. They have an affair, and we get to see her flaws through his "average guy" eyes. Rated R.

105m. **DIR:** Larry Peerce. **CAST:** Richard Benjamin, Ali MacGraw, Jack Klugman. **1969**

GOODBYE EMMANUELLE ★★ One of the *Emmanuelle* soft-core series, this one takes place on a tropical island and concerns a succession of personal and sexual relationships among half a dozen men and women. The dubbing is tolerable. Rated R for sexual situations. 92m. **DIR:** François Letterier. **CAST:** Sylvia Kristel, Umberto Orsini, Jean Pierre Bouvier. **1979 DVD**

GOODBYE GIRL, THE ★★★★1/2 Neil Simon's sparkling screenplay and the acting of Marsha Mason and Richard Dreyfuss combine to produce one of the best pure comedies since Hollywood's golden '30s. Mason and Dreyfuss are a mismatched pair of New Yorkers forced to become roommates. Rated PG. 110m. **DIR:** Herbert Ross. **CAST:** Richard Dreyfuss, Marsha Mason, Quinn Cummings. **1977 DVD**

GOODBYE LOVER ★★★1/2 This thoroughly demented drama is a macabre bit of *modern noir* that faithfully retains the atmosphere of classic 1950s B flicks, while injecting the wincing, ghastly humor that made *Pulp Fiction* and *Fargo* such guilty pleasures (credit Joel Coen's contributions to the script). A very bad girl has plenty of company in a Machiavellian murder scheme that starts as she dallies with two brothers, with murderous results. Mary-Louise Parker is superb as the other woman in this complex romantic rhombus, and Ellen DeGeneres steals the show as a cynical police detective forever belittling her Bible-thumping partner. Rated R for violence, profanity, nudity, and strong sexual content. 115m. **DIR:** Roland Joffe. **CAST:** Patricia Arquette, Dermot Mulroney, Ellen DeGeneres, Mary-Louise Parker, Don Johnson, Ray McKinnon. **1999 DVD**

GOODBYE, MISS 4TH OF JULY ★★★1/2 Inspirational true story of a young Greek immigrant who refuses to let her American dream be tarnished by bigotry in 1917 West Virginia. Roxana Zal plays spunky Niki Janus, who befriends Big John Creed (Lou Gossett Jr.) and thus attracts the wrath of the Ku Klux Klan. Made for the Disney Channel, this has high production values. Not rated; contains frightening scenes of night riders in action. 89m. **DIR:** George Miller. **CAST:** Roxana Zal, Louis Gossett Jr., Chris Sarandon, Chantal Contouri, Chynna Phillips, Mitchell Anderson. **1988**

GOODBYE, MR. CHIPS 🦃 Cash in this *Chips*. Rated G. 151m. **DIR:** Herbert Ross. **CAST:** Peter O'Toole, Petula Clark, Michael Redgrave, George Baker, Sian Phillips. **1969**

GOODBYE, MR. CHIPS ★★★★1/2 Robert Donat creates one of filmdom's most heartwarming roles as Chips, the Latin teacher of an English boys' school. The poignant movie follows Chips from his first bumbling, early teaching days until he becomes a beloved school institution. Greer Garson was introduced to American audiences in the rewarding role of Chips's loving wife. B&W; 114m. **DIR:** Sam Wood. **CAST:** Robert Donat, Greer Garson, John Mills. **1939**

GOODBYE, MY LADY ★★★ A young boy in the bayou country finds a lost dog and takes it to his heart, knowing that it probably belongs to someone else and that he might have to give it up. Director William Wellman transforms James Street's novel into a warm, enduring film. This uncluttered little gem features standout performances by Brandon de Wilde and Walter Brennan as the youngster and his uncle. B&W; 94m. **DIR:** William Wellman. **CAST:** Walter Brennan, Phil Harris, Brandon de Wilde, Sidney Poitier, William Hopper, Louise Beavers. **1956**

GOODBYE NEW YORK ★★★ In this amusing comedy, an insurance salesperson (Julie Hagerty) becomes fed up with her job and husband and leaves for Paris. After falling asleep on the plane, she wakes up in Israel with no money and no luggage. Rated R for language and very brief nudity. 90m. **DIR:** Amos Kollek. **CAST:** Julie Hagerty, Amos Kollek, David Topaz, Shmuel Shiloh. **1984**

GOODBYE, NORMA JEAN ★★★ A depiction of Norma Jean Baker's travels along the rocky road to superstardom as Marilyn Monroe. Her only motivation in life is her dream of becoming a star. Rated R for nudity. 95m. **DIR:** Larry Buchanan. **CAST:** Misty Rowe, Terrence Locke, Patch Mackenzie. **1975**

GOODBYE PEOPLE, THE ★★★★ This unashamedly sentimental film is a delight. Martin Balsam is memorable as a man attempting to realize the dream of many years by rebuilding his Coney Island hot-dog stand. Pamela Reed and Judd Hirsch, as the young people who help him, turn in outstanding performances, and the hot dog stand itself is a fantastic structure. 104m. **DIR:** Herb Gardner. **CAST:** Judd Hirsch, Martin Balsam, Pamela Reed, Ron Silver, Michael Tucker, Gene Saks. **1984**

GOODFELLAS ★★★★★ No punches are pulled in this violent, mesmerizing movie, which covers thirty years in the life of a Mafia family. Based on the book by Nicholas Pileggi, it features Ray Liotta as a half-Irish, half-Sicilian kid from Brooklyn who achieves his life's ambition of being a gangster when he is adopted by a local "family" headed by Paul Sorvino. Rated R for violence, profanity, and depictions of drug use. 148m. **DIR:** Martin Scorsese. **CAST:** Robert De Niro, Joe Pesci, Ray Liotta, Lorraine Bracco, Paul Sorvino. **1990 DVD**

GOODNIGHT, GOD BLESS 🦃 British entry in the slasher sweepstakes has a maniacal killer dressed in priest's garb. Not rated; contains violence and sexual suggestion. 100m. **DIR:** John Eyres. **CAST:** Emma Sutton, Frank Rozelaar Goleen. **1988**

GOOFY MOVIE, A ★★★1/2 Single parent Goofy tries some male bonding with teenage son Max. Kids will enjoy this slapstick-filled feature-length cartoon that attempts to address the frequent misunderstandings between teens and their parents. Rated G. 78m. **DIR:** Kevin Lima. **1995 DVD**

GOONIES, THE ★★★ This "Steven Spielberg production" is a mess. But it's sometimes an entertaining mess. The screenplay, taken from a story by Spielberg, concerns a feisty group of underprivileged kids—whose housing project is about to be destroyed—who find a treasure map, which could be the solution to all their problems. Rated PG for profanity. 111m. **DIR:** Richard Donner. **CAST:** Sean Astin, Josh Brolin, Jeff Cohen, Corey Feldman, Kerri Green, Martha Plimpton, Ke Huy-Quan. **1985 DVD**

GOOSE WOMAN, THE ★★★ Unusual drama, based on a novel by Rex Beach: a famous opera star, after giving birth to an illegitimate son, loses her standing and is reduced to poverty and drink. A contrived ending mars an otherwise sensitive outing for Louise Dresser and then-young director Clarence Brown. Silent. B&W; 90m. **DIR:** Clarence Brown. **CAST:** Louise Dresser, Jack Pickford, Constance Bennett. **1925**

GOOSEBUMPS: THE HAUNTED MASK ★★★★ Perfectly realized Halloween story based on R. L. Stine's popular series of books. Carly Beth is so proud of her new Halloween mask that she never takes it off. Then on Halloween night, she learns that she can't take it off—she has become a monster. Plenty of chills and mayhem ensue as Carly Beth seeks help for her unusual problem. Not rated. 44m. **DIR:** Timothy Bond. **CAST:** Kathryn Long, Cody Jones, Kathryn Short, Brenda Bazinet. **1995**

GOR ★★ A mild-mannered college professor is thrust through time and space to help a simple tribe recover its magical stone in this Conan-inspired sword-and-sorcery flick. Elaborate costumes and sets don't make up for the second-rate story. Rated PG for violence. 95m. **DIR:** Fritz Kiersch. **CAST:** Urbano Barberini, Rebecca Ferratti, Jack Palance, Paul Smith, Oliver Reed. **1987**

GORATH 🦃 An out-of-control planet headed for Earth is the subject of this Japanese science-fiction flick. 77m. **DIR:** Inoshiro Honda. **CAST:** None Credited. **1964**

GORDON'S WAR ★★1/2 Competent but uninspiring variation on *Death Wish* with an all-black cast. Paul Winfield is a Vietnam vet who avenges his wife's drug death. Rated R for violence, language, graphic drug use, and nudity. 90m. **DIR:** Ossie Davis. **CAST:** Paul Winfield, Carl Lee, David Downing, Tony King, Gilbert Lewis. **1978**

GORDY ★★ This live-action tale about a talking pig who becomes a tabloid celebrity and CEO of a rich conglomerate is slow-paced and the film's slaughterhouse finale may upset younger viewers. Rated G. 89m. **DIR:** Mark Lewis. **CAST:** Justin Garms, Doug Stone, Deborah Hobart, Kristy Young, Michael Roescher, Tom Lester, Ted Manson. **1995**

GORE VIDAL'S BILLY THE KID ★★ Uninspired retelling of the last years of Billy the Kid. Fine location cinematography enhance the realism, but the script and direction all but sink this TV movie. 92m. **DIR:** William A. Graham. **CAST:** Val Kilmer, Wilford Brimley. **1989**

GORE VIDAL'S LINCOLN ★★★★ Fine made-for-TV adaptation of Gore Vidal's novel depicting Lincoln as more of a politician than an idealist. Sam Waterston makes a decent Lincoln but Mary Tyler Moore delivers the performance of a lifetime as a mentally unstable Mary Todd Lincoln. The film focuses on the four years between Lincoln's presidential election and his assassination. Not rated; contains violence and gore in multiple Civil War battle scenes. 118m. **DIR:** Lamont Johnson. **CAST:** Sam Waterston, Mary Tyler Moore, Richard Mulligan, Ruby Dee, Steven Culp, Tom Brennan, Gregory Cooke. **1988**

GORGEOUS HUSSY, THE ★★ This tale of an innkeeper's daughter who wins the hearts of various political guests is the kind of movie that flickers in the bedrooms of insomniacs at three in the morning. B&W; 103m. **DIR:** Clarence Brown. **CAST:** Joan Crawford, Lionel Barrymore, Robert Taylor, Franchot Tone, Melvyn Douglas, James Stewart. **1936**

GORGO ★★★1/2 Unpretentious thriller from England has a dinosaur-type monster captured and put on display in London's Piccadilly Circus, only to have its towering two-hundred-foot parent destroy half the city looking for it. Brisk pacing and well-executed effects. 76m. **DIR:** Eugene Lourie. **CAST:** Bill Travers, William Sylvester, Vincent Winter, Martin Benson. **1961 DVD**

GORGON, THE ★★★ Peter Cushing and Christopher Lee take on a Medusa-headed monster in this British Hammer Films chiller. A good one for horror buffs. 83m. **DIR:** Terence Fisher. **CAST:** Peter Cushing, Christopher Lee, Richard Pasco, Barbara Shelley. **1964**

GORILLA, THE ★★ This is another one of those horror comedies that takes place in an old mansion and again wastes poor Bela Lugosi's acting talents. The Ritz Brothers were an acquired taste, to be sure. B&W; 66m. **DIR:** Allan Dwan. **CAST:** The Ritz Brothers, Bela Lugosi, Lionel Atwill. **1939 DVD**

GORILLA AT LARGE ★★ Silly murder mystery set against a carnival background came at the end of the 3-D craze. A cast of familiar faces looks properly embarrassed by the inane goings-on, thus making it fun to watch. 84m. **DIR:** Harmon Jones. **CAST:** Cameron Mitchell, Anne Bancroft, Lee J. Cobb, Raymond Burr, Charlotte Austin, Lee Marvin. **1954**

GORILLAS IN THE MIST ★★★★ Sigourney Weaver stars in this impressive biopic about Dian Fossey, the crusading primatologist whose devotion to the once nearly extinct mountain gorillas of central Africa led to her murder. Rather than present Fossey as a saint, the film takes great pains to show her complexity. Fossey's interaction with the gorillas provides unforgettable scenes. Rated PG-13 for profanity, suggested sex, and violence. 129m. **DIR:** Michael Apted. **CAST:** Sigourney Weaver, Bryan Brown, Julie Harris, John Omirah Miluwi. **1988 DVD**

GORKY PARK ★★1/2 In this maddeningly uninvolving screen version of Martin Cruz Smith's bestselling mystery novel, three mutilated bodies are found in the Moscow park, and it's up to Russian policeman Arkady Renko (a miscast William Hurt) to find the maniacal killer. Lee Marvin is quite good as a suave bad guy, as are Joanna Pacula and Brian Dennehy. Rated R for nudity, sex, violence, and profanity. 128m. **DIR:** Michael Apted. **CAST:** William Hurt, Lee Marvin, Joanna Pacula, Brian Dennehy, Ian Bannen, Alexander Knox. **1983**

GORP 🦃 Particularly unfunny summer-camp flick. Rated R for nudity and profanity. 91m. **DIR:** Joseph Ruben. **CAST:** Michael Lembeck, Philip Casnoff, Dennis Quaid, David Huddleston, Rosanna Arquette. **1980**

•GOSFORD PARK ★★★★ Fans of Agatha Christie–style mysteries and PBS classics such as *Upstairs, Downstairs* will adore this concoction which puts a massive ensemble cast through all sorts of delightful character interaction en route to investigating the murder that interrupts a weekend retreat in an English country mansion. The performances are somewhat mannered, the pacing definitely languid; the result won't appeal to everybody, but fans of such class-conscious comedy-dramas will think they've died and gone to heaven. And the cast is, in a word, amazing. Rated R (and rather needlessly) for profanity and mild sensuality. 137m. **DIR:** Robert Altman. **CAST:** Michael Gambon, Kristin Scott Thomas, Camilla Rutherford, Maggie Smith, Charles Dance, Alan Bates, Helen Mirren, Derek Jacobi, Emily Watson, Clive Owen, Ryan Phillippe, Stephen Fry. **2001 DVD**

GOSHOGUN—THE TIME STRANGER ★★★ Six friends defy death in this animated story of sacrifice and loyalty among a group of elite government agents. Don't let the shifting time lines throw you—there's more here than meets the eye. In Japanese with English subtitles. Not rated; contains violence, nudity, and profanity. 90m. **DIR:** Kunihiko Yuyama. **1985**

GOSPEL ★★★★ Featuring many of the top stars of black gospel music, this is a joyous, spirit-lifting music documentary that contains the highlights of a five-and-a-half-hour concert filmed in June 1981 at Oakland Paramount Theater. The spirited performances might even make a believer out of you—that is, if you aren't already. Rated G. 92m. **DIR:** David Levick, Frederick A. Rizenberg. **CAST:** Mighty Clouds of Joy, Clark Sisters, Walter Hawkins and the Hawkins Family, Shirley Caesar, Rev. James Cleveland. **1982**

GOSPEL ACCORDING TO SAINT MATTHEW, THE ★★★★ Pier Paolo Pasolini's visionary account of Jesus Christ's spiritual struggle against the afflictions of social injustice. Shot on location throughout southern Italy with a cast of nonprofessional actors who possess a natural quality. This highly acclaimed film received a special jury prize at the Venice Film Festival. In Italian with English subtitles. B&W; 136m. **DIR:** Pier Paolo Pasolini. **CAST:** Enrique Irazoque. **1964**

GOSPEL ACCORDING TO VIC, THE ★★★1/2 In this delightful comedy from Scotland, a teacher (Tom Conti) at a Glasgow parochial school finds that he can create miracles—even though he doesn't believe in them. Those who have reveled in the subtle, sly humor of *Gregory's Girl*, *Local Hero*, and other Scottish films will find similar joys in this. Rated PG-13 for adult content. 92m. **DIR:** Charles Gormley. **CAST:** Tom Conti, Helen Mirren, David Hayman, Brian Pettifer, Jennifer Black. **1986**

GOSSIP ★★1/2 Three college students start a nasty rumor as an exercise for a communications class, then the rumor gets out of hand and the innocent begin to suffer. The film has a kind of sinister energy, but it's shallow, casually vicious, and unconvincing, as if we're not expected to believe it but merely enjoy the trendy MTV-age hipness of it all. Rated R for profanity, sexual scenes, and brief violence. 90m. **DIR:** Davis Guggenheim. **CAST:** James Marsden, Lena Headey, Norman Reedus, Kate Hudson, Edward James Olmos, Eric Bogosian. **2000 DVD**

GOTCHA! ★★★★ In this entertaining mixture of coming-of-age comedy and suspense-thriller, a college boy (Anthony Edwards) goes to Paris in search of romance and adventure. He gets both when he meets a beautiful, mysterious woman (Linda Fiorentino) who puts both of their lives in danger. Rated PG-13 for slight nudity, suggested sex, profanity, and violence. 97m. **DIR:** Jeff Kanew. **CAST:** Anthony Edwards, Linda Fiorentino, Alex Rocco, Nick Corri, Marla Adams, Klaus Lowitsch. **1985**

GOTHAM ★★ A *film noir* thriller that's confusing, slow, and tediously melodramatic. Tommy Lee Jones is a Marlowesque detective hired as a go-between for a well-to-do husband and his murdered wife (Virginia Madsen). Romantically atmospheric and beautifully photographed, the film is marred by terrible dialogue and anemic acting. Rated R for nudity, simulated sex, violence, and profanity. 92m. **DIR:** Lloyd Fonvielle. **CAST:** Tommy Lee Jones, Virginia Madsen, Frederic Forrest. **1988**

GOTHIC ★★ Director Ken Russell returns to his favorite subject—the tortured artist—for this look at what may have happened that spooky evening in 1816 when Lord Byron, poet Percy Shelley, his fiancée Mary, her stepsister Claire, and Byron's ex-lover Dr. Polidori spent the evening together, attempting to scare each other. What the viewer gets is the usual Russell bag of tricks: insane hallucinations, group sex, scenes of gruesome murders, and much, much more. Rated R. 90m. **DIR:** Ken Russell. **CAST:** Gabriel Byrne, Julian Sands, Natasha Richardson, Timothy Spall. **1986 DVD**

GOTTI ★★★★ Armand Assante embraces the title role in this absorbing docudrama, as the Mafia "Teflon Don" who was just as loved by blue-collar New Yorkers as he was despised by the FBI. Based on *Gotti, Rise and Fall*, by Jerry Capeci and Gene Mustain, the story loosely follows Gotti's career from 1973 to the betrayal from within that finally brought him down. Assante convincingly sells Gotti as a suave clotheshorse, with a hair-trigger temper matched only by the savvy that maintained his growing power base. Compelling viewing. Rated R for violence and profanity. 116m. **DIR:** Robert Harmon. **CAST:** Armand Assante, William Forsythe, Richard Sarafian, Frank Vincent, Dominic Chianese, Anthony Quinn. **1996 DVD**

GOVERNESS, THE ★★1/2 Although you're bound to sympathize with an intelligent and well-bred nineteenth-century Jewish woman prompted to conceal her heritage due to a repressive environment, it's hard to get beyond this gal's self-destructive stupidity. The woman in question (Minnie Driver) takes a job as a governess but quickly initiates an affair with the child's father. Pretty tiresome for most of us. Rated R for nudity and strong sexual content. 114m. **DIR:** Sandra Goldbacher. **CAST:** Minnie Driver, Tom Wilkinson, Harriet Walter, Florence Hoath, Bruce Myers, Jonathan Rhys Meyers. **1998 DVD**

GOYA IN BORDEAUX ★★★1/2 Exiled in France, the great painter spends his last days reminiscing to his young daughter, with his past and present mingling in his mind. The film may confuse viewers unfamiliar with Goya, but the visual phantasmagoria of images from the artist's life and work is haunting and hard to dismiss. In Spanish with English subtitles. Rated R for mature themes, violent images, and brief sexual scenes. 94m. **DIR:** Carlos Saura. **CAST:** Francisco Rabal, José Coronado, Daphne Fernández, Maribel Verdu. **1999 DVD**

GRACE AND GLORIE ★★★1/2 Having left the fast-paced city life, Diane Lane plays a woman who finds hospice work very satisfying and peaceful. That peace is shattered by a new patient (Gena Rowlands) who forces her to confront her attraction to death and dying. Rowlands's scenes are more inspiring than depressing in this *Hallmark Hall of Fame* production. Smiles and tears are virtually guaranteed. Not rated; contains adult themes. 99m. **DIR:** Arthur Allan Seidelman. **CAST:** Gena Rowlands, Diane Lane, Neal McDonough, Chris Beetem. **1998**

GRACE OF MY HEART ★★1/2 Give writer-director Allison Anders credit: she obviously tried to take us inside the music business with this film about the career of a Carole King–style singer-songwriter. Indeed it is pretty much King's story up until she leaves New York for Los Angeles and starts up an affair with a surf-music genius/recluse. It is here that the film loses its pace and credibility. Illeana Douglas shines throughout, even when the screenplay begins to border on parody. Rated R for suggested sex and profanity. 116m. **DIR:** Allison Anders. **CAST:** Illeana Douglas, Matt Dillon, Eric Stoltz, John Turturro, Bruce Davison, Patsy Kensit, Chris Isaak, Bridget Fonda. **1996 DVD**

GRACE QUIGLEY ★★1/2 After witnessing the murder of her landlord, spinster Katharine Hepburn enlists the aid of freelance hit man Nick Nolte. Hepburn wants Nolte to end her life, but not before he puts to rest some of her elderly friends who feel it is time for them to die. Extremely black comedy doesn't have enough humor and warmth to rise above its gruesome subject matter. Rated R. 87m. **DIR:** Anthony Harvey. **CAST:** Katharine Hepburn, Nick Nolte, Elizabeth Wilson, Chip Zien, Christopher Murney. **1985**

GRADUATE, THE ★★★★1/2 Mike Nichols won an Academy Award for his direction of this touching, funny, unsettling, and unforgettable release about a young man (Dustin Hoffman, in his first major role) attempting to chart his future and develop his own set of values. He falls in love with Katharine Ross, but finds himself seduced by her wily, sexy mother, Anne Bancroft (as Mrs. Robinson). Don't forget the superb soundtrack of songs by Paul Simon and Art Garfunkel. 105m. **DIR:** Mike Nichols. **CAST:** Dustin Hoffman, Anne Bancroft, Katharine Ross. **1967 DVD**

GRADUATION DAY ★★ A high school runner dies during a competition. Soon someone begins killing all her teammates. Plenty of violence in this one. Rated R. 96m. **DIR:** Herb Freed. **CAST:** Christopher George, Michael Pataki, E. J. Peaker. **1981**

GRAFFITI BRIDGE ★★ Prince's hollow fantasy sequel to *Purple Rain* is about the conflicting values (artistic integrity versus commercial success) that ignite a power struggle between two nightclub co-owners (funksters Prince and Morris Day). Rated PG-13 for profanity and sexual themes. 111m. **DIR:** Prince. **CAST:** Prince, Morris Day, Jerome Benton, Ingrid Chavez. **1990**

GRAIN OF SAND, THE ★★★1/2 A struggling woman retreats to her hometown to search for an old love. Delphine Seyrig's strong performance is the highlight of this moving drama. In French with English subtitles. 90m. **DIR:** Pomme Meffre. **CAST:** Delphine Seyrig, Genevieve Fontanel. **1982**

GRAND CANYON ★★★★1/2 Writer-director Lawrence Kasdan picks up ten years later with the baby-boom generation he first examined in *The Big Chill*. Through a collection of vignettes of daily life, a superb cast portrays what it's like to be 40 in the nineties. No motion picture is flawless, but this funny, touching, and insightful character study comes pretty close. Rated R for profanity, nudity, and violence. 134m. **DIR:** Lawrence Kasdan. **CAST:** Danny Glover, Kevin Kline, Steve Martin, Mary McDonnell, Mary-Louise Parker, Alfre Woodard. **1991 DVD**

GRAND HOTEL ★★★★ World War I is over. Life in the fast lane has returned to Berlin's Grand Hotel, crossroads of a thousand lives, backdrop to as many stories. This anthology of life at various levels won an Oscar for best picture. B&W; 113m. **DIR:** Edmund Goulding. **CAST:** John Barrymore, Greta Garbo, Wallace Beery, Joan Crawford, Lionel Barrymore, Lewis Stone. **1932**

GRAND ILLUSION ★★★★★ Shortly before Hitler plunged Europe into World War II, this monumental French film tried to examine why men submit to warfare's "grand illusions." We are taken to a German prison camp in World War I, where it becomes quite easy to see the hypocrisy of war while watching the day-to-day miniworld of camp life. This classic by Jean Renoir is a must-see for anyone who appreciates great art. B&W; 95m. **DIR:** Jean Renoir. **CAST:** Jean Gabin, Pierre Fresnay, Erich Von Stroheim, Marcel Dalio, Julien Carette. **1937 DVD**

GRAND ISLE ★★★ While on vacation on an island paradise, Kelly McGillis discovers the passion inside of her reawakened when she encounters several men. Handsome production features a gorgeous cast and scenery. Contains nudity and simulated sex. 94m. **DIR:** Mary Lambert. **CAST:** Kelly McGillis, Julian Sands, Glenne Headly, Ellen Burstyn. **1991**

GRAND LARCENY ★★ A miscast Marilu Henner brings low this caper comedy about the American-raised daughter of a French thief, whose death results in her having to take over the "family business." Only the presence of debonair Ian McShane saves this from being a complete failure. Made for TV. 95m. **DIR:** Jeannot Szwarc. **CAST:** Marilu Henner, Ian McShane, Louis Jourdan, Omar Sharif. **1988**

GRAND PRIX ★★1/2 The cars, the drivers, and the race itself are the real stars of this international epic, beautifully filmed on locations throughout Europe. The four interrelated stories of professional adversaries and their personal lives intrude on the exciting footage of the real thing. Yves Montand, though, does a credible job in what is basically a big-budget soap opera with oil stains. 179m. **DIR:** John Frankenheimer. **CAST:** James Garner, Eva Marie Saint, Yves Montand, Toshiro Mifune, Brian Bedford, Jessica Walter, Antonio Sabato, Adolfo Celi. **1966**

GRAND THEFT AUTO ★★1/2 The basic plot of *It's a Mad Mad Mad Mad World* is given a retread by first-time director—and star—Ron Howard in this frantic 1977 car-chase comedy. Sadly, little of the style that made *Night Shift* and *Splash* such treats is evident here. Rated PG. 89m. **DIR:** Ron Howard. **CAST:** Ron Howard, Nancy Morgan. **1977 DVD**

GRAND TOUR: DISASTER IN TIME ★★★ Lawrence O'Donnell and C. L. Moore's classic science-fiction novella, *The Vintage Season*, is the basis of this intriguing made-for-cable drama, which finds innkeeper Jeff Daniels rather puzzled over the strange behavior of some new tourists... who, for example, clearly don't understand the principle behind tying shoes. Unfortunately, writer-director David N. Twohy ruins a good thing with his needlessly upbeat conclusion. Rated PG-13. 99m. **DIR:** David N. Twohy. **CAST:** Jeff Daniels, Ariana Richards, Emilia Crow, Jim Haynie. **1992**

GRANDMA'S BOY ★★★ Shy, young man wins the girl of his dreams with the help of his loving grandmother.

Through some time-worn plot devices, the timid fellow captures a local terror and takes on the bully who has plagued him most of his life, but it's satisfying fun and still holds up. Harold Lloyd scored his feature-length bull's-eye with this release and joined the pantheon of great silent comedians that included Charlie Chaplin and Buster Keaton. B&W; 49m. **DIR:** Fred Newmeyer. **CAST:** Harold Lloyd, Mildred Davis, Anna Townsend, Charles Stevenson, Dick Sutherland. **1922**

GRANDMA'S HOUSE ★★★1/2 Two orphaned teens sent to live with their grandparents suspect that this seemingly kindly old couple have a few skeletons in the closet. Cleverly written thriller has more than its share of surprises. Not rated, but violence makes this unsuitable for kids. 89m. **DIR:** Peter Rader. **CAST:** Eric Foster, Kim Valentine, Brinke Stevens. **1989**

GRANDVIEW, U.S.A. ★★ A coming-of-age study lacking in depth and characterization. Rated R for nudity, violence, and profanity. 97m. **DIR:** Randal Kleiser. **CAST:** Jamie Lee Curtis, C. Thomas Howell, Patrick Swayze, Jennifer Jason Leigh, Ramon Bieri, Carole Cook, Troy Donahue, William Windom. **1984**

GRANNY, THE ★★★ Stella Stevens chews up the scenery in this hilarious horror spoof, as a miserable, spiteful, wealthy old battle-ax whose conniving family hastens her departure for her fortune. Granny, though, has plans of her own. She acquires a mythical potion for eternal life that doesn't quite produce the results she expected. Rated R for nudity, violence, and profanity. 85m. **DIR:** Luca Bercovici. **CAST:** Stella Stevens, Shannon Whirry. **1994**

GRAPES OF WRATH, THE ★★★★★ Henry Fonda stars in this superb screen adaptation of the John Steinbeck novel about farmers from Oklahoma fleeing the Dust Bowl and poverty of their home state only to be confronted by prejudice and violence in California. It's a compelling drama beautifully acted by the director's stock company. B&W; 129m. **DIR:** John Ford. **CAST:** Henry Fonda, John Carradine, Jane Darwell, Russell Simpson, Charley Grapewin, John Qualen. **1940**

GRASS HARP, THE ★★1/2 This is based on Truman Capote's bittersweet memoir detailing a boyhood spent with his two maiden aunts. A strong supporting cast helps to define his eccentric southern family, but Edward Furlong is too understated as Capote's alter ego. There are some charming moments, but cloying sentimentalism undermines all. Rated PG for mild profanity. 107m. **DIR:** Charles Matthau. **CAST:** Walter Matthau, Jack Lemmon, Sissy Spacek, Piper Laurie, Mary Steenburgen, Edward Furlong, Charles Durning, Nell Carter, Roddy McDowall. **1995**

GRASS IS ALWAYS GREENER OVER THE SEPTIC TANK, THE ★★★1/2 Carol Burnett and Charles Grodin shine in this tale of the domestic horrors of suburban life taken from Erma Bombeck's bestseller. The comedy doesn't always work, but when it does it rivals Grodin's *The Heartbreak Kid* and some of the best moments of Burnett's TV show. No rating, but the equivalent of a PG for language. 98m. **DIR:** Robert Day. **CAST:** Carol Burnett, Charles Grodin, Alex Rocco, Linda Gray. **1978**

GRASS IS GREENER, THE ★★★1/2 Cary Grant and Deborah Kerr star as a married couple experimenting with extramarital affairs in this comedy. Some funny moments, but it's not hilarious. 105m. **DIR:** Stanley Donen. **CAST:** Cary Grant, Deborah Kerr, Jean Simmons, Robert Mitchum. **1960 DVD**

GRASSHOPPER, THE ★★★1/2 Jacqueline Bisset is riveting in this little-known film. She plays a young woman who abandons the security of her family for the glamour and excitement of the entertainment world. Unfortunately, her career hopes are shattered as each man in her life robs her of self-respect. Quirky ending warns viewers of the rapid descent one might take after rejecting morality. Equivalent to an R for sexual situations and seedy lifestyle. 95m. **DIR:** Jerry Paris. **CAST:** Jacqueline Bisset, Jim Brown, Joseph Cotten. **1970**

•GRATEFUL DAWG ★★★ Musical history comes alive in this film documenting the friendship between Grateful Dead lead guitarist Jerry Garcia and David Grisman, founder of Dawg music. Utilizing rare concert footage, home videos of private jams, and never-before-released recordings, Grisman takes us on a journey filled with musical insight, great songs, and plenty of nostalgia. You don't have to be a Grateful Dead or Dawg music fan to appreciate the effort. Rated PG-13 for language. 81m. **DIR:** Gillian Grisman. **CAST:** Jerry Garcia, David Grisman. **2000 DVD**

GRAVE, THE ★★★1/2 You'll have fun with this nasty little thriller. After hearing about a treasure supposedly buried beneath a grave, two good ol' boys bust out of prison, connect with some particularly dim-witted friends. Although warped and vicious, this will please viewers with a macabre sense of humor. Good twist ending, too. Rated R for profanity, violence, and simulated sex. 90m. **DIR:** Jonas Pate. **CAST:** Craig Sheffer, Gabrielle Anwar, Anthony Michael Hall, Josh Charles, Donal Logue, Keith David, Eric Roberts. **1995**

GRAVE INDISCRETION ★★★ A stuffy British archaeologist finds his world infiltrated and eventually overrun by a mysterious and ultimately menacing butler. Outstanding performances throughout. Also known as *Gentlemen Don't Eat Poets*. Rated R for nudity. 98m. **DIR:** John-Paul Davidson. **CAST:** Alan Bates, Theresa Russell, Sting, John Mills. **1996**

GRAVE OF THE FIREFLIES ★★★★ Those who doubt that animation can successfully tell serious, meaningful stories should watch this wonderful animated feature. Young Seita and his little sister, homeless and orphaned during the final days of World War II, try desperately to survive in a time when food and aid are scarce. This story will break your heart. In Japanese with English subtitles. Not rated, but suitable for most audiences. 88m. **DIR:** Isao Takahata. **1988 DVD**

GRAVE OF THE VAMPIRE 🦃 Baby bloodsucker grows up to search for his father and discover his birthright. 95m. **DIR:** John Hayes. **CAST:** William Smith, Michael Pataki. **1972**

GRAVE SECRETS ★★ A woman, tormented by what she believes are ghosts, hires a parapsychologist in this not-too-scary supernatural flick. Rated R for violence and profanity. 90m. **DIR:** Donald P. Borchers. **CAST:** Paul LeMat, Renee Soutendijk, David Warner, Lee Ving, John Crawford. **1989**

GRAVE SECRETS: THE LEGACY OF HILLTOP DRIVE ★★ The paranormal goings-on in this made-for-TV movie are pretty mild. Too much of a resemblance to the ghost story classic *Poltergeist*. 94m. **DIR:** John Patterson. **CAST:** Patty Duke, David Soul, David Selby, Kiersten Warren, Kimberly Cullum. **1992**

GRAVESEND ★★1/2 Young director Salvatore Stabile makes an impressive debut with this gritty tale of four Brooklyn teenagers trying to dispose of a body. Unfortunately, the cast isn't nearly as committed as the director, and they fail to command the situation or our attention. Rated R for language and violence. 86m. **DIR:** Salvatore Stabile. **CAST:** Thomas Brandise, Tom Malloy, Michael Parducci, Tony Tucci. **1997 DVD**

GRAVEYARD SHIFT 🦃 New York cabbie expects more than a tip. Rated R. 90m. **DIR:** Gerard Ciccoritti. **CAST:** Silvio Oliviero, Helen Papas. **1987**

GRAY LADY DOWN ★★★1/2 This adventure film starring Charlton Heston is action-packed and well-acted. The story concerns a two-man rescue operation of a sunken nuclear sub that has collided with a freighter. Beautiful photography and special effects. 111m. **DIR:** David Greene. **CAST:** Charlton Heston, David Carradine, Stacy Keach, Ned Beatty, Ronny Cox, Rosemary Forsyth. **1977 DVD**

GRAYEAGLE ★★ Disappointing reworking of John Wayne's *The Searchers*, with Alex Cord as the Cheyenne warrior Grayeagle, who kidnaps Lana Wood and is pursued by the girl's father, Ben Johnson. Rated PG for violence and mild nudity. 104m. **DIR:** Charles B. Pierce. **CAST:** Ben Johnson, Iron Eyes Cody, Lana Wood, Alex Cord, Jack Elam, Paul Fix. **1977**

GREASE ★★★ After they meet and enjoy a tender summer romance, John Travolta and Olivia Newton-John tearfully part. Surprisingly, they are reunited when she becomes the new girl at his high school. Around his friends, he must play Mr. Tough Guy, and her goody-two-shoes image doesn't quite fit in. Slight, but fun. Rated PG. 110m. **DIR:** Randal Kleiser. **CAST:** John Travolta, Olivia Newton-John, Stockard Channing, Jeff Conaway, Didi Conn, Eve Arden, Sid Caesar. **1978**

GREASE 2 ★★★ A sequel to the most successful screen musical of all time, *Grease 2* takes us back to Rydell High. The result is a fun little movie that seems to work almost in spite of itself. Rated PG for suggestive gestures and lyrics. 115m. **DIR:** Patricia Birch. **CAST:** Maxwell Caulfield, Michelle Pfeiffer, Adrian Zmed, Lorna Luft, Didi Conn. **1982**

GREASED LIGHTNING ★★★ *Greased Lightning* is a funny and exciting film. Richard Pryor is a knockout in the lead role, and the film is a real audience pleaser. Because the story is true, it carries a punch even *Rocky* couldn't match. Wendell Scott's story is more dramatic. Scott was the first black man to win a NASCAR Grand National stock car race. Rated PG. 96m. **DIR:** Michael Schultz. **CAST:** Richard Pryor, Pam Grier, Beau Bridges, Cleavon Little, Richie Havens. **1977**

GREASER'S PALACE ★★1/2 You'll either love or hate this one, a retelling of the passion of Christ set in a small western town. Sometimes inventive, sometimes maddening. Not rated. 91m. **DIR:** Robert Downey. **CAST:** Allan Arbus, Luana Anders, Herve Villechaize, Don Calfa. **1972 DVD**

GREAT ADVENTURE, THE ★★ Spin-off of *Call of the Wild* has an orphan boy, his dog, and a dance-hall queen take on a Yukon bully in gold-rush Dawson. Good family story with veterans Jack Palance and Joan Collins in prime form. Rated PG. 90m. **DIR:** Paul Elliotts. **CAST:** Joan Collins, Jack Palance, Fred Romer, Elisabetta Virgili. **1976 DVD**

GREAT AMERICAN SEX SCANDAL, THE ★★★ Enjoyable, made-for-television romp about a sex trial that has the whole world talking, especially the sequestered jury. When a nebbish accountant is brought to trial for embezzlement, the facts behind his case intrigue the media, his attorney, the jury, and even the accountant himself. While the world waits patiently to find out the facts, the jury members grapple with personal problems of their own. Likable cast of familiar faces. Rated PG-13 for adult situations. 94m. **DIR:** Michael Schultz. **CAST:** Stephen Baldwin, Barbara Bosson, Heather Locklear, Bronson Pinchot, Lynn Redgrave, Tracy Scoggins, Alan Thicke, Reginald Vel Johnson. **1989**

GREAT BALLS OF FIRE ★★★★ A landmark music bio. It's obvious how hard talented Dennis Quaid has worked on his piano playing (with hands, feet, head, and tail) and on his Jerry Lee Lewis hellion-touched-by-God mannerisms and he's sublime in the role. So is Alec Baldwin, playing it straight and righteous as Jerry Lee's famous cousin, Jimmy Swaggart. Some miraculous moments. Rated PG-13 for profanity and sexual themes. 110m. **DIR:** Jim McBride. **CAST:** Dennis Quaid, Winona Ryder, Alec Baldwin, Trey Wilson. **1989**

GREAT BANK HOAX, THE ★★1/2 It is doubtful that viewers today will think of Watergate when watching this comedy caper, but it was originally intended as a parable. When the pillars of the community find out that the bank has been embezzled, they decide to rob it. Great characterizations by all-star cast. Rated PG. 89m. **DIR:** Joseph Jacoby. **CAST:** Richard Basehart, Burgess Meredith, Paul Sand, Ned Beatty, Michael Murphy, Arthur Godfrey. **1977**

GREAT CARUSO, THE ★★★★ A number of factual liberties are taken in this lavish screen biography of the great Italian tenor, but no matter. Mario Lanza's voice is magnificent; Ann Blyth and Dorothy Kirsten sing like birds. Devotees of music will love the arias. 109m. **DIR:** Richard Thorpe. **CAST:** Mario Lanza, Ann Blyth, Dorothy Kirsten. **1950**

GREAT CHASE, THE ★★★★ Silent-film chases from several classics comprise the bulk of this compilation, including the running acrobatics of Douglas Fairbanks Sr. in *The Mark of Zorro*, the escape of Lillian Gish over the ice floes in *Way Down East*, and car chases and stunts of all descriptions from silent comedies. A large part of the film is devoted to Buster Keaton's locomotive chase from *The General*. B&W; 79m. **DIR:** Frank Gallop. **CAST:** Buster Keaton, Douglas Fairbanks Sr., Lillian Gish, Pearl White. **1963 DVD**

GREAT DAN PATCH, THE ★★★ The story of the greatest trotting horse of them all. Good racing scenes. An opera for horse lovers. B&W; 94m. **DIR:** Joseph M. Newman. **CAST:** Dennis O'Keefe, Gail Russell, Ruth Warrick, Charlotte Greenwood. **1949**

GREAT DAY ★★1/2 Eleanor Roosevelt's impending trip to Great Britain is the background for this tribute to England's women during wartime. Effective quasi-documentary. B&W; 94m. **DIR:** Lance Comfort. **CAST:** Eric Portman, Flora Robson, Sheila Sim. **1945**

GREAT DAY IN HARLEM, A ★★★★ In the summer of 1958, fifty-seven hard-core, nocturnal jazz musicians gathered in front of a Harlem brownstone stoop. The photograph taken that morning for *Esquire* magazine, which included such giants as Thelonious Monk, Count Basie, Gene Krupa, Marian McPartland, Charles Mingus, and Art Blakey, has become the most famous snapshot in jazz history. The event has been shaped into a warm valentine using home-movie footage, archival performances, interviews, and stills. Not rated. 60m. **DIR:** Jean Bach. **1995 DVD**

GREAT DICTATOR, THE ★★★★★ Charlie Chaplin stars in and directs this devastating lampoon of the Third Reich. The celebrated clown's first all-talking picture, it casts him in two roles—as his famous Little Tramp and as Adenoid Hynkel, the Hitler-like ruler of Tomania. As with the similarly themed *Duck Soup*, starring the Marx Brothers, the comedy was a little too whimsical for wartime audiences. But it has to be regarded as a classic. B&W; 128m. **DIR:** Charles Chaplin. **CAST:** Charlie Chaplin, Jack Oakie, Paulette Goddard. **1940 DVD**

GREAT ELEPHANT ESCAPE, THE ★★★ Plenty of adventure in this tale of a boy who joins his mother in Africa. There, he meets a local boy, and together they attempt to save a baby elephant from poachers. The two youths and the baby elephant set out on a trek across the Dark Continent, finding all kinds of adventure, fun, and danger. Exotic locale, likable characters, and a good story make this an enjoyable romp. Rated PG for violence. 95m. **DIR:** George Miller. **CAST:** Stephanie Zimbalist, Joseph Gordon-Levitt, Julian Sands. **1995**

GREAT ESCAPE, THE ★★★★★ If ever there was a movie that could be called pure cheer-the-heroes entertainment, it's *The Great Escape*. The plot centers around a German prison camp in World War II. The commandant has received the assignment of housing all the escape-minded Allied prisoners. The Germans are obviously playing with fire with this all-star group, and, sure enough, all hell breaks loose with excitement galore. 168m. **DIR:** John Sturges. **CAST:** Steve McQueen, James Garner, Charles Bronson, Richard Attenborough, James Coburn. **1963 DVD**

GREAT ESCAPE II, THE ★★ In World War II, seventy-five American and British soldiers tunnel themselves out of prison. This star-studded, made-for-television two-parter has been shortened considerably for video, but still plays well. 93m. **DIR:** Paul Wendkos, Jud Taylor. **CAST:** Christopher Reeve, Judd Hirsch, Donald Pleasence, Charles Haid. **1988**

GREAT EXPECTATIONS (1946) ★★★★1/2 A penniless orphan becomes a gentleman through the generosity of a mysterious patron. The second of three film versions of Charles Dickens's classic story. Made at the close of World War II, this version is by far the finest from all standpoints: direction, script, cast, photography, art direction. B&W; 118m. **DIR:** David Lean. **CAST:** John Mills, Alec Guinness, Valerie Hobson, Bernard Miles, Finlay Currie, Martita Hunt, Jean Simmons. **1946 DVD**

GREAT EXPECTATIONS (1983) ★★ Spotty though interesting-enough animated adaptation of Charles Dickens classic tale about a young man's lessons in maturity. There's a lot of tragedy here (as expected), which may catch the attention of older children, but small youngsters will no doubt find this too low-key. 72m. **DIR:** Jean Tych. **1983**

GREAT EXPECTATIONS (1988) ★★★★ Fine BBC production of Charles Dickens classic tale about a boy named Pip. This broadcast takes special care to include every plot convolution (and there are many!). While literary enthusiasts will rejoice in this, most casual viewers will be fidgeting with impatience. Best to watch this in two sittings! 300m. **DIR:** Julian Amyes. **CAST:** Stratford Johns, Gerry Sundquist, Joan Hickson. **1988**

GREAT EXPECTATIONS (1989) ★★★★1/2 First-rate, British-made miniseries of the Charles Dickens classic features outstanding performances, especially by Anthony Hopkins as Magwitch and Jean Simmons (Estella in director David Lean's 1946 version) as the mysterious and poignant Miss Haversham. Recommended for the whole family. 310m. **DIR:** Kevin O'Connor. **CAST:** Anthony Hopkins, Jean Simmons, John Rhys-Davies, Ray McAnally, Kim Thomson. **1989**

GREAT EXPECTATIONS (1998) ★★★1/2 Of all Dickens's best-known books, this one has the most timeless elements: a penniless, unsophisticated boy falls in love with a worldly, wealthy, slightly older girl who regards him as a toy. With the boy's subsequent efforts to level the playing field by "rising" to her station, he discovers that he has left behind those portions of his personality that defined him. This rendition begins in a small Florida town and eventually moves to New York City. Anne Bancroft has a field day as demented old Ms. Dinsmoor. Rated R for profanity, nudity, and strong sexual content. 111m. **DIR:** Alfonso Cuaron. **CAST:** Ethan Hawke, Gwyneth Paltrow, Chris Cooper, Anne Bancroft, Robert De Niro, Hank Azaria, Josh Mostel. **1998 DVD**

GREAT EXPECTATIONS—THE UNTOLD STORY ★★1/2 This story should *never* have been told. We follow Magwitch, the escaped convict who befriends the little boy in Charles Dickens's *Great Expectations*, as he changes to a rich gentleman in Australia. Not rated. 102m. **DIR:** Tim Burstall. **CAST:** John Stanton, Sigrid Thornton, Robert Coleby, Noel Ferrier. **1987**

GREAT FLAMARION, THE ★★★ Schemer Mary Beth Hughes suckers vaudeville trick-shot artist Erich Von Stroheim into murdering her husband and leaves him to take the fall while she flees with Dan Duryea. Nothing new in the plot line, but Von Stroheim's performance is reward enough. B&W; 78m. **DIR:** Anthony Mann. **CAST:** Erich Von Stroheim, Mary Beth Hughes, Dan Duryea. **1945**

GREAT GABBO, THE ★★★1/2 Cinema giant Erich Von Stroheim gives a tour-de-force performance as a brilliant but cold ventriloquist whose disregard for the feelings of others comes back to haunt him when he realizes that he has lost the affection of a girl he has come to love. This is a film that lingers in the memory and rates with other fine films about ventriloquism like *Dead Of Night* and *Magic*. B&W; 89m. **DIR:** James Cruze. **CAST:** Erich Von Stroheim, Betty Compson, Don Douglas. **1929**

GREAT GATSBY, THE ★★★ This is a well-mounted, well-acted film that is, perhaps, a bit overlong. However, Robert Redford, the mysterious title character, is marvelous as Gatsby. Bruce Dern is equally memorable as the man who always has been rich and selfish. Rated PG. 144m. **DIR:** Jack Clayton. **CAST:** Robert Redford, Mia Farrow, Karen Black, Sam Waterston, Bruce Dern. **1974 DVD**

GREAT GUNS ★★ Although it's a cut below their classics, *Sons of the Desert* fans will love it, and so will most—especially the young. Stan and Ollie have jobs guarding a rich man's playboy son. He gets drafted; the fellows join up to continue their work. The playboy gets along just fine in khaki. The boys get up to their ears in trouble with an archetypical sergeant. B&W; 74m. **DIR:** Monty Banks. **CAST:** Stan Laurel, Oliver Hardy, Sheila Ryan, Dick Nelson. **1941**

GREAT GUY ★★ Depression film about a feisty inspector crusading against corruption in the meat-packing business. Not vintage James Cagney . . . but okay. B&W; 75m. **DIR:** John G. Blystone. **CAST:** James Cagney, Mae Clarke, Edward Brophy. **1936**

GREAT IMPOSTOR, THE ★★★1/2 The amazing story of Ferdinand Demara is told in engrossing style by director Robert Mulligan. Demara, with natural charm and uncanny adaptability, successfully managed to pose as everything from a clergyman to a doctor. The role is a tour de force for Tony Curtis. Compelling and seasoned with dark humor. 112m. **DIR:** Robert Mulligan. **CAST:** Tony Curtis, Edmond O'Brien, Arthur O'Connell, Gary Merrill. **1960**

GREAT INDIAN RAILWAY, THE ★★★★ Gorgeous photography and extensive research turned this National Geographic production into a true enticement for armchair travelers. It leaves one with an understanding of the machinations of the largest train system in the world and its effects on Indian society. However, there is too much material for one film—occasionally dropped snippets of information leave one hungering for more. Narrated by Linda Hunt. Not rated. 111m. **DIR:** William Livingston. **1995**

GREAT LIE, THE ★★★ Prime soap opera in the tradition of Bette Davis's *The Old Maid*, but this time she is the bitchy one who takes over someone else's child. Mary Astor (an Oscar winner for supporting actress) plays a concert pianist who marries Davis's former lover, George Brent. The marriage turns out to be illegal, and, before they can get married again Brent crashes in the jungle. B&W; 102m. **DIR:** Edmund Goulding. **CAST:** Bette Davis, George Brent, Mary Astor, Hattie McDaniel, Lucile Watson, Jerome Cowan, Grant Mitchell. **1941**

GREAT LOCOMOTIVE CHASE, THE ★★★1/2 Fess Parker and his band of spies infiltrate the South and abscond with a railroad train. Jeffrey Hunter is the conductor who chases them to regain possession of the train. This is a straightforward telling of actual events, emphasizing action and suspense. 85m. **DIR:** Francis D. Lyon. **CAST:** Fess Parker, Jeffrey Hunter, Jeff York, John Lupton. **1956 DVD**

GREAT LOS ANGELES EARTHQUAKE, THE ★★1/2 The big one hits Los Angeles in this condensed version of the television miniseries. Characters get lost in the trim, leaving only victims of the overblown special effects. Joe Spano is especially embarrassing as the city official afraid to cry wolf. 106m. **DIR:** Larry Elikann. **CAST:** Joanna Kerns, Dan Lauria, Alan Autry, Ed Begley Jr., Joe Spano. **1990**

GREAT LOVE EXPERIMENT, THE ★★ This HBO Family Playhouse special features a nerdy teen who becomes the guinea pig for the in group. To her surprise, she is suddenly pursued by three cool guys and made over by the most popular girl in the senior class. For teens only. 45m. **DIR:** Claudia Weill. **CAST:** Tracy Pollan. **1982**

GREAT LOVER, THE ★★★★ This is top-notch Bob Hope. The story, as usual, is simple. While on a transatlantic steamship, a timid Boy Scout leader romances lovely Rhonda Fleming and tracks down a strangler. Comedic suspense is well played. B&W; 80m. **DIR:** Alexander Hall. **CAST:** Bob Hope, Rhonda Fleming, Roland Young, Jim Backus, Roland Culver, George Reeves. **1949 DVD**

GREAT MADCAP, THE ★★1/2 To cure a rich man of his profligate ways, his family tricks him into thinking that his fortune has been lost. One of director Luis Buñuel's least interesting films, this features satirical themes that he would later redo. In Spanish with English subtitles. B&W; 90m. **DIR:** Luis Buñuel. **CAST:** Fernando Soler, Ruben Rojo. **1949**

GREAT MAN VOTES, THE ★★★1/2 Drunken widower raises his two spunky kids in a rather unorthodox home. They are constantly harassed by the children of the more successful fathers until the party relies on Barrymore's vote to set the tone for other precincts. B&W; 72m. **DIR:** Garson Kanin. **CAST:** John Barrymore, Peter Holden, Virginia Weidler, Katharine Alexander. **1939**

GREAT MAN'S LADY, THE ★★1/2 It's all a bit much as Barbara Stanwyck stoically dedicates her life to a city founder who really doesn't deserve all that devotion. Stanwyck is her usual feisty self, but the film's structure suffers from trying to cover too much ground. Not rated. B&W; 91m. **DIR:** William Wellman. **CAST:** Barbara Stanwyck, Joel McCrea, Brian Donlevy, Thurston Hall, K. T. Stevens, Lloyd Corrigan. **1942**

GREAT MCGINTY, THE ★★★1/2 The ups and downs of hobo Brian Donlevy and his crooked cohort Akim Tamiroff make for very funny satire in this refreshing gem from the inventive Preston Sturges. The action is secondary to the great dialogue. The leads are fine and the rapport they share on screen is truly engaging. B&W; 83m. **DIR:** Preston Sturges. **CAST:** Brian Donlevy, Akim Tamiroff, Muriel Angelus, Louis Jean Heydt, Arthur Hoyt. **1940**

GREAT MISSOURI RAID, THE ★★ Another depiction of Frank and Jesse James and their pals the Younger brothers. This picture is good for a late-night view or while you're microwaving your dinner. Passable, but better accounts of the James boys are available. 83m. **DIR:** Gordon Douglas. **CAST:** Wendell Corey, Macdonald Carey, Ellen Drew, Ward Bond. **1950**

GREAT MOMENT, THE ★★ A nineteenth-century dentist promotes the use of ether as an anesthetic. Confusing blend of comedy and drama makes this bio-pic very uneven. B&W; 83m. **DIR:** Preston Sturges. **CAST:** Joel McCrea, Betty Field, William Demarest, Harry Carey, Grady Sutton, Franklin Pangborn, Jimmy Conlin, Louis Jean Heydt, Thurston Hall, Porter Hall. **1944**

GREAT MOUSE DETECTIVE, THE ★★★1/2 Disney's charming adaptation of Eve Titus's *Basil of Baker Street* involves a diminutive consulting detective's efforts to rescue a master toy maker from the evil clutches of dastardly Professor Ratigan. Sherlock Holmes riffs abound, as Basil and his faithful companion, Dr. Dawson, scour London streets in search of clues. Take note of the climactic battle between Basil and Ratigan in the thrashing gear works of Big Ben, Disney's first serious experiment with computer animation. Rated G. 73m. **DIR:** John Musker, Ron Clements, Dave Michener, Bunny Mattison. **1986**

GREAT MUPPET CAPER, THE ★★★★ Miss Piggy, Kermit the Frog, Fozzie Bear, and the Great Gonzo attempt to solve the mysterious theft of the fabulous Baseball Diamond in this, the second feature-length motion picture Muppet outing. Rated G. 95m. **DIR:** Jim Henson. **CAST:** Muppets, Diana Rigg, Charles Grodin, Peter Falk, Peter Ustinov, Jack Warden, Robert Morley. **1981 DVD**

GREAT, MY PARENTS ARE DIVORCING ★★★★ The French have a talent for dramatizing stories from a child's point of view. In this film, love and marriage and divorce are explored through the reactions of a group of children who unite as their real families are dissolving. Warmhearted film, offering laughs and wisdom in equal portions. In French with English subtitles. Not rated. 98m. **DIR:** Patrick Braoude. **CAST:** Patrick Braoude, Clementine Celarie, Patrick Bouchitey. **1992**

GREAT NORTHFIELD MINNESOTA RAID, THE ★★★ A strong cast of character actors propels this offbeat Western, which chronicles the exploits of the James-Younger gang. Cliff Robertson is an effectively world-weary and witty Cole Younger, and Robert Duvall sets off sparks as a crafty, calculating Jesse James. The film never quite satisfies as a whole though there are some terrific moments. Rated R for violence and profanity. 91m. **DIR:** Phil Kaufman. **CAST:** Cliff Robertson, Robert Duvall, Luke Askew, R. G. Armstrong, Dana Elcar, Donald Moffat, Jack Pearce, Matt Clark, Elisha Cook Jr. **1972**

GREAT OUTDOORS, THE ★★1/2 Another screwball comedy featuring former members of *Saturday Night Live* and *SCTV*, this stars Dan Aykroyd and John Candy as brothers-in-law battling to take charge of a family vacation in the country, where almost everything goes wrong. Aside from Aykroyd, all the characters are shallow. Rated PG for profanity. 90m. **DIR:** Howard Deutch. **CAST:** Dan Aykroyd, John Candy, Stephanie Faracy. **1988 DVD**

GREAT RACE, THE ★★★1/2 Set in the early 1900s, this film comically traces the daily events of the first New York–to–Paris car race. Unfortunately, two-and-a-half hours of silly spoofs will have even the most avid film fan yawning. 147m. **DIR:** Blake Edwards. **CAST:** Tony Curtis, Natalie Wood, Jack Lemmon, Peter Falk, Keenan Wynn, Larry Storch, Arthur O'Connell, Vivian Vance. **1965**

GREAT RIVIERA BANK ROBBERY, THE ★★★1/2 In 1976, a group of French right-wing terrorists called "The Chain," with the assistance of a gang of thieves, pulled off one of the largest heists in history. The step-by-step illustration of this bold operation proves to be interesting, and the fact that this incident really happened makes this film all the more enjoyable. 98m. **DIR:** Francis Megahy. **CAST:** Ian McShane, Warren Clarke, Stephen Greif, Christopher Malcolm. **1979**

GREAT ROCK AND ROLL SWINDLE, THE ★★★★ Free-form pseudodocumentary about legendary punk-rock band the Sex Pistols is just an excuse for promoter Malcolm McLaren to blow his own horn, though he does that quite entertainingly. Not rated; contains profanity. 103m. **DIR:** Julien Temple. **CAST:** Malcolm McLaren, Sid Vicious, John Lydon, Paul Cook, Steve Jones. **1980**

GREAT ST. LOUIS BANK ROBBERY, THE ★★★1/2 Underrated crime-drama in the *Asphalt Jungle* vein, featuring 19 year old Steve McQueen as a college athlete on the skids who joins a trio of experienced criminals planning to rob a bank. The film's modest budget works in its favor, lending a note of gritty realism (some of the extras were people who were at the real-life robbery who actually inspired this film!). B&W; 87m. **DIR:** Charles Guggenheim, John Stix. **CAST:** Steve McQueen, Crahan Denton, David Clarke. **1959 DVD**

GREAT ST. TRINIAN'S TRAIN ROBBERY, THE ★★★ The last in the series of British comedies based on Ronald Searle's cartoons depicting a girls' school populated by monstrously awful brats. In this one, the students prove more than a match for thieves who have hidden loot on the school premises. Not the best of the series, but fun nonetheless. 94m. **DIR:** Frank Launder, Sidney Gilliat. **CAST:** Frankie Howerd, Reg Varney, Dora Bryan. **1966**

GREAT SANTINI, THE ★★★★ Robert Duvall's superb performance in the title role is the most outstanding feature of this fine film. The story of a troubled family and its unpredictable patriarch (Duvall), it was released briefly in early 1980 and then disappeared. But thanks to the efforts of the New York film critics, it was rereleased with appropriate hoopla and did well at the box office. Rated PG for profanity and violence. 116m. **DIR:** Lewis John Carlino. **CAST:** Robert Duvall, Blythe Danner, Michael O'Keefe. **1980 DVD**

GREAT SCOUT AND CATHOUSE THURSDAY, THE ★★★ Eccentric Western-comedy involving a variety of get-rich-quick schemes concocted by an amusing band of rogues. Oliver Reed steals the show as a wacky American Indian whose double-crosses usually backfire. Not much plot and considerable silliness, but fun nonetheless. Rated PG for sexual situations. 102m. **DIR:** Don Taylor. **CAST:** Lee Marvin, Oliver Reed, Elizabeth Ashley, Robert Culp, Strother Martin, Kay Lenz. **1976**

GREAT SMOKEY ROADBLOCK, THE ★★1/2 Entertaining if somewhat hokey comedy-drama casts Henry Fonda as a trucker on the verge of losing his rig, when along comes a homeless entourage of prostitutes (led by Eileen Brennan), who persuade Henry to take them for a ride. Rated PG for language. 84m. **DIR:** John Leone. **CAST:** Henry Fonda, Eileen Brennan, John Byner, Dub Taylor, Susan Sarandon, Austin Pendleton. **1976**

GREAT TEXAS DYNAMITE CHASE, THE ★★ Bullets and bodies fly in this low-budget cult film about two female bank robbers who blast their way across the countryside. Look for Johnny Crawford, of *The Rifleman* fame, in a featured role. Violence and some nudity. Rated R. 90m. **DIR:** Michael Pressman. **CAST:** Claudia Jennings, Jocelyn Jones, Johnny Crawford, Chris Pennock. **1977 DVD**

GREAT TRAIN ROBBERY, THE ★★★★ Based on a true incident, this suspense-filled caper has plenty of hooks to keep you interested. Sean Connery is dashing and convincing as mastermind Edward Pierce. Lesley-Anne Down is stunning as his mistress, accomplice, and disguise expert. Add a pinch of Donald Sutherland as a boastful pickpocket and cracksman, and you have a trio of crooks that can steal your heart. Rated PG. 111m. **DIR:** Michael Crichton. **CAST:** Sean Connery, Lesley-Anne Down, Donald Sutherland, Alan Webb. **1979 DVD**

GREAT WALDO PEPPER, THE ★★★ The daredevil barnstorming pilots of the era between the world wars are sent a pleasant valentine by director George Roy Hill in this flying film. Robert Redford, in a satisfying low-key performance, is Waldo Pepper, a barnstormer who yearns for the action of the World War I dogfights. Rated PG. 108m. **DIR:** George Roy Hill. **CAST:** Robert Redford, Bo Svenson, Susan Sarandon, Bo Boundin. **1975 DVD**

GREAT WALL, A ★★★1/2 Not a documentary about the 1,500-mile structure that rolls wavelike through northern China. Instead, it is a warm comedy about the clash of cultures that results when a Chinese-American family returns to its homeland. It is also the first American movie to be made in the People's Republic of China. As such, it gives some fascinating insights into Chinese culture and often does so in a marvelously entertaining way. Rated PG. 100m. **DIR:** Peter Wang. **CAST:** Peter Wang, Sharon Iwai, Kelvin Han Yee. **1986**

GREAT WALLENDAS, THE ★★★ In this made-for-television movie, Lloyd Bridges stars as the head of the Wallenda family of high-wire artists. Bridges gives one of his most convincing performances as he keeps the spirit and determination of the family alive through their many tragedies. 104m. **DIR:** Larry Elikann. **CAST:** Lloyd Bridges, Britt Ekland, Taina Elg, John van Dreelen, Cathy Rigby, Michael McGuire. **1978**

GREAT WALTZ, THE ★★★★ This biography of Viennese waltz king Johann Strauss II may have no factual bearing whatever (and it doesn't), but it's great fun and cinematically quite stunning. Unfortunately, Oscar Hammerstein's new lyrics to the waltzes are entrusted to diva Miliza Korjus, whose weak voice and inept bel canto technique are quite awful. B&W; 103m. **DIR:** Julien Duvivier. **CAST:** Fernand Gravet, Luise Rainer, Miliza Korjus. **1938**

GREAT WHITE HOPE, THE ★★★ Compelling, emotional character study of the first black heavyweight champion, Jack Johnson, with a supercharged performance by James Earl Jones in the main role. Jones is supported by an equally great cast in this portrait of a man doomed by the prejudice of his society. Rated PG. 101m. **DIR:** Martin Ritt. **CAST:** James Earl Jones, Jane Alexander, Lou Gilbert, Hal Holbrook. **1970**

GREAT WHITE HYPE, THE ★★1/2 It's hard to satirize a blood sport that has already become an ugly parody of itself, but this chaotic boxing comedy produces a few laughs. When fight fans tire of watching two black boxers punch each other, a slippery promoter slyly markets a Caucasian challenger to battle the world's African-American champ. The film wants to be the *Spinal Tap* of pugilism but misses many punches. Rated R for language and violence. 91m. **DIR:** Reginald Hudlin. **CAST:** Damon Wayans, Peter Berg, Samuel L. Jackson, Jeff Goldblum, Jon Lovitz, Richard "Cheech" Marin, Jamie Foxx. **1996**

GREAT ZIEGFELD, THE ★★★★★ This Academy Award–winning best picture is a marvelous film biography of legendary showman Florenz Ziegfeld. William Powell is perfect in the title role and Oscar winner Luise Rainer is tremendous as the fabulous Anna Held. The sets, costumes, and production design are superb. This is Hollywood at its finest. B&W; 176m. **DIR:** Robert Z. Leonard. **CAST:** William Powell, Myrna Loy, Luise Rainer, Frank Morgan, Fanny Brice, Virginia Bruce, Reginald Owen, Dennis Morgan. **1936**

GREATEST, THE ★★ Muhammad Ali plays himself in this disjointed screen biography, which is poorly directed by Tom Gries. Even the supporting performances don't help much. Rated PG. 101m. **DIR:** Tom Gries. **CAST:** Muhammad Ali, Ernest Borgnine, John Marley, Robert Duvall, James Earl Jones, Roger E. Mosley. **1977 DVD**

GREATEST MAN IN THE WORLD, THE ★★★★ A droll adaptation of James Thurber's tale. Brad Davis is an uncouth amateur barnstormer who outperforms Charles Lindbergh by flying nonstop around the *world*... aided by a brilliant method of fuel conservation, and fortified—during the four-day trip—by a hunk of salami and a gallon of gin. Introduced by Henry Fonda; suitable for family viewing. 51m. **DIR:** Ralph Rosenblum. **CAST:** Brad Davis, Reed Birney, John McMartin, Howard DaSilva, Carol Kane, William Prince, Sudie Bond. **1980**

GREATEST SHOW ON EARTH, THE ★★★★ The 1952 Oscar winner for best picture succeeds in the same manner as its subject, the circus; it's enjoyable family entertainment. Three major stories of backstage circus life all work and blend well in this film. 153m. **DIR:** Cecil B. DeMille. **CAST:** Betty Hutton, James Stewart, Charlton Heston, Cornel Wilde, Dorothy Lamour, Gloria Grahame. **1952**

GREATEST STORY EVER TOLD, THE ★★★ Although this well-meant movie is accurate to the story of Jesus, the viewer tends to be distracted by its long running time and the appearance of Hollywood stars in unexpected roles. 141m. **DIR:** George Stevens. **CAST:** Max von Sydow, Charlton Heston, Carroll Baker, Angela Lansbury, Sidney Poitier, Telly Savalas, José Ferrer, Van Heflin, Dorothy McGuire, John Wayne, Ed Wynn, Shelley Winters. **1965 DVD**

GREED ★★★★★ One of the greatest silent films, this is the stark, brilliant study of the corruption of a decent, simple man by the specter of poverty and failed dreams. Gibson Gowland is superb as the bumbling self-taught dentist who marries spinster ZaSu Pitts, loses his trade, and succumbs to avarice-based hatred leading to murder. A masterpiece. Silent. B&W; 133m. **DIR:** Erich Von Stroheim. **CAST:** Gibson Gowland, ZaSu Pitts, Jean Hersholt. **1924**

GREEDY ★★★1/2 An aging Kirk Douglas is typically robust in this aptly named comedy. A group of scheming relatives recruit Douglas's favorite nephew, Michael J. Fox, to keep the rich old coot from throwing his millions away on a young mistress. It's only occasionally funny, but never boring. Phil Hartman is terrific as the nastiest family member. Rated PG-13 for profanity and suggested sex. 113m. **DIR:** Jonathan Lynn. **CAST:** Michael J. Fox, Kirk Douglas, Olivia D'Abo, Phil Hartman, Ed Begley Jr., Jere Burns, Colleen Camp, Bob Balaban, Joyce Hyser, Mary Ellen Trainor, Kevin McCarthy. **1994 DVD**

GREEK TYCOON, THE ★★1/2 When this film was first shown, it stimulated much controversy and interest, because it promised to tell all about the Aristotle Onassis and Jackie Kennedy romance. Anthony Quinn borrows from his *Zorba the Greek* role to be a convincingly macho and callous Greek shipping tycoon. Unfortunately, the plot was neglected and the story comes across as grade-B soap. Rated R. 106m. **DIR:** J. Lee Thompson. **CAST:** Anthony Quinn, Jacqueline Bisset, Raf Vallone, Edward Albert, Charles Durning, Camilla Sparv, James Franciscus. **1978**

GREEN ARCHER ★★ Detective Spike Holland tries to unravel the mystery of Garr Castle after he is called in to investigate the disappearance of Valerie Howett's sister, Elaine. Lots of sliding panels and silhouettes of the phantom bowman in this slow-moving chapterplay. B&W; 15 chapters. **DIR:** James W. Horne. **CAST:** Victor Jory, Iris Meredith, James Craven, Robert Fiske. **1940**

GREEN BERETS, THE ★★★ John Wayne's Vietnam war movie is better than its reputation would suggest. We were fully prepared to hate the film after having avoided it when originally released. However, it turned out to be an exciting and enjoyable (albeit typical) Wayne vehicle. Rated G. 141m. **DIR:** John Wayne, Ray Kellogg. **CAST:** John Wayne, David Janssen, Jim Hutton, Aldo Ray, Raymond St. Jacques, Bruce Cabot, Jack Soo, George Takei, Patrick Wayne. **1968 DVD**

GREEN CARD ★★★★ Delightful old-fashioned comedy-romance from Australian writer-director Peter Weir. Gérard Depardieu plays a French immigrant songwriter who attempts to stay in America by marrying Andie MacDowell, who needs a husband to land a choice apartment in Manhattan. Hilarious and heartwarming. Rated PG-13 for brief profanity. 108m. **DIR:** Peter Weir. **CAST:** Gérard Depardieu, Andie MacDowell, Bebe Neuwirth. **1990**

GREEN DOLPHIN STREET ★★ Plodding drama about two sisters, Lana Turner and Donna Reed, in romantic pursuit of the same man, Van Heflin. Special effects, including a whopper of an earthquake, won an Oscar, but do not a film make. B&W; 141m. **DIR:** Victor Saville. **CAST:** Lana Turner, Donna Reed, Van Heflin, Edmund Gwenn, Frank Morgan, Richard Hart. **1947**

GREEN FOR DANGER ★★★★ Mystery fans shouldn't miss this classic British whodunit, written and filmed with a dry sense of humor. Alastair Sim is a delight as the Scotland Yard detective trying to solve the riddle of a man who was murdered in a hospital—while he was being operated on! B&W; 91m. **DIR:** Sidney Gilliat. **CAST:** Alastair Sim, Sally Gray, Trevor Howard. **1946**

GREEN HORNET, THE (TV SERIES) ★★★ Based on the 1930s radio series created by George W. Trendle, this TV show was an attempt to cash in on the *Batman* phenomenon and is more compelling, less campy. Van Williams ably portrayed the heroic Britt Reid, crime fighter extraordinaire. This short-lived series showcased the martial arts wizardry and unique charisma of Bruce Lee, who played Reid's trusty sidekick, Kato. Two episodes are included per tape. All twenty-six episodes of the series are available. 60m. **DIR:** Various. **CAST:** Van Williams, Bruce Lee, Wende Wagner, Lloyd Gough, Walter Brooke. **1966–1967**

GREEN ICE ★★ Unconvincing tale of an emerald theft in Colombia. Ryan O'Neal engineers the robbery. Rated PG. 115m. **DIR:** Ernest Day. **CAST:** Ryan O'Neal, Anne Archer, Omar Sharif. **1981**

GREEN MAN, THE ★★★1/2 Albert Finney chews up the scenery in great style as an alcoholic innkeeper who tantalizes guests by suggesting that his bed-and-breakfast is haunted . . . and then discovers, with shock, that his unlikely yarns may have come true. A darkly comic novel by Kingsley Amis is the inspiration for this made-for-TV tale. Definitely not for the prudish. 150m. **DIR:** Elijah Moshinsky. **CAST:** Albert Finney, Michael Hordern, Sarah Berger, Linda Marlowe. **1991**

GREEN MANSIONS ★★★ Anthony Perkins is a South American aristocrat, fleeing a revolution, who is befriended by a native tribe. He is sent by them to a rain forest to hunt and kill a mystical vengeful goddess, Rima, the Bird Girl, but finds instead a young innocent (Audrey Hepburn) and her secretive grandfather (Lee J. Cobb). Starts off well but is overall a rather shallow working of William Henry Hudson's romantic novel. Location filming helps. 104m. **DIR:** Mel Ferrer. **CAST:** Audrey Hepburn, Anthony Perkins, Lee J. Cobb, Sessue Hayakawa, Henry Silva, Nehemiah Persoff. **1959**

GREEN MILE, THE ★★★★ Excellent acting keeps this overly long adaptation of Stephen King's 1996 serial novel from eroding into an emotionally sticky parable about racism, justice, resurrection, and the spiritual value of a pet death row mouse. Set mostly in a Depression-era penitentiary, the film slowly builds power as a cell-block superintendent bonds with a gentle-giant African American convicted of child murder. It's a rather old-fashioned story of good versus evil as shaped by some very surprising supernatural events. Rated R for profanity, violence, and a grisly execution. 180m. **DIR:** Frank Darabont. **CAST:** Tom Hanks, Michael Clarke Duncan, Michael Jeter, David Morse, Sam Rockwell, James Cromwell, Doug Hutchison, Barry Pepper, Bonnie Hunt. **1999 DVD**

GREEN PASTURES ★★★★ A fine all-black cast headed by Rex Ingram as de Lawd brings Marc Connelly's classic fable of life in heaven vividly to the screen. A unique viewing experience. B&W; 90m. **DIR:** William Keighley, Marc Connelly. **CAST:** Rex Ingram, Eddie "Rochester" Anderson. **1936**

GREEN PROMISE, THE ★★★ The hard life of farmers and their families is explored in this surprisingly involving and well-acted film. Walter Brennan gives his usual first-rate performance as the patriarch who toils over and tills the land. B&W; 93m. **DIR:** William D. Russell. **CAST:** Marguerite Chapman, Walter Brennan, Robert Paige, Natalie Wood. **1949**

GREEN ROOM, THE ★★ Based on the writings of Henry James, this is a lifeless and disappointing film by François Truffaut about a writer who turns a dilapidated chapel into a memorial for World War I soldiers. Not the French filmmaker at his best. In French with English subtitles. Rated PG. 93m. **DIR:** François Truffaut. **CAST:** François Truffaut, Nathalie Baye, Jean Dasté. **1978**

GREEN SLIME, THE A bit of alien green guck makes its way onto a space station, multiplies itself into ookie monsters. Laughable, with such poor special effects that no one asked to be listed in the credits. Not rated, but it won't scare the kids. 88m. **DIR:** Kinji Fukasaku. **CAST:** Robert Horton, Richard Jaeckel, Luciana Paluzzi. **1969**

GREEN WALL, THE ★★★★1/2 A young family, determined to escape the pressure of life in Lima, struggles against overwhelming obstacles to survive in the exotic, overgrown Peruvian jungle. Stunning cinematography by Mario Robles Godoy. In Spanish with English subtitles. 110m. **DIR:** Armando Robles Godoy. **CAST:** Julio Aleman. **1970**

•GREENFINGERS ★★1/2 Inmates at a British minimum-security prison take up gardening, going so far as to enter a big national competition. The result is too predictable and self-consciously "eccentric," but performances are decent. Rated R for profanity. 91m. **DIR:** Joel Hershman. **CAST:** Clive Owen, Helen Mirren, David Kelly, Natasha Little, Warren Clarke. **2000 DVD**

GREETINGS ★★★ Robert De Niro shines in his starring debut, an offbeat comedy about a young man's sexual odyssey through New York City. Director Brian De Palma takes a satirical overview on free love, the JFK assassination, and Vietnam. Made on a shoestring budget. Rated R for nudity and profanity. 85m. **DIR:** Brian De Palma. **CAST:** Robert De Niro, Jonathan Warden, Gerrit Graham, Allen Garfield. **1968**

GREGORY'S GIRL ★★★★1/2 In this utterly delightful movie from Scotland, a gangly, good-natured kid named Gregory—who has just gone through a five-inch growth spurt that has left him with the physical grace of a drunken stilt walker and made him a problem player on the school's winless soccer team—falls in love with the team's newest and best player: a girl named Dorothy. Not rated, the film has no objectionable content. 91m. **DIR:** Bill Forsyth. **CAST:** Gordon John Sinclair, Dee Hepburn, Chic Murray, Jake D'Arcy, Alex Norton, John Bett, Clare Grogan. **1981 DVD**

GREMLINS ★★★★ "Steven Spielberg Presentation" is highly wacky. It's one part *E.T.— The Extra-Terrestrial*, one part scary-funny horror film, one part Muppet movie, and one part Bugs Bunny–Warner Bros. cartoon. Sound strange? You got it. In the story, Billy Peltzer (Zach Galligan) gets a cute little pet from his inventor-father (Hoyt Axton) for Christmas. But there's a catch. Rated PG for profanity and stylized violence. 111m. **DIR:** Joe Dante. **CAST:** Zach Galligan, Phoebe Cates, Hoyt Axton, Frances Lee McCain, Polly Holliday, Glynn Turman, Dick Miller, Keye Luke, Scott Brady. **1984 DVD**

GREMLINS 2: THE NEW BATCH ★★★★ Those mischievous mutating creatures are back. This time they invade a futuristic New York office complex run by a Donald Trump–like billionaire. Playful, energetic, and much like the first movie in its use of visual gags, social satire, cartoonish mayhem, surprise in-jokes for film fans. Rated PG-13 for cartoon violence. 114m. **DIR:** Joe Dante. **CAST:** Zach Galligan, Phoebe Cates, John Glover, Robert Prosky, Robert Picardo, Christopher Lee, Dick Miller, Jackie Joseph. **1990**

GREY FOX, THE ★★★★★ Richard Farnsworth (*Comes a Horseman*) stars in this marvelously entertaining Canadian feature as the gentleman bandit Bill Miner who, as the movie poster proclaimed, "on June 17, 1901, after thirty-three years in San Quentin Prison for robbing stagecoaches, was released into the twentieth century." Rated PG for brief violence. 92m. **DIR:** Phillip Borsos. **CAST:** Richard Farnsworth, Jackie Burroughs, Ken Pogue, Timothy Webber. **1982**

GREY MATTER ★★ This metaphysical horror film is thought-provoking but hampered by bad acting and a small budget. Not rated; contains violence. 89m. **DIR:** Joy N. Houck Jr. **CAST:** James Best, Barbara Burgess, Gerald McRaney. **1973**

GREY OWL ★★★1/2 Despite handsome production values and beautiful Canadian scenery, this true-life adventure lacks a strong lead. Pierce Brosnan is miscast as trapper Archie Grey Owl, whose eventual marriage to a young Iroquois woman forces him to become a conservationist. Brosnan looks the part, but fails to connect with the film's spiritual center. Possibly one of the most expensive direct-to-video releases. Rated PG-13 for nudity and violence. 118m. **DIR:** Richard Attenborough. **CAST:** Pierce Brosnan, Annie Galipeau, Renée Asherson, Stephanie Cole, Nathaniel Arcand. **1999 DVD**

GREYFRIARS BOBBY ★★★ Somewhat lethargic tale of a dog that is befriended by an entire town after his owner dies. The plot drags, but the cast and the atmosphere of the settings make it worth watching. 91m. **DIR:** Don Chaffey. **CAST:** Donald Crisp, Laurence Naismith, Alex Mackenzie, Kay Walsh. **1961**

GREYSTOKE: THE LEGEND OF TARZAN, LORD OF THE APES ★★★1/2 Director Hugh Hudson made one of the few Tarzan movies to remain faithful to the books and original character created by Edgar Rice Burroughs. Tarzan in one dramatic leap, goes from the dank, dangerous rain forests of West Africa to claim his rightful heritage—a baronial mansion in Scotland and a title as the seventh Earl of Greystoke. Rated PG for nudity and violence. 129m. **DIR:** Hugh Hudson. **CAST:** Christopher Lambert, Andie MacDowell, Ian Holm, Ralph Richardson, James Fox, Cheryl Campbell. **1984**

GRIDLOCK'D ★★★★ This character-driven comedy-drama features Tupac Shakur and Tim Roth, as a pair of junkies who decide to get clean after a friend nearly dies of an overdose. Of course, our somewhat sullied heroes' path to a better life is fraught with problems. Not only can they not get into a rehab program without an immense hassle, but being in the wrong place at the wrong time puts them on the bad side of a group of gangsters. Rated R for nudity, profanity, and violence. 91m. **DIR:** Vondie Curtis-Hall. **CAST:** Tim Roth, Tupac Shakur, Thandie Newton, Charles Fleischer, Howard Hesseman, James Pickens Jr., John Sayles, Eric Payne. **1997 DVD**

GRIEF ★★★ A hectic, behind-the-scenes comedy about a week in the life of the people who bring *The Love Judge* to daytime television. Like *Soapdish*, director-writer Richard Glatzer's comedy is a pointed, hilarious exposé of the trials and tribulations that befall the people who get the show on the air every day. Alexis Arquette shines as the up-and-coming producer whose sexual preference gets him into hot water with a straight coworker. Not rated; contains adult language and situations. 86m. **DIR:** Richard Glatzer. **CAST:** Alexis Arquette, Jackie Beat, Craig Chester, Illeana Douglas. **1994**

GRIEVOUS BODILY HARM ★★1/2 This Australian drama is a well-woven tale about a police detective trying to find his missing wife. The acting is first-rate, as is the script, but director Mark Joffe lets the pace drag from time to time. Rated R. 135m. **DIR:** Mark Joffe.

CAST: Colin Friels, John Waters, Bruno Lawrence, Shane Briant. **1988**

GRIFFIN AND PHOENIX: A LOVE STORY ★★★1/2 Strange, haunting tearjerker about two dying people in love with one another and with life. Jill Clayburgh and Peter Falk in the title roles win hearts hands-down and lift spirits as gloom and doom close in. Made for TV. 100m. **DIR:** Daryl Duke. **CAST:** Peter Falk, Jill Clayburgh, Dorothy Tristan. **1976**

GRIFTERS, THE ★★★★ A savagely funny and often shocking adaptation by Donald E. Westlake of Jim Thompson's hardboiled novel, this black comedy is like a grotesque version of *The Sting*. Anjelica Huston, John Cusack, and Annette Bening are clever crooks who cheat their way through life until the inevitable catches up with them. Rated R for violence, nudity, and profanity. 119m. **DIR:** Stephen Frears. **CAST:** Anjelica Huston, John Cusack, Annette Bening, Pat Hingle, Henry Jones, J. T. Walsh, Charles Napier, Stephen Tobolowsky, Gailard Sartain. **1990 DVD**

GRIM PRAIRIE TALES ★★★ Two plains travelers, one a city dweller and the other a trail-weary bounty hunter, exchange stories of horror while they camp on the open prairie. Their freaky tales will test your ability to suspend belief, but all are fun to watch. Rated R for violence, profanity, and gore. 87m. **DIR:** Wayne Coe. **CAST:** James Earl Jones, Brad Dourif, William Atherton, Lisa Eichhorn, Marc McClure, Scott Paulin. **1990**

GRIM REAPER, THE ★★★ Absorbing crime-drama about the violent death of a prostitute—as told through three different people. Pier Paolo Pasolini's script recalls *Rashomon*, with its series of flashbacks. Bernardo Bertolucci's first feature film. In Italian with English subtitles. B&W; 100m. **DIR:** Bernardo Bertolucci. **CAST:** Francesco Rulu. **1962**

GRIND ★★1/2 A young man who cares more about racing cars than his dead-end job at a factory is drawn into an affair with his brother's frustrated wife. Some good performances and a feel for life in suburban New Jersey aren't enough to recommend this dreary melodrama. Rated R for profanity and sexual situations. 96m. **DIR:** Chris Kentis. **CAST:** Billy Crudup, Adrienne Shelly, Paul Schulze, Frank Vincent. **1996 DVD**

GRISBI ★★★★ A gangster classic that concentrates less on violence than on character. Jean Gabin plays an aging gangster who has stolen a fortune in gold bars that he hopes will allow him to live out the rest of his life in style. The problem is, hanging on to the loot proves to be harder than getting it. Look for Jeanne Moreau in a small part. Dubbed in English. B&W; 90m. **DIR:** Jacques Becker. **CAST:** Jean Gabin, Rene Dary, Dora Doll, Lino Ventura. **1953**

GRISSOM GANG, THE ★★★ Lurid crime-drama set in the 1920s. A wealthy heiress (Kim Darby) is kidnapped by a family of grotesque rednecks whose leader (Scott Wilson) falls in love with her. This gritty, violent film receives comically uneven direction from Robert Aldrich. Rated R. 127m. **DIR:** Robert Aldrich. **CAST:** Kim Darby, Scott Wilson, Irene Dailey, Tony Musante, Robert Lansing. **1971 DVD**

GRIZZLY ★★ Another "nature runs amok" film with Christopher George going up against an eighteen-foot killer bear this time out. Some taut action, but the movie has no style or pizzazz. Rated PG for violence. 92m. **DIR:** William Girdler. **CAST:** Christopher George, Andrew Prine, Richard Jaeckel. **1976 DVD**

GRIZZLY FALLS ★★★ A well-photographed family film about a young boy who is captured by a grizzly bear. Incredible scenery. Rated PG. **DIR:** Stewart Raffill. **CAST:** Bryan Brown, Tom Jackson, Oliver Tobias, Richard Harris. **1999 DVD**

GRIZZLY MOUNTAIN ★★1/2 *Grizzly Adams* star Dan Haggerty heads up this family fantasy about two kids who stumble into a cave and travel back in time. There, they meet mountain man Haggerty, who is trying to save the surrounding area from developers. Even though the film has a made-for-television look, it's lots of fun, especially for younger children who will appreciate the silly humor and kid angle. Rated G. 96m. **DIR:** Jeremy Haft. **CAST:** Dan Haggerty, Kim Morgan Greene, Nicole Lund, Martin Kove, Dyland Haggerty, Megan Haggerty. **1997**

•GROOVE ★★★1/2 A wannabe writer accepts an invitation to a rave, an underground party where young people dance to trance-inducing electronic music. If you have to be told what a rave is, this movie probably isn't for you, though it does an admirable job (on a minimal budget) of conveying the spirit of liberation that ravers seek. Rated R for drug use, profanity, and sexuality. 86m. **DIR:** Greg Harrison. **CAST:** Chris Ferreira, Elizabeth Sun, Steve Van Wormer. **2000 DVD**

GROOVE TUBE, THE ★★1/2 A sometimes funny and most times just silly—or gross—1974 takeoff on television by writer-director Ken Shapiro. The V.D. commercial is a classic, however. Look for Chevy Chase in his first, brief screen appearance. Rated R. 75m. **DIR:** Ken Shapiro. **CAST:** Ken Shapiro, Lane Sarasohn, Chevy Chase, Richard Belzer. **1974 DVD**

GROSS ANATOMY ★★★ Sort of a *Paper Chase* for med school, this focuses on the very likable son of a fisherman who must accept or reject the cutthroat competition among his peers. A bit contrived but still watchable. Rated PG-13 for profanity. 107m. **DIR:** Thom Eberhardt. **CAST:** Matthew Modine, Daphne Zuniga, Christine Lahti. **1989**

GROSS JOKES ★★ A group of comedians tell off-color and somewhat gross jokes culled from the book by Julius Alvin. Moderately funny. Not rated; contains adult language and humor. 53m. **DIR:** Bob Williams. **CAST:** George Wallace, Tommy Sledge, Sheryl Bernstein, Tim Jones, Barry Diamond, Joe Alaskey, Budd Friedman. **1985**

GROSSE POINTE BLANK ★★★★ This dark-hued romp is a career-maker for star John Cusack, a meticulous assassin who finds business conflicting with pleasure while attending his ten-year high-school reunion. When not dodging bullets, Cusack tries to patch things up with the girl he jilted long ago at the high-school prom. The script is sharp and sassy, the action fast and furious, and the comic tone too funny for words. Rated R for violence and profanity. 107m. **DIR:** George Armitage. **CAST:** John Cusack, Minnie Driver, Dan Aykroyd, Alan Arkin, Joan Cusack, Jeremy Piven, Hank Azaria. **1997 DVD**

GROTESQUE 🦃 Psychotic punks looking for a treasure. Rated R for violence and nudity. 80m. **DIR:** Joe Tornatore. **CAST:** Linda Blair, Tab Hunter, Charles Dierkop. **1987**

GROUND CONTROL ★★★1/2 In this direct-to-video drama, Jack Harris, a former controller still haunted by the crash of a plane, is called back into action when a storm takes out the tower in Phoenix, and he's forced to land the planes with no radar or contact. Gripping one moment, melodramatic the next, the film ultimately wins us over with decent performances and a traveler's common fear. Rated PG-13 for language. 98m. **DIR:** Richard Howard. **CAST:** Kiefer Sutherland, Robert Sean Leonard, Kelly McGillis, Henry Winkler, Kristy Swanson, Michael Gross, Margaret Cho. **1998 DVD**

GROUND ZERO ★★1/2 Political thriller that lacks the strike capability to give it a complete victory. While a cameraman investigates his father's death, he stumbles onto a cover-up by the British and Australian governments involving nuclear testing in the fifties. Aborigines, political influence, corruption, murder, and genocide are just some of the fallout from his investigation. Just enough to keep you interested, but ultimately misses the target. Rated PG-13 for violence and profanity. 100m. **DIR:** Michael Pattinson, Bruce Myles. **CAST:** Colin Friels, Jack Thompson, Donald Pleasence. **1988**

GROUNDHOG DAY ★★★1/2 Arrogantly self-centered TV weatherman Phil Connors (Bill Murray), practically convinced he *creates* the weather, stumbles into a time warp and winds up repeating the most insipid day of his life: twenty-four hours in Punxsutawney, Pennsylvania, during its annual Groundhog Day festivities. The film actually displays some heart in its last act. Rated PG for profanity. 103m. **DIR:** Harold Ramis. **CAST:** Bill Murray, Andie MacDowell, Chris Elliott, Stephen Tobolowsky. **1993 DVD**

GROUNDSTAR CONSPIRACY, THE ★★★1/2 This nifty thriller has gone unrecognized for years. George Peppard stars as a government investigator sent to uncover the security leak that led to the destruction of a vital—and secret—space laboratory, and the amnesia-stricken Michael Sarrazin is his only lead. The clever plot and excellent character interactions build to a surprising climax. Rated PG. 103m. **DIR:** Lamont Johnson. **CAST:** George Peppard, Michael Sarrazin, Christine Belford. **1972 DVD**

GROUP, THE ★★★ Based on the book by Mary McCarthy about the lives and loves of eight female college friends. Overlong, convoluted semi-sleazy fun. The impressive cast almost makes you forget it's just a catty soap opera. So watch it anyway. 150m. **DIR:** Sidney Lumet. **CAST:** Joan Hackett, Elizabeth Hartman, Shirley Knight, Joanna Pettet, Jessica Walter, James Broderick, Larry Hagman, Richard Mulligan, Hal Holbrook. **1966**

GROWN-UPS ★★ Originally made for cable TV, this theatre piece by cartoonist Jules Feiffer revolves around a writer (Charles Grodin) and his difficulties with his family. Feiffer's dialogue is sharply observed, but there's no real story, and the characters' continual bickering never leads anywhere. 106m. **DIR:** John Madden. **CAST:** Charles Grodin, Martin Balsam, Marilu Henner, Jean Stapleton. **1985**

GRUESOME TWOSOME 🦃 *Sweeney Todd*–style parody about a wig maker and her homicidal son. 72m. **DIR:** Herschell Gordon Lewis. **CAST:** Elizabeth David, Chris Martel. **1967 DVD**

GRUMPIER OLD MEN ★★★★ The second teaming of Jack Lemmon and Walter Matthau as cranky, lifelong neighbors provides—surprisingly—as many chuckles and guffaws as their first outing. This time, the two codgers agree on a temporary truce when newcomer Sophia Loren threatens to turn the local bait shop into an Italian restaurant. Once again, Burgess Meredith, as Lemmon's sex-obsessed father, gets most of the belly laughs. Rated PG-13 for vulgarity and suggested sex. 100m. **DIR:** Howard Deutch. **CAST:** Jack Lemmon, Walter Matthau, Ann-Margret, Sophia Loren, Burgess Meredith, Kevin Pollak, Daryl Hannah, Ann Guilbert. **1995 DVD**

GRUMPY OLD MEN ★★★★ A howlingly funny tale of two longtime rivals (Walter Matthau and Jack Lemmon) fighting over the affections of sexy new neighbor Ann-Margret. Lemmon and Matthau are in top form, but 84 year old Burgess Meredith, as Lemmon's irascible father, has the film's funniest lines. Be sure to catch the outtakes shown during the closing credits for a laugh-filled capper to this comic gem. Rated PG-13 for sexual references. 105m. **DIR:** Donald Petrie. **CAST:** Jack Lemmon, Walter Matthau, Ann-Margret, Daryl Hannah, Burgess Meredith, Kevin Pollak, Ossie Davis, Buck Henry. **1993 DVD**

GUADALCANAL DIARY ★★★★ Timely story of the U.S. Marine Corp's deadly struggle for this South Pacific island is one of the best wartime adventure films. B&W; 93m. **DIR:** Lewis Seiler. **CAST:** Preston Foster, Lloyd Nolan, William Bendix, Richard Conte, Anthony Quinn, Richard Jaeckel. **1943 DVD**

GUANTANAMERA! ★★★ Famous singer Yoyita returns to her hometown after fifty years and rekindles a passionate relationship with her first love. She dies in his arms, and the rest of this whimsical romantic comedy chronicles the journey of her coffin back to Havana under the escort of her lover, her unhappily married niece, and her niece's husband. In Spanish with English subtitles. Not rated; contains sexual references. 104m. **DIR:** Tomas Gutierrez Alea, Juan Carlos Tabio. **CAST:** Mirta Ibarra, Jorge Perugorria, Raul Eguren, Carlos Cruz, Conchito Brando, Pedro Fernandez. **1994 DVD**

GUARDIAN, THE 🦃 Los Angeles couple finds out the hard way that the attractive, charming nanny they've hired is a tree-worshiping druid. Rated R for language, violence, and nudity. 93m. **DIR:** William Friedkin. **CAST:** Jenny Seagrove, Dwier Brown. **1990 DVD**

GUARDIAN, THE ★★★1/2 When the tenants of an upper-class New York City apartment house become fed up with the violence of the streets intruding on their building, they hire a live-in guard (Louis Gossett Jr.). While he does manage to rid the building of lawbreakers, some begin to question his methods. This HBO made-for-cable film is notches above most cable fare. Profanity and violence. 102m. **DIR:** David Greene. **CAST:** Martin Sheen, Louis Gossett Jr., Arthur Hill. **1984**

GUARDIAN ANGEL ★★ Martial arts expert Cynthia Rothrock is back in this pedestrian effort about an ex-cop out to avenge the deaths of her partner and lover. She gets her chance when the killer breaks out of jail, and Rothrock is hired to protect the killer's next target. Novelty here is the killer is a woman. Anyone for a good cat fight? Rated R for violence, language, and adult situations. 98m. **DIR:** Richard W. Munchkin. **CAST:** Cynthia Rothrock, Daniel McVicar, Lydie Denier, Marshall Teague. **1993 DVD**

GUARDIAN OF THE ABYSS 🦃 Uneventful devil-worship flick from England. 50m. **DIR:** Don Sharp. **CAST:** Ray Lonnen. **1985**

GUARDING TESS ★★★★ Secret service agent Nicolas Cage wants out of his current assignment—looking after feisty former first lady Shirley MacLaine—but she has other ideas in this highly entertaining comedy-drama. MacLaine and Cage do not immediately spring to mind as a perfect pairing, but they work extremely well together. Intriguing characters, some genuine laughs, a few tears, and even a sprinkle of suspense. Rated PG-13 for profanity and light violence. 98m. **DIR:** Hugh Wilson. **CAST:** Shirley MacLaine, Nicolas Cage, Austin Pendleton, Edward Albert, James Rebhorn, Richard Griffiths, Harry J. Lennix. **1994 DVD**

GUARDSMAN, THE ★★★★ A movie landmark since it is the only film to costar Broadway's Alfred Lunt and Lynn Fontanne. This film also recorded their most successful roles for posterity. Ferenc Molnar wrote the original play about a man who tests his wife's faithfulness by posing as a macho, romantic Russian guardsman. B&W; 83m. **DIR:** Sidney Franklin. **CAST:** Alfred Lunt, Lynn Fontanne, Roland Young, ZaSu Pitts, Maude Eburne, Herman Bing. **1931**

GUESS WHO'S COMING TO DINNER ★★★ This final film pairing of Spencer Tracy and Katharine Hepburn was one of the first to deal with interracial marriage. Though quite daring at the time, this movie seems rather quaint today. Still, Tracy and Hepburn are fun to watch, and Sidney Poitier and Katharine Houghton make an appealing young couple. 108m. **DIR:** Stanley Kramer. **CAST:** Spencer Tracy, Katharine Hepburn, Sidney Poitier, Katharine Houghton, Cecil Kellaway, Beah Richards, Virginia Christine. **1967 DVD**

GUEST IN THE HOUSE ★★★ This grim melodrama features Anne Baxter as an emotionally disturbed girl who turns an idyllic household into a chaotic nightmare. An engrossing psychological thriller. B&W; 121m. **DIR:** John Brahm. **CAST:** Anne Baxter, Ralph Bellamy, Aline MacMahon, Ruth Warrick, Jerome Cowan. **1944**

GUEST WIFE ★★1/2 Claudette Colbert poses as foreign correspondent Don Ameche's wife to fool the boss, who thinks he's married. Funny and cute but not that funny and cute. B&W; 90m. **DIR:** Sam Wood. **CAST:** Claudette Colbert, Don Ameche, Dick Foran, Charles Dingle, Grant Mitchell, Irving Bacon. **1945**

GUIDE FOR THE MARRIED MAN, A ★★★1/2 Worldly Robert Morse tries to teach reluctant Walter Matthau the fundamentals of adultery. His lessons are acted out by a dazzling roster of top comedy stars. This episodic film provides a steady stream of laughs. The bit in which Joey Bishop is caught red-handed and practices the "deny, deny, deny" technique is a classic. 89m. **DIR:** Gene Kelly. **CAST:** Walter Matthau, Inger Stevens, Robert Morse, Sue Ane Langdon, Lucille Ball, Jack Benny, Joey Bishop, Art Carney, Jayne Mansfield, Carl Reiner, Sid Caesar, Phil Silvers, Jeffrey Hunter, Sam Jaffe. **1967**

GUIDE FOR THE MARRIED WOMAN, A ★★1/2 In this made-for-television movie, Cybill Shepherd plays a frustrated housewife who decides that life must hold more excitement than her current predictable situation. Though the cast includes many big names, this film never really takes off and is no match for the earlier *Guide for the Married Man.* 100m. **DIR:** Hy Averback. **CAST:** Cybill Shepherd, Charles Frank, John Hillerman, Elaine Joyce, Peter Marshall, Eve Arden. **1978**

GUILTY, THE ★★★ Bill Pullman delivers a dark performance as a lawyer whose sexual indiscretions could cost him a judgeship. When a firm secretary spurns his advances and threatens to expose him, he hires a local teen to kill her. Big mistake, as the teen has a hidden past that could destroy the attorney once and for all. Decent thriller with better-than-average performances. Rated R for adult situations, language, and violence. 112m. **DIR:** Anthony Waller. **CAST:** Bill Pullman, Gabrielle Anwar, Devon Sawa, Angela Featherstone, Joanne Whalley. **1999 DVD**

GUILTY AS CHARGED 🦃 Black comedy fans are in for a shock with this unfunny tale of a vigilante who tracks down criminals and gives them the hot seat in his homemade electric chair. Pull the plug on this puppy before it short-circuits. Rated R for violence. 93m. **DIR:** Sam Irvin. **CAST:** Rod Steiger, Lauren Hutton, Isaac Hayes, Heather Graham. **1991**

GUILTY AS SIN ★★ A courtroom melodrama about a lady lawyer who falls for her handsome client. But the movie is an uneven blend of star power and director's disinterest. 120m. **DIR:** Sidney Lumet. **CAST:** Rebecca DeMornay, Don Johnson, Stephen Lang, Jack Warden. **1993**

GUILTY BY SUSPICION ★★★★ Robert De Niro is marvelous as a Hollywood director who loses his home and ability to make a living after refusing to testify against his friends at a hearing of the House Un-American Activities Committee during the blacklist period of the fifties. Riveting film by producer-turned-writer-director Irwin Winkler. Rated PG-13 for profanity. 105m. **DIR:** Irwin Winkler. **CAST:** Robert De Niro, Annette Bening, George Wendt, Patricia Wettig, Sam Wanamaker, Ben Piazza, Gailard Sartain, Stuart Margolin, Martin Scorsese. **1991 DVD**

GUINEVERE ★★★ An insecure young woman has an affair with a middle-aged alcoholic who makes a practice of seducing and abandoning sweet young things. Writer-director Audrey Welles draws sincere, layered performances from her cast that compensate for the familiarity of the story and the patently false ending. Rated R for profanity and sexual scenes. 104m. **DIR:** Audrey Welles. **CAST:** Stephen Rea, Sarah Polley, Jean Smart, Gina Gershon, Paul Dooley. **1999 DVD**

GULAG ★★1/2 This engrossing tale of an American athlete shipped to a Soviet prison camp works at odd moments in spite of a preposterous script. On the other hand, the escape sequence is clever and quite exciting. 120m. **DIR:** Roger Young. **CAST:** David Keith, Malcolm McDowell. **1985**

GULLIVER IN LILLIPUT ★★ This British TV movie stays fairly close to the Jonathan Swift classic satire of small-minded people. Probably too close because it's not long before these bickering people stop being funny and start getting on your nerves. Not rated; contains no objectionable material. 107m. **DIR:** Barry Letts. **CAST:** Andrew Burt, Elizabeth Sladen. **1982**

GULLIVER'S TRAVELS ★★ Richard Harris seems lost in this meager retelling of the Jonathan Swift satire. The combination of live action and animation further detracts from the story. Rated G. 80m. **DIR:** Peter R. Hunt. **CAST:** Richard Harris, Catherine Schell. **1977**

GULLIVER'S TRAVELS ★★1/2 Made and issued as an answer to Disney's *Snow White and the Seven Dwarfs*, this full-length cartoon of the famous Jonathan Swift satire about an English sailor who falls among tiny people in a land called Lilliput is just so-so. Lanny Ross, Jessica Dragonette (voices). 74m. **DIR:** Dave Fleischer. **1939 DVD**

GULLIVER'S TRAVELS (1996) (TELEVISION) ★★★★ This made-for-TV miniseries cuts no corners in majestic sets, special effects, and an all-star cast. Remaining loyal to Jonathan Swift's satiric classic, we travel not only to the lands of giants and little people but also to a flying island of pseudointellectuals and an island ruled by horses. Ted Danson is superb as Gulliver. His adventures are told in flashbacks from an English insane asylum where he is committed for his "ravings." Not rated; not really suitable for small children due to violence and a scene in which Danson urinates to put out a fire. 175m. **DIR:** Charles Sturridge. **CAST:** Ted Danson, Mary Steenburgen, James Fox, Geraldine Chaplin, Edward Woodward, Ned Beatty, Peter O'Toole, Omar Sharif. **1996 DVD**

GUMBALL RALLY, THE ★★1/2 First film based on an anything-goes cross-country road race. Featuring some excellent stunt driving, with occasional laughs, it's much better than *Cannonball Run*. Rated PG for language. 107m. **DIR:** Chuck Bail. **CAST:** Michael Sarrazin, Gary Busey, Tim McIntire, Raul Julia, Normann Burton. **1976**

GUMBY THE MOVIE ★★★ Even die-hard Gumby fans will find this too much of a good thing. Unanswered plot questions will bother all but the youngest tots who will just enjoy watching Gumby and his pals. Dozens of new characters have been added to the cast from the 1960s TV show, but Gumby and Pokey are still the stars as they take on the greedy Blockheads. Rated G. 90m. **DIR:** Art Clokey. **1995**

GUMMO 🦃 A perfect example of why overhyped, precocious teenage directors should not be allowed to make films. There's nothing entertaining or redeeming about the two teenage slackers who need to get a life. Rated R for language, violence, and adult situations. 89m. **DIR:** Harmony Korine. **CAST:** Jacob Reynolds, Nick Sutton, Linda Manz, Max Perlich, Chloe Sevigny. **1997 DVD**

GUMSHOE ★★★1/2 Every hard-bitten private-eye film and *film noir* is saluted in this crime-edged comedy. Liverpool bingo caller Albert Finney finds himself in deep, murky water when he tries to live his fantasy of being a Humphrey Bogart–type shamus. Raymond Chandler and Dashiell Hammett fans will love every frame. Rated PG. 88m. **DIR:** Stephen Frears. **CAST:** Albert Finney, Billie Whitelaw, Frank Finlay, Janice Rule, Caroline Seymour. **1972**

GUMSHOE KID, THE ★★1/2 Wannabe gumshoe Jay Underwood quits school to join the family private eye business. Rated R for nudity and violence. 98m. **DIR:** Joseph Manduke. **CAST:** Jay Underwood, Tracy Scoggins, Vince Edwards. **1990**

GUN CODE ★★★ When the residents of Miller's Flats find themselves being coerced into paying protection money, Tim Haines (Tim McCoy) rides to the rescue, guns ablazing. Even the minuscule budgets of Producers Releasing Corporation couldn't stop McCoy from turning out above-average Westerns. B&W; 52m. **DIR:** Peter Stewart. **CAST:** Tim McCoy, Dave O'Brien. **1940**

GUN CRAZY ★★★1/2 Young man obsessed by guns teams up with a carnival sharpshooter who leads him into a life of robbery and murder. This odd little cult classic is fast and lean. MacKinlay Kantor wrote the original story and cowrote the screenplay. B&W; 86m. **DIR:** Joseph H. Lewis. **CAST:** Peggy Cummins, John Dall, Morris Carnovsky. **1950**

GUN FURY ★★★ Donna Reed is kidnapped. Rock Hudson chases the bad men and saves her from a fate worse than death in Arizona's mesmerizing Red Rock country. Villainy abounds. 83m. **DIR:** Raoul Walsh. **CAST:** Rock Hudson, Donna Reed, Lee Marvin, Philip Carey, Neville Brand. **1953**

GUN IN BETTY LOU'S HANDBAG, THE ★★1/2 In order to get into the spirit of this generally predictable screwball comedy, one has to accept screenwriter Grace Cary Bickley's premise that a neglected wife would claim to be a murderer to get her police-detective husband's attention. Breathlessly sincere performances by Penelope Ann Miller and Eric Thal make it as entertaining as it is dumb. Rated PG-13 for profanity and violence. 90m. **DIR:** Alan Moyle. **CAST:** Penelope Ann Miller, Eric Thal, Alfre Woodard, William Forsythe, Cathy Moriarty. **1992**

GUN IN THE HOUSE, A ★★★1/2 This TV movie stars Sally Struthers as a woman being tried for the handgun murder of a man who broke into her house. Struthers excels in the role. An above-average drama. 100m. **DIR:** Ivan Nagy. **CAST:** Sally Struthers, David Ackroyd, Jeffrey Tambor, Dick Anthony Williams, Millie Perkins. **1981**

GUN RIDERS, THE ★★ Genre fans may enjoy this violent adult Western, though others will find it nihilistic and sleazy. A sadistic gunman, nicknamed the Messenger of Death, is the center of a story pitting Indians, gunrunners, and settlers against each other. Photographed by Vilmos Zsigmond. Rated PG. 88m. **DIR:** Al Adamson. **CAST:** Robert Dix, Scott Brady, Jim Davis, John Carradine, Paula Raymond. **1969**

GUN SHY ★★ A stressed-out, undercover drug agent is persuaded to stay on the job for one more sting against a Colombian drug lord; meanwhile, he falls for a wisecracking nurse. This inane, confused comedy rambles in circles until the climax, where it all but disintegrates before your eyes. Rated R for violence, profanity, and brief nudity. 101m. **DIR:** Eric Blakeney. **CAST:** Liam Neeson, Oliver Platt, Sandra Bullock, Jose Zuniga. **2000 DVD**

GUN SMUGGLERS ★★★1/2 When an entire shipment of Gatling guns is stolen, Tim Holt must act fast. B&W; 61m. **DIR:** Frank McDonald. **CAST:** Tim Holt, Richard Martin, Martha Hyer, Paul Hurst, Gary Gray, Douglas Fowley. **1948**

GUNBUSTER—VOLS. 1–3 ★★ Japanese animation. A tedious, overwrought tale of duty and sacrifice in the Space Force. Quality animation. In Japanese with English subtitles. Not rated violence and illustrated nudity. **DIR:** Hideaki Anno. **1989**

GUNCRAZY (1950) 🦃 Small-town bad girl Drew Barrymore's love letters to young convict James LeGros brings him to town upon parole, whereupon the two shoot up the locals. Growin' up sure is hard to do. Rated R for violence, suggested sex, and profanity. 96m. **DIR:** Tamra Davis. **CAST:** Drew Barrymore, James LeGros, Rodney Harvey, Joe Dallesandro, Michael Ironside, Ione Skye. **1992**

GUNDOWN AT SANDOVAL ★★★ Texas John Slaughter faces overwhelming odds when he vows to avenge a friend's death and goes against the inhabitants of Sandoval, an infamous outlaw hideout. Featuring lots of hard riding and gunplay, this Disney television show was originally shown in Europe as a feature film. 72m. **DIR:** Harry Keller. **CAST:** Tom Tryon, Dan Duryea, Beverly Garland, Lyle Bettger, Harry Carey Jr. **1959**

GUNFIGHT, A ★★ Lifeless Western features the acting debut of country singer Johnny Cash. He is teamed with Kirk Douglas in a story of two long-in-the-tooth gunslingers. 90m. **DIR:** Lamont Johnson. **CAST:** Kirk Douglas, Johnny Cash, Jane Alexander, Karen Black, Raf Vallone. **1971**

GUNFIGHT AT THE O.K. CORRAL ★★★★ The Wyatt Earp–Doc Holliday legend got another going-over in this rather good Western. Burt Lancaster and Kirk Douglas portray these larger-than-life gunfighters, who shoot it out with the nefarious Clanton family in 1881 Tombstone. The movie effectively builds up its tension until the climactic gunfight. 122m. **DIR:** John Sturges. **CAST:** Burt Lancaster, Kirk Douglas, Rhonda Fleming, Jo Van Fleet, John Ireland, Lee Van Cleef, Frank Faylen. **1957**

GUNFIGHTER, THE (1950) ★★★★★ A notorious gunslinger (Gregory Peck) tries to settle down, but his reputation dogs him wherever he goes. Peck (though almost too young for his role) gives one of his best performances in this neglected classic. There's not much action, but it's an engrossing character study. B&W; 84m. **DIR:** Henry King. **CAST:** Gregory Peck, Helen Westcott, Millard Mitchell, Skip Homeier, Jean Parker, Karl Malden. **1950**

GUNFIGHTER (1997) ★★1/2 Old West gunslinger tale is more likely to cause saddle sores than jubilation for Western fans. Robert Carradine plays The Kid, a singer looking for work, who encounters The Stranger, who relates his deadly and colorful past, including a shoot-out with a bad guy named Tex. Now Tex wants revenge, and The Stranger must face down his old nemesis one more time. At least Carradine doesn't break out in song. Rated R for violence. 95m. **DIR:** Christopher Coppola. **CAST:** Martin Sheen, Robert Carradine, Clu Gulager. **1997 DVD**

GUNFIGHTER'S MOON ★★1/2 Gunfighter Frank Morgan (Lance Henriksen) returns to the town where he once lived to help the new sheriff. Complications ensue with the sheriff's wife (Morgan's former lover), and her daughter, who doesn't know that Morgan is her real father. Mix of Western and soap opera doesn't really work, despite a good performance by Henriksen. Rated PG-13 for violence. 95m. **DIR:** Larry Ferguson. **CAST:** Lance Henriksen, Kay Lenz. **1997**

GUNFIRE ★★★ More story than action in this tale of an outlaw who is pardoned on the condition he kill a rancher whose land the railroad wants. Problems set in when the gunfighter sympathizes with the rancher and falls in love with his wife. Convincing performances by Warren Oates, Fabio Testi, and Jenny Agutter make this better than average. Not rated; contains violence. 90m. **DIR:** Monte Hellman. **CAST:** Warren Oates, Jenny Agutter, Fabio Testi, Carlos Bravo, Sam Peckinpah. **1978**

GUNG HO! (1943) ★★1/2 Although not meant to be funny, this ultrapatriotic war film has its truly outrageous moments. It must have been a real booster for wartime filmgoers in America. Today it's almost embarrassing—particularly during the scene in which a recruit is accepted into a special team of commandos simply because he "hates Japs." B&W; 88m. **DIR:** Ray Enright. **CAST:** Randolph Scott, Grace McDonald, Alan Curtis, Noah Beery Jr., J. Carrol Naish, David Bruce, Robert Mitchum, Sam Levene. **1943**

GUNG HO (1985) ★★★★ Another winner from director Ron Howard and writers Lowell Ganz and Babaloo Mandel, who previously teamed on *Night Shift* and *Splash*. This is a pointed study of the cultural chaos that occurs when small-town Hadleyville's automobile plant is rescued by imported Japanese management. Rated PG-13 for language. 111m. **DIR:** Ron Howard. **CAST:** Michael Keaton, Gedde Watanabe, George Wendt, Mimi Rogers, John Turturro, Clint Howard. **1985**

GUNGA DIN ★★★★★ An acknowledged classic, this release has it all: laughs, thrills, and chills. Howard Hawks was originally set to direct it and played a large part in its creation. Plot: Three soldiers in nineteenth-century India put down a native uprising with the help of an Indian water carrier. B&W; 117m. **DIR:** George Stevens. **CAST:** Cary Grant, Victor McLaglen, Douglas Fairbanks Jr., Joan Fontaine, Sam Jaffe, Eduardo Ciannelli. **1939**

GUNMAN FROM BODIE ★★★1/2 The best of the many trio series Westerns of the 1930s and 40s, *The Rough Riders* teamed two of the genre's most charismatic stars, Buck Jones and Tim McCoy, with one of the best sidekicks in the business, Raymond Hatton. The second film in the series, *Gunman from Bodie,* is considered by most aficionados to be the best. The plot, about a trio of marshals who set out to capture a gang of cattle thieves, may be worn-out, but the star power makes this first-rate. B&W; 60m. **DIR:** Spencer Gordon Bennet. **CAST:** Buck Jones, Tim McCoy, Raymond Hatton, Dave O'Brien. **1941**

GUNMEN ★★★ Action-packed movie stars Mario Van Peebles as a New York detective who turns bounty hunter to bring down South American drug lord Patrick Stewart. Top-billed Christopher Lambert is the wacko brother of a drug runner, whose whereabouts may be the key to the mission. An oddball cop/buddy movie with touches of the spaghetti Western, it's weird and uneven, but entertaining. Rated R for violence, profanity, nudity, and simulated sex. 97m. **DIR:** Deran Sarafian. **CAST:** Christopher Lambert, Mario Van Peebles, Denis Leary, Patrick Stewart, Sally Kirkland, Kadeem Hardison, Richard Sarafian. **1994 DVD**

GUNRUNNER, THE ★★ Kevin Costner plans to make a fortune bootlegging liquor in order to buy guns for

China's downtrodden masses. Poor editing destroys the continuity of what might have been an intriguing film. Rated R for violence and a hint of sex. 92m. **DIR:** Nardo Castillo. **CAST:** Kevin Costner, Sara Botsford. **1989**

GUNS OF DIABLO ★★★ Wagon train guide Charles Bronson, accompanied by young Kurt Russell, rides into a strange town where he unexpectantly rekindles an old romance and is ambushed by ruthless outlaws. Edited from two episodes of the TV series *Travels of Jamie McPheeters*. 91m. **DIR:** Boris Ingster. **CAST:** Charles Bronson, Kurt Russell, Susan Oliver, Jan Merlin. **1964**

GUNS OF FORT PETTICOAT ★★★1/2 Cavalry officer Audie Murphy trains a group of women to defend their settlement against marauding Indians. Unusual twist on a tired plot. 82m. **DIR:** George Marshall. **CAST:** Audie Murphy, Kathryn Grant, Hope Emerson, Jeff Donnell, James Griffith. **1957**

GUNS OF HATE ★★★ When a prospector finds the fabled Lost Dutchman mine, outlaws try to steal it from him and his daughter. Tim Holt to the rescue in one of his best RKO outings. B&W; 62m. **DIR:** Lesley Selander. **CAST:** Tim Holt, Richard Martin, Steve Brodie, Nan Leslie, Myrna Dell. **1948**

GUNS OF NAVARONE, THE ★★★★ Along with *The Great Escape*, this film is one of the best World War II adventure yarns. Gregory Peck, David Niven, and Anthony Quinn are part of a multinational task force that is sent to Greece with a mission to destroy two huge German batteries that threaten a fleet of Allied troop transports. 145m. **DIR:** J. Lee Thompson. **CAST:** Gregory Peck, David Niven, Anthony Quinn, Stanley Baker, Anthony Quayle, James Darren, Irene Papas. **1961 DVD**

GUNS OF THE MAGNIFICENT SEVEN ★★★ George Kennedy, fresh from his success with *Cool Hand Luke*, steps in for Yul Brynner as Chris, a well-meaning gunfighter who has a bad habit of getting his friends killed while defending the downtrodden. This second sequel has some fine performances—particularly by Kennedy and James Whitmore—and some rousing action scenes, but the original *Seven* has yet to be equaled. Rated PG. 106m. **DIR:** Paul Wendkos. **CAST:** George Kennedy, Monte Markham, James Whitmore, Bernie Casey, Joe Don Baker, Michael Ansara. **1969**

GUNSHY ★★ The friendship between a writer and an Atlantic City mobster, who agree to share their knowledge with each other, fuels this pedestrian dramatic thriller. Their mutual interests also include the mobster's girlfriend. Things get complicated, but not enough to make the film more than it is. Rated R for adult situations, language, and violence. 105m. **DIR:** Jeff Celentano. **CAST:** William L. Petersen, Jeff Wincott, Diane Lane, Kevin Gage, Eric Schaeffer. **1998 DVD**

GUNSLINGER ★★★ Outlaw John Ireland is hired by land-grabbing saloon boss Allison Hayes to kill female sheriff, Beverly Garland. An early one from director Roger Corman, who has become somewhat of a cult figure. 83m. **DIR:** Roger Corman. **CAST:** John Ireland, Beverly Garland, Allison Hayes, Chris Alcaide, Dick Miller. **1956**

GUNSMOKE (TV SERIES) ★★★★ Television's finest Western series most important asset was the exquisite cast ensemble: James Arness as Marshal Matt Dillon, Amanda Blake as Kitty the saloon keeper, Dennis Weaver and Ken Curtis as well-meaning deputies, and Milburn Stone as the irascible Doc Adams. The best episodes are the half hours, which feature some of the tightest, most evocative storytelling ever to be presented. 60m. **DIR:** Various. **CAST:** James Arness, Milburn Stone, Amanda Blake, Dennis Weaver, Ken Curtis, Burt Reynolds, Glenn Strange, Buck Taylor. **1955–1975**

GUNSMOKE: RETURN TO DODGE ★★★ When Matt Dillon (James Arness), now retired from the job of town marshal, is badly wounded in a fight, Miss Kitty (Amanda Blake) leaves her new home in New Orleans to be at his side in Dodge, where an old enemy of theirs is also headed to exact revenge. Buoyed by a series of flashbacks from the series' twenty years of episodes. 96m. **DIR:** Vincent McEveety. **CAST:** James Arness, Amanda Blake, Buck Taylor, Steve Forrest, Earl Holliman. **1987**

GUS ★★★1/2 This Disney comedy has a mule named Gus delivering the winning kicks for a losing football team. Naturally, the rival team kidnaps the mule before the big game, and the search is on. Lots of slapstick comedy for the kids to enjoy in this one. Rated G. 96m. **DIR:** Vincent McEveety. **CAST:** Edward Asner, Don Knotts, Gary Grimes, Dick Van Patten. **1976**

GUY: AWAKENING OF THE DEVIL ★★ Our heroes in this animated tribute to sex and violence are a pair of hard-boiled soldiers of fortune, one of whom gains the ability to mutate into a giant, apparently invulnerable creature. In Japanese with English subtitles. Available rated R or unrated, both with nudity and violence; the unrated version contains explicit sex. 40m. **DIR:** Yorihisa Uchida. **1990**

GUY II: SECOND TARGET ★★1/2 Guy and Raina, the terrible twosome of fortune hunters, go after a fortune hidden in the temple of a bizarre cult in this animated feature. Fans of the transforming-monster subgenre will enjoy this one. In Japanese with English subtitles. Not rated; contains violence, profanity, and brief nudity. 33m. **DIR:** Yorihisa Uchida. **1992**

GUY NAMED JOE, A ★★★★ Enchanting film has a dead WWII pilot (Spencer Tracy) coming back to Earth from heaven to aid a young aviator (Van Johnson) with his love life and combat missions. MGM pulls out all the stops with a blockbuster cast and high production values. Tracy's performance is sublime. B&W; 120m. **DIR:** Victor Fleming. **CAST:** Spencer Tracy, Van Johnson, Irene Dunne, Ward Bond, Lionel Barrymore, James Gleason. **1943**

GUYANA TRAGEDY, THE: THE STORY OF JIM JONES ★★★★ Powers Boothe won an Emmy award for his gripping portrayal of the Reverend Jim Jones, whose growing megalomania led him to establish a camp in South America. There, in 1978, Jones led more than nine hundred followers in a mass suicide. Though made for television, this well-documented story features a conclusion that will shock most viewers, and is not suitable for younger children. 192m. **DIR:** William A. Graham. **CAST:** Powers Boothe, Ned Beatty, Irene Cara, Veronica Cartwright, Rosalind Cash, Brad Dourif, Meg Foster, Michael C. Gwynne, Diane Ladd, Ron O'Neal, Randy Quaid, Diana Scarwid, Brenda Vaccaro, LeVar Burton, Colleen Dewhurst, Clifton James, James Earl Jones. **1980**

GUYS AND DOLLS ★★★ This passable musical stars Marlon Brando and Frank Sinatra as New York gamblers with a gangster-like aura. Brando and Sinatra bet on whether or not a lovely Salvation Army soldier (Jean Simmons) is date bait. 150m. **DIR:** Joseph L. Mankiewicz. **CAST:** Marlon Brando, Frank Sinatra, Jean Simmons, Vivian Blaine, Stubby Kaye, Veda Ann Borg. **1955 DVD**

GUYVER, THE ★★★1/2 Japanese comic-book superhero jumps to the big screen in a film that's truly comic book in look and style. Jack Armstrong is a college student who stumbles across a helmet that transforms him into a superhero. Hot on his tail are a gang of mutants and a CIA agent. Outrageous special effects and tongue-in-cheek humor make this adventure film worthy of continuation. Rated PG-13 for violence. 92m. **DIR:** Screaming Mad George, Steve Wang. **CAST:** Mark Hamill, David Gale, Michael Berryman, Jack Armstrong. **1992**

GUYVER 2: DARK HERO ★★ Gooey monsters do battle with a metallic hero in this comic book–like film based on the popular comic-book series. The convoluted story is about thirty minutes too long, despite very entertaining battle choreography, some fine visual effects, and great monster makeup. Rated R for profanity, violence, and gore. 127m. **DIR:** Steve Wang. **CAST:** David Hayter, Kathy Christopherson, Christopher Michael. **1994**

GUYVER: OUT OF CONTROL ★★1/2 An early look at the origin of the Guyver superhero, this animated story tries to make up for its lack of detail with violent action but doesn't quite succeed. In Japanese with English subtitles. Not rated; contains violence and nudity. 55m. **DIR:** Hiroshi Watanabe. **1987**

GYMKATA Disappointing fist-and-foot actioner. Rated R for violence. 90m. **DIR:** Robert Clouse. **CAST:** Kurt Thomas, Tetchie Agbayani, Richard Norton. **1985**

GYPSY (1962) ★★★ Tries to surpass its hackneyed situation with an energetic musical score and a story about real people. In this case, the characters are stripper Gypsy Rose Lee and her backstage mother supreme, Rose. The music is excellent, but the characters are weakly defined. 149m. **DIR:** Mervyn LeRoy. **CAST:** Natalie Wood, Rosalind Russell, Karl Malden. **1962 DVD**

GYPSY (1993) ★★★★ Bette Midler struts her stuff in this engaging TV adaptation of the Broadway musical. She's Mama Rose, the boisterous, driven stage mother of June Havoc and Gypsy Rose Lee. It's a show-stopping performance, and Midler deftly shades her hard-edged but endearing character while belting out Jule Styne's memorable tunes with élan. Made for TV. 150m. **DIR:** Emile Ardolino. **CAST:** Bette Midler, Cynthia Gibb, Peter Riegert, Edward Asner. **1993 DVD**

GYPSY ANGELS Even die-hard fans eager to see Vanna White in a blink-and-you'll-miss-it topless scene won't care about this romance between an Atlanta stripper and a stunt pilot. Rated R. 92m. **DIR:** Alan Smithee. **CAST:** Vanna White, Gene Bicknell, Richard Roundtree, Tige Andrews, Marilyn Hassett, Lyle Waggoner. **1989**

GYPSY BLOOD ★★1/2 This adaptation of the Prosper Merimee story *Carmen* vaulted both director Ernst Lubitsch and star Pola Negri to the front rank of the European film scene. It has been called the first major post-war German release on the international scene. The title was changed to *Gypsy Blood* for American distribution. Silent. B&W; 104m. **DIR:** Ernst Lubitsch. **CAST:** Pola Negri. **1918**

GYPSY COLT ★★★ A good Americanized updating of *Lassie Come Home* with a girl and her horse. The exciting and well-filmed scenes of the horse, Gypsy, alone and in peril will hold the interest of children and adults. Fine Western scenery is a plus. 72m. **DIR:** Andrew Marton. **CAST:** Donna Corcoran, Ward Bond, Frances Dee, Larry Keating, Lee Van Cleef. **1954**

GYPSY WARRIORS, THE ★★ James Whitmore Jr. and Tom Selleck are two American soldiers in World War II who go behind enemy lines to capture a formula for germ warfare. The humor is bland and the action is déjà vu. Not rated. Has violence. 77m. **DIR:** Lou Antonio. **CAST:** James Whitmore Jr., Tom Selleck, Joseph Ruskin, Lina Raymond, Michael Lane, Ted Gehring, Albert Paulsen, Kenneth Tigar. **1978**

GYPSY WILDCAT ★★★ A colorful adventure set in medieval times with a plot similar to Westerns of the 1940s and a cast of once-popular Hollywood sex objects. 77m. **DIR:** Roy William Neill. **CAST:** Maria Montez, Jon Hall, Douglass Dumbrille, Leo Carrillo, Gale Sondergaard, Nigel Bruce, Curt Bois. **1944**

H

H-MAN, THE ★★★ Unintentional humor makes this low-budget Japanese monster movie a near comedy classic. A boat wanders into a nuclear-test zone, mutating a crew member into a horrible water monster. With some of the lamest special effects ever filmed, this is guaranteed to make even the most humorless individual crack a smile. Not rated, but suitable for all ages. 79m. **DIR:** Inoshiro Honda. **CAST:** Yumi Shirakawa. **1959**

H. P. LOVECRAFT'S NECRONOMICON: BOOK OF THE DEAD ★★1/2 When horror author H. P. Lovecraft visits a mysterious library, the stories he reads come to life in the form of these three horrific tales. Loaded with blood and guts, so-so horror film will entertain fans of the genre but won't win over anyone else. Rated R for horror violence. 97m. **DIR:** Brian Yuzna, Christophe Gans, Shusuke Kaneko. **CAST:** Jeffrey Combs, David Warner, Bruce Payne, Belinda Bauer. **1993**

HABIT ★★★ Rich in atmosphere and ambiguity, this tale of a man on the rebound who falls into the arms of a mysterious woman keeps you guessing. Close friends fear for his life: they suspect that the woman is a vampire. The film captures a dark underground world where nothing is what it seems. Not rated; contains violence, language, nudity, and adult situations. 112m. **DIR:** Larry Fessenden. **CAST:** Larry Fessenden, Meredith Snaider, Aaron Beall, Patricia Coleman, Heather Woodbury, Jesse Hartman. **1997 DVD**

HABITAT ★★★ The greenhouse effect really takes its toll on one family in this made-for-cable, science-fiction morality play about the evil mankind inflicts on the

Earth and one another. A high-school student watches his father's accelerated evolution experiment spiral out of control. Then Dad disappears, Mom turns into Mother Nature, and the house grows into a forest fortress. Rated R for adult situations, language, nudity, and violence. 103m. **DIR:** Renee Daalder. **CAST:** Balthazar Getty, Alice Krige, Tcheky Karyo, Lara Harris, Kenneth Walsh. **1996 DVD**

HABITATION OF DRAGONS, THE ★★★ Horton Foote's moving play about one family's secrets and cruelty. Frederic Forrest plays the complacent older brother whose life is about to fall apart when his wife's affair is revealed. Younger brother (Brad Davis) finally is allowed to reach out to him despite the strained years between them. Slow pace matches the painful effort the family makes in order to face the past and deal with the present. Not rated; contains adult themes. 94m. **DIR:** Michael Lindsay-Hogg. **CAST:** Frederic Forrest, Brad Davis, Jean Stapleton, Hallie Foote. **1992**

HACKERS ★★ Manhattan high-school cyberpunks surfing the net stumble onto an industrial extortion conspiracy. The leather-clad, rock 'n' roll hackers are framed for the crime but enlist the aid of the information-highway underground to make things right. Cyberspace becomes a neon wonderland, but the film's visual sizzle is dampened by a clumsy plot and awkward acting. Rated PG-13 for language and suggested sex. 95m. **DIR:** Iain Softley. **CAST:** Jonny Lee Miller, Angelina Jolie, Fisher Stevens, Lorraine Bracco. **1995 DVD**

HADLEY'S REBELLION ★★★ Low-key drama of the growing pains encountered by a country boy as he tries to adjust to a new life in California. Well-intentioned script lacks impact, and Griffin O'Neal makes for a bland hero. Rated PG. 96m. **DIR:** Fred Walton. **CAST:** Griffin O'Neal, William Devane, Charles Durning, Adam Baldwin. **1984**

•HAIKU TUNNEL 🦃 A law clerk rebels against office life by refusing to work. Josh Kornbluth trespasses on Woody Allen country with dull results in this amateurish vanity production, all too clearly adapted from a long stage monologue. Rated R for profanity and sexual humor. 88m. **DIR:** Jacob Kornbluth, Josh Kornbluth. **CAST:** Josh Kornbluth, Warren Keith, Helen Shumaker, Amy Resnick. **2001 DVD**

HAIL CAESAR 🦃 Director-star Anthony Michael Hall tries to prove his worth to his girlfriend's father so that he may pursue his first love: rock and roll. This *Caesar* takes a stab at comedy and misses. Rated PG for language and adult situations. 93m. **DIR:** Anthony Michael Hall. **CAST:** Anthony Michael Hall, Robert Downey Jr., Judd Nelson, Samuel L. Jackson, Frank Gorshin. **1994**

HAIL, HERO! ★★ Dated, uneven film features an overly rambunctious Michael Douglas (in his first film) returning home to announce his enlistment during the Vietnam War. Rated PG. 100m. **DIR:** David Miller. **CAST:** Michael Douglas, Arthur Kennedy, Peter Strauss, Teresa Wright. **1969**

HAIL MARY ★★★★ This story of the coming of Christ in modern times will offend only the most dogmatic Christians, or narrow-minded religious zealots. Godard's eye for the aesthetic gives this film a compassionate feel. *The Book of Mary*, a film by Anne-Marie Mieville, is the prologue and is equally beautiful. In French with English subtitles. Not rated; the equivalent of an R for nudity. 107m. **DIR:** Jean-Luc Godard. **CAST:** Myriem Roussel, Thierry Lacoste, Philippe Lacoste. **1985**

HAIL THE CONQUERING HERO ★★★★1/2 Defense plant worker Eddie Bracken is passed off by Marine buddies as the hero of Guadalcanal and his hometown goes overboard in adulation and tribute. Another winning satire from writer-director Preston Sturges. Fine family viewing. B&W; 101m. **DIR:** Preston Sturges. **CAST:** Eddie Bracken, Ella Raines, William Demarest, Raymond Walburn, Franklin Pangborn. **1944**

HAIR ★★★1/2 Neglected adaptation of the hit Broadway play about 1960s unrest. John Savage is the uptight Midwesterner who pals up with a group of (shudder) hippies celebrating the Age of Aquarius. Grand musical moments, due to Twyla Tharp's impressive choreography. Rated PG for nudity. 121m. **DIR:** Milos Forman. **CAST:** Treat Williams, John Savage, Beverly D'Angelo, Annie Golden, Charlotte Rae. **1979 DVD**

HAIRDRESSER'S HUSBAND, THE ★★★★ A 12 year old boy has his first experience with sensuality in the chair of a local hairdresser. The warmth of the shampoo and the closeness of her body give birth to a romantic notion that leads the adult Antoine (Jean Rochefort) to marry a hairdresser (Anna Galiena). French writer-director Patrice Leconte takes a whimsical approach to the story. In French with English subtitles. Not rated, the film has simulated sex. 84m. **DIR:** Patrice Leconte. **CAST:** Jean Rochefort, Anna Galiena, Roland Bertin. **1992**

HAIRSPRAY ★★★ Writer-director John Waters's ode to the dance craze of the Sixties features some outrageously campy performances. The story revolves around the desire of a pudgy teen (Ricki Lake) to be one of the featured stars on a Baltimore TV show in 1963. Rated PG. 87m. **DIR:** John Waters. **CAST:** Sonny Bono, Divine, Colleen (Vitamin C) Fitzpatrick, Deborah Harry, Ricki Lake, Leslie Ann Powers, Clayton Prince, Jerry Stiller, Mink Stole, Shawn Thompson, Pia Zadora. **1988**

HAIRY APE, THE ★★★ Eugene O'Neill's play about an animal-like coal stoker on an ocean liner. The hairy ape falls in love with a heartless socialite passenger who at once is captivated and repulsed by his coarse approach to life. William Bendix is fascinating in the title role. B&W; 90m. **DIR:** Alfred Santell. **CAST:** William Bendix, Susan Hayward, John Loder. **1944**

HALF A SIXPENCE ★★ A tuneful musical incarnation of H. G. Wells' novel, *Kipps*, as presented on Broadway with most of the original Broadway cast. The story of a British boy winning and losing a fortune, and winning, losing, and re-winning a girlfriend, is flashy and tuneful, but a mite long for one sitting. 149m. **DIR:** George Sidney. **CAST:** Tommy Steele, Julia Foster, Cyril Ritchard, Pamela Brown, James Villiers, Hilton Edwards, Penelope Horner. **1967**

HALF BAKED 🦃 Dopey comedy about three New York City potheads who sell stolen laboratory marijuana to raise bail for their jailed roommate. Rated R for drug use, language, nudity, and sexual content. 82m. **DIR:** Tamra Davis. **CAST:** Dave Chappelle, Guillermo Diaz, Jim Breuer, Harland Williams, Rachel True, Clarence Williams, III. **1998 DVD**

HALF-BREED, THE ★★1/2 Predictable oater about a saloon owner determined to drive Apaches off their land so he can mine the gold he's sure is there. 81m. **DIR:** Stuart Gilmore. **CAST:** Robert Young, Janis Carter, Jack Buetel, Reed Hadley, Barton MacLane. **1952**

HALF HUMAN 🦃 From the director of *Godzilla* comes an abominable snowman terrorizing Mount Fuji. B&W; 78m. **DIR:** Inoshiro Honda. **CAST:** John Carradine, Morris Ankrum. **1958**

HALF-MOON STREET ★★ Half-baked adaptation of Paul Theroux's *Doctor Slaughter*, which was equally flawed as a novel. Sigourney Weaver stars as an American abroad who decides to supplement her academic (but low-paid) government position by moonlighting as a sophisticated "escort." Rated R for nudity and sexual themes. 90m. **DIR:** Bob Swaim. **CAST:** Sigourney Weaver, Michael Caine, Patrick Kavanagh. **1986**

HALF OF HEAVEN ★★★★ A woman works her way up from poverty to power in this unusual import from Spain. Rosa (Angela Molina) almost seems to drift her way to the top as Madrid's most successful restaurateur, but there are deeper meanings in this often funny and always fascinating mix of magic, politics, and romance. Not rated, the film has brief violence. In Spanish with English subtitles. 127m. **DIR:** Manuel Gutiérrez Aragón. **CAST:** Angela Molina, Margarita Lozano, Fernando Fernán Gómez. **1987**

HALFBACK OF NOTRE DAME, THE ★★★ Clumsy Gabriel Hogan is a hulking school misfit in this family-oriented spin on Victor Hugo, with Emmanuelle Vaugier positively sparkling as the French exchange student who persuades him that piano lessons might be more fulfilling than football. It's a sweet little story, capably told. Rated PG for minor end-zone violence. 97m. **DIR:** René Bonniere. **CAST:** Gabriel Hogan, Scott Hylands, Allen Cutler, Sandra Nelson, Emmanuelle Vaugier. **1995**

HALFMOON ★★1/2 From his study in Tangiers, American author Paul Bowles (*The Sheltering Sky*) introduces three short films adapted from his work. All set in North Africa, the tales are mesmerizingly filmed even though their meanings may be hard to grasp. Not rated. 90m. **DIR:** Frieder Schlaich, Irene von Alberti. **CAST:** Samir Guesmi, Khaled Ksouri, Veronica Quilligan. **1995**

HALLELUJAH! ★★★★ Dated in technique but up-to-date in story and acting, this is the first major movie with an all-black cast. The plot revolves around a preacher who has lost his fight with temptation too many times. Irving Berlin wrote the song, "Waiting at the End of the Road," expressly for the film. B&W; 106m. **DIR:** King Vidor. **CAST:** Nina Mae McKinney, Daniel Hayner. **1929**

HALLELUJAH, I'M A BUM ★★★★ A charming Depression-day comedy and one of the few films with dialogue delivered in rhymed stanzas, this film boasts a name cast headed by Al Jolson as a hobo who tries to reform after he meets a beautiful woman. Rodgers and Hart wrote "You Are Too Beautiful" expressly for this film. The composer-lyricist team also appears as photographers. B&W; 82m. **DIR:** Lewis Milestone. **CAST:** Al Jolson, Madge Evans, Frank Morgan, Harry Langdon, Tyler Brooke, Edgar Connor. **1933 DVD**

HALLELUJAH TRAIL, THE ★★★ Those who fondly remember television's *F Troop* should adore this cavalry comedy, which finds Burt Lancaster and Jim Hutton leading a wagon-train load of liquor through Indian territory. Temperance leader Lee Remick wants it all destroyed. Overlong, but fun nonetheless. 167m. **DIR:** John Sturges. **CAST:** Burt Lancaster, Lee Remick, Jim Hutton, Brian Keith, Martin Landau, Donald Pleasence. **1965 DVD**

HALLOWEEN ★★★★1/2 This is a surprisingly tasteful and enjoyable slasher film. Director John Carpenter puts the accent on suspense and atmosphere rather than blood and guts, as in other films of this kind. The story revolves around the escape of a soulless maniac who returns to the town where he murdered his sister. Rated R. 93m. **DIR:** John Carpenter. **CAST:** Jamie Lee Curtis, Donald Pleasence, Nancy Loomis, P. J. Soles, Charles Cyphers. **1978 DVD**

HALLOWEEN II ★★★ This respectable sequel picks up where the original left off: with the boogeyman on the prowl and Jamie Lee Curtis running for her life. Rated R because of violence and nudity. 92m. **DIR:** Rick Rosenthal. **CAST:** Jamie Lee Curtis, Donald Pleasence, Charles Cyphers, Jeffrey Kramer, Lance Guest. **1981 DVD**

HALLOWEEN III: SEASON OF THE WITCH ★★1/2 A maniacal mask manufacturer in northern California provides kiddies with devilishly designed pumpkin masks. Not a true sequel to the gruesome *Halloween* twosome, but still watchable. Rated R. 96m. **DIR:** Tommy Lee Wallace. **CAST:** Tom Atkins, Stacey Nelkin, Dan O'Herlihy. **1983 DVD**

HALLOWEEN IV: THE RETURN OF MICHAEL MYERS ★★★ The makers of this third sequel to John Carpenter's ground-breaking *Halloween* obviously tried to create a quality horror film and for the most part they've succeeded. Director Dwight H. Little commendably puts the accent on atmosphere and suspense in detailing the third killing spree of Michael Myers (a.k.a. The Shape). Donald Pleasence returns as Myers's nemesis, Dr. Loomis, to hunt down this fiendish foe. Rated R for violence and profanity. 88m. **DIR:** Dwight H. Little. **CAST:** Donald Pleasence, Ellie Cornell, Danielle Harris. **1988 DVD**

HALLOWEEN: H20 ★★ This seventh entry in the slasher series has a knockout climax but focuses more on false alarms than true terror. Unstoppable zombie Michael Myers returns twenty years after his first murderous rampage as a child to stalk his sister Laurie, who is now the alcoholic headmistress of a private school. Rated R for violence, gore, profanity, and sexual situations. 85m. **DIR:** Steve Miner. **CAST:** Jamie Lee Curtis, Josh Harnett, Adam Arkin, LL Cool J, Joseph Gordon Levitt, Michelle Williams, Adam Hann-Byrd, Jodi Lyn O'Keefe. **1998 DVD**

HALLOWEEN: THE CURSE OF MICHAEL MYERS ★★★ Realizing this is the last outing for Michael Myers, the filmmakers have upped the ante in terms of suspense and gore. Michael returns to his old stomping grounds to put an end to his lineage. There are all kinds of subplots about devil worshipers and kids in trouble, plus enough scares to give even the strongest of wills a jolt. Rated R for violence, profanity, adult situations, and nudity. 88m. **DIR:** Joe Chappelle. **CAST:** Paul

Stephen Rudd, Marianne Hagan, Mitchell Ryan, Donald Pleasence. **1995 DVD**

HALLOWEEN TREE, THE ★★★★ Delightful animated version of the Ray Bradbury tale. A group of trick-or-treaters embark on an incredible journey as they chase the soul of a friend through Halloween's history. Written and narrated by Bradbury. Not rated, but suitable for all ages. 70m. **DIR:** Mario Piluso. **CAST:** Ray Bradbury, Leonard Nimoy, Annie Baker, Alex Greenwald, Edan Gross, Lindsay Crouse (voices). **1993**

HALLOWEEN V: THE REVENGE OF MICHAEL MYERS ★★ What started off as the story of a truly frightening killer (the unstoppable Michael Myers) has become a run-of-the-mill slasher series. Tedious. Rated R for violence. 89m. **DIR:** Dominique Othenin-Girard. **CAST:** Donald Pleasence, Ellie Cornell, Danielle Harris, Beau Starr. **1989 DVD**

HALLS OF MONTEZUMA ★★★1/2 There's a minimum of romance and lots of action in this oft-told story of American Marines at war in the South Pacific during World War II. Realistic adventure yarn. 113m. **DIR:** Lewis Milestone. **CAST:** Richard Widmark, Jack Palance, Jack Webb, Robert Wagner, Karl Malden, Reginald Gardiner, Philip Ahn. **1950 DVD**

HAMBONE AND HILLIE ★★★ A delightful story of love and loyalty between an old woman (Lillian Gish) and her dog and constant companion, Hambone. While boarding a flight in New York to return to Los Angeles, Hambone is accidentally lost. And so begins a three-thousand-mile cross-country trip filled with perilous freeways, wicked humans, and dangerous animals. Rated PG. 97m. **DIR:** Roy Watts. **CAST:** Lillian Gish, Timothy Bottoms, Candy Clark, O. J. Simpson, Robert Walker Jr. **1984**

HAMBURGER HILL ★★1/2 In dealing with one of the bloodiest battles of the Vietnam War, director John Irvin and screenwriter Jim Carabatsos have made a film so brutally real that watching it is an endurance test. Although well-acted and well made, it is more like a shocking documentary than a work of fiction. Rated R for violence and profanity. 112m. **DIR:** John Irvin. **CAST:** Anthony Barrile, Michael Patrick Boatman, Don Cheadle, Michael Dolan, Don James, Dylan McDermott, M. A. Nickles, Harry O'Reilly, Tim Quill, Courtney B. Vance, Steven Weber, Daniel O'Shea. **1987 DVD**

HAMBURGER—THE MOTION PICTURE 🦃 A very funny comedy could be made about the fast-food industry, but this isn't it. Rated R for profanity, nudity, suggested sex, and violence. 90m. **DIR:** Mike Marvin. **CAST:** Leigh McCloskey, Sandy Hackett, Randi Brooks, Charles Tyner, Chuck McCann, Dick Butkus. **1986**

HAMLET (1948) ★★★★★ In every way a brilliant presentation of Shakespeare's best-known play masterminded by England's foremost player. Superb in the title role, Laurence Olivier won the 1948 Oscar for best actor, and (as producer) for best picture. A high point among many is Stanley Holloway's droll performance as the First Gravedigger. B&W; 150m. **DIR:** Laurence Olivier. **CAST:** Laurence Olivier, Basil Sydney, Eileen Herlie, Jean Simmons, Felix Aylmer, Terence Morgan, Peter Cushing, Stanley Holloway. **1948 DVD**

HAMLET (1969) ★★★ Nicol Williamson gives a far more energetic portrayal of the famous Dane than the noted Oscar-winning performance of Laurence Olivier. Worth seeing for comparison of interpretations. An exceptional supporting cast adds to the allure of this low-budget adaptation. 113m. **DIR:** Tony Richardson. **CAST:** Nicol Williamson, Gordon Jackson, Anthony Hopkins, Judy Parfitt, Marianne Faithfull, Mark Dignam. **1969**

HAMLET (1990) ★★★★1/2 Kenneth Branagh's *Henry V* proved that Shakespeare adaptations could be accessible to mainstream audiences and still remain faithful to the source. Director Franco Zefirelli's *Hamlet* continues this tradition, with Mel Gibson bringing great vitality and physicality to the role of the Bard's most poignant hero. Rated PG for violence. 135m. **DIR:** Franco Zeffirelli. **CAST:** Mel Gibson, Glenn Close, Alan Bates, Ian Holm, Paul Scofield, Helena Bonham Carter. **1990**

HAMLET (1996) ★★★★★ This is the most impressive version of *Hamlet* ever to appear on the big screen. Filming William Shakespeare's play in its entirety, Kenneth Branagh added the depth long missing from previous screen versions. Each character springs to full life while Branagh brings the vitality and inventiveness to *Hamlet* that made his *Henry V* and *Much Ado About Nothing* so memorable. The story, of course, involves murder, incest, and revenge in the royal Danish court. Rated PG-13. 242m. **DIR:** Kenneth Branagh. **CAST:** Kenneth Branagh, Julie Christie, Derek Jacobi, Kate Winslet, Billy Crystal, Robin Williams, Jack Lemmon, Gérard Depardieu, Charlton Heston, Rufus Sewell, Brian Blessed. **1996**

HAMLET (2000) ★★★★ Director Michael Almereyda gives Shakespeare's tragedy an unusual interpretation, set in New York City at the "Denmark Corporation" and the "Hotel Elsinore." Freely cutting and rearranging, Almereyda illuminates the heart of the play, making some of the Bard's most familiar scenes startlingly new and fresh. The film also profits from Almereyda's gift for unusual casting (Kyle MacLachlan as Claudius, Bill Murray as Polonius, etc.). Rated R for violence. 112m. **DIR:** Michael Almereyda. **CAST:** Ethan Hawke, Kyle MacLachlan, Diane Venora, Bill Murray, Liev Schreiber, Julia Stiles. **2000 DVD**

HAMMERED: THE BEST OF SLEDGE ★★ Well-intentioned but flat takeoff of tough cop movies and TV shows, *Hammered* stars David Rasche as Detective Sledge Hammer, a man who talks to his gun and loves extreme and senseless violence. This is a compilation of four *Sledge Hammer* TV shows. 104m. **DIR:** Jackie Cooper, Gary Walkow, Martha Coolidge. **CAST:** David Rasche, Anne-Marie Martin, Harrison Page, John Vernon. **1986**

HAMMERSMITH IS OUT ★★★1/2 In this black comedy an insane criminal is sprung from an asylum by an ambitious attendant. Gaining strength and polish as the plot unfolds, the film promises a bit more than it actually offers. Rated R for profanity, sexual situations, and mild violence. 108m. **DIR:** Peter Ustinov. **CAST:** Elizabeth Taylor, Richard Burton, Peter Ustinov, Beau Bridges, George Raft, John Schuck. **1971**

HAMMETT ★★ A disappointing homage to mystery writer Dashiell Hammett, this Wim Wenders–directed and Francis Ford Coppola–meddled production was two years in the making and hardly seems worth it. The plot is nearly incomprehensible, something that could never be said of the real-life Hammett's works (*The Maltese Falcon*, *The Thin Man*, etc.). Rated PG. 97m. **DIR:** Wim Wenders. **CAST:** Frederic Forrest, Peter Boyle, Marilu Henner, Elisha Cook Jr., R. G. Armstrong. **1982**

HAND, THE 🦃 Thumbs down on this dull film. Rated R. 104m. **DIR:** Oliver Stone. **CAST:** Michael Caine, Andrea Marcovicci, Annie McEnroe, Bruce McGill. **1981**

HAND GUN ★★ The story of a bad guy (Seymour Cassel) and his son (Treat Williams) and the cops that are out to stop them. With an atmosphere just like that of TV's *NYPD Blue*, *Hand Gun* lacks the intelligence and depth that make the program work. Rated R for violence, profanity, and nudity. 90m. **DIR:** Whitney Ransick. **CAST:** Treat Williams, Seymour Cassel, Paul Schulze. **1994 DVD**

HAND THAT ROCKS THE CRADLE, THE ★★★1/2 Once you get past the utterly disgusting first ten minutes, this becomes an effective little suspense tale of a woman who gets revenge for her husband's death by posing as a nanny. Rebecca DeMornay is chilling as the menacing cradle rocker. Rated R for violence, profanity, and nudity. 110m. **DIR:** Curtis Hanson. **CAST:** Annabella Sciorra, Rebecca DeMornay, Matt McCoy, Ernie Hudson, John de Lancie. **1992 DVD**

HANDFUL OF DUST, A ★★★★ Based on Evelyn Waugh's masterpiece, this is a deliciously staged drama of actions and fate. Set in post–World War I England and the jungles of South America, the film presents two aristocrats searching along different paths for happiness. Superb ensemble playing. 118m. **DIR:** Charles Sturridge. **CAST:** James Wilby, Rupert Graves, Kristin Scott Thomas, Anjelica Huston, Alec Guinness. **1988**

HANDMAID'S TALE, THE ★★★★ Adapted from Margaret Atwood's chilling cautionary novel, this feminist horror story stars Natasha Richardson as one of the few remaining fertile women in a futuristic United States where ultraconservatives rule and mandate that all such women must "serve" to provide children for carefully selected members of the upper crust. Rated R for language and explicit sexual themes. 109m. **DIR:** Volker Schlöndorff. **CAST:** Natasha Richardson, Robert Duvall, Faye Dunaway, Aidan Quinn, Elizabeth McGovern, Victoria Tennant. **1990 DVD**

HANDS ACROSS THE TABLE ★★★1/2 Carole Lombard is charismatic and witty as a manicurist who must choose between charming-but-poor Fred MacMurray or wealthy-but-dull Ralph Bellamy. Lots of silly plot complications but sparkling performances. Not rated. B&W; 80m. **DIR:** Mitchell Leisen. **CAST:** Carole Lombard, Fred MacMurray, Ralph Bellamy, William Demarest, Astrid Allwyn, Ruth Donnelly, Marie Prevost. **1935**

HANDS OF A STRANGER ★★ Mediocre remake of *The Hands of Orlac*, the old chestnut about a pianist who receives the hands of a murderer after his own are mangled in an accident. The preposterously purple dialogue is a hoot. B&W; 86m. **DIR:** Newt Arnold. **CAST:** Paul Lukather, Joan Harvey, Irish McCalla, Barry Gordon. **1962**

HANDS OF ORLAC ★★★ In one of his finest roles, Conrad Veidt stars in this oft-filmed story of a concert pianist who is led to believe a killer's hands have been grafted onto his own after an accident. This Austrian silent is a top competitor in a field dominated by German terror films and remains a riveting entry. B&W; 82m. **DIR:** Robert Wiene. **CAST:** Conrad Veidt, Fritz Kortner, Carmen Cartellieri, Alexandra Sorina, Paul Askonas, Fritz Strassny. **1925**

HANDS OF STEEL 🦃 A cyborg assassin goes wrong and is pursued by police and baddies. Rated R for language and violence. 94m. **DIR:** Martin Dolman. **CAST:** Daniel Greene, Janet Agren, Claudio Cassinelli, George Eastman, John Saxon. **1986**

HANDS OF THE RIPPER ★★★1/2 First-rate period horror—the last great offering of Britain's Hammer Films—speculates what might have happened if Jack the Ripper had had a daughter who grew up unknowingly emulating her murderous dad. A literate script, fine performances, and astute direction by then-promising Peter Sasdy. Rated R. 85m. **DIR:** Peter Sasdy. **CAST:** Eric Porter, Angharad Rees, Jane Merrow. **1971**

HANG 'EM HIGH ★★★ Clint Eastwood's first stateside spaghetti Western is a good one, with the star out to get the vigilantes who tried to hang him for a murder he didn't commit. Pat Hingle is the hangin' judge who gives Clint his license to hunt, and Ben Johnson is the marshal who saves his life. Ed Begley Sr. is memorable as the leader of the vigilantes. Rated PG. 114m. **DIR:** Ted Post. **CAST:** Clint Eastwood, Inger Stevens, Ed Begley Sr., Pat Hingle, Arlene Golonka, Ben Johnson. **1968 DVD**

HANGAR 18 🦃 The story revolves around an alien spaceship that is accidentally disabled by a U.S. satellite. Rated PG. 93m. **DIR:** James L. Conway. **CAST:** Darren McGavin, Robert Vaughn, Gary Collins, Joseph Campanella, James Hampton. **1980**

HANGIN' WITH THE HOMEBOYS ★★★★ A multicultural *Wayne's World*, this features four young men—two black, two Puerto Rican—on the brink of nowhere. All unsuccessful, they gather for a boys' night out. Bittersweet, with both hilarious and tragic scenes. A low-budget gem. Rated R for nudity, violence, and profanity. 89m. **DIR:** Joseph B. Vasquez. **CAST:** Doug E. Doug, Mario Joyner, John Leguizamo. **1991**

HANGING GARDEN, THE ★★★ A man returns home after years of separation from his family to attend his sister's wedding, and is reminded why he left in the first place. He is constantly haunted by visions of a rotund, teenage boy dangling from a noose, and he struggles to make sense of what it means. The acting is good, and the themes are respectable, but the film has a habit of plodding along. Rated R for language and some violence. 91m. **DIR:** Thom Fitzgerald. **CAST:** Chris Leavins, Kerry Fox, Seana McKenna, Peter MacNeill. **1996**

HANGING ON A STAR 🦃 Deborah Raffin is the persistent and savvy road agent for a promising group of unknown musicians. Rated PG. 93m. **DIR:** Mike MacFarland. **CAST:** Lane Caudell, Deborah Raffin, Wolfman Jack. **1978**

HANGING TREE, THE ★★★★ A strange, haunting tale, with Gary Cooper as a withdrawn and secretive doctor in a mining town. When he cares for a blinded traveler (Maria Schell), the jealousy of the miners brings about violence and tragedy. All but ignored when released, this is worth a look. George C. Scott's movie debut. 106m. **DIR:** Delmer Daves. **CAST:** Gary Cooper, Maria Schell, Karl Malden, George C. Scott, Ben Pi-

azza, Virginia Gregg, Guy Wilkerson, Karl Swenson, King Donovan, John Dierkes. **1956**

HANGING UP ★★1/2 Buried somewhere inside this mess is a poignant, often shattering story of a woman who dearly loves her father, despite his having sunk into the babbling of senile dementia. Alas, director-costar Diane Keaton treats her film like a screwball comedy, which is at odds with the heartbreaking tragedies to be found in Delia and Nora Ephron's screenplay. The result, a mishmash of conflicting moods, will please nobody. Don't take this call. Rated PG-13 for profanity. 92m. **DIR:** Diane Keaton. **CAST:** Meg Ryan, Diane Keaton, Lisa Kudrow, Walter Matthau, Adam Arkin, Cloris Leachman. **2000 DVD**

HANGMAN'S KNOT ★★★1/2 Randolph Scott as a Confederate officer who hijacks a Union gold shipment and then learns the Civil War is over. While he decides what to do with their bounty, outlaws attack them at an isolated way station. 81m. **DIR:** Roy Huggins. **CAST:** Randolph Scott, Donna Reed, Lee Marvin, Richard Denning, Claude Jarman Jr. **1952**

HANGMEN ALSO DIE ★★★★ Brian Donlevy plays the assassin charged with killing a Nazi stooge in Prague. Gene Lockhart is the scapegoat. One of Fritz Lang's best movies. B&W; 134m. **DIR:** Fritz Lang. **CAST:** Brian Donlevy, Walter Brennan, Anna Lee, Gene Lockhart, Dennis O'Keefe. **1943 DVD**

HANGOVER SQUARE ★★★1/2 The director and star of *The Lodger* reunite for this similar tale of a schizophrenic composer who kills under the influence of certain sounds. An above-average thriller with strong music (by Bernard Herrmann), atmospheric photography, and a gripping performance by star Laird Cregar, who died before the film was released. B&W; 77m. **DIR:** John Brahm. **CAST:** Laird Cregar, Linda Darnell, George Sanders, Glenn Langan, Alan Napier. **1945**

HANK AARON: CHASING THE DREAM ★★★★1/2 Not what you expect, as '"Hammerin' Hank"' the sports hero is only part of the story. This encompasses the insidious pervasiveness of racism in American life by focusing on one athlete who helped break down the color lines. Interviews with sports figures, Aaron family members, and political leaders are seamlessly blended with reenactments and memorable archival footage. The result is both an exciting document of sports history and a searing comment on cultural bigotry. Not rated. B&W/color; 95m. **DIR:** Mike Tollin. **CAST:** Hank Aaron. **1995**

HANKY PANKY ★★ In an obvious takeoff on the Hitchcock suspense formula, this seldom funny comedy features Gene Wilder as an innocent man caught up in international intrigue and murder. Rated PG for violence and gore. 110m. **DIR:** Sidney Poitier. **CAST:** Gene Wilder, Gilda Radner, Richard Widmark, Kathleen Quinlan, Robert Prosky. **1982**

HANNA K. 🦃 Jill Clayburgh is an Israeli lawyer appointed to defend a man who entered the country illegally in an attempt to reclaim the land where he grew up. Rated R for coarse language. 110m. **DIR:** Constantin Costa-Gavras. **CAST:** Jill Clayburgh, Jean Yanne, Gabriel Byrne, David Clennon. **1984**

HANNAH AND HER SISTERS ★★★★★ A two-year study of a family held together by house-mother Mia Farrow. Hannah is best friend, trusted confidante, and sympathetic peacemaker for sisters Barbara Hershey and Dianne Wiest, husband Michael Caine, and parents Maureen O'Sullivan and Lloyd Nolan. Woody Allen is a hypochondriac who may get his fondest wish: a fatal disease. Rated PG-13 for sexual situations. 106m. **DIR:** Woody Allen. **CAST:** Woody Allen, Michael Caine, Mia Farrow, Carrie Fisher, Barbara Hershey, Maureen O'Sullivan, Dianne Wiest, Max von Sydow, Daniel Stern, Lloyd Nolan, Sam Waterston. **1986 DVD**

HANNA'S WAR ★★★1/2 Powerful true story of a brave Jewish girl who is recruited by the British to rescue captured British fliers during WWII. Maruschka Detmers plays the brave Hanna who, though tortured brutally after her own capture, refuses to divulge military secrets. Rated PG-13 for violence. 148m. **DIR:** Menahem Golan. **CAST:** Maruschka Detmers, Ellen Burstyn, Anthony Andrews, Donald Pleasence. **1988**

HANNIBAL ★★ The guilty pleasure of watching Anthony Hopkins chew up the scenery—and a few other things—is the only highlight of this disappointing sequel to *Silence of the Lambs*, which commits the heinous sin of betraying everything that we admired about Jodie Foster's Clarice Starling. Julianne Moore makes a poor substitute for Foster in this ponderous, stupid storyline, which comes to life only during the notorious Grand Guignol finale. Rarely have so many heavyweight talents—including scripters David Mamet and Steven Zaillian—labored to produce so little. Rated R for profanity, gore, violence, and graphic cannibalism. 135m. **DIR:** Ridley Scott. **CAST:** Anthony Hopkins, Julianne Moore, Ray Liotta, Gary Oldman, Frankie Faison, Giancarlo Giannini, Francesca Neri. **2001 DVD**

HANNIE CAULDER ★★1/2 Revenge Western has Raquel Welch learning to be a gunslinger with the help of laid-back Robert Culp, so that she can hunt down and kill the three maniacs (Ernest Borgnine, Jack Elam, and Strother Martin) who murdered her husband. Rated R for violence. 85m. **DIR:** Burt Kennedy. **CAST:** Raquel Welch, Robert Culp, Ernest Borgnine, Jack Elam, Strother Martin, Christopher Lee. **1972**

HANOI HILTON, THE 🦃 A prisoner-of-war camp during the Vietnam War. Rated R for profanity and extreme violence. 130m. **DIR:** Lionel Chetwynd. **CAST:** Michael Moriarty, Paul LeMat, David Soul, Jeffrey Jones, Lawrence Pressman. **1987**

HANOVER STREET ★★ Action director Peter Hyams is out of his element with this melodramatic World War II drama, which consists mostly of an unlikely tryst between American soldier Harrison Ford and (married) British nurse Lesley-Anne Down. Overblown and mawkish. Rated PG. 109m. **DIR:** Peter Hyams. **CAST:** Harrison Ford, Lesley-Anne Down, Christopher Plummer, Alec McCowen. **1979 DVD**

HANS BRINKER ★★★ This is the well-known tale of Hans Brinker and his silver skates. Made this time as a musical, it stars Robin Askwith as Hans with Eleanor Parker and John Gregson as his mother and invalid father, and there are some pleasant skating sequences. This film would make particularly good family viewing for the holidays. It is not rated, but would be considered a G. 103m. **DIR:** Robert Scheerer. **CAST:** Robin Askwith, Eleanor Parker, Richard Basehart, Roberta Torey, John Gregson, Cyril Ritchard. **1979**

HANS CHRISTIAN ANDERSEN ★★★1/2 Danny Kaye is superb as the famous storyteller, and Frank Loesser composed some wonderful songs for this glossy oversweet musical. Ballet great Jeanmaire is a knockout. This is top-notch family entertainment. 120m. **DIR:** Charles Vidor. **CAST:** Danny Kaye, Farley Granger, Zizi Jeanmaire, John Qualen. **1952 DVD**

HANS CHRISTIAN ANDERSEN'S THUMBELINA ★★★ Perhaps we've been spoiled by recent Disney works like *The Little Mermaid*, *Beauty and the Beast*, and *Aladdin*, but this telling of the famous children's tale seems awfully slight in the story and song departments. The animation is fine, although not up to Don Bluth's highest standards, but the adventures of its tiny heroine are a bit on the ho-hum side. That said, little girls will adore it. Rated G. 83m. **DIR:** Don Bluth, Gary Goldman. **1994**

HANUSSEN ★★★★ In this German import based on a true story, Klaus Maria Brandauer is at the peak of his powers as a clairvoyant whose hypnotic, frightening talent for predicting the future both shocks and arouses the apathetic German public in the 1920s and 1930s. When his prophecies bring him to the attention of Adolf Hitler and the Nazi party, he finds his life in danger. In German with English subtitles. Rated R for violence and nudity. 117m. **DIR:** István Szabó. **CAST:** Klaus Maria Brandauer, Erland Josephson, Walter Schmidinger. **1988**

HAPPIEST MILLIONAIRE, THE ★★★ The Disney version of a factual memoir of life in the Philadelphia household of eccentric millionaire Anthony J. Drexel Biddle. Lively light entertainment that hops along between musical numbers. 118m. **DIR:** Norman Tokar. **CAST:** Fred MacMurray, Tommy Steele, Greer Garson, Geraldine Page, Gladys Cooper, John Davidson. **1967**

HAPPILY EVER AFTER ★★ For some unknown reason, a seemingly happy wife and mother takes off with a bisexual male prostitute in this Brazilian film. After *Dona Flor and Her Two Husbands*, director Bruno Barreto again presents a woman who seems to need two very different men in her life. In Portuguese with English subtitles. Not rated; contains nudity and simulated sex. 108m. **DIR:** Bruno Barreto. **CAST:** Regina Duarte, Paulo Castelli. **1986**

HAPPINESS ★★ This perverse *Father Knows Best* as filtered through shock cinema is dangerously ambiguous and overwrought. It tries to turn the moral sewage of a pathetic extended New Jersey family (pedophilia, rape, murder, phone sex, mutilation, stalking) into a dark comedy. Not rated; contains graphic sexual situations, profanity, and nudity. 140m. **DIR:** Todd Solondz. **CAST:** Jane Adams, Dylan Baker, Justin Elvin, Cynthia Stevenson, Lara Flynn Boyle, Jared Harris, Philip Seymour Hoffman, Elizabeth Ashley, Camryn Manheim, Ben Gazzara, Louise Lasser. **1998 DVD**

•**HAPPY ACCIDENTS** ★★★1/2 Unlucky in love, Marisa Tomei meets a man (Vincent D'Onofrio) who seems perfect in every way but one: he thinks he's a time traveler from the twenty-fifth century. The offbeat mix of science fiction and relationship comedy scores a modest bull's-eye, with clever dialogue and fine performances by Tomei, D'Onofrio, and Holland Taylor as Tomei's shrink. Rated R for profanity. 110m. **DIR:** Brad Anderson. **CAST:** Marisa Tomei, Vincent D'Onofrio, Holland Taylor, Nadia Dajani, Tovah Feldshuh. **2001**

HAPPY BIRTHDAY, GEMINI ★★ A strong play about a sexual-identity crisis becomes a weak movie when the sexuality is toned down too much. The movie doesn't need graphic sex scenes, just some intelligent dialogue so the characters can communicate with each other. The story is about a newly graduated Harvard man who thinks he may be gay. The sparkling supporting cast keeps the movie moving. Rated R. 107m. **DIR:** Richard Benner. **CAST:** Madeline Kahn, Rita Moreno, David Marshall Grant, Robert Viharo. **1980**

HAPPY BIRTHDAY TO ME ★★ After surviving a tragic car accident that killed her mother, a young woman (Melissa Sue Anderson) suffers recurrent blackouts. During these lapses of consciousness, other students at her exclusive prep school are murdered in bizarre and vicious ways. Story coherence and credibility take a backseat to all the bloodletting. Rated R. 108m. **DIR:** J. Lee Thompson. **CAST:** Melissa Sue Anderson, Glenn Ford, Matt Craven. **1981**

HAPPY GILMORE ★★ A wannabe ice hockey player can scrap with the big boys better than he can skate. He discovers he can use his power puck swat to drive golf balls record distances and tries to win enough money on the PGA Tour to save his grandmother from the IRS. The laughs are patchy and Adam Sandler's sociopathic tantrums slice wildly off course. Rated PG-13 for language and violence. 92m. **DIR:** Dennis Dugan. **CAST:** Adam Sandler, Christopher McDonald, Julie Bowen, Frances Bay, Carl Weathers. **1996 DVD**

HAPPY GO LOVELY ★★★ Perky Vera-Ellen is a dancing darling in this lightweight musical with a very tired plot about a producer who hires a chorus girl with the idea that her boyfriend has money to invest in his show. It's all cute, but nothing startling. 87m. **DIR:** H. Bruce Humberstone. **CAST:** David Niven, Vera-Ellen, Cesar Romero. **1951 DVD**

HAPPY HOOKER, THE ★★★ After Xaviera Hollander's novel became a bestseller, Lynn Redgrave was cast as Hollander in this offbeat comedy. Redgrave recounts Hollander's rise from freelance prostitute to one of New York's most infamous madams. Viewers get a peek at the kinky scenes when they play the sex-for-hire game. Rated R for nudity and sex. 96m. **DIR:** Nicholas Sgarro. **CAST:** Lynn Redgrave, Jean-Pierre Aumont, Elizabeth Wilson, Tom Poston, Lovelady Powell, Nicholas Pryor. **1975**

HAPPY HOOKER GOES HOLLYWOOD, THE ★★ If you've ever wanted to see Adam (*Batman*) West in drag, here's your chance. Lots of other people embarrass themselves as well in this comedy that certainly tries hard for laughs (though it gets very few). Rated R, but it's all talk and no action. 85m. **DIR:** Alan Roberts. **CAST:** Martine Beswick, Chris Lemmon, Adam West, Phil Silvers, Richard Deacon, Edie Adams, Dick Miller. **1980**

HAPPY HOOKER GOES TO WASHINGTON, THE 🦃 Xaviera Hollander (Joey Heatherton) is called to Washington. Rated R. 89m. **DIR:** William A. Levey. **CAST:** Joey Heatherton, George Hamilton, Ray Walston, Jack Carter. **1977**

HAPPY HOUR ★★ Blah comedy about a chemist's discovery of a secret ingredient that makes beer irre-

sistible. A lot of T&A, and a good peformance by Rich Little as a superspy, but the premise keeps the film's comedic stock low. Not rated, coarse language. 88m. **DIR:** John DeBello. **CAST:** Richard Gilliland, Jamie Farr, Tawny Kitaen, Rich Little. **1986**

HAPPY LANDING ★★★1/2 One of Sonja Henie's most popular movies, and her costars get most of the credit. Two men compete for her affections between songs, dancing, and ice-skating routines. The songs are especially good, and the singers—Don Ameche, Ethel Merman, Peters Sisters, and Condos Brothers—are outstanding. B&W; 102m. **DIR:** Roy Del Ruth. **CAST:** Sonja Henie, Don Ameche, Cesar Romero, Ethel Merman, Lon Chaney Jr., Jean Hersholt, Wally Vernon, Billy Gilbert, El Brendel, Raymond Scott. **1938**

HAPPY NEW YEAR (1973) (LA BONNE ANNÉE) ★★★★ Delightful French crime caper mixed with romance and comedy. As two thieves plot a jewel heist, one (Lino Ventura) also plans a meeting with the lovely antique dealer (Françoise Fabian) who runs the shop next door to their target. Director Claude Lelouch's film blends suspense with engaging wit. Rated PG for profanity and sex. Available in French version or dubbed. 114m. **DIR:** Claude Lelouch. **CAST:** Lino Ventura, Françoise Fabian, Charles Gerard. **1974**

HAPPY NEW YEAR (1987) ★★★1/2 Another film that was the victim of the studio system; it received only a marginal theatrical release. Peter Falk deserves to be seen in his multirole performance. He and Charles Durning are a couple of con men planning a jewel heist in Florida. (Based on Claude Lelouch's 1973 French film of the same name.) Rated PG. 86m. **DIR:** John G. Avildsen. **CAST:** Peter Falk, Charles Durning, Tom Courtenay, Wendy Hughes. **1987**

HAPPY, TEXAS ★★★1/2 Two escaped convicts pose as a gay couple traveling the rural South organizing small-town beauty pageants. Their plans to rob a bank go awry when they both fall for local women. The film is modest, easygoing, and likable, just like the town of the title, with many amusing performances—especially Steve Zahn as a dim bulb who suddenly discovers his talent for choreography. Rated PG-13 for mild profanity and violence. 98m. **DIR:** Mark Illsley. **CAST:** Jeremy Northam, Steve Zahn, Ally Walker, Illeana Douglas, William H. Macy. **1999 DVD**

HAPPY TOGETHER ★★1/2 This college romance is basically a 1990s retread of *The Sterile Cuckoo,* with Helen Slater taking a spirited whirl at the Liza Minnelli role. Slater is a charming, underrated actress, but she tries too hard—as does the film as a whole. Rated PG-13. 102m. **DIR:** Mel Damski. **CAST:** Patrick Dempsey, Helen Slater. **1990 DVD**

HARD BOILED ★★★1/2 Nobody stages gun battles better than director John Woo, whose relentless scenes of violence have a lyrical, almost poetic style. With Woo's trademark character development we get to know tough cop Chow Yun-Fat before he's sent into the eye of the storm with a renegade cop in an attempt to stop a gun-smuggling operation and find the killer who iced his partner. Explosive action and carnage ensue. Not rated; contains graphic violence and adult situations. 127m. **DIR:** John Woo. **CAST:** Chow Yun-Fat, Tony Leung Chiu Wai, Teresa Mo. **1988 DVD**

HARD BOUNTY ★★ Jim Wynorski, possibly the busiest B-movie director working today, has corralled a better-than-usual cast for this Old West tale of murder and revenge with a female attitude. Rated R for violence, language, and adult situations. 90m. **DIR:** Jim Wynorski. **CAST:** Matt McCoy, Kelly LeBrock, Rochelle Swanson. **1995 DVD**

HARD CHOICES ★★★ Independently made low-budget feature starts out as a drama about a social worker's efforts to free a boy she believes has been unjustly imprisoned. But it loses plausibility when she falls in love with him and helps him escape. Not rated; contains nudity, violence, and profanity. 90m. **DIR:** Rick King. **CAST:** Margaret Klenck, Gary McCleery, John Seitz, John Sayles, Martin Donovan, Spalding Gray. **1984**

HARD CORE LOGO ★★★★ Frolicking, high-octane pseudodocumentary in the vein of *This Is Spinal Tap*. Here, director Bruce MacDonald chronicles a last-gasp reunion of punk band Hard Core Logo. It is up to front man Joe Dick to keep the band together, but the tensions and pitfalls of life on the road soon begin to take their toll on the band and anarchy results. The cast is uniformly good, but it is Hugh Dillon who takes the spotlight as Dick. A delight. Rated R for profanity, simulated sex, violence, and substance abuse. 92m. **DIR:** Bruce McDonald. **CAST:** Hugh Dillon, Callum Keith Rennie, Terry David Mulligan. **1996 DVD**

HARD COUNTRY ★★★1/2 Though it tries to make a statement about the contemporary cowboy lost in the modern world and feminism in the boondocks, this is really just lighthearted entertainment. A rockabilly love story of the macho man (Jan-Michael Vincent) versus the liberated woman (Kim Basinger). Rated PG. 104m. **DIR:** David Greene. **CAST:** Jan-Michael Vincent, Michael Parks, Kim Basinger, Tanya Tucker, Ted Neeley, Daryl Hannah. **1981**

HARD DAY'S NIGHT, A ★★★★★ Put simply, this is the greatest rock 'n' roll comedy ever made. Scripted by Alan Owen as a sort of day in the life of the Beatles, it's fast-paced, funny, and full of great Lennon-McCartney songs. Even more than thirty years after its release, it continues to delight several generations of viewers. B&W; 85m. **DIR:** Richard Lester. **CAST:** The Beatles, Wilfred Brambell, Victor Spinetti, Anna Quayle. **1964**

HARD DRIVE ★★1/2 In this Internet thriller, Leo Damian plays a former child star now resigned to communicating to the world through his computer. He begins an E-mail affair with a mysterious woman with a kinky sexual appetite, and they decide to meet. The mystery woman ends up dead; the former child star becomes the main suspect. Some plot twists keep this high-tech thriller from crashing. Not rated; contains nudity, violence, and strong language. 92m. **DIR:** James Meredino. **CAST:** Matt McCoy, Leo Damian, Christina Fulton, Edward Albert. **1994 DVD**

HARD EIGHT ★★★1/2 Casinos and hotel and motel rooms are the key settings of this seductive character study of two love-starved gamblers and a hooker. Seasoned high roller Sydney takes homeless lug John underwing and teaches him about gambling and personal style. When an extortion scam backfires on his rather dumb new friend, Sydney intervenes. The film crackles with superb dialogue, quiet desperation, and impending tragedy. Rated R for violence, language, and sexual-

ity. 101m. **DIR:** Paul Thomas Anderson. **CAST:** Philip Baker Hall, John C. Reilly, Gwyneth Paltrow, Samuel L. Jackson. **1997 DVD**

HARD EVIDENCE ★★ Gregory Harrison stands out in this tired action film about a married man who learns that his mistress's business is drug smuggling. Before he knows it, he shoots a DEA agent in self-defense. Then his wife is dragged into the mess. Rated R for nudity, violence, and language. 100m. **DIR:** Michael Kennedy. **CAST:** Gregory Harrison, Joan Severance, Cali Timmins, Andrew Airlie. **1994**

HARD HOMBRE ★★1/2 Easygoing cowpoke who promised his mother not to fight takes a job on a beautiful señorita's ranch and is mistaken for a notorious outlaw. Lots of humor with some riding and even a tussle or two thrown in for good measure. B&W; 65m. **DIR:** Otto Brower. **CAST:** Hoot Gibson, Lina Basquette, Skeeter Bill Robbins, Mathilde Comont, Jesse Arnold, Raymond Nye. **1931**

HARD JUSTICE ★★ Despite Greg Yaitanes's stylish direction, this tale of a cop who goes undercover in a prison to avenge his partner's death is just another mindless exercise in nonstop action. No surprises here. Rated R for strong violence and adult language. 95m. **DIR:** Greg Yaitanes. **CAST:** David Bradley, Charles Napier, Yuji Okumoto. **1995**

HARD PROMISES ★★★ A woman divorces her husband while he is away on a twelve-year trip, only to have him turn up right before she remarries. Rated PG for profanity. 95m. **DIR:** Martin Davidson. **CAST:** Sissy Spacek, William L. Petersen, Brian Kerwin, Mare Winningham, Jeff Perry. **1991**

HARD RAIN ★★ This shallow disaster-heist flick is not convincingly written or acted. A security guard is accosted by bandits when his armored car becomes stuck in a flooded small Midwestern town that is threatened by possible collapse of a nearby dam. The guard takes his $3 million cargo and sloshes into the night with a way-too-nice villain and his white-trash cronies pursuing on Jet-Skis and in motorboats. Rated R for language and violence. 98m. **DIR:** Mikael Salomon. **CAST:** Christian Slater, Morgan Freeman, Minnie Driver, Randy Quaid, Betty White. **1998 DVD**

HARD ROCK NIGHTMARE 🦃 Is a werewolf responsible for killing the members of a heavy metal band? Not rated; contains violence and brief nudity. 89m. **DIR:** Dominick Brascia. **CAST:** Martin Hansen, Gregory Joujon-Roche, Troy Donahue. **1989**

HARD ROCK ZOMBIES ★★1/2 The title pretty much says it all: After being murdered while on the road, the members of a heavy-metal band are brought back from the dead as zombies. Amusing in a goofy way, though shoddy special-effects makeup brings it down a notch. Rated R for violence and gore. 94m. **DIR:** Krishna Shah. **CAST:** E. J. Curcio, Sam Mann. **1985**

HARD TARGET ★★★1/2 For his first American film, Hong Kong film legend John Woo delivers an action movie that will please both fans of the genre and serious film buffs. Vietnam veteran Jean-Claude Van Damme comes up against bloodthirsty millionaires whose ultimate thrill is to hunt human game. Reminiscent of Walter Hill's earlier films—*The Driver*, for example—this thriller is somewhat short on character development, but for nonstop excitement it has few peers. Rated R for extreme violence and profanity. 92m. **DIR:** John Woo. **CAST:** Jean-Claude Van Damme, Lance Henriksen, Yancy Butler, Wilford Brimley, Arnold Vosloo, Kasi Lemmons. **1993 DVD**

HARD TICKET TO HAWAII 🦃 Drug enforcement in Hawaii. Rated R for plentiful nudity and sexual situations. 96m. **DIR:** Andy Sidaris. **CAST:** Dona Speir, Hope Marie Carlton, Ronn Moss. **1987 DVD**

HARD TIME ★★★ Talk about retro! Burt Reynolds returns to his favorite role: the tough-talking, world-weary investigator who never plays by the rules. This time he's a Florida cop framed for a murder he didn't commit. Mia Sara is laughably miscast as the attorney who agrees to defend our hero. Reynolds remains watchable but it's a shame to see him return to this fluff after proving his greater capabilities in *Boogie Nights*. Rated PG-13 for violence and drug use. 95m. **DIR:** Burt Reynolds. **CAST:** Burt Reynolds, Charles Durning, Mia Sara, Billy Dee Williams, Robert Loggia, Michael Buie. **1998**

HARD TIMES ★★★★1/2 This release is far and away one of Charles Bronson's best starring vehicles. In it he plays a bare-knuckles fighter who teams up with a couple of hustlers, James Coburn and Strother Martin, to "sting" some local hoods. Bronson's wife, Jill Ireland, is surprisingly good as the love interest. Rated PG. 97m. **DIR:** Walter Hill. **CAST:** Charles Bronson, James Coburn, Jill Ireland, Strother Martin. **1975 DVD**

HARD TO DIE 🦃 "Hard to watch" is a more appropriate title for this silly slashfest. Five girls taking inventory don sexy lingerie then become victims. Pictures on video box include two women who weren't even in the film. Rated R for nudity, profanity, violence, and gore. 81m. **DIR:** Jim Wynorski. **CAST:** Orville Ketchum, Robyn Harris, Melissa Moore, Debra Dare, Forrest J. Ackerman, Lindsay Taylor. **1990**

HARD TO HOLD ★★ In this highly forgettable film, Rick Springfield plays a music superstar who has everything except the woman (Janet Eilber) he loves. The first half hour is quite good, but from there it goes downhill into soap opera. Rated PG for brief nudity and profanity. 93m. **DIR:** Larry Peerce. **CAST:** Rick Springfield, Janet Eilber, Patti Hansen, Albert Salmi. **1984**

HARD TO KILL ★★★1/2 Solid action film stars martial arts expert Steve Seagal as an honest cop who falls prey to corruption. Crisply directed by Bruce Malmuth, this is a definite cut above most movies in its genre. Rated R for violence, profanity, and nudity. 95m. **DIR:** Bruce Malmuth. **CAST:** Steven Seagal, Kelly LeBrock. **1990 DVD**

HARD TRAVELING ★★ California, 1940. A struggling farm couple battle the odds to survive. Slow-moving saga. Rated PG. 99m. **DIR:** Dan Bessie. **CAST:** J. E. Freeman, Ellen Geer, Barry Corbin. **1985**

HARD TRUTH ★★★ Cop Michael Rooker and safecracker Eric Roberts team up to intercept a mob cash payment being made to a city councilman. But who is double-crossing whom, and who will get the girl (Lysette Anthony) both want? Better-than-average video thriller, with a plot that keeps you guessing right up to the end. Not rated; contains violence, nudity, sexual situations, and profanity. 100m. **DIR:** Kristine Peterson. **CAST:** Eric Roberts, Michael Rooker, Lysette Anthony, Ray Baker. **1994**

HARD WAY, THE (1942) ★★★★ Ida Lupino proved she could carry the whole show as a disgruntled woman who hates her life and wants to make sure her sister has a better one. She manipulates her sister's life and destroys just about everyone else around them. Hardcore melodrama and exceptionally good. B&W; 108m. **DIR:** Vincent Sherman. **CAST:** Ida Lupino, Joan Leslie, Dennis Morgan, Jack Carson, Roman Bohnen, Faye Emerson, Gladys George, Julie Bishop. **1942**

HARD WAY, THE (1979) ★★ Patrick McGoohan is an international terrorist who wants out of the business. Unfortunately for him, a former associate (Lee Van Cleef) wants him to do one more job and will have him killed if he doesn't. 88m. **DIR:** Michael Dryhurst. **CAST:** Patrick McGoohan, Lee Van Cleef, Donal McCann, Edna O'Brien. **1979**

HARD WAY, THE (1991) ★★★1/2 Formulaic buddy movie about a movie star attempting to research a cop role by hanging out with the real thing. Engaging performances by Michael J. Fox and James Woods. Rated R for profanity and violence. 95m. **DIR:** John Badham. **CAST:** Michael J. Fox, James Woods, Penny Marshall, Stephen Lang, Annabella Sciorra. **1991 DVD**

•HARDBALL ★★★1/2 This hard-edged little drama deserves plenty of credit for avoiding the light comedy and fairy-tale conclusions by which underdog sports sagas usually are known, and would deserve an even higher rating were it not for Keanu Reeves's wooden (as usual) performance in the lead role. He's a scruffy, self-destructive gambler who, in exchange for having a debt paid off, is forced to coach an inner-city Chicago Little League team. The story works just fine when it concentrates on Reeves's efforts to bond with his young players; a sidebar relationship involving Diane Lane is less successful. Don't pick this up expecting only sweetness and light; it could traumatize younger children. Rated PG-13 for profanity, violence, and dramatic intensity. 106m. **DIR:** Brian Robbins. **CAST:** Keanu Reeves, Diane Lane, John Hawkes, D. B. Sweeney, Mike McGlone, Graham Beckel. **2001 DVD**

HARDCORE ★★ This film stars George C. Scott as Jake Van Dorn, whose family leads a church-oriented life in their home in Grand Rapids, Michigan. When the church sponsors a youth trip to California, Van Dorn's daughter Kristen (Ilah Davis) is allowed to go. She disappears, so Van Dorn goes to Los Angeles and learns she's now making porno flicks. *Hardcore* is rated R, but is closer to an X. 108m. **DIR:** Paul Schrader. **CAST:** George C. Scott, Peter Boyle, Season Hubley, Dick Sargent, Ilah Davis. **1979**

HARDER THEY COME, THE ★★★★ Made in Jamaica by Jamaicans, this film has become an underground cult classic. In it, a rural boy comes to the big city to become a singer. There, he is forced into a life of crime. Rated R. 98m. **DIR:** Perry Henzell. **CAST:** Jimmy Cliff, Janet Barkley. **1973**

HARDER THEY FALL, THE ★★★1/2 This boxing drama is as mean and brutal as they come. A gentle giant is built up, set up, and brought down by a collection of human vultures while sportswriter Humphrey Bogart flip-flops on the moral issues. The ring photography is spectacular. Don't expect anything like *Rocky*. B&W; 109m. **DIR:** Mark Robson. **CAST:** Humphrey Bogart, Rod Steiger, Jan Sterling, Mike Lane, Max Baer, Jersey Joe Walcott. **1956**

HARDHAT AND LEGS ★★★ The scene is New York City. Kevin Dobson is a horseplaying Italian construction worker who whistles at nice gams. Sharon Gless is democratic upper class. The twain meet, and sparks fly. It's all cheerful and upbeat and works because of first-rate acting. Made for television. 104m. **DIR:** Lee Philips. **CAST:** Kevin Dobson, Sharon Gless. **1980**

HARDLY WORKING ★★ Jerry Lewis's 1980s screen comeback is passable family fare. As a middle-aged, out-of-work clown, he tries his hand at a number of jobs and flubs them all. His fans will love it; others need not apply. Rated PG. 91m. **DIR:** Jerry Lewis. **CAST:** Jerry Lewis, Susan Oliver, Roger C. Carmel, Deanna Lund, Harold J. Stone, Steve Franken. **1981**

HARDWARE A post-apocalypse salvage expert gives the remains of a robot to his lady friend unaware that the mechanical creature was programmed to kill humans. Rated R for violence, gore, nudity, and profanity. 95m. **DIR:** Richard Stanley. **CAST:** Dylan McDermott, Stacey Travis, John Lynch, Iggy Pop. **1990**

HAREM ★★★1/2 Nastassja Kinski is a stockbroker who is abducted by a wealthy OPEC oil minister (Ben Kingsley) and becomes a part of his harem. A bittersweet tale of a lonely dreamer and his passion for a modern woman. Not rated, but has violence, profanity, and nudity. 107m. **DIR:** Arthur Joffe. **CAST:** Nastassja Kinski, Ben Kingsley, Robbin Zohra Segal. **1985**

HARLAN COUNTY, U.S.A. ★★★★1/2 This Oscar-winning documentary concerning Kentucky coal miners is both tragic and riveting. Its gripping scenes draw the audience into the world of miners and their families. Superior from start to finish. Rated PG. 103m. **DIR:** Barbara Kopple. **1977**

HARLAN COUNTY WAR ★★★1/2 Holly Hunter was nominated for a Golden Globe for her performance as a coal miner's wife in this fact-based, made-for-cable original. It is 1973, and coal miners are still living in houses without plumbing, and still dying from black lung. They decide it's high time to form a union, but the owners and managers do their best to resist. Good acting and a good script carry most of the film, but it's ordinary in every other way. Not rated; contains profanity, violence, and brief nudity. 103m. **DIR:** Tony Bill. **CAST:** Holly Hunter, Stellan Skarsgard, Ted Levine, Wayne Robson. **2000 DVD**

HARLEM NIGHTS ★★★ This gangster movie has taken a tremendous critical bashing, but we found it enjoyable. Not only has writer-producer-director-star Eddie Murphy created an old-fashioned melodrama that, save for the continuous profanity, could just as easily have starred Humphrey Bogart or James Cagney but he has given fine roles to some of the industry's finest black performers. Rated R for profanity, violence, and suggested sex. 119m. **DIR:** Eddie Murphy. **CAST:** Eddie Murphy, Richard Pryor, Redd Foxx, Danny Aiello, Michael Lerner, Della Reese, Stan Shaw, Arsenio Hall. **1989 DVD**

HARLEM RIDES THE RANGE ★★1/2 Stale plot about stolen mine rights (to a radium mine this time) is secondary to the limited action and uniqueness of seeing an all-black cast in what had traditionally been the territory of white actors and actresses. B&W; 58m. **DIR:**

Richard Kahn. **CAST:** Herbert Jeffrey, Lucius Brooks. **1939**

HARLEY ★★★ Lou Diamond Phillips stars as Harley, an L.A. motorcycle hood who gets sent to a Texas ranch instead of a juvenile detention center. Good family film. Rated PG. 80m. **DIR:** Fred Holmes. **CAST:** Lou Diamond Phillips. **1985**

HARLEY DAVIDSON AND THE MARLBORO MAN ★★ Mickey Rourke is the hog-riding hero, Don Johnson the cowboy in 1996, when a drug called Crystal Dream is killing addicts by the thousands. So our heroes go to war with the pushers. It's hard to believe that the director who helmed the exquisite *Lonesome Dove* was responsible for this post-apocalyptic hogwash. Rated R for violence, profanity, and nudity. 98m. **DIR:** Simon Wincer. **CAST:** Mickey Rourke, Don Johnson, Chelsea Field, Giancarlo Esposito, Vanessa L. Williams, Julius W. Harris, Robert Ginty, Daniel Baldwin. **1991 DVD**

HARLOW ★★ One of two films made in 1965 that dealt with the life of the late film star and sex goddess Jean Harlow. Carroll Baker simply is not the actress to play Harlow, and the whole thing is a trashy mess. 125m. **DIR:** Gordon Douglas. **CAST:** Carroll Baker, Peter Lawford, Red Buttons, Mike Connors, Raf Vallone, Angela Lansbury, Martin Balsam, Leslie Nielsen. **1965**

HARMONISTS, THE ★★★1/2 As persecution in Hitler-era Europe spreads, the Comedian Harmonists—five Berlin singers and their pianist—were scrutinized by the Nazis for including Jews in their group. This fascinating musical biography about love, tolerance, patriotism, mass denial, and the tentacles of bigotry is both sweeping and intimate. In German with English subtitles. Rated R for brief nudity. 115m. **DIR:** Joseph Vilsmaier. **CAST:** Aldrich Noethen, Ben Becker, Meret Becker, Heino Firch, Heinrich Schafmeister, Max Tidof. **1999**

HARMONY CATS ★★ Mediocre morality play about an out-of-work symphony violinist who, as a last resort, teams up with a country and western group. Obviously out of his league, Jim Byrnes begins to get into the swing of things. Hee-haw! Not rated; contains strong language and adult situations. 104m. **DIR:** Sandy Wilson. **CAST:** Kim Coates, Jim Byrnes, Lisa Brokop. **1993**

HARMONY LANE ★★ Only the music saves this half-hearted account of composer Stephen Foster's tragic life from being classed a turkey. The sets are shoddy, the camera rarely moves, most of the acting is insipid, and the screenplay is one long string of music cues. B&W; 89m. **DIR:** Joseph Santley. **CAST:** Douglass Montgomery, Evelyn Venable, Adrienne Ames, William Frawley. **1935**

HAROLD AND MAUDE ★★★★★ Hal Ashby directed this delightful black comedy about an odd young man named Harold (Bud Cort) who devises some rather elaborate fake deaths to jar his snooty, manipulative mother (Vivian Pickles). Soon his attention turns to an octogenarian named Maude (Ruth Gordon), with whom he falls in love. Featuring a superb soundtrack of songs by Cat Stevens, this is one of the original cult classics—and deservedly so. Rated PG. 90m. **DIR:** Hal Ashby. **CAST:** Bud Cort, Vivian Pickles, Ruth Gordon, Cyril Cusack, Charles Tyner, Ellen Geer. **1972 DVD**

HAROLD LLOYD'S COMEDY CLASSICS ★★★ This nostalgic retrospective combines four of Harold Lloyd's prestardom shorts: *The Chef*, *The Cinema Director*, *Two Gun Gussie*, and *I'm On My Way*. Silent with musical score. Compiled after Lloyd's death. B&W; 47m. **DIR:** Harold Lloyd. **CAST:** Harold Lloyd, Bebe Daniels, Snub Pollard. **1919**

HARPER ★★★★1/2 Ross MacDonald's detective, Lew Archer, undergoes a name change but still survives as a memorable screen character in the capable hands of Paul Newman. This one ranks right up there with *The Maltese Falcon*, *The Big Sleep* (the Humphrey Bogart version), *Farewell My Lovely*, and *The Long Goodbye* as one of the best of its type. 121m. **DIR:** Jack Smight. **CAST:** Paul Newman, Lauren Bacall, Shelley Winters, Arthur Hill, Julie Harris, Janet Leigh, Robert Wagner. **1966**

HARPER VALLEY P.T.A. ★★ Based on the popular country song, this silly piece of fluff features Barbara Eden as the sexy woman who gives her gossiping neighbors their proper comeuppance. Rated PG. 102m. **DIR:** Richard Bennett. **CAST:** Barbara Eden, Ronny Cox, Nanette Fabray, Susan Swift, Ron Masak. **1978**

HARRAD EXPERIMENT, THE ★★ Uninvolving adaptation of Robert Rimmer's well-intentioned bestseller about an experimental college that makes sexual freedom the primary curriculum. The film is attractive as a novelty item because of erotic scenes between Don Johnson and Laurie Walters. Rated R. 88m. **DIR:** Ted Post. **CAST:** Don Johnson, James Whitmore, Tippi Hedren, Bruno Kirby, Laurie Walters. **1973**

HARRIET THE SPY ★★ Nickelodeon's maiden theatrical release disappoints by gearing itself directly to 10 year olds rather than to general audiences. That said, it does make some points about being different and how parents need to be actively involved in their children's lives. The sixth-grade sleuth follows her nanny's (Rosie O'Donnell) advice, writing down everything she sees and thinks. When her private notebook is exposed she must face the ostracism of her peers. Rated PG for cruelty. 97m. **DIR:** Bronwen Hughes. **CAST:** Michelle Trachtenberg, Rosie O'Donnell, Vanessa Lee Chester, Gregory Edward Smith, Eartha Kitt, J. Smith-Cameron. **1996**

HARRISON BERGERON ★★★1/2 Although it owes as much to C. M. Kornbluth's "The Marching Morons" as to Kurt Vonnegut's original short story, this intriguing thriller says a lot about the perils of enforced conformity. Sean Astin stars as a futuristic kid whose congenital intelligence cannot be suppressed by the gadgets all people wear to be "truly equal." Rated R for violence, profanity, simulated sex, and graphic newsreel footage. 99m. **DIR:** Bruce Pittman. **CAST:** Sean Astin, Miranda de Pencier, Christopher Plummer, Buck Henry, Eugene Levy, Howie Mandel, Andrea Martin. **1995**

•HARRISON'S FLOWERS ★★1/2 A loyal wife rushes to war-torn Yugoslavia, where her photojournalist husband is missing and presumed dead. Some superbly horrific scenes of the warfare in the Balkans in the early 1990s vie with a farfetched story and uninteresting characters; the film is obviously modeled on *The Killing Fields*, but is much less compelling. Rated R for war violence and profanity. 102m. **DIR:** Elie Chouraqui. **CAST:** Andie MacDowell, Elias Koteas, Brendan Gleeson, Adrien Brody, David Strathairn. **2000**

HARRY AND SON ★★★ A widower (Paul Newman) can land a wrecking ball on a dime but can't seem to make contact with his artistically inclined son, Howard (Robby Benson), in this superb character study. Directed, coproduced, and cowritten by Newman, it's sort of a male *Terms of Endearment*. Rated PG for nudity and profanity. 117m. **DIR:** Paul Newman. **CAST:** Paul Newman, Robby Benson, Joanne Woodward, Ellen Barkin, Ossie Davis, Wilford Brimley. **1984**

HARRY AND THE HENDERSONS ★★★ A shaggy *E.T.* story, this focuses on the plight of a family (headed by John Lithgow and Melinda Dillon) that just happens to run into Bigfoot one day. It's silly, outrageously sentimental, and a gentle poke in the ribs of Steven Spielberg, whose Amblin Productions financed the film. Rated PG for profanity and violence. 110m. **DIR:** William Dear. **CAST:** John Lithgow, Melinda Dillon, Don Ameche, Lainie Kazan, David Suchet. **1987**

HARRY AND TONTO ★★★★ Art Carney won an Oscar for his tour-de-force performance in this character study, directed by Paul Mazursky. In a role that's a far cry from his Ed Norton on Jackie Gleason's *The Honeymooners*, the star plays an older gentleman who, with his cat, takes a cross-country trip and lives life to the fullest. Rated R. 115m. **DIR:** Paul Mazursky. **CAST:** Art Carney, Ellen Burstyn, Chief Dan George, Geraldine Fitzgerald, Larry Hagman, Arthur Hunnicutt. **1974**

HARRY AND WALTER GO TO NEW YORK ★★1/2 James Caan and Elliott Gould appear to be having the time of their lives portraying two inept con men. Michael Caine and Diane Keaton are, as always, excellent. *Harry and Walter* is sort of like Chinese food—an hour later, you feel as if you haven't had anything. Rated PG. 123m. **DIR:** Mark Rydell. **CAST:** James Caan, Elliott Gould, Michael Caine, Diane Keaton, Charles Durning. **1976**

•HARRY POTTER AND THE SORCERER'S STONE ★★★★ A young orphan, Harry Potter, is rescued from the taunts and humiliation of his cruel relatives when he is sought out by the Hogwarts School of Witchcraft and Wizardry and discovers he is the son of two legendary conjurers who were the victims of the evil Lord Voldemort. He spends time in between classes seeking out the ancient artifact of the title while becoming aware that great things are expected of him and that his parents' killer is his nemesis as well. The film renders faithfully J. K. Rowling's book, a tactic that only occasionally works against the film, particularly in a supernatural sports match that plays more like a display of screen magic than a test of our young hero's courage. The three charming young leads get support from a superb cast of veterans. Be forewarned: Although based on a popular series of children's books, the movie may be too frightening for impressionable youngsters. Rated PG for scary stuff and language. 152m. **DIR:** Chris Columbus. **CAST:** Daniel Radcliffe, Rupert Grint, Emma Watson, Robbie Coltrane, Richard Harris, Maggie Smith, Alan Rickman, Tom Felton, Matthew Lewis, John Hurt, Ian Hart, Fiona Shaw, Richard Griffiths. **2001 DVD**

HARRY TRACY ★★★1/2 Bruce Dern plays the title role in this surprisingly amiable little Western, with the star as the last of a gentlemanly outlaw breed. Although he's a crafty character, Harry always seems to get caught. His mind is all too often on other things—in particular, a well-to-do woman (Helen Shaver). Rated PG. 100m. **DIR:** William A. Graham. **CAST:** Bruce Dern, Helen Shaver, Michael C. Gwynne, Gordon Lightfoot. **1982**

HARRY'S WAR ★★ In this cornball comedy, Harry Johnson (Edward Herrmann) takes on the Internal Revenue Service, which made a mistake on his return. Rated PG. 98m. **DIR:** Kieth Merrill. **CAST:** Edward Herrmann, Geraldine Page, Karen Grassle, David Ogden Stiers, Salome Jens, Elisha Cook Jr. **1981**

•HART'S WAR ★★1/2 Stone-cold stoic Bruce Willis pretty much destroys this somber, unsatisfying blend of *Stalag 17* and *The Great Escape*, which starts off like a WWII prisoner-of-war drama and then turns into a courtroom mystery. Neither genre is handled well, because director Gregory Hoblit never takes the time or trouble to make characters out of all these faceless Allied prisoners. You know that something's seriously wrong in a picture of this nature when the only interesting individual is the German camp commander. Rated R for violence and profanity. 123m. **DIR:** Gregory Hoblit. **CAST:** Bruce Willis, Colin Farrell, Terrence Howard, Cole Hauser, Marcel Iures, Linus Roache. **2002 DVD**

HARUM SCARUM ★★★ When a swashbuckling film star (Elvis Presley) visits a primitive Arabian country, he is forced to aid assassins in their bid to destroy the king. Simultaneously, he falls in love with the king's beautiful daughter (Mary Ann Mobley). Elvis manages to belt out nine tunes, including "Shake That Tambourine" and "Harem Holiday." His fans won't be disappointed. 85m. **DIR:** Gene Nelson. **CAST:** Elvis Presley, Mary Ann Mobley, Michael Ansara, Billy Barty. **1965**

HARVEST (1937) ★★★★ Simple but touching story of a man and woman struggling to survive in a deserted village. One of the great director's best loved films, though it does drag on a bit too long. In French with English subtitles. B&W; 129m. **DIR:** Marcel Pagnol. **CAST:** Gabriel Gabrio, Fernandel, Orane Demazis. **1937**

HARVEST, THE (1992) ★★1/2 While in Mexico investigating a series of killings, screenwriter Miguel Ferrer is abducted and drugged. When he awakens he finds out that one of his kidneys has been removed. Now black-market organ dealers want his second kidney. Interesting idea gets only a modicum of suspense from writer-director David Marconi, while familiar faces do their best to flesh out the background. Rated R for violence and language. 97m. **DIR:** David Marconi. **CAST:** Miguel Ferrer, Harvey Fierstein, Leilani Sarelle, Anthony Denison, Tim Thomerson, Henry Silva. **1992**

HARVEST OF FIRE ★★★1/2 A series of barn burnings, presumed to be hate crimes against the Amish in Iowa, brings a modern FBI agent into the Mennonite world in this moving *Hallmark Hall of Fame* production. An Amish widow opens her home and insights to the agent. More than a good mystery, this is a relationship film in which the two women find common ground. Compelling viewing on an enlightening topic. Made-for-TV, this is not rated, but contains violence. 90m. **DIR:** Arthur Allan Seidelman. **CAST:** Patty Duke, Lolita Davidovich, J. A. Preston, Jean Louisa Kelly, Eric Mabius, James Read. **1996**

HARVEY ★★★★1/2 James Stewart has one of his best screen roles as Elwood P. Dowd, a delightful drunk

whose companion is a six-foot rabbit named Harvey. Josephine Hull is the concerned relative who wants Elwood committed to a mental institution, and Cecil Kellaway is the psychiatrist who discovers there's more magic than madness to our hero's illusion. B&W; 104m. **DIR:** Henry Koster. **CAST:** James Stewart, Josephine Hull, Peggy Dow, Charles Drake, Cecil Kellaway. **1950 DVD**

HARVEY GIRLS, THE ★★★ Rousing fun marks this big, bustling musical, which is loosely tied to the development of pioneer railroad-station restaurateur Fred Harvey's string of eateries along the Santa Fe right-of-way. Judy Garland is the innocent who goes west to grow up, Angela Lansbury is the wise bad girl, and John Hodiak is the requisite gambler. 102m. **DIR:** George Sidney. **CAST:** Judy Garland, John Hodiak, Ray Bolger, Preston Foster, Virginia O'Brien, Angela Lansbury, Marjorie Main, Chill Wills, Cyd Charisse, Kenny Baker. **1945 DVD**

HASTY HEART ★★★1/2 Made for Showtime pay cable, this version of the 1949 movie with Ronald Reagan is corny as all get-out, but is still pretty effective. In an army hospital in Burma during WWII, a proud Scottish soldier (Gregory Harrison) doesn't know that he has only a few weeks to live. He refuses to accept the hospitality of the other soldiers in the ward, all of whom know of his approaching death. Get out your handkerchiefs! 135m. **DIR:** Martin Speer. **CAST:** Gregory Harrison, Cheryl Ladd, Perry King. **1983**

HATARI! ★★★ If only Howard Hawks had been able to do as he wanted and cast Clark Gable along with John Wayne in this story of zoo-supplying animal hunters in Africa, this could have been a great film. As it is, it's still enjoyable, with a fine blend of action, romance, and comedy. 159m. **DIR:** Howard Hawks. **CAST:** John Wayne, Elsa Martinelli, Red Buttons, Hardy Kruger. **1962 DVD**

HATBOX MYSTERY, THE ★★ In a scant 44 minutes private detective Tom Neal saves his secretary from prison, brings the guilty party to bay, and still has time to explain just what happened. Not great but a real curio, perhaps the shortest detective film ever sold as a feature. B&W; 44m. **DIR:** Lambert Hillyer. **CAST:** Tom Neal, Pamela Blake, Allen Jenkins, Virginia Sale. **1947**

HATE ★★★★1/2 Three youths of diverse backgrounds team up to fight gangs and police in the Paris suburbs. When one friend ends up in the hospital thanks to police brutality, another takes the law into his own hands and cements the destiny of all three. Gritty and unrelenting, the film packs quite a punch. In French with English subtitles. Not rated; contains violence and profanity. 95m. **DIR:** Mathieu Kassovitz. **CAST:** Vincent Cassel, Hubert Kounde, Said Taghmaoui. **1995**

HATFIELDS AND THE MCCOYS, THE ★★1/2 The great American legend of backwoods feuding long celebrated in song and story. Jack Palance and Steve Forrest make the most of portraying the clan patriarchs. The feud was reason enough to leave the hills and head west in the 1880s. Made for TV. 74m. **DIR:** Clyde Ware. **CAST:** Jack Palance, Steve Forrest, Richard Hatch, Joan Caulfield. **1975**

HAUNTED ★★★★ Aidan Quinn is a renowned debunker of spirit mediums and ghost stories who travels to a remote British estate at the request of a terrified elderly woman. Nothing is what it seems, but you probably won't be able to figure out the mystery before he does. Set in the Roaring Twenties, this beautifully shot adaptation of James Herbert's novel is rife with a sexuality and horror underscored by subtle direction. Rated R for nudity, sexual situations, and adult themes. 107m. **DIR:** Lewis Gilbert. **CAST:** Aidan Quinn, Kate Beckinsale, Anthony Andrews, John Gielgud, Anna Massey, Victoria Shalet. **1995 DVD**

HAUNTED CASTLE ★★★ Based on the novel by Rudolf Stratz, this complex chiller takes place in a northern German castle shrouded in a mysterious, haunting atmosphere. Great cinematography and set design make for an impressive spectacle. Silent. B&W; 56m. **DIR:** F. W. Murnau. **CAST:** Paul Hartmann, Olga Tschechowa. **1921**

HAUNTED GOLD ★★★1/2 John Wayne gives one of his best early performances in this enjoyable Warner Bros. B Western, in which a gold mine is haunted by a mysterious figure known as "The Phantom." Wayne and his saddle pal, Blue Washington, ride to the rescue of Sheila Terry, who is threatened by both the spooky villain and a gang of outlaws led by veteran heavy Harry Woods. An effective mix of genres. B&W; 58m. **DIR:** Mack V. Wright. **CAST:** John Wayne, Sheila Terry, Harry Woods, Erville Anderson, Otto Hoffman, Martha Mattox, Blue Washington, Slim Whitaker. **1932**

HAUNTED HONEYMOON Limp chiller spoof. Rated PG. 90m. **DIR:** Gene Wilder. **CAST:** Gene Wilder, Gilda Radner, Dom DeLuise, Jonathan Pryce, Paul Smith, Peter Vaughan. **1986 DVD**

HAUNTED PALACE, THE ★★★1/2 Although the title of this horror film, one of the best in a series of American-International Pictures releases directed by Roger Corman, was taken from a poem by Edgar Allan Poe; Charles Beaumont's screenplay was based on a story, "The Case of Charles Dexter Ward," written by H. P. Lovecraft. It's better than average Corman, with Vincent Price nicely subdued as the descendant of an ancient warlock. 85m. **DIR:** Roger Corman. **CAST:** Vincent Price, Debra Paget, Lon Chaney Jr., Elisha Cook Jr., Leo Gordon. **1963**

HAUNTED SEA, THE ★★ When a sea captain and his crew come across a deserted ship carrying Aztec treasure, they think their ship has come in. Unfortunately, the treasure is being guarded by an ancient creature that doesn't take kindly to looters. Silliness on the high seas. Rated R for language and violence. 73m. **DIR:** Daniel Patrick. **CAST:** Joanna Pacula, Krista Allen, James Brolin. **1997**

HAUNTED STRANGLER, THE ★★★1/2 Boris Karloff is well cast in this effective story of a writer who develops the homicidal tendencies of a long-dead killer he's been writing about. Gripping horror film. B&W; 81m. **DIR:** Robert Day. **CAST:** Boris Karloff, Anthony Dawson, Elizabeth Allan. **1958 DVD**

HAUNTED SUMMER ★★ Though visually stunning, this story of the meeting between Lord Byron and Percy Shelley (that eventually led to Mary Shelley's tale *Frankenstein*) is just too weird to be taken seriously. Full of sexual innuendo and drug-induced tripping, this is definitely one for fans of period pieces only. Rated R. 106m. **DIR:** Ivan Passer. **CAST:** Philip Anglim, Laura Dern, Alice Krige, Eric Stoltz, Alex Winter. **1988**

HAUNTING, THE (1963) ★★★★ Long considered one of the most masterly crafted tales of terror ever brought to the screen, this gripping triumph for Robert Wise still packs a punch. Julie Harris and Claire Bloom are outstanding as they recognize and finally confront the evil that inhabits a haunted house. Based on Shirley Jackson's classic *The Haunting of Hill House*. B&W; 112m. **DIR:** Robert Wise. **CAST:** Julie Harris, Claire Bloom, Richard Johnson, Russ Tamblyn, Fay Compton, Lois Maxwell. **1963**

HAUNTING, THE (1999) ★★★ Scientist Liam Neeson lures three insomniacs to a haunted house under the pretense of studying sleep deprivation when he's actually testing reactions to fear. Forget Robert Wise's classic film and Shirley Jackson's gripping, original story—both of which allowed the viewer to imagine the terror—and you may get a few thrills out of this blatant, special-effects-laden scarefest. Rated PG-13 for scary stuff and mild profanity. 113m. **DIR:** Jan De Bont. **CAST:** Liam Neeson, Catherine Zeta-Jones, Lili Taylor, Owen Wilson, Bruce Dern. **1999 DVD**

HAUNTING OF JULIA, THE ★★ A vague, confused story of a young mother whose daughter chokes to death. In this otherwise pedestrian film there are sporadic spots of quality, mostly in Tom Conti's scenes. Rated R for profanity. 96m. **DIR:** Richard Loncraine. **CAST:** Mia Farrow, Keir Dullea, Tom Conti. **1981**

HAUNTING OF MORELLA, THE 🦃 Bad acting and directing help to mutilate this movie in which a mother's curse is placed upon her baby daughter. Rated R for violence and nudity. 82m. **DIR:** Jim Wynorski. **CAST:** David McCallum, Nicole Eggert, Christopher Halsted. **1989**

HAUNTING OF SARAH HARDY, THE ★★★ A suspense story of a recently married heiress who returns to her estate after a fifteen-year absence. Fairly standard TV film. 92m. **DIR:** Jerry London. **CAST:** Sela Ward, Michael Woods, Roscoe Born, Morgan Fairchild, Polly Bergen. **1989**

HAUNTING OF SEA CLIFF INN, THE ★★1/2 A not-very-scary, made-for-cable original about a husband and wife who buy an old Victorian and start to convert it into a bed and breakfast, only to discover the house is haunted. Passable acting, but not much plot. Rated PG-13 for violence. 94m. **DIR:** Walter Klenhard. **CAST:** Ally Sheedy, William R. Moses, Louise Fletcher, Lucinda Weist, Tom McCleister. **1994**

HAUNTING PASSION, THE ★★ An uneven made-for-TV supernatural romance in which a ghost seduces housewife Jane Seymour. There are a few chills, but more often than not, it falls short of the mark. 98m. **DIR:** John Korty. **CAST:** Jane Seymour, Gerald McRaney, Millie Perkins, Ruth Nelson. **1983 DVD**

HAUNTS OF THE VERY RICH ★★ This TV movie brings together a handful of people who have had close calls with death. It's sort of a low-quality *Twilight Zone* version of *Fantasy Island*. 72m. **DIR:** Paul Wendkos. **CAST:** Lloyd Bridges, Donna Mills, Edward Asner, Cloris Leachman, Anne Francis, Tony Bill, Robert Reed, Moses Gunn. **1972**

HAV PLENTY ★★★ Lee Plenty is an aspiring novelist who comes to terms with his relationship with haughty New York businesswoman Havilland Savage. This profanity-laced visit with upwardly mobile African-American professionals begins clumsily before establishing a fresh, seductive comic charm. Rated R for profanity. 91m. **DIR:** Christopher Scott Cherot. **CAST:** Christopher Scott Cherot, Chenoa Maxwell, Tammi Jones, Robinne Lee, Reginald James. **1998 DVD**

HAVANA ★★ Despite a very promising and involving first hour, this *Casablanca*, Cuban style, bogs down in political polemics and a predictable plot as out-for-himself gambler Robert Redford finds himself falling in love with a politically involved widow (Lena Olin). Rated R for profanity, violence, and nudity. 130m. **DIR:** Sydney Pollack. **CAST:** Robert Redford, Lena Olin, Alan Arkin, Raul Julia, Tomas Milian, Tony Plana. **1990 DVD**

HAVE A NICE FUNERAL ★★★ Is Sartana a ghost or a magician? Whatever, he's an avenging angel who goes after an evil banker and his devious daughter. An over-the-top performance by John Garko makes this one of the best of the Sartana series. Not rated; contains violence. 90m. **DIR:** Anthony Ascot. **CAST:** John Garko, Antonio Vilar, Daniela Giordana, George Wang, Frank Ressel, Franco Pesce. **1971**

HAVE GUN, WILL TRAVEL (TV SERIES) ★★★★ One of the most popular TV Westerns of its day, this excellent series has been out of the public eye for nearly three decades. The erudite, black-clad Paladin (Richard Boone) is a hired gun with a conscience. Boone brings a precise, understated mix of strength, tenderness, menace, and irony to what remains his greatest role. Made for TV. B&W; 58m. **DIR:** Andrew V. McLaglen, Various. **CAST:** Richard Boone, Kam Tong, Lisa Lu. **1957–63**

HAVING A WONDERFUL CRIME ★★★ Pat O'Brien plays a lawyer who gets together with amateur sleuths Carole Landis and George Murphy to find out why a magician mysteriously disappeared. A murder mystery played for laughs with a cast who can put it across. B&W; 71m. **DIR:** A. Edward Sutherland. **CAST:** Pat O'Brien, Carole Landis, George Murphy, Gloria Holden, George Zucco. **1945**

HAVING A WONDERFUL TIME 🦃 Based on a Broadway stage hit, this was *supposed* to be romance and comedy at a famed Catskills resort hotel. B&W; 71m. **DIR:** Alfred Santell. **CAST:** Ginger Rogers, Douglas Fairbanks Jr., Red Skelton, Lucille Ball, Eve Arden, Lee Bowman, Jack Carson. **1938**

HAVING IT ALL ★★★ Dyan Cannon makes up for any script deficiencies with sheer exuberance. In this remake of *The Captain's Paradise*, the roles are reversed, and Cannon plays the bigamist. As a fashion designer, she is constantly traveling between New York and Los Angeles. She has a home and husband in each and manages to juggle the two. Made for TV, this is unrated. 100m. **DIR:** Edward Zwick. **CAST:** Dyan Cannon, Hart Bochner, Barry Newman, Sylvia Sidney, Melanie Chartoff. **1982**

HAWAII ★★★★ All-star epic presentation of Part III of James Michener's six-part novel of the same title. Excellent performances by Max von Sydow and Julie Andrews as the early 1800s missionaries to Hawaii, as well as by Richard Harris as the sea captain who tries to woo Andrews away. 171m. **DIR:** George Roy Hill. **CAST:** Julie Andrews, Max von Sydow, Richard Harris, Gene Hackman, Carroll O'Connor. **1966**

HAWK, THE ★★★ A wife who was once institutionalized starts to think her husband is a serial killer. Is she

going crazy again, or is she right? The plot has a few good twists, but it's too easy to figure out. Rated R for profanity and violence. 84m. **DIR:** David Hayman. **CAST:** Helen Mirren, George Costigan, Rosemary Leach, Owen Teale, Melanie Hill. **1992**

HAWK OF THE WILDERNESS ★★★ Wonderful nonsense about the son of a scientist who is shipwrecked on an unknown island and raised and protected by a giant native. The film is filled with earthquakes, exploding volcanoes, bloodthirsty manhunters, and greedy treasure seekers. The most exciting elements of the 1930s jungle/tropical paradise films mixed with the best self-sacrifice and revenge traditions of the day make this a grand serial. B&W; 12 chapters. **DIR:** William Witney, John English. **CAST:** Herman Brix, Noble Johnson, Mala, Monte Blue, Jill Martin, William Royle. **1938**

HAWK THE SLAYER ★★ In this sword-and-sorcery adventure, John Terry plays the good Hawk, who, with his band of warriors—a dwarf and an elf among them—fights Jack Palance, his evil older brother. Palance's performance saves the film from mediocrity. Not rated; has violence. 90m. **DIR:** Terry Marcel. **CAST:** Jack Palance, John Terry. **1980**

HAWKS ★★★★ This neglected treasure concerns a couple of feisty patients—Timothy Dalton and Anthony Edwards—in a hospital terminal ward. The macabre gallows humor may be difficult for mainstream tastes, but Dalton's often enraged battle with life is utterly compelling. With music by the Bee Gees (and Barry Gibb takes cocredit for the story idea). Rated R for profanity and brief nudity. 103m. **DIR:** Robert Ellis Miller. **CAST:** Timothy Dalton, Anthony Edwards. **1989**

HAWKS AND THE SPARROWS, THE ★★1/2 A father and his rambunctious son take a stroll that soon becomes a religious pilgrimage in this poetic comedy. The famous Italian comic Toto gives this lifeless story its brightest moments. In Italian with English subtitles. B&W; 90m. **DIR:** Pier Paolo Pasolini. **CAST:** Toto, Davoli Ninetto. **1966**

HAWK'S VENGEANCE ★★ Run-of-the-mill action film is the story of a soldier avenging the death of his brother. Rated R for violence and language. 96m. **DIR:** Marc Voizard. **CAST:** Gary Daniels, Jayne Heitmeyer, Vlasta Vrana, Cass Magda, Catherine Blythe. **1996**

HAWMPS! Old West cavalry unit uses camels instead of horses. Rated G. 120m. **DIR:** Joe Camp. **CAST:** James Hampton, Christopher Connelly, Slim Pickens, Denver Pyle, Jack Elam. **1976**

HAZEL CHRISTMAS SHOW, THE (TV SERIES) ★★1/2 The know-it-all housekeeper celebrates the Yuletide in two special episodes from the 1961–1966 series. "Just 86 Shopping Minutes Left Till Christmas" finds her employer, Mr. Baxter, deciding that the family should have an austere, noncommercialized Christmas. "Hazel's Christmas Shopping" has the spunky maid working part-time in a department store to save up money to buy gifts for the Baxters. Not rated. 60m. **DIR:** William D. Russell. **CAST:** Shirley Booth, Don DeFore, Whitney Blake, Bobby Buntrock, Karen Steele, Lauren Gilbert, Molly Dodd, Byron Foulger, Eleanor Andley, Helen Spring. **1961; 1965**

HE GOT GAME ★★1/2 This uneven drama is about ethnic pride, urban survival, and the corruption of American sports. Jake Shuttlesworth, an Attica inmate on a one-week furlough, can shave time off his manslaughter sentence by convincing his basketball-star son Jesus to enroll at the governor's alma mater. There's one problem: Jesus hates his dad. The film's often brilliant cinematic flourishes are undercut by a contrived script. Rated R for language, nudity, simulated sex, drug use, and domestic violence. 137m. **DIR:** Spike Lee. **CAST:** Denzel Washington, Ray Allen, Milla Jovovich, Rosario Dawson, Hill Harper. **1998 DVD**

HE KNOWS YOU'RE ALONE ★★ There's a killer on the loose, specializing in brides-to-be. His current target for dismemberment is pretty Amy (Caitlin O'Heaney). While stalking his special prey, the killer keeps his knife sharp by decimating the population of Staten Island. Rated R. 94m. **DIR:** Armand Mastroianni. **CAST:** Don Scardino, Caitlin O'Heaney, Elizabeth Kemp, Tom Hanks. **1981**

HE SAID, SHE SAID ★★★1/2 When telling friends how they got together, married directors Ken Kwapis and Marisa Silver were surprised to hear how much their stories differed. So they decided to make a movie about a courting couple (Kevin Bacon, Elizabeth Perkins) and the male/female opposing views of the romance. Slight, but charming. Rated PG-13 for profanity. 115m. **DIR:** Ken Kwapis, Marisa Silver. **CAST:** Kevin Bacon, Elizabeth Perkins, Sharon Stone, Nathan Lane, Anthony LaPaglia. **1990 DVD**

HE WALKED BY NIGHT ★★★★1/2 Richard Basehart is superb in this documentary-style drama as a killer stalked by methodical policemen. A little-known cinematic gem, it's first-rate in every department and reportedly inspired Jack Webb to create *Dragnet*. B&W; 79m. **DIR:** Alfred Werker, Anthony Mann. **CAST:** Richard Basehart, Scott Brady, Jack Webb, Roy Roberts, Whit Bissell. **1948**

HE WHO GETS SLAPPED ★★★1/2 One of Lon Chaney Sr.'s best performances as a brilliant scientist who becomes a circus clown after a personal tragedy. The very first film produced by MGM. Silent. B&W; 80m. **DIR:** Victor Sjöström. **CAST:** Lon Chaney Sr., Norma Shearer, John Gilbert. **1924**

HEAD, THE (1959) ★★ Magnificently atmospheric and surreal West German mad scientist shocker with a much stronger plot than most films of its ilk—notably the Edgar Wallace series—could boast. Classically gothic and fogbound, this fascinating oddity follows the horrific events that result when a mad scientist becomes victim of his most daring experiment. B&W; 92m. **DIR:** Victor Trivas. **CAST:** Horst Frank, Michel Simon. **1959**

HEAD (1968) ★★★ They get the funniest looks from everyone they meet. And it's no wonder. This film is truly bizarre. The Monkees were hurtled to fame in the aftershock of the Beatles' success. Their ingratiating series was accused of imitating *A Hard Day's Night*, but their innovative feature-film debut, *Head*, was ahead of its time. A free-form product of the psychedelic era. 86m. **DIR:** Bob Rafelson. **CAST:** Mickey Dolenz, David Jones, Mike Nesmith, Peter Tork, Teri Garr, Vito Scotti, Timothy Carey, Logan Ramsey. **1968 DVD**

HEAD AGAINST THE WALL ★★★ An unruly boy who blames his father for his mother's accidental death is sent to a mental hospital. Director Georges Franju shot much of this (his first feature-length film) in an actual

insane asylum, and the sense of fatalistic foreboding may be a bit too oppressive for many viewers. In French with English subtitles. B&W; 98m. **DIR:** Georges Franju. **CAST:** Jean-Pierre Mocky, Pierre Brasseur, Anouk Aimée, Charles Aznavour. **1958**

HEAD OFFICE ★★ A sometimes funny comedy about the son of an influential politician who upon graduating from college gets a high-paying job with a major corporation. Rated PG-13. 90m. **DIR:** Ken Finkleman. **CAST:** Judge Reinhold, Lori-Nan Engler, Eddie Albert, Merritt Butrick, Ron Frazier, Richard Masur, Rick Moranis, Jane Seymour, Danny DeVito. **1985**

HEAD OVER HEELS ★★ Romantic comedies don't come much dumber than this mindless trifle about a regular gal (Monica Potter) who moves in with four man-obsessed models and then falls in love with the guy in a neighboring building . . . who (horrors!) may have killed his previous girlfriend. Potter and costar Freddie Prinze Jr. have genuine chemistry, but it's lost amid this script's witless attempts at slapstick and gross-out humor. Rated PG-13 for sexual candor, profanity, and crude humor. 91m. **DIR:** Mark Waters. **CAST:** Monica Potter, Freddie Prinze Jr., Sarah O'Hare, Shalom Harlow, Ivana Milicevic, Tomiko Fraser, China Chow. **2001 DVD**

HEADIN' HOME ★★ A small-town lad smitten with the baseball bug earns the enmity of his community when his play helps a visiting team defeat the locals. Years later he returns to his family and best girl a baseball star. Well on his way to becoming a legend, Babe Ruth basically plays himself in his first film. Though missing enough footage to make the story hazy, it is a fabulous opportunity to see one of the great baseball figures of the 20th century playing at the legendary Polo Grounds. B&W; 56m. **DIR:** Lawrence Windom. **CAST:** Babe Ruth, Ruth Taylor, William Sheer, Margaret Sedden, Francis Victory. **1920**

HEADLESS BODY IN TOPLESS BAR The first film based on a *New York Post* headline and about as good as the source would indicate. Cheap, dreary, and unconvincing, it's about a deranged gunman who takes the pathetic denizens of a Manhattan strip bar hostage and the degrading psychological games he makes them play. Not rated; contains lots of nudity, violence, language, and erotic subject matter. 106m. **DIR:** James Bruce. **CAST:** Raymond J. Barry, Jennifer MacDonald, Taylor Nichols, David Selby, Paul Williams. **1996**

HEADLESS HORSEMAN, THE ★★1/2 The time-honored (but worn) story of lanky Yankee schoolmaster Ichabod Crane's rube-ish efforts to wed wealthy Katrina Van Tassel. Will Rogers looks the part of the homespun Crane and gives a fair impression of the character. Silent. B&W; 52m. **DIR:** Edward Venturini. **CAST:** Will Rogers, Lois Meredith. **1922**

HEADS ★★★ Talk about disappointments! This darkly satirical slice of small-town somnambulism opens brilliantly, but fails to fulfill its potential. Jon Cryer is perfect as a rookie reporter for the moribund *Dry Falls Daily Document*, the newspaper for a community brought to life when decapitated townsfolk start popping up. Sadly, events quickly collapse into a conventional (and boring) murder mystery. Rated R for gore, profanity, and simulated sex. 102m. **DIR:** Paul Shapiro. **CAST:** Jon Cryer, Edward Asner, Jennifer Tilly, Shawn Thompson, Roddy McDowall. **1994**

HEAR MY SONG ★★★★ A gentle satire in the style of *Local Hero* and *Gregory's Girl*, this English import tells the sly story of a promoter (Adrian Dunbar, who cowrote the screenplay) who attempts to fool the public one time too many. It's charming, heartwarming, and funny. Rated R for profanity, nudity, and brief violence. 104m. **DIR:** Peter Chelsom. **CAST:** Ned Beatty, Adrian Dunbar, Shirley Ann Field, Tara Fitzgerald, William Hootkins. **1991**

HEAR NO EVIL ★★★1/2 A deaf athletic trainer finds herself living a nightmare after a client plants a rare coin on her. Restaurant owner D. B. Sweeney tries to help while becoming sensitized to her handicap. The deaf angle gives this thriller a decent edge, but it's too predictable to be totally gripping. Rated R for violence and profanity. 98m. **DIR:** Robert Greenwald. **CAST:** Marlee Matlin, D. B. Sweeney, Martin Sheen. **1993**

HEARSE, THE This film is about a satanic pact between an old woman and her lover. Rated PG. 100m. **DIR:** George Bowers. **CAST:** Trish Van Devere, Joseph Cotten, David Gautreaux, Donald Hotton. **1980 DVD**

HEARST AND DAVIES AFFAIR, THE ★★★ From William Randolph Hearst's and Marion Davies's first meeting at the Ziegfeld Follies to his death, this made-for-TV original takes the viewer through their entire affair—told from Davies's point of view. The mise-en-scène is beautiful, since the film was shot on location at Hearst Castle. Both Robert Mitchum and Virginia Madsen deliver fine performances as the title couple. Not rated. 95m. **DIR:** David Lowell Rich. **CAST:** Robert Mitchum, Virginia Madsen, Fritz Weaver, Doris Belack. **1985**

HEART (1987) ★★ A down-and-out boxer (Brad Davis) makes a comeback. This is well-worn territory and *Heart* has little new to offer. Rated R for violence and profanity. 93m. **DIR:** James Lemmo. **CAST:** Brad Davis, Jesse Doran, Sam Gray, Robinson Frank Adu, Steve Buscemi, Frances Fisher. **1987**

•HEART (1999) ★★1/2 You would think that a successful heart transplant would be enough to make a man stand up and cheer. For the recipient, a charter pilot named Gary, it turns out to be a nightmare. First, his wife's ex-lover enters the picture, determined to get even for being jilted. Then Gary meets the donor's mother, an obsessive woman who also can't let go. There's a fair amount of suspense in this tight British thriller, which follows the straight and narrow but still manages to catch you by surprise. Rated R for adult situations, language, nudity, and violence. 81m. **DIR:** Charles McDougall. **CAST:** Chris Eccleston, Rhys Ifans, Saskia Reeves, Kate Hardie, Bill Paterson. **1999 DVD**

HEART AND SOULS ★★★1/2 Sentimental fantasy follows the misadventures of Robert Downey Jr., who, at the moment of his birth, is "adopted" by a quartet of ghosts. The spirits cut off all communication with him when he's ten, breaking the boy's heart. So he's not exactly happy to see them again when he's an adult and they're asking for help. Rated PG-13 for brief profanity, one sexy scene, and light violence. 104m. **DIR:** Ron Underwood. **CAST:** Robert Downey Jr., Charles Grodin,

Alfre Woodard, Kyra Sedgwick, Elisabeth Shue, Tom Sizemore, David Paymer. **1993 DVD**

HEART BEAT ★★★★ *Heart Beat* is a perfect title for this warm, bittersweet visual poem on the beat generation by writer-director John Byrum. It pulses with life and emotion, intoxicating the viewer with a rhythmic flow of stunning images and superb performances by Nick Nolte, Sissy Spacek, and John Heard. The story begins with the cross-country adventure that inspired Jack Kerouac's *On the Road*. Rated R. 109m. **DIR:** John Byrum. **CAST:** Nick Nolte, Sissy Spacek, John Heard, Ray Sharkey, Ann Dusenberry. **1980**

HEART CONDITION ★★★ By sheer force of talent, Bob Hoskins and Denzel Washington turn this formulaic movie into something worth watching. Hoskins is a racist cop who has a heart attack and is given recently deceased Washington's heart in a transplant operation. Rent this one on discount night, and it just may put a smile on your face. Rated R for profanity, sexual situations, and violence. 90m. **DIR:** James D. Parriott. **CAST:** Bob Hoskins, Denzel Washington, Chloe Webb, Roger E. Mosley. **1990**

HEART IS A LONELY HUNTER, THE ★★★★ This release features Alan Arkin in a superb performance, which won him an Academy Award nomination. In it, he plays a sensitive and compassionate man who is also a deaf-mute. Rated G. 125m. **DIR:** Robert Ellis Miller. **CAST:** Alan Arkin, Sondra Locke, Laurinda Barrett, Stacy Keach, Chuck McCann, Cicely Tyson. **1968**

HEART LIKE A WHEEL ★★★★ This top-notch film biography of racing-champion Shirley Muldowney features a marvelous performance by Bonnie Bedelia as the first woman to crack the National Hot Rod Association's embargo against female competitors. Rated PG for profanity. 113m. **DIR:** Jonathan Kaplan. **CAST:** Bonnie Bedelia, Beau Bridges, Leo Rossi, Hoyt Axton, Bill McKinney, Dean Paul Martin, Dick Miller. **1983**

HEART OF A CHAMPION: THE RAY MANCINI STORY ★★★ Made-for-TV movie of the life of Ray "Boom Boom" Mancini focuses on his quest for the lightweight boxing title. His drive is intensified by his desire to bring pride to his father, who could have had a shot at the title had he not been called to serve in World War II. Fight sequences staged by Sylvester Stallone. 100m. **DIR:** Richard Michaels. **CAST:** Robert Blake, Doug McKeon, Mariclare Costello. **1985**

HEART OF ARIZONA ★★ Belle Starr and daughter Jackie move near the Bar-20, and Hopalong Cassidy has his hands full. Belle and Jackie are pinned down by rustlers who are using her ranch. The outlaw queen bravely walks into a hail of bullets with her guns blazing before help arrives. B&W; 68m. **DIR:** Lesley Selander. **CAST:** William Boyd, George "Gabby" Hayes, Russell Hayden, Natalie Moorhead, John Elliot, Lane Chandler. **1938**

HEART OF DARKNESS ★★1/2 Slow-moving and sometimes incoherent made-for-TV interpretation of Joseph Conrad's novel concerning an ivory company representative who may or may not have gone mad at his isolated African outpost, and the steamboat captain sent to find him. Conrad's novel is served far better by director Francis Ford Coppola's *Apocalypse Now*. 104m. **DIR:** Nicolas Roeg. **CAST:** Tim Roth, John Malkovich, Isaach De Bankee, James Fox, Morten Faldaas, Iman. **1994**

HEART OF DIXIE, THE ★★ With its heart in the right place but its head lost in the clouds this film only manages to satisfy on two levels: its 1957 period details of the South, which is struggling to maintain its slipping grip on antebellum grandeur; and a small, tight performance by Treat Williams. The film centers on the activities of a group of sorority sisters at Alabama's Randolph University and their Big-Daddy-in-training lugs of boyfriends. Rated PG for mild violence and reasonably oblique sexual discussions. 110m. **DIR:** Martin Davidson. **CAST:** Ally Sheedy, Virginia Madsen, Phoebe Cates, Don Michael Paul, Treat Williams. **1989 DVD**

HEART OF DRAGON ★★★ Jackie Chan, in a departure from his usually good-natured hero, employs less humor and more pathos as a policeman unwillingly burdened by his retarded brother's daily antics. Director Sammo Hung costars, creating to perfection the childish sibling. Blood proves thicker than water when Chan's brother is falsely accused of a robbery, and Chan risks his life and career to protect him. In Chinese with English subtitles. Not rated; contains violence. 85m. **DIR:** Sammo Hung. **CAST:** Jackie Chan, Emily Chu, Sammo Hung. **1985 DVD**

HEART OF GLASS ★★★★1/2 One of director Werner Herzog's most haunting and mystifying films. In a small village in preindustrial Germany, a glassblower dies, and the secret for his unique ruby glass is lost forever leaving the townspeople in hysteria. A remarkable, visionary film. In German with English subtitles. Not rated. 93m. **DIR:** Werner Herzog. **CAST:** Josef Bierbichler. **1976 DVD**

HEART OF JUSTICE ★★★1/2 Engrossing drama follows a reporter's attempt to piece together the reason a popular author was murdered by a wealthy socialite. Film plays like an Alfred Hitchcock movie with very fine performances by all involved. 108m. **DIR:** Bruno Barreto. **CAST:** Dennis Hopper, Eric Stoltz, Jennifer Connelly, Bradford Dillman, William H. Macy, Dermot Mulroney, Vincent Price, Joanna Miles, Harris Yulin. **1993**

HEART OF MIDNIGHT ★★★ What begins as a disturbing haunted-house movie becomes a chilling whodunit. Jennifer Jason Leigh inherits a dilapidated ballroom with a steamy past. Grippingly weird. Rated R. 95m. **DIR:** Matthew Chapman. **CAST:** Jennifer Jason Leigh, Peter Coyote, Frank Stallone, Brenda Vaccaro. **1989**

HEART OF THE GOLDEN WEST ★★1/2 This modern-day adventure pits Roy Rogers and his fellow ranchers against cheating city slickers intent on defrauding the cowboys and putting them out of business. Enjoyable Western hokum. B&W; 65m. **DIR:** Joseph Kane. **CAST:** Roy Rogers, Smiley Burnette, George "Gabby" Hayes, Ruth Terry. **1942**

HEART OF THE ROCKIES ★★★★ Possibly the best of the Three Mesquiteers series as the trio find a vicious mountain family behind cattle rustling and the illegal trapping of game. B&W; 56m. **DIR:** Joseph Kane. **CAST:** Robert Livingston, Ray "Crash" Corrigan, Max Terhune, Yakima Canutt, Lynne Roberts. **1937**

HEART OF THE STAG ★★★★ The shocking subject matter—forced incest—could have resulted in an uncomfortable film to watch. However, New Zealander Michael Firth, who directed the movie and conceived the story, handles it expertly, and the result is a riveting viewing experience. Rated R for violence, profanity, and

sexual situations. 94m. **DIR:** Michael Firth. **CAST:** Bruno Lawrence, Terence Cooper, Mary Regan. **1983**

HEARTACHES ★★★ A touching, yet lighthearted, film about love, friendship, and survival follows the trials and tribulations of a young pregnant woman (Annie Potts), who is separated from her husband (Robert Carradine), and the kooky girlfriend she meets on the bus (Margot Kidder). The Canadian film is rated R for a minimal amount of sex, which is handled discreetly. 93m. **DIR:** Donald Shebib. **CAST:** Robert Carradine, Margot Kidder, Annie Potts, Winston Rekert, George Touliatos. **1981**

HEARTBEEPS ★★★ Andy Kaufman and Bernadette Peters play robots who fall in love and decide to explore the world around them. It's a good family film, and the kids will probably love it. Rated PG. 79m. **DIR:** Allan Arkush. **CAST:** Andy Kaufman, Bernadette Peters, Randy Quaid. **1981**

HEARTBREAK HOTEL ★★★ In this bit of none-too-convincing whimsy, Charlie Schlatter plays an aspiring rock guitarist who kidnaps Elvis Presley (David Keith). Keith does a terrific job of impersonating Presley, and director Chris Columbus's script has some warmly funny moments, but the movie cannot overcome its preposterous premise. Rated PG-13 for profanity and violence. 100m. **DIR:** Chris Columbus. **CAST:** David Keith, Tuesday Weld, Charlie Schlatter, Chris Mulkey. **1988**

HEARTBREAK HOUSE ★★★1/2 Rex Harrison is ideally cast as George Bernard Shaw's Captain Shotover. At Shotover's house the guests include his two daughters and a visiting young woman, each in the grip of romantic trauma. What is presented is essentially an ongoing collision of philosophies, but the able cast keeps the debate lively. Not rated, but with no objectionable material. 122m. **DIR:** Anthony Page. **CAST:** Rex Harrison, Amy Irving, Rosemary Harris. **1985**

HEARTBREAK KID, THE ★★★★ The lack of care or commitment in the modern marriage is satirized in this comedy. Charles Grodin plays a young man who's grown tired of his wife while driving to their honeymoon in Florida. By the time he sees beautiful Cybill Shepherd on the beach, his marriage has totally disintegrated. Jeannie Berlin, director Elaine May's daughter, is the big scene stealer as Grodin's whining bride. Rated PG. 104m. **DIR:** Elaine May. **CAST:** Charles Grodin, Cybill Shepherd, Jeannie Berlin, Eddie Albert, Audra Lindley. **1972 DVD**

HEARTBREAK RIDGE ★★★ Whoever thought Grenada would be the subject of cinematic war heroics? Though the film could use some trimming, the story of a hard-nosed Marine sergeant whipping a hopeless-looking unit into a crack fighting team is still compelling. Rated R. 126m. **DIR:** Clint Eastwood. **CAST:** Clint Eastwood, Marsha Mason, Everett McGill, Bo Svenson, Mario Van Peebles, Moses Gunn, Tom Villard. **1986**

HEARTBREAKERS (1984) ★★★1/2 Two men in their thirties, Arthur Blue (Peter Coyote) and Eli Kahn (Nick Mancuso), friends since childhood, find their relationship severely tested when each is suddenly caught up in his own fervent drive for success. Rated R for simulated sex and profanity. 106m. **DIR:** Bobby Roth. **CAST:** Peter Coyote, Nick Mancuso, Max Gail, Kathryn Harrold. **1984**

HEARTBREAKERS (2001) ★★★ A mother-and-daughter team runs a scam on a series of wealthy men: the mom marries them, the daughter seduces them, then they split Mom's divorce settlement. The script is only serviceable and the "surprise" twists are telegraphed way in advance, but the star power of the cast puts the film over in style. Rated PG-13 for mild profanity and sexual humor. 123m. **DIR:** David Mirkin. **CAST:** Sigourney Weaver, Jennifer Love Hewitt, Ray Liotta, Jason Lee, Gene Hackman. **2001 DVD**

HEARTBURN ★★★1/2 Uneven adaptation of Nora Ephron's novel (she also wrote the screenplay) and a thinly disguised account of her own separation from Watergate journalist Carl Bernstein. Jack Nicholson and Meryl Streep fall in love, get married, and drift apart. Its strength comes from the superb performances by the stars and an incredible supporting cast. Needlessly rated R for language. 108m. **DIR:** Mike Nichols. **CAST:** Meryl Streep, Jack Nicholson, Jeff Daniels, Maureen Stapleton, Stockard Channing, Richard Masur, Catherine O'Hara, Milos Forman. **1986**

HEARTLAND ★★★★ This is an excellent and deceptively simple story, of a widow (Conchata Ferrell) who settled, with her daughter and a homesteader (Rip Torn), in turn-of-the-century Wyoming. The film deals with the complex problems of surviving in nature and society. It's well worth watching. Rated PG. 96m. **DIR:** Richard Pearce. **CAST:** Conchata Ferrell, Rip Torn, Lilia Skala, Megan Folsom. **1979 DVD**

HEARTLESS ★★ Heartless, gutless, and brainless, this made-for-cable original is about a young woman who receives a heart transplant. Little does she know, the heart came from a murdered woman, and the story goes into a terminal coma from there. Not rated; contains violence and suggested sex. 95m. **DIR:** Judith Vogelsang. **CAST:** Madchen Amick, Louise Fletcher, David Packer, Tom Schanley, Pamela Bellwood, Bo Svenson. **1997 DVD**

HEARTS ADRIFT ★★ A woman and her daughter take a trip to San Diego, one to find love and the other to rekindle an old flame. This made-for-cable original has an artificial, soap-opera feel to it, and (considering the cast) it's no wonder. Not rated; contains suggested sex. 95m. **DIR:** Vic Sarin. **CAST:** Sydney Penny, Scott Reeves, Kathleen Noone, Nicolas Coster, Don Murray. **1996**

HEARTS AND ARMOUR ★★1/2 Warrior Orlando (Rick Edwards) seeks victory over the Moors and the rescue of his love (Tanya Roberts), while his female comrade-in-arms, Bradamante (Barbara de Rossi), falls in love with Ruggero (Ron Moss), the Moor whom Orlando is fated to kill. Unfortunately, the script is not strong enough to do justice to the complex plot. Not rated; has violence and nudity. 101m. **DIR:** Giacomo Battiato. **CAST:** Zenda Araya, Barbara de Rossi, Rick Edwards, Ronn Moss, Tanya Roberts. **1983**

HEARTS AND MINDS ★★★★★ Unforgettable Oscar-winning documentary about the effects of the Vietnam War on the people of that country. Without narration or commentary, filmmaker Peter Davis juxtaposes scenes of the ruined country with interviews of military leaders. Rated R. 112m. **DIR:** Peter Davis. **1974**

HEART'S DESIRE ★★ Richard Tauber, a popular tenor in British operetta, stars in this ho-hum musical as a Vi-

ennese waiter who becomes a star in London. In the end, true love brings him back home. B&W; 79m. **DIR:** Paul Stein. **CAST:** Richard Tauber, Leonora Corbett. **1935**

•HEARTS IN ATLANTIS ★★★★1/2 Scripter William Goldman's brilliant adaptation covers only the first half of Stephen King's book, but the result is a sweetly nostalgic coming-of-age saga much in the mold of *Stand by Me*. Anthony Hopkins is superb as the time-worn older gentleman who befriends our 11-year-old protagonist during the summer of 1960, and helps the boy make that difficult transition from childhood to young adulthood. Completely devoid of the book's supernatual elements, the film instead concentrates on the fascinating (and often difficult) relationships between children and adults, and between an overly sensitive boy and his self-centered mother. The result stands as one of the best film adaptations made from a King property. Rated PG-13 for violence and dramatic intensity. 101m. **DIR:** Scott Hicks. **CAST:** Anthony Hopkins, Anton Yelchin, Hope Davis, Mika Boorem, David Morse. **2001 DVD**

HEARTS OF DARKNESS ★★★★★ Draws on 60 hours of footage shot by Eleanor Coppola during the 238 days of principal photography in the Philippines for husband Francis's *Apocalypse Now* (as well as after-the-fact interviews with its cast and crew). Unprecedented insight into the moviemaking process and the on-location madness. A must-see for film buffs. Not rated; the film has profanity and graphic scenes of native rituals during which animals are slain. 96m. **DIR:** Fax Bahr, George Hickenlooper. **1992**

HEARTS OF FIRE 🦃 A girl who dreams of becoming a rock star. Rated R for brief nudity and profanity. 95m. **DIR:** Richard Marquand. **CAST:** Fiona, Bob Dylan, Rupert Everett, Julian Glover. **1987**

HEARTS OF THE WEST ★★★ Pleasant little comedy-drama about an aspiring writer from Iowa (Jeff Bridges) who, determined to pen masterful Westerns, winds up in Hollywood as a most reluctant cowboy. The setting is the early 1920s, and the story playfully explores many classic Western myths. Rated PG. 103m. **DIR:** Howard Zieff. **CAST:** Jeff Bridges, Alan Arkin, Blythe Danner, Andy Griffith. **1975**

HEARTS OF THE WORLD ★★★ This World War I epic, a propaganda film, was made to convince the United States to enter the conflict and aid Britain and France. Actual battle footage from both sides in the conflict is interwoven with the story of a young man going to war and the tragic effects on his family and village. Silent. B&W; 122m. **DIR:** D. W. Griffith. **CAST:** Lillian Gish, Dorothy Gish, Robert Harron, Ben Alexander. **1918**

HEARTSTOPPER ★★★ In this film based on his novel *The Awakening*, John Russo spins a fascinating tale of a surgeon accused and hanged for vampirism who returns from the grave as a real vampire. Acting is top-notch, as Russo paints an exciting story. 96m. **DIR:** John Russo. **CAST:** Kevin Kindlon, Jon Hall, Moon Zappa, Tom Savini. **1991**

HEAT ★★★1/2 If this cops-and-robbers tale had concentrated solely on the professional rivalry between police detective Al Pacino and thief Robert De Niro, *Heat* would have been a hands-down winner; however, too much screen time is allotted to their private lives. Nevertheless, the excellent cast makes it worth watching and the action scenes are top-notch. Rated R for violence, simulated sex, and profanity. 172m. **DIR:** Michael Mann. **CAST:** Al Pacino, Robert De Niro, Val Kilmer, Jon Voight, Tom Sizemore, Diane Venora, Amy Brenneman, Ashley Judd, Mykelti Williamson, Wes Studi, Natalie Portman. **1995 DVD**

HEAT (1972) ★★★ One of Andy Warhol's better film productions is this steamy tale of an unemployed actor (Joe Dallesandro) whose involvement with a neurotic has-been actress (Sylvia Miles) has tragicomic results. A low-budget homage to *Sunset Boulevard* that even non-Warhol fans may enjoy. Excellent music score composed and performed by John Cale. Rated R for nudity and language. 100m. **DIR:** Paul Morrissey. **CAST:** Sylvia Miles, Joe Dallesandro, Andrea Feldman, Pat Ast. **1972 DVD**

HEAT (1987) ★★1/2 A good try at an action thriller that doesn't succeed because of awkward pacing, uneven direction, and a mood that swings wildly from raw violence to good-buddy playfulness. Burt Reynolds is a Las Vegas–based troubleshooter with two problems: an old girlfriend who craves revenge and a mousy young executive (Peter MacNicol, stealing every scene he shared with Reynolds) who craves the ability to protect himself. Rated R for language and violence. 101m. **DIR:** Dick Richards. **CAST:** Burt Reynolds, Karen Young, Peter MacNicol, Howard Hesseman, Neill Barry, Diana Scarwid. **1987**

HEAT AND DUST ★★★★ Two love stories—one from the 1920s and one from today—are entwined in this classy, thoroughly enjoyable soap opera about two British women who go to India and become involved in its seductive mysteries. Julie Christie stars as a modern woman retracing the steps of her great-aunt (Greta Scacchi), who fell in love with an Indian ruler (played by the celebrated Indian star Shashi Kapoor). Rated R for nudity and brief violence. 130m. **DIR:** James Ivory. **CAST:** Julie Christie, Greta Scacchi, Shashi Kapoor, Christopher Cazenove, Julian Glover, Susan Fleetwood. **1983**

HEAT AND SUNLIGHT ★★★★ Electrifying, narratively risky drama featuring director Rob Nilsson as a photographer who is overwhelmed with jealousy and obsession. Visually stunning, with a great soundtrack by David Byrne and Brian Eno. Rated R for nudity and profanity. B&W; 98m. **DIR:** Rob Nilsson. **CAST:** Rob Nilsson. **1987**

HEAT OF DESIRE ★★ So many sex comedies are about married men who discover adultery brings new vitality, this plot has become a cinematic cliché. But this didn't stop director Luc Beraud from using it again in this disappointing film. In French with English subtitles. Not rated; the film has nudity and suggested sex. 91m. **DIR:** Luc Beraud. **CAST:** Patrick Dewaere, Clio Goldsmith, Jeanne Moreau, Guy Marchand. **1984**

HEAT WAVE ★★★1/2 Cable television film depicting the Watts riots of the early Seventies. Blair Underwood plays a young black *L.A. Times* employee given his chance at reporting when it becomes apparent that white journalists cannot get into the Watts area to cover the riots. Engrossing fact-based account. 96m. **DIR:** Kevin Hooks. **CAST:** Blair Underwood, Cicely Tyson, James Earl Jones, Margaret Avery. **1990**

HEATED VENGEANCE ★★ A U.S. serviceman (Richard Hatch) returns to Southeast Asia years after the Viet-

nam War to bring back his old flame (Jolina Mitchell-Collins). Former enemies abduct him and bring him back to their camp, where he finds that they are dealing with drugs. Not rated, has violence, profanity, sex, and nudity. 91m. **DIR:** Edward Murphy. **CAST:** Richard Hatch, Michael J. Pollard, Dennis Patrick, Mills Watson, Cameron Dye, Robert Walker Jr. **1987**

HEATHERS ★★★★ A *Dr. Strangelove* or *Blue Velvet* of the teen set, this brash black comedy tackles such typically adolescent issues as peer pressure, high school cliques, heterosexuality, and homosexuality—and even teen suicide—in ways that are inventive, irreverent, startling, and occasionally offensive. Rated R; with violence and profanity. 110m. **DIR:** Michael Lehmann. **CAST:** Winona Ryder, Christian Slater, Kim Walker. **1989 DVD**

HEAT'S ON, THE ★★1/2 After a three-year absence Mae West returned to the screen as a Broadway star caught between two rival producers. She shouldn't have bothered, since the firmly entrenched Hays Office knocked out the double entendres for which she was noted. Her last film until 1970's dismal *Myra Breckenridge*. B&W; 80m. **DIR:** Gregory Ratoff. **CAST:** Mae West, Victor Moore, William Gaxton, Lloyd Bridges, Lina Romay, Xavier Cugat, Hazel Scott. **1943**

HEATSEEKER ★★ Having beaten to death the kick-boxing formula in the here and now, the filmmakers behind this effort take the sport to the year 2019 when cyborgs rule the kick-boxing arena. There's only one human opponent left, and he refuses to fight. Yeah, right. Rated R for violence. 91m. **DIR:** Albert Pyun. **CAST:** Keith Cooke, Thom Mathews, Norbert Weisser, Gary Daniels. **1995**

HEATWAVE ★★★ Judy Davis plays an idealistic liberal opposed to proposed real estate developments. Davis's crusade leads to her involvement in a possible kidnap-murder and a love affair with the young architect of the housing project she's protesting. Not rated. 99m. **DIR:** Phillip Noyce. **CAST:** Judy Davis, Richard Moir, Chris Haywood, Bill Hunter, Anna Jemison. **1983**

HEAVEN (1987) ★★★ Weird collage assembled by actress Diane Keaton mixes footage from old movies with interviews of assorted oddballs who talk about what they think Heaven will be like. Love it or hate it, it's certainly different. Not rated. 80m. **DIR:** Diane Keaton. **1987**

HEAVEN (1998) ★★★★ Gruesomely violent and almost unbearably intense thriller scores on almost every level—from its fine performances to its tight editing to its gutsy dare-to-turn-your-eyes away direction. Recommended but not for everybody. Rated R for violence, profanity, and nudity. 103m. **DIR:** Scott Reynolds. **CAST:** Martin Donovan, Joanna Going, Patrick Malahide, Richard Schiff, Karl Urban, Danny Edwards, Michael Langley, Jeremy Birchall, Clint Sharplin. **1998 DVD**

HEAVEN AND EARTH (1991) ★★★ Imagine the battles of the great Akira Kurosawa samurai epics, but without the rich philosophical dimension or tragic aura. This film lacks the emotional staying power of the master's work, but it is still rich in splendor. In Japanese with English subtitles. Rated PG-13. 106m. **DIR:** Haruki Kadokawa. **CAST:** Takaaki Enoki. **1991**

HEAVEN AND EARTH (1993) ★★★ Oliver Stone returns to Vietnam to focus on one woman's Dickensian ordeals. She survives the French and American invasions, and then tackles life in the gluttonous United States after marrying a war-weary sergeant who, in a bit of near comical overkill, becomes violently homicidal. Actors in lead roles are sensational, but their characters are lost amid Stone's bombastic visual diatribes. Rated R for violence, profanity, nudity, and rape. 140m. **DIR:** Oliver Stone. **CAST:** Hiep Thi Le, Tommy Lee Jones, Joan Chen, Haing S. Ngor, Debbie Reynolds. **1993 DVD**

HEAVEN BEFORE I DIE ★★★ Likable low-budget feature about a Middle Easterner who comes to Toronto to pursue his dream of becoming a Charlie Chaplin impersonator. Giancarlo Giannini (*Swept Away*) steals the film as a petty thief who helps him get the hang of life in the New World. Rated PG. 98m. **DIR:** Izidore K. Musallam. **CAST:** Andy Velasquez, Giancarlo Giannini, Joanna Pacula. **1997**

HEAVEN CAN WAIT (1943) ★★★★★ Newly deceased Don Ameche meets "Your Excellency" (the devil) and reviews his roguish life. If ever you wondered what was meant by "the Lubitsch touch," *Heaven Can Wait* explains it. Quite simply this is the most joyful fantasy–love story ever filmed. 112m. **DIR:** Ernst Lubitsch. **CAST:** Don Ameche, Gene Tierney, Charles Coburn, Laird Cregar, Spring Byington, Eugene Pallette, Marjorie Main, Louis Calhern, Signe Hasso, Allyn Joslyn, Florence Bates. **1943**

HEAVEN CAN WAIT (1975) ★★★★1/2 In this charming remake of *Here Comes Mr. Jordan* (1941), Warren Beatty plays quarterback Joe Pendleton, who meets a premature demise when an overzealous angel takes the athlete's spirit out of his body after an accident. As it turns out, it wasn't Joe's time to die. However, in the interim, his body is cremated. Thus begins a quest to find a proper earthly replacement. Rated PG. 100m. **DIR:** Warren Beatty, Buck Henry. **CAST:** Warren Beatty, Julie Christie, Jack Warden, Dyan Cannon, Charles Grodin, James Mason, Buck Henry, Vincent Gardenia. **1978 DVD**

HEAVEN HELP US ★★ Donald Sutherland, John Heard, Wallace Shawn, and Kate Reid support the youthful cast of this comedy about a group of schoolboys (played by Andrew McCarthy, Kevin Dillon, Malcolm Dunarie, and Stephen Geoffreys) discovering the opposite sex and other adolescent pursuits. Rated R. 90m. **DIR:** Michael Dinner. **CAST:** Andrew McCarthy, Kevin Dillon, Malcolm Dunarie, Stephen Geoffreys, Donald Sutherland, John Heard, Wallace Shawn, Kate Reid. **1985**

HEAVEN IS A PLAYGROUND ★★★1/2 A Chicago slum has one thing going for it: a basketball coach determined to take kids off the streets and onto college campuses. Enter a young white lawyer who helps the coach vanquish an unethical promoter. Rated R for profanity and violence. 104m. **DIR:** Randall Fried. **CAST:** Mike Warren, D. B. Sweeney, Richard Jordan. **1991**

HEAVEN ON EARTH ★★★★ Scripters Margaret Atwood and Peter Pearson pay tribute to a bit of Canadian history with this poignant look at the thousands of orphaned "home children" shipped from England to work as indentured slaves . . . or, if they were lucky, to be adopted into loving families. Suitable for family viewing. 82m. **DIR:** Allan Kroeker. **CAST:** R. H. Thomson, Sian Leisa Davies. **1986**

HEAVEN OR VEGAS ★★ Life is a gamble, but this misguided tale of love and redemption comes up snake eyes. Richard Grieco is the high-rent gigolo and Yasmine Bleeth the part-time call girl looking for a better life and redemption in Montana. Things heat up when her younger sister threatens their newfound happiness. This direct-to-video effort is nothing more than a soap opera that leaves a nasty ring around the tub. Rated R for language and adult situations. 110m. **DIR:** Gregory C. Haynes. **CAST:** Richard Grieco, Yasmine Bleeth, Andy Romano, Monica Potter, Geoffrey Blake, Sarah Schaub. **1996**

HEAVEN TONIGHT ★★★1/2 This British import is a slick contemporary retelling of *A Star Is Born*, with John Waters as an aging rocker frustrated by his inability to generate the headlines he did twenty years earlier, and Guy Pearce as his capable, soft-spoken son, whose musical star is on the rise. Frank Howson and Alister Webb's script contains considerable truth and a lot of heart. Rated R for profanity and drug use. 97m. **DIR:** Pino Amenta. **CAST:** John Waters, Rebecca Gilling, Kim Gyngell, Guy Pearce. **1993**

HEAVENLY CREATURES ★★★★★ Two New Zealand schoolgirls conspire to murder one girl's mother in the mid-1950s when parental concerns about their obsessive friendship threaten to separate them forever. Surreal scenes set in an alternate universe inhabited by unicorns, giant butterflies, castles, and claymation-type knights are used to reimagine the emotional slide of the two teens into chilling action. This tragic, mesmerizing, and grisly character study is based on a true story about author Anne Perry. Rated R for language and violence. 99m. **DIR:** Peter Jackson. **CAST:** Melanie Lynskey, Kate Winslet. **1994**

HEAVENLY KID, THE ★★ *The Heavenly Kid* is earthbound. Cocky Bobby Fontana (Lewis Smith) bit the big one in a chicken race seventeen years ago: which would make it 1968, but the soundtrack and the wardrobe are definitely 1955—a basic problem rendering this otherwise simply stupid film completely unintelligible. Rated PG-13 for language, situations, and bare body parts. 90m. **DIR:** Cary Medoway. **CAST:** Lewis Smith, Jason Gedrick, Jane Kaczmarek, Richard Mulligan. **1985**

HEAVEN'S A DRAG ★★ This so wants to be the gay version of *Truly, Madly, Deeply*, but it's merely a pale copy. Ian Williams is too weak an actor to carry off his haunting of a former lover (Thomas Arklie) in this bittersweet love story. Makes a good point about facing your emotions, warts and all, but the script and the presentation buckle under their good intentions. Not rated; contains profanity and brief nudity. 96m. **DIR:** Peter Mackenzie Litten. **CAST:** Ian Williams, Thomas Arklie, Dillie Keane, Tony Slattery. **1994**

HEAVENS ABOVE ★★★1/2 Another low-key gem from the late Peter Sellers, this irreverent story of a clergyman with the common touch spoofs just about everything within reach, some of it brilliantly. Sellers shows his congregation the error of their selfish ways and engages them in some odd charities, often with hilarious results. B&W; 105m. **DIR:** John Boulting, Roy Boulting. **CAST:** Peter Sellers, Cecil Parker, Isabel Jeans, Eric Sykes. **1963**

HEAVEN'S BURNING ★★★1/2 Excitement abounds in this twisted tale of a young, bored Japanese bride honeymooning in Australia who fakes her own kidnapping only to be taken for real during a bank robbery. When the getaway-car driver kidnaps her from his accomplices to keep them from killing her, they head to the Outback to hide out. Clever *film noir* with lots of twists. Rated R for adult situations, language, and violence. 99m. **DIR:** Craig Lahiff. **CAST:** Russell Crowe, Youki Kudoh, Kenji Isomura, Ray Barrett. **1997 DVD**

HEAVEN'S GATE ★★1/2 Written and directed by Michael Cimino (*The Deer Hunter*), this $36 million epic Western about the land wars in Wyoming between the cattle barons and immigrant farmers, is awkward and overlong but at least makes sense in the complete video version. Rated R for nudity, sex, and violence. 219m. **DIR:** Michael Cimino. **CAST:** Kris Kristofferson, Christopher Walken, Isabelle Huppert, John Hurt, Sam Waterston, Brad Dourif, Jeff Bridges, Joseph Cotten. **1980 DVD**

HEAVEN'S PRISONERS ★★★★ Alec Baldwin gives an outstanding performance as ex-cop Dave Robicheaux, who finds himself drawn back into the sleazy underworld of New Orleans when a plane crashes in the waters near his bait shop. Adapted from the hardboiled detective novel by James Lee Burke, the film is deliberate in its pace and may disappoint some viewers, but excellent performances, stylish direction, and a blues-powered soundtrack make it a rich character study in a mystery setting. Rated R for violence, profanity, nudity, and sex. 132m. **DIR:** Phil Joanou. **CAST:** Alec Baldwin, Kelly Lynch, Mary Stuart Masterson, Eric Roberts, Teri Hatcher. **1996**

HEAVY ★★★ This moody, low-key drama is a *Marty* for the 1990s. Introverted, overweight pizza chef Victor lives with his mom and works at her dingy diner. He is befriended by a pretty college dropout with boyfriend problems who jump-starts his stagnant personal life. The film lays bare the insecurities and fantasies of a physically large but socially invisible loser and looks at the world through his wildly darting eyes. Not rated; contains strong language, nudity, and sex. 119m. **DIR:** James Mangold. **CAST:** Pruitt Taylor Vince, Liv Tyler, Shelley Winters, Deborah Harry, Evan Dando, Joe Grifasi. **1996 DVD**

HEAVY METAL ★★★ While this animated film, based on the French science-fiction comic book of the same name, has not aged particularly well, there are still some high points in its anthology of stories. Combining the sexy sci-fi art style pioneered by Frank Frazetta with an updated E. C. Comics approach to storytelling, it also features the rock music of Blue Oyster Cult, Black Sabbath, Cheap Trick, and others. Voices by John Candy, John Vernon, Harold Ramis, Eugene Levy, and Joe Flaherty. Rated R for sex and violence. 90m. **DIR:** Gerald Potterton. **1981 DVD**

HEAVY TRAFFIC ★★★ Ralph Bakshi's follow-up to *Fritz the Cat* is a mixture of live action and animation. Technically outstanding, but its downbeat look at urban life is rather unpleasant to watch. Rated R for profanity, nudity, and violence. 76m. **DIR:** Ralph Bakshi. **CAST:** Animated. **1973 DVD**

HEAVYWEIGHTS ★★ Chubby boys attending summer fat camp seeking sanctuary from the weight-conscious world are greeted with a jolt. The camp's new owner, a health guru, initiates a rigorous fitness regime that he

wants to film for an infomercial. Rated PG. 103m. **DIR:** Steven Brill. **CAST:** Ben Stiller, Tom McGowan, Leah Lail, Aaron Schwartz, Kenan Thompson, Tom Hodges, Shaun Weiss, Jerry Stiller, Anne Meara. **1995**

HECK'S WAY HOME ★★★1/2 After losing "his people" during a move from Winnipeg to Vancouver (in preparation for a sea voyage to Australia), a resourceful dog hits the road in a determined effort to find them again. Chris Haddock's script is a charmer all the way, and Alan Arkin lends considerable comic relief as a dogcatcher on the verge of retirement . . . but not before *finally* dealing with his long-term nemesis. Rated G. 92m. **DIR:** Michael Scott. **CAST:** Chad Krowchuk, Michael Riley, Shannon Lawson, Don Francks, Alan Arkin. **1995**

HEDD WYN ★★★★ Haunting, true tale of how a young Welsh farmer's dreams of winning a poetry contest are dashed when he signs up to fight in World War I. Before he goes off to fight in the war, Ellis Evans (Huw Garmon) submits a poem into competition under the pseudonym Hedd Wyn. Lying mortally wounded in a trench, Evans examines his life, his loves, and ultimately, his death. Lyrical, almost epic in proportion. In Welsh with English subtitles. Not rated. 123m. **DIR:** Paul Turner. **CAST:** Huw Garmon, Sue Roderick, Judith Humphreys, Nia Dryhurst. **1992**

HEDDA ★★★★ Screenwriter-director Trevor Nunn creates a fine adaptation of Henrik Ibsen's *Hedda Gabler*. Glenda Jackson presides as a coldhearted, power-hungry manipulator who toys with the lives and emotions of those around her. Jackson's costars—members of the Royal Shakespeare Company—match her fine performance. 103m. **DIR:** Trevor Nunn. **CAST:** Glenda Jackson, Timothy West, Peter Eyre, Patrick Stewart. **1975**

•HEDWIG AND THE ANGRY INCH ★★★★ An East German transsexual (writer-director John Cameron Mitchell) and her rock band play a series of seedy one-night stands, dogging the tour of the superstar who stole her songs. This flamboyant, offbeat rock musical, which may remind some of *The Rocky Horror Picture Show*, examines serious questions of love and identity while having fun, and gives a tour de force performance to boot. Stephen Trask's songs are marvelous. Rated R for profanity and sexual content. 95m. **DIR:** John Cameron Mitchell. **CAST:** John Cameron Mitchell, Michael Pitt, Miriam Shor, Stephen Trask, Andrea Martin. **2001 DVD**

HEIDI (1937) ★★★★ This classic stars a spunky Shirley Temple as the girl who is taken away from her kind and loving grandfather's home in the Swiss Alps and forced to live with her cruel aunt. B&W; 88m. **DIR:** Allan Dwan. **CAST:** Shirley Temple, Jean Hersholt, Arthur Treacher. **1937 DVD**

HEIDI (1965) ★★★★ Shirley Temple fans will disagree, but we think that the beautiful location scenes filmed in the Swiss Alps and the generally high level of production and performances make this the best version on video of the classic children's tale. It's been updated to the present day, but otherwise it is faithful to Johanna Spyri's book. Dubbed in English. 95m. **DIR:** Werner Jacobs. **CAST:** Eva Maria Singhammer. **1965**

HEIDI CHRONICLES, THE ★★★ Wendy Wasserstein adapted her Pulitzer Prize–winning play for cable, but it never loses that stagy feeling. Jamie Lee Curtis and Tom Hulce are fun and believable as college students whose friendship spans thirty years. Wasserstein makes a strong case for feminism and the dialogue is intelligent and witty, but the supporting roles are stereotypical and there are no dramatic surprises. Not rated; contains profanity and sexual situations. 94m. **DIR:** Paul Bogart. **CAST:** Jamie Lee Curtis, Tom Hulce, Kim Cattrall, Peter Friedman. **1995**

HEIDI FLEISS, HOLLYWOOD MADAME ★★★★ Award-winning documentary filmmaker Nick Broomfield turns his cameras on infamous Beverly Hills madam Heidi Fleiss, and the result is a fascinating look at a woman's fall from fame. Utilizing family home movies, news clips, and personal interviews, Broomfield depicts a woman on the fast track in Hollywood, serving a clientele of the rich and infamous. Neither pretty nor flattering, it's always engaging and juicy. Not rated; contains nudity, profanity, and adult situations. 106m. **DIR:** Nick Broomfield. **1995 DVD**

HEIDI'S SONG ★★ Only those 5 years old and younger will enjoy this feature-length cartoon adaptation of Johanna Spyri's classic children's tale. Rated G. 94m. **DIR:** Robert Taylor. **1982**

HEIRESS, THE ★★★★1/2 This moving drama takes place in New York City in the mid-1800s. Olivia de Havilland is excellent (she won an Oscar for this performance) as a plain but extraordinarily rich woman who is pursued by a wily gold digger (played by Montgomery Clift). Ralph Richardson is great as her straitlaced father. B&W; 115m. **DIR:** William Wyler. **CAST:** Olivia de Havilland, Montgomery Clift, Ralph Richardson, Miriam Hopkins, Vanessa Brown, Mona Freeman, Ray Collins. **1949**

HEIST, THE (1989) ★★★1/2 Fun revenge film features Pierce Brosnan as a framed con seeking to even the score with his former racetrack partner (Tom Skerritt). There are so many twists and turns in the plot that you will be guessing the final outcome until the closing shot. Not rated HBO film features violence. 97m. **DIR:** Stuart Orme. **CAST:** Pierce Brosnan, Tom Skerritt, Wendy Hughes. **1989**

•HEIST (2001) ★★★1/2 Gene Hackman gives his usual strong performance in this workmanlike crime-drama as the leader of a crew of expert thieves working for fence Danny DeVito. Forced to do one more job in order to collect his money, Hackman and company must execute a near-impossible heist. The robbery itself is well staged, and the film keeps the audience guessing. Although writer-director David Mamet's previous works in the genre—*House of Games* and *The Spanish Prisoner*—are superior to *Heist*, second-rate Mamet is better than most directors' best efforts. Rated R for profanity, violence, and brief sexuality. 111m. **DIR:** David Mamet. **CAST:** Gene Hackman, Danny DeVito, Delroy Lindo, Sam Rockwell, Rebecca Pidgeon, Ricky Jay. **2001 DVD**

HELD UP ★★ Chicago smart aleck and his fiancée stop at a rural convenience store while touring the Grand Canyon area in his vintage Studebaker Hawk. When she discovers he spent their house nest egg on the car, she hitches a ride to Las Vegas and he becomes a hostage of Mexican bandits in a poorly executed robbery. This comedy about a black man stranded in redneck country (locals mistake the lead character for Mike Tyson and

Puff Daddy) is more flat than funny. Rated PG-13 for language and sexual innuendo. 89m. **DIR:** Steve Rash. **CAST:** Jamie Foxx, Nia Long, Eduardo Yanez, Barry Corbin, John Cullum. **2000 DVD**

HELEN MORGAN STORY, THE ★★★ Largely fictional biography of the singing star of the 1920s, with Ann Blyth as the torch singer and Paul Newman as the hood who does her wrong. Ripe melodrama that at least provides more than a dozen great songs (actually sung by Gogi Grant). B&W; 118m. **DIR:** Michael Curtiz. **CAST:** Ann Blyth, Paul Newman, Richard Carlson, Gene Evans. **1959**

HELEN OF TROY ★★★ This Greek myth, about the woman whose face launched a thousand ships, is bogged down with 1950s attitudes but manages to entertain through sheer extravagance. A cast of thousands wages war over the illicit affair between Queen Helen and Prince Paris. Plenty of grand-scale battles. 141m. **DIR:** Robert Wise. **CAST:** Rossana Podesta, Jacques Sernas, Cedric Hardwicke, Stanley Baker, Niall MacGinnis. **1955**

HELL COMES TO FROGTOWN This laughable poverty-row quickie is set in one of those post-apocalyptic futures that allow a minimum of set design. Rated R for nudity, language, and violence. 88m. **DIR:** R. J. Kizer, Donald G. Jackson. **CAST:** Roddy Piper, Sandahl Bergman, Rory Calhoun. **1987 DVD**

HELL HARBOR ★★1/2 Sleazy descendant of a pirate wants to sell his daughter to the harbor's moneylender, but she has eyes for a handsome skipper and passage to Havana. B&W; 83m. **DIR:** Henry King. **CAST:** Lupe Velez, Jean Hersholt, Gibson Gowland, John Holland, Al St. John. **1930**

HELL HIGH Students playing cruel practical jokes pick on the wrong victim, who summons demons from her past to do her bidding. The real cruel joke is having to sit through this film. Rated R for violence. 84m. **DIR:** Douglas Grossman. **CAST:** Christopher Stryker, Christopher Cousins, Jason Brill, Maureen Mooney. **1986**

HELL HOUNDS OF ALASKA ★★ Action tale taking place in Alaska during the gold rush. Outlaws ambush and murder a miner and kidnap his son. When the deed is discovered, a friend of the slain man tries to rescue the boy. Beautiful scenery and direction make this a fine family film. Rated G. 90m. **DIR:** Harald Reinl. **CAST:** Doug McClure, Harold Leipnitz, Angelica Ott, Roberto Blanco. **1973**

HELL IN THE PACIFIC ★★★1/2 John Boorman directed this moody, somewhat trying drama about an American and a Japanese conducting their own private war on a deserted island at the end of World War II. Well acted. 103m. **DIR:** John Boorman. **CAST:** Lee Marvin, Toshiro Mifune. **1968 DVD**

HELL IS FOR HEROES ★★★★ This tense, gritty World War II drama is heaven for action fans. Director Don Siegel is at his riveting best, drawing the viewer into the claustrophobic, nightmarish atmosphere. B&W; 90m. **DIR:** Don Siegel. **CAST:** Steve McQueen, Bobby Darin, Fess Parker, James Coburn, Harry Guardino, Mike Kellin, Nick Adams, Bob Newhart. **1962 DVD**

HELL NIGHT ★★ Linda Blair (*The Exorcist*) returns to the genre that spawned her film career in this low-budget horror flick about fraternity and sorority pledges spending the night in a mansion "haunted" by a crazed killer. Rated R. 101m. **DIR:** Tom DeSimone. **CAST:** Linda Blair, Vincent Van Patten, Peter Barton, Jenny Neuman. **1981 DVD**

HELL ON FRISCO BAY ★★★ A 1930s-type hardboiled crime story of a framed cop who does his time, is released from prison, and goes after the bigwig gangster who set him up. Lots of action on San Francisco's streets and its famous bay. 98m. **DIR:** Frank Tuttle. **CAST:** Alan Ladd, Joanne Dru, Edward G. Robinson, William Demarest, Fay Wray. **1955**

HELL SHIP MUTINY ★★ South Seas programmer with captain Jon Hall battling smugglers who are exploiting island natives. Watchable only for the cast. B&W; 66m. **DIR:** Lee Sholem, Elmo Williams. **CAST:** Jon Hall, John Carradine, Peter Lorre, Roberta Haynes, Mike Mazurki. **1957**

HELL SQUAD Las Vegas show girls are recruited by the CIA. Rated R for nudity and gore. 88m. **DIR:** Kenneth Hartford. **CAST:** Bainbridge Scott, Glen Hartford, William Bryant, Marvin Miller. **1985**

HELL TO ETERNITY ★★★ A trimly told and performed antiprejudice, antiwar drama based on the life of World War II hero Guy Gabaldon, a Californian raised by Japanese-American parents. Jeffrey Hunter and Sessue Hayakawa share acting honors as the hero and the strong-minded Japanese commander who confronts him in the South Pacific. Lots of battle scenes. B&W; 132m. **DIR:** Phil Karlson. **CAST:** Jeffrey Hunter, David Janssen, Vic Damone, Patricia Owens, Sessue Hayakawa. **1960**

HELL TOWN ★★★1/2 Stepping up from his low-budget programmers for Republic and Monogram, John Wayne was cast in the last of Paramount's series of films based on the stories of Zane Grey. He plays a happy-go-lucky cowhand who falls in with rustlers. Also known as *Born to the West*. B&W; 50m. **DIR:** Charles Barton. **CAST:** John Wayne, Marsha Hunt, Johnny Mack Brown, Alan Ladd, James Craig, Monte Blue, Lucien Littlefield. **1938**

HELL UP IN HARLEM Violent, cheaply made sequel to *Black Caesar*. Rated R. 98m. **DIR:** Larry Cohen. **CAST:** Fred Williamson, Julius W. Harris, Gloria Hendry, Margaret Avery, D'Urville Martin. **1973 DVD**

HELLBENDERS, THE Story of a washed-out Confederate and his band of sons. 92m. **DIR:** Sergio Corbucci. **CAST:** Joseph Cotten, Norma Bengell, Julian Mateos, Angel Aranda. **1967**

HELLBORN Only the most masochistic Ed Wood fans will want to sit through this tape. B&W; 50m. **DIR:** Edward D. Wood Jr. **CAST:** Edward D. Wood Jr., Mona McKinnon. **1952–1993**

HELLBOUND ★★ Only Chuck Norris and his fists of steel can stop a Beelzebub clone set free in modern society. Rated R for violence, nudity, and language. 97m. **DIR:** Aaron Norris. **CAST:** Chuck Norris, Calvin Levels, Sheree Wilson, Christopher Neame. **1993**

HELLCAB ★★★ Will Kern's stage play becomes a film with most of its emotional core intact. Paul Dillon does an excellent job of steering this human-interest drama through the mean streets of Chicago, playing a cabdriver whose day is filled with all sorts of adventures, and interesting characters and situations. But we hardly get to know the man behind the wheel and this

keeps the film from becoming complete. Rated R for adult situations and language. 96m. **DIR:** Mary Cybulski, John Tintori. **CAST:** Paul Dillon, Gillian Anderson, John Cusack, Moira Harris, Michael Ironside, Laurie Metcalf, Julianne Moore, Kevin J. O'Connor. **1998**

HELLCATS OF THE NAVY ★★★ This none-too-exciting drama has one thing to attract viewers: President Ronald Reagan and First Lady Nancy co-star. B&W; 82m. **DIR:** Nathan Juran. **CAST:** Ronald Reagan, Nancy Davis, Arthur Franz, Harry Lauter. **1957**

HELLDORADO ★★ Roy and the boys exercise their fists and tonsils while breaking up a gang of black-market racketeers in postwar Las Vegas. The popular rodeo forms the backdrop as Roy, Dale, and Gabby entertain the likes of singer Eddie Acuff and future Lone Ranger Clayton Moore. B&W; 70m. **DIR:** William Witney. **CAST:** Roy Rogers, George "Gabby" Hayes, Dale Evans, Bob Nolan and the Sons of the Pioneers, LeRoy Mason, Paul Harvey, Rex Lease, Eddie Acuff, Clayton Moore. **1946**

HELLDORADO ★★ A penniless hitchhiker discovers a ghost town with a gold mine. The picture boasts an acclaimed director and a highly professional cast, but it is unpersuasively produced. B&W; 75m. **DIR:** James Cruze. **CAST:** Richard Arlen, Madge Evans, Henry B. Walthall, Ralph Bellamy, James Gleason, Helen Jerome Eddy. **1934**

HELLER IN PINK TIGHTS ★★1/2 Legendary nineteenth-century actress and love goddess Adah Issacs Menken inspired this odd film about a ragtag theatrical troupe wandering the West in the 1880s. Colorful but air-filled, it offers a busty blonde Sophia Loren with lusty Tony Quinn. 100m. **DIR:** George Cukor. **CAST:** Sophia Loren, Anthony Quinn, Margaret O'Brien, Edmund Lowe, Steve Forrest, Eileen Heckart, Ramon Novarro. **1960**

HELLFIGHTERS ★★ Once again the talents of John Wayne have been squandered. The Duke is cast as a high-priced fireman sent around the world to put out dangerous oil rig fires. Even hard-core Wayne fans may wince at this one. Rated PG. 121m. **DIR:** Andrew V. McLaglen. **CAST:** John Wayne, Katharine Ross, Vera Miles, Jim Hutton, Bruce Cabot. **1969 DVD**

HELLFIRE ★★★1/2 Solid, offbeat Western in which a ne'er-do-well gambler, William ("Wild Bill") Elliott, is shoved onto the path of righteousness when a preacher saves his life. A bit preachy at times, it still packs a solid wallop of entertainment. 79m. **DIR:** R. G. Springsteen. **CAST:** William Elliott, Marie Windsor, Forrest Tucker, Jim Davis, Grant Withers, Paul Fix, Denver Pyle. **1949**

HELLFIRE CLUB, THE ★★ Tepid historical swashbuckler, made in England, about a dashing swordsman who is the grown-up son of one of the founders of royalty's legendary sex-and-sin fellowship. Doesn't devote enough screen time to the title organization's nefarious activities. 88m. **DIR:** Robert S. Baker, Monty Berman. **CAST:** Keith Michell, Adrienne Corri, Peter Cushing. **1960**

HELLGATE ★★ A band of badly scripted teenagers on holiday search for adventure in a legendary ghost town—unfortunately peopled by the nasty living dancehall dead. Feeble camp humor and tepid special effects sink this lightly erotic post-teen horror. Rated R. 96m. **DIR:** William A. Levey. **CAST:** Ron Palillo, Abigail Wolcott, Evan J. Klisser. **1989**

HELLHOLE 🦃 A young woman witnesses her mother's murder and psychosomatically loses her memory. Rated R for violence and nudity. 90m. **DIR:** Pierre DeMoro. **CAST:** Ray Sharkey, Judy Landers, Marjoe Gortner, Edy Williams. **1985**

HELLMASTER 🦃 Long-thought-dead professor John Saxon returns to his alma mater to continue his experiments turning students into mutants. The final exam has got to be a bummer. Not rated; contains horror violence. 99m. **DIR:** Douglas Schulze. **CAST:** John Saxon, David Emge. **1990**

HELLO AGAIN ★★1/2 Suburban housewife Shelley Long chokes to death on a Korean meatball only to find herself brought back to life via a magic spell cast by her wacky sister (Judith Ivey). Screenplay by Susan Isaacs. Rated PG for profanity. 95m. **DIR:** Frank Perry. **CAST:** Shelley Long, Judith Ivey, Gabriel Byrne, Corbin Bernsen, Sela Ward, Austin Pendleton. **1987**

HELLO, DOLLY! 🦃 Barbra Streisand as an intrepid matchmaker. Rated G. 146m. **DIR:** Gene Kelly. **CAST:** Barbra Streisand, Walter Matthau, Michael Crawford, E. J. Peaker, Marianne McAndrew. **1969**

HELLO, FRISCO, HELLO ★★1/2 John Payne is a selfish Barbary Coast saloon owner who buys and marries his way to Nob Hill, deserting friends and a true love. A best-song Oscar for Harry Warren and Mack Gordon's "You'll Never Know." 99m. **DIR:** H. Bruce Humberstone. **CAST:** Alice Faye, John Payne, Jack Oakie, Lynn Bari, June Havoc, Laird Cregar, Ward Bond. **1943**

HELLO, MARY LOU: PROM NIGHT II 🦃 Another tedious exploitation flick about a girl who returns from the grave to get revenge on her killers. Rated R for violence, nudity, and language. 96m. **DIR:** Bruce Pittman. **CAST:** Lisa Schrage, Wendy Lyon, Michael Ironside. **1987**

HELLRAISER ★★1/2 In his directing debut, Clive Barker adapts his short story and proves even the author can't necessarily bring his work to life on the screen. The story is about a man who acquires a demonic Rubik's Cube. Although imbued with marvelous visuals, the film has little of the intensity of a Barker novel. Rated R for violence, sex, and adult language. 90m. **DIR:** Clive Barker. **CAST:** Andrew Robinson, Clare Higgins, Ashley Laurence. **1987 DVD**

HELLRAISER II: HELLBOUND ★★1/2 People without skin! If that doesn't either pique your interest or turn you away, nothing will. A psychiatric patient, who is lost in a world of puzzles, unleashes the nasty Cenobites (introduced in *Hellraiser*). Clive Barker protégé Tony Randel makes everything a bit overwhelming, but it's all good, clean, gruesome fun. Rated R for gore. 96m. **DIR:** Tony Randel. **CAST:** Clare Higgins, Ashley Laurence, Kenneth Cranham. **1988**

HELLRAISER 3: HELL ON EARTH ★★★ Pinhead returns, only this time he's brought some new friends and they don't want to go back where they came from. Combine gory (and very imaginative) special effects and a slightly off-center story and you have one that should please fans, but make others sick. Rated R for profanity, simulated sex, and graphic violence. 90m. **DIR:** Anthony Hickox. **CAST:** Terry Ferrell, Doug Bradley, Paula Marshall, Kevin Bernhardt, Ashley Laurence. **1992**

HELLRAISER: BLOODLINE ★★ This fourth installment in Clive Barker's highly successful series about the dark prince of Hell was controversial before it even came out. What is left is a by-the-numbers exercise in skinnings and death that treads none of the daring ground of its predecessors. Director Alan Smithee is really special-effects artist Kevin Yagher. Rated R for violence, profanity, and gore. 86m. **DIR:** Alan Smithee. **CAST:** Doug Bradley, Bruce Ramsay, Valentina Vargas. **1996**

•**HELLRAISER: INFERNO** ★★ Lackluster chapter in the popular horror series, hampered by the minimal onscreen appearance of the series' hero, Pinhead. Rated R for violence, nudity, and drug use. 99m. **DIR:** Scott Derrickson. **CAST:** Craig Sheffer, Nicholas Turturro, James Remar, Doug Bradley, Nicholas Sadler. **2000 DVD**

HELL'S ANGELS FOREVER ★★1/2 A documentary on the notorious biker organization; mostly a feature-length endorsement rather than an objective profile. Early portion, tracing the Hells Angels' origins in post–World War II, working-class California, is best. Rated R for profanity. 87m. **DIR:** Richard Chase, Kevin Keating, Leon Gast. **1983**

HELL'S ANGELS ON WHEELS ★★1/2 This is one of the better 1960s biker films, most notably because Jack Nicholson has a big role in it. Not a great work by any means, but if you like biker movies ... 95m. **DIR:** Richard Rush. **CAST:** Adam Roarke, Jack Nicholson, Sabrina Scharf, John Garwood, Jana Taylor. **1967**

HELL'S ANGELS '69 ★★ Two rich kids devise a plan to rob a gambling casino by infiltrating the Hell's Angels and then using the gang to create a diversion. The plan works until the bikers retaliate. Mediocre. 97m. **DIR:** Lee Madden. **CAST:** Tom Stern, Jeremy Slate, Conny Van Dyke, Sonny Barger, Terry the Tramp. **1969**

HELL'S BRIGADE 🦃 Rotten film concerning a commando raid on Hitler's Germany during World War II. 99m. **DIR:** Henry Mankiewirk. **CAST:** Jack Palance, John Douglas. **1980**

HELL'S HINGES ★★★ William S. Hart's trademark character, the good-bad man, loses his heart to the new minister's sister when she arrives in Hell's Hinges. The minister is corrupted and the church burned down, causing Hart to seek revenge. This grim story is perhaps Hart's best film, and certainly his most imitated. Silent. B&W; 65m. **DIR:** William S. Hart, Charles Swickard. **CAST:** William S. Hart, Clara Williams, Robert McKim. **1916**

HELL'S HOUSE ★★ Gangster and prison films in the 1930s had their junior counterparts. In this barely so-so example, an innocent boy does time in a harsh reformatory because he won't rat on an adult crook friend. Junior Durkin is the poor kid, Pat O'Brien is the crook—a bootlegger—and Bette Davis is his girl. B&W; 72m. **DIR:** Howard Higgin. **CAST:** Junior Durkin, Bette Davis, Pat O'Brien, Frank Coghlan Jr., Charley Grapewin, Emma Dunn. **1932**

HELLSTROM CHRONICLE, THE ★★★★ This 1971 pseudodocumentary features fantastic close-up cinematography of insects and their ilk underpinning a story line by Dr. Hellstrom (Lawrence Pressman), which contends the critters are taking over. Despite the dumb premise, *The Hellstrom Chronicle* remains a captivating film. Rated G. 90m. **DIR:** Walon Green. **CAST:** Lawrence Pressman. **1971**

HELLZAPOPPIN ★★★ Olsen and Johnson's famously frantic Broadway show was filmed with inconsistent results. Like the Marx Brothers' MGM films, this is hurt by the introduction of a vapid romantic subplot, and while the two comics take every possible opportunity to make fun of it on-screen, it constantly bogs down the film. B&W; 84m. **DIR:** H. C. Potter. **CAST:** Ole Olsen, Chic Johnson, Robert Paige, Jane Frazee, Lewis Howard, Martha Raye, Mischa Auer, Elisha Cook Jr., Richard Lane, Hugh Herbert, Shemp Howard, Billy Curtis. **1941**

HELP! ★★★★ Though neither as inventive nor as charming as *A Hard Day's Night*, this second collaboration between director Richard Lester and the Fab Four has energy, fun, and memorable songs. The slim plot has a bizarre religious cult trying to retrieve a sacrificial ring from Ringo. From the reverberating opening chord of the title tune, the movie sweeps you up in its irresistibly zesty spirit. 90m. **DIR:** Richard Lester. **CAST:** The Beatles, Leo McKern, Eleanor Bron, Victor Spinetti. **1965 DVD**

HELTER SKELTER ★★★★ The story of Charles Manson's 1969 murder spree is vividly retold in this excellent TV movie. Steve Railsback is superb as the crazed Manson. Based on prosecutor Vincent Bugliosi's book, this is high-voltage stuff. Not rated and too intense for the kids. 114m. **DIR:** Tom Gries. **CAST:** George DiCenzo, Steve Railsback, Nancy Wolfe, Marilyn Burns. **1976**

HELTER-SKELTER MURDERS, THE 🦃 Sensationalistic account of the Tate murders. Rated R for graphic violence. B&W/color; 83m. **DIR:** Frank Howard. **CAST:** Debbie Duff. **1988**

HENNESSY ★★★ After his family is killed by a bomb, an Irishman plots to assassinate the Queen of England in revenge. Fairly suspenseful thriller with a sympathetic performance by Rod Steiger, though the fact that we know the queen is still alive tends to ruin the suspense. Rated PG. 103m. **DIR:** Don Sharp. **CAST:** Rod Steiger, Lee Remick, Richard Johnson, Trevor Howard, Eric Porter. **1975**

HENRY & JUNE ★★1/2 Good direction doesn't offset mediocre acting and an excruciatingly boring script in this oft-melodramatic story about expatriate author Henry Miller and his personal problems with sex. Based on Anaïs Nin's memoirs, it was the first release under the NC-17 rating code, though could have squeaked through with an R. 136m. **DIR:** Phil Kaufman. **CAST:** Fred Ward, Uma Thurman, Maria de Medeiros, Kevin Spacey, Richard E. Grant. **1990 DVD**

HENRY FOOL ★★★★1/2 Henry is an unkempt, self-deluded ex-convict who moves into the basement of a home inhabited by geeky garbageman Simon Grim, his slutty sister, and their despondent mother. He is writing a lengthy "confession" and convinces Simon to capture his own thoughts on paper. Simon does and becomes a media sensation in this profane seriocomic myth about friendship, artistic license, celebrity, and cultural trends. Rated R for language, sexuality, and adult themes. 137m. **DIR:** Hal Hartley. **CAST:** Thomas Jay Ryan, James Urbaniak, Parker Posey, Maria Porter, Kevin Corrigan. **1998**

HENRY IV ★★★ This Italian TV film is based on a Luigi Pirandello play. A modern aristocrat is thrown from his horse and then believes he is Emperor Henry IV. Twenty years pass and his past lover and a psychiatrist devise a plan to shake him back to reality. It's interesting, but seems long. In Italian with English subtitles. 95m. **DIR:** Marco Bellocchio. **CAST:** Marcello Mastroianni, Claudia Cardinale, Leopoldo Trieste. **1984**

HENRY MILLER ODYSSEY ★★★★ This film biography is regulation for all fans and those who would know more about one of America's most controversial writers. Alive with Miller and close friends, it is a finely photographed documentary revealing his opinions and reflections, innate gentleness, beguiling charm, and vigorous lust for living. 60m. **DIR:** Robert Snyder. **CAST:** Henry Miller, Lawrence Durrell, Anaïs Nin, Alfred Perles. **1969**

HENRY V (1944) ★★★★★ The first of Olivier's three major film forays into Shakespeare (the others are *Hamlet* and *Richard III*), this production blazed across screens like a meteor. A stirring, colorful film, full of sound and fury, and all the pageantry one expects from English history brought to vivid life. Olivier won an honorary Oscar for acting, directing, and producing. In a word: superb. 137m. **DIR:** Laurence Olivier. **CAST:** Laurence Olivier, Robert Newton, Leslie Banks, Felix Aylmer, Renée Asherson, Leo Genn. **1944 DVD**

HENRY V (1989) ★★★★★ What star-adapter-director Kenneth Branagh has done with Shakespeare's *Henry V* on screen is nothing short of miraculous. Not better, but different, than Laurence Olivier's 1944 production, Branagh's version truly does "ascend the brightest heaven of invention," as promised in the film's stunning prologue. In chronicling young King Henry's war against France, Branagh has created a Shakespearean adaptation on an epic scale and one of the best films of its kind. Rated PG for violence. 138m. **DIR:** Kenneth Branagh. **CAST:** Kenneth Branagh, Derek Jacobi, Paul Scofield, Judi Dench, Ian Holm, Emma Thompson, Robert Stephens, Geraldine McEwan, Alec McCowen. **1989 DVD**

HENRY: PORTRAIT OF A SERIAL KILLER ★★★★ Chillingly real and brutally explicit, this profile of a murderous drifter and his former prison pal emerges as a quasi-documentary that dwells so deep in the psychopathic mind of its title character one almost expects disclaimers to parade across the screen. Not rated, but filled with violence and raw brutality. 90m. **DIR:** John McNaughton. **CAST:** Michael Rooker. **1990 DVD**

HER ALIBI ★★★ This clever comedy-mystery presents Tom Selleck as a suspense writer who provides an alibi for a beautiful murder suspect (Paulina Porizkova). Fans of director Bruce Beresford may think this ditty is beneath him, but only a curmudgeon can resist its daffy charms. Rated PG for profanity and comic violence. 110m. **DIR:** Bruce Beresford. **CAST:** Tom Selleck, Paulina Porizkova, William Daniels, Tess Harper, Patrick Wayne, Hurd Hatfield. **1989 DVD**

HERBIE GOES BANANAS ★★1/2 This is the corniest and least funny of Disney's "Love Bug" series. This time Herbie is headed for Brazil to compete in the Grand Primio. Rated G. 93m. **DIR:** Vincent McEveety. **CAST:** Cloris Leachman, Charles Martin Smith, John Vernon, Stephan W. Burns, Harvey Korman. **1980**

HERBIE GOES TO MONTE CARLO ★★★1/2 Herbie the VW falls in love with a sports car as they compete in a race from Paris to Monte Carlo. There are lots of laughs in this one. Rated G. 104m. **DIR:** Vincent McEveety. **CAST:** Dean Jones, Don Knotts, Julie Sommars, Eric Braeden, Roy Kinnear, Jacque Marin. **1977**

HERBIE RIDES AGAIN ★★★1/2 This Disney comedy-adventure is a sequel to *The Love Bug*. This time, Helen Hayes, Ken Berry, and Stephanie Powers depend on Herbie, the magical Volkswagen, to save them from an evil Keenan Wynn. Rated G. 88m. **DIR:** Robert Stevenson. **CAST:** Helen Hayes, Ken Berry, Stefanie Powers, Keenan Wynn. **1974**

HERCULES (ANIMATED) (1997) ★★★★ Hercules is very much the hero of his finger-snapping signature tune and a larger-than-life archetype who demands hyperbole and excess. Sensational contribution by lyricist David Zippel, who teams with composer and Academy Award magnet Alan Menken. Credit also goes to James Woods, tremendous with his vocal characterization of the villain, Hades. He's matched by Broadway star Susan Egan as Meg, a slinky femme fatale with husky radiance and sex appeal. Rated G; suitable for all ages. 86m. **DIR:** John Musker, Ron Clements. **1997 DVD**

HERCULES (1959) ★★1/2 The first and still the best of the Italian-made epics based on the mythical superhero. Steve Reeves looks perfect in the part as Hercules out to win over his true love, the ravishing Sylva Koscina. Some nice action scenes. 107m. **DIR:** Pietro Francisci. **CAST:** Steve Reeves, Sylva Koscina, Ivo Garrani. **1959 DVD**

HERCULES (1983) 🦃 Lou Ferrigno as the most famous muscle man of them all. Rated PG for violence. 98m. **DIR:** Lewis Coates. **CAST:** Lou Ferrigno, Sybil Danning, Brad Harris, Rossana Podesta. **1983**

HERCULES AND THE AMAZON WOMEN ★★★ Second of the TV movies based on the adventures of the legendary strongman introduces Herc to the feminist ways of the Amazons, a race of warrior women. It's a battle of the sexes with Hercules in the middle trying to prove that men and women can live together. Once again, Anthony Quinn is a delight to watch as Zeus, the king of the gods. Rated PG for violence and suggested sex. 87m. **DIR:** Bill L. Norton. **CAST:** Kevin Sorbo, Anthony Quinn, Roma Downey, Lucy Lawless, Michael Hurst. **1994**

HERCULES AND THE CAPTIVE WOMEN ★★1/2 Hercules, his stowaway son, the King of Thebes, and a midget sail toward the lost city of Atlantis searching for the answers to a string of mysterious occurrences. Cornball, campy, and a good deal of fun. An Italian and French production, but dubbed in English. Not rated. 95m. **DIR:** Vittorio Cottafari. **CAST:** Reg Park, Fay Spain. **1963**

HERCULES AND THE CIRCLE OF FIRE ★★★1/2 Exciting, old-fashioned adventure tale finds Hercules fighting to save humanity lest the torch of life be extinguished by Hera. For the third outing as Hercules, Kevin Sorbo really slips into the role and makes it his own, combining just the right amount of heroics, humor, and charm. The special effects and fight scenes are superb, and the influence of producer Sam Raimi shows in what is probably the best of the four movies. Rated PG for vio-

lence. 89m. **DIR:** Doug Lefler. **CAST:** Kevin Sorbo, Anthony Quinn, Tawny Kitaen. **1994**

HERCULES AND THE LOST KINGDOM ★★★ First of the four TV movies that led to the hit series *Hercules: The Legendary Journeys*, this film introduces the son of Zeus to a new generation by adding wacky camera angles and modern views to the proceedings. Here, Hercules must save a lost kingdom from the tyrannous rule of his stepmother Hera. Mindless but enjoyable fun that the whole family can watch. Rated PG for violence. 91m. **DIR:** Harley Cokliss. **CAST:** Kevin Sorbo, Anthony Quinn, Renee O'Connor, Eric Close. **1994**

HERCULES GOES BANANAS 🦃 Ridiculous piece of celluloid starring a very young Arnold Schwarzenegger as Hercules. 73m. **DIR:** Arthur Allan Seidelman. **CAST:** Arnold Schwarzenegger, Arnold Stang. **1972**

HERCULES IN THE HAUNTED WORLD ★★★ Easily the best of the many *Hercules* sequels, because it was designed and directed by famed Italian genre master Mario Bava (*Black Sabbath*). Ignore the brief, dopey comic relief and enjoy the escapist, action-filled plot, which sends Hercules on a journey through Hades. Breathtaking visuals. 83m. **DIR:** Mario Bava. **CAST:** Reg Park, Christopher Lee. **1961**

HERCULES IN THE UNDERWORLD ★★★ Fourth and final installment in the TV movies about the exploits of the legendary strongman pits Hercules against medusas and Cerberus in the underworld. Kevin Sorbo really gets the hang of his role as Hercules here, and Anthony Quinn is a wonderful Zeus. Rated PG for violence and some frightening scenes. 91m. **DIR:** Bill L. Norton. **CAST:** Kevin Sorbo, Anthony Quinn, Tawny Kitaen, Marley Shelton, Timothy Balme, Michael Hurst. **1994**

HERCULES, PRISONER OF EVIL ★★ Not bad for its type, this sword-and-sandal action spectacle is really part of the *Ursus* subgenre of Italian muscle-man movies; the Hercules moniker was slapped on when it was dubbed and released straight to U.S. TV. 90m. **DIR:** Anthony M. Dawson. **CAST:** Reg Park, Ettore Manni. **1964**

HERCULES UNCHAINED ★★ When the god of muscles sets his little mind on something, don't get in his way! In this one, he's out to rescue his lady fair. It's a silly but diverting adventure. Steve Reeves is still the best Hercules on film, dubbed voice and all. 101m. **DIR:** Pietro Francisci. **CAST:** Steve Reeves, Sylva Koscina, Primo Carnera, Sylvia Lopez. **1960 DVD**

HERE COME THE CO-EDS ★★1/2 Standard-issue Abbott and Costello romp of the mid-1940s, with our heroes cast as custodians of a prim girls' academy. High energy, low IQ comedy. B&W; 87m. **DIR:** Jean Yarbrough. **CAST:** Bud Abbott, Lou Costello, Peggy Ryan, Martha O'Driscoll, Lon Chaney Jr. **1945**

HERE COME THE GIRLS ★★★ Bumbling Bob Hope is taken from the chorus and made the star of a Broadway show, unaware he is a decoy for a jealous slasher infatuated with the leading lady. Some good gags and lots of musical numbers. 78m. **DIR:** Claude Binyon. **CAST:** Bob Hope, Arlene Dahl, Tony Martin, Rosemary Clooney, Millard Mitchell, William Demarest, Fred Clark, Robert Strauss. **1953**

HERE COME THE WAVES ★★★1/2 Bing Crosby stars as a famous singer who enlists in the navy with best friend Sonny Tufts. A fun musical that features Betty Hutton as twins—so that both leading men get the girl. "Accentuate the Positive" was written for this film. B&W; 100m. **DIR:** Mark Sandrich. **CAST:** Bing Crosby, Betty Hutton, Sonny Tufts. **1944**

HERE COMES MR. JORDAN ★★★★★ We all know that bureaucracy can botch up almost anything. Well, the bureaucrats of heaven can really throw a lulu at boxer Joe Pendleton (Robert Montgomery). The heavenly administrators have called Joe up before his time, and they've got to set things straight. B&W; 93m. **DIR:** Alexander Hall. **CAST:** Robert Montgomery, Evelyn Keyes, Claude Rains, Rita Johnson, Edward Everett Horton, James Gleason. **1941**

HERE COMES SANTA CLAUS 🦃 Two kids visit Santa at the North Pole to make a personal plea for the return of the boy's parents on Christmas. 78m. **DIR:** Christian Gion. **CAST:** Karen Cheryl, Armand Meffre. **1984**

HERE COMES THE GROOM ★★★ Bing Crosby stars as a reporter returning from France with two war orphans. Jane Wyman finds herself torn between Crosby and wealthy Franchot Tone. Director Frank Capra keeps the pace brisk and adds to an otherwise familiar tale. 114m. **DIR:** Frank Capra. **CAST:** Bing Crosby, Jane Wyman, Alexis Smith, Franchot Tone. **1951**

HERE COMES TROUBLE ★★★ Jewel thief Mona Barrie mistakenly involves Paul Kelly in a crime when she gives him a cigarette case containing some loot. A mixture of comedy and crime—a perfect hour-long time filler. B&W; 62m. **DIR:** Lewis Seiler. **CAST:** Paul Kelly, Arline Judge, Mona Barrie, Gregory Ratoff. **1936**

HERE ON EARTH ★★1/2 A rich kid at an East Coast prep school falls for a working-class girl despite the disapproval of his father. If that sounds familiar, it's because the film is a blatant rip-off of *Love Story*, right down to the mysterious fatal disease. The appealing young stars, a good supporting cast, and nice scenery make the film a tolerable tearjerker. Rated PG-13 for mild profanity. 97m. **DIR:** Mark Piznarski. **CAST:** Chris Klein, Leelee Sobieski, Josh Hartnett, Bruce Greenwood, Annette O'Toole, Annie Corley, Stuart Wilson, Elaine Hendrix, Michael Rooker. **2000 DVD**

HERITAGE OF THE DESERT ★★★ Donald Woods comes West to claim an inheritance and is soon mixed up with outlaws. Best of three screen versions based on the Zane Grey novel. B&W; 74m. **DIR:** Lesley Selander. **CAST:** Donald Woods, Russell Hayden, Evelyn Venable, Sidney Toler. **1939**

HERO, THE (1971) ★★ Richard Harris distinguishes himself neither as actor nor as director in this mawkish sports drama. He plays a soccer star getting on in years who agrees to throw a game for money. Not the freshest of story lines. Not rated. 97m. **DIR:** Richard Harris. **CAST:** Richard Harris, Romy Schneider, Kim Burfield. **1971**

HERO (1992) ★★★★1/2 This saucy spin on Frank Capra's *Meet John Doe* is an acerbic—and often tremendously funny—indictment of American hero-worship. Andy Garcia is revered for having rescued passengers from a stricken airplane; unfortunately, he's taking credit for an act actually performed by small-potatoes criminal Dustin Hoffman (who, looking more ferret-like than ever, is simply priceless). Rated PG-13 for profanity. 116m. **DIR:** Stephen Frears. **CAST:** Dustin

Hoffman, Geena Davis, Andy Garcia, Joan Cusack, Chevy Chase, Tom Arnold. **1992 DVD**

HERO AIN'T NOTHIN' BUT A SANDWICH, A ★★1/2 Heartfelt, uneven black soap opera—a typical latter-day Ralph Nelson production. The director of *Lilies of the Field* lays it on thick in this sentimental adaptation of Alice Childress's book about a black ghetto teen's drug problem. 105m. **DIR:** Ralph Nelson. **CAST:** Cicely Tyson, Paul Winfield, Larry B. Scott, Glynn Turman. **1978**

HERO AND THE TERROR ★★1/2 Chuck Norris gives a good performance in this otherwise disappointing thriller. He's a police officer suffering from deep trauma after confronting a brutal, demented killer called the Terror (Jack O'Halloran). When the Terror escapes from a mental ward, our hero must battle the monster again. Rated R for violence and profanity. 90m. **DIR:** William Tannen. **CAST:** Chuck Norris, Jack O'Halloran, Brynn Thayer, Jeffrey Kramer, Steve James. **1988**

HERO AT LARGE ★★★1/2 In this enjoyably lightweight film, John Ritter plays Steve Nichols, an out-of-work actor who takes a part-time job to promote a movie about a crusading superhero, *Captain Avenger*. Rated PG. 98m. **DIR:** Martin Davidson. **CAST:** John Ritter, Anne Archer, Bert Convy, Kevin McCarthy. **1980**

HEROES ★★★1/2 Henry Winkler is excellent in this compelling story of a confused Vietnam vet traveling cross-country to meet a few of his old war buddies. MCA Home Video has elected to alter the film's closing theme for this release. Removing the emotionally charged "Carry on Wayward Son" by Kansas in favor of a teary generic tune somewhat diminishes the overall impact of the movie. Rated PG for mild language and violence. 113m. **DIR:** Jeremy Paul Kagan. **CAST:** Henry Winkler, Sally Field, Harrison Ford, Val Avery. **1977 DVD**

HEROES DIE YOUNG 🦃 A suicide squad goes behind enemy lines to knock out an oil field in German-occupied Romania. Not rated. B&W; 76m. **DIR:** Gerald S. Shepard. **CAST:** Erika Peters, Scott Borland. **1960**

HEROES FOR SALE ★★★ Warner Bros., noted for gangster films, also turned out many social conscience dramas during the Great Depression, and this is a good one. Richard Barthelmess, more a Poor Soul than an Everyman, suffers from morphine addiction caused by war injuries, the loss of a business in the industrial revolution, the death of his wife in a labor riot, and unjust imprisonment as a radical. Grim going, but fine performances. B&W; 71m. **DIR:** William Wellman. **CAST:** Richard Barthelmess, Aline MacMahon, Loretta Young. **1933**

HEROES OF DESERT STORM ★★1/2 Flag-waving, made-for-TV movie looks at the men (and women) who fought in Desert Storm. Pedestrian effort shows how quick it was made to cash in on patriotism. 93m. **DIR:** Don Ohlmeyer. **CAST:** Daniel Baldwin, Angela Bassett, Marshall Bell, Kris Kamm, Tim Russ. **1992**

HEROES OF THE HEART ★★★ When an old woman tells the residents of a trailer park she has been given the power by God to make their dreams come true, they discuss with each other just what their dreams are. Odd but intriguing comedy-drama. Not rated; contains profanity. 101m. **DIR:** Daniel Boyd. **CAST:** Lina Basquette, Larry Groce, John McIntire. **1995**

HEROES STAND ALONE ★★★ A plane on a secret mission is shot down behind enemy lines. The not so distant future is the setting for this Vietnam-style war movie. Not rated but contains violence and nudity. 83m. **DIR:** Mark Griffiths. **CAST:** Chad Everett, Bradford Dillman. **1990**

HEROIC LEGEND OF ARISLAN ★★★ An interesting tale and appealing characters blend well in this East-meets-West animated hybrid where European-style knights (with Japanese-style hearts) pit their swords against evil. Very good animation. Dubbed in English. Not rated; contains violence. 59m. **DIR:** Mamoru Hamatsu. **1992 DVD**

HEROIC LEGEND OF ARISLAN: THE AGE OF HEROES ★★★ Continuing the adventures of the popular animal, *The Age of Heroes* recounts villain Silvermask's attempts to reclaim the sacred sword that once belonged to his father. Such reclaiming, however, brings about an ancient evil that threatens all of Pars. Beautifully animated, the film nicely bridges the previous series but fails to keep up its pace and action. Too much time is spent on political intrigue and not enough on the sword fights that constitute a heroic legend. Viewers may be confused by many name changes, but a brief prologue explains why this was done. Not rated; contains violence. 60m. **DIR:** Mamoru Hamatsu. **1995**

HESTER STREET ★★★★ Beautifully filmed look at the Jewish community in nineteenth-century New York City. Film focuses on the relationship of a young couple, he turning his back on the old Jewish ways while she fights to hold on to them. Fine performances and great attention to period detail make this very enjoyable. Rated PG. B&W; 92m. **DIR:** Joan Micklin Silver. **CAST:** Carol Kane, Steven Keats, Mel Howard. **1975**

HEXED ★★ A hotel desk clerk with pathological liar tendencies gets mixed up in a bizarre twist of mistaken identity. This wannabe curiosity comedy from the creator of the TV series *Sledge Hammer* doesn't quite know the difference between being outrageous and being absolutely tasteless. Rated R for violence, simulated sex, and language. 100m. **DIR:** Alan Spencer. **CAST:** Arye Gross, Claudia Christian, Adrienne Shelly, Norman Fell, Michael E. Knight, Ray Baker. **1993**

HEY ABBOTT! ★★★★ This is a hilarious anthology of high points from Abbott and Costello television programs. Narrated by Milton Berle, the distillation includes the now-legendary duo's classic routines: "Who's on First?," "Oyster Stew," "Floogle Street," and "The Birthday Party." B&W; 76m. **DIR:** Jim Gates. **CAST:** Bud Abbott, Lou Costello, Joe Besser, Phil Silvers, Steve Allen. **1978**

HEY, BABU RIBA ★★★1/2 Yugoslav version of *American Graffiti*. Poignant, funny reminiscence of four boys and a girl growing up in the early Fifties. The film has an easy charm. In Serbo-Croatian with English subtitles. Rated R for mild profanity, violence, and sex. 109m. **DIR:** Javan Acin. **CAST:** Gala Videnovic. **1986**

HEY GOOD LOOKIN' 🦃 Boring animated film about street gangs of New York City during the 1950s. Rated R. 86m. **DIR:** Ralph Bakshi. **1983**

HEY, I'M ALIVE! ★★1/2 TV movie based on a true story of two people who survived a plane crash in the Yukon, then struggled to stay alive until rescuers could locate them. Well-acted, though nothing you haven't seen be-

fore. 74m. **DIR:** Lawrence Schiller. **CAST:** Edward Asner, Sally Struthers. **1975**

HEY THERE, IT'S YOGI BEAR ★★★ With this movie, Hanna-Barbera Studios made the jump from TV to feature-length cartoon. The result is consistently pleasant. Mel Blanc, J. Pat O'Malley, Julie Bennett, Daws Butler, Don Messick (voices). Rated G. 89m. **DIR:** William Hanna, Joseph Barbera. **1964**

HI LIFE ★★ Eric Stoltz plays an unemployed actor who desperately needs $900 to pay off a loan shark or have his legs broken. A lie he creates in order to get the money from his girlfriend takes on a life all its own, putting the actor in an unwelcome spotlight. Quaint, but not as Runyonesque as writer-director Roger Hedden wants us to believe. Rated R for language. 82m. **DIR:** Roger Hedden. **CAST:** Eric Stoltz, Daryl Hannah, Campbell Scott, Charles Durning, Peter Riegert, Moira Kelly. **1998 DVD**

•HI-LINE, THE ★★★ Understated independent film about a young woman, trapped in a dull existence in a Montana town, whose life is thrown into turmoil by revelations made by a stranger. Rachel Leigh Cook is impressive in a more serious role than those in the usual teen comedies. Unfortunately, the movie is almost ruined by an awful ending. Rated PG. 95m. **DIR:** Ron Judkins. **CAST:** Rachael Leigh Cook, Ryan Alosio, Tantoo Cardinal, Tom Hanson, Margot Kidder, Stuart Margolin. **1999 DVD**

HI-LO COUNTRY, THE ★★★ Two cowboys (Woody Harrelson, Billy Crudup) raise hell and defy the tides of progress in post–World War II New Mexico, while one of them carries on with the married woman they both love. Based on a novel by Max Evans, good performances and atmospheric detail redeem the overfamiliar story and slow pacing. Rated R for profanity, violence, and sexual scenes. 114m. **DIR:** Stephen Frears. **CAST:** Woody Harrelson, Billy Crudup, Patricia Arquette, Penelope Cruz, Sam Elliott, Cole Hauser, James Gammon. **1999 DVD**

HI MOM ★★★ Robert De Niro reprises his role as a Vietnam vet in this award-winning comedy under the direction of a young Brian De Palma. In this semi-sequel to *Greetings*, De Niro continues his adventures as an amateur filmmaker in Greenwich Village. Rated R for nudity and profanity. 87m. **DIR:** Brian De Palma. **CAST:** Robert De Niro, Jennifer Salt, Allen Garfield. **1970**

HI-YO SILVER ★★1/2 A tyrant operating under government protection in the old Southwest is brought to justice by a masked rider and his companions. Feature version of the serial has five potential Lone Rangers, and the audience has to guess along with the bad guys which one it is. Only about one-third of the film remains after editing down fifteen episodes so the storyline is pretty jumpy, but a framing device with new footage added helps a bit. B&W; 69m. **DIR:** William Witney, John English. **CAST:** Lee Powell, Chief Thundercloud, Herman Brix, Hal Taliaferro, George Letz, Lane Chandler, Lynne Roberts, Stanley Andrews. **1940**

HIDDEN, THE ★★★1/2 When a bizarre series of crimes wreaks havoc in Los Angeles, police detective Michael Nouri finds himself paired with an FBI agent (Kyle MacLachlan) whose behavior becomes increasingly strange as they pursue what may be an alien intruder. This hybrid science fiction–adventure will delight those who like their entertainment upredictable. Rated R for violence, nudity, and profanity. 97m. **DIR:** Jack Sholder. **CAST:** Michael Nouri, Kyle MacLachlan, Ed O'Ross, Clu Gulager, Claudia Christian, Clarence Felder. **1987 DVD**

HIDDEN II, THE ★★ Poor sequel stars Raphael Sbarge as an intergalactic cop tracking down a particularly nasty alien who likes to jump from body to body, leaving behind a pile of corpses and a frustrated police force. While the special effects are up to par, film takes way too long to get up to speed, relying on a cameo by original star Michael Nouri to tie the two films together. Rated R for violence, language, and nudity. 95m. **DIR:** Seth Pinsker. **CAST:** Raphael Sbarge, Kate Hode, Michael Nouri. **1993**

HIDDEN AGENDA (1990) ★★★★ Frances McDormand is a member of a panel investigating British atrocities in Northern Ireland who is caught up in the coverup of the death of her boyfriend at the hands of British soldiers. This is a wonderful conspiracy flick concerning the rise to power of British Prime Minister Margaret Thatcher. An added touch of realism is supplied by director Kenneth Loach's documentary-style filmmaking. Rated R for violence and profanity. 105m. **DIR:** Kenneth Loach. **CAST:** Frances McDormand, Brian Cox, Brad Dourif, Mai Zetterling. **1990**

•HIDDEN AGENDA (1998) ★★ If only this film had an agenda, aside from drudging up every Cold War cliché. Kevin Dillon plays David McLean, who travels to Berlin to see his brother and winds up being the unwitting pawn in a tug of war over a computer disc. Despite the presence of such heavyweights as J. T. Walsh and Christopher Plummer, there's nothing to ground this confusing spy game except dumb dialogue, paper-thin characters, and listless direction. Rated R for language, nudity, and violence. 94m. **DIR:** Iain Paterson. **CAST:** Kevin Dillon, Andrea Roth, J. T. Walsh, Christopher Plummer, Michael Wincott. **1998 DVD**

HIDDEN ASSASSIN ★★ Action fans will most appreciate this routine thriller about a U.S. marshal sent to Prague to apprehend an assassin. He immediately suspects a professional hit woman and before long begins to fall for his prey. Rated R for violence, profanity, and nudity. 88m. **DIR:** Ted Kotcheff. **CAST:** Dolph Lundgren, Maruschka Detmers, John Ashton, Assumpta Serna. **1994**

HIDDEN FEARS ★★ After she witnesses her husband's murder, a woman (Meg Foster) tries to block it out, but those memories have come back to haunt her, forcing her to remember what she saw. And she realizes that the killers are still looking for her. A mundane exercise in make-believe. Not rated; contains violence. 90m. **DIR:** Jean Bodon. **CAST:** Meg Foster, Frederic Forrest, Bever-Leigh Banfield, Wally Taylor. **1992**

HIDDEN FORTRESS, THE ★★★★★ Toshiro Mifune stars in this recently reconstructed, uncut, and immensely entertaining 1958 Japanese period epic directed by Akira Kurosawa. George Lucas has openly admitted the film's influence on his *Star Wars* trilogy. *Hidden Fortress* deals with a strong-willed princess (à la Carrie Fisher in the space fantasy) and her wise, sword-wielding protector (Mifune in the role adapted for Alec Guinness). In Japanese with English subtitles. Not rated, the film has violence. B&W; 126m. **DIR:** Akira

Kurosawa. **CAST:** Toshiro Mifune, Minoru Chiaki. **1958 DVD**

HIDDEN GOLD ★★★ Hopalong Cassidy takes the job of ranch foreman for a girl to stop a crook who wants to steal a gold mine. B&W; 61m. **DIR:** Lesley Selander. **CAST:** William Boyd, Russell Hayden, Britt Wood, Roy Barcroft, Ruth Rogers. **1940**

HIDDEN IN AMERICA ★★★★ Beau Bridges gives a devastatingly real performance as a blue-collar single father of two trying to make ends meet after losing his job. Too proud to accept help from a compassionate doctor, Bridges obsesses on the role of besieged martyr . . . until malnutrition threatens his young daughter. Both kids are superb. Coproducer Jeff Bridges orchestrated this film to help raise awareness of a growing problem. Rated PG for intensity. 95m. **DIR:** Martin Bell. **CAST:** Beau Bridges, Bruce Davison, Shelton Dane, Jena Malone, Alice Krige, Josef Sommer, Frances McDormand, Jeff Bridges. **1996**

HIDDEN OBSESSION ★★ A news anchorwoman, stalked by an obsessive fan, falls for the likable deputy next door, but is he really what he seems? Slow. Rated R for nudity, violence, and simulated sex. 92m. **DIR:** John Stewart. **CAST:** Jan-Michael Vincent, Heather Thomas, Nicholas Celozzi. **1993**

HIDDEN VALLEY OUTLAWS ★★★★ Marshall Bill Elliott is duped by an outlaw leader—but only for a while—as he searches for the Whistler, an unemotional killer who whistles while he robs and plunders. B&W; 54m. **DIR:** Howard Bretherton. **CAST:** William Elliott, George "Gabby" Hayes, Anne Jeffreys, Roy Barcroft, LeRoy Mason. **1944**

HIDE AND GO SHRIEK ★★ Slasher film that's a cut above the others because of the acting. Eight high school seniors, four boys and four girls, celebrate their graduation by partying in a deserted furniture store. Their plans are interrupted by a psychotic killer. Not rated, contains nudity and extreme violence. 94m. **DIR:** Skip Schoolnik. **CAST:** George Thomas, Brittain Frye. **1987**

HIDE AND SEEK ★★★1/2 Chilling thriller about a couple who will do anything to have a child. George Gallo and Jennifer Tilly play Frank and Helen, a couple whose desperation leads them to kidnap pregnant Anne (Daryl Hannah). After faking Anne's death so no one will come looking for her, they hold her hostage until the baby's arrival. Tight direction, fine-tuned performances, and an edgy plot combine to create an intensely suspenseful film. Also released as *Cord*. Rated R for language and violence. 100m. **DIR:** Sidney J. Furie. **CAST:** Daryl Hannah, George Gallo, Jennifer Tilly, Bruce Greenwood. **2000 DVD**

HIDE IN PLAIN SIGHT ★★★1/2 James Caan is a tire factory laborer whose former wife marries a two-bit hoodlum. The hood turns informant and, under the Witness Relocation Program, is given a secret identity. Caan's former wife and their two children are spirited off to points unknown. Caan's subsequent quest for his kids becomes a one-man-against-the-system crusade in this watchable movie. Rated PG. 98m. **DIR:** James Caan. **CAST:** James Caan, Jill Eikenberry, Robert Viharo, Joe Grifasi. **1980**

HIDEAWAY ★★★ Good cast gets lost in this special effects–heavy thriller. What starts off promisingly enough succumbs to director Brett Leonard's obsession with computer imagery. Those images are used to convey the psychic link Jeff Goldblum shares with a serial killer. Thanks to a life-after-death experience, Goldblum sees everything the killer sees, including the stalking of his daughter, played by Alicia Silverstone. Rated R for violence, language, and nudity. 103m. **DIR:** Brett Leonard. **CAST:** Jeff Goldblum, Christine Lahti, Alicia Silverstone, Rae Dawn Chong, Jeremy Sisto, Alfred Molina. **1995 DVD**

HIDEAWAYS, THE ★★★ Two bored suburban kids spend a week hiding out in the Metropolitan Museum of Art. Interested in one of the statues, the duo tracks down its donor, an eccentric rich woman (Ingrid Bergman) who lives in a mansion in New Jersey. Fanciful tale won't appeal to all children, but it has a legion of admirers. Originally titled *From the Mixed-Up Files of Mrs. Basil E. Frankweiler*. Rated G. 105m. **DIR:** Fielder Cook. **CAST:** Ingrid Bergman, Sally Prager, Johnny Doran, George Rose, Richard Mulligan, Madeline Kahn. **1973**

HIDEOUS ★★ A monster born from toxic waste becomes the prize for a collector of oddities, who finds his latest acquisition is capable of mutating into little ferocious monsters who don't take kindly to strangers. Sick special effects and a sense of morbid fun save this from becoming an extended joke. Rated R for language, nudity, and violence. 82m. **DIR:** Charles Band. **CAST:** Michael Citrinti, Rhonda Griffin, Mel Johnson Jr., Tracie May. **1997 DVD**

HIDEOUS KINKY ★★★1/2 Single mother and her two young daughters swap a bleak existence in London for the wonders of 1972 Morocco in this exotic drama. The mother seeks self-discovery and wants her daughters to embrace a life of adventure, even as they struggle with abandonment issues. Then a street performer becomes lover, father figure, and mentor to the clan. Rated R for language, nudity, and sexual content. 101m. **DIR:** Gillies MacKinnon. **CAST:** Kate Winslet, Carrie Mullan, Bella Riza, Said Taghmaoui. **1999 DVD**

HIDEOUS SUN DEMON, THE 🦃 Robert Clarke directed and also stars as the scientist turned into a lizard-like monster by radiation. B&W; 74m. **DIR:** Robert Clarke. **CAST:** Robert Clarke, Patricia Manning. **1959 DVD**

HIDER IN THE HOUSE ★★ Unfortunately Gary Busey's wonderful portrayal of an ex-convict who builds a secret room in a stranger's house is not enough to save this poorly written film. Good cast, but just too unbelievable. Rated R for violence. 109m. **DIR:** Matthew Patrick. **CAST:** Gary Busey, Mimi Rogers, Michael McKean, Elizabeth Ruscio, Bruce Glover. **1989**

HIDING OUT ★★ Jon Cryer does some top-notch acting in this comedy-drama, and screenwriters Joe Menosky and Jeff Rothberg avoid the obvious clichés in their story of a Boston stockbroker (Cryer) hiding from the mob in a suburban Delaware high school. The result, however, is a collection of bits and pieces rather than a cohesive whole. Rated PG-13 for profanity and violence. 98m. **DIR:** Bob Giraldi. **CAST:** Jon Cryer, Keith Coogan, Annabeth Gish, Oliver Cotton, Claude Brooks, Ned Eisenberg. **1987 DVD**

HIDING PLACE, THE ★★1/2 A professional cast gives depth and feeling to this true story of two Dutch women

who are sent to a concentration camp for hiding Jews from the Nazis during World War II. This film was produced by Reverend Billy Graham's Evangelistic Association. 145m. **DIR:** James F. Collier. **CAST:** Julie Harris, Eileen Heckart, Arthur O'Connell. **1975**

HIGH AND LOW ★★★★★ From a simple but exquisitely devised detective story, Akira Kurosawa builds a stunning work of insight, humor, suspense, and social commentary. Toshiro Mifune is the businessman who must decide if he will pay a ransom to kidnappers who have taken his chauffeur's young son by mistake. A masterwork, featuring superb acting by two of the giants of Japanese cinema, Mifune and Tatsuya Nakadai. Based on Ed McBain's 87th Precinct novel *King's Ransom*. In Japanese with English subtitles. B&W; 143m. **DIR:** Akira Kurosawa. **CAST:** Toshiro Mifune, Tatsuya Nakadai, Tatsuya Mihashi, Tsutomu Yamazaki, Takashi Shimura. **1963 DVD**

HIGH AND THE MIGHTY, THE ★★★1/2 John Wayne stars as Dan Roman, a veteran pilot with a tragic past. Although slow-going at times, this *Grand Hotel* in the air has more than enough fine moments generated by a cast of familiar faces to keep the viewer's interest. 147m. **DIR:** William Wellman. **CAST:** John Wayne, Claire Trevor, Laraine Day, Robert Stack, Jan Sterling, Phil Harris, Robert Newton, David Brian, Paul Kelly, Sidney Blackmer, Julie Bishop, John Howard, Wally Brown, Ann Doran, John Qualen, Paul Fix, George Chandler, Douglas Fowley, Regis Toomey, Carl "Alfalfa" Switzer, William Schallert, Karen Sharpe, John Smith. **1954**

HIGH ANXIETY ★★ Mel Brooks successfully spoofed the horror film with *Young Frankenstein* and the Western with *Blazing Saddles*. However, this takeoff of the Alfred Hitchcock suspense movies falls miserably flat. Rated PG. 94m. **DIR:** Mel Brooks. **CAST:** Mel Brooks, Madeline Kahn, Cloris Leachman, Harvey Korman, Dick Van Patten, Ron Carey. **1977**

HIGH ART ★★★★ A devastating yet natural performance by Ally Sheedy makes this a worthwhile movie, even for some not normally enchanted by skinny lesbian junkies talking about semiotics. Sheedy, the once-great photographer for whom art and love are unbearably painful, is seduced back to work by a young magazine editor, with dire consequences for both women and anyone who cares for either of them. Rated R for skinny lesbian junkie stuff. 101m. **DIR:** Lisa Cholodenko. **CAST:** Ally Sheedy, Radha Mitchell, Patricia Clarkson. **1998**

HIGH-BALLIN' ★★ Peter Fonda and Jerry Reed are good old boys squaring off against the bad boss of a rival trucking company. The film has enough action and humor to make it a passable entertainment. Helen Shaver is its most provocative element. Rated PG. 100m. **DIR:** Peter Carter. **CAST:** Peter Fonda, Jerry Reed, Helen Shaver, Chris Wiggins, David Ferry. **1978**

HIGH COMMAND, THE ★★★ Rebellion, a new murder, and a 16 year old killing absorb the interest of officers and men at an isolated British outpost on an island off the coast of Africa during the fading days of the British empire. B&W; 84m. **DIR:** Thorold Dickinson. **CAST:** Lionel Atwill, Lucie Mannheim, James Mason. **1937**

HIGH COUNTRY, THE ★★ So-so production values drag down this tale of an escaping convict (Timothy Bottoms) and a wide-eyed girl (Linda Purl) in the Canadian Rockies. It's a clichéd story, although Bottoms turns in his usual accomplished performance. Not rated, but has violence and brief nudity. 99m. **DIR:** Harvey Hart. **CAST:** Timothy Bottoms, Linda Purl, George Sims, Jim Lawrence, Bill Berry, Walter Mills. **1980**

HIGH CRIME ★★ Narcotics cop vs. Mafia kingpin in the picturesque Italian seaport of Genoa. Full of action, but no surprises. Rated PG. 100m. **DIR:** Enzo G. Castellari. **CAST:** Franco Nero, James Whitmore, Fernando Rey. **1973**

•HIGH CRIMES ★★★ Scripters Yuri Zeltser and Cary Bickley's slick adaptation of Joseph Finder's novel is the cinematic equivalent of a good airplane read: fast-paced, cleverly constructed, and fun to watch . . . but you don't dare stop to consider details, because then the story falls apart. Ashley Judd stars as a Marin County attorney who believes herself married to the perfect guy, until he's dragged out of their house one day and accused of war crimes he supposedly committed during a covert armed forces operation fifteen years earlier. Morgan Freeman lends solid support as a former military attorney who'd love revenge against the system that hung him out to dry when his alcoholism got out of control. Rated PG-13 for profanity, violence, and sexual candor. 115m. **DIR:** Carl Franklin. **CAST:** Ashley Judd, Morgan Freeman, James Caviezel, Amanda Peet, Tom Bower. **2002 DVD**

HIGH DESERT KILL ★★ A group of deer hunters are stalked, a la *Predator*, in this third-rate knockoff. Marc Singer and Anthony Geary meet old man Chuck Connors in the high desert of Arizona and soon find the only animals left in their area are themselves. Made for cable. 93m. **DIR:** Harry Falk. **CAST:** Marc Singer, Anthony Geary, Chuck Connors, Micah Grant. **1989**

HIGH FIDELITY ★★★★ Spin this baby! *High Fidelity* is both a primer on the agonies of modern love and a keenly observed examination of music geeks and their universe. In this stream-of-consciousness study of one man's attempt to determine why his relationships never last, John Cusack is mocking, analytical, and self-deprecating. He becomes a turn-of-the-new-century Everyman: a likable cad in a comfortable rut, who wonders if life is moving on without him. Rarely has a late-entry approach to adulthood been portrayed so engagingly and convincingly. The screenplay, adapted by D. V. DeVincentis, Steve Pink, and Cusack, is based on Nick Hornby's novel. Rated R for profanity. 107m. **DIR:** Stephen Frears. **CAST:** John Cusack, Iben Hjejle, Todd Louiso, Jack Black, Lisa Bonet, Catherine Zeta-Jones, Joan Cusack, Tim Robbins, Lili Taylor, Sara Gilbert. **2000 DVD**

HIGH HEELS (1972) ★★★ A French comedy to make you chuckle more often than not. A medical student marries the homely daughter of a hospital president to ensure himself a job. In French with English subtitles. Not rated, but recommended for viewers over 18 years of age. 90m. **DIR:** Claude Chabrol. **CAST:** Laura Antonelli, Jean-Paul Belmondo, Mia Farrow. **1972**

HIGH HEELS (1991) ★★★★ In this black comedy, the incandescent Victoria Abril plays the neurotic daughter of a self-absorbed film and stage star. When the mother returns to Spain after several years in Mexico, both women find themselves suspects in a murder investiga-

tion. It's funny, suspenseful, and oh-so-sexy. In Spanish with English subtitles. Not rated; the film has nudity, simulated sex, and violence. 115m. **DIR:** Pedro Almodóvar. **CAST:** Victoria Abril, Marisa Paredes, Miguel Bosé. **1991**

HIGH HOPES ★★★★★ A biting satire of Margaret Thatcher's England, as viewed by three distinct, combative couples in modern London. Ruth Sheen and Philip Davis are memorable as two latter-day hippie leftists who name their cactus Thatcher because it's a pain in the you-know-where. 100m. **DIR:** Mike Leigh. **CAST:** Ruth Sheen, Philip Davis. **1989**

HIGH NOON (1952) ★★★★★ Gary Cooper won his second Oscar for his role of the abandoned lawman in this classic Western. It's the sheriff's wedding day, and the head of an outlaw band, who has sworn vengeance against him, is due to arrive in town at high noon. When Cooper turns to his fellow townspeople for help, no one comes forward. The suspense of this movie keeps snowballing as the clock ticks ever closer to noon. B&W; 84m. **DIR:** Fred Zinnemann. **CAST:** Gary Cooper, Grace Kelly, Lloyd Bridges, Thomas Mitchell, Katy Jurado, Otto Kruger, Lon Chaney Jr. **1952 DVD**

HIGH NOON (2000) ★★★1/2 First airing on TBS, this remake of the 1952 Western classic features Tom Skerritt as the newlywed ready to put down his badge to please his peace-loving bride but then finds himself forced to stand alone against a crazed killer and his gang. Not rated; contains violence and mature themes. 94m. **DIR:** Rod Hardy. **CAST:** Tom Skerritt, Suzanne Thompson, Maria Conchita Alonso, Reed Diamond. **2000 DVD**

HIGH NOON, PART TWO 🦃 This is a poor attempt at a sequel. 100m. **DIR:** Jerry Jameson. **CAST:** Lee Majors, David Carradine, J. A. Preston, Pernell Roberts, M. Emmet Walsh. **1980**

HIGH PLAINS DRIFTER ★★★ Star-director Clint Eastwood tried to revive the soggy spaghetti Western genre one more time, with watchable results. Eastwood comes to a frontier town just in time to make sure its sleazy citizens are all but wiped out by a trio of revenge-seeking outlaws. Although atmospheric, it's also confusing and sometimes just downright nasty. Rated R for violence, profanity, and suggested sex. 105m. **DIR:** Clint Eastwood. **CAST:** Clint Eastwood, Verna Bloom, Marianna Hill, Mitchell Ryan, Jack Ging, Geoffrey Lewis, John Mitchum. **1973 DVD**

HIGH RISK ★★1/2 While snatching $5 million from a South American drug smuggler (James Coburn), four amateur conspirators (James Brolin, Cleavon Little, Bruce Davison, and Chick Vennera) cross paths with a sleazy bandit leader (Anthony Quinn), hordes of Colombian soldiers, and plenty of riotous trouble. This preposterous adventure offers diversion, but a lot of it is just plain awful. Rated R. 94m. **DIR:** Stewart Raffill. **CAST:** James Brolin, Cleavon Little, Bruce Davison, Chick Vennera, Anthony Quinn, James Coburn, Ernest Borgnine, Lindsay Wagner. **1981 DVD**

HIGH ROAD TO CHINA ★★★ Tom Selleck stars as a World War I flying ace who, with the aid of his sidekick/mechanic, Jack Weston, helps a spoiled heiress (Bess Armstrong) track down her missing father (Wilford Brimley). It's just like the B movies of yesteryear: predictable, silly, and fun. Rated PG for violence. 120m. **DIR:** Brian G. Hutton. **CAST:** Tom Selleck, Bess Armstrong, Jack Weston, Wilford Brimley, Robert Morley, Brian Blessed. **1983**

HIGH SCHOOL CAESAR 🦃 A rich high school kid (John Ashley) is ignored by the father he idolizes, so he spends his time running a protection racket, selling exams, and rigging school elections. Neither good nor bad enough to be memorable. B&W; 72m. **DIR:** O'Dale Ireland. **CAST:** John Ashley, Gary Vinson, Lowell Brown. **1960**

HIGH SCHOOL CONFIDENTIAL! ★★1/2 A narcotics officer sneaks into a tough high school to bust hopheads. Incredibly naïve treatment of drug scene is bad enough, but it's the actors' desperate attempts to look "hip" that make the film an unintentional laugh riot. B&W; 85m. **DIR:** Jack Arnold. **CAST:** Russ Tamblyn, Jan Sterling, John Drew Barrymore, Mamie Van Doren. **1958**

HIGH SCHOOL HIGH ★★1/2 Producer David Zucker of *Naked Gun* and *Airplane!* fame returns with his trademark, rapid-fire, hit-and-miss sight gags and wacky one-liners. This time, optimistic Jon "That's the ticket!" Lovitz leaves a private academy to teach in a bleak inner-city high. Attempt to resolve social issues is a bit ambitious for this spoof. Rated PG-13 for profanity and violence. 85m. **DIR:** Hart Bochner. **CAST:** Jon Lovitz, Tia Carrere, Mekhi Phifer, Malinda Williams, Louise Fletcher. **1996 DVD**

HIGH SCHOOL, USA ★★ The fact that the dancing robot is the best actor in this film should tell you something. This made-for-TV feature is your typical teen flick, which is exceptional only because it doesn't rely on nudity and foul language to hold its audience's attention. 96m. **DIR:** Rod Amateau. **CAST:** Michael J. Fox, Dwayne Hickman, Angela Cartwright. **1983**

HIGH SEASON ★★★★ This delightfully pixilated comedy-mystery presents a group of people feuding, faking, laughing, and loving on a breathtaking Greek isle. Cowritten and directed by Clare Peploe, the wife of Bernardo Bertolucci, *High Season* offers Jacqueline Bisset as a photographer and James Fox as her sculptor husband. Rated R for brief nudity and adult themes. 104m. **DIR:** Clare Peploe. **CAST:** Jacqueline Bisset, Irene Papas, James Fox, Kenneth Branagh, Sebastian Shaw, Robert Stephens. **1988**

HIGH SIERRA ★★★★1/2 Humphrey Bogart is at his best as a bad guy with a heart of gold in this 1941 gangster film. Bogart pays for the operation that corrects pretty Joan Leslie's crippled foot, but he finds his love is misplaced. One of the finest of the Warner Bros. genre entries. B&W; 100m. **DIR:** Raoul Walsh. **CAST:** Humphrey Bogart, Ida Lupino, Alan Curtis, Arthur Kennedy, Joan Leslie, Henry Hull. **1941**

HIGH SOCIETY ★★★1/2 The outstanding cast in this film is reason enough to watch this enjoyable musical remake of *The Philadelphia Story*. The film moves at a leisurely pace, helped by some nice songs by Cole Porter. 107m. **DIR:** Charles Walters. **CAST:** Bing Crosby, Frank Sinatra, Grace Kelly, Louis Armstrong, Celeste Holm. **1956**

HIGH SPIRITS 🦃 Peter O'Toole tries to generate revenue for the ancient family castle by proclaiming it a haunted tourist trap. Rated PG-13 for language and mild sexual themes. 97m. **DIR:** Neil Jordan. **CAST:** Pe-

ter O'Toole, Steve Guttenberg, Daryl Hannah, Beverly D'Angelo, Jennifer Tilly, Liam Neeson. **1988**

HIGH STAKES (1986) ★★ Hoping to become a star reporter, a young daydreamer gets his chance when he uncovers a criminal plot to unearth a hidden Nazi treasure. His Walter Mitty–ish fantasies are the least appealing part of the movie, but some funny supporting characters and one-liners compensate. Not rated. 82m. **DIR:** Larry Kent. **CAST:** David Foley, Roberta Weiss, Winston Rekert. **1986**

HIGH STAKES (1989) ★★★ Sally Kirkland turns in a convincing portrayal as a burned-out hooker who meets a financial whiz dealing with his own personal crises. His fascination with Kirkland sweeps him into her sleazy world. Rated R for violence and profanity. 86m. **DIR:** Amos Kollek. **CAST:** Sally Kirkland, Robert LuPone, Richard Lynch. **1989**

HIGH STRUNG 🦃 Steve Oedekerk bombards his audience with screaming complaints about everything. About as much fun as sitting in the dentist chair and listening to the guy in the next cubicle having his teeth drilled. Megastar Jim Carrey appears mostly in brief flashes. Rated R for profanity. 93m. **DIR:** Roger Nygard. **CAST:** Steve Oedekerk, Thomas F. Wilson, Denise Crosby, Fred Willard, Jim Carrey. **1994**

HIGH TIDE ★★★★ Judy Davis gives a superb performance as a rock 'n' roll singer stranded in a small Australian town when she loses her job in a band and her car breaks down all in the same day. She winds up staying in a trailer park only to encounter by accident the teenage daughter she deserted following the death of her husband. The offbeat but moving film reunites Davis with her *My Brilliant Career* director, Gillian Armstrong, for some truly impressive results. Rated PG. 102m. **DIR:** Gillian Armstrong. **CAST:** Judy Davis, Jan Adele, Claudia Karvan, Colin Friels. **1987**

HIGH VELOCITY ★★ Run-of-the-mill feature made in Manila about two ex-Vietnam buddies hired to rescue the head of a big corporation from Asian terrorists. Rated PG. 106m. **DIR:** Remi Kramer. **CAST:** Ben Gazzara, Britt Ekland, Paul Winfield, Keenan Wynn, Alejandro Rey, Victoria Racimo. **1977**

HIGH VOLTAGE (1929) ★★1/2 Elements of *Stagecoach* are evident in this early Pathé sound film (made ten years before John Ford's classic) that teams a pre–Hopalong Cassidy William Boyd and a lovely young Carole Lombard as a world-wise couple who fall for each other while snowbound during a bus trip in California's Sierra Nevada. Worth watching for Lombard's fine performance. B&W; 57m. **DIR:** Howard Higgin. **CAST:** William Boyd, Carole Lombard, Owen Moore, Diane Ellis, Billy Bevan. **1929**

HIGH VOLTAGE (1997) ★★ This throwback to Bruce Lee martial arts films stars his daughter Shannon, who plays the girlfriend of an Asian crime lord and falls for a thief who has stolen her boyfriend's money. The attempt to infuse style falls flat as does the rest of the film. Rated R for language and violence. 92m. **DIR:** Isaac Florentine. **CAST:** Antonio Sabato Jr., Shannon Lee, George Cheung, William Zabka. **1997 DVD**

HIGHER AND HIGHER ★★ Frank Sinatra and the entire cast do a wonderful job in this practically plotless picture about a once-rich man teaming up with his servants in his quest to be wealthy once again. This is Sinatra's first major film effort, and he does a fine job with the first-rate songs. B&W; 90m. **DIR:** Tim Whelan. **CAST:** Frank Sinatra, Michèle Morgan, Jack Haley, Leon Errol, Victor Borge, Mel Torme. **1943**

HIGHER LEARNING ★★ Date rape. Racism. Sexism. Neo-Nazism. Elitism. This ambitious, issue-packed look at the social turbulence of a fictional college campus gets an A for effort while expounding on the waywardness of the modern world. The film's flurry of sociopolitical punches, however, is amateurishly strung together. Rated R for language and violence. 127m. **DIR:** John Singleton. **CAST:** Omar Epps, Kristy Swanson, Tyra Banks, Jennifer Connelly, Laurence Fishburne, Ice Cube, Michael Rapaport. **1995 DVD**

HIGHEST HONOR, THE ★★★★★ A World War II story of a unique friendship between two enemies: Captain Robert Page, an Australian army officer, and Winoyu Tamiya, a security officer in the Japanese army. This great war film, packed with high adventure and warm human drama, is also a true story. Rated R. 99m. **DIR:** Peter Maxwell. **CAST:** John Howard, Atsuo Nakamura, Stuart Wilson. **1984**

HIGHLANDER ★★ A sixteenth-century Scottish clansman discovers he is one of a small group of immortals destined to fight each other through the centuries. The movie is a treat for the eyes, but you'll owe your brain an apology. Rated R for violence. 110m. **DIR:** Russell Mulcahy. **CAST:** Christopher Lambert, Clancy Brown, Sean Connery. **1986 DVD**

HIGHLANDER: ENDGAME 🦃 TV and movie series clansmen Duncan and Connor MacLeod, respectively, must decide who will decapitate the other to magically gain the necessary strength to prevent a renegade from becoming Earth's only immortal in this incoherent, century-hopping, globe-trotting meeting of Good and Evil. Rated R for violence and sexuality. 88m. **DIR:** Douglas Aarnikoski. **CAST:** Christopher Lambert, Adrian Paul, Lisa Barbuscia, Bruce Payne, Donnie Yen, Jim Byrnes. **2000 DVD**

HIGHLANDER 2: THE QUICKENING ★★1/2 Christopher Lambert and Sean Connery reprise their roles as the Highlander and his mentor Ramirez who have been banished to Earth. Great special effects can't keep one from thinking that something is missing from the film—like a cohesive plot. Rated R for violence. 91m. **DIR:** Russell Mulcahy. **CAST:** Christopher Lambert, Virginia Madsen, Michael Ironside, Sean Connery, John C. McGinley. **1991 DVD**

HIGHLANDER: THE FINAL DIMENSION ★★ That sixteenth-century Scottish clansman (Christopher Lambert) is still roaming through time, still fighting the forces of evil (represented by Mario Van Peebles), and still speaking with an inexplicable French accent. The third entry in the series has no discernible plot and suffers greatly from the absence of Sean Connery as the Highlander's mentor. Rated R for violence. 99m. **DIR:** Andy Morahan. **CAST:** Christopher Lambert, Mario Van Peebles, Deborah Unger, Mako, Marc Neufield, Raul Trujillo. **1994 DVD**

HIGHLANDER: THE GATHERING ★★ This is a combination of two episodes from the TV series, which is why the plot seems disjointed. Duncan and Connor must battle the evil immortals. Mind-numbing. Rated PG-13 for nudity and violence. 98m. **DIR:** Thomas Wright, Ray

Austin. **CAST:** Adrian Paul, Alexandra Vandernoot, Stan Kirsch, Christopher Lambert, Richard Moll, Vanity. **1992**

HIGHPOINT 🦃 Confusing comedy-thriller about an accountant who becomes mixed up in a CIA plot. Rated R; contains profanity and violence. 88m. **DIR:** Peter Carter. **CAST:** Richard Harris, Christopher Plummer, Beverly D'Angelo, Kate Reid, Peter Donat, Saul Rubinek. **1980**

•HIGHWAY ★★★ Short on plot but long on good intentions, this road trip drama stars Jared Leto and Jake Gyllenhaal as two best friends who find themselves on the run from the mob. Jack (Leto) is a Las Vegas pool cleaner who gets caught in bed with a mobster's wife. Jack grabs his friend Pilot (Gyllenhaal) and hits the road running, heading to Seattle. En route, they encounter all sorts of eccentric characters and offbeat situations. Rated R for adult situations, drugs, language, and violence. 97m. **DIR:** James Cox. **CAST:** Jared Leto, Jake Gyllenhaal, Selma Blair, Jeremy Piven, John C. McGinley. **2001 DVD**

HIGHWAY 61 ★★★ A wacky, somewhat surreal road comedy about a small-town Canadian barber whose claim to fame is finding a dead body. When the corpse's sister—a refugee from a rock 'n' roll crew—appears, they go on a journey down one of North America's most famous highways. Rated R for profanity, simulated sex, and nudity. 105m. **DIR:** Bruce McDonald. **CAST:** Valerie Buhagiar, Don McKellar, Earl Pastko. **1992**

HIGHWAY TO HELL ★★★★ Two young lovers get caught in an inter-dimensional speed trap, and are sent straight to hell. Fast-paced writing and action, as well as large dashes of humor and sight gags, make this an entertaining thriller. Rated R for violence and profanity. 100m. **DIR:** Ate De Jong. **CAST:** Patrick Bergin, Chad Lowe, Kristy Swanson, Richard Farnsworth. **1991**

HIGHWAYMAN, THE ★★1/2 A down-on-his-luck telephone salesman finds his luck further diminished when a young woman claiming to be his daughter mysteriously appears. Not a bad rental for bargain night and Louis Gossett Jr. shines as usual. Rated R for violence and profanity. 97m. **DIR:** Keoni Waxman. **CAST:** Louis Gossett Jr., Jason Priestley, Laura Harris. **1998 DVD**

HIJACKING HOLLYWOOD ★★★ Henry Thomas is a boyish filmmaker who takes the abuse of being a production assistant. When he can't take it anymore, he steals a reel of expensive special-effects footage and holds it ransom. Small, low-budget independent effort works magic with its charm and spunk. Rated R for adult situations, language, and nudity. 93m. **DIR:** Neil Mandt. **CAST:** Henry Thomas, Carrot Top (Scott Thompson), Mark Metcalf. **1997 DVD**

HILARY AND JACKIE ★★★★ The need to separate the artist from the art is key to this fascinating drama, which concerns the life of celebrated English cellist Jacqueline du Pre. Jackie could do no wrong in the eyes of her fans, who were more than willing to forgive her shocking candor and her tendency, during performances, to sensuously embrace her cello as one might a paramour. But she also was a monster: insecure, selfish, self-centered, capriciously cruel and spiteful. We cannot possibly like this woman. Yet we can at least begin to understand her in this absorbing and thoughtful study of talent's fragility. Rated R for profanity, nudity, and sexual content. 125m. **DIR:** Anand Tucker. **CAST:** Emily Watson, Rachel Griffiths, David Morrissey, James Frain, Charles Dance, Celia Imrie. **1998 DVD**

HILL, THE ★★★★ Powerful drill-sergeant-from-hell film, this zeroes in on the psychological and mental agony faced by a group of British military prisoners. Sean Connery is excellent as the latest victim of the break-their-spirits program. 122m. **DIR:** Sidney Lumet. **CAST:** Sean Connery, Harry Andrews, Ian Hendry, Ossie Davis, Michael Redgrave. **1965**

HILL STREET BLUES (TV SERIES) ★★★★ Steven Bochco's landmark 1980s police drama forever redefined the way we view cop shows. Daniel J. Travanti collected a pair of well-deserved Emmy awards as Captain Frank Furillo, the precinct captain who served as the show's rock-hard anchor. No matter how grim the day's events, he'd usually wind up at home in the evening, sharing a bathtub with lover Veronica Hamel, who occasionally busted his chops by day fulfilling her duties as public defender. Mike Post's catchy theme became a top-forty hit, and the ensemble cast grew to include considerably more than two dozen ongoing roles. Michael Conrad, as Sergeant Esterhaus, always spoke the series' signature line: "Let's be careful out there." 47m. **DIR:** Various. **CAST:** Daniel J. Travanti, Michael Conrad, Michael Warren, Charles Haid, Veronica Hamel, Bruce Weitz, Rene Enriquez, Keil Martin, Taurean Blacque, James B. Sikking, Joe Spano, Betty Thomas. **1981–87**

HILLBILLYS IN A HAUNTED HOUSE 🦃 Unbelievably bad mishmash of country corn and horror humor. 88m. **DIR:** Jean Yarbrough. **CAST:** Ferlin Husky, Joi Lansing, Don Bowman, John Carradine, Lon Chaney Jr., Basil Rathbone, Molly Bee, Merle Haggard, Sonny James. **1967 DVD**

HILLS HAVE EYES, THE 🦃 City folk have inherited a silver mine and are stopping on their way to California to check it out. That's when a ghoulish family comes crawling out of the rocks. Rated R for violence and profanity. 89m. **DIR:** Wes Craven. **CAST:** Susan Lamer, Robert Houston, Virginia Vincent, Russ Grieve, Dee Wallace. **1977**

HILLS HAVE EYES, THE: PART TWO 🦃 This really lame sequel wouldn't scare the most timid viewer. Rated R for violence and profanity (mild by horror standards). 86m. **DIR:** Wes Craven. **CAST:** John Laughlin, Michael Berryman. **1984**

HILLS OF HOME ★★★★ Effective family fare about an aging doctor and his devoted collie, Lassie. While tending to the townspeople, the kindly physician attempts to cure his dog's fear of water only to need help himself. A satisfying tearjerker in the mold of *All Creatures Great and Small*. 97m. **DIR:** Fred M. Wilcox. **CAST:** Edmund Gwenn, Tom Drake, Janet Leigh, Donald Crisp, Rhys Williams, Reginald Owen, Alan Napier, Eileen Erskine. **1948**

HILLS OF OLD WYOMING ★★1/2 Cattle rustlers plaguing the local ranchers have been traced back to the Indian reservation by Hopalong Cassidy and his pals. With the law, rustlers, and the local Indians all after the Bar-20 boys, Hoppy saves their hides when he finds proof to convict the murdering thieves. B&W; 80m. **DIR:** Nate Watt. **CAST:** William Boyd, George "Gabby" Hayes, Russell Hayden, Morris Ankrum, Gail Sheridan, Chief Big Tree, Steve Clemento. **1937**

HILLS OF UTAH, THE ★★1/2 Harking back to a classic theme, Gene returns to the town where his father was killed and manages to settle a local feud as well as uncover the truth about his father's murder. Even with Pat Buttram, this is somber for a Gene Autry film. B&W; 70m. **DIR:** John English. **CAST:** Gene Autry, Pat Buttram, Elaine Riley, Onslow Stevens, Donna Martell. **1951**

HILLSIDE STRANGLERS, THE ★★★ A video release of a made-for-television flick concerning two of California's most wanted criminals. Richard Crenna is the hard-nosed detective. Dennis Farina and Billy Zane are the cousins holding Los Angeles in a stranglehold of fear. 95m. **DIR:** Steven Gethers. **CAST:** Richard Crenna, Dennis Farina, Billy Zane, Tony Plana. **1989**

•HIMALAYA ★★★ An annual yak caravan across the mountains threatens to turn into disaster as two factions of a Tibetan village refuse to agree either on a departure time or the path needed to avoid deadly snowstorms. Village life is further disrupted by the death of a chief's son and the power struggle that ensues. This languidly paced story of revenge, romance, the perpetuation of religious beliefs, human perseverance, and torch-passing is gorgeously photographed. In Tibetan with English subtitles. Not rated. 104m. **DIR:** Eric Valli. **CAST:** Thilen Lhondup, Gurgon Kyap, Karma Wangiel. **1999 DVD**

HIMATSURI ★★★★1/2 Metaphysical story about man's lustful and often destructive relationship with nature. Kinya Kitaoji plays a lumberjack in a beautiful seaboard wilderness which is about to be marred by the building of a marine park. Rated R for nudity and violence. 120m. **DIR:** Mitsuo Yanagimachi. **CAST:** Kinya Kitaoji. **1985**

HINDENBURG, THE 🦃 Another disaster movie whose major disaster is its own script. Rated PG. 125m. **DIR:** Robert Wise. **CAST:** George C. Scott, Anne Bancroft, William Atherton, Roy Thinnes, Burgess Meredith, Charles Durning. **1975 DVD**

•HIP-HOP WITCH MOVIE, DA 🦃 Various hip-hop music stars ad lib about their own life-threatening encounters with Da Hip-Hop Witch. Not funny, not scary, and certainly not worth watching. Rated R for language. 94m. **DIR:** Dale Anthony Resteghini. **CAST:** Vanilla Ice, Eminem, Colleen (Vitamin C) Fitzpatrick. **2000 DVD**

HIPS, HIPS, HOORAY ★★★ Clowns Bert Wheeler and Robert Woolsey liven up this early, somewhat blue, comedy-musical. The pair play havoc as they invade Thelma Todd's ailing cosmetic business. B&W; 68m. **DIR:** Mark Sandrich. **CAST:** Bert Wheeler, Robert Woolsey, Thelma Todd, Ruth Etting, George Meeker, Dorothy Lee. **1934**

HIRED HAND, THE ★★★1/2 This low-key Western follows two drifters, Peter Fonda and Warren Oates, as they return to Fonda's farm and the wife, Verna Bloom, he deserted seven years earlier. While working on the farm, Fonda and Bloom begin to rekindle their relationship. Beautiful cinematography and fine performances, especially by Oates, add greatly to this worthy entry in the genre. Rated R. 93m. **DIR:** Peter Fonda. **CAST:** Peter Fonda, Warren Oates, Verna Bloom, Severn Darden. **1971**

HIRED TO KILL ★★ Aimless violence permeates this action film concerning a soldier of fortune and his efforts to infiltrate a Third World island and free a prisoner. Trite and just plain silly. Rated R for violence, nudity, and adult language. 91m. **DIR:** Nico Mastorakis, Peter Rader. **CAST:** Brian Thompson, Oliver Reed, George Kennedy, José Ferrer. **1990**

HIROSHIMA ★★★★ A fascinating, ambitious film (made for cable TV) that provides both the American and Japanese perspective on the creation, use, and aftermath of the atomic bombs dropped on two Japanese cities in 1945. Archival footage increases the feeling that one is watching history, a feeling that the well-researched script deserves. In English and Japanese with English subtitles. Rated PG for violence. 190m. **DIR:** Koreyoshi Kurahara, Roger Spottiswoode. **CAST:** Wesley Addy, Jeffrey DeMunn, David Gow, Richard Masur. **1995 DVD**

HIROSHIMA, MON AMOUR ★★★★ A mind-boggling tale about two people: one, a Frenchwoman, the other, a male survivor of the blast at Hiroshima. They meet and become lovers. Together they live their pasts, present, and futures in a complex series of fantasies, and nightmares. In French with English subtitles. B&W; 88m. **DIR:** Alain Resnais. **CAST:** Emmanuelle Riva, Bernard Fresson, Eiji Okada. **1959**

HIROSHIMA: OUT OF THE ASHES ★★★★ This superior TV-movie rendition of the atomic bombing of Hiroshima allows us to see things from the perspective of those who were there. An ironic twist of fate places freed POWs among the ruins. Rated PG-13 for violence. 98m. **DIR:** Peter Werner. **CAST:** Max von Sydow, Judd Nelson, Noriyuki "Pat" Morita, Mako, Ben Wright. **1990**

HIS BODYGUARD ★★1/2 Industrial spies break into a research lab to steal a biomedical prototype and a deaf scientist and the female head of security are caught up in it all. This made-for-cable original features decent acting, but too much of the story is pointless chasing around. Rated PG-13 for violence. 95m. **DIR:** Artie Mandelberg. **CAST:** Mitzi Kapture, Anthony Natale, Michael Copeman, Robin Gammell, Robert Guillaume. **1998**

HIS BROTHER'S GHOST ★★★1/2 Sturdy entry in the Billy Carson series has Buster Crabbe as a two-fisted rancher bent on capturing the gang that killed his best friend. It's much better than it sounds, one of the best Crabbe made in the series, which originally starred Bob Steele as a whitewashed Billy the Kid. B&W; 54m. **DIR:** Sam Newfield. **CAST:** Buster Crabbe, Al St. John, Charles King, Karl Hackett. **1945**

HIS BUTLER'S SISTER ★★★★1/2 A delightful Deanna Durbin singfest with a stellar performance by Pat O'Brien as the butler of the title. Durbin sings both modern and classical opera every time there's a lull in the comic highjinks about a composer chasing a girl until she catches him. B&W; 94m. **DIR:** Frank Borzage. **CAST:** Deanna Durbin, Pat O'Brien, Franchot Tone, Akim Tamiroff, Evelyn Ankers. **1943**

HIS DOUBLE LIFE ★★★ Edwardian novelist Arnold Bennett's comedy about a wealthy recluse who finds a better life by becoming a valet when his valet dies and is buried under his name. Remade with Monty Woolley and Gracie Fields as *Holy Matrimony* in 1943. B&W; 67m. **DIR:** Arthur Hopkins, William C. de Mille. **CAST:** Lillian Gish, Roland Young. **1933**

HIS GIRL FRIDAY ★★★★★ Based on Ben Hecht and Charles MacArthur's *The Front Page*, Howard Hawks converted this gentle spoof of newspapers and reporters into a hilarious battle of the sexes. Rosalind Russell is the reporter bent on retirement, and Cary Grant is the editor bent on maneuvering her out of it—and winning her heart in the process. B&W; 92m. **DIR:** Howard Hawks. **CAST:** Cary Grant, Rosalind Russell, Ralph Bellamy, Gene Lockhart, Helen Mack, Ernest Truex. **1940 DVD**

HIS KIND OF WOMAN ★★★1/2 Entertaining chase film as two-fisted gambler Robert Mitchum breezes down to South America to pick up $50 thousand only to find out he's being set up for the kill. Jane Russell is in fine shape as the worldly gal with a good heart, and Vincent Price steals the show as a hammy Hollywood actor. B&W; 120m. **DIR:** John Farrow. **CAST:** Robert Mitchum, Jane Russell, Vincent Price, Tim Holt, Charles McGraw, Raymond Burr, Jim Backus, Marjorie Reynolds. **1951**

HIS MAJESTY O'KEEFE ★★★1/2 A rip-snortin' adventure movie with Burt Lancaster furnishing all the energy as the nineteenth century American businessman who sails to the South Seas and finds a fortune in copra waiting for him. He also teaches the natives how to use gunpowder, and the result is both exciting and hilarious. 92m. **DIR:** Byron Haskin. **CAST:** Burt Lancaster, Joan Rice, Abraham Sofaer, Philip Ahn. **1954**

HIS NAME WAS KING ★★ Spaghetti Western about a bounty hunter named King (Richard Harrison) who tracks down a ring of gunrunners near the Mexican border. Not rated, but equal to a PG. 90m. **DIR:** Don Reynolds. **CAST:** Richard Harrison, Klaus Kinski. **1983**

HIS PICTURE IN THE PAPERS ★★★1/2 This clever film has Douglas Fairbanks performing a variety of Herculean feats—all aimed at getting his picture on the front pages of the New York papers. This comedy helped to define Fairbanks's motion-picture persona as the boisterous, buoyant, devil-may-care, ultra-athletic young go-getter. Silent. B&W; 68m. **DIR:** John Emerson. **CAST:** Douglas Fairbanks Sr. **1916**

HIS PRIVATE SECRETARY ★★ Playboy son of a bill collector is put to work by his father but falls for the daughter of his first deadbeat, an impoverished cleric. John Wayne is long on enthusiasm and short on technique as he tackles the lead in his only independent film for Showmen's Pictures, a visible step beneath the Mascot serials and Monogram Westerns he was toiling in at the time. B&W; 61m. **DIR:** Philip H. Whitman. **CAST:** John Wayne, Evalyn Knapp, Reginald Barlow, Arthur Hoyt, Natalie Kingston, Al St. John. **1933**

HISTORY IS MADE AT NIGHT ★★★ A preposterous film, but . . . Colin Clive is a sadistic jealous husband whose wife, Jean Arthur, falls for Parisian headwaiter Charles Boyer. He tries to frame the headwaiter for a murder he himself committed. He fails. Insanely determined to destroy the lovers, he arranges for his superliner to hit an iceberg! B&W; 97m. **DIR:** Frank Borzage. **CAST:** Charles Boyer, Jean Arthur, Colin Clive, Leo Carrillo. **1937**

HISTORY OF THE WORLD, PART ONE, THE 🦃 Mel Brooks is lost in this collection of bits that emerge like unused footage from *Monty Python's The Meaning of Life*. Rated R for crude language. 86m. **DIR:** Mel Brooks. **CAST:** Mel Brooks, Dom DeLuise, Madeline Kahn, Harvey Korman, Gregory Hines, Cloris Leachman. **1981 DVD**

HIT! (1973) ★★1/2 This is a praiseworthy attempt to bring some legitimacy to the blaxploitation genre. Billy Dee Williams plays an American police detective who tracks drug dealers to Marseilles. Rated R for nudity, violence, and profanity. 134m. **DIR:** Sidney J. Furie. **CAST:** Billy Dee Williams, Paul Hampton, Richard Pryor, Gwen Welles. **1973**

HIT, THE (1984) ★★★★ The British seem to have latched on to the gangster film with a vengeance. First, they made the superb film *The Long Good Friday*, and now they've scored again with this gripping character study. John Hurt gives an unusually restrained (and highly effective) performance as a hit man assigned to take care of a squealer (Terence Stamp) who has been hiding in Spain after testifying against the mob. Rated R for violence. 97m. **DIR:** Stephen Frears. **CAST:** John Hurt, Terence Stamp, Tim Roth, Fernando Rey, Laura Del Sol, Bill Hunter. **1984**

HIT AND RUN ★★1/2 A New York cabdriver, obsessed with the death of his wife in a hit-and-run accident, becomes a pawn in a murder plot. Mystery fans will appreciate the nighttime atmosphere and carefully (if slowly) developed plot. Rated PG. 96m. **DIR:** Charles Braverman. **CAST:** Paul Perri, Claudia Cron, Bart Braverman. **1982 DVD**

•HIT AND RUNWAY ★★ Heterosexual Italian screenwriting student teams with gay Woody Allen–ish playwright to pen an action flick in this affectionate but contrived comedy about unlikely creative partnerships, ambition, artistic integrity, and fizzling relationships. Other players in this amateurish, occasionally amusing spin on the *Odd Couple* are an unconvincing female ugly duckling and a shallow male actor with a Hebrew fetish. Rated R for language, sex, and violence. 105m. **DIR:** Christopher Livingston. **CAST:** Michael Parducci, Peter Jacobson, Kerr Smith, Judy Prescott, John Fiore, Hoyt Richards. **2001**

HIT LADY ★★1/2 Entertaining twist on an old story has Yvette Mimieux as a hit lady who tries to retire, only to be blackmailed into taking on just one more job. Televison movie; contains some cleaned-up violence. 74m. **DIR:** Tracy Keenan Wynn. **CAST:** Yvette Mimieux, Dack Rambo, Clu Gulager, Joseph Campanella, Keenan Wynn. **1974**

HIT LIST (1988) ★★ The Mafia hires a hit man (Lance Henriksen) to stifle a key witness. The hit man gets the address wrong and ends up kidnapping Jan-Michael Vincent's son. Some familiar faces pop up in the supporting cast of this not-so-bad suspense-drama. Rated R for violence and profanity. 87m. **DIR:** William Lustig. **CAST:** Jan-Michael Vincent, Rip Torn, Lance Henriksen, Leo Rossi. **1988**

HIT LIST, THE (1992) ★★★★ High marks to this twisty thriller from scripter Reed Steiner. Jeff Fahey stars as an implacable assassin whose professional routine goes awry after meeting client Yancy Butler. Postdubbing is inexplicably awful for an American-made film. Rated R for extreme violence, profanity, simulated sex, and nudity. 97m. **DIR:** William Webb. **CAST:** Jeff Fahey, Yancy Butler, James Coburn, Michael Beach, Jeff Kober. **1992**

HIT THE DECK ★★1/2 Fancy-free sailors on shore leave meet girls, dance, sing, and cut up in this updated 1920s Vincent Youmans hit from Broadway. Good, time-filling eyewash. 112m. **DIR:** Roy Rowland. **CAST:** Jane Powell, Tony Martin, Debbie Reynolds, Vic Damone, Ann Miller, Russ Tamblyn, Walter Pidgeon, Gene Raymond. **1955**

HIT THE DUTCHMAN ★★1/2 A Jewish ex-convict wants to become involved with gangster Legs Diamond, but must first change his name. This run-of-the-mill gangster film drags on way too long. Rated R for profanity, violence, and nudity. 116m. **DIR:** Menahem Golan. **CAST:** Bruce Nozick, Will Kempe, Sally Kirkland. **1992**

HIT THE ICE ★★★ Abbott and Costello play a pair of photographers in this outing, eluding assorted crooks. Gags abound, but so do musical numbers, which always seem to grind these films to a halt. On a par with most of their other efforts, it guarantees a great time for A&C fans. B&W; 82m. **DIR:** Charles Lamont. **CAST:** Bud Abbott, Lou Costello, Patric Knowles, Elyse Knox. **1943**

HIT THE SADDLE ★★★ A gold digging fandango dancer (Rita Hayworth, née Cansino) comes between two of the Three Mesquiteers while they battle a sinister outlaw gang. B&W; 54m. **DIR:** Mack V. Wright. **CAST:** Robert Livingston, Ray "Crash" Corrigan, Max Terhune, Rita Hayworth. **1937**

HIT WOMAN: THE DOUBLE EDGE ★★1/2 Soap star Susan Lucci plays dual roles as an assassin and the FBI agent out to find her. The story is quite dull, but Lucci does a fine job portraying two radically different people. Rated R for violence. 94m. **DIR:** Stephen Stafford. **CAST:** Susan Lucci, Robert Urich, Michael Woods, Kevin Dunn, Paul Freeman, Kari Lizer, Robert Prosky. **1992**

HITCHER, THE ★★★ C. Thomas Howell plays a young, squeamish, California-bound motorist who picks up a hitchhiker, played by Rutger Hauer, somewhere in the desert Southwest. What transpires is action that will leave you physically and emotionally drained. If you thought *The Terminator* was too violent, this one will redefine the word for you. Rated R. 96m. **DIR:** Robert Harmon. **CAST:** Rutger Hauer, C. Thomas Howell, Jeffrey DeMunn, Jennifer Jason Leigh. **1986 DVD**

HITCHHIKER, THE (SERIES) ★★★ Stories culled from HBO anthology series are included in this compilation of tapes. The stories always have a supernatural background and a moral but sometimes are a bit shallow. Not rated; contains adult language, violence, and nudity. 90m. **DIR:** Roger Vadim, Paul Verhoeven, Carl Schenkel, Phillip Noyce, Mai Zetterling, Richard Rothstein, David Wickes, Mike Hodges. **CAST:** Page Fletcher, Harry Hamlin, Karen Black, Gary Busey, Geraldine Page, Margot Kidder, Darren McGavin, Susan Anspach, Peter Coyote, Barry Bostwick, Willem Dafoe, M. Emmet Walsh, Tom Skerritt, Steve Collins, Shannon Tweed, Robert Vaughn, Sybil Danning, Michael O'Keefe. **1985**

HITCHHIKERS 🦃 Female hitchhikers rob the motorists who stop to pick them up. Rated R for nudity, profanity, and simulated sex. 87m. **DIR:** Ferd Sebastian. **CAST:** Misty Rowe, Norman Klar, Linda Avery. **1971**

HITCHHIKER'S GUIDE TO THE GALAXY, THE ★★★★ While perhaps the least successful adaptation (behind the book and LP) of Douglas Adam's now-classic BBC radio series, this television incarnation nonetheless succeeds quite well. Simon Jones is perfect as bathrobe-garbed Arthur Dent, an insignificant ordinary citizen thrown into the adventure of his life after narrowly escaping the Earth's destruction by aliens annoyed at how our planet blocked their proposed spatial thoroughfare. 194m. **DIR:** Alan Bell. **CAST:** Peter Jones, Simon Jones, David Dixon, Joe Melia, Martin Benson. **1985 DVD**

HITLER ★★ Richard Basehart plays Adolf Hitler in this rather slow-moving, shallow account of *der Führer*'s last years. You're better off watching a good documentary on the subject. 107m. **DIR:** Stuart Heisler. **CAST:** Richard Basehart, Cordula Trantow, Maria Emo, John Mitchum. **1962**

HITLER—DEAD OR ALIVE 🦃 Paroled gangster and his henchmen accept a $1 million offer to assassinate Hitler. B&W; 72m. **DIR:** Nick Grindé. **CAST:** Ward Bond, Warren Hymer, Paul Fix. **1942**

HITLER, THE LAST TEN DAYS ★★ This film should hold interest only for history buffs. It is a rather dry and tedious account of the desperate closing days of the Third Reich. Alec Guinness gives a capable, yet sometimes overwrought, performance as the Nazi leader from the time he enters his underground bunker in Berlin until his eventual suicide. Rated PG. 108m. **DIR:** Ennio DeConcini. **CAST:** Alec Guinness, Simon Ward, Adolfo Celi, Diane Cilento. **1973**

HITLER'S CHILDREN ★★★★ A great love story is created with the horror of Nazi Germany as a background. This film shows a young German boy who falls in love with an American girl. The boy gets caught up in Hitler's enticing web of propaganda, while his girlfriend resists all of Hitler's ideas. B&W; 83m. **DIR:** Edward Dmytryk, Irving Reis. **CAST:** Tim Holt, Bonita Granville, Kent Smith, Otto Kruger. **1942**

HITLER'S DAUGHTER 🦃 Made-for-cable drama suggests one of Hitler's mistresses produced a girl-child, who was then trained by Nazi-nasties to revive the Fourth Reich in our United States. Rated R for language and violence. 88m. **DIR:** James A. Contner. **CAST:** Patrick Cassidy, Melody Anderson, Veronica Cartwright, Kay Lenz. **1990**

HITMAN, THE ★★★1/2 A police officer goes underground after being betrayed and shot by his crooked partner. Officially listed as dead, he becomes the "hit man" for a Seattle crime boss in order to bring down a sophisticated drug operation. Rated R for violence and profanity. 96m. **DIR:** Aaron Norris. **CAST:** Chuck Norris, Michael Parks, Al Waxman, Alberta Watson. **1991 DVD**

HITZ ★★ Melodramatic dramatization of kids killing kids among L.A. gangs loses credibility in the courtroom, with judges taking their work too personally. Muddled message film. Rated R for nudity, violence, and profanity. 90m. **DIR:** William Sachs. **CAST:** Emilia Crow, Richard Coca, Elliott Gould. **1992**

HOBBIT, THE ★★ Disappointing cartoon version of the classic J. R. R. Tolkien fantasy. Orson Bean provides the voice of the dwarflike Hobbit, Bilbo Baggins, and John Huston, at his stentorian best, is the wizard Gandalf. Unfortunately, all the creatures have a cutesy look, which doesn't gel with the story. An unrated TV movie. 78m. **DIR:** Arthur Rankin Jr., Jules Bass. **1978 DVD**

HOBSON'S CHOICE (1954) ★★★★★ Charles Laughton gives one of his most brilliant performances as a turn-of-the-century London shoemaker whose love for the status quo and his whiskey is shattered by the determination of his daughter to wed. This is the original 1954 movie version of the British comedy. Laughton is expertly supported by John Mills and Brenda de Banzie as the two who wish to marry. B&W; 107m. **DIR:** David Lean. **CAST:** Charles Laughton, John Mills, Brenda de Banzie, Daphne Anderson. **1954**

HOBSON'S CHOICE (1983) ★★★1/2 Sharon Gless is the main attraction in this quaint period drama, set in 1914 New Orleans. She's the spirited and capable eldest daughter of the irascible Henry Horatio Hobson (Jack Warden), seller of shoes and self-proclaimed "pillar of the community." Gless methodically arranges a marriage with his finest shoemaker (Richard Thomas). Not rated; suitable for family viewing. 100m. **DIR:** Gilbert Cates. **CAST:** Sharon Gless, Jack Warden, Richard Thomas, Bert Remsen, Robert Englund, Lillian Gish. **1983**

HOCUS POCUS ★★★1/2 While not much of a box-office hit, this cauldron's brew of thrills and laughs will delight children. Three witches, revived after 300 years, wreak havoc in modern-day Salem, Massachusetts. The movie is scary enough to involve youngsters but not so frightening as to give them nightmares. Rated PG for brief vulgarity and scary stuff. 96m. **DIR:** Kenny Ortega. **CAST:** Bette Midler, Sarah Jessica Parker, Kathy Najimy, Omri Katz, Thora Birch, Vinessa Shaw, Amanda Shepherd. **1993 DVD**

HOFFA ★★★★ Though it leaves several questions about its subject's past and family life unaddressed, this screen biography of labor leader Jimmy Hoffa is a tour de force. The film does not whitewash the events that led to Hoffa's rise to power but maintains a moral ambiguity. Screenplay by David Mamet. Rated R for profanity, violence, and nudity. 140m. **DIR:** Danny DeVito. **CAST:** Jack Nicholson, Danny DeVito, Armand Assante, J. T. Walsh, John C. Reilly, Frank Whaley, Kevin Anderson, John P. Ryan, Robert Prosky, Natalija Nogulich, Nicholas Pryor, Paul Guilfoyle, Karen Young, Cliff Gorman. **1992**

HOGAN'S HEROES (TV SERIES) ★★★ One of the better sitcoms from the late 1960s. During World War II, Col. Robert Hogan leads an international band of resistance fighters composed of prisoners of war interned in a Nazi POW camp, right under the noses of their bumbling German captors. Good writing, directing, and ensemble acting made the idea work for 168 shows. Made for TV. 50m. **DIR:** Various. **CAST:** Bob Crane, Werner Klemperer, John Banner, Robert Clary, Richard Dawson, Larry Hovis, Ivan Dixon, Kenneth Washington. **1965–70**

HOLCROFT COVENANT, THE ★★ In the closing days of World War II, three infamous Nazi officers deposit a large sum of money into a Swiss bank account to be withdrawn years later by their children. This slow but intriguing film, based on the novel by Robert Ludlum, will undoubtedly please spy-film enthusiasts, although others may find it tedious and contrived. Rated R for adult situations. 105m. **DIR:** John Frankenheimer. **CAST:** Michael Caine, Anthony Andrews, Victoria Tennant, Mario Adorf, Lilli Palmer. **1985 DVD**

HOLD 'EM JAIL ★★★ Fast-moving Wheeler and Woolsey burlesque puts them in prison with a warden (slow-burning Edgar Kennedy) whose passion is football. To get on his good side, they put together a prison football team and challenge a rival prison to a gridiron battle. B&W; 74m. **DIR:** Norman Taurog. **CAST:** Bert Wheeler, Robert Woolsey, Betty Grable, Robert Armstrong, Edgar Kennedy. **1932**

HOLD ME, THRILL ME, KISS ME ★★★1/2 Offbeat, slightly sleazy comedy about a drifter who hooks up with a sex-obsessed stripper and her sweet-natured sister only to find violence, depravity, and danger. Writer-director Joel Hershman set out to, in his words, "make a movie just as tasteless, vulgar and tacky as Hollywood for a lot less money." He's succeeded. Not rated, the film has profanity, nudity, simulated sex, and violence. 97m. **DIR:** Joel Hershman. **CAST:** Adrienne Shelly, Max Parrish, Sean Young, Diane Ladd, Andrea Naschak, Bela Lehoczky, Timothy Leary. **1993**

HOLD THAT GHOST ★★★1/2 Abbott and Costello score in this super comedy about two goofs (guess who) inheriting a haunted house where all kinds of bizarre events occur. You may have to watch this one a few times to catch all the gags. B&W; 86m. **DIR:** Arthur Lubin. **CAST:** Bud Abbott, Lou Costello, Richard Carlson, Joan Davis. **1941**

HOLD THE DREAM ★★★ This made-for-TV sequel to *A Woman of Substance* finds an aging Emma Harte (Deborah Kerr) turning over her department-store empire to her granddaughter, Paula (Jenny Seagrove). The rest of the family has plans to steal the business for themselves. Not as captivating as *Woman of Substance*, this sequel will still manage to entertain patrons of the soaps. 180m. **DIR:** Don Sharp. **CAST:** Jenny Seagrove, Deborah Kerr, Stephen Collins, James Brolin. **1986 DVD**

HOLD YOUR MAN ★★★★ One of the best examples of a movie that succeeds because of the vibes between its stars, this one holds your attention from start to finish. The two leads play a gangster and a gun moll who trade barbs, insults, and kisses with equal displays of passion. B&W; 87m. **DIR:** Sam Wood. **CAST:** Jean Harlow, Clark Gable, Dorothy Burgess, Guy Kibbee, Stu Erwin, Elizabeth Patterson. **1933**

HOLE IN THE HEAD, A ★★★ Frank Sinatra plays a Florida motel owner who never quite manages to get his life together, torn between his adoring son (Eddie Hodges) and his nagging brother (Edward G. Robinson). The veteran cast keeps this wispy comedy afloat, and its virtues include the Oscar-winning song "High Hopes." Not rated; suitable for the whole family. 120m. **DIR:** Frank Capra. **CAST:** Frank Sinatra, Edward G. Robinson, Eleanor Parker, Eddie Hodges, Carolyn Jones, Thelma Ritter, Keenan Wynn, Joi Lansing. **1959 DVD**

HOLES, THE ★★ Obscure French satire about a group of misanthropes who live in the Paris sewers. Francophiles will want to see it for the cast, but there's little else to recommend it. Dubbed in English. Not rated. 94m. **DIR:** Pierre Tchernia. **CAST:** Michel Serrault, Michel Galabru, Charles Denner, Philippe Noiret, Gérard Depardieu. **1973 DVD**

HOLIDAY ★★★★1/2 This delightful film was adapted from the Broadway play by Phillip Barry and features

Cary Grant as a nonconformist, who, for love's sake, must confront New York City's upper-class society. Indeed, he must make the ultimate sacrifice to please his fiancée (Doris Nolan) and join her father's banking firm. Only her sister (Katharine Hepburn) seems to understand Grant's need to live a different kind of life. B&W; 93m. **DIR:** George Cukor. **CAST:** Katharine Hepburn, Cary Grant, Doris Nolan, Lew Ayres, Edward Everett Horton, Binnie Barnes, Henry Daniell. **1938**

HOLIDAY AFFAIR (1949) ★★★ Two highly different men court a pretty widow with a young son in this Christmas season story. A warm and friendly film for devotees of romantic melodrama. B&W; 87m. **DIR:** Don Hartman. **CAST:** Janet Leigh, Robert Mitchum, Wendell Corey. **1949**

HOLIDAY AFFAIR (1996) ★★★ This made-for-cable remake is not much of an improvement on the story of two men vying for the attentions of one woman during the Christmas season. From the start, it's obvious whom Cynthia Gibb will end up with, and her barely credible performance gives no indication she is in emotional turmoil. The result is just dull. Not rated. 95m. **DIR:** Alan Myerson. **CAST:** Cynthia Gibb, David James Elliott, Tom Irwin. **1996**

HOLIDAY HOTEL ★★★ It's August, and all of France is going on vacation for the entire month. The cast of this fast-paced comedy is heading toward the Brittany coast. Michel Lang keeps the tempo moving with clever farcical bits and dialogue. Partially in English, the movie has an R rating due to nudity and profanity. 109m. **DIR:** Michel Lang. **CAST:** Sophie Barjac, Daniel Ceccaldi, Michel Grellier, Guy Marchand. **1978**

HOLIDAY IN MEXICO ★★★1/2 Song-filled feast, with widowed Walter Pidgeon as the Ambassador to Mexico. He and his daughter, Jane Powell, find the loves of their lives. Powell sings the "Italian Street Song" and a moving version of "Ave Maria." Jose Iturbi plays Chopin's "Polonaise." 127m. **DIR:** George Sidney. **CAST:** Walter Pidgeon, José Iturbi, Roddy McDowall, Ilona Massey, Jane Powell, Xavier Cugat, Hugo Haas, Linda Christian. **1946**

HOLIDAY INN ★★★★ Irving Berlin's music and the delightful teaming of Bing Crosby and Fred Astaire are the high points of this wartime musical. The timeless renditions of "White Christmas" and "Easter Parade" more than make up for a script that at best could be called fluff. B&W; 101m. **DIR:** Mark Sandrich. **CAST:** Bing Crosby, Fred Astaire, Marjorie Reynolds, Virginia Dale. **1942 DVD**

HOLLOW MAN ★★1/2 Andrew W. Marlowe's script is an uncredited update of H. G. Wells's *The Invisible Man*, with Kevin Bacon starring as the brilliant scientist driven mad by his own experiment. The story begins fairly well, but eventually degenerates into a farfetched slasher movie, with only first-rate special effects to recommend it. Rated R for violence and profanity. 114m. **DIR:** Paul Verhoeven. **CAST:** Elisabeth Shue, Kevin Bacon, Josh Brolin, Kim Dickens, William Devane. **2000 DVD**

HOLLOW POINT ★★1/2 Here's a switch: action hero Thomas Ian Griffith abandons his usual "style" and plays this explosive shoot-'em-up strictly for cartoon-style laughs. Unfortunately, neither Griffith nor costar Tia Carrere can manage the proper tongue-in-cheek tone; both are overshadowed by costar Donald Sutherland, who steals the film as an assassin with principles. Rated R for violence, profanity, and drug use. 103m. **DIR:** Sidney J. Furie. **CAST:** Thomas Ian Griffith, Tia Carrere, John Lithgow, Donald Sutherland. **1995**

HOLLOW REED ★★★1/2 A gay father's attempt to gain custody of his son after he suspects the child is being abused sparks controversy in this intense and topical drama. Martin Donovan is sensational as the father trying to start his new life after divorce only to have his lifestyle scrutinized when he attempts to investigate his son's abuse. Rated R for adult situations and language. 105m. **DIR:** Angela Pope. **CAST:** Martin Donovan, Joely Richardson, Ian Hart, Jason Flemyng, Sam Bould. **1995**

HOLLYWOOD BOULEVARD ★★★ A would-be actress goes to work for inept moviemakers in this comedy. This is the first film that Joe Dante (*Gremlins*) directed. Rated R. 83m. **DIR:** Joe Dante, Allan Arkush. **CAST:** Candice Rialson, Mary Woronov, Rita George, Jeffrey Kramer, Dick Miller, Paul Bartel. **1976 DVD**

HOLLYWOOD BOULEVARD II 🦃 Sleazoid trash takes place on a movie set. Rated R for nudity, profanity, and violence. 82m. **DIR:** Steve Barnett. **CAST:** Ginger Lynn Allen, Kelly Monteith, Eddie Deezen. **1989**

HOLLYWOOD CANTEEN ★★★ An all-star tribute to soldiers, sailors, and Marines who frequented the famed Hollywood Canteen during World War II. Bette Davis and John Garfield founded the USO haven, and just about everybody in show business donated his and her time to make the servicemen feel at ease. The slim storyline is about the one millionth soldier to visit the Canteen. B&W; 125m. **DIR:** Delmer Daves. **CAST:** Bette Davis, John Garfield, Joan Crawford, Ida Lupino, Errol Flynn, Olivia de Havilland, Joan Leslie, Jack Benny, Roy Rogers, Robert Hutton, Dane Clark, Sydney Greenstreet, Peter Lorre, Barbara Stanwyck, Alexis Smith, Eddie Cantor, Janis Paige. **1944**

HOLLYWOOD CAVALCADE ★★★★ A highly fictionalized history of early Hollywood with several comic veterans from the silent days on hand to do what they do best. 96m. **DIR:** Irving Cummings. **CAST:** Don Ameche, Alice Faye, Jed Prouty, Alan Curtis, Chick Chandler, Donald Meek, Al Jolson, Buster Keaton, Ben Turpin, Chester Conklin, Mack Sennett, The Keystone Kops. **1939**

HOLLYWOOD CHAINSAW HOOKERS ★★ Easily Fred Olen Ray's best film (which admittedly is saying very little), this is not the rip-off its title suggests. Ray delivers a campy, sexy, *very* bloody parody about attractive prostitutes who dismember their unsuspecting customers. Both gory and tedious. Rated R. 90m. **DIR:** Fred Olen Ray. **CAST:** Gunnar Hansen, Linnea Quigley. **1988 DVD**

HOLLYWOOD CONFIDENTIAL ★★ Mediocre mystery thiller about a team of detectives who clean up celebrity "messes." Plays like a failed television-series pilot. Rated R for sexual content and violence. 92m. **DIR:** Reynaldo Villalobos. **CAST:** Edward James Olmos, Charlize Theron, Rick Aiello. **1995 DVD**

HOLLYWOOD COP 🦃 Undercover cop battles the mob. Rated R for nudity and violence. B&W; 100m. **DIR:** Amir Shervan. **CAST:** David Goss, Jim Mitchum, Cameron

Mitchell, Troy Donahue, Aldo Ray, Lincoln Kilpatrick. **1987**

HOLLYWOOD DETECTIVE, THE ★★1/2 This chatty thriller bears all the earmarks of a failed television pilot, with Telly Savalas starring as a has-been TV actor rather improbably hired by jittery flake Helene Udy to find her missing boyfriend. Christopher Crowe's script is cute but nothing special; his few topical references to Malathion and Medflies do not a *Chinatown* make. 93m. **DIR:** Kevin Connor. **CAST:** Telly Savalas, Helene Udy, George Coe, Joe Dallesandro. **1991**

•**HOLLYWOOD ENDING** ★★★1/2 Woody Allen's latest will be adored by those who've waited for their hero to make another genuinely funny movie in the vein of early-career farces such as *Sleeper* and *Love and Death*. Allen stars as Oscar-winning film director Val Waxman, whose neurotic behavior has made him unemployable, but who nonetheless gets a plum assignment thanks to some intervention by ex-wife Téa Leoni. Alas, poor Val still has issues, and he winds up psychosomatically blind on the first scheduled day of shooting. Can a blind director successfully make a film? As one character dryly comments, "Have you *seen* some of the pictures coming out of Hollywood these days?" Tinsel Town insiders and behind-the-scenes fans will get more out of this than mainstream viewers, but it's still a pretty funny echo of classic screwball comedies. Rated PG-13 for drug references and mild sexual candor. 114m. **DIR:** Woody Allen. **CAST:** Woody Allen, Téa Leoni, Treat Williams, Mark Rydell, Debra Messing, George Hamilton, Tiffani-Amber Thiessen. **2002 DVD**

HOLLYWOOD HARRY ★★★1/2 Robert Forster stars in this comedy about a down-and-out detective who is forced to take his runaway niece on his investigations. Rated PG-13 for profanity. 99m. **DIR:** Robert Forster. **CAST:** Robert Forster, Joe Spinell, Shannon Wilcox, Kathrine Forster, Marji Martin, Mallie Jackson, Read Morgan. **1985**

HOLLYWOOD HEARTBREAK ★★1/2 Decent, but all too familiar, tale of a Hollywood hopeful. This time the twist is that instead of a gorgeous starlet, the protagonist is a male writer. Not rated; contains profanity. 80m. **DIR:** Lance Dickson. **CAST:** Mark Moses, Carol Mayo Jenkins, Ron Karabatsos. **1990**

HOLLYWOOD HOTEL ★★ Saxophonist Dick Powell wins a talent contest, gets a film contract, but gets the boot because he won't cozy up to bitchy star Lola Lane, preferring her sister instead. Songs by Johnny Mercer and Richard Whiting, including "Hooray for Hollywood," help bolster this otherwise average musical mishmash. B&W; 109m. **DIR:** Busby Berkeley. **CAST:** Dick Powell, Rosemary Lane, Lola Lane, Ted Healy, Alan Mowbray, Frances Langford, Hugh Herbert, Louella Parsons, Glenda Farrell, Edgar Kennedy. **1937**

HOLLYWOOD KNIGHTS, THE ★★★★ Despite the lowbrow antics, this nostalgic chestnut says a lot about male bonding. With their hamburger hangout ready to close on Halloween Eve, 1965, a local car club decides to have one last blowout to retaliate against the snobs. Funny, romantic, and emotionally in touch with the spirit of the era, the film includes many memorable moments and a soundtrack that keeps the joint jumping. Rated R for adult situations and language. 92m. **DIR:** Floyd Mutrux. **CAST:** Tony Danza, Michelle Pfeiffer, Robert Wuhl, Fran Drescher, Stuart Pankin, Richard Schaal, Leigh French. **1980 DVD**

HOLLYWOOD MEATCLEAVER MASSACRE 🦃 Cheesy hack-'em-up about a vengeful demon. Amateurish and inept. Rated R. 87m. **DIR:** Evan Lee. **CAST:** Christopher Lee, Larry Justin. **1975**

HOLLYWOOD OR BUST ★★1/2 One of Dean Martin and Jerry Lewis's lesser efforts concerns the boys' misadventures on a trip to Hollywood where movie nut Jerry hopes to meet his dream girl, Anita Ekberg (who plays herself). Starts off well, but stalls as soon as the musical interludes begin. The final teaming of Martin and Lewis. 95m. **DIR:** Frank Tashlin. **CAST:** Jerry Lewis, Dean Martin, Pat Crowley, Anita Ekberg. **1956**

HOLLYWOOD PARTY ★★★ Jimmy Durante's jungle series as "Schnarzan, the Conqueror" are box-office failures, so he hosts a large party to generate interest in them. That's it, but it opens the door for some lavish musical numbers and cameo appearances by Stan Laurel, Oliver Hardy, the Three Stooges, Jack Pearl (as Baron Muenchausen), and Mickey Mouse. A Walt Disney cartoon short is in color. B&W/color; 69m. **DIR:** Allan Dwan, Roy Rowland. **CAST:** Jimmy Durante, Stan Laurel, Oliver Hardy, Lupe Velez. **1934**

HOLLYWOOD SAFARI ★★1/2 A family of animal trainers tries to find their escaped mountain lion before it is killed by a trigger-happy deputy eager to substitute it for a lion that has been attacking local tourists. Adventure aimed at kids, who may not mind the jumpy plot and cheapo special effects. Rated PG for mild violence. 89m. **DIR:** Henri Charr. **CAST:** Ted Jan Roberts, Ryan J. O'Neill, David Leisure, Don "The Dragon" Wilson, Debby Boone. **1997**

HOLLYWOOD SHUFFLE ★★★1/2 In the style of *Kentucky Fried Movie*, writer-director-star Robert Townsend lampoons Hollywood's perception of blacks—and racial stereotypes in general. It's not always funny, but some scenes are hilarious. A private-eye spoof called "Death of a Break Dancer," and something entitled "Black Acting School" are the standouts. Rated R for profanity and adult content. 82m. **DIR:** Robert Townsend. **CAST:** Robert Townsend, Anne-Marie Johnson, Starletta Dupois. **1987 DVD**

HOLLYWOOD VICE SQUAD 🦃 A tepid affair about a runaway in the sleazoid areas of Hollywood. Rated R for nudity, profanity, and violence. 93m. **DIR:** Penelope Spheeris. **CAST:** Ronny Cox, Frank Gorshin, Leon Isaac Kennedy, Trish Van Devere, Carrie Fisher. **1986 DVD**

HOLOCAUST ★★★★1/2 This Emmy-winning miniseries is one of the finest programs ever produced for television. The story follows the lives of two German families during the reign of Hitler's Third Reich. Everyone in front of and behind the camera does a stunning job. This is a must-see. 570m. **DIR:** Marvin J. Chomsky. **CAST:** Tom Bell, Michael Moriarty, Tovah Feldshuh, Meryl Streep, Fritz Weaver, David Warner. **1978**

HOLOCAUST 2000 🦃 The Antichrist plans to destroy the world, using nuclear reactors. Rated R. 96m. **DIR:** Alberto De Martino. **CAST:** Kirk Douglas, Agostina Belli, Simon Ward, Anthony Quayle. **1978**

HOLY INNOCENTS ★★★★ This moving drama explores the social class struggles in a remote farming community during Franco's rule in Spain. It's a sensi-

tive and compelling look into the struggle of the rural lower class against the wealthy landowners. This critically acclaimed film earned acting awards at the Cannes Film Festival for Alfredo Landa and Francisco Rabal. In Spanish with English subtitles. 108m. **DIR:** Mario Camus. **CAST:** Alfredo Landa, Francisco Rabal. **1984**

HOLY MAN ★★ This comedy misfire is an unfocused assortment of half-baked ideas without the benefit of a star to hold it all together, since Eddie Murphy's participation is as vapid as the concept itself. He plays a spiritual innocent—or so we're led to believe—trying to save network executive Jeff Goldblum's soul, not that you're likely to care, since the stars have zero chemistry. Rated PG for mildly tasteless humor. 113m. **DIR:** Stephen Herek. **CAST:** Eddie Murphy, Jeff Goldblum, Kelly Preston, Robert Loggia, Jon Cryer. **1998 DVD**

HOLY MATRIMONY ★★1/2 Well-intentioned comedy has a moral and some good performances, but a formulaic chase story keeps it mired in mediocrity. Patricia Arquette dreams of becoming a star in Hollywood, so she helps her ne'er-do-well boyfriend rob a carnival owner only to find herself hiding out in a strict, religious Hutterite settlement. This leads to all sorts of rarely hilarious complications. Rated PG-13 for profanity, violence, and suggested nudity. 93m. **DIR:** Leonard Nimoy. **CAST:** Patricia Arquette, Armin Mueller-Stahl, Joseph Gordon-Levitt, Tate Donovan, John Schuck. **1994**

HOLY SMOKE ★★ An Australian family hires a deprogrammer (Harvey Keitel) to rescue their daughter (Kate Winslet) from an Indian religious cult. Director Jane Campion's over-the-top film flails around madly without ever lighting on a coherent idea; the age gap and lack of chemistry between Winslet and Keitel don't help. Rated R for nudity, profanity, and sexual scenes. 120m. **DIR:** Jane Campion. **CAST:** Kate Winslet, Harvey Keitel, Julie Hamilton, Sophie Lee, Pam Grier. **1999 DVD**

HOMAGE ★★1/2 The odd-couple friendship between a reclusive older woman (Blythe Danner) and the young man she hires to tend her estate (Frank Whaley) is disrupted when he becomes obsessed with her daughter, a sexy actress (Sheryl Lee). Quirky drama that never fully delivers on all the issues it raises. Rated R for profanity and sexual situations. 100m. **DIR:** Ross Kagan Marks. **CAST:** Blythe Danner, Frank Whaley, Sheryl Lee, Bruce Davison. **1996 DVD**

HOMBRE ★★★★ Paul Newman gives a superb performance as a white man raised by Indians who is enticed into helping a stagecoach full of settlers make its way across treacherous country. Richard Boone is the baddie who makes this chore difficult, but the racism Newman encounters in this Martin Ritt film provides the real—and thought-provoking—thrust. 111m. **DIR:** Martin Ritt. **CAST:** Paul Newman, Fredric March, Richard Boone, Diane Cilento, Cameron Mitchell, Barbara Rush, Martin Balsam. **1967**

HOME ALONE ★★★★ A child's eye view of *It's a Wonderful Life* in which youngsters are reminded of the importance of family and real values. It all begins when 8 year old Kevin McAllister (Macaulay Culkin) wishes his family would just go away, and they, unbeknownst to him, accidentally go on vacation without him. From there on it's a roller-coaster ride of chuckles and chills. Rated PG for brief vulgarity and silly violence. 100m. **DIR:** Chris Columbus. **CAST:** Macaulay Culkin, Joe Pesci, Daniel Stern, John Heard, Catherine O'Hara, Roberts Blossom, John Candy. **1990 DVD**

HOME ALONE 2: LOST IN NEW YORK ★★★★ Essentially a bigger-budgeted remake of the first film, this sequel is filled with belly laughs. Writer-producer John Hughes does tend to get a bit maudlin, but Macaulay Culkin's misadventures in the Big Apple, after being more believably separated from his parents this time, are more consistently entertaining than his first time *Home Alone*. Rated PG for profanity and slapstick violence. 113m. **DIR:** Chris Columbus. **CAST:** Macaulay Culkin, Joe Pesci, Daniel Stern, Catherine O'Hara, John Heard, Tim Curry, Brenda Fricker, Eddie Bracken. **1992 DVD**

HOME ALONE 3 ★★★1/2 Alex D. Linz fills in nicely as Alex Pruitt, who has to fend off a band of international crooks intent on retrieving a computer chip hidden inside one of his toys. Home with the chicken pox, Alex is forced to become resourceful when his mom steps out to get his medicine, and the crooks step in. Funny, endearing stuff. Rated PG. 102m. **DIR:** Raja Gosnell. **CAST:** Alex D. Linz, Haviland Morris, Lenny von Dohlen, Olek Krupa, Kevin Kilner, Rya Kihlstedt. **1997 DVD**

HOME AND THE WORLD ★★★★★ Satyajit Ray's critically acclaimed, harrowing account of the coming-of-age of an Indian woman. She falls in love with her husband's best friend, an organizer against British goods. This fascinating portrait of Bengali life was based on the Nobel Prize–winning novel by Rabindranath Tagore. In Bengali with English subtitles. Not rated. 130m. **DIR:** Satyajit Ray. **CAST:** Soumitra Chatterjee, Victor Banerjee. **1984**

HOME FOR CHRISTMAS ★★★ Unbelievable, yet touching, made-for-TV tale of a young girl's desire to receive a grandfather for Christmas. Mickey Rooney plays the homeless man she's chosen. 96m. **DIR:** Peter McCubbin. **CAST:** Mickey Rooney, Chantellese Kent, Simon Richards, Lesley Kelly. **1990 DVD**

HOME FOR THE HOLIDAYS (1972) (TELEVISION) ★★★ This TV movie focuses on a family that gathers for Christmas, only to learn they're being stalked by a psycho with a pitchfork. A chilling whodunit. 90m. **DIR:** John Llewellyn Moxey. **CAST:** Sally Field, Jessica Walter, Eleanor Parker, Julie Harris, Jill Haworth, Walter Brennan. **1972**

HOME FOR THE HOLIDAYS (1995) ★★1/2 The stressful, crisis-laden Thanksgiving weekend of a "typical" American family makes for a film with a split personality. The first half is overbearing and obnoxious, while the second half turns suddenly mushy and sentimental. The quiet moments are the best, but they're too few and too late. Rated PG-13 for mild profanity. 103m. **DIR:** Jodie Foster. **CAST:** Holly Hunter, Robert Downey Jr., Anne Bancroft, Dylan McDermott, Charles Durning, Geraldine Chaplin, Steve Guttenberg, Claire Danes. **1995 DVD**

HOME FRIES ★★★ Two brothers, after killing their philandering stepfather, decide to go after Dad's teenage mistress (Drew Barrymore)—until one brother falls in love with her. The amiably offbeat premise and the sweet, vulnerable performances of

Barrymore and Luke Wilson help to offset the meandering contrivances of the script and Dean Parisot's uneasy direction. Catherine O'Hara has some eerie moments as the boys' demented mother. Rated PG-13 for mild profanity. 96m. **DIR:** Dean Parisot. **CAST:** Drew Barrymore, Luke Wilson, Jake Busey, Catherine O'Hara, Shelley Duvall. **1998 DVD**

HOME FROM THE HILL ★★★★ Melodramatic film focuses on a wealthy but dysfunctional southern family. Robert Mitchum is the philandering patriarch. George Hamilton and George Peppard debut as Mitchum's grown sons. Downbeat but well acted and directed. 151m. **DIR:** Vincente Minnelli. **CAST:** Robert Mitchum, Eleanor Parker, George Hamilton, George Peppard, Luana Patten. **1959**

HOME IS WHERE THE HART IS 🦃 Lethargic, unfunny attempt at a black comedy. Rated PG-13. 85m. **DIR:** Rex Bromfield. **CAST:** Valri Bromfield, Stephen E. Miller, Eric Christmas, Leslie Nielsen, Martin Mull. **1987**

HOME MOVIES ★★ A little film produced with the help of Brian De Palma's filmmaking students at Sarah Lawrence College. A director, played by Kirk Douglas, gives "star therapy" to a young man who feels he is a mere extra in his own life. The film is quirky and fun at times, but as entertainment, it's quite tedious. Rated PG. 90m. **DIR:** Brian De Palma. **CAST:** Nancy Allen, Keith Gordon, Kirk Douglas, Gerrit Graham, Vincent Gardenia. **1980**

HOME OF OUR OWN, A ★★★ A single mother (Kathy Bates) and her six kids move into an abandoned farmhouse in Idaho, making a deal with the owner to fix it up and eventually buy it from him. There's a crisis every ten minutes, and not much happens that you haven't seen before, but the actors carry the film, especially Edward Furlong and Clarissa Lessig as the two older children. Rated PG. 102m. **DIR:** Tony Bill. **CAST:** Kathy Bates, Edward Furlong, Clarissa Lessig, Soon-Tek Oh, Tony Campisi. **1993 DVD**

HOME OF THE BRAVE ★★★ This is one of the first films dealing with blacks serving in the military during World War II. The story finds James Edwards on a mission in the Pacific and deals with the racial abuse that he encounters from his own men. The good plot of this film could use some more action, yet it is still worth watching. B&W; 85m. **DIR:** Mark Robson. **CAST:** James Edwards, Steve Brodie, Jeff Corey, Douglas Dick. **1949**

HOME REMEDY ★★★ A young New Jersey man retreats into his suburban house, where the noisy woman next door is his only obstacle to complete and blissful inertia. Odd, talky black comedy. Not rated, mild sexual situations. 92m. **DIR:** Maggie Greenwald. **CAST:** Seth Barrish, Maxine Albert. **1988**

HOME, SWEET HOME (1914) ★★1/2 Henry B. Walthall is John Howard Payne in this fanciful biography of the famous composer. Lillian Gish is his faithful, long-suffering sweetheart. Denied happiness in life, the lovers are united as they "fly" to heaven. Silent. B&W; 80m. **DIR:** D. W. Griffith. **CAST:** Henry B. Walthall, Lillian Gish, Dorothy Gish, Mae Marsh, Spottiswoode Aitken, Miriam Cooper, Robert Harron, Donald Crisp, Blanche Sweet, Owen Moore. **1914**

HOME SWEET HOME (1982) ★★★★ One in a series of films made by Mike Leigh in the 1970s and early 1980s for British television. A low-budget, bitter black comedy, it is an incisive bit of snoopery. Leigh reveals the isolation of the English working class by focusing on three postal workers who find their lives mingled, as one of them is sleeping with the wives of the other two. Leigh makes it clear that the Monty Pythoners didn't have to look far for their parodies. Not rated; contains profanity and adult themes. 90m. **DIR:** Mike Leigh. **CAST:** Eric Richard, Timothy Spall, Kay Stonham, Lorraine Brunning. **1982**

HOMEBODIES ★★★ A cast of aging screen veterans liven up this offbeat thriller about a group of senior citizens who turn into a hit squad when faced with eviction. Director Larry Yust keeps things moving at a lively pace and even manages a few bizarre twists in the final scenes. Rated PG for violence, language. 96m. **DIR:** Larry Yust. **CAST:** Douglas Fowley, Ruth McDevitt, Ian Wolfe. **1974**

HOMEBOY ★★ This slow-moving, moody drama about a washed-up cowboy prizefighter is engorged with down-and-out characters. Mickey Rourke stars as the maverick boxer who drinks, smirks, and mumbles his way to one last shot as a top middleweight contender. The raunchy, atmospheric soundtrack is by Eric Clapton and Michael Kamen. Rated R for profanity and violence. 118m. **DIR:** Michael Seresin. **CAST:** Mickey Rourke, Christopher Walken, Debra Feuer, Kevin Conway. **1988**

HOMEBOYS ★★ Mexican-Americans are portrayed as ruthless drug dealers in this urban piece about how a cop can be torn between his job and his love for his brother. The young cast does a fair job in this low-budget production. Not rated, but with nudity and profanity. 91m. **DIR:** Lindsay Norgard. **CAST:** Todd Bridges, David Garrison. **1992**

HOMEBOYS II: CRACK CITY ★★ A good kid falls in with a bad crowd when he moves to Harlem from the suburbs. Well-intentioned message movie is weighed down by too many ridiculous plot elements. It has nothing to do with *Homeboys*. Not rated, but an R equivalent for violence and nudity. 90m. **DIR:** Daniel Matmor. **CAST:** Brian Paul Stewart, Delia Sheppard. **1989**

HOMECOMING (1948) ★★ In this post–WWII melodrama, Clark Gable, Lana Turner, and Anne Baxter are glamorous. If they had something to do other than talk and stare, they might have had a better movie. It's about an army surgeon who has a romance with his nurse while both are in the trenches. Even with Gable and Turner as the illicit lovers, the movie isn't as good as it should have been. B&W; 113m. **DIR:** Mervyn LeRoy. **CAST:** Clark Gable, Lana Turner, Anne Baxter, John Hodiak, Ray Collins, Cameron Mitchell, Gladys Cooper, Marshall Thompson. **1948**

HOMECOMING (1996) ★★★1/2 When their mentally unstable mother simply wanders off one day, adolescent Kimberlee Peterson takes charge of three younger siblings and eventually guides them to an eccentric grandmother who scarcely knows them. Anne Bancroft steals the show as that estranged relative, but director Mark Jean wisely doesn't let her go over the top. Heartwarming entertainment, perfect for the entire family. Rated G. 105m. **DIR:** Mark Jean. **CAST:** Anne Bancroft, Kimberlee Peterson, Trever O'Brien, Hanna Hall, William Greenblatt, Bonnie Bedelia. **1996 DVD**

HOMECOMING, THE (1973) ★★★★ Michael Jayston brings his wife, Vivien Merchant, home to meet the family after several years of separation. His father and two brothers are no-holds-barred Harold Pinter characters. If you like drama and Pinter, you'll want to check out this American Film Theater production, which has outstanding direction by Peter Hall. 111m. **DIR:** Peter Hall. **CAST:** Cyril Cusack, Ian Holm, Michael Jayston, Vivien Merchant, Terrence Rigby, Paul Rogers. **1973**

HOMEGROWN ★★★ Enjoyable film with a terrific cast about a group of illicit marijuana farmers who decide to take over the business when their boss is gunned down. In order to do that, however, they have to pretend he's still alive. Rated R for profanity and nudity. 103m. **DIR:** Stephen Gyllenhaal. **CAST:** Billy Bob Thornton, Hank Azaria, Kelly Lynch, Jon Bon Jovi, Judge Reinhold, Ted Danson, John Lithgow, Jamie Lee Curtis. **1998 DVD**

HOMER AND EDDIE ★★★ Outstanding performance by James Belushi as a retarded man trying to return to his dying father despite the fact that his father has disowned him. Whoopi Goldberg plays a sociopathic woman who gives Belushi the ride of a lifetime. Rated R for profanity and violence. 102m. **DIR:** Andrei Konchalovsky. **CAST:** James Belushi, Whoopi Goldberg, Karen Black, Anne Ramsey. **1989**

HOMETOWN BOY MAKES GOOD ★★★ Waiter Anthony Edwards returns home to Minnesota for a visit and finds out that the little white lie he told his mother has spread. It seems the whole town thinks he's a famous psychiatrist, and pretty soon he's Doc Minnesota. Half the fun is watching Edwards cover his bases while continuing the sham. Good supporting cast pitches in to make this a fun outing. Not rated; contains adult language. 88m. **DIR:** David Burton Morris. **CAST:** Anthony Edwards, Grace Zabriskie, Chris Mulkey. **1993**

HOMEWARD BOUND: THE INCREDIBLE JOURNEY ★★★★1/2 The folks at Walt Disney Pictures take the animal adventure to artistic heights. A remake of Disney's *The Incredible Journey*, this highly entertaining movie gives voices (supplied by Sally Field, Michael J. Fox, and Don Ameche) and hilarious dialogue to two dogs and a cat, who attempt to make their way home through the untamed wilderness of a national forest. A delight for all ages. Rated G. 84m. **DIR:** Duwayne Dunham. **CAST:** Robert Hays, Kim Greist, Jean Smart, Veronica Lauren, Kevin Chevalia, Benj Thall. **1993 DVD**

HOMEWARD BOUND II: LOST IN SAN FRANCISCO ★★ American bulldog Chance, golden retriever Shadow, and Himalayan cat Sassy once again are separated from their family. This time they need to survive the bully pooches, pet nappers, and mean streets of San Francisco while trying to find their way back to their new Marin digs. Lacks the original film's breathtaking nature thrills and warm humor. Rated G. 97m. **DIR:** David R. Ellis. **CAST:** Robert Hays, Kim Greist, Veronica Lauren, Kevin Chevalia, Benj Thall. **1996 DVD**

HOMEWORK 🦃 High school teacher seduces one of her students. Rated R for nudity. 90m. **DIR:** James Beshears. **CAST:** Joan Collins, Shell Kepler, Wings Hauser, Betty Thomas. **1982**

HOMEWRECKER ★★★1/2 Scientist Robby Benson suffers a breakdown after accidentally killing a family during a military defense test. When he privately rebuilds his computer, he adds human traits, and the computer (voiced by Kate Jackson) takes on a very human, and jealous, persona. An imaginative plot, tight editing, and Benson's performance overcome the low budget. Rated PG-13 for profanity. 88m. **DIR:** Fred Walton. **CAST:** Robby Benson, Sydney Walsh, Sarah Rose Karr. **1992**

HOMICIDAL ★★★ Schlockmeister William Castle's best movie is this blatant *Psycho* takeoff that, unlike most such imitations, at least manages to add a few new twists. B&W; 87m. **DIR:** William Castle. **CAST:** Glenn Corbett, Patricia Breslin, Jean Aless, Eugenie Leontovich. **1961 DVD**

HOMICIDAL IMPULSE ★★1/2 Derivative thriller stars Scott Valentine as an assistant district attorney who gets involved with scheming intern Vanessa Angel, who's willing to do anything to rise to the top, including murder. Rated R for nudity and violence. 86m. **DIR:** David Tausik. **CAST:** Scott Valentine, Vanessa Angel, Charles Napier. **1992**

HOMICIDE ★★★1/2 A detective is assigned against his will to investigate the murder of an older Jewish woman killed at her shop in a predominantly black neighborhood. Crackling dialogue and a suspenseful atmosphere make up for a plot twist that doesn't quite ring true in this Chinese puzzle of a movie. Rated R for profanity and violence. 102m. **DIR:** David Mamet. **CAST:** Joe Mantegna, William H. Macy, Natalija Nogulich, Ving Rhames. **1991**

HONDO ★★★★ One of John Wayne's best films and performances, this 3-D Western overcomes the gimmicky process with excellent performances, plenty of action, and an uncommonly strong screenplay from frequent Wayne collaborator James Edward Grant. The Duke plays an army scout who adopts a widowed frontierswoman (Geraldine Page in her Oscar-nominated film debut) and her son. 84m. **DIR:** John Farrow. **CAST:** John Wayne, Geraldine Page, Ward Bond, Lee Aaker, James Arness, Michael Pate, Leo Gordon, Paul Fix. **1953**

HONDO AND THE APACHES ★★★ Based on the John Wayne film. Ralph Taeger is Indian scout, Hondo Lane. Three episodes of the *Hondo* TV series edited into feature form. 85m. **DIR:** Lee H. Katzin. **CAST:** Ralph Taeger, Robert Taylor, Noah Beery Jr., Michael Rennie, John Smith, Kathie Browne. **1967**

HONEY, I BLEW UP THE KID ★★★★ This is a delightful sequel to *Honey, I Shrunk the Kids*. The new adventure once again finds scientist Rick Moranis working on an experiment, only this time it's an enlargement ray that blows up his kid to 112 feet tall! The special effects are remarkable. Rated PG. 89m. **DIR:** Randal Kleiser. **CAST:** Rick Moranis, Marcia Strassman, Lloyd Bridges, Robert Oliveri, John Shea. **1992**

HONEY, I SHRUNK THE KIDS ★★★1/2 Old-fashioned Disney fun in the *Absent-Minded Professor* tradition gets contemporary special effects and solid bits of comedy. Rick Moranis is the scientist who invents a machine that, when accidentally triggered, shrinks his and the neighbors' kids to ant-size. Rated PG for slight profanity. 100m. **DIR:** Joe Johnston. **CAST:** Rick Moranis, Jared Rushton, Matt Frewer. **1989**

HONEY POT, THE ★★ Rex Harrison summons three of his former loves to his deathbed for the reading of his will. This bloated, star-studded extravaganza could lose thirty minutes from its first half and become an entertaining little whodunit. 131m. **DIR:** Joseph L. Mankiewicz. **CAST:** Rex Harrison, Susan Hayward, Cliff Robertson, Maggie Smith, Capucine, Edie Adams. **1967**

HONEY, WE SHRUNK OURSELVES ★★ Third, and weakest, entry in Disney's *Honey* series, this wisely was passed over for theatrical release, going straight to video. For a film that relies on special effects, there are too many computer graphics that just don't measure up. Rick Moranis, who shrinks himself and his brother (Stuart Pankin), seems to sleepwalk through his part of nutty inventor. Rated PG for juvenile misbehavior. 75m. **DIR:** Dean Cundey. **CAST:** Rick Moranis, Stuart Pankin, Eve Gordon, Bug Hall, Robin Bartlett. **1996**

HONEYBOY ★★ Erik Estrada is the boy, Morgan Fairchild the honey, in this watered-down compilation of every boxing cliché ever employed in the poor-boy-makes-good genre. Not rated and suitable for viewing by families with relatively strong stomachs. 100m. **DIR:** John Berry. **CAST:** Erik Estrada, Morgan Fairchild, Hector Elizondo, James McEachin, Phillip R. Allen. **1982**

HONEYMOON ★★★1/2 A Frenchwoman (Nathalie Baye) goes on what appears to be a carefree New York vacation with her boyfriend (Richard Berry). However, he is busted for smuggling cocaine, and she is set for deportation. She goes to an agency that arranges marriages of convenience. She is assured that she will never see her new American "husband"—only to have him show up and refuse to leave her alone. Rated R for profanity, nudity, and violence. 98m. **DIR:** Patrick Jamain. **CAST:** Nathalie Baye, John Shea, Richard Berry, Peter Donat. **1987**

HONEYMOON ACADEMY ★★ A secret agent (Kim Cattrall) marries unsuspecting Robert Hays. Reliance on sight gags and slapstick for laughs doesn't pan out. Rated PG-13 for violence. 94m. **DIR:** Gene Quintano. **CAST:** Robert Hays, Kim Cattrall, Leigh Taylor-Young, Jonathan Banks. **1990**

HONEYMOON IN VEGAS ★★★★ Private detective Nicolas Cage finally overcomes his fear of commitment and agrees to marry longtime love Sarah Jessica Parker. On their honeymoon, they go to Las Vegas where everything begins going wrong, and they end up in the clutches of gangster James Caan. More inspired madcap madness from writer-director Andrew Bergman. Rated PG-13. 100m. **DIR:** Andrew Bergman. **CAST:** James Caan, Nicolas Cage, Sarah Jessica Parker, Anne Bancroft, Peter Boyle, Noriyuki "Pat" Morita. **1992 DVD**

HONEYMOON KILLERS, THE ★★★ Grim story of a smooth-talking Lothario and his obese lover who befriend and murder vulnerable older women for their money is based on the infamous "lonely hearts killers" of the 1940s and 1950s. Not for the squeamish, but a solid entry in the growing file of true-crime films. 108m. **DIR:** Leonard Kastle. **CAST:** Tony Lo Bianco, Shirley Stoler, Mary Jane Higby. **1970**

HONEYMOON MACHINE, THE ★★1/2 Three sailors use the master computer of their cruiser in an attempt to beat the roulette at a casino in Venice. Dean Jagger is fun as a bellowing admiral. 87m. **DIR:** Richard Thorpe. **CAST:** Steve McQueen, Brigid Bazlen, Jim Hutton, Paula Prentiss, Dean Jagger, Jack Weston, Jack Mullaney. **1961**

HONEYMOONERS, THE: LOST EPISODES (TV SERIES) ★★★★1/2 For years, the thirty-nine filmed episodes of *The Honeymooners*, all created during the 1955–1956 season, were the only ones the public could view. Then, with a dramatic flourish, Jackie Gleason announced that he had uncovered dozens of other episodes, preserved on kinescope. The skits often matched the classic thirty-nine in the categories of heart and hilarity. At their worst, these sketches surpass ninety-nine percent of what passes for comedy on television today. Twenty-two volumes; two or three episodes per tape. B&W; 47—55. **DIR:** Frank Satenstein. **CAST:** Jackie Gleason, Art Carney, Audrey Meadows, Joyce Randolph. **1952–1957**

HONEYMOONERS, THE (TV SERIES) ★★★★★ A tacky apartment in Bensonhurst, Brooklyn, is the setting for the misadventures of bus driver Ralph Kramden, his wife Alice, and their best friends, the Nortons. When Alice derides Ralph's get-rich-quick schemes, he's apt to bellow, "One of these days—Pow! Right in the kisser!" But, Gleason tempers the bluster with childlike appeal and, by the end of the episode, contrite Ralph embraces Alice and proclaims, "Baby, you're the greatest!" Each of the thirty-nine filmed episodes is a comic gem. Two episodes per tape. B&W; 50m. **DIR:** Frank Satenstein. **CAST:** Jackie Gleason, Art Carney, Audrey Meadows, Joyce Randolph. **1955–1956**

HONEYSUCKLE ROSE ★★1/2 For his first starring role, country singer Willie Nelson is saddled with a rather stodgy film that all but sinks in the mire of its unimaginative handling and sappy story. Rated PG. 119m. **DIR:** Jerry Schatzberg. **CAST:** Willie Nelson, Dyan Cannon, Amy Irving, Slim Pickens. **1980**

HONG KONG '97 🦃 Dismal, low-budget thriller about an assassin trying to unravel China's takeover of Hong Kong in 1997 from Great Britain. Rated R for nudity, violence, and adult language. 91m. **DIR:** Albert Pyun. **CAST:** Robert Patrick, Tim Thomerson, Brian James, Ming-Na Wen. **1994**

HONKY TONK ★★★ A gambler fleeing tar and feathers meets a Boston beauty and her con man father on the train going to a new frontier town. He grows rich from graft and marries the beauty. Clark Gable and Lana Turner clicked as a team in this lively, lusty oater. B&W; 105m. **DIR:** Jack Conway. **CAST:** Clark Gable, Lana Turner, Frank Morgan, Claire Trevor, Marjorie Main, Albert Dekker, Henry O'Neill, Chill Wills, Veda Ann Borg. **1941**

HONKY TONK FREEWAY ★★★ Director John Schlesinger captures the comedy of modern American life in a small Florida town. The stars keep you laughing. Rated R. 107m. **DIR:** John Schlesinger. **CAST:** William Devane, Beverly D'Angelo, Beau Bridges, Geraldine Page, Teri Garr. **1981 DVD**

HONKYTONK MAN ★★★★ Clint Eastwood stars as an alcoholic, tubercular country singer headed for an audition at the Grand Ole Opry during the depths of the Depression. A bittersweet character study, it works remarkably well. You even begin to believe Eastwood in

the role. The star's son, Kyle Eastwood, makes an impressive film debut. Rated PG for strong language and sexual content. 122m. **DIR:** Clint Eastwood. **CAST:** Clint Eastwood, Kyle Eastwood, John McIntire. **1982**

HONOLULU ★★★★ More comedy than musical, this film was the last film George Burns made before his comeback in *The Sunshine Boys* more than a quarter of a century later. Robert Young plays a movie star and his twin brother, who change places and cause all sorts of mix-ups. Burns and Gracie Allen fill most of the time with choice one-liners. B&W; 83m. **DIR:** Edward Buzzell. **CAST:** Eleanor Powell, George Burns, Gracie Allen, Robert Young, Rita Johnson, Sig Ruman, Ruth Hussey, Eddie "Rochester" Anderson, Ann Morris, Clarence Kolb. **1939**

HONOR AMONG THIEVES ★★1/2 Charles Bronson plays a mercenary who is locked in a French bank over the weekend with Alain Delon, a doctor. Bronson is there to rob the bank of its 200 million francs, while Delon is there to replace some misappropriated securities. This is a little different type of picture for Bronson—a bit more subtle, a little slower-paced, and with more dialogue than action. Rated R. 93m. **DIR:** Jean Herman. **CAST:** Charles Bronson, Alain Delon, Brigitte Fossey. **1983 DVD**

HONOR THY FATHER ★★ A movie version of the real-life internal Mafia war that took place during the late 1960s among members of the Bonanno crime family. Weak. Not rated; contains violence. 97m. **DIR:** Paul Wendkos. **CAST:** Joseph Bologna, Brenda Vaccaro, Raf Vallone. **1973 DVD**

HONOR THY FATHER & MOTHER: THE MENENDEZ KILLINGS ★★ The better (and that's not saying much) of two made-for-television docudramas chronicling the murders of Jose and Kitty Menendez (James Farentino and Jill Clayburgh), who were allegedly murdered by their sons Erik and Lyle in order to inherit the family fortune. Film fails to add anything new to the tragic events that gripped America when the sons were brought to trial. Not rated; contains strong images of violence. 97m. **DIR:** Paul Schneider. **CAST:** James Farentino, Jill Clayburgh, Billy Warlock, David Beron. **1993**

HOODLUM ★★★1/2 When gangster Dutch Schultz begins to yank control of the Harlem numbers racket from its black caretakers, he steps on the toes of his organized crime associates. Bumpy Johnson then joins forces with the mob's Lucky Luciano to exterminate the greedy, swaggering renegade. This predictable, violent melodrama benefits from its 1930s Harlem setting and excellent cast. Rated R for violence, language, nudity, and suggested sex. 142m. **DIR:** Bill Duke. **CAST:** Laurence Fishburne, Tim Roth, Andy Garcia, Cicely Tyson, Vanessa L. Williams, Clarence Williams, III, Richard Bradford. **1997 DVD**

HOODLUM EMPIRE ★★ A racketeer's nephew decides to go straight after a tour of duty in World War II but runs into problems from both sides of the law. A very thinly disguised filmic depiction of the famous Estes Kefauver investigation into Frank Costello and his ties with organized crime, this docudrama is long on talent but short on style. B&W; 98m. **DIR:** Joseph Kane. **CAST:** Brian Donlevy, Claire Trevor, Forrest Tucker, Vera Hruba Ralston, Luther Adler, John Russell, Gene Lockhart, Grant Withers, Taylor Holmes, Richard Jaeckel. **1952**

HOODLUM PRIEST, THE ★★★1/2 Don Murray gives a sincere performance as Father Charles Dismis Clark, a Jesuit priest who devotes himself to helping newly released convicts reenter society. The focus is on one young parolee (Keir Dullea, in his debut) who has trouble finding his way. Murray coproduced. B&W; 101m. **DIR:** Irvin Kershner. **CAST:** Don Murray, Keir Dullea, Larry Gates, Logan Ramsey, Don Joslyn, Cindi Wood. **1961**

HOODS ★★1/2 A small group of gangsters is commissioned to put a hit out on a fellow that they've never heard of. When they finally track down the elusive target, the assassins discover that their target is just a kid. The group is thrown into confusion by this unexpected turn of affairs, but they soon find out that there is a lot to this kid that they do not know about. The cast is full of recognizable faces, but the film cannot decide whether it is a dark satire or a slapstick farce—it doesn't work as either. Rated R for language, violence, and sexual situations. 92m. **DIR:** Mark Malone. **CAST:** Joe Mantegna, Kevin Pollak, Joe Pantoliano, Jennifer Tilly. **1998 DVD**

HOOK ★★★1/2 For all its minor flaws, director Steven Spielberg's heartfelt continuation of James M. Barrie's *Peter Pan* is fine family entertainment. There are some dull spots, but it's doubtful they'll be as glaring on the small screen. Look for Glenn Close and singer David Crosby in brief bits as pirates on Hook's ship. Rated PG for vulgar language. 137m. **DIR:** Steven Spielberg. **CAST:** Robin Williams, Dustin Hoffman, Julia Roberts, Bob Hoskins, Maggie Smith, Charlie Korsmo, Phil Collins, Glenn Close, David Crosby. **1991 DVD**

HOOK, LINE AND SINKER ★★ Silly story of two nitwits who woo a mother and daughter. The popular comedy team of Wheeler and Woolsey did better work than this sort of a watered-down version of The Marx Brothers'. B&W; 71m. **DIR:** Eddie Cline. **CAST:** Bert Wheeler, Robert Woolsey, Dorothy Lee, Hugh Herbert, Natalie Moorhead. **1930**

HOOP DREAMS ★★★★★ This rich slice of the American Dream stretches into the realm of exhilarating Hollywood drama. Three white guys with a camera talked their way into the lives of two black youths in 1987 and emerged nearly five years later with a staggering urban saga. Hoping to eventually play in the NBA, the two 14 year olds accept sports scholarships to a high-profile Catholic high school. The recruitment is sweet, but the kids are faced with escalating pressures that alter their lives. Rated PG-13 for language. 171m. **DIR:** Steve James. **CAST:** William Gates, Arthur Agee. **1994**

HOOPER ★★★★ Fresh from their success with *Smokey and the Bandit*, director Hal Needham and stars Burt Reynolds and Sally Field are reunited for this humorous, knockabout comedy about Hollywood stuntmen. Jan-Michael Vincent adds to the film's impact as an up-and-coming fall guy out to best top-of-the-heap Reynolds. Good fun. Rated PG. 99m. **DIR:** Hal Needham. **CAST:** Burt Reynolds, Sally Field, Jan-Michael Vincent, Brian Keith. **1978 DVD**

HOOSIER SCHOOLBOY ★★★ A Depression-era melodrama that's as timely today as it was in the 1930s. The story is told through the eyes of a young schoolboy who

sees how many WWI veterans are treated by businessmen after the war is over. He realizes that's one reason why his father is an alcoholic. Good story despite maudlin treatment. B&W; 62m. **DIR:** William Nigh. **CAST:** Mickey Rooney, Anne Nagel, Frank Sheilds, Edward Pawley. **1937**

HOOSIERS ★★★★1/2 The most satisfying high school basketball movie in years. Gene Hackman is the new coach—with a mysterious past—at Hickory High. His unorthodox methods rankle the locals, his fellow teachers, and the undisciplined team members. But before you can say hoosiermania, the team is at the 1951 state championships. It doesn't hurt that the realistic script is based on a true Indiana Cinderella story. Rated PG. 114m. **DIR:** David Anspaugh. **CAST:** Gene Hackman, Barbara Hershey, Dennis Hopper, Sheb Wooley. **1986 DVD**

HOPALONG CASSIDY RETURNS ★★★ Cassidy pins on a sheriff's badge and lines up miners and ranchers to stop Blackie, a gang enforcer and murderer. Hoppy guns him down and bestows a last kiss on the dying saloon owner, Lilly. B&W; 74m. **DIR:** Nate Watt. **CAST:** William Boyd, George "Gabby" Hayes, Evelyn Brent, Stephen Morris, William Janney, Gail Sheridan. **1936**

HOPALONG RIDES AGAIN ★★★ Spring is in the air but with it comes danger for Hopalong Cassidy. A herd was stolen and friends murdered near Black Mesa and that's where the Bar-20 gang is now headed. Hoppy likes a woman there whose brother, an eccentric scientist, is actually the cold-blooded murderer. B&W; 65m. **DIR:** Lesley Selander. **CAST:** William Boyd, George "Gabby" Hayes, Russell Hayden, William Duncan, Lois Wilde, Billy King, Harry Worth. **1937**

HOPE ★★★★ This TNT original is about racial injustice in a small Mississippi town. The mouthpiece for the message is a spunky young girl (Jena Malone) who must choose between family and fairness. The subject matter is somber, but Malone and her sidekick (Lee Norris) inject mirthful moments as youthful outsiders. Not rated; contains profanity and racist remarks. 90m. **DIR:** Goldie Hawn. **CAST:** Jena Malone, Jeffrey Sams, J. T. Walsh, Christine Lahti, Catherine O'Hara, Lee Norris. **1997**

HOPE AND GLORY ★★★★1/2 Writer-producer-director John Boorman's much-praised film chronicles his boyhood experiences during the London blitz. Rather than the horror story one might expect, it is a marvelously entertaining, warm, and thoughtful look backward. Blessed with vibrant characters, cultural richness, and a fresh point of view, it never fails to fascinate. Rated PG-13 for profanity and suggested sex. 113m. **DIR:** John Boorman. **CAST:** Sarah Miles, David Hayman, Derrick O'Connor, Susan Wooldridge, Sammi Davis, Ian Bannen, Sebastian Rice Edwards, Jean-Marc Barr. **1987 DVD**

HOPE FLOATS ★★1/2 Housewife Birdee appears on a national TV talk show, where her best friend confesses she is having an affair with her husband. Humiliated, heartbroken, and in shock, Birdee moves into her eccentric mother's Texas home with her distraught daughter, where she mopes in her bathrobe before landing a job and dating a hayseed hunk. Rated PG-13 for mature themes and language. 110m. **DIR:** Forest Whitaker. **CAST:** Sandra Bullock, Harry Connick Jr., Gena Rowlands, Mae Whitman, Michael Paré. **1998 DVD**

HOPPITY GOES TO TOWN ★★★ Max and Dave Fleischer, of Betty Boop and Popeye fame, brought their distinctive style of animation to this feature about the insect residents of Bugtown. The Fleischers were better at making short cartoons—there's not enough plot or characterization here to justify a feature—but their style is always delightful. Adults may enjoy it more than kids. Kenny Gardner, Gwen Williams, Jack Mercer, Ted Pierce (voices). 77m. **DIR:** Dave Fleischer. **1941**

HOPPY SERVES A WRIT ★★1/2 Hopalong Cassidy in Oklahoma Territory. Strictly a formula series Western, but well mounted, breezy, and moves along at a fast clip with a good cast. B&W; 67m. **DIR:** George Archainbaud. **CAST:** William Boyd, Andy Clyde, Victor Jory, George Reeves, Robert Mitchum, Byron Foulger. **1943**

HOPSCOTCH ★★★★ Walter Matthau is wonderful in this fast-paced and funny film as a spy who decides to extract a little revenge on the pompous supervisor (Ned Beatty) who demoted him. Glenda Jackson has a nice bit as Matthau's romantic interest. Rated R. 104m. **DIR:** Ronald Neame. **CAST:** Walter Matthau, Ned Beatty, Glenda Jackson. **1980**

HORIZONTAL LIEUTENANT, THE ★★★ A bumbling World War II junior officer is assigned to catch an elusive supplies thief at a Pacific island storage base. Mild service comedy with likable stars. 90m. **DIR:** Richard Thorpe. **CAST:** Jim Hutton, Paula Prentiss, Jack Carter, Jim Backus, Charles McGraw, Miyoshi Umeki, Marty Ingels. **1962**

HORN BLOWS AT MIDNIGHT, THE ★★★ A comedy classic that has improved with age. Jack Benny ridiculed it because it flopped when first released. But his kidding elevated it to a cult status, and it is delightful to watch today. The plot about an angel sent to Earth to blow his trumpet and end the world may be a cliché, but Benny gives it style. B&W; 78m. **DIR:** Raoul Walsh. **CAST:** Jack Benny, Alexis Smith, Dolores Moran, John Alexander, Reginald Gardiner, Allyn Joslyn, Margaret Dumont, Guy Kibbee, Franklin Pangborn. **1945**

HORNET'S NEST ★★ Commando Rock Hudson leads a group of orphaned Italian boys in a raid on a Nazi-held dam. Some fair action scenes but pretty farfetched. Rated PG. 110m. **DIR:** Phil Karlson. **CAST:** Rock Hudson, Sylva Koscina. **1970**

HORRIBLE DOCTOR BONES, THE 🦃 The title says it all. Dr. Bones looks to take over the world with zombies controlled by hip-hop music. Rated R for violence, profanity, and sexual situations. 72m. **DIR:** Art Carnage. **CAST:** Darrow Igus, Larry Bates, Sarah Scott. **2000 DVD**

HORRIBLE DR. HICHCOCK, THE (TERROR OF DR. HICHCOCK, THE) ★★1/2 Robert Flemyng's naïve second wife is unaware of his plans to use her in a plot to revive her late predecessor. The U.S. version of this above-average Italian period-horror shocker is handicapped by its distributor's cutting of twelve minutes from the movie—mostly to eliminate details of the title character's obsession with necrophilia. The British release (also available as *The Terror of Dr. Hichcock*) is slightly longer. 76m. **DIR:** Robert Hampton (Riccardo Freda). **CAST:** Barbara Steele, Robert Flemyng. **1962**

HORRIBLE HORROR ★★1/2 Beloved 1950s *Shock Theater* host Zacherley (aka John Zacherle) is in vintage form for this direct-to-video compilation of clips, outtakes, and trailers from mostly awful horror movies. The dumb framing device will have you fast-forwarding through Zacherley's routines after about twenty minutes and slowing down to savor vignettes from *The Brainiac, Killers from Space, Devil Bat, She Demons*, and dozens more. Not rated. 110m. **DIR:** David Bergman. **CAST:** Zacherley. **1987**

HORROR EXPRESS ★★★★ Director Eugenio Martin creates a neat shocker about a prehistoric manlike creature terrorizing a trans-Siberian train when he is awakened from his centuries-old tomb. Lively cast includes a pre-Kojak Telly Savalas in the role of a crazed Russian Cossack intent on killing the thing. Rated R. 88m. **DIR:** Eugenio Martin. **CAST:** Peter Cushing, Christopher Lee, Telly Savalas. **1972 DVD**

HORROR HOSPITAL ★★ A crazy doctor (Michael Gough) performing gruesome brain experiments at a remote English hospital runs into trouble when a nosy young couple begins snooping around. Slow-moving gorefest. Rated R for violence and blood. 84m. **DIR:** Anthony Balch. **CAST:** Michael Gough, Robin Askwith, Dennis Price. **1973 DVD**

HORROR HOTEL ★★★ Christopher Lee is a sinister teacher who urges a female student to research a witchcraft thesis at a New England village that's the perfect embodiment of Lovecraftian isolation. A good cast, screenwriter George Baxt (*Circus of Horrors*), and some top technicians—including legendary cinematographer Desmond Dickinson (Olivier's *Hamlet*)—overcome a tiny budget and make this witchcraft saga a miniclassic of the British horror renaissance. B&W; 76m. **DIR:** John Llewellyn Moxey. **CAST:** Dennis Lotis, Betta St. John, Christopher Lee, Venetia Stevenson. **1960 DVD**

HORROR ISLAND 🦃 Goofballs search for treasure in a haunted castle. B&W; 61m. **DIR:** George Waggner. **CAST:** Dick Foran, Leo Carrillo, Peggy Moran, Fuzzy Knight, Iris Adrian. **1941**

HORROR OF DRACULA ★★★★1/2 This is the one that launched Hammer Films's popular Dracula series, featuring Christopher Lee in the first—and best—of his many appearances as the Count and Peter Cushing as his archnemesis Van Helsing. A stylish, exciting reworking of Bram Stoker's classic story of a bloodthirsty vampire on the prowl from Transylvania to London and back again. Genuinely scary film, with a hell of an ending, too. 82m. **DIR:** Terence Fisher. **CAST:** Christopher Lee, Peter Cushing, Michael Gough, Melissa Stribling, Miles Malleson. **1958**

HORROR OF FRANKENSTEIN ★★★★ Young medical student, fed up with school, decides to drop out and continue his studies alone. So what if his name just happens to be Frankenstein and he just happens to be making a monster? Good entry in the series has many ghoulish sequences, along with some welcome touches of humor. Recommended. Rated R. 95m. **DIR:** Jimmy Sangster. **CAST:** Ralph Bates, Kate O'Mara, Veronica Carlson, Dennis Price. **1970 DVD**

HORROR OF PARTY BEACH, THE 🦃 A really horrendous horror film about radioactive lizard-like monsters. 72m. **DIR:** Del Tenney. **CAST:** John Scott, Alice Lyon. **1964**

HORROR OF THE BLOOD MONSTERS 🦃 Astronauts land on mystery planet and find it inhabited by stock footage from Filipino monster movies. Rated R. 85m. **DIR:** Al Adamson. **CAST:** John Carradine, Robert Dix, Vicki Volante. **1970**

HORROR RISES FROM THE TOMB ★★ Five hundred years after an evil knight is beheaded, he returns to make trouble for his descendants when they visit the family castle. Tired shocks, though better than many of the slasher cheapies on the video racks. Not rated, with the usual violence and tepid gore. 80m. **DIR:** Carlos Aured. **CAST:** Paul Naschy, Emma Cohen. **1972**

HORROR SHOW, THE ★★1/2 Executed killer Brion James haunts the family of the cop who captured him, turning their dreams into deadly nightmares. Standard horror yarn goes for shocks at the expense of logic. Rated R for strong violence. 95m. **DIR:** James Isaac. **CAST:** Lance Henriksen, Brian James, Rita Taggart, Alvy Moore. **1989**

HORRORS OF THE BLACK MUSEUM ★★ Twisted mystery writer transforms his assistant into a homicidal monster, sells the stories he has written about the gruesome crimes, and adds the implements of death to his "museum." This sadistic shocker used a gimmick called "HypnoVision" to validate its excesses and saturated drive-in screens with the blood and gore found in the crime comics of the early 1950s. The opening sequence is still a stunner and hallmark of bad taste. Not rated; contains violence and brutal murders. 95m. **DIR:** Arthur Crabtree. **CAST:** Michael Gough, June Cunninghame, Graham Curnow, Shirley Ann Field, Geoffrey Keen. **1959**

•HORRORVISION ★★★ People who log on to the Web site horrorvision.com soon end up dead in this ultralow-budget shockfest. The film moves along briskly and the plot is more complex than usual for this type of film, but the abrupt ending leaves one wondering if a sequel was intended or if the filmmakers just ran out of ideas. Rated R for violence, profanity, and nudity. 70m. **DIR:** Danny Draven. **CAST:** Jake Leonard, Brinke Stevens, Ariauna Albright. **2001 DVD**

HORSE, THE ★★★ Grim tale of a father and son from a small village forced to travel to Istanbul to find work. Their struggles and the conditions in which the impoverished must live are realistically portrayed. Not rated, but far too bleak for kids. In Turkish with English subtitles. 116m. **DIR:** Ali Ozgenturk. **CAST:** Genco Erkal. **1982**

HORSE FEATHERS ★★★★★ The funniest of the films starring the four Marx Brothers, this features Groucho as the president of Huxley College, which desperately needs a winning football team. So Groucho hires Chico and Harpo to help him fix the season. Meanwhile, Groucho is competing for the attentions of the sexy college widow, Thelma Todd. The team's most outrageous and hilarious gagfest. B&W; 69m. **DIR:** Norman Z. McLeod. **CAST:** The Marx Brothers, Thelma Todd, David Landau. **1932 DVD**

HORSE FOR DANNY, A ★★★ A perfect tale for children who love horses. An orphaned girl who lives with her horse trainer uncle finds a horse she believes can become a champion. Sure enough, the horse proves to

be special, but there are those who want the horse stopped. Entertaining if somewhat bland family film has its heart in the right place. Rated PG. 92m. **DIR:** Dick Lowry. **CAST:** Robert Urich, Ron Brice, Gary Basaraba, Erik Jensen, Leelee Sobieski. **1995**

HORSE IN THE GRAY FLANNEL SUIT, THE ★★ This Disney film takes you back to America's early awareness of Madison Avenue and the many games and gimmicks it devises to get the almighty dollar. Dean Jones is an ad executive who develops an ad campaign around his daughter's devotion to horses. 113m. **DIR:** Norman Tokar. **CAST:** Dean Jones, Diane Baker, Lloyd Bochner, Fred Clark, Kurt Russell. **1968**

HORSE OF PRIDE, THE ★★ Unconvincing study of peasant life set in Brittany at the turn of the century, as seen through the eyes of a young boy. In French with English subtitles. Not rated. 118m. **DIR:** Claude Chabrol. **CAST:** Jacques Dufilho, Bernadette Lesache, François Cluzet. **1980**

HORSE SOLDIERS, THE ★★★★ Based on a true incident during the Civil War, this is a minor, but enjoyable, John Ford cavalry outing. John Wayne and William Holden play well-matched adversaries. 119m. **DIR:** John Ford. **CAST:** John Wayne, William Holden, Constance Towers, Hoot Gibson. **1959 DVD**

HORSE THIEF, THE ★★★★ The mysterious barren landscape of Tibet becomes the setting for a tribal drama of theft, ostracism, and horrible retribution. Beautifully photographed amidst a series of Buddhist rituals captured wordlessly. In Mandarin with English subtitles. Not rated. 88m. **DIR:** Tian Zhuangzhuang. **CAST:** Tseshang Rigzin. **1987**

HORSE WHISPERER, THE ★★★★★ This isn't a film, it's a symphony: a magnificent project that perfectly suits Robert Redford's taste, style, and abilities. The story's focus is a 14-year-old New York teenager who suffers a horrible accident with her favorite horse and loses her spirit along with one leg. The girl's career-oriented mother, galvanized by this tragedy, drags both the girl and the horse across the country to Montana, where she hopes for a miracle at the hands of a talented horse trainer. The subsequent romantic overtures between these two adults from different worlds play out against the Herculean task of helping the tormented girl and her terrified animal. Redford once again proves himself the most generous of directors; all the best scenes and lines go to his costars. This is, without question, 1998's most elegant and meticulously crafted picture. Rated PG-13 for the brutally intense accident that opens the story. 164m. **DIR:** Robert Redford. **CAST:** Robert Redford, Kristin Scott Thomas, Sam Neill, Dianne Wiest, Scarlett Johansson, Chris Cooper. **1998 DVD**

HORSE WITHOUT A HEAD, THE ★★★ Good old Disney fun as a group of boys give more trouble to a band of thieves than they can handle. An excellent cast headed by Leo McKern as a devious no-gooder. The whole family will enjoy this unrated film. 89m. **DIR:** Don Chaffey. **CAST:** Leo McKern, Jean-Pierre Aumont, Herbert Lom, Pamela Franklin, Vincent Winter. **1963**

HORSEMAN ON THE ROOF, THE ★★★ Immensely silly French romantic epic, in which a chivalrous Italian rebel escorts a Gallic noblewoman through a region plagued by cholera. A not-so-subtle AIDS metaphor gets overworked here, much to the detriment of the heroic atmosphere the filmmaker clearly wished to establish. Set in the 1830s, against gorgeous landscapes that won't look so good on video. In French with English subtitles. Rated R. 119m. **DIR:** Jean-Paul Rappeneau. **CAST:** Juliette Binoche, Olivier Martinez. **1995**

HORSEMASTERS ★★ Annette and Tommy team up once again in this average story about young Americans pursuing their careers in horse training among the great riding academies of Europe. 77m. **DIR:** William Fairchild. **CAST:** Annette Funicello, Janet Munro, Tommy Kirk, Donald Pleasence, Tony Britton. **1961**

HORSEMEN, THE In this dull action film, Omar Sharif, as an Afghan tribesman, attempts to outride his father. Rated PG. 109m. **DIR:** John Frankenheimer. **CAST:** Omar Sharif, Jack Palance, Leigh Taylor-Young, Peter Jeffrey, Eric Pohlmann. **1970**

HORSEPLAYER ★★ Strange tale, unremarkably told, of two takers (M. K. Harris and Sammi Davis) who use a disturbed man (Brad Dourif) for their own ends. Rated R for violence and profanity. 89m. **DIR:** Kurt Voss. **CAST:** Brad Dourif, Sammi Davis, M. K. Harris, Vic Tayback. **1990**

HORSE'S MOUTH, THE ★★★1/2 Star Alec Guinness, who also penned the script, romps in high comic style through this film version of Joyce Cary's mocking novel about an eccentric painter. 93m. **DIR:** Ronald Neame. **CAST:** Alec Guinness, Kay Walsh, Renee Houston, Michael Gough. **1958**

HOSPITAL, THE ★★★★1/2 You definitely don't want to check in. But if you like to laugh, you'll want to check it out. This 1971 black comedy did for the medical profession what . . . *And Justice for All* did for our court system and *Network* did for television. Paddy Chayefsky's Oscar-winning screenplay casts George C. Scott as an embittered doctor battling against the outrageous goings-on at the institution of the title. Rated PG. 103m. **DIR:** Arthur Hiller. **CAST:** George C. Scott, Diana Rigg, Barnard Hughes. **1971**

HOSPITAL MASSACRE Another *Halloween* clone, this one is set in a hospital where a psycho killer murders everyone in an attempt to get revenge on the girl who laughed at his Valentine's Day card twenty years before. Rated R for nudity and gore. 88m. **DIR:** Boaz Davidson. **CAST:** Barbi Benton, Chip Lucia, Jon Van Ness. **1982**

HOSTAGE (1987) Idiotic story of a South African farmer who must rescue his wife and child from evil Arabs. Rated R for language and violence. 94m. **DIR:** Hanro Möhr. **CAST:** Wings Hauser, Karen Black, Kevin McCarthy, Nancy Locke. **1987**

HOSTAGE (1992) ★★ Sam Neill stars as a James Bondish secret agent who finds retirement a rather harrowing option. Shooting and bombings pervade. Rated R for sex and violence. 100m. **DIR:** Robert Young. **CAST:** Sam Neill, Talisa Soto, James Fox. **1992**

HOSTAGE FOR A DAY ★★1/2 John Candy directed this made-for-television comedy about a henpecked husband who plans to run off with his girlfriend. That is, until he finds out his scheming wife has cleaned out his secret bank account. In order to get the money back, he stages a hostage situation in his house with himself as the victim. Likable cast helps save this mildly entertaining comedy. Rated PG. 92m. **DIR:** John Candy. **CAST:**

George Wendt, Robin Duke, John Vernon, John Candy, Christopher Templeton. **1994**

HOSTAGE HOTEL ★★ The last of three *Hard Time* movies made for cable starring Burt Reynolds as Logan McQueen, ex-cop and PI. In this, the worst of the bunch, he fights to save his partner and a congressman who are being held in a booby-trapped hotel by a deranged Vietnam veteran. The whole thing gives the impression of having been made up as they went along. Not rated; contains violence and mild profanity. 89m. **DIR:** Hal Needham. **CAST:** Burt Reynolds, Charles Durning, Keith Carradine, David Rasche, Ted McGinley. **1999**

HOSTAGE TOWER, THE ★★1/2 A successful international criminal sought by major police organizations puts together a special team of experts for his next spectacular crime, broadly hinted at in the title. Intrigue and private purposes abound in this action film, wherein the cast successfully outweighs the movie. Rated PG for violence. 97m. **DIR:** Claudio Guzman. **CAST:** Peter Fonda, Maud Adams, Billy Dee Williams, Rachel Roberts, Douglas Fairbanks Jr. **1980**

HOSTAGE TRAIN ★★ Much ado about nothing as cop Judge Reinhold tries to save his girlfriend and a trainload of passengers being held hostage by terrorists in a collapsed tunnel. No big deal, especially Reinhold's turn as an action star. Rated R for language and violence. 98m. **DIR:** Robert Lee. **CAST:** Judge Reinhold, Carol Alt, Michael Sarrazin. **1996**

HOSTAGES ★★1/2 Bernard MacLaverty's well-meaning made-for-cable account of the five-year hostage crisis in Lebanon suffers from simplified characters and events compressed past the point of conveying much drama. No doubt this superficial tone results from the lack of participation by those who were there. Director David Wheatley also elicits very little passion from his strong ensemble cast. The result is oddly uninvolving. 96m. **DIR:** David Wheatley. **CAST:** Colin Firth, Ciarán Hinds, Jay O. Sanders, Josef Sommer, Harry Dean Stanton, Kathy Bates, Natasha Richardson. **1993**

HOSTILE GUNS ★★ Incredible cast of veteran B-movie Western actors is the main attraction in this routine drama of two peace officers who transport an unsavory group of criminals to prison. 91m. **DIR:** R. G. Springsteen. **CAST:** George Montgomery, Tab Hunter, Yvonne De Carlo, Brian Donlevy, John Russell, Leo Gordon, Richard Arlen, Don Barry, Emile Meyer. **1967**

HOSTILE INTENT ★★ A group of computer hackers finds their weekend war game is the real thing after they tap into a secret government database, triggering the agency to hunt them down. They would have been better off downloading dirty pictures from the net. Rated R for language and violence. 90m. **DIR:** Jonathan Heap. **CAST:** Rob Lowe, Sofia Shinas, Saul Rubinek, John Savage. **1996**

HOSTILE INTENTIONS ★★ Good intentions land three women in hot water when they travel to Tijuana for girls' night out. There, they are forced to defend themselves against corrupt police and locals, and must use their wits in order to make it back across the border. Rated R for violence, drug abuse, and adult language. 90m. **DIR:** Catherine Cyran. **CAST:** Tia Carrere, Tricia Leigh Fisher, Lisa Dean Ryan, Carlos Gomez. **1994**

HOSTILE TAKE OVER ★★★1/2 Apt direction by George Mihalka elevates what would be another psycho-on-the-loose cheapie. David Warner plays a lonely employee who holds three colleagues hostage. A tense thriller rated R for nudity, profanity, and violence. 93m. **DIR:** George Mihalka. **CAST:** David Warner, Michael Ironside, Kate Vernon, Jayne Eastwood. **1988**

HOSTILE WATERS ★★★1/2 An actual 1986 incident involving a Soviet nuclear sub is the jumping-off point for this tense little drama, which strongly suggests that a near reactor meltdown resulted from a collision between Soviet and American subs involved in standard cat-and-mouse games in the Atlantic. Rutger Hauer and his crew struggle to avoid a nuclear incident while saving their own lives in this engrossing film. Rated PG-13 for profanity and violent peril. 95m. **DIR:** David Drury. **CAST:** Rutger Hauer, Martin Sheen, Colm Feore, Rob Campbell, Harris Yulin, Regina Taylor, Max von Sydow. **1997**

HOT BOX, THE ★★ Low-budget Filipino-shot women's-prison film was cowritten and produced by Jonathan Demme. Rated R; contains nudity, profanity, and violence. 85m. **DIR:** Joe Viola. **CAST:** Margaret Markov, Andrea Cagen, Charles Dierkop. **1972**

HOT CHOCOLATE ★★1/2 A French chocolate factory is going broke and a millionaire Texas cowgirl (Bo Derek) wants to buy it. Low-expectation fun. Rated PG-13 for violence. 93m. **DIR:** Josee Dayan. **CAST:** Robert Hays, Bo Derek, Francois Mathouret, Howard Hesseman. **1992**

HOT DOG . . . THE MOVIE ★★ David Naughton costars with onetime Playboy Playmate of the Year Shannon Tweed in this comedy about high jinks on the ski slopes. Rated R for nudity, profanity, and suggested sex. 96m. **DIR:** Peter Markle. **CAST:** David Naughton, Patrick Houser, Shannon Tweed. **1984**

HOT HEAD ★★1/2 Patrick Dewaere stars in this so-so French comedy about a freewheeling soccer athlete who gets kicked off the team after an incident with a star player, finds himself drifting in the streets, and eventually is framed for a rape he didn't commit. Dubbed (poorly) in English. Rated R for nudity. 90m. **DIR:** Jean-Jacques Annaud. **CAST:** Patrick Dewaere, France Dougnac, Dorothee Jemma. **1978**

HOT ICE 🦃 Extremely dull (and uncredited) Ed Wood script about jewel thieves at a ski lodge. Rated R for brief nudity. 85m. **DIR:** Stephen C. Apostolof. **CAST:** Harvey Shain, Patti Kelly. **1974**

HOT LEAD ★★★ Tim Holt must team up with an ex-con in order to stop a murderous gang of train robbers. B&W; 60m. **DIR:** Stuart Gilmore. **CAST:** Tim Holt, Richard Martin, John Dehner, Joan Dixon, Ross Elliott. **1951**

HOT LEAD AND COLD FEET ★★ This predictable, occasionally funny Western stars Jim Dale as twin brothers; one is a drunk who terrorizes the town and the other a missionary. Rated G. 89m. **DIR:** Robert Butler. **CAST:** Jim Dale, Karen Valentine, Don Knotts, Jack Elam, Darren McGavin. **1978**

HOT MILLIONS ★★★★ A wry comedy with a skillful cast that pokes fun at the computer age. A con man poses as a computer genius and gets a job with a million dollar corporation. He then transfers the company's funds into his own account. When he gets caught, he uses his wits to stay one step ahead. Rated G. 106m. **DIR:** Eric Till. **CAST:** Peter Ustinov, Bob Newhart, Mag-

gie Smith, Karl Malden, Robert Morley, Cesar Romero, Julie May, Melinda May. **1968**

HOT MOVES 🦃 Here's another teen lust comedy. Rated R. 80m. **DIR:** Jim Sotos. **CAST:** Michael Zorek, Adam Silbar, Jeff Fishman, Johnny Timko. **1985**

HOT PURSUIT ★★ In this comedy, a college student (John Cusack) misses the plane on which he was to join his girlfriend (Wendy Gazelle) and her wealthy parents on a vacation cruise. He then finds himself embarking on a series of wildly improbable misadventures as he attempts to catch up with them. Rated PG-13 for profanity and violence. 90m. **DIR:** Steven Lisberger. **CAST:** John Cusack, Robert Loggia, Wendy Gazelle, Jerry Stiller, Monte Markham. **1987 DVD**

HOT RESORT 🦃 *Airplane*-style takeoff on the resort industry. Rated R for nudity, profanity, and simulated sex. 92m. **DIR:** John Robins. **CAST:** Tom Parsekian, Michael Berz, Bronson Pinchot, Marcy Walker, Frank Gorshin. **1984**

HOT ROCK, THE ★★★★ A neatly planned jewelry heist goes awry and the fun begins. Peter Yates's direction is razor sharp. The cast is absolutely perfect. This movie is a crowd-pleasing blend of action, humor, and suspense. Rated PG. 105m. **DIR:** Peter Yates. **CAST:** Robert Redford, George Segal, Ron Leibman, Paul Sand, Zero Mostel, Moses Gunn, William Redfield, Charlotte Rae. **1972**

HOT SHOT ★★★1/2 More than just a soccer version of *The Karate Kid*, this film of a young man's conquest of adversity stands on its own. Jim Youngs is a rich kid who runs away to Rio de Janeiro, where he pursues his idol, Pelé, the greatest soccer player of all time. An enjoyable family film and a must for soccer fans. Rated PG. 94m. **DIR:** Rick King. **CAST:** Jim Youngs, Pelé, Billy Warlock, Weyman Thompson, Mario Van Peebles. **1986 DVD**

HOT SHOTS ★★★★ This hilarious parody of *Top Gun*–style films stars Charlie Sheen as a renegade navy pilot who must live with the stigma of his father's past. Look for scenes poking fun at movies as diverse as *The Fabulous Baker Boys*, *Gone With the Wind*, *Dances With Wolves*, and—in the film's funniest scene—*9 1/2 Weeks*. Rated PG-13 for brief profanity. 85m. **DIR:** Jim Abrahams. **CAST:** Charlie Sheen, Cary Elwes, Valeria Golino, Lloyd Bridges, Kevin Dunn, Jon Cryer, William O'Leary, Efrem Zimbalist Jr. **1991**

HOT SHOTS PART DEUX ★★★1/2 *Airplane* codirector Jim Abrahams is at it again with this slapstick sequel that blasts *Rambo*esque action flicks. Charlie Sheen leads the assault with fellow *Hot Shot*-ers Valeria Golino and Lloyd Bridges. Rated PG-13 for profanity and violence. 90m. **DIR:** Jim Abrahams. **CAST:** Charlie Sheen, Lloyd Bridges, Valeria Golino, Richard Crenna, Brenda Bakke. **1993**

HOT SPELL ★★★ Entertaining thoughts of leaving her for a younger woman, macho husband Anthony Quinn has anguishing housewife Shirley Booth sweating out this near remake of *Come Back, Little Sheba*. Booth invokes empathy, Quinn again proves his depth of talent, Shirley MacLaine shows why stardom soon was hers; but a soap opera is a soap opera. B&W; 86m. **DIR:** Daniel Mann. **CAST:** Shirley Booth, Anthony Quinn, Shirley MacLaine, Earl Holliman, Eileen Heckart. **1958**

HOT SPOT ★★1/2 Director Dennis Hopper keeps the *Hot Spot* on simmer when it needs to boil over with tension and excitement. Don Johnson is semicomatose as a low-life who drifts into a small Texas town where he robs the local bank and gets involved with two women, one bad (Virginia Madsen) and one innocent (Jennifer Connelly). Rated R for simulated sex, nudity, profanity, and violence. 129m. **DIR:** Dennis Hopper. **CAST:** Don Johnson, Virginia Madsen, Jennifer Connelly, Charles Martin Smith, Bill Sadler, Jerry Hardin, Barry Corbin. **1990 DVD**

HOT STUFF ★★★1/2 An entertaining, old-fashioned comedy that whips right along. Director-star Dom DeLuise makes the most of his dual role. The story concerns a government fencing operation for capturing crooks and the results are humorous. Rated PG. 87m. **DIR:** Dom DeLuise. **CAST:** Dom DeLuise, Jerry Reed, Suzanne Pleshette, Ossie Davis. **1979**

HOT TO TROT ★★1/2 Cute update on the Francis the Talking Mule comedies of the Fifties. This time we have a witty horse. What gets tiresome is the horse's dumb friend Fred (Bob Goldthwait). The best lines go to John Candy as the horse's voice. Rated PG for profanity. 83m. **DIR:** Michael Dinner. **CAST:** Bob Goldthwait, Dabney Coleman, Virginia Madsen, Cindy Pickett, Mary Gross. **1988**

HOT UNDER THE COLLAR ★★1/2 Poor Richard Gabai. He's so in love with Angela Visser that he'll follow her anywhere, even when she checks into the local convent. Desperate, Gabai disguises himself as a priest, and then a nun, and then must really go undercover when the convent is infiltrated by a gangster in search of hidden loot. Congenial comedy. Rated R. 87m. **DIR:** Richard Gabai. **CAST:** Angela Visser, Richard Gabai. **1991**

HOTEL ★★1/2 This film is based on Arthur Hailey's bestseller, which eventually spawned a TV series. In its *Airport*-style story, a number of characters and events unfold against the main theme of Melvyn Douglas's attempt to keep from selling the hotel to a tycoon who would modernize and change the landmark. 125m. **DIR:** Richard Quine. **CAST:** Rod Taylor, Catherine Spaak, Melvyn Douglas, Karl Malden, Richard Conte, Michael Rennie, Merle Oberon, Kevin McCarthy. **1967**

HOTEL COLONIAL 🦃 In this uncredited adaptation of Joseph Conrad's *Heart of Darkness*, John Savage searches the jungles of Colombia for his brother. Rated R for nudity and violence. 107m. **DIR:** Cinzia Torrini. **CAST:** John Savage, Robert Duvall, Rachel Ward, Massimo Troisi. **1987**

HOTEL DE LOVE ★★★1/2 Director-writer Craig Rosenberg's debut is a sweet and funny romantic comedy. Aden Young and Simon Bossell star as two brothers who fall in love with the same woman (a delicious Saffron Burrows), in high school. Ten years later they meet up at the Hotel de Love, where she has come to get married. Now it's up to the two brothers to stop her from walking down the aisle. Rated R for adult situations, language, and nudity. 93m. **DIR:** Craig Rosenberg. **CAST:** Aden Young, Simon Bossell, Saffron Burrows. **1996**

HOTEL NEW HAMPSHIRE, THE ★★ Based on John Irving's novel, this muddled motion picture has its moments. Beau Bridges stars as the head of a family that

weathers all sorts of disasters. Rated R for profanity. 110m. **DIR:** Tony Richardson. **CAST:** Beau Bridges, Jodie Foster, Rob Lowe, Nastassja Kinski, Amanda Plummer. **1984 DVD**

HOTEL PARADISO ★★★ Mild sex farce. Alec Guinness attempts a tryst with his neighbor's wife, but everything and everyone blocks his way. 96m. **DIR:** Peter Glenville. **CAST:** Alec Guinness, Gina Lollobrigida, Robert Morley, Akim Tamiroff. **1966**

HOTEL RESERVE ★★1/2 Intrigue and romance are the chief ingredients of this lightweight spy melodrama set just before the outbreak of World War II in a fancy resort hotel. B&W; 80m. **DIR:** Victor Hanbury. **CAST:** James Mason, Lucie Mannheim, Herbert Lom, Patricia Medina. **1944**

HOTEL ROOM ★★★★ One hotel room, three weird stories. David Lynch directed the two most effective tales. In one, Harry Dean Stanton is a cantankerous drunk with an eerie past. In the other, Crispin Glover embarks on an unsettling psychological journey with his unstable wife. Chelsea Field is fighting mad at shallow boyfriend Griffin Dunne in a slighter, more comic story. Not rated; contains adult themes, sexual situations, and violence. 96m. **DIR:** David Lynch, James Signorelli. **CAST:** Harry Dean Stanton, Glenne Headly, Griffin Dunne, Chelsea Field, Crispin Glover. **1992**

HOTEL TERMINUS: THE LIFE AND TIMES OF KLAUS BARBIE ★★★★1/2 A fascinating film chronicle of the life of Nazi SS Captain Klaus Barbie, the "Butcher of Lyon," responsible for the deportation and death of thousands of Jews, and the brutal torture of French Resistance members. Oscar winner as best documentary. In English and French, German, and Spanish with English subtitles. Not rated, but with graphic discussion of torture, so parental discretion is advised. B&W/color; 267m. **DIR:** Marcel Ophuls. **1988**

H.O.T.S. ★★ Drive-in special about two feuding sororities whose battles culminate in a topless football game. Cheerfully raunchy trash for those times when you're not quite up to Ingmar Bergman. Rated R for plentiful nudity. 95m. **DIR:** Gerald Sindell. **CAST:** Susan Kiger, Lisa London, Danny Bonaduce. **1979 DVD**

HOUDINI (1953) ★★★1/2 Tony Curtis is quite good in this colorful but sketchy account of the famed illusionist. Enjoyable fluff makes up for lack of substance with good period atmosphere and dandy reenactments of Houdini's most famous escapes. 106m. **DIR:** George Marshall. **CAST:** Tony Curtis, Janet Leigh, Ian Wolfe, Torin Thatcher. **1953**

HOUDINI (1998) ★★★ Those hoping for a definitive portrait of the celebrated magician and illusionist will leave disappointed, because this superficial and melodramatic biography turns Houdini into a shrill narcissist. This TNT original film has "TV movie" written all over it: The production values look cheap, and the most talented actors turn up in only brief supporting roles. Rated PG for dramatic intensity. 95m. **DIR:** Pen Densham. **CAST:** Johnathon Schaech, Stacy Edwards, Paul Sorvino, George Segal, Rhea Perlman, David Warner. **1998**

HOUND OF THE BASKERVILLES, THE (1939) ★★★★ The second best of the Basil Rathbone–Nigel Bruce Sherlock Holmes movies, this 1939 release marked the stars' debut in the roles for which they would forever be known. (*The Adventures of Sherlock Holmes*, which was made the same year, featured the on-screen detective team at its peak.) Holmes and Watson are called upon by Henry Baskerville to save him from a curse—in the form of a hound from hell—that has plagued his family for centuries. B&W; 84m. **DIR:** Sidney Lanfield. **CAST:** Basil Rathbone, Nigel Bruce, John Carradine, Lionel Atwill, Mary Gordon, E. E. Clive, Richard Greene. **1939**

HOUND OF THE BASKERVILLES, THE (1959) ★★★★ One of the better adaptations of Conan Doyle's moody novel, and particularly enjoyable for its presentation of Peter Cushing (as Sherlock Holmes) and Christopher Lee together in nonhorror roles. This British entry (from the Hammer House of Horror) caught more of the murky atmosphere than any other version of any other Holmes tale. Intelligent scripting, compelling acting, and spooky cinematography. 84m. **DIR:** Terence Fisher. **CAST:** Peter Cushing, Christopher Lee, Andre Morell, Marla Landi, Miles Malleson. **1959**

HOUND OF THE BASKERVILLES, THE (1977) 🦃 Truly abysmal send-up of the novel by Conan Doyle. 84m. **DIR:** Paul Morrissey. **CAST:** Dudley Moore, Peter Cook, Denholm Elliott, Joan Greenwood, Hugh Griffith, Terry-Thomas, Roy Kinnear. **1977**

HOUND OF THE BASKERVILLES, THE (1983) ★★★1/2 Ian Richardson makes a fine Sherlock Holmes in this enjoyable version of Sir Arthur Conan Doyle's oft-filmed tale. While we prefer the Basil Rathbone and Peter Cushing vehicles, there's certainly nothing wrong with this suspenseful, well-mounted and atmospheric thriller. 101m. **DIR:** Douglas Hickox. **CAST:** Ian Richardson, Donald Churchill, Denholm Elliott, Martin Shaw, Brian Blessed, Ronald Lacey, Eleanor Bron, Edward Judd, Glynis Barber. **1983 DVD**

HOUR OF THE ASSASSIN ★1/2 Action thriller set in the fictional South American country of San Pedro where Erik Estrada has been hired by the military forces to kill the president. Robert Vaughn plays the CIA agent who has to stop him. Although this film has its share of car crashes, gunfire, and explosions, it lacks any real suspense. Rated R. 96m. **DIR:** Luis Llosa. **CAST:** Erik Estrada, Robert Vaughn. **1986**

HOUR OF THE GUN, THE ★★★★ This sequel to *Gunfight at the O.K. Corral* deserves to be counted as a minor classic. James Garner is superb as an embittered and obsessed Wyatt Earp, who, with the help of an increasingly ailing Doc Holliday, sets out to bring Ike Clanton to justice. 100m. **DIR:** John Sturges. **CAST:** James Garner, Jason Robards Jr., Robert Ryan, Steve Ihnat, Albert Salmi, Charles Aidman, Michael Tolan, Frank Converse, Larry Gates, Karl Swenson, Jon Voight, Monte Markham, William Windom. **1967**

HOUR OF THE WOLF ★★★★ Ingmar Bergman's surreal, claustrophobic look into the personality of a tormented artist. Bizarre hallucinations shape the artist's world, creating a disturbing vision that seems at times completely out of control. Probably the closest Bergman has ever come to creating a horror film. In Swedish with English subtitles. B&W; 89m. **DIR:** Ingmar Bergman. **CAST:** Max von Sydow, Liv Ullmann, Ingrid Thulin. **1968**

HOURGLASS 🦃 A vanity piece for C. Thomas Howell, who struts through this muddled story of a powerful fashion designer who tosses away his life for a beautiful

woman (Sofia Shinas). Howell's directorial debut. Rated R for profanity, nudity, violence, and sexual situations. 91m. **DIR:** C. Thomas Howell. **CAST:** C. Thomas Howell, Sofia Shinas, Ed Begley Jr., Terry Kiser, Timothy Bottoms, Anthony Clark, Kiefer Sutherland. **1995**

HOURS AND TIMES ★★★★1/2 This short (60-minute) feature marks an auspicious debut for writer-director Christopher Munch. It's an impressive, wonderfully intimate drama that supposes what might have gone on between John Lennon and his manager, Brian Epstein, during a weekend in 1963, when they flee the insanity of Beatlemania for a little solitude in Barcelona. David Angus and Ian Hart are fabulous as the fabled rock star and his manager. B&W; 60m. **DIR:** Christopher Munch. **CAST:** David Angus, Ian Hart, Stephanie Pack. **1992**

HOUSE ★★1/2 A comedy-thriller about an author who moves into an old mansion left to him by an aunt who committed suicide. The cast is good, but the shocks are predictable, crippling the suspense. Rated R for violence and profanity. 93m. **DIR:** Steve Miner. **CAST:** William Katt, George Wendt, Kay Lenz, Richard Moll. **1986 DVD**

HOUSE II: THE SECOND STORY ★★ In this unwarranted sequel to *House*, a young man inherits a mansion and invites his best friend to move in with him. A series of humorous and mysterious events lead the two to exhume the grave of the young man's great-grandfather, who is magically still alive. Rated PG-13 for foul language and some violence. 88m. **DIR:** Ethan Wiley. **CAST:** Arye Gross, Jonathan Stark, Royal Dano, Bill Maher, John Ratzenberger. **1987**

HOUSE IV ★★1/2 A famous horror writer dies and leaves his wife and daughter the old family home, but his half brother has other plans. Soon the whole family is up to their necks in spooky goings on. Rated R for nudity and violence. 94m. **DIR:** Lewis Abernathy. **CAST:** Terri Treas, Scott Burkholder, William Katt. **1991**

HOUSE ACROSS THE BAY, THE ★★1/2 An airplane designer (Walter Pidgeon) swipes the waiting wife (Joan Bennett) of a gangster (George Raft) while Raft is paying his dues in the joint. Then he gets out.... Classic Raft film. Tense, exciting, but familiar. Lloyd Nolan plays a shyster very well. B&W; 86m. **DIR:** Archie Mayo. **CAST:** George Raft, Joan Bennett, Lloyd Nolan, Gladys George, Walter Pidgeon. **1940**

HOUSE ARREST ★★ There are very few laughs in this occasionally ugly and mean-spirited HBO comedy starring Jamie Lee Curtis and Kevin Pollak as a couple on the brink of divorce. Their kids decide the best way to keep the family together is to lock the parents in the basement and force-feed them a kind of marriage counseling. So silly you have to wonder for whom this was targeted. Rated PG for profanity. 109m. **DIR:** Harry Winer. **CAST:** Jamie Lee Curtis, Kevin Pollak, Jennifer Tilly, Ray Walston, Wallace Shawn, Christopher McDonald. **1995 DVD**

HOUSE BY THE CEMETERY ★★ One of the better latter-day spaghetti horrors, this merging of *The Amityville Horror* and *The Innocents* actually has some suspense to go along with the explicit gore. But don't let the kids see it. Rated R. 86m. **DIR:** Lucio Fulci. **CAST:** Katherine MacColl. **1981 DVD**

HOUSE BY THE RIVER ★★★ Fritz Lang explores one of his favorite themes: obsession. A moody chamber work about a man who kills his maid out of passionate rage, then implicates his own brother to relieve his guilt. Full of fascinating psychological touches that manage to create a disturbing atmosphere. B&W; 88m. **DIR:** Fritz Lang. **CAST:** Louis Hayward, Jane Wyatt, Lee Bowman, Ann Shoemaker, Kathleen Freeman. **1950**

HOUSE CALLS ★★★★1/2 Here's a romantic comedy reminiscent of films Spencer Tracy and Katharine Hepburn made together mostly because of the teaming of Walter Matthau and Glenda Jackson. A recently widowed doctor (Matthau) finds his bachelor spree cut short by a romantic encounter with a nurse (Jackson) who refuses to be just another conquest. A delightful battle of the sexes with two equally matched opponents. Rated PG. 96m. **DIR:** Howard Zieff. **CAST:** Walter Matthau, Glenda Jackson, Richard Benjamin, Art Carney. **1978**

HOUSE DIVIDED, A ★★★1/2 When a wealthy Georgian dies in this post–Civil War drama, a trial ensues to determine whether his mixed-ethnicity daughter or his brother inherits. It's an entertaining made-for-cable film that is somewhat predictable and doesn't say anything new about slavery or race relations. The lush and thorough production and the superb acting almost make up for the inadequacies. Rated R for profanity and violence. 101m. **DIR:** John Kent Harrison. **CAST:** Sam Waterston, Jennifer Beals, Lisa Gay Hamilton, Timothy Daly. **2000**

HOUSE IN THE HILLS, A ★★1/2 While house-sitting, an aspiring actress is taken hostage and falls in love with her captor. Very bizarre love story with an even more bizarre ending. Rated R for nudity, simulated sex, and profanity. 89m. **DIR:** Ken Wiederhorn. **CAST:** Michael Madsen, Helen Slater, James Laurenson, Elyssa Davalos, Jeffrey Tambor. **1993**

HOUSE OF ANGELS ★★★1/2 This offbeat comedy examines the culture clash that occurs when the leather-clad granddaughter of a recently deceased landowner roars into town on a motorcycle to claim her inheritance and shocks the stuffy locals with her openly decadent lifestyle. Not for all tastes. In Swedish with English subtitles. Rated R for profanity, nudity, and simulated sex. 119m. **DIR:** Colin Nutley. **CAST:** Helena Bergstrom, Rikard Wolff, Sven Wollter, Viveka Sidahl, Per Oscarsson. **1993**

HOUSE OF CARDS ★★★★ Strange but gripping drama about a young girl who retreats into her mind after seeing her father fall to his death. Frantic, her mother, Kathleen Turner, calls in psychiatrist Tommy Lee Jones to help reach the girl, but everything they try seems to make the situation worse. Heartrending. Rated PG-13 for adult situations. 109m. **DIR:** Michael Lessac. **CAST:** Kathleen Turner, Tommy Lee Jones, Asha Menina, Shiloh Strong, Esther Rolle, Park Overall, Michael Horse. **1993 DVD**

HOUSE OF DARK SHADOWS ★★★ Gore and murder run rampant throughout this film based on the TV soap *Dark Shadows*. Barnabas Collins (Jonathan Frid), a particularly violent vampire, will stop at nothing to be reunited with Josette, his fiancée 200 years ago. Rated PG for violence. 98m. **DIR:** Dan Curtis. **CAST:** Jonathan

Frid, Kathryn Leigh Scott, Grayson Hall, Joan Bennett. **1970**

HOUSE OF DRACULA ★★1/2 Scientist Onslow Stevens falls under the spell of Count Dracula while Larry Talbot, aka the Wolfman, seeks to end the horror once and for all. The movie's nostalgia value makes it fun to watch, but it is by no means a classic. B&W; 67m. **DIR:** Erle C. Kenton. **CAST:** Lon Chaney Jr., John Carradine, Martha O'Driscoll, Lionel Atwill, Onslow Stevens, Glenn Strange, Jane Adams, Ludwig Stossel. **1945**

HOUSE OF EXORCISM, THE 🦃 Incomprehensible. Rated R for profanity, nudity, gore, and violence. 93m. **DIR:** Mickey Lion, Mario Bava. **CAST:** Telly Savalas, Robert Alda, Elke Sommer. **1975 DVD**

HOUSE OF FEAR ★★★★ The last of the high-quality entries in the Universal Sherlock Holmes series has Holmes (Basil Rathbone) and Watson (Nigel Bruce) attempting to solve a series of murders among the guests at a Scottish mansion. It was based on Conan Doyle's "The Adventure of the Five Orange Pips" and combines atmosphere, pacing, fine acting, and sure direction. B&W; 69m. **DIR:** Roy William Neill. **CAST:** Basil Rathbone, Nigel Bruce, Aubrey Mather, Dennis Hoey. **1945**

HOUSE OF FRANKENSTEIN ★★★1/2 Universal Pictures' first all-star monsterfest may have signaled the beginning of the end of the company's reign of horror, but it's nevertheless an enjoyable film for fans of old-time chillers. Boris Karloff is excellent as the mad scientist who escapes from an insane asylum and proceeds to wreak havoc on his enemies with the expert help of Dracula, the Wolfman, and the Frankenstein monster. Good for a rainy night. B&W; 71m. **DIR:** Erle C. Kenton. **CAST:** Boris Karloff, J. Carrol Naish, Lon Chaney Jr., John Carradine, Lionel Atwill, George Zucco, Glenn Strange, Anne Gwynne, Elena Verdugo, Sig Ruman. **1944**

HOUSE OF GAMES ★★★★1/2 Pulitzer Prize–winning playwright David Mamet makes an impressive directorial debut with this suspense-thriller. Lindsay Crouse, the writer-director's wife, gives an effective performance as a psychiatrist who attempts to intercede with a con man (Joe Mantegna) on behalf of one of her patients, a compulsive gambler who owes him several thousand dollars. She is sucked into a world of mirrors where nothing is what it seems. Rated R for profanity and violence. 102m. **DIR:** David Mamet. **CAST:** Lindsay Crouse, Joe Mantegna, Lilia Skala. **1987 DVD**

HOUSE OF HORRORS ★★ An untalented sculptor simply decides to kill off his critics in this lame tale of unrequited love and revenge. Only interesting for Rondo Hatton's appearance as The Creeper. Hatton, who suffered from a disease of the pituitary gland, needed no makeup to play the monstrous bad guy, but he could have used acting lessons. Not rated. B&W; 65m. **DIR:** Jean Yarbrough. **CAST:** Rondo Hatton, Martin Kosleck, Virginia Grey, Bill Goodwin, Robert Lowery. **1946**

HOUSE OF MIRTH, THE ★★1/2 In this adaptation of Edith Wharton's novel, Lily Bart, a ravishing player in early 1900 New York society, faces financial ruin if she does not soon marry. Her flirtations with an attorney and contact with suitors, married men, and jealous peers feed a claustrophobic, emotionally parched melodrama that feels long and labored. This tale of sexual hypocrisy, inheritances, naïve investments (both economic and personal), and vicious backstabbing has the heavy ache of tragedy but is uninvolving. Rated PG. 140m. **DIR:** Terence Davies. **CAST:** Gillian Anderson, Eric Stoltz, Laura Linney, Jodhi May, Anthony LaPaglia, Terry Kinney, Dan Aykroyd, Elizabeth McGovern. **2000 DVD**

HOUSE OF 1,000 DOLLS ★★ Sexploitation potboiler, a British/Spanish coproduction starring Vincent Price as an illusionist who runs a white slavery racket on the side. Variously campy, sleazy, and boring. 83m. **DIR:** Jeremy Summers. **CAST:** Vincent Price, Martha Hyer, George Nader. **1967**

HOUSE OF PSYCHOTIC WOMEN 🦃 The "World's Worst Videos" version of this already cut (for U.S. release) Spanish shocker about a sex murderer. Rated R. 90m. **DIR:** Carlos Aured. **CAST:** Paul Naschy, Diana Lorys. **1973**

HOUSE OF SEVEN CORPSES, THE ★★1/2 Veteran cast almost saves this minor yarn about a film crew shooting a horror movie in a foreboding old mansion. Semi-entertaining nonsense. Rated PG. 90m. **DIR:** Paul Harrison. **CAST:** John Ireland, Faith Domergue, John Carradine. **1973 DVD**

HOUSE OF STRANGERS ★★★1/2 Well-acted, engrossing tale of the fall of a wealthy banker's family. Edward G. Robinson plays the patriarch whose four sons are now at odds with him and each other for various reasons. B&W; 101m. **DIR:** Joseph L. Mankiewicz. **CAST:** Edward G. Robinson, Luther Adler, Richard Conte, Susan Hayward. **1949**

HOUSE OF THE LONG SHADOWS ★★★ This is the good old-fashioned–type horror film that doesn't rely on blood and gore to give the viewer a scare. This gothic thriller is a great choice for horror fans who still like to use their imaginations. Rated PG. 102m. **DIR:** Pete Walker. **CAST:** Vincent Price, John Carradine, Christopher Lee, Desi Arnaz Jr., Peter Cushing. **1984**

HOUSE OF THE RISING SUN ★★ Technically sound but artistically soulless film that attempts to give an Eighties look to a Thirties murder mystery. Jamie Barrett is an aspiring reporter, willing to do anything to get the lowdown on pimp Frank Annese. Not rated; contains adult situations. 86m. **DIR:** Greg Gold. **CAST:** Frank Annese, Jamie Barrett, Tawny Moyer, Deborah Wakeham, James Daughton, John J. York. **1987**

HOUSE OF THE SEVEN GABLES, THE ★★★★1/2 The only rendition of the Nathaniel Hawthorne classic made during the talkie era thus far, and a good one. Vincent Price and George Sanders one-up each other with cynical dialogue and scenery chewing, and the script is faithful to the book. The story of a jealous man who sends an innocent man to prison is hauntingly photographed and uses replicas of the nineteenth-century New England house that inspired it. B&W; 90m. **DIR:** Joe May. **CAST:** Vincent Price, Margaret Lindsay, George Sanders, Nan Grey, Alan Napier, Dick Foran. **1940**

HOUSE OF THE SPIRITS, THE ★★1/2 Even a high-powered cast cannot save this sketchy depiction of seventy years in the history of an unnamed country (reportedly Chile) as seen by three generations of aristocracy. Not quite an all-out embarrassment, but close. Rated R

for violence, profanity, nudity, and simulated sex. 138m. **DIR:** Bille August. **CAST:** Jeremy Irons, Meryl Streep, Glenn Close, Winona Ryder, Antonio Banderas, Vanessa Redgrave, Armin Mueller-Stahl, Maria Conchita Alonso, Sarita Choudhury. **1994 DVD**

HOUSE OF USHER, THE 🦃 Boring retelling of the Edgar Allan Poe classic. Rated R for violence and profanity. 92m. **DIR:** Alan Birkinshaw. **CAST:** Oliver Reed, Donald Pleasence, Romy Windsor. **1990**

HOUSE OF WAX ★★★1/2 Vincent Price stars as a demented sculptor who, after losing the use of his hands in a fire, turns to murder in this above-average horror film. 88m. **DIR:** André de Toth. **CAST:** Vincent Price, Phyllis Kirk, Carolyn Jones. **1953**

HOUSE OF YES, THE ★★★ College student Josh Hamilton brings fiancée Tori Spelling home to meet his grotesquely dysfunctional family. The whole thing is too clever for its own good, but it's smoothly directed, with shrewd and witty acting. Spelling, who gives the standout performance, plays the only normal person in sight. Rated R for profanity and incest-related theme. 90m. **DIR:** Mark Waters. **CAST:** Parker Posey, Josh Hamilton, Genevieve Bujold, Tori Spelling, Freddie Prinze Jr. **1997 DVD**

HOUSE ON CARROLL STREET, THE ★★★ Commendable suspense film about a young accused communist (Kelly McGillis) who becomes involved in a Nazi smuggling ring in 1951 Washington, D.C. Jeff Daniels is one of the investigating FBI men who falls for McGillis. A good costume piece, and McGillis and Daniels turn in solid performances, along with Jessica Tandy as McGillis's crusty employer. Rated PG for language, violence, and slight nudity. 111m. **DIR:** Peter Yates. **CAST:** Kelly McGillis, Jeff Daniels, Jessica Tandy, Mandy Patinkin. **1988**

HOUSE ON GARIBALDI STREET ★★ Run-of-the-mill suspense tale chronicling the abduction of Nazi war criminal Adolf Eichmann by Israelis in South America. Effectively performed, though. 104m. **DIR:** Peter Collinson. **CAST:** Martin Balsam, Topol, Janet Suzman, Leo McKern. **1979**

HOUSE ON HAUNTED HILL (1958) ★★★ Vincent Price is at his most relaxed and confident in this fun fright flick about the wealthy owner of a creepy old fortress who offers a group a fortune if they can survive a night there. Humorous at times, deadly serious at others. B&W; 75m. **DIR:** William Castle. **CAST:** Vincent Price, Carol Ohmart, Richard Long, Elisha Cook Jr., Carolyn Craig, Alan Marshal. **1958 DVD**

HOUSE ON HAUNTED HILL (1999) ★★ Amusement-park impresario Geoffrey Rush invites five guests to spend the night in a former insane asylum, with those who stay until dawn receiving a $1 million prize. Even with its high-tech special effects, this remake of the 1958 William Castle film is tackier than the original. The supposedly sophisticated guests wander off by themselves despite the threatening atmosphere of the "house," exhibiting behavior we found difficult to accept even by teenagers in low-budget slasher movies. Rated R for violence, gore, profanity, and nudity. 96m. **DIR:** William Malone. **CAST:** Geoffrey Rush, Taye Diggs, Famke Janssen, Peter Gallagher, Chris Kattan, Bridgette Wilson, Max Perlich, Jeffrey Coombs, Peter Graves. **1999 DVD**

HOUSE ON 92ND STREET, THE ★★★★1/2 One of the first successful docudramas, the movie focuses on espionage activity in New York during World War II. As spies try to steal atomic secrets, the camera follows them every step of the way. B&W; 88m. **DIR:** Henry Hathaway. **CAST:** Signe Hasso, William Eythe, Lloyd Nolan, Gene Lockhart, Leo G. Carroll, Harry Bellaver. **1945**

HOUSE ON TOMBSTONE HILL, THE ★★ College students take up residence in a cursed mansion, and become prey to the old lady who guards the attic. Unknown cast gives their all in this creaky thriller. Not rated; contains nudity and violence. 92m. **DIR:** J. Riffel. **CAST:** Mark Zobian. **1988**

HOUSE PARTY ★★★★ This delightful rap musical was one of the sleeper hits of 1990. The plot is standard let's-have-a-party-while-my-folks-are-away stuff, but with a surprisingly fresh humor and some dynamite dance numbers. The R rating (for profanity) makes it unsuitable for small children, but for mature teens and adults it's a great good time. 105m. **DIR:** Reginald Hudlin. **CAST:** Kid'n'Play, Full Force, Robin Harris. **1990 DVD**

HOUSE PARTY 2 ★★1/2 Inferior sequel. The film, which is dedicated to the late comedian Robin Harris (seen in flashback scenes) and features Whoopi Goldberg in a brief cameo, has some funny moments, most of which are provided by Martin Lawrence as Kid 'N' Play's out-of-control disc jockey. Otherwise, it's pretty standard fare. Rated R for profanity and violence. 90m. **DIR:** Doug McHenry, George Jackson. **CAST:** Christopher Reid, Christopher Martin, Martin Lawrence, Tisha Campbell, Georg Stanford Brown, William Schallert. **1991 DVD**

HOUSE PARTY 3 ★★ Rappers Kid 'N' Play get lost in the cluttered shuffle of their own hip-hop comedy. Kid's bachelor party and the duo's management of an all-girl group hit a few snags. Rated R for profanity. 94m. **DIR:** Eric Meza. **CAST:** Christopher Reid, Christopher Martin, Bernie Mac, Angela Means, Khandi Alexander. **1994 DVD**

HOUSE THAT BLED TO DEATH, THE ★★ Marginally scary horror film about a house that is possessed. Possessed by what or who? Don't ask us—the film refuses to give up the reason for all the blood that keeps shooting out of the pipes, or the various bloody members that show up in the fridge now and then. Not rated, but would probably merit a PG for violence and gore. 50m. **DIR:** Tom Clegg. **CAST:** Nicholas Ball. **1985**

HOUSE THAT DRIPPED BLOOD, THE ★★★1/2 All-star horror-anthology high jinks adapted from the stories of Robert Bloch. It's not quite on a par with the pioneering British release *Dead of Night*, but it'll do. Best segment: a horror star (Jon Pertwee) discovers a vampire's cape and finds himself becoming a little too convincing in the role of a bloodsucker. Rated PG. 102m. **DIR:** Peter Duffell. **CAST:** Christopher Lee, Peter Cushing, Denholm Elliott, Jon Pertwee, Ingrid Pitt. **1970**

HOUSE THAT MARY BOUGHT, THE ★★★1/2 In this thriller, adapted from Tim Wynne-Jones's novel, *Odd's End*, a married couple settle into a gorgeous little home by the coast, only to discover that someone keeps breaking into the place and engaging in all sorts of mischief. Or is it one of them, trying to drive the other into a nervous breakdown? The luxurious Brittany and Luxem-

bourg settings are a poetic counterpoint to the creepy story. Rated PG for mild violence. 104m. **DIR:** Simon MacCorkindale. **CAST:** Susan George, Ben Cross, Maurice Thorogood, Vernon Dobtcheff, Jean-Paul Muel, Charlotte Valandrey. **1994**

HOUSE THAT VANISHED, THE ★★ Exploitative suspense tale about a woman who sees a murder but can't convince anyone that it happened. There's a lot of nudity and an underdeveloped plot in this British-made film, which was fifteen minutes longer when it was originally released as *Scream and Die*. Rated R. 84m. **DIR:** Joseph Larraz. **CAST:** Andrea Allan. **1973**

HOUSE WHERE EVIL DWELLS, THE ★★ Depressing little horror romp with a Japanese background. In a savagely violent opening, a young samurai swordsman discovers the amorous activities of his less-than-faithful wife, and a gory fight ensues. This traps some really angry spirits in the house, which Edward Albert and Susan George move into centuries later. Rated R for nudity, violence, and language. 91m. **DIR:** Kevin O'Connor. **CAST:** Edward Albert, Susan George, Doug McClure. **1985**

HOUSEBOAT ★★★ A minor entry in Cary Grant's *oeuvre* of romantic fluff, largely unremarkable because of its ho-hum script. With this sort of insubstantial material coming his way, it's little wonder Grant chose to retire eight years later. He lives on a houseboat *sans* wife; Sophia Loren is the housekeeper-maid with whom he falls in love. Not rated; suitable for family viewing. 110m. **DIR:** Melville Shavelson. **CAST:** Cary Grant, Sophia Loren, Martha Hyer, Harry Guardino. **1958**

HOUSEGUEST ★★ An editing disaster, this overlong series of sight gags and one-liners doesn't do Sinbad's multitalents justice. To avoid the mob, he poses as a distinguished dentist and stays with a troubled family that he attempts to help (à la *Uncle Buck*). Phil Hartman provides some chuckles as his totally unhip host. The ending attempts to bring it all together but, alas, it's just too little too late. Rated PG for cartoon-variety violence. 110m. **DIR:** Randall Miller. **CAST:** Sinbad, Phil Hartman, Jeffrey Jones, Kim Greist. **1994**

HOUSEHOLD SAINTS ★★★1/2 Not as well etched as director Nancy Savoca's debut *True Love*, but a well-meaning pleasure nonetheless. The lives and loves of three generations of Italian-American women living in New York's Little Italy, come alive thanks to excellent performances by Tracey Ullman, Judith Malina, and, most notably, Lili Taylor as the current bearer of the torch. Nicely woven tale of the human spirit. Rated R for adult situations, language, and nudity. 124m. **DIR:** Nancy Savoca. **CAST:** Tracey Ullman, Judith Malina, Lili Taylor, Vincent D'Onofrio. **1993**

HOUSEHOLDER, THE ★★★★ Engaging low-budget comedy about a naïve young man and woman learning to adjust to their arranged marriage. The first collaboration by the legendary team of producer Ismail Merchant, writer Ruth Prawer Jhabvala and director James Ivory, aided by an uncredited Satyajit Ray as editor. In English. B&W; 100m. **DIR:** James Ivory. **CAST:** Shashi Kapoor. **1963**

HOUSEKEEPER, THE ★★★ A slightly demented housekeeper is driven over the edge by a Bible-thumping ex-hooker and proceeds to kill the family she works for. A suspenseful atmosphere moves the film along. Rated R for violence. 97m. **DIR:** Ousama Rawi. **CAST:** Rita Tushingham, Rose Petty, Jackie Burroughs. **1987**

HOUSEKEEPING ★★★ Director Bill Forsyth makes superbly quirky movies, and *Housekeeping*, based on Marilynne Robinson's novel, is a worthy addition to his body of work. Christine Lahti plays a contented transient who comes to the Pacific Northwest to care for her two orphaned nieces. Lahti makes the offbeat moments resound with weird humor. Rated PG. 112m. **DIR:** Bill Forsyth. **CAST:** Christine Lahti, Andrea Burchill, Sarah Walker. **1987**

HOUSESITTER ★★★1/2 Architect Newton Davis (Steve Martin) is rebuffed in love, then finds a relative stranger (Goldie Hawn) posing as his wife. Hawn, Martin, and director Frank Oz manage to hit the funnybone consistently enough for this to be a fun romp. Rated PG. 102m. **DIR:** Frank Oz. **CAST:** Steve Martin, Goldie Hawn, Dana Delany, Julie Harris, Donald Moffat, Peter MacNicol. **1992 DVD**

HOUSEWIFE ★★ When a would-be rapist and thief breaks into the house of a well-to-do Beverly Hills couple, he unleashes the tensions that exist beneath the surface of their well-ordered lives. Exploitative drama with a cast that deserves better. Rated R for violence and sexual situations. 95m. **DIR:** Larry Cohen. **CAST:** Yaphet Kotto, Andrew Duggan, Joyce Van Patten, Jeannie Berlin. **1972**

HOW FUNNY CAN SEX BE? ★★1/2 Mediocre anthology featuring eight tales about love and sex. Giancarlo Giannini and Laura Antonelli liven up their segments, but you might want to fast-forward through some of the others. Rated R for nudity. 97m. **DIR:** Dino Risi. **CAST:** Giancarlo Giannini, Laura Antonelli. **1976**

HOW GREEN WAS MY VALLEY ★★★★★ This 1941 best-picture Oscar winner is a tribute to the lasting value of a family's love. Director John Ford also won an Oscar for the way he brings out the soul of Richard Llewellyn's bestseller, which concerns a Welsh mining family, as seen through the eyes of its youngest member (Roddy McDowall, in one of his most famous child-star roles). 118m. **DIR:** John Ford. **CAST:** Walter Pidgeon, Maureen O'Hara, Roddy McDowall, Donald Crisp, John Loder, Barry Fitzgerald. **1941 DVD**

•**HOW HIGH** 🦃 Two buddies turn Harvard into Party Central with help from the ghost of a deceased friend in this loud, profanity-riddled, poorly edited, and mostly unfunny stream of drug, sex, and racial humor that attempts to drag Cheech and Chong weed comedy into the twenty-first century. Rated R for drug use, language, and sexual content. 96m. **DIR:** Jesse Dylan. **CAST:** Method Man, Redman, Chuck Davis, Obba Babatundé, Spalding Gray. **2001 DVD**

HOW I GOT INTO COLLEGE 🦃 Uninspired and dull adolescent comedy. Rated PG-13. 98m. **DIR:** Savage Steve Holland. **CAST:** Anthony Edwards, Corey Parker. **1989**

HOW I WON THE WAR ★★★1/2 John Lennon had his only solo screen turn (away from the Beatles) in this often hilarious war spoof. Directed by Richard Lester, it features Michael Crawford as a military man who has a wacky way of distorting the truth as he reminisces about his adventures in battle. 109m. **DIR:** Richard Lester. **CAST:** Michael Crawford, John Lennon, Michael Hordern, Jack MacGowran. **1967 DVD**

HOW STELLA GOT HER GROOVE BACK ★★1/2 Forty year old stockbroker and single mom has a love affair with a twenty year old Jamaican while vacationing in the tropics. This reversal of Hollywood's usual coupling of older man/younger woman begins as a brisk comedy and then sputters down the stretch as a rather shallow, sentimental romance. Rated R for language, nudity, and simulated sex. 124m. **DIR:** Kevin Sullivan. **CAST:** Angela Bassett, Taye Diggs, Whoopi Goldberg, Regina King, Suzzanne Douglas, Michael J. Pagan. **1998 DVD**

HOW THE GRINCH STOLE CHRISTMAS ★★★1/2 The animated holiday perennial gets an opulent spin in this colorful live-action adaptation, which deserves kudos for the extraordinary set design. Looking at this film is a treat that cannot be repeated too often; unfortunately, the same cannot be said of the weak story elements. Jim Carrey is marvelous as the gleefully nasty Grinch, but costar Taylor Momsen makes a stiff and unconvincing Cindy-Lou Who. Even so, the final 20 minutes, apparently lifted directly from the 1966 Chuck Jones animated version, are pure magic. Rated PG for mild innuendo and comic mayhem. 104m. **DIR:** Ron Howard. **CAST:** Jim Carrey, Jeffrey Tambor, Christine Baranski, Bill Irwin, Taylor Momsen. **2000 DVD**

HOW THE WEST WAS FUN ★★★ It's fun on the range as the adorable Olsen twins join their father in an attempt to save a dude ranch that their mother once attended as a child. Kids will enjoy this harmless, made-for-television romp. Not rated. 92m. **DIR:** Stuart Margolin. **CAST:** Mary-Kate Olsen, Ashley Olsen, Martin Mull, Patrick Cassidy, Ben Cardinal. **1994**

HOW THE WEST WAS WON ★★★1/2 Any Western with this cast is worth a glimpse. Sadly, much of the grandeur of the original version is lost because it was released on the three-screen Cinerama process. For a taste of its original grandeur, check out the letter-boxed Laserdisc version, where the clear, sharp picture and excellent stereo sound do the film justice. 155m. **DIR:** Henry Hathaway, George Marshall, John Ford. **CAST:** Gregory Peck, Henry Fonda, James Stewart, John Wayne, Debbie Reynolds, Walter Brennan, Karl Malden, Richard Widmark, Robert Preston, George Peppard, Carolyn Jones, Carroll Baker. **1963 DVD**

HOW TO BE A WOMAN AND NOT DIE IN THE ATTEMPT ★★★1/2 Breezy Spanish comedy stars the fabulous Carmen Maura and Antonio Resines as a couple trying to make their marriage work. Told in four chapters based on the seasons, the film takes a comic look at a much-divorced journalist, whose recent marriage to a record producer is her last hurrah. The writer and director exploit the relationship for all it's worth, while the cast does its best to keep matters from slipping into sitcom territory. In Spanish with English subtitles. Not rated. 100m. **DIR:** Ana Belen. **CAST:** Carmen Maura, Antonio Resines, Juanjo Puigcorbe, Carmen Conesa. **1991 DVD**

HOW TO BEAT THE HIGH CO$T OF LIVING ★★ A great cast all dressed up with no place to go . . . except Jane Curtin, whose shopping-mall striptease is a marginal high point in a caper comedy not even up to the substandards of an average made-for-television movie. Tiresome and taxing. Rated PG. 110m. **DIR:** Robert Scheerer. **CAST:** Jessica Lange, Susan Saint James, Jane Curtin, Richard Benjamin, Fred Willard, Dabney Coleman. **1980**

HOW TO BREAK UP A HAPPY DIVORCE ★★★ Ex-wife Barbara Eden wants ex-husband Hal Linden back. To make him jealous, she dates a well-known playboy. Comic mayhem follows. Lots of sight gags. This is an unrated TV movie. 78m. **DIR:** Jerry Paris. **CAST:** Hal Linden, Barbara Eden, Harold Gould. **1976**

HOW TO FRAME A FIGG ★★★★ Classic, slapstick comedy starring Don Knotts as a naïve accountant who is set up as the patsy for a city council that's been stealing money from the city. A charming, very funny outing with a hysterical performance by Knotts. Rated G. 103m. **DIR:** Alan Rafkin. **CAST:** Don Knotts, Yvonne Craig, Elaine Joyce, Joe Flynn, Edward Andrews. **1971**

HOW TO GET AHEAD IN ADVERTISING ★★ During an ad campaign for a new pimple cream, a British advertising executive goes completely berserk when a boil erupts on his neck, grows into a human head, and spews forth abrasive slogans ad nauseam. This heavy-handed assault on the marketing of useless and even harmful commodities is ultimately more abrasive than fun. Rated PG-13. 94m. **DIR:** Bruce Robinson. **CAST:** Richard E. Grant, Rachel Ward, Jacqueline Tong, Susan Wooldridge. **1989**

HOW TO IRRITATE PEOPLE ★★★★★ Even before *Monty Python*, John Cleese's sense of aggressive humor was fully developed, as can be seen in this hilarious collection of skits. As in all of his best work, Cleese (who wrote this BBC special along with future *Python* mate Graham Chapman) mines humor from the disparity between the surface politeness of the English and the frustrated rage underneath. Not rated. 65m. **DIR:** Ian Fordyce. **CAST:** John Cleese, Graham Chapman, Michael Palin, Connie Booth, Tim Brooke-Taylor. **1968 DVD**

HOW TO MAKE A MONSTER 🦃 Hollywood makeup artist goes off the deep end. B&W/color; 75m. **DIR:** Herbert L. Strock. **CAST:** Robert H. Harris, Paul Brinegar, Gary Conway, Gary Clarke, Malcolm Atterbury. **1958**

HOW TO MAKE AN AMERICAN QUILT ★★★1/2 Based on Whitney Otto's celebrated book, the film has emotionally scarred women sharing their pain in an effort to show marriage-shy Winona Ryder the value of commitment. Some of the episodic tales succeed, while others seem trivial. It's a pleasure to see so many Hollywood icons in one project. Rated PG-13 for profanity, sexual candor, and drug use. 116m. **DIR:** Jocelyn Moorhouse. **CAST:** Winona Ryder, Maya Angelou, Anne Bancroft, Ellen Burstyn, Kate Nelligan, Jean Simmons, Lois Smith, Alfre Woodard, Dermot Mulroney, Rip Torn, Kate Capshaw, Claire Danes, Melinda Dillon, Samantha Mathis. **1995 DVD**

HOW TO MARRY A MILLIONAIRE ★★★ The stars, Marilyn Monroe, Lauren Bacall, and Betty Grable, are fun to watch in this comedy. However, director Jean Negulesco doesn't do much to keep our interest. The story in this slight romp is all in the title—with William Powell giving the girls a run for his money. 96m. **DIR:** Jean Negulesco. **CAST:** Lauren Bacall, Marilyn Monroe, Betty Grable, William Powell, Cameron Mitchell, David Wayne, Rory Calhoun. **1953 DVD**

HOW TO MURDER YOUR WIFE ★★1/2 Jack Lemmon plays a comic-strip artist whose well-structured life is

disrupted when he discovers he has married a beautiful woman after a night of drunken partying. Finding the situation intolerable, Lemmon contrives to take out his frustration by murdering his new bride in the comic strip. Some clever bits, but the premise and attitudes are unbelievably sexist. 118m. **DIR:** Richard Quine. **CAST:** Jack Lemmon, Virna Lisi, Terry-Thomas, Eddie Mayehoff, Claire Trevor, Sidney Blackmer, Jack Albertson, Mary Wickes. **1965**

HOW TO STEAL A MILLION ★★★★1/2 A delightful romp with sophisticated dialogue, excellent acting, and colorful sets and costumes. The plot revolves around a museum heist that's done to save the "honor" of a magnificent forger, by his daughter and a noted burglar. 127m. **DIR:** William Wyler. **CAST:** Audrey Hepburn, Peter O'Toole, Charles Boyer, Eli Wallach, Hugh Griffith. **1966**

HOW TO STUFF A WILD BIKINI ★★ It's no surprise to see Frankie Avalon and Annette Funicello together in this beach-party film. Dwayne Hickman tries his hand at romancing Annette in this one. Not much plot, but lots of crazy (sometimes funny) things are going on. 90m. **DIR:** William Asher. **CAST:** Frankie Avalon, Annette Funicello, Dwayne Hickman, Mickey Rooney, Buster Keaton. **1965 DVD**

HOW TO SUCCEED IN BUSINESS WITHOUT REALLY TRYING ★★★★★ A near-perfect musical based on the Pulitzer Prize–winning Broadway show, with most of the original cast intact. Robert Morse plays the window washer who plots his way to the top of the Worldwide Wicket Company. The musical numbers are staged with inventiveness and performed with exuberance. Maureen Arthur is a standout as the buxom beauty all the managers want in their secretarial pool. 121m. **DIR:** David Swift. **CAST:** Robert Morse, Rudy Vallee, Michele Lee, Anthony Teague, Maureen Arthur, Sammy Smith. **1967 DVD**

HOW U LIKE ME NOW ★★★ Extremely low-budget account of the struggles of a group of African-American friends on Chicago's South Side. The acting is uneven, but writer/director/producer Darryl Roberts turned out a gritty, honest, and funny script with enough warmth and humor to help you over the rough patches. Rated R for profanity and sexual situations. 109m. **DIR:** Darryl Roberts. **CAST:** Darnell Williams, Salli Richardson, Daniel Gardner, Raymond Whitfield, Darryl Roberts. **1992**

HOWARD THE DUCK 🦃 An extremely rotten egg. Unwisely rated PG, considering some smarmy sex scenes and frightening monster makeup. 111m. **DIR:** Willard Huyck. **CAST:** Lea Thompson, Jeffrey Jones, Tim Robbins, Ed Gale. **1986**

HOWARDS END ★★★★★ Two relatively liberated middle-class sisters become entangled with the members of an upper-crust British family. The creative team that adapted E. M. Forster's *Room with a View* and *Maurice* saved the best for this Forster adaptation, a gorgeous and engrossing story of the first decade of the twentieth century, propelled through distinctive characters, rich dialogue, delicious irony, and evocative locales. Rated PG. 140m. **DIR:** James Ivory. **CAST:** Emma Thompson, Anthony Hopkins, Vanessa Redgrave, Helena Bonham Carter, James Wilby, Samuel West. **1992 DVD**

HOWARDS OF VIRGINIA, THE ★★ Tiring, too-long retelling of the Revolutionary War centering on an aristocratic Virginia family. In the Cary Grant filmography, it is just plain awful. B&W; 117m. **DIR:** Frank Lloyd. **CAST:** Cary Grant, Martha Scott, Cedric Hardwicke, Alan Marshal, Richard Carlson, Paul Kelly, Anne Revere, Irving Bacon. **1940**

HOWLING, THE ★★★★ Every spooky scene you've ever seen, every horror movie cliché that's ever been overspoken, and every guaranteed-to-make-'em-jump, out-of-the-dark surprise that Hollywood ever came up with for its scary movies. It also has the best special effects since *Alien* and some really off-the-wall humor. Rated R for gruesome adult horror. 91m. **DIR:** Joe Dante. **CAST:** Dee Wallace, Christopher Stone, Patrick Macnee, Dennis Dugan, Slim Pickens, John Carradine. **1981 DVD**

HOWLING II . . . YOUR SISTER IS A WEREWOLF 🦃 Poor follow-up to *The Howling*. Rated R for nudity, blood, and gore. 91m. **DIR:** Philippe Mora. **CAST:** Christopher Lee, Reb Brown, Annie McEnroe, Sybil Danning. **1984**

HOWLING III ★★1/2 Werewolves turn up in Australia, only these are marsupials. A sociologist falls in love with one of them and tries to save the whole tribe. The story focuses more on character than gore, and you find yourself strangely engrossed. Rated PG-13 for brief nudity and violence. 95m. **DIR:** Philippe Mora. **CAST:** Barry Otto. **1987 DVD**

HOWLING IV 🦃 Werewolves are scarce in this third sequel about a woman haunted by the ghost of a nun who was killed by one of the lycanthropes. Rated R for violence and nudity. 94m. **DIR:** John Hough. **CAST:** Romy Windsor, Michael T. Weiss, Antony Hamilton. **1988**

HOWLING V—THE REBIRTH ★★★1/2 A group of people gather at a castle that has been shut for 500 years—for a rather fun game of who's the werewolf. Only the title has any relation to the previous movies in the series. Enjoyable. Rated R for violence and nudity. 99m. **DIR:** Neal Sundstrom. **CAST:** Philip Davis. **1989**

HOWLING VI: THE FREAKS ★★1/2 A carnival freak show is the scene of a battle between a vampire and the werewolf-drifter who pursues him. Special effects that leave a lot to be desired diminish this really strange entry in the long-running werewolf series. Rated R for violence and profanity. 102m. **DIR:** Hope Perello. **CAST:** Brendan Hughes, Michelle Matheson, Sean Gregory Sullivan, Antonio Fargas, Carol Lynley. **1990**

HOWLING, THE: NEW MOON RISING 🦃 Ridiculous follow-up to the popular werewolf film series. An undercover reporter investigates a series of bloody murders in an off-the-map town. Bad acting, nonexistent direction, and some really terrible country/western music performed by the cast. Rated R for profanity and werewolf violence. 90m. **DIR:** Clive Turner. **CAST:** John Ramsden, Ernest Kester, Clive Turner, John Hoff, Elizabeth She. **1994**

HUCK AND THE KING OF HEARTS ★★★ Credit scripter Christopher Sturgeon with an inventive idea: To redo *Huckleberry Finn* as a contemporary family adventure with clever echoes of Mark Twain. Thus, young Chauncey Leopardi flees a hard-hearted stepfather, joins forces with small-time grifter "Injun" Joe (Graham Greene), and heads for Las Vegas and a meeting with a

long-estranged grandfather (John Astin). Rated PG for violence. 98m. **DIR:** Michael Keusch. **CAST:** Chauncey Leopardi, Joe Piscopo, Dee Wallace, Gretchen Becker, John Astin, Graham Greene. **1993**

HUCKLEBERRY FINN (1974) ★★ The weakest version of the popular story, mainly because forgettable songs take the place of personality. The basic plot of a young boy learning about life from a runaway slave is there, but the players look and act bored. Rated G. 117m. **DIR:** J. Lee Thompson. **CAST:** Jeff East, Paul Winfield, David Wayne, Harvey Korman, Arthur O'Connell, Gary Merrill, Kim O'Brien. **1974**

HUCKLEBERRY FINN (1975) ★★★★ Ron Howard does a fine job as Mark Twain's mischievous misfit. This made-for-TV film is well worth watching. The supporting actors are fun to watch, too. 74m. **DIR:** Robert Totten. **CAST:** Ron Howard, Donny Most, Antonio Fargas, Merle Haggard, Jack Elam, Royal Dano, Sarah Selby. **1975**

HUCKSTERS, THE ★★ Exposé of the advertising business is as vapid as the products pushed by the advertisers in this overlong melodrama. A mature Clark Gable, recently returned from duty in World War II, heads a stunning but ultimately wasted cast that includes Deborah Kerr and Ava Gardner as the two gals who want him. B&W; 115m. **DIR:** Jack Conway. **CAST:** Clark Gable, Deborah Kerr, Sydney Greenstreet, Adolphe Menjou, Ava Gardner, Keenan Wynn, Edward Arnold, Frank Albertson, Douglas Fowley. **1947**

HUD ★★★★★ In one of his most memorable performances, Paul Newman stars as the arrogant ne'er-do-well son of a Texas rancher (Melvyn Douglas) who has fallen on hard times. Instead of helping his father, Hud drunkenly pursues the family's housekeeper (Patricia Neal), who wants nothing to do with him. When asked, Newman dubbed this one "pretty good." An understatement. B&W; 112m. **DIR:** Martin Ritt. **CAST:** Paul Newman, Patricia Neal, Melvyn Douglas, Brandon de Wilde. **1963**

HUDSON HAWK ★★★ Fans of Bruce Willis's wisecracking comedy style will enjoy this critically lambasted spoof of spy thrillers filled with slapstick comedy, unexpected musical numbers, and goofy supporting characters. Willis plays a cat burglar who is forced back into the biz. Rated R for profanity and violence. 95m. **DIR:** Michael Lehmann. **CAST:** Bruce Willis, Danny Aiello, Andie MacDowell, James Coburn, Richard E. Grant, Sandra Bernhard. **1991 DVD**

HUDSUCKER PROXY, THE ★★★1/2 This film falls a little short with its twisted send-up of Frank Capra's populist dramas of the 1930s and 1940s. Tim Robbins is a schnook who is promoted from the mailroom to the presidency of a corporation after his predecessor leaps to his death (presumably out of boredom). Paul Newman steals the movie as the main manipulator, while Jennifer Jason Leigh goes a little overboard as a tough gal reporter. Rated PG. 111m. **DIR:** Joel Coen. **CAST:** Tim Robbins, Paul Newman, Jennifer Jason Leigh, Charles Durning, John Mahoney, Jim True, Bill Cobbs, Bruce Campbell. **1994 DVD**

HUGO POOL ★★★1/2 Forced to rely on her dysfunctional parents to help meet an impossible deadline in her pool-cleaning business, a young woman spends a wild day among the rich and strange in Los Angeles. Some truly odd vignettes and a sweet subplot highlight this independent film. There's a lot of heart as well as strong performances and surprise cameos in this riveting little gem. Rated R. 92m. **DIR:** Robert Downey. **CAST:** Alyssa Milano, Patrick Dempsey, Malcolm McDowell, Robert Downey Jr., Cathy Moriarty, Richard Lewis, Sean Penn, Bert Remsen, Chuck Barris. **1997 DVD**

HULA ★★1/2 Clara Bow chews up the palm fronds as Hula, wild daughter of an Irish planter in Hawaii who defies domesticity until she falls for a starched-shirt, married engineer. This liberated love story had a surefire audience eager for anything by Jazz-Age wildcat Bow. A piece of fluff, but entertaining. B&W; 64m. **DIR:** Victor Fleming. **CAST:** Clara Bow, Clive Brook, Arlette Marchal, Arnold Kent, Maude Truax, Albert Gran. **1927**

HULLABALOO OVER GEORGE AND BONNIE'S PICTURES ★★1/2 British and American art dealers compete to gain access to a valuable art collection belonging to an Indian prince. A lesser effort from the team behind *A Room with a View*; gently funny in spots, but it never really goes anywhere. Not rated, but nothing objectionable. 85m. **DIR:** James Ivory. **CAST:** Peggy Ashcroft, Victor Banerjee, Saeed Jaffrey. **1976**

HUMAN COMEDY, THE ★★★1/2 California author William Saroyan's tender and touching story of life in a small valley town during World War II is a winner all around in this compassionate, now-nostalgic film. Mickey Rooney shines as the Western Union messenger verging on manhood. A sentimental slice of life, comic and tragic. B&W; 118m. **DIR:** Clarence Brown. **CAST:** Mickey Rooney, Frank Morgan, "Butch" Jenkins, Ray Collins, Darryl Hickman, Marsha Hunt, Fay Bainter, Donna Reed, James Craig, Van Johnson. **1943**

HUMAN CONDITION, THE, PART ONE: NO GREATER LOVE ★★★★ Based on a Japanese bestseller, this is the story of a sensitive, compassionate man who tries to maintain his humanity through the spiraling horrors of World War II. Part One opens in 1943. The film is quite long, but never dull, with breathtaking wide-screen photography (also available in a letter box video format). The fractured-English subtitles are the only drawback. Not rated. B&W; 200m. **DIR:** Masaki Kobayashi. **CAST:** Tatsuya Nakadai, Michiyo Aratama, Chikage Awashima. **1958**

HUMAN CONDITION, THE, PART TWO: THE ROADTO ETERNITY ★★★1/2 Director Masaki Kobayashi's epic film trilogy continues, with hero Kaji entering the imperial army in the closing months of World War II. Despite his doubts about Japanese war aims, he proves a good soldier and acquits himself bravely. Unlike the first film in the trilogy, this one ends with a cliff-hanger. Not rated, but not for children or squeamish adults. B&W; 180m. **DIR:** Masaki Kobayashi. **CAST:** Tatsuya Nakadai. **1959**

HUMAN CONDITION, THE, PART THREE: A SOLDIER'S PRAYER ★★★★ Director Masaki Kobayashi's magnum opus comes to its shattering conclusion as Kaji, his unit wiped out in battle, leads a band of stragglers and refugees through the Manchurian wilderness. Acting, cinematography, and editing are all first-rate in this heartwrenching tale of Japan's darkest days. Not rated. B&W; 190m. **DIR:** Masaki Kobayashi. **CAST:** Tatsuya Nakadai. **1961**

HUMAN DESIRE ★★★1/2 Broderick Crawford turns in a compelling performance as a hot-tempered husband who kills an innocent man with whom he suspects his wife of having an affair. Fritz Lang's remake of Jean Renoir's *La Bête Humaine*. B&W; 90m. **DIR:** Fritz Lang. **CAST:** Glenn Ford, Broderick Crawford, Gloria Grahame, Edgar Buchanan. **1954**

HUMAN DESIRES ★★1/2 Soft-core porn flick masquerading as a murder mystery. Keep your finger on the fast-forward button. Rated R for language, violence, nudity, and sexual situations. 94m. **DIR:** Ellen Earnshaw. **CAST:** Shannon Tweed, Christian Noble, Dawn Ann Billings, Ashby Adams, Peggy Trentini, Duke Stroud. **1996**

HUMAN DUPLICATORS, THE ★★ Alien giant Richard Kiel comes to Earth to create identical duplicates of its populace but falls in love instead. Hokey, cheap, and badly acted. 82m. **DIR:** Hugo Grimaldi. **CAST:** George Nader, Barbara Nichols, Hugh Beaumont, George Macready, Richard Arlen, Richard Kiel. **1965**

HUMAN FACTOR, THE ★★★ Nicol Williamson is a lower-grade British agent who because of personal ties to South Africa releases minor secrets to a Soviet-front organization there. When superiors start to investigate he sets about to defect to Russia although it is his assistant who initially comes under suspicion. A strangely remote working of Graham Greene's novel that never catches the suspense intended. Robert Morley is great as an investigator who makes snap decisions and acts upon them. Inexplicably rated R for minor sexual content. 115m. **DIR:** Otto Preminger. **CAST:** Nicol Williamson, Richard Attenborough, John Gielgud, Derek Jacobi, Robert Morley, Ann Todd, Iman. **1979**

HUMAN HEARTS ★★1/2 Old-fashioned story of a criminally manipulated big-city woman who comes between a devoted father and son. Set in a peaceful village in Arkansas. Handkerchief material. Silent. B&W; 99m. **DIR:** King Baggott. **CAST:** House Peters, Russell Simpson, Mary Philbin. **1922**

HUMAN MONSTER, THE (DARK EYES OF LONDON) ★★★ Creaky but sometimes clever suspense thriller about a humanitarian (Bela Lugosi) who may not be as philanthropic as he seems. Strange murders have been occurring in the vicinity of his charitable facility. This preposterous Edgar Wallace story has its moments. B&W; 73m. **DIR:** Walter Summers. **CAST:** Bela Lugosi, Hugh Williams, Greta Gynt, Edmon Ryan. **1939 DVD**

•**HUMAN NATURE** ★★★1/2 An uptight scientist (Tim Robbins), his hirsute girlfriend (Patricia Arquette), and his flirtatious lab assistant (Miranda Otto) try to rehabilitate a man raised in the wild as an ape (Rhys Ifans). Written by Charlie (Being John Malkovich) Kaufman, this oddball comedy has much of that earlier film's what-next wackiness and unpredictability, with some pretty trenchant comments on civilization and sex. Rated R for profanity, nudity, and sexual scenes. 96m. **DIR:** Michel Gondry. **CAST:** Tim Robbins, Patricia Arquette, Rhys Ifans, Miranda Otto, Rosie Perez, Mary Kay Place, Robert Forster. **2002 DVD**

HUMAN RESOURCES ★★★ A French college student takes a summer internship in his father's factory, where he becomes an unwitting pawn in the management's resistance to the thirty-five-hour work week. This slice of blue-collar life in France is earnest, thoughtful, and well-acted by a largely nonprofessional cast. In French with English subtitles. Not rated; suitable for mature audiences, with some profanity in subtitles. 100m. **DIR:** Laurent Cantet. **CAST:** Jalil Lespert, Jean-Claude Vallod, Chantal Barré, Lucien Longueville. **1999**

HUMAN SHIELD, THE 🦃 This boring, violent story revolves around an Iraqi general who tortures an American. Bad plot, bad acting. Rated R for violence. 92m. **DIR:** Ted Post. **CAST:** Michael Dudikoff, Tommy Hinkley, Steve Inwood. **1991**

HUMAN TRAFFIC ★★ Five Welsh teens drink, drug, and dance through a weekend pub and rave scene before staring into another mundane Monday. This kaleidoscopic recruitment poster for the "chemical generation" is surprisingly flat for a story propelled by pounding techno rock and hyper, surrealistic camera work. Characters include a store clerk troubled by impotency and a party girl rebounding from soured relationships. Rated R for strong sexuality, language, and drug use. 99m. **DIR:** Justin Kerrigan. **CAST:** John Simm, Lorraine Pilkington, Shaun Parkes, Nicola Reynolds, Danny Dyer. **2000 DVD**

HUMAN VAPOR, THE ★★ Essentially reworking the premise of the more interesting Honda film, *The H-Man*, this tells of a scientist transformed by a misbegotten experiment into a hideous, gaseous killer. Film dispenses with the draggy subplots of its forerunner, but still manages to outlast its welcome. 79m. **DIR:** Inoshiro Honda. **CAST:** Yoshio Tsuchiya. **1964**

HUMANOID, THE ★★★ Japanese animation set on a far-off and idyllic planet. The title character is a "young" humanoid that is just beginning to understand and participate in human relationships. Unfortunately, "her" life is suddenly disturbed by a scheming villain. In Japanese with English subtitles. 45m. **DIR:** Shin-Ichi Masaki. **1986**

HUMANOID DEFENDER 🦃 This movie is actually two episodes from a TV series that never made it, sort of a mix of *The Six Million Dollar Man* and *The Fugitive*. 94m. **DIR:** Ron Satlof. **CAST:** Terence Knox, Gary Kasper, Aimee Eccles, Marie Windsor. **1985**

HUMANOIDS FROM THE DEEP ★★ One of producer Roger Corman's own remakes for cable TV, this bears little resemblance to the earlier *Humanoids*, and is actually less graphic. But it's also pretty contrived, with just about everything ineptly borrowed from some better monster movie. Rated R for violence, gore, nudity, and profanity. 86m. **DIR:** Jeff Yonis. **CAST:** Robert Carradine, Emma Samms, Justin Walker, Clint Howard. **1996 DVD**

HUMONGOUS 🦃 Idiotic teenagers become shipwrecked on an island whose only inhabitant is a hairy, murderous mutant. Rated R for violence. 90m. **DIR:** Paul Lynch. **CAST:** Janet Julian, David Wallace. **1982**

HUMORESQUE ★★★★ Terrific dialogue highlights this wonderfully trashy story of a talented violinist (John Garfield) who sells his soul and body to a wealthy, older woman (Joan Crawford) who promises to further his career. Witty, sophisticated, and lavish in its production values, this is a weeper par excellence. 125m. **DIR:** Jean Negulesco. **CAST:** Joan Crawford, John Garfield, Oscar Levant, J. Carrol Naish, Craig Stevens. **1946**

HUNCHBACK ★★★1/2 Handsome TV adaptation of Victor Hugo's novel *The Hunchback of Notre Dame*,

with Anthony Hopkins in fine form as the tragic Quasimodo. Excellent supporting cast and stunning set design make this version of the classic one to cherish. 150m. **DIR:** Michael Tuchner. **CAST:** Anthony Hopkins, Derek Jacobi, Lesley-Anne Down, Robert Powell, John Gielgud, David Suchet, Tim Pigott-Smith. **1982**

HUNCHBACK OF NOTRE DAME, THE (1923) ★★★★1/2 Although it has been remade, with varying degrees of success, in the sound era, no film has surpassed the Lon Chaney version in screen spectacle or in the athletic excellence of moviedom's "man of a thousand faces." A musical score has been added. B&W; 108m. **DIR:** Wallace Worsley. **CAST:** Lon Chaney Sr., Patsy Ruth Miller, Ernest Torrence. **1923 DVD**

HUNCHBACK OF NOTRE DAME, THE (1939) ★★★★ In this horror classic, Charles Laughton gives a tour-de-force performance as the deformed bell-ringer who comes to the aid of a pretty gypsy (Maureen O'Hara). Cedric Hardwicke and Edmond O'Brien also give strong performances in this remake of the silent film. B&W; 117m. **DIR:** William Dieterle. **CAST:** Charles Laughton, Thomas Mitchell, Maureen O'Hara, Edmond O'Brien, Cedric Hardwicke. **1939 DVD**

HUNCHBACK, THE (1997) ★★★★ TNT hits pay dirt with Mandy Patinkin's excellent portrayal of Victor Hugo's Quasimodo. Patinkin's makeup and mannerisms hearken back to Charles Laughton's in the same role, allowing the character's pain to be fully revealed. Richard Harris is pathological as the sadistic priest, and Salma Hayek is luminescent as the beautiful gypsy who befriends Quasimodo. This is not made for children. Not rated; contains adult themes, cruelty, and sadism. **DIR:** Peter Medak. **CAST:** Mandy Patinkin, Richard Harris, Salma Hayek. **1997 DVD**

HUNCHBACK OF NOTRE DAME, THE (1997) ★★★★★ Disney's animated musical version of Victor Hugo's classic is the studio's most mature cartoon to date. Issues of prejudice, sexual obsession, and religious hypocrisy are at the foreground, yet there's enough action and spectacle to keep kids enchanted. Quasimodo himself is a little more cuddly than in the book, but other than that and the obligatory happy ending, the Disney animators are faithful to Hugo's pessimistic worldview. Of course, they create an astounding 15-century Paris. Rated G. 90m. **DIR:** Gary Trousdale, Kirk Wise. **1997 DVD**

HUNGARIAN FAIRY TALE, A ★★★★1/2 An imaginative and affecting tale from Hungary, blending myth, social satire, and a Dickensian story of a Budapest orphan. Filmed in stunning black and white, and employing little dialogue. In Hungarian with English subtitles. 97m. **DIR:** Gyula Gazdag. **CAST:** David Vermes. **1988**

HUNGER (1966) ★★★★ Hauntingly funny portrait of a starving writer in Norway, circa 1890. The would-be writer explores his fantasies as he stumbles through the streets penniless. Per Oscarsson turns in a brilliant performance that netted him the best actor award at the Cannes Film Festival. A must-see! In Swedish with English subtitles. B&W; 100m. **DIR:** Henning Carlsen. **CAST:** Per Oscarsson, Gunnel Lindblom. **1966**

HUNGER, THE (1983) ★★ Arty and visually striking yet cold, this kinky sci-fi horror film features French actress Catherine Deneuve as a seductive vampire. Her centuries-old boyfriend (David Bowie) is about to disintegrate, so she picks a new lover (Susan Sarandon). Rated R for gore, profanity, and nudity. 94m. **DIR:** Tony Scott. **CAST:** Catherine Deneuve, David Bowie, Susan Sarandon, Cliff De Young. **1983**

HUNGRY HILL ★★ A heavy-handed interpretation of Daphne duMaurier's novel set in nineteenth-century Britain where two Irish families fight over rights to the land. B&W; 92m. **DIR:** Brian Desmond Hurst. **CAST:** Jean Simmons, Dennis Price, Margaret Lockwood, Siobhan McKenna, Eileen Herlie. **1947 DVD**

HUNK A social outcast makes a deal with the devil. Rated PG. 90m. **DIR:** Lawrence Bassoff. **CAST:** John Allen Nelson, Steve Levitt, Rebeccah Bush, Robert Morse, James Coco, Avery Schreiber, Deborah Shelton. **1987 DVD**

HUNLEY, THE ★★ This TNT original chronicles the Confederate attempt to prevent the fall of Charleston to the Yankee navy in 1864. Their invention of a torpedo-wielding submarine puts the lives of its daring crew on the line. Flashbacks throughout and ghost-story overtones fail because we're never really grounded in the events that led to the sub's creation or the molding of the military leaders' characters. Not rated; contains violence. 90m. **DIR:** John Gray. **CAST:** Armand Assante, Donald Sutherland, Alex Jennings, Sebastian Roche. **1999**

HUNT, THE ★★★1/2 A powerful, uncompromising meditation on violence, about three veterans of the Spanish Civil War who hunt rabbits a generation later in the same hills across which they fought. In Spanish with English subtitles. Not rated; contains graphic violence. B&W; 92m. **DIR:** Carlos Saura. **CAST:** Ismael Merlo. **1954**

HUNT FOR RED OCTOBER, THE ★★★★1/2 In this edge-of-your-seat winner adapted from Tom Clancy's best-selling suspense novel, Sean Connery plays a Soviet submarine captain who uses Russia's ultimate underwater weapon as a means to defect to the West. A superb supporting cast enlivens this crackerjack thriller. Rated PG for brief violence. 132m. **DIR:** John McTiernan. **CAST:** Sean Connery, Alec Baldwin, Scott Glenn, James Earl Jones, Sam Neill, Richard Jordan, Tim Curry, Jeffrey Jones, Peter Firth, Joss Ackland. **1990 DVD**

HUNT FOR THE NIGHT STALKER ★★★ Involving made-for-television police drama that follows the exploits of the two detectives who diligently pursued serial killer Richard Ramirez, whose reign of terror put southern California in a panic. Good performances and painstaking detail. Also known as *Manhunt: Search for the Night Stalker*. 100m. **DIR:** Bruce Seth Green. **CAST:** Richard Jordan, A Martinez, Lisa Eilbacher. **1989**

HUNT THE MAN DOWN ★★1/2 A public defender has the difficult chore of defending a man who has been a fugitive from a murder charge for twelve years. In attempting to follow an ice-cold trail and prove his defendant innocent, Gig Young fights an uphill battle. B&W; 68m. **DIR:** George Archainbaud. **CAST:** Gig Young, Lynne Roberts, Mary Anderson, Willard Parker, Carla Balenda, Gerald Mohr, James Anderson, Harry Shannon, Cleo Moore. **1950**

HUNTED, THE (1995) ★★ An American businessman becomes Ninja bait. Howlingly awful at times and drenched in carnage, this action-fu flick reaches a pin-

nacle of delirious excess during a massacre and showdown aboard a speeding train. Rated R for violence, sex, and language. 110m. **DIR:** J. F. Lawton. **CAST:** Christopher Lambert, John Lone, Joan Chen, Yoshio Harada, Yoko Shimada. **1995 DVD**

HUNTED (1997) ★★1/2 An insurance investigator finds herself facing off with a madman when she journeys to a remote forest in search of missing millions. Run-of-the-mill chase-thriller with above-average performances. Rated R for violence. 96m. **DIR:** Stuart Cooper. **CAST:** Harry Hamlin, Madchen Amick. **1997**

HUNTER (1971) ★★1/2 A brainwashed agent is programmed to release a deadly virus. The scheme is discovered, and a good guy takes his place to catch the bad guys. Made for television. 73m. **DIR:** Leonard Horn. **CAST:** John Vernon, Steve Ihnat, Fritz Weaver, Edward Binns. **1971**

HUNTER, THE (1980) ★★ An uneven action film that focuses on a modern-day bounty hunter. Steve McQueen plays real-life troubleshooter Ralph "Papa" Thorson. Though old and a bit awkward, Thorson leads—at least on screen—a dangerous, action-filled life. Rated PG. 97m. **DIR:** Buzz Kulik. **CAST:** Steve McQueen, Eli Wallach, LeVar Burton, Ben Johnson, Kathryn Harrold. **1980 DVD**

HUNTER IN THE DARK ★★★ Japan circa 1750: dissatisfied with their corrupt government, Japanese warriors create underground groups that wield Mafia-type power. Some brilliant shots of Ezo, the perfect land acquisition. Letter-boxed, which makes reading subtitles easy. In Japanese with English subtitles. Not rated, contains nudity, violence, and profanity. 138m. **DIR:** Hideo Gosha. **CAST:** Tatsuya Nakadai. **1979**

HUNTER'S BLOOD *Deliverance*, but without any of that film's tension or acting. Rated R for language and violence. 101m. **DIR:** Robert C. Hughes. **CAST:** Sam Bottoms, Clu Gulager, Kim Delaney, Mayf Nutter, Ken Swofford, Joey Travolta. **1987**

HUNTER'S MOON Painful tale of a backwoods Georgia father, played by Burt Reynolds, hunting down the man who loves his daughter. Possibly the worst film Reynolds has ever made. Rated R for adult situations, language, nudity, and violence. 104m. **DIR:** Richard Weinman. **CAST:** Burt Reynolds, Keith Carradine, Hayley DuMond, Pat Hingle, Brian James, Charles Napier. **1999 DVD**

HUNTING ★★★ Torrid drama finds rich, attractive John Savage playing with the emotions of both friends and business associates. When he lures young, married Kerry Armstrong into an affair, blackmail, and murder ensue. Rated R for nudity and violence. 97m. **DIR:** Frank Howson. **CAST:** John Savage, Kerry Armstrong, Guy Pearce, Rebecca Rigg. **1991**

HUNTRESS, THE ★★★ When a woman's bounty-hunter husband is killed, she and her daughter take up the family business to pay off their debts. The result is nonstop comedy and action, as the two women start to bring in the bad guys, as well as look for whoever killed their husband and father. This made-for-cable original is supposedly based on a true story. Not rated; contains violence. 95m. **DIR:** Jeffrey Reiner. **CAST:** Annette O'Toole, Aleksa Palladino, Alanna Ubach, Vicki Lewis, Matthew Glave, Craig T. Nelson. **2000**

HUNTRESS: SPIRIT OF THE NIGHT ★★ A young woman returns to her homeland to claim her ancestral castle—and the family curse. The scary parts aren't scary and the sexy parts aren't anything to write home about either. Rated R for profanity and simulated sex. 86m. **DIR:** Mark S. Manos. **CAST:** Jenna Bodner. **1996**

HURLYBURLY ★★★1/2 David Mamet's acerbic play about Hollywood lowlifes finds its way to the big screen, and the results are just as unsavory. The problem isn't with the performers, who are at their best, but with the characters. There isn't a redeemable one in the bunch, and while it is interesting to watch them self-destruct, the outcome leaves a bad taste in your mouth. Sean Penn is exceptional as the casting director whose party days are getting the best of him. Rated R for adult situations, language, nudity, and violence. 123m. **DIR:** Anthony Drazan. **CAST:** Sean Penn, Kevin Spacey, Robin Wright, Chazz Palminteri, Garry Shandling, Anna Paquin, Meg Ryan. **1998 DVD**

HURRICANE, THE (1937) ★★★ One of early Hollywood's disaster films. The lives and loves of a group of stereotyped characters on a Pacific island are interrupted by the big wind of the title. The sequences involving people are labored, but the special effects of the hurricane make this picture worth watching. B&W; 102m. **DIR:** John Ford. **CAST:** Jon Hall, Dorothy Lamour, Raymond Massey, Mary Astor. **1937**

HURRICANE (1979) Another Dino de Laurentiis misfire, an awful remake of the John Ford classic. Rated PG. 119m. **DIR:** Jan Troell. **CAST:** Jason Robards Jr., Mia Farrow, Dayton Ka'ne, Max von Sydow, Trevor Howard. **1979**

HURRICANE, THE (1999) ★★1/2 Real-life boxer Rubin "Hurricane" Carter was convicted for the 1966 murder of three white bar patrons in Patterson, New Jersey. This film dramatizes his arrest, railroading, and incarceration, and the racism that soiled his case. It features a riveting performance from Denzel Washington, but Carter's complex personality and past feel too sanitized, and the script reinvents and oversimplifies his path to exoneration. Rated R for language and violence. 125m. **DIR:** Norman Jewison. **CAST:** Denzel Washington, Vicellous Reon Shannon, Deborah Unger, Liev Schreiber, John Hannah, Dan Hedaya. **1999 DVD**

HURRICANE EXPRESS ★★ Big John Wayne stars in his second serial for Mascot Pictures and plays an aviator on the trail of the mysterious "Wrecker." This feature, edited down from a twelve-chapter serial, displays a high level of energy and excitement, a great deal of it as a direct result of young Wayne's whole-hearted involvement in this basically simple chase film. B&W; 80m. **DIR:** Armand Schaefer, J. P. McGowan. **CAST:** John Wayne, Tully Marshall, Conway Tearle, Shirley Grey. **1932**

HURRICANE SMITH ★★1/2 Texas tough Carl Weathers blows into Australia like a hurricane when his sister is killed by drug lord Jurgen Prochnow. Watch Carl weather plenty of evil mates, teaching them a *Rocky* lesson in manners. Rated R for violence and nudity. 87m. **DIR:** Colin Budd. **CAST:** Carl Weathers, Jurgen Prochnow, Tony Bonner. **1991**

HURRICANE STREETS ★★ Brendan Sexton III is effective as a street punk desperate for a better life. He agrees to one more score to raise money to relocate to

New Mexico, but things turn sour. Familiar tale gets points for Morgan J. Freeman's direction that attempts to make it all matter. Rated R for language, violence, and adult situations. 86m. **DIR:** Morgan J. Freeman. **CAST:** Brendan Sexton III, Shawn Elliott, L. M. "Kit" Carson, Edie Falco, Antoine McLean, Mtume Gant. **1997**

HURRY UP OR I'LL BE 30 ★★★ Aimless comedy-drama will appeal to those with a fondness for slice-of-life movies. Set in Brooklyn, the movie follows an almost-thirty single guy (John Lefkowitz) who is frustrated over his life. Danny DeVito has a supporting part as a fellow Brooklynite. Rated R for sexual situations and profanity. 88m. **DIR:** Joseph Jacoby. **CAST:** John Lefkowitz, Linda De Coff, Danny DeVito. **1973**

HUSBANDS AND LOVERS 🦃 Seemingly endless and pointless film features Joanna Pacula as a selfish wife who demands weekends off to spend with her abusive lover. Comes in R and unrated versions, both containing violence and nudity. 94m. **DIR:** Mauro Bolognini. **CAST:** Julian Sands, Joanna Pacula, Tcheky Karyo. **1991**

HUSBANDS AND WIVES ★★★1/2 Off-camera events eclipsed this Woody Allen comedy-drama during its initial release, detracting from the power of an often brilliant study of marriages under stress. Judy Davis is simply magnificent as a fault-finding shrew. While the characters are uniformly excellent, the film is severely compromised by Carlo Di Palma's headache-inducing hand-held camera (intended to suggest a documentary approach). Rated R for profanity. 107m. **DIR:** Woody Allen. **CAST:** Woody Allen, Mia Farrow, Judy Davis, Sydney Pollack, Juliette Lewis, Liam Neeson. **1992 DVD**

HUSH ★★★ Jessica Lange ventures into Bette Davis territory playing Martha, the doting and obsessed mother of Jackson. When Jackson brings his girlfriend Helen home to the family horse ranch in Kentucky, Martha sees Helen as a threat to the hold she has on her son. The more Helen learns of the family history, the more she fears for her life. Not grand entertainment, but a cut above the usual Lifetime Channel stuff it resembles. Rated PG-13 for language and violence. 96m. **DIR:** Jonathan Darby. **CAST:** Jessica Lange, Gwyneth Paltrow, Johnathon Schaech, Nina Foch, Debi Mazar. **1998 DVD**

HUSH . . . HUSH, SWEET CHARLOTTE ★★★ Originally planned as a sequel to *What Ever Happened to Baby Jane?*, reuniting stars of that movie Bette Davis and Joan Crawford, this effort was filmed with Bette opposite her old Warner Bros. cellmate—Olivia de Havilland. This time they're on opposite sides of the magnolia bush, with Olivia trying to drive poor Bette, who's not all there to begin with, mad. B&W; 133m. **DIR:** Robert Aldrich. **CAST:** Bette Davis, Olivia de Havilland, Joseph Cotten, Agnes Moorehead, Cecil Kellaway, Mary Astor, Bruce Dern. **1965**

HUSH LITTLE BABY ★★1/2 In this made-for-cable movie, an adopted woman is located by her biological mother. They become friends, but she doesn't know that her mother tried to kill her when she was a child. This so-so film's story has been done much better before. Not rated; contains violence. 95m. **DIR:** Jorge Montesi. **CAST:** Diane Ladd, Wendel Meldrum, Geraint Wyn Davies, Illya Woloshyn, Ingrid Veninger. **1993 DVD**

HUSSY ★★ Both the talented British actress Helen Mirren and director Matthew Chapman (his debut) usually do much better work than in this dreary melodrama about a nightclub hostess and part-time prostitute. Chapman succeeds at re-creating the oppressive atmosphere of a seedy British nightclub all too well. Rated R for nudity. 95m. **DIR:** Matthew Chapman. **CAST:** Helen Mirren, John Shea. **1980**

HUSTLE ★★1/2 *Hustle* reteams director Robert Aldrich and actor Burt Reynolds after their box-office success with *The Longest Yard*. Fine character performances from Eddie Albert, Ernest Borgnine, and Jack Carter help to elevate the macho/action yarn, but it is Academy Award winner Ben Johnson who provides the real show. Rated R. 120m. **DIR:** Robert Aldrich. **CAST:** Burt Reynolds, Catherine Deneuve, Eddie Albert, Ernest Borgnine, Jack Carter, Ben Johnson. **1975**

HUSTLER, THE ★★★★★ This film may well contain Paul Newman's best screen performance. As pool shark Eddie Felson, he's magnificent. A two-bit hustler who travels from pool room to pool room taking suckers—whom he allows to win until the stakes get high enough, then wipes them out—Felson decides to take a shot at the big time. He challenges Minnesota Fats (nicely played by Jackie Gleason) to a big money match. B&W; 135m. **DIR:** Robert Rossen. **CAST:** Paul Newman, Jackie Gleason, Piper Laurie, George C. Scott, Murray Hamilton, Myron McCormick. **1961**

HUSTLING ★★★★ An investigative report delves into the world of big-city prostitution in this adult TV movie. Fine performances and a good script place this above the average TV film. 100m. **DIR:** Joseph Sargent. **CAST:** Lee Remick, Jill Clayburgh, Alex Rocco, Monte Markham. **1975**

HYPE! ★★★ Sympathetic documentary about Seattle's so-called "grunge" music scene, whose explosion in popularity in the early 1990s was less than welcomed by many of the bands involved. Filmmaker Doug Pray captures the essence of rock 'n' roll irony, in which the music is rendered meaningless by success. Give it an extra star if you're a fan of Soundgarden, the Melvins, Pearl Jam, or other bands who appear. Not rated; contains profanity. 84m. **DIR:** Doug Pray. **1997**

HYPER SAPIAN: PEOPLE FROM ANOTHER STAR ★★ Two youngsters from another star system escape their elders to visit Wyoming. Predictable, bland nonsense. Rated PG for violence. 95m. **DIR:** Peter R. Hunt. **CAST:** Ricky Paul Goldin, Sydney Penny, Keenan Wynn, Gail Strickland, Peter Jason. **1986**

HYPNOTIC EYE, THE ★★1/2 Surprisingly sleazy (for its time) thriller in which beautiful women who volunteer to help out in a stage hypnotist's act later mysteriously mutilate themselves. B&W; 79m. **DIR:** George Blair. **CAST:** Jacques Bergerac, Allison Hayes, Marcia Henderson, Merry Anders, Ferdinand Demara. **1960**

HYSTERIA ★★1/2 After their success in remaking old Universal horror movies, the folks at England's Hammer Films decided to try their luck with Hitchcockian suspense. This film is one of the results. Robert Webber plays an American amnesia victim in England. This unrated film contains some mild violence. B&W; 85m. **DIR:** Freddie Francis. **CAST:** Robert Webber, Lelia Goldoni, Maurice Denham, Jennifer Jayne. **1964**

HYSTERICAL ★★ Zany horror spoof generates a sprinkling of laughs. This movie was supposed to make the Hudson Brothers the Marx Brothers of the 1980s. Rated PG. 87m. **DIR:** Chris Bearde. **CAST:** William Hudson, Mark Hudson, Brett Hudson, Cindy Pickett, Richard Kiel, Julie Newmar, Bud Cort, Robert Donner, Murray Hamilton, Clint Walker. **1983 DVD**

I

I AM A CAMERA ★★★1/2 Julie Harris is perfect as the easy, good-time English bohemian Sally Bowles in this finely honed film clone of the play adapted by John Van Druten from novelist Christopher Isherwood's autobiographical stories about pre–World War II Berlin. The Broadway and screen versions ultimately became the musical *Cabaret*. 98m. **DIR:** Henry Cornelius. **CAST:** Julie Harris, Laurence Harvey, Shelley Winters, Ron Randell, Patrick McGoohan. **1955**

I AM A FUGITIVE FROM A CHAIN GANG ★★★★ Dark, disturbing, and effective Paul Muni vehicle. The star plays an innocent man who finds himself convicted of a crime and brutalized by a corrupt court system. An unforgettable film. B&W; 90m. **DIR:** Mervyn LeRoy. **CAST:** Paul Muni, Glenda Farrell, Helen Vinson, Preston Foster. **1932**

I AM CUBA ★★★★★ It's the artistry—not the politics—that makes this dreamy, somber propaganda film so exhilarating. This Russian-Cuban "friendship project" was to glorify the isle's liberation from Batista's dictatorship and Ugly Americanism. It ended up emphasizing a visually poetic style rather than romanticizing Communism. In Spanish, Russian, and dubbed English with English subtitles. Not rated. 141m. **DIR:** Mikhail K. Kalatozov. **CAST:** Luz Maria Collazo, Jose Gallardo, Sergio Corrieri, Mario Gonzales Broche, Raul Garcia, Jean Bouise, Celia Rodriguez, Luisa Maria Jimenez. **1964 DVD**

I AM CURIOUS BLUE ★★ Both *I Am Curious Yellow* and *Blue* were derived from the same footage, shot by director Vilgot Sjoman in the late Sixties. When the finished product turned out to be too long, he turned it into two movies instead. Ergo, *Curious Blue* is less a sequel than simply more of the same meandering inquiry into social issues, punctuated by an occasional naked body. In Swedish with English subtitles. Not rated; the movie features frank but unerotic sex. B&W; 103m. **DIR:** Vilgot Sjoman. **CAST:** Lena Nyman, Vilgot Sjoman, Borje Ahlstedt. **1968**

I AM CURIOUS YELLOW ★1/2 This Swedish import caused quite an uproar when it was released in the mid-1960s, because of its frontal nudity and sexual content. It seems pretty dull today. There isn't much of a plot built around the escapades of a young Swedish sociologist whose goal in life appears to be having sex in as many weird places as she can. In Swedish with English subtitles. B&W; 121m. **DIR:** Vilgot Sjoman. **CAST:** Lena Nyman, Borje Ahlstedt. **1967**

•**I AM SAM** ★★★ *Rain Man* meets *Kramer vs. Kramer* as Sam Dawson, a Starbucks busboy with the mental capability of a 7-year-old, raises his angelic, preciously precocious daughter until Social Services attempts to place her in a foster home. The emotional and legal struggles that ensue become contrived and message-heavy as a glamorous, upscale attorney, who has child-care issues of her own, carries Sam's torch into the courtroom. Excellent acting elevates the film above its sentimental, soap-opera platitudes in a daunting search for heart and truth. Rated PG-13 for mature themes and profanity. 130m. **DIR:** Jessie Nelson. **CAST:** Sean Penn, Michelle Pfeiffer, Dakota Fanning, Dianne Wiest. **2001 DVD**

I AM THE CHEESE ★★1/2 A teenager who has witnessed the death of his parents is confined to a psychiatric hospital where doctors try to get him to deal with his tragedy. The dime-store psychology is the only drawback to this well-played movie. Rated PG. 95m. **DIR:** Robert Jiras. **CAST:** Robert MacNaughton, Hope Lange, Don Murray, Robert Wagner, Cynthia Nixon, Lee Richardson. **1983**

I AM THE LAW ★★★ This slick but somewhat silly crime melodrama stars Edward G. Robinson as a crusading district attorney out to get a group of mobsters headed by a corrupt civic leader. B&W; 83m. **DIR:** Alexander Hall. **CAST:** Edward G. Robinson, Barbara O'Neil, John Beal, Wendy Barrie, Otto Kruger, Marc Lawrence. **1938**

I BURY THE LIVING ★★1/2 Rash of sudden deaths among cemetery plot owners gives mortuary manager Richard Boone grave suspicions he has the power to "put the lid" on his clients. Murder mystery with supernatural overtones is complemented by imaginative design and cinematography. B&W; 76m. **DIR:** Albert Band. **CAST:** Richard Boone, Theodore Bikel, Peggy Maurer, Herbert Anderson. **1958 DVD**

I, CLAUDIUS ★★★★★ This PBS series brilliantly recounts the history of the Roman Empire—the reign of Augustus, the infamous cruelty of Tiberius and his successor, Caligula, and the reign of the mild and amiable Claudius. One of the most popular *Masterpiece Theater* presentations. 780m. **DIR:** Herbert Wise. **CAST:** Derek Jacobi, Sian Phillips, Brian Blessed, John Hurt. **1976 DVD**

I COME IN PEACE ★★ Ridiculous subplot involving a preppie gang mars the first half of this sci-fi adventure. Dolph Lundgren must stop an alien's murderous rampage. The alien's method of sucking the endorphins of his victims' brains is pretty disgusting. Rated R for violence and gore. 90m. **DIR:** Craig R. Baxley. **CAST:** Dolph Lundgren, Brian Benben, Betsy Brantley. **1990**

I CONFESS ★★★ In spite of shortcomings, this is the film that best reflects many of Hitch's puritanical ethics. Montgomery Clift stars as a priest who takes confession from a man who—coincidentally—killed a blackmailer who knew of Clift's prevows relationship with Anne Baxter. (Whew!) Moody and atmospheric. B&W; 95m. **DIR:** Alfred Hitchcock. **CAST:** Montgomery Clift, Karl Malden, Anne Baxter, Brian Aherne. **1953**

I COULD GO ON SINGING ★★★ In this, her last film, with a disturbing true-to-her-life plot, Judy Garland plays a successful concert singer beset by personal problems. When Judy sings, the film lives. When she

doesn't, it's wistful, teary, and a bit sloppy. Strictly for Garland fanatics. 99m. **DIR:** Ronald Neame. **CAST:** Judy Garland, Dirk Bogarde, Jack Klugman, Aline MacMahon. **1963**

I COVER THE WATERFRONT ★★★ One, and one of the better, of a spate of newspaper stories that vied with gangster films on 1930s screens. In this one, a ruthless fisherman who smuggles Chinese into the United States doesn't think twice about pushing them overboard when approached by the Coast Guard. Claudette Colbert is his innocent daughter. Ace reporter Ben Lyon courts her in an effort to get at the truth. B&W; 70m. **DIR:** James Cruze. **CAST:** Claudette Colbert, Ernest Torrence, Ben Lyon, Wilfred Lucas, George Humbert. **1933**

I DIED A THOUSAND TIMES ★★1/2 Color remake of Raoul Walsh's *High Sierra* features Jack Palance as Mad Dog Earle, whose criminal tendencies are softened by a young woman (Lori Nelson) who needs surgery in order to lead a normal life. 110m. **DIR:** Stuart Heisler. **CAST:** Jack Palance, Shelley Winters, Lee Marvin, Lori Nelson, Earl Holliman, Lon Chaney Jr. **1955**

I DISMEMBER MAMA 🦃 Great title—horrible movie. Rated R for violence and nudity. 86m. **DIR:** Paul Leder. **CAST:** Zooey Hall, Greg Mullavey. **1972**

I DO! I DO! ★★★★ Lee Remick and Hal Linden step into the parts originally created on Broadway by Mary Martin and Robert Preston in this video of a performance taped before an audience. The play deals with the marriage of Michael to Agnes—from the night before their wedding to the day when they leave their home of forty years. Solid entertainment. 116m. **DIR:** Gower Champion. **CAST:** Lee Remick, Hal Linden. **1982**

I DON'T BUY KISSES ANYMORE ★★★1/2 Sweetheart of a romantic comedy. Jason Alexander stars as an overweight shoe salesman who thinks he's hit pay dirt when a college student shows an interest in him. What blossoms is true love and a film that revels in that celebration. Rated PG. 112m. **DIR:** Robert Mascarelli. **CAST:** Jason Alexander, Nia Peeples, Eileen Brennan, Lainie Kazan, Lou Jacobi. **1991**

I DON'T WANT TO TALK ABOUT IT ★★ On her daughter's second birthday, a wealthy Latin American widow plunges into denial that her only child is a dwarf and pressures town locals to never discuss the girl's small stature. Enter a mysterious, melancholy stranger who disrupts her reluctance to face reality. This languid contemplation of the mysteries of love, set in the 1930s, attempts to build with a fablelike tone, but never plumbs the full passion or depth of its characters. In Spanish with English subtitles. Rated PG-13. 102m. **DIR:** Maria Luisa Bemberg. **CAST:** Alejandra Podesta, Luisina Brando, Marcello Mastroianni. **1994**

I DOOD IT ★★1/2 A musical based on an old Buster Keaton silent comedy about a tailor's assistant (Red Skelton) going gaga over a dancer (Eleanor Powell). Powell's tap dancing is especially noteworthy. B&W; 102m. **DIR:** Vincente Minnelli. **CAST:** Red Skelton, Eleanor Powell, Lena Horne, Hazel Scott, Butterfly McQueen, Helen O'Connell, Bob Eberly, Sam Levene, John Hodiak, Morris Ankrum, Thurston Hall. **1943**

I DREAM TOO MUCH ★★1/2 This picture is more of a showcase for Lily Pons's vocal abilities in the operetta form. Henry Fonda and Pons are two performers who face career obstacles. The music is okay. B&W; 95m. **DIR:** John Cromwell. **CAST:** Henry Fonda, Lily Pons, Lucille Ball, Eric Blore. **1935**

I DREAMED OF AFRICA ★★1/2 An Italian divorcée homesteads on a farm in Africa with her new husband and young son. Based on the memoirs of Kuki Gallmann, the film plods monotonously through two decades on the veldt without working up much dramatic momentum. The earnest acting and beautiful African scenery help somewhat. Rated PG-13 for mild profanity and brief violence. 112m. **DIR:** Hugh Hudson. **CAST:** Kim Basinger, Vincent Perez, Eva Marie Saint, Liam Aiken, Winston Ntshona. **2000 DVD**

I DRINK YOUR BLOOD ★★1/2 Devil worshipers go berserk after they are fed the blood of a rabid dog. Ferociously violent film with elements of social commentary was severely cut after being threatened with an X rating: the restored version is available on video. Not rated; contains extreme violence and nudity. 83m. **DIR:** David E. Durston. **CAST:** Bhaskar, Jadine Wong, Ronda Fultz. **1971**

I GOT THE HOOK UP 🦃 Two low-life hustlers get into trouble when they sell off a carload of stolen cellular phones. Crude, racist, sexist, and abominably acted, this sorry mess is strictly for die-hard fans of hip-hop artist Master P, who starred and directed. Rated R for brief drug use, nudity, and incessant profanity. 94m. **DIR:** Michael Martin, Master P. **CAST:** Master P, A. J. Johnson, Gretchen Palmer, Tom "Tiny" Lister Jr., John Witherspoon. **1998 DVD**

I HEARD THE OWL CALL MY NAME ★★★1/2 In this mystical tale of love and courage, Tom Courtenay beautifully portrays Father Mark Brian, a young Anglican priest whose bishop, played by Dean Jagger, sends him to make his mark. He finds himself among the proud Indians of the Northwest. Rated G. 79m. **DIR:** Daryl Duke. **CAST:** Tom Courtenay, Dean Jagger, Paul Stanley. **1973**

I KNOW WHAT YOU DID LAST SUMMER ★★ Two teen couples have late-night sex on a North Carolina beach and then crash their car into a pedestrian on the way home. They dump the body off a pier to avoid legal hassles (their vehicle reeks of spilled booze) and swear not to discuss the incident with anyone—or even among themselves. Their secret comes back to stalk them literally in a dumb, brutal slasher movie that has huge morality play ambitions. Rated R for violence, language, nudity, and sex. 96m. **DIR:** Jim Gillespie. **CAST:** Jennifer Love Hewitt, Sarah Michelle Gellar, Ryan Philippe, Freddie Prinze Jr., Anne Heche. **1997 DVD**

I KNOW WHY THE CAGED BIRD SINGS ★★★1/2 Based on writer Maya Angelou's memoirs of her early life in the Depression years in the South. Often very touching and effective, this made-for-TV film details the author's reaction to her parents' divorce and the struggle of her grandparents to raise her and her brother. 100m. **DIR:** Fielder Cook. **CAST:** Diahann Carroll, Ruby Dee, Esther Rolle, Roger E. Mosley. **1979**

I LIKE IT LIKE THAT ★★1/2 An independent-minded Bronx woman takes a job in a record company to support her family after her bike-messenger husband is jailed for looting during a blackout. She's got three rowdy kids, a transvestite brother, and an overbearing

mother-in-law in this scrappy, randy take on ethnic neighborhood life where everyone is either sharing door stoops, lunging at each other's throats, or both. Gritty, comic, but uninvolving. Rated R for language, nudity, and simulated sex. 106m. **DIR:** Darnell Martin. **CAST:** Lauren Velez, Jon Seda, Lisa Vidal, Griffin Dunne, Rita Moreno. **1994**

I LIVE MY LIFE ★★★ A wealthy young woman falls in love with an archaeologist while on a cruise. Charming romantic drama. B&W; 97m. **DIR:** W. S. Van Dyke. **CAST:** Joan Crawford, Brian Aherne, Frank Morgan, Aline MacMahon. **1935**

I LIVE WITH ME DAD ★★★ Yes, the title is correct. That's what a poor Australian boy keeps repeating to the various child-welfare and police authorities who try to take him from his father. Not rated. 86m. **DIR:** Paul Moloney. **CAST:** Haydon Samuels, Rebecca Gibney. **1985**

I LOVE LUCY (TV SERIES) ★★★★★ The archetypical TV sitcom. Domestic squabbles have never been more entertaining. Ricky's accent and temper, Lucy's schemes and ambitions, Ethel's submissiveness, Fred's parsimoniousness, all added up to surefire hilarity. Classic moments include Lucy and Ethel toiling in a chocolate factory, Lucy stomping grapes, Lucy meeting William Holden, Ricky getting the news that he's a father, and Lucy selling a health tonic. 48m. **DIR:** William Asher. **CAST:** Lucille Ball, Desi Arnaz Sr., Vivian Vance, William Frawley. **1951–1956**

I LOVE MELVIN ★★★ Entertaining little MGM musical has Donald O'Connor pretending to be a man with connections so he can have a chance with perky Debbie Reynolds. The story is slight, but the laughs and songs are good, and O'Connor and Reynolds work well together. Entertaining and amusing. 76m. **DIR:** Don Weis. **CAST:** Debbie Reynolds, Donald O'Connor, Una Merkel, Allyn Joslyn, Noreen Corcoran, Richard Anderson, Jim Backus, Barbara Ruick. **1953**

I LOVE MY WIFE 🦃 The problems of an upper-class couple and their ridiculous attempts to solve them. Rated PG. 95m. **DIR:** Mel Stuart. **CAST:** Elliott Gould, Brenda Vaccaro, Angel Tompkins, Dabney Coleman, Joan Tompkins. **1970**

I LOVE N.Y. 🦃 Scott Baio plays a hotheaded photographer who falls for a famous actor's daughter. Rated R for profanity. 100m. **DIR:** Alan Smithee. **CAST:** Scott Baio, Christopher Plummer, Jennifer O'Neill. **1988**

I LOVE TROUBLE ★★★ Uneven mix of suspense-thriller and romantic comedy comes up short because of the lack of real chemistry between Julia Roberts and Nick Nolte, reporters from competing Chicago newspapers who solve the mystery of a derailed train. Still, there are enough effective moments to make it watchable. Rated PG for violence and profanity. 123m. **DIR:** Charles Shyer. **CAST:** Julia Roberts, Nick Nolte, Saul Rubinek, James Rebhorn, Robert Loggia, Kelly Rutherford, Olympia Dukakis, Marsha Mason, Eugene Levy, Charles Martin Smith. **1994 DVD**

I LOVE YOU AGAIN ★★★★ Master con artist William Powell awakes from a nine-year bout of amnesia and learns he has become a stuffy but successful small-town businessman about to be divorced by wife Myrna Loy. He recalls nothing of the nine years, yet wants to win back his wife and pull an oil scam on the town. Witty dialogue, hilarious situations, and just plain fun. B&W; 99m. **DIR:** W. S. Van Dyke. **CAST:** William Powell, Myrna Loy, Frank McHugh, Edmund Lowe, Carl "Alfalfa" Switzer. **1940**

I LOVE YOU ALICE B. TOKLAS! ★★★ Peter Sellers plays a lawyer-cum-hippie in this far-out comedy about middle-age crisis. Rated PG. 93m. **DIR:** Hy Averback. **CAST:** Peter Sellers, Leigh Taylor-Young, Jo Van Fleet. **1968**

I LOVE YOU, DON'T TOUCH ME! ★★★ A young woman looks for love in several wrong places, never having the good sense until the final fade-out to fall for the swell guy who adores her. An overfamiliar story is given a pleasant polish (and a welcome female perspective) by writer-director Julie Davis in her feature debut, aided immensely by the attractive performances of Marla Schaffel and Mitchell Whitfield in the two leads. Rated R for profanity and sexual scenes. 85m. **DIR:** Julie Davis. **CAST:** Marla Schaffel, Mitchell Whitfield, Meredith Scott Lynn, Michael Harris, Darryl Theirse. **1998**

I LOVE YOU (EU TE AMO) ★★★ This release, starring Brazilian sexpot Sonia Braga, is a high-class hardcore—though not close-up—sex film with pretensions of being a work of art. And if that turns you on, go for it. Not rated, the film has nudity and profanity. 104m. **DIR:** Arnaldo Jabor. **CAST:** Sonia Braga, Paulo Cesar Pereio. **1982**

I LOVE YOU TO DEATH ★★★★ Offbeat true-life murder comedy, in which loving wife Tracey Ullman decides to dispatch philandering husband Kevin Kline with the help of her mom (Joan Plowright), an admirer (River Phoenix), and two stoned-out hit men (William Hurt and Keanu Reeves). Funny, but not for all tastes. Rated R for profanity and violence. 96m. **DIR:** Lawrence Kasdan. **CAST:** Kevin Kline, Tracey Ullman, Joan Plowright, River Phoenix, William Hurt, Keanu Reeves, James Gammon, Victoria Jackson. **1990**

I, MADMAN ★★ A bookstore employee (Jenny Wright) becomes so engrossed in a horror novel that she begins living its terrors. This film provides the same kind of tacky entertainment found in such masterpieces of ineptitude as *Plan 9 from Outer Space* and *Robot Monster.* Rated R for violence, simulated sex, and profanity. 95m. **DIR:** Tibor Takacs. **CAST:** Jenny Wright, Clayton Rohner. **1989**

I MARRIED A CENTERFOLD ★★1/2 When a nerdish engineer bets $500 that he can meet Miss November, a centerfold, he not only finds her, but the two fall in love. Made for TV. 100m. **DIR:** Peter Werner. **CAST:** Teri Copley, Timothy Daly, Diane Ladd, Anson Williams. **1984**

I MARRIED A MONSTER ★★ Campy sci-fi flick about an alien race that comes to Earth to impregnate women. Noteworthy for some fine, unintentionally hilarious moments. Rated PG-13 for violence. 90m. **DIR:** Nancy Malone. **CAST:** Richard Burgi, Susan Walters, Tim Ryan, Richard Herd, Barbara Niven. **1998**

I MARRIED A MONSTER FROM OUTER SPACE ★★★ This riveting story is about aliens who duplicate their bodies in the form of Earth men in hopes of repopulating their planet. One earthwoman who unknowingly marries one of the aliens discovers the secret, but can't get anyone to believe her. B&W; 78m. **DIR:** Gene Fowler

Jr. **CAST:** Tom Tryon, Gloria Talbott, Ken Lynch, Maxie Rosenbloom. **1958**

I MARRIED A STRANGE PERSON ★★★★ Bill Plympton wrote, directed, and animated this hilarious venture into the surreal that involves a man with a very mundane existence. While watching television, a peculiar boil grows on the back of his neck—one that gives the man the power to bring whatever he thinks of into reality. This turns his marriage upside down, and now, the evil Smiley Corporation wants this fantastic power for itself. Witty and original, this bizarre tale is full of laughs and classic Bill Plympton animation techniques. Rated R for animated sex, violence, and language. 73m. **DIR:** Bill Plympton. **1997 DVD**

I MARRIED A VAMPIRE 🦃 Boring nonsense, more about a country girl's adventures in the big city than a horror flick. 85m. **DIR:** Jay Raskin. **CAST:** Rachel Golden, Brendan Hickey. **1983**

I MARRIED A WITCH ★★★1/2 The whimsy of humorist Thorne Smith (the author of *Topper*) shows its age, but watching Veronica Lake and Fredric March perform together is a treat in this very pre-*Bewitched* farce. Look for Susan Hayward in a small role. B&W; 76m. **DIR:** René Clair. **CAST:** Veronica Lake, Fredric March, Cecil Kellaway, Robert Benchley. **1942**

I MARRIED A WOMAN ★★ George Gobel plays an advertising man who is having difficulty holding on to both his biggest account and his wife, who feels he's not paying her enough attention. Angie Dickinson and John Wayne have walk-on parts. B&W/color; 80m. **DIR:** Hal Kanter. **CAST:** George Gobel, Diana Dors, Adolphe Menjou, Jessie Royce Landis, Nita Talbot, William Redfield, John McGiver. **1958**

I MARRIED AN ANGEL ★★ In this, their final film together, playboy Nelson Eddy dreams he courts and marries angel Jeanette MacDonald. *Leaden* and *bizarre* are but two of the words critics used. B&W; 84m. **DIR:** W. S. Van Dyke. **CAST:** Jeanette MacDonald, Nelson Eddy, Edward Everett Horton, Binnie Barnes, Reginald Owen. **1942**

I MARRIED JOAN (TV SERIES) ★★★ Joan Davis, following the popularity of *I Love Lucy*, starred in this sitcom involving a goofy housewife and the judge she married. B&W; 80m. **DIR:** Philip Rapp, Marc Daniels. **CAST:** Joan Davis, Jim Backus. **1952–1953**

I, MOBSTER ★★★1/2 Fast-moving gangster story recounted by mob boss Steve Cochran, looking back on his career while he testifies before the Senate Rackets Committee. Familiar stuff, but well-made. B&W; 81m. **DIR:** Roger Corman. **CAST:** Steve Cochran, Lita Milan, Robert Strauss, Celia Lovsky, Lili St. Cyr, Yvette Vickers, Robert Shayne. **1958**

I NEVER PROMISED YOU A ROSE GARDEN ★★★1/2 Kathleen Quinlan plays a schizophrenic teenager seeking treatment from a dedicated psychiatrist in this well-acted but depressing drama. Rated R. 96m. **DIR:** Anthony Page. **CAST:** Bibi Andersson, Kathleen Quinlan, Diane Varsi. **1977 DVD**

I NEVER SANG FOR MY FATHER ★★★★1/2 A depressing but finely crafted film about a man (Gene Hackman) who must deal with the care of his elderly father (Melvyn Douglas). Everyone in this touching film does a superb job. Based on a play of the same name by Robert Anderson. Rated PG. 93m. **DIR:** Gilbert Cates. **CAST:** Melvyn Douglas, Gene Hackman, Estelle Parsons, Dorothy Stickney. **1970**

I ONLY WANT YOU TO LOVE ME ★★★★ Fans of prolific but short-lived German filmmaker Rainer Werner Fassbinder shouldn't miss this rarely-seen film, made for German television. Like much of his work, it deals with the stress of modern life on someone who can't handle it, in this case a young lawyer who gets in over his head while trying to impress his unfeeling father. Not rated. In German with English subtitles. 104m. **DIR:** Rainer Werner Fassbinder. **CAST:** Vitus Zeplichal, Elke Aberle, Ernie Mangold. **1976**

I OUGHT TO BE IN PICTURES ★★★★ Neil Simon's best work since *The Goodbye Girl*, this heartwarming story stars Walter Matthau as a father who deserts his Brooklyn family. Dinah Manoff is the daughter who wants to be a movie star, and Ann-Margret is the woman who brings the two together. Rated PG for mild profanity and brief nudity. 107m. **DIR:** Herbert Ross. **CAST:** Walter Matthau, Ann-Margret, Dinah Manoff. **1982**

I POSED FOR PLAYBOY 🦃 Three women pose nude and must live with the repercussions. Slow, bland, and listless melodrama. Rated R for nudity and profanity. 103m. **DIR:** Stephen Stafford. **CAST:** Lynda Carter, Michele Greene, Amanda Peterson. **1991**

I REMEMBER MAMA ★★★1/2 Irene Dunne is Mama in this sentimental drama about an engaging Norwegian family in San Francisco. Definitely a feel-good film for the nostalgic-minded. Hearts of gold all the way! B&W; 148m. **DIR:** George Stevens. **CAST:** Irene Dunne, Barbara Bel Geddes, Oscar Homolka, Philip Dorn, Ellen Corby. **1948**

I SEE A DARK STRANGER ★★★1/2 Known in Great Britain as *The Adventuress*, this delightful picture tells of a high-strung yet charming Irish girl who, hating the British, helps a Nazi spy during World War II. Wry humor serves as counterpoint to the suspense. A class act. B&W; 98m. **DIR:** Frank Launder. **CAST:** Deborah Kerr, Trevor Howard, Raymond Huntley, Liam Redmond. **1947**

I SENT A LETTER TO MY LOVE ★★★ Simone Signoret and Jean Rochefort star as sister and brother in this absorbing study of love, devotion, loneliness, and frustration. After Signoret places a personal ad (requesting male companionship) in the local paper, Rochefort responds—and they begin a correspondence, via mail, that brings passion and hope to their otherwise empty lives. In French with English subtitles. 96m. **DIR:** Moshe Mizrahi. **CAST:** Simone Signoret, Jean Rochefort, Delphine Seyrig. **1981**

I SHOT A MAN IN VEGAS ★★ Four young people try to reconstruct the events leading up to the shooting death of their friend as they drive across the Nevada desert with his corpse in the trunk. Talky film filled with clunky dialogue, implausible plot revelations, and characters you wouldn't want to be stuck with in a car. Rated R for violence, adult situations, and language. 80m. **DIR:** Keoni Waxman. **CAST:** John Stockwell, Janeane Garofalo, Brian Dillinger, David Cubitt. **1995**

I SHOT ANDY WARHOL ★★★ More interested in recreating the surface sheen of Warhol's 1960s art scene than in understanding his coterie of cronies, Mary Harron's movie is a pretty conventional period piece, considering its outrageous subject matter. Lili Taylor is fe-

rocious as the mad, radical-feminist genius who did the title deed, but it's a performance that eventually wears on more than it illuminates. Not rated; contains foul language, drug use, and sex, with some minor violence and nudity. 106m. **DIR:** Mary Harron. **CAST:** Lili Taylor, Jared Harris, Stephen Dorff, Martha Plimpton. **1996 DVD**

I SPIT ON YOUR CORPSE 🦃 A team of larcenous females goes on a killing spree across the country. Not rated; contains nudity and violence. 88m. **DIR:** Al Adamson. **CAST:** Georgina Spelvin. **1974**

I SPIT ON YOUR GRAVE 🦃 After being brutally raped by a gang of thugs (one of whom is retarded), a young woman takes sadistic revenge. Most videotapes of this title contain the longer X-rated version. Rated R or X. 88m. **DIR:** Meir Zarchi. **CAST:** Camille Keaton. **1981 DVD**

I SPY (TV SERIES) ★★★★ Remember Bill Cosby before terminal cuteness and a bank account the size of Guam overwhelmed him? This classic TV series will remind you of his charm and ability. It also focuses much-deserved attention on the colossally cool and clever Robert Culp. There's plenty of fun and suspense as spies Kelly Robinson and Alexander Scott, under the guise of tennis pro and trainer, do battle against the international forces of evil. 60m. **DIR:** Richard C. Sarafian, Paul Wendkos. **CAST:** Robert Culp, Bill Cosby. **1965–1968 DVD**

I STAND CONDEMNED ★★★ A jealous suitor frames a rival in order to have a clear field for the affections of the woman both love. Not much here, except a young and dashing Laurence Olivier in one of his first films. B&W; 75m. **DIR:** Anthony Asquith. **CAST:** Harry Baur, Laurence Olivier, Robert Cochran. **1935**

I STILL KNOW WHAT YOU DID LAST SUMMER ★★ Although its predecessor contained a modicum of wit, genuine suspense, and restraint, this sequel is a bland, body-count endurance test which doesn't even try for logic or common sense as that guy with the baling hook is still after poor Jennifer Love Hewitt. Viewers can safely assume that any ancillary character is guaranteed to be impaled. Rated R for violence, gore, drug use, and profanity. 96m. **DIR:** Danny Cannon. **CAST:** Jennifer Love Hewitt, Freddie Prinze Jr., Brandy, Mekhi Phifer, Muse Watson, Bill Cobbs, Jeffrey Combs, Jennifer Esposito. **1998 DVD**

I, THE JURY 🦃 Armand Assante is a passable Mike Hammer in this sleazy hybrid of James Bond and *Death Wish II*. Rated R. 111m. **DIR:** Richard T. Heffron. **CAST:** Armand Assante, Barbara Carrera, Alan King. **1982**

I THINK I DO 🦃 College pals reunite several years after graduation as gay and straight romances blossom and crumble in awkward cliché-laden episodes. Rated R for sexuality, language, and drug use. 94m. **DIR:** Brian Sloan. **CAST:** Alexis Arquette, Christian Maelen, Tuc Watkins, Lauren Velez, Marianne Hagan. **1998 DVD**

I VITELLONI ★★★★ Five men in a small town on the Adriatic become discontented and restless. Stunning cinematography highlights this consideration of rootlessness, a central theme that runs throughout Fellini's work. In Italian with English subtitles. B&W; 104m. **DIR:** Federico Fellini. **CAST:** Franco Interlenghi, Alberto Sordi, Franco Fabrizi. **1953**

I WAKE UP SCREAMING ★★★ Laird Cregar's performance as a menacing and sinister detective bent on convicting an innocent Victor Mature for the murder of Carole Landis dominates this suspense-filled *film noir*. Betty Grable is surprisingly effective in her first nonmusical role as the victim's sister, who finds herself attracted to the chief suspect. A classy whodunit. B&W; 82m. **DIR:** H. Bruce Humberstone. **CAST:** Betty Grable, Victor Mature, Carole Landis, Laird Cregar, William Gargan. **1941**

I WALKED WITH A ZOMBIE ★★★★1/2 Director Jacques Tourneur made this classic horror film, involving voodoo and black magic, on an island in the Pacific. One of the best of its kind, this is a great Val Lewton production. B&W; 69m. **DIR:** Jacques Tourneur. **CAST:** Frances Dee, Tom Conway, James Ellison. **1943**

I WANNA HOLD YOUR HAND ★★★ A group of New Jersey teens try to get tickets to the Beatles' first appearance on the *Ed Sullivan Show*. This was one of the biggest money losers of 1978, but it's not that bad. Fast-paced and energetic, with a nice sense of period and some fine performances. Rated PG. 104m. **DIR:** Robert Zemeckis. **CAST:** Nancy Allen, Bobby DiCicco, Marc McClure, Theresa Saldana, Eddie Deezen, Will Jordan, Wendie Jo Sperber. **1978**

I WANT TO LIVE! ★★★ Pulling all stops out, Susan Hayward won an Oscar playing antiheroine B-girl Barbara Graham in this shattering real-life drama. Stupidly involved in a robbery-murder, Graham was indicted, railroaded to conviction, and executed at California's infamous San Quentin State Prison in 1955. To sit through this one you have to be steel-nerved or supremely callous, or both. B&W; 120m. **DIR:** Robert Wise. **CAST:** Susan Hayward, Simon Oakland, Virginia Vincent, Theodore Bikel. **1958 DVD**

I WANT WHAT I WANT ★★ The search for emotional and sexual identity is the focal point of this British production about a man who undergoes a sex-change operation and falls in love. Although the subject matter is still controversial today, this film is remarkably tame. 97m. **DIR:** John Dexter. **CAST:** Anne Heywood, Harry Andrews, Jill Bennett, Michael Coles, Nigel Flatley. **1972**

I WANT YOU ★★1/2 Michael Winterbottom's psychological thriller delivers lots of sexual heat and tension, but is so muddled you want to throw your arms up in surrender. Rachel Weisz is stunning as Helen, a shy hairdresser who has become the obsession of a teenage mute boy. After sabotaging her previous relationships, the young man meets his match when one of Helen's former lovers returns. Winterbottom lines the film with dark, twisted secrets and revelations, delivered with a heavy hand and little flair. Rated R for adult situations, language, nudity, and violence. 87m. **DIR:** Michael Winterbottom. **CAST:** Rachel Weisz, Alessandro Nivola, Luka Petrusic, Labina Mitevska. **1998**

I WAS A MALE WAR BRIDE ★★★★ Cary Grant plays Henri Rochard, a real-life French officer who married an American WAC in post–World War II Germany just as she was to return to the United States. A great farce from beginning to end, with Grant a riot in drag attempting to board a ship full of war brides bound for America. B&W; 105m. **DIR:** Howard Hawks. **CAST:**

Cary Grant, Ann Sheridan, Marion Marshall, Kenneth Tobey. **1949**

I WAS A TEENAGE FRANKENSTEIN ★★ A descendant of the infamous Dr. Frankenstein sets up shop in America and pieces together a new creature out of hotrod-driving teenagers. This follow-up to *I Was A Teenage Werewolf* is campy fun with mad scientist Whit Bissell uttering lines like "Answer me, you fool! I know you have a civil tongue in your head. I sewed it there myself!" B&W/color; 72m. **DIR:** Herbert L. Strock. **CAST:** Whit Bissell, Phyllis Coates, Robert Burton, Gary Conway. **1957**

I WAS A TEENAGE WEREWOLF ★★1/2 All things considered (the low budget, the demands of the teen/drive-in genre), this is a pretty good exploitation monster movie. Buoyed by Michael Landon's passionate performance and Gene Fowler Jr.'s energetic direction (which opens the film with a fist thrown straight at the audience). B&W; 70m. **DIR:** Gene Fowler Jr. **CAST:** Michael Landon, Yvonne Lime, Whit Bissell. **1957**

I WAS A TEENAGE ZOMBIE 🦃 A drug pusher is murdered and his body thrown into a river contaminated by a nuclear power plant. Not rated; contains violence, adult language, and brief nudity. 90m. **DIR:** John Elias Michalakis. **CAST:** Michael Rubin, Steve McCoy. **1986 DVD**

I WAS A ZOMBIE FOR THE FBI ★★ Intentionally (and sometimes winningly) campy satire about alien invaders who pollute the world's soft drink industry while seeking a top-secret cola formula. Contains a hokey, claymation monster and granite-jaw acting. B&W; 105m. **DIR:** Marius Penczner. **CAST:** James Raspberry, Larry Raspberry. **1982**

I WAS STALIN'S BODYGUARD ★★★★1/2 Fascinating, controversial documentary about the last surviving personal bodyguard of Josef Stalin. Filmmaker Semeon Arranovitch brilliantly weaves together firsthand testimony with rare footage, including Stalin's home movies, creating a penetrating glimpse into a violent, repressive era of the Soviet Union. In Russian with English subtitles. Not rated. 73m. **DIR:** Semeon Arranovitch. **1990**

I WENT DOWN ★★★ This wry Irish crime-comedy is an entertaining road movie featuring two mismatched hoods, hard luck ex-con Gil and hardcore goon Bunny. This shaggy-dog tale is more talk than action and lightly peppered with impending retribution. Rated R for language, violence, nudity, and suggested sex. 107m. **DIR:** Paddy Breathnach. **CAST:** Peter McDonald, Tony Doyle, Brendan Gleeson, Peter Caffrey. **1998**

I WILL FIGHT NO MORE FOREVER ★★★1/2 Effective and affecting story of how the Nez Percé Indian tribe, under Chief Joseph, were driven to war with the U.S. government in 1877. The Nez Percé tied up five thousand troops for more than eight months, even though fighting with only a hundred able-bodied warriors. Ned Romero is superb as the proud but wise Chief Joseph, and James Whitmore turns in a fine performance as the craggy General Howard. Made for TV. 106m. **DIR:** Richard T. Heffron. **CAST:** Ned Romero, James Whitmore, Sam Elliott, Linda Redfern. **1975**

I WILL, I WILL . . . FOR NOW 🦃 A Santa Barbara sex clinic where "nothing is unnatural." Rated R. 96m. **DIR:** Norman Panama. **CAST:** Elliott Gould, Diane Keaton, Paul Sorvino, Victoria Principal, Robert Alda, Warren Berlinger. **1976**

I WORSHIP HIS SHADOW 🦃 The first of a four-part film, *Tales from a Parallel Universe*, made for cable television, this overwrought space opera–parody gives every indication of having been made up as it was being filmed. The ensuing films in the series are even worse. Rated R for violence, profanity, and adult situations. 94m. **DIR:** Paul Donovan. **CAST:** Brian Downey, Eva Habermann, Michael McManus, Barry Bostwick. **1995**

I, ZOMBIE ★★★ Surprisingly good take on zombies from British director Andrew Parkinson. A journalist on assignment finds himself attacked by a woman who appears to be mutilated. Slowly, the man finds himself decaying and the need for blood becomes an increasing urge to suppress. The first film from Fangoria Video is gory but is made enjoyable by the filmmakers' talent and enthusiasm. Not rated; contains gore and violence. 89m. **DIR:** Andrew Parkinson. **CAST:** Giles Aspen, Ellen Softley. **1999 DVD**

ICE ★★ Jewel thief (Traci Lords) and her brother find themselves caught between two rival groups of gangsters after they steal a cache of diamonds from the head honcho of one of the gangs. Glitz and glitter can't hide the flaws in this one. Rated R for violence, nudity, and profanity. 90m. **DIR:** Brook Yeaton. **CAST:** Traci Lords, Zach Galligan, Phillip Troy. **1993**

•ICE AGE ★★★★1/2 Chris Wedge makes his big-screen directorial debut with a vengeance in this computer-animated feature with all the sass of *Shrek* and the frantic, slapstick pacing of a classic Warner Bros. cartoon. The story, set in prehistoric times, concerns a trio of unlikely heroes—a woolly mammoth, a sloth, and a saber-toothed tiger—who band together in an effort to reunite a human child with its tribe. Their subsequent adventures are both harrowing and hilarious, with even the most serious moments lightened by a fourth critter's single-minded (and forever unsuccessful) efforts to bury a prized acorn. This is definitely one for the permanent library. Rated PG for mild peril. 95m. **DIR:** Chris Wedge, Carlos Saldanha. **2002**

ICE CASTLES ★★1/2 Alexis Wintson (Lynn-Holly Johnson) is a girl from a small midwestern town who dreams of skating in the Olympics. No matter how fetching and believable Johnson may be, nothing can surmount the soggy sentimentality of this cliché-ridden work. Rated PG. 109m. **DIR:** Donald Wrye. **CAST:** Robby Benson, Lynn-Holly Johnson, Colleen Dewhurst, Tom Skerritt. **1979 DVD**

ICE CREAM MAN 🦃 The neighborhood ice cream man, recently released from an insane asylum, goes around town collecting unsuspecting youngsters to serve as ingredients in his gourmet ice cream. Ultra-low-budget gorefest for undiscriminating horror fans and celebrity watchers only. Not rated; contains many scenes of graphic horror. 87m. **DIR:** Norman Apstein. **CAST:** Clint Howard, Justin Isfeld, Anndi McAfee, JoJo Adams. **1995**

ICE PALACE ★★★1/2 Film adaptation of Edna Ferber's soap-opera saga about Alaska's statehood. Zeb Kennedy (Richard Burton) fights against statehood while Thor Storm (Robert Ryan) devotes his life to it. Beautifully acted, particularly by Carolyn Jones as the woman both men love. 144m. **DIR:** Vincent Sherman.

CAST: Richard Burton, Robert Ryan, Carolyn Jones, Martha Hyer, Jim Backus. **1960**

ICE PIRATES ★★★1/2 This entertaining and often funny sci-fi film takes place countless years from now, when the universe has run out of water. Rated PG for violence, profanity, scatological humor, and suggested sex. 91m. **DIR:** Stewart Raffill. **CAST:** Robert Urich, Mary Crosby, John Matuszak, Anjelica Huston, John Carradine. **1984**

ICE RUNNER ★★★ CIA agent (Edward Albert) is sentenced to a Russian gulag in Siberia for espionage. During transit by rail, he switches identities with a dead prisoner. When he runs afoul of the camp commandant, a war of wits and nerves begins. Strange mix of political intrigue and mysticism skates around the thin ice in the plot. Rated R for nudity, profanity, and violence. 114m. **DIR:** Barry Samson. **CAST:** Edward Albert, Victor Wong, Olga Kabo, Eugene Lazarev, Alexander Kurnitzov, Basil Hoffman. **1993**

ICE STATION ZEBRA ★★★ This long cold war cliffhanger about a submarine skipper awaiting orders while cruising to the North Pole under the ice was eccentric billionaire Howard Hughes's favorite film. The suspense comes with a British agent's hunt for the usual Russian spy. Rated G. 148m. **DIR:** John Sturges. **CAST:** Rock Hudson, Ernest Borgnine, Patrick McGoohan, Jim Brown, Tony Bill, Lloyd Nolan. **1968**

ICE STORM, THE ★★★ This film is based on Rick Moody's novel about Thanksgiving 1973 in a middle-class New England family, with adolescent children fumbling with puberty while their parents flounder in the backwash of the sexual revolution. Though expertly made and well acted, the film's characters are uptight and repellent, and the story is bleak and oversymbolic. More to be admired than enjoyed. Rated R for profanity and sexual themes. 113m. **DIR:** Ang Lee. **CAST:** Kevin Kline, Joan Allen, Christina Ricci, Sigourney Weaver, Elijah Wood, Tobey Maguire, Adam Hann-Byrd. **1997 DVD**

ICELAND ★★★1/2 A typical Sonja Henie musical with lots of music, romancing, and slapstick comedy. Henie plays an ice skater who falls in love with an American marine. She tells her parents she is going to marry him so her younger sister can marry the man of her dreams. (In their culture, the oldest daughter always marries first.) Now she has to make good on her promise. B&W; 79m. **DIR:** H. Bruce Humberstone. **CAST:** Sonja Henie, John Payne, Jack Oakie, Felix Bressart, Osa Massen, Fritz Feld, Joan Merrill, Adeline de Walt Reynolds, Sammy Kaye. **1942**

ICEMAN ★★★1/2 Timothy Hutton stars in this often gripping and always watchable movie as an anthropologist who is part of an arctic exploration team that discovers the body of a prehistoric man (John Lone), who is still alive. Hutton finds himself defending the creature from those who want to poke, prod, and even dissect their terrified subject. Rated PG for violence and profanity. 99m. **DIR:** Fred Schepisi. **CAST:** Timothy Hutton, Lindsay Crouse, John Lone, Josef Sommer. **1984**

ICICLE THIEF, THE ★★★★1/2 Writer-director-actor Maurizio Nichetti has been called the Woody Allen of Italy, so it's appropriate that he's now made a wonderful film combining some of the ideas of *Purple Rose of Cairo* with the technical virtuosity of *Zelig*. A delightfully inventive parody-satire, this explores the ability of movies to carry us into other worlds. In Italian with English subtitles. Not rated. 90m. **DIR:** Maurizio Nichetti. **CAST:** Maurizio Nichetti. **1990**

ICY BREASTS ★★★ Detective Alain Delon discovers that his beautiful client has been killing the men in her life. Effective suspense-drama. In French with English subtitles. 105m. **DIR:** Georges Lautner. **CAST:** Alain Delon, Mireille Darc. **1975**

IDAHO TRANSFER 🦃 Young scientists invent a time-travel machine. No rating. 90m. **DIR:** Peter Fonda. **CAST:** Keith Carradine, Kelly Bohannon. **1973**

•IDEAL HUSBAND, AN ★★★1/2 Oscar Wilde's wit-riddled play has been adapted into a rollicking romp through late 1800s romance and politics. Lord Goring, "the idlest man in London," is badgered by his crusty father to make something of himself and becomes entwined in a potential scandal that threatens to ruin a friend's virtuous name and career. The knotted plot turns a parliament vote on the construction of a canal in Argentina into a playful smorgasbord of blackmail, mistaken identities, sexual dalliance, and tainted pasts. Rated PG-13 for brief nudity and sexual content. 96m. **DIR:** Oliver Parker. **CAST:** Rupert Everett, Julianne Moore, Jeremy Northam, Cate Blanchett, Minnie Driver, John Wood, Lindsay Duncan, Peter Vaughan. **1999 DVD**

IDENTITY CRISIS ★★ A witch fuses the soul of a murdered fashion designer with a rapper's body in this fluffy comedy. Rated R for profanity and nudity. 98m. **DIR:** Melvin Van Peebles. **CAST:** Mario Van Peebles, Ilan Mitchell-Smith. **1990**

IDIOT, THE ★★★★★ Early gem by Akira Kurosawa based on the novel by Dostoyevski about the confrontation between a demented ruffian and a holy fool prince. Akira Kurosawa transports this tale of madness and jealousy to postwar Japan and places it among blizzards and claustrophobic, madly lit interiors. Highly recommended! In Japanese with English subtitles. B&W; 166m. **DIR:** Akira Kurosawa. **CAST:** Toshiro Mifune, Masayuki Mori, Setsuko Hara. **1951**

IDIOT'S DELIGHT ★★★1/2 An all-star cast makes memorable movie history in this, the last antiwar film produced before World War II erupted. Norma Shearer is at her best as a Garbo-like fake-Russian-accented mistress companion of munitions tycoon Edward Arnold. Clark Gable is her ex, a wisecracking vaudeville hoofer. With other types, they are stranded in a European luxury hotel as war looms. B&W; 105m. **DIR:** Clarence Brown. **CAST:** Clark Gable, Norma Shearer, Edward Arnold, Charles Coburn, Burgess Meredith, Laura Hope Crews, Joseph Schildkraut, Virginia Grey. **1938**

IDLE HANDS 🦃 This comedy-horror flick is more repulsive than funny or frightening as a demonic spirit takes over the right hand of a teen stoner who murders his parents and attacks everyone within reach. Rated R for gore, violence, drug use, sexual content, and language. 92m. **DIR:** Rodman Flender. **CAST:** Devon Sawa, Jessica Alba, Seth Green, Elden Henson. **1999 DVD**

IDOL DANCER, THE ★★1/2 A drunken Yankee beachcomber befriends a young native girl on an island in the South Seas. B&W; 76m. **DIR:** D. W. Griffith. **CAST:**

Richard Barthelmess, Clarine Seymour, Creighton Hale. **1920**

IDOLMAKER, THE ★★★★ This superior rock 'n' roll drama stands with a handful of pictures— *The Buddy Holly Story* and *American Hot Wax* among them—as one of the few to capture the excitement of rock music while still offering something in the way of a decent plot and characterization. Ray Sharkey is excellent as a songwriter-manager who pulls, pushes, punches, and plunders his way to the top of the music world. The score, by Jeff Barry, is top-notch. Rated PG. 119m. **DIR:** Taylor Hackford. **CAST:** Ray Sharkey, Tovah Feldshuh, Peter Gallagher, Maureen McCormick. **1980 DVD**

IF . . . ★★★★ This is British director Lindsay Anderson's black comedy about English private schools and the revolt against their strict code of behavior taken to the farthest limits of the imagination. Malcolm McDowell's movie debut. Rated R. 111m. **DIR:** Lindsay Anderson. **CAST:** Malcolm McDowell, David Wood, Richard Warwick. **1969**

IF EVER I SEE YOU AGAIN 🦃 Fresh from his success with *You Light Up My Life*, writer-director-composer Joe Brooks threw together this celluloid love poem to model Shelley Hack. Rated PG. 105m. **DIR:** Joseph Brooks. **CAST:** Joe Brooks, Shelley Hack, Jimmy Breslin, George Plimpton. **1978**

IF I HAD A MILLION ★★★★1/2 Wonderful episodic tale where wealthy Richard Bennett picks names from the telephone book, giving each person one million dollars. The two funniest segments star Charles Laughton and W. C. Fields. Both comic masterpieces. B&W; 90m. **DIR:** Various. **CAST:** Gary Cooper, W. C. Fields, Charles Laughton, George Raft, Richard Bennett, Mary Boland, Frances Dee, Jack Oakie, Gene Raymond, Charlie Ruggles, Alison Skipworth. **1932**

IF I WERE KING ★★★★ Ronald Colman makes a great François Villon in this story of "The Vagabond King" who takes the place of France's Louis XI when he wins a bet. B&W; 101m. **DIR:** Frank Lloyd. **CAST:** Ronald Colman, Basil Rathbone, Frances Dee, Ellen Drew, Henry Wilcoxon. **1938**

IF I WERE RICH ★★★ How to live and avoid paying bills while waiting for prosperity to return is the theme of this entertaining British comedy. Robert Donat falls for Wendy Barrie when he arrives to shut off her once-rich-but-now-bankrupt father Edmund Gwenn's electricity. The debonair Donat is a delight in this early pairing with Barrie. B&W; 63m. **DIR:** Zoltán Korda. **CAST:** Robert Donat, Wendy Barrie, Edmund Gwenn. **1933**

IF IT'S TUESDAY, THIS MUST BE BELGIUM ★★★1/2 Plenty of laughs with a group of Americans on a wild eighteen-day bus tour of Europe, running from one mishap to another. Added fun with lots of guest stars in surprise cameos. Rated G. 99m. **DIR:** Mel Stuart. **CAST:** Suzanne Pleshette, Ian McShane, Mildred Natwick, Murray Hamilton, Michael Constantine, Norman Fell, Peggy Cass, Marty Ingels, Pamela Britton, Sandy Baron. **1969**

IF LOOKS COULD KILL ★★★ Richard Grieco is a high school student mistaken for an undercover secret agent. As such, he enjoys all the frills (car, clothes, women) that go with the job. Unfortunately, he must also contend with bad guys. A wonderful, action-packed conclusion. Rated PG-13 for profanity and violence. 90m. **DIR:** William Dear. **CAST:** Richard Grieco, Linda Hunt, Roger Rees, Robin Bartlett, Roger Daltrey. **1991**

IF LUCY FELL 🦃 In this annoying, witless comedy, platonic roommates Sarah Jessica Parker and Eric Schaeffer vow to jump off the Brooklyn Bridge if they don't find true love within a month. Naturally, the characters end up together—but not at the bottom of the East River, where they belong. Rated R for profanity. 93m. **DIR:** Eric Schaeffer. **CAST:** Sarah Jessica Parker, Eric Schaeffer, Elle Macpherson, Ben Stiller. **1996 DVD**

IF THESE WALLS COULD TALK ★★★1/2 The abortion movement fuels this advocacy cinema, which tells three pivotal stories occurring within the same large house. Demi Moore is first-rate as a widowed nurse in the early 1950s, who lives in abject terror of the pregnancy she feels will ruin her life. Cher (also making her directorial debut) turns up in the 1990s segment as a compassionate clinic physician, who crosses picket lines. Ironically, the best segment—set in the 1970s—focuses on happily married Sissy Spacek and her crisis over a surprise pregnancy. Lacking the shrill tone and one-sided approach of the other two tales, it reaches an honest conclusion. Rated R for profanity, nudity, violence, and strong dramatic content. 95m. **DIR:** Cher, Nancy Savoca. **CAST:** Demi Moore, Sissy Spacek, Cher, Shirley Knight, C.C.H. Pounder, Xander Berkeley, Joanna Gleason, Anne Heche, Jada Pinkett. **1996 DVD**

IF YOU COULD SEE WHAT I HEAR ★★ The film is supposedly the biography of blind singer-composer Tom Sullivan. You'd have to be not only blind but deaf and, most of all, dumb to appreciate this one. Rated PG. 103m. **DIR:** Eric Till. **CAST:** Marc Singer, R. H. Thomson, Sarah Torgov, Shari Belafonte, Douglas Campbell. **1982**

IF YOU KNEW SUSIE ★★1/2 If you enjoy the comedy and musical stylings of Joan Davis and Eddie Cantor, you'll probably be pleased with this thin story of two entertainers who discover a will signed by George Washington. Dated and held together only by Cantor's sure touch and slick performance. B&W; 90m. **DIR:** Gordon Douglas. **CAST:** Eddie Cantor, Joan Davis, Allyn Joslyn. **1948**

IKE: THE WAR YEARS ★★ Robert Duvall is D-day commander General Dwight Eisenhower, and Lee Remick is his wartime romance Kay Summersby, in this tedious retelling of high-echelon soldiering and whitewashed hanky-panky during the European phase of World War II. Trimmed drastically from an original six-hour miniseries. 196m. **DIR:** Melville Shavelson, Boris Sagal. **CAST:** Robert Duvall, Lee Remick, J. D. Cannon, Darren McGavin. **1978**

IKIRU ★★★★1/2 *Ikiru* is the Japanese infinitive *to live*. The film opens with a shot of an X ray; a narrator tells us the man—an Everyman—is dying of cancer. But a dream flickers to life, and his last years are fulfilled by a lasting accomplishment. It packs a genuine emotional wallop. In Japanese with English subtitles. B&W; 143m. **DIR:** Akira Kurosawa. **CAST:** Takashi Shimura. **1952**

IL BIDONE ★★★ Broderick Crawford gives a strong performance in this nearly forgotten film by Federico Fellini, about an aging con man who realizes his lifetime of selfishness has only made his existence meaningless. In Italian with English subtitles. B&W; 92m. **DIR:** Fed-

erico Fellini. **CAST:** Broderick Crawford, Richard Basehart, Giulietta Masina, Franco Fabrizi. **1955 DVD**

IL GRIDO (OUTCRY, THE) ★★1/2 Drab film about a worker and his child wandering around rural Italy. Also known as *The Outcry*. In Italian with English subtitles. 102m. **DIR:** Michelangelo Antonioni. **CAST:** Steve Cochran, Alida Valli, Betsy Blair. **1957 DVD**

IL LADRO DI BAMBINI (STOLEN CHILDREN) ★★★★★ An 11-year-old girl and her younger brother are taken away from their mother, who has been supporting the family from her daughter's earnings as a prostitute. It falls to a young, good-hearted military officer to escort the youngsters to a children's home, and he turns the trip into a rediscovery of love and happiness for both of them. Both hard-edged and heartwarming, this is a brilliant motion picture. In Italian with English subtitles. 116m. **DIR:** Gianni Amelio. **CAST:** Enrico Lo Verso, Valentina Scalici, Guiseppe Ieracitano. **1992**

I'LL BE HOME FOR CHRISTMAS 🦃 Smug West Coast college student glued inside a Santa suit has several lame misadventures as he travels to join his family in New York for Christmas. Rated PG. 86m. **DIR:** Arlene Sanford. **CAST:** Jonathan Taylor Thomas, Jessica Biel, Adam LaVorgna, Gary Cole, Eve Gordon, Lauren Maltby. **1998 DVD**

I'LL CRY TOMORROW ★★★1/2 In addition to giving one of the most professional performances of her career, Susan Hayward sang (and very well) the songs in this screen biography of Lillian Roth. Her masterful portrayal, supported by a solid cast, won her a Cannes Film Festival award. B&W; 117m. **DIR:** Daniel Mann. **CAST:** Susan Hayward, Eddie Albert, Richard Conte, Jo Van Fleet, Don Taylor, Ray Danton. **1955**

I'LL DO ANYTHING ★★1/2 Writer-director James L. Brooks *badly* miscalculated in this saga of struggling Hollywood actor and single father Nick Nolte, whose stabs at cinematic fame are derailed by the need to care for his precocious daughter Whittni Wright. Although shooting for the vicious insider's humor of *The Player*, this overblown mess staggers beneath its own pretensions. Rated PG-13 for profanity and brief nudity. 115m. **DIR:** James L. Brooks. **CAST:** Nick Nolte, Albert Brooks, Julie Kavner, Joely Richardson, Tracey Ullman, Whittni Wright. **1994**

ILL MET BY MOONLIGHT ★★★ In 1944 on the island of Crete, the British hatch a plot to kidnap a German general and smuggle him to Cairo. This sets off a manhunt with twenty thousand German troops and airplanes pursuing the partisans through Crete's mountainous terrain. B&W; 105m. **DIR:** Michael Powell. **CAST:** Dirk Bogarde, Marius Goring, David Oxley, Cyril Cusack. **1957**

I'LL SEE YOU IN MY DREAMS ★★★1/2 This sugar-coated biography of lyricist Gus Kahn contains a truly warm performance by Danny Thomas, coupled with fine renditions of Kahn's songs ("Pretty Baby," "It Had To Be You," "Love Me Or Leave Me," etc.) B&W; 110m. **DIR:** Michael Curtiz. **CAST:** Danny Thomas, Doris Day, Frank Lovejoy, Patrice Wymore, James Gleason, Mary Wickes, Jim Backus. **1951**

I'LL TAKE SWEDEN ★★ Bob Hope takes a job in Sweden to break up his daughter's love affair and finds romance himself. Misfires all the way. 96m. **DIR:** Frederick de Cordova. **CAST:** Bob Hope, Tuesday Weld, Frankie Avalon, Dina Merrill, John Qualen. **1965**

ILLEGAL IN BLUE ★★ Pedestrian sex thriller dishes up the one about the clean cop in love with a woman who may be a murder suspect. Plenty of steamy rendezvous in the not-rated version. Rated R. Unrated version available. 94m. **DIR:** Stuart Segall. **CAST:** Stacey Dash, Dan Gauthier, Louis Giambalvo, Trevor Goddard. **1995**

ILLEGALLY YOURS 🦃 A bumbling jury member falls for the plaintiff in a murder case. Rated PG. 102m. **DIR:** Peter Bogdanovich. **CAST:** Rob Lowe, Colleen Camp, Kenneth Mars, Kim Myers. **1988**

ILLICIT ★★ A sexy title for a dull movie about a loose-living woman who tries to settle down until she gets bored with marriage. The same story is better presented in the Bette Davis remake called *Ex-Lady*. B&W; 81m. **DIR:** Archie Mayo. **CAST:** Barbara Stanwyck, Joan Blondell, Charles Butterworth, Ricardo Cortez, James Rennie. **1931**

ILLICIT BEHAVIOR ★★ Mediocre film with a twisted plot involving good and bad cops. Jack Scalia spends most of the movie either roughing up or killing people he dislikes, only to find out that he has severely tangled himself up in a conspiracy. Rated R for violence, nudity, and language. 101m. **DIR:** Worth Keeter. **CAST:** Robert Davi, Joan Severance, Jack Scalia, James Russo, Kent McCord, Jenilee Harrison. **1992**

ILLTOWN ★★ A Miami drug dealer becomes embroiled in a power struggle against a former friend just out of prison and nursing some long-held grudge. The film is so cryptic and pretentious, the characters so repellent, and the symbolism so smug and heavy-handed, that by the time writer-director Nick Gomez finally gets around to explaining what the grudge is, you probably won't care. Rated R for profanity, violence, scenes of drug use, and brief nudity. 103m. **DIR:** Nick Gomez. **CAST:** Michael Rapaport, Lili Taylor, Kevin Corrigan, Adam Trese, Tony Danza, Isaac Hayes. **1996**

ILLUMINATA 🦃 A playwright (John Turturro, who also directed, and badly) agonizes over his latest play while the members of his theater company fear he's about to abandon them. A good cast founders helplessly in a pretentious, bombastic script. Rated R for mature themes and brief nudity. 111m. **DIR:** John Turturro. **CAST:** John Turturro, Katherine Borowitz, Beverly D'Angelo, Susan Sarandon, Christopher Walken, Ben Gazzara, Rufus Sewell. **1998 DVD**

ILLUSION TRAVELS BY STREETCAR ★★★ Two employees of a municipal public transport company in Mexico City are dissatisfied with their superiors, so they withdraw an old tram, get drunk at a local festival, and take one last trip through the town. Light comedy from director Luis Buñuel during his prolific Mexican cinema period. In Spanish with English subtitles. 90m. **DIR:** Luis Buñuel. **CAST:** Lilia Prado, Carlos Navarro, Agustin Isunza. **1953**

ILLUSIONS ★★ Mediocre story in which a former mental patient (Heather Locklear) believes her sister-in-law is trying to drive her insane. Narration distracts the viewer and only exists to fill gaps in the plot. Not rated; contains nudity. 90m. **DIR:** Victor Kulle. **CAST:** Robert Carradine, Heather Locklear, Emma Samms, Ned Beatty, Paul Mantee, Susannah York. **1992**

ILLUSTRATED MAN, THE 🦃 Ponderous, dull, and overly talkie adaptation of the work of Ray Bradbury.

Rated PG for violence and partial nudity. 103m. **DIR:** Jack Smight. **CAST:** Rod Steiger, Claire Bloom, Robert Drivas. **1969**

ILSA, THE WICKED WARDEN 🦃 Also titled: *Greta the Mad Butcher, Ilsa—Absolute Power.* Rated R. 90m. **DIR:** Jess (Jesus) Franco. **CAST:** Dyanne Thorne, Lina Romay, Jess Franco. **1977 DVD**

I'M A FOOL ★★★ Ron Howard stars as a naïve young man who abandons his Ohio home for life on the road as a horse trainer. His desperate attempts to make himself worthy in the eyes of the opposite sex escalate until he's passing himself off as the son of a fabulously wealthy man. From a Sherwood Anderson story. Introduced by Henry Fonda; unrated and suitable for family viewing. 38m. **DIR:** Noel Black. **CAST:** Ron Howard, Amy Irving, John Light. **1976**

I'M ALL RIGHT JACK ★★★1/2 British comedies can be marvelously entertaining, especially when they star Peter Sellers, as in this witty spoof of the absurdities of the labor movement carried to its ultimate extreme. B&W; 101m. **DIR:** John Boulting. **CAST:** Peter Sellers, Terry-Thomas, Ian Carmichael. **1960**

I'M ALMOST NOT CRAZY: JOHN CASSAVETES—THE MAN AND HIS WORK ★★★★ Penetrating look at filmmaker-actor John Cassavetes, whose low-budget American movies earned the praise of film directors and critics internationally. His working methods are explored on the set of *Love Streams* (his final screen bid). Cassavetes's brutal, uncompromising approach to his craft is brilliantly captured by Michael Ventura. Not rated; contains some profanity. 60m. **DIR:** Michael Ventura. **1989**

I'M DANCING AS FAST AS I CAN 🦃 Based on documentary filmmaker Barbara Gordon's bestselling autobiography, which dealt with her valiant—and sometimes horrifying—struggle with Valium addiction. Rated PG for profanity. 107m. **DIR:** Jack Hofsiss. **CAST:** Jill Clayburgh, Nicol Williamson, Geraldine Page. **1981**

I'M DANGEROUS TONIGHT 🦃 An Aztec ceremonial cloak serves as a catalyst for murders in a small college town. Originally aired on cable TV. 92m. **DIR:** Tobe Hooper. **CAST:** Madchen Amick, R. Lee Ermey, Anthony Perkins, Dee Wallace. **1990**

I'M GONNA GIT YOU SUCKA! ★★★★ Keenen Ivory Wayans wrote and directed this uproariously funny parody of the blaxploitation flicks of the early Seventies. The gags run fast and loose, and the result is a satisfying laughfest. Rated R for language. 88m. **DIR:** Keenen Ivory Wayans. **CAST:** Keenen Ivory Wayans, Bernie Casey, Jim Brown, Isaac Hayes, Antonio Fargas, Steve James, John Vernon, Clu Gulager. **1989 DVD**

I'M LOSING YOU ★★ Writer Bruce Wagner adapts his own novel and directs this pedestrian effort starring Frank Langella trying to balance a wife, a mistress, his health, and his public appearance. Lots of missed opportunities and a waste of talent. Rated R for language. 100m. **DIR:** Bruce Wagner. **CAST:** Frank Langella, Amanda Donohoe, Elizabeth Perkins, Rosanna Arquette, Andrew McCarthy, Salome Jens. **1998 DVD**

I'M NO ANGEL ★★★★ One of her funniest films, Mae West had complete creative control over script, camera angles, costars, and director. She plays a circus performer who cons gullible old men out of their money. The highlight of the show is the courtroom scene with West acting as her own attorney and compromising the judge, as well as everyone else. B&W; 87m. **DIR:** Wesley Ruggles. **CAST:** Mae West, Cary Grant, Kent Taylor, Edward Arnold, Gregory Ratoff, Gertrude Michael, Dennis O'Keefe, Ralf Harolde. **1933 DVD**

I'M NOT RAPPAPORT ★★1/2 Two feisty octogenarians—African-American building superintendent Midge and Jewish left-wing radical Nate—spend time squabbling on a Central Park bench in this sometimes clunky rework of Herb Gardner's award-winning play. This meandering character study works best when Midge plays straight man to Nate's elaborate yarns. When they leave their bench to battle a park punk and a drug dealer, the film loses its wily comic realism. Rated PG-13 for brief violence and drug content. 131m. **DIR:** Herb Gardner. **CAST:** Walter Matthau, Ossie Davis, Amy Irving, Martha Plimpton, Craig T. Nelson. **1996**

I'M THE ONE THAT I WANT ★★ Comedian Margaret Cho's two November 1999 performances at San Francisco's Warfield Theater have been edited into a confessional concert that covers such topics as gay bars, straight pornography, lesbian sex, the Ku Klux Klan, alcoholism, and the ugly side of Hollywood. It's an alternately heartfelt, captivating, disposable but mostly raunchy spin on life by a woman who mixes modern taboos with stories of personal crisis and pain. Rated R for language and graphic sexual content. 96m. **DIR:** Lionel Coleman. **CAST:** Margaret Cho. **2000**

I'M THE ONE YOU'RE LOOKING FOR ★★★★ A beautiful model is raped, then becomes curiously obsessed with her attacker, willing to endure anything and anyone to find him. Set in the seedy, seething atmosphere of Barcelona, this is a fascinating exploration of the macabre aspect of human sexual longing. In Spanish with English subtitles. Rated R for nudity. 85m. **DIR:** Jaime Chavarri. **CAST:** Patricia Adrian. **1988**

IMAGE, THE ★★★★1/2 Ratings-hungry telejournalists turn a critical eye on themselves in this crackling topical drama—a study of a network news star who begins to believe his own reviews. This made-for-cable movie is unrated, but contains explicit language and brief nudity. 89m. **DIR:** Peter Werner. **CAST:** Albert Finney, John Mahoney, Kathy Baker, Swoosie Kurtz, Marsha Mason. **1990 DVD**

IMAGEMAKER, THE ★★★1/2 Intriguing exposé on the selling of American politicians. Michael Nouri plays a deposed political power maker whose life is threatened when he plans to tell all. Anne Twomey plays the TV reporter who had ruined his previous career. Rated R for nudity, violence, and profanity. 93m. **DIR:** Hal Weiner. **CAST:** Michael Nouri, Anne Twomey, Jerry Orbach, Jessica Harper, Farley Granger. **1985**

IMAGINARY CRIMES ★★★★ Harvey Keitel once again delivers a stunning performance as a con-man father who has been playing the game so long he is now conning his family and himself. Rated PG for language. 106m. **DIR:** Anthony Drazan. **CAST:** Harvey Keitel, Fairuza Balk, Kelly Lynch, Vincent D'Onofrio, Christopher Penn, Seymour Cassel. **1994 DVD**

IMAGINE: JOHN LENNON ★★★★★ Superb documentary chronicles the life, times, and untimely death of rock 'n' roll icon John Lennon. Carefully selected footage from the career of the Beatles is combined with

television interviews and never-before-seen film of Lennon's private life for a remarkably insightful and emotionally moving work. Rated R for nudity and profanity. 103m. **DIR:** Andrew Solt. **CAST:** John Lennon, Yoko Ono, George Harrison. **1988 DVD**

IMITATION OF LIFE ★★★1/2 Earnest performances and gifted direction make this soap-operaish, Fannie Hurst tearjerker tolerable viewing. Lana Turner is a fame-greedy actress who neglects her daughter for her career. Juanita Moore is her black friend whose daughter repudiates her heritage and breaks her mother's heart by passing for white. 124m. **DIR:** Douglas Sirk. **CAST:** Lana Turner, John Gavin, Sandra Dee, Dan O'Herlihy, Susan Kohner, Troy Donahue, Robert Alda, Juanita Moore. **1959**

IMMEDIATE FAMILY ★★★1/2 Unable to have children, a wealthy couple decide to adopt a teenager's baby. Meeting the girl and her boyfriend proves to be both touching and humorous. Rated PG-13 for adult topic. 100m. **DIR:** Jonathan Kaplan. **CAST:** Glenn Close, James Woods, Mary Stuart Masterson, Kevin Dillon. **1989**

IMMORTAL BACHELOR, THE ★★ A female juror hearing the case of a cleaning woman who killed her cheating husband fantasizes about the dead man. But for the well-known cast, this Italian comedy would never have been imported. Dubbed in English. Not rated, but a PG equivalent. 95m. **DIR:** Marcello Fondato. **CAST:** Giancarlo Giannini, Monica Vitti, Vittorio Gassman, Claudia Cardinale. **1979**

IMMORTAL BATTALION, THE (THE WAY AHEAD) ★★★1/2 Based on an idea conceived by Lt. Col. David Niven, this highly effective wartime semidocumentary follows his attempts to turn a group of newly activated civilians into a combat team. This gem skillfully mixes training and combat footage with filmed sequences to create a powerful mood while delicately balancing great performances. 91m. **DIR:** Carol Reed. **CAST:** David Niven, Stanley Holloway, Raymond Huntley, Peter Ustinov, Trevor Howard, Leo Genn, James Donald. **1944**

IMMORTAL BELOVED ★★1/2 After Ludwig van Beethoven's death, his assistant searches for the master composer's long-lost love who is to inherit Ludwig's music and estate. Through interviews with associates and possible lovers, the story speculates on the lady's identity and unearths a dark life of child abuse, womanizing, tormenting deafness, and bristling attitude. The film is gorgeously staged and photographed, but sluggishly paced. Rated R for language, violence, nudity, and simulated sex. 125m. **DIR:** Bernard Rose. **CAST:** Gary Oldman, Jeroen Krabbé, Valeria Golino, Isabella Rossellini, Johanna ter Steege. **1994 DVD**

IMMORTAL COMBAT ★★ Unintentional humor and inane plot twists keep this routine martial arts expo from beating itself to death. Roddy Piper and Sonny Chiba play Los Angeles police detectives who sneak onto an island fortress to stop a madwoman planning to take over the world. Meg Foster swallows the screen whole in her over-the-top portrayal of the deadly dragon lady. Lots of punching and kicking, and little else. Rated R for violence, language, and adult situations. 109m. **DIR:** Daniel Neira. **CAST:** Roddy Piper, Sonny Chiba, Meg Foster, Tom "Tiny" Lister Jr. **1994 DVD**

IMMORTAL SERGEANT, THE ★★★1/2 Henry Fonda gives a solid performance as a corporal in the Canadian army, attached to the British Eighth Army in North Africa during World War II. During a battle with Nazi troops, his squad sergeant is killed and he is forced into command. From a novel by John Brophy. B&W; 91m. **DIR:** John M. Stahl. **CAST:** Henry Fonda, Maureen O'Hara, Thomas Mitchell, Allyn Joslyn, Reginald Gardiner, Melville Cooper. **1943**

IMMORTAL STORY ★★★★ A powerful, cynical old man tries to turn a myth into reality by hiring people to enact it for his amusement. Made for French television, this adaptation of a short story by Isak Dinesen shows a subtler and more contemplative side of director Orson Welles, not the brash youth who made *Citizen Kane*. 63m. **DIR:** Orson Welles. **CAST:** Orson Welles, Jeanne Moreau, Roger Coggio, Fernando Rey. **1968**

IMMORTALS, THE ★★★ Although ostensibly a gory heist caper, this little thriller is oddly appealing. Nightclub manager Eric Roberts assembles eight men and women to rob four cash-laden suitcases from crime lord Tony Curtis, only to see the plan backfire when the subordinates realize what they all have in common. A refreshing change from the usual genre entries. Rated R for violence, profanity, drug use, and nudity. 92m. **DIR:** Brian Grant. **CAST:** Eric Roberts, Tia Carrere, Tony Curtis, Joe Pantoliano, Clarence Williams, III, William Forsythe. **1995 DVD**

IMPACT ★★ Shades of *Double Indemnity*! Unfaithful wife and lover plot to kill rich husband, but lover gets bumped instead. Interesting, but don't believe the title. B&W; 111m. **DIR:** Arthur Lubin. **CAST:** Brian Donlevy, Helen Walker, Tony Barrett, Ella Raines, Charles Coburn, Anna May Wong. **1948 DVD**

IMPLICATED ★★ Run-of-the-mill thriller about a supposedly nice guy named Tom who plans to kidnap his new girlfriend and his boss's daughter in a twisted game of revenge. It won't put you to sleep, or maybe it will. Rated R for language, violence, and adult situations. 95m. **DIR:** Irving Belateche. **CAST:** William McNamara, Amy Locane, Frederic Forrest, Priscilla Barnes, Philip Baker Hall. **1998**

IMPORTANCE OF BEING EARNEST, THE ★★★★★ A peerless cast of stage professionals brings this version of Oscar Wilde's classic Victorian Era comedy of manners to vivid life in high style. Once again, the problem of Mr. Worthing's cloakroom origins delights with hilarious results. A very funny film. 95m. **DIR:** Anthony Asquith. **CAST:** Michael Redgrave, Edith Evans, Margaret Rutherford, Joan Greenwood, Michael Denison, Dorothy Tutin, Richard Wattis. **1952**

IMPOSSIBLE SPY, THE ★★★★ This video is based on the true exploits of Elie Cohen, a spy for Israel's Mossad. Cohen, played by John Shea, is recruited by the Mossad in 1959 and sent to Argentina, where he works his way into the good graces of a group that is plotting to overthrow the Syrian government. He participates while sending information to Israel. The results of his work affect not only his family but the future of Israel. Made for British television, this is unrated. 96m. **DIR:** Jim Goddard. **CAST:** John Shea, Eli Wallach, Sasson Gabay. **1987 DVD**

IMPOSSIBLE YEARS, THE 🦃 Kids using bad words at school and having premarital sex, all done in bad taste.

Inexplicably rated G. 92m. **DIR:** Michael Gordon. **CAST:** David Niven, Lola Albright, Chad Everett, Ozzie Nelson, Cristina Ferrare, Jeff Cooper, Don Beddoe. **1968**

IMPOSTER, THE 🦃 Con artist in a private war against juvenile drug dealers. Not rated. 95m. **DIR:** Michael Pressman. **CAST:** Anthony Geary, Billy Dee Williams, Lorna Patterson, Penny Johnson, Jordan Charney. **1984**

•IMPOSTOR ★★ The year is 2079 and the Earth is engaged in constant warfare with invading Centaurian forces. An Earth Security Agency detective suspects weapons engineer Spence of being a suicide replicant bomber. In *The Fugitive*–like fashion, Spence escapes subjection to an extraction device that would rip the alleged bomb from one of his heart chambers and tries to prove his innocence. The ensuing chase is a poorly executed, padded, and overwrought adaptation of Philip K. Dick's 1953 short story. Rated PG-13 for language, violence, and sexual content. 96m. **DIR:** Gary Fleder. **CAST:** Gary Sinise, Madeleine Stowe, Vincent D'Onofrio, Tony Shalhoub, Mekhi Phifer. **2002**

IMPOSTORS, THE ★★★ Stanley Tucci and Oliver Platt play Depression-era actors desperately trying to stay alive between theater roles. Circumstance finds them stowaways onboard a ship of fools crawling with folks who aren't quite what they appear. Rated R for profanity and crude sexual candor. 102m. **DIR:** Stanley Tucci. **CAST:** Stanley Tucci, Oliver Platt, Alfred Molina, Lili Taylor, Tony Shalhoub, Steve Buscemi, Isabella Rossellini, Billy Connolly, Dana Ivey, Hope Davis. **1998 DVD**

IMPROMPTU ★★★★ George Sand, the female novelist with the men's pants and stylish cigars, and Frederic Chopin, the Polish composer, pianist, and all-around sensitive soul, were the talk of Paris as they embarked on a most unusual and passionate affair. That's the subject of this extravagant and entertaining period romance spiced with unexpected comedy and lovely music. Rated PG-13. 109m. **DIR:** James Lapine. **CAST:** Judy Davis, Hugh Grant, Mandy Patinkin, Bernadette Peters, Julian Sands, Emma Thompson. **1991 DVD**

IMPROPER CHANNELS ★★ Story of an overeager social worker who accuses a father (Alan Arkin) of child abuse. Rated PG for language. 92m. **DIR:** Eric Till. **CAST:** Alan Arkin, Mariette Hartley, Monica Parker. **1981**

IMPULSE (1974) 🦃 William Shatner plays an emotionally disturbed ex–mental patient with a penchant for murder. Not rated, but with several unconvincing murders and lots of phony blood. 85m. **DIR:** William Grefe. **CAST:** William Shatner, Ruth Roman, Harold Sakata. **1974**

IMPULSE (1984) ★★ This mildly interesting thriller takes place in a town where the inhabitants find they have increasing difficulties in controlling their urges. A hasty, unconvincing final ten minutes. Rated R for profanity and violence. 91m. **DIR:** Graham Baker. **CAST:** Tim Matheson, Meg Tilly, Hume Cronyn. **1984 DVD**

IMPULSE (1990) ★★★ Honest cop Theresa Russell yields to temptation while working undercover as a hooker, then tries to extricate herself from the ensuing investigation. Director Sondra Locke keeps the action tense through some pretty implausible plot twists. Rated R for violence and language. 109m. **DIR:** Sondra Locke. **CAST:** Theresa Russell, Jeff Fahey, George Dzundza. **1990**

IMPURE THOUGHTS ★★1/2 A group of friends who attended the same Catholic grammar school in the early Sixties meet after death and reminisce about their youths. Rated PG. 87m. **DIR:** Michael A. Simpson. **CAST:** Brad Dourif, Lane Davies, Terry Beaver, John Putch. **1986**

IN A GLASS CAGE ★★ Horrifying film about an ex–Nazi doctor, now confined to an iron lung, who is tracked down by a young man who survived his sexual tortures. Made with great skill but overwrought—few will be able to stomach it. In Spanish with English subtitles. Not rated; definitely not for children. 112m. **DIR:** Agustin Villaronga. **CAST:** Gunter Meisner, David Sust. **1986**

IN A LONELY PLACE ★★★★ Humphrey Bogart gives one of his finest performances in this taut psychological thriller. He plays a hard-drinking, fiercely opinionated screenwriter whose violent temper has more than once landed him in trouble. He has an affair with a sexy neighbor (Gloria Grahame) who begins to fear for her life when Bogart becomes the prime suspect in a murder case. B&W; 91m. **DIR:** Nicholas Ray. **CAST:** Humphrey Bogart, Gloria Grahame, Frank Lovejoy, Robert Warwick. **1950**

IN A SHALLOW GRAVE ★★ Michael Biehn stars as a disfigured World War II vet who returns to an empty home and life. Patrick Dempsey is a drifter who becomes a messenger between Biehn and his ex-fiancée (Maureen Mueller). The resulting love triangle, both heterosexual and homosexual, is too short on plot, and the movie ends without an ending. Rated R. 92m. **DIR:** Kenneth Bowser. **CAST:** Michael Biehn, Patrick Dempsey, Michael Beach, Maureen Mueller. **1988**

IN A STRANGER'S HANDS ★★★ Robert Urich is the private investigator tracking down a missing girl. The deeper he digs, the more complex the case gets, until he comes face-to-face with the kidnapper. Tough, gritty, and socially relevant, this made-for-cable thriller works, although some of the subject matter is grim. 93m. **DIR:** David Greene. **CAST:** Robert Urich, Megan Gallagher, Brett Cullen, Isabella Hoffmann. **1991**

IN A YEAR OF 13 MOONS ★★★1/2 A man undergoes a sex-change operation to please his male lover, only to be abandoned and forced to deal with the new life he has made for himself. Best appreciated by viewers already familiar with the work of the prolific German filmmaker Rainer Werner Fassbinder; others may find this bleak and visually off-putting film a chore to watch. In German with English subtitles. Not rated; not for kids. 129m. **DIR:** Rainer Werner Fassbinder. **CAST:** Volker Spengler, Ingrid Caven, Eva Mattes. **1978**

IN & OUT ★★★1/2 Kevin Kline is a literature and drama teacher in a small town in the Midwest whose life is turned topsy-turvy when he is "outed" by a former student during an Oscars telecast. Soon to be married and unaware of his more feminine characteristics, Kline recoils from this disclosure and sets out to prove how macho he is. But gay reporter Tom Selleck and the townsfolk won't let him forget his new reputation. Kline brings many funny and touching moments to the screen. Rated PG-13 for profanity. 90m. **DIR:** Frank Oz. **CAST:** Kevin Kline, Tom Selleck, Joan Cusack, Matt Dillon, Debbie Reynolds, Wilford Brimley, Bob Newhart, Deborah Rush. **1997 DVD**

IN COLD BLOOD ★★★★★ A chilling documentary-like re-creation of the senseless murder of a Kansas farm family. This stark black-and-white drama follows two ex-convicts (Robert Blake and Scott Wilson) from the point at which they hatch their plan until their eventual capture and execution. This is an emotionally powerful film that is not for the faint of heart. B&W; 134m. **DIR:** Richard Brooks. **CAST:** Robert Blake, Scott Wilson, John Forsythe, Jeff Corey. **1967**

IN COUNTRY ★★★1/2 A Kentucky teenager (Emily Lloyd) tries to understand the Vietnam War and why her father had to die in this uneven but well-intentioned and ultimately powerful film. Bruce Willis gives an effective performance as Lloyd's uncle, a Vietnam vet who has never fully recovered from his combat experience. Rated R for brief violence and profanity. 106m. **DIR:** Norman Jewison. **CAST:** Bruce Willis, Emily Lloyd, Joan Allen, Kevin Anderson, Richard Hamilton, Judith Ivey, Peggy Rea. **1989 DVD**

IN CROWD, THE 🦃 Dark secrets tumble from the closet with unintentionally laughable results when a doctor secures a job at a swank country club for a former female mental-hospital patient who looks like the missing sister of an evil-minded debutante. Rated R for language, sex, violence, and drug use. 108m. **DIR:** Mary Lambert. **CAST:** Lori Heuring, Susan Ward, Daniel Hugh Kelly, Matthew Settle. **2000 DVD**

IN CUSTODY ★★ An idealistic schoolteacher in India learns that his idol, renowned as the greatest living poet of the Urdu language, is really a sloppy, dissolute old drunkard. Any film with long passages of poetry will suffer in translation, but even so, this one is a terrible bore, belaboring every little point. In Hindi and Urdu with English subtitles. Not rated; contains mild profanity. 150m. **DIR:** Ismail Merchant. **CAST:** Om Puri, Shashi Kapoor. **1994**

IN DANGEROUS COMPANY 🦃 Unexciting, glitzy Sidney Sheldon-ish piece has Tracy Scoggins as a beautiful woman who uses her body to square one bad guy off against the other. Rated R for nudity, simulated sex, violence, and language. 92m. **DIR:** Reuben Preuss. **CAST:** Tracy Scoggins, Cliff De Young, Chris Mulkey, Henry Darrow, Richard Portnow, Steven Keats. **1988**

IN DARK PLACES ★★ Joan Severance stars in this standard erotic thriller as an artist who moves in with the brother she never knew after their father dies, then screws up his life with more-than-sisterly interest. The sex scenes are relatively tame, and the plot is predictable. Rated R for nudity, sexual situations, and profanity. 96m. **DIR:** James Burke. **CAST:** Joan Severance, Bryan Kestner, John Vargas. **1997**

IN DREAMS ★★1/2 A woman's dreams foretell the murder of her daughter, but the horror doesn't stop there—it seems the killer is actually stalking her through her psychic nightmares. Annette Bening is riveting as the dreamer, and director Neil Jordan gives everything an eerie, otherworld look, but the film suffers from a weak third act and the miscasting of Robert Downey Jr., unintentionally comical as the killer. Rated R for violence and profanity. 100m. **DIR:** Neil Jordan. **CAST:** Annette Bening, Robert Downey Jr., Aidan Quinn, Stephen Rea, Paul Guilfoyle. **1999 DVD**

IN EARLY ARIZONA ★★★1/2 In this big-budget B, Wild Bill Elliott tames the town of Tombstone by getting rid of the evil Harry Woods. A fine example of this type of Western lore. Plenty of action and energy. B&W; 53m. **DIR:** Joseph Levering. **CAST:** William Elliott, Harry Woods, Charles King. **1938**

IN GOLD WE TRUST 🦃 Renegade MIAs in Southeast Asia murder their own rescue party to steal the ransom money. Insipid. Not rated, contains profanity and violence. 89m. **DIR:** P. Chalong. **CAST:** Jan-Michael Vincent, Sam Jones, James Phillips, Michi McGee, Sherrie Rose. **1990**

IN HARM'S WAY ★★ John Wayne leads the United States Navy into a monumental struggle against the Japanese. Kirk Douglas is the antihero who stirs up a fuss. The ships are models and the battles are conducted in a bathtub. It's too big and too long. B&W; 167m. **DIR:** Otto Preminger. **CAST:** John Wayne, Kirk Douglas, Patricia Neal, Tom Tryon, Paula Prentiss, Brandon de Wilde, Stanley Holloway, Jill Haworth, Burgess Meredith, Henry Fonda, Dana Andrews, Franchot Tone, Patrick O'Neal. **1965 DVD**

IN HIS FATHER'S SHOES ★★★1/2 A young boy finds magical shoes and literally gets the opportunity to "walk in his father's footsteps." While shedding no new light on the battles between parent and child, the story demonstrates—without being shrill—just how much things have changed for black Americans. This one deserves to be watched by all members of the family, with its implications discussed later. Rated G; suitable for all ages. 105m. **DIR:** Vic Sarin. **CAST:** Louis Gossett Jr., Barbara Eve Harris, Rachel Crawford, Dejanet Sears, Robert Ri'chard. **1997**

•IN HIS LIFE: THE JOHN LENNON STORY ★★1/2 The legend of John Lennon comes to life in this made-for-television biography which examines the early years of the Beatles in Liverpool and opens up the famous icon's life enough to give us a peek into the mind of a brilliant musician and human being. Philip McQuillan does a decent job as the young Lennon, whose interest in music blossoms into a passion that eventually led to The Beatles. Hardly definitive, but entertaining nonetheless. Rated PG-13. 87m. **DIR:** David Carson. **CAST:** Philip McQuillan, Blair Brown, Christine Kavanagh, Daniel McGowan, Mark Rice-Oxley. **2000 DVD**

IN-LAWS, THE ★★★★ This delightful caper comedy mixes mystery and action with the fun. Vince Ricardo (Peter Falk) is the mastermind behind a bold theft of engravings of U.S. currency from a Treasury Department armored car. Sheldon Kornpett (Alan Arkin) is a slightly neurotic dentist. Soon they're off on a perilous mission. Falk and Arkin make a great team, playing off each other brilliantly. Rated PG. 103m. **DIR:** Arthur Hiller. **CAST:** Peter Falk, Alan Arkin, Penny Peyser, Michael Lembeck. **1979**

IN LIKE FLINT ★★★ James Coburn's smooth portrayal of super-secret agent Derek Flint is ample reason to catch this spy spoof, the sequel to *Our Man Flint*. An evil organization is substituting duplicates for all the world's leaders. Jerry Goldsmith contributes another droll jazz score. Not rated; suitable for family viewing. 114m. **DIR:** Gordon Douglas. **CAST:** James Coburn, Lee J. Cobb, Jean Hale, Andrew Duggan. **1967**

IN LOVE AND WAR (1991) ★★★ James Woods portrays navy pilot Jim Stockdale who is shot down over enemy territory and suffers POW camp tortures for nearly

eight years of war in Vietnam. This emotionally compelling story pays tribute to America's fighting men and the parts their resolute wives play in the politics of bringing their husbands home. Rated R for mature subject matter. 96m. **DIR:** Paul Aaron. **CAST:** James Woods, Jane Alexander, Haing S. Ngor. **1991**

IN LOVE AND WAR (1996) ★★1/2 This wartime romance between cub reporter Ernest Hemingway and older nurse Agnes is strong on gauzy atmosphere and weak on passion. Stationed in WWI Italy, Ernie is shot while lugging an Italian infantryman to safety. Agnes saves his leg and wins his heart in a fictionalized affair that plunges the aspiring writer into terminal bitterness. Rated PG-13 for graphic battle injuries and suggested sex. 115m. **DIR:** Richard Attenborough. **CAST:** Sandra Bullock, Chris O'Donnell, Ingrid Lacey, Emilio Bonnucci, Mackenzie Astin. **1996 DVD**

•IN LOVE AND WAR (2001) ★★★★ Outstanding *Hallmark Hall of Fame* presentation adapts Eric Newby's autobiographical account of his WWII mission in Italy. The film, focusing on his capture and romantic involvement, has a refreshing international feel. The two leads, Callum Blue as British Commando Newby and Barbora Bobulova as Wanda, connect with a charm and innocence reminiscent of Romeo and Juliet. Nicola Piovani's music enhances an already terrific story. Not rated; contains mature themes. 96m. **DIR:** John Kent Harrison. **CAST:** Callum Blue, Barbora Bobulova, Maurizio Donadoni, Nicola Pannelli. **2001 DVD**

IN LOVE WITH AN OLDER WOMAN ★★1/2 San Francisco lawyer John Ritter falls in love with a woman fifteen years older than him. They move in together. Made-for-TV movie (can't you tell?), though not bad. 96m. **DIR:** Jack Bender. **CAST:** John Ritter, Karen Carlson, Jamie Rose, Jeff Altman. **1982**

IN NAME ONLY ★★★1/2 This is a classic soap opera. Cary Grant is desperately in love with sweet and lovely Carole Lombard. Unfortunately, he's married to venomous Kay Francis. You can't help but get completely wrapped up in the skillfully executed story. B&W; 102m. **DIR:** John Cromwell. **CAST:** Carole Lombard, Cary Grant, Kay Francis, Charles Coburn, Helen Vinson, Peggy Ann Garner. **1939**

IN NOME DEL PAPA RE (IN THE NAME OF THE POPE-KING) ★★★★ A compelling drama of intrigue, political conflict, and murder. In 1867, as Italian patriots fight to unify their country, an affluent public official's resignation is complicated when his son becomes a prime suspect in the bombing of a military barracks. Nino Manfredi's performance netted him a best actor award at the Paris Film Festival. In Italian with English subtitles. Not rated; contains profanity and violence. 115m. **DIR:** Luigi Magni. **CAST:** Nino Manfredi. **1987**

IN OLD AMARILLO ★★★1/2 A severe range drought that threatens ranchers is compounded by a vicious ranch foreman who plans to profit from the disaster. Another in the ahead-of-their-time environmental Roy Rogers contemporary Westerns. B&W; 67m. **DIR:** William Witney. **CAST:** Roy Rogers, Estelita Rodriguez, Penny Edwards, Pinky Lee, Roy Barcroft. **1951**

IN OLD ARIZONA ★★ The first Western talkie and the first sound film made outdoors is also the first movie to spawn a series. Warner Baxter (in his Oscar-winning role) plays O. Henry's Mexican bandido, the Cisco Kid, changing the concept to suit his personality. The Cisco Kid was originally a parody on Billy the Kid. Baxter gave him an accent, an eagerness to enjoy life, and a girlfriend. The movie is slow by today's standards, so it is mostly a curiosity piece. B&W; 63m. **DIR:** Raoul Walsh, Irving Cummings. **CAST:** Warner Baxter, Dorothy Burgess, Edmund Lowe, J. Farrell MacDonald. **1929**

IN OLD CALIENTE ★★★★ The coming of the Americans to California provides the story to one of Roy Rogers's finest musical Westerns from the early years. Classic Rogers–Gabby Hayes duet, "We're Not Comin' Out Tonight." B&W; 54m. **DIR:** Joseph Kane. **CAST:** Roy Rogers, Lynne Roberts, George "Gabby" Hayes, Jack LaRue, Katherine DeMille. **1939**

IN OLD CALIFORNIA ★★★ In one of his numerous B-plus pictures for Republic Studios, John Wayne plays a mild-mannered pharmacist who is forced to take up arms when he settles down in a Western town run by the corrupt Albert Dekker. Director William McGann keeps things moving at a sprightly pace, which is more than one can say of the other films in the series. B&W; 88m. **DIR:** William McGann. **CAST:** John Wayne, Binnie Barnes, Albert Dekker, Helen Parrish, Patsy Kelly, Edgar Kennedy. **1942 DVD**

IN OLD CHICAGO ★★★★ Tyrone Power attempts to control Chicago through corruption and vice while his brother, Don Ameche, heads a reform movement. Fast-moving story leading to a spectacular re-creation of the 1871 fire. Supporting Oscar for Alice Brady as their mother (Mrs. O'Leary), who owns the cow that kicks over the lantern that . . . B&W; 95m. **DIR:** Henry King. **CAST:** Tyrone Power, Alice Faye, Don Ameche, Alice Brady, Andy Devine, Brian Donlevy, Phyllis Brooks, Tom Brown, Sidney Blackmer, Rondo Hatton. **1938**

IN OLD COLORADO ★★1/2 Ma Woods and her fellow "nesters" are fenced in and cut off from water by a big rancher who thinks they've been rustling his cattle. Hopalong Cassidy and the Bar-20 to the rescue. B&W; 65m. **DIR:** Howard Bretherton. **CAST:** William Boyd, Russell Hayden, Andy Clyde, Margaret Hayes, Morris Ankrum, Stanley Andrews. **1941**

IN OLD MEXICO ★★★ In this suspense-Western, a sequel to *Borderland*, Hopalong Cassidy solves a murder while working in Mexico. A good script plus fine direction and acting make this a sure-bet B Western. B&W; 62m. **DIR:** Edward Venturini. **CAST:** William Boyd, George "Gabby" Hayes, Russell Hayden, Jan Clayton, Glenn Strange. **1938**

IN OLD SANTA FE ★★★ As this film proves, Gene Autry was not the first singing cowboy no matter what he claims. Ken Maynard sings here as he'd done a few times before. Introductory Autry film has Gene and Smiley Burnette performing at a dance while Maynard stops the villain. B&W; 64m. **DIR:** David Howard. **CAST:** Ken Maynard, George "Gabby" Hayes, Evalyn Knapp, Gene Autry, Smiley Burnette. **1934**

IN PERSON ★★★ Vivacious, shrewish film star flees to a resort incognito and meets a handsome stranger who is totally unimpressed when he learns who she really is. Enjoyable. B&W; 85m. **DIR:** William A. Seiter. **CAST:** Ginger Rogers, George Brent, Alan Mowbray, Grant Mitchell, Samuel S. Hinds, Edgar Kennedy. **1935**

IN PRAISE OF OLDER WOMEN 🦃 A man's reflections on his various affairs. Rated R. 108m. **DIR:** George

Kaczender. **CAST:** Tom Berenger, Karen Black, Susan Strasberg, Alexandra Stewart. **1978**

IN PURSUIT ★ An innocent man is framed for murder in this dull, predictable, and sometimes downright ludicrous film. Rated R for language, sexual situations, and violence. 91m. **DIR:** Peter Pistor. **CAST:** Daniel Baldwin, Claudia Schiffer, Coolio, Dean Stockwell. **2000 DVD**

IN PURSUIT OF HONOR ★★★★ This thoughtful Depression-era drama is adapted from events concerning the disbanding of the U.S. Cavalry forces. When ordered to oversee the slaughter of their extra horses, an insubordinate lieutenant and sergeant steal the animals in an effort to somehow save their lives. Rated PG-13 for profanity and one horrendous scene of animal extermination. 110m. **DIR:** Ken Olin. **CAST:** Don Johnson, Craig Sheffer, Gabrielle Anwar, Bob Gunton, James B. Sikking, John Dennis Johnston, Rod Steiger. **1995 DVD**

IN SEARCH OF HISTORIC JESUS 🦃 Low-budget reenactments of key events in Jesus' life. Rated G. 91m. **DIR:** Henning Schellerup. **CAST:** John Rubinstein, John Anderson, Morgan Brittany, Nehemiah Persoff, John Hoyt. **1979**

IN SEARCH OF THE CASTAWAYS ★★★★ Young Hayley Mills enlists the aid of financial backers Maurice Chevalier and Wilfrid Hyde-White in search for her missing father, a ship captain. Superb special effects depict the many obstacles and natural disasters the searchers must overcome. 100m. **DIR:** Robert Stevenson. **CAST:** Hayley Mills, Maurice Chevalier, George Sanders, Wilfrid Hyde-White, Michael Anderson Jr. **1962**

IN SEARCH OF THE SERPENT OF DEATH 🦃 A *Raiders of the Lost Ark* rip-off. Rated R for violence. 97m. **DIR:** Anwar Kawadri. **CAST:** Jeff Fahey, Camilla More. **1989**

IN SELF DEFENSE 🦃 Linda Purl testifies against a crazed murderer after the police promise her protection they can't provide in this unimaginative, overacted thriller. Rated PG for substance abuse and violence. 94m. **DIR:** Bruce Seth Green. **CAST:** Linda Purl, Yaphet Kotto, Billy Drago. **1987**

IN SOCIETY ★★1/2 Abbott and Costello are mistaken for pillars of upscale society. Imagine the possibilities. Slick, fast-paced comedy from their initial Universal period. B&W; 75m. **DIR:** Jean Yarbrough. **CAST:** Bud Abbott, Lou Costello, Arthur Treacher, Marion Hutton, Kirby Grant. **1944**

IN THE AFTERMATH: ANGELS NEVER SLEEP ★★ Uneasy mixture of animation and live- action in this sci-fi story concerning an angel sent to assist an Earthman after the nuclear holocaust. The animation and the live action are good, but the two don't gel. A decent attempt to add life to an overworked genre, though. Contains rough language and violence. 85m. **DIR:** Carl Colpaert. **CAST:** Tony Markes, Rainbow Dolan. **1987**

IN THE ARMY NOW ★★ A goofy electronics-store sales clerk joins the military reserves, makes a mess of basic training, and is sent to the desert front lines of a Libyan war where he is befriended by a timid dentist and harassed by a special-forces bully. There are some wild, hilarious moments, but the bombs dropped here are not only by American war planes. Rated PG. 91m. **DIR:** Daniel Petrie Jr. **CAST:** Pauly Shore, David Alan Grier, Lori Petty, Andy Dick, Esai Morales. **1994**

IN THE COLD OF THE NIGHT 🦃 Jeff Lester is a man plagued by a nightmare in which he attempts to kill a mysterious woman. Rated R for nudity and violence. 112m. **DIR:** Nico Mastorakis. **CAST:** Jeff Lester, Adrienne Sachs, David Soul, Tippi Hedren. **1990**

IN THE COMPANY OF MEN ★★★★ Bloodied by relationships with women, emasculated by corporate cannibalism, and frustrated by injustices of the twentieth century, a duo of white-collar weasels is intoxicated with thoughts of revenge. Their whipping boy will be the first vulnerable woman they can romantically dupe and dump. This brutal look at misogyny, infected human dynamics, and the ugliness of life in today's business trenches makes no apologies for the evil that lurks in the hearts of men. Rated R for language. 93m. **DIR:** Neil LaBute. **CAST:** Aaron Eckart, Matt Malloy, Stacy Edwards. **1997 DVD**

IN THE COMPANY OF SPIES ★★★★ When one of their agents is arrested in North Korea, the CIA assembles a team to determine what critical piece of information he was trying to deliver, and how to extract him from the country. This made-for-cable original is tense and gritty, and gives a wonderfully accurate portrayal of the inner workings of the CIA (at least, according to the CIA). As an action film, it is easily the equal to Tom Clancy fare, and is chock-full of excitement for the viewer. Not rated; contains profanity and violence. 104m. **DIR:** Tim Matheson. **CAST:** Tom Berenger, Ron Silver, Alice Krige, Arye Gross, Elizabeth Arlen, Clancy Brown. **1999**

IN THE DEEP WOODS ★★1/2 Red herrings abound in this made-for-TV whodunit about a children's-book illustrator who may hold the key to a series of unexplained murders. Despite its hackneyed plot twists, the film remains notable for Anthony Perkins's final role, as a shady private investigator. 93m. **DIR:** Charles Correll. **CAST:** Rosanna Arquette, Anthony Perkins, Will Patton, D. W. Moffett, Christopher Rydell, Amy Ryan, Beth Broderick. **1992**

IN THE GLOAMING ★★★1/2 Christopher Reeve's directorial debut is a moving document of an AIDS-afflicted young man who returns home to die. But this disappointingly brief adaptation of Alice Elliott Dark's story leaves too many dramatic stones unturned, most notably the sister who feels left out by parents who always preferred her brother. Glenn Close is radiant as the mother who tries to grasp as much as she can before her son leaves her forever. Rated PG for theme. 60m. **DIR:** Christopher Reeve. **CAST:** Glenn Close, Robert Sean Leonard, David Strathairn, Bridget Fonda, Whoopi Goldberg. **1997**

IN THE GOOD OLD SUMMERTIME ★★★ Despite its title, most of the action of this remake of the classic romantic comedy *The Shop Around the Corner* takes place in winter. Judy Garland and Van Johnson work in the same music store. They dislike each other, but are unknowingly secret pen pals who have much in common. Truth wins out, but by the time it does, love has struck. Buster Keaton is wasted as comic relief. 102m. **DIR:** Robert Z. Leonard. **CAST:** Judy Garland, Van Johnson, S. Z. Sakall, Buster Keaton, Spring Byington. **1949**

IN THE HEAT OF PASSION ★★1/2 In this case, the end doesn't justify the means as Sally Kirkland leads Nick Corri on a wild sleazefest. She appears to be a bored but fabulously wealthy wife out to have forbidden pleasure

with a younger man. Comes in both R and an unrated version, both containing violence, nudity, and profanity. 93m. **DIR:** Rodman Flender. **CAST:** Sally Kirkland, Nick Corri, Jack Carter. **1991**

IN THE HEAT OF PASSION II: UNFAITHFUL When Barry Bostwick and his lover permanently dispose of his wife, they plan to take his inheritance money and live it up. A series of unexpected events, however, makes that plan somewhat impossible to execute and the tension builds to the point of explosion—and a surprise ending. Another erotic thriller that's much more predictable than it is sexy. Rated R for profanity, nudity, and sexual situations. 107m. **DIR:** Catherine Cyran. **CAST:** Barry Bostwick, Lesley-Anne Down, Teresa Hill. **1994**

IN THE HEAT OF THE NIGHT ★★★★ A rousing murder mystery elevated by the excellent acting of Rod Steiger and Sidney Poitier. Racial tension is created when a rural southern sheriff (Steiger) and a black northern detective reluctantly join forces to solve the crime. The picture received Oscars for best picture and Steiger's performance. 109m. **DIR:** Norman Jewison. **CAST:** Sidney Poitier, Rod Steiger, Warren Oates, Lee Grant. **1967 DVD**

IN THE LAND OF THE DEAF ★★★★ The title aptly sums up this excursion into a place few of us have ever visited. Director Nicolas Philibert reveals an entire culture that is perhaps more emotional, communicative, and expressive than that experienced by the hearing. He brings his camera into schools, a wedding, even an apartment-hunting expedition as he dispels misconceptions about the 130 million deaf people worldwide. Quite touching, thanks to sensitivity and truthfulness in every frame. In French with English subtitles. Not rated. 99m. **DIR:** Nicolas Philibert. **1993**

IN THE LINE OF DUTY: AMBUSH IN WACO ★★★1/2 Riveting, up-to-the-minute TV drama about self-proclaimed evangelical leader David Koresh, and his magnetic hold on his followers. Events depict Koresh's battle with the government, when he held the Bureau of Alcohol, Tobacco and Firearms at bay until a deadly showdown lit the skies of Waco, Texas. Powerful performances from Tim Daly as Koresh, and Dan Lauria as the bureau captain who takes control of the siege. Rated R for violence. 93m. **DIR:** Dick Lowry. **CAST:** Timothy Daly, Dan Lauria, William O'Leary. **1993**

IN THE LINE OF FIRE ★★★★1/2 This is the ultimate *Dirty Harry* movie. Even though Clint Eastwood plays Secret Service agent Frank Horrigan (instead of Harry Callahan), this film is to his cop movies what *Unforgiven* is to his Westerns. Fans of the detective series will recognize familiar plot elements as Eastwood attempts to prevent psycho John Malkovich from assassinating the president. Rated R for violence and profanity. 135m. **DIR:** Wolfgang Petersen. **CAST:** Clint Eastwood, John Malkovich, René Russo, Dylan McDermott, Gary Cole, Fred Dalton Thompson, John Mahoney. **1993 DVD**

IN THE MOOD ★★1/2 Patrick Dempsey plays a conniving teenager who becomes a media star by repeatedly marrying older women. Although this period (1940s) comedy has some funny bits and lines, the story is slapdash. Rated PG-13. 100m. **DIR:** Phil Alden Robinson. **CAST:** Patrick Dempsey, Talia Balsam, Beverly D'Angelo, Michael Constantine, Kathleen Freeman. **1987**

IN THE MOOD FOR LOVE ★★★ This dreamy, lush drama set in 1960s Hong Kong is about a man and a woman who move into an apartment house on the same day and discover their spouses (whom we never see) are having an affair. They then lean on each other for advice and emotional support, engage in melancholy playacting in which they pretend to be the unfaithful couple, and cautiously tiptoe around an affair of their own. In Cantonese and French with English subtitles. Rated PG. 98m. **DIR:** Kar-wai Wong. **CAST:** Maggie Cheung, Tony Leung Chin-Wai. **2000 DVD**

IN THE MOUTH OF MADNESS ★★★1/2 John Carpenter's creepy take on a popular horror author who mysteriously disappears and the private investigator hired to locate him after his latest book causes readers to go insane. Paired with the author's editor, the P.I. seeks out the author and finds him in the fictional town featured in the book. Carpenter draws a thin line between reality and illusion and keeps the audience guessing. Rated R for violence and language. 95m. **DIR:** John Carpenter. **CAST:** Sam Neill, Julie Carmen, Jurgen Prochnow, Charlton Heston. **1995 DVD**

IN THE NAME OF JUSTICE Citizens pose as government agents to get revenge on the drug lord who killed their loved ones. No-budget action film that slips into incompetence. Rated R for violence, profanity, nudity, and sex. 95m. **DIR:** John R. Poague. **CAST:** Jerry Trimble, Paul R. Ellis. **1998**

IN THE NAME OF THE FATHER ★★★★ This political thriller is based on the true story of Gerry Conlon, an Irish youth accused of a crime he didn't commit. Conlon is enjoying the freewheeling lifestyle of the swinging '60s in London and has an antiestablishment attitude, but he isn't guilty of the terrorist bombing for which he and his innocent father are arrested. Emma Thompson adds vitality to the courtroom scenes as she attempts to prove their innocence. Riveting and brilliantly acted. Rated R for violence and profanity. 125m. **DIR:** Jim Sheridan. **CAST:** Daniel Day-Lewis, Emma Thompson, Pete Postlethwaite. **1993**

IN THE PRESENCE OF MINE ENEMIES ★★★ Rod Serling's 1960 *Playhouse 90* television script has lost some of its edge since its original appearance. Armin Mueller-Stahl stars as a rabbi trying to retain his hope and dignity amid the atrocities committed by the Nazis who control the Warsaw ghetto where he lives. His attempt to find God's greater meaning in all acts of casual cruelty eventually drives him mad. Interesting, but more of a period piece at this point. Rated PG-13 for violence and dramatic intensity. 100m. **DIR:** Joan Micklin Silver. **CAST:** Armin Mueller-Stahl, Charles Dance, Elina Lowensohn, Don McKellar, Chad Lowe. **1997 DVD**

IN THE REALM OF PASSION ★★★ Nagisa Oshima, Japan's most controversial director, scores some high and low points with this erotic, metaphysical ghost story about a woman who, along with her lover, kills her husband only to suffer a haunting by his vengeful spirit. Excellent performances by both leads along with some impressive atmospheric cinematography. In Japanese with English subtitles. Not rated; contains nudity and violence. 108m. **DIR:** Nagisa Oshima. **CAST:** Kazuko Yoshiyuki, Tatsuya Fuji. **1980 DVD**

IN THE REALM OF THE SENSES ★★ Uneasy blend of pornography and art in this tale of sexual obsession. Di-

rector Nagisa Oshima delves into the mystery of human sexuality, but comes away with a shallow pretentious result. In Japanese with English subtitles. Rated X for its depiction of sex. 104m. **DIR:** Nagisa Oshima. **CAST:** Tatsuya Fuji, Elko Matsuda. **1976 DVD**

IN THE SHADOW OF KILIMANJARO 🦃 The supposedly true story of what happened in Kenya when ninety thousand baboons went on a killing spree because of the 1984 drought. Rated R for violence. 97m. **DIR:** Raju Patel. **CAST:** John Rhys-Davies, Timothy Bottoms, Irene Miracle, Michele Carey. **1986**

IN THE SHADOW OF THE SUN ★★1/2 Interesting but overlong experimental film by Derek Jarman. This multilayered, hypnotic, nonlinear film was shot in Super-8 at the cost of $200 and features a dizzying soundtrack with the music of Throbbing Gristle and Chris Carter. Not rated. 54m. **DIR:** Derek Jarman. **1974**

IN THE SHADOWS ★★1/2 Writer-director Meg Richman updates Henry James's *The Wings of the Dove*, and despite modern sensibilities, the translation fails to capture the heart of the story. A waitress agrees to take care of a terminally ill rich woman, played by Joely Richardson, and sees an opportunity to have her cake and eat it too. The film lacks the emotional impact of the 1997 version. Also released as *Under Heaven*. Rated R for adult situations and language. 112m. **DIR:** Meg Richman. **CAST:** Molly Parker, Joely Richardson, Aden Young. **1998 DVD**

IN THE SOUP ★★ Very bizarre movie in which an aspiring film writer finds an extremely strange man to help him finance his script. Don't expect to laugh during this film, unless you like off-the-wall humor. Not rated; contains nudity and profanity. 96m. **DIR:** Alexandre Rockwell. **CAST:** Seymour Cassel, Steve Buscemi, Jennifer Beals, Will Patton, Stanley Tucci, Pay Moya, Jim Jarmusch, Carol Kane. **1992**

IN THE SPIRIT ★★★1/2 Marlo Thomas stands out in a top-flight cast as a lovable New Age nut who involves a hapless married couple (Elaine May, Peter Falk) in murder and mayhem when her protégé, a prostitute (Jeannie Berlin), is found dead. Berlin, May's daughter, co-wrote the script. Rated R for profanity and violence. 95m. **DIR:** Sandra Seacat. **CAST:** Jeannie Berlin, Olympia Dukakis, Peter Falk, Melanie Griffith, Elaine May, Marlo Thomas. **1990**

IN THE TIME OF BARBARIANS 🦃 Doran, the good barbarian king of Armana, faces danger as he pursues an evil marauder across his lands and into present-day Los Angeles. Rated R for violence and nudity. 96m. **DIR:** Joseph L. Barmettler. **CAST:** Deron Michael McBee, Jo Ann Ayres. **1990**

IN THE TIME OF BARBARIANS II ★★ Wandering swordsman Galen finds service with the good guys as two sisters battle for the throne of a magical land. Falling in love with a beautiful princess, he soon finds that his employer is not as pure as he once thought. Rated R for violence and nudity. 85m. **DIR:** Ricardo Jacques Gale. **CAST:** Diana Frank, Lenore Andriel, Tom Schultz. **1992**

IN THE WHITE CITY ★★★ A naval mechanic leaves his ship in Lisbon. He wanders the city, photographing it with his Super-8 camera, and sends the films back to his wife to explain why he won't come home. An elegantly photographed but slow-moving mood piece. In French with English subtitles. Not rated. 108m. **DIR:** Alain Tanner. **CAST:** Bruno Ganz, Teresa Madruga. **1983**

IN THIS OUR LIFE ★★★1/2 The best Bette Davis movies are those in which she must work to keep the spotlight, such as when paired with skillful Olivia de Havilland. They play sisters in love with the same man (Dennis Morgan). Humphrey Bogart and the cast of *The Maltese Falcon* have walk-ons in a bar scene. B&W; 97m. **DIR:** John Huston. **CAST:** Bette Davis, Olivia de Havilland, Dennis Morgan, Charles Coburn, George Brent, Hattie McDaniel, Frank Craven, Billie Burke, Lee Patrick. **1942**

IN TOO DEEP ★★1/2 An undercover cop finds himself growing a little too close to the drug kingpin he's supposed to be working against. Smooth direction and first-rate acting almost—but not quite—overcome a dreary, cliché-ridden script. Rated R for violence and profanity. 104m. **DIR:** Michael Rymer. **CAST:** Omar Epps, Nia Long, LL Cool J, Veronica Webb, Pam Grier, Stanley Tucci. **1999 DVD**

IN WHICH WE SERVE ★★★★★ Noel Coward wrote, produced, directed, and acted in this, one of the most moving wartime portrayals of men at sea. It is not the stirring battle sequences that make this film stand out but the intimate human story of the crew, their families, and the ship they love. A great film in all respects. B&W; 115m. **DIR:** Noel Coward, David Lean. **CAST:** Noel Coward, John Mills, Michael Wilding. **1942**

INCIDENT, THE (1967) ★★★1/2 Gritty inner-city horror story takes place on a late-night subway ride as two young thugs (Martin Sheen and Tony Musante, in their first film) terrorize each of the passengers. Definitely worth a watch! Not rated; contains violence. B&W; 99m. **DIR:** Larry Peerce. **CAST:** Tony Musante, Martin Sheen, Beau Bridges, Donna Mills, Gary Merrill, Thelma Ritter, Ruby Dee. **1967**

INCIDENT, THE (1989) ★★★1/2 During World War II, a small-town lawyer (Walter Matthau) finds himself railroaded by a powerful judge (Harry Morgan) into defending an accused murderer (Peter Firth). The problem is that Matthau's client is a German soldier from a nearby POW camp, where he allegedly killed the town doctor (Barnard Hughes), who was also the lawyer's longtime friend. Well-done. Made for TV. 94m. **DIR:** Joseph Sargent. **CAST:** Walter Matthau, Harry Morgan, Robert Carradine, Susan Blakely, Peter Firth, Barnard Hughes. **1989**

INCIDENT AT DARK RIVER ★★ Predictable environmental-pollution teledrama is nonetheless enjoyable, due largely to reliable Mike Farrell (who also wrote the story). A battery factory is dumping nasty things in the river out back—and denying everything. 94m. **DIR:** Michael Pressman. **CAST:** Mike Farrell, Tess Harper, Helen Hunt. **1989**

INCIDENT AT DECEPTION RIDGE ★★★1/2 In this taut little thriller, newly released ex-con Michael O'Keefe gets involved with some nasty types trying to recover a suitcase filled with stolen cash, and the chase is on. Folks annoyed by this genre's frequent reliance on gore will be pleased by Randy Kornfield and Ken Hixon's script, which downplays needless violence in favor of genuine suspense. Rated PG-13 for profanity and mild violence. 94m. **DIR:** John McPherson. **CAST:**

Michael O'Keefe, Ed Begley Jr., Miguel Ferrer, Linda Purl, Michelle Johnson, Colleen Flynn. **1994**

INCIDENT AT OGLALA ★★★★ Director Michael Apted and the Native Americans interviewed in this documentary make a compelling case for a retrial of Leonard Peltier, a leader in the American Indian Movement who is now serving two consecutive life terms for his alleged murder of two FBI agents during a confrontation. Apted somewhat fictionalized the conflicts between traditionalist Indians and their "mixed-blood" tribal leaders in *Thunderheart*, which should be viewed before watching this heartrending documentary. Rated PG. 93m. **DIR:** Michael Apted. **1992 DVD**

INCOGNITO ★★1/2 This romance-thriller undercuts its suspense by exposing its ending and then flashing back to a caper gone sour. A globetrotting art forger negotiates with an oily trio of art dealers to paint a fake Rembrandt. He also discusses life's nuances with his ailing mentor father and has sex with a European art expert he mistakes for a student. The details of the art forgery are fascinating, but the forger's extracurricular activities are boring. Rated R for language, nudity, and suggested sex. 109m. **DIR:** John Badham. **CAST:** Jason Patric, Irène Jacob, Rod Steiger, Ian Richardson. **1998 DVD**

INCONVENIENT WOMAN, AN ★★ Dominick Dunne's celebrated novel arrives as a made-for-TV soap opera with murder, double crosses, and plenty of scenery chewing. Great cast makes the best of a mediocre situation. 126m. **DIR:** Larry Elikann. **CAST:** Rebecca DeMornay, Jason Robards Jr., Jill Eikenberry, Peter Gallagher. **1991**

INCREDIBLE HULK, THE ★★1/2 Bill Bixby is sincere in the role of Dr. David Banner, a scientist whose experiments with gamma rays result in his being transformed into a huge green creature (Lou Ferrigno) whenever something angers him. Pilot for the series is a lot of fun, with better production values than most TV efforts. Based on the Marvel Comics character. 100m. **DIR:** Kenneth Johnson. **CAST:** Bill Bixby, Susan Sullivan, Lou Ferrigno, Jack Colvin, Charles Siebert. **1977**

INCREDIBLE HULK RETURNS, THE ★★ First of three made-for-TV movies based on the series. The script dumbs down the muscle-bound Hulk and, in introducing fellow Marvel Comics hero Thor, creates an even dumber character. Not rated, but suitable for the kiddies. 96m. **DIR:** Nicholas Corea. **CAST:** Lou Ferrigno, Bill Bixby, Eric Allen Kramer, Charles Napier, Lee Purcell, Tim Thomerson. **1988**

INCREDIBLE JOURNEY, THE ★★★★1/2 This live-action Walt Disney film is the story of two dogs and a cat that make a treacherous journey across Canada to find their home and family. It's impossible to dislike this heartwarming tale. 80m. **DIR:** Fletcher Markle. **CAST:** Emile Genest, John Drainie. **1963**

INCREDIBLE JOURNEY OF DR. MEG LAUREL,THE ★★★1/2 In this made-for-television film, Lindsay Wagner stars as Meg Laurel. From humble beginnings as an orphan from the Appalachian Mountains, she becomes a doctor. After graduating from Harvard Medical School, she sets up practice in 1930s Boston. But Wagner decides to return to the mountain people and administer the latest in medical procedures. 150m. **DIR:** Guy Green. **CAST:** Lindsay Wagner, Jane Wyman, Dorothy McGuire, James Woods, Gary Lockwood, Charles Tyner, Andrew Duggan, Brock Peters, John C. Reilly. **1978**

INCREDIBLE MELTING MAN, THE ★★ Superb makeup by Rick Baker highlights this story of an astronaut (Alex Rebar) who contracts a strange ailment that results in his turning into a gooey, melting mess upon his return to Earth. Wild stuff. Rated R for terminal grossness. 86m. **DIR:** William Sachs. **CAST:** Alex Rebar, Burr DeBenning, Myron Healey, Ann Sweeney. **1978**

INCREDIBLE MR. LIMPET, THE ★★ What can you say about a film whose hero is a fishbowl fancier who wishes himself into a fish so he can help the U.S. Navy defeat enemy submarines during World War II? Don Knotts as Henry Limpet is guilty as charged. Although popular with children, this outré excursion into fantasy will leave most viewers scratching their scales and flapping their gills wondering why on earth it was ever made. 102m. **DIR:** Arthur Lubin. **CAST:** Don Knotts, Carole Cook, Jack Weston, Andrew Duggan, Larry Keating. **1964**

INCREDIBLE PETRIFIED WORLD, THE Stupefying concoction, set almost entirely in a diving bell. B&W; 78m. **DIR:** Jerry Warren. **CAST:** John Carradine, Phyllis Coates. **1958**

INCREDIBLE ROCKY MOUNTAIN RACE, THE ★★★ This Western with a comic touch is about a race used by townspeople to get rid of two troublemakers. These troublemakers include Mark Twain (Christopher Connelly) and his archenemy, Mike Fink (Forrest Tucker). There is more comedy as the snags increase and the problems get out of hand. Rated G. 97m. **DIR:** James L. Conway. **CAST:** Christopher Connelly, Forrest Tucker, Larry Storch, Jack Kruschen, Mike Mazurki. **1985**

INCREDIBLE SARAH, THE ★★ As the legendary French actress Sarah Bernhardt—in her time the toast of Paris, London, and New York—Glenda Jackson tears passions to tatters, to very rags. Theater history buffs may like this pseudobiography. 106m. **DIR:** Richard Fleischer. **CAST:** Glenda Jackson, Daniel Massey, Yvonne Mitchell. **1976**

INCREDIBLE SHRINKING MAN, THE ★★★★ Good special effects as a man (Grant Williams), exposed to a strange radioactive mist, finds himself becoming smaller . . . and smaller . . . and smaller. Well-mounted thriller from Universal with many memorable scenes, including the classic showdown with an ordinary house spider. B&W; 81m. **DIR:** Jack Arnold. **CAST:** Grant Williams, Randy Stuart, Paul Langton, April Kent. **1957**

INCREDIBLE SHRINKING WOMAN, THE ★★ This comedy, starring Lily Tomlin, falls prey to the law of diminishing returns. But to simply dismiss it as a failure would be inaccurate and unfair. This comic adaptation of Richard Matheson's classic science-fiction novel (*The Shrinking Man*) is not a bad movie. It's more like . . . well . . . the perfect old-fashioned Disney movie—a little corny and strained at times but not a total loss. Rated PG. 88m. **DIR:** Joel Schumacher. **CAST:** Lily Tomlin, Ned Beatty, Henry Gibson, Elizabeth Wilson, Charles Grodin, Pamela Bellwood, Mike Douglas, Mark Blankfield. **1981**

INCREDIBLE TWO-HEADED TRANSPLANT, THE A sadistic killer's head is grafted to the body of a dim-wit-

ted giant. Rated PG. 88m. **DIR:** Anthony M. Lanza. **CAST:** Bruce Dern, Pat Priest, Casey Kasem. **1971**

INCREDIBLY STRANGE CREATURES WHO STOPPED LIVING AND BECAME MIXED-UP ZOMBIES, THE 🦃 This movie doesn't live up to its title; how could it? It was later released as *Teenage Psycho Meets Bloody Mary*. 81m. **DIR:** Ray Dennis Steckler. **CAST:** Cash Flagg, Brett O'Hara, Carolyn Brandt, Atlas King. **1965**

INCREDIBLY TRUE ADVENTURE OF TWO GIRLS IN LOVE, THE ★★1/2 Two high-school students discover a flirtatious attraction that ripens into physical love. Writer-director Maria Maggenti tries for a lighthearted girl-meets-girl romance, but her writing is flat, her directing awkward, and the ending dissolves in chaos. Laurel Holloman and Nicole Parker are appealing in the title roles, but the supporting cast is largely inept. Rated R for profanity and nudity. 94m. **DIR:** Maria Maggenti. **CAST:** Laurel Holloman, Nicole Parker. **1995**

INDECENCY ★★★ A suspenseful whodunit about the murder of an ad agency owner. Was it the soon-to-be ex-husband, the partner who was sleeping with the husband, or the drug dealer? Good plot and good acting make this an enjoyable film. Rated PG-13 for sensuality and profanity. 88m. **DIR:** Marisa Silver. **CAST:** Jennifer Beals, Sammi Davis, James Remar, Barbara Williams, Christopher John Fields. **1992**

INDECENT OBSESSION, AN ★★★ A bleak, intense view of the results of war. Wendy Hughes is the compassionate nurse for shell-shocked British soldiers and other war-torn crazies. A sensitive adaptation of Colleen McCullough's bestseller. Not rated; contains violence, nudity, and profanity. 100m. **DIR:** Lex Marinos. **CAST:** Wendy Hughes, Gary Sweet, Richard Moir. **1985**

INDECENT PROPOSAL ★★1/2 Good performances cannot save this brainless soap opera. Extremely wealthy Robert Redford offers $1 million to married Demi Moore if she'll spend the night with him. Naturally, Moore and her hubby, a whining, less-than-effective Woody Harrelson, are in deep financial trouble and the rest of the film is just as predictable. Rated R for profanity, nudity, and simulated sex. 113m. **DIR:** Adrian Lyne. **CAST:** Robert Redford, Demi Moore, Woody Harrelson, Oliver Platt, Seymour Cassel. **1993 DVD**

INDEPENDENCE DAY (1983) ★★★★ Excellent little story about a young woman (Kathleen Quinlan) who wants to leave the stifling environment of her hometown. She's helped and hindered by a growing attachment to David Keith, a garage mechanic with his own problems. Rated R for violence and sex. 110m. **DIR:** Robert Mandel. **CAST:** David Keith, Kathleen Quinlan, Richard Farnsworth, Frances Sternhagen, Cliff De Young, Dianne Wiest. **1983**

INDEPENDENCE DAY (1996) ★★★★1/2 The best retro science-fiction epic since George Lucas released *Star Wars* is also a distant cousin to the 1970s disaster flick: a slam-bang, thrill-a-minute effort that truly puts the motion in "motion picture." With a nod to H. G. Wells's *War of the Worlds*, this film is a star-studded tale of extraterrestrial invasion, human dignity, and good ol' American know-how. Bill Pullman makes a grand United States president; Jeff Goldblum is the absentminded scientist who ultimately saves the day. But the Oscar-winning special effects carry this high-octane actionfest. Rated PG-13 for profanity and violence. 145m. **DIR:** Roland Emmerich. **CAST:** Will Smith, Bill Pullman, Jeff Goldblum, Mary McDonnell, Judd Hirsch, Margaret Colin, Randy Quaid, Robert Loggia, Brent Spiner. **1996 DVD**

•INDEPENDENT, THE ★★★1/2 Veteran comedian Jerry Stiller plays low-budget filmmaker Morty Fineman (a sort of combination of 1960s B-movie auteurs Roger Corman and Russ Meyer) in this amusing pseudo-documentary. Film buffs will love it; be sure to stick around for the closing credits, which include a hilarious list of Fineman's "classics." Rated R for profanity, some violence, and brief nudity. 85m. **DIR:** Stephen Kessler. **CAST:** Jerry Stiller, Janeane Garofalo, Max Perlich, Roger Corman, Ron Howard, Peter Bogdanovich. **2000 DVD**

INDESTRUCTIBLE MAN ★★ Lon Chaney looks uncomfortable in the title role of an electrocuted man brought back to life who seeks revenge on the old gang who betrayed him. Nothing new has been added to the worn-out story, unless you want to count the awful narration, which makes this passable thriller seem utterly ridiculous at times. B&W; 70m. **DIR:** Jack Pollexfen. **CAST:** Lon Chaney Jr., Marian Carr, Ross Elliott, Casey Adams. **1956 DVD**

INDIAN IN THE CUPBOARD, THE ★★★1/2 Children familiar with Lynne Reid Banks's original story may be disappointed with this big-screen adaptation, which leaves out several important characters and events. Judged on its own merits, however, this is an entertaining, sometimes fascinating tale of a young boy who discovers a way to bring his toys alive. Even adults will find it worth watching. Rated PG. 96m. **DIR:** Frank Oz. **CAST:** Hal Scardino, Litefoot, Lindsay Crouse, Richard Jenkins, Rishi Bhat, David Keith, Steve Coogan. **1995 DVD**

INDIAN RUNNER, THE ★★★1/2 As a first-time director, actor Sean Penn has fashioned a movie that's not unlike one of his better performances—edgy, rough-hewn, daring, passionate, and fascinating. His movie revolves around the conflicts arising from two brothers as unalike as Cain and Abel. Though a box-office failure, *The Indian Runner* offers hope for a substantial directorial career from Penn. Rated R, with profanity and violence. 125m. **DIR:** Sean Penn. **CAST:** David Morse, Viggo Mortensen, Valeria Golino, Patricia Arquette, Charles Bronson, Sandy Dennis. **1991 DVD**

INDIAN SUMMER ★★★ This amiable, warmhearted comedy is best described as *The Big Chill* goes to summer camp. An Ontario camp director invites his favorite kids from the "golden years" of the early 1970s back for a twenty-year reunion. It's a movie full of big grins and tolerable, skin-deep goo. Rated PG-13 for language, drug use, and simulated sex. 98m. **DIR:** Mike Binder. **CAST:** Alan Arkin, Matt Craven, Diane Lane, Bill Paxton, Elizabeth Perkins, Kevin Pollak, Sam Raimi, Vincent Spano, Julie Warner, Kimberly Williams. **1993**

INDIAN UPRISING ★★ The surrender of Apache Indian Chief, Geronimo—here, highly fictionalized to involve mercenary white men and heroic cavalry men. Although the cassette box lists 74 minutes, this is a severely edited print of an original color film. B&W; 60m. **DIR:** Ray Nazarro. **CAST:** George Montgomery, Audrey Long, Carl Benton Reid, Joe Sawyer. **1952**

INDIANA JONES AND THE LAST CRUSADE ★★★★1/2 In the last film of this entertaining cliff-hanger series, Indiana Jones embarks on a quest for the Holy Grail when his father disappears while on the same mission. Father and son are soon slugging it out with some nasty Nazis in this all-ages delight. Rated PG-13 for violence and profanity. 127m. **DIR:** Steven Spielberg. **CAST:** Harrison Ford, Sean Connery, Denholm Elliott, John Rhys-Davies, River Phoenix. **1989**

INDIANA JONES AND THE TEMPLE OF DOOM ★★★★ This sequel is almost as good as the original, *Raiders of the Lost Ark*. The story takes place before the events of *Raiders* with its two-fisted, whip-wielding hero, Dr. Indiana Jones (Harrison Ford) performing feats of derring-do in Singapore and India circa 1935. Parents may want to see this fast-paced and sometimes scary film before allowing their kids to watch it. Rated PG for profanity and violence. 118m. **DIR:** Steven Spielberg. **CAST:** Harrison Ford, Kate Capshaw. **1984**

INDICTMENT: THE MCMARTIN TRIAL ★★★★1/2 Producer Oliver Stone and cowriter Abby Mann positively excoriate the Los Angeles–area preschool legal and media circus that lasted 2,489 days, destroyed the lives of defendants, and ultimately failed to find any of them guilty. Overzealous prosecutors and a child therapist with questionable credentials emerge as the villains, while defense attorney James Woods eventually becomes galvanic with righteous indignation. The entire cast in this HBO-made film is excellent. Rated R for profanity and brief nudity. 132m. **DIR:** Mick Jackson. **CAST:** James Woods, Mercedes Ruehl, Sada Thompson, Henry Thomas, Shirley Knight, Lolita Davidovich. **1995**

INDIO ★★ Marvin Hagler stars as a half-breed Marine Corps officer who returns to his native land in the Amazon to find that developers have ravaged the countryside and his people. As a former U.S. army colonel, Brian Dennehy brings a little class to an otherwise routine *Rambo* rip-off. Rated R for violence and profanity. 94m. **DIR:** Anthony M. Dawson. **CAST:** Francesco Quinn, Brian Dennehy, Marvin Hagler. **1989**

INDIO 2: THE REVOLT 🦃 Marvelous Marvin Hagler isn't so marvelous as Sergeant Iron, a U.S. Marine leading Amazonian tribes against greedy developers. Not rated; contains violence. 104m. **DIR:** Anthony M. Dawson. **CAST:** Marvin Hagler, Charles Napier, Frank Cuervo. **1990**

INDISCREET (1931) 🦃 Gloria Swanson trying to conceal her questionable past. B&W; 92m. **DIR:** Leo McCarey. **CAST:** Gloria Swanson, Ben Lyon, Arthur Lake. **1931 DVD**

INDISCREET (1958) ★★1/2 Dated comedy about an on-again, off-again affair between rich actress Ingrid Bergman and playboy bachelor Cary Grant. These stars could make anything watchable, but this isn't one of their best. 100m. **DIR:** Stanley Donen. **CAST:** Cary Grant, Ingrid Bergman, Cecil Parker. **1958 DVD**

INDISCRETION OF AN AMERICAN WIFE ★★1/2 One hour and three minutes of emotional turmoil played out against the background of Rome's railway station as adultress Jennifer Jones meets her lover, Montgomery Clift, for the last time. B&W; 63m. **DIR:** Vittorio De Sica. **CAST:** Jennifer Jones, Montgomery Clift, Gino Cervi, Richard Beymer. **1954 DVD**

INDOCHINE ★★★★1/2 Set in French Indochina in 1930, this exquisite import chronicles the violent changes that led to the creation of Vietnam from the ruins of colonialism. Catherine Deneuve is superb in the pivotal role of an Asian-born, French-descended owner of a rubber plantation. In French with English subtitles. Rated PG-13 for violence, nudity, and profanity. 155m. **DIR:** Regis Wargnier. **CAST:** Catherine Deneuve, Vincent Perez, Dan Pham Linh, Jean Yanne. **1992 DVD**

INDUSTRIAL SYMPHONY NO. 1 THE DREAM OF THE BROKEN HEARTED ★★★1/2 Bizarre glimpse into a broken love affair set against the backdrop of an industrial wasteland from the director of *Eraserhead*, *Twin Peaks*, and *Wild At Heart*. This surreal opera was performed at The Brooklyn Academy of Music opera house and features an impressive score by composer Angelo Badalamenti, with lyrics by David Lynch. Not rated; contains some nudity. 50m. **DIR:** David Lynch. **CAST:** Laura Dern, Nicolas Cage, Julee Cruise. **1989**

INFAMOUS DOROTHY PARKER, THE ★★1/2 A quickie documentary put together for the release of *Mrs. Parker and the Vicious Circle*, this provides a decent background of Parker during her adult years. Entertaining and informative as this may be, the overly slick, intrusive graphics may cause you to scream. Ditto for host Wendy Lieberman. Made for A&E. Not rated. 49m. **DIR:** Robert Yuhas. **CAST:** Wendy Lieberman, Jennifer Jason Leigh, Alan Rudolph, Fran Lebowitz, Campbell Scott, Matthew Broderick, Gloria Steinem. **1994**

INFERNAL TRIO, THE ★★★1/2 Lurid, stylishly gruesome black comedy about a sociopathic lawyer (Michel Piccoli) who, after seducing two sisters, enlists them to marry and murder victims and defraud their insurance companies. Based on an actual police case. In French with English subtitles. Not rated; contains violence and nudity. 100m. **DIR:** Francis Girod. **CAST:** Romy Schneider, Michel Piccoli, Andrea Ferreol. **1974**

INFERNO (1980) ★★ This Italian horror flick is heavy on suspense but weak on plot. Leigh McCloskey is the hero who comes to help his sister when she discovers that her apartment is inhabited by an ancient evil spirit. Voices are dubbed, even American actor McCloskey's, and something may have been lost in the translation. Rated R for gore. 83m. **DIR:** Dario Argento. **CAST:** Eleonora Giorgi, Leigh McCloskey, Gabriele Lavia. **1980 DVD**

INFERNO (1998) ★★★★ Well-made disaster flick tells the story of a burst of radioactive heat from the sun that turns up the Earth's temperature to 145 degrees for several days. The story focuses on the lives of several people and how the heat wave affects them. Rated PG-13 for violence. 90m. **DIR:** Ian Barry. **CAST:** James Remar, Stephanie Niznik, Daniel Von Bargen, Jonathan LaPaglia. **1998**

INFESTED (TICKS) 🦃 Wood ticks pumped up on herbal steroids crawl under the skin of forest visitors in this low-budget horrorama. Rated R for violence, gore, and language. 85m. **DIR:** Tony Randel. **CAST:** Rosalind Allen, Ami Dolenz, Seth Green, Virginya Keehne, Ray Oriel, Alfonso Ribeiro, Peter Scolari, Dina Dayrit, Michale Medeiros, Barry Lynch, Clint Howard. **1993**

INFILTRATOR, THE ★★★ Israeli-American journalist Yaron Svoray's covert penetration of the modern Ger-

man neo-Nazi movement must have been incredibly perilous, but this screen adaptation makes the whole endeavor seem trite. Oliver Platt is properly dedicated in the central role, but the subject's deadly seriousness is ill-served by this simplistic adaptation of Svoray's book, *In Hitler's Shadow*. Rated R for profanity, violence, nudity, and rape. 102m. **DIR:** John Mackenzie. **CAST:** Oliver Platt, Arliss Howard, Tony Haygarth, Michael Byrne, Julian Glover, Peter Riegert, Alan King. **1995**

INFINITY ★★1/2 Star Matthew Broderick makes his directorial debut with this bio-pic of physicist Richard Feynman during World War II, who works on the Manhattan Project in New Mexico while spending weekends with his wife who is dying of tuberculosis. Clearly a labor of love, the film has several fine moments but succumbs to its own earnestly plodding pace and too many disease-of-the-week clichés. Rated PG for profanity and mild sensuality. 119m. **DIR:** Matthew Broderick. **CAST:** Matthew Broderick, Patricia Arquette, Peter Riegert. **1996 DVD**

INFORMANT, THE ★★★1/2 An IRA terrorist having unsuccessfully tried to "resign," is roped into a high-profile assassination and then gets caught. Faced with life in prison, he chooses instead to save his own hide by ratting out his former friends and associates. This adaptation of Gerald Seymour's *Field of Blood* becomes yet another intellectual analysis of the Irish "troubles," but this one wears its opinion on its sleeve, showing all IRA participants in a negative light. Rated R for profanity, nudity, rape, simulated sex, and violence. 105m. **DIR:** Jim McBride. **CAST:** Cary Elwes, Anthony Brophy, Timothy Dalton, Maria Lennon, Sean McGinley. **1997**

INFORMER, THE ★★★★ John Ford's classic about a slow-witted Irish pug (Victor McLaglen), who turns his friend in for money to impress his ladylove and gets his comeuppance from the IRA, has lost none of its atmospheric punch over the years. McLaglen is superb, and the movie lingers in your memory long after the credits roll. B&W; 91m. **DIR:** John Ford. **CAST:** Victor McLaglen, Heather Angel, Preston Foster. **1935**

INFRA-MAN ★★1/2 Mainly for kids, this *Ultraman* rip-off, about a giant superhero protecting the Earth from a bunch of crazy-looking monsters, still manages to succeed, despite the lame acting and hokey special effects. Ridiculous but enjoyable. Rated PG. 92m. **DIR:** Hua-Shan. **CAST:** Wang Hsieh. **1976**

INHERIT THE WIND (1960) ★★★★★ In this superb film based on the stage play of the notorious Scopes monkey trial, a biology teacher is put on trial for teaching the theory of evolution. The courtroom battle that actually took place between Clarence Darrow and Willian Jennings Bryan could not have been more powerful or stimulating than the acting battle put on by two of America's most respected actors—Spencer Tracy and Fredric March. 127m. **DIR:** Stanley Kramer. **CAST:** Spencer Tracy, Fredric March, Gene Kelly, Dick York, Claude Akins. **1960 DVD**

INHERIT THE WIND (1999) ★★★★ Time has not diminished the intensity of Jerome Lawrence and Robert E. Lee's grand play, and this film faithfully adapts the 1960 script for which Nedrick Young and Harold Jacob Smith received Oscar nominations. Jack Lemmon stands in for Spencer Tracy, and George C. Scott for Fredric March, in the slightly fictionalized but still-powerful Scopes monkey courtroom battle resulting from one schoolteacher's attempt to teach evolution in Hillsboro High School in 1925. (Indeed, it could be argued that this story became even more timely in the late 1990s.) Scott chews up the scenery grandly as the visiting prosecutor who preaches fire and brimstone, while Lemmon has the quieter—but far more piercing—role as the defender forced to challenge and even humiliate the man he once regarded as a good friend. Beau Bridges comments from the side as the cynical journalist (based on H. L. Mencken) who regarded the trial as the height of absurdity, and Piper Laurie is warm and dignified as Scott's wife. While not quite up to the original, this remake still packs quite a punch. Rated PG for dramatic content. 113m. **DIR:** Daniel Petrie. **CAST:** Jack Lemmon, George C. Scott, Lane Smith, Tom Everett Scott, Kathryn Morris, John Cullum, Piper Laurie, Beau Bridges. **1999**

INHERITORS, THE ★★1/2 A mean-spirited Austrian farmer, recently murdered, has left his farm to the ten peasants who work there—not because he likes them, but because he thinks they'll kill each other fighting over it. Meanwhile, the local landowners scheme to get the farm away from the peasants. Gloomy, turgid, pessimistic—writer-director Ruzowitzky seems to share the dead farmer's contempt for humanity. In German with English subtitles. Rated R for mature themes. 90m. **DIR:** Stefan Ruzowitzky. **CAST:** Simon Schwartz, Sophie Rois, Lars Rudolph, Julia Gschnitzer. **1998 DVD**

INHUMANOID 🦃 This blindingly inept sci-fi chiller opens with a ridiculously gratuitous sex scene, proceeds through the grotesque murder of a little girl, and then utilizes laughable cardboard sets during a protracted duel between a killer android and the world's dumbest female protagonist. Rated R for nudity, simulated sex, profanity, violence, and gore. 87m. **DIR:** Victoria Muspratt. **CAST:** Richard Grieco, Lara Harris, Corbin Bernsen. **1996**

INITIATION OF SARAH, THE ★★ Adequate TV movie features Kay Lenz as a young college girl being victimized by other students during initiation, and her subsequent revenge upon acquiring supernatural powers. Hokey thriller should have been better, judging from the cast. 100m. **DIR:** Robert Day. **CAST:** Kay Lenz, Shelley Winters, Kathryn Crosby, Morgan Brittany, Tony Bill. **1978**

INKWELL, THE ★★ This amateurish coming-of-age story has its heart in the right place, but it's a dramatic and comic mess. A decent but troubled African-American teen from New York City and his parents spend their 1976 summer vacation with affluent relatives on Martha's Vineyard. The fashions—especially the bell-bottomed, polyester jumpsuits—are a scream. But the film never draws a credible bead on its characters or their relationships. Rated R for language and suggested sex. 112m. **DIR:** Matty Rich. **CAST:** Larenz Tate, Suzzanne Douglas, Joe Morton, Glynn Turman, Jada Pinkett. **1994**

INN OF THE SIXTH HAPPINESS, THE ★★★★ Superb acting marks this heartwarming biography of China missionary Gladys Aylward (Ingrid Bergman). The movie opens with her determined attempt to enter the missionary service and follows her to strife-torn China.

The highlight is her cross-country adventure as she leads a group of orphans away from the war zone. 158m. **DIR:** Mark Robson. **CAST:** Ingrid Bergman, Curt Jurgens, Robert Donat. **1958**

INNER CIRCLE, THE ★★★1/2 This drama, released within weeks of the dismantling of the Soviet Union, comes along to remind us of the coldly cruel totalitarianism of Josef Stalin. Tom Hulce stars as Ivan Sanshin, a young KGB projectionist who is shocked and thrilled to find himself selected as chief projectionist for the movie buff and dictator. The fact that it's based on a true story, and was filmed entirely in the Kremlin and other parts of Russia, lends authenticity and impact. Rated PG-13. 137m. **DIR:** Andrei Konchalovsky. **CAST:** Tom Hulce, Lolita Davidovich, Bob Hoskins. **1991**

INNER SANCTUM ★★1/2 Wheelchair-bound wife Valerie Wildman suspects her husband and new nurse are plotting to drive her insane. The plot's not hot, but the sex in the unrated version is pretty steamy. Available in both a tamer R version and a soft-core unrated version. 90m. **DIR:** Fred Olen Ray. **CAST:** Joseph Bottoms, Margaux Hemingway, Tanya Roberts, Valerie Wildman, William Butler, Brett Clark. **1991**

INNER SANCTUM 2 🦃 Another erotic thriller lacking eroticism and thrills. Available in R-rated and unrated versions; both contain profanity, nudity, and sexual situations. 93m. **DIR:** Fred Olen Ray. **CAST:** Michael Nouri, Tracy Brooks Swope, Sandahl Bergman. **1994**

INNERSPACE ★★★★ Get this story line: Dennis Quaid is a rebel astronaut who is miniaturized in order to be injected into the body of a rabbit. By accident the syringe carrying Quaid ends up being injected into the body of hypochondriac Martin Short. Sound weird? It is. Sound funny? We thought so. Rated PG for profanity and violence. 130m. **DIR:** Joe Dante. **CAST:** Dennis Quaid, Martin Short, Meg Ryan, Kevin McCarthy, Fiona Lewis, Henry Gibson. **1987**

•INNOCENCE ★★★1/2 Lovers separated for over forty years reunite and rekindle their passion for each other in this restrained but engrossing Australian drama about adultery and other affairs of the heart. He is a widowed music teacher still enamored with his first love. She is now a svelte grandmother who is stuck in a marriage that has become routine at best and who wants love, not just sacrifice, from her emotionally distant first husband. Not rated; contains profanity, nudity, sex, and mature themes. 94m. **DIR:** Paul Cox. **CAST:** Charles Tingwell, Julia Blake, Terry Norris, Kristien Van Pellicom, Kenny Aernouts. **2000**

INNOCENCE UNPROTECTED ★★★★ Controversial Yugoslavian filmmaker Dusan Makavejev took a 1942 melodrama (the first feature film made in the Serb language), restored and recut it, and added new interviews with its director and cast. He then used it as the basis for a singular collage incorporating other elements of contemporary political importance. The result is alternately ironic, satirical, and serious, but always compelling. In Serb with English subtitles. Not rated. 78m. **DIR:** Dusan Makavejev. **1968**

INNOCENT, THE (1976) ★★★★ Some rate this as the most beautiful of all Luchino Visconti's films. Set in a nineteenth-century baronial manor, it's the old tale of the real versus the ideal, but beautifully done. In Italian with English subtitles. Rated R due to some explicit scenes. 115m. **DIR:** Luchino Visconti. **CAST:** Laura Antonelli, Giancarlo Giannini, Jennifer O'Neill. **1976**

INNOCENT, THE (1993) ★★★★1/2 Paranoia, fierce sexuality, and an unexpected murder merge in this unusual thriller set against the political backdrop of the cold war. Campbell Scott is the naïve Brit sent to Berlin to work on a top-secret engineering project but is tempted into deep waters by Isabella Rossellini. Anthony Hopkins joins them in an unholy alliance of secrecy and deceit. The little moments tell a lot in this story that heads in surprising directions. Rated R for profanity, nudity, violence, and sexual situations. 99m. **DIR:** John Schlesinger. **CAST:** Anthony Hopkins, Isabella Rossellini, Campbell Scott, Ronald Nitschke. **1993**

INNOCENT BLOOD ★★★ Director John Landis returns to his roots with this mostly amusing spin on vampire lore, which finds sultry Anne Parillaud as a selective bloodsucker who feeds only on those deserving to die. Rated R for gore, profanity, explicit sex, and nudity. 112m. **DIR:** John Landis. **CAST:** Anne Parillaud, Robert Loggia, Anthony LaPaglia, Don Rickles. **1992 DVD**

INNOCENT LIES ★★ Creepy thriller finds a detective investigating the death of his best friend. When he's drawn to the victim's sister, he learns that the family is hiding some dark secrets involving the girl and her overly protective brother. Incest theme is a bit touchy for such fare. Not rated; contains adult situations and language. 88m. **DIR:** Patrick DeWolf. **CAST:** Stephen Dorff, Gabrielle Anwar, Adrian Dunbar. **1995**

INNOCENT MAN, AN ★★★★ Jimmie Rainwood (Tom Selleck) is a decent guy; an airplane mechanic who likes his job and loves his wife. But a mistake by two overzealous undercover detectives changes his simple life into a nightmare. Well directed by Peter Yates, *An Innocent Man* has a solid dramatic story line, and fine performances. Rated R for violence and profanity. 113m. **DIR:** Peter Yates. **CAST:** Tom Selleck, F. Murray Abraham, Laila Robins, David Rasche. **1989**

INNOCENT VICTIM ★★★ Lauren Bacall stars as a woman recovering from a nervous breakdown visiting her daughter (Helen Shaver) in England. When Shaver's son dies suddenly, Bacall makes a fateful decision. Fine performances by Bacall and Shaver highlight this quirky little thriller, based on Ruth Rendell's *Tree of Hands*. Rated R for violence and profanity. 100m. **DIR:** Giles Foster. **CAST:** Lauren Bacall, Helen Shaver, Peter Firth. **1990**

INNOCENTS, THE ★★★★1/2 Henry James's *The Turn of the Screw* becomes a marvelously atmospheric period thriller in director Jack Clayton's hands. Deborah Kerr sparkles as a governess hired to watch over the two motherless young children who inhabit one of those oppressively gloomy British mansions; after spending some time with her new charges, our heroine begins to suspect that they've been possessed by the spirits of former servants who died under unhappy circumstances. Or is she simply imagining things? The film will keep you guessing and proves once and for all that considerable terror can be generated by what is merely suggested, rather than what is shown. Great stuff, but perhaps too intense for young viewers. 100m. **DIR:** Jack Clayton. **CAST:** Deborah Kerr, Michael Redgrave, Peter Wyngarde, Megs Jenkins, Pamela Franklin, Martin Stephens. **1961**

INQUIRY, THE ★★ Italian-made film about the investigation by a Roman official (Keith Carradine) into the resurrection of Christ. Carradine is fine but Harvey Keitel makes an uneasy Pontius Pilate because of his tough-guy accent. Not rated; contains some nudity and violence. 106m. **DIR:** Damiano Damiani. **CAST:** Keith Carradine, Harvey Keitel, Phyllis Logan. **1986**

INSECT WOMAN ★★★★ Sachiko Hidari gives an emotionally supercharged performance that gained her a best actress award at the Berlin Film Festival. In this harrowing drama, she plays an impoverished country girl who escapes a brutal existence by fleeing to Tokyo where she finds success as a madam. Director Shohei Imamura weaves a dark and often humorous story with shocking overtones. Winner of Japanese film awards for best actress, director, and film. In Japanese with English subtitles. B&W; 123m. **DIR:** Shohei Imamura. **CAST:** Sachiko Hidari. **1963**

INSERTS 🦃 Dreary film about a once-great 1930s film director now making porno movies. Rated R. 99m. **DIR:** John Byrum. **CAST:** Richard Dreyfuss, Jessica Harper, Bob Hoskins, Veronica Cartwright. **1976**

INSIDE ★★★ Scripter Bima Stagg's prison drama opens well but runs out of steam before a highly unsatisfying conclusion. The setting is South Africa in 1988; the game, a round of intense psychological warfare, involving a sadistic police official, his liberal white prisoner, and a black fellow prisoner later given the authority to investigate the situation. Too bad the story can't match the intensity of all three performances. Rated R for violence, torture, profanity, nudity, and simulated sex. 94m. **DIR:** Arthur Penn. **CAST:** Nigel Hawthorne, Eric Stoltz, Louis Gossett Jr. **1996 DVD**

INSIDE DAISY CLOVER ★★ Natalie Wood plays a teenager who wants to be a star. Robert Redford is the matinee idol she marries to get her name in the gossip columns. A grim story about Hollywood that has better performances than plot. 128m. **DIR:** Robert Mulligan. **CAST:** Natalie Wood, Robert Redford, Christopher Plummer, Roddy McDowall, Ruth Gordon. **1964**

INSIDE MAN, THE ★★★1/2 Inspired by a 1981 incident in which a Soviet submarine ran aground in Sweden, this exciting adventure film really moves. A CIA agent (Dennis Hopper) sets up a young ex-Marine (Gosta Ekman) as the inside man who must investigate the theft of a laser-submarine search device. Check this one out. It's unrated, but contains some strong language. 90m. **DIR:** Tom Clegg. **CAST:** Dennis Hopper, Hardy Kruger, Gosta Ekman, Celia Gregory. **1984 DVD**

INSIDE MONKEY ZETTERLAND ★★★ Monkey Zetterland is a former teen movie star turned scriptwriter. His extended family includes a mother who's a soap star, a hairdresser brother, a gay sister and her pregnant girlfriend, a pair of terrorists, and his wandering biker dad. The ensemble cast struggles gamely to rise above the erratic script. Rated R for adult situations, profanity, and brief violence. 93m. **DIR:** Jefery Levy. **CAST:** Steve Antin, Patricia Arquette, Sandra Bernhard, Sofia Coppola, Tate Donovan, Rupert Everett, Katherine Helmond, Bo Hopkins, Ricki Lake, Debi Mazar, Martha Plimpton. **1992**

INSIDE MOVES ★★★★ This is a film that grows on you as the heartwarming story unfolds. With a unique blend of humor and insight, director Richard Donner and screenwriters Valerie Curtin and Barry Levinson provide a captivating look into a very special friendship. John Savage plays a man who, after failing at suicide, succeeds at life with the help of some disabled friends. Rated PG. 113m. **DIR:** Richard Donner. **CAST:** John Savage, David Morse, Amy Wright, Tony Burton. **1980**

INSIDE OUT (1975) ★★★ An unlikely trio (Telly Savalas, Robert Culp, and James Mason) band together to recover $6 million in gold that Hitler had hidden. The action and suspense in this film should hold most viewers' attention. Rated PG. 98m. **DIR:** Peter Duffell. **CAST:** Telly Savalas, Robert Culp, James Mason, Aldo Ray. **1975**

INSIDE OUT (1986) ★★1/2 Compelling drama that tackles agoraphobia, the fear of open spaces. Elliott Gould stars as a man who fears leaving his New York apartment; his only contact with the outside world are the phone and delivery services. Rated R for profanity. 87m. **DIR:** Robert Taicher. **CAST:** Elliott Gould, Howard Hesseman, Jennifer Tilly, Dana Elcar. **1986**

INSIDE THE THIRD REICH ★★★1/2 This made-for-TV miniseries is based on the autobiography of Albert Speer, the German architect who became Hitler's chief builder. Rutger Hauer portrays Speer as a man obsessed with the opportunity to build extensively while being blissfully unaware of the horrors of war around him. 250m. **DIR:** Marvin J. Chomsky. **CAST:** Rutger Hauer, Derek Jacobi, Blythe Danner, John Gielgud, Ian Holm, Elke Sommer, Trevor Howard, Robert Vaughn. **1982**

INSIDER, THE ★★★★1/2 When the *60 Minutes* producer gets a tobacco-industry scientist to reveal the darkest secrets of his employers on camera, it seems CBS News has the story of the decade; however, executives at the network are not thrilled with this big scoop and attempt to use their power to influence the news department not to run the story, thus endangering the life of the scientist and his family. Russell Crowe, as the scientist, and Christopher Plummer, as Mike Wallace, give the standout performances, but everything about this drama is first class. Rated R for profanity and an atmosphere of danger. 157m. **DIR:** Michael Mann. **CAST:** Al Pacino, Russell Crowe, Christopher Plummer, Diane Venora, Gina Gershon, Lindsay Crouse. **1999 DVD**

INSIGNIFICANCE ★★ Michael Emil's absolutely wonderful impersonation of Albert Einstein makes this film worth seeing. In 1954 Marilyn Monroe comes to visit Einstein in his hotel room to explain the theory of relativity to him. Charming, but it eventually loses its uniqueness as it incorporates disjunctive symbolic flashbacks into the narrative. Rated R. 110m. **DIR:** Nicolas Roeg. **CAST:** Michael Emil, Theresa Russell, Gary Busey, Tony Curtis, Will Sampson. **1985**

INSOMNIA ★★★★ A former Swedish detective finds himself in Norway on a murder investigation in this harrowing exploration of one man's fall from grace. Jonas Engström, once a highly successful detective, is looking for personal redemption, but instead encounters his personal demons. In his debut, director Erik Skjoldbjærg has created a film that is both suspenseful and unnerving. Once the film casts its spell, you won't be able to close your eyes. In Swedish with English subtitles. Not rated; contains adult situations, language, and violence. 97m. **DIR:** Erik Skjoldbjærg. **CAST:** Stellan Skarsgard, Sverre Anker Ousdal. **1997 DVD**

INSPECTOR GADGET ★★★1/2 Thanks to leaping advancements in special effects and morphing technology, Disney's take on *Inspector Gadget* can be branded the very first wholly live-action cartoon, in every sense of the word (and we mean that as a compliment). Blessed with furious energy and impeccable comic timing, this is gobs o' fun, from the very first second—a spring-laden spoof of the familiar Disney logo—to the very last. The film is further blessed with suitably heroic protagonists, marvelously flamboyant villains, and a director who perfectly understands the nature of this project. Matthew Broderick, who has based his career on humanizing characters under odd or even extreme circumstances, makes a stalwart cyborg investigator, albeit one not taken seriously, and Rupert Everett is sublime as the nefarious Sanford Scolex. This one, to borrow one of its own phrases, is a wowser: lots of fun and wonderfully inventive. Rated PG for comic mayhem. 80m. **DIR:** David Kellogg. **CAST:** Matthew Broderick, Rupert Everett, Joely Fisher, Michelle Trachtenberg, Andy Dick, Cheri Oteri, Dabney Coleman. **1999 DVD**

INSPECTOR GENERAL, THE ★★★★ In this classic comedy set in Russia of the 1800s, Danny Kaye is the town fool who is mistaken for a confidant of Napoleon. The laughs come when Danny is caught up in court intrigue and really has no idea what is going on. Kaye's talents are showcased in this film. 102m. **DIR:** Henry Koster. **CAST:** Danny Kaye, Walter Slezak, Elsa Lanchester. **1949**

INSPECTOR MORSE (TV SERIES) ★★★★1/2 Colin Dexter's introspective and moody Chief Inspector Morse and his amiable assistant, Detective-Sergeant Lewis, are perfectly rendered in this British mystery series. Morse, an opera lover who enjoys his pints of bitter, is a lonely bachelor, but solves his murder cases with zeal and intelligence. Lewis, an affable family man, makes an excellent counterpart to his demanding boss. A well-paced set of stories set in Oxford. 52m. **DIR:** Peter Hammond, Brian Parker, Alastair Reid. **CAST:** John Thaw, Kevin Whately, Peter Woodthorpe, Norman Jones. **1987–1988**

INSPECTORS, THE ★★★ This valentine to our dedicated, resourceful, hardworking U.S. postal inspectors turns them into crack investigators on a par with the most seasoned FBI agent. Bruce Zimmerman's script is pure contrivance, but stars Lou Gossett Jr. and Jonathan Silverman give events dignity and credibility. Rated R for profanity, violence, sexual candor, and a grim autopsy scene. 102m. **DIR:** Brad Turner. **CAST:** Louis Gossett Jr., Jonathan Silverman, Gregory Thirloway, Tobias Mehler. **1998 DVD**

INSPIRATION ★★★ Greta Garbo plays a Parisian model and courtesan with whom an aspiring politician becomes infatuated, even though aware of and troubled by her past. The high rating is for the legion of Garbo fans; others may find it dated and dull. B&W; 74m. **DIR:** Clarence Brown. **CAST:** Greta Garbo, Robert Montgomery, Lewis Stone, Marjorie Rambeau. **1931**

INSTANT JUSTICE Michael Paré plays Marine Sergeant Youngblood, who has a penchant for headbutting. Rated R. 101m. **DIR:** Craig T. Rumar. **CAST:** Michael Paré, Tawny Kitaen, Charles Napier. **1986**

INSTANT KARMA A young creative consultant for a television network looks for love. Not rated. 91m. **DIR:** Roderick Taylor. **CAST:** Craig Sheffer, David Cassidy, Chelsea Noble, Alan Blumenfeld. **1990**

INSTINCT ★★★ Suggested by Daniel Quinn's novel *Ishmael*, this film is woefully derivative of *Silence of the Lambs* and *One Flew Over the Cuckoo's Nest*, with bits of *Gorillas in the Mist* thrown in. That said, the interactions between characters are all well sculpted and portrayed. Once again Anthony Hopkins is behind bars, ostensibly deranged but actually far smarter and craftier than both his captors and the compassionate but naïve psychiatrist sent to evaluate him. The issue is why Hopkins, a brilliant primatologist, would have killed several park rangers in Rwanda, where he was studying gorillas. Trust us: You'll figure it out long before the psychiatrist does. Rated R for violence and dramatic intensity. 124m. **DIR:** Jon Turteltaub. **CAST:** Anthony Hopkins, Cuba Gooding Jr., Donald Sutherland, Maura Tierney, George Dzundza, John Ashton. **1999 DVD**

INTERCEPTOR ★★★1/2 High marks to this spiffy airborne thriller, which finds a pilot as the sole "wild card" able to prevent a terrorist hijacking. Crisp direction and a good, high-tech script from John Brancato and Michael Ferris. Rated PG-13 for profanity and violence. 88m. **DIR:** Michael Cohn. **CAST:** Andrew Divoff, Elizabeth Morehead, Jurgen Prochnow. **1992 DVD**

INTERIORS ★★★★ Woody Allen tips his hat to Swedish director Ingmar Bergman with this very downbeat drama about a family tearing itself apart. Extremely serious stuff, with fine performances by all. Allen shows he can direct more than comedy. Rated R for language. 99m. **DIR:** Woody Allen. **CAST:** Diane Keaton, E. G. Marshall, Geraldine Page, Richard Jordan, Sam Waterston. **1978 DVD**

INTERMEZZO (1936) ★★★★ Original version of the story about an affair between young pianist Ingrid Bergman and married violinist Gosta Ekman. Long unseen (David O. Selznick suppressed it when he remade it in Hollywood three years later), this rediscovery is a video treasure for Bergman fans. In Swedish with English subtitles. B&W; 88m. **DIR:** Gustav Molander. **CAST:** Gosta Ekman, Ingrid Bergman. **1936 DVD**

INTERMEZZO (1939) ★★★★ A love affair between a married concert violinist and a young woman doesn't stray very far from the standard eternal love triangle. This classic weeper has more renown as the English-language debut of Ingrid Bergman. B&W; 70m. **DIR:** Gregory Ratoff. **CAST:** Leslie Howard, Ingrid Bergman, Cecil Kellaway. **1939**

INTERNAL AFFAIRS ★★★ Brutal, sexually charged thriller about an Internal Affairs investigator (Andy Garcia) who is obsessed with busting a degenerate street cop (Richard Gere). The unrelenting tension mounts as the pursuit of justice becomes a very personal vendetta. Gere is at his best here as a creep you'll just love to hate. Rated R for sex, violence, and profanity. 115m. **DIR:** Mike Figgis. **CAST:** Richard Gere, Andy Garcia, Nancy Travis, Laurie Metcalf, William Baldwin. **1990 DVD**

INTERNATIONAL HOUSE ★★★1/2 An offbeat, must-see film involving a melting pot of characters gathered at the luxurious International House Hotel to bid on the rights to the radioscope, an early version of television. As usual, a Russian muddies the waters with cunning and craft, while an American bumbles to the rescue. W.

C. Fields and Burns and Allen are in rare form throughout. B&W; 70m. **DIR:** A. Edward Sutherland. **CAST:** W. C. Fields, Peggy Hopkins Joyce, Baby Rose Marie, Cab Calloway, Stu Erwin, George Burns, Gracie Allen, Bela Lugosi, Franklin Pangborn, Sterling Holloway, Jeanne Marie. **1933**

INTERNATIONAL TOURNÉE OF ANIMATIONVOL. I, THE ★★★1/2 Fine collection of animated shorts from the nineteenth International Tournée of Animation. This video package features some award-winning animation by filmmakers from around the world. Some of the best selections from this compilation are Marv Newland's *Anijam,* John Canemaker's *Bottom's Dream,* Osamu Tezuka's *Jumping,* and the Academy Award–winning *Anna & Bella,* by Dutch cartoonist Borge Ring. Amusing and inventive. 88m. **DIR:** Various. **1988**

INTERNATIONAL TOURNÉE OF ANIMATIONVOL. II, THE ★★★★ Highly impressive collection of animated shorts from around the world featuring some of the best new animation around. Some of the compilations' best works are the Academy Award–winning short "A Greek Tragedy," from Belgium; "The Frog, The Dog and The Devil," from New Zealand; Bill Plympton's "Your Face"; and "Drawing on My Mind," by Bob Kurtz featuring dialogue and the voice of comic George Carlin. 86m. **DIR:** Various. **1989**

INTERNATIONAL VELVET ★★ A disappointing sequel to *National Velvet* (1944), with Tatum O'Neal only passable as the young horsewoman who rides to victory. Rated PG. 127m. **DIR:** Bryan Forbes. **CAST:** Tatum O'Neal, Christopher Plummer, Anthony Hopkins. **1978**

INTERNECINE PROJECT, THE ★★★ James Coburn plays an ambitious business tycoon who finds he has to kill four associates to meet a business agreement. The fashion in which he does this proves to be interesting. Worth a look for the trick ending. Rated PG. 89m. **DIR:** Ken Hughes. **CAST:** James Coburn, Lee Grant, Harry Andrews, Ian Hendry, Michael Jayston, Keenan Wynn. **1974**

INTERNS, THE ★★★ This melodrama of the lives of interns in an American hospital has it all. The new doctors must deal with death, drugs, abortions, and personal problems. Competently acted and directed. B&W; 130m. **DIR:** David Swift. **CAST:** Cliff Robertson, Michael Callan, James MacArthur, Nick Adams, Suzy Parker, Buddy Ebsen, Telly Savalas. **1962**

INTERNS CAN'T TAKE MONEY ★★★1/2 Gangstas, doctas, and dames in distress all figure into this genre-defying installment that launched the Dr. Kildare flicks. Joel McCrea is steady and handsome as the young doc, but this is Barbara Stanwyck's show as a wronged woman trying to salvage her life. Watch for Lloyd Nolan as a hoodlum with a sensitive streak. Not rated. B&W; 79m. **DIR:** Alfred Santell. **CAST:** Barbara Stanwyck, Joel McCrea, Lloyd Nolan, Stanley Ridges, Lee Bowman, Barry Macollum, Irving Bacon, Gaylord Pendelton. **1937**

INTERROGATION ★★★★ A cabaret singer is imprisoned after sleeping with a military officer. This is a harrowing drama of one woman's struggle to survive unyielding cruelty and atrocious living conditions. Upon completion, the movie was banned by the Polish government, until the director managed to smuggle it out of the country. A gem. In Polish with English subtitles. Not rated; the film has nudity and violence. 118m. **DIR:** Richard Bugajski. **CAST:** Krystyna Janda, Adam Ferency, Agnieszka Holland. **1982**

INTERRUPTED MELODY ★★★★1/2 An excellent movie biography of Australian opera singer Marjorie Lawrence. She was stricken with polio but continued her career in spite of her handicap. Eleanor Parker stars as Lawrence with vocals dubbed by opera star Eileen Farrell. 106m. **DIR:** Curtis Bernhardt. **CAST:** Eleanor Parker, Glenn Ford, Roger Moore, Cecil Kellaway, Stephen Bekassy. **1955**

INTERSECTION 🦃 Vancouver architect floundering in a midlife crisis watches chunks of his life pass before him during a nasty rural auto accident. Rated R for sex, nudity, and language. 105m. **DIR:** Mark Rydell. **CAST:** Richard Gere, Sharon Stone, Lolita Davidovich, Martin Landau, David Selby. **1994 DVD**

INTERVAL ★★ Merle Oberon's last feature film is a weepy story of a woman who tours the world trying to find her one true love while attempting to forget her past. Passable, but hardly a distinguished finale for Oberon's career. Rated PG. 84m. **DIR:** Daniel Mann. **CAST:** Merle Oberon, Robert Wolders, Claudio Brook, Russ Conway. **1973**

INTERVIEW WITH THE VAMPIRE ★★★★1/2 This adaptation of Anne Rice's bestseller features an unexpectedly dead-on performance by Tom Cruise as the decadent Lestat and a poignant one by Brad Pitt as his reluctant disciple. The story begins with reporter Christian Slater interviewing Pitt, who spins a tale of evil, corruption, and heartbreak, and ends in a pulse-pounding, high-speed pursuit. Fans of the genre will be well pleased; casual viewers will applaud the relative restraint used in the blood-and-gore category. Rated R for violence, gore, profanity, nudity, and sexual content. 122m. **DIR:** Neil Jordan. **CAST:** Tom Cruise, Brad Pitt, Antonio Banderas, Stephen Rea, Christian Slater, Kirsten Dunst. **1994 DVD**

INTERZONE 🦃 In a futuristic society the remaining humans battle mutants but fail to do anything original. Rated R for violence. 97m. **DIR:** Deran Sarafian. **CAST:** Bruce Abbott. **1988**

INTIMATE BETRAYAL ★★ Former friends engage in a battle of wits over the woman who left one for the other. Pretentious and lurid drama about the nature of male bonding. Rated R for nudity, sexual situations, strong profanity, and violence. 90m. **DIR:** Andrew Behar. **CAST:** Dwier Brown, Jessica Hecht, Richard Edson, Annabelle Gurwitch. **1996**

INTIMATE CONTACT ★★★ Claire Bloom and Daniel Massey are wonderful as an affluent couple confronted with the specter of AIDS. A sobering account of a family's attempt to deal with this tragic disease. Rate PG. 159m. **DIR:** Waris Hussein. **CAST:** Claire Bloom, Daniel Massey, Sylvia Syms, Mark Kingston, Maggie Steed. **1987**

INTIMATE OBSESSION 🦃 Bored wife meets dangerous stranger in this cheap "erotic mystery" that's as generic as its title. Rated R for nudity and sexual situations. 80m. **DIR:** Lawrence Unger. **CAST:** Jodie Fisher, James Quarter. **1992**

INTIMATE POWER ★★★ This is the true story of a French girl sold into slavery who becomes the sultan's favorite. She bears him a male heir and then proceeds

to instill in her son the rights of the Turkish people hoping for reform when he becomes sultan. Rated R for violence and nudity. 104m. **DIR:** Jack Smight. **CAST:** F. Murray Abraham, Maud Adams. **1989**

INTIMATE RELATIONS ★★1/2 When an affair develops between a frumpy English housewife and her young lodger, the woman's teenage daughter jealously moves to interfere. Based on a real-life 1950s case that ended in a double murder, Philip Goodhew's film is, on the one hand, jokey and overdone, while on the other hand plodding and listless. Acting is a saving grace—especially Julie Walters as the frustrated older woman. Rated R for sexual themes, some profanity, and climactic violence. 105m. **DIR:** Philip Goodhew. **CAST:** Julie Walters, Rupert Graves, Laura Sadler, Matthew Walker. **1996**

INTIMATE STRANGER ★★ Deborah Harry takes a part-time job on a sex phone line and meets up with the ultimate psycho. Now she must find him before he gets her. Rated R for profanity, nudity, and violence. 96m. **DIR:** Allan Holzman. **CAST:** Deborah Harry, James Russo, Tim Thomerson, Grace Zabriskie. **1991**

INTIMATE STRANGERS ★★ Dennis Weaver and Sally Struthers are a husband and wife who permit a lack of self-esteem to drag them into the dark areas of psychological warfare and wife beating. Melvyn Douglas is outstanding and Tyne Daly was nominated for an Emmy Award for her work in this made-for-TV film. 120m. **DIR:** John Llewellyn Moxey. **CAST:** Dennis Weaver, Sally Struthers, Tyne Daly, Larry Hagman, Melvyn Douglas. **1977**

•INTO THE ARMS OF STRANGERS ★★★★★ Oscar-winning documentary chronicles the little-known story of the Kindertransport, a British program that allowed 10,000 Jewish children to escape Nazi Germany in the months before the outbreak of World War II. Stirring and deeply moving, it's a tribute to British decency and further proof—as if any were needed—of the bottomless evil of the Third Reich. Rated PG. 122m. **DIR:** Mark Jonathan Harris. **2000 DVD**

INTO THE BADLANDS ★★ This trio of weird made-for-cable Western tales ranges from tepid to terrible. Rod Serling might have penned the first, with Helen Hunt and Dylan McDermott sharing a damned romance, on a bad day; the other two make absolutely no sense. Only Dern's engaging narration saves this mess from turkeydom. 93m. **DIR:** Sam Pillsbury. **CAST:** Bruce Dern, Mariel Hemingway, Helen Hunt, Dylan McDermott, Lisa Pelikan, Andrew Robinson. **1991 DVD**

INTO THE FIRE 🦃 A young drifter finds himself in the middle of deceit and treachery when he stops at a roadside diner. Rated R for nudity and violence. 88m. **DIR:** Graeme Campbell. **CAST:** Art Hindle, Olivia D'Abo, Lee Montgomery, Susan Anspach. **1988**

INTO THE HOMELAND ★★★ This HBO release is a topical but predictable story starring Powers Boothe as an ex-cop who endeavors to rescue his kidnapped daughter from a white supremacist organization headed by Paul LeMat. The shockingly real portrayal of the supremacists' ethics make this movie worth viewing. Not rated; contains violence and strong language. 120m. **DIR:** Lesli Linka Glatter. **CAST:** Powers Boothe, C. Thomas Howell, Paul LeMat, Cindy Pickett. **1987**

INTO THE NIGHT ★★1/2 Packed with cinematic in-jokes and guest appearances by more than a dozen film directors, this is a film fan's dream. Unfortunately, it might also be a casual viewer's nightmare. Jeff Goldblum and Michelle Pfeiffer stumble into international intrigue and share a bizarre and deadly adventure in contemporary Los Angeles. Rated R for violence and profanity. 115m. **DIR:** John Landis. **CAST:** Jeff Goldblum, Michelle Pfeiffer, Paul Mazursky, Kathryn Harrold, Richard Farnsworth, Irene Papas, David Bowie, Dan Aykroyd. **1985**

INTO THE SUN ★★★★ To research a role, an obnoxious movie star rides shotgun with a crack pilot in the Middle East. Some movies, by sheer force of the talent involved, turn out to be much better than anyone had a right to expect. Director Fritz Kiersch and his cast (including a hilarious Terry Kiser) make this one seem fresh and even innovative. Rated R for profanity and violence. 100m. **DIR:** Fritz Kiersch. **CAST:** Anthony Michael Hall, Michael Paré, Terry Kiser. **1992**

INTO THE WEST ★★★★ Here's a wonderful family film that kids will adore and adults will find fascinating. Two Irish boys find themselves off on an exciting journey after they are "adopted" by a magical horse. The lads are part of a little-known Irish subculture: the Travelers, a gypsylike clan descended from an ancient Celtic tribe. Rated PG for very brief profanity. 91m. **DIR:** Mike Newell. **CAST:** Gabriel Byrne, Ellen Barkin, Colm Meaney, Ciaran Fitzgerald, Rory Conroy, David Kelly, Johnny Murphy. **1993**

INTOLERANCE ★★★★ This milestone silent epic tells and blends four stories of injustice, modern and ancient. The sets for the Babylonian sequence were the largest ever built for a film. One scene alone involved 15,000 people and 250 chariots. The acting is dated, but the picture presents a powerful viewing experience. B&W; 123m. **DIR:** D. W. Griffith. **CAST:** Lillian Gish, Bessie Love, Mae Marsh, Elmo Lincoln, Tully Marshall, Eugene Pallette, Tod Browning, Monte Blue, Robert Harron, Constance Talmadge, Erich Von Stroheim. **1916 DVD**

INTRIGUE ★★ Robert Loggia plays a former CIA agent who has defected to the KGB. Realizing that he's terminally ill, he wants to return to the United States. Slow start, decent middle, and just okay ending sum up the quality of this made-for-TV spy flick. Rated PG for violence. 96m. **DIR:** David Drury. **CAST:** Scott Glenn, Robert Loggia, William Atherton. **1988**

INTRODUCING DOROTHY DANDRIDGE ★★★★ Star-producer Halle Berry shepherded this mesmerizing study of Dorothy Dandridge, the first black actress ever to garner an Academy Award nomination for Best Actress (in 1954's *Carmen Jones*) . . . a milestone event not even acknowledged by most film references. Adapted from the unabashed valentine of a biography by Earl Mills (played here by Brent Spiner), this melancholy drama follows Dandridge's rise from dancer and chanteuse to the fiery actress who blossomed on the big screen, under the guidance of director Otto Preminger. Unfortunately Preminger also wielded far too much influence over his protégé, and what should have been a meteoric career rise stalled when Dandridge began refusing roles she deemed offensive or token. Director Martha Coolidge's film gracefully moves back and forth via flashback, and Berry displays the same fire and grit that must have made Dandridge herself such a sensa-

tion. Spiner also is fine, as the manager/friend who carried a torch from afar. The script, alas, stalls when considering the ill-advised husbands—one reduced to little more than a footnote—who must have hurt Dandridge's career. Rated R for profanity, nudity, rape, and simulated sex. 115m. **DIR:** Martha Coolidge. **CAST:** Halle Berry, Brent Spiner, Obba Babatundé, Loretta Devine, Cynda Williams, Klaus Maria Brandauer, William Atherton, D. B. Sweeney. **1999 DVD**

INTRUDER, THE (1961) ★★★1/2 Gripping film about a racist (William Shatner) who attempts to block court-ordered integration in a small-town school. Shatner's performance is very good, and the finale is especially intense. A.k.a. *Shame* and *I Hate Your Guts*. Not rated. B&W; 80m. **DIR:** Roger Corman. **CAST:** William Shatner, Leo Gordon, Jeanne Cooper. **1961 DVD**

INTRUDER (1988) ★★ A bloodthirsty killer is locked in a supermarket with employees preparing for a going-out-of-business sale. Slasher fans should find this amusing. Rated R for violence and profanity. 90m. **DIR:** Scott Spiegel. **CAST:** Elizabeth Cox, Danny Hicks, René Estevez. **1988**

INTRUDER IN THE DUST ★★★★★ One of the best adaptations of a William Faulkner novel, this was one of the first movies to take a stand on racial issues. Basically, it's the story of the lynching of an African-American by rednecks in the South. It deals as much with the reaction of the white population as it does with that of the black community. B&W; 88m. **DIR:** Clarence Brown. **CAST:** David Brian, Juano Hernandez, Claude Jarman Jr., Will Geer, Elizabeth Patterson, Porter Hall, Charles Kemper. **1949**

INTRUDER WITHIN, THE 🦃 Cheesy *Alien*. Action takes place on an ocean oil-drilling rig instead of commercial spacecraft. 100m. **DIR:** Peter Carter. **CAST:** Chad Everett, Joseph Bottoms, Jennifer Warren. **1981**

INTRUDERS ★★★★ Two sisters, through hypnotic regression, convince a psychologist that they've been repeatedly abducted, since childhood, by aliens. The story moves suspensefully, exploring government conspiracies and theories why extraterrestrials are kidnapping humans. Made for TV, yet still effectively creepy. 163m. **DIR:** Dan Curtis. **CAST:** Richard Crenna, Mare Winningham, Susan Blakely, Daphne Ashbrook. **1992**

INVADER (1993) ★★ A reporter for a trashy tabloid discovers government officials and scientists working on a new computerized weapons system from an abandoned UFO. But no one will believe him, until the mega-computer tries to take control of military bases and personnel. Rated R for violence and profanity. 95m. **DIR:** Philip Cook. **CAST:** Hans Bachmann, A. Thomas Smith, Rick Foucheux, John Cooke, Ally Sheedy. **1993**

INVADER, THE (1996) ★★1/2 A visitor from another planet impregnates a human female in order to save his dying race. However, the visitor's mortal enemy wants to stop him. Silly but entertaining science fiction. Not rated; contains violence and profanity. 97m. **DIR:** Mark Rosman. **CAST:** Sean Young, Ben Cross, Daniel Baldwin, Nick Mancuso. **1996**

INVADERS, THE ★★★★ Based on the popular television series from the 1960s, this made-for-TV miniseries is suspenseful, well-acted, and eerily effective. Scott Bakula stars as a man who uncovers the invasion of Earth by an alien species but can't convince his fellow Earthlings, who think he's crazy. Not rated; contains mild violence and profanity. 180m. **DIR:** Paul Shapiro. **CAST:** Scott Bakula, Elizabeth Peña, Richard Thomas, Roy Thinnes, Delane Matthews, Richard Belzer. **1995**

INVADERS FROM MARS (1953) ★★★★ Everybody remembers this one. Kid sees a flying saucer land in a nearby field, only nobody will believe him. Some really weird visuals throughout this minor sci-fi classic. 78m. **DIR:** William Cameron Menzies. **CAST:** Helena Carter, Jimmy Hunt, Leif Erickson, Arthur Franz. **1953 DVD**

INVADERS FROM MARS (1986) ★★★ Director Tobe Hooper maintains the tone of the original; this version feels like a 1950s movie made with 1980s production values. Rated PG-13 for rather intense situations and ugly beasties. 94m. **DIR:** Tobe Hooper. **CAST:** Karen Black, Hunter Carson, Timothy Bottoms, Laraine Newman, James Karen, Louise Fletcher, Bud Cort. **1986 DVD**

•INVASION ★★1/2 Aliens come to earth to taste-test the inhabitants of a small town in this campy, pseudo-homage to alien invasion movies of yore. More spoof than alien *noir*, this movie is rife with puns, innuendo, and an absolutely bizarre cast worthy of a David Lynch production. Rated R for sex and violence. 92m. **DIR:** John Paizs. **CAST:** Campbell Scott, Tom Everett Scott, Fiona Loewi. **1999 DVD**

INVASION EARTH: THE ALIENS ARE HERE ★★ Comedic aliens take over a cinema presenting a sci-fi film festival, subverting humans into blank-eyed underwear-clad zombies. But some kids get wise to the scheme and try to put a stop to it before it's too late. Unfunny as comedy, but with great clips of classic sci-fi and horror films from years past. Not rated, but suitable for most age-groups. 84m. **DIR:** George Maitland. **CAST:** Janis Fabian, Christian Lee. **1987**

INVASION OF PRIVACY (1992) ★★ A worn-out story line about a psychotic ex-convict who goes to work for the journalist that he idolizes. Robby Benson still can't act, and Jennifer O'Neill doesn't do much better. Made for cable. 95m. **DIR:** Kevin Meyer. **CAST:** Robby Benson, Jennifer O'Neill, Ian Ogilvy. **1992**

INVASION OF PRIVACY (1996) ★★1/2 Nice girl thinks she meets the guy of her dreams, only to learn he's a petulant psychopath. At this point, Larry Cohen's script veers into truly bewildering waters, as our now-pregnant heroine is kidnapped by the guy and held in a mountain cabin until she's past the point of obtaining a legal abortion. The final act is strident, annoying, and just plain stupid. Rated R for profanity, nudity, rape, and violence. 95m. **DIR:** Anthony Hickox. **CAST:** Johnathon Schaech, Mili Avital, Naomi Campbell, Tom Wright, R. G. Armstrong, David Keith, Charlotte Rampling. **1996**

INVASION OF THE ANIMAL PEOPLE 🦃 Extraterrestrial visitors assume various forms. B&W; 73m. **DIR:** Virgil Vogel, Jerry Warren. **CAST:** Robert Burton, Barbara Wilson, John Carradine (narrator). **1962**

INVASION OF THE BEE GIRLS ★★★ Enjoyable film about strange female invaders doing weird things to the male population of a small town in California. Plot is not too important in this wacky sci-fi spoof. Not for kids. Rated PG. 85m. **DIR:** Denis Sanders. **CAST:** Victoria Vetri, William Smith, Cliff Osmond, Anitra Ford. **1973**

INVASION OF THE BODY SNATCHERS (1956) ★★★★★ Quite possibly the most frightening film ever made, this stars Kevin McCarthy as a small-town doctor

who discovers his patients, family, and friends are being taken over by cold, emotionless, human-duplicating pods from outer space. Not many films can be considered truly disturbing, but this one more than qualifies. Coming from the B-movie science-fiction boom of the 1950s, it has emerged as a cinema classic. B&W; 80m. **DIR:** Don Siegel. **CAST:** Kevin McCarthy, Dana Wynter, Carolyn Jones, King Donovan. **1956 DVD**

INVASION OF THE BODY SNATCHERS (1978) ★★★★ Excellent semisequel to Don Siegel's 1956 classic of the same name, with Donald Sutherland fine in the role originally created by Kevin McCarthy (who has a cameo here). This time the story takes place in San Francisco, with mysterious "seeds" from outer space duplicating—then destroying—San Francisco Bay Area residents at an alarming rate. Rated PG. 115m. **DIR:** Phil Kaufman. **CAST:** Donald Sutherland, Brooke Adams, Leonard Nimoy, Jeff Goldblum, Veronica Cartwright. **1978 DVD**

INVASION OF THE FLESH HUNTERS ★★★ A new twist on the zombie flick. This time these guys aren't dead. They just have a cannibalistic disease brought back from Southeast Asia. Good effects. Not rated. 90m. **DIR:** Anthony M. Dawson. **CAST:** John Saxon. **1982**

INVASION OF THE SAUCER MEN ★★★ Goofy-looking aliens with alcohol for blood battle hot-rodding teens. A minor camp classic that doesn't take itself seriously for a moment. B&W; 69m. **DIR:** Edward L. Cahn. **CAST:** Steve Terrell, Gloria Castillo, Frank Gorshin. **1957**

INVASION OF THE SPACE PREACHERS ★★1/2 Nerds camping in West Virginia help a beautiful female alien track bad guys from her planet. No big laughs, but a genial time waster. Rated R for nudity and profanity. 100m. **DIR:** Daniel Boyd. **CAST:** Jim Wolfe, Guy Nelson. **1990**

INVASION OF THE STAR CREATURES ★★ Two bumbling soldiers foil the efforts of statuesque beauties in high heels and their pot-grown vegetable men to conquer Earth. Any film that opens with "R. I. Diculous Presents" and credits its music as "electronic noise" is worth a watch. As a send-up of the space and science-fiction films from the early 1960s, this cheapo is a match for the worst of Ed Wood's movies; but the cast and crew were in on the joke. Annoyingly enjoyable. B&W; 81m. **DIR:** Bruno De Sota. **CAST:** Bob Ball, Frankie Ray, Gloria Victor, Dolores Reed, Slick Slavin, Mark Ferris, Jim Almanzar. **1962**

INVASION UFO ★★ Strictly for fans of the short-lived science-fiction TV series, whose title explains all. 97m. **DIR:** Gerry Anderson, David Lane, David Tomblin. **CAST:** Ed Bishop, George Sewell, Michael Billington. **1980**

INVASION USA (1952) 🦃 Tacky "red scare" movie about a Communist invasion of the United States. B&W; 74m. **DIR:** Alfred E. Green. **CAST:** Gerald Mohr, Peggie Castle, Dan O'Herlihy, Phyllis Coates, Noel Neill. **1952**

INVASION U.S.A. (1985) ★★★ Chuck Norris plays a one-man army (as always) who comes to the rescue of the good ol' U.S.A. and pummels the minions of psychotic spy Richard Lynch. Rated R for violence, gore, and profanity. 107m. **DIR:** Joseph Zito. **CAST:** Chuck Norris, Richard Lynch, Melissa Prophet. **1985 DVD**

INVENTING THE ABBOTTS ★★★1/2 Two rival working-class brothers mix it up sexually and romantically with the three rich Abbott girls. Set in the late 1950s, the story finds its true soul in the relationship between Jacey and Doug Holt, who live with their widowed mother in an Illinois town. The two siblings unravel the circumstances of their father's death and their mother's social isolation, slither into adulthood, and develop very different relationships with each of the Abbott women. The acting is potent and the emotional payoff is satisfying. Rated R for language, sex, and nudity. 105m. **DIR:** Pat O'Connor. **CAST:** Joaquin Phoenix, Billy Crudup, Joanna Going, Jennifer Tilly, Liv Tyler, Will Patton, Kathy Baker, Jennifer Connelly. **1997 DVD**

INVESTIGATION ★★★ When the village tannery owner (Victor Lanoux) kills his wife to marry his pregnant girlfriend (Valerie Mairesse), a meticulous inspector comes to investigate. His Columbo-ish tactics pick up the film's pace and turn a so-so melodrama into a delightful winner. In French with English subtitles. Rated R for violence. 116m. **DIR:** Etienne Perier. **CAST:** Victor Lanoux, Jean Carmet, Valerie Mairesse, Michel Robin. **1979**

•INVINCIBLE 🦃 Unbelievable: a kung fu film that talks you to death! Short on both action and adventure, this esoteric fantasy stars Billy Zane as a reformed Earth invader. Zane expounds ad nauseam on the role of four chosen humans who must combat evil shadow men. His monotonous mantra had us diving for the remote! Not rated; contains violence. 92m. **DIR:** Jefery Levi. **CAST:** Billy Zane, Tory Kittles, David Field, Byron Mann. **2001**

INVISIBLE ADVERSARIES ★★1/2 Controversial avant-garde film about a Viennese photographer who believes that extraterrestrial beings are taking over the minds of her fellow citizens while raising their level of human aggression. This dark satire is interesting but uneven. In German with English subtitles. Not rated; contains explicit nudity and graphic violence. 112m. **DIR:** Valie Export. **CAST:** Susanne Wild, Peter Weibel. **1977**

INVISIBLE AGENT ★★★ Universal Pictures recycles H. G. Wells's *The Invisible Man* again, this time as a World War II spy thriller. The result is above-average—crisply plotted and atmospheric. Jon Hall plays the dashing title character, but John P. Fulton's special effects are the real star. B&W; 81m. **DIR:** Edwin L. Marin. **CAST:** Ilona Massey, Jon Hall, Cedric Hardwicke, Peter Lorre. **1942**

INVISIBLE BOY, THE ★★ Sci-fi parable about a computer's scheme to rule the world. The special effects are okay, and Robby the Robot has a supporting role, but it was too dull even in the 1950s. B&W; 85m. **DIR:** Herman Hoffman. **CAST:** Richard Eyer, Diane Brewster, Philip Abbott. **1957**

INVISIBLE DAD ★★ The production team behind *Invisible Mom* rehashes the same formula, this time with Dad becoming the invisible member of the family. Same film, different name, with a much inferior script. Rated PG. 90m. **DIR:** Fred Olen Ray. **CAST:** Saran Noris, Mary Elizabeth McGlynn, Karen Black, Charles Dierkop. **1996**

INVISIBLE GHOST 🦃 Bela Lugosi is an unwitting murderer, used by his supposedly dead wife to further her schemes. B&W; 64m. **DIR:** Joseph H. Lewis. **CAST:** Bela Lugosi, Polly Ann Young, John McGuire, Betty Compson, Jack Mulhall. **1941 DVD**

INVISIBLE INVADERS 🦃 Moon monsters possess dead bodies to attack Earth. Invisible thrills. B&W; 67m. **DIR:**

Edward L. Cahn. **CAST:** John Agar, Jean Byron, John Carradine, Robert Hutton. **1959**

INVISIBLE KID, THE ★★ Geared for preteens, this sci-fi comedy about a boy who accidentally discovers an invisibility potion might be a little too juvenile for all audiences. Rated PG for language and nudity. 96m. **DIR:** Avery Crounse. **CAST:** Jay Underwood, Wally Ward, Mike Genovese, Karen Black. **1988**

INVISIBLE MAN, THE ★★★★1/2 Claude Rains goes unseen until the finish in his screen debut. He plays Jack Griffin, the title character in H. G. Wells's famous story of a scientist who creates an invisibility serum—with the side effect of driving a person slowly insane. Frightening film could initially be mistaken for a comedy, with large chunks of humor in the first half, turning deadly serious thereafter. B&W; 71m. **DIR:** James Whale. **CAST:** Claude Rains, Gloria Stuart, Una O'Connor, Henry Travers, E. E. Clive, Dwight Frye. **1933 DVD**

INVISIBLE MAN RETURNS ★★★ Convicted of his brother's murder and condemned to die, Vincent Price is injected with a serum that renders him invisible and aids in his effort to catch the real killer. John Fulton's special effects and a top-notch cast make this, the second in Universal's series, another one of their winning chillers. B&W; 81m. **DIR:** Joe May. **CAST:** Cedric Hardwicke, Vincent Price, Nan Grey, John Sutton, Alan Napier, Cecil Kellaway. **1940**

INVISIBLE MANIAC ★★ Tacky Fifties-style sci-fi pastiche has voyeuristic physics professor perfecting an invisibility potion for the purpose of ogling the high school cheerleading team. Titillating silliness has its camp moments. Rated R. 85m. **DIR:** Rif Coogan. **CAST:** Noel Peters. **1990**

INVISIBLE MAN'S REVENGE, THE ★★ A sequel to a sequel that boasts a better cast than script. Jon Hall is injected with an invisibility drug by John Carradine, who then refuses to reverse the process. Lackluster script and direction. Not rated. B&W; 65m. **DIR:** Ford Beebe. **CAST:** Jon Hall, Alan Curtis, Evelyn Ankers, Leon Errol, John Carradine. **1944**

INVISIBLE MOM ★★★ Dee Wallace is a delight both on and off the screen in this formulaic yet enjoyable romp. She's the harried wife of a science professor whose latest experiment has rendered her invisible. Lots of fun as Mom tries to run the household and Dad scrambles for a cure. Rated PG. 83m. **DIR:** Fred Olen Ray. **CAST:** Dee Wallace, Barry Livingston, Trent Knight, Russ Tamblyn, Christopher Stone, Stella Stevens. **1997 DVD**

INVISIBLE RAY, THE ★★★ Boris Karloff and Bela Lugosi are teamed in this interesting story. A brilliant research scientist (Karloff), experimenting in Africa, is contaminated by a hunk of radioactive meteor landing nearby and soon discovers that his mere touch can kill. Neat Universal thriller features first-rate effects and good ensemble acting. B&W; 81m. **DIR:** Lambert Hillyer. **CAST:** Boris Karloff, Bela Lugosi, Frances Drake, Frank Lawton. **1936**

INVISIBLE STRANGLER 🦃 A murderer on death row discovers he has a psychic power to make himself invisible. Not rated; contains graphic violence. 85m. **DIR:** John Florea. **CAST:** Robert Foxworth, Stefanie Powers, Elke Sommer. **1984 DVD**

INVISIBLE: THE CHRONICLES OF BENJAMIN KNIGHT 🦃 Dreadful foray into the *Invisible Man* genre presents nothing new, but borrows heavily from other films. Produced as a sequel to *Mandroid*. Rated R for violence, language, and nudity. 80m. **DIR:** Jack Ersgard. **CAST:** Brian Cousins, Jennifer Nash, Alan Oppenheimer, Aharon Ipale. **1994**

INVISIBLE WOMAN, THE ★★★ Featherweight sci-fi comedy as a scientist turns a fashion model invisible, but it's got the best cast of any Universal programmer of the 1940s. B&W; 72m. **DIR:** A. Edward Sutherland. **CAST:** John Barrymore, Virginia Bruce, John Howard, Charlie Ruggles, Margaret Hamilton, Oscar Homolka. **1941**

INVITATION AU VOYAGE ★★★1/2 Here is a strange but watchable French import with plenty of suspense and surprises for those willing to give it a chance to work its unusual magic. Peter Del Monte's film allows the viewer to make assumptions and then shatters those conceptions with a succession of inventive twists and revelations. In French with English subtitles. Rated R for adult content. 100m. **DIR:** Peter Del Monte. **CAST:** Laurent Malet, Aurore Clement, Mario Adorf. **1982**

INVITATION TO A GUNFIGHTER ★★ Studio-slick Western is short on action and long on dialogue as a hired professional killer comes to town and changes the balance of power. Everybody gets a chance to emote in this gabfest. 92m. **DIR:** Richard Wilson. **CAST:** Yul Brynner, George Segal, Janice Rule, Pat Hingle. **1964**

INVITATION TO HELL 🦃 A family visits a posh vacation resort, only to be seduced by a beautiful Satan worshiper. Bland telefilm. 96m. **DIR:** Wes Craven. **CAST:** Robert Urich, Joanna Cassidy, Susan Lucci, Kevin McCarthy. **1984**

INVITATION TO THE DANCE ★★★ Strictly for lovers of Terpsichore, this film tells three stories entirely through dance. It sort of drags until Gene Kelly appears in a live action-cartoon sequence about "Sinbad" of Arabian Nights fame. 93m. **DIR:** Gene Kelly. **CAST:** Gene Kelly. **1957**

INVITATION TO THE WEDDING ★★ A feeble little British tale about a young American college student who falls in love with his best friend's sister, who just so happens to be engaged to an English war hero. John Gielgud offers the only comic relief as an Englishman-turned-Southern evangelist. 89m. **DIR:** Joseph Brooks. **CAST:** John Gielgud, Ralph Richardson, Paul Nicholas, Elizabeth Shepherd. **1973**

IPCRESS FILE, THE ★★★★ First and by far the best of Michael Caine's three "Harry Palmer" films, this one introduces Len Deighton's reluctant thief-turned-secret agent. Caine, relentlessly serious behind owl-like spectacles, investigates the mystery of specialists kidnapped and relocated to parts unknown. John Barry's moody jazz score superbly counterpoints the action, and Sidney J. Furie's direction is taut and suspenseful. Not rated, suitable for family viewing. 108m. **DIR:** Sidney J. Furie. **CAST:** Michael Caine, Nigel Green, Guy Doleman, Gordon Jackson, Sue Lloyd. **1965 DVD**

IP5: THE ISLAND OF PACHYDERMS ★★ This beautiful but confusing film is about two Parisian street kids, a teenage Hispanic graffiti artist and an 11-year-old black street rapper. They steal a car, only to discover an elderly man (Yves Montand in his last performance)

asleep in the backseat. He teaches them mysterious lessons about nature and life. In French with English subtitles. 119m. **DIR:** Jean-Jacques Beineix. **CAST:** Yves Montand, Olivier Martinez, Sekkou Sail, Geraldine Pailhas. **1992**

IPHIGENIA ★★★★★ A stunning film interpretation of the Greek classic *Iphigenia in Aulis*. Irene Papas is brilliant as Clytemnestra, the caring and outraged mother. Intense score by Mikos Theodorakis. In Greek with English subtitles. No MPAA rating. 127m. **DIR:** Michael Cacoyannis. **CAST:** Irene Papas. **1978**

I.Q. ★★★★ Walter Matthau is an absolute delight as Albert Einstein, who plays cupid to his brainy niece, Meg Ryan, and a good-hearted garage mechanic, Tim Robbins. Ryan is all set to marry stuffy college professor Stephen Fry because he's "the proper kind of husband" for a member of the Einstein family, but Uncle Albert and his eccentric cronies have other ideas. Featuring top-notch performances in every role, this lighthearted romantic comedy recalls Hollywood's golden era. Rated PG for light profanity. 107m. **DIR:** Fred Schepisi. **CAST:** Meg Ryan, Tim Robbins, Walter Matthau, Stephen Fry, Lou Jacobi, Gene Saks, Joseph Maher, Charles Durning, Frank Whaley. **1994**

IRAN DAYS OF CRISIS ★★★ Fact-based account of the Iranian takeover of the American embassy in Tehran and the subsequent hostage crisis. Engrossing, thought-provoking film boasts good performances and realistic locales. Made for cable. 183m. **DIR:** Kevin Connor. **CAST:** Jeff Fahey, George Grizzard, Arliss Howard, Alice Krige, Tony Goldwyn, Daniel Gélin, Valerie Kaprisky. **1991**

IREZUMI (SPIRIT OF TATTOO) ★★★★1/2 An erotic tale of obsession that calls forth the rebirth of a near-dead art. A woman defies cultural taboos and gets her back elaborately tattooed to fulfill her mate's obsession. Rated R for nudity. 88m. **DIR:** Yoichi Takabayashi. **CAST:** Masayo Utsunomiya, Tomisaburo Wakayama. **1983**

IRIS BLOND ★★ Occasionally amusing tale of a middle-aged, washed-up pop singer whose lease on life is renewed when he visits a fortune-teller. Romeo dumps his girlfriend for a young muse who resembles the fortune-teller's prophecy. Sparked by his new love, Romeo learns that love and happiness don't always go hand in hand. The Italian-French coproduction tries to be hip, but the characters aren't very likable, while the film's look and feel are trashy. In French and Italian with English subtitles. Rated R for adult situations and language. 113m. **DIR:** Carlo Verdone. **CAST:** Carlo Verdone, Claudia Gerini, Andrea Ferreol. **1996**

IRISHMAN, THE ★★★1/2 Excellent Australian drama set in the 1920s. An immigrant Irish worker, who has made a living in rough territory with his team of horses, refuses to recognize progress in the form of a gas-driven truck that will put him out of business. His unwillingness to adapt tears apart his family, who wants to back him up but recognizes that he is wrong. 108m. **DIR:** Donald Crombie. **CAST:** Michael Craig, Simon Burke, Robyn Nevin, Lou Brown. **1978 DVD**

IRMA LA DOUCE ★★★ Gendarme Jack Lemmon gets involved with prostitute Shirley MacLaine in what director Billy Wilder hoped would be another MacLaine/Lemmon hit like *The Apartment*. It isn't. It's raw humor in glorious color. Send the "Silver Spoons" set off to bed before you screen this one. 142m. **DIR:** Billy Wilder. **CAST:** Shirley MacLaine, Jack Lemmon, Lou Jacobi, Herschel Bernardi. **1963 DVD**

IRMA VEP ★★★★ This playful swat at the egos, mechanics, and exasperations involved in filmmaking is shot in a breezy docudrama style. A Hong Kong action heroine is hired to star as a slinky cat burglar in a French remake of a silent black-and-white vampire serial. The production is in chaos, and the resilient actress is tossed into a sea of warring personalities. The title of the film is an anagram for vampire. In French with English subtitles. Not rated. 96m. **DIR:** Olivier Assayas. **CAST:** Maggie Cheung, Jean-Pierre Léaud, Nathalie Richard, Bulle Ogier, Lou Castel. **1996 DVD**

IRON & SILK ★★★ Mark Salzman's experiences in China to master martial arts jump from book to the big screen in a film that's filled with visual splendor and compelling characters. Cultures clash in a winning way as Salzman forsakes his western ways to become more in tune with his surroundings. Rated PG. 94m. **DIR:** Shirley Sun. **CAST:** Mark Salzman. **1990**

IRON DUKE, THE ★★★★ A thoroughly English stage actor, George Arliss did not make this, his first British film, until late in the decade he spent in the Hollywood studios. His Duke of Wellington, victor over Napoleon at Waterloo, is picture perfect. Buffs will particularly enjoy a younger Felix Aylmer, later Polonius in Laurence Olivier's 1948 *Hamlet*. B&W; 88m. **DIR:** Victor Saville. **CAST:** George Arliss, A. E. Matthews, Emlyn Williams, Felix Aylmer, Gladys Cooper. **1936**

IRON EAGLE ★★ A better name for this modern war movie might have been *Ramboy*, so shamelessly does it attempt to be a *Rambo* for the teen-age set. Jason Gedrick stars as an 18 year old would-be pilot who steals an F-16 fighter plane to rescue his father (Tim Thomerson), a prisoner of war in the Middle East. A terminally dull fantasy of blood lust. Rated PG-13 for violence and profanity. 115m. **DIR:** Sidney J. Furie. **CAST:** Louis Gossett Jr., Jason Gedrick, Tim Thomerson, David Suchet. **1986 DVD**

IRON EAGLE II 🦃 Ridiculous sequel to the preposterous original. Rated PG for violence and profanity. 105m. **DIR:** Sidney J. Furie. **CAST:** Louis Gossett Jr., Mark Humphrey, Stuart Margolin, Alan Scarfe. **1988 DVD**

IRON EAGLE IV ★★ Yet another retread of tired material, this time with Lou Gossett's stalwart military hero trying to turn twentysome-thing delinquents into crack fighter pilots. Completely ludicrous, and a waste of the star's talents. Rated PG-13 for profanity and violence. 95m. **DIR:** Sidney J. Furie. **CAST:** Louis Gossett Jr., Jason Cadieux, Al Waxman, Joanne Vannicola. **1995**

IRON GIANT, THE ★★★★ Working from the celebrated short story by England's Ted Hughes, coadaptor-director Brad Bird and screenwriter Tim McCanlies have crafted a positively enchanting tale of friendship and honesty. But the film also serves as something of a time capsule. The setting is 1957; the beeping Sputnik is silent observer to a large fireball that plunges from space into the ocean off the coast of bucolic Rockwell, Maine. The visitor turns out to be a massive robot, designed as a "living weapon" but disoriented enough to befriend a 9-year-old boy who, in turn, does everything possible to help this new comrade. All this unfolds via a

somewhat "flat" animation style that owes far more to the late 1950s and early 1960s than the lush three-dimensionality of modern Disney features. This is not a bad thing; Bird's stylistic decision greatly adds to the story's quaint, Norman Rockwell qualities. It's also one of the most intelligent animated parables we've seen in a while: a carefully crafted tale with heart and a shrewd moral. Rated PG for occasional dramatic intensity. 86m. **DIR:** Brad Bird. **1999 DVD**

IRON MAJOR, THE ★★1/2 Decent Hollywood bio-pic about disabled World War I hero Frank Cavanaugh, who became a trophy-winning college football coach. Loaded with sentiment, spunk, and humor. B&W; 90m. **DIR:** Ray Enright. **CAST:** Pat O'Brien, Ruth Warrick, Robert Ryan, Leon Ames. **1943**

IRON MASK, THE ★★★1/2 The last of Douglas Fairbanks's truly memorable series of historical adventures is a rousing version of the Dumas story of the later adventures of D'Artagnan and his efforts to restore the rightful king to the throne of France. Well-budgeted and full of good stunts and deadly encounters, this film was released with sound effects and a synchronized score. B&W; 87m. **DIR:** Allan Dwan. **CAST:** Douglas Fairbanks Sr., Nigel de Brulier, Marguerite de la Motte. **1929**

IRON MAZE ★★ Japanese tycoon buys a shut down steel plant in an economically depressed American town. Sparks fly when his impulsive American wife has an affair with a former employee of the plant. Meandering maze of cinematic clichés. Rated R for profanity, violence, and nudity. 102m. **DIR:** Hiroaki Yoshida. **CAST:** Jeff Fahey, Bridget Fonda, J. T. Walsh. **1991 DVD**

•IRON MONKEY ★★★1/2 Unable to capture the Robin Hood and Zorro-like bandit of the title and his female assistant, a corrupt governor forces a famed warrior to join the hunt by taking his son (the historical Chinese character Wong Fei-Hung) hostage. The dazzling wire-enhanced acrobatics and pitched battles involve assorted weapons and martial arts moves that are exuberantly announced ("Shadowless kick!" and "Flying sleeve!") before their execution, adding brisk comic relief. All lead to a final showdown atop large, flaming wooden posts. In Cantonese with English subtitles. Rated PG-13 for violence and sexuality. 85m. **DIR:** Woo-Ping Yuen. **CAST:** Donnie Yen, Yu Rongguang, Jean Wang, Tsang Sze-Man. **1993 DVD**

IRON TRIANGLE, THE ★★★ The Vietnam War seen through the eyes of a hardboiled American captain (Beau Bridges, fine as always). Haing S. Ngor (Oscar winner for *The Killing Fields*) plays a small part as a Cong officer. Solid, blood-and-guts war drama bogs down in the middle but ends with a well-staged climactic battle. Rated R for graphic combat scenes and profanity. 94m. **DIR:** Eric Weston. **CAST:** Beau Bridges, Haing S. Ngor, Johnny Hallyday. **1988**

IRON WARRIOR 🦃 *Conan*-type action flick with plenty of sabers, smoke, and skin. Rated R for violence and nudity. 82m. **DIR:** Al Bradley. **CAST:** Miles O'Keeffe, Savina Gersak, Tim Lane. **1987**

IRON WILL ★★★ Dakota teen enters the world's most grueling dogsled marathon to save the family farm and earn his college tuition in this gloriously old-fashioned adventure. Some events don't gel—the death of the kid's dad seems avoidable, the trek's final short cut isn't really *that* treacherous—but the action cracks along sharply, the bad guys are easy to hate, and a wry subtext about journalists working feverishly to define a race and man-child in legendary terms is entertaining. Rated PG. 97m. **DIR:** Charles Haid. **CAST:** Mackenzie Astin, Kevin Spacey, David Ogden Stiers, August Schellengberg, Brian Cox, Penelope Windust. **1993 DVD**

IRONCLADS ★★1/2 This TV movie dramatizes the historic sea battle between the *Monitor* and the *Merrimack*. History lesson is almost ruined with silly subplots. 94m. **DIR:** Delbert Mann. **CAST:** Virginia Madsen, Alex Hyde-White, Reed Edward Diamond, Philip Casnoff, E. G. Marshall, Fritz Weaver. **1991**

IRONWEED ★★★★1/2 William Kennedy's adaptation of his Pulitzer Prize–winning novel turns into a showcase for Jack Nicholson and Meryl Streep, both playing skid-row alcoholics. Director Hector Babenco superbly captures the grinding, hand-to-mouth dreariness of this Depression era tale, which traces the relationship of opportunity and convenience between the two leads. This may be Streep's finest hour; her complete descent into the part is riveting. Rated R for language, violence, and brief nudity. 144m. **DIR:** Hector Babenco. **CAST:** Jack Nicholson, Meryl Streep, Carroll Baker, Michael O'Keefe, Tom Waits, Fred Gwynne. **1987**

IRRECONCILABLE DIFFERENCES ★★1/2 Drew Barrymore plays a little girl who sues her self-centered, career-conscious parents—Ryan O'Neal and Shelley Long—for divorce. The laughs are few, but there are some effective scenes of character development. Rated PG for profanity and nudity. 101m. **DIR:** Charles Shyer. **CAST:** Drew Barrymore, Ryan O'Neal, Shelley Long. **1984**

IS PARIS BURNING? ★★★ A spectacular war movie that plays like a newsreel with famous stars in bit parts. The story of the liberation of Paris, and the Nazi attempt to burn it to the ground is dramatic, moving, and educational. B&W; 175m. **DIR:** René Clement. **CAST:** Kirk Douglas, Glenn Ford, Orson Welles, Jean-Paul Belmondo, Charles Boyer, Leslie Caron, Yves Montand, Simone Signoret, Robert Stack, Jean-Pierre Cassel, Claude Dauphin, Gert Fröbe, Daniel Gélin, Alain Delon. **1966**

ISADORA ★★★ A straightforward biography of American modern dance pioneer Isadora Duncan. Vanessa Redgrave ably carries the burden of bringing this eccentric, early flower child to life. Unfortunately she is often undone by a script that drags, becomes repetitious, and rambles. 138m. **DIR:** Karel Reisz. **CAST:** Vanessa Redgrave, James Fox, Jason Robards Jr. **1969**

ISHTAR 🦃 A bloated, disjointed, and ponderous megabuck vanity production. Rated PG-13 for language and brief nudity. 107m. **DIR:** Elaine May. **CAST:** Warren Beatty, Dustin Hoffman, Isabelle Adjani, Charles Grodin, Jack Weston, Tess Harper, Carol Kane. **1987**

ISLAND, THE (1962) ★★★★1/2 A family struggles to survive on an isolated island where they are the only inhabitants. Filmed with no dialogue, this is nevertheless an elegant and moving allegory of human life. B&W; 92m. **DIR:** Kaneto Shindo. **CAST:** Nobuko Otowa, Shinji Tanaka. **1962**

ISLAND, THE (1980) 🦃 Michael Caine as a reporter investigating the mysterious disappearances of pleasure craft and their owners in the Caribbean. Rated R.

113m. **DIR:** Michael Ritchie. **CAST:** Michael Caine, David Warner, Angela Punch McGregor. **1980**

ISLAND AT THE TOP OF THE WORLD, THE ★★★ A rich man ventures into the Arctic in search of his son. Unbelievably, he finds a Viking kingdom. Rated G. 93m. **DIR:** Robert Stevenson. **CAST:** David Hartman, Mako, Donald Sinden. **1974 DVD**

ISLAND CLAWS ★★ As science-fiction horror thrillers go, this one is about average. *Attack of the Killer Crabs* would have been a more appropriate title, though. Dr. McNeal (Barry Nelson) is a scientist who is experimenting to make larger crabs as a food source. Rated PG for violence. 91m. **DIR:** Hernan Cardenas. **CAST:** Robert Lansing, Barry Nelson, Steve Hanks, Nita Talbot. **1980**

ISLAND FURY 🦃 Hokey action film about two teenage girls who, as children, accidentally stumbled across a cache of mob money while vacationing on a small island. Now the mob wants them killed so the secret can be kept. Not rated; contains violence, language, and adult situations. 90m. **DIR:** Henri Charr. **CAST:** Monet Elizabeth, Tanya Louise, Michael Wayne, Ross Hamilton. **1994**

ISLAND IN THE SKY ★★1/2 Pilot John Wayne is forced to land his C-47 on the frozen, uncharted tundra of Labrador. Talky, slow-moving drama. B&W; 109m. **DIR:** William Wellman. **CAST:** John Wayne, Lloyd Nolan, Walter Abel, James Arness, Andy Devine, Allyn Joslyn, Jimmy Lydon, Harry Carey Jr., Hal Baylor, Sean McClory, Regis Toomey, Paul Fix, George Chandler, Bob Steele, Darryl Hickman, Mike Connors, Carl "Alfalfa" Switzer. **1953**

ISLAND OF DESIRE ★★ A trio become involved in a romantic triangle when they are marooned on an island during World War II. The whole thing is substandard, but Linda Darnell is still worth watching. 103m. **DIR:** Stuart Heisler. **CAST:** Linda Darnell, Tab Hunter, Donald Gray. **1952**

ISLAND OF DR. MOREAU, THE (1977) ★★ Remake of 1933's *Island of Lost Souls* isn't nearly as good. Burt Lancaster develops process of turning animals into half-humans on a desolate tropical island. Watchable only for Burt's sturdy performance and Richard Basehart's portrayal of one of the beasts. Rated PG. 104m. **DIR:** William Witney. **CAST:** Burt Lancaster, Michael York, Barbara Carrera, Richard Basehart. **1977**

ISLAND OF DR. MOREAU, THE (1996) 🦃 H. G. Wells's creepy morality tale about genetic research and man's infatuation with godlike power is reduced to tiresome "mad scientist" rubbish. Rated PG-13 for violence, gore, and horror special effects. 96m. **DIR:** John Frankenheimer. **CAST:** Marlon Brando, Val Kilmer, David Thewlis, Fairuza Balk, Ron Perlman. **1996 DVD**

ISLAND OF LOST SOULS ★★★★ This seminal horror melodrama of the 1930s still has the power to enthrall, thanks to its otherworldly atmosphere and sequences of unbridled, sadistic horror. H. G. Wells's *The Island of Dr. Moreau* is the basis for this tense chiller in which a shipwreck victim, the unwilling "guest" of the exiled doctor, discovers Moreau speeding up evolution to transform jungle beasts into humans . . . sort of. A classic. B&W; 70m. **DIR:** Erle C. Kenton. **CAST:** Charles Laughton, Richard Arlen, Leila Hyams, Bela Lugosi, Kathleen Burke, Stanley Fields. **1933**

ISLAND OF TERROR ★★★ On an island off the coast of Ireland, scientists battle lab-created, turtlelike mutants that live on human bone marrow. Fun thriller with some terrifically queasy sound effects. 87m. **DIR:** Terence Fisher. **CAST:** Peter Cushing, Edward Judd, Carole Gray. **1966**

ISLAND OF THE BLUE DOLPHINS ★★★ Alone on an island, a girl and her brother struggle to survive. When attacked by wild dogs, the girl manages to befriend the fiercest one. This adventure will be especially interesting for 7- to 12-year-olds. 93m. **DIR:** James B. Clark. **CAST:** Celia Kaye, George Kennedy, Larry Domasin. **1964**

ISLAND OF THE LOST ★★1/2 A scientist and his family become shipwrecked on an island inhabited by assorted beasts with genetic disorders. Not rated; contains mild violence. 92m. **DIR:** John Florea. **CAST:** Richard Greene, Luke Halpin, Mart Hulswit, Robin Mattson. **1968**

ISLAND TRADER ★★ A young boy on an island finds a wrecked airplane laden with gold bullion. He is then pursued by a dangerous criminal and a tugboat skipper, both of whom want the treasure. This potentially exciting adventure film is marred by amateurish direction, a low budget, and uninspired acting. 95m. **DIR:** Howard Rubie. **CAST:** John Ewart, Ruth Cracknell, Eric Oldfield. **1970**

ISLANDER, THE ★★★ A young girl grapples with sexism and diminished expectations in a quiet fishing village of Norwegian immigrants along the shores of Lake Michigan. Quaint coming-of-age film. Rated PG. 99m. **DIR:** Nany Thurow. **CAST:** Kit Wholihan, Jeff Weborg. **1988**

ISLANDS IN THE STREAM ★★★ This is really two movies in one. The first part is an affecting look at a broken family. The second is a cheap action-adventure. Thomas Hudson, a famous painter and sculptor, lives the life of a recluse in the Bahamas. His only companions are his seagoing crew. One summer, his three sons arrive to see him for the first time in four years. Rated PG for violence and profanity. 105m. **DIR:** Franklin J. Schaffner. **CAST:** George C. Scott, Julius W. Harris, David Hemmings, Brad Savage, Hart Bochner, Claire Bloom. **1977**

ISLE OF THE DEAD ★★★1/2 Atmospheric goings-on dominate this typically tasteful horror study from producer Val Lewton. A group of people are stranded on a Greek island during a quarantine. Star Boris Karloff is, as usual, outstanding. B&W; 72m. **DIR:** Mark Robson. **CAST:** Boris Karloff, Ellen Drew, Jason Robards Sr. **1945**

ISN'T SHE GREAT ★★ Soap-opera synopsis of Jacqueline Susann's life as a failed actress, disappointed mother, and outlandish, bestselling author fails on several levels. Bette Midler, as Susann, goes through an endless parade of flamboyant costumes which are supposed to define her character. Also, there is an uncomfortable blending of comedy and tragedy as she deals with her autistic son and breast cancer. Nathan Lane, as her manager and husband, and David Hyde Pierce, as her uptight editor, hint at what could have been a better film. Rated R for language and sexual innuendo. 95m. **DIR:** Andrew Bergman. **CAST:** Bette Midler, Nathan Lane, David Hyde Pierce. **2000 DVD**

ISTANBUL 🦃 A grungy American with a mysterious past meets a penniless student in Belgium and involves

him in a kidnapping. This English-dubbed thriller from France is hampered by the hammy overacting of Brad Dourif. Rated R for nudity, profanity, and sexual situations. 90m. **DIR:** Marc Didden. **CAST:** Brad Dourif, Dominique Deruddere, Ingrid De Vos. **1985**

ISTANBUL ★★ Limpid remake of 1947's *Singapore*, with Errol Flynn as the smuggler who finds more than mere memories of a lost love when he returns to Istanbul. Unfortunately, this is a *film noir* that forgot the *noir* and plays out like a melodrama. Casting did not help, as Flynn was too old for the part. Not rated. 85m. **DIR:** Joseph Pevney. **CAST:** Errol Flynn, Cornell Borchers, John Bentley, Nat King Cole, Leif Erickson, Peggy Knudsen, Martin Benson, Werner Klemperer, Torin Thatcher. **1956**

ISTANBUL: KEEP YOUR EYES OPEN ★★ A father searches for his daughter in this very odd drama. Director Mats Ahern leads his cast around and around, eventually leading them, and the audience, into confusion. Rated PG-13. 88m. **DIR:** Mats Ahern. **CAST:** Timothy Bottoms, Twiggy, Robert Morley. **1990**

IT (1927) ★★★ Advance promotion about *It* (read: sex appeal) made this clever little comedy about shop girl Clara Bow chasing and catching her boss Antonio Moreno a solid hit. It also boosted red-haired Brooklyn bombshell Clara to superstardom. Rising star Gary Cooper appears only briefly. Silent. B&W; 71m. **DIR:** Clarence Badger. **CAST:** Clara Bow, Antonio Moreno, William Austin, Lloyd Corrigan, Jacqueline Gadsden, Gary Cooper. **1927**

IT (1991) ★★★1/2 Although scripters Lawrence D. Cohen and Tommy Lee Wallace do a superb job setting up the events of Stephen King's lengthy bestseller, the ultimate payoff—when It is finally given a form—is quite disappointing. That's a shame, because this teleplay's first half is perhaps the best King adaptation ever lensed. Made for TV, but probably too intense for very young viewers. 192m. **DIR:** Tommy Lee Wallace. **CAST:** Harry Anderson, Dennis Christopher, Richard Masur, Annette O'Toole, Tim Reid, John Ritter, Richard Thomas, Tim Curry. **1991**

IT CAME FROM BENEATH THE SEA ★★★★ Ray Harryhausen's powerhouse special effects light up the screen in this story of a giant octopus from the depths of the Pacific that causes massive destruction along the North American coast as it makes its way toward San Francisco. A little talky at times, but the brilliantly achieved effects make this a must-see movie even on the small screen. B&W; 80m. **DIR:** Robert Gordon. **CAST:** Kenneth Tobey, Faith Domergue, Donald Curtis, Ian Keith. **1955**

IT CAME FROM OUTER SPACE ★★★★ Science-fiction author Ray Bradbury wrote the screenplay for this surprisingly effective 3-D chiller from the 1950s about creatures from outer space taking over the bodies of Earthlings. It was the first film to use this theme and still holds up today. B&W; 81m. **DIR:** Jack Arnold. **CAST:** Richard Carlson, Barbara Rush, Charles Drake. **1953**

IT CAME FROM THE SKY ★★★ Strange but occasionally affecting story with John Ritter and JoBeth Williams as the parents of a teenage boy who has been left partially paralyzed and speechless after an accident. Their troubled marriage is restored when they become the unwilling hosts to an odd couple whose plane crashes into their house. Kevin Zegers is particularly good as the boy who may have magical powers. Rated R for profanity. 92m. **DIR:** Jack Bender. **CAST:** John Ritter, JoBeth Williams, Christopher Lloyd, Yasmine Bleeth, Kevin Zegers. **1999 DVD**

IT CAME UPON A MIDNIGHT CLEAR ★★ Cornball story about a New York cop (Mickey Rooney) who dies from a heart attack but arranges with heavenly higher-ups to spend one last Christmas with his grandson (Scott Grimes). *It's a Wonderful Life* this is not. Made for television. 99m. **DIR:** Peter H. Hunt. **CAST:** Mickey Rooney, Scott Grimes, Barrie Youngfellow, George Gaynes, Hamilton Camp. **1984**

IT CONQUERED THE WORLD ★★ Paul Blaisdell's five-foot-high monster, which resembles an angry, upended cucumber that comes to a point at the top, looks better in the stills printed in monster magazines of the Sixties than in the movie itself—an above-average variation on *Invasion of the Body Snatchers*. A campy, frantic B movie. B&W; 68m. **DIR:** Roger Corman. **CAST:** Peter Graves, Beverly Garland, Lee Van Cleef. **1956**

IT COULD HAPPEN TO YOU ★★★1/2 Good-hearted beat cop Nicolas Cage promises to split his potential winnings on a lottery ticket with waitress Bridget Fonda when he's short of change for a tip. Of course, he wins the big prize, which causes all sorts of complications. This is a winning, unassuming little movie with the stars doing an outstanding job. Rated PG for light profanity. 101m. **DIR:** Andrew Bergman. **CAST:** Nicolas Cage, Bridget Fonda, Rosie Perez, Wendell Pierce, Isaac Hayes, Victor Rojas, Seymour Cassel, Stanley Tucci, Red Buttons. **1994 DVD**

IT HAPPENED AT THE WORLD'S FAIR ★★1/2 Adorable tyke plays matchmaker for Elvis Presley and Joan O'Brien at the Seattle World's Fair. It's a breezy romantic comedy with bouncy songs. Elvis hadn't yet reached the point where he was just going through the motions. He seems to be having fun and you will, too. 105m. **DIR:** Norman Taurog. **CAST:** Elvis Presley, Joan O'Brien, Gary Lockwood, Yvonne Craig. **1963**

IT HAPPENED IN BROOKLYN ★★ A modest musical made to capitalize on the hit-parade popularity of Frank Sinatra. The story concerns several Brooklynites trying to make the big time in show business. The only energy of note is Jimmy Durante. Passable. B&W; 105m. **DIR:** Richard Whorf. **CAST:** Frank Sinatra, Kathryn Grayson, Jimmy Durante, Peter Lawford, Gloria Grahame. **1947**

IT HAPPENED IN NEW ORLEANS ★★ Bobby Breen, the male Shirley Temple, stars as a Civil War orphan forced to leave his ex-slave mammy and go to New York. There, his Yankee relatives give him a hard time until his renditions of Stephen Foster tunes and his overwhelming cuteness win them over. Also known as *Rainbow on the River*. B&W; 83m. **DIR:** Kurt Neumann. **CAST:** Bobby Breen, May Robson, Charles Butterworth, Louise Beavers, Alan Mowbray, Benita Hume, Henry O'Neill, Eddie "Rochester" Anderson. **1936**

IT HAPPENED ONE NIGHT ★★★★★ Prior to *One Flew over the Cuckoo's Nest*, this 1934 comedy was the only film to capture all the major Academy Awards. Clark Gable stars as a cynical reporter on the trail of a runaway heiress, Claudette Colbert. They fall in love, of

course, and the result is vintage movie magic. B&W; 105m. **DIR:** Frank Capra. **CAST:** Clark Gable, Claudette Colbert, Ward Bond. **1934 DVD**

IT HAPPENS EVERY SPRING ★★★1/2 Great farce with chemistry professor Ray Milland accidentally developing a compound that, when applied, results in a baseball repulsing anything made of wood, including a bat. His major-league career as a pitcher is short-lived but lots of fun. B&W; 87m. **DIR:** Lloyd Bacon. **CAST:** Ray Milland, Jean Peters, Paul Douglas, Ed Begley Sr., Ted de Corsia, Ray Collins, Jessie Royce Landis, Alan Hale Jr. **1949**

IT LIVES AGAIN ★★★ In an effort to outdo the original *It's Alive!*, this film has three mutated babies on the loose, and everybody in a panic. Doesn't quite measure up to its predecessor, but still successful due to another fine makeup job by Rick Baker. Rated R. 91m. **DIR:** Larry Cohen. **CAST:** Frederic Forrest, Kathleen Lloyd, John P. Ryan, John Marley, Andrew Duggan. **1978**

IT RAINED ALL NIGHT THE DAY I LEFT ★★1/2 Tony Curtis and Lou Gossett Jr. play two small-time weapons salesmen who are ambushed in Africa. They go to work for a recently widowed woman (Sally Kellerman) who controls all the water in this extremely hot and dry region. Because she blames the natives for her husband's death, she rations their water. Rated R for sex and violence. 100m. **DIR:** Nicolas Gessner. **CAST:** Louis Gossett Jr., Sally Kellerman, Tony Curtis. **1978**

IT SHOULD HAPPEN TO YOU ★★★1/2 Judy Holliday plays an actress who's desperate to garner publicity and hopes splashing her name across billboards all over New York City will ignite her career. The movie provides steady chuckles. Jack Lemmon makes an amusing screen debut. Holliday is hard to resist. B&W; 81m. **DIR:** George Cukor. **CAST:** Judy Holliday, Peter Lawford, Jack Lemmon, Michael O'Shea, Vaughn Taylor. **1954**

IT STARTED IN NAPLES ★★ Clark Gable and Sophia Loren together sounds good on paper but doesn't work in this predictable comedy about an American man trying to get custody of his Italian nephew. 100m. **DIR:** Melville Shavelson. **CAST:** Clark Gable, Sophia Loren, Vittorio De Sica. **1960**

IT STARTED WITH A KISS ★★★ A show girl looking for a rich husband marries an air force sergeant instead, then wants the marriage kept platonic until she is sure. Fred Clark, as a general, again steals the show. 104m. **DIR:** George Marshall. **CAST:** Glenn Ford, Debbie Reynolds, Eva Gabor, Fred Clark, Edgar Buchanan, Harry Morgan. **1959**

IT STARTED WITH EVE ★★★★ Most of Deanna Durbin's movies have dated badly, but this comedy still retains a lot of charm. She plays a hatcheck girl who agrees to pose as the fiancée of multimillionaire Bob Cummings in order to grant the dying wish of his father. Problems start when the old man turns out not to be dying after all. B&W; 90m. **DIR:** Henry Koster. **CAST:** Deanna Durbin, Charles Laughton, Robert Cummings, Guy Kibbee. **1941**

IT TAKES A THIEF (TV SERIES) ★★★★ Suave and debonair Robert Wagner secured the television role of his career in this late-Sixties series, very loosely adapted from Alfred Hitchcock's *To Catch a Thief* (1955). Burglar Alexander Mundy put his talents to work for a supersecret government agency (the SIA). Actual European locales added to the show's luxurious tone, as did the occasional appearance of Fred Astaire (as Alexander's father, Alister, a retired thief). Delightful fun. 52m. **DIR:** Various. **CAST:** Robert Wagner, Malachi Throne, Fred Astaire. **1968–70**

IT TAKES TWO (1988) ★★ This young boy's fantasy features George Newbern as a reluctant bridegroom who has an affair with a fast car and a hot blonde car dealer. Only teens may fully appreciate this trite sex comedy. Rated PG-13 for profanity and sexual situations. 79m. **DIR:** David Beaird. **CAST:** George Newbern, Kimberly Foster. **1988**

IT TAKES TWO (1995) ★★1/2 A poor little rich girl and her orphan look-alike (identical twins Ashley and Mary-Kate Olsen) try to fix up the rich kid's widowed dad with the orphan's favorite social worker. *The Prince and the Pauper* meets *The Parent Trap* in a bland, inoffensive comedy for very small children. The Olsen twins perform dutifully but lack the experience to carry a whole film. Rated PG. 98m. **DIR:** Andy Tennant. **CAST:** Kirstie Alley, Steve Guttenberg, Mary-Kate Olsen, Ashley Olsen, Philip Bosco, Jane Sibbett. **1995**

IT! THE TERROR FROM BEYOND SPACE 🦃 Supposedly the inspiration for *Alien*, this is a dull tale of a spaceship returning from Mars in 1973, carrying a hitchhiking scaly being that disposes of the crew, one by one. B&W; 69m. **DIR:** Edward L. Cahn. **CAST:** Marshall Thompson, Ann Doran. **1958 DVD**

•ITALIAN FOR BEGINNERS ★★★★ This infectious romantic comedy blends old-fashioned roundelay charm with the Spartan tenets of the Dogme 95 film collective (handheld cameras, natural lighting, no special effects) as six lonely hearts gravitate to a Copenhagen Italian class. These people (including a priest, a shy hotel manager, a hot-tempered bar manager, and a klutzy pastry-shop clerk) search for intimate connections and deal with love, death, suicide, shaken religious faith, euthanasia, and generally bad hair days. In Danish and Italian with English subtitles. Rated R for language and sexual content. 99m. **DIR:** Lone Scherfig. **CAST:** Anders W. Berthelsen, Ann Eleonora Jorgensen, Anette Stovelbæk, Peter Gantzler, Lars Kaalund, Sara Indrio Jensen. **2000**

ITALIAN JOB, THE ★★★ An ex-con creates the world's biggest traffic jam in an attempt to steal millions in gold. The only problem is the mob doesn't like the idea. A fairly funny caper comedy. 99m. **DIR:** Peter Collinson. **CAST:** Michael Caine, Noel Coward, Benny Hill, Rossano Brazzi. **1969**

ITALIAN STRAW HAT, THE ★★★ The future happiness of newlyweds is threatened when the groom must find a replacement for a straw hat eaten by a horse. Failure means fighting a duel with the lover of the married woman who was wearing the hat. A silent classic with English intertitles and musical score. B&W; 72m. **DIR:** René Clair. **CAST:** Albert Préjean, Olga Tschechowa. **1927**

IT'S A BIG COUNTRY ★★★ This loving tribute to the United States is a grab bag of short stories glorifying the American way of life. The best has Ethel Barrymore set out to change our vital statistics because no one counted her in the last census. B&W; 89m. **DIR:** Clarence Brown, Don Hartman, John Sturges, Richard Thorpe, Charles Vidor, Don Weis, William Wellman.

CAST: Ethel Barrymore, Keefe Brasselle, Gary Cooper, Nancy Davis, Van Johnson, Gene Kelly, Janet Leigh, Marjorie Main, Fredric March, George Murphy, William Powell, S. Z. Sakall, Lewis Stone, James Whitmore, Keenan Wynn. **1951**

IT'S A DATE ★★★ A teenager competes with her widowed mother for a mature man. Corny plot, but it works because of the refreshing Deanna Durbin and her crystal-clear soprano voice. Remade with Jane Powell as *Nancy Goes to Rio* with different songs and didn't work nearly as well. B&W; 103m. **DIR:** William A. Seiter. **CAST:** Deanna Durbin, Walter Pidgeon, Kay Francis, Eugene Pallette, S. Z. Sakall, Fritz Feld, Samuel S. Hinds. **1940**

IT'S A DOG'S LIFE ★★ A scrappy bull terrier from the waterfront becomes the Bowery's paws-down champ under Jeff Richards's patronage, but cleans up his act when he comes under the influence of kindly Edmund Gwenn and his loving daughter Sally Fraser. Should warm the hearts of dog lovers everywhere. 88m. **DIR:** Herman Hoffman. **CAST:** Jeff Richards, Jarma Lewis, Edmund Gwenn, Dean Jagger, Sally Fraser, Richard Anderson. **1955**

IT'S A GIFT ★★★★★ In a class with the best of the comedies of the 1930s (including *Duck Soup*, *I'm No Angel*, *My Man Godfrey*), this classic was produced during the peak of Fields's association with Paramount and is his archetypal vehicle, peopled with characters whose sole purpose in life seems to be to annoy his long-suffering Harold Bissonette. A side-splitting series of visual delights. B&W; 73m. **DIR:** Norman Z. McLeod. **CAST:** W. C. Fields, Kathleen Howard, Baby LeRoy. **1934**

IT'S A GREAT FEELING ★★★ Doris Day's third movie is more of a comedy than a musical, but she still gets to sing a half-dozen sprightly songs. Jack Carson plays an obnoxious movie star. Cameo bits by Errol Flynn, Gary Cooper, Joan Crawford, Sydney Greenstreet, Jane Wyman, Edward G. Robinson, Ronald Reagan, Eleanor Parker, Patricia Neal, and Danny Kaye. 85m. **DIR:** David Butler. **CAST:** Doris Day, Dennis Morgan, Jack Carson, Bill Goodwin. **1949**

IT'S A GREAT LIFE ★★★ Dagwood and Blondie Bumstead sure could get away with silly story lines, and this is one of the silliest. Dagwood buys a horse because he misunderstood his instructions—he was told to buy a house. The players make it work. B&W; 75m. **DIR:** Frank Strayer. **CAST:** Penny Singleton, Arthur Lake, Danny Mummert, Hugh Herbert, Marjorie Ann Mutchie, Irving Bacon, Alan Dinehart. **1943**

IT'S A JOKE, SON! ★★ Radio's Senator Claghorn comes to life in the form of Kenny Delmar, whose bombastic talk and Old South attitude entertained millions on Fred Allen's popular network show. The blustering politician is hijacked by some underhanded rivals and only the strains of his beloved "Dixie" give him the strength to win the day. Cornball but fun. B&W; 63m. **DIR:** Ben Stoloff. **CAST:** Kenny Delmar, Una Merkel, June Lockhart, Kenneth Farrell, Douglass Dumbrille. **1947**

IT'S A MAD MAD MAD MAD WORLD ★★★★ Spencer Tracy and a cast made up of "Who's Who of American Comedy" are combined in this wacky chase movie to end all chase movies. Tracy is the crafty police captain who is following the progress of various money-mad citizens out to beat one another in discovering the buried hiding place of 350,000 stolen dollars. 154m. **DIR:** Stanley Kramer. **CAST:** Spencer Tracy, Milton Berle, Jonathan Winters, Buddy Hackett, Sid Caesar, Phil Silvers, Mickey Rooney, Peter Falk, Dick Shawn, Ethel Merman, Buster Keaton, Jimmy Durante, Edie Adams, Dorothy Provine, Terry-Thomas, William Demarest, Andy Devine. **1963 DVD**

IT'S A WONDERFUL LIFE ★★★★1/2 Have you ever wished you'd never been born? What if that wish were granted? That's the premise of Frank Capra's heartbreaking, humorous, and ultimately heartwarming *It's a Wonderful Life*. The story is about a good man who is so busy helping others that life seems to pass him by. B&W; 129m. **DIR:** Frank Capra. **CAST:** James Stewart, Donna Reed, Lionel Barrymore, Thomas Mitchell, Ward Bond, Henry Travers. **1946 DVD**

IT'S ALIVE! ★★★1/2 Camp classic about a mutated baby with a thirst for human blood has to be seen to be believed. Convincing effects work by Rick Baker and a fantastic score by Bernard Herrmann make this film one to remember. Rated PG. 91m. **DIR:** Larry Cohen. **CAST:** John P. Ryan, Sharon Farrell, Andrew Duggan, Guy Stockwell, Michael Ansara. **1974**

IT'S ALIVE III: ISLAND OF THE ALIVE ★★1/2 In this sequel, the mutant babies are sequestered on a desert island, where they reproduce and make their way back home to wreak havoc. Although this is a surprisingly strong entry in the *Alive* series, it suffers from some sloppy effects and mediocre acting. Rated R for violence. 95m. **DIR:** Larry Cohen. **CAST:** Michael Moriarty, Karen Black, Gerrit Graham, James Dixon. **1986**

IT'S ALL TRUE ★★★★1/2 This fresh glimpse of Orson Welles's three aborted 1942 docudramas about Latin American culture—commissioned to promote President Roosevelt's Good Neighbor Policy—sadly reminds us of all the great films Welles never made. His unfinished shorts about a Mexican boy and his bull, the samba, and four Brazilian fishermen on a social protest voyage are mixed with interviews of the legendary filmmaker and his associates. The result is part travelogue, part historic treasure, and part passion play. Rated G. 89m. **DIR:** Richard Wilson, Myron Meisel, Bill Krohn. **CAST:** Orson Welles. **1993**

IT'S ALWAYS FAIR WEATHER ★★★ World War II buddies Gene Kelly, Dan Dailey, and Michael Kidd meet a decade after discharge and find they actively dislike one another. Enter romance, reconciliation ploys, and attempted exploitation of their reunion on televison. Don't be surprised to realize it recalls *On the Town*. 102m. **DIR:** Gene Kelly, Stanley Donen. **CAST:** Gene Kelly, Dan Dailey, Michael Kidd, Cyd Charisse, Dolores Gray, David Burns. **1955**

IT'S GOOD TO BE ALIVE ★★★1/2 The tragedy of a great athlete being struck down in the prime of his career is dealt with in this story of Brooklyn Dodgers catcher Roy Campanella (Paul Winfield). Campanella had two spectacular seasons with the Dodgers before being permanently crippled from the waist down in a car accident in 1958. This film focuses on Campanella's struggle with self-respect after the wreck. A good companion piece to *Brian's Song*. 100m. **DIR:** Michael Lan-

don. **CAST:** Paul Winfield, Louis Gossett Jr., Ruby Dee, Ramon Bieri, Lloyd Gough. **1974**

IT'S IN THE BAG ★★★ The plot (if there ever was one) derives from the Russian fable about an impoverished nobleman on a treasure hunt. Continuity soon goes out the window, however, when the cast starts winging it in one hilarious episode after another. This is Fred Allen, acerbic and nasal as always, in his best screen comedy. B&W; 87m. **DIR:** Richard Wallace. **CAST:** Fred Allen, Jack Benny, Binnie Barnes, Robert Benchley, Victor Moore, Sidney Toler, Rudy Vallee, William Bendix, Don Ameche. **1945**

IT'S IN THE WATER ★★★1/2 In this independent comedy, Keri Jo Chapman plays a woman trapped in a loveless marriage, who has a lesbian affair with an old friend. As word gets out, the gossip induces hysteria in the small-town citizens who fear that there's something in the water. While some performances are rough around the edges and some dialogue is clumsy, the overall effect is one of joy and celebration. Simple, refreshing message delivered in a simple, refreshing manner. Not rated; contains adult situations and language. 100m. **DIR:** Kelli Herd. **CAST:** Keri Jo Chapman, Teresa Garrett, John Hallum. **1998 DVD**

IT'S MY PARTY ★★★1/2 Eric Roberts plays an architect with AIDS who, as death nears, gathers friends and family around him for a last farewell; unexpectedly, his ex-lover shows up as well. Much of the film tends toward predictable soap opera, but it avoids maudlin excess thanks to sensitive direction and fine acting. Rated R for profanity and mature themes. 110m. **DIR:** Randal Kleiser. **CAST:** Eric Roberts, Gregory Harrison, Margaret Cho, Bronson Pinchot, Lee Grant, Marlee Matlin, Olivia Newton-John, George Segal, Roddy McDowall, Paul Regina. **1996**

IT'S MY TURN ★★ Jill Clayburgh is a college professor confused about her relationship with live-in lover Charles Grodin, a Chicago real estate salesman. Then she meets baseball player Michael Douglas. They fall in love. The viewer yawns. Rated R. 91m. **DIR:** Claudia Weill. **CAST:** Jill Clayburgh, Michael Douglas, Beverly Garland, Charles Grodin. **1980**

IT'S PAT: THE MOVIE ★★ Another *Saturday Night Live* character limps to the big screen, and even though this film clocks in at a measly 78 minutes, it still seems 60 minutes too long. Some good laughs are derived from attempting to discover title character's gender, but Charles Rocket as an obsessed neighbor is way out there. Rated PG-13 for plenty of sexual innuendo. 78m. **DIR:** Adam Bernstein. **CAST:** Julia Sweeney, David Foley, Charles Rocket, Kathy Griffin, Julie Hayden. **1994**

IVAN THE TERRIBLE—PART I & PART II ★★★★★ Considered among the classics of world cinema, this epic biography of Russia's first czar was commissioned by Joseph Stalin to encourage acceptance of his harsh and historically similar policies. World-renowned director Sergei Eisenstein, instead, transformed what was designed as party propaganda into a panoramic saga of how power corrupts those seeking it. B&W; 188m. **DIR:** Sergei Eisenstein. **CAST:** Nikolai Cherkassov, Ludmila Tselikovskaya. **1945 DVD**

IVANHOE (1952) ★★★★ Robert Taylor stars as Sir Walter Scott's dashing knight Ivanhoe. His mission is to secure the ransom for King Richard the Lionhearted, who has been captured while returning from the Crusades. Action and swordplay abound as Ivanhoe strives for Richard's release and protects two very fair maidens (Elizabeth Taylor and Joan Fontaine) from the lecherous grasp of archvillain George Sanders. 106m. **DIR:** Richard Thorpe. **CAST:** Robert Taylor, Elizabeth Taylor, Joan Fontaine, George Sanders, Sebastian Cabot. **1952**

IVANHOE (1982) ★★★★ Lavish remake of the 1952 version of Sir Walter Scott's novel of chivalry and derring-do. This time, Anthony Andrews is the disinherited knight who joins ranks with Robin Hood to recapture King Richard's throne from the sniveling Prince John. Brilliant costuming and pageantry. Originally a TV miniseries. 180m. **DIR:** Douglas Camfield. **CAST:** Anthony Andrews, James Mason, Sam Neill, Olivia Hussey. **1982**

IVANHOE (1997) ★★★ Sir Walter Scott's classic about love and loyalty is remade, yet again, this time as a TV miniseries with an emphasis on the ill treatment afforded Jews in twelfth-century England. Remaining loyal to the displaced King Richard, Ivanhoe takes on Prince John and his minions. This forms the backdrop to his long-time romance with Rowena and new friendship with Rebecca as his heroism extends to protecting her and her father. Splendid pageantry and costuming. Not rated; contains violence and animal brutality. 180m. **DIR:** Stuart Orme. **CAST:** Steven Waddington, Susan Lynch, Victoria Smurfit, Ralph Brown. **1997 DVD**

I'VE ALWAYS LOVED YOU ★★★ A lavish musical featuring Arthur Rubinstein on the soundtrack performing selections by Rachmaninoff, Tchaikovsky, Beethoven, Chopin, Liszt, Wagner, and Mendelssohn—to underscore the romance of an arrogant orchestra conductor and the lady pianist who upstages him. The UCLA archivally restored print restores the vibrant Technicolor and provides a clean soundtrack. 117m. **DIR:** Frank Borzage. **CAST:** Catherine McLeod, Philip Dorn, Maria Ouspenskaya, Felix Bressart, Elizabeth Patterson, Vanessa Brown, Adele Mara, Fritz Feld, Stephanie Bachelor, Cora Witherspoon. **1946**

I'VE BEEN WAITING FOR YOU ★★★ Effective adaptation of Lois Duncan's novel *Gallows Hill*, a reincarnation/witchcraft chiller set in a high school. Here, the descendants of those who participated in a witch trial are compelled to relive the event. Rated PG-13 for violence. 90m. **DIR:** Christopher Leitch. **CAST:** Sarah Chalke, Christian Campbell, Soleil Moon Frye, Markie Post. **1998 DVD**

I'VE HEARD THE MERMAIDS SINGING ★★★ A slight but often engaging story about a naïve photographer (Sheila McCarthy) who longs to be a part of the elitist art world. The cloyingly whimsical ending is the only thunk in this nifty debut from director Patricia Rozema. Rated PG. 83m. **DIR:** Patricia Rozema. **CAST:** Sheila McCarthy, Paule Viallargeon, Anne-Marie Macdonald. **1987**

IVORY-HANDLED GUN, THE ★★1/2 Buck Ward and the Wolverine Kid have a score to settle that goes back to their father's time and they each have one ivory-handled gun and want the other. Released with a serial chapter, cartoon, and newsreel. B&W; 59m. **DIR:** Ray Taylor. **CAST:** Buck Jones, Charlotte Wynters, Walter Miller, Carl Stockdale, Frank Rice, Bob Kortman, Stanley Blystone. **1935**

IVORY HUNTERS ★★★1/2 Powerful made-for-cable drama reveals the horrors of elephants mutilated for their tusks. Manages to make its point without overt preaching. John Lithgow plays an author in Nairobi looking for his missing researcher. There he meets a dedicated field biologist (Isabella Rossellini) and a police inspector (James Earl Jones) waging their own wars against poachers. 94m. **DIR:** Joseph Sargent. **CAST:** John Lithgow, Isabella Rossellini, James Earl Jones, Tony Todd. **1990**

IZZY & MOE ★★★1/2 Together for the last time, Jackie Gleason and Art Carney are near-perfect as ex-vaudevillians who become New York Prohibition agents in this made-for-TV movie based on actual characters. The two stars still worked beautifully together after all those years. 100m. **DIR:** Jackie Cooper. **CAST:** Jackie Gleason, Art Carney, Cynthia Harris, Zohra Lampert. **1985**

J

J. LYLE ★★★ Best known for his distinctive pencil-sketch animation, filmmaker Bill Plympton retains much of his bizarre humor in his first live-action film (which features some animated segments). But like his previous (all-animated) feature, *The Tune*, this tale of a greedy lawyer who has a change of heart while trying to evict the residents of an apartment complex has a few too many dull stretches mixed in with the flashes of wit. Not rated; contains nothing objectionable. 75m. **DIR:** Bill Plympton. **CAST:** Richard Kuranda, Jennifer Corby, John Bader. **1996**

JABBERWOCKY ★★1/2 Monty Python fans will be disappointed to see only one group member, Michael Palin, in this British film. Palin plays a dim-witted peasant during the Dark Ages. A monster called Jabberwocky is destroying villages all over the countryside, so Palin tries to destroy the monster. There are some funny moments but nothing in comparison with true Python films. No MPAA rating. 100m. **DIR:** Terry Gilliam. **CAST:** Michael Palin, Max Wall, Deborah Fallender. **1977 DVD**

J'ACCUSE ★★★★ Director Abel Gance's remake of this classic silent film shows the horrors of war as it affects two friends, soldiers in love with the same woman. Cinematically rich, with an unforgettable sequence showing war casualties rising from their graves. In French with English subtitles. B&W; 95m. **DIR:** Abel Gance. **CAST:** Victor Francen, Jean Max. **1938**

JACK ★★★ Robin Williams adds another misfit to his résumé in this mostly lighthearted fantasy–tragedy about a little boy with an unusual disease that causes premature aging. James DeMonaco and Gary Nadeau's script too often takes the easy way out, focusing on the comedic aspects of a boy trapped inside a man's body, rather than dwelling on the situation's truly tragic aspects. Rated PG-13 for profanity and blue humor. 113m. **DIR:** Francis Ford Coppola. **CAST:** Robin Williams, Diane Lane, Jennifer Lopez, Brian Kerwin, Fran Drescher, Bill Cosby. **1996**

JACK AND SARAH ★★★ A recently widowed London attorney (Richard E. Grant) impulsively hires an American waitress (Samantha Mathis) as nanny to his infant daughter. This affable romantic comedy-drama tends to wander from scene to scene and juggles a few more plot threads than it can handle; still, it never becomes predictable, and the surprising rapport between Grant and Mathis (along with the excellent supporting cast) carries the day. Rated R for profanity and brief nudity. 100m. **DIR:** Tim Sullivan. **CAST:** Richard E. Grant, Samantha Mathis, Judi Dench, Ian McKellen, David Swift, Eileen Atkins, Cherie Lunghi. **1996 DVD**

JACK BE NIMBLE ★★1/2 Some creepy moments aren't enough to distinguish this supernatural thriller from the rest of the pack. As babies, Jack and Dora were abandoned and split up by adoption. Dora uses her extrasensory powers to locate Jack and finds that he is in danger. Not rated; contains intense situations. 93m. **DIR:** Garth Maxwell. **CAST:** Alexis Arquette, Sarah Kennedy, Bruno Lawrence. **1994 DVD**

JACK BENNY PROGRAM, THE (TV SERIES) ★★★★ Following the formula that had made him a smash on radio, Jack Benny became a fixture on TV. Bolstered by the top-notch character actors who popped up on the show, Benny held the spotlight with a pregnant pause, a hand on the chin, or a shift of the eyes. Comic bits frequently revolved around Benny's stinginess and deadly violin playing. Video appearances include Ernie Kovacs, Jayne Mansfield, Johnny Carson, Connie Francis, The Smothers Brothers, George Burns, Humphrey Bogart, Kirk Douglas, Fred Allen, Ann-Margret, and Bob Hope. B&W; 30m. **DIR:** Frederick de Cordova. **CAST:** Jack Benny, Mary Livingstone, Eddie "Rochester" Anderson, Dennis Day, Don Wilson, Mel Blanc. **1950–1965**

JACK BULL, THE ★★★★ This unusual Western focuses on one man's quest for justice. When two of Myrl Redding's (John Cusack) horses and one of his workers are abused by the richest man in the territory of Wyoming, Redding seeks justice, first through the law, then by his own means. Politics and loyalties work against Redding's quest, but in the end he triumphs . . . at great cost. This made-for-cable original is based on a true story, and contains enough grit and moral dilemma to chew on for a week. Excellent performances by the entire cast enhance the offbeat story of one man's justice. Rated R for profanity and violence. 116m. **DIR:** John Badham. **CAST:** John Cusack, John Goodman, L. Q. Jones, Miranda Otto, John C. McGinley, John Savage. **1999 DVD**

JACK FROST (1997) ★★ When a serial killer is accidentally exposed to experimental genetic materials, he is transformed into a murderous snowman. Horror spoof is too gruesome to be funny and too goofy to be scary—and features some of the phoniest snow you've ever seen. Rated R for gruesome violence and profanity. 89m. **DIR:** Michael Cooney. **CAST:** Christopher Allport, Scott McDonald, F. William Parker. **1997 DVD**

JACK FROST (1998) Decent special effects can't salvage this sappy disaster. Michael Keaton plays a blues singer who becomes a better dad to his son when he is reincarnated as a talking snowman who throws a mean snowball. Rated PG for a sexual situation. 100m.

DIR: Troy Miller. **CAST:** Michael Keaton, Kelly Preston, Mark Addy, Joseph Cross. **1998 DVD**

•JACK FROST 2 ★★ Jack, the killer snowman, returns to commit mass carnage at a tropical island resort, which is of course, the perfect spot for vacationing homicidal balls of ice. Extremely campy and silly, this movie falls into the so-bad-it's-good category. Rated R for graphic violence, language, and nudity. 91m. **DIR:** Michael Cooney. **CAST:** Christopher Allport, Eileen Seeley. **2000 DVD**

JACK KNIFE MAN, THE ★★★★ A lonely old river rat finds his life changed for the better by an orphan boy left in his care. Better than the hokey plot sounds, with believable characterizations and impressively atmospheric direction by a young King Vidor. Silent with musical score. B&W; 86m. **DIR:** King Vidor. **CAST:** Fred Turner, Harry Todd, Bobby Kelso, Florence Vidor. **1920**

JACK LONDON ★★ Episodic, fictionalized account of one of America's most popular authors is entertaining, but one wishes for a more definitive biography. Heavily influenced by the anti-Japanese sentiment rampant at the time of its release, the tragic tale of the poor boy who gained and alienated the love of America and the world cries out to be remade in today's more permissive atmosphere. B&W; 94m. **DIR:** Alfred Santell. **CAST:** Michael O'Shea, Susan Hayward, Osa Massen, Harry Davenport, Frank Craven, Virginia Mayo. **1943**

JACK-O 🦃 Land developers unearth an ancient demon, who continues his centuries-old quest for blood. *Pumpkinhead* did it first and much better. Rated R for violence and adult language. 90m. **DIR:** Steve Latshaw. **CAST:** Linnea Quigley, Rebecca Wicks, Gary Doles, John Carradine. **1995 DVD**

JACK THE BEAR ★★★★ The joys and horrors of childhood are explored in this insightful film in which a local TV personality, who hosts monster movies, attempts to raise his two sons after the tragic death of his wife. The title character is his eldest son, a preteen whose adventures with first love and new friends are darkened by the specter of a psychotic neighbor. Rated PG for brief profanity and violence. 99m. **DIR:** Marshall Herskovitz. **CAST:** Danny DeVito, Robert J. Steinmiller, Miko Hughes, Gary Sinise, Art La Fleur, Stefan Gierasch, Erica Yohn, Julia Louis-Dreyfus, Reese Witherspoon, Bert Remsen. **1993**

JACK THE GIANT KILLER ★★★1/2 A delightful reworking of "Jack and the Beanstalk," with many innovative special effects to give it adult appeal. Kerwin Mathews of Ray Harryhausen's *Sinbad* movies fights giants and monsters molded by Harryhausen's disciple, Jim Danforth. Lots of fun. 94m. **DIR:** Nathan Juran. **CAST:** Kerwin Mathews, Torin Thatcher, Judi Meredith. **1962**

JACK THE RIPPER (1959) ★★ This thoroughly fictionalized rendering of the exploits of Whitechapel's mass murderer hasn't aged well. B&W; 84m. **DIR:** Robert S. Baker, Monty Berman. **CAST:** Lee Patterson, Eddie Byrne, George Rose. **1959**

JACK THE RIPPER (1979) ★★ Klaus Kinski plays Jack the Ripper, and Josephine Chaplin is Cynthia, the Scotland Yard inspector's girlfriend. Jack the Ripper is terrorizing London by killing women and disposing of their bodies in the Thames River. Rated R for violence and nudity. 82m. **DIR:** Jess (Jesus) Franco. **CAST:** Klaus Kinski, Josephine Chaplin. **1979 DVD**

JACK THE RIPPER (1988) ★★★★ For more than a century the enigma of Jack the Ripper and why he disemboweled five prostitutes in 1888 London has plagued criminologists and historians. In this fine teleplay, all who have been suspect are introduced and examined. Director David Wickes comes up with what is both a possible and probable solution as to why he has never been identified. Michael Caine is outstanding as Frederick Abberline, the alcoholic Scotland Yard inspector in charge of the investigation. Not rated; surprisingly little gore, but not for the kids. 200m. **DIR:** David Wickes. **CAST:** Michael Caine, Armand Assante, Ray McAnally, Susan George, Jane Seymour, Lewis Collins, Ken Bones, Harry Andrews. **1988**

JACKAL, THE ★★★1/2 Events have been updated and key points have been modified in this absorbing remake of *The Day of the Jackal*. As before, this is a disturbing parable on a free society's vulnerability to terrorists and the shocking ease with which a methodical killer—in this case, Bruce Willis—could snuff any of our public figures. Sleek, intelligent, well cast, and always fun to watch. Rated R for violence and profanity. 124m. **DIR:** Michael Caton-Jones. **CAST:** Bruce Willis, Richard Gere, Sidney Poitier, Diane Venora, Mathilda May. **1997 DVD**

JACKER 2: DESCENT TO HELL 🦃 This low-budget horror movie is nothing short of mind-numbing as an unkillable carjacker runs rampant on a spree of destruction and mayhem. Not rated; contains profanity, violence, nudity, and simulated sex. 89m. **DIR:** Barry Gaines. **CAST:** Philip Herman, Barry Gaines, Ben Stanski, Nancy Feliciano. **1999**

JACKIE BROWN ★★★★ At long last, the immensely talented Pam Grier gets her due as the star of this crime caper, based on the novel *Rum Punch* by Elmore Leonard. This tense thriller, full of surprises and outstanding performances, is no *Pulp Fiction*, but it'll do just fine for fans of the filmmaker's offbeat style. Rated R for violence, profanity, and nudity. 155m. **DIR:** Quentin Tarantino. **CAST:** Pam Grier, Samuel L. Jackson, Robert Forster, Bridget Fonda, Michael Keaton, Robert De Niro, Michael Bowen, Chris Tucker, Lisa Gay Hamilton, Tom "Tiny" Lister Jr. **1997**

JACKIE CHAN'S FIRST STRIKE ★★★ There are plenty of thrills, chills, and spills in this Jackie Chan movie, which also is known as *Police Story 4: First Strike*. But by editing it for American audiences, the distributors have taken all the sense out of the story and left our globe-trotting hero bouncing from one life-or-death encounter to another. *Rumble in the Bronx* was a better example of making a Hong Kong release into watchable U.S. fare. Rated PG-13 for violence. 88m. **DIR:** Stanley Tong. **CAST:** Jackie Chan, Jackson Lou. **1996 DVD**

JACKIE CHAN'S POLICE FORCE 🦃 A lame, comedic kung fu mixture. Rated PG-13 for violence. 101m. **DIR:** Jackie Chan. **CAST:** Jackie Chan, Brigitte Lin. **1986**

JACKIE COLLINS' LUCKY CHANCES ★★1/2 This TV miniseries combines two of Jackie Collins's steamy novels. The first and better half traces crime boss Gino Santangelo's rise to power, while the remainder of the film is devoted to his headstrong and not very endearing daughter, Lucky (Nicollette Sheridan), and her quest to win Dad's approval. Predictable and melodramatic, but

you'll get hooked anyway. Not rated; contains mild sex and violence. 285m. **DIR:** Buzz Kulik. **CAST:** Nicollette Sheridan, Vincent Irizarry, Michael Nader. **1990**

JACKIE ROBINSON STORY, THE ★★★★ This is one of the best baseball films ever—the biography of Jackie Robinson, first black to play in the major leagues. The performances (including Mr. Robinson as himself) are very good, and the direction is sharp. B&W; 76m. **DIR:** Alfred E. Green. **CAST:** Jackie Robinson, Ruby Dee, Minor Watson, Louise Beavers. **1950 DVD**

JACKKNIFE ★★★★ Ed Harris and Kathy Baker star as brother and sister in this drama about veterans who suffer from post-Vietnam stress syndrome. Robert De Niro plays another vet who comes into their lives, causing volatile changes. Rated R, with profanity and violence. 102m. **DIR:** David Jones. **CAST:** Robert De Niro, Ed Harris, Kathy Baker. **1989**

JACKPOT, THE ★★★★ A satire on radio quiz programs that pokes fun at public reaction more than industry greed and has the cast to put it over. B&W; 87m. **DIR:** Walter Lang. **CAST:** James Stewart, Barbara Hale, James Gleason, Natalie Wood, Tommy Rettig, Patricia Medina. **1950**

•JACKPOT ★★1/2 Would-be country singer Jon Gries abandons his wife and child to hit the karaoke circuit and try to break into the big time. Can one really hit the big time singing karaoke, or is that just an intended irony here? In any case, performances are good, the atmosphere convincingly seedy, but the film is slow-moving and unpleasant. Rated R for profanity and sexual scenes. 96m. **DIR:** Michael Polish. **CAST:** Jonathan Gries, Garrett Morris, Daryl Hannah. **2001 DVD**

JACK'S BACK ★★★ Not a splatter film, but a fairly thoughtful suspense melodrama. James Spader portrays twin brothers in this tale of a Jack-the-Ripper copycat killer operating in modern-day Los Angeles. Rated R for gore. 90m. **DIR:** Rowdy Herrington. **CAST:** James Spader, Cynthia Gibb, Robert Picardo, Rod Loomis, Chris Mulkey. **1988**

JACKSON COUNTY JAIL ★★★1/2 This chase film is pretty good. Yvette Mimieux escapes from jail with fellow inmate Tommy Lee Jones. Audiences can't help but sympathize with Mimieux, because she was unfairly arrested and then raped by her jailer. Rated R. 89m. **DIR:** Michael Miller. **CAST:** Yvette Mimieux, Tommy Lee Jones, Robert Carradine. **1976 DVD**

JACKSONS, THE: AN AMERICAN DREAM ★★★1/2 Though slanted in favor of its title characters, this made-for-TV movie features excellent performances by a star-studded cast as they act out the saccharine history of one of America's most talented dysfunctional families. Main attraction Michael is played by fifteen different actors as he ages. Not rated. 225m. **DIR:** Karen Arthur. **CAST:** Holly Robinson, Angela Bassett, Billy Dee Williams, Margaret Avery, Lawrence Hilton-Jacobs, Vanessa L. Williams. **1992**

JACOB I HAVE LOVED ★★★ Fine adaptation of Katherine Paterson's Newbery Award–winning book. Bridget Fonda portrays a tomboy who plays second fiddle to her glamorous and talented twin sister. Resentment turns to hatred until Fonda befriends an old sea captain. Originally shown on PBS's *Wonderworks* series. 57m. **DIR:** Victoria Hochberg. **CAST:** Bridget Fonda, Jenny Robertson, John Kellogg. **1989**

JACOB TWO-TWO MEETS THE HOODED FANG ★★★1/2 Delightful tale of a boy nicknamed Jacob Two-Two because he has to say everything twice when talking to grownups. (They never listen to him the first time.) Fed up with adults, he dreams that he is sentenced to Slimer's Island, a children's prison where his guard is the Hooded Fang (a funny performance by Alex Karras). The low budget shows, but most of the humor of Mordecai Richler's book is retained. Rated G. 80m. **DIR:** Theodore J. Flicker. **CAST:** Stephen Rosenberg, Alex Karras. **1979 DVD**

JACOB'S LADDER ★★★ A spiritual tale about a Vietnam veteran who is plagued by strange nightmares and, after a while, daymares. Is it the aftereffects of a drug tested on soldiers? Is a parallel universe of demons invading our own? Does the film get a little carried away with all this "other-side" stuff? You decide for yourself. Rated R for violence, nudity, and profanity. 115m. **DIR:** Adrian Lyne. **CAST:** Tim Robbins, Elizabeth Peña, Danny Aiello, Matt Craven, Jason Alexander, Macaulay Culkin. **1990 DVD**

JADE Assistant district attorney David Caruso finds himself compromised when his investigation into the murder of a prominent figure seems to lead to the wife of a longtime friend. It's pure, unadulterated trash. Rated R for violence, profanity, nudity, sex, and rape. 90m. **DIR:** William Friedkin. **CAST:** David Caruso, Linda Fiorentino, Chazz Palminteri, Michael Biehn, Richard Crenna, Kevin Tighe. **1995 DVD**

JADE MASK, THE ★★ *Charlie Chan* programmer from cheapie Monogram period. Charlie seeks an inventor's murderer. Routine. B&W; 66m. **DIR:** Phil Rosen. **CAST:** Sidney Toler, Mantan Moreland, Edwin Luke, Janet Warren, Frank Reicher. **1945**

JAGGED EDGE ★★1/2 A publishing magnate (Jeff Bridges) is accused of the ritualistic slaying of his wife; an attorney (Glenn Close) is hired to defend him. They fall in love, conduct an affair during the trial(!), which is not noticed by the ambitious prosecutor (Peter Coyote) (!), and generally behave like total fools; during this, we and Close ponder the burning question: Did Bridges do the dirty deed? Too bad the story doesn't measure up. Rated R for violence. 108m. **DIR:** Richard Marquand. **CAST:** Glenn Close, Jeff Bridges, Peter Coyote, Robert Loggia, Leigh Taylor-Young. **1985 DVD**

JAIL BAIT (1954) ★★ Delightfully awful crime melodrama from everyone's favorite bad auteur, Ed *(Plan 9 From Outer Space)* Wood. Hardboiled punk Tim Farrell involves the son of a famous plastic surgeon in a robbery, then forces the doctor to help him escape from the police. There's lots of ridiculous dialogue, cheap sets, a final plot twist you'll spot a mile away, and one of the most god awful droning musical scores you'll ever hear. A must-see for camp aficionados. B&W; 70m. **DIR:** Edward D. Wood Jr. **CAST:** Timothy Farrell, Dolores Fuller, Lyle Talbot, Herbert Rawlinson, Steve Reeves. **1954 DVD**

JAILBAIT (1992) ★★ C. Thomas Howell is the burnt-out cop who gets involved with a teenage runaway who witnessed a murder. Pretty seedy affair corrals all of the clichés. Not rated and R-rated versions available. Rated R for nudity, violence, and language; unrated version has more nudity. 100/103. **DIR:** Rafal Zielinski. **CAST:** C. Thomas Howell, Renee Humphrey. **1992**

•JAILBAIT (2000) ★★ An 18-year-old jock is seduced by the school floozy and unintentionally impregnates her in this mild satire of teen sexuality. When it is discovered that she is only sixteen, the young man is arrested and accused of statutory rape, which in turn leads to an exaggerated legal battle. While pretending to take a witty look at real teen issues, this movie glamorizes teen sexuality more than it promotes safe sexual practices. Rated R for nudity and sexual situations. 94m. **DIR:** Alan Moyle. **CAST:** Matt Frewer, Mary Gross, Kevin Mundy. **2000 DVD**

JAILHOUSE ROCK ★★★★ Quite possibly Elvis Presley's best as far as musical sequences go, this 1957 film is still burdened by a sappy plot. Good-hearted Presley gets stuck in the slammer, only to hook up with a conniving manager (Mickey Shaughnessy). Forget the plot and enjoy the great rock 'n' roll songs. B&W; 96m. **DIR:** Richard Thorpe. **CAST:** Elvis Presley, Mickey Shaughnessy, Dean Jones, Judy Tyler. **1957 DVD**

JAKE SPANNER PRIVATE EYE ★★ Robert Mitchum plays Jake Spanner, a retired private detective in this mediocre made-for-cable movie. A group of senior citizens decide to help Jake find the double-crossing Ernest Borgnine before an evil drug queen does. 95m. **DIR:** Lee H. Katzin. **CAST:** Robert Mitchum, Ernest Borgnine, John Mitchum, Richard Yniguez, Jim Mitchum, Dick Van Patten, Stella Stevens, Kareem Abdul-Jabbar, Edie Adams. **1989**

JAKE SPEED ★★★1/2 Quirky little adventure thriller, from the folks involved with the equally deft *Night of the Comet*. When Karen Kopins's younger sister is kidnapped and threatened with white slavery by John Hurt's delightfully oily villain, Speed (Wayne Crawford) and his associate Remo (Dennis Christopher) materialize and offer to help. Rated PG for mild violence. 100m. **DIR:** Andrew Lane. **CAST:** Wayne Crawford, Dennis Christopher, Karen Kopins, John Hurt, Leon Ames, Donna Pescow, Barry Primus, Monte Markham. **1986 DVD**

JAKOB THE LIAR ★★ Widowed, melancholy cafe owner hides a child from the Gestapo and brings hope to the inhabitants of a Jewish Ghetto in Nazi-occupied 1944 Poland by sharing news he allegedly hears on a secreted radio. The first-rate set designs, costumes, cinematography, and score of this seriocomic Holocaust fable establish a bleak Euroscape. The film nonetheless collapses in a heavy-breathing marriage of irony and unearned sentiment. Rated PG-13 for violence. 113m. **DIR:** Peter Kassovitz. **CAST:** Robin Williams, Alan Arkin, Bob Balaban, Liev Schreiber, Armin Mueller-Stahl, Hannah Taylor Gordon. **1999 DVD**

JAMAICA INN ★★★ Not one of Alfred Hitchcock's best directorial efforts. But the cast makes it, just the same. Charles Laughton is Squire Pengallon, the evil chief of a band of cutthroats in Victorian England. Maureen O'Hara is a beautiful damsel in distress. B&W; 98m. **DIR:** Alfred Hitchcock. **CAST:** Charles Laughton, Maureen O'Hara, Leslie Banks, Emlyn Williams, Robert Newton, Mervyn Johns. **1939 DVD**

JAMES AND THE GIANT PEACH ★★★★ Roald Dahl's classic children's story gets ambitious treatment from director Henry Selick. Young Paul Terry loses his parents and endures the contempt of two outrageously cruel aunts, until encountering an old beggar with magical, luminescent "crocodile tongues." They infect a dying peach tree, which produces a stadium-sized fruit; once James climbs inside, the live-action performers are replaced by huge, animated insects. James and his new friends experience all sorts of adventures while en route to New York City, none better than an ocean encounter with an impressively frightening mechanical shark. Rated PG for occasional intensity. 80m. **DIR:** Henry Selick. **CAST:** Paul Terry, Joanna Lumley, Miriam Margolyes, Pete Postlethwaite. **1996 DVD**

JAMES DEAN—A LEGEND IN HIS OWN TIME ★★1/2 Lackluster dramatization of actor James Dean's life as seen through the eyes of a friend. Stephen McHattie qualifies as a James Dean look-alike and gives a solid performance. This film features a fine supporting cast. 99m. **DIR:** Robert Butler. **CAST:** Michael Brandon, Stephen McHattie, Candy Clark, Amy Irving, Meg Foster, Jayne Meadows, Brooke Adams. **1976**

JAMES DEAN STORY, THE ★★1/2 Robert Altman's first feature film was this unexceptional documentary about the late actor that relies heavily on clips from his films and television appearances. Not rated. 79m. **DIR:** Robert Altman, George W. George. **1957 DVD**

•JAMES DEAN (2001) ★★★ Decent bio-flick made for TNT features James Franco as America's symbolic icon for teen restlessness and rebellion. The focus is on his tragic childhood in which Mom dies and Dad rejects him. Determined to become a great actor, he takes on Broadway en route to Hollywood. Franco presents Dean as needy with sharp mood swings. Director Mark Rydell steps in smoothly to play studio head Jack Warner. Not rated; contains sexual situations and adult themes. 95m. **DIR:** Mark Rydell. **CAST:** James Franco, Michael Moriarty, Valentina Cervi, Enrico Colantoni. **2001 DVD**

JAMES JOYCE'S WOMEN ★★★★1/2 A delicious, verbally erotic movie. With Joyce as the writer and Fionnula Flanagan (writer and producer) as interpreter, things are bound to be intense. The film is virtually a one-woman show, with Flanagan portraying seven different characters from Joyce's life and works. The humor and sensuality will thrill Joyce fans. Rated R for nudity and sexual situations. 89m. **DIR:** Michael Pearce. **CAST:** Fionnula Flanagan, Timothy E. O'Grady, Chris O'Neill. **1985**

JAMON, JAMON ★★1/2 In a provincial Spanish town, a well-to-do young man falls in love with the daughter of the town prostitute. His mother disapproves (of course) and hires a male model to woo the girl away from her son. This film was named best picture at the Venice Film Festival, but we thought it was little more than a silly sex comedy with a soap-opera-style plot. In Spanish with English subtitles. Not rated, the film has nudity, simulated sex, profanity, and violence. 95m. **DIR:** Bigas Luna. **CAST:** Anna Galiena, Stefania Sandrelli, Javier Bardem, Penelope Cruz. **1993**

JANE AND THE LOST CITY ★★★1/2 World War II British comic-strip heroine, Jane, comes to life in the form of lovely Kristen Hughes. She must help England's war effort by finding the diamonds of Africa's Lost City before the Nazis get them. A treasure trove of chuckles. Rated PG for profanity. 94m. **DIR:** Terry Marcel. **CAST:** Kristen Hughes, Maud Adams, Sam Jones. **1987 DVD**

JANE AUSTEN IN MANHATTAN ★★ The team responsible for *A Room with a View* comes up empty with this

satire about two off-Broadway producers battling for the rights to a little-known play written by Jane Austen when she was 12 years old. The infighting among the theatrical community is amusing, but the movie is predominantly cold and unmoving. Not rated. 108m. **DIR:** James Ivory. **CAST:** Anne Baxter, Robert Powell, Sean Young, Tim Choate. **1980**

JANE AUSTEN'S MAFIA ★★1/2 Director Jim Abrahams gives the *Airplane!* treatment to *The Godfather* (not to mention *Casino, Forrest Gump, The English Patient,* and *Showgirls*). There are a few good laughs, but not enough to overcome the duds and misfires. Alternate title: *Mafia!* Rated PG-13 for risqué humor. 84m. **DIR:** Jim Abrahams. **CAST:** Jay Mohr, Billy Burke, Christina Applegate, Pamela Gidley, Olympia Dukakis, Lloyd Bridges, Tony Lo Bianco. **1998**

JANE EYRE (1934) ★★ A willing second-tier cast and the passage of time make something of a curiosity of this classic story of a young orphan girl who grows up to become a governess. Tolerable. B&W; 70m. **DIR:** Christy Cabanne. **CAST:** Colin Clive, Virginia Bruce. **1934**

JANE EYRE (1944) ★★★★ Devotee's of Charlotte Brontë's romantic novel about a young woman leaving an orphans' home and being placed as a governess may be disappointed. But for others, the movie really starts with the appearance of Orson Welles and his interpretation of the moody and mysterious Edward Rochester. B&W; 96m. **DIR:** Robert Stevenson. **CAST:** Orson Welles, Joan Fontaine, Margaret O'Brien, Peggy Ann Garner, John Sutton, Sara Allgood, Henry Daniell, Agnes Moorehead, Elizabeth Taylor. **1944**

JANE EYRE (1983) ★★★★ This marvelous BBC production honors Charlotte Brontë's classic tale of courage and romance. A thrilling and thorough adaptation. Zelah Clarke plays the orphaned, mistreated, and unloved Jane who later falls for the darkly mysterious Mr. Rochester (Timothy Dalton). 239m. **DIR:** Julian Amyes. **CAST:** Timothy Dalton, Zelah Clarke. **1983**

JANE EYRE (1996) ★★★★ The only drawback in this adaptation of Charlotte Brontë's classic novel of unlikely romance is its brevity. Anna Paquin is properly spirited as the young orphan abandoned in a sepulchral girls' school by distant relatives; she matures into the equally vigorous Charlotte Gainsbourg, who accepts a position as governess for the ward of brooding Edward Rochester (William Hurt). Amid secrets involving an insolent maid and long-unglimpsed rooms, Jane unwisely falls in love with Rochester. Although faithfully capturing the massive book's middle section, this film concludes with dissatisfying abruptness. Rated PG. 112m. **DIR:** Franco Zeffirelli. **CAST:** William Hurt, Charlotte Gainsbourg, Joan Plowright, Anna Paquin, Geraldine Chaplin, Billie Whitelaw, Maria Schneider, Fiona Shaw, Elle Macpherson, John Wood. **1996**

JANIS ★★★ The most comprehensive documentary study of flower child Janis Joplin, this is filled with poignant memories and electrifying performances. Rated R for language. 96m. **DIR:** Howard Alk, Seaton Findlay. **1974**

JANUARY MAN, THE ★★ Whew! We've seen some weird movies in our time, but this one deserves a special place in some museum. John Patrick Shanley (*Moonstruck*) wrote this goofy mystery about a former police detective (Kevin Kline) who is drafted back into service when a serial killer begins to terrorize New York City. Rated R for profanity and violence. 110m. **DIR:** Pat O'Connor. **CAST:** Kevin Kline, Susan Sarandon, Mary Elizabeth Mastrantonio, Harvey Keitel, Danny Aiello, Alan Rickman, Rod Steiger. **1989 DVD**

JASON AND THE ARGONAUTS (1963) ★★★★ The captivating special effects by master Ray Harryhausen are the actual stars of this movie. This is the telling of the famous myth of Jason (Todd Armstrong), his crew of derring-doers, and their search for the Golden Fleece. 104m. **DIR:** Don Chaffey. **CAST:** Todd Armstrong, Gary Raymond, Honor Blackman. **1963 DVD**

JASON AND THE ARGONAUTS (2000) ★★ Despite lavish costuming and special effects, this big-budget, TV miniseries disappoints viewers. Acting ranges from emotionless line reading to corny melodrama, while battles with assorted creatures will only dazzle preteens. Stick with Ray Harryhausen's 1963 version. Not rated; contains violence. 180m. **DIR:** Nick Willing. **CAST:** Jason London, Dennis Hopper, Natasha Henstridge. **2000 DVD**

JASON GOES TO HELL: THE FINAL FRIDAY ★★★ Fans of the *Friday the 13th* films will enjoy this ninth and final (?) trip to the infamous Crystal Lake. We wouldn't reveal anything by saying Jason is killed in this movie. He's been killed so often it is hard to keep track. But some loose ends are made tighter, and an intriguing explanation for Jason's evil is offered. Watch to the very end. Rated R for violence, profanity, and plenty of gore. 88m. **DIR:** Adam Marcus. **CAST:** John D. LeMay, Kari Keegan, Kane Hodder, Steven Williams, Steven Culp, Erin Gray, Allison Smith, Kipp Marcus. **1993**

JASON'S LYRIC ★★1/2 Jason is a store clerk who dates a waitress while attending to the emotional needs of his widowed mother and the welfare of his ex-con, gang-linked brother. This hard-edged African-American romance is punctuated with flashbacks to a fatal domestic altercation, resulting in a disturbing vision of life on the edge of a Texas ghetto. The acting and script that propel the film's courtship are weak. Rated R for violence, nudity, language, and simulated sex. 119m. **DIR:** Doug McHenry. **CAST:** Allen Payne, Bokeem Woodbine, Jada Pinkett, Forest Whitaker, Suzzanne Douglas. **1994 DVD**

JAWBREAKER ★★★ When a birthday prank proves deadly for high-school power brokers, their ruthless leader devises the perfect cover-up. The plot thickens a bit when an awkward nerd discovers the murder. Dark comedy seeks redemption with the perfect comeuppance. Rated R for violence, language, sexual innuendo, and sexual situations. 87m. **DIR:** Darren Stein. **CAST:** Rebecca Gayheart, Rose McGowan, Julie Benz, Judy Greer. **1999 DVD**

JAWS ★★★★★ A young Steven Spielberg (27 at the time) directed this 1975 scare masterpiece based on the Peter Benchley novel. A large shark is terrorizing the tourists at the local beach. The eerie music by John Williams heightens the tension to underscore the shark's presence and scare the audience right out of their seats. Roy Scheider, Robert Shaw, and Richard Dreyfuss offer outstanding performances. Rated PG. 124m. **DIR:** Steven Spielberg. **CAST:** Roy Scheider, Robert Shaw, Richard Dreyfuss, Lorraine Gary, Murray Hamilton. **1975 DVD**

JAWS 3 ★★ Among those marked for lunch in this soggy, unexciting sequel are Lou Gossett Jr., Dennis Quaid, and Bess Armstrong. They look bored. You'll be bored. Rated PG. 97m. **DIR:** Joe Alves. **CAST:** Louis Gossett Jr., Dennis Quaid, Bess Armstrong, Simon MacCorkindale. **1983**

JAWS OF DEATH, THE ★★ Low-rent *Jaws* clone features Jaeckel as a shark breeder who rents his finny friends out to Florida aquariums. But when he finds out that the sharks are being exploited, he seeks revenge. Better than *Jaws: The Revenge*, but not by much. 93m. **DIR:** William Grefe. **CAST:** Richard Jaeckel, Jennifer Bishop, Harold Sakata. **1976**

JAWS: THE REVENGE 🦃 This third sequel is lowest-common-denominator filmmaking, a by-the-numbers effort. Rated PG-13. 89m. **DIR:** Joseph Sargent. **CAST:** Lorraine Gary, Lance Guest, Michael Caine, Mario Van Peebles, Karen Young. **1987 DVD**

JAWS 2 ★★★ Even though it's a sequel, *Jaws 2* delivers. Police chief Martin Brody (Roy Scheider) believes there's a shark in the waters off Amity again, but his wife and employers think he's crazy. Rated PG. 120m. **DIR:** Jeannot Szwarc. **CAST:** Roy Scheider, Lorraine Gary, Murray Hamilton, Jeffrey Kramer. **1978 DVD**

•**JAY AND SILENT BOB STRIKE BACK** ★★ Foul language and crude sex gags are the heart and soul of this raunchy road trip. Drug-dazed buddies Jay and Silent Bob learn that a movie is being made about their comic-book alter egos, Bluntman and Chronic, and that they and the upcoming production are being criticized on the Internet. They then head from New Jersey to Miramax's Southern California studio to shut down the movie. This sleazy, cheesy mockery of All Things Hollywood features numerous cameos including Ben Affleck, Matt Damon, and Gus Van Sant as themselves. Rated R for language, sexual references, and drug use. 99m. **DIR:** Kevin Smith. **CAST:** Jason Mewes, Kevin Smith. **2001 DVD**

JAYHAWKERS, THE ★★★ A routine Western story line enhanced by strong personalities in leading roles. Jeff Chandler and Fess Parker come to blows in a power struggle, and French actress Nicole Maurey is caught in the middle. 100m. **DIR:** Melvin Frank. **CAST:** Jeff Chandler, Fess Parker, Nicole Maurey, Henry Silva, Herbert Rudley. **1959**

JAYNE MANSFIELD STORY, THE ★★ Loni Anderson gives only an average performance as 1950s blonde sex bomb Mansfield. Made for television. 100m. **DIR:** Dick Lowry. **CAST:** Loni Anderson, Arnold Schwarzenegger, Kathleen Lloyd. **1980**

JAZZ SINGER, THE (1927) ★★★1/2 Generally considered the first talking film, this milestone in motion-picture history is really a silent film with a musical score and a few spoken lines. Al Jolson plays the son of an orthodox cantor who wants his son to follow in his footsteps. Jolson, though touched by his father's wishes, feels he must be a jazz singer. B&W; 89m. **DIR:** Alan Crosland. **CAST:** Al Jolson, May McAvoy, Warner Oland, William Demarest, Roscoe Karns, Myrna Loy. **1927**

JAZZ SINGER, THE (1953) ★★★1/2 Danny Thomas is a cantor's son who chooses a show-business career over a traditional life in a synagogue. Forget this is a remake of Al Jolson's historic first talkie and view it on its own musical merits. You will be surprised at Thomas's easy way with a song and wonder why he and Peggy Lee were never used to such good advantage again. 107m. **DIR:** Michael Curtiz. **CAST:** Danny Thomas, Peggy Lee, Mildred Dunnock, Eduard Franz, Tom Tully, Allyn Joslyn. **1953**

JAZZ SINGER, THE (1980) 🦃 Mushy mishmash that only Diamond's most devoted fans will love. Rated PG. 115m. **DIR:** Richard Fleischer. **CAST:** Neil Diamond, Laurence Olivier, Lucie Arnaz. **1980 DVD**

JAZZMAN ★★★1/2 Good-humored, accessible story about a classically trained Soviet musician who tries to start a jazz combo in the 1930s. In Russian with English subtitles. Not rated. 95m. **DIR:** Karen Chakhnazarov. **CAST:** Igor Skoliar, Alexandre Pankratov-Tchiorny. **1983**

J.D.'S REVENGE ★★★1/2 A gangster, murdered in 1940s New Orleans, returns from the dead thirty-five years later, possessing the body of a law student in his quest for revenge. Surprisingly well-crafted low-budget thriller. Rated R for strong violence and profanity. 95m. **DIR:** Arthur Marks. **CAST:** Glynn Turman, Joan Pringle, Louis Gossett Jr. **1976 DVD**

JE VOUS AIME (I LOVE YOU ALL) ★★ Some films are so complicated and convoluted you need a viewer's guide while watching them. So it is with this flashback-ridden French import. About a 35 year old woman, Alice (Catherine Deneuve), who finds it impossible to keep a love relationship alive, it hops, skips, and jumps back and forth through her life. No MPAA rating; the film has sexual situations and nudity. 105m. **DIR:** Claude Berri. **CAST:** Catherine Deneuve, Jean-Louis Trintignant, Serge Gainsbourg, Gérard Depardieu. **1981**

JEAN DE FLORETTE ★★★★★ This is a sort of French *Days of Heaven*, an epic set close to the land, specifically the hilly farm country of Provence. Land is the central issue around which the action swirls. Yves Montand is spellbinding as an ambitious, immoral farmer who dupes his city-bred neighbor Jean de Florette (played by the equally impressive Gérard Depardieu). The rest of the story is told in *Manon of the Spring*. In French with English subtitles. Rated PG. 122m. **DIR:** Claude Berri. **CAST:** Yves Montand, Gérard Depardieu, Daniel Auteuil. **1987 DVD**

•**JEEPERS CREEPERS** ★★1/2 Siblings Darius and Trish take the long, rural way home from college during spring break and are terrorized by a madman driving a fortified truck (even the windows are covered with steel plates). All hell breaks loose when the two co-eds see the driver dump sheet-wrapped bodies down a large drain pipe. The first half of this sadistic, preposterous movie is well crafted and scary. The latter half is pure creature-feature rubbish that introduces a human-organ-eating monster. Rated R for language, violence, and gore. 87m. **DIR:** Victor Salva. **CAST:** Justin Long, Gina Phillips, Patricia Belcher, Jonathan Breck, Brandon Smith, Eileen Brennan. **2001 DVD**

JEEVES AND WOOSTER (TV SERIES) ★★★★ P. G. Wodehouse fans will love these faithful renditions of tales about bumbling Bertie Wooster and his all-knowing retainer, Jeeves, who always manages to pull his master's bacon out of the most improbable fires. Aside from Wodehouse's piquant verbal byplay, there's nothing more delightful than watching Jeeves puncture the

balloons of his aristocratic, stuffed-shirt employer . . . who never even perceives he's been humbled. 52m. **DIR:** Robert Young. **CAST:** Stephen Fry, Hugh Laurie. **1990**

JEFFERSON IN PARIS ★★1/2 Sumptuous but plodding account of Thomas Jefferson's tenure as American minister to France (1784–1789). The film dawdles over decor and can't decide whether to focus on Jefferson's personal life or the social unrest in pre-Revolutionary France. Rated PG-13 for mature themes. 144m. **DIR:** James Ivory. **CAST:** Nick Nolte, Greta Scacchi, Thandie Newton, Gwyneth Paltrow, Simon Callow, James Earl Jones, Seth Gilliam, Michel Lonsdale, Lambert Wilson. **1995**

JEFFREY ★★★1/2 A gay man gives up sex for fear of AIDS, then meets his HIV-positive Mr. Right. Paul Rudnick's brilliantly witty off-Broadway hit gets a faithful (though rather stage-bound) screening, with an excellent all-star cast and Rudnick's hilarious lines compensating for awkward direction and a preening performance by Steven Weber in the title role. Rated R for profanity and frank dialogue. 94m. **DIR:** Christopher Ashley. **CAST:** Steven Weber, Patrick Stewart, Michael T. Weiss, Bryan Batt, Sigourney Weaver, Olympia Dukakis, Kathy Najimy, Nathan Lane. **1995**

JEKYLL & HYDE ★★★ Michael Caine dons two faces in this remake. Familiar tale gets few new plot twists in this made-for-television thriller. Rated R for horror, violence. 95m. **DIR:** David Wickes. **CAST:** Michael Caine, Cheryl Ladd, Joss Ackland, Lionel Jeffries. **1990**

JEKYLL & HYDE—TOGETHER AGAIN ★★★ If you like offbeat, crude, and timely humor, you'll enjoy this 1980s-style version of Robert Louis Stevenson's horror classic. Though the film needs some editing, Mark Blankfield is a riot as the mad scientist. Rated R for heavy doses of vulgarity and sexual innuendo. 87m. **DIR:** Jerry Belson. **CAST:** Mark Blankfield, Bess Armstrong, Krista Erickson. **1982**

JENNIFER ★★ A carbon copy of *Carrie*—but with snakes. Jennifer is a sweet, innocent child on a poor-kid's scholarship at an uppity school for rich girls. She is tormented until she is harassed into a frenzy. What's the catch? Jennifer was raised by a cult of religious fanatics who believe that God has given her the power to command reptiles. Rated PG. 90m. **DIR:** Brice Mack. **CAST:** Lisa Pelikan, Bert Convy, Nina Foch, John Gavin, Wesley Eure. **1978**

JENNIFER 8 ★★★1/2 A solid, inventive ending and crisp dialogue help this sometimes contrived thriller, in which burned-out L.A. cop Andy Garcia joins former partner Lance Henriksen on a small-town police force only to find himself on the trail of a serial killer. Rated R for violence, profanity, and nudity. 127m. **DIR:** Bruce Robinson. **CAST:** Andy Garcia, Uma Thurman, John Malkovich, Lance Henriksen, Kathy Baker, Graham Beckel, Kevin Conway, Perry Lang, Lenny von Dohlen. **1992 DVD**

JENNY LAMOUR ★★★★ Without each other's knowledge, a venal cabaret singer and her doting husband try to cover up what they believe to be their involvement in a murder. But a dogged policeman (a wonderfully sardonic performance by Louis Jouvet) is determined to discover the truth. Witty, atmospheric, and professional. Dubbed. B&W; 105m. **DIR:** Henri-Georges Clouzot. **CAST:** Louis Jouvet, Suzy Delair, Bernard Blier. **1947**

JENNY'S WAR ★★1/2 When her son, an RAF pilot, is shot down over Germany during World War II, Jenny Baines (Dyan Cannon) disguises herself as a man and heads to Germany to find him. It may have been based on a real story, but this lengthy made-for-TV movie is utterly preposterous. Not rated; contains no objectionable material. 192m. **DIR:** Steven Gethers. **CAST:** Dyan Cannon, Elke Sommer, Robert Hardy, Christopher Cazenove, Hugh Grant. **1985**

JEREMIAH JOHNSON ★★★★ Robert Redford plays Johnson, a simple man who has no taste for cities. We see him as he grows from his first feeble attempts at survival to a hunter who has quickened his senses with wild meat and vegetation—a man who is a part of the wildlife of the mountains. Gives a sense of humanness to a genre that had, up until its release, spent time reworking the same myths. Rated PG. 107m. **DIR:** Sydney Pollack. **CAST:** Robert Redford, Will Geer, Charles Tyner, Stefan Gierasch, Allyn Ann McLerie. **1972 DVD**

JERICHO ★★★1/2 Paul Robeson plays a black soldier who is convicted of manslaughter for the accidental murder of his sergeant. He takes advantage of the kindness of officer Henry Wilcoxon to escape across the African desert and begin a new life. Absorbing study of revenge and human dignity. B&W; 77m. **DIR:** Thornton Freeland. **CAST:** Paul Robeson, Henry Wilcoxon, Wallace Ford. **1937**

JERICHO FEVER ★★★ In this made-for-cable original, two doctors must battle an unknown disease that was accidentally brought into the United States by terrorists. Now the terrorists must be captured to obtain the cure. A solid plot and good acting make this enjoyable. Not rated; contains violence. 95m. **DIR:** Sandor Stern. **CAST:** Stephanie Zimbalist, Perry King, Branscombe Richmond, Alan Scarfe, Ari Barak, Elyssa Davalos, Kario Salem. **1993**

JERICHO MILE, THE ★★★★ This tough, inspiring TV movie tells the story of a man, serving a life sentence at Folsom Prison, who dedicates himself to becoming an Olympic-caliber runner. Director Michael Mann makes sure the film is riveting and realistic at all times. 100m. **DIR:** Michael Mann. **CAST:** Peter Strauss, Roger E. Mosley, Brian Dennehy, Billy Green Bush, Ed Lauter, Beverly Todd. **1979**

JERK, THE ★★★★ Steve Martin made a very funny starring debut in this wacky comedy. Nonfans probably won't like it, but for those who think he's hilarious, the laughs just keep on coming. Rated R. 94m. **DIR:** Carl Reiner. **CAST:** Steve Martin, Bernadette Peters, Bill Macy, Jackie Mason. **1979 DVD**

JERRY AND TOM ★★★★ Adapted from a play, this well-written film follows a decade in the lives of two car salesmen who double as paid killers. But don't be fooled into thinking this is another Tarantino imitation: the violence is not sensationalized, and there are choice parts for a bevy of first-rate actors. Rated R for profanity and violence. 92m. **DIR:** Saul Rubinek. **CAST:** Joe Mantegna, Sam Rockwell, William H. Macy, Maury Chaykin, Ted Danson, Charles Durning, Peter Riegert, Sarah Polley. **1998 DVD**

JERRY MAGUIRE ★★★★1/2 This frothy comedy-drama mixes perceptive social commentary, witty dia-

logue, and a touching love affair. Tom Cruise is an ultra-slick sports agent who one night realizes that quality should be more important than quantity; Renee Zellweger is an agency secretary and single mother who comes along when he abandons the fast-lane lifestyle for his own firm. He has but one client: an Arizona Cardinals wide receiver—Cuba Gooding Jr., delivering an Academy Award–winning performance—with as much attitude as natural talent. At least three major storylines occupy this picture, but Cameron Crowe keeps a firm handle on each. Rated R for profanity, nudity, and strong sexual content. 138m. **DIR:** Cameron Crowe. **CAST:** Tom Cruise, Cuba Gooding Jr., Renee Zellweger, Kelly Preston, Jerry O'Connell, Jonathan Lipnicki. **1996 DVD**

JERSEY GIRL ★★★1/2 Winning fairy tale about Jersey girl Jami Gertz looking for Mr. Right in Manhattan. She literally runs into him when she sideswipes Dylan McDermott's Mercedes. He's everything she's looking for, but she reminds him of everything he's worked so hard to leave behind. But you know what they say about opposites. The fun is watching Gertz pursue her man against all odds. Funny, warm, and sweet. Rated PG-13 for language and adult situations. 95m. **DIR:** David Burton Morris. **CAST:** Jami Gertz, Dylan McDermott, Joseph Bologna, Star Jasper, Molly Price, Aida Turturro. **1993**

JERUSALEM ★★★★ In turn-of-the-century Sweden, a rural village is torn apart by the preachings of a charismatic faith healer, who leads his followers to resettle in the Holy Land. Director Bille August (adapting a novel by Nobel Prize winner Selma Lagerlof) tells his story of alienation, suffering, and redemption through the lives of two young lovers. The film is slow-moving and overlong, but psychologically complex and superbly acted. In Swedish with English subtitles. Rated PG-13 for brief nudity and mature themes. 166m. **DIR:** Bille August. **CAST:** Maria Bonnevie, Ulf Friberg, Pernilla August, Lena Endre, Sven-Bertil Taube, Max von Sydow, Olympia Dukakis. **1996**

JESSE ★★ By-the-numbers TV movie based on a true story about a small-town nurse who provides medical care in place of the often-absent regional doctor. The contrived dramatic conflict renders much of the story unbelievable. 100m. **DIR:** Glenn Jordan. **CAST:** Lee Remick, Scott Wilson, Richard Marcus, Albert Salmi. **1988**

JESSE JAMES ★★★1/2 Tyrone Power is Jesse, and Henry Fonda is Frank in this legend-gilding account of the life and misdeeds of Missouri's most famous outlaw. Bending history, the film paints Jesse as a peaceful man driven to a life of crime by heartless big business in the form of a railroad, and a loving husband and father murdered for profit by a coward. 105m. **DIR:** Henry King. **CAST:** Tyrone Power, Henry Fonda, Nancy Kelly, Randolph Scott, Henry Hull, Jane Darwell, Brian Donlevy, Donald Meek, John Carradine, Slim Summerville, J. Edward Bromberg. **1939**

JESSE JAMES AT BAY ★★1/2 Roy Rogers is a fictionalized Jesse James who rides not against the railroads, but against one evil bunch misrepresenting the railroad and stealing the land of poor, honest farmers. A top contender for *the* most farfetched, fallacious frontier foolishness ever filmed. B&W; 56m. **DIR:** Joseph Kane. **CAST:** Roy Rogers, George "Gabby" Hayes, Sally Payne. **1941**

JESSE JAMES MEETS FRANKENSTEIN'S DAUGHTER 🦃 The feeble plot pits hero Jesse James against the evil daughter of the infamous doctor of the title. 88m. **DIR:** William Beaudine. **CAST:** John Lupton, Estelita, Cal Bolder, Jim Davis. **1966**

JESSE OWENS STORY, THE ★★★ This made-for-TV movie of the Olympic hero provides a provocative insight into the many behind-the-scenes events that plague people who are thrust into public admiration. Dorian Harewood is perfect in his performance of the not-always-admirable hero, a victim of his own inabilities and the uncontrollable events surrounding him. This film also holds up a mirror to our society's many embarrassing racial attitudes. 180m. **DIR:** Richard Irving. **CAST:** Dorian Harewood, Debbi Morgan, George Kennedy, Georg Stanford Brown, Tom Bosley, LeVar Burton. **1984**

JESUS ★★ More a Bible study than entertainment; this film is narrated by Alexander Scourby and the words are taken from the Good News Bible, the Book of Luke. Filmed in the Holy Land. 117m. **DIR:** Peter Sykes, John Kirsh. **CAST:** Brian Deacon, Rivka Noiman. **1979 DVD**

JESUS CHRIST, SUPERSTAR ★★★1/2 Believe it or not, this could be the ancestor of such rock videos as Michael Jackson's "Thriller." The movie illustrates segments of Jesus Christ's later life by staging sets and drama to go along with the soundtrack. This will not offer any religious experiences in the traditional sense, but is interesting nonetheless. Rated G. 103m. **DIR:** Norman Jewison. **CAST:** Ted Neeley, Carl Anderson, Yvonne Elliman. **1973 DVD**

JESUS OF MONTREAL ★★★★1/2 Denys Arcand, the French-Canadian writer-director, finds original things to say with a not totally original idea—that the actor playing Jesus in a modern-day passion play may, in fact, *be* Jesus. Lothaire Bluteau is superb in the title role. In French with English subtitles. Rated R for profanity. 119m. **DIR:** Denys Arcand. **CAST:** Lothaire Bluteau, Denys Arcand. **1990**

JESUS OF NAZARETH ★★★★ This vivid TV movie of the life of Jesus is beautifully directed by the poetic genius Franco Zefferelli. An outstanding cast gives warm and sensitive performances in what is the finest film to date of the familiar Bible story. It fills *three* cassettes but well worth the time. 371m. **DIR:** Franco Zeffirelli. **CAST:** Robert Powell, Anne Bancroft, James Mason, Rod Steiger, Olivia Hussey. **1976 DVD**

JESUS' SON ★★★★ Denis Johnson's short story collection about bad behavior, addiction, and redemption is faithfully adapted into this stream of tattered, dreamy vignettes. A wandering doper narrates his own journey through mental and moral chaos to rediscovered compassion. He shares his heart and heroin with his girlfriend in 1971 Iowa and transcendental experiences with an assortment of weird, wacky characters in a nonlinear gust of deadpan humor and lyrical imagery. Rated R for language, sexuality, drug use, and violence. 110m. **DIR:** Alison Maclean. **CAST:** Billy Crudup, Samantha Morton, Jack Black, Dennis Hopper, Denis Leary, Will Patton, Holly Hunter. **2000 DVD**

JET ATTACK 🦃 John Agar tries to rescue an American scientist captured by the North Koreans. B&W; 68m.

DIR: Edward L. Cahn. **CAST:** John Agar, Audrey Totter, Gregory Walcott. **1958**

JET BENNY SHOW, THE ★★1/2 Peculiar spoof stars Jack Benny impersonator Steve Norman as a Buck Rogers–type hero accompanied on his adventures in outer space by a Rochester-like robot. The concept is as elusive as the humor, though fans of the old Jack Benny TV show may want to check it out. Not rated. 77m. **DIR:** Roger D. Evans. **CAST:** Steve Norman, Kevin Dees. **1975**

JET LI'S THE ENFORCER ★★1/2 The formula in this 1995 Hong Kong import still works. Jet Li plays an undercover Beijing cop whose public and private lives are about to clash on his latest assignment. The pedestrian plot deals with traditional themes like the loss of a loved one and loyalty, but it is Li who gives the film the punch it needs. Reedited from *My Father Is a Hero*. Rated R for violence. 100m. **DIR:** Corey Yuen. **CAST:** Jet Li, Anita Mui, Tse Miu. **1995 DVD**

JETSONS: THE MOVIE ★★ Those futuristic Flintstones—George, Jane, Judy, and Elroy Jetson—get the big-screen treatment with a movie that suffers from too many commercial tie-ins and songs by Tiffany (who voices Judy Jetson). Still there are some funny moments in the story, which has Mr. Spacely (a last bow by the late Mel Blanc) transferring George and family to an outpost in outer space. Rated G. 87m. **DIR:** William Hanna, Joseph Barbera. **1990**

JEWEL IN THE CROWN, THE ★★★★★ Based on Paul Scott's *Raj Quartet*, this Emmy Award–winning series first aired on British television in fourteen episodes. It is a wonderful epic that depicts Britain's last years of power in India (1942–1947). The story revolves around the love of an Indian man for a white woman, and the repercussions of their forbidden romance. The love-hate relationship of the English and the Indians is well depicted. 700m. **DIR:** Christopher Morahan, Jim O'Brien. **CAST:** Tim Pigott-Smith, Geraldine James, Peggy Ashcroft, Charles Dance, Susan Wooldridge, Art Malik, Judy Parfitt. **1984 DVD**

JEWEL OF THE NILE, THE ★★★1/2 This generally enjoyable sequel to *Romancing the Stone* details the further adventures of novelist Joan Wilder (Kathleen Turner) and soldier of fortune Jack Colton (Michael Douglas) in the deserts of North Africa. Danny DeVito supplies the laughs. Rated PG. 106m. **DIR:** Lewis Teague. **CAST:** Michael Douglas, Kathleen Turner, Danny DeVito, Avner Eisenberg. **1985 DVD**

JEZEBEL ★★★★ Bette Davis gives one of her finest performances as a spoiled southern belle in this release. Directed by William Wyler, it brought Davis her second best-actress Oscar—and a well-deserved one at that. She's superb as the self-centered "Jezebel" who takes too long in deciding between a banker (Henry Fonda) and a dandy (George Brent) and loses all. B&W; 103m. **DIR:** William Wyler. **CAST:** Bette Davis, Henry Fonda, George Brent, Spring Byington. **1938 DVD**

JEZEBEL'S KISS ★★ Steamy, sleazy thriller about a beautiful young woman who seeks revenge for the death of her grandfather. Inept. Rated R for nudity, violence, and profanity. 95m. **DIR:** Harvey Keith. **CAST:** Katherine Barrese, Malcolm McDowell, Everett McGill, Meredith Baxter-Birney, Meg Foster, Bert Remsen. **1990**

JFK ★★★★ Director Oliver Stone's fascinating examination of the assassination of President John F. Kennedy attempts to disprove the contention that Lee Harvey Oswald was the lone killer. Kevin Costner stars as Jim Garrison, the New Orleans district attorney who attempted to prosecute a local businessman for conspiracy in the Nov. 22, 1963, murder. Stone, a master of overstatement, is on his best behavior, but there are moments of unnecessary sensationalism. Rated R for violence, profanity, and suggested sex. 190m. **DIR:** Oliver Stone. **CAST:** Kevin Costner, Sissy Spacek, Joe Pesci, Tommy Lee Jones, Gary Oldman, Jay O. Sanders, Michael Rooker, Laurie Metcalf, Gary Grubbs, John Candy, Jack Lemmon, Walter Matthau, Edward Asner, Donald Sutherland, Kevin Bacon, Brian Doyle-Murray, Sally Kirkland. **1991 DVD**

JFK: RECKLESS YOUTH ★★★ Patrick Dempsey delivers an exceptional performance as the young Kennedy, long before the White House. The conflicts that permeated his life, from his decision to disobey his father's wishes to the women and illness that plagued his life, come to the forefront in this made-for-TV miniseries. The emotional impact and production values are better-than-average. Not rated. 182m. **DIR:** Harry Winer. **CAST:** Patrick Dempsey, Terry Kinney, Loren Dean, Diana Scarwid, Andrew Lowery. **1993**

JIGSAW MAN, THE ★★★★ Michael Caine plays a British secret agent who has defected, under orders, to Russia. Before leaving, he discovered a list of Soviet spies operating in England and hid it. After forty years, he returns to England in order to get the list with spies from both countries hot on his trail. This is a wonderfully entertaining puzzle of a movie. Rated PG for violence and profanity. 90m. **DIR:** Freddie Francis. **CAST:** Michael Caine, Laurence Olivier, Susan George, Robert Powell, Charles Gray. **1984**

JIGSAW MURDERS, THE 🦃 A psycho killer leaves body parts around L.A. 98m. **DIR:** Jag Mundhra. **CAST:** Chad Everett, Yaphet Kotto, Michelle Johnson, Michael Sabatino. **1988**

JILL THE RIPPER ★★1/2 An alcoholic cop is on the trail of a serial killer. Not very believable but, as usual, it's fun to watch Dolph Lundgren in action. Rated R for violence, profanity, nudity, and gore. 94m. **DIR:** Anthony Hickox. **CAST:** Dolph Lundgren, Danielle Brett. **1999 DVD**

JIM THORPE—ALL AMERICAN ★★★ This well-intentioned bio-pic stretches much of the truth in the sad story of American Indian athlete Jim Thorpe, Olympic medalist and professional baseball, football, and track star. Director Michael Curtiz places most of the sympathy with Burt Lancaster, sidestepping Thorpe's personal demons. Burt is in fine physical shape as he recreates some of Thorpe's feats for the camera. B&W; 107m. **DIR:** Michael Curtiz. **CAST:** Burt Lancaster, Charles Bickford, Steve Cochran, Phyllis Thaxter, Dick Wesson. **1951**

JIMI HENDRIX ★★★★ Jimi Hendrix, the undisputed master of psychedelia, is captured brilliantly through concert footage and candid film clips in this excellent all-around 1973 rockumentary. The film explores Hendrix's career through interviews and rare concert footage of his performances from London's Marquee Club in 1967, and the Monterey Pop, Woodstock, and

Isle of Wight festivals. Director Gary Weis was responsible for some great film shorts on *Saturday Night Live*. 103m. **DIR:** Gary Weis. **CAST:** Jimi Hendrix, Billy Cox, Mitch Mitchell, Eric Clapton, Pete Townshend, Little Richard, Dick Cavett. **1973 DVD**

JIMMY CLIFF—BONGO MAN ★★1/2 This little-known documentary is a tribute to reggae singer-songwriter Jimmy Cliff. The film attempts, somewhat confusingly, to portray him as a man of the people, a champion of human rights during a period of racial and political turbulence in Jamaica. Cliff's other movie vehicle, *The Harder They Come*, a crudely shot musical-drama, remains stronger than *Bongo Man*. 89m. **DIR:** Stefan Paul. **CAST:** Jimmy Cliff. **1985**

JIMMY HOLLYWOOD ★★ A struggling, manic actor, who goes ballistic when his car is burglarized, becomes America's first video vigilante by taping criminals at work and leaving the evidence and tied-up crooks for the cops. The self-obsessed thespian tries to parlay his new Bronson-with-a-camcorder fame into a career of sorts. This meandering, oddball comedy about the down side of Tinsel Town stardom never gels. Rated R for language and violence. 110m. **DIR:** Barry Levinson. **CAST:** Joe Pesci, Christian Slater, Victoria Abril. **1994**

•JIMMY NEUTRON, BOY GENIUS ★★★ Feature-length animated film by Nickelodeon opens the door to toys, games, and a new TV series. That said, the wee ones will be amused by Jimmy's scientific gadgets and remarkable wits. All come into play after the town's adults are abducted by aliens. Jimmy leads an army of youngsters on a rescue mission to the enemies' planet. Jimmy's robotic dog provides a few chuckles. Among the cast of voice talents are Martin Short, Patrick Stewart, Andrea Martin, and David Lander. Rated G. 82m. **DIR:** John A. Davis. **2001 DVD**

JIMMY THE KID ★★ Paul LeMat leads a band of bungling criminals in an attempt to kidnap the precocious son (Gary Coleman) of extremely wealthy singers (Cleavon Little and Fay Hauser). To everyone's surprise, Jimmy doesn't mind being kidnapped. Yawn. Rated PG. 85m. **DIR:** Gary Nelson. **CAST:** Paul LeMat, Gary Coleman, Cleavon Little, Fay Hauser, Dee Wallace. **1983**

JINGLE ALL THE WAY ★★★ Arnold Schwarzenegger displays his comedic skills as a dad determined to fulfill his son's Christmas wish. Sinbad, as a mailman with plenty of time on his hands, becomes his archenemy as the two scour the city for the last Turbo Man toy available. Meanwhile, Schwarzenegger's wife is pursued by their sleazy neighbor. This film makes a fine satire of Christmas's commercialization. Rated PG for comic-book violence. 91m. **DIR:** Brian Levant. **CAST:** Arnold Schwarzenegger, Sinbad, Rita Wilson, Phil Hartman, Robert Conrad, James Belushi. **1996 DVD**

JINXED ★★1/2 Bette Midler is in peak form as a would-be cabaret singer who enlists the aid of a blackjack dealer (Ken Wahl) in a plot to murder her gambler boyfriend (Rip Torn) in this often funny black comedy. If it weren't for Midler, you'd notice how silly and unbelievable it all is. Rated R for profanity and sexual situations. 103m. **DIR:** Don Siegel. **CAST:** Bette Midler, Ken Wahl, Rip Torn, Benson Fong. **1982**

JIT ★★★★ A young country boy tries to win the love of a sophisticated city girl in this charming and sometimes surprising African comedy. He tries to overcome his biggest hurdle, the exorbitant bride price demanded by her father, with the help of a "Jukwa," his guiding spirit who would rather he return to his village. The first major film produced in Zimbabwe. Not rated; contains no objectionable material. 98m. **DIR:** Michael Raeburn. **CAST:** Dominic Makuvachurna, Sibongile Nene. **1990**

JIVE JUNCTION ★★1/2 Weird World War II musical about high school music students who give up playing the classics and turn to jazz in order to help the war effort. How? By opening up a canteen where soliders can dance their troubles away. Written by future novelist Irving Wallace. B&W; 62m. **DIR:** Edgar G. Ulmer. **CAST:** Dickie Moore, Tina Thayer. **1943**

JO JO DANCER, YOUR LIFE IS CALLING ★★★★1/2 In this show-biz biography, Richard Pryor plays Jo Jo Dancer, a well-known entertainer at the peak of his popularity and the depths of self-understanding and love. A drug-related accident puts Jo Jo in the hospital and forces him to reexamine his life. Rated R for profanity, nudity, suggested sex, drug use, and violence. 100m. **DIR:** Richard Pryor. **CAST:** Richard Pryor, Debbie Allen, Art Evans, Fay Hauser, Barbara Williams, Carmen McRae, Paula Kelly, Diahnne Abbott, Scoey Mitchell, Billy Eckstine, Wings Hauser, Michael Ironside. **1986 DVD**

JOAN OF ARC (1948) ★★★ Ingrid Bergman is touching and devout in this by-the-book rendering of Maxwell Anderson's noted play, but too much talk and too little action strain patience and buttocks. 100m. **DIR:** Victor Fleming. **CAST:** Ingrid Bergman, José Ferrer, Francis L. Sullivan, J. Carrol Naish, Ward Bond. **1948**

•JOAN OF ARC (1999) ★★★ Fine miniseries take on the legend proves to be more interesting than the bigger budgeted and touted *The Messenger: The Story of Joan of Arc*. Through its strong supporting cast and its focus on the political and spiritual aspects of the legend, the film overcomes the weak performance by Leelee Sobieski in the lead. Charlotte Church lends her voice to the haunting vocals. Rated PG for violence. 139m. **DIR:** Christian Duguay. **CAST:** Leelee Sobieski, Chad Willett, Neil Patrick Harris, Olympia Dukakis, Peter O'Toole, Shirley MacLaine, Jacqueline Bisset, Powers Boothe, Maximilian Schell, Peter Strauss, Robert Loggia. **1999 DVD**

JOAN OF PARIS ★★ Allied fliers parachute into Nazi-held France and enlist a local barmaid to help them find their way to British Intelligence. It all made sense back in 1942, and this melodrama is strong on love, duty, and sacrifice, and thick with snarling Nazis and long-winded patriots. B&W; 93m. **DIR:** Robert Stevenson. **CAST:** Michèle Morgan, Paul Henreid, Thomas Mitchell, Laird Cregar, May Robson, Alan Ladd. **1942**

JOCKS 🦃 A tennis coach must make his goofy team champions. Rated R for nudity and obscenities. 90m. **DIR:** Steve Carver. **CAST:** Scott Strader, Perry Lang, Mariska Hargitay, Richard Roundtree, Christopher Lee. **1986 DVD**

JOE ★★★ Peter Boyle stars in this violent film about a bigot who ends up associating much more closely with the people he hates. Falling short in the storytelling, *Joe* is nevertheless helped along by top-notch acting. Rated R. 107m. **DIR:** John G. Avildsen. **CAST:** Peter Boyle, Dennis Patrick, Susan Sarandon. **1970 DVD**

•JOE DIRT 🦃 Trailer-trash poster boy abandoned by his folks during a childhood trip to the Grand Canyon

becomes a celebrated folk hero while working as a janitor at a Los Angeles radio station in this alleged comedy. Rated PG-13 for language and crude sex-related humor. 93m. **DIR:** Dennie Gordon. **CAST:** David Spade, Brittany Daniel, Dennis Miller, Kid Rock. **2001 DVD**

JOE GOULD'S SECRET ★★★1/2 *New Yorker* writer Joseph Mitchell strikes up an odd friendship with an eccentric, exasperating street bohemian who claims to be working on a vast oral history of modern times. Based on two articles by the real Mitchell, "Professor Sea Gull" and "Joe Gould's Secret," the film is a loving eulogy to the friendlier Manhattan of the 1940s, with a bravura performance by Ian Holm and a more subdued but equally good one from Stanley Tucci. Rated R for profanity. 108m. **DIR:** Stanley Tucci. **CAST:** Ian Holm, Stanley Tucci, Patricia Clarkson, Hope Davis, Susan Sarandon, Steve Martin. **1999 DVD**

JOE KIDD ★★★1/2 While not exactly a thrill-a-minute movie, this Western has a number of memorable moments. Director John Sturges has been better, but Clint Eastwood and Robert Duvall are at the peak of their forms in this story of a gunman (Eastwood) hired by a cattle baron (Duvall) to track down some Mexican-Americans who are fighting back because they've been cheated out of their land. Rated PG. 88m. **DIR:** John Sturges. **CAST:** Clint Eastwood, Robert Duvall, John Saxon, Don Stroud. **1972 DVD**

JOE LOUIS STORY, THE ★★ Real-life boxer Coley Wallace brings some sense of authenticity to this all-too-familiar Hollywood sketch of an athlete's rise to fame. Newsreel footage elevates this otherwise routine low-budget bio-pic. B&W; 88m. **DIR:** Robert Gordon. **CAST:** Coley Wallace, Paul Stewart, Hilda Simms, James Edwards, John Marley. **1953 DVD**

•JOE SOMEBODY ★★ When corporate Milquetoast Tim Allen gets beaten up in front of his daughter, he plots revenge on the company bully who slapped him around. A clichéd, illogical, and disorganized script combines with clumsy pacing to sink a game and talented cast. Rated PG. 98m. **DIR:** John Pasquin. **CAST:** Tim Allen, Julie Bowen, Hayden Panettiere, James Belushi, Greg Germann, Kelly Lynch. **2001 DVD**

JOE TORRE: CURVEBALLS ALONG THE WAY ★★★ Lightweight reenactment of the events surrounding baseball manager Joe Torre's career-topping efforts to bring the New York Yankees to the World Series. Paul Sorvino displays aw-shucks charm and instinctive talent as Torre, a guy with baseball in the blood who nonetheless rates family above all else. And he gets a full plate, as one beloved brother dies mere months into this all-important season, and another (Robert Loggia) declines and winds up hospitalized. While not up to the quality or emotional punch of *Bang the Drum Slowly*, scripter Philip Rosenberg delivers a heartfelt little story. Rated PG for dramatic intensity. 85m. **DIR:** Sturla Gunnarsson. **CAST:** Paul Sorvino, Robert Loggia, Barbara Williams, Isaiah Washington, Kenneth Welsh. **1997**

JOE VERSUS THE VOLCANO ★★★1/2 You have to be in the right mood to enjoy this featherweight comedy from writer-director John Patrick Shanley. When a millionaire offers Tom Hanks an expense account and a leisurely trip to the South Seas, Hanks accepts—even though it means jumping into a volcano. Meg Ryan is superb in three hilarious supporting roles. Rated PG for brief profanity. 94m. **DIR:** John Patrick Shanley. **CAST:** Tom Hanks, Meg Ryan, Lloyd Bridges, Robert Stack, Abe Vigoda, Dan Hedaya, Ossie Davis. **1990 DVD**

JOE'S APARTMENT ★★ An Iowa farm boy (Jerry O'Connell) moves to New York and makes acquaintances of the millions of singing, dancing cockroaches inhabiting his apartment. The five-minute MTV short is blown up to feature length and loses all its meager charm. The roach musical numbers are actually rather entertaining; it's all the stuff with the humans that stinks. O'Connell seems never to have washed his face during shooting. Rated PG-13 for crude humor. 80m. **DIR:** John Payson. **CAST:** Jerry O'Connell, Megan Ward, Robert Vaughn. **1996 DVD**

JOEY ★★★ Delightful family tale about a young boy who finds a baby kangaroo and makes his way to Sydney to reunite the joey with his family. Unbeknown to the boy, the young kangaroo's family has been captured by poachers who plan on using them in an illegal kangaroo-boxing scheme. Rated PG. 97m. **DIR:** Ian Barry. **CAST:** Alex McKenna, Ed Begley Jr. **1997**

JOEY BREAKER ★★★ An obnoxious, smooth-talking agent on the fast track to money and power falls in love with a waitress who is striving to complete her education as a nurse. Quirky, offbeat film benefits from the performances of its talented cast members. Rated R for nudity and profanity. 92m. **DIR:** Steven Starr. **CAST:** Richard Edson, Cedella Marley, Erik King, Gina Gershon. **1992**

JOHN AND THE MISSUS ★★★ The beautiful coast of Newfoundland provides the backdrop for this otherwise depressing Canadian film. A town loses its source of income when the local mine is closed. Gordon Pinsent plays a stubborn, courageous man who refuses the meager resettlement money the government offers. Rated PG for mature themes. 98m. **DIR:** Gordon Pinsent. **CAST:** Gordon Pinsent, Jackie Burroughs, Timothy Webber. **1987**

JOHN & YOKO: A LOVE STORY ★★ Episodic account of the John Lennon–Yoko Ono relationship—from the famous "Christ" remark in 1966 to his assassination in 1980—is marred by unbelievable characters and a condensed mix of fact and fabrication. The technical adviser was Lennon's friend, Elliot Minz (played briefly by David Baxt). Not rated. 180m. **DIR:** Sandor Stern. **CAST:** Mark McGann, Kim Miyori, Peter Capaldi, Richard Morant. **1989**

JOHN CARPENTER PRESENTS: BODY BAGS ★★1/2 Although this *Tales from the Crypt* wannabe is laced with the appropriate gore, two of the three stories are strictly dullsville. The third, blessed with a grand performance by Stacy Keach as a fellow horrified by encroaching baldness, brings new meaning to a full-bodied head of hair. Rated R for profanity, nudity, simulated sex, and gobs o' gore. 95m. **DIR:** John Carpenter. **CAST:** Robert Carradine, Stacy Keach, David Warner, Sheena Easton, Deborah Harry, Mark Hamill, Twiggy. **1993 DVD**

JOHN CARPENTER'S ESCAPE FROM L.A. ★★1/2 Bigger doesn't exactly mean better, as proved by this fifteen-years-later sequel. Featuring essentially the same plot as Carpenter's lower-budgeted but superior *Escape from New York*, it once again puts laconic Snake

Plissken in a do-or-die situation involving the president and national security. Rated R for violence and profanity. 101m. **DIR:** John Carpenter. **CAST:** Kurt Russell, Stacy Keach, Steve Buscemi, Valeria Golino, Peter Fonda, Pam Grier, Cliff Robertson, Michelle Forbes, Georges Corraface, Bruce Campbell, A. J. Langer. **1996 DVD**

JOHN CARPENTER'S VAMPIRES ★★1/2 Although James Woods is brilliantly cast as a foul-mouthed, Vatican-backed vampire slayer who heads an enthusiastic team of mercenaries, the film turns sour when our "hero" abandons his common sense while seeking vengeance against a 600 year old vampire master. The storyline becomes ludicrously arbitrary is *not* scary. Rated R for gore, violence, profanity, and nudity. 107m. **DIR:** John Carpenter. **CAST:** James Woods, Daniel Baldwin, Sheryl Lee, Thomas Ian Griffith, Tim Guinee, Maximilian Schell. **1998 DVD**

JOHN HUSTON—THE MAN, THE MOVIES, THE MAVERICK ★★★★★ A wonderful, robust, and entertaining documentary biography of the great director, compiled from rare home movies, film clips, and interviews, narrated by Robert Mitchum (who speaks from a fantasy attic of engrossing Huston memorabilia). John Huston was an utterly fascinating eccentric and adventurer. This TV biography is a superb tribute. 129m. **DIR:** Frank Martin. **1989**

JOHN PAUL JONES ★★1/2 John Farrow's direction is as wooden as Robert Stack's performance in this lackluster attempt to chronicle the life of America's first naval hero. Lots of familiar faces in cameo appearances, e.g., Bette Davis as Catherine the Great. 127m. **DIR:** John Farrow. **CAST:** Robert Stack, Marisa Pavan, Charles Coburn, Macdonald Carey, Jean-Pierre Aumont, Peter Cushing, Bruce Cabot, David Farrar, Bette Davis. **1959**

•JOHN Q ★★★1/2 Although shamelessly contrived and marred by an almost laughably melodramatic third act, this slice of advocacy cinema still gets high marks for Denzel Washington's gripping performance as a distraught parent whose young son may be denied proper medical coverage because of a work-related insurance snafu. Given the late twentieth-century meltdown of the American health-care system, it's impossible to ignore many of the plot elements in the initially intelligent script; it's just a shame that it switches midstream to a riff on *Dog Day Afternoon*. Even so, this film has considerable food for thought, and Washington definitely sells it. Rated PG-13 for brief profanity, brief violence, and emergency room intensity. 118m. **DIR:** Nick Cassavetes. **CAST:** Denzel Washington, Robert Duvall, James Woods, Anne Heche, Eddie Griffin, Kimberly Elise, Shawn Hatosy, Ray Liotta. **2002 DVD**

JOHN WOO'S ONCE A THIEF ★★★ Action director John Woo helms an American remake of his own earlier hit with mixed results; while the players are engaging and the plot suitably fast-paced, the stunts are subdued in deference to this film's made-for-television origins. Ex-thieves turned undercover form an unlikely romantic triangle, while participating in a caper involving a former friend-turned-rival. Wholly preposterous but fun to watch. Rated PG for violence. 95m. **DIR:** John Woo. **CAST:** Sandrine Holt, Ivan Sergei, Nicholas Lea, Robert Ito, Michael Wong, Jennifer Dale. **1996**

JOHNNY & CLYDE ★★★ Johnny's a kid left in charge of the house one day, while Clyde is a cute but slobbering bloodhound who prompts all sorts of havoc. Undemanding children will have a lot of fun with this silly little tale. Suitable for all ages. 84m. **DIR:** William Bindley. **CAST:** Michael Rooker, Johnny White, Sam Malkin, David B. Nichols. **1995**

JOHNNY ANGEL ★★★ Above-average gangster film provides some nice moments. George Raft seeks the killer of his father while busting up the mob. Nothing special, but fun to watch. B&W; 79m. **DIR:** Edwin L. Marin. **CAST:** George Raft, Claire Trevor, Signe Hasso, Hoagy Carmichael. **1945**

JOHNNY APOLLO ★★★★ Tyrone Power's father is exposed as a white-collar criminal; bitter Tyrone turns to crime himself and winds up in the same cell block as Dad. Tough, engrossing crime melodrama is solid entertainment all the way. B&W; 93m. **DIR:** Henry Hathaway. **CAST:** Tyrone Power, Dorothy Lamour, Edward Arnold, Lloyd Nolan, Charley Grapewin, Lionel Atwill. **1940**

JOHNNY BE GOOD 🦃 Anthony Michael Hall is a high school football player who is heavily recruited by every major college in the United States. Rated R for language, partial nudity, and sexual situations. 86m. **DIR:** Bud Smith. **CAST:** Anthony Michael Hall, Robert Downey Jr., Paul Gleason, Uma Thurman, Steve James, Seymour Cassel, Michael Greene, Robert Downey Sr. **1988**

JOHNNY BELINDA ★★★★ Jane Wyman won an Oscar for her remarkable performance as a deaf-mute farm girl. Her multidimensional characterization lifts this movie over mere melodrama. The many disasters that befall its put-upon heroine, including rape and trying to raise the resulting offspring in the face of community pressure, would be scoffed at in a lesser actress. B&W; 103m. **DIR:** Jean Negulesco. **CAST:** Jane Wyman, Lew Ayres, Charles Bickford, Agnes Moorehead. **1948**

JOHNNY CARSON: HIS FAVORITE MOMENTS ★★★★★ Four-tape collection chronicles the best and sometimes the worst of the King of Late Night. Carefully selected highlights from almost thirty years of *The Tonight Show* capture the very essence of Carson and his trademark reactions as he weathers classic comedians, wrangles out-of-control animals, and introduces a stellar line-up of guests. The first three tapes are broken down by decade, while the last tape is a complete copy of the last episode. Not rated. 50m. **DIR:** Not credited. **CAST:** Johnny Carson, Ed McMahon. **1962–1992**

JOHNNY COME LATELY ★★★ A good showcase for James Cagney's feisty personality with a wholesome touch not often seen in today's movies. He plays a vagrant who happens onto a job on a small-town newspaper, and winds up playing cupid to the publisher's daughter and her boyfriend. B&W; 97m. **DIR:** William K. Howard. **CAST:** James Cagney, Grace George, Hattie McDaniel, Marjorie Lord, Marjorie Main. **1943**

JOHNNY DANGEROUSLY 🦃 In this fitfully funny spoof of 1930s gangster movies, Michael Keaton and Joe Piscopo play rival crime lords. Directed by Amy Heckerling, it leaves the viewer with genuinely mixed feelings. Rated PG-13 for violence and profanity. 90m. **DIR:** Amy Heckerling. **CAST:** Michael Keaton, Joe Piscopo, Marilu Henner, Maureen Stapleton. **1984**

JOHNNY EAGER ★★★★1/2 When the DA's daughter falls for a good-looking mobster, sparks fly. Few cops-and-robbers movies are as well cast as this one. Robert Taylor was no longer known as a pretty boy after playing the role of the gangster, and Lana Turner established her image as a sizzling sex symbol. Van Heflin earned a best-supporting-actor's Oscar for his role of the gangster with a conscience. B&W; 107m. **DIR:** Mervyn LeRoy. **CAST:** Lana Turner, Robert Taylor, Robert Sterling, Edward Arnold, Glenda Farrell, Patricia Dane, Barry Nelson, Van Heflin. **1941**

JOHNNY GOT HIS GUN ★★1/2 Featuring Timothy Bottoms as an American World War I soldier who loses his legs, eyes, ears, mouth, and nose after a German artillery shell explodes, this is a morbid, depressing antiwar film with flashes of brilliance. Rated PG. 111m. **DIR:** Dalton Trumbo. **CAST:** Timothy Bottoms, Marsha Hunt, Jason Robards Jr., Donald Sutherland, Diane Varsi, David Soul, Anthony Geary. **1971**

JOHNNY GUITAR ★★★1/2 A positively weird Western, this Nicholas Ray film features the ultimate role reversal. Bar owner Joan Crawford and landowner Mercedes McCambridge shoot it out while their gun-toting boyfriends (Sterling Hayden and Scott Brady) look on. 110m. **DIR:** Nicholas Ray. **CAST:** Joan Crawford, Mercedes McCambridge, Sterling Hayden, Scott Brady, Ward Bond, Ernest Borgnine, John Carradine. **1954**

JOHNNY HANDSOME ★★★1/2 Mickey Rourke plays a badly disfigured criminal double-crossed during a robbery and sent to prison, where plastic surgery is performed on his face as part of a new rehabilitation program. Once released, he plots revenge on those responsible for his capture. Be warned: the violence is extreme. Rated R for violence, language, and nudity. 93m. **DIR:** Walter Hill. **CAST:** Mickey Rourke, Elizabeth McGovern, Ellen Barkin, Lance Henriksen, Morgan Freeman, Forest Whitaker. **1989**

JOHNNY MNEMONIC ★★★1/2 Few motion pictures have captured the storytelling style of comic books as well as this futuristic adventure about a human computer in a race against time. Keanu Reeves is appropriately downbeat as the title character, whose childhood memories have been replaced with a computer chip that allows him to smuggle highly classified information. Rated R for violence, profanity, and nudity. 98m. **DIR:** Robert Longo. **CAST:** Keanu Reeves, Dolph Lundgren, Takeshi Kitano, Ice T, Dina Meyer, Denis Akiyama, Henry Rollins. **1995 DVD**

JOHNNY MYSTO ★★ Silliness abounds in this tale of a young aspiring magician who accidentally makes his sister disappear. His attempt to find her involves an old magician, time travel, and a stint in King Arthur's court to defeat an evil wizard. Rated PG. 87m. **DIR:** Jeff Burr. **CAST:** Toran Caudell, Patrick Renna, Amber Tamblyn, Michael Ansara, Ian Abercrombie, Russ Tamblyn. **1996**

JOHNNY RENO ★★ Another in producer A. C. Lyles's anachronistic, mid-Sixties Paramount Westerns featuring old-time sagebrush stars in an old-fashioned oater. Relentlessly corny, but watchable. 83m. **DIR:** R. G. Springsteen. **CAST:** Dana Andrews, Jane Russell, Lon Chaney Jr., John Agar, Lyle Bettger, Tom Drake, Richard Arlen, Robert Lowery. **1966**

JOHNNY SHILOH ★★★1/2 After his parents are killed during the Civil War, young Johnny Shiloh joins up with a group of soldiers led by the crusty Brian Keith. The performances are good and it's pure Walt Disney adventure. 90m. **DIR:** James Neilson. **CAST:** Brian Keith, Kevin Corcoran, Darryl Hickman, Skip Homeier. **1963**

JOHNNY STECCHINO ★★ This is a silly slapstick farce of mistaken identity that was the most popular film at the Italian box office up till that time. Roberto Benigni directs and plays the dual roles of a tough mafioso and a timid look-alike bus driver. When the shy driver is mistaken for a mob boss, his life is changed dramatically. The overlong film offers wacky, simplistic humor, not unlike a Jerry Lewis movie with an Italian accent. In Italian with English subtitles. 122m. **DIR:** Roberto Benigni. **CAST:** Roberto Benigni, Nicoletta Braschi, Paolo Bonacelli. **1992**

JOHNNY SUEDE ★★1/2 Brad Pitt plays a lackluster, aimless adolescent who discovers a purpose in life when he's literally hit on the head with a pair of suede shoes. This low-budget comedy is from the surreal, off-the-wall school, and owes much to the early work of Jim Jarmusch (for whom Tom DiCillo was once a cinematographer). Only fans of cult films and the preciously weird need apply. 97m. **DIR:** Tom DiCillo. **CAST:** Brad Pitt, Catherine Keener, Calvin Levels, Alison Moir, Nick Cave, Tina Louise. **1992**

JOHNNY TIGER ★★1/2 Chad Everett is a half-breed Seminole, Robert Taylor is a sympathetic teacher, and Geraldine Brooks is a sympathetic doctor, all trying to reach some valid conclusion about the American Indians' role in the modern world. It's nothing to get excited about. 102m. **DIR:** Paul Wendkos. **CAST:** Robert Taylor, Geraldine Brooks, Chad Everett. **1966**

JOHNNY TREMAIN ★★★1/2 Colorful Walt Disney Revolutionary War entry is a perfect blend of schoolboy heroics and Hollywood history, with young Johnny Tremain an apprentice silversmith caught up in the brewing American Revolution. Heavy on the patriotism, with picture-book tableaus of the Boston Tea Party, Paul Revere's ride, and the battles at Concord. Infectious score throughout. 80m. **DIR:** Robert Stevenson. **CAST:** Hal Stalmaster, Luana Patten, Sebastian Cabot, Richard Beymer. **1957**

JOHNNY 2.0 ★★★ In a future where everything is run by a faceless but sinister corporation, a scientist wakes up after fifteen years in a coma to find that his memory has been removed and transplanted. This made-for-cable production has enough interesting concepts to keep sci-fi buffs happy despite the so-so special effects. Rated PG-13 for violence and sexuality. 95m. **DIR:** Neill L. Fearnley. **CAST:** Jeff Fahey, Tahnee Welch, Michael Ironside, John Neville. **1998 DVD**

JOHNNY'S GIRL ★★1/2 After her mother dies, a teenage girl moves in with and tries to reform her father, a small-time Alaskan con artist. Decent, even heartfelt performances can't overcome an uneven script and muddled direction in this made-for-TV flick. Not rated; contains profanity. 120m. **DIR:** John Kent Harrison. **CAST:** Treat Williams, Mia Kirshner. **1995**

JOHNS ★★ A day in the life of two male hustlers plying the sun-bleached wastes of Santa Monica Boulevard. The day, with arch symbolism, happens to be Christmas Eve, and that should give you an idea of how things will

end up. Writer-director Scott Silver's first film is shallow and self-conscious—supposedly based on the stories of real hustlers, but crammed with familiar clichés. Rated R for mature themes, profanity, and simulated sex. 96m. **DIR:** Scott Silver. **CAST:** Lukas Haas, David Arquette, Arliss Howard, Keith David, Elliott Gould, John C. McGinley. **1996 DVD**

JOHNSONS, THE ★★★ Bizarre Danish film in which a young girl is haunted by the titular brothers. The Johnsons worship a fertility god named Xangadix and require the pubescent girl for a ceremony. Director Rudolf Van Den Berg fills the film with atmosphere, but some scenes may be too much for the fainthearted. In Danish with English subtitles. Not rated; contains violence, gore, and sexual situations. 103m. **DIR:** Rudolf Van Den Berg. **CAST:** Monique van de Ven, Esmee De La Bretonere. **1992 DVD**

JOKE OF DESTINY ★★ Italian audiences may have laughed uproariously at this new film by director Lina Wertmuller. However, American viewers are unlikely to get the joke. In Italian with English subtitles. Rated PG for profanity. 105m. **DIR:** Lina Wertmuller. **CAST:** Ugo Tognazzi, Piera Degli Esposti, Gastone Moschin. **1984**

JOLLY CORNER, THE ★★★ The uncertainties of diverging career paths lie at the heart of this TV adaptation of the moody Henry James short story. Fritz Weaver returns to turn-of-the-century America after having lived abroad for thirty-five years, and he becomes obsessed by the memories contained within his ancestral home. Introduced by Henry Fonda; unrated and suitable for family viewing. 43m. **DIR:** Arthur Barron. **CAST:** Fritz Weaver, Salome Jens. **1975**

JOLSON SINGS AGAIN ★★1/2 Larry Parks again does the great and incomparable Al Jolson to a turn; Jolson himself again sings his unforgettable standards. But the film, trumped up to cash in, hasn't the class, charm, or swagger of the original. 96m. **DIR:** Henry Levin. **CAST:** Larry Parks, Barbara Hale, William Demarest, Bill Goodwin, Ludwig Donath, Myron McCormick. **1949**

JOLSON STORY, THE ★★★★ The show-business life story of vaudeville and Broadway stage great Al Jolson gets all-stops-out treatment in this fast-paced, tune-full film. Larry Parks acts and lip-synchs the hard-driving entertainer to a T. Jolson himself dubbed the singing. 128m. **DIR:** Alfred E. Green. **CAST:** Larry Parks, William Demarest, Evelyn Keyes, Bill Goodwin, Ludwig Donath. **1946**

JON JOST'S FRAMEUP ★★ This tale of two losers on the road has been done before and done better. Writer-director Jon Jost filmed this low-rent morality play in just ten days, and it looks it. Jost may capture the tragicomic aspects of the relationship between a dim waitress and her ex-con lover, but the style is more student film than cutting edge. Not rated; contains profanity, violence, sexual situations, nudity, and adult themes. B&W; 91m. **DIR:** Jon Jost. **CAST:** Howard Swain, Nancy Carlin. **1993**

JONAH WHO WILL BE 25 IN THE YEAR 2000 ★★★1/2 A provocative, Swiss-French character study, centering on eight people thrust together by the social and political events of the late 1960s. The title obliquely refers to the unborn child carried by the pregnant Myriam Boyer. Mature, playful, and entertaining, it is bookended by the same director's *No Man's Land*. In French with English subtitles. Rated PG. 115m. **DIR:** Alain Tanner. **CAST:** Jean-Luc Bideau, Rufus, Miou-Miou, Jacques Denis, Dominique Labourier, Myriam Boyer, Roger Jendly. **1976**

JONATHAN LIVINGSTON SEAGULL 🦃 Overblown and laughable. Rated G. 120m. **DIR:** Hall Bartlett. **1973**

JORY ★★★ A surprisingly sensitive film for the genre finds Robby Benson, in his first film role, as a 15-year-old boy who must learn to go it alone in the Wild West after his father is senselessly murdered. While remaining exciting and suspenseful, the film takes time to make commentary about manhood and machismo in an adult, thoughtful manner. Rated PG. 97m. **DIR:** Jorge Fons. **CAST:** Robby Benson, John Marley, B. J. Thomas, Linda Purl. **1972**

JOSEPH ★★★1/2 The talents and larger than life presence of Ben Kingsley and Martin Landau put this biblical epic a notch above other Turner Pictures endeavors. Landau plays Joseph's doting father while Kingsley becomes his Egyptian slave owner after his jealous brothers sell him. Not rated; contains violence and sexual situations. 180m. **DIR:** Roger Young. **CAST:** Paul Mercurio, Ben Kingsley, Martin Landau, Lesley Ann Warren. **1995**

JOSEPH ANDREWS ★★ The adventures of Joseph Andrews (Peter Firth) as he rises from lowly servant to personal footman. This is director Tony Richardson's second attempt to transform a Henry Fielding novel to film. Unfortunately, the first-rate cast cannot save this ill-fated attempt to restage *Tom Jones*. Rated R for sex and profanity. 99m. **DIR:** Tony Richardson. **CAST:** Ann-Margret, Peter Firth, Beryl Reid, Michael Hordern, Jim Dale, John Gielgud, Hugh Griffith, Wendy Craig, Peggy Ashcroft. **1977**

JOSEPHA ★★ Infidelity ruins the professional and personal lives of a married pair of actors. Writer Christopher Frank adapted his own novel but can't get this self-serious drama to work on screen. French, dubbed in English. Not rated; sexual situations. 100m. **DIR:** Christopher Frank. **CAST:** Claude Brasseur, Miou-Miou, Bruno Cremer. **1983**

JOSEPHINE BAKER STORY, THE ★★★★ Lynn Whitfield *owns* this ambitious, unblushingly sexy HBO biography of singer and dancer Josephine Baker, who scandalized the States with her uninhibited personality and erotic choreography. Rubén Blades and David Dukes are fine as two of the significant men in her life. Craig T. Nelson's riveting cameo as Walter Winchell reveals the newscaster in far less than his usual flattering light. Rated R for nudity. 134m. **DIR:** Brian Gibson. **CAST:** Lynn Whitfield, Rubén Blades, David Dukes, Kene Holiday, Craig T. Nelson, Louis Gossett Jr. **1991 DVD**

JOSH AND S.A.M. ★★1/2 Teenager Josh convinces his younger brother, Sam, that he is "S.A.M.," a Strategically Altered Mutant who has been sold to the government by their estranged parents and turned into a robotic child warrior. During one shuffle between Mom and Dad, the troubled youths run away to Canada on an adventure of self-discovery. Part road movie and part domestic drama, this uneven story of adolescent angst has an engaging, offbeat charm. Rated PG-13 for language and violence. 97m. **DIR:** Billy Weber. **CAST:** Jacob Tierney, Noah Fleiss, Martha Plimpton, Stephen Tobolowsky, Joan Allen, Christopher Penn. **1993**

JOSH KIRBY, TIME WARRIOR (SERIES) ★★1/2 In this direct-to-video serial, young Josh Kirby is caught up in a race to save the universe from ultimate destruction. While some episodes make it, others may bore the youngsters at whom the series is aimed. Episode titles include *Planet of the Dino-Knights, The Human Pets, Trapped on Toy World, Eggs from 70 Million B.C., Journey to the Magic Cavern,* and *Last Battle for the Universe*. Rated PG for violence. 8893. **DIR:** Ernest Farino, Frank Arnold. **CAST:** Corbin Allred, Derek Webster, Jennifer Burns, Barrie Ingham. **1995**

JOSHUA THEN AND NOW ★★★★1/2 Based by screenwriter Mordecai Richler (*The Apprenticeship of Duddy Kravitz*) on his autobiographical novel of the same name, this little-known gem is blessed with humor, poignancy, and insight. Jewish writer Joshua Shapiro's life seems to be in shambles. Surviving an embarrassing upbringing by a gangster father, Joshua nearly meets his match in the snobbish high society of his WASP wife. Rated R for profanity, nudity, suggested sex. 118m. **DIR:** Ted Kotcheff. **CAST:** James Woods, Alan Arkin, Gabrielle Lazure, Michael Sarrazin, Linda Sorenson. **1985**

JOSIE AND THE PUSSYCATS ★★ Power-pop songs keep this live-action, dumbed-down version of the Saturday-morning cartoon and Archie Comics series from being unbearable. The title characters are rockers who lament the lameness of pop trends (especially prefab boy groups) and place individuality, teamwork, and friendship above materialism. They get a shot at stardom with help from two slithery record-company executives and uncover a conspiracy to weave subliminal messages into pop recordings. Rated PG-13 for language and sexuality. 98m. **DIR:** Harry Elfont, Deborah Kaplan. **CAST:** Rachael Leigh Cook, Rosario Dawson, Tara Reid, Parker Posey, Alan Cumming. **2001 DVD**

JOUR DE FÊTE ★★1/2 Jacques Tati is the focal point of this light comedy loosely tied to the arrival of a carnival in a small village. As François, the bumbling postman, Tati sees a film on the heroism of the American postal service and tries to emulate it on his small rural route. In French with subtitles. B&W; 81m. **DIR:** Jacques Tati. **CAST:** Jacques Tati, Guy Decomble, Paul Frankeur. **1949**

JOURNEY ★★★1/2 This *Hallmark Hall of Fame* TV special focuses on a boy who struggles to come to terms with his restless mother and her abandonment of him and his sister. His grandparents take on the parental responsibilities and attempt to create their own family and history. Strong message about the fragile nature of the family unit and the inner strength that must be tapped in a crisis. Strong performances delivered by all. Not rated; contains mature themes. 100m. **DIR:** Tom McLoughlin. **CAST:** Jason Robards Jr., Brenda Fricker, Max Pomeranc, Meg Tilly, Eliza Dushku. **1995**

JOURNEY BACK TO OZ ★★1/2 This cartoon version sequel to *The Wizard of Oz* leaves the Wizard out. The voices of famous stars help maintain adult interest. Rated G. 90m. **DIR:** Hal Sutherland. **1974**

JOURNEY FOR MARGARET ★★★ A childless journalist in war-ravaged England falls for two little orphans, and he and his wife become involved with their future. Margaret O'Brien pushes all the emotional buttons in a phenomenal film debut. This is solid MGM wartime filmmaking at its propagandistic best. B&W; 81m. **DIR:** W. S. Van Dyke. **CAST:** Robert Young, Laraine Day, Fay Bainter, Nigel Bruce, Margaret O'Brien. **1942**

JOURNEY INTO FEAR (1942) ★★★★ A sometimes confusing but always suspenseful World War II tale of an American ordnance expert (Joseph Cotten) targeted for assassination in Istanbul. Like *The Magnificent Ambersons*, this faulted classic was started by Orson Welles but was taken over by RKO. Uncredited Welles partly directed and, with Cotten, adapted this Eric Ambler mystery for the screen. Remade in 1975. B&W; 69m. **DIR:** Norman Foster, Orson Welles. **CAST:** Joseph Cotten, Orson Welles, Dolores Del Rio, Ruth Warrick, Agnes Moorehead, Everett Sloane, Edgar Barrier, Hans Conried. **1942**

JOURNEY INTO FEAR (1975) ★★ Canadian remake of Orson Welles's 1942 spy drama is occasionally intriguing but ultimately ambiguous and lacking in dramatic punch. Sam Waterston's portrayal of a research geologist, and wide-ranging European locations, help sustain interest. Rated PG. 103m. **DIR:** Daniel Mann. **CAST:** Sam Waterston, Zero Mostel, Yvette Mimieux, Scott Marlowe, Ian McShane, Joseph Wiseman, Shelley Winters, Stanley Holloway, Donald Pleasence, Vincent Price. **1975**

JOURNEY OF AUGUST KING, THE ★★★ Jason Patric is the widowed, nineteenth-century farmer who crosses paths with an exotic runaway slave, played with delicate sensibility by Thandie Newton. As much about her trek north as the emotional journey both undertake, this is surprising in its realism. The visuals are impressive, but this needed more intensity from Patric and a less-relaxed pace to keep from slowly fading. Rated PG-13 for off-screen violence and implied sexual situations. 92m. **DIR:** John Duigan. **CAST:** Jason Patric, Thandie Newton, Larry Drake, Sam Waterston. **1995**

JOURNEY OF HONOR ★★ Historic tale of feuding Japanese warlords in 1602 has epic written all over it, but comes across trite and clichéd. Visuals are the only saving grace. Rated PG-13 for violence. 107m. **DIR:** Gordon Hessler. **CAST:** Sho Kosugi, Christopher Lee, Norman Lloyd, John Rhys-Davies, Toshiro Mifune. **1991**

JOURNEY OF HOPE ★★★★ Swiss director Xavier Koller's Oscar-winning film chronicles the harrowing journey of a family of Kurds who attempt to leave the abject poverty of their Turkish village for the "promised land" of Switzerland. Based in part on fact and in part on Koller's imaginings, this is nevertheless a gripping motion picture. In Kurdish, Turkish, German, and Italian. Not rated; contains subject matter too harsh for children. 110m. **DIR:** Xavier Koller. **CAST:** Necmettin Cobanoglu. **1990**

JOURNEY OF NATTY GANN, THE ★★★★★ With this superb film, the Disney Studios returned triumphantly to the genre of family films. Meredith Salenger stars as Natty, a 14-year-old street urchin who must ride the rails from Chicago to Seattle during the Depression to find her father (Ray Wise). Rated PG for light violence. 101m. **DIR:** Jeremy Paul Kagan. **CAST:** Meredith Salenger, Ray Wise, John Cusack, Lainie Kazan, Scatman Crothers. **1985**

JOURNEY TO SPIRIT ISLAND ★★★1/2 A teenage Native American girl takes up her grandmother's quest to save a sacred island, used to bury their ancestors, from

unscrupulous developers. Above-average family adventure, beautifully photographed in the Pacific Northwest by Vilmos Zsigmond. Rated PG. 93m. **DIR:** Laszlo Pal. **CAST:** Bettina, Maria Antoinette Rodgers, Brandon Douglas. **1988**

JOURNEY TO THE CENTER OF THE EARTH (1959) ★★★ Jules Verne story was impressive when first released, but it looks pretty silly these days. However, James Mason is always fascinating to watch, production values are high, and kids should enjoy its innocent fun. 132m. **DIR:** Henry Levin. **CAST:** James Mason, Pat Boone, Arlene Dahl, Diane Baker. **1959**

JOURNEY TO THE CENTER OF THE EARTH (1987) 🦃 There's little Jules Verne in this hopelessly muddled adventure, notable only for some impressive sets. Rated PG. 79m. **DIR:** Rusty Lemorande. **CAST:** Nicola Cowper, Ilan Mitchell-Smith, Paul Carafotes, Kathy Ireland, Emo Philips. **1987**

JOURNEY TO THE CENTER OF TIME (TIME WARP) ★★1/2 A group of scientists working on a time-travel device are accidentally propelled five thousand years into the future following an equipment malfunction. Once there, they discover an alien civilization (headed by a young Lyle Waggoner) attempting to take over the world. Low-budget film features passable special effects, but the dialogue and acting are subpar. 82m. **DIR:** David L. Hewitt. **CAST:** Scott Brady, Gigi Perreau, Anthony Eisley, Abraham Sofaer, Lyle Waggoner. **1967 DVD**

JOURNEY TO THE FAR SIDE OF THE SUN ★★★1/2 Extremely clever sci-fi thriller concerns the discovery of a planet rotating in Earth's orbit, but always hidden from view on the other side of the Sun. Thoughtful, literate, and fascinating, this effort is marred only by a needlessly oblique and frustrating conclusion. Not rated; suitable for family viewing. 99m. **DIR:** Robert Parrish. **CAST:** Roy Thinnes, Lynn Loring, Herbert Lom, Patrick Wymark, Ian Hendry. **1969 DVD**

JOURNEY'S END: THE SAGA OF STAR TREK:THE NEXT GENERATION ★★★ Only fans of this *Star Trek* spin-off series will appreciate the behind-the-scenes segments. In addition, host Jonathan Frakes makes an appearance at a *Star Trek* convention and Marina Sirtis conducts the series' score. Clips from the final episode and the feature film *Generations* hint that the voyages of the *Enterprise 1701-D* will continue, at least through theatrical releases. Not rated. 46m. **DIR:** Donald R. Beck. **CAST:** Jonathan Frakes, Marina Sirtis, Patrick Stewart, John de Lancie. **1994**

JOY HOUSE ★★1/2 Spooky and interesting, but ultimately only mildly rewarding, this film features Jane Fonda in one of her sexy French roles as a free-spirited waif attempting to seduce her cousin's chauffeur (Alain Delon). 98m. **DIR:** René Clement. **CAST:** Jane Fonda, Alain Delon, Lola Albright, Sorrell Booke. **1964 DVD**

JOY LUCK CLUB, THE ★★★★★ Employing multiple flashbacks that never become confusing, this film, based on Amy Tan's best-selling novel, explores the turbulent lives of four Chinese women, each of whom emerges from mainland China's male-dominated society to face the challenge of coping with a now-grown daughter raised in the United States. Each vignette manages to be more poignant and compelling than its predecessor. Rated R for violence, profanity, and strong sexual themes. 138m. **DIR:** Wayne Wang. **CAST:** Kieu Chinh, Ming-Na Wen, Tamlyn Tomita, Tsai Chin, France Nuyen, Lauren Tom, Lisa Lu, Rosalind Chao. **1993**

JOY OF LIVING ★★★ Engaging screwball musical-comedy about a playboy who will stop at nothing to win the affection of a bright singing star. Great songs by Jerome Kern. B&W; 90m. **DIR:** Tay Garnett. **CAST:** Irene Dunne, Douglas Fairbanks Jr., Lucille Ball. **1938**

JOY OF SEX, THE ★★ This comedy, about the plight of two virgins, male and female, in a sex-crazy age, has few offensive elements. But there is one problem: it isn't funny. Rated R for profanity, suggested sex, and scatological humor. 93m. **DIR:** Martha Coolidge. **CAST:** Michelle Meyrink, Cameron Dye, Lisa Langlois. **1984**

•JOY RIDE ★★★★ This marvelously taut little thriller may not look like much at first blush, but director John Dahl really tightens the screws for a genuinely suspenseful final act. Nice guy Paul Walker hopes to get closer to potential girlfriend Leelee Sobieski during a cross-country road trip, but he makes the mistake of bringing troublemaking sibling Steve Zahn along. Goaded by his brother into pulling a nasty CB-oriented trick on a lonely trucker, our hero lives to regret this thoughtless prank . . . and *then* some. Rated R for profanity, violence, and brief nudity. 96m. **DIR:** John Dahl. **CAST:** Steve Zahn, Paul Walker, Leelee Sobieski, Jessica Bowman. **2001**

JOY STICKS 🦃 A wealthy businessman wants to shut down the local video game room. Rated R. 88m. **DIR:** Greydon Clark. **CAST:** Joe Don Baker, Leif Green, Logan Ramsey. **1983**

JOYLESS STREET ★★★ Greta Garbo has her first starring role as a young woman who succumbs to hard times in the decadent Vienna of World War I. Look for Marlene Dietrich in a cameo. B&W; 65m. **DIR:** G. W. Pabst. **CAST:** Greta Garbo, Asta Nielsen. **1925**

JOYRIDE (1977) ★★1/2 Four second-generation actors acquit themselves fairly well in this loosely directed drama about a quartet of youngsters who start off in search of adventure and find themselves turning to crime. Rated R. 92m. **DIR:** Joseph Ruben. **CAST:** Desi Arnaz Jr., Robert Carradine, Melanie Griffith, Anne Lockhart, Tom Ligon. **1977**

JOYRIDE (1997) ★★ Trying to escape her pimp, a hooker and her innocent boyfriend make the mistake of stealing the car of a hit woman whose most recent victim is still in the trunk. Flashy direction doesn't compensate for a tired script that asks more of a second-rate cast than it can deliver. Rated R for profanity, violence, and sexual situations. 92m. **DIR:** Quinton Peeples. **CAST:** Tobey Maguire, Wilson Cruz, Adam West, Benicio Del Toro. **1997**

JU DOU ★★★★★ This Oscar-nominated Chinese film is a lovely, sensual, ultimately tragic tale of illicit love in the strict, male-dominated feudal society of rural China, circa 1920. On visual imagery alone, the film would be worthy of attention. In Chinese with English subtitles. Not rated. 93m. **DIR:** Yimou Zhang. **CAST:** Gong Li, Li Baotian. **1990 DVD**

JUAREZ ★★★★ Warner Bros. in the 1930s and '40s seemed to trot out veteran actor Paul Muni every time they attempted to film a screen biography. This re-creation of the life of Mexico's famous peasant leader was no exception. Surrounded by an all-star cast, including

Bette Davis and Brian Aherne, this big budget bio is well mounted and well intentioned. B&W; 132m. **DIR:** William Dieterle. **CAST:** Paul Muni, Bette Davis, Brian Aherne, Claude Rains, John Garfield. **1939**

JUBAL ★★★1/2 Adult Western finds drifter Jubal Troop (Glenn Ford) enmeshed in just about everybody's problems when he signs on with rancher Ernest Borgnine. Beautifully photographed and well acted, this tale of jealousy and revenge is standout entertainment. 101m. **DIR:** Delmer Daves. **CAST:** Glenn Ford, Ernest Borgnine, Valerie French, Rod Steiger, Charles Bronson, Noah Beery Jr., Felicia Farr. **1956**

JUBILEE ★★ Avant-garde filmmaker Derek Jarman's surreal fantasy about a futuristic England, a postpunk-Thatcherian wasteland where civilization is in anarchaic terrorism. Highly uneven. Not rated; contains nudity and graphic violence. 105m. **DIR:** Derek Jarman. **CAST:** Jenny Runacre, Jordan, Little Nell, Richard O'Brien, Adam Ant. **1978**

JUBILEE TRAIL ★★ Tired romantic triangle in old California is short on action and long on melodrama as a young woman has to choose among the rough-hewn men who court her. This fine cast can't drag the film out of the syrupy mire it settles into. Director Joseph Kane had a lot more luck with Gene Autry and Roy Rogers programmers. 103m. **DIR:** Joseph Kane. **CAST:** Forrest Tucker, Vera Hruba Ralston, Joan Leslie, John Russell, Jim Davis, Pat O'Brien, Barton MacLane, Ray Middleton, Buddy Baer, Jack Elam. **1953**

JUD SUSS ★★ This film, *The Jew, Suss*, is infamous as the most rabid of the anti-Semitic films made by the Nazis under personal supervision of propaganda minister Joseph Goebbels. It depicts "the Jewish menace" in both symbolic and overt terms in a story about a wandering Jew who enters a small European country and nearly brings it to ruin. Any serious student of cinema should see it as an example of the medium's enormous power to proselytize. In German with English subtitles. B&W; 97m. **DIR:** Veidt Harlan. **CAST:** Ferdinand Marian, Werner Krauss. **1940**

JUDAS KISS ★★★ A few small-time criminals decide to try something bigger than they're used to—a four million dollar kidnapping scheme. With federal agents on their trail, each player must decide who he can trust, and who he can betray. The pacing and acting is good, but the occasionally forced homage to *film noir* is completely unnecessary. Rated R for nudity, violence, and language. 108m. **DIR:** Sebastian Gutierrez. **CAST:** Emma Thompson, Gil Bellows, Hal Holbrook, Alan Rickman, Carla Gugino, Til Schweiger. **1998**

JUDAS PROJECT, THE ★★ Well-meaning but preachy film about the last three years of Jesus Christ's life, presented in a modern-day setting. Director-writer James H. Barden has struck upon a novel idea, but his execution is too heavy-handed and the untalented cast doesn't help. Rated PG-13 for violence. 97m. **DIR:** James H. Barden. **CAST:** John O'Banion, Ramy Zada, Richard Herd, Gerald Gordon, Jeff Corey. **1992**

JUDE ★★★★1/2 This adaptation of Thomas Hardy's classic tragedy is as haunting as it is beautiful. Christopher Eccleston is the title character trapped by the convents and social hierarchy of the late nineteenth century. Spirited, intellectual Kate Winslet is the soul mate who aids his downfall. The novel's sensibilities are captured equally by visuals and faultless performances, but the supporting roles are weak. Rated R for nudity, sexual situations, and a graphic childbirth scene. 122m. **DIR:** Michael Winterbottom. **CAST:** Chris Eccleston, Kate Winslet. **1996 DVD**

JUDEX ★★★1/2 This remake of a serial from the early days of cinema will make you laugh out loud one moment and become misty-eyed with nostalgia the next. Based on an old potboiler by Feuillade and Bernede, *Judex* ("the judge") is an enjoyable adventure of a superhero who is lovable, human, and fallible. In French with English subtitles. B&W; 103m. **DIR:** Georges Franju. **CAST:** Channing Pollock, Jacques Jouanneau, Edith Scob, Michel Vitold, Francine Berge. **1963**

JUDGE AND JURY ★★1/2 An executed criminal returns from the dead to get revenge on the innocent man he blames for the death of his wife. Action-packed thriller benefits from a fun performance by David Keith as the unstoppable maniac. Rated R for violence and profanity. 90m. **DIR:** John Eyres. **CAST:** David Keith, Martin Kove, Laura Johnson. **1997 DVD**

JUDGE AND THE ASSASSIN, THE ★★★ In nineteenth century France, a rural judge tries to ascertain whether a serial killer is insane or merely faking to escape execution. Interesting but ultimately vague (at least to American eyes) historical drama. In French with English subtitles. Not rated; brief nudity. 130m. **DIR:** Bertrand Tavernier. **CAST:** Philippe Noiret, Michel Galabru, Jean-Claude Brialy, Isabelle Huppert. **1976**

JUDGE DREDD ★★★1/2 Sylvester Stallone stars as British-created superhero, Judge Dredd, a judge, jury, and executioner in the twenty-second century. Big, loud, and jam-packed with special effects, the movie took a critical lambasting in its theatrical release, but it's not as bad as its reputation would suggest. Rated R for violence and profanity. 96m. **DIR:** Danny Cannon. **CAST:** Sylvester Stallone, Armand Assante, Diane Lane, Rob Schneider, Joan Chen, Jurgen Prochnow, Max von Sydow, Joanna Miles, Balthazar Getty. **1995 DVD**

JUDGE PRIEST ★★★1/2 A slice of Americana, and a good one. Life and drama in an old southern town, with all the clichés painted brilliantly. Will Rogers is fine. Stepin Fetchit is properly Uncle Tom. John Ford's sensitive direction makes this film one for the books. A touching, poignant portrait of community life lost and gone forever. B&W; 71m. **DIR:** John Ford. **CAST:** Will Rogers, Anita Louise, Stepin Fetchit, Henry B. Walthall, Tom Brown, Hattie McDaniel. **1934**

JUDGE STEPS OUT, THE ★★★1/2 A Boston judge (Alexander Knox) runs away from his increasingly empty life to find happiness as a short-order cook in California. He falls in love and must choose between responsibility and pleasure. B&W; 91m. **DIR:** Boris Ingster. **CAST:** Alexander Knox, Ann Sothern, George Tobias, Florence Bates, Frieda Inescort. **1949**

JUDGMENT ★★★★ The Catholic church takes a beating in this gripping teledrama, loosely lifted from an actual court case. The setting is a small-town Louisiana parish filled with staunch Catholics who idolize local priest David Strathairn (superb in a chilling role). Alas, the good father regards his altar boys with decidedly unhealthy affection. Rated PG-13 for frank sexual themes. 90m. **DIR:** Tom Topor. **CAST:** Keith Carradine, Blythe

Danner, David Strathairn, Michael Faustino, Mitchell Ryan, Robert Joy, Jack Warden. **1990 DVD**

JUDGMENT AT NUREMBERG ★★★★ An all-star cast shines in this thoughtful social drama. During the late stages of the Nazi war crimes trial, an American judge (Spencer Tracy) must ponder the issue of how extensive is the responsibility of citizens for carrying out the criminal orders of their governments. B&W; 178m. **DIR:** Stanley Kramer. **CAST:** Spencer Tracy, Burt Lancaster, Maximilian Schell, Richard Widmark, Marlene Dietrich, Montgomery Clift, Judy Garland. **1961**

JUDGMENT DAY 🦃 Fragments of a splintered meteor threaten the Earth, and only a spiritual rebel in South America can save the world from oblivion. This movie is abhorrently worse than a dozen or so films with the same plot. Rated R for violence and language. 90m. **DIR:** John Terlesky. **CAST:** Ice T, Suzy Amis, Tom "Tiny" Lister Jr., Coolio, Mario Van Peebles. **1999 DVD**

JUDGMENT IN BERLIN ★★★ Intelligent courtroom drama in the *Inherit the Wind* and *Judgment at Nuremberg* vein. An East German hijacks a Polish airliner and has it fly to West Berlin, where he seeks political asylum. Instead of offering safety, the U.S. government puts him on trial for terrorism. Martin Sheen as the no-nonsense judge carries the film. Rated PG for language. 110m. **DIR:** Leo Penn. **CAST:** Martin Sheen, Sam Wanamaker, Max Gail, Sean Penn. **1988**

JUDGMENT NIGHT ★★★ Four buddies get lost in Chicago on the way to a boxing match and end up being chased by a vicious gang in this above-average urban thriller, with high-voltage villain Denis Leary as the main attraction. Rated R for profanity and violence. 109m. **DIR:** Stephen Hopkins. **CAST:** Emilio Estevez, Cuba Gooding Jr., Denis Leary, Stephen Dorff, Jeremy Piven, Peter Greene, Michael DeLorenzo, Michael Wiseman. **1993 DVD**

JUDICIAL CONSENT ★★★ In this courtroom thriller, hard-line judge Bonnie Bedelia tries a case involving the murder of an associate, and gradually realizes that *she* is being framed for the crime. The strong cast provides more credibility than this film deserves, considering the idiotic behavior in the climax. Rated R for nudity, simulated sex, profanity, and violence. 100m. **DIR:** William Bindley. **CAST:** Bonnie Bedelia, Billy Wirth, Will Patton, Lisa Blount, Dabney Coleman, Kevin McCarthy. **1995**

JUDITH OF BETHULIA ★★★ The first American four-reel film designed for feature-length exhibition, this lavish biblical spectacle of deep emotional conflict and deception brings together two stories: (1) the forty-day siege of the great Judean walled city of Bethulia and (2) the innocent lovers the siege engulfs and threatens. A brilliant example of early film drama presaging Cecil B. DeMille. Silent with musical score. B&W; 65m. **DIR:** D. W. Griffith. **CAST:** Blanche Sweet, Henry B. Walthall, Mae Marsh, Robert Harron, Lillian Gish, Dorothy Gish. **1914**

JUDY BERLIN ★★★1/2 A solar eclipse in a Long Island town catches a number of the local inhabitants with their quirks showing, and the film follows them as they wander around town—a lonely schoolteacher (Barbara Barrie), her starstruck daughter Judy (Edie Falco, in an exquisite performance), a former classmate of Judy's (Aaron Harnick, representing writer-director Eric Mendelsohn), and his flighty mother (the late Madeline Kahn, wistful and touching in her last film). All but plotless, the film is nevertheless a minor gem, affectionate and observant. Rated R for mature themes and mild profanity. B&W; 93m. **DIR:** Eric Mendelsohn. **CAST:** Edie Falco, Aaron Harnick, Madeline Kahn, Bob Dishy, Barbara Barrie. **1999 DVD**

JUDY GARLAND AND FRIENDS ★★★★ Back in 1963, a then 21 year old pre-*Funny Girl* singer named Barbra Streisand got her first television exposure on this classic *Judy Garland Show*. Besides her young daughter Liza Minnelli, Garland also welcomes the grande dame of Broadway, Ethel Merman. The singing (including an eight-song medley with Streisand) is superb, and is a tribute to the talent and personality of Garland. B&W; 55m. **DIR:** Bill Hobin. **1963**

JUGGERNAUT (1936) ★★1/2 In this low-budget mystery-drama filmed in England, Boris Karloff plays Dr. Sartorius, a brilliant (but cracked) specialist on the verge of perfecting a cure for paralysis. He makes a deal with a patient to murder her husband. B&W; 64m. **DIR:** Henry Edwards. **CAST:** Boris Karloff. **1936**

JUGGERNAUT (1974) ★★★★1/2 Here's a first-rate, suspenseful thriller about demolitions expert Richard Harris attempting to deactivate a bomb aboard a luxury liner. Richard Lester elevates the familiar plot line with inspired direction, and Lester regular Roy Kinnear is on hand to add some deft bits of comedy. Rated PG. 109m. **DIR:** Richard Lester. **CAST:** Richard Harris, Omar Sharif, David Hemmings, Anthony Hopkins, Shirley Knight, Ian Holm, Roy Kinnear. **1974**

JUGULAR WINE ★★★ After being seduced and bitten by a beautiful vampire, an anthropologist becomes obsessed with death. Obviously a low-budget production, this film succeeds due to its impressive cast of illustrious celebrities, as well as first-time writer and director Blair Murphy's panache. Rated R for violence, nudity, and profanity. 95m. **DIR:** Blair Murphy. **CAST:** Shaun Irons, Stan Lee, Frank Miller, Henry Rollins, Lisa Malkiewicz, Vladimir Kehkaial, Michael Colyar. **1994**

JUICE ★★★1/2 Spike Lee's cinematographer, Ernest R. Dickerson, makes his directorial debut with this gritty, downbeat chronicle of life on the streets of Harlem. Four friends edge around the outside of the law until the fateful moment when they finally step over the line and find themselves on the run. It's not unlike an inner-city version of *The Wild Bunch*. Rated R for profanity, violence, and suggested sex. 96m. **DIR:** Ernest R. Dickerson. **CAST:** Omar Epps, Jermaine "Huggy" Hopkins, Khalil Kain, Tupac Shakur. **1992 DVD**

JULES AND JIM ★★★★★ Superb character study, which revolves around a bizarre ménage à trois. It is really a film about wanting what you can't have and not wanting what you think you desire once you have it. In French with English subtitles. B&W; 104m. **DIR:** François Truffaut. **CAST:** Oskar Werner, Jeanne Moreau, Henri Serre. **1961 DVD**

JULIA ★★★★1/2 Alvin Sargent won an Oscar for his taut screen adaptation of the late Lillian Hellman's bestselling memoir *Pentimento*. It's a harrowing tale of Hellman's journey into Germany to locate her childhood friend who has joined in the resistance against the Nazis. Great performances by all cast members. Rated PG. 118m. **DIR:** Fred Zinnemann. **CAST:** Jane Fonda,

Vanessa Redgrave, Jason Robards Jr., Maximilian Schell, Meryl Streep. **1977**

JULIA AND JULIA 🦃 Dreary Italian-made, English-language movie is an uninspired rehash of the parallel-worlds plot from the old science-fiction pulp magazines. Rated R for profanity, nudity, and violence. 95m. **DIR:** Peter Del Monte. **CAST:** Kathleen Turner, Gabriel Byrne, Sting, Gabriele Ferzetti. **1988**

JULIA HAS TWO LOVERS 🦃 Daphna Kastner was unknown as a writer and actress before this horrid film, whose title is self-explanatory, and hopefully she will never be heard from again. Rated R for nudity and simulated sex. 87m. **DIR:** Bashar Shbib. **CAST:** Daphna Kastner, David Duchovny, David Charles. **1990**

JULIA MISBEHAVES ★★★★ Delightful farce with Greer Garson as a London chorine, long separated from stuffy husband Walter Pidgeon and their refined daughter, Elizabeth Taylor, coming back into their lives for the marriage of the latter. Garson is wonderful in her only comic role, even allowing herself to become foil to a group of acrobats. B&W; 99m. **DIR:** Jack Conway. **CAST:** Greer Garson, Walter Pidgeon, Peter Lawford, Elizabeth Taylor, Cesar Romero, Lucile Watson, Nigel Bruce, Mary Boland, Henry Stephenson, Ian Wolfe, Veda Ann Borg. **1948**

JULIAN PO ★★ A nondescript young man (Christian Slater) wanders into a small mountain town, and the locals are suspicious. But when they learn he's come to kill himself, they become suddenly respectful and solicitous. First-time filmmaker Alan Wade transplants a Serbo-Croatian story to rural Appalachia, and the result is like a weird mixture of Franz Kafka, Samuel Beckett, and Mark Twain. Slater is earnest, but like the rest of the cast he's hampered by the heavy-handed allegory of the script. Rated PG-13 for mild profanity. 78m. **DIR:** Alan Wade. **CAST:** Christian Slater, Robin Tunney, Michael Parks, Harve Presnell, Dina Spybey, Zeljko Ivanek. **1997**

JULIE ★★ Campy melodrama with Doris Day as an airline stewardess who realizes that her second husband is a psychopath who killed her first husband—and may do the same to her. You'll find it hard to keep a straight face during the ridiculous finale in which Doris has to land a jumbo jet by herself. B&W; 99m. **DIR:** Andrew L. Stone. **CAST:** Doris Day, Louis Jourdan, Barry Sullivan, Frank Lovejoy, Jack Kruschen. **1956**

JULIET OF THE SPIRITS ★★★★★ The convoluted plot in this classic centers around a wealthy wife suspicious of her cheating husband. Giulietta Masina (in real life, Mrs. Fellini) has never been so tantalizingly innocent with her Bambi eyes. This is Fellini's first attempt with color. 148m. **DIR:** Federico Fellini. **CAST:** Giulietta Masina, Sandra Milo, Valentina Cortese, Sylva Koscina. **1965 DVD**

JULIUS CAESAR (1953) ★★★★ Cool, confident, starbright performances mark this stirring, memorable mounting of Shakespeare's great classic of honor and the struggle for power in ancient Rome. A superb blend of eloquent language and judicious camera art. Standouts: John Gielgud as the cunning Cassius and Marlon Brando, whose fire-hot/ice-cold portrayal of Mark Antony alone makes the film worthwhile. B&W; 120m. **DIR:** Joseph L. Mankiewicz. **CAST:** Louis Calhern, Marlon Brando, James Mason, John Gielgud, Edmond O'Brien, Greer Garson, Deborah Kerr. **1953**

JULIUS CAESAR (1970) ★★ A good cast, but Shakespeare loses in this so-so rendering of ambition, greed, jealousy, and politics in toga Rome. 117m. **DIR:** Stuart Burge. **CAST:** Charlton Heston, Jason Robards Jr., John Gielgud, Robert Vaughn, Richard Chamberlain, Diana Rigg, Christopher Lee. **1970**

JUMANJI ★★★1/2 Terrific computer-generated effects highlight this fantasy about youngsters who find their lives taken over by a bizarre and all-powerful board game. Robin Williams is fine in a *Hook*-style role as an adult involved in the games, but it is David Allen Grier, as a hapless policeman, who provides the laughs. Heartwarming and fun. Rated PG. 104m. **DIR:** Joe Johnston. **CAST:** Robin Williams, Bonnie Hunt, Kirsten Dunst, Bradley Pierce, Bebe Neuwirth, Jonathan Hyde, David Alan Grier, Patricia Clarkson. **1995 DVD**

JUMBO ★★ A big-budget circus-locale musical that flopped, despite Rodgers and Hart songs, William Daniels photography, a Sidney Sheldon script from a Hecht and MacArthur story, and a cast that should have known better. 125m. **DIR:** Charles Walters. **CAST:** Doris Day, Stephen Boyd, Jimmy Durante, Martha Raye, Dean Jagger. **1962**

•JUMP TOMORROW ★★1/2 On his way to an arranged marriage with a childhood acquaintance, a shy young man finds himself smitten with a woman he meets in an airport. Writer-director Joel Hopkins's first feature, a familiar romantic road comedy, gets off to an uncertain start but becomes more endearing, and the performances more assured, as it goes along. Rated PG. 97m. **DIR:** Joel Hopkins. **CAST:** Tunde Adebimpe, Hippolyte Girardot, Natalia Verbeke. **2001**

JUMPIN' AT THE BONEYARD ★★1/2 Two brothers accidentally meet for the first time in years and try to connect again. One is divorced and unemployed, the other a drug-addicted thief, and their visit to the Bronx slum where they grew up mirrors their bleak lives. Sometimes compelling but ultimately pointless and downbeat. Rated R for profanity and drug use. 107m. **DIR:** Jeff Stanzler. **CAST:** Tim Roth, Alexis Arquette, Danitra Vance, Samuel L. Jackson, Luis Guzman. **1992**

JUMPIN' JACK FLASH ★★1/2 Whoopi Goldberg's inspired clowning is the only worthwhile element in her first big-screen comedy. She plays a computer operator who finds herself involved in international intrigue. Rated R for profanity and violence. 100m. **DIR:** Penny Marshall. **CAST:** Whoopi Goldberg, Stephen Collins, John Wood, Carol Kane, James Belushi, Annie Potts, Peter Michael Goetz, Roscoe Lee Browne, Jeroen Krabbé, Jonathan Pryce. **1986**

JUMPING JACKS ★★★ It's all Jerry Lewis antics as two nightclub entertainers join the parachute corps. Not on a par with *At War With The Army*. B&W; 96m. **DIR:** Norman Taurog. **CAST:** Dean Martin, Jerry Lewis, Mona Freeman, Don DeFore, Robert Strauss, Ray Teal. **1952**

JUNE BRIDE ★★★1/2 A noted correspondent is forced to work for his ex-flame, now an editor of a woman's magazine. His cynicism causes complications with the bride and her family. Robert Montgomery, as the reporter, steals the show. B&W; 97m. **DIR:** Bretaigne Win-

dust. **CAST:** Bette Davis, Robert Montgomery, Fay Bainter, Tom Tully, Mary Wickes, Jerome Cowan. **1948**

JUNE NIGHT ★★★1/2 Ingrid Bergman gives a harrowing performance in this well-crafted melodrama about a young woman who changes her identity in order to escape the scars of a violent incident at the hands of a former lover. This poignant film gives viewers a chance to experience a young Bergman before her success in Hollywood. In Swedish with English subtitles. B&W; 90m. **DIR:** Per Lindberg. **CAST:** Ingrid Bergman. **1940 DVD**

JUNGLE BOOK (1942) ★★★★ This one's for fantasy fans of all ages. Sabu stars in Rudyard Kipling's tale of a boy raised by wolves in the jungle of India. Beautiful color presentation holds the viewer from start to finish. Rated G. 109m. **DIR:** Zoltán Korda. **CAST:** Sabu, Joseph Calleia, John Qualen. **1942 DVD**

JUNGLE BOOK, THE (1967) ★★★★ Phil Harris's Baloo the Bear steals the show in this rendition of Rudyard Kipling's *Mowgli* stories, the last full-length animated film that reflected Walt Disney's personal participation. Although not as lavishly illustrated as earlier Disney efforts, *The Jungle Book* benefits from its clever songs ("The Bare Necessities," among others) and inspired vocal casting. 78m. **DIR:** Wolfgang Reitherman. **1967 DVD**

JUNGLE CAPTIVE ★★ Acquanetta's missing from this second and last sequel to *Captive Wild Woman*, replaced by Vicky Lane as the ape-turned-woman who kills when upset. B&W; 63m. **DIR:** Harold Young. **CAST:** Otto Kruger, Amelita Ward, Phil Brown, Vicky Lane. **1945**

JUNGLE FEVER ★★★ Writer-director Spike Lee's story of an interracial romance between a married black architect (Wesley Snipes) and his single Italian-American secretary (Annabella Sciorra) has some terrific performances and unforgettable moments. Sad to say, you have to wade through quite a bit of tedium to get to them. Rated R for profanity, violence, and nudity. 135m. **DIR:** Spike Lee. **CAST:** Wesley Snipes, Annabella Sciorra, Spike Lee, Anthony Quinn, Ossie Davis, Ruby Dee, Lonette McKee, John Turturro, Tim Robbins, Brad Dourif. **1991 DVD**

JUNGLE HEAT ★★ Dr. Evelyn Howard (Deborah Raffin), an anthropologist from L.A., hires an alcoholic ex–Vietnam vet (Peter Fonda) to fly her into the jungles of South America. There she looks for an ancient tribe of pygmies but finds instead monsters that greatly resemble the Creature from the Black Lagoon. Rated PG for language and gore. 93m. **DIR:** Gus Trikonis. **CAST:** Peter Fonda, Deborah Raffin, John Amos. **1984**

JUNGLE JIM ★★★ The first entry in Columbia's long-running series starring Johnny Weissmuller finds Alex Raymond's comic-strip hero helping a female scientist search for a rare drug that can help cure polio. Future Superman George Reeves plays the heavy. B&W; 73m. **DIR:** William Berke. **CAST:** Johnny Weissmuller, Virginia Grey, George Reeves, Lita Baron, Rick Vallin. **1948**

JUNGLE PATROL ★★ This is a routine World War II story about a squadron of fliers commanded by a young officer who has been ordered to hold an airfield against the Japanese. The subplot is a silly romance between the officer and a USO performer. Best ingredient: the music score by Emil Newman and Arthur Lange. B&W; 72m. **DIR:** Joseph M. Newman. **CAST:** Kristine Miller, Arthur Franz, Ross Ford, Tommy Noonan, Gene Reynolds, Richard Jaeckel, Harry Lauter. **1948**

JUNGLE RAIDERS ★★ Christopher Connelly plays an adventurer–con man hired to find the Ruby of Gloom in Malaysia. This *Raiders of the Lost Ark* rip-off is too plodding for most viewers. It includes a few fun, action-filled moments but stick to the Lucas-Spielberg classic. Rated PG for violence and profanity. 102m. **DIR:** Anthony M. Dawson. **CAST:** Christopher Connelly, Marina Costa, Lee Van Cleef. **1985**

JUNGLE 2 JUNGLE ★★1/2 Tim Allen plays a New York stockbroker who discovers he's a father while seeking a divorce in a Venezuelan jungle. Returning to the big city with his son, he gains a better perception of what is important in life. Mildly humorous with some gorgeous rain-forest shots. Otherwise, predictable Disney fare reminiscent of the *Love Bug* series era. Rated PG for sexual innuendo. 95m. **DIR:** John Pasquin. **CAST:** Tim Allen, Sam Huntington, JoBeth Williams, Bob Dishy, Martin Short, Lolita Davidovich, David Ogden Stiers. **1997**

JUNGLE WARRIORS ★★1/2 The idea of a group of female models in Peru for a shoot in the jungle is quite absurd. If you can overlook the premise, though, this action film is modestly satisfying. It's rather like an episode of *Miami Vice* but with scantily dressed women packing machine guns. Rated R for violence, profanity, and nudity. 96m. **DIR:** Ernst R. von Theumer. **CAST:** Sybil Danning, Marjoe Gortner, Nina Van Pallandt, Paul Smith, John Vernon, Alex Cord, Woody Strode, Kai Wulfe, Dana Elcar. **1983**

JUNGLE WOMAN ★★ Lots of footage from *Captive Wild Woman* is used to pad out this sequel that, beginning with scientist J. Carrol Naish reviving ape-woman Acquanetta, has essentially the same plot. B&W; 60m. **DIR:** Reginald LeBorg. **CAST:** Acquanetta, Evelyn Ankers, J. Carrol Naish, Samuel S. Hinds, Milburn Stone. **1944**

JUNGLEGROUND ★★ Roddy Piper plays a police lieutenant who gets trapped inside "Jungleground," the worst crime-ridden area of the city. Apprehended by the local gang's vicious leader, Piper is set loose for a nasty game of cat and mouse. Rated R for violence and language. 90m. **DIR:** Don Allan. **CAST:** Roddy Piper, Tori Higginson, Peter Williams. **1994 DVD**

JUNIOR ★★★1/2 Arnold Schwarzenegger follows in the footsteps of Billy Crystal (*Rabbit Test*) as "the world's first pregnant man." The big guy pokes fun at his macho image by playing an absentminded scientist coerced into embryo implantation by not-so-ethical colleague Danny DeVito, complicating a budding romance with accident-prone scientist Emma Thompson. The film never quite achieves the heights of hilarity trod by *Twins*, but it does have its moments. Rated PG-13 for mature situations. 109m. **DIR:** Ivan Reitman. **CAST:** Arnold Schwarzenegger, Danny DeVito, Emma Thompson, Frank Langella, Pamela Reed, Judy Collins, James Eckhouse, Aida Turturro. **1994 DVD**

JUNIOR BONNER ★★★ A rodeo has-been, Steve McQueen, returns home for one last rousing performance in front of the home folks. McQueen is quite good as the soft-spoken cowboy who tries to make peace with his family. Robert Preston is a real scene stealer as his

hard-drinking carouser of a father. Rated PG. 103m. **DIR:** Sam Peckinpah. **CAST:** Steve McQueen, Robert Preston, Ida Lupino, Ben Johnson, Joe Don Baker. **1972 DVD**

JUNIOR'S GROOVE ★★★ Engaging tale of a piano prodigy who escapes his urban world through elaborate fantasy. When his home life becomes desperate, he's forced to team up with a kid from the streets in order to survive both what is real and imaginary. Lynn Whitfield is excellent as the prodigy's mother. Rated R for language, violence, and adult situations. 91m. **DIR:** Clement Virgo. **CAST:** Lynn Whitfield, Margot Kidder, Martin Villafana, Clark Johnson, Rainbow Sun Francks. **1997 DVD**

JUNIPER TREE, THE ★★★ Adaptation of a story by the Brothers Grimm about two sisters who use magical powers to battle for the affections of a widower. Probably only released in America because of the presence of alternative music star Bjork (here using her full name), this is a bleakly filmed tale that may appeal to art-house buffs, but which certainly will bore children to tears. Not rated; contains nothing objectionable. 78m. **DIR:** Nietzchka Keene. **CAST:** Bjork Gudmundsdottir, Byrndia Petra Bragadottir, Vladimir Orn Flygenring. **1987 DVD**

JUNKMAN, THE 🦃 From the makers of *Gone in 60 Seconds*, this sequel is tagged as the "chase film for the '80s." Rated PG. 99m. **DIR:** H. B. Halicki. **CAST:** Christopher Stone, Susan Shaw, Lang Jeffries, Lynda Day George. **1982 DVD**

JUNO AND THE PAYCOCK ★★1/2 Sean O'Casey's famous play gets the Hitchcock treatment, and the result is an intriguing blend of Irish melodrama and sinister moods. The setting is the Dublin uprising, the characters members of a poor family with more than its share of grief. A young unwed mother, an anticipated inheritance, and an unwise young man are the focus for various sorts of tragedy. B&W; 85m. **DIR:** Alfred Hitchcock. **CAST:** Sara Allgood, Edward Chapman, Sidney Morgan. **1929**

JUPITER'S DARLING ★★★ If you are in a lighthearted mood, this spoof of Hannibal's siege of Rome is a perfect way to pass time. Witty songs and situations coupled with a likable cast. 96m. **DIR:** George Sidney. **CAST:** Esther Williams, Howard Keel, George Sanders, Marge Champion, Gower Champion, Richard Haydn. **1955**

JUPITER'S THIGH ★★★★1/2 The delightful *Dear Inspector* duo is back in this delicious sequel directed by Philippe de Broca (*King of Hearts*). This time, the lady detective (Annie Girardot) and her Greek archaeologist lover (Philippe Noiret) get married and honeymoon—where else?—in Greece. But they aren't there long before they find themselves caught up in mayhem. It's great fun, served up with sophistication. In French with English subtitles. 90m. **DIR:** Philippe de Broca. **CAST:** Annie Girardot, Philippe Noiret. **1983**

JUPITER'S WIFE ★★★★★ When filmmaker Michel Negroponte met Maggie, a fortysomething homeless woman who lived in Manhattan's Central Park with her dogs, he was struck by her good cheer and the complexity of her seemingly incoherent ramblings. So he spent two years meeting with and filming her, gradually uncovering the history that led to her situation. After watching this utterly compelling documentary, you'll never again view "those people" as faceless nuisances. Not rated. 78m. **DIR:** Michel Negroponte. **1995**

JURASSIC PARK ★★★★ In this adaptation from the novel by Michael Crichton, dinosaurs are genetically re-created to populate the ultimate theme park, and a special few are allowed a sneak preview. Awe and wonder soon turns to terror as the creatures break out of their confines and go on a rampage. Rated PG-13 for violence. 120m. **DIR:** Steven Spielberg. **CAST:** Sam Neill, Laura Dern, Jeff Goldblum, Richard Attenborough, Bob Peck, Martin Ferrero, B. D. Wong, Samuel L. Jackson, Wayne Knight, Joseph Mazzello, Ariana Richards. **1993 DVD**

•JURASSIC PARK III ★★ Talk about diminished expectations; with the single exception of Sam Neill, returning as the first film's Dr. Alan Grant, the human cast members of this suspenseless dud *deserve* to be eaten . . . and as rapidly as possible, particularly shrieking female lead Téa Leoni. They're among a half-dozen folks who land on Isla Sorna—breeding facility for the dinosaurs that wreaked havoc in the first two films—due to the flimsiest of reasons, and thereafter attempt to dodge dinos with less intelligence than we'd expect from any cub scout. Don't bother. Rated PG-13 for intense sci-fi terror and violence. 92m. **DIR:** Joe Johnston. **CAST:** Sam Neill, William H. Macy, Téa Leoni, Alessandro Nivola, Trevor Morgan, Michael Jeter. **2001 DVD**

JUROR, THE ★★1/2 A juror on a high-profile Mafia trial is terrorized by a hoodlum (Alec Baldwin) who wants her to hang the jury. The film is hokey and contrived, and its resemblance to *Trial by Jury* (1994) may be more than coincidental, but this version of the story is a marginal improvement, sparked by Baldwin's succulently hammy performance. Rated R for violence, profanity, and brief nudity. 107m. **DIR:** Brian Gibson. **CAST:** Demi Moore, Alec Baldwin, James Gandolfini, Joseph Gordon-Levitt, Anne Heche, Lindsay Crouse. **1996 DVD**

JURY DUTY ★★ Cashing in on America's obsession with the O. J. Simpson murder trial, this spoofs the jury system in general and the sequestering of jurors in particular. Pauly Shore portrays a goofy loser who parlays his position as juror number six into a luxury vacation. Rated PG-13 for profanity. 88m. **DIR:** John Fortenberry. **CAST:** Pauly Shore, Tia Carrere, Stanley Tucci, Brian Doyle-Murray, Abe Vigoda, Charles Napier. **1995**

JUST A GIGOLO 🦃 Prussian aristocrat ends up as a disillusioned male prostitute. 96m. **DIR:** David Hemmings. **CAST:** David Bowie, Sydne Rome, Kim Novak, David Hemmings, Marlene Dietrich, Maria Schell, Curt Jurgens. **1978**

JUST ANOTHER GIRL ON THE I.R.T. ★★★1/2 Powerful debut from director Leslie Harris, who draws a memorable performance out of Ariyan Johnson as a determined Brooklyn high-school student attempting to make a better life for herself. Her dreams of higher education take a backseat to reality when she finds herself pregnant. Excellent slice-of-life drama is sometimes funny, sometimes sad, but always interesting and well directed. Rated R for language and adult situations. 96m. **DIR:** Leslie Harris. **CAST:** Ariyan Johnson, Kevin Thigpen. **1993**

JUST AROUND THE CORNER ★★★ This bucket of sap has nearly too-sweet Shirley Temple ending the Depression by charming a crusty sourpussed millionaire into providing new jobs. The ridiculous becomes sublime when Shirley dances with the incomparable Bill Robinson. B&W; 70m. **DIR:** Irving Cummings. **CAST:** Shirley Temple, Joan Davis, Charles Farrell, Bill Robinson, Bert Lahr. **1938**

JUST BEFORE DAWN ★★ Same old, same old as characters head into the wilderness—after being warned not to—where they are besieged by mountain men. Deborah Benson delivers a performance that is far better than this film deserves. Rated R for violence and profanity. 90m. **DIR:** Jeff Lieberman. **CAST:** Deborah Benson, George Kennedy, Chris Lemmon. **1982**

JUST BETWEEN FRIENDS ★★★1/2 Mary Tyler Moore stars in this big-screen soap opera as a homemaker happily married to Ted Danson. She meets TV news reporter Christine Lahti and they become friends. They have a lot in common—including being in love with the same man. Rated PG-13 for profanity and suggested sex. 115m. **DIR:** Allan Burns. **CAST:** Mary Tyler Moore, Christine Lahti, Sam Waterston, Ted Danson, Mark Blum. **1986**

JUST CAUSE ★★★1/2 Law professor Sean Connery is coaxed into action when a condemned killer appeals to his sense of justice. Part *Silence of the Lambs* and part *Cape Fear*, this is an effective suspense thriller. High-voltage performances by a strong cast and sleight-of-hand direction by Arne Glimcher keep the viewer involved despite the familiarity of some of the story elements and a couple of contrived plot twists (taken directly from John Katzenbach's original novel). Rated R for violence and profanity. 102m. **DIR:** Arne Glimcher. **CAST:** Sean Connery, Laurence Fishburne, Kate Capshaw, Blair Underwood, Ed Harris, Christopher Murray, Ruby Dee, Scarlett Johansson, Daniel J. Travanti, Ned Beatty, Liz Torres, Kevin McCarthy, Hope Lange, Chris Sarandon, George Plimpton. **1995 DVD**

JUST FOR THE HELL OF IT ★★ Teen vandals terrorize a Florida town. Not rated, but unsuitable for young children. 88m. **DIR:** Herschell Gordon Lewis. **CAST:** Rodney Bedell, Ray Sager, Nancy Lee Noble. **1967 DVD**

JUST IMAGINE ★★ Cornball character from 1930 is suspended for fifty years and wakes up in New York of 1980. Trifling plot takes a backseat to the special effects created in part by some of the team from *King Kong* and later used in the *Flash Gordon* serials. Incredibly silly, this science-fiction musical has one plus: a beautiful Maureen O'Sullivan in one of her first roles. They don't make 'em like this anymore, and it's amazing that they ever did. B&W; 108m. **DIR:** David Butler. **CAST:** El Brendel, Maureen O'Sullivan, John Garrick, Kenneth Thompson, Mischa Auer, Ivan Lino, Marjorie White, Hobart Bosworth. **1930**

JUST LIKE A WOMAN ★★★ Breezy performances punctuate this offbeat comedy about cross-dressing. An American businessman in London falls for his landlady who finds her new tenant quite an eyeful. When they finally get together, she learns of his desire to wear women's clothing. How they come to grips with his desire while maintaining a normal relationship provides plenty of insight and laughter. Rated R for language. 102m. **DIR:** Christopher Monger. **CAST:** Julie Walters, Adrian Pasdar, Paul Freeman. **1992**

JUST LOOKING ★★★ A teenager in the 1950s devotes his summer to trying to watch a couple—any couple—having sex. Director Jason Alexander (of TV's *Seinfeld*) covers coming-of-age material with an actor's flair for sitcom shtick, while the good performances gloss over the unsettling fact that the young hero is a budding Peeping Tom. Rated R for profanity and sexual scenes. 97m. **DIR:** Jason Alexander. **CAST:** Ryan Merriman, Joey Franquinha, Peter Onorati, Gretchen Mol, Amy Braverman, Patti LuPone. **1999 DVD**

JUST ONE OF THE GIRLS 🦃 Lowbrow teen fantasy has Corey Haim cross-dressing on campus to avoid the school bully and get closer to the bully's sister. Exactly what you'd expect, but worse. Rated R for nudity and language. 94m. **DIR:** Michael Keusch. **CAST:** Corey Haim, Nicole Eggert, Cameron Bancroft, Gabe Khouth. **1993**

JUST ONE OF THE GUYS ★★★ A sort of reverse *Tootsie*, this surprisingly restrained teen-lust comedy stars Joyce Hyser as an attractive young woman who switches high schools and sexes. The premise is flimsy and forced, but director Lisa Gottlieb and her cast keep the viewer entertained. Rated PG-13 for nudity, violence, and profanity. 88m. **DIR:** Lisa Gottlieb. **CAST:** Joyce Hyser, Clayton Rohner, Billy Jacoby, Toni Hudson. **1985**

JUST ONE TIME ★★1/2 Director-writer Lane Janger stars as Anthony, a New York firefighter who wants his girlfriend to consent to a three-way with another woman before their upcoming wedding. She agrees to go along with the plan if her husband will share their bed with another man. The complications that ensue are neither as funny nor as dramatic as Janger would lead us to believe. Guillermo Diaz stands out as the gay neighbor who has his eye on the firefighter. Rated R for adult situations and language. 111m. **DIR:** Lane Janger. **CAST:** Lane Janger, Joelle Carter, Guillermo Diaz, Jennifer Esposito. **1999 DVD**

JUST TELL ME WHAT YOU WANT ★★ Alan King gives a fine performance in this otherwise forgettable film as an executive who attempts to get his mistress (Ali MacGraw) back. She's in love with a younger man (Peter Weller). Rated R. 112m. **DIR:** Sidney Lumet. **CAST:** Alan King, Ali MacGraw, Peter Weller, Myrna Loy, Keenan Wynn, Tony Roberts, Dina Merrill. **1980**

JUST THE TICKET ★★ Dull comedy-romance is sabotaged by a complete lack of chemistry between stars Andy Garcia and Andie MacDowell. Rated R for profanity. 112m. **DIR:** Richard Wenk. **CAST:** Andy Garcia, Andie MacDowell, Elizabeth Ashley, Ron Leibman, Chris Lemmon, Don Novello, Abe Vigoda. **1998 DVD**

JUST THE WAY YOU ARE ★★1/2 Kristy McNichol gives a fine performance as a pretty flautist who cleverly overcomes the need to wear a leg brace. But this deception brings an unexpected moment of truth. Even the plodding direction of Edouard Molinaro can't prevent this well-written work from occasionally being witty, and touching. Rated PG. 95m. **DIR:** Edouard Molinaro. **CAST:** Kristy McNichol, Michael Ontkean, Kaki Hunter. **1984**

•JUST VISITING ★★★1/2 This remake of the 1993 blockbuster *Les Visiteurs* (nine Cesar nominations)

transports a twelfth-century nobleman and his servant into modern Chicago. The Dark Age duo meet one of the count's descendants and must return home in the only time corridor that allows them to save the life of the nobleman's fiancée. This fish-out-of-water story about culture clash and self-assertion is as clunky as the count's armor but very funny. Rated PG-13 for language, crude humor, and violence. 88m. **DIR:** Jean-Marie Gaubert. **CAST:** Jean Reno, Christian Clavier, Christina Applegate, Tara Reid, Matthew Ross, Bridgette Wilson-Sampras, Malcolm McDowell. **2001 DVD**

JUST WILLIAM'S LUCK ★★ Based on a series of children's books that were popular in Great Britain, this isn't likely to do as well with American kids. William and his pals are mischief-makers who spend most of the film getting into various sorts of trouble. 87m. **DIR:** Val Guest. **CAST:** William Graham, Garry Marsh. **1947**

JUST WRITE ★★★1/2 Beverly Hills tour-bus driver finds a new focus to his life when he meets the actress he adores and she mistakes him for a screenwriter. Feel-good romantic comedy is a movie lover's delight filled with interesting characters and the usual setbacks before the final fade-out. This one is really like "the kind they used to make." Rated PG-13 for mild profanity and adult situations. 95m. **DIR:** Andrew Gallerani. **CAST:** Jeremy Piven, Sherilyn Fenn, JoBeth Williams, Jeffrey Sams, Alex Rocco, Wallace Shawn, Costas Mandylor, Yeardley Smith. **1997 DVD**

JUST YOU AND ME, KID ★★ The delights of George Burns as an ex–vaudeville performer do not mask the worthless plot in this tale of Burns's attempt to hide a young runaway (Brooke Shields) fleeing a drug dealer. Shields's inability to move with Burns's rhythm rapidly becomes annoying. Rated PG for mild language and brief nudity. 93m. **DIR:** Leonard Stern. **CAST:** George Burns, Brooke Shields, Ray Bolger, Lorraine Gary, Burl Ives. **1979**

JUST YOUR LUCK ★★1/2 In this Quentin Tarantino wannabe, patrons of an all-night diner try to decide what to do with a $6 million lottery ticket after its owner has a heart attack. A good ensemble cast can't do much with the weak dialogue and weaker plot. Rated R for violence and profanity. 88m. **DIR:** Gary Auerbach. **CAST:** Virginia Madsen, Sean Patrick Flanery, Ernie Hudson, Alanna Ubach, Vince Vaughn, Jon Favreau, Jon Polito, Mike Starr, Carroll Baker, John Lurie, Flea, Bill Erwin. **1996**

JUSTIN MORGAN HAD A HORSE ★★★ Agreeable Disney film focuses on the ingenuity and foresight of a poor Vermont schoolteacher following the Revolutionary War. He trained and bred the first Morgan horse, which was noted for its speed, strength, and stamina. 91m. **DIR:** Hollingsworth Morse. **CAST:** Don Murray, Lana Wood, Gary Crosby. **1972**

JUSTINE ★★ This compression of four volumes of Laurence Durrell's *Alexandria Quartet* into one film tells the story of a Middle Eastern prostitute who rises to a position of power in her country. Fans of the novels will be disappointed; those unfamiliar with the story will be confused. Rated R for nudity and sexual situations. 117m. **DIR:** George Cukor. **CAST:** Anouk Aimée, Dirk Bogarde, Robert Forster, Anna Karina, Philippe Noiret, Michael York, John Vernon, Jack Albertson, Cliff Gorman, Michael Constantine, Severn Darden. **1969**

K

K-9 ★★★ James Belushi is terrific as a maverick cop whose single-minded pursuit of a drug dealer (Kevin Tighe) makes him a less-than-desirable partner. Enter Jerry Lee, a feisty police dog who proves to be more than a match for Belushi. Rated PG-13 for profanity and violence. 95m. **DIR:** Rod Daniel. **CAST:** James Belushi, Mel Harris, Kevin Tighe. **1989 DVD**

•K-PAX ★★1/2 A transient in a mental institution (Kevin Spacey) claims to be from outer space; his psychiatrist (Jeff Bridges) thinks there's more to him than meets the eye. The acting is good but the script is too solemn and sentimental, the ending too carefully ambiguous to be satisfying. Rated PG-13 for brief violence and mild profanity. 120m. **DIR:** Iain Softley. **CAST:** Kevin Spacey, Jeff Bridges, Mary McCormack, Alfre Woodard, David Patrick Kelly. **2001 DVD**

KADOSH ★★1/2 Two sisters in an Orthodox Jewish community are victimized by their patriarchal society—one is forced into a loveless marriage, the other ostracized for failing to bear children. The humanism is admirable, but the message is dulled by shallow characters, redundant dialogue, and leaden pacing. Rather than showing spirits crushed by tradition, the film portrays a culture with no spirit in the first place. In Hebrew with English subtitles. Not rated; contains several sexual scenes. 110m. **DIR:** Amos Gitai. **CAST:** Yael Abecassis, Yussuf Abu-Warda, Meital Barda, Yoram Hattab, Sami Hori. **1999 DVD**

KAFKA ★★★1/2 This odd, tongue-in-cheek thriller will delight some viewers and annoy others. About an insurance claims clerk in Prague, circa 1919, it's a study in paranoia, with the title character being thrust into a world of plots and counterplots. It has little to do with the life and writings of Franz Kafka. Rated PG-13 for violence. 98m. **DIR:** Steven Soderbergh. **CAST:** Jeremy Irons, Theresa Russell, Joel Grey, Ian Holm, Jeroen Krabbé, Armin Mueller-Stahl, Alec Guinness, Brian Glover, Keith Allen, Robert Flemyng. **1992**

KAGEMUSHA ★★★★★ A 70 year old Akira Kurosawa outdoes himself in this epic masterpiece about honor and illusion. Kurosawa popularized the samurai genre—which has been described as the Japanese equivalent of the Western—in America with his breathtaking, action-packed films. This is yet another feast for the eyes, heart, and mind. Rated PG. 159m. **DIR:** Akira Kurosawa. **CAST:** Tatsuya Nakadai. **1980**

KALIFORNIA ★★★★1/2 This *Bad Lands* for the 1990s is a tense, chilling psychodrama and darkly comic road movie. While visiting America's most infamous murder sites to develop material for a book, a liberal journalist and his photographer lover share a convertible and traveling expenses with a white-trash sociopath and his incredibly dumb girlfriend. The characters are brilliantly developed and interconnected during the trek. Rated R for sex, violence, and profanity. 117m. **DIR:** Do-

minic Sena. **CAST:** Brad Pitt, Juliette Lewis, David Duchovny, Michelle Forbes. **1993 DVD**

KAMA SUTRA: A TALE OF LOVE ★★1/2 This exotic adult fable is rich in mythic sixteenth-century Indian atmosphere, but plays like a harem soap opera. Tara is a spoiled princess who marries into royalty. Maya is her sensuous servant who seduces Tara's husband on their wedding night and reenters her court as chief courtesan for Tara's decadent spouse. The film's attempt to connect with the spiritual embodiment of *The Kama Sutra of Vatsayana* only partly succeeds. Not rated; contains strong language, nudity, sex, and violence. 114m. **DIR:** Mira Nair. **CAST:** Indira Varma, Sarita Choudhury, Naveen Andrews, Ramon Tikaram. **1996 DVD**

KAMERADSCHAFT ★★★1/2 The story development is slow, but the concept is so strong and the sense of cross-cultural camaraderie so stirring that the film remains impressive. The story concerns French miners getting trapped by a mine disaster, with German miners attempting a daring rescue. In German and French with English subtitles. B&W; 87m. **DIR:** G. W. Pabst. **CAST:** George Chalia, David Mendaille, Ernest Busch. **1931**

KAMIKAZE 89 ★★★ The late Rainer Werner Fassbinder stars in this bizarre fantasy-thriller set in a decadent German city in 1989. A bomb has been planted in the headquarters of a giant conglomerate and a police lieutenant (Fassbinder) has very little time to locate it. In German with English subtitles. 90m. **DIR:** Wolf Gremm. **CAST:** Rainer Werner Fassbinder, Gunther Kaufmann, Brigitte Mira, Franco Nero. **1983**

KANAL ★★★★ Andrzej Wajda's compelling war drama about the Polish resistance fighters during World War II brought international acclaim to the Polish cinema. This film explores the dreams, the despair, and the struggle of a generation who refused to be held captive in their own land by the Nazi war machine in 1944. In Polish with English subtitles. B&W; 96m. **DIR:** Andrzej Wajda. **CAST:** Teresa Izewska. **1957**

•**KANDAHAR** ★★★★ Lone artificial legs ride parachutes into a desert Red Cross camp along the Iran-Afghan border. Little girls are instructed to pretend to be ants if their home imprisonment under Taliban rule is unbearable. These and other images resonate throughout this compelling docudrama as expatriate Afghan journalist Nafas reenters her native land in search of a sister who lost both legs in a land-mine explosion and plans to commit suicide. Bandits and Taliban repression interrupt the rescue mission as Nafas treks through an overload of human misery. In Farsi with English subtitles. Not rated. 85m. **DIR:** Mohsen Makhmalbaf. **CAST:** Niloufar Pazira, Hassan Tantai, Sadou Teymouri. **2001**

KANDYLAND ★★★ Fairly interesting story centers around a girl's desire to make a living at exotic dancing. The nice thing about this film is that it concentrates on the people involved, not the dances. Rated R for nudity, profanity, and violence. 94m. **DIR:** Robert Schnitzer. **CAST:** Sandahl Bergman, Kim Evenson. **1987**

KANGAROO ★★★★ Real-life husband and wife Colin Friels and Judy Davis give superb performances in this Australian film adaptation of the semiautobiographical novel by D. H. Lawrence. Writer Richard Somers (Friels), a thinly veiled version of Lawrence, finds himself vilified by critics in his native England for writing sexually suggestive novels and, with his German-born wife Harriet (Davis), journeys down under in search of a better life. Rated R for violence, nudity, and profanity. 100m. **DIR:** Tim Burstall. **CAST:** Colin Friels, Judy Davis, John Walton, Hugh Keays-Byrne. **1986**

KANSAN, THE ★★★ Tough, two-fisted Richard Dix sets his jaw and routs the baddies in a wide-open prairie town but must then contend with a corrupt official in this enjoyable Western, the third to pair him with Jane Wyatt and heavies Victor Jory and Albert Dekker. B&W; 79m. **DIR:** George Archainbaud. **CAST:** Richard Dix, Jane Wyatt, Victor Jory, Albert Dekker, Eugene Pallette, Robert Armstrong. **1943**

KANSAS ★★ Lethargic melodrama has fresh-faced Andrew McCarthy teaming up with sleazy Matt Dillon, who cons him into robbing a bank. Rated R for profanity and violence. 105m. **DIR:** David Stevens. **CAST:** Matt Dillon, Andrew McCarthy, Leslie Hope, Kyra Sedgwick. **1988 DVD**

KANSAS CITY ★★ Robert Altman's ode to his jazz roots is an absolute mess, a film that wastes a good cast and comes alive only during its musical interludes. The ridiculous plot involves a working-class girl who hopes to leverage her lover from a crime lord by kidnapping a stoned socialite. Any potential drama is lost during interminable speeches—all deadly dull. Rated R for violence, profanity, and drug use. 115m. **DIR:** Robert Altman. **CAST:** Jennifer Jason Leigh, Miranda Richardson, Harry Belafonte, Michael Murphy, Dermot Mulroney, Steve Buscemi. **1996**

KANSAS CITY CONFIDENTIAL ★★★ Four masked men pull a split-second-timed bank heist and get away while innocent ex-con John Payne gets the third degree. After the police lose interest in him, Payne follows the robbers to Guatemala. Good photography and atmosphere, but overlong. B&W; 98m. **DIR:** Phil Karlson. **CAST:** John Payne, Coleen Gray, Preston Foster, Lee Van Cleef, Neville Brand, Jack Elam. **1952**

KANSAS CITY MASSACRE, THE ★★★ Dale Robertson reprises his role of the outlandish Melvin Purvis that he originated in 1974's *Melvin Purvis, G-Man*. Practically every notorious gangster who ever lived meets the unstoppable G-Man in this made-for-TV film. Watch for the acting debut of the notorious ex-governor of Georgia, Lester Maddox. Here he's governor of Oklahoma. 120m. **DIR:** Dan Curtis. **CAST:** Dale Robertson, Bo Hopkins, Robert Walden, Mills Watson, Scott Brady, Harris Yulin. **1975**

KANSAS CYCLONE ★★★ A crooked mine owner is holding up gold ore shipments from other mines and running the ore back through his dummy mine. Don Barry, an undercover marshal, poses as a geologist to catch the bandits. The action, under the capable hands of Yakima Canutt, and a couple of interesting subplots from screenwriter Oliver Drake lift this one above the average. B&W; 58m. **DIR:** George Sherman. **CAST:** Don Barry, Lynn Merrick. **1941**

KANSAS PACIFIC ★★1/2 Railroad drama set in pre–Civil War days has rangy Sterling Hayden romancing Eve Miller and battling pro-Confederate saboteurs. 73m. **DIR:** Ray Nazarro. **CAST:** Sterling Hayden, Eve Miller, Barton MacLane, Douglas Fowley, Myron Healey, Clayton Moore, Reed Hadley. **1953 DVD**

KANSAS TERRORS ★★★ The Three Mesquiteers must recover gold paid them for selling a herd of horses. They encounter a tyrant who rules an island in the Caribbean. B&W; 57m. **DIR:** George Sherman. **CAST:** Robert Livingston, Duncan Renaldo, Raymond Hatton, Jacqueline Wells, Howard Hickman. **1939**

KAOS ★★★1/2 Italian writer-directors Paolo and Vittorio Taviani adapted four short stories by Luigi Pirandello for this sumptuously photographed film about peasant life in Sicily. For all its beauty and style, this is a disappointing, uneven work. The first two stories are wonderful, but the final pair leave a lot to be desired. In Italian with English subtitles. Rated R for nudity and violence. 188m. **DIR:** Paolo Taviani, Vittorio Taviani. **CAST:** Margarita Lozano, Enrica Maria Mudugno, Omero Antonutti. **1986**

KARATE COP 🦃 Futuristic chop-socky about the last cop on Earth and a beautiful scientist who team up to find a precious stone. Rated R for violence and language. 91m. **DIR:** Alan Roberts. **CAST:** Ron Marchini, Carrie Chambers, David Carradine, Michael Bristow. **1992**

KARATE KID, THE ★★★★1/2 A heartwarming, surefire crowd pleaser, this believable and touching work about the hazards of high school days and adolescence will have you cheering during its climax and leave you with a smile on your face. You'll find yourself rooting for the put-upon hero, Daniel (Ralph Macchio), and booing the bad guys. Rated PG for violence and profanity. 126m. **DIR:** John G. Avildsen. **CAST:** Ralph Macchio, Noriyuki "Pat" Morita, Elisabeth Shue. **1984 DVD**

KARATE KID PART II, THE ★★★1/2 This second in the *Karate Kid* series begins moments after the conclusion of the first film. Mr. Miyagi (Noriyuki "Pat" Morita) receives word that his father, residing in Okinawa, is dying, so he drops everything and heads for home, with young Daniel (Ralph Macchio) along for the ride. Once in Okinawa, Miyagi encounters an old rival and an old love, while Daniel makes a new enemy and a new love. Rated PG for mild violence. 113m. **DIR:** John G. Avildsen. **CAST:** Ralph Macchio, Noriyuki "Pat" Morita, Nobu McCarthy, Martin Kove, William Zabka. **1986**

KARATE KID PART III, THE ★★ Back for the third time as Daniel "The Karate Kid" LaRusso, Ralph Macchio prepares to defend his championship. Even the watchable Pat Morita can't make this one a winner. Rated PG. 111m. **DIR:** John G. Avildsen. **CAST:** Ralph Macchio, Noriyuki "Pat" Morita, Martin Kove. **1989**

•KATE AND LEOPOLD ★★★1/2 Delightful romantic comedy links an uptight advertising executive (Meg Ryan) with a nineteenth-century duke. Reacting to current technology and morality, Hugh Jackman resurrects a bit of Cary Grant's magic and charm. Ryan, unfortunately, maintains a "bad hair day" throughout most of the film in direct contrast to her impeccable love interest. Breckin Meyer, as Ryan's underachieving sibling, adds warmth and chuckles to this time-traveling love story. Rated PG-13 for language. 115m. **DIR:** James Mangold. **CAST:** Meg Ryan, Hugh Jackman, Breckin Meyer, Liev Schreiber. **2001 DVD**

KATHERINE ★★★ This television movie follows Sissy Spacek from a middle-class young student to a social activist and finally to an underground terrorist. Spacek is very convincing in this demanding role. The movie tends to remind one of the Patty Hearst case and features good, solid storytelling. 100m. **DIR:** Jeremy Paul Kagan. **CAST:** Sissy Spacek, Art Carney, Henry Winkler, Jane Wyatt, Julie Kavner. **1975**

KATIE'S PASSION ★★ The story of a poor country girl's struggle to survive in Holland during the economic crisis of the 1880s. Director Paul Verhoeven misses the mark with this saga. Rutger Hauer delivers a rather lackluster performance as a vain banker. Not much passion, or anything else here. In Dutch with English subtitles. 107m. **DIR:** Paul Verhoeven. **CAST:** Rutger Hauer, Monique van de Ven. **1988**

KAVIK THE WOLF DOG ★★★ This average made-for-TV movie is the story of Kavik, a brave sled dog who journeys back to the boy he loves when a ruthless, wealthy man transports him from Alaska to Seattle. 104m. **DIR:** Peter Carter. **CAST:** Ronny Cox, John Ireland, Linda Sorenson, Andrew Ian McMillan, Chris Wiggins. **1980**

KAZAAM ★★ Basketball superstar Shaquille O'Neal is a likable genie prepared to deliver three wishes to a troubled boy. The plot is overly involved with the boy's estranged father's illegal dealings, his mother's desire to remarry, and a gang of hoodlums making his life miserable. There are as many tense scenes as comic ones, which gives the film a split personality unlikely to satisfy either the fluff or action seeker. Uneven performances by many of the key players don't help either. Rated PG for violence. 90m. **DIR:** Paul Michael Glaser. **CAST:** Shaquille O'Neal, Francis Capra, Ally Walker, James Acheson. **1996**

KEATON RIDES AGAIN/RAILROADER ★★★★ Coupled delightfully in this Buster Keaton program are a biographical profile with interviews, and a solo opus of Buster in trouble on a handcar rolling along the seemingly endless tracks of the Canadian National Railway. Both were lovingly produced by the National Film Board of Canada less than a year before the great comic's life ended. B&W; 81m. **DIR:** John Spotton, Gerald Potterton. **CAST:** Buster Keaton. **1965**

KEATON'S COP ★★ Former mobster Abe Vigoda is on a hit list and requires police protection. Lee Majors becomes his macho bodyguard in this shoot-'em-up that can't decide whether it's a comedy or actioner. Rated R for profanity and violence. 95m. **DIR:** Robert Burge. **CAST:** Lee Majors, Abe Vigoda, Don Rickles. **1990**

KEEP, THE ★★ A centuries-old presence awakens in an old castle. Rated R for nudity and violence. 96m. **DIR:** Michael Mann. **CAST:** Ian McKellen, Alberta Watson, Scott Glenn, Jurgen Prochnow. **1983**

KEEP THE CHANGE ★★★1/2 An uninspired artist (William L. Petersen) realizes he needs to return to his family's ranch in Montana to get back to his roots. Not rated; contains implied sex. 95m. **DIR:** Andy Tennant. **CAST:** William L. Petersen, Lolita Davidovich, Rachel Ticotin, Jack Palance, Buck Henry, Fred Dalton Thompson, Jeff Kober, Lois Smith. **1992**

KEEPER, THE ★★ The owner of an insane asylum preys on the wealthy families of his charges. Rated R. 96m. **DIR:** T. Y. Drake. **CAST:** Christopher Lee, Sally Gray. **1984**

KEEPER OF THE CITY ★★1/2 Anthony LaPaglia flips out—too much abuse as a child—and embarks on a one-man crusade to rid Chicago of its aging crime lords. Lou Gossett's hardened and weary cop lifts this routine

made-for-cable thriller slightly above other genre entries, no thanks to Gerald DePego's pedestrian adaptation of his own novel. 95m. **DIR:** Bobby Roth. **CAST:** Louis Gossett Jr., Anthony LaPaglia, Peter Coyote, Renee Soutendijk. **1992**

KEEPER OF THE FLAME ★★★★ In this second teaming of Spencer Tracy and Katharine Hepburn, he is a noted journalist who plans to write a tribute to a respected and admired patriot killed in a vehicle accident; she is the patriot's widow. Fine adult drama. B&W; 100m. **DIR:** George Cukor. **CAST:** Spencer Tracy, Katharine Hepburn, Richard Whorf, Margaret Wycherly, Forrest Tucker, Percy Kilbride, Darryl Hickman, Donald Meek, Howard DaSilva. **1942**

KEEPING THE FAITH ★★★★ First-time director Edward Norton's scrumptious romantic triangle begins stiffly but soon settles into a consistent groove: The broad gestures mellow out, and the character interaction becomes more important than attempts to milk laughs from Stuart Blumberg's improbable tale, which involves a Roman Catholic priest, a rabbi, and the vivacious, corporate executive who has reentered their lives after a two-decade absence. As children, these three had been inseparable; the question now is whether the new element of romantic tension will strengthen or shatter their close rapport. What eventually occurs proves amusing, poignant, and surprisingly believable. Rated PG-13 for sexual candor. 129m. **DIR:** Edward Norton. **CAST:** Ben Stiller, Edward Norton, Jenna Elfman, Anne Bancroft, Eli Wallach, Ron Rifkin, Milos Forman, Holland Taylor. **2000 DVD**

KEEPING TRACK ★★★1/2 Superior action thriller follows Michael Sarrazin and Margot Kidder as two innocent bystanders who witness a murder and a robbery. Once they find the $5 million, they must learn to trust one another because everyone is after them, including the CIA and Russian spies. This one will keep you guessing. Rated R. 102m. **DIR:** Robin Spry. **CAST:** Michael Sarrazin, Margot Kidder, Alan Scarfe, Ken Pogue. **1985**

KELLY'S HEROES ★★★ An amiable rip-off of *The Dirty Dozen*, this 1970 war comedy was funnier at the time of its original release. Stoic Clint Eastwood is stuck with a bunch of goof-offs (Telly Savalas, Donald Sutherland, Don Rickles, and Gavin McLeod) as he searches for Nazi treasure. Sutherland's World War II hippie ("Give me those positive waves, man") is a little tough to take these days, but this caper picture still has its moments. Rated PG. 145m. **DIR:** Brian G. Hutton. **CAST:** Clint Eastwood, Telly Savalas, Donald Sutherland, Don Rickles, Gavin MacLeod, Carroll O'Connor. **1970 DVD**

KENNEDY (TV MINISERIES) ★★★★ This outstanding made-for-TV miniseries is even more enjoyable when viewed in one sitting. This upfront portrait of John F. Kennedy from presidential campaign to assassination shows the warts as well as the charm and mystique of the entire Kennedy clan. The cast is excellent. An easy-to-swallow history lesson on Camelot. 278m. **DIR:** Jim Goddard. **CAST:** Martin Sheen, John Shea, Blair Brown, E. G. Marshall, Geraldine Fitzgerald, Vincent Gardenia. **1983 DVD**

KENNEL MURDER CASE, THE ★★★★ A classic detective thriller, this features William Powell as the dapper Philo Vance solving a locked-door murder. The supporting players complement his suave characterization perfectly. Dated, but good. B&W; 73m. **DIR:** Michael Curtiz. **CAST:** William Powell, Mary Astor, Eugene Pallette, Ralph Morgan, Jack LaRue. **1933 DVD**

KENT STATE ★★★★ Disturbing docudrama traces the events leading up to the killing of four students by National Guardsmen during a 1970 antiwar protest. Objectively filmed, this TV movie is a memorable and effective history lesson. 180m. **DIR:** James Goldstone. **CAST:** Jane Fleiss, Charley Lang, Talia Balsam, Keith Gordon, John Getz, Jeff McCracken. **1981**

KENTUCKIAN, THE ★★★ Pushing west in the 1820s, Burt Lancaster bucks all odds to reach Texas and begin a new life. A good mix of history, adventure, romance, and comedy makes this one worth a family watching. 104m. **DIR:** Burt Lancaster. **CAST:** Burt Lancaster, Diana Lynn, Dianne Foster, Walter Matthau, John Carradine, Una Merkel. **1955 DVD**

KENTUCKY FRIED MOVIE ★★★ The first film outing of the creators of *Airplane!* is an on-again, off-again collection of comedy skits. Directed by John Landis, the best bits involve a Bruce Lee takeoff and a surprise appearance by Wally and the Beaver. Rated R. 78m. **DIR:** John Landis. **CAST:** Evan Kim, Master Bong SooHan, Bill Bixby, Donald Sutherland. **1977 DVD**

KENTUCKY KERNELS ★★1/2 Wheeler and Woolsey (a now-forgotten early Thirties comedy team) and *Our Gang/Little Rascals* star Spanky McFarland travel to the heart of Dixie to claim an inheritance. Breezy, slapstick comedy has aged surprisingly well. One of the first features directed by George Stevens. B&W; 75m. **DIR:** George Stevens. **CAST:** Bert Wheeler, Robert Woolsey, Mary Carlisle, Spanky McFarland. **1934**

KENTUCKY RIFLE ★★1/2 Pioneers going west are stranded in Comanche country. They must barter the Kentucky long rifles in their wagons for safe passage. Passable oater. 80m. **DIR:** Carl K. Hittleman. **CAST:** Chill Wills, Jeanne Cagney, Cathy Downes, Lance Fuller, Sterling Holloway. **1955**

KEROUAC ★★★ Reenactments, interviews, and early television clips are used to probe the mental illness and alcoholism of Beat writer Jack Kerouac. The old TV clips are more intriguing and revealing than the cheesy scenes filmed with an actor. This touches all the bases but doesn't provide much insight, even if it did garner awards when first released. Narrated by Peter Coyote. Not rated; contains profanity. B&W/color; 73m. **DIR:** John Antonelli. **CAST:** Jack Kerouac, William S. Burroughs, Allen Ginsberg, Jack Coulter. **1984**

KEY, THE ★★1/2 A strange, moody curio, directed in somber tones by British filmmaker Carol Reed, and noteworthy as the first British film to star Sophia Loren. She plays a kept woman who comes with the London flat belonging to a succession of tugboat captains during World War II. B&W; 125m. **DIR:** Carol Reed. **CAST:** William Holden, Sophia Loren, Trevor Howard, Oscar Homolka, Bernard Lee. **1958**

KEY EXCHANGE ★★★ This movie is a good study of modern-day relationships. Brooke Adams and Ben Masters play a couple making a firm commitment in their relationship. Daniel Stern is hilarious as a friend of the couple who is going through his own domestic crisis. Rated R for language, sex, and nudity. 96m. **DIR:** Barnet

Kellman. **CAST:** Brooke Adams, Ben Masters, Daniel Stern, Danny Aiello, Tony Roberts. **1985**

KEY LARGO ★★★★ Humphrey Bogart is one of a group of dissimilar individuals held in a run-down Florida Keys hotel by a band of hoodlums on the lam. Lauren Bacall looks to him as her white knight, but as a disillusioned war vet he has had enough violence. That is, until a crime kingpin (Edward G. Robinson) pushes things a little too far. B&W; 101m. **DIR:** John Huston. **CAST:** Humphrey Bogart, Lauren Bacall, Edward G. Robinson, Claire Trevor, Lionel Barrymore. **1948 DVD**

KEY TO REBECCA, THE ★★1/2 Ken Follett's best-selling World War II-set novel becomes a rather stodgy TV movie, with David Soul as a Nazi spy involved in a battle of wits with British officer Cliff Robertson. It all looks pretty fake, though at least Follett's story holds your attention. 192m. **DIR:** David Hemmings. **CAST:** Cliff Robertson, David Soul, Season Hubley, Anthony Quayle, David Hemmings, Robert Culp. **1985**

KEY TO THE CITY ★★★1/2 Prim Loretta Young and roughneck Clark Gable meet at a mayor's convention in San Francisco, and a wacky and rocky romance follows. A much underrated movie with hilarious situations handled expertly by pros. Marilyn Maxwell's striptease is a hoot. B&W; 101m. **DIR:** George Sidney. **CAST:** Clark Gable, Loretta Young, Marilyn Maxwell, Frank Morgan, Lewis Stone, Raymond Burr, James Gleason, Raymond Walburn, Pamela Britton, Clinton Sundberg. **1950**

KEYS TO THE KINGDOM, THE ★★★1/2 Gregory Peck is a Scottish priest in this bleak tale of poverty and despotism in 1930s war-torn China. As the missionary who bests the odds, Peck is fine. B&W; 137m. **DIR:** John M. Stahl. **CAST:** Gregory Peck, Vincent Price, Thomas Mitchell, Roddy McDowall. **1944**

KEYS TO TULSA ★★1/2 This pulp crime-drama is also a dark multiple character study. The black sheep son of an oil tycoon returns to Tulsa after an unexplained absence; gets involved with a blackmail scheme; resurrects his relationship with an old flame, her gun-crazy brother, and druggie husband; and falls in lust with a zonked-out stripper. The film, like its characters, is all attitude with no real soul. Rated R for violence, nudity, sex, language, and drug use. 113m. **DIR:** Leslie Greif. **CAST:** Eric Stoltz, James Spader, Deborah Unger, Joanna Going, Michael Rooker, Mary Tyler Moore, James Coburn. **1996 DVD**

KEYSTONE COMEDIES: VOL. 1–5 ★★★ The Mack Sennett Studios produced some of the most celebrated slapstick of the silent screen. In these volumes great comic performers display some of their finest talents for some marvelous movie mayhem and magic. Silent. B&W; 4258. **DIR:** Roscoe Arbuckle. **CAST:** Roscoe "Fatty" Arbuckle, Mabel Normand, Edgar Kennedy, Minta Durfee, Al St. John, Louise Fazenda, Joe Bordeaux, Alice Davenport, Dora Rogers, Owen Moore, Glen Cavender, Ford Sterling, Mae Busch. **1915**

KHARTOUM ★★★★ Underrated historical adventure-drama recalls the British defeat in northern Africa by Arab tribesmen circa 1833. Location filming, exciting battle scenes, and fine acting raise this spectacle to the level of superior entertainment. 134m. **DIR:** Basil Dearden. **CAST:** Laurence Olivier, Charlton Heston, Ralph Richardson, Richard Johnson, Alexander Knox. **1966 DVD**

KICK OR DIE ★★ Predictable campus psycho film has coeds on the run from a sadistic rapist. Enter Kevin Bernhardt as a former kick-boxing champ. Rated R for profanity, violence, and nudity. 87m. **DIR:** Charles Norton. **CAST:** Kevin Bernhardt. **1987**

KICKBOXER ★★1/2 This flick looks a little like *Rocky* and a lot like *The Karate Kid*, but it is a step up for Jean-Claude Van Damme in the acting department. Good action scenes and a fun plot. Rated R for violence and language. 97m. **DIR:** Mark DiSalle, David Worth. **CAST:** Jean-Claude Van Damme, Dennis Alexio, Dennis Chan. **1989 DVD**

KICKBOXER 2: THE ROAD BACK 🦃 With more kick-you-in-the-face action, this sequel, sans original star Jean-Claude Van Damme, is weak in the joints. Rated R for violence. 90m. **DIR:** Albert Pyun. **CAST:** Sasha Mitchell, Peter Boyle, Dennis Chan, John Diehl. **1990**

KICKBOXER 3: ART OF WAR ★★ While in Rio de Janeiro for a kick-boxing exhibition, America's champion Sasha Mitchell rescues a kidnapped girl. Standard martial arts flick. Rated R for strong violence and profanity. 92m. **DIR:** Rick King. **CAST:** Sasha Mitchell, Dennis Chan. **1992**

KICKBOXER 4: AGGRESSOR, THE ★★ By-the-book martial arts showcase, with handsome Sasha Mitchell as the high-kicking David Sloan. This outing, Sloan is in prison after being framed for murder but makes a deal with the DEA: To win his freedom he must track down his longtime nemesis, Tong Po. It doesn't take much persuasion when Sloan finds out that his wife has been abducted by Po. Sloan enters a martial arts tournament at the evil master's guarded fortress in order to rescue her. Rated R for violence and language. 90m. **DIR:** Albert Pyun. **CAST:** Sasha Mitchell, Kamel Krifia, Brad Thornton. **1993**

KICKBOXER 5: REDEMPTION ★★1/2 Another sequel, another star. This one features Mark Dacascos as a martial artist out to avenge the murder of a friend. Although kick boxing is all that this film has in common with its predecessors, it's better than the first three in the series. Rated R for violence. 87m. **DIR:** Kristine Peterson. **CAST:** Mark Dacascos, James Ryan, Geoff Meed, Tony Caprari. **1994**

KICKED IN THE HEAD 🦃 A slacker airhead (Kevin Corrigan, who cowrote the atrocious script) alternates adventures in his "voyage of self-discovery" with shady errands for his disreputable uncle (James Woods). Woods (who could energize a funeral even when playing the corpse) is the only asset in this aimless, pointless, and brainless film. Rated R for profanity, drug use, and mild violence. 87m. **DIR:** Matthew Harrison. **CAST:** Kevin Corrigan, Linda Fiorentino, Michael Rapaport, James Woods, Lili Taylor, Burt Young. **1997 DVD**

KICKING AND SCREAMING ★★★ Four college roommates, terrified of "real life," continue frittering their lives away after graduation—sulking and pouting. A little kicking and screaming might have made these selfish crybabies more interesting. Still, the wickedly clever dialogue and the talented cast help keep the lead-balloon premise afloat. Rated R for profanity. 96m. **DIR:** Noah Baumbach. **CAST:** Josh Hamilton, Olivia

D'Abo, Carlos Jacott, Eric Stoltz, Parker Posey, Jason Wiles, Christopher Eigeman. **1995**

KID, THE (1921)/THE IDLE CLASS ★★★★ A skillful blend of comedy and pathos, *The Kid*, the first of Charles Chaplin's silent feature films, has his famous tramp alter ego adopting an abandoned baby boy whose mother, years later, suddenly appears to claim him. Chaplin is magnificent. Coogan's performance in the title role made him the first child superstar. Also on the bill: *The Idle Class*, a satire on the leisure of the rich involving mistaken identity. Silent. B&W; 86m. **DIR:** Charles Chaplin. **CAST:** Charlie Chaplin, Edna Purviance, Jackie Coogan. **1921 DVD**

KID (1990) ★★★1/2 Exciting thriller about a mysterious stranger (C. Thomas Howell) who wants revenge for his parents' deaths. Great editing and terrific sound effects help make this film quite entertaining. Rated R for violence and profanity. 94m. **DIR:** John Mark Robinson. **CAST:** C. Thomas Howell, Sarah Trigger, Brian Austin Green, R. Lee Ermey. **1990 DVD**

KID, THE (2000) ★★★★1/2 Just before his fortieth birthday, a successful but emotionally dead image consultant (Bruce Willis) gets a magical visit from his 8 year old self (Spencer Breslin), giving him a second chance at happiness. Reminiscent of Charles Dickens's *A Christmas Carol*, this Disney production works wonderfully well, with Willis continuing to stretch and amaze as an actor and young Breslin matching him scene for scene. A treasure. Rated PG. 104m. **DIR:** Jon Turtletaub. **CAST:** Bruce Willis, Spencer Breslin, Emily Mortimer, Lily Tomlin, Chi McBride, Jean Smart, Dana Ivey. **2000 DVD**

KID CALLED DANGER, A ★★★ Looking to follow in the steps of his police-officer father, a young teen and his friends try to capture a jewel thief they have spotted in the neighborhood. Suspenseful, made-for-video adventure aimed at young teens. Rated PG for mild violence. 90m. **DIR:** Eric Hendershot. **CAST:** Clayton Taylor, Mac Melonas, Devin Gardner. **1999 DVD**

KID FOR TWO FARTHINGS, A ★★★★ A young London boy buys a goat with only one horn and believes it is a unicorn that has the power to work magic. It's a magical movie, directed by Carol Reed with the same zest he later brought to *Oliver*. 91m. **DIR:** Carol Reed. **CAST:** Jonathan Ashmore, Celia Johnson, Diana Dors, David Kossoff. **1956**

KID FROM BROOKLYN, THE ★★★ Danny Kaye is fine as the comedy lead in this remake of Harold Lloyd's *The Milky Way*. He plays the milkman who becomes a prizefighter. Good family entertainment. 104m. **DIR:** Norman Z. McLeod. **CAST:** Danny Kaye, Virginia Mayo, Vera-Ellen, Steve Cochran, Eve Arden. **1946**

KID FROM LEFT FIELD, THE ★★★ Gary Coleman plays a batboy who leads the San Diego Padres to victory through the advice of his father (a former baseball great). Ed McMahon costars in this remake of the 1953 Dan Dailey version. Made for TV. 100m. **DIR:** Adell Aldrich. **CAST:** Gary Coleman, Tab Hunter, Gary Collins, Ed McMahon. **1979**

KID GALAHAD (1937) ★★★1/2 Solid gangster tale has fight promoter Edward G. Robinson discovering a boxer in bellhop Wayne Morris. It's prime Warner Bros. melodrama, deliciously played. Because of the Elvis Presley remake, this was retitled *The Battling Bellhop* for television. B&W; 101m. **DIR:** Michael Curtiz. **CAST:** Edward G. Robinson, Bette Davis, Humphrey Bogart, Wayne Morris, Harry Carey, Jane Bryan, William Haade, Ben Welden, Veda Ann Borg, Frank Faylen. **1937**

KID GALAHAD (1962) ★★1/2 Remake of a film of the same title made in 1937 starring Edward G. Robinson, Bette Davis, and Humphrey Bogart. In this version, Elvis Presley is a boxer who prefers life as a garage mechanic. Presley fans will enjoy this one, of course. 95m. **DIR:** Phil Karlson. **CAST:** Elvis Presley, Gig Young, Lola Albright, Joan Blackman, Ned Glass. **1962**

KID IN KING ARTHUR'S COURT, A ★★★ Kids will get a kick out of this lightweight adaptation of Mark Twain's *A Connecticut Yankee in King Arthur's Court* in which our young hero thwarts the villains with the help of Rollerblades and a CD player. However, adults may not be so charmed. Rated PG. 89m. **DIR:** Michael Gottlieb. **CAST:** Thomas Ian Nicholas, Joss Ackland, Art Malik, Paloma Baeza, Kate Winslet, Ron Moody. **1995**

KID MILLIONS ★★ The fifth of six elaborate musicals produced with Eddie Cantor by Samuel Goldwyn. Banjo Eyes inherits a fortune and becomes the mark for a parade of con artists. Lavish Busby Berkeley musical numbers help to salvage an otherwise inane plot. B&W; 90m. **DIR:** Roy Del Ruth. **CAST:** Eddie Cantor, Ethel Merman, Ann Sothern, George Murphy, Warren Hymer. **1934**

KID RANGER ★★★ Trouble begins when a ranger shoots a man he wrongly believes to be part of an outlaw gang. Two-fisted hero Bob Steele must track down the real gang. B&W; 56m. **DIR:** Robert N. Bradbury. **CAST:** Bob Steele, Joan Barclay, William Farnum, Charles King. **1936**

KID WHO LOVED CHRISTMAS, THE ★★★★ Heartwarming Christmas tale about an orphan who will do anything to be with his adopted father for the holidays. With an all-star cast and a wonderful message, this made-for-TV drama is pure magic. 100m. **DIR:** Arthur Allan Seidelman. **CAST:** Trent Cameron, Cicely Tyson, Mike Warren, Sammy Davis Jr., Gilbert Lewis, Della Reese. **1990**

KID WITH THE BROKEN HALO, THE ★★ Sort of a *Different Strokes* meets *It's A Wonderful Life*, this television movie tells of a little angel forced to earn his wings by making things right for people in three vignettes. The film was actually an unsold pilot, and the fare is sweet and gentle enough. 100m. **DIR:** Leslie Martinson. **CAST:** Gary Coleman, Robert Guillaume, June Allyson, Ray Walston, Mason Adams, Telma Hopkins, Georg Stanford Brown, John Pleshette. **1982**

KID WITH THE 200 I.Q., THE ★★ In this predictable TV movie, Gary Coleman plays a 13 year old genius who enters college. Mildly amusing at best. 96m. **DIR:** Leslie Martinson. **CAST:** Gary Coleman, Robert Guillaume, Dean Butler, Kari Michaelson, Harriet Nelson. **1983**

KID WITH X-RAY EYES, THE ★★★ Surprisingly entertaining film in the *Home Alone* mode that succeeds mostly due to the performance of Justin Berfield, starring as a youngster who discovers a pair of glasses that allow him to see through most anything. Rated PG. 84m. **DIR:** Sherman Scott. **CAST:** Justin Berfield, Robert Carradine, Ross Hagen, Martin Jarvis. **1999 DVD**

KIDNAP SYNDICATE, THE ★★ James Mason plays a millionaire whose child has been kidnapped. Luc

Merenda is the poor father of a child who has been taken along with Mason's. Director Fernando Di Leo tries to juxtapose the irony of the two fathers, but it comes off like a trite melodrama with lots of blood spilling and profanity. 105m. **DIR:** Fernando Di Leo. **CAST:** James Mason, Luc Merenda, Valentina Cortese. **1976**

KIDNAPPED ★★★ Walt Disney takes a shot at this Robert Louis Stevenson eighteenth-century adventure. A young man (James MacArthur) is spirited away to sea just as he is about to inherit his family's estate. Plenty of swashbuckling for children of all ages. 94m. **DIR:** Robert Stevenson. **CAST:** James MacArthur, Peter Finch. **1960 DVD**

KIDNAPPED IN PARADISE ★★1/2 Pirates kidnap a woman's sister, and she sets off to save her only sibling. This made-for-cable original falls victim to predictability and the only surprise here is how little action there is in this "action" film. Not rated; contains violence. 95m. **DIR:** Rob Hedden. **CAST:** Joely Fisher, Charlotte Ross, Rob Knepper, David Beecroft. **1999**

KIDNAPPING OF THE PRESIDENT, THE ★★★★ As the title implies, terrorists kidnap the president and hold him hostage in this excellent action-thriller. The acting is excellent, the suspense taut, and the direction tightly paced. Rated R. 120m. **DIR:** George Mendeluk. **CAST:** William Shatner, Hal Holbrook, Van Johnson, Ava Gardner. **1979 DVD**

KIDS ★★★1/2 Scripter Harmony Korine follows a pack of inner-city kids through an average day of sex, drugs, and rock 'n' roll, focusing on a young man who "lives to seduce virgins" and doesn't realize that he's infected with AIDS. The dialogue is brutal, the contempt for humanity is appalling, and the sexual content is rough. This frightening wake-up call should be required viewing for every parent and politician in the land. Not rated, but equivalent to an NC-17 for profanity, nudity, drug use, and simulated sex. 90m. **DIR:** Larry Clark. **CAST:** Leo Fitzpatrick, Justin Pierce, Chloe Sevigny, Sarah Henderson. **1995 DVD**

KIDS ARE ALRIGHT, THE ★★★1/2 More a documentary detailing the career of British rock group the Who than an entertainment, this film by Jeff Stein still manages to capture the spirit of rock 'n' roll. Rated PG. 108m. **DIR:** Jeff Stein. **CAST:** The Who, Ringo Starr, Steve Martin, Tom Smothers. **1979**

KIDS IN THE HALL: BRAIN CANDY ★★ Canadian TV-comedy players Kids in the Hall make their theatrical film debut in this satirical story of a miracle feel-good drug unleashed on the public before its full effects are known. A halfway-decent idea for a brief sketch is dragged out far beyond its merits, with few laughs. The Kids' modest talents may play better on video than on the big screen. Rated R for profanity. 97m. **DIR:** Kelly Makin. **CAST:** David Foley, Bruce McCulloch, Kevin McDonald, Mark McKinney, Carrot Top (Scott Thompson). **1996**

KIKA ★★★★ Nominally about a none-too-bright woman who loves both a photographer and his American stepfather, who may be a murderer, the story is just an excuse to poke fun at our morbid, media-fed fascination with serial criminals. The film includes what can only be called the silliest rape scene ever staged, though it's likely to outrage many viewers. In English and Spanish with English subtitles. Not rated, with lots of slapstick sex, nudity, and some violence. 95m. **DIR:** Pedro Almodóvar. **CAST:** Veronica Forque, Peter Coyote, Victoria Abril, Alex Casanovas, Rossy De Palma. **1993 DVD**

•KIKUJIRO ★★★1/2 Japanese cult icon "Beat" Takeshi Kitano, known in the West only for violent cop movies like *Brother* and *Boiling Point*, shows another side of his personality with this offbeat road comedy inspired by *The Wizard of Oz*. He plays a retired *yakuza* whose wife forces him to help a young boy find his mother. The *yakuza*, who is hardly warm and cuddly, may shock audiences with some of his behavior. The film's slow pace and unpredictable comic tone may also not appeal, but those with a taste for something different are encouraged to seek this out. In Japanese with English subtitles. Rated PG-13 for mild violence. 121m. **DIR:** Takeshi Kitano. **CAST:** Takeshi Kitano, Yusuke Sekiguchi, Kayoko Kishimoto, Great Gidayu, Rakkyo Ide. **1999 DVD**

KILL, THE ★★ Richard Jaeckel plays a world-weary, womanizing private eye in this overly familiar story of a hunt for stolen money in the byways of the Orient. The locale is Macao, famed gambling haven across the bay from Hong Kong. No rating, but contains violence and nudity. 81m. **DIR:** Rolf Bamer. **CAST:** Richard Jaeckel. **1973**

KILL AND KILL AGAIN ★★ Kung fu champ James Ryan repeats his starring role from *Kill or Be Killed*. This time, martial arts master Steve Chase (Ryan) has been hired to rescue a Nobel Prize–winning chemist from the clutches of a demented billionaire. Rated R. 100m. **DIR:** Ivan Hall. **CAST:** James Ryan, Anneline Kriel. **1981 DVD**

KILL CASTRO (CUBA CROSSING, MERCENARIES, SWEET VIOLENT TONY) Implausible adventure yarn. Rated R. 90m. **DIR:** Peter Barton. **CAST:** Stuart Whitman, Caren Kaye, Robert Vaughn, Woody Strode, Albert Salmi, Michael Gazzo, Sybil Danning, Raymond St. Jacques. **1978**

KILL CRUISE ★★ Spur of the moment decision by an alcoholic yachtsman to sail to Barbados with two young British women leads to the predictable clash of passions. Listless voyage propelled only by capable performances and a twist ending. Rated R for violence, profanity, and nudity. 99m. **DIR:** Peter Keglevic. **CAST:** Jurgen Prochnow, Patsy Kensit, Elizabeth Hurley. **1990 DVD**

KILL ME AGAIN ★★ A fairly suspenseful thriller about a private eye who gets caught up in plot twist after plot twist after a woman asks him to fake her death. Predictable, but there are worse ways to spend an hour and a half. Rated R for violence. 94m. **DIR:** John Dahl. **CAST:** Val Kilmer, Joanne Whalley, Michael Madsen, Jonathan Gries, Michael Greene, Bibi Besch. **1990 DVD**

•KILL ME LATER ★★★1/2 Refreshingly dark comedy about a bank teller and a bank robber who connect at the most unexpected times in their lives. When Shawn heads to the roof to end it all, she's intercepted by robber Charlie, who takes her hostage and uses her to evade the law. On the run, Charlie and Shawn bring out the best in each other and create a perplexing dynamic. Filled with offbeat dialogue and engaging perfor-

mances, this little gem sparkles every chance it gets. Rated R for language. 89m. **DIR:** Dana Lustig. **CAST:** Selma Blair, Max Beesley, D. W. Moffett, O'Neal Compton. **2001 DVD**

KILL-OFF, THE ★★★★ Despite being bedridden, smalltown gossip Luanne (Loretta Gross) is able to wield an evil influence, making more than a few enemies who wouldn't mind seeing her dead. One of the best adaptations of the work of pulp novelist Jim Thompson (*After Dark, My Sweet; The Grifters*), this is a film whose low budget works in its favor, evoking the oppressively fatalistic atmosphere at which Thompson excelled. Rated R for profanity, violence, and brief nudity. 100m. **DIR:** Maggie Greenwald. **CAST:** Loretta Gross, Jackson Sims, Cathy Haase, Steve Monroe. **1990**

KILL OR BE KILLED ★★ A former Nazi pits himself against the Japanese master who defeated him in an important tournament during World War II. Run-of-the-mill martial arts nonsense. James Ryan shows a glimmer of personality to go with his physical prowess. Rated PG. 90m. **DIR:** Ivan Hall. **CAST:** James Ryan, Norman Combes, Charlotte Michelle. **1980**

•**KILL SHOT** ★ Not the slasher/T&A flick you may expect from the cover art but rather a grim story of five university students and their various struggles. Rated R for sexuality and violence. 92m. **DIR:** Nelson McCormick. **CAST:** Jack Scalia, Sally Kellerman, Elliott Gould, Casper Van Dien, Denise Richards. **1995 DVD**

KILL ZONE 🦃 Totally derivative war film has wigged-out Colonel Wiggins, played by David Carradine, pushing his platoon one mission too far. Director Cirio Santiago pushed this genre one film too far. Rated R for language and violence. 95m. **DIR:** Cirio H. Santiago. **CAST:** David Carradine, Tony Dorsett, Rob Youngblood, Vic Trevino. **1993**

KILLER, THE ★★★★★ John Woo's best film features Chow Yun-Fat as an honorable assassin trying to get out of the business. Impeccable pacing and incredible action choreography create an operatic intensity that leaves you feeling giddy. Available both dubbed and in Cantonese with English subtitles. Not rated; very strong violence. 102m. **DIR:** John Woo. **CAST:** Chow Yun-Fat, Sally Yeh, Danny Lee. **1989 DVD**

KILLER: A JOURNAL OF MURDER ★★★ In the 1920s, a hardened criminal (James Woods) tells the story of his life to an idealistic young prison guard (Robert Sean Leonard). Based on the diaries of a psychopathic killer, this is an excellent vehicle for Woods, though the story isn't as interesting as the character. Rated R for graphic violence and profanity. B&W/color; 91m. **DIR:** Tim Metcalfe. **CAST:** James Woods, Robert Sean Leonard, Ellen Greene, Steve Forrest. **1996**

•**KILLER BUD** 🦃 Two losers tempt two attractive girls with the promise of getting high, and then spend the rest of the night looking for marijuana. The losers are played by Corin Nemec and David Faustino, whose performances are more deadly than the killer buds they are trying to score. Rated R for adult situations, drugs, and language. 92m. **DIR:** Karl T. Hirsch. **CAST:** Corin Nemec, David Faustino, Danielle Harris, Caroline Keenan, Robert Stack. **2001 DVD**

KILLER ELITE, THE ★★1/2 Secret service agent James Caan is double-crossed by his partner (Robert Duvall) while guarding a witness. Disabled by a bullet wound, he has to begin a long process of recovery. He wants revenge. There are some good action scenes. However, considering all the top-flight talent involved, it is a major disappointment. Rated PG. 120m. **DIR:** Sam Peckinpah. **CAST:** James Caan, Robert Duvall, Arthur Hill, Bo Hopkins, Mako, Burt Young, Gig Young. **1975 DVD**

KILLER EYE, THE 🦃 A scientist accidentally opens a gateway to another dimension and unleashes the killer eye, a giant eyeball with hypnotic powers and a penchant for the ladies, in this absolutely ludicrous thriller. Rated R for violence and nudity. 80m. **DIR:** Richard Chasen. **CAST:** Jacqueline Lovell, Blake Bailey. **1998**

KILLER FISH 🦃 Bad acting and lousy Spanish accents help to make this a total bust. Rated PG, but contains violence and some nudity. 101m. **DIR:** Anthony M. Dawson. **CAST:** Lee Majors, Karen Black, Margaux Hemingway, Marisa Berenson, James Franciscus. **1978**

KILLER FLICK ★★★ Don't try to make sense of *Killer Flick*; just enjoy the ride, for nothing is what it seems in this wicked homage to Oliver Stone's *Natural Born Killers*. What starts off as a road trip turns into an examination of violence for kicks, pitting four filmmakers against a society they disdain. Headed for Hollywood, the foursome—a director, writer, cameraman, and composer—make the film as they go, using ordinary people as their actors and forcing them into compromising positions before dispatching them. Tragically funny, *Killer Flick* is also absurdist filmmaking. You don't watch it for entertainment; you watch it to find out where it's headed. Not rated; contains adult language and violence. 93m. **DIR:** Mark Weidman. **CAST:** Emmett Grennan, Sheri Hellard, Christian Leffler, Zen Todd, Kathleen Walsh. **1998**

KILLER FORCE ★★ Diamond security officer fakes a theft to secure the confidence of a ruthless smuggling ring. Predictable heist film. Rated R. 100m. **DIR:** Val Guest. **CAST:** Telly Savalas, Peter Fonda, Hugh O'Brian, O. J. Simpson, Maud Adams, Christopher Lee. **1983**

KILLER IMAGE 🦃 Confusing film with a complete lack of continuity starts with the murder of a photographer who just happens to capture a murderer on film. Now his brother is pursued by the psycho. Rated R for violence and profanity. 97m. **DIR:** David Winning. **CAST:** Michael Ironside, M. Emmet Walsh, John Pyper-Ferguson, Krista Erickson. **1992**

KILLER INSIDE ME, THE ★★★ Stacy Keach plays a schizophrenic sheriff in a small town. A tightly woven plot offers the viewer plenty of surprises. Rated R for violence and profanity. 99m. **DIR:** Burt Kennedy. **CAST:** Stacy Keach, Susan Tyrrell, Tisha Sterling, Keenan Wynn, Charles McGraw, John Dehner, Pepe Serna, Royal Dano, John Carradine, Don Stroud. **1975 DVD**

KILLER INSTINCT ★★★ Two brothers toughing it out during the 1920s Prohibition become gangsters and take on the mob. Handsome production values and some close-to-the-cuff performances, but this story has been told before, and better. Rated R for violence, language, and nudity. 101m. **DIR:** Greydon Clark, Ken Stein. **CAST:** Ken Stein, Chris Bradley, Rachel York, Bruce Nozick. **1992**

KILLER KLOWNS FROM OUTER SPACE ★★★1/2 Lon Chaney once opined that "there is nothing more frightening than a clown after midnight." This sci-fi–horror

thriller proves that claim with a mixture of camp, comedy, and chills. The title says it all, but the results are more entertaining than one might expect. Rated PG-13 for profanity and violence. 90m. **DIR:** Stephen Chiodo. **CAST:** Grant Cramer, Suzanne Snyder, John Allen Nelson, Royal Dano, John Vernon. **1988 DVD**

KILLER SHREWS, THE 🦃 Crackpot scientist on an isolated island breeds shrews the size and shape of large, bewigged dogs that eat everything (and everyone) in their path. B&W; 69m. **DIR:** Ray Kellogg. **CAST:** James Best, Ingrid Goude, Ken Curtis, Baruch Lumet. **1959 DVD**

KILLER TOMATOES EAT FRANCE ★★★ Part four of the killer tomato trilogy is a cute spoof on just about everything. Dr. Mortimer Gangreen, played wonderfully by John Astin, breaks out of prison and tries to put a fake King Louie on the throne of France. Not rated; contains humorous violence. 90m. **DIR:** John DeBello. **CAST:** Marc Price, Angela Visser, Steve Lundquist, John Astin. **1991**

KILLER TOMATOES STRIKE BACK 🦃 Third installment of the killer tomato saga features John Astin as Professor Gangreen attempting—once again—to dominate the world. Beyond corny, this reduces the original to an all-time low. Not rated. 88m. **DIR:** John DeBello. **CAST:** John Astin. **1990**

KILLER TONGUE ★★ If it weren't for the film's over-the-top premise and execution, this affair would deserve a tongue-lashing. Melinda Clarke gets more than she bargained for when she swallows an alien life-form in her soup. Instead of getting a stomachache, she develops a ten-foot killer tongue with an insatiable taste for blood. Totally silly, this low-budget film gets points for effort. Not rated; contains adult situations, language, nudity, and violence. 97m. **DIR:** Alberto Sciamma. **CAST:** Melinda Clarke, Robert Englund, Jason Durr, Mapi Galan. **1996 DVD**

KILLERS, THE ★★★ Two hit men piece together a story on the man they've just killed. A tense thriller loosely based on a short story by Ernest Hemingway. This remake of the 1946 classic emphasizes violence rather than storytelling. Ronald Reagan is excellent as an unscrupulous business tycoon. Rated PG; contains graphic violence. 95m. **DIR:** Don Siegel. **CAST:** Lee Marvin, John Cassavetes, Angie Dickinson, Ronald Reagan. **1964 DVD**

KILLERS FROM SPACE 🦃 Bug-eyed men from outer space. B&W; 68m. **DIR:** W. Lee Wilder. **CAST:** Peter Graves, James Seay. **1954**

KILLERS IN THE HOUSE ★★ When a family visits a house they just inherited, they are taken hostage by a group of bank robbers who thought the house was empty. This made-for-cable original has mostly dumb dialogue and flat acting. Rated R for violence. 95m. **DIR:** Michael Schultz. **CAST:** Mario Van Peebles, Holly Robinson, Andrew Divoff, Hal Linden. **1998**

KILLER'S KISS ★★ A boxer rescues a singer from the lecherous clutches of her boss. This ultra-low-budget melodrama is a curiosity piece primarily because Stanley Kubrick wrote, photographed, directed, and edited it. 67m. **DIR:** Stanley Kubrick. **CAST:** Jamie Smith, Irene Kane, Frank Silvera. **1955 DVD**

KILLING, THE ★★★★ Strong *noir* thriller from Stanley Kubrick has Sterling Hayden leading a group of criminals in an intricately timed heist at a racetrack. Excellent performances and atmospheric handling of the subject matter mark Kubrick, even at this early stage of his career, as a filmmaker to watch. B&W; 83m. **DIR:** Stanley Kubrick. **CAST:** Sterling Hayden, Coleen Gray, Jay C. Flippen, Marie Windsor, Timothy Carey, Vince Edwards, Elisha Cook Jr. **1956 DVD**

KILLING AFFAIR, A ★★★ Exceptional psychological drama about a young woman (Kathy Baker) who befriends a stranger (Peter Weller). As it turns out, he killed her husband to avenge the death of his own wife and family. The relationship between the two intensifies to an unexpected, terrifying conclusion. Rated R for nudity and violence. 100m. **DIR:** David Saperstein. **CAST:** Peter Weller, Kathy Baker, John Glover, Bill Smitrovich. **1988**

KILLING AT HELL'S GATE ★★★ Made-for-TV action film about a group of people, including a controversial U.S. senator, who take a raft trip only to find that the bullets are harder to dodge than the jagged rocks. This ain't no *Deliverance*, but it's watchable. 96m. **DIR:** Jerry Jameson. **CAST:** Robert Urich, Deborah Raffin, Lee Purcell, Joel Higgins, George DiCenzo, Paul Burke, Brian James, John Randolph. **1981**

KILLING CARS ★★ A car designer finds that the Berlin company he works for is going to shelve his environmentally safe automobile, so he sets out to sell the plans to someone who will manufacture the machine. Rated R for violence, nudity, and profanity. 104m. **DIR:** Michael Verhoeven. **CAST:** Jurgen Prochnow, Senta Berger, Bernhard Wicki, William Conrad, Daniel Gélin. **1986**

KILLING EDGE, THE ★★ Fairly decent low-budget account of one man's search through a nuclear wasteland for his wife and son. The acting is good and the writing is solid, but the film occasionally gets bogged down in repetition. Not rated, contains violence and language. 90m. **DIR:** Lindsay Shonteff. **CAST:** Bill French, Marv Spencer. **1986**

KILLING 'EM SOFTLY ★★ George Segal is a down-and-out musician who kills the friend of a young singer (Irene Cara) in an argument over the death of his dog. While attempting to prove that Segal is not the killer, Cara falls in love with him. An interesting and well-acted story bogs down in the attempt to turn this film into a music video. The music is good, but it overpowers the story. Filmed in Canada. 90m. **DIR:** Max Fischer. **CAST:** George Segal, Irene Cara, Joyce Gordon, Barbara Cook. **1985**

KILLING FIELDS, THE ★★★★★ Here's an unforgettable motion picture. Based on the experiences of *New York Times* correspondent Sidney Schanberg during the war in Cambodia and his friendship with Cambodian guide and self-proclaimed journalist Dith Pran (whom Schanberg fights to save from imprisonment), it is a tale of love, loyalty, political intrigue, and horror. The viewer cannot help but be jarred and emotionally moved by it. Rated R for violence. 142m. **DIR:** Roland Joffe. **CAST:** Sam Waterston, Haing S. Ngor, John Malkovich, Julian Sands, Craig T. Nelson. **1984 DVD**

KILLING FLOOR, THE ★★★ Honest and forthright depiction of union squabbles in the Chicago stockyards during World War II. Credible performances and a well-honed script add to a realistic picture of working life in the sticky goo of a slaughterhouse operating under

Dickensian stringency. Not rated. 117m. **DIR:** Bill Duke. **CAST:** Damien Leake, Moses Gunn, Alfre Woodard, Clarence Felder. **1984**

KILLING GAME, THE 🦃 Made-for-video movie tries to evoke a cynical, hardboiled style but lacks the talent behind (and in front of) the camera. Not rated, but featuring nudity and substantial violence. 83m. **DIR:** Joseph Merhi. **CAST:** Chad Hayward, Cynthia Killion. **1988**

KILLING HEAT ★★1/2 Uneven acting and a general lack of atmosphere hinder the screen adaptation of Doris Lessing's novel *The Grass is Singing*. Karen Black plays a city woman who marries a small-time farmer and slowly goes insane while trying to adapt herself to the rural life-style. Set in South Africa in the early 1960s. Not rated; contains nudity and violence. 104m. **DIR:** Michael Raeburn. **CAST:** Karen Black, John Thaw, John Kani. **1984**

KILLING HOUR, THE ★★ Elizabeth Kemp plays a clairvoyant art student who, through her drawings, becomes involved in a series of murders. The story is a rip-off of *The Eyes of Laura Mars*. With that said, suspense is achieved during the last fifteen minutes of the film. Rated R for violence, nudity, and profanity. 97m. **DIR:** Armand Mastroianni. **CAST:** Perry King, Elizabeth Kemp, Norman Parker, Kenneth McMillan. **1984 DVD**

KILLING IN A SMALL TOWN ★★ Based on a true case, this just passable TV murder-of-the-week entry falls flat with Barbara Hershey internalizing the drab exterior of her character—ignoring the fact that she is also a passionate ax murderess. 95m. **DIR:** Stephen Gyllenhaal. **CAST:** Barbara Hershey, Brian Dennehy, John Terry, Richard Gilliland. **1990**

KILLING JAR, THE ★★★ When Michael Sanford drives by the scene of a brutal murder, images of the slaying converge with dreams from a repressed childhood trauma, causing him to doubt his sanity. Things heat up when Michael becomes the main suspect in a series of murders, keeping us in suspense until the shocking finale. Rated R for violence, language, and nudity. 101m. **DIR:** Evan Crooke. **CAST:** Brett Cullen, Tamlyn Tomita, Brian James, Wes Studi, M. Emmet Walsh. **1996 DVD**

KILLING MAN, THE ★★ Yawner about a professional killer (Jeff Wincott) who is double-crossed by the mob and becomes a government operative. Rated R for violence and adult language. 100m. **DIR:** David Mitchell. **CAST:** Jeff Wincott, Terri Hawkes, David Bolt, Michael Ironside. **1994 DVD**

KILLING MIND, THE 🦃 A young girl witnesses a murder and grows up to become a homicide investigator so that she can reopen the case. This murder-mystery plot is so old and tired it would be a bigger mystery why anyone would have trouble figuring it out in this made-for-cable film. 96m. **DIR:** Michael Ray Rhodes. **CAST:** Stephanie Zimbalist, Daniel Roebuck, Tony Bill. **1991**

KILLING MR. GRIFFIN ★★★1/2 Following the events of Lois Duncan's teen thriller closely, this above-average TV movie manages to capture nuances of the story such as how important fitting in is in high school. Fine performances by the young leads boost the film, although Mario Lopez is predictably stiff. Jay Thomas's dead-on portrayal of Mr. Griffin makes the character someone that you hate and feel compassion for simultaneously. Look for several hot young stars in early roles here. Rated PG-13 for mild violence. 92m. **DIR:** Jack Bender. **CAST:** Amy Jo Johnson, Scott Bairstow, Mario Lopez, Michelle Williams, Jay Thomas. **1997 DVD**

KILLING OF A CHINESE BOOKIE ★★★1/2 Downbeat character study stars Ben Gazzara as a small-time nightclub owner who finds himself in big-time trouble when he's coerced into murdering a Chinese crime lord to pay off a debt. Director John Cassavetes's most accessible film is nevertheless a meandering character study with shaky cinematography and a bit too much improvisation. At least it goes somewhere. Rated R for violence and profanity. 113m. **DIR:** John Cassavetes. **CAST:** Ben Gazzara, Timothy Carey, Seymour Cassel. **1976 DVD**

KILLING OF ANGEL STREET, THE ★★ The misleading title and packaging of *The Killing of Angel Street* makes it look like a teenage slasher flick, but the title refers to an actual street in a neighborhood in Australia. The plot involves the citizens' struggle to keep their homes from demolition by corrupt businessmen. 100m. **DIR:** Donald Crombie. **CAST:** Liz Alexander, John Hargreaves, Reg Lye. **1981**

KILLING OF RANDY WEBSTER, THE ★★ Hal Holbrook and Dixie Carter, his real-life wife, portray parents searching desperately for meaning in the death of their troubled teenage son. The boy steals a van, then leads Houston police on a wild chase. They fire as the boy pulls a gun. Or did he? Made for television. 90m. **DIR:** Sam Wanamaker. **CAST:** Hal Holbrook, Dixie Carter, Jennifer Jason Leigh, Sean Penn. **1985**

KILLING OF SISTER GEORGE, THE ★★1/2 Now that the initial controversy that swirled around this film's honest depiction of a lesbian relationship has died away, a retrospective viewing shows a passable yet uninspired story and wooden acting in its central performances. This stage play of an aging actress whose career and relationships are crumbling around her was not brought to the screen with much spirit. Rated R for nudity. 140m. **DIR:** Robert Aldrich. **CAST:** Beryl Reid, Susannah York, Coral Browne. **1968 DVD**

KILLING SPREE ★★ This low-budget bloodfest about a jealous husband who kills the imagined suitors of his wife does contain some unique death scenes. But the lighting is often overbearing, and it's hard to hear what the actors (who aren't very good anyway) are saying. Not rated; contains violence. 88m. **DIR:** Tim Ritter. **CAST:** Asbestos Felt. **1987 DVD**

KILLING STREETS ★★ Michael Paré takes on the dual roles of a government operative kidnapped in Lebanon and his twin brother who leads an attempt to rescue him in this sometimes exciting, but ultimately mediocre, shoot-'em-up. Not rated; contains violence and profanity. 106m. **DIR:** Stephen Cornwell. **CAST:** Michael Paré, Lorenzo Lamas, Jennifer Runyon. **1991**

KILLING TIME, THE (1987) ★★★★ Kiefer Sutherland is a killer posing as a new deputy sheriff in a small resort town. Beau Bridges is to be the new sheriff upon the retirement of Joe Don Baker. But there is much more to be discovered in this tense drama of murder, deception, and suspicion. Rated R for violence and profanity. 94m. **DIR:** Rick King. **CAST:** Beau Bridges, Kiefer Sutherland, Wayne Rogers, Joe Don Baker. **1987**

KILLING TIME (1996) ★★★1/2 Crafty thriller stars Bruce Fairbrass as a cop who hires a professional hit woman to kill the scum who killed his partner. When he realizes he can't afford to pay off the assassin, he hires a

cheaper hit man to kill her. Then the real fun begins. Nice, tidy stab at *film noir*. Rated R for language and violence. 91m. **DIR:** Bharat Nalluri. **CAST:** Bruce Fairbrass, Kendra Torgan, Peter Harding, Neil Armstrong. **1996**

•KILLING YARD, THE ★★★ The atrocities of Attica prison and the subsequent riot in 1971 are brought to light in this made-for-cable original. We see little of the actual events—instead, we follow the trial of one of the prisoners accused of murdering a fellow inmate during the riot. While it is a unique way of recounting the events, hearing about the riot secondhand removes a lot of the emotional impact. Uninspired acting only makes this flat movie more so. Not rated; contains profanity, violence, and nudity. 110m. **DIR:** Euzhan Palcy. **CAST:** Alan Alda, Morris Chestnut, Rose McGowan, Christopher Heyerdahl. **2001**

KILLING ZOE ★★ When a Paris bank robbery goes sour, the robbers begin killing indiscriminately. No plot twists, no character revelations, just a slow buildup to a long parade of violence and gore. Rated R for extreme violence. 96m. **DIR:** Roger Avary. **CAST:** Eric Stoltz, Jean-Hugues Anglade, Julie Delpy. **1994 DVD**

KILLING ZONE, THE ★★ Daron McBee of television's *American Gladiators* stars in this actioner as the convict nephew of an ex–DEA agent. Not rated; contains violence and profanity. 90m. **DIR:** Addison Randall. **CAST:** Deron Michael McBee. **1990**

KIM ★★★1/2 Rudyard Kipling's India comes to life in this colorful story of the young son of a soldier and his adventures with a dashing secret operative in defense of queen and country. Dean Stockwell is one of the finest and most believable of child stars, and the great Errol Flynn is still capable of personifying the spirit of adventure and romance in this one-dimensional but entertaining story. 113m. **DIR:** Victor Saville. **CAST:** Errol Flynn, Dean Stockwell, Paul Lukas, Thomas Gomez, Cecil Kellaway. **1951**

KIMAGURE ORANGE ROAD, VOLS. 1—4 ★★★ Japanese animation. It is difficult to categorize this engrossing series as there are so many different elements involved in the stories. Essentially, this is a drama centering around a young man's relationship with two different girls. In Japanese with English subtitles. Not rated; contains nudity. 50m. **DIR:** Morikawa Shigeru. **1988**

KIMAGURE ORANGE ROAD: THE MOVIE ★★★1/2 Japanese animation. Two of the young characters from the Orange Road series have gone on to college where they confront their feelings for one another, much to the dismay of the third corner of their love triangle. Absorbing drama series. In Japanese with English subtitles. Not rated; contains nudity. 70m. **DIR:** Mochizuki Tomomichi. **1988**

KIND HEARTS AND CORONETS ★★★★ A young man (Dennis Price) thinks up a novel way to speed up his inheritance—by killing off the other heirs. This is the central premise of this arresting black comedy, which manages to poke fun at mass murder and get away with it. Alec Guinness plays all eight victims. 104m. **DIR:** Robert Hamer. **CAST:** Dennis Price, Alec Guinness, Valerie Hobson. **1949**

KIND OF LOVING, A ★★ This British romance features Alan Bates as a young man infatuated with a cute blonde at work. When she gets pregnant, he marries her and realizes how ill-prepared he was for this commitment. Not rated, this contains nudity and adult themes equivalent to an R. B&W; 107m. **DIR:** John Schlesinger. **CAST:** Alan Bates, Thora Hird, June Ritchie. **1962**

KINDERGARTEN ★★★1/2 Poet Yevgenii Yevtushenko wrote and directed this film based on his own childhood memories of life in Moscow during World War II, especially the evacuation of the city as the Nazis approached. The chaos as seen through childlike eyes is compelling, even strangely beautiful. In Russian with English subtitles. Not rated. 159m. **DIR:** Yevgenii Yevtushenko. **1983**

KINDERGARTEN COP ★★★1/2 High-concept comedy has big Arnold Schwarzenegger playing an undercover narcotics detective who has to pose as a kindergarten teacher to get the goods on a nasty drug lord (Richard Tyson). If it weren't for all the violence, this could have been a fun film for the whole family. As it is, Schwarzenegger is often funny, and Pamela Reed does a bang-up job as his unpredictable partner. Rated PG-13 for violence. 111m. **DIR:** Ivan Reitman. **CAST:** Arnold Schwarzenegger, Penelope Ann Miller, Pamela Reed, Linda Hunt, Richard Tyson, Carroll Baker, Cathy Moriarty. **1990 DVD**

KINDRED, THE 🦃 Derivative horror film, which steals its creature from *Alien* and its plot from any one of a hundred run-of-the-razor slasher flicks. Rated R for profanity, violence, and gore. 95m. **DIR:** Jeffrey Obrow, Stephen Carpenter. **CAST:** David Allen Brooks, Amanda Pays, Rod Steiger, Kim Hunter. **1987**

KING ★★★★ Paul Winfield and Cicely Tyson star as the Rev. Martin Luther King Jr. and Coretta Scott King in this outstanding docudrama of the martyred civil rights leader's murder-capped battle against segregation and for black human dignity. Director Abby Mann, who also scripted, interpolated actual newsreel footage with restaged confrontation incidents for maximum dramatic impact. 272m. **DIR:** Abby Mann. **CAST:** Paul Winfield, Cicely Tyson, Ossie Davis, Roscoe Lee Browne, Howard Rollins Jr., Cliff De Young, Dolph Sweet, Lonny Chapman. **1978**

KING AND FOUR QUEENS, THE ★★★1/2 This blend of mystery, comedy, and romance takes place in a western ghost town where stagecoach robbery gold is hidden. Desperado Clark Gable plays up to four women in hopes of finding the money. B&W; 86m. **DIR:** Raoul Walsh. **CAST:** Clark Gable, Eleanor Parker, Jo Van Fleet, Jean Willes, Barbara Nichols, Sara Shane, Roy Roberts, Jay C. Flippen, Arthur Shields. **1956**

KING AND I, THE (1956) ★★★★1/2 Yul Brynner and Deborah Kerr star in this superb 1956 Rodgers and Hammerstein musicalization of *Anna and the King of Siam*. Kerr is the widowed teacher who first clashes, then falls in love, with the King (Brynner). 133m. **DIR:** Walter Lang. **CAST:** Yul Brynner, Deborah Kerr, Rita Moreno. **1956 DVD**

KING AND I, THE (1999) 🦃 Taken on its own, this animated version of the Rodgers and Hammerstein classic is merely third-rate, but the way it trashes a masterpiece of American musical theater makes it one of the most despicable acts of artistic vandalism in movie history. Rent the 1956 movie instead; even your kids will like it better. Rated G. 88m. **DIR:** Richard Rich. **CAST:**

Miranda Richardson, Martin Vidnovic, Ian Richardson. **1999 DVD**

KING ARTHUR, THE YOUNG WARLORD ★★ *King Arthur, the Young Warlord* follows the English legend in his early years through subplots that lead nowhere. It must be noted that the violence displayed may not be some people's idea of good ol' G-rated fun despite the MPAA approval. 96m. **DIR:** Sidney Hayers, Pat Jackson, Peter Sasdy. **CAST:** Oliver Tobias, Michael Gothard, Jack Watson, Brian Blessed, Peter Firth. **1975**

KING COBRA 🦃 This rip-off of *Jaws* and everything that came after features a giant rubber snake and a lot of bad acting. The scariest thing about the film is that it got made. Rated PG-13 for language and violence. 93m. **DIR:** David Hillenbrand, Scott Hillenbrand. **CAST:** Noriyuki "Pat" Morita, Hoyt Axton, Scott Hillenbrand, Courtney Gains. **1999 DVD**

KING CREOLE ★★★★ A surprisingly strong Elvis Presley vehicle, this musical, set in New Orleans, benefits from solid direction from Michael Curtiz and a first-rate cast. 116m. **DIR:** Michael Curtiz. **CAST:** Elvis Presley, Carolyn Jones, Dolores Hart, Dean Jagger, Walter Matthau. **1958 DVD**

KING DAVID ★★★ Only biblical scholars will be able to say whether the makers of *King David* remained faithful to the Old Testament. As a big-screen production, however, it is impressive. Directed by Australian filmmaker Bruce Beresford, it is one of the few responsible attempts at filming the Bible. Rated PG-13 for nudity and violence. 115m. **DIR:** Bruce Beresford. **CAST:** Richard Gere, Edward Woodward, Alice Krige, Denis Quilley. **1985**

KING IN NEW YORK, A ★★1/2 Supposedly anti-American, this 1957 film by Charles Chaplin, not seen in the United States until 1973, was a big letdown to his fans, who had built their worship on *Easy Street*, *City Lights*, *Modern Times*, and *The Great Dictator*. It pokes fun at the 1950s, with its witch-hunts and burgeoning postwar technology. It is not the Chaplin of old, but just old Chaplin, and too much of him. B&W; 105m. **DIR:** Charles Chaplin. **CAST:** Charlie Chaplin, Dawn Addams, Michael Chaplin. **1957 DVD**

KING KONG (1933) ★★★★★ This classic was one of early sound film's most spectacular successes. The movie, about the giant ape who is captured on a prehistoric island and proceeds to tear New York City apart until his final stand on the Empire State Building, is the stuff of which legends are made. Its marriage of sound, music, image, energy, pace, and excitement made *King Kong* stand as a landmark film. B&W; 100m. **DIR:** Merian C. Cooper, Ernest B. Schoedsack. **CAST:** Robert Armstrong, Fay Wray, Bruce Cabot, Frank Reicher, Noble Johnson. **1933**

KING KONG (1976) ★★ This remake, starring Jeff Bridges and Jessica Lange, is a pale imitation of the 1933 classic. For kids only. Rated PG for violence. 135m. **DIR:** John Guillermin. **CAST:** Jeff Bridges, Jessica Lange, Charles Grodin. **1976 DVD**

KING KONG LIVES 🦃 Romance of the resuscitated Kong and his new love, Lady Kong. Rated PG-13 for violence. 105m. **DIR:** John Guillermin. **CAST:** Brian Kerwin, Linda Hamilton, John Ashton, Peter Michael Goetz. **1986**

KING KONG VS. GODZILLA ★★ King Kong and Godzilla duke it out atop Mount Fuji in this East meets West supermonster movie. Here, though, Kong is a junkie hooked on some wild jungle juice. The bouts are quite humorous. Not rated. 91m. **DIR:** Inoshiro Honda. **CAST:** Michael Keith, Tadao Takashima, Kenji Sahara. **1963 DVD**

KING LEAR (1971) ★★★1/2 Sturdy but truncated film adaptation of Shakespeare's play about a mad king and his cruel, power-hungry children. The Danish set location lends a disturbing air to this production, which features a powerful portrayal from Paul Scofield. 137m. **DIR:** Peter Brook. **CAST:** Paul Scofield, Irene Worth, Jack MacGowran, Alan Webb, Cyril Cusack, Patrick Magee. **1971**

KING LEAR (1982) ★★★ A good stage production of what is possibly Shakespeare's most tragic of tales. Mike Kellen is very good as the aging Lear, betrayed by his daughters, but acting honors go to Charles Aidman as the tortured Gloucester. David Groh is interesting as his plotting bastard son, Edmund. A Bard Productions Ltd. release. 182m. **DIR:** Alan Cooke. **CAST:** Mike Kellen, Darryl Hickman, Charles Aidman, David Groh, Joel Baily. **1982**

KING LEAR (1984) ★★★★ Produced for television, this version of Shakespeare's great tragedy of greed and lust for power became an instant classic, and promptly won an Emmy. A career-crowning achievement for Laurence Olivier. 158m. **DIR:** Michael Elliot. **CAST:** Laurence Olivier, Diana Rigg, Anna Calder-Marshall, Dorothy Tutin, Leo McKern, John Hurt, Robert Lindsay. **1984 DVD**

KING LEAR (1988) ★★★1/2 Patrick Magee stars in this Shakespearean tragedy about a foolish king who surrounds himself with treacherous flatterers while banishing those who remain true to him. Fine acting and glorious costumes and sets make this British television production most watchable. 110m. **CAST:** Patrick Magee, Ray Smith, Ronald Radd. **1988**

KING OF COMEDY, THE ★★★★ This is certainly one of the most unusual movies of all time; a sort of black-comedy variation on creator Martin Scorsese's *Taxi Driver*. The star of that film, Robert De Niro, stars as aspiring comic Rupert Pupkin. In order to get his big break on television, Pupkin kidnaps a talk-show host (Jerry Lewis). Rated PG. 109m. **DIR:** Martin Scorsese. **CAST:** Robert De Niro, Jerry Lewis, Sandra Bernhard. **1983**

KING OF HEARTS ★★★★1/2 Philippe de Broca's wartime fantasy provides delightful insights into human behavior. A World War I Scottish infantryman (Alan Bates) searching for a hidden enemy bunker enters a small town that, after being deserted by its citizens, has been taken over by inmates of an insane asylum. In French with English subtitles. No MPAA rating. 102m. **DIR:** Philippe de Broca. **CAST:** Alan Bates, Genevieve Bujold. **1966 DVD**

KING OF JAZZ, THE ★★★ Lavish big-budget musical revue chock-full of big production numbers and great songs. Shot in early two-color Technicolor. Imaginative settings and photography make this last of the all-star extravaganzas most impressive. 93m. **DIR:** John Murray Anderson. **CAST:** Paul Whiteman, John Boles, Bing Crosby. **1930**

KING OF KINGS, THE (1927) ★★★ Cecil B. DeMille was more than ready when he made this one. It's silent, but Hollywood's greatest showman displays his gift for telling a story with required reverence. Naturally, since it's by DeMille, the production is a lavish one. B&W; 115m. **DIR:** Cecil B. DeMille. **CAST:** H. B. Warner, Ernest Torrence, Jacqueline Logan, William Boyd, Joseph Schildkraut. **1927**

KING OF KINGS (1961) ★★★ Well-told tale of the life of Christ, performed with understanding and compassion, though flawed by too much attention to the spectacular, rather than the spiritual. Has its moving moments, nonetheless. Narrated by Orson Welles. 168m. **DIR:** Nicholas Ray. **CAST:** Jeffrey Hunter, Siobhan McKenna, Robert Ryan, Hurd Hatfield, Viveca Lindfors, Rita Gam, Rip Torn, Royal Dano, George Coulouris. **1961**

KING OF MARVIN GARDENS, THE ★★★ Jack Nicholson and Bruce Dern, at the peak of their young careers, play brothers involved in an Atlantic City swindle. Some entertaining theatrics, but once the novelty wears off, the film is overpoweringly depressing. Rated R for profanity, and brief nudity. 104m. **DIR:** Bob Rafelson. **CAST:** Jack Nicholson, Bruce Dern, Ellen Burstyn, Scatman Crothers. **1972 DVD**

KING OF MASKS, THE ★★★★1/2 This fascinating, gorgeously photographed melodrama about sexism in 1930s China is both blatantly manipulative and deeply moving. Old street performer Wang is befriended by a female impersonator from the Sichuan opera who urges him to pass along his artistic secrets before he dies. Wang buys a child at a slave market to live aboard his small houseboat and become the heir of his illusions involving silk face masks. Their relationship becomes a hotbed of complications and shredded emotions. In Mandarin with English subtitles. Not rated. 101m. **DIR:** Wu Tianming. **CAST:** Zhu Xu, Zhou Renying, Zhao Zhigang. **1999 DVD**

KING OF NEW YORK ★★★1/2 Overlooked gangster film follows a New York drug kingpin's attempts to reclaim territory lost during his stay in prison. Cult director Abel Ferrara pulls out all the stops in this violent, fast-paced crime-drama. Rated R for violence, language, drug use, and nudity. 103m. **DIR:** Abel Ferrara. **CAST:** Christopher Walken, Laurence Fishburne, David Caruso, Victor Argo, Wesley Snipes, Janet Julian. **1990 DVD**

KING OF THE BULLWHIP ★★1/2 Looking every bit like Humphrey Bogart's twin brother in a black hat, Lash LaRue was the whip-wielding westerner in a series of low-budget shoot-'em-ups in the 1950s. This, his first for a major distributor, was one of his better efforts. Lash and his sidekick Al St. John must go undercover when a bandit pretends to be our hero while robbing a bank. 60m. **DIR:** Ron Ormond. **CAST:** Lash LaRue, Al St. John, Jack Holt, Dennis Moore, Tom Neal, Anne Gwynne. **1951**

KING OF THE CARNIVAL 🦃 The serial in America was settling into rigor mortis when this stock-footage-fest about circus aerialists battling counterfeiters limped into a television-saturated theater market and died. B&W; 12 chapters. **DIR:** Franklin Adreon. **CAST:** Harry Lauter, Fran Bennett, Keith Richards, Robert Shayne, Gregory Gay, Rick Vallin. **1955**

KING OF THE COWBOYS ★★★★ Roy Rogers at his best as a government agent working undercover as a rodeo performer infiltrating a ring of WWII saboteurs. B&W; 54m. **DIR:** Joseph Kane. **CAST:** Roy Rogers, Smiley Burnette, Peggy Moran, Sons of the Pioneers, Gerald Mohr. **1943**

KING OF THE GRIZZLIES ★★1/2 Wahb, a grizzly cub, loses his mother and sister to cattlemen protecting their herd. He quickly gets into trouble but is rescued by John Yesno, a Cree Indian. Average animal adventure film in the Disney mold. Rated G. 93m. **DIR:** Ron Kelly. **CAST:** John Yesno, Chris Wiggins, Hugh Webster. **1969**

KING OF THE GYPSIES ★★★ Dave Stepanowicz (Eric Roberts) is the grandson of King Zharko Stepanowicz (Sterling Hayden), the patriarch of a gypsy tribe who is both intelligent and violent. Though Dave renounces his gypsy heritage, he is unable to escape it. The performances are uniformly excellent. Director Frank Pierson is the only one who can be held responsible for the film's lack of power. Rated R. 112m. **DIR:** Frank Pierson. **CAST:** Eric Roberts, Sterling Hayden, Susan Sarandon, Annette O'Toole, Brooke Shields, Shelley Winters. **1978**

KING OF THE HILL ★★★★★ A. E. Hotchner's Depression-era memoirs are the basis for this poignant study of childhood strength in the face of escalating tragedy. Young Jesse Bradford watches as his family is scattered, and then—when his father accepts a distant job—becomes the sole occupant of their seedy hotel rooms. This enthralling tale is populated with eclectic characters, all rendered splendidly by a masterful ensemble cast. Rated PG-13 for mild profanity and dramatic intensity. 103m. **DIR:** Steven Soderbergh. **CAST:** Jesse Bradford, Jeroen Krabbé, Lisa Eichhorn, Spalding Gray, Elizabeth McGovern, Karen Allen. **1993**

KING OF THE MOUNTAIN ★★ The quest for success by a trio of buddies leads mostly to unexciting night races on Hollywood's winding Mulholland Drive and clichéd back-stabbing in the music business. Rated PG. 90m. **DIR:** Noel Nosseck. **CAST:** Harry Hamlin, Richard Cox, Joseph Bottoms, Dennis Hopper. **1981**

KING OF THE PECOS ★★★ John Wayne uses his law school training and a proficiency with firearms to exact revenge on the land robber who killed our hero's father. Standard B Western plot is enhanced by plenty of action, and Wayne's increasing skill in front of the camera. B&W; 54m. **DIR:** Joseph Kane. **CAST:** John Wayne, Muriel Evans, Cy Kendall, Jack Clifford, Yakima Canutt. **1936 DVD**

KING OF THE ROARING TWENTIES ★★ The career (supposedly) of the notorious bookie who, among other things, fixed the 1919 World Series. No excitement or conviction; David Janssen is miscast. Not rated, but with the usual gangster gunplay. B&W; 106m. **DIR:** Joseph M. Newman. **CAST:** David Janssen, Dianne Foster, Jack Carson, Diana Dors, Mickey Rooney. **1961**

KING OF THE ROCKETMEN ★★★ This chapterplay precursor to the *Commando Cody* television series has longtime baddie Tristram Coffin joining the good guys for a change. Strapping on his flying suit, he does battle with evil conspirators. Good fun for serial fans, with highly implausible last-minute escapes. B&W; 12 chap-

ters. **DIR:** Fred Brannon. **CAST:** Tristram Coffin, Mae Clarke, Dale Van Sickel, Tom Steele. **1949**

KING OF THE WIND ★★★1/2 Rousing family entertainment based on the popular novel by Marguerite Henry. Teenager Navin Chowdhry tames a wild Arabian horse. The horse is sent from Northern Africa to the King of France, and Chowdhry follows. When he discovers that the magnificent creature will be sent to war, he attempts to steal it. The youth lands in jail, and his only way out is to ride the horse in a special race. Exciting and enthralling every hoof step of the way. Not rated. 101m. **DIR:** Peter Duffell. **CAST:** Richard Harris, Glenda Jackson, Jenny Agutter, Navin Chowdhry. **1993**

KING OF THE ZOMBIES 🦃 Typical mad scientist–zombie movie with evil genius attempting to create an invulnerable army of mindless slaves. B&W; 67m. **DIR:** Jean Yarbrough. **CAST:** Dick Purcell, Joan Woodbury, Mantan Moreland, John Archer. **1941 DVD**

KING, QUEEN AND KNAVE 🦃 Even with the wonderful grace and charm of David Niven, this story authored by Vladimir Nabokov is a dud. Not rated. 92m. **DIR:** Jerzy Skolimowski. **CAST:** David Niven, Gina Lollobrigida, John Moulder-Brown, Mario Adorf. **1972**

KING RALPH ★★★ When a freak accident wipes out the entire royal family, Las Vegas entertainer John Goodman is the sole heir to the English crown. With the help of Peter O'Toole and Richard Griffiths (in fine performances), Goodman's good-natured, lovable slob attempts to rise to the occasion. Amiably entertaining comedy. Rated PG for brief profanity. 97m. **DIR:** David S. Ward. **CAST:** John Goodman, Peter O'Toole, John Hurt, Camille Courdi, Richard Griffiths. **1991 DVD**

KING RAT ★★★★ A Japanese prison camp in World War II is the setting for this stark drama of survival of the fittest, the fittest in this case being "King Rat" (George Segal), the opportunistic head of black-market operations within the compound. B&W; 133m. **DIR:** Bryan Forbes. **CAST:** George Segal, Tom Courtenay, James Fox, John Mills. **1965**

KING RICHARD AND THE CRUSADERS 🦃 George Sanders is far from kingly in this rip-off of Sir Walter Scott's *The Talisman*. The uninspired cast drags the show down. 114m. **DIR:** David Butler. **CAST:** George Sanders, Rex Harrison, Virginia Mayo, Laurence Harvey. **1954**

KING RICHARD II ★★★1/2 David Birney is quite effective as Shakespeare's scheming, then remorseful Richard, in this well-made, filmed stage production. Acting honors are shared by Paul Shenar as his cousin, the betrayed and vengeful Bolingbroke (later Henry IV), and Peter MacLean as their uncle, the Duke of York. A Bard Productions Ltd. release. 172m. **DIR:** William Woodman. **CAST:** David Birney, Paul Shenar, Peter MacLean, Mary Joan Negro, Logan Ramsey, Nan Martin, Jay Robinson, Nicholas Hammond. **1982 DVD**

KING SOLOMON'S MINES (1937) ★★★1/2 H. Rider Haggard's splendid adventure story received its first sound-film treatment here. This version is superior in many respects to the more famous 1950 color remake. The action and battle sequences (many shot on location with real tribesmen) rival the best early MGM Tarzan films for costumes and feel. B&W; 79m. **DIR:** Robert Stevenson. **CAST:** Cedric Hardwicke, Paul Robeson, Roland Young, John Loder, Anna Lee. **1937 DVD**

KING SOLOMON'S MINES (1950) ★★★★★ The "great white hunter" genre of adventure films has been a movie staple for ages, yet only this one rates as a cinema classic. Stewart Granger guides a party through darkest Africa in search of a lady's husband. On the way, the hunter and the lady (Deborah Kerr) become fast friends. 102m. **DIR:** Compton Bennett, Andrew Marton. **CAST:** Stewart Granger, Deborah Kerr, Hugo Haas. **1950**

KING SOLOMON'S MINES (1985) 🦃 A crime against H. Rider Haggard's classic adventure novel—a compendium of cornball clichés and stupid slapstick. Rated PG-13 for violence and profanity. 100m. **DIR:** J. Lee Thompson. **CAST:** Richard Chamberlain, Sharon Stone, John Rhys-Davies, Herbert Lom, Ken Gampu. **1985**

KING SOLOMON'S TREASURE 🦃 This mindless adventure features a stuttering David McCallum pursuing treasure in Africa's Forbidden City. 90m. **DIR:** Alvin Rakoff. **CAST:** David McCallum, Britt Ekland, Patrick Macnee, John Colicos. **1976**

KING TUT: THE FACE OF TUTANKHAMUN ★★★1/2 The four 50-minute segments of this documentary produced for A&E are hosted by series writer and historian Christopher Frayling. The length stretches somewhat beyond the material, but some dazzling artifacts are showcased as the historical and apocryphal aspects of the boy king are unraveled. Not rated. 200m. **DIR:** Derek Towers, David Wallace. **1992**

KINGDOM, THE ★★★ Creepy tale about a busy Danish hospital and the ghost that haunts it, searching for redemption. Eerie, well-acted, and visually stunning film runs way too long. In Danish with English subtitles (but imagery is so rich that viewers won't want to read at the same time). Not rated, but features horrific images and gory pieces of medical footage. 265m. **DIR:** Lars von Trier. **CAST:** Ernst-Hugo Jaregard, Kirsten Rolffes, Holger Juul Ransen, Soren Pilmark, Ghita Norby, Jens Okking, Otto Brandenburg, Udo Kier. **1994**

•KINGDOM COME ★★ An extended family comes together for a patriarch's funeral and works through a multitude of private and public issues, squabbles, and feelings for the deceased in this lumbering, broadly comic drama. The script—based on *Dearly Departed*, a play by David Dean Bottrell and Jessie Jones—feebly wrings spiritual inspiration from stereotypical and superficial characters and a family closet packed to the rafters with soiled relationships and bruised emotions. Rated PG. 95m. **DIR:** Doug McHenry. **CAST:** LL Cool J, Whoopi Goldberg, Vivica A. Fox, Cedric the Entertainer, Jada Pinkett Smith, Toni Braxton, Loretta Devine. **2001 DVD**

KINGDOM OF THE SPIDERS ★★★ William Shatner stars in this unsuspenseful thriller with lurid special effects. The title tells it all. Rated PG. 94m. **DIR:** John "Bud" Cardos. **CAST:** William Shatner, Tiffany Bolling, Woody Strode. **1977**

KINGDOM OF THE VAMPIRE ★★ Made for less money than a used car, this film follows a vampire who works in a liquor store. The acting ranges from bad to mediocre, but at least the production tries. Not rated; contains violence and profanity. 75m. **DIR:** J. R. Bookwalter. **CAST:**

Matthew Jason Walsh, Cherie Patry, Shannon Doyle. **1991**

KINGFISH: A STORY OF HUEY P. LONG ★★★1/2 John Goodman delivers a full-bodied performance as Democratic Louisiana Sen. Huey P. Long, whose days of drinking and loving are captured here as entertainment. Evenhanded script and Goodman's strong presence make this made-for-cable movie more about the man than the madness. 97m. **DIR:** Thomas Schlamme. **CAST:** John Goodman, Matt Craven, Anne Heche, Ann Dowd, Jeff Perry. **1995**

KINGPIN ★★ Washed-up pro bowler Woody Harrelson grooms Amish farmboy Randy Quaid for the "big time" in Reno. Directing brothers Peter and Bobby Farrelly recycle the story from their own *Dumb and Dumber,* with the earlier film's greatest assets—stars Jim Carrey and Jeff Daniels—conspicuously missing. This time there are only a few scattered laughs and more than a few repulsive moments. Rated PG-13 for mild profanity and sexual humor. 113m. **DIR:** Peter Farrelly, Bobby Farrelly. **CAST:** Woody Harrelson, Randy Quaid, Vanessa Angel, Bill Murray, Chris Elliott. **1996 DVD**

KINGS AND DESPERATE MEN: A HOSTAGE INCIDENT ★★★ Improbable but engrossing account of terrorists taking over a radio talk show to present their case to the public. Patrick McGoohan lends his commanding presence as the abrasive, cynical talk-show host. A strange, almost cinema vérité portrayal, the title comes from a John Donne poem that's quoted by McGoohan. Rated PG-13 for language and violence. 117m. **DIR:** Alexis Kanner. **CAST:** Patrick McGoohan, Alexis Kanner, Andrea Marcovicci, Margaret Trudeau. **1989**

KINGS GO FORTH ★★★★ A World War II melodrama with social consciousness. Frank Sinatra and Tony Curtis play two skirt chasers in the army who fall for the same girl (Natalie Wood). When they find out one of her parents is black, the true colors of the soldiers are revealed. B&W; 110m. **DIR:** Delmer Daves. **CAST:** Tony Curtis, Frank Sinatra, Natalie Wood, Leora Dana. **1958 DVD**

KINGS OF THE ROAD ★★★★ This is the film that put the new-wave German cinema on the map. Wim Wenders's classic road tale of wanderlust in Deutschland centers on a traveling movie projectionist-repairman who encounters a hitchhiker who is depressed following the collapse of his marriage. The men form an unusual relationship while en route from West to East Germany. A truly astonishing film with a great rock 'n' roll score. In German with English subtitles. B&W; 176m. **DIR:** Wim Wenders. **CAST:** Rudiger Vogler, Hanns Zischler, Lisa Kreuzer. **1976**

KING'S ROW ★★★★★ A small American town at the turn of the century is the setting where two men (Ronald Reagan and Robert Cummings) grow up to experience the corruption and moral decay behind the facade of a peaceful, serene community. This brilliantly photographed drama is close to being a masterpiece, thanks to exceptional performances by many of Hollywood's best character actors. B&W; 127m. **DIR:** Sam Wood. **CAST:** Ann Sheridan, Robert Cummings, Ronald Reagan, Claude Rains, Charles Coburn, Betty Field, Judith Anderson. **1941**

KING'S WHORE, THE ★★★ A European king is obsessed with a happily married woman who wants nothing to do with him. Good acting, but the story drags on too long. Rated R for profanity, nudity, and violence. 111m. **DIR:** Axel Corti. **CAST:** Timothy Dalton, Valeria Golino, Stephane Freiss, Margaret Tyzack, Feodor Chaliapin, Eleanor David, Paul Crauchet, Robin Renucci. **1990**

KINJITE (FORBIDDEN SUBJECTS) 🦃 Again Charles Bronson plays a vigilante who deals out his own brand of justice. Rated R for nudity, profanity, and violence. 96m. **DIR:** J. Lee Thompson. **CAST:** Charles Bronson, Perry Lopez, Peggy Lipton. **1989**

KIPPERBANG ★★1/2 This is another World War II coming-of-age saga, in the same category as *Hope and Glory*, *Empire of the Sun*, and *Au Revoir les Enfants*. Charming and wistful at times, it doesn't quite reach the heights. Rated PG. 80m. **DIR:** Michael Apted. **CAST:** John Albasiny, Alison Steadman. **1982**

KISMET (1944) ★★ Ronald Colman plays the beggar-of-beggars who cons his way into the Caliph's palace and romances Marlene Dietrich. The musical version has the same story line and the advantage of Borodin's music to make it more romantic. 100m. **DIR:** William Dieterle. **CAST:** Ronald Colman, Marlene Dietrich, Edward Arnold, James Craig, Joy Page, Hugh Herbert, Florence Bates, Harry Davenport, Robert Warwick, Hobart Cavanaugh. **1944**

KISMET (1955) ★★1/2 The Borodin-based Arabian Nights fantasy, a hit on Broadway, is stylishly staged and ripe with "Baubles, Bangles, and Beads" and Dolores Gray's show-stopping "Bagdad." Sadly, however, the shift to film loses the snap and crackle despite great singing by Howard Keel, Vic Damone, and Ann Blyth. The earlier Ronald Colman version (1944) is more fun and half a star better. 113m. **DIR:** Vincente Minnelli. **CAST:** Howard Keel, Ann Blyth, Monty Woolley, Vic Damone, Dolores Gray. **1955**

KISS, THE (1929) ★★★★ The kind of smooth, stylish, and sophisticated production that best represents the apex of the silent-film period. Irene (Greta Garbo) gets caught up in a messy domestic tangle of infidelity and murder. The highly stylized courtroom scenes (redolent of German Expressionism) and flashback sequences give the film a flamboyant, visually arresting look. B&W; 70m. **DIR:** Jacques Feyder. **CAST:** Greta Garbo, Conrad Nagel. **1929**

KISS, THE (1988) ★★ An African voodoo priestess (Joanna Pacula) is looking for an heir. So she invades the lives of her dead sister's family. That old black magic just ain't there. Rated R for nudity and violence. 105m. **DIR:** Pen Densham. **CAST:** Joanna Pacula, Meredith Salenger. **1988**

KISS BEFORE DYING, A ★★1/2 Psychotic Matt Dillon stalks Sean Young in this all-too-familiar tale—derived from Ira Levin's novel. Still, the leads are fine, especially Young in a dual role as sisters. The 1956 adaptation is better. Rated R for violence, nudity, and profanity. 93m. **DIR:** James Dearden. **CAST:** Matt Dillon, Sean Young, Max von Sydow, Diane Ladd, James Russo. **1991**

KISS DADDY GOOD NIGHT ★★ Uma Thurman stars as a struggling model who survives by picking up wealthy men in bars, then drugging and robbing them. She finds the situation reversed when an obsessive suitor decides that he wants her all to himself. Moody,

ultimately incomprehensible thriller. Rated R for nudity and violence. 89m. **DIR:** Peter Ily Huemer. **CAST:** Uma Thurman, Paul Dillon, Paul Richards. **1988**

KISS DADDY GOODBYE 🦃 Two psychic kids reanimate their father's corpse for some revenge in this tepid entry. Not rated; contains violence and profanity. 81m. **DIR:** Patrick Regan. **CAST:** Fabian Forte, Marilyn Burns. **1981**

KISS ME A KILLER 🦃 A young wife and a drifter plot to eliminate her older husband. This is the Hispanic version of *The Postman Always Rings Twice*. The final irony this time out isn't nearly as satisfying. Rated R for nudity and profanity. 91m. **DIR:** Marcus De Leon. **CAST:** Julie Carmen, Robert Beltran, Guy Boyd, Ramon Franco, Charles Boswell. **1991**

KISS ME DEADLY ★★★1/2 Robert Aldrich's adaptation of Mickey Spillane's Mike Hammer novel was hailed by French new wave film critics in the 1960s as a masterpiece. Brutal and surrealistic, it has Hammer attempting to protect a woman (Cloris Leachman) from the men who want to kill her. B&W; 105m. **DIR:** Robert Aldrich. **CAST:** Ralph Meeker, Albert Dekker, Cloris Leachman, Paul Stewart. **1955 DVD**

KISS ME GOODBYE ★★★ Sally Field plays a widow of three years who has just fallen in love again. Her first husband was an electrifying Broadway choreographer named Jolly (James Caan). Her husband-to-be is a slightly stuffy Egyptologist (Jeff Bridges). Before her wedding day, she receives a visit from Jolly's ghost, who is apparently upset about the approaching wedding. Rated PG for profanity and sexual situations. 101m. **DIR:** Robert Mulligan. **CAST:** Sally Field, James Caan, Jeff Bridges, Claire Trevor. **1982**

KISS ME GUIDO ★★★★ Frankie Zito is an aspiring actor who lives with his family and works in their pizza joint. When he catches his brother fooling around with his fiancée, he decides to move out. Naïve Frankie answers a classified ad for a GWM roommate, not realizing that it stands for Gay White Male. When Frankie realizes that his roommate is gay, a lack of funds forces him to stay leading to a hilarious series of events. Rated R for adult situations and language. 90m. **DIR:** Tony Vitale. **CAST:** Nick Scotti, Anthony Barrile, Anthony De Sando. **1997 DVD**

KISS ME KATE ★★★ That which is Shakespeare's *Taming of the Shrew* in the original is deftly rendered by Cole Porter, scripter Dorothy Kingsley, and George Sidney's graceful direction, by way of some fine performances by Howard Keel and Kathryn Grayson as a married pair whose onstage and offstage lives mingle. 109m. **DIR:** George Sidney. **CAST:** Howard Keel, Kathryn Grayson, Keenan Wynn, James Whitmore, Ann Miller, Tommy Rall, Bobby Van, Bob Fosse. **1953**

KISS ME, STUPID ★★★1/2 A skirt-chasing boozing singer (Dean Martin) stops in the town of Climax, Nevada, and is waylaid by a would-be songwriter. This sex farce is on its way to cult status. When released it was condemned by the Legion of Decency and panned by critics and the general public; but it's worth a second look. Scripted by I. A. L. Diamond and director Billy Wilder. B&W; 126m. **DIR:** Billy Wilder. **CAST:** Dean Martin, Kim Novak, Ray Walston, Felicia Farr, Cliff Osmond, Alice Pearce. **1964**

KISS MEETS THE PHANTOM OF THE PARK 🦃 Flaccid made-for-TV movie about the heavy-metal group and a loony amusement park handyman. 100m. **DIR:** Gordon Hessler. **CAST:** Peter Criss, Ace Frehley, Gene Simmons, Paul Stanley. **1978**

KISS OF DEATH (1947) ★★★★1/2 Finely crafted gangster film deals with convict Victor Mature infiltrating a gang run by psychopath Richard Widmark (in his film debut) so that Mature can obtain evidence on Widmark. Contains the now-famous scene of Widmark gleefully pushing a wheelchair-bound woman to her death down a flight of stairs. B&W; 98m. **DIR:** Henry Hathaway. **CAST:** Victor Mature, Richard Widmark, Brian Donlevy, Karl Malden, Coleen Gray. **1947**

KISS OF DEATH (1995) ★★★1/2 David Caruso is excellent as the tortured Jimmy Kilmartin, a small-time car thief whose attempts to go straight are thwarted by a psychopath. Despite the impending clash between these two, scripter Richard Price gets far more mileage out of the complicated, strange and wonderful relationship between Caruso and Samuel L. Jackson's police investigator. Rated R for violence, profanity, and nudity. 101m. **DIR:** Barbet Schroeder. **CAST:** David Caruso, Samuel L. Jackson, Nicolas Cage, Helen Hunt, Kathryn Erbe, Stanley Tucci, Michael Rapaport, Ving Rhames. **1995**

KISS OF FIRE ★★ A decent performance by Christina Applegate as a young woman trying to forget a difficult past is the only worthwhile aspect of this meandering, pointless drama. The provocative box, which shows Applegate as a stripper, is misleading. Also released as *Claudine's Return*. Rated R for sexual situations, violence, nudity, and profanity. 92m. **DIR:** Antonio Tibaldi. **CAST:** Christina Applegate, Stefano Dionisi, Matt Clark. **1998 DVD**

•KISS OF THE DRAGON ★★★ Luc Besson (the auteur of *La Femme Nikita* and *The Fifth Element*) produced and cowrote the screenplay for this bloody, breathless martial arts–conspiracy film. A Beijing police operative kicks butt all over Paris with deadly precision after being framed for murder by a sadistic French inspector. A North Dakota farm girl turned heroin-addicted prostitute is the weakest link in plot points that are at times blurrier than star Jet Li's flying feet. Rated R for language, violence, sexual content, and drug use. 98m. **DIR:** Chris Nahon. **CAST:** Jet Li, Tcheky Karyo, Bridget Fonda, Max Ryan. **2001 DVD**

KISS OF THE SPIDER WOMAN ★★★★ This first English-language film by Hector Babenco is a somber, brilliantly acted tale about a gay window dresser, Molina (William Hurt), and a revolutionary, Valentin (Raul Julia), who slowly begin to care for each other and understand each other's viewpoint while imprisoned together in a South American prison. It is stark, violent, and daring. Rated R for profanity, violence, and suggested sex. 119m. **DIR:** Hector Babenco. **CAST:** William Hurt, Raul Julia, Sonia Braga. **1985**

KISS OF THE VAMPIRE ★★★1/2 A solidly creepy British vampire flick from Hammer Studios that really has some bite to it, even if Noel Willman is a Christopher Lee clone. A period piece set around the turn of the century, this has a few tricks up its bloody sleeve. Also released in a heavily edited U.S. version, *Kiss of Evil*. Not rated; contains implied violence. 88m. **DIR:** Don Sharp. **CAST:** Clifford Evans, Edward DeSouza, Noel Willman, Jennifer Daniel. **1963 DVD**

KISS OR KILL ★★1/2 Australian lovers lure businessmen into motel rooms for sex and then drug and rob them in this edgy but pointless slice of outback *noir.* They become the target of a sprawling manhunt when one of their tricks dies and they flee the scene with a videotape that incriminates a local soccer legend as an active pedophile. The outlaw sweethearts are pursued as the body count grows. An irritating exercise in jump-cut editing. Rated R for nudity, sex, language, and violence. 96m. **DIR:** Bill Bennett. **CAST:** Frances O'Connor, Matt Day, Chris Haywood, Barry Langrishe, Barry Otto, Andrew S. Gilbert. **1997**

KISS SHOT ★★★ Single mom struggles after being laid off. In desperation she hustles pool while being wooed by both her manager and a playboy. Solid performances and well-paced plot development maintain viewer interest. Rated PG for violence. 88m. **DIR:** Jerry London. **CAST:** Whoopi Goldberg, Dennis Franz, Dorian Harewood. **1989 DVD**

KISS THE GIRLS ★★★1/2 Morgan Freeman, a forensic psychologist on the Washington, D.C., police force, is drawn to Durham, North Carolina, when his niece becomes the latest victim of a serial killer. But is she dead? According to the only victim to escape, our villain kills only those women who won't follow the rules of his fantasy game. Although there is a lack of mystery to the identity of the villain, there's still plenty of suspense. Rated R for violence, profanity, nudity, and suggested sex. 120m. **DIR:** Gary Fleder. **CAST:** Morgan Freeman, Ashley Judd, Cary Elwes, Tony Goldwyn, Jay O. Sanders, Bill Nunn, Brian Cox, Alex McArthur, Richard T. Jones, Jeremy Piven, William Converse-Roberts. **1997 DVD**

KISS THE GIRLS GOODBYE ❤ Repulsive exploitation about a man who kidnaps a young woman and bends her to his will. Not rated; contains strong violence, profanity, sexual situations, and substance abuse. 92m. **DIR:** Lee Karaim. **CAST:** Frankie Ray, Stephanie Smith, Ann O'Leary. **1997**

KISS THE SKY ★★1/2 On a business trip to the Philippines, Jeff and Marty decide to dump their humdrum jobs and families for a chance to rediscover the irresponsibility of their youth, but paradise turns ugly when their previous lives and a beautiful woman surface. Gorgeous cinematography and a sense of wonderment go a long way. Rated R for adult situations, language, nudity, and violence. 105m. **DIR:** Roger Young. **CAST:** William L. Petersen, Gary Cole, Sheryl Lee, Patricia Charbonneau, Terence Stamp. **1998 DVD**

•KISS TOLEDO GOODBYE ★★ An ordinary guy (Michael Rapaport) gets thrust into the role of a mob boss when the untimely death of his previously unknown biological father (Robert Forster) opens up that position in the "family" business. Other than a few good lines, mainly from Christopher Walken, this movie is mostly dull and uninteresting and is certainly not worth the cast assembled. Rated R for violence and language. 96m. **DIR:** Lyndon Chubbuck. **CAST:** Michael Rapaport, Christopher Walken, Robert Forster, Christine Taylor, Nancy Allen. **1999 DVD**

KISS TOMORROW GOODBYE ★★★ Violent, fast-paced gangster film brings back the days of the B movie. James Cagney is cast once again as a ruthless gangster who knows no limits. A rogue's gallery of character actors lends good support to this overlooked entry into the genre. 102m. **DIR:** Gordon Douglas. **CAST:** James Cagney, Luther Adler, Ward Bond, Barbara Payton, Barton MacLane, Neville Brand, Kenneth Tobey, Steve Brodie. **1950**

KISSED ★★1/2 A young girl shows a morbid fascination with dead animals; as an adult she becomes an apprentice embalmer, and her fascination grows into a sexual obsession with her "patients." Writer-director Lynne Stopkewich's first feature film (adapted from a story by Canadian writer Barbara Gowdy) avoids sensationalizing its grim subject, but it's so resolutely tactful that the heroine's obsession never seems deeply felt. Not rated; contains frontal nudity and graphic scenes of necrophiliac sex. 72m. **DIR:** Lynne Stopkewich. **CAST:** Molly Parker, Peter Outerbridge, Jay Brazeau, Natasha Morley, James Timmons. **1996**

KISSES FOR MY PRESIDENT ★★★ With a little more care, this could have been a great comedy. As it is, there is some fun when Fred MacMurray, as the husband of the first woman president of the United States (Polly Bergen), falls heir to many of the tasks and functions handled by our first ladies. B&W; 113m. **DIR:** Curtis Bernhardt. **CAST:** Fred MacMurray, Polly Bergen, Arlene Dahl, Edward Andrews. **1964**

KISSIN' COUSINS ★★ Would Elvis in dual roles double the fun? Divide it by two is closer to the truth. This time he is both an air force lieutenant and a *blond* hillbilly. He manages to fall in love while belting a few country tunes such as "Smokey Mountain Boy" and "Barefoot Ballad." 96m. **DIR:** Gene Nelson. **CAST:** Elvis Presley, Arthur O'Connell, Jack Albertson. **1964**

KISSING A FOOL ★★ An egotistical TV personality (David Schwimmer) tests the fidelity of his fiancée (Mili Avital) by asking his best friend (Jason Lee) to try to seduce her. The clichéd premise has some mild possibilities, but none is developed in this dumb, unfunny comedy. Schwimmer's character is obnoxious, Lee's is a whiner, and Avital's seems too good for either of them. In a stunning misjudgment, director Doug Ellin gives away the "surprise" ending in the very first shot. Rated R for profanity. 105m. **DIR:** Doug Ellin. **CAST:** David Schwimmer, Jason Lee, Mili Avital, Bonnie Hunt, Kari Wuhrer. **1998 DVD**

KISSING BANDIT, THE ★★★ A shy eastern-bred nerd tries to carry on the legend of his bandit father, a Casanova of the West. Made at the low point of Frank Sinatra's first career and recommended only as a curiosity piece for his fans. Ricardo Montalban, Ann Miller, and Cyd Charisse are teamed for one dance number. 102m. **DIR:** Laslo Benedek. **CAST:** Frank Sinatra, Kathryn Grayson, Mildred Natwick, J. Carrol Naish, Billy Gilbert, Ricardo Montalban, Ann Miller, Cyd Charisse. **1948**

KISSING PLACE, THE ★★★★ An absolutely chilling performance by Meredith Baxter-Birney sparks this made-for-TV thriller. She's a woman who has kidnapped a boy to replace her dead child. All goes well for nearly eight years until unsettling dreams force the boy to question his identity. 88m. **DIR:** Tony Wharmby. **CAST:** Meredith Baxter-Birney, David Ogden Stiers, Nathaniel Moreau, Victoria Snow. **1989**

KISSINGER AND NIXON ★★ Need a nap? Ten minutes of this talkfest and REM will have a whole new meaning.

Strong performances by Beau Bridges as Richard Nixon and Ron Silver as Henry Kissinger cannot save this behind-the-scenes look at the negotiations to end the war in Vietnam. They talk in conference, they negotiate in Paris, they chat in the Oval Office, and they'll put you to sleep. Made for cable. Not rated; contains profanity. 90m. **DIR:** Daniel Petrie. **CAST:** Beau Bridges, Ron Silver, Matt Frewer, George Takei, Ron White. **1995**

KIT CARSON ★★★1/2 This lively Western about the two-fisted frontiersman gave Jon Hall one of his best roles. Good action scenes. B&W; 97m. **DIR:** George B. Seitz. **CAST:** Jon Hall, Dana Andrews, Lynn Bari. **1940**

KITCHEN TOTO, THE ★★★★ Powerful, uncompromising drama about a 10 year old black boy who becomes hopelessly caught in the middle of racial violence between East African tribesmen and white British colonists in 1952 Kenya. Brilliantly performed and directed. Rated PG. Contains violence and nudity. 90m. **DIR:** Harry Hook. **CAST:** Bob Peck, Phyllis Logan. **1988**

KITTY AND THE BAGMAN ★★1/2 Overambitious period piece about two Australian crime queens battling for control. The Roaring Twenties sets and the constant shifts back and forth from broad comedy to drama to shoot-'em-up action should entertain some viewers. Not rated. 95m. **DIR:** Donald Crombie. **CAST:** John Stanton, Liddy Clark. **1982**

KITTY FOYLE ★★★★ Ginger Rogers, who became a star in comedies and musicals, went dramatic (and won an Oscar) in this three-hanky tearjerker about the troubled love life of an attractive secretary. Pure soap opera, but splendidly presented. B&W; 107m. **DIR:** Sam Wood. **CAST:** Ginger Rogers, Dennis Morgan, James Craig, Eduardo Ciannelli, Gladys Cooper, Ernest Cossart. **1940**

KLANSMAN, THE 🦃 Lee Marvin and Richard Burton fight the Klan in a southern town. Rated R. 112m. **DIR:** Terence Young. **CAST:** Lee Marvin, Richard Burton, Cameron Mitchell, O. J. Simpson, Lola Falana, Linda Evans. **1974**

KLEPTOMANIA ★★★ This intriguing—albeit flawed—character study pairs a street hustler with a bored, bulimic society wife. They become each other's lifeline, share a fetish for stealing, and could use some strong counseling. Although it's interesting to speculate where the script is heading, the film's conclusion is both disappointing and unlikely. Rated R for profanity, rape, nudity, and violence. 90m. **DIR:** Don Boyd. **CAST:** Amy Irving, Patsy Kensit, Victor Garber, Gregg Baker, Delbert McClinton. **1993**

KLONDIKE ANNIE ★★★1/2 Mae West stars in this comedy as a shady lady who leaves the Barbary Coast for Alaska, where she takes on the identity of a zealous nun and finds out religion isn't as much of a sham as she thought. It's unusual for West, but she keeps it respectable—and so did the overzealous censors, who cut out all of her double-entendres. B&W; 78m. **DIR:** Raoul Walsh. **CAST:** Mae West, Victor McLaglen, Helen Jerome Eddy, Phillip Reed, Harold Huber. **1936 DVD**

KLUTE ★★★★ Jane Fonda dominates every frame in this study of a worldly call girl. Her Oscar-winning performance looks into the hidden sides of a prostitute's lifestyle; the dreams, fear, shame, and loneliness of her world are graphically illustrated. Donald Sutherland costars as an out-of-town cop looking for a missing friend. He feels Fonda holds the key to his whereabouts. Rated R. 114m. **DIR:** Alan J. Pakula. **CAST:** Jane Fonda, Donald Sutherland, Roy Scheider. **1971 DVD**

KNACK . . . AND HOW TO GET IT, THE ★★★★ Ray Brooks plays the lad with a knack for handling the ladies. Michael Crawford is the novice who wants to learn. Rita Tushingham is the lass caught in the middle. A British sex comedy produced before sex comedies were fashionable, meaning there's more talk than action. But the talk is witty, the direction zesty and the acting close to perfection. B&W; 85m. **DIR:** Richard Lester. **CAST:** Michael Crawford, Ray Brooks, Donal Donnelly, Rita Tushingham, Charlotte Rampling, Peter Copley. **1965**

KNICKERBOCKER HOLIDAY ★★ A plodding, lackluster rendition of the Kurt Weill/Maxwell Anderson musical about Peter Stuyvesant and Dutch New York. The best song, "September Song," was originally sung by Walter Huston. Unfortunately, he's not in the film. B&W; 85m. **DIR:** Harry Brown. **CAST:** Nelson Eddy, Charles Coburn, Shelley Winters, Chester Conklin, Constance Dowling, Percy Kilbride. **1944**

KNIFE IN THE HEAD ★★★ When an innocent man is shot in the head during a police attack on a political rally, he loses his memory and physical coordination. His difficult recovery is slowed when the police, who need to justify their actions, accuse him of being a terrorist. Bruno Ganz is excellent in the lead role, but the ambitious film may be difficult to follow for American viewers unfamiliar with German politics. In German with English subtitles. 112m. **DIR:** Reinhard Hauff. **CAST:** Bruno Ganz, Angela Winkler, Hans Brenner. **1978**

KNIFE IN THE WATER ★★★★ Absolutely fascinating feature-film debut for director Roman Polanski. A couple off for a sailing holiday encounter a young hitchhiker and invite him along. The resulting sexual tension is riveting, the outcome impossible to anticipate. In many ways, this remains one of Polanski's finest pictures. In Polish with English subtitles. Not rated; the film has sexual situations. B&W; 94m. **DIR:** Roman Polanski. **CAST:** Leon Niemczyk, Jolanta Umecka, Zygmunt Malanowicz. **1962**

•KNIGHT CHILLS ★★ An obsessed role-playing game enthusiast dies in a freak car accident, and then returns from the grave as the ghost of his gaming character, hell-bent on wreaking vengeance upon the other players that had wronged him in life. Almost falling into that so-bad-it's-good category, the cheeseball premise is nothing compared to the hilariously poor acting by the ensemble cast. Not rated; contains some scenes of graphic violence and harsh language. 90m. **DIR:** Katherine Hicks. **CAST:** Tim Jeffrey, Laura Alexander, DJ Perry. **2002**

KNIGHT MOVES ★★ At an international chess tournament in the Pacific Northwest one of the top touring masters becomes the prime suspect in a macabre, ritual murder. This atmospheric thriller makes less sense the more one thinks about it, but it certainly isn't dull. Rated R for violence and language. 110m. **DIR:** Carl Schenkel. **CAST:** Christopher Lambert, Diane Lane, Tom Skerritt, Daniel Baldwin. **1993 DVD**

KNIGHT WITHOUT ARMOUR ★★★ This melodrama, about a British national caught up in the Russian Revolution and his attempts to save aristocrat Marlene Dietrich, is filled with beautiful photography but remains

basically a curiosity, one of the few American films to depict communism in the 1930s. Robert Donat is an unassuming, gentle hero. B&W; 107m. **DIR:** Jacques Feyder. **CAST:** Robert Donat, Marlene Dietrich, Miles Malleson, David Tree. **1937**

KNIGHTRIDERS ★★★ What was supposed to be a modern-day look at the lost Code of Honor comes across on screen as a bunch of weirdos dressed in armor riding motorcycles in a traveling circus. At a length of almost two-and-a-half hours, there isn't enough to hold the viewer's interest. Rated PG. 145m. **DIR:** George A. Romero. **CAST:** Ed Harris, Tom Savini, Amy Ingersoll. **1981 DVD**

KNIGHTS ★★★ Vampiric cyborgs in futuristic Taos see people as a handy source of fuel. Hoping to save humankind, robot Kris Kristofferson teaches kick-boxing champ Kathy Long all the right moves. Aside from the weak ending and a laughable battle scene (featuring a dismembered Kristofferson), this sword-and-sorcery cheapo isn't bad. Rated R for violence and profanity. 89m. **DIR:** Albert Pyun. **CAST:** Kris Kristofferson, Lance Henriksen, Kathy Long. **1992**

KNIGHTS AND ARMOR ★★★ A seamless blend of interviews with well-versed historians, this provides a couple of intriguing biographies of famous knights, as well as a rundown of the Middle Ages. There is even a quick lesson concerning the complications of armor and heraldry. Easily digestible and informative, but with little crossover appeal if you aren't interested in this subject. Made for A&E. Not rated. 100m. **DIR:** Andy Stevenson. **1994**

KNIGHTS AND EMERALDS ★★★1/2 A young drummer in a marching band in working-class Birmingham defies the racism of his family and friends when he takes up with a competing band of black youths. Original and endearing, sidestepping countless clichés into which it could easily have fallen. A good family item. Rated PG. 94m. **DIR:** Ian Emes. **CAST:** Christopher Wild, Beverly Hills, Warren Mitchell. **1986**

KNIGHTS OF THE CITY 🦃 A New York street gang is also a pop musical group. Rated R. 89m. **DIR:** Dominic Orlando. **CAST:** Leon Isaac Kennedy, Nicholas Campbell, John Mengatti, Wendy Barry, Stoney Jackson, The Fat Boys, Michael Ansara. **1987**

KNIGHTS OF THE ROUND TABLE ★★1/2 Colorful wide-screen epic of King Arthur's court is long on pageantry but lacks the spirit required to make this type of film work well. 115m. **DIR:** Richard Thorpe. **CAST:** Robert Taylor, Ava Gardner, Mel Ferrer, Stanley Baker, Felix Aylmer, Robert Urquhart. **1953**

KNIGHT'S TALE, A ★★ A medieval squire posing as a knight becomes a star on the European jousting circuit. The film is cheerfully anachronistic, making tournaments into a sort of World Wrestling Federation and setting it all to a modern rock score ("We Will Rock You," "The Boys Are Back in Town"). The novelty wears off quickly, though, and the film settles down to a trite story of a young man pursuing his dream. Rated PG-13 for tournament combat scenes. 132m. **DIR:** Brian Helgeland. **CAST:** Heath Ledger, Mark Addy, Rufus Sewell, Shannyn Sossamon, Alan Tudyk. **2001**

KNOCK OFF ★★★ Watchable action-adventure film plays a bit like a cheap kung fu movie but, thanks to a screenplay by actionmeister Steven E. De Souza and sharp direction by Tsui Hark, it's entertaining. Rated R for violence and language. 91m. **DIR:** Tsui Hark. **CAST:** Jean-Claude Van Damme, Rob Schneider, Lela Rochon, Michael Fitzergald, Paul Sorvino. **1998 DVD**

KNOCK ON ANY DOOR ★★★1/2 Before John Derek became a Svengali for Ursula Andress, Linda Evans, and Bo Derek, he was an actor—and a pretty good one, too, as he proves in this courtroom drama directed by Nicholas Ray. He's a kid who can't help having gotten into trouble, and Humphrey Bogart is the attorney who attempts to explain his plight to the jury. B&W; 100m. **DIR:** Nicholas Ray. **CAST:** John Derek, Humphrey Bogart, Susan Perry, Allene Roberts. **1949**

KNOCKING ON DEATH'S DOOR ★★1/2 Newly wed paranormal investigators spend their honeymoon at a haunted house in Maine, where the resident ghosts take a particular interest in the young bride. Filmed in Ireland, this Roger Corman production at least looks good, and has a few shocks mixed into a largely predictable plot. Rated R for nudity, sexual situations, and violence. 92m. **DIR:** Mitch Marcus. **CAST:** Brian Bloom, Kimberly Rowe, David Carradine, John Doe. **1997 DVD**

KNOCKOUT ★★★ Good intentions abound in this female Hispanic *Rocky*, starring Sophia Adella Hernandez as Belle, who wants to follow in her father's boxing footsteps. She's good in the ring, but is she good enough to beat the rival who put her best friend in the hospital? While the pedestrian script fails to reach a KO, the cast adds punch. Rated PG-13 for language and violence. 100m. **DIR:** Lorenzo Doumani. **CAST:** Sophia Adella Hernandez, Maria Conchita Alonso, Paul Winfield, Tony Plana, William McNamara. **2000 DVD**

KNUTE ROCKNE—ALL AMERICAN ★★★ This is an overly sentimental biography of the famous Notre Dame football coach. But if you like football or you want to see Ronald Reagan show off his moves, it could hold your interest. Pat O'Brien has the central role, and he plays it with real gusto. B&W; 84m. **DIR:** Lloyd Bacon. **CAST:** Ronald Reagan, Pat O'Brien, Donald Crisp. **1940**

KOJIRO ★★★★ This first-rate semisequel to director Hiroshi Inagaki's *Samurai Trilogy* casts Tatsuya Nakadai as the fabled master swordsman, Musashi Miyamoto, whose exploits made up the three previous films. But he is not the main character here. Instead, the focus is on Kojiro (Kikunosuke Onoe), whose goal is to become the greatest swordsman in all Japan and thus follow the trail blazed by Miyamoto. In Japanese with English subtitles. Not rated; the film contains violence. 152m. **DIR:** Hiroshi Inagaki. **CAST:** Kikunosuke Onoe, Yuriko Hoshi, Tatsuya Nakadai. **1967**

KOKO: A TALKING GORILLA ★★★ Does a gorilla that has been taught a three-hundred-plus-word vocabulary have civil rights? That's one of the arguments raised as this film looks at the efforts of a psychology researcher to keep the ape, borrowed from the San Francisco Zoo, which she has taught to "speak" (via sign language). 82m. **DIR:** Barbet Schroeder. **1978**

KOLOBOS ★★ Offered the chance to appear on a "reality" TV show, a group of teens heads for a remote location where they are stalked and slaughtered by a monster. This gruesome tale is a slight notch above average low-budget horror, but the unsatisfying ending is annoying. Not rated; contains violence, gore, and profanity. 87m. **DIR:** Daniel Liatowitsch, David Todd Ocvirk.

CAST: Amy Weber, Promise LeMarco, Linnea Quigley. **1999 DVD**

KOLYA ★★★★★ The 1996 Academy Award winner for best foreign film is an enchanting tale of a lonely man brought out of his shell by a wholly unexpected housemate. A down-on-his-luck Czech cellist, reduced to performing for funerals, accepts some quick cash via an arranged marriage with a young Russian woman who desires Czech citizenship. Scarcely days after this illegal transaction is completed, she flees into the arms of her German lover (a trip made possible by her new papers), leaving behind a confused 6 year old son. Although the man and boy don't even speak each other's language, they eventually bond under droll circumstances. Rated PG-13 for mild sensuality. 105m. **DIR:** Jan Sverák. **CAST:** Zdenek Sverak, Andrej Chalimon, Ondrez Vetchy, Stella Zazvorkova. **1996**

KOMODO ★★★1/2 A town is attacked by ten-foot-long dragons from the island of Komodo. Surprisingly entertaining *Jaws/Anaconda* clone with superb special effects and some genuine thrills and chills. Rated PG-13 for violence and profanity. 90m. **DIR:** Michael Lantieri. **CAST:** Jill Hennessy, Billy Burke, Kevin Zegers, Paul Gleason, Nina Landis, Simon Westaway. **1999 DVD**

KONGA ★★ Botanist Michael Gough develops a serum that causes his chimpanzee, Konga, to grow into a monstrous ape who kills at Gough's bidding. This sleazy British monster movie isn't too bad until the climax, which is ruined by laughable special effects. B&W; 90m. **DIR:** John Lemont. **CAST:** Michael Gough, Margo Johns, Jess Conrad, Claire Gordon. **1960**

KOROSHI ★★1/2 Patrick McGoohan's popular *Secret Agent* television series is poorly represented by this attempt to string two episodes into a full-length feature. The color photography—the series was B&W—is the only legitimate appeal; the episodes themselves are rather weak. For serious fans only. Not rated; suitable for family viewing. 100m. **DIR:** Michael Truman, Peter Yates. **CAST:** Patrick McGoohan, Kenneth Griffith, Amanda Barrie, Ronald Howard. **1966**

KOSTAS ★★1/2 A tormented Greek-Cypriot tries to find love with an Australian girl in England. Director Paul Cox has created a character study with little depth and too much tedium. Not for the easily bored. Rated R for suggested sex. 110m. **DIR:** Paul Cox. **CAST:** Takis Emmanuel, Wendy Hughes. **1979**

KOTCH ★★★★ Walter Matthau is in top form as a feisty senior citizen who takes to the road when his family tries to put him in a retirement home. First-time director Jack Lemmon does himself proud with this alternately witty and warmly human comedy. Rated PG. 113m. **DIR:** Jack Lemmon. **CAST:** Walter Matthau, Deborah Winters, Felicia Farr, Charles Aidman. **1971**

KOUNTERFEIT ★★ Mildly diverting tale of two low-life hoods who try to hit the big time by cashing in $3 million of counterfeit money for a million of the real thing. Their simple transaction attracts the attention of cops, hit men, and a woman with a vendetta. Rated R for language and violence. 87m. **DIR:** John Mallory Asher. **CAST:** Bruce Payne, Corbin Bernsen, Hilary Swank, Michael Gross, Mark Paul Gosselaar. **1996**

KOVACS ★★★★ Ernie Kovacs was one of the most innovative forces in the early days of television. His ingenious approach to comedy revolutionized the medium, and its impact can still be felt today. This definitive anthology contains some of his best moments, including his famous "Mack the Knife" blackout segments. His career on television lasted from 1950 to 1962, when his life was cut short by a fatal car accident. B&W; 85m. **DIR:** Ernie Kovacs. **CAST:** Ernie Kovacs. **1971**

KOYAANISQATSI ★★★★ The title is a Hopi Indian word meaning "crazy life, life in turmoil, life disintegrating, life out of balance, a state of life that calls for another way of living." In keeping with this, director Godfrey Reggio contrasts scenes of nature to the hectic life of the city. There is no plot or dialogue. Instead, the accent is on the artistic cinematography, by Ron Fricke, and the score, by Philip Glass. It's a feast for the eyes and ears. No MPAA rating. 87m. **DIR:** Godfrey Reggio. **1983**

KRAMER VS. KRAMER ★★★★ Dustin Hoffman and Meryl Streep star in the Academy Award–winning drama about a couple who separate, leaving their only son in the custody of the father, who is a stranger to his child. Just when the father and son have learned to live with each other, the mother fights for custody of the child. *Kramer vs. Kramer* jerks you from tears to laughs and back again—and all the while you're begging for more. Rated PG. 104m. **DIR:** Robert Benton. **CAST:** Dustin Hoffman, Meryl Streep, Jane Alexander, Howard Duff, JoBeth Williams. **1979 DVD**

KRAYS, THE ★★★★ From British filmmaker Peter Medak comes this compelling, chilling portrait of Ronald and Reginald Kray, psychotic twins who ruled the London underworld in the 1960s. Features first-rate performances. Rated R for profanity and violence. 119m. **DIR:** Peter Medak. **CAST:** Billie Whitelaw, Gary Kemp, Martin Kemp, Susan Fleetwood. **1990**

KRIEMHILDE'S REVENGE ★★★★ This is a perfect sequel to the splendid *Siegfried*. Watch them both in one sitting if you get the chance. Siegfried's vengeful lover Kriemhilde raises an army to atone for his death. Beautifully photographed and edited, this international success placed German cinema in the vanguard of filmmaking. Silent. B&W; 95m. **DIR:** Fritz Lang. **CAST:** Margarete Schon, Rudolf Klein-Rogge, Paul Richter, Bernhard Goetzke. **1925**

KRIPPENDORF'S TRIBE ★★ This wincingly awkward misfire further emphasizes the notion that Richard Dreyfuss—here playing an anthropologist forced to "fabricate" an undiscovered tribe in New Guinea—remains one of our most inconsistent actors. The premise is moronic and the characters too far removed from reality. Rated PG-13 for mild profanity and sexuality. 94m. **DIR:** Todd Holland. **CAST:** Richard Dreyfuss, Jenna Elfman, Natasha Lyonne, Gregory Edward Smith, Carl Michael Lindner, Lily Tomlin. **1998**

KRONOS ★★★ In this alien invasion film, a giant, featureless robot is sent to Earth. The robot absorbs all forms of energy and grows as it feeds. The scientists must find a way to destroy the giant before it reaches the high-population areas of southern California. Although the special effects are nothing by today's filmmaking standards, this picture is one of the best from a decade dominated by giant monsters and alien invaders. B&W; 78m. **DIR:** Kurt Neumann. **CAST:** Jeff Morrow, Barbara Lawrence. **1957 DVD**

KRULL In this poor sci-fi–sword-and-sorcery film, a young man is called upon to do battle with a master of

evil to save a beautiful princess. Rated PG for violence. 117m. **DIR:** Peter Yates. **CAST:** Ken Marshall, Freddie Jones, Lysette Anthony. **1983 DVD**

KRUSH GROOVE Lame rap musical. Rated R. 95m. **DIR:** Michael Schultz. **CAST:** Blair Underwood, Sheila E., Kurtis Blow, The Fat Boys, Run DMC. **1985**

K2 ★★ This disappointing adventure, adapted from Patrick Meyers's successful stage play, rehashes every mountain-climbing movie cliché. An obnoxious attorney (Michael Biehn) and his physicist pal (Matt Craven) join a team that climbs the second highest and most treacherous mountain in the world. Rated R for violence and profanity. 104m. **DIR:** Franc Roddam. **CAST:** Michael Biehn, Matt Craven, Raymond J. Barry, Patricia Charbonneau, Hiroshi Fujioka, Luca Bercovici. **1992**

KUFFS ★★★1/2 When police officer Bruce Boxleitner is killed, his ne'er-do-well brother, Christian Slater, takes over the family-owned, patrol-special business in hopes of finding the killer. Director Bruce A. Evans uses a crisp, tongue-in-cheek storytelling style, mixing action, romance, and comedy. Rated PG-13 for profanity and violence. 106m. **DIR:** Bruce A. Evans. **CAST:** Christian Slater, Tony Goldwyn, Milla Jovovich, Bruce Boxleitner. **1992**

KULL THE CONQUEROR ★★ Kull, a muscular slave-warrior turned king, discovers his sensual young bride is a 3,000 year old witch who has been reincarnated to kill him. He then journeys to the Isle of Ice to save the world. This moronic, sanitized version of Conan author Robert E. Howard's pulp fiction superhero of the 1930s also features an irritating heavy-metal rock score. Rated PG-13 for violence and sensuality. 95m. **DIR:** John Nicolella. **CAST:** Kevin Sorbo, Tia Carrere, Karina Lombard, Joe Shaw, Roy Brocksmith, Harvey Fierstein, Litefoot, Edward Tudor Pole. **1997 DVD**

KUNDUN ★★ This visually gorgeous film, complemented by equally opulent costumes, is about as interesting as waiting for paint to dry. No matter how limited your knowledge of China, Tibet, and the fourteenth Dalai Lama, the film will not shed additional insight. For all the depth of Melissa Mathison's script, this endurance test could have been compressed into a fifteen-minute newsreel short. Rated PG-13 for violence. 135m. **DIR:** Martin Scorsese. **CAST:** Tenzin Thuthob Tsarong, Sonam Phuntsok, Lobsang Samten, Gyatso Lukhang, Gyurme Tethong. **1997 DVD**

KUNG FU (1971) ★★★ The pilot of the 1970s television series starring David Carradine has its moments for those who fondly remember the show. Carradine plays a Buddhist monk roaming the Old West. When his wisdom fails to mollify the bad guys, he is forced to use martial arts to see justice done. 75m. **DIR:** Jerry Thorpe. **CAST:** David Carradine, Keye Luke, Philip Ahn, Keith Carradine, Barry Sullivan, Radames Pera. **1971**

KUNG FU—THE MOVIE (1986) ★★ David Carradine returns to his decade-old hit TV series, as Kwai Chang Caine, a fugitive Buddhist monk. Caine is still on the run from Chinese assassins. Brandon Lee also stars as his son under the spell of an evil sorcerer to kill his father. (Carradine's role as Caine in the TV series was originally offered to Bruce Lee, Brandon Lee's father.) 92m. **DIR:** Richard Lang. **CAST:** David Carradine, Brandon Lee, Kerrie Keane, Mako, Bill Lucking, Luke Askew, Keye Luke, Benson Fong. **1986**

•KUNG POW!: ENTER THE FIST Director-star Steve Oedekerk steals Woody Allen's *What's Up, Tiger Lily?* idea, dubbing a new sound track on a crummy martial arts movie. Not a single laugh, however, and Oedekerk is no Jackie Chan. Rated PG-13 for comic violence and sexual humor. 81m. **DIR:** Steve Oedekerk. **CAST:** Steve Oedekerk, Jennifer Tung, Tad Horino, Philip Tan. **2002**

KURT VONNEGUT'S MONKEY HOUSE ★★★ This made-for-cable production features three Kurt Vonnegut short stories. Sociological debate and brutal danger make "All the King's Men" the strongest tale: A U.S. ambassador must use his family and military advisers in a human chess game against a communist rebel leader. Other tales: "Next Door" and "The Euphio Question." Mild violence, but otherwise suitable for family viewing. 90m. **DIR:** Allan Winton King, Paul Shapiro, Gilbert Shilton. **CAST:** Len Cariou, Miguel Fernandes, Gordon Clapp, Donnelly Rhodes. **1991**

KWAIDAN ★★★★ An anthology of ghost stories adapted from books by Lafcadio Hearn, an American writer who lived in Japan in the late nineteenth century. Colorful, eerie, and quite unique, it's one of the most visually stunning horror films ever produced. The movie isn't for children, though—it could induce nightmares. In Japanese with English subtitles. 164m. **DIR:** Masaki Kobayashi. **CAST:** Michiyo Aratama, Keiko Kishi, Tatsuya Nakadai. **1963**

L

LA BALANCE ★★★★ This is an homage of sorts to the American cop thriller. It turns the genre inside out, however, by focusing on the plight of two unfortunates—a prostitute (Nathalie Baye) and a petty criminal (Philippe Léotard)—who get caught in a vise between the cops and a gangland chief. The result is a first-rate crime story. In French with English subtitles. Rated R for nudity, profanity, and violence. 102m. **DIR:** Bob Swaim. **CAST:** Nathalie Baye, Philippe Léotard, Richard Berry, Maurice Ronet. **1982**

LA BAMBA ★★★★ At the age of 17, with three huge hits under his belt, Ritchie Valens joined Buddy Holly and the Big Bopper on an ill-fated airplane ride that killed all three and left rock 'n' roll bereft of some giant talent. In this biography, *Zoot Suit* writer-director Luis Valdez achieves a fine blend of rock 'n' roll and soap opera. Rated PG-13 for language. 108m. **DIR:** Luis Valdez. **CAST:** Lou Diamond Phillips, Rosana De Soto, Esai Morales, Danielle von Zerneck, Elizabeth Peña. **1987 DVD**

LA BELLE NOISEUSE ★★★★ As one wag put it, this art film is *really* about watching paint dry. Yet, it's also a fascinating examination of the creative process. Its subject is the relationship between a gorgeous woman and the retired painter she inspires to return to painting. The scenes in which he nervously contemplates reentering the painful world of creation make the four-hour

running time a small price to pay. In French with English subtitles. 240m. **DIR:** Jacques Rivette. **CAST:** Michel Piccoli, Jane Birkin, Emmanuelle Beart, Marianne Denicourt, David Bursztein. **1991**

LA BÊTE HUMAINE ★★★★1/2 Remarkable performances by Jean Gabin, Fernand Ledoux, and Simone Simon, along with Jean Renoir's masterful editing and perfectly simple visuals, elevate a middling and grim Emile Zola novel to fine cinema. The artistry of this film about duplicity and murder transcends what could have been a seedy little tale. In French with English subtitles. B&W; 99m. **DIR:** Jean Renoir. **CAST:** Jean Gabin, Julien Carette, Fernand Ledoux, Jean Renoir, Simone Simon. **1938**

LA BOUM ★★★ A teenager (Sophie Marceau) discovers a whole new world open to her when her parents move to Paris. Her new set of friends delight in giving "boums"—French slang for big parties. Although this film seems overly long, many scenes are nevertheless tender and lovingly directed by Claude Pinoteau. In French with English subtitles. No MPAA rating. 100m. **DIR:** Claude Pinoteau. **CAST:** Sophie Marceau, Brigitte Fossey, Claude Brasseur. **1980**

L.A. BOUNTY ★★ Wings Hauser was born to play wigged-out pyschos, and he's a standout in this otherwise pedestrian cop thriller. Rated R for violence and profanity. 85m. **DIR:** Worth Keller. **CAST:** Wings Hauser, Sybil Danning, Henry Darrow. **1989**

LA CAGE AUX FOLLES ★★★★ A screamingly funny French comedy and the biggest-grossing foreign-language film ever released in America, this stars Ugo Tognazzi and Michel Serrault as lovers who must masquerade as husband and wife so as not to obstruct the marriage of Tognazzi's son to the daughter of a stuffy bureaucrat. In French with English subtitles. Rated PG for mature situations. 110m. **DIR:** Edouard Molinaro. **CAST:** Ugo Tognazzi, Michel Serrault. **1978 DVD**

LA CAGE AUX FOLLES II ★★ This follow-up to the superb French comedy is just more proof "sequels aren't equals." In French with English subtitles. Rated PG for mature situations. 101m. **DIR:** Edouard Molinaro. **CAST:** Ugo Tognazzi, Michel Serrault. **1981 DVD**

LA CAGE AUX FOLLES III, THE WEDDING 🦃 Pathetic and dreadful second sequel to *La Cage Aux Folles*. In French with English subtitles. Rated PG-13. 88m. **DIR:** Georges Lautner. **CAST:** Michel Serrault, Ugo Tognazzi, Stéphane Audran. **1986**

LA CÉRÉMONIE ★★★★ Antagonism between social classes escalates from verbal sparring and malicious surveillance to bloodshed in this sinfully clever suspense yarn. The female owner of a chic gallery on France's northern coast hires an oddly passive maid to care for her home and family. The maid is befriended by the local psycho postmistress and a sinister conspiracy evolves as they share dark secrets. Wait for the final credits or you'll miss the punch line. In French with English subtitles. Not rated; contains profanity and violence. 111m. **DIR:** Claude Chabrol. **CAST:** Sandrine Bonnaire, Isabelle Huppert, Jacqueline Bisset, Virginie Ledoyen, Valentin Merlet, Jean-Pierre Cassel. **1995**

LA CHIENNE ★★★★ Jean Renoir's first sound feature stars Michel Simon as a married man who finds himself involved with a prostitute after rescuing her from a beating by her pimp. Remade by Fritz Lang in 1945 as *Scarlet Street*. In French with English subtitles. B&W; 95m. **DIR:** Jean Renoir. **CAST:** Michel Simon, Janie Mareze. **1931**

LA CHUTE DE LA MAISON USHER ★★★1/2 Avant-garde artist Jean Epstein turned to filmmaking for this memorable adaptation of the famous Edgar Allan Poe story, in which a man is haunted by the sister he caused to be buried alive. The stylized images and photographic techniques were unusual at the time, and if they no longer seem so fresh, this short, silent film is still compelling. B&W; 48m. **DIR:** Jean Epstein. **CAST:** Marguerite Gance, Jean Debucourt. **1928**

LA CIUDAD ★★★★★ This four-part movie about Latino immigrants in New York City emulates Italian neorealist films like *The Bicycle Thief*. Most of the performers are nonprofessionals, and the stories are largely based on the lives of people who might otherwise pass beneath our attention. Beautifully scored and filmed in black-and-white. In Spanish with English subtitles. Not rated. B&W; 88m. **DIR:** David Riker. **CAST:** Cipriano García, Leticia Herrera, José Rabelo, Silvia Goiz, Ricardo Cuevas. **1998**

L.A. CONFIDENTIAL ★★★★1/2 The seamy side of Hollywood in the 1950s is explored in this multilayered film based on James Ellroy's novel, which centers around the activities of the L.A. police force and a muckraking magazine publisher (Danny DeVito). Kevin Spacey is a high-profile cop who benefits from DeVito's busts of movie stars and political figures, while Russell Crowe steals the film as the straight-arrow detective who finds himself caught up in the corruption of the city's underbelly because, in part, of his love affair with a high-priced hooker (Oscar-winning Kim Basinger). Rated R for violence, profanity, and suggested sex. 136m. **DIR:** Curtis Hanson. **CAST:** Kevin Spacey, Russell Crowe, Guy Pearce, Danny DeVito, James Cromwell, David Strathairn, Kim Basinger, Graham Beckel, Paul Guilfoyle. **1997 DVD**

L.A. CRACKDOWN ★★ An undercover cop (Pamela Dixon) battles crack dealers and blows away bad guys by the dozen. Made-for-video cheapie that is more concerned with showing sexy women than their problems. The sequel followed so fast, it was probably made at the same time. Not rated; nudity, violence. 84m. **DIR:** Joseph Merhi. **CAST:** Pamela Dixon, Tricia Parks. **1988**

L.A. CRACKDOWN II ★★ More of the same, with Pamela Dixon and her new partner stalking a serial killer with a penchant for bar girls. Not rated; nudity, strong violence. 87m. **DIR:** Joseph Merhi. **CAST:** Pamela Dixon, Anthony Gates. **1988**

LA CUCARACHA ★★★ A struggling writer is approached to murder someone for money but soon finds the tables turned on him. From that point on, his life becomes one bent on revenge. Bizarre film isn't for everyone, but features a delightfully over-the-top performance by star Eric Roberts. Rated R for violence and profanity. 95m. **DIR:** Jack Perez. **CAST:** Eric Roberts, Joaquim de Almeida, Tara Crespo, James McManus. **1998 DVD**

LA DOLCE VITA ★★★★ Federico Fellini's surreal journey through Rome follows a society journalist (Marcello Mastroianni) as he navigates a bizarre world in which emotions have been destroyed by surface reali-

ties, moral conventions, and unresolved guilts. This film is considered a landmark in cinematic achievement. In Italian with English subtitles. Not rated. B&W; 175m. **DIR:** Federico Fellini. **CAST:** Marcello Mastroianni, Anouk Aimée, Anita Ekberg, Barbara Steele, Nadia Gray. **1960**

LA FEMME NIKITA ★★★★ Luc Besson's stylishly inventive, ultraviolent, high-energy thriller about the recruitment of a convicted drug addict to be a secret service assassin. This visceral thriller isn't for the squeamish, but action fans who also like to think and who have a sense of style ought to love it. In French with English subtitles. Rated R. 117m. **DIR:** Luc Besson. **CAST:** Anne Parillaud, Jean-Hugues Anglade, Tcheky Karyo. **1991 DVD**

L.A. GODDESS ★★ Lust on a movie set as a studio executive falls for a star's stunt double. The comedic tone seems an afterthought to shore up the soft-core erotica. Available in R and unrated versions; contains sex and profanity. **DIR:** Jag Mundhra. **CAST:** David Heavener, Kathy Shower, Jeff Conaway, Joe Estevez. **1993**

LA GRANDE BOURGEOISE ★★ This should be a suspenseful film about a brother who murders his sister's lackluster husband. However, the movie's primary concern is with costume and soft-focus lenses so that even the lukewarm emotions are overshadowed. In Italian with English subtitles. 115m. **DIR:** Mauro Bolognini. **CAST:** Catherine Deneuve, Giancarlo Giannini, Fernando Rey. **1974**

LA GRANDE VADROUILLE ★★★ Three Royal Air Force members are shot down over occupied France in this humorous film. Unfortunately, half of the French and German spoken is not translated into English. In English, French, and German with English subtitles. Not rated. 122m. **DIR:** Gerard Oury. **CAST:** Courvil, Bourvil, Louis de Funes, Claudio Brook, Andrea Parisy, Collette Brosset, Mike Marshall. **1964**

L.A. LAW ★★★1/2 Above-average television movie introduced the cast of characters of the successful series. Set in a high-powered Los Angeles law firm, this is both compelling and humorous. A must for fans of the series. 97m. **DIR:** Gregory Hoblit. **CAST:** Harry Hamlin, Susan Dey, Jimmy Smits, Michael Tucker, Jill Eikenberry, Richard Dysart, Corbin Bernsen, Alan Rachins, Susan Ruttan. **1987**

LA LECTRICE (THE READER) ★★★ Clever comedy for ultraliterary types, with Miou-Miou at her charming best as a woman who hires herself out as a professional reader. She becomes a confidante, booster, adviser, and friend to a collection of loners, loonies, and emotionally unstable individuals. In French with English subtitles. 98m. **DIR:** Michel Deville. **CAST:** Miou-Miou, Maria Casares, Patrick Chesnais. **1989**

LA MACHINE ★★ Psychiatrist Gérard Depardieu invents a machine that allows him to exchange personalities with other people and tests it on a criminal psychopath. Subtitles are the only difference between this and dozens of other hokey mad-scientist movies. Not rated; contains graphic violence, nudity, sexual situations, adult situations, and profanity. In French with English subtitles. 96m. **DIR:** Francois Dupeyron. **CAST:** Gérard Depardieu, Nathalie Baye, Didier Bourdon. **1994**

LA MARSEILLAISE ★★★★ Though its plot is somewhat uneven, this film contains many beautiful sequences. The documentary-like story (and Jean Renoir's call to his countrymen to stand fast against the growing threat of Hitler) parallels the rise of the French Revolution with the spread of the new rallying song as 150 revolutionary volunteers from Marseilles march to Paris and join with others to storm the Bastille. In French with English subtitles. B&W; 130m. **DIR:** Jean Renoir. **CAST:** Pierre Renoir, Louis Jouvet, Julien Carette. **1937**

LA NUIT DE VARENNES ★★1/2 An ambitious and imaginative, but ultimately disappointing, film of King Louis XVI's flight from revolutionary Paris in 1791 as seen through the sensibilities of Casanova (Marcello Mastroianni), Restif de la Bretonne (Jean-Louis Barrault), and Tom Paine (Harvey Keitel). All these folks do is talk, talk, talk. In French with English subtitles. Rated R for nudity, sex, and profanity. 133m. **DIR:** Ettore Scola. **CAST:** Marcello Mastroianni, Jean-Louis Barrault, Harvey Keitel. **1983**

LA PASSANTE ★★1/2 Romy Schneider is featured in a dual role as Elsa, a German refugee, and as Lina, the wife of a contemporary world leader. The story centers on the relationship of two lovers caught up in a drama of political intrigue in France. Both Schneider and Michel Piccoli give excellent performances in this otherwise slow-moving thriller. In French with English subtitles. Contains nudity and violence; recommended for adult viewing. 106m. **DIR:** Jaques Rouffio. **CAST:** Romy Schneider, Michel Piccoli, Maria Schell. **1983**

LA PROMESSE ★★★ The son of a Belgian slumlord gets the first stirrings of a conscience when one of the illegal aliens his father is exploiting dies in an accident and the boy feels responsible for the man's widow and child. This film has the air of tough street realism and the feel of actual behavior caught on camera almost by accident. Despite a weak and inconclusive ending, it's well acted. In French with English subtitles. Not rated; suitable for mature audiences. 90m. **DIR:** Jean-Pierre Dardenne, Luc Dardenne. **CAST:** Jeremie Renier, Olivier Gourmet, Assita Ouedraogo, Rasmane Ouedraogo. **1996 DVD**

LA PURITAINE ★★★★ Penetrating drama played out in an empty theater where the artistic manager prepares for the homecoming of the daughter who ran away a year earlier. He ensembles a group of young actresses of his troupe in order to have them impersonate behavioral aspects of his daughter. Brilliant cinematography by William Lubtchansky. In French with English subtitles. Not rated, but is recommended for adult viewers. 90m. **DIR:** Jacques Doillon. **CAST:** Michel Piccoli, Sandrine Bonnaire. **1986**

LA RONDE ★★★ It would be hard to imagine any film more like a French farce than *La Ronde,* in spite of its Austrian origins. This fast-paced, witty look at amours and indiscretions begins with the soldier (Serge Reggiani) and lady of easy virtue (Simone Signoret). Their assignation starts a chain of events that is charmingly risqué. In French with English subtitles. B&W; 97m. **DIR:** Max Ophüls. **CAST:** Anton Walbrook, Serge Reggiani, Simone Simon, Simone Signoret, Daniel Gélin, Danielle Darrieux. **1950**

LA SCORTA ★★★ Four state policemen are assigned to protect a prosecuting magistrate from the violent wrath of Sicilian hoods in this intimate, compelling tale about determined idealism and male bonding under duress. The film paints an ugly picture of how coalitions between the Mafia and greedy government factions have corrupted rural and urban Italian life. In Italian with English subtitles. Not rated. 92m. **DIR:** Ricky Tognazzi. **CAST:** Carlo Checchi, Claudio Amendola, Enrico Lo Verso, Tony Sperandeo, Ricky Memphis. **1994**

LA SEPARATION ★★1/2 Pierre and Anne seem to have it all, including an infant son, yet passion has disappeared from their marriage. When Anne takes on a lover, the revelation takes its toll on Pierre. While it's not definitive, the film manages to explore the fragile landscape traveled by a couple in trouble. In French with English subtitles. Not rated; contains adult situations and language. 85m. **DIR:** Christian Vincent. **CAST:** Isabelle Huppert, Daniel Auteuil. **1994 DVD**

LA SIGNORA DI TUTTI ★★ A famous actress attempts suicide, and we are taken on a retrospective journey through her life. Her beauty enchants and intoxicates men, who go as far as committing suicide to prove their love. Tacky, dated, and laughable at times, but with a hint of naïve historical charm that just barely saves it from the dreaded poultry symbol. In Italian with English subtitles. B&W; 89m. **DIR:** Max Ophüls. **CAST:** Isa Miranda. **1934**

L.A. STORY ★★★★ In writer Steve Martin's *Manhattan*-style comedy about Los Angeles, a wacky weatherman (Martin) becomes disillusioned with his television job, his status-crazy girlfriend (Marilu Henner), and life in general until a British journalist (Martin's wife Victoria Tennant) brings romance back into his world. Great fun for Martin's fans, with a hilarious supporting performance by Sarah Jessica Parker as a gum-popping Valley Girl. Rated PG-13 for profanity. 95m. **DIR:** Mick Jackson. **CAST:** Steve Martin, Victoria Tennant, Richard E. Grant, Marilu Henner, Sarah Jessica Parker. **1991 DVD**

LA STRADA ★★★★★ This is Fellini's first internationally acclaimed film. Gelsomina (Giulietta Masina), a simpleminded peasant girl, is sold to a circus strongman (Anthony Quinn), and as she follows him on his tour through the countryside, she falls desperately in love with him. She becomes the victim of his constant abuse and brutality until their meeting with an acrobat (Richard Basehart) dramatically changes the course of their lives. B&W; 94m. **DIR:** Federico Fellini. **CAST:** Giulietta Masina, Anthony Quinn, Richard Basehart. **1954**

LA TRAVIATA ★★★★ Franco Zeffirelli set out to make a film of Verdi's opera that would appeal to a general audience as well as opera buffs, and he has handsomely succeeded. He has found the right visual terms for the pathetic romance of a courtesan compelled to give up her aristocratic lover. The score is beautifully sung by Teresa Stratas, as Violetta and Placido Domingo, as Alfredo. In Italian with English subtitles. Rated G. 112m. **DIR:** Franco Zeffirelli. **CAST:** Teresa Stratas, Placido Domingo. **1982 DVD**

LA TRUITE (THE TROUT) ★★★ Sometimes disjointed story of a young girl who leaves her rural background and arranged marriage to climb the rocky path to success in both love and business. Although director Joseph Losey generally has the right idea, in the end, it lacks warmth and a sense of cohesion. In French with English subtitles. Rated R. 100m. **DIR:** Joseph Losey. **CAST:** Lissette Malidor, Isabelle Huppert, Jacques Spiesser. **1982**

L.A. VICE ★★ Detective Jon Chance quits the L.A.P.D. when an old friend is killed, but comes back to solve the case. Sequel to *L.A. Heat* is an improvement, but still not particularly memorable. Not rated, but an R equivalent for violence, profanity, and sexual situations. 83m. **DIR:** Joseph Merhi. **CAST:** Lawrence Hilton-Jacobs, William Smith, Jean Levine, Jastereo Covaire, R. W. Munchkin. **1989**

LA VIE CONTINUE ★★ Soap-operaish story about a woman trying to build a new life for herself and her children after her husband dies suddenly. The American remake, *Men Don't Leave*, was actually much better. French, dubbed in English. Not rated. 93m. **DIR:** Moshe Mizrahi. **CAST:** Annie Girardot, Jean-Pierre Cassel, Pierre Dux, Michel Aumont. **1981**

LABOR PAINS ★★ Cutesy romantic comedy suffers from sitcom dialogue and situations. Kyra Sedgwick stars as a columnist desperate to hide her pregnancy from her family and ex-boyfriend. Everything is played for a joke in this flat, uninteresting direct-to-video effort. Rated R for adult themes and language. 89m. **DIR:** Tracey Alexson. **CAST:** Kyra Sedgwick, Rob Morrow, Mary Tyler Moore, Robert Klein, Lela Rochon. **2000**

LABYRINTH ★★★ A charming fantasy that combines live actors with another impressive collection of Jim Henson's Muppets. Jennifer Connelly wishes for the Goblin King (David Bowie) to kidnap her baby brother; when that idle desire is granted, she must journey to an enchanted land and solve a giant maze in order to rescue her little brother. Rated PG for mild violence. 101m. **DIR:** Jim Henson. **CAST:** David Bowie, Jennifer Connelly, Toby Froud. **1986 DVD**

LABYRINTH OF PASSION ★★ Unengaging screwball comedy about the misadventures of a nympho punk rockette, an incestuous gynecologist, and a desperate empress in search of sperm from a member of the imperial family of Iran. In Spanish with English subtitles. Rated R for nudity and profanity. 100m. **DIR:** Pedro Almodóvar. **CAST:** Celia Roth, Imanol Arias, Antonio Banderas. **1983**

LACEMAKER, THE ★★★1/2 Isabelle Huppert had her first major role here as a shy young Parisian beautician who falls in love with a university student while on vacation. But when they try to keep the affair going back in Paris, class differences drive them apart. Huppert's sympathetic performance pulls the film through occasional patches of pathos. In French with English subtitles. Not rated; the film features sexual situations. 107m. **DIR:** Claude Goretta. **CAST:** Isabelle Huppert, Yves Beneyton. **1977**

LADIES CLUB ★★ A policewoman and a female doctor organize a support group to help rape victims deal with their feelings of rage and disgust. The club of the title soon turns into a vigilante group with the women punishing repeat offenders. Rated R for violence and gore. 86m. **DIR:** A. K. Allen. **CAST:** Karen Austin, Diana Scarwid, Christine Belford, Beverly Todd. **1987**

LADIES' MAN, THE (1961) ★★ Jerry Lewis plays a houseboy for an all-female boardinghouse in Hollywood.

Lewis wrote, directed, and stars in this silly slapstick farce. Watch for an amusing cameo by George Raft. 106m. **DIR:** Jerry Lewis. **CAST:** Jerry Lewis, Helen Traubel, Kathleen Freeman, Hope Holiday, Pat Stanley. **1961**

LADIES MAN, THE (2000) 🦃 Another *Saturday Night Live* sketch futilely tries to stretch to feature length in this lame comedy as radio talk-show host Leon Phelps, a self-proclaimed expert on females and seduction, crosses paths with a former lover and a group of men who want to kill him for having sex with their wives. Rated R for language, violence, nudity, and sexual content. 84m. **DIR:** Reginald Hudlin. **CAST:** Tim Meadows, Karyn Parsons, Billy Dee Williams, Tiffani-Amber Thiessen, Lee Evans, Will Ferrell, Eugene Levy, Julianne Moore. **2000 DVD**

LADIES OF LEISURE ★★★ Gold-digger Barbara Stanwyck snares a rich fiancé, but her past reputation gets in the way. Dated melodrama, but worth seeing for the young Stanwyck. B&W; 98m. **DIR:** Frank Capra. **CAST:** Barbara Stanwyck, Ralph Graves, Lowell Sherman, Marie Prevost. **1930**

LADIES OF THE CHORUS ★★ The story of a chorus girl who tries to keep her young daughter from making romantic mistakes is pure detergent drama. A minor Marilyn Monroe musical, but her first major role so it's a curiosity piece. Adele Jergens is fine as the mother. B&W; 61m. **DIR:** Phil Karlson. **CAST:** Marilyn Monroe, Adele Jergens, Rand Brooks. **1949**

LADIES ON THE ROCKS ★★★ Had Thelma and Louise taken to the stage instead of a life of crime, their adventures might have resembled this amusing low-key comedy. Two women tour rural Denmark with their male-bashing cabaret show. In Danish with English subtitles. Not rated; contains adult themes and sexual situations. 100m. **DIR:** Christian Braad Thomsen. **CAST:** Helle Ryslinge, Annemarie Helger. **1983**

LADIES SING THE BLUES, THE ★★★★ Some of the finest ladies of blues are beautifully represented here in great archival footage. Even though the narration is weak, the music is powerful and sweet. Standout Billie Holiday is backed by brilliant sidemen Coleman Hawkins, Lester Young, and Ben Webster as they groove together on "Fine and Mellow." 60m. **DIR:** Tom Jenz. **CAST:** Billie Holiday, Dinah Washington, Bessie Smith, Lena Horne, Peggy Lee, Sarah Vaughan. **1989 DVD**

LADIES THEY TALK ABOUT ★★★ Bank robber Barbara Stanwyck is rehabilitated in prison by good-hearted Preston Foster. Pre-Production Code movie, adapted from the play *Women in Prison*, raised some eyebrows with its frank dialogue. B&W; 69m. **DIR:** Howard Bretherton, William Keighley. **CAST:** Barbara Stanwyck, Lyle Talbot, Preston Foster, Lillian Roth. **1933**

LADY AND THE DOG, THE ★★★ Anton Chekhov's short story is transformed into a Victorian melodrama about two wealthy people with too much time on their hands. In Russian with English subtitles. B&W; 89m. **DIR:** Josef Heifitz. **CAST:** Iya Savvina, Alexei Batalov. **1960**

LADY AND THE TRAMP ★★★★ One of the sweetest animated tales from the Disney canon, this fantasy concerns a high-bred cocker spaniel (Lady) and the adventures she has with a raffish mongrel stray (The Tramp). Since Disney originally had the film released in CinemaScope, more attention has been given to the lush backgrounds. Not rated; suitable for family viewing. 75m. **DIR:** Hamilton Luske, Clyde Geronimi, Wilfred Jackson. **1955 DVD**

LADY AND THE TRAMP II: SCAMP'S ADVENTURE ★★1/2 This disappointing sequel to Disney's classic canine love story combines animation with computer-animated images along with a now-formula songfest which, in this case, is rather annoying. The direct-to-video release focuses on Lady and the Tramp's wayward pup who chooses the streets over the security of home. The "oohs" and "aahs" of the original have been replaced with a heavy-handed "teach a lesson" feel. Rated G. 69m. **DIR:** Darrell Rooney, Jeannine Roussel. **2001 DVD**

LADY AVENGER ★★ Tough Peggie Sanders busts out of prison to get even with her brother's murderers. Forgettable made-for-video cheap thrills. Rated R for sexual situations, profanity, and violence. 82m. **DIR:** David DeCoteau. **CAST:** Peggie Sanders, Tony Josephs, Jacolyn Leeman, Michelle Bauer, Daniel Hirsch. **1989**

LADY BE GOOD ★★★1/2 A lively musical version of a George Gershwin Broadway show using a different plot and only part of the original score. Some Gershwin classics are presented with originality. But the best tune, "The Last Time I Saw Paris," was written by Gershwin's competitor, Jerome Kern who won an Oscar for it; it has been associated with this musical ever since. B&W; 112m. **DIR:** Norman Z. McLeod. **CAST:** Ann Sothern, Robert Young, Dan Dailey, Virginia O'Brien, Red Skelton, Lionel Barrymore, Eleanor Powell, Phil Silvers. **1941**

LADY BEWARE ★★ Decent but unriveting film along the lines of *Fatal Attraction*, with a psychotic pursuing pretty window dresser Diane Lane. The rest of the cast and situations are stereotypical and fairly mundane. Rated R for nudity and violence. 108m. **DIR:** Karen Arthur. **CAST:** Diane Lane, Michael Woods, Cotter Smith. **1987**

LADY BY CHOICE ★★★ The sequel to *Lady for a Day*, remade as *Pocketful of Miracles*, with Carole Lombard as a do-gooder who turns May Robson into a proper lady. Witty Depression comedy. B&W; 80m. **DIR:** David Burton. **CAST:** Carole Lombard, May Robson, Roger Pryor, Walter Connolly, Arthur Hohl. **1934**

LADY CAROLINE LAMB ★★ Without shame, this banal film victimizes the wife of an English politician who openly carried on with poet and womanizer Lord Byron. Writer-director Robert Bolt created this fiasco. 118m. **DIR:** Robert Bolt. **CAST:** Sarah Miles, Richard Chamberlain, John Mills, Laurence Olivier, Ralph Richardson, Margaret Leighton, Jon Finch. **1972**

LADY CHATTERLEY'S LOVER (1959) ★★ Cinematic telling of D. H. Lawrence's risqué novel. It concerns the wife of a crippled and impotent mine owner who has an affair with a handsome gamekeeper. It's not very good in any respect. A British-French coproduction. B&W; 101m. **DIR:** Marc Allegret. **CAST:** Danielle Darrieux, Leo Genn, Erno Crisa. **1959**

LADY CHATTERLEY'S LOVER (1981) ★★ A beautifully staged, but banal, version of the D. H. Lawrence classic. Rated R. 105m. **DIR:** Just Jaeckin. **CAST:** Sylvia Kristel, Nicholas Clay. **1981**

LADY DRAGON ★★ Weak kickboxing effort succeeds only due to presence of star Cynthia Rothrock. She's a bundle of dynamite playing a former government agent, who is ambushed and left for dead while trying to avenge her husband's death. She's saved by a martial-arts expert who nurses her back to health and then retrains her to finish the job. Rated R for violence, nudity, and strong language. 90m. **DIR:** David Worth. **CAST:** Cynthia Rothrock, Richard Norton. **1992 DVD**

LADY DRAGON 2 ★★ The stakes are higher, but it's still pretty much the same old thing. This time kickboxing champ Cynthia Rothrock sets out to recover $25 million in diamonds from bad guy Billy Drago. Fans will get a kick out of this workable sequel. Rated R for violence, strong language, and adult situations. 95m. **DIR:** David Worth. **CAST:** Cynthia Rothrock, Billy Drago, Sam Jones. **1993**

LADY EVE, THE ★★★★ Barbara Stanwyck, Henry Fonda, and Charles Coburn are first-rate in this romantic comedy, which was brilliantly written and directed by Preston Sturges. Fonda is a rather simpleminded millionaire, and Stanwyck is the conniving woman who seeks to snare him. The results are hilarious. B&W; 94m. **DIR:** Preston Sturges. **CAST:** Barbara Stanwyck, Henry Fonda, Charles Coburn, William Demarest. **1941**

LADY FOR A DAY ★★★★ An elderly beggar woman elicits the aid of a petty mobster and an oddball assortment of New York down-and-outers. She needs to palm herself off as a society matron in order to convince a Spanish noble family to accept her daughter as a suitable mate for their son. Remade by Frank Capra as *Pocketful of Miracles*. B&W; 95m. **DIR:** Frank Capra. **CAST:** May Robson, Warren William, Guy Kibbee, Glenda Farrell, Walter Connolly. **1933 DVD**

LADY FOR A NIGHT 🦃 John Wayne plays second fiddle to Joan Blondell. She's a saloon singer fighting for a measure of respectability. B&W; 87m. **DIR:** Leigh Jason. **CAST:** John Wayne, Joan Blondell, Ray Middleton. **1941**

LADY FRANKENSTEIN 🦃 Joseph Cotten ill-used as Baron Frankenstein attempting once again to create life in yet another silly-looking assemblage of spare parts. Rated R for violence. 84m. **DIR:** Mel Welles. **CAST:** Joseph Cotten, Mickey Hargitay. **1971 DVD**

LADY FROM LOUISIANA ★★ John Wayne is a crusading lawyer in this middling Republic period piece. B&W; 82m. **DIR:** Bernard Vorhaus. **CAST:** John Wayne, Ray Middleton, Ona Munson. **1941**

LADY FROM SHANGHAI ★★★1/2 Orson Welles and Rita Hayworth were husband and wife when they made this taut, surprising thriller about a beautiful, amoral woman, her crippled, repulsive lawyer husband, his partner, and a somewhat naïve Irish sailor made cat's-paw in a murder scheme. Under Welles's inventive direction, Everett Sloane and the camera steal the show with a climactic scene in the hall of mirrors at San Francisco's old oceanfront Playland. B&W; 87m. **DIR:** Orson Welles. **CAST:** Rita Hayworth, Orson Welles, Everett Sloane, Glenn Anders, Erskine Sanford, Ted de Corsia. **1948 DVD**

LADY FROM YESTERDAY, THE ★★ Made-for-TV movie with a less-than-original plot: an ex-soldier, now a happily married businessman, is shocked when the Vietnamese woman he had an affair with shows up on his doorstep, complete with the child he never knew they had. Viewers will be somewhat less surprised. 98m. **DIR:** Robert Day. **CAST:** Wayne Rogers, Bonnie Bedelia, Pat Hingle, Tina Chen. **1985**

LADY GODIVA 🦃 Tiresome historical spectacle with Maureen O'Hara as history's most famous nudist—and no, you don't see anything. 89m. **DIR:** Arthur Lubin. **CAST:** Maureen O'Hara, George Nader, Victor McLaglen. **1955**

LADY ICE ★★ Donald Sutherland is an investigator for an insurance firm and Jennifer O'Neill is his romantic interest. The catch is that her father is a crook who sells stolen gems. Rated PG. 93m. **DIR:** Tom Gries. **CAST:** Donald Sutherland, Robert Duvall, Jennifer O'Neill, Patrick Magee. **1973**

LADY IN A CAGE ★★★★ Superb shocker may finally get the recognition it deserves, thanks to home video. Olivia de Havilland is terrorized by a gang of punks when she becomes trapped in an elevator in her home. Good acting, especially by a young James Caan, and excellent photography help make this film really something special. Very violent at times. B&W; 93m. **DIR:** Walter Grauman. **CAST:** Olivia de Havilland, James Caan, Ann Sothern. **1964**

LADY IN CEMENT ★★ Sequel to *Tony Rome* misses the mark. Once again private eye Frank Sinatra is immersed into the underbelly of Miami, this time with rather undistinguished results. 93m. **DIR:** Gordon Douglas. **CAST:** Frank Sinatra, Raquel Welch, Richard Conte, Dan Blocker, Lainie Kazan, Martin Gabel. **1968**

LADY IN QUESTION ★★★ Brian Aherne plays a French merchant who acts as a juror on a murder trial where young Rita Hayworth is the defendant. After her eventual release, Aherne takes pity on her and brings her to his home to work and live while keeping her identity a secret from his family. Remake of the French film *Gribouille*. B&W; 78m. **DIR:** Charles Vidor. **CAST:** Brian Aherne, Rita Hayworth, Glenn Ford, Irene Rich, George Coulouris, Lloyd Corrigan, Evelyn Keyes. **1940**

LADY IN RED ★★★1/2 A splendid screenplay by John Sayles energizes this telling of the Dillinger story from the distaff side, with Pamela Sue Martin as the gangster's moll enduring the results of a life of crime. Director Lewis Teague keeps things moving right along. Rated R for profanity, nudity, and violence. 93m. **DIR:** Lewis Teague. **CAST:** Pamela Sue Martin, Robert Conrad, Robert Forster, Louise Fletcher, Robert Hogan. **1979**

LADY IN THE LAKE ★★★ Director-star Robert Montgomery's adaptation of Raymond Chandler's mystery is a failed attempt at screen innovation. Montgomery uses a subjective camera to substitute for detective Philip Marlowe's first-person narrative of his efforts to find a missing wife. A clever but ineffectual whodunit. B&W; 103m. **DIR:** Robert Montgomery. **CAST:** Robert Montgomery, Audrey Totter, Lloyd Nolan, Jayne Meadows, Tom Tully, Leon Ames. **1946**

LADY IN WHITE ★★★★ A high-grade suspenser. A grade-school boy (Lukas Haas) is locked in his classroom closet. While there, he sees the ghost of one of ten children who've been molested and killed in the past ten years. He also sees (but not clearly) the murderer, who then begins pursuing him. Now the question: Who

did it? Well worth a watch! Rated PG-13 for violence and obscenities. 112m. **DIR:** Frank LaLoggia. **CAST:** Lukas Haas, Len Cariou, Alex Rocco, Katherine Helmond. **1988 DVD**

LADY IS WILLING, THE ★★★1/2 Marlene Dietrich wants to adopt an abandoned baby she found but needs a husband of convenience. She decides on Fred MacMurray, a handy pediatrician. Lightweight comedy but the stars shine. B&W; 92m. **DIR:** Mitchell Leisen. **CAST:** Marlene Dietrich, Fred MacMurray, Aline MacMahon, Stanley Ridges, Arline Judge. **1942**

LADY JANE ★★★1/2 Excellent costume political soap opera about Lady Jane Grey, accidental successor to the English throne. Helena Bonham Carter glows as Lady Jane, the strong-willed suffragist who engages in a power struggle with Mary I for the throne of England. Rated PG-13 for adult situations and violence. 140m. **DIR:** Trevor Nunn. **CAST:** Helena Bonham Carter, Cary Elwes, John Wood, Michael Hordern, Jill Bennett, Jane Lapotaire, Sara Kestleman, Patrick Stewart. **1985**

LADY KILLER ★★★1/2 The stars of the smash-hit *Public Enemy*, James Cagney and Mae Clarke, were reunited for this less-popular gangster film. Watching Cagney go from theater usher to hotshot hood to movie star is a real hoot. B&W; 74m. **DIR:** Roy Del Ruth. **CAST:** James Cagney, Mae Clarke, Margaret Lindsay, Henry O'Neill, Raymond Hatton, Russell Hopton, Douglass Dumbrille. **1933**

LADY KILLERS 🦃 Lady Killers, a male strip joint, attracts police attention when one of the performers is murdered. A good-looking officer goes undercover as a stripper to solve the crime. Unbelievably bad! Not rated, contains nudity and violence. 93m. **DIR:** Robert Lewis. **CAST:** Marilu Henner, Susan Blakely, Lesley-Anne Down, Thomas Calabro. **1988**

LADY L ★★ Too much style and not enough substance, with the preposterous premise that Sophia Loren would enter an in-name-only marriage with David Niven while dallying with anarchist Paul Newman. The movie is all posturing and posing and leads absolutely nowhere. 124m. **DIR:** Peter Ustinov. **CAST:** Sophia Loren, Paul Newman, Peter Ustinov, David Niven, Marcel Dalio, Claude Dauphin, Michel Piccoli. **1965**

LADY MOBSTER 🦃 Susan Lucci wallows in excess as a woman hell bent on revenge when her parents are murdered by the mob, in this made-for-cable film. 94m. **DIR:** John Llewellyn Moxey. **CAST:** Susan Lucci, Michael Nader, Roscoe Born, Thomas Bray. **1988**

LADY OF BURLESQUE ★★★ Slick and amusing adaptation of Gypsy Rose Lee's clever mystery novel of top bananas, blackouts, and strippers, *The G-String Murder*. Interesting look into an aspect of show business that now exists only in fading memories. B&W; 91m. **DIR:** William Wellman. **CAST:** Barbara Stanwyck, Michael O'Shea, J. Edward Bromberg, Iris Adrian, Pinky Lee. **1943 DVD**

LADY OF THE HOUSE ★★ Dyan Cannon stars in this TV dramatization of the life of Sally Stanford, Mayor of Sausalito, California. Cannon gives a better performance than usual, and Armand Assante is even better. 90m. **DIR:** Ralph Nelson, Vincent Sherman. **CAST:** Dyan Cannon, Armand Assante, Zohra Lampert, Susan Tyrrell. **1978**

LADY OF THE LAKE ★★★★ Beautifully shot, sensuous fantasy from Canadian filmmaker Maurice Devereaux took five years to film, but the end result is well worth it. The lady here is a medieval gypsy witch named Viviane, who was murdered by a spiteful knight. Upon the death of his uncle, a man inherits a house by the lady's lake and discovers the secrets within. Second Fangoria video release. Rated R for violence, profanity, and simulated sex. 85m. **DIR:** Maurice Devereaux. **CAST:** Tennyson Loeh, Erik Rutherford, Chris Piggins. **1999 DVD**

LADY ON A TRAIN ★★★★★ A delightful mystery-comedy with Deanna Durbin as the heroine who sees a murder committed through a train window. The police ignore her so she decides to solve the murder herself. The upshot, when her snooping leads her to an especially nutty family, is both suspenseful and witty. B&W; 95m. **DIR:** Charles David. **CAST:** Deanna Durbin, Ralph Bellamy, David Bruce, Edward Everett Horton, Patricia Morison, Dan Duryea, William Frawley, George Coulouris. **1945**

LADY ON THE BUS ★★ Story of a shy bride who is frigid on her wedding night. She first turns to her husband's friends and then strangers she meets on buses. Marginal comedy. In Portuguese with English subtitles. Rated R for sex. 102m. **DIR:** Neville D'Almeida. **CAST:** Sonia Braga. **1978**

LADY SCARFACE ★★1/2 Role reversal is the order of the day for this story of a hardened dame who spits lead and asks questions later, ruling her gang with a velvet glove and leading the police and authorities on a grim chase. Atmospheric but pretentious, this isn't as good as it could have been despite the presence of classy Judith Anderson. B&W; 66m. **DIR:** Frank Woodruff. **CAST:** Judith Anderson, Dennis O'Keefe, Frances Neal, Eric Blore, Marc Lawrence. **1941**

LADY SINGS THE BLUES ★★★1/2 Diana Ross made a dynamic screen debut in this screen biography of another singing great, Billie Holiday, whose career was thwarted by drug addiction. Rated R. 144m. **DIR:** Sidney J. Furie. **CAST:** Diana Ross, Billy Dee Williams, Richard Pryor. **1972**

LADY TAKES A CHANCE, A ★★★ John Wayne is a rough-'n'-ready, not-the-marrying kind, rodeo star. Jean Arthur is an innocent girl from New York City out west. He falls off a horse into her lap, she falls for him, and the chase is on. *It Happened One Night* with spurs. B&W; 86m. **DIR:** William A. Seiter. **CAST:** Jean Arthur, John Wayne, Phil Silvers, Charles Winninger, Grady Sutton, Hans Conried, Grant Withers, Mary Field. **1943**

LADY TERMINATOR ★★ Enjoyably bad blood 'n' sex saga. An American anthropology student in the South Seas is possessed by the vengeful spirit of a long-dead queen. Rated R for strong violence and nudity. 83m. **DIR:** Jalil Jackson. **CAST:** Barbara Anne Constable, Christopher J. Hart. **1989**

LADY VANISHES, THE ★★★★★ Along with *The Thirty-nine Steps*, this is the most admired film from Alfred Hitchcock's early directorial career. The comedy-suspense-thriller centers around a group of British types on a train trip from central Europe to England. A young woman (Margaret Lockwood) seeks the aid of a fellow passenger (Michael Redgrave) in an attempt to locate a charming old lady (Dame May Whitty) she had

met earlier on the train and who now is apparently missing. B&W; 97m. **DIR:** Alfred Hitchcock. **CAST:** Margaret Lockwood, Michael Redgrave, May Whitty. **1938 DVD**

LADY VANISHES, THE 🦃 A better title for this remake might be *The Plot Vanishes*. Rated PG. 95m. **DIR:** Anthony Page. **CAST:** Elliott Gould, Cybill Shepherd, Angela Lansbury, Herbert Lom, Arthur Lowe, Ian Carmichael. **1979**

LADY WINDERMERE'S FAN ★★★★1/2 This is a dynamite version of Oscar Wilde's play. The very enigmatic Mrs. Erlynne comes close to scandalizing all of London society. This is one of Ernst Lubitsch's best silent films. B&W; 80m. **DIR:** Ernst Lubitsch. **CAST:** Ronald Colman, May McAvoy, Irene Rich. **1925**

LADYBIRD, LADYBIRD ★★★1/2 A single mother (Crissy Rock, in an electrifying acting debut) battles with social services for custody of her four kids, and for two others she has with a gentle Paraguayan expatriate (Vladimir Vega). The film gives a 1990s update to the working-class anger of British plays and films of forty years ago. The mother's anger is uncontrollable and self-destructive, and the film is powerful and, ultimately, frustrating. Not rated; contains brief violence and extensive profanity. 102m. **DIR:** Kenneth Loach. **CAST:** Crissy Rock, Vladimir Vega, Ray Winstone, Sandie Lavelle. **1994**

LADYBUGS ★★ Dangerfield is an inept girls' soccer coach who convinces his fiancée's son to dress up like a girl and help run the team. Dangerfield's trademark one-liners are the best things about the film. Rated PG-13 for brief profanity and sexual innuendo. 91m. **DIR:** Sidney J. Furie. **CAST:** Rodney Dangerfield, Jackée, Jonathan Brandis, Ilene Graff, Vinessa Shaw, Tom Parks. **1992**

LADYHAWKE ★★★1/2 In this 700 year old legend of love and honor, Rutger Hauer and Michelle Pfeiffer are lovers separated by an evil curse. Hauer, a valiant knight, is aided by a wisecracking thief, Matthew Broderick, in his quest to break the spell by destroying its creator. This is a lush and lavish fantasy that will please the young and the young at heart. Rated PG-13 for violence. 124m. **DIR:** Richard Donner. **CAST:** Matthew Broderick, Rutger Hauer, Michelle Pfeiffer, Leo McKern, John Wood. **1985 DVD**

LADYKILLER (1992) ★★★1/2 An ex-police detective turned evidence photographer (Mimi Rogers) becomes obsessed with a murder case. She joins a computer dating service, only to be matched with the prime murder suspect. Good acting all around. Made for cable. 91m. **DIR:** Michael Scott. **CAST:** Mimi Rogers, John Shea, Tom Irwin, Alice Krige, Bob Gunton, Bert Remsen. **1992**

LADYKILLER (1996) ★★ Ben Gazzara's world-weary detective is the only good thing about this otherwise routine police thriller, which involves a serial maniac who kills his nubile victims by stuffing them with absurd amounts of loose change. As befits producer Roger Corman, there's plenty of gratuitous nudity. Rated R for violence, profanity, nudity, and simulated sex. 90m. **DIR:** Terence H. Winkless. **CAST:** Ben Gazzara, Alex McArthur, Stephen Davies, Terri Treas. **1996**

LADYKILLERS, THE ★★★★1/2 England had a golden decade of great comedies during the 1950s. *The Ladykillers* is one of the best. Alec Guinness and Peter Sellers are teamed as a couple of small-time criminals who have devised what they believe to be the perfect crime. Unfortunately, their plans are thwarted by the sweetest, most innocent little old landlady you'd ever want to meet. Great fun! 87m. **DIR:** Alexander Mackendrick. **CAST:** Alec Guinness, Peter Sellers, Cecil Parker. **1955**

L'AGE D'OR ★★★★★ Banned for years in many countries, this satire remains a shocking but funny film. A couple trying to make love (in a most unromantic way) are thwarted by every possible repressive social institution—although in the mocking eyes of director Luis Buñuel, *every* social institution is repressive. The film's surreal nature makes it a fresh viewing experience despite its age. Though he is credited as codirector, Salvador Dalí (who earlier collaborated with Buñuel on the short *Un Chien Andalou*) had nothing to do with this film. 60m. **DIR:** Luis Buñuel. **CAST:** Gaston Modot, Lya Lys. **1930**

LAGUNA HEAT ★★★1/2 This well-written script was made for HBO cable. Harry Hamlin is an ex–L.A. cop who lives with his father in Laguna Beach. He soon gets involved in a murder investigation. Director Simon Langton keeps the action moving and the plot twisting. 110m. **DIR:** Simon Langton. **CAST:** Harry Hamlin, Jason Robards Jr., Rip Torn, Catharine Hicks, Anne Francis, James Gammon. **1987**

LAIR OF THE WHITE WORM 🦃 Ken Russell writhes again, disgustingly perverse and snidely campy. Rated R. 99m. **DIR:** Ken Russell. **CAST:** Amanda Donohoe, Hugh Grant, Sammi Davis, Catherine Oxenberg, Peter Capaldi. **1988 DVD**

LAKE CONSEQUENCE ★★1/2 Arty smut-maven Zalman King turns producer for this melodramatic tale of a suburban housewife (Joan Severance) who slips into debauched sex with the tightly wired stud (Billy Zane) pruning the trees in her neighborhood. Lots of bare skin. Rated R for nudity and profanity. 85m. **DIR:** Rafael Eisenman. **CAST:** Billy Zane, Joan Severance, May Karasun. **1993**

LAKE PLACID ★★★1/2 This mainstream monster movie opens with a supremely gory moment, just to show that it means business, and then introduces its heroes and settles back for the acerbic, eccentric character banter that we'd expect of writer-producer David E. Kelley, best known for TV creations *The Practice* and *Ally McBeal*. The monster in question resides in tranquil Black Lake, in the backwoods of Maine, where it routinely chomps on anybody foolish enough to fall into the water. But, deft script and engaging characters aside, something must have gone wrong during production, because the film concludes—*very* abruptly—just as it has kicked into gear. Matters are resolved so quickly that you're likely to feel cheated. Let's therefore call this one suspenseful, skillfully scripted, well-performed, and quite entertaining . . . for two-thirds of a movie. Rated R for violence, profanity, and dollops of gore. 80m. **DIR:** Steve Miner. **CAST:** Bill Pullman, Bridget Fonda, Oliver Platt, Brendan Gleeson, Betty White, Meredith Salenger. **1999 DVD**

LAKOTA WOMAN: SIEGE AT WOUNDED KNEE ★★★ Good but preachy account of how one Lakota woman took a stand at Wounded Knee, South Dakota, in 1973 in order to regain her dignity. Irene Bedard makes a fine

debut as Mary Crow Dog, a woman ignorant of her heritage until she took part in the bloody siege that proved a turning point for American Indians. Made-for-cable film tries too hard to be politically correct. Not rated; contains violence. 113m. **DIR:** Frank Pierson. **CAST:** Irene Bedard, August Schellengberg, Joseph Running Fox, Floyd Red Crow Westerman, Tantoo Cardinal. **1994**

LAMBADA ★★ This attempt to exploit the sensuous dance from Brazil (do you know anyone who's actually "done" this dance?) is slightly better than *The Forbidden Dance*, which was released simultaneously—but that's not saying much. There is some nice choreography by Shabba-Doo. Rated PG. 97m. **DIR:** Joel Silberg. **CAST:** J. Eddie Peck, Melora Hardin, Dennis Burkley. **1990**

L'AMERICA ★★★★ Two Italian scam artists have hopes of securing government grants for their phony shoe factory in desperately poor post-communist Albania. They pluck a feeble-minded old man from a prison camp to act as the company's puppet chairman only to have him disappear into the flood of refugees escaping to Italy. This haunting story about the realities of mass immigration is told with documentary-like sweep. In Italian with English subtitles. Not rated. 116m. **DIR:** Gianni Amelio. **CAST:** Enrico Lo Verso, Michele Placido, Carmelo Di Mazzarelli, Piro Mikani. **1996**

LANCELOT OF THE LAKE ★★★★★ With characteristic austerity, Robert Bresson recounts the breakup of King Arthur's fabled Round Table as the ideals of chivalry give way to petty squabbles and sexual philandering. In French with English subtitles. Not rated. 85m. **DIR:** Robert Bresson. **CAST:** Luc Simon, Laura Duke Condominas. **1974**

LAND AND FREEDOM ★★★ An interesting approach to the Spanish Civil War—from the point of view of a naïve English Marxist who sees the Stalinists undercutting their anti-Fascist allies—that gets bogged down in political rhetoric and clichéd characterizations. A beautifully filmed tale of wartime disillusionment that could have been more intellectually and emotionally captivating. Not rated; contains military violence, language, and a sex scene. 110m. **DIR:** Kenneth Loach. **CAST:** Ian Hart. **1995**

LAND BEFORE TIME, THE ★★★★ This terrific animated film from director Don Bluth follows the journey of five young dinosaurs as they struggle to reach the Great Valley, the only place on Earth as yet untouched by a plague that has ravaged the world. On the way, they have several funny, suspenseful, and life-threatening adventures. The result is a wonderful film for the younger set. Rated G. 66m. **DIR:** Don Bluth. **1988 DVD**

LAND BEFORE TIME II, THE ★★ Some rather awful songs litter an otherwise bland direct-to-video sequel that likely will bore all but the very youngest of viewers. In this one, Littlefoot the dinosaur and his mischievous friends find unexpected perils in their happy valley home. Rated G. 72m. **DIR:** Roy Allen Smith. **1994**

LAND BEFORE TIME III, THE ★★★ Littlefoot and pals face new danger in this third entry in the animated movie series. In this direct-to-video release, their water supply is cut off, forcing the dinosaurs to ration, with conflicts and greed resulting. Bullying adolescents and bickering parents contrast sharply with the caring, sharing little ones. Animation, though passable, doesn't measure up to the original theatrical release. Rated G. 71m. **DIR:** Roy Allen Smith. **1995**

LAND GIRLS, THE ★★1/2 In this silly soap opera–sex farce, three lovely London lasses head to rural Dorset to pitch in while the men are off fighting World War II. They all illogically have affairs with the farmer's sullen son, who doesn't deserve any of them. This romantic piffle truly has no clue as to what it's really about. Rated R for sex, language, and mild violence. 112m. **DIR:** David Leland. **CAST:** Catherine McCormack, Rachel Weisz, Anna Friel, Steven Mackintosh. **1997**

LAND OF FARAWAY, THE ★★ An orphaned 11 year old boy is rescued from his dreary, dismal existence and spirited away to *The Land of Faraway.* The boy's father turns out to be the king of Faraway, and he finds the joy in life that he's been missing. But he has to earn his new inheritance by destroying the evil knight, Kato. Poor production values and sloppy direction spoil an otherwise good fairy tale. Rated PG. 95m. **DIR:** Vladimir Grammatikor. **CAST:** Timothy Bottoms, Susannah York, Christopher Lee. **1987**

LAND OF THE MINOTAUR ★★ Peter Cushing, in one of his few truly villainous roles, plays the leader of a bloodthirsty devil cult that preys on tourists in modern Greece. Already slow-paced, this low-budget creature feature is gravely handicapped by its American distributor's decision to cut six minutes of nudity and violence, thereby ensuring a PG rating. What remains is picturesque but tame. Brian Eno composed and performs the eerie electronic score. 88m. **DIR:** Costa Carayiannis. **CAST:** Peter Cushing, Donald Pleasence. **1976**

LAND OF THE OPEN RANGE ★★1/2 Sheriff Tim Holt has his hands full of ex-cons when a local no-good dies and leaves his ranch open to a land rush. However, to qualify for a homestead, each man must have served two years or more in prison. A different twist on the standard B land grab plot, and one of Holt's better prewar efforts. B&W; 60m. **DIR:** Edward Killy. **CAST:** Tim Holt, Ray Whitley, Roy Barcroft. **1942**

LAND OF THE PHARAOHS ★★1/2 Joan Collins plays the cunning villainess in a story about ancient Egypt. Talky but colorful historical drama with a visual tour of Egypt in all its splendor. 106m. **DIR:** Howard Hawks. **CAST:** Jack Hawkins, Joan Collins, Sydney Chaplin, James Robertson Justice, Dewey Martin. **1955**

LAND RAIDERS 🦃 Spanish-made violent oater with Telly Savalas as the Indian-hating town boss. 101m. **DIR:** Nathan Juran. **CAST:** Telly Savalas, George Maharis, Arlene Dahl. **1970**

LAND THAT TIME FORGOT, THE ★★ Poor Edgar Rice Burroughs, his wonderful adventure books for kids rarely got the right screen treatment. This British production tries hard, but the cheesy special effects eventually do it in. A sequel, *The People That Time Forgot*, fared no better. Rated PG. 90m. **DIR:** Kevin Connor. **CAST:** Doug McClure, Susan Penhaligon, John McEnery. **1975**

LAND UNKNOWN, THE ★★ A navy helicopter forced down in the Antarctic lands in a warm-water region where prehistoric animals still live. The production is better than the average B movie, but the dinosaurs are cheesy. B&W; 79m. **DIR:** Virgil Vogel. **CAST:** Jock Mahoney, Shawn Smith, William Reynolds. **1957**

LAND WITHOUT BREAD ★★★ A powerful documentary from director Luis Buñuel about the impoverished people living in the Las Hurdes region of Spain. In Spanish with English subtitles. B&W; 45m. **DIR:** Luis Buñuel. **1932**

LANDLADY, THE ★★ Talia Shire stars as Melanie Leroy, a desperate woman whose pursuit of a perfect life is shattered when she catches her husband cheating. After dispatching him, Melanie becomes the landlady of an apartment building, a position she uses to find the ideal husband. Instead, she's forced to dispatch those who get in the way of her happiness. And all 3-C wanted to do was borrow some butter. Pedestrian thrills fail to rise above that level. Rated R for violence and language. 98m. **DIR:** Robert Malenfant. **CAST:** Talia Shire, Jack Coleman, Melissa Behr, Susie Singer, Bette Ford, Bruce Weitz. **1997 DVD**

LANDSLIDE ★★★ Intriguing mystery follows young geologist Anthony Edwards's trek back to a small town he left years ago. Several of the locals try to figure out if he's the mysterious stranger who disappeared after a fatal car crash that killed the town leader and his family. Director Jean-Claude Lord guides his attractive cast through their paces with a tight reign. Rated PG-13 for violence. 95m. **DIR:** Jean-Claude Lord. **CAST:** Anthony Edwards, Tom Burlinson, Joanna Cassidy, Melody Anderson, Lloyd Bochner. **1992**

L'ANGE (THE ANGEL) ★★★ Strange concoction of the bizarre and grotesque make up this metaphysical animation feature depicting murderous phantasms stuck in a parallel universe. This film contains some dazzling images; too bad they found their way into an incoherent movie. In French with English subtitles. Not rated; contains nudity and violence. 70m. **DIR:** Patrick Bokanowski. **1982**

LANGOLIERS, THE ★★★1/2 A planeload of familiar faces find themselves trapped in a time vortex that is quickly collapsing. When ten passengers on a red-eye flight from Los Angeles to Boston awaken, they find that everyone else has disappeared. When they land, they discover a world where time stands still, and ferocious little critters eat everything in sight. This television miniseries, based on a Stephen King novella, is a little long in the tooth, but fascinating nonetheless. 180m. **DIR:** Tom Holland. **CAST:** Patricia Wettig, Dean Stockwell, Bronson Pinchot, David Morse, Mark Lindsay Chapman, Christopher Collet, Kate Maberly. **1995 DVD**

L'ANNÉE DES MEDUSES 🦃 If Jackie Collins were French, she'd probably be churning out stuff like this. On the Riviera, a young girl competes with her mother for the pick of the season's hunk crop. In French with English subtitles. Not rated, but loaded with nudity and soft-core sex. 110m. **DIR:** Christopher Frank. **CAST:** Valerie Kaprisky, Bernard Giraudeau, Caroline Cellier. **1986**

LANSKY ★★ This low-key made-for-cable original about Mafia financial whiz Meyer Lansky suffers from a staggering cast of characters and confusion over what is happening in each scene (rapid dialogue and obscure references account for this). Pepper this mess with trite and clichéd dialogue, and the film simply falls flat. Rated R for profanity, violence, and nudity. 116m. **DIR:** John McNaughton. **CAST:** Richard Dreyfuss, Eric Roberts, Max Perlich, Matthew Settle, Beverly D'Angelo, Anthony LaPaglia. **1999 DVD**

•LANTANA ★★★ It would be tempting to dismiss this often tedious drama as overlong and dull, but that would be unfair; after a slow start, the character interplay becomes intriguing enough to hold one's interest. Anthony LaPaglia heads a fine ensemble cast, and Andrew Bovell's script plays on the notion that complete strangers can be drawn together by random events. Alas, sticking with this needlessly protracted picture eventually becomes difficult, particularly during the three or four false endings. Rated R for profanity and sexual candor. 120m. **DIR:** Ray Lawrence. **CAST:** Anthony LaPaglia, Geoffrey Rush, Barbara Hershey, Kerry Armstrong, Rachael Blake. **2001**

LANTERN HILL ★★★★ A brilliant new *Wonderworks* production partially filmed on Prince Edward Island in Canada. Marion Bennett is Jane Stewart, a young girl whose powers are revealed in uniting her estranged parents in the mysterious Maritime Islands. A classic tale of family love. Made for television. 120m. **DIR:** Kevin Sullivan. **CAST:** Zoe Caldwell, Sam Waterston, Colleen Dewhurst, Marion Bennett, Sarah Polley. **1991**

•LARA CROFT: TOMB RAIDER ★★★ Wealthy British aristocrat and adventurer Angelina Jolie discovers that her deceased father (played by Jolie's real-life dad, Jon Voight) has left her a filmed message. She is to retrieve an ancient artifact before it falls into the hands of a secret society, which plans to use it as a means to control the world when the solar system's planets align. Fast-paced and heavily laden with special effects yet somehow simultaneously lightweight and bombastic, the film may appeal more to fans of the video game on which it is based than to casual viewers. Rated PG for violence and sexy costumes. 100m. **DIR:** Simon West. **CAST:** Angelina Jolie, Jon Voight, Iain Glen, Noah Taylor, Daniel Craig, Richard Johnson. **2001 DVD**

L'ARGENT ★★★★★ Robert Bresson's last film, almost a fable, charts the inexorable moral degradation of a man condemned for a crime he didn't commit. Like all of this great director's work, it demands close attention, but rewards it with unforgettable images of overpowering emotional resonance. In French with English subtitles. Not rated. 90m. **DIR:** Robert Bresson. **CAST:** Christian Patey, Sylvie van den Elsen. **1983**

LARGER THAN LIFE ★★ Slick motivational speaker inherits a female circus elephant from his deceased clown father. He takes the huge orphan across America by train, truck, and foot and plans to sell her on the West Coast either to a kind animal researcher or a mean-spirited circus boss. The film is sometimes amusing, but the elephant is given nothing special to do other than trumpet and raise a leg. This road comedy adds up to just peanuts for audiences expecting big and frequent laughs. Rated PG. 93m. **DIR:** Howard Franklin. **CAST:** Bill Murray, Linda Fiorentino, Matthew McConaughey, Janeane Garofalo, Pat Hingle. **1996**

LARKS ON A STRING ★★★1/2 Love blooms for a young couple in a reeducation camp, and their fellow detainees decide to give them a wedding and honeymoon under the noses of the camp authorities. This high-spirited comedy was banned by Soviet authorities until Glasnost. In Czech with English subtitles. Not

rated. B&W; 96m. **DIR:** Jiri Menzel. **CAST:** Vera Kresadlova, Vaclav Neckar. **1969**

LAS VEGAS HILLBILLYS 🦃 Hillbilly Ferlin Husky inherits a failing Las Vegas bar and makes it a success by turning it into Vegas's only country-and-western nightclub. The 1967 sequel *Hillbillys in a Haunted House*, is equally dismal. 90m. **DIR:** Arthur C. Pierce. **CAST:** Ferlin Husky, Jayne Mansfield, Mamie Van Doren, Sonny James, Richard Kiel. **1966 DVD**

LAS VEGAS LADY 🦃 Lame plot about a big money heist. 87m. **DIR:** Noel Nosseck. **CAST:** Stella Stevens, Stuart Whitman, George DiCenzo, Lynne Moody, Linda Scruggs. **1976 DVD**

LAS VEGAS STORY, THE 🦃 Las Vegas loser. B&W; 88m. **DIR:** Robert Stevenson. **CAST:** Jane Russell, Victor Mature, Vincent Price, Hoagy Carmichael, Jay C. Flippen, Brad Dexter. **1952**

LAS VEGAS WEEKEND ★★ After getting kicked out of college, a nerdy computer whiz decides to take his foolproof blackjack system to Las Vegas. Mild comedy could have been funnier. Rated R for brief nudity. 82m. **DIR:** Dale Trevillion. **CAST:** Barry Hickey, Ray Dennis Steckler. **1985**

LASER MAN, THE ★★★ A funny and inventive melting-pot comedy about a Chinese-American laser researcher living in Manhattan. However, the comedy is tempered by an incongruously serious subplot about arms dealers and the morality of scientific research. Not a total success, but worth seeing. 93m. **DIR:** Peter Wang. **CAST:** Marc Hayashi, Maryann Urbano, Tony Leung Chiu Wai, Peter Wang, Sally Yeh. **1988**

LASER MISSION ★★ The largest and most precious diamond in the world has been stolen. Ernest Borgnine is a professor with the know-how to turn that power into a destructive laser. Enter Bruce Lee's son Brandon, who saves the world from total destruction without once breaking into sweat. Rated R for violence. 90m. **DIR:** Beau Davis. **CAST:** Brandon Lee, Ernest Borgnine. **1990 DVD**

LASER MOON ★★ Former porn star Traci Lords gets down and dirty again as an undercover policewoman using herself as bait to trap a killer. Of note, the killer uses a laser on his victims, and then indulges his fantasies. Not rated, contains nudity, violence, and adult language. 90m. **DIR:** Douglas K. Grimm. **CAST:** Traci Lords, Crystal Shaw, Harrison Leduke, Bruce Carter. **1992 DVD**

LASERBLAST ★★ Dreadful low-budget film with some excellent special effects by David Allen. Story concerns a young man who accidentally lays his hands on an alien ray gun. Rated PG. 90m. **DIR:** Michael Raye. **CAST:** Kim Milford, Cheryl Smith, Roddy McDowall, Keenan Wynn. **1978 DVD**

LASERHAWK ★★1/2 A teenager with an overactive imagination has the fate of the world in his hands when he can't persuade anyone to believe what he has discovered—an alien plan to take over the world. Young teens are the target audience for this so-so sci-fi adventure with a not-very-believable plot and merely adequate special effects. Rated PG-13 for mild profanity and violence. 102m. **DIR:** Jack Pellerin. **CAST:** Jason James Richter, Mark Hamill, Gordon Currie, Melissa Galianos. **1997 DVD**

LASSIE ★★★1/2 Solid family entertainment has the cuddly collie coming to the aid of a disaffected teen dismayed by his family's move from the city to the country. Soon, our young hero learns something about old-fashioned values as he helps his folks stand up to an unscrupulous rival in the sheep-ranching business. It's just what you'd expect from a Lassie movie—no more, no less. Rated PG for light violence. 92m. **DIR:** Daniel Petrie. **CAST:** Tom Guiry, Helen Slater, Jon Tenney, Brittany Boyd, Frederic Forrest, Richard Farnsworth, Michelle Williams. **1994 DVD**

LASSIE COME HOME ★★★★ Heart-tugging story of a boy forced to give up the pet he loves is family drama at its best. An impeccable cast, beautiful photography, and intelligent scripting of Eric Knight's timeless novel highlight this wonderful tale of unsurmountable obstacles overcome by kindness and fidelity. 88m. **DIR:** Fred M. Wilcox. **CAST:** Roddy McDowall, Donald Crisp, Elizabeth Taylor, Nigel Bruce, Elsa Lanchester, May Whitty, Edmund Gwenn. **1943**

LASSITER ★★★ Tom Selleck stars as yet another jewel thief in the 1930s who attempts to steal a cache of uncut diamonds from the Nazis. Good-but-not-great entertainment. Rated R for nudity, suggested sex, violence, and profanity. 100m. **DIR:** Roger Young. **CAST:** Tom Selleck, Jane Seymour, Lauren Hutton, Bob Hoskins. **1984**

LAST ACTION HERO, THE ★★1/2 An 11 year old movie buff gets a magic ticket and finds himself thrust into the big-screen adventures of his hero, Jack Slater. Although not a total turkey, this bloated movie-within-a-movie has some serious flaws. The last half is plagued by lapses in logic and sappy sentimentality. Rated PG-13 for violence and brief profanity. 130m. **DIR:** John McTiernan. **CAST:** Arnold Schwarzenegger, F. Murray Abraham, Art Carney, Charles Dance, Frank McRae, Tom Noonan, Robert Prosky, Anthony Quinn, Mercedes Ruehl, Joan Plowright, Austin O'Brien. **1993 DVD**

LAST AMERICAN HERO, THE ★★★★ An entertaining action film about the famous whiskey runner from North Carolina who becomes a legend when he proves himself a great stock-car driver. Jeff Bridges's portrait of the rebel Junior Jackson is engaging, but Art Lund steals the show as Johnson's bootlegger father. Rated PG for profanity and sex. 95m. **DIR:** Lamont Johnson. **CAST:** Jeff Bridges, Valerie Perrine, Geraldine Fitzgerald, Ned Beatty, Gary Busey, Art Lund, Ed Lauter, William Smith. **1973**

LAST ANGRY MAN, THE ★★★1/2 Paul Muni, one of Hollywood's most respected actors, gave his final screen performance in this well-made version of Gerald Greene's novel about an aging family doctor in Brooklyn. The sentiment gets a little thick occasionally, but Muni's performance keeps it all watchable. Look for Godfrey Cambridge in a small role. Not rated, but suitable for the whole family. B&W; 100m. **DIR:** Daniel Mann. **CAST:** Paul Muni, David Wayne, Betsy Palmer, Luther Adler, Joby Baker. **1959**

LAST ASSASSINS ★★ How many times are they going to make this movie? Nancy Allen stars as an ex-CIA agent who is lured back into the business for one more mission with her old commander. Of course, he's a bad guy who is blackmailing her, so she steals his top-secret

plans. Then he kidnaps her daughter, and.... The plot elements might be tweaked a little, but it's all too familiar. Rated R for violence and language. 90m. **DIR:** William H. Molina. **CAST:** Nancy Allen, Lance Henriksen, Scott Lincoln, Dean Scofield, Floyd Red Crow Westerman. **1996 DVD**

LAST BEST YEAR, THE ★★★★ Mary Tyler Moore and Bernadette Peters are excellent in this heartbreaking story. Peters plays Jane Murray, a woman who only has six months left to live. Mary Tyler Moore plays Wendy Haller, a psychologist who reaches out to Jane. Together they find strength in each other, and a reason to live. This made-for-television weeper is a cut above the rest. Rated PG for adult content. 88m. **DIR:** John Erman. **CAST:** Mary Tyler Moore, Bernadette Peters, Carmen Mathews, Kate Reid, Kenneth Welsh, Dorothy McGuire. **1990**

LAST BOY SCOUT, THE ★★★★ A private detective must team up with an ex-football star to catch the killer of a topless dancer. Bruce Willis bounced back nicely from the *Hudson Hawk* debacle with this rip-roaring action movie in the style of the *Die Hard* films. Rated R for violence, profanity, nudity, and suggested sex. 105m. **DIR:** Tony Scott. **CAST:** Bruce Willis, Damon Wayans, Chelsea Field, Noble Willingham, Taylor Negron, Bruce McGill. **1991 DVD**

LAST BREATH ★★★ Creepy thriller about a devoted husband who will do anything to save the life of his wife. When his wife is struck down by a debilitating lung disease, Martin Devoe (Luke Perry) does what every conscientious husband would do: he begins dating. The only hitch is he plans to use his new girlfriend as a donor for his wife. And they say secondhand smoke kills. Rated R for adult situations, language, and violence. 90m. **DIR:** P.J. Posner. **CAST:** Luke Perry, Gia Carides, David Margulies, Francie Swift. **1996 DVD**

LAST BROADCAST, THE ★★★ Four men travel into the New Jersey Pine Barrens in an attempt to video the fabled Jersey Devil. Everything goes wrong, and only one of them escapes with his life. A year later, a documentary filmmaker tries to piece together the events of that fateful night to decide once and for all whether the lone survivor or something else was behind the vicious slayings. It is rumored that this movie inspired *The Blair Witch Project*. Rated R for violence and language. 87m. **DIR:** Stefan Avalos, Lance Weiler. **CAST:** David Beard, Jim Seward, Rein Clabbers, Michele Pulaski. **1997 DVD**

LAST BUTTERFLY, THE ★★★★ Haunting drama is about an actor and mime forced by the Germans to perform in Terezin, a model city, as a facade to show the world how well the Nazis are treating the imprisoned Jews. When he finds out that the children in his show are destined for the gas chambers, he decides to give the Nazis a show they won't forget. Not rated; contains violence. 106m. **DIR:** Karel Kachyna. **CAST:** Tom Courtenay, Brigitte Fossey, Freddie Jones, Linda Jablonska. **1994**

LAST CALL ★★ William Katt has a business deal go sour, so he and Shannon Tweed pair up for a little sex and vengeance in this confusing drama about greed. Too much sex and not enough plot. Not rated; contains violence and profanity. 90m. **DIR:** Jag Mundhra. **CAST:** William Katt, Shannon Tweed, Joseph Campanella, Stella Stevens. **1990 DVD**

LAST CALL AT MAUD'S ★★★ Informative, sentimental documentary covering the closing of the famous San Francisco lesbian bar is actually a funny, sad history of lesbianism over the last fifty years. Utilizing nostalgic newsreels, newspaper clippings, and documentary footage, this fond farewell remains a positive statement despite its sad subject. Not rated; contains mature themes. 77m. **DIR:** Paris Poirer. **1993 DVD**

•LAST CASTLE, THE ★★1/2 By refusing to follow orders, a highly respected army general causes the death of soldiers under his command. As a result, he is sentenced to serve time in a military prison where he becomes the leader of a revolt against the sadistic commander of the facility. Predictable, yes, but the cast is top-notch, and there are some fine action sequences. While lacking the qualities that made *The Great Escape* and *Stalag 17* classics of the genre, it manages to be mildly entertaining. Rated R for profanity and violence. 131m. **DIR:** Rod Lurie. **CAST:** Robert Redford, James Gandolfini, Mark Ruffalo, Steve Burton, Delroy Lindo, Paul Calderon, Samuel Ball, Jeremy Childs. **2001 DVD**

LAST CHASE, THE ★★1/2 Made at the end of the OPEC oil crisis, this film assumes the crisis only got worse until there was a civil war in America and the eastern states banned all cars and planes. Lee Majors plays an aged race-car driver who flees New York to California with a runaway (Chris Makepeace). Confusing at times, and the Orwellian touches have been done so often that all the scare has left them. Not rated. 106m. **DIR:** Martyn Burke. **CAST:** Lee Majors, Chris Makepeace, Burgess Meredith. **1980**

LAST COMMAND, THE (1928) ★★★★ German star Emil Jannings's second U.S. film has him portraying a czarist army commander who flees the Russian Revolution to America. Here, he sinks into poverty and winds up as a Hollywood extra. Art imitates life when he is cast to play a Russian general in a film directed by a former revolutionary (and former rival in love). William Powell plays the director, a stiff, unbending sadist bent upon humiliating Jannings. Silent. B&W; 80m. **DIR:** Josef von Sternberg. **CAST:** Emil Jannings, William Powell, Evelyn Brent. **1928**

LAST COMMAND, THE (1955) ★★1/2 This is a watchable Western about the famed last stand at the Alamo during Texas's fight for independence from Mexico. Jim Bowie (Sterling Hayden), Davy Crockett (Arthur Hunnicutt), and Colonel Travis (Richard Carlson) are portrayed in a more realistic manner than they were in John Wayne's *The Alamo*, but the story is still mostly hokum. 110m. **DIR:** Frank Lloyd. **CAST:** Sterling Hayden, Richard Carlson, Anna Maria Alberghetti, Ernest Borgnine, Arthur Hunnicutt, Jim Davis, J. Carrol Naish. **1955**

LAST CONTRACT, THE ★★ In this violent film, Jack Palance stars as an artist and a hit man who is hired to kill his best friend. Unable to do it, he is ordered to assassinate a rival crime lord. When he kills the wrong man, the deadly game of hit and counterhit gets out of hand. Rated R. 85m. **DIR:** Allan A. Buckhantz. **CAST:** Jack Palance, Rod Steiger, Bo Svenson, Richard Roundtree, Ann Turkel. **1986**

LAST DANCE ★★1/2 Sharon Stone plays a death-row inmate awaiting execution; Rob Morrow is the attorney

who tries to get her sentence commuted to life in prison. Stone tears into her showy role with hardboiled relish, but the script plays more like a catalogue of prison-movie clichés than a genuine statement on capital punishment. Well-directed by Bruce Beresford, but Morrow's bland, pedestrian performance is, like the script, a major liability. Rated R for profanity and brief violence. 107m. **DIR:** Bruce Beresford. **CAST:** Sharon Stone, Rob Morrow, Peter Gallagher, Randy Quaid, Jack Thompson. **1996**

LAST DAYS, THE ★★★★1/2 Five survivors of the Holocaust—a grandmother, teacher, businessman, artist, and congressman from California—vividly recount and reflect on the roundup and massacre of Hungarian Jews in 1944. This powerful, Oscar-winning documentary ties individual human faces, intimate testimony, and archival footage to the horrors of genocide and makes a lucid case that pure evil does exist on Earth. Not rated. 88m. **DIR:** James Moll. **1998 DVD**

LAST DAYS OF CHEZ NOUS, THE ★★★★ Quirky, European-style comedy-drama from Australian director Gillian Armstrong focuses on a writer and her relationships with a French-born husband, troubled sister, and crochety father. Armstrong's low-key, believable and touching handling of the subject matter is what makes *The Last Days of Chez Nous* such a treasure. Not rated, the film has profanity and brief nudity. 96m. **DIR:** Gillian Armstrong. **CAST:** Lisa Harrow, Bruno Ganz, Kerry Fox, Miranda Otto, Kiri Paramore, Bill Hunter. **1993**

LAST DAYS OF DISCO, THE ★★★1/2 It's the early 1980s. Shy Alice and bitchy Charlotte are editorial assistants who frequent Manhattan's disco scene. In this nostalgic comedy, they and several friends discuss feelings, philosophies, sex, and relationships with polished, deadpan sincerity. A subplot misfires, but this invasion of yesteryear's tribal stomping grounds is mostly fun. Rated R for sexual content, nudity, and drug use. 113m. **DIR:** Whit Stillman. **CAST:** Chloe Sevigny, Kate Beckinsale, Christopher Eigeman, Matt Keeslar. **1998 DVD**

LAST DAYS OF FRANK AND JESSE JAMES ★★★ Once you get past the country-western motif, this is an honorable biography of the notorious Wild West hoodlums. Kris Kristofferson and Johnny Cash are convincingly brotherly, and director William A. Graham adds just enough grittiness to make them a little less than heroic. 97m. **DIR:** William A. Graham. **CAST:** Kris Kristofferson, Johnny Cash, Willie Nelson. **1988**

LAST DAYS OF FRANKIE THE FLY, THE ★★1/2 Yet another Quentin Tarantino clone, this violent gangster-comedy-thriller is worth seeing mostly for Dennis Hopper as a non-too-smart mob underling who embezzles his boss's money to finance a porn film. Rated R for profanity and violence. 96m. **DIR:** Peter Markle. **CAST:** Dennis Hopper, Kiefer Sutherland, Michael Madsen, Daryl Hannah, Dayton Callie. **1997**

LAST DAYS OF MAN ON EARTH, THE ★★★1/2 Kinetic adaptation of Michael Moorcock's weird little novel, *The Final Programme*, the first of his adventures featuring Jerry Cornelius. Jon Finch plays Jerry as a smart-assed James Bond, and the prize he fights for is a microfilm containing the secret to self-replicating beings . . . highly useful in case of nuclear war. Finch encounters a variety of oddball characters, none stranger than Jenny Runacre, an enigmatic adversary who absorbs her lovers. Rated R for violence and sex. 73m. **DIR:** Robert Fuest. **CAST:** Jon Finch, Sterling Hayden, Patrick Magee, Jenny Runacre, Hugh Griffith. **1973**

LAST DAYS OF PATTON, THE ★★★ A three-star adaptation of Ladislas Farago's book, which follows four-star General George S. Patton's 1945 peacetime career as commander of the Third Army, military governor of Bavaria, and finally as head of the Fifteenth Army. This made-for-TV sequel to George C. Scott's Oscar-winner lacks much of its predecessor's blood and guts. 146m. **DIR:** Delbert Mann. **CAST:** George C. Scott, Erika Hoffman, Eva Marie Saint, Richard Dysart, Murray Hamilton, Ed Lauter. **1985 DVD**

LAST DAYS OF POMPEII (1960) ★★ A different scenario than the 1935 original. Steve Reeves plays a hero in the Roman army stationed in Greece who tries to save a group of Christians that has been jailed and condemned to death. The story is interesting, but the action scenes are rather dumb. 93m. **DIR:** Mario Bonnard. **CAST:** Steve Reeves, Fernando Rey, Christine Kaufmann, Barbara Carroll, Angel Aranda. **1960**

LAST DAYS OF POMPEII, THE (1935) ★★★ Roman blacksmith Preston Foster becomes a gladiator after tragedy takes his wife and baby. En route to fortune, he adopts the young son of one of his victims. In Judea, he sees but refuses to help Christ, who cures the boy following serious injury. Touched by Jesus, the boy grows up to help runaway slaves. Tremendous special effects. B&W; 96m. **DIR:** Ernest B. Schoedsack. **CAST:** Preston Foster, Basil Rathbone, Alan Hale Sr., Louis Calhern. **1935**

•LAST DEBATE, THE ★★★1/2 Based on a book by Jim Lehrer, this made-for-cable movie depicts a presidential debate that uncovers serious character flaws in one of the candidates. The four journalists responsible for revealing this information are at first reviled, then revered for their actions. Meanwhile, an objective reporter searches for the origin of the character assassination. This interesting political drama raises a lot of questions about the media's role in our government. Not rated; contains profanity. 96m. **DIR:** John Badham. **CAST:** James Garner, Peter Gallagher, Audra McDonald, Donna Murphy, Marco Sanchez. **2000**

LAST DETAIL, THE ★★★★ Two veteran navy men (Jack Nicholson and Otis Young) are assigned to transport a young sailor to the brig for theft. They take pity on the naïve loser (Randy Quaid) and decide to show him one last good time. By opening the youngster's eyes to the previously unknown world around him, their kindness is in danger of backfiring in this drama. Rated R. 105m. **DIR:** Hal Ashby. **CAST:** Jack Nicholson, Otis Young, Randy Quaid, Michael Moriarty, Nancy Allen. **1973 DVD**

LAST DON, THE ★★★1/2 Danny Aiello is excellent as the mob boss whose daughter ends up marrying the son of his rival, igniting a long-simmering vendetta. Video version of the miniseries, based on the Mario Puzo novel, is a leaner and meaner effort. Rated R for adult situations, language, nudity, and violence. 148m. **DIR:** Graeme Clifford. **CAST:** Danny Aiello, Joe Mantegna, Jason Gedrick, Daryl Hannah, Kirstie Alley, Penelope Ann Miller. **1997 DVD**

LAST DRAGON, THE ★★★1/2 Produced by Motown Records man Berry Gordy, this is lively, unpretentious

nonsense about a shy karate champ (Taimak) fending off villains threatening a disc jockey (Vanity). Good, silly fun. Rated PG-13 for violence. 109m. **DIR:** Michael Schultz. **CAST:** Taimak, Vanity, Christopher Murney. **1985 DVD**

LAST EMBRACE, THE ★★★1/2 A CIA agent must track down an obsessed, methodical killer. A complex, intelligent thriller in the Hitchcock style with skilled performances, a lush music score, and a cliff-hanging climax at Niagara Falls. Rated R for nudity and violence. 102m. **DIR:** Jonathan Demme. **CAST:** Roy Scheider, Janet Margolin, Sam Levene, Marcia Rodd, Christopher Walken, John Glover, Charles Napier. **1979**

LAST EMPEROR, THE ★★★★★ An awe-inspiring epic that tells a heartrending, intimate story against a backdrop of spectacle and history. The screenplay by Mark Peploe and director Bernardo Bertolucci dramatizes the life of Pu Yi (John Lone), China's last emperor. When he was taken from his home at the age of 3 to become the all-powerful Qing Emperor, the youngster was ironically condemned to a lifetime of imprisonment. Rated PG-13 for violence, brief nudity, and frank sexuality. 160m. **DIR:** Bernardo Bertolucci. **CAST:** John Lone, Peter O'Toole, Joan Chen, Ying Ruocheng, Victor Wong, Dennis Dun. **1987 DVD**

LAST EXIT TO BROOKLYN ★★★★ Uli Edel's film is a dark, unflinching drama about mislaid dreams, unfulfilled expectations, and gritty survival, set in the midst of waterfront labor unrest in the Brooklyn of the early Fifties. Adapted from the cult 1964 novel by Hubert Selby Jr. Rated R, with strong violence and profanity. 102m. **DIR:** Uli Edel. **CAST:** Stephen Lang, Jennifer Jason Leigh, Peter Dobson, Ricki Lake, Jerry Orbach. **1990**

LAST EXIT TO EARTH ★★ The "Great Feminist Revolution" eventually leads to male sterility in this sci-fi cheapie from producer Roger Corman, which concerns a quartet of women from the year 2500 who travel back in time to abduct some male breeding stock. Plot and dialogue are trite, predictable, and poorly realized by a disinterested cast. Rated R for nudity, violence, and profanity. 90m. **DIR:** Katt Shea Ruben. **CAST:** Kim Greist, Costas Mandylor, Amy Hathaway, David Groh, Hilary Shephard. **1996**

LAST FIVE DAYS, THE ★★★1/2 During the Nazi reign, a brother and sister are placed in jail to be questioned. The sister encounters Else, a prison clerk, who is awaiting her own trial. The viewer experiences the despair of the sister's last five days and her emotional encounter with Else and other anti-Hitler sympathizers. In German with English subtitles. Not rated, suitable for all audiences. 115m. **DIR:** Percy Adlon. **CAST:** Irm Hermann, Lena Stolze, Will Spindler, Hans Hirschmuller, Philip Arp, Joachim Bernhard. **1982**

LAST FLIGHT OF NOAH'S ARK ★★★ This is the story of an unemployed pilot (Elliott Gould) who, against his better judgment, agrees to fly a plane full of farm animals to a Pacific island for a young missionary (Genevieve Bujold). This film, while not one of Disney's best, does offer clean, wholesome fun for the younger (and young-at-heart) audience. Rated G. 97m. **DIR:** Charles Jarrott. **CAST:** Elliott Gould, Genevieve Bujold, Rick Schroder, Vincent Gardenia. **1980 DVD**

LAST FLIGHT TO HELL 🦃 Mundane chase flick has hunky Reb Brown tracking down a group of terrorists who have kidnapped a South American drug lord. Why? Rated R. 84m. **DIR:** Paul D. Robinson. **CAST:** Reb Brown, Chuck Connors. **1991**

LAST FLING, THE ★★★ Cute made-for-TV movie about a philanderer (John Ritter) who finally finds his perfect match (Connie Sellecca) only to have her disappear. His attempts to find her are usually funny and often hilarious. 95m. **DIR:** Corey Allen. **CAST:** John Ritter, Connie Sellecca, Scott Bakula, Paul Sand, John Bennett Perry. **1986**

LAST GAME, THE ★★ Maudlin tale of an attractive and responsible clean-cut college kid who works two jobs, goes to school, and takes care of his blind father while his father dreams that one day his boy will play pro football. This movie is just too banal for recommendation. No MPAA rating, but equal to a PG for sex and profanity. 107m. **DIR:** Martin Beck. **CAST:** Howard Segal, Ed L. Grady, Terry Alden, Joan Hotchkis. **1980 DVD**

LAST GASP ★★ Deceitful contractor Robert Patrick murders a Mexican Indian interfering with a project, and is "rewarded" by a curse which turns him into a feral killer forced to slice up a new victim every twenty days. Only plucky Joanna Pacula stands in his way, in this trite and predictable thriller. Rated R for violence, gore, nudity, simulated sex, and profanity. 90m. **DIR:** Scott McGinnis. **CAST:** Robert Patrick, Joanna Pacula, Vyto Ruginis, Mimi Craven. **1995**

LAST GOOD TIME, THE ★★1/2 An elderly violinist (Armin Mueller-Stahl) strikes up an unusual friendship with a young woman (Olivia d'Abo) on the run from her abusive boyfriend. Low-key and muted, the film is reminiscent of Louis Malle's *Atlantic City* but not nearly as good. Rated R for profanity and brief nudity. 89m. **DIR:** Bob Balaban. **CAST:** Armin Mueller-Stahl, Olivia D'Abo, Maureen Stapleton, Lionel Stander, Adrian Pasdar. **1995**

LAST GUN, THE ★★ In this Italian Western dubbed into English, a gunfighter tired of killing hangs up his pistols and settles down in a small town. The story is classic. The acting and directing are not. 98m. **DIR:** Serge Bergone. **CAST:** Cameron Mitchell, Frank Wolff, Carl Mohner. **1964**

LAST HIT, THE ★★★ A government assassin wants to retire, but is told he must first kill one more person. He falls in love with the woman he purchased his house from, and then realizes his target is her father. A few good twists and good acting will keep you watching. Not rated, made for cable, but contains violence. 95m. **DIR:** Jan Egleson. **CAST:** Bryan Brown, Brooke Adams, Daniel Von Bargen, Sally Kemp, Rider Strong, Harris Yulin. **1993**

LAST HOLIDAY ★★★★ Alec Guinness is magnificent as a failed salesman told he has only months to live. He plans to quietly live out his time at a resort hotel, but becomes an important influence on the guests and staff. Bittersweet, witty story by J. B. Priestley. B&W; 88m. **DIR:** Henry Cass. **CAST:** Alec Guinness, Beatrice Campbell, Kay Walsh, Bernard Lee, Wilfrid Hyde-White. **1950**

LAST HORROR FILM, THE 🦃 Mama's boy obsessed with a horror-movie actress goes on a killing spree at the Cannes Film Festival. Rated R for violence. 87m.

DIR: David Winters. **CAST:** Caroline Munro, Joe Spinell. **1984**

LAST HOUR, THE ★★ A cop tries to rescue his ex-wife from mobsters. Low-budget rip-off of *Die Hard*. Rated R for violence, profanity, nudity, and simulated sex. 85m. **DIR:** William Sachs. **CAST:** Michael Paré, Shannon Tweed, Bobby DiCicco. **1991**

LAST HOUSE ON THE LEFT 🦃 Two teenage girls are tortured and killed by a sadistic trio. Graphic torture and humiliation scenes rate this one an R at best. 91m. **DIR:** Wes Craven. **CAST:** David Hess, Lucy Grantham, Sandra Cassel. **1972**

LAST HUNT, THE ★★1/2 A downer disguised as an upper. This outdoor drama has more talk than action, as buffalo try to escape from crafty white men. Stewart Granger makes a weak hero, but Robert Taylor is pretty good as the villain. 108m. **DIR:** Richard Brooks. **CAST:** Robert Taylor, Stewart Granger, Constance Ford, Debra Paget, Lloyd Nolan, Joe De Santis, Russ Tamblyn. **1955**

LAST HURRAH, THE ★★★★ Spencer Tracy gives a memorable performance as an Irish-Catholic mayor running for office one last time. Jeffrey Hunter is Tracy's nephew, a cynical reporter who comes to respect the old man's values and integrity. B&W; 111m. **DIR:** John Ford. **CAST:** Spencer Tracy, Jeffrey Hunter, Dianne Foster, Pat O'Brien, Basil Rathbone, Donald Crisp, James Gleason, Edward Brophy, John Carradine, Wallace Ford, Frank McHugh, Jane Darwell. **1958 DVD**

LAST INNOCENT MAN, THE ★★★★ When a talented young district attorney meets a mysterious and beautiful woman in a bar, their ensuing affair entangles him in a web of deceit. This suspenseful courtroom drama provides a number of intriguing plot twists and makes for a delicious combination of action and suspense. Produced by Home Box Office; has brief nudity and sexual situations. 114m. **DIR:** Roger Spottiswoode. **CAST:** Ed Harris, Roxanne Hart, David Suchet, Bruce McGill. **1987**

LAST LAUGH, THE ★★★★ Historically recognized as the first film to exploit the moving camera, this silent classic tells the story of a lordly luxury hotel doorman who is abruptly and callously demoted to the menial status of a washroom attendant. Deprived of his job and uniform, his life slowly disintegrates. Emil Jannings gives a brilliant performance. B&W; 74m. **DIR:** F. W. Murnau. **CAST:** Emil Jannings. **1924 DVD**

LAST LIGHT ★★★★★ A masterful character study from first-time director Kiefer Sutherland, who also stars as an unrepentant killer. While waiting on death row, he finds an unlikely friend in prison guard Forest Whitaker. Robert Eisele's script offers no apologies for the murderer's brutality but makes a case for treating even the most heinous individual with dignity. You'll be riveted from the first few shocking frames. Rated R for violence and profanity. 104m. **DIR:** Kiefer Sutherland. **CAST:** Forest Whitaker, Kiefer Sutherland, Amanda Plummer, Kathleen Quinlan, Lynne Moody, Clancy Brown. **1993**

LAST MAN ON EARTH, THE ★★★1/2 In this nightmarish tale, a scientist (Vincent Price) is a bit late in developing a serum to stem the tide of a plague epidemic. He becomes the last man on Earth and lives in fear of the walking dead, who crave his blood. This paranoid horror film (based on Richard Matheson's *I Am Legend*) is more chilling than its higher-budget remake, *The Omega Man*. B&W; 86m. **DIR:** Sidney Salkow. **CAST:** Vincent Price, Franca Bettoia, Emma Danieli, Giacomo Rossi-Stuart. **1964**

LAST MAN STANDING (1988) ★★★★ Surprisingly good prizefight film in which Vernon Wells plays a down-and-out boxer who attempts to find work outside the ring. The brutality of the fight game is well captured. Rated R for profanity and violence. 92m. **DIR:** Damien Lee. **CAST:** Vernon Wells, William Sanderson, Franco Columbu. **1988**

LAST MAN STANDING (1994) ★★★ Smartly-directed action picture stars Jeff Wincott as a cop who risks it all to stop a group of dirty policemen who have worked out a look-the-other-way deal with a drug czar. Great action sequences and stunts are enhanced by a better-than-average screenplay and performances. Rated R for violence, profanity, nudity, and sexual situations. 95m. **DIR:** Joseph Merhi. **CAST:** Jeff Wincott, Jillian McWhirter, Steve Eastin, Jonathan Fuller, Jonathan Banks. **1994**

LAST MAN STANDING (1996) ★★★★ Dashiell Hammett's *Red Harvest* comes full circle, from feudal Japan (in Akira Kurosawa's *Yojimbo*) and the Old West (in Sergo Leone's *A Fistful of Dollars*) back to America in the 1920s. Bruce Willis pits two rival gangs against each other to break their reign of terror in a small town. Walter Hill's fans will love it, but the impartial will not be impressed. Rated R for violence, profanity, and suggested sex. 100m. **DIR:** Walter Hill. **CAST:** Bruce Willis, Christopher Walken, Bruce Dern, Alexandra Powers, David Patrick Kelly, William Sanderson, Karina Lombard, R. D. Call. **1996 DVD**

LAST MARRIED COUPLE IN AMERICA, THE 🦃 Lame-brained little sex farce about one perfect couple's struggle to hold their own marriage together. Rated R for profanity and nudity. 103m. **DIR:** Gilbert Cates. **CAST:** Natalie Wood, George Segal, Arlene Golonka, Bob Dishy, Priscilla Barnes, Dom DeLuise, Valerie Harper. **1980**

LAST METRO, THE ★★★1/2 Catherine Deneuve and Gérard Depardieu star in this drama about a Parisian theatrical company that believes "the show must go on" despite the restrictions and terrors of the Nazis during their World War II occupation of France. This film has several nice moments and surprises that make up for its occasional dull spots and extended running time. Rated PG. 133m. **DIR:** François Truffaut. **CAST:** Catherine Deneuve, Gérard Depardieu, Jean Poiret. **1980 DVD**

LAST MILE, THE ★★★ No-win prison film (based on a stage play) is a claustrophobic foray into death row. This archetypal prison-break melodrama has a quiet dignity that elevates the dialogue between the inmates. Preston Foster as Killer Miles plays the toughest con in the block and the leader of the break attempt. B&W; 70m. **DIR:** Sam Bischoff. **CAST:** Preston Foster, Howard Phillips, George E. Stone, Paul Fix. **1932**

LAST MOVIE, THE (CHINCHERO) 🦃 Dennis Hopper's abysmal follow-up to *Easy Rider* wastes a talented cast in this incoherent story about a film crew after they pull out of a small Peruvian village. Rated R for nudity and profanity. 108m. **DIR:** Dennis Hopper. **CAST:** Dennis Hopper, Julie Adams, Peter Fonda, Kris Kristofferson,

Sylvia Miles, John Phillip Law, Samuel Fuller, Dean Stockwell. **1971**

LAST NIGHT ★★★ At midnight the world will end and everyone seems to know it. What people decide to do with their last hours on Earth is up to them—some stories are funny, and others poignant. Rated R for sex, violence, and language. 96m. **DIR:** Don McKellar. **CAST:** Don McKellar, Sandra Oh, Callum Keith Rennie, Sarah Polley, David Cronenberg, Genevieve Bujold. **1998 DVD**

LAST NIGHT AT THE ALAMO ★★★★ On the night before the demolition of a run-down Houston bar, the regulars gather to mourn its passing. The satire of Kim Henkel's script, which targets machismo, is balanced by a real affection for these losers who depend on beer and bull to face the world. Recommended. Not rated, the film features plentiful profanity. 82m. **DIR:** Eagle Pennell. **CAST:** Sonny Davis. **1983**

LAST OF ENGLAND, THE ★★★★★ Painter-poet-filmmaker Derek Jarman has created a stunning visionary work that is a mysterious, well-crafted montage of image and sound, evoking a world of apocalyptic fury—filmed in Belfast and London. With a British strain of convulsive romanticism Jarman uses Super-8 lyricism, gay erotica, and old home movies to illustrate the fall of England. Not rated; contains nudity and violence. B&W/color; 87m. **DIR:** Derek Jarman. **CAST:** Tilda Swinton, Spencer Leigh. **1987**

LAST OF HIS TRIBE, THE ★★★ Graham Greene contributes a moving and dignified interpretation of Ishi, the last free-living Yahi Indian who in 1911 was taken to San Francisco and placed under the care of Professor Albert Kroeber. Made for cable, with graphic surgical footage. Rated PG-13 for sexual frankness and explicit medical procedures. 90m. **DIR:** Harry Hook. **CAST:** Jon Voight, Graham Greene, David Ogden Stiers, Jack Blessing, Anne Archer. **1992**

LAST OF MRS. CHENEY, THE ★★★ Jewel thieves in high society. This star-studded remake of Norma Shearer's 1929 hit version of Frederick Lonsdale's evergreen comedy falls a mite short, but is nonetheless worth watching. As always, Robert Montgomery and William Powell are urbanity in spades. Good show. B&W; 98m. **DIR:** Richard Boleslawski. **CAST:** Robert Montgomery, Joan Crawford, William Powell, Frank Morgan, Jessie Ralph, Benita Hume, Nigel Bruce. **1937**

LAST OF MRS. LINCOLN, THE ★★★★ Julie Harris shines in her portrayal of Mary Todd Lincoln during the last seventeen years of her life. Bearing enormous debts accumulated during her stay in the White House and denied a pension by the Senate because of her Southern heritage, she eventually falls into penury and insanity. Michael Cristofer and Robby Benson play the two surviving Lincoln sons. Made for television. 117m. **DIR:** George Schaefer. **CAST:** Julie Harris, Michael Cristofer, Robby Benson, Patrick Duffy, Denver Pyle, Priscilla Morrill. **1984**

LAST OF PHILIP BANTER, THE ★★1/2 Scott Paulin gives a stunning performance in this lurid psychodrama. He's a self-destructive alcoholic whose life degenerates into madness after the discovery of some mysterious manuscripts. Rated R; contains profanity and violence. 100m. **DIR:** Herve Hachuel. **CAST:** Scott Paulin, Irene Miracle, Gregg Henry, Kate Vernon, Tony Curtis. **1986**

LAST OF SHEILA, THE ★★★★ A cleverly planned, very watchable whodunit. Because of some unusual camera angles and subtle dialogue, the audience is drawn into active participation in the mystery. A sundry collection of Hollywood types are invited on a yachting cruise by James Coburn. It seems one of them has been involved in the death of Coburn's wife. Rated PG. 120m. **DIR:** Herbert Ross. **CAST:** James Coburn, Dyan Cannon, James Mason, Raquel Welch, Richard Benjamin. **1973**

LAST OF THE BLONDE BOMBSHELLS, THE ★★★★ Judi Dench won a Golden Globe for her portrayal of a widow trying to reunite her swing band from World War II in this made-for-cable original. After her husband dies, Dench dusts off her saxophone and starts playing again, which prompts her granddaughter's request to bring the band back together for a school dance. Along the way, Dench finds a new sense of purpose and a new romance. Good acting, a good script, and interesting characters make this an enjoyable film. Rated PG-13 for profanity. 83m. **DIR:** Gillies MacKinnon. **CAST:** Judi Dench, Ian Holm, Leslie Caron, Olympia Dukakis, Cleo Laine, Joan Sims, Billie Whitelaw, June Whitfield. **2000 DVD**

LAST OF THE COMANCHES ★★ Tough cavalry sergeant has to lead a stagecoach load of passengers to safety across the desert following an Indian raid. Broderick Crawford was woefully miscast in the handful of Westerns he did. B&W; 85m. **DIR:** André de Toth. **CAST:** Broderick Crawford, Barbara Hale, Lloyd Bridges. **1953**

LAST OF THE DOGMEN ★★★1/2 Modern-day outlaw tracker Tom Berenger goes after three fugitives in the wilds of Montana only to find himself confronting ghostly warriors from the past. Director Tab Murphy builds suspense nicely in the first third of the film; so much so that the eventual revelation is something of a disappointment. But things pick up again, and the result is an old-fashioned piece of entertainment that will please those who worry that "they don't make 'em like they used to." Rated PG. 117m. **DIR:** Tab Murphy. **CAST:** Tom Berenger, Barbara Hershey, Kurtwood Smith, Steve Reevis, Andrew Miller. **1995 DVD**

LAST OF THE FINEST, THE ★★ Four Los Angeles undercover cops (led by burly Brian Dennehy) are temporarily suspended. When one member of this elite squad gets murdered, the other three seek revenge. This standard shoot-'em-up is rated R for language and violence. 106m. **DIR:** John Mackenzie. **CAST:** Brian Dennehy, Joe Pantoliano, Jeff Fahey, Bill Paxton, Michael C. Gwynne, Henry Darrow. **1990**

LAST OF THE MOHICANS, THE (1920) ★★★1/2 The most faithful version of James Fenimore Cooper's story with some surprisingly strong dramatic moments. Almost none of this was shot in a studio, and the location filming is still impressive, now that the film has been restored by the Eastman House. Silent. B&W; 72m. **DIR:** Clarence Brown, Maurice Tourneur. **CAST:** Wallace Beery, Barbara Bedford, Albert Roscoe. **1920 DVD**

LAST OF THE MOHICANS, THE (1936) ★★★★ Blood, thunder, and interracial romance during the French and Indian War are brought to life from James Fenimore

Cooper's novel. Randolph Scott is the intrepid Hawkeye; Robert Barrat is the noble Chingachgook; Binnie Barnes is Alice Monroe. The star-crossed lovers are Phillip Reed, as Uncas, the title character, and Heather Angel, as Cora Monroe. B&W; 100m. **DIR:** George B. Seitz. **CAST:** Randolph Scott, Binnie Barnes, Heather Angel, Robert Barrat, Phillip Reed, Henry Wilcoxon, Bruce Cabot. **1936**

LAST OF THE MOHICANS (1985) ★★1/2 In this TV film based on James Fenimore Cooper's classic, a small party headed for a fort is deserted by their guide and must turn to Hawkeye and Chingachgook to bring them to safety. When two of the party are captured, our heroes must rescue them and battle the leader of the Indians. 97m. **DIR:** James L. Conway. **CAST:** Steve Forrest, Ned Romero, Andrew Prine, Robert Tessier. **1985**

LAST OF THE MOHICANS, THE (1992) ★★★★★ A classy romance angle and director Michael Mann's sweeping vision highlight this retelling of James Fenimore Cooper's novel of colonial America. A first-class production all the way, this historic tale never feels dated, and the action scenes are state-of-the-art. Rated R for violence. 120m. **DIR:** Michael Mann. **CAST:** Daniel Day-Lewis, Madeleine Stowe, Russell Means, Eric Schweig, Jodhi May, Steven Waddington, Maurice Roeves, Wes Studi, Patrice Chereau. **1992 DVD**

LAST OF THE PONY RIDERS ★★★1/2 Gene Autry's last feature film concerns the old West transition period from pony express to stagecoach and telegraph. Action-packed ending to Autry's twenty years of B-Western films. B&W; 59m. **DIR:** George Archainbaud. **CAST:** Gene Autry, Smiley Burnette, Dick Jones, Kathleen Case. **1953**

LAST OF THE RED HOT LOVERS 🦃 A married man uses his mother's apartment for amorous dalliances. Rated PG. 98m. **DIR:** Gene Saks. **CAST:** Alan Arkin, Paula Prentiss, Sally Kellerman. **1972**

LAST OF THE REDMEN ★★★ Low-budget remake of James Fenimore Cooper's immortal *Last of the Mohicans* story with Michael O'Shea sorely miscast as an Irish Hawkeye. The French-Indian wars rage in gorgeous Cinecolor as Hawkeye and Rick Vallin as Uncas, the last of the Mohicans, brave danger to rescue two sisters from warring Iroquois Indians. 79m. **DIR:** George Sherman. **CAST:** Jon Hall, Michael O'Shea, Buster Crabbe, Evelyn Ankers, Julie Bishop, Rick Vallin. **1947**

•LAST ORDERS ★★1/2 Four Englishmen respect the final request of a pub pal and take a road trip to scatter his ashes off the pier of a seaside resort in this classy but dry, lackluster trip down memory lane. Flashbacks of the deceased's life unfurl secrets, dreams, weaknesses, betrayals, and the trials of friendship. The story about closure and moving forward is adapted from Graham Swift's novel. Rated R for language and sexual content. 109m. **DIR:** Fred Schepisi. **CAST:** Michael Caine, Bob Hoskins, David Hemmings, Ray Winstone, Tom Courtenay, Helen Mirren, Laura Morelli. **2001**

LAST OUTLAW, THE (1936) ★★★★1/2 Possibly Harry Carey's best film as a star, this is a delightful remake of a John Ford story of the silent era. Carey is a former outlaw released from prison, only to find that the West he knew is gone. Hoot Gibson is Carey's old saddle pal, and they soon take on a group of modern-day outlaws. B&W; 62m. **DIR:** Christy Cabanne. **CAST:** Harry Carey, Hoot Gibson, Henry B. Walthall, Tom Tyler. **1936**

LAST OUTLAW, THE (1993) ★★1/2 After a prologue stolen from *The Wild Bunch*, this laughably macho revenge saga becomes an exercise in sadistic gore . . . no surprise, considering the involvement of scripter Eric Red (*The Hitcher*). Betrayed by his own gang, outlaw Mickey Rourke joins the posse hunting his former associates . . . just so he can kill them, one by one. Rated R for profanity and extreme violence. 90m. **DIR:** Geoff Murphy. **CAST:** Mickey Rourke, Dermot Mulroney, Ted Levine, John C. McGinley. **1993**

LAST PARTY, THE ★★★1/2 Robert Downey Jr. is the host of this satiric, in-your-face documentary chronicling the 1992 presidential race. Downey finds plenty to poke fun at and recruits some famous names and faces to help him try to find meaning at the Democratic and Republican National Conventions. You know the participants in this celluloid mirror are politicians because they keep making donkeys out of themselves. Not rated; contains strong language. 96m. **DIR:** Martin Benjamin, Marc Levin. **1993**

LAST PICTURE SHOW, THE ★★★★★ Outstanding adaptation of Larry McMurtry's novel about a boy's rites of passage in a small Texas town during the 1950s. Virtually all the performances are excellent due to the deft direction of Peter Bogdanovich, who assured his fame with this picture. Ben Johnson, as a pool-hall owner, and Cloris Leachman, as a lonely wife, deservedly won Oscars for their supporting performances. Rated R for brief nudity and adult situations. B&W; 118m. **DIR:** Peter Bogdanovich. **CAST:** Timothy Bottoms, Ben Johnson, Jeff Bridges, Cloris Leachman, Cybill Shepherd, Randy Quaid, Eileen Brennan. **1971 DVD**

LAST PLANE OUT 🦃 Poor rip-off of *Under Fire*. Rated R. 98m. **DIR:** David Nelson. **CAST:** Jan-Michael Vincent, Lloyd Batista, Julie Carmen. **1983**

LAST POLKA, THE ★★★★ This made-for-HBO special features the unique Second City comedy of Yosh (John Candy) and Stan (Eugene Levy) Schmenge, a delightful pair of polka bandleaders, as they reminisce about their checkered musical careers. Fellow *SCTV* troupe members Catherine O'Hara and Rick Moranis add to this adept send-up of *The Last Waltz*, Martin Scorsese's documentary chronicling the final concert of real-life rock legends The Band. 60m. **DIR:** John Blanchard. **CAST:** John Candy, Eugene Levy, Catherine O'Hara, Rick Moranis. **1984**

LAST PROSTITUTE, THE ★★★★ This heartwarming made-for-cable coming-of-age drama features two teenage boys seeking the services of an infamous prostitute. They're disappointed to find her retired from the business. Fine acting and directing make this an unforgettable gem. 93m. **DIR:** Lou Antonio. **CAST:** Sonia Braga, Wil Wheaton, Cotter Smith, David Kaufman. **1991**

LAST REMAKE OF BEAU GESTE, THE 🦃 Vapid foreign legion comedy. Rated PG—sexual situations. 84m. **DIR:** Marty Feldman. **CAST:** Marty Feldman, Michael York, Ann-Margret, Trevor Howard. **1977**

LAST RESORT (1985) ★★1/2 Charles Grodin and family are off on vacation to Club Sand. Amid slapstick jokes and Grodin's exasperated yelling is an intermittently entertaining movie. Rated R for sex and language. 80m.

DIR: Zane Buzby. **CAST:** Charles Grodin, Jon Lovitz, Robin Pearson Rose, Megan Mullally, John Ashton. **1985 DVD**

LAST RESORT (2000) ★★★★ When a Russian mother and her son arrive in London to live with her boyfriend, he fails to pick them up, and they find themselves living in a refugee camp where their hope for freedom rests in the hands of a kindly stranger. A splendid and entertaining portrayal of the disorientation and loneliness faced by immigrants arriving in a new country. Not rated; contains adult situations, language, and violence. 76m. **DIR:** Paul Paulikovski. **CAST:** Dina Korzun, Artyom Strelnikov, Paddy Considine. **2000**

LAST RIDE, THE (1991) ★★1/2 Recently paroled ex-convict innocently accepts a ride from a psychotic truck driver, only to have it turn into the ride of his life. Doesn't put the pedal to the metal, but grabs your interest. 84m. **DIR:** Karl Krogstad. **CAST:** Dan Ranger. **1991**

LAST RIDE, THE (1994) ★★ Mickey Rourke is Frank T. Wells, outlaw rodeo rider, always living on the edge. Lori Singer is an unstable woman on the run from the law. When their worlds collide, there's an explosion of passion and bullets. Good cast is wasted in this weak action film. Rated R for violence, nudity, and language. 102m. **DIR:** Michael Karbelnikoff. **CAST:** Mickey Rourke, Lori Singer, Brian James, Rodney A. Grant, Peter Berg. **1994 DVD**

LAST RIDE OF THE DALTON GANG, THE ★★1/2 When two former Dalton Gang train robbers are reunited in Hollywood in 1934, they relive the early days as they share a bottle of whiskey. 146m. **DIR:** Dan Curtis. **CAST:** Jack Palance, Larry Wilcox, Dale Robertson, Bo Hopkins, Cliff Potts. **1979**

LAST RITES (1988) ★★ A young Italian priest (Tom Berenger) runs afoul of the Mafia when he grants sanctuary to a woman (Daphne Zuniga) who has witnessed a murder. Interesting but the story turns silly when priest and witness fall in love. Rated R for violence, nudity, and profanity. 103m. **DIR:** Donald P. Bellisario. **CAST:** Tom Berenger, Daphne Zuniga, Paul Dooley. **1988**

LAST RITES (1998) ★★ Randy Quaid is electrifying as a death-row prisoner whose electric chair experience leaves him a changed man. Once a mean-spirited killer, Jeremy Dillon undergoes a transformation when a power outage interrupts his execution, sending only a partial charge through his body. Now it's up to a psychiatrist to prove he's telling the truth. Interesting idea gets bogged down by flat script and supporting cast. Rated R for language and violence. 88m. **DIR:** Kevin Dowling. **CAST:** Randy Quaid, Embeth Davidtz, A Martinez. **1998**

LAST ROUND-UP ★★★★ Gene Autry's first for his own production company at Columbia Pictures is his personal favorite. Set in the modern West, Gene must relocate a tribe of Indians when their homeland is marked for an aqueduct project. B&W; 77m. **DIR:** John English. **CAST:** Gene Autry, Bobby Blake, Jean Heather, Ralph Morgan. **1947**

LAST SAFARI ★★ Director Henry Hathaway's trademark machismo got the better of him in this dreary drama about an aging big-game hunter who escorts a young couple to Africa. 110m. **DIR:** Henry Hathaway. **CAST:** Stewart Granger, Kaz Garas. **1967**

LAST SEDUCTION, THE ★★★1/2 Though amoral and bereft of sympathetic characters, *The Last Seduction* is absorbing; credit the energetic performances, stylish direction, and mellow jazz soundtrack. Bored city gal Linda Fiorentino cons husband Bill Pullman into a one-time drug sale, after which she flees (with the cash) into upstate New York . . . where she intrigues good ol' boy Peter Berg. Her hubbie, of course, follows her. Rated R for profanity, nudity, violence, and simulated sex. 110m. **DIR:** John Dahl. **CAST:** Linda Fiorentino, Peter Berg, Bill Pullman, J. T. Walsh, Bill Nunn. **1993 DVD**

•LAST SEPTEMBER, THE ★★1/2 An Irish country house in the late 1920s is the setting for a drama about the end of Britain's rule over that country. The aristocratic owners play host to a variety of characters who represent various elements of national and international society. Adapted from Elizabeth Bowen's novel, the film tries to pack far too much into a standard running time: viewers who lack a strong grasp of twentieth-century British history are likely to be confused by the whole thing. Rated R for some violence and sexuality. 103m. **DIR:** Deborah Warner. **CAST:** Michael Gambon, Maggie Smith, Keeley Hawes, Fiona Shaw, Tom Hickey, Jane Birkin. **1999 DVD**

LAST STAND AT SABER RIVER ★★★★ Returning from the Civil War as a Confederate hero, Tom Selleck reunites with wife Suzy Amis, only to find that his youngest child is dead and that she wants to go home to Arizona, where Confederate soliders are not considered heroes. But return they do—to fight for their land and their way of life. Adapted from the Elmore Leonard novel. Made for TV. 96m. **DIR:** Dick Lowry. **CAST:** Tom Selleck, Suzy Amis, David Carradine, Keith Carradine, Harry Carey Jr., Rex Linn, Patrick Kilpatrick. **1997**

LAST STARFIGHTER, THE ★★★★ In this enjoyable comedy–science-fiction film, a young man (Lance Guest) beats a video game called the Starfighter and soon finds himself recruited by an alien (Robert Preston) to do battle in outer space. Thanks to its witty dialogue and hilarious situations, this hybrid is a viewing delight. Rated PG for violence and profanity. 100m. **DIR:** Nick Castle. **CAST:** Lance Guest, Robert Preston, Dan O'Herlihy, Catherine Mary Stewart, Barbara Bosson. **1984 DVD**

LAST STOP ★★★ Fairly entertaining thriller about a group of strangers, snowed in at a small greasy spoon, who discover there are bank robbers/murderers in their midst. But who is who? Rated R for profanity, violence, and sexuality. 94m. **DIR:** Mark Malone. **CAST:** Adam Beach, Jurgen Prochnow, Rose McGowan, Amy Adamson. **2000 DVD**

LAST SUMMER ★★1/2 Engrossing tale of teen desires, frustrations, and fears, played out in disturbingly dark fashion. Bruce Davison and Cathy Burns are especially memorable in unusual roles. Rated R. 97m. **DIR:** Frank Perry. **CAST:** Richard Thomas, Barbara Hershey, Bruce Davison, Cathy Burns, Ralph Waite, Conrad Bain. **1969**

LAST SUMMER IN THE HAMPTONS ★★★★ As an extended family of theater professionals prepare a stage performance for an invitation-only audience, their own lives become kindred spirits to the work of playwright Anton Chekhov and filmmaker Jean Renoir. This ensemble piece bites rapturously into the dynam-

ics of blood relations as well as art. Not rated. 105m. **DIR:** Henry Jaglom. **CAST:** Victoria Foyt, Viveca Lindfors, Jon Robin Baitz, Melissa Leo, Martha Plimpton, Nick Gregory, Andre Gregory, Holland Taylor. **1995**

LAST SUPPER, THE (1976) ★★★ Uncompromising drama based on an incident from eighteenth-century Cuban history about a petit-bourgeois slaveholder who decides to improve his soul by instructing his slaves in the glories of Christianity. He invites twelve of them to participate in a reenactment of the Last Supper in hopes of instilling Christian ideals. In Spanish with English subtitles. Not rated; contains violence and nudity. 110m. **DIR:** Tomas Gutierrez Alea. **CAST:** Nelson Villagra. **1976**

LAST SUPPER, THE (1996) ★★★ Marginally successful political satire in which a houseful of Iowa graduate students invites repulsive right-wing ideologues to dinner and poisons them. Inevitably, our politically-correct avengers succumb to infighting and paranoia. Director Stacy Title doesn't seem certain whether Dan Rosen's stagey scenario is a comedy, an ironic morality play, or an important social statement. Rated R. 94m. **DIR:** Stacy Title. **CAST:** Cameron Diaz, Annabeth Gish, Ron Eldard, Jonathan Penner, Courtney B. Vance, Ron Perlman. **1996**

LAST TANGO IN PARIS ★★★ A middle-aged man (Marlon Brando) and a young French girl (Maria Schneider) have a doomed love affair. This pretentious sex melodrama is mainly notable for being banned when it first came out. Rated NC-17 for sex. 129m. **DIR:** Bernardo Bertolucci. **CAST:** Marlon Brando, Maria Schneider, Jean-Pierre Léaud. **1972 DVD**

LAST TEMPTATION OF CHRIST, THE ★★★ This adaptation of Nikos Kazantzakis's controversial novel contains some unnecessary scenes of nudity and simulated sex. Nevertheless, what emerges is a heartfelt work that has some moments of true power—especially when the story's reluctant savior accepts his divine nature and performs miracles. Rated R for nudity and violence. 164m. **DIR:** Martin Scorsese. **CAST:** Willem Dafoe, Harvey Keitel, Barbara Hershey, Harry Dean Stanton, David Bowie, Verna Bloom, Andre Gregory. **1988 DVD**

LAST TIME I COMMITTED SUICIDE, THE ★★★★ Life story of Beat-movement pioneer Neal Cassady is stylish and entertaining and features a standout performance by Keanu Reeves as one of Cassady's friends. Rated R for language. 93m. **DIR:** Stephen Kay. **CAST:** Thomas Jane, Keanu Reeves, Adrien Brody, Claire Forlani, Marg Helgenberger. **1996**

LAST TIME I SAW PARIS, THE ★★★ The Metro-Goldwyn-Mayer glitter shows clearly in this dramatic account of post–World War II Paris. This Paris, though, is filled with divorce, domestic quarrels, and jaded lives. Donna Reed gives the best performance. 116m. **DIR:** Richard Brooks. **CAST:** Van Johnson, Elizabeth Taylor, Donna Reed, Walter Pidgeon, Eva Gabor. **1954 DVD**

LAST TRAIN FROM GUN HILL ★★★1/2 In this hybrid suspense-Western, a marshal (Kirk Douglas) is searching for the man who raped and murdered his wife. When the culprit (Earl Holliman) turns out to be the son of a wealthy rancher (Anthony Quinn), our hero holes up in a hotel room and takes on all comers until the next train arrives. A minor classic. 94m. **DIR:** John Sturges. **CAST:** Kirk Douglas, Anthony Quinn, Carolyn Jones, Earl Holliman, Brad Dexter. **1959**

LAST TRAIN HOME ★★★ When a Canadian family is broken up by its father's participation in a barroom brawl, the teenage son treks cross-country seeking his fleeing dad. The family dog, an adorable Benji lookalike, steals every scene. Made for the Family Channel. 92m. **DIR:** Randy Bradshaw. **CAST:** Noam Zylberman, Ron White, Nick Mancuso, Ned Beatty. **1990**

LAST TYCOON, THE ★★★ Tantalizing yet frustrating, this slow-moving attempt to film F. Scott Fitzgerald's last (and unfinished) book is a conglomeration of talent at all levels, but appears as a confusing collection of scenes and confrontations. Robert De Niro plays Monroe Starr, the sickly motion picture magnate and the "last tycoon." Rated PG. 125m. **DIR:** Elia Kazan. **CAST:** Robert De Niro, Robert Mitchum, Tony Curtis, Jeanne Moreau, Jack Nicholson, Donald Pleasence, Peter Strauss, Ray Milland, Ingrid Boulting, Dana Andrews, John Carradine, Theresa Russell. **1976**

LAST UNICORN, THE ★★★1/2 Well-written and nicely animated feature about a magical unicorn who goes on a quest to find the rest of her kind. Strong characters and a sprightly pace make this a gem, which features the voices of Alan Arkin, Jeff Bridges, Mia Farrow, Tammy Grimes, Robert Klein, Angela Lansbury, Christopher Lee, and Keenan Wynn. It's a class act. Rated G. 85m. **DIR:** Arthur Rankin Jr., Jules Bass. **1982**

LAST VALLEY, THE ★★★ Impressive and thought-provoking adventure epic about a warrior (Michael Caine) who brings his soldiers to a peaceful valley that, in the seventeenth century, has remained untouched by the Thirty Years War. Rated R. 128m. **DIR:** James Clavell. **CAST:** Michael Caine, Omar Sharif. **1971 DVD**

LAST VOYAGE, THE ★★★★ Director Andrew L. Stone has taken a fairly suspenseful disaster-at-sea tale, making it a completely absorbing and fascinating movie. Filmed aboard the famous luxury liner, *Ile de France*, before it was scrapped. 91m. **DIR:** Andrew L. Stone. **CAST:** Robert Stack, Dorothy Malone, George Sanders, Edmond O'Brien, Woody Strode. **1960**

LAST WALTZ, THE ★★★★ Director Martin Scorsese's (*Taxi Driver*) superb film of The Band's final concert appearance is an unforgettable celebration of American music. Rated PG. 117m. **DIR:** Martin Scorsese. **CAST:** The Band, Bob Dylan, Neil Young, Joni Mitchell, Van Morrison, Eric Clapton, Neil Diamond, Muddy Waters. **1978**

LAST WARNING, THE ★★★1/2 A mysterious caped and masked murderer terrorizes a Broadway theater's cast and crew in this stylish thriller, which employs all sorts of gimmickry to good effect. Originally released with sound, this visually stimulating whodunit exists now only in its silent version and is considered must-see viewing among film historians and aficionados. Silent, with musical accompaniment. B&W; 78m. **DIR:** Paul Leni. **CAST:** Laura LaPlante, Montagu Love, John Boles, Roy D'Arcy, Bert Roach, Margaret Livingston, Mack Swain. **1929**

LAST WARRIOR, THE (1989) ★★★★ Two Marines, one American, the other Japanese, are left on an island in the closing days of World War II. What ensues is a tightly directed, action-packed fight to the death. Rated

R for violence and brief nudity. 94m. **DIR:** Martin Wragge. **CAST:** Gary Graham. **1989**

•LAST WARRIOR, THE (2000) ★★1/2 Not bad, but not great, sci-fi/action film about an air force captain who, in the year 2006, must lead a group of earthquake survivors off the Island of California and back to safety. Rated PG-13 for violence. 95m. **DIR:** Sheldon Lettich. **CAST:** Dolph Lundgren, Sherri Alexander, Joe Michael Burke, Rebecca Cross. **2000 DVD**

LAST WAVE, THE ★★★1/2 In this suspenseful, fascinating film, Richard Chamberlain plays a lawyer defending a group of aborigines on trial for murder. His investigation into the incident leads to a frightening series of apocalyptic visions. Rated PG. 106m. **DIR:** Peter Weir. **CAST:** Richard Chamberlain, Olivia Hamnett. **1977 DVD**

LAST WAY OUT, THE ★★★★ Low-budget *film noir* hits the mark, because it's packed with all the necessary elements. Kurt Johnson is the former career criminal forced back into business by his old partners. Not rated; contains adult situations, language, and violence. B&W; 88m. **DIR:** Mark Steensland. **CAST:** Kurt Johnson, Kevin Reed, Katie Brown, John Lamb, David Pierini. **1996**

LAST WINTER, THE 🦃 Kathleen Quinlan and Yona Elian are wives of Israeli soldiers missing in action during the Yom Kippur War of 1973. Rated R. 92m. **DIR:** Riki Shelach. **CAST:** Kathleen Quinlan, Yona Elian, Stephen Macht. **1984**

LAST WORD, THE (1979) ★★★ When police try to evict him and his family from a run-down apartment building, inventor Danny Travis (Richard Harris) takes a police officer hostage. His goal is to get the attention of the newspapers so that he can expose the governor's crooked real estate racket and save his home. Likable comedy-drama in the Frank Capra mold. Rated PG. 105m. **DIR:** Roy Boulting. **CAST:** Richard Harris, Karen Black, Martin Landau, Dennis Christopher, Biff McGuire, Christopher Guest, Penelope Milford, Michael Pataki. **1979**

LAST WORD, THE (1995) ★★★ An investigative journalist falls in love with a stripper/hooker and then finds that the relationship impairs his ability to transform his underworld exposés into a coherent film script. Although acceptable, the film would have benefited by concentrating on central characters. Rated R for profanity, nudity, and simulated sex. 95m. **DIR:** Tony Spiridakis. **CAST:** Timothy Hutton, Joe Pantoliano, Michelle Burke, Richard Dreyfuss, Tony Goldwyn, Chazz Palminteri, Cybill Shepherd, Jimmy Smits. **1995 DVD**

LAST YEAR AT MARIENBAD ★★★ This film provides no middle ground—you either love it or you hate it. The confusing story is about a young man (Giorgio Albertazzi) finding himself in a monstrous, baroque hotel trying to renew his love affair with a woman who seems to have forgotten that there is an affair to renew. The past, present, and future all seem to run parallel, cross over, and converge. In French with English subtitles. B&W; 93m. **DIR:** Alain Resnais. **CAST:** Delphine Seyrig, Giorgio Albertazzi, Sacha Pitoeff. **1962 DVD**

LATCHO DROM ★★★★★ Generically referred to as "gypsies," the Rom people of Europe have been wanderers through their long history, often in reaction to efforts of different countries to destroy them. In this documentary, various members tell the history of their people in song. The music itself is richly satisfying, but the lyrics, which are subtitled in English, are what make the film so compelling. Not rated. 88m. **DIR:** Tony Gatlif. **1996**

LATE CHRYSANTHEMUMS ★★★★★ With limited options available to them, four aging geisha try to plan for their futures. Beautifully acted, realistic but never melodramatic; a wonderful film from Mikio Naruse, an overlooked (outside of his own country) master of the Japanese cinema. In Japanese with English subtitles. B&W; 101m. **DIR:** Mikio Naruse. **CAST:** Haruko Sugimura. **1954**

LATE FOR DINNER ★★★★ In what is sort of a cross between *Back to the Future* and *Of Mice and Men*, Brian Wimmer and Peter Berg drive from Santa Fe, New Mexico, to Pomona, California, in 1962 only to wake up twenty-nine years later in 1991 with no idea what happened. What begins as a wacky, offbeat romp becomes a profoundly moving story about loss and reconciliation. Rated PG for violence. 106m. **DIR:** W. D. Richter. **CAST:** Brian Wimmer, Peter Berg, Marcia Gay Harden, Colleen Flynn, Kyle Secor, Michael Beach, Peter Gallagher. **1991**

•LATE LAST NIGHT ★★1/2 Jeff (Steven Weber) takes his friend Dan (Emilio Estevez), whose wife has left him, out for a night on the town. One mishap after another befalls the party-going duo, as they constantly tread the thin line between life, death, sobriety, and hilarity. Estevez and Weber make for a likable pair but get smothered with predictable, plot-driven clichés. Rated R for language, sex, and drug use. 90m. **DIR:** Steven Brill. **CAST:** Emilio Estevez, Steven Weber, Catherine O'Hara. **1999 DVD**

LATE SHIFT, THE ★★★ This HBO "docu-comedy," based on Bill Carter's book, details the network war that erupted when NBC-TV finally replaced Johnny Carson as host of *The Tonight Show*. David Letterman wanted the job; Jay Leno wound up with it. This adaptation demonstrates the industry's callous venality and absence of loyalty, and captures Rich Little's dead-on Johnny Carson imitation. Rated R for profanity. 96m. **DIR:** Betty Thomas. **CAST:** Kathy Bates, John Michael Higgins, Daniel Roebuck, Bob Balaban, Ed Begley Jr., Peter Jurasik, Reni Santoni, Treat Williams, Rich Little. **1995**

LATE SHOW, THE ★★★★1/2 Just prior to directing *Kramer vs. Kramer*, Robert Benton created this little gem. It stars Art Carney as an aging private eye out to avenge the death of his partner (Howard Duff) with the unwanted help of wacky Lily Tomlin. Loosely lifted from Sam Peckinpah's *Ride the High Country* and John Huston's *The Maltese Falcon*, this detective story is a bittersweet, sometimes tragic, takeoff on the genre. That it works so well is a credit to all involved. Rated PG. 94m. **DIR:** Robert Benton. **CAST:** Art Carney, Howard Duff, Lily Tomlin, Bill Macy, John Considine. **1977**

LATE SPRING ★★★★★ Afraid that his grown daughter will become an old maid, a widower pretends that he wishes to remarry to persuade her to leave home. Yasujiro Ozu made a number of films with a similar theme, but this is the best. In Japanese with English subtitles. 107m. **DIR:** Yasujiro Ozu. **CAST:** Setsuko Hara, Chishu Ryu. **1949**

LATIN LOVERS ★★ A movie with a few musical numbers, but not enough to make it move, this is one of Lana Turner's self-indulgent romances. She plays a woman looking for true love while touring South America and not able to find it anywhere. Not until she matches wits with Ricardo Montalban. Colorful settings, but colorless acting. 104m. **DIR:** Mervyn LeRoy. **CAST:** Lana Turner, Ricardo Montalban, John Lund, Louis Calhern, Rita Moreno, Jean Hagen, Beulah Bondi, Eduard Franz. **1953**

LATINO ★★ Master cinematographer Haskell Wexler tries his hand at writing and directing in this story of a Chicago Green Beret who questions the activities required of him in the Nicaraguan war. This is a fairly routine war story, with the exception of the protagonist being a Latin American. 108m. **DIR:** Haskell Wexler. **CAST:** Robert Beltran, Annette Cardona, Tony Plana. **1985**

LATITUDE ZERO ★★1/2 Jules Verne-style fantasy about a scientist (Joseph Cotten) who has built a research city on the bottom of the ocean. This Japanese movie would be better if only the special effects (batmen, giant rats, and flying lion with a human brain) weren't so cheesy, though Cesar Romero makes a nicely hissable villain. Rated G. 99m. **DIR:** Inoshiro Honda. **CAST:** Joseph Cotten, Cesar Romero, Richard Jaeckel, Patricia Medina, Linda Haynes, Akira Takarada. **1969**

LAUGH FOR JOY (PASSIONATE THIEF) (1954) ★★★ Delightful comedy of errors set on New Year's Eve. Anna Magnani plays a film extra who complicates things for a pickpocket (Ben Gazzara). Also released on videocassette under the title *Passionate Thief*, which is dubbed in English. In Italian with English subtitles. B&W; 106m. **DIR:** Mario Monicelli. **CAST:** Anna Magnani, Ben Gazzara, Toto, Fred Clark. **1954**

LAUGHING POLICEMAN, THE ★★★1/2 Little-known police thriller that deserved far better than it got at the box office. Walter Matthau and Bruce Dern are a pair of cops seeking a mass murderer who preys on bus passengers. Taut drama, taken from the superb thriller by Maj Sjowall and Per Wahloo. Rated R for violence. 111m. **DIR:** Stuart Rosenberg. **CAST:** Walter Matthau, Bruce Dern, Louis Gossett Jr., Albert Paulsen, Cathy Lee Crosby, Anthony Zerbe. **1974**

LAUGHING SINNERS ★★1/2 In the first of their eight screen teamings, Clark Gable is a Salvation Army officer who "saves" Joan Crawford after she has been seduced and abandoned by a fast-talking traveling salesman. B&W; 72m. **DIR:** Harry Beaumont. **CAST:** Joan Crawford, Clark Gable, Neil Hamilton, Marjorie Rambeau, Roscoe Karns, Guy Kibbee, Cliff Edwards. **1931**

•LAUGHTER ON THE 23RD FLOOR ★★★ Nathan Lane plays a TV comic star in the 1950s, whose life is as wild and crazy as the characters he plays. This made-for-cable film, based on a play by Neil Simon, follows the slow decline of the show and how it affects the writers behind the scenes. Good lines and acting, but there's a lack of purpose about the story that leaves the film flat. Rated R for profanity. 102m. **DIR:** Richard Benjamin. **CAST:** Nathan Lane, Mark Linn-Baker, Victor Garber, Saul Rubinek, Peri Gilpin, Dan Castellaneta. **2000**

LAURA ★★★★★ A lovely socialite (Gene Tierney) is apparently murdered, and the police detective (Dana Andrews) assigned to the case is up to his neck in likely suspects. To compound matters, he has developed a strange attraction for the deceased woman through her portrait. So starts one of the most original mysteries ever to come from Hollywood. B&W; 88m. **DIR:** Otto Preminger. **CAST:** Gene Tierney, Dana Andrews, Vincent Price, Judith Anderson, Clifton Webb. **1944**

LAUREL AND HARDY CLASSICS: VOL. 1–9 ★★★ Stan Laurel and Oliver Hardy demonstrate why most consider them one of the funniest comedy teams of the silver screen. This standout compilation of their shorts contains *Another Fine Mess*, *The Music Box*, *Hog Wild*, *The Fixer-Uppers*, *Night Owls*, *Any Old Port*, *Oliver the Eighth*. Silent. B&W. **DIR:** James Parrott, Charles R. Rogers, George Marshall, Lloyd French, James W. Horne, Lewis R. Foster. **CAST:** Stan Laurel, Oliver Hardy, Billy Gilbert, Charlie Hall, Stanley Sanford, Mae Busch, James Finlayson, Walter Long, Edgar Kennedy, Anita Garvin, Jean Harlow. **1930–1938**

LAUREL AVENUE ★★★★ Compelling saga focuses on a close-knit family's struggle with changing values and increasing inner-city crime. Spanning three generations and an emotionally charged weekend, we're given a vivid—at times painful—glimpse into the struggles of each member. An HBO miniseries, with violence, profanity, drug use, and sexual situations. 160m. **DIR:** Carl Franklin. **CAST:** Mary Alice, Jay Brooks, Juanita Jennings, Scott Lawrence, Dan Martin. **1993**

LAVENDER HILL MOB, THE ★★★★★ Fun, fun, and more fun from this celebrated British comedy. Alec Guinness is a mousy bank clerk. He has a plan for intercepting the bank's armored-car shipment. With the aid of a few friends he forms an amateur robbery squad. Lo and behold, they escape with the loot. After all, the plan was foolproof. Or was it? B&W; 82m. **DIR:** Charles Crichton. **CAST:** Alec Guinness, Stanley Holloway, Sidney James, Alfie Bass. **1951**

L'AVENTURA ★★★★ A girl disappears on a yachting trip, and while her lover and best friend search for her, they begin a wild romantic affair. Antonioni's penetrating study of Italy's bored and idle bourgeoisie contains some staggering observations on spiritual isolation and love. Winner of the Special Jury Award at Cannes. Italian with English subtitles. B&W; 145m. **DIR:** Michelangelo Antonioni. **CAST:** Monica Vitti, Gabriele Ferzetti, Lea Massari. **1960**

LAW AND JAKE WADE, THE ★★1/2 A robust Western with Richard Widmark chewing the scenery as the bad guy looking for buried treasure and conning good guy Robert Taylor into helping him. *Star Trek's* DeForest Kelley has an important supporting role. 86m. **DIR:** John Sturges. **CAST:** Robert Taylor, Richard Widmark, Patricia Owens, Robert Middleton, DeForest Kelley, Henry Silva. **1958**

LAW AND ORDER ★★★★ In a story coscripted by John Huston, Walter Huston gets one of the best roles of his career as a Wyatt Earp–style lawman. Harry Carey and Raymond Hatton are superb as his ready-for-anything sidekicks in an excellent Western that still seems fresh and innovative today. B&W; 70m. **DIR:** Edward L. Cahn. **CAST:** Walter Huston, Harry Carey, Raymond Hatton, Andy Devine. **1932**

LAW FOR TOMBSTONE ★★1/2 Buck and his fellow Texas Rangers head to Tombstone to get the draw on Twin-Gun Jack, but they have to do it cautious-like

'cause Jack's got plenty of crooks on his side. Released with a serial chapter, cartoon, and newsreel. B&W; 59m. **DIR:** Buck Jones, B. Reeves "Breezy" Eason. **CAST:** Buck Jones, Muriel Evans, Harvey Clark, Carl Stockdale, Earle Hodgins, Alexander Cross. **1937**

LAW OF DESIRE ★★★ Spain's Pedro Almodóvar likes to play with the clichés of movie melodrama in a manner that endears him to movie buffs. This film, which first gained him wide attention in the U.S., deals with a gay movie director who wants to live as passionately as his transsexual brother (now his sister). He gets his wish in this topsy-turvy farce. In Spanish with English subtitles. Not rated, but an R equivalent. 100m. **DIR:** Pedro Almodóvar. **CAST:** Eusebio Poncela, Carmen Maura, Antonio Banderas, Miguel Molina. **1986**

LAW OF THE PAMPAS ★★★ South-of-the-border action. This is a good Hopalong Cassidy with all the right elements and an exotic locale to boot. B&W; 74m. **DIR:** Nate Watt. **CAST:** William Boyd, Russell Hayden, Sidney Blackmer, Sidney Toler, Pedro De Cordoba, Glenn Strange. **1939**

LAW OF THE SEA ★★★ Wreck survivors are rescued by a sadistic sea captain, whose lust drives a woman to suicide. Creaky curiosity. B&W; 60m. **DIR:** Otto Brower. **CAST:** William Farnum. **1932**

LAW WEST OF TOMBSTONE ★★★1/2 Enjoyable, folksy Western has the marvelous Harry Carey starring as a con artist who becomes the law in Tombstone. Tim Holt, in a strong film debut, is the young hothead he befriends and reforms. Look for Allan "Rocky" Lane in a brief bit at the beginning as Holt's saddle pal. B&W; 72m. **DIR:** Glenn Tryon. **CAST:** Harry Carey, Tim Holt, Evelyn Brent, Ward Bond, Allan "Rocky" Lane. **1938**

LAWLESS FRONTIER ★★1/2 A Mexican bandit (Earl Dwire) manages to evade the blame for a series of crimes he's committed because the sheriff is sure that John Wayne is the culprit. The Duke, of course, traps the bad guy and clears his good name in this predictable B Western. B&W; 59m. **DIR:** Robert N. Bradbury. **CAST:** John Wayne, Sheila Terry, George "Gabby" Hayes, Earl Dwire. **1935 DVD**

LAWLESS NINETIES, THE ★★★ When outlaws use underhanded tactics to keep the citizens of Wyoming from voting for statehood, it's up to government agent John Wayne and his men to put a stop to it. Gabby Hayes has an uncharacteristic role as a Southern gentleman. It's predictable, but a notch above many oaters. B&W; 55m. **DIR:** Joseph Kane. **CAST:** John Wayne, Ann Rutherford, Lane Chandler, Harry Woods, George "Gabby" Hayes, Snowflake, Charles King. **1936**

LAWLESS STREET, A ★★★ Randolph Scott portrays a no-nonsense marshal in Medicine Bend until the arrival of an old flame (Angela Lansbury) and the evil plottings of a power-hungry citizen (Warner Anderson) threaten to cost him his job—and maybe his life. Some amusing quips from Scott and the involving climax make this one worth watching. 78m. **DIR:** Joseph H. Lewis. **CAST:** Randolph Scott, Angela Lansbury, Warner Anderson, Jean Parker, Wallace Ford, John Emery, Michael Pate, Don Megowan. **1955**

LAWLESS VALLEY ★★★★ Prison parolee George O'Brien returns home to clear his name and put the true guilty parties behind bars in this solid series Western. In a nice touch, Fred Kohler Sr. and Fred Kohler Jr. play father-and-son heavies. B&W; 59m. **DIR:** Bert Gilroy. **CAST:** George O'Brien, Kay Sutton, Walter Miller, Fred Kohler Sr., Fred Kohler Jr., Chill Wills. **1938**

LAWMAN ★★ There's no fire in Burt Lancaster this time around. He plays a marshal who is determined to bring in the bad guys, despite the protestations of an entire town. The story has promise, but doesn't deliver. Robert Ryan is worth watching, cast against type as a meek sheriff. Rated PG. 98m. **DIR:** Michael Winner. **CAST:** Burt Lancaster, Robert Ryan, Lee J. Cobb, Robert Duvall, Sheree North, Richard Jordan, Ralph Waite, John Hillerman, J. D. Cannon, Albert Salmi. **1971 DVD**

LAWMAN IS BORN, A ★★1/2 Former football star Johnny Mack Brown is a two-fisted good guy who foils the nefarious plans of an outlaw gang. This time, the baddies are after land (as opposed to the alternate formulas of cattle, money, gold, or horses). It's fun for fans. B&W; 58m. **DIR:** Sam Newfield. **CAST:** Johnny Mack Brown, Iris Meredith, Al St. John. **1937**

LAWN DOGS ★★★ Sexual tensions rise in this steamy tale of a small gated community. While their husbands pursue professional status, the lonely wives have affairs. The comfortable facade is destroyed when a young stud named Trent enters: Trent does more than just mow their lawns; he forces the residents into an emotional showdown. Rated R for nudity, language, and adult situations. 101m. **DIR:** John Duigan. **CAST:** Sam Rockwell, Christopher McDonald, Kathleen Quinlan, Mischa Barton. **1997 DVD**

LAWNMOWER MAN, THE ★★★1/2 The mind-blowing special effects of this film lose a little in the translation to the small screen. But they still are the highlight of this story about a scientist (Pierce Brosnan) who uses computer "virtual reality" to turn a simpleminded gardener (Jeff Fahey) into a psychopathic genius. Some of the most outstanding computer animation since Disney's *Tron*. Rated R for violence, profanity, and nudity. 148m. **DIR:** Brett Leonard. **CAST:** Jeff Fahey, Pierce Brosnan, Jenny Wright, Geoffrey Lewis. **1992 DVD**

LAWNMOWER MAN 2: JOBE'S WAR (LAWNMOWER MAN: BEYOND CYBERSPACE) Not only is the title character different from that in the original *Lawnmower Man*, as Matt Frewer has stepped into Jeff Fahey's shoes, but we are now magically transferred to a future where nothing makes sense—not the plot, the costumes, the lousy sets, or the point of this supposed sequel. Rated PG-13 for profanity and violence. 93m. **DIR:** Farhad Mann. **CAST:** Patrick Bergin, Matt Frewer, Ely Pouget, Austin O'Brien, Kevin Conway. **1995**

LAWRENCE OF ARABIA ★★★★★ Director David Lean brings us an expansive screen biography of T. E. Lawrence, the complex English leader of the Arab revolt against Turkey in World War I. This is a tremendous accomplishment in every respect. Peter O'Toole is stunning in his first major film role as Lawrence. A definite thinking person's spectacle. 222m. **DIR:** David Lean. **CAST:** Peter O'Toole, Alec Guinness, Anthony Quinn, Arthur Kennedy, Omar Sharif. **1962 DVD**

LAWRENCEVILLE STORIES, THE ★★★1/2 Award-winning miniseries takes a humorous look at a turn-of-the-century boarding school. Owen Johnson's delightful short story collection sets the stage for endless pranks

perpetuated by teenage boys. 180m. **DIR:** Allan A. Goldstein, Robert Iscove. **CAST:** Zach Galligan, Edward Herrmann, Robert Joy, Nicholas Rowe. **1988**

LAZARUS SYNDROME, THE ★★ When the illicit practices of a hospital administrator drive another practitioner to distraction, he joins forces with a patient who just happens to be a journalist in order to expose the bad guy and his lackeys. Made for television. 90m. **DIR:** Jerry Thorpe. **CAST:** Louis Gossett Jr., Ronald Hunter, E. G. Marshall, Sheila Frazier. **1976**

LBJ: THE EARLY YEARS ★★★★ This superlative made-for-TV movie is the story of Lyndon Johnson from 1934, when he was first entering politics as a congressman's aide, to his swearing in as president aboard *Air Force One*. Randy Quaid and Patti LuPone as LBJ and Lady Bird are outstanding. 144m. **DIR:** Peter Werner. **CAST:** Randy Quaid, Patti LuPone, Morgan Brittany, Pat Hingle, Kevin McCarthy, Charles Frank. **1986**

LE BAL ★★★★ European history of the last half century is reduced to some fifty popular dance tunes—and a variety of very human dancers—in this innovative and entertaining film. The unusual import eschews dialogue for tangos, fox trots, and jazz to make its points. Ettore Scola chronicles the dramatic changes in political power, social behavior, and fashion trends from the 1930s to the present without ever moving his cameras out of an art deco ballroom. No MPAA rating; the film has brief violence. 109m. **DIR:** Ettore Scola. **1983**

LE BEAU MARIAGE ★★★★ A young woman decides it is high time she got married. She chooses the man she wants, a busy lawyer, and tells her friends of their coming wedding. He knows nothing of this, but she is confident. By French director Eric Rohmer. In French with English subtitles. Rated R. 100m. **DIR:** Eric Rohmer. **CAST:** Beatrice Romand, Arielle Dombasle, André Dussolier. **1982**

LE BEAU SERGE ★★ An ailing theology student, home for a rest cure, is reunited with his boyhood friend, who is now an alcoholic stuck in an unhappy marriage. Vague drama is of interest only as an early example of the French new wave. In French with English subtitles. Not rated. 97m. **DIR:** Claude Chabrol. **CAST:** Gerard Blain, Jean-Claude Brialy, Bernadette Lafont. **1958**

LE BONHEUR ★★ Extremely boring story about happiness. A husband is happy with his wife, but becomes even happier when he takes a mistress. In French with English subtitles. Not rated; contains nudity and graphic sex. 77m. **DIR:** Agnes Varda. **CAST:** Jean-Claude Druou, Claire Druou, Marie-France Boyer. **1976**

LE BOUCHER (THE BUTCHER) ★★★★ French director Claude Chabrol's mini-masterwork about a hunt for a serial killer in provincial France. Jean Yanne is the ex–army butcher who may or may not be the murderer. Prim schoolmistress Stéphane Audran (director Chabrol's wife) is irresistibly drawn to him. There are a few affectionate Hitchcock touches, but mostly, this ball-of-twine thriller is Chabrol's own, and that is its considerable strength. English subtitles (beware of the dubbed version). Rated R for violence. 94m. **DIR:** Claude Chabrol. **CAST:** Stéphane Audran, Jean Yanne, Antonio Passalia, Mario Beccaria. **1969**

LE BOURGEOIS GENTILHOMME ★★ This adaptation of Molière's satire about a social climber is a recording of the stage performance, and will seem static and overacted to most viewers. Worth checking out for Molière enthusiasts and French language classes, but not recommended for general audiences. In French with English subtitles. 97m. **DIR:** Jean Meyer. **CAST:** Jean Meyer, Louis Seigner, Jacques Charon. **1958**

LE CAS DU DR. LAURENT ★★1/2 Dated tale about a kindly old doctor who tries to introduce modern methods of medicine and sanitation to the residents of a small farming village. In particular, he tries to ease the suffering of women as they endure childbirth. Noteworthy for the performance of Gabin as the doctor and for footage of an actual childbirth. In French. B&W; 88m. **DIR:** Jean-Paul Le Chanois. **CAST:** Jean Gabin, Nicole Courcel, Sylvia Monfort. **1957**

LE CAVALEUR ★★★★ A poignantly philosophical, yet witty and often hilarious farce about the perils of a middle-aged heartbreak kid. Our cad about town is unerringly portrayed by Jean Rochefort as a classical pianist trying to juggle his art and the many past, present, and possible future women in his life. Nudity but generally innocent adult situations. 106m. **DIR:** Philippe de Broca. **CAST:** Jean Rochefort, Annie Girardot. **1980**

LE CHÈVRE (THE GOAT) ★★1/2 The stars of *Les Compéres*, Pierre Richard and Gérard Depardieu, romp again in this French comedy as two investigators searching for a missing girl in Mexico. While this import may please staunch fans of the stars, it is far from being a laugh riot. In French with English subtitles. Not rated; the film has profanity and violence. 91m. **DIR:** Francis Veber. **CAST:** Pierre Richard, Gérard Depardieu, Michel Robin, Pedro Armendariz Jr. **1981**

LE COMPLOT (THE CONSPIRACY) ★★★1/2 Complex political thriller, based on true events, about an explosive game of espionage between leftist rebels, the police, and Gaullist patriots. Quite suspenseful. In French with English subtitles. Rated R for profanity and violence. 120m. **DIR:** René Gainville. **CAST:** Jean Rochefort, Michel Bouquet, Marina Vlady. **1973**

LE CORBEAU (THE RAVEN) ★★★★ Citizens of a French provincial town are upset to find that someone is on to all their guilty secrets and is revealing them in a series of poison pen letters. An intelligent, involving thriller, remade in the United States as *The Thirteenth Letter*. In French with English subtitles. 91m. **DIR:** Henri-Georges Clouzot. **CAST:** Pierre Fresnay, Pierre Larquey. **1943**

LE DÉPART ★★★ Jean-Pierre Léaud, best known from François Truffaut's semiautobiographical films *The 400 Blows* and *Love on the Run*, stars as another disaffected youth. He's desperately trying to borrow or rent a Porsche so that he can enter a race. Zany comedy is noteworthy for Léaud's performance and as an early effort by Polish director Jerzy Skolimowski. In French with English subtitles. Not rated. B&W; 89m. **DIR:** Jerzy Skolimowski. **CAST:** Jean-Pierre Léaud, Catherine Isabelle Duport. **1967**

LE DOULOS ★★★★ Outstanding, complex crime-drama about a police informer who attempts to expose a violent underworld crime ring. An excellent homage to American gangster films of the 1940s. Brilliant cinematography and sizzling performances by a great cast make this suspenseful thriller a film classic. In French with English subtitles. B&W; 105m. **DIR:** Jean-Pierre

Melville. **CAST:** Jean-Paul Belmondo, Serge Reggiani, Michel Piccoli. **1961**

LE GAI SAVOIR (THE JOY OF KNOWLEDGE) ★★ Incomprehensible film about two aliens. The poor extraterrestrials may have had better luck if they hadn't landed in this movie. In French with English subtitles. 96m. **DIR:** Jean-Luc Godard. **CAST:** Jean-Pierre Léaud, Juliet Berto. **1965**

LE GENTLEMAN D'ESPOM (DUKE OF THE DERBY) ★★★ This lighthearted look at the sport of kings gives veteran French film star Jean Gabin ample chance to shine as the title character, an aged, suave snob living by his wits and luck handicapping and soliciting bets from the rich. Everything is fine until, eager to impress an old flame, he passes a bad check. B&W; 83m. **DIR:** Jacques Juranville. **CAST:** Jean Gabin, Madeleine Robinson, Paul Frankeur. **1962**

LE GRAND CHEMIN (THE GRAND HIGHWAY) ★★★★ A delightful film about an 8 year old Parisian boy's summer in the country. Along with his friend Martine (Vanessa Guedj), Louis (played by director Jean-Loup Hubert's son Antoine) learns about the simple pleasures and terrors of life and love. This is great cinema for old and young alike, despite some nudity. In French with English subtitles. 104m. **DIR:** Jean-Loup Hubert. **CAST:** Vanessa Guedj, Antoine Hubert, Richard Bohringer, Anemone. **1988**

LE JOUR SE LEVE (DAYBREAK) ★★★ An affecting, atmospheric French melodrama by the director of the classic *Children of Paradise*. Jean Gabin plays a man provoked to murder his lover's seducer. There is some brilliant, sensuous moviemaking here. The existing print lacks sufficient subtitling but is still worth viewing. B&W; 85m. **DIR:** Marcel Carné. **CAST:** Jean Gabin, Jules Berry, Arletty, Jacqueline Laurent. **1939**

LE MAGNIFIQUE ★★★ A writer of spy novels imagines himself as his own character, a James Bond type, with the girl next door as his trusty sidekick. Though it never builds up a full head of steam, this French comedy holds your interest through the dull stretches. Written by Francis Verber (*La Cage Aux Folles, Three Fugitives*). In French with English subtitles. 93m. **DIR:** Philippe de Broca. **CAST:** Jean-Paul Belmondo, Jacqueline Bisset. **1974 DVD**

•LE MANS ★★★1/2 Incredibly well-photographed and brilliantly edited film about the world-famous twenty-four-hour auto race. Told in a unique documentary-like style with virtually no storyline, *Le Mans* is about the race and only the race. We never get to know any of the characters, but the film draws you into the action so well that you don't mind. Rated G. 106m. **DIR:** Lee H. Katzin. **CAST:** Steve McQueen, Siegfried Rauch, Elga Andersen, Ronald Leigh-Hunt. **1971**

LE MILLION ★★★★ Made more than fifty years ago, this delightful comedy about the efforts of a group of people to retrieve an elusive lottery ticket is more applicable to American audiences of today than it was when originally released. René Clair's classic fantasy-adventure is freewheeling and fun. French, subtitled in English. B&W; 85m. **DIR:** René Clair. **CAST:** Annabella, René Lefévre. **1931 DVD**

LE PETIT AMOUR ★★1/2 Romantic comedy based on a short story by Jane Birkin about a 40 year old divorcée who falls for a 15 year old schoolboy. Mediocre, but with good performances. In French with English subtitles. Rated R for nudity. 80m. **DIR:** Agnes Varda. **CAST:** Jane Birkin, Mathieu Demy, Charlotte Gainsbourg. **1987**

LE PLAISIR ★★1/2 Max Ophüls (*La Ronde*) adapts three ironic stories by Guy de Maupassant with his customary style, most evident in his extremely mobile camera work. However, the stories themselves are mediocre and not really up to the elaborate treatment. In French with English subtitles. B&W; 97m. **DIR:** Max Ophüls. **CAST:** Jean Gabin, Danielle Darrieux, Simone Simon. **1952**

LE REPOS DU GUERRIER (WARRIOR'S REST) ★★★★ Brigitte Bardot plays a proper French girl who rescues a sociopathic drifter from a suicide attempt. The drifter immediately takes over Bardot's life, ruining her reputation and abusing her verbally and emotionally, yet denying her attempts to form a real relationship. This is a precursor of *The Servant*, *9 1/2 Weeks*, and other frank observations of sexual obsession. In French. 98m. **DIR:** Roger Vadim. **CAST:** Brigitte Bardot, Robert Hossein, James Robertson Justice, Jean-Marc Bory. **1962**

LE ROUGE ET LE NOIR ★★★ The great French novel fails to come to life in this lavish but vacant adaptation, which follows the career of Julien Sorel, a social climber who enters the priesthood in order to rise above his family's social status. Also known as *The Red and the Black*. In French with English subtitles. 170m. **DIR:** Claude Autant-Lara. **CAST:** Gérard Philipe, Danielle Darrieux. **1954**

LE SAMOURAI ★★★★★ John Woo's *The Killer* was largely inspired by this classic that can be enjoyed both as a gripping thriller and as a muted but wholly intoxicating exercise in cinematic style. Alain Delon is the quintessence of cool as the hired killer who lets himself be weakened by emotion. In French with English subtitles. Not rated; contains violence. 95m. **DIR:** Jean-Pierre Melville. **CAST:** Alain Delon, François Perier, Nathalie Delon. **1967**

LE SCHPOUNTZ ★★★1/2 Country doofus Fernandel, convinced that he's the next Charles Boyer, tries to break into the movies in this consistently funny satire of the film world. In French with English subtitles. B&W; 140m. **DIR:** Marcel Pagnol. **CAST:** Fernandel, Orane Demazis, Charpin, Robert Vattier, Pierre Brasseur. **1938**

LE SECRET ★★★ Jean-Louis Trintignant plays an escapee from a psychiatric prison who finds shelter with a reclusive writer and his wife by persuading them that he has been tortured for information. Fine performances, a tense atmosphere, and music by Ennio Morricone make this worth your while. In French with English subtitles. Not rated. 100m. **DIR:** Robert Enrico. **CAST:** Jean-Louis Trintignant, Marlene Jobert, Philippe Noiret. **1974**

LE SEX SHOP ★★★★ Wry, satirical film about an owner of a failing little bookstore, who converts his business into a sex shop, where he peddles pornographic books and sexual devices in order to make ends meet. Excellent social-sexual satire. In French with English subtitles. Not rated; contains nudity and profanity. 90m. **DIR:** Claude Berri. **CAST:** Claude Berri, Juliet Berto. **1973**

LE VOYAGE IMAGINAIRE ★★1/2 A daydreaming clerk imagines a fantasy where he vies for the love of his coworker against the office Romeos. His dream takes them to a land of abandoned fairies where magic changes the young lovers into animals; when the dream ends the spell doesn't. Surreal French comedy. B&W; 66m. **DIR:** René Clair. **CAST:** Jean Borlin, Dolly Davys, Albert Préjean, Jim Geralds. **1925**

LEADER OF THE BAND ★★★ In this charming comedy Steve Landesberg plays an unemployed musician who becomes the band instructor for a group of misfits. Too much footage is devoted to marching-band performances, but all in all this film has general appeal. Rated PG for profanity. 90m. **DIR:** Nessa Hyams. **CAST:** Steve Landesberg, Gailard Sartain, Mercedes Ruehl. **1987**

LEADING MAN, THE ★★★★ American action-film hero Robin Grange is cast as an assassin torn between love and duty in a London play written by Felix Webb. When Grange discovers that the writer wants to leave his spouse for a young actress, he offers to seduce Webb's wife to expedite the situation. Webb agrees and soon finds his life being rewritten by his ruthless coconspirator. Rated R for language and sexuality. 96m. **DIR:** John Duigan. **CAST:** Jon Bon Jovi, Lambert Wilson, Thandie Newton, Anna Galiena, David Warner, Barry Humphries. **1998 DVD**

LEAGUE OF GENTLEMEN, THE ★★★★ A British army officer assembles a group of other military retirees and plots a perfect robbery. One of those lighthearted thrillers where the joy comes from watching professionals pull off an incredibly detailed crime. B&W; 114m. **DIR:** Basil Dearden. **CAST:** Jack Hawkins, Nigel Patrick, Roger Livesey, Richard Attenborough, Bryan Forbes, Kieron Moore. **1961 DVD**

LEAGUE OF THEIR OWN, A ★★★1/2 Director Penny Marshall's tribute to the first women's baseball league is a nice little movie that runs out of steam a bit in the last 45 minutes. Geena Davis is superb as "the natural" who finds herself caught in a battle of wills with sister/pitcher Lori Petty and the team's rummy coach, Tom Hanks, a one-time baseball great. The comedy bits by Madonna, Rosie O'Donnell, Megan Cavanaugh, and (seen all too briefly) Jon Lovitz help to buoy the film's melodramatic plotline. Rated PG. 118m. **DIR:** Penny Marshall. **CAST:** Tom Hanks, Geena Davis, Madonna, Lori Petty, Jon Lovitz, David Strathairn, Garry Marshall, Megan Cavanaugh, Rosie O'Donnell, Tracy Reiner, Bill Pullman. **1992 DVD**

LEAN ON ME ★★★★ Morgan Freeman gives a superb performance as real-life high school principal Joe Clark, who almost single-handedly converted Eastside High in Paterson, New Jersey, from a den of drugs, gangs, and corruption into an effective place of learning. Director John Avildsen has created a feel-good movie that conveys a timely message. Rated PG-13 for profanity and violence. 104m. **DIR:** John G. Avildsen. **CAST:** Morgan Freeman, Robert Guillaume, Beverly Todd. **1989 DVD**

LEAP OF FAITH ★★★1/2 The glorious gospel music is the main reason to catch Steve Martin's act as a dancin' preacher who decides to con the residents of a small town. Debra Winger plays the cynical right-hand man to Martin's phony faith healer. *Leap of Faith* pours on the sentimentality a bit thick, but the music—hallelujah! Rated PG-13 for profanity. 108m. **DIR:** Richard Pearce. **CAST:** Steve Martin, Debra Winger, Liam Neeson, Lolita Davidovich, Lukas Haas, Meat Loaf, Philip Seymour Hoffman, M. C. Gainey, Delores Hall, John Toles-Bey, Albertina Walker. **1992**

LEAPIN' LEPRECHAUNS ★★★ Kids will enjoy this fun, magical romp that takes its cue from vintage Walt Disney efforts like *Darby O'Gill and the Little People* and *The Gnome-Mobile*. Four leprechauns are forced into action when an ambitious American plans to turn their homeland into an amusement park called "Ireland-Land." They do whatever it takes, including befriending the developer's young daughter. Rated PG. 84m. **DIR:** Ted Nicolaou. **CAST:** John Bluthal, Grant Cramer, Sharon Lee Jones, Sylvester McCoy, James Ellis, Gregory Edward Smith. **1994**

LEARNING TREE, THE ★★★★ In adapting his own novel about the coming-of-age of a young black man in Kansas circa 1920, photographer-turned-filmmaker Gordon Parks not only wrote and directed, but also produced the project and composed its musical score. The result is a uniquely personal vision. Rated PG for violence, profanity, and racial epithets. 107m. **DIR:** Gordon Parks Jr. **CAST:** Kyle Johnson, Alex Clarke, Estelle Evans, Dana Elcar. **1969**

LEATHER BOYS, THE ★★ Considered adult and controversial when first released in England, this slice-of-life drama about teenagers who marry for sex and settle into drab existences doesn't carry the weight it once did. Rather depressing, this film is an interesting look at life in London in the early 1960s, but it has dated badly. B&W; 108m. **DIR:** Sidney J. Furie. **CAST:** Rita Tushingham, Dudley Sutton, Colin Campbell. **1963 DVD**

LEATHER BURNERS, THE ★★1/2 In this oddball series Western, Hopalong Cassidy (William Boyd) and his sidekick, California (Andy Clyde), are framed for murder by a calculating cattle rustler (Victor Jory). It's up to a junior detective (Bobby Larson) to prove our heroes' innocence in time to allow them to participate in the final showdown. B&W; 58m. **DIR:** Joseph E. Henabery. **CAST:** William Boyd, Andy Clyde, Victor Jory, Bobby Larson, Robert Mitchum. **1943**

LEATHER JACKET LOVE STORY ★★ David DeCoteau's attempt at a romantic comedy aimed at the gay market falls shy of the mark. While the film has likable characters and a solid story, the actors bring down the rest of the film with their poor work. Not rated; contains nudity and profanity. B&W; 85m. **DIR:** David DeCoteau. **CAST:** Sean Tataryn, Chris Bradley, Mink Stole, Nicholas Worth. **1997**

LEATHER JACKETS ★★ A one-dimensional blue-collar vehicle for leading man Cary Elwes. Rated R for violence, profanity, nudity, and some strongly suggestive sex scenes involving former porn queen Ginger Lynn Allen. 90m. **DIR:** Lee Drysdale. **CAST:** Bridget Fonda, Cary Elwes, D. B. Sweeney, Ginger Lynn Allen. **1992**

LEATHERFACE—THE TEXAS CHAINSAW MASSACRE III ★★1/2 Some light comedy helps break up the terror in this story of two travelers who make the mistake of stopping in Texas for directions. Not as scary as the first film in the series and not as bloody as the second. Rated R for violence. 87m. **DIR:** Jeff Burr. **CAST:** Viggo Mortensen, William Butler, Ken Foree. **1989**

LEAVE 'EM LAUGHING ★★★★1/2 Mickey Rooney is outstanding portraying real-life Chicago clown Jack Thum. Thum and his wife (played by Anne Jackson) cared for dozens of unwanted children. When Thum realizes he has terminal cancer, he falls apart and his wife must help him regain his inner strength and deal with reality. A real tearjerker! Made for TV, this is unrated. 104m. **DIR:** Jackie Cooper. **CAST:** Mickey Rooney, Anne Jackson, Red Buttons, William Windom, Elisha Cook Jr. **1981**

LEAVE HER TO HEAVEN ★★★★★ A fine translation of the Ben Ames Williams novel about a jealous woman who causes more torment to those she loves than to those she doesn't care about—going so far as to destroy herself if it causes her husband to suffer. Very stylish and beautifully acted. 110m. **DIR:** John M. Stahl. **CAST:** Gene Tierney, Cornel Wilde, Jeanne Crain, Vincent Price, Darryl Hickman, Mary Philips. **1945**

LEAVE IT TO BEAVER ★★★1/2 This successful update of the popular 1957–1963 television series retains the family love and moral integrity that hallmarked the show. Christopher McDonald projects genuine warmth as the world's most perfect dad, but Janine Turner is less successful as Mom, the sole character to exhibit just-plain-dumb throwback behavior (vacuuming the house while dressed for the opera). Modern kids may find this too wholesome, but it'll be good for 'em. Rated PG for mild profanity. 88m. **DIR:** Andy Cadiff. **CAST:** Christopher McDonald, Janine Turner, Cameron Finley, Erik von Detten, Adam Zolotin. **1997 DVD**

LEAVES FROM SATAN'S BOOK ★★ Carl Dreyer's second film is a surprising mixture of leering and posturing clichés. The story tells of Satan's appearance in four different disguises to perform his unholy temptations. Beautiful sets and effective character types, but hopelessly melodramatic stereotypes. Silent. B&W; 165m. **DIR:** Carl Dreyer. **CAST:** Heige Nissen, Jacob Texiere. **1919**

LEAVING LAS VEGAS ★★★★1/2 Nicolas Cage took home an Oscar for his all-stops-out performance as a failed Hollywood player determined to drink himself to death. After cashing out his entire life and relocating to Las Vegas, he encounters soft-hearted hooker Elisabeth Shue, who falls in love with him. The powerhouse performances are complemented by director Mike Figgis's quasi-surreal blend of Vegas flash-trash and *film noir* smokiness. Rated R for violence, profanity, nudity, and rape. 112m. **DIR:** Mike Figgis. **CAST:** Nicolas Cage, Elisabeth Shue, Julian Sands. **1995 DVD**

LEAVING NORMAL ★★★ In what could unkindly be called *Thelma and Louise II*, a tough, no-nonsense waitress (Christine Lahti) and a naïve young woman (Meg Tilly) fleeing an abusive husband go on a road trip from Normal, Wyoming, to the wilds of Alaska. The performances and a few surprises on the way help mitigate a now-too-familiar story. Rated R for profanity, violence, and nudity. 110m. **DIR:** Edward Zwick. **CAST:** Christine Lahti, Meg Tilly, Lenny von Dohlen, James Gammon. **1992**

L'ECOLE BUISSONNIERE ★★★1/2 A teacher with modern ideas goes to work for a small village, and now the once bored students are excited about going to school. A few elders in the village decide that the new teacher is a bad influence on the children; they make a bet with him, the stakes being his job. You'll be rooting for the teacher in this nicely portrayed, neo-realist film. In French with English subtitles. B&W; 84m. **DIR:** Jean-Paul Le Chanois. **CAST:** Bernard Blier, Juliette Faber, Pierre Coste. **1951**

LEECH WOMAN, THE ★★ The neglected wife of a cosmetics researcher discovers an African potion that can restore her faded youth, but she has to kill young men to obtain the "secret ingredient." Coleen Gray gives an all-out performance, but there's too much setup and too little payoff. B&W; 77m. **DIR:** Edward Dein. **CAST:** Coleen Gray, Grant Williams, Gloria Talbott. **1959**

LEFT BEHIND ★★★ When millions of people suddenly vanish into thin air, a television news reporter discovers that the Rapture may be at hand. Well-made and surprisingly restrained religious film. Rated PG-13 for violence. 95m. **DIR:** Vic Sarin. **CAST:** Kirk Cameron, Brad Johnson, Chelsea Noble, Clarence Gilyard. **2000 DVD**

LEFT FOR DEAD 🦃 Contrived murder drama, staged in a series of flashbacks. Not rated; contains violence, profanity, and nudity. 88m. **DIR:** Murray Markowitz. **CAST:** Elke Sommer, Donald Pilon, Chuck Shamata, George Touliatos. **1978**

LEFT HAND OF GOD, THE ★★★1/2 Humphrey Bogart is an American forced to pose as a priest while on the run from a renegade Chinese warlord (Lee J. Cobb). It's not the fastest-moving adventure story, but Bogart and Cobb are quite good, and Gene Tierney is an effective heroine. The result is worthy entertainment. 87m. **DIR:** Edward Dmytryk. **CAST:** Humphrey Bogart, Lee J. Cobb, Gene Tierney, Agnes Moorehead. **1955**

LEFT HANDED GUN, THE ★★★1/2 Effective Western follows the exploits of Billy the Kid from the Lincoln County cattle wars until his death at the hands of Pat Garrett. One of the best of several Westerns to deal with the legend of Billy the Kid. B&W; 102m. **DIR:** Arthur Penn. **CAST:** Paul Newman, John Dehner, James Best, Hurd Hatfield, Lita Milan. **1958**

•LEFT LUGGAGE ★★★★ Emotionally satisfying tale of a young woman trying to come to grips with being Jewish. Laura Fraser is touching as Chaja, a student of philosophy at odds with her concentration camp parents over her identity and religion. When Chaja becomes a nanny for a Hasidic family with five children, she slowly begins to understand what it means to hold on to tradition and values. Vital to Chaja's redemption is her relationship with the family's youngest son, who doesn't speak. With the help of the boy's mother (Isabella Rossellini), both Chaja and the son learn to accept who they are. Excellent cast, a sharp screenplay, and inviting direction. Not rated. 100m. **DIR:** Jeroen Krabbe. **CAST:** Isabella Rossellini, Maximilian Schell, Marianne Sagebrecht, Laura Fraser, Topol, David Bradley. **1998 DVD**

LEGACY, THE ★★ A young American couple (Katharine Ross and Sam Elliott) staying at a mysterious English mansion discover that the woman has been chosen as the mate for some sort of ugly, demonic creature upstairs. Rated R for violence and language. 100m. **DIR:** Richard Marquand. **CAST:** Katharine Ross, Sam Elliott, John Standing, Roger Daltrey. **1979**

LEGACY FOR LEONETTE ★★ Romance Theatre tries a murder mystery but devotes too much time to the love angle. A young woman goes to England to investigate

her father's mysterious death but is distracted by her handsome lawyer. Episodic and mildly entertaining. Not rated; contains no objectionable material. 99m. **DIR:** Jim Drake. **CAST:** Loyita Chapel, Michael Anderson Jr., Dinah Anne Rogers, Shane McCamey. **1982**

LEGACY OF HORROR Another of Andy Milligan's lethally dull and thoroughly amateurish shockers, a remake of his own *The Ghastly Ones*. Rated R. 90m. **DIR:** Andy Milligan. **CAST:** Elaine Bois, Chris Broderick. **1978**

LEGACY OF LIES ★★ Michael Ontkean portrays a good Chicago cop who is caught up in a politically motivated murder. Martin Landau plays his father, a crooked Chicago police officer who's willing to take the fall to prevent his son from becoming corrupt. Weak story line undermines this made-for-cable drama. 91m. **DIR:** Bradford May. **CAST:** Michael Ontkean, Martin Landau, Joe Morton, Patricia Clarkson, Chelcie Ross, Eli Wallach. **1992**

LEGAL DECEIT ★★1/2 A lawyer agrees to join a coworker's plan to boost their careers by blackmail only to regret it when she finds he is willing to extend his criminal actions to murder. Second-rate thriller is notable only as a starring vehicle for Lela Rochon before she made *Waiting to Exhale*. Not rated. 93m. **DIR:** Monika Harris. **CAST:** Lela Rochon, Phil Morris, John Stockwell. **1995**

LEGAL EAGLES ★★★1/2 This comedy-mystery features Robert Redford as an assistant district attorney and Debra Winger as a defense attorney. The two partner in a complex case involving art theft and a loopy performance artist, played by Daryl Hannah. Redford and Winger keep things moving with energy and charisma. Rated PG for mild adult situations. 114m. **DIR:** Ivan Reitman. **CAST:** Robert Redford, Debra Winger, Daryl Hannah, Brian Dennehy, Terence Stamp, Steven Hill, Jennie Dundas, Roscoe Lee Browne. **1986 DVD**

LEGALESE ★★★★ High-profile courtroom high jinks get lambasted in this cynical drama about modern celebrity trials. James Garner has a reputation for being able to get *anybody* off, maybe even a flamboyant celebrity accused of killing her sister's husband. This film doesn't say much for the current state of justice in American courts, but that's the point. Rated R, for profanity. 95m. **DIR:** Glenn Jordan. **CAST:** James Garner, Gina Gershon, Mary-Louise Parker, Edward Kerr, Kathleen Turner. **1998**

•LEGALLY BLONDE ★★★1/2 Reese Witherspoon is wonderful as the "Malibu Barbie" of Harvard Law School. After earning a fashion degree, she follows her boyfriend to the ultimate Ivy League institution and develops a touching friendship with a depressed manicurist. The contrast between preppy snobs and the chihuahua-toting Witherspoon results in a laughfest. Rated PG-13 for sexual innuendo and profanity. 96m. **DIR:** Robert Luketic. **CAST:** Reese Witherspoon, Luke Wilson, Matthew Davis, Selma Blair. **2001 DVD**

LEGEND Tom Cruise simply looks embarrassed as a forest-living lad who joins a quest to save a unicorn, keeper of his world's Light. Rated PG for mild violence. 89m. **DIR:** Ridley Scott. **CAST:** Tom Cruise, Tim Curry, Mia Sara, David Bennent, Billy Barty. **1986**

•LEGEND, THE ★★★★ In one of Jet Li's biggest Hong Kong hits, he plays the traditional hero Fong Sai Yuk as a young man (and a bit of a brat). It's as much a comedy as an action movie, with some spectacular fight scenes that are as funny as they are thrilling. Watch for the scene in which Li and his opponent fight while running on the heads of the crowd watching them! Josephine Siao nearly steals the show as Fong's overprotective mother, who poses as a man to do some fighting of her own. Dubbed in English. Rated R for violence. 100m. **DIR:** Corey Yuen. **CAST:** Jet Li, Michelle Reis, Josephine Siao. **1993 DVD**

LEGEND OF BAGGER VANCE, THE ★★★★ If *A River Runs Through It* was director Robert Redford's ode to the Zen of fly-fishing, then this luxurious adaptation of Steven Pressfield's novel turns golf into a similar metaphor for life. Matt Damon stars as an F. Scott Fitzgerald–style golden boy who "loses his swing" (and therefore his soul) when he returns home to Savannah following World War I. With the help of a mysterious trickster figure played with laid-back charm by Will Smith, our hero attempts to regain both during a climactic golf tournament. A bit slow, but well worth the effort. Rated PG-13 for profanity, sensuality, and war violence. 127m. **DIR:** Robert Redford. **CAST:** Will Smith, Matt Damon, Charlize Theron, Bruce McGill, Joel Gretsch, J. Michael Moncrief, Jack Lemmon. **2000 DVD**

LEGEND OF BILLIE JEAN, THE A girl from Texas (Helen Slater) becomes an outlaw. Rated PG-13 for language and violence. 92m. **DIR:** Matthew Robbins. **CAST:** Helen Slater, Keith Gordon, Christian Slater, Peter Coyote. **1985**

LEGEND OF BOGGY CREEK ★★ One of the better "mystery of" docudramas, which were the rage of the early 1970s, this supposedly true story focuses on a monster that lurks in the swamps of Arkansas. Rated PG. 95m. **DIR:** Charles B. Pierce. **CAST:** Willie E. Smith, John P. Nixon. **1972**

LEGEND OF CRYSTANIA ★★★ Following the events of *Record of Lodoss War*, parts one and two, this animated fantasy focuses on the Black Knight Ashram as he leads the people of Marmo to Crystania where they are beset by the Gods' King, an insane deity who possesses the knight. The animation is shoddy and the story at times too ploddingly placed; yet the film still manages to capture some of the excitement of its predecessors. Not rated; contains violence. 85m. **DIR:** Nakamura Ryutaro. **1996 DVD**

LEGEND OF FRENCHIE KING, THE Muddled Western about a gang of female outlaws falls flat. Rated R for profanity, violence, and adult situations. 97m. **DIR:** Christian-Jaque. **CAST:** Brigitte Bardot, Claudia Cardinale, Guy Casaril, Michael J. Pollard. **1971**

LEGEND OF GATOR FACE, THE ★★★ Move the suburban setting to swamp country, and replace an alien visitor with a friendly alligator/human hybrid, and you've got this odd little spin on *E.T.* The story moves along reasonably well while the two young stars attempt to inject some life into their sleepy small town, but things go downhill after we finally get a glimpse of the badly conceived title creature. Suitable for all ages. 100m. **DIR:** Vic Sarin. **CAST:** John White, Dan Warry-Smith, Charlotte Sullivan, C. David Johnson, Paul Winfield. **1996**

LEGEND OF HELL HOUSE, THE ★★★1/2 Richard Matheson's riveting suspense tale of a group of re-

searchers attempting to survive a week in a haunted house in order to try to solve the mystery of the many deaths that have occurred there. Jarring at times, with very inventive camera shots and a great cast headed by Roddy McDowall as the only survivor of a previous investigation. Rated PG for violence. 95m. **DIR:** John Hough. **CAST:** Roddy McDowall, Pamela Franklin, Gayle Hunnicutt, Clive Revill. **1973 DVD**

LEGEND OF HILLBILLY JOHN, THE ★★ When a young man's grandfather challenges the devil and loses, he decides to take on the master of Hell himself, armed with only his guitar. Flawed low-budget production with intermittent charms. Rated G. 86m. **DIR:** John Newland. **CAST:** Hedge Capers, Severn Darden, Denver Pyle. **1973**

LEGEND OF 1900, THE ★★★1/2 Baby boy abandoned on a transatlantic ocean liner is named for the year of his birth. He matures into a famous pianist without venturing onto dry land, is challenged to a keyboard duel by an arrogant Jelly Roll Morton, and is tempted to jump ship in pursuit of a young muse. The tale is narrated by a trumpet player who tries to help 1900 find his true niche in life. This overly long fable is full of magical moments that do not quite gel into a wondrous whole. Rated R for language. 119m. **DIR:** Giuseppe Tornatore. **CAST:** Tim Roth, Pruitt Taylor Vince, Clarence Williams, III, Bill Nunn, Melanie Thierry. **1999**

LEGEND OF SLEEPY HOLLOW, THE (1949) ★★★★ One of the finest of the Disney "novelette" cartoons, this adaptation is given a properly sepulchral tone by narrator Bing Crosby. Reasonably scary, particularly for small fry, who might get pretty nervous during poor Ichabod Crane's final, fateful ride. 49m. **DIR:** Jack Kinney, Clyde Geronimi, James Algar. **1949**

LEGEND OF SURAM FORTRESS, THE ★★★★ Idiosyncratic retelling of a medieval Georgian legend about the attempt to build a fortress to repel invaders. Difficult to comprehend (unless you know a lot about Georgian folklore), the film's many striking images make for a memorable viewing experience. In Georgian with English subtitles. 87m. **DIR:** Sergi Parajanov, Dodo Abashidze. **CAST:** Levan Uchaneishvili. **1984 DVD**

LEGEND OF THE EIGHT SAMURAI ★★ Shizu is the princess who leads her warriors into battle against a giant centipede, ghosts, and a nearly immortal witch. An interesting story line, but derivative, slow in spots, badly dubbed, and disappointing. Not rated; contains moderate violence. 130m. **DIR:** Haruki Kadokawa. **CAST:** Hiroku Yokoshimaru, Sonny Chiba. **1984 DVD**

LEGEND OF THE FOREST ★★ The story is inconsequential in this awkward tribute to Disney's *Fantasia* that strives for experimental depth but doesn't deliver. Using a typically Western animation setting (the forest), the evolution of animation style from the last sixty years unfolds to music from Tchaikovsky's Fourth Symphony. High concept with only limited results. In Japanese with English subtitles. Not rated. 26m. **DIR:** Osamu Tezuka. **1987**

LEGEND OF THE LONE RANGER, THE 🦃 While kids may slightly enjoy this often corny, slow-paced Western—adults will probably be falling asleep. Rated PG. 98m. **DIR:** William Fraker. **CAST:** Klinton Spilsbury, Michael Horse, Jason Robards Jr. **1981 DVD**

LEGEND OF THE LOST ★★ Cornball adventure-romance borrows several themes from *Treasure of the Sierra Madre* and doesn't improve upon them. John Wayne is a cynical soldier of fortune who escorts idealist Rossano Brazzi and prostitute Sophia Loren through the desert in search of ancient treasure. 107m. **DIR:** Henry Hathaway. **CAST:** John Wayne, Sophia Loren, Rossano Brazzi, Kurt Kasznar. **1957**

LEGEND OF THE LOST TOMB ★★★ Amiable family-style adventure, smartly adapted from Walter Dean Myers's *Tales of a Dead King,* about two teenagers searching for the mysterious treasure promised by a lost scroll, while battling the evil minions of antiquities thief Stacy Keach. Broadly played and mostly good-natured fun, allowing for a few genuinely frightening scenes involving scorpions. Rated PG for mild violence. 93m. **DIR:** Jonathan Winfrey. **CAST:** Brock Pierce, Kimberlee Peterson, Rick Rossovich, Stacy Keach, Khaled El Sawy. **1997**

LEGEND OF THE NORTH WIND, THE ★★1/2 In seventeenth-century Newfoundland, three children try to prevent an unscrupulous explorer from unleashing an evil spirit as part of his plan to capture whales. This well-intentioned but corny animated film is for young children only. Rated G. 74m. **1995**

•LEGEND OF THE RED DRAGON ★★★ Traditional martial arts action and storytelling distinguish this dubbed epic. Jet Li stars as Kwun, a master warrior who is devastated when his wife and entire village are murdered by evil Manchu soldiers. With his son Ting, the only survivor of the massacre, Kwun makes his way across ancient China looking for revenge. His quest takes him to the home of a wealthy man who has raised five Shaolin masters. When the Manchu soldiers arrive, it's up to Kwun, Ting, and the masters to end their reign of terror. Rated R for violence. 83m. **DIR:** Wong Jing. **CAST:** Jet Li, Sung Young Chen, Cheun-Hua Chi, Damian Lau. **1994 DVD**

LEGEND OF THE SPIRIT DOG ★★★ A mysterious wolf-dog is rescued in the Alaska wilderness by a female environmentalist and her young son. When a company begins illegal dumping on a sacred mountain, Spirit helps his new family save the day. Panoramic location photography, a rousing plot, and family and earth values add to this spiritual adventure. Rated PG for violence. 90m. **DIR:** Michael Spence, Martin Goldman. **CAST:** Morgan Brittany, Martin Balsam, Martin Landau, David Richards. **1994**

LEGEND OF THE WEREWOLF ★★ Peter Cushing's ever-professional performance is the only noteworthy element. British werewolf movie. Not rated, but the equivalent of PG-13. 90m. **DIR:** Freddie Francis. **CAST:** Peter Cushing, Ron Moody, Hugh Griffith. **1974**

LEGEND OF VALENTINO ★★ TV movie released close to the fiftieth anniversary of the fabled actor's death adheres to some facts concerning the archetypal Latin lover, but still presents an unsatisfying and incomplete portrait. But this film still leaves too many questions either unanswered or glossed over. Not too bad for a TV movie. 100m. **DIR:** Melville Shavelson. **CAST:** Franco Nero, Suzanne Pleshette, Judd Hirsch, Lesley Ann Warren, Milton Berle, Yvette Mimieux, Harold J. Stone. **1975**

LEGEND OF WALKS FAR WOMAN, THE 🦃 Badly miscast Raquel Welch portrays an Indian heroine facing the perils of the Indian versus white man's culture

clash. 150m. **DIR:** Mel Damski. **CAST:** Raquel Welch, Bradford Dillman, George Clutsei, Nick Mancuso, Nick Ramos. **1982**

LEGENDS OF THE AMERICAN WEST (SERIES) ★★★1/2 Rare photos, diaries, interviews with relatives of the legends, movie clips, and reenactments are used to give a factual account of the American West and the famous characters we have known through myth and legend. *Jesse James, Billy The Kid,* and *Wyatt Earp and the Gunfighters* are the best with fine use of memorabilia, photos, and new facts. The uneven *Cowboys and Indians* emphasizes truth over movie distortion, and the Indians get a fair shake for once. *The West Remembered* is disappointing. Not rated. 30m. **DIR:** Marina Amoruso. **1992**

LEGENDS OF THE FALL ★★★★ Sprawling, old-fashioned melodrama about disillusioned U.S. Cavalry officer raising three sons near the remote Montana Rockies. War, politics, Prohibition, and the love of a fickle woman turn brother against brother, and father against son. Director Edward Zwick handles the Shakespearean tragedy without descending into bathos, and John Toll's cinematography is exquisite. Rated R for profanity, violence, and simulated sex. 134m. **DIR:** Edward Zwick. **CAST:** Brad Pitt, Anthony Hopkins, Aidan Quinn, Julia Ormond, Henry Thomas. **1994 DVD**

LEGENDS OF THE NORTH ★★ A hidden cache of gold buried in a Canadian lake sparks a race for ownership. Randy Quaid plays the fortune hunter, who seeks advice from the son of the man who hid the gold. Gorgeous scenery fills the screen, but the action and acting are pretty mundane. Rated PG. 98m. **DIR:** Rene Manzor. **CAST:** Georges Corraface, Randy Quaid, Macha Grenon, Bill Merasty. **1994**

LEGION OF THE NIGHT ★★1/2 Grim, disturbing film has soldier Tim Lovelace learning of a government experiment with cybernetic zombie assassins and running afoul of drug-running gangsters. Not rated; contains gore, violence, and profanity. 85m. **DIR:** Matt Jaissle. **CAST:** Tim Lovelace, Ron Asheton, Heather Fine, Bill Hinzman. **1995**

LEGIONNAIRE ★★ Standard-issue French Foreign Legion dust drama jumps from one worn-out cliché to the next, with Jean-Claude Van Damme playing a boxer who is forced to join the Legion when he refuses to throw a fight and is hunted down by a mob boss. Even at ninety-nine minutes the film feels long and drawn out. Rated R for violence, language, and adult situations. 99m. **DIR:** Peter MacDonald. **CAST:** Jean-Claude Van Damme, Steven Berkoff, Adewale Akinnuoye-Agbaje, Daniel Caltagirone, Nicolas Farrell. **1998 DVD**

LEMON DROP KID, THE ★★★ Great group of character actors makes this Damon Runyon story of an incompetent bookie work like a charm. Fast-talking Bob Hope has the tailor-made leading role. Deadly Lloyd Nolan plays the guy putting the screws to Hope, and Marilyn Maxwell plays the girl caught in the middle. B&W; 91m. **DIR:** Sidney Lanfield. **CAST:** Bob Hope, Marilyn Maxwell, Lloyd Nolan, Jane Darwell, Andrea King, Fred Clark, Jay C. Flippen, William Frawley. **1951 DVD**

LEMON SISTERS, THE ★★ Engaging characters are in desperate need of a coherent story as three middle-aged, part-time lounge singers find their show-biz dreams slipping away in 1982 Atlantic City. Hollow comedy-cum-drama. Rated PG-13. 100m. **DIR:** Joyce Chopra. **CAST:** Diane Keaton, Carol Kane, Kathryn Grody, Rubén Blades, Aidan Quinn, Elliott Gould. **1990 DVD**

LEMORA—LADY DRACULA ★★★1/2 Shot in black-and-white, this atmospheric vampire film is an oddity in that it is a period piece made on a fraction of the budget of much larger films. Future exploitation star Cheryl "Rainbeaux" Smith appears as the Singing Angel, on whom just about everyone wants to get their hands. Rated PG for violence. 80m. **DIR:** Richard Blackburn. **CAST:** Lesley Glib, Cheryl Smith. **1973**

LENA'S HOLIDAY ★★1/2 Decent romantic thriller. A newly freed East German on vacation in Los Angeles becomes inadvertently involved with diamond thieves and must run for her life. Rated PG-13. 97m. **DIR:** Michael Keusch. **CAST:** Felicity Waterman, Chris Lemmon, Michael Sarrazin, Nick Mancuso. **1990 DVD**

L'ENFER ★★★★ One man's descent into madness is explored in this harrowing film, whose production history was equally harrowing. Shot and reshot over a period of thirty years, the final product is a testament to endurance. Paul and Nelly have a wonderful life. Paul works at a resort hotel, a job he has held for the past fifteen years. When Paul makes the bold step to buy the hotel, the couple's life begins to crumble as Paul slips into madness and extreme jealousy. In French with English subtitles. 105m. **DIR:** Claude Chabrol. **CAST:** François Cluzet, Emmanuelle Beart, Natalie Cardone. **1994 DVD**

LENNY ★★★★★ Bob Fosse brilliantly directed this stark biography of self-destructive, controversial persecuted comic talent Lenny Bruce. Dustin Hoffman captures all those contrary emotions in his portrayal of the late 1950s and '60s stand-up comedian. Valerie Perrine is a treasure in her low-key role as Bruce's stripper wife. Rated R. B&W; 112m. **DIR:** Bob Fosse. **CAST:** Dustin Hoffman, Valerie Perrine, Jan Miner. **1974 DVD**

LENNY BRUCE PERFORMANCE FILM, THE ★★★★ This simple, straightforward solo showcases Lenny Bruce, the master of bitter satire, in all his gritty brilliance. Bruce was an original, a pioneer who paved the way for George Carlin, Richard Pryor, and all the rest. Also included is Bruce's color-cartoon parody of the Lone Ranger, "Thank You Masked Man." Otherwise, black and white. Rated R for language. 70m. **DIR:** John Magnuson. **CAST:** Lenny Bruce. **1968**

LEO TOLSTOY'S ANNA KARENINA ★★ The novel of upper-class adultery in czarist Russia takes its worst beating yet in this turgid, disjointed shambles. Alfred Molina hogs the action as Levin, spouting dense passages of Tolstoyan philosophy. Meanwhile, Sophie Marceau plays the tragic Anna as a selfish neurotic; James Fox, as her husband, is far more sympathetic. Rated PG-13 for mature themes and brief simulated sex. 110m. **DIR:** Bernard Rose. **CAST:** Sophie Marceau, Sean Bean, Alfred Molina, Mia Kirshner, James Fox, Danny Huston, Saskia Wickham, Fiona Shaw. **1997**

LEOLO ★★★★ This surreal memoir of growing up poor in Montreal's ghetto alternates between images of great beauty and great coarseness. The boy at the center of the story is fed up with a bizarre family life. He creates a fantasy background, concluding that he was accidentally fathered by an Italian peasant in a wacky

accident that has to be seen to be believed. Though original and audacious, this film is not for the easily offended. In French with English subtitles. Rated R, with profanity, scatological humor, and sexual situations. 107m. **DIR:** Jean-Claude Lauzon. **CAST:** Maxime Collin, Ginetta Reno, Julien Guiomar. **1993**

LEON THE PIG FARMER ★★★1/2 Good intentions and goofy humor ease this little film past its duller moments. Mark Frankel is a London Jew who discovers his real father raises pigs. Already at odds with his career, sex life, and identity, this news nearly pushes poor Leon over the edge. Not as funny as it wants to be, but it's consistently amusing and infectiously bubbly. Some scenes could have been lifted right out of a Monty Python skit. Not rated; contains mild profanity. 98m. **DIR:** Vadim Jean, Gary Sinyor. **CAST:** Mark Frankel, Janet Suzman, Brian Glover, Connie Booth, David de Keyser, Maryam D'Abo. **1992**

LEONARD PART 6 Bill Cosby, forced into saving the world, does so, but he can't save the picture. Rated PG. 83m. **DIR:** Paul Weiland. **CAST:** Bill Cosby, Tom Courtenay, Joe Don Baker, Moses Gunn. **1987**

LEOPARD, THE ★★★★ Luchino Visconti's multigenerational spectacle of nineteenth-century Sicily has been restored on video, replacing the dubbed version that was cut by 40 minutes and presented to confused American audiences in the mid-1960s. Burt Lancaster is surprisingly effective as the formidable head of an Italian (!) dynasty. 205m. **DIR:** Luchino Visconti. **CAST:** Burt Lancaster, Alain Delon, Claudia Cardinale. **1963**

LEOPARD IN THE SNOW ★★ Silly romance between a spoiled rich girl and a maimed former race-car driver. The dialogue is slow and some scenes lead nowhere. The pluses include the driver's pet leopard and his butler Bolt (Jeremy Kemp). Rated PG for one scene in which our lovebirds *almost* become passionate. 89m. **DIR:** Gerry O'Hara. **CAST:** Keir Dullea, Susan Penhaligon, Kenneth More, Billie Whitelaw, Jeremy Kemp. **1977**

LEOPARD MAN, THE ★★★1/2 This Val Lewton–produced thriller depicts the havoc and killing that begin when a leopard escapes and terrorizes a New Mexico village. B&W; 59m. **DIR:** Jacques Tourneur. **CAST:** Dennis O'Keefe, Isabel Jewell. **1943**

LEOPARD SON, THE ★★★★ The Discovery Channel's first theatrically released film is a combination of documentary and storyline narrated by John Gielgud. Naturalist Hugo van Lawick captured two years in the life of a Serengeti leopard cub. Although viewers are not spared the harsh realities of surviving in the animal kingdom, they are also made privy to all its joy and wonderment as the male cub learns to be self-sufficient. Fabulous footage of a multitude of species with appropriate soundtrack for each. Not rated. 85m. **DIR:** Hugo van Lawick. **1996**

LEPKE ★★★ Tony Curtis gives an effective performance in the lead role of this gangster drama. He's the head of Murder Inc. The story sticks close to the facts. It's no classic, but watchable. Rated R. 110m. **DIR:** Menahem Golan. **CAST:** Tony Curtis, Anjanette Comer, Michael Callan, Warren Berlinger, Milton Berle, Vic Tayback. **1975**

LEPRECHAUN No luck of the Irish for writer-director Mark Jones, whose abysmal little fright flick concerns a nasty Lucky Charms refugee. Nothing but blarney. Rated R for violence and profanity. 92m. **DIR:** Mark Jones. **CAST:** Warwick Davis, Jennifer Aniston, Ken Olandt, Mark Holton. **1993 DVD**

LEPRECHAUN 2 ★★ In search of a bride, the wily leprechaun goes to America where he causes the usual mayhem (including killing an irritating waiter with his own espresso machine). Some cleverness manages to struggle through briefly before being bludgeoned to death by the dead-end story. Rated R for violence, nudity, and profanity. 84m. **DIR:** Rodman Flender. **CAST:** Warwick Davis, Charlie Heath, Shevonne Durkin, Clint Howard. **1994 DVD**

LEPRECHAUN 3 Unless you loved *Leprechaun* and *Leprechaun 2*, you won't want to watch this version in which the leprechaun terrorizes Las Vegas. Rated R for profanity, violence, nudity, and simulated sex. 93m. **DIR:** Brian Trenchard-Smith. **CAST:** Warwick Davis, John Gatins, Lee Armstrong. **1995 DVD**

LEPRECHAUN 4 IN SPACE ★★★ The vicious little leprechaun's third outing takes place in a distant galaxy, where the leprechaun is holding an alien princess hostage until he can marry her. Headed from Earth is a spaceship filled with space marines intent on saving the princess. The leprechaun sneaks aboard and starts killing them one by one. New setting and gory special effects breathe new life into the franchise. Rated R for violence and language. 98m. **DIR:** Brian Trenchard-Smith. **CAST:** Warwick Davis, Rebekah Carlton, Debbe Dunning. **1996 DVD**

LEPRECHAUN IN THE HOOD The dastardly, diminutive demon finally runs out of steam in a film that wants to be funny and scary, but winds up neither. Setting the film in the hood fails to generate anything new or exciting. Time to make a wish and send this guy packing. Rated R for adult situations, language, and violence. 90m. **DIR:** Robert Spera. **CAST:** Warwick Davis, Ice T, Coolio, Postmaster P, Stray Bullet. **1999 DVD**

LES ABYSSES ★★★ Straightforward adaptation of the notorious murder case that inspired Jean Genet's *The Maids*. Two sisters try to stop the sale of a vineyard that is their only means of support; when they fail, they kill the owner for whom they have worked all their lives. In French with English subtitles. B&W; 90m. **DIR:** Nico Papatakis. **CAST:** Francine Berge, Colette Berge. **1963**

LES BICHES ★★★ This story revolves around Frederique and Why, two lesbian lovers in love with the same man. Good music, but the acting could be better. In French with English subtitles. Not rated; contains profanity. 104m. **DIR:** Claude Chabrol. **CAST:** Jean-Louis Trintignant, Jacqueline Sassard, Stéphane Audran. **1968**

LES CARABINIERS ★★★1/2 One of Jean-Luc Godard's strangest films, an extreme attack on the absurdity of war seen through the eyes of two morons who enlist as mercenaries. Not rated. In French with English subtitles. B&W; 80m. **DIR:** Jean-Luc Godard. **CAST:** Marino Masé, Albert Juross. **1962 DVD**

LES CHOSES DE LA VIE (THINGS IN LIFE, THE) ★★★1/2 A hospitalized businessman, injured in an automobile accident, reflects on his relationship with his wife and mistress. Mediocre drama gets a lift from a strong cast. In French with English subtitles. 90m. **DIR:**

Claude Sautet. **CAST:** Romy Schneider, Michel Piccoli, Lea Massari. **1970**

LES COMPERES ★★★★ Pierre Richard and Gérard Depardieu star in this madcap French comedy as two strangers who find themselves on the trail of a runaway teenager. Both think they're the father—it was the only way the boy's mother could think of to enlist their aid. In French with English subtitles. Rated PG for profanity and brief violence. 90m. **DIR:** Francis Veber. **CAST:** Pierre Richard, Gérard Depardieu. **1984**

LES COUSINS ★★★1/2 Innocent country lad, in Paris for the first time to attend university, moves in with his unscrupulous cousin. Melancholy study of big-city decadence directed with a cold, clear eye by Claude Chabrol. In French with English subtitles. Not rated. 110m. **DIR:** Claude Chabrol. **CAST:** Gerard Blain, Jean-Claude Brialy, Juliette Mayniel. **1958**

LES ENFANTS TERRIBLES ★★★1/2 Jean Cocteau wrote (but did not direct) this drama as a companion piece to his earlier *Les Parents Terribles*. In a similarly claustrophobic story, the nearly incestuous relationship between a teenage brother and sister destroys them when it is shattered by other people of their same age. Director Jean-Pierre Melville, then at the beginning of his career, turns the low budget to his stylistic advantage. Also known as *The Strange Ones*. In French with English subtitles. B&W; 100m. **DIR:** Jean-Pierre Melville. **CAST:** Nicole Stephane, Edouard Dermithe. **1949**

LES GIRLS ★★★★ Gene Kelly is charming, Mitzi Gaynor is funny, Taina Elg is funnier, Kay Kendall is funniest in this tale of a libel suit over a published memoir. Three conflicting accounts of what was and wasn't emerge from the courtroom. A witty film with Cole Porter music and stylish direction by George Cukor. 114m. **DIR:** George Cukor. **CAST:** Gene Kelly, Kay Kendall, Taina Elg, Mitzi Gaynor, Jacques Bergerac. **1957**

LES GRANDES GUEULES (JAILBIRDS' VACATION) ★★1/2 This comedy-drama about parolees working on a backwoods sawmill would be better if it were shorter and the extended fistfight scenes were cut measurably. Otherwise, the "jailbirds" are a lively, entertaining bunch. In French with English subtitles. 125m. **DIR:** Robert Enrico. **CAST:** Lino Ventura, Bourvil, Marie Dubois. **1965**

LES LIAISONS DANGEREUSES ★★★ Complex, amoral tale of a diplomat and his wife whose open marriage and numerous affairs eventually lead to tragedy. Well photographed and acted (especially by Jeanne Moreau), this adult and downbeat film fluctuates at times between satire and comedy and depression, but overall the experience is pretty grim. In French with English subtitles. B&W; 108m. **DIR:** Roger Vadim. **CAST:** Gérard Philipe, Jeanne Moreau, Jeanne Valerie, Annette Vadim, Simone Renant, Jean-Louis Trintignant. **1959**

LES MISÉRABLES (1935) ★★★★ The most watchable and best acted of the many versions of Victor Hugo's story of good and evil. Fredric March steals a loaf of bread to survive, only to undergo a lifetime of torment. Charles Laughton is absolutely frightening as the personification of an uncaring legal system. B&W; 108m. **DIR:** Richard Boleslawski. **CAST:** Fredric March, Charles Laughton, Cedric Hardwicke, Florence Eldridge. **1935**

LES MISÉRABLES (1959) ★★★★ The length weakens the story, but this is probably the most complete film version of Victor Hugo's novel. The story of a detective's relentless pursuit of a man for stealing bread inspired many modern chase films. In French with English subtitles. B&W; 210m. **DIR:** Jean-Paul Le Chanois. **CAST:** Jean Gabin, Daniele Delorme, Bourvil, Bernard Blier, Gianni Esposito. **1957**

LES MISÉRABLES (1978) ★★★1/2 Lavish television version of Victor Hugo's classic tale of a petty thief's attempt to forget his past only to be hounded through the years by a relentless police inspector. Richard Jordan as the thief turned mayor and Anthony Perkins as his tormentor are extremely good. 150m. **DIR:** Glenn Jordan. **CAST:** Richard Jordan, Anthony Perkins, John Gielgud, Cyril Cusack, Flora Robson, Claude Dauphin. **1978**

LES MISÉRABLES (1995) ★★★ This loose weaving of Victor Hugo's 1862 novel into the twentieth century unfolds as two parallel epics. When an illiterate Frenchman helps a wealthy Jewish family flee Nazi persecution, he discovers that his life mirrors that of Jean Valjean, and that he shares Valjean's desperate struggle to assert the dignity of man. The film is saturated with soap-opera sensibilities and seductive historical resonance. In French with English subtitles. Rated R for violence, language, and sex. 174m. **DIR:** Claude Lelouch. **CAST:** Jean-Paul Belmondo, Michel Boujenah, Alessandra Martines, Annie Girardot, Philippe Léotard. **1995**

LES MISÉRABLES (1998) ★★★★ Until the third act, this opulent adaptation of Victor Hugo's classic superbly re-creates Javert's maniacal pursuit of Jean Valjean, the ex-convict who wishes only to forge a new life of compassion and dignity. The lead players are excellent: Liam Neeson is believably powerful as Valjean; hawk-nosed Geoffrey Rush is positively chilling as the implacable Javert. Details are meticulous, but the long-awaited conclusion lacks closure and is irritatingly abrupt. Getting there, however, is the stuff of great melodrama. Rated PG-13 for violence and dramatic intensity. 129m. **DIR:** Bille August. **CAST:** Liam Neeson, Geoffrey Rush, Uma Thurman, Claire Danes, Hans Matheson, Reine Brynolfsson, Peter Vaughan. **1998 DVD**

LES PARENTS TERRIBLES ★★★★ Unwilling to let her son escape her clutches, a domineering middle-class woman tries to interfere with his upcoming marriage, not knowing that her son's fiancée is also her henpecked husband's mistress. In adaptating his own stage play, director Jean Cocteau maintains the stage setting (which consists of only two scenes) in order to emphasize the claustrophobic lives these people live. A subtle but effective drama. Also known as *The Storm Within*. In French with English subtitles. B&W; 98m. **DIR:** Jean Cocteau. **CAST:** Jean Marais, Yvonne de Bray, Gabrielle Dorziat. **1948**

LES PATTERSON SAVES THE WORLD ★★★ Barry Humphries, the immensely popular Australian comic best known here for his character Dame Edna Everage, plays both the good dame and Sir Les Patterson, a fat, flatulent, drunken ambassador from down under. The plot, a spy-movie spoof, holds together a string of outrageous slapstick gags involving bodily functions, ethnic humor, and sexual etiquette. Not rated; it's not for kids.

105m. **DIR:** George Miller. **CAST:** Barry Humphries, Pamela Stephenson. **1987**

LES RENDEZ-VOUS D'ANNA ★★★★ Anna is a film director who lives a life of desultory detachment while traveling through Europe. She indulges in anonymous sex and is plagued by people talking relentlessly about themselves, to whom she listens with comically placid disinterest. A fascinating movie, shot with flawless fluidity. In French with English subtitles. Rated R for nudity. 120m. **DIR:** Chantal Akerman. **CAST:** Aurore Clement, Helmut Griem, Magali Noel, Lea Massari, Jean-Pierre Cassel. **1978**

LES TRICHEURS ★★1/2 A roulette addict tries to break his habit with the help of a woman he meets at the tables. Lackluster gambling drama, set in the casinos of Europe. In French with English subtitles. Not rated. 93m. **DIR:** Barbet Schroeder. **CAST:** Jacques Dutronc, Bulle Ogier, Kurt Raab. **1984**

LES VIOLONS DU BAL ★★★ Clever movie combines the story of director-star Michel Drach's childhood (in France under the Nazi occupation) and his attempts as an adult to film the story. Engaging coming-of-age story. In French with English subtitles. 108m. **DIR:** Michel Drach. **CAST:** Michel Drach, Jean-Louis Trintignant, Marie-Jose Nat. **1974**

LES VISITEURS DU SOIR ★★★ In medieval France, the devil sends two of his servants to disrupt the engagement party of a baron's daughter. A handsome but lightweight morality play. In French with English subtitles. B&W; 110m. **DIR:** Marcel Carné. **CAST:** Arletty, Jules Berry, Marie Dea, Alain Cuny. **1942**

LES VOLEURS ★★★ French filmmaker Andre Techine recyles the old brothers-on-opposite-sides-of-the-law plot, dressing it up with *Pulp Fiction*-style flashing back and forth in time. The result is well acted (especially by Laurence Cote) but overlong. Catherine Deneuve, as a lesbian professor in love with Cote, is wasted in a glorified cameo. In French with English subtitles. Rated R for violence, profanity (in subtitles), nudity, and simulated sex. 113m. **DIR:** André Téchiné. **CAST:** Daniel Auteuil, Catherine Deneuve, Laurence Cote, Benoit Magimel. **1996**

LESS THAN ZERO A movie meant to illuminate the meaninglessness of Los Angeles's post-college-crowd cool. Rated R for violence and profanity. 100m. **DIR:** Marek Kanievska. **CAST:** Andrew McCarthy, Jami Gertz, Robert Downey Jr., James Spader, Tony Bill, Nicholas Pryor, Michael Bowen. **1987 DVD**

LESSER EVIL, THE ★★★ A quartet of men are reunited when the police begin to reinvestigate a crime in which they were involved as teenagers. The cast is the best reason to see this suspense drama, though too much of the film consists of flashbacks to their teenage years. Rated R for profanity, violence, and brief nudity. 96m. **DIR:** David Mackay. **CAST:** David Paymer, Arliss Howard, Tony Goldwyn, Colm Feore. **1998**

LESSON IN LOVE, A ★★★ Gunnar Björnstrand plays a philandering gynecologist who realizes that his long-suffering wife is the woman he loves the most, and he sets out to win her back. This is a little ponderous for a true romantic comedy, but good writing and good acting move the film along and provide some funny yet realistic situations. In Swedish with subtitles. B&W; 97m. **DIR:** Ingmar Bergman. **CAST:** Gunnar Björnstrand, Eva Dahlbeck, Harriet Andersson. **1954**

LET FREEDOM RING ★★★ In the West of the 1880s, Nelson Eddy leads homesteaders against the selfish interests of a group of tycoons. Unadorned flag-waving written by Ben Hecht, but it works as Eddy sings many familiar American standards. B&W; 100m. **DIR:** Jack Conway. **CAST:** Nelson Eddy, Virginia Bruce, Victor McLaglen, Lionel Barrymore, Edward Arnold, Guy Kibbee, Charles Butterworth, H. B. Warner, Raymond Walburn. **1939**

LET HIM HAVE IT ★★★★★ One of the best films of 1991—a powerful tale of a miscarriage of justice in the London of 1952, based on the true story of two teens convicted of murdering a policeman. Peter Medak's film details how one of the kids, a sweet-natured, simpleminded adolescent, ended up on death row, when he shouldn't even have been tried. Rated R, with profanity and violence. 110m. **DIR:** Peter Medak. **CAST:** Chris Eccleston, Paul Reynolds, Tom Courtenay. **1991**

LET IT BE ★★★1/2 The last days of the Beatles are chronicled in this cinema verité production, which was originally meant to be just a documentary on the recording of an album. What emerges, however, is a portrait of four men who have outgrown their images and, sadly, one another. There are moments of abandon, in which they recapture the old magic, but overall, the movie makes it obvious that the Beatles would never get back to where they once belonged. Rated G. 80m. **DIR:** Michael Lindsay-Hogg. **CAST:** The Beatles. **1970**

LET IT RIDE ★★★1/2 One last binge at the racetrack by a chronic gambler (Richard Dreyfuss), who can't resist a hot tip on the horses, turns into a riotous fiasco in this breezy, modest comedy. Rated PG-13. 91m. **DIR:** Joe Pytka. **CAST:** Richard Dreyfuss, Teri Garr, David Johansen, Allen Garfield, Jennifer Tilly. **1989 DVD**

LET IT ROCK ★★ This ludicrous behind-the-scenes view of the music business features Dennis Hopper as a manic rock-music promoter. Rated R for nudity, profanity, and violence. 75m. **DIR:** Roland Klick. **CAST:** Dennis Hopper, Terrance Robay, David Hess. **1988**

L'ETAT SAUVAGE (THE SAVAGE STATE) ★★★ Engrossing political thriller set in 1960s Africa after independence from colonial rule. A government official returns looking for his wife, who is living with a powerful black minister in the new government. A genuine sexual potboiler. In French with English subtitles. Not rated; contains nudity and violence. 111m. **DIR:** Francis Girod. **CAST:** Jacques Dutronc, Marie-Christine Barrault, Michel Piccoli. **1978**

LETHAL CHARM ★★ Familiar tale has White House correspondent Barbara Eden playing mentor to novice Heather Locklear, only to have Locklear take over Eden's life, her son, and eventually her job. When Locklear becomes volatile, Eden uses her investigative skills to get to the bottom of things. Ho-hum made-for-TV affair. Not rated. 92m. **DIR:** Richard Michaels. **CAST:** Barbara Eden, Heather Locklear. **1990**

LETHAL GAMES Citizens of a small town band together to fight off the mob. They turn to ex-Vietnam vet Frank Stallone for assistance. Yeah, right! 83m. **DIR:** John Bowen. **CAST:** Frank Stallone, Brenda Vaccaro. **1991**

LETHAL LOLITA—AMY FISHER: MY STORY Trashy sensationalized made-for-TV movie about an im-

mature 16 year old girl and her scandalous affair with a married man. 93m. **DIR:** Bradford May. **CAST:** Ed Marinaro, Noelle Parker, Boyd Kestner, Pierrette Lynch, Kathleen Laskey. **1992**

LETHAL NINJA ★★ Ex-CIA agent journeys to Africa to rescue his wife from evil Ninjas in the employ of a Nostradamus-inspired fanatic out to poison the world's water supply. (Yes, *that* old story again!) For kick-boxing fans only. Rated R for strong violence. 83m. **DIR:** Yossi Wein. **CAST:** Ross Kettle, Karyn Hill, Frank Notaro. **1993**

LETHAL OBSESSION 🦃 Contrived suspense yarn about drugs and murder. Rated R; contains nudity, profanity, and violence. 100m. **DIR:** Peter Patzack. **CAST:** Tahnee Welch, Elliott Gould, Michael York, Peter Maffay. **1987**

LETHAL TENDER ★★ Dreary and familiar tale of terrorists holding the department of water hostage as a diversionary tactic to steal millions in bonds. Jeff Fahey looks tired as the cop jumping through bad guy Gary Busey's hoops in order to save the day. Rated R for language and violence. 93m. **DIR:** John Bradshaw. **CAST:** Jeff Fahey, Kim Coates, Gary Busey. **1996**

LETHAL WEAPON ★★★★ This fast, frantic, and wholly improbable police thriller owes its success to the chemistry between the two leads. Mel Gibson is fine as the cop on the edge (the weapon of the title). Danny Glover is equally good as his laid-back, methodical partner. Rated R for violence. 105m. **DIR:** Richard Donner. **CAST:** Mel Gibson, Danny Glover, Gary Busey, Mitchell Ryan, Tom Atkins, Darlene Love. **1987 DVD**

LETHAL WEAPON 2 ★★★1/2 Mel Gibson and Danny Glover return as odd-couple police officers Riggs and Murtaugh in this enjoyable action sequel. This time, our mismatched heroes are up against some bad guys from South Africa. Predictable but fun. Rated R for violence, profanity, nudity, and simulated sex. 110m. **DIR:** Richard Donner. **CAST:** Mel Gibson, Danny Glover, Joe Pesci, Joss Ackland, Patsy Kensit. **1989 DVD**

LETHAL WEAPON 3 ★★★1/2 More madness and mayhem from the lethal team of Mel Gibson and Danny Glover as they, with the help of comic relief Joe Pesci, go after a renegade cop who is selling formerly confiscated weapons to L.A. street gangs. It's almost too much of a good thing, as director Richard Donner and his collaborators pack the movie with every gag, shoot-out, and chase they can come up with. Rated R for violence and profanity. 117m. **DIR:** Richard Donner. **CAST:** Mel Gibson, Danny Glover, Joe Pesci, René Russo, Stuart Wilson, Darlene Love. **1992 DVD**

LETHAL WEAPON 4 ★★1/2 Maverick cops Mel Gibson and Danny Glover are back again, this time battling an Asian gangster (Hong Kong action star Jet Li) who is smuggling immigrants and counterfeit Chinese currency. The series has become a bloated, bizarre mix of slapstick and high explosives, but Gibson and Glover are as appealing as ever, and director Richard Donner somehow keeps things moving along. Rated R for violence and profanity. 125m. **DIR:** Richard Donner. **CAST:** Mel Gibson, Danny Glover, René Russo, Joe Pesci, Chris Rock, Jet Li. **1998 DVD**

LETHAL WOMAN ★★ A rape victim takes revenge by luring all involved to her island and killing them. Not rated but contains nudity, violence, and gore. 96m. **DIR:** Christian Marnham. **CAST:** Robert Lipton, Merete VanKamp, Shannon Tweed. **1989**

LET'S DANCE ★★ A listless, disappointing musical. A miscast Betty Hutton and Fred Astaire stumble through the tired story of a song-and-dance team that splits up and reunites. 112m. **DIR:** Norman Z. McLeod. **CAST:** Betty Hutton, Fred Astaire, Roland Young, Ruth Warrick. **1950**

LET'S DO IT AGAIN ★★★1/2 After scoring with *Uptown Saturday Night*, Sidney Poitier and Bill Cosby decided to reteam for this tale of a couple of lodge brothers taking on the gangsters. Rated PG. 112m. **DIR:** Sidney Poitier. **CAST:** Sidney Poitier, Bill Cosby, Jimmie Walker, Calvin Lockhart, John Amos. **1975**

LET'S GET HARRY ★★1/2 When an American (Mark Harmon) is kidnapped during a South American revolution, a group of his friends decide to bring him home. They hire a soldier of fortune (Robert Duvall) to lead them into the jungles of Colombia where, against all odds, they fight to bring Harry home. Rated R for violence and language. 98m. **DIR:** Alan Smithee. **CAST:** Robert Duvall, Gary Busey, Mark Harmon, Glenn Frey, Michael Schoeffling. **1986**

LET'S MAKE IT LEGAL ★★★ Claudette Colbert and Zachary Scott are the best players in this sophisticated comedy about marriage, divorce, and friendship. Marilyn Monroe shines in a supporting role. B&W; 74m. **DIR:** Richard Sale. **CAST:** Claudette Colbert, Marilyn Monroe, Macdonald Carey, Zachary Scott, Robert Wagner. **1951**

LET'S MAKE LOVE ★★★ A tasty soufflé filled with engaging performances. Yves Montand plays a millionaire who wants to stop a musical show because it lampoons him. When he meets cast member Marilyn Monroe, he changes his mind. He hires Milton Berle to teach him comedy, Gene Kelly to teach him dance, and Bing Crosby as a vocal coach. Monroe's "My Heart Belongs to Daddy" number is a highlight. 118m. **DIR:** George Cukor. **CAST:** Marilyn Monroe, Yves Montand, Tony Randall, Wilfrid Hyde-White. **1960**

LET'S SCARE JESSICA TO DEATH ★★ A young woman staying with some odd people out in the country witnesses all sorts of strange things, like ghosts and blood-stained corpses. Is it real, or some kind of elaborate hoax? The title tells it all in this disjointed terror tale, though it does contain a few spooky scenes. Rated PG. 89m. **DIR:** John Hancock. **CAST:** Zohra Lampert, Barton Heyman. **1971**

LET'S SPEND THE NIGHT TOGETHER ★★★1/2 In this concert film, directed by Hal Ashby, the Rolling Stones are seen rockin' and rollin' in footage shot during the band's 1981 American tour. It's a little too long—but Stones fans and hard-core rockers should love it. Rated PG for suggestive lyrics and behavior. 94m. **DIR:** Hal Ashby. **CAST:** The Rolling Stones. **1982**

LETTER, THE ★★★★ Bette Davis stars in this screen adaptation of Somerset Maugham's play as the coldly calculating wife of a rubber plantation owner (Herbert Marshall) in Malaya. In a fit of pique, she shoots her lover and concocts elaborate lies to protect herself. With tension mounting all the way, we wonder if her evil ways will eventually lead to her downfall. B&W; 95m. **DIR:** William Wyler. **CAST:** Bette Davis, Herbert Marshall, James Stephenson. **1940**

LETTER FROM AN UNKNOWN WOMAN ★★★ Disregarding the fact that concert pianist Louis Jourdan uses her without pity, beautiful Joan Fontaine stupidly continues to love him through the years. Romantic direction and smooth performances make the clichés work. B&W; 90m. **DIR:** Max Ophüls. **CAST:** Joan Fontaine, Louis Jourdan, Mady Christians, Art Smith, Erskine Sanford. **1948**

LETTER OF INTRODUCTION ★★★★ An enjoyable melodrama, this is the story of a young actress (Andrea Leeds) who seeks out the advice of an old actor (Adolphe Menjou). The aging star encourages her in her various endeavors. The relationship between the two lead characters is so real, so warm that it carries the film. B&W; 100m. **DIR:** John M. Stahl. **CAST:** Adolphe Menjou, Andrea Leeds, Edgar Bergen, George Murphy, Eve Arden, Rita Johnson, Ernest Cossart, Ann Sheridan. **1938**

LETTER TO BREZHNEV ★★★1/2 This wistful, spunky little movie presents two young women of Liverpool who befriend a couple of Russian sailors. Teresa (played by Liverpool comedienne Margi Clarke) is just after some fun, but Elaine (Alexandra Pigg) falls in love with her sailor. Peter Firth plays Elaine's love and he's the quintessence of sweetness. Alexandra Pigg gives the film some street-talking sass, and Firth imbues it with adorable innocence. 95m. **DIR:** Chris Bernard. **CAST:** Alexandra Pigg, Alfred Molina, Peter Firth, Margi Clarke. **1985**

LETTER TO MY KILLER ★★1/2 An average couple try their hand at simple blackmail in this made-for-cable original, only to find themselves in a nightmare of consequences. Starts out slow and never picks up speed. Rated PG-13 for violence. 92m. **DIR:** Janet Mayers. **CAST:** Mare Winningham, Nick Chinlund, Rip Torn. **1995**

LETTER TO THREE WIVES, A ★★★1/2 Three wives receive a letter from a friend saying that she has run off with one of their husbands. The viewer is then shown three stories that tell why each of the women's husbands might have left them. Very interesting screenplay and superb acting make this an enjoyable film. B&W; 103m. **DIR:** Joseph L. Mankiewicz. **CAST:** Jeanne Crain, Linda Darnell, Ann Sothern, Kirk Douglas, Paul Douglas, Barbara Lawrence, Jeffrey Lynn. **1949**

LETTERS FROM THE PARK ★★★★ Charming love story à la *Cyrano de Bergerac* features Victor La Place as a sensitive man who writes letters professionally in Cuba in 1913. Hired by an awkward young man who prefers hot air balloons to poetry, he begins a romantic correspondence which becomes real for him. Originally made for Spanish television, this contains mature themes. In Spanish with English subtitles. 85m. **DIR:** Tomas Gutierrez Alea. **CAST:** Victor La Place, Ivonne Lopez, Miguel Paneque. **1988**

LETTERS TO AN UNKNOWN LOVER ★★★ A soldier who has been carrying on a romance through the mail with a Frenchwoman he has never met dies. When his friend escapes from a Nazi prison camp, he pretends to be the dead man in order to get the woman and her sister to hide him. This engrossing tale, a French and British coproduction, is unrated; it contains some nudity and sexual situations. 100m. **DIR:** Peter Duffell. **CAST:** Cherie Lunghi, Yves Beneyton, Mathilda May. **1985**

LETTING THE BIRDS GO FREE ★★ Slow-moving and passionless Romance Theatre production features a homely woman who shares the endless duties of her family's small farm. Amid her daily drudgery, a mysterious stranger comes to work on their machinery. Her attraction to him is a desperate attempt to escape her boring life. Never romantic. Not rated; contains no objectionable material. 60m. **DIR:** Moira Armstrong. **CAST:** Carolyn Pickles, Tom Wilkinson, Martin Stone, Lionel Jeffries. **1987**

LEVIATHAN ★★ The crew of an undersea mining platform comes across a sunken Soviet ship that has been scuttled in an effort to keep some genetic experiment gone awry away from the world. What the miners encounter is part *Alien,* part *20,000 Leagues Under the Sea,* part *The Thing.* Since these other films are so much better, it's best to leave this one alone. Rated R for violence. 98m. **DIR:** George Pan Cosmatos. **CAST:** Peter Weller, Richard Crenna, Amanda Pays, Daniel Stern, Ernie Hudson, Meg Foster, Lisa Eilbacher, Hector Elizondo. **1989 DVD**

L'HOMME BLESSÉ (THE WOUNDED MAN) ★★★1/2 Lurid sexual psychodrama about a withdrawn young man's obsession for a street hustler he meets by chance. His frustrated lust builds until it finds its shocking release. A powerful and disturbing piece of cinema for adults only. In French with English subtitles. Not rated; contains profanity, nudity, and violence. 90m. **DIR:** Patrice Chereau. **CAST:** Jean-Hugues Anglade, Vittorio Mezzogiorno, Roland Bertin, Lisa Kreuzer. **1988**

•LIAM ★★★ When an Irish worker in 1930s Liverpool loses his job, he becomes easy prey for street-corner Fascists railing against the Jews; meanwhile, his wife copes with poverty by becoming preoccupied with their 5-year-old son's approaching first Communion. Acting is excellent, but the overly familiar story is similar to *Angela's Ashes* and suffers in comparison. Rated R for profanity and brief nudity. 91m. **DIR:** Stephen Frears. **CAST:** Ian Hart, Claire Hackett, Anthony Borrows, David Hart, Megan Burns. **2000 DVD**

LIANNA ★★★★ The problem with most motion pictures about gays is they always seem to be more concerned with sex than love. In comparison, this film, written and directed by John Sayles stands as a remarkable achievement. About a married housewife named Lianna (Linda Griffiths) who decides to have an affair with, and eventually move in with, another woman (Jane Halloren), it is a sensitive study of one woman's life and loves. Rated R for nudity, sex, and profanity. 110m. **DIR:** John Sayles. **CAST:** Linda Griffiths, Jane Halloren, Jon De Vries, Jo Henderson. **1983**

LIAR, LIAR ★★★★ This comedy with heart provides the perfect showcase for star Jim Carrey. He's a successful lawyer who finds himself magically committed to speaking only the truth, the result of a son's birthday wish. Carrey's rubber-man gyrations make the film move, but the on-target screenplay holds it all together. Rated PG-13. 87m. **DIR:** Tom Shadyac. **CAST:** Jim Carrey, Maura Tierney, Jennifer Tilly, Swoosie Kurtz, Amanda Donohoe, Jason Bernard, Cary Elwes, Mitchell Ryan, Anne Haney, Justin Cooper, Randall "Tex" Cobb. **1997 DVD**

LIARS, THE ★★ A woman and her lover pose as mother and son to gain the confidence of a rich man and then murder him for his money. Dreary melodrama. In French with English subtitles. B&W; 92m. **DIR:** Edmond Gréville. **CAST:** Dawn Addams, Jean Servais, Claude Brasseur. **1964**

LIARS' CLUB, THE ★★1/2 Somewhat interesting tale about a group of high-school friends who try to cover up a rape and end up involved in a murder. The more they try to conceal their crimes, the deeper they sink. Rated R for nudity and language. 91m. **DIR:** Jeffrey Porter. **CAST:** Wil Wheaton, Brian Krause, Michael Cudutz, Bruce Weitz. **1993**

LIAR'S MOON ★★★1/2 Two young lovers encounter unusually hostile resistance from their parents. Their elopement produces many of the expected problems faced by youths just starting out: limited finances, inexperience, and incompatibility. Rated PG for language. 106m. **DIR:** David Fisher. **CAST:** Matt Dillon, Cindy Fisher, Christopher Connelly, Hoyt Axton, Yvonne De Carlo, Susan Tyrrell. **1983 DVD**

LIBELED LADY ★★★★★ Their fame as Nick and Nora Charles in the *Thin Man* series notwithstanding, this is the finest film to have paired William Powell and Myrna Loy. They take part in a deliciously funny tale of a newspaper that, when faced with a libel suit from an angered woman, attempts to turn the libel into irrefutable fact. Spencer Tracy and Jean Harlow lend their considerable support, and the result is a delight from start to finish. B&W; 98m. **DIR:** Jack Conway. **CAST:** William Powell, Myrna Loy, Spencer Tracy, Jean Harlow. **1936**

LIBERATION OF L. B. JONES, THE 🦃 A wealthy black man is deluded into divorcing his wife because of her believed infidelity with a white cop. Rated R. 102m. **DIR:** William Wyler. **CAST:** Lola Falana, Roscoe Lee Browne, Lee J. Cobb, Lee Majors, Barbara Hershey. **1970**

LIBERTY AND BASH ★★ *Tarzan*-star Miles O'Keeffe and *Hercules/Hulk* Lou Ferrigno are featured in this typically on-par action flick about two war buddies out to stop murderous Miami drug runners. Rated R for language. 92m. **DIR:** Myrl A. Schreibman. **CAST:** Miles O'Keeffe, Lou Ferrigno. **1989**

LIBERTY HEIGHTS ★★★★ Baltimore in 1954 is the setting of this intimate, bittersweet trip down memory lane. A Jewish teen makes friends with an upper-class black girl and has his loyalty tested. His college-age brother learns that dream girl and worst nightmare can describe the same date. Their father runs a numbers racket and a burlesque club, and their mother tries to keep ethnic tradition alive in the family. This lush, warmly detailed story about issues and distinctions of race, religion, and social class gives us plenty to feel, think, and grin about. Rated R for language and sexual content. 122m. **DIR:** Barry Levinson. **CAST:** Ben Foster, Adrien Brody, Joe Mantegna, Rebekah Johnson, Carolyn Murphy, Bebe Neuwirth. **1999 DVD**

LICENSE TO DRIVE ★★★ Wildly improbable yet frenetically funny account of how young Les (Corey Haim) flunks his driver's license exam yet steals his grandfather's Cadillac for a hot date. Richard Masur is perfect as the quiet, sane father trying to deal with insanity. Rated PG-13 for profanity. 88m. **DIR:** Greg Beeman. **CAST:** Corey Haim, Corey Feldman, Carol Kane, Richard Masur, Heather Graham. **1988**

LICENSE TO KILL ★★★★ Timothy Dalton, in his second outing as James Bond, seeks revenge when his pal, former CIA-agent-turned-DEA-man Felix Leiter, is maimed and Leiter's bride is murdered. Uncommonly serious tone is a boost to the once-formulaic series, and Dalton comes into his own as the modern 007. Rated PG-13. 135m. **DIR:** John Glen. **CAST:** Timothy Dalton, Robert Davi, Carey Lowell. **1989 DVD**

•L.I.E. ★★1/2 A Long Island teenager, neglected by his father since his mother's death, comes under the wing of a neighbor, a sexual predator who preys on teenage boys. Well-acted, especially by Brian Cox as the neighbor, and unsensational (despite the rating), the film is also sluggish and shapeless, with some pivotal implausibilities in the story. Rated NC-17 for profanity and sexual themes. 97m. **DIR:** Michael Cuesta. **CAST:** Brian Cox, Paul Franklin Dano, Billy Kay, Bruce Altman, James Costa. **2001**

LIE DOWN WITH DOGS ★★★1/2 Film-school graduate Wally White wrote, directed, and stars in this hilarious exposé of one man's outrageous summer in Provincetown. White plays a reserved gay man whose job passing out handbills is going nowhere. He joins some friends for the summer, trying to get a job as a houseboy to pay his bills. Although not to everyone's taste, this film is funny and fresh. Rated R for adult situations and language. 84m. **DIR:** Wally White. **CAST:** Wally White, Kevin Mayes, Darren Dryden, Bash Halow. **1995**

LIEBELEI ★★★★ A young lieutenant's love for a Viennese girl is disrupted when he is provoked to a duel by a baron (who mistakenly believes the young man in love with his wife). One of the first masterworks by Max Ophüls, a touching evocation of imperial Vienna. A minor masterpiece. In German with English subtitles. B&W; 88m. **DIR:** Max Ophüls. **CAST:** Magda Schneider, Wolfgang Liebeneiner. **1933**

LIEBESTRAUM ★★★ A strange tale comparable to the stylings of director David Lynch. Here a young architect is enmeshed in an ill-fated love triangle when he becomes obsessed with an old office building. Rated R for sexual situations and violence. 105m. **DIR:** Mike Figgis. **CAST:** Kevin Anderson, Pamela Gidley, Kim Novak, Bill Pullman. **1991 DVD**

LIES (1986) ★★★★ Ann Dusenberry plays a starving actress who gets sucked into a complicated and treacherous plan to gain the inheritance of a rich patient in a mental hospital. The plot is complicated and the good acting balances the intensity. The best part: a great performance by Gail Strickland, who plays a character you'll love to hate. Rated R for violence, sex, nudity, and profanity. 93m. **DIR:** Ken Wheat, Jim Wheat. **CAST:** Ann Dusenberry, Gail Strickland, Bruce Davison, Clu Gulager, Terence Knox, Bert Remsen. **1986**

•LIES (1999) ★★★★ Banned in Korea, this explicit examination of a teenage girl's journey into womanhood features outstanding performances that make this more of a film about people than sex. Lee Sang Hyun and Kim Tae Yeon are both bold and beautiful as the forty-year-old sculptor named J who agrees to help 18-year-old student Y lose her virginity. What begins as a story about sexual awakening turns into an exploration

of the power sex has on its participants. In Korean with English subtitles. Not rated; contains explicit adult situations. 112m. **DIR:** Jang Sun Woo. **CAST:** Lee Sang Hyun, Kim Tae Yeon, Hye Jin Jeon, Kwon Taek Han. **1999**

LIES & WHISPERS ★★★★ Gripping drama that deals with the pain and embarrassment that a couple faces when the woman discovers that her grandfather was a Nazi war criminal. Dr. Lauren Graham, a child psychologist, meets and falls in love with a Czech author who is a candidate for minister of culture. Their romance is threatened when Graham uncovers her grandfather's secret past. This film deals with the consequences with intelligence and humanity. Rated R for language and violence. 95m. **DIR:** Roger L. Simon. **CAST:** Gina Gershon, Rade Serbedzija, Patricia Hodge, Otakar Brousek, Gordon Lovitt. **1998 DVD**

LIES BEFORE KISSES ★★★ Above-average made-for-TV vengefest features Ben Gazzara being framed for the murder of a beautiful blackmailer. The setup is obvious, but who hates him enough to do this must be revealed. Satisfying ending. 93m. **DIR:** Lou Antonio. **CAST:** Jaclyn Smith, Ben Gazzara, Nick Mancuso, Greg Evigan. **1991**

LIES MY FATHER TOLD ME ★★★1/2 Sympathetic tale of a Jewish boy growing up in a Montreal ghetto during the 1920s. Young David sees through the eyes of wonderment as his simple grandfather passes on his stories, a rich tapestry of tradition and family. Rated PG. 102m. **DIR:** Ján Kadár. **CAST:** Yossi Yadin, Jeffrey Lynas, Len Birman, Marilyn Lightstone. **1975**

LIES OF THE TWINS ★★1/2 Aidan Quinn has a field day playing identical twin psychiatrists (or *are* they actually two different people?), the gentler of whom falls in love with fashion model Isabella Rossellini. Things keep us guessing; alas, concluding events are just plain silly. Made for cable. 93m. **DIR:** Tim Hunter. **CAST:** Aidan Quinn, Isabella Rossellini, Iman, Hurd Hatfield. **1991**

LIFE ★★ Small-time hustler Eddie Murphy and innocent bystander Martin Lawrence get railroaded for a murder in 1932 Mississippi, and wind up in a hard-time prison that looks an awful lot like a country club, given how much our two stars *don't* suffer. It's all nonsense, and utterly lacking in humor: yet another Eddie Murphy vehicle that shoots for the lowest common denominator . . . and scores. Rated R for profanity and violence. **DIR:** Ted Demme. **CAST:** Eddie Murphy, Martin Lawrence, Obba Babatundé, Nick Cassavetes, Anthony Anderson. **1999 DVD**

LIFE AND ASSASSINATION OF THE KINGFISH, THE ★★★ A docudrama chronicling the life of flamboyant Louisiana politician Huey Long (Edward Asner). Told as a flashback, during the time Long lay dying from an assassin's bullet, this is an insightful look at an unforgettable time in U.S. history. 96m. **DIR:** Robert Collins. **CAST:** Edward Asner, Nicholas Pryor. **1976**

LIFE AND DEATH OF COLONEL BLIMP, THE ★★★★★ A truly superb film chronicling the life and times of a staunch for-king-and-country British soldier. Sentimentally celebrating the human spirit, it opens during World War II and unfolds through a series of flashbacks that reach as far back as the Boer War. Roger Livesey is excellent in the title role. Deborah Kerr portrays the four women in his life across four decades with charm and insight. Definitely a keeper. 163m. **DIR:** Michael Powell, Emeric Pressburger. **CAST:** Roger Livesey, Deborah Kerr, Anton Walbrook. **1943**

LIFE AND NOTHING BUT ★★★★★ This antiwar film, which focuses on a group of people attempting to find the bodies of dead soldiers—husbands, fathers, and other loved ones—after World War I, has all the elements of a true classic: unforgettable characters, romance, suspense, and magnificent visuals. Philippe Noiret adds a great characterization to his list of credits. In French with English subtitles. Rated PG. 135m. **DIR:** Bertrand Tavernier. **CAST:** Philippe Noiret, Sabine Azema. **1989**

LIFE AND NOTHING MORE . . . ★★★★ Blurring the line between fiction and reality, this exquisite Iranian film is set shortly after an earthquake that killed 50,000 people. As a filmmaker and his son search for two boys who had appeared in one of the man's films, they see how people are coping with this devastation. American viewers may initially find this rather slow, but the lyrical quality keeps building. In Iranian with English subtitles. Not rated. 91m. **DIR:** Abbas Kiarostami. **CAST:** Farhad Kheradmad, Puya Payvar. **1992**

LIFE AND TIMES OF GRIZZLY ADAMS, THE ★★ Fur trapper Dan Haggerty heads for the hills when he's unjustly accused of a crime. There he befriends an oversized bear and they live happily ever after. Rated G. 93m. **DIR:** Richard Friedenberg. **CAST:** Dan Haggerty, Don Shanks, Lisa Jones, Marjory Harper, Bozo. **1976**

LIFE AND TIMES OF HANK GREENBERG, THE ★★★1/2 An entertaining review of the career of baseball star Hank Greenberg, with an emphasis on Greenberg's inspiration to Jewish children as well as on his grappling with Depression-era anti-Semitism. Greenberg speaks for himself in interviews from throughout his career. Not rated; suitable for all audiences. 89m. **DIR:** Aviva Kempner. **CAST:** Hank Greenberg, Walter Matthau, Bob Feller, Alan M. Dershowitz, Charlie Gehringer. **1998 DVD**

LIFE AND TIMES OF JUDGE ROY BEAN, THE ★★★ Weird Western with Paul Newman as the fabled hanging judge. It has some interesting set pieces among the strangeness. Stacy Keach is outstanding as Bad Bob. Rated PG. 120m. **DIR:** John Huston. **CAST:** Paul Newman, Stacy Keach, Victoria Principal, Jacqueline Bisset, Ava Gardner. **1972**

•LIFE AS A HOUSE ★★★★ Kevin Kline does his finest work as a man forced to confront—and, hopefully, improve upon—the decisions he has made through life, in this contrived but poignant screenplay. The catalyst is a Hollywood favorite (the fatal disease), and Kline uses his last summer to renew relationships with his ex-wife (Kristin Scott Thomas) and estranged teenage son (Hayden Christensen). Slowly but surely, the three bond while fulfilling our hero's long-standing dream of building his own house on an outcropping of land overlooking the Pacific Ocean. Before long, everybody in the neighborhood is involved . . . as are we. Rated R for profanity, drug use, and sexual candor. 124m. **DIR:** Irwin Winkler. **CAST:** Kevin Kline, Kristin Scott Thomas, Hayden Christensen, Jamey Sheridan, Sam Robards, Scott Bakula, Jena Malone, Mary Steenburgen. **2001 DVD**

LIFE BEGINS FOR ANDY HARDY ★★★ Andy Hardy, fresh out of high school, tries on New York City for size, comes to grips with a mature woman, and learns a few big-city lessons before deciding college near home and hearth is best. The eleventh and one of the best in the series. B&W; 100m. **DIR:** George B. Seitz. **CAST:** Mickey Rooney, Judy Garland, Lewis Stone, Fay Holden, Ann Rutherford, Sara Haden. **1941**

LIFE IN THE THEATER, A ★★★1/2 Wonderful acting by Jack Lemmon and Matthew Broderick and a witty script by David Mamet highlight this look at theatrical actors. Lemmon and Broderick deliver all the dialogue as the old pro and the promising newcomer. A real treat to watch. Made for TV. 94m. **DIR:** Gregory Mosher. **CAST:** Jack Lemmon, Matthew Broderick. **1993**

LIFE IS BEAUTIFUL ★★★★★ This film begins as a delightful romantic comedy before taking a startling detour. The setting is WWII-era Italy, with star-director-cowriter Roberto Benigni cast as a Jewish waiter named Guido, who marries a beautiful young schoolteacher. After several years, with Italy now overrun by German soldiers, the couple and their young son are hurled into a concentration camp. Determined to shield the boy, Guido employs his quick wit to persuade the impressionable child that it is an elaborate escapade, one filled with countless traps to "trick" and "fool" lesser players into losing. Benigni's audaciousness is damn near unparalleled, because he has done the impossible by setting a film in a Jewish concentration camp and retaining both a sense of humor and the triumph of human spirit. Rated PG-13 for dramatic intensity. 115m. **DIR:** Roberto Benigni. **CAST:** Roberto Benigni, Nicoletta Braschi, Giorgio Cantarini, Giustino Durano, Sergio Bustric, Horst Buchholz. **1998 DVD**

LIFE IS SWEET ★★★★1/2 Writer-director Mike Leigh is a social visionary, who prior to his first movie *High Hopes*, enthralled and captivated Britain with his made-for-television plays. This, his second movie, is a superlative portrait of a British family: a nurturing mother, a lovably blundering father, and two daughters. The complete spectrum of human emotion is covered and evoked as we observe the family members interact. Rated R for profanity, nudity, and simulated sex. 103m. **DIR:** Mike Leigh. **CAST:** Timothy Spall, Jane Horrocks, Alison Steadman, Jim Broadbent. **1991**

LIFE LESS ORDINARY, A ★★★1/2 This manic contemporary screwball comedy will either delight or utterly baffle viewers. Put-upon janitor Ewan McGregor, seeking revenge after being fired, "kidnaps" the boss's daughter with more than a little assistance from the lady in question. It's all orchestrated by a pair of "celestial cops" who've been ordered by God to make these two young people fall in love. What follows is part musical, part comedy, part pathos, and all madness. Rated R for profanity and violence. 103m. **DIR:** Danny Boyle. **CAST:** Ewan McGregor, Cameron Diaz, Holly Hunter, Delroy Lindo, Ian Holm, Ian McNeice, Stanley Tucci, Dan Hedaya, Tony Shalhoub. **1997 DVD**

LIFE OF BRIAN ★★★★ Religious fanaticism gets a real drubbing in this irreverent and often sidesplitting comedy, which features and was created by those Monty Python crazies. Graham Chapman plays the title role of a reluctant "savior" born in a manger just down the street from Jesus Christ's. Rated R for nudity and profanity. 93m. **DIR:** Terry Jones. **CAST:** Terry Jones, John Cleese, Eric Idle, Michael Palin, Terry Gilliam, Graham Chapman. **1979 DVD**

LIFE OF EMILE ZOLA, THE ★★★★ Paul Muni is excellent in the title role of the nineteenth-century novelist who championed the cause of the wrongly accused Captain Dreyfus (Joseph Schildkraut). A lavish production! B&W; 93m. **DIR:** William Dieterle. **CAST:** Paul Muni, Joseph Schildkraut, Gale Sondergaard, Gloria Holden, Donald Crisp, Louis Calhern. **1937**

LIFE OF HER OWN, A ★★ Can a career woman find love and still have a life of her own? If she looks like Lana Turner, she obviously can in this tearjerker about two models who want careers and husbands in that order. Sluggish pacing and pretentious dialogue make this movie look like a TV soap opera. B&W; 108m. **DIR:** George Cukor. **CAST:** Lana Turner, Ray Milland, Ann Dvorak, Barry Sullivan, Louis Calhern, Tom Ewell, Jean Hagen, Sara Haden, Phyllis Kirk. **1950**

LIFE OF OHARU ★★★★1/2 All but unknown in the U.S., Japanese director Kenji Mizoguchi was one of the great artists of the cinema. This story, of a woman in feudal Japan who, after disgracing the honor of her samurai father, is sold into prostitution, may seem somewhat melodramatic to Western audiences. But Mizoguchi's art rested in his formalistic visual style, consisting of carefully composed shots, long takes, and minimal editing. In Japanese with English subtitles. B&W; 136m. **DIR:** Kenji Mizoguchi. **CAST:** Kinuyo Tanaka, Toshiro Mifune. **1952**

LIFE ON A STRING ★★★1/2 A blind musician can regain his sight only by so devoting his life to music that he breaks one thousand strings while playing his banjo. While the plot of this Chinese fable is occasionally obscure, director Chen Kaige (*Farewell My Concubine*) provides breathtaking scenery and an unforgettable battle scene. Not rated; contains no objectionable material. 110m. **DIR:** Chen Kaige. **CAST:** Liu Zhong Yuan, Huang Lei. **1990 DVD**

LIFE ON THE MISSISSIPPI ★★★ A veteran riverboat pilot takes on a young apprentice. Good ensemble acting and beautiful location photography enhance this TV movie based on Mark Twain's novel about his own experiences during the glorious days of riverboats. 115m. **DIR:** Peter H. Hunt. **CAST:** Robert Lansing, David Knell, James Keane, Donald Madden. **1980**

LIFE 101 ★★★ Though predictable, you should still find yourself caught up in this sweetly goofy look at the life of a college frosh (Corey Haim) in the 1960s. There is nothing new to the life lessons here, but both Haim and Keith Coogan charm their way through this romantic comedy. Not rated; contains profanity and sexual situations. 95m. **DIR:** Redge Mahaffey. **CAST:** Corey Haim, Keith Coogan, Ami Dolenz, Louis Mandylor, Kyle Cody, Traci Adell. **1995**

•LIFE OR SOMETHING LIKE IT ★★ Angelina Jolie is laughably, ludicrously miscast as a Seattle TV feature reporter, who decides to reevaluate her life after a homeless street seer predicts that she'll die the following week. Jolie's TV newsroom persona and working environment are just as unbelievable as the notion that a real-world individual would pay the slightest attention to such claptrap, and she shares no chemistry with romantic costar Edward Burns. This one's little more than

a waste of time. Rated PG-13 for profanity, brief violence, and sexual candor. 104m. **DIR:** Stephen Herek. **CAST:** Angelina Jolie, Edward Burns, Tony Shalhoub, Stockard Channing, Christian Kane, Melissa Errico. **2002 DVD**

LIFE STINKS ★★1/2 A kinder, gentler Mel Brooks directed, cowrote, and stars in this message movie about a rich land developer who bets he can spend a month on the streets of Los Angeles. Even though the film is quite funny, he unfortunately tends to be a tad preachy. Rated PG-13 for profanity and suggested sex. 91m. **DIR:** Mel Brooks. **CAST:** Mel Brooks, Lesley Ann Warren, Jeffrey Tambor, Stuart Pankin, Howard Morris. **1991**

LIFE WITH FATHER ★★★★ A warm, witty, charming, nostalgic memoir of life and the coming of age of author Clarence Day in turn-of-the-century New York City. Centering on his staid, eccentric father (William Powell), the film is a 100 percent delight. Based on the long-running Broadway play. 118m. **DIR:** Michael Curtiz. **CAST:** William Powell, Irene Dunne, Edmund Gwenn, ZaSu Pitts, Jimmy Lydon, Elizabeth Taylor, Martin Milner. **1947 DVD**

LIFE WITH MIKEY ★★★1/2 The story of a former child star who runs a talent agency has built-in laugh spots. Especially with Michael J. Fox as the agent who needs a child star for a commercial or his agency will go under. Fox has a handle on comic reactions and gets to use them. Rated PG. 106m. **DIR:** James Lapine. **CAST:** Michael J. Fox, Nathan Lane, Cyndi Lauper, Christina Vidal. **1993**

•LIFE WITHOUT DICK ★★ You really want to love this charming little dark comedy, but by the time it ends the affair is so over. When Colleen (Sarah Jessica Parker) learns that her boyfriend Dick (Johnny Knoxville) has been unfaithful, she decides to scare him with a gun, which accidentally goes off and kills him. His death then causes problems for novice hit man Daniel (Harry Connick Jr.), who has been hired to whack Dick. As Colleen and Daniel begin a passionate love affair, they must decide what to do with the stiff. Sounds better than it is. Rated PG-13 for language and violence. 96m. **DIR:** Bix Skahill. **CAST:** Sarah Jessica Parker, Harry Connick Jr., Johnny Knoxville, Teri Garr, Craig Ferguson. **2000 DVD**

LIFEBOAT ★★★1/2 A microcosm of American society, survivors of a World War II torpedoing, adrift in a lifeboat, nearly come a cropper when they take a Nazi aboard. Dumbly dismissed as an artistic failure by most critics, it has some ridiculous flaws, but is nonetheless an interesting and engrossing film. Tunnel-voiced Tallulah Bankhead is tops in this seagoing *Grand Hotel*. Look for Hitchcock's pictorial trademark in a newspaper. B&W; 96m. **DIR:** Alfred Hitchcock. **CAST:** Tallulah Bankhead, John Hodiak, William Bendix, Walter Slezak, Henry Hull, Canada Lee, Hume Cronyn, Heather Angel. **1944**

LIFEFORCE ★★ In this disappointing and disjointed science-fiction–horror film by director Tobe Hooper (*Poltergeist*), ancient vampires from outer space return to Earth via Halley's Comet to feed on human souls. Rated R for violence, gore, nudity, profanity, and suggested sex. 96m. **DIR:** Tobe Hooper. **CAST:** Steve Railsback, Peter Firth, Mathilda May, Frank Finlay, Michael Gothard. **1985 DVD**

LIFEFORCE EXPERIMENT, THE ★★★1/2 Scientist Donald Sutherland is working on a top-secret project, and the CIA sends agent Mimi Kuzyk to investigate. Appalled by what she discovers, Kuzyk wants her bosses to stop the experiment, but they have other plans. Good, but not great made-for-cable adaptation of the Daphne du Maurier story. 96m. **DIR:** Piers Haggard. **CAST:** Donald Sutherland, Mimi Kuzyk, Vlasta Vrana, Corin Nemec, Hayley Reynolds, Miguel Fernandes, Michael Rudder, Michael J. Reynolds. **1994**

LIFEFORM ★★★ Okay *Alien* knockoff begins when a lost Mars probe returns to Earth with an alien egg attached. Before you can say "space-pod," the little dickens has hatched and a tiny monster with an attitude becomes a big monster with a body count. Slow at times but otherwise engaging film. Rated R for violence, profanity, and gore. 90m. **DIR:** Mark H. Baker. **CAST:** Cotter Smith, Deirdre O'Connell, Robert Wisdom, Ryan Philippe. **1995**

LIFEGUARD ★★1/2 After his fifteen-year high school reunion, Sam Elliott begins to feel twinges of fear and guilt. How long can he go on being a lifeguard? Shouldn't he be making the move into a career with a future? The film is likable and easygoing, like its star. If your interest starts to drift, Elliott's charisma will pull you back. Rated PG. 96m. **DIR:** Daniel Petrie. **CAST:** Sam Elliott, Anne Archer, Kathleen Quinlan, Parker Stevenson, Stephen Young. **1976**

LIFELINE ★★ This mildly interesting, but wholly unrealistic, made-for-cable original is about a woman's quest to find her daughter, who has been kidnapped by a white-slave cartel. Not rated; contains violence. 95m. **DIR:** Fred Gerber. **CAST:** Lorraine Bracco, Lisa Jakub, Jean-Marc Barr, Stephen Shellen, Victor Lanoux. **1995 DVD**

LIFEPOD ★★★ It's Alfred Hitchcock's *Lifeboat* in outer space as eight people are trapped in a crippled escape pod after an intergalactic passenger ship is blown up en route. Supplies are short and communications down, plus one of the survivors seems intent on killing off the others. Good special effects and performances help make this film involving, though unexceptional. Made for TV. 90m. **DIR:** Ron Silver. **CAST:** Robert Loggia, Ron Silver, Jessica Tuck, Stan Shaw, Adam Storke, Kelli Williams, Ed Gale, C.C.H. Pounder. **1993**

LIFT, THE ★★★ Grizzly supernatural thriller about a demonic elevator that mysteriously claims the lives of innocent riders. The film mixes dark humor with the macabre. This Dutch-made horror film was a major box-office hit in Europe. Rated R for nudity and graphic violence. In Dutch with English subtitles. Also available in a dubbed version. 95m. **DIR:** Dick Maas. **CAST:** Huub Stapel. **1985**

LIGHT AT THE END OF THE WORLD, THE 🦃 Kirk Douglas is a lighthouse keeper whose isolated island is invaded by ruthless pirates. Tedious. Not rated, contains violence and sexual suggestions. 126m. **DIR:** Kevin Billington. **CAST:** Kirk Douglas, Yul Brynner, Samantha Eggar, Jean-Claude Druou, Fernando Rey. **1971**

LIGHT IN THE FOREST, THE ★★1/2 James MacArthur stars as a young man who had been captured and raised by the Delaware Indians and is later returned to his white family. Generally a good story with adequate acting, the ending is much too contrived and trite. 92m.

DIR: Herschel Daugherty. **CAST:** James MacArthur, Fess Parker, Wendell Corey, Joanne Dru, Carol Lynley. **1958**

LIGHT IN THE JUNGLE, THE 🦃 Malcolm McDowell plays Dr. Albert Schweitzer as he brings medicine and music to Africa. Schweitzer, who won the Nobel Peace Prize in 1953, deserves a better bio than this static, sentimental, and unfulfilling bit of window dressing. Rated PG. 91m. **DIR:** Gary Hofmeyr. **CAST:** Malcolm McDowell, Susan Strasberg. **1990**

LIGHT IT UP ★★1/2 Decorated New York cop brings a troubled past to his new job as security guard. He becomes a hostage when an altercation fueled by unbearable conditions at a Queens high school escalates into a standoff between students and police. It's a cautionary tale about tolerance, bureaucratic neglect, and emotional baggage and plays better than it sometimes deserves due to its highly talented cast. Rated R for violence and language. 100m. **DIR:** Craig Bolotin. **CAST:** Forest Whitaker, Usher Raymond, Robert Ri'chard, Clifton Collins Jr., Rosario Dawson, Sara Gilbert, Judd Nelson. **1999 DVD**

LIGHT OF DAY ★★1/2 The dead-end lives of a Cleveland bar band. There's Michael J. Fox as the guitarist willing to compromise in life for some stability. And there's his nihilistic sister (Joan Jett), the leader of the group who says that the beat of the music is all-important. Rated PG-13. 107m. **DIR:** Paul Schrader. **CAST:** Michael J. Fox, Gena Rowlands, Joan Jett, Jason Miller, Michael McKean. **1987**

LIGHT SLEEPER ★★★ 40 year old drug delivery boy (Willem Dafoe) must come to terms with his future when his boss (Susan Sarandon) decides to shut down her upscale drug service. A very moody piece, with fine performances by Dafoe and Sarandon. Rated R for profanity and violence. 103m. **DIR:** Paul Schrader. **CAST:** Willem Dafoe, Susan Sarandon, Dana Delany, David Clennon, Mary Beth Hurt, Victor Garber, Jane Adams. **1992 DVD**

LIGHTHORSEMEN, THE ★★★1/2 Vivid dramatization of the encounter between the Australian and Turkish forces at Beersheba in the North African desert during World War I. Film's main focus is on a young recruit who cannot bring himself to kill in battle. Beautiful cinematography and fine performances by the entire cast make this one a winner. Rated PG. 110m. **DIR:** Simon Wincer. **CAST:** Jon Blake, Peter Phelps, Tony Bonner, Bill Kerr, John Walton, Sigrid Thornton. **1988**

LIGHTNIN' CRANDALL ★★★★ Bob Steele buys a ranch that is sandwiched between two feuding cattle ranches. Terrific action and stunt work make this one a cavalcade of fast thrills, and one of Steele's best. B&W; 60m. **DIR:** Sam Newfield. **CAST:** Bob Steele, Lois January, Dave O'Brien, Charles King. **1937**

LIGHTNING INCIDENT, THE 🦃 Absolutely laughable saga of a psychic woman (Nancy McKeon) whose newborn son is kidnapped by voodoo cultists. Moderately violent; made for cable. Rated R for language and violence. 90m. **DIR:** Michael Switzer. **CAST:** Nancy McKeon, Tantoo Cardinal, Elpidia Carrillo, Polly Bergen, Tim Ryan. **1991**

LIGHTNING JACK ★★★ Easygoing outlaw Paul Hogan justs wants to be wanted—by the law—but his attempts at infamy are continually thwarted. It's the mild, mild West, with Cuba Gooding Jr. supplying most of the laughs as Hogan's mute sidekick in a pleasant movie that should please the star's fans. Rated PG-13 for suggested sex and light violence. 98m. **DIR:** Simon Wincer. **CAST:** Paul Hogan, Cuba Gooding Jr., Beverly D'Angelo, Kamala Dawson, Pat Hingle, Richard Riehle, L. Q. Jones, Frank McRae. **1994 DVD**

LIGHTNING OVER WATER ★★★1/2 This haunting film chronicles the final days in the life of American film director Nicholas Ray, whose movies include *Rebel Without a Cause*, *Johnny Guitar*, and *In a Lonely Place*. Wim Wenders presents a warm and gentle portrait of the director as he slowly dies from cancer. Filmed on location in Ray's loft in New York City. Poignant and unforgettable. 91m. **DIR:** Wim Wenders. **CAST:** Nicholas Ray, Wim Wenders. **1980**

LIGHTNING, THE WHITE STALLION 🦃 In this disappointing family film, Mickey Rooney plays a down-on-his-luck gambler who owns a champion jumper. Rated PG. 93m. **DIR:** William A. Levey. **CAST:** Mickey Rooney, Susan George. **1986**

LIGHTS, CAMERA, ACTION, LOVE ★★ This Romance Theatre production about an actress who must choose between a cameraman and her director could easily be dismissed for its poor acting, inane dialogue, and contrived plot. Its soap-opera style, however, may appeal to those hooked on either soaps or Harlequin romances. Introduced by Louis Jourdan. Not rated; contains no objectionable material. 97m. **DIR:** Jim Balden. **CAST:** Laura Johnson, Gary Hudson, Kathleen Nolan, Elissa Leeds, Robert Phelps. **1972**

LIGHTS OF OLD SANTA FE ★★★ A sneaky rival rodeo owner has his eyes on Dale Evans's show, and her, too! Roy Rogers and sidekick Gabby Hayes to the rescue. No dramatic climax, just a big rodeo finale weakens this one. B&W; 78m. **DIR:** Frank McDonald. **CAST:** Roy Rogers, George "Gabby" Hayes, Dale Evans, Tom Keene, Lloyd Corrigan. **1944**

LIGHTSHIP, THE ★★ The chief interest in this allegorical suspense drama is in seeing Robert Duvall play an over-the-top villain. But the story itself—a trio of sadistic bank robbers hijack a floating, anchored lighthouse and the ship's pacifist captain (Klaus Maria Brandauer) tries to stop his crew from fighting back—is short on suspense. Rated R. 90m. **DIR:** Jerzy Skolimowski. **CAST:** Robert Duvall, Klaus Maria Brandauer, Michael Lyndon. **1986**

LIKE FATHER, LIKE SON ★★ Father and son (Dudley Moore and Kirk Cameron) accidentally transfer brains. The film too often sinks to tasteless and juvenile stunts to spice up the lone idea. Rated PG-13. 99m. **DIR:** Rod Daniel. **CAST:** Dudley Moore, Kirk Cameron, Margaret Colin, Catharine Hicks, Sean Astin, Patrick O'Neal. **1987**

LIKE WATER FOR CHOCOLATE ★★★★ Romance, fantasy, comedy, and drama blend in delicious fashion. Based on the celebrated novel by Laura Esquivel, the movie depicts a young woman whose engagement is thwarted by her selfish mother. The frustrated woman transfers her passion into her cooking, which takes on a supernatural quality. There is a magical aura to the film, which is also extremely sensual. In Spanish with English subtitles. Rated R for nudity and suggested sex. 113m. **DIR:** Alfonso Arau. **CAST:** Lumi Cavazos, Marco

Leonardi, Regina Torne, Mario Ivan Martinez. **1993 DVD**

LI'L ABNER (1940) ★★ The first of two filmed versions of Al Capp's popular comic strip boasts a great cast of silent film's best clowns. B&W; 78m. **DIR:** Albert S. Rogell. **CAST:** Granville Owen, Martha Driscoll, Buster Keaton, Kay Sutton, Edgar Kennedy, Chester Conklin, Billy Bevan, Al St. John. **1940**

LI'L ABNER (1959) ★★★★ A perfectly delightful combination of satire, music, and cartoonish fun based on the popular Broadway musical with most of the original cast. The highlight is the Sadie Hawkins Day race in which the women in Dogpatch get to marry the man they catch. With such songs as "Bring Them Back the Way They Was," "The Country's in the Very Best of Hands," and "I'm Past My Prime." 112m. **DIR:** Melvin Frank. **CAST:** Peter Palmer, Leslie Parrish, Julie Newmar, Stubby Kaye, Stella Stevens, Howard St. John, Billie Hayes, Robert Strauss. **1959**

LILACS IN THE SPRING (LET'S MAKE UP) 🦃 Errol Flynn is much too braggadocio-like in this English-made musical about a highborn lady trying to decide which suitor to marry. Flynn looks embarrassed and well he should be with this script. 94m. **DIR:** Herbert Wilcox. **CAST:** Errol Flynn, Anna Neagle, David Farrar. **1954**

LILI ★★★★ "Hi Lili, Hi Lili, Hi Low," the famous song by composer Bronislau Kaper, is just one of the delights in this musical fantasy about a French orphan who tags along with a carnival and a self-centered puppeteer. A certified pleasure to keep your spirits up. 81m. **DIR:** Charles Walters. **CAST:** Leslie Caron, Mel Ferrer, Zsa Zsa Gabor, Jean-Pierre Aumont. **1953**

LILI MARLEEN ★★★1/2 The popular song of the Forties and the wartime adventures of the singer of the song, who became known as Lili to the German troops, are the basis for this engrossing film. In German with English subtitles. Rated R because of nudity and implied sex. 120m. **DIR:** Rainer Werner Fassbinder. **CAST:** Hanna Schygulla, Giancarlo Giannini, Mel Ferrer. **1981**

LILIES ★★ A Catholic bishop, lured to a prison to hear a dying inmate's confession, is treated instead to a reenactment of scenes from his own past, when he and the inmate were students together. Pretentious, contrived, and amateurishly acted, with nearly incoherent dialogue, this affected film inexplicably won several awards. Not rated; contains mature themes, sexual content, and brief nudity. 95m. **DIR:** John Greyson. **CAST:** Ian D. Clark, Marcel Sabourin, Jason Cadieux, Danny Gilmore, Brent Carver, Matthew Ferguson. **1996 DVD**

LILIES OF THE FIELD ★★★★ Sidney Poitier won an Academy Award for his portrayal of a handyman who happens upon a group of nuns who have fled from East Germany and finds himself building a chapel for them. With little or no buildup, the movie went on to become a big hit. B&W; 93m. **DIR:** Ralph Nelson. **CAST:** Sidney Poitier, Lilia Skala. **1963 DVD**

LILIES OF THE FIELD ★★ Corinne Griffith loses custody of her child and finds a new life as a show girl. A real weeper in the most mawkish tarnished-woman tradition. Stolid and overwrought. B&W; 65m. **DIR:** Alexander Korda. **CAST:** Corinne Griffith, Ralph Forbes. **1930**

LILITH ★★ This is an intriguing, somber, frequently indecipherable journey into the darker depths of the human psyche. Warren Beatty is a young psychiatric therapist at a mental institute who falls in love with a beautiful schizophrenic patient (Jean Seberg), with tragic results. Visually impressive, it remains dramatically frustrating due to its ambiguous blending of sanity and madness. B&W; 114m. **DIR:** Robert Rossen. **CAST:** Warren Beatty, Jean Seberg, Peter Fonda, Kim Hunter, Anne Meacham, Jessica Walter, Gene Hackman. **1964**

LILLIE ★★★★ The fascinating, fashionable, passionate, scandal-marked life of Edwardian beauty Lillie Langtry, international stage star and mistress of Edward, Prince of Wales, heir to Queen Victoria, is colorfully told in this excellent PBS series of manners and mannerisms. **DIR:** Tony Wharmby. **CAST:** Francesca Annis, Peter Egan, Anton Rodgers. **1977 DVD**

LILY DALE ★★1/2 Horton Foote's claustrophobic stageplay makes an unwieldy transition to the screen. The result is an awkward series of confrontations between people who explain neither themselves nor their motives during an estranged son's visit with his mother and high-strung sister. Rated PG. 95m. **DIR:** Peter Masterson. **CAST:** Mary Stuart Masterson, Sam Shepard, Stockard Channing, Tim Guinee, John Slattery, Jean Stapleton. **1996 DVD**

LILY IN LOVE ★★★★ Christopher Plummer is superb as an aging, egocentric actor who disguises himself as a younger man in an attempt to snag a plum role in a film written by his wife (Maggie Smith), and succeeds all too well. *Lily in Love* is a marvelously warm and witty adult comedy. Not rated, the film has some profanity. 105m. **DIR:** Karoly Makk. **CAST:** Christopher Plummer, Maggie Smith, Elke Sommer, Adolph Green. **1985**

LIMBIC REGION, THE ★★1/2 Dedicated cop Edward James Olmos alienates family and friends while obsessing over a serial murderer clearly patterned on San Francisco's Zodiac killer, in this mildly intriguing but ultimately boring drama. Scripters Todd Johnson and Patrick Ranahan spend too much time with the reenacted murders and not enough with Olmos; the flashback narration is also intrusive. Rated R for violence, profanity, nudity, and simulated sex. 95m. **DIR:** Michael Pattinson. **CAST:** Edward James Olmos, George Dzundza, Roger R. Cross, Gwynyth Walsh. **1996**

LIMBO ★★★ The plot here scarcely does the fascinating characters justice, and the unexpectedly abrupt fade-out is infuriatingly oblique. The story, set in modern-day Alaska, concerns a fisherman turned land-based handyman after a decades-old tragedy from which he still hasn't recovered. He catches the eye of a perky lounge singer who's got problems of her own when it comes to handling her clearly troubled teenage daughter. Unexpected circumstances isolate this trio, and what begins as an interesting ensemble character drama transforms into a fight for survival. Rated R for profanity, earthy dialogue, and brief violence. 126m. **DIR:** John Sayles. **CAST:** David Strathairn, Mary Elizabeth Mastrantonio, Vanessa Martinez, Kris Kristofferson, Casey Siemaszko. **1999 DVD**

LIMELIGHT ★★★1/2 Too long and too much Charlie Chaplin (who trimmed Buster Keaton's part when it became obvious he was stealing the film), this is neverthe-

less a poignant excursion. Chaplin is an aging music hall comic on the skids who saves a ballerina (Claire Bloom) from suicide and, while bolstering her hopes, regains his confidence. The score, by Chaplin, is haunting. B&W; 145m. **DIR:** Charles Chaplin. **CAST:** Charlie Chaplin, Claire Bloom, Buster Keaton, Sydney Chaplin, Nigel Bruce. **1952 DVD**

LIMEY, THE ★★★★ Upon his release from a British prison, a professional thief (Terence Stamp) journeys to Southern California, where he hopes to learn the truth about his daughter's mysterious death. The trail leads him to a high-rolling record producer (Peter Fonda) involved with underworld figures. Stylishly directed by Steven Soderbergh and filled with outstanding performances. Rated R for violence, profanity, and brief nudity. 90m. **DIR:** Steven Soderbergh. **CAST:** Terence Stamp, Peter Fonda, Lesley Ann Warren, Luis Guzman, Barry Newman, Joe Dallesandro, Nicky Katt, Bill Duke, Amelia Heinle, Melissa George. **1999 DVD**

LIMIT UP ★★ Nancy Allen stars as a woman who wants to be a trader with Chicago's Mercantile Exchange. She's enticed by one of Satan's disciples into a contract for her soul. Harmless, predictable. Watch for cameos by Sally Kellerman and Ray Charles. Rated PG-13 for profanity. 88m. **DIR:** Richard Martini. **CAST:** Nancy Allen, Dean Stockwell, Brad Hall, Danitra Vance. **1989**

LINCOLN ASSASSINATION, THE ★★★★ A two-part History Channel production that is as addictive as any fictional drama. Everyone knows the basics, but this painstakingly outlines the events up to and after the assassination, including far-reaching effects. Narrated by Tom Berenger and featuring historical photographs, combined with interviews of both historians and descendants of some of the participants. Not rated. 100m. **DIR:** Laura Verklan. **1995**

LINDA ★★★★ In this made-for-cable movie based on a John D. MacDonald novella, two neighborhood couples become good friends and go on vacation together. Tensions build and one wife shoots the other couple. Thus starts one very twisted plot. Good acting and a suspenseful plot keep the viewer watching. Rated PG-13 for violence. 88m. **DIR:** Nathaniel Gutman. **CAST:** Virginia Madsen, Richard Thomas, Ted McGinley, Laura Harrington, T. E. Russell. **1993**

LINDBERGH KIDNAPPING CASE, THE ★★★ Still another look at one of this century's most famous and fascinating tragedies, this made-for-television version is above average. Anthony Hopkins rates four stars as Bruno Hauptmann, the man convicted and executed for the crime. 150m. **DIR:** Buzz Kulik. **CAST:** Cliff De Young, Anthony Hopkins, Joseph Cotten, Denise Alexander, Sian Barbara Allen, Martin Balsam, Peter Donat, Dean Jagger, Walter Pidgeon. **1976**

LINE KING, THE ★★★★ Al Hirschfeld, the cartoonist whose distinctive ink caricatures have graced *The New York Times* and other publications for seventy years, is the subject of this appealing documentary. While Hirschfeld's rich and varied life makes this an appealing film for most audiences, it is especially recommended to theater buffs, as many Broadway luminaries can be seen paying tribute to the artist. Not rated. 87m. **DIR:** Susan W. Dryfoos. **1996**

LINGUINI INCIDENT, THE ★★ David Bowie's even performance as a man desperate to get married can't compensate for Rosanna Arquette's annoyingly brittle portrayal of a would-be escape artist. The two join with hilarious Eszter Balint to rob an ultra-trendy restaurant. Rated R for profanity. 93m. **DIR:** Richard Shepard. **CAST:** Rosanna Arquette, David Bowie, Eszter Balint, Andre Gregory, Buck Henry, Marlee Matlin. **1992**

LINK ★★1/2 A student (Elisabeth Shue) takes a job with an eccentric anthropology professor (Terence Stamp) and finds herself menaced by a powerful, intelligent ape named Link. The story leaves a number of questions unanswered, but the film can be praised for taking the old cliché of an ape being on the loose and making it surprisingly effective. Rated R for profanity, brief nudity, and violence. 103m. **DIR:** Richard Franklin. **CAST:** Terence Stamp, Elisabeth Shue. **1986 DVD**

LION AND THE HAWK, THE ★★★ Turkey in 1923 is the backdrop for this film about a young rebel (Simon Dutton) who runs off with a woman betrothed to a powerful regional governor's nephew. Not rated; has sex, nudity, and violence. 105m. **DIR:** Peter Ustinov. **CAST:** Peter Ustinov, Herbert Lom, Simon Dutton, Leonie Mellinger, Denis Quilley, Michael Elphick. **1983**

LION IN WINTER, THE ★★★★1/2 Acerbic retelling of the clash of wits between England's King Henry II (Peter O'Toole) and Eleanor of Aquitaine (Katharine Hepburn), adapted by James Goldman from his Broadway play. Hepburn won an Oscar for her part, and it's quite well played. The story's extended power struggle rages back and forth, with Henry and Eleanor striking sparks throughout. Rated PG. 135m. **DIR:** Anthony Harvey. **CAST:** Katharine Hepburn, Peter O'Toole, Anthony Hopkins, John Castle, Timothy Dalton, Nigel Terry. **1968 DVD**

LION IS IN THE STREETS, A ★★★1/2 An overlooked, and neglected, movie with James Cagney as a southern hustler and con artist, making it big in politics, stepping on anyone and everyone he meets. In lesser hands than Cagney's, and his favorite director Raoul Walsh, this would be only so-so, but with them it packs a wallop. 88m. **DIR:** Raoul Walsh. **CAST:** James Cagney, Barbara Hale, Anne Francis, Jeanne Cagney, Lon Chaney Jr. **1953**

LION KING, THE ★★★★1/2 Yet another winner from the modern-day Disney animation masters focuses on a young cub sent into exile when his father is betrayed and killed by a power-hungry sibling. Combining some surprisingly hard-edged moments with plenty of comedy and music, *The Lion King* sets another high-water mark for animated storytelling. Jeremy Irons is outstanding as the voice of the treacherous and scheming Uncle Scar. Rated G. 87m. **DIR:** Roger Allers, Rob Minkoff. **1994**

•LION KING II: SIMBA'S PRIDE ★★★1/2 Thoroughly enjoyable direct-to-video sequel reunites the original voice talent from the first film, and while the music and animation aren't nearly as sharp, a grand sense of adventure and excellent life lessons bring the film into focus. Despite Simba and Nala's insistence that their new daughter Kiara stay away from the Outlands, she sneaks away and meets exiled lion cub Kovu. Kovu's mother, Zira, sees the budding relationship as a way to exact revenge on Simba, and sets into motion a plan to have him killed and take over the pride. Everyone's favorite characters make appearances, while the new additions only

add to the fun. Features the voice talents of Matthew Broderick, Neve Campbell, James Earl Jones, Andy Dick, Nathan Lane, Ernie Sabella, Robert Guillaume, and James Marsden. Rated G. 81m. **DIR:** Rob LaDuca, Darrell Rooney. **1998 DVD**

LION OF AFRICA, THE ★★ This HBO action film is long-winded and a tad too derivative of *Romancing the Stone*. Odd couple Brian Dennehy and Brooke Adams race across Africa with a hot rock that attracts a host of bad guys. Not rated, has violence and profanity. 110m. **DIR:** Kevin Connor. **CAST:** Brian Dennehy, Brooke Adams, Don Warrington, Carl Andrews, Katharine Schofield. **1987**

LION OF THE DESERT ★★★1/2 This epic motion picture gives an absorbing portrait of the 1929–31 war in the North African deserts of Libya when Bedouin troops on horseback faced the tanks and mechanized armies of Mussolini. Anthony Quinn is Omar Mukhtar, the desert lion who became a nationalist and a warrior at the age of 52 and fought the Italians until they captured and hanged him twenty years later. Rated PG. 162m. **DIR:** Moustapha Akkad. **CAST:** Anthony Quinn, Oliver Reed, Rod Steiger. **1981 DVD**

LION, THE WITCH AND THE WARDROBE, THE ★★★1/2 Four children pass through a wardrobe into a wondrous land of mythical creatures where an evil Ice Queen has been terrorizing her subjects. This enjoyable made-for-television cartoon was based on C. S. Lewis's *Chronicles of Narnia*. 95m. **DIR:** Bill Melendez. **1979**

LIONHEART (1986) ★★★ On his way to join King Richard's crusade in France, a young knight is joined by a ragtag band of kids on the run from the evil Black Prince. It's enjoyable and suitable for children. It's also captioned for the hearing impaired. Rated PG. 105m. **DIR:** Franklin J. Schaffner. **CAST:** Eric Stoltz, Gabriel Byrne, Nicola Cowper, Dexter Fletcher. **1986**

LIONHEART (1991) ★★ In this lackluster Jean-Claude Van Damme vehicle, he plays a foreign legionnaire who comes to the U.S. after his brother is killed—all just an excuse for the usual string of martial arts battles. Rated R for violence, profanity, and nudity. 105m. **DIR:** Sheldon Lettich. **CAST:** Jean-Claude Van Damme, Harrison Page, Deborah Rennard, Lisa Pelikan, Ashley Johnson. **1991 DVD**

LIP SERVICE (1988) ★★★1/2 This HBO film exposes the decline of TV news shows in an offbeat, at times hilarious, style. Old-timer Paul Dooley is forced to share his early morning show with a brash, brainless youngster (Griffin Dunne) who specializes in cheap theatrics. Contains profanity. 77m. **DIR:** W. H. Macy. **CAST:** Griffin Dunne, Paul Dooley. **1988**

L.I.P. SERVICE (1999) 🦃 Soft-core romp has three private eyes following a porn star for a client in this poor excuse for coupling. Available in two editions, R-rated and not rated; both feature nudity and simulated sex. 90m. **DIR:** Art Carnage. **CAST:** Zoe Paul, Venessa Blair, Elina Madison. **1999**

LIPSTICK 🦃 Model is sexually molested by a composer. Rated R. 89m. **DIR:** Lamont Johnson. **CAST:** Margaux Hemingway, Mariel Hemingway, Anne Bancroft, Perry King, Chris Sarandon. **1976**

LIPSTICK CAMERA ★★ An aspiring television newscaster uses a miniature camera to get a scoop and impress her idol. But after novice reporter Ele Keats has the film developed, someone makes every attempt to silence her and retrieve the film. Pedestrian and underexposed. Rated R for nudity, adult situations, and violence. 93m. **DIR:** Mike Bonifer. **CAST:** Brian Wimmer, Ele Keats, Terry O'Quinn, Sandahl Bergman, Charlotte Lewis, Corey Feldman. **1993 DVD**

LIQUID SKY ★★★1/2 An alien spaceship lands on Earth in search of chemicals produced in the body during sex. One of the aliens enters the life of a new wave fashion model and feeds off her lovers, most of whom she's more than happy to see dead. *Liquid Sky* alternately shocks and amuses us with this unusual, stark, and ugly—but somehow fitting—look at an American subculture. Rated R for profanity, violence, rape, and suggested sex. 112m. **DIR:** Slava Tsukerman. **CAST:** Anne Carlisle, Paula E. Sheppard. **1983 DVD**

LISA ★★ A teenage girl plays flirtatious sex games on the telephone, unaware that her latest "partner" is a vicious serial killer. Implausible plot, cheap thrills. Rated PG-13. 95m. **DIR:** Gary A. Sherman. **CAST:** Cheryl Ladd, D. W. Moffett, Staci Keanan. **1990**

•LISA PICARD IS FAMOUS ★★1/2 *Waiting for Guffman* raised the bar on fake documentaries so high in 1997 that this comedy about show business feels thin and only mildly amusing. A filmmaker selects an aspiring—and promising—actress as the subject of his latest documentary. He can then chronicle the changes in her life down to the way she walks that celebrity walk and talks that celebrity talk. Her only companions are a nerdy boyfriend and a gay who launches a one-man way off-Broadway show about homophobia. The film also features cameos from several famous movie stars as themselves. Not rated. 90m. **DIR:** Griffin Dunne. **CAST:** Laura Kirk, Nat DeWolf, Daniel London, Griffin Dunne. **2001**

LISBON ★★ Maureen O'Hara's husband is in a communist prison. International gentleman thief Claude Rains hires Ray Milland to rescue him. Not James Bond caliber. Not *To Catch a Thief* classy. Not really worth much. 90m. **DIR:** Ray Milland. **CAST:** Ray Milland, Claude Rains, Maureen O'Hara, Francis Lederer, Percy Marmont. **1956**

LISBON STORY ★★★1/2 Commissioned to make a film portrait of Lisbon, German director Wim Wenders turned the occasion into an excuse to make a diverting comedy about his usual preoccupations, the nature and history of cinema. The story, about a sound engineer who comes to Portugal to work on a film only to find that the director has disappeared, is little more than a frame for a lot of talk mixed with lovely cityscapes. Quite diverting for Wenders buffs. Not rated; contains mild profanity. 103m. **DIR:** Wim Wenders. **CAST:** Rudiger Vogler, Patrick Bauchau, Teresa Salgueiro. **1994**

LIST OF ADRIAN MESSENGER, THE ★★★★1/2 Excellent suspenser has a mysterious stranger visiting an English estate and the puzzling series of murders that coincide with his arrival. Crisp acting, coupled with John Huston's taut direction, make this crackerjack entertainment. With cameo appearances by Kirk Douglas, Tony Curtis, Burt Lancaster, Robert Mitchum, Frank Sinatra. B&W; 98m. **DIR:** John Huston. **CAST:** George C. Scott, Dana Wynter, Clive Brook, Herbert Marshall. **1963**

LISTEN ★★ Two girls eavesdropping on callers to a phone-sex line discover that one of them is a serial killer. Well-made but uninvolving (and overlong) erotic thriller. Rated R for nudity and violence. 104m. **DIR:** Gavin Wilding. **CAST:** Brooke Langton, Sarah Buxton, Gordon Currie. **1997**

LISTEN, DARLING ★★★ A clever family comedy with Judy Garland introducing "Zing Went the Strings of My Heart," one of her trademark tunes. She also sings "Nobody's Baby" while she and her teenaged brother (Freddie Bartholomew) search for the right mate for their widowed mother. An enjoyable musical. B&W; 70m. **DIR:** Edwin L. Marin. **CAST:** Judy Garland, Freddie Bartholomew, Mary Astor, Walter Pidgeon, Charley Grapewin, Scotty Beckett, Gene Lockhart. **1938**

LISTEN TO ME 🦃 Members of a college debating team take time out to find romance. Rated PG-13. 107m. **DIR:** Douglas Day Stewart. **CAST:** Kirk Cameron, Jami Gertz, Roy Scheider, Anthony Zerbe. **1989**

LISTEN TO YOUR HEART ★★★ This cute but predictable romantic comedy features a book editor (Tim Matheson) falling in love with his art director (Kate Jackson). Made for TV, this is unrated. 104m. **DIR:** Don Taylor. **CAST:** Kate Jackson, Tim Matheson, Cassie Yates, George Coe, Tony Plana. **1983**

LISZTOMANIA 🦃 Hokey screen biography of composer Franz Liszt. Rated R. 105m. **DIR:** Ken Russell. **CAST:** Roger Daltrey, Sara Kestleman, Paul Nicholas, Fiona Lewis, Ringo Starr. **1975**

LITTLE ANNIE ROONEY ★★★ The title character is a teenaged street kid in braids, but America's Sweetheart, Mary Pickford, who played her, was 32 at the time. Pickford gets away with it—as she did in many of her films. As the daughter of a widowed New York cop, Annie keeps house, runs a street gang, and anguishes when her father is killed and her boyfriend is wrongly accused of the crime. Silent. B&W; 60m. **DIR:** William Beaudine. **CAST:** Mary Pickford, Spec O'Donnell, Hugh Fay. **1925**

LITTLE BIG HORN ★★★★ A small patrol of cavalry men attempt to get through hostile Indian Territory to warn Custer's Seventh Cavalry of the impending Sioux-Cheyenne ambush. Highly suspenseful. B&W; 86m. **DIR:** Charles Marquis Warren. **CAST:** Lloyd Bridges, John Ireland, Marie Windsor, Reed Hadley, Hugh O'Brian, Jim Davis. **1951**

LITTLE BIG LEAGUE ★★★★ There's a lot of heart in this smart, funny, and respectful fable about a 12 year old kid who inherits the Minnesota Twins baseball team. When his grandfather dies and leaves him the team, Billy Heywood fires the abusive manager and takes over the job himself. How Billy works through his problems and those of the team makes for engaging viewing. Like *The Sandlot* and *The Bad News Bears* before it, *Little Big League* emerges as a film about kids and baseball that speaks to the child in all of us. Rated PG. 120m. **DIR:** Andrew Scheinman. **CAST:** Luke Edwards, Timothy Busfield, John Ashton, Ashley Crow, Kevin Dunn, Jonathan Silverman, Dennis Farina. **1994**

LITTLE BIG MAN ★★★★ Dustin Hoffman gives a bravura performance as Jack Crabbe, a 121 year old survivor of Custer's last stand. An offbeat Western-comedy, this film chronicles, in flashback, Crabbe's numerous adventures in the Old West. It's a remarkable film in more ways than one. Rated PG. 150m. **DIR:** Arthur Penn. **CAST:** Dustin Hoffman, Chief Dan George, Faye Dunaway, Martin Balsam, Jeff Corey, Richard Mulligan. **1970**

LITTLE BIGFOOT ★★★ Kids will enjoy this outdoor adventure about a family on vacation that discovers a baby Bigfoot. Young Payton Shoemaker (Ross Malinger) is looking for a little excitement while spending his summer vacation with his family in the wilderness. He gets his wish when he stumbles across the title creature. It's up to Payton and his family to save the infant from a ruthless logging company owner and his band of thugs. Rated PG for violence and language. 99m. **DIR:** Art Camacho. **CAST:** Ross Malinger, P. J. Soles, Kenneth Tigar, Kelly Packard, Don Stroud, Matt McCoy. **1995**

LITTLE BOY LOST ★★★ Newspaperman Bing Crosby can't tell which kid is his as he searches for his son in a French orphanage following World War II. Get out the Kleenex. 95m. **DIR:** George Seaton. **CAST:** Bing Crosby, Claude Dauphin, Nicole Maurey. **1953**

LITTLE BUDDHA ★★1/2 This reverent epic is really two different films rather clumsily patched together. One half, about the ancient Prince Siddhārtha (Keanu Reeves) and his spiritual transformation into Buddha, the Enlightened One, is interesting and enjoyable. The other half, about the modern-day search for the reincarnation of a venerated Buddhist monk, is dull and lifeless. Rated PG. 123m. **DIR:** Bernardo Bertolucci. **CAST:** Keanu Reeves, Chris Isaak, Bridget Fonda, Alex Wiesendanger, Ying Ruocheng, Jigme, Kunsang, Raju Lai, Greishma Makar Singh. **1994 DVD**

LITTLE CAESAR ★★★ Historically, this is an important film. Made in 1930, it started the whole genre of gangster films. As entertainment, this veiled biography of Al Capone is terribly dated. Edward G. Robinson's performance is like a Warner Bros. cartoon in places, but one has to remember this is the original. B&W; 80m. **DIR:** Mervyn LeRoy. **CAST:** Edward G. Robinson, Douglas Fairbanks Jr. **1930**

LITTLE CITY ★★★ Amusing, complicated romantic drama about six people who leave more than their hearts in San Francisco. An exciting cast fleshes out this tale of friends, roommates, and lovers who wind up sharing each other's company and beds before the end of the film. Filled with sparkling dialogue and engaging performances, *Little City* proves that New York isn't the only city that never sleeps. Rated R for language and adult situations. 90m. **DIR:** Roberto Benabib. **CAST:** Jon Bon Jovi, Josh Charles, Joanna Going, Penelope Ann Miller, Annabella Sciorra, JoBeth Williams. **1998 DVD**

LITTLE COLONEL, THE ★★★1/2 Grandpa Lionel Barrymore is on the outs with daughter Evelyn Venable as the South recovers from the Civil War. Adorable Shirley Temple smoothes it all over. Film's high point is her step dance with Mr. Bojangles, Bill Robinson. B&W; 80m. **DIR:** David Butler. **CAST:** Shirley Temple, Lionel Barrymore, Evelyn Venable, Bill Robinson, Sidney Blackmer. **1935**

LITTLE DARLINGS ★★ A story of the trials and tribulations of teen-age virginity, this film too often lapses into chronic cuteness. *Little Darlings* follows the antics of two 15 year old outcasts—rich, sophisticated Ferris Whitney (Tatum O'Neal) and poor, belligerent Angel

Bright (Kristy McNichol)—as they compete to "score" with a boy first. Rated R. 95m. **DIR:** Ronald F. Maxwell. **CAST:** Tatum O'Neal, Kristy McNichol, Matt Dillon, Armand Assante. **1980**

LITTLE DEATH, THE ★★★ A young musician finds himself falling in love with his stepmother after his father is suddenly murdered. However, the affair uncovers more than lust—there seems to be a conspiracy at hand as well. Almost completely predictable thriller is still watchable thanks to performances by Pamela Gidley and Brent Fraser. Rated R for profanity, violence, and nudity. 90m. **DIR:** Jan Verheyen. **CAST:** Pamela Gidley, J. T. Walsh, Dwight Yoakam, Brent Fraser, D. W. Moffett, Richard Beymer. **1995**

LITTLE DORRIT ★★★★★ Told in two parts, "Nobody's Fault" and "Little Dorrit's Story," this is a splendid six-hour production of Charles Dickens's most popular novel of his time. Derek Jacobi plays Arthur Clennam, a businessman whose life is forever changed when he meets the good-hearted heroine of the title (newcomer Sarah Pickering). An epic of human suffering, compassion, and triumph. Rated G. 356m. **DIR:** Christine Edzard. **CAST:** Alec Guinness, Derek Jacobi, Sarah Pickering, Joan Greenwood, Roshan Seth. **1988**

LITTLE DRUMMER GIRL, THE ★★1/2 Director George Roy Hill did everything he could to make this adaptation of John Le Carré's best-seller a fast-paced, involving political thriller. However, his work is thwarted by an unconvincing lead performance by Diane Keaton, who plays an actress recruited by an Israeli general (Klaus Kinski) to help trap a terrorist. Rated R for violence, profanity, suggested sex, and nudity. 130m. **DIR:** George Roy Hill. **CAST:** Diane Keaton, Yorgo Voyagis, Klaus Kinski. **1984**

LITTLE FOXES, THE ★★★★ The ever-fascinating, ever-unique Bette Davis dominates this outstanding rendering of controversial playwright Lillian Hellman's drama of amoral family greed and corruption down South. Davis's ruthless matriarch, Regina, is the ultimate Edwardian bitch, for whom murder by inaction is not beyond the pale when it comes to achieving her desires. B&W; 116m. **DIR:** William Wyler. **CAST:** Bette Davis, Herbert Marshall, Teresa Wright, Richard Carlson, Dan Duryea. **1941 DVD**

LITTLE GHOST ★★ Mildly diverting tale of a 12 year old boy who teams with a girl ghost to save her castle from becoming an exclusive resort. Rated G. 88m. **DIR:** Linda Shayne. **CAST:** Kristine Wayborn, James Fitzpatrick, Sally Kirkland, Linda Bruneau, Trishalee Hardy. **1997**

LITTLE GIANT ★★ Title refers to a vacuum cleaner that Lou Costello sells door to door. Bud Abbott's in the movie, too, but they don't have any scenes together. Were they feuding? Whatever the reason, the gimmick doesn't work. B&W; 91m. **DIR:** William A. Seiter. **CAST:** Bud Abbott, Lou Costello, Brenda Joyce. **1946**

LITTLE GIANTS ★★★1/2 The *Bad News Bears* formula gets a first-class, kid-pleasing shift to the football field. Put-upon younger brother Rick Moranis decides to challenge the supremacy of sports hero, older brother Ed O'Neill by putting together a ragtag team of rejects to compete for a local championship. There are few surprises here, but there is something to be said for a movie that delivers exactly what it promises. Rated PG for kiddie-style toilet humor. 105m. **DIR:** Duwayne Dunham. **CAST:** Rick Moranis, Ed O'Neill, John Madden, Shawna Waldron, Mary Ellen Trainor, Brian Haley. **1994**

LITTLE GIRL WHO LIVES DOWN THE LANE, THE ★★★1/2 A remarkably subdued film from a genre that has existed primarily on gore, violence, and audience manipulation. Jodie Foster gives an absorbingly realistic performance in the title role. Martin Sheen is the child molester who menaces her. It's a well-acted chiller. Rated PG. 94m. **DIR:** Nicolas Gessner. **CAST:** Jodie Foster, Martin Sheen, Alexis Smith. **1976**

LITTLE GLORIA, HAPPY AT LAST ★★★★ This TV miniseries focuses on the unhappy childhood of Gloria Vanderbilt and the tug-of-war surrounding her custody trial in 1934. It's hard not to pity the poor little rich girl as portrayed in William Haney's bestseller and adapted in this teleplay. Definitely worth a watch! 208m. **DIR:** Waris Hussein. **CAST:** Martin Balsam, Bette Davis, Michael Gross, Lucy Gutteridge, Glynis Johns, Angela Lansbury, Maureen Stapleton. **1982**

LITTLE HEROES ★★1/2 Adorable tale of a little girl and her trusty mutt, who prove to a small town that miracles can still come true. There's a lot of heart and some great messages in this family film. 78m. **DIR:** Craig Clyde. **CAST:** Raeanin Simpson. **1991 DVD**

LITTLE HOUSE ON THE PRAIRIE (TV SERIES) ★★★ The long-running series was based on Laura Ingalls Wilder's novels about her family's adventures on the Kansas frontier. Michael Landon portrayed Charles Ingalls, the idealistic, sensitive husband and father. Episodes tend to be genuinely heartwarming. Each episode 60m. (Special TV-movies are 100 minutes.) **DIR:** Michael Landon. **CAST:** Michael Landon, Karen Grassle, Melissa Gilbert, Melissa Sue Anderson, Lindsay and Sidney Greenbush, Victor French, Dean Butler, Matthew Laborteaux. **1974–1984**

LITTLE INDIAN, BIG CITY ★★1/2 Disney's English-dubbed version of the 1994 French hit features a Parisian businessman off in the jungles of Venezuela to get his long-departed wife to sign their divorce papers. He brings back a tribal 13 year old son he didn't know he had sired and is soon up to his eyeballs in adventure. The film is a little rough for the kiddies and only marginally funny. Rated PG. 90m. **DIR:** Herve Palud. **CAST:** Ludwig Briand, Thierry Lhermitte, Miou-Miou, Arielle Dombasle, Patrick Timsit. **1996**

LITTLE KIDNAPPERS ★★★1/2 Remake of 1954 British film about two orphans living with their grandfather in turn-of-the-century Canada. Feeling ignored and desperate for family, the two boys kidnap a baby so they can raise it themselves. Heartfelt and honest portrayal of family values. Not rated. 93m. **DIR:** Donald Shebib. **CAST:** Patricia Gage, Bruce Greenwood, Charlton Heston, Charles Miller, Leo Wheatley. **1990**

LITTLE LADIES OF THE NIGHT ★★ Linda Purl plays a teenage runaway who is forced into prostitution. TV-movie sexploitation. 100m. **DIR:** Marvin J. Chomsky. **CAST:** Linda Purl, David Soul, Louis Gossett Jr., Carolyn Jones, Paul Burke, Dorothy Malone. **1977**

LITTLE LORD FAUNTLEROY ★★★★ This is the made-for-television version of the heartwarming classic about a poor young boy (Rick Schroder) whose life is

dramatically changed when his wealthy grandfather (Alec Guinness) takes him in. Well-done. 120m. **DIR:** Jack Gold. **CAST:** Rick Schroder, Alec Guinness, Eric Porter, Colin Blakely, Connie Booth. **1980**

LITTLE LORD FAUNTLEROY ★★★★ Far from a syrupy-sweet child movie, this is the affecting tale of a long-lost American heir (Freddie Bartholomew) brought to live with a hard-hearted British lord (C. Aubrey Smith) whose icy manner is warmed by the cheerful child. B&W; 98m. **DIR:** John Cromwell. **CAST:** Freddie Bartholomew, C. Aubrey Smith, Dolores Costello, Jessie Ralph, Mickey Rooney, Guy Kibbee. **1936 DVD**

LITTLE MAN TATE ★★★★ For her directorial debut, actress Jodie Foster joins forces with screenwriter Scott Frank to dramatize the struggle between a working-class mother and a wealthy educator for custody of a gifted child. It isn't often that a family film is both heartwarming and thought-provoking, but this little gem is one of the exceptions. Rated PG for brief profanity. 106m. **DIR:** Jodie Foster. **CAST:** Jodie Foster, Dianne Wiest, Adam Hann-Byrd, Harry Connick Jr., David Pierce, Josh Mostel. **1991 DVD**

LITTLE MEN (1935) ★★ A sentimental tale about a boys' school, and the wayward youths who live there is told with honesty and sincerity but not much personality. This is a poor man's *Boys Town* and needs the likes of a Mickey Rooney or Spencer Tracy to make it come alive. B&W; 56m. **DIR:** Phil Rosen. **CAST:** Frankie Darro, Erin O'Brien-Moore, Ralph Morgan, Junior Durkin, Dickie Moore, Richard Quine. **1935**

LITTLE MEN (1940) 🦃 Louisa May Alcott's classic of childhood turned into a travesty. B&W; 84m. **DIR:** Norman Z. McLeod. **CAST:** Jack Oakie, Kay Francis, George Bancroft, Jimmy Lydon, Ann Gillis, William Demarest, Sterling Holloway, Isabel Jewell. **1940**

LITTLE MEN (1998) ★★★★ Surprisingly rich tale of a home for boys and the trials and tribulations therein. Based on the book by Louisa May Alcott, who also penned *Little Women*. Rated PG. 98m. **DIR:** Rodney Gibbons. **CAST:** Mariel Hemingway, Michael Caloz, Ben Cook, Chris Sarandon. **1998**

LITTLE MERMAID, THE (1979) ★★ Not to be confused with the Disney classic, this is a passably animated version of the Hans Christian Andersen story, and it hews closer to the original tale. Children may be disappointed by the downbeat ending. Rated G. 71m. **DIR:** Tim Reid. **1979**

LITTLE MERMAID, THE (1989) ★★★★★ This adaptation of the Hans Christian Andersen story is, in our opinion, even better than the celebrated movies produced during Walt Disney's heyday. Writer-directors John Musker and Ron Clements, with invaluable assistance from producer Howard Ashman and his songwriting partner Alan Menken, have created the best screen fairy tale of them all. Even the songs are integral to the story, which has some of the most memorable characters to grace an animated film. Rated G. 76m. **DIR:** John Musker, Ron Clements. **1989 DVD**

LITTLE MINISTER, THE ★★★1/2 An early effort in the career of Katharine Hepburn. This charming story, of a proper Scottish minister who falls in love with what he believes is a gypsy girl, is not just for Hepburn fans. B&W; 110m. **DIR:** Richard Wallace. **CAST:** Katharine Hepburn, Donald Crisp, John Beal, Andy Clyde. **1934**

LITTLE MISS BROADWAY ★★★ Orphan Shirley Temple is placed with the manager of a theatrical hotel whose owner, crusty Edna May Oliver, dislikes show people. When she threatens to ship Shirley back to the orphanage, nephew George Murphy sides with the actors. Along the way, Shirley dances with Murphy and clowns with hotel guest Jimmy Durante. B&W; 70m. **DIR:** Irving Cummings. **CAST:** Shirley Temple, George Murphy, Jane Darwell, Edna May Oliver, Jimmy Durante, El Brendel, Donald Meek. **1938**

LITTLE MISS MARKER (1934) ★★★★ Delightful Shirley Temple vehicle has our heroine left as an I.O.U. on a gambling debt and charming hard-hearted racetrack denizens into becoming better people. The best of the screen adaptations of Damon Runyon's story. B&W; 88m. **DIR:** Alexander Hall. **CAST:** Adolphe Menjou, Shirley Temple, Dorothy Dell, Charles Bickford, Lynne Overman. **1934**

LITTLE MISS MARKER (1980) 🦃 Turgid remake. Rated PG. 103m. **DIR:** Walter Bernstein. **CAST:** Walter Matthau, Julie Andrews, Tony Curtis, Bob Newhart, Sara Stimson, Lee Grant. **1980**

LITTLE MISS MILLIONS ★★ Winsome comedy finds poor-little-rich-girl Jennifer Love Hewitt looking for her real mother, while greedy stepmother Anita Morris hires private eye Howard Hesseman to find her. He does, but then Morris claims he kidnapped the girl. The two hit the road to clear their names and find Hewitt's real mom. Congenial fun. Rated PG. 90m. **DIR:** Jim Wynorski. **CAST:** Howard Hesseman, Jennifer Love Hewitt, Anita Morris, Steve Landesberg. **1993**

LITTLE MONSTERS 🦃 Irritating, ugly monsters living in a dark, chaotic netherworld pop out from under unsuspecting children's beds at night. Rated PG, but it's definitely not Disney fare. 103m. **DIR:** Richard Alan Greenburg. **CAST:** Fred Savage, Howie Mandel, Daniel Stern, Frank Whaley, Margaret Whitton, Ben Savage. **1989**

LITTLE MOON & JUD MCGRAW 🦃 Comedy-Western that has James Caan as a falsely accused man hunting for the real crook. Rated R, contains nudity and violence. 92m. **DIR:** Bernard Girard. **CAST:** James Caan, Stefanie Powers, Sammy Davis Jr., Aldo Ray, Barbara Werle, Robert Walker Jr. **1978**

LITTLE MURDERS ★★★★ Jules Feiffer's savagely black comedy details the nightmarish adventures of a mild-mannered New Yorker (Elliott Gould) who finds the world becoming increasingly insane and violent. What seemed like bizarre fantasy when *Little Murders* was originally released is today all too close to reality. Strangely, this makes the film easier to watch while taking away none of its bite. Rated PG for violence and profanity. 107m. **DIR:** Alan Arkin. **CAST:** Elliott Gould, Marcia Rodd, Vincent Gardenia, Elizabeth Wilson, Donald Sutherland, Lou Jacobi, Alan Arkin. **1971**

LITTLE NELLIE KELLY ★★★ Charles Winninger is a stubborn Irishman who refuses to recognize the marriage of his daughter Judy Garland to George Murphy. Based on George M. Cohan's Broadway musical-comedy. Fine renditions of many old standards. B&W; 100m. **DIR:** Norman Taurog. **CAST:** Judy Garland, George Murphy, Charles Winninger, Arthur Shields. **1940**

LITTLE NEMO: ADVENTURES IN SLUMBERLAND ★★★ In this fairly entertaining animated movie, Little Nemo is a youngster whose dreams lead him into Slumberland, where the Dream King has plans for the boy to be his successor. Meanwhile, the mischievous Flip (voiced by Mickey Rooney) leads our hero to unintentionally unleash the Nightmare King. Rated G. 83m. **DIR:** Masanori Hata, William Hurtz. **1992**

LITTLE NICKY When two of Satan's heirs go AWOL in Manhattan after their dad once again delays his retirement, the netherworld patriarch sends his sweet, simpleton son Nicky to bring them back in this crude, unfunny comedy. Rated R for language and sexual humor. 86m. **DIR:** Steven Brill. **CAST:** Adam Sandler, Patricia Arquette, Harvey Keitel, Tom "Tiny" Lister Jr., Rhys Ifans. **2000 DVD**

LITTLE NIGHT MUSIC, A ★★1/2 Based on Ingmar Bergman's comedy about sexual liaisons at a country mansion, this musical version doesn't quite come to life. Rated PG. 124m. **DIR:** Harold Prince. **CAST:** Elizabeth Taylor, Diana Rigg, Lesley-Anne Down. **1978**

LITTLE NIKITA ★★★1/2 Well-crafted, old-fashioned espionage story about the awakening of "sleeper" agents (planted by the Soviets twenty years earlier in San Diego). Sidney Poitier is the FBI agent tracking the situation, and River Phoenix plays a teenager caught in the middle. Richard Bradford is great as a manipulative but likable KGB agent. Rated PG for language and violence. 98m. **DIR:** Richard Benjamin. **CAST:** Sidney Poitier, River Phoenix, Richard Jenkins, Caroline Kava, Richard Bradford, Richard Lynch, Loretta Devine, Lucy Deakins. **1988**

LITTLE NINJAS ★★1/2 Slight, derivative kiddy romp about three karate-chopping youngsters who come into possession of a treasure map while on vacation. When they return home to Los Angeles, they must join forces to fight off the bad guys who have come for the map. Kids will enjoy this mindless exercise. Rated PG. 85m. **DIR:** Emmett Alston. **CAST:** Jon Anzaldo, Steven Nelson. **1993**

LITTLE NOISES ★★ Low-budget, seemingly pointless film. A talentless writer sells the poems of a mute man as his own. Now he must deal with his conscience. Not rated. 80m. **DIR:** Jane Spencer. **CAST:** Crispin Glover, Tatum O'Neal, Rik Mayall, Tate Donovan. **1991**

LITTLE ODESSA ★★★1/2 Although bleak to the point of total despair, writer-director James Gray's feature debut is a contemporary, Russian-Jewish spin on *The Godfather*: a mesmerizing study of a small-time gangster trying to reconcile estranged family ties. Tim Roth is chilling as the wholly amoral killer, whose return to New York's Brighton Beach proves disastrous for the parents and younger brother he left behind. Gray's matter-of-fact approach to this violent tale is positively haunting. Rated R for violence, profanity, and nudity. 111m. **DIR:** James Gray. **CAST:** Tim Roth, Maximilian Schell, Vanessa Redgrave, Edward Furlong, Moira Kelly. **1995 DVD**

LITTLE ORPHAN ANNIE ★★1/2 The first sound version featuring the adventures of Harold Gray's pupilless, precocious adolescent. A good cast and engaging score by Max Steiner add to the charm of this undeservedly neglected comic-strip adaptation. B&W; 60m. **DIR:** John S. Robertson. **CAST:** Mitzi Green, Edgar Kennedy, Buster Phelps, May Robson. **1932**

LITTLE PATRIOT, THE ★★ Colonial miniepic tells the story of a young boy and his family and their trials and tribulations in the new land that would become New York City. Rated PG. 88m. **DIR:** J. Christian Ingvordsen. **CAST:** Dan Haggerty, John Christian, Rick Washburne, Jacqueline Knox. **1992**

LITTLE PRINCE, THE ★★ Aviator Richard Kiley teaches an alien boy about life and love. This picture has a great cast, beautiful photography, and is based on the children's classic by Antoine de Saint-Exupéry. Unfortunately, it also has a poor musical score by Alan J. Lerner and Frederick Loewe. Rated G. 88m. **DIR:** Stanley Donen. **CAST:** Richard Kiley, Steven Warner, Bob Fosse, Gene Wilder. **1974**

LITTLE PRINCESS, THE (1939) ★★★1/2 The 1930s supertyke Shirley Temple had one of her very best vehicles in this Victorian-era tearjerker. In it, she's a sweet-natured child who is mistreated at a strict boarding school when her father disappears during the Boer War. Get out your handkerchiefs. B&W; 93m. **DIR:** Walter Lang. **CAST:** Shirley Temple, Richard Greene, Anita Louise, Ian Hunter, Cesar Romero, Arthur Treacher. **1939 DVD**

LITTLE PRINCESS, A (1986) ★★1/2 Melodramatic tale of an indulged girl who, having lived in India with her lively, free-spending father, is enrolled in a prissy English boarding school. The girl's constant sermonizing about her plight is most annoying. A lesser WonderWorks production. 174m. **DIR:** Carol Wiseman. **CAST:** Amelia Shankley, Nigel Havers, Maureen Lipman. **1986**

LITTLE PRINCESS, A (1995) ★★★★★ This magical, visually intoxicating drama and hankie twister is about a young girl who is uprooted from India to a grim New York City boarding school. The story focuses on the power of imagination and inner spirit, and the film's critical relationship between Dad and daughter has a powerful beauty not often found in movies today. Rated G. 98m. **DIR:** Alfonso Cuaron. **CAST:** Liesel Matthews, Eleanor Bron, Liam Cunningham, Vanessa Lee Chester, Rusty Schwimmer. **1995 DVD**

LITTLE RASCALS, THE ★★1/2 This re-creation of yesteryear's *Our Gang* comedies substitutes gross humor for charm. Example: When members of the He-Man Woman Haters' Club decide to dissuade Alfalfa from courting Darla, one of their tricks is to put used kitty litter in his peanut-butter sandwiches. This is a kids' movie? That said, youngsters will probably love it, and there is some nostalgic fun in seeing the most memorable characters from the series join forces in a big-screen romp. Rated PG for toilet humor. 82m. **DIR:** Penelope Spheeris. **CAST:** Travis Tedford, Bug Hall, Brittany Ashton Holmes, Kevin Jamal Woods, Zachary Mabry, Ross Elliot Bagley, Mel Brooks, Whoopi Goldberg, Daryl Hannah, Reba McEntire. **1994 DVD**

LITTLE RIDERS, THE ★★★★ This made-for-cable production, based on Margareth Shemin's novel, concerns a little girl's efforts to save a Dutch town's soul from the Nazis. Half-American Noley Thornton lives with her grandparents, and helps care for the horseriding figurines that signal each hour from the clocktower. When an occupational Nazi leader decides to melt down the figurines as a means to destroy local spirit, she and

her grandparents concoct a desperate scheme. Rated PG for violence. 108m. **DIR:** Kevin Connor. **CAST:** Paul Scofield, Rosemary Harris, Noley Thornton, Benedick Blythe, Luke Edwards, Malcolm McDowell, Derek de Lint. **1996**

LITTLE ROMANCE, A ★★★★1/2 Everyone needs *A Little Romance* in their life. This absolutely enchanting film by director George Roy Hill has something for everyone. Its story of two appealing youngsters (Thelonious Bernard and Diane Lane) who fall in love in Paris is full of surprises, laughs, and uplifting moments. Rated PG. 108m. **DIR:** George Roy Hill. **CAST:** Thelonious Bernard, Diane Lane, Laurence Olivier, Sally Kellerman, Broderick Crawford, David Dukes. **1979**

LITTLE SEX, A ★★ A New York director of television commercials can't keep his hands off his actresses, even though he's married to a beautiful, intelligent woman. This is a tepid romantic comedy. Rated R. 95m. **DIR:** Bruce Paltrow. **CAST:** Tim Matheson, Kate Capshaw, Edward Herrmann. **1982**

LITTLE SHOP OF HORRORS, THE (1960) ★★★★ Dynamite Roger Corman superquickie about a meek florist shop employee (Jonathan Haze) who inadvertently creates a ferocious man-eating plant. This horror-comedy was filmed in two days and is one of the funniest ever made. B&W; 72m. **DIR:** Roger Corman. **CAST:** Jonathan Haze, Mel Welles, Jackie Joseph, Jack Nicholson, Dick Miller. **1960 DVD**

LITTLE SHOP OF HORRORS (1986) ★★★★1/2 This totally bent musical–horror–comedy was based on director Roger Corman's bizarre horror cheapie from 1960. Rick Moranis is wonderful as the schnook who finds and cares for a man-eating plant set on conquering the world. Uproariously funny, marvelously acted, spectacularly staged, and tuneful. Rated PG-13 for violence. 94m. **DIR:** Frank Oz. **CAST:** Rick Moranis, Ellen Greene, Vincent Gardenia, Steve Martin, James Belushi, John Candy, Bill Murray, Christopher Guest. **1986 DVD**

LITTLE SISTER ★★1/2 Likable comedy with Jonathan Silverman as a love-struck student who dons women's clothing in order to sneak into a sorority. Been-there, done-that comedy still manages to be quite entertaining. Rated PG-13 for sexual content. 94m. **DIR:** Jimmy Zeilinger. **CAST:** Jonathan Silverman, Alyssa Milano, George Newbern. **1991**

LITTLE SWEETHEART ★★★ Not since *The Bad Seed* have we seen a little girl as deadly as 9 year old Thelma (played by newcomer Cassie Barasch). She delves in blackmail of a couple on the run from a bank embezzlement job. Rated R for violence. 93m. **DIR:** Anthony Simmons. **CAST:** John Hurt, Karen Young, Cassie Barasch, Barbara Bosson. **1990**

LITTLE THEATRE OF JEAN RENOIR, THE ★★★ The great director's last film (actually made for television) is better seen as a postscript to his long career. The three segments (plus a musical interlude from Jeanne Moreau) remind the viewer of his best work rather than recapitulating it. In French with English subtitles. 100m. **DIR:** Jean Renoir. **CAST:** Jeanne Moreau, Jean Carmet, Fernand Sardou, Pierre Olaf, Françoise Arnoul. **1969**

LITTLE THIEF, THE ★★★★ François Truffaut was working on this script, sort of a female version of *The 400 Blows*, at the time of his death; it was completed and filmed by his friend Claude Miller. Charlotte Gainsbourg gives a strong performance as a rebellious adolescent girl, struggling to raise herself after she is abandoned by her mother. In French with English subtitles. Not rated; features adult themes. 104m. **DIR:** Claude Miller. **CAST:** Charlotte Gainsbourg, Didier Bezace. **1989**

LITTLE TREASURE ★★★ While the synopsis on the back of the box may give one the impression this release is a rip-off of *Romancing the Stone*, only the rough outline of the story is lifted from the 1984 hit. The Margot Kidder/Ted Danson team is not a copy of the Kathleen Turner/Michael Douglas couple; these characters are more down-home. And the concentration on domestic drama almost fills the gap left by the absence of action. Rated R for nudity and language. 95m. **DIR:** Alan Sharp. **CAST:** Margot Kidder, Ted Danson, Burt Lancaster. **1985**

LITTLE VAMPIRE, THE ★★★ A 9 year old California boy (Jonathan Lipnicki) feels lonely and misplaced in Scotland until he befriends a vampire and his family. Lipnicki decides to help his new pals complete their centuries-old quest to become human again. Cute family entertainment provides only intermittent laughs. Rated PG for scary vampire nightmares and an even scarier vampire hunter. 91m. **DIR:** Uli Edel. **CAST:** Jonathan Lipnicki, Richard E. Grant, Rollo Weeks, Alice Krige. **2000 DVD**

LITTLE VEGAS ★★★★ A fantastic movie about a man (Anthony Denison) trying to escape from the mob-like life of his family. After the death of a matronly woman who was taking care of him, he must contend with the other residents of a small desert town who see him as a gigolo. Rated R for nudity and profanity. 91m. **DIR:** Perry Lang. **CAST:** Anthony Denison, Catherine O'Hara, Anne Francis, Michael Nouri, Perry Lang, John Sayles, Bruce McGill, Jerry Stiller. **1990**

LITTLE VERA ★★★ Glasnost takes a front-row-center seat in this angst-ridden drama about the thoroughly modern Moscovite Vera. Her alcoholic father and ineffectual mother constantly worry about Vera's untraditional ways. She falls in love and moves her fiancé into the family's tight quarters. This is the first widely released Soviet film to show present-day teenage culture—plus—simulated sex. In Russian with English subtitles. Not rated. 130m. **DIR:** Vasily Pichul. **CAST:** Natalya Negoda. **1989 DVD**

•LITTLE VOICE ★★★★ This odd British fantasy deserves far better than it received during an eye-blink theatrical release in the United States, if only because of star Jane Horrocks's frankly jaw-dropping performance as the title character. She plays a reclusive young woman who lives in the shadow of her spiteful mother (Oscar-nominated Brenda Blethyn), and communicates by mimicking performances by torch singers such as Judy Garland and Shirley Bassey. The premise is captivating all by itself; the fact that Horrocks does all her own singing is astonishing. Michael Caine also shines in a small role as a scheming cad who'd love to exploit this young woman's unusual talent. Although achingly melancholy at times, the film (and Horrocks) have enough spirit and spunk to carry the day. Rated R for profanity and brief nudity. 96m. **DIR:** Mark Herman.

CAST: Brenda Blethyn, Jane Horrocks, Ewan McGregor, Philip Jackson, Annette Badland, Michael Caine. **1998 DVD**

LITTLE WHITE LIES ★★★ While on vacation in Rome, surgeon Tim Matheson and detective Ann Jillian meet and fall in love. Harmless fluff, pleasant diversion for a made-for-television feature. 95m. **DIR:** Anson Williams. **CAST:** Tim Matheson, Ann Jillian. **1989**

LITTLE WITCHES ★★ Catholic schoolgirls discover the uses and abuses of black magic in this rip-off of *The Craft.* If you liked that, you'll probably like this—just not as much. Rated R for violence and nudity. 91m. **DIR:** Jane Simpson. **CAST:** Jennifer Rubin, Jack Nance, Zelda Rubinstein, Sheeri Rappaport. **1996 DVD**

LITTLE WOMEN (1933) ★★★★1/2 George Cukor's *Little Women* is far and away the best of the four film versions of Louisa May Alcott's timeless story of the March family. Katharine Hepburn is excellent as the tomboyish Jo. B&W; 115m. **DIR:** George Cukor. **CAST:** Katharine Hepburn, Spring Byington, Joan Bennett, Frances Dee, Jean Parker. **1933 DVD**

LITTLE WOMEN (1949) ★★1/2 Textbook casting and intelligent performances make this a safe second rendering of Louisa May Alcott's famous story of maturing young women finding romance in the nineteenth century. Technicolor is an enhancement, but the 1933 original is vastly superior. 121m. **DIR:** Mervyn LeRoy. **CAST:** June Allyson, Peter Lawford, Elizabeth Taylor, Mary Astor, Janet Leigh, Margaret O'Brien. **1949**

LITTLE WOMEN (1994) ★★★★ This adaptation of Louisa May Alcott's American classic is a triumph of casting and period authenticity, if perhaps possessed of too much feminism for its era. Jo is once again the cinematic focus, as she defies the passive female stereotypes of the 1860s to pursue a writing career. The production design is perfect, and you can almost feel the cozy family's love jumping out from the screen. Rated PG for dramatic intensity. 119m. **DIR:** Gillian Armstrong. **CAST:** Winona Ryder, Susan Sarandon, Trini Alvarado, Eric Stoltz, Christian Bale, Gabriel Byrne, Claire Danes, Kirsten Dunst. **1994 DVD**

LITTLE WORLD OF DON CAMILLO, THE ★★★ The emotional and often grim struggle between Church and State has never been more humanely or lovingly presented than in the novels of Giovanni Guareschi, expertly brought to life in this gentle, amusing film. The great French comedian Fernandel captures the essence of the feisty priest who is a perpetual thorn in the side of the communist mayor of his village and parish. B&W; 96m. **DIR:** Julien Duvivier. **CAST:** Fernandel, Gino Cervi, Sylvie, Franco Interlenghi. **1953**

LITTLEST ANGEL, THE ★★ This made-for-TV musical fantasy loses something in its video translation. A young shepherd finds his transition into heaven difficult to accept. 77m. **DIR:** Joe Layton. **CAST:** Johnny Whitaker, Fred Gwynne, Connie Stevens, James Coco, E. G. Marshall, Tony Randall. **1969**

LITTLEST HORSE THIEVES, THE ★★★ At the turn of the century, some children become alarmed that the ponies working in the coal mines are to be destroyed. The children decide to steal the ponies. Rather predictable but with good characterizations and a solid period atmosphere. Rated G. 104m. **DIR:** Charles Jarrott. **CAST:** Alastair Sim, Peter Barkworth, Maurice Colbourne, Susan Tebbs, Andrew Harrison, Chloe Franks. **1976 DVD**

LITTLEST OUTLAW, THE ★★★ This Walt Disney import from Mexico tells a familiar but pleasant story of a young boy who befriends a renegade horse and saves him from destruction. The kids should like it, and this one will appeal to the adults as well. 73m. **DIR:** Roberto Gavaldon. **CAST:** Pedro Armendariz, Joseph Calleia, Rodolfo Acosta, Andres Velasquez. **1954**

LITTLEST REBEL, THE ★★★1/2 Prime Shirley Temple, in which, as the daughter of a Confederate officer during the Civil War, she thwarts a double execution by charming President Lincoln. The plot stops, of course, while she and Bojangles dance. B&W; 70m. **DIR:** David Butler. **CAST:** Shirley Temple, John Boles, Jack Holt, Bill Robinson, Karen Morley, Guinn Williams, Willie Best. **1935**

LITTLEST VIKING, THE ★★ Very slow-moving tale about a young boy and his family's violent feud with the neighbors in the fjord next door. Quite a few moral lessons are given in the film, but you'll have to stay awake. Rated PG. 85m. **DIR:** Knut W. Jorfald, Lars Rasmussen, Paul Trevor Bale. **CAST:** Kristian Tonby, Per Jansen, Terje Stromdahl, Rulle Smit. **1989**

LIVE A LITTLE, LOVE A LITTLE 🦃 The interesting thing about this Elvis vehicle is that the sexual innuendos are more blatant than in his other romantic comedies. Rated PG for mild profanity. 89m. **DIR:** Norman Taurog. **CAST:** Elvis Presley, Michele Carey, Don Porter, Dick Sargent. **1968**

LIVE AND LET DIE ★★ The first Roger Moore (as James Bond) adventure is a hodgepodge of the surrealistic and the slick that doesn't quite live up to its Connery-powered predecessors. The chase-and-suspense formula wears thin. Rated PG. 121m. **DIR:** Guy Hamilton. **CAST:** Roger Moore, Jane Seymour, Yaphet Kotto, Geoffrey Holder. **1973 DVD**

LIVE BY THE FIST 🦃 Boring choreography and an annoying, trite script drop-kick this martial-arts fistfest right into the turkey pile. Rated R for violence. 77m. **DIR:** Cirio H. Santiago. **CAST:** Jerry Trimble, George Takei. **1993**

LIVE FLESH ★★★★ When a young man finishes his prison sentence for shooting and crippling a cop, he hovers uncomfortably close to the cop and his wife. Is it just coincidence, or does he have some subtle plan in mind? Loosely adapted from a novel by English mystery writer Ruth Rendell the basic idea veers in a completely different direction, and the result is erotic, psychologically complex, and entirely unpredictable. In Spanish with English subtitles. Rated R for profanity (in subtitles) and sexual situations. 101m. **DIR:** Pedro Almodóvar. **CAST:** Javier Bardem, Francesca Neri, Liberto Rabal, Angela Molina. **1997 DVD**

LIVE! FROM DEATH ROW ★★★ In this skillfully directed made-for-TV nail biter, Bruce Davison gives a high-powered performance as a condemned murderer who takes a tabloid reporter and her crew hostage just before his scheduled execution. Not rated; contains adult situations. 94m. **DIR:** Patrick Duncan. **CAST:** Bruce Davison, Joanna Cassidy, Jason Tomlins, Kathleen Wilhoite, Art La Fleur. **1992**

LIVE NUDE GIRLS ★★★1/2 Engaging ensemble film about a group of women who throw their friend a party in

honor of her third trip down the aisle. The fun and games spill over into a slumber party, where each of the women unveils her deepest and darkest desires, fears, and fantasies. It's *The Big Chill* on estrogen, a funny and enlightening comedy-drama where women bare their souls more than their bodies. Rated R for profanity and nudity. 100m. **DIR:** Julianna Lavin. **CAST:** Cynthia Stevenson, Kim Cattrall, Olivia D'Abo, Laila Robins. **1995**

LIVE WIRE ★★★ A bomb kills a senator, but no traces of an explosive can be found. An FBI agent (Pierce Brosnan) must find the cause of the explosion while fighting his own inner battles. Very good acting by Brosnan and Ron Silver, who plays a corrupt senator, but the plot is predictable. Rated R for violence, profanity, and nudity. 85m. **DIR:** Christian Duguay. **CAST:** Pierce Brosnan, Ron Silver, Ben Cross, Lisa Eilbacher, Brent Jennings, Tony Plana, Al Waxman. **1992**

LIVE WIRE: HUMAN TIMEBOMB ★★ Mediocre sequel finds special agent Jim Parker being abducted by the Cuban government, whose ruthless general installs a microchip in the agent's neck. Now under the command of the general, Parker becomes his country's most feared enemy. Ho hum. Rated R for violence and adult language. 98m. **DIR:** Mark Roper. **CAST:** Bryan Genesse, Joe Lara, J. Cynthia Brooks. **1995**

LIVES OF A BENGAL LANCER, THE ★★★★1/2 One of the great adventure films, this action-packed epic stars Gary Cooper and Franchot Tone as fearless friends in the famed British regiment. Their lives become complicated when they take the commander's son (Richard Cromwell) under their wings and he turns out to be less than a model soldier. B&W; 109m. **DIR:** Henry Hathaway. **CAST:** Gary Cooper, Franchot Tone, Richard Cromwell, Guy Standing, C. Aubrey Smith, Monte Blue, Kathleen Burke. **1935**

LIVIN' LARGE ★★1/2 In this hit-and-miss comedy, Terrence "T. C." Carson plays a young man devoted to getting on television. When his big break comes, his devotion to his career threatens to alienate his longtime friends. Rated R for profanity and violence. 96m. **DIR:** Michael Schultz. **CAST:** Terrence "T. C." Carson, Lisa Arrindell, Nathaniel Hall, Blanche Baker, Julia Campbell. **1991**

LIVING DAYLIGHTS, THE ★★★1/2 Timothy Dalton adds a dimension of humanity to James Bond in his screen bow as the ultimate spy hero. The silly set pieces and gimmicks that marred even the best Roger Moore entries in the series are gone. Instead, the filmmakers have opted for a strong plot about a phony KGB defector (Jeroen Krabbé) and a renegade arms dealer (Joe Don Baker). Rated PG. 130m. **DIR:** John Glen. **CAST:** Timothy Dalton, Maryam D'Abo, Jeroen Krabbé, Joe Don Baker, John Rhys-Davies, Art Malik, Desmond Llewellyn. **1987 DVD**

LIVING DEAD GIRL ★★1/2 French director Jean Rollin's films rarely make much sense, but they are always sumptuously made as evidenced by this tale of a girl and her sudden taste for the flesh of the living. In French with English subtitles. Not rated; contains violence and nudity. 85m. **DIR:** Jean Rollin. **CAST:** Francoise Blanchard, Carina Baron. **1982 DVD**

LIVING END, THE ★★★★ This hard-core, unsentimental road movie/romance between two HIV-positive gay men manages to be bizarre, bitter, *and* intriguing. Figuring they have nothing to lose, Craig Gilmore and Mike Dytri hit the road and act out their bad-boy fantasies amid provocative conversations. Tough to watch, but nihilism rarely looks this good. Not rated, but includes profanity, violence, nudity, and sexual situations. 85m. **DIR:** Gregg Araki. **CAST:** Craig Gilmore, Mike Dytri, Darcy Marta, Scot Goetz, Johanna Went, Mary Woronov. **1992**

LIVING FREE ★★ Disappointing sequel to *Born Free*, with Elsa the lioness now in the wilderness and raising three cubs. The chemistry just isn't here in this film. 91m. **DIR:** Jack Couffer. **CAST:** Susan Hampshire, Nigel Davenport, Geoffrey Keen. **1972**

LIVING IN A BIG WAY ★★ A comedy-drama about a wartime marriage that goes sour, this movie uses music for all the wrong reasons. It works up to a point, mainly because Gene Kelly is such an exuberant dancer. His costar, Marie McDonald, looks a lot better than she acts. B&W; 102m. **DIR:** Gregory La Cava. **CAST:** Gene Kelly, Marie McDonald, Charles Winninger, Spring Byington, Phyllis Thaxter, Clinton Sundberg. **1947**

LIVING IN OBLIVION ★★★1/2 Low-budget gem focuses on the endless mishaps likely to occur on a low-budget film set. The harried director vainly attempts to ease tensions between his female lead and the male "prima donna" hired simply for his name. Slow start makes a dramatic recovery with numerous gut-splitting scenes of hilarious absurdity. Satisfying on a multitude of levels. Rated R for sex, nudity, and profanity. B&W/color; 90m. **DIR:** Tom DiCillo. **CAST:** Dermot Mulroney, Catherine Keener, James LeGros, Steve Buscemi. **1995**

LIVING IN PERIL ★★★ Familiar faces help elevate this pedestrian whodunit about an architect who finds himself framed for murder. Rob Lowe stars as Walter, the architect hired by millionaire James Belushi to build his new home. When a woman ends up dead in his apartment, Walter suspects that someone is trying to ruin him. Moderately entertaining with the prerequisite plot elements. Rated R for language and violence. 95m. **DIR:** Jack Ersgard. **CAST:** Rob Lowe, James Belushi, Dean Stockwell, Dana Wheeler-Nicholson. **1998**

LIVING ON TOKYO TIME ★★★★ Explores an Asian-American culture clash from the Japanese point of view. Kyoko (Minako Ohashi), a young woman, comes from Japan to San Francisco. She agrees to a marriage of convenience with a junk-food-eating Japanese-American who wants to be a rock star. The result is a warm-hearted character study blessed with insight and humor. In English and Japanese with subtitles. Not rated. 83m. **DIR:** Steven Okazaki. **CAST:** Minako Ohashi, Ken Nakagawa. **1987**

LIVING OUT LOUD ★★★1/2 A recently divorced New Yorker's path crosses that of the doorman in her apartment building just as both are trying to rebuild their lives. Loosely adapted from two Chekhov short stories, the film never overcomes the fact that it's telling two unrelated tales. Still, there are many pleasures and fine moments. Rated R for profanity and sexual themes. 93m. **DIR:** Richard LaGravanese. **CAST:** Holly Hunter, Danny DeVito, Queen Latifah, Martin Donovan, Elias Koteas. **1998 DVD**

LIVING PROOF: THE HANK WILLIAMS Jr., STORY 🦃 A miscast made-for-television stink bomb. 100m. **DIR:**

Dick Lowry. **CAST:** Richard Thomas, Clu Gulager, Allyn Ann McLerie. **1983**

LIVING THE BLUES ★★ White suburban boy who wants to be a blues guitarist pesters the uncle of his inner-city girlfriend for a spot in his band. Well-intended but amateurish. Not rated; contains mild sexual situations. 78m. **DIR:** Alan Gorg. **CAST:** Michael Kerr, Galyn Görg, Sam Taylor, Gwyn Gorg, Martin Raymond. **1986**

LIVING TO DIE ★★ Private eye Nick Carpenter is called upon to stop an embezzling scheme that involves a Las Vegas luminary. The Vegas backdrop enlivens what is essentially a dreary story. Rated R for nudity and violence. 92m. **DIR:** Wings Hauser. **CAST:** Wings Hauser, Darcy Demiss. **1990**

LIVING VENUS ★★ Harvey Korman probably would like to forget that he made his debut in this melodrama loosely based on the story of Hugh Hefner and *Playboy* magazine. Not rated; contains adult situations. B&W; 71m. **DIR:** Herschell Gordon Lewis. **CAST:** William Kerwin, Danica D'Hondt, Harvey Korman. **1959**

LIZARD IN A WOMAN'S SKIN, A ★★1/2 In this thriller from Italian goremeister Lucio Fulci, a woman may or may not be part of a gruesome murder. Did she really do it? Is this real or a hallucination? At times the film can be slow, but Fulci makes up for it with wild camera work. Rated R for violence and gore. 105m. **DIR:** Lucio Fulci. **CAST:** Florinda Balkan. **1971**

LLOYD'S OF LONDON ★★★★ An old-fashioned look at how the big business developed. Freddie Bartholomew is top-billed as the lad who grows up to be the hero of England's insurance industry. Highly entertaining. B&W; 115m. **DIR:** Henry King. **CAST:** Tyrone Power, George Sanders, Madeleine Carroll, Freddie Bartholomew, C. Aubrey Smith, Virginia Field. **1936**

LOADED ★★ Murky murder mystery takes place on the set of a low-budget horror movie being shot in rural England. It's the directorial debut of Jane Campion's sister Anna, who seems more interested in letting her characters yak about their personal feelings than in telling a story. Rated R for profanity, nudity, and sexual situations. 96m. **DIR:** Anna Campion. **CAST:** Catherine McCormack, Thandie Newton, Matthew Eggleton. **1996**

LOADED PISTOLS ★★★★ Well-handled, typical B-Western plot finds Gene Autry safeguarding young cowpoke Russell Arms (of TV's "Your Hit Parade") wrongly accused of murder. B&W; 77m. **DIR:** John English. **CAST:** Gene Autry, Barbara Britton, Jack Holt, Russell Arms, Chill Wills, Robert Shayne. **1948**

LOBSTER FOR BREAKFAST ★★1/2 Screwball comedy Italian style about the loves and misadventures of a toilet salesman. In Italian with English subtitles. Not rated; contains profanity and nudity. 93m. **DIR:** Giorgio Capitani. **CAST:** Janet Agren, Claudine Auger. **1982**

LOBSTER MAN FROM MARS ★★ A sometimes funny comedy about a movie producer who, in need of a tax-sheltering flop, calls upon an amateur filmmaker and his sci-fi flick to save him. Old and overused jokes and sight gags cause this parody to flop more often than fly. Rated PG. 84m. **DIR:** Stanley Sheff. **CAST:** Tony Curtis, Deborah Foreman, Patrick Macnee, Billy Barty. **1990**

LOCAL HERO ★★★★1/2 A wonderfully offbeat comedy by Bill Forsyth. Burt Lancaster plays a Houston oil baron who sends Peter Riegert to the west coast of Scotland to negotiate with the natives for North Sea oil rights. As with *Gregory's Girl*, which was about a gangly, good-natured boy's first crush, this film is blessed with sparkling little moments of humor, unforgettable characters, and a warmly human story. Rated PG for language. 111m. **DIR:** Bill Forsyth. **CAST:** Burt Lancaster, Peter Riegert, Fulton MacKay. **1983 DVD**

LOCH NESS ★★★ So-so drama sends yet another scientist (Ted Danson) to Scotland to investigate the Loch Ness creature's possible existence. This is overshadowed by Danson's romance with a pretty innkeeper. Gorgeous location shots are really a plus, but the limited screen time allotted to the creatures is quite a disappointment. Rod Stewart's tribute to his homeland, "Rhythm of My Heart," provides a fitting finale. Rated PG for violence. 160m. **DIR:** John Henderson. **CAST:** Ted Danson, Joely Richardson, Kirsty Graham, Ian Holm, James Frain. **1996**

LOCH NESS HORROR, THE 🦃 Japan isn't the only country that has monsters that look like muppets. Rated PG. Has some violence. 93m. **DIR:** Larry Buchanan. **CAST:** Barry Buchanan, Sandy Kenyon. **1982**

LOCK AND LOAD ★★ Members of the 82nd Airborne Special Forces group are stealing large sums of cash and jewels and killing themselves. One such member, haunted by dreams, wants to know why. Interesting premise. Rated R for violence. 89m. **DIR:** David A. Prior. **CAST:** Jack Vogel. **1990**

LOCK, STOCK AND TWO SMOKING BARRELS ★★1/2 This darkly cheeky crime caper hops from bloody shoot-outs to torture scenes with quick winks and nudges to all that is Tarantino. The plot nearly ties itself in knots as four London lads lose a high-stakes poker game to a porn king and then rob other crooks to repay the underworld loan. Rated R for language, violence, drug content, and brief nudity. 103m. **DIR:** Guy Ritchie. **CAST:** Nick Moran, Jason Statham, Dexter Fletcher, Jason Flemyng, P. H. Moriarty, Vinnie Jones, Lenny McLean. **1999 DVD**

LOCK UP ★★★1/2 Sylvester Stallone gives one of his best performances in this melodramatic prison drama, which is reminiscent of similarly themed Warner Bros. movies of the Thirties and Forties. Stallone is a model prisoner who, just before he is about to be released, finds himself transferred to a high-security facility run by an old enemy (Donald Sutherland) who wants to see him dead. Rated R for profanity, violence, and suggested sex. 106m. **DIR:** John Flynn. **CAST:** Sylvester Stallone, Donald Sutherland, John Amos, Darlanne Fluegel. **1989 DVD**

LOCKED IN SILENCE ★★★ Two brothers are forced to share a terrible secret in this somewhat unconvincing drama; the younger boy retreats behind a wall of hysterical muteness, a condition that proves vexing to parents who grow desperate. Bruce Davison has the difficult role, as the father who means well but is quick to anger. But the basic premise in David A. Simons and Dalene Young's script never quite gels; it's difficult to imagine, for example, that the boy would maintain his self-imposed silence even when his mother's life is at stake . . . and the resolution—the reason behind it all—is dissatisfying and anticlimactic. Rated PG for dramatic inten-

sity. 94m. **DIR:** Bruce Pittman. **CAST:** Bonnie Bedelia, Bruce Davison, Marc Donato, Bill Switzer, Steven McCarthy, Helen Hughes, Dan Hedaya. **1999**

LOCUSTS, THE ★★★ John Steinbeckesque tale of a drifter and his war of grit against a disturbed female beef farmer. Excellent performances buoy this ultimately depressing flick. Rated R for sexual situations and profanity. 125m. **DIR:** John Patrick Kelley. **CAST:** Kate Capshaw, Jeremy Davies, Vince Vaughn, Paul Rudd, Daniel Meyer, Ashley Judd. **1997 DVD**

LODGER, THE ★★★★ Alfred Hitchcock's first signature thriller remains a timeless piece of wonder, showcasing the unique visual and stylistic tricks that would mark his work for years to come. Ivor Novello stars as a man who checks into a boardinghouse and becomes the object of scrutiny when a series of murders plague the area. Silent. B&W; 75m. **DIR:** Alfred Hitchcock. **CAST:** Ivor Novello, Malcolm Keen, Marie Ault. **1926 DVD**

LOGAN'S RUN ★★★ Popular but overlong sci-fi film concerning a futuristic society where people are only allowed to live to the age of 30, and a policeman nearing the limit who searches desperately for a way to avoid mandatory extermination. Nice production is enhanced immeasurably by outlandish sets and beautiful, imaginative miniatures. Rated PG. 120m. **DIR:** Michael Anderson. **CAST:** Michael York, Jenny Agutter, Peter Ustinov, Richard Jordan. **1976 DVD**

LOIS GIBBS AND THE LOVE CANAL ★★1/2 Marsha Mason is good as the housewife-turned-activist who fought for justice for residents of Niagara Falls after it was discovered that their homes were built over a toxic waste dump. But this made-for-TV movie tends to trivialize that real-life tragedy. 95m. **DIR:** Glenn Jordan. **CAST:** Marsha Mason, Bob Gunton, Penny Fuller. **1982**

LOLA (1960) ★★★★ Jacques Demy adapts the intoxicating camera pyrotechnics and style of Max Ophüls (to whom the film is dedicated) in this unjustly forgotten new wave classic starring Anouk Aimée as a cabaret singer romantically involved with three men. A delight. In French with English subtitles. Not rated. 91m. **DIR:** Jacques Demy. **CAST:** Anouk Aimée, Marc Michel. **1960**

LOLA (1982) ★★★★ Viewers can't help but be dazzled and delighted with the late Rainer Werner Fassbinder's offbeat remake of *The Blue Angel*. Centering his story on a singer-prostitute named Lola (Barbara Sukowa), Fassbinder reveals a cynical view of humanity. Rated R. In German with English subtitles. 114m. **DIR:** Rainer Werner Fassbinder. **CAST:** Barbara Sukowa, Armin Mueller-Stahl, Mario Adorf. **1982**

LOLA MONTES ★★★★★ A dazzlingly beautiful film. Mirroring the fragmented flashbacks in which the heroine, now reduced to a circus act, recounts her love affairs through nineteenth-century Europe, Max Ophüls's camera swoops and spins through the entire span of the expanded screen, retained in the video's letter box format. In French with English subtitles. Not rated. 110m. **DIR:** Max Ophüls. **CAST:** Martine Carol, Peter Ustinov, Anton Walbrook, Oskar Werner. **1955 DVD**

LOLA'S GAME 🦃 Shoddily made, poorly plotted thriller of a cop searching for the killer of his girlfriend. The pits. Rated R for nudity, sexual situations, profanity, and violence. 75m. **DIR:** Tim Andrew. **CAST:** Doug Jeffrey, Elise Miller, Antonio Guma, Joe Estevez. **1998**

LOLITA (1962) ★★★ A man's unconventional obsession for a "nymphet" is the basis for this bizarre satire. James Mason and Sue Lyon are the naughty pair in this film, which caused quite a stir in the 1960s but seems fairly tame today. B&W; 152m. **DIR:** Stanley Kubrick. **CAST:** James Mason, Sue Lyons, Shelley Winters, Peter Sellers. **1962 DVD**

LOLITA (1997) ★★★★ In this absorbing adaptation of Vladimir Nabokov's controversial novel, Jeremy Irons portrays the doomed and tragic Humbert Humbert. Employing a somber and self-critical voice-over, Irons introduces himself as damaged goods: a man who never fully left adolescence, thanks to the unexpected death of a childhood sweetheart. He therefore finds redemption of the damned upon meeting teenaged Lolita while seeking lodging in a 1947 New England town; from that point onward, the atmosphere of impending doom intensifies with the slow-motion horror of a train wreck. Despite her sexpot tendencies, inherited from a man-hungry mother, it's obvious that Lolita is anything but happy. Make no mistake: This is not a happy story. Rated R for profanity, nudity, violence, and extremely strong sexual content. 137m. **DIR:** Adrian Lyne. **CAST:** Jeremy Irons, Dominique Swain, Melanie Griffith, Frank Langella. **1997 DVD**

LONDON KILLS ME ★★★ True-to-life portrayal of a London drug dealer who wants to get a real job, but must first buy decent shoes. If you can sit through the gritty first half, you'll actually start rooting for the main character. Rated R for violence and nudity. 107m. **DIR:** Hanif Kureishi. **CAST:** Justin Chadwick, Steven Mackintosh, Emer McCourt, Roshan Seth, Fiona Shaw, Brad Dourif. **1992**

LONDON MELODY ★★★ Intrigued by her beauty and spunk, a kindhearted diplomat secretly helps a struggling cockney street singer realize her ambitions by financing her musical training. Charming slice of London nightlife before World War II. B&W; 71m. **DIR:** Herbert Wilcox. **CAST:** Anna Neagle, Tullio Carminati. **1937**

LONE DEFENDER, THE ★★ Two prospectors are ambushed and one of them, Rin Tin Tin's master, is murdered. For the next twelve installments of this early sound serial, Rinty chases and is chased by the Cactus Kid and his low-down thievin' gang. B&W; 12 chapters. **DIR:** Richard Thorpe. **CAST:** Rin Tin Tin, Walter Miller. **1930**

LONE JUSTICE ★★ So much for truth in packaging. This is only the first portion of the *Ned Blessing* television miniseries. Soon after star Daniel Baldwin arrives on screen to play the Western gunfighter as an adult, the tape screeches to a halt without resolving any plot elements. Don't be suckered by this one. Rated PG-13 for violence and profanity. 94m. **DIR:** Peter Werner. **CAST:** Daniel Baldwin, Luis Avalos, Chris Cooper, Julia Campbell, René Auberjonois, Jeff Kober. **1993**

LONE JUSTICE 2 ★★★ Stalwart gunfighter Ned Blessing is back, although his sidekick (Crecencio) is the only continuity between this and the previous installment. Even Blessing is played by somebody else! The good news is that Brad Johnson is far more believable in the role, but Bill Wittliff's screenplay provides no more closure than we found in part one. Rated PG for vio-

lence and mild profanity. 93m. **DIR:** Jack Bender. **CAST:** Brad Johnson, Luis Avalos, Brenda Bakke, Rob Campbell, Wes Studi. **1993**

LONE RANGER, THE (1938) ★★★1/2 One of America's most popular heroes rode out of the radio and onto the screen in one of the best and most fondly remembered serials of all time. The ballyhoo that accompanied the release of this exciting chapterplay made it an overwhelming hit at the box office. Thought to be lost until recently, most versions of this serial feature two chapters in French, the only copy available. B&W; 15 chapters. **DIR:** William Witney, John English. **CAST:** Lee Powell, Chief Thundercloud, Bruce Bennett, Lynne Roberts, William Farnum, Lane Chandler, George Montgomery, Hal Taliaferro, George Cleveland. **1938**

LONE RANGER, THE (1956) ★★★1/2 The first color feature film based on the legend of the Lone Ranger is a treat for the kids and not too tough for the adults to sit through. Clayton Moore and Jay Silverheels reprise their television roles and find themselves battling white settlers, led by an evil Lyle Bettger, and the much put-upon Indians, riled up by a surly Michael Ansara. 86m. **DIR:** Stuart Heisler. **CAST:** Clayton Moore, Jay Silverheels, Lyle Bettger, Bonita Granville. **1956 DVD**

LONE RANGER, THE (TV SERIES) ★★★1/2 Emerging from a cloud of dust, with a hearty "Hi-yo Silver!" the Lone Ranger, with his faithful Indian companion, Tonto, leads the fight for law and order in the Old West. Wearing a black mask fashioned from the vest of his murdered brother, the former Texas Ranger uses silver bullets to remind him of the value of human life. He sought justice, not vengeance, and became a hero to millions of youngsters. Now, these two-episode videocassettes enable you to return to those thrilling days of yesteryear. 55m. **DIR:** Various!. **CAST:** Clayton Moore, Jay Silverheels. **1949–1965**

LONE RANGER AND THE LOST CITY OF GOLD, THE ★★1/2 The Lone Ranger and Tonto, as immortalized by Clayton Moore and Jay Silverheels, expose the murderers who hold a clue to a fabulously wealthy lost city's location. 80m. **DIR:** Lesley Selander. **CAST:** Clayton Moore, Jay Silverheels, Douglas Kennedy, Noreen Nash, John Miljan. **1958 DVD**

LONE RUNNER 🦃 Our hero runs around a desert with a Rambo crossbow (complete with exploding arrows). Rated PG for violence and profanity. 84m. **DIR:** Ruggero Deodato. **CAST:** Miles O'Keeffe, Savina Gersak, Donal Hodson, Ronald Lacey. **1986**

LONE STAR (1952) ★★★ This rip-roaring Western disguised as a historical document works as both. Lionel Barrymore steals every scene he's in as the aging Andrew Jackson. He sends no-nonsense cattleman (Clark Gable) to keep Sam Houston from establishing Texas as a republic. Good action and lots of glamour from the stars. B&W; 94m. **DIR:** Vincent Sherman. **CAST:** Clark Gable, Ava Gardner, Broderick Crawford, Lionel Barrymore, Beulah Bondi, Ed Begley Sr. **1952**

LONE STAR (1996) ★★★1/2 An ambitious drama that combines a mystery story with social commentary, set amid three cultures—anglo, Mexican, black—in a Texas border town. Chris Cooper stars as a sheriff whose investigation into a decades-old murder may involve his father, the late, legendary former sheriff in town. Director John Sayles is also a novelist, and this is his most novel-like screenplay; in fact, it may be too broad based; the storyline sometimes meanders. 130m. **DIR:** John Sayles. **CAST:** Chris Cooper, Kris Kristofferson, Elizabeth Peña, Matthew McConaughey, Joe Morton, Clifton James. **1996 DVD**

LONE STAR RAIDERS ★★ The Three Mesquiteers try to save an old lady's ranch from bankruptcy by selling a herd of wild horses. Weak Mesquiteers entry burdened by too much stock footage. B&W; 54m. **DIR:** George Sherman. **CAST:** Robert Livingston, Bob Steele, Rufe Davis, Sarah Padden. **1940**

LONE STAR TRAIL ★★★1/2 In this entertaining oater, Johnny Mack Brown is framed in a robbery case. Obviously upset, he hits the trail to find the real perpetrators. In the process, he meets up with outlaw Robert Mitchum, and one of the great fistfights in movie history is the result. Certainly worth a view. B&W; 77m. **DIR:** Ray Taylor. **CAST:** Johnny Mack Brown, Tex Ritter, Fuzzy Knight, Robert Mitchum. **1943**

LONE TIGER 🦃 A skilled martial artist dons a cheesy-looking tiger mask to avenge his father's death against a vile fight promoter. Hilariously poor choreography can't help enliven this stinker. Not rated; may be too violent for children. 90m. **DIR:** Warren A. Stevens. **CAST:** Timothy Bottoms, Richard Lynch, Bruce Locke, Robert Z'Dar. **1999**

LONE WOLF ★★ Small-town students investigate a series of gory murders and discover a werewolf. Better than many such low-budget efforts, but barely worth seeing unless you're an avid lycanthrophile. Not rated, the film has some violence and gore. 96m. **DIR:** John Callas. **CAST:** Dyann Brown, Kevin Hart, Jamie Newcomb, Ann Douglas, Tom Henry. **1989**

LONE WOLF AND CUB: SWORD OF VENGEANCE ★★★★ The first entry in the Japanese series, previously seen in America only as *Shogun Assassin,* which reedited scenes from several of the films. The films are known to fans as the "Baby Cart" series because the hero, a former shogun executioner, pulls his infant son along in a baby cart while he wanders, searching for his wife's murderers. Newly subtitled and letterboxed, these films are all classics of the Japanese cinema, though the squeamish can't be warned too strongly about the intense violence. Not rated; contains graphic violence and nudity. 83m. **DIR:** Kenji Misumi. **CAST:** Tomisaburo Wakayama, Fumio Watanabe. **1973**

LONE WOLF MCQUADE ★★★1/2 Chuck Norris plays a Texas Ranger who forgets the rules in his zeal to punish the bad guys. Norris meets his match in David Carradine, the leader of a gun-smuggling ring. The worth-waiting-for climax is a martial arts battle between the two. Rated PG for violence and profanity. 107m. **DIR:** Steve Carver. **CAST:** Chuck Norris, L. Q. Jones, R. G. Armstrong, David Carradine, Barbara Carrera. **1983 DVD**

LONELINESS OF THE LONG DISTANCE RUNNER, THE ★★★★★ Powerful British drama about a youth in a reform school who runs in order to escape his dreary surroundings. Tom Courtenay is superb as Colin, a troubled youth who finds freedom of the mind with every step he runs. Michael Redgrave plays the governor of the reform school who sees opportunity in the boy's ability. Colin agrees to run in a race against another reform school in exchange for more freedom and how that

decision affects his beliefs brings the film to a natural yet frustrating conclusion. 104m. **DIR:** Tony Richardson. **CAST:** Tom Courtenay, Michael Redgrave, Avis Bunnage, Peter Madden, James Fox, Alec McCowen. **1962**

LONELY ARE THE BRAVE ★★★★ A "little" Hollywood Western set in modern times has a lot to offer those who can endure its heavy-handed message. Kirk Douglas is just right as the cowboy out of step with his times. His attempts to escape from jail on horseback in contrast to the mechanized attempts to catch him by a modern police force are handled well. B&W; 107m. **DIR:** David Miller. **CAST:** Kirk Douglas, Walter Matthau, Gena Rowlands. **1962**

LONELY GUY, THE ★★★ Steve Martin stars in this okay comedy as a struggling young writer. One day he comes home to find his live-in mate (Robyn Douglass) in bed with another man and becomes the "Lonely Guy" of the title. Only recommended for Steve Martin fans. Rated R for brief nudity and profanity. 90m. **DIR:** Arthur Hiller. **CAST:** Steve Martin, Robyn Douglass, Charles Grodin, Merv Griffin, Dr. Joyce Brothers. **1984 DVD**

LONELY HEARTS (1981) ★★★★1/2 A funny, touching Australian romantic comedy about two offbeat characters who fall in love. Peter (Norman Kaye) is a 50 year old mama's boy who doesn't know what to do with his life when his mother dies. Then he meets Patricia (Wendy Hughes), a woman who has never had a life of her own. It's a warmly human delight. Rated R. 95m. **DIR:** Paul Cox. **CAST:** Norman Kaye, Wendy Hughes, Julia Blake. **1981 DVD**

LONELY HEARTS (1991) ★★★1/2 Eric Roberts plays an unscrupulous swindler who wines and dines lonely women before taking all their assets for bogus investments. Beverly D'Angelo cramps his style by clinging desperately to him. Suspenseful made-for-cable thriller. 109m. **DIR:** Andrew Lane. **CAST:** Eric Roberts, Beverly D'Angelo, Joanna Cassidy, Herta Ware. **1991**

LONELY IN AMERICA ★★★1/2 Bittersweet comedy concerns an East Indian man's rude awakening to the less inviting aspects of immigrating to the United States. Some of his experiences are more painful than hilarious and, as such, send home a message about compassion and tolerance. Rated PG-13 for sexual situations. 96m. **DIR:** Barry Alexander Brown. **CAST:** Ranjit Chowdhry, Adelaide Miller, Robert Kessler. **1990**

LONELY LADY, THE 🦃 Pia Zadora as an aspiring writer who is used and abused by every man she meets. Rated R for violence, nudity, and profanity. 92m. **DIR:** Peter Sasdy. **CAST:** Pia Zadora, Lloyd Bochner, Bibi Besch. **1983**

LONELY MAN, THE ★★★ Interesting, but not exciting, this tautly directed oater is about a gunfighter, bent on reforming, who returns to his family after a seventeen-year hiatus. A brooding Jack Palance is the gunfighter. He is not warmly welcomed home by his deserted son, brooding Anthony Perkins. B&W; 87m. **DIR:** Henry Levin. **CAST:** Jack Palance, Anthony Perkins, Neville Brand, Robert Middleton, Elisha Cook Jr., Lee Van Cleef. **1957**

LONELY PASSION OF JUDITH HEARNE, THE ★★★★ Maggie Smith gives a superb, seamless performance as Judith Hearne, an Irish spinster in the 1950s sequestered from the carnal world by plainness and Catholicism. When she meets an Americanized Irishman (brilliantly portrayed by Bob Hoskins, New York accent and all), parts of her character's dormant personality spring to life. Rated R. 115m. **DIR:** Jack Clayton. **CAST:** Maggie Smith, Bob Hoskins, Marie Kean, Wendy Hiller. **1987**

LONELY TRAIL, THE ★★★ When former Yankee soldier John Wayne returns to his Texas ranch after the Civil War, he is greeted with suspicion and open hostility by his neighbors, whose sympathies were on the side of the Confederacy. Solid sagebrush saga. B&W; 58m. **DIR:** Joseph Kane. **CAST:** John Wayne, Ann Rutherford, Cy Kendall, Snowflake, Bob Kortman, Dennis Moore, Yakima Canutt. **1936**

LONELYHEARTS ★★ A perfect example of how Hollywood can ruin great material. Montgomery Clift is tortured, Robert Ryan is cynical, and Maureen Stapleton is pitifully sex-starved in this disappointing adaptation of Nathaniel West's brilliant novel about an agony columnist who gets too caught up in a correspondent's life. Baloney! B&W; 101m. **DIR:** Vincent J. Donehue. **CAST:** Montgomery Clift, Robert Ryan, Myrna Loy, Maureen Stapleton, Dolores Hart, Jackie Coogan, Mike Kellin, Frank Overton, Onslow Stevens. **1958**

LONESOME DOVE ★★★★★ Superb miniseries adapted from the sprawling novel by Larry McMurtry and originally written as a screenplay for John Wayne, Jimmy Stewart, and Henry Fonda. This is truly one of the great Westerns. Robert Duvall and Tommy Lee Jones give what are arguably the finest performances of their careers as a pair of aging Texas Rangers who go on one last adventure: a treacherous cattle drive to Montana. 384m. **DIR:** Simon Wincer. **CAST:** Robert Duvall, Tommy Lee Jones, Danny Glover, Diane Lane, Robert Urich, Frederic Forrest, D. B. Sweeney, Rick Schroder, Anjelica Huston, Chris Cooper, Timothy Scott, Glenne Headly, Barry Corbin, William Sanderson. **1989 DVD**

LONG AGO TOMORROW ★★★ Malcolm McDowell stars in this in-depth story about an arrogant soccer player who is paralyzed by a mysterious disease. A pretty young woman who shares the same disability is able to help him adapt. McDowell keeps the plot alive with a very believable performance. Rated PG. 116m. **DIR:** Bryan Forbes. **CAST:** Malcolm McDowell, Nanette Newman, Georgia Brown, Gerald Sim, Bernard Lee, Michael Flanders. **1970**

LONG DAY CLOSES, THE ★★★★1/2 This is another masterful and affecting stream-of-consciousness movie memoir from the creator of *Distant Voices/Still Lives*. Once again, he explores his rough-and-tumble, working-class English childhood. This later film spotlights his much warmer and loving feelings about his mother. Once again, colorful family members come and go, and the world is spiced with lovingly re-created songs of memory. Davies's movies are an acquired taste, but one well worth acquiring. 84m. **DIR:** Terence Davies. **CAST:** Marjorie Yates, Leigh McCormack, Anthony Watson. **1993**

LONG DAY'S JOURNEY INTO NIGHT (1962) ★★★★★ This superb film was based on Eugene O'Neill's play about a troubled turn-of-the-century New England family. Katharine Hepburn is brilliant as the drug-addict wife. Ralph Richardson is equally good as her husband, a self-centered actor. One of their sons is an alcoholic, while the

other is dying of tuberculosis. Although depressing, it is an unforgettable viewing experience. B&W; 136m. **DIR:** Sidney Lumet. **CAST:** Katharine Hepburn, Ralph Richardson, Jason Robards Jr., Dean Stockwell. **1962**

LONG DAY'S JOURNEY INTO NIGHT (1987) ★★★★ Excellent television adaptation of Eugene O'Neill's harrowing drama about a New England family in deep crisis. The stunning direction by Jonathan Miller makes this almost the equal of the 1962 film. Jack Lemmon turns in another powerful performance. Recommended for mature audiences. 169m. **DIR:** Jonathan Miller. **CAST:** Jack Lemmon, Bethel Leslie, Peter Gallagher, Kevin Spacey. **1987**

LONG GONE ★★★★ This very likable film follows the exploits of a minor-league baseball team and their manager (William Petersen) during one magical season in Florida during the early Fifties. Insightful HBO-produced movie is not unlike *Bull Durham* in that both take a loving look at America's favorite pastime while dissecting other societal concerns. 110m. **DIR:** Martin Davidson. **CAST:** William L. Petersen, Virginia Madsen, Henry Gibson. **1987**

LONG GOOD FRIDAY, THE ★★★★★ This superb British film depicts the struggle of an underworld boss (Bob Hoskins, in a brilliant performance) to hold on to his territory. It's a classic in the genre on a par with *The Godfather*, *The Public Enemy*, and *High Sierra*. Rated R for nudity, profanity, and violence. 114m. **DIR:** John Mackenzie. **CAST:** Bob Hoskins, Helen Mirren, Pierce Brosnan. **1980 DVD**

LONG GOODBYE, THE ★★★★ In this revisionist, haunting telling of the Raymond Chandler detective novel, "It's okay with me" is the easygoing credo of private eye Philip Marlowe as he drifts among the rich and nasty. This multilayered movie adapted by Leigh Brackett is not for all tastes, but a must-see in our book. Rated R for violence and profanity. 112m. **DIR:** Robert Altman. **CAST:** Elliott Gould, Nina Van Pallandt, Sterling Hayden, Henry Gibson, Mark Rydell, Jim Bouton, David Carradine, David Arkin, Warren Berlinger. **1973**

LONG GRAY LINE, THE ★★★ John Ford stock company regulars Maureen O'Hara and Ward Bond join heartthrob Tyrone Power in this sentimental tale of a celebrated West Point athletic trainer, and his years of devoted service to the academy and its plebes before cheating scandals and racial bigotry. 138m. **DIR:** John Ford. **CAST:** Tyrone Power, Maureen O'Hara, Robert Francis, Ward Bond, Donald Crisp, Betsy Palmer. **1955**

LONG HAUL ★★ Blond bombshell Diana Dors entices unhappily married trucker Victor Mature into nefarious schemes. Limp British drama. B&W; 100m. **DIR:** Ken Hughes. **CAST:** Victor Mature, Patrick Allen, Diana Dors. **1957**

LONG HOT SUMMER, THE (1958) ★★★★ Paul Newman drifts into a Mississippi town and sets hearts aflutterin' and tongues awaggin' as he fascinates the womenfolk, alienates the menfolk, and aggravates Big Daddy Varner, the town's monied redneck. Based on parts of two short stories and one novel by William Faulkner, this hodgepodge of sex, scandal, and suspicion is great fun. 115m. **DIR:** Martin Ritt. **CAST:** Paul Newman, Joanne Woodward, Orson Welles, Anthony Franciosa, Lee Remick, Angela Lansbury. **1958**

LONG HOT SUMMER, THE (1985) ★★★1/2 Don Johnson is a drifter who comes to a small southern town and upsets the routine of a family clan headed by patriarch Jason Robards. As well as being a moving, steamy tale of lust and greed, it also shows that director Stuart Cooper can get above-average performances from the likes of Johnson and Cybill Shepherd. This telemovie was originally shown in two parts. 208m. **DIR:** Stuart Cooper. **CAST:** Don Johnson, Jason Robards Jr., Cybill Shepherd, Judith Ivey, Ava Gardner, Wings Hauser. **1985**

LONG JOHN SILVER ★★★ Avast me hearties, Robert Newton is at his scene-chewing best in this otherwise unexceptional (and unofficial) sequel to Disney's *Treasure Island*. 109m. **DIR:** Byron Haskin. **CAST:** Robert Newton, Connie Gilchrist, Kit Taylor, Grant Taylor. **1954**

LONG KISS GOODNIGHT, THE ★★★★ OK, so this story, about a suburban mom with amnesia who discovers she's a highly trained, remorseless assassin, is pure hokum. If you can forget the implausibility of the premise, it's great fun for action fans, as star Geena Davis and her reluctant companion, Samuel L. Jackson, get out of one tight scrape after another. Director Renny Harlin keeps his tongue planted firmly in cheek throughout. Rated R for violence and profanity. 120m. **DIR:** Renny Harlin. **CAST:** Geena Davis, Samuel L. Jackson, Patrick Malahide, Craig Bierko, Brian Cox, David Morse, G. D. Spradlin. **1996 DVD**

LONG LIVE YOUR DEATH ★★ A fake prince, a fake Mexican revolutionary hero, and a journalist try to locate a hidden treasure. A comedy-spaghetti Western set in Mexico with some good sight gags and dialogue. Eli Wallach is at his best. Not rated; contains violence. 98m. **DIR:** Duccio Tessari. **CAST:** Franco Nero, Eli Wallach, Lynn Redgrave, Marilu Tolo, Eduardo Fajardo. **1974**

LONG LONG TRAIL ★★★ Hooter is the Ramblin' Kid in a typical, but above-average, lighthearted Gibson Western. This one's a racehorse story. Love interest Sally Eilers became the real Mrs. Gibson a few months later. B&W; 60m. **DIR:** Arthur Rosson. **CAST:** Hoot Gibson, Sally Eilers, Walter Brennan. **1929**

LONG, LONG TRAILER, THE ★★★ You might not love Lucy in this one, but you'll sure like her a lot. Ball and Desi Arnaz portray a couple not unlike the Ricardos. Their honeymoon trip is complicated by an impossibly long trailer. Once their dream vehicle, this trailer becomes a nightmare. 103m. **DIR:** Vincente Minnelli. **CAST:** Lucille Ball, Desi Arnaz Sr., Marjorie Main, Keenan Wynn. **1954**

LONG RIDERS, THE ★★★1/2 Film about the James-Younger Gang has a few deficiencies. Character development and plot complexity are ignored in favor of lots of action. This is partly offset by the casting of real-life brothers. While it sounds like a gimmick, it actually adds a much-needed dimension of character to the picture. Rated R for violence. 100m. **DIR:** Walter Hill. **CAST:** David Carradine, Keith Carradine, Robert Carradine, Stacy Keach, James Keach, Nicholas Guest, Christopher Guest, Dennis Quaid, Randy Quaid. **1980 DVD**

LONG ROAD HOME, THE ★★1/2 A family of Texas migrant workers, led by a former rodeo star, longs to escape their existence and move into their own house. There are some good performances in this heartfelt

made-for-cable drama, but it's no *Grapes of Wrath*. Not rated; contains mild violence. 88m. **DIR:** John Korty. **CAST:** Mark Harmon, Lee Purcell, Morgan Weisser, Leon Russom. **1991 DVD**

•**LONG RUN, THE** ★★1/2 Familiar tale of a crusty running coach who alienates everyone around him. Armin Mueller-Stahl plays to type as Berry Bohmer, a German immigrant who works at a South African brick factory. When he's not working, Berry trains the workers to compete in the rugged Comrades Marathon. After Berry is laid off, he offers to train South African refugee Christine for the race. Their relationship is filled with every sports cliché on record, but the actors manage to reach the finish line nonetheless. Rated R for adult language and nudity. 115m. **DIR:** Jean Stewart. **CAST:** Armin Mueller-Stahl, Nthati Moshesh, Paterson Joseph. **2000 DVD**

LONG VOYAGE HOME, THE ★★★★1/2 Life in the merchant marines as experienced and recalled by Nobel Prize–winning playwright Eugene O'Neill. The hopes and dreams and comradeship of a group of seamen beautifully blended in a gripping, moving account of men, a ship, and the ever-enigmatic sea. The major characters are superbly drawn by those playing them. Definitely a must-see, and see-again, film. Classic. B&W; 105m. **DIR:** John Ford. **CAST:** John Wayne, Barry Fitzgerald, Thomas Mitchell, Mildred Natwick. **1940**

LONG WALK HOME, THE ★★★★ Superb performances by Sissy Spacek and Whoopi Goldberg highlight this absorbing drama about the first civil rights action: the Montgomery, Alabama, bus boycott of 1956. Rated PG for racial epithets and brief violence. 97m. **DIR:** Richard Pearce. **CAST:** Sissy Spacek, Whoopi Goldberg, Dwight Schultz, Ving Rhames, Dylan Baker. **1990**

LONG WAY HOME, THE ★★★ Director Michael Apted turns his cameras on Russian rock 'n' roller Boris Grebenshikov, whose musical odyssey is both tune-filled and inspirational. From Leningrad to New York to Los Angeles, the cameras document Russia's equivalent of Bruce Springsteen. Musical cameos by Dave Stewart, Annie Lennox, and Chrissie Hynde. Not rated. 82m. **DIR:** Michael Apted. **1989**

LONG WEEKEND ★★★1/2 This Australian film is a must-see for environmentalists. We are introduced to a couple who carelessly start a forest fire, run over a kangaroo, senselessly destroy a tree, shoot animals for the sport of it, and break an eagle's egg. Then nature avenges itself. Not rated, this contains obscenities, nudity, and gore. 95m. **DIR:** Colin Eggleston. **CAST:** John Hargreaves, Briony Behets. **1986**

LONGEST DAY, THE ★★★★★ A magnificent re-creation of the Allied invasion of Normandy in June of 1944 with an all-star cast, this epic war film succeeds where others may fail—*Midway* and *Tora! Tora! Tora!*, for example. A big-budget film that shows you where the money was spent, it's first-rate in all respects. B&W; 180m. **DIR:** Ken Annakin, Andrew Marton, Bernhard Wicki. **CAST:** John Wayne, Robert Mitchum, Henry Fonda, Richard Burton, Rod Steiger, Sean Connery, Robert Wagner. **1963 DVD**

LONGEST DRIVE, THE ★★1/2 Culled from the 1976 television series, *The Quest*, this passable Western features Kurt Russell and Tim Matheson as two young brothers who help save an Irish rancher's herd, land, and fiery reputation. 92m. **DIR:** Bernard McEveety. **CAST:** Kurt Russell, Tim Matheson, Dan O'Herlihy, Keenan Wynn, Woody Strode, Erik Estrada. **1976**

LONGEST HUNT, THE ★★ A legendary gunfighter named Stark is hired by a wealthy Mexican landowner to bring back his rebellious son who has joined a gang of American bandits. Stark succeeds but a surprise awaits when he finds out the boy is not the landowner's son. A good story twist makes this an enjoyable film. Not rated; contains violence. 89m. **DIR:** Frank B. Corlish. **CAST:** Brian Kelly, Keenan Wynn, Erica Blanc, Fred Munroe, Virginia Field, Duane Rowland. **1968**

LONGEST YARD, THE ★★★★ An ex–professional football quarterback (Burt Reynolds) is sent to a Florida prison for stealing his girlfriend's car. The warden (Eddie Albert) forces Reynolds to put together a prisoner team to play his semipro team made up of guards. Great audience participation film with the last third dedicated to the game. Rated R for language and violence. 123m. **DIR:** Robert Aldrich. **CAST:** Burt Reynolds, Eddie Albert, Michael Conrad, Bernadette Peters, Ed Lauter. **1974**

LONGHORN ★★★★ Rancher Bill Elliott tries to drive Herefords backward on the Oregon Trail to mate with Texas longhorns and form a tough new breed of cattle. Along the way he battles Indians, discontent cowhands, and a treacherous partner. The first, and possibly best, of Elliott's later Allied Artists films after leaving Republic where he'd starred in 34 Westerns over an eight-year period. B&W; 70m. **DIR:** Lewis D. Collins. **CAST:** William Elliott, Phyllis Coates, Myron Healey, John Hart. **1951**

LONGSHOT (1981) 🦃 A soccer star turns down a scholarship at a prestigious university in order to attend the football championships in Europe. 100m. **DIR:** E. W. Swackhamer. **CAST:** Leif Garrett, Ralph Seymour, Zoe Chaveau, Linda Manz. **1981**

LONGSHOT, THE (1985) 🦃 Dreck about small-time horse players. Rated PG. 110m. **DIR:** Paul Bartel. **CAST:** Tim Conway, Harvey Korman, Jack Weston, Ted Wass, Anne Meara, Stella Stevens, Jonathan Winters. **1985**

LONGTIME COMPANION ★★★★ An accessible and affecting film that puts a much-needed human face on the tragedy of AIDS. An ensemble piece following the lives and relationships among nine gay New Yorkers and one woman friend over nine years. The cast is superb, with Bruce Davison especially memorable. The perceptive script is by playwright Craig Lucas. Rated R for profanity. 96m. **DIR:** Norman René. **CAST:** Bruce Davison, Campbell Scott, Dermot Mulroney, Mark Lamos, Patrick Cassidy, John Dossett, Mary-Louise Parker. **1990**

LOOK BACK IN ANGER (1958) ★★★★1/2 This riveting look into one of the "angry young men" of the 1950s has Richard Burton and Claire Bloom at their best. Burton exposes the torment and frustration these men felt toward their country and private life with more vividness than you may want to deal with, but if you're looking for a realistic re-creation of the period, look no further. B&W; 99m. **DIR:** Tony Richardson. **CAST:** Richard Burton, Claire Bloom. **1958 DVD**

LOOK BACK IN ANGER (1980) ★★ Jimmy Porter is a failed trumpet player and lower-class intellectual who turns his dashed hopes into a symphony of verbal abuse played upon his wife and best friend. McDowell serves up a Porter who is smug and easy to despise, but his portrayal lacks the powerful rage of Richard Burton in the 1958 film version of this mid-Fifties stage smash. 101m. **DIR:** Lindsay Anderson. **CAST:** Malcolm McDowell, Lisa Banes, Fran Brill, Robert Brill, Raymond Hardie. **1980**

LOOK BACK IN ANGER (1989) ★★★★ Kenneth Branagh is brilliant as a detestable young man who constantly lashes out at his wife and business partner. This spellbinding adaptation of John Osborne's play was produced for British television. Not rated; contains profanity. 114m. **DIR:** David Jones. **CAST:** Kenneth Branagh, Emma Thompson, Gerard Horan, Siobhan Redmond. **1989**

LOOK FOR THE SILVER LINING ★★★ This supposed biography of Marilyn Miller is a familiar vaudeville-to-Broadway story. Take it as such and enjoy the songs from that era. Ray Bolger, as Miller's mentor, has some very good numbers. 100m. **DIR:** David Butler. **CAST:** June Haver, Ray Bolger, Gordon MacRae, Charlie Ruggles, Rosemary DeCamp, S. Z. Sakall, Walter Caltett, Will Rogers Jr. **1949**

LOOK WHO'S LAUGHING ★★ Pretty weak comedy featuring radio favorites Edgar Bergen and Fibber McGee and Molly. Rather lean on laughs, except when Charlie McCarthy takes the spotlight. B&W; 78m. **DIR:** Allan Dwan. **CAST:** Edgar Bergen, Jim Jordan, Marion Jordan, Lucille Ball, Harold Peary. **1941**

LOOK WHO'S TALKING ★★★★ Hilarious adventure of an unmarried woman (Kirstie Alley) seeking the perfect father for her baby. John Travolta becomes the baby's unconventional sitter. Baby Mikey's humorous impressions from conception to age one are relayed through the offscreen voice of Bruce Willis. PG-13 for an opening sex-ed sequence of Mikey's conception. 100m. **DIR:** Amy Heckerling. **CAST:** Kirstie Alley, John Travolta, Olympia Dukakis, George Segal. **1989 DVD**

LOOK WHO'S TALKING NOW 🦃 Precocious family dogs spar with voices supplied by Danny DeVito and Diane Keaton in this tired, insulting sequel. Rated PG-13. 97m. **DIR:** Tom Ropelewski. **CAST:** John Travolta, Kirstie Alley. **1993**

LOOK WHO'S TALKING TOO 🦃 A totally unfunny sequel that reunites the original cast but can't come up with the spark that made the first so enjoyable. Also featuring the voices of Bruce Willis, Roseanne Barr, and Damon Wayans. Rated PG-13. 81m. **DIR:** Amy Heckerling. **CAST:** John Travolta, Kirstie Alley, Olympia Dukakis, Elias Koteas. **1990 DVD**

LOOKALIKE, THE ★★★1/2 Kate Wilhelm's thoughtful story becomes an absorbing made-for-cable thriller. Melissa Gilbert stars as a young woman not entirely convinced of her sanity, following the death of her young daughter. It all builds to a stylish climax, with a few well-hidden surprises. Brief violence. Rated PG-13. 88m. **DIR:** Gary Nelson. **CAST:** Melissa Gilbert, Diane Ladd, Thaao Penghlis, Frances Lee McCain. **1990**

LOOKER ★★ Writer-director Michael Crichton describes this movie as "a thriller about television commercials," but it's really a fairly simpleminded suspense film. Plastic surgeon Albert Finney discovers a plot by evil mastermind James Coburn to clone models for television commercials. This is fiction? Rated PG because of nudity and violence. 94m. **DIR:** Michael Crichton. **CAST:** Albert Finney, James Coburn, Susan Dey, Leigh Taylor-Young. **1981**

LOOKIN' TO GET OUT ★★★ This offbeat comedy stars Jon Voight and Burt Young as a couple of compulsive gamblers out to hit the fabled "big score" in Las Vegas. It does drag a bit in the middle. However, the first hour zips by before you know it, and the ending is a humdinger. Rated R for violence and profanity. 104m. **DIR:** Hal Ashby. **CAST:** Jon Voight, Burt Young, Ann-Margret, Bert Remsen. **1982**

LOOKING FOR MIRACLES ★★★1/2 The summer of 1935 marks the reunion of two brothers separated by poverty. Heartwarming family entertainment originally made for the Disney Channel. 104m. **DIR:** Kevin Sullivan. **CAST:** Greg Spottiswood, Zachary Bennett, Joe Flaherty. **1990**

LOOKING FOR MR. GOODBAR ★★ A strong performance by star Diane Keaton almost saves this dismal character study about a woman drawn to sleazy sex and low-lifes. Rated R. 135m. **DIR:** Richard Brooks. **CAST:** Diane Keaton, Tuesday Weld, Richard Gere, Richard Kiley, Tom Berenger. **1977**

LOOKING FOR RICHARD ★★1/2 Al Pacino's attempt to bring Shakespeare to the masses is a vanity production that sags beneath the star-director's incessant mugging. Intended as a primer to *Richard III*, this opus instead becomes an exercise in frustration; every time we get involved in the play's drama and intrigue, Pacino drags us right back out. Not rated, but equivalent to a PG for profanity. 109m. **DIR:** Al Pacino. **CAST:** Al Pacino, Harris Yulin, Penelope Allen, Alec Baldwin, Kevin Spacey, Estelle Parsons, Winona Ryder, Aidan Quinn. **1996**

LOOKING FOR TROUBLE ★★ A girl who longs for a pet tries to save an abused elephant from a circus. Third-rate kids' fare whose only virtue is inoffensiveness. Rated PG. 73m. **DIR:** Jay Aubrey. **CAST:** Holly Butler, Shawn McAllister, Susan Gallagher. **1996**

LOOKING GLASS WAR, THE ★★ This plodding adaptation of John Le Carré's espionage novel about a Pole sent to get the scam on a rocket in East Berlin never gets off the ground. Most of the acting is as wooden as bleacher seating. Where's Smiley when we need him? Rated PG. 106m. **DIR:** Frank Pierson. **CAST:** Christopher Jones, Pia Degermark, Ralph Richardson, Anthony Hopkins. **1970**

LOONEY, LOONEY, LOONEY BUGS BUNNY MOVIE ★★★1/2 This follow-up to the *Bugs Bunny/Road Runner Movie* lacks the earlier film's inventiveness, but then Chuck Jones was always the most cerebral of the Warner Bros. cartoon directors. Friz Freleng, on the other hand, only tried to make people laugh. This collection of his cartoons—which feature Daffy Duck, Porky Pig, Tweety Pie, and Yosemite Sam, among others, in addition to Bugs—does just that with general efficiency. Rated G. 79m. **DIR:** Friz Freleng. **1981**

LOOPHOLE ★★1/2 In yet another heist film, unemployed architect Albert Finney concocts an ambitious plan to break into a highly guarded and impenetrable London bank. There is a bit of snap in the scenario and dialogue, but ultimately the film loses its freshness. Su-

sannah York gives a fine performance. Not rated. 105m. **DIR:** John Quested. **CAST:** Albert Finney, Martin Sheen, Susannah York, Colin Blakely. **1980**

LOOSE CANNONS ★★ Gene Hackman stars as a hard-nosed career policeman who gets stuck with the deranged Dan Aykroyd as a partner. Only a few funny scenes provided by Aykroyd, including one in which he imitates the Road Runner, save this uneven cop comedy. Rated R for profanity and violence. 90m. **DIR:** Bob Clark. **CAST:** Gene Hackman, Dan Aykroyd, Dom DeLuise, Ronny Cox, Nancy Travis, Robert Prosky, Paul Koslo. **1990**

LOOSE CONNECTIONS ★★★1/2 In this cult comedy, an Englishwoman (Lindsay Duncan) builds a car with two female friends so that they can attend a feminist convention in Germany. At the last minute, her friends back out, and she is forced to accept a goofy substitute (Stephen Rea) as her traveling companion. Offbeat entertainment. Rated PG for profanity. 90m. **DIR:** Richard Eyre. **CAST:** Stephen Rea, Lindsay Duncan. **1984**

LOOSE SHOES Failed attempt to spoof B movies. Rated R. 73m. **DIR:** Ira Miller. **CAST:** Buddy Hackett, Howard Hesseman, Bill Murray, Susan Tyrrell, Avery Schreiber. **1977**

LOOT ★★ A hearse driver and his friend rob a bank and store the loot inside a coffin, setting off a slapstick, cliché-ridden comedy complete with a runaway funeral procession—and every graveyard quip in the book. Dated now, this was probably racy in its day. Not rated. 102m. **DIR:** Silvio Narizzano. **CAST:** Lee Remick, Richard Attenborough, Milo O'Shea, Hywel Bennett. **1972**

LORD JIM ★★★★ Joseph Conrad's complex novel of human weakness has been simplified for easier appreciation and brought to the screen in a lavish visual style. Peter O'Toole is Jim, a sailor in Southeast Asia who is adopted by a suppressed village as its leader in spite of a past clouded by allegations of cowardice. The belief shown in him by the native villagers is put to the test by a group of European thugs. 154m. **DIR:** Richard Brooks. **CAST:** Peter O'Toole, James Mason, Eli Wallach. **1965**

LORD LOVE A DUCK ★★★1/2 A cynic's delight that makes a big joke out of greed, lust, and egomania. Roddy McDowall plays a high school senior who helps classmate Tuesday Weld con her father, marry a hunk, become a movie star and—when she gets bored with everything else—become a widow. A lot of laughs, but not for every taste. B&W; 105m. **DIR:** George Axelrod. **CAST:** Roddy McDowall, Tuesday Weld, Lola Albright, Ruth Gordon, Max Showalter, Martin Gabel, Harvey Korman, Donald Murphy, Sarah Marshall. **1966**

LORD OF ILLUSIONS Horror impresario Clive Barker's nasty little shocker, intended to be a suspenseful marriage of Lovecraft and detective *film noir*, emerges instead as an incoherent mess with a hero who behaves like a daft fool at all times. Rated R for violence, profanity, and gore. 108m. **DIR:** Clive Barker. **CAST:** Scott Bakula, Kevin J. O'Connor, Famke Janssen, Vincent Schiavelli. **1995 DVD**

LORD OF THE FLIES (1963) ★★★★ William Golding's grim allegory comes to the screen in a near-perfect adaptation helmed by British stage director Peter Brook. English schoolboys, stranded on an island and left to their own devices, gradually revert to the savage cruelty of wild animals. Visually hypnotic and powerful, something you just can't tear your eyes away from. The cast is outstanding, and what the film fails to take from Golding's symbolism, it compensates for with raw energy. B&W; 91m. **DIR:** Peter Brook. **CAST:** James Aubrey, Hugh Edwards, Tom Chapin. **1963 DVD**

LORD OF THE FLIES (1989) ★★ This 1989 Americanization of Sir William Golding's apocalyptic novel has the external trappings of a good film—lush scenery, and a fine cast of unknowns. But the depth and sensitivity of the 1963 Peter Brook version are blatantly missing. Rated R for profanity and violence. 120m. **DIR:** Harry Hook. **CAST:** Balthazar Getty. **1989 DVD**

LORD OF THE RINGS, THE J.R.R. Tolkien's beloved epic fantasy is trashed in this animated film. Rated PG. 133m. **DIR:** Ralph Bakshi. **1978 DVD**

•LORD OF THE RINGS, THE: FELLOWSHIP OF THE RING ★★★★★ In this glorious screen adaptation of J.R.R. Tolkien's beloved fantasy epic, a sweet-natured hobbit named Frodo finds himself chosen to be the "bearer" of a powerful ring capable of instilling its curse of evil intent in nearly all who possess it. Only the purity of his innocence protects our frail, little hero as he, with the help of a "fellowship" of nine, faces horrific dangers as he carries it to the one place its powers can be nullified for all time: Mount Doom, the domain of the villainous sorcerer who gave it life. This first installment in a three-part series is so entrancing that it hardly seems nearly three hours long. Perfect casting, superb filmmaking, and special effects that seem astounding in these seen-it-all times make it a film to treasure. Rated PG-13 for violence and scary stuff. 178m. **DIR:** Peter Jackson. **CAST:** Elijah Wood, Alan Howard, Noel Appleby, Billy Boyd, Ian McKellan, Viggo Mortensen, Dominic Monaghan, Sean Astin, Sala Baker, Liv Tyler, Ian Holm, Orlando Bloom, Christopher Lee, Cate Blanchett. **2001 DVD**

LORDS OF DISCIPLINE, THE ★★★1/2 A thought-provoking film, *Lords* contains many emotionally charged and well-played scenes. David Keith stars as a student at a military academy who puts his life in danger by helping a black cadet being hazed. Rated R for profanity, nudity, and violence. 102m. **DIR:** Franc Roddam. **CAST:** David Keith, Robert Prosky, G. D. Spradlin, Rick Rossovich. **1983**

LORDS OF FLATBUSH, THE ★★1/2 Of all the leads, only Paul Mace didn't go on to bigger things. The film provides a fairly satisfying blend of toughness and sentimentality, humor and pathos, as it tells a story of coming-of-age in 1950s New York. Rated PG. 88m. **DIR:** Stephen F. Verona, Martin Davidson. **CAST:** Perry King, Sylvester Stallone, Henry Winkler, Paul Mace, Susan Blakely. **1974 DVD**

LORDS OF THE DEEP Poverty-row quickie, designed solely to cash in on the underwater menace subgenre spearheaded by *The Abyss*. Inexplicably rated PG-13. 79m. **DIR:** Mary Ann Fisher. **CAST:** Bradford Dillman, Priscilla Barnes. **1989**

LORENZO'S OIL ★★★★★ In a switch from his *Mad Max* films, doctor-turned-director George Miller uses the full force of his knowledge and skills to make gripping this emotionally powerful tale about a couple fighting for the life of their seriously ill son. In refusing to accept the verdict of a stodgy, entrenched medical

establishment, the parents use every means possible to find a cure. Based on a true story. Rated PG-13 for profanity. 135m. **DIR:** George Miller. **CAST:** Nick Nolte, Susan Sarandon, Peter Ustinov, Kathleen Wilhoite. **1992**

LORNA DOONE ★★★1/2 Beautiful, made-for-British-television adaptation of R. D. Blackmore's romantic novel stars Sean Bean and Polly Walker as star-crossed lovers whose union adds some kinks to a family feud. After his parents are killed, John Ridd vows to kill the Doone family, but unexpectedly falls for their daughter Lorna. Wonderfully romantic and steeped in period detail. Rated PG. 90m. **DIR:** Andrew Grieve. **CAST:** Sean Bean, Polly Walker, Clive Owen, Billie Whitelaw. **1990 DVD**

LOS OLVIDADOS ★★★★★ Luis Buñuel marks the beginning of his mature style with this film. Hyperpersonal, shocking, erotic, hallucinogenic, and surrealistic images are integrated into naturalistic action: two youths of the Mexican slums venture deeper and deeper into the criminal world until they are beyond redemption. In Spanish with English subtitles. B&W; 88m. **DIR:** Luis Buñuel. **CAST:** Alfonso Mejia, Roberto Cobo. **1950**

LOSER ★★★ Hick Jason Biggs finds trouble fitting in after getting accepted to a big-city college. Solace comes from an eccentric young woman who doesn't worry about peer pressure but has problems of her own: namely, the narcissistic professor with whom she's having an affair. Watching these two young folks stumble into a relationship has moments of genuine poignance, but overall the film lacks the punch of writer-director Amy Heckerling's earlier efforts. Rated PG-13 for drug content, profanity, and coarse sexual references. 98m. **DIR:** Amy Heckerling. **CAST:** Jason Biggs, Mena Suvari, Zak Orth, Thomas Sadoski, Jimmi Simpson, Greg Kinnear, Dan Aykroyd. **2000 DVD**

LOSERS, THE 🦃 Imagine *Rambo* made as a biker film and you'll have *The Losers*. Rated R for violence and nudity. 95m. **DIR:** Jack Starrett. **CAST:** William Smith, Bernie Hamilton, Adam Roarke. **1970**

LOSIN' IT ★★★ Better-than-average teen exploitation flick, this one has four boys off to Tijuana for a good time. Shelley Long ("Cheers") adds interest as a runaway wife who joins them on their journey. Rated R. 104m. **DIR:** Curtis Hanson. **CAST:** Tom Cruise, Shelley Long, Jackie Earle Haley, John Stockwell. **1982 DVD**

LOSING CHASE ★★★1/2 Helen Mirren dominates this character study, as a depressed wife trying to regain her stability following a public nervous breakdown. Her attentive husband hires a "mother's helper" to keep the two young children in line, but the newcomer proves more beneficial to Mirren. Anne Meredith's thoughtful script builds to an unexpected twist but then stops too soon; it would be nice to see what happens next. Rated PG-13 for profanity and dramatic content. 95m. **DIR:** Kevin Bacon. **CAST:** Helen Mirren, Kyra Sedgwick, Beau Bridges, Michael Yarmush, Lucas Denton. **1996**

LOSING ISAIAH ★★1/2 Adoptive Caucasian parents of an abandoned African American crack baby land in court when the kid's rehabbed, biological mom tries to get him back. The performances are first-rate, but the film feels just as manipulative as its dueling attorneys. Rated R for language and drug use. 108m. **DIR:** Stephen Gyllenhaal. **CAST:** Jessica Lange, Halle Berry, David Strathairn, Samuel L. Jackson, Cuba Gooding Jr. **1995**

LOSS OF SEXUAL INNOCENCE, THE ★★1/2 This plot-free film plays like a stream of dreams. The downside is that it also feels like a film-school experiment driven by Calvin Klein ad aesthetics. The core story is about a filmmaker who has lost much more than the film's provocative title suggests. Scenes in which a curious child evolves to a jaded adult are also intercut with a modern version of Adam and Eve in which a black man and white woman emerge from a small lake. There's enough philosophical and cinematic doodling here for several films. Rated R for nudity, sexuality, language, and violence. 101m. **DIR:** Mike Figgis. **CAST:** Julian Sands, Jonathan Rhys-Meyers, Saffron Burrows, Femi Ogumbanjo, Hanne Klintoe. **1999 DVD**

LOST! ★★★1/2 Even though it contains no nudity or violence, this is a movie that you should be careful about letting children see. Based on a true incident, it tells of three people adrift in the Pacific Ocean on an overturned boat. One, a religious zealot, feels that their plight is a test of God, and that they should do nothing to try to help themselves. Not rated. 94m. **DIR:** Peter Rowe. **CAST:** Kenneth Walsh, Helen Shaver, Michael Hogan. **1986**

•LOST AND DELIRIOUS ★★★★ This poetic and heartbreaking adaptation of Susan Swan's *The Wives of Bath* is fueled by Piper Perabo's strong performance as a self-destructive young woman who (borrowing the film's Shakespearean overtones) loves wisely, but not too well. A shy new student at a girls' school must forge her own identity after learning how *not* to behave by observing her two roommates, whose lesbian relationship comes to a tragic end. The metaphysical final scene is needlessly contrived, but everything else in this film feels achingly authentic. Rated R for profanity, nudity, and strong sexual content. 100m. **DIR:** Léa Pool. **CAST:** Piper Perabo, Jessica Paré, Mischa Barton, Jackie Burroughs, Graham Greene, Mimi Kuzyk. **2001 DVD**

LOST AND FOUND (1979) ★★ After teaming up successfully for *A Touch of Class*, writer-director Melvin Frank and his stars, Glenda Jackson and George Segal, tried again. But the result was an unfunny comedy about two bickering, cardboard characters. Rated PG. 112m. **DIR:** Melvin Frank. **CAST:** Glenda Jackson, George Segal, Maureen Stapleton. **1979**

LOST & FOUND (1999) 🦃 David Spade plays a loser who kidnaps the dog of a beautiful French woman in order to win her heart. Go figure. One highlight: Spade doing his Neil Diamond impression. Rated PG-13 for language, sexual innuendo, and partial nudity. 97m. **DIR:** Jeff Pollack. **CAST:** David Spade, Sophie Marceau, Artie Lange, Patrick Bruel. **1999 DVD**

LOST ANGELS ★★★★ Adam Horovitz ("King Ad Rock" of the Beastie Boys) makes an impressive dramatic debut as Tim Doolan, a misguided teenager who winds up in a Los Angeles psychiatric counseling center, where one of the staff psychiatrists wants to see the troubled youngsters properly treated. Rated R for language and violence. 121m. **DIR:** Hugh Hudson. **CAST:** Adam Horovitz, Donald Sutherland, Amy Locane, Don Bloomfield, Celin Weston, Graham Beckel. **1989**

LOST BOYS, THE ★★ In this vampire variation on *Peter Pan*, director Joel Schumacher seems more inter-

ested in pretty shots and fancy costumes than atmosphere and plot. The story has Jason Patric falling in with a group of hip bloodsuckers led by Kiefer Sutherland. Rated R for violence, suggested sex, and profanity. 98m. **DIR:** Joel Schumacher. **CAST:** Jason Patric, Dianne Wiest, Corey Haim, Barnard Hughes, Edward Herrmann, Kiefer Sutherland, Jami Gertz, Corey Feldman. **1987 DVD**

LOST CAPONE, THE 🦃 Al Capone and his little-known brother, who became a lawman in Nebraska and fought the bootleggers sent by Brother Al. Dull television movie. 93m. **DIR:** John Gray. **CAST:** Adrian Pasdar, Ally Sheedy, Eric Roberts, Jimmie F. Skaggs. **1990**

LOST CHILD, THE ★★★★ Riveting *Hallmark Hall of Fame* feature follows a woman's journey back to her family. Following the deaths of the Jewish couple who raised her, she discovers that she is actually a Navajo Indian. Thriving on the loving reunion with her biological family, she seems oblivious to the challenges her husband and daughters face on the reservation. Great acting complements the fact-based script. Not rated; contains mature themes. 100m. **DIR:** Karen Arthur. **CAST:** Mercedes Ruehl, Jamey Sheridan, Tantoo Cardinal, Ned Romero, Irene Bedard. **2000**

LOST CITY, THE ★★ Incredibly bad serial becomes an incredible feature as crazy Zolok, maniacal ruler of a lost African city, uses a kidnapped scientist to wreak havoc on the rest of the world. Laughable thriller. B&W; 74m. **DIR:** Harry Revier. **CAST:** William "Stage" Boyd, Kane Richmond, George "Gabby" Hayes. **1935**

LOST COMMAND ★★★ A good international cast and fine direction bring to vivid life this story of French-Algerian guerrilla warfare in North Africa following World War II. Anthony Quinn is especially effective. Great action scenes. 130m. **DIR:** Mark Robson. **CAST:** Anthony Quinn, Alain Delon, George Segal, Michèle Morgan, Claudia Cardinale. **1966**

LOST CONTINENT, THE (1951) ★★ Air Force pilot Cesar Romero teams up with scientist John Hoyt to find a rocket ship that crash-landed on an uncharted island. They discover death and dinosaurs instead. Mild adventure-fantasy. 83m. **DIR:** Sam Newfield. **CAST:** Cesar Romero, Hillary Brooke, Chick Chandler, John Hoyt, Acquanetta, Sid Melton, Whit Bissell, Hugh Beaumont. **1951 DVD**

LOST CONTINENT, THE (1968) ★★1/2 Hammer adaptation of Dennis Wheatley's novel *Uncharted Seas* is a film that should have played more with adventure. Not up to the standards set by other Hammer productions. Rated G. 89m. **DIR:** Michael Carreras. **CAST:** Eric Porter, Suzanna Leigh. **1968 DVD**

LOST EMPIRE, THE 🦃 Inept, hokey film about the island stronghold of a mysterious ruler. Rated R for some nudity and violence. 86m. **DIR:** Jim Wynorski. **CAST:** Melanie Vincz, Raven De La Croix, Angela Aames, Paul Coufos, Robert Tessier. **1983 DVD**

LOST HIGHWAY ★★★ This weird, disturbing creep show is part nightmare, part surreal mystery. Fred Madison is a jazz saxophonist with a paranoia problem. The film's unofficial first act ends as Fred is arrested for his wife's murder. In act two, Fred morphs into a young car mechanic while on death row. He is released and begins a different life that intersects with his own past, a volatile crime boss, and a powder-faced sorcerer. Rated R for language, nudity, sex, and violence. 135m. **DIR:** David Lynch. **CAST:** Bill Pullman, Patricia Arquette, Balthazar Getty, Robert Loggia, Robert Blake. **1996**

LOST HONOR OF KATHARINA BLUM, THE ★★★ Angela Winkler's performance as Katharina Blum is the central force behind Schlondörff's interpretation of Heinrich Boll's novel. Katharina Blum is a poor, young housekeeper who spends one night with a suspected political terrorist. Her life is thereby ruined by the police and the media. In German with English subtitles. Rated R. 97m. **DIR:** Volker Schlöndorff. **CAST:** Angela Winkler. **1977**

LOST HORIZON ★★★★ Novelist James Hilton's intriguing story of a group of disparate people who survive an air crash and stumble onto a strange and haunting Tibetan land. One of the great classic films of the late 1930s. Long-missing footage has recently been restored, along with so-called lost scenes. B&W; 132m. **DIR:** Frank Capra. **CAST:** Ronald Colman, Jane Wyatt, John Howard, Edward Everett Horton, Margo, Sam Jaffe, Thomas Mitchell, Isabel Jewell, H. B. Warner. **1937 DVD**

LOST IN A HAREM ★★★ Abbott and Costello as traveling magicians attempt to save a singer from the clutches of a sheikh. Best bit is Costello locked up with a murderer who explains: "S-l-o-w-l-y, I turned." 89m. **DIR:** Charles F. Riesner. **CAST:** Bud Abbott, Lou Costello, Marilyn Maxwell, Douglass Dumbrille. **1944**

LOST IN ALASKA ★★ Gambling, mining, the Alaska gold rush, and anything else the writers could think of is tossed into this mess of a comedy, one of Abbott and Costello's weakest. B&W; 76m. **DIR:** Jean Yarbrough. **CAST:** Bud Abbott, Lou Costello, Tom Ewell, Mitzi Green. **1952**

LOST IN AMERICA ★★★★1/2 *Lost in America* is Albert Brooks' funniest film to date. Some viewers may be driven to distraction by Brooks's all-too-true study of what happens when a "successful" and "responsible" married couple chucks it all and goes out on an *Easy Rider*–style trip across the country. Brooks makes movies about the things most adults would consider their worst nightmare. If you can stand the pain, the pleasure is well worth it. Rated R for profanity and adult situations. 92m. **DIR:** Albert Brooks. **CAST:** Albert Brooks, Julie Hagerty, Garry Marshall. **1985 DVD**

LOST IN SPACE (1998) ★★★ The special effects in this big-screen re-creation of the tacky TV series are admittedly impressive, as is costar Matt LeBlanc's turn as the no-nonsense pilot. Otherwise, this version of *Swiss Family Robinson* in space is a convoluted affair, with a time-travel subplot that gets weirder and less convincing as it goes along. It's nice to see the quickie appearances by the original TV cast, but youngsters are sure to love it whether they know the old series or not. Rated PG-13 for violence. 131m. **DIR:** Stephen Hopkins. **CAST:** William Hurt, Mimi Rogers, Gary Oldman, Heather Graham, Lacey Chabert, Jack Johnson, Matt LeBlanc, Mark Goddard, June Lockhart, Edward Fox, Marta Kristen, Angela Cartwright. **1998 DVD**

LOST IN SPACE (TV SERIES) ★★★ The Robinson family volunteers to help Earth solve its overpopulation problem by exploring space. That incessantly fussy saboteur, Colonel Zachary Smith, thwarts their mission. Terrifically tacky special effects and loads of campy hu-

mor earned the show a cult following. The robot proved to be the most endearing personality on board. 60m. **DIR:** Leo Penn, Alexander Singer, Tony Leader. **CAST:** Guy Williams, June Lockhart, Mark Goddard, Jonathan Harris, Marta Kristen, Angela Cartwright, Billy Mumy. **1965–1968**

LOST IN THE BERMUDA TRIANGLE 🦃 How come really bad movies about the Bermuda Triangle never get lost in there? When his pregnant wife Mary disappears while on a cruise through the Triangle, husband Brian turns to a scientist for help. Their journey takes them to a parallel universe where flat acting, direction, and writing are as prevalent as bad movies about the Bermuda Triangle. Rated PG. 97m. **DIR:** Norberto Barba. **CAST:** Graham Beckel, Ron Canada, Christina Haag, Tom Verica. **1998**

LOST IN YONKERS ★★★★ Playwright Neil Simon wrote the screenplay for this adaptation of his Pulitzer and Tony Award–winning play about two brothers left with their crotchety old grandmother in the 1930s. Mercedes Ruehl is fabulous as the boys' aunt, a slightly dimwitted woman living with her mother (Irene Worth). Richard Dreyfuss also makes a fine impression as the boys' gangster uncle. Rated PG for adult themes. 110m. **DIR:** Martha Coolidge. **CAST:** Richard Dreyfuss, Mercedes Ruehl, Irene Worth, David Strathairn, Brad Stoll. **1993**

LOST LANGUAGE OF CRANES, THE ★★★ Set in England, this film deals with a homosexual who decides to tell his parents the truth, only to find out that his father has suppressed his own homosexuality for years. Eileen Atkins wonderfully portrays the mother who cannot accept her son's lifestyle and then loses her husband. Not rated; contains homosexual activity. 85m. **DIR:** Nigel Finch. **CAST:** Brian Cox, Eileen Atkins, Angus MacFadyen, Corey Parker, René Auberjonois, John Schlesinger, Cathy Tyson, Richard Warwick. **1992**

LOST MISSILE, THE ★★★ Scientists race to destroy an unmanned alien missile that, at a temperature of one million degrees, is melting everything in its path—and is heading for Manhattan. Reasonably tense low-budget sci-fi thriller with a good performance from its star, a very young Robert Loggia. B&W; 65m. **DIR:** Lester Berke. **CAST:** Robert Loggia, Ellen Parker, Philip Pine, Larry Kerr. **1958**

LOST MOMENT, THE ★★★1/2 A low-key, dark, offbeat drama based on Henry James's novel *The Aspern Papers*, which was based on a true story. A publisher (Robert Cummings), seeking love letters written by a long-dead great poet, goes to Italy to interview a very old lady and her niece. The old lady is spooky, the niece neurotic, the film fascinating. Those who know Cummings only from his TV series will be pleasantly surprised with his serious acting. B&W; 88m. **DIR:** Martin Gable. **CAST:** Robert Cummings, Susan Hayward, Agnes Moorehead, Eduardo Ciannelli. **1947**

LOST PATROL, THE ★★★★ An intrepid band of British cavalrymen lost in the Mesopotamian desert are picked off by the Arabs, one by one. Brisk direction and top-notch characterizations make this a winner—though it is grim. B&W; 65m. **DIR:** John Ford. **CAST:** Victor McLaglen, Boris Karloff, Wallace Ford, Reginald Denny, Alan Hale Sr., J. M. Kerrigan, Billy Bevan. **1934**

LOST PLANET, THE ★★ Interplanetary nonsense for the grammar-school set is the order of the day as reporters Judd Holdren and Vivian Mason lock electrons with an evil scientist and his allies from the planet Ergro. Suitably silly serial. B&W; 15 chapters. **DIR:** Spencer Gordon Bennet. **CAST:** Judd Heldren, Vivian Mason. **1953**

LOST SOULS 🦃 Desperate waif Winona Ryder tries to convince celebrity atheist Ben Chaplin that he's been chosen to be the Antichrist. This unholy spawn of *The Exorcist* out of *Rosemary's Baby* is dreary going indeed, even when it becomes unintentionally hilarious. Rated R for violence and profanity. 97m. **DIR:** Janusz Kaminski. **CAST:** Winona Ryder, Ben Chaplin, Sarah Wynter, Philip Baker Hall, John Hurt, Elias Koteas. **2000 DVD**

LOST SQUADRON ★★★ Mystery-adventure about the "accidental" deaths of former World War I pilots engaged as stunt fliers for the movies. Full of industry "in-jokes," breezy dialogue, and good stunts, this is a fun film—especially for anyone with an interest in stunt flying or aviation in general. B&W; 79m. **DIR:** George Archainbaud. **CAST:** Richard Dix, Mary Astor, Erich Von Stroheim, Joel McCrea, Dorothy Jordan, Robert Armstrong. **1932**

LOST STOOGES, THE ★★★ Leonard Maltin narrates this compilation of early film appearances by Ted Healy and the Three Stooges in MGM musicals and two-reel fillers—before Moe Howard, Larry Fine, and Curly Howard broke off to make their successful series of shorts for Columbia. These excerpts are primarily of interest for their historical value. Not rated, this direct-to-video release has Stooges-type violence. B&W; 68m. **DIR:** Mark Lamberti. **CAST:** Moe Howard, Larry Fine, Curly Howard, Ted Healy. **1990**

LOST WEEKEND, THE ★★★★★ Gripping, powerful study of alcoholism and its destructive effect on one man's life. Arguably Ray Milland's best performance (he won an Oscar) and undeniably one of the most potent films of all time. Forty years after its release, the movie has lost none of its importance or effectiveness. Additional Oscars for best picture, director, and screenplay. B&W; 101m. **DIR:** Billy Wilder. **CAST:** Ray Milland, Jane Wyman, Philip Terry, Howard DaSilva, Frank Faylen. **1945 DVD**

LOST WORLD, THE (1925) ★★★★ Silent version of Arthur Conan Doyle's classic story of Professor Challenger and his expedition to a desolate plateau roaming with prehistoric beasts. The movie climaxes with a brontosaurus running amok in London. An ambitious production, interesting as film history and quite entertaining, considering its age. B&W; 60m. Also available in a restored 102m. **DIR:** Harry Hoyt. **CAST:** Bessie Love, Lewis Stone, Wallace Beery. **1925 DVD**

LOST WORLD, THE (1992) ★★ Lackluster adaptation of Sir Arthur Conan Doyle's fanciful tale of a lost land where dinosaurs still roam. The film's low budget betrays its aspirations, making this period piece seem cheap and undermined. A group led by Professor Challenger (John Rhys-Davies) and zoological expert David Warner encounters cave men, the elements, and unconvincing dinosaurs. Not rated; contains some violence. 99m. **DIR:** Timothy Bond. **CAST:** David Warner, John Rhys-Davies, Eric McCormack, Tamara Gorski. **1992**

LOST WORLD, THE: JURASSIC PARK ★★★ In this weak sequel to *Jurassic Park*, Jeff Goldblum returns as the wisecracking, chaos-theory scientist, who this time leads a small team to investigate the doings at "Site B," the "nursery" where the dinosaurs were bred and later shipped to the first film's ill-fated park. The script bears little resemblance to Michael Crichton's novel, and matters really go to hell when our heroes are joined by a team of mercenaries bent on capturing dinosaurs and hauling them off to the San Diego Zoo. Rated PG-13 for profanity, violence, and gore. 134m. **DIR:** Steven Spielberg. **CAST:** Jeff Goldblum, Julianne Moore, Pete Postlethwaite, Arliss Howard, Richard Attenborough, Vince Vaughn, Vanessa Lee Chester. **1997 DVD**

LOTS OF LUCK ★★ Made for Disney's cable channel, this mildly funny family film exposes the darker side of striking it rich. A family (Martin Mull and Annette Funicello play dad and mom) suddenly wins the lottery. Unfortunately they lose their friends and privacy. 88m. **DIR:** Peter Baldwin. **CAST:** Martin Mull, Annette Funicello, Fred Willard, Polly Holliday, Mia Dillon, Tracey Gold. **1985**

LOTTO LAND ★★★★ Enjoyable, upbeat drama about how a missing New York lottery ticket worth $27 million sets a small Brooklyn neighborhood on its ear. Director-writer John Rubino has created a modern-day fable about hope and opportunity that's contagious. Larry Gilliard Jr. shines as a confused teenager trying to make sense of his life. The film has the most engaging characters and situations. Not rated; contains profanity and adult situations. 90m. **DIR:** John Rubino. **CAST:** Lawrence Gilliard Jr., Wendell Holmes, Suzanne Costallos, Barbara Gonzales. **1994 DVD**

LOTUS EATERS, THE ★★★1/2 Bittersweet comedy chronicles the loss of innocence of a family on a British Columbian island. While the husband falls under the spell of a sexy new teacher, the teenage daughter experiments with sex. These changes affect the 10 year old daughter, through whose eyes much is revealed. Both compelling and shocking to see the family's rapid, negative metamorphosis. Winner of multiple Genie and Atlantic Film Festival awards. Rated PG-13 for nudity and profanity. 101m. **DIR:** Paul Shapiro. **CAST:** Sheila McCarthy, Aloka McLean, R. H. Thomson, Tara Frederick, Michele-Barbara Pelletier. **1993**

LOUIS L'AMOUR'S CROSSFIRE TRAIL ★★★★ Keeping a deathbed promise, Tom Selleck comes to the aid of a widow (Virginia Madsen) in this intriguing TNT Western based on Louis L'Amour's action-packed story. Heroic Selleck takes on a wicked Mark Harmon who has his eye on Madsen and her land. Big shoot-out finale is well worth the wait. Not rated; contains violence. 97m. **DIR:** Simon Wincer. **CAST:** Tom Selleck, Virginia Madsen, Mark Harmon, Wilford Brimley. **2000**

LOUISIANA 🦃 Southern belle manages to destroy the lives of all around her. Made for television. 206m. **DIR:** Philippe de Broca. **CAST:** Margot Kidder, Ian Charleson, Victor Lanoux, Andrea Ferreol. **1984**

LOUISIANA PURCHASE ★★★1/2 Attempts are made to frame an honest fuddy-duddy senator (Victor Moore). Moore is a joy, but it is Bob Hope's classic filibuster that is the highlight of the movie. Based on an Irving Berlin musical; a few good songs were retained. 98m. **DIR:** Irving Cummings. **CAST:** Bob Hope, Vera Zorina, Victor Moore, Dona Drake, Raymond Walburn, Maxie Rosenbloom, Frank Albertson. **1941**

LOUISIANA STORY, THE ★★★ This last film by noted documentarian Robert Flaherty dramatizes the effect of oil development on the lives of a young boy, his family, and his pet raccoon in Louisiana. Score by Virgil Thomson, played by the Philadelphia Symphony Orchestra. B&W; 79m. **DIR:** Robert Flaherty. **1948**

LOULOU ★★★1/2 In this mixture of unabashed eroticism and deeply felt romanticism Isabelle Huppert and Gérard Depardieu play lovers who embark on a free-wheeling relationship. Lustful, explosive sexual psychodrama. In French with English subtitles. Rated R for nudity and profanity. 110m. **DIR:** Maurice Pialat. **CAST:** Isabelle Huppert, Gérard Depardieu, Guy Marchand. **1980 DVD**

LOVE ★★★★ Rich character study of two long-suffering women thrown together to enact the final chapter of the older woman's life. Lili Darvas is excellent as the fragile but feisty elder. In Hungarian with English subtitles. B&W; 92m. **DIR:** Karoly Makk. **CAST:** Lili Darvas, Mari Torocsik. **1971**

LOVE AFFAIR (1939) ★★★★ Romantic drama is at once sensitive, poignant, heartbreaking, and heartening. It tells the story of two jaded people who meet on shipboard, fall in love, part, agree to get together six months later, and are thwarted and tested by fate in the form of an accident. The plot is corn syrup, but the charm, grace, and razor-sharp timing of the stars raise it to minor classic status. Remade in 1957 as *An Affair to Remember*. 88m. **DIR:** Leo McCarey. **CAST:** Irene Dunne, Charles Boyer, Maria Ouspenskaya, Lee Bowman. **1939 DVD**

LOVE AFFAIR (1994) ★★★ A remake of Cary Grant and Deborah Kerr's 1957 *An Affair to Remember*, this film fails to temper the melodrama down for today's more cynical audiences. This time, Warren Beatty is a philandering fiancé (to Kate Capshaw) who's suddenly compelled to change his life in order to woo Annette Bening. Both Beatty and Bening are appealing but the sappy plot isn't to be believed. Rated PG-13 for adult themes and sexual situations. 95m. **DIR:** Glenn Gordon Caron. **CAST:** Warren Beatty, Annette Bening, Pierce Brosnan, Katharine Hepburn, Kate Capshaw, Garry Shandling. **1994 DVD**

LOVE AMONG THE RUINS ★★★★ In this made-for-TV comedy-romance, Katharine Hepburn plays opposite Laurence Olivier. The delightful story focuses on the plight of an aging actress who is being sued by a young gigolo for breach of promise. Her situation is further complicated when the prominent barrister handling her defense turns out to be a lovestruck former suitor. 100m. **DIR:** George Cukor. **CAST:** Katharine Hepburn, Laurence Olivier, Leigh Lawson, Joan Sims. **1975**

LOVE & A .45 ★★★★ A hot musical soundtrack and hot young stars make this modern-day Bonnie and Clyde tale a fast-and-furious treat. Gil Bellows and Renee Zellweger are sensational as the young lovers who tire of their small Texas town and turn to a life of crime. When a young girl is murdered during a robbery, the outlaw couple makes a run for the border, followed in hot pursuit by the law. Similar in theme to *Natural Born Killers* minus the acid trip. Rated R for violence, adult situations, and language. 120m. **DIR:** Darin Scott.

CAST: Gil Bellows, Renee Zellweger, Rory Cochrane. **1994**

LOVE AND ANARCHY ★★★★★ Giancarlo Giannini gets to eat up the screen with this role. Comic, tragic, and intellectually stimulating, this is Wertmuller's best film. Giannini is bent on assassinating Mussolini right after the rise of fascism but somehow gets waylaid. A classic. Rated R for sexual situations, language, and some nudity. 117m. **DIR:** Lina Wertmuller. **CAST:** Giancarlo Giannini, Mariangela Melato. **1973 DVD**

LOVE AND BASKETBALL ★★★ Childhood sweethearts enter into an extended rocky romance while chasing dreams of becoming professional hoop stars. Though well-acted, this romantic drama's many conflicts are too slickly developed and resolved to be deeply moving. The film was a huge hit at the Sundance Film Festival. Rated PG-13 for sexuality and language. 118m. **DIR:** Gina Prince-Bythewood. **CAST:** Sanaa Lathan, Omar Epps, Alfre Woodard, Dennis Haysbert, Debbi Morgan. **2000 DVD**

LOVE AND BULLETS Charles Bronson is hired to snatch Jill Ireland from crime lord Rod Steiger. Rated PG for violence. 103m. **DIR:** Stuart Rosenberg. **CAST:** Charles Bronson, Rod Steiger, Strother Martin, Bradford Dillman, Henry Silva, Jill Ireland. **1979**

LOVE AND DEATH ★★★★ This comedy set in 1812 Russia is one of Woody Allen's funniest films. Diane Keaton is the high-minded Russian with assassination (of Napoleon) in mind. Allen is her cowardly accomplice with sex on the brain. The movie satirizes not only love and death, but politics, classic Russian literature (Tolstoy's *War and Peace*), and foreign films, as well. Use of Prokofiev music enhances the piece. Rated PG. 82m. **DIR:** Woody Allen. **CAST:** Woody Allen, Diane Keaton, Harold Gould, Alfred Lutter, Zvee Scooler. **1975 DVD**

LOVE AND DEATH ON LONG ISLAND ★★★★ John Hurt plays an esoteric English writer—so out of tune with modern times that he doesn't even know a VCR needs a television to work—who becomes unexpectedly obsessed with a small-time American film actor (Jason Priestley). He even moves to New York to be near the object of his affection. Odd and offbeat, with many sensitive touches, this quiet little film sneaks up on you. Rated PG-13 for brief profanity. 103m. **DIR:** Richard Kwietniowski. **CAST:** John Hurt, Jason Priestley, Fiona Loewi, Sheila Hancock, Maury Chaykin. **1997 DVD**

LOVE AND HATE ★★★ Based on *A Canadian Tragedy*, by Maggie Siggins, this powerful film looks at the life of a prominent Saskatchewan family. Kate Nelligan plays the battered wife who finally leaves, only to be terrorized by her husband (Kenneth Welsh). Not rated. 176m. **DIR:** Francis Mankiewicz. **CAST:** Kate Nelligan, Kenneth Welsh, Leon Pownall, Brent Carver. **1989**

LOVE AND HUMAN REMAINS ★★ Quebec filmmaker Denys Arcand's first English-language film loses something in the translation. Sporadically funny dark comedy follows a bunch of young urban adults in pursuit of their kaleidoscopic sexual preferences, fears, and fetishes. Rated R for sex, violence, nudity, language, and drug use. 99m. **DIR:** Denys Arcand. **CAST:** Thomas Gibson, Ruth Marshall, Cameron Bancroft, Mia Kirshner, Rick Roberts, Joanne Vannicola. **1994**

LOVE AND MURDER ★★1/2 Decent low-budget thriller features a struggling photographer suddenly involved in a girl's questionable suicide. Rated R for violence and profanity. 87m. **DIR:** Steven H. Stern. **CAST:** Todd Waring. **1988**

LOVE AND OTHER CATASTROPHES ★★★★ This contemporary screwball comedy follows a quintet of Australian university students during an average day of love, lust, and library fines. One woman enters a Kafkaesque bureaucratic maze while attempting to switch departments; another tries to spark romantic flames with a philosophical gigolo, while remaining blind to the puppy love of a second fellow. This $37,000 wonder is loads more entertaining than most million-dollar Hollywood misfires. Rated R for profanity, drug use, and strong sexual content. 76m. **DIR:** Emma-Kate Croghan. **CAST:** Matt Day, Matthew Dyktynski, Alice Garner, Frances O'Connor, Radha Mitchell. **1996**

LOVE & SEX ★★ A neurotic magazine writer and her artist boyfriend break up but can't let go. The resemblance to *Annie Hall* is deliberate but purely superficial; the appealing stars are trapped in a movie you've seen a hundred times before, reciting clumsy lines such as, "Love is agony and ecstasy, freedom and imprisonment." Not rated; contains profanity, mature themes, and sexual scenes. 82m. **DIR:** Valerie Breiman. **CAST:** Famke Janssen, Jon Favreau, Noah Emmerich, Ann Magnuson, Cheri Oteri. **2000 DVD**

LOVE AND THE FRENCHWOMAN ★★★ Seven short films about women at different stages of life. Lightweight stuff, but not without some charming and comical moments. Dubbed. B&W; 135m. **DIR:** Henri Decoin, Jean Delannoy, Michel Boisrone, René Clair, Henri Verneuil, Christian-Jaque. **CAST:** Annie Girardot, Martine Lambert, Michel Serrault, Jean-Paul Belmondo. **1960 DVD**

LOVE AND WAR ★★★ An account of navy pilot Jim Stockdale's eight-year imprisonment in a North Vietnamese prison camp. James Woods is excellent as Stockdale, conveying uncertainty behind his undying patriotic loyalty. Painful but enlightening made-for-TV movie. 96m. **DIR:** Paul Aaron. **CAST:** James Woods, Jane Alexander, Haing S. Ngor. **1987**

LOVE AT FIRST BITE ★★★★ The Dracula legend is given the comedy treatment in this amusing parody of horror films. George Hamilton plays the campy Count, who has an unorthodox way with the ladies. (In this case, it's Susan Saint James, much to the chagrin of her boyfriend, Richard Benjamin.) Even though the humor is heavy-handed in parts, you find yourself chuckling continually in spite of yourself. Rated PG. 96m. **DIR:** Stan Dragoti. **CAST:** George Hamilton, Susan Saint James, Richard Benjamin, Dick Shawn, Arte Johnson. **1979**

LOVE AT FIRST SIGHT Dan Aykroyd tries for laughs as a blind man in love with a girl whose family won't have him for a son-in-law. Rated PG. 85m. **DIR:** Rex Bromfield. **CAST:** Mary Ann McDonald, Dan Aykroyd, Barry Morse. **1977**

LOVE AT LARGE ★★★★ Writer-director Alan Rudolph serves up a deliciously offbeat spoof of the mystery movie with his tale of a private eye (Tom Berenger) hired by a mysterious woman (Anne Archer). It's funny and intriguing; a movie buff's delight. Rated R for pro-

fanity and violence. 97m. **DIR:** Alan Rudolph. **CAST:** Tom Berenger, Elizabeth Perkins, Anne Archer, Kate Capshaw, Annette O'Toole, Ted Levine, Ann Magnuson, Neil Young. **1990**

LOVE AT STAKE 🦃 Attempted spoof of witchcraft and black-magic films is a dismal failure. Rated R for nudity and profanity. 88m. **DIR:** John Moffitt. **CAST:** Barbara Carrera, Bud Cort, Dave Thomas, Patrick Cassidy, Stuart Pankin. **1988**

LOVE AT THE TOP ★★★★ In this delightful film, Glynnis (Janis Paige) is at the top of her career as a lingerie designer. While being considered for promotion, she finds herself pitted against the son-in-law of the boss, a very romantic young man. Excellent. 105m. **DIR:** John Bowab. **CAST:** Janis Paige, Richard Young, Jim McKrell. **1982**

LOVE BUG, THE (1969) ★★★1/2 This is a delightful Disney comedy. A family film about a Volkswagen with a mind of its own and some special talents as well, it was the first of the four "Herbie" films. Rated G. 107m. **DIR:** Robert Stevenson. **CAST:** Michele Lee, Dean Jones, Buddy Hackett, Joe Flynn. **1969**

LOVE BUG, THE (1997) ★★1/2 Made-for-television remake of the lovable family film about Herbie, a Volkswagen Bug with a mind of its own. Unfortunately, it's clear after several adventures that Herbie is trapped in a lackluster remake. While the cast is game, they're not nearly as engaging as the original cast, which included Dean Jones (who turns up briefly here). Bruce Campbell is the new driver, with former "Monkee" Mickey Dolenz as his sidekick. There's little race action, and the notion that the villain drives a Satanic version of Herbie is silly. Still, children will find this a pleasant diversion. Not rated. 88m. **DIR:** Peyton Reed. **CAST:** Bruce Campbell, John Hannah, Mickey Dolenz, Alexandra Wentworth, Kevin J. O'Connor, Dana Gould, Dean Jones. **1997**

LOVE, CHEAT & STEAL ★★★1/2 Financial wizard John Lithgow returns to his roots to help save his father's bank and uncovers a drug-tinged money-laundering scheme. As if that weren't bad enough, he gets a visit from the "brother" of his attractive new wife . . . whom we know is actually her dangerously vengeful first husband. This complex yarn of double and triple crosses is quite fun. Rated R for profanity, violence, and nudity. 96m. **DIR:** William Curran. **CAST:** John Lithgow, Eric Roberts, Madchen Amick, Richard Edson, Donald Moffat, David Ackroyd. **1993**

LOVE CHILD ★★★★ Although its ads gave *Love Child* the appearance of a cheapo exploitation flick, this superb prison drama is anything but. Directed by Larry Peerce, it is the gripping story of a young woman, Terry Jean Moore (Amy Madigan), who became pregnant by a guard in a women's prison in Florida and fought for the right to keep her baby. Rated R for profanity, nudity, sex, and violence. 96m. **DIR:** Larry Peerce. **CAST:** Amy Madigan, Beau Bridges, Mackenzie Phillips. **1982**

•LOVE COME DOWN ★★★ Larenz Tate delivers a poignant, powerful performance as Neville Carter, a former addict and thief who turns his life around and becomes a stand-up comedian. Even though Carter seems to be on the road to recovery, he still has to combat his inner demons that summon him back to his old life and cause tension between Carter and his new girlfriend. The film admirably explores Carter's emotional battlefield, creates sympathetic characters, and makes statements without standing on a soapbox. Rated R for adult situations, drugs, language, and nudity. 102m. **DIR:** Clement Virgo. **CAST:** Larenz Tate, Deborah Cox, Martin Cummins, Jennifer Dale. **2000 DVD**

LOVE CRAZY ★★★★ Crazy is right, in this screwball comedy where innocent William Powell is found by his wife (Myrna Loy) in a compromising situation with an old flame. She sues for divorce; he feigns insanity to keep her, carrying the act all the way to a lunacy hearing. B&W; 99m. **DIR:** Jack Conway. **CAST:** William Powell, Myrna Loy, Gail Patrick, Jack Carson, Florence Bates, Sidney Blackmer, Sig Ruman. **1941**

LOVE CRIMES ★★ For most of its brief running time, this movie, about the capture of a clever con man–rapist, is a gripping thriller with erotic overtones—then it ends abruptly, leaving the viewer wondering exactly what happened. This is because the studio nixed director Lizzie Borden's original ending and a quick fix was substituted. Rated R for nudity, violence, and profanity. 85m. **DIR:** Lizzie Borden. **CAST:** Sean Young, Patrick Bergin, Arnetia Walker, James Read, Ron Orbach. **1992**

LOVE FEAST, THE 🦃 Ed Wood was at the bottom of the barrel when he starred in this sex comedy his fans would best avoid. Not rated; contains nudity and sexual situations. 63m. **DIR:** Joseph F. Robertson. **CAST:** Edward D. Wood Jr., Linda Coplin. **1969**

LOVE FIELD ★★★★ Michelle Pfeiffer is a 1960s Dallas housewife who models herself after Jacqueline Kennedy. When President John F. Kennedy is assassinated, Pfeiffer decides she has to attend the funeral. On the way, she encounters Dennis Haysbert, a black man traveling with his daughter. Pfeiffer and Haysbert (in a role originally given to Denzel Washington, who left the picture) are superb. Rated PG-13 for profanity and violence. 104m. **DIR:** Jonathan Kaplan. **CAST:** Michelle Pfeiffer, Dennis Haysbert, Stephanie McFadden, Brian Kerwin, Louise Latham, Peggy Rea. **1992 DVD**

LOVE FINDS ANDY HARDY ★★★ In this fourth film of the series, the love that finds Mickey Rooney as Andy Hardy is then-teenager Lana Turner. As usual, it's an all-innocent slice of small-town American family life. B&W; 90m. **DIR:** George B. Seitz. **CAST:** Mickey Rooney, Lewis Stone, Fay Holden, Judy Garland, Cecilia Parker, Lana Turner, Ann Rutherford. **1938**

LOVE FROM A STRANGER (1937) ★★1/2 A suave killer who woos wealthy women and does away with them after the nuptials raises the suspicions of a lottery winner he chooses as his next victim. Whether one views this film as a first-class, melodramatic thriller or hilarious camp, it's an entertaining gem from the "forgotten horrors" catalogue. B&W; 90m. **DIR:** Rowland V. Lee. **CAST:** Ann Harding, Basil Rathbone, Binnie Hale, Bruce Seton, Jean Cadell, Bryan Powley. **1937**

LOVE FROM A STRANGER (1947) ★★★ Just-married woman suspects her new husband is a murderer and that she will be his next victim in this suspense-thriller in the vein of *Suspicion*. B&W; 81m. **DIR:** Richard Whorf. **CAST:** Sylvia Sidney, John Hodiak, John Howard, Isobel Elsom, Ernest Cossart. **1947**

LOVE GOD?, THE ★★ Meek Don Knotts is turned into a Hugh Hefner-ish "swinger" by shady Edmond O'Brien, who wants to turn Knotts's bird-lovers' magazine into a

porno mag. This feeble comedy was dated even when it first came out. Rated PG for suggestive situations. 101m. **DIR:** Nat Hiken. **CAST:** Don Knotts, Anne Francis, Edmond O'Brien, James Gregory, Maureen Arthur. **1969**

LOVE HAPPY ★★ The last Marx Brothers movie, this 1949 production was originally set to star only Harpo, but Chico and, later, Groucho were brought in to beef up its box-office potential. They should've known better. Only Groucho's ogling of then-screen-newcomer Marilyn Monroe makes it interesting for movie buffs. B&W; 91m. **DIR:** David Miller. **CAST:** The Marx Brothers, Marilyn Monroe, Raymond Burr. **1949**

LOVE HAS MANY FACES 🦃 Anachronistic, tame sex opera—filmed in Acapulco—with Lana Turner, Cliff Robertson and Hugh O'Brian. Unwatchable. 105m. **DIR:** Alexander Singer. **CAST:** Lana Turner, Cliff Robertson, Hugh O'Brian, Ruth Roman, Stefanie Powers, Virginia Grey. **1965**

LOVE, HONOR & OBEY ★★★ Gripping crime-drama stars Jude Law as the nephew of a London mob boss. Jonny Lee Miller plays his best friend who gets his wish to be part of the gangster life. Trouble brews when the new recruit attempts to flame a war with a rival mob, setting off an incendiary chain of events. The filmmakers invest a lot of black humor into the proceedings, creating a film that looks tough but never takes itself seriously. Rated R for adult situations, language, and violence. 93m. **DIR:** Dominic Anciano, Ray Burdis. **CAST:** Jude Law, Jonny Lee Miller, Sadie Frost, Ray Winstone, Sean Pertwee, Rhys Ifans. **2000 DVD**

LOVE HURTS ★★ Womanizer is forced into dealing with his irresponsible past when he finds his ex-wife and kids have moved in with his parents. Rated R for profanity and suggested sex. 110m. **DIR:** Bud Yorkin. **CAST:** Jeff Daniels, Judith Ivey, John Mahoney, Cynthia Sikes, Amy Wright, Cloris Leachman. **1989**

LOVE IN GERMANY, A ★★ During World War II, the Germans bring in Polish POWs to do menial labor. Frau Kopp (Hanna Schygulla) hires a young Polish POW. The first half of the film is effective, but the second half receives an excessively sensational treatment, ultimately diminishing the flavor and appeal. In French with English subtitles. Rated R for violence and nudity. 107m. **DIR:** Andrzej Wajda. **CAST:** Hanna Schygulla, Marie-Christine Barrault, Bernhard Wicki. **1984**

LOVE IN THE AFTERNOON ★★★★ Audrey Hepburn shares fantastic chemistry with both Maurice Chevalier and Gary Cooper in this film classic, which explores the love interests of an American entrepreneur and his lopsided involvement with a young French ingenue. When her doting father (a detective) is asked to investigate the American's love life, it makes for a touching, charming bit of entertainment that never loses its appeal. 130m. **DIR:** Billy Wilder. **CAST:** Gary Cooper, Audrey Hepburn, Maurice Chevalier, John McGiver. **1957 DVD**

LOVE IN THE PRESENT TENSE ★★1/2 Millie Perkins adds style and class to this Romance Theatre soap. A former model returns to New York to promote her daughter's career and falls for an irresistible photographer. Made for TV. 97m. **DIR:** Tony Mordente. **CAST:** Millie Perkins, Thomas MacGreevy, Deborah Foreman, Doris Roberts. **1982**

LOVE IS A GUN ★★★ Eric Roberts plays a police photographer whose involvement with a mystery woman turns his simple life upside down. When Roberts finds a photo of model Kelly Preston in his locker, he's instantly smitten. His dream lover becomes his nightmare when she ends up dead, and he's the only suspect. Atmospheric thriller is served well by star Roberts, who delivers a riveting performance. Rated R for violence, adult situations, and language. 92m. **DIR:** David Hartwell. **CAST:** Eric Roberts, Kelly Preston, Eliza Roberts, R. Lee Ermey, Joseph Sirola. **1994**

LOVE IS A MANY-SPLENDORED THING ★★★ Clichéd story of ill-starred lovers from two different worlds who don't make it. Jennifer Jones is a Eurasian doctor who falls in love with war correspondent William Holden during the Korean conflict. 102m. **DIR:** Henry King. **CAST:** Jennifer Jones, William Holden, Isobel Elsom, Richard Loo. **1955 DVD**

LOVE IS ALL THERE IS 🦃 Two competing catering companies play out a comedic modern-day version of *Romeo and Juliet* that is buffoonish, stereotypical, frantic, and loud. Rated R for profanity and implied sexuality. 105m. **DIR:** Renee Taylor, Joseph Bologna. **CAST:** Lainie Kazan, Joseph Bologna, Barbara Carrera, Paul Sorvino, Renee Taylor, Abe Vigoda, Connie Stevens, Dick Van Patten. **1996**

LOVE IS BETTER THAN EVER ★★1/2 Elizabeth Taylor is a children's dancing-school teacher out to hook a hard-boiled talent agent, Larry Parks. The songs are completely forgettable. Tom Tully, as Taylor's father, saves the movie. B&W; 81m. **DIR:** Stanley Donen. **CAST:** Elizabeth Taylor, Larry Parks, Josephine Hutchinson, Tom Tully, Ann Doran, Kathleen Freeman. **1952**

LOVE IS THE DEVIL ★★★ British painter Francis Bacon and the decadent art scene of 1960s London are the subjects of this unsettling movie. Bacon, the film tells us, was a tortured genius who vented his anger on those around him. John Maybury was denied the use of Bacon's vivid, misshapen paintings, so he makes the whole film look like one of the artist's canvases, shooting through mirrors and distorting glass. Not rated; contains profanity, mature themes, and scenes of sadomasochism. 91m. **DIR:** John Maybury. **CAST:** Derek Jacobi, Daniel Craig, Tilda Swinton, Anne Lambton. **1998 DVD**

LOVE JONES ★★★1/2 Boy meets girl, and they almost lose each other because neither one wants to be the first to utter the dreaded " *L* word." This romantic "dramedy" compensates for a slender plot with good writing, appealing performances, and the refreshing novelty of seeing the courtship ritual played out by middle-class African Americans. Rated R for profanity. 108m. **DIR:** Theodore Witcher. **CAST:** Larenz Tate, Nia Long, Isaiah Washington, Lisas Nicole Carson, Khalil Kain, Leonard Roberts, Bernadette L. Clarke, Bill Bellamy. **1997 DVD**

LOVE KILLS (1991) ★★ Increasingly chaotic plot twists muddy this otherwise tedious made-for-cable thriller, which features Virginia Madsen as a professional photographer led to believe that her criminal psychologist husband has hired a maniac to kill her. Madsen sighs and pouts a lot, but she really doesn't make us care. Rated PG-13 for mild profanity and sexual themes. 92m.

DIR: Brian Grant. **CAST:** Virginia Madsen, Lenny von Dohlen, Erich Anderson, Jim Metzler. **1991**

LOVE KILLS (1999) ★★★ Mario Van Peebles is a con man who dupes rich widows out of their inheritances. When he tries to pull a scam on Lesley Ann Warren, he starts to have second thoughts. In the meantime, family members, friends, and brief acquaintances try to outwit each other in the attempt to find a cache of gems somewhere on her estate. When Daniel Baldwin shows up, anarchy reigns supreme. Rated R for sex, violence, and language. 95m. **DIR:** Mario Van Peebles. **CAST:** Mario Van Peebles, Lesley Ann Warren, Daniel Baldwin, Louise Fletcher. **1999 DVD**

LOVE LAUGHS AT ANDY HARDY ★★ America's all-American, lovable, irritating, well-meaning wimp comes home from World War II and plunges back into the same adolescent rut of agonizing young love. The change of times has made this cookie-cutter film very predictable, but it's fun anyway. B&W; 93m. **DIR:** Willis Goldbeck. **CAST:** Mickey Rooney, Lewis Stone, Fay Holden, Sara Haden, Bonita Granville. **1946**

LOVE LEADS THE WAY ★★★★ This Disney TV movie features Timothy Bottoms in the true story of Morris Frank, the first American to train with a Seeing-Eye dog. Blinded while boxing, Frank at first refuses to accept his handicap and later resents the dog who offers to be his eyes. Fortunately, he adapts and later lobbies for acceptance of Seeing-Eye dogs throughout the United States. Bottoms turns in an exceptional performance as the struggling Frank. 99m. **DIR:** Delbert Mann. **CAST:** Timothy Bottoms, Eva Marie Saint, Arthur Hill, Susan Dey. **1984**

LOVE LETTER, THE (1998) ★★ Disappointing *Hallmark Hall of Fame* drama about love that crosses the time barrier is both sappy and unbelievable. A modern man obsessed with the Civil War era buys an antique desk that contains the romantic longings of a nineteenth-century woman. He responds with a letter of his own, thus igniting their literary love affair. Naturally, this wreaks havoc with his current relationship to his fiancée. Unfortunately, there is little chemistry between any of the three leads. Not rated; contains adult situations. 90m. **DIR:** Dan Curtis. **CAST:** Campbell Scott, Jennifer Jason Leigh, Daphne Ashbrook, David Dukes, Estelle Parsons. **1998 DVD**

LOVE LETTER, THE (1999) ★★★ Kooky little romance includes surreal moments as a small Massachusetts town is transformed by an anonymous love letter. The heart-stopping note makes its way into many people's hands and each believes it was intended for him or her. Amusing and slow paced, this is not for action fans. Rated PG-13 for language and sexual situations. 89m. **DIR:** Peter Ho-Sun Chan. **CAST:** Kate Capshaw, Tom Everett Scott, Tom Selleck, Ellen DeGeneres. **1999 DVD**

LOVE LETTERS ★★★★ In this impressive character study, the heroine, played by Jamie Lee Curtis, wonders aloud to her friend (Amy Madigan): "Sometimes it's right to do the wrong thing, isn't it?" Probing the emotions that lead to infidelity, this is a true adult motion picture. This concept is intelligently explored by writer-director Amy Jones. Rated R for graphic sex. 98m. **DIR:** Amy Jones. **CAST:** Jamie Lee Curtis, Amy Madigan, Bud Cort, James Keach. **1983 DVD**

LOVE, LIES AND MURDER ★★★ Made as a TV miniseries, this violent thriller is based on a 1985 murder. It appears at first to be clear-cut. However, there were actually two murderers and one Manson-like manipulator behind the ugly scenes. Talk about dysfunctional families! 200m. **DIR:** Robert Markowitz. **CAST:** Clancy Brown, Sheryl Lee, Moira Kelly, John Ashton. **1991**

LOVE MACHINE, THE ★★ A lust for power drives a television newscaster into the willing arms of the network president's wife. Pessimistic tale of the motivations that move the wheels of television news. Sexy, soapy adaptation of the Jacqueline Susann novel. Rated R. 108m. **DIR:** Jack Haley Jr. **CAST:** Dyan Cannon, John Phillip Law, Robert Ryan, Jackie Cooper, David Hemmings, Shecky Greene, William Roerick. **1971**

LOVE MATTERS ★★★ In spite of some preachiness, this little melodrama makes a few perceptive points on the hard work and dedication required for a successful marriage. Unfortunately, we don't see enough of distanced lovers Griffin Dunne and Annette O'Toole; too much time is wasted on the selfish antics of a shallow friend (Tony Goldwyn) and his latest sexual conquest. Rated R for profanity, nudity, and simulated sex. 97m. **DIR:** Eb Lottimer. **CAST:** Griffin Dunne, Tony Goldwyn, Annette O'Toole, Gina Gershon, Kate Burton, Gerrit Graham. **1993**

LOVE ME OR LEAVE ME ★★★★ This musical bio-pic about ambitious singer Ruth Etting and her crude and domineering racketeer husband found usually cute Doris Day and old pro James Cagney scorching the screen with strong performances. Along with biting drama, a record-setting thirteen Doris Day solos, including the title song and "Ten Cents a Dance," are served. The story won an Oscar. 122m. **DIR:** Charles Vidor. **CAST:** James Cagney, Doris Day, Cameron Mitchell, Robert Keith, Tom Tully. **1955**

LOVE ME TENDER ★★★ Western drama takes place in Texas after the Civil War, with Elvis and his brother fighting over Debra Paget. The most distinguishing characteristic of this movie is the fact that it was Elvis's first film. Elvis fans will, of course, enjoy his singing the ballad "Love Me Tender." B&W; 89m. **DIR:** Robert D. Webb. **CAST:** Elvis Presley, Debra Paget, Richard Egan. **1956**

LOVE ME TONIGHT ★★★★★ A romantic musical that set a pattern for many that followed. Rodgers and Hart wrote the music, and most are still being played. This is the film that introduced "Lover," "Mimi," and "Isn't It Romantic?" all sung by Maurice Chevalier with verve and style. Pure charm. B&W; 104m. **DIR:** Rouben Mamoulian. **CAST:** Jeanette MacDonald, Maurice Chevalier, Myrna Loy, Charlie Ruggles, Charles Butterworth, C. Aubrey Smith, Elizabeth Patterson. **1932**

LOVE MEETINGS ★★ Messy, unorganized documentary that explores the sexual attitudes of Italians in the early 1960s. Featuring interviews with philosophers, poets, students, clergymen, farmers, factory workers, and children. Dated material with completely unreadable English subtitles. B&W; 90m. **DIR:** Pier Paolo Pasolini. **1964**

LOVE NEST ★★1/2 An ex-GI returns home to find that his wife has purchased a run-down apartment building whose tenants come to dominate their lives. Mild comedy, mostly of interest to Marilyn Monroe completists.

B&W; 84m. **DIR:** Joseph M. Newman. **CAST:** William Lundigan, June Haver, Frank Fay, Marilyn Monroe, Jack Paar. **1951**

LOVE OF JEANNE NEY ★★★ A romance between a French girl and a Russian Communist is thwarted at every turn. Lots of action in this Russian Revolution–set tale. Silent. B&W; 102m. **DIR:** G. W. Pabst. **CAST:** Brigitte Helm. **1926 DVD**

LOVE ON THE DOLE ★★★1/2 Based on Walter Greenwoods's novel, this film is about a London family trying to subsist during the Depression. A classy cast gives top-notch performances. 89m. **DIR:** John Baxter. **CAST:** Deborah Kerr, Clifford Evans, Mary Merrall. **1941**

LOVE ON THE RUN (1936) ★★★ When a foreign correspondent helps a publicity-shy heiress flee from her own wedding ceremony (sound familiar?), they become involved with spies and intrigue. Good escapism. B&W; 80m. **DIR:** W. S. Van Dyke. **CAST:** Joan Crawford, Clark Gable, Franchot Tone, Reginald Owen, William Demarest, Donald Meek, Billy Gilbert. **1936**

LOVE ON THE RUN (1979) ★★★1/2 François Truffaut's tribute to himself. *Love on the Run* is the fifth film (*400 Blows*; *Love at Twenty*; *Stolen Kisses*; *Bed & Board*) in the series for character Antoine Doinel (Jean-Pierre Léaud). Now in his thirties and on the eve of divorce, Doinel rediscovers women. Light romantic work filled with humor and compassion. In French with English subtitles. Rated PG. 93m. **DIR:** François Truffaut. **CAST:** Jean-Pierre Léaud, Claude Jade, Marie-France Pisier. **1979 DVD**

LOVE OR MONEY? ★★ A rising young real estate turk wrestles with his conscience. Should he nail the big deal or follow his heart down the path of love with his client's daughter? Trite comedy. Rated PG-13. 90m. **DIR:** Todd Hallowell. **CAST:** Timothy Daly, Haviland Morris, Kevin McCarthy, Shelley Fabares, David Doyle. **1988**

LOVE POTION #9 ★★★★ Dweeb, zero-charisma scientists Tate Donovan and Sandra Bullock trade in their beakers for romance when they down that famous love potion from gypsy Anne Bancroft. Funny, charming comedy finds new avenues for laughter. The complications are pretty typical, but the script and direction by Dale Launer are sharp and on the money. Rated PG-13 for sexual situations and language. 99m. **DIR:** Dale Launer. **CAST:** Tate Donovan, Sandra Bullock, Dale Midkiff, Anne Bancroft. **1992 DVD**

LOVE SERENADE ★★★ When a famous Australian disc jockey moves to a tiny outback town in the middle of nowhere, he disrupts the quietly desperate lives of the sisters who live next door. Another quirky, oddball Australian comedy, but this time the quirkiness runs out of steam and the characters become distasteful before the contrived ending. Still, there are compensating pleasures, chief among them Rebecca Frith's performance as the more outgoing (and more desperate) older sister. Rated R for sexual themes. 100m. **DIR:** Shirley Barrett. **CAST:** Miranda Otto, Rebecca Frith, George Shevtsov, John Alansu. **1995**

LOVE SONGS (PAROLES ET MUSIQUE) ★★ Christopher Lambert plays a bisexual rock singer having an affair with a woman (Catherine Deneuve). Pointless and frequently incomprehensible. Dubbed (execrably) into English. 107m. **DIR:** Elie Chouraqui. **CAST:** Catherine Deneuve, Christopher Lambert, Nick Mancuso, Richard Anconina, Jacques Perrin. **1985**

LOVE SPELL 🦃 A dud based on the legend of Tristan and Isolde and their doomed love. 90m. **DIR:** Tom Donavan. **CAST:** Richard Burton, Kate Mulgrew, Nicholas Clay, Cyril Cusack. **1979**

LOVE STINKS ★★ This lumbering sex farce blends the worst elements of a TV sitcom with enough tiresome profanity to keep it off the networks for a while. It's mostly a starring vehicle for television actor French Stewart, admittedly funny as a writer-producer unlucky enough to get stuck with The Shrew from Hell. Mostly, though, this is a weary retread of *The War of the Roses*. Rated R for profanity and strong sexual candor. 94m. **DIR:** Jeff Franklin. **CAST:** French Stewart, Bridgette Wilson, Bill Bellamy, Tyra Banks, Jason Bateman, Tiffani-Amber Thiessen, Colleen Camp. **1999 DVD**

LOVE STORY ★★★★ Unabashedly sentimental and manipulative, this film was a box-office smash. Directed by Arthur Hiller and adapted by Erich Segal from his bestselling novel, it features Ryan O'Neal and Ali MacGraw as star-crossed lovers who meet, marry, make it, and then discover she is dying. Rated PG. 99m. **DIR:** Arthur Hiller. **CAST:** Ryan O'Neal, Ali MacGraw, Ray Milland, John Marley. **1970 DVD**

LOVE STREAMS ★★ A depressing story of a writer who involves himself in the lives of lonely women for inspiration, and his emotionally unstable sister, whom he takes in after a difficult divorce has left her without possession of her child. There are some funny moments and some heartfelt scenes, as well, but John Cassavetes's direction is awkward. Rated PG-13 for language and adult situations. 122m. **DIR:** John Cassavetes. **CAST:** John Cassavetes, Gena Rowlands, Diahnne Abbott, Seymour Cassel. **1984**

LOVE TO KILL ★★★ Mob hit men Moe (Tony Danza) and Franco (Michael Madsen) are ready to retire. Moe wants to settle down with his new girlfriend, Monica, but a gun deal gone wrong and an old mob vendetta keep him busy. When Monica discovers her sister's dead body at Moe's, she comes after him, too. Quirky, offbeat story of love and vengeance. Rated R for adult situations, language, and violence. 102m. **DIR:** James Bruce. **CAST:** Tony Danza, Michael Madsen, Elizabeth Barondes, James Russo, Louise Fletcher. **1997 DVD**

LOVE! VALOUR! COMPASSION! ★★★ A group of gay men spend three country weekends together over the course of a summer. The film moves from Memorial Day to Labor Day, tracing the ups and downs of everyone's lives. Essentially plotless, but has a witty script and first-rate acting. Especially good are Jason Alexander as a lonely HIV-positive man, and John Glover, who gives a tour de force as identical twin brothers—one a saint, the other a scoundrel. Rated R for profanity, nudity, and sexual situations. 115m. **DIR:** Joe Mantello. **CAST:** Jason Alexander, Randy Becker, Stephen Bogardus, John Glover, John Benjamin Hickey, Justin Kirk, Stephen Spinella. **1997**

LOVE WITH A PERFECT STRANGER ★★ Chance encounters on a train, exotic international locations, carriage rides, curiously abandoned fine restaurants, and luxury hotels all create an atmosphere for romance. This Harlequin Romance has dialogue and interplay patterned after the popular books. Not rated British

television production is suitable for any age. 98m. **DIR:** Desmond Davis. **CAST:** Marilu Henner, Daniel Massey. **1988**

LOVE WITH THE PROPER STRANGER ★★★★ This neatly crafted tale of a pregnant young woman (Natalie Wood) and a restless trumpet player (Steve McQueen) offers generous portions of comedy, drama, and romance. Wood is at her most captivating. McQueen, veering a bit from his trademark cool, gives a highly engaging performance. Their relationship creates ample sparks. 100m. **DIR:** Robert Mulligan. **CAST:** Natalie Wood, Steve McQueen, Edie Adams, Herschel Bernardi, Tom Bosley. **1963**

LOVE YOUR MAMA ★★ If good intentions and a conscientious heart were all it took, *Love Your Mama* would be a classic. *Love Your Mama* is a rough-hewn, amateurish-looking drama about a black family in the Chicago ghetto, held together through the love and hard work of the mother. It's too bad it wasn't more polished. Rated PG-13, with profanity. 92m. **DIR:** Ruby L. Oliver. **CAST:** Carol E. Hall, Audrey Morgan. **1993**

LOVED ONE, THE ★★★★1/2 A naïve British poet finds himself in the California funeral industry, which includes human and animal customers. The all-star cast includes Jonathan Winters in a dual role as an unscrupulous clergyman and the director of a pet cemetery. Brilliantly written by Christopher Isherwood and Terry Southern. B&W; 116m. **DIR:** Tony Richardson. **CAST:** Robert Morse, Rod Steiger, Robert Morley, Jonathan Winters, Tab Hunter, Milton Berle, Lionel Stander, Anjanette Comer, Liberace, James Coburn, John Gielgud. **1965**

LOVELESS, THE ★★ This could have been called *The Senseless* thanks to its lack of plot and emphasis on violence. It's a biker picture set in the 1950s and stars Willem Dafoe, who gives a good performance with the scant dialogue he's given. Though a poor tribute to *The Wild One*, this film does have a cult following. Rated R for violence, nudity, and sex scenes. 85m. **DIR:** Kathryn Bigelow, Monty Montgomery. **CAST:** Willem Dafoe, Robert Gordon, Marin Kanter. **1984**

LOVELIFE ★★★1/2 Director Jon Harmon Feldman's intricate and insightful screenplay guides a splendid cast through this tale of love and life. The campus of a graduate school is the breeding ground for romance and betrayal as student Saffron Burrows cheats on her boyfriend with a professor. The relationship causes a chain reaction that forces everyone involved to examine their priorities. Sharply written and executed. Rated R for adult situations and language. 96m. **DIR:** Jon Harmon Feldman. **CAST:** Sherilyn Fenn, Saffron Burrows, Jon Tenney, Bruce Davison, Matthew Letscher. **1997**

LOVELY TO LOOK AT ★★★★ Jerome Kern's Broadway and movie hit *Roberta* gets a face-lift with a charismatic cast, Technicolor, and inventive staging. Marge and Gower Champion dance "I Won't Dance" as a ballet. All in all, a musical treat, although the story about a trio of men inheriting a dress shop strains credibility. 105m. **DIR:** Mervyn LeRoy. **CAST:** Kathryn Grayson, Howard Keel, Red Skelton, Marge Champion, Gower Champion, Ann Miller, Zsa Zsa Gabor, Kurt Kasznar. **1952**

LOVER, THE ★★★ Although director-coscenarist Jean-Jacques Annaud gives Marguerite Duras's infamous bestseller the serious treatment it deserves, the aggravatingly sparse story line seems mere window-dressing. French schoolgirl Jane March enters a relationship with twentysomething Chinese gentleman Tony Leung. Considerable arty coupling. Rated R for nudity and simulated sex. 110m. **DIR:** Jean-Jacques Annaud. **CAST:** Jane March, Tony Leung Chiu Wai, Frederique Meininger. **1992 DVD**

LOVER COME BACK ★★★★ Rock Hudson and Doris Day are rival advertising executives battling professionally, psychologically, and sexually. A bright comedy that builds nicely. One of their best. Silly, innocent fun with a great supporting cast. 107m. **DIR:** Delbert Mann. **CAST:** Rock Hudson, Doris Day, Tony Randall, Edie Adams, Jack Oakie, Jack Kruschen, Ann B. Davis, Joe Flynn, Jack Albertson. **1961**

LOVERBOY 🦃 Lame sex farce. Rated PG-13 for profanity and sexual situations. 98m. **DIR:** Joan Micklin Silver. **CAST:** Patrick Dempsey, Kate Jackson, Carrie Fisher, Barbara Carrera, Kirstie Alley, Robert Ginty. **1989**

LOVERS, THE (1958) ★★ Notorious in the early Sixties, when it was prosecuted in the U.S. for obscenity, this French drama looks mighty tame now. All the fuss was over an extended lovemaking scene between rich wife Jeanne Moreau and a young man she has just met. What little interest the film retains is in its wide-screen photography, which is lost in the transfer to home video, anyway. In French with English subtitles. B&W; 90m. **DIR:** Louis Malle. **CAST:** Jeanne Moreau, Alain Cuny, Jean-Marc Bory. **1958**

LOVERS (1992) ★★★★ Just out of General Franco's army, a young soldier makes wedding plans with his virginal fiancée—when he's not involved in steamy sex and shady scams with his new landlady. In Spanish with English subtitles. Not rated; contains profanity, nudity, and violence. 103m. **DIR:** Vicente Aranda. **CAST:** Victoria Abril, Jorge Sanz, Maribel Verdu. **1992**

LOVERS AND LIARS ★★1/2 The first thing that occurs to you while watching this film is a question: What's Goldie Hawn doing in a dubbed Italian sex comedy? Costarring Giancarlo Giannini it is a modestly entertaining piece of fluff tailored primarily for European tastes and, therefore, will probably disappoint most of Hawn's fans. Rated R. 96m. **DIR:** Mario Monicelli. **CAST:** Goldie Hawn, Giancarlo Giannini, Laura Betti. **1979 DVD**

LOVERS AND OTHER STRANGERS ★★★1/2 A funny film about young love, marriage, and their many side effects on others. Marks Diane Keaton's debut in pictures. The late Gig Young is a delight. Rated R. 106m. **DIR:** Cy Howard. **CAST:** Gig Young, Diane Keaton, Bea Arthur, Bonnie Bedelia, Anne Jackson, Harry Guardino, Richard Castellano, Michael Brandon, Cloris Leachman, Anne Meara. **1970**

LOVER'S KNOT ★★★ Cupid sends a caseworker (Tim Curry) to Earth to help a couple who are fated to be together but just can't seem to get going. Average romantic comedy benefits from many whimsical touches à la *Annie Hall*. Rated R for brief nudity, sexual situations, adult situations, and profanity. 85m. **DIR:** Pete Shaner. **CAST:** Bill Campbell, Jennifer Grey, Tim Curry, Adam Baldwin. **1995**

LOVERS' LOVERS ★★ Limp sex fantasy finds a couple trying to spice up their relationship by bringing another couple into their bedroom. They should have tried coun-

seling. Rated R for nudity and language. 90m. **DIR:** Serge Rodnunsky. **CAST:** Serge Rodnunsky, Jennifer Ciesar, Cindy Parker, Ray Bennett. **1993**

LOVERS OF THE ARCTIC CIRCLE ★★★★ Saga of two people with intertwining destinies, where random happenings can turn into life-changing events. While chasing a lost ball, a young boy happens upon a girl hiding in the woods. This unexpected encounter is just the beginning of a life of chance meetings and coincidental occurrences between the two of them. A movie about near misses, this is one film that always stays on target. In Spanish with English subtitles. Rated R for sex and some violence. 108m. **DIR:** Julio Medem. **CAST:** Najwa Nimri, Fele Martinez. **1998**

LOVERS OF THEIR TIME ★★ In this passable film, a married man (Edward Petherbridge) leads a boring life until he meets his dream love. 60m. **DIR:** Robert Knights. **CAST:** Edward Petherbridge, Cheryl Prime. **1986**

LOVERS ON THE BRIDGE ★★★★ This audacious film elevates the story of two homeless lovers to an artful exploration of love, need, and values. Beautifully crafted, the film follows the on-again, off-again relationship of two people who live on Paris's Pont-Neuf Bridge, when they're not trying to find food or emotional sustenance in the cold world. In French with English subtitles. 126m. **DIR:** Léos Carax. **CAST:** Denis Lavant, Juliette Binoche. **1992**

•LOVER'S PRAYER ★★1/2 Director Reverge Anselmo fails to capture the spirit and ultimate tragedy of Ivan Turgenev's story "First Love" about a young Russian man who falls in love with his neighbor's daughter. Nick Stahl is an odd choice to play young Vladimir, home from school for the summer, who immediately falls under the charms of Zinaida (Kirsten Dunst), a young beauty who has several admirers. While Vladimir believes he has a chance, his hopes are dashed when he learns Zinaida is having an affair with his father. The filmmakers don't handle the tempest in a teapot very well, and the actors seem bored. Rated PG-13 for adult situations. 106m. **DIR:** Reverge Anselmo. **CAST:** Kirsten Dunst, Julie Walters, Nick Stahl, James Fox, Geraldine James, Nathaniel Parker. **2000 DVD**

LOVES AND TIMES OF SCARAMOUCHE, THE 🦃 Michael Sarrazin, as Scaramouche, stumbles through this ridiculous swashbuckler. 92m. **DIR:** Enzo G. Castellari. **CAST:** Michael Sarrazin, Ursula Andress, Aldo Maccioni, Gian Carlo Prete. **1976**

LOVE'S LABOUR'S LOST ★★★★ Writer-director Kenneth Branagh continues to enliven Shakespeare with his penchant for creative risk. Moving this tale to 1930s England and adding classic songs and dance sequences from that era, Branagh recounts the adventures of four friends who swear an oath to three years of celibacy and devotion to intellectual study. While initially disconcerting, this unorthodox musical-comedy soon becomes infectious. It will especially please film fans who delighted in the filmmaker's similar adaptation of *Much Ado about Nothing*. Rated PG. 93m. **DIR:** Kenneth Branagh. **CAST:** Kenneth Branagh, Alessandro Nivola, Alicia Silverstone, Natascha McElhone, Matthew Lillard, Adrian Lester, Timothy Spall, Nathan Lane, Stefania Rocca. **2000 DVD**

LOVES OF A BLONDE ★★★1/2 This dark comedy from Milos Forman centers on a young girl working in a small-town factory who pursues a musician. Often hilarious. In Czech with English subtitles. B&W; 88m. **DIR:** Milos Forman. **CAST:** Hana Brejchova, Josef Sebanek. **1965 DVD**

LOVES OF CARMEN, THE ★★ Rita Hayworth plays an immoral gypsy hussy who ruins the life of a young Spanish officer (Glenn Ford). It's melodramatic and corny at times but still fun to see sparks fly between Hayworth as the beautiful vixen and an ever-so-handsome Ford. 98m. **DIR:** Charles Vidor. **CAST:** Rita Hayworth, Glenn Ford, Ron Randell, Victor Jory, Luther Adler, Arnold Moss. **1948 DVD**

LOVES OF THREE QUEENS ★★ A three-hour Italian epic starring Hedy Lamarr as three of history's most memorable women—Guinevere, Empress Josephine, Helen of Troy—was chopped down to less than half its original length for American release, so don't expect it to make a lot of sense. Dubbed. 80m. **DIR:** Marc Allegret. **CAST:** Hedy Lamarr. **1953**

LOVE'S SAVAGE FURY 🦃 TV-movie attempt to re-create the passion of *Gone with the Wind*. 100m. **DIR:** Joseph Hardy. **CAST:** Jennifer O'Neill, Perry King, Raymond Burr, Connie Stevens. **1979**

LOVESICK ★★★ You won't fall out of your seat laughing or grab a tissue to dab away the tears. But this movie, about a psychiatrist's (Dudley Moore) obsession with his patient (Elizabeth McGovern) does have its moments. Rated PG. 95m. **DIR:** Marshall Brickman. **CAST:** Dudley Moore, Elizabeth McGovern, Alec Guinness, John Huston. **1983 DVD**

LOVING COUPLES ★★ The plot is that old and tired one, about two couples who swap partners for a temporary fling only to reunite by film's end happier and wiser for the experience. It's a premise that's been worn thin and is badly in need of retirement. Rated PG. 97m. **DIR:** Jack Smight. **CAST:** Shirley MacLaine, James Coburn, Susan Sarandon, Stephen Collins. **1980**

•LOVING JEZEBEL ★★★ Hill Harper is the main reason to see this occasionally amusing romantic comedy about a man who constantly falls for the wrong kind of woman. Theodorus Melville has always had a thing for the opposite sex, but inevitably falls for someone unavailable. As told in flashbacks, Theo looks for answers in his past, hoping to find a woman he can love without exception. Instead of being objects of desire, the women in his life are actually engaging characters who teach him several life lessons. Rated R for adult situations and language. 87m. **DIR:** Kwyn Bader. **CAST:** Hill Harper, Laurel Holloman, Nicole Ari Parker, Phylicia Rashad. **1999 DVD**

LOVING YOU ★★★ This better-than-average Elvis Presley vehicle features him as a small-town country boy who makes good when his singing ability is discovered. It has a bit of romance but the main attraction is Elvis singing his rock 'n' roll songs, including the title tune. 101m. **DIR:** Hal Kanter. **CAST:** Elvis Presley, Lizabeth Scott, Wendell Corey, Dolores Hart. **1957**

LOW BLOW 🦃 A private investigator tries to rescue a millionaire's daughter from a religious cult. Rated R for violence and profanity. 85m. **DIR:** Frank Harris. **CAST:** Leo Fong, Cameron Mitchell, Troy Donahue, Akosua Busia, Stack Pierce. **1986**

LOW DOWN DIRTY SHAME, A ★★1/2 Shame, a former L.A. cop who was unfairly discredited, struggles to make it as a private detective only to find himself right back in the middle of the case that ruined his law-enforcement career. Jada Pinkett's animated performance as Shame's fast-talking girl Friday is one of the few outstanding elements in this otherwise so-so spoof of blaxploitation pictures. Rated R for violence, profanity, nudity, and simulated sex. 100m. **DIR:** Keenen Ivory Wayans. **CAST:** Keenen Ivory Wayans, Charles Dutton, Jada Pinkett, Salli Richardson, Andrew Divoff, Corwin Hawkins, Gary Cervantes, Gregory Sierra. **1994**

LOW LIFE, THE ★★1/2 Mopey college grad Rory Cochrane drifts around the fringes of L.A., working dead-end jobs and hoping to become a screenwriter. Director George Hickenlooper has a nice feel for the seedy atmosphere, and the ensemble cast is strong, but the script is as aimless and off-putting as the characters it describes. Sean Astin, as Cochrane's earnest, lonely roommate, gives the film's most interesting and sympathetic performance. Rated R for profanity. 99m. **DIR:** George Hickenlooper. **CAST:** Rory Cochrane, Kyra Sedgwick, Sean Astin, Christian Meoli, Sara Melson. **1996**

LOWER DEPTHS (1936) ★★★★ Another poignant observation by Jean Renoir about social classes. This time the director adapts Maxim Gorky's play about an impoverished thief (brilliantly performed by Jean Gabin) who meets a baron and instructs him in the joys of living without material wealth. In French with English subtitles. 92m. **DIR:** Jean Renoir. **CAST:** Jean Gabin, Louis Jouvet. **1936**

LOWER DEPTHS, THE (1957) ★★★★ Brilliant adaptation of Maxim Gorky's play about a group of destitute people surviving on their tenuous self-esteem, while living in a ghetto. Akira Kurosawa explores this crippled society with tolerance, biting humor, and compassion. In Japanese with English subtitles. B&W; 125m. **DIR:** Akira Kurosawa. **CAST:** Toshiro Mifune. **1957**

LOWER LEVEL ★★★ A psychotic security guard manipulates elevators, doors, and alarms to set up the perfect date with his object of obsession. Surprisingly watchable. Rated R for nudity, violence, and gore. 85m. **DIR:** Kristine Peterson. **CAST:** David Bradley, Elizabeth Gracen, Jeff Yagher. **1990 DVD**

LOYALTIES ★★ In this Canadian-made drama, an upper-class Englishwoman reluctantly moves to a small town in one of the northwest territories, where she becomes friends with her housekeeper, a hell-raising half-Indian woman. The story of the two women is well-handled, but the movie turns into an unbelievable melodrama about the wife having to suffer for her husband's indiscretions. Rated R for violence and sexual situations. 98m. **DIR:** Anne Wheeler. **CAST:** Susan Wooldridge, Tantoo Cardinal, Kenneth Welsh. **1987**

LT. ROBIN CRUSOE, U.S.N. Modern-day story of Robinson Crusoe, poorly done and with few laughs. Rated G. 113m. **DIR:** Byron Paul. **CAST:** Dick Van Dyke, Nancy Kwan, Akim Tamiroff. **1966**

LUCAS ★★★★ Charming tale of young love, leagues above the usual teen-oriented fare due to an intelligent and compassionate script by writer-director David Seltzer. Corey Haim stars as a 14 year old whiz kid "accelerated" into high school who falls in love, during the summer between terms, with 16 year old Kerri Green. Rated PG-13 for language. 100m. **DIR:** David Seltzer. **CAST:** Corey Haim, Kerri Green, Charlie Sheen, Courtney Thorne-Smith, Winona Ryder. **1986**

•LUCK OF THE DRAW ★★1/2 James Marshall plays a man, down on his luck, who finds himself suddenly in possession of counterfeit $100 bill printing plates. The opposing forces, each of which thinks the other has been hiding its knowledge of those plates, soon realize that he has them, and then the real manhunt begins. A veritable panoply of B-movie acting and clichés makes for a show that quickly stagnates. Rated R for violence, language, and sexual situations. 101m. **DIR:** Luca Bercovici. **CAST:** James Marshall, Dennis Hopper, William Forsythe, Michael Madsen, Ice T, Eric Roberts. **2000 DVD**

LUCKY JIM ★★★ High jinks and antics at a small British university as a young lecturer tries to improve his lot by sucking up to his superior, but continually goofs. Acceptable adaptation of the Kingsley Amis novel. 95m. **DIR:** John Boulting. **CAST:** Ian Carmichael, Terry-Thomas, Hugh Griffith. **1957**

LUCKY LUCIANO ★★ The last years of one of crime land's most "influential" bosses. The film started out to be an important one for Francesco Rosi, but the distributors of the English edition went in for the sensationalism with too graphic subtitles and/or dubbing, depending on the version. Not a bad film if you know Italian. If you don't, stick with *The Godfather*. Rated R for profanity and violence. 110m. **DIR:** Francesco Rosi. **CAST:** Gian Maria Volonté, Rod Steiger, Edmond O'Brien, Vincent Gardenia, Charles Cioffi. **1974**

LUCKY LUKE ★★ Don't expect to laugh while watching this mediocre comedy-Western about a sheriff who's "faster than his shadow." Roger Miller lends his voice as the narrating horse. Not rated; contains mild violence. 91m. **DIR:** Terence Hill. **CAST:** Terence Hill, Nancy Morgan, Roger Miller, Fritz Sperberg. **1994 DVD**

LUCKY LUKE: THE BALLAD OF THE DALTONS ★★ Overlong yarn of the Old West starring an all-American cowboy (complete with immovable cigarette on the lower lip): Lucky Luke. References to killing are taken in stride, but for the most part this is harmless cartoon fare. Not rated. 82m. **DIR:** René Goscinny. **1978**

LUCKY ME ★★ The title does not mean the viewer. Love finds an unemployed Florida chorus girl seeking work. Only the caliber of the cast keeps this matte-finished song-and-dancer from being a complete bomb. Angie Dickinson's film debut. 100m. **DIR:** Jack Donohue. **CAST:** Doris Day, Robert Cummings, Phil Silvers, Eddie Foy Jr., Nancy Walker, Martha Hyer, Angie Dickinson. **1954**

LUCKY NUMBERS ★★ Edgy dark comedy with irregular lighting and sporadic production values robs viewers of relaxed enjoyment in this let's-rob-the-lottery farce. John Travolta plays a likable, debt-riddled weatherman who teams up with a foul-mouthed lottery-ball puller (Lisa Kudrow) to hatch an ingenious plot. Greed and violence dominate, leaving little room for laughs. Disappointing. Rated R for sex, profanity, and violence. 102m. **DIR:** Nora Ephron. **CAST:** John Travolta, Lisa Kudrow, Tim Roth, Ed O'Neill. **2000 DVD**

LUCKY PARTNERS ★★★ Artist Ronald Colman wishes passing errand girl Ginger Rogers good luck, thereby touching off a chain of events ending in romance. Lightweight comedy with, for the time, raw touches. Ginger's naïve charm and Ronald's urbanity make for interesting interplay. B&W; 99m. **DIR:** Lewis Milestone. **CAST:** Ginger Rogers, Ronald Colman, Spring Byington, Jack Carson, Harry Davenport. **1940**

LUCKY STIFF ★★★ Lovelorn Joe Alaskey can't believe his luck when he's picked up by gorgeous Donna Dixon and invited to her family's home for Christmas dinner. What he doesn't know is that he's the entree-to-be for this cannibal clan. Writer Pat Profft provides plenty of hilariously demented characters and funny one-liners. Rated PG. 82m. **DIR:** Anthony Perkins. **CAST:** Joe Alaskey, Donna Dixon, Jeff Kober. **1988**

LUCKY TEXAN ★★★ Gold miners John Wayne and Gabby Hayes strike it rich. But before they can cash in their claim, Hayes is falsely accused of robbery and murder. Of course, the Duke rides to his aid. Creaky, but fun for fans. B&W; 56m. **DIR:** Robert N. Bradbury. **CAST:** John Wayne, Barbara Sheldon, George "Gabby" Hayes. **1934 DVD**

•LUCKYTOWN BLUES ★★1/2 Lidda Doyles (Kirsten Dunst) and her poker-loving boyfriend (Vincent Kartheiser) travel to Las Vegas in search of her father (James Caan)—a man she never knew. Once there, the naïve young couple gets swept up in the glitzy high-stakes nature of Sin City, and teeters on the edge of corruption. The young stars are good at what they do, but they still can't dig their way out of this painfully mediocre film. Rated R for violence, sex, language, and drugs. 101m. **DIR:** Paul Nicholas. **CAST:** Kirsten Dunst, Vincent Kartheiser, James Caan, Luis Guzman. **2000 DVD**

LUCY AND DESI: A HOME MOVIE ★★★★1/2 This revealing film about Lucille Ball and Desi Arnaz—which won an Emmy after airing on NBC in 1993 and is now extended by thirteen minutes—delves into their once-happy marriage and the dissolution caused by the pressures of Hollywood. Upbeat footage of the successful Desilu production company helps to balance the pain of watching two people drift apart in this documentary of surprising depth. Not rated; contains mild profanity. B&W/Color. 111m. **DIR:** Lucie Arnaz. **CAST:** Lucille Ball, Desi Arnaz Sr., Lucie Arnaz, Desi Arnaz Jr. **1994**

LUCY AND DESI: BEFORE THE LAUGHTER ★★★ A warts-and-all portrayal of America's favorite couple of the 1960s, particularly distinguished by Frances Fisher's passionate turn as the redheaded queen of comedy. Not recommended for those who maintain the *I Love Lucy* image. Not rated. 96m. **DIR:** Charles Janot. **CAST:** Frances Fisher, Maurice Bernard. **1991**

LUGOSI, THE FORGOTTEN KING ★★★★ Forrest J. Ackerman hosts this comprehensive look at the life and career of Bela Lugosi, featuring outtakes, trailers, and interviews with some of his costars (including John Carradine and Ralph Bellamy). Not rated. B&W/color. 55m. **DIR:** Mark S. Gilman Jr., Dave Stuckey. **1983**

LULLABY OF BROADWAY ★★1/2 Musical-comedy with show girl Doris Day returning from England, believing her mother to be a Broadway star, learning she is over-the-hill, singing and boozing in a bar. Many old standards by George Gershwin, Cole Porter, Harry Warren, etc. 92m. **DIR:** David Butler. **CAST:** Doris Day, Gene Nelson, Gladys George, Billy DeWolfe, S. Z. Sakall, Florence Bates. **1951**

LULU ON THE BRIDGE ★★★1/2 Writer Paul Auster (*Blue in the Face*) makes an auspicious debut as director with a stylish slice of *film noir*. Harvey Keitel is excellent as jazz saxophonist Izzy Maurer, whose near-death experience leads him down a rabbit hole filled with dark and sinister characters. Mira Sorvino is luminous as a film actress whose life inadvertently becomes entangled with Izzy's. Moody and unexpected. Rated PG-13 for language and violence. 103m. **DIR:** Paul Auster. **CAST:** Harvey Keitel, Mira Sorvino, Willem Dafoe, Gina Gershon, Mandy Patinkin, Vanessa Redgrave. **1998 DVD**

LUMIERE 🦃 The only thing this film illuminates is Jeanne Moreau's pretentiousness. In French. 95m. **DIR:** Jeanne Moreau. **CAST:** Jeanne Moreau, Francine Racette, Bruno Ganz, François Simon, Lucia Bose, Keith Carradine. **1976**

LUMINARIAS ★★1/2 Sitcom meets soap opera in this sometimes amateurish but scrappy production. Four Latina professionals grapple with stormy relationships as the fallout of marital infidelity and interracial couplings affects their lives. The title refers to the restaurant where the quartet's conversation, lubricated with liquor and punctuated with profanity, is free to roam wherever the moment takes it. Evelina Fernandez adapted the script from her play. Rated R for language, adult themes, and sex. 100m. **DIR:** Jose Luis Valenzuela. **CAST:** Evelina Fernandez, Scott Bakula, Marta DuBois, Angela Moya, Dyana Ortelli, Seidy Lopez, Sal Lopez, Robert Beltran. **2000 DVD**

•LUMUMBA ★★★1/2 Congo Prime Minister Patrice Lumumba is introduced as he is transported by car caravan to his own January 1961 execution just several months after Belgium loosened its colonial grip on the country. The narration stitches together a sometimes dry and skeletal but compelling story about the price of freedom and volatility of an entire nation. The film establishes a convincing time and place as it flashes back to Lumumba's political career and then to his grisly execution, dismemberment, and cremation. In French with English subtitles. Not rated; contains graphic violence. 115m. **DIR:** Raoul Peck. **CAST:** Eriq Ebouaney, Alex Descas, Théophile Sowié, Maka Kotto, Dieudonné Kabongo. **2000**

LUNA PARK ★★★★ Riveting, at times harrowing portrait of Russian skinheads. Interesting plot twist comes when one of the gang discovers that his father was a Jewish composer. In Russian with English subtitles. Not rated; contains strong images of violence. 105m. **DIR:** Pavel Lounguine. **CAST:** Oleg Borisou, Andrei Goutine, Natalie Egorova. **1991**

LUNATIC, THE ★★★ Delicious comedy stars Paul Campbell as the title character, a freewheeling, free-loving reggae man who talks to trees and is generally considered an annoyance. Excellent musical soundtrack enhances the lush, natural beauty of the film and characters. Rated R for sexual situations. 93m. **DIR:** Lol Creme. **CAST:** Julie T. Wallace, Paul Campbell. **1992 DVD**

LUNATICS: A LOVE STORY ★★★ Lunatic Theodore Raimi (brother of writer-director Sam) hides out in his apartment, afraid of the real world. When he accidentally connects on the phone with on-the-run Deborah Foreman, he sees his chance to escape his mental cell. Pretty wacky stuff, including some outrageous special effects. Rated PG-13 for language and surreal violence. 87m. **DIR:** Josh Becker. **CAST:** Theodore Raimi, Deborah Foreman, Bruce Campbell. **1992**

LUNATICS & LOVERS ★★ Tepid morality play stars Marcello Mastroianni as a wealthy aristocrat whose delusions upset the locals. When a musician attempts to replace his imaginary wife with the real thing, chaos ensues. In Italian with English subtitles. Rated PG. 92m. **DIR:** Flavio Mogherini. **CAST:** Marcello Mastroianni, Lino Toffalo, Claudia Mori, Lino Morelli. **1975**

LUNCH WAGON ★★1/2 The vehicle of the title belongs to three enterprising young women who set up near a construction site. Spirited drive-in comedy offers more laughs than most of its ilk along with the requisite jiggle. Rated R for nudity and profanity. 88m. **DIR:** Ernest Pintoff. **CAST:** Pamela Bryant, Rose Marie. **1980**

LUPIN III: TALES OF THE WOLF (TV SERIES) ★★★ Taken from the popular Japanese series, these episodes feature the animated adventures of cunning cat-burglar Wolf and his crafty comrades. With plenty of action and lighthearted fun, *Lupin* will be enjoyed by animation fans who value cleverness over graphic violence. Dubbed in English. Not rated, but suitable for most audiences (some brief illustrated nudity). 30m. **DIR:** Hayao Miyazaki. **1977**

LUPO ★★★ In this warmhearted comedy from Israel, Yuda Barkan is charming as Lupo, a cart driver. Like a modern Fiddler on the Roof, he's caught in the currents of change. His horse is killed by a car, his daughter is wooed by a rich banker's son, and the city plans to demolish the old shack he calls home. Rated G. 100m. **DIR:** Menahem Golan. **CAST:** Yuda Barkan, Gabi Amrani, Esther Greenberg. **1970**

LURED INNOCENCE ★★ Tired, generic, and predictable thriller about a small-town waitress on trial for the murder of her lover's wife. One of the waitress's young admirers, who leaves town to become a reporter, returns to cover her trial. Little suspense and flat acting make this a struggle to sit through. Rated R for adult situations and language. 99m. **DIR:** Kikuo Kawasaki. **CAST:** Marley Shelton, Dennis Hopper, Devon Gummersall, Talia Shire, Cheri Oteri. **1999 DVD**

LURKERS 🦃 Hopelessly meandering tale about an abused young girl haunted by the forces of evil. Rated R for violence and nudity. 95m. **DIR:** Roberta Findlay. **CAST:** Christine Moore, Gary Warner. **1988**

LURKING FEAR ★★ Evil creatures are eating the inhabitants of a small town in this movie adapted from a story by H. P. Lovecraft. Bad acting, directing, and dialogue, and lots of gore. Not rated; contains violence and profanity. 76m. **DIR:** C. Courtney Joyner. **CAST:** Jon Finch, Blake Bailey, Ashley Lauren, Jeffrey Combs, Allison Mackie, Vincent Schiavelli. **1994**

•**LUSCIOUS (1997)** 🦃 A young woman (Kari Wuhrer) helps get her boyfriend's artistic juices flowing by having sex with him on paint-strewn canvases. Not even Kari Wuhrer's omnipresent lack of clothing can make up for having no story and terrible acting. Rated R for sex and constant nudity. 90m. **DIR:** Evan Georgiades. **CAST:** Kari Wuhrer, Stephen Shellen. **1997 DVD**

•**LUSH** ★★ The South may rise again, but this melodrama set in New Orleans is about as wobbly as its lead character, Lionel "Ex" Exley, a former PGA pro who has stumbled from grace and into a bottle of booze. When a drinking buddy who has named him in his will disappears, Ex finds himself the main suspect, and takes flight. Two high society sisters offer Ex shelter from the storm, but not without consequences. There's more talk than action in this pointless character study, and even then the dialogue is thin. Rated R for adult situations, drugs, and language. 94m. **DIR:** Mark Gibson. **CAST:** Campbell Scott, Jared Harris, Laura Linney, Laurel Holloman. **1999 DVD**

LUSH LIFE ★★★★ Best friends Jeff Goldblum and Forest Whitaker are hardworking jazz "session men" (the anonymous fellows lending background support for better-known stars). After providing a fascinating glimpse of this taxing profession, the story kicks into gear when Whitaker is diagnosed with a brain tumor; he decides to go out in style by throwing the world's biggest jazz party. Watch for actual jazz greats such as Jack Sheldon, Ernie Andrews, and Charlie Heath. Rated R for profanity, simulated sex, and drug use. 96m. **DIR:** Michael Elias. **CAST:** Jeff Goldblum, Forest Whitaker, Kathy Baker, Tracey Needham, Lois Chiles. **1994**

LUST FOR A VAMPIRE ★★★ All-girls school turns out to be a haven for vampires, with a visiting writer (Michael Johnson) falling in love with one of the undead students (Yutte Stensgaard). Atmospheric blending of chills and fleshy eroticism combined with a terrific ending. Rated R. 95m. **DIR:** Jimmy Sangster. **CAST:** Suzanna Leigh, Michael Johnson, Ralph Bates, Barbara Jefford, Yutte Stensgaard. **1970 DVD**

LUST FOR GOLD ★★★1/2 Based on the true story of the Lost Dutchman mine, told in flashbacks and recounting the double dealings of Glenn Ford, Ida Lupino, and husband Gig Young as they plot against one another. B&W; 90m. **DIR:** S. Sylvan Simon. **CAST:** Glenn Ford, Ida Lupino, Edgar Buchanan, Will Geer, Gig Young. **1949**

LUST FOR LIFE ★★★1/2 A standout performance by Kirk Douglas, in the role of artist Vincent van Gogh, creates a rare, affecting portrait of a tormented man driven by the frenzied energy of passion. Unfortunately this overblown Hollywood production fails to exploit the beauty of some of the locations that inspired the paintings. 123m. **DIR:** Vincente Minnelli. **CAST:** Kirk Douglas, Anthony Quinn, James Donald, Pamela Brown. **1956**

LUST IN THE DUST ★★ Tab Hunter and female impersonator Divine (who's anything but), who first teamed in *Polyester*, star in this so-so spoof of spaghetti Westerns, directed by Paul Bartel. The ad blurb tells all: "He rode the West. The girls rode the rest. Together they ravaged the land." Rated R for nudity, suggested sex, and violence. 86m. **DIR:** Paul Bartel. **CAST:** Tab Hunter, Divine, Lainie Kazan, Geoffrey Lewis, Henry Silva, Cesar Romero. **1985**

LUSTY MEN, THE ★★★★ The world of rodeo cowboys is explored in this well-made film directed by cult fa-

vorite Nicholas Ray. Robert Mitchum has one of his best roles as a broken-down ex–rodeo star who gets a second chance at the big money by tutoring an egotistical newcomer on the circuit, well played by Arthur Kennedy. B&W; 113m. **DIR:** Nicholas Ray. **CAST:** Robert Mitchum, Susan Hayward, Arthur Kennedy, Arthur Hunnicutt. **1952**

LUTHER ★★★ Stacy Keach's gripping performance as Martin Luther is more than enough reason to see this otherwise turgid version of John Osborne's play (minimally adapted for this American Film Theater presentation) about the founder of Protestantism. Rated G. 108m. **DIR:** Guy Green. **CAST:** Stacy Keach, Patrick Magee, Hugh Griffith, Leonard Rossiter, Judi Dench, Maurice Denham. **1974**

LUTHER, THE GEEK A chicken-clucking killer terrorizes a Midwestern family. For geeks only. Rated R for violence, nudity, and profanity. 92m. **DIR:** Carlton J. Albright. **CAST:** Edward Terry, Joan Roth, J. Jerome Clarke, Tom Mills. **1994**

LUV ★★ When talent the caliber of Jack Lemmon, Peter Falk, and Elaine May cannot breathe life into a film, then nothing can. The plot concerns three New York intellectuals and their tribulations. Who cares? 95m. **DIR:** Clive Donner. **CAST:** Jack Lemmon, Elaine May, Peter Falk, Severn Darden. **1967**

LUXURY LINER ★★1/2 Jane Powell plays Cupid for her widowed sea-captain father. Forget the plot. Enjoy the music. 98m. **DIR:** Richard Whorf. **CAST:** George Brent, Jane Powell, Lauritz Melchior, Frances Gifford, Xavier Cugat, Connie Gilchrist, Richard Derr. **1948**

•LUZHIN DEFENCE, THE ★★★★ Exquisite period drama loosely based on the Vladimir Nabokov novel stars John Turturro as the emotionally scarred chess master Alexander Luzhin. Unable to connect with people, Luzhin turns all of his attention to his game. During a chess championship in Italy, Luzhin begins to fall for Natalia, a young woman who could be his salvation. Emily Watson shines as the only person who can help him face his former mentor, who is intent on destroying Luzhin. The performances are as rich and detailed as the production design. Rated PG-13 for adult situations. 106m. **DIR:** Marleen Gorris. **CAST:** John Turturro, Emily Watson, Stuart Wilson, Geraldine James, Christopher Thompson. **2000 DVD**

LUZIA ★★1/2 Modern Western features a young woman seeking revenge for her parents' murder. She begins working as a cowhand at the ranch of the powerful men responsible for making her an orphan. Slow moving and a bit too melodramatic. Not rated, contains nudity, violence, and profanity. In Portuguese with English subtitles. 112m. **DIR:** Fabio Barreto. **CAST:** Claudia Ohana, Thales Pan Chacon, Luzia Falcao. **1988**

LYDIA ★★★1/2 This sentimental treatment of the highly regarded French film *Carnet du Bal* is well acted and directed. It's the story of an elderly woman who has a reunion with four of her former loves. Merle Oberon's performance is one of her best. B&W; 104m. **DIR:** Julien Duvivier. **CAST:** Merle Oberon, Joseph Cotten, Edna May Oliver, Alan Marshal. **1941**

M

M ★★★★★ A child-killer is chased by police, and by other criminals who would prefer to mete out their own justice. Peter Lorre, in his first film role, gives a striking portrayal of a man driven by uncontrollable forces. A classic German film, understated, yet filled with haunting images. Beware of videocassettes containing badly translated, illegible subtitles. In German with English subtitles. Not rated. B&W; 99m. **DIR:** Fritz Lang. **CAST:** Peter Lorre, Gustav Grundgens. **1931 DVD**

M. BUTTERFLY ★★ Playwright David Henry Hwang's 1988 Tony-winning play, *M. Butterfly*, was based on the true story of a French diplomat tried and convicted of espionage in 1986 after having a twenty-year affair with a Chinese opera singer who turned out to be a spy—and a man. It's a fascinating tale, but one that is more suited to the illusions of the stage than the harsh reality of the camera. Rated R for profanity, simulated sex, and violence. 101m. **DIR:** David Cronenberg. **CAST:** Jeremy Irons, John Lone, Barbara Sukowa, Ian Richardson. **1993**

MA AND PA KETTLE AT HOME ★★1/2 Ma and Pa tidy up the farm to impress the college official checking out their request for a scholarship for their son. A rainstorm ruins their home so Ma and Pa use their wits to get that scholarship in one of the funnier titles in the series. B&W; 81m. **DIR:** Charles Lamont. **CAST:** Marjorie Main, Percy Kilbride, Brett Halsey, Mary Wickes, Alan Mowbray. **1954**

MA AND PA KETTLE (THE FURTHER ADVENTURES OF MA AND PA KETTLE) ★★★ *The Egg and I* scene stealers Marjorie Main and Percy Kilbride were such a hit as the displaced Washington-state "hillbillies," Ma and Pa Kettle, their own series was inevitable. In the opener Pa wins a futuristic home in a slogan contest. An obvious but well-used tool to introduce many good sight gags. Corny, but fun. B&W; 76m. **DIR:** Charles Lamont. **CAST:** Marjorie Main, Percy Kilbride, Richard Long, Meg Randall, Patricia Alphin, Esther Dale, Barry Kelley, O. Z. Whitehead. **1949**

MA AND PA KETTLE AT THE FAIR ★★★ This fourth series entry has Ma intending to enter the jam-making contest at the state fair but in error registering Pa's plow horse in the harness race. The gags and situations are still lowbrow, but you'll laugh in spite of yourself. B&W; 79m. **DIR:** Charles Barton. **CAST:** Marjorie Main, Percy Kilbride, Lori Nelson, James Best, Esther Dale, Russell Simpson, Emory Parnell. **1951**

MA AND PA KETTLE AT WAIKIKI ★★★ Notable primarily because it marks Percy Kilbride's last appearance as Pa Kettle. B&W; 79m. **DIR:** Lee Sholem. **CAST:** Percy Kilbride, Marjorie Main, Byron Palmer, Lori Nelson, Hilo Hattie. **1955**

MA AND PA KETTLE BACK ON THE FARM ★★★ In this third entry in the series the Kettles become grandparents, meet their stuffy Boston in-laws, and when Pa seemingly discovers uranium on the old farm he be-

comes radioactive. The gags include an arithmetic lesson "borrowed" from Universal Studio coworkers, Abbott and Costello. Still corny, still funny. B&W; 81m. **DIR:** Edward Sedgwick. **CAST:** Marjorie Main, Percy Kilbride, Richard Long, Meg Randall, Ray Collins, Esther Dale, Barbara Brown, Emory Parnell, Peter Leeds. **1951**

MA AND PA KETTLE GO TO TOWN ★★★1/2 A typical fish-out-of-water story with Ma and Pa at their countrified best. They get involved with a gangster, lose the gangster's money, and meddle in their children's lives in between chase scenes in the Big Apple. B&W; 79m. **DIR:** Charles Lamont. **CAST:** Marjorie Main, Percy Kilbride, Richard Long, Meg Randall, Jim Backus, Charles McGraw, Elliott Lewis. **1950**

MA AND PA KETTLE ON VACATION ★★ Corn-pone humor and Paris society don't mix, but the Kettles manage to keep the film afloat with predictable gags and grimaces. B&W; 75m. **DIR:** Charles Lamont. **CAST:** Marjorie Main, Percy Kilbride, Sig Ruman, Teddy Hart, Ray Collins, Rita Moreno. **1953**

MA BARKER'S KILLER BROOD ★★ Sweet, grandmotherly Lurene Tuttle, delivering an absolutely ferocious, chop-licking portrayal of Ma Barker, lends fleeting interest to this otherwise overlong gangster cheapie. B&W; 82m. **DIR:** Bill Karn. **CAST:** Lurene Tuttle, Tristram Coffin, Paul Dubov. **1960**

MA SAISON PREFERÉE ★★★ A doctor (Daniel Auteuil) and his lawyer sister (Catherine Deneuve) grapple with their precarious relationship as their mother's health begins to fail. The plot smacks of soap opera, but Auteuil and Deneuve have extraordinary rapport. An extraneous subplot slows the action. In French with English subtitles. Not rated; contains brief nudity and mature themes. 125m. **DIR:** André Téchiné. **CAST:** Daniel Auteuil, Catherine Deneuve, Marthe Villalonga, Anthony Prada, Chiara Mastroianni, Carmen Chaplin. **1993**

MA VIE EN ROSE ★★★1/2 A French boy is convinced that when he grows up he will be a girl and marry the son of his father's boss; in the meantime, his innocent certainty causes confusion and perplexity among his family and their suburban middle-class neighbors. The film's whimsical charm and fine acting compensate for occasional slips into broad sitcom exaggeration. In French with English subtitles. Rated R for some profanity and mature themes of sexual identity. 88m. **DIR:** Alain Berliner. **CAST:** Georges Du Fresne, Michele Laroque, Jean-Philippe Ecoffey, Hélène Vincent, Julien Riviere. **1997 DVD**

MAC ★★★★ Writer-director-star John Turturro's tribute to the life and work ethic of his father, is a collection of real-life vignettes superbly acted and visualized. While not for all tastes, *Mac* is obviously a labor of love. Set in Queens in 1954 and focusing on three brothers who make the heartbreaking mistake of going into business together, it is an offbeat yet sometimes intensely moving film. Rated R for profanity, violence, and simulated sex. 118m. **DIR:** John Turturro. **CAST:** John Turturro, Michael Badalucco, Carl Capotoro, Katherine Borowitz, Ellen Barkin, John Amos, Olek Krupa. **1993**

MAC AND ME 🦃 Imagine the most product-friendly film ever made and you have (Big) *Mac and Me*. To be fair, the film stars the courageous Jade Calegory, a paraplegic wheelchair-bound since birth, and a share of the producer's net profits will be donated to Ronald McDonald's Children's Charities. But the plot rips off everything in sight. Rated PG. 101m. **DIR:** Stewart Raffill. **CAST:** Jade Calegory, Christine Ebersole, Jonathan Ward. **1988**

MACABRE SERENADE ★★ One of the four Mexican films featuring footage of Boris Karloff but assembled after his death (see *Sinister Invasion*), this is the best of a bad lot. He plays a toy maker whose creations seek revenge on his evil relatives after his death. There's a sloppily cut version also on video called *Dance of Death*; it originally played theatres as *House of Evil*. 75m. **DIR:** Juan Ibanez, Jack Hill. **CAST:** Boris Karloff. **1968**

MACAO ★★ Jane Russell is a singer in the fabled Oriental port and gambling heaven of Macao, across the bay from Hong Kong. She's in love with Robert Mitchum, a good guy caught in a web of circumstance. Russell is the only thing about this film that isn't flat. B&W; 80m. **DIR:** Josef von Sternberg. **CAST:** Jane Russell, Robert Mitchum, William Bendix, Gloria Grahame, Thomas Gomez. **1952**

MACARIO ★★★★ Excellent poetic fable based on a story by the mysterious author B. Traven (*The Treasure of the Sierra Madre*). Tarso Ignacio Lopez gives a deeply felt performance as an impoverished woodcutter. One of the most honored Mexican films, and the first to earn an Oscar nomination. In Spanish with English subtitles. B&W; 91m. **DIR:** Roberto Gavaldon. **CAST:** Tarso Ignacio Lopez, Pina Pellicer. **1960**

MACARONI ★★★★1/2 Wonderful Italian comedy-drama from the director of *A Special Day* and *Le Bal*. This one concerns an American executive (Jack Lemmon) who returns to Naples for a business meeting forty years after his stay there with the army. He is visited by an old friend (Marcello Mastroianni). Both Lemmon and Mastroianni deliver brilliant performances. Rated PG for profanity. 104m. **DIR:** Ettore Scola. **CAST:** Jack Lemmon, Marcello Mastroianni, Daria Nicolodi. **1985**

MACARTHUR ★★★ Gregory Peck is cast as the famous general during the latter years of his long military career. It begins with his assumption of command of the Philippine garrison in World War II and continues through his sacking by President Truman during the Korean conflict. The film takes a middle ground in its depiction of this complex man and the controversy that surrounded him. Peck's performance is credible, but the film remains uneven. Rated PG. 130m. **DIR:** Joseph Sargent. **CAST:** Gregory Peck, Dan O'Herlihy, Ed Flanders. **1977 DVD**

MACARTHUR'S CHILDREN ★★ This import deals with effects of Japan's occupation by America, on a group of youngsters and adults living on a tiny Japanese island. Rated PG for profanity and suggested sex. In Japanese with English subtitles. 120m. **DIR:** Masahiro Shinoda. **CAST:** Takaya Yamauchi, Yoshiyuki Omori. **1984**

MACBETH ★★1/2 Allowing for this being a film of a stage production, it is a disappointing and somewhat slow-moving telling of Shakespeare's tale. Interesting and offbeat casting. A Bard Productions Ltd. release. 150m. **DIR:** Arthur Allan Seidelman. **CAST:** Jeremy Brett, Piper Laurie, Simon MacCorkindale, Barry

Primus, Millie Perkins, Alan Oppenheimer, Jay Robinson, Johnny Crawford. **1981 DVD**

MACBETH ★★★1/2 As the crown-hungry Scottish thane Macbeth, Maurice Evans is superb and superbly abetted by Dame Judith Anderson, as the grasping, conniving Lady Macbeth. Another in the developing series of made-for-television *Hallmark Hall of Fame* programs being released on videocassette. B&W; 103m. **DIR:** George Schaefer. **CAST:** Maurice Evans, Judith Anderson. **1961**

MACBETH ★★★1/2 The violent retelling of this classic story was commissioned and underwritten by publisher Hugh Hefner. Shakespeare's tragedy about a man driven to self-destruction by the forces of evil is vividly brought to life by director Roman Polanski. Grim yet compelling, this version of one of our great plays is not for everyone and contains scenes that make it objectionable for children (or squeamish adults). 140m. **DIR:** Roman Polanski. **CAST:** Jon Finch, Francesca Annis, Martin Shaw, Nicholas Selby, John Stride. **1971 DVD**

MACBETH ★★★ Shakespeare's noted tragedy, filmed according to a script by Orson Welles. Interesting movie—made on a budget of $700,000 in three weeks. Welles is an intriguing Macbeth, but Jeanette Nolan as his lady is out of her element. Edgar Barrier and Dan O'Herlihy are fine as Banquo and Macduff. B&W; 105m. **DIR:** Orson Welles. **CAST:** Orson Welles, Roddy McDowall, Jeanette Nolan, Edgar Barrier, Dan O'Herlihy. **1948**

•MACH 2 🦃 Laughable action-thriller stars Brian Bosworth as a terrorist specialist who finds himself trapped on a hijacked plane with a vice presidential candidate and a stunning publicist. The action and dialogue are as stilted as the performances, while the direction of Fred Olen Ray is nonexistent. Rated R for violence. 94m. **DIR:** Fred Olen Ray. **CAST:** Brian Bosworth, Shannon Whirry, Bruce Weitz, Cliff Robertson, Lance Guest, Michael Dorn. **2000 DVD**

MACHINE-GUN KELLY ★★1/2 Grade-B bio-pic about the famed Depression-era hoodlum, with an excellent performance by Charles Bronson in the title role and an intelligent script by R. Wright Campbell. One of Roger Corman's best early features. B&W; 84m. **DIR:** Roger Corman. **CAST:** Charles Bronson, Susan Cabot, Morey Amsterdam. **1958**

MACHINE GUN KILLERS ★★ A falsely accused Union officer is given thirty days to prove that he was not the thief of a machine gun that ended up in Confederate hands. Tight direction and acting place this spaghetti Western a cut above. Rated PG. 98m. **DIR:** Paolo Bianchini. **CAST:** Robert Woods, John Ireland, Evelyn Stewart, Claudie Lange, Gerard Herter, Roberto Camardiel. **1968**

MACHO CALLAHAN ★★★ David Janssen convincingly portrays Macho Callahan, a man hardened by his confinement in a horrid Confederate prison camp. When he kills a man (David Carradine) over a bottle of champagne, the man's bride (Jean Seberg) seeks revenge. Rated R for violence and gore. 99m. **DIR:** Bernard Kowalski. **CAST:** David Janssen, Jean Seberg, Lee J. Cobb, James Booth, David Carradine, Bo Hopkins. **1970**

MACISTE IN HELL ★★ Italian muscle-hero Maciste (Kirk Morris), the *real* hero of dozens of sword-and-sorcery epics with bogus Hercules titles appended for U.S. release, anachronistically pops up in medieval Scotland(!), where he combats a vengeful witch. 78m. **DIR:** Riccardo Freda. **CAST:** Kirk Morris, Helene Chanel. **1962**

MACK, THE ★★ Typical of the blaxploitation films of the early 1970s, a broadly overacted story about a southern California pimp. It gets two stars only because it's a fair example of the genre. Rated R for violence and language. 110m. **DIR:** Michael Campus. **CAST:** Richard Pryor, Max Julien, Roger E. Mosley, Don Gordon. **1973**

MACK THE KNIFE 🦃 The subtle refinements of Bertolt Brecht and Kurt Weill's *Threepenny Opera* have been unceremoniously trashed in this dull-edged bore of a musical. Rated PG-13, with moderate violence and adult situations. 122m. **DIR:** Menahem Golan. **CAST:** Raul Julia, Julia Migenes-Johnson, Richard Harris, Julie Walters, Roger Daltrey. **1990**

MACKENNA'S GOLD ★★ Disappointing "big" Western follows search for gold. Impressive cast cannot overcome a poor script and uninspired direction. 128m. **DIR:** J. Lee Thompson. **CAST:** Gregory Peck, Omar Sharif, Telly Savalas, Julie Newmar, Lee J. Cobb. **1969 DVD**

MACKINTOSH MAN, THE ★★★ A cold war spy thriller with all the edge-of-seat trimmings: car chases, beatings, escapes, and captures. Trouble is, it has been done before, before, and before. Paul Newman is the agent; wily and wonderful James Mason is the communist spy he must catch. Rated PG. 98m. **DIR:** John Huston. **CAST:** Paul Newman, James Mason, Dominique Sanda, Ian Bannen, Nigel Patrick. **1973**

MACON COUNTY JAIL 🦃 Star power isn't enough to salvage this derivative made-for-cable collision of *Jackson County Jail* and *Macon County Line*. Rated R for violence, language, and nudity. 88m. **DIR:** Victoria Muspratt. **CAST:** Ally Sheedy, David Carradine, Charles Napier. **1997**

MACON COUNTY LINE ★★★ A very effective little thriller based on a true incident. Set in Georgia in the 1950s, the story concerns three youths hunted by the law for a murder they did not commit. Producer Max Baer Jr. has a good eye for detail and the flavor of the times. Rated R. 89m. **DIR:** Richard Compton. **CAST:** Alan Vint, Max Baer Jr., Geoffrey Lewis. **1974 DVD**

MACROSS PLUS ★★ Technically brilliant animation scenes are wasted on a trite story wherein a hotshot pilot becomes a hotshot test pilot. If you thought *Top Gun* was the greatest movie ever made, you might enjoy this as well. In Japanese with English subtitles. Not rated; contains profanity. 40m. **DIR:** Shoji Kawamori, Shinichiro Watanabe. **1994**

MAD ABOUT MAMBO ★★★★ Absolutely adorable Irish romantic comedy stars a winning William Ash as Danny Mitchell, an aspiring soccer player looking for a way to improve his game. When a Brazilian player arrives and shows off his moves, Danny decides to take dance lessons to gain rhythm and footwork. There he meets and falls in love with Lucy McLoughlin, the privileged girlfriend of the soccer-team captain. Lots of local color and a sweet, endearing script give the cast plenty to work with. They excel at every turn. Rated PG-13 for language. 92m. **DIR:** John Forte. **CAST:** William Ash,

Keri Russell, Brian Cox, Theo Fraser Steele, Julian Littman. **2000**

MAD ABOUT MUSIC ★★★★1/2 An early Deanna Durbin vehicle that uses her youthful appearance and mature voice to advantage. She plays the daughter of a socialite who doesn't want people to know about her teenage offspring. Daughter loses herself in a fantasy world to impress her schoolmates and winds up playing cupid for her mother. B&W; 96m. **DIR:** Norman Taurog. **CAST:** Deanna Durbin, Gail Patrick, Herbert Marshall, Marcia Mae Jones, Arthur Treacher, William Frawley. **1938**

MAD ABOUT YOU ★★ Barely watchable heiress-on-the-move flick, features a millionaire's daughter dating three men simultaneously. Rated PG. 92m. **DIR:** Lorenzo Doumani. **CAST:** Claudia Christian, Joe Gian, Adam West, Shari Shattuck. **1988**

MAD AT THE MOON ★★ Bizarre, confused horror-Western stars Mary Stuart Masterson as a young woman forced by her mother into marriage with a well-to-do rancher. When her husband turns out to be a werewolf, it's up to the man she loves to save her life. An arty misfire. Rated R for violence, simulated sex, and nudity. 98m. **DIR:** Martin Donovan. **CAST:** Mary Stuart Masterson, Hart Bochner, Fionnula Flanagan, Cec Verrell, Stephen Blake. **1992**

MAD BOMBER, THE Bert I. Gordon wrote, produced, and directed this mess. It's not even up to his usual low standards. Rated R for violence. 91m. **DIR:** Bert I. Gordon. **CAST:** Vince Edwards, Chuck Connors, Neville Brand. **1973**

MAD BULL ★★1/2 A wrestler struggles to escape the sensationalism of his profession. Alex Karras is believable as a man haunted by the assassination of his tag-team brother. Schmaltzy at times, but enjoyable nonetheless. 100m. **DIR:** Walter Doniger, Len Steckler. **CAST:** Alex Karras, Susan Anspach, Nicholas Colasanto, Elisha Cook Jr., Danny Dayton. **1977**

MAD CITY ★★★1/2 Dustin Hoffman is a nearly washed-up television news reporter who stumbles onto the story of a lifetime: a disgruntled ex-employee (John Travolta) takes over a city museum at gunpoint. All Travolta wants is his job back or, at least, someone to listen to his side of the story, while Hoffman parlays the working stiff's plight into a comeback to national prominence. The film's message—about the power of the media and the egos that manipulate it—is pounded home so mercilessly that what might have been an insightful drama becomes a one-dimensional political statement. Rated R for violence and profanity. 114m. **DIR:** Constantin Costa-Gavras. **CAST:** John Travolta, Dustin Hoffman, Mia Kirshner, Alan Alda, Robert Prosky, Blythe Danner, William Atherton, Ted Levine. **1997 DVD**

MAD DOCTOR OF MARKET STREET, THE ★★ Lionel Atwill hams enjoyably as a doctor who persuades the natives of a tropical island that he can revive the dead. Director Joseph H. Lewis has a cult following for some of his later B movies, but this one is pretty uninspired. B&W; 60m. **DIR:** Joseph H. Lewis. **CAST:** Lionel Atwill, Una Merkel, Nat Pendleton, Claire Dodd, Anne Nagel, Noble Johnson. **1942**

MAD DOG AND GLORY ★★★★ Police photographer-detective Robert De Niro inadvertently saves the life of gangster Bill Murray and finds himself the recipient of a special favor: one week of the live-in charms of Uma Thurman. At first, De Niro wants no part of it, then he begins falling in love with Thurman—much to the chagrin of Murray. De Niro, Thurman, and Murray are excellent. Rated R for violence, profanity, and nudity. 97m. **DIR:** John McNaughton. **CAST:** Robert De Niro, Uma Thurman, Bill Murray, Kathy Baker, David Caruso, Mike Starr, Tom Towles. **1993 DVD**

MAD DOG MORGAN ★★1/2 Dennis Hopper plays an Australian bush ranger in this familiar tale of a man forced into a life of crime. Good support from aborigine David Gulpilil and Australian actor Jack Thompson help this visually stimulating film, but Hopper's excesses and a muddled ending weigh against it. Early prison sequences and scattered scenes are brutal. Rated R. 102m. **DIR:** Philippe Mora. **CAST:** Dennis Hopper, Jack Thompson, David Gulpilil, Michael Pate. **1976**

MAD DOGS AND ENGLISHMEN ★★★1/2 Joe Cocker and friends, including Rita Coolidge and Leon Russell, put together one of the zaniest rock tours ever in the early 1970s, leaving a legendary trail of drugs and groupies in their wake. Fortunately, the superstar group was also able to function on stage, and this movie effectively captures the spirit of the 1970 tour. Performances of "With a Little Help from My Friends," "Superstar," and "Feeling Alright" can be considered rock classics. 118m. **DIR:** Pierre Adidge. **CAST:** Joe Cocker, Leon Russell, Rita Coolidge. **1972**

MAD EXECUTIONERS, THE ★★1/2 After *Dark Eyes of London*, this is probably the quintessential Edgar Wallace–style chiller from West Germany (albeit based on a story by his son, Bryan). A vigilante court is executing elusive criminals, while in an unrelated subplot, a mad scientist is beheading women! Ignore the dubbing and concentrate on the pulpy thrills and creepy set design. B&W; 94m. **DIR:** Edward Willeg. **CAST:** Wolfgang Preiss, Harry Riebauer, Chris Howland. **1963**

MAD GHOUL, THE A cast of unknown (over)actors and offscreen special effects rule in this silliness about a "poisonous vapor" that turns men into monsters and puts them under a scientist's power. Not rated. B&W; 65m. **DIR:** James Hogan. **CAST:** David Bruce, George Zucco, Evelyn Ankers, Turhan Bey, Charles McGraw. **1943**

MAD LOVE Great title but a pathetic tale of a high-school senior drawn like a moth to a flame to manic-depressive Drew Barrymore, whose performance is little more than an annoying twitch. Rated PG-13 for profanity and sexual situations. 99m. **DIR:** Antonia Bird. **CAST:** Chris O'Donnell, Drew Barrymore. **1995 DVD**

MAD LOVE ★★★1/2 Colin Clive plays a gifted pianist who loses his hands in a rail accident and finds that the hands miraculously grafted to his wrists by Peter Lorre belonged to a murderer and follow the impulses of the former owner. This complex story of obsession is a murder mystery with an odd twist. A compelling study of depravity. B&W; 67m. **DIR:** Karl Freund. **CAST:** Peter Lorre, Colin Clive, Frances Drake, Ted Healy, Sara Haden, Edward Brophy, Keye Luke. **1935**

MAD, MAD MONSTERS, THE A gruesome conglomeration of ghoulies gathers for the wedding celebration

of Frankenstein's monster. 60m. **DIR:** Arthur Rankin Jr., Jules Bass. **1972**

MAD MAX ★★★1/2 Exciting sci-fi adventure features Mel Gibson as a fast-driving cop who has to take on a gang of crazies in the dangerous world of the future. Rated R. 93m. **DIR:** George Miller. **CAST:** Mel Gibson, Joanne Samuel, Hugh Keays-Byrne, Tim Burns, Roger Ward. **1979 DVD**

MAD MAX BEYOND THUNDERDOME ★★★1/2 Mad Max is back—and he's angrier than ever. Those who enjoyed *Road Warrior* will find more of the same in director George Miller's third post-apocalypse, action-packed adventure film. This time the resourceful futuristic warrior (Mel Gibson) confronts evil ruler Tina Turner. Rated PG-13 for violence and profanity. 109m. **DIR:** George Miller, George Ogilvie. **CAST:** Mel Gibson, Tina Turner, Helen Buday, Frank Thring, Bruce Spence. **1985 DVD**

MAD MISS MANTON, THE ★★★ A group of high-society ladies led by Miss Manton (Barbara Stanwyck) help solve a murder mystery with comic results—sometimes. The humor is pretty outdated, and the brand of romanticism, while being in step with the 1930s, comes off rather silly in the latter part of the twentieth century. Henry Fonda plays a newspaper editor who falls in love with the mad Miss Manton. B&W; 80m. **DIR:** Leigh Jason. **CAST:** Barbara Stanwyck, Henry Fonda, Sam Levene, Frances Mercer, Stanley Ridges. **1938**

MAD MONSTER 🦃 Scientist George Zucco is mad and Glenn Strange is the monster he creates in order to get even with disbelievers. B&W; 77m. **DIR:** Sam Newfield. **CAST:** Johnny Downs, George Zucco, Anne Nagel, Glenn Strange. **1942**

MAD MONSTER PARTY ★★1/2 An amusing little puppet film; a lot more fun for genre buffs who will understand all the references made to classic horror films. Worth seeing once, as a novelty. 94m. **DIR:** Jules Bass. **CAST:** Boris Karloff, Phyllis Diller, Ethel Ennis, Gale Garnett. **1967**

MAD WEDNESDAY (SEE ALSO SIN OF HAROLD DIDDLEBOCK) ★★1/2 The great silent comedian Harold Lloyd stars in an update of his famous brash, go-getting 1920s straw-hatted, black-rimmed-glasses character. A good, but not well executed, idea. Originally issued in 1947 as *The Sin of Harold Diddlebock* in the director's version. This was producer Howard Hughes's "improved" version. B&W; 90m. **DIR:** Preston Sturges. **CAST:** Harold Lloyd, Frances Ramsden, Jimmy Conlin, Raymond Walburn, Arline Judge, Lionel Stander, Rudy Vallee, Edgar Kennedy. **1950**

MADAME BEHAVE ★★1/2 A struggling young architect can't seem to stay out of women's clothes as he goes from one wild situation to another in an attempt to get his girl an engagement ring and win her away from a foppish suitor. Lots of clever captions and cross-dressing in this fast-paced farce by the only actor to make a film (and stage) career as a female impersonator in America, Julian Eltinge. B&W; 54m. **DIR:** Scott Sidney. **CAST:** Julian Eltinge, Ann Pennington, Lionel Belmore, David James, Jack Duffy, Tom Wilson. **1925**

MADAME BOVARY ★★★★ This gorgeously filmed, spectacularly designed adaptation of Gustave Flaubert's once-controversial novel features a stunning performance by Isabelle Huppert as Emma Bovary, who uses marriage to escape the boredom of a provincial life and then turns into an adultress when seeking escape from her unimaginative spouse. A soap opera to be sure, but on a grand, impressive scale. In French with English subtitles. Not rated; this import has suggested sex. 131m. **DIR:** Claude Chabrol. **CAST:** Isabelle Huppert, Jean-François Balmer, Christophe Malavoy. **1991**

MADAME BOVARY ★★★ Emma Bovary is an incurable romantic whose affairs of the heart ultimately lead to her destruction. Jennifer Jones is superb as Emma. Louis Jourdan plays her most engaging lover. Van Heflin portrays her betrayed husband. James Mason portrays Gustave Flaubert, on whose classic French novel the film is based. B&W; 115m. **DIR:** Vincente Minnelli. **CAST:** Jennifer Jones, Louis Jourdan, Van Heflin, James Mason. **1949**

MADAME BOVARY ★★★ Valentine Tessier is superb in the role of a woman who is half swan and half goose in director Jean Renoir's charming offbeat version of Flaubert's great novel. In French with English subtitles. B&W; 96m. **DIR:** Jean Renoir. **CAST:** Pierre Renoir, Valentine Tessier. **1934**

MADAME BUTTERFLY ★★★1/2 Puccini's classic opera, of the Japanese geisha seduced and abandoned by an American naval officer in turn-of-the-century Nagasaki, makes a graceful, and surprisingly stirring film. Sumptuous cinematography and a lush rendition of Puccini's beautiful music are two of the many pleasures in this lovely, melodic film. A French production, sung in Italian with English subtitles. Not rated; suitable for general audiences. 129m. **DIR:** Frederic Miterrand. **CAST:** Ying Huang, Richard Troxell, Ning Liang, Richard Cowan, Jing-Ma Fan, Christopheren Noimura, Constance Hauman, Yo Kuskabe. **1996 DVD**

MADAME CURIE ★★★★1/2 An excellent biography of the woman who discovered radium, balanced by a romantic retelling of her private life with her husband. The show belongs to Greer Garson and Walter Pidgeon in the third film to costar them and make the most of their remarkable chemistry. B&W; 124m. **DIR:** Mervyn LeRoy. **CAST:** Greer Garson, Walter Pidgeon, May Whitty, Henry Travers, Albert Basserman, Robert Walker, C. Aubrey Smith, Victor Francen, Reginald Owen, Van Johnson, Margaret O'Brien. **1943**

MADAME ROSA ★★★★★ This superbly moving motion picture features Simone Signoret in one of her greatest roles. It is a simple, human story that takes place six flights up in a dilapidated building where a once-beautiful prostitute and survivor of Nazi concentration camps cares for the children of hookers. No MPAA rating. 105m. **DIR:** Moshe Mizrahi. **CAST:** Simone Signoret, Sammy Den Youb, Claude Dauphin. **1977**

MADAME SATAN ★★★ A wealthy socialite tries to win her husband back from the arms of a chorus girl. Bizarre extravaganza in which the story only gets in the way of a lot of DeMille spectacularizing. B&W; 115m. **DIR:** Cecil B. DeMille. **CAST:** Kay Johnson, Reginald Denny, Lillian Roth, Roland Young. **1930**

MADAME SIN ★★★ Undistinguished film in which Bette Davis plays a female Fu Manchu opposite Robert Wagner's sophisticated hero. Written expressly for the actress, it was the most expensive made-for-TV movie of its time and won high ratings. 73m. **DIR:** David Greene.

CAST: Robert Wagner, Bette Davis, Roy Kinnear, Paul Maxwell, Denholm Elliott, Gordon Jackson. **1971**

MADAME SOUSATZKA ★★★ A flamboyant star turn from Shirley MacLaine fuels this gentle story about an eccentric piano teacher and the gifted prodigy who comes to her for lessons in both music and life. The adaptation of Bernice Rubens's novel devotes equal time to richly drawn supporting characters: Peggy Ashcroft's wistful landlady and Twiggy's aspiring singer, among others. Rated PG-13 for language. 122m. **DIR:** John Schlesinger. **CAST:** Shirley MacLaine, Navin Chowdhry, Peggy Ashcroft, Twiggy. **1988**

MADAME X ★★★ In this sentimental old chestnut, filmed six times since 1909, a woman is defended against murder charges by an attorney who is not aware he is her son. Lana Turner is good and is backed by a fine cast, but Technicolor and a big budget make this one of producer Ross Hunter's mistakes. Constance Bennett's last film. 100m. **DIR:** David Lowell Rich. **CAST:** Lana Turner, John Forsythe, Constance Bennett, Ricardo Montalban, Burgess Meredith. **1966**

MADAME X ★★★ One of the few versions of the famous stage play that relies on acting and characterization more than glamour and pretense. Character actress Gladys George adds heart, soul, and a lot of acting technique to the story of a diplomat's daughter who has a brief affair and is forced into prostitution because of it. B&W; 75m. **DIR:** Sam Wood. **CAST:** Gladys George, Warren William, John Beal, Reginald Owen, Henry Daniell, Phillip Reed, Ruth Hussey, Emma Dunn, Lynne Carver, Luis Alberni, George Zucco, Cora Witherspoon. **1937**

M.A.D.D.: MOTHERS AGAINST DRUNK DRIVING ★★1/2 True story of Candy Lightner and her struggle to establish M.A.D.D., the national anti-drunk-driving organization. A convincing performance by Mariette Hartley as the California housewife whose life is thrown into turmoil and tragic heartbreak when her daughter is killed by a drunk driver. Above-average TV movie. 100m. **DIR:** William A. Graham. **CAST:** Mariette Hartley, Paula Prentiss, Bert Remsen, John Rubinstein, Cliff Potts, David Huddleston, Grace Zabriskie, Nicolas Coster. **1983**

MADDENING, THE 🦃 A scenery-chewing, vindictive-spewing Burt Reynolds kidnaps Mia Sara so that his wacko wife, played by a mummified Angie Dickinson, will have company in their swamp-front home. Rated R for profanity and violence. 97m. **DIR:** Danny Huston. **CAST:** Burt Reynolds, Angie Dickinson, Mia Sara, Brian Wimmer, Josh Mostel, William Hickey. **1995**

•MADE ★★★1/2 A small-time L.A. hood (Jon Favreau) and his mouthy, stupid pal (Vince Vaughn) are sent to New York on a mysterious errand, wondering all the while exactly what they're getting into. The two leads are excellent and Favreau's direction is smooth and natural, all of which compensates for a slightly unfocused and anticlimactic final third. Rated R for profanity, drug use, and sexual scenes. 94m. **DIR:** Jon Favreau. **CAST:** Jon Favreau, Vince Vaughn, Sean "Puffy" Combs, Peter Falk, Famke Janssen. **2001 DVD**

MADE FOR EACH OTHER ★★★★ This is a highly appealing comedy-drama centering on the rocky first years of a marriage. The young couple (Carole Lombard and James Stewart) must do battle with interfering in-laws, inept servants, and the consequences of childbirth. The real strength of this film lies in the screenplay, by Jo Swerling. It gives viewers a thoughtful and tasteful picture of events that we can all relate to. B&W; 100m. **DIR:** John Cromwell. **CAST:** Carole Lombard, James Stewart, Charles Coburn, Lucile Watson, Harry Davenport. **1939 DVD**

MADE IN AMERICA ★★★ Some of the funniest slapstick scenes ever filmed are in this movie, but they are used to cover up its serious themes rather than clarify them. The story is of a black teenager who wants a father so badly she seeks out his identity against her mother's wishes. When the teen finds out her father was a sperm bank donor and is white, to boot, sparks fly in every direction. Rated PG. 118m. **DIR:** Richard Benjamin. **CAST:** Whoopi Goldberg, Ted Danson, Will Smith, Nia Long, Paul Rodriguez, Jennifer Tilly, Peggy Rea. **1993 DVD**

MADE IN HEAVEN ★★ This silly English comedy stars a very young Petula Clark. Following a tradition started by Henry VI, a local village holds an annual contest to determine if a couple can survive one year of unmarried married bliss. The hiring of a flirtatious, Hungarian maid complicates the matter. 90m. **DIR:** John Paddy Carstairs. **CAST:** David Tomlinson, Petula Clark, Sonja Ziemann, A. E. Matthews. **1948**

MADE IN HEAVEN 🦃 Timothy Hutton stars as a lad who dies heroically, winds up in Heaven, and falls in love with unborn spirit Kelly McGillis. Rated PG for brief nudity. 103m. **DIR:** Alan Rudolph. **CAST:** Timothy Hutton, Kelly McGillis, Maureen Stapleton, Mare Winningham, Ellen Barkin, Debra Winger. **1987**

MADE IN USA ★★1/2 Bonnie and Clyde–style drama about a couple of drifters who leave their brutal job as coal miners in Pennsylvania for the sunny horizon of California. While en route west they encounter sexy hitchhiker Lori Singer and embark on a crime spree. Good cast fails to lift this overdone crime-drama above mediocrity. Pretty disappointing. Rated R. 82m. **DIR:** Ken Friedman. **CAST:** Adrian Pasdar, Christopher Penn, Lori Singer. **1988**

MADELINE ★★★ The title character is an outspoken British orphan who is the littlest and bravest of twelve girls living in a Paris boarding school under supervision of a nun. This update of Ludwig Bemelman's stories shapes disparate elements of the series that began in 1939 into a whimsical outing. Rated PG. 89m. **DIR:** Daisy von Scherler Mayer. **CAST:** Hatty Jones, Frances McDormand, Nigel Hawthorne. **1998 DVD**

MADEMOISELLE ★★★1/2 A lusty melodrama tailor-made for international sex-goddess Jeanne Moreau. She makes the most of her role as a sexually repressed schoolteacher who works out her frustration by committing a variety of crimes. She then seduces a woodcutter and claims he raped her and is the real crime doer in the community. *Then* she goes after the woodcutter's teenaged son. Outlandish but fascinating. B&W; 103m. **DIR:** Tony Richardson. **CAST:** Jeanne Moreau, Ettore Manni, Umberto Orsini, Keith Skinner, Mony Rey. **1966 DVD**

MADEMOISELLE FIFI ★★1/2 An allegory about Nazis inspired by two different Guy de Maupassant short stories. A bullish Prussian gets his comeuppance from a French laundress during the Franco-Prussian War. Al-

luring performances, but very predictable. B&W; 69m. **DIR:** Robert Wise. **CAST:** Kurt Kreuger, Simone Simon, John Emery, Alan Napier, Jason Robards Sr., Norma Varden. **1944**

MADEMOISELLE STRIPTEASE ★★1/2 Lightweight comedy made just before Brigitte Bardot became an international sensation. She plays a free spirit sent to Paris, where romance and trouble lurk. Brief nudity scenes were trimmed for American release (and this video). French, dubbed in English. B&W; 100m. **DIR:** Marc Allegret. **CAST:** Brigitte Bardot, Daniel Gélin, Robert Hirsch. **1956**

MADHOUSE ★★ Yuppie couple Kirstie Alley and John Larroquette find their dream house invaded and destroyed by unwanted houseguests. Only the game performances of Larroquette and Alley save this painful-to-watch comedy. Rated PG-13 for profanity and simulated sex. 100m. **DIR:** Tom Ropelewski. **CAST:** John Larroquette, Kirstie Alley, Alison La Placa, John Diehl, Jessica Lundy, Dennis Miller, Robert Ginty. **1990**

MADHOUSE ★★★ Vincent Price and Peter Cushing share more screen time in their third film together (following *Scream and Scream Again* and *Dr. Phibes Rises Again*), thus lifting it above most horror movies of its decade. In a story slightly reminiscent of the superior *Theatre of Blood*, Price plays an actor who is released from a hospital after suffering a nervous breakdown, only to discover that his TV-series alter ego, Dr. Death, is living up to his name. Rated PG for violence. 92m. **DIR:** Jim Clark. **CAST:** Vincent Price, Peter Cushing, Robert Quarry, Adrienne Corri, Linda Hayden. **1972**

MADHOUSE ★★1/2 When a woman's deranged twin escapes from the loony bin and crashes her sibling's party, you can imagine the bloodfest that results. Although the story sounds simple, there are some surprises. Stylishly filmed and well acted, with a bigger budget this might have been a classic. As it is, it's worth a look. Not rated; contains violence. 93m. **DIR:** Ovidio Assonitis (Oliver Hellman). **CAST:** Trish Everly, Michael MacRae. **1987**

MADIGAN ★★★1/2 Well-acted, atmospheric police adventure-drama pits tough Brooklyn cop Richard Widmark and New York's finest against a crazed escaped murderer. Realistic and exciting, this is still one of the best of the "behind-the-scenes" police films. 101m. **DIR:** Don Siegel. **CAST:** Richard Widmark, Henry Fonda, Harry Guardino, James Whitmore, Inger Stevens, Michael Dunn, Steve Ihnat, Sheree North. **1968 DVD**

MADIGAN'S MILLIONS ❤ Only the most fanatical Dustin Hoffman fans need bother with this tedious spy farce. 86m. **DIR:** Stanley Prager. **CAST:** Dustin Hoffman, Elsa Martinelli, Cesar Romero. **1967**

MADNESS OF KING GEORGE, THE ★★★1/2 Alan Bennett's play about the periodic dementia that afflicted Britain's George III comes to the screen in an elegant, well-acted production. The film focuses on the petty political maneuvers to fill the vacuum left by the king's illness, with the royal health taking a backseat to parliamentary self-preservation. Not rated; contains mild profanity and suggested sexual situations. 107m. **DIR:** Nicholas Hytner. **CAST:** Nigel Hawthorne, Helen Mirren, Ian Holm, Amanda Donohoe, Rupert Graves, Rupert Everett. **1994 DVD**

MADO ★★★1/2 The midlife crisis of a French businessman sparks this complex, intelligent look at social unrest in modern France. In French with English subtitles. Not rated; contains sexual situations. 130m. **DIR:** Claude Sautet. **CAST:** Michel Piccoli, Romy Schneider, Charles Denner, Ottavia Piccolo. **1976**

MADONNA: INNOCENCE LOST ★★ So-so telling of the phenomenally successful pop star's life features a dead-on performance by Terumi Matthews as Madonna but is sabotaged by a hokey script and clichéd dialogue. Made for TV and based upon the book *Madonna Unauthorized* by Christopher Andersen. Not rated, but features mild profanity and adult situations. 90m. **DIR:** Bradford May. **CAST:** Terumi Matthews, Wendie Malick, Jeff Yagher, Diana LeBlanc, Dean Stockwell. **1994**

MADOX-01 ★★★ Japanese animation. Havoc ensues when a university student trapped in a high-tech military attack unit (Madox-01) runs afoul of a psychotic tank commander. Superior animation. In Japanese with English subtitles. Not rated, with violence and mild profanity. 48m. **DIR:** Aramaki Nobuyuki. **1989**

MADRON ★★1/2 You've heard of the spaghetti Western. Well here's an Israeli Western. The story involves a nun and a gunslinger who, after a typical wagon-train massacre, are chased by a band of Apaches. The actors are good, but the story is pedestrian. Rated PG. 93m. **DIR:** Jerry Hopper. **CAST:** Richard Boone, Leslie Caron, Paul Smith, Gabi Amrani. **1970 DVD**

MADWOMAN OF CHAILLOT, THE ★★ Self-conscious story about an eccentric who feels the world is better off without the greed of mercenary interests. Everyone looks embarrassed. Rated G because it is completely innocuous. 132m. **DIR:** Bryan Forbes. **CAST:** Katharine Hepburn, Charles Boyer, Yul Brynner, Danny Kaye, John Gavin, Nanette Newman, Giulietta Masina, Richard Chamberlain, Edith Evans, Paul Henreid, Donald Pleasence, Margaret Leighton, Oscar Homolka. **1969**

MAE WEST ★★★1/2 This TV biography features a very convincing Ann Jillian as siren Mae West. (Some poetic license has been taken in order to make this complimentary to West.) Roddy McDowall, as a female impersonator, trains West to be sultry, alluring, and ultradesirable while James Brolin plays the longtime love who offers her stability. 100m. **DIR:** Lee Philips. **CAST:** Ann Jillian, James Brolin, Roddy McDowall, Piper Laurie. **1982**

MAEDCHEN IN UNIFORM ★★★★ At once a fascinating and emotionally disturbing film, this German classic turns mainly on the love of a sexually repressed young girl for a compassionate female teacher in a state-run school. Remade in 1958 with Romy Schneider and Lili Palmer. In German with English subtitles. B&W; 90m. **DIR:** Leontine Sagan. **CAST:** Emilia Unda, Dorothea Wieck. **1931**

MAFIA PRINCESS ❤ Susan Lucci plays the spoiled daughter of a Mafia crime lord. Made for TV. 100m. **DIR:** Robert Collins. **CAST:** Tony Curtis, Susan Lucci, Kathleen Widdoes, Chuck Shamata. **1986**

MAFIA: THE HISTORY OF THE MOB IN AMERICA ★★ Only an occasionally interesting segment makes this rather repetitive tracing of mob growth watchable. Sections of note include the early days of the Kennedy clan, the failure of Prohibition, and the rise of labor unions.

Some graphic images taken from photographs may not be suitable for younger viewers. 200m. **DIR:** David Royle, Edward Gray, David Meyer. **1993 DVD**

MAGDALENE ★★ This film plays like a Barbara Cartland romance novel with Nastassja Kinski as a beautiful woman who spurns the love of a powerful baron. Corny. Rated R for nudity. 89m. **DIR:** Monica Teuber. **CAST:** Nastassja Kinski, David Warner, Steve Bond, Franco Nero. **1990**

MAGIC ★★★1/2 Will make your skin crawl. The slow descent into madness of the main character, Corky (Anthony Hopkins), a ventriloquist-magician, is the most disturbing study in terror to hit the screens since *Psycho*. Rated R. 106m. **DIR:** Richard Attenborough. **CAST:** Anthony Hopkins, Burgess Meredith, Ed Lauter, Ann-Margret. **1978 DVD**

MAGIC BOW, THE ★★ A superficial film biography of nineteenth-century composer and violinist Niccolo Paganini. The story goes into more detail than necessary about the composer's romance with a wealthy woman. Too many lulls between musical numbers, but the music is gorgeous. B&W; 106m. **DIR:** Bernard Knowles. **CAST:** Stewart Granger, Phyllis Calvert, Jean Kent, Cecil Parker, Dennis Price, Yehudi Menuhin. **1946**

MAGIC CHRISTIAN, THE ★★★ A now-dated comedy about the world's wealthiest man (Peter Sellers) and his adopted son (Ringo Starr) testing the depths of degradation to which people will plunge themselves for money still has some funny scenes and outrageous cameos by Christopher Lee (as Dracula), Raquel Welch, and Richard Attenborough. Rated PG. 93m. **DIR:** Joseph McGrath. **CAST:** Peter Sellers, Ringo Starr, Christopher Lee, Raquel Welch, Richard Attenborough, Yul Brynner. **1970**

MAGIC FLUTE, THE ★★★★ Ingmar Bergman's highly imaginative and richly stylized presentation of Mozart's last opera. The camera starts from a position within the audience at an opera house, but after the curtain rises, it moves freely within and around the stage. The adaptation remains highly theatrical, and quite magical, and the music, of course, is glorious. Sung in Swedish with English subtitles. Not rated. 150m. **DIR:** Ingmar Bergman. **1974 DVD**

MAGIC GARDEN, THE ★★★ Charming South African comedy featuring an amateur cast. A sum of money stolen from a church keeps finding its way into the hands of people who need it! A good family movie. Also known as *Pennywhistle Blues*. B&W; 63m. **DIR:** Donald Swanson. **CAST:** Tommy Ramokgopa. **1952**

MAGIC HUNTER ★★1/2 The director of the arthouse hit *My 20th Century* lets his ambition get the better of him in this inventive but frustrating exercise. At the center is a folk story of a hunter who sells his soul in exchange for seven bullets guaranteed to hit their targets. But the continual jumps between different times and places in this vague political allegory simply wear out the viewer. In Hungarian with English subtitles. Not rated. 106m. **DIR:** Ildiko Enyedi. **CAST:** Gary Kemp, Sadie Frost, Alexander Kaidanovsky, Peter Vallai. **1996**

MAGIC IN THE MIRROR ★★1/2 This version of *Alice Through the Looking Glass* features colorful characters and enough magical mayhem to entertain kids, but adults will see right through this looking-glass adventure. When young Mary Margaret steps through the antique mirror once owned by her grandmother, she's transported to a magical world. Now Mary Margaret has to find a way back. Rated G. 86m. **DIR:** Ted Nicolaou. **CAST:** Jamie Renée Smith, Kevin Wixted, Saxon Trainor, David Brooks. **1996**

MAGIC IN THE WATER, THE ★★★1/2 Enjoyable family film about a work-obsessed psychiatrist who doesn't realize what a mess he's making of his life, to say nothing of his relationship with his children, until a magical creature intervenes. Rated PG. 98m. **DIR:** Rick Stevenson. **CAST:** Mark Harmon, Harley Jane Kozak, Joshua Jackson, Sarah Wayne. **1995**

MAGIC KID ★★★ As the kick-boxing title character, young Ted Jan Roberts does little but frown and fight goons in this pleasant, cartoonish fantasy (which, at times, seems little more than a plug for Universal Studios theme park). The film is rescued from oblivion by jittery Stephen Furst, simply wonderful as the boy's uncle, a washed-up Hollywood agent in debt to mob boss Joseph Campanella. Rated PG for violence. 87m. **DIR:** Joseph Merhi. **CAST:** Stephen Furst, Billy Hufsey, Ted Jan Roberts, Shonda Whipple, Joseph Campanella, Don "The Dragon" Wilson. **1993**

MAGIC KID 2 ★★1/2 This sequel isn't helped by the clearly inexperienced direction of star Stephen Furst (who also cowrote the simplistic script). Kick-boxing youngster and his hapless uncle are now stuck in the Hollywood star-making system. Rated PG for mild violence. 86m. **DIR:** Stephen Furst. **CAST:** Stephen Furst, Ted Jan Roberts, Jennifer Savidge, Dana Barron, Donald Gibb. **1994**

MAGIC OF LASSIE, THE ★★1/2 Like the Disney live-action films of yore, *The Magic of Lassie* tries to incorporate a little of everything: heartwarming drama, suspense, comedy, and even music. But here the formula is bland. The story is okay, but it is all too long. Rated G. 100m. **DIR:** Don Chaffey. **CAST:** James Stewart, Mickey Rooney, Pernell Roberts, Stephanie Zimbalist, Michael Sharrett, Alice Faye, Gene Evans, Lane Davies, Mike Mazurki, Lassie. **1978**

MAGIC STONE, THE ★★1/2 Not one of writer-director Pamela Berger's best. She could not overcome a low budget in this telling of an Irish slave brought to North America in the late tenth century by Vikings. Based on historical research and actual archaeological findings, this sweet film has much to say about cultural acceptance. Too many directorial glitches undermine the script's romance and adventure. Rated PD-M for violence. 95m. **DIR:** Pamela Berger. **CAST:** Christopher Johnson, Robert McDonough, Eva Kim, Jonah Ming Lee, Gino Montesinos, Robert Mason Ham. **1994**

MAGIC SWORD, THE ★★ Young Gary Lockwood is on a quest to free an imprisoned princess and fights his way through an ogre, dragon, and other uninspired monsters with the help of the witch in the family, Estelle Winwood. Basil Rathbone makes a fine old evil sorcerer, relishing his foul deeds and eagerly planning new transgressions. The kids might like it, but it's laughable. 80m. **DIR:** Bert I. Gordon. **CAST:** Gary Lockwood, Anne Helm, Basil Rathbone, Estelle Winwood, Liam Sullivan. **1962**

MAGIC TOWN ★★ After successfully collaborating with Frank Capra on some of his finest films, writer Robert Riskin teamed with director William Wellman

for this mildly entertaining but preachy tale. An advertising executive (James Stewart) finds the perfect American community, which is turned topsy-turvy when the secret gets out. B&W; 103m. **DIR:** William Wellman. **CAST:** James Stewart, Jane Wyman, Ned Sparks. **1947**

MAGIC VOYAGE, THE ★★ This mediocre animated film is meant to be a history lesson about Christopher Columbus's voyage to America, but it's actually just a love story between a wood worm and a firefly. Rated G. 80m. **DIR:** Michael Schoemann. **1994 DVD**

MAGICAL MYSTERY TOUR ★★ This is a tour by bus and by mind. Unfortunately, the minds involved must have been distorted at the time that the film was made. Occasional bursts of wit and imagination come through, but sometimes this chunk of psychedelic pretension is a crashing bore. Good songs, though. 60m. **DIR:** The Beatles. **CAST:** The Beatles, Bonzo Dog Band. **1967 DVD**

MAGICAL TWILIGHT ★★ A pair of good student witches are sent to Earth as part of their final exam while, unknown to them, a third witch (this one evil) also has been sent for the same purpose, but with an opposing goal in mind. In Japanese with English subtitles. Not rated; contains nudity and sexual situations. 25m. **DIR:** Toshiaki Kobayashi. **1994**

MAGICIAN, THE ★★★ Dark and somber parable deals with the quest for an afterlife by focusing on confrontation between a mesmerist and a magician. This shadowy allegory may not be everyone's idea of entertainment, but the richness of ideas and the excellent acting of director Ingmar Bergman's fine stable of actors make this a compelling film. Swedish, subtitled in English. B&W; 102m. **DIR:** Ingmar Bergman. **CAST:** Max von Sydow, Ingrid Thulin, Gunnar Björnstrand, Bibi Andersson. **1959**

MAGICIAN OF LUBLIN, THE 🦃 Superficial adaptation of Isaac Bashevis Singer's novel about a Jewish traveling magician in nineteenth-century Europe. Rated R for nudity. 105m. **DIR:** Menahem Golan. **CAST:** Alan Arkin, Louise Fletcher, Valerie Perrine, Shelley Winters, Lou Jacobi, Warren Berlinger, Lisa Whelchel. **1979**

MAGNETIC MONSTER, THE ★★★ Intelligent sci-fi thriller with a unique monster—an energy-consuming isotope (created by research scientists, of course) that turns energy into matter and doubles in size every twelve hours. B&W; 76m. **DIR:** Curt Siodmak. **CAST:** Richard Carlson, King Donovan, Jean Byron, Harry Ellerbe, Strother Martin. **1953**

MAGNIFICENT AMBERSONS, THE ★★★★★ Orson Welles's legendary depiction of the decline of a wealthy midwestern family and the comeuppance of its youngest member is a definite must-see motion picture. Much has been made about the callous editing of the final print by studio henchmen, but that doesn't change the total impact. It's still a classic. Special notice must be given to Welles and cameraman Stanley Cortez for the artistic, almost portraitlike, look of the film. B&W; 88m. **DIR:** Orson Welles. **CAST:** Joseph Cotten, Tim Holt, Agnes Moorehead. **1942 DVD**

MAGNIFICENT OBSESSION ★★★ Rock Hudson, a drunken playboy, blinds Jane Wyman in an auto accident. Stricken, he reforms and becomes a doctor in order to restore her sight in this melodramatic tearjerker. First filmed in 1935, with Irene Dunne and Robert Taylor. 108m. **DIR:** Douglas Sirk. **CAST:** Jane Wyman, Rock Hudson, Agnes Moorehead, Otto Kruger. **1954**

MAGNIFICENT SEVEN, THE ★★★★ Japanese director Akira Kurosawa's *The Seven Samurai* served as the inspiration for this enjoyable Western, directed by John Sturges (*The Great Escape*). It's the rousing tale of how a group of American gunfighters come to the aid of a village of Mexican farmers plagued by bandits. 126m. **DIR:** John Sturges. **CAST:** Yul Brynner, Steve McQueen, Charles Bronson, James Coburn, Eli Wallach, Robert Vaughn. **1960 DVD**

MAGNIFICENT SEVEN, THE (TV SERIES) ★★★1/2 After the Civil War, a band of renegade Confederate soldiers terrorize a community consisting of Seminole Indians and runaway slaves, and it's up to the title characters to ride to the rescue. Because this pilot for the television series bears the burden of introducing its main characters, the first half is slow. But once the seven heroes charge into action, the plot picks up. Ron Perlman, as a "spiritual man," stands out in a surprisingly solid cast. Made for TV. 90m. **DIR:** Geoff Murphy. **CAST:** Michael Biehn, Eric Close, Ron Perlman, Dale Midkiff, Andrew Ravovit, Anthony Starke, Rick Worthy, Kurtwood Smith, Laurie Holden, Tony Burton, Michael Greyeyes, Ned Romero. **1999**

MAGNIFICENT YANKEE, THE ★★★1/2 Moving film biography of the Washington years of Oliver Wendell Holmes. The movie opens with his appointment to the Supreme Court in 1902 (at age 61) and closes just before his retirement in 1933. This also happens to be a charming love story. Louis Calhern was Oscar nominated for his portrayal. B&W; 80m. **DIR:** John Sturges. **CAST:** Louis Calhern, Ann Harding, Eduard Franz, Philip Ober, Ian Wolfe, Richard Anderson, Jimmy Lydon. **1950**

MAGNOLIA ★★★ This brilliant mess interweaves the lives of a dozen characters during a random twenty-four-hour period in the San Fernando Valley. By turns fascinating and compelling, tiresome and repulsive, audacious and self-indulgent, the film is too long, and enduring the final act will be more than many viewers can stand. The plot explores the notion that we're all interconnected by random events, spontaneous friendships, and undisclosed blood ties. Interesting thought, but the film is a series of one-acts in search of a binding thread that ultimately isn't present. Rated R for profanity and drug use. 180m. **DIR:** P. T. Anderson. **CAST:** Jeremy Blackman, Tom Cruise, Philip Baker Hall, Philip Seymour Hoffman, William H. Macy, Julianne Moore, John C. Reilly, Jason Robards Jr., Melora Walters. **1999 DVD**

MAGNUM FORCE ★★★ This is the second and least enjoyable of the five Dirty Harry films. Harry (Clint Eastwood) must deal with vigilante cops as well as the usual big-city scum. Clint is iron-jawed and athletic, but the film still lacks something. Rated R for language, violence, nudity, and gore. 124m. **DIR:** Ted Post. **CAST:** Clint Eastwood, Hal Holbrook, David Soul, Tim Matheson, Robert Urich, Suzanne Somers. **1973 DVD**

MAHABHARATA, THE ★★★★ An exquisite six-part Shakespearean-style production made in Paris for public television of the eighteen-book Sanskrit epic of mankind's search for Dharma (truth). Dealing with the fortunes of rival ruling families, the Kauravas and Pan-

davas, this tale weaves historical elements and myth to expose man's ultimate choice between destiny and freedom. 222m. **DIR:** Peter Brook. **CAST:** Robert Langton-Lloyd. **1989**

MAHLER ★★1/2 Ken Russell's fantasy film about the biography of composer Gustav Mahler. Robert Powell's portrayal of Mahler as a man consumed with passion and ambition is a brilliant one. Georgina Hale as Alma, Mahler's wife, is also well played. Unfortunately, the cast cannot give coherence to the script. 115m. **DIR:** Ken Russell. **CAST:** Robert Powell, Georgina Hale, Richard Morant. **1974 DVD**

MAHOGANY ★★ The highlight of this unimpressive melodrama is Diana Ross's lovely wardrobe. She plays a poor girl who makes it big as a famous model and, later, dress designer after Anthony Perkins discovers her. This one jerks more yawns than tears. Rated PG. 109m. **DIR:** Berry Gordy. **CAST:** Diana Ross, Anthony Perkins, Billy Dee Williams. **1975**

MAID, THE ★★★ Businessman Martin Sheen falls for businesswoman Jacqueline Bisset and becomes her maid to get closer to her in this sometimes predictable, but always entertaining, romantic comedy. Rated PG for mild profanity. 91m. **DIR:** Ian Toynton. **CAST:** Martin Sheen, Jacqueline Bisset, Jean-Pierre Cassel, James Faulkner. **1991**

MAID TO ORDER ★★1/2 This modern retelling of the Cinderella fable isn't much of a star vehicle for Ally Sheedy, who's constantly upstaged by the supporting players. She's a spoiled little rich girl whose hip fairy godmother (Beverly D'Angelo) turns her into a nonentity, forced to work for an honest dollar. Rated PG for language and brief nudity. 96m. **DIR:** Amy Jones. **CAST:** Ally Sheedy, Beverly D'Angelo, Michael Ontkean, Valerie Perrine, Dick Shawn, Tom Skerritt. **1987**

MAID'S NIGHT OUT, THE ★★ This energetic comedy tells of a millionaire's son (Allan Lane) who becomes a milkman for a month to win a bet with his self-made millionaire father (George Irving). Along the way, he meets Joan Fontaine. Lowbrow but fun. B&W; 64m. **DIR:** Ben Holmes. **CAST:** Joan Fontaine, Hedda Hopper, Allan "Rocky" Lane, Cecil Kellaway. **1938**

MAIN EVENT, THE 🦃 A limp boxing comedy that tried unsuccessfully to reunite the stars of *What's Up Doc?* Rated PG. 112m. **DIR:** Howard Zieff. **CAST:** Barbra Streisand, Ryan O'Neal, Paul Sand. **1979**

MAIN STREET TO BROADWAY ★★ The story of a young playwright's rise to success on Broadway is nothing you haven't seen before. The only attraction here is an endless array of cameo appearances by Ethel and Lionel Barrymore, Shirley Booth, Rex Harrison, Rodgers and Hammerstein, Mary Martin, Lilli Palmer, Cornel Wilde, and other notables of the theater world. B&W; 102m. **DIR:** Tay Garnett. **CAST:** Tom Murton, Mary Murphy, Agnes Moorehead, Rosemary DeCamp, Tallulah Bankhead. **1953**

•**MAINLINE RUN** ★★ Fresh out of prison, a small potatoes drug runner signs up for a new caper with his old cronies, a job that soon goes bad and has them all fighting for their lives. Grim crime tale recommended only to those who like plenty of violent gunfights. Not rated. 96m. **DIR:** Howard Ford. **CAST:** Hugo Speer, Andrew Joseph, Nelson E. Ward. **1994 DVD**

MAITRESSE ★★★ A normal young man becomes involved with a professional dominatrix. Odd film is neither exploitative nor pornographic, but it sure is peculiar. In French with English subtitles. Not rated, but the subject matter marks it as adults-only territory. 110m. **DIR:** Barbet Schroeder. **CAST:** Gérard Depardieu, Bulle Ogier, Andre Rouyer. **1975**

•**MAJESTIC, THE** ★★ A Hollywood writer (Jim Carrey) during the Blacklisted 1950s develops amnesia following a car accident and is mistaken for a small-town war hero, long missing in action. Stitched together from remnants of *The Front*, *Hail the Conquering Hero*, and *Cinema Paradiso*, the film is earnestly acted but long-winded and solemn, with false nostalgia oozing from every scene. Rated PG. 152m. **DIR:** Frank Darabont. **CAST:** Jim Carrey, Laurie Holden, Martin Landau, Allen Garfield, David Ogden Stiers, James Whitmore. **2001 DVD**

MAJOR BARBARA ★★★1/2 In the title role as a Salvation Army officer, Wendy Hiller heads a matchless cast in this thoughtful film of George Bernard Shaw's comedy about the power of money and the evils of poverty. Rex Harrison, as her fiancé, and Robert Newton, as a hard case with doubts about the honesty and motives of do-gooders, are excellent. B&W; 136m. **DIR:** Gabriel Pascal. **CAST:** Wendy Hiller, Rex Harrison, Robert Morley, Robert Newton, Emlyn Williams, Sybil Thorndike, Deborah Kerr. **1941**

MAJOR DUNDEE ★★★ This is a flawed but watchable Western directed with typical verve by Sam Peckinpah. The plot follows a group of Confederate prisoners who volunteer to go into Mexico and track down a band of rampaging Apache Indians. 124m. **DIR:** Sam Peckinpah. **CAST:** Charlton Heston, Richard Harris, James Coburn, Jim Hutton, Warren Oates, Ben Johnson. **1965**

MAJOR LEAGUE ★★★1/2 In this often funny but clichéd baseball comedy, the Cleveland Indians find themselves headed for oblivion when the new owner, former show girl Margaret Whitton, decides to put together the worst possible team. Tom Berenger, Charlie Sheen, and Corbin Bernsen are fine as three inept players, and character actor James Gammon shines as their coach. Rated R for profanity and violence. 95m. **DIR:** David S. Ward. **CAST:** Tom Berenger, Charlie Sheen, Corbin Bernsen, Margaret Whitton, James Gammon. **1989**

MAJOR LEAGUE II ★★ The sequel to the 1989 baseball hit is more of the same, with an almost identical plot and nearly the entire cast reprising their original roles (Omar Epps replaces Wesley Snipes). This time, though, the zest is gone—everyone looks tired and just a little embarrassed. Rated PG, but with profanity some may find offensive. 105m. **DIR:** David S. Ward. **CAST:** Charlie Sheen, Tom Berenger, Corbin Bernsen, James Gammon, David Keith, Omar Epps. **1994 DVD**

MAJOR LEAGUE: BACK TO THE MINORS ★★ The *Major League* franchise continues despite the trade and retirement of some of its most notable players. Scott Bakula steps up to the plate, playing a veteran minor-league pitcher at the end of his career. An opportunity to manage a Triple A team inspires him, until he learns that the players are a mess. The writers slow-pitch every cliché in the game book, while the director

fails to rally the fans. The actors are okay, but even they seem to know the season's over. Rated PG-13 for language. 100m. **DIR:** John Warren. **CAST:** Scott Bakula, Corbin Bernsen, Dennis Haysbert, Jensen Daggett, Ted McGinley. **1998 DVD**

MAJOR PAYNE ★★ Gung ho Marine is discharged by the military—"there's no one left to kill, he's killed them all"—and takes a job training junior ROTC at a private academy in this predictable band-of-misfits comedy. Rated PG-13 for language. 97m. **DIR:** Nick Castle. **CAST:** Damon Wayans, Karyn Parsons, William Hickey, Michael Ironside, Albert Hall. **1995 DVD**

MAJOR ROCK ★★ The plot about a rescue team sent to save five centerfolds and the president's daughter from South American terrorists is a thin excuse for plentiful sex and nudity (even more in the unrated version, which is 12 minutes longer). Rated R for nudity, sexual situations, and profanity. 78m. **DIR:** Charles Allen. **CAST:** Tabitha Stevens, Don Fisher, Buck Adams. **1999**

MAJORETTES, THE ★★ Written before *Halloween* but not produced until well after that film, this slasher film has an edge on the competition in that it has a plot that involves more than just the killings of the titular cheerleaders. Scripted by John Russo. Rated R for violence, profanity, and nudity. 92m. **DIR:** Bill Hinzman. **CAST:** Kevin Kindlon, Terrie Godfrey, Sueanne Seamens. **1987**

MAJORITY OF ONE, A ★★★★ In spite of miscasting, the charm and wit of Leonard Spiegelgass's Broadway play shine through. Rosalind Russell tries to play a typical Jewish mother and this just calls attention to her WASPishness. Sir Alec Guinness drops his "l's" and rolls his "r's" as a Japanese gentleman and gets laughs in the wrong places. Very predictable but fun. 156m. **DIR:** Mervyn LeRoy. **CAST:** Rosalind Russell, Alec Guinness, Madlyn Rhue, Ray Danton, Mae Questel, Sharon Hugeny, Alan Mowbray, Gary Vinson, Marc Mamo. **1961**

MAKE A WISH 🦃 Basil Rathbone is a jolly good composer. Henry Armetta, Leon Errol, and Donald Meek want to steal Basil's latest operetta. B&W; 80m. **DIR:** Kurt Neumann. **CAST:** Bobby Breen, Basil Rathbone, Marion Claire, Henry Armetta, Leon Errol, Donald Meek. **1937**

MAKE HASTE TO LIVE ★★★ A mobster, framed for killing his wife, is finally released. Now he wants revenge from the one woman who escaped his grasp by outsmarting him. Compact, chilling thriller. B&W; 90m. **DIR:** William A. Seiter. **CAST:** Dorothy McGuire, Stephen McNally, Edgar Buchanan. **1954**

MAKE ME AN OFFER 🦃 A young woman makes her way to the top by becoming a quick study in the California real estate business. Made for television. 100m. **DIR:** Jerry Paris. **CAST:** Susan Blakely, Patrick O'Neal, Stella Stevens, John Rubinstein. **1980**

MAKE MINE MINK ★★★★ Bright dialogue and clever situations make this crazy comedy from Britain highly enjoyable. An ex-officer, a dowager, and a motley crew of fur thieves team to commit larceny for charity. Gap-toothed Terry-Thomas is in top form in this one. 100m. **DIR:** Robert Asher. **CAST:** Terry-Thomas, Athene Seyler, Billie Whitelaw. **1960**

MAKE ROOM FOR TOMORROW ★★★ More a collection of mildly humorous events than an out-and-out comedy. Victor Lanoux plays a father going through a midlife crisis. Rated R for language and nudity. 104m. **DIR:** Peter Kassovitz. **CAST:** Victor Lanoux, Jane Birkin, Georges Wilson. **1982**

MAKE THEM DIE SLOWLY 🦃 South American cannibals. Not rated; contains nudity, profanity, and extreme violence. 92m. **DIR:** Umberto Lenzi. **CAST:** John Morghen, Lorainne DeSelle. **1980 DVD**

MAKING CONTACT ★★ After his father dies, a little boy begins to exhibit telekinetic powers and begins giving life to his favorite toys. Obviously aimed at children, this film is quite imaginative. 82m. **DIR:** Roland Emmerich. **CAST:** Joshua Morell, Eve Kryll. **1985**

MAKING LOVE ★★ Kate Jackson discovers that her husband (Michael Ontkean) is in love with another . . . man (Harry Hamlin). Rated R because of adult subject matter, profanity, and implicit sexual activity. 113m. **DIR:** Arthur Hiller. **CAST:** Kate Jackson, Michael Ontkean, Harry Hamlin. **1982**

MAKING MR. RIGHT ★★1/2 This mild satire, about a female image consultant who falls for the android she's supposed to be promoting, doesn't come close to the energy level of director Susan Seidelman's *Desperately Seeking Susan*. Rated PG-13. 98m. **DIR:** Susan Seidelman. **CAST:** John Malkovich, Ann Magnuson, Ben Masters, Glenne Headly, Laurie Metcalf, Polly Bergen, Hart Bochner. **1987**

MAKING THE GRADE ★★1/2 A rich kid pays a surrogate to attend prep school for him. Typical teen-exploitation fare. Rated R. 105m. **DIR:** Dorian Walker. **CAST:** Judd Nelson, Jonna Lee, Carey Scott. **1984 DVD**

MALAREK ★★★ Victor Malarek's biographical novel (*Hey, Malarek*) exposes the abuse of teens in the Montreal Detention Center. As a rookie reporter, Malarek witnessed the cold-blooded shooting of an escaped teen. His investigation inspired his book and this film. Rated R for violence and profanity. 105m. **DIR:** Roger Cardinal. **CAST:** Elias Koteas, Kerrie Keane, Al Waxman, Michael Sarrazin. **1988**

MALCOLM ★★★★1/2 An absolutely charming Australian entry that swept that country's Oscars the year it was released. Colin Friels has the title role as an emotionally immature young man who, after he loses his job with a local rapid-transit company (for building his own tram with company parts), finds himself among thieves and loves it. 90m. **DIR:** Nadia Tess. **CAST:** Colin Friels, John Hargreaves, Lindy Davies, Chris Haywood. **1986**

MALCOLM X ★★★★★ Writer-director Spike Lee's most passionate film may also be his greatest. In chronicling the life of the black activist from his Harlem gangster years to his 1965 assassination at the age of 39 by followers of Elijah Muhammad, Lee pays scrupulous attention to detail and avoids the rambling, self-indulgent qualities that hampered his previous projects. At the heart of the film is a superb performance in the title role by Denzel Washington. Brilliant! Rated PG-13 for violence, suggested sex, and profanity. 193m. **DIR:** Spike Lee. **CAST:** Denzel Washington, Spike Lee, Angela Bassett, Albert Hall, Al Freeman Jr., Delroy Lindo, Kate Vernon, Lonette McKee, Karen Allen. **1992 DVD**

MALE AND FEMALE ★★★ Cecil B. DeMille yarn from his best period of exotic, erotic fables. Loosely derived from James M. Barrie's play, *The Admirable Crichton*. For DeMille fans, it's quintessential fun. Silent. B&W; 100m. **DIR:** Cecil B. DeMille. **CAST:** Gloria Swanson, Thomas Meighan, Lila Lee. **1919 DVD**

MALENA ★★★★ In a small Sicilian village during World War II, a luscious war widow arouses the hormones of the boys, the lust of the men, and the hatred of the women. Although this epic of growing up in Fascist Italy starts out funny but forced, like warmed-over Fellini, it grows into something wiser, sadder, and more thoughtful—a rueful reflection on the lost dreams of adolescence. In Italian with English subtitles. Rated R for nudity, profanity (in subtitles), sexual scenes, and brief violence. 92m. **DIR:** Giuseppe Tornatore. **CAST:** Monica Bellucci, Giuseppe Sulfaro, Luciano Federico, Pietro Notarianni. **2000 DVD**

MALEVOLENCE ★★ Unpleasant film about a racist convict who is used as a pawn in the assassination of a black politician. Rated R for profanity, violence, and sexuality. 95m. **DIR:** Belle Avery. **CAST:** Joe Cortese, Michael McGrady, Brian James, Lou Rawls, Michael Stone. **1996**

MALIBU BIKINI SHOP, THE 🦃 An exploitative romp about two brothers who inherit a bikini shop. Rated R for nudity and profanity. 90m. **DIR:** David Wechter. **CAST:** Michael David Wright, Bruce Greenwood, Barbara Horan, Debra Blee, Jay Robinson. **1985**

MALICE ★★★ When a serial killer begins murdering female students in a New England college town, the institution's mild-mannered dean becomes involved in the investigation while simultaneously wondering about the cocky surgeon who has taken a room in his house. And when the dean's wife unexpectedly winds up in the hospital, things *really* get interesting. This thriller starts off extremely well, but then settles into television-style drama. Even so, it never gets boring. Rated R for profanity, violence, and simulated sex. 106m. **DIR:** Harold Becker. **CAST:** Alec Baldwin, Nicole Kidman, Bill Pullman, Bebe Neuwirth, George C. Scott, Anne Bancroft, Peter Gallagher, Josef Sommer. **1993 DVD**

MALICIOUS ★★★1/2 Italian beauty Laura Antonelli is hired as a housekeeper for a widower and his three sons. Not surprisingly, she becomes the object of affection for all four men—particularly 14-year-old Nino. Rated R. 98m. **DIR:** Salvatore Samperi. **CAST:** Laura Antonelli, Turi Ferro, Alessandro Momo, Tina Aumont. **1974**

MALICIOUS ★★ Only for people who want to see Molly Ringwald naked. She plays a complete psycho trying to land a college-baseball player with whom she shared a one-night stand. An unimaginative *Fatal Attraction* rip-off that is hardly enhanced by Ringwald's mouth-breathing, out-of-control harpy. Rated R for profanity, sexual situations, nudity, and violence. 92m. **DIR:** Ian Corson. **CAST:** Molly Ringwald, John Vernon, Patrick McGaw, Sarah Lassez. **1995**

MALL RATS 🦃 In this crude, dull misadventure, two guys spend a day at a shopping mall trying to reconcile with the girlfriends who dumped them. Rated R for profanity, nudity, and sex. 97m. **DIR:** Kevin Smith. **CAST:** Jason Lee, Jeremy London, Shannen Doherty, Claire Forlani, Michael Rooker. **1995 DVD**

MALONE ★★★1/2 In this modern-day Western, Burt Reynolds is in top form as Malone, an ex-CIA hit man on the run. Underneath all the car chases, big-bang explosions, and the blitz fire of automatic weapons is the simplest of all B-Western plots—in which a former gunfighter is forced out of retirement by the plight of settlers forced off their land by black-hatted villains. Rated R for profanity, violence, and suggested sex. 92m. **DIR:** Harley Cokliss. **CAST:** Burt Reynolds, Cliff Robertson, Kenneth McMillan, Scott Wilson, Lauren Hutton, Cynthia Gibb. **1987**

MALOU ★★★ Moving drama of a woman's search for the truth about the marriage between her French mother and a German Jew during Hitler's terrifying reign. The story unfolds through a rich tapestry of flashbacks. In German with English subtitles. Not rated. 94m. **DIR:** Jeanine Meerapfel. **CAST:** Ingrid Caven, Helmut Griem. **1983**

MALTA STORY, THE ★★★ Set in 1942, this is about British pluck on the island of Malta while the British were under siege from the Axis forces and the effect the war has on private lives. Flight Lieutenant Ross's (Alec Guinness) love for a native girl (Muriel Pavlow) goes unrequited when his commanding officer (Anthony Steel) sends him on a dangerous mission. B&W; 103m. **DIR:** Brian Desmond Hurst. **CAST:** Alec Guinness, Jack Hawkins, Anthony Steel, Muriel Pavlow. **1953**

MALTESE FALCON, THE ★★★★★ One of the all-time great movies, John Huston's first effort as a director is the definitive screen version of Dashiell Hammett's crime story. In a maze of double crosses and back stabbing, Humphrey Bogart, as Sam Spade, fights to get hold of a black bird, "the stuff that dreams are made of." B&W; 100m. **DIR:** John Huston. **CAST:** Humphrey Bogart, Mary Astor, Sydney Greenstreet, Peter Lorre, Elisha Cook Jr., Ward Bond. **1941 DVD**

MAMA, THERE'S A MAN IN YOUR BED ★★★★ This is a somewhat unlikely but sweet and funny romantic tale of a white Parisian executive and his unexpected love for the black cleaning woman at his office. Daniel Auteuil (the slow-witted nephew Ugolin in *Jean de Florette*) stars. In French with English subtitles. Not rated but of a PG-13 quality, with adult situations. 108m. **DIR:** Coline Serreau. **CAST:** Daniel Auteuil, Fir-mine Richard. **1990**

MAMA TURNS 100 ★★★ A comparatively lighthearted attack on Franco's Spain from Carlos Saura. He reunites the cast of his 1972 *Anna and the Wolves* for this similar story of a greedy family battling among themselves. The humor is hit-and-miss, and the social analysis may be lost on American audiences. In Spanish with English subtitles. Not rated. 115m. **DIR:** Carlos Saura. **CAST:** Geraldine Chaplin. **1979**

MAMBO ★★ Dated B movie features Silvano Mangano as an impoverished Venetian who seeks wealth and fame, first as a dancer and then as a count's wife. She has an annoying habit of thinking aloud rather than showing her emotions. B&W; 94m. **DIR:** Robert Rossen. **CAST:** Silvana Mangano, Michael Rennie, Shelley Winters, Vittorio Gassman. **1954**

MAMBO CAFÉ ★★1/2 With their Spanish Harlem café in jeopardy of closing, the owners and their college-

bound daughter cook up a scheme to bring in business. They invite a mob boss to dinner hoping that he'll get killed in their café. When he does, business picks up, but so does interest from the Feds and the mob. Interesting idea doesn't get the respect it deserves, although the cast is better than the script. Rated PG-13 for adult situations and language. 98m. **DIR:** Reuben Gonzalez. **CAST:** Thalia, Paul Rodriguez, Rosanna DeSoto, Danny Aiello. **1999 DVD**

MAMBO KINGS, THE ★★★★ Oscar Hijuelos's Pulitzer Prize–winning novel of Cuban immigrants, has been brought to the screen with great passion, energy and style. An engrossing story of brotherhood and cultural pride, and a vibrant showcase for magnificent Cuban music, it spotlights Armand Assante and Antonio Banderas, who charms in his first English-language role. Rated R, with profanity, violence, and nudity. 125m. **DIR:** Arne Glimcher. **CAST:** Armand Assante, Antonio Banderas, Cathy Moriarty, Maruschka Detmers, Desi Arnaz Jr., Tito Puente. **1992**

MAME You won't love Lucy in this one. Rated PG. 131m. **DIR:** Gene Saks. **CAST:** Lucille Ball, Robert Preston, Jane Connell, Bea Arthur. **1974**

MAMMA DRACULA A horror–black comedy that fails on both counts. Not rated; contains nudity and adult situations. 93m. **DIR:** Boris Szulzinger. **CAST:** Louise Fletcher, Maria Schneider, Marc-Henri Wajnberg, Alexander Wanberg, Jess Hahn. **1988**

MAMMA ROMA ★★★ Anna Magnani's larger-than-life performance is the best reason to see this somewhat dated melodrama. She plays a prostitute in Rome who tries to get out of the business and raise her son to be a respectable middle-class citizen. Filmmaker Pier Paolo Pasolini has a great eye for location filming. In Italian with English subtitles. B&W; 110m. **DIR:** Pier Paolo Pasolini. **CAST:** Anna Magnani, Franco Citti, Ettore Garofolo. **1962**

MAN, A WOMAN AND A BANK, A ★★ An odd little caper flick that never quite gets off the ground. A couple of guys decide to rob a bank via computer, and—of course—things don't work out as planned. Rated PG. 100m. **DIR:** Noel Black. **CAST:** Donald Sutherland, Brooke Adams, Paul Mazursky. **1979**

MAN ALONE, A ★★★ Ray Milland's first directorial effort finds him hiding from a lynch mob in a small Western town. And who is he hiding with? The sheriff's daughter! Not too bad, as Westerns go. 96m. **DIR:** Ray Milland. **CAST:** Ray Milland, Mary Murphy, Ward Bond, Raymond Burr, Lee Van Cleef. **1955**

MAN AND A WOMAN, A ★★★★ This is a superbly written, directed, and acted story of a young widow and widower who fall in love. Anouk Aimée and race-car driver Jean-Louis Trintignant set this film on fire. A hit in 1966 and still a fine picture. French, dubbed into English. 102m. **DIR:** Claude Lelouch. **CAST:** Anouk Aimée, Jean-Louis Trintignant, Pierre Barouh, Valerie Lagrange. **1966**

MAN AND A WOMAN, A: 20 YEARS LATER The director of this movie took his 1966 *A Man and a Woman* and, after twenty years, assembled the original lead actors and created a monster. In French. Rated PG. 112m. **DIR:** Claude Lelouch. **CAST:** Anouk Aimée, Jean-Louis Trintignant, Richard Berry. **1986**

MAN AND BOY ★★1/2 Bill Cosby and his family try to make a go of it by homesteading on the prairie. The story provides ample opportunity for some Cosbyesque explanations about the black experience of that period. Rated G. 98m. **DIR:** E. W. Swackhamer. **CAST:** Bill Cosby, Gloria Foster, George Spell, Leif Erickson, Yaphet Kotto, Douglas Turner Ward, John Anderson, Henry Silva, Dub Taylor. **1971**

MAN AND THE MONSTER, THE ★★ The Mexican monster movies that were made in the late 1950s at the Churubusco-Azteca Studios are an acquired taste. Their crisp, black-and-white photography is richly atmospheric, but production values are meager and acting is mediocre. This one, a Jekyll-Hyde potboiler involving a musician who changes into a hairy beast at inconvenient times, is directed by the man who made this odd subgenre's best films. B&W; 74m. **DIR:** Rafael Baledon. **CAST:** Enrique Rabal, Abel Salazar. **1958**

MAN BEAST A search for the Abominable Snowman. B&W; 72m. **DIR:** Jerry Warren. **CAST:** Rock Madison, Virginia Maynor. **1955**

MAN BITES DOG ★★ Several brilliant cinematic shots cannot justify this sick spoof of the documentary. A camera crew follows a cold-blooded killer on his brutal daily routine. Unsettling and difficult to watch. Rated NC-17, it contains countless acts of violence as well as profanity, sex, and gore. In French with English subtitles. B&W; 96m. **DIR:** Rémy Belvaux. **CAST:** Benoit Poelvoorde, Rémy Belvaux, Jenny Drye, Malou Madou. **1992**

MAN CALLED ADAM, A A world-class jazz trumpet player can't live with the guilt of accidentally killing his wife and child. B&W; 103m. **DIR:** Leo Penn. **CAST:** Sammy Davis Jr., Louis Armstrong, Peter Lawford, Mel Torme, Frank Sinatra Jr., Lola Falana, Ossie Davis, Cicely Tyson. **1966**

MAN CALLED FLINTSTONE, A ★★★1/2 The Ralph Kramden and Ed Norton of the kiddie-set, Fred Flintstone and Barney Rubble are featured in this full-length animated cartoon. Fred takes over for lookalike secret agent, Rack Slag, and goes after the "Green Goose" and his henchmen, SMIRK agents. Great fun for the kids. 87m. **DIR:** William Hanna, Joseph Barbera. **1966**

MAN CALLED HORSE, A ★★★ Richard Harris (in one of his best roles) portrays an English aristocrat who's enslaved and treated like a pack animal by Sioux Indians in the Dakotas. He loses his veneer of sophistication and finds the core of his manhood. This strong film offers an unusually realistic depiction of American Indian life. Rated PG. 114m. **DIR:** Elliot Silverstein. **CAST:** Richard Harris, Judith Anderson, Jean Gascon, Corinna Tsopei, Dub Taylor. **1970**

MAN CALLED NOON, THE ★★★★ The Louis L'Amour classic remains faithful to the book. A bounty hunter and a female rancher help Jubal Noon, a gunfighter with amnesia, unravel his identity while seeking vengeance for the deaths of his wife and child. Great photography, direction, and score make this one of the best. Rated R for violence. 90m. **DIR:** Peter Collinson. **CAST:** Richard Crenna, Stephen Boyd, Farley Granger, Rosanna Schiaffino, Patty Shepard. **1974**

MAN CALLED PETER, A ★★★1/2 This warm, winning film biography tells the story of Scottish clergyman Peter Marshall, who was appointed chaplain of the U.S. Senate. Beautifully played by Richard Todd and Jean

Peters. 117m. **DIR:** Henry Koster. **CAST:** Richard Todd, Jean Peters, Marjorie Rambeau, Les Tremayne. **1955**

MAN CALLED SARGE, A World War II misfits against Rommel's desert forces. Rated PG-13. 88m. **DIR:** Stuart Gillard. **CAST:** Gary Kroeger, Gretchen German, Jennifer Runyon, Marc Singer. **1990**

MAN ESCAPED, A ★★★★ Engrossing drama based on the true story of a French resistance officer's escape from a Nazi prison. Director Robert Bresson heightens our participation with attention to the most minute details, including a detailed reconstruction of the actual prison cell. In French with English subtitles. Not rated; contains no objectionable material. B&W; 102m. **DIR:** Robert Bresson. **CAST:** Francois Leterrier, Charles Le Clainche, Roland Monot. **1956**

MAN FACING SOUTHEAST ★★★1/2 A haunting, eerie mystery in which an unknown man—possibly an alien—inexplicably appears in the midst of a Buenos Aires psychiatric hospital. Rich with Christian symbolism, this film leaves one wondering who is really sick—society or those society finds insane. Some nudity and sexual situations. In Spanish with English subtitles. 105m. **DIR:** Eliseo Subiela. **CAST:** Lorenzo Quinteros, Hugo Soto. **1987**

MAN FOR ALL SEASONS, A ★★★★★ This splendid film, about Sir Thomas More's heartfelt refusal to help King Henry VIII break with the Catholic church and form the Church of England, won the best-picture Oscar in 1966. Paul Scofield, who is magnificent in the title role, also won best actor. Directed by Fred Zinnemann and written by Robert Bolt, the picture also benefits from memorable supporting performances by an all-star cast. 120m. **DIR:** Fred Zinnemann. **CAST:** Paul Scofield, Wendy Hiller, Robert Shaw, Orson Welles, Susannah York. **1966 DVD**

MAN FROM ATLANTIS, THE ★★1/2 The pilot for the 1977 TV sci-fi series. Patrick Duffy plays the man from beneath the waves, recruited by the navy to retrieve a top-secret submarine. Belinda Montgomery is the marine biologist who holds Duffy's reins. 60m. **DIR:** Lee H. Katzin. **CAST:** Patrick Duffy, Belinda Montgomery, Victor Buono, Art Lund, Lawrence Pressman. **1977**

MAN FROM BEYOND, THE ★★★ Legendary escape artist Harry Houdini wrote and starred in this timeless story of a man encased in a block of ice for one hundred years who is discovered, thawed out, and thrust into twentieth-century life. While the special effects lack sophistication and the acting seems pretty broad, this is one of the few existing examples of Houdini's film work. Silent. B&W; 50m. **DIR:** Burton King. **CAST:** Harry Houdini. **1921**

MAN FROM COLORADO, THE ★★★ A great cast and solid performances elevate this post–Civil War psychological Western about a former northern colonel (Glenn Ford) who becomes a federal judge in Colorado. William Holden plays his friend. 99m. **DIR:** Henry Levin. **CAST:** Glenn Ford, William Holden, Ellen Drew, Ray Collins, Edgar Buchanan, Jerome Courtland, Denver Pyle. **1948**

MAN FROM LARAMIE, THE ★★★★1/2 Magnificent Western has James Stewart as a stranger who finds himself at odds with a powerful ranching family. The patriarch (Donald Crisp) is going blind, so the running of the ranch is left to his psychotic son (Alex Nicol) and longtime ranch foreman (Arthur Kennedy). Possibly the summit of director Anthony Mann's career; certainly Stewart's finest Western performance. 101m. **DIR:** Anthony Mann. **CAST:** James Stewart, Arthur Kennedy, Donald Crisp, Alex Nicol, Cathy O'Donnell, Jack Elam. **1955 DVD**

MAN FROM LEFT FIELD, THE ★★★ Burt Reynolds directed and stars in this heartfelt made-for-TV drama about a homeless man who ends up coaching a ragtag kids' baseball team. Although a mystery to the locals and even himself, he begins to unlock his past and learns how he lost everything. Reba McEntire has some nice moments as a mom who helps him. Not too sweet, but inspiring. 96m. **DIR:** Burt Reynolds. **CAST:** Burt Reynolds, Reba McEntire. **1993**

MAN FROM MONTEREY, THE ★★★ Swashbuckling action mixes with gunplay in this enjoyable Warner Bros. B Western set in Old California. American army officer John Wayne rides to the rescue of a Spanish aristocrat, while silent-screen veteran Francis Ford (brother of director John) adds class as the chief heavy. Luis Alberni provides a few chuckles in comic support. B&W; 57m. **DIR:** Mack V. Wright. **CAST:** John Wayne, Ruth Hall, Francis Ford, Donald Reed, Lafe McKee, Luis Alberni, Slim Whitaker. **1933**

MAN FROM MUSIC MOUNTAIN ★★★ Gene Autry thwarts unscrupulous land developers attempting to sell worthless mining stock. Routine. B&W; 54m. **DIR:** Joseph Kane. **CAST:** Gene Autry, Smiley Burnette, Carol Hughes, Sally Payne, Earl Dwire. **1938**

MAN FROM NOWHERE, THE ★★★1/2 A henpecked small-town man seizes the opportunity to move to Rome and start a new life when he is mistakenly reported dead. Stylish, ironic comedy, based on a Luigi Pirandello novel and (unusual, for the time) filmed on location in Italy. In French with English subtitles. B&W; 98m. **DIR:** Pierre Chenal. **CAST:** Pierre Blanchar, Isa Miranda, Ginette Leclerc. **1937**

MAN FROM PAINTED POST, THE ★★★1/2 Early Fairbanks actioner about a good bad man. Great stunts on horseback and with the lasso. Silent. 55m. **DIR:** Joseph E. Henabery. **CAST:** Douglas Fairbanks Sr., Eileen Percy, Frank Campeau. **1917**

MAN FROM PLANET X, THE ★★★ Creepy sets and a strong, offbeat story set this low-budget film apart. When a space traveler lands in the foggy moors of the Scottish highlands, his intentions are anything but evil—until he gets a lesson in just how venal some members of the human race can be. B&W; 70m. **DIR:** Edgar G. Ulmer. **CAST:** Robert Clarke, Margaret Field, Raymond Bond, William Schallert. **1951 DVD**

MAN FROM SNOWY RIVER, THE ★★★★ If you've been looking for an adventure film for the whole family, this Australian Western about the coming-of-age of a mountain man (Tom Burlinson) is it. Rated PG, the film has no objectionable material. 115m. **DIR:** George Miller. **CAST:** Tom Burlinson, Kirk Douglas, Jack Thompson, Bruce Kerr. **1982**

MAN FROM THE ALAMO, THE ★★★1/2 An exciting, well-acted story of a soldier (Glenn Ford) who escapes from the doomed Alamo in an effort to warn others about Santa Ana's invasion of Texas. After the Alamo falls, he is branded a traitor and deserter and must prove his mettle to the Texicans. Historically inaccu-

rate, but exciting and fun. 79m. **DIR:** Budd Boetticher. **CAST:** Glenn Ford, Julie Adams, Victor Jory, Chill Wills, Hugh O'Brian, Neville Brand. **1953**

MAN FROM U.N.C.L.E., THE (TV SERIES) ★★★1/2 This tongue-in-cheek spy series was one of the mid-Sixties' hottest cult phenomena. The central character, Napoleon Solo, was suavely rendered by Robert Vaughn. Solo was assisted by Illya Kuryakin (David McCallum), and both answered to Leo G. Carroll's paternalistic Alexander Waverly, who dispatched his agents on their global peacekeeping missions. The episodes taken from the show's debut season are by far the best. *Star Trek* fans should take note of "The Project Strigas Affair," which includes William Shatner and Leonard Nimoy. Each tape contains two hour-length episodes. 104m. **DIR:** John Brahm, Alf Kjellin, Joseph Sargent. **CAST:** Robert Vaughn, David McCallum, Leo G. Carroll. **1964–68**

MAN FROM UTAH, THE ★★ Low, low-budget Western with a very young John Wayne as a lawman going undercover to catch some crooks using a rodeo to bilk unsuspecting cowboys. The rodeo footage was used over and over again by the film company, Monogram Pictures, in similar films. B&W; 57m. **DIR:** Robert N. Bradbury. **CAST:** John Wayne, Polly Ann Young, George "Gabby" Hayes, Yakima Canutt, George Cleveland. **1934 DVD**

MAN HUNT (1941) ★★★★ Based on *Rogue Male*, Geoffrey Household's crackerjack suspense novel about a British big-game hunter who wants to see if it's possible to assassinate Hitler, this is one of Fritz Lang's tensest American films. Dudley Nichols's script and Walter Pidgeon's performance lend authority and conviction, and the only shortcoming is a sentimental subplot with Joan Bennett. B&W; 105m. **DIR:** Fritz Lang. **CAST:** Walter Pidgeon, George Sanders, Joan Bennett. **1941**

MAN I LOVE, THE ★★★1/2 A moody melodramatic movie that benefits from sexy stars and sensational music by George Gershwin, Jerome Kern, and Johnny Green. Ida Lupino is sensuous as a streetwise cabaret singer who keeps mobsters at arm's length in order to protect her family. Not much story, but plenty of sophistication. B&W; 96m. **DIR:** Raoul Walsh. **CAST:** Ida Lupino, Robert Alda, Andrea King, Bruce Bennett, Dolores Moran, John Ridgely, Martha Vickers, Alan Hale Sr., Craig Stevens. **1946**

MAN IN GREY, THE ★★★ A tale of attempted husband-stealing that worked well to make the prey, James Mason, a star. Margaret Lockwood is the love thief who proves to intended victim Phyllis Calvert that with her for a friend she needs no enemies. Mason is a stand-out as the coveted husband. B&W; 116m. **DIR:** Leslie Arliss. **CAST:** Margaret Lockwood, James Mason, Phyllis Calvert, Stewart Granger, Martita Hunt. **1943**

MAN IN LOVE, A 🦃 European actress finds herself involved in an affair with an egotistical American film star. Rated R for nudity, profanity, and simulated sex. 108m. **DIR:** Diane Kurys. **CAST:** Peter Coyote, Greta Scacchi, Peter Riegert, Jamie Lee Curtis, Claudia Cardinale, John Berry. **1987**

MAN IN THE ATTIC, THE ★★★ In this fascinating tale of obsessive love, Neil Patrick Harris plays Edward, the young man caught up in a love affair with married woman Anne Archer. Lover by day, Edward retreats to a secret attic hideaway at night when hubby is home. This goes on for several years until Edward finally cracks. Good performances make it all seem plausible in this made-for-cable drama. Rated PG-13 for adult situations and language. 104m. **DIR:** Graeme Campbell. **CAST:** Anne Archer, Neil Patrick Harris, Len Cariou, Alex Carter. **1994**

MAN IN THE EIFFEL TOWER, THE ★★★★ A rarely seen little gem of suspense: an intriguing plot, a crafty police inspector (Charles Laughton), an equally crafty murderer (Franchot Tone), and an exciting conclusion. Well acted. 97m. **DIR:** Burgess Meredith. **CAST:** Charles Laughton, Franchot Tone, Burgess Meredith, Robert Hutton, Jean Wallace. **1949**

MAN IN THE GLASS BOOTH ★★★★ Robert Shaw's electrifying play was brought to the screen as part of the experimental American Film Theater series, and even though the video is hard to find, the experience is well worth it. Maximilian Schell is outstanding as Arthur Goldman, whose life becomes a living nightmare when he's kidnapped by Israeli soldiers and deported to face charges of being an ex-Nazi. Placed in a glass booth for the duration of his trial, Goldman's story slowly unfolds as the truth comes out. Director Arthur Hiller deftly sidesteps the theatrical flourishes to tell the story of one man's frightening odyssey. Not rated. 117m. **DIR:** Arthur Hiller. **CAST:** Maximilian Schell, Lois Nettleton, Luther Adler, Lawrence Pressman, Lloyd Bochner. **1975**

MAN IN THE GRAY FLANNEL SUIT, THE ★★★1/2 The title of Sloan Wilson's novel became a catchphrase to describe the mind-set of corporate America in the 1950s. Considering that, it's a pleasant surprise to find that Nunnally Johnson's film has hardly dated at all. 153m. **DIR:** Nunnally Johnson. **CAST:** Gregory Peck, Jennifer Jones, Fredric March, Marisa Pavan, Lee J. Cobb, Keenan Wynn, Gene Lockhart. **1956**

MAN IN THE IRON MASK, THE ★★★1/2 D'Artagnan and the legendary musketeers once more come to life in this sumptuous adaptation, played here by veteran actors who acquit themselves far better than Leonardo DiCaprio, somewhat miscast as the young, villainous King of France. This marks the directorial debut of Randall Wallace, and while all the elements are properly in place and Wallace works with a cast that most directors would kill for, the results are rather slow. Rated PG-13 for violence, discreet nudity, and suggested sex. 117m. **DIR:** Randall Wallace. **CAST:** Leonardo DiCaprio, Jeremy Irons, John Malkovich, Gérard Depardieu, Anne Parillaud, Judith Godreche. **1998 DVD**

MAN IN THE IRON MASK, THE ★★★ Louis Hayward plays twin brothers—a fop and a swashbuckler—in this first sound version of Dumas's classic novel of malice, mayhem, intrigue, and ironic revenge in eighteenth-century France. Separated at birth, one brother becomes the king of France, the other a sword-wielding cohort of the Three Musketeers. Their clash makes for great romantic adventure. B&W; 110m. **DIR:** James Whale. **CAST:** Louis Hayward, Joan Bennett, Warren William, Alan Hale Sr., Joseph Schildkraut. **1939**

MAN IN THE IRON MASK, THE ★★★ This is the Alexandre Dumas tale of twin brothers, separated at birth. One becomes the wicked king of France, the other, a heroic peasant. The story receives a top-drawer treatment in this classy TV movie. Richard Chamber-

lain proves he's the most appealing swashbuckler since Errol Flynn retired his sword. 100m. **DIR:** Mike Newell. **CAST:** Richard Chamberlain, Patrick McGoohan, Louis Jourdan, Jenny Agutter, Ralph Richardson. **1977**

MAN IN THE MOON, THE ★★★★ About two sisters who fall in love with the same boy, this coming-of-age movie skillfully captures all the angst, joy, and heartbreak of adolescence and first love. It might have been a simple tearjerker if not for its remarkable sense of realism and honesty. Rated PG-13 for suggested sex and mature themes. 103m. **DIR:** Robert Mulligan. **CAST:** Sam Waterston, Tess Harper, Gail Strickland, Reese Witherspoon, Jason London, Emily Warfield. **1991 DVD**

MAN IN THE SADDLE ★★★★ Insanely jealous Alexander Knox tries to run Randolph Scott off the range after Scott's former girl, Joan Leslie, decides to marry Knox. One of director André de Toth's best Westerns. Memorable for its prolonged well-staged fight between Scott and John Russell. 87m. **DIR:** André de Toth. **CAST:** Randolph Scott, Joan Leslie, John Russell, Alexander Knox, Ellen Drew, Cameron Mitchell. **1951**

MAN IN THE SANTA CLAUS SUIT, THE ★★★ In one of his last performances, Fred Astaire plays seven characters who enrich the lives of everybody in a small community. This made-for-TV production is a delightful Christmastime picture. 100m. **DIR:** Corey Allen. **CAST:** Fred Astaire, John Byner, Nanette Fabray, Gary Burghoff, Bert Convy, Harold Gould. **1978**

MAN IN THE WHITE SUIT, THE ★★★★★ In *The Man in the White Suit*, Alec Guinness is the perfect choice to play an unassuming scientist who invents a fabric that can't be torn, frayed, or stained! Can you imagine the furor this causes in the textile industry? This uniquely original script pokes fun at big business and big labor as they try to suppress his discovery. Joan Greenwood is a treasure in a supporting role. B&W; 84m. **DIR:** Alexander Mackendrick. **CAST:** Alec Guinness, Joan Greenwood, Cecil Parker. **1952**

MAN IN THE WILDERNESS ★★★1/2 Exciting outdoor adventure film follows the exploits of a trapper left for dead by his fellow hunters after a bear attack. Gritty film is beautifully filmed and acted. Rated R for violence. 105m. **DIR:** Richard C. Sarafian. **CAST:** Richard Harris, John Huston, John Bindon, Prunella Ransome, Henry Wilcoxon. **1971**

MAN IN UNIFORM, A ★★★★ Eerie, compelling, and startling drama about an actor (Tom McCamus) who can't stop playing the cop he portrays on TV, even after the cameras have stopped rolling. In his off-hours, he haunts the streets, slowly but surely immersing himself in a world that eventually will swallow him. Creepy but effective performances and a shockingly realistic atmosphere make this riveting. Rated R for violence and profanity. 102m. **DIR:** David Wellington. **CAST:** Tom McCamus, Brigitte Bako, David Hemblen, Kevin Tighe. **1993 DVD**

MAN INSIDE, THE ★★1/2 In this so-so film, James Franciscus is a Canadian vice squad agent who works his way into the organization of a major heroin dealer. In the course of his assignment he has the opportunity to split with $2 million, and is tempted to do so. This Canadian film is unrated. 96m. **DIR:** Gerald Mayer. **CAST:** James Franciscus, Stefanie Powers, Jacques Godin, Len Birman, Donald Davis, Allan Royale. **1984**

MAN INSIDE, THE ★★ Well-intentioned drama about a crusader (Jurgen Prochnow) who goes undercover to expose a corrupt, muckraking West German newspaper that goes over the top a bit too often. Rated R for violence and profanity. 93m. **DIR:** Bobby Roth. **CAST:** Jurgen Prochnow, Peter Coyote, Dieter Laser, Nathalie Baye. **1990**

MAN IS NOT A BIRD ★★★★ In his first feature, Yugoslav director Dusan Makavejev *(Montenegro)* mixes documentary footage of a grimy copper factory with a fictional story of an engineer who works there and his relationship with a woman. Makavejev's "guerrilla" mixture of stylistic techniques makes the film continually engrossing. In Serbian with English subtitles. B&W; 80m. **DIR:** Dusan Makavejev. **CAST:** Milena Dravic, Janez Vrhovec. **1965**

MAN MADE MONSTER (THE ATOMIC MONSTER) ★★★ Scientist Lionel Atwill, who envisions a race of superhuman killers fueled by electricity, chooses hapless Lon Chaney Jr. as his glowing guinea pig. Chaney brings class to this unusual, and intriguing, little B flick. Not rated. B&W; 59m. **DIR:** George Waggner. **CAST:** Lon Chaney Jr., Lionel Atwill, Frank Albertson, Anne Nagel, Ben Taggart, Samuel S. Hinds. **1941**

MAN OF A THOUSAND FACES ★★1/2 Sentimentalized, soap-opera bio-pic of Lon Chaney Sr., the screen's greatest horror star, dwells too much on his troubled private life and too little on films. James Cagney turns in a moving performance in the title role. Chaney's films, currently available on video, speak more eloquently without dialogue. 122m. **DIR:** Joseph Pevney. **CAST:** James Cagney, Dorothy Malone, Jane Greer, Marjorie Rambeau, Jim Backus, Robert Evans, Jeanne Cagney, Snub Pollard. **1957 DVD**

MAN OF FLOWERS ★★★★★ Kinky, humorous, and touching, this winner from Australia affirms Paul Cox (of *Lonely Hearts* fame) as one of the wittiest and most sensitive directors from Down Under. Norman Kaye is terrific as an eccentric old man who collects art and flowers and watches pretty women undress. To him these are things of beauty that he can observe but can't touch. Rated R for nudity. 90m. **DIR:** Paul Cox. **CAST:** Norman Kaye, Alyson Best, Chris Haywood, Werner Herzog. **1984 DVD**

MAN OF IRON ★★★★ This work of fiction set against the backdrop of stark truth in Communist Poland shows the dramatic events that bridged the Gdansk student rebellions of the 1960s and the Solidarity strikes of 1980. The story is told through the eyes of a journalism student looking for evidence of political skulduggery. In Polish with English subtitles. Rated PG. 140m. **DIR:** Andrzej Wajda. **CAST:** Jerzy Radziwilowicz, Krystyna Janda, Marian Opiana, Irene Byrska. **1981**

MAN OF LA MANCHA For those who loved the hit Broadway musical and those who heard about how wonderful it was, this adaptation is a shameful and outrageous letdown. Rated G. 130m. **DIR:** Arthur Hiller. **CAST:** Peter O'Toole, Sophia Loren, James Coco, Harry Andrews. **1972**

MAN OF MARBLE ★★★★ Epic film that reconstructs the life of a Polish laborer, a forgotten heroic figure, through his political efforts against the Stalinist power

structure of the 1950s. Engrossing. In Polish with English subtitles. Not rated. B&W/color; 160m. **DIR:** Andrzej Wajda. **CAST:** Jerzy Radziwilowicz, Krystyna Janda. **1977**

MAN OF NO IMPORTANCE, A ★★★ In 1963 Dublin, a repressed homosexual busman (Albert Finney) with a fixation on Oscar Wilde, meets persecution from a former friend when he attempts to mount a production of Wilde's banned *Salomé* with the cast taken from the passengers on his bus. Finney's bravura performance dominates this well-acted but slight, rather meandering film. Rated R for mature themes and a brief scene of simulated sex. 98m. **DIR:** Suri Krishnamma. **CAST:** Albert Finney, Brenda Fricker, Michael Gambon, Tara Fitzgerald, Rufus Sewell. **1994**

MAN OF PASSION, A ★★ Typical story of a young boy's coming-of-age. The young boy is left with his grandfather, a famous painter. There he learns about life and sex. Not rated; contains nudity and simulated sex. 95m. **DIR:** J. Anthony Loma. **CAST:** Anthony Quinn, Maud Adams, Ramon Sheen, Ray Walston, Elizabeth Ashley. **1989**

MAN OF THE FOREST ★★★★ This is one of two very good Westerns made by Randolph Scott in a year that produced many fine films. Based on Zane Grey's novel, Scott plays a cowboy who kidnaps a young woman to keep her from the clutches of a bad guy. Zesty and action-packed. B&W; 62m. **DIR:** Henry Hathaway. **CAST:** Randolph Scott, Harry Carey, Buster Crabbe, Noah Beery Sr., Guinn Williams. **1933**

MAN OF THE FRONTIER (RED RIVER VALLEY) ★★1/2 This early entry in the Gene Autry series features Gene as an undercover agent out to stop a gang bent on sabotaging construction of a much-needed dam. Very enjoyable, and a nice example of the kind of film Autry could make but didn't have to after a while. B&W; 60m. **DIR:** B. Reeves "Breezy" Eason. **CAST:** Gene Autry, Smiley Burnette, Frances Grant. **1936**

MAN OF THE HOUSE ★★1/2 When his divorced mom (Farrah Fawcett) considers marriage to a lawyer (Chevy Chase), a young boy (Jonathan Taylor Thomas of TV's *Home Improvement*) sulks and schemes to get rid of the newcomer. Rated PG. 98m. **DIR:** James Orr. **CAST:** Jonathan Taylor Thomas, Chevy Chase, Farrah Fawcett, George Wendt. **1995**

MAN OF THE WEST ★★★★ Reformed outlaw Gary Cooper reluctantly falls in with former boss Lee J. Cobb to save innocent hostages from Cobb's gang. This tense, claustrophobic Western takes place almost entirely indoors. A minor classic. 100m. **DIR:** Anthony Mann. **CAST:** Gary Cooper, Lee J. Cobb, Julie London, Arthur O'Connell, Jack Lord, John Dehner. **1958**

MAN OF THE YEAR ★★★1/2 When a model is chosen *Playgirl* magazine's "Man of the Year," he gets to spend a year as the fantasy of every woman—as long as no one finds out he's gay. Beneath the humor of this clever "mockumentary" is a lot of provocative commentary about sexual stereotyping and role-playing in American life. Not rated. 85m. **DIR:** Dirk Shafer. **CAST:** Dirk Shafer. **1995 DVD**

MAN ON A STRING ★★1/2 An undercover government agent tries to break up two mob factions by setting them against each other. Predictable made-for-TV movie. Not rated; contains no objectionable material. 74m. **DIR:** Joseph Sargent. **CAST:** Christopher George, William Schallert, Joel Grey, Keith Carradine, Kitty Winn, Jack Warden, James B. Sikking. **1972**

MAN ON FIRE 🦃 Scott Glenn plays an ex-CIA agent hired to protect the daughter of a wealthy American couple. Glenn is the film's only redemption. Rated R for language and graphic violence. 92m. **DIR:** Elie Chouraqui. **CAST:** Scott Glenn, Brooke Adams, Danny Aiello, Joe Pesci, Jonathan Pryce. **1987**

MAN ON THE MOON ★★★1/2 Jim Carrey stars in the life of Andy Kaufman, the oddball comic who amused millions as Latka Gravas on *Taxi*, then irritated many of those same people with his other routines and his abrasive alter ego, lounge singer Tony Clifton. People never knew quite what to make of Kaufman, and in a way the film doesn't either. Still, Carrey's performance is uncanny, and because Carrey is so naturally funny, Kaufman's other antics come off as funnier and less annoying than we remember them. Rated R for profanity. 118m. **DIR:** Milos Forman. **CAST:** Jim Carrey, Danny DeVito, Courtney Love, Paul Giamatti. **1999 DVD**

MAN ON THE ROOF ★★★★ Gripping adaptation of the novel by Mal Sjöwall and Per Wahloo starring Carl-Gustav Linstedt as veteran detective Martin Beck, who is called upon to find a killer with a grudge against cops. While many of the naturalistic techniques pioneered in this thriller have become commonplace, it doesn't dilute this film's power. In Swedish with English subtitles. 109m. **DIR:** Bo Widerberg. **CAST:** Carl-Gustav Linstedt, Halan Serner, Sven Wollter. **1976**

MAN RAY CLASSIC SHORTS ★★1/2 Abstract photographer-artist Man Ray uses animation, superimposition, and lens distortions in these early silent experimental films shot in and around 1920s Paris. Interesting cinematography gets redundant at times. With French subtitles. Silent. B&W; 45m. **DIR:** Man Ray. **1924–1926**

MAN THAT CORRUPTED HADLEYBURG, THE ★★★★★ Robert Preston shows up in Hadleyburg with a sack of gold. Would-be saints and holier-than-thou guardians of public decency are exposed as ordinary people with quite human failings in this delightfully sly adaptation of Mark Twain's acerbic story. Henry Fonda's introduction includes rare film footage of Twain. Not rated and suitable for family viewing. 40m. **DIR:** Ralph Rosenblum. **CAST:** Robert Preston, Fred Gwynne, Frances Sternhagen, Tom Aldredge. **1980**

MAN THEY COULD NOT HANG, THE ★★★ Boris Karloff's fine performance carries this fast-paced tale of a scientist executed for murder and brought back to life and his bizarre plan of revenge on the judge and jury who convicted him. B&W; 72m. **DIR:** Nick Grindé. **CAST:** Boris Karloff, Lorna Gray, Robert Wilcox. **1939**

MAN TROUBLE ★★ A terrific cast is wasted in this inept comedy about a down-on-his-luck security expert. Jack Nicholson mugs shamelessly, while Beverly D'Angelo gives this supposed comedy's only funny performance. Rated PG-13 for profanity, simulated sex, and violence. 100m. **DIR:** Bob Rafelson. **CAST:** Jack Nicholson, Ellen Barkin, Harry Dean Stanton, Beverly D'Angelo, Michael McKean, Saul Rubinek, Viveka Davis, Veronica Cartwright, David Clennon, Paul Mazursky. **1992**

MAN UPSTAIRS, THE ★★ An awkward performance by Ryan O'Neal doesn't help this stagy made-for-TV comedy about a prison escapee who hides in the home of an elderly woman (Katharine Hepburn). It's not an inspired teaming; their timing is off and the frequent attempts at humor fall flat. 95m. **DIR:** George Schaefer. **CAST:** Katharine Hepburn, Ryan O'Neal, Henry Beckman, Helena Carroll, Brenda Forbes. **1992**

MAN WHO BROKE 1000 CHAINS, THE ★★★★1/2 An excellent retelling of *I am a Fugitive from a Chain Gang* with Val Kilmer in the Paul Muni role. Kilmer's performance is as sharp as Muni's, and the supporting players, notably Charles Durning, are superb. Not rated, has violence and profanity. 113m. **DIR:** Daniel Mann. **CAST:** Val Kilmer, Sonia Braga, Charles Durning, Kyra Sedgwick, James Keach. **1987**

MAN WHO CAME TO DINNER, THE ★★★★★ The classic George Kaufman and Moss Hart farce features Monty Woolley in his original Broadway role. High camp and high comedy result when a cynical newspaper columnist falls and supposedly breaks his leg. Bette Davis has a straight role as the secretary. Wacky and lots and lots of fun. 112m. **DIR:** William Keighley. **CAST:** Monty Woolley, Bette Davis, Ann Sheridan, Jimmy Durante, Mary Wickes, Reginald Gardiner, Grant Mitchell, Richard Travis, Billie Burke. **1941**

MAN WHO CAPTURED EICHMANN, THE ★★★★ Robert Duvall gives a chilling performance as Nazi war criminal Eichmann in this story about an Israeli team and its efforts to bring him to justice. Not rated; contains adult language. 95m. **DIR:** William A. Graham. **CAST:** Robert Duvall, Arliss Howard, Jeffrey Tambor, Joel Brooks, Jack Laufer, Nicolas Surovy, Sam Robards. **1997**

MAN WHO CHEATED HIMSELF, THE ★★★1/2 The man of the title is the police lieutenant who falls in love with a woman who accidentally shot her husband. He helps her get rid of the body in an atmospheric murder mystery that capitalizes on suspense more than violence. Good acting and clever writing. B&W; 81m. **DIR:** Felix Feist. **CAST:** Jane Wyatt, Lee J. Cobb, John Dall, Lisa Howard, Terry Frost. **1950**

MAN WHO COULD WORK MIRACLES, THE ★★★1/2 A timid department store clerk suddenly finds he possesses the power to do whatever he desires. Roland Young is matchless as the clerk, and is supported by a first-rate cast in this captivating fantasy. B&W; 82m. **DIR:** Lothar Mendes. **CAST:** Roland Young, Ralph Richardson, Joan Gardner, George Zucco. **1937**

•**MAN WHO CRIED, THE** ★★★ A Jewish refugee (Christina Ricci) is adopted by a British family, then grows up to find herself trapped in Paris when the Nazis march in. Deliberate and slightly ponderous, the film suffers from Ricci's blank performance; Cate Blanchett easily steals the show as a Russian expatriate who takes Ricci under her wing. Rated R for sexual scenes. 97m. **DIR:** Sally Potter. **CAST:** Christina Ricci, Cate Blanchett, Johnny Depp, John Turturro, Harry Dean Stanton. **2000 DVD**

MAN WHO FELL TO EARTH, THE ★★★★ A moody, cerebral science-fiction thriller about an alien (David Bowie) who becomes trapped on our planet. Its occasional ambiguities are overpowered by sheer mind-tugging bizarreness and directorial brilliance. Rated R. 140m. **DIR:** Nicolas Roeg. **CAST:** David Bowie, Rip Torn, Candy Clark, Buck Henry. **1976 DVD**

MAN WHO HAD POWER OVER WOMEN, THE ★★ This British picture, adapted from Gordon Williams's novel, takes a semiserious look at a talent agency. A passable time filler, with some unexpected touches. Rated R. 89m. **DIR:** John Krish. **CAST:** Rod Taylor, James Booth, Carol White. **1970**

MAN WHO HAUNTED HIMSELF, THE ★★★1/2 Freaky melodrama about a car crash with unexpected side effects. Recovering from the wreck, a man (Roger Moore) begins to question his sanity when it appears that his exact double has assumed his position in the world. Imaginative film keeps the viewer involved from start to finish. Rated PG. 94m. **DIR:** Basil Dearden. **CAST:** Roger Moore, Hildegard Neil. **1970**

MAN WHO KNEW TOO LITTLE, THE ★★★★ Bill Murray, a naïve American visitor to England whose vulgar ways almost upset a crucial business deal being set up by his brother, is cleverly sent off on a "Theater of Life" spy adventure. The only problem is, Murray ends up in the middle of a real life-or-death situation while thwarting his assailants through sheer nonchalance and ineptitude. Fans of the star will love it, and some classic sequences should win over the skeptical. Rated PG-13 for violence and profanity. 94m. **DIR:** Jon Amiel. **CAST:** Bill Murray, Peter Gallagher, Joanne Whalley, Alfred Molina, John Standing. **1997 DVD**

MAN WHO KNEW TOO MUCH, THE ★★★★★ The remake with James Stewart can't hold a candle to this superb suspense film about a man (Leslie Banks) who stumbles onto a conspiracy and then is forced into action when his child is kidnapped to ensure his silence. This is Hitchcock at his best, with Peter Lorre in fine fettle as the sneering villain. B&W; 83m. **DIR:** Alfred Hitchcock. **CAST:** Leslie Banks, Peter Lorre, Edna Best, Nova Pilbeam. **1934 DVD**

MAN WHO KNEW TOO MUCH, THE ★★★ James Stewart and Doris Day star in this fairly entertaining Hitchcock thriller as a married couple who take a vacation trip to Africa and become involved in international intrigue when they happen on the scene of a murder. It's no match for the original, but the director's fans no doubt will enjoy it. 120m. **DIR:** Alfred Hitchcock. **CAST:** James Stewart, Doris Day, Carolyn Jones. **1955 DVD**

MAN WHO LAUGHS, THE ★★★ In this adaptation of a Victor Hugo novel, the king orders that a rebellious nobleman's infant son be surgically mutilated to wear an external grin. Given to gypsies, who cast him adrift a few years later, he saves an infant girl he finds in the arms of her dead mother. A traveling carnival performer takes them in and turns the boy into a comedy star. This long-winded story of intrigue and perversion in the court of England plays against the tender love story of the tragic actor and the young, blind girl he rescued. Action, melodrama, and sweeping spectacle make this one of the more interesting films from the end of the silent era. Silent, with musical score. B&W; 110m. **DIR:** Paul Leni. **CAST:** Conrad Veidt, Mary Philbin, Olga Baclanova, Brandon Hurst, Cesare Gravine, Stuart Holms, Sam de Grasse. **1928**

MAN WHO LIVED AGAIN, THE ★★★ One of Karloff's rare British films of the 1930s, this is an initially slow-moving, mad scientist melodrama about mind transfer-

ence, which gradually builds to a potent second half. B&W; 61m. **DIR:** Robert Stevenson. **CAST:** Boris Karloff, Anna Lee, John Loder. **1936**

MAN WHO LOVED CAT DANCING, THE 🦃 Burt Reynolds is wasted in this tale of a train robber. Rated PG. 114m. **DIR:** Richard C. Sarafian. **CAST:** Burt Reynolds, Sarah Miles, George Hamilton, Lee J. Cobb, Jack Warden. **1973**

MAN WHO LOVED WOMEN, THE ★★★★ The basis for a 1983 Blake Edwards film starring Burt Reynolds, this comedy-drama from François Truffaut has more irony and bite than the remake. Beginning with the protagonist's funeral, the movie examines why he wants and needs women so much, and why they respond to him as well. Like most Truffaut films, it has a deceptively light tone. In French with English subtitles. 119m. **DIR:** François Truffaut. **CAST:** Charles Denner, Brigitte Fossey, Leslie Caron, Nathalie Baye. **1977**

MAN WHO LOVED WOMEN, THE ★★★ The first collaboration of Burt Reynolds, Julie Andrews, and her director hubby, Blake Edwards, didn't sound like the kind of thing that would make screen history. And it isn't. But it is a pleasantly entertaining—and sometimes uproariously funny—adult sex comedy. The always likable Reynolds plays a guy who just can't say no to the opposite sex. Rated R for nudity and profanity. 110m. **DIR:** Blake Edwards. **CAST:** Burt Reynolds, Julie Andrews, Marilu Henner, Kim Basinger, Barry Corbin. **1983**

MAN WHO NEVER WAS, THE ★★★1/2 British intelligence pulls the wool over Nazi eyes in this intriguing true tale of World War II espionage involving fake invasion plans planted on a corpse dressed as a British officer. 102m. **DIR:** Ronald Neame. **CAST:** Clifton Webb, Gloria Grahame, Robert Flemyng, Stephen Boyd, Laurence Naismith, Michael Hordern. **1955**

MAN WHO SAW TOMORROW, THE ★★★1/2 Orson Welles narrates and appears in this fascinating dramatization of the prophecies of sixteenth-century poet, physician, and psychic Michel de Nostradamus. Nostradamus was astonishingly accurate and, in some cases, actually cited names and dates. His prediction for the future is equally amazing—and, sometimes, terrifying. Rated PG. 90m. **DIR:** Robert Guenette. **1981**

MAN WHO SHOT LIBERTY VALANCE, THE ★★★★★ This release was director John Ford's bittersweet farewell to the Western. John Wayne reprises his role of the western man of action, this time with a twist. James Stewart's part could well be called *Mr. Smith Goes to Shinbone*, it draws so much on his most famous image. Combined with Ford's visual sense and belief in sparse dialogue, as well as fine ensemble playing in supporting roles, it adds up to a highly satisfying film. B&W; 119m. **DIR:** John Ford. **CAST:** John Wayne, James Stewart, Vera Miles, Lee Marvin, Edmond O'Brien, Woody Strode, Andy Devine, Strother Martin, Lee Van Cleef. **1962 DVD**

MAN WHO WASN'T THERE, THE 🦃 Espionage and invisibility. This was originally released in 3-D. Rated R for nudity and language. 111m. **DIR:** Bruce Malmuth. **CAST:** Steve Guttenberg, Jeffrey Tambor, Lisa Langlois, Art Hindle, Vincent Baggetta. **1983**

•MAN WHO WASN'T THERE, THE (2001) ★★★★1/2 Small-town barber Billy Bob Thornton blackmails his wife's lover (James Gandolfini) to get the money for a get-rich-quick scheme, but events quickly slip out of his control. Filmmaking brothers Joel and Ethan Coen revisit the film *noir* world of their early success *Blood Simple*, with sleek and stylish results. In a sterling cast, Tony Shalhoub steals the show as a slick lawyer. Rated R for mature themes and brief but intense violence. B&W; 116m. **DIR:** Joel Coen. **CAST:** Billy Bob Thornton, Frances McDormand, James Gandolfini, Michael Badalucco, Tony Shalhoub, Scarlett Johansson. **2001 DVD**

MAN WHO WOULD BE KING, THE ★★★★1/2 A superb screen adventure, this is loosely based on Rudyard Kipling's story and was made at the same time Sean Connery and John Huston starred in the other sand-and-camel flick, the excellent *The Wind and the Lion*. Both are classics in the adventure genre. Rated PG. 129m. **DIR:** John Huston. **CAST:** Sean Connery, Michael Caine, Christopher Plummer. **1975 DVD**

MAN WITH A GUN ★★★ Appealing cast fleshes out this predictable tale of a hit man (Michael Madsen) asked to kill his boss's scheming wife Rena (Jennifer Tilly). Unfortunately, the hit man is in love with Rena and struggles with the assignment. Then Rena suggests he kill her twin sister instead, a decision that sends John down a road of self-discovery, where his conscience is tested to the limit. Rated R for violence, profanity, and nudity. 96m. **DIR:** David Wyles. **CAST:** Michael Madsen, Jennifer Tilly, Gary Busey, Robert Loggia. **1994**

MAN WITH BOGART'S FACE, THE ★★1/2 A modern-day Humphrey Bogart–type mystery. Film has fun with the genre while avoiding outright parody. A warm-hearted homage. Enjoyable, but of no great importance. Rated PG. 106m. **DIR:** Robert Day. **CAST:** Robert Sacchi, Michelle Phillips, Olivia Hussey, Franco Nero, Misty Rowe, Victor Buono, Herbert Lom, Sybil Danning, George Raft, Mike Mazurki. **1980 DVD**

MAN WITH ONE RED SHOE, THE ★★★1/2 An American remake of the French comedy *The Tall Blond Man with One Black Shoe*, this casts Tom Hanks as a concert violinist who is pursued by a group of spies. Hanks is nearly the whole show. Jim Belushi (as his practical-joke-loving buddy) and Carrie Fisher (as an overly amorous flute player) also provide some hearty laughs. Rated PG for profanity and violence. 96m. **DIR:** Stan Dragoti. **CAST:** Tom Hanks, Dabney Coleman, Charles Durning, Lori Singer, James Belushi, Carrie Fisher, Edward Herrmann. **1985**

MAN WITH THE GOLDEN ARM, THE ★★★ This dated film attempts to be *The Lost Weekend* of drug-addiction movies. Frank Sinatra is the loser on the needle and the nod in sleazy Chicago surroundings. Eleanor Parker is his crippled wife. Kim Novak, in an early role, is the girl who saves him. As a study of those who say yes, it carries a small jolt. B&W; 119m. **DIR:** Otto Preminger. **CAST:** Frank Sinatra, Eleanor Parker, Kim Novak, Arnold Stang, Darren McGavin, Robert Strauss. **1955 DVD**

MAN WITH THE GOLDEN GUN, THE ★★ In spite of the potentially sinister presence of Christopher Lee as the head baddie, this is the most poorly constructed of all the Bond films. Roger Moore sleepwalks through the entire picture, and the plot tosses in every cliché. Rated PG—some violence. 125m. **DIR:** Guy Hamilton. **CAST:** Roger Moore, Christopher Lee, Britt Ekland, Maud

Adams, Herve Villechaize, Bernard Lee, Lois Maxwell. **1974 DVD**

MAN WITH THE PERFECT SWING, THE ★★1/2 Lighthearted and low-budget comedy-drama about a middle-aged man who sees his life as a failure, until he comes up with a new golf swing that can make anyone a golf pro. The hard part comes in trying to convince everyone that the one-time loser is now a winner. Rated PG-13 for profanity. 93m. **DIR:** Michael Hovis. **CAST:** James Black, Suzanne Savoy, Marco Perella, James Belcher. **1995**

MAN WITH TWO BRAINS, THE ★★★★ Steve Martin stars in this generally amusing takeoff of 1950s horror-sci-fi flicks as a scientist with a nasty wife (Kathleen Turner) and a sweet patient (the voice of Sissy Spacek). There's only one problem with the latter: all that's left of her is her brain. Rated R for nudity, profanity, and violence. 93m. **DIR:** Carl Reiner. **CAST:** Steve Martin, Kathleen Turner, David Warner, Paul Benedict. **1983 DVD**

MAN WITH TWO HEADS This semiremake of *Dr. Jekyll & Mr. Hyde* is loaded with gore and guts. Rated R. 80m. **DIR:** Scott Williams. **1982**

MAN WITHOUT A FACE, THE ★★★★ Touching drama about a 12-year-old boy who dreams of attending a prestigious military academy. When he fails to pass the entrance exam, the lad turns to a reclusive former teacher, whose scarred face and tragic past have caused him to be viewed as a monster by the other kids living in their coastal village. Rated PG-13 for brief profanity and sexual undertones. 114m. **DIR:** Mel Gibson. **CAST:** Mel Gibson, Margaret Whitton, Fay Masterson, Gaby Hoffman, Geoffrey Lewis, Richard Masur, Nick Stahl, Michael DeLuise. **1993**

MAN WITHOUT A STAR ★★★ With charm, fists, and guns, foreman Kirk Douglas swaggers through this stock story of rival ranchers. Jeanne Crain is his beautiful boss; Claire Trevor is, as usual, a big-hearted saloon hostess. 89m. **DIR:** King Vidor. **CAST:** Kirk Douglas, Jeanne Crain, Claire Trevor, Richard Boone, Jack Elam, Mara Corday. **1955**

MAN, WOMAN AND CHILD ★★★1/2 Here's a surprisingly tasteful and well-acted tearjerker written by Erich Segal. Martin Sheen stars as a married college professor who finds out he has a son in France, the result of an affair ten years before. Sheen decides to bring his son to America, which causes complications. Rated PG for language and adult situations. 99m. **DIR:** Dick Richards. **CAST:** Martin Sheen, Blythe Danner, Sebastian Dungan. **1983**

MANAGUA A good cast is wasted in this confusing, sex-soaked thriller about American agents infiltrating Latin American drug cartels. Rated R for nudity, violence, profanity, substance abuse, and sexual situations. 108m. **DIR:** Michele Taverna. **CAST:** Louis Gossett Jr., Assumpta Serna, John Savage, John Diehl, Robert Beltran, Michael Moriarty. **1997**

MANCE LIPSCOMB: A WELL-SPENT LIFE ★★★★ Les Blank's stirring portrait of Texas songster Mance Lipscomb is a moving tribute to a legendary bluesman. Lipscomb's crafty, bottleneck-slide guitar style is reminiscent of country-blues giant Furry Lewis and contemporary Texas-blues great Lightnin' Hopkins. 44m. **DIR:** Les Blank. **1981**

MANCHURIAN CANDIDATE, THE ★★★★1/2 This cold-war black comedy is still topical, chilling, and hilarious. Frank Sinatra gives a superbly controlled performance as a Korean War veteran who begins to believe that the honored heroics of a former member of his squad (Laurence Harvey) may be the product of brainwashing by an enemy with even more sinister designs. A delicate balance between hilarity and horror. Not rated, the film has violence. B&W; 126m. **DIR:** John Frankenheimer. **CAST:** Frank Sinatra, Laurence Harvey, Janet Leigh, Angela Lansbury, James Gregory, Leslie Parrish. **1962 DVD**

MANDELA ★★★ Although Danny Glover and Alfre Woodard put heart and soul into their interpretations of South African activists Nelson and Winnie Mandela, Ronald Harwood's poorly balanced script sets events in a one-sided vacuum. A less involving drama than Richard Attenborough's *Cry Freedom*. Not rated; suitable for family viewing. 135m. **DIR:** Philip Saville. **CAST:** Danny Glover, Alfre Woodard, Warren Clarke, Julian Glover. **1987 DVD**

MANDELA AND DE KLERK ★★★★ This made-for-cable original portrays Nelson Mandela's struggle to attain freedom for the blacks in South Africa. Sydney Poitier is a natural as Mandela, exuding the force of character and strength of conviction that sustained the title character during his twenty-seven years in prison. And while the story may not be entertaining, it is a fascinating study of history and how one man can make a difference. Not rated; contains violence. 113m. **DIR:** Joseph Sargent. **CAST:** Sidney Poitier, Michael Caine, Tina Lifford. **1997**

MANDINGO Sick film concerning Southern plantations before the Civil War and the treatment of the black slaves. Rated R. 127m. **DIR:** Richard Fleischer. **CAST:** James Mason, Susan George, Perry King, Richard Ward, Brenda Sikes. **1975**

MANDROID ★★★ Scientists and the CIA struggle for control of a powerful, man-made element with both curative and destructive powers—depending on who has it. Covers every sci-fi detail from invisibility to a mad doctor in an iron mask! Just don't ponder the details. Rated R for violence, profanity, and brief nudity. 81m. **DIR:** Jack Ersgard. **CAST:** Brian Cousins, Janette Allyson Caldwell, Michael DellaFemina, Curt Lowens, Patrick Ersgard. **1993**

MANFISH Probably the only low-budget attempt to cash in on calypso music using Edgar Allan Poe, boats, and fish. 76m. **DIR:** W. Lee Wilder. **CAST:** John Bromfield, Lon Chaney Jr., Victor Jory, Barbara Nichols. **1956**

MANGLER, THE Massive industrial laundry-pressing device is possessed by evil spirits and begins folding people into lumps of grisly pulp. Rated R for violence, gore, and language. 106m. **DIR:** Tobe Hooper. **CAST:** Robert Englund, Ted Levine, Daniel Matmore, Jeremy Crutchley. **1995**

•MANGLER 2, THE ★★ Original creator Stephen King's name is nowhere to be found on this mangled direct-to-video sequel. When a nasty virus infects the security system of a private college, it starts killing off the student body. More of an excuse to kill people than to scare an audience. Rated R for language and violence. 100m. **DIR:** Michael Hamilton-Wright. **CAST:** Chelse

Swain, Philippe Bergeron, Lance Henriksen. **2001 DVD**

MANHANDLED ★★1/2 Disappointing vehicle for Gloria Swanson. Believe it or not, she's a department store salesclerk—but never fear, Swanson gets ample opportunities to model exotic gowns as she impersonates a Russian countess. Slick but routine. Silent. B&W; 70m. **DIR:** Allan Dwan. **CAST:** Gloria Swanson, Tom Moore. **1924**

MANHATTAN ★★★★★ Reworking the same themes he explored in *Play It Again, Sam* and *Annie Hall*, Woody Allen again comes up with perhaps his greatest masterpiece. Diane Keaton returns as the object of his awkward but well-meaning affections. It's heartwarming, insightful, screamingly funny, and a feast for the eyes. The black-and-white cinematography of long-time Allen collaborator Gordon Willis recalls the great visuals of *Citizen Kane* and *The Third Man*. Rated R. B&W; 96m. **DIR:** Woody Allen. **CAST:** Diane Keaton, Woody Allen, Michael Murphy, Mariel Hemingway, Meryl Streep. **1979 DVD**

MANHATTAN BABY An archaeologist's daughter is possessed by an Egyptian demon. This film lacks the style and substance of some other Italian horror features. Not rated, but with lots of fake blood. 90m. **DIR:** Lucio Fulci. **CAST:** George Hacker, Christopher Connelly, Martha Taylor. **1983 DVD**

MANHATTAN MELODRAMA ★★★★ In MGM's best version of an oft-told story, two boyhood pals (Clark Gable, William Powell) end up on opposite sides of the law as adults but maintain their friendship and friendly competition for the affections of Myrna Loy. The wonderful cast makes it delicious, old-fashioned movie fun. Historical note: this is the movie John Dillinger was watching before he was shot down by the FBI outside the Biograph Theatre in Chicago. B&W; 93m. **DIR:** W. S. Van Dyke. **CAST:** Clark Gable, William Powell, Myrna Loy, Mickey Rooney, Leo Carrillo, Isabel Jewell, Nat Pendleton. **1934**

MANHATTAN MERENGUE ★★ Tired tale of an illegal immigrant who dreams of dancing on Broadway and comes close when he becomes a janitor at a dance school. When Miguel attracts the attention of the head instructor, she wants to see all of his moves, on the floor and in bed. Their affair creates havoc for the dancer, who now must contend with immigration authorities and a jealous instructor. Rated PG-13 for adult situations and language. 94m. **DIR:** Joseph B. Vasquez. **CAST:** George Perez, Lumi Cavazos, Marco Leonardi, Alyson Reed. **1994 DVD**

MANHATTAN MERRY-GO-ROUND ★★1/2 Incredible lineup of popular performers is the main attraction of this catchall production about a gangster who takes over a recording company. This oddity runs the gamut from Gene Autry's country crooning to the jivin' gyrations of legendary Cab Calloway. B&W; 80m. **DIR:** Charles F. Riesner. **CAST:** Gene Autry, Phil Regan, Leo Carrillo, Ann Dvorak, Tamara Geva, Ted Lewis, Cab Calloway, Joe DiMaggio, Louis Prima, Henry Armetta, Max Terhune, Smiley Burnette, James Gleason. **1938**

MANHATTAN MURDER MYSTERY ★★★★ Joyous reunion for Woody Allen and Diane Keaton presents them as a married couple at odds over whether a neighbor has committed murder. She's sure of it, he thinks she's gone off the deep end, and the audience is almost too busy laughing to care. A cleverly constructed howdunit from Allen and Marshall Brickman, who previously collaborated on *Annie Hall* and *Manhattan*. Rated PG for brief violence. 108m. **DIR:** Woody Allen. **CAST:** Woody Allen, Diane Keaton, Alan Alda, Anjelica Huston, Jerry Adler, Joy Behar, Ron Rifkin. **1993 DVD**

MANHATTAN PROJECT, THE ★★★ Contemporary comedy-adventure-thriller concerns a high-school youth (Christopher Collet) who, with the aid of his idealistic girlfriend (Cynthia Nixon), steals some plutonium and makes his own nuclear bomb. There's a pleasing balance of humor and suspense. Rated PG for violence. 115m. **DIR:** Marshall Brickman. **CAST:** John Lithgow, Christopher Collet, Cynthia Nixon, Jill Eikenberry. **1986**

MANHUNT (1973) (THE ITALIAN CONNECTION) ★★ Unbeknownst to him, a small-time Milano crook is framed as a big-time drug dealer, which results in the murder of his wife. He sets out in search of an explanation and revenge. Mediocre action picture was retitled *The Italian Connection* to cash in on the success of *The French Connection*. Dubbed in English. Rated R. 93m. **DIR:** Fernando Di Leo. **CAST:** Mario Adorf, Henry Silva, Woody Strode, Adolfo Celi, Luciana Paluzzi, Sylva Koscina, Cyril Cusack. **1973**

MANHUNT FOR CLAUDE DALLAS ★★1/2 True-life made-for-television adventure traces the exploits of mountain man Claude Dallas, whose murder spree and eventual capture made headlines. Fascinating look at law enforcement. 100m. **DIR:** Jerry London. **CAST:** Matt Salinger, Claude Akins, Lois Nettleton, Rip Torn. **1986**

MANHUNTER ★★★★1/2 Thoroughly engrossing tale of an FBI man (William Petersen) following a trail of blood through the southeast left by a ruthless, calculating psychopath known only as "The Tooth Fairy," for reasons made shockingly clear. Rated R for violence and various adult contents. 118m. **DIR:** Michael Mann. **CAST:** William L. Petersen, Kim Greist, Brian Cox, Dennis Farina, Joan Allen. **1986**

MANIA ★★★1/2 After *The Body Snatcher* (1945), this powerful British melodrama is the best fictional reworking of the scandalous saga of Edinburgh's Dr. Robert Knox and his clandestine pact with grave robbers Burke and Hare. Cushing, as Knox, is dagger-sharp as always, and the direction of John Gilling evenly balances the requisite sensationalism with a mature script. B&W; 87m. **DIR:** John Gilling. **CAST:** Peter Cushing, June Laverick, Donald Pleasence. **1959**

MANIAC (1934) ★★ Legendary film about a mad doctor and his even madder assistant knocked 'em dead at the men's clubs and exploitation houses in the 1930s and 1940s, but it seems pretty mild compared to today's color gorefests. Not rated. B&W; 52m. **DIR:** Dwain Esper. **CAST:** Bill Woods, Horace Carpenter. **1934 DVD**

MANIAC (1962) ★★★ Spooky mystery film about a madman on the loose in France, with Kerwin Mathews perfect as an American artist whose vacation there turns out to be anything but. Chilling atmosphere. B&W; 86m. **DIR:** Michael Carreras. **CAST:** Kerwin Mathews, Nadia Gray, Donald Houston. **1962**

MANIAC (1980) A plethora of shootings, stabbings, decapitations, and scalpings. Rated R for every excess imaginable. 87m. **DIR:** William Lustig. **CAST:** Joe

Spinell, Caroline Munro, Gail Lawrence, Kelly Piper, Tom Savini. **1980 DVD**

MANIAC COP 🦃 A deranged killer cop is stalking the streets of New York. Rated R for violence, nudity, and adult situations. 92m. **DIR:** William Lustig. **CAST:** Tom Atkins, Bruce Campbell, Richard Roundtree, William Smith, Sheree North. **1988 DVD**

MANIAC COP 2 ★★★ This sequel resurrects the homicidal cop out to avenge his unwarranted incarceration in Sing-Sing. Viciously maimed in prison, he sets out to dispatch any responsible party (and a few just for the hell of it). Rated R for violence, profanity, and gore. 90m. **DIR:** William Lustig. **CAST:** Robert Davi, Claudia Christian, Michael Lerner, Bruce Campbell, Clarence Williams, III, Leo Rossi. **1990**

MANIAC COP 3: BADGE OF SILENCE ★★★ When a fellow police officer is wounded in action and then framed, the undead Maniac Cop sets out to clear her name, systematically eliminating all those who stand in the way. He seems to be rather inexact in his methods (to be expected from a moldering corpse, we suppose). Rated R for violence. 85m. **DIR:** William Lustig. **CAST:** Robert Davi, Robert Z'Dar, Caitlin Dulany, Gretchen Becker, Jackie Earle Haley. **1993**

MANIFESTO ★★★1/2 A colorful, eccentric comedy from the director of *Montenegro* and *The Coca-Cola Kid*. It's a wacky tale of revolutionaries trying to alter the political system in a picturesque European country, circa 1920. Romance, misguided idealism, and ineptitude get in the way of all their efforts, but viewers have a lot of fun along the way. 96m. **DIR:** Dusan Makavejev. **CAST:** Camilla Soeberg, Alfred Molina, Eric Stoltz, Simon Callow, Lindsay Duncan. **1988**

MANIONS OF AMERICA, THE ★★★★ A bit sudsy at times, this was originally televised as a miniseries. It is an absolutely absorbing saga of a rebellious Irish lad's life as an immigrant in the United States. His hotheadedness can only be matched by the willfulness and determination of his British wife. 360m. **DIR:** Joseph Sargent. **CAST:** Pierce Brosnan, Kate Mulgrew, David Soul, Linda Purl. **1981**

MANIPULATOR, THE 🦃 Schizophrenic movie makeup man abducts an actress. Rated R for violence, profanity, and nudity. 91m. **DIR:** Yabo Yablonsky. **CAST:** Mickey Rooney, Luana Anders, Keenan Wynn. **1971**

MANITOU, THE 🦃 Hilariously hokey film about a woman who by some strange trick of chance is growing an ancient Indian out of her neck! Rated PG. 104m. **DIR:** William Girdler. **CAST:** Tony Curtis, Susan Strasberg, Michael Ansara, Ann Sothern, Burgess Meredith, Stella Stevens. **1978**

MANKILLERS 🦃 The FBI hires a band of twelve ruthless female prisoners to dispose of an ex-agent turned renegade. Not rated. 90m. **DIR:** David A. Prior. **CAST:** Edd Byrnes, Gail Fisher, Edy Williams. **1987**

MANNEQUIN (1937) ★★★ Poor working girl sees only the riches of a self-made millionaire as a way to happiness, yet lets herself be manipulated by a cad. Pros at work. The song "Always And Always" was Oscar-nominated. B&W; 95m. **DIR:** Frank Borzage. **CAST:** Joan Crawford, Spencer Tracy, Alan Curtis, Ralph Morgan. **1937**

MANNEQUIN (1987) 🦃 MTV glitz and worn-out comedy bits. Rated PG. 90m. **DIR:** Michael Gottlieb. **CAST:** Andrew McCarthy, Kim Cattrall, Estelle Getty, G. W. Bailey, Meshach Taylor. **1987 DVD**

MANNEQUIN TWO: ON THE MOVE ★★ William Ragsdale is a modern-day descendant of royalty who discovers that a department-store mannequin is really alive. Good comic turns by Terry Kiser as a dastardly count and Meshach Taylor, who reprises his role as an effeminate art director. Rated PG. 98m. **DIR:** Stewart Raffill. **CAST:** Kristy Swanson, William Ragsdale, Terry Kiser, Stuart Pankin, Meshach Taylor. **1991**

MANNY & LO ★★1/2 Two young sisters on the run kidnap a maternity-store clerk to help with the older sister's impending childbirth. Writer-director Lisa Krueger's film is sweet and gentle-hearted but also contrived and rather cloying. It benefits greatly from the warm, no-nonsense performance of Mary Kay Place as the kidnap victim. Rated R for profanity. 90m. **DIR:** Lisa Krueger. **CAST:** Scarlett Johansson, Aleksa Palladino, Mary Kay Place, Glenn Fitzgerald, Angie Phillips. **1996**

MANNY'S ORPHANS (COME THE TIGERS) 🦃 Another *Bad News Bears* movie, but of course not within striking distance of the original. 90m. **DIR:** Sean S. Cunningham. **CAST:** Richard Lincoln. **1978**

MANON ★★1/2 Disappointing update of a classic love story takes place during the German occupation of France. The two stars are rather wan, leaving the gritty depiction of war-torn Paris as the film's sole saving grace. In French with English subtitles. Not rated. 90m. **DIR:** Henri-Georges Clouzot. **CAST:** Cecile Aubrey, Michel Auclair. **1951**

MANON OF THE SPRING ★★★★★ For its visual beauty alone, this sequel to *Jean de Florette* is a motion picture to savor. But it has a great deal more to offer. Chief among its pleasures are superb performances by Yves Montand and Daniel Auteuil. A fascinating tale of revenge and unrequited love. In French with English subtitles. Rated PG-13 for nudity. 113m. **DIR:** Claude Berri. **CAST:** Yves Montand, Daniel Auteuil, Emmanuelle Beart, Elisabeth Depardieu. **1987 DVD**

MAN'S BEST FRIEND (1993) ★★ A genetically engineered guard dog runs amok when a crusading TV reporter, thinking she is rescuing him from vivisection, smuggles him home. Plenty of nasty shocks, with dumb characters doing the usual dumb things and getting their throats ripped out. Rated R for violence. 87m. **DIR:** John Lafia. **CAST:** Ally Sheedy, Lance Henriksen. **1993**

MAN'S FAVORITE SPORT? ★★★ Comedy about a nonfishing outdoor-sports columnist who finds himself entered in an anglers' contest is fast and funny and provides Rock Hudson with one of his best roles. Screwball Paula Prentiss spends most of her time gumming up the works for poor Rock. The situations and dialogue are clever and breezy, employing director Howard Hawks's famous overlapping dialogue to maximum advantage. 120m. **DIR:** Howard Hawks. **CAST:** Rock Hudson, Paula Prentiss, John McGiver, Roscoe Karns, Maria Perschy, Charlene Holt. **1964**

MANSFIELD PARK ★★★ Fanny Price, perhaps the meekest and least admirable of Jane Austen's various heroines, has been given something of a makeover in filmmaker Patricia Rozema's adaptation of *Mansfield Park*; the results are mixed. Now more a late twentieth-century feminist than an early nineteenth-century rebel, this change completely mutates the story's dy-

namics. Fanny gets the opportunity to blossom when removed from her poor childhood environment to be raised by wealthy, condescending relatives, and she has more decency and good breeding than most. But the film itself is slow—even for this genre of gentility—and rather dreary, and the script a poor condensation of Austen's novel. Rated PG-13 for the brutal contents of a sketchbook. 110m. **DIR:** Patricia Rozema. **CAST:** Embeth Davidtz, Jonny Lee Miller, Alessandro Nivola, Frances O'Connor, Harold Pinter. **1999 DVD**

MANSION OF THE DOOMED Uncredited remake of *Eyes without a Face* that is notable only as the first film for producer Charles Band, actor Lance Henriksen, special effects man Stan Winston, and future action director Andrew Davis. Not rated; contains violence and gore. 89m. **DIR:** Michael Pataki. **CAST:** Richard Basehart, Gloria Grahame, Lance Henriksen. **1975**

MANSTER, THE ★★1/2 Peter Dyneley plays a skirt-chasing, alcoholic reporter who falls victim to a Japanese mad scientist's experiments, eventually becoming a two-headed monster. A trash film must-see, with a welcome bonus: it's genuinely creepy in addition to being lurid. It's also got a unique *technical* hook: it's not a dubbed import, but one of the first international coproductions. B&W; 72m. **DIR:** George Breakston, Kenneth Crane. **CAST:** Peter Dyneley, Jane Hylton. **1962**

MANXMAN, THE Afternoon soap operas are nothing compared to this howler, the last of director Alfred Hitchcock's silent films. B&W; 70m. **DIR:** Alfred Hitchcock. **CAST:** Carl Brisson, Malcolm Keen, Anny Ondra. **1929 DVD**

MAP OF THE HUMAN HEART ★★★★ With great cinematic panache, director Vincent Ward tells the epic story of a young Eskimo who falls in love with a woman of mixed race. Through decades, they encounter obstacles to their romance. Anne Parillaud is particularly compelling as the object of the naïve Eskimo lad's desire. The WWII flying sequences are dazzling. The film reminds us of the value of primitive cultures. Rated R for nudity and suggested sex. 95m. **DIR:** Vincent Ward. **CAST:** Anne Parillaud, Patrick Bergin, Jason Scott Lee, John Cusack, Jeanne Moreau. **1993**

MAP OF THE WORLD, A ★★★1/2 A Wisconsin farm wife sees her life unravel when, first, a friend's daughter drowns in her pond and, next, she is accused of sexually abusing a local boy. Adapted from Jane Hamilton's novel, the film relies too much on voice-over narration, especially in the last third. But the acting is strong throughout, and the central role is a real showcase for Sigourney Weaver. Rated R for profanity, nudity, and brief sexual scenes. 127m. **DIR:** Scott Elliott. **CAST:** Sigourney Weaver, Julianne Moore, David Strathairn, Arliss Howard, Chloe Sevigny, Louise Fletcher. **1999 DVD**

MAPP & LUCIA ★★★ Filmed in the mid-1980s and set in the late 1920s, this frothy Channel Four British import has long been a cult favorite of Anglophiles and satirists. Lucia is played by Geraldine McEwan, an affected village doyenne in constant battle with the equally formidable Mapp (Prunella Scales). All five parts in the series deftly exhibit the brio and bull twaddle of E. F. Benson's widely read novel. Not rated. 260m. **DIR:** Donald McWhinnie. **CAST:** Geraldine McEwan, Prunella Scales, Nigel Hawthorne. **1984**

MARAT/SADE ★★★★ Glenda Jackson made her film debut in this terrifying adaptation of Peter Weiss's play about a performance staged by some inmates of a French insane asylum, under the direction of the Marquis de Sade. Peter Brook's direction is superb, as he creates a dark, claustrophobic atmosphere. Great ensemble acting. Not for the squeamish. 115m. **DIR:** Peter Brook. **CAST:** Patrick Magee, Glenda Jackson, Ian Richardson. **1966 DVD**

MARATHON ★★1/2 In this comic examination of midlife crisis, Bob Newhart becomes enamored of a woman he sees at a local running event, only to discover his true feelings. The uninspired direction and screenplay weaken the efforts of a veteran cast. Rated PG for mild language. 97m. **DIR:** Jackie Cooper. **CAST:** Bob Newhart, Herb Edelman, Dick Gautier, Anita Gillette, Leigh Taylor-Young, John Hillerman. **1985**

MARATHON MAN ★★★★ A young student (Dustin Hoffman) unwittingly becomes involved in the pursuit of an ex-Nazi war criminal (Laurence Olivier) in this chase thriller. The action holds your interest throughout. Rated R. 125m. **DIR:** John Schlesinger. **CAST:** Dustin Hoffman, Laurence Olivier, Roy Scheider, William Devane, Marthe Keller. **1976 DVD**

MARCH OF THE WOODEN SOLDIERS (BABES IN TOYLAND (1934)) ★★★★ This film features Stan Laurel and Oliver Hardy as the toy maker's assistants in the land of Old King Cole. Utterly forgettable songs slow down an otherwise enjoyable fantasy film. Stan and Ollie are integrated well into the storyline, finally saving the town from the attack of the boogeymen. B&W; 73m. **DIR:** Gus Meins. **CAST:** Stan Laurel, Oliver Hardy, Charlotte Henry. **1934 DVD**

MARCH OR DIE ★★1/2 Old-fashioned epic adventure that reminds us of *Beau Geste* and *The Charge of the Light Brigade*, but lacks credibility and style. Gene Hackman stars as an iron-willed major in the French foreign legion, who defends a desert outpost in Africa from marauding Arabs. Catherine Deneuve provides the romance. Not rated, but equivalent to an R for violence and mature situations. 104m. **DIR:** Dick Richards. **CAST:** Gene Hackman, Terence Hill, Max von Sydow, Catherine Deneuve. **1977**

MARCIANO ★★ This made-for-TV bio-film concentrates far too much on the private life of the only boxer ever to retire from the pugilistic sport world undefeated—Rocky Marciano. More footage should have been devoted to his professional fighting career. There's nothing special here. 100m. **DIR:** Bernard Kowalski. **CAST:** Tony Lo Bianco, Belinda Montgomery, Vincent Gardenia, Richard Herd. **1979**

MARCO POLO Don Diamont stars in the title role as a man who finds adventure and fights a shoddily dressed Jack Palance bent on world domination. Full of cheesy action scenes, this movie contains no mention of anything for which the historical character is actually known. Also released as *The Incredible Adventures of Marco Polo*. Rated PG-13 for adventure violence. 97m. **DIR:** George Erschbamer. **CAST:** Don Diamont, Jack Palance, Herbert Lom, Oliver Reed. **1998 DVD**

MARCO POLO JR. ★★ An ancient prophecy sends a young man on a musical mission to the fabled kingdom of Xanadu. The soundtrack is reminiscent of those

moldy Bobby Vinton albums hidden away in your attic. 82m. **DIR:** Eric Porter. **1972**

MARDI GRAS FOR THE DEVIL ★★1/2 Twenty years after his father was killed, a cop finds that the murderer, who rips his victims' hearts out, is after him. Unfortunately, the killer is the devil, who just may be unstoppable. Don't even try to find a plot. Not rated; contains nudity and graphic sex. 95m. **DIR:** David A. Prior. **CAST:** Robert Davi, Michael Ironside, Lesley-Anne Down, Lydie Denier, Mike Starr, Lillian Lehman, Margaret Avery, John Amos. **1993**

MARGARET'S MUSEUM ★★★★ The treacherous, tough life of a coal miner takes center stage in this haunting tale of lost love. Helena Bonham Carter is captivating as Margaret MacNeil, whose love for coal miner Clive Russell upsets her mother, who lost her own husband in a mining accident. Eternal love takes on new meaning when Russell is killed in an accident and Margaret is left to sort out her life. Set in Canada during the 1940s, this exquisite period piece deals with emotional issues in a most unusual way. Rated R for language and nudity. 118m. **DIR:** Mort Ransen. **CAST:** Helena Bonham Carter, Kate Nelligan, Clive Russell, Kenneth Welsh. **1995**

MARIANNE & JULIANE ★★★ Tie between two estranged sisters develops when one is imprisoned for revolutionary anarchy. The more conservative sister can't resist rebuilding their childhood camaraderie. Strange but engrossing with flashbacks indicating that the two had swapped personalities at some point in their lives. Stark, artful, and sometimes painful to watch. In German with English subtitles. Not rated; contains nudity and gore. 103m. **DIR:** Margarethe von Trotta. **CAST:** Barbara Sukowa, Jutta Lampe, Rudiger Vogler, Doris Schade. **1981**

MARIA'S LOVERS 🦃 A former World War II prisoner of war and his loving wife. Rated R for profanity, nudity, suggested sex, and violence. 105m. **DIR:** Andrei Konchalovsky. **CAST:** Nastassja Kinski, John Savage, Keith Carradine, Robert Mitchum, Vincent Spano, Bud Cort. **1985 DVD**

MARIE ★★★ Sissy Spacek plays real-life heroine Marie Ragghianti, whose courage and honesty brought about the fall of a corrupt administration in Tennessee. Marie is a battered housewife who leaves her cruel husband. Struggling to raise her three children, she eventually works her way up to becoming the state's first female parole board head. Rated PG-13 for violence and profanity. 100m. **DIR:** Roger Donaldson. **CAST:** Sissy Spacek, Jeff Daniels, Keith Szarabajka. **1986**

MARIE ANTOINETTE ★★★ A regal rendition of the queen who lost her head, but not her stature in history. The film traces the life of the Austrian princess who became queen of France, and covers the period when she had a romantic attachment for the Swedish Count Axel de Fersen (Tyrone Power). B&W; 149m. **DIR:** W. S. Van Dyke. **CAST:** Norma Shearer, Tyrone Power, Robert Morley, John Barrymore, Joseph Schildkraut, Gladys George, Anita Louise, Reginald Gardiner. **1938**

MARIE BAIE DES ANGES ★★ A sexually adventurous 15-year-old turns an American navy outpost on the French Riviera into her own personal playground when she meets and mates with a young sociopath. This swirl of colorful nonlinear narrative and ominous moral decay is seductively crafted but glorifies juvenile angst while failing to get under the skin of its characters. In French with English subtitles. Rated R for violence, nudity, profanity, sexual assault, and sexual situations. 90m. **DIR:** Manuel Pradal. **CAST:** Vahina Giocante, Frederic Malgras. **1998**

MARILYN & BOBBY: HER FINAL AFFAIR 🦃 This made-for-cable original is just another boring, poorly acted account of the last days of Marilyn Monroe. Not rated. 95m. **DIR:** Bradford May. **CAST:** Melody Anderson, James F. Kelly, Jonathan Banks, Kristoffer Tabori, Geoffrey Blake, Thomas Wagner, Ian Buchanan, Tomas Millan, Richard Dysart. **1993**

MARINE RAIDERS ★★1/2 Tough but fair-minded Marine commanding officer tries to steer his favorite captain away from the rocky reefs of romance but finally relents and lets love lead the lucky couple to the altar. B&W; 90m. **DIR:** Harold Schuster. **CAST:** Pat O'Brien, Robert Ryan, Ruth Hussey, Frank McHugh, Barton MacLane, Richard Martin. **1944**

MARIUS ★★★ This French movie is a marvelous view of the working class in Marseilles between the wars. The story revolves around Marius (Pierre Fresnay) and his love for Fanny (Orane Demazis), the daughter of a fish store proprietess. The poetic essence of the film is captured with style as Marius ships out to sea, unknowingly leaving Fanny with child. In French with English subtitles. B&W; 125m. **DIR:** Alexander Korda. **CAST:** Raimu, Pierre Fresnay, Orane Demazis, Alida Rouffe. **1931**

MARJOE ★★★1/2 The life of evangelist-turned-actor Marjoe Gortner is traced in this entertaining documentary. Film offers the viewer a peek into the world of the traveling evangelist. When Marjoe gets his act going, the movie is at its best. At times a little stagy, but always interesting. Rated PG for language. 88m. **DIR:** Howard Smith, Sarah Kernochan. **CAST:** Marjoe Gortner. **1972**

MARJORIE MORNINGSTAR ★★★ Natalie Wood and Gene Kelly give fine performances in this adaptation of the novel by Herman Wouk. Wood falls for show biz and for carefree theatrical producer Kelly. As Wood's eccentric uncle, Ed Wynn almost steals the show. A fine score by Max Steiner. 123m. **DIR:** Irving Rapper. **CAST:** Gene Kelly, Natalie Wood, Ed Wynn, Claire Trevor, Everett Sloane, Martin Milner, Carolyn Jones. **1958 DVD**

MARK OF CAIN ★★★ Though this film overdoes the eerie music and protracted conversations, it is a compelling tale about twin brothers. A graphic murder sets the plot in motion. A lovely old home surrounded by breathtaking winter scenery is the principal setting. 90m. **DIR:** Bruce Pittman. **CAST:** Robin Crew, Wendy Crewson, August Schellengberg. **1984**

MARK OF THE BEAST, THE 🦃 An anthropologist avenges her twin sister's ritual murder. Ineptly written and acted. Not rated; contains nudity, profanity, violence, and simulated sex. 88m. **DIR:** Jeff Hathcock. **CAST:** Bo Hopkins, Richard Hill, Sheila Cann. **1990**

MARK OF THE DEVIL 🦃 A sadistic German-British film about an impotent, overachieving witch finder. Notorious as the only movie in history to offer free stomach-distress bags to every patron. Rated R. 96m. **DIR:** Michael Armstrong. **CAST:** Herbert Lom, Udo Kier, Reggie Nalder. **1970 DVD**

MARK OF THE DEVIL, PART 2 🦃 After the frolic of the original *Mark of the Devil*, what's left for this sequel to

the notorious, medieval witch-hunting saga? Not much. Rated R. 88m. **DIR:** Adrian Hoven. **CAST:** Anton Diffring, Jean-Pierre Zola, Reggie Nalder, Erica Blanc. **1972**

MARK OF THE HAWK, THE ♥ African man struggles to integrate his people into the societal mainstream. A snooze. 84m. **DIR:** Michael Audley. **CAST:** Sidney Poitier, Juano Hernandez, Eartha Kitt, John McIntire. **1958**

MARK OF THE VAMPIRE ★★★1/2 MGM's atmospheric version of *Dracula*, utilizing the same director and star. This time, though, it's Count Mora (Bela Lugosi) terrorizing the residents of an old estate along with his ghoulish daughter (Carol Borland). Lionel Barrymore is the believer who tries to put an end to their nocturnal activities. B&W; 61m. **DIR:** Tod Browning. **CAST:** Lionel Barrymore, Elizabeth Allan, Bela Lugosi, Lionel Atwill, Carol Borland. **1935**

MARK OF ZORRO, THE (1920) ★★★1/2 Douglas Fairbanks took a chance in 1920 and jumped from comedy-adventures to *costumed* comedy-adventures; with this classic film, he never turned back. Fairbanks made the character of Zorro his own and quickly established himself as an American legend. Silent. B&W; 90m. **DIR:** Fred Niblo. **CAST:** Douglas Fairbanks Sr., Marguerite de la Motte, Noah Beery Sr., Robert McKim. **1920 DVD**

MARK OF ZORRO, THE (1940) ★★★★1/2 Glossy MGM swashbuckler is stylishly directed by Rouben Mamoulian, with Tyrone Power well cast as the foppish aristocrat who lives a secret life as the masked avenger, Zorro, in old California. The inspired casting of Basil Rathbone, Eugene Pallette, and Montagu Love in supporting roles recalls the Errol Flynn classic, *The Adventures of Robin Hood*, while Power's duel with Rathbone almost outdoes it. B&W; 93m. **DIR:** Rouben Mamoulian. **CAST:** Tyrone Power, Basil Rathbone, J. Edward Bromberg, Linda Darnell, Gale Sondergaard, Eugene Pallette, Montagu Love, Robert Lowery. **1940**

MARKED FOR DEATH ★★1/2 Suburbia is infested with Jamaican drug pushers led by the fearsome, dreadlocked Screwface (Basil Wallace) until a no-nonsense, retired DEA agent (Steven Seagal) decides to clean up the neighborhood. Bone-cruncher Seagal makes a great action-fu star. But this isn't one of his best. Rated R for language and violence. 93m. **DIR:** Dwight H. Little. **CAST:** Steven Seagal, Keith David, Basil Wallace, Joanna Pacula. **1990 DVD**

MARKED MAN ★★1/2 So-so action film is the story of a convict who witnesses the murder of a mob boss in prison by a pair of guards. From that point on, he fits the description of the title character, with the law, the Mafia, and a whole slew of unsavory characters trying to track him down and put a bullet through his memory. Lots of action, some decent performances, and a quick pace make this watchable. Rated R for profanity and violence. 94m. **DIR:** Marc Voizard. **CAST:** Roddy Piper, Jane Wheeler, Alina Thompson, Miles O'Keeffe. **1996**

MARKED WOMAN ★★★ Iron-hided district attorney Humphrey Bogart, in one of his early good-guy roles, convinces Bette Davis and other ladies of the evening to squeal on their boss, crime kingpin Eduardo Ciannelli. B&W; 99m. **DIR:** Lloyd Bacon. **CAST:** Bette Davis, Humphrey Bogart, Eduardo Ciannelli, Lola Lane, Isabel Jewell, Allen Jenkins. **1937**

MARLENE ★★★★ In this documentary, director Maximilian Schell pulls off something close to a miracle: he creates an absorbing and entertaining study of Marlene Dietrich without ever having her on camera during the interviews. (She refused to be photographed.) Instead, we hear her famous husky voice talking about her life, loves, and movies as scenes from the latter—as well as newsreels and TV clips—play onscreen. 95m. **DIR:** Maximilian Schell. **CAST:** Marlene Dietrich, Maximilian Schell. **1985 DVD**

MARLOWE ★★★1/2 In this adaptation of Raymond Chandler's *The Little Sister*, James Garner makes a spiffy Philip Marlowe. This time, the noble detective is hired to find a missing man, and Bruce Lee, in an early but sparkling film appearance, is one of several interested parties who wants our hero to drop the case. 95m. **DIR:** Paul Bogart. **CAST:** James Garner, Gayle Hunnicutt, Carroll O'Connor, Rita Moreno, Sharon Farrell, William Daniels, Jackie Coogan, Bruce Lee. **1969**

MARNIE ★★★1/2 Unsung Alfred Hitchcock film about a strange young woman (Tippi Hedren) who isn't at all what she appears to be, and Sean Connery as the man determined to find out what makes her tick. Compelling, if overlong, but in the best Hitchcock tradition. 129m. **DIR:** Alfred Hitchcock. **CAST:** Sean Connery, Tippi Hedren, Diane Baker, Martin Gabel, Bruce Dern. **1964 DVD**

MAROC 7 ★★1/2 Generic, British-made robbery tale with Gene Barry as a secret agent hot on the trail of a shrewd thief. Efficient, but routine. 91m. **DIR:** Gerry O'Hara. **CAST:** Gene Barry, Elsa Martinelli, Cyd Charisse. **1967**

MAROONED ♥ Tale of three astronauts unable to return to Earth and the ensuing rescue attempt. Rated PG. 134m. **DIR:** John Sturges. **CAST:** Gregory Peck, Richard Crenna, David Janssen, Gene Hackman, James Franciscus, Lee Grant. **1969**

MARQUIS ★★★ Weird, weird, weird French satire based on the writings of de Sade, in which the marquis and his jailers are played by actors in animal masks and his stories are enacted (quite graphically in some instances) with Claymation figures. In French with English subtitles. Not rated, but definitely not for kids. 88m. **DIR:** Henri Xhonneux. **CAST:** Philippe Bizot, Gabrielle van Damme. **1989**

MARRIAGE CIRCLE, THE ★★★★★ Arguably Ernst Lubitsch's best American silent. A comedy of erotic manners ensues when a professor tries to divorce his wife after seeing her flirt with the husband of her best friend. Silent. B&W; 104m. **DIR:** Ernst Lubitsch. **CAST:** Florence Vidor, Monte Blue, Marie Prevost, Adolphe Menjou. **1924 DVD**

MARRIAGE ITALIAN STYLE ★★★1/2 Sophia Loren and Marcello Mastroianni are perfectly cast in this bawdy farce about the efforts of a longtime mistress to get her lover to marry her. It's openly sexual in a way that American films of the time were not, which shows off Loren to best advantage. Dubbed in English. 102m. **DIR:** Vittorio De Sica. **CAST:** Sophia Loren, Marcello Mastroianni, Marilu Tolo. **1964**

MARRIAGE OF MARIA BRAUN, THE ★★1/2 Probably Rainer Werner Fassbinder's easiest film to take because it's basically straightforward and stars the sensual and comedic Hanna Schygulla. She plays Maria Braun, a

tough cookie who marries a Wehrmacht officer whom she loses to the war and then prison. The film is full of Fassbinder's overly dramatic, sordid sexual atmosphere. It can be both funny and perverse. In German. Rated R. 120m. **DIR:** Rainer Werner Fassbinder. **CAST:** Hanna Schygulla, Klaus Lowitsch, Ivan Desny. **1979**

MARRIED MAN, A ★★ A love triangle leads to murder in this oh-so-British boudoir-and-drawing-room tale. Expect to yawn frequently during this made-for-TV feature. 200m. **DIR:** John Davies. **CAST:** Anthony Hopkins, Ciaran Madden, Lise Hilboldt, John Le Mesurier. **1984**

MARRIED PEOPLE, SINGLE SEX ★★★ Three couples find themselves struggling with their love lives. One couple wants to end their marriage. One wife turns outside her marriage for thrills, while another husband finds pleasure on the phone. It's *thirtysomething* with plenty of nudity and sex as everyone tries to come to terms with their impending mid-life crisis. Literate and sexy. Available in rated R and unrated version; both contain plenty of adult language, situations, and nudity. 110m. **DIR:** Mike Sedan. **CAST:** Chase Masterson, Joseph Pilato, Bob Rudd, Darla Slavens, Teri Thompson. **1993**

MARRIED TO IT ★★1/2 Three New York City couples become friends while planning a school play for their children. Some funny and poignant bits, but ultimately doesn't live up to the sum of its parts. Rated R for profanity and nudity. 105m. **DIR:** Arthur Hiller. **CAST:** Beau Bridges, Stockard Channing, Robert Sean Leonard, Mary Stuart Masterson, Cybill Shepherd, Ron Silver. **1991**

MARRIED TO THE MOB ★★★★1/2 This concoction includes humor, oddball set design, eccentric characters galore, and music that sets the scene and the audience in motion. Michelle Pfeiffer plays a beautiful, innocent-yet-fatal femme, here doing her darnedest to extricate herself from the Long Island mob scene after her mobster husband is "iced"; Dean Stockwell is the threatening Don Juan don; Matthew Modine is the savior-nerd. Rated R for language and adult situations. 106m. **DIR:** Jonathan Demme. **CAST:** Michelle Pfeiffer, Matthew Modine, Dean Stockwell, Mercedes Ruehl. **1988 DVD**

MARRIED TOO YOUNG ★★ An uncredited Ed Wood contributed to the script of this drab potboiler about a teen couple whose life together goes downhill after they quit high school to get married. B&W; 76m. **DIR:** George Moskov. **CAST:** Harold Lloyd Jr., Trudy Marshall, Anthony Dexter. **1962**

MARRIED WOMAN, A ★★★ One of Jean-Luc Godard's most conventional films, a study of a Parisian woman who doesn't know if the father of her unborn child is her husband or her lover. In French with English subtitles. 94m. **DIR:** Jean-Luc Godard. **CAST:** Macha Meril, Philippe Leroy, Bernard Noel. **1964**

MARRYING MAN, THE ★★1/2 Neil Simon's screenplay sprinkles laughs into the romance between a toothpaste heir and a torch singer. Stand-up comedian Paul Reiser does a fine job of delivering the best zingers as he narrates their on-again, off-again love story. Rated R for profanity, violence, and simulated sex. 115m. **DIR:** Jerry Rees. **CAST:** Kim Basinger, Alec Baldwin, Robert Loggia, Elisabeth Shue, Armand Assante, Paul Reiser, Fisher Stevens, Peter Dobson. **1991**

MARS ATTACKS! ★★ Iconoclastic director Tim Burton finally bites off more than he can chew with this mean-spirited freak show of a film. Based loosely on an infamous series of early 1960s trading cards, the plot concerns Earth's invasion by bubble-headed Martians who apparently grew up gleefully ripping the wings off Martian flies. There's no plot to speak of, just a series of depraved sight gags involving big-name stars getting tortured or killed by the giggling little invaders. Rated PG-13 for profanity and quite graphic violence. 103m. **DIR:** Tim Burton. **CAST:** Jack Nicholson, Glenn Close, Annette Bening, Pierce Brosnan, Danny DeVito, Martin Short, Sarah Jessica Parker, Lukas Haas, Natalie Portman. **1996 DVD**

MARS NEEDS WOMEN 🦃 Laughable science-fiction yarn featuring Tommy Kirk as a Martian who invades Earth in search of female mates. Ridiculous costumes and special effects only add to the campy effect. Not rated. 80m. **DIR:** Larry Buchanan. **CAST:** Tommy Kirk. **1966 DVD**

MARSHAL LAW ★★ Jimmy Smits's engaging debut as an action hero is overshadowed by director Stephen Cornwell's extremely annoying "video verité" camera work, in this otherwise-routine kill-or-be-killed saga. Cornwell clearly watched Oliver Stone's *Natural Born Killers* too many times. Rated R for violence, profanity, drug use, and simulated sex. 95m. **DIR:** Stephen Cornwell. **CAST:** Jimmy Smits, James LeGros, Vonte Sweet, Scott Plank, Kristy Swanson. **1996**

MARSHAL OF CEDAR ROCK ★★★ Marshal Rocky Lane lets a young man escape from prison in order to lead him to money the man apparently stole in a bank robbery. Instead, the trail leads him straight into a railroad land-grab swindle. B&W; 54m. **DIR:** Harry Keller. **CAST:** Allan "Rocky" Lane, Phyllis Coates, Roy Barcroft, William Henry, Robert Shayne, Eddy Waller. **1953 DVD**

MARSHAL OF CRIPPLE CREEK ★★★★ Last of the Republic Red Ryder series is one of the fastest-paced, most action-packed of the twenty-three they produced. The discovery of gold in Cripple Creek causes the boomtown to be overrun by a lawless element. B&W; 54m. **DIR:** R. G. Springsteen. **CAST:** Allan "Rocky" Lane, Robert Blake, Gene Roth, Trevor Bardette. **1947**

MARSHAL OF MESA CITY ★★★★ Outstanding series Western features George O'Brien as a retired lawman who rides into a town ruled by a corrupt sheriff (Leon Ames) and stays on to end his reign of terror. Excellent character development and plot twists. B&W; 62m. **DIR:** David Howard. **CAST:** George O'Brien, Virginia Vale, Leon Ames, Henry Brandon. **1939**

MARTIAL LAW ★★ Two policemen use hands and feet to fight crime. A film geared entirely to the martial arts viewing public. Rated R for violence. 90m. **DIR:** S. E. Cohen. **CAST:** Chad McQueen, Cynthia Rothrock, David Carradine. **1990**

MARTIAL LAW TWO—UNDERCOVER 🦃 Martial arts expert Cynthia Rothrock goes undercover to catch a cop killer. Nothing revealing here. Rated R for nudity, violence, and profanity. 92m. **DIR:** Kurt Anderson. **CAST:** Jeff Wincott, Cynthia Rothrock, Billy Drago. **1991**

MARTIAL OUTLAW ★★ Brothers Jeff Wincott and Gary Hudson find themselves on opposite sides of the law. Wincott's a DEA agent assigned to infiltrate a $20 million drug deal; Hudson is a crooked cop with a piece of the action. The two stars show off their martial-arts skills, but the story stinks. Rated R for violence. 89m. **DIR:** Kurt Anderson. **CAST:** Jeff Wincott, Gary Hudson, Richard Jaeckel. **1993**

MARTIAN CHRONICLES, PARTS I-III, THE ★★★ Mankind colonizes Mars in this adaptation of the Ray Bradbury classic. As this was originally a TV miniseries, the budget was low and it shows in the cheap sets and poor special effects. The acting is very good, however. 314m. **DIR:** Michael Anderson. **CAST:** Rock Hudson, Darren McGavin, Gayle Hunnicutt, Bernadette Peters, Nicholas Hammond, Roddy McDowall. **1979**

MARTIANS GO HOME 🦃 Some wisecracking aliens come to Earth. Rated PG-13 for adult language. 89m. **DIR:** David Odell. **CAST:** Randy Quaid, Margaret Colin, John Philbin, Anita Harris. **1990**

MARTIN ★★★ Director George Romero creates a good chiller with a lot of bloodcurdling power about a young man who thinks he's a vampire. This is very well-done. Rated R. 95m. **DIR:** George A. Romero. **CAST:** John Amplas, Lincoln Maazel. **1978 DVD**

MARTIN CHUZZLEWIT ★★★★★ Charles Dickens's stinging and hilarious satire is exquisitely presented in this lush three-part BBC import. Paul Scofield heads an extended, self-involved family panting after, and plotting for, his vast fortune. From the actors' intriguing faces to the elaborately detailed costumes, this is an impeccable production much enhanced by a brilliant cast. So cunningly adapted and performed it can be watched easily in one sitting, regardless of the length. Not rated; contains implied violence. 288m. **DIR:** Pedr James. **CAST:** Paul Scofield, John Mills, Pete Postlethwaite, Julia Sawalha. **1994**

MARTIN LUTHER ★★1/2 This biography of the cleric who broke with the Catholic Church and founded Protestantism is handsomely photographed but overly respectful—Luther seems too saintly, wasting the talents of Old Vic veteran Niall MacGinnis. B&W; 104m. **DIR:** Irving Pichel. **CAST:** Niall MacGinnis, John Ruddock. **1953 DVD**

MARTIN'S DAY ★★1/2 Richard Harris plays an escaped convict who kidnaps young Justin Henry but ends up being his friend in this Canadian production. A good idea with a pedestrian resolution. Rated PG. 98m. **DIR:** Alan Gibson. **CAST:** Richard Harris, Lindsay Wagner, John Ireland, James Coburn, Justin Henry, Karen Black. **1984**

MARTY (1953) (TELEVISION) ★★★★ The original *Marty*, written for the *Goodyear Playhouse* by Paddy Chayefsky in 1953. Rod Steiger is tremendously sincere in his first starring role as the lonely butcher who meets a plain schoolteacher (Nancy Marchand) one night at the Waverly ballroom. Powerful, low-key drama, hardly hurt by the poor technical standards of the time. Hosted by Eva Marie Saint; interviews with the stars and the director thrown in for good measure. B&W; 60m. **DIR:** Delbert Mann. **CAST:** Rod Steiger, Nancy Marchand, Esther Minciotti, Joe Mantell, Betsy Palmer, Nehemiah Persoff. **1953**

MARTY (1955) ★★★★★ This heartwarming movie about a New York butcher captured the Academy Award for best picture and another for Ernest Borgnine's poignant portrayal. Two lonely people manage to stumble into romance in spite of their own insecurities and the pressures of others. B&W; 91m. **DIR:** Delbert Mann. **CAST:** Ernest Borgnine, Betsy Blair. **1955 DVD**

MARVELOUS LAND OF OZ, THE ★★★ This teleplay, based on the works of L. Frank Baum, is an excellent means of introducing children to the experience of live theater. It boasts marvelous costuming and presentation by the Minneapolis Children's Theatre Company and School. 101m. **DIR:** John Driver, John Clark Donohue. **CAST:** Wendy Lehr, Christopher Passi. **1981**

MARVIN AND TIGE ★★★★ Touching story of a runaway (Gibran Brown) who finds a friend in a poor and lonely man (John Cassavetes). Cassavetes's beautiful loser character works so well with Brown's streetwise pomp that the tension created by the clash of personalities makes their eventual deep relationship that much more rewarding. Rated PG for a few profane words. 104m. **DIR:** Eric Weston. **CAST:** John Cassavetes, Gibran Brown, Billy Dee Williams, Denise Nicholas, Fay Hauser. **1982**

MARVIN'S ROOM ★★ Scott McPherson's intimate little play becomes a treacly, disease-of-the-week sudser helped not at all by Meryl Streep or Diane Keaton. The latter is a saintly woman who has spent twenty years caring for family members, only to discover she has leukemia. This forces a reunion with estranged sister Streep and wayward nephew Leonardo DiCaprio. What follows is the sort of smarmy nonsense that wouldn't be believed by *Love Story* fans. Rated PG-13 for profanity and medical candor. 98m. **DIR:** Jerry Zaks. **CAST:** Meryl Streep, Diane Keaton, Leonardo DiCaprio, Robert De Niro, Hume Cronyn, Gwen Verdon. **1996 DVD**

MARY AND JOSEPH: A STORY OF FAITH 🦃 One can wish for a good telling of the story of Mary, she of the Immaculate Conception, and the devout Joseph, chosen "parents" of Christ, but this TV movie is not it. Dull, badly acted, and sustains no interest either historically or religiously. 146m. **DIR:** Eric Till. **CAST:** Blanche Baker, Jeff East, Lloyd Bochner, Colleen Dewhurst. **1979**

MARY HARTMAN, MARY HARTMAN (TV SERIES) ★★★★ Full of whimsy and satire, this off-the-wall show plunged into subjects considered taboo by normal sitcoms, such as impotence and marijuana. Louise Lasser, as Mary, fashioned a unique character with which a wide audience empathized. This series is worth another look. 70m. **DIR:** Joan Darling, Jim Drake. **CAST:** Louise Lasser, Greg Mullavey, Mary Kay Place, Graham Jarvis, Victor Kilian, Debralee Scott, Martin Mull. **1976**

MARY, MARY, BLOODY MARY ★★ A bloody and grisly film depicting the horror of vampirism and mass murder. A beautiful vampire and artist, Mary (Cristina Ferrare), goes to Mexico to fulfill her need for blood. This film is rated R for nudity, violence, and gore. 95m. **DIR:** Juan Lopez Moctezuma. **CAST:** Cristina Ferrare, David Young, Helena Rojo, John Carradine. **1987**

MARY MY DEAREST ★★ A magician converts a thief, marries him, and has him join her in a traveling show. She inadvertently hitches a ride with people being

transported to an insane asylum where she becomes trapped. Poorly acted and very depressing. In Spanish with English subtitles. Not rated; contains nudity and suggested sex. 100m. **DIR:** Jaime Humberto Hermosillo. **CAST:** Maria Rojo, Hector Bonilla, Ana Ofelia Morguia. **1983**

MARY OF SCOTLAND ★★★★ Katharine Hepburn plays one of history's tragic figures in director John Ford's biography of the sixteenth-century queen of Scotland. Fredric March is Bothwell, her supporter (and eventual lover) in her battle for power. The last scene, where Mary confronts her English accusers in court, is so well acted and photographed, it alone is worth the price of the rental. B&W; 123m. **DIR:** John Ford. **CAST:** Katharine Hepburn, Fredric March, John Carradine. **1936**

MARY POPPINS ★★★★★ Here's Julie Andrews in her screen debut. She plays a nanny who believes that "a spoonful of sugar makes the medicine go down." Andrews is great in the role and sings ever so sweetly. The song and dance numbers are attractively laid on, with Dick Van Dyke, as Mary's Cockney beau, giving an amusing performance. Rated G. 140m. **DIR:** Robert Stevenson. **CAST:** Julie Andrews, Dick Van Dyke, David Tomlinson, Glynis Johns, Karen Dotrice, Matthew Garber, Jane Darwell, Ed Wynn, Arthur Treacher, Hermione Baddeley. **1964 DVD**

MARY REILLY ★★ The oft-told tale of Dr. Jekyll and Mr. Hyde (John Malkovich), seen through the eyes of Jekyll's adoring housemaid (Julia Roberts). Murky, mushy, glacially slow, and devoid of suspense, with one-note performances from the stars. Roberts, unable to deploy her trademark smile, cowers like a scared rabbit, while Malkovich inexplicably plays Jekyll and Hyde as looking and sounding almost exactly alike. Rated R for brief but intense violence. 118m. **DIR:** Stephen Frears. **CAST:** Julia Roberts, John Malkovich, Glenn Close, Michael Gambon, George Cole, Kathy Staff. **1996**

MARY SHELLEY'S FRANKENSTEIN ★★1/2 Kenneth Branagh's retelling of Mary Shelley's story is a major disappointment. The emphasis seems to be more on the lavish sets than the characters, despite the efforts of cast and director. Like the monster Victor Frankenstein creates, this movie is an often awkward patchwork. Give us *Bride of Frankenstein* any day. Rated R for violence, gore, simulated sex, and nudity. 123m. **DIR:** Kenneth Branagh. **CAST:** Robert De Niro, Kenneth Branagh, Tom Hulce, Helena Bonham Carter, Aidan Quinn, Ian Holm, John Cleese. **1994 DVD**

MARZIPAN PIG, THE ★★★ Tim Curry narrates this animated food chain fable about the effect of a candy pig on the mouse who ate him and the owl who ate the mouse. Seems a harsh metaphor for the 5- to 8-year-olds it's aimed at, but ends on a light, upbeat note. 30m. **DIR:** Michael Sporn. **1990**

MASADA ★★★★ A spectacular TV movie based on the famous battle of Masada during the Roman domination of the known world. Fine acting, especially by Peter O'Toole, and excellent production values elevate this one far above the average small-screen movie. Not rated. 131m. **DIR:** Boris Sagal. **CAST:** Peter O'Toole, Peter Strauss, Barbara Carrera. **1984**

MASALA ★★★★ Silliness abounds in this delightfully funny domestic comedy. A distraught Indian woman living in Canada summons a Hindu god to help her dysfunctional family. Before the day is done, various family members will confront terrorists, marital woes, government agents, and a son who arrives with some interesting news. Multicultural effort is in English. Not rated; contains adult situations, nudity, and strong language. 105m. **DIR:** Srinivas Krishna. **CAST:** Saeed Jaffrey, Srinivas Krishna, Zohra Seghal. **1992**

MASCARA 🦃 Luridly exploitative film about a sister and brother with a very kinky relationship. Rated R for nudity, profanity, and violence. 99m. **DIR:** Patrick Conrad. **CAST:** Charlotte Rampling, Michael Sarrazin, Derek de Lint. **1987**

MASCULINE FEMININE ★★★ Jean-Luc Godard's eleventh film is an uneven attempt at exploring the relationship between a young Parisian radical, effectively portrayed by Jean-Pierre Leaud, and a slightly promiscuous woman (Chantal Goya) in fifteen discontinuous, contrapuntal vignettes. Good camera work and interesting screenplay lose strength in a muddled and disjointed story. In French with English subtitles. B&W; 103m. **DIR:** Jean-Luc Godard. **CAST:** Jean-Pierre Léaud, Chantal Goya, Catherine Isabelle Duport, Marlene Jobert. **1966**

M*A*S*H ★★★★1/2 Fans of the television series of the same name and *Trapper John, M.D.* may have a bit of trouble recognizing their favorite characters, but this is the original. One of eccentric film director Robert Altman's few true artistic successes, this release is outrageous good fun. Rated PG. 116m. **DIR:** Robert Altman. **CAST:** Elliott Gould, Donald Sutherland, Sally Kellerman, Tom Skerritt, Robert Duvall, Jo Ann Pflug, Bud Cort, Gary Burghoff. **1970 DVD**

M*A*S*H (TV SERIES) ★★★★ Nobody expected director Robert Altman's wry 1970 war comedy to translate well on the small screen, but a decade's worth of episodes and an impressive string of Emmy Awards proved the folly of that particular prediction. Alan Alda and Wayne Rogers became perfectly acceptable substitutes for Elliott Gould and Donald Sutherland, and the series also introduced many supporting players—notably McLean Stevenson, as Lieutenant Colonel Henry Blake—who eventually went on to successes of their own. (Gary Burghoff's anticipatory Corporal Radar O'Reilly was the only carryover from film to series.) This television classic owes most of its success to Larry Gelbart's thoughtful scripts. Each tape includes two half-hour episodes. 52m. **DIR:** Hy Averback, Jackie Cooper, Gene Reynolds. **CAST:** Alan Alda, Wayne Rogers, McLean Stevenson, Loretta Swit, Larry Linville, Gary Burghoff. **1972–1983**

MASK, THE 🦃 Low-budget chiller, shot in 3-D, about a psychiatrist who discovers an ancient ritual mask that causes violent hallucinations. B&W; 85m. **DIR:** Julian Roffman. **CAST:** Paul Stevens, Claudette Nevins. **1961**

MASK (1985) ★★★★★ They used to call them moving pictures, and few films fit this phrase as well as this one, starring Cher, Sam Elliott, and Eric Stoltz. The story of a teenage boy coping with a disfiguring disease, it touches the viewer's heart as few movies have ever done. *Mask* rises above simple entertainment with its uplifting true-life tale. Rated PG-13. 120m. **DIR:** Peter

Bogdanovich. **CAST:** Cher, Sam Elliott, Eric Stoltz, Laura Dern. **1985 DVD**

MASK, THE ★★★★ A good-hearted, put-upon bank employee discovers a mask that frees his inhibitions and gives him eye-popping magical powers. Star Jim Carrey is marvelous in this cartoon-style film that salutes the groundbreaking animated shorts made at Warner Bros. and MGM by Tex Avery and Bob Clampett. Cameron Diaz is a real knockout, even keeping pace with the rubber-legged Carrey in a dance sequence that has to be seen to be believed. Rated PG-13 for violence and profanity. 101m. **DIR:** Charles Russell. **CAST:** Jim Carrey, Cameron Diaz, Peter Riegert, Peter Greene, Amy Yasbeck, Richard Jeni. **1994 DVD**

MASK OF DEATH ★★★ Better-than-average Lorenzo Lamas vehicle has the macho action star doing double duty, portraying a ruthless murderer plus the undercover detective who undergoes plastic surgery to replace the killer after he's murdered. Lamas actually emotes as detective Dan McKenna, who becomes two-faced in order to avenge the murder of his wife. Decent action and cast keep this one on its toes. Rated R for language, nudity, and violence. 89m. **DIR:** David Mitchell. **CAST:** Lorenzo Lamas, Rae Dawn Chong, Billy Dee Williams, Conrad Dunn. **1997 DVD**

MASK OF FU MANCHU, THE ★★★1/2 The best of all the movies adapted from Sax Rohmer's novels about an evil mastermind intent on taking over the world features Boris Karloff as the title character and Lewis Stone as his Sherlock Holmes–style nemesis, Nayland Smith. If one can overlook the unfortunate racial stereotypes (Rohmer often referred to Fu Manchu as "The Yellow Peril"), this film makes for fun viewing. B&W; 72m. **DIR:** Charles Babin. **CAST:** Boris Karloff, Lewis Stone, Karen Morley, Myrna Loy, Charles Starrett, Jean Hersholt. **1932**

MASK OF ZORRO, THE ★★★★★ Expertly crafted action entertainment. Anthony Hopkins plays the aged California folk hero who trains Antonio Banderas to take up the sword against corrupt Spanish officials. Fantastic fencing, spectacular stunts, a good dose of comedy, and even some moving acting make this the best filmed incarnation yet of the Mexican masked man. Executive produced by Steven Spielberg, who obviously had a lot of say in the film's shaping. Rated PG-13 for violence. 137m. **DIR:** Martin Campbell. **CAST:** Antonio Banderas, Anthony Hopkins, Catherine Zeta-Jones, Stuart Wilson, Matthew Letscher. **1998 DVD**

MASKED MARVEL, THE ★★1/2 The mysterious Masked Marvel comes to the aid of the World-Wide Insurance Company to battle the evil Sakima, a former Japanese envoy, and his gang of saboteurs, who are threatening the security of America. Practically nonstop action and top stunt work highlight this wartime Republic serial, which is about as patriotic as a serial can be. B&W; 12 chapters. **DIR:** Spencer Gordon Bennet. **CAST:** William Forrest, Louise Currie, Johnny Arthur. **1943**

MASKS OF DEATH ★★★ Twenty-seven years after playing Sherlock Holmes in the Hammer Films version of *The Hound of the Baskervilles*, Peter Cushing returned to the role for this enjoyable thriller. This time, the Great Detective and Dr. Watson (John Mills) investigate a series of bizarre murders, which leave their victims' faces frozen in expressions of terror. 80m. **DIR:** Roy Ward Baker. **CAST:** Peter Cushing, John Mills, Anne Baxter, Ray Milland. **1986**

MASQUE OF THE RED DEATH, THE (1964) ★★★ The combination of Roger Corman, Edgar Allan Poe, and Vincent Price meant first-rate (though low-budget) horror films in the early 1960s. This was one of the best. Price is deliciously villainous. 86m. **DIR:** Roger Corman. **CAST:** Vincent Price, Hazel Court, Jane Asher, David Weston, Patrick Magee. **1964**

MASQUE OF THE RED DEATH (1989) ★★★ A fine rendition of the classic Edgar Allan Poe story of paranoia and death. Producer Roger Corman adds a smattering of sex and violence, but what elevates this film are the sumptuous sets and costumes. Rated R. 83m. **DIR:** Larry Brand. **CAST:** Patrick Macnee, Jeff Osterhage. **1989**

MASQUERADE ★★★1/2 Bizarre psychodrama about a famous young actor who, disillusioned by his popularity, escapes into a world where reality and fantasy become obscured. Unconventional, stylistic approach by director Janusz Kijowski (one of Poland's new-wave filmmakers). In Polish with English subtitles. 102m. **DIR:** Janusz Kijowski. **CAST:** Boguslaw Linda. **1986**

MASQUERADE ★★1/2 Overblown variation on Hitchcock's *Suspicion* with Rob Lowe playing the devious but attractive husband who may be after heiress Meg Tilly's money. Some new plot twists are introduced, but unfortunately these don't save *Masquerade* from playing a lot like *Dallas*. Rated R for language, nudity, simulated sex, and violence. 98m. **DIR:** Bob Swaim. **CAST:** Rob Lowe, Meg Tilly, Kim Cattrall, Doug Savant, John Glover, Dana Delany. **1988**

MASS APPEAL ★★★★1/2 A first-rate discussion of the dichotomy between private conscience and mass appeal, this film finds a mediocre and worldly priest, Father Tim Farley (Jack Lemmon), walking a political tightrope between the young seminarian (Zeljko Ivanek) he has befriended and his superior, Monsignor Burke (Charles Durning). At times both comic and tragic, it is not only a fine memorial but also a splendid motion picture. Rated PG. 99m. **DIR:** Glenn Jordan. **CAST:** Jack Lemmon, Zeljko Ivanek, Charles Durning, Louise Latham, James Ray. **1984**

MASSACRE AT CENTRAL HIGH ★★★ Low-budget production has a teenager exacting his own brand of revenge on tough gang members who are making things hard for the students at a local high school. This violent drama has a lot going for it, except for some goofy dialogue. Otherwise, nicely done. Rated R. 85m. **DIR:** Renee Daalder. **CAST:** Andrew Stevens, Kimberly Beck, Derrel Maury, Robert Carradine. **1976**

MASSACRE AT FORT HOLMAN (REASON TO LIVE . . . A REASON TO DIE, A) ★1/2 Spaghetti Western of marginal interest. Eight condemned men led by James Coburn get a chance to redeem themselves by overtaking a rebel fort. Plenty of action can't help the worn-out plot or Western clichés. Rated PG for violence and profanity. 90m. **DIR:** Tonino Valerii. **CAST:** James Coburn, Telly Savalas, Bud Spencer. **1984**

MASSACRE IN ROME ★★★1/2 Chilling drama about a priest (Marcello Mastroianni) opposing a Nazi colonel (Richard Burton) who must execute hundreds of Roman citizens in retaliation for the death by partisans of

some Nazi troops. Rated PG for violence. 103m. **DIR:** George Pan Cosmatos. **CAST:** Richard Burton, Marcello Mastroianni, Leo McKern, John Steiner. **1973**

MASSIVE RETALIATION 🦃 A group of friends gathers at their own civil-defense fort during a national emergency. Not rated; has profanity and violence. 90m. **DIR:** Thomas A. Cohen. **CAST:** Tom Boyer, Karlene Crockett, Peter Donat, Marilyn Hassett, Jason Gedrick. **1984**

MASTER HAROLD AND THE BOYS ★★★★ An intense movie filmed in a single setting with a cast of three. Matthew Broderick gives a moving performance as a white English boy in 1950s South Africa. Zakes Mokae, in a brilliant portrayal as a black servant, tries to lead the boy gently toward manhood. Not rated; contains profanity. 90m. **DIR:** Michael Lindsay-Hogg. **CAST:** Matthew Broderick, Zakes Mokae, John Kani. **1984**

MASTER OF BALLANTRAE, THE ★★ Errol Flynn's disappointing swan song as a swashbuckler is about two brothers who take different sides in squabbles over the British throne. 89m. **DIR:** William Keighley. **CAST:** Errol Flynn, Anthony Steel, Roger Livesey, Beatrice Campbell, Yvonne Furneaux. **1953**

MASTER OF THE HOUSE (DU SKAL AERE DIN HUSTRU) ★★★★ In this funny satire of middle-class life, a wife runs away from her husband, a chauvinist pig who treats her brutally. Later, the wife is reunited with her husband after an old nurse has taught him a lesson. Silent. B&W; 81m. **DIR:** Carl Dreyer. **CAST:** Johannes Meyer, Astrid Holm. **1925**

MASTER OF THE WORLD ★★★ Jules Verne's tale brought excitingly to the screen. Vincent Price plays a self-proclaimed god trying to end all war by flying around the world in a giant airship, blowing ships from the water, etc. Lots of fun. 104m. **DIR:** William Witney. **CAST:** Vincent Price, Charles Bronson, Henry Hull. **1961**

MASTER RACE, THE ★★★ Hitler's Third Reich collapses. A dedicated Nazi officer escapes. His refusal to accept defeat becomes an engrossing study of blind obedience to immorality. B&W; 96m. **DIR:** Herbert J. Biberman. **CAST:** George Coulouris, Stanley Ridges, Osa Massen, Lloyd Bridges. **1944**

MASTERMIND ★★★ Zero Mostel spoofs Charlie Chan in this 1969 comedy that wasn't released until 1976. It's better than it sounds, with in-jokes for old-movie buffs and lots of slapstick for the whole family. It's even rated G! 84m. **DIR:** Alex March. **CAST:** Zero Mostel, Bradford Dillman, Jules Munshin. **1976**

MASTERMINDS ★★1/2 When the students at an upper-crust private school are held hostage by their new security consultant, only one student, a recently expelled computer-hacking troublemaker, stands between the villain and a $650 million ransom. Silly, farfetched, and way over-the-top, it's sort of a children's production of *Die Hard* crossed with *The Rock*, with plenty of violence but no blood or death—which isn't very convincing, but at least it protects the PG-13 rating. Patrick Stewart's lip-smacking gusto as the chief bad guy is the film's main asset. Rated PG-13 for violent action. 106m. **DIR:** Roger Christian. **CAST:** Patrick Stewart, Vincent Kartheiser, Brenda Fricker, Bradley Whitford, Matt Craven. **1997**

MASTERS OF MENACE ★★★ Cameos by Jim Belushi, John Candy, George Wendt, and Dan Aykroyd help this story of a young lawyer who must follow a motorcycle gang around and make sure they don't get into any trouble. He doesn't have any luck. Rated PG-13 for violence and profanity. 97m. **DIR:** Daniel Raskov. **CAST:** David Rasche, Catherine Bach, David L. Lander, Teri Copley, Ray Baker. **1990**

MASTERS OF THE UNIVERSE ★★1/2 Those toy and cartoon characters come to life on the silver screen, and all things considered, the translation is fairly successful. He-Man and friends are exiled to Earth, where they befriend a teenage couple and battle Skeletor's evil minions. A small amount of foul language and one scene of graphic violence may be deemed unsuitable for young children by some parents. Rated PG. 106m. **DIR:** Gary Goddard. **CAST:** Dolph Lundgren, Frank Langella, Courteney Cox, James Tolkan, Meg Foster. **1987**

MATA HARI ★★★ Casting Greta Garbo as history's most alluring spy proved to be big box office. She captivated Ramon Novarro—*and* the audience! The legend's throaty voice is hypnotic. B&W; 90m. **DIR:** George Fitzmaurice. **CAST:** Greta Garbo, Ramon Novarro, Karen Morley, Lionel Barrymore, Lewis Stone. **1931**

MATA HARI ★★ Liberally sprinkled with action, erotica, and existentialism, *Mata Hari* is one of Sylvia (*Emmanuelle*) Kristel's better works. This story traces the erotic dancer from Indonesia as she unwittingly becomes the tool of the German government during World War II. Rated R for sex and nudity. 103m. **DIR:** Curtis Harrington. **CAST:** Sylvia Kristel, Christopher Cazenove, Oliver Tobias. **1985**

MATADOR ★★★★ Mind-boggling psychosexual melodrama carried to hilarious extremes by director Pedro Almodóvar. The story centers around a lame ex-bullfighter who derives sexual gratification from murder. In Spanish with English subtitles. Rated R for nudity and violence. 107m. **DIR:** Pedro Almodóvar. **CAST:** Assumpta Serna, Antonio Banderas, Carmen Maura. **1988**

MATCH, THE ★★★1/2 Clichés abound in this charming Scottish comedy about two pubs that celebrate an annual ritual of squaring off against each other in a soccer game. The stakes on the one hundredth anniversary are high. The losing pub must close forever, fulfilling a century-old feud between the original owners. The underdogs find a miracle in a local milkman with great athletic skill. The film breathes new life into the clichés, while the wonderful cast makes the characters engaging. Rated PG-13 for language. 96m. **DIR:** Mick Davis. **CAST:** Tom Sizemore, Ian Holm, Richard E. Grant, Laura Frasser. **1999**

MATCHMAKER, THE ★★★★ Gabby Shirley Booth takes it upon herself to find a wife for rich merchant Paul Ford, but finds herself attracted to the stuffy old crank, and they end up an item. Young Anthony Perkins and Shirley MacLaine fall in love along the way, and everything ends up swell. This pleasant little comedy was written for the stage by Thornton Wilder, and it found its way to the stage and the screen again as *Hello Dolly*. B&W; 101m. **DIR:** Joseph Anthony. **CAST:** Shirley Booth, Paul Ford, Anthony Perkins, Shirley MacLaine, Robert Morse, Wallace Ford, Rex Evans, Russell Collins, Gavin Gordon. **1958**

MATCHMAKER, THE ★★★★ Comedian-turned-actress Janeane Garofalo is totally delightful as a Boston congressional aide who is sent to Ireland to dig up some history on her boss. Instead, she stumbles into a small village's matchmaker festival, where she learns about love and herself. David O'Hara shines as one of the locals who steals her heart, while Denis Leary checks in as an ungrateful political assistant. A feel-goody comedy with lots of heart and laughs. Rated R for language. 97m. **DIR:** Mark Joffe. **CAST:** Janeane Garofalo, David O'Hara, Milo O'Shea, Denis Leary, Jay O. Sanders. **1997 DVD**

MATERNAL INSTINCTS ★★1/2 A woman who desperately wants to have a baby becomes obsessed with ruining her doctor's life after undergoing an emergency hysterectomy. The acting in this made-for-cable original is stiff and unconvincing. Rated PG-13 for violence. 92m. **DIR:** George Kaczender. **CAST:** Delta Burke, Beth Broderick, Garwin Sanford. **1996**

MATEWAN ★★★★1/2 Writer-director John Sayles's masterpiece about the massacre of striking West Virginia coal miners in 1920 has both heart and humor. Chris Cooper is the soft-spoken union organizer who tries to avoid violence. James Earl Jones is the leader of a group of black workers who were shocked to find, too late, that they were brought in as scabs. And David Strathairn is memorable as the town sheriff who attempts to keep the peace. Rated PG-13 for violence and profanity. 132m. **DIR:** John Sayles. **CAST:** Chris Cooper, Will Oldham, Mary McDonnell, James Earl Jones, David Strathairn, Josh Mostel. **1987 DVD**

MATILDA (1978) ★★★1/2 A cute comedy about a boxing kangaroo who becomes a legend in the sport. Elliott Gould plays a small-time booking agent who becomes the manager of the heavyweight marsupial. Sentimental at times and a bit corny, too, but worth the time. Recommended for family viewing. Rated G. 105m. **DIR:** Daniel Mann. **CAST:** Elliott Gould, Robert Mitchum, Clive Revill, Harry Guardino, Roy Clark, Lionel Stander, Art Metrano. **1978**

MATILDA (1996) ★★★★ In this dark comedy and modern-day fable, resourceful Matilda develops her telekinetic powers to even the odds between herself and a sadistic school principal, while distancing herself from her ill-mannered, uneducated, and unethical parents by immersing herself in the world of books. Powerful messages delivered without obvious preaching. Rated PG for simulated child abuse. 93m. **DIR:** Danny DeVito. **CAST:** Mara Wilson, Danny DeVito, Rhea Perlman, Pam Ferris, Embeth Davidtz. **1996 DVD**

MATINEE ★★★★ Charlie Haas's screenplay is set during the Cuban Missile Crisis in Key West, where John Goodman is staging a premiere of his latest masterwork: *Mant*—"Half Man, Half Ant, All Terror!" while the populace deals with the fear of impending nuclear war. Goodman's deft performance is complemented by a well-played, coming-of-age story. Rated PG for profanity. 97m. **DIR:** Joe Dante. **CAST:** John Goodman, Cathy Moriarty, Simon Fenton, Omri Katz, Kellie Martin, Lisa Jakub, Jesse White, Dick Miller, John Sayles, William Schallert, Robert Cornthwaite. **1993 DVD**

MATING GAME, THE ★★★★ A straight-as-an-arrow tax collector finds himself being wooed by both the farmer and his daughter, who have never seen any good reason to pay taxes. Great comedy, exceptional cast, with special mention for Fred Clark as the evil head of the Internal Revenue Service. 101m. **DIR:** George Marshall. **CAST:** Debbie Reynolds, Tony Randall, Paul Douglas, Fred Clark, Una Merkel, Philip Ober. **1951**

MATING HABITS OF THE EARTHBOUND HUMAN, THE ★★★1/2 David Hyde Pierce narrates this take on nature documentaries, where we follow the sex lives of two humans in their natural habitats, including a typical human-meeting facility—the nightclub. This hilarious farce parodies all of those animal shows seen on PBS in a new, creative way. Rated R for sexual situations. 90m. **DIR:** Jeff Abugov. **CAST:** Mackenzie Astin, Carmen Electra, David Hyde Pierce. **1999**

MATING SEASON, THE ★★★ An enjoyable romantic comedy set among the flora and fauna commonly inhabited by bird-watchers. When an emotional lady attorney resorts to bird-watching for relaxation, she meets a charming businessman. Affable little TV movie. 96m. **DIR:** John Llewellyn Moxey. **CAST:** Lucie Arnaz, Laurence Luckinbill, Swoosie Kurtz, Diane Stilwell, Joel Brooks. **1986**

MATRIX, THE ★★★★ This slick cyberpunk tale, which boasts an ingenious plot and bravura filmmaking, is a first-class head trip that's both fun to watch and intellectually stimulating. The story's focus is a conservative, buttoned-down software programmer (Keanu Reeves) with an after-hours fixation on a hacker's legend—somebody named Morpheus—reputed to know "great things" about cyberspace. That proves to be the understatement of the century, when our hero finds himself the target of powerful and sinister "agents" of some oblique government entity. The mesmerizing blend of hyperspeed imagery and slow-motion flourish will keep you dazzled for days. And yet, however wild things get, it all makes sense. Rated R for violence, profanity, and special effects. 138m. **DIR:** Larry Wachowski, Andy Wachowski. **CAST:** Keanu Reeves, Laurence Fishburne, Carrie-Anne Moss, Hugo Weaving, Joe Pantoliano. **1999 DVD**

MATT THE GOOSEBOY ★★★1/2 Beautifully detailed animation garnishes this presentation of a classic Hungarian folktale, wherein a young peasant boy must act to end the oppression of his people and country. 77m. **DIR:** Attila Durgay, Luis Elman. **1978**

MATTER OF DEGREES, A ★★★ When a college threatens to change its progressive campus radio station to a more laid-back listening format, staff members and students revolt. Rated R for sexual situations. 90m. **DIR:** W. T. Morgan. **CAST:** Arye Gross, Judith Hoag, Tom Sizemore. **1990**

MATTER OF PRINCIPLE, A ★★★★ Delightful tale about a selfish tyrant (Alan Arkin) who is suddenly overthrown by his much-put-upon wife (Barbara Dana, Arkin's real-life wife). She takes their eleven children after he destroys their first Christmas tree. Finally, he must wake up and think about someone besides himself. Not rated, but fine family entertainment. 60m. **DIR:** Gwen Arner. **CAST:** Alan Arkin, Barbara Dana, Tony Arkin. **1983**

MATTER OF TIME, A 🦃 A penniless countess takes a country-bumpkin-come-to-the-big-city hotel chambermaid in hand. Rated PG. 99m. **DIR:** Vincente Minnelli.

CAST: Liza Minnelli, Ingrid Bergman, Charles Boyer, Spiro Andros, Isabella Rossellini. **1976**

MATTERS OF THE HEART ★★ Made-for-cable melodrama concerning a talented college musician (Christopher Gartin) who falls in love with a world-famous pianist (Jane Seymour at her bitchiest) . . . who, naturally, has cancer! Brief nudity. 94m. **DIR:** Michael Ray Rhodes. **CAST:** Jane Seymour, Christopher Gartin, James Stacy, Geoffrey Lewis. **1990**

MAURICE ★★★ Based on E. M. Forster's long-suppressed, semiautobiographical novel, this film details the love of a middle-class college student (James Wilby) for his aristocratic classmate (Hugh Grant). A minor, but handsome film. Rated R for nudity and implied sex. 140m. **DIR:** James Ivory. **CAST:** James Wilby, Hugh Grant, Rupert Graves, Denholm Elliott. **1987**

MAUVAISE GRAINE (BAD SEED) ★★★1/2 Fans of Billy Wilder (and what film buff isn't?) will give thanks that this early feature by the director has been unearthed. Made in France while the young Wilder was in the process of emigrating to the United States from his native Germany, this is a surprisingly racy look at criminal life in Paris during the Jazz Age. In French with English subtitles. B&W; 76m. **DIR:** Billy Wilder, Alexander Esway. **CAST:** Pierre Mingand, Raymond Galle, Danielle Darrieux. **1933**

MAVERICK ★★★★1/2 This big-screen adaptation of the TV series features Mel Gibson as gambler and reluctant hero Bret Maverick. James Garner, the first actor to play the title character, costars as a lawman who anticipates Maverick's every move. Sexy grifter Jodie Foster keeps our hero preoccupied in other ways, as this unlikely trio heads for a high-stakes poker competition. It's great fun for Western fans, since a number of TV and movie cowboys make cameo appearances. Rated PG for violence. 129m. **DIR:** Richard Donner. **CAST:** Mel Gibson, Jodie Foster, James Garner, James Coburn, Graham Greene, Alfred Molina, Max Perlich, Leo Gordon, Danny Glover, Margot Kidder, Robert Fuller, Denver Pyle, Dennis Fimple, Bert Ramson, Doug McClure, Will Hutchins, Waylon Jennings. **1994 DVD**

MAVERICK (TV SERIES) ★★★★ One of the best TV Western series, this tongue-in-cheek show starred James Garner and Jack Kelly as the Maverick brothers, Bret and Bart, and after Garner left, Roger Moore as British cousin Beau. The first two episodes to be released on video are classics. "Shady Deal at Sunny Acres" has Bret and Bart outwitting corrupt banker John Dehner with the help of the series' semiregular shady characters. "Duel at Sundown" features a young Clint Eastwood as a trigger-happy character. B&W; 49m. **DIR:** Leslie Martinson, Arthur Lubin. **CAST:** James Garner, Jack Kelly, Roger Moore, Clint Eastwood, Efrem Zimbalist Jr., Richard Long, Diane Brewster, John Dehner, Leo Gordon, Edgar Buchanan, Abby Dalton. **1958–1962**

MAVERICK QUEEN, THE ★★★ Sparks erupt when a Pinkerton detective works undercover at a Wyoming gambling hotel that is a hangout for an outlaw gang. Barbara Stanwyck is cast aptly as the beauty who owns the hotel and is caught between her jealous lover and the lawman. 90m. **DIR:** Joseph Kane. **CAST:** Barbara Stanwyck, Barry Sullivan, Scott Brady, Mary Murphy, Wallace Ford. **1955**

MAX AND HELEN ★★★1/2 Thoughtful, often heartbreaking story looks at two victims of the Holocaust. Max (Treat Williams) tells his story to famed Nazi hunter Simon Wiesenthal (Martin Landau), who has located the camp commandant where Max and his fiancée Helen (Alice Krige) were held. Made for cable TV. No rating, but contains scenes of torture and rape. 79m. **DIR:** Philip Saville. **CAST:** Martin Landau, Treat Williams, Alice Krige. **1990**

MAX DUGAN RETURNS ★★1/2 After spending many years in jail and gambling to big winnings, Max Dugan (Jason Robards) seeks his daughter (Marsha Mason) to bestow gifts upon her and her son. Though grateful, she finds it difficult to explain to her policeman-boyfriend, Donald Sutherland. The charm of this Neil Simon fable wears thin. Rated PG. 98m. **DIR:** Herbert Ross. **CAST:** Jason Robards Jr., Marsha Mason, Donald Sutherland. **1983**

MAX HEADROOM ★★★1/2 The original British production, later remade as a short-lived American TV series. Post-apocalypse newsman discovers an insidious form of advertising that causes viewers to explode. After being murdered by network executives, he's reborn as a computer-generated figure named Max Headroom. A sly parody of ratings-hungry television, the film is visually superb. 60m. **DIR:** Rocky Morton, Annabel Jankel. **CAST:** Matt Frewer, Nickolas Grace, Hilary Tindall, Morgan Shepherd, Amanda Pays. **1986**

MAX IS MISSING ★★★1/2 You'll enjoy this kid-oriented adventure saga, which stars Toran Caudell as a 12-year-old American boy who clashes with artifact thieves while visiting Peru's Machu Picchu ruins. After befriending a local boy (Victor Rojas), our resourceful hero struggles to deliver a priceless Inca amulet to its rightful heirs. Great fun, intelligently executed, and highlighted by credible performances from both boys. Rated PG for mild violence. 95m. **DIR:** Mark Griffiths. **CAST:** Toran Caudell, Victor Rojas, Matthew Sullivan, Alexandra Hedison, Rick Dean, Charles Napier. **1995**

•MAX KEEBLE'S BIG MOVE 🦃 An adolescent spends his last week at school playing nasty tricks on all the bullies who tormented him—then finds out his family isn't moving away after all. One of Disney's all-time worst—badly written, overacted, ugly to look at, and ugly in spirit. Rated PG. 86m. **DIR:** Tim Hill. **CAST:** Alex D. Linz, Larry Miller, Zena Grey, Nora Dunn, Robert Carradine, Josh Peck. **2001 DVD**

MAX MON AMOUR ★★★1/2 A proper Frenchwoman falls in love with a chimpanzee in this unusually civilized comedy about the limits of civilization. Not rated; contains adult themes. 94m. **DIR:** Nagisa Oshima. **CAST:** Charlotte Rampling, Anthony Higgins, Victoria Abril. **1986**

MAXIE ★★ Cute but not particularly impressive fantasy about a conservative secretary (Glenn Close) who becomes possessed by the spirit of a flamboyant flapper (Close, too). The star is wonderful, but the predictable plot and the uninspired direction let her—and the viewer—down. Rated PG for suggested sex. 98m. **DIR:** Paul Aaron. **CAST:** Glenn Close, Mandy Patinkin, Ruth Gordon, Barnard Hughes, Valerie Curtin. **1985**

MAXIMUM FORCE ★★ Three crackerjack cops go undercover to infiltrate a crime lord and destroy him. The only thing maximum about this action-adventure is the

title. Rated R for profanity, nudity, and violence. 90m. **DIR:** Joseph Merhi. **CAST:** John Saxon, Mickey Rooney, Sam Jones, Jason Lively, Richard Lynch, Sherrie Rose. **1992**

MAXIMUM IMPACT ★★ Upon witnessing the brutalizing of a teen prostitute, a man steals her and takes her to safety, thus bringing the wrath of a gang down on his family. After his family is killed he becomes a loose cannon. Full of brutal violence but little style or excitement. Not rated; contains violence. 70m. **DIR:** Lance Randas. **CAST:** Ken Jarosz, James Black, Jo Norcia, Bill Morrison. **1992**

MAXIMUM OVERDRIVE 🦃 Chaotic mess, loosely based on Stephen King's short story "Trucks." 97m. **DIR:** Stephen King. **CAST:** Emilio Estevez, Pat Hingle, Laura Harrington, Yeardley Smith, Ellen McElduff, J. C. Quinn. **1986 DVD**

MAXIMUM RISK ★★★ Action star Jean-Claude Van Damme investigates the murder of the twin brother he never knew he had, and his search takes him to New York's Little Odessa and the Russian mafia. A better-than-average script, along with the usual outlandish violence, makes this slugfest one of Van Damme's best efforts. Rated R for profanity and violence. 126m. **DIR:** Ringo Lam. **CAST:** Jean-Claude Van Damme, Natasha Henstridge, Jean-Hugues Anglade, Stéphane Audran. **1996 DVD**

MAXIMUM SECURITY 🦃 An unjustly imprisoned cop battles nuclear-armed terrorists in a high-tech prison in this made-for-video thriller that is almost dumb enough to be entertaining—but not quite. Rated R for violence, profanity, nudity, and sexual situations. 80m. **DIR:** Fred Olen Ray. **CAST:** Paul Michael Robinson, Landon Hall, George Franklin. **1996**

MAY FOOLS ★★★★ An upper-class French family (and a few hangers-on) gather for their mother's funeral at a country estate, just as the 1968 Paris student riots seem to be setting off another French Revolution. A leisurely comedy-drama from director Louis Malle (cowriting with Jean-Claude Carrière). Rated R for profanity, nudity, and simulated sex. 105m. **DIR:** Louis Malle. **CAST:** Michel Piccoli, Miou-Miou, Michel Duchaussoy, Harriet Walter, Bruno Carette, Paulette Dubost. **1989**

MAY WINE ★★★ Pleasant bedroom romp features a Parisian gynecologist (Guy Marchand) being shamelessly pursued by two Americans. The twist is that the two women are mother (Joanna Cassidy) and daughter (Lara Flynn Boyle). Contrived, but guaranteed to elicit a giggle or two. Rated R for nudity and language. 88m. **DIR:** Carol Wiseman. **CAST:** Joanna Cassidy, Guy Marchand, Lara Flynn Boyle, Paul Freeman. **1990**

MAYA ★★★ A boy living with his hunter father in India feels neglected and takes off with a native boy to deliver a sacred white elephant to a remote holy city. Preteens will enjoy this; location filming is a plus. 91m. **DIR:** John Berry. **CAST:** Clint Walker, Jay North, I. S. Johar. **1966**

MAYBE, MAYBE NOT ★★1/2 A philandering young rake, thrown out by his long-suffering girlfriend, is taken in by a gay friend. Predictable and presumably hilarious complications ensue. The film is stylish and handsomely mounted, but the characters remain two-dimensional and the premise hackneyed. In German with English subtitles. Rated R for mature themes, profanity, and brief nudity. 96m. **DIR:** Sonke Wortmann. **CAST:** Til Schweiger, Katja Riemann, Joachim Król, Rufus Beck. **1995**

MAYERLING ★★★ Fine-tuned, convincing performances mark this French-made romantic tragedy based upon Austrian Crown Prince Rudolph's ill-starred clandestine love for court lady-in-waiting Countess Marie Vetsera, in 1889. A 1969 British remake stinks by comparison. In French with English subtitles. B&W; 91m. **DIR:** Anatole Litvak. **CAST:** Charles Boyer, Danielle Darrieux, Suzy Prim. **1936**

MAYFLOWER MADAM ★★ TV-movie bio of Mayflower descendant and debutante Sydney Biddle Barrows. Though allegedly based on fact, the events depicted here seem strictly soap-operaish. 96m. **DIR:** Lou Antonio. **CAST:** Candice Bergen, Chris Sarandon, Chita Rivera. **1987**

MAYTIME ★★★1/2 A curio of the past. A penniless tenor meets and falls in love with an opera star suffering in a loveless marriage to her adoring and jealous teacher and mentor. The hands Fate deals are not pat. See if you can tell that John Barrymore is reading his lines from idiot boards off-camera. This film is one of the Eddy/MacDonald duo's best. B&W; 132m. **DIR:** Robert Z. Leonard. **CAST:** Jeanette MacDonald, Nelson Eddy, John Barrymore, Sig Ruman. **1937**

•**MAZE** ★★★ Unexpected romantic drama about an introverted artist suffering from Tourette's syndrome who is forced to face his fears and weaknesses after he begins to fall for one of his models. Lyle Maze (Rob Morrow) is elated when his best friend's fiancée agrees to pose for him, and comes to her rescue when his best friend takes a walk. Morrow successfully evokes the loneliness of Lyle, while Laura Linney shines as the jilted fiancée. But the script fails to avoid the common clichés and pitfalls of the genre, which turn what could have been a gem into a diamond in the rough. Rated R for adult situations, language, and nudity. 98m. **DIR:** Rob Morrow. **CAST:** Rob Morrow, Laura Linney, Craig Sheffer, Rose Gregorio, Gia Carides. **2000 DVD**

MAZES AND MONSTERS ★★ TV movie portrays the lives of several college students whose interest in a Dungeons and Dragons type of role-playing game becomes hazardous. If you're into this sword-and-sorcery stuff, rent *Ladyhawke* instead. 103m. **DIR:** Steven H. Stern. **CAST:** Tom Hanks, Chris Makepeace, Wendy Crewson, David Wallace, Lloyd Bochner, Peter Donat, Louise Sorel, Susan Strasberg. **1982**

MCBAIN 🦃 It's hard to keep track of what's going on in this lamebrained action-adventure flick involving a mercenary team out to dethrone a Central American dictator. Rated R for profanity and violence. 104m. **DIR:** James Glickenhaus. **CAST:** Christopher Walken, Maria Conchita Alonso, Michael Ironside. **1991**

MCCABE AND MRS. MILLER ★★★★ Life in the turn-of-the-century Northwest is given a first-class treatment in director Robert Altman's visually perfect comedy-drama. Sparkling performances by Warren Beatty, as a small-town wheeler-dealer, and Julie Christie, as a whore with a heart that beats to the jingle of gold. Rated R. 121m. **DIR:** Robert Altman. **CAST:** Warren Beatty, Julie Christie, Shelley Duvall, Keith Carradine. **1971**

MCCINSEY'S ISLAND ★★ Former secret agent Hulk Hogan and cult leader Grace Jones battle to find a hid-

den treasure buried on a tropical island. This tame thriller is intended primarily for young viewers, who won't appreciate the sheer weirdness of its casting. Rated PG for mild violence. 94m. **DIR:** Sam Firstenberg. **CAST:** Hulk Hogan, Grace Jones, Todd Sheeler, Robert Vaughn. **1998**

MCCONNELL STORY, THE ★★1/2 Run-of-the-mill romanticized bio-pic of real-life jet-test pilot has Alan Ladd acting like a stick, June Allyson as his devoted wife tearfully waiting on the tarmac. 107m. **DIR:** Gordon Douglas. **CAST:** Alan Ladd, June Allyson, James Whitmore, Frank Faylen. **1955**

MCGUFFIN, THE ★★★ British suspense-drama begins like Alfred Hitchcock's *Rear Window*, which is well and good, considering its title is taken from a phrase coined by Hitchcock himself! Charles Dance offers an excellent portrayal of a movie critic who becomes embroiled in a government cover-up. Brief nudity and sexual situations. 104m. **DIR:** Colin Bucksey. **CAST:** Charles Dance, Brian Glover, Ritza Brown, Francis Matthews, Phyllis Logan, Jerry Stiller. **1985**

MCHALE'S NAVY 🦃 This mirthless action-comedy is an insult to its silly 1960s TV sitcom namesake, as retired naval officer McHale protects a sleepy Caribbean island and the world's leaders from an East German terrorist. Rated PG. 105m. **DIR:** Bryan Spicer. **CAST:** Tom Arnold, Debra Messing, Bruce Campbell, Dean Stockwell, David Alan Grier, Tim Curry. **1997**

MCLINTOCK! ★★★1/2 Broad Western-comedy stars John Wayne as a prosperous rancher who attempts to keep the peace between settlers and landowners while fighting a war of his own with headstrong Maureen O'Hara. A bit overlong, the film still features some priceless scenes. 127m. **DIR:** Andrew V. McLaglen. **CAST:** John Wayne, Maureen O'Hara, Yvonne De Carlo, Patrick Wayne, Stefanie Powers, Jack Kruschen, Chill Wills, Jerry Van Dyke, Edgar Buchanan, Bruce Cabot, Perry Lopez, Michael Pate, Strother Martin, Leo Gordon, Robert Lowery, Hank Worden. **1963 DVD**

MCQ ★★★1/2 The success of *Dirty Harry* and the slow death of the Western prompted John Wayne to shed his Stetson and six-guns for cop clothes. While this John Sturges film doesn't quite match the Clint Eastwood–Don Siegel production that inspired it, there are some good scenes and suspense. Rated PG. 116m. **DIR:** John Sturges. **CAST:** John Wayne, Al Lettieri, Eddie Albert, Diana Muldaur, Clu Gulager, Colleen Dewhurst. **1974**

MCVICAR ★★★ In this interesting British film, Roger Daltrey (lead singer for the Who) portrays John McVicar, whose real-life escape from the high-security wing of a British prison led to him being named "public enemy No. 1." Rated R. 111m. **DIR:** Tom Clegg. **CAST:** Roger Daltrey, Adam Faith, Jeremy Blake. **1980**

MD GEIST ★★ In this animated story, Geist, a bio-engineered superman exiled because of his particularly dangerous nature, engages in a little private warfare after he manages to return to "civilization." Not rated; contains violence, nudity, and profanity. 41m. **DIR:** Ikeda Hayato. **1986**

ME AND HIM ★★ You'd think a comedy about a staid businessman who gets life lessons from his newly loquacious penis would offer a few laughs, and this does. *Very* few. There are songs, too, though not from *him*. Rated R for nudity and sexual situations. 94m. **DIR:** Doris Dörrie. **CAST:** Griffin Dunne, Ellen Greene, Carey Lowell, Craig T. Nelson, Mark Linn-Baker. **1987**

ME AND THE KID ★★ Two burglars attempt to rob a mansion, but all they find is an empty safe and a neglected rich kid, whom they decide to kidnap. When one of the burglars attempts to return the victim, the boy doesn't want to go home. Unfortunately, the story drags a bit. Not rated; contains violence and profanity. 95m. **DIR:** Dan Curtis. **CAST:** Danny Aiello, Joe Pantoliano, Cathy Moriarty, Alex Zuckerman, David Dukes, Anita Morris, Rick Aiello. **1993**

ME AND THE MOB ★★★ Sometimes too silly but often just-funny-enough spoof of life in the mob. Rated R for language and violence. 86m. **DIR:** Frank Rainone. **CAST:** Sandra Bullock, John Castelloe, Tony Darrow, James Lorinz. **1994**

ME & VERONICA 🦃 False sentiment as hard-living Patricia Wettig dumps her kids with sister Elizabeth McGovern just before she heads off to jail. Slow and uninteresting. Rated R for adult situations and language. 97m. **DIR:** Don Scardino. **CAST:** Elizabeth McGovern, Patricia Wettig, Michael O'Keefe. **1992**

ME, MYSELF & I 🦃 Irritating comedy finds writer George Segal trying to make sense of neighbor JoBeth Williams's twin personalities. Dull and uninteresting. Rated R for language and adult situations. 97m. **DIR:** Pablo Ferro. **CAST:** George Segal, JoBeth Williams, Shelley Hack, Don Calfa. **1992**

ME, MYSELF & IRENE ★★1/2 A too-nice Rhode Island State Trooper (Jim Carrey) reacts to years of mistreatment by developing an alternate personality named Hank, who doesn't take any guff from anyone. The premise gives Carrey plenty of opportunity for the kind of rubber-faced comedy only he does so well. But the plot—Carrey escorting a woman (Renée Zellweger) back to New York to face charges, with both of his personalities falling for her on the way—is distended and uninvolving. Laughs are only scattered. Rated R for profanity and raunchy humor. 116m. **DIR:** Bobby Farrelly, Peter Farrelly. **CAST:** Jim Carrey, Renée Zellweger, Robert Forster, Chris Cooper, Richard Jenkins. **2000 DVD**

ME MYSELF I ★★★★ This clever Australian fantasy, superficially reminiscent of *Sliding Doors*, charts its own course while painting an intriguing picture of an alternate life. With the onset of another birthday, an investigative journalist suddenly decides that her life is meaningless without the husband, children, dog, and mortgage in the suburbs that traditionally define success. Then, one morning, she encounters . . . herself: a *different* self, the one who married the "guy who got away" a decade earlier. Suddenly the other self vanishes, leaving our heroine to cope with the life she might have had. But since she still remembers her previous existence, she can't help messing with the established order of things. The results—alternately fascinating, poignant, and triumphant—are always entertaining. Rated R for profanity, nudity, and sexual content. 104m. **DIR:** Pip Karmel. **CAST:** Rachel Griffiths, David Roberts, Sandy Winton, Yael Stone, Shaun Loseby, Trent Sullivan. **2000 DVD**

•ME YOU THEM ★★ In rural Brazil, a woman establishes a casual ménage with her elderly husband, his

dim-bulb cousin, and a handsome drifter. Regina Casé as the woman has dignity and weary grace, but other characters make no impression, and the film moves at a numbing crawl. In Portuguese with English subtitles. Rated PG-13 for sexual themes. 104m. **DIR:** Andrucha Waddington. **CAST:** Regina Casé, Lima Duarte, Stênio Garcia. **2000 DVD**

MEAN GUNS ★★★ In this bizarre but undeniably lively futuristic thriller, a hundred violent felons are taken to an abandoned prison, armed with baseball bats and guns, and told that $10 million will be divided up among three of them—the last three survivors. Rated R for violence and profanity. **DIR:** Albert Pyun. **CAST:** Christopher Lambert, Ice T, Kimberly Warren. **1997 DVD**

MEAN JOHNNY BARROWS 🦃 Fred Williamson plays a Vietnam war hero, dishonorably discharged for striking an officer. Rated R. 80m. **DIR:** Fred Williamson. **CAST:** Fred Williamson, Roddy McDowall, Stuart Whitman, Elliott Gould. **1976**

MEAN SEASON, THE ★★★1/2 Miami crime reporter Kurt Russell finds himself the unwilling confidant of a maniacal killer in this exciting thriller. The film occasionally relies on stock shocks. Still, it is fast-paced and inventive enough to overcome the clichés. Rated R for violence. 109m. **DIR:** Phillip Borsos. **CAST:** Kurt Russell, Richard Jordan, Mariel Hemingway, Richard Masur. **1985**

MEAN STREAK ★★ Suspense thriller strikes out due to clumsy plotting and tired performances. Scott Bakula plays a bigoted maverick cop forced to team up with black FBI agent Leon in order to find a serial killer intent on stopping a baseball player from breaking a record. Contrived every step of the way. The script, filled with every cliché in the book, gets no help from Tim Hunter's sluggish direction. Made for television. Rated R for violence. 97m. **DIR:** Tim Hunter. **CAST:** Scott Bakula, Leon, Bridgid Coulter, Howard Dell. **1999**

MEAN STREAK ★★ A thoroughly predictable and completely lackluster cop drama is given some extra juice by making its central character (Scott Bakula) something of a racist, and then forcing him to team up with a black partner; the resulting interaction isn't nearly as provocative as writers David F. Ryan and John Fasano intended. Television police shows tell better stories, and they're also better directed. Rated R for violence, profanity, nudity, and simulated sex. 97m. **DIR:** Tim Hunter. **CAST:** Scott Bakula, Leon, Bridgid Coulter, Ron McLarty, Howard Dell. **1999**

MEAN STREETS ★★★★1/2 This impressive film by director Martin Scorsese has criminal realism and explosive violence. Robert De Niro gives a high-energy performance as a ghetto psycho in New York's Little Italy who insults a Mafia loan shark by avoiding payment. He then rips off the friend who tries to save him. This study of street life at its most savage is a cult favorite. Rated R. 110m. **DIR:** Martin Scorsese. **CAST:** Robert De Niro, Harvey Keitel, Amy Robinson, Robert Carradine, David Carradine. **1973 DVD**

MEANEST MAN IN THE WORLD, THE ★★★1/2 Jack Benny's best picture. He plays a lawyer who can't win a case, and decides the only way to get ahead in the world is to be rotten to people. The film is good satire that still holds true, and Benny plays the role to the hilt. B&W; 57m. **DIR:** Sidney Lanfield. **CAST:** Jack Benny, Priscilla Lane, Eddie "Rochester" Anderson, Edmund Gwenn, Anne Revere, Tor Johnson. **1943**

MEANTIME ★★★★ British filmmaker Mike Leigh's drama about life under Thatcherism may be a bit vague to American audiences who aren't familiar with the issues involved. But it is typically well acted, especially Tim Roth as a slow-witted unemployed youth and Gary Oldman as his skinhead friend (it was the film debut of both). Made for British television. Not rated; contains mature themes and profanity. 103m. **DIR:** Mike Leigh. **CAST:** Marion Bailey, Phil Daniels, Tim Roth, Gary Oldman, Pam Ferris, Alfred Molina. **1983 DVD**

•MEAT LOAF: TO HELL AND BACK ★★★★ Terrific dramatization of rock singer Meat Loaf's autobiography, which covers his tumultuous youth, his quest for rock stardom, and the peaks and valleys he faced when he finally got to the top. Honest, eye-opening and very well made. Features original songs performed by Meat Loaf. Rated PG-13 for substance abuse and brief violence. 90m. **DIR:** Jim McBride. **CAST:** W. Earl Brown, Dedee Pfeiffer, Zachary Thorne. **2000**

MEATBALLS ★★★1/2 Somehow, this *Animal House*–style comedy's disjointedness is easier to swallow than it should be. Elmer Bernstein's music gets sentimental in the right places, and star Bill Murray is fun to watch. Rated PG. 92m. **DIR:** Ivan Reitman. **CAST:** Bill Murray, Harvey Atkin, Kate Lynch, Chris Makepeace. **1979 DVD**

MEATBALLS PART II 🦃 Pitifully unfunny high jinks at summer camp. Rated PG for sexual references. 87m. **DIR:** Ken Wiederhorn. **CAST:** Richard Mulligan, Kim Richards, John Mengatti, Misty Rowe. **1984**

MEATBALLS III 🦃 Lousy. Rated R for nudity, profanity, and suggested sex. 94m. **DIR:** George Mendeluk. **CAST:** Sally Kellerman, Patrick Dempsey, Al Waxman, Shannon Tweed. **1987**

MEATBALLS 4 🦃 Hey kids, it's the old let's-save-the-summer-camp scenario one more time. Boring. Rated R for nudity and language. 84m. **DIR:** Bob Logan. **CAST:** Corey Feldman, Jack Nance, Sarah Douglas. **1992**

MECHANIC, THE ★★1/2 A professional hit man (Charles Bronson) teaches his craft to a young student (Jan-Michael Vincent). Slow-moving for the most part, with a few good action scenes. Rated R for violence and language. 100m. **DIR:** Michael Winner. **CAST:** Charles Bronson, Jan-Michael Vincent, Jill Ireland, Keenan Wynn. **1972**

MEDEA ★★★★ Maria Callas enacts the title role in this film adaptation of Euripides' tragedy. The diva is an exciting screen presence. In Italian with English subtitles. Rated R for nudity and violence. 100m. **DIR:** Pier Paolo Pasolini. **CAST:** Maria Callas. **1970**

MEDICINE HAT STALLION, THE ★★ Decent TV movie about a young lad (Leif Garrett) who, with the help of Indian Chief Red Cloud (Ned Romero), runs off to join the Pony Express. Well acted, but overlong, and the commercial breaks are jarring and obvious. 85m. **DIR:** Michael O'Herlihy. **CAST:** Leif Garrett, Mitchell Ryan, Bibi Besch, John Anderson, Charles Tyner, John Quade, Milo O'Shea, Ned Romero. **1977**

MEDICINE MAN ★★★ For those of us who could derive enjoyment in watching Sean Connery in a dog-food commercial, this muddled adventure-drama will do just

fine. While one would expect better from director John McTiernan, there's not much even Howard Hawks could do with this "politically correct" story about a crotchety scientist who finds and then loses a cure for cancer in the threatened rain forests of Brazil. Rated PG-13 for violence and profanity. 104m. **DIR:** John McTiernan. **CAST:** Sean Connery, Lorraine Bracco, José Wilker. **1992 DVD**

MEDICINE RIVER ★★1/2 Amiable comedy about a photojournalist named Will, a Blackfeet Indian who returns home to Medicine River after a twenty-year absence to attend his mother's funeral. Set in his ways, Will becomes involved with a rascal named Harlen Bigbear, who helps him regain his lost identity. Good cast, interesting situations, and sense of self-discovery make this Canadian import worth a look. Rated PG. 96m. **DIR:** Stuart Margolin. **CAST:** Graham Greene, Tom Jackson, Sheila Tousey, Jimmy Herman, Raul Trujillo. **1992**

MEDITERRANEO ★★★★ In 1941, several misfit soldiers arrive on a Greek isle. The men, none very gung ho about their mission, are to hold and protect the island for Mussolini and the cause of fascism. A pleasant, bittersweet fable. In Italian with English subtitles. Not rated; the film has profanity and nudity. 90m. **DIR:** Gabriele Salvatores. **CAST:** Diego Abatantuono, Claudio Biagli, Giuseppi Cederna, Claudio Bisio. **1991**

MEDIUM COOL ★★★★1/2 Robert Forster stars as a television news cameraman in Chicago during the 1968 Democratic convention. All the political themes of the 1960s are here—many scenes were filmed during the riots. Cinematographer Haskell Wexler's first try at directing is a winner. Highly recommended. Rated R for nudity and language. 110m. **DIR:** Haskell Wexler. **CAST:** Robert Forster, Verna Bloom, Peter Bonerz. **1969 DVD**

MEDUSA TOUCH, THE ★★★ Born with the power to kill by will, Richard Burton goes completely out of control after someone almost beats him to death. This is a strange, disturbing film. Burton is effective, but Lee Remick is out of place as his psychiatrist. Rated R. 110m. **DIR:** Jack Gold. **CAST:** Richard Burton, Lee Remick, Gordon Jackson, Lino Ventura, Harry Andrews. **1978**

MEET DANNY WILSON ★★1/2 A low-grade Frank Sinatra vehicle with old standards instead of new songs. The story is old hat as well. Sinatra is the singer who falls in love with his mobster boss's girlfriend. B&W; 86m. **DIR:** Joseph Pevney. **CAST:** Frank Sinatra, Raymond Burr, Shelley Winters, Alex Nicol. **1952**

MEET DR. CHRISTIAN ★★ Folksy Jean Hersholt enacts the title role, meeting and besting medical crisis after medical crisis, in this first of six films translated from the popular 1930s radio series. B&W; 63m. **DIR:** Bernard Vorhaus. **CAST:** Jean Hersholt, Dorothy Lovett, Robert Baldwin, Paul Harvey, Marcia Mae Jones, Jackie Moran. **1939**

MEET JOE BLACK ★★★1/2 This provocative remake of 1934's *Death Takes a Holiday* is nearly undone by its absurd length. That said, viewers cannot help being intrigued by the premise: Death Incarnate, en route to collecting another mortal whose time on Earth has come to an end, allows himself to be distracted by fleshly concerns. Wanting to better understand earthly motivations, Death takes human form and, thus concealed, walks among us. Complications ensue when Death falls in love with his host's daughter but great human truths are at the heart of what follows. Rated PG-13 for profanity and sensuality. 180m. **DIR:** Martin Brest. **CAST:** Brad Pitt, Anthony Hopkins, Claire Forlani, Jake Webber, Marcia Gay Harden, Jeffrey Tambor. **1998 DVD**

MEET JOHN DOE ★★★★ A penniless drifter (Gary Cooper) gets caught up in a newspaper publicity stunt. He is groomed and presented as the spokesman of the common man by powerful men who manipulate his every action for their own purposes. When he finally resists, he is exposed as a fraud. His fellow common men turn against him, or do they? Barbara Stanwyck is the newspaperwoman who first uses him and with whom he predictably falls in love. B&W; 132m. **DIR:** Frank Capra. **CAST:** Gary Cooper, Barbara Stanwyck, Walter Brennan, Spring Byington. **1941 DVD**

MEET ME IN LAS VEGAS ★★1/2 Dan Dailey romances ballerina Cyd Charisse in this inoffensive time killer. A number of star cameos (Paul Henreid, Lena Horne, Frankie Laine, Jerry Colonna) add some fun, but the film is more belly flop than big splash. 112m. **DIR:** Roy Rowland. **CAST:** Dan Dailey, Cyd Charisse, Agnes Moorehead, Lili Darvas, Jim Backus. **1956**

MEET ME IN ST. LOUIS ★★★★ Here's a fun-filled entertainment package made at the MGM studios during the heyday of their musicals. This nostalgic look at a family in St. Louis before the 1903 World's Fair dwells on the tension when the father announces an impending transfer to New York. Judy Garland's songs remain fresh and enjoyable today. 112m. **DIR:** Vincente Minnelli. **CAST:** Judy Garland, Margaret O'Brien, Tom Drake. **1944**

MEET THE APPLEGATES A family of insects disguised as humans. Rated R for profanity and sexual themes. 90m. **DIR:** Michael Lehmann. **CAST:** Ed Begley Jr., Stockard Channing, Bobby Jacoby, Dabney Coleman. **1989**

MEET THE DEEDLES ★★ Twin surfer dudes with saltwater for brains are sent to a Wyoming summer boot camp by their filthy-rich father for a taste of discipline. They escape from the camp commander's pickup truck and are mistaken for rookie female park rangers who are en route to save Yellowstone Park from a prairie dog infestation. They then uncover a plot by a deranged former ranger to harness Old Faithful as his own theme park. Rated PG. 96m. **DIR:** Steve Boyum. **CAST:** Paul Walker, Steve Van Wormer, A. J. Langer, Dennis Hopper, John Ashton, Eric Braeden. **1998**

MEET THE FEEBLES ★★★ Like his early gore epics *Bad Taste* and *Dead Alive*, this Peter Jackson film is bound to offend at least someone. Essentially this is a raunchy version of the Muppets. Onstage they are cute and fuzzy. Offstage they are anything but. Highly over the top. Not rated; contains violence, profanity, gore, and simulated sex. 96m. **DIR:** Peter Jackson. **1989 DVD**

MEET THE HOLLOWHEADS ★★ Five minutes of introduction would have saved viewers the first twenty minutes of confusion as we enter the lives of a family living in an unknown place and at an undisclosed time. Things don't really pick up until Mr. Hollowhead brings his villainous boss home to dinner. Rated PG-13 for sexual innuendo and gore. 87m. **DIR:** Tom Burman. **CAST:** John

Glover, Nancy Mette, Richard Portnow, Anne Ramsey. **1988**

MEET THE NAVY ★★★ This British musical fell into obscurity because the cast contains no star names. That's because they're all from the Royal Canadian Navy revue, a troupe of drafted performers. However, there are enough talented singers, dancers, and funnymen here to make you wonder why none went on to greater success. B&W; 81m. **DIR:** Alfred Travers. **CAST:** Lionel Murton, Margaret Hurst. **1946**

MEET THE PARENTS ★★★★ Hilarious spoof zooms in on the painful introduction of a suitor (Ben Stiller) to his future in-laws. Robert De Niro is marvelous as the former CIA agent/father who goes to great lengths, including lie-detector tests and video monitors, to discredit Stiller. Stiller's position as the outsider occasionally warrants more tears than laughter. Rated PG-13 for adult situations and language. 108m. **DIR:** Jay Roach. **CAST:** Ben Stiller, Robert De Niro, Teri Polo, Blythe Danner. **2000 DVD**

MEET WALLY SPARKS ★★ In this spoof of talk TV, Rodney Dangerfield plays an outrageous show host who ends up staying with the governor who wants him off TV. Parade of talk-show hosts make cameo appearances. There's also a parade of situation-comedy stars. Sexual wisecracks are tiresome, but other genuinely funny scenes make the film bearable. Rated R for language and sexual situations. 102m. **DIR:** Peter Baldwin. **CAST:** Rodney Dangerfield, David Ogden Stiers, Debi Mazar, Cindy Williams, Burt Reynolds, Alan Rachins. **1996 DVD**

MEETING AT MIDNIGHT 🦃 Flat, dark, dreary *Charlie Chan* programmer from the Monogram Pictures period. Charlie investigates fortune tellers and mediums. A bore. B&W; 67m. **DIR:** Phil Rosen. **CAST:** Sidney Toler, Mantan Moreland, Frances Chan. **1944**

MEETING VENUS ★★1/2 Glenn Close enters the rarefied air of opera for a romantic film in the tradition of Ingrid Bergman's high-class romance, *Intermezzo*. She plays a world-class diva who falls hard for her conductor during the hectic rehearsals for a Parisian production of *Tannhauser*. The film, however, frequently has more in common with soap opera than grand opera. Rated PG-13. 120m. **DIR:** István Szabó. **CAST:** Glenn Close, Neils Arestrup. **1991**

MEETINGS WITH REMARKABLE MEN ★★★★ The quest for spiritual truth and self-realization by Russian philosopher G. I. Gurdjieff (Dragan Maksimovic) is the subject of this intriguing work. Director Peter Brook concentrates on Gurdjieff's early days. Not rated. 102m. **DIR:** Peter Brook. **CAST:** Dragan Maksimovic, Mikica Dimitrijevic, Terence Stamp, Athol Fugard, Gerry Sundquist, Warren Mitchell. **1979**

MEGAFORCE 🦃 Dull sci-fi adventure about a rapid-deployment defense unit that galvanizes into action whenever freedom is threatened. PG for no discernible reason. 99m. **DIR:** Hal Needham. **CAST:** Barry Bostwick, Michael Beck, Persis Khambatta, Henry Silva. **1982**

MEGAVILLE ★★ In the world of the future, intimacy is reviled, openness is frowned upon, and commercial TV is a capital offense. Enter Megaville, a television-free zone that the government must send an experimental supersoldier to eliminate. An overblown plot. Rated R for violence, profanity, and nudity. 96m. **DIR:** Peter Lehner. **CAST:** Billy Zane, J. C. Quinn, Grace Zabriskie, Daniel J. Travanti. **1991**

MELANIE ★★★ This drama about an illiterate Arkansas woman trying to regain custody of her son from her ex-husband in California is full of clichés but works anyway thanks to sincere direction and performances. Singer Burton Cummings plays a washed-up rock star who helps Melanie and is redeemed in the process; he also contributed the musical score. Not rated, but the equivalent of a PG-13. 109m. **DIR:** Rex Bromfield. **CAST:** Glynnis O'Connor, Burton Cummings, Paul Sorvino, Don Johnson. **1982**

MELO ★★★ An offering of quiet, subtle charms, one of those typically French chamber romances in which small gestures or glances speak volumes. It's a straightforward exploration of a romantic triangle, set in the world of contemporary classical music, and features a memorable, César-winning performance by Sabine Azema. In French with English subtitles. 112m. **DIR:** Alain Resnais. **CAST:** Sabine Azema, Pierre Arditi, Fanny Ardant, André Dussolier. **1988**

MELODIE EN SOUS-SOL (THE BIG GRAB) (ANY NUMBER CAN WIN) ★★★ Fresh from prison, aging gangster Jean Gabin makes intricate and elaborate plans to score big by robbing a major Riviera gambling casino. Alain Delon joins him in conniving their way to the casino vault by seducing a showgirl to gain vital backstage access. Gabin, as the cool, experienced ex-convict, and Delon, as his young, upstart, eager partner, are part-perfect. In French with English subtitles. B&W; 118m. **DIR:** Henri Verneuil. **CAST:** Jean Gabin, Alain Delon, Viviane Romance, Carla Marlier. **1963 DVD**

MELODY ★★ A cute story, completely destroyed by montage after montage set to a musical score by the Bee Gees. Not enough dialogue here to carry this innocent tale about two 10-year-olds who fall in love and decide to get married. Slow. 130m. **DIR:** Waris Hussein. **CAST:** Jack Wild, Mark Lester, Tracy Hyde, Roy Kinnear, Kate Williams, Ken Jones. **1972**

MELODY CRUISE ★★1/2 Two millionaires enjoy cruising with a bevy of willing babes. All goes well until the bachelor (Charlie Ruggles) falls hard for a sweet little schoolmarm. This dated romp has its moments. B&W; 75m. **DIR:** Mark Sandrich. **CAST:** Charlie Ruggles, Phil Harris, Helen Mack. **1933**

MELODY FOR THREE ★★ In the last (and weakest) of the Dr. Christian movies, the compassionate MD branches out into psychology by restoring a family torn apart by divorce. Gratuitous musical numbers only make this short feature seem longer than it is. 67m. **DIR:** Erle C. Kenton. **CAST:** Jean Hersholt, Fay Wray, Irene Ryan. **1941**

MELODY MASTER (THE GREAT AWAKENING) (NEW WINE) ★★ This film is another one in a long line of tortured-composer melodramas. Alan Curtis gives a bland portrayal of Franz Schubert. There are some good comedy spots supplied by Binnie Barnes and Billy Gilbert. B&W; 80m. **DIR:** Reinhold Schunzel. **CAST:** Alan Curtis, Ilona Massey, Albert Basserman, Binnie Barnes, Billy Gilbert, Sterling Holloway, John Qualen, Sig Arno, Forrest Tucker. **1941**

MELODY RANCH ★★1/2 The creative forces at Republic Studios decided to team Gene Autry with Jimmy Durante and Ann Miller, replace Smiley Burnette with

Gabby Hayes, and pretend nothing was different. Venerable heavy Barton MacLane provides the menace as a local gangster intent on running honorary sheriff Gene Autry out of town, but there isn't enough action. B&W; 80m. **DIR:** Joseph Santley. **CAST:** Gene Autry, Jimmy Durante, Ann Miller, Barton MacLane, George "Gabby" Hayes. **1940**

MELODY TRAIL ★★1/2 The fifth Gene Autry–Smiley Burnette film is a pleasant story about a rodeo rider who loses his winnings and is forced to work for a rancher with a romantic daughter. B&W; 60m. **DIR:** Joseph Kane. **CAST:** Gene Autry, Smiley Burnette, Ann Rutherford. **1935**

MELVIN AND HOWARD ★★★★★ This brilliantly directed slice-of-life film works marvelously well on two levels. On the surface, it's the entertaining tale of how Melvin Dummar (Paul LeMat) met Howard Hughes (Jason Robards)—or did he? Underneath, it's a hilarious spoof of our society. Mary Steenburgen costars in this triumph of American filmmaking, a rare gem that deserves to be seen and talked about. Rated R. 95m. **DIR:** Jonathan Demme. **CAST:** Paul LeMat, Jason Robards Jr., Mary Steenburgen, Pamela Reed. **1980 DVD**

MELVIN PURVIS: G-MAN ★★★ In the tradition of the Warner Bros. gangster films of the Thirties, Melvin Purvis (Dale Robertson) holds nothing back in this fictionalized account of the all-consuming search for Machine Gun Kelly. Wild and fast-paced, this made-for-TV film is exciting and entertaining. 78m. **DIR:** Dan Curtis. **CAST:** Dale Robertson, Harris Yulin, Margaret Blye, Dick Sargent. **1974**

MEMBER OF THE WEDDING, THE ★★★★ Julie Harris plays an awkward 12-year-old who is caught between being a child and growing up. She yearns to belong and decides to join her brother and his bride on their honeymoon. Her total introversion allows her to ignore the needs of her motherly nanny (brilliantly played by Ethel Waters) and her loyal cousin (Brandon de Wilde). Depressing but riveting. B&W; 91m. **DIR:** Fred Zinnemann. **CAST:** Julie Harris, Ethel Waters, Brandon de Wilde, Arthur Franz. **1953**

MEMBER OF THE WEDDING, THE ★★★ Carson McCullers's novel emerges as a peculiar film, rendered almost boring by its heavy reliance on dialogue, and our inability to empathize with the self-centered adolescent girl who draws her excitement vicariously. Anna Paquin establishes a presence as this precocious lass, but her performance is too mannered to seem genuine. Rated PG for mild profanity. 95m. **DIR:** Fielder Cook. **CAST:** Alfre Woodard, Anna Paquin, Corey Dunn, Enrico Colantoni, Anne Tremko, Pat Hingle. **1996**

•MEMENTO ★★★★ This artfully structured thriller begins with a Polaroid snapshot of blood-splattered tiles that fades and gets sucked back into its camera. It ends with an ambiguous twist to a murder mystery. In between, each scene of this sort of back-to-the-future crime story ends where the previous scene began in a tidal regression and progression of story and character. A one-sided phone conversation (filmed in black-and-white) bridges the scenes as an insurance investigator handicapped by the loss of his short-term memory tries to track down his wife's killer. Rated R for language, violence, and drug use. 116m. **DIR:** Christopher Nolan. **CAST:** Guy Pearce, Carrie-Anne Moss, Joe Pantoliano. **2000 DVD**

MEMOIRS OF AN INVISIBLE MAN ★★★★ Terrific special effects and inventive comedy combine to make this adaptation of the book by H. F. Saint much more than just another Chevy Chase vehicle. Chase plays an executive who turns invisible as the result of a freak accident, and finds himself pursued by a ruthless spy (Sam Neill). Thanks to top-notch direction by John Carpenter, plenty of suspense and excitement. Rated PG-13, for violence and nudity. 99m. **DIR:** John Carpenter. **CAST:** Chevy Chase, Daryl Hannah, Sam Neill, Michael McKean, Stephen Tobolowsky. **1992**

MEMORIAL DAY ★★★ Made-for-TV movie with stirring, sensitive performances by Mike Farrell, Robert Walden, and Edward Hermann. Farrell portrays a successful attorney who has a reunion with his former Vietnam combat buddies. The reunion awakens painful memories and a dark secret. Shelley Fabares plays Farrell's psychologist wife. Rated PG. 95m. **DIR:** Joseph Sargent. **CAST:** Mike Farrell, Shelley Fabares, Robert Walden, Edward Herrmann, Danny Glover, Bonnie Bedelia. **1988**

MEMORIES OF A MARRIAGE ★★★★ Sensitive film allows a mild-mannered husband to reflect on his married life through a series of revealing flashbacks. In each scene, his wife is passionate, stubborn, or charitable—but never lukewarm. In Danish with English subtitles. Not rated, contains mature themes. 90m. **DIR:** Kaspar Rostrup. **CAST:** Ghita Norby, Frits Helmuth, Rikke Bendsen, Henning Moritzen. **1989**

MEMORIES OF ME ★★ A New York doctor (Billy Crystal) has a heart attack and decides to reevaluate his priorities as well as his stormy relationship with his father (Alan King). Rated PG-13 for profanity and adult situations. 104m. **DIR:** Henry Winkler. **CAST:** Billy Crystal, Alan King, JoBeth Williams. **1988**

MEMORIES OF MURDER ★★ A wealthy Seattle socialite wakes up one morning to find she has been leading an alternate life for two years. 94m. **DIR:** Robert Lewis. **CAST:** Nancy Allen, Vanity, Robin Thomas, Olivia Brown, Donald Davis. **1990**

MEMORIES OF UNDERDEVELOPMENT ★★★ In the early 1960s, a Europeanized Cuban intellectual too lazy to leave Miami and too eccentric to fit into Cuban society engages in a passionate sexual affair with a beautiful young woman. A scathing satire on sex and politics. In Spanish with English subtitles. B&W; 97m. **DIR:** Tomas Gutierrez Alea. **CAST:** Sergio Corrieri. **1968**

MEMPHIS ★★★ Engrossing thriller follows the kidnapping of the son of a black banker by three whites in the 1950s. Film boasts strong performances and a real eye for period detail. Made for cable. 93m. **DIR:** Yves Simoneau. **CAST:** Cybill Shepherd, J. E. Freeman, Richard Brooks, Moses Gunn. **1992**

MEMPHIS BELLE ★★★★ This spectacular British-American production about U.S. pilots in World War II was based on the 1943 documentary made during the war by Hollywood director William Wyler. The story concerns the twenty-fifth and final mission of the crew of the Memphis Belle, a giant B17 bomber that was known as a flying fortress in its day. Top-flight. Rated PG-13 for brief profanity and violence. 101m. **DIR:** Michael Caton-Jones. **CAST:** Matthew Modine, Eric Stoltz, Tate

Donovan, D. B. Sweeney, Billy Zane, Sean Astin, Harry Connick Jr., Courtney Gains, John Lithgow, David Strathairn. **1990 DVD**

MEN, THE (1950) ★★★★ Marlon Brando's first film, this is about a paralyzed World War II vet trying to deal with his injury. A sensitive script and good acting make this film a classic. Better than *Coming Home* in depicting vets' feelings and attitudes about readjusting to society. B&W; 85m. **DIR:** Fred Zinnemann. **CAST:** Marlon Brando, Jack Webb, Teresa Wright. **1950**

MEN . . . (1985) ★★★★ In this tongue-in-cheek anthropological study by German writer-director Doris Dörrie, a hotshot advertising executive, who has been having a fling with his secretary, is outraged to discover that his wife has a lover. Devastated at first, he finally decides to get even, and his revenge is one of the most inventive and hilarious ever to grace the screen. In German with English subtitles. Not rated; the film has profanity. 99m. **DIR:** Doris Dörrie. **CAST:** Uwe Ochsenknecht, Ulrike Kriener, Heiner Lauterbach. **1985**

MEN (1997) ★★1/2 Sean Young turns in a strong, sexy performance as a woman bored with her dreary New York existence and alcoholic, impotent boyfriend. As Stella, Young gets her groove back when she jets to Los Angeles and encounters numerous eccentric characters, both givers and takers. Director Zoe Clarke-Williams is obviously trying for something more serious than the usual straight-to-video sex drama, and she almost always succeeds. Rated R for language, nudity, and adult situations. 93m. **DIR:** Zoe Clarke-Williams. **CAST:** Sean Young, Dylan Walsh, Richard Hillman, Karen Black, John Heard. **1997 DVD**

MEN AT WORK ★★ Cool garbagemen discover a nefarious plot to pollute the environment in what is best described as *Police Academy Meets Big Green*. Better luck next time, boys! Rated PG-13 for violence and profanity. 98m. **DIR:** Emilio Estevez. **CAST:** Charlie Sheen, Emilio Estevez, Leslie Hope, Keith David, Dean Cameron, John Getz. **1990**

MEN DON'T LEAVE ★★★★ Jessica Lange struggles to raise two precocious sons after their father dies in a freak accident. The death of a loved one is no laughing matter—unless we're referring to this remarkable movie from Paul Brickman, who waited six years after hitting it big with *Risky Business* to make his second film. Rated PG-13 for adult themes. 120m. **DIR:** Paul Brickman. **CAST:** Jessica Lange, Arliss Howard, Joan Cusack, Tom Mason, Kathy Bates. **1990**

MEN IN BLACK ★★★★1/2 This science-fiction-comedy, about an unofficial government agency that regulates and polices the secret immigration of outer-space aliens living on Earth, is an enticing romp based on a little-known comic-book series. Tommy Lee Jones is the ultimate straight man, playing against Will Smith, a darling of contemporary cinema. One of the most flat-out entertaining films of the decade. The only reason it doesn't deserve five stars is because, well, it isn't quite on the level of *Citizen Kane*. Rated PG-13 for language and violence. 98m. **DIR:** Barry Sonnenfeld. **CAST:** Tommy Lee Jones, Will Smith, Linda Fiorentino, Vincent D'Onofrio, Rip Torn, Tony Shalhoub. **1997 DVD**

MEN IN LOVE ★★★1/2 Shot on video, this film presents a human, honest approach to the subject of AIDS. Sensitive, inspiring tale of a gay man who returns his lover's ashes to Hawaii for dispersal. There he meets his lover's friends, who console him. 87m. **DIR:** Marc Huestis. **CAST:** Doug Self, Joe Tolbe, Emerald Starr. **1990**

MEN IN WAR ★★★★ This outstanding Korean War action film with Robert Ryan and Aldo Ray fighting the Chinese and each other is one of the very best "war is hell" films. B&W; 104m. **DIR:** Anthony Mann. **CAST:** Robert Ryan, Aldo Ray, Vic Morrow. **1957 DVD**

MEN OF BOYS TOWN ★★★ Spencer Tracy and Mickey Rooney are back again as Father Flanagan and Whitey Marsh in this sentimental sequel to MGM's *Boys Town*. Here a completely reformed Rooney is involved in rehabilitating kids and raising the money to keep the institution operating. Good family entertainment. B&W; 107m. **DIR:** Norman Taurog. **CAST:** Spencer Tracy, Mickey Rooney, Bobs Watson, Larry Nunn, Darryl Hickman, Lee J. Cobb, Mary Nash. **1941**

MEN OF HONOR ★★1/2 Cuba Gooding Jr. plays real-life hero Carl Brashear, first African American in the U.S. Navy's elite diving corps, with Robert De Niro as a fictitious redneck instructor whose bigotry he must overcome. Performances are grimly earnest, but the lengthy film has too many climaxes too far apart, and the men's respective wives don't get much to do. Rated R for profanity. 129m. **DIR:** George Tillman Jr. **CAST:** Robert De Niro, Cuba Gooding Jr., Michael Rapaport, Charlize Theron, Aunjanue Ellis, Hal Holbrook. **2000 DVD**

MEN OF RESPECT ★★ With Francis Ford Coppola making *The Godfather Part III* into a gangster version of Shakespeare's *King Lear*, it probably made sense to writer-director William Reilly to adapt *Macbeth* for a similarly styled film. Unlike Coppola's majestic movie, however, *Men of Respect* is dreary, overacted, and overwrought. Rated R for violence, profanity, and nudity. 122m. **DIR:** William Reilly. **CAST:** John Turturro, Katherine Borowitz, Dennis Farina, Peter Boyle, Rod Steiger, Lilia Skala, Steven Wright, Stanley Tucci. **1991**

MEN OF SHERWOOD FOREST ★★ The inspirational saga of nobleman-turned-outlaw receives scant embellishment in this ho-hum addition to the Robin Hood canon. Produced by fledgling Hammer Studios hard on the heels of the popular Walt Disney feature and the syndicated Richard Greene television show. 77m. **DIR:** Val Guest. **CAST:** Don Taylor, Reginald Beckwith. **1954**

MEN OF THE FIGHTING LADY ★★★1/2 Based on two separate factual articles for the *Saturday Evening Post* by James Michener and Navy Commander Harry A. Burns, this story of a jet fighter squadron off the coast of Korea was fashioned to fit Van Johnson. Exciting battle scenes. Not rated. 80m. **DIR:** Andrew Marton. **CAST:** Van Johnson, Walter Pidgeon, Louis Calhern, Dewey Martin, Keenan Wynn, Frank Lovejoy, Robert Horton. **1954**

MEN OF WAR ★★★ OK action film stars muscle-bound Dolph Lundgren as a mercenary assigned to "convince" a group of islanders it's time to move to the mainland (so greedy developers can exploit the island's abundance of guano). Lundgren, however, winds up befriending the islanders and coming to their defense. Lots of action and machismo make up for lack of story. Rated R for violence and profanity. 102m. **DIR:** Perry Lang. **CAST:** Dolph Lundgren, Charlotte Lewis, B. D.

Wong, Anthony Denison, Tom "Tiny" Lister Jr., Kevin Tighe, Perry Lang. **1994 DVD**

MEN WITH GUNS ★★1/2 A widowed, wealthy physician in a nameless Latin-American country sets off to visit his old students in rural villages and finds the countryside awash in persecution and murder. An abandoned boy, an army deserter, and a defrocked priest join him on the journey. This laborious, slow-paced drama about the sociopolitical toll of ignorance, denial, and government-supported brutality is haunting but repetitious. In Spanish, English, and Indian dialects with English subtitles. Rated R for language and violence. 128m. **DIR:** John Sayles. **CAST:** Federico Luppi, Damian Delgado, Dan Rivera Gonzales, Tania Cruz, Damian Alcazar. **1998**

MENACE ON THE MOUNTAIN ★★1/2 This lesser Disney coming-of-age film features Mitch Vogel as a spunky 14-year-old forced to become the man of the house. While his Confederate dad fights the Yankees during the Civil War, Vogel must face thieving deserters who threaten his family. The plot is weak, the dialogue insipid. Not rated; contains violence. 89m. **DIR:** Vincent McEveety. **CAST:** Mitch Vogel, Pat Crowley, Albert Salmi, Charles Aidman. **1970**

MENACE II SOCIETY ★★★★ Sobering, insightful film about the horrors of inner-city life focuses on the moral crisis confronting a teenage gang member who attempts to turn his life around with the help of a no-nonsense teacher and a straitlaced young woman. The filmmakers and actors do an excellent job of showing the audience the predicaments, pressure, and prejudices that can turn a basically decent kid into a cold-blooded killer. Powerful stuff. Rated R for violence, profanity, and simulated sex. 104m. **DIR:** Allen Hughes, Albert Hughes. **CAST:** Tyrin Turner, Jada Pinkett, Larenz Tate, Bill Duke, Charles Dutton, Samuel L. Jackson, Glenn Plummer. **1993 DVD**

MÉNAGE ★★★ Two down-and-outers (Michel Blanc and Miou-Miou) are taken in by a flamboyant thief (Gérard Depardieu), who introduces them to a life of crime and kinky sex in this alternately hilarious and mean-spirited comedy. The first half of this bizarre work is enjoyable, but the acceptance of the last part will depend on the taste—and tolerance—of the viewer. In French with English subtitles. Not rated; the film has profanity, violence, nudity, and simulated sex. 84m. **DIR:** Bertrand Blier. **CAST:** Gérard Depardieu, Michel Blanc, Miou-Miou, Bruno Cremer. **1986**

MEN'S CLUB, THE ★★★ Fine performances by an all-star cast in this offbeat and disturbing film about a boy's night out that is turned into an exploration of men's attitudes toward women. The changes remain hidden inside the characters, although we can guess what has happened by their actions. Rated R for nudity, profanity, suggested sex, and violence. 93m. **DIR:** Peter Medak. **CAST:** Roy Scheider, Frank Langella, Harvey Keitel, Treat Williams, Richard Jordan, David Dukes, Craig Wasson, Stockard Channing, Ann Wedgeworth, Jennifer Jason Leigh, Cindy Pickett. **1986**

MEPHISTO ★★★★★ Winner of the 1981 Academy Award for best foreign-language film, this brilliant movie, by Hungarian writer-director Istvan Szabo, examines the conceits of artists with devastating honesty and insight. Klaus Maria Brandauer, in a stunning performance, plays an actor whose overwhelming desire for artistic success leads to his becoming a puppet of the Nazi government. The film has nudity and violence. In German with English subtitles. 135m. **DIR:** István Szabó. **CAST:** Klaus Maria Brandauer, Krystyna Janda. **1981 DVD**

MEPHISTO WALTZ, THE ★★ Satanism and the transfer of souls are at the heart of this needlessly wordy and laughably atmospheric chiller. The thin material—and the viewer's patience—are stretched about twenty minutes too long. Rated R for violence. 108m. **DIR:** Paul Wendkos. **CAST:** Alan Alda, Jacqueline Bisset, Curt Jurgens. **1971**

MERCENARY 🦃 The muddled script and direction don't help an overacting John Ritter as a billionaire who wages war against a Middle East terrorist (Martin Kove in thick pancake makeup and thicker phony accent). Rated R for profanity, violence, and nudity. 97m. **DIR:** Avi Nesher. **CAST:** John Ritter, Olivier Gruner, Robert Culp, Ed Lauter, Martin Kove. **1996**

MERCENARY FIGHTERS ★★ U.S. mercenaries (Peter Fonda and company) are hired to get rid of tribesmen who are blocking the building of a new dam. When they discover the dam would force the tribe off its homeland, the mercenaries begin to fight among themselves. The actors took some heat for participating in this film, which was made in South Africa and the results are certainly nothing you'd want to put your career on the line for. 91m. **DIR:** Riki Shelach. **CAST:** Peter Fonda, Reb Brown, Ron O'Neal, Jim Mitchum, Robert DoQui. **1986**

MERCENARY 2: THICK AND THIN 🦃 Some movies beg for a sequel. *Mercenary* wasn't one of them. Rated R for adult situations, language, and violence. 100m. **DIR:** Philippe Mora. **CAST:** Olivier Gruner, Robert Townsend, Claudia Christian, Nicholas Turturro. **1997**

MERCHANT OF FOUR SEASONS, THE ★★ Melodramatic character study about a fruit peddler who drinks himself to death. This slice-of-life soap opera gone amok lacks emotional power. In German with English subtitles. Not rated; contains nudity and profanity. 88m. **DIR:** Rainer Werner Fassbinder. **CAST:** Irm Hermann, Hanna Schygulla. **1972**

MERCI LA VIE ★★ Even one of France's greatest filmmakers, Bertrand Blier, is entitled to an occasional miscue. This saga of two young women on an odyssey of self-discovery is often aimless, frequently enigmatic, and surreal in its use of time shifts. It romps through a confusing world of the mind. In French with English subtitles. Not rated. 117m. **DIR:** Bertrand Blier. **CAST:** Charlotte Gainsbourg, Anouk Grinberg, Gérard Depardieu, Michel Blanc, Jean-Louis Trintignant. **1991**

MERCURY RISING ★★★1/2 In this thriller, Bruce Willis plays another world-weary lone wolf. The central character is an autistic 9-year-old boy unable to comprehend the danger he's in after he accidentally decodes a government communications cipher. Rather than invest in a new cipher, NSA bad guy Alec Baldwin elects to eliminate the kid. Young Miko Hughes is almost uncanny in his ability to play a kid who's there-but-not-quite-there. Rated R for violence, profanity, and peril directed at a helpless child. 110m. **DIR:** Harold Becker. **CAST:** Bruce Willis, Alec Baldwin, Miko Hughes, Chi McBride, Kim Dickens. **1998 DVD**

MERCY (1996) ★★1/2 A powerful millionaire finds out that he has less control over the world than he thought when his daughter is kidnapped. The script has a bit more depth than Mel Gibson's *Ransom* (which came out at the same time), but it soon becomes predictable as the rich man is humiliated by his tormentors. Rated R. 85m. **DIR:** Richard Shepard. **CAST:** John Rubinstein, Amber Kain, Sam Rockwell, Jane Lanier, Maura Tierney. **1996**

MERCY (1999) ★★ *Mercy* is what the filmmakers should have had on the viewers instead of subjecting them to this tiresome effort about a homicide detective investigating a nasty serial killer who preys on members of an elite lesbian club. Her search leads her into a kinky, sexual underworld where trust is in short supply. Julian Sands costars as a transvestite. Oh mercy! Rated R for adult situations, language, nudity, and violence. 94m. **DIR:** Damian Harris. **CAST:** Ellen Barkin, Julian Sands, Wendy Crewson, Peta Wilson, Karen Young. **1999 DVD**

MERCY MISSION (THE RESCUE OF FLIGHT 711) ★★★ Excellent performances salvage this tale of courage and heroism. Scott Bakula plays the pilot of a small Cessna who gets lost over the Pacific Ocean when his compass malfunctions. Robert Loggia shines as the pilot of a commercial airliner who comes to his rescue, risking his and his passengers' lives. The stars make this made-for-television melodrama fly. Rated PG for intensity. 92m. **DIR:** Roger Young. **CAST:** Robert Loggia, Scott Bakula. **1993**

MERIDIAN (KISS OF THE BEAST) ★★★1/2 This Italian throwback to their horror flicks of the Sixties comes complete with haunted castle and the group of wandering sideshow performers who focus on the beautiful castle mistress (Sherilyn Fenn). The added twist is a Beauty and the Beast theme with British actor Malcolm Jamieson playing twins—one evil, one good. Rated R for nudity, violence, and gore. 90m. **DIR:** Charles Band. **CAST:** Sherilyn Fenn, Malcolm Jamieson, Hilary Mason, Alex Daniels. **1990**

MERLIN (1992) ★★ Reporter Christy Lake (Nadia Cameron) learns that she's the reincarnated daughter of legendary magician Merlin, and she must guard a powerful sword from an evil wizard who is chasing her through time. This confusing film relies too heavily on gimmicks and mediocre special effects. Rated PG-13 for violence and adult situations. 112m. **DIR:** Paul Hunt. **CAST:** Nadia Cameron, Richard Lynch, Peter Phelps, James Hong. **1992**

•MERLIN (1998) ★★★★1/2 Opulent fantasy details the life of King Arthur's court wizard Merlin from the events behind his conception to the entrusting of the sword of Excalibur. Unlike previous films about Camelot, *Merlin* is all about the magic. And what magic it is. Jim Henson's Creature Shop contributes astounding special effects that are even more entertaining than the wonderful performances from the all-star cast. A triumph. Rated PG for mild violence. 140m. **DIR:** Steve Barron. **CAST:** Sam Neill, Miranda Richardson, Martin Short, Helena Bonham Carter, Isabella Rossellini, Rutger Hauer, James Earl Jones, John Gielgud. **1998 DVD**

MERLIN & THE SWORD Retelling of the King Arthur legend. Not rated, contains mild sex and violence. 94m. **DIR:** Clive Donner. **CAST:** Malcolm McDowell, Candice Bergen, Edward Woodward, Dyan Cannon, Rupert Everett. **1982**

MERLIN OF THE CRYSTAL CAVE ★★★ Although slow at times, this film redeems itself through fabulous hillside photography and decent special effects. Adapted from Mary Stewart's book, this BBC production chronicles Merlin's life before young Arthur became his protégé. As a child, Merlin suffered the fate of being the royal "bastard" and turned to a wise hermit for guidance and an introduction to mysterious powers. Not rated; contains violence. 159m. **DIR:** Michael Darlow. **CAST:** George Winter, Thomas Lambert, Jody David, Robert Powell, Trevor Peacock. **1992**

MERLIN'S SHOP OF MYSTICAL WONDERS ★★1/2 In this film set in the present day, Merlin, his wife, and some magical creatures open up a shop with the hope of bringing magic and wonder to all who enter. Complications ensue when a snoopy reporter sets out to prove the proprietor isn't really Merlin. Kids will enjoy this little romp. FAB Rating: PD (Parental discretion). 92m. **DIR:** Kenneth J. Burton. **CAST:** George Milan, Bunny Summers, John Terrence, Patricia Sansone, Ernest Borgnine. **1996**

MERMAIDS ★★★1/2 Terrific performances by Cher, Bob Hoskins, and Winona Ryder highlight this uneven but generally entertaining and decidedly offbeat comedy. Ryder is the confused 15-year-old daughter of the unpredictable Cher. A sort of *Harold and Maude* of the mother-daughter set, this one is not for all tastes. Rated PG-13 for profanity. 115m. **DIR:** Richard Benjamin. **CAST:** Cher, Bob Hoskins, Winona Ryder, Michael Schoeffling, Christina Ricci. **1990 DVD**

MERRY CHRISTMAS, MR. LAWRENCE ★★★1/2 Set in a prisoner-of-war camp in Java in 1942, this film, by Nagisa Oshima, focuses on a clash of cultures—and wills. Oshima's camera looks on relentlessly as a British officer (David Bowie), who refuses to cooperate or knuckle under, is beaten and tortured by camp commander Ryuichi Sakomoto. Rated R for violence, strong language, and adult situations. 122m. **DIR:** Nagisa Oshima. **CAST:** David Bowie, Ryuichi Sakamoto, Tom Conti. **1983**

MERRY-GO-ROUND, THE ★★ A mismatched love affair between a count and a hurdy-gurdy operator with the backdrop of World War I. Silent. B&W; 115m. **DIR:** Rupert Julian. **CAST:** Norman Kerry, Mary Philbin. **1923**

MERRY WAR, A ★★★★ Delightful romp about a copywriter at an advertising firm in London during the 1930s. Dissatisfied with his situation, Gordon Comstock quits his job to become a poet. His decision plays havoc with his girlfriend's desire to get married. How Gordon comes to realize his self-worth is just part of the joy of this film based on the best-selling novel *Keep the Aspidistra Flying* by George Orwell. Rated R for adult situations. 101m. **DIR:** Robert Bierman. **CAST:** Richard E. Grant, Helena Bonham Carter, Harriet Walter. **1998 DVD**

MERRY WIDOW, THE ★★★ A carefully chosen cast, a witty script, an infectious score, lavish sets, and the fabled Lubitsch touch at the helm make this musical-comedy sparkle. Maurice Chevalier and Jeanette MacDonald are perfect. B&W; 99m. **DIR:** Ernst Lubitsch. **CAST:** Maurice Chevalier, Jeanette MacDonald, Una Merkel, Edward Everett Horton. **1934**

MERRY WIDOW, THE ★★★1/2 If ever a film deserved to be called "quirky," this adaptation of a once-popular operetta is it. Director Erich Von Stroheim undercuts his story about two European princes fighting for the love of an American showgirl with so much odd slapstick that you never know when you should be taking anything seriously. B&W; 111m. **DIR:** Erich Von Stroheim. **CAST:** Mae Murray, John Gilbert, Roy D'Arcy. **1925**

MERRY WIVES OF WINDSOR, THE ★★ A slow-moving stage production of Shakespeare's comedy of morals with the colorful Sir John Falstaff (Leon Charles) out to seduce two married women and have them support his habits. Interesting casting of Gloria Grahame as Mistress Page, but, overall, disappointing. A Bard Productions Ltd. release. 160m. **DIR:** Jack Manning. **CAST:** Leon Charles, Gloria Grahame, Valerie Sedle Snyder, Dixie Neyland, Joel Asher, John Houseman. **1970 DVD**

MERTON OF THE MOVIES ★★★★ Red Skelton enlivens a very dated script with the help of comedy genius Buster Keaton. Both of them devised the slapstick routines that freshen the story of a movie-theater usher who climbs Hollywood's ladder of success with a gentle push from his friends. The show-business atmosphere is amiable and authentic, and the comedic timing is terrific. B&W; 83m. **DIR:** Robert Alton. **CAST:** Red Skelton, Virginia O'Brien, Gloria Grahame, Leon Ames, Alan Mowbray, Hugo Haas. **1947**

MESMERIZED (SHOCKED) ★★1/2 In this modern takeoff on *Svengali*, Jodie Foster plays a young orphan whose marriage to an older man (John Lithgow) proves stifling. Her imagination turns to murder, with the lovely New Zealand landscape in perfect contrast to her dreary thoughts. Not rated, contains mild profanity and sexual innuendo. 90m. **DIR:** Michael Laughlin. **CAST:** Jodie Foster, John Lithgow, Michael Murphy, Dan Shor. **1984 DVD**

MESSAGE, THE (MOHAMMAD, MESSENGER OF GOD) ★★1/2 Viewers expecting to see Mohammad in this three-hour epic will be disappointed.... He never appears on the screen. Instead, we see Anthony Quinn, as Mohammad's uncle, struggling to win religious freedom for Mohammad. The film tends to drag a bit and is definitely overlong. Rated PG. 180m. **DIR:** Moustapha Akkad. **CAST:** Anthony Quinn, Irene Papas, Michael Ansara, Johnny Sekka. **1977 DVD**

MESSAGE IN A BOTTLE ★★★ This mawkish tale, adapted from Nicholas Sparks's equally dissatisfying novel puts audiences through the wringer and concludes in a way intended to be "spiritually uplifting"... a buzz phrase for "sadder than all get-out." This is just sudsy melodrama: very well performed and beautifully filmed on North Carolina's Outer Banks, but wholly dissatisfying and damn near pointless. The final scenes are discordantly jarring enough to feel as though they've been yanked from some other story. Robin Wright Penn's a *Chicago Tribune* researcher who finds a bottle on the beach, and becomes obsessed by locating the man who wrote the exquisitely romantic note inside; when she does find him, they begin a tentative relationship... two wounded birds attempting to find happiness together. But it will not, alas, be that easy. Rated PG-13 for profanity and dramatic content. 132m. **DIR:** Luis Mandoki. **CAST:** Kevin Costner, Robin Wright, Paul Newman, John Savage, Illeana Douglas, Robbie Coltrane. **1998 DVD**

MESSENGER: THE STORY OF JOAN OF ARC, THE ★★ Director Luc Besson takes a roaring blood-and-thunder crack at the career of the Maid of Orleans. Joan anguishes over the horrors of war, but that doesn't keep Besson from wallowing in several endless battle scenes and the rape and murder of a fictitious sister of Joan's. Performances are arch and overstated, except for Timothy West as Joan's chief inquisitor, who is restrained and oddly sympathetic. Rated R for violence. 141m. **DIR:** Luc Besson. **CAST:** Milla Jovovich, John Malkovich, Faye Dunaway, Dustin Hoffman, Timothy West. **1999 DVD**

MESSENGER, THE ★★★1/2 Director Norman Loftis has infused this independent, urban remake of Vittorio De Sica's *The Bicycle Thief* with a realism and urgency seldom found in Hollywood films. A minuscule budget and some scenery chewing by lead actor Richard Barboza are detractions, but this is just stylish and gritty enough to hold your attention. Not rated; contains profanity and violence. 80m. **DIR:** Norman Loftis. **CAST:** Richard Barboza, Carolyn Kinebrew, Scott Ferguson. **1994**

MESSENGER OF DEATH ★★1/2 Middling Charles Bronson vehicle features the star in a convincing portrayal of a newspaper reporter investigating the bizarre murder of a Mormon family. A strong, suspenseful opening degenerates into a routine thriller. However, J. Lee Thompson does elicit believable performances from the cast. Rated R for violence and profanity. 98m. **DIR:** J. Lee Thompson. **CAST:** Charles Bronson, Trish Van Devere, John Ireland, Jeff Corey, Laurence Luckinbill, Marilyn Hassett. **1988**

MESSIN' WITH THE BLUES ★★★★ Recorded live on June 28, 1974, at the Montreux Jazz Festival in Switzerland, this fine documentary records master bluesman Muddy Waters leading his disciples (Junior Wells, Buddy Guy, Pinetop Perkins, and Bill Wyman) through a fine set of Chicago boogie. A set by Wells and Guy kicks off the tape. 54m. **DIR:** Jean Bovon. **1974**

METALSTORM: THE DESTRUCTION OF JARED-SYN An outer-space ranger takes on the powerful villain of the title. Rated PG for violence. 84m. **DIR:** Charles Band. **CAST:** Jeffrey Byron, Mike Preston, Tim Thomerson, Kelly Preston. **1983**

METAMORPHOSIS: THE ALIEN FACTOR ★★ Splashy special effects highlight this pedestrian science-fiction entry about a lab scientist who begins to mutate after being bitten by a frog injected with a mysterious serum from outer space. Will his co-workers cure him before they become lunch? Rated R for gore, nudity, language, and violence. 92m. **DIR:** Glen Takakjian. **CAST:** George Gerard, Tony Gigante, Katherine Romaine. **1993**

METEOR A comet strikes an asteroid, and sends a huge chunk of rock hurtling on a collision course with Earth. Rated PG. 103m. **DIR:** Ronald Neame. **CAST:** Sean Connery, Natalie Wood, Karl Malden, Brian Keith, Henry Fonda. **1979 DVD**

METEOR MAN ★★★ A timid schoolteacher in a crime-ridden inner-city neighborhood acquires superpowers. There are some very funny moments in this uneven, family-oriented comedy, especially as our hero learns about his new abilities. Good cast, too. Rated PG for

light violence. 100m. **DIR:** Robert Townsend. **CAST:** Robert Townsend, Marla Gibbs, Robert Guillaume, James Earl Jones, Bill Cosby, Eddie Griffin, Sinbad, Frank Gorshin, Nancy Wilson. **1993**

METEOR MONSTER (TEENAGE MONSTER) 🦃 Former Universal horror siren Anne Gwynne shielding her idiot son—who has been changed into a hairy monster by a meteor shower. B&W; 65m. **DIR:** Jacques Marquette. **CAST:** Anne Gwynne, Stuart Wade, Gloria Castillo. **1958 DVD**

METEORITES! ★★ This made-for-cable original is a pale knockoff of the bigger hit of the year, *Armageddon*. A stream of meteorites bombards a small town, and everyone must put aside his problems and try to survive. Much of the story is unbelievable and has little to no impact. Rated PG-13 for violence. 95m. **DIR:** Chris Thomson. **CAST:** Roxanne Hart, Tom Wopat, Pato Hoffman. **1998**

METRO ★★ A hostage negotiator on the San Francisco police force (Eddie Murphy) tangles with a psychotic jewel thief. After a good opening scene, the hostage negotiation angle goes out the window, and the film becomes *Beverly Hills Cop* with cable cars, with Murphy once again playing the kind of unappealing loudmouth he parodied as Buddy Love in *The Nutty Professor*. Rated R for violence and profanity. 117m. **DIR:** Thomas Carter. **CAST:** Eddie Murphy, Michael Rapaport, Michael Wincott, Carmen Ejogo. **1996 DVD**

METROLAND ★★★ A London suburbanite begins to question his middle-class contentment when an old chum sneers at him for selling out. Based on a novel by Julian Barnes, the film is forthright and sincere, aided greatly by the performances of Emily Watson and Elsa Zylberstein. Rated R for profanity, nudity, and sexual scenes. 101m. **DIR:** Philip Saville. **CAST:** Christian Bale, Emily Watson, Lee Ross, Elsa Zylberstein. **1997 DVD**

METROPOLIS (1926) ★★★★★ Fritz Lang's 1926 creation embodies the fine difference between classic and masterpiece. Using some of the most innovative camera work in film of any time, it's also an uncannily accurate projection of futuristic society. It is a silent-screen triumph. B&W; 120m. **DIR:** Fritz Lang. **CAST:** Brigitte Helm, Alfred Abel. **1926 DVD**

METROPOLIS (1984 MUSICAL VERSION) ★★★★★ Fritz Lang's 1926 silent science-fiction classic has been enhanced with special individual coloring and tints, recently recovered scenes, storyboards, and stills. The rock score, supervised by Giorgio Moroder, features Pat Benatar, Bonnie Tyler, Loverboy, Billy Squier, Adam Ant, Freddie Mercury, Jon Anderson, and Cycle V. 87m. **DIR:** Fritz Lang, Giorgio Moroder. **CAST:** Brigitte Helm, Alfred Abel. **1984**

METROPOLITAN ★★★★1/2 This deliciously different, independently made movie allows viewers a glimpse at the fading preppie-debutante social scene of New York by introducing a middle-class outsider into this rarefied world. An accidental meeting brings him into the "Sally Fowler Rat Pack" where a nice girl develops a crush on him. Rated PG-13 for profanity. 107m. **DIR:** Whit Stillman. **CAST:** Carolyn Farina, Edward Clements, Christopher Eigeman, Taylor Nicholas. **1990**

MEXICALI ROSE ★★★★ Radio singer Gene Autry discovers the oil company sponsoring his radio show is involved in a stock promotion fraud. Among their victims is an orphanage run by a girl. One of Autry's best. B&W; 60m. **DIR:** George Sherman. **CAST:** Gene Autry, Smiley Burnette, Noah Beery Sr., William Farnum, Luana Walters. **1939**

MEXICAN, THE ★★★1/2 Although much was made of the celestial pairing of Julia Roberts and Brad Pitt in this pleasantly weird romantic drama, the two stars don't share many scenes. Pitt's low-level bagman is sent to Mexico to recover a priceless (but cursed) antique pistol, while girlfriend Roberts heads to Las Vegas in a state of abandoned fury. Nothing goes right for either character, and the seriocomic tone becomes more entertaining as the story progresses. The best scenes are those between Roberts and James Gandolfini's unexpectedly refined and compassionate hit man. Rated R for profanity and violence. 123m. **DIR:** Gore Verbinski. **CAST:** Julia Roberts, Brad Pitt, James Gandolfini, J. K. Simmons, Bob Balaban, Gene Hackman. **2001 DVD**

MEXICAN HAYRIDE ★★ Lou Costello chases swindler Bud Abbott to Mexico and dim-wittedly aids him. Substandard entry in the series. B&W; 77m. **DIR:** Charles Barton. **CAST:** Bud Abbott, Lou Costello, Virginia Grey, John Hubbard, Pedro De Cordoba, Fritz Feld. **1948**

MEXICAN SPITFIRE ★★★1/2 This is one of a series of second-feature comedies about a youngish businessman and his temperamental Mexican wife. Though the stars are Lupe Velez and Donald Woods, the simplistic plot shifts early on to the young man's accident-prone uncle Matt and his rich and proper boss Lord Epping, both of whom were played by the spaghetti-legged Ziegfeld comic Leon Errol. He's in top form here. B&W; 75m. **DIR:** Leslie Goodwins. **CAST:** Lupe Velez, Donald Woods, Leon Errol. **1939**

MGM'S THE BIG PARADE OF COMEDY ★★ Disappointing and disjointed; an incoherent grab bag of short scenes from comic silent and sound films, compiled by the usually dependable Robert Youngson. B&W; 100m. **DIR:** Robert Youngson. **CAST:** Stan Laurel, Oliver Hardy, Bud Abbott, Lou Costello, Marion Davies. **1963**

MI VIDA LOCA ★★★ Three interrelated stories set among female gang members living in the Echo Park barrio of Los Angeles. The first and third stories are more dramatically compelling than the second, which causes the film's pace to slacken. Still, it's a vivid, well-acted group portrait of young women trying to live decent lives amid violence and despair. Rated R for profanity. 92m. **DIR:** Allison Anders. **CAST:** Angel Aviles, Seidy Lopez, Jacob Vargas, Panchito Gomez, Jesse Borrego. **1994**

MIAMI BLUES ★★1/2 A sociopath (Alec Baldwin) goes on a crime spree in Miami, hooks up with a trusting hooker (Jennifer Jason Leigh) and eludes a slow-witted cop (Fred Ward). Director George Armitage was trying for something stylishly offbeat and ended up with something that was mostly off. Rated R for violence, nudity, and profanity. 96m. **DIR:** George Armitage. **CAST:** Fred Ward, Alec Baldwin, Jennifer Jason Leigh, Nora Dunn, Charles Napier. **1990**

MIAMI COPS 🦃 This boring Italian film features a seasoned cop attempting to break up an international drug-smuggling ring. B&W; 103m. **DIR:** Al Bradley. **CAST:** Richard Roundtree. **1989**

MIAMI HORROR 🦃 Poorly dubbed Italian thriller about scientists who believe that Earth life originated

from bacteria on meteorites from outer space. 88m. **DIR:** Martin Herbert. **CAST:** David Warbeck, Laura Trotter, John Ireland. **1985**

MIAMI HOT TALK ★★1/2 The on-air sex fantasies of a Miami radio host cause problems for both her and her listeners. Slightly better than average soft-core sexploitation. Rated R for nudity, sexual situations, and profanity. 80m. **DIR:** Andrew Blake. **CAST:** Seana Ryan, Frank Rodriguez, Tiffany Berlingame. **1996**

MIAMI HUSTLE ★★ Supermodel Kathy Ireland makes her starring debut in this failed caper thriller as a supposedly shrewd con artist who uses her body to help separate marks from their assets. Alas, Ireland can't act a lick. Philip Collins and Daniel Miller's script begins reasonably well, but the final act is ridiculous. *The Sting* it ain't. Rated PG-13 for nudity and mild profanity. 81m. **DIR:** Lawrence Lanoff. **CAST:** Kathy Ireland, John Enos, Audie England, Richard Sarafian, Eduardo Yanez, Allan Rich. **1995**

MIAMI RHAPSODY ★★★ Writer-director David Frankel's big-screen debut is so strongly reminiscent of Woody Allen and Neil Simon that he should pay royalties. Perky Sarah Jessica Parker, nervous about tying the knot with her fiancé, confers with family members... only to find each one involved in an extramarital affair. Clever dialogue and amusing one-liners abound, but the whole is somewhat less than the sum of its talented parts. Rated PG-13 for profanity and sexual candor. 95m. **DIR:** David Frankel. **CAST:** Sarah Jessica Parker, Gil Bellows, Antonio Banderas, Mia Farrow, Paul Mazursky, Kevin Pollak, Carla Gugino. **1995 DVD**

MIAMI SUPERCOPS 🦃 The stars of *They Call Me Trinity* ditch the Old West for Miami in this Italian import that's so bad, it's unbearable. Rated PG. 97m. **DIR:** Bruno Corbucci. **CAST:** Terence Hill, Bud Spencer. **1985**

MIAMI VICE ★★★★ This pilot for the popular NBC series is slam-bang entertainment. A New York City cop (Philip Michael Thomas) on the trail of the powerful drug kingpin who killed his brother traces him to Miami, running into a vice cop (Don Johnson) who's after the same guy. All the trademarks of the series are here: great music, rapid-fire editing, gritty low-key performances, and bursts of sporadic violence. The only real flaw in this tape is the sound quality, which, even in hi-fi stereo, is muffled. 97m. **DIR:** Thomas Carter. **CAST:** Don Johnson, Philip Michael Thomas, Saundra Santiago, Michael Talbott, John Diehl, Gregory Sierra, Bill Smitrovich, Belinda Montgomery, Martin Ferrero, Mykelti Williamson, Olivia Brown, Miguel Pinero. **1984**

MIAMI VICE: "THE PRODIGAL SON" ★★★ The pastel duo, Crockett (Don Johnson) and Tubbs (Philip Michael Thomas), trek up to New York in search of the bad guys in this watchable second-season opener. 99m. **DIR:** Paul Michael Glaser. **CAST:** Don Johnson, Philip Michael Thomas, Edward James Olmos, Olivia Brown, Penn Jillette, Pam Grier. **1985**

MICHAEL ★★★1/2 John Travolta is the title character, an angel come to Earth for one last visit to set straight a pair of cynical journalists, Andie MacDowell and William Hurt. With Bob Hoskins on hand to add hilarity as their ethically challenged publisher, *Michael* is fun to watch, just not very memorable. Rated PG. 105m. **DIR:** Nora Ephron. **CAST:** John Travolta, Andie MacDowell, William Hurt, Bob Hoskins, Robert Pastorelli, Jean Stapleton, Teri Garr. **1996 DVD**

MICHAEL COLLINS ★★★★ Director Neil Jordan creates a magnificent epic glorifying IRA militant Michael Collins. His only filmmaking weakness appears in a lack of background to support the extreme violence that consumes much of the film. Liam Neeson brilliantly brings the title character to a larger-than-life existence. Aidan Quinn plays his closest friend, with Julia Roberts as their mutual love interest. Rated R for violence and profanity. 135m. **DIR:** Neil Jordan. **CAST:** Liam Neeson, Aidan Quinn, Julia Roberts, Alan Rickman, Ian Hart, Stephen Rea. **1996 DVD**

MICHAEL JACKSON MOONWALKER ★★★★1/2 Spectacle is what we expect of Michael Jackson, and he delivers a stunning twenty-first-century Saturday-morning special that runs the course from Disney to Claymation to sizzling sci-fi effects. But what makes it such a treat is the sensational show of humor as Jackson parodies his own treatment by the tabloids, his kooky fetishes, even his own success. 84m. **DIR:** Jerry Kramer, Collin Chivers. **CAST:** Michael Jackson, Sean Lennon. **1988**

MICKEY BLUE EYES ★★★★ A proper English auctioneer falls in love with a New York schoolteacher only to find out that she's the daughter of a Mafia kingpin. It's as much a comedy of mistaken identity as it is a send-up of mob pictures, with Hugh Grant in top form as the clumsy, embarrassed hero who is out of his depth. The highlight is Grant's marbles-in-the-mouth attempt to master mobster jargon. Reminiscent of *The Freshman*, it features James Caan, an alumnus of *The Godfather*, as "the bad guy," and an amiable, wink-of-the-eye quality. Rated PG-13 for profanity, violence, and suggested sex. 101m. **DIR:** Kelly Makin. **CAST:** Hugh Grant, James Caan, Jeanne Tripplehorn, Burt Young, James Fox, Joe Viterelli, Gerry Becker, Maddie Corman, Tony Darrow, Paul Lazar, Vincent Pastore, Frank Pelligrino. **1999 DVD**

MICKI & MAUDE ★★★★1/2 In this hysterically funny comedy Dudley Moore stars as a television personality who tries to juggle marriages to two women, Amy Irving and Ann Reinking. Directed by Blake Edwards, it's a triumph for filmmaker and cast alike. Rated PG-13 for profanity and suggested sex. 96m. **DIR:** Blake Edwards. **CAST:** Dudley Moore, Amy Irving, Ann Reinking, George Gaynes, Wallace Shawn. **1984**

MICROCOSMOS ★★★★1/2 This amazing, intimate venture into the insect kingdom includes birth, death, survival, romance, decapitations, comedy, high drama, and stunning beauty. High-tech close-ups of the French countryside unveil an amazing bugscape. Caterpillars parade like seasoned Shriners. Raindrops fall like bombs. Snails entwine to rapturous music. And a lush soundtrack plays second fiddle to the munching, buzzing, and scratching of daily insect activity. The nonchalant squishing of bugs will never be the same. Rated G. 77m. **DIR:** Claude Nuridsnay, Marie Perennou. **1996**

MIDAS TOUCH, THE ★★ Lighthearted kiddie tale about a young boy who strikes a deal with a witch so that everything he touches literally turns to gold. Then young Billy turns his grandmother into a golden statue, and thieves steal her. Young children will appreciate the am-

ple antics as Billy and his friends save the day. Rated PG. 92m. **DIR:** Peter Manoogian. **CAST:** Trever O'Brien, Ashley Lyn Cafagna, Joey Simmrin, David Jeremiah. **1997**

MIDDLE-AGE CRAZY ★★★ Bruce Dern lives the lyrics of this pop song–turned-film, playing a fellow who shorts out upon reaching the mid-life crisis of his fortieth birthday. Wife Ann-Margret is abandoned for a football cheerleader, and the family car is pushed aside by a Porsche. Director John Trent resists the easy opportunity for cheap comedy, however, and treats the material with surprising compassion. Rated PG. 95m. **DIR:** John Trent. **CAST:** Bruce Dern, Ann-Margret, Graham Jarvis. **1980**

MIDDLE OF THE NIGHT ★★★ A melodrama about marriage that symbolized a moral awakening for middle-aged America in the late 1950s. Fine-tuned film treatment of Paddy Chayefsky's stage play. B&W; 119m. **DIR:** Delbert Mann. **CAST:** Fredric March, Kim Novak, Glenda Farrell, Martin Balsam, Lee Grant, Joan Copeland. **1959**

MIDDLEMARCH ★★★1/2 In spite of fine acting and impeccable production values, the didactic tone of George Eliot's 1871–72 novel never lets you forget you are in BBC land. Still, this three-cassette, PBS miniseries is richly detailed, lushly photographed, and contemporary in spirit. The letter-box strip across the bottom broadens the ratio without reducing the players to puppets on the screen. Not rated. 357m. **DIR:** Anthony Page. **CAST:** Juliet Aubrey, Robert Hardy, Douglas Hodge, Michael Hordern, Peter Jeffrey, Patrick Malahide, Trevyn McDowell, Rufus Sewell. **1994**

MIDNIGHT (1934) ★★ Based on a well-received stage play, this rather implausible melodrama concerns a jury foreman who insists on a death verdict in the case of a young woman who killed a cruel lover. The juror then has to turn his own daughter over to the authorities for the same crime. Its main appeal now is Humphrey Bogart in a supporting role as a slick gangster. B&W; 74m. **DIR:** Chester Erskine. **CAST:** O. P. Heggie, Sidney Fox, Henry Hull, Lynne Overman, Margaret Wycherly, Humphrey Bogart, Richard Whorf. **1934 DVD**

MIDNIGHT (1939) ★★★★1/2 One of the movies that made 1939 Hollywood's best year, this comic romp is about a con woman who's hired to pose as a rich countess to come between a playboy and her employer's wife. And what a job she does! The movie proves that graphic sex isn't necessary to make a sexy movie. B&W; 94m. **DIR:** Mitchell Leisen. **CAST:** Claudette Colbert, Don Ameche, John Barrymore, Mary Astor, Francis Lederer, Monty Woolley, Hedda Hopper. **1939**

MIDNIGHT (1980) 🦃 Two college guys and a female hitchhiker end up in a town plagued by a family of Satan worshipers. Rated R for violence and profanity. 91m. **DIR:** John Russo. **CAST:** Lawrence Tierney, Melanie Verlin, John Amplas. **1980**

MIDNIGHT (1989) ★★1/2 A sultry hostess who introduces horror movies is pursued by a struggling actor and fan. On the soundtrack: some listenable original songs and a nice version of "Low Spark of High-Heeled Boys," sung by Jim Capaldi. Rated R for language. 90m. **DIR:** Norman Thaddeus Vane. **CAST:** Lynn Redgrave, Tony Curtis, Frank Gorshin, Wolfman Jack. **1989**

MIDNIGHT 2 ★★ Writer-director John Russo's sequel to his 1980 film is better than the first in a variety of ways, but still falls way short of the standard of excellence set by the groundbreaking *Night of the Living Dead*. Here, Russo uses his low budget to the benefit of the tale of college kids getting knocked off in a small town. Not rated; contains violence, profanity, nudity, and simulated sex. 72m. **DIR:** John Russo. **CAST:** Matthew Jason Walsh. **1993**

MIDNIGHT CABARET 🦃 Satanic time waster. Rated R for nudity and violence. 93m. **DIR:** Pece Dingo. **CAST:** Lisa Hart Carroll, Michael Des Barres, Paul Drake, Laura Harrington. **1988**

MIDNIGHT CLEAR, A ★★★★ Based on William Wharton's autobiographical novel, this compelling antiwar drama is about a group of young American soldiers sent on a reconnaissance mission into enemy territory during World War II. This impressive film recalls the impact and filmmaking technique of Stanley Kubrick's *Paths of Glory*. Rated R for profanity and violence. 107m. **DIR:** Keith Gordon. **CAST:** Ethan Hawke, Kevin Dillon, Peter Berg, Arye Gross, Frank Whaley, Gary Sinise, John C. McGinley. **1992**

MIDNIGHT COWBOY ★★★★★ In this tremendous film, about the struggle for existence in the urban nightmare of New York's Forty-second Street area, Jon Voight and Dustin Hoffman deliver brilliant performances. The film won Oscars for best picture, best director, and best screenplay. Voight plays handsome Joe Buck, who arrives from Texas to make his mark as a hustler, only to be outhustled by everyone else, including the crafty, sleazy "Ratso," superbly played by Hoffman. Rated R. 113m. **DIR:** John Schlesinger. **CAST:** Jon Voight, Dustin Hoffman, Sylvia Miles, Barnard Hughes, Brenda Vaccaro. **1969 DVD**

MIDNIGHT CROSSING 🦃 Poorly written and realized film about four people on a treasure hunt into Cuba. Rated R for language, violence, and nudity. 104m. **DIR:** Roger Holzberg. **CAST:** Faye Dunaway, Daniel J. Travanti, Kim Cattrall, John Laughlin, Ned Beatty. **1988**

MIDNIGHT DANCER (1987) ★★★ A young ballerina balances her artistic yearning with a night job in the chorus line of Club Paradise. Hints of gangsters, drugs, and seedy sex give this Australian film an honest coating of grit—rare among dance movies. Rated R. 97m. **DIR:** Pamela Gibbons. **CAST:** Deanne Jeffs, Mary Regan. **1987**

MIDNIGHT DANCER (1994) ★★★ Three brothers work as go-go boys in a sleazy Manila sex club to help keep their family together. This world of dirty dancing and prostitution is seen through the eyes of the youngest brother, who dances by night, and tries to keep his mother from worrying about her sons the rest of the time. The brothers consider themselves heterosexual, but often engage in homosexual activity. Tough viewing. In Filipino with English subtitles. Not rated; contains nudity, profanity, and violence. 118m. **DIR:** Mel Chionglo. **CAST:** Alex Del Rosario, Gandong Cervantes, Lawrence David, Perla Bautista. **1994**

MIDNIGHT EDITION 🦃 A real snoozer of a movie about a reporter who becomes obsessed with a death-row inmate. Rated R for nudity, violence, and profanity. 98m. **DIR:** Howard Libov. **CAST:** Will Patton, Michael DeLuise, Clare Wren, Nancy Moore Atchison. **1993**

MIDNIGHT EXPRESS ★★★★1/2 This is the true story of Billy Hayes, who was busted for trying to smuggle hashish out of Turkey and spent five years in the squalor

and terror of a Turkish prison. *Midnight Express* is not an experience easily shaken. Yet it is a film for our times that teaches a powerful and important lesson. Rated R. 121m. **DIR:** Alan Parker. **CAST:** Brad Davis, John Hurt, Randy Quaid. **1978 DVD**

MIDNIGHT HEAT ★★ Tim Matheson fails to score as Tyler Grey, a football player who is having an affair with the team owner's wife. When the team owner ends up dead, Grey finds himself framed for the murder. Watch him do the quarterback shuffle as he tries to prove his innocence. Rated R for violence, nudity, and adult language. 97m. **DIR:** Harvey Frost. **CAST:** Tim Matheson, Mimi Craven, Stephen Mendel. **1994**

MIDNIGHT HOUR ★★★ High school students recite an ancient curse as a Halloween prank and unintentionally release demons from hell and the dead from their graves. Enjoyable cross between *Night of the Living Dead* and *An American Werewolf in London*, helped along by humor and a lively cast. Rated R for gore, violence, and profanity. 87m. **DIR:** Jack Bender. **CAST:** Shari Belafonte, LeVar Burton, Lee Montgomery, Dick Van Patten, Kevin McCarthy. **1986 DVD**

MIDNIGHT IN THE GARDEN OF GOOD AND EVIL ★★★ Clint Eastwood's fascination with southern Gothic surfaces in service of this enigmatic, captivating, and frustrating adaptation of John Berendt's equally puzzling novel. Based on actual events, this is a study of a young New York–based writer who becomes the journalist of choice when a wealthy Savannah, Georgia, aristocrat is charged with homicide. Alas, the film's eccentric characters eventually overwhelm it. Rated R for violence, profanity, and sexual candor. 135m. **DIR:** Clint Eastwood. **CAST:** Kevin Spacey, John Cusack, Jude Law, Jack Thompson, Paul Hipp, Alison Eastwood, Irma P. Hall, The Lady Chablis. **1997 DVD**

MIDNIGHT KISS ★★ A murderer who removes the blood from his victims is running loose, so a female detective is used as bait and is attacked. She cannot believe that vampires exist, until she becomes one herself. Extremely bad dialogue and horrible acting really take a bite out of this picture. In R-rated and unrated versions; contains profanity, violence, and nudity. 85m. **DIR:** Joel Bender. **CAST:** Michelle Owens, Gregory A. Greer, Michael McMillin, Robert Milano, B. J. Gates, Michael Shawn. **1992**

MIDNIGHT LACE ★★★ A fine mystery with a cast that makes the most of it. Doris Day is an American living in London and married to successful businessman Rex Harrison. She soon finds her life in danger. Some viewers may find it less sophisticated than present-day thrillers, but there's plenty of suspense and plot twists to recommend it. 100m. **DIR:** David Miller. **CAST:** Doris Day, Rex Harrison, John Gavin, Myrna Loy, Roddy McDowall, Herbert Marshall, Natasha Perry. **1960**

MIDNIGHT MADNESS 🦃 A midnight scavenger hunt. Rated PG. 110m. **DIR:** David Wechter, Michael Nankin. **CAST:** David Naughton, Debra Clinger, Eddie Deezen, Stephen Furst. **1980 DVD**

MIDNIGHT MAN ★★1/2 So-so action-adventure, based on the novel by Jack Higgins. A former terrorist is enlisted by the British government to help stop a terrorist's attack on the royal family. Rated R for violence and profanity. 104m. **DIR:** Lawrence Gordon Clark. **CAST:** Rob Lowe, Kenneth Cranham, Deborah Moore. **1998**

MIDNIGHT MOVIE MASSACRE ★★★ This is definitely a candidate for the midnight-movie cult crowd—set in 1956 while an audience of outrageous characters are watching a sci-fi movie. A real flying saucer lands outside, and the monster invades the theater. Gross fun, a crowd pleaser with surprisingly good photography and production. Not rated, with graphic violence and simulated sex. 86m. **DIR:** Mark Stock. **CAST:** Robert Clarke, Ann Robinson. **1986**

MIDNIGHT MURDERS ★★★ Rod Steiger stars as a David Koresh–like religious fanatic who is arrested for tax evasion. He begins gathering weapons to protect his "people" from the government and the feds respond in kind. Fast-paced and controversial action-thriller. Rated R for violence. 95m. **DIR:** Dick Lowry. **CAST:** Rod Steiger, Michael Gross, Gary Basaraba. **1991**

MIDNIGHT RIDE ★★ Michael Dudikoff stars as a cop whose estranged wife is kidnapped by madman Mark Hamill and taken on the wildest ride of her life. So-so chase film is hampered by Dudikoff's lifeless performance but buoyed by Hamill's over-the-top insanity, a cameo by Robert Mitchum, and some exciting action sequences. Rated R for profanity and violence. 93m. **DIR:** Bob Bralver. **CAST:** Michael Dudikoff, Mark Hamill, Robert Mitchum, Savina Gersak. **1992**

MIDNIGHT RUN ★★★★ Robert De Niro is wonderfully funny as a bounty hunter charged with bringing in fugitive Charles Grodin. The latter is hiding out after stealing $15 million from a crime boss and giving it to charity. Mixing laughs, surprises, and oodles of action, Martin Brest has come up with the perfect follow-up to his megahit, *Beverly Hills Cop*. Rated R for profanity and violence. 125m. **DIR:** Martin Brest. **CAST:** Robert De Niro, Charles Grodin, Yaphet Kotto, John Ashton, Dennis Farina. **1988 DVD**

MIDNIGHT WITNESS ★★ After a fight with his live-in girlfriend, Paul can't sleep, so he decides to play with his new video camera. Shooting out his window, he videotapes the police beating up a suspect. Now he and his girlfriend must run for their lives. Try not to fall asleep due to the bad plot and poor acting. Not rated; contains violence, nudity, and simulated sex. 90m. **DIR:** Peter Foldy. **CAST:** Paul Johansson, Maxwell Caulfield, Karen Moncrieff, Jan-Michael Vincent, Mick Murray, Mark Pellegrino, Virginia Mayo. **1992**

MIDNIGHT'S CHILD ★★ Run-of-the-mill made-for-TV thriller with cult member Olivia D'Abo taking a job as a nanny in order to abduct her charge to be the bride of Satan. She doesn't rock the cradle but manages to stir up the household a bit. Not rated. 89m. **DIR:** Colin Bucksey. **CAST:** Marcy Walker, Cotter Smith, Olivia D'Abo, Elisabeth Moss. **1992**

MIDSUMMER NIGHT'S DREAM, A (1935) ★★★★ Warner Bros. rolled out many of its big-name contract stars during the studio's heyday for this engrossing rendition of Shakespeare's classic comedy. Enchantment is the key element in this fairy-tale story of the misadventures of a group of mythical mischief makers. B&W; 117m. **DIR:** Max Reinhardt. **CAST:** James Cagney, Olivia de Havilland, Dick Powell, Mickey Rooney. **1935**

MIDSUMMER NIGHT'S DREAM, A (1968) ★★1/2 Special effects and countryside locales strangely distract from the overall hilarity of Shakespeare's spoof on love. Some of the most pun-filled lines are lost as some of the

cast members confuse talking fast for authentic articulation. Diana Rigg is rather pathetic as the lovelorn Helena while Ian Holm's Puck provides laughs. Not rated; features Judi Dench as the Fairy Queen in very scanty attire. 124m. **DIR:** Peter Hall. **CAST:** Diana Rigg, David Warner, Ian Holm, Judi Dench, Ian Richardson. **1968**

MIDSUMMER NIGHT'S SEX COMEDY, A ★★1/2 Woody Allen's sometimes dull cinematic treatise—albeit sweet-natured, and beautifully photographed by Gordon Willis—on the star-writer-director's favorite subjects: sex and death. That's not to say *A Midsummer Night's Sex Comedy* doesn't have its humorous moments. Allen's fans will undoubtedly enjoy it. Rated PG for adult themes. 88m. **DIR:** Woody Allen. **CAST:** Woody Allen, Mia Farrow, José Ferrer, Julie Hagerty, Tony Roberts, Mary Steenburgen. **1982 DVD**

MIDWAY ★★★ An all-star cast was assembled to bring to the screen this famous sea battle of World War II. Midway became famous as the site of the overwhelming victory of American carrier forces, which shifted the balance of power in the Pacific. As a historical drama, this film is accurate and maintains interest. However, a romance subplot is totally out of place. Rated PG. 132m. **DIR:** Jack Smight. **CAST:** Henry Fonda, Charlton Heston, Robert Mitchum, Hal Holbrook, Edward Albert, Cliff Robertson. **1976 DVD**

MIDWINTER'S TALE, A ★★1/2 A group of theatrical misfits tries to stage a production of *Hamlet* in a deserted country church. Director Kenneth Branagh's breakneck pace can't quite conceal the hey-kids-let's-put-on-a-show clichés of his own script, and much of the dialogue is unintelligible to American ears. The talented cast, however, is a major asset. Rated R for profanity. B&W; 98m. **DIR:** Kenneth Branagh. **CAST:** Michael Maloney, Jennifer Saunders, Joan Collins, Richard Briers, Nicolas Farrell, Ann Davies. **1996**

MIFUNE ★★★★ In this beguiling drama-romance about hidden pasts and family ties, a married Copenhagen yuppie returns alone to his family's farm to bury his father and care for his mentally challenged brother. He hires a housekeeper who has a troubled brother of her own. The film embraces the Danish Dogma 95 film collective's "vow of chastity," which dictates the use of handheld cameras, and natural lighting and sound. In Danish with English subtitles. Rated R for sexuality, language, and violence. 99m. **DIR:** Soeren Kragh-Jacobsen. **CAST:** Anders W. Berthelsen, Jesper Asholt, Iben Hjejle, Emil Tarding, Sofie Grabol. **2000 DVD**

MIGHTY, THE ★★★★ Great "small" film in which two young boys, both considered outcasts, find new strength in their friendship. Exceptional cast is terrific in this heartwarming tearjerker. Rated PG-13. 100m. **DIR:** Peter Chelsom. **CAST:** Sharon Stone, Harry Dean Stanton, Gillian Anderson, Kieran Culkin, Gena Rowlands, Meat Loaf, Elden Henson. **1998 DVD**

MIGHTY APHRODITE ★★★1/2 A deliciously comic performance by Mira Sorvino as a naïve prostitute is the main attraction in this middleweight comedy from actor-writer-director Woody Allen, whose screen character becomes obsessed with discovering the identity of his adopted son's mother. A bizarre Greek chorus periodically comments on events. Rated R for profanity and sexual situations. **DIR:** Woody Allen. **CAST:** Woody Allen, Helena Bonham Carter, Mira Sorvino, Michael Rapaport, F. Murray Abraham, Claire Bloom, Olympia Dukakis, David Ogden Stiers, Jack Warden, James Woods, Dan Moran. **1995 DVD**

MIGHTY DUCKS, THE ★★★1/2 Fast-living lawyer Emilio Estevez is assigned 500 hours of community service after being convicted on a drunk-driving arrest, and he finds himself coaching a hockey team made up of league misfits. *The Bad News Bears* on ice. Rated PG for brief vulgarity. 93m. **DIR:** Stephen Herek. **CAST:** Emilio Estevez, Joss Ackland, Lane Smith, Heidi Kling. **1992 DVD**

MIGHTY JOE YOUNG (1949) ★★★1/2 In this timeless fantasy from the creator of *King Kong* (Willis O'Brien with his young apprentice, Ray Harryhausen), the story follows the discovery of a twelve-foot gorilla in Africa by a fast-talking, money-hungry nightclub owner (Robert Armstrong), who schemes to bring the animal back to Hollywood. B&W; 94m. **DIR:** Ernest B. Schoedsack. **CAST:** Terry Moore, Ben Johnson, Robert Armstrong, Frank McHugh. **1949**

MIGHTY JOE YOUNG (1998) ★★★★ Faithful remake of the 1949 classic has a few 1990s updates including a wild-animal sanctuary meant to protect the lovable giant gorilla. Bill Paxton plays a zoologist who's gaga over both the beast and the girl. Ruthless poachers create strong, clear-cut villains at which to hiss. There is a seamless blend of stop-motion, computer-generated images, blue screen, full-size animatronics, and the man in a gorilla suit thrown in for good measure. This film socks home a strong "save the wildlife" message. Rated PG-13 for violence. 114m. **DIR:** Ron Underwood. **CAST:** Charlize Theron, Bill Paxton, Rade Serbedzija, Naveen Andrews, David Paymer. **1998 DVD**

MIGHTY MORPHIN POWER RANGERS: THE MOVIE ★★ Cheesy, big-screen version of the kiddie TV series is nothing but a feature-length commercial for the tie-in toys. Special effects are cheap, and the Power Rangers are played by blandly pretty faces. With broad acting and infantile comic relief, it's strictly for undemanding toddlers—except that their parents may well object to the film's nonstop (though cartoonish) violence. Rated PG. 96m. **DIR:** Bryan Spicer. **CAST:** Karan Ashley, Johnny Yong Bosch, Steve Cardenas, Jason David Frank, Amy Jo Johnson, David Yost, Paul Freeman. **1995**

MIGHTY PEKING MAN ★★★ Some movies are so bad they're funny. This is one of them. After an earthquake destroys a small village, an expedition is formed to track down a legendary ape man in the Himalayan jungles. The giant ape man has nothing to do with the earthquake. It's just a device to bring him down off his mountaintop home. When the expedition arrives, they not only discover the ape man, but his female friend, a buxom blonde who was orphaned and grew up in the jungle. This 1977 Hong Kong effort apes the *King Kong* legend for all it's worth, inducing laughter with shameful special effects, dreadful dialogue, and even worse dubbing. Rated PG-13 for adult situations and violence. 90m. **DIR:** Ho Meng-Hua. **CAST:** Danny Lee, Evelyne Kraft, Hsiao Yao, Ku Feng. **1977 DVD**

MIGHTY QUINN, THE ★★★ A quirky, entertaining mystery story, set in the reggae world of a Caribbean island. Denzel Washington plays the local police chief—"The Mighty Quinn"—who is on the trail of a murderer.

Director Carl Schenkel contributes an inventive visual style and makes ample use of a wonderful reggae score. Rated R, with profanity, violence, and mild sexual situations. 95m. **DIR:** Carl Schenkel. **CAST:** Denzel Washington, Robert Townsend, James Fox, Sheryl Lee Ralph, Mimi Rogers. **1989**

MIGRANTS, THE ★★★★ Nominated for six Emmy Awards, this moving adaptation of Tennessee Williams's story accurately depicts the trials and tribulations of migrant farm workers. Cloris Leachman brilliantly portrays Viola, who has seen too much suffering but maintains a glimmer of hope for her children. Despite major setbacks, Ron Howard, as her oldest son, tries to fulfill her dreams. Not rated; contains adult themes. 83m. **DIR:** Tom Gries. **CAST:** Cloris Leachman, Ron Howard, Sissy Spacek, Cindy Williams, Lisa Lucas. **1973**

MIKADO, THE (1939) ★★★★1/2 Members of the D'Oyly Carte Opera Company perform in this colorful British-made movie of the Gilbert and Sullivan operetta. Kenny Baker furnishes the American influence, but the real stars are the music, fanciful sets, and gorgeous Technicolor cinematography. As enjoyable as a professional staging. 90m. **DIR:** Victor Schertzinger. **CAST:** Kenny Baker, Martyn Green, Jean Colin. **1939 DVD**

MIKADO, THE (1987) ★★★1/2 Gilbert and Sullivan's delightfully amusing light opera is majestically performed at the London Coliseum by the English National Opera. Eric Idle dominates as Lord High Executioner of the town of Titipu. Special optical effects and camera angles add to the fun. 131m. **DIR:** John Michael Phillips. **CAST:** Eric Idle, Bonaventura Bottone, Lesley Garrett. **1987**

MIKE'S MURDER ★★★ This could have been an interesting tale of a small-time Los Angeles drug dealer and part-time tennis pro involved in a drug rip-off. But a string of confusing plot devices doesn't work. Rated R for violence, language, and nudity. 97m. **DIR:** James Bridges. **CAST:** Debra Winger, Mark Keyloun, Darrell Larson. **1984**

MIKEY ★★★1/2 Talk about problem children. Young Mikey, played by Brian Bonsall, has a real attitude problem. When he feels unloved, he murders his parents, and then moves on to the next foster home. This bad seed continues his reign of terror until he falls for the girl next door. Rated R for violence, nudity, and language. 92m. **DIR:** Dennis Dimster-Denk. **CAST:** John Diehl, Lyman Ward, Brian Bonsall, Josie Bissett. **1992 DVD**

MIKEY AND NICKY ★★★ The story of a fateful day and the relationship of two small-time crooks who have been best friends since childhood. This hauntingly funny film slowly builds to its climax in the Elaine May tradition. Great acting from Peter Falk and John Cassavetes. Rated R for profanity. 119m. **DIR:** Elaine May. **CAST:** Peter Falk, John Cassavetes, Ned Beatty, Joyce Van Patten. **1976**

MILAGRO BEANFIELD WAR, THE ★★★ There are fine perfomances in this slight, but enjoyable comedy-drama in which a group of citizens from a small town attempt to save their way of life by fighting big-money interests. The story is simplistic but a real spirit lifter. Rated R for violence and profanity. 117m. **DIR:** Robert Redford. **CAST:** Rubén Blades, Richard Bradford, Sonia Braga, Julie Carmen, James Gammon, Melanie Griffith, John Heard, Daniel Stern, Christopher Walken, Chick Vennera. **1988**

MILDRED PIERCE ★★★★ Bored housewife Joan Crawford parlays waiting tables into a restaurant chain and an infatuation with Zachary Scott. Her spoiled daughter, Ann Blyth, hits on him. Emotions run high and taut as everything unravels in this A-one adaptation of James M. Cain's novel of murder and cheap love. Her performance in the title role won Joan Crawford an Oscar for best actress. B&W; 109m. **DIR:** Michael Curtiz. **CAST:** Joan Crawford, Jack Carson, Zachary Scott, Eve Arden, Ann Blyth, Bruce Bennett, George Tobias, Lee Patrick. **1945**

MILES FROM HOME ★★ Richard Gere and Kevin Anderson star as brothers in this uneven drama about tragic rural figures. The brothers' farm is lost to foreclosure. They respond by torching the place and heading off on a confused odyssey of crime and misadventure. Rated R for profanity and violence. 103m. **DIR:** Gary Sinise. **CAST:** Richard Gere, Kevin Anderson. **1988**

MILES TO GO ★★★ When she learns she is dying of cancer, a woman lays plans for the future of her family by seeking her own "replacement." Unusual premise is handled tastefully in this TV movie. 98m. **DIR:** David Greene. **CAST:** Jill Clayburgh, Tom Skerritt, Mimi Kuzyk. **1986**

MILK MONEY ★★★1/2 An adolescent boy heads into the big bad city with some friends, intending to trade lunch money for a glimpse of a hooker's breasts, and winds up bringing perky Melanie Griffith home to meet his single father. R. J. Stewart's screenplay gets renewed mileage from the hooker-with-a-heart-of-gold stereotype, thanks mostly to clever dialogue and Griffith's warmhearted performance. Rated PG-13 for profanity, brief nudity, and violence. 108m. **DIR:** Richard Benjamin. **CAST:** Melanie Griffith, Ed Harris, Michael Patrick Carter, Malcolm McDowell. **1994**

MILKY WAY, THE (1936) ★★★★ In this superb compendium of gags flowing from his character of a milkman who innocently decks the champion during a brawl, the great Harold Lloyd amply proves why he was such a success. Lloyd was a master comic craftsman. This is the finest of his few talking films. B&W; 83m. **DIR:** Leo McCarey. **CAST:** Harold Lloyd, Adolphe Menjou, Helen Mack. **1936**

MILKY WAY, THE (1970) ★★★★ Haunting comedy about two men making a religious pilgrimage through France. Excellent supporting cast and outstanding direction by Luis Buñuel. French dialogue with English subtitles. Not rated. 102m. **DIR:** Luis Buñuel. **CAST:** Paul Frankeur, Laurent Terzieff, Alain Cuny, Bernard Verley, Michel Piccoli, Delphine Seyrig. **1970**

MILL OF THE STONE WOMEN ★★★ A fascinating one-shot, made in Holland by French and Italian filmmakers, about a mad professor who turns women into statues. Visually innovative, scary, and original. 63m. **DIR:** Giorgio Ferroni. **CAST:** Pierre Brice, Wolfgang Preiss, Scilla Gabel. **1960**

MILL ON THE FLOSS, THE ★★★1/2 Geraldine Fitzgerald is Maggie and James Mason is Tom Tolliver in this careful and faithful adaptation of novelist George Eliot's story of ill-starred romance. B&W; 77m. **DIR:** Tim Whelan. **CAST:** Geraldine Fitzgerald, James Mason. **1939**

MILLE BOLLE BLU ★★★★ One day in the life of the residents of an Italian apartment building in 1961, as they wait for a total eclipse of the sun. Like an Italian *Slacker,* the film's invisible star is the endlessly gliding camera that moves us effortlessly from person to person. A memorable debut from director Leone Pompucci, who gets an astonishing range of life into a brief film. Not rated; contains profanity. In Italian with English subtitles. 83m. **DIR:** Leone Pompucci. **CAST:** Paolo Bonacelli, Stefania Montorsi, Stefano Dionisi, Nicoletta Boris. **1993**

MILLENNIUM (1989) Terrible time-travel story has Kris Kristofferson as an air-disaster troubleshooter, who meets a mysterious woman from the future. Rated PG-13 for violence and suggested sex. 110m. **DIR:** Michael Anderson. **CAST:** Kris Kristofferson, Cheryl Ladd, Daniel J. Travanti, Robert Joy. **1989 DVD**

MILLENNIUM (1996) ★★★1/2 Chris Carter, the producer of the cult hit *The X-Files*, attacked an unsuspecting populace with this second TV outing, a dark thriller about the approaching turn of the century and the corresponding rise in crime. What ensued was a somewhat depressing but always fascinating look at the human condition. The tape includes the pilot and the second episode, "Gehenna." Not rated; contains graphic and disturbing content. 88m. **DIR:** David Nutter. **CAST:** Lance Henriksen, Megan Gallagher, Terry O'Quinn, Bill Smitrovich, Brittany Tiplady. **1996**

MILLER'S CROSSING ★★★★ Corrupt political boss (Albert Finney) of an eastern city severs ties with his best friend and confidant (Gabriel Byrne) in 1929 when they both fall for the same woman and find themselves on opposing sides of a violent gang war. An underworld code of ethics, protocol, and loyalty provides the ground rules for this very entertaining, slightly bent homage to past mobster films. Rated R for language and violence. 115m. **DIR:** Joel Coen. **CAST:** Gabriel Byrne, Marcia Gay Harden, John Turturro, Albert Finney, Jon Polito. **1990**

MILLION DOLLAR DUCK, THE ★★ A duck is accidentally given a dose of radiation that makes it produce eggs with solid gold yolks. Dean Jones and Sandy Duncan, as the owners of the duck, use the yolks to pay off bills until the Treasury Department gets wise. Mildly entertaining comedy in the Disney tradition. Rated G. 92m. **DIR:** Vincent McEveety. **CAST:** Dean Jones, Sandy Duncan, Joe Flynn, Tony Roberts. **1971**

MILLION DOLLAR HOTEL ★★ Despite a high-powered cast led by Mel Gibson as an FBI agent trying to solve a murder, this offbeat mystery fails to impress. There's plenty of deception and little honor among the guests, who do their best to keep things interesting. Unfortunately, the actors look lost. Big waste of talent and time. Rated R for adult situations, language, and violence. 122m. **DIR:** Wim Wenders. **CAST:** Mel Gibson, Milla Jovovich, Jimmy Smits, Peter Stormare, Amanda Plummer, Tim Roth, Gloria Stuart. **2000 DVD**

MILLION DOLLAR MERMAID ★★ Esther Williams swims through her role as famous early distaff aquatic star Annette Kellerman, who pioneered one-piece suits and vaudeville tank acts. Victor Mature woos her in this highly fictionalized film biography. The Busby Berkeley production numbers are a highlight. 115m. **DIR:** Mervyn LeRoy. **CAST:** Esther Williams, Victor Mature, Walter Pidgeon, David Brian, Jesse White. **1952**

MILLION DOLLAR MYSTERY A gimmick film that originally offered $1 million to the first audience member who could put the movie's clues together. Rated PG. 95m. **DIR:** Richard Fleischer. **CAST:** Jamie Alcroft, Royce D. Applegate, Tom Bosley, Eddie Deezen, Rich Hall, Mack Dryden. **1987**

MILLION TO JUAN, A ★★ Comedian Paul Rodriguez plays a Hispanic father in L.A. working for his green card who receives a million-dollar check. The catch: he can only "use" it, not cash it. The film is well-intentioned, but the script (loosely adapted from a Mark Twain story) tries to be too many things—romantic comedy, social satire, rags-to-riches fantasy—and winds up a mess. Rated PG. 93m. **DIR:** Paul Rodriguez. **CAST:** Paul Rodriguez, Edward James Olmos, Richard "Cheech" Marin, Rubén Blades, Polly Draper. **1994**

MILLIONAIRE'S EXPRESS (SHANGHAI EXPRESS) ★★★★1/2 Deliriously entertaining action comedy featuring Sammo Hung. He plays a rogue who tries to hijack a train filled with rich people to his hometown, hoping they'll spend money there. But he has to do battle with bandits who want all that money for themselves. Something of a tribute to the Westerns of Sergio Leone, this is hurt only by a sloppy story. Not rated; contains comic violence. 107m. **DIR:** Sammo Hung. **CAST:** Sammo Hung, Rosamund Kwan, Yuen Biao, Cynthia Rothrock, Yukari Oshima. **1986 DVD**

MILLIONS ★★ Spoiled young man whose ambitions outstrip his brainpower decides to make his fortune. Lots of sex cheapens the plot. Rated R for nudity and profanity. 90m. **DIR:** Carlo Vanzina. **CAST:** Billy Zane, Lauren Hutton, Carol Alt, Donald Pleasence, Alexandra Paul. **1991**

MILO If this movie were any more of a dog it would have fleas. You'll still wind up scratching your head wondering why the filmmakers thought we needed another *Halloween* rip-off about a woman who believes that her childhood attacker has come back to finish the job. Rated R for violence and language. 91m. **DIR:** Pascal Franchot. **CAST:** Paula Cale, Vincent Schiavelli, Antonio Fargas, Jennifer Jostyn. **1998 DVD**

MIMIC ★★★1/2 Mexican director Guillermo del Toro has made his American film debut an exciting, old-fashioned monster movie that unapologetically harkens back to the "giant bug" epics of the 1950s. Genetic engineers concoct a "designer predator" to combat a virulent disease carried by New York City cockroaches; unfortunately, after three years the cure proves much worse than the affliction. The film's first half is intriguing science and character development, leading to a slam-bang suspense finale in the bowels of the city subway system. Rated R for violence, gore, and profanity. 105m. **DIR:** Guillermo del Toro. **CAST:** Mira Sorvino, Jeremy Northam, Josh Brolin, Charles Dutton, Giancarlo Giannini, F. Murray Abraham. **1997 DVD**

•MIMIC 2 ★★1/2 A giant mutant cockroach has the ability to morph itself into human form in this mediocre direct-to-video sequel. This movie focuses on Remy and her peculiar love/hate relationship with this big bug. While not a good movie, *Mimic 2* stays fairly true to the first one. Rated R for gory violence and language. 82m.

DIR: Jean de Segonzac. **CAST:** Alix Koromzay, Bruno Campos, Will Estes. **2001 DVD**

MIN AND BILL ★★★ Their first picture together as a team puts Marie Dressler and Wallace Beery to the test when the future of the waif (Dorothy Jordan) she has reared on the rough-and-tumble waterfront is threatened by the girl's disreputable mother, Marjorie Rambeau. Her emotional portrayal won Marie Dressler an Oscar for best actress and helped make the film the box-office hit of its year. B&W; 70m. **DIR:** George Hill. **CAST:** Marie Dressler, Wallace Beery, Dorothy Jordan, Marjorie Rambeau. **1931**

MINA TANNENBAUM ★★★1/2 À la *Entre Nous* or *Beaches*, this French drama chronicles the relationship between two young girls and how it changes as they face the challenges of adulthood. Well acted and engrossingly written, it suffers only from some overreaching on the part of first-time writer-director Martine Dugowson. In French with English subtitles. 124m. **DIR:** Martine Dugowson. **CAST:** Romane Bohringer, Elsa Zylberstein, Florence Thomassin. **1994**

MINBO, OR THE GENTLE ART OF JAPANESE EXTORTION ★★★ A hotel owner tries to escape the *yakuza*—Japanese mobsters—who have infiltrated his building and are driving away his customers. Filmmaker Juzo Itami had his own trouble with *yakuza*, and this film is an act of revenge, though it's a subpar effort. Still, there are enough amusing tangents to keep viewers entertained. In Japanese with English subtitles. Not rated; contains violence, nudity, and profanity. 123m. **DIR:** Juzo Itami. **CAST:** Nobuko Miyamoto, Akira Takarada, Takehiro Murata, Yasuo Daichi. **1992**

MIND FIELD ★★1/2 When cop Michael Ironside starts hallucinating, he traces the cause of his delusions to a secret CIA experiment involving LSD. Rated R for violence. 92m. **DIR:** Jean-Claude Lord. **CAST:** Michael Ironside, Sean McCann, Christopher Plummer, Lisa Langlois. **1990**

MIND KILLER ★★ A nerdy library worker uncovers a manuscript about the power of positive thinking. Soon he has the power to control minds and to lift objects mentally. But the power has its drawbacks, turning him into a monster. The movie is low-budget, but the filmmakers try hard. Not rated; contains adult language and situations. 84m. **DIR:** Michael Krueger. **CAST:** Joe McDonald. **1987**

MIND RIPPER ★★ Low-budget thriller about a government experiment gone awry and the former supervisor who is called back into action to kill the manmade creature. Even though most of the action takes place in an underground laboratory, this film isn't nearly claustrophobic enough. Rated R for violence and adult language. 90m. **DIR:** Joe Gayton. **CAST:** Lance Henriksen, John Diehl, Natasha Gregson Wagner, Dan Blom, Claire Stansfield. **1995**

MIND SNATCHERS, THE ★★★ Christopher Walken plays a nihilistic U.S. soldier in West Germany who is admitted to a mental institution. He finds out later the hospital is actually a laboratory where a German scientist is testing a new form of psychological control. Walken's performance is excellent and the idea is an interesting one, but the film moves slowly. Rated PG for violence and profanity. 94m. **DIR:** Bernard Girard. **CAST:** Christopher Walken, Ronny Cox, Joss Ackland, Ralph Meeker. **1972**

MINDGAMES ★★★ Taut thriller features Maxwell Caulfield as a psychotic hitchhiker who attaches himself to an unhappy couple and their son. What follows is a series of violent and unnerving mind games. Rated R for violence. 93m. **DIR:** Bob Yari. **CAST:** Maxwell Caulfield, Edward Albert, Shawn Weatherly. **1989**

MINDTWISTER 🦃 Schlockmeister Fred Olen Ray refurbishes one of his soft-core quickies by adding disparate scenes with Telly Savalas, who undoubtedly had no control over how his footage was used. Beware this cut-and-paste rubbish. Rated R for nudity, simulated sex, violence, and profanity. 95m. **DIR:** Fred Olen Ray. **CAST:** Telly Savalas, Suzanne Slater, Gary Hudson, Erika Nann, Richard Roundtree. **1993**

MINDWALK ★★★ A trio of archetypes—a scientist (Liv Ullmann), a politician (Sam Waterston), and a poet (John Heard)—discuss the current "crisis in perspective," which comes from the discovery, in physics, that the old, "mechanistic" way of looking at life (thinking about living things in terms of their components) should be replaced by a more holistic view. More of a lecture than a movie, *Mindwalk* will fascinate those who appreciate novelist-turned-screenwriter Fritjof Capra's theories. Rated PG. 111m. **DIR:** Berndt Capra. **CAST:** Liv Ullmann, Sam Waterston, John Heard, Ione Skye. **1991**

MINDWARP ★★★1/2 After a nuclear war, randomly chosen individuals dwell in underground bunkers, living their lives out in computer-generated fantasies. But when one girl rebels, she is exiled to the surface. Low-budget, but fun gross-out action-thriller. Rated R for nudity, profanity, and violence. 91m. **DIR:** Steve Barnett. **CAST:** Bruce Campbell, Angus Scrimm, Elizabeth Kent. **1991**

MINE OWN EXECUTIONER ★★★ Noted psychiatrist Burgess Meredith accepts ex–fighter pilot and Japanese prisoner of war Kieron Moore as a patient. He finds himself in the thick of a schizophrenic's hell, resulting in murder and suicide. Top-notch suspense. B&W; 105m. **DIR:** Anthony Kimmins. **CAST:** Burgess Meredith, Kieron Moore, Dulcie Gray. **1948**

MINES OF KILIMANJARO ★★ *Raiders of the Lost Ark* imitation with an American college student in Africa searching for the lost diamond mines of Kilimanjaro. Trying to stop him are the Nazis, Chinese gangsters, and native tribesmen. The action footage is badly choreographed, the music is strident, and the historical accuracy is a laugh. Not rated; contains violence. 88m. **DIR:** Mino Guerrini. **CAST:** Tobias Hoesl, Elena Pompei, Christopher Connelly. **1987**

MINGUS ★★★ Revealing portrait of Charles Mingus, the great bassist, considered to be one of the most influential figures in jazz. Most of this film was shot in his cluttered New York loft as he awaited eviction in the wake of a legal tangle with the city. B&W; 58m. **DIR:** Thomas Reichmann. **1968**

MINION, THE 🦃 In what may be his worst movie ever, hulking Dolph Lundgren plays a heavenly warrior called into action when the gateway that will let Satan onto Earth is sundered. Also released as *Fallen Knight*. Rated R for horror, violence, and profanity. 96m. **DIR:**

Jean-Marc Piché. **CAST:** Dolph Lundgren, Françoise Robertson. **1998**

MINISTRY OF VENGEANCE 🦃 Loathsome in every respect—a minister reverts to his military training to seek revenge on terrorists. Rated R for violence. 93m. **DIR:** Peter Maris. **CAST:** John Schneider, Ned Beatty, James Tolkan, Apollonia Kotero, Robert Miano, Yaphet Kotto, George Kennedy. **1989**

MINIVER STORY, THE ★★1/2 Post–World War II sequel to the popular *Mrs. Miniver* has Greer Garson putting her family's affairs in order while hiding the fact that she is dying. Good performances by the stars, but it is really just pure soap opera. B&W; 104m. **DIR:** H. C. Potter. **CAST:** Greer Garson, Walter Pidgeon, John Hodiak, Leo Genn, Cathy O'Donnell, Reginald Owen, Peter Finch, Henry Wilcoxon. **1950**

MINOR MIRACLE, A ★★1/2 A heartwarming story about a group of orphaned children and their devoted guardian (John Huston), who band together to save the St. Francis School for Boys. If you liked *Going My Way* and *Oh God!* you'll like this G-rated movie. 100m. **DIR:** Raoul Lomas. **CAST:** John Huston, Pelé, Peter Fox. **1983**

MINUS MAN, THE ★★★ An amiable drifter befriends strangers, soothes them with drawling small talk, then kills them with a painless, fast-acting poison. The film hints at deep waters under the killer's placid surface, but never plumbs them. It's disconnected and a little frustrating to watch, but the film's elusiveness seems to embody that of the central character. Rated R for mature themes. 112m. **DIR:** Hampton Fancher. **CAST:** Owen Wilson, Brian Cox, Janeane Garofalo, Dwight Yoakam, Mercedes Ruehl, Dennis Haysbert, Sheryl Crow. **1999 DVD**

MINUTE TO PRAY, A SECOND TO DIE, A ★★ This is a routine Western with Alex Cord as an outlaw trying to turn himself in when amnesty is declared by the governor of New Mexico (played by Robert Ryan). Arthur Kennedy, as the marshal, has other plans. Rated R for violence. 99m. **DIR:** Franco Giraldi. **CAST:** Alex Cord, Arthur Kennedy, Robert Ryan, Nicoletta Machiavelli. **1967**

MIRACLE, THE (1959) ★★★ In Spain in the early 1800s, a postulant nun deserts her order to search for a soldier she loves and becomes a noted gypsy, singer, and courtesan. Tries for deep religious meaning but misses the mark. 120m. **DIR:** Irving Rapper. **CAST:** Carroll Baker, Roger Moore, Walter Slezak, Vittorio Gassman, Katina Paxinou, Dennis King. **1959**

MIRACLE, THE (1990) ★★★ Two Irish teenagers (Niall Byrne and Lorraine Pilkington) while away their days fantasizing about people they encounter. When a mysterious woman (Beverly D'Angelo) arrives, Byrne takes it a step further only to find out that she's the mother he never knew. A pleasant surprise. Rated PG for profanity. 100m. **DIR:** Neil Jordan. **CAST:** Beverly D'Angelo, Niall Byrne, Donal McCann, Lorraine Pilkington. **1990**

MIRACLE AT MIDNIGHT ★★★★ Sam Waterston and Mia Farrow star in this movie based on a true story about a Danish family that helped Jews escape from a Denmark under siege by the Nazis. During one fateful evening they attempt to sneak out a few Jewish families right under the nose of a watchful enemy army. While not as gripping as say, *Schindler's List*, this movie is quite good and is suitable for all ages. Not rated. 89m. **DIR:** Ken Cameron. **CAST:** Sam Waterston, Mia Farrow, Justin Whalin. **1998**

MIRACLE BEACH ★★★ Delightful fantasy unfolds when an all-around loser finds a genie who can grant all his wishes. Rated R for nudity and simulated sex. 88m. **DIR:** Skott Snider. **CAST:** Dean Cameron, Ami Dolenz, Felicity Waterman, Noriyuki "Pat" Morita. **1991**

MIRACLE DOWN UNDER ★★★1/2 This moving drama is actually *A Christmas Carol* Australian style. Only a small boy's kindness can rekindle an evil miser's Christmas spirit. This fine family film contains no objectionable material. 106m. **DIR:** George Miller. **CAST:** Dee Wallace, John Waters, Charles Tingwell, Bill Kerr, Andrew Ferguson. **1987**

MIRACLE IN LANE 2 ★★★★ Inspirational, true-life story about a paralyzed boy who overcomes adversity to become a soapbox-derby champion. Frankie Muniz shines as Justin Yoder, the 12-year-old boy who uses optimism and humor to get by. Envious of his brother's numerous athletic trophies, Justin sets out to win one of his own. His quest lands him in the driver's seat of the soapbox derby, where he excels despite his disability. This made-for-television Disney movie is filled with strong performances, an encouraging message, and enough hope and spirit to push it past the finish line. Honestly affecting underdog tale. Not rated. 89m. **DIR:** Greg Beeman. **CAST:** Frankie Muniz, Rick Rossovich, Molly Hagan, Patrick Levis, Roger Aaron Brown. **2000**

MIRACLE IN MILAN ★★★1/2 A baby found in a cabbage patch grows up to be Toto the Good, who organizes a shantytown into the perfect commune. Or so he had hoped, but it is not to be—even with the help of the old lady who found him, now an angel of mercy. This fantasy by Vittorio De Sica also delivers a message of social satire and innocence. Winner of the Cannes Grand Prix and the New York Film Critics' Circle best foreign film awards. In Italian with English subtitles. B&W; 96m. **DIR:** Vittorio De Sica. **CAST:** Francesco Golisano, Paolo Stoppa. **1951**

MIRACLE IN ROME ★★★ Spanish TV film adaptation of Gabriel Garcia Marquez's intriguing tale of one man's struggle with sainthood. Frank Ramirez plays the bereaved father who's lost his vivacious 7-year-old daughter. Heartwarming, though morbid, insight into a man's undying love and devotion for his innocent child. In Spanish with English subtitles. 76m. **DIR:** Lisandro Duque Naranjo. **CAST:** Frank Ramirez. **1988**

MIRACLE IN THE WILDERNESS ★★ Heavy-handed message film spreads the "give peace a chance" motto. When settlers (Kris Kristofferson and Kim Cattrall) are kidnapped by vengeful Blackfeet Indians, Kristofferson's violent attempts to save his wife and child are in vain. Only Cattrall's gentle ways can free them. Preachy and unbelievable made-for-cable drama. 88m. **DIR:** Kevin James Dobson. **CAST:** Kris Kristofferson, Kim Cattrall, John Dennis Johnston. **1991**

MIRACLE MILE ★★★★ A fascinatingly frightful study of mass hysteria centered on a spreading rumor that a nuclear holocaust is imminent. Anthony Edwards accidentally overhears a phone conversation that "the button has been pushed." He learns that Los Angeles is seventy minutes from destruction and must scramble about, trying to discover the truth and possibly save

himself and others. Superb. Rated R. 87m. **DIR:** Steve DeJarnett. **CAST:** Anthony Edwards, Mare Winningham, John Agar. **1989**

MIRACLE OF MORGAN'S CREEK, THE ★★★★1/2 All comic hell breaks loose when Betty Hutton finds herself pregnant following an all-night party, can't recall who the father is, and eventually gives birth to sextuplets. An audacious, daring Bronx cheer at American morals and ideals, this rollicking farce, cram-jammed with comic lines, is a real winner. B&W; 99m. **DIR:** Preston Sturges. **CAST:** Betty Hutton, Eddie Bracken, William Demarest, Diana Lynn, Brian Donlevy, Akim Tamiroff, Jimmy Conlin, Porter Hall. **1944**

MIRACLE OF OUR LADY OF FATIMA, THE ★★★1/2 Remarkably well-told story of the famous appearance of the Virgin Mary in the small town of Fatima, Portugal. The Virgin appears to some farm children and they try to spread her word to a skeptical world. Not rated, but equivalent to a G. 102m. **DIR:** John Brahm. **CAST:** Gilbert Roland, Frank Silvera, Sherry Jackson. **1952**

MIRACLE OF THE BELLS, THE ★★★ A miracle takes place when a movie star is buried in her coal-mining hometown. Hard-bitten press agent Fred MacMurray turns mushy to see "the kid" gets the right send-off. The story is trite and its telling too long, but the cast is earnest and the film has a way of clicking. B&W; 120m. **DIR:** Irving Pichel. **CAST:** Fred MacMurray, Alida Valli, Frank Sinatra, Lee J. Cobb. **1948**

MIRACLE OF THE HEART ★★★ Made-for-TV sequel to the 1938 *Boys Town*, which featured Spencer Tracy as Father Flanagan. This time, Art Carney plays one of Flanagan's boys, who is now an older priest. Touching and heartwarming. 96m. **DIR:** Georg Stanford Brown. **CAST:** Art Carney, Casey Siemaszko, Jack Bannon, Darrell Larson. **1986**

MIRACLE OF THE WHITE STALLIONS ★★ True story of the evacuation of the famed Lipizzan stallions from war-torn Vienna doesn't pack much of a wallop; kids and horse fans should enjoy it. 92m. **DIR:** Arthur Hiller. **CAST:** Robert Taylor, Lilli Palmer, Curt Jurgens, Eddie Albert, James Franciscus, John Larch. **1963**

MIRACLE ON ICE ★★1/2 This made-for-TV movie reenacts the American hockey victory at the 1980 Lake Placid Olympic Games. Karl Malden plays his usual tough-but-fair persona to the hilt as character-building coach Herb Brooks. 140m. **DIR:** Steven H. Stern. **CAST:** Karl Malden, Andrew Stevens, Steve Guttenberg, Jessica Walter. **1981**

MIRACLE ON 34TH STREET (1947) ★★★★★ In this, one of Hollywood's most delightful fantasies, the spirit of Christmas is rekindled in a young girl (Natalie Wood) by a department store Santa. Edmund Gwenn is perfect as the endearing Macy's employee who causes a furor when he claims to be the real Kris Kringle. Is he or isn't he? That is for you to decide in this heartwarming family classic. B&W; 96m. **DIR:** George Seaton. **CAST:** Natalie Wood, Edmund Gwenn, Maureen O'Hara. **1947 DVD**

MIRACLE ON 34TH STREET (1994) ★★★★ Young Mara Wilson *owns* this heartfelt remake of George Seaton's holiday classic, as a precocious little girl who'd like to believe in Santa Claus... if only her overly practical mother would permit it. Richard Attenborough is the angelic Kris Kringle, whose tenure as a department-store Santa prompts all sorts of holiday magic. Rated PG. 114m. **DIR:** Les Mayfield. **CAST:** Richard Attenborough, Elizabeth Perkins, Dylan McDermott, Mara Wilson, J. T. Walsh, James Remar, Jane Leeves, Simon Jones, William Windom, Robert Prosky. **1994 DVD**

MIRACLE WORKER, THE (1962) ★★★★1/2 Anne Bancroft and Patty Duke are superb when re-creating their acclaimed Broadway performances in this production. Patty Duke is the untamed and blind deaf-mute Helen Keller and Bancroft is her equally strong-willed, but compassionate, teacher. Their harrowing fight for power and the ultimately touching first communication make up one of the screen's great sequences. B&W; 107m. **DIR:** Arthur Penn. **CAST:** Anne Bancroft, Patty Duke, Andrew Prine. **1962 DVD**

MIRACLE WORKER, THE (1979) ★★★1/2 This made-for-TV biography features Patty Duke as Anne Sullivan, teacher and friend of a disturbed deaf and blind girl. Melissa Gilbert takes the role of Helen Keller, which garnered an Oscar for Duke in 1962. This version is not quite as moving as the earlier one, but it's still worth watching. 100m. **DIR:** Paul Aaron. **CAST:** Patty Duke, Melissa Gilbert, Charles Siebert. **1979**

MIRACLES ★★1/2 This film involves a sick little girl in a remote Mexican jungle, a doctor and his recently divorced wife in L.A., and a bungling burglar. The story revolves around the sometimes funny circumstances that bring all these characters together. Rated PG for language and mild violence. 90m. **DIR:** Jim Kouf. **CAST:** Tom Conti, Teri Garr, Paul Rodriguez, Christopher Lloyd. **1986 DVD**

MIRAGE (1965) ★★★ Some really fine scenes and top-notch actors enliven this slow but ultimately satisfying mystery thriller. Gregory Peck is David Stillwell, a man who has lost his memory. Occasionally snappy dialogue, with an interesting but overdone use of flashbacks. B&W; 108m. **DIR:** Edward Dmytryk. **CAST:** Gregory Peck, Diane Baker, Walter Matthau, Kevin McCarthy, Jack Weston, George Kennedy, Leif Erickson, Walter Abel. **1965**

MIRAGE (1995) ★★★ An ex-cop is hired to protect a mysterious, beautiful woman and they find themselves drawn to each other. Amid their passion, however, a hidden, sinister plot exposes itself. Entertaining mystery-thriller offers a gritty performance from Edward James Olmos and an intriguing turn by Sean Young. Rated R for profanity, violence, and nudity. 92m. **DIR:** Paul Williams. **CAST:** Edward James Olmos, Sean Young, James Andronica. **1995**

MIRROR, THE ★★★★ A young boy is hypnotized in an attempt to cure a chronic stutter in this poetic mixture of dream and reality by the Soviet Union's most visionary film director, Andrei Tarkovsky. Brilliant use of color and black-and-white cinematography. Mesmerizing. In Russian with English subtitles. 90m. **DIR:** Andrei Tarkovsky. **CAST:** Margarita Terekhova. **1976 DVD**

MIRROR CRACK'D, THE ★★ Elizabeth Taylor, Kim Novak, and Tony Curtis seem to be vying to see who can turn in the worst performance in this tepid adaptation of the Agatha Christie murder mystery. Angela Lansbury makes an excellent Miss Marple, and Edward Fox is top-notch as her Scotland Yard inspector nephew. Rated PG. 105m. **DIR:** Guy Hamilton. **CAST:** Elizabeth Taylor, Kim Novak, Tony Curtis, Angela Lansbury, Edward Fox, Rock Hudson. **1980 DVD**

MIRROR CRACK'D FROM SIDE TO SIDE, THE ★★★1/2 This Agatha Christie mystery is an enjoyable puzzle filled with red herrings. Miss Marple must help her nephew, Inspector Craddock, find the murderer. Not rated; suitable for family viewing. 100m. **DIR:** Norman Stone. **CAST:** Joan Hickson, Claire Bloom, Barry Newman, Glynis Barber, John Castle, Judy Cornwell, David Horovitch. **1992**

MIRROR HAS TWO FACES, THE ★★★ Typical Barbra Streisand "Am I pretty?" neurosis is pleasantly showcased in this romantic comedy. A good date film, this features Streisand as a prof pursued by a sexy math whiz (Jeff Bridges) who seeks a platonic marital relationship. Frustrated by their lack of intimacy, Streisand sells out by transforming herself into a hot looker. Rated PG-13 for language and sexual situations. 125m. **DIR:** Barbra Streisand. **CAST:** Barbra Streisand, Jeff Bridges, Pierce Brosnan, George Segal, Mimi Rogers, Lauren Bacall, Brenda Vaccaro. **1996 DVD**

MIRROR MIRROR ★★1/2 An awkward teenage girl uses black magic, gained from an arcane mirror, to avenge herself on her cruel classmates. The film tries hard, but there's no payoff. Rated R for violence and profanity. 105m. **DIR:** Marina Sargenti. **CAST:** Karen Black, Rainbow Harvest, Yvonne De Carlo, William Sanderson. **1990**

MIRROR, MIRROR 2: RAVEN DANCE ★★ Ballerina Tracy Wells, recovering from a bad fall at a nunnery, comes across the haunted mirror and unleashes the terrors within. The actors chew the scenery, while everything else just trudges along at a ho-hum pace. Rated R for violence. 91m. **DIR:** Jimmy Lifton. **CAST:** Tracy Wells, Sally Kellerman, Roddy McDowall, Sarah Douglas, Veronica Cartwright, William Sanderson. **1993 DVD**

MIRROR OF DEATH An abused woman takes up voodoo as therapy. Not rated, but has violence, gore, and profanity. 85m. **DIR:** Deryn Warren. **CAST:** Julie Merrill. **1987**

MIRRORS ★★1/2 An aspiring ballerina must choose between the love of her straitlaced boyfriend and her struggle to become a dancer in New York. Her small-town values are challenged by the free-spirited theatrical gypsies wtih whom she works. The idea is riveting, but plot twists seem contrived. Not rated; contains nudity. 99m. **DIR:** Harry Winer. **CAST:** Marguerite Hickey, Timothy Daly, Shanna Reed, Antony Hamilton, Keenan Wynn. **1985**

MISADVENTURES OF BUSTER KEATON, THE ★★ The world-famous "Great Stone Face" has his moments in this sound version of one of his classic silent comedies but falls short of what he did in his prime. Still, Keaton running a small theater, bumbling and fumbling at every turn, is a delight to behold. B&W; 65m. **DIR:** Arthur Hilton. **CAST:** Buster Keaton, Marcia Mae Jones. **1950**

MISADVENTURES OF MERLIN JONES, THE ★★1/2 Tommy Kirk stars as a boy genius whose talents for mind reading and hypnotism land him in all sorts of trouble. Entertaining for the young or indiscriminate; pretty bland for everybody else. 88m. **DIR:** Robert Stevenson. **CAST:** Tommy Kirk, Annette Funicello, Leon Ames, Stu Erwin, Alan Hewitt. **1964**

MISADVENTURES OF MR. WILT, THE ★★★1/2 Screwball British comedy about a man trying to explain to the police that he didn't kill his wife, but a life-size blow-up doll. Told in flashback, this is an effective little film that is hampered only by a disappointing ending. Rated R for profanity. 84m. **DIR:** Michael Tuchner. **CAST:** Griff Rhys Jones, Mel Smith, Alison Steadman, Diana Quick. **1989**

MISCHIEF ★★★ In this disarming coming-of-age comedy, Doug McKeon (*On Golden Pond*) plays Jonathan, whose hopes of romance are thwarted until Gene (Chris Nash, in an impressive debut), a kid from the big city, shows him how. Rated R for violence, profanity, nudity, and simulated sex. 93m. **DIR:** Mel Damski. **CAST:** Doug McKeon, Catherine Mary Stewart, Chris Nash, Kelly Preston, D. W. Brown. **1985**

MISERY ★★★★ In this black-comedy thriller, James Caan stars as a popular novelist, who is kept captive by his most ardent fan (Kathy Bates, who scored a best-actress Oscar)—who just happens to be a psychopath. As written by Academy Award–winner William Goldman, it's the best Stephen King adaptation since Rob Reiner's *Stand by Me*. Rated R for profanity and violence. 104m. **DIR:** Rob Reiner. **CAST:** James Caan, Kathy Bates, Richard Farnsworth, Frances Sternhagen, Lauren Bacall. **1990 DVD**

MISFIT BRIGADE, THE ★★★ Oliver Reed and David Carradine have cameo roles in this takeoff on *The Dirty Dozen*. Bruce Davison, David Patrick Kelly, and their buddies are assorted criminals from a Nazi penal brigade. The cast has a lot of fun with the tongue-in-cheek action. Rated R. 99m. **DIR:** Gordon Hessler. **CAST:** Bruce Davison, David Patrick Kelly, D. W. Moffett, Oliver Reed, David Carradine, Jay O. Sanders. **1987**

MISFITS, THE ★★★ Arthur Miller's parable of a hope-stripped divorcée and a gaggle of her boot-shod cowpoke boyfriends shagging wild horses in the Nevada desert, this film was the last hurrah for Marilyn Monroe and Clark Gable. The acting is good, but the story line is lean. B&W; 124m. **DIR:** John Huston. **CAST:** Marilyn Monroe, Clark Gable, Montgomery Clift, Thelma Ritter, Eli Wallach, Estelle Winwood. **1961 DVD**

MISFITS OF SCIENCE ★★1/2 Dean Paul Martin stars as the ringleader of a group of individuals possessing unique abilities. He rallies them together to combine their powers. No rating. This was the first installment in the failed television series. 96m. **DIR:** James D. Parriott. **CAST:** Dean Paul Martin, Kevin Peter Hall, Mark Thomas Miller, Courteney Cox. **1986**

MISHIMA: A LIFE IN FOUR CHAPTERS ★★★★ By depicting this enigmatic writer's life through his art, filmmaker Paul Schrader has come close to illustrating the true heart of an artist. This is not a standard narrative biography but a bold attempt to meld an artist's life with his life's work. The movie is, as suggested in the title, divided into four parts: "Beauty," "Art," "Action," and the climactic "A Harmony of Pen and Sword." Rated R for sex, nudity, violence, and adult situations. 121m. **DIR:** Paul Schrader. **CAST:** Ken Ogata, Ken Swada, Yasusuka Brando. **1985 DVD**

MISPLACED ★★★ A modest but appealing independent film about the hurdles facing a teenage immigrant, newly arrived in America. Set in 1981, *Misplaced* is part

coming-of-age tale and part cross-cultural drama. Not rated. 98m. **DIR:** Louis Yansen. **CAST:** John Cameron Mitchell, Elzbieta Czyzewska, Viveca Lindfors. **1991**

MISS ANNIE ROONEY ★★ The highlight of this film comes when Dickie Moore gives Shirley Temple her first screen kiss. The rest of this average picture involves a poor girl who falls in love with a rich dandy. No sparks here. 84m. **DIR:** Edwin L. Marin. **CAST:** Shirley Temple, William Gargan, Guy Kibbee, Dickie Moore, Peggy Ryan, Gloria Holden. **1942**

MISS CONGENIALITY ★★★★ Perfect Sandra Bullock vehicle allows her to fill this action-packed comedy with pratfalls galore. As a frumpy-looking FBI agent, she goes undercover to compete in a beauty contest targeted by a serial bomber. Michael Caine delights as the makeover genius hired to transform her. Rated PG-13 for violence and profanity. 111m. **DIR:** Donald Petrie. **CAST:** Sandra Bullock, Michael Caine, Candice Bergen, Benjamin Bratt. **2000 DVD**

MISS EVERS' BOYS ★★★★ Recent American history is filled with atrocities, and this remains one of the worst: the 1932 "Tuskegee Study" that took place in Macon County, Alabama, and traced the development of untreated syphilis in the African American male. Alfre Woodard plays the title character in this HBO production, a nurse who fully understands the consequences of what she condones by her silence, but rationalizes that the "study" somehow contributes to a greater good. Your heart will ache for the trusting men who naïvely believed they were being cured. Rated PG-13 for profanity and sexual candor. 120m. **DIR:** Joseph Sargent. **CAST:** Alfre Woodard, Laurence Fishburne, Craig Sheffer, Joe Morton, Obba Babatundé, E. G. Marshall, Ossie Davis. **1996 DVD**

MISS FIRECRACKER ★★★★ A wacky, colorful, feel-good movie about a young Mississippi woman whose hunger for self-respect takes her through the rigors of her hometown Yazoo City Miss Firecracker Contest. Holly Hunter is marvelous as the misguided woman, while Mary Steenburgen shines as her cousin. From the off-Broadway play by Beth (*Crimes of the Heart*) Henley. Rated PG. 102m. **DIR:** Thomas Schlamme. **CAST:** Holly Hunter, Mary Steenburgen, Tim Robbins, Alfre Woodard, Scott Glenn. **1989**

MISS GRANT TAKES RICHMOND ★★★ Lucille Ball plays a dizzy secretary who outwits a band of thieves and wins handsome William Holden (who looks just as baffled as he did years later guest-starring on *I Love Lucy*). Agreeable star vehicle has a stalwart supporting cast. B&W; 87m. **DIR:** Lloyd Bacon. **CAST:** Lucille Ball, William Holden, Janis Carter, James Gleason, Frank McHugh. **1949**

MISS JULIE (1950) ★★ An impetuous young Swedish countess rejected by her fiancé flirts with and then seduces a handsome servant. Brooding melodrama based on a Strindberg play becomes a very tedious experience. In Swedish with English subtitles. Not rated; contains nudity. B&W; 90m. **DIR:** Alf Sjoberg. **CAST:** Anita Bjork, Ulf Palme, Max von Sydow. **1950**

MISS JULIE (1999) ★★ A haughty young Swedish countess is irresistibly drawn to her father's valet. August Strindberg's play, a groundbreaker for its sexual frankness one hundred years ago, has not retained its cutting edge and it's frankly an excruciating bore. Rated R for sexual content and some profanity. 100m. **DIR:** Mike Figgis. **CAST:** Saffron Burrows, Peter Mullan, Maria Doyle Kennedy. **1999 DVD**

MISS LULU BETT ★★★ Miss Lulu is the family drone who is tricked into marriage and seemingly loses her chance at happiness with the man she loves. How she liberates herself from a life of servitude is a surprisingly frank look at an unmarried woman's role in the first decades of the twentieth century and is one of the best-remembered vehicles of pioneer women's rights activist Lois Wilson. B&W; 65m. **DIR:** William C. de Mille. **CAST:** Lois Wilson, Theodore Roberts, Milton Sills, Helen Ferguson, Mary Girachi, Mabel Van Buren, Taylor Graves. **1921**

MISS MARY ★★★1/2 A good knowledge of the history of Argentina—specifically between the years 1930 and 1945—will help viewers appreciate this biting black comedy. Julie Christie gives a marvelous performance as a British governess brought to the South American country to work for a wealthy family. Through her eyes, in a series of flashbacks, we see how the corrupt aristocracy slowly falls apart. In both English and Spanish. Rated R for profanity, nudity, and suggested and simulated sex. 100m. **DIR:** Maria Luisa Bemberg. **CAST:** Julie Christie, Nacha Guevara, Tato Pavlovsky. **1987**

MISS RIGHT ★★ This vignettish, uneven sex comedy strongly resembles TV's *Love American Style*. A UPI correspondent in Rome (William Tepper) becomes involved with several beautiful women. Rated R for profanity and nudity. 98m. **DIR:** Paul Williams. **CAST:** William Tepper, Karen Black, Margot Kidder, Virna Lisi, Marie-France Pisier, Clio Goldsmith. **1988**

MISS ROSE WHITE ★★★★ *Hallmark Hall of Fame* movie starring Kyra Sedgwick as a young Jewish career woman forced to confront her family's heritage and tragic past. Heartwarming with captivating performances by the entire cast. 95m. **DIR:** Joseph Sargent. **CAST:** Kyra Sedgwick, Maximilian Schell, Amanda Plummer, D. B. Sweeney, Penny Fuller, Milton Selzer. **1992**

MISS SADIE THOMPSON ★★1/2 A remake of *Rain*, the 1932 adaptation of Somerset Maugham's novel with Joan Crawford and Walter Huston, this production (with music) is notable only for the outstanding performance by Rita Hayworth in the title role. 91m. **DIR:** Curtis Bernhardt. **CAST:** Rita Hayworth, José Ferrer, Aldo Ray. **1953**

MISSILE TO THE MOON 🦃 Silly story of renegade expedition to the Moon. B&W; 78m. **DIR:** Richard Cunha. **CAST:** Richard Travis, Cathy Downes, K. T. Stevens, Michael Whalen, Tommy Cook, Gary Clarke. **1958 DVD**

MISSILES OF OCTOBER, THE ★★★★1/2 This is a superbly cast, well-written, excitingly directed made-for-TV film dealing with the crucial decisions that were made during the Cuban missile crisis of October 1962. It follows the hour-by-hour situations that occurred when the U.S. government discovered that the Soviet Union was installing offensive missiles in Cuba. Gripping and realistic. 175m. **DIR:** Anthony Page. **CAST:** William Devane, Ralph Bellamy, Martin Sheen, Howard DaSilva. **1974 DVD**

MISSING ★★★★★ A superb political thriller directed by Costa-Gavras, this stars Jack Lemmon and

Sissy Spacek as the father and wife of a journalist who disappears during a bloody South American coup. Rated R for violence, nudity, and profanity. 122m. **DIR:** Constantin Costa-Gavras. **CAST:** Jack Lemmon, Sissy Spacek, John Shea, Melanie Mayron, Janice Rule, David Clennon. **1982**

MISSING IN ACTION ★★★1/2 Chuck Norris is a one-man army in this Vietnam-based action film. Anyone else might be laughable in such a role. But the former karate star makes it work. The story focuses on an attempt by Col. James Braddock (Norris), a former Vietnam prisoner of war, to free the other Americans he believes are still there. Rated R for profanity, violence, and brief nudity. 101m. **DIR:** Joseph Zito. **CAST:** Chuck Norris, M. Emmet Walsh, Lenore Kasdorf, James Hong. **1984 DVD**

MISSING IN ACTION 2: THE BEGINNING ★★1/2 Following on the heels of the previous year's surprise hit, this "prequel" is really the same movie, only it tells the story of how Colonel Braddock (Chuck Norris) and his men escaped their Vietnam prison camp after ten years of torture. The acting is nonexistent, the action predictable and violent. Rated R for violence. 95m. **DIR:** Lance Hool. **CAST:** Chuck Norris, Cosie Costa, Soon-Tek Oh, Steven Williams. **1985**

MISSING LINK ★★★1/2 A beautifully photographed story of a man-ape's journey across the desolate African plain after his people are killed by the encroachment of man. A pseudo-documentary style offers a breathtaking view of some of Earth's strangest creatures. First-rate man-ape makeup by Academy Award–winner Rick Baker. Rated PG. 92m. **DIR:** David Hughes, Carol Hughes. **CAST:** Peter Elliott, Michael Gambon. **1988**

MISSING PIECES (1994) ★★1/2 An ancient riddle sends two friends on a quest for fame and fortune in this so-so comedy. Eric Idle plays Wendell, a greeting-card writer whose life is in a slump—then he inherits an ancient riddle from a Chinese relative. It sets the scene for a madcap chase across the United States, ending up in San Francisco. Rated PG. 93m. **DIR:** Leonard Stern. **CAST:** Eric Idle, Robert Wuhl, Lauren Hutton, Richard Belzer. **1994**

MISSING PIECES (2000) ★★★1/2 Based on Ron Hansen's novel *Atticus*, this suspenseful *Hallmark Hall of Fame* film focuses on a parent's inability to accept his estranged son's apparent suicide. Determined to find out what really happened to his son in Mexico, he begins his own investigation. Despite a slow start, the plot's many twists reel viewers in for a surprising, satisfying conclusion. Not rated; contains mature themes. 99m. **DIR:** Carl Schenkel. **CAST:** James Coburn, Paul Kersey, Lisa Zane. **2000**

MISSION, THE ★★★1/2 Jeremy Irons plays a Spanish Jesuit who goes into the South American wilderness to build a mission in the hope of converting the Indians of the region. Robert De Niro plays a slave hunter who is converted and joins Irons in his mission. When Spain sells the colony to Portugal, they are forced to defend all they have built against the Portuguese aggressors. Rated PG for violence and sex. 125m. **DIR:** Roland Joffe. **CAST:** Jeremy Irons, Robert De Niro, Liam Neeson, Ray McAnally, Aidan Quinn. **1986 DVD**

MISSION GALACTICA: THE CYLON ATTACK ★★1/2 Feature-length reediting of episodes from TV's *Battlestar Galactica* finds crew of this extremely simplistic, juvenile space opera under attack from their mortal enemy, the Cylons. 108m. **DIR:** Vince Edwards. **CAST:** Lorne Greene, Dirk Benedict. **1979**

MISSION: IMPOSSIBLE ★★★★ A crack team of American undercover agents is assigned to set up operations in Prague to catch a double agent in the act. Based on the 1960s television series, this film keeps viewers wondering what's going to happen next, right up to the spectacular, climactic train sequence. Rated PG-13 for violence and profanity. 110m. **DIR:** Brian De Palma. **CAST:** Tom Cruise, Jon Voight, Emmanuelle Beart, Emilio Estevez, Vanessa Redgrave, Harry Czerny, Jean Reno, Ving Rhames, Kristin Scott Thomas. **1996 DVD**

MISSION: IMPOSSIBLE 2 ★★★★ Trust legendary action director John Woo to revitalize this big-screen franchise, which got off to a rocky start with the morose and overly complicated events of its predecessor. This time out, covert operative Ethan Hunt (Tom Cruise) reprises a story line lifted from Alfred Hitchcock's *Notorious* by recruiting a civilian (Thandie Newton), falling for her, and then reluctantly ordering her to patch things up with—and spy on—a former lover who's threatening the world with a super-virus. The twisty love triangle carries more depth than you'd expect, and pleasantly occupies us until Woo's all-stops-out climax. Cruise fits superbly with the director's signature flourishes; the result is a high-octane action epic that doesn't have much to do with the original TV series, but is nonetheless exciting and entertaining. Rated PG-13 for violence and sensuality. 126m. **DIR:** John Woo. **CAST:** Tom Cruise, Dougray Scott, Thandie Newton, Richard Roxburgh, Ving Rhames, John Polson, Brendan Gleeson, Rade Sherbedgia. **2000 DVD**

MISSION IN MOROCCO ★★ Lex Barker stars as an American oil executive whose murdered partner possessed a microfilm that shows the location of oil in Morocco. Tired adventure yawner shot on location in Morocco. B&W; 79m. **DIR:** Anthony Squire. **CAST:** Lex Barker, Juli Redding. **1959**

MISSION MARS 🦃 Danger-in-outer-space adventure has a trio of astronauts coping with mysterious forces while on the way to Mars. 95m. **DIR:** Nicholas Webster. **CAST:** Darren McGavin, Nick Adams. **1968**

MISSION OF JUSTICE ★★★ A large city is plagued with crime, but the woman who is running for mayor has a new solution: the Peacemakers—a group of disadvantaged youths who roam the streets and prevent crime. At first glance, this film looks pretty bad, but you'll keep watching. Rated R for violence and profanity. 95m. **DIR:** Steve Barnett. **CAST:** Jeff Wincott, Brigitte Nielsen, Luca Bercovici, Matthias Hues. **1992**

MISSION OF THE SHARK ★★★ Though compelling, this film doesn't develop the characters of the Americans aboard the USS *Indianapolis* before they're struck by Japanese torpedoes in July 1945. Stacy Keach plays Captain Charles McVay, who ultimately is blamed for the deaths of over 800 men. Terrifying scenes of the men's struggle to survive for five days without food or water in the shark-infested ocean. Not rated; contains violence. 92m. **DIR:** Robert Iscove. **CAST:** Stacy Keach, Richard Thomas, Carrie Snodgress. **1991**

MISSION STARDUST ★★ Only die-hard fans of Italian space operas are likely to seek out this adaptation of one of the Perry Rhodan pulp novels. And that's a shame, because, given its meager budget and indifferent dubbing, this is still one of the more imaginative European sci-fi adventures. 90m. **DIR:** Primo Zeglio. **CAST:** Essy Persson, Gianni Rizzo. **1965**

MISSION TO GLORY 🦃 The true story of Father Francisco Kin, the Spanish padre who helped develop California in the late seventeenth century. Rated PG for violence. 97m. **DIR:** Ken Kennedy. **CAST:** Ricardo Montalban, Cesar Romero, Rory Calhoun, Michael Ansara, Keenan Wynn, Richard Egan. **1979**

MISSION TO MARS ★★1/2 If a half century of science-fiction films could evaporate overnight, this might be an impressive little picture. But we cannot pretend that far superior efforts like *Close Encounters of the Third Kind* and *Contact* never happened. Director Brian De Palma paces this routine mysterious-red-planet saga with the slow, self-important deliberation of 1950s efforts such as *Destination Moon*, in a style that today seems lethargic, dreary, and old-fashioned. Rated PG for brief violence. 113m. **DIR:** Brian De Palma. **CAST:** Gary Sinise, Tim Robbins, Don Cheadle, Connie Nielsen, Jerry O'Connell. **2000 DVD**

MISSIONARY, THE ★★★1/2 Monty Python's Michael Palin, who also wrote the script, plays a well-meaning American minister assigned the task of saving the souls of London's fallen women. Not a nonstop, gag-filled descent into absurdity like the Monty Python movies. It is, instead, a warmhearted spoof with the accent on character and very sparing but effective in its humor. Rated R. 90m. **DIR:** Richard Loncraine. **CAST:** Michael Palin, Maggie Smith, Denholm Elliott, Trevor Howard, Michael Hordern. **1982**

MISSISSIPPI ★★★1/2 A delightful mixture of music and personality with Bing Crosby at his best singing Rodgers and Hart's "It's Easy to Remember But So Hard to Forget." He boards a showboat run by rascally W. C. Fields. The plot comes from Booth Tarkington's novel *Magnolia*, but the personalities are pure Hollywood. B&W; 73m. **DIR:** A. Edward Sutherland. **CAST:** Bing Crosby, W. C. Fields, Joan Bennett, Gail Patrick, Queenie Smith, John Miljan, Ann Sheridan. **1935**

MISSISSIPPI BLUES ★★★★★ French film director Bertrand Tavernier joins American author Robert Parrish on a spellbinding odyssey through the deep South. Tavernier and his French camera crew beautifully capture the true spirit of the South through the religious fervor of the black evangelical movement. Some great location photography laced with a rich blues soundtrack. In English and French with English subtitles. 92m. **DIR:** Bertrand Tavernier, Robert Parrish. **CAST:** Roosevelt Barnes, Joe Cooper, Hayword Mills. **1987**

MISSISSIPPI BURNING ★★★★ As the master of dramatic propaganda, Alan Parker presents this hair-raising account of what *might* have happened back in 1964 when three civil rights activists turned up missing in Mississippi. Laid-back Gene Hackman and by-the-book Willem Dafoe are the FBI agents in charge of the investigation. If good intentions excuse execution, then this is worthy fiction; at the very least, it allows Hackman to demonstrate his considerable range. Definitely not for the squeamish. Rated R for language and brutal violence. 125m. **DIR:** Alan Parker. **CAST:** Gene Hackman, Willem Dafoe, Frances McDormand, Brad Dourif, R. Lee Ermey. **1988 DVD**

MISSISSIPPI MASALA ★★★★ Director Mira Nair manages to achieve something of a miracle with this story of love between a black businessman (Denzel Washington) and an Indian immigrant (Sarita Choudhury) who become outcasts in the Deep South. A serious, insightful examination of racial prejudice wedded with heartwarming and sexy romance. Washington is particularly impressive. Rated R for profanity, nudity, and violence. 117m. **DIR:** Mira Nair. **CAST:** Denzel Washington, Roshan Seth, Sarita Choudhury, Charles Dutton, Tico Wells, Joe Seneca. **1991**

MISSISSIPPI MERMAID ★★★ Interesting drama about a wealthy industrialist living on an island who orders a bride by mail. All this eventually leads to deception and murder. Solid performances by Jean-Paul Belmondo and Catherine Deneuve. In French with English subtitles. Not rated. 123m. **DIR:** François Truffaut. **CAST:** Jean-Paul Belmondo, Catherine Deneuve, Michel Bouquet. **1969**

MISSOURI BREAKS, THE ★★ For all its potential, this Western really lets you down. Jack Nicholson is acceptable as the outlaw trying to ply his trade. Marlon Brando, on the other hand, is inconsistent as a relentless bounty hunter. Rated PG. 126m. **DIR:** Arthur Penn. **CAST:** Marlon Brando, Jack Nicholson, Kathleen Lloyd, Harry Dean Stanton. **1976**

MISSOURIANS, THE ★★★★ A band of vicious killers, known as the Missourians, attempt to hide out in a town where the leader's Polish immigrant mother and brother live; only complicating matters for them as the town already holds malice against foreigners. Strong story line and good action make this one of Monte Hale's best. B&W; 60m. **DIR:** George Blair. **CAST:** Monte Hale, Paul Hurst, Roy Barcroft. **1950**

MR. ACCIDENT ★★ An accident-prone egg-factory employee uncovers a fiendish plot by the new owners. Typical Yahoo Serious nonsense loaded with slapstick that is often just not very funny. Way, way over-the-top. Rated PG-13 for cartoonish violence. 89m. **DIR:** Yahoo Serious. **CAST:** Yahoo Serious, Helen Dallimore, David Field, Grant Piro. **2000 DVD**

MR. ACE ★★ Potboiler about a spoiled society woman (Sylvia Sidney) who uses a gangster (George Raft) to win a congressional election goes through the motions but very little else. B&W; 84m. **DIR:** Edwin L. Marin. **CAST:** George Raft, Sylvia Sidney, Stanley Ridges, Sara Haden, Jerome Cowan. **1946 DVD**

MR. AND MRS. BRIDGE ★★★★ Adapted from the novels *Mr. Bridge* and *Mrs. Bridge* by Evan S. Connell, this slice of Americana presents an affecting chronicle of the lives of an upper-class WASP family. Composed of vignettes in the characters' lives, some of which are more compelling than others, it nonetheless adds up to a satisfying motion picture. Rated PG-13 for profanity. 127m. **DIR:** James Ivory. **CAST:** Paul Newman, Joanne Woodward, Blythe Danner, Simon Callow, Kyra Sedgwick, Robert Sean Leonard, Austin Pendleton. **1990 DVD**

MR. AND MRS. LOVING ★★★1/2 Timothy Hutton and Lela Rochon generate sympathy as the working-class title characters whose pursuit for dignity changed

the very fabric of the United States. After being thrown out of their native state of Virginia because their mixed-race marriage violated racist antimiscegenation laws—and this in the early 1960s!—the Supreme Court ruled on the issue and forever abolished such heinous restrictions. Sadly, we learn absolutely nothing about how the Lovings survived the arduous process needed to *reach* the Supreme Court. Rated PG-13 for simulated sex and mild profanity. 95m. **DIR:** Richard Friedenberg. **CAST:** Timothy Hutton, Lela Rochon, Ruby Dee, Bill Nunn, Corey Parker, Isaiah Washington. **1996**

MR. AND MRS. SMITH ★★★★ This film deals with the love-hate-love relationship of Carole Lombard and Robert Montgomery, who play a couple who discover their marriage isn't legal. The bouncy dialogue by Norman Krasna is justly famous and includes some of the most classic comedy scenes ever. Directing this enjoyable farce, in his only pure comedy, is Alfred Hitchcock. B&W; 95m. **DIR:** Alfred Hitchcock. **CAST:** Carole Lombard, Robert Montgomery, Gene Raymond, Jack Carson. **1941**

MR. ARKADIN (CONFIDENTIAL REPORT) ★★1/2 Actor-writer-director Orson Welles confuses the audience more than he entertains them in this odd story of an amnesiac millionaire financier who hires an investigator to find his past. The intriguing story fails to translate effectively to the screen; even the efforts of a fine cast couldn't help Welles turn this into a critical or commercial success. B&W; 99m. **DIR:** Orson Welles. **CAST:** Orson Welles, Michael Redgrave, Akim Tamiroff, Patricia Medina, Mischa Auer. **1955 DVD**

MR. BASEBALL ★★★ Tom Selleck mugs his way through this fish-out-of-water comedy about an American major league baseball player who is sent to play in Japan. Rated PG-13 for profanity. 110m. **DIR:** Fred Schepisi. **CAST:** Tom Selleck, Ken Takakura, Dennis Haysbert. **1992 DVD**

MR. BEAN ★★★★ Rowan Atkinson's Mr. Bean is a hapless little nebbish who contrives outlandish solutions to everyday problems. Some episodes are lengthy dramas; others feature several short blackout sketches. Many are poignant and some are cruel, but they're always hysterical; be on the lookout for wayward swimming trunks in a public pool, and Mr. Bean's adventures in a fancy hotel. Not rated, but suitable for all ages. 60m. **DIR:** John Birkin, John Howard Davies. **CAST:** Rowan Atkinson, Robin Driscoll, Matilda Ziegler. **1989–1995**

MR. BILLION ★★1/2 Sappy but seductive story about a humble Italian mechanic (Terence Hill) who will inherit a financial empire if he can get to the signing over of his uncle's will before a gang of kidnappers or the corporation's chairman (Jackie Gleason) gets to him first. Rated PG for violence and sex. 89m. **DIR:** Jonathan Kaplan. **CAST:** Terence Hill, Valerie Perrine, Jackie Gleason, Slim Pickens, William Redfield, Chill Wills, Dick Miller. **1977**

MR. BLANDINGS BUILDS HIS DREAM HOUSE ★★★★ In this screwball comedy, Cary Grant plays a man tired of the hustle and bustle of city life. He decides to move to the country, construct his private Shangri-La, and settle back into a serene rural life-style. His fantasy and reality come into comic conflict. Myrna Loy is cast as his ever-patient wife in this very fine film. B&W; 94m. **DIR:** H. C. Potter. **CAST:** Cary Grant, Myrna Loy, Melvyn Douglas. **1948**

MR. CORBETT'S GHOST ★★★ New Year's Eve, 1767, somewhere in England and young Ben Partridge has a choice to make: desire or duty. His decision on which road to pursue forms the basis of this fine atmospheric ghost story, produced for TV. 75m. **DIR:** Danny Huston. **CAST:** John Huston, Paul Scofield, Burgess Meredith, Mark Farmer. **1986**

MR. DEATH: THE RISE AND FALL OF FRED A. LEUCHTER JR. ★★★★1/2 This documentary is a complex yet lucid character study that evolves into a meditation on the roots of evil. Fred Leuchter Jr. is a self-taught execution expert who worked on gas chambers, lethal injection systems, and a gallows until he was hired by a Holocaust revisionist to refute the existence of gas chambers at Auschwitz. The film strings Leuchter's deadpan monologues, archival photos, reenactments, and grainy home movies into a riveting story about corrupted ideals, flawed scientific logic, and the fragility of truth. Rated PG-13 for mature themes. 96m. **DIR:** Errol Morris. **2000 DVD**

MR. DEEDS GOES TO TOWN ★★★★★ The quiet unassuming world of a contented New Englander (Gary Cooper) is severely tested when he inherits a fortune in this classic Frank Capra comedy. An amusing series of misadventures results when our hero's straightforward values are caught in a tug-of-war with the corruption of big city money and snobbishness. B&W; 120m. **DIR:** Frank Capra. **CAST:** Gary Cooper, Jean Arthur, Douglass Dumbrille, Lionel Stander, George Bancroft. **1936 DVD**

MR. DESTINY ★★1/2 James Belushi plays a pencil pusher who believes he is a failure. Michael Caine, who can shape people's lives, shows him differently in this passable comedy that reminds one of *It's a Wonderful Life*. Rated PG-13 for profanity. 117m. **DIR:** James Orr. **CAST:** James Belushi, Linda Hamilton, Jon Lovitz, Hart Bochner, Michael Caine. **1990**

MR. FROST ★★★1/2 After being arrested for twenty-four murders by an English detective (Alan Bates), the mysterious Mr. Frost (Jeff Goldblum) refuses to speak for three years until a psychiatrist (Kathy Baker) attempts to reach him. That's when Frost begins claiming he is Satan. Intriguing blend of suspense and black comedy. Rated R for violence and profanity. 92m. **DIR:** Philip Setbon. **CAST:** Jeff Goldblum, Alan Bates, Kathy Baker. **1990**

MR. HALPERN AND MR. JOHNSON ★★★ Laurence Olivier plays a recently widowed Jewish manufacturer who, to his surprise, is asked to join a stranger named Johnson (Jackie Gleason) for a drink after the funeral. It seems that Johnson was once in love with the late Mrs. Halpern. What's more, they carried on a friendship for a number of years right up to just before her death. And therein lies the drama of this slight tale. 57m. **DIR:** Alvin Rakoff. **CAST:** Laurence Olivier, Jackie Gleason. **1983**

MR. HOBBS TAKES A VACATION ★★★ Somewhat against his better judgment, ever-patient James Stewart takes his wife Maureen O'Hara and their children and grandchildren on vacation. They wind up in a ramshackle old house on the Pacific Coast, and he winds up more hassled than when home or at work. Good acting

and a clever script make this thin-plotted comedy amusing. 116m. **DIR:** Henry Koster. **CAST:** James Stewart, Maureen O'Hara, Marie Wilson, Fabian, John Saxon. **1962**

MR. HOLLAND'S OPUS ★★★★ In this wonderful family film, Richard Dreyfuss gives an outstanding performance as a music teacher who struggles to have a positive effect on the lives of his students despite complications at home. We don't want to give away any more of the story than this. Suffice it to say, this is a feel-good movie in the best sense, with accolades deserved by all involved. Rated PG-13 for profanity and adult themes. 142m. **DIR:** Stephen Herek. **CAST:** Richard Dreyfuss, Glenne Headly, Alicia Witt, Jay Thomas, Olympia Dukakis, William H. Macy, Jean Louisa Kelly. **1995 DVD**

MR. HORN ★★★ A bittersweet, near-melancholy chronicle of the exploits of Horn (David Carradine), who is shown first as an idealistic young man helping an old-timer (Richard Widmark) track down Geronimo and later as a cynical gunman hired to eliminate some rustlers. 200m. **DIR:** Jack Starrett. **CAST:** David Carradine, Richard Widmark, Karen Black, Richard Masur, Jeremy Slate, Pat McCormick, Jack Starrett. **1979**

MR. HULOT'S HOLIDAY ★★★1/2 A delightfully lighthearted film about the natural comedy to be found in vacationing. Jacques Tati plays the famous Monsieur Hulot, who has some silly adventures at a seaside resort. Although partially dubbed in English, this film has a mime quality that is magical. B&W; 86m. **DIR:** Jacques Tati. **CAST:** Jacques Tati, Nathale Pascaud. **1953 DVD**

MR. IMPERIUM ★★ A musical that misses because there's no chemistry whatsoever between the leads. Ezio Pinza's Broadway charm isn't photogenic so it's difficult to relate to Lana Turner's attraction to him. They sing such songs as "My Love and My Mule" in a willy-nilly attempt to tug the audience's heartstrings. 87m. **DIR:** Don Hartman. **CAST:** Lana Turner, Ezio Pinza, Marjorie Main, Debbie Reynolds, Barry Sullivan, Keenan Wynn. **1951**

MR. INSIDE/MR. OUTSIDE ★★ Hal Linden and Tony LoBianco are fine in this made-for-television cop thriller as two New York City detectives attempting to foil a smuggling ring. Director William Graham's pacing makes you forget how much this movie is like so many other works created for TV. 74m. **DIR:** William A. Graham. **CAST:** Hal Linden, Tony Lo Bianco, Phil Bruns, Paul Benjamin, Stefan Schnabel. **1973**

MR. JEALOUSY ★★1/2 Cute but claustrophobic romantic comedy about a jealous boyfriend who can't stand the fact that his latest girlfriend had a life before him. When his jealousy consumes their relationship, he joins the therapy group of his girlfriend's ex-boyfriend, unwittingly bringing the couple back together again. Witty dialogue and a decent cast help make this exercise in yuppy angst bearable. Rated R for language and adult situations. 100m. **DIR:** Noah Baumbach. **CAST:** Eric Stoltz, Annabella Sciorra, Christopher Eigeman, Bridget Fonda, Marianne Jean-Baptiste. **1998 DVD**

MISTER JOHNSON ★★★★ A poignant drama about the clash of cultures in the colonial western Africa of the 1920s. Adapted from Joyce Cary's 1939 novel, it follows the tragicomic exploits of a black African clerk named Johnson as he attempts to ingratiate himself into the lives and society of the ruling white colonialists. Rated PG-13. 102m. **DIR:** Bruce Beresford. **CAST:** Maynard Eziashi, Pierce Brosnan, Edward Woodward. **1991 DVD**

MR. JONES ★★ Doctor-patient romances don't get much more unconvincing than this. A wild-eyed, mysterious manic-depressive so infatuates a hospital shrink that she sacrifices her professional ethics for offscreen sex with her emotionally kinetic charge. The film's two stars keep the film promising, but the sterile love story doesn't do justice to its serious themes of emotional alienation and mental care. It's a tantalizing puzzle that has several missing pieces. Rated R for profanity. 110m. **DIR:** Mike Figgis. **CAST:** Richard Gere, Lena Olin. **1993 DVD**

MR. KLEIN ★★★1/2 Dark-sided character study of a Parisian antique dealer who buys artwork and personal treasures from Jews trying to escape Paris in 1942. He (Alain Delon) finds himself mistaken for a missing Jew of the same name. Rated PG. Available in French version. 123m. **DIR:** Joseph Losey. **CAST:** Alain Delon, Jeanne Moreau, Juliet Berto, Michel Lonsdale, Jean Bouise, Francine Berge. **1976**

MR. LOVE ★★1/2 Slow-moving yet interesting study of a middle-aged man who wins the love of women by being caring and encouraging. Barry Jackson is the soft-spoken British gardener who, stuck in a loveless marriage, seeks to befriend the lonesome women he encounters. Rated PG-13. 91m. **DIR:** Roy Battersby. **CAST:** Barry Jackson, Maurice Denham, Margaret Tyzack. **1985**

MR. LUCKY ★★★ Cary Grant is a gambler attempting to bilk money from a charity relief program. He changes his tune when he falls for a wealthy society girl, Laraine Day. This is a slick piece of wartime fluff. The plot has nothing you haven't seen before, but the charm of Grant makes it watchable. B&W; 100m. **DIR:** H. C. Potter. **CAST:** Cary Grant, Laraine Day. **1943**

MR. MAGOO 🦃 Give director Stanley Tong, of Jackie Chan's *Super Cop* and *Rumble in the Bronx*, a wacky comedy and what do you get? A series of kung fu fights and a lack of Magoo-like madness. The limited plot has Magoo (Leslie Nielsen) being drawn into an international plot to steal a world-renowned gem. Within thirty minutes, you'll be wishing that you were as nearsighted as Magoo and didn't have to witness this celluloid disaster. Rated PG for violence. 86m. **DIR:** Stanley Tong. **CAST:** Leslie Nielsen, Kelly Lynch, Ernie Hudson, Stephen Tobolowsky, Nick Chinlund. **1997 DVD**

MR. MAGOO'S CHRISTMAS CAROL ★★★★★ Mr. Magoo is Ebenezer Scrooge in this first-rate animated musical of Charles Dickens's holiday classic, which remains the best animated adaptation to date. The songs by Jule Styne and Bob Merrill are magnificent. 53m. **DIR:** Abe Levitow. **1962 DVD**

MR. MAJESTYK ★★★1/2 In this better-than-average Charles Bronson vehicle, he's a watermelon grower (!) coming up against gangster Al Lettieri (in a first-rate performance). Rated R. 103m. **DIR:** Richard Fleischer. **CAST:** Charles Bronson, Al Lettieri, Linda Cristal, Lee Purcell, Paul Koslo. **1974**

MR. MOM ★★★★ Michael Keaton is hilarious as an engineer who loses his job at an automobile manufacturing plant and, when wife Teri Garr gets a high-paying

job at an advertising agency, becomes a hopelessly inept househusband. The story is familiar and predictable, but Keaton's off-the-wall antics and boyish charm make it all seem fresh and lively. Rated PG for light profanity. 91m. **DIR:** Stan Dragoti. **CAST:** Michael Keaton, Teri Garr, Ann Jillian, Martin Mull. **1983 DVD**

MR. MOTO IN DANGER ISLAND ★★1/2 The globe-trotting detective goes to Puerto Rico to crack a diamond-smuggling ring. This was the last of the eight Mr. Moto movies, and it shows: Peter Lorre, tired of the character, often seems to be just going through the paces. B&W; 64m. **DIR:** Herbert Leeds. **CAST:** Peter Lorre, Jean Hersholt, Amanda Duff, Richard Lane, Leon Ames. **1939**

MR. MOTO TAKES A CHANCE ★★1/2 Mr. Moto gets to exercise his mastery of disguise as he investigates a potentially murderous cult in Indochina. The fourth Mr. Moto movie, this suffers from an overstuffed plot. B&W; 63m. **DIR:** Norman Foster. **CAST:** Peter Lorre, Rochelle Hudson, Robert Kent, J. Edward Bromberg. **1938**

MR. MOTO TAKES A VACATION ★★1/2 Too busy fighting international criminals to take a real vacation, Mr. Moto is actually posing as a tourist in order to trap a thief who's after the jewels of the Queen of Sheba. One of the lesser Mr. Moto movies. B&W; 65m. **DIR:** Norman Foster. **CAST:** Peter Lorre, Joseph Schildkraut, Lionel Atwill, Virginia Field, Willie Best. **1939**

MR. MOTO'S GAMBLE ★★★ Aided by students from a detective class he is teaching, Mr. Moto investigates the murder of a boxer. An unusual entry in the series in that it was supposed to be a Charlie Chan movie until Warner Oland died in the middle of filming! B&W; 71m. **DIR:** James Tinling. **CAST:** Peter Lorre, Keye Luke, Dick Baldwin, Maxie Rosenbloom, Ward Bond, Lon Chaney Jr. **1938**

MR. MOTO'S LAST WARNING ★★★ One of the last in the low-budget series that produced eight films in less than three years. This time out, the detective gets involved with terrorist spies intent on blowing up the French fleet in the Suez Canal. Enjoyable, quaint entertainment with a good supporting cast. B&W; 71m. **DIR:** Norman Foster. **CAST:** Peter Lorre, Ricardo Cortez, Virginia Field, John Carradine, George Sanders. **1939**

MR. MURDER ★★★1/2 Solid TV miniseries adaptation of Dean Koontz's bestseller. Stephen Baldwin plays a successful author of murder mysteries whose life is thrown upside down when a man who looks just like him shows up and claims to be him. While some events have been added or expanded upon from the novel, the general feel of the book comes through on the small screen. Not rated; contains violence. 193m. **DIR:** Dick Lowry. **CAST:** Stephen Baldwin, Julie Warner, Thomas Haden Church, James Coburn. **1999 DVD**

MR. MUSIC ★★ Bing Crosby is an easygoing songwriter living beyond his means. Nancy Olson is hired to handle his finances. Slow-moving, completely forgettable songs, and wasted guest stars. B&W; 113m. **DIR:** Richard Haydn. **CAST:** Bing Crosby, Nancy Olson, Charles Coburn, Ruth Hussey, Robert Stack, Tom Ewell, Peggy Lee, Groucho Marx, Richard Haydn. **1950**

MR. NANNY ★★ A retired professional wrestler (Hulk Hogan) wants work as a bodyguard but winds up babysitting two neglected kids. Hogan is no Anthony Hopkins, but he is likable on screen; too bad the film, with a labored plot and unfunny gags, doesn't give him the support he needs. Rated PG. 83m. **DIR:** Michael Gottlieb. **CAST:** Hulk Hogan, Austin Pendleton, Sherman Hemsley, David Johansen. **1993**

MR. NICE GUY ★★★ A celebrity TV chef/martial arts expert is chased through Melbourne by Australian gangsters seeking an incriminating videotape made by a local reporter. The plot is thin, but the film's exhilarating chases and acrobatics include brawls aboard a horse-drawn carriage and inside a delivery van and a battle at a construction site. In English and Cantonese with English subtitles. Rated PG-13 for violence. 83m. **DIR:** Sammo Hung. **CAST:** Jackie Chan, Richard Norton, Gabrielle Fitzpatrick, Miki Lee, Karen McLynont. **1998 DVD**

MR. NORTH ★★★1/2 In this fantasy a young Yale graduate arrives in elite Newport, Rhode Island as a tutor and ends up touching the citizens in seemingly magical ways. Based on Thornton Wilder's novel, *Theophilus North*, and directed by the late John Huston's son, Danny, this small-scale piece of whimsy is a winner. Rated PG. 92m. **DIR:** Danny Huston. **CAST:** Anthony Edwards, Robert Mitchum, Lauren Bacall, Harry Dean Stanton, Anjelica Huston. **1988**

MR. PEABODY AND THE MERMAID ★★ This is *Splash*, 1940s-style. A married New Englander (William Powell) snags an amorous mermaid while fishing and transfers her to his swimming pool, with the expected results. B&W; 89m. **DIR:** Irving Pichel. **CAST:** William Powell, Ann Blyth, Irene Hervey. **1948**

MR. RELIABLE ★★★1/2 True stories are always the strangest, as proven by this depiction of Australia's first hostage crisis in the summer of 1968. An unwed mom moves in with a petty criminal, but an addled police force thinks she and the baby are captives. Sparkling, offbeat humor is deftly woven into more serious scenes, maintaining a consistent level of weirdness. Rated PG-13 for profanity and sexual situations. 109m. **DIR:** Nadia Tass. **CAST:** Colin Friels, Jacqueline McKenzie, Paul Sonkkila. **1996**

•MR. RICE'S SECRET ★★★ David Bowie portrays the recently deceased Mr. Rice, a character we see mostly in flashback sequences. The movie centers around Mr. Rice's young neighbor friend Owen (Bill Switzer), to whom Mr. Rice had bequeathed a treasure map, the hidden treasure being the secret of longevity. On his quest, Owen learns a few valuable lessons and a fundamental appreciation of life. This movie has its morals in the right place, and really only suffers from trying to fill a half-hour's worth of story into 113 minutes. Rated PG for mild language and bullying. 113m. **DIR:** Nicholas Kendall. **CAST:** David Bowie, Bill Switzer. **2000 DVD**

MISTER ROBERTS ★★★★1/2 A navy cargo ship well outside the World War II battle zone is the setting for this hit comedy-drama. Henry Fonda is Lieutenant Roberts, the first officer who helps the crew battle their ceaseless boredom and tyrannical captain (James Cagney). Jack Lemmon began his road to stardom with his sparkling performance as the irrepressible con-man Ensign Pulver. 123m. **DIR:** John Ford, Mervyn LeRoy. **CAST:** Henry Fonda, James Cagney, Jack Lemmon, William Powell, Ward Bond. **1955 DVD**

MR. ROBINSON CRUSOE ★★★ Dashing Douglas Fairbanks Sr. bets he can survive like Crusoe on a South Sea island. Just how he does it makes for great fun. Fairbanks was just short of 50 when he made this film, but he was still the agile, athletic swashbuckler whose wholesome charm made him the idol of millions. B&W; 76m. **DIR:** A. Edward Sutherland. **CAST:** Douglas Fairbanks Sr., William Farnum, Maria Alba. **1932**

MR. SATURDAY NIGHT ★★★★ Billy Crystal gives a smashing performance in this poignant comedy chronicling fifty years in the life of a stand-up comedian. Costar David Paymer almost steals Crystal's show as his brother-manager who must put up with the increasingly irritating comic. Rated R for profanity. 119m. **DIR:** Billy Crystal. **CAST:** Billy Crystal, David Paymer, Julie Warner, Helen Hunt, Ron Silver, Jerry Orbach. **1992 DVD**

MR. SKEFFINGTON ★★★ Selfish and self-centered Bette Davis goes from reigning society beauty to hag in this typical soap opera of the upper crust—ranging across decades through feast and famine, indulgence and deceit. Time takes its toll on her. Then comes her one chance to do the right thing. Davis's performance is splendid. B&W; 147m. **DIR:** Vincent Sherman. **CAST:** Bette Davis, Claude Rains, Walter Abel, George Coulouris, Jerome Cowan, Gigi Perreau. **1944**

MR. SKITCH ★★★ Will Rogers, broke after a bank failure, heads West hoping to recoup at a gambling casino. A dollar wins him a bundle—that wife ZaSu Pitts promptly loses. Typical Rogers comedy fare sprinkled with quick quips and homespun philosophy. B&W; 70m. **DIR:** James Cruze. **CAST:** Will Rogers, ZaSu Pitts, Rochelle Hudson, Eugene Pallette. **1933**

MR. SMITH GOES TO WASHINGTON ★★★★★ This Frank Capra classic is the story of a naïve senator's fight against political corruption. James Stewart stars as Jefferson Smith, the idealistic scoutmaster who is appointed to fill out the term of a dead senator. Upon arriving in the capitol, he begins to get a hint of the corruption in his home state. His passionate filibuster against this corruption remains one of the most emotionally powerful scenes in film history. B&W; 129m. **DIR:** Frank Capra. **CAST:** James Stewart, Jean Arthur, Claude Rains. **1939 DVD**

MR. STITCH ★★★ Surrealistic film about a mad doctor who creates his own creature using the body parts of eighty-eight men and women. The result is a patchwork quilt of a human who is supposed to be completely controllable. Instead, the creature has flashbacks into the lives of some of the people who made up his being and begins to question the experiment. Final third of the movie takes an unbelievable turn. Interesting comment on scientific research. Rated R for violence. 80m. **DIR:** Roger Avary. **CAST:** Rutger Hauer, Wil Wheaton, Nia Peeples. **1995**

MR. SUPERINVISIBLE ★★ Disney-like comedy with Dean Jones as the scientist who stumbles upon a virus that causes invisibility. Cute in spots; kids should like it. 90m. **DIR:** Anthony M. Dawson. **CAST:** Dean Jones, Gastone Moschin, Ingeborg Schoener, Rafael Alonso, Peter Carsten. **1973**

MR. SYCAMORE A mailman decides to turn into a tree. Peculiar and pointless. Not rated. 87m. **DIR:** Pancho Kohner. **CAST:** Jason Robards Jr., Sandy Dennis, Jean Simmons, Mark Miller. **1975**

MR. VAMPIRE (VOL. 1–4) ★★★1/2 This Chinese vampire movie is a surreal and hilarious romp filled with remarkable martial arts and bizarre special effects laced with great slapstick and vampire erotica. Director Lau Koon Wai has created a bloodsucker who sports long purple fingernails and yellow fangs and, when not levitating, hops like a bunny. In Chinese with English subtitles. Not rated; contains violence and nudity. 375m. **DIR:** Wong Kee Hung, Law Lit, Sung Kam Shing. **CAST:** Ricky Hui, Yuen Biao, Richard Ng, Lam Ching Ying. **1986–1988 DVD**

MR. WINKLE GOES TO WAR ★★★ Edward G. Robinson is a henpecked bookkeeper who gets drafted into the army during World War II. As the saying goes, the army makes a man out of him. Like so many films of its time, *Mr. Winkle Goes to War* was part of the war effort, and as such, hasn't worn very well; what was considered heartfelt or patriotic back in the 1940s is now rendered maudlin or just corny. Still, the acting is excellent. B&W; 80m. **DIR:** Alfred E. Green. **CAST:** Edward G. Robinson, Ruth Warrick, Richard Lane, Robert Armstrong. **1944**

MR. WONDERFUL ★★★★ Fine acting highlights this insightful study of relationships. Matt Dillon plays a Con Edison electrical worker who is being strapped by alimony payments; fiancée Mary-Louise Parker suspects he's still in love with ex-wife Annabella Sciorra. Rated PG-13 for brief profanity and simulated sex. 101m. **DIR:** Anthony Minghella. **CAST:** Matt Dillon, Annabella Sciorra, Mary-Louise Parker, William Hurt, Vincent D'Onofrio, David Barry Gray, Bruce Kirby, Dan Hedaya, Luis Guzman, Joanna Merlin, Jessica Harper, Adam LeFevre. **1993 DVD**

MR. WONG, DETECTIVE ★★★ First of five Mr. Wong films starring Boris Karloff as Hugh Wiley's black-suited sleuth is a notch above most of Monogram Pictures programmers. Mr. Wong attempts to solve the deaths of three industrialists, which have baffled the authorities and have the government and media in an uproar. Fun for mystery and detective fans. B&W; 69m. **DIR:** William Nigh. **CAST:** Boris Karloff, Grant Withers, Evelyn Brent, Maxine Jennings, Lucien Prival. **1938 DVD**

MR. WONG IN CHINATOWN ★★ A Chinese princess and her bodyguards are killed while she is trying to buy defense planes for her homeland, and Mr. Wong steps in to find the culprits. Tepid entry to a tolerable series. B&W; 70m. **DIR:** William Nigh. **CAST:** Boris Karloff, Grant Withers, Marjorie Reynolds. **1939 DVD**

MR. WRITE ★★ Likable Paul Reiser is ill served by this forced comedy, adapted by Howard J. Morris from what must have been an excruciating play. Reiser's would-be playwright toils amid the horrors of television commercials, while concocting a stage epic just as shrill and bizarre as this whole film. Rated PG-13 for profanity and suggested sex. 89m. **DIR:** Charlie Loventhal. **CAST:** Paul Reiser, Jessica Tuck, Doug Davidson, Wendie Jo Sperber, Martin Mull. **1994**

MR. WRONG ★★★ Lonely and single Ellen DeGeneres meets a sexy guy (Bill Pullman) who seems too good to be true; by the time she realizes what a loser he is, she can't get rid of him. The script is predictable and Nick Castle's direction is only adequate, but De-

Generes's personal charm and a few inspired gags make it all worthwhile. Rated PG-13 for mild profanity and comic violence. 92m. **DIR:** Nick Castle. **CAST:** Ellen DeGeneres, Bill Pullman, Joan Cusack, Dean Stockwell, Joan Plowright. **1996**

MISTRAL'S DAUGHTER ★★ This sudsy adaptation of Judith Krantz's novel features Stefanie Powers as the model and then mistress of a cynical artist (Stacy Keach). Made for television, this miniseries is unrated but contains partial nudity and simulated sex. 300m. **DIR:** Douglas Hickox. **CAST:** Stefanie Powers, Stacy Keach, Lee Remick, Timothy Dalton, Robert Urich, Stéphane Audran. **1984**

MISTRESS, THE (1953) ★★★1/2 Tragic tale of a Japanese woman trapped in a life as mistress to a greedy Shylock. When she falls in love with a medical student, her reputation causes nothing but heartache and sorrow. In Japanese with English subtitles. B&W; 106m. **DIR:** Shiro Toyoda. **CAST:** Hideko Takamine, Hiroshi Akutagawa. **1953**

MISTRESS (1987) ★★ Sudsy coming-of-age melodrama about a mistress who must support herself after her wealthy lover dies. Made for TV, this contains adult themes. 96m. **DIR:** Michael Tuchner. **CAST:** Victoria Principal, Don Murray, Joanna Kerns, Kerrie Keane. **1987**

MISTRESS (1992) ★★★ A writer (Robert Wuhl) tries to get his long forgotten script made into a movie, while a trio of wealthy men attempt to get their mistresses shoehorned into acting roles. Barry Primus directs from his own story and deftly captures the games Hollywood wannabes play; similar to Robert Altman's *The Player*. Look for comic shenanigans from Robert De Niro. Rated PG. 109m. **DIR:** Barry Primus. **CAST:** Robert Wuhl, Robert De Niro, Martin Landau, Danny Aiello, Eli Wallach, Laurie Metcalf, Sheryl Lee Ralph, Jean Smart, Ernest Borgnine, Christopher Walken. **1992 DVD**

MISTRIAL ★★1/2 Writer-director Heywood Gould's positively ludicrous script finds veteran cop Bill Pullman dissatisfied with a controversial courtroom verdict . . . so he holds judge, jury, and defendant at gunpoint and forces all concerned to reenact the trial. And they do! Sincere concerns about flaws in the U.S. justice system are wholly overshadowed by the ridiculous premise. Rated R for violence and profanity. 89m. **DIR:** Heywood Gould. **CAST:** Bill Pullman, Robert Loggia, Blair Underwood, Leo Burmester, Roma Maffia, James Rebhorn, Josef Sommer. **1996**

•MISTS OF AVALON, THE ★★★ To enjoy this TNT miniseries, viewers must set aside the Arthurian legend traditionally espoused. Based on Marion Zimmer Bradley's bestseller, this version presents the dark side of Camelot in which women wield the power behind the throne. Anjelica Huston, as the leader, tries to retain her sect's power by manipulating her successor, Morgaine (Julianna Margulies). The women are fearless but Arthur is sadly uninformed and therefore weak. Decent costuming, special effects, and a fine soundtrack make viewing pleasant despite some sick plot twists. Not rated; contains nudity, violence, and sexual situations. 184m. **DIR:** Uli Edel. **CAST:** Julianna Margulies, Anjelica Huston, Joan Allen, Michael Vartan. **2001 DVD**

MISTY ★★★ A thoroughly enjoyable family film about two youngsters who teach a young horse new tricks. Film version of Marguerite Henry's bestseller *Misty of Chincoteague*. Filmed on an island off the Virginia coast, so the scenery is a selling point. 92m. **DIR:** James B. Clark. **CAST:** David Ladd, Arthur O'Connell, Anne Seymour, Pam Smith. **1961**

MISUNDERSTOOD (1984) 🦃 A rich businessman raises two young sons who are traumatized by the sudden death of their mother. Rated PG for profanity. 91m. **DIR:** Jerry Schatzberg. **CAST:** Gene Hackman, Henry Thomas, Huckleberry Fox. **1984**

MISUNDERSTOOD (1988) ★★ This is an Italian production of the U.S. film release that starred Gene Hackman. The slow, depressing story did not need to be done twice. In this version, Anthony Quayle is a British consul in Italy. He is trying to raise his two sons following the death of his wife. The focus is on the father's relationship with the older son, which lacks understanding and compassion. The director, Luigi Comencini, takes far too long to reach the too late conclusion. Rated PG for adult themes. 101m. **DIR:** Luigi Comencini. **CAST:** Anthony Quayle, Stefano Colagrande, Georgia Moll. **1988**

MIXED BLOOD ★★1/2 Paul Morrissey, the man who brought you Andy Warhol's versions of *Frankenstein* and *Dracula*, has made a serious film about the Alphabet City drug subculture and its inherent violent nature. Here the surroundings are brutal and unforgiving, and the cheap film stock gives the movie a newsreel feeling. Not rated; contains violence and profanity. 98m. **DIR:** Paul Morrissey. **CAST:** Marilia Pera, Richard Ulacia, Linda Kerridge, Geraldine Smith, Angel David, Rodney Harvey. **1985**

MIXED NUTS 🦃 No one dies laughing in this strained comedy about Christmas Eve day at a Venice Beach suicide-prevention center staffed by misfits who are about to be evicted. Rated PG-13 for language. 97m. **DIR:** Nora Ephron. **CAST:** Steve Martin, Madeline Kahn, Juliette Lewis, Robert Klein, Adam Sandler, Rita Wilson, Rob Reiner, Garry Shandling. **1994 DVD**

MO' BETTER BLUES ★★1/2 Writer-director Spike Lee was trying to make a movie about a jazz musician that was free of the usual clichés—primarily in response to Clint Eastwood's *Bird*—but only Wesley Snipes's volatile performance as a sax-playing rival energizes this lackadaisical affair about a successful, slick, and attractive trumpeter (Denzel Washington). Rated R for profanity, nudity, and violence. 120m. **DIR:** Spike Lee. **CAST:** Denzel Washington, Spike Lee, Wesley Snipes, Giancarlo Esposito, Robin Harris, Joie Lee, Cynda Williams, Bill Nunn, John Turturro, Rubén Blades, Dick Anthony Williams. **1990**

MO' MONEY ★★★1/2 Damon Wayans wrote and stars in this comedy about a small-time street hustler who falls in love and tries to go straight. There are some terrific moments of hilarity in this fast-paced, fun flick, which also features an impressive feature-film acting debut by Marlon Wayans. Rated R for profanity, nudity, and violence. 97m. **DIR:** Peter MacDonald. **CAST:** Damon Wayans, Marlon Wayans, Stacey Dash, Joe Santos, John Diehl. **1992**

MOB BOSS ★★1/2 Sometimes funny gangster story about an aging don (William Hickey) who calls upon his absolutely useless son (Eddie Deezen) to take over the family business. Deezen's training as a mobster is hilarious. Rated R for nudity and profanity. 93m. **DIR:** Fred

Olen Ray. **CAST:** Morgan Fairchild, Eddie Deezen, William Hickey, Don Stroud, Jack O'Halloran, Mike Mazurki, Stuart Whitman. **1990**

MOB JUSTICE ★★1/2 Unspoken peace agreement between the mob and law enforcement agencies is broken when a small-time hood kills an undercover federal agent. Tony Danza is convincing as the killer who must hide out from both the law and his employers. Rated R for violence and profanity. 95m. **DIR:** Peter Markle. **CAST:** Tony Danza, Ted Levine, Dan Lauria, Nicholas Turturro, Samuel L. Jackson. **1991**

MOB STORY ★★1/2 A moderately funny comedy-drama. A mob kingpin escapes to Winnipeg to stay with relatives. His attempts to train his nephew in the fine art of crime run afoul as his enemies track him down. Rated PG-13. 98m. **DIR:** Jancarlo Markiw, Gabriel Markiw. **CAST:** Margot Kidder, John Vernon, Kate Vernon, Al Waxman. **1989 DVD**

MOB WAR 🦃 Bargain-basement flick about a young mob turk. Rated R for violence and profanity. 96m. **DIR:** J. Christian Ingvordsen. **CAST:** Johnny Stumper, Jake La Motta. **1988 DVD**

MOBSTERS ★★ In what might be called *Young Guns in the Roaring Twenties*, Christian Slater plays Lucky Luciano and Patrick Dempsey is Meyer Lansky in yet another gangster movie. It's no *GoodFellas*, but there's plenty of action, with F. Murray Abraham and Anthony Quinn adding class. Rated R for violence and profanity. 110m. **DIR:** Michael Karbelnikoff. **CAST:** Christian Slater, Patrick Dempsey, Richard Grieco, F. Murray Abraham, Anthony Quinn. **1991**

MOBY DICK (1956) ★★★★1/2 Director John Huston's brilliant adaptation of Herman Melville's classic novel features Gregory Peck in one of his best performances as the driven Captain Ahab. 116m. **DIR:** John Huston. **CAST:** Gregory Peck, Richard Basehart, Leo Genn, Orson Welles. **1956 DVD**

MOBY DICK (1998) ★★★★ Rich, extremely well acted adaptation of the classic Herman Melville novel offers breathtaking sets and scenery, impressive special effects, and a complex cast of fascinating characters. Rated PG. 145m. **DIR:** Franc Roddam. **CAST:** Patrick Stewart, Henry Thomas, Ted Levine, Gregory Peck. **1998 DVD**

MOCKERY ★★1/2 Silent-screen master of menace Lon Chaney Sr. stars in this MGM melodrama set during the Russian Revolution. Modern viewers may find it slow-going. Worth seeing for Chaney in a straight role, however, and for the stylish direction of Benjamin Christensen, which includes a chilling opening shot. B&W; 90m. **DIR:** Benjamin Christensen. **CAST:** Lon Chaney Sr., Barbara Bedford, Ricardo Cortez, Mack Swain. **1927**

MOD SQUAD, THE ★★ This update of the 1960s TV series is a mess from the outset, stranding the talented young stars and a strong supporting cast in a half-baked story that makes absolutely no sense—beginning with the fact that it's set in the 1990s, when nobody uses words like *mod* anymore. Rated R for violence and profanity. 94m. **DIR:** Scott Silver. **CAST:** Claire Danes, Giovanni Ribisi, Omar Epps, Dennis Farina, Josh Brolin, Michael Lerner. **1999 DVD**

MOD SQUAD, THE (TV SERIES) ★★★1/2 Three youths are busted for minor crimes and then recruited to go undercover. Pete is a poor little rich boy who's rebelling against his Beverly Hills parents. Linc is a ghetto black who seethes beneath a stoic exterior. Julie, the sensitive blonde, is the daughter of a prostitute. The series effectively combined action, positive messages, and a mildly antiestablishment bent. 60m. **DIR:** Various!. **CAST:** Michael Cole, Clarence Williams, III, Peggy Lipton, Tige Andrews. **1968–1973**

•MODEL BEHAVIOR ★★ In this movie inspired by *The Prince and the Pauper*, Maggie Lawson plays two roles—one a glamorous teen model who longs for the simple life, and the other a bored, lonely teenager who dreams of fame and glory. They meet and briefly switch identities. Justin Timberlake plays the starlet's love interest, and her mother is portrayed by Kathie Lee Gifford. Cody Gifford turns in a groaningly nepotistic cameo appearance, but other than that, this movie is harmless, tepid family entertainment. Not rated. 89m. **DIR:** Mark Rosman. **CAST:** Maggie Lawson, Kathie Lee Gifford, Justin Timberlake. **2000**

MODEL BY DAY ★★1/2 After her roommate is attacked, a model decides to do her part to rid the city of crime. The film has some good comedic moments, but the plot is unbelievable. Rated R for nudity and violence. 89m. **DIR:** Christian Duguay. **CAST:** Famke Janssen, Stephen Shellen, Shannon Tweed, Sean Young, Clark Johnson, Traci Lind, Kim Coates. **1993**

MODERN AFFAIR, A ★★★ Businesswoman Lisa Eichhorn decides to have a baby via artificial insemination. But after she's pregnant, she becomes consumed with curiosity about her unborn child's anonymous father and decides to find him. Likable romantic comedy. Rated R for sexual situations and profanity. 91m. **DIR:** Vern Oakley. **CAST:** Lisa Eichhorn, Stanley Tucci, Caroline Aaron, Mary Jo Salerno, Robert Joy, Tammy Grimes. **1994**

MODERN GIRLS ★★★ Cynthia Gibb, Virginia Madsen, and Daphne Zuniga turn in fine individual performances as the *Modern Girls*, but this well-edited and visually striking film has some slow scenes among the funny. However, younger viewers should find it enjoyable overall. Rated PG-13 for profanity and sexual situations. 82m. **DIR:** Jerry Kramer. **CAST:** Cynthia Gibb, Virginia Madsen, Daphne Zuniga, Clayton Rohner, Stephen Shellen, Chris Nash. **1987**

MODERN LOVE ★★ Robby Benson's ideal concept of marital bliss is marred by the realities of daily life. Some funny bits, but Benson's fantasies get unbelievably out of hand. (His real wife, Karla DeVito, is great as his harried film wife and a new mother.) Rated R for nudity. 110m. **DIR:** Robby Benson. **CAST:** Robby Benson, Karla DeVito, Burt Reynolds, Rue McClanahan. **1990**

MODERN PROBLEMS ★★ In this passable comedy, directed by Ken (*The Groove Tube*) Shapiro, Chevy Chase plays an air traffic controller who may be permanently out to lunch. Rated PG because of its brief nudity and sexual theme. 91m. **DIR:** Ken Shapiro. **CAST:** Chevy Chase, Patti D'Arbanville, Mary Kay Place. **1981**

MODERN ROMANCE ★★★★ Love may be a many-splendored thing for some people, but it's sheer torture for Robert Cole (Albert Brooks) in this contemporary comedy. Brooks wrote, directed, and starred in this very entertaining, often hilarious story about a self-indulgent, narcissistic Hollywood film editor whose love life

has the stability of Mount St. Helens. Rated R. 93m. **DIR:** Albert Brooks. **CAST:** Albert Brooks, Kathryn Harrold, Bruno Kirby. **1981**

MODERN TIMES ★★★★ Charlie Chaplin must have had a crystal ball when he created *Modern Times*. His satire of life in an industrial society has more relevance today than when it was made. Primarily it is still pure Chaplin, with his perfectly timed and edited sight gags. The story finds the Little Tramp confronting all the dehumanizing inventions of a futuristic manufacturing plant. B&W; 89m. **DIR:** Charles Chaplin. **CAST:** Charlie Chaplin, Paulette Goddard. **1936 DVD**

MODERNS, THE ★★ This ironic look at the Paris art scene of the Twenties just isn't funny *enough*. Director Alan Rudolph is always poised at the crossroads of humorous seriousness, but in *The Moderns* he's got his vision in limbo too much of the time. Keith Carradine is good as an expatriate painter, and Wallace Shawn has the best lines as a gossip columnist. Not rated. 126m. **DIR:** Alan Rudolph. **CAST:** Keith Carradine, Linda Fiorentino, John Lone, Wallace Shawn, Genevieve Bujold, Geraldine Chaplin, Kevin J. O'Connor. **1988**

MOGAMBO ★★★ This remake of the film classic *Red Dust* stars Clark Gable as the great white hunter who dallies with a sophisticated married woman (Grace Kelly), only to return to the arms of a jaded lady (Ava Gardner, who is quite good in the role of the woman with a past). It's not great John Ford, but it'll do. 115m. **DIR:** John Ford. **CAST:** Clark Gable, Grace Kelly, Ava Gardner. **1953**

MOHAWK ★1/2 Cornball story about love between settler Scott Brady and Indian Rita Gam must have been inspired by access to footage from John Ford's classic *Drums Along the Mohawk*. 79m. **DIR:** Kurt Neumann. **CAST:** Scott Brady, Rita Gam, Neville Brand, Lori Nelson, Allison Hayes, Ted de Corsia. **1956 DVD**

MOJAVE FIREBRAND ★★★ Wild Bill Elliott helps old pal Gabby Hayes protect his silver mine from a lawless element. B&W; 56m. **DIR:** Spencer Gordon Bennet. **CAST:** William Elliott, George "Gabby" Hayes, Anne Jeffreys, LeRoy Mason. **1944**

MOJAVE MOON ★★★ Decent cast struggles to overcome oddball script and weak direction in this misguided character study. Danny Aiello stars as a Los Angeles car salesman so desperate for love that he agrees to drive a young woman to her home in the Mojave Desert. Once there, he becomes involved with the girl's mom and her wacky boyfriend, who recruits Aiello into his paranoid world. Rated R for adult situations, language, nudity, and violence. 95m. **DIR:** Kevin Dowling. **CAST:** Danny Aiello, Anne Archer, Angelina Jolie, Michael Biehn. **1996**

MOLE PEOPLE, THE ★★ Explorers discover a lost civilization of albino Sumerians living under a mountain. For fright-night nostalgists only. B&W; 78m. **DIR:** Virgil Vogel. **CAST:** John Agar, Hugh Beaumont, Alan Napier. **1956**

MOLL FLANDERS (1996) ★★★★ Sumptuous, triumphant feminist adaptation of Daniel Defoe's eighteenth-century novel. Robin Wright's Moll is a plucky lass whose spirit is never broken, though class prejudice, prostitution, and melodramatic tragedy all conspire to do the poor woman in. Even better, American Wright keeps her cockney accent consistent. Essentially a costume soap opera, but a stirring one. Rated PG-13. 123m. **DIR:** Pen Densham. **CAST:** Robin Wright, Morgan Freeman, Stockard Channing, John Lynch. **1996**

MOLL FLANDERS (1996) ★★★★1/2 Comely Alex Kingston climbs into the role of Daniel Defoe's adventures with such sexual force and strength of personality that one is instantly caught up in Flanders's rich life story. A very spirited and surprisingly erotic Masterpiece Theater production that communicates the novel's sentiment while convincingly re-creating the early 1700s. Released as a two-tape set. Not rated; contains profanity, nudity, and sexual situations. 220m. **DIR:** David Attwood. **CAST:** Alex Kingston, Daniel Craig, Diana Rigg, Ronald Fraser. **1996 DVD**

MOLLY ★★1/2 An institutionalized young woman gets an operation that frees her from her mental illness—but only temporarily. Director John Duigan's film was delayed for nearly a year and shows the signs of editing-room tinkering; even so, it's hard to see how it could ever have been anything but a derivative retread of films like *Charly* and *Awakenings*. Rated PG-13 for brief nudity. 89m. **DIR:** John Duigan. **CAST:** Elisabeth Shue, Aaron Eckhart, Jill Hennesy, Thomas Jane, D. W. Moffett. **1999 DVD**

MOLLY & GINA ★★ Female bonding films are all the rage since *Thelma & Louise*, but you wouldn't want to drive off a cliff with Molly and Gina. Frances Fisher and Natasha Gregson Wagner play the girlfriends of two dead Los Angeles punks. When they attempt to investigate, they are met with the usual parade of bullets, bad guys, and close calls on the mean streets of L.A. Familiar faces can't save this routine thriller. Rated R for violence and nudity. 93m. **DIR:** Paul Leder. **CAST:** Frances Fisher, Natasha Gregson Wagner, Peter Fonda, Bruce Weitz, Stella Stevens. **1993**

MOLLY MAGUIRES, THE ★★★ The Molly Maguires were a group of terrorists in the 1870s who fought for better conditions for the Pennsylvania coal miners. In this dramatization, Sean Connery is their leader and Richard Harris is a Pinkerton detective who infiltrates the group. The film gives a vivid portrayal of the miners' dreadful existence. Performances are first-rate. A little long, but worth checking out. 123m. **DIR:** Martin Ritt. **CAST:** Sean Connery, Richard Harris, Samantha Eggar, Frank Finlay, Art Lund. **1970**

MOM A television reporter tries to protect his family and the community from his mother, a flesh-eating ghoul. Rated R for violence and profanity. 95m. **DIR:** Patrick Rand. **CAST:** Mark Thomas Miller, Art Evans, Mary McDonough, Jeanne Bates. **1990**

MOM AND DAD ★★ Don't know nuthin' 'bout birthin' no babies? Then see this once-banned road-show classic that toured the country for decades. Not rated. B&W; 83m. **DIR:** William Beaudine. **CAST:** Hardie Albright, Lois Austin, June Carlson. **1947**

MOM AND DAD SAVE THE WORLD ★★★1/2 Kids will get plenty of howls out of this goofy comedy, in which an American family is whisked away to the planet Spengo—in the station wagon. The result is a latter-day version of those so-bad-they're-funny sci-fi flicks of the 1950s. Rated PG for silly violence. 87m. **DIR:** Greg Beeman. **CAST:** Teri Garr, Jeffrey Jones, Jon Lovitz, Eric Idle, Wallace Shawn, Thalmus Rasulala. **1992**

MOMMIE DEAREST ★★★1/2 At times this trashy screen version of Christina Crawford's controversial autobiography—which stars Faye Dunaway in an astounding performance as Joan Crawford—is so harrowing and grotesque you're tempted to stop the tape. But it's so morbidly fascinating you can't take your eyes off the screen. Rated PG. 129m. **DIR:** Frank Perry. **CAST:** Faye Dunaway, Diana Scarwid, Steve Forrest. **1981 DVD**

MOMMY ★★ *Bad Seed* Patty McCormack grows up to become the *Mommy*, a woman so possessive of her daughter that she will do anything to protect her. Good chance for the actors to chew scenery and not much more. Rated PG-13 for language and violence. 89m. **DIR:** Max Allan Collins. **CAST:** Patty McCormack, Jason Miller, Brinke Stevens, Majel Barrett. **1994 DVD**

MOMMY 2: MOMMY'S DAY Unjustifiable sequel to the already poor *Mommy* is nearly impossible to watch. Psycho mother Patty McCormack, upon her release from prison, goes after everyone who tries to keep her away from the daughter she nearly murdered in the first film. Low-budget disaster. Not rated; contains violence. 89m. **DIR:** Max Allan Collins. **CAST:** Patty McCormack, Paul Petersen, Gary Sandy, Brinke Stevens. **1996 DVD**

MON ONCLE ANTOINE ★★★1/2 Above-average coming-of-age story about a boy in rural Canada during the 1940s. In French with English subtitles. Not rated, but fine for the entire family. 110m. **DIR:** Claude Jutra. **CAST:** Jacques Gagnon, Claude Jutra. **1971**

MON ONCLE D'AMERIQUE ★★★★ In this bizarre French comedy, director Alain Resnais works something close to a miracle: he combines intelligence with entertainment. On one level, a delectable farce with the requisite ironies, surprise complications, and bittersweet truths. Underneath, it is a thought-provoking scientific treatise—by biologist Henri Laborit—on the human condition. In French with English subtitles. Rated PG. 123m. **DIR:** Alain Resnais. **CAST:** Gérard Depardieu, Nicole Garcia, Roger Pierre. **1980**

MONA LISA ★★★★1/2 Bob Hoskins is Britain's answer to Humphrey Bogart and James Cagney. In this crime-thriller, Hoskins plays a simple but moral man whose less than honest endeavors have landed him in prison. Upon his release, he goes to his former boss (Michael Caine) in search of a job. Not rated; the film has profanity, suggested sex, and violence. 100m. **DIR:** Neil Jordan. **CAST:** Bob Hoskins, Cathy Tyson, Michael Caine, Clark Peters. **1986**

•MONDAY NIGHT MAYHEM ★★1/2 Decent TNT docudrama about the inception of prime-time network football is actually a valentine to Howard Cosell. John Turturro, who convincingly portrays the verbose announcer, feels like an outsider around his jock coannouncers. They're often left scratching their heads as Cosell's rapid wit zips past them. In the limelight, Cosell faces both accolades and prejudice while longing to report serious news. Intriguing look at football and a surprisingly complex man. Not rated; contains profanity. 98m. **DIR:** Ernest R. Dickerson. **CAST:** John Turturro, Brad Beyer, Kevin Anderson, John Heard. **2001**

MONDO ★★★ A homeless boy with no memory of his past becomes the center of a loose-knit community of outsiders in the French seaport town of Nice. Filmmaker Tony Gatlif (*Latcho Drom*, *Gadjo Dilo*) used mostly nonactors to create this visually pleasing but rather naïve fable. In French with English subtitles. Not rated; contains nudity. 80m. **DIR:** Tony Gatlif. **CAST:** Ovidiu Balan, Philippe Petit. **1995**

MONDO CANE II ★★ Disappointing sequel to the controversial and bizarre cult documentary released in 1963. Again the strange and fascinating world of human ritual is explored but without the intensity or the humor that the first film managed to create. Not rated; contains violence and nudity. 90m. **DIR:** Gualtiero Jacopetti. **1964**

MONDO TRASHO This is not a sync-sound movie, and the 1950s rock 'n' roll, along with the occasional wild dubbed-over dialogue, gets tiresome after twenty minutes. Not rated, but this is equivalent to an X for violence, gore, and sex. 130m. **DIR:** John Waters. **CAST:** Divine, Mary Vivian Pearce, Mink Stole, David Lochary. **1971**

MONEY ★★ Pedestrian thriller about a man willing to do whatever it takes to retrieve his father's stolen money. Eric Stoltz is oddly cast in this Italian-French effort as the son who teams up with some eccentric characters to track down the culprits. The plot is all over the map. The scenery is nice, but who wants to sit through a financial thriller travelogue? Not rated; contains adult situations and violence. 117m. **DIR:** Steven H. Stern. **CAST:** F. Murray Abraham, Eric Stoltz, Maryam D'Abo, Christopher Plummer. **1990**

MONEY FOR NOTHING ★★★★ The fact-based story of Joey Coyle, an unemployed Philadelphia dock worker who finds $1.2 million when it falls out of an armored car on its way to an Atlantic City casino. The film bends the facts somewhat—it has the satiric feel of a 1940s Preston Sturges farce—but it makes fine entertainment, fast-paced and well acted by an excellent cast. Rated R for profanity. 100m. **DIR:** Ramon Menendez. **CAST:** John Cusack, Debi Mazar, Michael Madsen, Maury Chaykin. **1993**

MONEY KINGS ★★★1/2 High-profile cast elevates this pedestrian thriller about a bar owner and one of his customers who decide to take on the Boston mob. Peter Falk is Vinnie, the owner of the pub who runs an illegal gambling den in the back. When the mob wants a piece of his action, they send a young, ambitious collector to oversee his operation and things get out of hand. Rated R for language, violence, and adult situations. 96m. **DIR:** Graham Theakston. **CAST:** Peter Falk, Timothy Hutton, Freddie Prinze Jr., Lauren Holly, Tyne Daly, Colm Meaney. **1999 DVD**

MONEY PIT, THE ★★ In this gimmicky, contrived Steven Spielberg production, Tom Hanks plays a rock 'n' roll lawyer who falls in love with musician Shelley Long. When these lovebirds buy a fixer-upper, they encounter all sorts of problems. Rated PG for profanity and suggested sex. 90m. **DIR:** Richard Benjamin. **CAST:** Tom Hanks, Shelley Long, Alexander Godunov, Maureen Stapleton, Joe Mantegna, Philip Bosco, Josh Mostel. **1986**

MONEY TALKS ★★1/2 When fast-talking street hustler Chris Tucker is unwittingly involved in a jailbreak that leaves several cops dead, he turns to maverick TV newsman Charlie Sheen to help him clear his name and find the real killers. Although it is a hopeless mess, with a jumbled plot ending with everyone practically demol-

ishing the L.A. Coliseum, Tucker manages to inject the film with some energy, and he and Sheen have a few good scenes. Rated R for violence and nonstop profanity. 95m. **DIR:** Brett Ratner. **CAST:** Chris Tucker, Charlie Sheen, David Warner, Heather Locklear, Paul Sorvino. **1997 DVD**

MONEY TO BURN ★★ Plodding action-thriller stars McQueen and Swayze (not Steve and Patrick but Chad and Don), who seem right at home in this predictable combination of sex and violence. The guys go on a spending spree with $5 million a friend has given them—do they ever stop and wonder where the money came from? Of course, it belongs to the mob, who have sent one of their best hit men to retrieve it. No-brainer from the first frame. Rated R for nudity, language, and violence. 96m. **DIR:** John Sjorgen. **CAST:** Chad McQueen, Don Swayze, Joe Estevez. **1993**

MONEY TRAIN ★★1/2 Two foster brothers (Wesley Snipes, Woody Harrelson) work as transit cops in New York City and continually run afoul of their sadistic supervisor (Robert Blake). Enjoyable in its funny, fast-paced first half, this film takes a turn for the worse halfway through, causing us to lose sympathy for the main characters and doubt the sanity of the filmmakers. Blake is terrific, however. Rated R for violence, profanity, and simulated sex. 110m. **DIR:** Joseph Ruben. **CAST:** Wesley Snipes, Woody Harrelson, Jennifer Lopez, Robert Blake, Chris Cooper, Joe Grifasi. **1995 DVD**

MONEYTREE, THE ★★ A marijuana grower attempts to ply his trade despite a materialistic, disapproving girlfriend, cops, and rip-off artists. There are some bright moments among the predictable, poorly improvised, and preachy pro-drug ones. Not rated; the film has profanity, violence, and nudity. 94m. **DIR:** Alan Dienstag. **CAST:** Christopher Dienstag. **1991**

MONIKA ★★ Young Harriet Andersson is Monika, a sultry, precocious teenager who escapes her poverty with the help of a young man. Pretty dull stuff. Also known by the title *Summer With Monika*. In Swedish with English subtitles. B&W; 82m. **DIR:** Ingmar Bergman. **CAST:** Harriet Andersson. **1952**

MONKEY BUSINESS (1931) ★★★★1/2 The Marx Brothers are stowaways on a cruise ship, deflating pomposity and confusing authority. This movie dispenses with needless subplots and stagy musical numbers. It's undiluted Marx zaniness, and one of the team's best films. B&W; 77m. **DIR:** Norman Z. McLeod. **CAST:** The Marx Brothers, Thelma Todd, Ruth Hall. **1931 DVD**

MONKEY BUSINESS (1952) ★★★★ A romping screwball comedy about a genius chemist (Cary Grant) who invents a formula that delays the aging process. A chimpanzee in the lab pours the formula in the public water fountain, causing all concerned to revert to adolescence. A minor classic. B&W; 97m. **DIR:** Howard Hawks. **CAST:** Cary Grant, Marilyn Monroe, Ginger Rogers, Charles Coburn, Hugh Marlowe, Larry Keating. **1952 DVD**

MONKEY GRIP ★★★1/2 One year in the life of a divorced mother as she struggles to keep some sense of herself while trying to support herself and her child and maintain a relationship with a drug-addicted musician. Possibly too slow for some tastes, but overall this Australian film offers a probing look at contemporary life-styles. Not rated; the film contains frank discussions of sex. 100m. **DIR:** Ken Cameron. **CAST:** Noni Hazlehurst, Colin Friels, Christina Amphlett. **1982**

MONKEY SHINES: AN EXPERIMENT IN FEAR ★★★ A virile young man doesn't take too readily to becoming a paralytic overnight, immobilized and wheelchair-bound. Enter Ella, a superintelligent (through the miracle of modern science) monkey who is brought in to help with absolutely everything, including revenge. Genuine amusement—and some decent chills—for aficionados of the genre. Rated R for violence, sex, and terror. 115m. **DIR:** George A. Romero. **CAST:** Jason Beghe, Kate McNeil, John Pankow, Joyce Van Patten. **1988 DVD**

MONKEY TROUBLE ★★★★ Delightful film about a youngster (Thora Birch) who finds a capuchin monkey, whom she calls Dodger. Soon both of them are dodging cops, criminals, and befuddled parents because the cute little monkey is actually a well-trained jewel thief. His original master (Harvey Keitel) needs him back to make good on a promise to a powerful and ruthless mobster. Rated PG for brief profanity and light violence. 95m. **DIR:** Franco Amurri. **CAST:** Thora Birch, Harvey Keitel, Mimi Rogers, Christopher McDonald, Kevin Scannell, Alison Elliott, Robert Miranda, Victor Argo. **1994**

MONKEYBONE ★★ This is what happens when a film suffers from being *too* unrestrained. What should've been a clever dark fantasy about a comic-book artist who enters his own world is instead a textbook case of style over substance. Director Henry Selick—so wonderful with puppet animation—hasn't the faintest idea how to manipulate live human beings, which leaves stars Brendan Fraser and Bridget Fonda looking woefully bad. Rated PG-13 for brief nudity and crude humor. 92m. **DIR:** Henry Selick. **CAST:** Brendan Fraser, Bridget Fonda, Chris Kattan, Giancarlo Esposito, Rose McGowan, Whoopi Goldberg. **2001 DVD**

MONKEYS GO HOME 🦃 Stupid monkeyshines. Rated G. 89m. **DIR:** Andrew V. McLaglen. **CAST:** Maurice Chevalier, Dean Jones, Yvette Mimieux. **1966**

MONKEY'S UNCLE, THE ★★ This sequel to *The Misadventures of Merlin Jones* finds whiz kid Tommy Kirk up to no good with a flying machine and a sleep-learning technique employed on a monkey. More of the same from Disney, really: mild slapstick, and G-rated romance with Annette Funicello. For young minds only. 87m. **DIR:** Robert Stevenson. **CAST:** Tommy Kirk, Annette Funicello, Leon Ames, Arthur O'Connell, Frank Faylen. **1965**

MONOLITH ★★ Two cops who dislike each other discover a government secret—an alien being that grows more powerful every day. Extremely bad acting and not much of a plot. Rated R for profanity and violence. 96m. **DIR:** John Eyres. **CAST:** Bill Paxton, Lindsay Frost, John Hurt, Louis Gossett Jr. **1993**

MONOLITH MONSTERS, THE ★★★ Fragments of a meteor grow to enormous proportions when exposed to moisture in the Arizona desert. The good script has a novel premise, but B production values hold it back. B&W; 78m. **DIR:** John Sherwood. **CAST:** Grant Williams, Lola Albright, Les Tremayne. **1957**

MONSIEUR BEAUCAIRE ★★★1/2 Bob Hope is King Louie XV's barber, tricked into impersonating a court

dandy, not knowing an assassination is planned. Joan Caulfield is a beautiful chambermaid. Lots of laughs. Very loosely based on Booth Tarkington's novel. B&W; 93m. **DIR:** George Marshall. **CAST:** Bob Hope, Joan Caulfield, Patric Knowles, Marjorie Reynolds, Cecil Kellaway, Joseph Schildkraut, Reginald Owen, Constance Collier, Hillary Brooke. **1946**

MONSIEUR HIRE ★★★★ A grouchy recluse, already suspected of murder, spies on his lovely neighbor; is he working up to kill again? Slow-moving but suspenseful, beautifully photographed and acted. In French with English subtitles. Rated PG-13 for subtle eroticism. 88m. **DIR:** Patrice Leconte. **CAST:** Michel Blanc, Sandrine Bonnaire, Luc Thuillier, Eric Berenger. **1990**

MONSIEUR VERDOUX ★★★★ A trend-setting black comedy in which a dandified, Parisian Bluebeard murders wives for their money. Wry humor abounds. Charlie Chaplin is superb in the title role. But it's Martha Raye who steals the film—most decidedly in the rowboat scene. The genius that made Chaplin famous the world over shows throughout. B&W; 123m. **DIR:** Charles Chaplin. **CAST:** Charlie Chaplin, Martha Raye, Isobel Elsom, Marilyn Nash, William Frawley. **1947 DVD**

MONSIEUR VINCENT ★★★★ Winner of a special Academy Award, this is a moving, beautifully photographed biography of St. Vincent de Paul, patron saint of social workers. Even if you don't think you'd be interested in the subject matter, it's worth seeing for the performance of Pierre Fresnay, one of France's greatest actors. In French with English subtitles. 73m. **DIR:** Maurice Cloche. **CAST:** Pierre Fresnay, Aimée Clariond, Jean Debucourt. **1949**

MONSIGNOR 🦃 A Vatican priest seduces a student nun and makes deals with the Mafia to help the Church's finances. Rated R for profanity, nudity, and violence. 122m. **DIR:** Frank Perry. **CAST:** Christopher Reeve, Genevieve Bujold, Fernando Rey, Jason Miller. **1982**

MONSIGNOR QUIXOTE ★★★1/2 When a newly appointed monsignor (Alec Guinness) sets out on a holiday with a confirmed Communist (Leo McKern), the two form a strong friendship. Together they challenge corruption within the church. Guinness, playing Don Quixote's grandson, is an innocent idealist while McKern plays the crusty cynic. Made for HBO. 123m. **DIR:** Rodney Bennett. **CAST:** Alec Guinness, Leo McKern, Ian Richardson. **1985**

MONSOON 🦃 An American finds love in the arms of his fiancée's mysterious, jungle-wandering sister. 79m. **DIR:** Rod Amateau. **CAST:** Ursula Thiess, George Nader, Myron Healey, Diana Douglas, Ellen Corby. **1953 DVD**

•MONSOON WEDDING ★★★★1/2 A familiar story—the major and minor crises of the days leading up to a wedding—gets an exotic, colorful telling in this exuberant movie. The crowd of characters is a bit confusing at first, but they're all so interesting and most are so likable that we take to them right away. In English, Hindi, and Punjabi, with English subtitles. Rated R for mature themes and profanity. 114m. **DIR:** Mira Nair. **CAST:** Naseeruddin Shah, Vasundhara Das, Parvin Dabas, Shefali Shetty, Vijay Raaz. **2001**

MONSTER, THE (1925) ★★★ Horror buffs who grew up seeing tantalizing stills from this Lon Chaney Sr. vehicle in monster magazines may be disappointed initially to find that it's a comedy. But there is atmosphere to spare, and Chaney—as a mad scientist and the title fiend—is a bonus. B&W; 86m. **DIR:** Roland West. **CAST:** Lon Chaney Sr., Gertrude Olmstead. **1925**

MONSTER, THE (1996) ★★ A small-time nobody is mistaken for a sex-crazed serial killer and unwittingly stumbles deeper in trouble with the police. The jokes keep coming, but most haven't been funny since the long-ago heyday of burlesque. If sheer physical effort could make someone funny, the frenetic Benigni would be Buster Keaton—but it can't, and he isn't. In Italian with English subtitles. Not rated; contains brief nudity, suggested violence, and much sexual humor. 110m. **DIR:** Roberto Benigni. **CAST:** Roberto Benigni, Michel Blanc, Nicoletta Braschi, Dominique Lavanant, Jean-Claude Brialy. **1996 DVD**

MONSTER AND THE GIRL, THE ★★1/2 White slavery is an intriguing, *noir*ish theme before the sci-fi element spins the story out of control when a criminal's brain is transplanted into an ape's skull. Not rated. B&W; 65m. **DIR:** Stuart Heisler. **CAST:** George Zucco, Ellen Drew, Robert Paige, Paul Lukas. **1941**

MONSTER CLUB, THE ★★★1/2 Better-than-average series of horror tales by Ronald Chetwynd-Hayes, linked by a sinister nightclub where the guys 'n' ghouls can hang out. All the stories keep tongue firmly in cheek and involve imaginary creatures of mixed parentage, such as a "shadmonk," born of a vampire and werewolf. Rated PG for violence. 97m. **DIR:** Roy Ward Baker. **CAST:** Vincent Price, John Carradine, Donald Pleasence, Stuart Whitman, Britt Ekland, Simon Ward. **1981**

MONSTER DOG 🦃 Alice Cooper's music video, shown in the first five minutes of the film, is the only part of this release worth watching. Not rated; the film has violence. 88m. **DIR:** Clyde Anderson. **CAST:** Alice Cooper, Victoria Vera. **1986**

MONSTER FROM A PREHISTORIC PLANET ★★ A bit of added humanity makes this more than just another Japanese big-rubber-monster movie. Parents of a captive baby monster smash across the countryside trying to find him. Plenty of smashed models and bad dialogue make this a must for fans of this genre. Rated PG. 90m. **DIR:** Haruyasu Noguchi. **CAST:** Tarrin. **1967**

MONSTER FROM GREEN HELL ★★ Giant rubber wasps on the rampage in Africa. Our heroes battle a lethargic script to the death. In an attempt to revive the audience, the last reel of the movie was filmed in color. Big deal. B&W/color; 71m. **DIR:** Kenneth Crane. **CAST:** Jim Davis, Barbara Turner, Eduardo Ciannelli. **1957**

MONSTER FROM THE OCEAN FLOOR, THE 🦃 A legendary sea monster is discovered off the coast of Mexico. B&W; 64m. **DIR:** Wyott Ordung. **CAST:** Anne Kimball, Stuart Wade, Wyott Ordung. **1954 DVD**

MONSTER IN A BOX ★★★★ Nobody can sit and talk to the camera like Spalding Gray. In this, the monologist's second filmed stage performance, Gray discusses his brushes with life and death as he wrote his pseudoautobiographical novel *Impossible Vacation*.

Rated PG-13 for profanity. 90m. **DIR:** Nick Broomfield. **CAST:** Spalding Gray. **1991**

MONSTER IN THE CLOSET ★★1/2 Horror spoof about a music-loving, bloodthirsty mutant that inhabits people's closets. Some jokes bomb, but most hit home. John Carradine is priceless in his short role. Rated PG for profanity and brief nudity. 100m. **DIR:** Bob Dahlin. **CAST:** Donald Grant, Denise Dubarry, Claude Akins, Henry Gibson, John Carradine, Stella Stevens. **1987 DVD**

MONSTER MAKER, THE ★★ A scientist conducting experiments in glandular research injects a pianist with a serum that causes his body to grow abnormally large, especially his hands. Low-budget thriller does very little. B&W; 64m. **DIR:** Sam Newfield. **CAST:** J. Carrol Naish, Ralph Morgan, Wanda McKay, Sam Flint, Glenn Strange. **1944 DVD**

MONSTER OF PIEDRAS BLANCAS, THE 🦃 This monstrosity features a human-shaped sea creature with a penchant for separating humans from their heads. B&W; 71m. **DIR:** Irvin Berwick. **CAST:** Les Tremayne, Forrest Lewis. **1958**

MONSTER OF THE ISLAND, THE 🦃 The "Monster" in this cheap, misleadingly titled Italian crime-drama is the ruthless head of a drug-smuggling ring. B&W; 87m. **DIR:** Roberto Montero, Alberto Vecchietti. **CAST:** Boris Karloff. **1953**

MONSTER ON THE CAMPUS ★★ The blood of a prehistoric fish turns a university professor into a murderous ape-beast. Below-average effort from sci-fi specialist Jack Arnold. B&W; 77m. **DIR:** Jack Arnold. **CAST:** Arthur Franz, Joanna Moore, Judson Pratt, Troy Donahue. **1959**

MONSTER SQUAD, THE ★★★ A group of kids form a club to help combat an infiltration of monsters in their town. What unfolds is a clever mixture of Hollywood sci-fi monster effects and a well-conceived spoof of horror movies, past and present. Rated PG-13 for violence. 82m. **DIR:** Fred Dekker. **CAST:** Andre Gower, Duncan Regehr, Stan Shaw, Tommy Noonan. **1987**

MONSTER THAT CHALLENGED THE WORLD, THE ★★ This late-1950s sci-fi programmer is set apart by only one thing: the giant monster, which is life-size (not a miniature) and given plenty of screen time. Hero Tim Holt is ludicrous as a navy commander battling huge, caterpillar-like creatures and romancing a young widow. B&W; 83m. **DIR:** Arnold Laven. **CAST:** Tim Holt, Audrey Dalton, Hans Conried. **1957**

MONSTER WALKS, THE ★★1/2 This independently produced creaker contains most of the elements popular in old-house horror shows of the late 1920s and early 1930s, including deadly apes, secret passages, gloomy storms, and thoroughly petrified ethnic types. Tolerably funny if you overlook the racist portrayal by Sleep 'n' Eat (Willie Best). B&W; 57m. **DIR:** Frank Strayer. **CAST:** Rex Lease, Vera Reynolds, Mischa Auer, Sheldon Lewis, Willie Best. **1932**

•MONSTER'S BALL ★★★★1/2 This gripping drama, which deals with characters authentic enough to be otherworldy, illustrates the shallowness of most cinematic endeavors. The question at the heart of Milo Addica and Will Rokos's absorbing story is whether redemption is possible, or whether conventional wisdom—that a leopard cannot change its spots—will doom everybody here to more pain and suffering. Billy Bob Thornton plays a racist Georgia death row prison guard who has, of necessity, bricked in all his feelings; Halle Berry is the recent widow of a felon he helped execute. A crisis brings these two together, whereupon they embark on a tentative, highly unlikely but hopeful relationship. Make no mistake: This is a deeply disturbing film, a portrait of ordinary citizens at the absolute ragged edge of despair. Rated R for nudity, strong sexual content, dramatic intensity, profanity, and unpleasant racism. 108m. **DIR:** Marc Forster. **CAST:** Billy Bob Thornton, Halle Berry, Heath Ledger, Peter Boyle, Sean "Puffy" Combs, Coronji Calhoun. **2001 DVD**

•MONSTERS, INC. ★★★★ Delightful film with an intriguing premise: the energy that powers the city of Monstropolis is generated by the screams of children frightened by the monsters who hide in their closets. Big Sulley (voiced by John Goodman) and his pal Mike (Billy Crystal) are dismayed by a downturn in productivity, which is further threatened when a child manages to find her way into their secret city. The monsters, you see, are just as afraid of youngsters as the kids are of them—maybe more so. It's funny, suspenseful, and even touching; an entertainment gem for all ages. Rated G. 92m. **DIR:** Peter Docter, David Silverman, Lee Unkrich. **2001 DVD**

MONTANA ★★1/2 Kyra Sedgwick and Robin Tunney are the main reasons to sit through this formulaic thriller about a professional female assassin named Claire (Sedgwick) and her boss's runaway girlfriend, whom she's assigned to bring back. It's a low-level job, one that Claire resents, but when Kitty (Tunney) ends up killing someone while in her custody, the two find themselves on the run from both sides of the law. Some spirited moments don't add up to a whole. Rated R for violence, language, and adult situations. 96m. **DIR:** Jennifer Leitzes. **CAST:** Kyra Sedgwick, Stanley Tucci, Robin Tunney, Robbie Coltrane, John Ritter, Philip Seymour Hoffman. **1997**

MONTANA ★★1/2 Very slow-paced story of a Montana cattle-ranching family torn between the old values of the land and selling out to coal developers. Film loses its focus early on. Hit-and-miss script by Larry McMurtry doesn't help. Made for cable. 73m. **DIR:** William A. Graham. **CAST:** Richard Crenna, Gena Rowlands, Lea Thompson, Justin Deas, Elizabeth Berridge, Scott Coffey, Darren Calton, Peter Fonda. **1990**

MONTANA BELLE ★★1/2 Jane Russell plays notorious Belle Starr, the female bandit who rode with the Dalton Gang. As Western programmers go, this is not bad, but Jane in a blonde wig just doesn't cut it! Originally filmed in color, but video copies are in black and white. B&W; 81m. **DIR:** Allan Dwan. **CAST:** Jane Russell, George Brent, Scott Brady, Forrest Tucker. **1951**

MONTE CARLO ★★ Tacky TV miniseries features Joan Collins as a singing spy during World War II. If you enjoy soap operas, you won't mind. Scenery is a plus. 205m. **DIR:** Anthony Page. **CAST:** Joan Collins, George Hamilton, Lauren Hutton, Malcolm McDowell. **1986**

MONTE WALSH ★★★1/2 Sad but satisfying Western about a couple of saddle pals (Lee Marvin, Jack Palance) attempting to make the transition to a new age and century. Cinematographer William Fraker made an impressive directorial debut with this fine

film. Rated R for violence. 106m. **DIR:** William Fraker. **CAST:** Lee Marvin, Jack Palance, Jeanne Moreau, Mitchell Ryan, Jim Davis. **1970**

MONTENEGRO ★★★★ Susan Anspach stars as a discontented housewife who wanders into a Yugoslavian nightclub, finds herself surrounded by sex and violence, and discovers she rather likes it, in this outlandish, outrageous, and sometimes shocking black comedy. The laughs come with the realization that this movie is totally bonkers. Rated R because of profanity, nudity, sex, and violence. 98m. **DIR:** Dusan Makavejev. **CAST:** Susan Anspach, John Zacharias. **1981 DVD**

MONTEREY POP ★★★★ Despite its ragged sound by today's digital standards, *Monterey Pop* is a historical masterpiece. A chance to see legendary Sixties soloists and groups in their prime far outweighs any technical drawbacks. This was the concert that kicked off 1967's Summer of Love, and with it, a generation of mega-performer shows that culminated in Woodstock. 72m. **DIR:** D. A. Pennebaker. **CAST:** Jimi Hendrix, Otis Redding, The Who, The Animals, Jefferson Airplane, Janis Joplin, Country Joe and the Fish, The Mamas and the Papas, Booker T. and the MGs, Ravi Shankar. **1969**

MONTH BY THE LAKE, A ★★★ At an Italian resort before World War II, a middle-aged spinster vies with a pretty American governess for the attention of a stuffy retired soldier. Details of the story and period don't always ring true, and director John Irvin maintains a too-hectic pace, but the acting is good and the film's warmth is real. Rated PG. 97m. **DIR:** John Irvin. **CAST:** Vanessa Redgrave, Edward Fox, Uma Thurman, Alessandro Gassman, Carlo Cartier, Alida Valli. **1995**

MONTH IN THE COUNTRY, A ★★★ Two emotionally scarred World War I veterans find themselves working for a month in a small Yorkshire village. The acting is flawless, but a gripping plot never quite materializes. Rated PG. 96m. **DIR:** Pat O'Connor. **CAST:** Colin Firth, Kenneth Branagh, Natasha Richardson. **1987**

MONTY PYTHON AND THE HOLY GRAIL ★★★1/2 The Monty Python gang assault the legend of King Arthur and his knights in this often uproariously funny, sometimes tedious, movie. Rated PG. 90m. **DIR:** Terry Gilliam. **CAST:** Terry Jones, Graham Chapman, John Cleese, Terry Gilliam, Michael Palin. **1974 DVD**

MONTY PYTHON LIVE AT THE HOLLYWOOD BOWL ★★★★ Hold on to your sides! Those Monty Python crazies are back with more unbridled hilarity. Rated R for profanity, nudity, and the best in bad taste. 73m. **DIR:** Terry Hughes. **CAST:** John Cleese, Eric Idle, Graham Chapman, Terry Jones, Michael Palin, Terry Gilliam. **1982**

MONTY PYTHON'S FLYING CIRCUS (TV SERIES) ★★★★ This is a series of videos featuring highlights from the popular English TV show of the early 1970s. All the madcap characters remain intact along with the innovative and trendsetting animation by Terry Gilliam. You don't have to be British to enjoy the various political asides and lampoons. You do have to like fast-paced, off-the-wall craziness. The talented cast also conceived and wrote all of the material. 60m. **DIR:** Ian McNaughton. **CAST:** Graham Chapman, John Cleese, Terry Gilliam, Eric Idle, Terry Jones, Michael Palin. **1970–1972 DVD**

MONTY PYTHON'S THE MEANING OF LIFE ★★★★ Those Monty Python goons perform a series of sketches on the important issues of life. According to Michael Palin, the film "ranges from philosophy to history to medicine to halibut—especially halibut." This heady mixture of satiric and surreal bits about the life cycle from birth to death may prove offensive to some and a sheer delight to others. Rated R for offensive goings-on. 103m. **DIR:** Terry Jones. **CAST:** John Cleese, Eric Idle, Graham Chapman, Terry Jones, Terry Gilliam. **1983 DVD**

MONUMENT AVE. ★★★ A small-time hoodlum begins to question the worth of his aimless life among the Irish gangs of South Boston. The film has a documentary feel and some of the muttered dialogue is almost unintelligible; but the story is believably low-key and the acting excellent. Not rated; contains drug use, violence, and extensive profanity. 93m. **DIR:** Ted Demme. **CAST:** Denis Leary, Colm Meaney, Martin Sheen, Billy Crudup, Ian Hart. **1998 DVD**

•MOOD SWINGERS ★★★ Based on the Martin Amis novel *Dead Babies*, this is the story of a group of college students who gather at a secluded mansion to partake in a weekend of illegal drug experimenting. What starts out as an over-the-top party ends in murder and perhaps even more. A fine cast holds your interest until the last frame. Rated R for drug content, violence, and nudity. 105m. **DIR:** William Marsh. **CAST:** Paul Bettany, Katy Carmichael, Hayley Carr, Charlie Condou, Olivia Williams. **2000 DVD**

MOON AND SIXPENCE, THE ★★★1/2 One of the better movies based on a Somerset Maugham novel. George Sanders is appropriately disillusioned as artist Charles Strickland, a character loosely based on real-life painter Paul Gauguin. He moves to Tahiti to fulfill his ambitions when the constrictions of European society get him down. B&W; 89m. **DIR:** Albert Lewin. **CAST:** George Sanders, Herbert Marshall, Florence Bates, Doris Dudley, Elena Verdugo, Albert Basserman, Eric Blore. **1942**

MOON 44 ★★1/2 Michael Paré is an internal affairs cop for a large corporation investigating the theft of giant outer-space mining rigs in this passable sci-fi adventure. Good flying effects. Rated R for violence and profanity. 102m. **DIR:** Roland Emmerich. **CAST:** Michael Paré, Lisa Eichhorn, Malcolm McDowell, Stephen Geoffreys, Roscoe Lee Browne. **1990 DVD**

MOON IN THE GUTTER, THE 🦃 A pretentious, self-consciously artistic bore that seems to defy any viewer to sit through it. Rated R for profanity, nudity, and violence. In French with subtitles. 126m. **DIR:** Jean-Jacques Beineix. **CAST:** Gérard Depardieu, Nastassja Kinski, Victoria Abril. **1983**

MOON IS BLUE, THE ★★ It's hard to believe this comedy, based on a stage hit, was once considered highly controversial. We doubt that even your grandmother would be offended by this very moral film. The thin plot concerns a young woman who fends off two slightly aging playboys by repeatedly vowing to remain a virgin until married. B&W; 95m. **DIR:** Otto Preminger. **CAST:** William Holden, David Niven, Maggie McNamara, Tom Tully, Dawn Addams. **1953**

MOON OF THE WOLF ★★ Another ABC Movie of the Week makes it to video. Disappointing yarn of the search for a werewolf on the loose in Louisiana. Good acting by the leads, but there's not enough action or excitement to sustain interest. 73m. **DIR:** Daniel Petrie. **CAST:** David Janssen, Barbara Rush, Bradford Dillman, John Beradino. **1972**

MOON OVER BROADWAY ★★★1/2 Documentarians D. A. Pennebaker and Chris Hegedus follow the development of a Broadway play (Ken Ludwig's *Moon over Buffalo*, starring Carol Burnett and Philip Bosco) from first rehearsals to opening night. It's a rare glimpse behind the curtain of big-time theater, with all its pleasures, squabbles, and insecurities. All are to be commended for allowing such a generous look at the often awkward creative process. Not rated; suitable for all audiences. 97m. **DIR:** Chris Hegedus, D. A. Pennebaker. **CAST:** Carol Burnett, Philip Bosco, Ken Ludwig, Tom Moore. **1997 DVD**

MOON OVER HARLEM ★★1/2 Uneven melodrama featuring an all-black cast. The unlikely director is German émigré Edgar G. Ulmer, the visionary film poet who worked with F. W. Murnau and other German Expressionists. Ulmer has a considerable reputation among French critics. B&W; 77m. **DIR:** Edgar G. Ulmer. **CAST:** Bud Harris. **1939 DVD**

MOON OVER MIAMI ★★★ Texas sisters Betty Grable and Carole Landis arrive in Miami to hunt for rich husbands. After a suitable round of romantic adventures, they snare penniless Don Ameche and millionaire Robert Cummings. A fun film that helped establish Grable. 91m. **DIR:** Walter Lang. **CAST:** Don Ameche, Robert Cummings, Betty Grable, Carole Landis, Charlotte Greenwood, Jack Haley. **1941**

MOON OVER PARADOR ★★1/2 This misfired comedy thrusts Richard Dreyfuss, who plays a modestly successful actor, into the role of his career: impersonating the recently deceased dictator of an anonymous Caribbean country. Political strongman Raul Julia wants the charade to continue until he can take over smoothly. Everything rattles to a most unconvincing conclusion. Rated PG-13 for language and mild sexual themes. 105m. **DIR:** Paul Mazursky. **CAST:** Richard Dreyfuss, Raul Julia, Sonia Braga, Jonathan Winters, Fernando Rey, Polly Holliday. **1988**

MOON PILOT ★★★1/2 Tom Tryon gets volunteered to become the first astronaut to circle the moon. Good script, with satire and laughs in ample quantities. Rated G. 98m. **DIR:** James Neilson. **CAST:** Tom Tryon, Brian Keith, Edmond O'Brien, Dany Saval. **1962**

MOON TRAP 🦃 Two astronauts find a race of resourceful mechanical aliens on the lunar surface. Rated R for language and nudity. 92m. **DIR:** Robert Dyke. **CAST:** Walter Koenig, Bruce Campbell. **1989**

MOONBASE ★★ In the year 2045, inhabitants of Earth have resorted to using the moon as a dump. That's the good news. The bad news is that some vicious criminals have escaped from an orbiting prison and have landed on the moon. They plan to use the nuclear weapons buried there as their ticket back to Earth. OK effects, but no big deal. Rated R for language and violence. 89m. **DIR:** Paolo Mazzucato. **CAST:** Scott Plank, Jocelyn Seagrave, Kurt Fuller, Robert O'Reilly. **1997**

MOONCHILD ★★1/2 Arguably Todd Sheets's best film, this tale of genetically created werewolves could have been an intriguing sci-fi shocker. Instead, what we get is a gore flick with little plot interest. Not rated; contains violence, gore, and profanity. 102m. **DIR:** Todd Sheets. **CAST:** Auggi Alvarez, Kathleen McSweeney. **1994**

MOONCUSSERS ★★1/2 Kevin Corcoran stars as a boy who discovers the secrets of the Mooncussers—pirates who work on moonless nights to draw ships to their doom by means of false signal lamps on shore. 85m. **DIR:** James Neilson. **CAST:** Oscar Homolka, Kevin Corcoran, Robert Emhardt, Joan Freeman. **1962**

MOONDANCE ★★★ The bond between two brothers is stretched to the breaking point when they fall in love with the same beautiful young girl. Well-acted film features songs by Van Morrison. Rated R for nudity, sexual situations, and profanity. 96m. **DIR:** Dagmar Hirtz. **CAST:** Ruaidhri Conroy, Ian Shaw, Julie Brendler, Marianne Faithfull. **1994**

MOONLIGHT AND VALENTINO ★★ Recent widow receives solace from her sister, best friend, and ex-stepmother. The film should be a powerhouse of female bonding, but the script is aimless and dithering, and no one—least of all director David Anspaugh—knows what to do with it. Rated R for profanity and brief nudity. 104m. **DIR:** David Anspaugh. **CAST:** Elizabeth Perkins, Gwyneth Paltrow, Kathleen Turner, Whoopi Goldberg, Jon Bon Jovi, Josef Sommer, Peter Coyote. **1995**

MOONLIGHTING (1983) ★★★★1/2 This film, a political parable criticizing the Soviet Union's suppression of Solidarity in Poland, may sound rather heavy, gloomy, and dull. It isn't. Written and directed by Jerzy Skolimowski, it focuses on four Polish construction workers remodeling a flat in London. Give it a look. In Polish with English subtitles. Rated PG for very brief nudity. 97m. **DIR:** Jerzy Skolimowski. **CAST:** Jeremy Irons, Eugene Lipinski. **1983**

MOONLIGHTING (1985) (TV PILOT) ★★★★ This is the pilot film for the delightfully offbeat ABC series. Maddie, a supersuccessful model, suddenly finds herself facing poverty, thanks to an embezzler. She decides to sell off all her assets, including a money-losing detective agency. David, a fast-talking, irresistible eccentric, tries to talk her into making a career of sleuthing instead. Bruce Willis is dazzling as David. And the chemistry beween Willis and Cybill Shepherd heats up to just the right temperature. 97m. **DIR:** Robert Butler. **CAST:** Cybill Shepherd, Bruce Willis, Allyce Beasley. **1985 DVD**

MOONRAKER 🦃 The James Bond series hit absolute rock bottom in 1979 with this outer-space adventure. Rated PG. 126m. **DIR:** Lewis Gilbert. **CAST:** Roger Moore, Lois Chiles, Michel Lonsdale. **1979 DVD**

MOONRISE ★★ Being the son of a man hanged for murder isn't easy, and Danny (Dane Clark) has grown up with quite a chip on his shoulder. Very melodramatic. B&W; 90m. **DIR:** Frank Borzage. **CAST:** Dane Clark, Gail Russell, Lloyd Bridges, Ethel Barrymore. **1948**

MOONSHINE COUNTY EXPRESS ★★ In this bogus action flick, William Conrad has his hands full with the three vengeful daughters of a man he just murdered. Rated PG for mild language and violence. 95m. **DIR:**

Gus Trikonis. **CAST:** John Saxon, Susan Howard, William Conrad, Dub Taylor. **1977**

MOONSHINE HIGHWAY ★★★1/2 This tale of illicit love and illegal alcohol is set in Tennessee in 1957, during the days when dry states still offered outlets to those who manufactured black-market moonshine. Restless Kyle MacLachlan divides his time between playing highway tag with the Feds and romancing the local sheriff's wife. Eventually, he's forced to make choices. Rated PG-13 for profanity and violence. 96m. **DIR:** Andy Armstrong. **CAST:** Kyle MacLachlan, Randy Quaid, Maria Del Mar, Alex Carter, Jeremy Ratchford, Gary Farmer. **1995**

MOONSPINNERS, THE ★★★ A young girl (Hayley Mills) becomes involved in a jewel theft in Crete. The best features of this film are the appearance of a "grownup" Hayley Mills and the return to the screen of Pola Negri. The film is essentially a lightweight melodrama in the Hitchcock mold. 118m. **DIR:** James Neilson. **CAST:** Hayley Mills, Eli Wallach, Pola Negri, Peter McEnery, Joan Greenwood, Irene Papas. **1964**

MOONSTRUCK ★★★★1/2 Cher, Nicolas Cage, and a superb supporting cast enliven this delightful comedy about a group of Italian-Americans who find amore when the moon shines bright. Director Norman Jewison and screenwriter John Patrick Shanley make one hilarious complication follow another. Rated PG for profanity and suggested sex. 102m. **DIR:** Norman Jewison. **CAST:** Cher, Nicolas Cage, Vincent Gardenia, Olympia Dukakis, Danny Aiello, Julie Bovasso, John Mahoney, Feodor Chaliapin. **1987 DVD**

MORAN OF THE LADY LETTY ★★★ A shanghaied socialite meets and falls in love with a tough seafarer, who turns out to be a woman in disguise. Dandy location photography around Catalina. A change of pace for Valentino purists. Silent. B&W; 70m. **DIR:** George Melford. **CAST:** Rudolph Valentino. **1922**

MORE ★★★1/2 A German youth, on the road after finishing college, becomes enamored of a free-spirited American girl in Paris. Barbet Schroeder's first film as a director, this grim portrait of directionless young people is ironically best remembered for its Pink Floyd score. In English. Not rated, contains nudity. 110m. **DIR:** Barbet Schroeder. **CAST:** Mimsy Farmer, Klaus Grunberg. **1969**

MORE AMERICAN GRAFFITI ★★ Sequel to George Lucas's high-spirited, nostalgic *American Graffiti* lacks the charm of the original as it follows up on the lives of the various characters. There are a few bright moments, but a split-screen technique that didn't work when the film was initially released is even more annoying on video. Rated PG. 111m. **DIR:** B.W.L. Norton. **CAST:** Ron Howard, Paul LeMat, Candy Clark, Bo Hopkins, Cindy Williams, Charles Martin Smith, Mackenzie Phillips, Harrison Ford, Scott Glenn, Mary Kay Place, Rosanna Arquette. **1979**

MORE THE MERRIER, THE ★★★★ This delightful comedy is set in Washington, D.C., during the hotel and housing shortage of the hectic World War II years. Charles Coburn earned a supporting Oscar as the old curmudgeon trying to cope with the housing problem while advising Joel McCrea and Jean Arthur on how to handle their love life. (Cary Grant played Coburn's character when this was remade as *Walk, Don't Run*.) B&W; 104m. **DIR:** George Stevens. **CAST:** Joel McCrea, Jean Arthur, Charles Coburn. **1943**

MORE WILD WILD WEST ★★1/2 TV movie is a pale reminder of the irresistible original series. The Old West's most invincible secret service agents, James West and Artemus Gordon, again come out of retirement, this time to rescue the world from an invisibility plot. Jonathan Winters hams it up as the villainous Albert Paradine II. There's too much silly comedy, not enough excitement. 94m. **DIR:** Burt Kennedy. **CAST:** Robert Conrad, Ross Martin, Jonathan Winters, Harry Morgan, René Auberjonois, Liz Torres, Victor Buono, Dr. Joyce Brothers, Emma Samms. **1980**

MORGAN ★★★★ In this cult favorite, Vanessa Redgrave decides to leave her wacky husband (David Warner). He's a wild man who has a thing for gorillas (this brings scenes from *King Kong*). Nevertheless, he tries to win her back in an increasingly unorthodox manner. Deeply imbedded in the 1960s, this film still brings quite a few laughs. B&W; 97m. **DIR:** Karel Reisz. **CAST:** Vanessa Redgrave, David Warner, Robert Stephens, Irene Handl. **1966 DVD**

MORGAN STEWART'S COMING HOME ★★ Made before *Pretty in Pink* but released after it to take advantage of the impression Jon Cryer made in that John Hughes teen comedy. The young actor stars in this tepid comedy as a preppie who tries to reorder his family's priorities. Cryer has some good moments, and Lynn Redgrave is top-notch as his mom, but the laughs just aren't there. Rated PG-13. 92m. **DIR:** Alan Smithee. **CAST:** Jon Cryer, Lynn Redgrave, Viveka Davis, Paul Gleason, Nicholas Pryor. **1987**

MORGAN THE PIRATE ★★★ This fictionalized account of the adventures of the historical Henry Morgan (with muscle man Steve Reeves in the title role) is perhaps the most entertaining of that actor's many Italian-made features. Even by current standards, there is plenty of action and romance. 93m. **DIR:** André de Toth, Primo Zeglio. **CAST:** Steve Reeves, Valerie Lagrange, Ivo Garbani. **1961**

MORITURI ★★1/2 Marlon Brando portrays a spy working for the British who, through a series of moral equations involving anti-Nazism versus Nazism, convinces the captain of a German freighter on a voyage from Japan to Germany to side with the Allies. The concept is good, but the script gets weaker and weaker as the film progresses. B&W; 128m. **DIR:** Bernhard Wicki. **CAST:** Marlon Brando, Yul Brynner, Janet Margolin, Trevor Howard, Wally Cox, William Redfield. **1965**

MORK & MINDY (TV SERIES) ★★★1/2 Sitcom that launched stand-up comic Robin Williams to superstardom. Playing Mork from the planet Ork, he makes zany observations and assessments of Earth life and customs. Some of his funniest bits were unscripted ad-lib. Pam Dawber plays it straight as his kindly and informative roommate. Four volumes, each containing two episodes and lasting approximately 50m. **DIR:** Howard Storm, Jeff Chambers. **CAST:** Robin Williams, Pam Dawber, Conrad Janis, Elizabeth Kerr, Tom Poston, Jay Thomas. **1978–1982**

MORNING AFTER, THE ★★★1/2 An alcoholic ex–movie star (Jane Fonda) wakes up one morning in bed next to a dead man and is unable to remember what happened the night before. Fonda is terrific as the hero-

ine-victim, and Jeff Bridges gives a solid performance as the ex-cop who comes to her aid. The result is an enjoyable thriller in the style of *Jagged Edge*. Rated R for profanity. 103m. **DIR:** Sidney Lumet. **CAST:** Jane Fonda, Jeff Bridges, Raul Julia, Diane Salinger, Richard Foronjy. **1986**

MORNING GLORY (1933) ★★1/2 A naïve young actress comes to New York to find fame and romance. Based on the Zoe Akins play, the stagy film version hasn't aged well. But Katharine Hepburn is charismatic as the actress. She won her first Academy Award for this showy performance. B&W; 74m. **DIR:** Lowell Sherman. **CAST:** Katharine Hepburn, Adolphe Menjou, Douglas Fairbanks Jr., C. Aubrey Smith. **1933**

MORNING GLORY (1992) ★★1/2 Based on a book by LaVyrle Spencer, an ex-con applies for a job as the husband of a reclusive woman. Just when they fall in love, he's charged with killing a floozy. Unfortunately the story is very slow and boring. Rated PG-13 for profanity. 96m. **DIR:** Steven H. Stern. **CAST:** Christopher Reeve, Deborah Raffin, Lloyd Bochner, Nina Foch, Helen Shaver, J. T. Walsh. **1992**

MOROCCO ★★★ The fabulous and fabled Marlene Dietrich in her first Hollywood film. She's a cabaret singer stranded in exotic, sinister Morocco, who must choose between suave, rich Adolphe Menjou, or dashing French Legionnaire Gary Cooper. The scene at the oasis is classic 1930s cinematography. B&W; 92m. **DIR:** Josef von Sternberg. **CAST:** Gary Cooper, Adolphe Menjou, Marlene Dietrich. **1930**

MORONS FROM OUTER SPACE ★★1/2 Four aliens from a distant planet crash-land on Earth, but their arrival is not a secret and they soon become international celebrities. The comedy comes from the fact that they're idiots and act accordingly. Unfortunately, the morons are not as funny as the viewer would hope. Rated PG for language. 78m. **DIR:** Mike Hodges. **CAST:** Griff Rhys Jones, Mel Smith, James B. Sikking, Dindsdale Landen. **1985 DVD**

MORRISON MURDERS, THE ★★★1/2 This made-for-cable original, based on a true story, focuses on two brothers who try to cope with the savage murders of their parents and younger brother. Hard times await both of them, as grief is soon followed by accusations that one of them is the killer. Good acting by John Corbett and company in this engaging story. Not rated; contains violence. 95m. **DIR:** Chris Thomson. **CAST:** John Corbett, Jonathon Scarfe, Maya McLaughlin, Gordon Clapp. **1996**

MORTAL KOMBAT ★★1/2 Yet another tiresome video-game-turned-film, this one highlighted mostly by its shrill shock-rock soundtrack. The plot is stolen shamelessly from *Enter the Dragon*, with three stalwart heroes battling extraterrestrial champions over the fate of Earth. Christopher Lambert looks particularly silly as a wise sage who speaks in fortune-cookie riddles. Rated PG-13 for surprisingly savage violence. 101m. **DIR:** Paul Anderson. **CAST:** Robin Shou, Linden Ashby, Bridgette Wilson, Cary-Hiroyuki Tagawa, Talisa Soto, Christopher Lambert. **1995 DVD**

MORTAL KOMBAT: ANNIHILATION ★★ The song lyric "Everybody was kung fu fighting" summarizes the plot, character, and theme of this video game spinoff. The chosen defenders of Earth must defeat the evil minions of an alternate dimension. Elaborate special effects can't compensate for the mediocre acting and near plotless premise. This loud music/video arcade combo is just an excuse for nonstop violence. Rated PG-13 for violence. 95m. **DIR:** John R. Leonetti. **CAST:** Robin Shou, Talisa Soto, Brian Thompson, Sandra Hess, Lynn Red Williams. **1997 DVD**

MORTAL KOMBAT: THE ANIMATED MOVIE ★★1/2 The *Mortal Kombat* franchise becomes an animated, direct-to-video movie that's sure to please fans of the video game. Using computer-generated animation, this film depicts the origins of the series' characters and engages them in plenty of action and mayhem. Rated PG for animated violence. 60m. **DIR:** Joe Franck. **1995**

MORTAL PASSIONS A slut plots to murder her wealthy husband with the help of her sheepish boyfriend. Rated R for violence, nudity, and profanity. 96m. **DIR:** Andrew Lane. **CAST:** Zach Galligan, Krista Erickson, Luca Bercovici, Michael Bowen. **1990**

MORTAL SINS (1990) (DANGEROUS OBSESSION) ★★1/2 Private eye Brian Benben becomes embroiled in a series of murders that lead to television ministries and the mysterious daughter of a powerful television evangelist. Rated R for violence and nudity. 85m. **DIR:** Yuri Sivo. **CAST:** Debrah Farentino, Brian Benben, Anthony LaPaglia, James Harper. **1990**

MORTAL SINS (1992) ★★★ It appears that a priest is murdering young women, then giving them last rites. Father Thomas (Christopher Reeve) hears the confession of the murderer and starts to play detective. A few good twists keep the viewer guessing. Not rated, made for cable, but contains violence. 95m. **DIR:** Bradford May. **CAST:** Christopher Reeve, Roxann Biggs, Francis Guinan, Weston McMillan, Phillip R. Allen, Lisa Vultaggio, George Touliatos, Mavor Moore, Karen Kondazian. **1992**

MORTAL STORM, THE ★★★★ Phyllis Bottome's famous novel about the rise of Nazism makes good screen fare in spite of the screenwriter's apparent reluctance to call a spade a spade. Germany is never identified even though it is quite obvious in this story about a schoolteacher's family in the early days of World War II. Very well acted. B&W; 100m. **DIR:** Frank Borzage. **CAST:** James Stewart, Margaret Sullavan, Robert Young, Bonita Granville, Frank Morgan, Irene Rich, Dan Dailey, Tom Drake, Robert Stack, Maria Ouspenskaya, Gene Reynolds, Ward Bond. **1940**

MORTAL THOUGHTS ★★★ Demi Moore and Glenne Headly give strong performances in this relentlessly downbeat and disturbing drama. Director Alan Rudolph and screenwriters William Reilly and Claude Kerven explore the possible murder of an abusive, foul-mouthed, drug-addicted husband (Bruce Willis) by his wife (Headly) and her best friend (Moore). Rated R for violence and profanity. 104m. **DIR:** Alan Rudolph. **CAST:** Demi Moore, Glenne Headly, Bruce Willis, John Pankow, Harvey Keitel, Billie Neal, Frank Vincent. **1991 DVD**

MORTUARY ACADEMY ★★ Academic comedy fails to advance to the head of the class. The brothers Grimm (yes, that's their last name) must make it through the dreaded academy in order to inherit big bucks. Typical. Rated R for nudity, language, and some violence. 86m.

DIR: Michael Schroeder. **CAST:** Christopher Atkins, Tracey Walter, Lynn Danielson, Mary Woronov, Perry Lang. **1992**

MOSCOW DOES NOT BELIEVE IN TEARS ★★★★ For all its rewards, this film requires a bit of patience on the part of the viewer. The first hour of the tragic comedy is almost excruciatingly slow. But once it gets deeper into the story, you're very glad you toughed it out. MPAA unrated, but contains brief nudity and brief violence. 152m. **DIR:** Vladimir Menshov. **CAST:** Vera Alentova, Irina Muravyova. **1980 DVD**

MOSCOW ON THE HUDSON ★★★★1/2 Robin Williams stars in this sweet, funny, sad, and sexy comedy as a Russian circus performer who, while on tour in the United States, decides to defect after experiencing the wonders of Bloomingdale's department store in New York. Paul Mazursky cowrote and directed this touching character study. Rated R for profanity, nudity, suggested sex, and violence. 115m. **DIR:** Paul Mazursky. **CAST:** Robin Williams, Maria Conchita Alonso, Cleavant Derricks. **1984 DVD**

MOSES (1975) ★★★ This biblical screen story of the Hebrew lawgiver is fairly standard as such films go. Burt Lancaster is well suited to play the stoic Moses. However, in trimming down this six-hour TV miniseries for video release, its makers lost most of the character development in the supporting roles. 141m. **DIR:** Gianfranco De Bosio. **CAST:** Burt Lancaster, Anthony Quayle, Irene Papas, Ingrid Thulin, William Lancaster. **1975**

MOSES (1996) ★★★ In this TNT original miniseries, Ben Kingsley shines as a stuttering, self-effacing, reluctant leader to the Hebrews. He leads his people out of Egypt and slavery and then his real problems begin. His people whine and grumble incessantly during their forty years in the desert. Special effects are OK but not spectacular and the dialogue is often insipid. Not rated; contains violence. 170m. **DIR:** Roger Young. **CAST:** Ben Kingsley, Frank Langella, David Suchet, Maurice Roeves, Philip Stone, Christopher Lee, Enrico Lo Verso, Geraldine McEwan. **1996**

MOSQUITO ★★ Dopey mutant-bug movie saved by hokey special effects and a fondness for the genre. They're big, they're bad, and they suck human blood. Rated R for violence and language. 92m. **DIR:** Gary Jones. **CAST:** Gunnar Hansen, Ron Asheton, Steve Dixon, Rachel Loiselle, Tim Lovelace. **1994 DVD**

MOSQUITO COAST, THE ★★★ In spite of the top-notch talent involved, this remains a flawed endeavor. Allie Fox (Harrison Ford) is a monomaniacal genius who can't bear what he perceives to be the rape of the United States, so he drags his wife and four children to the untamed wilderness of the Mosquito Coast in a self-indulgent attempt to mimic the Swiss Family Robinson. Rated PG. 117m. **DIR:** Peter Weir. **CAST:** Harrison Ford, Helen Mirren, River Phoenix, Conrad Roberts, Andre Gregory, Martha Plimpton. **1986 DVD**

MOST DANGEROUS GAME, THE ★★★1/2 This sister production to *King Kong* utilizes the same sets, same technical staff, and most of the same cast to tell the story of Count Zaroff, the insane ruler of a secret island who spends his time hunting the victims of the ships that he wrecks. Filmed many times since and used as a theme for countless television plots, this original is still the standard to measure all the others by. Nonstop action for sixty-three tight minutes. B&W; 63m. **DIR:** Ernest B. Schoedsack, Irving Pichel. **CAST:** Joel McCrea, Fay Wray, Leslie Banks, Robert Armstrong. **1932 DVD**

MOST WANTED ★★1/2 So-so pilot for Robert Stack's TV series. As the head of a special police unit, he works with a computer whiz, psychologist, and undercover detective to crack the most difficult cases. Here, they find a psychopath who has been raping and murdering nuns. Aside from Stack, many of the costars (including Tom Selleck) did not stay with the show. Made-for-TV, this is unrated but contains violence. 78m. **DIR:** Walter Grauman. **CAST:** Robert Stack, Tom Selleck, Leslie Charleson, Shelly Novack. **1976**

MOTEL HELL ★★1/2 "It takes all kinds of critters to make Farmer Vincent Fritters!" Ahem! This above-average horror-comedy stars Rory Calhoun (who overplays grandly) as a nice ol' farmer who has struck gold with his dried pork treats. His secret ingredient happens to be human flesh. Rated R for violence. 102m. **DIR:** Kevin Connor. **CAST:** Rory Calhoun, Nancy Parsons, Paul Linke, Nina Axelrod, Elaine Joyce. **1980**

MOTHER (1952) ★★★★ This is a beautifully shot black-and-white movie about a working-class mother who must raise her family after her husband's death in post–World War II. While the story appears to be simple, there is great depth in each character. This was voted Japan's best film in 1952. In Japanese with English subtitles. B&W; 98m. **DIR:** Mikio Naruse. **CAST:** Kinuyo Tanaka. **1952**

MOTHER (1994) ★★★ Tension builds when an obsessive mom (Diane Ladd) believes she's losing her son to a girlfriend, college, etc. She'll do anything to keep him. Not surprisingly there's more to this little family than meets the eye, making Mom more wacko than originally assumed. Olympia Dukakis plays the lecherous neighbor who has the hots for the son. Rated R for profanity, violence, and gore. 95m. **DIR:** Frank LaLoggia. **CAST:** Diane Ladd, Olympia Dukakis, Morgan Weisser, Ele Keats, Matt Clark, Scott Wilson. **1994**

MOTHER ★★★★ Hilarious twist to the traditional coming-of-age film features Albert Brooks as a forty-something writer who returns to his childhood home seeking answers to his personal failures from his mom (Debbie Reynolds). Her penny-pinching ways and sly remarks are meant as constructive criticism but inevitably lead to future psychosis. Brooks reverts to his troubled youth, challenging his mother's every move while avoiding her attempts to send him packing. Unlikely scenario is the film's running joke, and it's a surprisingly good one! Rated PG-13 for language. 97m. **DIR:** Albert Brooks. **CAST:** Debbie Reynolds, Albert Brooks, Rob Morrow. **1996 DVD**

MOTHER AND THE LAW, THE ★★★★★ One of the undisputed masterpieces of the silent cinema. This is the rarely seen complete version of the so-called modern episode to D. W. Griffith's *Intolerance*. A young husband (Bobby Harron) is unjustly indicted for murder and is saved only at the last minute in one of Griffith's most sensational last-minute-rescue climaxes. Silent. B&W; 93m. **DIR:** D. W. Griffith. **CAST:** Mae Marsh, Robert Harron. **1914**

MOTHER AND THE WHORE, THE ★★★1/2 Considered a masterpiece by those on its wavelength, this long, talky film is not for all viewers. Not unlike *Last Tango in Paris*, it dissects modern soullessness through the sexual yearnings of a male character and the women involved with him. It's a grim challenge, recommended for serious film enthusiasts. In French with English subtitles. Not rated; contains sexual situations and nudity. B&W; 215m. **DIR:** Jean Eustache. **CAST:** Jean-Pierre Léaud, Bernadette Lafont, Francoise Lebrun. **1973**

MOTHER, JUGS, AND SPEED ★★★ Hang on tight! This is a fast and furious black comedy about a rundown ambulance service that puts body count ahead of patient welfare in the race to the hospital. Bill Cosby and Raquel Welch make an odd combination that clicks. There's also some scene-stealing hilarity from Larry Hagman as an oversexed driver. Rated R. 95m. **DIR:** Peter Yates. **CAST:** Bill Cosby, Raquel Welch, Larry Hagman, Harvey Keitel. **1976**

MOTHER KUSTERS GOES TO HEAVEN ★★★ When a German factory worker kills his boss and then commits suicide, his widow must deal with the convoluted aftermath. Emotionally and politically charged, this potent, pro-communist tract was banned by the Berlin Film Festival. In German with English subtitles. Rated R for adult themes. 108m. **DIR:** Rainer Werner Fassbinder. **CAST:** Brigitte Mira, Ingrid Caven, Margit Carstensen. **1975**

MOTHER LODE ★★ Although this modern-day adventure yarn about a search for gold boasts a feasible plot and fine acting by Charlton Heston (who also directed) and John Marley, its liabilities far outweigh its assets. Rated PG, the film contains occasional obscenities and violence. 101m. **DIR:** Charlton Heston. **CAST:** Charlton Heston, John Marley, Nick Mancuso, Kim Basinger. **1982**

MOTHER NIGHT ★★ This creaky psychological thriller, based on Kurt Vonnegut's novel, is about an American spy (Nick Nolte) who poses as a successful German propaganda minister during World War II, only to worry he may have become his own creation. Alan Arkin livens up the mood as a sympathetic and personable painter. Another plus is John Goodman's dangerous but cuddly military man. Rated R for profanity, nudity, and sexual situations. 113m. **DIR:** Keith Gordon. **CAST:** Nick Nolte, Sheryl Lee, Alan Arkin, John Goodman, Kirsten Dunst. **1996 DVD**

MOTHER TERESA ★★★★★ Many consider her to be a living saint and her selfless dedication to the world's sick of heart, body, mind, and soul seems to justify that claim. Mother Teresa is, at the very least, a heroic figure who simply believes that "we must all be holy in what we do." Five years in the making, this documentary lets an extraordinary life speak for itself. Not rated, this film has shocking scenes of poverty and starvation. 83m. **DIR:** Ann Petrie, Jeanette Petrie. **1987**

MOTHER WORE TIGHTS ★★★★ This landmark musical is the story of two vaudeville performers who meet, marry, have a family, and continue with their careers. The musical score won an Oscar, and stars Betty Grable and Dan Dailey became a popular movie team. 107m. **DIR:** Walter Lang. **CAST:** Betty Grable, Dan Dailey, Mona Freeman, Connie Marshall, William Frawley, Kathleen Lockhart, Robert Arthur, Señor Wences. **1947**

MOTHER'S BOYS ★★1/2 A mentally unbalanced woman is willing to go to terrible lengths to get back the husband and three sons she abandoned years before. Everything-but-the-kitchen-sink thriller is stylish and effective, but has a nasty edge that keeps the supense from being pleasurable. Rated R for violence. 96m. **DIR:** Yves Simoneau. **CAST:** Jamie Lee Curtis, Peter Gallagher, Joanne Whalley, Vanessa Redgrave, Joss Ackland. **1994 DVD**

MOTHER'S PRAYER, A ★★1/2 A mediocre, drawn-out, made-for-cable original about a widow who is looking to find a family for her son before she dies of AIDS. Not rated; contains profanity. 94m. **DIR:** Larry Elikann. **CAST:** Linda Hamilton, Noah Fleiss, Bruce Dern, Kate Nelligan, RuPaul. **1995**

•MOTHMAN PROPHECIES, THE ★★1/2 This messy but eerie paranormal thriller was "inspired" by real-life events. The wife of *Washington Post* reporter John Klein crashes their car after being distracted by a large, winged phenomenon. Under odd circumstances, John later discovers that the people in Point Pleasant, West Virginia, also claim to have seen the creepy creature. He investigates with the help of a local cop in a story that offers more tone than answers but generally entertains. Rated PG-13 for mature themes, profanity, and sexuality. 119m. **DIR:** Mark Pellington. **CAST:** Richard Gere, Laura Linney, Debra Messing, Alan Bates, Will Patton. **2002 DVD**

MOTHRA ★★★ Two six-inch-tall princesses are taken from their island home to perform in a Tokyo nightclub. A native tribe prays for the return of the princesses, and their prayers hatch a giant egg, releasing a giant caterpillar. The caterpillar goes to Tokyo searching for the princesses and turns into a giant moth while wrecking the city. Although the story may sound corny, this is one of the best of the giant-monster movies to come out of Japan. 100m. **DIR:** Inoshiro Honda. **CAST:** Lee Kresel, Franky Sakai, Hiroshi Koizumi. **1962**

MOTORAMA ★★★★ Ten-year-old Jordan Christopher Michael takes off in a stolen car, questing for Motorama game cards and instant wealth. This darkly funny, extremely bizarre road movie features a strange supporting cast and gallons of imagination. For unusual tastes only. Rated R for profanity and brief nudity. 90m. **DIR:** Barry Shils. **CAST:** Jordan Christopher Michael, Flea, Meat Loaf, Drew Barrymore, Garrett Morris, Michael J. Pollard, Mary Woronov, Martha Quinn. **1991 DVD**

MOTORCYCLE GANG ★★ Cut-rate variation on *The Wild One* (and every other teen-J.D. movie cliché they could cram in) runs on too long, but is still lurid fun. Yes, Carl Switzer is indeed "Alfalfa," captured here shortly before his violent offscreen death. B&W; 78m. **DIR:** Edward L. Cahn. **CAST:** Anne Neyland, Steve Terrell, John Ashley, Carl "Alfalfa" Switzer. **1957**

MOUCHETTE ★★★★ Director Robert Bresson's unique cinematic style has never been more evident than in this heartfelt drama. The story depicts the hardships of a young peasant girl who desperately attempts to transcend a brutal household where she lives with her alcoholic, bootlegger father and brothers. In

French with English subtitles. Not rated. 90m. **DIR:** Robert Bresson. **CAST:** Nadine Nortier. **1966**

MOULIN ROUGE (1952) ★★★★ Overlooked gem by director John Huston, with José Ferrer memorable as Henri de Toulouse-Lautrec, the famous nineteenth-century Parisian artist whose growth was stunted by a childhood accident. Lavish photography and Oscar-winning art direction and costumes make this a feast for the eyes. 123m. **DIR:** John Huston. **CAST:** José Ferrer, Zsa Zsa Gabor, Suzanne Flon, Christopher Lee, Peter Cushing. **1952**

•MOULIN ROUGE (2001) ★★★★1/2 Director Baz Luhrmann's audacious 2001 Best Picture nominee, nothing less than a masterful reworking of the classic Hollywood musical, is a visual spectacle for the eyes, ears, and heart. The story is set in Paris circa 1900, with Nicole Kidman starring as notorious nightclub courtesan Satine, dubbed "The Sparkling Diamond." Ewan McGregor is the young writer who falls under her spell, only to learn that Satine hasn't the luxury of indulging true love, but instead must answer to the nightclub's decadent financial backers. The production design, costumes, and choreography are awesome, and (surprise, surprise!) Kidman and McGregor do their own singing for the soundtrack's jaw-dropping covers of dozens upon dozens of pop hits. This is the sort of film that puts the "motion" back in motion pictures! Rated PG-13 for sexual content. 127m. **DIR:** Baz Luhrmann. **CAST:** Nicole Kidman, Ewan McGregor, John Leguizamo, Jim Broadbent, Richard Roxburgh. **2001 DVD**

MOUNTAIN, THE ★★★ Though this moralistic drama lacks punch, the fine performances of Spencer Tracy and Robert Wagner make it worth watching. They play mountaineering brothers risking a treacherous climb to find the wreckage of a passenger plane. 105m. **DIR:** Edward Dmytryk. **CAST:** Spencer Tracy, Robert Wagner, Claire Trevor, William Demarest, Richard Arlen, E. G. Marshall. **1956**

MOUNTAIN FAMILY ROBINSON ★★1/2 *Mountain Family Robinson* delivers exactly what it sets out to achieve. Predictable and a bit corny. The cast displays an affability that should charm the children and make this film a relaxing, easy time passer for parents as well. Rated G. 100m. **DIR:** John Cotter. **CAST:** Robert Logan, Susan D. Shaw, Heather Rattray, Ham Larsen. **1979**

MOUNTAIN MEN, THE A buddy movie about two bickering fur trappers who get involved in Indian uprisings. Rated R. 102m. **DIR:** Richard Lang. **CAST:** Charlton Heston, Brian Keith, Victoria Racimo, Stephen Macht. **1980**

MOUNTAINS OF THE MOON ★★★★1/2 Bob Rafelson's robust African adventure about the search for the source of the Nile is also an engrossing and intelligent portrait of the charismatic explorer Sir Richard Burton. A film of epic scope and exotic textures, a superbly entertaining re-creation of the Victorian Age of exploration, and the story of a most complex and colorful explorer. Rated R, with violence, as well as a brief reminder that Burton was also obsessed with erotica. 130m. **DIR:** Bob Rafelson. **CAST:** Patrick Bergin, Iain Glen, Roger Rees, Fiona Shaw. **1990 DVD**

MOUSE AND HIS CHILD, THE ★★ Muddled cartoon feature about a pair of windup toys who attempt to escape from the tyranny of an evil rat. It's an uneasy combination of a simple children's story with a heavy-handed metaphor. The voices are provided by Peter Ustinov, Cloris Leachman, Andy Devine, and Sally Kellerman. Rated G. 82m. **DIR:** Fred Wolf, Charles Swenson. **1977**

MOUSE HUNT ★★★1/2 Dreamworks pulled out all the stops to tickle our funny bones in this delightful farce. Nathan Lane and Lee Evans play Laurel-and-Hardy-ish brothers determined to rid their recently inherited house of a pesky little rodent. Their insane attempts at extermination are constantly outwitted by the clever mouse. Endless sight gags come fast and furious, allowing those that fail to be quickly replaced by ones that don't. Rated PG for sexual situations and comic-book violence. 100m. **DIR:** Gore Verbinski. **CAST:** Nathan Lane, Lee Evans, Christopher Walken. **1997 DVD**

MOUSE THAT ROARED, THE ★★★★ Any film that features Peter Sellers at his peak can't help but be funny. In this British movie, a tiny European nation devises a foolproof method of filling its depleted treasury. It declares war on the United States with the intention of losing and collecting war reparations from the generous Americans. Even foolproof plans don't always go as expected . . . in this case with hilarious results. 83m. **DIR:** Jack Arnold. **CAST:** Peter Sellers, Jean Seberg, Leo McKern. **1958**

MOVERS AND SHAKERS ★★ This star-studded film starts off well but quickly falls apart. Walter Matthau plays a Hollywood producer who begins work on a movie project with only the title, *Love in Sex*, to start with. Charles Grodin plays the screenwriter who is commissioned to write the script, which is intended as a tribute to love. But with serious marital problems, Grodin is hardly the proper candidate. Rated PG for profanity. 80m. **DIR:** William Asher. **CAST:** Walter Matthau, Charles Grodin, Vincent Gardenia, Tyne Daly, Bill Macy, Gilda Radner, Steve Martin, Penny Marshall. **1985**

MOVIE MOVIE ★★★1/2 Clever, affectionate spoof of 1930s pictures presents a double feature: *Dynamite Hands* is a black-and-white boxing story; *Baxter's Beauties of 1933* is a lavish, Busby Berkeley–type extravaganza. This nostalgic package even includes a preview of coming attractions. Rated PG. 107m. **DIR:** Stanley Donen. **CAST:** George C. Scott, Trish Van Devere, Eli Wallach, Red Buttons, Barry Bostwick, Harry Hamlin, Barbara Harris, Art Carney, Ann Reinking, Kathleen Beller. **1978**

MOVIE STRUCK (PICK A STAR) ★★ Typical story about a young girl trying to break into pictures is brightened by a brief appearance by Stan Laurel and Oliver Hardy, who demonstrate the effectiveness of breakaway glass during a barroom confrontation with a tough. Strange musical numbers and some witty dialogue buoy this thin story a little, but Stan and Ollie are still the main reasons to catch this one—and there just isn't that much of them. B&W; 70m. **DIR:** Edward Sedgwick. **CAST:** Stan Laurel, Oliver Hardy, Jack Haley, Patsy Kelly. **1937**

MOVING ★★ Chalk this up as another disappointment from Richard Pryor. Pryor plays an out-of-work mass-transit engineer who finds a job in Idaho and must move his family from their home in New Jersey. Rated R for profanity and violence. 90m. **DIR:** Alan Metter. **CAST:**

Richard Pryor, Beverly Todd, Dave Thomas, Dana Carvey, Randy Quaid, Rodney Dangerfield. **1988**

MOVING FINGER, THE ★★★1/2 The sleepy village of Lymston loses its serenity when residents begin receiving nasty anonymous letters; the situation so upsets the vicar's wife that she summons her good friend Miss Marple (Joan Hickson). This tale is highlighted by its engaging characters. Not rated; suitable for family viewing. 102m. **DIR:** Roy Boulting. **CAST:** Joan Hickson, Michael Culver, Sandra Payne, Richard Pearson, Andrew Bicknell. **1984**

MOVING TARGET (1990) 🦃 Linda Blair plays a woman on the run who has witnessed the murder of her boyfriend. Pathetic. Rated R for violence and language. 85m. **DIR:** Marius Mattei. **CAST:** Ernest Borgnine, Linda Blair. **1990**

MOVING TARGET (1996) ★★ Typical action flick brings nothing new to the genre. The only real fun comes from watching Billy Dee Williams and fondly remembering his days as Lando Calrissian. Rated R for violence, profanity, and sexuality. 106m. **DIR:** Damien Lee. **CAST:** Michael Dudikoff, Billy Dee Williams. **1996 DVD**

MOVING THE MOUNTAIN ★★★★★ If you thought it was electrifying to watch a lone man face a line of tanks in Tiananmen Square in 1989, wait until you hear the rest of the story. Director Michael Apted fashioned together newsreel footage, dramatic reenactments, and heart-wrenching interviews with many of the student leaders. He not only brings this historic episode to life, but infuses it with a current edge. Apted captures our hearts by wisely depending on simple talking heads to reveal the pain and guilt of the now-exiled student leaders. Not rated. 83m. **DIR:** Michael Apted. **1994 DVD**

MOVING VIOLATION ★★1/2 Another southern car-chase movie from the Roger Corman factory, this one features some pretty good high-speed pyrotechnics. (Those scenes were done by second-unit director Barbara Peeters.) The plot, which is merely an excuse for the chases, has an innocent couple being pursued by a corrupt sheriff. Rated PG. 91m. **DIR:** Charles S. Dubin. **CAST:** Stephen McHattie, Kay Lenz, Eddie Albert, Lonny Chapman, Will Geer, Dick Miller. **1976**

MOVING VIOLATIONS ★★ Neal Israel and Pat Proft, who brought us *Police Academy* and *Bachelor Party*, writhe again with another "subject" comedy—this time about traffic school. Star John Murray does a reasonable job of imitating his older brother, Bill. Rated PG-13 for profanity and suggested sex. 90m. **DIR:** Neal Israel. **CAST:** John Murray, Jennifer Tilly, James Keach, Wendie Jo Sperber, Sally Kellerman, Fred Willard. **1985**

MOZART BROTHERS, THE ★★1/2 This surrealistic film about a zany director's insane production of *Don Giovanni* owes far more to the Marx Brothers than the music of Mozart. Étienne Glaser is splendid as the spacy director. However refreshing, the plot is not developed beyond the initial sniggers. In Swedish with English subtitles. Not rated. 111m. **DIR:** Suzanne Osten. **CAST:** Étienne Glaser, Philip Zanden. **1988**

MOZART STORY, THE ★★1/2 Though produced in Austria, this Mozart biography plays as loose with the facts as any Hollywood bio-pic. You'll only want to see it for the music, played by the Vienna Philharmonic Orchestra and Vienna State Opera. Includes excerpts from all of Mozart's best-known works. Curt Jurgens (billed as Curd Juergens) plays Emperor Joseph II. Dialogue dubbed in English. B&W; 95m. **DIR:** Carl Hartl. **CAST:** Hans Holt, Winnie Markus, Curt Jurgens. **1937**

MRS. BROWN ★★1/2 The true story of the bond between the widowed Queen Victoria (Judi Dench) and her Scottish stableman John Brown (Billy Connolly) is given a stately *Masterpiece Theater* treatment, but the result is unconvincing, primarily because of the lack of chemistry between Dench and Connolly. Dench's Victoria is dour and haughty, Connolly's Brown is coarse and loutish; both are decades too old for their roles. Rated PG. 103m. **DIR:** John Madden. **CAST:** Judi Dench, Billy Connolly, Antony Sher, Geoffrey Palmer, Richard Pasco, David Westhead. **1997 DVD**

MRS. BROWN YOU'VE GOT A LOVELY DAUGHTER ★★ England's Herman's Hermits star in this film, named after one of their hit songs. The limited plot revolves around the group acquiring a greyhound and deciding to race it. Caution: Only for hard-core Hermits fans! Rated G. 110m. **DIR:** Saul Swimmer. **CAST:** Herman's Hermits, Stanley Holloway. **1968**

MRS. DALLOWAY ★★★★1/2 This marvelous adaptation of Virginia Woolf's classic novel portrays a day in the life of a wealthy Englishwoman, with flashbacks to the days when she had her whole life before her. This lyrical film miraculously draws the two worlds of Clarissa Dalloway, the gulf of years that separates them, and the poignant memories that unite them. Rated PG-13 for brief nudity and mature themes. 97m. **DIR:** Marleen Gorris. **CAST:** Vanessa Redgrave, Natascha McElhone, Rupert Graves, Michael Kitchen, John Standing, Lena Headey. **1997 DVD**

MRS. DOUBTFIRE ★★★★ Robin Williams is a howl as a father so desperate to be near his kids after separating from his wife that he masquerades as their elderly Irish nanny. Sally Field proves to be a terrific "straight man" for her costar. Rated PG-13 for brief profanity and scatological humor. 125m. **DIR:** Chris Columbus. **CAST:** Robin Williams, Sally Field, Pierce Brosnan, Harvey Fierstein, Polly Holliday, Lisa Jakub, Matthew Lawrence, Mara Wilson, Robert Prosky, Anne Haney, Sydney Walker, Martin Mull. **1993 DVD**

MRS. MINIVER ★★★★ This highly sentimental story of the English home front during the early years of World War II is one of the best examples of cinematic propaganda ever produced. It follows the lives of the Miniver family, especially Mrs. Miniver (Greer Garson), as they become enmeshed in a series of attempts to prove that there will always be an England. It won seven Academy Awards, including best picture. B&W; 134m. **DIR:** William Wyler. **CAST:** Greer Garson, Walter Pidgeon, Teresa Wright, May Whitty, Richard Ney, Henry Travers, Henry Wilcoxon, Reginald Owen. **1942**

MRS. MUNCK ★★1/2 Diane Ladd directed and scripted this vanity project, which teams her with former offscreen husband Bruce Dern. He's an embittered, crippled, and unloved old man; she's his betrayed ex-lover who takes him in, for possibly vengeful purposes that are never clearly explained. Rated PG-13 for profanity, brief nudity, and simulated sex. 99m. **DIR:** Diane Ladd. **CAST:** Diane Ladd, Bruce Dern, Kelly Preston, Shelley Winters. **1995**

MRS. PARKER AND THE VICIOUS CIRCLE ★★★1/2 It may be clever and sentient, but this biopic of Dorothy Parker and her witty companions plays like a Who's Who of the literati. Jennifer Jason Leigh gets under your skin emotionally in a performance that is at once brilliant and arch. Rated R for profanity, nudity, and sexual situations. 124m. **DIR:** Alan Rudolph. **CAST:** Jennifer Jason Leigh, Matthew Broderick, Campbell Scott, Andrew McCarthy, Stephen Gallagher, Stephen Baldwin, Gwyneth Paltrow, Lili Taylor. **1994**

MRS. PARKINGTON ★★★1/2 Over a sixty-year period a poor girl from a Nevada mining town becomes the matriarch of a powerful New York family. Fine performances from an outstanding cast, witty dialogue, and interesting subplots. Oscar nominations for Greer Garson and, in support, Agnes Moorehead. B&W; 124m. **DIR:** Tay Garnett. **CAST:** Greer Garson, Walter Pidgeon, Agnes Moorehead, Edward Arnold, Cecil Kellaway, Gladys Cooper, Frances Rafferty, Dan Duryea, Hugh Marlowe, Lee Patrick, Tom Drake, Rod Cameron, Selena Royle, Peter Lawford. **1944**

MRS. SANTA CLAUS ★★★ Irrepressible Angela Lansbury stars in the title role of this musical. Feeling unappreciated by her famous spouse (Charles Durning), she takes off with the reindeer! Landing in New York in 1910, she becomes involved with the suffrage rights movement and child labor reform. Frothy fun is capped by a customary happy holiday ending. Rated G. 91m. **DIR:** Terry Hughes. **CAST:** Angela Lansbury, Charles Durning, Michael Jeter, David Norona, Lynsey Bartilson, Debra Wiseman. **1996**

MRS. SOFFEL ★★1/2 We assume Australian director Gillian Armstrong's intent was to make more than a simple entertainment about a warden's wife (Diane Keaton) who helps two prisoners (Mel Gibson and Matthew Modine) escape. But she creates a shapeless "statement" about the plight of women at the turn of the century. Even the stars' excellent performances can't save it. Rated PG-13 for violence, suggested sex, and profanity. 112m. **DIR:** Gillian Armstrong. **CAST:** Diane Keaton, Mel Gibson, Matthew Modine, Edward Herrmann, Trini Alvarado. **1984 DVD**

MRS. WIGGS OF THE CABBAGE PATCH ★★ This sentimental twaddle about a poor but optimistic family from the wrong side of the tracks is a throwback to nineteenth-century stage melodrama, saved only by the presence of the great W. C. Fields, ZaSu Pitts, and a fine cast of character actors. If you are a Fields fan, beware—the much-put-upon comedian only appears in the last part of the film. Creaky. B&W; 80m. **DIR:** Norman Taurog. **CAST:** Pauline Lord, W. C. Fields, ZaSu Pitts, Evelyn Venable, Kent Taylor, Charles Middleton, Donald Meek. **1934**

MRS. WINTERBOURNE ★★1/2 Pregnant, unmarried Ricki Lake is mistaken for the new wife of a recently deceased millionaire and welcomed into the bosom of his aristocratic family. The Cornell Woolrich mystery novel *I Married a Dead Man* is rather grotesquely mutated into a rehash with a talented cast struggling against the strained, predictable script. Rated PG-13 for mild profanity. 104m. **DIR:** Richard Benjamin. **CAST:** Shirley MacLaine, Ricki Lake, Brendan Fraser, Loren Dean, Miguel Sandoval. **1996 DVD**

MS. BEAR ★★★ A lost bear cub looking for its mother escapes the clutches of a hunter and is adopted by a young girl. Against the wishes of her father, the girl keeps the bear cub, who eventually becomes a member of the family. When the hunter shows up, she helps the bear escape once again. Lots of fun for the family, this is a comedy with heart. Rated G. 95m. **DIR:** Paul Ziller. **CAST:** Ed Begley Jr., Shaun Johnston, Kaitlyn Burke, Kimberly Warnat. **1997**

MS. .45 ★★★★ An attractive mute woman is raped and beaten twice in the same evening. She slips into madness and seeks revenge with a .45 pistol. A female version of *Death Wish* with an ending at a Halloween costume party that will knock your socks off. Not for all tastes. Rated R for violence, nudity, rape, language, and gore. 90m. **DIR:** Abel Ferrara. **CAST:** Zoe Tamerlis. **1981 DVD**

MS. SCROOGE ★★ This modernized, made-for-cable retelling of Charles Dickens's classic is one of the most lackluster and watered-down versions out there. Cicely Tyson's Ebonita Scrooge is so tight-lipped that she's barely understandable, and much of the original tale simply doesn't translate well into the present day. Rated G. 95m. **DIR:** John Korty. **CAST:** Cicely Tyson, Michael Beach, John Bourgeois, Katherine Helmond. **1997**

MUCH ADO ABOUT NOTHING ★★★★ Kenneth Branagh again brings energy, accessibility, and cinematic style to one of William Shakespeare's classic stories. Confirmed bachelor Benedick trades barbs with the caustic Beatrice, and young Claudio suspects duplicity on the part of the innocent Hero. Great fun! Rated PG-13 for brief nudity and suggested sex. 110m. **DIR:** Kenneth Branagh. **CAST:** Kenneth Branagh, Michael Keaton, Robert Sean Leonard, Keanu Reeves, Emma Thompson, Denzel Washington, Kate Beckinsale, Brian Blessed, Imelda Staunton, Phyllida Law. **1993 DVD**

MUDHONEY ★★★★ A cult favorite from Russ Meyer about the exploits of some rural folks involved in the pursuit of cheap thrills and the meaning of life. Considered an adults-only film when released, it now seems quite tame. Plot has a local scum terrorizing Antoinette Cristiani, a deaf-and-dumb beautiful blonde until her rescue by Hal Hopper. Not rated, but an R rating would be in order because of some nudity and adult themes. B&W; 92m. **DIR:** Russ Meyer. **CAST:** Hal Hopper, Antoinette Cristiani. **1965**

MUGSY'S GIRLS A predictable bit of fluff about a sorority out to earn rent money through mud wrestling. Rated R for nudity and profanity. 87m. **DIR:** Kevin Brodie. **CAST:** Ruth Gordon, Laura Branigan, Eddie Deezen. **1985**

MULAN ★★★★1/2 Chinese design elements and storytelling simplicity make this one of the better latter-day Disney animated features. Humor, action, romance, social commentary, and musical interludes are balanced perfectly in this medieval tale of an awkward young woman who disguises herself as a man to take her aged warrior father's place in battle. More than any previous Disney cartoon, this plays like a well-crafted adventure film that just happens to be animated. Rated G. 87m. **DIR:** Barry Cook, Tony Bancroft. **1998 DVD**

MULE TRAIN ★★1/2 Gene Autry helps a pal keep a valuable cement claim from crooked businessman, Bob Livingston. Classic song incorporated into a so-so plot with an actionless windup. Sidekick Pat Buttram and Shelia Ryan were real-life man and wife. B&W; 70m. **DIR:** John English. **CAST:** Gene Autry, Pat Buttram, Sheila Ryan, Robert Livingston, Gregg Barton. **1950**

•**MULHOLLAND DRIVE** ★★1/2 This darkly comic *noir* mystery is strange, erotic, perverse, cryptic, disturbing, wacky, and impervious to mainstream demands. It begins as a voluptuous amnesia victim and a perky wannabe actress try to uncover the nameless femme fatale's identity. It later veers into an alternate world as the actors become new characters or establish new relationships with each other. This enigmatic maze about female exploitation, gay sexual awakening, paranoia, contagious emotions, and the illusions of cinema is intriguing but should feel fresher and be more fun. Rated R for language, violence, nudity, and sex. 146m. **DIR:** David Lynch. **CAST:** Naomi Watts, Laura Harring, Justin Theroux, Ann Miller. **2001 DVD**

MULHOLLAND FALLS ★★★1/2 Gritty period detective movie stars Nick Nolte as the leader of The Hat Squad, an elite quartet of Los Angeles police detectives who answer to no one as they rid the city of mobsters. When Nolte's former mistress is found murdered, the trail leads to a possible government cover-up. Strong performances and suspense throughout. Rated R for violence, profanity, nudity, and simulated sex. 107m. **DIR:** Lee Tamahori. **CAST:** Nick Nolte, Melanie Griffith, Chazz Palminteri, Michael Madsen, Christopher Penn, Treat Williams, Jennifer Connelly, Daniel Baldwin, Andrew McCarthy, John Malkovich, Bruce Dern, William L. Petersen, Rob Lowe, Louise Fletcher, Ed Lauter. **1996**

MULTIPLE MANIACS A homage to gore king Herschell Gordon Lewis's *Two Thousand Maniacs*. Not rated, but the equivalent of an X. B&W; 70m. **DIR:** John Waters. **CAST:** Divine, Mink Stole, Paul Swift, Cookie Mueller, David Lochary, Mary Vivian Pearce, Edith Massey. **1971**

MULTIPLICITY ★★★1/2 Michael Keaton revives his *Mr. Mom* persona with a twist; unable to keep up with a job and a home life, he has himself cloned. Then the executive Keaton decides he needs a clone and it begins. Keaton is a master clown, and he gets terrific support from Andie MacDowell, Harris Yulin, Richard Masur, and the rest of the cast. While not a comedy classic, it does provide plenty of chuckles and complications. Rated PG-13 for suggested sex. 117m. **DIR:** Harold Ramis. **CAST:** Michael Keaton, Harris Yulin, Andie MacDowell, Richard Masur, Eugene Levy, Anne Cusack, John de Lancie, Brian Doyle-Murray, Julie Bowen. **1996 DVD**

MUMFORD ★★★★ A small-town psychologist (Loren Dean) dispenses common-sense advice to his patients, inspiring unexpected results. Meanwhile, there's something odd about the good doctor, who just happens to have the same name as the town and operates in a highly unorthodox fashion. In this quirky comedy-drama, writer-director Lawrence Kasdan creates characters and situations that offer insight into the human condition while keeping the viewer well entertained. Rated R for profanity and sexual situations. 96m. **DIR:** Lawrence Kasdan. **CAST:** Loren Dean, Sofie Crisp, Jason Lee, Alfre Woodard, Mary McDonnell, Pruitt Taylor Vance, Zooey Deschanel, Martin Short, David Paymer, Jane Adams, Dana Ivey, Kevin Tighe, Ted Danson, Jason Ritter, Elisabeth Moss. **1999 DVD**

MUMMY, THE (1932) ★★★★ First-rate horror-thriller about an Egyptian mummy returning to life after 3,700 years. Boris Karloff plays the title role in one of his very best performances. Superb makeup, dialogue, atmosphere, and direction make this one an all-time classic. B&W; 73m. **DIR:** Karl Freund. **CAST:** Boris Karloff, Zita Johann, David Manners, Edward Van Sloan. **1932 DVD**

MUMMY, THE (1959) ★★★1/2 Excellent updating of the mummy legend. Christopher Lee is terrifying as the ancient Egyptian awakened from his centuries-old sleep to take revenge on those who desecrated the tomb of his beloved princess. Well-photographed, atmospheric production is high-quality entertainment. 88m. **DIR:** Terence Fisher. **CAST:** Peter Cushing, Christopher Lee, Yvonne Furneaux. **1959**

MUMMY, THE (1999) ★★★1/2 Few films successfully walk the line when trying to be all things to all people, but this reboot of the venerable Universal monster franchise manages that difficult task: It's definitely scary, unquestionably funny, and a rousing good adventure yarn. The forces of virtue are led by a dashing foreign legionnaire who returns to the ruined city of Hamunaptra with a curvaceous but clumsy Egyptologist and her ne'er-do-well brother. Events get out of hand and an "ancient evil" is unleashed upon the world . . . until and unless our heroes can bottle it up again. It's all handled with impressive panache and grand pacing by a director who's equally comfortable with hair's-breadth-escape action, pratfallish belly laughs, and creepy moments of suspense. Rated PG-13 for violence and cursed evil doings. 127m. **DIR:** Stephen Sommers. **CAST:** Brendan Fraser, Rachel Weisz, John Hannah, Arnold Vosloo, Kevin J. O'Connor. **1999 DVD**

MUMMY AND THE CURSE OF THE JACKALS, THE This Las Vegas–based monster mess was unfinished and theatrically unreleased, and remains unwatchable. Not rated. 86m. **DIR:** Oliver Drake. **CAST:** Anthony Eisley, Martina Pons, John Carradine. **1967**

MUMMY RETURNS, THE ★★1/2 Brendan Fraser and Rachel Weisz, the stars of the 1999 hit, are back, battling the resurrected priest Imhotep (Arnold Vosloo) and his evil cohorts. The action never lets up, and neither do the glib wisecracks or the computer-generated special effects. It's all a bit forced and frantic, and becomes exhausting well before the final fade-out. Rated PG-13 for violent action. 121m. **DIR:** Stephen Sommers. **CAST:** Brendan Fraser, Rachel Weisz, John Hannah, Arnold Vosloo, Oded Fehr. **2001**

MUMMY'S CURSE, THE ★★1/2 In Universal's final *Mummy* movie, the monster turns up in the Louisiana bayou, where high priests Peter Coe and Martin Kosleck send him on a rampage. Unoriginal but creepy and fast-paced. B&W; 62m. **DIR:** Leslie Goodwins. **CAST:** Lon Chaney Jr., Peter Coe, Virginia Christine, Martin Kosleck. **1944**

MUMMY'S GHOST, THE ★★1/2 Universal Pictures' screenwriters used one new wrinkle in each of their otherwise routine *Mummy* chillers. In this one, the gimmick is the climactic fate of the heroine. Also, check out John Carradine as the mad high priest. B&W; 60m. **DIR:** Reginald LeBorg. **CAST:** Lon Chaney Jr., John Carradine, Ramsay Ames, Robert Lowery. **1944**

MUMMY'S HAND, THE ★★★ A pair of carnival barker archaeologists team up with a magician's daughter and go into the grave-robbing business. Their efforts bring them within a bandage width of the shambling mummy and the evil priest who brings the dead back to life. Tom Tyler makes a good mummy and the film has chills. B&W; 67m. **DIR:** Christy Cabanne. **CAST:** Dick Foran, Peggy Moran, Wallace Ford, Eduardo Ciannelli, Tom Tyler, George Zucco. **1940**

MUMMY'S SHROUD, THE ★★1/2 After a slow and overly long opening, this film picks up as an archaeological expedition removes the mummy from its tomb and unleashes the beast by accident. The plot is clichéd and full of enough holes to nearly sink it, but the acting saves it. 90m. **DIR:** John Gilling. **CAST:** Andre Morell, John Phillips, David Buck, Elizabeth Sellars, Maggie Kimberley. **1967 DVD**

MUMMY'S TOMB, THE ★★1/2 This sequel to *The Mummy's Hand* was Lon Chaney Jr.'s first *Mummy* movie for Universal. Egyptian high priest Turhan Bey revives the Mummy at a New England museum and sends him on a rampage. Note: This 1993 video release is missing the scene in which Mary Gordon is murdered. B&W; 61m. **DIR:** Harold Young. **CAST:** Lon Chaney Jr., Elyse Knox, John Hubbard, Turhan Bey. **1942**

MUNCHIE 🦃 In this silly sequel, a magical imp (the voice of Dom DeLuise) helps an unpopular youngster through some difficult childhood traumas. Although adults may find little substance here, children may be mildly entertained. Rated PG for violence. 85m. **DIR:** Jim Wynorski. **CAST:** Loni Anderson, Andrew Stevens, Arte Johnson. **1991**

MUNCHIE STRIKES BACK 🦃 Why? Even the target audience, young children, will find this low-budget effort derivative and boring. Rated PG. 80m. **DIR:** Jim Wynorski. **CAST:** Lesley-Anne Down, Andrew Stevens. **1994**

MUNCHIES 🦃 Harvey Korman has dual parts as an archaeologist who discovers a junk-food-eating creature, and as a con artist who kidnaps the little critters. Rated PG for sexual innuendo. 83m. **DIR:** Bettina Hirsch. **CAST:** Harvey Korman, Charles Stratton, Alix Elias. **1987**

MUNSTERS' REVENGE, THE ★★★ More schlock than shock and chock full of predictable puns, this munster mash is super Saturday-morning fun. Most of the original players from the TV series are back, with outstanding guests like Sid Caesar as the curator of a wax museum. 96m. **DIR:** Don Weis. **CAST:** Fred Gwynne, Yvonne De Carlo, Al Lewis, Sid Caesar. **1981 DVD**

MUPPET CHRISTMAS CAROL, THE ★★★1/2 Kermit the Frog as Bob Crachit? Director Brian Henson somehow makes it work in this family-oriented telling of the classic Charles Dickens tale. It's no match for the acclaimed 1951 version starring Alastair Sim, but Michael Caine makes a fine Scrooge. Rated G. 86m. **DIR:** Brian Henson. **CAST:** Michael Caine. **1992**

MUPPET MOVIE, THE ★★★1/2 Though there is a huge all-star guest cast, the Muppets are the real stars of this superior family film in which the characters trek to Hollywood in search of stardom. Rated G. 94m. **DIR:** James Frawley. **CAST:** Muppets, Edgar Bergen, Milton Berle, Mel Brooks, James Coburn, Dom DeLuise, Elliott Gould, Bob Hope, Madeline Kahn, Carol Kane, Cloris Leachman, Steve Martin, Richard Pryor, Telly Savalas, Orson Welles, Paul Williams. **1979 DVD**

MUPPET TREASURE ISLAND ★★★ Robert Louis Stevenson's classic story about loyalty and pirate loot has become an entertaining mix of adventure, music, and Muppet madness. The film closely follows the book's journey from a grungy English seaside inn to a tropical paradise with the brisk clip of a blustery trade wind. Rated G. 99m. **DIR:** Brian Henson. **CAST:** Tim Curry, Kevin Bishop, Billy Connolly, Jennifer Saunders. **1996**

MUPPETS FROM SPACE ★★★★ This, like all Muppet endeavors, is that most perfect of family pleasures: a film silly enough and flamboyantly colorful enough to delight the small fry, and funny enough—without ever turning crass—to keep adults captivated. The story centers on Gonzo, one of the few Muppet regulars not based on a recognizable Terran life-form, and that's the crux of the matter. Obsessed by a search for his roots, Gonzo is excited when his breakfast cereal starts spelling out messages, but such contact from afar does not sit well with a paranoid government operative (Jeffrey Tambor), who is convinced that life out there means us harm. Subsequent adventures tweak everything from *Hitchhiker's Guide to the Galaxy* to *The X-Files*: all in all, a lot of fun. Rated G; suitable for all ages. 82m. **DIR:** Tim Hill. **CAST:** Jeffrey Tambor, F. Murray Abraham, Ray Liotta, Andie MacDowell, Rob Schneider. **1999 DVD**

MUPPETS TAKE MANHATTAN, THE ★★★ Jim Henson's popular puppets take a bite of the Big Apple in their third and least effective screen romp. Playwright Kermit and his pals try to get their musical on the Broadway stage. Rated G. 94m. **DIR:** Frank Oz. **CAST:** Muppets, Art Carney, Dabney Coleman, Joan Rivers, Elliott Gould, Liza Minnelli, Brooke Shields. **1984 DVD**

MURDER ★★★ An early Alfred Hitchcock thriller, and a good one, although it shows its age. Herbert Marshall, a producer-director, is selected to serve on a murder-trial jury. He believes the accused, an aspiring actress, is innocent of the crime and takes it upon himself to apprehend the real killer. B&W; 92m. **DIR:** Alfred Hitchcock. **CAST:** Herbert Marshall, Norah Baring. **1930 DVD**

MURDER AHOY ★★1/2 Threadbare mystery has Miss Marple (Margaret Rutherford) investigating murder aboard ship. This was the last film in the British series, although it was released in America before the superior *Murder Most Foul*. Despite her considerable talents, Rutherford could not raise this sinking ship above the level of mediocrity. B&W; 74m. **DIR:** George Pollock. **CAST:** Margaret Rutherford, Lionel Jeffries, Stringer Davis, Charles Tingwell. **1964**

MURDER AT 1600 ★★1/2 After a bloody female corpse is found in a White House restroom, a civil-war buff/homicide cop smells a cover-up, and teams up with a sharpshooter secret-service agent to sift through the

case. The action ends with a ludicrous romp through tunnels that Lincoln had built under the White House. Rated R for violence, language, nudity, and sexuality. 106m. **DIR:** Dwight H. Little. **CAST:** Wesley Snipes, Daniel Benzali, Diane Lane, Alan Alda, Ronny Cox, Dennis Miller. **1997 DVD**

MURDER AT THE GALLOP ★★★★ Margaret Rutherford has her best Miss Marple outing in this adaptation of Agatha Christie's Hercule Poirot mystery, *After the Funeral.* She and Robert Morley play off each other beautifully in this comedy-laced tale, which has Marple insinuating herself into a murder investigation. Her assistant, Mr. Stringer, is played by Rutherford's real-life husband, Stringer Davis. B&W; 81m. **DIR:** George Pollock. **CAST:** Margaret Rutherford, Robert Morley, Flora Robson, Stringer Davis, Charles Tingwell. **1963**

MURDER AT THE VANITIES ★★★1/2 A musical whodunit, this blend of comedy and mystery finds tenacious Victor McLaglen embroiled in a murder investigation at Earl Carroll's Vanities, a popular and long-running variety show of the 1930s and 1940s. Musical numbers and novelty acts pop up between clues in this stylish oddity. Lots of fun. B&W; 89m. **DIR:** Mitchell Leisen. **CAST:** Jack Oakie, Kitty Carlisle, Victor McLaglen, Carl Brisson, Donald Meek, Gail Patrick, Jessie Ralph, Duke Ellington, Ann Sheridan. **1934**

MURDER AT THE VICARAGE ★★★★ Originally published in 1930, this Agatha Christie story introduced the elderly, spinster detective Miss Marple. This BBC production perfectly captures the cozy English village of St. Mary Mead, where Miss Marple resides. Commenting on a missing pound note in the collection box, and a well-planned murder, our white-haired heroine says, "There is a great deal of wickedness in village life." A must-see for any mystery buff. Rated G. 102m. **DIR:** Julian Amyes. **CAST:** Joan Hickson, Paul Eddington, Cheryl Campbell, David Horovitch. **1986**

MURDER BY DEATH ★★★★ Mystery buffs will get a big kick out of this spoof of the genre, penned by Neil Simon. Peter Sellers, Peter Falk, David Niven, Maggie Smith, and James Coco play thinly disguised send-ups of famed fictional detectives who are invited to the home of Truman Capote to solve a baffling murder. Rated PG. 94m. **DIR:** Robert Moore. **CAST:** Peter Sellers, Peter Falk, David Niven, Maggie Smith, James Coco, Alec Guinness. **1976 DVD**

MURDER BY DECREE ★★★1/2 Excellent cast stylishly serves up this Sherlock Holmes mystery. Christopher Plummer and James Mason are well suited to the roles of Holmes and Dr. Watson. The murky story deals with Jack the Ripper. Rated R for violence and gore. 121m. **DIR:** Bob Clark. **CAST:** Christopher Plummer, James Mason, Donald Sutherland, Genevieve Bujold, Susan Clark, David Hemmings, John Gielgud, Anthony Quayle. **1979**

MURDER BY MOONLIGHT Detective thriller set in a colony on the Moon, circa 2105. NASA agent Brigitte Nielsen joins Russian counterpart Julian Sands to solve a murder in this low-budget effort. Rated PG-13 for violence. 100m. **DIR:** Michael Lindsay-Hogg. **CAST:** Julian Sands, Brigitte Nielsen, Brian Cox, Gerald McRaney. **1989**

MURDER BY NUMBERS (1989) A dud. Rated PG-13. 91m. **DIR:** Paul Leder. **CAST:** Sam Behrens, Shari Belafonte, Dick Sargent, Cleavon Little, Jayne Meadows, Ronee Blakley. **1989**

•MURDER BY NUMBERS (2002) ★★★ Scripter Tony Gayton's twisty little thriller desperately aspires to the high level of *Seven* or *Silence of the Lambs*, but frequently misses because of star Sandra Bullock's inability to credibly play a tightly wound homicide investigator and crime-scene specialist. Her character's behavior is too often unlikely or flat-out ridiculous, which destroys the mood generated by Ryan Gosling and Michael Pitt, genuinely creepy as the two young students who—very much in the mold of Hitchcock's *Rope*—decide to demonstrate their superior intellect by killing somebody and planting false clues to confuse the cops. Sadly, Bullock just doesn't have the acting chops to make this film succeed. Rated R for profanity, violence, drug use, and sexual candor. 121m. **DIR:** Barbet Schroeder. **CAST:** Sandra Bullock, Ben Chaplin, Ryan Gosling, Michael Pitt, Agnes Bruckner, Christopher Penn, R. D. Call. **2002 DVD**

MURDER BY PHONE ★★★ In this okay shocker, Richard Chamberlain is cast as an environmentalist whose lecture engagement in New York City turns out to be an opportunity to investigate the gruesome death of one of his students. Rated R. 79m. **DIR:** Michael Anderson. **CAST:** Richard Chamberlain, John Houseman. **1980**

MURDER BY TELEVISION ★★ Bela Lugosi plays an inventor in this low-budget murder mystery. Television was still something out of *Science and Invention* back in 1935, so it was fair game as a contrivance used to commit the crime. B&W; 60m. **DIR:** Clifford Sanforth. **CAST:** Bela Lugosi, June Collyer, George Meeker, Hattie McDaniel. **1935**

MURDER ELITE ★★ Ali MacGraw plays a woman who, after losing all her money in America, comes back to her native England to start fresh. Meanwhile, there is a killer on the loose. The two stories ultimately collide, but MacGraw's uninspired acting and the poor direction make the film rather plodding. Not rated. 104m. **DIR:** Claude Whatham. **CAST:** Ali MacGraw, Billie Whitelaw, Hywel Bennett, Ray Lonnen. **1985**

MURDER IN COWETA COUNTY ★★★1/2 Andy Griffith is outstanding as a Georgia businessman who thinks he can get away with murder. Johnny Cash plays the determined sheriff who's willing to go to any lengths to prove Griffith's guilt. This made-for-TV suspense-drama was based on an actual Georgia murder that took place in 1948. 104m. **DIR:** Gary Nelson. **CAST:** Andy Griffith, Johnny Cash, Earl Hindman. **1983**

MURDER IN MIND ★★★ An amnesiac is the chief suspect in her husband's murder, and the police recruit a noted therapist to hypnotize her and unlock her memory. They get more than they bargain for when her recollection of the event differs from the facts. The fun comes in trying to separate the fact from the fiction. Rated R for adult situations, language, and violence. 89m. **DIR:** Andy Morahan. **CAST:** Nigel Hawthorne, Mary-Louise Parker, Jimmy Smits, Jason Scott Lee, Gailard Sartain. **1997**

MURDER IN NEW HAMPSHIRE ★★1/2 Passable TV killer-of-the-week saga focuses on a video production teacher's plot to use her student as her husband's assassin. At times unbelievable, although this is based on

fact. 93m. **DIR:** Joyce Chopra. **CAST:** Helen Hunt, Chad Allen, Larry Drake, Ken Howard, Howard Hesseman. **1992 DVD**

MURDER IN SPACE ★★ As you watch this made-for-TV whodunit, you must immediately look for clues. If not, you'll get bored and the long-awaited solution won't make sense to you. Wilford Brimley as the head of Mission Control tries to put the pieces together. 95m. **DIR:** Steven H. Stern. **CAST:** Wilford Brimley, Michael Ironside, Martin Balsam, Arthur Hill. **1985**

MURDER IN TEXAS ★★★★ Absorbing TV docudrama based on a true story. Sam Elliott is Dr. John Hill, a prominent plastic surgeon accused of murdering his socialite wife. A gripping study of psychopathic behavior. Good performances all around, including Farrah Fawcett and Andy Griffith, who reaped an Emmy nomination. 200m. **DIR:** William Hale. **CAST:** Farrah Fawcett, Sam Elliott, Katharine Ross, Andy Griffith, Bill Dana. **1983**

MURDER IN THE FIRST ★★★1/2 Dan Gordon's gritty and memorable script concerns the actual Alcatraz convict whose three straight years in solitary confinement paved the way for prison reform. Kevin Bacon plays the Depression-era youth who wound up among hardened killers after stealing five dollars to feed his younger sister. The entire U.S. penal system is put on trial after Bacon murders a prison snitch. Rated R for profanity, violence, torture, and explicit sexual content. 120m. **DIR:** Marc Rocco. **CAST:** Christian Slater, Kevin Bacon, Gary Oldman, Embeth Davidtz, Brad Dourif, William H. Macy, R. Lee Ermey. **1995 DVD**

MURDER IS ANNOUNCED, A ★★★1/2 The sedate personals column of Chipping Cleghorn's *North Benham Gazette*, usually filled with pleas regarding lost dogs and bicycles for sale, is enlivened by a classified announcing a murder, which then takes place, as scheduled. Miss Marple (Joan Hickson) is summoned by the village constabulary. This is one of Agatha Christie's more convoluted stories. Not rated; suitable for family viewing. 153m. **DIR:** David Giles. **CAST:** Joan Hickson, Ursula Howells, Renée Asherson, John Castle, Sylvia Syms, Joan Sims. **1984**

MURDER MOST FOUL ★★★1/2 Like *Murder at the Gallop*, this is another Miss Marple adventure fashioned out of a Hercule Poirot mystery (*Mrs. McGinty's Dead*). The plot is only a framework for Margaret Rutherford's delightful antics. This time, she is the only dissenting member of a jury in a murder case. B&W; 91m. **DIR:** George Pollock. **CAST:** Margaret Rutherford, Ron Moody, Charles Tingwell, Stringer Davis, Francesca Annis, Dennis Price. **1964**

MURDER MY SWEET ★★★★ In the mid-1940s, Dick Powell decided to change his clean-cut crooner image by playing Raymond Chandler's hardboiled detective, Philip Marlowe. It worked marvelously, with Powell making a fine white knight in tarnished armor on the trail of killers and blackmailers. B&W; 95m. **DIR:** Edward Dmytryk. **CAST:** Dick Powell, Claire Trevor, Anne Shirley. **1944**

MURDER OF CROWS, A ★★★★ A lawyer, wrongfully disbarred, writes a novel about his experiences and opens a floodgate of trouble when the horrific incidents in his novel mimic those of a bloodthirsty serial killer. Requires a solid suspension of disbelief but is entertaining and peppered with fantastic performances. Rated R for violence, profanity, nudity, and sexual situations. 101m. **DIR:** Rowdy Herrington. **CAST:** Cuba Gooding Jr., Tom Berenger, Marianne Jean-Baptiste, Eric Stoltz. **1999 DVD**

MURDER OF MARY PHAGAN, THE ★★★★ True story of 1913 Georgia governor John Slaton's fight to free a factory manager accused of killing a young girl. He has to fight a lynch mob determined to hang the factory manager because he was Jewish. This TV movie is long, but well worth seeing. 250m. **DIR:** William Hale. **CAST:** Jack Lemmon, Peter Gallagher, Richard Jordan, Robert Prosky, Kevin Spacey, Kathryn Walker, Paul Dooley, Rebecca Miller. **1988**

MURDER OF THE CENTURY ★★★★ In this era of media overkill, it is surprising to learn that one week after the murder of architect Stanford White by millionaire Harry K. Thaw over the affections of Thaw's wife, Evelyn Nesbit, there was a silent-film version in the theaters. Narrated by David Ogden Stiers with Blair Brown providing the voice of Nesbit, and illustrated by scores of photos and early film clips, this provides a fascinating glimpse at turn-of-the-century America. Made for PBS. Not rated. B&W/color; 60m. **DIR:** Carl Charlson. **1995**

MURDER ON FLIGHT 502 ★★ A mad bomber threatens to blow an international airliner to pieces. He is thwarted by Robert Stack and other reluctant heroes. Reminiscent of *Airport* and a half-dozen sequels. The cast alone keeps this made-for-TV potboiler from falling flat on its baggage carousel. 120m. **DIR:** George McCowan. **CAST:** Ralph Bellamy, Polly Bergen, Robert Stack, Theodore Bikel, Sonny Bono, Dane Clark, Laraine Day, Fernando Lamas, George Maharis, Farrah Fawcett, Hugh O'Brian, Brooke Adams, Walter Pidgeon, Molly Picon. **1975 DVD**

MURDER ON LINE ONE ★★ Standard horror flick set in London. This time, the murderer films the killings and gets his kicks rewatching his work—transgressor of the VCR age. Rated R for violence and bloodshed. 103m. **DIR:** Anders Palm. **CAST:** Emma Jacobs, Peter Blake. **1990**

MURDER ON THE BAYOU ★★★1/2 German director Volker Schlondörff examines the American South, specifically the Bayou country of Louisiana, where an elderly black man (Lou Gossett Jr.) is suspected of killing a white racist. Marvelously well-acted TV movie, rich in character moments, and surprisingly upbeat given its subject matter. 91m. **DIR:** Volker Schlöndorff. **CAST:** Louis Gossett Jr., Richard Widmark, Holly Hunter, Joe Seneca, Will Patton, Woody Strode. **1987**

MURDER ON THE ORIENT EXPRESS ★★★★1/2 Belgian detective Hercule Poirot solves a murder on a train in this stylish prestige picture based on the Agatha Christie mystery. Albert Finney is terrific as the detective and is supported by an all-star cast. Rated PG. 127m. **DIR:** Sidney Lumet. **CAST:** Albert Finney, Ingrid Bergman, Lauren Bacall, Sean Connery, Vanessa Redgrave, Michael York, Jacqueline Bisset. **1974**

MURDER 101 ★★★★ Pierce Brosnan's considerable charm works perfectly in this cable-TV mystery by writer-director Bill Condon. Brosnan stars as a college writing instructor teaching his students the fundamentals of suspense fiction; naturally, somebody adopts his lesson plan and makes the poor professor Suspect Num-

ber One in a deft murder. Rated PG-13. 93m. **DIR:** Bill Condon. **CAST:** Pierce Brosnan, Dey Young, Raphael Sbarge, Kim Thomson. **1991 DVD**

MURDER OVER NEW YORK ★★ The world's most famous Asian detective, Charlie Chan (Sidney Toler), goes after a gang of saboteurs plaguing the airways after a Scotland Yard inspector is felled by poisonous gas. Although cast with plenty of top-flight character actors, this one falls a little flat. The formula was wearing pretty thin after twenty-four films. B&W; 64m. **DIR:** Harry Lachman. **CAST:** Sidney Toler, Marjorie Weaver, Robert Lowery, Ricardo Cortez, Donald MacBride, Melville Cooper, Kane Richmond, Clarence Muse, John Sutton. **1940**

MURDER SHE PURRED ★★★ Ricki Lake is delightful as author Rita Mae Brown's snoop, who teams up with Tucker the Dog and Mrs. Murphy the Cat to solve crimes. This made-for-television Walt Disney feature is an enjoyable romp for kids and adults. Not rated. 88m. **DIR:** Simon Wincer. **CAST:** Ricki Lake, Linden Ashby, Blythe Danner, Anthony Clark, Bruce McGill, Ed Begley Jr. **1998**

MURDER SHE SAID ★★★★ Now that Joan Hickson has brought Agatha Christie's Miss Marple to life in the superb BBC series, it has become common for mystery buffs to denigrate the four films starring Margaret Rutherford as Marple. We beg to differ. Rutherford makes a delightful screen sleuth, and this adaptation of *4:50 to Paddington* is quite enjoyable. The first entry in the series, it has Marple witnessing a murder on a train. B&W; 87m. **DIR:** George Pollock. **CAST:** Margaret Rutherford, Arthur Kennedy, Charles Tingwell, Muriel Pavlow, James Robertson Justice, Thorley Walters, Joan Hickson. **1961**

MURDER SO SWEET ★★★ Better-than-average network teleflic "based on actual events," with dependable Harry Hamlin starring as hunkish good ol' boy Steve Catlin, an unrepentant ladies' man who loved 'em and left 'em . . . dead. Plucky Helen Shaver decides to take him down. Lurid boxart suggests otherwise, but this is pretty tame stuff. Rated PG for mild profanity. 94m. **DIR:** Larry Peerce. **CAST:** Harry Hamlin, Helen Shaver, Terence Knox, Ed Lauter, Faith Ford, Eileen Brennan. **1993**

MURDER STORY ★★★1/2 In this little-known gem, an aspiring mystery writer (Bruce Boa) involves his mentor-hero (Christopher Lee) in a real-life killing. The story is a trifle contrived but generally enjoyable. Lee gets a rare chance to play a heroic character and makes the most of it. A must-see for fans of the genre. Rated PG. 90m. **DIR:** Eddie Arno, Markus Innocenti. **CAST:** Christopher Lee, Bruce Boa. **1989**

MURDER WITH MIRRORS ★★★ Inspired casting saves an otherwise pedestrian TV adaptation of Agatha Christie. Helen Hayes (never the best Miss Marple) comes to the aid of an old friend (Bette Davis), whose ancestral home is threatened. Although noteworthy as the only time Hayes and Davis appeared in the same project, George Eckstein's script is pretty ho-hum. 100m. **DIR:** Dick Lowry. **CAST:** Helen Hayes, Bette Davis, John Mills, Leo McKern. **1985**

MURDER WITHOUT MOTIVE ★★★ Subtitled *The Edmund Perry Story* and based on Robert Sam Anson's book *Best Intentions*, this is the tragic account of a Harlem honor student's loneliness and frustration at an exclusive private high school. Curtis McClarin is convincing in the lead. Not rated; contains violence and drug use. 93m. **DIR:** Kevin Hooks. **CAST:** Curtis McClarin, Anna Maria Horsford, Carla Gugino, Christopher Daniel Barnes. **1991**

MURDERCYCLE ★★1/2 Some films have a great concept but a weak plot to back it up. This is the dilemma of *Murdercycle*: the tale of an evil alien entity that takes the form of a motorcycle armed to the extreme with high-tech weaponry. Everything about the film seems to run on cruise control from there on out. Rated PG-13 for violence and profanity. 90m. **DIR:** Thomas L. Callaway. **CAST:** Charles Wesley. **1999**

MURDERED INNOCENCE ★★ An escaped con and an ex-con come toe-to-toe to finish what they began twenty years ago when one of their mothers was murdered. Comically clichéd thriller is way overdone in the style department and is further marred by an unnecessarily convoluted screenplay. Rated R for violence and sexual situations. 77m. **DIR:** Frank Coraci. **CAST:** Jason Miller, Fred Carpenter, Jacqueline Macario, Gary Aumiller. **1994**

MURDERERS AMONG US: THE SIMON WIESENTHAL STORY ★★★1/2 Powerful HBO reenactment of real-life Nazi concentration camp victim Simon Wiesenthal's postwar search for Nazi leaders. Among those he brings to justice are the notorious Adolf Eichmann and Franz Murer. Ben Kingsley is unforgettable as Wiesenthal. 155m. **DIR:** Brian Gibson. **CAST:** Ben Kingsley, Renee Soutendijk, Craig T. Nelson. **1989**

MURDERERS' ROW ★★1/2 This entry into the Matt Helm secret agent series is pretty dismal. Dean Martin has been much better in other films. The Matt Helm series was an attempt to grab the Bond and Flint audience, but Martin just couldn't cut it as a superspy. 108m. **DIR:** Henry Levin. **CAST:** Dean Martin, Ann-Margret, Karl Malden, James Gregory. **1966**

MURDEROUS VISION ★★1/2 A missing-persons investigator (Bruce Boxleitner) teams with a reluctant psychic (Laura Johnson) to track down a psychotic killer with a penchant for severed heads. Writer Paul Joseph Gulino borrows pretty heavily from Thomas Harris's *Silence of the Lambs* for this chaotic made-for-cable thriller. Rated R for violence and language. 93m. **DIR:** Gary A. Sherman. **CAST:** Bruce Boxleitner, Laura Johnson, Robert Culp. **1991**

MURDERS IN THE RUE MORGUE (1932) ★★1/2 Very little of Edgar Allan Poe's original story is evident in this muddled and perverse story of Dr. Mirakle and his efforts to mate his companion (an ape) with the leading lady of the film. Bela Lugosi as the evil doctor grimaces often and wears a black cape. B&W; 62m. **DIR:** Robert Florey. **CAST:** Bela Lugosi, Sidney Fox, Leon Ames, Arlene Francis, Noble Johnson. **1932**

MURDERS IN THE RUE MORGUE (1971) ★★ Members of a horror theatre troupe in nineteenth-century Paris are dispatched systematically by a mysterious fiend. Good cast, nice atmosphere, but confusing and altogether too artsy for its own good. Rated PG. 87m. **DIR:** Gordon Hessler. **CAST:** Jason Robards Jr., Herbert Lom, Michael Dunn, Lilli Palmer, Christine Kaufmann, Adolfo Celi. **1971**

MURDERS IN THE RUE MORGUE (1986) ★★★ Here again: the Poe tale of a grisly double murder in nine-

teenth-century Paris. Solid performances by a top-notch cast, along with fine atmospheric cinematography give this made-for-television production a lift. Rated PG. 100m. **DIR:** Jeannot Szwarc. **CAST:** George C. Scott, Rebecca DeMornay, Ian McShane, Neil Dickson. **1986**

MURDERS IN THE ZOO ★★★ Wild, pre-Code horror from Paramount. Lionel Atwill is a zookeeper who's also a jealous husband. In the first scene, set in the Asian jungle, he sews his wife's lover's mouth shut, leaving him to die in the jungle. Back home, he dumps one victim into a crocodile pool, and kills another with snake venom. Lurid fun—not for the kiddies, even now. B&W; 64m. **DIR:** A. Edward Sutherland. **CAST:** Lionel Atwill, Charlie Ruggles, Randolph Scott, Gail Patrick, John Lodge, Kathleen Burke. **1933**

MURIEL ★★★★ Like *Last Year at Marienbad*, this stylized Alain Resnais film is largely about the burden of memory, as experienced by four interlinked characters. Difficult and demanding, it is composed of many short, overlapping scenes. But for those who accept its challenge, the emotional payoff can be extraordinary. In French with English subtitles. 116m. **DIR:** Alain Resnais. **CAST:** Delphine Seyrig, Jean-Pierre Kérien, Nita Klein. **1963**

MURIEL'S WEDDING ★★★★ Fans of *Strictly Ballroom* and *The Adventures of Priscilla Queen of the Desert* will adore this equally flamboyant Australian comedy that stars Toni Collette as a socially inept ugly duckling desperate to become a swan. She's a melancholy fixture in the small town of Porpoise Spit and a young woman so out of touch that she worships the tunes of 1970s pop group Abba. Rated R for profanity and brief nudity. 105m. **DIR:** P. J. Hogan. **CAST:** Toni Collette, Bill Hunter, Rachel Griffiths, Jeanie Drynan, Gennie Nevinson, Matt Day. **1994 DVD**

MURMUR OF THE HEART ★★★ Director Louis Malle's story of a sickly French teenager and his youthful, free-spirited mother in the 1950s gets off to a wonderful start, then runs out of steam in its second half as the two check into a health resort. Still, it has charm, wit, and style to spare. Not rated, but Malle's treatment of a single act of incest may raise American eyebrows, although the subject is very tastefully handled. In French with English subtitles. 118m. **DIR:** Louis Malle. **CAST:** Lea Massari, Benoit Ferreux, Daniel Gélin, Michel Lonsdale. **1971**

MURPH THE SURF ★★1/2 In this based-on-real-life thriller, two Florida beachniks connive to do the impossible: steal the fabled 564-carat Star of India sapphire out of New York's American Museum of Natural History. Re-creation of the 1964 crime induces sweat, along with a good speedboat chase, but the picture never really catches a wave. 101m. **DIR:** Marvin J. Chomsky. **CAST:** Robert Conrad, Don Stroud, Donna Mills, Luther Adler. **1975**

MURPHY'S LAW 🦃 Charles Bronson is a cop framed for the murder of his ex-wife. Rated R. 101m. **DIR:** J. Lee Thompson. **CAST:** Charles Bronson, Carrie Snodgress, Kathleen Wilhoite. **1986**

MURPHY'S ROMANCE ★★★★ This sweet little love story marks the finest performance by James Garner. He's a crusty small-town pharmacist, a widower with no shortage of home-cooked meals but little interest in anything more permanent. Garner and Sally Field are great together, and the result is a complete charmer. Rated PG-13. 107m. **DIR:** Martin Ritt. **CAST:** Sally Field, James Garner, Brian Kerwin, Corey Haim. **1985 DVD**

MURPHY'S WAR ★★★ World War II sea drama follows a British seaman, sole survivor of a brutal massacre of his ship's crew by a German U-boat, as he seeks revenge. Peter O'Toole gives a hard-hitting, no-holds-barred performance as the outraged, bloodthirsty Murphy. Rated PG. 108m. **DIR:** Peter Yates. **CAST:** Peter O'Toole, Sian Phillips, Horst Janson, Philippe Noiret, John Hallam. **1971**

MURROW ★★★★ Compassionate HBO film about the famous radio and television journalist Edward R. Murrow, played brilliantly by Daniel Travanti. The film devotes most of its running time to the journalist's struggle against McCarthyism. 114m. **DIR:** Jack Gold. **CAST:** Daniel J. Travanti, Dabney Coleman, Edward Herrmann, John McMartin, David Suchet, Kathryn Leigh Scott. **1985**

MUSCLE BEACH PARTY ★★ Everyone's favorite surfing couple, Frankie and Annette, and their beach buddies return for more fluff in the sun. This features the first screen appearance of Little Stevie Wonder. 94m. **DIR:** William Asher. **CAST:** Frankie Avalon, Annette Funicello, Buddy Hackett, Luciana Paluzzi, Don Rickles, John Ashley, Jody McCrea, Morey Amsterdam. **1964**

MUSE, THE ★★★★ When a screenwriter (Albert Brooks) is told that he's "lost his edge," he takes the advice of another scripter and gets himself a muse (Sharon Stone). Allegedly descended from the goddesses of ancient Greece, this unusually demanding woman makes his life in the Hollywood jungle even more frantic and bewildering than it already was, bringing welcome laughs and an inside peek into the fickle world of Hollywood. Writer-director Brooks's fans will love this smart, knowing movie, as he continues to chronicle the lives and changing perspectives of baby boomers. The uninitiated may need to watch some of his earlier films to get in the groove. Rated PG-13 for profanity. 97m. **DIR:** Albert Brooks. **CAST:** Albert Brooks, Sharon Stone, Andie MacDowell, Jeff Bridges, Mark Fuerstein, Steven Wright, Bradley Whitford, Mario Opinato, Cybill Shepherd, Lorenzo Lamas, Jennifer Tilly, Rob Reiner, James Cameron, Martin Scorsese, Wolfgang Puck. **1999 DVD**

MUSIC BOX, THE ★★★1/2 An American lawyer is called upon to defend her Hungarian immigrant father when he is accused of having committed heinous war crimes during World War II in Nazi-occupied Hungary. Jessica Lange is excellent in this mystery with a message. Rated PG-13 for profanity. 123m. **DIR:** Constantin Costa-Gavras. **CAST:** Jessica Lange, Armin Mueller-Stahl, Frederic Forrest, Lukas Haas. **1989**

MUSIC FROM ANOTHER ROOM ★★1/2 A high-profile cast can't salvage this whimsical romantic drama. Danny, as a boy, helped his father deliver a little girl named Anna and then announced he would marry her one day. Years later, Danny bumps into Anna, now a grown-up beauty. Unfortunately, she is saddled with a dying mother and a dysfunctional family that demands her time. Will Danny be able to sway Anna to leave her responsibilities and get a life of her own? Rated PG-13 for language and adult situations. 104m. **DIR:** Charlie Peters. **CAST:** Jude Law, Gretchen Mol, Jennifer Tilly,

Martha Plimpton, Brenda Blethyn, Jon Tenney, Jeremy Piven. **1997**

MUSIC LOVERS, THE ★★ A tasteless movie biography of Tchaikovsky, that gets two stars for the way the music is presented, not story or acting. Director Ken Russell overdoes it with phallic symbols and homoerotic references that are embarrassing to watch. 124m. **DIR:** Ken Russell. **CAST:** Glenda Jackson, Richard Chamberlain, Christopher Gable, Max Adrian, Kenneth Colley. **1971**

MUSIC MAN, THE ★★★★1/2 They sure don't make musicals like this anymore, a smashing adaptation of Meredith Willson's Broadway hit. Robert Preston reprises the role of his life as a smooth-talkin' salesman who cajoles the parents of River City, Iowa, into purchasing band instruments and uniforms for their children. 151m. **DIR:** Morton Da Costa. **CAST:** Robert Preston, Shirley Jones, Buddy Hackett, Ron Howard, Paul Ford, Hermione Gingold. **1962 DVD**

MUSIC OF CHANCE, THE ★★★ Dreamers Mandy Patinkin and James Spader enter a high-stakes poker game with two eccentric gamblers. When they lose, they are forced to build a wall to pay off their debt—once construction begins, all rhyme and reason end. Interesting cast makes this gambler's bluff pay off. Rated R for strong language. 98m. **DIR:** Philip Haas. **CAST:** James Spader, Mandy Patinkin, M. Emmet Walsh, Joel Grey, Charles Durning, Samantha Mathis. **1993**

MUSIC OF THE HEART ★★★ This drama, based on the 1995 Oscar-nominated documentary *Small Wonders*, is more reverent than compelling or exhilarating. It chronicles the efforts of teacher-musician Roberta Guaspari-Tzvaras to establish a violin program in the public schools of East Harlem. The tenacious teacher/mentor brings a sense of pride and accomplishment to her students while battling racism and a budget crunch that threatens to terminate her classes. Rated PG. 123m. **DIR:** Wes Craven. **CAST:** Meryl Streep, Aidan Quinn, Gloria Estefan, Cloris Leachman, Angela Bassett. **1999 DVD**

MUSIC SCHOOL, THE ★★★ The mathematical precision of music as a metaphor for the ideal life unattainable by mere mortals is the driving force behind this John Updike story. Ron Weyand stars as a typically angst-ridden Updike hero. The story unfolds through Updike's off-camera commentary. Introduced by Henry Fonda; aside from fleeting nudity, suitable for family viewing. 30m. **DIR:** John Korty. **CAST:** Ron Weyand, Dana Larsson, Cathleen Bauer. **1974**

MUSIC TEACHER, THE ★★★★★ Belgian director and co-scenarist Gerard Corbiau weave an incredibly sensual story of the love of a gifted singer (Anne Roussel) for her music teacher (José Van Dam). Superb acting, exquisite cinematography, and great music. In French with English subtitles. Rated PG for suggested sex. 100m. **DIR:** Gerard Corbiau. **CAST:** José Van Dam, Anne Roussel, Philippe Volter. **1989**

•**MUSKETEER, THE** ★★★ This aptly titled film focuses on the exploits of young D'Artagnan, all but ignoring his celebrated elders in the swashbuckling trade. Instead, we watch as the would-be musketeer exhibits his uncanny fighting prowess, goes on a secret mission with the queen, woos the winsome Francesca, and searches for the scoundrel who killed his parents. Tim Roth has a high time as the assassin Febre, and Catherine Deneuve delights as a royal who doesn't mind jumping into the fray. The kung fu–style fighting scenes seem somewhat out of place, but as long as you're going to be irreverent, you might as well go all the way. Rated PG-13 for violence and suggested sex. 105m. **DIR:** Peter Hyams. **CAST:** Catherine Deneuve, Justin Chambers, Mena Suvari, Stephen Rea, Tim Roth, Daniel Mesguich, Nick Moran, Stephen Spiers. **2001 DVD**

MUSSOLINI AND I ★★★ A weak and confusing narrative hinders this HBO film about the Fascist leader and his family's struggle with power. Bob Hoskins plays the Italian premier with a British accent; ditto for Anthony Hopkins who portrays Galeazzo Ciano, Italy's minister of foreign affairs and the dictator's brother-in-law. Still, the story is kept interesting despite its length. Not rated, but the equivalent of a PG for violence. 130m. **DIR:** Alberto Negrin. **CAST:** Anthony Hopkins, Susan Sarandon, Bob Hoskins, Annie Girardot, Barbara de Rossi, Vittorio Mezzogiorno, Fabio Testi, Kurt Raab. **1985**

MUTANT 🦃 Idiocy. Rated R for violence. 100m. **DIR:** John "Bud" Cardos. **CAST:** Bo Hopkins, Wings Hauser, Jennifer Warren, Cary Guffey, Lee Montgomery. **1983**

MUTANT ON THE BOUNTY ★★ Silly yet sometimes amusing sci-fi spoof about a research team on a spaceship. Not rated. 93m. **DIR:** Robert Torrance. **CAST:** John Roarke, Deborah Benson, John Furey. **1989**

MUTANT SPECIES ★★ A team of mercenaries enters a forest in search of an alien symbiont/weapon. When the weapon combines itself with one of the soldiers, creating an unfeeling killing machine, soldiers begin to die at a very rapid pace. Ludicrous and overplayed feature offers a thrill or two. Rated R for violence and profanity. 100m. **DIR:** David A. Prior. **CAST:** Leo Rossi, Powers Boothe, Wilford Brimley, Denise Crosby, Grant Gelt. **1995**

MUTANTS IN PARADISE ★★1/2 Campus loser, roped into an experiment to create a "nuke-proof" man, becomes a local celebrity. Rambling student-made film has cute ideas but lacks the budget to flesh them out. For one thing, there aren't any mutants. Not rated; contains no objectionable material. 77m. **DIR:** Scott Apostolou. **CAST:** Brad Greenquist, Anna Nicholas, Edith Massey, Ray "Boom Boom" Mancini. **1985**

MUTATOR ★★ Mediocre nature-run-amok/genetic-experiment thriller with only so-so hairy monster effects. Here, the lab must be sealed off to keep the monsters from getting out. The sole point of interest is Brion James in a rare hero role. Rated R for violence. 91m. **DIR:** John R. Bowey. **CAST:** Brian James, Carolyn Ann Clark. **1991**

MUTE WITNESS ★★★★ Being scared is rarely this much fun. Russian actress Marina Sudina is fab in the title role as a speechless special-effects woman working a low-budget American-movie gig in Russia. Sudina, who would have made a great silent-screen actress, so articulates her terror upon witnessing a crime that you'll soon shift to the edge of your seat. The overall effect is furiously suspenseful. Watch for Alec Guinness in an unbilled cameo. Rated R for profanity, violence, and nudity. 98m. **DIR:** Anthony Waller. **CAST:** Marina Sudina, Fay Ripley, Evan Richards, Oleg Jankovskij, Alec Guinness. **1994**

MUTINY IN OUTER SPACE ★★ After exploring caves on the moon, astronauts become infected with an alien fungus. Overplotted sci-fi potboiler bears some similarity to *Alien*, though not enough to make it interesting. B&W; 80m. **DIR:** Hugo Grimaldi. **CAST:** William Leslie, Dolores Faith, Pamela Curran, Richard Garland, Harold Lloyd Jr., Glenn Langan. **1965**

MUTINY ON THE BOUNTY ★★ This years-later remake hits the South Seas with a gigantic belly flop. Trevor Howard is commanding as the tyrannical Captain Bligh, but Marlon Brando as mutiny leader Fletcher Christian? Yucko! 179m. **DIR:** Lewis Milestone. **CAST:** Marlon Brando, Trevor Howard, Richard Harris, Hugh Griffith, Richard Haydn, Gordon Jackson. **1962**

MUTINY ON THE BOUNTY ★★★★ The first and best known of three versions of the now-classic account of mutiny against the tyranny of Captain William Bligh during a worldwide British naval expedition in 1789. Charles Laughton is superb as the merciless Bligh, Clark Gable unquestionably fine as the leader of the mutiny, Fletcher Christian. The film won an Oscar for best picture and still entertains today. B&W; 132m. **DIR:** Frank Lloyd. **CAST:** Charles Laughton, Clark Gable, Franchot Tone, Dudley Digges, Eddie Quillan, Donald Crisp, Henry Stephenson. **1935**

MUTUAL NEEDS ★★ An ambitious junior executive rises in the ranks after the hooker he hired to pose as his wife impresses his boss. But his luck turns when she decides she deserves a piece of his good fortune. An erotic thriller whose plot mostly just fills time between heavy-breathing scenes with Rochelle Swanson. Rated R for profanity, nudity, sex, and violence. 88m. **DIR:** Robert Angelo. **CAST:** Eric Woods, Richard Grieco, Rochelle Swanson, Charlotte Lewis. **1997**

•MVP2: MOST VERTICAL PRIMATE ★★ Jack the chimp is back, hanging up his ice hockey skates for another extreme sport: skateboarding. In this direct-to-video sequel, Jack is booted out of the hockey league and teams up with a homeless boy to win a skateboarding championship. Strictly for the little ones. Not rated. 87m. **DIR:** Robert Vince. **CAST:** Richard Karn, Cameron Bancroft, Scott Goodman, Bob Burnquist. **2001 DVD**

MY AMERICAN COUSIN ★★★★ This delightful Canadian comedy-drama focuses on what happens when the dull life of 12-year-old Sandra (played by feisty newcomer Margaret Langrick) is invaded by her high-spirited 17-year-old relative, Butch (John Wildman), from California. A warm character study with a number of funny moments, this is a refreshing antidote to the mindless teen flicks so common today. Rated PG for mild sexuality. 110m. **DIR:** Sandy Wilson. **CAST:** Margaret Langrick, John Wildman, Richard Donat. **1986**

MY ANTONIA ★★★ Willa Cather's novels about frontier life tend to translate smoothly to video, and this is no exception. Neil Patrick Harris is the orphaned teenager who falls for a poor immigrant girl. The land is as much a character as the people in this enjoyable family picture. Rated PG for adult themes. 92m. **DIR:** Joseph Sargent. **CAST:** Neil Patrick Harris, Jan Triska, Jason Robards Jr., Eva Marie Saint, Norbert Weisser. **1994**

MY BEAUTIFUL LAUNDRETTE ★★★★1/2 In modern-day England, a young Pakistani immigrant is given a laundrette by his rich uncle and, with the help of his punk-rocker boyfriend turns it into a showplace. A racist gang decides to close them down. British director Stephen Frears keeps things from becoming too heavy by adding deft touches of comedy. Rated R for profanity, suggested and simulated sex, and violence. 103m. **DIR:** Stephen Frears. **CAST:** Saeed Jaffrey, Roshan Seth, Daniel Day-Lewis, Gordon Warnecke, Shirley Ann Field. **1985**

MY BEST FRIEND IS A VAMPIRE ★★ Teen romance with a twist: Our hero has just become a vampire. Abundant car-chase scenes should intrigue teen viewers. Rated PG for Jeremy's seduction by the sexy vampire. 90m. **DIR:** Jimmy Huston. **CAST:** Robert Sean Leonard, Cheryl Pollak, René Auberjonois, Fannie Flagg. **1986**

MY BEST FRIEND'S GIRL ★★★ A philosophical comedy about two best but very different friends who find themselves in love with the same girl. Isabelle Huppert marvelously plays the sultry object of both men's desire, but the real gem of this film is the performance of Coluche, who falls in love with his best friend's girl. In French with English subtitles. Nudity and simulated sex. 99m. **DIR:** Bertrand Blier. **CAST:** Isabelle Huppert, Thierry Lhermitte, Coluche. **1984**

MY BEST FRIEND'S WEDDING ★★★ Julia Roberts realizes she's in love with her best friend of ten years (Dermot Mulroney), when he announces his engagement to wonderful rich girl Cameron Diaz. Roberts's attempts to sabotage the wedding lack comic energy, while the film explores emotional issues only superficially. Rupert Everett almost saves the show as Roberts's gay boss, reluctantly posing as her lover. Rated PG-13. 105m. **DIR:** P. J. Hogan. **CAST:** Julia Roberts, Dermot Mulroney, Cameron Diaz, Rupert Everett. **1997 DVD**

MY BLOODY VALENTINE ★★ Candy boxes stuffed with bloody human hearts signal the return of a legendary murderous coal miner to Valentine Bluffs. This film provides a few doses of excitement and a tidal wave of killings. Rated R. 91m. **DIR:** George Mihalka. **CAST:** Paul Kelman, Lori Hallier, Neil Affleck. **1981**

MY BLUE HEAVEN ★★★ Steve Martin and Rick Moranis are fun to watch in this gangster comedy, which has Martin as a mob informer in the witness protection program and Moranis as the FBI agent assigned to watch over him. Don't expect to laugh uproariously. Rated PG-13 for profanity and violence. 95m. **DIR:** Herbert Ross. **CAST:** Steve Martin, Rick Moranis, Joan Cusack, Melanie Mayron, Carol Kane, Bill Irwin, Deborah Rush. **1990 DVD**

MY BODYGUARD ★★★★★ This is a wonderfully funny and touching movie. Fifteen-year-old Clifford Peache (Chris Makepeace) must face the challenges of public high school after nine years of private education. His classes are easy. It's his schoolmates who cause problems. Specifically, there's Moody (Matt Dillon), a nasty young thug who extorts money from the other students. Rated PG. 96m. **DIR:** Tony Bill. **CAST:** Chris Makepeace, Matt Dillon, Martin Mull, Ruth Gordon, Adam Baldwin. **1980 DVD**

MY BOYFRIEND'S BACK ★★★1/2 When love-struck nerd Andrew Lowery is shot saving Traci Lind's life, his dying wish is that she will accompany him to the prom. She agrees; he dies. Lowery keeps his date by returning from the dead, setting off some hilarious complications. Humor is derived mainly from his home life, and the interaction of his goofy parents. Rated PG-13 for comic gore and adult language. 85m. **DIR:** Bob Balaban. **CAST:** Andrew Lowery, Traci Lind, Mary Beth Hurt, Edward Herrmann, Paul Dooley, Cloris Leachman. **1993**

MY BOYS ARE GOOD BOYS ★★ It's good to see veteran actors Ralph Meeker and Ida Lupino again, but it's too bad the occasion is this low-budget effort. They play parents of juvenile delinquents who rob an armored car. Pretty mediocre. Rated PG. 90m. **DIR:** Bethel Buckalew. **CAST:** Ralph Meeker, Ida Lupino, Lloyd Nolan, David Doyle. **1978**

MY BRILLIANT CAREER ★★★★1/2 A superb Australian import, *My Brilliant Career* is about a young woman clearly born before her time. It is the waning years of the nineteenth century, when the only respectable status for a woman is to be married. Sybylla Melvyn (Judy Davis), who lives with her family in the Australian bush, does not want to marry. She has "immortal longings." Rated G. 101m. **DIR:** Gillian Armstrong. **CAST:** Judy Davis, Sam Neill, Wendy Hughes. **1979**

MY BROTHER'S WIFE ★★ John Ritter lends some heart to this tired tale of a man who spends two decades pursuing his sister-in-law. Ritter helps save this made-for-television comedy, based on A. R. Gurney's play *The Middle Ages*. 100m. **DIR:** Jack Bender. **CAST:** John Ritter, Mel Harris, Polly Bergen. **1989**

MY CHAUFFEUR ★★1/2 In this better-than-average (for the genre) soft-core sex comedy, an aggressive, slightly kooky young woman upsets things at an all-male limousine company. Rated R for oodles of nudity, leering dirty old men by the truckload, suggested sex, and profanity. Don't let the kids rent this while you're out playing poker. 97m. **DIR:** David Beaird. **CAST:** Deborah Foreman, Sam Jones, Howard Hesseman, E. G. Marshall, Sean McClory. **1986 DVD**

MY COUSIN VINNY ★★★★ A fledgling Brooklyn lawyer attempts to free his cousin, who has been arrested on a murder charge in backward Wahzoo City, Alabama. It's a movie you won't want to miss. Joe Pesci is terrific, and so is Marisa Tomei as his gum popping fiancée. Rated R for profanity and brief violence. 116m. **DIR:** Jonathan Lynn. **CAST:** Joe Pesci, Ralph Macchio, Marisa Tomei, Mitchell Whitfield, Fred Gwynne, Lane Smith, Austin Pendleton, Bruce McGill, Maury Chaykin. **1991**

MY DARLING CLEMENTINE ★★★★1/2 The epic struggle between good and evil is wrapped up in this classic retelling of the shoot-out at the O.K. Corral, between the Earps and the lawless Clanton family. Henry Fonda gives his Wyatt Earp a feeling of believability, perfectly matched by Walter Brennan's riveting portrayal of villainy as the head of the Clanton gang. B&W; 97m. **DIR:** John Ford. **CAST:** Henry Fonda, Victor Mature, Walter Brennan, Linda Darnell, Ward Bond, Tim Holt. **1946**

MY DATE WITH THE PRESIDENT'S DAUGHTER ★★1/2 Complications abound in this cute, funny, made-for-television comedy about what happens when the daughter of the president of the United States wants to start dating. Dabney Coleman has some nice moments as the president, who realizes that his daughter is growing up. Clean, innocent fun for the whole family. Not rated. 90m. **DIR:** Alex Zamm. **CAST:** Dabney Coleman, Will Friedle, Elisabeth Harnois, Mimi Kuzyk, Jay Thomas. **1998**

MY DAUGHTER'S KEEPER ★★1/2 British entry into *The Hand That Rocks the Cradle* subgenre features (surprise) a psychotic nanny who takes over the household, her charge, and finally the husband. Some chilling moments, but it all seems derivative at this point in the game. Not rated; contains violence, nudity, and adult language. 109m. **DIR:** Heinrich Dahms. **CAST:** Nicholas Guest, Ana Padrao, Jocelyn Broderick, Kelly Westhof. **1993**

MY DEAR SECRETARY ★★1/2 A comedy battle of quips and wits between writer Kirk Douglas and best-selling author Laraine Day. Both lose the picture to Keenan Wynn, who is a droll delight. B&W; 94m. **DIR:** Charles Martin. **CAST:** Laraine Day, Kirk Douglas, Helen Walker, Keenan Wynn, Alan Mowbray. **1948**

MY DEMON LOVER ★★★1/2 Scott Valentine is delightful as a lovable bum who is possessed by the devil. His infatuation with a very gullible Denny (Michelle Little) becomes complicated when he is transformed into a demon every time he gets amorous. Rated PG for simulated sex and mild gore. 87m. **DIR:** Charlie Loventhal. **CAST:** Scott Valentine, Michelle Little, Robert Trebor, Gina Gallego, Alan Fudge. **1987**

MY DINNER WITH ANDRE ★★★★★ One of the most daring films ever made, this fascinating work consists almost entirely of a dinner conversation between two men. It's a terrific little movie. You'll be surprised how entertaining it is. No MPAA rating. The film has no objectionable material. 110m. **DIR:** Louis Malle. **CAST:** Andre Gregory, Wallace Shawn. **1981 DVD**

MY DOG SKIP ★★★★ This sentimental tale of a boy and his dog, based on Willie Morris's bestselling memoir, is adapted with sparkle and a rich tapestry of memorable characters. Everything is perfect, from Gail Gilchriest's poignant script to narrator Harry Connick Jr.'s honeyed southern drawl, which whisks us back to 1942, to the small town of Yazoo, Mississippi. The story concerns Willie, an undersized 8-year-old only child (Frankie Muniz), who has been badly sheltered from life's possible traumas by a gruff father. Only after an enthusiastic canine is introduced into the house does this pattern change and Willie finds himself able to make those connections into solid boyhood that had, until now, eluded him. The result is a slice of cinema heaven: a film with the narrative depth of *To Kill a Mockingbird* and the sentimental intensity of that killer-of-all-killer family films, *Old Yeller*. Rated PG for dramatic intensity. 93m. **DIR:** Jay Russell. **CAST:** Frankie Muniz, Diane Lane, Kevin Bacon, Luke Wilson. **2000 DVD**

MY DREAM IS YOURS ★★★ Doris Day becomes a radio star in a snappy musical-comedy based on Dick Powell's 1934 hit, *Twenty Million Sweethearts*. Day plays the role Powell played in the original, a would-be singer who makes the big time in radio. A dream sequence

with Bugs Bunny is a highlight. 101m. **DIR:** Michael Curtiz. **CAST:** Doris Day, Jack Carson, Lee Bowman, Adolphe Menjou, Eve Arden, S. Z. Sakall, Edgar Kennedy, Sheldon Leonard, Franklin Pangborn. **1949**

MY FAIR LADY ★★★★1/2 *Pygmalion*, the timeless George Bernard Shaw play, has been a success in every form in which it has been presented. This Oscar-winning 1964 movie musical adaptation is no exception. Rex Harrison, as Professor Henry Higgins, is the perfect example of British class snobbishness. Audrey Hepburn gives a fine performance as Eliza Doolittle (with Marni Nixon supplying the singing). 170m. **DIR:** George Cukor. **CAST:** Rex Harrison, Audrey Hepburn, Stanley Holloway. **1964 DVD**

MY FAMILY ★★★ An intimate epic covering sixty years of a Mexican-American family's struggles, triumphs, and absurdities. The narrative is, unfortunately, spread too thin, and only the all-Latino ensemble's best actors (Jimmy Smits, Edward James Olmos) manage to make their characters rise above symbolic status. Rated R for language, violence, sex, nudity, and drugs. 130m. **DIR:** Gregory Nava. **CAST:** Jimmy Smits, Esai Morales, Eduardo Lopez Rojas, Jenny Gago, Elpidia Carrillo, Edward James Olmos, Constance Marie. **1995**

MY FATHER IS COMING ★★★ A young German woman living in Manhattan pretends to be married when her father pays a visit, then watches in amazement as the supposedly stuffy old man has an affair with a sex therapist. Amusing exploration of modern sexuality. Not rated; contains nudity and frank sexual discussions. B&W; 82m. **DIR:** Monika Treut. **CAST:** Shelley Kastner, Alfred Edel, Annie Sprinkle. **1991**

MY FATHER, THE HERO ★★★1/2 Genial, goofy Disney comedy is obviously intended to increase French superstar Gérard Depardieu's popularity in America. Though at first seemingly miscast, Depardieu is fine as the father of a feisty teenage girl. She tries to pass him off as her older lover while they're on vacation in order to appear sexy and sophisticated to a young suitor. It's charming, corny, and humorous all at the same time. Rated PG. **DIR:** Steve Miner. **CAST:** Gérard Depardieu, Katherine Heigl, Dalton James, Faith Prince, Stephen Tobolowsky, Emma Thompson. **1994**

MY FATHER'S GLORY ★★★★★ French filmmaker Yves Robert's remarkable film is the unforgettable chronicle of author and filmmaker Marcel Pagnol's idyllic remembrances of his childhood. The most commonplace events are made to seem magical in this import and its sequel, *My Mother's Castle*. Not since *Jean de Florette* and *Manon of the Spring* has a French filmmaker so artfully mined a literary source. Bravo! In French with English subtitles. Rated G. 110m. **DIR:** Yves Robert. **CAST:** Philippe Caubère, Nathalie Roussel, Thérèse Liotard, Didier Pain. **1991**

MY FAVORITE BLONDE ★★★★ Funny outing with cowardly vaudeville star Bob Hope on his way to Hollywood. (His trained penguin just won a contract.) He becomes involved with a British secret agent and assassinations. B&W; 78m. **DIR:** Sidney Lanfield. **CAST:** Bob Hope, Madeleine Carroll, Gale Sondergaard, George Zucco. **1942**

MY FAVORITE BRUNETTE ★★★★1/2 Classic Bob Hope comedy with Bob as a photographer who, thanks to a case of mistaken identity, makes No. 1 on the death list of a gang of thugs, played beautifully by Peter Lorre, Lon Chaney Jr., John Hoyt, and Elisha Cook Jr. Bob tries every trick in the book to save his neck, as well as Dorothy Lamour's. A scream! B&W; 87m. **DIR:** Elliott Nugent. **CAST:** Bob Hope, Dorothy Lamour, Peter Lorre, Lon Chaney Jr., John Hoyt. **1947 DVD**

MY FAVORITE MARTIAN ★★★ Remaining faithful to the TV series, this plays out as more of a sequel than a remake. Jeff Daniels stumbles on the ship after being dumped by the boss's spoiled brat and plunges into an endless series of problems after the martian moves in with him. Physical humor and sight gags get a bit tiresome. Rated PG for comic-book violence and sexual innuendo. 91m. **DIR:** Donald Petrie. **CAST:** Jeff Daniels, Christopher Lloyd, Daryl Hannah, Elizabeth Hurley, Ray Walston. **1999 DVD**

MY FAVORITE WIFE ★★★★★ Cary Grant and Irene Dunne teamed up for many hilarious films, but the best is this often-copied comedy. Grant is a widower about to be remarried when his long-lost and presumed-dead wife (Dunne) is rescued after years on an island with a handsome young scientist (Randolph Scott). The delightful complications that result make this one of the 1940s' best comedies. B&W; 88m. **DIR:** Garson Kanin. **CAST:** Cary Grant, Irene Dunne, Randolph Scott. **1940**

MY FAVORITE YEAR ★★★★1/2 This warmhearted, hilarious comedy is an affectionate tribute to the frenzied Golden Age of television, that period when uninhibited comics like Sid Caesar faced the added pressure of performing live. With superb performances all around and on-the-money direction by Richard Benjamin, it's a real treasure. Rated PG for slight profanity and sexual situations. 92m. **DIR:** Richard Benjamin. **CAST:** Peter O'Toole, Mark Linn-Baker, Joseph Bologna, Lainie Kazan, Bill Macy. **1982**

MY FELLOW AMERICANS ★★★★ In James Garner, Jack Lemmon finds as worthy a comic partner as Walter Matthau in what could just as easily have been called *Grumpy Old Presidents*. Longtime rivals Lemmon, a Republican, and Garner, a Democrat, find themselves thrown together in a life-or-death situation when the current president decides he wants them dead. There have been some dirty dealings at the White House, and the new prez wants to pin it on someone else. Rated PG-13 for suggested sex, profanity, and violence. 101m. **DIR:** Peter Segal. **CAST:** Jack Lemmon, James Garner, Dan Aykroyd, John Heard, Sela Ward, Wilford Brimley, Everett McGill, Lauren Bacall, Bradley Whitford, James Rebhorn, Esther Rolle, Conchata Ferrell. **1996 DVD**

•MY FIRST MISTER ★★★1/2 A disaffected, multiple-pierced teenager (Leelee Sobieski) befriends a frumpy middle-aged clothing salesman (Albert Brooks). The story, seen more from the viewpoint of the adult than of the teenager, veers into melodrama in the last act, but the compensations include fine acting and interesting characters. Rated R for profanity. 108m. **DIR:** Christine Lahti. **CAST:** Leelee Sobieski, Albert Brooks, Carol Kane, Mary Kay Place, Michael McKean, John Goodman. **2001 DVD**

MY FIRST WIFE ★★★1/2 In the tradition of *Ordinary People*, *Kramer vs. Kramer*, and *Smash Palace* comes another film about the dissolution of a marriage. The

story deals with a classical music programmer/composer who finds that his wife doesn't love him anymore. Rated PG for adult situations and language. 95m. **DIR:** Paul Cox. **CAST:** John Hargreaves, Wendy Hughes. **1985**

MY 5 WIVES ★★ Someone should ban Sidney J. Furie from directing comedies in the future. His heavy-handed approach all but ruins this silly farce. Rodney Dangerfield still gets no respect, but mostly from a director who uses a sundial for comic timing. Dangerfield plays an entrepreneur so desperate for a prime piece of real estate that he engages in a weird religion and ends up with five wives. The jokes are as limp as soggy paper and just as thin. Rated R for adult situations and language. 100m. **DIR:** Sidney J. Furie. **CAST:** Rodney Dangerfield, Jerry Stiller, Molly Shannon, Andrew Dice Clay, John Byner. **2000 DVD**

MY FOOLISH HEART ★★★★ One of the most popular romances from WW II years, this movie inspired a popular song and helped establish the romantic image that made Susan Hayward famous. A woman falls in love with a soldier about to be shipped out and carries his child in this romantic melodrama. B&W; 98m. **DIR:** Mark Robson. **CAST:** Susan Hayward, Dana Andrews, Robert Keith, Gigi Perreau, Kent Smith, Lois Wheeler. **1949**

MY FORBIDDEN PAST ★★ Set in steamy New Orleans in 1890, this one's about Ava Gardner's cold-blooded attempts to buy married-man Robert Mitchum's affections with the help of an unexpected inheritance. His wife is killed. He's accused of her murder. Gardner, revealing her unsavory past in order to save him, wins his love. B&W; 81m. **DIR:** Robert Stevenson. **CAST:** Robert Mitchum, Ava Gardner, Janis Carter, Melvyn Douglas, Lucile Watson. **1951**

MY FRIEND FLICKA ★★★1/2 A young boy raises and nourishes a sickly colt despite his father's warning that the horse came from wild stock and could be unstable. Fine rendition of Mary O'Hara's timeless novel and one of the best of a genre that flourished in the 1940s before Disney cornered the market a few years later. 89m. **DIR:** Harold Schuster. **CAST:** Roddy McDowall, Preston Foster, Rita Johnson, James Bell, Jeff Corey, Diana Hale, Arthur Loft. **1943**

MY FRIEND IRMA ★★1/2 The plan to transpose a popular radio show about the "dumbest" of all "dumb blondes" to the screen went astray when it became the vehicle to introduce the team of Dean Martin and Jerry Lewis. The creator of the radio show, Cy Howard, coscripted, but he and his star, the lovely Marie Wilson, were all but lost in the shuffle. B&W; 113m. **DIR:** George Marshall. **CAST:** John Lund, Diana Lynn, Don DeFore, Marie Wilson, Dean Martin, Jerry Lewis, Hans Conried. **1949**

MY GEISHA ★★★ A Hollywood actress disguises herself as a geisha to convince her producer-husband to cast her in his Japan-based production of *Madame Butterfly.* Shirley MacLaine is delightful in an *I Love Lucy* sort of plot. 120m. **DIR:** Jack Cardiff. **CAST:** Shirley MacLaine, Yves Montand, Edward G. Robinson, Robert Cummings. **1962**

MY GIANT ★★ Small-time agent Billy Crystal discovers what he thinks is his ticket to the big time in a towering Romanian peasant (NBA star Gheorghe Muresan). Gradually the gentle giant brings out the human side of the cynical agent. The only laughs come in the first few minutes. The film gradually dissolves into mushy sentiment. Rated PG. 103m. **DIR:** Michael Lehmann. **CAST:** Billy Crystal, Gheorghe Muresan, Kathleen Quinlan, Joanna Pacula, Zane Carney, Harold Gould, Doris Roberts, Steven Seagal. **1998 DVD**

MY GIRL ★★★★ A genuinely touching, frequently hilarious and heartfelt film about the difficult adjustments forced on an 11-year-old girl who secretly fears that she was responsible for her mother's death. Lovable characters and the essence of truth make this a good film for families to watch and discuss afterward. Rated PG for brief vulgarity. 90m. **DIR:** Howard Zieff. **CAST:** Dan Aykroyd, Jamie Lee Curtis, Macaulay Culkin, Anna Chlumsky, Richard Masur, Griffin Dunne. **1991 DVD**

MY GIRL 2 🦃 Vada Sultenfuss, the hypochondriac daughter of a widowed mortician, hits her teens in this terminally dull sequel as she researches the life of the mother she never knew. Rated PG. 99m. **DIR:** Howard Zieff. **CAST:** Anna Chlumsky, Austin O'Brien, Dan Aykroyd, Jamie Lee Curtis, Richard Masur. **1994**

MY GIRL TISA ★★1/2 Tired story of a pretty, diligent immigrant girl's efforts to bring her father to New York from the old country. B&W; 95m. **DIR:** Elliott Nugent. **CAST:** Lilli Palmer, Sam Wanamaker, Akim Tamiroff, Alan Hale Sr., Stella Adler. **1948**

MY GRANDPA IS A VAMPIRE 🦃 Grandpa (Al Lewis) does not meet vampire criteria. He's able to survive in sunlight, doesn't suck blood, and performs a number of magic tricks. This film, made in New Zealand, takes the bite out of the would-be vampire thus reducing him to an ET-ish ghoul. Not rated, contains violence. 92m. **DIR:** David Blyth. **CAST:** Al Lewis. **1991**

MY HEROES HAVE ALWAYS BEEN COWBOYS ★★★★ The themes explored in Sam Peckinpah's *Junior Bonner* get a reworking in this surprisingly effective film about a rodeo bull rider (Scott Glenn) who comes home to heal his injuries and ends up rescuing his father (Ben Johnson) from a retirement home. Wonderful performances and strong character development even make up for the expected *Rocky*-style ending. Rated PG for brief profanity and violence. 106m. **DIR:** Stuart Rosenberg. **CAST:** Scott Glenn, Kate Capshaw, Ben Johnson, Tess Harper, Gary Busey, Mickey Rooney, Balthazar Getty, Clarence Williams, III, Dub Taylor, Clu Gulager. **1991**

•**MY HORRIBLE YEAR** ★★★1/2 An almost-16-year-old girl tries to deal with the various changes and realities in her life. Irreverent narration by Allison Mack adds spice to the tale of loves and tragedies, adventures and misfortunes. This made-for-cable original is enjoyable family fare, with a playful story and decent acting. Not rated; suitable for all audiences. 92m. **DIR:** Eric Stoltz. **CAST:** Karen Allen, Allison Mack, Caterina Scorsone, Dan Petronijevic, Eric Stoltz. **2001**

MY LEFT FOOT ★★★★★ Everything is right in the screen biography of handicapped Irish writer-artist Christy Brown who was afflicted with cerebral palsy from birth. Writer-director Jim Sheridan and coscripter Shane Connaughton tell Brown's story without once succumbing to cliché or audience manipulation. Oscar-winner Daniel Day-Lewis gives what may be the perfor-

mance of his career. Rated R for profanity and violence. 119m. **DIR:** Jim Sheridan. **CAST:** Daniel Day-Lewis, Ray McAnally, Brenda Fricker, Fiona Shaw, Hugh O'Connor, Cyril Cusack. **1989 DVD**

MY LIFE ★★★ A career-obsessed public relations executive, dying of cancer, spends his last months making peace with his parents and videotaping himself for his unborn child. Solid, surefire performances from stars Michael Keaton and Nicole Kidman redeem this predictable disease-of-the-week tearjerker. Rated PG-13 for mild profanity and mature themes. 114m. **DIR:** Bruce Joel Rubin. **CAST:** Michael Keaton, Nicole Kidman, Michael Constantine, Haing S. Ngor. **1993**

MY LIFE AND TIMES WITH ANTONIN ARTAUD ★★★★ Exquisitely photographed and performed tale of poet Antonin Artaud, who founded the infamous "Theater of Cruelty." When Artaud is released from a Parisian mental institution in 1946, he is befriended by young poet Jacques Prevel. This haunting tale, which details their tumultuous relationship is uncomfortable at times, but always watchable. In French with English subtitles. Not rated; contains profanity and mature themes. 93m. **DIR:** Gérard Mordillat. **CAST:** Sami Frey, Marc Barbé, Julie Jézéquel, Valerie Jeannet. **1993**

MY LIFE AS A DOG ★★★★★ This charming, offbeat, and downright lovable import from Sweden is a big surprise. It tells of a young boy in 1950s Sweden who's shipped off to a country village when his mother becomes seriously ill. There, as he tries to come to terms with his new life, he encounters a town filled with colorful eccentrics and a young tomboy who becomes his first love. In Swedish with English subtitles. 101m. **DIR:** Lasse Hallstrom. **CAST:** Anton Glanzelius. **1987 DVD**

MY LIFE SO FAR ★★★1/2 Rich, privileged clan and their servants gather at an idyllic country estate in 1920 Scotland. The central character is a 10-year-old boy who is introduced to the mysteries of the flesh when he raids a secret attic library. His relationship with his inventor father and both their lives are complicated when an uncle brings his young French fiancée for a visit. This both dark and whimsical family portrait is based on the memoirs of Royal Opera House director Denis Forman. Rated PG-13 for sexual content. 93m. **DIR:** Hugh Hudson. **CAST:** Robert Norman, Colin Firth, Malcolm McDowell, Irène Jacob. **1999 DVD**

MY LIFE TO LIVE ★★★ Early piece of groundbreaking cinema by Jean-Luc Godard features Anna Karina as a young woman who leaves her husband to become an actress but eventually turns to prostitution. As with any Jean-Luc Godard film, the point is not so much the plot as the director's relentless experimentation with film technique and probing of social issues. In French with English subtitles. B&W; 85m. **DIR:** Jean-Luc Godard. **CAST:** Anna Karina, Saddy Rebbot. **1963 DVD**

MY LIFE'S IN TURNAROUND 🦃 If you like profanity and plotless stories, you'll love this film about two guys trying to make a movie about their lives. Rated R for profanity and nudity. 84m. **DIR:** Eric Schaeffer, Donald Lardnerward. **CAST:** Eric Schaeffer, Donald Lardnerward, Lisa Gerstein. **1994**

MY LITTLE CHICKADEE ★★★★★ W. C. Fields and Mae West enter a marriage of convenience in the Old West. It seems the card sharp (Fields) and the tainted lady (West) need to create an aura of respectability before they descend upon an unsuspecting town. That indicates trouble ahead for the town, and lots of fun for viewers. B&W; 83m. **DIR:** Eddie Cline. **CAST:** W. C. Fields, Mae West, Dick Foran, Joseph Calleia. **1940**

MY LITTLE GIRL ★★ Familiar tale of a do-good rich kid's introduction to the real world. Mary Stuart Masterson stars as a 16-year-old high school student who volunteers to spend a summer working at a state-run shelter. The performances raise this (just barely) to the tolerable level. Rated R for violence and profanity. 118m. **DIR:** Connie Kaiserman. **CAST:** James Earl Jones, Geraldine Page, Mary Stuart Masterson, Anne Meara. **1986**

MY LITTLE PONY: THE MOVIE ★★★ Darling ponies are threatened by the evil witch family. Children under 7 should enjoy this, but older children and adults may feel it's too long. Danny DeVito, Madeline Kahn, Cloris Leachman, Rhea Perlman, Tony Randall (voices). Rated G. 85m. **DIR:** Michael Joens. **1986**

MY LOVE FOR YOURS (HONEYMOON IN BALI) ★★★ An eager cast and a witty script make a passable entertainment of this otherwise trite story of a cool, self-assured career girl thawed by love. B&W; 99m. **DIR:** Edward H. Griffith. **CAST:** Madeleine Carroll, Fred MacMurray, Allan Jones, Helen Broderick, Akim Tamiroff, Osa Massen, John Qualen. **1939**

MY LUCKY STAR ★★★★ Sonja Henie skates like a dream as a student working at a department store to pay for college. She falls for teacher Richard Greene, flirts with department-store heir Cesar Romero and performs in an "Alice in Wonderland" ice ballet to help the department store out of a jam. B&W; 81m. **DIR:** Roy Del Ruth. **CAST:** Sonja Henie, Richard Greene, Cesar Romero, Gypsy Rose Lee, Buddy Ebsen, Billy Gilbert, Arthur Treacher. **1938**

MY MAGIC DOG ★★ An invisible dog that only an 8-year-old boy can see saves the day when he thwarts bullies and an evil aunt out to make off with the kid's inheritance. Only the youngest of children will appreciate the predictable format. Not rated. 98m. **DIR:** John Putch. **CAST:** Leo Millbrook, Russ Tamblyn, John Phillip Law. **1997**

MY MAN (MON HOMME) ★★★★ The perennial bad boy of French cinema, Bertrand Blier shows he hasn't mellowed much since his Oscar-winning *Get Out Your Handkerchiefs*. The failure of the sexes to understand each other, as well as men's fear of female sexuality, remain his favorite subjects in this occasionally surreal comedy about a happy hooker who fashions a homeless bum into a successful pimp. In French with English subtitles. Not rated; the film features strong sexual content. 95m. **DIR:** Bertrand Blier. **CAST:** Anouk Grinberg, Gerard Lanvin, Valeria Bruni Tedeschi, Olivier Martinez, Mathieu Kassovitz. **1997**

MY MAN ADAM ★★ Daydreaming teenager Raphael Sbarge gets a chance to live out his fantasies when he uncovers a sinister plot at school. Disappointing comedy has some clever moments but the plot seems slapped together. Rated R, though there's nothing really offensive. 84m. **DIR:** Roger L. Simon. **CAST:** Raphael Sbarge, Page Hannah, Dave Thomas, Veronica Cartwright. **1985**

MY MAN GODFREY ★★★★★ *My Man Godfrey* is one of the great screwball comedies of the 1930s. Carole

Lombard plays the most eccentric member of an eccentric family. William Powell is the relatively sane portion of the formula. Carole finds him when she is sent to find a "lost man." Powell seems to fit the bill, since he's living a hobo's life on the wrong side of the tracks. B&W; 95m. **DIR:** Gregory La Cava. **CAST:** Carole Lombard, William Powell, Gail Patrick, Alice Brady, Eugene Pallette. **1936 DVD**

MY MAN GODFREY ★★1/2 Passable but otherwise doomed updating of the 1936 classic screwball comedy will play better for those not familiar with the original. The stars try. 92m. **DIR:** Henry Koster. **CAST:** June Allyson, David Niven, Jessie Royce Landis, Robert Keith, Eva Gabor, Jay Robinson, Jeff Donnell, Martha Hyer. **1957**

MY MOM'S A WEREWOLF ★★ When a bored housewife (Susan Blakely) succumbs to a charming stranger (John Saxon), she is horrified to find herself transforming into a werewolf. Now her daughter and her ghoulish pal must figure out how to transform Blakely back into dear old mom. PG for profanity and violence. 90m. **DIR:** Michael Fischa. **CAST:** Susan Blakely, John Saxon, Katrina Caspary, Ruth Buzzi. **1988 DVD**

MY MOTHER'S CASTLE ★★★★★ More glorious adventures for young Marcel Pagnol in the exquisite sequel to *My Father's Glory*. Once again, filmmaker Yves Robert brings out all of the suspense, humor, and heartbreak in this autobiographical tale. In French with English subtitles. Rated PG. 98m. **DIR:** Yves Robert. **CAST:** Philippe Caubère, Nathalie Roussel, Thérèse Liotard, Didier Pain, Jean Rochefort. **1991**

MY MOTHER'S SECRET LIFE ★★ Long-lost daughter turns up on Mom's doorstep. To her horror, Mom (Loni Anderson) turns out to be an expensive call girl. Hard to believe and just barely watchable. 94m. **DIR:** Robert Markowitz. **CAST:** Loni Anderson, Paul Sorvino, Amanda Wyss. **1984**

MY NAME IS BARBRA ★★★★ Barbra Streisand fans have a real treasure awaiting them in *My Name Is Barbra*. Shown in 1965, shot in black and white, and featuring no guests, it was Streisand's first television special. It's a wonderful opportunity to see this exceptional performer early in her career. Viewers will also be treated to knockout versions of "When the Sun Comes Out" and "My Man." 60m. **DIR:** Dwight Hemion. **CAST:** Barbra Streisand. **1965**

MY NAME IS BILL W ★★★1/2 Impressive made-for-TV drama depicts the personal tragedies of Bill Wilson (James Woods) that led to the founding of Alcoholics Anonymous. It is difficult to watch at times, specifically in the scenes where Wilson's life and career turn sour because of excessive drinking. But this, of course, is the point of the film. Outstanding performances by a fine cast. Made for TV. 100m. **DIR:** Daniel Petrie. **CAST:** James Woods, James Garner, JoBeth Williams, Gary Sinise, Fritz Weaver, Robert Harper, George Coe. **1989**

MY NAME IS IVAN ★★★★ The title character is a 12-year-old boy who works as a scout for the Soviet army during World War II. An affecting study of the horrors of war. Young Kolya Burlaiev is remarkable as Ivan. In Russian with English subtitles. Not rated. 84m. **DIR:** Andrei Tarkovsky. **CAST:** Kolya Burlaiev, Valentin Zubkov. **1963**

MY NAME IS JOE ★★★★ Recovering Glasgow alcoholic coaches a ragtag soccer team and falls in love. His sober life is jeopardized when he tries to free one of his players from debts to a local crime lord. This realistic drama escorts us into a social rat's nest in which unemployment and domestic violence run rampant, and people rely on street savvy for survival. In thick Scottish accents with English subtitles. Rated R for language, violence, nudity, and sex. 105m. **DIR:** Kenneth Loach. **CAST:** Peter Mullan, Louise Goodall, David McKay, David Hayman, Anne-Marie Kennedy. **1999**

MY NAME IS NOBODY ★★★1/2 This is a delightful spoof of the Clint Eastwood spaghetti Westerns. Terence Hill is a gunfighter who worships old-timer Henry Fonda, who merely wishes to go away and retire. Rated PG. 115m. **DIR:** Tonino Valerii. **CAST:** Henry Fonda, Terence Hill, Leo Gordon, Geoffrey Lewis. **1974**

MY NEIGHBOR TOTORO ★★★1/2 Pleasant animated diversion from Japan will appeal to younger children, who will find its colorful animation and adorable title character enchanting. Totoro is a funny little blue forest spirit, who takes two small sisters on a magical journey. Better-than-average dubbing and a universal story make this film better than most. Rated G. 86m. **DIR:** Hayao Miyazaki. **1988**

MY NEIGHBORHOOD ★★★ An offbeat comedy with a dark tone featuring director-actor Michell Kriegman as neurotic pub owner who invites strangers off the street to view bizarre, homemade videos. Original and recommended. 28m. **DIR:** Michael Kriegman. **CAST:** Michael Kriegman. **1982**

MY NEW GUN ★★1/2 This droll comedy doesn't quite deliver on its entertaining premise, but it satisfies modestly, thanks to the principal players. Diane Lane stars as a yuppie housewife who doesn't quite know how to react when her husband (Stephen Collins) gives her a gun for protection. 100m. **DIR:** Stacy Cochran. **CAST:** Diane Lane, Stephen Collins, James LeGros, Tess Harper. **1992**

MY NEW PARTNER ★★★★ Walrus-faced Philippe Noiret is hilarious in this French comedy that swept the César Awards (the French Oscars). He plays a corrupt but effective police detective who is saddled with a new partner, an idealistic young police-academy graduate. Hollywood would never make a comedy this cynical about police work; they've seldom made one as funny either. In French with English subtitles. Rated R for nudity and sexual situations. 106m. **DIR:** Claude Zidi. **CAST:** Philippe Noiret, Thierry Lhermitte, Regine. **1984**

MY NIGHT AT MAUD'S ★★★★ The first feature by Eric Rohmer to be shown in the United States. It is the third film of the cycle he called *Six Moral Tales*. A man is in love with a woman, but his eyes wander to another. However, the transgression is only brief, for, according to Rohmer, the only true love is the love ordained by God. Beautifully photographed in black and white, the camera looks the actors straight in the eye and captures every nuance. In French with English subtitles. B&W; 105m. **DIR:** Eric Rohmer. **CAST:** Jean-Louis Trintignant, Françoise Fabian, Marie-Christine Barrault. **1970 DVD**

MY OLD MAN ★★★★ Excellent made-for-television adaptation of a short story by Ernest Hemingway about

a down-on-his-luck horse trainer (Warren Oates) and the daughter (Kristy McNichol) who loves him even more than horses. Oates gives a fabulous performance; certainly one of the best of his too-brief career. Eileen Brennan lends support as a sympathetic waitress. Not rated; suitable for family viewing. 104m. **DIR:** John Erman. **CAST:** Warren Oates, Kristy McNichol, Eileen Brennan. **1979**

MY OLD MAN'S PLACE ★★ Outdated cliché-ridden melodrama about a soldier's return home from Vietnam bringing two army friends with him. The inevitable clash of wills and personalities leads to the film's deadly conclusion. Rated R for nudity, profanity, and violence. 92m. **DIR:** Edwin Sherin. **CAST:** Arthur Kennedy, Mitchell Ryan, William Devane, Michael Moriarty. **1973**

MY OTHER HUSBAND ★★★★ At first, this French import starring the marvelous Miou-Miou seems rather like a scatterbrained, faintly funny retread of the old person-with-two-spouses comedy plot. But it goes on to become an affecting, sweetly sad little treasure. In French with English subtitles. Rated PG-13 for profanity. 110m. **DIR:** Georges Lautner. **CAST:** Miou-Miou, Roger Hanin, Eddy Mitchell. **1981**

MY OWN COUNTRY ★★★1/2 The story, told with perhaps too much brevity, follows Dr. Abraham Verghese as he becomes one of the first AIDS experts while tending patients in Johnson City, Tennessee. The episodic screenplay focuses on several cases, how they affect the lives of loved ones, and how Verghese finds himself consumed by trying to understand the implacable disease. Rated PG-13 for profanity and strong dramatic content. 106m. **DIR:** Mira Nair. **CAST:** Naveen Andrews, Glenne Headly, Hal Holbrook, Swoosie Kurtz, Marisa Tomei, Adam Tomei. **1998**

MY OWN PRIVATE IDAHO ★★★★ Stylishly photographed road movie about two young male street hustlers on their own personal vision quest. River Phoenix gives a heartfelt performance as a street prostitute who suffers from narcolepsy. Keanu Reeves plays a troubled bisexual youth from an affluent family. Moving, bittersweet movie. Rated R for nudity, profanity, and violence. 110m. **DIR:** Gus Van Sant. **CAST:** Keanu Reeves, River Phoenix, William Richert. **1991**

MY PAL, THE KING ★★★ Cowboy Tom Mix befriends boy king Mickey Rooney and teaches him the ways of the West. Mix's Wild West Show takes center stage for some entertaining passages, and cliff-hanger action keeps the story moving along. B&W; 74m. **DIR:** Kurt Neumann. **CAST:** Tom Mix, Mickey Rooney. **1932**

MY PAL TRIGGER ★★★1/2 One of the most fondly remembered and perhaps the best of all the Roy Rogers movies, this gentle story centers on Roy's attempts to mate his mare with a superb golden stallion. Villain Jack Holt is responsible for the death of the mare, and Roy is blamed and incarcerated. B&W; 79m. **DIR:** Frank McDonald. **CAST:** Roy Rogers, George "Gabby" Hayes, Dale Evans, Jack Holt. **1946**

MY SAMURAI ★★ A reluctant martial arts student learns the value of his lessons when his master takes on gang members. As martial arts flicks go, this is watchable with some very impressive fight scenes. Not rated; contains plenty of violence. 87m. **DIR:** Fred Dresch. **CAST:** Julian Lee, Mako, Bubba Smith, Terry O'Quinn, Jim Turner, John Kallo. **1992**

MY SCIENCE PROJECT ★★ John Stockwell finds some UFO debris abandoned (!) by the military in 1959. The doohickey quickly rages out of control sending Stockwell and chums to battle dinosaurs and futuristic soldiers. Rated PG for profanity. 94m. **DIR:** Jonathan Betuel. **CAST:** John Stockwell, Danielle von Zerneck, Fisher Stevens, Dennis Hopper, Richard Masur. **1985 DVD**

MY SIDE OF THE MOUNTAIN ★★★★ File this in that all-too-small category of films that both you and your kids can enjoy. A 13-year-old Toronto boy decides to prove his self-worth by living in a Quebec forest for one year with no resources other than his own wits. Gus the Raccoon steals the show, but you'll be charmed and entertained by the rest of the movie as well. Rated G. 100m. **DIR:** James B. Clark. **CAST:** Teddy Eccles, Theodore Bikel. **1969**

MY SISTER EILEEN ★★★★ Fast-moving musical remake of the 1940 stage play about two small-town sisters overwhelmed by New York's Greenwich Village and its inhabitants. Jack Lemmon joins Betty Garrett in a knockout rendition of "It's Bigger Than You or Me." 108m. **DIR:** Richard Quine. **CAST:** Janet Leigh, Betty Garrett, Jack Lemmon, Bob Fosse, Kurt Kasznar, Dick York, Hal March, Queenie Smith, Richard Deacon, Tommy Rall. **1955**

MY SISTER, MY LOVE (THE MAFU CAGE) ★★★ Offbeat story concerns two loving, but unbalanced, sisters who eliminate anyone who tries to come between them. Good acting all around and a perverse sense of style are just two elements that make this movie click. Rated R. 99m. **DIR:** Karen Arthur. **CAST:** Carol Kane, Lee Grant, Will Geer, James Olson. **1979**

MY SON THE FANATIC ★★★ Pakistani taxi driver in northern England self-destructs after being goaded into leading a more hedonistic lifestyle by a kinky German businessman. He has an affair with a prostitute and his life is further destabilized as his son embraces Islamic fundamentalism and invites a religious leader into their home. Hanif Kureishi adapted this dark and sometimes funny tale of displacement, racism, and culture clashes from his own 1994 short story. Rated R for language and sexual content. 86m. **DIR:** Udayan Prasad. **CAST:** Om Puri, Stellan Skarsgard, Rachel Griffiths, Akbar Kurtha. **1999 DVD**

MY STEPMOTHER IS AN ALIEN ★★1/2 A beautiful alien (Kim Basinger) comes to Earth to reverse the effects of a ray that has changed the gravity of her planet. Unfortunately, the creator of the ray (Dan Aykroyd) doesn't know how to re-create it. Thinking he is lying, she marries him to get the secret. A so-so farce with a predictably sweet ending. Rated PG-13. 108m. **DIR:** Richard Benjamin. **CAST:** Dan Aykroyd, Kim Basinger, Jon Lovitz, Alyson Hannigan. **1988 DVD**

MY STEPSON, MY LOVER ★★ A nurse marries an older, wealthy businessman, and a few months later she starts eyeing her husband's twentysomething hunk of a son. Poor acting and a wishy-washy plot line kill this made-for-cable original before it can get off the ground. Not rated. 95m. **DIR:** Mary Lambert. **CAST:** Rachel Ward, Joshua Morrow, Al Wiggins, Terry O'Quinn. **1997**

MY SUMMER STORY ★★★1/2 Eleven years separated this droll little comedy from its predecessor, *A*

Christmas Story, but humorist-essayist Jean Shepherd's childhood reminiscences are every bit as pungent and wacky. He has the gift of making viewers nostalgic for a childhood they never personally experienced. Rated PG for mild profanity. 86m. **DIR:** Bob Clark. **CAST:** Charles Grodin, Kieran Culkin, Mary Steenburgen, Christian Culkin, Al Mancini, Glenn Shadix. **1994**

MY SWEET CHARLIE ★★★★ The fine performances of Patty Duke and Al Freeman Jr. make this made-for-TV drama especially watchable. Duke plays a disowned, unwed mom-to-be who meets a black lawyer being pursued by the police. They hit it off and manage to help each other. A must-see for viewers interested in drama with a social comment. 97m. **DIR:** Lamont Johnson. **CAST:** Patty Duke, Al Freeman Jr., Ford Rainey. **1969**

MY SWEET SUICIDE ★★★ When a depressed man is unable to kill himself, he enlists the aid of a sympathetic girl in committing the perfect suicide. This black comedy has its technical drawbacks, but may interest fans of indie movies. Not rated; contains mature themes and profanity. 79m. **DIR:** David Michael Flanagan. **CAST:** Matthew Aldrich, Michelle Thompson. **1998 DVD**

MY TEACHER'S WIFE 🦃 Every generation deserves its own "Hey, I'm having sex with my teacher's wife" comedy. Here's to the class of 1999. A.k.a. *Learning Curves*. Rated R for language and adult situations. 90m. **DIR:** Bruce Leddy. **CAST:** Jason London, Tia Carrere, Christopher McDonald, Jeffrey Tambor. **1995 DVD**

MY TUTOR 🦃 A young man gets an education in more than just reading, writing, and 'rithmetic. Rated R for nudity and implied sex. 97m. **DIR:** George Bowers. **CAST:** Matt Lattanzi, Caren Kaye, Kevin McCarthy. **1983 DVD**

MY 20TH CENTURY ★★★★ Two long-separated twins are reunited on the Orient Express on New Year's Eve, 1899. Though completely different—one is a vain young woman, the other a fiery revolutionary—both are lovers of the same man. A witty look at the genesis of our era, with two wonderful performances by Dorotha Segda as both sisters. In Hungarian with English subtitles. Not rated. B&W; 104m. **DIR:** Ildiko Enyedi. **CAST:** Dorotha Segda, Oleg Jankovskij. **1988**

MY UNCLE (MON ONCLE) ★★★★ The second of Jacques Tati's cinematic romps as Mr. Hulot (the first was the famous *Mr. Hulot's Holiday*), this delightful comedy continues Tati's recurrent theme of the common man confronted with an increasingly mechanized and depersonalized society. (It's also the only Tati film to win the Academy Award for best foreign film.) 116m. **DIR:** Jacques Tati. **CAST:** Jacques Tati, Jean-Pierre Zola. **1958 DVD**

MY WICKED, WICKED WAYS ★★ Errol Flynn's fast-paced life is slowed down a bit for this TV movie. It seems to have lost its zest in the translation. But choosing Duncan Regehr to play Flynn was an inspiration. 142m. **DIR:** Don Taylor. **CAST:** Duncan Regehr, Barbara Hershey, Darren McGavin, Hal Linden. **1984**

MYRA BRECKENRIDGE ★★ Infamous film version of Gore Vidal's satiric novel about a gay movie buff who has a sex-change operation (turning him into Raquel Welch!). Not very good, but the prententious psychedelic style and parade of old movie stars in cameo roles make it a must-see for camp enthusiasts and Sixties nostalgists. Originally rated X, the brief nudity and sexual concerns would barely earn this an R today. 94m. **DIR:** Michael Sarne. **CAST:** Raquel Welch, Mae West, John Huston, Rex Reed, John Carradine, Farrah Fawcett, Tom Selleck. **1970**

MYSTERIANS, THE ★★1/2 An alien civilization attempts takeover of Earth after its home planet is destroyed. Massive destruction from the director of *Godzilla*. Quaint Japanese-style special effects look pretty silly these days, but the film can be fun if seen in the right spirit. 85m. **DIR:** Inoshiro Honda. **CAST:** Kenji Sahara. **1959**

MYSTERIES ★★★ Rutger Hauer plays an affluent foreigner in a seaside village who becomes obsessed by a local beauty. This intriguing drama is hampered by poorly dubbed dialogue. Not rated, but has sex and nudity. 93m. **DIR:** Paul de Lussanet. **CAST:** Sylvia Kristel, Rutger Hauer, David Rappaport, Rita Tushingham, Andrea Ferreol. **1984**

MYSTERIOUS DESPERADO ★★★ Tim Holt's sidekick is heir to a large estate. Ruthless land grabbers have other plans for the property and frame Chito's cousin on a murder charge. B&W; 60m. **DIR:** Lesley Selander. **CAST:** Tim Holt, Richard Martin, Edward Norris, Robert Livingston. **1949**

MYSTERIOUS DR. FU MANCHU ★★1/2 Former humanitarian Dr. Fu Manchu vows vengeance on the "white devils" who killed his wife and son during the Boxer Rebellion. Using the child of a dead missionary as his hypnotized agent, Fu tracks down those he holds responsible and murders them by devious means until he comes to a reckoning with nemesis Nayland-Smith. First talking Fu Manchu film is a bit long but fluid, action-packed, and sprinkled with lines like, "I assure you that your body, if it is found, will be quite unrecognizable." B&W; 85m. **DIR:** Rowland V. Lee. **CAST:** Warner Oland, Jean Arthur, Neil Hamilton, O. P. Heggie, William Austin, Noble Johnson. **1929**

MYSTERIOUS DR. SATAN ★★★ Eduardo Cianelli unleashes his death-dealing robot upon a helpless public. Chockful of great stunts, last-minute escapes, and logic that defies description, this prime chapterplay from Republic's thrill factory had just about everything a juvenile audience could ask for and then some. B&W; 15 chapters. **DIR:** William Witney, John English. **CAST:** Eduardo Ciannelli, Robert Wilcox, William Newell, C. Montague Shaw, Dorothy Herbert, Ella Neal, Jack Mulhall, Edwin Stanley. **1940**

MYSTERIOUS ISLAND ★★★★ Fantasy-adventure based on Jules Verne's novel about a group of Civil War prisoners who escape by balloon and land on an uncharted island in the Pacific, where they must fight to stay alive against incredible odds. With fantastic effects work by Ray Harryhausen and a breathtaking Bernard Herrmann score. 101m. **DIR:** Cy Endfield. **CAST:** Michael Craig, Joan Greenwood, Michael Callan, Gary Merrill, Herbert Lom. **1961**

MYSTERIOUS LADY, THE ★★★1/2 Greta Garbo plays Tania, a Russian spy who falls in love with an Austrian soldier, calling into question her political loyalties. Early Garbo vehicle whose preposterous love story and willfully arbitrary plot machinations nonetheless make for great fun. Silent. B&W; 84m. **DIR:** Fred Niblo. **CAST:** Greta Garbo, Conrad Nagel, Gustav von Seyffertitz. **1928**

MYSTERIOUS MR. MOTO ★★1/2 Mr. Moto comes to the aid of Scotland Yard by infiltrating the League of Assassins before they can murder an industralist needed in the war effort. B&W; 62m. **DIR:** Norman Foster. **CAST:** Peter Forre, Mary Maguire, Henry Wilcoxon, Leon Ames. **1938**

MYSTERIOUS MR. WONG, THE ★★ Not to be confused with the Mr. Wong detective series that starred Boris Karloff, this low-budget mystery has Bela Lugosi in the title role, portraying a fiendish criminal bent on possessing twelve coins connected with Confucius. B&W; 68m. **DIR:** William Nigh. **CAST:** Bela Lugosi, Wallace Ford, Arline Judge. **1935**

MYSTERIOUS MUSEUM ★★1/2 Average family fantasy about two teens being sucked into a magical painting at a museum. Once inside the medieval world of the painting, they help the locals retrieve the Jewel of Polaris, the only thing that can stop an evil warlord. The production is competent, but the story uninspired. Rated PG for violence. 80m. **DIR:** David Schmoeller. **CAST:** Andrew James Trauth, Brianna Brown. **1999**

MYSTERIOUS STRANGER, THE ★★★★ A wonderful adaptation of a Mark Twain story about a printer's apprentice who daydreams he is back in the sixteenth century. Add to this a magical stranger and a not so magical alchemist, and you have fun for the whole family. Not rated. 89m. **DIR:** Peter H. Hunt. **CAST:** Chris Makepeace, Lance Kerwin, Fred Gwynne, Bernhard Wicki. **1982**

MYSTERY, ALASKA ★★★1/2 In an out-of-the-way town in Alaska obsessed with hockey, a former resident sets up a nationally televised game pitting the locals against professional pucksters, the New York Rangers, as part of what he hopes to be a triumphant homecoming. Of course, he causes more consternation than jubilation among the locals. What starts as a typical sports movie about underdogs getting their big chance is enriched by fine performances and an above-average script by David E. Kelley. Rated R for profanity, brief nudity, and sexual references. 118m. **DIR:** Jay Roach. **CAST:** Russell Crowe, Hank Azaria, Mary McCormack, Burt Reynolds, Colm Meaney, Lolita Davidovich, Maury Chaykin, Ron Eldard, Judith Ivey, Mike Meyers, Ryan Northcott, Michael Buie, Kevin Durand, Scott Grimes, Rachel Wilson. **1999 DVD**

MYSTERY DATE ★★1/2 This teenage version of Martin Scorsese's *After Hours* is only moderately funny and is saved from total video-shelf hell by young star Ethan Hawke. Rated PG-13 for violence and profanity. 90m. **DIR:** Jonathan Wacks. **CAST:** Ethan Hawke, Teri Polo, Brian McNamara, Fisher Stevens, B. D. Wong. **1991**

MYSTERY ISLAND ★★★ When four children whose boat has run out of gas discover what appears to be a deserted island, they promptly name it Mystery Island. The children find a case of counterfeit money which belongs to villains, who later return to the island for it. The best part about this children's film is the beautiful underwater photography. 75m. **DIR:** Gene Scott. **CAST:** Jayson Duncan, Niklas Juhlin. **1981**

MYSTERY MAN ★★★ Hopalong Cassidy and his pals foil an outlaw gang's attempt to rob a bank. For revenge, the gang steals Hoppy's cattle and turns him over to the sheriff as the real outlaw leader. The most action-packed of all the Cassidy series. B&W; 60m. **DIR:** George Archainbaud. **CAST:** William Boyd, Andy Clyde, Jimmy Rogers, Eleanor Stewart. **1944**

MYSTERY MEN ★★★ When Champion City's greatest superhero, Captain Amazing (Greg Kinnear), is captured by his arch rival, Cassanova Frankenstein (Geoffrey Rush), a group of second-rate, wannabe crime fighters—Blue Raja (Hank Azaria), Bowler (Janeane Garofalo), Shoveler (William H. Macy), Invisible Boy (Kel Mitchell), Spleen (Paul Reubens), Mr. Furious (Ben Stiller), and Sphinx (Wes Studi)—attempt to save the day. Adapted from the Dark Horse comic book, there are some very funny moments in this movie, which tries too hard to be hip and is encumbered by an overlong running time. Still, it's better than *Howard the Duck*. Rated PG-13 for profanity, scatological humor, and light violence. 120m. **DIR:** Kinka Usher. **CAST:** Hank Azaria, Janeane Garofalo, William H. Macy, Kel Mitchell, Paul Reubens, Ben Stiller, Wes Studi, Greg Kinnear, Geoffrey Rush, Lena Olin, Tom Waits, Eddie Izzard, Louise Lasser. **1999 DVD**

MYSTERY, MR. RA ★★ Filmmaker Frank Cassenti captures Sun Ra and his band during rehearsals and rare concert footage from Sun Ra's remarkable Afro-psychedelic music circus. Disappointing look at the thirty-five-year career of this remarkable musician, bandleader, philosopher, and shaman. 51m. **DIR:** Frank Cassenti. **CAST:** Sun Ra. **1983**

MYSTERY MONSTERS ★★ Low-budget affair tries to make up in imagination what it lacks in production values, but there's not much here to recommend. When they're not being held captive by television host Cap'n Mike, three magical monsters pose as puppets on a daytime kiddie show. When an evil witch arrives to steal the monsters, it's up to the show's kid stars to save them. Rated PG for violence. 81m. **DIR:** Robert Talbot. **CAST:** Ashley Lyn Cafagna, Ted Redwine, Daniel Hartley, Michael Dennis. **1997**

MYSTERY OF ALEXINA, THE ★★★★ True story of a sexually ambiguous young man, raised in the nineteenth century as a woman, who becomes aware of his true identity only when he falls in love with a young woman. The script doesn't answer all the questions it raises, but there's more than enough to compel your interest. In French with English subtitles. 84m. **DIR:** René Feret. **CAST:** Philippe Vullemin, Valerie Stroh. **1985**

MYSTERY OF EDWIN DROOD, THE ★★★ An unfinished Charles Dickens story is the basis for this moody suspense drama about a drug-addicted choirmaster who is accused of killing his nephew. Claude Rains is fine as suspect John Jasper, whose infatuations with his nephew's fiancée helps seal his fate. Nothing is what it seems in this Victorian thriller. Not rated. 86m. **DIR:** Stuart Walker. **CAST:** Claude Rains, Douglass Montgomery, Heather Angel, David Manners. **1935**

MYSTERY OF PICASSO, THE ★★★★★ Pablo Picasso conceives, prepares, sketches, and paints fifteen canvasses—all of which were destroyed after the film was completed. A one-of-a-kind look at the artistic process, sensitively directed with exquisite music and photography (by Claude Renoir). In French with English subtitles. 85m. **DIR:** Henri-Georges Clouzot. **1956**

MYSTERY OF RAMPO, THE ★★★ Surreal, sometimes confusing tale of a mystery writer who suspects

that his latest novel has taken on a life all its own. When he reads an account of a woman who murdered her husband, the writer notices startling similarities to his latest manuscript. When his curiosity gets the best of him, he's swept into a world where reality collides with fantasy. In Japanese with English subtitles. Not rated; contains violence, nudity, and adult situations. 101m. **DIR:** Kazuyoshi Okuyama. **CAST:** Naoto Takenaka, Michiko Hada, Masahiro Motoki. **1994**

MYSTERY OF THE HOODED HORSEMEN ★★1/2 One of Tex Ritter's most popular oaters. A group of night riders in dark hoods and cloaks add just a touch of the supernatural to an otherwise standard story of land greed and cattle conniving. B&W; 60m. **DIR:** Ray Taylor. **CAST:** Tex Ritter, Iris Meredith, Charles King, Forrest Taylor, Earl Dwire, Lafe McKee, Hank Worden, Joe Girard. **1937**

MYSTERY OF THE MARIE CELESTE, THE (THE PHANTOM SHIP) ★★★ On December 4, 1872, the brigantine *Marie Celeste*, said to have been jinxed by death, fire, and collision since its launching in 1861, was found moving smoothly under half-sail, completely deserted, east of the Azores. No trace of the crew was ever found. To this day, what happened remains a true mystery of the sea. This account offers one explanation. B&W; 64m. **DIR:** Dension Clift. **CAST:** Bela Lugosi, Shirley Grey. **1937**

MYSTERY OF THE WAX MUSEUM ★★★ Dated but interesting tale of a crippled, crazed sculptor (the ever-dependable Lionel Atwill) who murders people and displays them in his museum as his own wax creations. Humorous subplot really curbs the attention, but stick with it. One of the earliest color films, it is often shown on television in black and white. 77m. **DIR:** Michael Curtiz. **CAST:** Lionel Atwill, Fay Wray, Glenda Farrell, Frank McHugh. **1933**

MYSTERY RANCH ★★★1/2 Crazed rancher holds his dead partner's daughter against her will in order to marry her, but a stalwart lawman takes it upon himself to save her and break the grip of fear the madman and his henchmen have on the territory. Spooky Western with mystery overtones is one of the finest of its kind. B&W; 65m. **DIR:** David Howard. **CAST:** George O'Brien, Cecilia Parker, Charles Middleton, Roy Stewart, Noble Johnson, Charles Stevens, Forrester Harvey. **1932**

MYSTERY SCIENCE THEATRE 3000: THE MOVIE ★★★ The popular series from cable-TV's Comedy Central (known as *MST3K* to fans) comes to the big screen with its premise intact (a human and two whimsical robots make fun of a cheesy sci-fi film). The object of their derision, 1955's *This Island Earth* (see our listing for details), is better than most of the cable series' targets, but there are still ample opportunities for the impudent wisecracks that made the series such irresistible fun. Rated PG-13 for some sexual humor. 87m. **DIR:** James Mallon. **CAST:** Michael J. Nelson, Trace Beaulieu. **1996 DVD**

MYSTERY SQUADRON ★★1/2 Mascot Studios continued its effort to be the best producer of serials with this fast-moving story of the sinister Mystery Squadron and its fanatical leader, the Black Ace. Bob Steele and "Big Boy" Williams trade in their chaps and horses for parachutes and planes as they do their utmost to apprehend the Black Ace, a deadly saboteur. B&W; 12 chapters. **DIR:** Colbert Clark, David Howard. **CAST:** Bob Steele, Guinn Williams, Lucille Brown, Jack Mulhall, Purnell Pratt. **1933**

MYSTERY TRAIN ★★★1/2 Offbeat character study that takes place in Memphis. The film centers around a couple of Japanese tourists with a penchant for Elvis nostalgia, an Italian woman who arrives to bury her murdered husband, and an unemployed Englishman who is breaking up with his American girlfriend. Some hilarious moments. Rated R for nudity and profanity. 110m. **DIR:** Jim Jarmusch. **CAST:** Youki Kaudoh, Masatoshi Nagase, Joe Strummer, Screamin' Jay Hawkins. **1990 DVD**

MYSTIC PIZZA ★★★1/2 This coming-of-age picture has all of the right ingredients of a main-course favorite. The antics involve three women—two sisters and a friend—who work at a pizza parlor in the resort town of Mystic, Connecticut. The superb young players and the dazzling New England scenery are a slice of heaven. Rated R for language. 102m. **DIR:** Donald Petrie. **CAST:** Annabeth Gish, Julia Roberts, Lili Taylor, Vincent D'Onofrio, William R. Moses, Adam Storke, Matt Damon. **1988 DVD**

MYTH OF FINGERPRINTS, THE ★★★ Thanksgiving reunion ticks like a time bomb as one of New England's covertly dysfunctional families works its way through a hellish gathering of the tribe. This frosty drama explores the cracks in blood and flesh relationships amid a patriarchal repression that allows old resentments to gnaw away the soul of a family. Rated R for sex, nudity, and language. 93m. **DIR:** Bart Freundlich. **CAST:** Roy Scheider, Blythe Danner, Noah Wyle, Julianne Moore, Michael Vartan, Laurel Holloman, Arija Bareikis, Hope Davis, James LeGros, Brian Kerwin. **1997 DVD**

N

NADINE ★★★ A cute caper comedy. Kim Basinger is a not-so-bright hairdresser who finds herself involved in murder and mayhem. She enlists the aid of her estranged husband (Jeff Bridges). Rip Torn gives a fine performance as the chief villain. Rated PG for light violence and profanity. 95m. **DIR:** Robert Benton. **CAST:** Jeff Bridges, Kim Basinger, Rip Torn, Gwen Verdon, Glenne Headly, Jerry Stiller. **1987**

NADJA ★★ The female offspring of a famous vampire stalks New York looking for fresh blood. Uncredited semiremake of *Dracula's Daughter* (1936) is amateurish, and its low budget is all too apparent. Scenes in "Pixelvision" (actually shot with a cheap toy camera) are more annoying than arresting. Rated R for violence. B&W; 92m. **DIR:** Michael Almereyda. **CAST:** Elina Lowensohn, Peter Fonda, Martin Donovan, Suzy Amis, Galaxy Craze. **1995**

NAILS ★★ Bad boy Dennis Hopper's *way*-over-the-top performance as a brutal cop barely saves Larry Ferguson's humdrum script from turkeydom. Rated R for nudity, profanity, and considerable violence. 96m. **DIR:**

John Flynn. **CAST:** Dennis Hopper, Anne Archer, Tomas Milian, Keith David, Cliff De Young. **1992**

NAIROBI AFFAIR ★★ Charlton Heston plays a safari photographer who is having an affair with his son's ex-wife (Maud Adams). Rated PG for violence. 95m. **DIR:** Marvin J. Chomsky. **CAST:** John Savage, Maud Adams, Charlton Heston. **1986**

NAIS ★★★ A hunchbacked laborer helps the girl he loves in her romance with the son of a rich landowner. Though he only wrote the screenplay (adapted from an Émile Zola story), this touching film bears the unmistakable stamp of Marcel Pagnol. In French with English subtitles. B&W; 95m. **DIR:** Raymond Leboursier. **CAST:** Fernandel, Jacqueline Pagnol. **1945**

NAKED ★★★★ A bleak, stark drama about Johnny, a homeless young man who roams the streets of London in search of sex and shelter, both of which he gets often. Numerous characters come and go, and most of them are emotionally manipulated or machinated by our young antihero. Disturbing and dazzling. Rated R for nudity and violence. 126m. **DIR:** Mike Leigh. **CAST:** David Thewlis, Lesley Sharp, Katrin Cartlidge, Greg Cruttwell. **1994**

NAKED AND THE DEAD, THE ★★★ This action-packed World War II film is based on Norman Mailer's famous book. Not nearly as good as the book, nevertheless the film is still quite powerful and exciting. Worth a watch. 131m. **DIR:** Raoul Walsh. **CAST:** Aldo Ray, Joey Bishop, Cliff Robertson, Raymond Massey. **1958**

NAKED CITY, THE ★★★★1/2 Detailed story of a police investigation into the murder of a model takes the backseat to the star of this movie—New York City. Pace-setting location filming helps this interesting crime-drama that was the basis for the superior and long-running TV series. Producer-narrator Mark Hellinger died shortly before the premier showing. B&W; 96m. **DIR:** Jules Dassin. **CAST:** Barry Fitzgerald, Howard Duff, Dorothy Hart, Don Taylor, Ted de Corsia, House Jameson, James Gregory, Paul Ford. **1948 DVD**

NAKED CIVIL SERVANT, THE ★★★1/2 Exceptional film based on the biography of the famous English homosexual Quentin Crisp. John Hurt's remarkable performance earned him a British Academy Award for his sensitive portrayal. Not rated, but recommended for mature audiences. 80m. **DIR:** Jack Gold. **CAST:** John Hurt, Patricia Hodge. **1975**

NAKED COUNTRY, THE ★★★ A rancher, his lonely wife, and an alcoholic policeman form a deadly triangle in Australia's outback. Set in 1955, this beautifully filmed story is rooted in soap opera, but becomes a violent struggle with the aborigines that resonates with remorse. Rated R for nudity, profanity, and violence. 90m. **DIR:** Tim Burstall. **CAST:** John Stanton, Rebecca Gilling. **1992**

NAKED EDGE, THE ★★★ Familiar, slow-moving story of a wife who suspects her husband is a murderer. Lots of red herrings. Gary Cooper's last film. B&W; 97m. **DIR:** Michael Anderson. **CAST:** Gary Cooper, Deborah Kerr, Eric Portman, Diane Cilento, Hermione Gingold, Peter Cushing, Michael Wilding. **1961**

NAKED FACE, THE ★★★ A psychiatrist (Roger Moore) finds himself the target of murder in this enjoyable suspense film. The police think he's the killer, as the first attempt on his life results in the death of a patient who had borrowed his raincoat. Rated R for violence and profanity. 98m. **DIR:** Bryan Forbes. **CAST:** Roger Moore, Rod Steiger, Elliott Gould, Art Carney, Anne Archer. **1984**

NAKED GUN, THE ★★★★ Fans of the short-lived television series *Police Squad!* will love this full-length adventure featuring Leslie Nielsen's stiff-lipped Frank Drebin, the toughest—and clumsiest—cop in the universe. This parody of 1960s television cop shows is riddled with countless sight gags, outrageous puns, and over-the-top characterizations. Rated PG-13 for language and mild sexual coarseness. 85m. **DIR:** David Zucker. **CAST:** Leslie Nielsen, George Kennedy, Priscilla Presley, Ricardo Montalban, O. J. Simpson, Nancy Marchand. **1988 DVD**

NAKED GUN 2 1/2, THE ★★★1/2 The loony *Police Squad* gang is back in this wacky sequel to the smash-hit police parody. In this saga, the amazingly brain-dead Lt. Frank Drebin (Leslie Nielsen) gets involved in efforts to bust a criminal hatching a nefarious antiecology crime. The film lacks the zip of the original, but it's still a nutty romp. Rated PG-13 for profanity and adult humor. 88m. **DIR:** David Zucker. **CAST:** Leslie Nielsen, Priscilla Presley, Robert Goulet, George Kennedy, O. J. Simpson. **1991 DVD**

NAKED GUN 33 1/3, THE—THE FINAL INSULT ★★1/2 TV's *Police Squad!* originators make their third regurgitation of comic chaos as klutzy cop Lt. Frank Drebin comes out of brief retirement to nab a mad bomber. This film climaxes with Drebin being mistaken for Phil Donahue as he brings an Oscars telecast to its knees. Cameo surprises abound, but this romp is not as funny as its predecessors. Rated PG-13 for suggested sex and language. 83m. **DIR:** Peter Segal. **CAST:** Leslie Nielsen, Priscilla Presley, Fred Ward, George Kennedy, O. J. Simpson. **1994 DVD**

NAKED HEART, THE ★★ After five years in a convent, a young woman returns to her home in the frozen Canadian north and tries to decide which of her three suitors to marry. Filmed in Europe, this slow, somewhat depressing tale has little going for it. B&W; 96m. **DIR:** Marc Allegret. **CAST:** Michèle Morgan, Kieron Moore, Françoise Rosay. **1950**

NAKED IN NEW YORK ★★★1/2 An eclectic supporting cast and a breezy screenplay lend support to this romantic comedy about a pair of college sweethearts attempting to make the best of a long-distance relationship. Rated R for adult situations and language. 89m. **DIR:** Dan Algrant. **CAST:** Eric Stoltz, Mary-Louise Parker, Ralph Macchio, Jill Clayburgh, Kathleen Turner, Whoopi Goldberg. **1994**

NAKED IN THE SUN ★★1/2 Osceola (James Craig), war chief of the Seminole Indians, must battle unscrupulous whites, the United States government, and his own tribe to live in dignity. This is well-acted and effective in evoking audience sympathy. 79m. **DIR:** R. John Hugh. **CAST:** James Craig, Barton MacLane, Lita Milan, Tony Hunter. **1957**

NAKED JUNGLE, THE ★★ In this studio soap opera made from the short story *Leninnen Versus the Ants*, Charlton Heston is slightly out of place but still powerful as the South American plantation owner. Eleanor Parker is ridiculous as his new wife, and a young, thin William Conrad is along for the ride. Not rated, contains

slight violence. 95m. **DIR:** Byron Haskin. **CAST:** Charlton Heston, Eleanor Parker, Abraham Sofaer, William Conrad, Romo Vincent, Douglas Fowley. **1953**

NAKED KISS, THE ★★★1/2 An ex-hooker makes a break and winds up in a small town only to discover more evil and trouble. Constance Towers as the girl who begins to find herself is a standout; the cast includes former veteran star Patsy Kelly and the silent screen's *Peter Pan*, Betty Bronson. Gritty *film noir* mystery. B&W; 90m. **DIR:** Samuel Fuller. **CAST:** Constance Towers, Anthony Eisley, Michael Dante, Virginia Grey, Patsy Kelly, Betty Bronson. **1965 DVD**

NAKED LUNCH ★★★ A nightmare brought to life with sometimes nauseating intensity, director David Cronenberg's adaptation of William S. Burroughs's novel weds incidents from the author's life into the fantastical, drug-induced hallucinations that comprised the book. Peter Weller is the exterminator who, through the encouragement of wife Judy Davis, becomes addicted to bug powder and ends up in Interzone. Utterly bizarre and not for all tastes. Rated R for profanity, violence, and nudity. 115m. **DIR:** David Cronenberg. **CAST:** Peter Weller, Judy Davis, Ian Holm, Julian Sands, Roy Scheider. **1992**

NAKED MAJA, THE ★★ Dull telling of the eighteenth-century romance between artist Francisco Goya and the duchess of Alba which led to their fall from grace with the Spanish court and the Catholic Church. 111m. **DIR:** Henry Koster. **CAST:** Ava Gardner, Anthony Franciosa, Amadeo Nazzari, Gino Cervi. **1958**

NAKED MAN, THE ★★★ Director J. Todd Anderson throws everything but the kitchen sink into this madcap collection of bizarre characters and even more bizarre circumstances. Michael Rapaport is hysterically funny as a young chiropractor who moonlights as a professional wrestler. Cowriter Ethan Coen helps blend outrageous comedy with unforgettable characters into a frenzied farce. Direct-to-video. Rated R for language, violence, and adult situations. 98m. **DIR:** J. Todd Anderson. **CAST:** Michael Rapaport, Michael Jeter, Rachael Leigh Cook, Joe Grifasi. **1998**

NAKED OBSESSION ★★ When a councilman samples his city's red-light district, he's framed for murder. This sexually explicit film plays faintly as a dark comic buddy picture. Not rated, but with considerable nudity and profanity. 85m. **DIR:** Dan Golden. **CAST:** William Katt, Maria Ford, Rick Dean, Roger Craig, Elena Sahagun. **1990**

NAKED PREY, THE ★★★★ An African safari takes a disastrous turn and Cornel Wilde winds up running naked and unarmed through the searing jungle as a large band of native warriors keeps on his heels, determined to finish him off. This is an amazingly intense adventure of man versus man and man versus nature. Wilde does a remarkable job, both as star and director. 94m. **DIR:** Cornel Wilde. **CAST:** Cornel Wilde, Gert Van Den Bergh, Ken Gampu. **1966**

NAKED SOULS ★★1/2 Memory researcher Brian Krause would rather perfect a means to transfer consciousness than pay attention to sexy girlfriend Pamela Anderson Lee—silly boy!—and winds up working with sinister millionaire David Warner. Frank Dietz's script covers familiar genre territory, and not all that well. Rated R for nudity, violence, profanity, and simulated sex. 85m. **DIR:** Lyndon Chubbuck. **CAST:** Brian Krause, Pamela Anderson Lee, David Warner, Clayton Rohner, Dean Stockwell. **1995**

NAKED SPUR, THE ★★★★1/2 Superb Western finds bounty hunter James Stewart chasing bad guy Robert Ryan through the Rockies. Once captured, Ryan attempts to cause trouble between Stewart and his sidekicks. 91m. **DIR:** Anthony Mann. **CAST:** James Stewart, Janet Leigh, Robert Ryan, Ralph Meeker, Millard Mitchell. **1953**

NAKED TANGO ★★★ In the 1920s, a young woman comes to Buenos Aires as a mail-order bride, only to find that she has been sold into white slavery by her intended husband. The film is an overheated melodrama of male-domination fantasies, but dark, moody photography and strong acting make it engrossing and hard to dismiss. Rated R for violence and sexual situations. 90m. **DIR:** Leonard Schrader. **CAST:** Vincent D'Onofrio, Mathilda May, Esai Morales, Fernando Rey, Josh Mostel. **1991**

NAKED TRUTH (YOUR PAST IS SHOWING) ★★1/2 This oddball British comedy involves a group of loonies who are brought together to get rid of the editor of a smutty magazine. Peter Sellers is good as a disgusting television celebrity and Terry-Thomas is very effective as a politician. 92m. **DIR:** Mario Zampi. **CAST:** Terry-Thomas, Dennis Price, Peter Sellers, Shirley Eaton. **1957 DVD**

NAKED VENUS ★★ Famed cult director Edgar G. Ulmer's last film is a slow-moving drama about an American artist whose marriage to a nudist-model is torn apart by his wealthy mother. The film explores the barriers of prejudice concerning nudist colonies. Not rated; contains nudity. B&W; 80m. **DIR:** Edgar G. Ulmer. **CAST:** Patricia Conelle. **1958**

NAKED YOUTH ★★ A good kid gets involved with a bad apple and together they wind up in prison—and then break out. It's hardly the camp classic the distributors would have you believe. B&W; 80m. **DIR:** John Schreyer. **CAST:** Robert Hutton, John Goddard, Carol Ohmart. **1961**

NAME OF THE ROSE, THE ★★★ In this passable screen adaptation of Umberto Eco's bestseller, Sean Connery stars as a monkish Sherlock Holmes trying to solve a series of murders in a fourteenth-century monastery. Connery is fun to watch, but the plot is rather feeble. Rated R for nudity, simulated sex, and violence. 118m. **DIR:** Jean-Jacques Annaud. **CAST:** Sean Connery, F. Murray Abraham, Christian Slater, Elya Baskin, Feodor Chaliapin, William Hickey, Michel Lonsdale, Ron Perlman. **1986**

NAMU, THE KILLER WHALE ★★★1/2 A well-made family film that isn't as sinister as its title. It's based on the true story of a whale in a public aquarium. Namu was so friendly and intelligent it was set free. The 1993 movie, *Free Willy*, was inspired by this film. 86m. **DIR:** Laslo Benedek. **CAST:** Robert Lansing, Lee Meriwether, John Anderson, Richard Erdman, Robin Mattson. **1966**

NANA ★★1/2 Adaptation of Émile Zola's oft-filmed story about the girl who will do anything to get out of the slums. This handsomely produced vehicle for Martine Carol (wife of director Christian-Jacque) is otherwise undistinguished. In French with English subtitles.

120m. **DIR:** Christian-Jaque. **CAST:** Martine Carol, Charles Boyer. **1955**

NANCY GOES TO RIO ★★★ Nancy (Jane Powell) wins the leading role in a musical play that her mother (Ann Sothern) has her eye on. Both old standards and original songs fill in the slight plot. 99m. **DIR:** Robert Z. Leonard. **CAST:** Ann Sothern, Jane Powell, Louis Calhern, Barry Sullivan, Carmen Miranda. **1950**

NANNY, THE ★★★ A strong performance in the title role by Bette Davis marks this story of a jealous, guilt-ridden nursemaid pitted against a mentally disturbed 10-year-old in a classic battle of wills ending in attempted murder. 93m. **DIR:** Seth Holt. **CAST:** Bette Davis, Wendy Craig, Jill Bennett, William Dix, Maurice Denham. **1965**

NANOOK OF THE NORTH ★★★★ Crude and primitive as the conditions under which it was made, this direct study of Eskimo life set the standard for and has remained the most famous of the early documentary films. A milestone in stark realism; the walrus hunt sequence is especially effective. B&W; 55m. **DIR:** Robert Flaherty. **1922 DVD**

NAPOLEON (1927) ★★★★★ Over a half century after its debut this film remains a visual wonder, encompassing a number of filmmaking techniques, some of which still seem revolutionary. The complete film—as pieced together by British film historian Kevin Brownlow over a period of twenty years—is one motion picture event no lover of the art form will want to miss even on the small screen without the full effect of its spectacular three-screen climax. B&W; 235m. **DIR:** Abel Gance. **CAST:** Albert Dieudonné, Antonin Artaud. **1927**

NAPOLEON (1955) 🦃 Boring. 115m. **DIR:** Sacha Guitry. **CAST:** Orson Welles, Maria Schell, Yves Montand, Erich Von Stroheim. **1955 DVD**

NAPOLEON (1995) ★★★ Family film starring an adorable golden retriever puppy that gets into all sorts of predicaments. When Muffin accidentally falls into a hot air balloon, he is whisked off to the forest, where he must make his way back home. All ages will enjoy this all-animal adventure. Rated G. 81m. **DIR:** Mario Andreacchio. **1995 DVD**

NAPOLEON AND JOSEPHINE: A LOVE STORY 🦃 TV miniseries. Armand Assante plays Napoleon from his pregeneral days until his exile. Jacqueline Bisset is his loving Josephine. 300m. **DIR:** Richard T. Heffron. **CAST:** Jacqueline Bisset, Armand Assante, Anthony Perkins, Stephanie Beacham. **1987**

NAPOLEON AND SAMANTHA ★★★1/2 This Disney film features Johnny Whitaker as Napoleon, an orphan who decides to hide his grandpa's body when the old man dies and care for their pet lion, Major. When a college student/goat herder named Danny (Michael Douglas) helps bury Grandpa, Napoleon decides to follow him to his flock. Samantha (Jodie Foster) joins him and the lion as they face the dangers of a fierce mountain lion and a bear. Rated G. 91m. **DIR:** Bernard McEveety. **CAST:** Johnny Whitaker, Jodie Foster, Michael Douglas, Will Geer, Arch Johnson, Henry Jones. **1972 DVD**

NARROW MARGIN, THE (1952) ★★★1/2 Tight crime entry has tough cop Charles McGraw assigned to transport the widow of a gangster to trial despite threats of hit men. Action takes place on a speeding train as McGraw and the hit men play a deadly cat-and-mouse game. Unrelenting suspense makes this one of the better films made in the Fifties. B&W; 70m. **DIR:** Richard Fleischer. **CAST:** Charles McGraw, Marie Windsor, Jacqueline White, Queenie Leonard. **1952**

NARROW MARGIN (1990) ★★★ An update of the 1952 thriller, this absorbing drama's lapses in logic are compensated for by two gripping performances by Gene Hackman and Anne Archer. She's a frightened murder witness hiding out in the wilderness; he's the Los Angeles deputy district attorney determined to bring her back. Great fun, until its rather abrupt conclusion. Rated R for language and violence. 97m. **DIR:** Peter Hyams. **CAST:** Gene Hackman, Anne Archer, James B. Sikking, M. Emmet Walsh. **1990 DVD**

NARROW TRAIL, THE ★★★ "Better a painted pony than a painted woman" was the slogan selling this above-average Western about a cowboy's love for his horse. One of early-Western star William S. Hart's many pictures, this one was something of a paean to his great horse, Fritz. Like all Hart films, this one is marked by his scrupulous attention to authenticity of setting, scenery, and costume. Silent. B&W; 56m. **DIR:** Lambert Hillyer. **CAST:** William S. Hart. **1917**

NASHVILLE ★★★★★ Robert Altman's classic study of American culture is, on the surface, a look into the country-western music business. But underneath, Altman has many things to say about all of us. Great ensemble acting by Keith Carradine, Lily Tomlin, Ned Beatty, and Henry Gibson, to name just a few, makes this one of the great films of the 1970s. Rated R for language and violence. 159m. **DIR:** Robert Altman. **CAST:** Keith Carradine, Lily Tomlin, Ned Beatty, Henry Gibson, Karen Black, Ronee Blakley. **1975**

NASTY GIRL, THE ★★★★★ This Oscar-nominated film is the most highly original movie to come out of Germany since the glory days of Fassbinder and Herzog. And the key to its freshness is its unique blend of charming, upbeat comedy with a serious topic: the scars and guilt from the Nazi era that still run deep in modern German life. In German with English subtitles. Not rated. 96m. **DIR:** Michael Verhoeven. **CAST:** Lena Stolze. **1990**

NASTY HABITS ★★ *Nasty Habits* promises much more than it delivers. As a satire of the Watergate conspiracy, placed in a convent, it relies too heavily on the true incident for its punch. Rated PG, with some profanity. 96m. **DIR:** Michael Lindsay-Hogg. **CAST:** Glenda Jackson, Sandy Dennis, Susan Penhaligon, Edith Evans, Melina Mercouri. **1977**

NASTY HERO ★★ An ex-con comes to Miami to get revenge on the hoods who sent him to prison. Car chases substitute for solid storytelling, but some of the actors are quite good. Rated PG-13. 79m. **DIR:** Nick Barwood. **CAST:** Scott Feraco, Robert Sedgwick, Raymond Serra. **1987**

NASTY RABBIT ★★ Stilted *Blazing Saddles*–type parody is a curiosity piece, featuring Mexican bandits, Japanese soldiers, Nazi troopers, Indians, cowboys, and circus freaks, all rolled into one long-winded mess. 85m. **DIR:** James Landis. **CAST:** Arch Hall Jr., Richard Kiel. **1964**

NATE AND HAYES ★★★ Tommy Lee Jones as a good pirate, Michael O'Keefe as his missionary accomplice,

and Max Phipps as their cutthroat nemesis make this a jolly movie. Set in the South Seas of the late nineteenth century, it's unpretentious, old-fashioned movie fun. Rated PG for violence. 100m. **DIR:** Ferdinand Fairfax. **CAST:** Tommy Lee Jones, Michael O'Keefe, Max Phipps. **1983**

NATIONAL LAMPOON'S ATTACK OF THE 5' 2" WOMEN ★★ A made-for-cable double feature starring comic Julie Brown in parodies of Tonya Harding and Lorena Bobbitt. Despite an impressive supporting cast, both minifeatures are crude, mean-spirited, and only rarely funny. Brown is often annoying enough to make you reach for the stop button on the nearest remote control. Rated R for profanity and sexual situations. 83m. **DIR:** Richard Wenk. **CAST:** Julie Brown, Sam McMurray, Adam Storke, Priscilla Barnes. **1994**

NATIONAL LAMPOON'S CHRISTMAS VACATION ★★★ Chevy Chase glides charmingly through this frantic farce. This sequel to the two Lampoon *Vacation* flicks has the Griswold family staying home for the holidays and being invaded by bickering relatives. Randy Quaid excels as the ultimate slob. Rated PG-13 for scatological humor and profanity. 97m. **DIR:** Jeremiah S. Chechik. **CAST:** Chevy Chase, Beverly D'Angelo, Randy Quaid, Diane Ladd, John Randolph, E. G. Marshall, Juliette Lewis. **1989 DVD**

NATIONAL LAMPOON'S CLASS OF '86 ★★★ You've got to be in a *National Lampoon* frame of mind to enjoy this comedy revue, which means embracing the off-the-wall humor for which the magazine is noted. Though unrated, it's strictly adult fare. 86m. **DIR:** Jerry Adler. **CAST:** Rodger Bumpass, Veanne Cox, Annie Golden, Tommy Koenig, John Michael Higgins, Brian O'Connor. **1986**

NATIONAL LAMPOON'S CLASS REUNION The graduating class of 1972 returns to wreak havoc on its alma mater. Rated R for nudity. 84m. **DIR:** Michael Miller. **CAST:** Gerrit Graham, Stephen Furst, Zane Buzby, Michael Lerner. **1982 DVD**

NATIONAL LAMPOON'S EUROPEAN VACATION The sappy sequel to *Vacation*. Rated PG-13 for profanity. 95m. **DIR:** Amy Heckerling. **CAST:** Chevy Chase, Beverly D'Angelo, Dana Hill, Jason Lively, Eric Idle, Victor Lanoux, John Astin. **1985 DVD**

NATIONAL LAMPOON'S FAVORITE DEADLY SINS ★★★ Lust, greed, and anger are the focus of this compilation film's three vignettes. Denis Leary's fixation on a gorgeous neighbor quickly becomes tiresome, while Andrew Clay's rendition of chronic rage is little more than a blackout sketch. But Joe Mantegna scores as a venal TV miniseries producer. Rated R for profanity, nudity, violence, and simulated sex. 100m. **DIR:** David Jablin, Denis Leary. **CAST:** Denis Leary, Annabella Sciorra, Andrew Clay, Joe Mantegna, Cassidy Rae, Brian Keith, William Ragsdale, Gerrit Graham. **1995**

NATIONAL LAMPOON'S GOLF PUNKS ★★ Well-intentioned slob comedy stars Tom Arnold as a former golf pro leading a group of ragtag young players in a tournament against the snobs. Some laughs, but film suffers from a serious case of déjà vu. Rated PG for language. 92m. **DIR:** Harvey Frost. **CAST:** Tom Arnold, James Kirk, Rene Tardif, Gregory Thirloway. **1998 DVD**

NATIONAL LAMPOON'S LAST RESORT Made-for-video lame duck take on the old, "Hey gang, let's save the summer camp" premise. Teen has-beens Corey Haim and Corey Feldman save the day. Who will save us? Rated PG-13 for language and sexual situations. 91m. **DIR:** Rafal Zielinski. **CAST:** Corey Feldman, Corey Haim, Geoffrey Lewis, Robert Mandan. **1994 DVD**

NATIONAL LAMPOON'S LOADED WEAPON 1 It's amazing that an action-comedy parody under the *National Lampoon* banner could be so lame and deadly dull, but this cop-action satire is a misfired groanfest. Rated PG-13 for violence and language. 97m. **DIR:** Gene Quintano. **CAST:** Emilio Estevez, Samuel L. Jackson, Jon Lovitz, Tim Curry, William Shatner, Whoopi Goldberg, Bruce Willis, Charlie Sheen, Kathy Ireland. **1993**

NATIONAL LAMPOON'S SENIOR TRIP High school's senior slackers write a letter to the U.S. president about public education and are manipulated to become reform-bill poster kids in this offensive tripe. Rated R for language, suggested sex, and nudity. 93m. **DIR:** Kelly Makin. **CAST:** Rob Moore, Jeremy Renner, Valerie Mahaffey, Fiona Loewi, Matt Frewer, Tommy Chong. **1995**

NATIONAL LAMPOON'S VACATION ★★★ Clark Griswold (Chevy Chase) goes on a disastrous vacation with his wife, Ellen (Beverly D'Angelo), and kids, Rusty (Anthony Michael Hall) and Audrey (Dana Barron). Rated R for nudity and profanity. 98m. **DIR:** Harold Ramis. **CAST:** Chevy Chase, Beverly D'Angelo, Anthony Michael Hall, Dana Barron, Christie Brinkley, John Candy. **1983 DVD**

NATIONAL VELVET ★★★★ This heartwarming tale of two youngsters determined to train a beloved horse to win the famed Grand National Race is good for the whole family, especially little girls who love horses and sentimentalists who fondly recall Elizabeth Taylor when she was young, innocent, and adorable. Have Kleenex on hand. 125m. **DIR:** Clarence Brown. **CAST:** Mickey Rooney, Elizabeth Taylor, Donald Crisp, Anne Revere, Angela Lansbury, Reginald Owen. **1944 DVD**

NATIVE AMERICANS, THE ★★★★★ Informative and entertaining, this fast-moving, TBS production is told exclusively from the viewpoint of American Indians. It is kept lively and relevant by the exploration of oral histories, myths, art, and the spirituality of the past. Rich in detail and emotions, it delves into painful memories and makes intriguing, intelligent analogies. Each of the six episodes rates an A+ for high production values and disarming honesty. Not rated. 52m. **DIR:** John Borden, Phil Lucas, George Burdeau. **1994**

NATIVE SON (1950) ★★1/2 Seeing author Richard Wright playing his fictional character, Bigger Thomas, is the chief interest of this low-budget adaptation of his groundbreaking novel. B&W; 91m. **DIR:** Pierre Chenal. **CAST:** Richard Wright, Jean Wallace, Gloria Madison. **1950**

NATIVE SON (1986) ★★1/2 In this screen adaptation of Richard Wright's 1940 novel, a 19-year-old black youth takes a job as a chauffeur to a wealthy white couple. His hopes for a brighter future are shattered when a tragic accident leads to the death of their daughter and he is accused of murder. Rated R for nudity, suggested sex, violence, and gore. 101m. **DIR:** Jerrold Freedman. **CAST:** Victor Love, Geraldine Page, Elizabeth McGovern, Matt Dillon, Oprah Winfrey, Akosua Busia, Carroll

Baker, Art Evans, David Rasche, Lane Smith, John McMartin. **1986**

NATIVITY, THE ★★ Nicely filmed but dramatically unimpressive TV movie about Joseph's (John Shea) wooing of Mary (Madeline Stowe). Leo McKern is the mad King Herod. Not one of the top Biblical epics by a long shot. 97m. **DIR:** Bernard Kowalski. **CAST:** John Shea, Madeleine Stowe, Jane Wyatt, Paul Stewart, Leo McKern, John Rhys-Davies, Kate O'Mara. **1978**

NATURAL, THE ★★★★ A thoroughly rewarding, old-fashioned screen entertainment, this adaptation of Bernard Malamud's novel about an unusually gifted baseball player is a must-see. With its brilliant all-star cast, superb story, unforgettable characters, sumptuous cinematography, and sure-handed direction, this film recalls the Golden Age of Hollywood at its best. Rated PG for brief violence. 134m. **DIR:** Barry Levinson. **CAST:** Robert Redford, Robert Duvall, Glenn Close, Kim Basinger, Wilford Brimley, Richard Farnsworth, Robert Prosky, Joe Don Baker. **1984**

NATURAL BORN KILLERS 🦃 Writer-director Oliver Stone's bombastic study of mass murder is a self-indulgent, migraine-inducing mess that shrilly indicts the incestuous, bread-and-circus relationship between violence and media celebrity as if it were something new. Less a coherent film and more a masturbatory, MTV-style assault on the senses. Rated R for graphic violence, gore, profanity, gruesome images, and deviant sexuality. 120m. **DIR:** Oliver Stone. **CAST:** Woody Harrelson, Juliette Lewis, Robert Downey Jr., Tommy Lee Jones, Rodney Dangerfield. **1994 DVD**

NATURAL CAUSES ★★ When a woman journeys to Thailand to visit her mother, she finds herself in the midst of a violent political conspiracy that only she has the power to stop. Dull thriller offers just enough story to keep dedicated viewers awake but will put most everyone else fast asleep. Rated PG-13 for violence and profanity. 90m. **DIR:** James Becket. **CAST:** Linda Purl, Cary-Hiroyuki Tagawa, Will Patton, Tim Thomerson, Ali MacGraw. **1993**

NATURAL ENEMIES ★★★★ Excellent study of domestic murder. Hal Holbrook plays a successful magazine editor who murders his wife and three children. Louise Fletcher is great as Holbrook's emotionally unstable wife. Depressing, to be certain, but worth watching. Rated R for violence, profanity, sex, nudity, and adult subject matter. 100m. **DIR:** Jeff Kanew. **CAST:** Hal Holbrook, Louise Fletcher, Viveca Lindfors, José Ferrer, Patricia Elliott. **1979**

NATURAL ENEMY ★★1/2 Donald Sutherland and William McNamara are fine as the stockbroker and the student intent on ruining his business in this made-for-cable effort. Even though the film travels down a well-worn path, the stars keep you interested, especially McNamara once again playing a psycho. Not rated; contains violence. 88m. **DIR:** Douglas Jackson. **CAST:** Donald Sutherland, William McNamara, Lesley Ann Warren, Joe Pantoliano, Tia Carrere. **1997**

NATURE OF THE BEAST ★★ Two men, a businessman and a drifter, hook up for one psychotic road trip. One is probably the thief who lifted a cool mil from the mob, the other is probably a serial killer who favors hatchets. But which man is the killer? Who cares? Rated R for profanity, violence, sexual situations, brief nudity, drug use, and dismemberment. 91m. **DIR:** Victor Salva. **CAST:** Eric Roberts, Lance Henriksen, Brian James. **1995**

NAUGHTY MARIETTA ★★★ This warm, vibrant rehash of Victor Herbert's tuneful 1910 operetta established leads Jeanette MacDonald and Nelson Eddy as the screen's peerless singing duo. The plot's next to nothing—a French princess flees to America and falls in love with an Indian scout—but the music is stirring, charming, and corny. B&W; 106m. **DIR:** W. S. Van Dyke. **CAST:** Jeanette MacDonald, Nelson Eddy, Frank Morgan, Douglass Dumbrille, Elsa Lanchester, Akim Tamiroff. **1935**

NAUGHTY NINETIES, THE ★★ Suitably attired for the period, the always eager Bud and Lou find themselves hip-deep in Mississippi riverboat gamblers. The pair's usual ripostes, including "Who's on First," prevail. The finale is tried-and-true slapstick. B&W; 76m. **DIR:** Jean Yarbrough. **CAST:** Bud Abbott, Lou Costello, Joe Sawyer, Alan Curtis, Rita Johnson, Lois Collier. **1945**

NAVAJO BLUES 🦃 Everyone looks bored in this listless thriller about a Las Vegas cop hiding from the mob on a Navajo reservation. Rated R for violence, sexual situations, and profanity. 87m. **DIR:** Joey Travolta. **CAST:** Steven Bauer, Charlotte Lewis, Irene Bedard. **1997**

NAVIGATOR, THE (1924) ★★★★1/2 Buster Keaton used a condemned ocean liner as the set for this feature where he plays a millionaire stuck on an abandoned ship with only one other person: the woman who just rejected his proposal of marriage. There are many memorable gags, but our favorite features Buster taking a walk on the ocean floor. This tape also contains two Keaton shorts, *The Boat* and *The Love Nest*. B&W; 110m. **DIR:** Donald Crisp, Buster Keaton. **CAST:** Buster Keaton, Kathryn McGuire. **1924 DVD**

NAVIGATOR: A MEDIEVAL ODYSSEY, THE ★★★★1/2 A visionary film from New Zealand that involves a medieval quest through time. The film opens in Cumbria in 1348, in the midst of the terrifying Black Plague. A village of miners tries to appease what they view as a vengeful God by vowing to travel a great distance to fulfill a child's vision. The adventurers travel through the center of the Earth—and surface in a modern-day New Zealand town. Astonishingly original. In B&W and color. 91m. **DIR:** Vincent Ward. **CAST:** Bruce Lyons, Chris Haywood. **1989**

NAVY BLUE AND GOLD ★★★ Familiar but entertaining story of three Annapolis middies learning (by way of the annual Army-Navy football game) the meaning of esprit de corps. Billie Burke is a particular delight. B&W; 94m. **DIR:** Sam Wood. **CAST:** Robert Young, James Stewart, Lionel Barrymore, Florence Rice, Billie Burke, Tom Brown, Samuel S. Hinds, Paul Kelly, Frank Albertson, Minor Watson. **1937**

NAVY SEALS ★★ When Middle Eastern terrorists acquire some American stinger missiles, it's up to the rough-and-ready Navy SEALS (Sea, Air and Land) to blow them up. Director Lewis Teague cannot overcome the tedium of the predictable screenplay, although the action scenes are robust. Rated R for violence and profanity. 118m. **DIR:** Lewis Teague. **CAST:** Charlie Sheen, Michael Biehn, Joanne Whalley, Rick Rossovich. **1990 DVD**

NAVY VS. THE NIGHT MONSTERS, THE 🦃 Homicidal plants scheme to take over the world. 90m. **DIR:**

Michael Hoey. **CAST:** Mamie Van Doren, Anthony Eisley, Pamela Mason, Bobby Van. **1966**

NAZARIN ★★★★★ A priest is cast out of his church for giving shelter to a prostitute. A remarkable film by Luis Buñuel that presents a clever variation of the Don Quixote theme, applied to religion and hypocrisy. This surrealistic comedy won the Grand Prize at the Cannes Film Festival. In Spanish with English subtitles. B&W; 92m. **DIR:** Luis Buñuel. **CAST:** Francisco Rabal. **1958**

NEA (A YOUNG EMMANUELLE) ★★★ In this French sex comedy, a young girl, Sybille Ashby (Ann Zacharias), stifled by the wealth of her parents, turns to anonymously writing erotic literature via firsthand experience. A relatively successful and entertaining film of its kind, it has sex and adult themes. In French with English subtitles. Rated R. 103m. **DIR:** Nelly Kaplan. **CAST:** Sami Frey, Ann Zacharias, Micheline Presle. **1978**

NEANDERTHAL MAN, THE 🦃 Serum from a prehistoric fish turns a scientist into the titular beastie. B&W; 77m. **DIR:** E. A. Dupont. **CAST:** Robert Shayne, Richard Crane, Doris Merrick, Robert Long. **1953**

NEAR DARK ★★★1/2 A stylish story of nomadic vampires. A girl takes a fancy to a young stud and turns him into a vampire, forcing him to join the macabre family. His problem is that he can't bring himself to make his first kill. It's the character development and acting that make this movie worthwhile. Rated R for violence and language. 95m. **DIR:** Kathryn Bigelow. **CAST:** Adrian Pasdar, Jenny Wright, Tim Thomerson, Jenette Goldstein, Lance Henriksen, Bill Paxton. **1987**

NEAR MISSES ★★1/2 Executive Judge Reinhold balances two wives and a secretary-girlfriend on the side, but his troubles really begin when he asks fellow coworker Casey Siemaszko to impersonate him when his yearly army reserve duty comes up. Rated PG-13 for profanity. 92m. **DIR:** Baz Taylor. **CAST:** Judge Reinhold, Casey Siemaszko, Rebecca Pauley, Cecile Paoli. **1990**

'NEATH ARIZONA SKIES ★★1/2 Formula B Western has John Wayne as the protector of the heir to rich oil lands, a little Indian girl. Of course, the baddies try to kidnap her and the Duke rides to the rescue. Low-budget and predictable. B&W; 57m. **DIR:** Henry Frazer. **CAST:** John Wayne, Sheila Terry, Yakima Canutt, George "Gabby" Hayes. **1934**

NECESSARY PARTIES ★★★★ Clever film about a teenager who refuses to accept his parents' divorce. With the help of an idealistic part-time lawyer/full-time auto mechanic, the boy sues his folks as an affected third party. This sensitive presentation from TV's *Wonderworks* offers occasional chuckles. 109m. **DIR:** Gwen Arner. **CAST:** Alan Arkin, Mark Paul Gosselaar, Barbara Dana, Donald Moffat, Adam Arkin, Julie Hagerty. **1988**

NECESSARY ROUGHNESS ★★★★ While the premise of this football comedy is familiar—a group of losers banding together against almost impossible odds—the execution seems fresh. Not only is this a very funny comedy, it has something to say about the state of college athletics. Rated PG-13 for profanity. 104m. **DIR:** Stan Dragoti. **CAST:** Scott Bakula, Robert Loggia, Harley Jane Kozak, Sinbad, Hector Elizondo, Jason Bateman, Kathy Ireland, Larry Miller. **1991**

NECROMANCER ★★ A sorceress possesses a young woman, using her to kill men and steal their life forces. Violence and bloodshed abound unfortunately, but not much suspense. Rated R for graphic violence and nudity. 88m. **DIR:** Dusty Nelson. **CAST:** Elizabeth Cayton, Russ Tamblyn. **1988**

NEEDFUL THINGS ★★★★ In Castle Rock, Maine, a mysterious stranger opens a curio shop that seems to have something for everyone. Just one problem: The owner is actually the devil, and he only trades for souls. He turns the locals against each other, setting off a chain reaction of murder and mayhem that culminates in an explosive finale between evil and the law. Viciously tongue-in-cheek. Rated R for strong violence and adult language. 113m. **DIR:** Fraser Heston. **CAST:** Max von Sydow, Ed Harris, Bonnie Bedelia, J. T. Walsh, Amanda Plummer. **1993 DVD**

NEGATIVES ★★★ Quirky satire of a married couple (Glenda Jackson and Peter McEnery) whose fantasy world of playacting and charades is interrupted by the intrusive overtures of a third person. Peter Medak's direction is sharp, and the fantasy sequences are pungently imaginative. 99m. **DIR:** Peter Medak. **CAST:** Glenda Jackson, Peter McEnery. **1968**

NEGOTIATOR, THE ★★★★ Gripping thriller about a police hostage negotiator who takes a few hostages himself after being framed for killing his partner. The script, though taut, has its logic lapses. But Samuel L. Jackson, as the distraught but cagey suspect, and Kevin Spacey, as the second negotiator brought in to finesse the crisis, play it for all it's worth, and because of them there's never a down moment. Rated R for violence and language. 135m. **DIR:** F. Gary Gray. **CAST:** Samuel L. Jackson, Kevin Spacey, Ron Rifkin, John Spencer, J. T. Walsh. **1998 DVD**

NEIGHBOR, THE ★★★ Earnest performances give Kurt Wimmer's predictable script far more power than it deserves. Linda Kozlowski is properly sympathetic as a pregnant woman who fears next-door neighbor Rod Steiger might be more than a beloved, small-town obstetrician. Naturally, hubby Ron Lea dismisses her concerns as second-trimester hysteria. Steiger, for once subdued, delivers his best work in years. Rated PG for intensity and mild violence. 93m. **DIR:** Rodney Gibbons. **CAST:** Linda Kozlowski, Ron Lea, Rod Steiger. **1993**

NEIGHBORS ★★★1/2 This is a strange movie. John Belushi plays a suburban homeowner whose peaceful existence is threatened when his new neighbors (played by Dan Aykroyd and Cathy Moriarty) turn out to be complete wackos. It isn't a laugh-a-minute farce, but there are numerous chuckles and a few guffaws along the way. Rated R because of profanity and sexual content. 94m. **DIR:** John G. Avildsen. **CAST:** John Belushi, Dan Aykroyd, Cathy Moriarty, Kathryn Walker, Tim Kazurinsky. **1981**

NELL ★★★★ Jodie Foster shines as a young woman raised apart from civilization in the backwoods of North Carolina. Nell is left to fend for herself when the woman who raised her dies, and it's up to the sympathetic town doctor to help her adjust to the increasingly intruding outside world. Gripping and emotionally rewarding, this offbeat story never compromises its clear-eyed point of view. Rated PG-13 for nudity and profanity. 113m. **DIR:** Michael Apted. **CAST:** Jodie Foster, Liam

Neeson, Natasha Richardson, Richard Libertini, Nick Searcy, Robin Mullins. **1994**

NELLY AND MONSIEUR ARNAUD ★★★★★ A wealthy, aging judge hires a beautiful young divorcée to type up his memoirs; they stir complex feelings in each other that neither can quite fathom or bear. Director Claude Sautet's understanding of the vagaries of the human heart has never been more acute, and the lead actors are marvels of poise, originality, and honesty. In French with English subtitles. Not rated, but addresses thoroughly adult issues and has a brief sex scene. 106m. **DIR:** Claude Sautet. **CAST:** Emmanuelle Beart, Michel Serrault, Jean-Hugues Anglade. **1995 DVD**

NEMESIS (1986) ★★★1/2 Joan Hickson's Miss Marple becomes the "unbeatable rival no man may escape" in this adaptation of Agatha Christie's last novel. The English countryside forms the backdrop for this clever story. Not rated; suitable for family viewing. 102m. **DIR:** David Tucker. **CAST:** Joan Hickson, Margaret Tyzack, Anna Cropper, Valerie Lush, Peter Tilbury, Bruce Payne, Helen Cherry. **1986**

NEMESIS (1993) ★★ In the year 2027, an ex-L.A.P.D. detective must determine whether the humans or the cyborgs are his enemy. He has three days to complete his mission or else the bomb in his heart will explode. Rated R for violence and profanity. 92m. **DIR:** Albert Pyun. **CAST:** Olivier Gruner, Tim Thomerson, Cary-Hiroyuki Tagawa, Merle Kennedy, Yuji Okumoto, Marjorie Monaghan, Brian James, Deborah Shelton. **1993 DVD**

NEMESIS 2 🦃 Strictly low-rent affair about a cyborg sent to kill a woman who holds the secret to save humanity. If this is our future, then humanity doesn't need saving. Rated R for violence. 83m. **DIR:** Albert Pyun. **CAST:** Sue Price, Tina Cote, Earl White, Chad Stahelski. **1995**

NEMESIS 3: TIME LAPSE ★★ Nothing new in this continuing tale about evil cyborgs intent on wiping out mankind. A woman with superhuman DNA holds the key to the world's salvation. Rated R for violence, profanity, and nudity. 91m. **DIR:** Albert Pyun. **CAST:** Sue Price, Tim Thomerson, Norbert Weisser, Xavier Declie. **1995**

NEMESIS 4 🦃 Fourth and final(?) chapter in this tale of cyborgs with heart is short on acting talent, budget, and running time. Rated R for violence, nudity, gore, and profanity. 65m. **DIR:** Albert Pyun. **CAST:** Andrew Divoff, Sue Price, Norbert Weisser. **1995 DVD**

NEO-TOKYO ★★ This collection of short animated stories is a rather uneven showcase for three of Japan's premiere animation directors. Two of the features are merely exercises in self-indulgence, but the last, "An Order to Stop Construction" from *Akira* director Katsuhiro Otomo, is definitely worth seeing. In Japanese with English subtitles. Not rated; contains some graphic violence. 50m. **DIR:** Rin Taro, Yoshiaki Kawajiri, Katsuhiro Otomo. **1986**

NEON BIBLE, THE ★★★★1/2 Charismatic Gena Rowlands struts her stuff as a radio singer who shores up a sad nephew desperate for both affection and a connection to a different life. This film, which captures the insulation and poverty of the American South, is so visually arresting you can't shake it free. Not rated; contains violence and profanity. 92m. **DIR:** Terence Davies. **CAST:** Gena Rowlands, Denis Leary, Diana Scarwid, Jacob Tierney. **1994 DVD**

NEON CITY ★★1/2 In order to get to the fabled Neon City, a group of travelers must cross a barren wasteland where they are in constant danger of solar flares and attacks by mutant bandits. Some great stunt work helps this futuristic adventure. Rated R for violence and profanity. 107m. **DIR:** Monte Markham. **CAST:** Michael Ironside, Vanity, Lyle Alzado, Richard Sanders. **1991**

NEON EMPIRE, THE ★★ This tedious, cut-down version of a four-hour made-for-cable gangster flick merely wastes the talents of performers who sleepwalk through their parts. Pete Hamill's pedestrian screenplay should have been the stuff of intrigue and crackling suspense. Not rated but contains profanity and considerable violence. 120m. **DIR:** Larry Peerce. **CAST:** Ray Sharkey, Gary Busey, Linda Fiorentino, Martin Landau, Dylan McDermott, Julie Carmen, Harry Guardino. **1989**

NEON MANIACS ★★1/2 Ancient evil beings are released into present-day San Francisco, killing everyone in their path. Three teenagers learn the demons' weakness and go on a crusade to destroy them. With good special effects, original creatures, and lots of scares, this film is worth a look. Rated R for violence. 90m. **DIR:** Joseph Mangine. **CAST:** Allan Hayes, Leilani Sarelle. **1985**

NEPTUNE FACTOR, THE ★★ Ben Gazzara stars as the commander of an experimental deep-sea submarine. He is called in to rescue an aquatic research team trapped in the remains of their lab on the ocean floor. Why they built it in the middle of a quake zone is the first in a series of dumb plot ideas. Rated G. 94m. **DIR:** Daniel Petrie. **CAST:** Ben Gazzara, Yvette Mimieux, Walter Pidgeon, Ernest Borgnine. **1973**

NEPTUNE'S DAUGHTER ★★1/2 Big-budgeted aquatic musical from MGM studios has Esther Williams playing a (what else?) swimsuit designer on holiday in South America floating in and out of danger with Red Skelton. The plot isn't important as long as you can keep time with Xavier Cugat's mambo beat. Harmless, enjoyable nonsense. 93m. **DIR:** Edward Buzzell. **CAST:** Esther Williams, Red Skelton, Keenan Wynn, Ricardo Montalban, Betty Garrett, Mel Blanc, Mike Mazurki, Ted de Corsia, Xavier Cugat. **1949**

NERVOUS TICKS ★★★ Airline employee Bill Pullman tries to run off to Rio with married Julie Brown. Interesting for having been shot in "real time," but the plot is just too wacky. Rated R for violence, profanity, and nudity. 95m. **DIR:** Rocky Lang. **CAST:** Bill Pullman, Peter Boyle, Julie Brown, Brent Jennings, James LeGros. **1991**

NEST, THE (1981) ★★1/2 *The Nest* is the story of a tragic relationship between a 60-year-old widower and a 12-year-old girl. The movie takes a far too romantic view of the widower's sacrifices to the friendship. Hector Alterio as the older man has a warm and inviting face and voice. He is the one who enlists our sympathies. In Spanish with English subtitles. 109m. **DIR:** Jaime De Arminan. **CAST:** Hector Alterio, Ana Torrent. **1981**

NEST, THE (1988) ★★★1/2 A skin-rippling tale of a genetic experiment gone awry. Flesh-eating cockroaches are on the verge of overrunning a small island and they are not about to let anything stand in their way. What's worse, they're mutating into the form of whatever they

consume. Special effects are above par and definitely not for the squeamish. Rated R. 88m. **DIR:** Terence H. Winkless. **CAST:** Robert Lansing, Lisa Langlois, Franc Luz, Stephen Davies, Nancy Morgan. **1988**

NESTING, THE ★★ Tolerable haunted-house film about a writer (Robin Groves) who rents a house in the country so as to get some peace and quiet. But guess what? You got it—the house is plagued with undead spirits. Rated R for nudity and violence. 104m. **DIR:** Armand Weston. **CAST:** Robin Groves, Christopher Loomis, John Carradine, Gloria Grahame. **1980**

NET, THE ★★★ Sandra Bullock, once again cast as the most personable lonely woman in the world, brings more credibility to this film than Michael Ferris and John Brancato's often-silly script really deserves. She's a genius computer hacker who stumbles upon some dangerous software, and then finds herself targeted by a suave assassin who quite sadistically toys with her. The plot is illogical enough to stretch credibility. Rated PG-13 for profanity and violence. 112m. **DIR:** Irwin Winkler. **CAST:** Sandra Bullock, Jeremy Northam, Dennis Miller, Diane Baker. **1995 DVD**

NETHERWORLD ★★★ The heir to a Louisiana mansion is asked to bring his father back from the dead as a condition of the deed. The film creates a sort of ornithological voodooist mythology. Not rated, but has profanity and brief nudity. 87m. **DIR:** David Schmoeller. **CAST:** Michael Bendetti, Denise Gentile, Anjanette Comer. **1991 DVD**

NETWORK ★★★★★ "I'm mad as hell and I'm not going to take it anymore!" Peter Finch (who won a posthumous Academy Award for best actor), William Holden, Faye Dunaway, Robert Duvall, and Ned Beatty give superb performances in this black comedy about the world of television as penned by Paddy Chayefsky. It's a biting satire on the inner workings of this century's most powerful medium. Rated R. 121m. **DIR:** Sidney Lumet. **CAST:** Peter Finch, William Holden, Faye Dunaway, Robert Duvall, Ned Beatty, Beatrice Straight. **1976 DVD**

NEUROTIC CABARET ★★★ A strange and entertaining movie. The plot revolves around two people's attempts to get their movie made. Tammy Stones, who also penned the script, stars as a strip-joint dancer. An amusing vehicle played tongue in cheek. Rated R for nudity. 97m. **DIR:** John Woodward. **CAST:** Tammy Stones, Dennis Worthington. **1990**

NEVADA ★★★★ When a mysterious woman stumbles into a tiny town, some of the local women there embrace her—while others are suspicious. Excellent performances and crisp writing and direction make this an involving, riveting film. Rated R for profanity. 109m. **DIR:** Gary Teche. **CAST:** Amy Brenneman, Kirstie Alley, Gabrielle Anwar, Saffron Burrows, Angus MacFadyen, Kathy Najimy, Dee Wallace, James Wilder, Bridgette Wilson. **1997**

NEVADA SMITH ★★★ Steve McQueen, in the title role, is butcher's-freezer–cold, calculating, and merciless in this hard-hitting, gripping Western. The focus is on a senseless, vicious double murder and the revenge taken by the son of the innocent victims. Story and characters are excerpted from a section of Harold Robbins's sensational novel *The Carpetbaggers* not used in the 1964 film. 135m. **DIR:** Henry Hathaway. **CAST:** Steve McQueen, Karl Malden, Brian Keith, Arthur Kennedy, Suzanne Pleshette, Raf Vallone, Pat Hingle, Howard DaSilva, Martin Landau. **1966**

NEVADAN, THE ★★★1/2 Government agent Randolph Scott works undercover with outlaw Forrest Tucker to retrieve stolen gold. Originally filmed in color, only B&W prints seem to exist today. B&W; 81m. **DIR:** Gordon Douglas. **CAST:** Randolph Scott, Dorothy Malone, Forrest Tucker, George Macready, Jock Mahoney. **1950**

NEVER A DULL MOMENT 🦃 Dick Van Dyke doing his sophisticated version of Jerry Lewis at his worst. Rated G. 100m. **DIR:** Jerry Paris. **CAST:** Dick Van Dyke, Edward G. Robinson, Dorothy Provine, Henry Silva. **1968**

NEVER BEEN KISSED ★★1/2 Drew Barrymore stars as a shy *Chicago Sun Times* copy editor, whose passion to become a "real" reporter bears fruit when she's sent undercover to a local high school and ordered to find a sizzling story on today's teenagers. For Barrymore, this is like returning to the Seventh Level of Hell; her original high-school experiences were an unrelenting series of base and humiliating traumas. Unfortunately, this film can't quite decide what it wants to be when it grows up: romantic comedy or exaggerated farce. Rated PG-13 for mild profanity and sexual content. 107m. **DIR:** Raja Gosnell. **CAST:** Drew Barrymore, David Arquette, Molly Shannon, John C. Reilly, Leelee Sobieski, Jeremy Jordan, Garry Marshall, Michael Vartan. **1999 DVD**

NEVER CRY WOLF ★★★★★ Carroll Ballard made this breathtakingly beautiful, richly rewarding Disney feature about a lone biologist (Charles Martin Smith) learning firsthand about the white wolves of the Yukon by living with them. It's an extraordinary motion picture in every sense of the word. Rated PG for brief nudity. 105m. **DIR:** Carroll Ballard. **CAST:** Charles Martin Smith, Brian Dennehy. **1983 DVD**

NEVER FORGET ★★★1/2 Fact-based TV account of Jewish concentration camp survivor Mel Mermelstein's fight against the Institute for Historical Review, an organization that refused to accept the fact that the Holocaust ever took place. Leonard Nimoy has never been better. 94m. **DIR:** Joseph Sargent. **CAST:** Leonard Nimoy, Blythe Danner, Dabney Coleman, Paul Hampton. **1991**

NEVER GIVE A SUCKER AN EVEN BREAK ★★★★ This is a wild and woolly pastiche of hilarious gags and bizarre comedy routines revolving around W. C. Fields's attempt to sell an outlandish script to a movie studio. Some of the jokes misfire, but the absurdity of the situations makes up for the weak spots. B&W; 71m. **DIR:** Eddie Cline. **CAST:** W. C. Fields, Gloria Jean, Leon Errol. **1941**

NEVER LET GO ★★ Peter Sellers bombs out in his first dramatic role as a ruthless criminal in this thin story about car stealing. The sure acting of Mervyn Johns, longtime dependable supporting player, helps things but cannot begin to save the film. Nor can Richard Todd's efforts. B&W; 90m. **DIR:** John Guillermin. **CAST:** Peter Sellers, Richard Todd, Elizabeth Sellars, Carol White, Mervyn Johns. **1960**

NEVER LET ME GO ★★★ Clark Gable, a correspondent in post–World War II Russia, marries ballerina

Gene Tierney just before he is expelled from the country. When authorities detain her, he sets about to help her escape. B&W; 94m. **DIR:** Delmer Daves. **CAST:** Clark Gable, Gene Tierney, Bernard Miles, Richard Haydn, Belita, Kenneth More, Theodore Bikel. **1953**

NEVER LOVE A STRANGER 🦃 John Drew Barrymore as a young hustler whose success puts him on a collision course with his old boss and an eager district attorney. 91m. **DIR:** Robert Stevens. **CAST:** John Drew Barrymore, Lita Milan, Steve McQueen. **1958**

NEVER ON SUNDAY ★★★★ A wimpy egghead tries to make a lady out of an earthy, fun-loving prostitute. The setting is Greece; the dialogue and situations are delightful. Melina Mercouri is terrific. 91m. **DIR:** Jules Dassin. **CAST:** Melina Mercouri, Jules Dassin. **1960**

NEVER ON TUESDAY ★★★ Two best friends, leaving their boring hometown for sunny L.A., are stranded for two days in the desert with a beautiful girl. Unexpected cameo appearances by Charlie Sheen and Emilio Estevez. Rated R for nudity and simulated sex. 90m. **DIR:** Adam Rifkin. **CAST:** Claudia Christian, Andrew Lauer, Peter Berg. **1988**

NEVER SAY GOODBYE ★★ An outdated comedy about marriage and morals, this movie takes advantage of Errol Flynn's reputation as a womanizer to get laughs. He plays a divorced man courting his wife again. A few laughs and lots of clichéd comments. B&W; 96m. **DIR:** James V. Kern. **CAST:** Errol Flynn, Eleanor Parker, Donald Woods, Peggy Knudsen, Forrest Tucker, S. Z. Sakall, Hattie McDaniel. **1946**

NEVER SAY NEVER AGAIN ★★★★1/2 Sean Connery returns to the role of James Bond in this high-style, tongue-in-cheek remake of *Thunderball*. Once again, agent 007 goes up against the evil Largo, the sexy and deadly Fatima, and the ever-present head of SPECTRE, Blofeld. Action-packed and peppered with laughs. Rated PG for violence and nudity. 137m. **DIR:** Irvin Kershner. **CAST:** Sean Connery, Klaus Maria Brandauer, Max von Sydow, Barbara Carrera, Kim Basinger, Edward Fox, Bernie Casey, Alec McCowen. **1983 DVD**

NEVER SO FEW ★★★ Adroitly led by a group of American officers, a band of Burmese guerrillas fight a series of vicious battles against invading Japanese troops in this World War II action picture. The battle scenes are quite good, but the film is marred at times by the philosophizing of U.S. Army officer Frank Sinatra. It's good, but talky. 124m. **DIR:** John Sturges. **CAST:** Frank Sinatra, Gina Lollobrigida, Peter Lawford, Steve McQueen, Paul Henreid, Charles Bronson, Richard Johnson, Brian Donlevy, Dean Jones. **1959**

NEVER STEAL ANYTHING SMALL ★★1/2 Unbelievable musical-comedy-drama about a good-hearted union labor leader is saved by the dynamic James Cagney, who was always enough to make even the most hackneyed story worth watching. 94m. **DIR:** Charles Lederer. **CAST:** James Cagney, Shirley Jones, Roger Smith, Cara Williams, Nehemiah Persoff, Royal Dano, Horace McMahon. **1959**

NEVER TALK TO STRANGERS ★★ A criminal psychologist gets picked up in a grocery market by a charming yet dangerous Latino. When creepy things start happening, she hires a private detective to trail her new lover and sift through his murky identity. The psychologist's tormented past leads to a daring but unconvincing finale. Rated R for language, nudity, sex, and violence. 102m. **DIR:** Peter Hall. **CAST:** Rebecca DeMornay, Antonio Banderas, Dennis Miller, Len Cariou, Harry Dean Stanton. **1995 DVD**

NEVER 2 BIG ★★★ A man, accused of killing his superstar sister, must uncover the conniving record producer who's really behind the murder. Not bad but often contrived and over-the-top thriller. Rated R for violence, profanity, and nudity. 100m. **DIR:** Peter Gathings Bunche. **CAST:** Ernie Hudson, Nia Long, Donnie Wahlberg, Shermar Moore. **1998 DVD**

NEVER TOO LATE ★★★1/2 The villain, a conniving jail official, cleverly frames the handsome young hero in order to steal his girl in this classic melodrama. Originally, on the stage, the play resulted in sweeping reforms in the British penal system in the mid–nineteenth century. B&W; 67m. **DIR:** David MacDonald. **CAST:** Tod Slaughter. **1937 DVD**

NEVER WAVE AT A WAC (PRIVATE WORE SKIRTS, THE) ★★★ Ancestor of *Private Benjamin*, with Rosalind Russell as a spoiled socialite who joins the Women's Army Corps. Russell may be a bit old for the part, but she and dumb-blonde sidekick Marie Wilson provide some laughs. B&W; 87m. **DIR:** Norman Z. McLeod. **CAST:** Rosalind Russell, Marie Wilson, Paul Douglas, Louise Beavers. **1952**

NEVERENDING STORY, THE ★★★★1/2 This is a superb fantasy about a sensitive 10-year-old boy named Bastian (Barrett Oliver) who takes refuge in a fairy tale. In reading it, he's swept off to a land of startlingly strange creatures and heroic adventures where a young warrior, Atreyu (Noah Hathaway), does battle with the Nothing, a force that threatens to obliterate the land of mankind's hopes and dreams—and only Bastian has the power to save the day. Rated PG for slight profanity. 92m. **DIR:** Wolfgang Petersen. **CAST:** Barret Oliver, Noah Hathaway. **1984 DVD**

NEVERENDING STORY II, THE ★★1/2 Disappointing sequel to director Wolfgang Petersen's original has a new actor (Jonathan Brandis) as Bastian, the young reader/hero who is once again called upon to save the magical world of Fantasia. Rated PG for scary stuff. 90m. **DIR:** George Miller. **CAST:** Jonathan Brandis, Kenny Morrison, Clarissa Burt, John Wesley Shipp. **1991 DVD**

NEVERENDING STORY III, THE: ESCAPE TO FANTASIA ★★★1/2 Bastian, a teenager who can't stand his new stepsister or his new school, seeks refuge in the school library, where he escapes into his favorite book, *The Neverending Story*. Swept away to the magical city of Fantasia, he meets a cast of unusual characters brought to life by the Jim Henson Creature Shop. Kids will enjoy this live-action adventure-filled comedy. Rated G. 95m. **DIR:** Peter MacDonald. **CAST:** Jason James Richter, Melody Kay, Jack Black, Freddie Jones, Tony Robinson, Moya Brandy. **1994**

NEW ADVENTURES OF CHARLIE CHAN, THE (TV SERIES) ★★★ What do you get when you have an Irish actor (J. Carrol Naish) playing a retired Chinese detective? Unintentional but nonetheless delightful camp. Each of the three volumes released thus far contains three episodes of this British TV mystery series. B&W; 90m. **DIR:** Charles Haas. **CAST:** J. Carrol Naish, James Hong. **1957**

NEW ADVENTURES OF PIPPI LONGSTOCKING, THE ★★ Something has been lost in the film adaptation of Astrid Lindgren's tale. This time spunky but lovable Pippi is a brat who manages to give adult viewers a headache and children ideas about driving adults over the edge. A few catchy tunes but nothing else to recommend this. Rated G. 100m. **DIR:** Ken Annakin. **CAST:** Tami Erin, Eileen Brennan, Dennis Dugan, Dianne Hull. **1988 DVD**

NEW ADVENTURES OF TARZAN ★★1/2 For the first time on film, Edgar Rice Burroughs's immortal jungle lord spoke and behaved the way he had been created. This sometimes slow, but basically enjoyable twelve-episode chapterplay wove a complex story about a search for Tarzan's missing friend and a treacherous agent intent on stealing an ancient Mayan stone. B&W; 12 chapters. **DIR:** Edward Kull, W. F. McGaugh. **CAST:** Bruce Bennett, Ula Holt, Frank Baker, Dale Walsh, Harry Ernest. **1935**

NEW AGE, THE ★★1/2 Film is supposed to be a scathing dark comedy about commercialism and consumerism, but emerges as a dry, overlong whining contest between stars Peter Weller and Judy Davis. A successful married couple gets a dose of reality when he quits his job and she loses her designing firm. Instead of coping rationally, they open a boutique in the trendy Melrose section of Hollywood. Much ado about nothing. Rated R for nudity, adult situations, and language. 106m. **DIR:** Michael Tolkin. **CAST:** Peter Weller, Judy Davis, Adam West, John Diehl. **1994**

NEW BLOOD ★★★★ Writer-director Michael Hurst breathes new life into an old formula, creating a hybrid that manages to rise above the rest. Danny is a gangster wannabe who uses his own crew for a kidnapping that goes wrong. Wounded and on the run from the local mob, Danny seeks shelter at the home of his estranged father, who sees opportunity in Danny's condition. Unexpected twists, compelling dialogue, and strong direction create fireworks. Rated R for adult situations, language, and violence. 92m. **DIR:** Michael Hurst. **CAST:** John Hurt, Nick Moran, Carrie-Anne Moss, Joe Pantoliano, Shawn Wayans. **1999 DVD**

NEW CENTURIONS, THE ★★★★ A blend of harsh reality and soap opera. The moral seems to be "It is no fun being a cop." Watching George C. Scott and Stacy Keach get their lumps, we have to agree. Rated R. 103m. **DIR:** Richard Fleischer. **CAST:** George C. Scott, Stacy Keach, Jane Alexander, Erik Estrada. **1972**

NEW CRIME CITY: LOS ANGELES 2020 ★★★ In the future, when crime has run rampant, a cop is assigned the duty of tracking down and destroying a vial containing a dangerous virus. Violent, gritty, and intriguing sci-fi trash. Rated R for violence and nudity. 95m. **DIR:** Jonathan Winfrey. **CAST:** Rick Rossovich, Stacy Keach, Sherrie Rose, Rick Dean. **1994**

NEW CUTEY HONEY, THE ★★1/2 Veteran comic creator Go Nagai's animated, ever-changing female superhero is weakly updated. Pitted against a shadowy arch villain in a battle for the control of her city, Honey-chan must defeat creatures and cutthroats with the aid of her motley sidekicks. Too much formula action does nothing to set it apart from the low end of the genre. In Japanese with English subtitles. Not rated; contains nudity, sexual situations, and violence. 65m. **DIR:** Yasuchika Nagaoka. **1994**

NEW DOMINION TANK POLICE ★★★ With first-rate animation and action, the "Tank Police" from *Dominion* are back and under fire from both slick crooks and irate citizens. This time, our heroine and her beloved minitank "Bonaparte" must battle a villain with an uncanny knowledge of the police force's strengths and weaknesses. Not rated; contains some profanity. 60m. **DIR:** Furuse Noboru. **1995**

NEW EDEN ★★★ This science-fiction spin on *The Road Warrior* has all the earmarks of a failed television pilot, from squeaky-clean action scenes to slow blackouts every twenty minutes. Catch it for an early look at Stephen Baldwin, cast as Adams, the first "civilized man" to utilize technology in the desert wastelands of some nameless prison planet. Lisa Bonet makes a pretty vacuous Eve. Needlessly rated R for minimal violence and suggested sex. 89m. **DIR:** Alan Metzger. **CAST:** Stephen Baldwin, Lisa Bonet, Tobin Bell, Michael Bowen. **1994**

NEW FACES ★★1/2 This is a filmed version of the 1952 smash Broadway revue with a thin story line added. Ronny Graham is very good in a parody of *Death of a Salesman*. Eartha Kitt became a star through this vehicle and Robert Clary, Paul Lynde, and Alice Ghostley are used to good advantage. 99m. **DIR:** Harry Horner. **CAST:** Ronny Graham, Eartha Kitt, Paul Lynde, Robert Clary, Alice Ghostley, Carol Lawrence. **1954**

NEW FRONTIER ★★1/2 In a familiar plot, John Wayne is the son of a murdered sheriff out to find the baddies who did the dirty deed. Creaky but fun for fans. B&W; 59m. **DIR:** Carl Pierson. **CAST:** John Wayne, Muriel Evans, Mary McLaren, Murdock McQuarrie, Warner Richmond, Sam Flint, Earl Dwire. **1935**

NEW JACK CITY ★★★★ Wesley Snipes gives an explosive performance as a powerful Harlem drug lord who is targeted to be brought down by two undercover cops (rap singer Ice T and Judd Nelson). Director Mario Van Peebles delivers all the thrills, chills, and suspense the action crowd craves while still creating an effective anti-drug movie. Rated R for profanity, violence, and nudity. 97m. **DIR:** Mario Van Peebles. **CAST:** Wesley Snipes, Ice T, Chris Rock, Mario Van Peebles, Judd Nelson. **1991 DVD**

NEW JERSEY DRIVE ★★★ This study of ghetto youth whose main thrill in life is joyriding in stolen cars finds itself going in circles rather early. Though gritty and authentic-seeming, the cycle of thoughtless self-destructiveness and vindictive police brutality gets tedious. Rated R for violence, language, and drug use. 97m. **DIR:** Nick Gomez. **CAST:** Sharron Corley, Gabriel Casseus, Saul Stein. **1995 DVD**

NEW KIDS, THE 🦃 Two easygoing kids try to make friends at a new high school. Their attempt is thwarted by the town bully. Rated R for profanity, nudity, and violence. 96m. **DIR:** Sean S. Cunningham. **CAST:** Shannon Presby, Lori Loughlin, James Spader. **1985**

NEW KIND OF LOVE, A ★★ A minor romantic comedy that gets one star for showcasing the real-life vibes between Paul Newman and Joanne Woodward. It gets another star for having Maurice Chevalier sing "Mimi" and "Louise." The rest of it gets zilch. 110m. **DIR:** Melville Shavelson. **CAST:** Paul Newman, Joanne Woodward,

Maurice Chevalier, Thelma Ritter, Eva Gabor, George Tobias, Marvin Kaplan. **1963**

NEW LAND, THE ★★★★1/2 The displaced Swedish farmers introduced in *The Emigrants* return in this outstanding sequel. It is 1850 Minnesota and they are ready to "work the ground" where they settle. The two films, as a whole, are a true epic of faith and determination. Oscar-nominated for best foreign-language film. Swedish, dubbed in English. Rated PG. 161m. **DIR:** Jan Troell. **CAST:** Max von Sydow, Liv Ullmann. **1972**

NEW LEAF, A ★★★★ A rare (and wonderful) triple play from an American female talent: writer-director-star Elaine May makes an impressive mark with this latter-day screwball comedy, about a bankrupt rogue (Walter Matthau) who must find a rich woman to marry—within six weeks. His target turns out to be a clumsy botanist (May) seeking immortality by finding a new specimen of plant life (hence one element of the title). Rated PG for adult situations. 102m. **DIR:** Elaine May. **CAST:** Walter Matthau, Elaine May, Jack Weston, James Coco, William Redfield. **1971**

NEW LIFE, A ★★★ This amusing examination of life after divorce features a couple who stumbles into other relationships after an agreeable separation. Rated PG-13 for language and sexual themes. 104m. **DIR:** Alan Alda. **CAST:** Alan Alda, Ann-Margret, Hal Linden, Veronica Hamel, John Shea, Mary Kay Place, Beatrice Alda. **1988**

NEW MOON ★★★ This melodramatic romance, which takes place during the French Revolution, features Jeanette MacDonald as a spoiled aristocrat who falls for an extraordinary bondsman (Nelson Eddy). Some comic moments, and Eddy comes off looking much better than MacDonald in this one, one of eight love stories they brought to the screen. B&W; 106m. **DIR:** Robert Z. Leonard. **CAST:** Jeanette MacDonald, Nelson Eddy, Mary Boland, George Zucco. **1940**

NEW ROSE HOTEL ★★ Scattershot telling of the William Gibson tale in which two men train a woman to seduce their competition and steal his industrial secrets. Rated R for profanity, violence, and nudity. 92m. **DIR:** Abel Ferrara. **CAST:** Christopher Walken, Willem Dafoe, Annabella Sciorra, Gretchen Mol. **1998 DVD**

NEW WORLD DISORDER ★★1/2 A police coroner and an FBI agent team up to retrieve an invaluable computer encryption program from a terrorist. Straight-to-video thriller is slightly better than it sounds; worth a look if you're a Rutger Hauer buff. Rated R for violence and profanity. 93m. **DIR:** Richard Spence. **CAST:** Rutger Hauer, Andrew McCarthy, Tara Fitzgerald. **1999 DVD**

NEW YEAR'S DAY ★★★1/2 This gentle movie is a fairly intimate, if familiar, character study about three women who aren't quite ready to move out of the New York apartment that Henry Jaglom has recently leased. The film explores younger women's attachments to older men, and vice versa. May be too slow paced for some people. Rated R for nudity and profanity. 90m. **DIR:** Henry Jaglom. **CAST:** Henry Jaglom, Maggie Jakobson, Gwen Welles, Irene Moore, Milos Forman. **1990**

NEW YEAR'S EVIL 🦃 A crazy killer stalks victims at a televised New Year's Eve party. Rated R for all the usual reasons. 90m. **DIR:** Emmett Alston. **CAST:** Roz Kelly, Kip Niven, Chris Wallace. **1980**

NEW YORK COP ★★ An NYPD detective bonds with the street gang he's assigned to infiltrate. Serviceable crime opus, with a high body count and appropriately hammy acting. Rated R for violence, strong language, and adult situations. 88m. **DIR:** Toru Murakawa. **CAST:** Toru Nakamura, Chad McQueen, Andreas Katsulas, Mira Sorvino, Conan Lee, Tony Sirico. **1995**

NEW YORK, NEW YORK ★★★1/2 This is a difficult film to warm to, but worth it. Robert De Niro gives a splendid performance as an egomaniacal saxophonist who woos sweet-natured singer Liza Minnelli. The songs (especially the title tune) are great, and those with a taste for something different in musicals will find it rewarding. Rated PG. 163m. **DIR:** Martin Scorsese. **CAST:** Robert De Niro, Liza Minnelli, Lionel Stander, Georgie Auld, Mary Kay Place. **1977**

NEW YORK RIPPER, THE 🦃 Explicitly gory—yet dull—Italian horror about a sex murderer. R rating (four minutes were cut to avoid an X). 88m. **DIR:** Lucio Fulci. **CAST:** Jack Hedley. **1982 DVD**

NEW YORK STORIES ★★★★1/2 Here's a wonderful creation that provides three terrific movies for the price of one. Woody Allen's *Oedipus Wrecks* marks his return to comedy. Starring Allen as a lawyer who cannot escape his mother's overbearing influence, it's a hilarious vignette. Francis Coppola's *Life Without Zoe* is a light but charming fantasy about a sophisticated youngster named Zoe and her adventures in New York City. The best of this splendid trio is Martin Scorsese's *Life Lessons*, about the obsessive love of a celebrated painter for his protégée. Rated PG for profanity. 119m. **DIR:** Woody Allen, Francis Ford Coppola, Martin Scorsese. **CAST:** Woody Allen, Rosanna Arquette, Mia Farrow, Giancarlo Giannini, Julie Kavner, Heather McComb, Nick Nolte, Don Novello, Patrick O'Neal, Talia Shire. **1989**

NEW YORK THE WAY IT WAS ★★★★ The use of vintage footage and interviews with Alan King, Joe Franklin, and Mario Cuomo makes you feel as if you grew up in the Big Apple. This sentimental nostalgia trip won a much deserved Emmy when it aired on PBS, but it's packaged in a boxed set with two other easily missed, 58-minute documentaries, *The Old Neighborhood* and *Wish You Were Here!*. Not rated. 58m. **DIR:** Fred Fischer. **1993**

NEWMAN'S LAW 🦃 George Peppard plays a good cop accused of corruption and suspended from the force. Rated PG for violence. 98m. **DIR:** Richard T. Heffron. **CAST:** George Peppard, Roger Robinson, Abe Vigoda, Eugene Roche. **1974**

NEWS AT ELEVEN ★★★★ Martin Sheen plays a news anchorman whose integrity is threatened by the demands of his ratings-crazed news director. This is a jolting reminder of the enormous power of the press, with Sheen delivering a superior performance. 95m. **DIR:** Mike Robe. **CAST:** Martin Sheen, Barbara Babcock, Sheree Wilson, Peter Riegert. **1985**

NEWS FROM HOME 🦃 Sandwiched between the spectacular and seedy elements of New York, there is the mundane, to which we are treated in huge elongated slices. If you want something exciting to happen while watching this, look out the window. In French with Eng-

lish subtitles. Not rated. 85m. **DIR:** Chantal Akerman. **1991**

•NEWSBREAK 🦃 Michael Rooker stars as a news reporter trying to dig up dirt on a wealthy power company mogul played by Judge Reinhold. Lackadaisical acting and a trite storyline make for a painfully long hour and a half. Rated R for violence and language. 95m. **DIR:** Serge Rodnunsky. **CAST:** Judge Reinhold, Michael Rooker, Robert Culp. **2000 DVD**

NEWSFRONT ★★★★ A story of a newsreel company from 1948 until technology brought its existence to an end, this is a warm and wonderful film about real people. It's an insightful glimpse at the early days of the news business, with good character development. Rated PG. 110m. **DIR:** Phillip Noyce. **CAST:** Bill Hunter, Wendy Hughes, Gerald Kennedy. **1978**

NEWSIES ★★★ While this Disney production may not fulfill its promise to resurrect the movie musical, it is an entertaining picture for the whole family. The songs of Academy Award–winning composer Alan Menken propel the story of the 1899 newspaper boys strike. Rated PG for violence. 120m. **DIR:** Kenny Ortega. **CAST:** Christian Bale, David Moscow, Bill Pullman, Luke Edwards, Max Casella, Michael Lerner, Ann-Margret, Robert Duvall. **1992 DVD**

NEWTON BOYS, THE ★★1/2 Between 1919 and 1924, Willis Newton and his three brothers robbed more than eighty banks from Texas to Canada, then capped their career with America's largest train robbery. Unfortunately these four actors aren't given more than a shred of depth between them. Fast-forward to the closing credits footage of actual Newtons who are much more captivating than the fictitious younger selves portrayed here. Rated PG for mild violence and profanity. 113m. **DIR:** Richard Linklater. **CAST:** Matthew McConaughey, Ethan Hawke, Skeet Ulrich, Dwight Yoakam, Vincent D'Onofrio, Julianna Margulies. **1998 DVD**

NEXT BEST THING, THE ★★ When a woman (Madonna) gets pregnant after a one-night stand with her gay best friend (Rupert Everett), the two decide to raise the kid together as platonic housemates. This self-deluded fantasy is smarmy and false every inch of the way, from the unbelievable premise to the ludicrous happily-ever-after ending. Rated PG-13 for mature themes and mild profanity. 107m. **DIR:** John Schlesinger. **CAST:** Madonna, Rupert Everett, Benjamin Bratt, Josef Sommer, Lynn Redgrave. **2000 DVD**

NEXT DOOR ★★★ College professor James Woods unleashes the wrath of neighbor Randy Quaid, a butcher with no fondness for educators, and matters quickly get out of control. Scripter Barney Cohen's study of neighborhood warfare begins well, but suffers from an identity crisis. The darkly satirical mood is sabotaged by a far-too-serious climax that also escalates events past the point of credibility. Even so, the opening act is guaranteed to generate discomfort. Rated R for profanity and violence. 95m. **DIR:** Tony Bill. **CAST:** James Woods, Randy Quaid, Kate Capshaw, Lucinda Jenney. **1994**

NEXT FRIDAY ★★ In this sequel to and retread of the 1995 comedy *Friday*, a pot-smoking South Central Los Angeles slacker flees to the suburban home of his uncle when the neighborhood thug he helped send to prison escapes and seeks revenge. Some scattered, funny moments amid the film's raunchy misadventures. The soundtrack features the first song in nearly a decade from N.W.A. (with Snoop Dogg replacing the late Eazy-E). Rated R for drug use, language, nudity, and sexual content. 98m. **DIR:** Steve Carr. **CAST:** Ice Cube, John Witherspoon, Mike Epps, Don (DC) Curry, Tom "Tiny" Lister Jr. **2000 DVD**

NEXT KARATE KID, THE ★★ The fourth film in the series is an improvement over the third, but that's not saying much. Noriyuki "Pat" Morita is back, but the original "kid," Ralph Macchio, has grown up and moved on. This time, the old master teaches martial arts and self-respect to (gasp!) a girl—and that's about the only new twist on the old formula. Rated PG. 97m. **DIR:** Christopher Cain. **CAST:** Noriyuki "Pat" Morita, Hilary Swank, Michael Ironside, Constance Towers, Chris Conrad. **1994 DVD**

NEXT OF KIN ★★★1/2 A young man suffering from boredom and dissatisfaction with his upper-middle-class family undergoes video therapy with his parents. He becomes fascinated by a videotape of an Armenian family who feel guilty about surrendering their infant son to a foster home. Poignant look at a young WASP's displacement and response to his upper-middle-class role in Canadian society. Highly original filmmaking. Not rated. 74m. **DIR:** Atom Egoyan. **CAST:** Patrick Tierney. **1984 DVD**

NEXT OF KIN ★★ When his younger brother (Bill Paxton) is killed by a local mobster (Adam Baldwin), Patrick Swayze, as a Chicago cop from the "hollers" of Kentucky, takes justice in his own hands. Formula flick with a preposterous ending. Rated R for profanity and violence. 111m. **DIR:** John Irvin. **CAST:** Patrick Swayze, Liam Neeson, Adam Baldwin, Helen Hunt, Bill Paxton. **1989 DVD**

NEXT ONE, THE 🦃 A prophet from the future suddenly appears on the beach of a Greek island. Not rated. 105m. **DIR:** Nico Mastorakis. **CAST:** Keir Dullea, Adrienne Barbeau, Jeremy Licht, Peter Hobbs. **1981**

NEXT STOP, GREENWICH VILLAGE ★★★★ One of writer-director Paul Mazursky's first attempts to dramatize his youth, this film is a seriocomic study of the eccentricities of Greenwich Villagers. Unique as well as entertaining. 109m. **DIR:** Paul Mazursky. **CAST:** Lenny Baker, Shelley Winters, Ellen Greene, Christopher Walken, Jeff Goldblum, Lou Jacobi, Lois Smith. **1976**

NEXT STOP WONDERLAND ★★★1/2 Independent film focuses on a Boston night-shift nurse who, having just been dumped by her boyfriend, has decided that Fate is overrated and defiantly defends her now-single lifestyle. Her mother, not buying this nonsense, places a newspaper personal ad for her daughter . . . which generates sixty-four responses. The subsequent adventures in the dating scene prove a fertile ground for some zesty dialogue. All told, this is a genuinely delightful romantic comedy. Rated R for brief profanity. 96m. **DIR:** Brad Anderson. **CAST:** Hope Davis, Alan Gelfant, Philip Seymour Hoffman, Callie Thorne, Holland Taylor, Robert Klein. **1998 DVD**

NEXT SUMMER ★★★1/2 This romantic comedy features some of France's top stars in a story about a family in which personal frustrations conflict with passions in the quest for power and beauty. Excellent performances by a top-notch cast. In French with English sub-

titles. Not rated. 100m. **DIR:** Nadine Trintignant. **CAST:** Claudia Cardinale, Fanny Ardant, Philippe Noiret, Marie Trintignant, Jean-Louis Trintignant. **1986**

NEXT TIME I MARRY ★★★ A madcap comedy about marriage with Lucille Ball as an heiress who marries the first man she sees in order to get her inheritance. Ball has a ball, and it's contagious. B&W; 80m. **DIR:** Garson Kanin. **CAST:** Lucille Ball, Lee Bowman, James Ellison, Mantan Moreland. **1938**

NEXT VOICE YOU HEAR, THE ★★1/2 Man's-man director William Wellman was an odd choice to direct this preachy tract—typical of Dore Schary's well-meaning but ponderous message pictures of the Fifties—in which the voice of God speaks to mankind via a radio broadcast. The solid performances by James Whitmore and Jeff Corey lend the film what strength it has. B&W; 83m. **DIR:** William Wellman. **CAST:** James Whitmore, Nancy Davis, Jeff Corey. **1950**

NEXT YEAR IF ALL GOES WELL ★★★ Innocuous comedy about a pair of cohabitating lovers trying to decide whether to take the leap into marriage. Likable performances by Isabelle Adjani and Thierry Lhermitte. Dubbed. Rated R for brief nudity. 95m. **DIR:** Jean-Loup Hubert. **CAST:** Isabelle Adjani, Thierry Lhermitte. **1981**

NIAGARA ★★★1/2 A sexy, slightly sleazy, and sinister Marilyn Monroe plots the murder of husband Joseph Cotten in this twisted tale of infidelity and greed, shot against the pulsing scenic grandeur of Niagara Falls. But plans go awry and the falls redeem a killer. Excellent location camera work adds to the thrills. 89m. **DIR:** Henry Hathaway. **CAST:** Marilyn Monroe, Joseph Cotten, Jean Peters. **1953**

NIAGARA NIAGARA ★★ Robin Tunney and Henry Thomas play two misfit teenagers who take off for Canada on a feckless search for a particular kind of doll, falling into petty crime on the way. The acting is excellent, but it's not enough to redeem what is yet another young-outlaw-lovers-on-the-run film. Rated R for profanity, violence, and sexual scenes. 93m. **DIR:** Bob Gosse. **CAST:** Henry Thomas, Robin Tunney, Michael Parks, Stephen Lang, John McKay. **1997**

NICE DREAMS ★★★ Cheech and Chong are the counterculture kings of drug-oriented comedy. Their third feature film doesn't have quite as many classic comic gems as its predecessors, but it's more consistently entertaining. Rated R for nudity and profanity. 87m. **DIR:** Thomas Chong. **CAST:** Cheech and Chong, Evelyn Guerrero, Pee-Wee Herman, Stacy Keach. **1981 DVD**

NICE GIRL LIKE ME, A Dated Sixties comedy that was considered risqué for its time, but now seems silly and contrived. Rated PG. 91m. **DIR:** Desmond Davis. **CAST:** Barbara Ferris, Harry Andrews, Gladys Cooper. **1969**

NICE GIRLS DON'T EXPLODE ★★ Droll, slow-moving comedy about a girl (Michelle Meyrink) who causes spontaneous combustion of objects. William O'Leary as her current boyfriend is exceptional. Rated PG, the film contains some strong language and mild nudity. 92m. **DIR:** Chuck Martinez. **CAST:** Barbara Harris, Michelle Meyrink, William O'Leary, Wallace Shawn. **1987**

NICHOLAS AND ALEXANDRA ★★ This is an overlong, overdetailed depiction of the events preceding the Russian Revolution until the deaths of Czar Nicholas (Michael Jayston), his wife (Janet Suzman) and family. Some of the performances are outstanding, and the sets and costumes are top-notch. However, the film gets mired in trying to encompass too much historical detail. Rated PG. 183m. **DIR:** Franklin J. Schaffner. **CAST:** Michael Jayston, Janet Suzman, Tom Baker, Laurence Olivier, Michael Redgrave. **1971 DVD**

NICHOLAS NICKLEBY ★★★1/2 Proud but penniless young Nicholas Nickleby struggles to forge a life for himself and his family while contending with a money-mad scheming uncle and lesser villains. Good acting and authentic Victorian settings bring this classic Dickens novel to vivid screen life. Not quite in the mold of *Great Expectations*, but well above average. B&W; 108m. **DIR:** Alberto Cavalcanti. **CAST:** Derek Bond, Cedric Hardwicke, Sally Ann Howes, Cathleen Nesbitt. **1947 DVD**

NICK KNIGHT ★★★ Pilot movie for the TV series stars Rick Springfield as a vampire turned detective for the Los Angeles Police Department. 94m. **DIR:** Farhad Mann. **CAST:** Rick Springfield, John Kapelos, Robert Harper, Richard Fancy, Laura Johnson, Michael Nader. **1991**

NICK OF TIME ★★★1/2 This clever thriller plays itself out in "real time"; that is, the entire action takes place during the time required to watch it. Devoted father Johnny Depp is forced to become an unwilling assassin when his daughter is kidnapped after their arrival at Los Angeles's Union train station; either he kills the governor of California during a speech-making appearance, or the little girl dies. Although the premise is wholly improbable, you'll be too absorbed to care. Rated R for violence and profanity. 104m. **DIR:** John Badham. **CAST:** Johnny Depp, Christopher Walken, Charles Dutton, Peter Strauss, Roma Maffia, Gloria Reuben, Courtney Chase, Marsha Mason. **1995 DVD**

NICKEL & DIME ★★ C. Thomas Howell, a con artist who tries to match "long lost" heirs with unclaimed estates, is saddled with obnoxious accountant Wallace Shawn. A jumble, but Shawn and Howell forge a strangely endearing odd-couple relationship. Rated PG for profanity. 96m. **DIR:** Ben Moses. **CAST:** C. Thomas Howell, Wallace Shawn. **1992**

•NICO AND DANI ★★★ Two teenage Spanish boys spend a summer in sexual experimentation with each other, but one is really interested in girls and the other isn't. The script avoids most of the growing-up-gay movie clichés, and acting is very good, especially by Marieta Orozco and Esther Nubiola as two neighbor girls. In Spanish with English subtitles. Rated R for profanity (in subtitles), teen drug use, and sexual scenes. 90m. **DIR:** Cesc Gay. **CAST:** Fernando Ramallo, Jordi Vilches, Marieta Orozco, Esther Nubiola. **2001 DVD**

NICO ICON ★★★1/2 Documentary chronicles the life of Nico from her teen glory days as lovely French *Vogue* fashion model to her final years as ravaged drug addict. In between she became a Warhol Factory "superstar" and sang with the 1960s rock group the Velvet Underground. Through home movies, interviews, performance clips, and photographs, her self-destructive path as irresponsible mother and casual lover is spread before us in lurid detail without grandstanding or moralizing. In English, German, and French with English subtitles. Not rated; contains drug-related material. 75m. **DIR:** Suzanne Ofteringer. **1995 DVD**

NIGHT AFTER NIGHT ★★★★ Mae West's first movie is one of her funniest, and she only has a brief supporting role. The real star is George Raft as a rich hoodlum who tries to break into New York society during the Depression. West plays one of the hoodlum's former girlfriends, and she flounces in to turn society on its ear in this delightfully witty farce. B&W; 70m. **DIR:** Archie Mayo. **CAST:** George Raft, Constance Cummings, Alison Skipworth, Mae West, Wynne Gibson, Louis Calhern. **1932**

NIGHT AMBUSH ★★★1/2 Suspenseful World War II drama set in Crete, about a group of British soldiers who kidnap a German general right under the noses of his fellow officers. Solid performances. B&W; 93m. **DIR:** Michael Powell. **CAST:** Dirk Bogarde, Marius Goring, David Oxley, Cyril Cusack. **1957**

NIGHT AND DAY ★★★1/2 The meter's constantly running during this sharp-edged comedy about a woman who keeps two lovers. They're both cab drivers—one works the night shift, the other the day shift. She alternates between them and finds that she actually loves both men and her situation. Erotic and unconventional. In French with English subtitles. Not rated; contains sexual situations. 90m. **DIR:** Chantal Akerman. **CAST:** Guilaine Londez, Thomas Langmann, Francois Negret. **1991**

NIGHT AND DAY ★★★★ There was no way Hollywood could make an accurate biography of Cole Porter in those days—it had to play footsie with his ruthless social lionizing and sexual proclivities—but the film stands out as a remarkable document of the performers and performances available to the cameras at the time. Where else can you see Mary Martin doing "My Heart Belongs to Daddy" and Monte Woolley declaiming "Miss Otis Regrets"? 132m. **DIR:** Michael Curtiz. **CAST:** Cary Grant, Alexis Smith, Alan Hale Sr., Mary Martin, Monty Woolley. **1946**

NIGHT AND THE CITY (1950) ★★★★ Director Jules Dassin's drama is *film noir* at its best. Richard Widmark is the fight promoter, hustling up some action in London's East End, trying to make the score of a lifetime while keeping ahead of his debtors. Gene Tierney is splendid as the loyal girlfriend being taken for a ride. Plenty of mood and atmosphere permeate this entry. B&W; 95m. **DIR:** Jules Dassin. **CAST:** Richard Widmark, Gene Tierney, Googie Withers, Herbert Lom, Hugh Marlowe, Mike Mazurki. **1950**

NIGHT AND THE CITY (1992) ★★★1/2 Director Irwin Winkler's remake of Jules Dassin's 1950 *film noir* benefits from strong performances by Robert De Niro, Jessica Lange, and a distinguished cast of supporting players. The downbeat story has lawyer De Niro romancing the wife (Lange) of bar owner and longtime buddy Cliff Gorman while attempting to scam his way into the big time. Not a classic, but worth watching. Rated R for profanity and violence. 104m. **DIR:** Irwin Winkler. **CAST:** Robert De Niro, Jessica Lange, Cliff Gorman, Alan King, Jack Warden, Eli Wallach, Barry Primus, Gene Kirkwood. **1992**

NIGHT AND THE MOMENT, THE ★★ Lush production values and European settings do little to enhance this weary romantic drama. Willem Dafoe stars as a writer out to seduce Lena Olin, and uses tales of his previous liaisons as foreplay. It all looks pretty, but the actors and director never ignite a flame of passion. Rated R for adult situations, language, and nudity. 90m. **DIR:** Anna Maria Tato. **CAST:** Willem Dafoe, Lena Olin, Miranda Richardson. **1994**

NIGHT ANGEL ★★ Predictable horror fare about a soul-searching seductress raising some hell when she poses as a fashion model. She violently dispatches plenty of weak-willed men. Rated R for nudity. 90m. **DIR:** Dominique Othenin-Girard. **CAST:** Isa Andersen, Linden Ashby, Debra Feuer, Karen Black. **1990**

NIGHT AT THE OPERA, A ★★★★★ Despite the songs and sappy love story, the Marx Brothers (minus Zeppo) are in peak form in this classic musical comedy, which costars the legendary Margaret Dumont. B&W; 92m. **DIR:** Sam Wood. **CAST:** The Marx Brothers, Margaret Dumont, Kitty Carlisle, Allan Jones, Sig Ruman. **1935**

NIGHT AT THE ROXBURY, A ★★ Like numerous other attempts to bring *Saturday Night Live* characters to the big screen, this fails to maintain consistent humor and viewer interest. The head-bobbing Butabi brothers (Will Ferrell and Chris Kattan) try to make their mark on the nightclub scene despite their father's best efforts to turn them into responsible adults. Rated PG-13 for sexual situations. 82m. **DIR:** John Fortenberry. **CAST:** Will Ferrell, Chris Kattan, Dan Hedaya, Molly Shannon, Loni Anderson. **1998 DVD**

NIGHT BEFORE, THE ★★★ A senior prom date turns into a hilarious nightmare in this riveting, offbeat comedy. After waking up in an alley, a young man (Keanu Reeves) finds his date and wallet missing along with his father's sports car. And then things get surreal—in the style of *After Hours.* Rated R for language and violence. 85m. **DIR:** Thom Eberhardt. **CAST:** Keanu Reeves, Lori Loughlin, Theresa Saldana, Trinidad Silva. **1988**

NIGHT BREED ★★ Great monsters, fantastic makeup effects, exploding action—and very little plot. Horror writer Clive Barker's second turn as director lacks cohesion as the plot runs through the Canadian wilderness in search of a serial killer and an ancient tribe of monsters called the Night Breed. Rated R for violence. 97m. **DIR:** Clive Barker. **CAST:** Craig Sheffer, David Cronenberg, Charles Haid. **1989**

NIGHT CALLER FROM OUTER SPACE ★★1/2 Here's another one of those perennial sci-fi plots: outer space alien from a dying world comes to Earth looking for human women to serve as breeding stock. (With a planet named Ganymede, it's no wonder they're dying out!) A little British reserve keeps this in check; not bad of its type. B&W; 84m. **DIR:** John Gilling. **CAST:** John Saxon, Maurice Denham, Patricia Haines, Alfred Burke. **1965 DVD**

NIGHT CREATURE Grade-Z film has Donald Pleasence playing a half-crazed adventurer who captures a killer leopard and brings the creature to his private island. Rated PG. 83m. **DIR:** Lee Madden. **CAST:** Donald Pleasence, Nancy Kwan, Ross Hagen. **1978**

NIGHT CROSSING ★★★1/2 This Disney film is about a real-life escape from East Germany by two families in a gas-filled balloon. Unfortunately, minor flaws, such as mismatched accents and Americanized situations, prevent it from being a total success. Rated PG for violence. 106m. **DIR:** Delbert Mann. **CAST:** John Hurt, Jane Alexander, Beau Bridges, Ian Bannen. **1981**

NIGHT FALLS ON MANHATTAN ★★★ While exploring the gray areas that shape personal and professional lives, this film unleashes several fine performances. When police try to arrest a Harlem drug lord, the ensuing shoot-out leaves three cops dead. A young New York assistant district attorney then sifts through police dirty laundry while trying the case in court. Rated R for language and violence. 114m. **DIR:** Sidney Lumet. **CAST:** Andy Garcia, Lena Olin, Richard Dreyfuss, Ian Holm, Ron Leibman, James Gandolfini, Colm Feore, Shiek Mahmud-Bey. **1997 DVD**

NIGHT FIRE ★★ Video vixen Shannon Tweed stars as a wealthy businesswoman whose plans for a romantic weekend alone with her husband are shattered when a strange couple arrives at her country home. Amidst much sex and double crossing, a murderous plot is uncovered. Mildly entertaining trash isn't one of Tweed's best and her supporting cast hams its way through in a most embarrassing manner. Surprise ending is more of an anticlimax than a revelation. Rated R for nudity, sexual situations, and violence. 97m. **DIR:** Mike Sedan. **CAST:** Shannon Tweed, John Laughlin, Martin Hewitt. **1994 DVD**

NIGHT FLIER, THE ★★★ In adapting Stephen King's short story, the filmmakers added new characters and plot points while maintaining the feel of the original tale. Miguel Ferrer plays a tabloid reporter who is hot on the trail of a mysterious Cessna that lands at small airports then vanishes after everyone is murdered. While the vampire monster is a little bit cheesy looking, the film has a creepy feel that gets to you. Rated R for gore, profanity, and violence. 97m. **DIR:** Mark Pavia. **CAST:** Miguel Ferrer, Julie Entwisle. **1997 DVD**

NIGHT FLIGHT FROM MOSCOW ★★★ A decent, if overly talky, espionage film with a strong cast. Yul Brynner is a Russian diplomat who engages in a complicated plan to defect to the West. Rated PG. 113m. **DIR:** Henri Verneuil. **CAST:** Henry Fonda, Yul Brynner, Farley Granger, Dirk Bogarde, Virna Lisi, Philippe Noiret. **1973**

NIGHT FRIEND 🦃 A crusading priest becomes involved in organized crime. Rated R for profanity, nudity, and violence. 94m. **DIR:** Peter Gerretsen. **CAST:** Art Carney, Chuck Shamata. **1987**

NIGHT FULL OF RAIN, A ★★ After a series of stunning successes in the early Seventies, Italian director Lina Wertmuller began a downward slide with this film, her first attempt at an English-language movie. It details the ins and outs of the relationship between an independent woman (Candice Bergen) and her old-fashioned husband (Giancarlo Giannini). 104m. **DIR:** Lina Wertmuller. **CAST:** Giancarlo Giannini, Candice Bergen, Jill Eikenberry. **1978**

NIGHT GALLERY ★★★ Pilot for the TV series. Three tales of terror by Rod Serling told with style and flair. Segment one is the best, with Roddy McDowall eager to get his hands on an inheritance. Segment two features Joan Crawford as a blind woman with a yearning to see. Segment three, involving a paranoid war fugitive, is the least of the three. 98m. **DIR:** Boris Sagal, Steven Spielberg, Barry Shear. **CAST:** Roddy McDowall, Joan Crawford, Richard Kiley. **1969**

NIGHT GAME ★★1/2 Familiar story of a police officer (Roy Scheider) attempting to track down a serial killer before he can claim another female victim. The predictable ending is a bummer. Good performances, though. Rated R for violence and profanity. 95m. **DIR:** Peter Masterson. **CAST:** Roy Scheider, Karen Young, Richard Bradford, Paul Gleason, Carlin Glynn. **1989**

NIGHT GAMES ★★★ This film, which was originally made for television, led to the *Petrocelli* TV series for Barry Newman. He plays a lawyer who defends Stefanie Powers when she's accused of her husband's murder. There's enough intrigue and suspense in this film to capture most viewers' attention. Rated R. 78m. **DIR:** Don Taylor. **CAST:** Barry Newman, Susan Howard, Albert Salmi, Luke Askew, Ralph Meeker, Stefanie Powers. **1974**

NIGHT HAS EYES, THE ★★★1/2 This suspense film from war-weary Great Britain focuses on a schoolmarm who searches for a colleague who is missing on a mist-shrouded moor. Joyce Howard is excellent as the teacher-sleuth and the young James Mason does a credible job as a disturbed composer. B&W; 79m. **DIR:** Leslie Arliss. **CAST:** James Mason, Joyce Howard, Wilfrid Lawson. **1942**

NIGHT HUNTER ★★ Chop-socky star Don "The Dragon" Wilson adds guns and silver bullets to his arsenal of martial arts moves to battle vampires. A few good action scenes amid a lot of tedium. Rated R for violence and brief nudity. 86m. **DIR:** Rick Jacobson. **CAST:** Don "The Dragon" Wilson, Nicholas Guest, Maria Ford, Melanie Smith. **1996**

NIGHT IN CASABLANCA, A ★★★ Although the formula was wearing thin by 1946, Groucho's wisecracks and the incomparable antics of Chico and Harpo still carry the film. Joining forces in post-WWII Casablanca, the brothers wreak havoc in the staid Hotel Casablanca. B&W; 85m. **DIR:** Archie Mayo. **CAST:** The Marx Brothers, Charles Drake, Lisette Verea, Lois Collier. **1946**

NIGHT IN HEAVEN, A 🦃 College teacher falls in lust with student-male stripper. Rated R for nudity, slight profanity, and simulated sex. 80m. **DIR:** John G. Avildsen. **CAST:** Lesley Ann Warren, Christopher Atkins, Robert Logan, Carrie Snodgress. **1983**

NIGHT IN THE LIFE OF JIMMY REARDON, A 🦃 Jimmy Reardon is a teenage sex fiend in 1962 Evanston, Illinois. Rated R for profanity and leering sexual content. 92m. **DIR:** William Richert. **CAST:** River Phoenix, Meredith Salenger, Ione Skye, Louanne, Ann Magnuson. **1988 DVD**

NIGHT IS MY FUTURE ★★★1/2 In this early Ingmar Bergman film, a film that at the same time is dark in mood but bright with promise of things to come, we meet a blinded military veteran (Birger Malmsten) who is at war with the world and with himself due to his handicap. Through the selfless efforts of a maid, he learns to accept his problems and make a new life for himself. In Swedish with English subtitles. B&W; 87m. **DIR:** Ingmar Bergman. **CAST:** Mai Zetterling, Birger Malmsten. **1947**

NIGHT LIFE ★★★1/2 Four teenage corpses come back to life to haunt a young mortuary employee in this funny zombie picture. The corpses just want to party, and that they do until Scott Grimes can do away with them in grisly fashion. Rated R for violence, profanity, and gore. 92m. **DIR:** David Acomba. **CAST:** Scott Grimes, Cheryl

Pollak, Anthony Geary, Alan Blumenfeld, John Astin. **1990**

NIGHT MONSTER ★★★ Bela Lugosi has a small but effective role as a butler in this thriller about the mysterious murders of doctors treating bedridden patient Ralph Morgan. Old-fashioned thriller will please fans of Universal monster movies. B&W; 80m. **DIR:** Ford Beebe. **CAST:** Bela Lugosi, Lionel Atwill, Ralph Morgan, Irene Hervey, Don Porter, Nils Asther, Leif Erickson. **1942**

'NIGHT, MOTHER ★★ Playwright Marsha Norman's argument in favor of suicide is incredibly depressing material. Sissy Spacek plays a woman who has chosen to end her life. She decides to commit the act in her mother's house, with her mother there. We are only shown Spacek's unhappiness, and this limited manipulative view leaves us with nothing to do but wait uncomfortably for the outcome. Rated PG-13. 97m. **DIR:** Tom Moore. **CAST:** Sissy Spacek, Anne Bancroft. **1986**

NIGHT MOVES ★★★★ A dark and disturbing detective study with Gene Hackman superb as the private eye trying to solve a baffling mystery. This release was unfairly overlooked when in theaters—but you don't have to miss it now. Rated R. 95m. **DIR:** Arthur Penn. **CAST:** Gene Hackman, Susan Clark, Melanie Griffith. **1975**

NIGHT MUST FALL ★★★★ A suspenseful stage play makes a superbly suspenseful movie by letting the audience use its imagination. Robert Montgomery neatly underplays the role of the mad killer who totes his victim's head in a hatbox. Rosalind Russell is the girl who believes in him, but slowly learns the truth. B&W; 117m. **DIR:** Richard Thorpe. **CAST:** Robert Montgomery, Rosalind Russell, May Whitty, Alan Marshal, E. E. Clive, Kathleen Harrison. **1937**

NIGHT NURSE ★★★ No-nonsense Barbara Stanwyck plays the title role, using underworld contacts to safeguard two small children. A tough, taut melodrama that still works, thanks to its intriguing personalities. B&W; 73m. **DIR:** William Wellman. **CAST:** Barbara Stanwyck, Clark Gable, Ben Lyon, Joan Blondell, Charles Winninger. **1931**

NIGHT OF DARK SHADOWS ★★ The new owner of a spooky mansion is haunted by his ancestors. Barnabas Collins is nowhere to be found in this second film based on the original *Dark Shadows* TV series. Given that the series itself is on video, there's no reason to bother with this tired leftover. Rated PG. 97m. **DIR:** Dan Curtis. **CAST:** David Selby, Lara Parker, Kate Jackson, Grayson Hall. **1971**

NIGHT OF TERROR 🦃 Forgettable murder mystery with Bela Lugosi cast, as he was all too often, in a supporting role as a red herring. B&W; 65m. **DIR:** Ben Stoloff. **CAST:** Bela Lugosi, George Meeker, Tully Marshall, Bryant Washburn. **1933**

NIGHT OF THE COBRA WOMAN ★★ Former underground filmmaker Andrew Meyer (not to be confused with the utterly untalented Andy Milligan) coauthored and directed this sleazy, often boring, but nonetheless watchable drive-in horror flick, shot in the Philippines for Roger Corman. Rated R. 85m. **DIR:** Andrew Meyer. **CAST:** Marlene Clark, Joy Bang. **1972**

NIGHT OF THE COMET ★★★1/2 The passage of the comet wipes out all but a few people on our planet. The survivors, mostly young adults, are hunted by a pair of baddies, played by Geoffrey Lewis and Mary Woronov. It all adds up to a zesty low-budget spoof of science-fiction movies. Rated PG-13. 94m. **DIR:** Thom Eberhardt. **CAST:** Geoffrey Lewis, Mary Woronov, Catherine Mary Stewart, Kelli Maroney. **1984**

NIGHT OF THE CREEPS ★★★1/2 A film derived from virtually every horror movie ever made, this does a wonderful job paying homage to the genre. The story involves an alien organism that lands on Earth and immediately infects someone. Some thirty years later, when this contaminated individual is accidentally released, he wanders into a college town spreading these organisms in some rather disgusting ways. Not rated; contains violence. 89m. **DIR:** Fred Dekker. **CAST:** Jason Lively, Steve Marchall, Jill Whitlow, Tom Atkins, Dick Miller. **1986**

NIGHT OF THE CYCLONE 🦃 Chicago detective stumbles onto a murder when he travels to the Caribbean. Rated R for profanity, nudity, and violence. 90m. **DIR:** David Irving. **CAST:** Kris Kristofferson, Jeff Meek, Marisa Berenson. **1989**

NIGHT OF THE DEATH CULT ★★1/2 This is one of a popular series of Spanish horror movies concerning the Templars, blind medieval priests who rise from the dead when their tombs are violated. The film contains nudity, violence, and gore, though as a whole it is more subdued than American zombie movies. 85m. **DIR:** Amando de Ossorio. **CAST:** Victor Petit, Maria Kosti. **1975**

NIGHT OF THE DEMON 🦃 This is a boring little bomb of a movie with an intriguing title and nothing else. 97m. **DIR:** James C. Wasson. **CAST:** Michael Cutt, Jay Allen. **1983**

NIGHT OF THE DEMONS ★★★ A great creaky-house movie about a group of teenagers who hold a séance in an abandoned mortuary. What they conjure up from the dead is more than they bargained for. Rated R for violence and nudity. 90m. **DIR:** Kevin S. Tenney. **CAST:** William Gallo. **1989**

NIGHT OF THE DEMONS 2 ★★1/2 Inventive special effects and occasional flashes of wit elevate this haunted-house sequel above most gorefests, but the rigid formula has got pretty tiresome: good girls and boys survive the demonic carnage, while bad things happen to all their promiscuous friends. Rated R for violence, nudity, suggested sex, and profanity. 96m. **DIR:** Brian Trenchard-Smith. **CAST:** Bobby Jacoby, Amelia Kinkade, Zoe Trilling, Christi Harris. **1994**

NIGHT OF THE DEMONS 3 ★★ Another group of stereotypical teens meets the demon Angela and gets turned into zombies. If you've seen the first two, then don't bother with this one. Not rated; contains violence, profanity, nudity, and simulated sex. 85m. **DIR:** James Kaufman. **CAST:** Amelia Kinkade. **1997**

NIGHT OF THE DEVILS 🦃 Tepid modern-vampire melodrama. It's based on the same Tolstoy story that inspired the Boris Karloff sequence in *Black Sabbath*. No rating, but contains moderate violence and sex. English dubbed. 82m. **DIR:** Giorgio Ferroni. **CAST:** Gianni Garko, Agostina Belli, Mark Roberts. **1972**

NIGHT OF THE FOLLOWING DAY, THE ★★★ Three men and a woman abduct an heiress as she returns home to France. Marlon Brando plays the compassionate Bud, who is tired of being a criminal. His coconspirators include a drug addict, an old washed-up criminal,

and a sadist. The story line moves slowly but becomes very suspenseful near the end. Rated R for violence and nudity. 93m. **DIR:** Hubert Cornfield. **CAST:** Marlon Brando, Richard Boone, Rita Moreno, Pamela Franklin, Jess Hahn. **1968**

NIGHT OF THE FOX ★★ Preposterous adaptation of Jack Higgins's WWII-set thriller about an undercover mission to rescue an American officer from German-occupied territory. Choppily edited from a six-hour miniseries, leaving nothing but the clichés. 95m. **DIR:** Charles Jarrott. **CAST:** George Peppard, Deborah Raffin, Michael York, David Birney, John Mills. **1990**

NIGHT OF THE GENERALS 🦃 Lurid WWII murder mystery, revolving around a group of Nazi generals. 148m. **DIR:** Anatole Litvak. **CAST:** Peter O'Toole, Omar Sharif, Tom Courtenay, Donald Pleasence, Joanna Pettet, Christopher Plummer. **1967**

NIGHT OF THE GHOULS ★★ From the director of *Plan 9 from Outer Space* and *Glen or Glenda* comes a film so bad it was never released. Not nearly as enjoyably bad as Edward Wood's other work, but definitely worth a look for movie buffs. For the record, two young innocents stumble upon a haunted house (filled with some very tiresome bad actors). B&W; 75m. **DIR:** Edward D. Wood Jr. **CAST:** Kenne Duncan, Criswell. **1958 DVD**

NIGHT OF THE GRIZZLY, THE ★★★★ In order to maintain a peaceful standing in the rugged Old West, big Clint Walker must fight all the local bad guys (who should have known better) as well as a giant grizzly bear who moves in and out of camera range on a wheeled dolly. Nice outdoor sets and some good characterization help this no-frills family story. 102m. **DIR:** Joseph Pevney. **CAST:** Clint Walker, Martha Hyer, Ron Ely, Jack Elam. **1966**

NIGHT OF THE HOWLING BEAST ★★ The Wolfman meets the Abominable Snowman. Paul Naschy is the horror king of Spain, but after his movies have been chopped up and dubbed for American release, it's pretty hard to see why. Not rated, but the equivalent of a light R. 87m. **DIR:** Miguel Iglesias Bonns. **CAST:** Paul Naschy. **1975**

NIGHT OF THE HUNTED 🦃 French director Jean Rollin's shocker about the disintegration of the minds of the residents in an apartment complex is a thin excuse for coupling. Not rated; contains simulated sex, nudity, and violence. 93m. **DIR:** Jean Rollin. **CAST:** Vincent Gardère, Brigitte Lahaie. **1980 DVD**

NIGHT OF THE HUNTER ★★★★1/2 Absolutely the finest film from star Robert Mitchum, who is cast as a suave, smooth-talking—and absolutely evil—preacher determined to catch and kill his stepchildren. The entire film is eerie, exquisitely beautiful, and occasionally surreal; watch for the graceful, haunting shot of the children's freshly killed mother. B&W; 93m. **DIR:** Charles Laughton. **CAST:** Robert Mitchum, Shelley Winters, Lillian Gish, James Gleason. **1955 DVD**

NIGHT OF THE IGUANA, THE ★★★ In this film, based on Tennessee Williams's play, Richard Burton is a former minister trying to be reinstated in his church. Meanwhile, he takes a menial job as a tour guide, from which he gets fired. His attempted suicide is foiled and confusing. Finally, he finds other reasons to continue living. Sound dull? If not for the cast, it would be. B&W; 118m. **DIR:** John Huston. **CAST:** Richard Burton, Ava Gardner, Deborah Kerr, Sue Lyons. **1964**

NIGHT OF THE JUGGLER ★★ Psychopath kidnaps little girl for ransom. It's the wrong little girl. Her daddy's an ex-cop with no money and lots of rage. The movie, buoyed by James Brolin's potent performance, initially grabs viewers' attention. Eventually, it wheezes to a predictable conclusion. Rated R. 101m. **DIR:** Robert Butler. **CAST:** James Brolin, Cliff Gorman, Richard Castellano, Abby Bluestone, Linda G. Miller, Mandy Patinkin. **1980**

NIGHT OF THE LIVING DEAD ★★★1/2 This remake, directed by makeup master Tom Savini and produced by George Romero, combines all the terror of the 1968 original with 1990 special effects. Surprisingly, Savini, known for his realistic effects in *Dawn of the Dead* and *Friday the 13th*, doesn't pile the blood on. Rated R for violence, profanity, and gore. 96m. **DIR:** Tom Savini. **CAST:** Tony Todd. **1990 DVD**

NIGHT OF THE LIVING DEAD ★★★★ This gruesome low-budget horror film still packs a punch for those who like to be frightened out of their wits. It is an unrelenting shockfest laced with touches of black humor that deserves its cult status. B&W; 96m. **DIR:** George A. Romero. **CAST:** Duane Jones, Judith O'Dea, Keith Wayne. **1968 DVD**

NIGHT OF THE RUNNING MAN ★★★ While not long on logic, this compelling little thriller is fueled by Scott Glenn's stylish performance as an implacable professional killer. Cabby Andrew McCarthy stupidly flees with ill-gotten mob money, only to find Glenn at every port of call. John Glover also shines as Glenn's cheerfully sadistic partner. Rated R for profanity, violence, torture, nudity, and simulated sex. 93m. **DIR:** Mark L. Lester. **CAST:** Scott Glenn, Andrew McCarthy, Janet Gunn, Wayne Newton, John Glover. **1994**

NIGHT OF THE SCARECROW ★★★ Creative plot twists elevate this a notch above the average slasher film. This time the small town is being terrorized by a harmless-looking scarecrow that has an odd assortment of weapons and magic at his disposal. Actually, he's a warlock imprisoned generations ago now seeking revenge and restoration of his powers from his captors' ancestors. Rated R for nudity, sex, profanity, violence, and gore. 83m. **DIR:** Jeff Burr. **CAST:** Elizabeth Barondes, John Mese, Stephen Root, Bruce Glover, Gary Lockwood, Dirk Blocker, John Lazar, Howard Swain. **1995**

NIGHT OF THE SHARKS ★★1/2 Blackmail and intrigue, washed prettily in the lustrous clear water of Cancun, Mexico, compensate somewhat for the predictable post-*Jaws* approach, in which a one-eyed monster shark makes tropical snorkeling sticky. Rated R. 87m. **DIR:** Anthony Richmond. **CAST:** Treat Williams, Antonio Fargas, Christopher Connelly. **1989**

NIGHT OF THE SHOOTING STARS ★★1/2 Made by Paolo and Vittorio Taviani, this Italian import is about the flight of peasants from their mined village in pastoral Tuscany during the waning days of World War II. Despite its subject matter, the horrors of war, it is a strangely unaffecting—and ineffective—motion picture. In Italian with English subtitles. Not rated; the film has violence. 116m. **DIR:** Paolo Taviani, Vittorio Taviani. **CAST:** Omero Antonutti, Margarita Lozano. **1982**

NIGHT OF THE WARRIOR ★★ Lorenzo Lamas plays the photographer-nightclub proprietor-kick boxer extraordinaire who's been making a fortune for fight promoter Anthony Geary. When Lamas wants to quit fighting, Geary frames him for murder. Rated R for nudity, profanity, and violence. 96m. **DIR:** Rafal Zielinski. **CAST:** Lorenzo Lamas, Anthony Geary, Kathleen Kinmont, Arlene Dahl. **1990 DVD**

NIGHT OF THE ZOMBIES 🦃 It's just one long cannibal feast. Rated R for violence and gore. 101m. **DIR:** Bruno Mattei. **CAST:** Frank Garfield, Margie Newton. **1983**

NIGHT OF THE ZOMBIES 🦃 More socially conscious gore from the director of *Bloodsucking Freaks*. Not rated; contains violence, language, and gore. 88m. **DIR:** Joel M. Reed. **CAST:** Jamie Gillis, Ryan Hilliard, Samantha Grey. **1981**

NIGHT ON EARTH ★★★ Episodic film about four cabdrivers and their oddball encounters with an array of passengers on the same night in different countries. As with most of director Jim Jarmusch's films, the determinedly low-key and offbeat *Night on Earth* is a cinematic non sequitur, and only his fans will find it completely satisfying. Rated R for profanity. 128m. **DIR:** Jim Jarmusch. **CAST:** Gena Rowlands, Winona Ryder, Armin Mueller-Stahl, Giancarlo Esposito, Rosie Perez, Roberto Benigni. **1992**

NIGHT OWL ★★ The first offense of this film is false advertising as neither Caroline Munro nor John Leguizamo are major characters despite top billing. Second offense is that the movie is dull. Not rated; contains gore and profanity. B&W; 77m. **DIR:** Jeffrey Arsenault. **CAST:** James Raftery, John Leguizamo, Caroline Munro. **1994**

NIGHT PATROL 🦃 A bumbling rookie policeman doubles as "The Unknown Comic," cracking jokes in Los Angeles comedy clubs while wearing a paper bag over his head. Rated R. 84m. **DIR:** Jackie Kong. **CAST:** Linda Blair, Pat Paulsen, Jaye P. Morgan, Jack Riley, Billy Barty, Murray Langston. **1985**

NIGHT PORTER, THE 🦃 Sordid outing about an ex-Nazi and the woman he used to abuse sexually in a concentration camp. Lots of kinky scenes, including lovemaking on broken glass. Rated R for violence, nudity, and profanity. 115m. **DIR:** Lilliana Cavani. **CAST:** Dirk Bogarde, Charlotte Rampling, Philippe Leroy, Gabriele Ferzetti, Isa Miranda. **1974 DVD**

NIGHT RIDE HOME ★★★ This *Hallmark Hall of Fame* film features a family torn apart after the only son dies while horseback riding. Rebecca DeMornay plays the despicably self-centered mother who cares little for her grief-stricken husband or daughter. Acting is good but topic may make some uncomfortable. Not rated; contains mature topics. 98m. **DIR:** Glenn Jordan. **CAST:** Rebecca DeMornay, Keith Carradine, Thora Birch, Ellen Burstyn. **1999**

NIGHT RIDERS, THE ★★1/2 The Three Mesquiteers (John Wayne, Ray Corrigan, and Max Terhune) make like Zorro by donning capes and masks to foil a villain's attempt to enforce a phony Spanish land grant. Good formula Western fun. B&W; 58m. **DIR:** George Sherman. **CAST:** John Wayne, Ray "Crash" Corrigan, Max Terhune, Doreen McKay, Ruth Rogers, Tom Tyler, Kermit Maynard. **1939**

NIGHT SCHOOL 🦃 Students are (literally) losing their heads with worry over their grades. Rated R for graphic, but sloppy, violence. 88m. **DIR:** Ken Hughes. **CAST:** Leonard Mann, Rachel Ward, Drew Snyder, Joseph R. Sicari. **1981**

NIGHT SHIFT ★★★★ When a nerdish morgue attendant (Henry Winkler) gets talked into becoming a pimp by a sweet hooker (Shelley Long) and his crazed coworker (Michael Keaton), the result is uproarious comedy. While the concept is a little weird, director Ron Howard packs it with so many laughs and such appealing characters that you can't help but like it. Rated R for nudity, profanity, sex, and violence. 105m. **DIR:** Ron Howard. **CAST:** Henry Winkler, Shelley Long, Michael Keaton. **1982 DVD**

NIGHT STALKER, THE (1971) ★★★★ A superb made-for-television chiller about a modern-day vampire stalking the streets of Las Vegas. Richard Matheson's teleplay is tight and suspenseful, with Darren McGavin fine as the intrepid reporter on the bloodsucker's trail. 73m. **DIR:** John Llewellyn Moxey. **CAST:** Darren McGavin, Carol Lynley, Claude Akins. **1971 DVD**

NIGHT STALKER, THE (1986) ★★★ A Vietnam veteran hits the street, brutally murdering prostitutes. An over-the-hill, alcoholic police detective pursues him. The acting is uneven, but the suspense is solid. Worth a look. Rated R for nudity, profanity, and graphic violence. 91m. **DIR:** Max Kleven. **CAST:** Charles Napier, Michelle Reese, Joe Gian, Leka Carlin. **1986**

NIGHT STALKER, THE: TWO TALES OF TERROR (TV SERIES) ★★★★ Two episodes ("The Ripper" and "The Vampire") from the fascinating but gruesome series feature Darren McGavin as a reporter who is forever abandoning his assigned stories in favor of the latest offbeat police report. This time he tracks down Jack the Ripper in Chicago and a female vampire in L.A. Not rated; contains violence and gore. 98m. **DIR:** Allen Baron, Don Weis. **CAST:** Darren McGavin, Simon Oakland, Beatrice Colen, William Daniels, Suzanne Charney, Jan Murray, Kathleen Nolan. **1974**

NIGHT STRANGLER, THE ★★★ Newsman with a nose for the macabre unearths a centenarian killer in Seattle's underground city. Second *Kolchak* feature made for television is as fun and lively as its predecessor and led to a network series featuring the seedy monster hunter. Not rated. 74m. **DIR:** Dan Curtis. **CAST:** Darren McGavin, Simon Oakland, Wally Cox, Richard Anderson, Jo Ann Pflug, John Carradine, Margaret Hamilton, Al Lewis. **1972 DVD**

NIGHT TERROR ★★ Tepid made-for-TV suspense with Valerie Harper as terrified motorist pursued by madman Richard Romanus. Strictly by-the-numbers. 78m. **DIR:** E. W. Swackhamer. **CAST:** Valerie Harper, Richard Romanus, Nicholas Pryor. **1977**

NIGHT THAT NEVER HAPPENED, THE 🦃 Thin sex fantasy from the Playboy Channel about three guys treating their best friend to a night on the town before his wedding. Not rated; contains adult situations, language, and nudity. 95m. **DIR:** James Winner. **CAST:** Colleen McDermott, Lissa Boyle, Joshua D. Comen, Scott Coppola, Judd Dunning. **1997 DVD**

NIGHT THE CITY SCREAMED, THE ★★ Made-for-TV movie shows how different urban characters react to a power blackout on a hot summer night. The best subplot follows rookie cops David Cassidy and Clifton Davis as they try to contain an outbreak of looting. Rated PG

for mild violence. 96m. **DIR:** Harry Falk. **CAST:** Georg Stanford Brown, Raymond Burr, David Cassidy, Robert Culp, Clifton Davis, Don Meredith, Linda Purl. **1980**

NIGHT THE LIGHTS WENT OUT IN GEORGIA, THE ★★★1/2 Gutsy, lusty, and satisfying film about a country singer (Dennis Quaid) with wayward appetites and his levelheaded sister-manager (Kristy McNichol) who run into big trouble while working their way to Nashville. The gritty Deep South settings, fine action, a cast of credible extras, some memorable musical moments, and a dramatic script with comic overtones add up to above-average entertainment. Rated PG. 120m. **DIR:** Ronald F. Maxwell. **CAST:** Kristy McNichol, Mark Hamill, Dennis Quaid, Don Stroud. **1981**

NIGHT THEY RAIDED MINSKY'S, THE ★★★1/2 Director William Friedkin's tale of a religious girl's (Britt Ekland) involvement, much to her father's dismay, with a burlesque comic (Jason Robards). It's a nice look at what early burlesque was like, with good performances by all. Rated PG. 99m. **DIR:** William Friedkin. **CAST:** Britt Ekland, Jason Robards Jr., Elliott Gould. **1968**

NIGHT THEY SAVED CHRISTMAS, THE ★★★★ In this excellent made-for-television film, three kids strive to protect Santa's toy factory from being destroyed by an oil company. Art Carney is delightful as Saint Nick. 100m. **DIR:** Jackie Cooper. **CAST:** Jaclyn Smith, Art Carney, Paul LeMat, Mason Adams, June Lockhart, Paul Williams. **1984**

NIGHT TIDE ★★★ Dennis Hopper stars in this surreal fantasy about a young sailor on leave who falls in love with a mysterious woman posing as a mermaid in a seafront carnival. Avant-garde filmmaker Curtis Harrington, in his first feature, manages to create a mystical and nightmarish world in which his characters' true motivations are often obscured. Recommended for connoisseurs of the offbeat. B&W; 84m. **DIR:** Curtis Harrington. **CAST:** Dennis Hopper, Linda Lawson, Gavin Muir. **1961 DVD**

NIGHT TO DISMEMBER, A ★★ A must for bad-movie buffs, this insanely disjointed slasher movie features almost no dialogue, actors whose hairstyles and clothes change in mid-scene, and a tacked-on narration desperately trying to make sense of it all. Not rated, but with nudity and hilariously bad gore effects. 70m. **DIR:** Doris Wishman. **CAST:** Samantha Fox. **1983 DVD**

NIGHT TO REMEMBER, A (1943) ★★★★ This is a very interesting comedy-whodunit about a Greenwich Village mystery author and his wife who try to solve a real murder. Performances are wonderful and the direction is taut. B&W; 91m. **DIR:** Richard Wallace. **CAST:** Loretta Young, Brian Aherne, Jeff Donnell, William Wright, Sidney Toler, Gale Sondergaard. **1943**

NIGHT TO REMEMBER, A (1958) ★★★★ Authenticity and credibility mark this documentarylike enactment of the sinking of the luxury passenger liner H.M.S. *Titanic* in deep icy Atlantic waters in April, 1912. Novelist Eric Ambler scripted from historian Walter Lord's meticulously detailed account of the tragedy. B&W; 123m. **DIR:** Roy Ward Baker. **CAST:** Kenneth More, Jill Dixon, David McCallum, Laurence Naismith, Honor Blackman, Frank Lawton, Alec McCowen, George Rose. **1958 DVD**

NIGHT TRAIN TO KATMANDU ★★ Standard family fare about two youngsters who are uprooted from their comfortable suburban home in the United States to live with their anthropologist parents in Nepal. There they get involved in the quest for the legendary City That Never Was. Nothing special. Not rated. 102m. **DIR:** Robert Wiemer. **CAST:** Pernell Roberts, Eddie Castrodad. **1988**

NIGHT TRAIN TO MUNICH (NIGHT TRAIN) ★★★★1/2 Based on Gordon Wellesley's novel *Report on a Fugitive*, this taut thriller concerns a British agent (Rex Harrison) trying to rescue a Czech scientist who has escaped from the Gestapo. Along with a fine cast and superb script and direction, this film is blessed with the moody and wonderful photography of Otto Kanturek. B&W; 93m. **DIR:** Carol Reed. **CAST:** Rex Harrison, Margaret Lockwood, Paul Henreid, Basil Radford, Naunton Wayne. **1940**

NIGHT TRAIN TO TERROR ★★ Segments from three bad horror movies are condensed (which improves them considerably) and introduced by actors playing God and Satan. It's still pretty bad, but the edited stories are fast-moving and sleazily entertaining. See if you can recognize Richard "Bull" Moll (in two segments) with his hair. Rated R for nudity, graphic violence, and gore. 93m. **DIR:** John Carr, Jay Schlossberg-Cohen. **CAST:** Cameron Mitchell, John Phillip Law, Marc Lawrence, Richard Moll. **1985 DVD**

NIGHT TRAIN TO VENICE 🦃 Hugh Grant is a journalist dogged by neo-Nazis as he travels to Venice in this mindless and melodramatic oddity. Rated R for violence, profanity, sexual situations, and nudity. 98m. **DIR:** Carlo U. Quinterio. **CAST:** Hugh Grant, Malcolm McDowell, Tahnee Welch. **1993**

NIGHT VISITOR, THE (1970) ★★★ Revenge is the name of the game in this English-language Danish production. Max von Sydow plays an inmate in an insane asylum who comes up with a plan to escape for a single night and take revenge on the various people he believes are responsible for his current predicament. Performances are fine. Rated PG. 106m. **DIR:** Laslo Benedek. **CAST:** Max von Sydow, Liv Ullmann, Trevor Howard, Per Oscarsson, Rupert Davies. **1970 DVD**

NIGHT VISITOR (1989) ★★ When a compulsive liar (Derek Rydall) witnesses a Satanic murder committed by his history teacher, no one believes him. Rydall's childish whining is inconsistent with his role. Rated R for nudity, violence, and profanity. 93m. **DIR:** Rupert Hitzig. **CAST:** Derek Rydall, Allen Garfield, Michael J. Pollard, Shannon Tweed, Elliott Gould, Richard Roundtree. **1989**

NIGHT WALKER, THE ★★★1/2 Robert Bloch's intriguing script is the chief attraction of this moody little thriller, definitely among the best of director-producer William Castle's gimmick horror films. Wealthy Barbara Stanwyck can't stop dreaming about her dead husband, and the recurring nightmares prove to have an unusual cause. 86m. **DIR:** William Castle. **CAST:** Barbara Stanwyck, Robert Taylor, Lloyd Bochner. **1964**

NIGHT WARNING ★★ As in many gory movies, the victims and near victims have a convenient and unbelievable way of hanging around despite clear indications they are about to get it. Consequently, in spite of good performances, this is an unremarkable splatter film.

Rated R for violence. 96m. **DIR:** William Asher. **CAST:** Jimmy McNichol, Bo Svenson, Susan Tyrrell. **1982**

NIGHT WATCH ★★ In this so-so suspense–thriller, Elizabeth Taylor stars as a wealthy widow recovering from a nervous breakdown. From her window, she seems to witness a number of ghoulish goings-on. But does she? The operative phrase here after a while is "Who cares?" Rated PG. 98m. **DIR:** Brian G. Hutton. **CAST:** Elizabeth Taylor, Laurence Harvey, Billie Whitelaw, Robert Lang, Tony Britton. **1973**

NIGHT WE NEVER MET, THE ★★★1/2 A sophisticated comedy with strong players who understand the meaning of teamwork. Kevin Anderson time-shares his New York apartment to help pay the rent. Would-be lothario Matthew Broderick and unhappily married Annabella Sciorra rent on alternate days. You know in advance that they will find each other, but the fun is finding out how. Delightful dialogue. 99m. **DIR:** Warren Light. **CAST:** Matthew Broderick, Annabella Sciorra, Kevin Anderson, Jeanne Tripplehorn, Justine Bateman, Garry Shandling, Louise Lasser, Katharine Houghton. **1993**

NIGHT ZOO ★★★ An impressive, quirky French-Canadian film that brings together the unlikely combination of a tough, visceral, urban thriller and a sensitive, bittersweet story about the renewed love between a dying father and his grown son. The film moves from the dark streets of nighttime Montreal to a strange encounter with an elephant during a nocturnal visit to the zoo. Rated R, with strong violence and profanity. 107m. **DIR:** Jean-Claude Lauzon. **CAST:** Gilles Maheu, Roger Le Bel. **1987**

NIGHTBREAKER ★★★★ Effective message film takes us behind the scenes of nuclear tests on military personnel in Nevada, 1956. The atomic bomb horrors are both realistic and terrifying. Made for TV. 99m. **DIR:** Peter Markle. **CAST:** Emilio Estevez, Martin Sheen, Lea Thompson. **1989**

NIGHTCOMERS, THE ★★1/2 Strange prequel to *The Turn of the Screw*, this uneven effort contains some fine acting and boasts some truly eerie scenes, but is hampered by Michael Winner's loose direction and a nebulous story line. Marlon Brando is in good form as the mysterious catalyst, but this murky melodrama still lacks the solid story and cohesiveness that could have made it a true chiller. Rated R. 96m. **DIR:** Michael Winner. **CAST:** Marlon Brando, Stephanie Beacham, Thora Hird, Harry Andrews. **1971**

NIGHTFALL 🦃 David Birney is the ruler of a land that has never known night. Rated PG-13, but contains abundant nudity and violence. 83m. **DIR:** Paul Mayersberg. **CAST:** David Birney, Sarah Douglas. **1988**

NIGHTFLYERS ★★★ A motley crew of space explorers search for an ancient and mysterious entity. Their ship is controlled by a computer, programmed from the brain patterns of an abused, jealous, and telepathic woman. This film's only weaknesses are inconsistent special effects and an ending that leaves you hanging. Sci-fi fans should find this entertaining. Rated R for violence and language. 90m. **DIR:** T. C. Blake. **CAST:** Catherine Mary Stewart, Michael Praed, John Standing, Lisa Blount, Michael Des Barres. **1987**

NIGHTFORCE ★★ Linda Blair as a commando. A group of kids venture to Central America to free the kidnapped daughter of a prominent American politician. Rated R for violence. 82m. **DIR:** Lawrence D. Foldes. **CAST:** Linda Blair, Claudia Udy, James Van Patten, Richard Lynch, Chad McQueen, Cameron Mitchell. **1987**

NIGHTHAWKS ★★★★1/2 From its explosive first scene to the breathtakingly suspenseful denouement, *Nighthawks*, about a police detective hunting a wily terrorist, is a thoroughly enjoyable, supercharged action film. Rated R for violence, nudity, and profanity. 99m. **DIR:** Bruce Malmuth. **CAST:** Sylvester Stallone, Billy Dee Williams, Rutger Hauer, Lindsay Wagner. **1981 DVD**

NIGHTJOHN ★★★★1/2 Inspirational tale of a young slave girl named Sarny, whose prayer for knowledge is answered when her master brings home a new slave named Nightjohn. When Nightjohn defies tradition by teaching Sarny to read, her new skill opens up a whole new world to her, teaching her important lessons about life and the human spirit. Outstanding performances and period detail make this made-for-cable production a moving experience. Rated PG-13 for violence. 96m. **DIR:** Charles Burnett. **CAST:** Beau Bridges, Carl Lumbly, Allison Jones, Lorraine Toussaint, Bill Cobbs. **1996**

NIGHTKILL ★★★ Largely unreleased in theaters, this is a tidy little cat-and-mouse thriller with former Charlie's Angel Jaclyn Smith as a conniving widow and Robert Mitchum as the world-weary investigator who gets caught up in her scheme. Despite some inept direction, the last half hour is a nail biter, particularly scenes in a bathroom shower. Rated R for violence, nudity, and profanity. 97m. **DIR:** Ted Post. **CAST:** Jaclyn Smith, Robert Mitchum, James Franciscus. **1983**

NIGHTLIFE ★★★1/2 A doctor finds a beautiful patient with a strange taste for blood in this funny and scary horror show, made for cable. Keith Szarabajka, as a doctor, steals the show by being both spooky and comically warped. Great fun. 90m. **DIR:** Daniel Taplitz. **CAST:** Maryam D'Abo, Ben Cross, Keith Szarabajka. **1989**

NIGHTMAN, THE ★★★ Steamy southern romantic thriller. A woman suspects she's being stalked by a former lover who spent eighteen years in prison for the murder of her mother. In flashbacks, she recalls the events and the passion that led to a bitter love triangle and the killing. Rated R for simulated sex, nudity, violence, and profanity. 96m. **DIR:** Charles Haid. **CAST:** Joanna Kerns, Jenny Robertson, Latanya Richardson, Lou Walker. **1993**

NIGHTMARE ★★★ Dreams and visions haunt a teenager who begins to think she is losing her mind. Or is it all a plot to drive her crazy? Intriguing Hammer Studios thriller with enough red herrings and devious characters to keep you guessing. Not rated; contains implied violence. B&W; 83m. **DIR:** Freddie Francis. **CAST:** David Knight, Moira Redmond, Brenda Bruce, John Welsh. **1964**

NIGHTMARE ★★ Average made-for-television thriller about a girl who is abducted by a serial killer, escapes, and then has to face the nightmare all over again when the killer is caught and released on a technicality. No surprises here. Rated PG-13 for intense situations. 95m. **DIR:** John Pasquin. **CAST:** Victoria Principal, Paul

Sorvino, Jonathan Banks, Danielle Harris, Gregg Henry. **1991**

NIGHTMARE AT BITTERCREEK ★★ Nazi survivalists stalk a group of women camping in the mountains. The mediocre script offers a few chills and a modicum of suspense, but overall leaves one feeling unsatisfied. Made for TV. 92m. **DIR:** Tim Burstall. **CAST:** Lindsay Wagner, Tom Skerritt, Constance McCashin, Joanna Cassidy. **1990**

NIGHTMARE AT NOON 🦃 A group of renegade scientists testing a germ-warfare virus. Rated R for violence. 96m. **DIR:** Nico Mastorakis. **CAST:** Wings Hauser, Bo Hopkins, George Kennedy, Brian James. **1987 DVD**

NIGHTMARE BEFORE CHRISTMAS, THE ★★★★ Literally years in the making, Tim Burton's warped holiday fantasy is a true stunner. Employing a blend of conventional stop-motion and replacement animation (the latter rarely seen beyond George Pal's efforts), Burton and scripter Caroline Thompson spin a wonderfully weird tale about Halloweentown-hero Jack Skellington's efforts to redefine Christmas. While not for average tastes, this is one of those rare films with "sense of wonder" to spare. Rated G. 75m. **DIR:** Henry Selick. **1993 DVD**

NIGHTMARE CASTLE ★★ Barbara Steele plays two roles in this lurid Italian shocker about a faithless wife and the gory revenge exacted by her jealous husband. Routine theatrics, atmospherically photographed—and cut by fifteen minutes for its U.S. release. B&W; 90m. **DIR:** Mario Caiano. **CAST:** Barbara Steele, Paul Muller, Helga Line. **1965**

NIGHTMARE CIRCUS (BARN OF THE LIVING DEAD) (TERROR CIRCUS) ★★ A young man who was abused as a child abducts women and chains them in the family barn. This graphically violent low-budget R-rater was the first theatrical feature by the now highly respected director Alan Rudolph. 86m. **DIR:** Alan Rudolph. **CAST:** Andrew Prine, Sherry Alberoni. **1973**

NIGHTMARE HOUSE 🦃 Previously available on video under its original title *Scream, Baby, Scream*, the movie is rated R for violence and brief nudity. 83m. **DIR:** Joseph Adler. **CAST:** Ross Harris. **1969**

NIGHTMARE IN BLOOD ★★ A film that's fun for genre fans only. A horror-movie star appears at a horror convention that people are dying to get into. The twist is he isn't just playing a vampire in his films; he *is* one. The cassette box says "filmed in and around picturesque San Francisco," and most viewers will think that's the best thing about it. Not rated; contains mild bloodletting. 92m. **DIR:** John Stanley. **CAST:** Jerry Walter, Barrie Youngfellow, Kerwin Mathews. **1975**

NIGHTMARE IN WAX (CRIMES IN THE WAX MUSEUM) 🦃 Cameron Mitchell plays a disfigured ex–makeup man running a wax museum in Hollywood. Rated PG. 91m. **DIR:** Bud Townsend. **CAST:** Cameron Mitchell, Anne Helm, Scott Brady. **1969**

NIGHTMARE ON ELM STREET, A ★★★★ Wes Craven directed this clever shocker about a group of teenagers afflicted with the same bad dreams. Horror movie buffs, take note. Rated R for nudity, violence, and profanity. 91m. **DIR:** Wes Craven. **CAST:** John Saxon, Ronee Blakley, Heather Langenkamp, Robert Englund. **1984 DVD**

NIGHTMARE ON ELM STREET 2, A: FREDDY'S REVENGE 🦃 Another teen exploitation film. Rated R for nudity, language, and gore. 83m. **DIR:** Jack Sholder. **CAST:** Mark Patton, Kim Myers, Clu Gulager, Hope Lange. **1985 DVD**

NIGHTMARE ON ELM STREET 3, A: THE DREAM-WARRIORS 🦃 Freddy is at it again. Rated R. 97m. **DIR:** Charles Russell. **CAST:** Robert Englund, Heather Langenkamp, Patricia Arquette, Craig Wasson. **1987 DVD**

NIGHTMARE ON ELM STREET 4, A: THE DREAM-MASTER ★★ America's favorite child-molesting burn victim Freddy Krueger (Robert Englund) is back in this fourth installment of the hit series. Freddy's favorite pastime, killing teenagers in their dreams, is played to the hilt with fantastic special effects. Rated R for violence and gore. 97m. **DIR:** Renny Harlin. **CAST:** Robert Englund, Lisa Wilcox. **1988 DVD**

NIGHTMARE ON ELM STREET 5, A: THE DREAM CHILD ★★★ This fifth installment in the series is a wild ride filled with gruesome makeup effects and mind-blowing visuals. Never mind that Freddy's return is not explained. (He was supposedly killed in part 4.) This time he enters the dreams of the heroine's unborn child, attempting to place the souls of those he kills into the fetus. Rated R for violence, profanity, and plenty o' gore. 91m. **DIR:** Stephen Hopkins. **CAST:** Robert Englund, Lisa Wilcox. **1989 DVD**

NIGHTMARE ON THE 13TH FLOOR 🦃 Haunted hotel chiller. This made-for-cable movie has minimal violence. Rated PG-13. 85m. **DIR:** Walter Grauman. **CAST:** Michele Greene, Louise Fletcher, James Brolin, John Karlen. **1990**

NIGHTMARE YEARS, THE ★★★★ William L. Shirer's first-person account of the rise of Hitler comes to life in this made-for-cable bio. Sam Waterston plays the daring American reporter in Berlin, Vienna, and France from 1934 to 1940. 474m. **DIR:** Anthony Page. **CAST:** Sam Waterston, Marthe Keller, Kurtwood Smith. **1989**

NIGHTMARES ★★ Four everyday situations are twisted into tales of terror in this mostly mediocre horror film in the style of *Twilight Zone—the Movie* and *Creepshow*. Rated R for violence and profanity. 99m. **DIR:** Joseph Sargent. **CAST:** Cristina Raines, Emilio Estevez, Lance Henriksen. **1983 DVD**

NIGHTS IN WHITE SATIN ★★1/2 Hokey Cinderella story has Prince Charming as an ace fashion photographer. The glass slippers are snapshots of a rags-dressed beauty who lives among the poor just a motorcycle ride from the photographer's elegant loft. Rated R for nudity. 99m. **DIR:** Michael Bernard. **CAST:** Kenneth Gilman, Priscilla Harris. **1987**

NIGHTS OF CABIRIA ★★★★ Federico Fellini's seventh film can be hailed as a tragicomic masterpiece. The story focuses on an impoverished prostitute (Giulietta Masina) living on the outskirts of Rome, who is continuously betrayed by her faith in human nature. Masina gives an unforgettable performance. In Italian with English subtitles. B&W; 110m. **DIR:** Federico Fellini. **CAST:** Giulietta Masina, Amadeo Nazzari, François Perier. **1957 DVD**

NIGHTSCARE ★★★ When a vicious serial killer is administered an experimental drug, it releases him from the prison of his earthly body so he can renew his bloodshed through the dreams of his victims. Sometimes at-

mospheric, sometimes overly bloody, horror film features plenty of jolts and a surprisingly good performance from model Elizabeth Hurley who stars as the inventor of the treatment serum. Rated R for violence, profanity, and sexual situations. 89m. **DIR:** Vadim Jean. **CAST:** Elizabeth Hurley, Craig Fairbrass, Keith Allen, Anita Hobson, Craig Kelly. **1993**

NIGHTSIEGE-PROJECT: SHADOWCHASER 2 ★★ Plenty of sci-fi action and some decent special effects aren't enough to breathe life into this tired premise. Three unlikely heroes are brought together in order to stop an android that has the capability of turning the planet into toast. Utter nonsense dressed up with no place to go. R-rated and unrated versions; both contain extreme violence and adult language. 97/98. **DIR:** John Eyres. **CAST:** Bryan Genesse, Beth Toussaint, Frank Zagarino. **1994**

NIGHTSTICK ★★★ A fast-paced thriller with Bruce Fairbairn as an unorthodox cop who is hunting down two ex-convict brothers. The deadly duo are placing bombs in banks and threatening to blow them up unless a ransom is met. A good cast and above-average script make this one worth renting. Equivalent to an R, violent! 94m. **DIR:** Joseph L. Scanlan. **CAST:** Bruce Fairbairn, Robert Vaughn, Kerrie Keane, John Vernon, Leslie Nielsen. **1987**

NIGHTTIME IN NEVADA ★★★ Remorse-ridden killer Grant Withers, to cover up a murder he committed sixteen years ago, plans to steal Roy Rogers's cattle to pay off and make amends to the dead man's daughter. B Western bad-man logic. B&W; 67m. **DIR:** William Witney. **CAST:** Roy Rogers, Andy Devine, Adele Mara, Grant Withers, Bob Nolan and the Sons of the Pioneers. **1948**

NIGHTWATCH ★★1/2 A young law student (Ewan McGregor), while working as a night watchman at the city morgue, finds himself the prime suspect in a series of grisly murders. The actors are good (though McGregor's American accent comes and goes), and there are some genuinely creepy scenes, but the story is full of holes and the plot twists are telegraphed a mile in advance. Rated R for nudity, profanity, and gore. 105m. **DIR:** Ole Bornedal. **CAST:** Ewan McGregor, Nick Nolte, Josh Brolin, Patricia Arquette, Brad Dourif. **1998 DVD**

NIGHTWING 🦃 Absolutely laughable tale, derived from an abysmal Martin Cruz Smith novel, about a flock (herd? pack?) of vampire bats. Rated PG. 105m. **DIR:** Arthur Hiller. **CAST:** David Warner, Kathryn Harrold, Nick Mancuso, Strother Martin. **1979**

NIGHTWISH ★★ A team of graduate student dream researchers explores supernatural phenomena in a house haunted by a sinister alien presence. There are some good effects, and a fairly imaginative ending given the confused story line. Not rated, but with partial nudity and profanity. 96m. **DIR:** Bruce R. Cook. **CAST:** Clayton Rohner, Jack Starrett, Robert Tessier, Brian Thompson. **1990**

NIJINSKY ★★★ George de la Pena stars as the legendary dancer and Alan Bates is his lover, a Ballet Russe impresario. Herbert Ross (*The Turning Point*) is no stranger to ballet films. Here, he has assembled an outstanding cast and filmed them beautifully. Rated R. 125m. **DIR:** Herbert Ross. **CAST:** Alan Bates, George de la Pena, Leslie Browne, Jeremy Irons. **1980**

NIKKI, WILD DOG OF THE NORTH ★★★ The rugged wilderness of northern Canada provides the backdrop to this story of a dog that is separated from his owner. 73m. **DIR:** Jack Couffer. **CAST:** Don Haldane, Jean Coutu, Emile Genest. **1961 DVD**

NIL BY MOUTH ★★★★ This gritty skid through squalid working-class South London is a ferocious slice of social realism that slithers into dark, dysfunctional family relationships. Raymond is a human time bomb fueled by alcohol. His abuse of his wife and drug-addicted brother-in-law leads to several harrowing moments in a life bloodied by ugly machismo, self-loathing, and self-pity. Rated R for language, domestic violence, nudity, and graphic drug use. 128m. **DIR:** Gary Oldman. **CAST:** Ray Winstone, Kathy Burke, Charlie Creed-Miles, Laila Morse, Edna Dore. **1998**

NINA TAKES A LOVER ★★★★ Funny, enlightening, and involving romance stars Laura San Giacomo as a young woman wondering what to do with her spare time since her husband is on the road so often. She opts for an unusual affair. Well acted, written, and directed, film hits the bull's-eye more often than not. Rated R for profanity and sexuality. 100m. **DIR:** Alan Jacobs. **CAST:** Laura San Giacomo, Paul Rhys, Michael O'Keefe, Cristi Conaway, Fisher Stevens. **1995**

NINE DAYS A QUEEN ★★★ This well-acted historical drama picks up after the death of Henry VIII and follows the frenzied and often lethal scramble for power that went on in the court of England. Lovely Nova Pilbeam plays Lady Jane Grey, the heroine of the title who is taken to the headsman's block by Mary Tudor's armies after a pathetic reign of only nine days. Tragic and moving, this British film was well received by critics when it premiered but is practically forgotten today. B&W; 80m. **DIR:** Robert Stevenson. **CAST:** Cedric Hardwicke, Nova Pilbeam, John Mills, Sybil Thorndike, Leslie Perrins, Felix Aylmer, Miles Malleson. **1936**

976-EVIL ★★★1/2 Actor Robert Englund makes his directorial debut with this tale of a wimpish teenager who slowly becomes possessed by a 976 "Horrorscope" number. Englund gives his film a genuinely eerie feel without missing his chance to throw in a little comedy. Rated R for violence. 92m. **DIR:** Robert Englund. **CAST:** Jim Metzler, Stephen Geoffreys, Sandy Dennis, Robert Picardo. **1989**

976-EVIL II: THE ASTRAL FACTOR ★★ An occult-oriented telephone service assists a murderer in astrally projecting himself from jail so that he may continue his killing spree. A fair sequel. Rated R for graphic violence, profanity, and nudity. 93m. **DIR:** Jim Wynorski. **CAST:** Rene Assa, Brigitte Nielsen, Patrick O'Bryan. **1991**

NINE LIVES OF ELFEGO BACA, THE ★★★ Robert Loggia, as the long-lived hero of the Old West, faces one of his most harrowing perils as he confronts scores of gunmen. Lots of action and fun for the whole family. Rated G. 78m. **DIR:** Norman Foster. **CAST:** Robert Loggia, Robert F. Simon, Lisa Montell, Nestor Paiva. **1958**

NINE LIVES OF FRITZ THE CAT ★★1/2 A streetwise alley cat tries to escape his mundane existence in the sequel to the 1972 cult favorite, *Fritz the Cat*. Fritz is his usual witty, horny self. The animation is excellent and the film is written with a hip sense of humor. This is not Saturday-morning material, however, as there is a distinctly erotic tone to virtually every scene. Rated R for

adult theme and language. 77m. **DIR:** Robert Taylor. **1974 DVD**

NINE MONTHS ★★1/2 So-so comedy about a young couple, Hugh Grant and Julianne Moore, nervously on the verge of parenthood. More to the point, she's looking forward to being a mother, but he is panic-stricken at the thought of becoming a father. It's watchable enough, although annoying "friendly" parents played by Tom Arnold and Joan Cusack sabotage some of the film's potentially best scenes. Rated PG-13 for light profanity. 103m. **DIR:** Chris Columbus. **CAST:** Hugh Grant, Julianne Moore, Tom Arnold, Joan Cusack, Jeff Goldblum, Robin Williams. **1995**

NINE TO FIVE ★★★★ In this delightful comedy, Jane Fonda almost ends up playing third fiddle to two marvelous comediennes, Lily Tomlin and Dolly Parton. (That's right, Dolly Parton!) The gifted singer-songwriter makes one of the brightest acting debuts ever in this hilarious farce about three secretaries who decide to get revenge on their sexist, egomaniacal boss (Dabney Coleman). Rated PG. 110m. **DIR:** Colin Higgins. **CAST:** Jane Fonda, Lily Tomlin, Dolly Parton, Dabney Coleman. **1980**

9 1/2 NINJAS ★★★ A slapstick spoof of ninja movies and *9 1/2 Weeks.* A nonexistent plot, but solid hilarity. Michael Phenice is terrific. Rated R for nudity. 82m. **DIR:** Aaron Worth. **CAST:** Michael Phenice. **1990**

9 1/2 WEEKS ★★ Somewhere between toning down the bondage and liberating the heroine, this movie's story definitely loses out to the imagery. Mickey Rourke is quite believable in the lead role of the masochistic seducer, but Kim Basinger does little more than look pretty. This couple makes steamy work of simple things like dressing and eating. Rated R for sex and violence. 113m. **DIR:** Adrian Lyne. **CAST:** Mickey Rourke, Kim Basinger, Margaret Whitton, David Branski, Karen Young. **1986 DVD**

90 DAYS ★★★ A fine little comedy shot in documentary style. The narrator has sent for a Korean pen pal to come to be his wife in Canada. The resultant cultural differences are humorously explored. Not rated. 100m. **DIR:** Giles Walker. **CAST:** Stefas Wodoslavsky, Sam Grana. **1986**

NINETY DEGREES IN THE SHADE ★★ Strange combination of sex drama and morality tale about a grocery-store clerk whose loyalty to her boss leads to tragic consequences. The Anglo-Czech coproduction attempts to be daring in its mid-1960s depiction of forbidden lust, yet it seems tame and tiresome by today's standards. Not rated; contains adult situations. B&W; 90m. **DIR:** Jiri Weiss. **CAST:** Anne Heywood, James Booth, Rudolf Hrusínsky, Jirina Jiraskova. **1965**

99 AND 44/100 PERCENT DEAD 🦃 A hit man is hired to rub out a gangland boss. Rated PG for violence. 98m. **DIR:** John Frankenheimer. **CAST:** Richard Harris, Chuck Connors, Edmond O'Brien, Bradford Dillman, Ann Turkel. **1974**

99 WOMEN 🦃 Eurojunk set in a women's prison with all the usual stereotypes. Rated R. 90m. **DIR:** Jess (Jesus) Franco. **CAST:** Maria Schell, Mercedes McCambridge, Herbert Lom, Luciana Paluzzi. **1969**

92 IN THE SHADE ★★★ This wild and hilarious adaptation of first-time director Thomas McGuane's prize-winning novel concerns rival fishing-boat captains in Florida. Entire cast is first-rate in this sleeper. Rated R. 93m. **DIR:** Thomas McGuane. **CAST:** Peter Fonda, Warren Oates, Margot Kidder, Harry Dean Stanton, Burgess Meredith, Elizabeth Ashley, Sylvia Miles. **1975**

NINOTCHKA ★★★★★ "Garbo laughs," proclaimed the ads of its day; and so will you in this classic screen comedy. Greta Garbo is a Soviet commissar sent to Paris to check on the lack of progress of three bumbling trade envoys who have been seduced by the decadent trappings of capitalism. Melvyn Douglas, as a Parisian playboy, meets Garbo at the Eiffel Tower and plans a seduction of his own, in this most joyous of Hollywood comedies. B&W; 110m. **DIR:** Ernst Lubitsch. **CAST:** Greta Garbo, Melvyn Douglas, Bela Lugosi. **1939**

NINTH CONFIGURATION, THE ★★★★1/2 This terse, intense film is not for everyone, but the plot, screenplay, and acting are top-notch. Stacy Keach plays a psychiatrist caring for Vietnam War veterans who suffer from acute emotional disorders. Rated R for profanity and violence. 115m. **DIR:** William Peter Blatty. **CAST:** Stacy Keach, Scott Wilson, Jason Miller, Ed Flanders, Neville Brand, George DiCenzo, Moses Gunn, Robert Loggia, Joe Spinell, Alejandro Rey, Tom Atkins. **1979**

NINTH GATE, THE ★★★ Despite an intriguing premise and a solid first act, this supernatural tale eventually sinks beneath its own arty pretensions; director Roman Polanski works this film far beyond what most viewers will endure. That's a shame; Johnny Depp's lead performance and the production design are superb. Depp plays a cheerfully mercenary New York "book broker" who agrees to authenticate a seventeenth-century satanic text rumored to give its owner the ability to summon the devil himself. Judging by its surface gloss, this film should have been mesmerizing from start to finish... but, then, you can't always judge a book by its cover. Rated R for violence, profanity, nudity, and sexual content. 133m. **DIR:** Roman Polanski. **CAST:** Johnny Depp, Frank Langella, Lena Olin, Emmanuelle Seigner, Barbara Jefford. **2000 DVD**

NITTI: THE ENFORCER ★★1/2 Made-for-TV portrait of Frank Nitti (played with conviction by Anthony LaPaglia), who became Al Capone's right-hand man and enforcer in Chicago. Stunning period piece looks great, and supporting cast all do their best. 100m. **DIR:** Michael Switzer. **CAST:** Anthony LaPaglia, Trini Alvarado, Bruno Kirby, Michael Moriarty, Michael Russo. **1988**

NIXON ★★1/2 Many of Richard Nixon's family and associates criticized this portrayal of his life, but you don't have to be a Nixon admirer to be put off by this turgid, melodramatic film. Nixon becomes here a sweaty, glowering gnome, skulking drunkenly around the White House, obsessed with the assassination of JFK. Stone's depiction is long, uninvolving, and largely fanciful. Rated R for profanity. 190m. **DIR:** Oliver Stone. **CAST:** Anthony Hopkins, Joan Allen, Powers Boothe, Ed Harris, Bob Hoskins, E. G. Marshall, David Paymer, David Hyde Pierce, Paul Sorvino, Mary Steenburgen, J. T. Walsh, James Woods. **1995 DVD**

NO ALIBI ★★ Two men find themselves misled and manipulated by the same woman. Strong cast makes it better than it should be. Rated R for violence, profanity,

and sexual situations. 90m. **DIR:** Bruce Pittman. **CAST:** Dean Cain, Eric Roberts, Lexa Doig. **1999 DVD**

NO BIG DEAL ★★ Kevin Dillon plays an underprivileged punk who makes a lot of nice friends between trips to juvenile hall. Low production values and limited acting don't help matters. 90m. **DIR:** Robert Charlton. **CAST:** Kevin Dillon, Christopher Gartin, Mary Joan Negro, Sylvia Miles, Tammy Grimes. **1984**

•NO CODE OF CONDUCT ★★ The novelty of watching Martin and Charlie Sheen playing father and son cops wears out its welcome almost as fast as this painfully obvious law-enforcement drama. Martin plays Bill, the by-the-book cop who expects the same commitment from his son Jake (Charlie), who hates living in the shadow of his old man. The murder of a cop and a drug bust gone bad bring the two together, but not before the filmmakers expose us to every cop cliché on the beat. Rated R for drug use, language, and violence. 92m. **DIR:** Bret Michaels. **CAST:** Charlie Sheen, Martin Sheen, Mark Dacascos, Paul Gleason. **1998 DVD**

NO CONTEST ★★1/2 Although Shannon Tweed is a wholly unbelievable substitute for Bruce Willis, this *Die Hard* rip-off remains reasonably entertaining due to sheer momentum. Tweed, on the loose in a barricaded skyscraper, is the only one capable of stopping terrorists holed up with hostage beauty contestants. Although her fights are badly doubled, the wonderfully reprehensible villains give the story some additional juice. Rated R for violence and profanity. 98m. **DIR:** Paul Lynch. **CAST:** Shannon Tweed, Robert Davi, Andrew Clay, Roddy Piper, Nicholas Campbell, John Colicos. **1994**

NO DEAD HEROES 🦃 Another post–Vietnam War film where our heroes go in and kick some commie tail. Not rated. 86m. **DIR:** J. C. Miller. **CAST:** John Dresden, Max Thayer, Dave Anderson, Nick Nicholson, Mike Monte, Toni Nero. **1986**

NO DEPOSIT, NO RETURN ★★ Two kids decide to escape from their multimillionaire grandfather (David Niven) and visit their mother in Hong Kong. On their way to the airport, they end up in a getaway car with two incompetent safecrackers. It is unrealistic and not very believable, with occasional bits of real entertainment. Rated G. 115m. **DIR:** Norman Tokar. **CAST:** David Niven, Don Knotts, Darren McGavin, Herschel Bernardi, Barbara Feldon. **1976**

NO DESSERT DAD UNTIL YOU MOW THE LAWN ★★★ When parents Robert Hays and Joanna Kerns attempt to kick the smoking habit by way of self-hypnosis tapes their neglected kids alter the tapes, giving their parents a more youthful outlook on life. Watching their transformation from strung-out chain-smokers to vibrant, healthy parents is both funny and poignant. Rated PG. 93m. **DIR:** Howard McCain. **CAST:** Robert Hays, Joanna Kerns, Larry Linville, Joshua Schaefer, Allison Mack, Jimmy Marsden, Richard Moll. **1994**

NO DRUMS, NO BUGLES ★★★ Because he refuses to kill, a West Virginian farmer (Martin Sheen) spends three years during the Civil War hiding in the Blue Ridge Mountains. Generally the movie is excellent; Sheen commands your interest in what is essentially a one-man show, and the nature photography is striking. It's ruined for the home viewer, though, by a terrible film-to-video transfer in which much of the wide-screen dimension has been compressed into the square television ratio. What a waste! Rated PG. 85m. **DIR:** Clyde Ware. **CAST:** Martin Sheen. **1971**

NO ESCAPE ★★★ In the year 2022, decorated soldier Ray Liotta is sent to prison for shooting his commanding officer. When he fails to follow the rules, Liotta is dropped on a prison island where a tribe of grungy killers called the "Outsiders" do battle with the more civilized "Insiders." It's diverting and action-packed, but little more. Rated R for violence and gore. 118m. **DIR:** Martin Campbell. **CAST:** Ray Liotta, Lance Henriksen, Stuart Wilson, Kevin Dillon, Ernie Hudson, Michael Lerner, Kevin J. O'Connor. **1994 DVD**

NO ESCAPE, NO RETURN ★★ Recognizable faces flesh out this typical actioner. Three rogue cops are sent undercover to bring down a vicious drug lord. Pedestrian effort adds nothing new to the genre. Rated R for violence, language, and sexual situations. 96m. **DIR:** Charles Kanganis. **CAST:** Michael Nouri, John Saxon, Maxwell Caulfield, Denise Loveday, Kevin Benton. **1993**

NO HIGHWAY IN THE SKY ★★★ An adventure about flying safety instead of airplane crashes, this movie benefits more from the chemistry between its players than the development of the plot. B&W; 98m. **DIR:** Henry Koster. **CAST:** James Stewart, Marlene Dietrich, Glynis Johns, Dora Bryan, Jack Hawkins. **1951**

NO HOLDS BARRED ★★ Muscle-bound rip-off of *Rocky III*. Rated PG-13 for violence and profanity. 92m. **DIR:** Thomas Wright. **CAST:** Hulk Hogan, Joan Severance, Tiny Lester. **1989**

NO JUSTICE ★★ Rival factions battle for power in a small Southern town. Everything you'd expect from a movie apparently made for the drive-in market. Rated R for violence. 91m. **DIR:** Richard Wayne Martin. **CAST:** Bob Orwig, Cameron Mitchell, Steve Murphy, Philip Newman, Donald Farmer. **1989**

NO LAUGHING MATTER ★★1/2 A teenage boy forces his mother to quit drinking after her addiction has ruined both of their lives. Credible performances from both Suzanne Somers and Chad Christ, but this made-for-cable original just doesn't inspire like it should. Rated PG-13. 95m. **DIR:** Michael Elias. **CAST:** Suzanne Somers, Chad Christ, Selma Blair, Robert Desiderio. **1997**

NO LOOKING BACK ★★★★ Drifting mechanic returns home and tries to resurrect the glory days of a failed romance with a bitter diner waitress who is living with one of his childhood buddies. The emotional texture and working-class roots of this melancholy drama are strengthened by a moody sound track featuring songs by Bruce Springsteen and his wife, Patti Scialfa. Rated R for profanity and sexual situations. 96m. **DIR:** Edward Burns. **CAST:** Edward Burns, Lauren Holly, Jon Bon Jovi, Blythe Danner, Ben Affleck. **1998 DVD**

NO LOVE FOR JOHNNIE ★★★ This oddly titled drama is about a member of the British Parliament beset by problems in his personal and professional lives. Enjoyable for the performances by the outstanding character actors. B&W; 111m. **DIR:** Ralph Thomas. **CAST:** Peter Finch, Stanley Holloway, Mary Peach, Donald Pleasence, Billie Whitelaw, Dennis Price. **1961**

NO MAN OF HER OWN ★★★★ A big-time gambler marries a local girl on a bet and tries to keep her innocent of his activities. This vintage film has everything

the average film fan looks for—drama, romance, and comedy. B&W; 85m. **DIR:** Wesley Ruggles. **CAST:** Clark Gable, Carole Lombard. **1932**

•**NO MAN'S LAND (1987)** ★★1/2 Predictable police melodrama, with D. B. Sweeney as a young undercover cop tracking a Porsche theft ring in Los Angeles, headed by smoothie Charlie Sheen. The dialogue is sometimes childish, but the film has pace and economy. Rated R for language and violence. 107m. **DIR:** Peter Werner. **CAST:** Charlie Sheen, D. B. Sweeney, Randy Quaid, Lara Harris, Bill Duke, Arlen Dean Snyder. **1987**

NO MAN'S LAND (2001) ★★★★ Absurdity and grim reality are joined at the hip in this bracing, dourly satiric war-is-hell story. A Bosnian soldier survives a field artillery explosion. He awakens atop a land mine in a trench between two battling forces where his comrade and an enemy Serb soldier have also taken refuge. As a news crew and a United Nations peacekeeping squadron monitor their plight, this tale of modern madness questions the possibility of true neutrality when organized murder may be masquerading as civil war. In Bosnian with English subtitles. Rated R for language and violence. 97m. **DIR:** Danis Tanovic. **CAST:** Branko Djuric, Rene Bitorajac, Filip Sovagovic, Simon Callow, Katrin Cartlidge. **2001 DVD**

NO MERCY ★★ A rapid-paced thriller about a Chicago cop (Richard Gere) who travels to New Orleans to avenge the murder of his partner. Kim Basinger is the Cajun woman who is Gere's link to the villain. Rated R for violence, language, and sexual situations. 107m. **DIR:** Richard Pearce. **CAST:** Richard Gere, Kim Basinger, Jeroen Krabbé, George Dzundza, William Atherton, Terry Kinney, Bruce McGill, Ray Sharkey, Gary Basaraba. **1986 DVD**

NO, NO NANETTE ★★★1/2 A cute and clever version of the 1925 stage hit about a financially troubled old man and his doting niece. The story takes a backseat to Vincent Youmans's songs, chiefly "Tea for Two" and "I Want to Be Happy." Good cast, including some of Hollywood's veteran comics. B&W; 96m. **DIR:** Herbert Wilcox. **CAST:** Anna Neagle, Victor Mature, Richard Carlson, ZaSu Pitts, Roland Young, Eve Arden, Tamara, Billy Gilbert, Helen Broderick, Keye Luke. **1940**

NO ONE CRIES FOREVER ★★★ Don't let the confusing start discourage you—this one gets better! An innocent South African girl is forced into prostitution. When she falls in love with a charming conservationist, her madam has her face disfigured and her boyfriend sets out in search of her. Contains violence and gore. 96m. **DIR:** Jans Rautenbach. **CAST:** Elke Sommer, Howard Carpendale, James Ryan. **1985**

•**NO ONE SLEEPS** ★★1/2 Detective thriller with an alternative lifestyle twist, set against the backdrop of the AIDS crisis. Tom Wlaschiha stars as Stephen Hein, the son of a prominent medical researcher. Before his father's death, Stephen learns that AIDS had been deliberately introduced into the general population, and that everyone connected with the experiment was either dead or dying. As Stephen cruises the streets of San Francisco looking for answers, everyone he comes in contact with is murdered. Is there really a conspiracy, or is Stephen looking for redemption? Smart dialogue, decent performances, and a fresh perspective make up for the film's low budget. Rated R for adult situations, language, nudity, and violence; unrated version also available. 104m. **DIR:** Jochen Hick. **CAST:** Tom Wlaschiha, Irit Levi, Jim Thalman. **2000 DVD**

NO PLACE TO HIDE ★★★ Taut thriller finds hard-edged cop Kris Kristofferson attempting to protect Drew Barrymore, who has been targeted for death by the man who killed her sister. The unlikely pair find themselves on the run, trying to stay alive while Kristofferson tracks down the killer. Good performances including Martin Landau as a police chief with an attitude, and fine writing and direction distinguish this entry. Rated R for violence, language, and adult situations. 95m. **DIR:** Richard Danus. **CAST:** Kris Kristofferson, Drew Barrymore, Martin Landau, O. J. Simpson, Dey Young, Bruce Weitz. **1993**

NO REGRETS FOR OUR YOUTH ★★★★ Poignant drama of feminist self-discovery set against the backdrop of a militarist Japanese society. Setsuko Hara gives a harrowing performance as a spoiled housewife who becomes enlightened to the hypocrisy of politics when her lover, a disaffected leftist, is arrested and executed for espionage. In Japanese with English subtitles. B&W; 110m. **DIR:** Akira Kurosawa. **CAST:** Setsuko Hara, Takashi Shimura. **1946**

NO RETREAT, NO SURRENDER 🦃 An uninspired cross between *The Karate Kid* and *Rocky IV*. 85m. **DIR:** Corey Yuen. **CAST:** Kurt McKinney, J. W. Fails, Ron Pohnel, Jean-Claude Van Damme. **1985**

NO RETREAT, NO SURRENDER II ★★1/2 An American attempts to rescue his abducted Thai fiancée, who is being held by Russian and Vietnamese troops in the jungles of Southeast Asia. This is a cross between the *Rambo* movies and *Star Wars*, with the addition of whirling legs, kicking feet, and fists flying fast and furious. Rated R for violence. 92m. **DIR:** Corey Yuen. **CAST:** Loreen Avedon, Max Thayer. **1987**

NO RETREAT, NO SURRENDER 3: BLOOD BROTHERS ★★★ In this largely enjoyable martial arts action film, two rival siblings must avenge their father's murder. Well-choreographed fight scenes, which are a thrill a minute. Rated R for profanity and violence. 97m. **DIR:** Lucas Lo. **CAST:** Loreen Avedon, Keith Vitali, Joseph Campanella. **1990**

NO SAFE HAVEN 🦃 Wings Hauser plays a CIA agent whose family is killed by Bolivian drug smugglers. Rated R for violence, nudity, and suggested sex. 92m. **DIR:** Ronnie Rondell. **CAST:** Wings Hauser, Robert Tessier. **1987**

NO SMALL AFFAIR ★★1/2 A 16-year-old amateur photographer named Charles Cummings (Jon Cryer) falls in love with an up-and-coming 23-year-old rock singer, Laura Victor (Demi Moore). A mixture of delightfully clever and unabashedly stupid elements. Rated R for nudity, violence, and profanity. 102m. **DIR:** Jerry Schatzberg. **CAST:** Jon Cryer, Demi Moore. **1984**

NO SURRENDER ★★ Eccentric British film about a New Year's Eve party at a run-down nightclub in Liverpool. There is a moral subtext here, but little else that is engaging. Rated R. Contains violence and profanity. 100m. **DIR:** Peter Smith. **CAST:** Michael Angelis, Avis Bunnage, James Ellis, Tom Georgeson, Bernard Hill, Ray McAnally, Joanne Whalley, Elvis Costello. **1986**

NO TELLING ★★1/2 Somber independent film about a husband and wife spending the summer in the country: she tries to do some painting, but he (a medical researcher) locks himself in the barn and conducts experiments on wild animals he's captured. His final masterpiece is probably the most pitiful thing you've ever seen. Not rated; contains profanity and simulated sex. 93m. **DIR:** Larry Fessenden. **CAST:** Miriam Healy-Louie, Stephen Ramsey, David Van Tieghem. **1991 DVD**

NO TIME FOR SERGEANTS ★★★★ In this hilarious film version of the Broadway play by Ira Levin, young Andy Griffith is superb as a country boy drafted into the service. You'll scream with laughter as good-natured Will Stockdale (as portrayed by Andy on stage as well as here) proceeds to make a complete shambles of the U.S. Air Force through nothing more than sheer ignorance. B&W; 119m. **DIR:** Mervyn LeRoy. **CAST:** Andy Griffith, Nick Adams, Myron McCormick, Murray Hamilton, Don Knotts. **1957**

NO TIME FOR SERGEANTS (TELEVISION) ★★1/2 Andy Griffith turns in a good performance as a Georgia hick drafted into the army in this 1955 comedy written especially for television. Unfortunately, this type of physical comedy needs lots of rehearsal, something to which live television did not lend itself. Also, the innocent-turning-the-establishment-on-its-ear storyline dates the play. In this case, the theatrical movie is better. B&W; 60m. **DIR:** Alex Segal. **CAST:** Andy Griffith, Harry Clark, Robert Emhardt, Eddie Le Roy, Alexander Clark. **1955**

NO WAY BACK ★★ A cop goes up against a group of white supremacists and their cohorts in this loud, overdone action-adventure film. Rated R for violence and profanity. 92m. **DIR:** Frank Cappello. **CAST:** Russell Crowe, Helen Slater, Michael Lerner, Etsushi Toyokawa. **1996 DVD**

NO WAY HOME ★★★1/2 Tim Roth delivers a powerful performance as Joey, just out of prison for murder. His attempt to stay straight is complicated when he moves in with his criminal brother and his stripper wife. It doesn't take long before Joey's brother tries to entice him back into a life of crime. Better than one would expect from a straight-to-video effort. Rated R for adult situations, language, nudity, and violence. 101m. **DIR:** Buddy Giovinazzo. **CAST:** Tim Roth, James Russo, Deborah Unger, Saul Stein. **1996**

NO WAY OUT ★★★1/2 In this gripping, sexy, and surprising suspense thriller, Kevin Costner stars as a morally upright naval hero who accepts a position with the secretary of defense (Gene Hackman) and his somewhat overzealous assistant (Will Patton, who walks away with the film). Things become a bit sticky when the secretary becomes involved in murder. Rated R for nudity, sexual situations, language, and violence. 116m. **DIR:** Roger Donaldson. **CAST:** Kevin Costner, Gene Hackman, Sean Young, Will Patton, Howard Duff, Iman. **1987 DVD**

NO WAY TO TREAT A LADY ★★★★ Excellent thriller with a tour-de-force performance by Rod Steiger, who dons various disguises and personas to strangle women and imprint them with red lipstick lips. Superb script, adapted from William Goldman's novel, and a skilled supporting cast: George Segal as a mothered cop, Eileen Heckart as his delightfully pick-pick-picking mother, and Lee Remick as the attractive love interest. Rated PG for violence. 108m. **DIR:** Jack Smight. **CAST:** Rod Steiger, George Segal, Lee Remick, Eileen Heckart, Michael Dunn, Murray Hamilton. **1968**

NOAH ★★★★ Tony Danza scores in this update of the biblical story, playing a crooked construction company owner who is approached by a stranger to build an ark. The film handles all three stages of disbelief with aplomb: First, he's skeptical, then his children, then the townsfolk. With a little bit of faith and the love of his three sons, can a sinner change his ways and create a miracle? Excellent family values and a sense of adventure flood every frame of this made-for-television film. Not rated. 92m. **DIR:** Ken Kwapis. **CAST:** Tony Danza, Jane Sibbett, Wallace Shawn, Chris Marquette, Jesse Moss, Michal Suchanek. **1998**

NOAH'S ARK ★★★ A silent epic that uses the Old Testament story of Noah as a simile for World War I. Several animals and bit players actually drowned during the spectacular flood sequence so the torment shown is authentic. The story is corny, but the special effects are excellent. B&W; 127m. **DIR:** Michael Curtiz. **CAST:** George O'Brien, Dolores Costello, Myrna Loy, Noah Beery Sr., Guinn Williams, Louise Fazenda. **1929 DVD**

NOBODY LOVES ME ★★★1/2 Being single and pushing age thirty is eating Fanny Fink alive. The attractive airport-security agent is both alone and lonely. Then she meets a gay black psychic and torch singer who looks into her future and changes her life. This exasperating search for a soul mate comically chomps at late-life relationships and a social climate starved for true romance. In German with English subtitles. Not rated; contains adult fare. 104m. **DIR:** Doris Dörrie. **CAST:** Maria Schrader, Pierre Sanoussi-Bliss, Michael Von Au, Elisabeth Trissenaar. **1996**

NOBODY'S CHILDREN ★★★ This made-for-cable movie is based on the true story of an American couple who go to Romania to adopt a child. They must struggle with corrupt politicians, the black market, and the Romanian government bureaucracy. The story is all right, but too long. Not rated; contains graphic news footage. 95m. **DIR:** David Wheatley. **CAST:** Ann-Margret, Jay O. Sanders, Dominique Sanda, Reiner Schoene, Clive Owen. **1994**

NOBODY'S FOOL ★★★★ As a 60-year-old construction worker at odds with his family, his boss, and the world in general, Paul Newman is at the peak of his form. This insightful character study, based on Richard Russo's novel, also features topflight support from Jessica Tandy, Bruce Willis, and Melanie Griffith, but make no mistake—it's Newman's own. Rated R for profanity, nudity, and brief violence. 124m. **DIR:** Robert Benton. **CAST:** Paul Newman, Jessica Tandy, Bruce Willis, Melanie Griffith, Dylan Walsh, Pruitt Taylor Vince, Gene Saks, Josef Sommer, Philip Bosco. **1994**

NOBODY'S FOOL 🦃 Despite its pedigree—a screenplay by playwright Beth Henley (*Crimes of the Heart*)—this film is a real disappointment. Rated PG-13 for mild violence. 107m. **DIR:** Evelyn Purcell. **CAST:** Rosanna Arquette, Eric Roberts, Mare Winningham, Jim Youngs, Louise Fletcher. **1986**

NOBODY'S GIRLS ★★★★ Filmmaker Mirra Bank dramatizes the actual lives of five adventurous women who helped settle our last frontier with archival photos,

rare film footage, journal entries, and reenactments shot on location in New Mexico and Montana. Cloris Leachman steals the show as a mother-turned-madam, but all involved bring their portrayals to life. Made for PBS, this film boasts high production values. Not rated; contains brief nudity and adult themes. 90m. **DIR:** Mirra Bank. **CAST:** Cloris Leachman, Esther Rolle, Tantoo Cardinal, Angela Alvarado, Bai Ling. **1995**

NOBODY'S PERFECT ★★1/2 *Some Like it Hot* redux. This time, the boy behind the skirt (Chad Lowe) is posing as the new girl on the tennis team. Rated PG-13 for language. 90m. **DIR:** Robert Kaylor. **CAST:** Chad Lowe, Gail O'Grady, Robert Vaughn. **1989**

NOBODY'S PERFEKT ★★ Three friends all undergoing psychoanalysis (Gabe Kaplan, Robert Klein, and Alex Karras) decide to extort $650.00 from the city of Miami to pay for their car, which was totaled because they ran into a large pothole. Along the way, they become heroes by capturing armored-car robbers. 96m. **DIR:** Peter Bonerz. **CAST:** Gabe Kaplan, Alex Karras, Robert Klein, Susan Clark, Paul Stewart, Alex Rocco. **1981**

NOCTURNA 🦃 This fourth-rate imitation of *Old Dracula* and *Love at First Bite* has Dracula's granddaughter moving to Manhattan. Rated R for nudity. 85m. **DIR:** Harry Tampa. **CAST:** Nai Bonet, John Carradine, Yvonne De Carlo, Sy Richardson. **1979**

NOCTURNE ★★★ Somewhat deliberate but involving mystery yarn has police detective George Raft risking his career to prove that a composer's apparent suicide was actually murder. Colorful characters and good dialogue. B&W; 88m. **DIR:** Edwin L. Marin. **CAST:** George Raft, Lynn Bari, Virginia Huston, Joseph Pevney. **1946**

NOISES OFF ★★★★ Hilarious adaptation of the play by Michael Frayn presents Michael Caine as a director struggling to get a saucy comedy and its sometimes sauced performers ready. Director Peter Bogdanovich and his all-star cast capture the total mania of a classic Marx Brothers movie. Rated PG-13 for humorous violence, brief profanity, and suggestive double entendres. 104m. **DIR:** Peter Bogdanovich. **CAST:** Carol Burnett, Michael Caine, Denholm Elliott, Julie Hagerty, Marilu Henner, Mark Linn-Baker, Christopher Reeve, John Ritter, Nicollette Sheridan. **1992**

NOMADS ★★★ In this thought-provoking and chilling shocker, Pierce Brosnan is a French anthropologist who discovers a secret society of malevolent ghosts living in modern-day Los Angeles. In doing so, he incurs their wrath and endangers the life of a doctor (Lesley-Anne Down). Rated R for profanity, nudity, and violence. 95m. **DIR:** John McTiernan. **CAST:** Lesley-Anne Down, Pierce Brosnan, Adam Ant, Mary Woronov. **1986 DVD**

NOMADS OF THE NORTH ★★1/2 A trapper and his beloved flee to the farthest reaches of the wilderness to escape imprisonment for an accidental murder. But it's the moral struggle of a Canadian Mountie that's at the heart of this picture. This was Lon Chaney's first starring role. B&W; 78m. **DIR:** David M. Hartford. **CAST:** Lon Chaney Sr., Betty Blythe, Lewis Stone, Francis McDonald. **1920**

NONE BUT THE BRAVE ★★1/2 Story about American and Japanese soldiers stranded on an island during World War II is an interesting premise, but does not make compelling film fare. Frank Sinatra, fine in a small role as a doctor, made his directing debut in this film, the first joint American-Japanese production. 105m. **DIR:** Frank Sinatra. **CAST:** Frank Sinatra, Clint Walker, Tommy Sands, Brad Dexter, Tony Bill. **1965**

NONE BUT THE LONELY HEART ★★★ Old pro Ethel Barrymore won an Oscar for her sympathetic portrayal of a moody, whining cockney as Cary Grant's mother Ma Mott in this murky drama of broken dreams, thwarted hopes, and petty crime in the slums of London in the late 1930s. Nothing else like it in the Grant filmography. B&W; 113m. **DIR:** Clifford Odets. **CAST:** Cary Grant, Ethel Barrymore, Barry Fitzgerald, Jane Wyatt, June Duprez, Dan Duryea. **1944**

NOON WINE ★★★★1/2 The fickle nature of human opinion and its ability to savage a victim already down on his luck are the bitter lessons in this adaptation of Katharine Anne Porter's perceptive tale. Porter establishes a stable protagonist (Fred Ward) whose life eventually collapses after he generously provides work on his turn-of-the-century Texas farm for a taciturn loner (Stellan Skarsgard). Suitable for family viewing. 81m. **DIR:** Michael Fields. **CAST:** Fred Ward, Lise Hilboldt, Stellan Skarsgard, Pat Hingle, Jon Cryer. **1985**

NOOSE HANGS HIGH, THE ★★ One of the comedy team's lesser efforts, and they take a backseat to veteran laugh-getters in the supporting cast. The plot is about $50,000 of stolen money, with Abbott and Costello trying to get it back. B&W; 77m. **DIR:** Charles Barton. **CAST:** Bud Abbott, Lou Costello, Leon Errol, Cathy Downes, Mike Mazurki, Joseph Calleia, Fritz Feld. **1948**

NORMA JEAN AND MARILYN ★★★1/2 This study of Marilyn Monroe's rise from obscurity to stardom concerns the duality between hardscrabble Norma Jean (Ashley Judd), who'd do anything to succeed, and insecure Marilyn (Mira Sorvino), who just wants people to love her. Even after Norma Jean "becomes" Marilyn, the former hangs around as a nagging conscience; thus, both actresses give their own spin to events in the latter half of this woman's life, but watching her become famous is more intriguing. Rated R for nudity, rape, simulated sex, drug use, profanity, and violence. 133m. **DIR:** Tim Fywell. **CAST:** Ashley Judd, Mira Sorvino, Josh Charles, Ron Rifkin, David Dukes, Peter Dobson, Lindsay Crouse. **1996**

NORMA RAE ★★★★ Sally Field won her first Oscar for her outstanding performance as a southern textile worker attempting to unionize the mill with the aid of organizer Ron Leibman. Film is based on a true story and has good eyes and ears for authenticity. Entire cast is first-rate. Rated PG, some language, minor violence. 113m. **DIR:** Martin Ritt. **CAST:** Sally Field, Ron Leibman, Pat Hingle, Beau Bridges. **1979**

NORMAL LIFE ★★★1/2 This fascinating made-for-cable original, based on a true story, chronicles the descent of an ex-cop (Luke Perry) and his drug-dependent wife (Ashley Judd) into debt and crime. Perry and Judd deliver fine performances, and you can't help but pity their characters. The movie would have been better without the numerous and pointless nude scenes. Rated R for violence and nudity. 102m. **DIR:** John McNaughton. **CAST:** Ashley Judd, Luke Perry, Jim True. **1996**

NORMAN CONQUESTS, THE, EPISODE 1: TABLE MANNERS ★★★1/2 Alan Ayckbourn's clever trilogy is set in a family home in a small English town. Each segment takes place in a different part of the house but encompasses the same span of time. Furthermore, each part is complete in itself, but blends with the others. In the dining room, Norman tries to seduce his two sisters-in-law and draws the rest of the family into the tangle with surprising results. Sara is a treat as she tries to organize meals and control the others. 108m. **DIR:** Herbert Wise. **CAST:** Richard Briers, Penelope Keith, Tom Conti, David Troughton, Fiona Walker, Penelope Wilton. **1980**

NORMAN CONQUESTS, THE, EPISODE 3: ROUND AND ROUND THE GARDEN ★★★1/2 A garden setting rounds out a zany weekend at an English house. As Norman (Tom Conti) pursues his wife's sister, Tom (David Troughton), the visiting vet, misinterprets the goings-on and embarrasses himself in the bargain. 106m. **DIR:** Herbert Wise. **CAST:** Richard Briers, Penelope Keith, Tom Conti, David Troughton, Fiona Walker, Penelope Wilton. **1980**

NORMAN CONQUESTS, THE, EPISODE 2: LIVING TOGETHER ★★★1/2 The parlor is the setting as the family gathers for the weekend. Norman (Tom Conti) keeps everyone on the run as he drinks, manipulates, and seduces. 93m. **DIR:** Herbert Wise. **CAST:** Richard Briers, Penelope Keith, Tom Conti, David Troughton, Fiona Walker, Penelope Wilton. **1980**

NORMAN . . . IS THAT YOU? ★★ This embarrassing look at homophobia has a skillful cast that deserved better. Redd Foxx tries too hard to be funny as a father who finds out his son is gay. The Motown soundtrack is much better than the plot. Rated PG for its discreet handling of an R-rated topic. 91m. **DIR:** George Schlatter. **CAST:** Redd Foxx, Pearl Bailey, Michael Warren, Jayne Meadows, Dennis Dugan. **1976**

NORMAN LOVES ROSE ★★★1/2 In this Australian-made comedy, Tony Owen plays a love-struck teenager who is enamored of his sister-in-law, Carol Kane. When she gets pregnant, the question of paternity arises. Lots of laughs in this one! Rated R. 98m. **DIR:** Henri Safran. **CAST:** Carol Kane, Tony Owen, Warren Mitchell. **1982**

NORSEMAN, THE This low-budget story of the Vikings is full of stupid historical errors. Rated PG. 90m. **DIR:** Charles B. Pierce. **CAST:** Lee Majors, Charles B. Pierce Jr., Cornel Wilde, Mel Ferrer. **1978**

NORTH ★★1/2 Neglected "perfect son" Elijah Wood decides to become a free agent and trade in his parents for a more attentive couple, in this unsatisfying adaptation of Alan Zweibel's fanciful novel. Despite several dozen weighty cameo appearances, the parental "trial runs" generate no emotion, and a subplot involving a scheming young friend is quite irritating. Only Bruce Willis lends charm, as an unusual guardian angel. Rated PG for mild violence and profanity. 88m. **DIR:** Rob Reiner. **CAST:** Elijah Wood, Bruce Willis, Jon Lovitz, Matthew McCurley. **1994**

NORTH AND SOUTH ★★★1/2 Epic, all-star TV miniseries detailing the events leading up to the Civil War springs vividly to life from the pages of John Jakes's bestselling historical novel. The human drama unfolds on both sides of the conflict, inside the war rooms and bedrooms, and tears apart two friends, played by Patrick Swayze and James Read. Not rated. 561m. **DIR:** Richard T. Heffron. **CAST:** Patrick Swayze, James Read, Kirstie Alley, David Carradine, Lesley-Anne Down, Robert Guillaume, Hal Holbrook, Gene Kelly. **1985**

NORTH AVENUE IRREGULARS, THE ★★1/2 Average Disney film about a young priest (Edward Herrmann) who wants to do something about crime. He enlists a group of churchgoing, do-good women to work with him. Quality cast is wasted on marginal script. Rated G. 100m. **DIR:** Bruce Bilson. **CAST:** Edward Herrmann, Barbara Harris, Cloris Leachman, Susan Clark, Karen Valentine, Michael Constantine, Patsy Kelly, Virginia Capers. **1979 DVD**

NORTH BY NORTHWEST ★★★★★ Cary Grant and Eva Marie Saint star in this classic thriller by the master himself, Alfred Hitchcock, who plays (or preys) on the senses and keeps the action at a feverish pitch. The story is typical Hitchcock fare—a matter of mistaken identity embroils a man in espionage and murder. 136m. **DIR:** Alfred Hitchcock. **CAST:** Cary Grant, Eva Marie Saint, James Mason, Martin Landau. **1959 DVD**

NORTH DALLAS FORTY ★★★★1/2 Remarkably enough, *North Dallas Forty* isn't just another numbingly predictable sports film. It's an offbeat, sometimes brutal, examination of the business of football. A first-rate Nick Nolte stars. Rated R. 119m. **DIR:** Ted Kotcheff. **CAST:** Nick Nolte, Bo Svenson, G. D. Spradlin, Dayle Haddon, Mac Davis. **1979**

NORTH OF THE RIO GRANDE ★★★ When Hopalong Cassidy's brother is murdered, he, Lucky, and Windy travel to Cottonwood Gulch to find the killers. There's a full-blown Irish musical number tucked into this winner and a saloon girl with a heart for Hoppy who exclaims "It's funny . . . all my life men like Cassidy have been saying good-bye to me!" as the three friends ride off into the distance. B&W; 67m. **DIR:** Nate Watt. **CAST:** William Boyd, George "Gabby" Hayes, Russell Hayden, Stepen Morris, Lee J. Cobb. **1937**

NORTH SHORE ★★1/2 Matt Adler plays an Arizona teen who desperately wants to make it in Hawaii's North Shore surfing pipeline. The pipeline shots are terrific. Rated PG for mild violence. 92m. **DIR:** William Phelps. **CAST:** Matt Adler, Nia Peeples, John Philbin, Gregory Harrison. **1987**

NORTH SHORE FISH ★★★ This film adaptation of Israel Horovitz's stage play concerns the last day of a struggling Gloucester fish-packing plant and its impact on the already downsized staff. It's a slight piece that may have played well in front of a live audience but seems quaint and somewhat forced in this format; the half-dozen female employees are characterized by little beyond their curses, delivered in impeccable Massachusetts accents, and their contempt for lady-killing manager Tony Danza. Rated R for profanity. 93m. **DIR:** Steve Zuckerman. **CAST:** Mercedes Ruehl, Peter Riegert, Tony Danza, Carroll Baker, Wendie Malick. **1997**

NORTH STAR, THE (1943) ★★★★ This is a well-done World War II film about Russian peasants battling Nazi invaders during the early days of the German invasion of Russia in 1941. It's a bit corny and sentimental in places, but the battle scenes have the usual Milestone high-quality excitement. B&W; 105m. **DIR:** Lewis Mile-

stone. **CAST:** Ruth Gordon, Walter Huston, Anne Baxter, Dana Andrews. **1943**

NORTH STAR (1996) ★★ The production values are surprisingly decent and the scenery quite pleasing, but a weak script and lousy casting pull this apart at the plot seams. James Caan plays the corrupt miner pitted against a half-Indian trapper (Christopher Lambert) in this revisionist thriller set in Alaska. Rated R for violence, profanity, nudity, and sexual situations. 89m. **DIR:** Nils Gaup. **CAST:** James Caan, Christopher Lambert, Catherine McCormack, Burt Young, Jacques François. **1996**

NORTH TO ALASKA ★★★★ Rather than a typical John Wayne Western, this is a John Wayne Northern. It's a rough-and-tumble romantic comedy. Delightfully tongue-in-cheek, it presents the Duke at his two-fisted best. 122m. **DIR:** Henry Hathaway. **CAST:** John Wayne, Stewart Granger, Capucine, Fabian, Ernie Kovacs. **1960**

NORTHEAST OF SEOUL ★★ Three unlikely down-and-outers join forces and end up double-crossing each other in their pursuit of an ancient mystical sword. Very routine. Rated PG for violence. 84m. **DIR:** David Lowell Rich. **CAST:** Anita Ekberg, John Ireland, Victor Buono. **1972**

NORTHERN EXPOSURE (TV SERIES) ★★★★ This little drama began as a routine fish-out-of-water tale and matured into a densely layered, delightful account of the history and ongoing vitality of fictitious Cicely, Alaska (pop. 813). Rob Morrow is a droll bundle of neuroses forced into temporary servitude to repay the state of Alaska for medical school. To catch this program's rhythm, you'll do better to rent or buy all of the episodes. 52m. **CAST:** Rob Morrow, Janine Turner, Barry Corbin, John Corbett, Darren E. Burrows, John Cullum, Cynthia Geary, Elaine Miles, Peg Phillips. **1990–93**

NORTHERN EXTREMES ★★★ A tiny island secedes from Canada after losing its fishing rights and uses a deserted Soviet submarine to underscore the situation. Sharp satire of government and some quirky characterizations, but the tiny budget gets in the way. A good-hearted little comedy, even if the technical quality is extremely uneven. Rated PG for violence and sexual situations. 90m. **DIR:** Paul Donovan. **CAST:** Paul Gross, Denise Virieux. **1993**

NORTHERN LIGHTS ★★★★ Produced, directed, and edited by Rob Nilsson and John Hanson, this independently made feature presents the rich chronicle of a group of Swedish farmers in North Dakota during the winter of 1915–16. Though the budget was a slight $330,000, the film is a triumph of craft and vision. No MPAA rating. B&W; 98m. **DIR:** John Hanson, Rob Nilsson. **CAST:** Robert Behling, Joe Spano. **1979**

NORTHERN PASSAGE ★★ Animals and wildlife are gorgeously photographed, but when people enter they're merely talking heads. A woman with roots in both the white and native worlds tries to find her place in this tale of life in the Canadian frontier. Jeff Fahey, who is given top billing, merely rides through a couple of times. Rated PG-13 for profanity and violence. 97m. **DIR:** Arnaud Selignac. **CAST:** Jeff Fahey, Neve Campbell, Lorne Brass, Jacques Weber, Genevieve Rochette. **1994**

NORTHERN PURSUIT ★★★ Despite Raoul Walsh's capable direction, this film, about a German heritage Canadian Mountie (Errol Flynn) who feigns defection and guides a party of Nazi saboteurs is pure claptrap. It marked the beginning of Flynn's slow descent into obscurity and, eventually, illness. B&W; 94m. **DIR:** Raoul Walsh. **CAST:** Errol Flynn, Julie Bishop, Tom Tully. **1943**

NORTHWEST MOUNTED POLICE ★★★★ Predictable but loads of fun, the story is set in the Canadian Rockies. The hero is a Texas Ranger. One of the heroines is a half-breed, another a frontier woman with an English accent. 125m. **DIR:** Cecil B. DeMille. **CAST:** Gary Cooper, Paulette Goddard, Madeleine Carroll, Robert Preston, Akim Tamiroff, Robert Ryan, Preston Foster, Lon Chaney Jr., Lynne Overman. **1940**

NORTHWEST OUTPOST ★★ Nelson Eddy's last movie is not up to snuff. The setting of a Russian village in nineteenth-century California is colorful, and the prospect of an Indian attack on the Russian fort is suspenseful. But the story is downright dull. So is the music, even though it was composed by Rudolf Friml. B&W; 91m. **DIR:** Allan Dwan. **CAST:** Nelson Eddy, Ilona Massey, Joseph Schildkraut, Elsa Lanchester, Hugo Haas, Lenore Ulric. **1947**

NORTHWEST PASSAGE ★★★1/2 Spencer Tracy is the hard-driving, intrepid leader of Roger's Rangers, slogging through swamps and over mountains to open new territory in colonial America. Greenhorns Robert Young and Walter Brennan endure his wrath along the way. Adventure abounds. 125m. **DIR:** King Vidor. **CAST:** Spencer Tracy, Robert Young, Walter Brennan, Ruth Hussey, Nat Pendleton. **1940**

NORTHWEST TRAIL ★★★ Mountie Bob Steele uncovers a plot to rob the Canadian government by taking gold from an old mine and flying it across the border. 62m. **DIR:** Derwin Abrahams. **CAST:** Bob Steele, Joan Woodbury, John Litel. **1945**

NOSFERATU ★★★★ A product of the German Expressionist era, this is a milestone in the history of world cinema. Director F. W. Murnau seems to make the characters jump out at you. With his skeletal frame, rodent face, long nails, and long, pointed ears, Max Schreck is the most terrifying of all screen vampires. Silent. B&W; 63m. **DIR:** F. W. Murnau. **CAST:** Max Schreck, Gustav von Waggenheim. **1922 DVD**

NOSTALGHIA ★★★ Andrei Tarkovsky's first film made outside his native Russia is this highly personal work about a Russian poet on a research project in Italy who attempts to turn his longing for his home and family into a positive experience. Tarkovsky's seemingly unblinking stare (you've never seen a camera move so slowly) can yield moments of intense beauty, but you have to be in the mood for it. In Russian and Italian with English subtitles. Not rated. B&W/color; 120m. **DIR:** Andrei Tarkovsky. **CAST:** Oleg Yankovsky, Erland Josephson. **1983 DVD**

NOSTRADAMUS 🦃 The life of the fabled medieval physician and seer is turned into a ridiculous, unbelievable bore. If Nostradamus was such a great prophet, why didn't he warn us about films like this? Rated R for nudity. 118m. **DIR:** Roger Christian. **CAST:** Tcheky Karyo, Amanda Plummer, Rutger Hauer, F. Murray Abraham. **1994**

NOSTRADAMUS KID, THE ★★★ Amusing Australian period piece about a religious youth who believes his preacher's word that the world is coming to an end. Afraid that he will die a virgin, young Ken Elkin breaks free of his conservative background and sets out to experience life and love, and love, and love. Then he meets the right girl, who happens to have the wrong father, who just might end Elkin's world for real. Funny and touching. Rated R for nudity, adult situations, and language. 120m. **DIR:** Bob Ellis. **CAST:** Noah Taylor, Miranda Otto, Arthur Dingham, Peter Gwynn. **1992**

NOT A PENNY MORE, NOT A PENNY LESS ★★★1/2 A merciless business tycoon fleeces four investors residing in England, one of whom is a transplanted American college instructor. Refusing to remain a victim, the professor gathers the other three and proposes they regain all their losses—not a penny more, nor a penny less—by whatever means necessary. Solid TV adaptation of the Jeffrey Archer novel. 180m. **DIR:** Clive Donner. **CAST:** Ed Begley Jr., Edward Asner, François-Eric Gendron, Brian Protheroe, Nicholas Jones, Maryam D'Abo, Jenny Agutter. **1990**

•**NOT ANOTHER TEEN MOVIE** 🦃 This crude, lewd, and lame comedy attempts to lampoon recent high-school flicks the way that *Scary Movie* skewered the slasher genre, as a popular jock makes a bet that he can turn a female social outcast into a prom queen. Rated R for profanity, nudity, and sexual content. 85m. **DIR:** Joel Gallen. **CAST:** Chyler Leigh, Jaime Pressly, Chris Evans, Mia Kirshner, Randy Quaid, Ed Lauter, Cerina Vincent. **2001 DVD**

NOT AS A STRANGER ★★★★ A testament to the medical profession that doesn't skirt on those with lack of ethics. Olivia de Havilland is somewhat self-conscious in a blond wig and Swedish accent. But she tries hard as the nurse willing to put medical student Robert Mitchum through school by marrying him and caring for him. B&W; 135m. **DIR:** Stanley Kramer. **CAST:** Olivia de Havilland, Robert Mitchum, Charles Bickford, Frank Sinatra, Gloria Grahame, Lee Marvin, Broderick Crawford, Lon Chaney Jr., Harry Morgan, Virginia Christine. **1955**

NOT FOR PUBLICATION ★★1/2 A writer and a photographer attempt to break out of sleazy tabloid journalism by doing an investigative piece about high-level corruption. Playful, but not as distinctive as Paul Bartel's other works, such as *Eating Raoul* and *Lust in the Dust*. Rated PG for profanity. 87m. **DIR:** Paul Bartel. **CAST:** Nancy Allen, David Naughton, Laurence Luckinbill. **1984**

NOT IN THIS TOWN ★★★1/2 This made-for-cable drama, based on a true story, is a gripping examination of hate crimes and how one town stood together against the perpetrators. Fine performances from both Kathy Baker and Adam Arkin and an inspiring solution to the problem make this a powerful statement and good entertainment. Rated PG-13 for violence. 95m. **DIR:** Donald Wrye. **CAST:** Kathy Baker, Adam Arkin, Ed Begley Jr. **1997**

NOT LIKE US 🦃 Producer Roger Corman is releasing some pretty dreadful stuff these days, and this extremely wet little comedy—concerning aliens who skin human beings in order to walk among us unseen—really scrapes the bottom of the barrel. Rated R for gore, violence, nudity, simulated sex, and profanity. 90m. **DIR:** David Payne. **CAST:** Joanna Pacula, Peter Onorati, Rainer Grant, Morgan Englund. **1995**

NOT MY KID ★★★ Not just another disease-of-the-week vehicle. This telefilm is a well-written look at teenage drug abuse and the havoc it wreaks in a family. 100m. **DIR:** Michael Tuchner. **CAST:** George Segal, Stockard Channing, Andrew Robinson, Tate Donovan. **1985**

NOT OF THIS EARTH (1988) ★★★ Purposely trashy remake of a Roger Corman sci-fi classic from the Fifties. Plenty of action, campy comedy, and sex to hold your interest. Traci Lords is a private nurse assigned to administer blood transfusions to a mysterious, wealthy patient. Once she starts nosing around, the fun starts. Rated R for nudity, simulated sex, and violence. 82m. **DIR:** Jim Wynorski. **CAST:** Traci Lords, Arthur Roberts. **1988**

NOT OF THIS EARTH (1995) ★★★ Intentionally low-budget remake enjoys healthy special effects, a fun script, and decent performances. Michael York plays an alien who has come to Earth in search of blood. At first he just helps himself, but when he starts meeting resistance, he resorts to all sorts of fiendish ways to extract the crimson gold. Then he meets Amanda, and his whole world is turned upside down. Rated R for nudity, violence, profanity, and adult situations. 92m. **DIR:** Terence H. Winkless. **CAST:** Michael York, Parker Stevenson, Richard Belzer, Elizabeth Barondes. **1995**

NOT ONE LESS ★★★★ A 13-year-old substitute teacher in a rural Chinese school goes in search of one of her students who has run away to find work in the city. Master director Zhang Yimou offers a change of pace in this surprisingly nimble and sweet-tempered comedy, with charming, natural performances from the children in the school (all of whom use their real names as the names of their characters). In Mandarin with English subtitles. Rated G. 106m. **DIR:** Zhang Yimou. **CAST:** Wei Minzhi, Zhang Huike, Tian Zhenda, Gao Enman, Sun Zhimei, Feng Yuying, Li Fanfan. **1999 DVD**

NOT QUITE HUMAN ★★★ Made for the Disney Channel, this is the first of a trilogy of films about a likable android (Jay Underwood) and his eccentric creator (Alan Thicke). After completing his "project," Thicke flees with his daughter and new "son" to escape toy-company leaders who want to transform the android into the ultimate war toy. Underwood is terrific as the amiable robot. Fun family viewing. 95m. **DIR:** Steven H. Stern. **CAST:** Alan Thicke, Jay Underwood, Robyn Lively, Joseph Bologna, Robert Harper. **1987**

NOT QUITE HUMAN 2 ★★★1/2 This second film in the Disney trilogy about Chip the android (Jay Underwood) is the most hilarious and heartwarming. Chip goes to college and falls in love with a beautiful android. He must also contend with a computer virus that threatens to destroy him. The gentle romance upgrades an otherwise zany family film. 92m. **DIR:** Eric Luke. **CAST:** Jay Underwood, Alan Thicke, Robyn Lively, Katie Barberi, Dey Young. **1989**

NOT QUITE PARADISE ★★ A disparate group of people from around the world volunteer to work on an Israeli kibbutz. Surprisingly mean-spirited movie resembles a teens-at-camp comedy, though it offers some laughs in spite of itself. Rated R for sexual humor. 105m.

DIR: Lewis Gilbert. **CAST:** Sam Robards, Joanna Pacula. **1986**

NOT WANTED ★★★1/2 Former actress Ida Lupino made her uncredited start as the director of this intelligent melodrama (which she also cowrote and coproduced), replacing Elmer Clifton when he had a heart attack three days into production. Sally Forrest plays a waitress who finds herself an outcast when she bears a child out of wedlock. B&W; 94m. **DIR:** Elmer Clifton, Ida Lupino. **CAST:** Sally Forrest, Keefe Brasselle, Leo Penn. **1949**

NOT WITHOUT MY DAUGHTER ★★★1/2 The true story of Betty Mahmoody, a Michigan housewife who accompanied her Iranian doctor-husband to his home country for a visit and found herself a prisoner. A terrific performance by Sally Field in the lead role makes it worth the watch. Rated PG-13 for violence and profanity. 115m. **DIR:** Brian Gilbert. **CAST:** Sally Field, Alfred Molina, Sheila Rosenthal, Roshan Seth. **1991 DVD**

NOTHING BUT A MAN ★★★★1/2 Originally released in 1964, this stark tale of class problems within the black community, as compounded by racial pressures, was far ahead of its time. Ivan Dixon is a laborer who falls for Abbey Lincoln, the educated daughter of a preacher. Their social standings, along with the corrosive and wearisome effects of discrimination, put undue strain on their relationship. Not only a superb drama, but an astonishingly astute social history. Not rated. B&W; 92m. **DIR:** Michael Roemer. **CAST:** Ivan Dixon, Abbey Lincoln, Gloria Foster, Yaphet Kotto. **1964**

NOTHING BUT TROUBLE (1944) ★★1/2 Stan Laurel and Oliver Hardy are the chef and the table server, bringing havoc to a society partygiver. Some good sight gags, but not enough. B&W; 69m. **DIR:** Sam Taylor. **CAST:** Stan Laurel, Oliver Hardy, Mary Boland. **1944**

NOTHING BUT TROUBLE (1991) ★★ Disappointing, gross comedy—aimed by writer-director Dan Aykroyd at the *Police Academy/Porky's* crowd—about New Yorkers Chevy Chase and Demi Moore setting off for Atlantic City and being arrested. Rated PG-13 for profanity and gore. 90m. **DIR:** Dan Aykroyd. **CAST:** Chevy Chase, Dan Aykroyd, John Candy, Demi Moore. **1991 DVD**

NOTHING IN COMMON ★★★1/2 Tom Hanks plays a hotshot advertising executive who must deal with his increasingly demanding parents, who are divorcing after thirty-four years of marriage. Jackie Gleason gives a subtle, touching portrayal of the father. The film succeeds at making the difficult shift from zany humor to pathos. Rated PG for profanity and suggested sex. 120m. **DIR:** Garry Marshall. **CAST:** Tom Hanks, Jackie Gleason, Eva Marie Saint, Hector Elizondo, Barry Corbin, Bess Armstrong, Sela Ward. **1986 DVD**

NOTHING PERSONAL (1980) 🦃 A romantic comedy about the fight to stop the slaughter of baby seals? Rated PG. 97m. **DIR:** George Bloomfield. **CAST:** Donald Sutherland, Suzanne Somers, Lawrence Dane, Roscoe Lee Browne, Dabney Coleman, Saul Rubinek, John Dehner. **1980**

NOTHING PERSONAL (1997) ★★★ In 1975 Belfast, a bombing escalates the state of violence between terrorist factions. This tale of the dehumanizing effects of "the troubles" is well acted but doesn't add much to other films on the subject. Rated R for violence and profanity. 85m. **DIR:** Thaddeus O'Sullivan. **CAST:** James Frain, Ian Hart, Michael Gambon, John Lynch. **1997**

NOTHING SACRED ★★★★ Ace scriptwriter Ben Hecht's cynical mixture of slapstick and bitterness, perfectly performed by Fredric March and Carole Lombard, makes this satirical comedy a real winner. Vermont innocent, Lombard, is mistakenly thought to be dying of a rare disease. A crack New York reporter (March) pulls out all the stops in exploiting her to near-national sainthood. The boy-bites-man scene is priceless. 75m. **DIR:** William Wellman. **CAST:** Carole Lombard, Fredric March, Walter Connolly, Charles Winninger. **1937 DVD**

NOTHING TO LOSE ★★1/2 This misfired buddy "road comedy" apparently didn't grow much beyond its inspired teaming of Martin Lawrence and Tim Robbins, who are undeniably funny together. Robbins is a totally square advertising exec who returns home unexpectedly one afternoon only to hear the sounds of betrayal coming from the bedroom; his subsequent near-catatonia behind the wheel is interrupted by high-strung carjacker Lawrence, actually a "decent family man" trying to put food on the table (right). Writer-director Steve Oedekerk winds up with wasted supporting characters and thumpingly unfunny distractions. Rated R for profanity and violence. 97m. **DIR:** Steve Oedekerk. **CAST:** Martin Lawrence, Tim Robbins, John C. McGinley, Giancarlo Esposito, Kelly Preston, Michael McKean. **1997 DVD**

NOTHING UNDERNEATH 🦃 A ranger from Yellowstone goes to Italy, to investigate the disappearance of his kid sister. Not rated; contains violence and nudity. 96m. **DIR:** Carlo Vanzina. **CAST:** Tom Schanley, Renée Simonson, Donald Pleasence. **1987**

NOTORIOUS ★★★★1/2 *Notorious* is among the finest Alfred Hitchcock romantic thrillers. Cary Grant, as an American agent, and Ingrid Bergman, as the "notorious" daughter of a convicted traitor, join forces to seek out Nazis in postwar Rio. Claude Rains gives one of his greatest performances. B&W; 101m. **DIR:** Alfred Hitchcock. **CAST:** Cary Grant, Ingrid Bergman, Claude Rains, Louis Calhern. **1946 DVD**

NOTORIOUS NOBODIES ★★★1/2 Eight vignettes based on true events take place on the same day in different countries and show the range of human-rights violations that occur every day. The film's power comes from its widespread canvas. While individual scenes may be dramatically weak, the cumulative effect is much more than the sum of its parts. Subtitled. Not rated; contains violence. 102m. **DIR:** Stanislav Stanojevic. **1985**

NOTTING HILL ★★★★1/2 You just can't do much better than this extraordinarily charming and entertaining romantic comedy. Circumstances bring together the owner of a barely successful travel bookstore with an elegant American film star who has grown weary of the pretense and insincerity of everybody in her own social circle. But even if such opposites attract, can they stay together? What follows is a winning mixture of sly wit and touching romantic *frisson*. Rated PG-13 for sexual candor and earthy content. 123m. **DIR:** Roger Michell. **CAST:** Julia Roberts, Hugh Grant, Hugh Bonneville, Emma Chambers, James Dreyfuss, Rhys Ifans. **1999 DVD**

NOUS N'IRONS PLUS AU BOIS ★★ A group of young French Resistance fighters harass German troops in a forest held by the Germans. They capture a young German soldier who falls in love with a French girl. Aside from the presence of Marie-France Pisier, there's little here likely to interest an American audience. In French with English subtitles. 90m. **DIR:** Georges Dumoulin. **CAST:** Marie-France Pisier, Siegfried Rauch, Richard Leduc. **1969**

NOVEMBER CONSPIRACY, THE ★★★ Political intrigue highlights this familiar tale of a woman reporter assigned to cover a presidential candidate. What should have been a simple assignment turns into a deadly cat-and-mouse chase as the reporter dodges political assassins and deals with the murder of her boyfriend. This direct-to-video effort features a high-profile cast of B-list actors and C-grade plotting. Rated R for language and violence. 103m. **DIR:** Conrad Janis. **CAST:** Paige Turco, Dirk Benedict, George Segal, Elliott Gould, Bo Hopkins. **1995**

NOVEMBER MEN, THE ★★★ When a Hollywood director goes to work on a film about an assassin planning to kill George Bush during the 1992 presidential campaign, his girlfriend starts to suspect that the movie is only a blueprint for the real thing. A true independent movie from filmmaker Paul Williams (*Dealing*); what this lacks in polish it makes up for in ideas. Rated PG for profanity and violence. 98m. **DIR:** Paul Williams. **CAST:** Paul Williams, Leslie Bevis, James Andronica, Robert Davi. **1994**

•NOVOCAINE ★★★ Dentist Frank Sangster becomes a victim of his own dark desires when new patient Susan lures him into a dental chair after normal business hours for sex. Sangster gets involved in "one small lie" that unravels his entire life, jeopardizes his marriage plans to a wholesome obsessive-compulsive hygienist, and plunges him into a web of drug theft, betrayal, and murder. This macabre, crafty, and comic crime story includes surrealist flourishes such as X-ray images of masticating skulls. Rated R for language, drug use, violence, and sexuality. 95m. **DIR:** David Atkins. **CAST:** Steve Martin, Helena Bonham Carter, Laura Dern, Scott Caan, Elias Koteas. **2001 DVD**

NOW AND FOREVER A boutique owner comes back from a clothes-buying trip to find that her husband has been accused of rape. Rated R for violence. 93m. **DIR:** Adrian Carr. **CAST:** Cheryl Ladd, Robert Coleby, Carmen Duncan. **1983**

NOW AND THEN ★★1/2 Four female childhood friends reunite in Indiana to witness the birth of one chum's baby and yak about the summer of 1970 when they all turned 12 years old. Most of the film is a nostalgia-sweetened flashback, a sort of female *Stand by Me* with *Big Chill* bookends. Rated PG-13 for language and partial nudity. 98m. **DIR:** Lesli Linka Glatter. **CAST:** Christina Ricci, Thora Birch, Gaby Hoffman, Ashleigh Aston Moore, Rosie O'Donnell, Melanie Griffith, Demi Moore, Rita Wilson. **1995 DVD**

NOW, VOYAGER ★★★1/2 Bette Davis plays a neurotic, unattractive spinster named Charlotte Vale; an ugly duckling, who, of course, blossoms into a beautiful swan. And it's all thanks to the expert counsel of her psychiatrist (Claude Rains) and a shipboard romance with a married man (Paul Henreid). Directed by Irving Rapper, it features the famous cigarette-lighting ritual that set a trend in the 1940s. B&W; 117m. **DIR:** Irving Rapper. **CAST:** Bette Davis, Claude Rains, Paul Henreid. **1942 DVD**

NOW YOU SEE HIM, NOW YOU DON'T ★★ Kurt Russell discovers a formula that will make a person or item invisible. Bad guy Cesar Romero attempts to hijack the discovery for nefarious purposes, which leads to disastrous results. Rated G. 85m. **DIR:** Robert Butler. **CAST:** Kurt Russell, Joe Flynn, Jim Backus, Cesar Romero, William Windom. **1972**

NOWHERE ★★ The final part of a loose trilogy about whacked-out, culture-obsessed modern teens (following *Totally F***ked Up* and *The Doom Generation*), *Nowhere* is a plotless film about obnoxious L.A. kids. Though intended at least partly as a parody/satire, it is all but unwatchable for any viewers other than the under-25s to whom it panders. Rated R for profanity, drug usage, violence, and sexual situations. 85m. **DIR:** Gregg Araki. **CAST:** James Duval, Christina Applegate, Rachel True, Debi Mazar, Chiara Mastroianni, Heather Graham, Traci Lords, Shannen Doherty, John Ritter. **1997**

NOWHERE LAND ★★ In a remote mountain cabin, a female FBI agent and an ex-con battle the hired killers who want to keep him from testifying against their boss. Adequate but utterly unmemorable. Rated R for profanity and violence. 88m. **DIR:** Rupert Hitzig. **CAST:** Peter Dobson, Dina Meyer, Jon Polito, Francesco Quinn, Martin Kove. **1998 DVD**

NOWHERE TO HIDE ★★★★ Amy Madigan stars in this exciting adventure of relentless pursuit. Her husband, a marine officer, has uncovered a defective part that is causing accidents in his helicopter squadron. Before he can go public, he is killed. The assassins believe Madigan has the damaging evidence, and the chase is on. An exhilarating climax. Not rated. 100m. **DIR:** Mario Azzopardi. **CAST:** Amy Madigan, Michael Ironside, John Colicos, Daniel Hugh-Kelly. **1987 DVD**

NOWHERE TO RUN (1989) ★★ This coming-of-age film is based on an actual series of murders in Caddo, Texas, during 1960. When a paroled con (David Carradine) goes on a killing spree for revenge, six high school seniors find themselves swept into a world of corrupt politicians, crooked cops, and their own hormones. Rated R for violence and profanity. 87m. **DIR:** Carl Franklin. **CAST:** David Carradine, Jason Priestley, Henry Jones. **1989**

NOWHERE TO RUN (1993) ★★1/2 Jean-Claude Van Damme flexes his biceps and slowly progressing acting ability as an escaped convict who helps a widow save her ranch. Some witty dialogue here and there. Rated R for violence, profanity, and nudity. 90m. **DIR:** Robert Harmon. **CAST:** Jean-Claude Van Damme, Rosanna Arquette, Kieran Culkin, Ted Levine, Joss Ackland. **1993 DVD**

NUDE BOMB, THE (RETURN OF MAXWELL SMART, THE) ★★ Maxwell Smart (Don Adams), of the *Get Smart!* television series, gets the big-screen treatment in this barely watchable spy spoof about a crazed villain's attempt at world domination—by vaporizing all clothing. This film endured some editing-room "touching up" by *Robot Monster* director Phil Tucker. Rated PG. 94m. **DIR:** Clive Donner. **CAST:** Don Adams, Andrea Howard, Vittorio Gassman, Dana Elcar,

Rhonda Fleming, Sylvia Kristel, Joey Forman, Norman Lloyd. **1980**

NUDIST COLONY OF THE DEAD ★★1/2 They sing, they dance, they're dead. Nudists commit mass suicide when a church shuts down their colony. When teens show up later at the site, now a religious camp, the nudists rise from the dead and the fun begins. Some hilarious songs enliven this groaner. Not rated; contains nudity and violence. 90m. **DIR:** Mark Pirro. **CAST:** Deborah Stern, Rachel Latt, Braddon Mendelson, Forrest J. Ackerman. **1992**

NUDO DI DONNA (PORTRAIT OF A WOMAN, NUDE) ★★★ Nino Manfredi stars in this Italian comedy as a husband shocked to discover his wife (Eleonora Giorgi) may have posed nude for a painting. Told the model was a hooker, the skeptical Manfredi attempts to discover the truth in this madcap import. In Italian with English subtitles. Not rated. 112m. **DIR:** Nino Manfredi. **CAST:** Nino Manfredi, Eleonora Giorgi. **1982**

NUEBA YOL ★★★★ An immigrant's fragile dreams have seldom been better illustrated than in this story of a man from Santo Domingo who takes a chance to emigrate to the United States. Life in New York City turns out to be rougher than he had imagined, but he works as best he can to fit in. A charming film filled with gentle humor that makes for excellent family viewing. Not rated; contains no offensive material. In Spanish with English subtitles. 105m. **DIR:** Angel Muniz. **CAST:** Luisito Marti, Raul Carbonell. **1995**

NUMBER ONE FAN ★★ More *Fatal Attraction*–lite as a sexy actor sleeps with a fan, believing it to be a one-night stand. Then the fan becomes obsessed and people start disappearing. Formula thriller has become a genre unto itself. Rated R for language, nudity, and violence. 93m. **DIR:** Jane Simpson. **CAST:** Chad McQueen, Catherine Mary Stewart, Renee Ammann, Hoyt Axton, Nina Blackwood. **1994**

NUMBER ONE OF THE SECRET SERVICE ★★★ In this enjoyable spoof of James Bond films, secret agent Charles Blind attempts to stop evil Arthur Loveday from killing prominent international financiers. Rated PG. 87m. **DIR:** Lindsay Shonteff. **CAST:** Nicky Henson, Richard Todd, Aimi MacDonald, Geoffrey Keen, Sue Lloyd, Dudley Sutton, Jon Pertwee. **1970**

NUMBER ONE WITH A BULLET ★★ Uninspired police thriller-buddy movie suffers from a contrived script. Rated R for violence, profanity, and nudity. 103m. **DIR:** Jack Smight. **CAST:** Robert Carradine, Billy Dee Williams, Valerie Bertinelli, Peter Graves, Doris Roberts. **1987**

NUMBER 17 ★★1/2 Seldom-seen thriller from Alfred Hitchcock is a humorous departure from his later more obsessive films, but it still maintains his wry touches and unusual characters. Once again an unsuspecting innocent (in this case, a hobo) comes across something that places him in jeopardy (a gang of jewel thieves). B&W; 83m. **DIR:** Alfred Hitchcock. **CAST:** Leon M. Lion, Anne Grey, Donald Calthrop, Barry Jones. **1932 DVD**

NUN, THE (LA RELIGIEUSE) ★★ Forced into a nunnery by her family's poverty, a young woman tries to maintain her personal dignity despite physical and sexual abuse. While this is new-wave director Jacques Rivette's most accessible film, it still isn't easygoing. A serious film that is a chore to watch. In French with English subtitles. B&W; 140m. **DIR:** Jacques Rivette. **CAST:** Anna Karina, Lilo Pulver, Francisco Rabal. **1965**

NUNS ON THE RUN ★★★★ In this hilarious farce, Eric Idle and Robbie Coltrane play lower-echelon English crooks who decide to rip off their boss and fly to Brazil. When their plan goes awry, they are forced to hide in a convent and disguise themselves as nuns. What writer-director Jonathan Lynn and his actors do with the premise will have you gasping for breath after fits of uproarious laughter, Rated PG-13 for profanity and sexual humor. 90m. **DIR:** Jonathan Lynn. **CAST:** Eric Idle, Robbie Coltrane, Janet Suzman. **1990**

NUN'S STORY, THE ★★★ A record of a devoted nun's ultimate rebellion against vows of chastity, obedience, silence, and poverty, this Audrey Hepburn starrer was one of the big box-office hits of the 1950s. The wistful and winning Miss Hepburn shines. The supporting cast is excellent. 152m. **DIR:** Fred Zinnemann. **CAST:** Audrey Hepburn, Edith Evans, Peter Finch, Dean Jagger, Beatrice Straight, Colleen Dewhurst, Peggy Ashcroft, Mildred Dunnock. **1959**

NUREMBERG ★★★★ Based on Joseph E. Persico's *Nuremberg: Infamy on Trial*, this TNT miniseries delivers a spellbinding account of the trial of high-ranking Nazi war criminals. Actual footage and photos of the atrocities at Auschwitz and Belsen as well as riveting performances by all make this stand against inhumanity hauntingly unforgettable. Not rated, but definitely aimed at mature audiences. 185m. **DIR:** Yves Simoneau. **CAST:** Alec Baldwin, Brian Cox, Jill Hennessy, Christopher Plummer. **2000 DVD**

NURSE, THE ★★★ Wicked genre thriller about a woman seeking revenge on the man who pushed her father into killing himself and his family. Laura has waited for the right moment to get even with Bob Martin. That moment arrives when he has a sudden stroke, and Laura signs on as his personal nurse. Poor Bob. Rated R for adult situations, language, nudity, and violence. 94m. **DIR:** Robert Malenfant. **CAST:** Lisa Zane, John Stockwell, Janet Gunn, William R. Moses, Nancy Dussault, Jay Underwood. **1996**

NURSE BETTY ★★★★ When she witnesses the brutal murder of her husband, a waitress (Renée Zellweger) retreats into a fantasy in which she is romantically involved with her favorite soap-opera character (Greg Kinnear). She then sets out on a pilgrimage to Hollywood, unaware that her car is loaded with drugs and that the two killers (Morgan Freeman, Chris Rock) are hot on her trail. This offbeat tale delivers, thanks in large part to memorable performances by Zellweger and Freeman. Rated R for violence, profanity, and sex. 109m. **DIR:** Neil LaBute. **CAST:** Morgan Freeman, Renée Zellweger, Chris Rock, Greg Kinnear, Aaron Eckhart, Tia Texada, Crispin Glover, Pruitt Taylor Vince, Allison Janney, Kathleen Wilhoite, Elizabeth Mitchell. **2000 DVD**

NURSE EDITH CAVELL ★★★ The story of England's second most famous nurse, who helped transport refugee soldiers out of German-held Belgium during World War I. The film delivered a dramatically satisfying antiwar message just as World War II got under way. B&W; 95m. **DIR:** Herbert Wilcox. **CAST:** Anna Neagle, Edna May Oliver, George Sanders, ZaSu Pitts, H. B.

Warner, May Robson, Robert Coote, Martin Kosleck, Mary Howard. **1939**

NUT, THE ★★1/2 Eccentric socialite tries to win the girl of his dreams by helping her in her scheme to rehabilitate underprivileged children. Douglas Fairbanks spoofs social work in an uneven mix of gangsters, gags, innovative filming, and pedestrian humor. Silent. B&W; 87m. **DIR:** Ted Reed. **CAST:** Douglas Fairbanks Sr., Marguerite de la Motte, William Lowery, Barbara La Marr. **1921**

NUTCRACKER PRINCE, THE ★★1/2 Animated version of E.T.A. Hoffman's book *The Nutcracker and the Mouse King* benefits greatly from the voice talents of Kiefer Sutherland, Megan Follows, Peter O'Toole, Mike McDonald, and Phyllis Diller, who bring life to this fanciful tale of a young girl who joins the Nutcracker in his battle against the evil Mouse King. Rated G. 75m. **DIR:** Paul Schibli. **1990**

NUTS ★★★★ Star-producer Barbra Streisand chaperoned Tom Topor's deft play to the big screen and gave herself a meaty starring role in the process. She's a high-toned prostitute facing a murder charge who may not get her day in court, because her mother and stepfather would rather bury her in an insane asylum. Rated R for language and sexual themes. 116m. **DIR:** Martin Ritt. **CAST:** Barbra Streisand, Richard Dreyfuss, Maureen Stapleton, Eli Wallach, Robert Webber, James Whitmore, Karl Malden. **1987**

NUTTY PROFESSOR, THE (1963) ★★★★ Jerry Lewis's funniest self-directed comedy, this release—a takeoff on Robert Louis Stevenson's *Dr. Jekyll and Mr. Hyde*—is about a klutz who becomes a smoothie when he drinks a magic formula. Reportedly, this was Lewis's put-down of former partner Dean Martin. 107m. **DIR:** Jerry Lewis. **CAST:** Jerry Lewis, Stella Stevens, Kathleen Freeman. **1963 DVD**

NUTTY PROFESSOR, THE (1996) ★★★★ Eddie Murphy comes back with a vengeance in this remake of the 1963 Jerry Lewis comedy. As shy, overweight professor Sherman Klump, Murphy discovers a formula that allows him to shed pounds and inhibitions. It comes just in time, as Sherman has fallen in love with beautiful grad student Jada Pinkett, whom he can now romance—without revealing his true identity—as a slender man-about-town. Unfortunately, Sherman's chemical concoction proves to be anything but stable, bringing plenty of laughs to this surprisingly heartwarming tale. Rated PG-13 for profanity and scatological humor. 95m. **DIR:** Tom Shadyac. **CAST:** Eddie Murphy, Jada Pinkett, James Coburn, Larry Miller, Dave Chappelle, John Ales. **1996 DVD**

NUTTY PROFESSOR II: THE KLUMPS ★★ Disappointing sequel to the Eddie Murphy tour de force once again features the star in multiple roles. The accent on toilet humor and sexual innuendo, however, makes this movie unfit for its target audience: youngsters. This time, Prof. Sherman Klump, horrified to find his alter ego still present in his DNA, takes drastic measures that lead to the usual complications. It's too bad the filmmakers chose to go below the belt for their laughs, obscuring Murphy's talents in a torrent of distasteful scenes. Rated PG-13 for scatological humor and sex. 106m. **DIR:** Peter Segal. **CAST:** Eddie Murphy, Janet Jackson, Larry Miller, John Ales, Richard Gant. **2000 DVD**

NYMPHOID BARBARIAN IN DINOSAUR HELL, A The best thing about this film is its title. Not rated; contains violence and nudity. 84m. **DIR:** Brett Piper. **CAST:** Linda Corwin. **1990 DVD**

O

•O ★★★ William Shakespeare's *Othello* is updated and set in a high-tone prep school, with the Moor of Venice transformed into a star basketball player (Mekhi Phifer), Desdemona into the dean's daughter (Julia Stiles), and Iago into the coach's resentful son (Josh Hartnett). The script follows the Bard scene for scene, and acting is very strong; if nothing else, it makes an excellent introduction to Shakespeare for high-school students. Rated R for profanity, violence, and sexual content. 95m. **DIR:** Tim Blake Nelson. **CAST:** Mekhi Phifer, Josh Hartnett, Julia Stiles, Martin Sheen, John Heard. **2001 DVD**

O. J. SIMPSON STORY, THE ★★1/2 Tabloid-TV addicts can delight in the cheap thrills contained in this quickly produced made-for-television movie. Not rated; contains violence. 90m. **DIR:** Alan Smithee. **CAST:** Bobby Hosea, Jessica Tuck, David Roberson, Bruce Weitz, James Handy, Kimberly Russell. **1995**

O LUCKY MAN! ★★★★ Offbeat, often stunning story of a young salesman (Malcolm McDowell) and his efforts and obstacles in reaching the top rung of the success ladder. Allegorical and surrealistic at times, this film takes its own course like a fine piece of music. Great acting by a great cast (many of the principals play multiple roles) makes this a real viewing pleasure. Some adult situations and language. Rated R. 173m. **DIR:** Lindsay Anderson. **CAST:** Malcolm McDowell, Rachel Roberts, Ralph Richardson, Alan Price, Lindsay Anderson. **1973**

O PIONEERS! ★★★1/2 Eons distant from her film debut in Kong's palm, a self-assured, strong Jessica Lange bests male sibling opposition and competition and the rigors of Nebraska farm life to win and prevail. The gait is slow, the mood a mite somber, but the aim is true. 100m. **DIR:** Glenn Jordan. **CAST:** Jessica Lange, David Strathairn, Tom Aldredge, Anne Heche, Heather Graham. **1992**

OBJECT OF BEAUTY, THE ★★ The best things in life may be free, but you can't prove it to the Gold Card–flashing Jake and Tina, a jet-setting duo who've been living a life of incredible luxury. Played by John Malkovich and Andie MacDowell, they're the central characters in this inconsistent and somewhat flat comedy from writer-director Michael Lindsay-Hogg. Rated R. 110m. **DIR:** Michael Lindsay-Hogg. **CAST:** John Malkovich, Andie MacDowell, Rudi Davies. **1991 DVD**

OBJECT OF MY AFFECTION, THE ★★★ A young social worker (Jennifer Aniston) finds herself falling in love with her gay roommate (Paul Rudd) just as she becomes pregnant by her insensitive boyfriend (John

Pankow). This glossy, unusual romantic comedy has an intelligent script by Pulitzer Prize–winning playwright Wendy Wasserstein, deft direction by Nicholas Hytner, and an appealing cast. Rated R for profanity and mature themes. 111m. **DIR:** Nicholas Hytner. **CAST:** Jennifer Aniston, Paul Rudd, John Pankow, Alan Alda, Allison Janney, Nigel Hawthorne. **1998 DVD**

OBJECT OF OBSESSION 🦃 Run-of-the-mill sex thriller about two strangers who ignite each other's passions, driving them to extremes. Simple and silly. Rated R for nudity, violence, and adult language. 91m. **DIR:** Alexander Gregory Hippolyte. **CAST:** Scott Valentine, Erika Anderson, Liza Whitcraft, Robert Keith. **1994 DVD**

OBJECTIVE, BURMA! ★★1/2 During World War II a tough bunch of paratroopers are dropped into Burma to destroy a radar station and kill Japanese—but even with Errol Flynn in charge, they run into trouble. Overlong action film. B&W; 142m. **DIR:** Raoul Walsh. **CAST:** Errol Flynn, William Prince, James Brown, George Tobias, Henry Hull, Warner Anderson, Richard Erdman, Anthony Caruso, Hugh Beaumont. **1945**

OBLIVION ★★ Briefly glimpsed stop-motion monsters cannot save this inept science-fiction Western that exists only to give paychecks to B-actors trading on their old television roles. It's pretty embarrassing to watch George Takei cradle a bottle of whiskey and slur, "Jim . . . beam me up!" Rated PG-13 for violence and profanity. 94m. **DIR:** Sam Irvin. **CAST:** Richard Joseph Paul, Jackie Swanson, Meg Foster, Isaac Hayes, Julie Newmar, George Takei. **1994**

OBLIVION 2: BACKLASH ★★ Low-budget nonsense set in Badlands, a real wild West located in another galaxy. There, in the small rustic town of Oblivion, a bounty hunter named Sweeney is trying to keep his prisoner safe from an evil warlord. Lots of dusty, tumbleweed performances and so-so makeup effects do little to inspire the weak story. Rated PG-13 for violence. 82m. **DIR:** Sam Irvin. **CAST:** Richard Joseph Paul, Jackie Swanson, Andrew Divoff, Meg Foster, Isaac Hayes, Julie Newmar, George Takei. **1995**

OBLOMOV ★★★★ This thoroughly delightful film has as its main character Oblomov, a man who has chosen to sleep his life away. Then along comes a childhood friend who helps him explore a new meaning of life. A beautifully crafted triumph for director Nikita Mikhalkov (*A Slave of Love*). In Russian with English subtitles. MPAA not rated. 146m. **DIR:** Nikita Mikhalkov. **CAST:** Oleg Tabakov, Elena Soloyei. **1980**

OBLONG BOX, THE ★★ This little gothic horror, taken from an Edgar Allan Poe short story, can't escape the clichés of its genre: grave robbers, screaming women, lots of cleavage, and the hero's bride to be, who is unaware of her betrothed's wrongdoings. Sound familiar? Rated R (but more like a PG by today's standards) for violence. 91m. **DIR:** Gordon Hessler. **CAST:** Vincent Price, Christopher Lee, Rupert Davies, Sally Geeson. **1969**

OBSESSED ★★★1/2 After her son is accidentally struck and killed by the car of an American businessman, a Montreal woman feels improperly served by the legal system and plots revenge. Intelligently written drama about grief and responsibility. Rated PG-13. 103m. **DIR:** Robin Spry. **CAST:** Kerrie Keane, Daniel Pilon, Saul Rubinek, Colleen Dewhurst, Alan Thicke. **1988**

OBSESSION ★★★★ This is director Brian De Palma's tour de force. Bernard Hermann scores again, his music as effective as that in *Taxi Driver*. The script, about a widower who meets his former wife's exact double, was written by Paul Schrader (in collaboration with De Palma). Critics enthusiastically compare this with prime Hitchcock, and it more than qualifies. Rated PG. 98m. **DIR:** Brian De Palma. **CAST:** Cliff Robertson, Genevieve Bujold, John Lithgow. **1976**

OBSESSION: A TASTE FOR FEAR 🦃 Tacky, tasteless, disgusting Italian film about the brutal murders of women starring in bondage-type porno films. 90m. **DIR:** Piccio Raffanini. **CAST:** Virginia Hey, Gerard Darmon. **1989**

OBSESSIVE LOVE ★★1/2 *Fatal Attraction*–like made-for-TV thriller has soap-opera star Simon MacCorkindale fending off fan Yvette Mimieux. Handsome leads and topical story make up for an overly familiar plot. Not rated; contains adult language and situations. 97m. **DIR:** Steven H. Stern. **CAST:** Yvette Mimieux, Simon MacCorkindale, Constance McCashin, Lainie Kazan, Kin Shriner. **1984**

O.C. & STIGGS ★★★ Inspired by characters from *National Lampoon*, this offbeat film has two teenagers whose goal is to make life completely miserable for the local bigot (Paul Dooley), an obnoxious insurance magnate. Another energetic iconoclastic comedy from Robert Altman. Not rated. 109m. **DIR:** Robert Altman. **CAST:** Daniel H. Jenkins, Neill Barry, Paul Dooley, Jane Curtin, Martin Mull, Dennis Hopper, Ray Walston, Jon Cryer, Melvin Van Peebles. **1987**

OCCASIONAL HELL, AN ★★1/2 Not-bad thriller with Tom Berenger as a college professor who reverts to his former career as a cop when a colleague's widow (Valeria Golino) is accused of murder. The storyline is overly crowded, but it does hold your attention. Rated R for nudity, profanity, substance abuse, and sexual situations. 93m. **DIR:** Salome Breziner. **CAST:** Tom Berenger, Valeria Golino, Kari Wuhrer, Robert Davi, Stephen Lang. **1997 DVD**

OCCULTIST, THE 🦃 Pseudocampy adventure about a private eye hired to protect a visiting Caribbean leader from voodoo and assassins. Not rated, it has mild violence and suggestiveness. 80m. **DIR:** Tim Kincaid. **CAST:** Rick Gianasi, Joe Derrig, Jennifer Kanter, Matt Mitler. **1987**

OCCURRENCE AT OWL CREEK BRIDGE, AN ★★★1/2 This fascinating French film looks at the last fleeting moments of the life of a man being hanged from the bridge of the title during the American Civil War. This memorable short film works on all levels. B&W; 22m. **DIR:** Robert Enrico. **CAST:** Roger Jacquet, Anne Cornaly. **1962**

OCEAN'S ELEVEN ★★★ A twist ending, several stars, and good production values save this tale of an attempted robbery in Las Vegas. Frank Sinatra is the leader of the gang, and his now-famous "rat pack" are the gang members. Lightweight but pleasant. 127m. **DIR:** Lewis Milestone. **CAST:** Frank Sinatra, Dean Martin, Sammy Davis Jr., Peter Lawford, Angie Dickinson, Cesar Romero. **1960 DVD**

•OCEAN'S ELEVEN (2001) ★★★★ Upon his release from prison, career thief Danny Ocean begins planning the caper of a lifetime: the robbing of three casinos in Las Vegas. Unbeknownst to the team of ten specialists he assembles to do the job, he has a personal reason for pulling the heist, one that has more to do with matters of the heart than a desire for money. This stylish, thoroughly involving soufflé of pure entertainment more than eclipses the 1960 original. Expert use is made of the big-name cast, with adept touches of character added to what easily could have been caricatures. Rated PG-13 for profanity and suggested sex. 116m. **DIR:** Steven Soderbergh. **CAST:** George Clooney, Brad Pitt, Julia Roberts, Matt Damon, Andy Garcia, Carl Reiner, Elliott Gould, Scott Caan, Bernie Mac, Casey Affleck. **2001 DVD**

OCEANS OF FIRE ★★ Predictable formula adventure-saga about five ex-cons and head honcho, Gregory Harrison, putting up an oil rig off the South American coast. Only a star-studded cast saves this one from the depths of mediocrity. Rated PG. 93m. **DIR:** Steve Carver. **CAST:** Gregory Harrison, Billy Dee Williams, Lyle Alzado, Tony Burton, Ray "Boom Boom" Mancini, Ken Norton, Lee Ving, Cynthia Sikes, David Carradine. **1987**

OCTAGON, THE ★★ This "kung fu" flick stars Chuck Norris as a bodyguard for Karen Carlson. Norris naturally takes on multiple opponents and beats them easily. Rated R. 103m. **DIR:** Eric Karson. **CAST:** Chuck Norris, Karen Carlson, Lee Van Cleef, Jack Carter. **1980**

OCTAMAN ★★ Dull low-budget effort with a group of vacationers under attack by a funny-looking walking octopus-man created by a very young Rick Baker, who has since gone on to much bigger and better things. Rated PG for mild violence. 90m. **DIR:** Harry Essex. **CAST:** Kerwin Mathews, Pier Angeli, Jeff Morrow. **1971**

OCTAVIA 🦃 A ridiculously sappy fairy tale that quickly falls into an exploitation mode. Rated R. 93m. **DIR:** David Beaird. **CAST:** Susan Curtis, Neil Kinsella, Jake Foley. **1982**

OCTOBER SKY ★★★★ Heroes sometimes come in deceptive packages, and that's the case with this uplifting and fact-based story of Homer H. Hickam Jr., a West Virginia coal miner's son who stared up into the sky during that fateful day when the Soviet satellite Sputnik first passed overhead, and decided to become something other than an early candidate for death by black lung. Encouraged by a high-school teacher, Homer and several friends develop an interest in rocketry. Scripter Lewis Colick, working from Hickam's biography, *Rocket Boys*, fashions a tale that initially, makes us sympathetic disbelievers, just like Homer's classmates. But we're slowly won over with small and credible triumphs of Homer and his friends. This one's a winner: a film about real people who overcame unimaginable obstacles. Rated PG for mild profanity. 108m. **DIR:** Joe Johnston. **CAST:** Jake Gyllenhaal, Chris Cooper, William Lee Scott, Chris Owen, Chad Lindberg, Natalie Canerday, Laura Dern. **1999 DVD**

OCTOBER (TEN DAYS THAT SHOOK THE WORLD) ★★★★ This contribution to the tenth anniversary of the Russian Revolution of 1917 is as dazzling in its imagery as it is obscure in its storyline. The events leading up to the Cossacks' storming of the Winter Palace are refracted through a sensibility more interested in "Intellectual Cinema" than in routine plot formulas—making it perhaps more interesting to film history buffs than casual viewers. Silent. B&W; 85m. **DIR:** Sergei Eisenstein. **CAST:** V. Nikandrov, N. Popov. **1928 DVD**

•OCTOPUS (2000) ★★ A giant octopus, mutated from radiation from a sunken Russian nuclear submarine, wreaks havoc in this tired sci-fi flick. Hampered by a poor script and poorly executed computer effects, *Octopus* fails to rise higher than bargain-bin cheapie. Rated PG-13 for violence and profanity. 96m. **DIR:** John Eyres. **CAST:** Carolyn Lowery, Jay Harrington. **2000 DVD**

OCTOPUSSY ★★★1/2 Roger Moore returns as James Bond in the thirteenth screen adventure of Ian Fleming's superspy. It's like an adult-oriented *Raiders of the Lost Ark*: light, fast-paced, funny, and almost over before you know it—almost, because the film tends to overstay its welcome just a bit. Rated PG for violence and suggested sex. 130m. **DIR:** John Glen. **CAST:** Roger Moore, Maud Adams, Louis Jourdan. **1983**

ODD ANGRY SHOT, THE ★★★ This low-key film about Australian soldiers stationed in Vietnam during the undeclared war is a good attempt to make sense out of a senseless situation as Bryan Brown and his comrades attempt to come to grips with the morality of their involvement in a fight they have no heart for. Odd, sometimes highly effective blend of comedy and drama characterize this offbeat war entry. Some violence; adult situations and language. 89m. **DIR:** Tom Jeffrey. **CAST:** Bryan Brown, John Hargreaves, Graham Kennedy. **1979**

ODD COUPLE, THE ★★★★ Walter Matthau as Oscar Madison and Jack Lemmon as Felix Unger bring Neil Simon's delightful stage play to life in this comedy. They play two divorced men who try living together. The biggest laughs come from the fact that Felix is "Mr. Clean" and Oscar is a total slob—they're constantly getting on each other's nerves. Rated G. 105m. **DIR:** Gene Saks. **CAST:** Walter Matthau, Jack Lemmon, John Fiedler, Herb Edelman. **1968**

ODD COUPLE II, THE ★★★ In the wake of both *Grumpy Old Men* films and *Out to Sea*, the old dogs (Jack Lemmon and Walter Matthau) don't have any tricks that we haven't already seen repeatedly. Felix Unger and Oscar Madison reunite, after seventeen years, for the wedding of the former's daughter to the latter's son (stolen without so much as a by-your-leave from the aforementioned *Grumpy Old Men* sagas). Rated PG-13 for profanity and mild vulgarity. 97m. **DIR:** Howard Deutch. **CAST:** Jack Lemmon, Walter Matthau, Christine Baranski, Barnard Hughes, Jonathan Silverman, Jean Smart. **1998 DVD**

ODD JOB, THE ★★1/2 Monty Python's Graham Chapman wrote and starred in this comedy about a depressed businessman who hires a hit man to kill him. When he decides that life is worth living after all, he finds that he can't cancel his contract. Full of oddball characters and silly situations, but somehow it never builds up a full head of steam. Not rated. 86m. **DIR:** Peter Medak. **CAST:** Graham Chapman, David Jason, Diana Quick, Bill Paterson, Simon Williams. **1978**

ODD MAN OUT ★★★★ Carol Reed directed this suspenseful drama about a wounded IRA gunman (James Mason) on the run in Belfast and the people who help and hinder his escape. One of the hallmarks of postwar

British cinema. B&W; 113m. **DIR:** Carol Reed. **CAST:** James Mason, Robert Newton, Kathleen Ryan, Dan O'Herlihy. **1946 DVD**

ODD OBSESSION ★★ An aging man hopes to revive his waning potency. In Japanese with often incomplete or confusing English subtitles. Not rated, it contains off-camera sex. 107m. **DIR:** Kon Ichikawa. **CAST:** Machiko Kyo, Tatsuya Nakadai. **1960**

ODDBALL HALL 🦃 Jewel thieves masquerade as members of a fraternal order of do-gooders in this flat comedy of mistaken identities. Rated PG. 87m. **DIR:** Jackson Hunsicker. **CAST:** Don Ameche, Burgess Meredith, Bill Maynard. **1990**

ODDBALLS 🦃 Confusing comedy. Rated PG for obscenities and sexual situations. 92m. **DIR:** Miklos Lente. **CAST:** Foster Brooks, Michael Macdonald. **1984**

ODE TO BILLY JOE ★★★ For those who listened to Bobbie Gentry's hit song and wondered why Billy Joe jumped off the Talahatchie Bridge, this movie tries to provide one hypothesis. Robby Benson plays Billy Joe with just the right amount of innocence and confusion to be convincing as a youth who doubts his sexual orientation. Rated PG. 108m. **DIR:** Max Baer. **CAST:** Robby Benson, Glynnis O'Connor, Joan Hotchkis. **1976**

ODESSA FILE, THE ★★ Frederick Forsyth wrote the bestselling novel, but little of the zip remains in this weary film adaptation. German journalist Jon Voight learns of a secret file that may expose some former Nazis. Rated PG for violence. 128m. **DIR:** Ronald Neame. **CAST:** Jon Voight, Maximilian Schell, Derek Jacobi, Maria Schell. **1974 DVD**

ODYSSEY, THE ★★★ Armand Assante, properly Homeric in the central role, evolves from arrogant warrior to mature leader over a twenty-year period. Faithful wife Penelope never wavers in her devotion, while he is seduced by a witch and a beautiful goddess, and fights strange creatures on his long voyage home. Great location shots, fine costumes, and decent special effects make this very watchable. The only flaw is a lack of character development, due to the ambitious desire to cram Homer's twenty-four books into a two-night extravaganza. Not rated; contains violence and sexual situations. 180m. **DIR:** Andrei Konchalovsky. **CAST:** Armand Assante, Greta Scacchi, Isabella Rossellini, Eric Roberts, Bernadette Peters, Vanessa L. Williams. **1997 DVD**

OEDIPUS REX ★★ Disappointing adaptation of Sophocles' tragedy, offered in both contemporary and historical settings. Visually satisfying, but too excessive and unengaging. In Italian with English subtitles. Not rated; contains nudity and violence. 110m. **DIR:** Pier Paolo Pasolini. **CAST:** Franco Citti, Silvana Mangano, Alida Valli, Julian Beck. **1967**

OEDIPUS REX ★★1/2 Good adaptation of Sophocles's tragedy. Douglas Rain plays Oedipus, the doomed hero, who kills his father and marries his mother in fulfillment of the prophecy. 87m. **DIR:** Tyrone Guthrie. **CAST:** Douglas Rain, Douglas Campbell. **1957**

OF HUMAN BONDAGE ★★★★1/2 A young doctor (Leslie Howard) becomes obsessed with a sluttish waitress (Bette Davis), almost causing his downfall. Fine acting by all, with Davis an absolute knockout. No rating, but still a little adult for the kiddies. B&W; 83m. **DIR:** John Cromwell. **CAST:** Bette Davis, Leslie Howard, Alan Hale Sr., Frances Dee. **1934 DVD**

OF HUMAN BONDAGE ★★★★1/2 Excellent remake of the 1934 film with Bette Davis. This time Kim Novak plays Mildred Rogers, the promiscuous free spirit who becomes the obsession of Philip Carey (Laurence Harvey). Harvey's performance is wonderfully understated, and Novak plays the slut to the hilt without overdoing it. B&W; 100m. **DIR:** Ken Hughes. **CAST:** Kim Novak, Laurence Harvey, Robert Morley, Siobhan McKenna, Roger Livesey, Nanette Newman, Ronald Lacey. **1964**

OF HUMAN HEARTS ★★★1/2 A fine piece of Americana features Walter Huston as a backwoods traveling preacher whose son doesn't understand his faith and dedication to others. You'll even forgive the hokey ending with Abraham Lincoln (John Carradine) chiding selfish James Stewart for neglecting his mother. B&W; 100m. **DIR:** Clarence Brown. **CAST:** Walter Huston, James Stewart, Beulah Bondi, Guy Kibbee, Charles Coburn, John Carradine, Ann Rutherford, Charley Grapewin, Gene Lockhart, Clem Bevans, Gene Reynolds. **1938**

OF LOVE AND SHADOWS 🦃 Like *The House of the Spirits*, this is a potboiler based on a novel by Isabel Allende that tried to mix sociopolitical analysis of Chile with trashy soap opera. Rated R for violence, profanity, and sexual situations. 109m. **DIR:** Betty Kaplan. **CAST:** Antonio Banderas, Jennifer Connelly, Camille Gallardo, Stefania Sandrelli. **1994**

OF MICE AND MEN (1981) ★★★1/2 Robert Blake is George, Randy Quaid is big, dim-witted Lenny in this Blake-produced TV remake of the classic 1939 Burgess Meredith/Lon Chaney Jr. rendition of John Steinbeck's morality tale. While not as sensitive as the original, this version merits attention and appreciation. 125m. **DIR:** Reza S. Badiyi. **CAST:** Robert Blake, Randy Quaid, Lew Ayres, Pat Hingle, Cassie Yates. **1981**

OF MICE AND MEN (1992) ★★★★★ Actor-director Gary Sinise, working with a superb script from Horton Foote, delivers a hauntingly poignant adaptation of John Steinbeck's melancholy study of Depression-era California migrant workers. John Malkovich steals the film as the hulking Lenny, an inarticulate simpleton equally fascinated by puppies and pretty girls. Rated PG-13 for profanity and violence. 110m. **DIR:** Gary Sinise. **CAST:** Gary Sinise, John Malkovich, Casey Siemaszko, Ray Walston, Sherilyn Fenn. **1992 DVD**

OF PURE BLOOD ★★ A hoot of a made-for-television movie that wastes the talents of star Lee Remick who plays the distraught mother of a man killed in Germany. When she investigates her son's death, she immediately is thrown into a conspiracy involving Nazis and a genetic-breeding program. One-dimensional characters, corny dialogue, and laughable situations. 100m. **DIR:** Joseph Sargent. **CAST:** Lee Remick, Patrick McGoohan, Gottfried John, Richard Munch, Edith Schneider. **1986**

OF UNKNOWN ORIGIN ★★1/2 Flashes of unintentional humor enliven this shocker, about a suburban family terrorized in their home by a monstrous rat. Contains some inventive photography and effects, but mediocre acting and forgettable music. Bring on the exterminator! Rated R. 88m. **DIR:** George Pan Cosmatos.

CAST: Peter Weller, Jennifer Dale, Lawrence Dane. **1983**

OFF AND RUNNING ★★ This witless romantic comedy sat on the shelf for five years before winning pay-cable release, and it's easy to see why. Mitch Glazer's ridiculous script doesn't even begin to make sense, and leads Cyndi Lauper and David Keith have zero chemistry. They become involved with the death of a champion racehorse, a kidnapped kid, and a standard-issue assassin. Rated PG-13 for profanity and violence. 91m. **DIR:** Edward Bianchi. **CAST:** Cyndi Lauper, David Keith, Johnny Pinto, Jose Perez, David Thornton, Richard Belzer. **1990**

OFF BEAT ★★ This attempt at an old-fashioned romantic comedy succeeds as a romance, but as a comedy, it elicits only an occasional chuckle. One gains instant sympathy for captivating Meg Tilly's vulnerable big-city police officer. Rated PG. 100m. **DIR:** Michael Dinner. **CAST:** Meg Tilly, Judge Reinhold, Cleavant Derricks, Harvey Keitel. **1986**

OFF LIMITS (1953) ★★ Marilyn Maxwell adds a little "oomph" to this otherwise silly story of two army buddies and their antics. B&W; 89m. **DIR:** George Marshall. **CAST:** Bob Hope, Mickey Rooney, Marilyn Maxwell, Marvin Miller. **1953**

OFF LIMITS (1988) ★★★ Saigon, 1968, makes a noisy and violent background for this murder mystery. Willem Dafoe and Gregory Hines are a pair of military investigators assigned to find the high-ranking killer of local prostitutes. The two leads have good chemistry, Amanda Pays is credible as a sympathetic nun, and Scott Glenn is superb as a warped, messianic infantry colonel. Don't expect the plot to make much sense. Rated R for extreme language, violence, and brief nudity. 102m. **DIR:** Christopher Crowe. **CAST:** Willem Dafoe, Gregory Hines, Fred Ward, Amanda Pays, Scott Glenn. **1988**

OFF THE MARK ★★★ This off-the-wall comedy centers around Mark Neely, who once hosted a Russian boy (Terry Farrell) in his home for a year. Now they're both grown up and competing in a triathlon. The two leads are a delight. 81m. **DIR:** Bill Berry. **CAST:** Mark Neely, Terry Farrell, Virginia Capers, Jon Cypher, Barry Corbin. **1986**

OFF THE WALL A Tennessee speed demon (Rosanna Arquette) picks up two handsome hitchhikers. Rated R. 86m. **DIR:** Rick Friedberg. **CAST:** Paul Sorvino, Patrick Cassidy, Rosanna Arquette, Billy Hufsey, Mickey Gilley, Monte Markham. **1982**

OFFENCE, THE ★★★1/2 A series of child molestations causes London detective Sean Connery to go over the edge. Director Sidney Lumet tells the story in what is essentially a three-act play of Connery's confrontations with superior officer Trevor Howard, disillusioned wife Vivien Merchant, and suspect Ian Bannen. It's a superbly played, disturbing character study. Rated R for violence and profanity. 122m. **DIR:** Sidney Lumet. **CAST:** Sean Connery, Trevor Howard, Vivien Merchant, Ian Bannen, Derek Newark. **1973**

OFFICE KILLER ★★★ A meek and mild-mannered office employee, Dorine, uses her job as a copy editor for a consumer magazine to escape her horrid home life with her mother. When word filters down that employee downsizing is needed, Dorine, fearing for her job, begins a little housecleaning of her own, killing her coworkers. Dastardly funny, *Office Killer* is just the ticket for someone who has either been abused or ignored at his job. Rated R for violence, language, and adult situations. 83m. **DIR:** Cindy Sherman. **CAST:** Carol Kane, Jeanne Tripplehorn, Molly Ringwald. **1997**

OFFICE ROMANCES ★★ Slow-moving British soap. A plain, lonely country girl comes to work in London and is seduced by a selfish, married coworker. Ironically, she feels lucky to have been chosen by him. Not rated. 48m. **DIR:** Mary McMurray. **CAST:** Judy Parfitt, Ray Brooks. **1981**

OFFICE SPACE ★★★ This crude but funny whack at life in the white-collar trenches is about a computer programmer who begins dropping out of the rat race when his hypnotherapist drops dead during their first session. His sudden professional nonchalance and candid conversations with company consultants lead to promotions as he dates a waitress and stages a computer swindle. Rated R for language and sexual situations. 90m. **DIR:** Mike Judge. **CAST:** Ron Livingston, Jennifer Aniston, Stephen Root, Gary Cole. **1999 DVD**

OFFICER AND A DUCK, AN (LIMITED GOLD EDITION 2) ★★★★1/2 Six exceptional animated treats. Donald Duck turns unwilling soldier in these rarely seen entries, from his first days of "Donald Gets Drafted" to his ambitious scheme to go AWOL in "The Old Army Game," a plan that backfires with hilarious results. 50m. **DIR:** Walt Disney. **1942–1943**

OFFICER AND A GENTLEMAN, AN ★★★★1/2 Soap opera has never been art. However, this funny, touching, corny, and predictable movie, starring Richard Gere and Debra Winger, takes the genre as close to it as any of the old three-handkerchief classics. Director Taylor Hackford keeps just the right balance between the ridiculous and the sublime, making *An Officer and a Gentleman* one of the best of its kind. Rated R for nudity, profanity, and simulated sex. 125m. **DIR:** Taylor Hackford. **CAST:** Richard Gere, Debra Winger, Louis Gossett Jr., David Keith, Harold Sylvester. **1982**

OFFICIAL DENIAL ★★★1/2 Parker Stevenson believes he's been abducted and examined by extraterrestrials, but no one will believe him, including wife Erin Gray. Then a spacecraft crashes near his home, leaving an alien stranded, and the military decides to let Stevenson attempt to communicate with it. A well-acted and thought-provoking science-fiction thriller. Made for cable. 96m. **DIR:** Brian Trenchard-Smith. **CAST:** Parker Stevenson, Erin Gray, Dirk Benedict, Chad Everett. **1993**

OFFICIAL STORY, THE ★★★★★ This winner of the Oscar for best foreign-language film unforgettably details the destruction of a middle-class Argentinian family. The beginning of the end comes when the wife (brilliantly played by Norma Aleandro) suspects that her adopted baby daughter may be the orphan of parents murdered during the "dirty war" of the 1970s. In Spanish with English subtitles. Not rated, the film has violence. 110m. **DIR:** Luis Puenzo. **CAST:** Norma Aleandro, Hector Alterio, Analia Castro. **1985 DVD**

OFFSPRING, THE ★★★★ Four scary and original short stories are tied together by the narration of an old man (Vincent Price) who lives in a small town that seems to make people kill. Well written and acted, with decent special effects. Horror fans will love this. Rated

R for violence and brief nudity. 99m. **DIR:** Jeff Burr. **CAST:** Vincent Price, Clu Gulager, Terry Kiser. **1986**

OH, ALFIE 🦃 Alan Price is an uncaring ladies' man. Rated R for nudity. 99m. **DIR:** Ken Hughes. **CAST:** Alan Price, Jill Townsend, Joan Collins, Rula Lenska, Hannah Gordon. **1975**

OH! CALCUTTA! ★★ Only historians of the 1960s will have any reason to watch this, a videotaped performance of the musical revue that became infamous because it dealt with sex and featured onstage nudity. None of the sketches retain any humor or bite, a disappointment considering that the writers included Sam Shepard, John Lennon, Jules Feiffer, and Dan Greenberg. Not rated. 108m. **DIR:** Guillaume Martin Aucion. **CAST:** Raina Barrett, Mark Dempsey, Samantha Harper, Bill Macy. **1972**

OH DAD, POOR DAD—MAMA'S HUNG YOU IN THE CLOSET AND I'M FEELING SO SAD ★★★1/2 A cult favorite, and deservedly so. The plot has something to do with an odd young man (Robert Morse) whose mother (Rosalind Russell) drags him off on a vacation in the tropics with the boy's dead father. Morse excels in this unique, well-written, often hilarious film. 86m. **DIR:** Richard Quine. **CAST:** Rosalind Russell, Robert Morse, Barbara Harris, Jonathan Winters, Lionel Jeffries. **1967**

OH, GOD! ★★★★ God is made visible to a supermarket manager in this modern-day fantasy. The complications that result make for some predictable humor, but the story is kept flowing by some inspired casting. Ageless George Burns is a perfect vision of a God for Everyman in his tennis shoes and golf hat. John Denver exudes the right degree of naïveté as the put-upon grocer. Rated PG. 104m. **DIR:** Carl Reiner. **CAST:** George Burns, John Denver, Teri Garr, Ralph Bellamy. **1977**

OH, GOD! BOOK II ★★ George Burns, as God, returns in this fair sequel and enters a little girl's life, assigning her the task of coming up with a slogan that will revive interest in him. So she comes up with "Think God" and begins her campaign. It's passable family fare. Rated PG. 94m. **DIR:** Gilbert Cates. **CAST:** George Burns, Suzanne Pleshette, David Birney, Louanne, Howard Duff. **1980**

OH, GOD, YOU DEVIL! ★★★1/2 George Burns is back as the wisecracking, cigar-smoking deity. Only this time he plays a dual role—appearing as the devil. Ted Wass is the songwriter who strikes a Faustian bargain with Burns's bad side. This delightful comedy-with-a-moral is guaranteed to lift your spirits. Rated PG for suggested sex and profanity. 96m. **DIR:** Paul Bogart. **CAST:** George Burns, Ted Wass, Roxanne Hart, Ron Silver, Eugene Roche. **1984**

OH, HEAVENLY DOG! ★★ Chevy Chase should have known better. This movie is an overly silly cutesy about a private eye (Chase) who is murdered and then comes back as a dog (Benji) to trap his killers. Kids, however, should enjoy it. Rated PG. 103m. **DIR:** Joe Camp. **CAST:** Benji, Chevy Chase, Jane Seymour, Omar Sharif, Robert Morley. **1980**

OH! SUSANNA! ★★★ Gene Autry is mistaken for a bad man and must clear his name. B&W; 59m. **DIR:** Joseph Kane. **CAST:** Gene Autry, Smiley Burnette, Frances Grant. **1936**

OH, WHAT A NIGHT ★★★ Nostalgic soundtrack and innocent teen pranks highlight this better-than-average period piece about some 1950s teens trying to sow their wild oats. Young Corey Haim gets more than he bargained for when he falls for older woman Barbara Williams. Unexpectedly warm and sensitive. Made in Canada. Not rated; contains adult situations. 93m. **DIR:** Eric Till. **CAST:** Corey Haim, Barbara Williams, Keir Dullea, Robbie Coltrane, Genevieve Bujold. **1992**

O'HARA'S WIFE ★★ Trite little tale about a businessman whose dead wife returns from the grave to help him along in life. Made for television. 87m. **DIR:** William Bartman. **CAST:** Edward Asner, Mariette Hartley, Jodie Foster, Tom Bosley. **1982**

OKEFENOKEE ★★ The Florida swamplands are the setting for this forgettable story about smugglers who use the Seminole Indians to help bring drugs into the country. When the Indians are pushed too far, they strike back. What swamp did they dig this one out of? 78m. **DIR:** Roul Haig. **CAST:** Peter Coe, Henry Brandon. **1960**

OKLAHOMA! ★★★★ This movie adaptation of Rodgers and Hammerstein's Broadway musical stars Shirley Jones as a country girl (Laurie) who is courted by Curly, a cowboy (Gordon MacRae). Rod Steiger plays a villainous Jud, who also pursues Laurie. A very entertaining musical. 140m. **DIR:** Fred Zinnemann. **CAST:** Shirley Jones, Gordon MacRae, Rod Steiger, Eddie Albert, Gloria Grahame. **1956 DVD**

OKLAHOMA ANNIE 🦃 Judy Canova chases varmints out of town and brings decency to her community. 90m. **DIR:** R. G. Springsteen. **CAST:** Judy Canova, John Russell, Grant Withers, Allen Jenkins, Almira Sessions, Minerva Urecal. **1952**

OKLAHOMA KID, THE ★★★ Definitely one of the oddest of all major sagebrush sagas, this film, about a feared gunman (James Cagney) taking revenge on the men who hanged his innocent father, boasts a great cast of familiar characters as well as a musical interlude with Cagney singing "I Don't Want to Play in Your Yard" to the accompaniment of a honky-tonk piano and pair of six-shooters. A competent curio. B&W; 85m. **DIR:** Lloyd Bacon. **CAST:** James Cagney, Humphrey Bogart, Rosemary Lane, Donald Crisp, Charles Middleton, Ward Bond, Harvey Stephens. **1939**

OKLAHOMAN, THE ★★ Run-of-the-trail Western with Joel McCrea riding point to protect the rights of an outcast Indian against white-eyed crooks. 80m. **DIR:** Francis D. Lyon. **CAST:** Joel McCrea, Barbara Hale, Brad Dexter, Douglas Dick, Verna Felton. **1957**

OLD BOYFRIENDS 🦃 A woman decides to exact revenge on those men who made her past miserable. Rated R for profanity and violence. 103m. **DIR:** Joan Tewkesbury. **CAST:** Talia Shire, Richard Jordan, Keith Carradine, John Belushi, John Houseman, Buck Henry. **1979**

OLD CORRAL ★★★ Sheriff Gene Autry pursues a group of singing bandits, the Sons of the Pioneers, and battles tommy gun-wielding gangsters in order to save a runaway lounge singer who witnessed a murder. Noteworthy as the B Western where Autry fights Roy Rogers and forces Rogers to yodel. B&W; 54m. **DIR:** Joseph Kane. **CAST:** Gene Autry, Smiley Burnette, Roy

Rogers, Bob Nolan and the Sons of the Pioneers, Hope Manning, Lon Chaney Jr. **1936**

OLD CURIOSITY SHOP, THE ★★★ This enjoyable British-made follow-up to *Scrooge*, the successful musical adaptation of Charles Dickens's *A Christmas Carol*, adds tunes to the author's *The Old Curiosity Shop* and casts songwriter-singer Anthony Newley as the villain. Rated PG. 118m. **DIR:** Michael Tuchner. **CAST:** Anthony Newley, David Hemmings, David Warner, Michael Hordern, Jill Bennett. **1975**

OLD CURIOSITY SHOP, THE ★★★★ Handsome production of Charles Dickens's popular tale of Nell Trent, a precocious girl who's on the run with her grandfather from their sinister landlord, Quilp. Outstanding production design, a literate script, and an excellent cast headed by Sir Peter Ustinov as the grandfather and Tom Courtenay as Quilp make this *Hallmark* TV presentation a must-see. Rated G. 190m. **DIR:** Kevin Connor. **CAST:** Peter Ustinov, Tom Courtenay, James Fox, Sally Walsh. **1994**

OLD DARK HOUSE, THE (1932) ★★★★ A superb cast of famous faces enlivens this deliciously dark, comic tale of travelers stranded in a spooky mansion during a storm. On a par with director James Whale's very best—*Frankenstein*, *The Invisible Man*, and *Bride of Frankenstein*—this was long thought to be a lost film; its rediscovery is cause for celebration among film fans everywhere. B&W; 75m. **DIR:** James Whale. **CAST:** Boris Karloff, Melvyn Douglas, Charles Laughton, Gloria Stuart, Lilian Bond, Ernest Thesiger, Raymond Massey. **1932 DVD**

OLD DARK HOUSE, THE (1963) ★★ This messy, comedy-cum-chills rehash of the 1932 James Whale horror classic (which is still unavailable except in bootleg video versions) demonstrates mainly that William Castle, who directed the film, and Hammer Films, which coproduced it, were unsuited to collaboration. 86m. **DIR:** William Castle. **CAST:** Tom Poston, Robert Morley, Janette Scott, Joyce Grenfell, Mervyn Johns. **1963**

OLD ENOUGH 🦃 A prepubescent "coming-of-age" movie. Rated PG. 91m. **DIR:** Marisa Silver. **CAST:** Sarah Boyd, Rainbow Harvest, Neill Barry, Danny Aiello. **1984**

OLD EXPLORERS ★★1/2 Family adventure about two senior citizens who refuse to let old age stand in their way of having a full, exciting life. Using their imaginations, they span the globe, taking in such sights as the Sahara and the jungles of South America. Rated PG. 91m. **DIR:** William Pohlad. **CAST:** José Ferrer, James Whitmore. **1990**

OLD GRINGO, THE ★★★ Based on the novel by Carlos Fuentes. Jane Fonda hesitantly portrays an American schoolteacher on a quest for adventure with Pancho Villa's army during the 1910 Mexican revolution. Gregory Peck is an aging expatriate journalist traveling along for the last ride of his life. This project shows more aesthetic sensitivity during battle scenes than in dialogue sequences. Rated R for adult language. 120m. **DIR:** Luis Puenzo. **CAST:** Jane Fonda, Gregory Peck, Jimmy Smits. **1989**

OLD IRONSIDES ★★ This big-budget, action-packed yarn of wooden ships and iron men besting pirates in the Mediterranean has a big director, big stars, big scenes, and was ballyhooed at its premiere, but it was scuttled by a lackluster script. Silent. B&W; 88m. **DIR:** James Cruze. **CAST:** Charles Farrell, Esther Ralston, Wallace Beery, George Bancroft, Fred Kohler Sr., Boris Karloff. **1926**

OLD LADY WHO WALKED IN THE SEA, THE ★★★★ An aging con artist defies her partner in crime when she brings in a young man. Lady M., anxious to pass along her tricks of the trade to the new student, hopes to make him her last, great love. Her passion clouds her judgment and jeopardizes the team's final con game. In French with English subtitles. Not rated; contains profanity and adult situations. 94m. **DIR:** Laurent Heynemann. **CAST:** Jeanne Moreau, Michel Serrault, Luc Thuillier. **1994**

OLD MAID, THE ★★★1/2 Tearjerking film version of the Zoe Akins play based on the Edith Wharton novel about an unwed mother (Bette Davis) who gives up her daughter to be raised by a married cousin (Miriam Hopkins), and suffers the consequences. Hopkins works hard to upstage Davis. A solid box-office winner. B&W; 95m. **DIR:** Edmund Goulding. **CAST:** Bette Davis, Miriam Hopkins, George Brent, Donald Crisp. **1939**

OLD MAN ★★★1/2 In this *Hallmark Hall of Fame* adaptation of a William Faulkner short story, a convict gets a second chance at life when he becomes an unlikely hero during the great Mississippi flood of 1927. Well-told study of poor southerners whose normally difficult lives suddenly seem impossible. Not rated, but will appeal primarily to mature audiences. 90m. **DIR:** John Kent Harrison. **CAST:** Arliss Howard, Jeanne Tripplehorn, Leo Burmester. **1997**

OLD MAN AND THE SEA, THE (1958) ★★ Direction and script faithfully follow Ernest Hemingway's classic about a tired old fisherman who fights the unforgiving sea and giant prey only to win by losing. Spencer Tracy, in the title role, is overwhelmingly disappointing. The score won an Oscar, so buy the CD. 86m. **DIR:** John Sturges. **CAST:** Spencer Tracy, Felipe Pazos, Harry Bellaver. **1958 DVD**

OLD MAN AND THE SEA, THE (1990) ★★★1/2 Ernest Hemingway's saga is revitalized by Anthony Quinn's stirring performance as the old fisherman. Catching a fish is a symbol of his usefulness in the world but when sharks destroy his catch, he has to come to terms with his philosophy of life. Made for TV. 95m. **DIR:** Jud Taylor. **CAST:** Anthony Quinn, Patricia Clarkson, Alexis Cruz. **1990 DVD**

OLD SPANISH CUSTOM, AN ★★1/2 Set in Spain and filmed in England, this Buster Keaton sound comedy feature is best appreciated by diehard Keaton fans. Keaton is a bumbling yachtsman pursuing a scheming senorita. B&W; 56m. **DIR:** Adrian Brunel. **CAST:** Buster Keaton. **1935**

OLD SWIMMIN' HOLE, THE ★★ Easygoing homage to small-town America focuses on young Jackie Moran's plans to become a doctor, and his and his mother's life in simpler times. Modest and pleasant enough. B&W; 78m. **DIR:** Robert McGowan. **CAST:** Marcia Mae Jones, Jackie Moran, Leatrice Joy, Charles Brown. **1940**

OLD YELLER ★★★★ Here's a live-action Walt Disney favorite. A big yellow mongrel is taken in by a southwestern family. The warm attachment and numerous adventures of the dog and the two boys of the family are

sure to endear this old mutt to your heart. A few tears are guaranteed to fall at the conclusion, so you'd best have a hankie. 83m. **DIR:** Robert Stevenson. **CAST:** Dorothy McGuire, Fess Parker, Tommy Kirk, Chuck Connors. **1957 DVD**

OLDEST CONFEDERATE WIDOW TELLS ALL ★★★★ A lonely young girl (Diane Lane) marries a deranged Confederate vet (Donald Sutherland), who is at least three times her age, and spends much of their married years mothering him. Lane is a standout in this fine miniseries that was nominated for nine Emmy Awards. Anne Bancroft takes over the title role as she recounts her youth from the confines of her rest home. Cicely Tyson plays Lane's friend and confidante to perfection. Not rated; contains violence and sexual situations. 183m. **DIR:** Ken Cameron. **CAST:** Diane Lane, Donald Sutherland, Cicely Tyson, Anne Bancroft. **1994**

OLDEST LIVING GRADUATE, THE ★★★★ *The Oldest Living Graduate* features a memorable performance by Henry Fonda as the oldest living member of a prestigious Texas military academy. Cloris Leachman shines in her role of the colonel's daughter-in-law. The final moments of this teleplay are poignantly realistic. 90m. **DIR:** Jack Hofsiss. **CAST:** Henry Fonda, George Grizzard, Harry Dean Stanton, Penelope Milford, Cloris Leachman, David Ogden Stiers, Timothy Hutton. **1983**

OLDEST PROFESSION, THE ★★1/2 Jean-Luc Godard's contribution, the final of six segments in this omnibus comedy about prostitution through the ages, is worth seeing. But the rest resembles a Gallic version of *Love, American Style*. In French with English subtitles. Not rated. 97m. **DIR:** Franco Indovina, Mauro Bolognini, Philippe de Broca, Michel Pfleghar, Claude Autant-Lara, Jean-Luc Godard. **CAST:** Elsa Martinelli, Gastone Moschin, Raquel Welch, Anna Karina, Jean-Pierre Léaud. **1967**

OLEANNA ★★★★ David Mamet directed his powerful stage production for the big screen, and the results are equally powerful. William H. Macy plays a professor whose life is falling apart. He seeks redemption through a female student who desperately needs his help. Things heat up when the student accuses the professor of sexual harassment. Mamet carefully explores both sides of the coin before coming up with a conclusion. Rated R for language. 89m. **DIR:** David Mamet. **CAST:** William H. Macy, Debra Eisenstadt. **1994**

OLIVER ★★★★★ Charles Dickens never was such fun. *Oliver Twist* has become a luxurious musical and multiple Oscar-winner (including best picture). Mark Lester is the angelic Oliver, whose adventures begin one mealtime when he pleads, "Please, sir, I want some more." Jack Wild is an impish Artful Dodger, and Ron Moody steals the show as Fagin. Oliver Reed prevents the tale from becoming *too* sugarcoated. Rated G. 153m. **DIR:** Carol Reed. **CAST:** Ron Moody, Oliver Reed, Hugh Griffith, Shani Wallis, Mark Lester, Jack Wild. **1968 DVD**

OLIVER & COMPANY ★★★1/2 Disney's feature animation renaissance of the 1990s actually began with this charming reworking of Charles Dickens's *Oliver Twist*, which concerns a precocious kitten "adopted" by a gang of mischievous mutts. Superstar lyricist Howard Ashman, who later collected Oscars, makes an early mark with the tune—"Once Upon a Time in New York City"—which opens this film. Excellent voice "performances" turned in by Billy Joel, Richard Mulligan, and Bette Midler. Rated G. 73m. **DIR:** George Scribner. **1988 DVD**

OLIVER TWIST (1922) ★★★ Young Jackie Coogan, teamed with the legendary "Man of a Thousand Faces" Lon Chaney to portray, respectively, abused orphan Oliver Twist and literature's great manipulator of thieving children, Fagin, in this loose adaptation of Charles Dickens's enduring classic. Something of an oddity, this is one of at least eight film versions of the world-famous novel. Silent. B&W; 77m. **DIR:** Frank Lloyd. **CAST:** Jackie Coogan, Lon Chaney Sr., Gladys Brockwell, Esther Ralston. **1922 DVD**

OLIVER TWIST (1933) ★★ Low-budget version of the popular Charles Dickens story features some interesting performances and a few effective moments. This is a curiosity for students of literature or early sound film. Print quality is marginal. B&W; 77m. **DIR:** William Cowen. **CAST:** Dickie Moore, Irving Pichel, William "Stage" Boyd, Barbara Kent. **1933**

OLIVER TWIST (1948) ★★★★ Alec Guinness and Robert Newton give superb performances as the villains in this David Lean adaptation of the Charles Dickens story about a young boy who is forced into a life of thievery until he's rescued by a kindly old gentleman. B&W; 105m. **DIR:** David Lean. **CAST:** Alec Guinness, Robert Newton, John Howard Davies. **1948 DVD**

OLIVER TWIST (1978) ★★★★ A well-cast version of the Charles Dickens classic made for TV. The young hero symbolizes the state of English society in the nineteenth century when poverty, crime, and government neglect cried out for social reform. George C. Scott makes an effective Fagin. 100m. **DIR:** Clive Donner. **CAST:** George C. Scott, Tim Curry, Lysette Anthony, Michael Hordern, Timothy West, Eileen Atkins. **1982**

OLIVER TWIST (1997) ★★★1/2 Originally aired on the *Wonderful World of Disney*, this rendition of Charles Dickens's classic novel is surprisingly frank about the horrors faced by kids on the street. Oliver is befriended by the Artful Dodger after being thrown out of an orphanage. He is turned over to the tutelage of the seemingly benevolent, but highly manipulative, Fagin. Fagin's deadly associate, Bill Sikes, may give the wee ones nightmares. Not rated; contains violence and mental cruelty. 88m. **DIR:** Tony Bill. **CAST:** Richard Dreyfuss, Alex Trench, Elijah Wood, David O'Hara. **1997**

OLIVER'S STORY 🦃 Even if you loved *Love Story*, you'll find it difficult to like this lame sequel. Rated PG. 92m. **DIR:** John Korty. **CAST:** Ryan O'Neal, Candice Bergen, Nicola Pagett, Edward Binns, Ray Milland. **1978**

OLIVIER, OLIVIER ★★★★ An unusual French mystery of loss and identity, exploring themes similar to those in *The Return of Martin Guerre* and *Sommersby*. Once again, a person returns to a family after an absence of several years, and questions arise about his identity. Is he who we desperately want to believe he is? The contemporary story incorporates elements of fable and parapsychology. Rated R, with profanity, violence, and sexual material, including incest. 110m. **DIR:** Agnieszka Holland. **CAST:** Gregoire Colin, Marina Golovine. **1992**

OLLIE HOPNOODLE'S HAVEN OF BLISS ★★★★ Fans of Jean Shepherd's autobiographical *A Christmas Story* will be equally delighted by this sequel, in which the author's childhood alter ego has grown (but not matured) into a teenager. Various events conspire against the family's annual cabin outing. As always, Shepherd's witty narration evokes both whimsy and nostalgia. Made-for-cable; family fare. 90m. **DIR:** Richard Bartlett. **CAST:** Jerry O'Connell, James B. Sikking, Dorothy Lyman, Jason Adams, Jean Shepherd. **1988**

OMAHA (THE MOVIE) ★★1/2 First-time writer-director Dan Mirvish shows promise by relying on his savvy imagination to overcome a zero budget. Hughston Walkinshaw is the young Omahan who hits the road every time technology overwhelms him. Several elements, however, block his path to spiritual fulfillment, from a band of Colombian jewel thieves to a family hooked on factoid TV programs. Uneven, but clever, this valentine is energetic and endearing. Not rated; contains profanity. 85m. **DIR:** Dan Mirvish. **CAST:** Hughston Walkinshaw, Jill Anderson, Dick Mueller. **1994**

OMAR KHAYYAM ★★ Big-budget costume epic with Cornel Wilde as the Persian hero. Unfortunately, the producers skimped on the Saturday-matinee script, which is very weak. 100m. **DIR:** William Dieterle. **CAST:** Cornel Wilde, Debra Paget, John Derek, Raymond Massey, Yma Sumac, Michael Rennie, Sebastian Cabot. **1957**

OMEGA COP Futuristic story of a cop struggling to get three women back to the safety of police headquarters. Rated R for violence. 89m. **DIR:** Paul Kyriazi. **CAST:** Ron Marchini, Adam West, Meg Thayer, Stuart Whitman, Troy Donahue. **1990**

OMEGA DOOM Yet another apocalyptic movie about a cyborg warrior who gains cyberreligion and helps Earth fight against ultimate doom. Rated PG-13 for language and violence. 84m. **DIR:** Albert Pyun. **CAST:** Rutger Hauer, Shannon Whirry, Tina Cote, Norbert Weisser. **1996 DVD**

OMEGA MAN, THE ★★★ Charlton Heston does a last-man-on-Earth number in this free adaptation of Richard Matheson's *I Am Legend*. The novel's vampirism has been toned down, but Chuck still is holed up in his high-rise mansion by night, and killing robed (and sleeping) zombies by day. Although this is no more faithful to Matheson's work than 1964's *The Last Man on Earth*, it has enough throat-grabbing suspense to keep it moving. Rated PG—considerable violence. 98m. **DIR:** Boris Sagal. **CAST:** Charlton Heston, Anthony Zerbe, Rosalind Cash. **1971 DVD**

OMEGA SYNDROME ★★ Ken Wahl is a single parent who teams up with his old Vietnam war buddy (George DiCenzo) to track down his daughter's abductors. A very manipulative screenplay makes the film hard to take seriously. Rated R for violence and profanity. 90m. **DIR:** Joseph Manduke. **CAST:** Ken Wahl, George DiCenzo, Doug McClure, Ron Kuhlman, Patti Tippo. **1986**

OMEN, THE ★★★★ This, first of a series of movies about the return to Earth of the devil, is a real chiller. In the form of a young boy, Damien, Satan sets about reestablishing his rule over man. A series of bizarre deaths points to the boy. Rated R. 111m. **DIR:** Richard Donner. **CAST:** Gregory Peck, Lee Remick, Billie Whitelaw, David Warner. **1976**

OMEN IV: THE AWAKENING Made-for-TV continuation finds the devil continuing his reign of terror. 97m. **DIR:** Jorge Montesi, Dominique Othenin-Girard. **CAST:** Michael Lerner, Faye Grant, Michael Woods. **1992**

ON A CLEAR DAY, YOU CAN SEE FOREVER A psychiatrist discovers that one of his patients has lived a former life and can recall it under hypnosis. Rated G. 129m. **DIR:** Vincente Minnelli. **CAST:** Barbra Streisand, Yves Montand, Bob Newhart, Larry Blyden, Jack Nicholson. **1970**

ON AN ISLAND WITH YOU ★★ Lightweight story of navy flyer Peter Lawford pursuing actress Esther Williams while on location in the South Seas. Jimmy Durante's comedy and Cyd Charisse's dancing are the highlights. 117m. **DIR:** Richard Thorpe. **CAST:** Esther Williams, Peter Lawford, Ricardo Montalban, Jimmy Durante, Cyd Charisse. **1948**

ON APPROVAL ★★★ Former Sherlock Holmes Clive Brook displays a confident hand at directing in this enjoyable farce about women who exchange boyfriends. Fun and breezy with terrific performances by some of England's best talents, this film gave beloved Beatrice Lillie one of her best screen roles. B&W; 80m. **DIR:** Clive Brook. **CAST:** Beatrice Lillie, Clive Brook, Googie Withers, Roland Culver. **1943 DVD**

ON BORROWED TIME ★★★1/2 Lionel Barrymore is concerned about the future of his orphaned grandson. When death (Mr. Brink) calls, he tricks him up a tree and delays the inevitable. A rewarding fantasy. B&W; 98m. **DIR:** Harold S. Bucquet. **CAST:** Lionel Barrymore, Cedric Hardwicke, Beulah Bondi, Una Merkel, Bobs Watson, Henry Travers. **1939**

ON DANGEROUS GROUND (1951) ★★1/2 Robert Ryan does a credible job as a crime-weary patrol cop who takes out his frustrations on the men he arrests and winds up transferred after bloodying one too many suspects. B&W; 82m. **DIR:** Nicholas Ray. **CAST:** Robert Ryan, Ida Lupino, Ward Bond, Ed Begley Sr., Cleo Moore, Olive Carey. **1951**

ON DANGEROUS GROUND (1995) ★★ Jack Higgins's bestselling thriller is ill served by this low-rent adaptation, which compounds its problems by miscasting Rob Lowe as a rogue IRA-terrorist-turned-good-guy. He and the remaining protagonists seem clueless about the labyrinthine plot, which involves the Mafia, assassination attempts, and a priceless document that might keep Hong Kong out of Chinese hands for another century. A total snooze. Rated PG-13 for violence and profanity. 166m. **DIR:** Lawrence Gordon Clark. **CAST:** Rob Lowe, Kenneth Cranham, Deborah Moore, Ingeborga Dapkounaite, Daphne Cheung, Jurgen Prochnow. **1995**

ON DEADLY GROUND ★★1/2 Director-star Steven Seagal has come up with a martial arts movie with an environmental message. As you might guess, it's an uneasy combination, although action fans will find Seagal in top form as a one-man army out to stop oil tycoon Michael Caine (in a delightfully over-the-top role) from turning Alaska into one big ecological disaster. Rated R for violence and profanity. 98m. **DIR:** Steven Seagal. **CAST:** Steven Seagal, Michael Caine, Joan Chen, John

C. McGinley, R. Lee Ermey, Irvin Brink, Richard Hamilton. **1994 DVD**

ON GOLDEN POND ★★★★★ Henry Fonda, Katharine Hepburn, and Jane Fonda are terrific in this warm, funny, and often quite moving film, written by Ernest Thompson, about the conflicts and reconciliations among the members of a family that take place during a fateful summer. Rated PG because of brief profanity. 109m. **DIR:** Mark Rydell. **CAST:** Henry Fonda, Katharine Hepburn, Jane Fonda, Doug McKeon. **1981 DVD**

ON HER MAJESTY'S SECRET SERVICE ★★★★ With Sean Connery temporarily out of the James Bond series, Australian actor George Lazenby stepped into the 007 part for this entry—and did remarkably well. Director Peter Hunt keeps this moving at an incredibly fast pace, and this story about everyone's favorite superspy falling in love with an heiress (Diana Rigg) is one of author Ian Fleming's best. Rated PG. 140m. **DIR:** Peter R. Hunt. **CAST:** George Lazenby, Diana Rigg, Telly Savalas. **1969 DVD**

ON HOSTILE GROUND ★★★ Decent disaster film focuses on an underground sinkhole big enough to devour New Orleans. By the way, it's Mardi Gras and the geologist who wants to stop the festivities is at odds with his girlfriend who works for the mayor. Riveting, with plenty of close calls and body bags. Not rated; contains violence. 91m. **DIR:** Mario Azzopardi. **CAST:** John Corbett, Jessica Steen, Brittany Daniel. **2000**

ON MOONLIGHT BAY ★★★ Small-town setting, circa World War I, with tomboyish Doris Day falling for a college hero who is concerned about upcoming army service. Booth Tarkington's *Penrod* series set to music. Many fine songs of the era. 95m. **DIR:** Roy Del Ruth. **CAST:** Doris Day, Gordon MacRae, Leon Ames, Rosemary DeCamp, Billy Gray, Jack Smith, Mary Wickes, Ellen Corby. **1951**

ON THE AVENUE ★★★1/2 Dick Powell spoofs a noted spoiled heiress in his musical play. She buys out the backers and tries to sabotage the show and his reputation. Ah, but love steps in. Wonderful songs by Irving Berlin. Some cassettes open with an "added feature," a comedy sketch with Alice Faye and the Ritz Brothers. B&W; 88m. **DIR:** Roy Del Ruth. **CAST:** Dick Powell, Madeleine Carroll, Alice Faye, The Ritz Brothers, George Barbier, Cora Witherspoon, Alan Mowbray, Walter Catlett, Joan Davis, Stepin Fetchit, Sig Ruman, Billy Gilbert. **1937**

ON THE BEACH (1959) ★★★★ The effect of a nuclear holocaust on a group of people in Australia makes for engrossing drama in this film. Gregory Peck is a submarine commander who ups anchor and goes looking for survivors as a radioactive cloud slowly descends upon this apparently last human enclave. Director Stanley Kramer is a bit heavy-handed in his moralizing and the romance between Peck and Ava Gardner is distracting, yet the film remains a powerful antiwar statement. B&W; 133m. **DIR:** Stanley Kramer. **CAST:** Gregory Peck, Ava Gardner, Fred Astaire, Anthony Perkins. **1959 DVD**

ON THE BEACH (2000) ★★★ A nuclear holocaust destroys the northern half of the world, leaving Australia as the sole surviving civilization on the planet. But radioactive winds are coming, and one last hope lies in submarine captain Armand Assante, who agrees to lead a mission north to find habitable land. Both the acting and the production are excellent, but this lengthy update of the 1959 film winds up being more message than entertainment. Not rated; contains profanity, violence, and nudity. 195m. **DIR:** Russell Mulcahy. **CAST:** Armand Assante, Rachel Ward, Bryan Brown, Jacqueline McKenzie, Grant Bowler. **2000**

ON THE BLOCK ★★1/2 Baltimore strip joints threatened by a greedy land developer. This low-budget film would have been better if they had cut back on the dance acts. Rated R for nudity, profanity, and violence. 96m. **DIR:** Steve Yeager. **CAST:** Marilyn Jones, Michael Gabel, Howard Rollins Jr. **1991**

ON THE BOWERY ★★★★ Gritty, uncompromising docudrama, dealing with life among the tragic street people of the Lower East Side in New York City. An extraordinary, agonizing glimpse into the world of the depraved alcoholic nomads whose lives become a constant daily struggle. Excellent black-and-white cinematography. B&W; 65m. **DIR:** Lionel Rogosin. **CAST:** Ray Sayler, Gorman Hendricks, Frank Mathews. **1956**

ON THE EDGE ★★★1/2 Bruce Dern gives a solid performance as a middle-aged runner hoping to regain the glory that escaped him twenty years earlier when he was disqualified from the 1964 Olympic trials. The race to test his ability is the grueling 14.2-mile annual Cielo Sea Race over California's Mount Tamalpais. The mobile camera action in the training and race sequences is very effective. Rated PG. 95m. **DIR:** Rob Nilsson. **CAST:** Bruce Dern, Bill Bailey, Jim Haynie, John Marley, Pam Grier. **1985**

ON THE LINE (1987) ★★1/2 David Carradine smuggles aliens across the Mexican border. Scott Wilson pledges to nail Carradine and his operation. This mediocre adventure is not rated. 103m. **DIR:** José Luis Borau. **CAST:** David Carradine, Scott Wilson, Victoria Abril, Jeff Delger, Paul Richardson, Jesse Vint, Sam Jaffe. **1987 DVD**

•ON THE LINE (2001) ★★ Lance Bass of N'SYNC plays a young man who meets his dream woman on the Chicago el train, then tries to find her again without even knowing her name. The movie is sloppy, the story contrived and frustrating—if the characters behaved with normal intelligence, the misunderstanding could be cleared up in ten minutes and there would be no movie. Rated PG. 85m. **DIR:** Eric Bross. **CAST:** James Lance Bass, Emmanuelle Chriqui, Joey Fatone, Jerry Stiller, David Foley, Al Green. **2001 DVD**

ON THE MAKE ★★1/2 Well-intended but preachy movie about dating in the AIDS era. Teens obsessed with scoring at the local disco are heedless of such consequences as disease, pregnancy, and emotional numbness. Rated R for sexual situations and brief nudity. 74m. **DIR:** Samuel Herwitz. **CAST:** Steve Irlen, Mark McKelvey, Teresina, Kirk Baltz, Tara Leigh. **1989**

ON THE NICKEL ★★1/2 Ralph Waite, of TV's *The Waltons,* wrote, produced, and directed this drama about derelicts on L.A.'s skid row. It's a well-intentioned effort that is too unfocused and sentimental to work, though Donald Moffat's performance as a cleaned-up drunk is worth seeing. Rated R for rough language. 96m. **DIR:** Ralph Waite. **CAST:** Donald Moffat, Ralph Waite, Hal Williams, Jack Kehoe, Ellen Geer. **1980**

ON THE RIGHT TRACK ★★ Gary Coleman (of television's "Diff'rent Strokes") plays a tyke with a talent for picking the winners in horse races. Without Coleman, this would be an awful movie. Even with him, it is nothing to shout about. Rated PG. 98m. **DIR:** Lee Philips. **CAST:** Gary Coleman, Maureen Stapleton, Michael Lembeck, Norman Fell. **1981**

ON THE TOWN ★★★★ This is a classic boy-meets-girl, boy-loses-girl fable set to music. Three sailors are on a twenty-four-hour leave and find themselves (for the first time) in the big city of New York. They seek romance and adventure—and find it. 98m. **DIR:** Gene Kelly, Stanley Donen. **CAST:** Gene Kelly, Frank Sinatra, Ann Miller, Vera-Ellen, Jules Munshin, Betty Garrett. **1949 DVD**

ON THE WATERFRONT ★★★★★ Tough, uncompromising look at corruption on the New York waterfront. Marlon Brando is brilliant as Terry Malloy, a one-time fight contender who is now a longshoreman. Led into crime by his older brother (Rod Steiger), Terry is disgusted by the violent tactics of boss Lee J. Cobb. Yet if he should turn against the crooks, it could mean his life. A classic film with uniformly superb performances. B&W; 108m. **DIR:** Elia Kazan. **CAST:** Marlon Brando, Eva Marie Saint, Karl Malden, Lee J. Cobb, Rod Steiger. **1954 DVD**

ON THE YARD ★★ Subpar prison melodrama pits John Heard against a prison-yard boss. Some good peformances help, but this never gets going, nor does it ring true. Rated R. 102m. **DIR:** Raphael D. Silver. **CAST:** John Heard, Mike Kellin, Richard Bright, Thomas Waites, Joe Grifasi. **1979**

ON VALENTINE'S DAY ★★1/2 Horton Foote created this small-town love story about his own parents. A young couple (William Converse and Hallie Foote) tries to make ends meet after eloping. Her parents haven't spoken to her since they ran away, but all that is about to change. Rated PG. 106m. **DIR:** Ken Harrison. **CAST:** William Converse-Roberts, Hallie Foote, Michael Higgins, Steven Hill, Rochelle Oliver, Matthew Broderick. **1986**

ON WINGS OF EAGLES ★★★ Well-acted, long-form TV production about what happens when two business executives are imprisoned in Tehran just before the fall of the shah of Iran. Burt Lancaster is top-notch as the grizzled ex-military man who trains the company's other executives for a raid on the prison. Richard Crenna's take-charge tycoon in this fact-based film was modeled on Ross Perot. 221m. **DIR:** Andrew V. McLaglen. **CAST:** Burt Lancaster, Richard Crenna, Paul LeMat, Jim Metzler, Esai Morales, Constance Towers. **1986**

ONASSIS: THE RICHEST MAN IN THE WORLD ★★1/2 Mediocre made-for-TV biography of Aristotle Onassis's life focusing on his rise to wealth and power and unhappy marriages. Raul Julia stands out in the lead but has little support from his female counterparts. 120m. **DIR:** Waris Hussein. **CAST:** Raul Julia, Jane Seymour, Anthony Quinn, Francesca Annis, Anthony Zerbe. **1990**

ONCE A HERO ★★ Yesteryear's comic-book superhero, Captain Justice, is slowly fading away. His fans are deserting him, so he decides to cross from his world of fantasy to our world of today with predictable but occasionally amusing results. Not rated. 74m. **DIR:** Claudia Weill. **CAST:** Jeff Lester, Robert Forster, Milo O'Shea. **1988**

ONCE A THIEF ★★★1/2 Raised from childhood to be master art thieves, three friends are double-crossed by their former mentor. John Woo's equivalent to Hitchcock's *To Catch a Thief* is a genial, relatively lighthearted film compared to *The Killer*, aided by the boundless charms of his regular star, Chow Yun-Fat. And there are enough action and stunt scenes to keep regular Woo fans happy. Not rated; contains violence. 108m. **DIR:** John Woo. **CAST:** Chow Yun-Fat, Leslie Cheung, Cherie Chung. **1991 DVD**

ONCE AROUND ★★★1/2 If it weren't for off-putting, vulgar language and some skimpy character development, this offbeat comedy in the style of *Moonstruck* would be a real winner. As it is, there are some truly delightful and hilarious moments in its tale of a Boston woman (Holly Hunter) who finds romance in the arms of an oddball, middle-aged millionaire (Richard Dreyfuss). Rated R for profanity. 115m. **DIR:** Lasse Hallstrom. **CAST:** Richard Dreyfuss, Holly Hunter, Danny Aiello, Laura San Giacomo, Gena Rowlands. **1991**

ONCE BITTEN ★★★ Sly little vampire film about an ancient bloodsucker (Lauren Hutton) who can remain young and beautiful only by periodically supping on youthful male virgins. Likable Jim Carrey is her latest target, and their first few encounters (three's the magic number) leave him with an appetite for raw hamburgers and a tendency to sleep during the day so as to avoid sunlight. Rated PG-13 for sexual situations. 92m. **DIR:** Howard Storm. **CAST:** Lauren Hutton, Jim Carrey, Karen Kopins, Cleavon Little. **1985**

ONCE IN PARIS ★★★ Effervescent romantic comedy about a script doctor (Wayne Rogers) called to Paris to repair a screenplay. Once there, he falls in love and ends up ignoring his work. Sparkling writing perks up an old story. Rated PG for adult situations. 100m. **DIR:** Frank D. Gilroy. **CAST:** Wayne Rogers, Gayle Hunnicutt, Jack Lenoir, Tanya Lopert, Doris Roberts. **1978**

•ONCE IN THE LIFE ★★★1/2 Laurence Fishburne delivers a powerful performance in this tale of a drug heist that leads to tragic consequences. Fishburne plays 20/20 Mike, a street hood in need of some quick cash. He recruits his half brother Torch to rip off a drug lord of four bags of heroin, but when the heist goes wrong and the bullets start flying, the men find themselves trapped in an abandoned building. Things go from bad to worse when Mike's former partner in crime is coerced into killing them. The story is a little difficult to follow thanks to a hopscotch time line, but the performances more than make up for diversion. Rated R for drugs, language, and violence. 107m. **DIR:** Laurence Fishburne. **CAST:** Laurence Fishburne, Titus Welliver, Eamonn Walker, Annabella Sciorra, Gregory Hines, Paul Calderon. **2000 DVD**

ONCE IS NOT ENOUGH 🦃 Trash based on Jacqueline Susann's novel of jet-set sex. Rated R. 121m. **DIR:** Guy Green. **CAST:** Kirk Douglas, Alexis Smith, David Janssen, Deborah Raffin, George Hamilton, Melina Mercouri, Brenda Vaccaro. **1975**

ONCE UPON A CRIME ★★ Obnoxious, all-star comedy about murder and mayhem in Monte Carlo. The few moments of funny work by the cast members make it tolerable, but why did director Eugene Levy have the actors

scream nearly every line at the top of their lungs? Rated PG for profanity and goofy violence. 94m. **DIR:** Eugene Levy. **CAST:** John Candy, James Belushi, Cybill Shepherd, Sean Young, Richard Lewis, Ornella Muti, Giancarlo Giannini, George Hamilton. **1992**

ONCE UPON A FOREST ★★1/2 This eco-friendly animated tale concerns a trio of cute little animals who must save a friend from the deadly effects of poisonous gas. Rated G. 71m. **DIR:** Charles Grosvenor, Dave Michener. **1993**

ONCE UPON A HONEYMOON ★★1/2 In this travesty, one Cary Grant preferred to forget, he plays a newspaperman trying to get innocent stripteaser Ginger Rogers out of Europe as the German army advances. This amusing adventure-comedy is a bit dated, but Grant fans won't mind. B&W; 117m. **DIR:** Leo McCarey. **CAST:** Ginger Rogers, Cary Grant, Walter Slezak, Albert Dekker, Albert Basserman, Harry Shannon, John Banner. **1942**

ONCE UPON A TIME IN AMERICA (LONG VERSION) ★★★★ Italian director Sergio Leone's richly rewarding gangster epic; a $30 million production starring Robert De Niro in a forty-five-year saga of Jewish gangsters in New York City. Leone is best-known for his spaghetti westerns. This release culminates ten years of planning and false starts by the filmmaker. It was well worth the wait. Rated R for profanity, nudity, suggested sex, and violence. 225m. **DIR:** Sergio Leone. **CAST:** Robert De Niro, James Woods, Elizabeth McGovern, Tuesday Weld, Treat Williams, Burt Young. **1984**

ONCE UPON A TIME IN CHINA ★★★1/2 The beauty and action filling the screen in this martial arts epic yield a film that transcends the genre. Jet Li commands the screen as legendary nineteenth-century martial arts expert Wong Fei-Hung, fighting desperately to cleanse his village of corrupt Western influences. His task is complicated by his aunt's eagerness to spread the gospel on her return from America. Li is at his best fighting the various gangsters and foreigners intent on tainting his homeland. Rated R for violence. 134m. **DIR:** Tsui Hark. **CAST:** Jet Li, Yuen Biao, Rosamund Kwan. **1993 DVD**

ONCE UPON A TIME IN CHINA II ★★★★ In 1895, as China struggles to cast off the influence of England, Wong Fie-Hung battles the White Lotus Clan, an extremist group that is determined to obliterate any trace of foreign influence in China. Colorful, comical, and action-packed, this entertaining movie features two spectacular fight scenes between the boyishly charming Jet Li and Donnie Yen, another top Chinese martial arts star. In Chinese with English subtitles. Not rated; contains violence. 108m. **DIR:** Tsui Hark. **CAST:** Jet Li, Rosamund Kwan, Donnie Yen, David Chiang. **1992 DVD**

ONCE UPON A TIME IN CHINA III ★★★★ The action in this third film in the series revolves around a Lion Dance competition. The final competition is as spectacular as the martial arts stunts, which are often comical (especially one fought on an oil-covered floor). There's also a romantic thread as Wong Fei-Hung seeks to propose to his girlfriend. Not rated; contains violence. 107m. **DIR:** Tsui Hark. **CAST:** Jet Li, Rosamund Kwan, Mok Siu Chung. **1993 DVD**

ONCE UPON A TIME IN THE WEST ★★★★★ This superb film is the only spaghetti Western that can be called a classic. A mythic tale about the coming of the railroad and the exacting of revenge with larger-than-life characters, it is a work on a par with the best by great American Western film directors. Like *The Wild Bunch*, it has a fervent—and well-deserved—cult following in America. Rated PG. 165m. **DIR:** Sergio Leone. **CAST:** Claudia Cardinale, Henry Fonda, Charles Bronson, Jason Robards Jr., Jack Elam, Woody Strode, Lionel Stander. **1969**

ONCE UPON A TIME . . . WHEN WE WERE COLORED ★★★★ A loving, honorable film based on African American writer Clifton L. Taulbert's memoir of his rural Mississippi childhood in the years between World War II and the Civil Rights Movement of the 1960s. Director Tim Reid struggles with the script's uneventful, episodic structure, which makes the film seem longer than it is, but the acting is excellent and the essential decency of the story shines through. Rated PG. 112m. **DIR:** Tim Reid. **CAST:** Al Freeman Jr., Phylicia Rashad, Leon, Paula Kelly, Willie Norwood Jr., Damon Hines, Polly Bergen, Richard Roundtree. **1996**

ONCE WERE WARRIORS ★★★★1/2 Maori mother of five reevaluates her eighteen-year marriage to her alcoholic, volcanically tempered husband when his barroom vice and violence slop tragically into their home life. It's a raw, passionate story that has the electricity and visual wallop usually reserved for straight action pictures. Rated R for violence, sex, and language. 92m. **DIR:** Lee Tamahori. **CAST:** Rena Owen, Temuera Morrison, Julian Arahanga, Taungaroa Emile, Mamaengaroa Kerr-Bell. **1995**

•ONE, THE ★★1/2 Madman sets out to destroy all of his parallel selves, gaining strength with each kill. His last "self," an L.A. sheriff, proves to be his greatest challenge. Jet Li plays his many selves convincingly and the complex plot elevates this high-kicking shoot-'em-up. Rated PG-13 for violence. 88m. **DIR:** James Wong. **CAST:** Jet Li, Delroy Lindo, Carla Gugino, Jason Statham. **2001 DVD**

ONE AGAINST THE WIND ★★★★ A British socialite (Judy Davis) risks her life to guide Allied soldiers through Nazi-occupied France in this *Hallmark Hall of Fame* drama. Based on an actual person, Davis is captivating as the complex woman whose life disintegrates as she saves lives, using only her wits and impeccable manners. Made for TV. 96m. **DIR:** Larry Elikann. **CAST:** Judy Davis, Sam Neill. **1991**

ONE AND ONLY, THE ★★★ Writer Steve Gordon got started with this tale of an obnoxious college show-off who eventually finds fame as a wrestling showboater. Henry Winkler was still struggling to find a big-screen personality, but his occasional character flaws often are overshadowed by Gordon's deft little script. Rated PG. 98m. **DIR:** Carl Reiner. **CAST:** Henry Winkler, Kim Darby, Herve Villechaize, Harold Gould, Gene Saks, William Daniels. **1978**

ONE AND ONLY, GENUINE, ORIGINAL FAMILY BAND, THE ★★1/2 This period comedy, set in the Dakota territories, features Walter Brennan—who struggles to keep his family's band together in order to get invited to the Democratic convention in St. Louis. This is a lightweight movie but is, nonetheless, moderately enjoyable

for the whole family. Rated G. 110m. **DIR:** Michael O'Herlihy. **CAST:** Walter Brennan, Buddy Ebsen, Lesley Ann Warren, John Davidson, Goldie Hawn. **1967**

ONE ARABIAN NIGHT ★★ Heavy-handed screen version of the stage pantomine, *Sumurun*, by Max Reinhardt. The title character is the mistress of a sheikh who prefers romance with his son. Silent. B&W; 85m. **DIR:** Ernst Lubitsch. **CAST:** Pola Negri. **1920**

ONE BODY TOO MANY ★★1/2 Snappy dialogue and a memorable cast make this fast-paced whodunit worth a watch. Wisecracking Jack Haley is mistaken for a private investigator and finds himself in the thick of murder and intrigue. Bela Lugosi is again typecast as a menace. Nothing special, but not too bad for a low-budget programmer. B&W; 75m. **DIR:** Frank McDonald. **CAST:** Bela Lugosi, Jack Haley, Jean Parker, Blanche Yurka, Lyle Talbot, Douglas Fowley. **1944**

ONE COOKS, THE OTHER DOESN'T ★★ Suzanne Pleshette is the driving force behind this TV movie about a woman who finds herself having to share quarters with her ex-husband and his youthful bride-to-be when he is unable to make ends meet in the realty business. Though high in dimple quotient, it's engaging enough. 100m. **DIR:** Richard Michaels. **CAST:** Suzanne Pleshette, Rosanna Arquette, Joseph Bologna, Oliver Clark. **1983**

ONE CRAZY NIGHT ★★★★ Five Australian teens are trapped in the basement of a Melbourne hotel housing the Beatles in 1964. During the course of the night, these very different people swap their ideas on hero worship, sexual fantasies, fears, and expectations. It has that *Breakfast Club* feel, but bittersweet humor and a fresh cast make for an appealing diversion. Rated PG-13 for profanity. 92m. **DIR:** Michael Pattinson. **CAST:** Beth Champion, Malcolm Kennard, Dannii Minogue, Willa O'Neill, Noah Taylor. **1991**

ONE CRAZY SUMMER ★★1/2 Star John Cusack and writer-director Savage Steve Holland of *Better Off Dead* are reunited in this weird, slightly sick, and sometimes stupidly funny comedy about a college hopeful (Cusack) who must learn about love to gain entrance to an institute of higher learning. If you accept that silly premise, then you may get a few laughs. Rated PG. 94m. **DIR:** Savage Steve Holland. **CAST:** John Cusack, Demi Moore, Curtis Armstrong, Bob Goldthwait, Joe Flaherty, Tom Villard. **1986**

ONE DARK NIGHT ★★1/2 Meg Tilly and Adam "Batman" West star in this story of a young woman (Tilly) who is menaced by an energy-draining ghost. Rated R. 89m. **DIR:** Tom McLoughlin. **CAST:** Meg Tilly, Adam West, Robin Evans, Elizabeth Daily. **1983**

ONE DAY IN THE LIFE OF IVAN DENISOVICH ★★★ Tom Courtenay does a fine job as the title character, a prisoner in a Siberian labor camp. The famed novel by Alexander Solzhenitsyn is beautifully and bleakly photographed. Not an uplifting story, but a significant one. 100m. **DIR:** Caspar Wrede. **CAST:** Tom Courtenay, Espen Skjonberg, James Maxwell, Alfred Burke. **1971**

ONE DEADLY SUMMER ★★★ Isabelle Adjani stars as a promiscuous young woman who returns to a small village to seek revenge on three men who beat and raped her mother many years before. Exceptionally well acted, especially by Alain Souchon as her sympathetic boyfriend, and veteran European actress Suzanne Flon as his slightly crazy aunt. In French with English subtitles. Rated R for nudity and violence. 133m. **DIR:** Jean Becker. **CAST:** Isabelle Adjani, Alain Souchon, François Cluzet, Suzanne Flon, Manuel Gelin. **1983**

ONE DOWN, TWO TO GO ★★ Kung fu fighter (Jim Kelly) suspects a tournament is fixed and calls on his buddies (Jim Brown and director Fred Williamson) for help in this low-budget, theatrically unreleased sequel to *Three the Hard Way*. Some actors are hopelessly amateurish, and the story is a mere sketch. Not rated, the film has violence. 84m. **DIR:** Fred Williamson. **CAST:** Fred Williamson, Jim Brown, Jim Kelly, Richard Roundtree. **1983**

ONE-EYED JACKS ★★★★ Star Marlon Brando took over the reins of directing this Western from Stanley Kubrick midway through production, and the result is a terrific entry in the genre. Superb supporting performances help this beautifully photographed film about an outlaw seeking revenge on a double-dealing former partner. 141m. **DIR:** Marlon Brando. **CAST:** Marlon Brando, Karl Malden, Katy Jurado, Ben Johnson, Slim Pickens, Elisha Cook Jr. **1961 DVD**

ONE FALSE MOVE ★★★1/2 Terrific crime drama chronicles the exploits of three criminals, two men and a woman, from their initial cocaine rip-off in Los Angeles to a slam bang finale in a small Arkansas town. Entire cast is excellent under first-time director Carl Franklin's sure hand. Rated R for violence and language. 104m. **DIR:** Carl Franklin. **CAST:** Bill Paxton, Cynda Williams, Michael Beach, Jim Metzler. **1992 DVD**

ONE FINE DAY ★★★ George Clooney and Michelle Pfeiffer are a couple of single parents thrown together during a particularly hectic working day; of necessity, each watches the other's respective child when required. Clooney's daughter is a perfectly reasonable individual, but Pfeiffer's monster of a son brings this otherwise sweet-tempered story to a thudding halt. Rated PG for mild sensuality. 108m. **DIR:** Michael Hoffman. **CAST:** Michelle Pfeiffer, George Clooney, Mae Whitman, Alex D. Linz, Charles Durning. **1996 DVD**

ONE FLEW OVER THE CUCKOO'S NEST ★★★★★ Not since Capra's *It Happened One Night* had a motion picture swept all the major Academy Awards. Jack Nicholson sparkles as Randall P. McMurphy, a convict who is committed to a northwestern mental institution for examination. While there, he stimulates in each of his ward inmates an awakening spirit of self-worth and frees them from their passive acceptance of the hospital authorities' domination. Louise Fletcher is brilliant as the insensitive head nurse. Rated R. 133m. **DIR:** Milos Forman. **CAST:** Jack Nicholson, Louise Fletcher, Will Sampson, Danny DeVito, Christopher Lloyd, Scatman Crothers, Brad Dourif. **1975 DVD**

ONE FRIGHTENED NIGHT ★★ A stormy night, a spooky mansion, an eccentric millionaire, and a group of people stranded together was about all it used to take to make a scary movie. A good cast and some witty dialogue help, but there's only so much that can be done with this kind of mystery. B&W; 69m. **DIR:** Christy Cabanne. **CAST:** Wallace Ford, Mary Carlisle, Hedda Hopper, Charley Grapewin. **1935**

ONE FROM THE HEART ★★ This Francis Coppola film is a ballet of graceful and complex camera movements

occupying magnificent sets—but the characters get lost in the process. Teri Garr and Frederic Forrest play a couple flirting with two strangers (Raul Julia and Nastassja Kinski), but they fade away in the flash and fizz. Rated R. 100m. **DIR:** Francis Ford Coppola. **CAST:** Teri Garr, Frederic Forrest, Raul Julia, Nastassja Kinski, Harry Dean Stanton, Allen Garfield, Luana Anders. **1982**

ONE GOOD COP ★★★ When his partner is killed in a shoot-out with a drug-crazed criminal, detective Michael Keaton and his wife take in the partner's three daughters. Familiar material is handled well by a committed cast. Rated R for violence and profanity. 106m. **DIR:** Heywood Gould. **CAST:** Michael Keaton, René Russo, Anthony LaPaglia, Kevin Conway, Rachel Ticotin, Tony Plana. **1991**

ONE GOOD TURN ★★★ Better-than-average revenge thriller about a couple who invites a stranger into their house with deadly results. Matt agrees to let the man who saved his life twelve years ago stay in his home. Little does he realize that the stranger has a grudge he's been harboring all those years. Decent cast and taut direction elevate the mundane into suspense. Rated R for violence, profanity, and adult situations. 90m. **DIR:** Tony Randel. **CAST:** Lenny von Dohlen, James Remar, Suzy Amis, John Savage. **1995 DVD**

ONE HUNDRED AND ONE DALMATIANS (1961) ★★★★ Walt Disney animated charmer, concerning a family of Dalmations—far fewer than 101, at least initially—which runs afoul of the deliciously evil Cruella de Vil. In keeping with the jazzier soundtrack, the animation has rougher edges and more vibrant colors, rather than the pastels that marked the studio's earlier efforts. 79m. **DIR:** Wolfgang Reitherman, Hamilton Luske, Clyde Geronimi. **1961 DVD**

101 DALMATIANS (1996) ★★★ Although this is a delightful time passer, it is not the equal of the original Disney classic since here the animals are restricted to meaningful glances, head nods, and tail wags rather than the zesty dialogue allowed in the animated format. The pups play second fiddle to a sexy, though deranged Cruella De Vil. In this update, De Vil is the ruthless owner of a fashion house with Anita playing employee rather than former classmate. Roger now designs video games instead of writing songs. Still, young viewers can relax and enjoy! Rated G. 90m. **DIR:** Stephen Herek. **CAST:** Glenn Close, Jeff Daniels, Joely Richardson, Joan Plowright. **1996 DVD**

187 ★★1/2 Dedicated Brooklyn high-school science teacher moves to California after he is nearly stabbed to death by a student. He finds the West Coast public school system is also under a state of siege and adopts a warped interpretation of the Serenity Prayer to validate vigilante justice. This feverish thriller begins with a jolt but becomes progressively muddled. The film's title refers to the penal code for homicide. Rated R for language, violence, drug use, suggested sex, and nudity. 121m. **DIR:** Kevin Reynolds. **CAST:** Samuel L. Jackson, John Heard, Kelly Rowan, Clifton Gonzalez, Lobo Sebastian, Karina Arroyave. **1997 DVD**

•100 GIRLS ★★★1/2 Matthew (Jonathan Tucker) had an intimate encounter with a mystery woman in a school elevator during a power outage, and now all he has are memories and a pair of her panties. Masquerading as the girls' dorm fix-it guy, he infiltrates every room to hunt for his personal Cinderella's matching bra by causing maintenance problems, and then promptly showing up to repair them. A cute premise and a likable ensemble cast make this a better-than-average teen sex comedy. Rated R for sexual content, graphic language, and some violence. 95m. **DIR:** Michael Davis. **CAST:** Jonathan Tucker, Emmanuelle Chriqui, Katherine Heigl, Jaime Pressly, Marissa Ribisi. **2000 DVD**

ONE HUNDRED MEN AND A GIRL ★★★★1/2 Story of go-getting Deanna Durbin arranging a sponsor and a guest conductor for her unemployed symphony musician father (Adolphe Menjou) and his friends is a joyful musical feast. Oscar for the music department of Charles Previn and a nomination for the original story by William A. Wellman and Robert Carson. B&W; 84m. **DIR:** Henry Koster. **CAST:** Deanna Durbin, Leopold Stokowski, Adolphe Menjou, Alice Brady, Eugene Pallette, Mischa Auer, Billy Gilbert, Frank Jenks. **1937**

100 RIFLES ★★ The picture stirred controversy over Raquel Welch's interracial love scene with Jim Brown. But at this point, who cares? We're left with a so-so Western yarn. Rated R. 110m. **DIR:** Tom Gries. **CAST:** Burt Reynolds, Raquel Welch, Jim Brown, Fernando Lamas, Dan O'Herlihy. **1969**

102 DALMATIANS This misbegotten mutt of a movie wastes the time and talent of all involved, and may well remain an embarrassing low point for Gérard Depardieu and Glenn Close, both of whom overact to the point of hysterical absurdity. Disney hasn't released a film this bad in years. Rated G despite considerable mayhem and scenes of puppies in peril. 101m. **DIR:** Kevin Lima. **CAST:** Glenn Close, Gérard Depardieu, Ioan Gruffudd, Alice Evans, Tim McInnerny. **2000 DVD**

ONE IN A MILLION ★★★ Sonja Henie's film debut is only slightly dated. The center of the movie is her skating ability, and no one has ever topped her. She plays an unknown skater recruited to save a traveling show and winds up at Madison Square Garden with a proud papa, a handsome boyfriend, and an adoring public. B&W; 95m. **DIR:** Sidney Lanfield. **CAST:** Sonja Henie, Don Ameche, Adolphe Menjou, The Ritz Brothers, Jean Hersholt, Arline Judge, Ned Sparks, Dixie Dunbar, Borrah Minevich, Bess Flowers, Leah Ray. **1936**

ONE KILL ★★★ A female marine captain is charged with murder when she shoots a major with whom she once had an affair. This fact-based, made-for-cable original makes for decent drama, but doesn't reach beyond its story limitations. Anne Heche and company put in solid performances. Not rated; contains profanity and violence. 96m. **DIR:** Christopher Menaul. **CAST:** Anne Heche, Sam Shepard, Eric Stoltz, Kate McNeil. **1999**

ONE LAST RUN ★★ Male bonding theme is just an excuse for endless ski stunts. Not rated, contains profanity. 80m. **DIR:** Glenn Gebhard, Peter Winograd. **CAST:** Russell Todd, Craig Branham, Nels Van Patten, Ashley Laurence, Chuck Connors, Tracy Scoggins. **1990**

ONE MAGIC CHRISTMAS ★★★★1/2 Mary Steenburgen stars in this touching, feel-good movie as a young mother who has lost the spirit of Christmas. She regains it with the help of a Christmas angel (played by that terrific character actor Harry Dean Stanton). Rated G. 95m. **DIR:** Phillip Borsos. **CAST:** Mary Steenburgen,

Harry Dean Stanton, Gary Basaraba, Arthur Hill, Ken Pogue. **1985 DVD**

ONE MAN ARMY 🦃 Low-rent kick-boxing effort pits champ Jerry Trimble against the crooked small-town officials who killed his grandfather, but doesn't bring anything new to the arena. Rated R for violence and strong language. 90m. **DIR:** Cirio H. Santiago. **CAST:** Jerry Trimble, Melissa Moore, Dennis Hayden, Yvonne Michelle, Rick Dean. **1994**

ONE-MAN FORCE ★★★ John Matuszak plays an L.A. cop seeking to avenge his partner's murder. Good action drama. Rated R for violence and profanity. 90m. **DIR:** Dale Trevillion. **CAST:** John Matuszak, Ronny Cox, Charles Napier. **1989**

ONE MAN'S HERO ★★1/2 Set in the 1840s during the Mexican-American War, this tale of prejudice, freedom, romance, and tragedy chronicles the formation of St. Patrick's Battalion, a group of mostly Irish Catholics who desert the bigoted American army and fight with the Mexicans. This neglected, compelling slice of history is dramatized with uneven results. The dialogue is stiff and battles are awkwardly staged. Rated R for violence. 122m. **DIR:** Lance Hool. **CAST:** Tom Berenger, Daniela Romo, Joaquim de Almeida. **1999 DVD**

ONE MAN'S JUSTICE ★★1/2 A routine vengeance saga that concerns a military man's search for the maniac who killed his wife and young daughter. Enlivened slightly by Brian Bosworth's charm and Dejuan Guy, who stands out as a streetwise kid. Rated R for violence, profanity, and drug use. 101m. **DIR:** Kurt Wimmer. **CAST:** Brian Bosworth, Bruce Payne, Jeff Kober, DeJuan Guy, Hammer. **1995 DVD**

ONE MAN'S WAR ★★★ A superb ensemble cast does not compensate for the bewildering lack of punch to Mike Carter and Sergio Toledo's fact-based account of a family's battle with the corrupt government of 1976 Paraguay. Anthony Hopkins is mesmerizing as the proud and stubborn Dr. Joel Filartiga, who believes political "connections" will protect his family. Made for cable TV. 91m. **DIR:** Sergio Toledo. **CAST:** Anthony Hopkins, Norma Aleandro, Fernanda Torres, Rubén Blades. **1991**

ONE MAN'S WAY ★★★ More a tribute than an in-depth biography of clergyman Norman Vincent Peale and his early ministry. Don Murray is fine in the title role and there is passion when he delivers some of Peale's actual sermons. Good insight into the questions raised by other clerics over his book, *The Power of Positive Thinking*. B&W; 105m. **DIR:** Denis Sanders. **CAST:** Don Murray, Diana Hyland, William Windom, Virginia Christine, Veronica Cartwright, Ian Wolfe. **1964**

ONE MILLION B.C. ★★ D. W. Griffith reportedly directed parts of this prehistoric-age picture before producer Hal Roach and his son took over. Victor Mature, Carole Landis, and Lon Chaney Jr. try hard—and there are some good moments—but the result is a pretty dumb fantasy film. B&W; 80m. **DIR:** Hal Roach, Hal Roach Jr. **CAST:** Victor Mature, Carole Landis, Lon Chaney Jr. **1940**

ONE MINUTE TO ZERO ★★ Sluggish film about the Korean War benefits from some good acting by the male leads. The romantic subplot doesn't help much, but then not much could help this barely serviceable story about servicemen. B&W; 105m. **DIR:** Tay Garnett. **CAST:** Robert Mitchum, Ann Blyth, William Talman, Charles McGraw, Richard Egan. **1952**

ONE MORE SATURDAY NIGHT ★★★1/2 Al Franken and Tom Davis, who were writers and semiregulars on the original *Saturday Night Live* TV show, star in this enjoyable comedy, which they also wrote, about the problems encountered by adults and teenagers when trying to get a date on the most important night of the week. In its humane and decidedly offbeat way, *One More Saturday Night* is about the human condition in all its funny/sad complexity. Rated R for profanity and simulated sex. 95m. **DIR:** Dennis Klein. **CAST:** Al Franken, Tom Davis, Moira Harris. **1986**

•ONE NIGHT AT MCCOOL'S ★★★ Sexy con artist drives men to do outrageous things in the name of love. After losing his job, home, and self-respect, an exasperated Matt Dillon decides to end the madness by hiring a hit man. Michael Douglas, a producer of this film, steps in front of the camera to steal every scene as the killer for hire. This dark comedy offers plenty of wacky sight gags. Rated R for sex, crime, and violence. 93m. **DIR:** Harald Zwart. **CAST:** Matt Dillon, Liv Tyler, John Goodman, Michael Douglas. **2001 DVD**

ONE NIGHT IN THE TROPICS ★★1/2 Comics Abbott and Costello were brought in to enliven this revue-style romance with a few of their routines. They stole the movie, and it launched their screen careers. The nominal story line centers on a love triangle and Oscar Hammerstein, Jerome Kern, and Dorothy Fields wrote the songs. B&W; 82m. **DIR:** A. Edward Sutherland. **CAST:** Allan Jones, Nancy Kelly, Robert Cummings, Bud Abbott, Lou Costello, Leo Carrillo. **1940**

ONE NIGHT OF LOVE ★★★ The prototype of the operatic film cycle of the 1930s, it bolstered the flagging fortunes of opera star Grace Moore, who had been making movies since 1930, and successfully blended classical numbers with more "popular" song stylings. Film composer Louis Silvers won an Oscar for his score. B&W; 95m. **DIR:** Victor Schertzinger. **CAST:** Grace Moore, Lyle Talbot. **1934**

ONE NIGHT STAND ★★ Affluent Los Angeles commercial director returns to his wife after having a torrid fling with a New York woman and slides into a midlife funk. A year later he crosses paths with his lover and reignites their relationship. A rather bogus rationalization of the main characters' actions takes the bite out of a seductively photographed story about infidelity, friendship, and terminal illness. Rated R for nudity, sex, drug use, violence, and language. 103m. **DIR:** Mike Figgis. **CAST:** Wesley Snipes, Nastassja Kinski, Robert Downey Jr., Ming-Na Wen, Kyle MacLachlan. **1997 DVD**

ONE NIGHT STAND ★★ Talia Shire made her director's debut with this pedestrian erotic thriller about a bored Ally Sheedy looking for Mr. Perfect. Instead, she settles for Mr. One Night Stand, played by A Martinez. He's great in bed and he's got killer looks, but there's something about him that disturbs Sheedy. Ho-hum sexual game of cat and mouse. Not rated; contains nudity, adult language, and strong sexuality. 92m. **DIR:** Talia Shire. **CAST:** Ally Sheedy, A Martinez, Frederic Forrest, Gina Hecht, Diane Salinger, Jodi Thelen. **1995**

1-900 ★★★ Director Theo van Gogh's sexually frank comedy about two lonely professionals who meet

through a sex line. What begins as a one-time fantasy escalates into a weekly habit. Ariane Schluter and Ad van Kempen are honest and sincere as the two strangers who never meet, yet share every detail of their lives over the phone. In Dutch with English subtitles. Not rated; contains adult situations and profanity. 80m. **DIR:** Theo van Gogh. **CAST:** Ariane Schulter, Ad Van Kempen. **1995 DVD**

ONE OF OUR AIRCRAFT IS MISSING ★★★★ This British production is similar to *Desperate Journey* (1942) with Errol Flynn and Ronald Reagan. The story concerns an RAF crew who are shot down over Holland during World War II and who try to escape to England. High-caliber suspense. B&W; 106m. **DIR:** Michael Powell, Emeric Pressburger. **CAST:** Godfrey Tearle, Eric Portman, Pamela Brown, Hugh Williams, Googie Withers, Peter Ustinov. **1941**

ONE OF OUR DINOSAURS IS MISSING ★★1/2 In this moderately entertaining comedy-spy film, Peter Ustinov plays a Chinese intelligence agent attempting to recover some stolen microfilm. Helen Hayes plays a nanny who becomes involved in trying to get the film to the British authorities. Rated G. 101m. **DIR:** Robert Stevenson. **CAST:** Peter Ustinov, Helen Hayes, Derek Nimmo, Clive Revill. **1975**

ONE ON ONE ★★★★ The harsh world of big-time college athletics is brought into clearer focus by this unheralded "little film." Robby Benson is a naïve small-town basketball star who has his eyes opened when he wins a scholarship to a large western university. He doesn't play up to his coach's expectations, and the pressure is put on to take away his scholarship. Rated R. 98m. **DIR:** Lamont Johnson. **CAST:** Robby Benson, Annette O'Toole, G. D. Spradlin. **1980**

ONE RAINY AFTERNOON ★★ Silly movie about a young man who causes a furor when he kisses the wrong girl during a performance in the theater. It's a pretty slight premise, but under the skillful hands of director Rowland V. Lee (*The Count of Monte Cristo*, *Son of Frankenstein*), it becomes entertaining fare. A fine supporting cast helps flesh out the thin story, and a young Ida Lupino makes for a lovely leading lady. B&W; 79m. **DIR:** Rowland V. Lee. **CAST:** Francis Lederer, Ida Lupino, Roland Young, Hugh Herbert, Erik Rhodes, Mischa Auer. **1936**

ONE RIOT, ONE RANGER ★★★ Decent pilot for Chuck Norris's TV series *Walker, Texas Ranger* features the martial artist taking on a ruthless gang of bank robbers. His new partner (Clarence Gilyard Jr.) steals a number of scenes, but fights between lesser characters are poorly staged. Rated PG-13 for violence. 95m. **DIR:** Virgil Vogel. **CAST:** Chuck Norris, Clarence Gilyard Jr., Sheree Wilson, Gailard Sartain, Floyd Red Crow Westerman. **1993**

ONE RUSSIAN SUMMER 🦃 In czarist Russia of the eighteenth century, an anarchist peasant arrives at the estate of a brutish landowner to seek revenge. Rated R. 112m. **DIR:** Antonio Calenda. **CAST:** Oliver Reed, John McEnery, Claudia Cardinale, Carole André, Raymond Lovelock. **1973**

ONE SHOE MAKES IT MURDER ★★1/2 In this made-for-television movie, reminiscent in plot of *Out of the Past*, Robert Mitchum plays a world-weary detective who is hired by a crime boss (Mel Ferrer) to find his wayward wife (Angie Dickinson). Mitchum is watchable, but the story and direction never achieve a level of intensity. 97m. **DIR:** William Hale. **CAST:** Robert Mitchum, Angie Dickinson, Mel Ferrer, Jose Perez, John Harkins, Howard Hesseman. **1982**

ONE SINGS, THE OTHER DOESN'T ★★1/2 Labeled early on as a feminist film, this story is about a friendship between two different types of women spanning 1962 to 1976. When they meet again at a women's rally after ten years, they renew their friendship. 105m. **DIR:** Agnes Varda. **CAST:** Valerie Mairesse, Thérèse Liotard. **1977**

ONE STEP TO HELL ★★ On their way to a South African jail, a trio of killers escape and head for the jungle in search of a hidden gold mine, with police officer Ty Hardin hot on their trail. Not bad, but you wouldn't want to expend a lot of effort looking for it. 94m. **DIR:** Sandy Howard. **CAST:** Ty Hardin, Pier Angeli, Rossano Brazzi, George Sanders. **1968**

ONE THAT GOT AWAY, THE ★★★★ Excellent adaptation of the book by Kendal Burt and James Leasor about a captured German aviator who keeps escaping from a multitude of British prisoner-of-war camps. Based on a true story and especially well directed and performed, this adventure is highly recommended. B&W; 106m. **DIR:** Roy Ward Baker. **CAST:** Hardy Kruger, Colin Gordon, Michael Goodliffe. **1958**

1492: THE CONQUEST OF PARADISE ★★ Gérard Depardieu, so effective in character studies, is miscast as Christopher Columbus in this bloated epic. Beautifully filmed by director Ridley Scott and well acted by a strong cast. Rated PG-13 for violence and nudity. 152m. **DIR:** Ridley Scott. **CAST:** Gérard Depardieu, Armand Assante, Sigourney Weaver, Angela Molina, Fernando Rey, Tcheky Karyo, Frank Langella, Michael Wincott, Loren Dean, Kevin Dunn. **1992**

1900 ★★ This sprawling, self-conscious, exhausting film seems to revel in violence for its own sake. An insincere mishmash of scenes, *1900* chronicles the adventures of two young men set against the backdrop of the rise of fascism and socialism in Italy. The performances of Gérard Depardieu, Robert De Niro, and Dominique Sanda are lost in all the flashiness and bravado of Bernardo Bertolucci's direction. Rated R. 240m. **DIR:** Bernardo Bertolucci. **CAST:** Robert De Niro, Gérard Depardieu, Dominique Sanda, Burt Lancaster. **1976**

1918 ★★★ Minor-key slice-of-life film focuses on the denizens of a small Texas town in 1918. After introducing the main characters (including some based on members of his own family), screenwriter Horton Foote details the effects of a devastating epidemic of influenza that ravaged the town that year. The result is an almost academic but well-acted look at a bygone era. Rated PG. 94m. **DIR:** Ken Harrison. **CAST:** William Converse-Roberts, Hallie Foote, Matthew Broderick, Rochelle Oliver, Michael Higgins. **1984**

1984 (1955) ★★ Workmanlike adaptation of George Orwell's famous novel that, in spite of a good stab at Winston Smith by Edmond O'Brien, just doesn't capture the misery and desolation of the book. Frankly, this plays more like a postwar polemic than a drama, and great liberties have been taken with the story line. B&W; 91m. **DIR:** Michael Anderson. **CAST:** Edmond O'Brien, Jan Sterling, Michael Redgrave, Donald Pleasence. **1955**

1984 ★★★★1/2 A stunning adaptation of George Orwell's novel, which captures every mote of bleak despair found within those pages. John Hurt looks positively emaciated as the forlorn Winston Smith, the tragic figure who dares to fall in love in a totalitarian society where emotions are outlawed. Richard Burton, in his last film role, makes a grand interrogator. Rated R for nudity and adult themes. 123m. **DIR:** Michael Radford. **CAST:** John Hurt, Richard Burton, Suzanna Hamilton, Cyril Cusack. **1984**

1941 🦃 Steven Spielberg laid his first multimillion-dollar egg with this unfunny what-if comedy about the Japanese attacking Los Angeles during World War II. Rated PG. 118m. **DIR:** Steven Spielberg. **CAST:** John Belushi, Dan Aykroyd, Toshiro Mifune, Christopher Lee, Slim Pickens, Ned Beatty, John Candy, Nancy Allen, Tim Matheson, Murray Hamilton, Treat Williams. **1979 DVD**

1990: THE BRONX WARRIORS 🦃 Near the end of the 1980s, the Bronx becomes a kind of no-man's-land ruled by motorcycle gangs. Rated R for violence and language. 89m. **DIR:** Enzo G. Castellari. **CAST:** Vic Morrow, Christopher Connelly, Mark Gregory. **1983**

1969 ★★★ Writer-director Ernest Thompson's reminiscences of the flower-power era feature Kiefer Sutherland and Robert Downey Jr. as high school buddies who face the challenges of college and the abyss of military service in Vietnam. Thompson goes for too many larger-than-life moments in his directorial debut. But Sutherland and Bruce Dern create sparks as son and father, and the other actors are fine, too. Rated R for profanity, nudity, and violence. 105m. **DIR:** Ernest Thompson. **CAST:** Kiefer Sutherland, Robert Downey Jr., Bruce Dern, Mariette Hartley, Winona Ryder, Joanna Cassidy. **1988 DVD**

1001 RABBIT TALES ★★★★ Fourteen classic cartoons are interwoven with new footage to make another feature-length film out of the well-known Warner Bros. characters. This time the theme is fairy tales. Bugs and the gang spoof "Goldilocks and the Three Bears," "Jack and the Bean Stalk," and "Little Red Riding Hood," among others. This one also contains Chuck Jones's "One Froggy Evening," one of the greatest cartoons ever! Rated G. 76m. **DIR:** Friz Freleng, Chuck Jones. **1982**

1776 ★★★★ Broadway's hit musical about the founding of the nation is brought to the screen almost intact. Original cast members William Daniels, as John Adams, and Howard da Silva, as Benjamin Franklin, shine anew in this unique piece. Rated G. 141m. **DIR:** Peter H. Hunt. **CAST:** William Daniels, Howard da Silva, Ken Howard, Blythe Danner. **1972**

ONE TOUCH OF VENUS ★★ The Pygmalion myth gets the Hollywood treatment, long before *My Fair Lady*, although this is a wee bit diluted. Robert Walker plays a window decorator who becomes smitten, predictably, when a display statue of Venus comes to life in the form of Ava Gardner. The potentially entertaining premise is left flat by a script that lacks originality and wit. B&W; 90m. **DIR:** William A. Seiter. **CAST:** Robert Walker, Ava Gardner. **1948**

ONE TOUGH COP ★★★★ Excellent, gritty cop film tells a familiar story in an exceptional way. The title cop finds himself wedged between a lifelong friendship to the town mobster and a pair of overzealous FBI agents who want to use him as a tool to get to his buddy. Fine performances, taut direction, and razor-sharp writing throughout. Rated R for violence, profanity, and nudity. 90m. **DIR:** Bruno Barreto. **CAST:** Stephen Baldwin, Christopher Penn, Gina Gershon, Mike McGlone, Paul Guilfoyle. **1998 DVD**

ONE TRICK PONY ★★★1/2 This good little movie looks at life on the road with a has-been rock star. Paul Simon is surprisingly effective as the rock star who finds both his popularity slipping and his marriage falling apart. Rated R for nudity. 98m. **DIR:** Robert M. Young. **CAST:** Paul Simon, Lou Reed, Rip Torn, Blair Brown, Joan Hackett. **1980**

ONE TRUE THING ★★★1/2 This adaptation of Anna Quindlen's autobiographical novel of white upper-middle-class angst is about a grown child who makes a great show of wanting not to become like her parents, only to discover that she has fallen into familiar patterns—a solemn and familiar topic. There's no question that the heavyweight cast worked hard to produce something more powerful than the disease-of-the-month clichés of *Love Story*, and yet that very level of triteness occasionally overcomes the goodwill generated by the brilliant actors. Rated R for brief profanity and dramatic content. 120m. **DIR:** Carl Franklin. **CAST:** Meryl Streep, Renee Zellweger, William Hurt, Tom Everett Scott, Lauren Graham, Nicky Katt. **1998 DVD**

ONE, TWO, THREE ★★★1/2 James Cagney's "retirement" film (and his only movie with famed director Billy Wilder) is a nonstop, madcap assault on the audience. Wilder's questionable humor and odd plot about the clash between capitalism and communism could have spelled catastrophe for any other leading man, but veteran Cagney pulls it off with style. B&W; 108m. **DIR:** Billy Wilder. **CAST:** James Cagney, Arlene Francis, Horst Buchholz, Pamela Tiffin, Lilo Pulver, Red Buttons. **1961**

ONE WILD MOMENT ★★★★ In French director Claude Berri's warm and very sensitive film, a middle-aged man (Jean-Pierre Marielle) is told by his best friend's daughter that she's in love with him. Enjoy the story (which was adapted by director Stanley Donen for *Blame it on Rio*) as it should be told, as delicately and thoughtfully handled by Berri. In French with English subtitles. Not rated; the film has nudity, and profanity. 90m. **DIR:** Claude Berri. **CAST:** Jean-Pierre Marielle, Victor Lanoux. **1980**

ONE WOMAN OR TWO ★★★1/2 Gérard Depardieu plays an anthropologist digging for "the missing link." Dr. Ruth debuts as a philanthropist whose money will continue the search. And Sigourney Weaver is the advertising executive who almost ruins the entire project. Wonderful acting and superb dialogue are the highlights of this French turn on *Bringing Up Baby*. In French with English subtitles. 95m. **DIR:** Daniel Vigne. **CAST:** Sigourney Weaver, Gérard Depardieu, Dr. Ruth Westheimer. **1987**

ONEGIN ★★★★ When a nineteenth-century Russian nobleman visits the country estate he inherited from his uncle, he meets his neighbor, a young woman who falls in love with him. He spurns her love, and lives to regret his callous action when she marries another. A beautifully conceived adaptation of a work by Alek-

sandr Pushkin, superb in every aspect save one: a weak performance by Liv Tyler as the female lead. Rated R for violence and sexual themes. 106m. **DIR:** Martha Fiennes. **CAST:** Ralph Fiennes, Liv Tyler, Martin Donovan, Lena Headey. **1999 DVD**

ONIBABA ★★★★1/2 Director Kaneto Shindo's brilliantly photographed, savage tale of lust and survival in war-ravaged medieval Japan. A mother and daughter are drawn into deep conflict over a cunning warrior, who seduces the younger one, causing the mother to seek violent revenge. In Japanese with English subtitles. Not rated; contains nudity and is recommended for adults. B&W; 103m. **DIR:** Kaneto Shindo. **CAST:** Nobuko Otowa. **1964**

ONION FIELD, THE ★★★★ Solid screen version of Joseph Wambaugh's book about a cop (John Savage) who cracks up after his partner is murdered. James Woods and Franklyn Seales are memorable as the criminals. While not for all tastes, this film has a kind of subtle power and an almost documentary-like quality that will please those fascinated by true-crime stories. Rated R. 124m. **DIR:** Harold Becker. **CAST:** John Savage, James Woods, Franklyn Seales, Ted Danson, Ronny Cox, Dianne Hull. **1979**

ONIONHEAD ★★ One of the few Andy Griffith comedies that doesn't work, but it's not his fault. He plays a country boy in the coast guard who is sent to the galley to learn to cook. Walter Matthau is his teacher, and their scenes together are fine. It's the silly slapstick scenes involving love-starved girls that turn the movie topsy-turvy. B&W; 110m. **DIR:** Norman Taurog. **CAST:** Andy Griffith, Walter Matthau, Erin O'Brien, Ray Danton, Felicia Farr, Joey Bishop, Joe Mantell, James Gregory, Claude Akins, Roscoe Karns. **1958**

ONLY ANGELS HAVE WINGS ★★★★ Director Howard Hawks at his best tells yet another tale of professionals: pilots who fly the mail through treacherous weather and terrain in South America. Snappy dialogue and no-nonsense characters are handled deftly by the entire cast. It's great stuff, with Rita Hayworth getting a career-starting, glamorous role. B&W; 121m. **DIR:** Howard Hawks. **CAST:** Cary Grant, Jean Arthur, Richard Barthelmess, Rita Hayworth, Thomas Mitchell, John Carroll, Sig Ruman, Allyn Joslyn, Noah Beery Jr. **1939 DVD**

ONLY LOVE ★★1/2 Another *Love Story* from author Erich Segal, this one starring Rob Morrow and Mathilda May as doctors who fall in love, but when she's torn from his side, he marries the lovely Marisa Tomei. Then May returns with a debilitating illness that only Morrow can cure. If it sounds like the substance of a made-for-television soap opera, it is. Not rated. 130m. **DIR:** John Erman. **CAST:** Rob Morrow, Mathilda May, Marisa Tomei, Jeroen Krabbé, Paul Freeman. **1998**

ONLY ONE NIGHT ★★★1/2 Ingrid Bergman plays a woman courted by a circus performer who feels he is really beneath her station. She thinks so, too, and makes sure he doesn't forget it. One of her last Swedish films, and one of the films her new Hollywood bosses didn't dare remake because of the suggestive material. B&W; 89m. **DIR:** Gustav Molander. **CAST:** Ingrid Bergman, Edvin Adolphson. **1939**

ONLY THE BRAVE ★★★ For those who like particularly brutal coming-of-age stories. Two teenage girls live bleak lives in the shadow of an Australian oil refinery and forge a turbulent friendship that soon crosses all boundaries as they find themselves trapped in a nihilistic vortex. This may be startling for its realism, but it's just too dark for its own good. Letter-boxed. Not rated; contains profanity and violence. 62m. **DIR:** Ana Kokkinos. **CAST:** Elena Mandalis, Dora Kaskanis, Maude Davy. **1994**

ONLY THE LONELY ★★★1/2 Those *Home Alone* guys, writer John Hughes and director Chris Columbus, cooked up this follow-up to their surprise box-office smash. John Candy stars as a 38-year-old beat cop who falls in love with a mortician's daughter (Ally Sheedy), much to the disapproval of his feisty, opinionated Irish mother (a delightful performance by scene-stealer Maureen O'Hara). Rated PG-13 for profanity. 110m. **DIR:** Chris Columbus. **CAST:** John Candy, Maureen O'Hara, Ally Sheedy, Anthony Quinn, James Belushi, Kevin Dunn, Milo O'Shea, Bert Remsen, Macaulay Culkin. **1991**

ONLY THE STRONG ★★★ A world-class, martial-arts champion pits his strength and know-how against juvenile gangs and teaches them self-respect. The martial-arts sequences using the Brazilian Capoeira techniques are exciting to watch, and the story, though predictable, is well staged and well acted. Rated R for violence and profanity. 112m. **DIR:** Sheldon Lettich. **CAST:** Mark Dacascos, Stacey Travis, Paco Christian Prieto, Tod Susman, Richard Coca, Geoffrey Lewis. **1993**

ONLY THE VALIANT ★★1/2 Cavalry captain Gregory Peck is saddled not only with problems with Native Americans but irritability among his own troops. Produced by Cagney Productions, this Western is predictable but entertaining. B&W; 105m. **DIR:** Gordon Douglas. **CAST:** Gregory Peck, Ward Bond, Barbara Payton, Gig Young. **1951**

ONLY THRILL, THE ★★ True love never runs smooth, but this romantic drama is like riding an inner tube over Niagara Falls. Diane Keaton and Sam Shepard are wasted in this plain-Jane romance about two neighbors afraid of commitment who spend twenty-five years flirting with each other. When their children fall in love, they must reconcile their feelings. Robert Patrick and Diane Lane are miscast as the lovelorn children; the film lacks chemistry between the leads. Rated R for language. 103m. **DIR:** Peter Masterson. **CAST:** Diane Keaton, Sam Shepard, Diane Lane, Robert Patrick. **1997**

ONLY TWO CAN PLAY ★★★1/2 Peter Sellers is fabulous as a frustrated but determined Don Juan with aspirations of wooing society woman Mai Zetterling. As in so many of his roles, Sellers is funny and appealing in every move and mood. And Zetterling is the perfect choice for the haughty object of his attentions. 106m. **DIR:** Sidney Gilliat. **CAST:** Peter Sellers, Mai Zetterling, Richard Attenborough, Virginia Maskell. **1962**

ONLY WHEN I LAUGH ★★★ A brilliant but self-destructive actress (Marsha Mason) and her daughter (Kristy McNichol) reach toward understanding in this sometimes funny, sometimes tearful, but always entertaining adaptation by Neil Simon of his play *The Gingerbread Lady*. Rated R for profanity. 121m. **DIR:** Glenn Jordan. **CAST:** Marsha Mason, Kristy McNichol, James Coco, Joan Hackett. **1981**

ONLY WITH MARRIED MEN ★★ This TV movie is a pleasant yet thoroughly predictable light sex comedy about a woman (Michele Lee) who decides she will only date married men. She mistakes a bachelor (David Birney) for his married partner. 74m. **DIR:** Jerry Paris. **CAST:** David Birney, Michele Lee, Dom DeLuise, Judy Carne, Gavin MacLeod. **1974**

ONLY YOU (1991) ★★★ Enjoyable romantic romp features an adorable cast and some witty dialogue. Andrew McCarthy takes time off from his busy schedule to be with gorgeous Kelly Preston at a scenic seaside resort, where he meets cute Helen Hunt. Director Betty Thomas keeps everything light and charming. Rated PG-13 for language. 85m. **DIR:** Betty Thomas. **CAST:** Andrew McCarthy, Kelly Preston, Helen Hunt. **1991**

ONLY YOU (1994) ★★★★ Marisa Tomei makes an adorable Audrey Hepburn-type heroine for the 1990s in this hilarious love hunt with some ties to Hepburn's *Roman Holiday*. Tomei plays a soon-to-be-wed schoolteacher who flies to Rome hoping to find her fated lover before she weds a reserved podiatrist. Once there, she finds Robert Downey Jr., who appears to be her missing half. Don't miss the fun! Rated PG for sexual situations. 99m. **DIR:** Norman Jewison. **CAST:** Marisa Tomei, Robert Downey Jr., Bonnie Hunt, Joaquim de Almeida, Fisher Stevens, Billy Zane, John Benjamin Hickey. **1994 DVD**

OPEN CITY ★★★★1/2 Stunning study of resistance and survival in World War II Italy was the first important film to come out of postwar Europe and has been considered a classic in realism. Co-scripted by a young Federico Fellini, this powerful story traces the threads of people's lives as they interact and eventually entangle themselves in the shadow of their Gestapo-controlled "open city." In Italian with English subtitles. B&W; 105m. **DIR:** Roberto Rossellini. **CAST:** Aldo Fabrizi, Anna Magnani. **1946 DVD**

OPEN DOORS ★★★★ A sturdy and slow-moving but engrossing Italian drama about a stubbornly determined judge attempting to establish justice in a courtroom dominated by Fascist dictates. It earned an Oscar nomination as best foreign-language film. In Italian with English subtitles. 109m. **DIR:** Gianni Amelio. **CAST:** Gian Maria Volonté. **1991**

OPEN HOUSE This slasher movie features some particularly repellent and sadistic murders, along with nudity and sexual situations. A definite R. 95m. **DIR:** Jag Mundhra. **CAST:** Joseph Bottoms, Adrienne Barbeau, Rudy Ramos, Tiffany Bolling. **1987**

OPEN SEASON ★★★★ Very funny, biting film about what happens when the television-ratings system gets screwed up, and—for a short while—it appears TV audiences have learned to appreciate class and culture. Written and directed by Robert Wuhl. Rated R for profanity and nudity. 105m. **DIR:** Robert Wuhl. **CAST:** Robert Wuhl, Rod Taylor, Gailard Sartain, Helen Shaver. **1996**

OPEN YOUR EYES ★★★★★ A handsome young playboy is horribly disfigured when a spurned lover commits suicide by driving her car into a wall with him in the passenger seat. But is he going crazy, or is she not really dead? This stylish, wildly original psychological thriller, fiendishly clever and intricately plotted, will keep you guessing right up to the end. In Spanish with English subtitles. Rated R for nudity, sexual scenes, brief violence, and profanity (in subtitles). 117m. **DIR:** Alejandro Amenabar. **CAST:** Eduardo Noriega, Penelope Cruz, Fele Martinez, Najwa Nimri. **1997 DVD**

OPENING NIGHT ★★★ Gena Rowlands delivers a potent performance as an actress coming to grips with her life on the opening night of her new play. Director John Cassavetes guides Rowlands through this emotional roller coaster with his usual improvisational style, giving Rowlands every opportunity to shine. The events leading up to and following the actual production provide the fine cast with plenty of room to strut their stuff. Rated PG-13 for language. 144m. **DIR:** John Cassavetes. **CAST:** Gena Rowlands, Ben Gazzara, Joan Blondell, Paul Stewart, Zohra Lampert. **1977 DVD**

OPERA DO MALANDRO ★★★ A homage to the Hollywood musicals of the Forties, this vibrant, stylish film is set in Rio's seedy backstreets on the eve of the Pearl Harbor invasion. The story is about a gangster whose search for the American dream is disrupted by his love for a beautiful Brazilian girl. In Portuguese with English subtitles. 108m. **DIR:** Ruy Guerra. **CAST:** Edson Celulari, Claudia Ohana. **1987**

OPERATION AMSTERDAM ★★★ It's 1940 and Allied spies penetrate Holland to prevent the invading Nazis from getting their hands on Amsterdam's rich cache of diamonds. Filmed in a semidocumentary style, this movie is standard but well acted and produced. B&W; 105m. **DIR:** Michael McCarthy. **CAST:** Peter Finch, Eva Bartok, Tony Britton, Alexander Knox. **1960**

OPERATION C.I.A. ★★1/2 Political intrigue in Vietnam before the United States's full involvement finds a youthful Burt Reynolds as an agent assigned to derail an assassination attempt. Good location photography and Reynolds's enthusiasm and believability mark this film as one of the best chase films of the mid-1960s. B&W; 90m. **DIR:** Christian Nyby. **CAST:** Burt Reynolds, Kieu Chinh, Danielle Aubry, John Hoyt. **1965**

OPERATION CONDOR (1997) Don "The Dragon" Wilson heads up yet another mindless exercise in violence, playing a cop hot on the trail of his partner's killer in India. Wilson has played this role so many times he could do it in his sleep, which is the case here. Rated R for adult situations, language, and violence. 88m. **DIR:** Fred Olen Ray. **CAST:** Don "The Dragon" Wilson. **1997**

OPERATION CONDOR (1997) ★★★ International soldier of fortune Jackie Chan accepts an assignment to locate a huge cache of gold supposedly buried by Nazis beneath the Sahara during the closing days of World War II. Our hero's adventures involve the usual clumsy villains and decorative women, and everything climaxes in an impressive subterranean Nazi stronghold that provides Chan with opportunities for his trademarked fight sequences with "convenient" objects. Rated PG-13 for violence and brief nudity. 90m. **DIR:** Jackie Chan. **CAST:** Jackie Chan, Carol Cheng, Eva Cobo De Garcia, Shoko Ikeda. **1997 DVD**

OPERATION CROSSBOW ★★★★ A trio of specially trained commandos are sent to head off Hitler's rapidly developing rocket program. Suspenseful and exciting, with a top-notch international cast, fine special effects. 116m. **DIR:** Michael Anderson. **CAST:** George Peppard, Sophia Loren, Trevor Howard, John Mills, Richard Johnson, Tom Courtenay, Lilli Palmer, Jeremy

Kemp, Paul Henreid, Helmut Dantine, Richard Todd, Sylvia Syms. **1965**

OPERATION DELTA FORCE Awful action film about a group of terrorists planning to release an Armageddon disease to the world. Talented cast deserves better. Rated R for violence and profanity. 93m. **DIR:** Sam Firstenberg. **CAST:** Ernie Hudson, Jeff Fahey, Frank Zagarino, Hal Holbrook, Reb Stewart. **1996**

OPERATION DELTA FORCE 2 The original *Delta Force* franchise with Chuck Norris wasn't that good to begin with. Do we really need another rip-off sequel? Rated R for violence and language. 98m. **DIR:** Yossi Wein. **CAST:** Michael McGrady, Simon Jones, K. Kenneth Campbell, Dale Dye. **1997 DVD**

OPERATION DUMBO DROP ★★★ Danny Glover and Ray Liotta play American officers in Vietnam who set out to obtain an elephant for a friendly native village. The Vietnam War makes an unorthodox background for a lightweight family comedy, but the film is pleasant entertainment. Slapstick is efficiently mixed with sentiment. Rated PG for war action and mild profanity. 102m. **DIR:** Simon Wincer. **CAST:** Danny Glover, Ray Liotta, Denis Leary, Corin Nemec, Doug E. Doug. **1995**

OPERATION GOLDEN PHOENIX Laughable codswallop involving two medallions and a hidden treasure fuels this low-rent Canadian-Lebanese martial arts opus. Director-star Jalal Merhi wears two hats too many; he may kick with style, but he couldn't emote to save his life . . . and doesn't know the first thing about helming a film. Rated R for violence and profanity. 95m. **DIR:** Jalal Merhi. **CAST:** Jalal Merhi, Loreen Avedon, James Hong. **1994**

OPERATION INTERCEPT ★★ A pair of American fighter pilots attempt to stop a Russian scientist out for revenge. An interesting characterization by Natasha Andreichenko as the mad Russian is all that keeps this cheapo thriller from being completely forgettable. Rated R for profanity and violence. 94m. **DIR:** Paul Levine. **CAST:** Bruce Payne, Natasha Andreichenko, John Stockwell, Lance Henriksen, Corinne Bohrer. **1995**

OPERATION 'NAM ★★ Run-of-the-mill tale about a group of bored Vietnam vets going back to Vietnam to rescue their leader, still held in a POW camp. Notable only for the appearance of Ethan Wayne, one of John's sons. Not rated; contains violence, language, and nudity. 85m. **DIR:** Larry Ludman. **CAST:** Oliver Tobias, Christopher Connelly, Manfred Lehman, John Steiner, Ethan Wayne, Donald Pleasence. **1985**

OPERATION PACIFIC ★★★1/2 Action, suspense, comedy, and romance are nicely mixed in this fact-based film about the rush to perfect American torpedoes during World War II. John Wayne and Ward Bond are the navy men frustrated by the nonexploding, submerged missiles, and Patricia Neal is the nurse who can't quite decide whether or not she loves Wayne. B&W; 111m. **DIR:** George Waggner. **CAST:** John Wayne, Patricia Neal, Ward Bond, Scott Forbes, Philip Carey, Paul Picerni, Martin Milner, Jack Pennick, William Campbell. **1951**

OPERATION PETTICOAT ★★★★ The ageless Cary Grant stars with Tony Curtis in this wacky service comedy. They are captain and first officer of a submarine that undergoes a madcap series of misadventures during World War II. Their voyage across the Pacific is further complicated when a group of navy women is forced to join the crew. 124m. **DIR:** Blake Edwards. **CAST:** Cary Grant, Tony Curtis, Dina Merrill, Gene Evans, Arthur O'Connell, Dick Sargent. **1959 DVD**

OPERATION THUNDERBOLT ★★ Another film, like *The Raid on Entebbe*, dealing with the Israeli commando raid in Uganda in 1976 to free 104 hijacked airline passengers. Overly sentimental, with routine action sequences. No MPAA rating. 125m. **DIR:** Menahem Golan. **CAST:** Yehoram Gaon, Klaus Kinski, Assaf Dayan. **1977**

OPERATION WAR ZONE Courier lost in Vietnam possesses a document that could affect the outcome of the war. Too bad it wasn't the script for this film. 89m. **DIR:** David A. Prior. **CAST:** David Marriott, Joe Spinell. **1989**

OPERATIVE, THE ★★ Brian Bosworth continues his quest for movie-star status in this derivative and low-budget thriller about an ex-CIA agent who returns home to pick up the pieces of his life following an extended stay in a Soviet gulag. His recuperation is cut short when he becomes involved in a plot involving a stolen painting. Suspense and character arcs are nowhere to be found. Rated R for language and violence. 97m. **DIR:** Robert Lee. **CAST:** Brian Bosworth, Bob Dawson, John Tench, Jerry Wasserman. **2000 DVD**

•OPERATOR, THE ★★ An immoral man meets his match when he angers an information operator who makes his life hell by exposing secrets, tampering with credit reports, etc. Average thriller tries to be more than that by adding a level of philosophical depth but never quite makes it. Rated R for violence and nudity. 102m. **DIR:** Jon Dichter. **CAST:** Michael Laurence, Jacqueline Kim, Stephen Tobolowsky, Christa Miller, Brion James. **2000**

OPERATOR 13 ★★★ Two of Hollywood's most glamorous players get in a romantic clinch similar to Scarlett O'Hara and Rhett Butler's five years before *Gone with the Wind*. Marion Davies plays a Yankee spy during the Civil War. Gary Cooper is a southern sympathizer. They square off against each other and love blooms. Very romantic, very flashy, and slightly dated. B&W; 86m. **DIR:** Richard Boleslawski. **CAST:** Marion Davies, Gary Cooper, Jean Parker, Katharine Alexander, Ted Healy, Hattie McDaniel, Russell Hardie, Fuzzy Knight, Douglass Dumbrille. **1934**

OPPONENT, THE ★★1/2 A boxer rescues a mob boss's daughter, only to be swept up in her father's corrupt world. Now he's fighting for his life in a film that plays like a low-budget *Rocky*. Rated R for violence. 102m. **DIR:** Sergio Martino. **CAST:** Daniel Greene, Ernest Borgnine, Mary Stavin. **1990 DVD**

OPPORTUNISTS, THE ★★1/2 Reformed safecracker turned auto mechanic Victor Kelly comes out of retirement for one more heist in this promising but mostly dull crime story. When his mounting debts devour his better judgment, he teams up with a young Irish immigrant, two low-rent Queens security cops, and an oddball locksmith for a robbery. Rated R for language and violence. 90m. **DIR:** Myles Connell. **CAST:** Christopher Walken, Peter McDonald, Donal Logue, Jose Zuniga,

Cyndi Lauper, Tom Noonan, Vera Farmiga, Anne Pitoniak. **2000**

OPPORTUNITY KNOCKS ★★★ Mixing elements from *Trading Places* and *The Sting*, this is a big-screen sitcom designed to show off the talents of *Saturday Night Live* regular Dana Carvey. It does its job well. Carvey is a hoot as a con-man who lucks into a big score while hiding from a revenge-minded gangster. Rated PG-13 for profanity and adult humor. 95m. **DIR:** Donald Petrie. **CAST:** Dana Carvey, Robert Loggia, Todd Graff, Julia Campbell, Milo O'Shea, James Tolkan. **1990**

OPPOSING FORCE ★★1/2 In this average action-adventure movie, a group of soldiers undergo simulated prisoner-of-war training. When the commanding officer (Anthony Zerbe) goes insane, he rapes the sole female soldier (Lisa Eichhorn) and sets into motion a chain of violent events. Rated R for profanity and violence. 97m. **DIR:** Eric Karson. **CAST:** Tom Skerritt, Lisa Eichhorn, Anthony Zerbe, Richard Roundtree, John Considine. **1986**

OPPOSITE CORNERS ★★★ Gritty drama about a mafioso and the son he relentlessly pushes toward the dream he himself could never achieve: that of a championship boxer. That relentlessness, and a dark secret, may eventually push the two forever apart. Rated R for profanity, violence, and sexual situations. 106m. **DIR:** Louis D'Esposito. **CAST:** Cathy Moriarty, Anthony Dennison, Billy Warlock, Frankie Valli, Ray "Boom Boom" Mancini, Jay Acovone. **1996**

OPPOSITE OF SEX, THE ★★1/2 This audacious skewering of straight and gay relationships, dysfunctional families, and manipulative movie conventions is wickedly funny for half its run and then gradually withers. A trailer-park Lolita is the catalyst of an outrageous soap opera in which she runs away from home, seduces and marries her gay half-brother's lover, becomes pregnant, and cheats on her new spouse. Rated R for language and sexuality. 105m. **DIR:** Don Roos. **CAST:** Christina Ricci, Martin Donovan, Lisa Kudrow, Lyle Lovett, Ivan Sergei. **1998 DVD**

OPPOSITE SEX, THE (1956) ★★1/2 An uninspired remake of Clare Boothe's *The Women*, a good satire about woman's inhumanity to woman. They diluted it by adding macho male stereotypes instead of just talking about them like the first version did. 117m. **DIR:** David Miller. **CAST:** June Allyson, Ann Sheridan, Joan Blondell, Joan Collins, Ann Miller, Charlotte Greenwood, Jim Backus, Dolores Gray, Agnes Moorehead, Leslie Nielsen, Jeff Richards. **1956**

OPPOSITE SEX (AND HOW TO LIVE WITH THEM), THE (1993) 🦃 A waste of time and talent. The sexcapades of young singles are exploited more than they are explained in a laughless comedy about people who can't keep their hormones under control. The big scene is a "Strip Twister" dance scene followed by group wine tasting. Rated R for obvious reasons. 86m. **DIR:** Matthew Meshekoff. **CAST:** Arye Gross, Courteney Cox, Kevin Pollak, Julie Brown, Mitchell Ryan, Jack Carter, Phil Bruns, Mitzi McCall, B. J. Ward. **1993**

OPTIONS ★★ Modest little comedy features a nerdish contract man for TV movies treading the wilds of Africa—in complete suit and tie, plus briefcase!—to get the option on another life story. Rated PG for violence. 105m. **DIR:** Camilo Vila. **CAST:** Matt Salinger, Joanna Pacula, John Kani. **1988**

ORACLE, THE ★★ A woman discovers that the last occupant of her new apartment was a murder victim. Reaching out from beyond the grave, he tries to force her to avenge his death. Better than average for this sort of low-budget chiller, with some effective shocks and a few interesting plot twists. Rated R for gore. 94m. **DIR:** Roberta Findlay. **CAST:** Caroline Capers Powers, Roger Neil. **1985**

•ORANGE COUNTY ★★ An affluent, dysfunctional family gradually pulls together to get a reformed surf-bum sibling into college in this big-hearted, broad, and often flat comedy. After an incompetent high-school counselor sends the wrong transcript to Stanford, an ambitious wannabe writer, his girlfriend, and his stoner brother visit the institute of higher education to rectify the mistake. The film is fattened with cameos (Lily Tomlin, Ben Stiller, Chevy Chase, Harold Ramis, Kevin Kline) and not-quite infectious enthusiasm. Rated PG-13 for sexual content, profanity, and crude humor. 120m. **DIR:** Jake Kasdan. **CAST:** Colin Hanks, Schuyler Fisk, Jack Black, Catherine O'Hara, John Lithgow. **2002 DVD**

ORANGES ARE NOT THE ONLY FRUIT ★★★★ Made for British television, this adaptation of Jeanette Winterson's novel follows the growing pains of Jess, a teenager in a Northern England mill town where everyone belongs to a strict fundamentalist church. Jess's discovery that she is a lesbian will cause her banishment from the flock (and her zealous mother's house) if it is divulged. Richly drawn characters and splashes of rueful humor makes this an intelligent film with which any viewer can sympathize. Not rated; contains sexual situations. 165m. **DIR:** Beeban Kidron. **CAST:** Charlotte Coleman, Geraldine McEwan, Kenneth Cranham, Celia Imrie. **1990**

ORCA ★★★ Where *Jaws* was an exaggerated horror story, *Orca* is based on the tragic truth. Motivated by profit, Richard Harris and his crew go out with a huge net and find a family of whales. He misses the male and harpoons the female, who dies and aborts, leaving her huge mate to wreak havoc on the tiny seaport. Rated PG. 92m. **DIR:** Michael Anderson. **CAST:** Richard Harris, Keenan Wynn, Will Sampson, Bo Derek, Robert Carradine, Charlotte Rampling. **1977**

ORCHESTRA REHEARSAL ★★1/2 Subpar Fellini film, made for Italian television, has squabbling members of an orchestra rebel against their dictatorial conductor. This political allegory is at best vague and at worst incomprehensible to those unschooled in Italian current events. Not rated; contains some profanity. In Italian with English subtitles 72m. **DIR:** Federico Fellini. **CAST:** Balduin Bass, Clara Colosimo. **1979 DVD**

ORCHESTRA WIVES ★★★ Taking second place to the wonderful music of Glenn Miller and his orchestra is a story about the problems of the wives of the band members, both on and off the road. Academy Award nomination for Harry Warren and Mack Gordon's "I've Got A Gal In Kalamazoo." B&W; 98m. **DIR:** Archie Mayo. **CAST:** Glenn Miller, Lynn Bari, Carole Landis, George Montgomery, Cesar Romero, Ann Rutherford. **1942**

ORDEAL BY INNOCENCE ★★ In this production of yet another Agatha Christie novel, the cast may be stellar,

but the performances are almost all phoned in. Donald Sutherland plays a man who is certain that justice has been ill served in a small British community. Rated PG-13 for language and nudity. 91m. **DIR:** Desmond Davis. **CAST:** Donald Sutherland, Sarah Miles, Christopher Plummer, Ian McShane, Diana Quick, Faye Dunaway. **1984**

ORDEAL IN THE ARCTIC ★★★ Made-for-cable adventure stars Richard Chamberlain as the pilot of a military transport plane that crashes in the outer regions of the Arctic. A rescue attempt is aborted when a severe storm moves into the area. Human drama involves the survivors and their quest to stay alive. Exciting action sequences and a decent cast hold this familiar tale together. Rated PG. 93m. **DIR:** Mark Sobel. **CAST:** Richard Chamberlain, Melanie Mayron, Catherine Mary Stewart. **1997**

ORDEAL OF DR. MUDD, THE ★★★1/2 The true story of Dr. Samuel Mudd, who innocently aided the injured, fleeing John Wilkes Booth following Lincoln's assassination and was sent to prison for alleged participation in the conspiracy. Dennis Weaver's fine portrayal of the ill-fated doctor makes this film well worthwhile. More than a century passed before Mudd was cleared, thanks to the efforts of a descendant, newscaster Roger Mudd. Rated PG. 143m. **DIR:** Paul Wendkos. **CAST:** Dennis Weaver, Susan Sullivan, Richard Dysart, Arthur Hill. **1980**

•**ORDER, THE** ★★1/2 Extremely silly but surprisingly engaging action-adventure that pits martial arts star Jean-Claude Van Damme against a secret religious cult in Jerusalem. Van Damme plays a thief who specializes in religious artifacts. When his archeologist father is kidnapped after stumbling across an ancient scripture of a mysterious religious order, Van Damme swings into action, aided by a female Israeli cop. Enjoyable as long as you never take any of it seriously. Rated R for violence. 86m. **DIR:** Sheldon Lettich. **CAST:** Jean-Claude Van Damme, Charlton Heston, Ben Cross, Sofia Milos. **2001 DVD**

ORDER OF THE BLACK EAGLE ★★ Ian Hunter is the James Bondish main character, Duncan Jax, abetted in destroying a neo-Nazi group by his sidekick, a baboon, and a band of misfits. Rated R for violence and language. 93m. **DIR:** Worth Keeter. **CAST:** Ian Hunter, Charles K. Bibby, William T. Hicks, Jill Donnellan, Anna Rappagna, Flo Hyman. **1987**

ORDER OF THE EAGLE ★★★ On a camping trip in the woods, a Boy Scout discovers computer discs in a plane wreck. They contain secret military plans that bad guy Frank Stallone wants back. Well-written thriller. Not rated; contains mild violence. 82m. **DIR:** Thomas Baldwin. **CAST:** Frank Stallone, William Zipp, Casey Hirsch. **1989**

ORDET ★★★★1/2 Possibly the greatest work of Carl Dreyer, the Danish director whose films (*The Passion of Joan of Arc, Day of Wrath*) demonstrate an intellectual obsession with the nature of religious faith in the modern world. In this drama, based on a play written by a priest who was murdered by the Nazis, characters in a small, God-fearing town wrestle between two varieties of faith, one puritanical, the other life affirming. In Danish with English subtitles. B&W; 125m. **DIR:** Carl Dreyer. **CAST:** Henrik Malberg. **1955**

ORDINARY HEROES ★★★ A moving love story about a young couple torn apart when the man (Richard Dean Anderson) is drafted into the army and sent to Vietnam. He returns from combat blinded and attempts to piece his broken life back together with his former girlfriend (Valerie Bertinelli). This absorbing drama gets its strength from strong performances by both leads. Rated PG. 90m. **DIR:** Peter H. Cooper. **CAST:** Richard Dean Anderson, Valerie Bertinelli, Doris Roberts. **1986**

ORDINARY MAGIC ★★★ Inspiring family film stars Ryan Reynolds as an orphan who must leave India and live with his aunt in Canada. His interest in Indian culture and his practice of yoga make him a prime target for ridicule. When his aunt's house is scheduled for demolition, he wages a personal battle to save his new home. Glenne Headly lends nice support as the withdrawn aunt who comes alive. Not rated. 96m. **DIR:** Giles Walker. **CAST:** Glenne Headly, David Fox, Paul Anka, Ryan Reynolds. **1993**

ORDINARY PEOPLE ★★★★1/2 This moving human drama, which won the Academy Award for best picture of 1980, marked the directorial debut of Robert Redford . . . and an auspicious one it is, too. Redford elicits memorable performances from Mary Tyler Moore, Donald Sutherland, Timothy Hutton, and Judd Hirsch and makes the intelligent, powerful script by Alvin Sargent seem even better. Rated R for adult situations. 123m. **DIR:** Robert Redford. **CAST:** Mary Tyler Moore, Donald Sutherland, Timothy Hutton, Judd Hirsch, Elizabeth McGovern, Dinah Manoff, James B. Sikking. **1980**

ORGANIZATION, THE ★★★ This is the third and last installment of the Virgil Tibbs series based on the character Sidney Poitier originated in *In the Heat of the Night*. Tibbs is out to break up a ring of dope smugglers. A pretty good cop film, with some exciting action scenes. Rated PG; some strong stuff for the kids. 107m. **DIR:** Don Medford. **CAST:** Sidney Poitier, Barbara McNair, Raul Julia, Sheree North. **1971**

ORGANIZER, THE ★★★★ An Oscar nominee for best original screenplay, this is an effective period drama from director Mario Monicelli, better known for comedies like *Big Deal on Madonna Street*. Marcello Mastroianni stars as an unemployed teacher who helps organize a labor union at a factory in turn-of-the-century Turin. Not rated. In Italian with English subtitles. 127m. **DIR:** Mario Monicelli. **CAST:** Marcello Mastroianni, Renato Salvatori, Annie Giradot, Bernard Blier. **1964**

ORGAZMO 🦃 A nice Mormon boy stumbles into the porno business, where he becomes a star playing Orgazmo, a well-endowed superhero. This incompetent, humor-free comedy drew protests and pickets from the Mormon Church, but despite the free publicity it deservedly sank at the box office. Rated NC-17 for profanity, nudity, and raunchy jokes. 95m. **DIR:** Trey Parker. **CAST:** Trey Parker, Dian Bachar, Robyn Lynne Raab, Michael Dean Jacobs. **1998 DVD**

ORGUSS, VOLS. 1–4 ★★ Japanese animation. Mediocre series involving a young soldier who is transplanted suddenly from his own world into a parallel dimension. Standard television-series entry. Not rated, with brief nudity. 55–80. **DIR:** Noboru Ishiguro, Yasuyoshi Mikamoto. **1983**

ORGY OF THE DEAD 🦃 There's no plot to speak of, as the "Emperor of the Dead" (Criswell) holds court in a

graveyard. Not rated. 82m. **DIR:** A. C. Stephen. **CAST:** Criswell, Pat Barringer, William Bates. **1965**

ORIANE ★★★ A taut gothic romance about a young woman who returns to a hacienda inherited from her aunt only to find herself caught up in a mystery concerning past events. Fina Torres scores some high marks in her first feature film that won the coveted Camera d'Or at Cannes in 1985. In Spanish and French with English subtitles. Not rated; contains nudity. 88m. **DIR:** Fina Torres. **CAST:** Doris Wells. **1985**

ORIGINAL GANGSTAS ★★ Retired football hero returns to his economically struggling hometown when his father is assaulted after witnessing a drive-by killing. The gridiron great and his former "'Buds in the Hood'" reband to wipe out a vicious, heavily armed mob that has evolved from their old neighborhood clique. The movie tries both to transcend and exploit its action roots with uneven, predictable results. Rated R for language and violence. 99m. **DIR:** Larry Cohen. **CAST:** Fred Williamson, Pam Grier, Jim Brown, Ron O'Neal, Richard Roundtree, Wings Hauser, Oscar Brown Jr. **1996 DVD**

ORIGINAL INTENT ★★ Preachy, heavy-handed film about a yuppie lawyer becoming aware of the homeless problem and trying to save a shelter from a greedy developer. Rated PG for profanity. 97m. **DIR:** Robert Marcarelli. **CAST:** Jay Richardson, Candy Clark, Martin Sheen, Kris Kristofferson, Vince Edwards, Robert DoQui. **1991**

ORIGINAL KINGS OF COMEDY, THE ★★★ Four African American comedians who have toured together since 1977 are filmed both onstage and backstage during their 1990 live Charlotte Coliseum performances. The material veers from the nostalgic (an homage to "old school" music) to the raunchy (Pryoresque spins on the use of profanities), to poking fun at the differences between "black and white folk." Some segments are marred by poor sound quality; others produce monster laughs. Rated R for language and sexual references. 113m. **DIR:** Spike Lee. **CAST:** Steve Harvey, D. L. Hughley, Cedric the Entertainer, Bernie Mac. **2000 DVD**

•ORIGINAL SIN ★★★ A nineteenth-century Cuban planter (Antonio Banderas) discovers that his mail-order bride (Angelina Jolie) isn't quite what—or even who—she pretends to be. This adaptation of Cornell Woolrich's novel *Waltz into Darkness*—filmed before as François Truffaut's *Mississippi Mermaid*—is unevenly paced, but the photogenic stars and sultry tropical atmosphere make it worth seeing. Rated R for sexual scenes and violence. 116m. **DIR:** Michael Cristofer. **CAST:** Antonio Banderas, Angelina Jolie, Thomas Jane, Jack Thompson. **2001 DVD**

ORIGINAL SINS ★★★ Bound to tick off at least someone—especially Catholics—this little indie flick is a satirical look at faith as three devout teenagers meet a mysterious salesman (who may be the savior) and proceed to faint. They wake up to find they've been taken advantage of. Nothing is sacred as the directors take a shot at just about every institution possible and prove that the indie scene is very much alive. Not rated; contains nudity, violence, and profanity. 108m. **DIR:** Matthew Howe, Howard Berger. **CAST:** Cheryl Clifford, Angelique de Rochambeau, Faustina, Scooter McCrae. **1994**

ORLANDO ★★ The plight of women throughout the ages is examined in director Sally Potter's smug, off-putting screen adaptation of the novella by Virginia Woolf. It's visually stunning, but woe to anyone who expects to be entertained. Worst of all, Potter misuses gifted actress Tilda Swinton, who is expected to portray both a man and a woman. Balderdash. Rated PG-13 for violence, nudity, and suggested sex. 93m. **DIR:** Sally Potter. **CAST:** Tilda Swinton, Billy Zane, John Wood, Charlotte Valandrey, Heathcote Williams, Quentin Crisp, Peter Eyre, Thom Hoffman, Dudley Sutton. **1993 DVD**

ORPHAN BOY OF VIENNA, AN ★★ The only reason to see this hokey tearjerker about a boy who struggles to adjust to life in a German orphanage is the presence of the famous Vienna Boys' Choir, accompanied in several performances by the Vienna Philharmonic. In German with English subtitles. B&W; 90m. **DIR:** Max Neufeld. **CAST:** Ferdinand Materhofer. **1937**

ORPHAN TRAIN ★★★1/2 Inspirational tale of a young woman's desire to help thousands of orphans who were roaming the streets of New York in the 1850s. Realizing that her soup kitchen can't keep the kids out of trouble, she takes a group out west in hopes of finding farming families willing to adopt them. Originally shown on TV. 150m. **DIR:** William A. Graham. **CAST:** Jill Eikenberry, Kevin Dobson, Linda Manz, Glenn Close. **1979**

ORPHANS ★★★★ Based on the play by Lyle Kessler, this compact drama is a psychological thriller with a poignant twist. Albert Finney effectively portrays an affluent American gangster who does more than merely befriend two homeless young men—Treat, an angry delinquent (Matthew Modine), and Phillips (Kevin Anderson), his helpless younger brother. In a short time, he changes their lives. Rated R. 115m. **DIR:** Alan J. Pakula. **CAST:** Albert Finney, Matthew Modine, Kevin Anderson. **1987 DVD**

ORPHANS OF THE STORM ★★★1/2 Film's first master director blends fact and fiction, mixing the French Revolution with the trials and tribulations of two sisters—one blind and raised by thieves, the other betrayed by self-saving aristocrats. The plot creaks with age, but the settings and action spell good entertainment. Silent. B&W; 125m. **DIR:** D. W. Griffith. **CAST:** Lillian Gish, Dorothy Gish, Sidney Herbert, Sheldon Lewis, Monte Blue, Joseph Schildkraut, Creighton Hale, Morgan Wallace. **1922 DVD**

ORPHEUS ★★★1/2 Jean Cocteau's surreal account of the Greek myth with Jean Marais as Orpheus, the successful, envied, and despised poet who thrusts himself beyond mortality. Maria Casares costars as the lonely, troubled, passionate Death. Cocteau's poetic imagery will pull you deep into the fantasy. In French with English subtitles. B&W; 86m. **DIR:** Jean Cocteau. **CAST:** Jean Marais, Maria Casares. **1949 DVD**

ORPHEUS DESCENDING ★★★1/2 Fascinatingly horrifying made-for-cable adaptation of Tennessee Williams's slice-of-southern-Gothic stage play. Vanessa Redgrave fails at an Italian accent, but when she abandons an overused hysterical laugh, she delivers her usual fine performance. Not rated, contains nudity, profanity, and violence. 117m. **DIR:** Peter Hall. **CAST:**

Vanessa Redgrave, Kevin Anderson, Brad Sullivan. **1990**

OSAKA ELEGY ★★★★ Excellent dramatic comedy that realistically shows the exploitation of women in Japanese society. Isuzu Yamada plays a tough, sassy working girl who is continuously taken advantage of by men notorious for their greed and spinelessness. In Japanese with English subtitles. B&W; 75m. **DIR:** Kenji Mizoguchi. **CAST:** Isuzu Yamada. **1936**

OSCAR (1991) ★★★ This farce features a perfectly capable comic performance from Sylvester Stallone as a gangster who promises his dying father (Kirk Douglas in a hilarious cameo) that he'll go straight. But complications make keeping his vow difficult. An all-star supporting cast help buoy the story, which often drags under John Landis's laid-back direction. Rated PG for brief profanity. 110m. **DIR:** John Landis. **CAST:** Sylvester Stallone, Ornella Muti, Peter Riegert, Vincent Spano, Tim Curry, Chazz Palminteri, Marisa Tomei, Elizabeth Barondes, Kirk Douglas, Don Ameche, Yvonne De Carlo, Eddie Bracken, Martin Ferrero, Harry Shearer, Linda Gray, William Atherton. **1991**

OSCAR, THE (1966) 🦃 An unscrupulous actor advances his career at the expense of others. 119m. **DIR:** Russell Rouse. **CAST:** Stephen Boyd, Elke Sommer, Tony Bennett, Eleanor Parker, Ernest Borgnine, Joseph Cotten. **1966**

•OSCAR & LUCINDA ★★★★ A deft mix of human drama and adventure in this tale of one man's quest to win the heart of the woman he loves. Ralph Fiennes is moving as Oscar, a former ministry student whose love of gambling takes him from Devon, England, to Australia's outback. En route he meets Lucinda, played with headstrong charm by Cate Blanchett, a young woman with an inheritance and a lust for gambling. Even though they're perfect for each other, it takes a grand act on behalf of Oscar to show Lucinda just how much he loves her. Reminiscent of Werner Herzog's *Fitzcarraldo*, this film is filled with memorable images and indelible characters. Rated R for adult situations and language. 132m. **DIR:** Gillian Armstrong. **CAST:** Ralph Fiennes, Cate Blanchett, Tom Wilkinson, Ciarán Hinds, Clive Russell, Billie Brown. **1997**

•OSMOSIS JONES ★★★ If the live action were as entertaining and creative as Piet Kroon's whimsical animation, this would be a marvelous little picture ... but, alas, that's not the case. Voice talents Chris Rock and David Hyde Pierce become unlikely partners as a white blood cell and a twelve-hour cold capsule, who team up to hunt down and destroy a deadly virus that has infected their host body; Bill Murray (the host in question) is merely repulsive. Live-action directors Peter and Bobby Farrelly go for their signature gross and disgusting humor, at the expense of anything credible or even funny while costars Molly Shannon and Chris Elliott turn in some of the worst work we've ever seen. Rated PG (rather generously) for extremely crude humor. 83m. **DIR:** Bobby Farrelly, Peter Farrelly, Piet Kroon. **CAST:** Bill Murray, Molly Shannon, Chris Elliott. **2001 DVD**

OSSESSIONE ★★★★★ James M. Cain's *The Postman Always Rings Twice* as adapted to Italian locations. The fatal triangle here is a dissatisfied wife, a vulgar husband, and the inevitable charming stranger. A landmark in the development of both *film noir* and Italian neorealism. In Italian with English subtitles. B&W; 135m. **DIR:** Luchino Visconti. **CAST:** Clara Calamai, Massimo Girotti. **1942**

OSTERMAN WEEKEND, THE ★★ Sam Peckinpah's last is a confusing action movie with scarce viewing rewards for the filmmaker's fans. Based on Robert Ludlum's novel, it tells a complicated and convoluted story of espionage, revenge, and duplicity. Rated R for profanity, nudity, sex, and violence. 102m. **DIR:** Sam Peckinpah. **CAST:** Rutger Hauer, John Hurt, Burt Lancaster, Dennis Hopper, Chris Sarandon, Meg Foster. **1983**

OTAKU NO VIDEO ★★★ Incredibly dense with inside jokes and industry references, this tongue-in-cheek animated entry may be too esoteric for the casual viewer but any rabid animation fan (or *otaku*) will find it funny. The Japanese subculture of animation enthusiasts (somewhat comparable to *Star Trek* fans in the U.S.) is examined through an animated story interspersed with live, mock interviews of fans and statistical charts. In Japanese with English subtitles. Not rated; contains nudity. 100m. **DIR:** Mori Takeshi. **1991 DVD**

OTELLO ★★★★★ As with his screen version of *La Traviata*, Franco Zeffirelli's *Otello* is a masterpiece of filmed opera. In fact, it may well be the best such motion picture ever made. Placido Domingo is brilliant in the title role, both as an actor and a singer. And he gets able support from Katia Ricciarelli as Desdemona and Justino Diaz as Iago. Rated PG for stylized violence. 122m. **DIR:** Franco Zeffirelli. **CAST:** Placido Domingo, Katia Ricciarelli, Justino Diaz, Urbano Barberini. **1987**

OTHELLO (1922) ★★★★ Despite the silence of this early version of the Shakespeare tragedy, the essence of the drama is effectively conveyed by memorable quotes on title cards, elaborate sets and costuming, and fine performances. Silent. B&W; 81m. **DIR:** Dimitri Buchowetzki. **CAST:** Emil Jannings, Werner Krauss, Lya de Putti. **1922 DVD**

OTHELLO (1952) ★★★★1/2 Months of high-tech restoration have done much to reverse the damage done by years of neglect to Orson Welles's cockeyed masterpiece. Shot entirely out of sequence over four years and under the most inhospitable circumstances, *Othello*, nevertheless, bears the unmistakable mark of the American genius. The sparest cinematography, the monumental sets, the stark choral and instrumental music, and the reduced essence of Shakespeare are melded by the alchemist Welles into an unforgettable film experience. Best feature film, 1952 Cannes Film Festival. B&W; 91m. **DIR:** Orson Welles. **CAST:** Orson Welles, Suzanne Cloutier, Micheal MacLiammoir, Robert Coote, Fay Compton. **1952 DVD**

OTHELLO (1965) ★★★★ Laurence Olivier offers the most humanized portrayal of Shakespeare's vengeful Moor in this film, adapted from a stage production that Olivier had just appeared in. Its stage-to-film origins are obvious but forgotten thanks to superb performances by Olivier, Maggie Smith as Desdemona, and Frank Finlay as Iago. Not rated. 166m. **DIR:** Stuart Burge. **CAST:** Laurence Olivier, Frank Finlay, Maggie Smith, Derek Jacobi. **1965**

OTHELLO (1982) ★★★1/2 A fine stage production with William Marshall impressive as the valiant, but tragic Moor of Venice, Othello, tricked into madness and murder by his jealous aide, Iago (Ron Moody). Moody is magnificent as Shakespeare's greatest villain. Released by Bard Productions Ltd. 195m. **DIR:** Frank Melton. **CAST:** William Marshall, Ron Moody, Jenny Agutter, DeVeren Bookwalter, Peter MacLean, Jay Robinson. **1982**

OTHELLO (1996) ★★★ The fifth major film version of Shakespeare's tragedy (heavily edited by director Oliver Parker) is the first to feature an African American actor (Laurence Fishburne) in the title role. Fishburne is a fine actor, but he seems uncomfortable, both with Shakespeare's poetry and with Othello's volatile jealousy. Kenneth Branagh, as Iago, is more at ease with the Bard, and easily dominates the film. Rated R for violence, nudity, and simulated sex. 125m. **DIR:** Oliver Parker. **CAST:** Laurence Fishburne, Kenneth Branagh, Irène Jacob, Nathaniel Parker, Michael Maloney. **1996 DVD**

OTHER, THE ★★★1/2 Screenwriter Thomas Tryon, adapting his bestselling novel, raises plenty of goose bumps. This supernatural tale of good and evil, as personified by twin brothers, creates a genuinely eerie mood. Legendary acting coach Uta Hagen contributes a compelling performance. Director Robert Mulligan, keeping the emphasis on characterizations, never allows the suspense to lag. 100m. **DIR:** Robert Mulligan. **CAST:** Uta Hagen, Diana Muldaur, Chris Udvarnoky, Martin Udvarnoky, John Ritter. **1972**

OTHER PEOPLE'S MONEY ★★★1/2 Danny DeVito has a field day as a ruthless corporate raider conniving to take over upstanding Gregory Peck's business while romancing Peck's daughter. It's a modern-day version of a Capra film, but in the Nineties it is not a foregone conclusion that the good guys will win. Adapted by screenwriter Alvin Sargent from the play by Jerry Sterner. Rated R for profanity. 103m. **DIR:** Norman Jewison. **CAST:** Danny DeVito, Gregory Peck, Penelope Ann Miller, Piper Laurie, Dean Jones. **1991**

OTHER SIDE OF MIDNIGHT, THE 🦃 Glossy soap opera derived from schlockmaster Sidney Sheldon's bestselling novel. Rated R. 165m. **DIR:** Charles Jarrott. **CAST:** Marie-France Pisier, John Beck, Susan Sarandon, Raf Vallone, Clu Gulager. **1977**

OTHER SIDE OF THE MOUNTAIN, THE ★★★ Absolutely heart-wrenching account of Jill Kinmont, an Olympic-bound skier whose career was cut short by a fall that left her paralyzed. Marilyn Hassett, in her film debut, makes Kinmont a fighter whose determination initially backfires and prompts some to have unreasonable expectations of her limited recovery. Rated PG. 103m. **DIR:** Larry Peerce. **CAST:** Marilyn Hassett, Beau Bridges. **1975**

OTHER SIDE OF THE MOUNTAIN, PART II, THE ★★ A sequel to the modest 1975 hit, the film continues the story of Jill Kinmont, a promising young skier who was paralyzed from the shoulders down in an accident. The tender romance, well-played by Hassett and Bottoms, provides some fine moments. Rated PG. 100m. **DIR:** Larry Peerce. **CAST:** Marilyn Hassett, Timothy Bottoms, Nan Martin, Belinda Montgomery. **1978**

OTHER WOMAN, THE ★★ In this silly story about political corruption, an investigative reporter thinks her husband is having an affair with a hooker and later finds herself sexually attracted to the woman. Sam Jones is a corrupt politician with a punk hairdo. Rated R for nudity. 92m. **DIR:** Jag Mundhra. **CAST:** Sam Jones, Adrian Zmed, Lee Anne Beaman. **1992**

•OTHERS, THE ★★★★★ This ultraspooky ghost story begins with a scream, bores deep into a tale of restless spirits and psychological terror, and ends with a creepy twist. On an English Channel island at the end of World War II, a woman waits with her two children for the return of her soldier husband. The kids are apparently allergic to sunlight and the female sibling insists that supernatural intruders are wandering the manor halls. Rated PG-13 for thematic elements and frightening moments. 104m. **DIR:** Alejandro Amenabar. **CAST:** Nicole Kidman, Fionnula Flanagan, Chris Eccleston, Eric Sykes, Elaine Cassidy, James Bentley, Alakina Mann. **2001 DVD**

OUR DAILY BREAD ★★1/2 This vintage Depression social drama about an idealistic man organizing community farms and socialistic society is pretty creaky despite director King Vidor. Lead actor Tom Keene did better in cowboy films. B&W; 74m. **DIR:** King Vidor. **CAST:** Tom Keene, Karen Morley, John Qualen, Addison Richards. **1934 DVD**

OUR DANCING DAUGHTERS ★★★ One of the most famous flaming-youth movies of the late 1920s, and the one that really got Joan Crawford on her way as a top star for MGM. She plays Diana, a vivacious flapper who jiggles a lot and takes frequent belts from her hip flask. Silent. B&W; 86m. **DIR:** Harry Beaumont. **CAST:** Joan Crawford, Johnny Mack Brown, Nils Asther. **1928**

OUR FAMILY BUSINESS ★★ Two sons take different tacks in surviving within a Mafia family. Sam Wanamaker and Ray Milland give strong performances in this generally slow, uninspired twist on the *Godfather* theme. Made for television. 74m. **DIR:** Robert Collins. **CAST:** Ted Danson, Sam Wanamaker, Vera Miles, Ray Milland. **1981**

OUR FRIEND, MARTIN ★★★ Fascinating all-star feature that combines lively animation with the life story of Dr. Martin Luther King Jr. Rated G. 60m. **DIR:** Vincenzo Trippetti, Rob Smiley. **CAST:** Ed Asner, Angela Bassett, Lucas Black, LeVar Burton, Danny Glover, Whoopi Goldberg, Samuel L. Jackson, James Earl Jones, Ashley Judd, Dexter King, Yolanda King, Robert Ri'chard, Susan Sarandon, John Travolta, Jaleel White, Oprah Winfrey. **1998**

OUR HOSPITALITY ★★★★ Based on the legendary Hatfield-McCoy feud, this period comedy has Buster Keaton as innocent and unsuspecting Willie McKay journeying south to claim his inheritance. Keaton's comic and daredevil antics are brilliant. Silent. B&W; 74m. **DIR:** Buster Keaton, John G. Blystone. **CAST:** Buster Keaton, Natalie Talmadge, Ralph Bushman, Michael Keaton, Buster Keaton Jr. **1923 DVD**

•OUR LADY OF THE ASSASSINS ★★1/2 A Colombian writer picks up a teenage hit man in a homosexual bordello, and together they face the misery and despair of life in cocaine-driven Medellín. Director Barbet Schroeder shoots on high-definition video with gritty realism, drawing good performances from his cast, but the

squalor of this story of a child molester and a murderer quickly becomes oppressive. In Spanish with English subtitles. Rated R for profanity (in subtitles), sexual scenes, drug use, and violence. 98m. **DIR:** Barbet Schroeder. **CAST:** Germán Jaramillo, Anderson Ballesteros, Juan David Restrepo. **2001 DVD**

OUR LITTLE GIRL ★★★ Curly-top Shirley's physician father (Joel McCrea) is away so much that his lovely wife (Rosemary Ames) seeks solace from neighbor Lyle Talbot. Shirley is so distressed by this turn of events that she runs away, forcing her parents to reunite in their search for her. Fine melodrama. B&W; 63m. **DIR:** John S. Robertson. **CAST:** Shirley Temple, Rosemary Ames, Joel McCrea, Lyle Talbot. **1935**

OUR MAN FLINT ★★★1/2 Of the numerous imitators who followed James Bond's footsteps in the spy-crazed 1960s, Derek Flint of ZOWIE was by far the best. Ultracool and suavely sophisticated, James Coburn puts his earsplitting grin to good use as a renegade secret agent. One sequel followed: *In Like Flint*. Not rated; suitable for family viewing. 107m. **DIR:** Daniel Mann. **CAST:** James Coburn, Lee J. Cobb, Gila Golan, Edward Mulhare. **1966**

OUR MISS BROOKS (TV SERIES) ★★★ Desilu, basking in the success of *I Love Lucy*, adapted this likable vehicle for comedienne Eve Arden. The show, previously a hit on radio, stars Arden as Connie Brooks, a well-meaning English teacher at Madison High. Miss Brooks goes to extremes to earn the affection—or even the attention—of biology instructor Philip Boynton (Robert Rockwell). 30m. **DIR:** Al Lewis. **CAST:** Eve Arden, Gale Gordon, Robert Rockwell, Richard Crenna, Gloria McMillan, Jane Morgan. **1952–1957**

OUR MODERN MAIDENS ★★★ Jazz-age drama of love and infidelity bears more than a passing resemblance to *Our Dancing Daughters*, with Joan Crawford once again a flapper who makes a bad marriage. Ignore the story and enjoy the art deco sets and elaborate Adrian costumes. B&W; 75m. **DIR:** Jack Conway. **CAST:** Joan Crawford, Douglas Fairbanks Jr., Rod La Rocque, Anita Page. **1929**

OUR MOTHER'S MURDER ★★ A divorced woman with two teenage daughters marries an abusive alcoholic. Unfortunately, they have a child together, so she sticks with him, despite the worsening situation. This made-for-cable drama is based on a true story, but sophomoric narration and an overbearing message squash whatever entertainment value it had. Rated PG-13 for violence. 97m. **DIR:** Bill L. Norton. **CAST:** Holly Marie Combs, Roxanne Hart, Sarah Chalke, James Wilder. **1997**

OUR RELATIONS ★★★1/2 Stan Laurel and Oliver Hardy play two sets of twins. One set are sailors; the other are happily married civilians. When the boys' ship docks in the same city, a hilarious case of mistaken identity occurs. Highly enjoyable, the film doesn't lag at all. It features excellent performances by James Finlayson, Alan Hale, and Sidney Toler. B&W; 74m. **DIR:** Harry Lachman. **CAST:** Stan Laurel, Oliver Hardy, James Finlayson, Alan Hale Sr., Sidney Toler. **1936**

•OUR SONG ★★★★ In late summer, three Brooklyn girls who perform with a Crown Heights marching band make life-altering decisions. Lanisha is dumped by her boyfriend and looks to her separated parents for emotional support. Maria becomes pregnant. Jocelyn, who lives with her party-girl mother, slowly distances herself from the others and makes new best friends. The film captures the trio's growing pains and the gnawing complexities of inner-city life with compelling naturalism and intimacy. The fabulous Jackie Robinson Steppers appear as themselves. Rated R for language and drug use. 96m. **DIR:** Jim McKay. **CAST:** Kerry Washington, Melissa Martinez, Anna Simpson. **2001**

OUR SONS ★★★1/2 Touching portrait of a mother's attempt to cope when she learns her son is homosexual. Julie Andrews is splendid as the San Diego businesswoman who discovers her son is gay. When she learns that his lover is HIV positive, she visits the man's mother, a cocktail waitress in Arkansas, played by Ann-Margret. The cast in this made-for-television movie shines, while the writers make every attempt to steer clear of clichés. 96m. **DIR:** John Erman. **CAST:** Julie Andrews, Ann-Margret, Hugh Grant, Zeljko Ivanek, Tony Roberts. **1991**

OUR TOWN ★★★★ Superb performances from a top-flight cast add zest to this well-done adaptation of Thornton Wilder's play about life in a small town. B&W; 90m. **DIR:** Sam Wood. **CAST:** Frank Craven, William Holden, Martha Scott, Thomas Mitchell, Fay Bainter. **1940 DVD**

OUR TOWN ★★★1/2 Not as good as the 1940s theatrical version, this TV version of the award-winning play by Thornton Wilder is notable for the fine performance of Hal Holbrook. The simple telling of the day-to-day life of Grover's Corners is done with remarkable restraint. 100m. **DIR:** Franklin J. Schaffner. **CAST:** Ned Beatty, Sada Thompson, Ronny Cox, Glynnis O'Connor, Robby Benson, Hal Holbrook, John Houseman. **1980**

OUR VINES HAVE TENDER GRAPES ★★★★★ A shining example of a sentimental movie that doesn't go overboard, this film is set in Wisconsin among Scandinavian immigrants. The focus is on the relationship between two youngsters and their very wise father with lots of witty dialogue and plenty of humorous situations. B&W; 105m. **DIR:** Roy Rowland. **CAST:** Edward G. Robinson, Margaret O'Brien, "Butch" Jenkins, Agnes Moorehead, James Craig, Frances Gifford, Sara Haden. **1945**

OUT ★★ You may want out before the final countdown of this offbeat, surrealistic action film. Peter Coyote is an urban guerrilla who starts out in Greenwich Village and goes cross-country on assignments from a mysterious commander. This comedy-action pastiche tries very hard to be artsy. Rated PG. 88m. **DIR:** Eli Hollander. **CAST:** Peter Coyote, Danny Glover, O-Lan Shephard, Gail Dartez, Jim Haynie, Scott Beach. **1983**

OUT CALIFORNIA WAY ★★1/2 Monte Hale, a cowboy looking for work in Hollywood, comes to the attention of a movie producer. Hale's debut film. Guest Stars: Allan "Rocky" Lane, Roy Rogers, Dale Evans, Don Barry. 67m. **DIR:** Lesley Selander. **CAST:** Monte Hale, Adrian Booth, Robert Blake, John Dehner. **1946**

OUT COLD (1989) ★★★ Dark comedy featuring Teri Garr as a sultry housewife who enlists the aid of John Lithgow after she puts her philandering husband on ice. Some hilarious moments in an otherwise uneven movie. Rated R for sexual situations and violence. 92m. **DIR:**

Malcolm Mowbray. **CAST:** John Lithgow, Teri Garr, Randy Quaid. **1989**

•OUT COLD (2001) A big-time developer shakes up the free-and-easy life at a ski resort in rural Alaska. Snowboarders might enjoy the scenes on the slopes, but even they will find the moronic humor a bore; all others, stay away. Rated PG-13 for profanity and crude sexual humor. 89m. **DIR:** Brendan Malloy, Emmett Malloy. **CAST:** Jason London, Lee Majors, A. J. Cook, Willie Garson. **2001 DVD**

OUT FOR BLOOD ★★★ Martial arts revenge saga, with Don "The Dragon" Wilson typically charming as a lawyer determined to punish the drug dealers who murdered his wife and son. Although the story is one extended cliché—down to the wise old-timer—events occur rapidly enough to avoid becoming boring. Closing dialogue hints at a sequel. Rated R for violence and profanity. 86m. **DIR:** Richard W. Munchkin. **CAST:** Don "The Dragon" Wilson, Shari Shattuck, Michael De Lano, Ron Steelman, Aki Aleong, Todd Curtis. **1993**

OUT FOR JUSTICE ★★★★1/2 Steven Seagal is topnotch as a maverick police detective out to avenge the death of his partner. The best fist-and-foot-style action film to date, this release has pure adrenaline-pumping, jaw-dropping thrills and chills from beginning to end. Rated R for violence, drug use, profanity, and nudity. 90m. **DIR:** John Flynn. **CAST:** Steven Seagal, William Forsythe, Jerry Orbach. **1991 DVD**

OUT IN FIFTY ★★ Clichéd film about a recently released ex-con who wants only to live the clean life but is harassed by a detective who's certain he's going to go bad again. Rated R for violence, sexual situations, and profanity. 100m. **DIR:** Bojesse Christopher, Scott Leet. **CAST:** Balthazar Getty, Christina Applegate, Mickey Rourke, Scott Leet. **1999 DVD**

OUT OF AFRICA ★★★★1/2 Robert Redford and Meryl Streep are at the peaks of their considerable talents in this 1985 Oscar winner for best picture, a grand-scale motion picture also blessed with inspired direction, gorgeous cinematography, and a haunting score. This epic romance, based on the life and works of Isak Dinesen, concerns the love of two staunch individualists for each other and the land in which they live. Rated PG for a discreet sex scene. 160m. **DIR:** Sydney Pollack. **CAST:** Robert Redford, Meryl Streep, Klaus Maria Brandauer, Michael Kitchen, Malick Bowens, Michael Gough, Suzanna Hamilton. **1985 DVD**

OUT OF ANNIE'S PAST Try to stay awake while watching this made-for-cable original about a woman whose past comes back to haunt her. Rated R for violence. 95m. **DIR:** Stuart Cooper. **CAST:** Catherine Mary Stewart, Scott Valentine, Dennis Farina. **1994**

OUT OF BOUNDS A naïve Iowa boy journeys to Los Angeles and accidentally switches luggage with a nasty heroin smuggler. Rated R for extreme violence. 93m. **DIR:** Richard Tuggle. **CAST:** Anthony Michael Hall, Jenny Wright, Jeff Kober, Glynn Turman, Raymond J. Barry. **1986**

OUT OF CONTROL A group of teenagers take off for an exciting weekend on a private island. Rated R for obscenities, nudity, and violence. 78m. **DIR:** Allan Holzman. **CAST:** Martin Hewitt, Betsy Russell, Jim Youngs. **1984**

•OUT OF LINE ★★ A parole officer falls in love with a parolee and the twosome find themselves embroiled in danger and deceit. Mild crime story never really grabs the viewers' attention despite an appealing performance by Jennifer Beals. Rated R for language, violence, and sexuality. 96m. **DIR:** Johanna Demetrakas. **CAST:** Jennifer Beals, Holt McCallany, Michael Moriarty, Christopher Judge, William B. Davis. **2001 DVD**

OUT OF SEASON ★★ This British mood piece is full of atmosphere, but its strange love story, about a man who returns to England to find the woman with whom he had an affair twenty years before, is nothing more than average. Rated R. 90m. **DIR:** Alan Bridges. **CAST:** Vanessa Redgrave, Cliff Robertson, Susan George. **1975**

OUT OF SIGHT ★★★★ During an escape an imprisoned hunk of a bank robber encounters a female federal marshal who is torn between tracking down and getting down with the felon. Once out, the criminal plans a jewel heist with a number of unsavory characters and his hopeful paramour close behind. A character-driven caper film, this is a surprisingly funny movie, a cross between *Pulp Fiction* and *Get Shorty*. It features what is probably the funniest fatal-head-wound scene ever filmed. Rated R for violence. 110m. **DIR:** Steven Soderbergh. **CAST:** George Clooney, Jennifer Lopez, Ving Rhames, Don Cheadle, Dennis Farina, Albert Brooks. **1998 DVD**

OUT OF SIGHT OUT OF MIND Confusing tale involving a serial killer. A real waste of time. Rated R for violence. 94m. **DIR:** Greydon Clark. **CAST:** Susan Blakely, Edward Albert, Lynn-Holly Johnson, Wings Hauser. **1991**

OUT OF SYNC ★★ As if he isn't in enough trouble for failing to pay his bookie, an L.A. nightclub deejay falls for the girlfriend of a vicious drug dealer. Slow-moving and stiffly acted film takes too long to go nowhere. Rated R for profanity, sexual situations, and nudity. 105m. **DIR:** Debbie Allen. **CAST:** LL Cool J, Victoria Dillard, Yaphet Kotto, Howard Hesseman, Aries Spears. **1995 DVD**

OUT OF THE BLUE ★★★ A not-very-innocent young woman passes out in a naïve married man's apartment, making all sorts of trouble in this entertaining romantic comedy of errors and such. B&W; 84m. **DIR:** Leigh Jason. **CAST:** George Brent, Virginia Mayo, Ann Dvorak, Turhan Bey, Carole Landis. **1947**

•OUT OF THE COLD ★★★ Set in World War II Estonia, this love story about a former Broadway star *cum* cabaret entertainer examines love, intolerance, and the devastating effect of the war. Works on many levels and features an outstanding performance by Keith Carradine. Rated R for profanity and violence. 111m. **DIR:** Aleksandr Buravsky. **CAST:** Keith Carradine, Mercedes Ruehl, Mia Kirshner, Brian Dennehy, Kim Hunter, Judd Hirsch, Bronson Pinchot. **1999 DVD**

OUT OF THE DARK Contrived thriller about a psychotic killer who systematically eliminates beautiful women who work at an erotic phone service. Rated R for profanity, nudity, and violence. 89m. **DIR:** Michael Schroeder. **CAST:** Cameron Dye, Karen Black, Bud Cort, Divine, Paul Bartel. **1989**

OUT OF THE DARKNESS ★★★ Fine reenactment of the New York police chase of the serial killer known as

Son of Sam. Martin Sheen plays the man responsible for his capture. Made for TV. 96m. **DIR:** Jud Taylor. **CAST:** Martin Sheen, Hector Elizondo, Matt Clark. **1985**

OUT OF THE PAST ★★★★1/2 This film, which stars Robert Mitchum, is perhaps the quintessential example of *film noir*. A private eye (Mitchum, in a role intended for Bogart) allows himself to be duped by the beautiful but two-faced mistress (Jane Greer) of a big-time gangster (Kirk Douglas). It's a forgotten masterwork. B&W; 97m. **DIR:** Jacques Tourneur. **CAST:** Robert Mitchum, Jane Greer, Kirk Douglas, Richard Webb, Rhonda Fleming, Dickie Moore, Steve Brodie. **1947**

OUT OF THE RAIN ★★ A drifter returns home to find his brother murdered and too many questions regarding his death. Although the movie offers a few surprises, it tries too hard to be a taut suspense-thriller, rarely delivering. Not rated; contains violence, profanity, and brief nudity. 91m. **DIR:** Gary Winick. **CAST:** Bridget Fonda, Michael O'Keefe, John E. O'Keefe, John Seitz. **1990**

OUT OF TOWNERS, THE (1970) ★★★ Jack Lemmon and Sandy Dennis star in this Neil Simon comedy of a New York City vacation gone awry. It's a good idea that doesn't come off as well as one would have hoped. Rated PG for language. 97m. **DIR:** Arthur Hiller. **CAST:** Jack Lemmon, Sandy Dennis, Sandy Baron, Anne Meara, Billy Dee Williams. **1970**

OUT-OF-TOWNERS, THE (1999) ★★1/2 This is an amnesia movie: By the following morning, you won't even remember having seen it. Remade from a 1970 Neil Simon script that frankly wasn't too good to begin with, this update is bland, occasionally amusing, and utterly lacking in outstanding features. It does have the good sense to make its central characters likable and sympathetic but absent the talented Steve Martin and Goldie Hawn, this tale of midwesterners out of their depth in big, bad New York City wouldn't have much going for it. The film's best moments revolve around Martin's attempts to control his near-apoplectic fury. Rated PG-13 for mild profanity, mild sexual content, and comedic drug use. 92m. **DIR:** Sam Weisman. **CAST:** Steve Martin, Goldie Hawn, John Cleese. **1999 DVD**

OUT ON A LIMB ★★1/2 This TV film recounts Shirley MacLaine's move into metaphysics, discovering who she is and where she came from. Much too long, but if you like MacLaine, you might be amused. 159m. **DIR:** Robert Butler. **CAST:** Shirley MacLaine, Charles Dance, John Heard, Anne Jackson, Jerry Orbach. **1986**

OUT ON A LIMB ★★ There are few laughs in this comedy about a corporate executive (Matthew Broderick) who has a disaster-fraught journey from the big city to his rural hometown. The rest of the cast seems to be struggling to ignore how ridiculous the whole thing is. Rated PG for profanity, nudity, and violence. 83m. **DIR:** Francis Veber. **CAST:** Matthew Broderick, Jeffrey Jones, Heidi Kling, John C. Reilly, Marian Mercer, Larry Hankin, David Margulies. **1992**

OUT ON BAIL ★★1/2 Sort of a redneck version of *A Fistful of Dollars.* Drifter Robert Ginty turns the tables on small-town bad guys who try to force him to do their dirty work. Too bad it doesn't go all the way into spaghetti territory. Rated R for sexual situations and violence. 102m. **DIR:** Gordon Hessler. **CAST:** Robert Ginty, Kathy Shower, Tom Badal, Sidney Lassick, Leo Sparrowhawk. **1989**

OUT THERE ★★ Bill Campbell and a host of cameo players are grievously wasted in this inept tale of extraterrestrials who slowly take over Earth, by pervasively dulling our senses with Muzak. Too stupid to be taken seriously, but not clever enough to succeed as satire. Rated PG for profanity. 97m. **DIR:** Sam Irvin. **CAST:** Bill Campbell, Wendy Schaal, Rod Steiger, Jill St. John, June Lockhart, Bill Cobbs, Paul Dooley, David Rasche. **1995**

OUT TO SEA ★★★1/2 Two battling brothers-in-law pose as dance hosts on a Caribbean cruise ship to meet—and hopefully fleece—the wealthy women on board. No comedy milestones but if you're a fan of Lemmon and Matthau, you will find both actors in fine form. The supporting cast is first-rate. Rated PG-13 for language. 106m. **DIR:** Martha Coolidge. **CAST:** Jack Lemmon, Walter Matthau, Dyan Cannon, Gloria De Haven, Brent Spiner, Elaine Stritch, Hal Linden, Donald O'Connor, Edward Mulhare. **1997**

OUTBREAK ★★★★1/2 Top-notch thriller stars Dustin Hoffman as an army doctor battling a devastating virus and government cover-up, each of which threatens to wipe out the population of a small town. Featuring a first-rate supporting cast, it's edge-of-your-seat entertainment of the first order. Rated R for violence, profanity, and gore. 127m. **DIR:** Wolfgang Petersen. **CAST:** Dustin Hoffman, René Russo, Morgan Freeman, Kevin Spacey, Cuba Gooding Jr., Donald Sutherland, Patrick Dempsey. **1995 DVD**

OUTCAST, THE ★★ Before he became disenchanted with acting and turned to still photography, John Derek made a number of mostly mediocre films, this one among them. In this standard Western, he fights to win his rightful inheritance. Justice prevails, of course, but you know that going in. B&W; 90m. **DIR:** William Witney. **CAST:** John Derek, Joan Evans, Jim Davis. **1954**

OUTER LIMITS, THE (TV SERIES) ★★★1/2 This television classic of science fiction produced some fine morality plays. Assisted by the control voice that promised "there is nothing wrong with your television set," viewers experienced compelling *film noir* science fiction. With literate and absorbing scripts, the episodes hold up quite well today. The best is "Demon with a Glass Hand." Other noteworthy episodes include "The Sixth Finger," in which a Welsh coal miner takes a trip into his own biologic future, and "The Man Who Was Never Born." Suitable for family viewing, although a bit intense for small fry. B&W; 52m. **DIR:** Laslo Benedek, John Erman, James Goldstone, Charles Haas, Byron Haskin, Leonard Horn, Gerd Oswald. **CAST:** Robert Culp, Bruce Dern, Robert Duvall, Cedric Hardwicke, Shirley Knight, Martin Landau, David McCallum, Vera Miles, Edward Mulhare, Donald Pleasence, Cliff Robertson, Martin Sheen, Robert Webber. **1964**

OUTER LIMITS: SANDKINGS ★★★ George R. R. Martin's science-fiction shocker makes an uneasy transition to the screen, as the opening installment of cable's updated *Outer Limits* franchise. Obsessed scientist Beau Bridges smuggles home dangerous extraterrestrial eggs but quickly learns the folly of his actions when the ant-sized critters multiply rapidly . . . and start growing. Viewers may be intrigued by the novelty casting,

which features three generations of the Bridges family. Rated PG for violence. 93m. **DIR:** Stuart Gordon. **CAST:** Beau Bridges, Lloyd Bridges, Helen Shaver, Dylan Bridges. **1995**

OUTFIT, THE 🦃 Boring mishmash about Dutch Schultz, Legs Diamond, and Lucky Luciano creaks under the weight of macho posturing and a script shot full of holes. Rated R for violence, nudity, and profanity. 92m. **DIR:** J. Christian Ingvordsen. **CAST:** Lance Henriksen, Billy Drago, Martin Kove. **1993**

OUTLAND ★★★★ Sean Connery stars as the two-fisted marshal in this thoroughly enjoyable outer-space remake of *High Noon* directed by Peter Hyams. Much of the credit for that goes to Connery. As he has proved in many pictures, he is one of the few actors today who can play a fully credible adventure hero. Rated R. 109m. **DIR:** Peter Hyams. **CAST:** Sean Connery, Peter Boyle, Frances Sternhagen. **1981 DVD**

OUTLAW, THE ★★ This once-notorious Western now seems almost laughable. Jane Russell keeps her best attributes forward, but one wonders what Walter Huston and Thomas Mitchell are doing in this film. Only for those who want to know what all the fuss was about. 103m. **DIR:** Howard Hughes, Howard Hawks. **CAST:** Jane Russell, Walter Huston, Thomas Mitchell, Jack Buetel. **1943 DVD**

OUTLAW AND HIS WIFE, THE ★★★ In nineteenth-century Iceland a farmer is accused of stealing sheep and must retreat to the hills to escape capture. An amazing work for its time, this silent movie from Sweden was restored in 1986 and dons a full orchestral score. Not rated. B&W; 73m. **DIR:** Victor Sjöström. **CAST:** Victor Sjöström. **1917**

OUTLAW BLUES ★★1/2 Yet another of Peter Fonda's harmless but rather bland light comedies. He's an ex-con with a talent for songwriting but little in the way of industry smarts; he naïvely allows established country-western star James Callahan to make off with a few hits. Aided by backup singer Susan Saint James, in a charming little part, Fonda figures out how to succeed on his own. Rated PG for light violence and brief nudity. 100m. **DIR:** Richard T. Heffron. **CAST:** Peter Fonda, Susan Saint James, James Callahan, Michael Lerner. **1977**

OUTLAW FORCE ★★ It had to happen. Somebody crossed *Rambo* with *Urban Cowboy*. A gang run out of town by a handsome country singer (David Heavener) gets revenge when they rape and kill his wife, then kidnap his daughter and return to (where else?) Hollywood. Heavener, a Vietnam vet, takes justice into his own hands. Rated R for violence. 95m. **DIR:** David Heavener. **CAST:** David Heavener, Paul Smith, Frank Stallone, Warren Berlinger. **1987**

OUTLAW JOSEY WALES, THE ★★★★1/2 This Western is a masterpiece of characterization and action. Josey Wales is a farmer whose family is murdered by Red Legs, a band of cutthroats allied with the Union Army. Wales joins the Confederacy to avenge their deaths. After the war, everyone in his troop surrenders to the victorious Union except Wales. Rated PG. 135m. **DIR:** Clint Eastwood. **CAST:** Clint Eastwood, Sondra Locke, Chief Dan George, Bill McKinney, John Vernon, John Mitchum, John Russell. **1976 DVD**

OUTLAW OF GOR 🦃 Boring follow-up to the Conan-style original, *Gor*. Rated PG-13 for violence. 90m. **DIR:** John "Bud" Cardos. **CAST:** Urbano Barberini, Rebecca Ferratti, Jack Palance. **1987**

OUTLAWS OF SONORA ★★1/2 A vicious outlaw captures his exact double: Bob Livingston of the Three Mesquiteers. When the outlaw leader then robs a bank and murders the banker, the other Mesquiteers believe their pal has turned killer. B&W; 56m. **DIR:** George Sherman. **CAST:** Robert Livingston, Ray "Crash" Corrigan, Max Terhune, Jack Mulhall. **1938**

OUTLAWS OF THE DESERT ★★ Hopalong Cassidy and his pals travel to Arabia (Hoppy in a burnoose is a sight!) to buy horses for the government and encounter warring tribes and kidnappers. Doesn't measure up to the usual quality of the series. The print material on this title is dark and most of the scenes at night are barely discernible. B&W; 53m. **DIR:** Howard Bretherton. **CAST:** William Boyd, Andy Clyde, Brad King, Duncan Renaldo, Jean Phillips, Forrest Stanley. **1941**

OUTPOST IN MOROCCO ★★ George Raft is out of his element as a French legionnaire assigned to stop the activities of desert rebels only to find himself falling in love with the daughter (Marie Windsor) of their leader (Akim Tamiroff). Pure hokum and slow moving, too. B&W; 92m. **DIR:** Robert Florey. **CAST:** George Raft, Marie Windsor, Akim Tamiroff. **1949 DVD**

OUTRAGE! (1986) ★★★1/2 Compelling courtroom drama that takes on the judicial system with a vengeance. Robert Preston is superb as a man who readily admits to killing his daughter's murderer. Beau Bridges shines as his attorney. This made-for-television film tackles important issues without flinching. 100m. **DIR:** Walter Grauman. **CAST:** Robert Preston, Beau Bridges, Anthony Newley, Burgess Meredith, Linda Purl. **1986 DVD**

OUTRAGE (1994) ★★1/2 After taking murderous revenge on three men who raped her, a circus performer is forced to live as a fugitive. Subpar effort from veteran Spanish filmmaker Carlos Saura. Not rated; contains violence, nudity, and sexual situations. In Spanish with English subtitles. 108m. **DIR:** Carlos Saura. **CAST:** Antonio Banderas, Francesca Neri, Walter Vidarte. **1994 DVD**

OUTRAGEOUS ★★★★ A very offbeat and original comedy-drama concerning a gay nightclub performer's relationship with a pregnant mental patient. A different kind of love story, told with taste and compassion. Female impersonator Craig Russell steals the show. Take a chance on this one. Rated R. 100m. **DIR:** Richard Benner. **CAST:** Craig Russell, Hollis McLaren, Richert Easley. **1977**

OUTRAGEOUS FORTUNE ★★★★ Yet another delightfully inventive adult comedy from Disney's Touchstone arm, highlighted by a show-stealing performance by the Mae West of the 1980s: Bette Midler. Her strutting, strident would-be actress is a scream, a word that also describes the level at which she delivers her rapid-fire dialogue. Rated R for profanity. 100m. **DIR:** Arthur Hiller. **CAST:** Bette Midler, Shelley Long, Peter Coyote, Robert Prosky, John Schuck, George Carlin. **1987 DVD**

OUTSIDE CHANCE OF MAXIMILIAN GLICK, THE ★★★★ Delightfully engaging character study of a young Jewish boy's introduction to real life. He wants to enter a dual piano competition with a pretty gentile girl.

But his parents disapprove of this relationship, and try to keep him from seeing her. Rated G. 95m. **DIR:** Allan A. Goldstein. **CAST:** Saul Rubinek, Jan Rubes, Fairuza Balk. **1989**

OUTSIDE OZONA ★★★ An eclectic collection of characters finds itself slowly drawn together during a serial killer's spree. Rated R for profanity and violence. 99m. **DIR:** J. S. Cardone. **CAST:** Robert Forster, Kevin Pollak, Sherilyn Fenn, David Paymer, Penelope Ann Miller, Swoosie Kurtz, Taj Mahal, Meat Loaf, Lucy Webb. **1998**

OUTSIDE PROVIDENCE ★★★1/2 A blue-collar misfit attempts to redeem himself in this amiable coming-of-age saga, adapted from an earthy, semiautobiographical novel by filmmaker Peter Farrelly. Set in Rhode Island during the 1970s, where high-school senior Timothy Dunphy is rapidly trashing his life with loser friends, our hero winds up at preppy Cornwall Academy, where he decides to teach the anal-retentive administrators a thing or three. And, oh yes, he also falls in love. This is not a story for prudes; marijuana is as plentiful here as the incessant profanity. But the tale has a solid heart, and those with open minds are apt to be surprised by its poignance. Rated R for profanity and drug use. 102m. **DIR:** Michael Corrente. **CAST:** Shawn Hatosy, Alec Baldwin, Amy Smart, George Wendt, Gabriel Mann, Jonathan Brandis, Tommy Bone. **1999 DVD**

OUTSIDE THE LAW (1921) ★★★ Director Tod Browning's long association with the greatest of all character actors and one of the biggest stars of the silent screen began in 1921 when Lon Chaney supported female star Priscilla Dean in this crime-drama. The incomparable Chaney plays Black Mike, the meanest and smarmiest of hoodlums, as well as an old Chinese man, the faithful retainer to Miss Dean. Silent. B&W; 77m. **DIR:** Tod Browning. **CAST:** Priscilla Dean, Lon Chaney Sr., Ralph Lewis, Wheeler Oakman. **1921 DVD**

OUTSIDE THE LAW (1994) ★★ David Bradley plays a cop on the edge who is falling for the prime suspect in a murder investigation. Decent production values help save this direct-to-video crime-thriller, but lackluster writing and direction make the clichés hard to swallow. Rated R for violence, nudity, and language. 95m. **DIR:** Boaz Davidson. **CAST:** David Bradley, Anna Thomson. **1994**

OUTSIDERS, THE 🦃 Based on S. E. Hinton's popular novel, this is a simplistic movie about kids from the wrong side of the tracks. Rated PG for profanity and violence. 91m. **DIR:** Francis Ford Coppola. **CAST:** C. Thomas Howell, Matt Dillon, Ralph Macchio, Emilio Estevez, Tom Cruise, Leif Garrett, Patrick Swayze, Diane Lane. **1983 DVD**

OVER HER DEAD BODY ★★ Black comedy features Elizabeth Perkins and Judge Reinhold as adulterers who kill in self-defense when they're caught in the act. The whole film centers around Perkins's attempts to dump the body and make it look like an accident. Rated R for profanity and violence. 105m. **DIR:** Maurice Phillips. **CAST:** Elizabeth Perkins, Judge Reinhold, Maureen Mueller, Jeffrey Jones, Rhea Perlman. **1989**

OVER THE BROOKLYN BRIDGE ★★1/2 Elliott Gould stars in this occasionally interesting but mostly uneven slice-of-life story about a slovenly, diabetic Jewish luncheonette owner who dreams of getting out by buying a restaurant in downtown Manhattan. Rated R for nudity and profanity. 108m. **DIR:** Menahem Golan. **CAST:** Elliott Gould, Shelley Winters, Sid Caesar, Carol Kane, Burt Young, Margaux Hemingway. **1983**

OVER THE EDGE ★★★★ An explosive commentary on the restlessness of today's youth, this film also serves as an indictment against America's hypocritically permissive society. The violence that was supposedly caused by the release of gang films like *The Warriors*, *Boulevard Nights*, and *The Wanderers* caused the movie's makers to shelve it. However, Matt Dillon, who made his film debut herein, is now a hot property, and that's why this deserving movie is out on video. Rated R. 95m. **DIR:** Jonathan Kaplan. **CAST:** Matt Dillon, Michael Kramer, Pamela Ludwig. **1979**

OVER THE HILL ★★1/2 Unwanted widow Olympia Dukakis takes a road trip in the Australian outback. Its very oddness works in its favor, but the action drags and the ending is melodramatic. Rated PG for brief nudity. 102m. **DIR:** George Miller. **CAST:** Olympia Dukakis, Sigrid Thornton, Derek Fowlds, Aden Young. **1992**

OVER THE LINE 🦃 A college professor's life is turned upside down when she enters into a sexual relationship with a student. Rated R for adult situations, language, nudity, and violence. 108m. **DIR:** Oliver Hellman. **CAST:** Lesley-Anne Down, John Enos, Lady B. Pearl. **1993**

OVER THE TOP ★★ Thoroughly silly effort. Sylvester Stallone stars as a compassionate trucker who only wants to spend time with the son (David Mendenhall) whom he left, years before, in the custody of his wife (Susan Blakely, in a thankless role) and her rich, iron-willed father (Robert Loggia, as a one-note villain). This clichéd story has little of interest. Rated PG for mild violence. 94m. **DIR:** Menahem Golan. **CAST:** Sylvester Stallone, Robert Loggia, Susan Blakely, David Mendenhall. **1987**

OVERBOARD 🦃 A haughty heiress falls off her yacht and loses her memory. Rated PG. 106m. **DIR:** Garry Marshall. **CAST:** Goldie Hawn, Kurt Russell, Edward Herrmann, Katherine Helmond. **1988 DVD**

OVERCOAT, THE ★★★ Based on a story by Gogol, this Russian film tells the story of an office clerk who is content with his modest life and ambitions until he buys a new overcoat and enters on an upward track. Entertaining satire. In Russian with English subtitles. B&W; 78m. **DIR:** Alexi Batalov. **CAST:** Rolan Bykov. **1960**

OVEREXPOSED ★★ Gorefest surrounds a beautiful soap opera star (Catherine Oxenberg) when the people closest to her are killed one after another. Rated R for nudity, violence, and gore. 80m. **DIR:** Larry Brand. **CAST:** Catherine Oxenberg, David Naughton, Jennifer Edwards, Karen Black. **1990**

OVERINDULGENCE ★★ Tame rendition of the scandalous 1940s South African murder trial that shocked the world. A sordid tale of adultery, drugs, and child abuse is told by Juanita Carberry, one of the daughters of the decadent British settlers. Sir Jock Broughton is the accused murderer, and only Juanita knows the truth. This dramatic story is done in by a lightweight script, amateurish direction, and mediocre acting. For substance, sophistication, and style on the subject, check out *White Mischief*. Rated PG-13. 95m. **DIR:** Ross Devenish. **CAST:** Denholm Elliott, Holly Aird, Michael Bryne, Kathryn Pogson. **1987**

OVERKILL 🦃 How many more inept remakes of Richard Connell's "The Most Dangerous Game" must

we endure? Aaron Norris slouches through the jungle here, while avoiding the laughably demented Michael Nouri and his minions. Rated R for profanity and violence. 88m. **DIR:** Dean Ferrandini. **CAST:** Aaron Norris, Michael Nouri, Pamela Dickerson, David Rowe, Kenny Moskow. **1996**

OVERLAND STAGE RAIDERS ★★1/2 Louise Brooks made her last big-screen appearance in this series Western, which has the Three Mesquiteers investing in an airport used by gold miners to ship ore. Of course, our heroes must battle a group of crooks attempting to rob the shipments. B&W; 55m. **DIR:** George Sherman. **CAST:** John Wayne, Louise Brooks, Ray "Crash" Corrigan, Max Terhune. **1938**

OVERNIGHT DELIVERY ★★★ Chaos ensues when a college student suspects that his hometown girlfriend is cheating on him. To retaliate, he sends her a letter through an overnight delivery service. When he learns he's wrong, he makes a valiant attempt to retrieve the letter with the help of a friendly stripper. Lots of fun. Rated PG-13 for adult situations and language. 87m. **DIR:** Jason Bloom. **CAST:** Reese Witherspoon, Paul Rudd, Christine Taylor. **1997**

OVERSEAS ★★★1/2 Three French sisters share their joys and tragedies over an eighteen-year period (1946–1964) in Algeria. The native uprising forces each to say good-bye to her innocence. Lively musical score and touching moments are marred by confusing time jumps. Not rated; contains nudity, violence, and profanity. In French with English subtitles. 96m. **DIR:** Brigitte Rouan. **CAST:** Nicole Garcia, Marianne Basler, Brigitte Rouan, Philippe Galland. **1992**

OWL AND THE PUSSYCAT, THE ★★★★ Barbra Streisand plays a street-smart but undereducated prostitute who teams up with intellectual snob and bookstore clerk George Segal. The laughs abound as the two express themselves, through numerous debates. Rated R. 95m. **DIR:** Herbert Ross. **CAST:** Barbra Streisand, George Segal, Robert Klein. **1970 DVD**

OX-BOW INCIDENT, THE ★★★★1/2 One of the finest Westerns ever made, this thought-provoking drama stars Henry Fonda and Harry Morgan as a pair of drifters who try to stop the lynching of three men (Dana Andrews, Anthony Quinn, and Francis Ford) who may be innocent. Seldom has the terror of mob rule been so effectively portrayed. B&W; 75m. **DIR:** William Wellman. **CAST:** Henry Fonda, Dana Andrews, Mary Beth Hughes, Anthony Quinn, William Eythe, Harry Morgan, Jane Darwell, Frank Conroy, Harry Davenport. **1943**

OXFORD BLUES ★★ Rob Lowe plays a brash American attending England's Oxford University. Writer-director Robert Boris has even worked in the sports angle, by making Lowe a rowing champ who has to prove himself. A formula picture. Rated PG-13. 93m. **DIR:** Robert Boris. **CAST:** Rob Lowe, Amanda Pays. **1984**

OXYGEN ★★★ A rich woman is kidnapped and buried alive with approximately twenty-four hours worth of air. Her husband must get the ransom money in the kidnapper's hands, and then the location of the interred woman will be revealed. But the husband panics and contacts the authorities. This thriller is full of twists—some expected and others unpredictable. Rated R for violence and language. 92m. **DIR:** Richard Shepard. **CAST:** Adrien Brody, Maura Tierney, Dylan Baker, Terry Kinney. **1998 DVD**

OZONE ★★1/2 Perhaps given a larger budget, this could have been a great movie. As it is, the low budget definitely hinders this ambitious film. Even gunshots are dubbed. Not rated; contains violence and profanity. 83m. **DIR:** J. R. Bookwalter. **CAST:** James Black, Tom Hoover, Bill Morrison, James L. Edwards. **1993**

P

PACIFIC CONNECTION, THE Move over *Plan 9 from Outer Space*—this may just be the worst film ever made. Martial arts champ Roland Dantes saves his impressive skills for the final scene in this hodgepodge of inconsistencies, poor acting, and inane plot. Dantes must avenge the deaths of his parents by a corrupt Spanish governor and his foppish sons (one of whom is Dean Stockwell in a best forgotten role). Not rated; contains nudity, violence, and sex. 87m. **DIR:** Luis Nepomuceno. **CAST:** Roland Dantes, Nancy Kwan, Guy Madison, Alejandro Rey, Dean Stockwell, Gilbert Roland. **1960**

PACIFIC HEIGHTS ★★★★ When a yuppie couple purchases a Victorian apartment house in San Francisco, they figure they've found the home of their dreams. Then a secretive tenant moves in without permission and begins slowly destroying their property. An intelligent and gripping thriller that holds you right up to the climax. Rated R for profanity and violence. 107m. **DIR:** John Schlesinger. **CAST:** Melanie Griffith, Matthew Modine, Michael Keaton, Beverly D'Angelo, Nobu McCarthy, Laurie Metcalf, Carl Lumbly, Dorian Harewood, Luca Bercovici, Tippi Hedren. **1990 DVD**

PACIFIC INFERNO ★★1/2 This war adventure film is set in the Philippines during the final fall and capture of U.S. and Filipino soldiers. Jim Brown and Richard Jaeckel are American navy prisoners. Good, steady action follows. Not rated. 90m. **DIR:** Rolf Bayer. **CAST:** Jim Brown, Richard Jaeckel, Tim Brown, Tad Horino, Wilma Redding, Vic Diaz. **1985 DVD**

PACK, THE ★★ Slightly above-average horror film about a pack of dogs that goes wild and tries to kill two families. Rated R. 99m. **DIR:** Robert Clouse. **CAST:** Joe Don Baker, Hope Alexander Willis, Richard B. Shull, R. G. Armstrong. **1977**

PACK UP YOUR TROUBLES ★★★ Stan Laurel and Oliver Hardy join the army in World War I, with the usual disastrous results. After being discharged, they assume responsibility for a fallen comrade's young daughter and search for her grandparents. The plot line and scripting aren't as solid as in other films, but the boys squeeze out every laugh possible. B&W; 68m. **DIR:** George Marshall. **CAST:** Stan Laurel, Oliver Hardy. **1932**

PACKAGE, THE ★★★★ In this taut thriller, skillfully directed by Andrew Davis, Gene Hackman gives one of his best performances as a soldier assigned to take a

prisoner (Tommy Lee Jones) from Berlin to Washington, D.C. When his prisoner escapes, Hackman finds himself in the middle of a conspiracy whose masterminds want him out of the way. Rated R for violence and profanity. 109m. **DIR:** Andrew Davis. **CAST:** Gene Hackman, Tommy Lee Jones, Joanna Cassidy, John Heard, Dennis Franz, Pam Grier. **1989 DVD**

PACKIN' IT IN ★★★1/2 When Gary and Dianna Webber (Richard Benjamin and Paula Prentiss) flee from the pollution and crime of Los Angeles, they find themselves living among survivalists in Woodcrest, Oregon. The laughs begin as these city folks, including their punked-out daughter (played by Molly Ringwald), try to adjust to life in the wilderness. 92m. **DIR:** Jud Taylor. **CAST:** Richard Benjamin, Paula Prentiss, Molly Ringwald, Tony Roberts, Andrea Marcovicci. **1982**

•PACT, THE ★★1/2 Greg Sherman (Adam Frost) retreats to the safety of a private school after his parents are murdered right in front of him. Lenny (Rider Strong) infiltrates the school with the intention of finding Greg and killing him. They unwittingly become good friends before Lenny discovers just who his target is. This movie carefully straddles the line between excitement and tedium. Rated R for violence. 94m. **DIR:** Rodney Gibbons. **CAST:** Adam Frost, Rider Strong, John Heard, Nick Mancuso. **1999 DVD**

PADDY ★★1/2 Excellent performances by all the actors, especially Des Cave in the title role, cannot save this rather confused coming-of-age comedy. Despite moments of true hilarity, the film remains at best mildly amusing. 97m. **DIR:** Daniel Haller. **CAST:** Des Cave, Milo O'Shea, Peggy Cass. **1969**

PADRE PADRONE ★★★1/2 Although slow-moving, this low-budget film is a riveting account of a young Sardinian's traumatizing relationship with his overbearing father in a patriarchal society. The son bears the brutality, but eventually breaks the emotional bonds. This quietly powerful film depends on the actors for its punch. In Sardinian (Italian dialect) with English subtitles. 114m. **DIR:** Vittorio Taviani, Paolo Taviani. **CAST:** Omero Antonutti, Saverio Marioni. **1977 DVD**

PAGAN LOVE SONG ★★ Watered-down love story about American schoolteacher Howard Keel who falls for native girl Esther Williams is just another excuse for singing, swimming, and a tired old plot line. 76m. **DIR:** Robert Alton. **CAST:** Esther Williams, Howard Keel, Minna Gombell, Rita Moreno. **1950**

PAGEMASTER, THE ★★ Seeking sanctuary from a storm, a neurotic kid scurries into a huge library where paintings on the ceiling splash down and turn the precocious lad and his surroundings into a cartoon. He teams up with caricatures of a pirate, a fairy godmother, and a fraidy-cat goblin and dives into the pages of several classics. But the adventure lacks vitality. Rated G. 75m. **DIR:** Joe Johnston, Maurice Hunt. **CAST:** Macaulay Culkin, Christopher Lloyd, Whoopi Goldberg, Patrick Stewart, Leonard Nimoy, Frank Welker, Phil Hartman. **1994**

PAIN IN THE A—, A ★★ A professional hit man (Lino Ventura) arrives in Montpellier to kill a government witness who is set to testify against the mob. This unfunny slapstick comedy was adapted by director Billy Wilder for the equally disappointing *Buddy, Buddy* with Jack Lemmon and Walter Matthau. In French with English subtitles. Rated PG for light violence. 90m. **DIR:** Edouard Molinaro. **CAST:** Lino Ventura, Jacques Brel. **1973**

PAINT IT BLACK ★★★1/2 Talented young sculptor (Rick Rossovich) is under bondage to an unscrupulous gallery owner (Sally Kirkland). He meets a slightly off-center art collector (Doug Savant) who complicates his life with favors. Impressive little thriller. Rated R for violence, nudity, and adult situations. 101m. **DIR:** Tim Hunter. **CAST:** Rick Rossovich, Sally Kirkland, Martin Landau, Julie Carmen, Doug Savant. **1989**

PAINT JOB, THE ★★1/2 Margaret has a problem. She's in love with two men. One is her husband. One is a painter who also happens to be her neighbor. Her husband also happens to be the neighbor's boss. Torn between two lovers, she could be torn apart when she finds out that one of them is a serial killer. Interesting cast makes this confusing thriller click. Rated R for violence, language, and adult situations. 90m. **DIR:** Michael Taav. **CAST:** Will Patton, Bebe Neuwirth, Robert Pastorelli. **1992**

PAINT YOUR WAGON ★★★1/2 Clint Eastwood and Lee Marvin play partners during the California gold rush era. They share everything, including a bride (Jean Seberg) bought from a Mormon traveler (John Mitchum), in this silly, but fun musical. Rated PG. 166m. **DIR:** Joshua Logan. **CAST:** Clint Eastwood, Lee Marvin, Jean Seberg, Harve Presnell, John Mitchum. **1969 DVD**

PAINTED DESERT, THE ★★1/2 The future Hopalong Cassidy, William Boyd, plays a foundling who grows up on the other side of the range from his ladylove and must decide between the family feud and the cattle or Helen Twelvetrees and the cattle. A young Clark Gable plays the dark cloud that is menacing the future of these two nice kids. B&W; 75m. **DIR:** Howard Higgin. **CAST:** William Boyd, Helen Twelvetrees, William Farnum, J. Farrell MacDonald, Clark Gable. **1931**

PAINTED FACES ★★★★ Many of Hong Kong's top stars trained at the Peking Opera School. This docudrama tribute to the now-closed school, set in the 1960s, shows the rigorous training and strict discipline students received there, as well as the amazing results. In Cantonese with English subtitles. Not rated. 100m. **DIR:** Alex Law. **CAST:** Sammo Hung, Kam-bo, Chang Peipei. **1987**

PAINTED HERO ★★★1/2 Country singer Dwight Yoakam gives a laconic but convincing performance in this decidedly offbeat character study as a rodeo clown/bullfighter whose reluctant reentry into the big time brings him face-to-face with the past and the people he's tried to leave behind. It's a real sleeper. Rated R for profanity, simulated sex, nudity, and violence. 105m. **DIR:** Terry Benedict. **CAST:** Dwight Yoakam, Bo Hopkins, Michelle Joyner, Kiersten Warren, Cindy Pickett, John Getz. **1995**

PAINTED HILLS, THE ★★★1/2 A sentimental tale with Lassie starring as an intelligent canine who doesn't let human beings get away with anything. Set in the 1870s with greedy gold miners killing partners and rivals. But Lassie knows who the real good guys are! Well-photographed and nicely choreographed with a beautifully edited performance by Lassie that will make an animal lover out of just about anybody. 65m. **DIR:**

Harold F. Kress. **CAST:** Gary Gray, Paul Kelly, Bruce Cowling, Ann Doran, Chief Yowlachie, Andrea Virginia Lester. **1951**

PAINTED STALLION, THE ★★ History-bending serial finds Kit Carson, Davy Crockett, and Jim Bowie coming to the aid of Hoot Gibson as he leads a wagon train to Santa Fe. Lots of action and plot reversals. B&W; 12 chapters. **DIR:** William Witney, Ray Taylor. **CAST:** Ray "Crash" Corrigan, Hoot Gibson, Sammy McKim, Jack Perrin, Hal Taliaferro, Duncan Renaldo, LeRoy Mason, Yakima Canutt. **1937**

PAINTED VEIL, THE ★★★ A better-than-average Garbo melodrama because it has a better-than-average source. Somerset Maugham wrote the novel that inspired this sophisticated love story about a woman who cheats on her husband, then tries to make amends. B&W; 85m. **DIR:** Richard Boleslawski. **CAST:** Greta Garbo, George Brent, Herbert Marshall, Warner Oland, Jean Hersholt, Keye Luke, Cecilia Parker, Beulah Bondi. **1934**

PAIR OF ACES ★★ Kris Kristofferson and Willie Nelson star in this made-for-television modern-day Western. Kristofferson plays a Texas Ranger tracking down a serial killer while trying to keep tabs on a safecracker in his custody, played by Nelson. Not rated. 100m. **DIR:** Aaron Lipstadt. **CAST:** Willie Nelson, Kris Kristofferson, Rip Torn, Helen Shaver, Jane Cameron. **1990**

PAISAN ★★★1/2 Six separate stories of survival are hauntingly presented by writer Federico Fellini and director Roberto Rossellini in this early postwar Italian film. Shot on the streets and often improvised, the strong drama exposes the raw nerves brought on by living in a battleground. B&W; 90m. **DIR:** Roberto Rossellini. **CAST:** Carmela Sazio, Robert Van Loon, Gar Moore. **1946**

PAJAMA GAME, THE ★★★★ This, one of the best film versions yet made of a Broadway musical, features John Raitt (his only big-screen appearance) in his stage role as the workshop superintendent who must deal with a union demand for a 7-cent-per-hour raise. Doris Day plays the leader of the grievance committee, who fights and then falls for him. Broadway dancer Carol Haney also repeats her supporting role. 101m. **DIR:** George Abbott, Stanley Donen. **CAST:** Doris Day, John Raitt, Eddie Foy Jr., Carol Haney, Barbara Nichols, Reta Shaw. **1957 DVD**

PAL JOEY ★★★★ Frank Sinatra plays the antihero of this Rodgers and Hart classic about a hip guy who hopes to open a slick nightclub in San Francisco. With love interests Rita Hayworth and Kim Novak vying for Ol' Blue Eyes, and George Sidney's fast-paced direction, the picture is an enjoyable romp. The Rodgers and Hart score is perhaps their finest. 111m. **DIR:** George Sidney. **CAST:** Frank Sinatra, Rita Hayworth, Kim Novak, Barbara Nichols. **1957 DVD**

PALAIS ROYALE ★★ The Hollywood gangster is viewed through a peculiarly Canadian prism in this Toronto-made *film noir*. Matt Craven plays an ambitious advertising executive, circa 1959, who stumbles into a world of gangsters and goons. Slovenly. 100m. **DIR:** Martin Lavut. **CAST:** Dean Stockwell, Kim Cattrall, Matt Craven. **1988**

PALE BLOOD ★★ A suave vampire tries to catch the psycho giving his breed a bad name. Usual vampire exploitation flick, this bloodsucker begins on a creepy note but falters under a lousy script and a lopsided amount of violence against women. Rated R for profanity, violence, and nudity. 93m. **DIR:** Dachin Hsu. **CAST:** George Chakiris, Wings Hauser, Pamela Ludwig. **1990**

PALE RIDER ★★★1/2 Star-producer-director Clint Eastwood donned six-guns and a Stetson for the first time since the classic *The Outlaw Josey Wales* (1976) for this enjoyable Western. The star is a mysterious avenger who comes to the aid of embattled gold prospectors in the Old West. Rated R for violence and profanity. 113m. **DIR:** Clint Eastwood. **CAST:** Clint Eastwood, Michael Moriarty, Carrie Snodgress, Christopher Penn, Richard Dysart, Richard Kiel, John Russell. **1985 DVD**

PALEFACE, THE ★★★★ Hope stars as a cowardly dentist who marries Calamity Jane (Jane Russell in rare form) and becomes, thanks to her quick draw, a celebrated gunslinger. It inspired a sequel, *Son of Paleface*, and a remake, *The Shakiest Gun in the West*, with Don Knotts, but the original is still tops. 91m. **DIR:** Norman Z. McLeod. **CAST:** Bob Hope, Jane Russell, Robert Armstrong. **1948 DVD**

PALERMO CONNECTION, THE ★★★ Political intrigue surrounds New York's mayoral candidate after he proposes drug legalization. On his honeymoon, he's framed by the mob. Now he must choose between accepting the status quo and challenging the Sicilian Mafia. Not rated, contains violence, profanity, and nudity. 100m. **DIR:** Francesco Rosi. **CAST:** James Belushi, Mimi Rogers, Joss Ackland, Vittorio Gassman. **1989**

PALLBEARER, THE ★★★★ David Schwimmer stars in this offbeat comedy as a college graduate who can't get started on his career in architecture, but this is nothing compared with the pickle he gets himself into when he agrees to attend the funeral of "the best friend" he doesn't remember. This character study boasts fine performances and some moments of sheer hilarity. Rated PG-13 for profanity and suggested sex. 97m. **DIR:** Matt Reeves. **CAST:** David Schwimmer, Gwyneth Paltrow, Michael Rapaport, Barbara Hershey, Toni Collette, Carol Kane. **1996 DVD**

PALM BEACH ★★★ Four different stories concerning troubled Australian teens converge at the title location, a popular Aussie beach. Fans of the new Australian cinema will want to take a look, though the accents may be a bit thick for others. Not rated. 88m. **DIR:** Albie Thomas. **CAST:** Nat Young, Ken Brown, Amanda Berry, Bryan Brown. **1979**

PALM BEACH STORY, THE ★★★★ Preston Sturges was perhaps the greatest of all American writer-directors. This light story of an engineer's wife (Claudette Colbert) who takes a vacation from marriage in sunny Florida and encounters one of the oddest groupings of talented characters ever assembled may well be his best film. B&W; 90m. **DIR:** Preston Sturges. **CAST:** Claudette Colbert, Joel McCrea, Rudy Vallee, Mary Astor, Sig Arno, William Demarest, Franklin Pangborn, Jimmy Conlin. **1942**

PALM SPRINGS WEEKEND ★★ It's sun, fun, and romance as some wild guys and cool chicks take a break from higher education and Watusi themselves silly during spring break. Harmless fun. 100m. **DIR:** Norman

Taurog. **CAST:** Troy Donahue, Connie Stevens, Stefanie Powers, Robert Conrad, Ty Hardin, Jack Weston, Andrew Duggan. **1963**

PALMETTO 🦃 Hollywood has perpetrated a crime against novelist James Hadley Chase's work. Chase's unflinching violence has been replaced with laughable sex scenes between characters clearly unable to articulate their mock-sultry dialogue without looking as though they're about to burst into laughter. The story concerns a newspaper reporter who gets in over his head with a larcenous femme fatale. Try not to fall asleep. Rated R for profanity, violence, and strong sexual content. 112m. **DIR:** Volker Schlöndorff. **CAST:** Woody Harrelson, Elisabeth Shue, Gina Gershon, Rolf Hoppe, Michael Rapaport, Chloe Sevigny. **1998 DVD**

PALOMBELLA ROSSA ★★★1/2 A Fellini-inspired water-polo game becomes the waiting room for a politician's life after he has an auto accident. Michele (Nanni Moretti) finds himself searching for life's answers, while desperately trying to stay afloat during the game of his life. Truly inspired moments set against a surreal backdrop make this comedy a winner. In Italian with English subtitles. Not rated. 87m. **DIR:** Nanni Moretti. **CAST:** Nanni Moretti, Alfonso Santagata, Claudio Morganti, Asia Argento. **1989**

PALOOKA ★★1/2 First filmed version of Ham Fisher's popular *Joe Palooka* is an okay little film about country bumpkin Stu Erwin's rise to the top in the fight game. This film shares a niche with the other seldom-seen comic-strip film adaptations of the 1930s, and its availability on video is a pleasant gift to the fan who loves those tough and slightly goofy movies of the early 1930s. B&W; 86m. **DIR:** Ben Stoloff. **CAST:** Jimmy Durante, Stu Erwin, Lupe Velez, Marjorie Rambeau, Robert Armstrong, William Cagney, Thelma Todd, Mary Carlisle. **1934**

PALOOKAVILLE ★★★★ Most crooks get the basics right. You set up a jewelry store; you rob a jewelry store; but not the three likable Jersey City losers, the soul of this gentle caper comedy, who mistakenly rob the bakery next door and then plan to hold up an armored car. These sad-sack schemers hold court in seedy coffee shops and struggle with romance in a stubbornly nonviolent update of Italo Calvino's folksy 1940s short stories about economic survival in postwar Italy. Rated R for language. 92m. **DIR:** Alan Taylor. **CAST:** William Forsythe, Adam Trese, Vincent Gallo, Gareth Williams, Kim Dickens, Lisa Gay Hamilton, Frances McDormand, Bridgit Ryan. **1996**

PALS ★★★ George C. Scott and Don Ameche are delightful as two senior citizens who stumble across a cache of drug money. Made-for-television. 100m. **DIR:** Lou Antonio. **CAST:** George C. Scott, Don Ameche, Sylvia Sidney. **1986**

PALS OF THE SADDLE ★★1/2 The Three Mesquiteers (John Wayne, Ray Corrigan, and Max Terhune) help a woman government agent (Doreen McKay) trap a munitions ring in this enjoyable B Western series entry. B&W; 60m. **DIR:** George Sherman. **CAST:** John Wayne, Ray "Crash" Corrigan, Max Terhune, Doreen McKay, Frank Milan, Jack Kirk. **1938**

PANAMA DECEPTION, THE ★★★★ This blistering, Oscar-winning documentary chronicles the events leading to the U.S. invasion of Panama, actually a crusade designed to renegotiate the treaty that would have given Panama control of the strategically critical Panama Canal by the year 2000. Although these often grim images are laced with explicit footage of burned children and civilians crushed by tanks, the most chilling fact to emerge is that the U.S. mainstream media were duped into reporting only what the Reagan and Bush administrations wanted them to see. Not rated; contains graphic violence. 91m. **DIR:** Barbara Trent. **1992**

PANAMA HATTIE ★★ Take one hit musical play about a Panama nightclub owner, throw out all but a couple of Cole Porter tunes, refashion it for Red Skelton, then subdue him, and you have this lackluster movie that sat on the shelf for over a year before being released. Saved only by the debut of Lena Horne. B&W; 79m. **DIR:** Norman Z. McLeod. **CAST:** Red Skelton, Ann Sothern, Marsha Hunt, Virginia O'Brien, Lena Horne. **1942**

PANAMA LADY ★★ Lucille Ball does her best to liven up this tired story about a saloon dancer stuck in the tropics with her pick of the local sweat-soaked swains. Future Saturday-matinee cowboy favorite Allan "Rocky" Lane plays the two-fisted hombre who whisks everybody's favorite redhead off to the romantic oil fields in the jungle that he calls home. This is a remake of *Panama Flo* (1932). B&W; 65m. **DIR:** Jack B. Hively. **CAST:** Lucille Ball, Allan "Rocky" Lane, Donald Briggs, Evelyn Brent, Abner Biberman. **1939**

PANCHO BARNES ★★★1/2 The incredible true-life story of little-known Florence Pancho Barnes, portrayed fabulously by Valerie Bertinelli. This remarkable woman raced against Amelia Earhart, became a stunt pilot, and trained some of the most famous army boys to fly. Made for TV. 180m. **DIR:** Richard T. Heffron. **CAST:** Valerie Bertinelli, Ted Wass, James Stephens, Cynthia Harris, Geoffrey Lewis, Sam Robards. **1988**

PANCHO VILLA ★★ Telly Savalas plays the famous bandit to the hilt and beyond. Clint Walker runs guns for him. Chuck Connors postures as a stiff and stuffy military type. You'll soon see why the title role forever belongs to Wallace Beery. It all builds to a rousing head-on train wreck. Rated R. 92m. **DIR:** Eugenio Martin. **CAST:** Telly Savalas, Clint Walker, Chuck Connors, Anne Francis. **1972**

PANDEMONIUM ★★★ After attacks on cheerleading camps across the nation, there is only one place left to learn—Bambi's Cheerleading School. In this parody of slasher movies, Carol Kane steals the show as Candy, a girl with supernatural powers who just wants to have fun. Tom Smothers is a displaced Canadian Mountie; Paul Reubens (Pee-Wee Herman) plays his assistant. Rated PG for obscenities. 82m. **DIR:** Alfred Sole. **CAST:** Carol Kane, Tom Smothers, Debralee Scott, Candy Azzara, Miles Chapin, Tab Hunter, Paul Reubens. **1980**

PANDORA AND THE FLYING DUTCHMAN ★★★1/2 Lush photography gives this legendary love story an edge. Ava Gardner is exotically beautiful as a self-centered woman romantically involved with a race-car driver, a matador, and the ghost of a man doomed to sail the oceans until he meets a woman who loves him enough to die for him. The pace is slow, but the romantic appeal is exceptional. 122m. **DIR:** Albert Lewin. **CAST:** Ava Gardner, James Mason, Nigel Patrick, Harry Warrender. **1951 DVD**

PANDORA PROJECT, THE 🦃 It took two directors, including infamous low-budget impresario Jim Wynorsky,

to churn out this awful mess about a renegade commando who has stolen a top-secret weapon. It's one of those movies where even if you didn't pay to see it, you'd still want your money back. Not rated; contains violence. 92m. **DIR:** Jim Wynorsky, John Terlesky. **CAST:** Daniel Baldwin, Erika Eleniak, Richard Tyson, Tony Todd. **1998 DVD**

PANDORA'S BOX ★★★★1/2 Here is a gem from the heyday of German silent screen Expressionism. The film follows a winning yet amoral temptress, Lulu (a sparkling performance by Louise Brooks). Without concerns or inhibitions, Lulu blissfully ensnares a variety of weak men, only to contribute to their eventual downfall. B&W; 131m. **DIR:** G. W. Pabst. **CAST:** Louise Brooks, Fritz Kortner. **1929**

PANIC ★★★★1/2 Torn by a midlife crisis, a fretful family man (William H. Macy) wants to get out of the family business—he's a contract killer. This offbeat, domestic *film noir* is subtle and quietly spellbinding. Macy is excellent, as is the entire cast—especially Donald Sutherland as his monstrous father and Neve Campbell as the young woman with whom Macy's character becomes obsessed. Rated R for mature themes, profanity, sexual scenes, and brief violence. 90m. **DIR:** Henry Bromell. **CAST:** William H. Macy, Donald Sutherland, Neve Campbell, Tracey Ullman, John Ritter, Barbara Bain. **2000 DVD**

PANIC BUTTON ★★ Looking for a tax loss, a gangster bankrolls a film sure to be so bad that he'll lose money on it. Did Mel Brooks see this obscure comedy before he made *The Producers* (which is much funnier)? B&W; 90m. **DIR:** George Sherman. **CAST:** Maurice Chevalier, Eleanor Parker, Jayne Mansfield, Mike Connors, Akim Tamiroff. **1964**

PANIC IN NEEDLE PARK ★★★★ Still one of the best films ever made about drug abuse, as a likable young couple destroy their lives when they become hooked on heroin. Al Pacino is excellent in his first starring role, in a film that is almost queasily realistic in its depiction of urban drug culture. Rated R for drug use. 110m. **DIR:** Jerry Schatzberg. **CAST:** Al Pacino, Kitty Winn, Alan Vint, Richard Bright, Raul Julia, Paul Sorvino. **1971**

PANIC IN THE STREETS ★★★★ Oscar- winning story focuses on a New Orleans criminal who is unknowingly the carrier of a deadly virus. The police attempt to capture him before he can infect others. Taut thriller. B&W; 93m. **DIR:** Elia Kazan. **CAST:** Richard Widmark, Jack Palance, Paul Douglas, Barbara Bel Geddes, Zero Mostel. **1950**

PANIC IN THE YEAR ZERO ★★★1/2 Low-budget yet extremely effective tale of paranoia from producer Roger Corman. Ray Milland, who also directed, stars as the head of a family attempting to leave Los Angeles when the bombs drop. Outside the city limits, the family runs into massive chaos when panicking citizens take the law into their own hands. Their biggest fear isn't the bombs, but man himself. 95m. **DIR:** Ray Milland. **CAST:** Ray Milland, Joan Freeman, Frankie Avalon, Jean Hagen, Richard Garland. **1962**

•PANIC ROOM ★★★1/2 When three burglars invade their apartment, a woman and her daughter (Jodie Foster, Kristen Stewart) take refuge in the "panic room" (a self-contained, impregnable shelter)—but what the intruders want is in there with them. The film is well made and effective, although the suspense is nerve-racking and ultimately rather unpleasant. Rated R for profanity and violence. 108m. **DIR:** David Fincher. **CAST:** Jodie Foster, Forest Whitaker, Jared Leto, Dwight Yoakam, Kristen Stewart. **2002**

PANIQUE ★★★1/2 Based on a thriller by Georges Simenon, this gripping story features Michel Simon as a stranger who is framed for murder. A taut film comparable to the best of the chase *noir* genre so prevalent in French and American cinema of the mid-1940s. In French with English subtitles. B&W; 87m. **DIR:** Julien Duvivier. **CAST:** Michel Simon, Viviane Romance. **1946**

PANTALOONS ★★★ In this period comedy, horse-faced Fernandel gets a chance to fill in for his master, Don Juan. Unfortunately, the circumstances are so hectic that he can't take advantage of any of the women who so want to be conquered by the great lover, even if he looks somewhat less dashing than they'd imagined. Dubbed. 93m. **DIR:** John Berry. **CAST:** Fernandel, Carmen Seville, Fernando Rey. **1957**

PANTHER ★★ Whitewashed urban action-movie approach to the Sixties black-power party's story. The Black Panthers are portrayed as less complex, and less violent, than they really were, and the film's thesis that the FBI and the mob teamed up to destroy them with cheap drugs is, well, cheap propaganda. Rated R for violence, language, and drug use. 93m. **DIR:** Mario Van Peebles. **CAST:** Kadeem Hardison, Bokeem Woodbine, Courtney B. Vance, Marcus Chong, Joe Don Baker, M. Emmet Walsh. **1995 DVD**

PAPA'S DELICATE CONDITION ★★1/2 Somewhat stolid but pleasant enough story of family life in a small Texas town and the sometimes unpleasant notoriety brought to a family by their alcoholic patriarch, Jackie Gleason. Not as good a film as it was considered when released, this is still an enjoyable movie. 98m. **DIR:** George Marshall. **CAST:** Jackie Gleason, Glynis Johns, Charlie Ruggles, Laurel Goodwin, Charles Lane, Elisha Cook Jr., Juanita Moore, Murray Hamilton. **1963**

PAPER, THE ★★★★ Michael Keaton stars as an editor in this ensemble comedy-drama about a New York daily tabloid newspaper. He has only a few hours to get the scoop on a murder and stop cost-conscious managing editor Glenn Close from printing a sensationalistic cover that implies two innocent youngsters are guilty. Rated R for profanity and violence. 110m. **DIR:** Ron Howard. **CAST:** Michael Keaton, Glenn Close, Marisa Tomei, Randy Quaid, Robert Duvall, Jason Robards Jr., Jason Alexander, Spalding Gray, Catherine O'Hara, Jack Kehoe, Clint Howard. **1994 DVD**

PAPER BRIGADE, THE ★★★ When his family moves to the suburbs, a big city teen takes a paper route to make some money and finds out that the 'burbs aren't always as peaceful as everyone says. Enjoyable kids' comedy. Rated PG for mild violence. 89m. **DIR:** Blair Treu. **CAST:** Kyle Howard, Travis Wester, Robert Englund. **1996**

PAPER CHASE, THE ★★★★ John Houseman won the Oscar for best actor in a supporting role in 1973 with his first-rate performance in this excellent film. Timothy Bottoms stars as a law student attempting to earn his law degree in spite of a stuffy professor (Houseman).

Rated PG. 111m. **DIR:** James Bridges. **CAST:** Timothy Bottoms, John Houseman, Lindsay Wagner. **1973**

PAPER LION ★★★1/2 Based on George Plimpton's book, this film tells the story of the author's exploits when he becomes an honorary team member of the Detroit Lions pro football team. Alan Alda is fine as Plimpton and Alex Karras is a standout in his support. 107m. **DIR:** Alex March. **CAST:** Alan Alda, Lauren Hutton, Alex Karras, David Doyle, Ann Turkel, Roger Brown. **1968**

PAPER MARRIAGE (1988) ★★1/2 Martial arts star Sammo Hung plays an out-of-work Chinese boxer in Canada who reluctantly accepts a promise to marry a Hong Kong girl. Though highly uneven, the film has some funny moments. In Cantonese with English subtitles. Not rated; contains violence. 102m. **DIR:** Sammo Hung. **CAST:** Sammo Hung, Maggie Cheung. **1988**

PAPER MARRIAGE (1992) ★★ Silly tale of a Polish girl arriving in London to marry her fiancé. When his mom disapproves of the union, she marries an unemployed man. Problems naturally result in their bizarre marriage, but these are nothing compared to the effect that the emotionless actors have on the film. Not rated, contains sex, violence, and profanity. 90m. **DIR:** Krzysztof Lang. **CAST:** Gary Kemp, Joanna Trepechinska, Rita Tushingham. **1992**

PAPER MASK ★★★ Intriguing British thriller features Paul McGann as an ambitious young man who poses as an emergency room doctor. His lack of training has a deadly effect on a female patient (Barbara Leigh-Hunt). The nurse on duty (Amanda Donohoe) may cover up for or expose him. Rated R for nudity and violence. 105m. **DIR:** Christopher Morahan. **CAST:** Paul McGann, Amanda Donohoe, Frederick Treves, Tom Wilkinson, Barbara Leigh-Hunt. **1989**

PAPER MOON ★★★★★ Critic-turned-director Peter Bogdanovich ended his four-film winning streak—which included *Targets*, *The Last Picture Show*, and *What's Up Doc?*—with this comedy, starring Ryan O'Neal and Tatum O'Neal as a con man and a kid in the 1930s who get involved in some pretty wild predicaments and meet up with a variety of wacky characters. It's delightful entertainment from beginning to end. Rated PG. B&W; 102m. **DIR:** Peter Bogdanovich. **CAST:** Ryan O'Neal, Tatum O'Neal, Madeline Kahn, John Hillerman. **1973**

PAPER TIGER ★★ Stiffly British David Niven is tutor to the son (Ando) of a Japanese ambassador (Toshiro Mifune). He and his young charge are kidnapped by terrorists for political reasons. Derring-do follows, but it's all lukewarm and paplike. Rated PG. 99m. **DIR:** Ken Annakin. **CAST:** David Niven, Toshiro Mifune, Ando, Hardy Kruger. **1976**

PAPER WEDDING ★★★1/2 In order to save a political refugee from being deported, a single woman agrees to marry him. But the name-only marriage becomes real when the couple is forced to live together. This strong comedy was made before the similar *Green Card*, and the acting is excellent. Not rated, the film has suggested sex. 95m. **DIR:** Michel Brault. **CAST:** Genevieve Bujold, Manuel Aranguiz, Dorothee Berryman. **1989 DVD**

PAPERBACK ROMANCE ★★★ A young romance writer (Gia Carides) meets a handsome man (Anthony LaPaglia) at the library, but with her leg in a brace from childhood polio, she's too self-conscious to encourage him. When she breaks the afflicted leg, she uses the cast as "cover," never thinking what she'll do when the break heals. Similarly, writer-director Ben Lewin doesn't seem to have thought about how to develop his offbeat premise. On the plus side is the sexy rapport of the two stars (married in real life) and several unexpectedly funny scenes. Originally released in Australia at 94 minutes, with the wittier title *Lucky Break*. Not rated; suitable for mature audiences. 87m. **DIR:** Ben Lewin. **CAST:** Gia Carides, Anthony LaPaglia, Rebecca Gibney, Jacek Koman. **1994**

PAPERBOY, THE ★★1/2 A deranged teenager turns his crush on a neighbor into a murderous rampage. Typical thriller is slightly better if you turn off the sound—Marc Marut (as the paperboy) has a voice that is as caustic as battery acid. Rated R for violence and profanity. 93m. **DIR:** Douglas Jackson. **CAST:** Alexandra Paul, Marc Marut, William Katt, Frances Bay. **1994**

PAPERHOUSE ★★★★ In this original film from England, a lonely, misunderstood 11-year-old girl (Charlotte Burke) begins retreating into a fantasy world. Her world turns nightmarish when it starts to take over her dreams and a flu-like disease keeps making her faint. Visually impressive, well-acted, and intelligent fare. Rated PG-13 for violence. 94m. **DIR:** Bernard Rose. **CAST:** Charlotte Burke, Glenne Headly, Ben Cross. **1989**

PAPILLON ★★★★1/2 Unfairly criticized, this is a truly exceptional film biography of the man who escaped from Devil's Island. Steve McQueen gives an excellent performance, and Dustin Hoffman is once again a chameleon. Director Frank Schaffner invests the same gusto here that he did in *Patton*. Rated PG. 150m. **DIR:** Franklin J. Schaffner. **CAST:** Steve McQueen, Dustin Hoffman, Victor Jory, Don Gordon. **1973 DVD**

PARADE ★★1/2 Sadly, the great comedian Jacques Tati's last film is his least distinguished work. He plays host to a group of circus performers in this semidocumentary that is little more than a footnote in his filmography. In French with English subtitles. 85m. **DIR:** Jacques Tati. **CAST:** Jacques Tati. **1974**

PARADINE CASE, THE ★★ Even the Master of Suspense can't win 'em all. Obviously chafing under the rein of mentor David O. Selznick, Alfred Hitchcock produced one of his few failures—a boring, talky courtroom drama that stalls long before its conclusion. Not rated; suitable for family viewing. B&W; 112m. **DIR:** Alfred Hitchcock. **CAST:** Gregory Peck, Ann Todd, Charles Laughton, Ethel Barrymore, Charles Coburn, Louis Jourdan, Alida Valli, Leo G. Carroll, John Williams. **1947 DVD**

PARADISE (1982) ★★ Willie Aames and Phoebe Cates star as two teenagers who, as members of a caravan traveling from Baghdad to Damascus in the nineteenth century, escape a surprise attack by a sheikh intent on adding Cates to his harem. Rated R for frontal male and female nudity. 100m. **DIR:** Stuart Gillard. **CAST:** Willie Aames, Phoebe Cates, Tuvia Tavi. **1982**

PARADISE (1991) ★★★1/2 When a 10-year-old boy spends the summer with an emotionally estranged couple, they all help each other overcome personal tragedies. This film, adapted from the French *Le Grand Chemin* (*The Grand Highway*), has some very touch-

ing and funny moments. Rated PG-13 for profanity and nudity. 104m. **DIR:** Mary Agnes Donoghue. **CAST:** Don Johnson, Melanie Griffith, Elijah Wood, Thora Birch, Sheila McCarthy, Eve Gordon, Louise Latham. **1991**

PARADISE ALLEY 🦃 Turgid mess about three brothers hoping for a quick ride out of the slums. Rated PG for violence. 107m. **DIR:** Sylvester Stallone. **CAST:** Sylvester Stallone, Armand Assante, Lee Canalito. **1978**

PARADISE HAWAIIAN STYLE ★★1/2 Elvis Presley returns to Hawaii after his 1962 film, *Blue Hawaii*. This time he plays a pilot who makes time for romance while setting up a charter service. Some laughs and lots of songs. 91m. **DIR:** Michael Moore. **CAST:** Elvis Presley, Suzanna Leigh. **1966**

PARADISE LOST: THE CHILD MURDERS AT ROBIN HOOD HILLS ★★★★ First shown on HBO, this is one of the most important documentaries of the 1990s. When three young boys are horribly murdered in a small Tennessee town, the residents immediately suspect three teens who are the local oddballs. Although filmmakers Joe Berlinger and Bruce Sinofsky remain nonjudgmental, their record of the trial offers a devastating indictment of the justice system. Not rated, but not recommended for young children. 150m. **DIR:** Joe Berlinger, Bruce Sinofsky. **1997**

PARADISE MOTEL ★★★ Another teen romp, but with a surprise: the appealing cast can act. Gary Herschberger is a student whose father keeps moving the family around in pursuit of his get-rich schemes. The latest venture is the Paradise Motel. To gain acceptance, Herschberger loans out one of the rooms to the class stud. Rated R for language and nudity. 87m. **DIR:** Cary Medoway. **CAST:** Gary Herschberger, Robert Krantz, Joanna Leigh Stack. **1985**

PARADISE ROAD ★★★1/2 Bruce Beresford's heartfelt account of a little-known chapter in World War II ultimately suffers from being *too* tragic; his film doesn't maintain the dignity—or conclude with the triumph—of Spielberg's *Schindler's List*. His portrayal of British and ANZAC women imprisoned in a Japanese concentration camp does not address the subject with the proper depth. The top-lined stars portray compelling characters, but many of the supporting players and their eventual fates fail to generate the appropriate passion. Rated R for violence, torture, and nudity. 115m. **DIR:** Bruce Beresford. **CAST:** Glenn Close, Pauline Collins, Cate Blanchett, Frances McDormand, Julianna Margulies, Jennifer Ehle. **1997 DVD**

PARALLAX VIEW, THE ★★★★ This fine film offers a fascinating study of a reporter, played by Warren Beatty, trying to penetrate the cover-up of an assassination in which the hunter becomes the hunted. Rated R. 102m. **DIR:** Alan J. Pakula. **CAST:** Warren Beatty, Paula Prentiss, William Daniels. **1974 DVD**

PARALLEL LIVES ★★★1/2 An impressive ensemble cast is the best reason to watch director Linda Yellin's follow-up to *Chantilly Lace*, which employs the same technique of actor improvisation on a sketchy plot. The setting is a multigenerational sorority/fraternity reunion that allows old friends and foes the opportunity for one last encounter. It's great fun until the third act, which is marred by the needless intrusion of a murder investigation. Rated R for profanity and simulated sex. 105m. **DIR:** Linda Yellen. **CAST:** James Belushi, Liza Minnelli, JoBeth Williams, Jill Eikenberry, Gena Rowlands, Ben Gazzara, Ally Sheedy, Helen Slater, LeVar Burton, Treat Williams, Patricia Wettig, Jack Klugman, Paul Sorvino, Lindsay Crouse, James Brolin, Robert Wagner, Dudley Moore. **1994**

PARAMEDICS ★★1/2 A good guys–bad guys flick disguised as a sex comedy. Two paramedics are transferred to a nasty part of the city where a vicious gang is killing people to sell their organs. The comedy comes in the form of a mysterious beauty with a rather fatal sex drive. Rated PG-13 for sexual references. 91m. **DIR:** Stuart Margolin. **CAST:** George Newbern, Christopher McDonald, Lawrence Hilton-Jacobs, John Pleshette, James Noble, John P. Ryan. **1987**

PARANOIA (1969) 🦃 American widow makes the mistake of taking an evil young couple into her isolated villa. Originally rated X for nudity and sexual situations, but a tame R equivalent now. 91m. **DIR:** Umberto Lenzi. **CAST:** Carroll Baker, Lou Castel, Colette Descombes. **1969**

PARANOIA (1998) ★★ In this by-the-numbers thriller, Larry Drake plays Calvin Hawks, incarcerated for sadistically killing a woman's family. Since then she has been a recluse, using her home computer to communicate with the outside world. Then Calvin starts sending threatening E-mails that he's getting out soon. Rated R for violence, language, and adult situations. 86m. **DIR:** Larry Brand. **CAST:** Larry Drake, Brigitte Bako, Sally Kirkland, Scott Valentine, Stephen Gevedon. **1998 DVD**

PARANOIAC ★★1/2 An overwrought Oliver Reed is surprised to see his long-dead brother return to the family mansion. Too much Sturm und Drang weighs down this unwieldly thriller from Hammer Studios. Not rated; contains implied violence. B&W; 80m. **DIR:** Freddie Francis. **CAST:** Oliver Reed, Janette Scott, Alexander Davion, Liliane Brousse, Sheila Burrell, Maurice Denham. **1963**

PARASITE ★★1/2 If director Charles Band intended a film that would sicken its audience, he succeeded. Memorable scenes include parasites bursting through the stomach of one victim and the face of another. Rated R. 85m. **DIR:** Charles Band. **CAST:** Robert Glaudini, Demi Moore, Luca Bercovici, Vivian Blaine, Tom Villard. **1982 DVD**

PARATROOP COMMAND ★★1/2 World War II drama set in North Africa, where a paratrooper tries to make amends after he accidentally shoots a member of his own squadron. Effective action direction lifts this above the pedestrian. B&W; 71m. **DIR:** William Witney. **CAST:** Dick Bakalyan. **1959**

PARDON MON AFFAIRE ★★★★ Enjoyable romantic comedy about a middle-class, happily married man (Jean Rochefort) who pursues his fantasy of meeting a beautiful model (Anny Duperey) and having an affair. Later remade in America as *The Woman in Red*. In French with English subtitles. Rated PG. 105m. **DIR:** Yves Robert. **CAST:** Jean Rochefort, Claude Brasseur, Anny Duperey, Guy Bedos, Victor Lanoux. **1976**

PARDON MON AFFAIRE, TOO! ★★ Lukewarm comedy of infidelity and friendship. The focus is on four middle-aged men who share their troubles and feelings about their marriages and sex lives. No real laughs. In French with English subtitles. 110m. **DIR:** Yves Robert.

CAST: Jean Rochefort, Claude Brasseur, Guy Bedos, Victor Lanoux, Daniele Delorme. **1977**

PARDON MY SARONG ★★★ Two Chicago bus drivers are hired by a playboy to drive him to California, and somehow they end up on his yacht sailing the seas. Good musical interludes (including the Ink Spots) contribute to the success of this early A&C outing. B&W; 83m. **DIR:** Erle C. Kenton. **CAST:** Bud Abbott, Lou Costello, Robert Paige, Virginia Bruce, Lionel Atwill, William Demarest, Samuel S. Hinds. **1942**

PARDON MY TRUNK (HELLO ELEPHANT!) ★★1/2 An Italian schoolteacher (Vittorio De Sica), struggling against poverty does a good deed for a visiting Hindu prince. In gratitude, the Indian sends him a gift: a baby elephant. De Sica's performance elevates what otherwise would have been merely a silly slapstick exercise. Dubbed in English. B&W; 85m. **DIR:** Gianni Franciolini. **CAST:** Vittorio De Sica, Maria Mereader, Sabu, Nando Bruno. **1952**

PARDON US ★★★★ Stan Laurel and Oliver Hardy are sent to prison for selling home-brewed beer. They encounter all the usual prison stereotypical characters and play off them to delightful comedy effect. During an escape, they put on black faces and pick cotton along with blacks and Ollie sings "Lazy Moon." B&W; 55m. **DIR:** James Parrott. **CAST:** Stan Laurel, Oliver Hardy, Wilfred Lucas. **1931**

PARENT TRAP, THE (1961) ★★★★ Walt Disney doubled the fun in this comedy when he had Hayley Mills play twins. Mills plays sisters who meet for the first time at camp and decide to reunite their divorced parents (Brian Keith and Maureen O'Hara). 124m. **DIR:** David Swift. **CAST:** Hayley Mills, Brian Keith, Maureen O'Hara, Joanna Barnes. **1961**

PARENT TRAP, THE (1998) ★★★1/2 Although formulaic, at times uneven, and needlessly slapstick during the introductory scenes, this update of Disney's 1961 film grows on you. Like its new young star, Lindsay Lohan, this film wins over its audience through charm and personality. Lohan plays twins separated shortly after birth, and raised by divorced parents who never really fell out of love with each other. Once reunited at a summer camp, the girls scheme to bring their folks back together, a plan given extra urgency because Dad has been targeted by a money-hungry shark in Cute Young Thing's clothing. Nothing new here, but the result is certain to please all ages. Rated PG for no particular reason. 124m. **DIR:** Nancy Meyers. **CAST:** Dennis Quaid, Natasha Richardson, Lindsay Lohan, Elaine Hendrix, Lisa Ann Walter, Simon Kunz. **1998 DVD**

PARENTHOOD ★★★★★ In this heartwarming comedy, Steve Martin and Mary Steenburgen are superb as model parents coping with career and kids. There's fine support from Rick Moranis as a yuppie who pushes his 3-year-old daughter to learn Kafka and karate, Dianne Wiest as a Woodstock-goer coping with three troubled teens, and Jason Robards as the granddad who discovers that parenthood is a job for life. Rated PG-13 for profanity and sexual themes. 110m. **DIR:** Ron Howard. **CAST:** Steve Martin, Mary Steenburgen, Tom Hulce, Jason Robards Jr., Dianne Wiest, Rick Moranis, Martha Plimpton, Keanu Reeves. **1989 DVD**

PARENTS 🦃 Black comedy about a cannibalistic couple and their relationship with their suspicious young son. Rated R. 90m. **DIR:** Bob Balaban. **CAST:** Randy Quaid, Mary Beth Hurt, Sandy Dennis, Bryan Madorsky. **1989 DVD**

PARIAH ★★ When his African-American girlfriend is raped and driven to suicide by skinheads, a young man infiltrates the gang that did it; soon he finds himself adopting their twisted outlook on life. At least that seems to be writer-director Randolph Kret's intention, but the script lacks definition, the pacing is sluggish, and acting is amateurish. Not rated; contains profanity (including racial slurs), violence, nudity, and sexual scenes. 105m. **DIR:** Randolph Kret. **CAST:** Damon Jones, Dave Oren Ward, David Lee Wilson, Aimee Chaffin. **1998**

PARIS BELONGS TO US ★★ The first film directed by Jacques Rivette and the first feature-length release in the French new wave. Quite a *cause célèbre* in 1957, it stands as a testament to the initial, highly self-conscious experimentations of the generation. The incomprehensible plot seems to be the story of a young actress who becomes involved in a murderous intrigue hatched by an American novelist. In French with English subtitles. B&W; 135m. **DIR:** Jacques Rivette. **CAST:** Betty Schneider, Daniel Crohem, Jean-Claude Brialy. **1957**

PARIS BLUES ★★★1/2 Duke Ellington's superb jazz score enhances this drama. The action takes place in Paris where two jazz musicians (Paul Newman and Sidney Poitier) fall for two lovely tourists (Joanne Woodward and Diahann Carroll). What the plot lacks in originality is amply made up for by the fine music and outstanding cast. 98m. **DIR:** Martin Ritt. **CAST:** Paul Newman, Joanne Woodward, Diahann Carroll, Sidney Poitier, Louis Armstrong, Serge Reggiani. **1961**

PARIS EXPRESS, THE ★★1/2 Based on acclaimed mystery writer Georges Simenon's novel, this film details the exploits of a finance clerk (Claude Rains) who turns embezzler. Hoping to travel the world with his ill-gotten gains, he runs into more trouble and adventure than he can handle. 80m. **DIR:** Harold French. **CAST:** Claude Rains, Marta Toren, Anouk Aimée, Marius Goring, Herbert Lom. **1953**

PARIS FRANCE ★★★1/2 Unadulterated kink is the highlight of this nonflinching dark comedy about one woman's quest for sexual fulfillment. When her husband fails to satisfy her, Lucy, played by the alluring Leslie Hope, turns to a young stranger to punch her buttons. Their sexual escapades escalate until they explode in a very unconventional finale. Rated NC-17 for nudity, sexual situations, and adult language. 96m. **DIR:** Gerard Ciccoritti. **CAST:** Leslie Hope, Victor Ertmanis. **1993**

PARIS HOLIDAY ★★ Film-within-a-film show business story featuring Bob Hope and French comic Fernandel never gets off the ground. Statuesque Anita Ekberg succeeds in diverting attention from the two uncomfortable comedians. 101m. **DIR:** Gerd Oswald. **CAST:** Bob Hope, Fernandel, Anita Ekberg, Martha Hyer, Preston Sturges. **1957**

PARIS IS BURNING ★★★★ This superb documentary takes us through the public and private domain of poor black and Hispanic gays in New York City who vamp at lavish balls. At these events, participants imitate fashion models, Marines, Wall Street brokers, and other figures culled from magazine advertisements. Rated R for some nudity. 78m. **DIR:** Jennie Livingston. **1990**

PARIS, TEXAS ★★★★1/2 *Paris, Texas* is a haunting vision of personal pain and universal suffering, with Harry Dean Stanton impeccable as the weary wanderer who returns after four years to reclaim his son (Hunter Carson) and search for his wife (Nastassja Kinski). It is the kind of motion picture we rarely see, one that attempts to say something about our country and its people—and succeeds. Rated R for profanity and adult content. 144m. **DIR:** Wim Wenders. **CAST:** Harry Dean Stanton, Nastassja Kinski, Dean Stockwell, Aurore Clement, Hunter Carson. **1984**

PARIS TROUT ★★1/2 Pete Dexter's bleak take on 1949 Georgia gets first-cabin treatment but remains as inexplicably pointless as his novel. Dennis Hopper stars as the titular character, a venal and paranoid storekeeper who shoots and kills a young black girl and then dismisses the act as "nothing scandalous." Made-for-cable drama includes shocking violence and coarse language. 100m. **DIR:** Stephen Gyllenhaal. **CAST:** Dennis Hopper, Barbara Hershey, Ed Harris. **1991**

PARIS WAS A WOMAN ★★★ The community of women artists, writers, and intellectuals who took up residence in Paris's Left Bank in the 1920s is a fascinating subject. Unfortunately, this documentary is hampered by a lack of film footage of its subjects, resulting in too many talking heads and too much attention paid to lesser lights simply because there was footage of them available. You'd be better off reading a book on the subject. Not rated. 75m. **DIR:** Greta Schiller. **1996**

PARIS WHEN IT SIZZLES ★★★ Uneven story-within-a-story about a screenwriter (William Holden) who "creates" a Parisian fantasyland for himself and the assistant (Audrey Hepburn) with whom he's fallen in love. As the story progresses, they—and the viewer—have an increasingly difficult time distinguishing fact from scripted fiction. 110m. **DIR:** Richard Quine. **CAST:** William Holden, Audrey Hepburn, Noel Coward, Gregoire Aslan, Marlene Dietrich. **1954**

PARK IS MINE, THE ★★1/2 After his friend is killed, unstable Vietnam vet (Tommy Lee Jones) invades New York's Central Park and proclaims it to be his. Predictable ending. Pretty farfetched stuff. An HBO Film. 102m. **DIR:** Steven H. Stern. **CAST:** Tommy Lee Jones, Helen Shaver, Yaphet Kotto. **1985**

PARKER ADDERSON, PHILOSOPHER ★★★★ Man's ability to inflict torment even on those with nothing left to lose is the theme of this deft adaptation of the Ambrose Bierce short story. Harris Yulin stars as a Yankee spy caught red-handed by the ragtag troops of Douglas Watson's Confederate general. Introduced by Henry Fonda; suitable for family viewing. 39m. **DIR:** Arthur Barron. **CAST:** Harris Yulin, Douglas Watson, Darren O'Connor. **1974**

PARLOR, BEDROOM AND BATH ★★★ Some genuine belly laughs buoy this slight comedy about a bewildered bumpkin (Buster Keaton) at the mercy of some society wackos. Charlotte Greenwood works well with the Great Stone Face. B&W; 75m. **DIR:** Edward Sedgwick. **CAST:** Buster Keaton, Charlotte Greenwood, Reginald Denny, Cliff Edwards, Dorothy Christy, Joan Peers, Sally Eilers, Natalie Moorhead, Edward Brophy. **1932**

PARRISH ★★ Lust among the young and greed among the old in the tobacco fields of Connecticut. Karl Malden saves this. 140m. **DIR:** Delmer Daves. **CAST:** Troy Donahue, Claudette Colbert, Karl Malden, Dean Jagger, Connie Stevens, Diane McBain, Dub Taylor. **1961**

PARTING GLANCES ★★★★ Nick (Steve Buscemi), a rock singer, discovers he is dying of AIDS. Writer-director Bill Sherwood charts the effect this discovery has on Nick and his estranged lover, Michael (Richard Ganoung), who now lives with Robert (John Bolger). Subject matter aside, *Parting Glances* has a number of funny moments and is a life-affirming look at the gay lifestyle. 90m. **DIR:** Bill Sherwood. **CAST:** Richard Ganoung, John Bolger, Steve Buscemi, Adam Nathan, Kathy Kinney, Patrick Tull. **1986**

PARTNER ★★★ Bernardo Bertolucci apes Godard with less than optimal results in this story of a shy youth who creates an alternative self that possesses the qualities he lacks. Occasionally incoherent. In Italian and French with English subtitles. Not rated. 112m. **DIR:** Bernardo Bertolucci. **CAST:** Pierre Clementi, Tina Aumont, Stefania Sandrelli. **1968**

PARTNERS (1982) ★★★ Ryan O'Neal and John Hurt are two undercover detectives assigned to pose as lovers in order to track down the murderer of a gay man in this warm, funny, and suspenseful comedy-drama written by Francis Veber (*La Cage aux Folles*). Rated R for nudity, profanity, violence, and adult themes. 98m. **DIR:** James Burrows. **CAST:** Ryan O'Neal, John Hurt. **1982**

•PARTNERS (2000) ★★1/2 A computer programmer steals his company's next big program in an attempt to sell it to the highest bidder. When a street-smart drifter enters the picture, the programmer reluctantly realizes—like it or not—he's got a new partner in crime. Not bad little road-type movie benefits from another fine performance by David Paymer and an above-average performance from Casper Van Dien. Rated R for profanity and violence. 93m. **DIR:** Joey Travolta. **CAST:** Casper Van Dien, Vanessa Angel, David Paymer. **2000 DVD**

PARTNERS IN CRIME A disgraced ex-policeman turned private detective must turn to his ex-wife, a beautiful FBI agent, to help exonerate him from a kidnapping and murder rap. If you can believe former model Paulina Porizkova as the FBI agent, you might buy the rest of this claptrap. Rated R for adult situations, language, and violence. 90m. **DIR:** Jennifer Warren. **CAST:** Rutger Hauer, Paulina Porizkova, Andrew Dolan, Frank Gerrish. **2000 DVD**

PARTNERS IN CRIME (SECRET ADVERSARY) (TV SERIES) ★★★1/2 Agatha Christie's high-society private detectives, Tommy and Tuppence, are introduced in the feature-length WWI-era tale, *The Secret Adversary*; lacking personal finances or steady jobs after having left war service, they advertise their services as amateur sleuths. Series highlights include "Finessing the King," where sharp-eyed viewers will find all the clues necessary to match wits with the detectives; "The Affair of the Pink Pearl," in which their "guaranteed twenty-four-hour-service" is put to the test; and "The Case of the Missihg Lady," where Tuppence's attempts to work undercover become particularly amusing. 51m. **DIR:** Paul Annett, Christopher Hodson, Tony Wharmby. **CAST:** Francesca Annis, James Warwick, Reece Dinsdale. **1982–1983 DVD**

PARTY, THE ★★★ The closest Peter Sellers ever came to doing a one-man show on film. He plays an actor from India who mistakenly gets invited to a plush Hollywood party, where he falls all over himself and causes more mishaps and pratfalls than the Three Stooges. 99m. **DIR:** Blake Edwards. **CAST:** Peter Sellers, Claudine Longet, Denny Miller, Marge Champion, Gavin MacLeod. **1968**

PARTY CAMP ★★ Andrew Ross takes a job as a camp counselor with the object of turning the militarylike operation into party time for all. Just another teen romp with the usual caricatures, obligatory nudity, and titillation. Rated R. 96m. **DIR:** Gary Graver. **CAST:** Andrew Ross, Kerry Brennan, Peter Jason. **1986**

PARTY GIRL (1958) ★★★1/2 Crime-drama with lawyer Robert Taylor as a cunning mouthpiece for the mob in 1930s Chicago. All hell breaks loose when he decides to go legit. Familiar, but well-produced. 99m. **DIR:** Nicholas Ray. **CAST:** Robert Taylor, Cyd Charisse, Lee J. Cobb, John Ireland, Kent Smith. **1958**

PARTY GIRL (1995) ★★★ A painfully hip New York scenester discovers that her real purpose in life is to become a librarian. Sassy star Parker Posey's irrepressible sardonic charm triumphs over the precious concept and sometimes amateurish staging. Rated R for language, drug use, sex, and brief nudity. 98m. **DIR:** Daisy von Scherler Mayer. **CAST:** Parker Posey, Omar Townsend, Sasha von Scherler, Guillermo Diaz. **1995**

PARTY LINE 🦃 Disconnected nonsense about telephone party-line callers who turn up dead. Rated R for violence, profanity, and nudity. 91m. **DIR:** William Webb. **CAST:** Richard Hatch, Leif Garrett, Richard Roundtree. **1988**

PASCALI'S ISLAND ★★★★ A quietly enigmatic film about town loyalties, hypocrisy, and broader philosophical issues of art and romanticism, as represented by three characters on a Greek island in 1908. Ben Kingsley is brilliant as a low-level bureaucrat and semispy who will never challenge what he does or why, even when it threatens to destroy everything he cares about. Rated PG-13. 101m. **DIR:** James Dearden. **CAST:** Ben Kingsley, Helen Mirren, Charles Dance. **1988**

PASS THE AMMO ★★★1/2 Tim Curry's deliciously scheming evangelist is merely one of the delights in this inventive satire of television sermonizing. Bill Paxton and Linda Kozlowski play a couple of good ol' folks who plot to "steal back" some inheritance money the televangelist bilked from her family. Rated PG-13 for language and violence. 93m. **DIR:** David Beaird. **CAST:** Tim Curry, Bill Paxton, Linda Kozlowski, Annie Potts, Glenn Withrow, Dennis Burkley. **1987**

PASSAGE TO INDIA, A ★★★★★ After an absence from the screen of fourteen years, British director David Lean returned triumphantly, with the brilliant *A Passage to India*. Based on the 1924 novel by E. M. Forster, this brilliant screen adaptation compares favorably with David Lean's finest films. Ostensibly about the romantic adventures of a young Englishwoman in "the mysterious East" that culminate in a court trial (for attempted rape), it is also a multilayered, symbolic work about "the difficulty of living in the universe." Rated PG. 163m. **DIR:** David Lean. **CAST:** Judy Davis, Victor Banerjee, Alec Guinness, Peggy Ashcroft. **1984 DVD**

PASSAGE TO MARSEILLES ★★★ The performances of Humphrey Bogart, Claude Rains, Sydney Greenstreet, and Peter Lorre are all that's good about this muddled film about an escape from Devil's Island during World War II. Directed by Michael Curtiz, its flashback-within-flashback scenes all but totally confuse the viewer. B&W; 110m. **DIR:** Michael Curtiz. **CAST:** Humphrey Bogart, Claude Rains, Sydney Greenstreet, Peter Lorre. **1944**

PASSED AWAY ★★★ In this black comedy written and directed by Charlie Peters, members of an Irish family must set aside differences when the 70-year-old patriarch (Jack Warden) dies unexpectedly. The performances by a terrific cast of character actors make this movie worth seeing. Rated PG-13 for profanity. 96m. **DIR:** Charlie Peters. **CAST:** Bob Hoskins, Blair Brown, Tim Curry, Frances McDormand, William L. Petersen, Pamela Reed, Peter Riegert, Maureen Stapleton, Nancy Travis, Jack Warden. **1992**

PASSENGER, THE (1963) ★★★1/2 A chance meeting between two women—one a former guard at Auschwitz, the other one of her prisoners—triggers painful, unresolved memories of the Holocaust. Director Andrej Munk was killed in an auto accident before he could finish this film; the footage was assembled by a colleague who used still photos to approximate the rest of it. Had it been completed, it likely would have been a masterpiece. What is here is a mesmerizing (albeit frustrating) work. In Polish with English subtitles. Not rated; contains violence, adult situations, and nudity. B&W; 63m. **DIR:** Andrej Munk. **CAST:** Aleksandra Slaska, Anna Ciepielewska, Marek Walczewski. **1963**

PASSENGER, THE (1975) ★★ Billed as a suspense-drama, this is a very slow-moving tale about a disillusioned TV reporter (Jack Nicholson) working in Africa. He becomes involved with arms smugglers. Rated R. 119m. **DIR:** Michelangelo Antonioni. **CAST:** Jack Nicholson, Maria Schneider, Jenny Runacre, Ian Hendry. **1975**

PASSENGER 57 ★★★★1/2 Slam-bang action film is an airborne variation on *Die Hard*. This time, the hero is an airline security expert who is caught on a plane skyjacked by terrorists. Featuring a strong lead performance by Wesley Snipes, this little gem is so exciting, funny, suspenseful, and packed with great bits that you don't dare take your eyes off the screen for a second. Rated R for violence and profanity. 85m. **DIR:** Kevin Hooks. **CAST:** Wesley Snipes, Bruce Payne, Tom Sizemore, Bruce Greenwood, Robert Hooks, Michael Horse. **1992 DVD**

PASSING GLORY ★★★★ Andre Braugher shines as an activist priest in this uplifting tale, set in Louisiana circa 1965, which concerns efforts to integrate the local high-school basketball league. Our central character—who teaches history but is pressed to become a basketball coach—shares the frustration of his players, who believe that white teams don't deserve "bragging rights" until they've played *all* local challengers. The ensemble cast delivers the goods in this exciting underdog tale. Rated PG for mild profanity. 95m. **DIR:** Steve James. **CAST:** Andre Braugher, Rip Torn, Ruby Dee, Sean Squire, Bill Nunn. **1999**

PASSION (1919) ★★★ Combining realism with spectacle, this account of famous eighteenth-century French courtesan Madame Du Barry was the first Ger-

man film to earn international acclaim after World War I. As a result, the director and the stars received Hollywood contracts. The film is still recognized as the best of seven made about the subject between 1915 and 1954. Silent. B&W; 134m. **DIR:** Ernst Lubitsch. **CAST:** Pola Negri, Emil Jannings. **1919**

PASSION (1954) ★★ Colorful hokum about a hot-blooded adventurer (Cornel Wilde) and his quest for vengeance in old California. Directed by veteran filmmaker Allan Dwan, this okay adventure boasts a nice cast of character actors. 84m. **DIR:** Allan Dwan. **CAST:** Cornel Wilde, Yvonne De Carlo, Raymond Burr, Lon Chaney Jr., John Qualen. **1954**

PASSION FISH ★★★★★ This superb character study focuses on a soap-opera actress who is left paralyzed after being hit by a cab in New York City. Embittered, she returns to her childhood home in the Louisiana swamplands where a succession of live-in nurses leads to friendship between two emotionally scarred and scared women. David Strathairn adds heart to this touching, but unsentimental story. Rated R for profanity. 134m. **DIR:** John Sayles. **CAST:** Mary McDonnell, Alfre Woodard, David Strathairn, Vondie Curtis-Hall, Angela Bassett, Maggie Renzi. **1992 DVD**

PASSION FLOWER ★★1/2 In Singapore, a young playboy banker gets tangled up with the married daughter of a prominent financial figure in the British and American business community. Nicol Williamson is dandy as a sadistic and manipulative father who has his daughter's lover right where he wants him. This made-for-television movie contains mild profanity. 95m. **DIR:** Joseph Sargent. **CAST:** Bruce Boxleitner, Barbara Hershey, Nicol Williamson. **1985**

PASSION FOR LIFE ★★★ An enthusiastic young teacher in a provincial school fights resistance from parents and his fellow teachers to introduce more effective new methods. Unsurprising but effective drama. In French with English subtitles. B&W; 89m. **DIR:** Jean-Paul Le Chanois. **CAST:** Bernard Blier, Juliette Faber. **1949**

PASSION IN THE DESERT ★★★ Earnest, somewhat insane study of a Napoleonic soldier who, lost in the Egyptian desert, has a meaningful relationship with a leopard. Something about man's capacity for animalistic behavior is being explored here, and the big cat is a magnficent beast. But for all its heartfelt love of nature, this movie offers too many scenes that dare you not to laugh at them. Based on a Balzac short story. Rated PG-13 for nudity and violence. 93m. **DIR:** Lavinia Currier. **CAST:** Ben Daniels, Michel Piccoli. **1998**

PASSION OF ANNA, THE ★★★★1/2 One of Ingmar Bergman's greatest works is also one of his bleakest; an unflinching look into man's capacity for self-destruction. Four people are thrown together on an isolated island. Their interactions reveal their needs and insecurities, as well as the defenses they have developed. Bergman distances viewers from the film just as the characters try to distance themselves from others. In Swedish with English subtitles. Not rated. 101m. **DIR:** Ingmar Bergman. **CAST:** Liv Ullmann, Bibi Andersson, Max von Sydow, Erland Josephson. **1969**

PASSION OF AYN RAND, THE ★★1/2 This pretentious claptrap, clearly a view of Ayn Rand as seen by fatuous admirers, does little but dishonor the memory and career of a progressive social thinker who may well have been the manipulative shrew Helen Mirren makes her here, but who nonetheless deserves better. Scripters Howard Korder and Mary Gallagher, working from Barbara Branden's book, have fashioned a tedious, talky drama in which condescending characters play at being holier-than-thou while justifying their own selfishness and lust. The result is tiresome, boring, and intellectually dishonest. Rated R for profanity, nudity, and simulated sex. 104m. **DIR:** Chris Menaul. **CAST:** Helen Mirren, Eric Stoltz, Julie Delpy, Peter Fonda, Sybil Temchen, Tom McCamus. **1998 DVD**

PASSION OF DARKLY NOON, THE ★★★ Darkly Noon, the only survivor of a religious community, is taken in by a free-spirited woman who lives in a secluded forest house. Unable to deal with his repressed sexuality, he approaches madness when his hostess's absent lover returns. Rated R for graphic violence, nudity, and sexual situations. 106m. **DIR:** Philip Ridley. **CAST:** Brendan Fraser, Ashley Judd, Viggo Mortensen, Loren Dean, Grace Zabriskie. **1995**

PASSION OF JOAN OF ARC, THE ★★★★★ This is simply one of the greatest films ever made. Its emotional intensity is unsurpassed. Faces tell the tale of this movie. Maria Falconetti's Joan is unforgettable. Silent. B&W; 114m. **DIR:** Carl Dreyer. **CAST:** Maria Falconetti, Eugene Silvain, Antonin Artaud. **1928 DVD**

PASSION OF LOVE ★★★★ In 1862 Italy just after the war, a decorated captain (Bernard Giraudeau) is transferred to a faraway outpost, where he becomes the love object of his commander's cousin (Valeria D'Obici). What follows is a fascinating study of torment. Dubbed in English. Not rated. 117m. **DIR:** Ettore Scola. **CAST:** Valeria D'Obici, Bernard Giraudeau, Laura Antonelli, Bernard Blier, Jean-Louis Trintignant, Massimo Girotti. **1982**

PASSION OF MIND ★★1/2 A widowed mother of two (Demi Moore) living in France dreams at night that she's an unattached, high-powered New York literary agent—or is it the other way around, a lonely agent dreams she lives in France with her kids? The mystery dissipates quickly as Moore's two lives grow redundant. On the plus side are good performances by a strong cast and beautiful cinematography, especially in the French half of the heroine's double life. Rated PG-13 for sexual scenes. 105m. **DIR:** Alain Berliner. **CAST:** Demi Moore, Stellan Skarsgard, William Fichtner, Sinead Cusack, Peter Riegert. **2000 DVD**

PASSION TO KILL, A ★★★ Erotic thriller about a psychiatrist (Scott Bakula) who succumbs to the temptations of his best friend's wife. They keep the tryst a secret, which works to their advantage when the husband ends up dead. Now Bakula must discern whether he's making love to a murderer or not. Nice plot twist at the end. Rated R for nudity, violence, adult situations, and language. 93m. **DIR:** Rick King. **CAST:** Scott Bakula, Chelsea Field, Sheila Kelly, John Getz, Rex Smith. **1993**

PASSIONATE THIEF, THE ★ This less-than-hilarious Italian comedy is poorly dubbed. Ben Gazzara plays a thief at a New Year's Eve party. His suave attempts at removing the jewels are thwarted when Anna Magnani shows up and decides that he's interested in her. Monotonous. B&W; 100m. **DIR:** Mario Monicelli. **CAST:** Ben

Gazzara, Anna Magnani, Toto, Fred Clark, Edy Vessel. **1961**

PASSPORT TO PIMLICO ★★★1/2 One of a number of first-rate comedies turned out by Britain in the wake of World War II. A salty group of characters form their own self-governing enclave smack in the middle of London. Sly Margaret Rutherford and Stanley Holloway divide comedy chores with cricket-crazy Basil Radford and Naunton Wayne. B&W; 85m. **DIR:** Henry Cornelius. **CAST:** Margaret Rutherford, Stanley Holloway, Hermione Baddeley, Basil Radford, Naunton Wayne. **1948**

PAST MIDNIGHT ★★★ Rutger Hauer stars as a parolee trying to get a new start after serving fifteen years in prison. Natasha Richardson is the social worker assigned to ease him back into society. But someone doesn't want Hauer free and starts terrorizing Richardson. Fine performances by Hauer and Richardson keep your attention away from the overworked plot. Rated R for nudity, violence, and profanity. 100m. **DIR:** Jan Eliasberg. **CAST:** Rutger Hauer, Natasha Richardson, Clancy Brown, Guy Boyd. **1991**

PAST PERFECT ★★1/2 Intriguing philosophical questions get lost amid the sloppy scripting and truly ludicrous violence of this science-fiction thriller, which concerns agents from the future who return to our present, assigned to kill young thugs before they blossom into multiple murderers. Even undiscriminating viewers will be bothered by the countless time-travel paradoxes. Rated R for violence, profanity, and drug use. 92m. **DIR:** Jonathan Heap. **CAST:** Eric Roberts, Nick Mancuso, Saul Rubinek, Laurie Holden, Mark Hildreth. **1996**

PAST TENSE ★★★★ High marks to this inventive thriller, where nothing is quite what it seems. During evenings, a would-be novelist hatches complicated plots over his typewriter; by day, he's a methodical police detective. His intriguing fantasies mimic his own personal experiences, but with endless twists . . . and always involving his enigmatic neighbor. Rated R for violence, nudity, profanity, and simulated sex. 91m. **DIR:** Graeme Clifford. **CAST:** Scott Glenn, Anthony LaPaglia, Lara Flynn Boyle, David Ogden Stiers. **1994**

PAST THE BLEACHERS ★★★1/2 Moving story of a father who has just lost his son. Richard Dean Anderson stars as Bill Parish, who coaches a Little League baseball team to help ease his pain. When Parish meets a boy with natural talent, he takes him under his wing. Eventually Parish finds it in himself to open up again. This made-for-television drama punches the right buttons. Rated PG. 120m. **DIR:** Michael Switzer. **CAST:** Richard Dean Anderson, Barnard Hughes, Grayson Fricke, Glynnis O'Connor. **1995**

PASTIME ★★★★ Wonderfully entertaining film deals with a minor-league relief pitcher in the twilight of his career and his relationship with a shy rookie pitcher who appears to have the stuff to make the big leagues. William Russ gives a beautiful performance as the aging pitcher. Rated PG. 91m. **DIR:** Robin B. Armstrong. **CAST:** William Russ, Glenn Plummer, Noble Willingham, Jeffrey Tambor, Scott Plank, Deirdre O'Connell. **1991**

PAT AND MIKE ★★★ Cameo appearances by a host of tennis and golf greats, including Babe Didrikson and Don Budge, stud this five-iron tale of athlete Katharine Hepburn and promoter-manager Spencer Tracy at odds with each other on a barnstorming golf and tennis tour. As always, the Tracy and Hepburn chemistry assures good comedy. B&W; 95m. **DIR:** George Cukor. **CAST:** Spencer Tracy, Katharine Hepburn, Aldo Ray, William Ching. **1952**

PAT GARRETT AND BILLY THE KID ★★★★1/2 Sam Peckinpah's last masterpiece—in this "Restored Director's Cut"—begins with a stunning, never-before-seen ten-minute credit sequence that finally puts the film in focus. Other restored sequences make sense of what happens later between the main characters, Pat Garrett and Billy, and feature a who's who of character actors doing what they do best. Rated R for violence, nudity, and profanity. 122m. **DIR:** Sam Peckinpah. **CAST:** James Coburn, Kris Kristofferson, Bob Dylan, Jason Robards Jr., Barry Sullivan, John Beck, Chill Wills, Slim Pickens, Katy Jurado, Harry Dean Stanton, Jack Elam, Luke Askew, Richard Bright, R. G. Armstrong, Matt Clark, Elisha Cook Jr., Dub Taylor. **1973**

PATCH ADAMS ★★★ Although amiable and competent, this fact-based drama also is two-dimensional and predictable. Hunter "Patch" Adams is a doctor and audacious rebel with a clown's gift for raising smiles who routinely challenges the conventional wisdom of the established medical hierarchy. The choice of Robin Williams in the title role is indicative of the film's greater problems: Everything is superficial and simplistic, up to and including a performance that Williams has . . . um . . . patched together from pictures such as *Good Morning, Vietnam* and *Dead Poets Society*. You'll laugh a little and shed a tear or two, but not for a moment will you believe that this is anything but a fairy tale. Rated PG-13 for profanity. 120m. **DIR:** Tom Shadyac. **CAST:** Robin Williams, Monica Potter, Daniel London, Philip Seymour Hoffman, Bob Gunton. **1998 DVD**

PATCH OF BLUE, A ★★★1/2 A blind white girl who does not know her compassionate boyfriend is black, and her overprotective mother, are deftly brought together in this corn-filled but touching story. Shelley Winters as the mother won her second Oscar. B&W; 105m. **DIR:** Guy Green. **CAST:** Sidney Poitier, Elizabeth Hartman, Shelley Winters, Wallace Ford, Ivan Dixon. **1965**

PATCHWORK GIRL OF OZ, THE ★★★ One of the many sequels to L. Frank Baum's now-classic fantasy story, this film version tells the story of a poor Munchkin boy's adventures en route to Oz's Emerald City. The Patchwork Girl is just one of many strange and wonderful characters encountered. Silent, with musical score. B&W; 81m. **DIR:** J. Farrell McDonald. **1914**

PATERNITY ★★1/2 Buddy Evans (Burt Reynolds) decides to have a son—without the commitment of marriage—and recruits a music student working as a waitress (Beverly D'Angelo) to bear his child in this adult comedy. The first two-thirds provide belly laughs and chuckles. The problem comes with the unoriginal and predictable romantic ending. Rated PG because of dialogue involving sex and childbirth. 94m. **DIR:** David Steinberg. **CAST:** Burt Reynolds, Beverly D'Angelo, Norman Fell, Elizabeth Ashley, Lauren Hutton. **1981**

PATH TO PARADISE ★★★ The events leading to the World Trade Center bombing are detailed in this docu-

drama, which purports to demonstrate just how naïve Americans are and how easy it is to invade the United States. Arty camerawork and cinema verité stylings distract from the fascinating story. The final message is that we got off lucky that time and shouldn't expect the next terrorists to be so stupid. Rated R for violence and profanity. 91m. **DIR:** Leslie Libman, Larry Williams. **CAST:** Peter Gallagher, Art Malik, Ned Eisenberg, Marcia Gay Harden, Andreas Katsulas, Jeffrey DeMunn. **1997**

PATHER PANCHALI ★★★★ The first part of Satyajit Ray's *Apu* trilogy shows Apu's boyhood in an impoverished Bengal village after his father is forced to leave the family in order to seek work. Ray, who had no experience in filmmaking when he began, commands your attention with a lack of cinematic trickery, telling a universal story with a pure and unaffected style. The trilogy also includes *Aparajito* and *The World of Apu*. In Bengali with English subtitles. 112m. **DIR:** Satyajit Ray. **CAST:** Subir Banerji, Karuna Banerji. **1954**

PATHFINDER (1987) ★★★1/2 Brutal film about peaceful tribesmen being ruthlessly slaughtered by a savage group of scavengers. Action takes place in icy Norway with a treacherous chase through snow-covered mountains. In Lapp with English subtitles. Not rated, contains violence and nudity. 88m. **DIR:** Nils Gaup. **CAST:** Mikkel Gaup. **1987**

PATHFINDER, THE (1996) ★★ A gorgeously lensed, but spiritually empty, adaptation of James Fenimore Cooper's classic. The restored ships and forts give the production a sanitized luster wholly at odds with the gritty adventure yarn. Add phony French accents and "Native Americans" apparently recruited from Venice Beach, and the result is often unintentionally funny. Rated PG for mild violence. 105m. **DIR:** Donald Shebib. **CAST:** Kevin Dillon, Graham Greene, Laurie Holden, Jaimz Woolvett, Michael Hogan, Russell Means, Stacy Keach. **1996**

PATHS OF GLORY ★★★★★ A great antiwar movie! Kirk Douglas plays the compassionate French officer in World War I who must lead his men against insurmountable enemy positions, and then must defend three of them against charges of cowardice when the battle is lost. Adolphe Menjou and George Macready perfectly portray Douglas's monstrous senior officers. B&W; 86m. **DIR:** Stanley Kubrick. **CAST:** Kirk Douglas, Adolphe Menjou, George Macready, Timothy Carey, Ralph Meeker. **1957 DVD**

PATLABOR: THE MOBILE POLICE ★★★1/2 In a future metropolis where "labors" are giant robots designed for heavy construction use, the police have their hands full investigating a seemingly random plague of malfunctions that send the normally compliant machines into destructive rampages. Tasty animation combined with a nice science-fiction mystery. In Japanese with English subtitles. Not rated; contains profanity. 98m. **DIR:** Mamoru Oshii. **1989**

PATRICK ★★1/2 This film revolves around Patrick, who has been in a coma for four years. He is confined to a hospital, but after a new nurse comes to work on his floor he begins to exhibit psychic powers. Some violence, but nothing extremely bloody. Rated PG. 96m. **DIR:** Richard Franklin. **CAST:** Susan Penhaligon, Robert Helpmann. **1979**

PATRIOT (1986) 🦃 Underwater commandos fight terrorists. Rated R for nudity and violence. 90m. **DIR:** Frank Harris. **CAST:** Gregg Henry, Simone Griffeth, Michael J. Pollard, Jeff Conaway, Stack Pierce, Leslie Nielsen. **1986**

PATRIOT, THE (1998) ★★ Give Steven Seagal credit for caring about the environment and his country, but when will he learn that preaching doesn't make for very palatable entertainment? This time, he's a scientific genius (!) who must kick some butt as he struggles to find a cure for a lethal virus spread by a white supremacist. Only for die-hard fans of the star, although it does feature a nice turn by stalwart character actor L. Q. Jones. Rated R for violence. 90m. **DIR:** Dean Semler. **CAST:** Steven Seagal, Gailard Sartain, L. Q. Jones, Silas Weir Mitchell, Camilla Belle, Dan Beene, Damon Collazo, Whitney Yellow Robe. **1998 DVD**

PATRIOT, THE (2000) ★★1/2 A South Carolina planter (Mel Gibson) joins the American Revolution to avenge the murder of his son at the hands of a British officer. Robert Rodat's script falsifies everything about the period, from the behavior of the British to the status of slaves, and is shamelessly manipulative—there's no one the film won't kill to get us worked up. Director Roland Emmerich plays the melodrama for all it's worth, but he leans too heavily on Caleb Deschanel's beautiful cinematography and John Williams's bombastic music to sustain our interest throughout the lengthy film. Rated R for violence. 137m. **DIR:** Roland Emmerich. **CAST:** Mel Gibson, Heath Ledger, Chris Cooper, Jason Isaacs, Joely Richardson. **2000 DVD**

PATRIOT GAMES ★★★★1/2 First-rate suspense-thriller has Harrison Ford taking over the role of novelist Tom Clancy's CIA analyst Jack Ryan from Alec Baldwin, who played the character in *The Hunt for Red October*. This time Ryan must save his wife and daughter from renegade Irish terrorists. Taut and exciting, especially during the nail-biting climax. Rated R for profanity and violence. 118m. **DIR:** Phillip Noyce. **CAST:** Harrison Ford, Anne Archer, Patrick Bergin, Sean Bean, James Earl Jones, Richard Harris, James Fox. **1992 DVD**

PATSY, THE ★★1/2 A very minor Jerry Lewis comedy, though the stellar supporting cast is fun to watch. This one is for Lewis fans only; new viewers to Jerry's type of comedy should take in *The Errand Boy* or *The Nutty Professor* first. 101m. **DIR:** Jerry Lewis. **CAST:** Jerry Lewis, Everett Sloane, Ina Balin, Keenan Wynn, Peter Lorre, John Carradine. **1964**

PATTERNS ★★★1/2 Ed Begley dominates this Rod Serling drama of manipulation and machinations in the executive suite. The classic corporate-power-struggle story has changed in recent years, dating this film somewhat, but the games people play to climb to the top is still fascinating. B&W; 83m. **DIR:** Fielder Cook. **CAST:** Van Heflin, Everett Sloane, Ed Begley Sr., Beatrice Straight. **1956**

PATTES BLANCHES (WHITE PAWS) ★★★★ Engrossing melodrama about a reclusive aristocrat ridiculed in a small fishing community over a pair of white shoes he is fond of wearing. A well-crafted film by Jean Gremillon. In French with English subtitles. 92m. **DIR:** Jean Gremillon. **CAST:** Paul Bernard, Suzy Delair. **1987**

PATTI ROCKS ★★★★ Controversial sequel to 1975's *Loose Ends* picks up twelve years later. Bill (Chris Mulkey) has been having an affair with Patti Rocks (Karen Landry), who has informed him that she is pregnant. A very human story with a genuine twist. Rated R for profanity, nudity, and simulated sex. 86m. **DIR:** David Morris. **CAST:** Chris Mulkey, John Jenkins, Karen Landry. **1987**

PATTON ★★★★★ Flamboyant, controversial General George S. Patton is the subject of this Oscar-winning picture. George C. Scott is spellbinding in the title role. Scott's brilliant performance manages to bring alive this military hero, who strode a fine line between effective battlefield commander and demigod. Rated PG. 169m. **DIR:** Franklin J. Schaffner. **CAST:** George C. Scott, Karl Malden, Stephen Young, Tim Considine. **1970 DVD**

PATTY HEARST ★★★ Paul Schrader provides a restless, relentless, and often moving story of revolutionary idealism gone amok in this documentary-style drama of the kidnapping and subversion of Patty Hearst (Natasha Richardson). Performances are top notch, yet the film leaves a lot of questions unanswered. Rated R for profanity, nudity, and violence. 108m. **DIR:** Paul Schrader. **CAST:** Natasha Richardson, William Forsythe, Ving Rhames, Frances Fisher. **1988**

PAULIE ★★ Talking parrot is exiled to the basement of a research lab after embarrassing a scientist in front of his colleagues. Befriended by a Russian janitor, Paulie (via the voice of Jay Mohr) tells his life story. The janitor is touched by the bird's history and helps him find his original owner. The film's flashbacks want to be poignant, but Paulie just wants to wisecrack. Rated PG. 87m. **DIR:** John Roberts. **CAST:** Tony Shalhoub, Bruce Davison, Gena Rowlands, Richard "Cheech" Marin, Buddy Hackett. **1998 DVD**

PAULINE AT THE BEACH ★★★★ The screen works of French writer-director Eric Rohmer are decidedly unconventional. In this, one of his "Comedies and Proverbs," the 14-year-old title character (Amanda Langlet) shows herself to have a better sense of self and reality than the adults around her. In French with English subtitles. Rated R for nudity. 94m. **DIR:** Eric Rohmer. **CAST:** Amanda Langlet, Arielle Dombasle, Pascal Greggory, Feodor Atkine. **1983**

PAUL'S CASE ★★ Eric Roberts's impassioned portrayal of the working-class youth from turn-of-the-century Pittsburgh is the only draw. The outcome will leave viewers wondering. Introduced by Henry Fonda; suitable for family viewing. 52m. **DIR:** Lamont Johnson. **CAST:** Eric Roberts, Michael Higgins, Lindsay Crouse. **1980**

PAWNBROKER, THE ★★★★★ This is a somber and powerfully acted portrayal of a Jewish man who survived the Nazi Holocaust, only to find his spirit still as bleak as the Harlem ghetto in which he operates a pawnshop. Rod Steiger gives a tour-de-force performance as a man with dead emotions who is shocked out of his zombielike existence by confronting the realities of modern urban life. B&W; 116m. **DIR:** Sidney Lumet. **CAST:** Rod Steiger, Geraldine Fitzgerald, Brock Peters. **1965**

PAY IT FORWARD ★★★★ When a seventh-grade social studies teacher asks his class to devise a plan to change the world for the better and to implement it, one of his students takes him at his word and creates a chain reaction of good deeds. Refusing to shy away from tough issues and featuring memorable performances, this film is an uncommonly moving motion picture that only cynics will be able to resist. That said, some viewers may feel betrayed after watching it. But like any life-changing experience, one may need time to fully absorb its impact. Rated PG-13 for brief violence, profanity, suggested sex, and mature themes concerning substance abuse. 123m. **DIR:** Mimi Leder. **CAST:** Kevin Spacey, Helen Hunt, Haley Joel Osment, Jay Mohr, Jon Bon Jovi, Kathleen Wilhoite. **2000 DVD**

PAY OR DIE ★★★1/2 Ernest Borgnine plays the fabled leader of the Italian Squad, New York's crack police detectives who dealt with the turn-of-the-century Black Hand. Borgnine and his fellow Italian-Americans use force and intimidation to combat the savage Mafia-connected hoodlums who extort and murder their own people in Little Italy. An underrated crime film. B&W; 110m. **DIR:** Richard Wilson. **CAST:** Ernest Borgnine, Zohra Lampert, Al Austin. **1960**

PAYBACK (1990) ★★★1/2 Prison detail escapee falls in love with a small-town sheriff's daughter. Rated R for language and delicate seduction scenes. 94m. **DIR:** Russell Solberg. **CAST:** Corey Michael Eubanks, Michael Ironside, Don Swayze, Teresa Blake, Bert Remsen. **1990**

PAYBACK (1994) ★★★ Complicated plot twists keep the suspense turned up high in this tale of lust and revenge. C. Thomas Howell plays a prisoner who promises a dying old-timer that he will take care of the guard who beat him in exchange for the location of some buried loot. Years later, all of the pieces begin to fall into place for the final showdown. Rated R for violence, nudity, adult situations, and language. 93m. **DIR:** Anthony Hickox. **CAST:** C. Thomas Howell, Joan Severance, R. G. Armstrong, Marshall Bell. **1994**

PAYBACK (1999) ★★★1/2 One of Donald E. Westlake's early novels gets a second workout in this updated remake of *Point Blank*. Mel Gibson makes an unstoppable force in this nasty tale of a burglar whose chutzpah is larger than his common sense, and who stubbornly takes on the entire big-city criminal empire in order to retrieve what he perceives is his share of a recent heist. The story is wholly improbable and violent as hell, but Gibson's irresistible . . . even as a bad guy. Rated R for violence, profanity, torture, nudity, and drug use. 104m. **DIR:** Brian Helgeland. **CAST:** Mel Gibson, Gregg Henry, Maria Bello, David Paymer, Deborah Unger, William Devane. **1999 DVD**

PAYDAY ★★★★ Bravura performance by Rip Torn as a hard-drinking, ruthless country singer who's bent on destroying himself and everyone around him. Gripping, emotionally draining drama. Rarely seen in theaters, this one is definitely worth viewing on tape. Rated R for language, nudity, sexual situations. 103m. **DIR:** Daryl Duke. **CAST:** Rip Torn, Ahna Capri, Elayne Heilveil, Michael C. Gwynne. **1973**

PAYOFF ★★★1/2 Keith Carradine is sympathetic as an affable fellow forever haunted by the memory of—while a child—having unknowingly delivered a bomb that killed his parents. Earnest performances and slick pacing hide the plot flaws in this engaging little thriller. Made for cable, with violence and brief nudity. 111m.

DIR: Stuart Cooper. **CAST:** Keith Carradine, Kim Greist, Harry Dean Stanton, John Saxon, Robert Harper. **1991**

PCU ★★ At small Port Charles University (PCU, get it?), every special-interest group has its pet cause, and the ultrasensitive president (Jessica Walter) is persecuting the only fraternity that wants to have fun. It's a 1990s *Animal House*—only without John Belushi, and with too few laughs. Rated PG-13. 81m. **DIR:** Hart Bochner. **CAST:** Jeremy Piven, Chris Young, David Spade, Megan Ward, Sarah Trigger, Jessica Walter. **1994**

PEACEMAKER (1990) ★★1/2 An interplanetary serial killer is hunted down on Earth by a policeman from back home—but which one is which? Limp effects and dull direction may weaken your concern. Rated R. 90m. **DIR:** Kevin S. Tenney. **CAST:** Robert Forster, Lance Edwards, Robert Davi. **1990**

PEACEMAKER, THE (1997) ★★★★ It's a fine suspense thriller. Reviewers couldn't resist taking a swipe at Steven Spielberg and his partners for this relatively low-key first Dreamworks production, ignoring the strong pacing of director Mimi Leder and writing of Michael Schiffer. George Clooney and Nicole Kidman are first-rate as the lone duo aware of a world-threatening conspiracy involving nuclear weapons. Rated R for violence and profanity. 123m. **DIR:** Mimi Leder. **CAST:** George Clooney, Nicole Kidman, Michael Iures, Armin Mueller-Stahl, Jim Haynie. **1997 DVD**

PEANUT BUTTER SOLUTION, THE ★★1/2 Remember sitting around a campfire when you were a kid and creating a story that just went on and on? This is a campfire movie. Part of the *Tales for All* series, it combines old houses, ghosts, an evil madman, enforced child labor, and a main character with a real hairy problem, all mixed together in sort of a story. 96m. **DIR:** Michael Rubbo. **CAST:** Mathew Mackay, Siluk Saysanasy, Helen Hughes. **1985**

PEARL, THE ★★ John Steinbeck's heavy-handed parable about the value of wealth when compared with natural treasures is beautifully photographed and effectively presented, but the film suffers from the same shortcoming inherent in the book. The plight of the loving couple and their desperately ill son is relentlessly hammered home. 77m. **DIR:** Emilio Fernandez. **CAST:** Pedro Armendariz, Maria Elena Marques. **1948**

•PEARL HARBOR ★★★ Although not as bad as the vitriolic reviews would suggest, this depiction of the "date which will live in infamy" is at times laughably melodramatic, particulary with respect to the callow love triangle that sometimes seems more important than Japan's sneak attack on American soil. Lead Ben Affleck and Kate Beckinsale don't share a whit of chemistry, and the dialogue becomes even more turgid when Josh Hartnett comes between them. On the other hand, Cuba Gooding Jr. is sensational in his depiction of real-life seaman third class Dorie Miller; it's a shame the film doesn't spend more time with him. Then, too, the actual early morning attack is a masterpiece of Hollywood pyrotechnics, and powerfully poignant to boot. Rated PG-13 for profanity, violence, intense war sequences, and mild sensuality. 182m. **DIR:** Michael Bay. **CAST:** Ben Affleck, Josh Hartnett, Kate Beckinsale, William Lee Scott, Cuba Gooding Jr., Greg Zola, Ewen Bremner, Alec Baldwin, James King, Mako, Cary-Hiroyuki Tagawa, Colm Feore, Dan Aykroyd. **2001 DVD**

PEARL OF DEATH, THE ★★★★ Director Roy William Neill fashions Arthur Conan Doyle's "The Six Napoleons" into a rip-snorting screen adventure for Holmes (Basil Rathbone) and Watson (Nigel Bruce). They're tracking a trio of criminals: Giles Conover (Miles Mander), Naomi (Evelyn Ankers), and the Creeper (Rondo Hatton). Good stuff. B&W; 69m. **DIR:** Roy William Neill. **CAST:** Basil Rathbone, Nigel Bruce, Evelyn Ankers, Miles Mander, Dennis Hoey, Mary Gordon, Ian Wolfe, Rondo Hatton. **1944**

PEARL OF THE SOUTH PACIFIC A dull film about murder in the tropics. 86m. **DIR:** Allan Dwan. **CAST:** Virginia Mayo, Dennis Morgan, David Farrar, Murvyn Vye. **1955 DVD**

PEARLS OF THE CROWN, THE ★★★1/2 This featherweight historical extravaganza was presented as a celebration of the coronation of England's George VI, but it was clearly an excuse for writer-codirector Sacha Guitry to concoct choice scenes for some of the best theatrical actors in France. Some of the bits are delightful, but some drag on. In English, and in French and Italian with English subtitles. B&W; 120m. **DIR:** Sacha Guitry, Christian-Jaque. **CAST:** Sacha Guitry, Renée Saint-Cyr, Arletty, Raimu. **1937**

PEBBLE AND THE PENGUIN, THE ★★★ So-so musical score and uneven plot jumps mar this Don Bluth production. Martin Short gives voice to the likable but lovelorn Hubie, yet it is Jim Belushi's savvy Rocko who manages to steal the show. Rated G. 74m. **DIR:** Appel Gyorgy. **1995 DVD**

PECKER ★★1/2 A cheerful teenage amateur photographer (Edward Furlong) is discovered by the trendy Manhattan art scene, and the resulting celebrity all but ruins his life. Writer-director John Waters makes a none-too-subtle comment on his own career, but he flatters himself. Despite an appealing cast, the predictable story and amateurish production soon wear out their welcome. Rated R for brief but graphic nudity. 87m. **DIR:** John Waters. **CAST:** Edward Furlong, Christina Ricci, Lili Taylor, Mary Kay Place, Martha Plimpton. **1998 DVD**

PECK'S BAD BOY ★★★ Jackie Coogan shines as the mischievous scamp who commits all manner of mayhem, yet miraculously escapes the lethal designs his victims must harbor. Silent. B&W; 54m. **DIR:** Sam Wood. **CAST:** Jackie Coogan, Wheeler Oakman, Doris May, Raymond Hatton, Lillian Leighton. **1921**

PECK'S BAD BOY WITH THE CIRCUS ★★ Tommy Kelly, the mischievous Peck's Bad Boy, and his ragamuffin gang of troublemakers (including an aging Spanky MacFarland) wreak havoc around the circus. Comedy greats Edgar Kennedy and Billy Gilbert are the best part of this kids' film. B&W; 78m. **DIR:** Eddie Cline. **CAST:** Tommy Kelly, Ann Gillis, Edgar Kennedy, Billy Gilbert, Benita Hume, Spanky McFarland, Grant Mitchell. **1938**

PEDESTRIAN, THE ★★★1/2 The directorial debut for Maximilian Schell, this is a disturbing near masterpiece of drama exploring the realm of guilt and self-doubt that surrounds ex–World War II Nazis. Gustav Rudolph Sellner's haunting and quiet performance as an aging industrialist who is exposed as an ex-Nazi is a little

tedious but thought-provoking in the outcome—much like the film itself. 97m. **DIR:** Maximilian Schell. **CAST:** Gustav Rudolph Sellner, Peter Hall, Maximilian Schell. **1974**

PEE-WEE HERMAN SHOW, THE ★★1/2 Adult fans of Pee-Wee Herman will fit right into his childish but risqué playhouse. Others will no doubt wonder what planet he's from. Not rated, but some of the humor is sexual in nature. 58m. **DIR:** Marty Callner. **CAST:** Pee-Wee Herman, Phil Hartman, Brian Seff. **1981**

PEE-WEE'S BIG ADVENTURE ★★★1/2 You want weird? Here it is. Pee-Wee Herman made the jump from television to feature films with this totally bizarre movie about a man-size, petulant, 12-year-old goofball (Herman) going on a big adventure after his most prized possession—a bicycle—is stolen by some nasties. Rated PG for a scary scene and some daffy violence. 90m. **DIR:** Tim Burton. **CAST:** Pee-Wee Herman, Elizabeth Daily, Mark Holton, Diane Salinger. **1985 DVD**

PEEPING TOM ★★★1/2 Carl Boehm gives a chilling performance as a lethal psychopath who photographs his victims as they are dying. This film outraged both critics and viewers alike when it was first released, and rarely has been revived since. Not for all tastes, to be sure, but if you're adventurous, give this one a try. Rated R. 109m. **DIR:** Michael Powell. **CAST:** Carl Boehm, Moira Shearer, Anna Massey. **1960 DVD**

PEGGY SUE GOT MARRIED ★★★★1/2 Wistful, and often joyously funny, this delightful film features Kathleen Turner as Peggy, a 43-year-old mother of two who is facing divorce. When she attends her twenty-fifth annual high school reunion, she is thrust back in time and gets a chance to change the course of her life. Rated PG-13 for profanity and suggested sex. 103m. **DIR:** Francis Ford Coppola. **CAST:** Kathleen Turner, Nicolas Cage, Barry Miller, Catharine Hicks, Joan Allen, Kevin J. O'Connor, Lisa Jane Persky, Barbara Harris, Don Murray, Maureen O'Sullivan, Leon Ames, John Carradine. **1986 DVD**

PEKING OPERA BLUES ★★★★1/2 The circuslike Peking Opera provides an appropriately colorful backdrop for this period adventure that brings three dissimilar young women together to battle an evil general. High-spirited fun. In Cantonese with English subtitles. Not rated; contains violence. 98m. **DIR:** Tsui Hark. **CAST:** Lin Ching Hsia, Sally Yeh, Cherie Chung. **1986 DVD**

PELICAN BRIEF, THE ★★★1/2 Overlong but suspenseful adaptation of the bestselling novel by John Grisham casts Julia Roberts as a student who accidently stumbles onto the truth behind the killings of two Supreme Court justices, a discovery that puts her life in danger. Charismatic Denzel Washington plays the investigative reporter who comes to her aid. Rated R for violence and profanity. 141m. **DIR:** Alan J. Pakula. **CAST:** Julia Roberts, Denzel Washington, Sam Shepard, John Heard, John Lithgow, Hume Cronyn, Tony Goldwyn, James B. Sikking, William Atherton, Robert Culp, Stanley Tucci. **1993 DVD**

PELLE THE CONQUEROR ★★★★★ Bille August's superb drama casts Max von Sydow as a Swedish widower who takes his young son to Denmark in the hope of finding a better life. Once there, they must endure even harder times. In Danish and Swedish with English subtitles. Not rated, the film has nudity, violence, and profanity. 138m. **DIR:** Bille August. **CAST:** Max von Sydow, Pelle Hvenegaard. **1988 DVD**

PENDULUM ★★ In this rather confusing mystery, police captain George Peppard must acquit himself of a murder charge and catch the real culprit. A good cast perks things up some, but the story is too full of holes to be taken seriously. Some violence and adult situations. Rated PG. 106m. **DIR:** George Schaefer. **CAST:** George Peppard, Richard Kiley, Jean Seberg, Charles McGraw. **1969 DVD**

PENITENT, THE ★★ Raul Julia is a member of the Penitents, a religious cult that remembers the suffering of Christ by affixing one of its members to a cross and leaving him in the desert sun for an entire day—often to die as "God's will." Exploration of this intriguing milieu is set aside in favor of a silly soap opera about Julia's problem with his young wife and lusty pal. Rated PG for suggested sex. 90m. **DIR:** Cliff Osmond. **CAST:** Raul Julia, Armand Assante, Julie Carmen. **1988**

PENITENTIARY ★★ Leon Isaac Kennedy dons boxing gloves as the black Rocky to triumph over pure evil in this lurid, but entertaining, movie. 94m. **DIR:** Jamaa Fanaka. **CAST:** Leon Isaac Kennedy, Thommy Pollard. **1979 DVD**

PENITENTIARY II 🦃 A retread. Rated R for violence and profanity. 108m. **DIR:** Jamaa Fanaka. **CAST:** Leon Isaac Kennedy, Glynn Thurman, Ernie Hudson, Mr. T. **1982 DVD**

PENITENTIARY III 🦃 Lock this one up in solitary confinement. 91m. **DIR:** Jamaa Fanaka. **CAST:** Leon Isaac Kennedy, Anthony Geary, Steve Antin, Ric Mancini, Jim Bailey. **1987**

PENN & TELLER GET KILLED ★★★ Your appreciation for this bizarre comedy will depend upon your reaction to Penn & Teller, an abrasive comedy-magic team who specialize in fake gory magic tricks. While engaging in sick humor and magician debunking, our heroes discover that someone is trying to kill them. Like it or hate it, you have to admit that it's different. Rated R for violence and profanity. 90m. **DIR:** Arthur Penn. **CAST:** Penn Jillette, Teller, Caitlin Clarke, David Patrick Kelly. **1989**

PENNIES FROM HEAVEN ★★★1/2 Steve Martin and Bernadette Peters star in this downbeat musical. The production numbers are fabulous, but the dreary storyline—with Martin as a down-and-out song-plugger in Depression-era Chicago—may disappoint fans of the genre. Rated R for profanity and sexual situations. 107m. **DIR:** Herbert Ross. **CAST:** Steve Martin, Bernadette Peters, Jessica Harper. **1981**

PENNY SERENADE ★★★★ Cary Grant and Irene Dunne are one of the most fondly remembered comedy teams in films such as *The Awful Truth* and *My Favorite Wife*. This 1941 film is a radical change of pace, for it is a ten-hankie tearjerker about a couple's attempt to have children. They are excellent in this drama far removed from their standard comic fare. B&W; 125m. **DIR:** George Stevens. **CAST:** Cary Grant, Irene Dunne, Edgar Buchanan. **1941 DVD**

PENPAL MURDERS 🦃 A man's pen pal comes for a visit and unfortunately waits until the end of this stinker to kill the cast. Not rated. 118m. **DIR:** Steve

Postal. **CAST:** Jay Brockman, Jennifer Tuck, Angela Shepard. **1991**

PENTAGON WARS, THE ★★★★ A wonderful adaptation of Col. James G. Burton's book, which described the U.S. military's invention of a scout tank that neither fulfilled its function nor protected the soldiers inside. Kelsey Grammer is deliciously stubborn and egomaniacal as the driving force behind the Bradley Fighting Vehicle, while Cary Elwes is the White House–authorized "analyst" who refuses to approve it until satisfied by tests . . . every one continually sabotaged by those in charge, who want only to get the thing into production. Made-for-cable-film is a fascinating story. Rated R for profanity. 103m. **DIR:** Richard Benjamin. **CAST:** Kelsey Grammer, Cary Elwes, Viola Davis, John C. McGinley, Clifton Powell, Olympia Dukakis, Richard Benjamin. **1998**

PENTATHLON ★★ Silly Cold War thriller with Dolph Lundgren as an East German athlete who defects to the United States. Years later, his spiteful ex-coach, a neo-Nazi, takes drastic measures to ruin his big comeback. Rated R for violence and language. 101m. **DIR:** Bruce Malmuth. **CAST:** Dolph Lundgren, David Soul, Roger E. Mosley, Renee Colman. **1994**

PENTHOUSE, THE 🦃 Oh, boy, another woman-in-jeopardy thriller. This one has Robin Givens trapped in her high-rise with a fanatical ex-boyfriend. 93m. **DIR:** David Greene. **CAST:** Robin Givens, David Hewlett, Robert Guillaume, Cedric Smith. **1993**

PEOPLE, THE ★★ This TV movie is a fair interpretation of the science-fiction stories of Zenna Henderson about psychically talented aliens whose home world has been destroyed and who must survive on Earth. The script gives Henderson's subtle themes a heavy-handed and unbalanced treatment. 74m. **DIR:** John Korty. **CAST:** William Shatner, Dan O'Herlihy, Diane Varsi, Kim Darby. **1971**

PEOPLE ARE FUNNY ★★1/2 From the Pine-Thomas B unit at Paramount comes this agreeable little comedy. Jack Haley is a small-town radio announcer who has aspirations to be a big-time radio personality. Inspired by the radio program that later became a successful television series with Art Linkletter as the host. B&W; 94m. **DIR:** Sam White. **CAST:** Jack Haley, Rudy Vallee, Ozzie Nelson, Art Linkletter, Helen Walker, Frances Langford. **1946**

PEOPLE THAT TIME FORGOT, THE ★★ Edgar Rice Burroughs probably would have been outraged by this and its companion piece, *The Land That Time Forgot*. Doug McClure gets rescued by friend Patrick Wayne from a fate worse than death on a strange island circa 1919. Laughable rubber-suited monsters mix it up with ludicrous wire-controlled beasties. Rated PG. 90m. **DIR:** Kevin Connor. **CAST:** Doug McClure, Patrick Wayne, Sarah Douglas, Thorley Walters. **1977 DVD**

PEOPLE UNDER THE STAIRS, THE ★★★ A young boy from the ghetto gets more than he bargained for when he breaks into a house looking for money to help his cancer-stricken mother. It seems the home owners are a couple, with more than a few screws loose, who keep a group of boys locked in their basement. Hybrid of *Dawn of the Dead* and *Die Hard*. Rated R for violence and profanity. 102m. **DIR:** Wes Craven. **CAST:** Brandon Adams, Everett McGill, Wendy Robie, Ving Rhames, Kelly Jo Minter. **1991**

PEOPLE VS. JEAN HARRIS ★★ A sedate reenactment of a lengthy trial transcript, shot entirely inside a courtroom. A long, long, boring trial. Made for TV. 147m. **DIR:** George Schaefer. **CAST:** Ellen Burstyn, Martin Balsam, Richard Dysart, Peter Coyote. **1981**

PEOPLE VS. LARRY FLYNT, THE ★★ This seriocomic, bio-pic pits Flynt—the flamboyant pope of pornography—against the religious right and state censorship. But this film makes a feeble case for Flynt. It soft pedals *Hustler* as a blue-collar *Playboy* by calling it more honest—something this film needs to be. Rated R for language, nudity, sexual content, and drug use. 103m. **DIR:** Milos Forman. **CAST:** Woody Harrelson, Courtney Love, Edward Norton, Brett Harrelson, James Cromwell. **1996 DVD**

PEOPLE WILL TALK ★★★★1/2 Wonderful witty story of a doctor whose mysterious background is being investigated by jealous peers at his university. Meanwhile, he marries a young girl who is about to have another man's child. Yes, it is a comedy, and a great one. B&W; 110m. **DIR:** Joseph L. Mankiewicz. **CAST:** Cary Grant, Jeanne Crain, Finlay Currie, Hume Cronyn, Walter Slezak, Sidney Blackmer, Will Wright, Margaret Hamilton, Billy House. **1951**

PEOPLE'S HERO ★★★ Taken as a hostage during someone else's botched bank holdup, a cunning gangster turns the situation to his advantage. Hong Kong thriller downplays the usual firepower for plot, though the ending is explosive. In Cantonese with English subtitles. Not rated; contains strong violence. 82m. **DIR:** Yee Tung-shing. **CAST:** Ti Lung, Tony Leung Chiu Wai, Ronald Wong. **1987**

PEPE LE MOKO ★★★1/2 Algiers criminal Pepe Le Moko (Jean Gabin) is safe just as long as he remains in the city's picturesque, squalid native quarter. His passionate infatuation with a beautiful visitor from his beloved Paris, however, spells his doom. In French with English subtitles. B&W; 93m. **DIR:** Julien Duvivier. **CAST:** Jean Gabin, Mireille Balin, Gabriel Gario, Marcel Dalio. **1937**

PEPI, LUCI, BOM AND OTHER GIRLS ★★★ The plot, a satirical pastiche of melodramatic clichés, is less important than the nonstop swipes at bourgeois society in Pedro Almodóvar's first film. Crudely made on an amateur budget, this will be of interest mainly to fans of his later films. In Spanish with English subtitles. Not rated; contains sexual situations. 80m. **DIR:** Pedro Almodóvar. **CAST:** Carmen Maura, Felix Rotaeta. **1980**

PEPPERMINT SODA ★★★1/2 The first of French director Diane Kurys's semiautobiographical films (the best known of which is *Entre Nous*) depicts the growing pains of two teenage sisters. The setting is Paris, 1963, when society seems to be going through as many upheavals as the two girls. Meandering but generally delightful. In French with English subtitles. Rated PG. 100m. **DIR:** Diane Kurys. **CAST:** Eleonore Klarwein, Odile Michel. **1977**

PERCY & THUNDER ★★★★ The underbelly of professional boxing is exposed in this riveting drama. Courtney B. Vance stars as a middleweight boxer who has what it takes to go all the way. James Earl Jones costars as his trainer, a former boxer who knows what it takes to

win the title. Billy Dee Williams plays the stumbling block, a seedy character who controls the boxing game, and is willing to let anyone in for a price. Fine performances distinguish this exciting made-for-cable drama. Not rated. 90m. **DIR:** Ivan Dixon. **CAST:** Courtney B. Vance, James Earl Jones, Billy Dee Williams, Zakes Mokae, Robert Wuhl. **1992**

PEREZ FAMILY, THE ★★★★ A romantic fable set against the backdrop of the 1980 Mariel boatlift of Cuban refugees. A twenty-year resident of Castro's prisons comes to Miami in hopes of finding his long-gone wife and daughter. Circumstances team him up with a fiery young woman while his wife—who thinks he didn't make the last boat—finally lets herself fall in love with a new man. Rated R for sex, language, and mild violence. 112m. **DIR:** Mira Nair. **CAST:** Marisa Tomei, Alfred Molina, Anjelica Huston, Chazz Palminteri. **1995**

PERFECT ★★ In this irritatingly uneven and unfocused film, John Travolta stars as a *Rolling Stone* reporter out to do an exposé on the health-club boom. Jamie Lee Curtis is the aerobics instructor he attempts to spotlight in his story. Just another moralizing mess about journalistic ethics. Rated R for profanity, suggested sex, and violence. 120m. **DIR:** James Bridges. **CAST:** John Travolta, Jamie Lee Curtis, Jann Wenner, Marilu Henner, Laraine Newman. **1985**

PERFECT ALIBI ★★★ What starts off as a standard-issue thriller builds up steam thanks to a talented cast and director Kevin Meyer's crafted screenplay. Kathleen Quinlan plays a woman who wants to get back to work, and hires a nanny for the children. It doesn't take long before everyone suspects hubby and the new nanny of doing more than watching the kids. Those who get too nosy end up dead in this made-for-cable thriller. Not rated; contains violence. 100m. **DIR:** Kevin Meyer. **CAST:** Kathleen Quinlan, Teri Garr, Hector Elizondo, Alex McArthur. **1994**

PERFECT BLUE ★★★★ Imagine that Walt Disney made a film directed by Italian horror maestro Dario Argento and you might have a good idea of just how effective this animated shocker is. *Perfect Blue* tells the tale of Mima Kirigoe, a pop singer who leaves her band in order to pursue a career in acting. Once the change has been made, her life becomes a nightmare as she discovers the lengths to which some fans will go. A top-notch script and stylish animation help to sustain the mood of this dark, disturbing film. Not rated; contains graphic violence, nudity, profanity, and adult situations. 80m. **DIR:** Satoshi Kon. **1997 DVD**

PERFECT BRIDE, THE ★★ Nut-cake Sammi Davis, reacting violently to a childhood trauma (finally revealed after three ponderous flashbacks), repeatedly becomes engaged to nice young fellows, only to murder them on the eve of the wedding day. Plucky Kelly Preston senses something amiss. Made-for-cable chiller. 90m. **DIR:** Terrence O'Hara. **CAST:** Sammi Davis, Kelly Preston, Linden Ashby, John Agar. **1991**

PERFECT CRIME ★★★1/2 After a long weekend, a woman Marine turns up missing, and her soon-to-be ex-husband is suspected of killing her. But military investigators have a difficult time collecting any evidence to convict the guy. This made-for-cable mystery is based on a true story and does a fine job following the investigation. Good acting and a good story, but something's still lacking. Rated PG-13 for violence. 95m. **DIR:** Robert Lewis. **CAST:** Mitzi Kapture, Nick Searcy, Scott Lawrence, Jasmine Guy. **1997**

PERFECT DAUGHTER, THE ★★★ Two years after she left her parents' house and disappeared from their lives, a young woman turns up in a hospital with a head injury. She returns home, but the past she can't remember returns to haunt her. This made-for-cable original has an engaging plot and pretty good acting. Not rated; contains violence. 95m. **DIR:** Harry S. Longstreet. **CAST:** Tracey Gold, Bess Armstrong, Mark Joy, Kerrie Keane. **1996**

PERFECT FAMILY ★★ A young, widowed mother hires a housekeeper who moves in along with her brother; incidentally, his family died in a mysterious accident. The story is ruined in the middle, and there's really no reason to finish watching. Not rated, made for cable, but contains violence. 95m. **DIR:** E. W. Swackhamer. **CAST:** Bruce Boxleitner, Jennifer O'Neill, Juliana Hansen, Shiri Appleby, Joanna Cassidy. **1992**

PERFECT FURLOUGH ★★ Perfectly forgettable fluff about soldier Tony Curtis (who is taking the leave for his entire unit, which is stationed in the Arctic). At least he gets to meet and eventually win Janet Leigh (Mrs. Tony Curtis at that time). 93m. **DIR:** Blake Edwards. **CAST:** Tony Curtis, Janet Leigh, Keenan Wynn, Linda Cristal, Elaine Stritch, Troy Donahue. **1958**

PERFECT HARMONY ★★★★ Heartwarming film about enlightenment in a sleepy South Carolina town and its exclusive boys' prep school in 1959. A Yankee schoolteacher exposes the boys to non-Southern views of the Civil War, equality, etc. Amidst this awakening, a friendship blossoms between the caretaker's grandson and one of the privileged students. Not rated, this Disney-channel film uses a minimum of violence and racial slurs to prove its point. 93m. **DIR:** Will Mackenzie. **CAST:** Peter Scolari, Darren McGavin, Moses Gunn, Justin Whalin, David Faustino. **1990**

PERFECT LITTLE MURDER, A ★★ Amiable made-for-cable comedy stars Teri Garr as a housewife who overhears a murder plot in her small town and then must go undercover to prove it. Pleasant diversion as Garr and husband Robert Urich deal with her harebrained schemes. Rated PG for sexual innuendo. 94m. **DIR:** Anson Williams. **CAST:** Teri Garr, Robert Urich. **1990**

PERFECT MARRIAGE ★★ On their tenth wedding anniversary Loretta Young and David Niven suddenly decide they can't stand each other and go their separate, flirtatious ways. Dull. B&W; 87m. **DIR:** Lewis Allen. **CAST:** Loretta Young, David Niven, Eddie Albert, Charlie Ruggles, Virginia Field, Rita Johnson, ZaSu Pitts, Jerome Cowan, Ann Doran. **1947**

PERFECT MATCH, THE ★★ Although Marc McClure and Jennifer Edwards create some funny moments, the pacing and the dialogue are iffy in this romantic hodgepodge. The couple meets through a misleading personal ad—with both parties claiming to be something they're not. Rated PG for no apparent reason. 93m. **DIR:** Mark Deimel. **CAST:** Marc McClure, Jennifer Edwards, Diane Stilwell, Rob Paulsen, Karen Witter. **1987**

PERFECT MURDER, A ★★★ This contemporary riff on Hitchcock's 1954 *Dial M for Murder* is a string of wicked conspiracy twists that lead to a rather weak finale. Money and infidelity, the top two contributing ele-

ments to spousal murder, drive a rich Manhattan industrialist to plot the demise of his unfaithful heiress wife. Pure evil also surfaces as the slighted husband dangles a carrot of his own in front of his wife's lover. Rated R for simulated sex, nudity, language, and violence. 107m. **DIR:** Andrew Davis. **CAST:** Michael Douglas, Gwyneth Paltrow, Viggo Mortensen. **1998 DVD**

PERFECT STORM, THE ★★★★ Sebastian Junger's nonfiction bestseller about the killer storm of October 1991 comes to the screen as a harrowing, white-knuckle thriller, centering on an ill-fated fishing boat skippered by George Clooney with Mark Wahlberg and John C. Reilly among the crew. Director Wolfgang Petersen and a throng of special effects artists make the storm—the worst of the century, by all accounts—a horrifying experience. The sheer scale of the film may suffer on home video, but the tension and suspense will still come through. Rated PG-13 for profanity and intense action. 129m. **DIR:** Wolfgang Petersen. **CAST:** George Clooney, Mark Wahlberg, Diane Lane, John C. Reilly, William Fichtner, Karen Allen, Bob Gunton, Mary Elizabeth Mastrantonio. **2000 DVD**

PERFECT STRANGERS ★★1/2 A hired assassin loses his cool when he discovers that an infant boy witnessed his last contract. An uneven but gritty suspense film with many nice touches and effective use of grungy Manhattan locations. Rated R for violence. 90m. **DIR:** Larry Cohen. **CAST:** Anne Carlisle, Brad Rijn, Stephen Lack. **1984**

PERFECT TENANT, THE ★★ A woman rents out her guest house to a seemingly perfect tenant, not realizing that he plans to kill her because he blames her for causing his father's suicide. Maxwell Caulfield's hammy performance as the psycho renter doesn't keep this film from being a waste of time. Rated R for profanity and violence. 93m. **DIR:** Doug Campbell. **CAST:** Linda Purl, Maxwell Caulfield, Melissa Behr, Earl Holliman. **2000 DVD**

PERFECT WEAPON ★★1/2 Standard martial arts action, as our strong, silent hero (Jeff Speakman) goes after the killers of an old family friend. Fans of the genre will like this one; the fight scenes are quite well staged. Rated R for violence. 90m. **DIR:** Mark DiSalle. **CAST:** Jeff Speakman, Mako. **1991**

PERFECT WITNESS ★★★★1/2 This crackling suspenser, first aired on HBO, puts family man Aidan Quinn into a crime-infested nightmare. After witnessing a mob-style execution and telling the police what he knows, Quinn receives threats; but when he backs down, special attorney Brian Dennehy tosses him into jail for perjury. Terry Curtis Fox and Ron Hutchinson have scripted the ultimate horror—personal vs. social responsibility—and Quinn plays the part to frustrated perfection. 104m. **DIR:** Robert Mandel. **CAST:** Brian Dennehy, Aidan Quinn, Stockard Channing, Laura Harrington. **1989**

PERFECT WORLD, A ★★★★ Escaped convict Kevin Costner takes a young boy hostage and flees with Texas Ranger Clint Eastwood hot on his trail. That this serious-sounding film contains moments of comedy is one of the many pleasant surprises in an essentially downbeat morality play. Costner plays against type, and Eastwood successfully tries a John Wayne turn as an aged-in-the-saddle professional. Rated R for violence, profanity, and lewdness. 136m. **DIR:** Clint Eastwood. **CAST:** Kevin Costner, Clint Eastwood, Laura Dern, T. J. Lowther, Keith Szarabajka. **1993**

PERFECTLY NORMAL ★★★1/2 This is a relaxed, offkilter Canadian comedy showcasing the entertaining Scottish comic actor, Robbie Coltrane. He plays Alonzo Turner, a mysterious, eccentric stranger who enlivens the life of a dull brewery worker. Original and offbeat. Rated R for profanity. 101m. **DIR:** Yves Simoneau. **CAST:** Robbie Coltrane, Michael Riley. **1990**

PERFORMANCE ★★★★ Mick Jagger, the leader of the Rolling Stones rock group, stars in this bizarre film as Turner, a rock singer who decides to switch identities with a hunted hit man (James Fox). Codirected by Nicolas Roeg and Donald Cammell, the film is a chilling, profoundly disturbing cinematic nightmare about the dark side of man's consciousness. Rated R for profanity, nudity, and violence. 105m. **DIR:** Nicolas Roeg, Donald Cammell. **CAST:** Mick Jagger, James Fox, Anita Pallenberg. **1970**

PERFUMED NIGHTMARE ★★★★ Hilarious, poignant view of the impact of American cultural colonialism through the eyes of a young Philippines man. Brilliant meditation on the American dream shot on super 8mm for less than $10,000. Winner of the International Critics Award at the Berlin Film Festival. In Tagalog with English dialogue and subtitles. 91m. **DIR:** Kidlat Tahimik. **1983**

PERIL ★★ Nicole Garcia plays the wife of a wealthy businessman who is having an affair with their daughter's guitar instructor (Christophe Malavoy). Filmmaker Michel Deville aims too high in his direction with French new wave–like scene cuts. In French with English subtitles. Rated R for nudity, violence, profanity, and adult subject matter. 100m. **DIR:** Michel Deville. **CAST:** Christophe Malavoy, Nicole Garcia, Richard Bohringer, Anemone, Michel Piccoli. **1985 DVD**

PERILS OF PAULINE, THE (1933) ★★ Sound serial version of the famous Pearl White cliff-hanger retains only the original title. The daughter of a prominent scientist and her companion struggle to keep the formula for a deadly gas out of the hands of evil Dr. Bashan and his slimy assistant Fang. This serial lacks the charisma of later efforts from Universal Studios. B&W; 12 chapters. **DIR:** Ray Taylor. **CAST:** Evalyn Knapp, Robert Allen, James Durkin, John Davidson, Sonny Ray. **1933**

PERILS OF PAULINE, THE (1947) ★★★ Betty Hutton plays Pearl White, the queen of the silent serials, in this agreeable little movie. The old-style chase scenes and cliff-hanger situations make up for the overdose of sentimentality. 96m. **DIR:** George Marshall. **CAST:** Betty Hutton, John Lund, Billy DeWolfe, William Demarest, Constance Collier, Frank Faylen. **1947 DVD**

PERIOD OF ADJUSTMENT ★★★1/2 Newlyweds Jane Fonda and Jim Hutton start marriage on the wrong foot. Friend Anthony Franciosa, whose own marriage is on the rocks, attempts to straighten them out. Fine performances in a rare light comedy from Tennessee Williams. B&W; 111m. **DIR:** George Roy Hill. **CAST:** Anthony Franciosa, Jane Fonda, Jim Hutton, Lois Nettleton, John McGiver, Jack Albertson. **1962**

PERMANENT MIDNIGHT ★★★ Writer-director David Veloz's film is based on fact (TV writer Jerry Stahl's memoir about his own drug addiction), but it hits every

monkey-on-my-back cliché with clockwork precision. Ben Stiller's tour-de-force performance as Stahl—frantic, mercurial, reckless, harrowing—makes the familiar tale worth watching. Rated R for profanity, drug use, and sexual scenes. 85m. **DIR:** David Veloz. **CAST:** Ben Stiller, Elizabeth Hurley, Maria Bello, Owen Wilson. **1998 DVD**

PERMANENT RECORD ★★1/2 This drama stars Keanu Reeves as Chris, whose best friend, a popular, talented, seemingly well-adjusted high school senior, commits suicide. The film focuses on the effects the suicide has on his closest friends and how they come to accept it. Rated PG-13. 92m. **DIR:** Marisa Silver. **CAST:** Keanu Reeves, Alan Boyce, Richard Bradford. **1988**

PERMISSION TO KILL ★★ An exiled politician (Bekim Fehmiu) from an Eastern bloc nation living in Austria decides to return to his native country. A Western intelligence agent (Dirk Bogarde) must stop him. Rated PG for violence, profanity, and nudity. 96m. **DIR:** Cyril Frankel. **CAST:** Dirk Bogarde, Ava Gardner, Bekim Fehmiu, Timothy Dalton, Nicole Calfan, Frederic Forrest. **1975**

PERSECUTION 🦃 This tale of murder and deception never shows minimal signs of life. Rated R. 92m. **DIR:** Don Chaffey. **CAST:** Lana Turner, Trevor Howard, Ralph Bates. **1974**

PERSONA ★★★ Liv Ullmann gives a haunting performance as an actress who suddenly becomes mute and is put in the charge of a nurse (Bibi Andersson). The two women become so close that they change personalities. Ingmar Bergman's use of subtle split-screen effects dramatizes the metaphorical quality of this quiet film. In Swedish with English subtitles. B&W; 81m. **DIR:** Ingmar Bergman. **CAST:** Liv Ullmann, Bibi Andersson, Gunnar Björnstrand. **1966**

PERSONAL BEST ★★★★ Oscar-winning screenwriter Robert Towne wrote, directed, and produced this tough, honest, and nonexploitive story about two women who are friends, teammates, and sometimes lovers (Mariel Hemingway, Patrice Donnelly) preparing for the 1980 Olympics. Hemingway's and Donnelly's stunning performances make the film an impressive achievement. Rated R for nudity, strong language, and drug use. 124m. **DIR:** Robert Towne. **CAST:** Mariel Hemingway, Patrice Donnelly, Scott Glenn. **1982**

PERSONAL PROPERTY ★★★1/2 A clever comedy designed to make the most of two fiery sex symbols of their time, this comedy-drama marks the only teaming of Robert Taylor and Jean Harlow. The story is a silly setup of contrivances to get the two together. It works as a personality piece. B&W; 85m. **DIR:** W. S. Van Dyke. **CAST:** Jean Harlow, Robert Taylor, Reginald Owen, Una O'Connor, E. E. Clive, Cora Witherspoon. **1937**

PERSONAL SERVICES ★★★ The true-life story of Christine Painter, a British waitress who happened into a very successful career as a brothel madam. Julie Walters gives an all-out performance that's fascinating, but the movie's bluntness may be off-putting to most American viewers. It's rated R for language. 105m. **DIR:** Terry Jones. **CAST:** Julie Walters, Alec McCowen, Shirley Stelfox. **1987**

PERSONALS, THE ★★★1/2 Entertaining light comedy about a recently divorced Minneapolis man (Bill Schoppert) trying to get back in the dating game. Schoppert has the characteristics of Woody Allen, showing both pathos and a knack for one-liners. Rated PG for profanity. 90m. **DIR:** Peter Markle. **CAST:** Bill Schoppert, Karen Landry, Paul Eiding, Michael Laskin. **1983**

PERSONS UNKNOWN ★★★1/2 A beautiful blonde uses Joe Mantegna, the owner of a security agency, to get at money belonging to one of his clients. At least that's how it first appears, in this twisty, low-key thriller where you can never be sure who's zooming whom. Rated R for violence, drug use, profanity, and sex. 99m. **DIR:** George Hickenlooper. **CAST:** Joe Mantegna, Kelly Lynch, Jon Favreau, J. T. Walsh, Xander Berkeley, Naomi Watts. **1996**

PERSUADERS, THE (TV SERIES) ★★★ This tongue-in-cheek adventure series lasted just one season on ABC, but it offers a fair bit of action, humor, and style. Set in the glamour spots of Europe, the show follows two dashing playboys: Brett Sinclair (Roger Moore), a British lord, and Daniel Wilde (Tony Curtis), a self-made millionaire from the Bronx. Moore and Curtis are fun to watch in these tailor-made roles, smoothly handling the roughhousing, rivalry, and romance. 60m. **DIR:** Basil Dearden, Val Guest. **CAST:** Roger Moore, Tony Curtis, Laurence Naismith. **1972**

PERSUASION (1995) ★★★★1/2 A young woman (Amanda Root) still loves the suitor she foolishly rejected years before (Ciaran Hinds); now she watches in agony as he courts her brother-in-law's younger sister. Jane Austen's last novel is given a first-class filming. Root's character blossoms from an amiable wallflower to a confident beauty. Rated PG. 102m. **DIR:** Roger Michell. **CAST:** Amanda Root, Ciarán Hinds, Susan Fleetwood, Corin Redgrave, Fiona Shaw. **1995 DVD**

PERSUASION (1971) ★★ A BBC production so subtle you might just mistake it for dry and dull. This lacks effective sound quality and camera work; one can spot displaced shadows and hear an occasional flubbed line. This is very confined, even when the action moves outdoors, and none of the performances will inspire you to endure its length. Not rated. 225m. **DIR:** Howard Baker. **CAST:** Ann Firbank, Bryan Marshall. **1971**

PEST, THE 🦃 Imagine a manic Jim Carrey or Jerry Lewis at warp speed and you have John Leguizamo as the most appropriately named title character. The anorexic plot, which is just an excuse for his lightning-speed barrage of costume and character changes, features Leguizamo agreeing to become the human prey for wealthy hunters. Enough ethnic and sexual-orientation jokes to offend just about everyone. Rated PG-13 for language and bad taste. 84m. **DIR:** Paul Miller. **CAST:** John Leguizamo, Jeffrey Jones, Edoardo Ballerini, Freddy Rodriguez, Charles Hallahan. **1997 DVD**

PET SEMATARY ★★★1/2 This scarefest is the most faithful film adaptation of a Stephen King novel yet. A young doctor moves his family to an idyllic setting in the Maine woods. The calm is shattered when first the family's cat and then their son are killed on the nearby highway. If you can bear this, you'll love the all-out terror that follows. Rated R for violence. 102m. **DIR:** Mary Lambert. **CAST:** Dale Midkiff, Fred Gwynne, Denise Crosby. **1989**

PET SEMATARY TWO ★★ This disappointing gorefest returns to that cryptic Maine burial ground. Young Edward Furlong hopes to return his mother to life . . . in

spite of having seen his best friend's dog and stepfather revived as savage killers. So much for common sense. Rated R for violence and profanity. 102m. **DIR:** Mary Lambert. **CAST:** Edward Furlong, Anthony Edwards, Clancy Brown, Jared Rushton, Jason McGuire. **1992 DVD**

PET SHOP ★★★ Anyone who ever wanted a pet as a child will enjoy this lighthearted comedy about a Brooklyn family who must move to Arizona after the father testifies against a mobster. The children are delightful, but the story falls a bit short. Not rated, but suitable for all audiences. 88m. **DIR:** Hope Perello. **CAST:** Leigh Ann Orsi, Spencer Vrooman, Joanne Baron, David Wagner, Jane Morris, Jeff Michalski, Shashawnee Hall, Terry Kiser. **1994**

PETE KELLY'S BLUES ★★1/2 Guys, gals, gangsters, gin, and Dixieland jazz are done to a turn in this ultra-realistic re-creation of the Roaring Twenties. 95m. **DIR:** Jack Webb. **CAST:** Jack Webb, Janet Leigh, Edmond O'Brien, Jayne Mansfield, Lee Marvin, Peggy Lee, Ella Fitzgerald, Martin Milner, Andy Devine. **1955**

PETE 'N' TILLIE ★★ Bloated, morose mess features a chronically depressed Carol Burnett married to skirt chaser Walter Matthau. Matthau and Burnett never click, and fans of the duo are warned to steer clear. Rated PG for profanity. 100m. **DIR:** Martin Ritt. **CAST:** Walter Matthau, Carol Burnett, Geraldine Page, Barry Nelson. **1972**

PETER AND THE WOLF ★★★★★ Originally intended as the centerpiece for Walt Disney's planned sequel to *Fantasia*, this luxuriously animated rendition of Prokofiev's musical fable was instead repackaged as part of 1946's *Make Mine Music*. Sterling Holloway's narration adds a bit of contemporary humor to the gentle fable of a small Russian boy who goes wolf hunting. 30m. **DIR:** Walt Disney. **1946**

PETER GUNN (TV SERIES) ★★★1/2 Blake Edwards earned his Hollywood reputation with this stylish television detective series. Star Craig Stevens established an image that was endlessly imitated: suave, urbane, and self-mocking in the face of certain peril. Despite temptations, Gunn always remained true to his steady girl, Edie (Lola Albright), who worked as a singer in a waterfront nightclub dubbed Mother's. The most fun resulted from Gunn's contacts: an outrageous assortment of snitches, all willing to sing for a discreetly tendered sawbuck. Composer Henry Mancini began a trend with his jazzy themes. Each volume includes two episodes; the best are "Death House Testament" and "The Comic" (which earned Edwards an award from the Mystery Writers of America). B&W; 55m. **DIR:** Blake Edwards, Boris Sagal. **CAST:** Craig Stevens, Lola Albright, Herschel Bernardi, Hope Emerson. **1958–1961**

PETER PAN (1924) ★★★★ First and perhaps best of the three versions of this fantasy classic contains all the elements familiar to modern audiences while retaining the charm of an era long gone. Author James Barrie personally chose young Betty Bronson for the lead and kept a watchful eye on his best-known property, insuring just the right tone and mood for what was to become one of the great film hits of the 1920s. Skillful mix of theater (actors in costumes for all animal roles) and the best film effects available at the time blend beautifully in this beloved children's favorite. Silent, with tinted sequences and orchestral score. B&W; 101m. **DIR:** Herbert Brenon. **CAST:** Betty Bronson, Ernest Torrence, Mary Brian, Esther Ralston, Virginia Brown Faire, Philippe deLacey, Jack Murphy, Anna May Wong. **1924 DVD**

PETER PAN (1953) ★★★1/2 While this 1953 Disney release doesn't qualify as one of the studio's animated classics, it is nonetheless an entertaining version of James M. Barrie's children's play about Never-Never-Land, and the three Darling children taken there by Peter Pan and his fairy companion, Tinker Bell. Rated G. 77m. **DIR:** Hamilton Luske, Clyde Geronimi, Wilfred Jackson. **1953 DVD**

PETER PAN (1960) ★★★★ The magic is still there, remarkably, in this 1960 NBC Television production of the musical based on the book by James M. Barrie. Mary Martin stars in her most beloved role. Unusually high-quality release from GoodTimes Video, which has added four minutes of footage not seen in twenty years. 100m. **DIR:** Vincent J. Donehue. **CAST:** Mary Martin, Cyril Ritchard, Sondra Lee, Margalo Gilmore. **1960 DVD**

PETER'S FRIENDS ★★★1/2 A *Big Chill*–style reunion of English theatrical types in this humorous and touching soufflé from Kenneth Branagh. Costar-screenwriter Rita Rudner's script doesn't always hit the mark, but the cast does. Rated R for profanity and nudity. 102m. **DIR:** Kenneth Branagh. **CAST:** Kenneth Branagh, Emma Thompson, Rita Rudner, Stephen Fry, Hugh Laurie, Imelda Staunton, Alphonsia Emmanuel, Tony Slattery, Phyllida Law, Alex Lowe. **1993**

PETE'S DRAGON ★★1/2 Only the kiddies will get a kick out of this Disney feature, which combines live action with animation. In Maine, circa 1908, a 9-year-old boy (Sean Marshall) escapes his overbearing foster parents with the aid of the pet dragon that only he can see. Sort of a children's version of *Harvey*, it's generally lackluster and uninspired. Rated G. 134m. **DIR:** Don Chaffey. **CAST:** Mickey Rooney, Jim Dale, Helen Reddy, Red Buttons, Jim Backus, Sean Marshall. **1977**

PETRIFIED FOREST, THE ★★★★1/2 This adaptation of the Robert Sherwood play seems a bit dated at first. It's about a gangster (Humphrey Bogart, in one of his first important screen roles) who holds a writer (Leslie Howard), a waitress (Bette Davis), and others hostage in a diner. The first-rate story, exquisite ensemble acting and taut direction by Archie Mayo soon mesmerize the viewer. B&W; 83m. **DIR:** Archie Mayo. **CAST:** Humphrey Bogart, Leslie Howard, Bette Davis, Dick Foran. **1936**

PETTICOAT PLANET ★★ A bunch of men crash-land on a planet full of women who live in a Wild West–like environment. The usual soft-core couplings occur. For fans of this type of film only. Rated R for nudity and simulated sex. 78m. **DIR:** David DeCoteau. **CAST:** Troy Vincent, Betsy Lyn George, Elizabeth Kaitan. **1996 DVD**

PETULIA ★★★★ A story of complex relationships that centers around a prominent doctor (George C. Scott) who gets involved with a kooky young socialite (Julie Christie). A brilliant tragicomedy, one of Richard Lester's major achievements. Rated R. 105m. **DIR:** Richard Lester. **CAST:** George C. Scott, Julie Christie, Richard Chamberlain, Shirley Knight, Joseph Cotten, Arthur Hill. **1968**

PEYTON PLACE ★★★★ A landmark movie from a landmark novel with Lana Turner in her Oscar-nominated role of unwed mother Constance MacKenzie. She lives a lie so that her daughter, Alison, will never know the facts of her life. But Alison discovers facts of her own as the movie explores the morals of small-town life. 160m. **DIR:** Mark Robson. **CAST:** Lana Turner, Diane Varsi, Lloyd Nolan, Betty Field, Hope Lange, Arthur Kennedy, David Nelson, Terry Moore, Lee Philips, Russ Tamblyn, Leon Ames, Mildred Dunnock, Barry Coe, Lorne Greene. **1957**

PHANTASM ★★1/2 This strange mixture of horror and science fiction, while not an outstanding film by any account, does provide viewers with several thrills and unexpected twists. If you like to jump out of your seat, watch this alone with all the lights out. R-rated after scenes were cut from the original X-rated version. 87m. **DIR:** Don Coscarelli. **CAST:** Michael Baldwin, Bill Thornbury, Reggie Bannister. **1979 DVD**

PHANTASM II ★★ After ten years, the Tall Man (Angus Scrimm) is back, and he's nastier than ever. No longer is he merely looting cemeteries to enslave the dead for his fiendish purposes. He's also going after the living. But the heroes from the first film are hot on his trail. Lacks the wit, style, and originality of its predecessor. Rated R for nudity, profanity, and graphic violence. 90m. **DIR:** Don Coscarelli. **CAST:** James LeGros, Reggie Bannister, Angus Scrimm. **1988**

PHANTASM III: LORD OF THE DEAD ★★1/2 As is true of its predecessors, sheer momentum keeps this weird horror film going in spite of the ridiculous story. Our heroes are still after the wonderfully malevolent Tall Man. Young Kevin Conners brings enthusiasm to his performance as an orphaned boy determined to avenge his whole community's disappearance. Rated R for gore, profanity, nudity, and simulated sex. 91m. **DIR:** Don Coscarelli. **CAST:** Reggie Bannister, Michael Baldwin, Angus Scrimm, Gloria Lynn Henry, Kevin Conners. **1994**

PHANTASM IV: OBLIVION ★★★ The Tall Man returns to transform more corpses into his zombie slaves. More campy horror fun from the creators of the first three *Phantasm* movies. Doesn't make a lick of sense but has more style and humor than one might expect. Rated R for profanity, horror, and violence. 90m. **DIR:** Don Coscarelli. **CAST:** Michael Baldwin, Reggie Bannister, Bill Thornbury, Heidi Marnhout, Bob Ivy, Angus Scrimm. **1998 DVD**

PHANTOM, THE (1931) ★★ Creaky thriller about a mysterious prison escapee with scores to settle and the rookie reporter who cracks the case boasts one of the silliest villains on film. B&W; 62m. **DIR:** Alvin J. Neitz. **CAST:** Guinn Williams, Allene Ray, Niles Welch, Tom O'Brien, Wilfred Lucas, Sheldon Lewis. **1931**

PHANTOM, THE (1996) ★★★ Leisurely screen adaptation of Lee Falk's comic strip about "The Ghost Who Walks" and his alter ego, Kit Walker, in a story that pits the masked, purple-clad avenger against a power-crazed villain. Set in the 1930s, the movie has a fine period flavor and pokes fun at itself without becoming campy. Rated PG for violence. 100m. **DIR:** Simon Wincer. **CAST:** Billy Zane, Kristy Swanson, Treat Williams, Catherine Zeta Jones, Samantha Eggar, Patrick McGoohan, James Remar, Cary-Hiroyuki Tagawa. **1996 DVD**

PHANTOM BROADCAST, THE ★★★ The murder of a popular radio crooner reveals he was little more than the handsome lip-synching front for the real offstage singer, a twisted hunchback with a velvet voice. Cleverly plotted drama. B&W; 68m. **DIR:** Phil Rosen. **CAST:** Ralph Forbes, Gail Patrick, Guinn Williams, George "Gabby" Hayes. **1933**

PHANTOM CHARIOT ★★ The legend of the Coachman of Death being replaced each year by the last man to die on December 31 is used here to drive home a sermon on the evils of drink. In its day the use of multiple-layered flashbacks and double-exposure techniques made this Swedish silent a great success; today, alas, it only seems tedious and unendurably slow-paced. Silent. B&W; 83m. **DIR:** Victor Sjöström. **CAST:** Victor Sjöström. **1920**

PHANTOM CREEPS, THE ★★1/2 This Saturday-afternoon crowd pleaser features a crazed scientist, a giant robot, an invisibility belt, and a meteorite fragment that can render an entire army immobile—just about anything a kid can ask for in a serial. Good fun. B&W; 12 chapters. **DIR:** Ford Beebe, Saul Goodkind. **CAST:** Bela Lugosi, Regis Toomey. **1939 DVD**

PHANTOM EMPIRE (1935) ★★★ Gene Autry, with the aid of Frankie Darro, champion rider Betsy King Ross, and the Junior Thunder Riders, overcomes threats from greedy crooks and the deadly threat of Murania, the futuristic city twenty thousand feet beneath the ground. Plenty of action, the wonders of the "city of the future," and good special effects (including a death ray) make this one of Mascot Films's best serials. B&W; 12 chapters. **DIR:** Otto Brewer, B. Reeves "Breezy" Eason. **CAST:** Gene Autry, Frankie Darro, Betsy King Ross, Smiley Burnette. **1935**

PHANTOM EMPIRE, THE (1986) ★★★ Fans of old serials and Fifties sci-fi adventures will want to check out this good-natured parody. The plot, about a group of adventurers trying to salvage a cache of diamonds from a mutant-infested cavern, is a thin frame for lots of tongue-in-cheek dialogue and in-jokes. Rated R for nudity. 83m. **DIR:** Fred Olen Ray. **CAST:** Ross Hagen, Jeffrey Combs, Russ Tamblyn, Sybil Danning. **1986**

PHANTOM LOVE ★★★ The fact that this soft-core romp doesn't take itself seriously raises this piece of fluff above the rest of the pack. When a romance novelist goes to Italy to find inspiration for her next novel, she discovers a diary left in a bed-and-breakfast. It tells the story of a rebellious cousin who returns to the family estate in Italy, causing a stir with the "modern" ways she learned during her trip to America. Sexy and fun. Available in R and unrated versions; both contain nudity and simulated sex. 82m. **DIR:** Madison Monroe. **CAST:** Griffin Drew, Michelle von Flotow. **2000 DVD**

PHANTOM OF DEATH ★★ A concert pianist, dying of a rare disease that causes rapid aging, takes out his frustration on women from his past by hacking them to pieces. Donald Pleasence and Michael York are old pros, but the direction is flat and any suspense is worn quickly into the ground. Not rated; contains nudity and violence. 95m. **DIR:** Ruggero Deodato. **CAST:** Michael York, Edwige Fenech, Donald Pleasence. **1987**

PHANTOM OF LIBERTY, THE ★★ A kaleidoscope of satirical vignettes composed of outrageous riddles,

jokes, and associations all mocking mankind's inexplicable willingness to enslave itself in order to be "free." A big disappointment from Luis Buñuel whose use of tricks from his other films make this one seem clichéd. In French with English subtitles. 104m. **DIR:** Luis Buñuel. **CAST:** Jean-Claude Brialy, Adolfo Celi, Michel Piccoli, Monica Vitti. **1974**

PHANTOM OF THE MALL—ERIC'S REVENGE ★★ A killer seeks revenge on the developers who burned down his house and accidentally disfigured him while clearing the way for a new shopping mall. Good characters make this slasher flick marginally entertaining. Rated R for nudity. 91m. **DIR:** Richard Friedman. **CAST:** Derek Rydall, Jonathan Goldsmith, Rob Estes, Morgan Fairchild. **1988**

PHANTOM OF THE OPERA (1925) ★★★★★ Classic silent horror with Lon Chaney Sr. in his most poignant and gruesome role. This 1925 sample of Chaney's brilliance—he was truly the "man of a thousand faces"—still has enough power to send chills up your spine. Enjoy. B&W; 79m. **DIR:** Rupert Julian. **CAST:** Lon Chaney Sr., Mary Philbin, Norman Kerry. **1925 DVD**

PHANTOM OF THE OPERA (1943) ★★★ Overabundance of singing hurts this otherwise good remake of the 1925 silent. The well-known story concerns a Paris opera house being terrorized by a disfigured composer (Claude Rains) whose best works have been stolen. Acting is great, production values are high, but that singing has got to go! 92m. **DIR:** Arthur Lubin. **CAST:** Claude Rains, Susanna Foster, Nelson Eddy, Edgar Barrier, Miles Mander, Hume Cronyn. **1943 DVD**

PHANTOM OF THE OPERA (1962) ★★1/2 Herbert Lom plays the title role as much for sympathy as scares in this low-key remake from England's Hammer Studios. Otherwise, the plot doesn't vary much from the preceding versions. 84m. **DIR:** Terence Fisher. **CAST:** Herbert Lom, Heather Sears, Thorley Walters, Michael Gough. **1962**

PHANTOM OF THE OPERA (1989) ★★ This muddled retread owes more to the slasher genre than to Gaston Leroux. Although Jill Schoelen makes an appealing heroine, she seems far too intelligent to so casually accept the attention of the heard-but-not-seen guardian angel who lurks beneath the Opera House. He, of course, is none other than serial killer Robert Englund—hiding behind a suitably gory facial-skin mask. Rated R for violence and brief nudity. 93m. **DIR:** Dwight H. Little. **CAST:** Robert Englund, Jill Schoelen, Alex Hyde-White. **1989**

PHANTOM OF THE OPERA (1998) 🦃 In this, Dario Argento's version of the classic story, Julian Sands plays the mysterious half man, half monster, who is lurking around underneath the opera house, lusting after a talented singer played by Asia Argento. Nepotism aside, this ghastly take on *Phantom* fails to capture any of the drama and romance of the original tale. Rated R for gore and violence. 100m. **DIR:** Dario Argento. **CAST:** Julian Sands, Asia Argento. **1998 DVD**

PHANTOM OF THE PARADISE ★★1/2 Before he became obsessed with Hitchcock *hommages* and ultraviolent bloodbaths, director Brian De Palma did this odd little blend of Faust and *Phantom of the Opera*. William Finley sells his soul to Paul Williams and learns the dangers of achieving fame too quickly. Wildly erratic, with tedious dialogue alternating with droll visual bits. Rated PG—mild violence. 92m. **DIR:** Brian De Palma. **CAST:** Paul Williams, William Finley, Jessica Harper. **1974**

PHANTOM OF THE PLAINS ★★★ A pompous, polished crook whose specialty is marrying wealthy women is about to dupe the duchess until Red Ryder steps in to expose his con game. B&W; 56m. **DIR:** Lesley Selander. **CAST:** William Elliott, Robert Blake, Alice Fleming, Ian Keith, Virginia Christine. **1945**

PHANTOM OF THE RITZ ★★1/2 Taking its cue from *Phantom of the Opera* and *Phantom of the Paradise*, this campy little comedy kicks off in 1952 with a drag race that ends in tragedy. Then it's off to 1992, with entrepreneur Peter Bergman reopening the infamous Ritz theater. His plans for a gala opening are jeopardized when he realizes that an evil presence is making the rounds. Fun in a cheap sort of way, with the legendary Coasters lending musical support. Rated R for violence. 89m. **DIR:** Allen Plone. **CAST:** Peter Bergman, Deborah Van Valkenburgh. **1988**

PHANTOM THUNDERBOLT ★★1/2 The Thunderbolt Kid is hired by a town's citizens to round up a lawless gang. B&W; 63m. **DIR:** Alan James. **CAST:** Ken Maynard, Frances Dade, Bob Kortman. **1933**

PHANTOM 2040 (TV SERIES) ★★★1/2 The Phantom, guardian of his jungle domain, carries his ecological concerns into the future as descendants of the original comic-book hero take on the mantle of "The Ghost That Walks." Nontraditional character design and thoughtful stories boost this animated series a step above most Saturday-morning programming. 50m. **DIR:** Vincent Bassol, Michel Lyman, Mike Kaweski, Bertrand Tager Kagan. **1994**

PHANTOMS ★★ Dr. Jenny Pailey returns to her Colorado mountain village with her sister. The ladies notice that all the townsfolk are dead or missing and cross paths with a sheriff and his lecherous deputy. The quartet is then terrorized by a supernatural power responsible for mass human disappearances throughout history. Rated R for language, gore, and violence. 91m. **DIR:** Joe Chappelle. **CAST:** Joanna Going, Rose McGowan, Ben Affleck, Peter O'Toole, Liev Schreiber. **1997 DVD**

PHAR LAP ★★★★1/2 Absolutely chilling (and true) account of the superb Australian racehorse that chewed up the track in the 1920s and early 1930s. Tom Burlinson stars as the stable boy who first believed in, and then followed to fame, the indefatigable Phar Lap. This film's indictment of early horse-racing practices will make you shudder. Rated PG—very intense for younger children. 106m. **DIR:** Simon Wincer. **CAST:** Tom Burlinson, Ron Leibman, Martin Vaughn. **1984**

PHARAOH'S ARMY ★★★★ A quiet antiwar film that explores the far-reaching effects of the Civil War on a stoical Kentucky woman trying to protect her teenage son and their hardscrabble farm from the Yanks. An understanding slowly builds between her and a Yankee invader that is touching not only for what they have in common, but because they can never find common ground. Rated PG-13 for violence and mild profanity. 90m. **DIR:** Robby Henson. **CAST:** Chris Cooper, Patricia Clarkson, Will Lucas, Richard Tyson, Robert Joy, Kris Kristofferson, Huckleberry Fox. **1995**

PHASE IV ★★★1/2 An interesting sci-fi mood piece from 1973 about scientists (Nigel Davenport, Michael Murphy) attempting to outwit superintelligent mutant

ants. Good effects and fine acting. Rated PG. 86m. **DIR:** Saul Bass. **CAST:** Nigel Davenport, Michael Murphy, Lynne Frederick. **1974**

PHAT BEACH ★★★ Entertaining if loopy comedy about a pair of friends who head out to the beach for their summer vacation. Problem is, they've got no money, they "borrowed" Dad's Mercedes, and only one of them is responsible enough to realize this could mean trouble. Rated R for profanity and nudity. 88m. **DIR:** Doug Ellin. **CAST:** Jermaine "Huggy" Hopkins, Coolio, Brian Hooks, Tom "Tiny" Lister Jr. **1996 DVD**

PHEDRE ★★1/2 The performance of Marie Bell, the great French tragedienne, is the only reason to dig out this abbreviated adaptation of the Greek myth about the queen who fell in love with her stepson and caused her husband's death. The production is stagy. Poorly served by the subtitles. In French with English subtitles. 93m. **DIR:** Pierre Jourdan. **CAST:** Marie Bell, Jacques Dacqumine, Claude Giraud. **1968**

PHENOMENON ★★★★ Sweet-natured, small-town resident George Malley gets quite a shock on his thirty-seventh birthday, when a blinding light leaves him with heightened awareness and an insatiable appetite for knowledge. John Travolta is wonderful as the amiable fellow wholly unable to cope with his rapidly escalating intellect. Mostly, he'd just like to get closer to Kyra Sedgwick, a quiet single mom with an aversion to new love interests. Rated PG for mild sensuality. 117m. **DIR:** Jon Turteltaub. **CAST:** John Travolta, Kyra Sedgwick, Forest Whitaker, Robert Duvall, David Gallagher, Brent Spiner. **1996 DVD**

PHILADELPHIA ★★★★ Tom Hanks's Oscar-winning portrayal of an AIDS-infected attorney battling for his rights is the main draw in this heartfelt drama. Denzel Washington is equally good as the homophobic attorney who must confront his own prejudice and ignorance after he agrees to take on the case, in which Hanks alleges that he lost his job at a prestigious law firm because of discrimination. Rated PG-13 for profanity and mature subject matter. 119m. **DIR:** Jonathan Demme. **CAST:** Tom Hanks, Denzel Washington, Jason Robards Jr., Mary Steenburgen, Antonio Banderas, Ron Vawter, Robert Ridgely, Charles Napier, Lisa Summerour. **1993 DVD**

PHILADELPHIA EXPERIMENT, THE ★★★1/2 Reportedly based on a true incident during World War II involving an antiradar experiment that caused a naval battleship to disappear in Virginia, this entertaining science-fiction film stars Michael Paré as a sailor on that ship. But instead of ending up in Virginia, he finds himself in the modern world of 1984. Rated PG for violence and profanity. 102m. **DIR:** Stewart Raffill. **CAST:** Michael Paré, Nancy Allen, Bobby DiCicco, Eric Christmas. **1984**

PHILADELPHIA EXPERIMENT 2, THE ★★★ Although it bears little relation to its predecessor, Kevin Rock and Nick Paine have scripted an engaging time-travel thriller that explores the consequences of a stealth bomber unexpectedly landing in Nazi hands during World War II. Brad Johnson makes a suitably wholesome hero, and Gerrit Graham is amusing as a reckless scientist. Rated PG-13 for violence. 98m. **DIR:** Stephen Cornwell. **CAST:** Brad Johnson, Marjean Holden, Gerrit Graham, John Christian Graas. **1993**

PHILADELPHIA STORY, THE ★★★★★ This is one of the best comedies to come out of Hollywood. From the first scene, where Tracy Lord (Katharine Hepburn) deposits her ex-husband's (Cary Grant) golf clubs in a heap at her front door and in return, Grant deposits Hepburn in a heap right next to the clubs, the 1940s version of *The Taming of the Shrew* proceeds at a blistering pace. Grand entertainment. B&W; 112m. **DIR:** George Cukor. **CAST:** Katharine Hepburn, Cary Grant, James Stewart, Ruth Hussey, John Howard. **1940 DVD**

PHILBY, BURGESS AND MACLEAN: SPY SCANDAL OF THE CENTURY ★★★★ Yes, you can have an exciting spy story without James Bond chases and gimmicks. This riveting film spins the quiet, chilling tale of three of Britain's most notorious spies. They attended college together, were recruited by the Russians, and held high government security posts for thirty years before their discovery. Not rated. 83m. **DIR:** Gordon Flemyng. **CAST:** Anthony Bate, Derek Jacobi, Michael Culver, Ingrid Hafner, Elizabeth Seal. **1986**

PHOBIA 🦃 An almost-unwatchable nonthrilling thriller that combines psychobabble with murder. Rated R. 90m. **DIR:** John Huston. **CAST:** Paul Michael Glaser, Susan Hogan, John Colicos, Patricia Collins. **1980**

PHOENIX ★★★★ In this *film noir* of crooked cops in Phoenix, tensions rise as detective Harry Collins tries to get his gambling addiction under control. When a local loan shark sets out to collect his debt, Harry and his cop friends are forced into pulling off a dangerous heist that could end all of their problems. Filled with dark, interesting characters and escalating tension, Danny Cannon's film punches all the right buttons. Rated R for violence, language, and adult situations. 107m. **DIR:** Danny Cannon. **CAST:** Ray Liotta, Anthony LaPaglia, Anjelica Huston, Daniel Baldwin, Jeremy Piven, Kari Wuhrer. **1997 DVD**

PHOENIX THE WARRIOR 🦃 In the distant future germ warfare has killed all the men, and women have become warriors. Not rated; contains violence. 90m. **DIR:** Robert Hayes. **CAST:** Persis Khambatta. **1987**

PHONE CALL FROM A STRANGER ★★★ Fine acting by a stellar cast lifts this soap opera above the bubbles. Gary Merrill plays confessor to various fellow passengers on an ill-fated airline flight, and brings comfort and understanding to their families when most are killed in the crash. B&W; 96m. **DIR:** Jean Negulesco. **CAST:** Shelley Winters, Gary Merrill, Michael Rennie, Keenan Wynn, Bette Davis, Craig Stevens, Hugh Beaumont. **1952**

PHOTOGRAPHING FAIRIES ★★★1/2 Toby Stephens delivers a haunting performance as photographer Charles Castle who is presented with a photograph of supposedly real fairies that a woman says her two daughters took. His subsequent intervention with the woman, her two daughters, and her skeptical husband set into motion a tragic series of events. Based on the novel of the same name by Steve Szilagyi. Rated R for nudity, adult situations, and language. 107m. **DIR:** Nick Willing. **CAST:** Toby Stephens, Emily Woof, Ben Kingsley, Frances Barber, Philip Davis, Edward Hardwicke. **1997**

PHYSICAL EVIDENCE ★★1/2 Polished performances by Theresa Russell and Burt Reynolds are wasted in this convoluted police thriller. Russell is a public defender assigned to defend Reynolds, a cop accused of murder. A threadbare, erratic plot and haphazard direction by Michael Crichton ruin what could have been a first-rate film. Rated R for adult situations, violence, and profanity. 100m. **DIR:** Michael Crichton. **CAST:** Burt Reynolds, Theresa Russell, Ned Beatty, Kay Lenz. **1989**

PI ★★★★★ Max Cohen is a math genius who is going nuts. He lives in a squalid Manhattan apartment crammed with high-tech electronics and is obsessed with harnessing the chaos of the universe. Between bouts of paranoia and crippling migraines he is stalked by a shady brokerage firm and a Hasidic cabal. This microbudget study in madness uses bleached out black-and-white imagery as a Kafkaesque search for absolute truth blends reality with cyberpunk myth. Rated R for language and disturbing images. 85m. **DIR:** Darren Aronofsky. **CAST:** Sean Gullette, Mark Margolis, Samia Shoaib, Pam Hart, Ben Shenkman, Stephen Pearlman. **1998 DVD**

PIANO, THE ★★★★★ Jane Campion's mesmerizing film is about a mute-by-choice Scotswoman (Oscar-winner Holly Hunter) who journeys to the jungles of nineteenth-century New Zealand to marry Sam Neill, a man she's never met. Once there, she is horrified to find her beloved piano left on the beach until a neighbor (Harvey Keitel) offers to let her play it in exchange for romantic favors. Electrifying and offbeat, this is for lovers of original cinema. Rated R for nudity, simulated sex, and brief violence. 121m. **DIR:** Jane Campion. **CAST:** Holly Hunter, Harvey Keitel, Sam Neill, Anna Paquin. **1993 DVD**

PIANO FOR MRS. CIMINO, A ★★★★ Blessed with great humor and a terrific performance by Bette Davis, this made-for-television film about growing old with dignity is manipulative at times. In light of all the wonderful moments, however, the contrivances don't seem so bad. Davis plays a widow who is institutionalized for senility. The film follows her through her recovery and her rebirth as a single, self-sufficient woman. 96m. **DIR:** George Schaefer. **CAST:** Bette Davis, Keenan Wynn, Alexa Kenin, Penny Fuller, Christopher Guest, George Hearn. **1982**

PIANO LESSON, THE ★★★★ Powerful Pulitzer Prize–winning play by August Wilson is expertly adapted to film in this *Hallmark Hall of Fame* production. Controversy centers around an ornate piano, carved with ancestral images, that has been in the central family for eighty years. Not rated; may be too strong for young viewers. 95m. **DIR:** Lloyd Richards. **CAST:** Charles Dutton, Alfre Woodard, Carl Gordon, Courtney B. Vance, Tommy Hollis. **1995**

PICK-UP ARTIST, THE An absolute mess. Rated PG-13 for language and sexual content. 81m. **DIR:** James Toback. **CAST:** Molly Ringwald, Robert Downey Jr., Dennis Hopper, Harvey Keitel. **1987**

PICKING UP THE PIECES ★★1/2 Bizarre film about a murdered woman's hand that becomes a sacred idol in a small Mexican town. Wild characters inhabit this not-so-wild, uneven comedy that's sometimes funny but more often is just weird. Rated R for language, violence, and nudity. 95m. **DIR:** Alfonso Arau. **CAST:** Woody Allen, Maria Grazia Cucinotta, Richard "Cheech" Marin, David Schwimmer, Kiefer Sutherland. **1999 DVD**

PICKLE, THE This film is just as bad as the film-within-a-film that has-been director Danny Aiello makes in an attempt to revive his career. Extremely dreadful considering its pedigree. Rated R for language and nudity. 103m. **DIR:** Paul Mazursky. **CAST:** Danny Aiello, Dyan Cannon, Shelley Winters, Christopher Penn. **1993**

PICKPOCKET ★★★★1/2 Inspired by *Crime and Punishment*, this is one of the best films from the French master Robert Bresson, whose work is marked by an unblinking austerity that requires a little getting used to for American audiences. An intelligent young man decides to make a career of petty crime, despite his knowledge of the immorality of his actions. In French with English subtitles. Not rated; contains no offensive material. B&W; 75m. **DIR:** Robert Bresson. **CAST:** Martin LaSalle, Marika Green. **1959**

PICKUP ON SOUTH STREET ★★★★ Samuel Fuller's lean and mean thriller about a pickpocket (Richard Widmark) who accidentally lifts a roll of top-secret microfilm and becomes a target for espionage agents. It's prime Fuller: suspenseful, tough, and violent. B&W; 80m. **DIR:** Samuel Fuller. **CAST:** Richard Widmark, Jean Peters, Thelma Ritter. **1953**

PICKWICK PAPERS, THE ★★★ Arguably the best cinema condensation of Charles Dickens. Here recorded are the clever antics of Samuel Pickwick, Alfred Jingle, and Sam Weller as they move through their corner of mid-nineteenth-century England. 109m. **DIR:** Noel Langley. **CAST:** James Hayter, James Donald, Joyce Grenfell, Nigel Patrick, Hermione Baddeley. **1954 DVD**

PICNIC ★★★★ This is one of the best films about small-town life ever lensed, blessed with a cast that makes it even more credible. William Holden plays a drifter who, while visiting old school chum Cliff Robertson, falls for his friend's fiancée (Kim Novak). Derived from the William Inge stage play. 115m. **DIR:** Joshua Logan. **CAST:** William Holden, Kim Novak, Rosalind Russell, Susan Strasberg, Arthur O'Connell, Cliff Robertson, Nick Adams. **1956 DVD**

PICNIC AT HANGING ROCK ★★★★1/2 Surreal, hypnotic suspense story revolves around the mysterious disappearance of a group of students from an all-girls' school at the turn of the century in Australia. Director Peter Weir fashions a truly unsettling motion picture. His fans will rank it among his best. 110m. **DIR:** Peter Weir. **CAST:** Rachel Roberts, Dominic Guard, Helen Morse, Jacki Weaver. **1975 DVD**

PICNIC ON THE GRASS ★★★ Director Jean Renoir's tribute to French Impressionism takes place in the beautiful countryside as a scientific outing turns into a drunken reverie. In French with English subtitles. 92m. **DIR:** Jean Renoir. **CAST:** Paul Meurisse, Catherine Rouvel, Jacqueline Morane. **1959**

PICTURE BRIDE ★★1/2 After the death of her parents in 1916, a young Japanese woman emigrates to Hawaii as the mail-order bride of a sugarcane worker. Thoroughly researched, interesting—but uninvolving. Partially in English, mostly in Japanese with English subtitles. Rated PG-13 for mature themes. 94m. **DIR:** Kayo

Hatta. **CAST:** Youki Kudoh, Akira Takayama, Tamlyn Tomita, Cary-Hiroyuki Tagawa, Toshiro Mifune. **1995**

PICTURE MOMMY DEAD ★★ The tragic death of her mother causes a young girl to lose her memory. Afterward, she is possessed by the spirit of her late mommy. Ooh! Meanwhile the father, Don Ameche, marries again. Thus a rather silly battle ensues between stepmom and stepdaughter. Good acting; too bad the script isn't better. 88m. **DIR:** Bert I. Gordon. **CAST:** Don Ameche, Martha Hyer, Zsa Zsa Gabor, Signe Hasso, Susan Gordon. **1966**

PICTURE OF DORIAN GRAY, THE ★★★★ The classic adaptation of Oscar Wilde's famous novel, this features Hurd Hatfield giving a restrained performance in the title role of a young man whose portrait ages while he remains eternally youthful. Though talky and slow-moving, this film nevertheless keeps you glued to the screen. A few key scenes shot in Technicolor for effect. B&W/color; 110m. **DIR:** Albert Lewin. **CAST:** George Sanders, Hurd Hatfield, Donna Reed, Angela Lansbury, Peter Lawford. **1945**

PICTURE PERFECT ★★ Single working woman tries to snag a promotion at an advertising agency by faking she has a fiancé. Complications arise when the guy she pretends to be marrying turns out to be a much nicer guy than the corporate alley cat she sleeps with on the sly. Rated PG-13 for language and suggested sex. 101m. **DIR:** Glenn Gordon Caron. **CAST:** Jennifer Aniston, Jay Mohr, Illeana Douglas, Kevin Bacon, Olympia Dukakis, Kevin Dunn. **1997 DVD**

PICTURE WINDOWS ★★1/2 A talented cast and several experienced directors manage to add up to almost no surprises in this made-for-cable trilogy. All three stories represent a reflection on romance, but only the third, directed by Jonathan Kaplan, evokes much emotion. Rated R for violence, nudity, and profanity. 95m. **DIR:** Norman Jewison, Peter Bogdanovich, Jonathan Kaplan. **CAST:** Alan Arkin, Rosana De Soto, Dan Hedaya, George Segal, Sally Kirkland, Brooke Adams, Michael Lerner, Tamara Gorski, Joel Bissonnette. **1995 DVD**

PIE IN THE SKY ★★★ Harmless little romantic comedy in which a young man obsessed with traffic woos the girl of his dreams over a number of years, thousands of cars, and a brief encounter with his idol—the king of traffic reporters. Outrageous performance by Christine Lahti is a highlight. Rated R for profanity and sexual situations. 94m. **DIR:** Bryan Gordon. **CAST:** Josh Charles, Anne Heche, Peter Riegert, Christine Ebersole, Christine Lahti, John Goodman, Brent Spiner. **1995**

PIECE OF THE ACTION, A ★★★ Third entry in the Bill Cosby–Sidney Poitier partnership (after *Uptown Saturday Night* and *Let's Do It Again*), this one showing Poitier's greater comfort on both sides of the camera. The story concerns a pair of rascals given one of Life's Awful Choices: prison, or a team-up with some social workers to help a group of ghetto kids. Rated PG. 135m. **DIR:** Sidney Poitier. **CAST:** Sidney Poitier, Bill Cosby, Denise Nicholas, James Earl Jones. **1977**

PIECES 🦃 This movie promises, "You don't have to go to Texas for a chain-saw massacre!" While not rated by the MPAA, the picture would probably qualify for an X. 85m. **DIR:** Juan Piquer Simon. **CAST:** Christopher George, Lynda Day George, Edmund Purdom. **1983**

PIERROT LE FOU ★★★1/2 Complex drama about a man who leaves his rich wife and runs off with a beautiful young woman who is fleeing some gangsters. Shot on location throughout the south of France, this existential character drama will fascinate some viewers while boring others. In French with English subtitles. 110m. **DIR:** Jean-Luc Godard. **CAST:** Jean-Paul Belmondo, Anna Karina, Samuel Fuller, Jean-Pierre Léaud. **1965 DVD**

PIGS (DADDY'S DEADLY DARLING) 🦃 Mental patient meets human-scarfing swine. Not rated, film contains violence. 79m. **DIR:** Marc Lawrence. **CAST:** Jesse Vint, Jim Antonio, Marc Lawrence. **1973**

PIG'S TALE, A ★★ Low-budget *Meatballs* rip-off has a group of social rejects engaging in a battle of pranks, relay races, and bathroom humor against a group of spoiled rich brats. You've seen it done better before. Rated PG for mild profanity and crude humor. 94m. **DIR:** Paul Tassie. **CAST:** Joe Flaherty, Sean Babb, Mike Damus, Jonathan Hilario, Lisa Jakub, Andrew Harrison Leeds. **1994**

PIGSTY ★★★ This dark fable of bourgeois repression links the stories of two extremely unconventional people—a medieval soldier forced into cannibalism and a modern young man whose alienation from society leads him to bestiality. Skillfully made, though obscure. In Italian with English subtitles. Not rated; contains strong material and is not for children. 90m. **DIR:** Pier Paolo Pasolini. **CAST:** Pierre Clementi, Franco Citti, Jean-Pierre Léaud, Ugo Tognazzi. **1969**

PILLOW BOOK, THE ★★★★ Another exquisitely composed, artsy outrage from England's Peter Greenaway (*The Cook, the Thief, His Wife & Her Lover*), though more accessible than many of his recent works. A young Japanese woman is sexually excited by having calligraphy drawn on her nude body. When she finds an Englishman who lets her write on him, she likes it even more. Then, as is typical of Greenaway, things go from sensual to gruesome. Not rated; contains sex, nudity, violence, drug use, and you name it. 126m. **DIR:** Peter Greenaway. **CAST:** Vivian Wu, Ewan McGregor, Yoshi Oida. **1996 DVD**

PILLOW OF DEATH ★★ In the last *Inner Sanctum* mystery, Lon Chaney Jr. is a lawyer in love with his secretary and suspected of having smothered his wife to death. It's the only entry in the series in which Chaney turns out to be guilty—sort of. B&W; 65m. **DIR:** Wallace Fox. **CAST:** Lon Chaney Jr., Brenda Joyce, J. Edward Bromberg. **1945**

PILLOW TALK ★★★★ If you like the fluffy light comedy of Doris Day and Rock Hudson, this is their best effort. The ever-virginal Miss Day is keeping the wolves at bay. Tony Randall is excellent as the suitor who never wins the girl. 105m. **DIR:** Michael Gordon. **CAST:** Doris Day, Rock Hudson, Tony Randall, Thelma Ritter. **1959 DVD**

PILOT, THE ★★1/2 Cliff Robertson directed and starred in this film about an airline pilot's struggle with alcohol. Robertson's directing is not as convincing as his acting. Rated PG for profanity. 98m. **DIR:** Cliff Robertson. **CAST:** Cliff Robertson, Frank Converse, Diane Baker, Gordon MacRae, Dana Andrews, Milo O'Shea, Edward Binns. **1979**

PIMPERNEL SMITH ★★★ Star Leslie Howard, who also produced, brought his 1934 role in *The Scarlet Pimpernel* up to modern times in this anti-Nazi thriller involving a daring rescue of important scientists from prison. B&W; 122m. **DIR:** Leslie Howard. **CAST:** Leslie Howard, David Tomlinson, Philip Friend, Hugh McDermott, Mary Morris. **1942**

PIN ★★★1/2 Superb psychological thriller from the screenwriter of *The Amityville Horror* about a schizophrenic youth who develops a mad fixation with a medical dummy called Pin. David Hewlett is excellent as the manic youth torn between fantasy and reality. Rated R for nudity and violence. 103m. **DIR:** Sandor Stern. **CAST:** David Hewlett, Terry O'Quinn. **1989 DVD**

PIN-UP GIRL ★★★ Another in the series of happy musical comedies Betty Grable starred in during World War II, *Pin-Up Girl* logically took its title from her status with GIs. This time, a secretary falls for a sailor. To be near him, she pretends to be a Broadway star. 83m. **DIR:** H. Bruce Humberstone. **CAST:** Betty Grable, John Harvey, Martha Raye, Joe E. Brown, Eugene Pallette. **1944**

•PINERO ★★1/2 Junkie poet and playwright "Mikey" Pinero says that he has to be bad to make his writing good. He steals, mainlines heroin, hustles, lives on the street, betrays his friends, and goes to prison. Is he serious? Or just trying to justify his self-indulgent, recklessly criminal lifestyle? The film never makes it clear if the Manhattan underbelly dweller and Puerto Rican precursor of rap and poetry slams has a real clue about the value of his talent. For that misstep, this stream of nonlinear impressions is neither tragic nor heroic nor deeply dramatic, and fails to illuminate Pinero's character and lurid life. Rated R for profanity, nudity, sexual content, violence, and drug use. 95m. **DIR:** Leon Ichaso. **CAST:** Benjamin Bratt, Talisa Soto, Giancarlo Esposito, Rita Moreno, Mandy Patinkin. **2001**

PING PONG ★★ A young lawyer must gather the feuding members of a large family in order to administer a dead man's will. The plot is merely an excuse to guide us around the Chinese section of London. Modestly appealing. Rated PG. 100m. **DIR:** Po-Chih Leong. **CAST:** Lucy Sheen, David Yip. **1988**

PINK ANGELS ★★1/2 *Easy Rider* meets *The Adventures of Priscilla, Queen of the Desert*. Rated R for profanity and violence. 81m. **DIR:** Larry Brown. **CAST:** John Alderman, Tom Basham, Bruce Kimball, Michael Pataki, Dan Haggerty. **1971**

PINK CADILLAC ★★ Clint Eastwood returns to the *Every Which Way But Loose*–style action-comedy with this mediocre effort, in which he plays a skip tracer out to nab the bail-jumping Bernadette Peters. There are some good lines in this formula film, but it is predictable, overdone, and ultimately boring. Rated PG-13 for violence, profanity, and suggested sex. 122m. **DIR:** Buddy Van Horn. **CAST:** Clint Eastwood, Bernadette Peters, John Dennis Johnston, William Hickey, Geoffrey Lewis, Bill McKinney. **1989**

PINK FLAMINGOS ★★ The story of Babs Johnson (Divine), the "filthiest person alive," and Connie and Raymond Marble (Mink Stole and David Lochary), two challengers who are jealous of Babs's notoriety. As in all of Waters"s films, the point here is to shock. If this doesn't, nothing will. Rated NC-17 for violence, nudity, and very poor taste. 95m. **DIR:** John Waters. **CAST:** Divine, Mink Stole, David Lochary, Mary Vivian Pearce, Edith Massey. **1972**

PINK FLOYD: THE WALL ★★ For all its apparent intent, this visually impressive film, which has very little dialogue but, rather, uses garish visual images to the accompaniment of the British rock band's music, ends up being more of a celebration of insanity and inhumanity than an indictment of it as intended. Rated R for violence. 99m. **DIR:** Alan Parker. **CAST:** Bob Geldof, Christine Hargreaves, Bob Hoskins. **1982 DVD**

PINK MOTEL Phyllis Diller and Slim Pickens as owners of a less than prosperous motel. Not rated, this contains sexual situations. 90m. **DIR:** Mike MacFarland. **CAST:** Phyllis Diller, Slim Pickens, Terri Berland, Squire Fridell. **1982**

PINK NIGHTS Yet another teen sex comedy. Rated PG for profanity. 87m. **DIR:** Phillip Koch. **CAST:** Shaun Allen, Kevin Anderson. **1985**

PINK PANTHER, THE ★★★1/2 Peter Sellers is featured in his first bow as Inspector Jacques Clouseau, the inept French detective, on the trail of a jewel thief known as the Phantom in this, the original *Pink Panther*. This release has some good—and even hilarious—moments. But the sequel, *A Shot in the Dark*, is better. 113m. **DIR:** Blake Edwards. **CAST:** Peter Sellers, David Niven, Capucine, Claudia Cardinale, Robert Wagner. **1964 DVD**

PINK PANTHER STRIKES AGAIN, THE ★★★1/2 Peter Sellers's fourth time out as the clumsy Inspector Clouseau. Clouseau's former supervisor, Herbert Lom, cracks up and tries to destroy the world with a superlaser. Meanwhile, he's hired a team of international killers to do away with Clouseau. One turns out to be Lesley-Anne Down, who falls in love with the diminutive Frenchman. Rated PG. 103m. **DIR:** Blake Edwards. **CAST:** Peter Sellers, Herbert Lom, Lesley-Anne Down, Burt Kwouk, Colin Blakely. **1976 DVD**

PINKY ★★★1/2 Still powerful story of a light-skinned black girl. She has been passing for white, but her status becomes known when she returns home to a small Mississippi town. Straightforward handling and presentation of what was then rather explosive material. Outstanding performances. B&W; 102m. **DIR:** Elia Kazan. **CAST:** Jeanne Crain, Ethel Barrymore, Ethel Waters, William Lundigan, Arthur Hunnicutt. **1949**

PINOCCHIO ★★★★ An excellent adaptation of the classic tale about a wooden puppet who turns into a real boy. This *Faerie Tale Theatre* production, as with most of the others, will be best appreciated—and understood—by adults. It's blessed with just the right touch of humor, and Lainie Kazan is wonderful as the "Italian" fairy godmother. 51m. **DIR:** Peter Medak. **CAST:** James Coburn, Carl Reiner, Pee-Wee Herman, James Belushi, Lainie Kazan, Don Novello. **1983**

PINOCCHIO ★★★★★ In this timeless Walt Disney animated classic, a puppet made by a lonely old man gets the chance to become a real boy. *Pinocchio* is one of those rare motion pictures that can be enjoyed over and over again by adults as well as children. If you remember it as a "kid's show," watch it again. You'll be surprised at how wonderfully entertaining it is. Rated G. 87m. **DIR:** Walt Disney. **1940 DVD**

PINOCCHIO AND THE EMPEROR OF THE NIGHT ★★ This scary continuation of the classic tale features an

incorrigible Pinocchio who manages to lose his father's prized jewel box as well as his own right to be a real boy. Animation is okay, but somehow you feel as though you're watching an overlong Saturday-morning cartoon. Edward Asner, Tom Bosley, James Earl Jones, Don Knotts, William Windom (voices). Rated G. 91m. **DIR:** Hal Sutherland. **1987**

PINOCCHIO'S REVENGE ★★★1/2 This ain't no fairy tale. When a possessed wooden Pinocchio doll falls into the hands of an impressionable 8-year-old girl, he begins a vicious reign of terror. Rated R for violence and language. 96m. **DIR:** Kevin S. Tenney. **CAST:** Rosalind Allen, Lewis Van Bergen, Janet MacLachlan, Thomas Wagner, Brittany Alyse-Smith. **1996**

PIONEER WOMAN ★★1/2 In this passable made-for-television movie, the trials and tribulations of homesteading in Wyoming during the 1860s are told through the point of view of a wife and mother. After her husband is killed, she must make the difficult decision about staying on or going back east. 78m. **DIR:** Buzz Kulik. **CAST:** Joanna Pettet, William Shatner, David Janssen, Lance LeGault, Helen Hunt. **1973**

PIPE DREAMS 🦃 A wife moves to Alaska to win back her estranged man who is working on the pipeline. Rated PG for violence, profanity, and adult subject matter. 89m. **DIR:** Stephen F. Verona. **CAST:** Gladys Knight, Barry L. Hankerson, Bruce French, Wayne Tippitt. **1976**

PIPPI LONGSTOCKING ★★ The adventures of the spunky, irrepressible heroine of Astrid Lindgren's popular children's books are turned into an inoffensive but inert animated feature, produced in Sweden and revamped in Canada for English-speaking audiences. The animation is colorful but flat, and the soundtrack is threadbare, with sparse sound effects and dinky orchestrations that fail to pump life into the forgettable musical score. Rated G. 75m. **DIR:** Bill Giggie, Michael Schaack, Clive Smith. **1997**

PIRANHA (1978) ★★★ Director Joe Dante and writer John Sayles sent up *Jaws* in this nifty, gag-filled horror film. Full of scares and chuckles. Rated R. 92m. **DIR:** Joe Dante. **CAST:** Bradford Dillman, Kevin McCarthy, Heather Menzies, Keenan Wynn. **1978 DVD**

PIRANHA (1995) ★★ The 1978 original had the intelligence to emerge as a parody, but this inept remake tries to play it straight... with lamentable results. Alexandra Paul and William Katt try to stop mutant killer fish from devouring campers. Rated R for gore, nudity, and profanity. 81m. **DIR:** Scott Levy. **CAST:** Alexandra Paul, William Katt, Darleen Carr, Soleil Moon Frye, James Karen, Monte Markham. **1995**

PIRANHA PART TWO: THE SPAWNING ★★ Sequel to *Piranha* by the man who would later grace us with *The Terminator*. A mutated strain of piranha (with the ability to fly, no less) launches an air and sea tirade of violence against a group of vacationers at a tropical resort. Rated R for mild gore. 88m. **DIR:** James Cameron. **CAST:** Tricia O'Neil, Steve Marachuk, Lance Henriksen, Leslie Graves. **1981**

PIRATE, THE ★★★★ This splashy, though at times narratively weak, musical features Judy Garland and Gene Kelly singing and dancing their way through a Cole Porter score. It features a terrific dance sequence titled "Be a Clown" featuring clown-pirate-acrobat Kelly and the marvelous Nicholas Brothers. Watch it for the songs and the dances. 102m. **DIR:** Vincente Minnelli. **CAST:** Judy Garland, Gene Kelly, Gladys Cooper, Reginald Owen, Walter Slezak. **1948**

PIRATE MOVIE, THE ★★ This rock 'n' roll adaptation of Gilbert and Sullivan's *The Pirates of Penzance* is passable entertainment. Expect a lot of music, a lot of swashbuckling, and a little sappy romance. This film is rated PG for slight profanity and sexual innuendo. 99m. **DIR:** Ken Annakin. **CAST:** Christopher Atkins, Kristy McNichol, Ted Hamilton, Bill Kerr. **1982**

PIRATES 🦃 A turgid, overblown mess. Rated PG-13 for vulgarity. 117m. **DIR:** Roman Polanski. **CAST:** Walter Matthau, Cris Campion, Charlotte Lewis, Roy Kinnear. **1986**

PIRATES OF DARK WATERS, THE: THE SAGA BEGINS ★★★ Animated high seas adventure about a young prince who must restore his kingdom by discovering the secrets of thirteen hidden treasures. Voices by Dick Gautier, Hector Elizondo, Brock Peters, Tim Curry, Darleen Carr, and Roscoe Lee Browne. Not rated; contains violence. 90m. **DIR:** Don Lusk. **1991**

PIRATES OF PENZANCE, THE ★★★★ Stylized sets and takeoffs of Busby Berkeley camera setups give *Pirates* a true cinematic quality. Add to that outstanding work by the principals, some nice bits of slapstick comedy, and you have an enjoyable film for the entire family. Rated G. 112m. **DIR:** Wilford Leach. **CAST:** Angela Lansbury, Kevin Kline, Linda Ronstadt, Rex Smith, George Rose. **1983 DVD**

PIRATES OF SILICON VALLEY ★★★1/2 This TNT original paints an unflattering picture of the meteoric rise of Steve Jobs (Noah Wyle) at Apple Computers and the equally astounding expansion of Bill Gates (Anthony Michael Hall) and Microsoft Computers. Though the two men have different lifestyles, neither's image is unscathed as they "pirate" from any and all to get ahead. Good acting by the principals and a fourth-wall technique which allows the actors to step outside the story to reflect make this very watchable. Humor, sprinkled throughout, doesn't hurt either. Not rated; contains drug use and sexual situations. 90m. **DIR:** Martyn Burke. **CAST:** Noah Wyle, Anthony Michael Hall, John DiMaggio, Joey Slotnick. **1999**

PIRATES OF THE HIGH SEAS ★★ Buster Crabbe plays a rugged adventurer who sails to the aid of an old friend whose freight line is being sabotaged. This serial is pretty long in the tooth and if it weren't for the welcome presence of the heroic Crabbe, it would barely be worth watching. B&W; 15 chapters. **DIR:** Spencer Gordon Bennet, Thomas Carr. **CAST:** Buster Crabbe, Lois Hall, Tommy Farrell, Gene Roth, Tristram Coffin. **1950**

PIRATES OF THE PRAIRIE ★★★ Deputy marshal Tim Holt is assigned to go undercover as a gunsmith and find out why vigilantes have been terrorizing the citizens of East Spencerville. Solid effort from director Howard Bretherton in a series that managed to maintain an impressive standard of quality for its entire run. B&W; 57m. **DIR:** Howard Bretherton. **CAST:** Tim Holt, Cliff Edwards, Roy Barcroft. **1942**

PIRATES ON HORSEBACK ★★1/2 A gang murders a prospector before it finds where his diggings are. Hopalong Cassidy, Lucky, and California Carlson (a distant relative of the prospector) start their own search and

take on the crime boss and his gang. B&W; 69m. **DIR:** Lesley Selander. **CAST:** William Boyd, Russell Hayden, Andy Clyde, Evelyn Stewart, Morris Ankrum. **1941**

PISTOL, THE: THE BIRTH OF A LEGEND ★★★★ Writer Darrel Campbell did a fantastic job of transforming the life of basketball great Pistol Pete Maravich into a delightful film. Adam Guier does a great job as the young Pistol and has the viewer rooting for him the entire time. Rated G. 104m. **DIR:** Frank C. Schroeder. **CAST:** Millie Perkins, Nick Benedict, Adam Guier. **1990**

PIT AND THE PENDULUM, THE (1961) ★★★ More stylish, low-budget Edgar Allan Poe–inspired terror with star Vincent Price and director Roger Corman reteaming for this release. This is for fans of the series only. 80m. **DIR:** Roger Corman. **CAST:** Vincent Price, John Kerr, Barbara Steele, Luana Anders, Anthony Carbone. **1961**

PIT AND THE PENDULUM, THE (1991) ★★ Gorefest claims to be based on Edgar Allan Poe's short story, but actually bears little resemblance to it. When a sympathetic woman tries to stop the beating of a small boy by Spanish Inquisition guards, she's imprisoned for witchcraft. Rated R for nudity, profanity, torture, and gore. 97m. **DIR:** Stuart Gordon. **CAST:** Lance Henriksen, Rona De Ricci, Jonathan Fuller, Jeffrey Combs. **1991 DVD**

PITCH BLACK ★★1/2 A starship crash-lands on a desert planet with three suns. The planet is also inhabited by carnivorous creatures that thrive on darkness—and a rare solar eclipse is on the way. Director David Twohy has an excellent visual flair (the film really does seem to be on another planet) and performances are strong. Unfortunately, all are defeated by the script, a banal and predictable rehash of *Alien*. Rated R for violence. 107m. **DIR:** David N. Twohy. **CAST:** Vin Diesel, Radha Mitchell, Cole Hauser, Keith David, Lewis Fitz-Gerald, Claudia Black, Rhiana Griffith. **2000 DVD**

PITFALL ★★★ A tightly directed melodrama about a married man who strays and gets involved in a murder. Dick Powell made this one as a follow-up to *Murder, My Sweet*. This is the last movie Byron Barr made under that name; he changed it to Gig Young for future films. B&W; 84m. **DIR:** André de Toth. **CAST:** Dick Powell, Jane Wyatt, Lizabeth Scott, John Litel, Gig Young, Ann Doran, Raymond Burr, Dick Wessel. **1948**

PITTSBURGH ★★★ John Wayne dominates the screen as Pittsburgh Markham, an ambitious coal miner who risks it all to make his dreams come true. Interestingly, Pittsburgh is more of an opportunist than a hero. Somewhat slow and awkward, this is still a step up from most of Wayne's would-be Republic A-pictures from the same era. B&W; 90m. **DIR:** Lewis Seiler. **CAST:** Marlene Dietrich, Randolph Scott, John Wayne, Frank Craven, Louise Allbritton, Thomas Gomez, Shemp Howard, Ludwig Stossel, Paul Fix. **1942**

PIXOTE ★★★★ In Rio, half the population is younger than 18. Kids, only 10 or 12 years old, become thieves, beggars, and prostitutes. This is the story of one of these unfortunates. For some viewers it may be too powerful and disturbing, yet it is not the least bit exploitative or exaggerated. Rated R for violence, explicit sex, and nudity. 127m. **DIR:** Hector Babenco. **CAST:** Fernando Ramos Da Silva, Marilia Pera. **1981**

PIZZA MAN ★★★ Pizza delivery guy Elmo Bunn is caught in the middle of a campy worldwide conspiracy. Occasionally clever political satire. Not rated, but with some violence. 90m. **DIR:** J. D. Athens. **CAST:** Bill Maher, Annabelle Gurwitch. **1992**

P.K. & THE KID ★★★ Molly Ringwald, in one of her earliest films, is running away from her abusive father, Alex Rocco. She hitches up with Paul LeMat, who is driving to California for the annual arm-wrestling championships. The characters are well developed, and you can see a star in the making. 90m. **DIR:** Lou Lombardo. **CAST:** Paul LeMat, Molly Ringwald, Alex Rocco, Esther Rolle, John Madden. **1985**

•PLACE CALLED CHIAPAS, A ★★★★ Chiapas is a region in southern Mexico populated largely by indigenous people, who for years have been repressed by the Mexican government. This documentary charts the 1994 uprising in the region by the Zapatistas who chose to defy the government and demand self-determination. The film is rough and occasionally confusing for viewers who know little about the situation, but filmmaker Nettie Wild, who was able to get into the Zapatista strongholds, is to be commended for working to bring this crisis to larger attention. In English and Spanish with English subtitles. Not rated. 92m. **DIR:** Nettie Wild. **1998**

PLACE CALLED TODAY, A 🦃 Political drama laid in a city beset by racial strife. Also on video as *City in Fear*. Rated R for nudity and violence. 103m. **DIR:** Don Schain. **CAST:** J. Herbert Kerr Jr., Lana Wood, Cheri Caffaro. **1972**

PLACE CALLED TRINITY, A 🦃 A gunfighting gambler and his brother, a Mormon preacher, have different ideas on how to spend their sizable inheritance, but first they have to find the bandits who stole it. This idiotic comedy-Western filmed in Spain shows why spaghetti Westerns got their undeserved reputation. Only for the easily entertained. Not rated. 97m. **DIR:** James London. **CAST:** Richard Harrison, Donald O'Brien, Anna Zinneman, Rick Boyd. **1972**

PLACE FOR ANNIE, A ★★★★ This *Hallmark Hall of Fame* feature will restore your faith in mankind as Sissy Spacek brilliantly portrays a nurse whose heart is big enough not only for an HIV-positive infant but for the baby's rather unsavory mother as well. Top rate, not to be missed. Not rated; contains mature themes. 95m. **DIR:** John Gray. **CAST:** Sissy Spacek, Mary-Louise Parker, Joan Plowright, S. Epatha Merkerson, Jack Noseworthy. **1994**

PLACE IN THE SUN, A ★★★★ Elizabeth Taylor, Montgomery Clift, and Shelley Winters are caught in a tragic love triangle, based on Theodore Dreiser's *An American Tragedy*. All three artists give first-rate performances. The story of a working-class man who falls for a wealthy girl is a traditional one, yet the eroticism conveyed in the scenes between Taylor and Clift keeps this production well above the standard. B&W; 122m. **DIR:** George Stevens. **CAST:** Elizabeth Taylor, Montgomery Clift, Shelley Winters, Keefe Brasselle, Raymond Burr, Anne Revere. **1951**

PLACE OF WEEPING ★★★1/2 The first film about the South African struggle made by South Africans, this drama follows the battle of one woman who, with the help of a white reporter, stands against the system of apartheid. Although this film is a bit slow-moving and obviously made on a low budget, its political importance cannot be denied. Rated PG. 88m. **DIR:** Darrell Roodt.

CAST: James Whylie, Gcina Mhlophe, Charles Comyn. **1986**

PLACE VENDOME ★★★ Marianne Malivert, trapped in a loveless marriage, exudes a glacial beauty and an alluring depth of character that even her alcoholism cannot fully drown. Her husband's suicide leaves Marianne in possession of five stolen diamonds that hasten her reentry into sobriety and reconnect her to a checkered past in a seductive tale of fluctuating dignity, intrigue, and fractured relationships. In French with English subtitles. No MPAA rating. 105m. **DIR:** Nicole Garcia. **CAST:** Catherine Deneuve, Bernard Fresson, Jean-Pierre Bacri, Emmanuelle Seigner, Jacques Dutronc. **2000**

PLACES IN THE HEART ★★★★★ Based on Robert Benton's childhood memories in Waxahachie, Texas, this film stars Sally Field, who plays Edna Spalding, a mother of two who is suddenly widowed. Almost immediately, she is pressured by the bank to sell her home and the surrounding property. Rated PG for suggested sex, violence, and profanity. 110m. **DIR:** Robert Benton. **CAST:** Sally Field, Ed Harris, Lindsay Crouse, John Malkovich, Danny Glover. **1984 DVD**

PLAGUE, THE ★★★★ The bubonic plague strikes a city in South America. A doctor (William Hurt), with the help of a French reporter and her videographer, battles both the disease and the local government. Raul Julia brilliantly portrays a local cab driver who isn't quite what he seems. A gripping story, well acted and directed. Rated R for nudity and violence. 105m. **DIR:** Luis Puenzo. **CAST:** William Hurt, Robert Duvall, Raul Julia, Sandrine Bonnaire, Jean-Marc Barr. **1993**

PLAGUE DOGS, THE ★★★★1/2 This animated film is definitely *not* for children. It is a powerfully disturbing film that makes an unforgettable statement about animal rights. In it, two dogs escape from an experimental veterinary lab in which they had both been subjected to cruel and senseless operations and tests. Once free, they are hunted by both the "white coats" (lab doctors) and the nearby sheep owners. Rated PG. 99m. **DIR:** Martin Rosen. **1984**

PLAGUE OF THE ZOMBIES ★★★1/2 A couple of years before George Romero awoke the dead, Hammer produced this nifty little chiller. Here the zombies are resurrected by voodoo in order to work as slaves on a plantation mine in a Cornish village. The dead are stylishly presented, sets are high quality, and the direction captures the gloom and atmosphere of the surroundings. Recommended for fans of Hammer *and* zombie movies. 90m. **DIR:** John Gilling. **CAST:** Andre Morell, Diane Clare, Brook Williams, Jacqueline Pearce. **1966 DVD**

PLAIN CLOTHES ★★★1/2 A 24-year-old police detective (Arliss Howard) goes undercover as a high school student. From this not-very-promising plot, director Martha Coolidge and screenwriter A. Scott Frank have fashioned a marvelously tongue-in-cheek hybrid of mystery, teen comedy, and suspense thriller. Rated PG for profanity and violence. 100m. **DIR:** Martha Coolidge. **CAST:** Arliss Howard, Suzy Amis, George Wendt, Seymour Cassel, Abe Vigoda, Robert Stack, Harry Shearer. **1988**

PLAINSMAN, THE ★★★ If you can imagine a scenario uniting George Custer, Wild Bill Hickok, Calamity Jane, and Abraham Lincoln and you're willing to suspend historical disbelief, you should enjoy this stylish Cecil B. DeMille shoot-'em-up. Gary Cooper as Wild Bill Hickok does his best to keep Charles Bickford from selling guns to the Indians. B&W; 113m. **DIR:** Cecil B. DeMille. **CAST:** Gary Cooper, Jean Arthur, Charles Bickford, George "Gabby" Hayes. **1936**

PLAN B ★★★ Generation Xers realize their lives are going nowhere and consider moving on to Plan B. Jon Cryer is the novelist who is at a stalemate. He tags up with four of his friends on holiday and they sit around and wonder what went wrong. Angst-driven vehicles have been driven down this road before, but this one manages to make it to the end. Rated R for language. 102m. **DIR:** Gary Leva. **CAST:** Jon Cryer, Lance Guest, Lisa Darr, Mark Mathieson, Sara Mornell. **1997**

PLAN 9 FROM OUTER SPACE ★★★ Ever see a movie that was so bad it was funny? Well, this low-budget 1950s program is considered to be the very worst picture ever made, and it's hilarious. Written and directed by Edward D. Wood, it's a ponderous science-fiction cheapie that attempts to deliver an antiwar message as well as thrills and chills. It does neither. Even worse than the atrocious acting, cardboard sets, and moronic dialogue, Bela Lugosi is top-billed even though he had died months before. Undaunted, Wood used silent home-movie footage of the once-great horror film star. B&W; 79m. **DIR:** Edward D. Wood Jr. **CAST:** Bela Lugosi, Gregory Walcott, Tom Keene, Duke Moore, Mona McKinnon. **1959 DVD**

PLAN 10 FROM OUTER SPACE 🦃 Despite the title, this would-be cult movie about alien Mormons has nothing to do with Ed Wood's anticlassic *Plan 9*—or anything else, as far as we could tell. Not rated; contains brief nudity and profanity. 85m. **DIR:** Trent Harris. **CAST:** Karen Black, Stefene Russell. **1996**

PLANES, TRAINS AND AUTOMOBILES ★★★★ Although it tends to lose momentum in the last half, this screamingly funny film features Steve Martin and John Candy at the peak of their comedic powers. Martin is an uptight marketing executive en route from New York to Chicago to celebrate Thanksgiving with his family, only to end up on a bizarre cross-country odyssey with an obnoxious bozo played by Candy. Rated R for profanity. 100m. **DIR:** John Hughes. **CAST:** Steve Martin, John Candy, Michael McKean, Laila Robins, Martin Ferrero, Charles Tyner. **1987**

PLANET EARTH ★★ After the original *Star Trek* went off the air but before it was revived on the big screen, creator Gene Roddenberry experimented with several failed television series pilots. *Planet Earth*, essentially Woody Allen's *Sleeper* as straight drama, was one of the silliest. Lead hunk John Saxon goes under in 1979 and awakens in 2133, only to discover that a "great catastrophe" has fragmented people into a series of iconoclastic colonies. 74m. **DIR:** Marc Daniels. **CAST:** John Saxon, Janet Margolin, Ted Cassidy, Diana Muldaur. **1974**

PLANET OF BLOOD (QUEEN OF BLOOD) ★★ Curtis Harrington's two-week wonder is the best of a handful of space operas cobbled together using footage from the late Fifties Soviet sci-fi epic, *Planet of Storms*. An expedition rescues a strange, mute alien, not realizing she's the vampire who wiped out a previous ship from Earth! Slow-paced but oddly fascinating. 81m. **DIR:** Curtis

Harrington. **CAST:** John Saxon, Basil Rathbone, Judi Meredith, Dennis Hopper, Florence Marly. **1966**

PLANET OF THE APES ★★★★ Here is the first and best of the *Planet of the Ape* sci-fi series. Four American astronauts crash on a far-off planet and discover a culture where evolution has gone awry. The dominant form of primates are apes and gorillas. Man is reduced to a beast of burden. Much of the social comment is cutesy and forced, but this remains an enjoyable fantasy. Rated G. 112m. **DIR:** Franklin J. Schaffner. **CAST:** Charlton Heston, Kim Hunter, Roddy McDowall, Maurice Evans. **1968**

•PLANET OF THE APES (2001) ★★ An astronaut crash-lands a one-man space pod on a planet ruled by talking simians. His capture and flight for freedom is set mostly in a dark rainforest that stifles rather than enhances the intended excitement and suspense of the film, as race, human rights, and beast-of-burden themes are delivered with sledgehammer delicacy. Pierre Boulle's novel has been given a new surprise ending and spectacular special effects, but the action, humor, and social commentary do not gel into exhilarating cinema. Rated PG-13 for violence. 118m. **DIR:** Tim Burton. **CAST:** Mark Wahlberg, Estella Warren, Helena Bonham Carter, Tim Roth, Michael Clarke-Duncan, Kris Kristofferson. **2001 DVD**

PLANET OF THE DINOSAURS ★★ A spacecraft crash-lands on a planet inhabited by dinosaurs. Juvenile time killer with decent animation effects. Rated PG. 85m. **DIR:** James K. Shea. **CAST:** James Whitworth. **1978**

PLANET OF THE VAMPIRES ★★ After landing on a mysterious planet, astronauts are possessed by formless alien vampires trying to reach Earth. An Italian-Spanish production, also known as *Demon Planet*. The film is plodding and poorly dubbed. Watch director Mario Bava's *Black Sunday* instead. 86m. **DIR:** Mario Bava. **CAST:** Barry Sullivan, Norma Bengell, Angel Aranda. **1965 DVD**

PLANET PATROL ★★ The adventures of the youthful planet patrol include encounters with giant robots, living dinosaur skeletons, and a giant rubber monster. One section condenses all of *Kraa! The Sea Monster* into twenty minutes. Awful. Rated PG for violence. 80m. **DIR:** Russ Mazzolla. **CAST:** Alison Lohman, Anthony Furlong, J. W. Perra, Teal Marchande. **1999**

PLANTS ARE WATCHING, THE ★★1/2 Originally titled *The Kirlian Witness*, this low-budget melodrama is a well-intentioned fantasy about a clairvoyant woman who taps into the "minds" of plants. She uses the gift to learn the identity of the murderer of her sister. Clever and original, if unexciting. Not rated. 100m. **DIR:** Jonathan Sarno. **CAST:** Nancy Snyder, Joel Colodner, Nancy Boykin. **1978**

PLATINUM BLONDE ★★★★ Jean Harlow's namesake film shows her self-mocking style to advantage. She plays a rich girl who marries a poor newspaper reporter and drags herself up to his level of humanity. The story is similar to *It Happened One Night* but predated it by three years. B&W; 89m. **DIR:** Frank Capra. **CAST:** Jean Harlow, Loretta Young, Robert Williams. **1931**

PLATINUM HIGH SCHOOL ★★ Overheated nonsense, good for a few laughs. Mickey Rooney as a grieving father trying to uncover the conspiracy of silence behind his son's "accidental" death at an exclusive school. B&W; 93m. **DIR:** Charles Haas. **CAST:** Mickey Rooney, Terry Moore, Dan Duryea, Yvette Mimieux, Conway Twitty. **1960**

PLATOON ★★★★★ Writer-director Oliver Stone's Oscar-winning work is not just the best film made on the subject of Vietnam; it is a great cinematic work that stands high among the finest films ever made. Charlie Sheen is the well-meaning youth who volunteers for military service to become a real person instead of, in his words, "a fake human being." Not only does every step and noise bring the threat of death, but there is an intercompany war going on. Rated R for profanity, gore, and violence. 120m. **DIR:** Oliver Stone. **CAST:** Tom Berenger, Willem Dafoe, Charlie Sheen, Forest Whitaker, Francesco Quinn, John C. McGinley, Richard Edson. **1986 DVD**

PLATOON LEADER 🦃 Leaden bore. Rated R for violence. 93m. **DIR:** Aaron Norris. **CAST:** Michael Dudikoff, Robert F. Lyons, Rick Fitts, William Smith. **1988**

PLAY IT AGAIN, CHARLIE BROWN ★★★1/2 Lucy and Schroeder are featured in this animated Peanuts special that combines strong animation with some classic gags on unrequited love. Beethoven-loving Schroeder refuses to even notice Lucy, until she gets him a performing gig for a PTA benefit show. One major problem: he's been told to play rock music! Not rated. 25m. **DIR:** Bill Melendez. **1971**

PLAY IT AGAIN, SAM ★★★★1/2 Woody Allen plays a movie columnist and feature writer who lives his life watching movies. Humphrey Bogart is his idol, and the film commences with the final scenes from *Casablanca*. Allen's wife leaves him, and the film revolves around some unsuccessful attempts by his friends (Diane Keaton and Tony Roberts) to set him up with a girl. In an age when funny movies may make you smile at best, this is an oasis of sidesplitting humor. Rated PG. 87m. **DIR:** Herbert Ross. **CAST:** Woody Allen, Diane Keaton, Tony Roberts, Jerry Lacy, Susan Anspach. **1972 DVD**

PLAY IT TO THE BONE 🦃 In this stale road comedy, two middleweight boxing buddies hitch a ride from Los Angeles to Las Vegas with a woman who has dated them and then fight each other on the opening card for a Mike Tyson bout. Rated R for language, violence, and simulated sex. 125m. **DIR:** Ron Shelton. **CAST:** Woody Harrelson, Antonio Banderas, Lolita Davidovich, Tom Sizemore. **2000 DVD**

PLAY MISTY FOR ME ★★★★ A suspenseful shocker in which director-star Clint Eastwood, playing a disc jockey, is stalked by a crazed fan (Jessica Walter). It puts goose bumps on your goose bumps and marked an auspicious directorial debut for the squinty-eyed star. Rated R. 102m. **DIR:** Clint Eastwood. **CAST:** Clint Eastwood, Jessica Walter, Donna Mills, John Larch, Irene Hervey. **1971 DVD**

PLAY NICE ★★ A game of cat and mouse is played by an angry cop and a brutal serial killer. Predictable thriller. Rated R for violence and language. 89m. **DIR:** Terri Treas. **CAST:** Ed O'Ross. **1992**

PLAYBACK ★★ Erotic video star Shannon Whirry plays a conniving businesswoman who will stop at nothing to rise to the top. With the help of a private detective, she begins her smear campaign on a rising executive whose

position she wants. Predictable payoff. Rated R for nudity, adult situations, and language. 91m. **DIR:** Oley Sassone. **CAST:** Charles Grant, Shannon Whirry, George Hamilton, Tawny Kitaen, Harry Dean Stanton. **1995**

PLAYBOY OF THE WESTERN WORLD ★★★★ Everything about this story is fresh and inspiring, especially the dialogue and accents. A wonderful adaptation of the classic Irish play about a young woman and her fellow villagers falling in love with a handsome roguish stranger. 100m. **DIR:** Brian Desmond Hurst. **CAST:** Siobhan McKenna, Gary Raymond, Michael O'Brian. **1962**

PLAYBOYS, THE ★★★★ A sense of foreboding runs through this period piece based on coscreenwriter Shane Connaughton's childhood reminiscences of traveling troupes who performed at Irish villages in the 1950s. Robin Wright is splendid as the freethinking single mother who comes into conflict with the locals—until she's rescued from her situation by a flamboyant actor (Aidan Quinn). Rated PG-13 for profanity and violence. 113m. **DIR:** Gillies MacKinnon. **CAST:** Albert Finney, Aidan Quinn, Robin Wright, Milo O'Shea, Alan Devlin. **1992**

PLAYER, THE ★★★★★ Robert Altman uses Michael Tolkin's screenplay to savage the motion-picture industry in a deft dark comedy about a sleazy studio executive who fears for his life when a screenwriter starts sending a series of threatening postcards. A must-see for movie buffs. Rated R for profanity, violence, and nudity. 123m. **DIR:** Robert Altman. **CAST:** Tim Robbins, Greta Scacchi, Fred Ward, Whoopi Goldberg, Peter Gallagher, Brian James, Cynthia Stevenson, Vincent D'Onofrio, Dean Stockwell, Richard E. Grant, Sydney Pollack, Lyle Lovett, Dina Merrill. **1992 DVD**

PLAYERS Ali MacGraw is the bored mistress of Maximilian Schell; she falls for tennis pro Dean Paul Martin. Rated PG—sexual situations. 120m. **DIR:** Anthony Harvey. **CAST:** Ali MacGraw, Dean Paul Martin, Maximilian Schell. **1979**

PLAYERS CLUB, THE ★★ A single parent works her way through college as a stripper in the South. She is dubbed Diamond by a greedy boss who spends the entire film dodging a loan shark. Diamond tries to keep her cousin out of trouble when she also starts gyrating at the club. The film has a sassy, gritty realism that is burdened with stereotypical characters and a jaded message: "Make the money. Don't let the money make you." Rated R for language, sexual content, and violence. 103m. **DIR:** Ice Cube. **CAST:** Lisa Raye, Chrystale Wilson, Bernie Mac, Jamie Foxx, Monica Calhoun, Ice Cube. **1998 DVD**

PLAYING BY HEART ★★★★ Terrific romantic comedy about a family and their lives with excellent performances throughout, especially by Gillian Anderson, Jon Stewart, and Sean Connery in a decidedly different role. Rated R for profanity. 121m. **DIR:** Willard Carroll. **CAST:** Sean Connery, Gena Rowlands, Gillian Anderson, Jon Stewart, Ryan Phillippe. **1998 DVD**

PLAYING FOR KEEPS Teenagers inherit a dilapidated hotel and turn it into a rock 'n' roll resort for kids. Rated PG-13 for profanity, violence, nudity, and suggested sex. 103m. **DIR:** Bob Weinstein, Harvey Weinstein. **CAST:** Daniel Jordano, Matthew Penn, Leon W. Grant, Harold Gould, Jimmy Baio. **1986**

PLAYING FOR TIME ★★★★ This outstanding TV drama won numerous Emmy Awards. It's the true story of Fania Fenelon (Vanessa Redgrave) and a group of women prisoners in Auschwitz who survived by forming a small orchestra and performing for the Nazi officers. 148m. **DIR:** Daniel Mann. **CAST:** Vanessa Redgrave, Jane Alexander, Maud Adams, Viveca Lindfors, Shirley Knight. **1980**

PLAYING GOD ★★ Unlicensed L.A. surgeon performs surgery on a shooting victim in a bar. He then becomes the personal physician for a sleazy smuggler, falls in love with the hoodlum's girlfriend, and is dogged by federal investigators before stumbling into redemption. The premise is smart and spooky, but this overly bloody thriller is more worried about being cool than convincing. Rated R for violence, language, and drug use. 94m. **DIR:** Andy Wilson. **CAST:** David Duchovny, Timothy Hutton, Angelina Jolie. **1997 DVD**

PLAYMAKER ★★ Would-be starlet Jennifer Rubin seeks cinematic glory in this turgid erotic thriller, whose climactic plot twists cannot compensate for a first hour laden with pretentious pop psychology and unfocused execution. By the time the story smartens up, you'll be long past caring. Rated R for nudity, profanity, and violence. 91m. **DIR:** Yuri Zeltser. **CAST:** Colin Firth, Jennifer Rubin, John Getz, Jeff Perry. **1994**

PLAYMATES ★★★★ This is a very good romantic comedy about two divorced men who become friends and then secretly begin to date each other's ex-wife, with crazy results. Good cast, fine direction, and an energized screenplay by Richard Baer make this TV movie sparkle. 73m. **DIR:** Theodore J. Flicker. **CAST:** Alan Alda, Connie Stevens, Barbara Feldon, Doug McClure, Severn Darden, Roger Bowen, Eileen Brennan. **1972**

PLAYROOM ★★ Bizarre plot unfolds when an immortal prince draws a young archaeologist back to the site of his parents' murder. Adequate. Rated R for nudity, profanity, violence, and gore. 87m. **DIR:** Manny Coto. **CAST:** Lisa Aliff, Aron Eisenberg, Christopher McDonald, Vincent Schiavelli. **1989**

PLAYTIME ★★★1/2 Mr. Hulot is back again in this slapstick comedy as he attempts to keep an appointment in the big city. Paris and all of its buildings, automobiles, and population seem to conspire to thwart Mr. Hulot at every turn, and there are plenty of visual gags. The subtitled American release version is over thirty minutes shorter than the original French release. 108m. **DIR:** Jacques Tati. **CAST:** Jacques Tati. **1967 DVD**

PLAZA SUITE ★★★★1/2 Walter Matthau is at his comic best as he re-creates three separate roles from Neil Simon's stage comedy. The movie is actually three tales of what goes on in a particular suite. Rated PG. 115m. **DIR:** Arthur Hiller. **CAST:** Walter Matthau, Maureen Stapleton, Barbara Harris, Lee Grant. **1971**

PLEASANTVILLE ★★★★★ This sly, provocative allegory reveals the shortcomings of 1950s-style sitcom "utopias" in a manner that is as subversive as the ingenious storyline. During the film's first half, you'll giggle and gasp at the execution of the witty premise: two modern-day teens get zapped back into the black-and-white universe of a vintage television situation comedy,

where they're unable to resist "meddling" with the quaintly idealistic values found within the picture-perfect setting. The film initially exaggerates these old-fashioned conventions, and it's hard not to laugh... until we see what happens when *any* establishment grows uneasy about change. It's astonishing to consider that 1998 brought us this film and *The Truman Show*, two similarly creative and enlightening allegories, with each disclosing the limitations of artificially ideal environments. Rated PG-13 for profanity and sexual candor. 124m. **DIR:** Gary Ross. **CAST:** Tobey Maguire, Jeff Daniels, Reese Witherspoon, Joan Allen, William H. Macy, J. T. Walsh. **1998 DVD**

PLEASE DON'T EAT MY MOTHER! ★★ Uncredited remake of *Little Shop of Horrors* is even worse—and almost as funny. Middle-aged Henry Fudd (Buck Kartalian, who also directed under a pseudonym) takes time out from being a peeping Tom to feed murder victims to his man- (and woman-) eating plant. Cheesy but fun. Also known as *Hungry Pets*. Not rated; plentiful nudity. 98m. **DIR:** Jack Beckett. **CAST:** Buck Kartalian. **1972 DVD**

PLEASE DON'T EAT THE DAISIES ★★★ Witty David Niven meets his match when he crosses Doris Day's path and questions her ambitions. A clever comedy about a drama critic who copes with his wife's remodeling plans and a conniving actress friend at the same time. Based on Jean Kerr's bestseller and the basis for a TV series during the 1960s. 111m. **DIR:** Charles Walters. **CAST:** Doris Day, David Niven, Janis Paige, Spring Byington, Margaret Lindsay, Richard Haydn, Patsy Kelly, Jack Weston. **1960**

PLEASURE PALACE ★★ No, this is not a porno flick—the characters in this made-for-TV movie are more like old-fashioned melodrama icons. Hope Lange plays an honest widowed casino owner (yea!) who is afraid she will lose her casino to an influential oil baron (boo!). Despite the lack of subtlety in characters, some of the gambling scenes have real tension in them. Not rated, but the equivalent of a PG for violence. 92m. **DIR:** Walter Grauman. **CAST:** Omar Sharif, Victoria Principal, Walter Grauman, J. D. Cannon, Gerald S. O'Loughlin, José Ferrer, Hope Lange. **1980**

PLEASURE UNLIMITED A woman leaves her husband and tries to deal with the sexual revolution in this potboiler written by Ed Wood. Not rated; contains nudity and strong sexual situations. 72m. **DIR:** A. C. Stephen. **CAST:** Angela Carnon, Terry Johnson, Lynn Harris. **1973**

PLEDGE, THE ★★★ Shopworn, retiring cop promises the mother of a mutilated, murdered little girl that he will find the killer. The pledge grows into an obsession when he buys a rural gas station in the vicinity of a similar crime and befriends a barmaid whose daughter resembles the two previous victims. Haunting performances and moody direction keep contrived elements of the plot at bay. Rated R for violence and language. 124m. **DIR:** Sean Penn. **CAST:** Jack Nicholson, Robin Wright, Aaron Eckhart, Benicio Del Toro, Helen Mirren, Tom Noonan, Vanessa Redgrave. **2001 DVD**

PLEDGE NIGHT ★★★1/2 A nicely original horror movie about a group of fraternity guys who are menaced by the ghost of a pledge killed in their house twenty years ago. Inspired special effects keep this from being just another dead-slasher movie. Not rated; contains violence, nudity, and profanity. 90m. **DIR:** Paul Ziller. **CAST:** Todd Eastland, Shannon McMahon, Joey Belladonna, Will Kempe. **1988**

PLENTY ★★★★ In this difficult but rewarding film, Meryl Streep is superb as a former member of the French Resistance who finds life in her native England increasingly maddening during the postwar reconstruction period. Rated R for profanity, suggested sex, and violence. 120m. **DIR:** Fred Schepisi. **CAST:** Meryl Streep, Charles Dance, Sam Neill, Tracey Ullman, John Gielgud, Sting, Ian McKellen. **1985 DVD**

PLOT AGAINST HARRY, THE ★★★★ Shot in a casual black-and-white style that matches the material, this is a tale of the misadventures of an amiable Jewish racketeer, freshly released from prison. Witty satire on middle-class Jewish immigrant life. Not rated, but of PG-13 tone. B&W; 81m. **DIR:** Michael Roemer. **CAST:** Martin Priest. **1969**

PLOT TO KILL HITLER, THE ★★★1/2 Moderately entertaining thriller documents the attempted coup to overthrow Adolf Hitler. Not rated. 93m. **DIR:** Lawrence Schiller. **CAST:** Brad Davis, Madolyn Smith, Ian Richardson, Kenneth Colley, Jonathan Hyde, Rupert Everett. **1990**

PLOUGHMAN'S LUNCH, THE ★★ A morality piece about opportunism and exploitation portrayed through the world of journalism. The problem is that almost everyone in the film is a weasel. The point is to call attention to this fact, but it doesn't make for very enjoyable movie watching. Rated R. 107m. **DIR:** Richard Eyre. **CAST:** Jonathan Pryce, Tim Curry, Rosemary Harris, Frank Finlay, Charlie Dore. **1984**

PLOW THAT BROKE THE PLAINS, THE ★★★★ Written, directed, and produced by master documentarian Pare Lorentz, with a musical score by Virgil Thomson, this cornerstone film is a moving and dramatic account of man's abuse of America's Great Plains: Grass is its heroine, sun and wind its villain, its players nameless farmers whose farming practices produced the Dust Bowl and the Oklahoma-Kansas-Nebraska exodus. Coupled with it is "Night Mail," the John Grierson film tribute to the British postal and railway systems. B&W; 49m. **DIR:** Pare Lorentz. **1934–1936**

PLUMBER, THE ★★★1/2 A slightly unhinged plumber completely destroys a young couple's bathroom and begins to terrorize the woman of the house during his visits to make the repairs. A very black comedy-horror-film from the director of *Witness*. Originally made for Australian television. No rating; contains some strong language. 76m. **DIR:** Peter Weir. **CAST:** Ivar Kants, Judy Morris, Robert Coleby. **1980**

PLUNDER ROAD ★★ This ingenious update to *The Great Train Robbery* leaves five men on the run with $10 million in gold. The crime-does-not-pay theme prevails. The acting is not the greatest. B&W; 76m. **DIR:** Hubert Cornfield. **CAST:** Gene Raymond, Wayne Morris, Jeanne Cooper. **1957**

PLUNKETT & MACLEANE ★★1/2 Two rogues become known in 1748 London as the Gentlemen Highwaymen. Their story relies heavily on predictable Western contours as the scoundrels slowly bond while robbing filthy rich aristocrats. They soon attain mythic reputations and are pursued by a sadistic lawman who likes to gouge

out the eyes of his captives. This sometimes rousing crime-adventure is thick with atmosphere and cinematic flash but thin on character development and credible romance. Rated R for violence, language, and sex. 95m. **DIR:** Jake Scott. **CAST:** Robert Carlyle, Jonny Lee Miller, Ted Stott, Liv Tyler. **1999 DVD**

POCAHONTAS (1994) ★★★ One of several recent releases about a peace-loving Indian girl, this is an Enchanted Tale presented by Golden Films. Despite a lack of big bucks found in the Disney production, this manages to have decent animation and pleasant original tunes. Pocahontas, here, has a talking canoe, an eagle, and a hawk as advisers. Her adventures in England are also covered, along with her romance with John Smith. 48m. **DIR:** Kamoon Song. **1994**

POCAHONTAS (1995) ★★★★ While not an instant classic on a par with other contemporary animated musicals from the Disney Studios, *Pocahontas* is still a genuine pleasure, with fine songs (by Alan Menken and Stephen Schwartz), superb animation, and a story that will entertain young and old alike. Enjoy another triumph from the studio that makes the world's finest feature-length cartoons. Rated G. 87m. **DIR:** Mike Gabriel, Eric Goldberg. **1995 DVD**

POCKET MONEY ★★1/2 Cowpoke Paul Newman and con man Lee Marvin fall in with a calculating cattleman and spend the rest of the film getting themselves out of it. Likable enough but really doesn't go anywhere. 102m. **DIR:** Stuart Rosenberg. **CAST:** Paul Newman, Lee Marvin, Christine Belford, Strother Martin, Kelly Jean Peters, Wayne Rogers. **1972**

POCKETFUL OF MIRACLES ★★★ The term Capracorn could have been coined in response to this overly sentimental picture, basically a remake of the director's 1933 *Lady for a Day.* But Bette Davis is a delight as Apple Annie and Glenn Ford is winningly earnest as the producer who tries to turn her into a lady. Ann-Margret's film debut. 136m. **DIR:** Frank Capra. **CAST:** Bette Davis, Glenn Ford, Hope Lange, Thomas Mitchell, Peter Falk, Edward Everett Horton, Jack Elam, Ann-Margret. **1961 DVD**

POCKETFUL OF RYE, A ★★1/2 Agatha Christie's Miss Marple (Joan Hickson) arrives late in this mystery, which concerns a murder that is somehow connected with a nursery rhyme. Not rated, suitable for family viewing. 102m. **DIR:** Guy Slater. **CAST:** Joan Hickson, Peter Davison, Fabia Drake, Timothy West, Tom Wilkinson, Clive Merrison. **1984**

POETIC JUSTICE ★★ Director John Singleton's follow-up to *Boyz N the Hood* is essentially a self-indulgent mess about the offbeat love affair between a self-styled poet (Janet Jackson, in her film debut) and a troubled young man (Tupac Shakur). Jackson's inexpressive performance is further hampered by her inappropriate, overdubbed readings of Maya Angelou's poetry. Rated R for profanity, simulated sex, and violence. 108m. **DIR:** John Singleton. **CAST:** Janet Jackson, Tupac Shakur, Regina King, Joe Torry, Tyra Ferrell, Maya Angelou. **1993 DVD**

POINT, THE ★★★★1/2 The cartoon adventures of Oblio, a little boy who is banished from his homeland because (unlike everyone else there) his head doesn't come to a point. Completely irresistible for kids and grownups, with narration by Ringo Starr and songs by Harry Nilsson (including "Me and My Arrow"). Made for TV. 74m. **DIR:** Fred Wolf. **1971**

POINT BLANK ★★★★ This brutal crime-drama is one of the finest films of its type. Gangster Lee Marvin is double-crossed by his wife and crime partner, who shoot him and leave him for dead on Alcatraz Island—only to have him turn up a few years later, bent on revenge. Entire cast pulls out all of the stops; it's one of Lee Marvin's strongest performances. Rated R. 92m. **DIR:** John Boorman. **CAST:** Lee Marvin, Angie Dickinson, Lloyd Bochner, Keenan Wynn, Carroll O'Connor, John Vernon. **1967**

POINT BLANK ★★ When a busload of death-row inmates is ambushed and taken over by the prisoners, the jailbreak catches the attention of former cop turned mercenary Rudy Ray who has a brother on board the bus. Things heat up when the inmates take a mall hostage, leaving Ray and his former partner the only two people who can get inside and save the day. Been there, done that. Rated R for violence, language, and adult situations. 90m. **DIR:** Matt Earl Beesley. **CAST:** Mickey Rourke, Frederic Forrest, Kevin Gage, Michael Wright, Danny Trejo, James Gammon. **1998 DVD**

POINT BREAK ★★★1/2 For most of its running time, this release, about two FBI agents (Keanu Reeves, Gary Busey) attempting to catch the perpetrators (who may be led by surfer/guru Patrick Swayze) behind a series of bank robberies, is a terrific action movie. But *Point Break* tends to overstay its welcome with more false endings than we've ever seen. Rated R for violence and profanity. 125m. **DIR:** Kathryn Bigelow. **CAST:** Patrick Swayze, Keanu Reeves, Gary Busey, Lori Petty, John C. McGinley, James LeGros. **1991**

POINT OF IMPACT ★★1/2 A talented cast is wasted in this humdrum cop thriller where plot exists only to fill the spaces between the energetic coupling by Michael Paré and Barbara Carrera. He's a former U.S. Customs agent, she's a crime lord's wife needing protection from parties never adequately specified. Available in both R and unrated versions, each with considerable profanity, violence, nudity, and simulated sex. 96m. **DIR:** Bob Misiorowski. **CAST:** Michael Paré, Barbara Carrera, Michael Ironside, Lehua Reid. **1993**

POINT OF NO RETURN ★★★ American, scene-for-scene remake of French director Luc Besson's *La Femme Nikita* lacks the subtlety and poignance of the original. Instead, director John Badham puts the emphasis on violence, with street punk Bridget Fonda drafted as an assassin by a supersecret government organization. Fonda's committed performance is the only high-quality element in this no-excuses action romp. Rated R for violence, profanity, nudity, and simulated sex. 108m. **DIR:** John Badham. **CAST:** Bridget Fonda, Gabriel Byrne, Dermot Mulroney, Anne Bancroft, Harvey Keitel, Miguel Ferrer, Olivia D'Abo, Richard Romanus, Geoffrey Lewis. **1993 DVD**

POINTSMAN, THE ★★★ A lady from Holland mysteriously disembarks from a train in the Scottish Highlands. The only person at the depot is the point man who resides at this isolated outpost. This most unusual film requires patience, but it has a strangely compelling attraction. The interesting characters, the fine photography, and the sensual development between the two leads keep you rapt until the end. Rated R for

nudity and adult situations. 95m. **DIR:** Jos Stelling. **CAST:** Stephane Excoffier. **1988**

POIROT (SERIES) ★★★★★ Agatha Christie's endearing and eccentric private detective, Hercule Poirot—a Belgian policeman who fled to England in 1914 as a refugee—is perfectly portrayed by David Suchet in this engaging series of mysteries faithfully dramatized by Clive Exton. Poirot—joined by his faithful companion Captain Hastings and loyal and efficient secretary Miss Lemon—solves a variety of murder mysteries with panache. Highlights include "Murder in the Mews," in which Poirot and his friend, Inspector Japp of Scotland Yard, work together to solve a murder; "Triangle at Rhodes," filmed on location in the beautiful Greek islands, with a wonderfully tricky plot and an intriguing cast of characters; and "Problem at Sea," where Poirot and Hastings's Mediterranean cruise soon turns into a busman's holiday. 52m. **DIR:** Edward Bennett, Renny Rye. **CAST:** David Suchet, Hugh Fraser, Philip Jackson, Pauline Moran. **1989 DVD**

POISON ★★ Disturbing, at times disgusting, trilogy of stories spliced together jumping back and forth from one horror to the next. In one, a seven year old murders his father; another features a mad scientist whose experiment transforms him into a leper; and finally there's a cruel glimpse into a sadistic homosexual relationship behind prison bars. Not rated, contains nudity, violence, and profanity. 85m. **DIR:** Todd Haynes. **CAST:** Edith Meeks, Larry Maxwell, Susan Norman, Scott Renderer, James Lyons. **1990 DVD**

POISON IVY (1985) ★★ Top talents save this banal TV movie about life at a summer camp. Michael J. Fox is the hip counselor; Nancy McKeon is an assistant nurse and Fox's love interest; and Robert Klein is the bombastic camp director. All right for star watching. 97m. **DIR:** Larry Elikann. **CAST:** Michael J. Fox, Nancy McKeon, Robert Klein, Caren Kaye, Jason Bateman, Adam Baldwin. **1985**

POISON IVY (1992) ★★★1/2 Drew Barrymore makes a heck of an impact in a very adult role as Ivy, a sleazy teen who is taken in by a wealthy family. Ivy likes what she sees, especially dad (Tom Skerritt), whom she slowly seduces as she works to make the family her own. Rated R for profanity and suggested sex. 92m. **DIR:** Katt Shea Ruben. **CAST:** Drew Barrymore, Sara Gilbert, Tom Skerritt, Cheryl Ladd. **1992 DVD**

POISON IVY: THE NEW SEDUCTION ★★ Pointless sequel covers pretty much the same territory as the previous two entries in this sagging franchise. Newcomer Jaime Pressly stars as Violet, the evil sister of the original Ivy, who returns to her hometown to wreak havoc on the family she believes betrayed her sister. Violet systematically seduces her best friend's father and fiancé as retribution. Just another excuse to rehash a once-popular formula. R-rated and unrated versions; both contain nudity, violence, and language. 93/95. **DIR:** Kurt Voss. **CAST:** Jaime Pressly, Michael Des Barres, Megan Edwards, Greg Vaughan, Susan Tyrrell. **1997 DVD**

POISON IVY 2: LILY ★★ Former child actress Alyssa Milano takes another step to erase her goody-goody image. Here she plays an art student who stumbles across the diary of Ivy from the first film. Ivy's words inspire her to explore her own sexual desires. Rated R for nudity and adult language. Unrated version also available. 112m. **DIR:** Anne Goursand. **CAST:** Alyssa Milano, Xander Berkeley, Jonathan Scaech. **1995 DVD**

POKÉMON THE FIRST MOVIE: MEWTWO STRIKES BACK ★★ Japan's animated pocket monsters and human trainers leap from TV into feature films with this preachy adventure about fighting being the wrong way to settle issues. The mysterious Mew, a powerful Pokémon, is cloned by scientists into the even more powerful Mewtwo. When Mewtwo realizes he is a man-made freak and decides humans are evil, he raises havoc with an army of clones. Rated G. 69m. **DIR:** Kunihiko Yuyama. **1999 DVD**

POKÉMON THE MOVIE 2000 ★★ This "movie" combines *Pikachu's Rescue Adventure*, a 22-minute short, with *The Power of One*, a 63-minute feature that introduces six new Pokémon. The adventures have more action and less preaching than *Pokémon The First Movie* but suffer from cheesy plotting. Pikachu's journey takes us into an underground rain forest. In *Power*, Pokémon trainer Ash Ketchum tries to save the Earth after a Pokémon collector disrupts the harmony of nature. Rated G. 85m. **DIR:** Kunihiko Yuyama, Michael Haigney. **2000 DVD**

•POKÉMON 3 ★★ This animated sequel is actually two adventures under one title. The film short *Pikachu and Pichu* plays like a watercolor hallucination in which the popular Japanese pocket monsters run amok in a big city over a jazz/pop soundtrack. In the feature-length *Spell of the Unknown*, trainer Ash and his cohorts attempt to rescue his mother and the orphan Molly from a dreamworld prison where the Unknowns turn human thought and emotions into reality. The lengthy battles here become tiresome in a film that says Pokémon love to battle but also know when to quit. Rated G. 93m. **DIR:** Michael Haigney, Kunihiko Yuyama. **2001 DVD**

POKER ALICE ★★1/2 A nifty supporting cast outclasses Elizabeth Taylor in this poky TV movie. Liz seems bored playing a New Orleans gambler who travels to the Old West and wins a bordello in a poker game. 109m. **DIR:** Arthur Allan Seidelman. **CAST:** Elizabeth Taylor, Tom Skerritt, George Hamilton, Susan Tyrrell, Richard Mulligan, David Wayne. **1987**

POLAR BEAR KING, THE ★★★ In this slow-moving fairy tale, a prince is turned into a polar bear by a wicked witch. He travels north and encounters a young woman. They fall in love and battle the evil crone together. Rated PG. 87m. **DIR:** Ola Solum. **CAST:** Maria Bonnevie, Jack Fieldstad, Tobias Hoesl, Anna-Lotta Larsson, Jon Laxdal, Monica Nordquist. **1992**

POLICE ★★1/2 Dull crime-drama about a tough French cop (Gérard Depardieu), who becomes emotionally involved with a beautiful drug dealer (Sophie Marceau). Not much chemistry between the central characters. In French with English subtitles. Not rated; contains nudity and profanity. 113m. **DIR:** Maurice Pialat. **CAST:** Gérard Depardieu, Sophie Marceau, Richard Anconina, Sandrine Bonnaire. **1985**

POLICE ACADEMY ★★ Here's another *Animal House*–style comedy that tries very hard to be funny. Sometimes it is, and sometimes it isn't. Rated R for nudity, violence, and profanity. 95m. **DIR:** Hugh Wilson. **CAST:** Steve Guttenberg, George Gaynes, Kim Cattrall,

Bubba Smith, Michael Winslow, Andrew Rubin. **1984 DVD**

POLICE ACADEMY II: THEIR FIRST ASSIGNMENT ★★ Those inept would-be officers from Hugh Wilson's *Police Academy* return in this less funny but still box office–potent production. Episodic and silly. Rated PG-13 for profanity. 90m. **DIR:** Jerry Paris. **CAST:** Steve Guttenberg, Bubba Smith, David Graf, Michael Winslow, Bruce Mahler, Colleen Camp, Marion Ramsey, Howard Hesseman, George Gaynes. **1985**

POLICE ACADEMY III: BACK IN TRAINING Moronic. Rated PG for silly violence and references to body parts. 90m. **DIR:** Jerry Paris. **CAST:** Steve Guttenberg, Bubba Smith, David Graf, Michael Winslow, Marion Ramsey, Leslie Easterbrook, Art Metrano, Tim Kazurinsky, Bob Goldthwait, George Gaynes. **1986**

POLICE ACADEMY 4: CITIZENS ON PATROL Let's just say that if you liked the first three, there's no reason you shouldn't like the fourth. Rated PG for mild profanity. 87m. **DIR:** Jim Drake. **CAST:** Steve Guttenberg, Bubba Smith, Michael Winslow, David Graf, Tim Kazurinsky, Sharon Stone, G. W. Bailey, Bob Goldthwait. **1987**

POLICE ACADEMY 5: ASSIGNMENT: MIAMI BEACH Silly fifth entry in the series. Rated PG for language and ribald humor. 90m. **DIR:** Alan Myerson. **CAST:** Bubba Smith, David Graf, Michael Winslow, Leslie Easterbrook, Marion Ramsey, Janet Jones, René Auberjonois. **1988**

POLICE ACADEMY 6: CITY UNDER SIEGE Rated PG for violence and profanity. 87m. **DIR:** Peter Bonerz. **CAST:** Bubba Smith, Kenneth Mars, George Gaynes, David Graf, Michael Winslow, G. W. Bailey. **1989**

POLICE ACADEMY: MISSION TO MOSCOW Totally unfunny sequel finds the remaining inept recruits helping Moscow solve its problems. The only laugh is that they shot this turkey on location. Did someone say Cold War? Rated PG for slapstick violence. 83m. **DIR:** Alan Metter. **CAST:** George Gaynes, Michael Winslow, David Graf, Leslie Esterbrook, Charlie Schlatter. **1994**

POLICE SQUAD! ★★★★ Originally a 1982 summer TV show, with only six episodes aired, this is now a minor cult classic. The folks who made *Airplane!* went all out on this. Each one of the episodes is hilarious, much funnier than the popular film *Police Academy*. 75m. **DIR:** Jim Abrahams, David Zucker, Jerry Zucker, Joe Dante, Reza S. Badiyi. **CAST:** Leslie Nielsen, Alan North. **1982**

POLICE STORY III—SUPER COP ★★★★ With fantastic stunts, snappy touches of comedy, international locales, and a likable lead actor, this Hong Kong import comes extremely close to matching action films such as *Lethal Weapon*. Jackie Chan is a Hong Kong cop who goes undercover in Communist China in an effort to flush out a nasty drug lord. Chan—who does all his own stunts—really makes this a winner. In Cantonese with English subtitles. Not rated; contains violence and brief profanity. 100m. **DIR:** Stanley Tong. **CAST:** Jackie Chan, Michelle Yeoh, Maggie Cheung, Ken Tsang, Yuen Wah, Bill Tung, Josephine Koo. **1992**

POLISH VAMPIRE IN BURBANK, A ★★1/2 Low-budget, sophomoric horror-comedy that, nonetheless, provides a few laughs. Mark Pirro plays a "virgin" vampire. His sultry sister, another vampire, takes him out one night for a bite. One of those films that you giggle at, then feel very sheepish. Not rated; contains sexual suggestion and some ghoulish violence. 84m. **DIR:** Mark Pirro. **CAST:** Mark Pirro, Lori Sutton, Eddie Deezen. **1985**

POLISH WEDDING ★★1/2 In Chicago, the sexual maturity of a teenage girl causes consternation for her Polish-American family, headed by Lena Olin (who is Swedish) and Gabriel Byrne (Irish). *Polish Wedding* wants to be to Polish Americans what *Moonstruck* was to Italian Americans but wholly lacks that film's sense of whimsy and romance. Rated PG-13 for profanity and sexual situations. 101m. **DIR:** Theresa Connelly. **CAST:** Claire Danes, Lena Olin, Gabriel Byrne, Rade Serbedzija. **1998 DVD**

POLLOCK ★★★ Alcoholic painter Jackson Pollock, with his drip-pour-slash-and-splash paintings, became a sensation as well as whipping post for all things wrong with modern art. This uneven but unnerving look at his life and art is just as frustrating and nonrevelatory as it is vivid and explosive. It escorts us through the 1940s and 1950s up to Pollock's death in a car wreck at the age of 44. Rated R for profanity and sexual situations. 122m. **DIR:** Ed Harris. **CAST:** Ed Harris, Marcia Gay Harden, Amy Madigan, Jennifer Connelly, Jeffrey Tambor, Bud Cort. **2000 DVD**

POLLYANNA (1920) ★★★1/2 Mary Pickford (at age 27 in 1920) portrays 12-year-old Pollyanna, and she melts the hearts of everyone. If you admire silent films or Pickford, or both, you should see this one. B&W; 78m. **DIR:** Paul Powell. **CAST:** Mary Pickford, Katharine Griffith, Howard Ralston. **1920**

POLLYANNA (1960) ★★★1/2 Walt Disney's version of this classic childhood book is good entertainment for the whole family. Hayley Mills is the energetic and optimistic young girl who improves the lives of everyone she meets. Jane Wyman, Agnes Moorehead, and Adolphe Menjou head an exceptional supporting cast for this film. 134m. **DIR:** David Swift. **CAST:** Hayley Mills, Jane Wyman, Agnes Moorehead, Adolphe Menjou, Karl Malden, Nancy Olson. **1960 DVD**

POLTERGEIST ★★★★★ The ultimate screen ghost story, this is guaranteed to raise goose pimples while keeping viewers marvelously entertained. A sort of *Close Encounters* of the supernatural, it's a scary story about the plight of a suburban family whose home suddenly becomes a house of horrors. Rated PG for tense situations. 114m. **DIR:** Tobe Hooper. **CAST:** Craig T. Nelson, JoBeth Williams, Beatrice Straight, Dominique Dunne. **1982 DVD**

POLTERGEIST II: THE OTHER SIDE ★★ Mere months (screen time) after their last film adventure, the stalwart Freeling family is up to its eyeballs in spooks again—although the ghosts stay backstage while another collection of effects parades before the audience. The whole project collapses under its own weight. Rated PG-13 for violence. 92m. **DIR:** Brian Gibson. **CAST:** JoBeth Williams, Craig T. Nelson, Heather O'Rourke, Oliver Robins, Zelda Rubinstein, Will Sampson, Geraldine Fitzgerald. **1986**

POLTERGEIST III Little Carol Ann (Heather O'Rourke) moves to Chicago to attend a school for gifted children with mental disorders. Rated PG-13 for violence. 90m. **DIR:** Gary A. Sherman. **CAST:** Tom

Skerritt, Nancy Allen, Heather O'Rourke, Zelda Rubinstein. **1988**

POLTERGEIST: THE LEGACY ★★★ This moderately entertaining cable-series pilot has nothing to do with the *Poltergeist* series. Dedicated good guy Derek de Lint assembles a crew of resourceful demon chasers to track an evil entity that has impregnated an unsuspecting woman; the delivery of that infant must be seen to be believed. Rated R for nudity, rape, violence, gore, and profanity. 90m. **DIR:** Stuart Gillard. **CAST:** Derek de Lint, Martin Cummins, Robbi Chong, Patrick Fitzgerald, Alexandra Purvis, Helen Shaver, Bill Sadler. **1996**

POLYESTER ★★ Anyone for bad taste? Female impersonator Divine and 1950s heartthrob Tab Hunter play lovers in this film by writer-producer-director John Waters (*Pink Flamingos*). A special gimmick called "Odorama" allowed viewers to experience the story's various smells via a scratch-and-sniff card. Rated R. 86m. **DIR:** John Waters. **CAST:** Divine, Tab Hunter, Edith Massey, Mary Garlington. **1981**

POLYMORPH ★★★1/2 Exciting action-based sci-fi film that has a meteor crashing on Earth and bringing with it an organism that can emulate its victims. Into the woods comes a group of people who run into a drug runner infected with the organism. What follows is a clever tale of paranoia that has everyone questioning who is still himself. Not rated; contains violence, profanity, and gore. 86m. **DIR:** J. R. Bookwalter. **CAST:** James L. Edwards, Ariauna Albright, Sasha Graham, Joseph Daw, Jennifer Huss. **1996**

POMPATUS OF LOVE, THE ★★★ Four New York twentysomething men confront their feelings about love and commitment in this talky but engaging comedy-drama that benefits from a likable cast. Rated R for nudity, profanity, and adult situations. 99m. **DIR:** Richard Schenkman. **CAST:** Jon Cryer, Arabella Field, Tim Guinee, Adrian Pasdar, Adam Oliensis, Mia Sara, Jennifer Tilly, Kristin Scott Thomas, Michael McKean. **1996 DVD**

PONETTE ★★★★1/2 Brilliant, is the only way to describe the powerful performance of Victoire Thivisol, a 4-year-old actress at the heart of Jacques Doillon's haunting film about the loss of a parent. Except for an ending that seems to lose track of the film's message, *Ponette* is filled with heart and heartbreak. Little Ponette doesn't understand why her mother has been taken away from her, and spends most of the film looking for her, or at least the spirit of the woman who loved her so much. An exceptional, rare experience. In French with English subtitles. Not rated. 97m. **DIR:** Jacques Doillon. **CAST:** Victoire Thivisol, Delphine Schiltz, Matiaz Bureau Caton, Marie Trintignant. **1996 DVD**

PONTIAC MOON ★★ It's a painful sight when the most animated thing on the screen is Ted Danson's hairpiece. Inspired by the Apollo XI astronauts, eccentric Danson takes his sheltered son on a road trip. Mary Steenburgen deserves respect for making the most of her awkwardly scripted role as an agoraphobic mother. Rated PG-13 for a fistfight and profanity. 108m. **DIR:** Peter Medak. **CAST:** Ted Danson, Mary Steenburgen, Cathy Moriarty, Eric Schweig. **1994**

PONY EXPRESS ★★★ Bigger than they were in life, Western legends Buffalo Bill Cody and Wild Bill Hickok battle stagecoach station owners and Cheyenne Indians to establish the short-lived but glamorous pony express mail route in the early 1860s. Rousing good action for the historical Western fan who doesn't check every fact. 101m. **DIR:** Jerry Hopper. **CAST:** Charlton Heston, Rhonda Fleming, Jan Sterling, Forrest Tucker. **1953**

PONY EXPRESS RIDER ★★★★ A young man joins the pony express to find those responsible for the murder of his father. Solid performances from a host of veteran Western character actors. 100m. **DIR:** Hal Harrison Jr. **CAST:** Stewart Peterson, Henry Wilcoxon, Buck Taylor, Joan Caulfield, Maureen McCormick, Ken Curtis, Slim Pickens, Dub Taylor, Jack Elam. **1976**

PONY SOLDIER ★★ An obvious effort to regenerate Tyrone Power's lagging career, this Western relies on old cowboy-and-Indian ideas instead of an original story. It's set in the Canadian mountains to give it a different look, but the stories and characters are straight out of old-time Saturday-afternoon Westerns. 82m. **DIR:** Joseph M. Newman. **CAST:** Tyrone Power, Penny Edwards, Thomas Gomez, Robert Horton, Cameron Mitchell. **1952**

POODLE SPRINGS ★★★1/2 Novelist Robert Parker did a superb job of completing Raymond Chandler's last unfinished Philip Marlowe novel, which screenwriter Tom Stoppard efficiently brings to the screen. James Caan is rumpled and tired as the aging Marlowe, a man out of time in 1963, with modern technology soon to render his brand of sleuthing obsolete. But he's still got the juice, and this little thriller delivers plenty of twists while showcasing a new side of the P.I. as he adjusts to marriage with a wealthy lawyer half his age. Rated PG-13 for violence and brief nudity. 100m. **DIR:** Bob Rafelson. **CAST:** James Caan, Dina Meyer, David Keith, Tom Bower, Julia Campbell, Brian Cox, Joe Don Baker. **1998**

POOL HUSTLERS, THE ★★★ Comedy-drama about an amateur pool player out to take the title away from the national champion. In Italian with English subtitles. Not rated, the film has sexual situations. 101m. **DIR:** Maurizio Ponzi. **CAST:** Francesco Nuti. **1983**

POOR LITTLE RICH GIRL, THE (1917) ★★★ Mary Pickford's main claim to fame was her uncanny ability to convincingly portray females many years her junior. She stunted her range by doing so again and again, but the public loved it and willingly paid for it. She earned high critical acclaim demonstrating her range in this sentimental comedy-drama. One critic said that she was 8 years old, then a haughty 16, with no warning or motivation for the mercurial change. Silent, with organ music. B&W; 64m. **DIR:** Maurice Tourneur. **CAST:** Mary Pickford. **1917**

POOR LITTLE RICH GIRL (1936) ★★★★ A strong supporting cast makes this Shirley Temple vehicle one of her finest. She plays a motherless child who gets lost. Befriended by vaudevillians Alice Faye and Jack Haley, she joins the act, wows 'em, and wins 'em. As movie musicals go this one is tops. B&W; 72m. **DIR:** Irving Cummings. **CAST:** Shirley Temple, Alice Faye, Jack Haley, Michael Whalen, Gloria Stuart, Henry Armetta, Sara Haden, Jane Darwell. **1936**

POOR LITTLE RICH GIRL: THE BARBARA HUTTON STORY 🦃 Farrah Fawcett plays the title role in this shallow but well-dressed biography of the unhappy American heiress. Edited down from a 250-minute TV

miniseries, this is extremely choppy and superficial. Not rated; contains profanity. 98m. **DIR:** Charles Jarrott. **CAST:** Farrah Fawcett, Bruce Davison, Kevin McCarthy, James Read. **1987**

POOR WHITE TRASH Yankee architect clashes with the business (and moral) ethics of Louisiana developers. Not rated, but with nudity and violence. B&W; 90m. **DIR:** Harold Daniels. **CAST:** Peter Graves, Lita Milan, Douglas Fowley, Timothy Carey, Jonathan Haze. **1961 DVD**

POOR WHITE TRASH II Not really a sequel to *Poor White Trash,* just another lousy thriller about an insane Vietnam veteran who starts slaughtering people. Rated R for violence. 83m. **DIR:** S. F. Brownrigg. **CAST:** Gene Ross. **1976**

•POOTIE TANG Adapted from a skit on Chris Rock's cable TV show, this hopeless, cheap-looking mess doesn't even have enough laughs or story to fill its paltry 79-minute running time. Rated PG-13 for sexual humor and some profanity. 79m. **DIR:** Louis C. K. **CAST:** Lance Crouther, J. B. Smoove, Jennifer Coolidge, Robert Vaughn, Chris Rock. **2001 DVD**

POP & ME ★★★1/2 In an effort to better understand the relationship he shares with his father, filmmaker Chris Roe joins his dad on a globe-hopping trip to find the answers. The resulting documentary is an engaging, funny, and occasionally sad portrait of the bond between fathers and sons. Roe uses the camera as a therapist, hoping to gain wisdom and insight. He succeeds. The interviews with various fathers and sons are connected by a universal thread, which the filmmaker weaves into a fascinating film. Rated PG-13 for language. 91m. **DIR:** Chris Roe. **1999 DVD**

POPCORN ★★★1/2 A film student discovers her weird dreams are rooted in an old horror flick. Wonderfully entertaining chiller set during a festival of scare movies. Tom Villard is both humorous and frightening as a classmate who tries to kill the entire class. Rated R for violence and profanity. 93m. **DIR:** Mark Herrier. **CAST:** Jill Schoelen, Tom Villard, Dee Wallace, Kelly Jo Minter, Tony Roberts, Ray Walston. **1991 DVD**

POPE JOHN PAUL II ★★★★ Albert Finney is superb as the charismatic pontiff in this enactment of the Polish priest's adult life—from battles with Nazis and communism to his ascension to the throne of the Catholic church. Made for TV but with big-screen production values, the film represented Finney's American TV debut. 150m. **DIR:** Herbert Wise. **CAST:** Albert Finney, Nigel Hawthorne, Brian Cox, John McEnery, Ronald Pickup. **1984**

POPE MUST DIET, THE As a comedy, *The Pope Must Die* (retitled *The Pope Must Diet*) is about as unfunny as you can get. Director Peter Richardson delivers a pastiche of gags that will have you hitting the fast-forward button to find the good parts. There aren't any. Rated R for violence, profanity, and nudity. 90m. **DIR:** Peter Richardson. **CAST:** Robbie Coltrane, Beverly D'Angelo, Alex Rocco, Paul Bartel, Herbert Lom, Balthazar Getty, Peter Richardson. **1991**

POPE OF GREENWICH VILLAGE, THE ★★★1/2 This watchable film focuses on the hard-edged misadventures of two Italian cousins, Paulie (Eric Roberts) and Charlie (Mickey Rourke). Paulie is a not-so-bright dreamer who's obviously headed for trouble, and Charlie, who is smart enough to know better, always seems to get caught up in the middle of his cousin's half-baked and dangerous rip-off schemes. Rated R for profanity and violence. 120m. **DIR:** Stuart Rosenberg. **CAST:** Eric Roberts, Mickey Rourke, Daryl Hannah, Geraldine Page. **1984**

POPEYE ★★★ This adaptation of the famous comic strip by director Robert Altman is the cinematic equivalent of the old "good news, bad news" routine. The good news is that Robin Williams makes a terrific Popeye, and Shelley Duvall was born to play Olive Oyl. The bad news is that it's often boring. Still, it's hard to really dislike *Popeye*—it's so wonderfully weird to look at and so much fun at times. Rated PG. 114m. **DIR:** Robert Altman. **CAST:** Robin Williams, Shelley Duvall, Ray Walston, Paul Smith, Paul Dooley, Richard Libertini, Wesley Ivan Hurt, Bill Irwin. **1980 DVD**

POPI ★★1/2 Alan Arkin is Popi (Pappa), a hard-working if somewhat irresponsible Puerto Rican immigrant who comes up with a plan to provide his two young boys with new lives as Cuban refugees. Offbeat dramatic comedy, recommended only for families with older children. Rated G, although there is some violence and partial nudity. 115m. **DIR:** Arthur Hiller. **CAST:** Alan Arkin, Rita Moreno. **1969**

POPPY IS ALSO A FLOWER, THE ★★ Ian Fleming wrote the original story for this movie about efforts to destroy an international drug ring. Many in the huge cast worked for scale as a protest against drug abuse, but it backfired. So many stars pop up in small roles that they overwhelm the plot. Originally made for television, later released theatrically with added footage. Not rated; contains violence. 105m. **DIR:** Terence Young. **CAST:** E. G. Marshall, Trevor Howard, Gilbert Roland, Rita Hayworth, Anthony Quayle, Angie Dickinson, Yul Brynner, Eli Wallach, Marcello Mastroianni, Omar Sharif, Grace Kelly. **1966**

PORK CHOP HILL ★★★★ This no-win look at the Korean conflict features tough yet vulnerable Gregory Peck as the man forced to hold an insignificant mound of earth against overwhelming hordes of communist Chinese. A great cast and master director Lewis Milestone elevate this story to epic status. B&W; 97m. **DIR:** Lewis Milestone. **CAST:** Gregory Peck, Harry Guardino, Rip Torn, Woody Strode, George Peppard, Bob Steele, James Edwards. **1959 DVD**

PORKY'S Teenagers in a fateful trip to a redneck dive called Porky's. Rated R for vulgarity, nudity, and adult themes. 94m. **DIR:** Bob Clark. **CAST:** Dan Monahan, Mark Herrier, Wyatt Knight, Roger Wilson, Kim Cattrall, Scott Colomby. **1981 DVD**

PORKY'S II: THE NEXT DAY This time, the lustful kids of Angel Beach High battle with the Ku Klux Klan. Rated R for the usual garbage. 95m. **DIR:** Bob Clark. **CAST:** Dan Monahan, Wyatt Knight, Mark Herrier, Roger Wilson, Kaki Hunter, Scott Colomby, Nancy Parsons, Edward Winter. **1983**

PORKY'S REVENGE It's just more of the same stupidity. Rated R for profanity, suggested sex, and nudity. 90m. **DIR:** James Komack. **CAST:** Dan Monahan, Wyatt Knight, Tony Ganios, Mark Herrier, Kaki Hunter, Scott Colomby. **1985**

PORNOGRAPHERS, THE ★★★★ A small-time porno filmmaker struggles to cope with the corrupt sexual

ways of his family, the world outside, and himself. A brilliant black comedy that explores contemporary Japanese society with a kinky, perverse, irrational vision. In Japanese with English subtitles. B&W; 128m. **DIR:** Shohei Imamura. **CAST:** Shoichi Ozawa. **1966**

PORT OF CALL ★★★ When a seaman begins working on the docks, he falls in love with a suicidal young woman. The woman has had an unhappy childhood and a wild past, which has given her a bad reputation. This drama seems dated today. In Swedish with English subtitles. B&W; 100m. **DIR:** Ingmar Bergman. **CAST:** Nine-Christine Jonsson, Bengt Eklund. **1948**

PORT OF NEW YORK ★★1/2 A female narcotics smuggler decides to play ball with the police and deliver her former colleagues to them. Yul Brynner is the head smuggler who wants to stop the squealing—fast. Gritty and engrossing. B&W; 82m. **DIR:** Laslo Benedek. **CAST:** Scott Brady, Richard Rober, K. T. Stevens, Yul Brynner. **1949**

PORTNOY'S COMPLAINT ★★ Amazing that anyone had the nerve to attempt to translate Philip Roth's infamous novel to the screen. The neurotic Jewish boy, who has a strange relationship with his mother and an obsession with sex, should be neutered. It's worth viewing only as a curiosity. Rated R for profanity and sex. 101m. **DIR:** Ernest Lehman. **CAST:** Richard Benjamin, Karen Black, Lee Grant, Jack Somack, Jeannie Berlin, Jill Clayburgh. **1972**

PORTRAIT, THE ★★★ Sentimental story focuses on the twilight years of an elderly couple, while their daughter attempts to finish a portrait of the two. It's nice to see two great stars at work. Considering the wealth of talent involved, this film is a disappointment. 108m. **DIR:** Arthur Penn. **CAST:** Gregory Peck, Lauren Bacall, Cecilia Peck, Paul McCrane. **1993**

PORTRAIT OF A LADY, THE ★★★ This adaptation of Henry James's novel is about a headstrong Victorian woman (Nicole Kidman) who meets her match in duplicitous Barbara Hershey (nominated for best supporting actress for this role). In an attempt to marry for love, Kidman is paired with a controlling monster (John Malkovich). Sounds fascinating, but the slow pace and plot development make this a seemingly endless film. Rated PG-13 for brief nudity and sexual fantasies. 144m. **DIR:** Jane Campion. **CAST:** Nicole Kidman, John Malkovich, Barbara Hershey, John Gielgud, Shelley Winters, Shelley Duvall. **1996 DVD**

PORTRAIT OF A SHOWGIRL ★★ This made-for-television film is another attempt to chronicle the life of Las Vegas show girls. They meet men, they lose men. They lose jobs, they get jobs. 100m. **DIR:** Steven H. Stern. **CAST:** Lesley Ann Warren, Rita Moreno, Dianne Kay, Tony Curtis, Barry Primus, Howard Morris. **1982**

PORTRAIT OF A STRIPPER ★★ A dancer is forced to strip to support her fatherless son, causing the authorities to label her an unfit mother. Originally made for TV, timid presentation will, no doubt, disappoint many drooling video renters. 100m. **DIR:** John A. Alonzo. **CAST:** Lesley Ann Warren, Edward Herrmann, Vic Tayback, Sheree North. **1979**

PORTRAIT OF JENNIE ★★★★ A talented, unsung artist achieves fame and success after meeting a mysterious young girl who just might not be real in this charming, somewhat supernatural love story based on Robert Nathan's novel. A first-rate cast and high production values. B&W; 86m. **DIR:** William Dieterle. **CAST:** Jennifer Jones, Joseph Cotten, Ethel Barrymore, Lillian Gish, David Wayne, Henry Hull. **1948**

PORTRAIT OF TERESA ★★★1/2 Controversial emotionally charged drama about a disenchanted housewife who becomes involved with political and cultural groups in a postrevolutionary Cuban society. In Spanish with English subtitles. Not rated; contains profanity and violence. 115m. **DIR:** Pastor Vega. **CAST:** Daisy Granados. **1979**

PORTRAIT OF THE ARTIST AS A YOUNG MAN, A ★★★ Fair adaptation of James Joyce's autobiographical novel about the coming-of-age of a young man while attending a Dublin university. The character intensely questions the morals of his day, which include the Catholic Church and the tyranny of family and state. Excellent ensemble acting by a superb cast. Not rated. 93m. **DIR:** Joseph Strick. **CAST:** Bosco Hogan, T. P. McKenna, John Gielgud. **1977 DVD**

POSEIDON ADVENTURE, THE ★★★ It's New Year's Eve on the passenger liner *Poseidon*. A tidal wave overturns the ship, and from here on out the all-star cast, special effects, and imaginative sets take over. It's a fairly watchable disaster flick, nothing more. Rated PG. 117m. **DIR:** Ronald Neame. **CAST:** Gene Hackman, Ernest Borgnine, Shelley Winters, Roddy McDowall, Red Buttons, Stella Stevens. **1972 DVD**

POSITIVE I.D. ★★1/2 Slow-developing story about a suburban housewife (Stephanie Rascoe) who, after being raped, assumes another identity to escape her past life. Rascoe makes a remarkable transformation from plain housewife to knockout, and the twist ending is ample reward for those patient enough to sit through the first hour of the film. Rated R for language and nudity. 93m. **DIR:** Andy Anderson. **CAST:** Stephanie Rascoe, John Davies, Steve Fromholz. **1988**

POSITIVELY TRUE ADVENTURES OF THE ALLEGED TEXAS CHEERLEADER-MURDERING MOM, THE ★★★1/2 Trashy tabloid docudramas, and the media feeding-frenzy that creates them, are indicted in this often hilarious made-for-cable account of the Texas housewife (superbly played by Holly Hunter) who placed a contract on her daughter's cheerleading rival. Director Michael Ritchie maintains the darkly farcical tone against which his stars chew up the scenery. Rated R for profanity. 99m. **DIR:** Michael Ritchie. **CAST:** Holly Hunter, Beau Bridges, Swoosie Kurtz, Gregg Henry, Matt Frewer. **1993**

POSSE (1975) ★★ Sheriff Kirk Douglas uses his pursuit of bandit Burce Dern to boost his career. This disappointing message Western juxtaposes the evil of political ambition against the basic honesty of traditional law-breaking. 94m. **DIR:** Kirk Douglas. **CAST:** Kirk Douglas, Bruce Dern, James Stacy, Bo Hopkins, Luke Askew, David Canary, Alfonso Arau, Katherine Woodville, Mark Roberts. **1975**

POSSE (1993) ★★★★ A rip-snortin' Western with a twist. Black infantrymen desert their unit after the Spanish-American War, and their sadistic commanding officer goes after them. Fine acting by an unusual cast and plenty of action (including a love scene that caused rating problems) add up to a highly charged adventure. Rated R for violence, profanity, nudity, and simulated

sex. 107m. **DIR:** Mario Van Peebles. **CAST:** Mario Van Peebles, Stephen Baldwin, Charles Lane, Tom "Tiny" Lister Jr., Tone Loc, Big Daddy Kane, Billy Zane, Salli Richardson, Melvin Van Peebles, Richard Jordan, Blair Underwood, Pam Grier, Richard E. Grant, Isaac Hayes, Reginald Vel Johnson, Woody Strode. **1993 DVD**

POSSESSED (1931) ★★★1/2 Wonderful melodrama featuring Joan Crawford as a beautiful gold digger who becomes Clark Gable's mistress. When he has a chance to run for governor, she must choose between her luxurious lifestyle and his chance for a political career. Don't confuse this with Crawford's efforts as a schizophrenic in the 1947 *Possessed.* This gem was released to celebrate MGM's Diamond Jubilee. B&W; 77m. **DIR:** Clarence Brown. **CAST:** Joan Crawford, Clark Gable, Wallace Ford. **1931**

POSSESSED (1947) ★★★ A cold and clinical account of loveless marriage, mysterious suicide, frustrated love for a scoundrel, murder, and schizophrenia. The much-maligned Joan Crawford heads a fine, mature cast and gives one of her finer performances as a mentally troubled nurse. Extremely watchable. The opening scene is a real grabber. B&W; 108m. **DIR:** Curtis Bernhardt. **CAST:** Van Heflin, Joan Crawford, Raymond Massey, Geraldine Brooks, Stanley Ridges. **1947**

POSSESSED, THE (1977) ★★ A not-too-scary *Exorcist* clone. James Farentino is a defrocked priest who travels around in search of evil and is drawn to a girls' school. Made-for-TV demonic possession flick. 75m. **DIR:** Jerry Thorpe. **CAST:** James Farentino, Claudette Nevins, Eugene Roche, Harrison Ford, Ann Dusenberry, Diana Scarwid, Joan Hackett. **1977**

POSSESSED BY THE NIGHT ★★1/2 A sizzling thriller about a strange talisman that unleashes a writer's most erotic and dangerous desires. While in a tender relationship with wife Sandahl Bergman, Ted Prior tests the limits of his control by bedding sensual Shannon Tweed. When he becomes uncontrollable, the fireworks really begin to explode. Rated R for nudity, language, and violence; unrated version contains more sex. 87m. **DIR:** Fred Olen Ray. **CAST:** Ted Prior, Shannon Tweed, Sandahl Bergman, Chad McQueen, Henry Silva. **1993**

POSSUMS ★★★ Mac Davis plays a small-town radio announcer who, like many of his neighbors, is upset when the mayor disbands the high-school team (even if they have gone thirteen years without scoring a point). So he continues to broadcast imaginary games, in which the team starts to win. Likable entertainment for the whole family. Rated PG. 97m. **DIR:** J. Max Burnett. **CAST:** Mac Davis, Cynthia Sikes, Andrew Prine, Jay Underwood. **1999**

POST COITUM ★★1/2 A comfortably married French publisher (director and cowriter Brigitte Rouan) has an affair with the handsome young friend of one of her writers. When he dumps her, her life falls apart. This romantic comedy–drama has some good scenes, but Rouan's incessant wailing and blubbering over her lost love is monotonous and exasperating. Get over it, already! In French with English subtitles. Not rated; contains nudity, profanity (in subtitles), and sexual situations. 97m. **DIR:** Brigitte Rouan. **CAST:** Brigitte Rouan, Patrick Chesnais, Boris Terral, Nils Tavernier. **1997**

POSTAL INSPECTOR ★★ Story of a bankrupt nightclub owner and the fearless agent who brings him to justice is a paean to the post office and its fraud investigators. Highlight of this slow-moving programmer is a speedboat chase through a flooded city. B&W; 58m. **DIR:** Otto Brewer. **CAST:** Ricardo Cortez, Bela Lugosi, Patricia Ellis, Michael Loring. **1936**

POSTCARDS FROM THE EDGE ★★★★ Meryl Streep lets it all hang out in this outrageous adaptation of Carrie Fisher's bestselling autobiographical book. A superb supporting cast contributes to this tale of an actress whose drug dependence is getting out of hand, and so is her relationship with her show-biz mom. The result is a movie that sparkles with wit, energy, and surprises. Rated R for profanity, drug use, and suggested sex. 106m. **DIR:** Mike Nichols. **CAST:** Meryl Streep, Shirley MacLaine, Dennis Quaid, Gene Hackman, Richard Dreyfuss, Rob Reiner, Mary Wickes, Conrad Bain, Annette Bening, Gary Morton, C.C.H. Pounder. **1990 DVD**

POSTMAN, THE ★★★1/2 Kevin Costner positions himself as no less than the one man who might restore civilization to a badly fragmented, near-future (year 2013) United States decimated by war, ecological disaster, and the Messianic fervor of a disenfranchised lunatic who rallies like-minded white men in a campaign against all things technological. In such a world, with good citizens literally starving for hope and rationality, it would be easy for a symbol—a U.S. mail carrier—to take root and grow into a near-unstoppable force for good. The premise is so clever, so ennobling, that even an egomaniac such as Costner can't really blunt its power. We still need our heroes, and this film is a nice statement in a cynical age that could use a few beacons of hope. Rated R for violence, nudity, and simulated sex. 180m. **DIR:** Kevin Costner. **CAST:** Kevin Costner, Will Patton, Larenz Tate, Olivia Williams, James Russo, Tom Petty. **1997 DVD**

POSTMAN ALWAYS RINGS TWICE, THE (1946) ★★★★ If you wondered what went wrong in the sometimes steamily sexy and all too often soggy 1981 screen version of James M. Cain's celebrated novel, you need only watch this 1946 adaptation. John Garfield and Lana Turner play the lovers who murder the husband who stands in the way of their lust and suffer the consequences. B&W; 113m. **DIR:** Tay Garnett. **CAST:** John Garfield, Lana Turner, Cecil Kellaway, Hume Cronyn. **1946**

POSTMAN ALWAYS RINGS TWICE, THE (1981) ★★★ Jack Nicholson plays the drifter whose lust for a married woman (Jessica Lange) leads to murder in this disappointing remake based on James M. Cain's hard-boiled novel of sex and violence. After an electric first hour, it begins to ramble and ends abruptly, leaving the viewer dissatisfied. Rated R for graphic sex and violence. 123m. **DIR:** Bob Rafelson. **CAST:** Jessica Lange, Jack Nicholson, John Colicos, Michael Lerner, John P. Ryan, Anjelica Huston. **1981 DVD**

POSTMAN, THE (IL POSTINO) ★★★★1/2 A sweetly dim-witted Italian mailman (Massimo Troisi) makes friends with the exiled Chilean poet Pablo Neruda; in the process he discovers unexpected poetic depths in himself. This tender, sun-drenched Mediterranean tragicomedy is just about irresistible, with sensitive, first-rate performances. It was the first international

success for Troisi, a popular star in Italy who, sadly, died the day after filming was complete. In Italian with English subtitles. Rated PG. 115m. **DIR:** Michael Radford. **CAST:** Massimo Troisi, Philippe Noiret, Maria Grazia Cucinotta, Linda Moretti. **1994 DVD**

POT O' GOLD ★★ An amusing time passer based on a one-time popular radio show. The plot concerns an enthusiastic young man's effort to get Horace Heidt and his orchestra on his uncle's radio program. Gee! B&W; 86m. **DIR:** George Marshall. **CAST:** James Stewart, Paulette Goddard, Horace Heidt, Charles Winninger, Mary Gordon. **1941 DVD**

P.O.W.: THE ESCAPE ★★1/2 David Carradine's considerable acting talents are wasted once again in this *Rambo* rip-off that is missing everything but action. Rated R for profanity and violence. 90m. **DIR:** Gideon Amir. **CAST:** David Carradine, Mako, Charles R. Floyd, Steve James. **1986**

POWAQQATSI ★★★★ Director Godfrey Reggio's follow-up to *Koyaanisqatsi* is a sumptuous treat for the eyes and the ears. Subtitled *Life in Transformation*, it combines gorgeous cinematography with exquisite music by Philip Glass. Like its predecessor, it's an engaging but sobering look at the cost of what some call progress. 99m. **DIR:** Godfrey Reggio. **1988**

POWDER ★★★ A child born of lightning and forced to live in darkness is discovered after his caretaker dies. When Powder, an enigmatic white-skinned albino, emerges from the shadows, his strange looks and eagerness to be accepted put him at odds with the locals. It doesn't help his cause when they learn that he has advanced intelligence and the ability to transfer thoughts. This tale of understanding and friendship is occasionally heartwarming. Rated PG-13 for adult situations, language, nudity, and violence. 111m. **DIR:** Victor Salva. **CAST:** Mary Steenburgen, Sean Patrick Flanery, Lance Henriksen, Jeff Goldblum, Susan Tyrrell, Missy Crider. **1995 DVD**

POWDERKEG ★★ Mildly entertaining Western about two barnstorming adventurers (Rod Taylor and Dennis Cole) hired by a railroad owner to liberate a train taken hostage by a Mexican bandit. This was the pilot for the mid-Seventies TV series *The Bearcats*. 88m. **DIR:** Douglas Heyes. **CAST:** Rod Taylor, Dennis Cole, Fernando Lamas, Michael Ansara, Tisha Sterling, Luciana Paluzzi. **1976**

POWDERSMOKE RANGE ★★1/2 Despite its impressive all-star cast of Western players, this is just an average B Western. Its significance lies in it being the first film to feature William Colt MacDonald's Three Mesquiteers. 71m. **DIR:** Wallace Fox. **CAST:** Harry Carey, Hoot Gibson, Bob Steele, Tom Tyler, Guinn Williams, William Farnum, William Desmond. **1935**

POWER, THE (1980) Aztec idol is unearthed by some youngsters, who must face the consequences. Rated R for profanity, violence, and gore. 87m. **DIR:** Jeffrey Obrow, Stephen Carpenter. **CAST:** Susan Stokey, Warren Lincoln, Lisa Erickson. **1980**

POWER (1986) ★★★★ Sidney Lumet, who directed *Network*, once again takes viewers into the bowels of an American institution with this hard-edged study of the manipulation of the political process by market research and advertising. Richard Gere gives one of his better performances as a ruthless hustler who is given pause when the one politician he believes in (E. G. Marshall) becomes a pawn in the political power trade. Rated R for profanity, violence, and suggested sex. 111m. **DIR:** Sidney Lumet. **CAST:** Richard Gere, Julie Christie, Gene Hackman, Kate Capshaw, Denzel Washington, E. G. Marshall, Beatrice Straight. **1986 DVD**

POWER OF ATTORNEY ★★ Routine crime-thriller about a mob boss on trial for murder. A handpicked idealistic young defense attorney is seduced by power and money until his conscience finally catches up with him. By then, it may be too late. Rated R for violence and language. 96m. **DIR:** Howard Himelstein. **CAST:** Danny Aiello, Elias Koteas, Rae Dawn Chong, Nina Siemaszko, Roger Wilson. **1995**

POWER OF ONE, THE ★★★★1/2 Remarkably effective epic about a young man's fight against prejudice in South Africa. Set in the Thirties and Forties, the film details the adventures of an English boy who survives being tormented by youthful Afrikaners with the help of two mentors, one white and one black. Director John Avildsen uses the same combination of sports excitement and characterization that made *Rocky* so satisfying, and the result is stunning. Rated PG-13 for violence and profanity. 127m. **DIR:** John G. Avildsen. **CAST:** Stephen Dorff, Armin Mueller-Stahl, Morgan Freeman, John Gielgud, Fay Masterson, Daniel Craig, Dominic Walker, Alois Moyo, Ian Roberts, Marius Weyers. **1992 DVD**

POWER, PASSION, AND MURDER ★★ Hollywood of the late Thirties is the setting for a rising star's tragic affair with a married man. This telefilm is marred by daydreams of wannabes and has-beens. 104m. **DIR:** Paul Bogart. **CAST:** Michelle Pfeiffer, Brian Kerwin, Hector Elizondo. **1987 DVD**

POWER WITHIN, THE ★★1/2 A high-school martial artist comes into possession of a ring with mystical powers. Well-intentioned but slow-moving *Karate Kid* clone. Rated PG-13 for violence. 99m. **DIR:** Art Camacho. **CAST:** Ted Jan Roberts, Karen Valentine, Keith Coogan, John O'Hurley, William Zabka, Gerald Okamura, P. J. Soles, Ed O'Ross, Don "The Dragon" Wilson. **1995**

POWWOW HIGHWAY ★★★1/2 Taking a lighthearted look at a serious subject isn't easy, but this film does an excellent job. The subject is mistreatment of Indians on American reservations, from poor housing and bad job conditions to deprivation of tribal cultures and history. Though not rated, this is geared to an adult audience. 91m. **DIR:** Jonathan Wacks. **CAST:** A Martinez, Gary Farmer, Amanda Wyss. **1988**

PRACTICAL MAGIC ★★ Nothing could be less interesting than a story that makes stuff up as it goes along, fails to establish any parameters for reasonable behavior, and then wraps everything up with some thumpingly anticlimactic, *deus ex machina* intervention. All charges apply to this dim-bulb fantasy-comedy, which fritters away the talents of its four stars and does no justice at all to Alice Hoffman's source novel. Sandra Bullock and Nicole Kidman star as a pair of witches whose "white magic" proves incapable of properly dispatching a nasty fellow with a tendency to rise from the dead. Forget this misfire; it's practically incomprehensible. Rated PG-13 for violence and sensuality. 103m. **DIR:** Griffin Dunne. **CAST:** Sandra Bullock, Nicole Kidman,

Dianne Wiest, Stockard Channing, Aidan Quinn. **1998 DVD**

PRAIRIE RUSTLERS ★★★ Buster Crabbe is accused of his outlaw cousin's crimes because of their dead-ringer resemblance. B&W; 56m. **DIR:** Sam Newfield. **CAST:** Buster Crabbe, Al St. John, Evelyn Finley, Karl Hackett. **1945**

PRANCER ★★★ With some movies you have to hang in there. So it is with this film about a troubled girl who finds an injured reindeer just before Christmas. It takes nearly an hour for the story to engage the viewer fully, but from then on *Prancer* is very satisfying. Rated G. 100m. **DIR:** John Hancock. **CAST:** Sam Elliott, Cloris Leachman, Abe Vigoda, Michael Constantine. **1989 DVD**

PRAY FOR DEATH ★★★ A Ninja movie with a plot? What a concept! Kick master Sho Kosugi plays a loving husband and father who moves from Japan to the United States. Here he encounters gangsters who must be dealt with. Rated R for violence. 93m. **DIR:** Gordon Hessler. **CAST:** Sho Kosugi, James Booth, Donna Kei Benz, Normann Burton, Kane Kosugi, Shane Kosugi. **1985**

PRAY FOR THE WILDCATS 🦃 Three businessmen on a macho motorcycle trip in the desert. Made for TV. 100m. **DIR:** Robert Michael Lewis. **CAST:** Andy Griffith, William Shatner, Angie Dickinson, Janet Margolin, Robert Reed, Marjoe Gortner, Lorraine Gary. **1974**

PRAY TV (1980) ★★1/2 Dabney Coleman plays Marvin Fleece, penny-ante con man, who takes faltering TV station KRUD and turns it into K-GOD. A really funny satire on religion and television, betrayed only by a weak ending. Rated PG for language and general tastelessness. 92m. **DIR:** Rick Friedberg. **CAST:** Dabney Coleman, Archie Hahn, Joyce Jameson, Nancy Morgan, Roger E. Mosley, Marcia Wallace. **1980**

PRAY TV (1982) ★★1/2 Interesting TV movie about a young minister (John Ritter) who comes under the spell of a charismatic televangelist (Ned Beatty). Beatty is superb, but Ritter's performance is lackluster. 96m. **DIR:** Robert Markowitz. **CAST:** John Ritter, Ned Beatty, Richard Kiley, Madolyn Smith, Louise Latham. **1982**

PRAYER FOR THE DYING, A ★★ An overwrought adaptation of Jack Higgins's exciting thriller which sounds preachy even when trying to be suspenseful. Mickey Rourke is an IRA assassin who finds his conscience after unintentionally killing some schoolchildren; he flees to London and engages natty Alan Bates to help him out of the country. Rated R for language and violence. 107m. **DIR:** Mike Hodges. **CAST:** Mickey Rourke, Bob Hoskins, Alan Bates, Sammi Davis. **1987**

PRAYER IN THE DARK, A ★★★ Two escaped convicts take a family of Quakers hostage and demand that the mother take $4 million from the bank where she works, or her family will die. This made-for-cable original is a taut thriller with some interesting nonviolent solutions to the situation, but the acting is a little stilted, and the story not credible at parts. Rated PG-13 for violence. 95m. **DIR:** Gerard Ciccoritti. **CAST:** Lynda Carter, Teri Polo, Colin Ferguson. **1997**

PRAYER OF THE ROLLERBOYS ★★1/2 The Rollerboys are a gang of fascistic, drug-running teens who terrorize Los Angeles of the near future, zipping around on Rollerblades. Good stunt work and a *Blade Runner*–like look at the future make up for a too-familiar plot. Rated R for violence. 94m. **DIR:** Rick King. **CAST:** Corey Haim, Patricia Arquette, Christopher Collet, J. C. Quinn. **1991**

PRAYING MANTIS ★★★ In this made-for-cable original, a woman (Jane Seymour) who was abused as a child by her father kills her husbands on their wedding nights. Now she has fallen in love with a bookstore owner (Barry Bostwick), whose son and sister-in-law (Frances Fisher) don't trust her. Very good acting by Bostwick and Fisher, but the plot is on the predictable side. Rated PG-13 for violence. 90m. **DIR:** James Keach. **CAST:** Jane Seymour, Barry Bostwick, Chad Allen, Frances Fisher. **1993**

PRE-MADONNAS (SOCIAL SUICIDE) ★★ A rebellious debutante chooses a blue-collar boy as her escort to a haughty deb ball. Routine teenage farce intended for nondiscriminating fans of *Clueless* and *Beverly Hills 90210*. Shot in 1987. Rated PG-13 for sexual situations and strong language. 98m. **DIR:** Lawrence D. Foldes. **CAST:** Shannon Sturges, Peter Anthony Elliott, Bobbie Bresee, Kenn Cooper, Dan Cashman. **1995**

PREACHER'S WIFE, THE ★★★★ Director Penny Marshall has come up with what deserves to be a holiday perennial. The story is about Dudley, an angel sent from heaven to save the marriage of a pastor and the wife he seems to have shut out of his life. Dudley can't convince the reverend that he's the real article, but the title character certainly notices his gentle ways and healing touch. It's a love triangle straight from heaven. Rated PG. 124m. **DIR:** Penny Marshall. **CAST:** Denzel Washington, Whitney Houston, Courtney B. Vance, Gregory Hines, Jenifer Lewis, Lionel Ritchie. **1996**

PRECIOUS FIND ★★1/2 The California Gold Rush takes to the heavens in this futuristic action-thriller. In 2049 a whole new gold rush is taking place in outer space. A young miner, who has the ability to sniff it out, travels to a nearby planet with a card shark and space pilot, where they battle a claim jumper and her gang of bandits. Some thrills. Rated R for language and violence. 90m. **DIR:** Philippe Mora. **CAST:** Rutger Hauer, Harold Pruett, Joan Chen, Brian James. **1996**

PREDATOR ★★★★1/2 Sort of an earthbound *Alien*, *Predator* stars Arnold Schwarzenegger as a commando out to terminate a kill-crazy creature in a Latin American jungle. Although it sounds derivative, this film delivers a pulse-pounding tale. Rated R for profanity and violence. 107m. **DIR:** John McTiernan. **CAST:** Arnold Schwarzenegger, Carl Weathers, Elpidia Carrillo, Bill Duke, Sonny Landham, Richard Chaves, R. G. Armstrong, Kevin Peter Hall, Jesse Ventura. **1987 DVD**

PREDATOR 2 🦃 This sequel lacks the creativity. Rated R for violence, profanity, nudity, and gore. 108m. **DIR:** Stephen Hopkins. **CAST:** Danny Glover, Gary Busey, Rubén Blades, Maria Conchita Alonso, Bill Paxton, Robert Davi, Adam Baldwin, Kent McCord, Morton Downey Jr. **1990**

PREFONTAINE ★★★ Biography of Olympic runner Steve Prefontaine combines live action, interviews, and news footage for a decent docudrama. The focus throughout is on Pre's (Jared Leto) obsession with being the best while rebelling against the press and track association. Standout performances by Ed O'Neill and R. Lee Ermey as university coaches elevate the film a

notch. Rated PG-13 for profanity and violence. 107m. **DIR:** Steve James. **CAST:** Jared Leto, R. Lee Ermey, Ed O'Neill, Amy Locane. **1997**

PREHISTORIC BIMBOS IN ARMAGEDDON CITY 🦃 After World War III, the world is reduced to a wasteland full of cyborgs and warrior bimbos in this dopey sci-fi comedy. Not rated; contains violence, nudity, and profanity. 75m. **DIR:** Todd Sheets. **CAST:** Holly Star, Jenny Admire, Veronica Orr, Robert Vollrath, Tonia Monahan. **1993**

PREHISTORIC WOMEN 🦃 A dreadful film about a tribe of phallus-worshipping women. 91m. **DIR:** Michael Carreras. **CAST:** Martine Beswick. **1967 DVD**

PREHYSTERIA ★★★★ The plot may be derivative, but this solid slice of kiddie entertainment has surprisingly imaginative dialogue. A comic-book bad guy tries to strong-arm a farming family into handing over five dino eggs they accidentally acquired. A lot of fun for the kids, especially the pygmy dinos. Rated PG for mild profanity. 86m. **DIR:** Charles Band, Albert Band. **CAST:** Austin O'Brien, Brett Cullen, Samantha Mills. **1993**

PREHYSTERIA 2 ★★1/2 Fans of the first outing will enjoy this sequel that dishes up more of the same. The five miniature dinosaurs are back for more fun, this time helping a young boy thwart the plans of his evil governess to send him to military school, while helping the boy and his friend restore his father's prized train set. The critters are playful creations, providing plenty of adventure and mayhem. Rated PG. 81m. **DIR:** Albert Band. **CAST:** Kevin R. Connors, Jennifer Harte, Dean Scofield, Owen Bush, Larry Hankin. **1994**

PREHYSTERIA! 3 ★★ The kids might get a kick out of this third entry for the tiny dinosaurs, but adults may want to take the time to read a book. This time they help a girl save a mini-putt from a rival country club. Rated PG for humorous pranks. 85m. **DIR:** Julian Breen. **CAST:** Fred Willard, Whitney Anderson. **1995**

PRELUDE TO A KISS ★★★★ It's a dream marriage for both Alec Baldwin and Meg Ryan when they finally tie the knot, which begins to unravel in seminightmarish fashion when the bride is kissed by an old man with whom she swaps souls. A charming, low-key romance with nice performances from Baldwin and Ryan. Rated PG-13. 105m. **DIR:** Norman René. **CAST:** Alec Baldwin, Meg Ryan, Kathy Bates, Ned Beatty, Patty Duke, Sydney Walker. **1992**

PREMATURE BURIAL, THE ★★ A medical student's paranoia about being buried alive causes his worst fears to come true. Roger Corman's only Poe-derived film without Vincent Price. Lacking Price's playful and hammy acting style, it all seems too serious. 81m. **DIR:** Roger Corman. **CAST:** Ray Milland, Hazel Court, Richard Ney, Heather Angel. **1962**

PREMONITION, THE (1975) ★★1/2 Well-written but turgidly directed terror film about a young adopted girl kidnapped by her natural mother. The girl's adoptive parents turn to ESP to locate her, and fall into a strange world. Not rated, but has intense situations and some violence. 94m. **DIR:** Robert Schnitzer. **CAST:** Sharon Farrell, Richard Lynch, Jeff Corey, Danielle Brisebois. **1975**

PREMONITION (1998) ★★★ Entertaining but ultimately nonsensical film about a woman whose rescue from a plane crash becomes the one incident that could destroy the world as we know it. Also released as *Convergence*. Rated R for profanity and nudity. 99m. **DIR:** Gavin Wilding. **CAST:** Christopher Lloyd, Cyndy Preston, Adrian Paul. **1998 DVD**

PREP SCHOOL ★★1/2 This comedy-drama about a coed prep school in New England has the usual cast of characters. Familiar, but nicely performed. Rated PG-13 for profanity. 97m. **DIR:** Paul Almond. **CAST:** Leslie Hope, Andrew Sabiston. **1981**

PREPPIE MURDER, THE ★★★ William Baldwin is convincingly creepy as convicted killer Robert Chambers in this chilling made-for-TV crime-drama. After he strangles his girlfriend, played by Lara Flynn Boyle, in Central Park, his perfect life begins to unravel, and a portrait of a monster begins to surface. Danny Aiello is the detective who pieces it all together. Not rated; contains adult situations. 94m. **DIR:** John Herzfeld. **CAST:** Danny Aiello, William Baldwin, Lara Flynn Boyle, Joanna Kerns. **1990**

PREPPIES 🦃 R-rated sexploitation. Rated R for nudity, simulated sex, and profanity. 90m. **DIR:** Chuck Vincent. **CAST:** Nitchie Barrett, Dennis Drake, Steven Holt, Katt Shea. **1984**

PRESENCE, THE ★★ After narrowly escaping a plane crash on a small desert island, a group of castaways discovers a mysterious, abandoned laboratory, and begins to mutate and die one by one. Silly sci-fi/horror flick is made watchable only by its above-average performances and bizarre but definitely unique music score. Rated PG-13 for violence and profanity. 90m. **DIR:** Tommy Lee Wallace. **CAST:** Lisa Banes, Richard Beymer, Gary Graham, Kathy Ireland. **1992**

PRESENTING LILY MARS ★★ Stagestruck girl plugs her way to stardom. High points are when Judy Garland sings and the Tommy Dorsey and Bob Crosby bands. B&W; 104m. **DIR:** Norman Taurog. **CAST:** Judy Garland, Van Heflin, Richard Carlson, Marta Eggerth, Connie Gilchrist, Fay Bainter, Spring Byington, Marilyn Maxwell, Tommy Dorsey, Bob Crosby. **1943**

PRESIDENT'S ANALYST, THE ★★★★ Vastly underappreciated satire from writer-director Theodore J. Flicker, who concocts a wild tale concerning a psychiatrist (James Coburn) selected to be our president's "secret shrink." Coburn walks away with the picture, his wicked smile and piercing eyes becoming more and more suspicious as he falls prey to the paranoia of his elite assignment. Not rated; adult themes. 104m. **DIR:** Theodore J. Flicker. **CAST:** James Coburn, Godfrey Cambridge, Pat Harrington, Will Geer. **1967**

PRESIDENT'S PLANE IS MISSING, THE ★★★ Crisis after crisis occurs when *Air Force One* disappears with the president on board. This story of indecision and desire for control against a background of international crisis is an engaging suspense yarn. A very good story is helped by a veteran cast. 100m. **DIR:** Daryl Duke. **CAST:** Buddy Ebsen, Peter Graves, Arthur Kennedy, Raymond Massey, Mercedes McCambridge, Rip Torn, Dabney Coleman. **1971**

PRESIDIO, THE ★★★ An old-fashioned star vehicle, this murder mystery features Sean Connery as a military provost marshal at San Francisco's Presidio. Police detective Mark Harmon, who once served under Connery and still bears a grudge, is assigned to work with his former commanding officer. Forget the plot and en-

joy seeing Connery excel in a tailor-made role. Rated R for violence and profanity. 97m. **DIR:** Peter Hyams. **CAST:** Sean Connery, Mark Harmon, Meg Ryan, Jack Warden, Dana Gladstone, Mark Blum. **1988 DVD**

PRESSURE POINT ★★★1/2 During World War II, a black psychiatrist is assigned to evaluate a bigoted prisoner, jailed for sedition as a member of the American Nazi party. Interesting drama, fine performances, with a special nod to the underrated Bobby Darin. B&W; 91m. **DIR:** Hubert Cornfield. **CAST:** Sidney Poitier, Bobby Darin, Peter Falk, Carl Benton Reid. **1962**

PRESUMED INNOCENT ★★★★1/2 Director Alan J. Pakula's superb version of Scott Turow's critically acclaimed bestseller features Harrison Ford as a prosecuting attorney who finds himself under suspicion when his mistress is murdered. Even if you've read the novel, you'll want to watch this gripping thriller. Rated R for violence, profanity, and nudity. 124m. **DIR:** Alan J. Pakula. **CAST:** Harrison Ford, Brian Dennehy, Bonnie Bedelia, Greta Scacchi, Raul Julia, Paul Winfield, John Spencer. **1990 DVD**

PRETTY BABY ★★★★ Forcing the audience to reexamine accepted concepts is just one of the effects of this brilliant work by Louis Malle. He is fascinated by Violet (Brooke Shields), the girl we see growing up in a whorehouse in New Orleans. For Violet, all that goes on around her is normal. Rated R. 109m. **DIR:** Louis Malle. **CAST:** Brooke Shields, Susan Sarandon, Keith Carradine, Frances Faye, Antonio Fargas. **1978**

PRETTY IN PINK ★★★★ Molly Ringwald is wonderful as a young woman "from the poor side of town" who falls in love with rich kid Andrew McCarthy. The feeling is mutual, but their peers do everything they can to keep them apart. It is that rare teenage-oriented release that can be enjoyed by adults. Rated PG-13 for profanity and violence. 96m. **DIR:** Howard Deutch. **CAST:** Molly Ringwald, Harry Dean Stanton, Jon Cryer, Andrew McCarthy, Annie Potts, James Spader. **1986**

PRETTY KILL A madam involved with a police detective hires a hooker who just happens to have a multiple-personality disorder. Rated R for violence and nudity. 95m. **DIR:** George Kaczender. **CAST:** David Birney, Season Hubley, Yaphet Kotto. **1987**

PRETTY POISON ★★★★ Anthony Perkins gives one of his finest performances in this bizarre drama about a troubled arsonist who enlists a sexy high school girl (Tuesday Weld) in a wild scheme. This surreal black comedy is sparked by Weld's vivid performance and a highly original screenplay by Lorenzo Semple Jr. Not rated. 89m. **DIR:** Noel Black. **CAST:** Anthony Perkins, Tuesday Weld, Beverly Garland. **1968**

PRETTY WOMAN ★★★★ Imagine Cinderella as a young Hollywood hooker. Now put Prince Charming in a fancy sports car driving down the strip. Welcome to this fluffy, funny comedy about the unlikeliest of love mates: a runaway (Julia Roberts) and a corporate raider (Richard Gere). Rated R for profanity and sex. 119m. **DIR:** Garry Marshall. **CAST:** Richard Gere, Julia Roberts, Ralph Bellamy, Laura San Giacomo. **1990 DVD**

PREY, THE Six young hikers go up into the woods, where they run into a ghoul. Yum. Rated R for nudity and violence. 80m. **DIR:** Edwin Scott Brown. **CAST:** Debbie Thurseon, Steve Bond, Lori Lethin, Jackie Coogan. **1980**

PREY FOR THE HUNTER A lame reworking of *The Most Dangerous Game*, as businessmen hunt down a photographer deep in the African jungle. Dull presentation of an overused plot. Rated R for violence and profanity. 90m. **DIR:** John H. Parr. **CAST:** Todd Jensen, André Jacobs. **1992**

PREY OF THE CHAMELEON ★★★ Escaped mental patient Daphne Zuniga adopts the identity and personality of each woman she meets and kills, much to the frustration of pursuing FBI agents. Good ol' boy James Wilder, making a mess of his reconciliation with girlfriend Alexandra Paul (nicely credible as a small-town deputy sheriff), unwittingly gives a ride to the wrong hitchhiker. Made-for-cable mystery. 91m. **DIR:** Fleming B. Fuller. **CAST:** Daphne Zuniga, James Wilder, Alexandra Paul, Don Harvey. **1992**

PRICE ABOVE RUBIES, A ★★★★1/2 Renee Zellweger plays an Orthodox Jewish wife who, stifled by the traditions of her tight-knit community, risks ostracism by building a career for herself as a jewelry buyer. An unusual, provocative story is sensitively told, with touches of magic realism that enhance the emotional texture of this haunting and compassionate film. Rated R for sexual scenes and brief nudity. 117m. **DIR:** Boaz Yakin. **CAST:** Renee Zellweger, Chris Eccleston, Glenn Fitzgerald, Allen Payne, Julianna Margulies. **1998 DVD**

PRICE OF GLORY ★★1/2 A failed boxer (Jimmy Smits) tries to attain the fame and fortune that eluded him by making prizefighters of his three sons. Smits gives a good performance, supported by a strong cast. But his character is a selfish, detestable bully and—worse yet—the script is a parade of groan-inducing clichés. Rated PG-13 for mild profanity. 118m. **DIR:** Carlos Avila. **CAST:** Jimmy Smits, Maria Del Mar, Jon Seda, Clifton Collins Jr., Ernesto Hernandez, Ron Perlman, Louis Mandylor, Sal Lopez. **2000 DVD**

•PRICE OF MILK, THE ★★★ A New Zealand dairy farmer and his girlfriend decide to marry in spite of unresolved issues. The film dips into surrealism and becomes loose-ended and perplexing in spots, but writer-director Harry Sinclair's whimsical wit keeps it lighthearted and watchable. Rated PG-13 for mature themes and nudity. 87m. **DIR:** Harry Sinclair. **CAST:** Danielle Cormack, Karl Urban, Willa O'Neill, Michael Lawrence. **2000**

PRICELESS BEAUTY Italian-style *I Dream of Jeannie*. Rated R for nudity and profanity. 94m. **DIR:** Charles Finch. **CAST:** Christopher Lambert, Diane Lane, Francesco Quinn, J. C. Quinn. **1989**

PRICK UP YOUR EARS ★★★★ The poignant love story at the center will be touching to some and shocking to others. But this film about the rise to prominence of British playwright Joe Orton (Gary Oldman) and his relationship with Kenneth Halliwell (Alfred Molina) never fails to fascinate. Rated R for profanity and scenes of graphic sex. 110m. **DIR:** Stephen Frears. **CAST:** Gary Oldman, Alfred Molina, Vanessa Redgrave, Julie Walters, Wallace Shawn. **1987**

PRIDE AND PREJUDICE (1940) ★★★★ This film is an adaptation of Jane Austen's famous novel. The story takes place in nineteenth-century England with five sisters looking for suitable husbands. B&W; 116m. **DIR:**

Robert Z. Leonard. **CAST:** Greer Garson, Laurence Olivier, Maureen O'Sullivan, Marsha Hunt. **1940**

PRIDE AND PREJUDICE (1985) ★★★★ Marvelous BBC adaptation of Jane Austen's classic romance. Comic moments abound as a silly mother desperately tries to marry off her five daughters. Period costumes and English countryside and manor houses are authentic. 226m. **DIR:** Cyril Coke. **CAST:** Elizabeth Garvie, David Rintoul, Moray Watson, Priscilla Morgan. **1985**

PRIDE AND PREJUDICE (1996) ★★★★★ Positively addictive. The cast and crew capture Jane Austen's timeless wit and cutting observations of the class system and human foibles. The costumes and settings are delicious and Colin Firth and Jennifer Ehle dominate this comedy of manners in which a wedding band is the ultimate goal. Originally shown on cable. Not rated. 300m. **DIR:** Simon Langton. **CAST:** Colin Firth, Jennifer Ehle, Alison Steadman, Benjamin Whitrow, Susannah Harker, Crispin Bonham Carter, Anna Chancellor, Julia Sawalha, David Bamber, David Bark-Jones. **1996 DVD**

PRIDE AND THE PASSION, THE ★★ Here is a supreme example of how miscasting can ruin a movie's potential. Frank Sinatra is horrible as the Spanish peasant leader of a guerrilla army during the Napoleonic era. He secures the services of a gigantic cannon and a British navy officer (Cary Grant) to fire it. Sophia Loren is also in the cast, primarily as window dressing. 132m. **DIR:** Stanley Kramer. **CAST:** Frank Sinatra, Cary Grant, Sophia Loren, Theodore Bikel. **1957 DVD**

PRIDE OF JESSE HALLMAN, THE ★★ This is a well-meant but sluggish account of the quest for literacy by the title character, who is played by country singer-songwriter Johnny Cash. Made for television. 99m. **DIR:** Gary Nelson. **CAST:** Johnny Cash, Brenda Vaccaro, Eli Wallach, Ben Marley, Guy Boyd. **1981**

PRIDE OF ST. LOUIS, THE ★★1/2 The ups and downs of popular St. Louis Cardinals baseball player Dizzy Dean are affectionately chronicled in this warm and humorous sandlot-to-big-league bio. Dan Dailey is amusing and believable as the word-fracturing Dean. B&W; 92m. **DIR:** Harmon Jones. **CAST:** Dan Dailey, Joanne Dru, Richard Crenna, Hugh Sanders. **1952**

PRIDE OF THE BOWERY ★★ This offshoot of the famous Dead End Kids features Leo Gorcey and Bobby Jordan, two of the original "kids," along with Gorcey's brother David, who continued on and off for the rest of the series. Not quite as bad as their later efforts, this film still needs a dyed-in-the-wool East Side Kids fan to really enjoy it. B&W; 63m. **DIR:** Joseph H. Lewis. **CAST:** Leo Gorcey, Bobby Jordan, Donald Haines, Carleton Young, Kenneth Howell, David Gorcey. **1940**

PRIDE OF THE CLAN, THE ★★★★ Picturesque, crisply photographed saga of the Scottish Highlands. To those viewers who know Mary Pickford's later costume pictures in the 1920s, the spunky character and the action pacing will be a welcome surprise. Silent. B&W; 70m. **DIR:** Maurice Tourneur. **CAST:** Mary Pickford, Matt Moore. **1917**

PRIDE OF THE YANKEES, THE ★★★★★ Gary Cooper gives one of his finest performances as he captures the courageous spirit of New York Yankee immortal Lou Gehrig. This 1942 drama is a perfect blend of an exciting sports biography and a touching melodrama as we follow Gehrig's baseball career from its earliest playground beginnings until an illness strikes him down in his prime. Teresa Wright is just right in the difficult role of his loving wife. B&W; 127m. **DIR:** Sam Wood. **CAST:** Gary Cooper, Teresa Wright, Babe Ruth, Walter Brennan, Dan Duryea, Ludwig Stossel. **1942 DVD**

PRIEST ★★★ A conservative young priest in working-class Liverpool tries to control his own carnal nature while ministering to the spiritual needs of his parish. It's a genuinely entertaining melodrama about a crisis of faith. Rated R for mature themes, profanity, and homosexual love scenes. 105m. **DIR:** Antonia Bird. **CAST:** Linus Roache, Tom Wilkinson, Cathy Tyson, Robert Carlyle, Robert Pugh. **1994 DVD**

PRIEST OF LOVE ★★★★ The culmination of a decade-long quest to film the life of D. H. Lawrence results in a film that is absorbing, brilliantly acted, and stunningly photographed. It deals with Lawrence's exile from his native England, where his books were generally reviled; his relationship with wife Frieda; and their final time together in Italy. Rated R for profanity and sex. 125m. **DIR:** Christopher Miles. **CAST:** Ian McKellen, Janet Suzman, Ava Gardner, John Gielgud, Penelope Keith, Jorge Rivero, Maurizio Merli. **1981**

PRIMAL FEAR ★★★★1/2 A high-caliber thriller, this keeps you guessing right up to the shocking ending. Red herrings and duplicitous plot twists are woven tightly into this intelligent script about a hotshot attorney who goes looking for the limelight and finds it filled with shadows. A compelling performance by newcomer Edward Norton really makes this film believable, though Richard Gere does a masterful job of underplaying an arrogant but brilliant criminal lawyer. Rated R for violence, profanity, nudity, and sexual situations. 131m. **DIR:** Gregory Hoblit. **CAST:** Richard Gere, Laura Linney, Edward Norton, John Mahoney, Alfre Woodard, Frances McDormand. **1996 DVD**

PRIMAL SCREAM ★★ A futuristic psychological thriller that's heavy on psychology and weak on script and acting, but with some pretty neat special effects. Rated R for profanity, violence, and some nudity. 95m. **DIR:** William Murray. **CAST:** Kenneth McGregor. **1987**

PRIMAL SECRETS ★★1/2 Dark family secrets come to the surface in this made-for-cable suspense drama about an artist who's hired by a wealthy socialite. It's a dream job until the artist learns that she resembles her employer's daughter, who died under mysterious circumstances. What follows is a sometimes-interesting psychological drama with a disappointing finale. Rated PG-13. 93m. **DIR:** Ed Kaplan. **CAST:** Ellen Burstyn, Meg Tilly, Paxton Whitehead, Barnard Hughes. **1994**

PRIMARY COLORS ★★★★ Not since 1976's *All the President's Men* has a mainstream political drama demanded so much of its audience. Yet this film is fascinating: a full-throttle, all-stops-pulled-out analysis of the compromise-laden political scene. Its story turns on the moral question: To what degree can we forgive the failings of a politician whose intentions seem noble? This fictionalized account of President Clinton's primary race is galvanized by John Travolta's dead-on impersonation of the Prez; he and the picture itself are compelling from start to finish. Rated R for profanity and sexual content. 135m. **DIR:** Mike Nichols. **CAST:** John Travolta, Emma Thompson, Billy Bob Thornton,

Kathy Bates, Adrian Lester, Maura Tierney, Larry Hagman. **1998 DVD**

PRIMARY MOTIVE ★★★ Judd Nelson comes on strong as a young press secretary who uncovers some dirt about his candidate's opposition. Business as usual in the political arena: double crosses, lies, intrigue. Rated R for language. 98m. **DIR:** Daniel Adams. **CAST:** Judd Nelson, Richard Jordan, Sally Kirkland, Justine Bateman, John Savage. **1992**

PRIMARY TARGET ★★ Vietnam 1977: a wealthy American's wife is kidnapped. Anyone watching for inconsistencies will have a field day, but writer-director Clark Henderson plays it soft with likable heroes and equally nefarious villains. Rated R for violence. 85m. **DIR:** Clark Henderson. **CAST:** John Calvin, Miki Kim, Joey Aresco. **1990**

PRIME CUT ★★ Sissy Spacek made her film debut in this sleazy but energetic crime thriller about big-time gangsters and the slaughterhouse they use to convert their enemies into sausage. The talents of Lee Marvin and Gene Hackman elevate this essentially tasteless offering. Rated R for nudity, gore, and violence. 86m. **DIR:** Michael Ritchie. **CAST:** Lee Marvin, Gene Hackman, Angel Tompkins, Gregory Walcott, Sissy Spacek. **1972**

PRIME EVIL ★★1/2 A band of priests in New York City are actually disciples of Satan. A bloody sacrifice every thirteen years grants them immortality. Passable horror film has decent suspense and contains violent acts without being awash in gore. Rated R. 87m. **DIR:** Roberta Findlay. **CAST:** William Beckwith, Christine Moore. **1989 DVD**

•**PRIME GIG, THE** ★★1/2 Even though it dials up a modicum of suspense, this character study about telemarketers eventually reaches a wrong number. Vince Vaughn is fine as Pendleton "Penny" Wise, an ace con man looking for his next gig. When he learns that legendary con man Kelly Grant (Ed Harris) is setting up a big score, he's anxious to join the team. Grant's femme fatale girlfriend Caitlin (Julia Ormond) lends incentive, but Penny can't make up his mind if he's playing or being played. Lacks the intensity of *Boiler Room*, but there are engaging characters and an unrelenting mood of suspicion. Rated R for adult situations and language. 97m. **DIR:** Gregory Mosher. **CAST:** Vince Vaughn, Ed Harris, Julia Ormond, Wallace Shawn, Rory Cochrane. **2000 DVD**

PRIME OF MISS JEAN BRODIE, THE ★★★★★ Maggie Smith's first Oscar-winning performance fuels this character study of a late 1930s Edinburgh schoolteacher who steers her young charges past the rocky shoals of life, interlacing their studies with priceless descriptions of her affairs. Jay Presson Allen's deft script is drawn from Muriel Spark's novel, and rarely has the spirit of a book been so well captured on screen. Rated PG for frank dialogue. 166m. **DIR:** Ronald Neame. **CAST:** Maggie Smith, Robert Stephens, Celia Johnson, Pamela Franklin, Gordon Jackson. **1969**

PRIME RISK ★★★1/2 Two frustrated young people (Lee Montgomery and Samuel Bottoms) devise a scheme to rip off automatic teller machines. Trouble arises when they stumble on to a greater conspiracy involving foreign agents. Nonstop action with Keenan Wynn as a suitable villain. Rated PG-13 for mature situations and language. 98m. **DIR:** Michael Frakas. **CAST:** Lee Montgomery, Sam Bottoms, Toni Hudson, Keenan Wynn, Clu Gulager. **1984**

PRIME SUSPECT (1982) (FEATURE) 🦃 A young girl is murdered. A decent, honest, hardworking citizen becomes the prime suspect in the case. 100m. **DIR:** Noel Black. **CAST:** Mike Farrell, Teri Garr, Veronica Cartwright, Lane Smith, Barry Corbin, James Sloyan, Charles Aidman. **1982 DVD**

PRIME SUSPECT 1 ★★★★★ Author Lynda La Plante's outspoken Detective Chief Inspector Jane Tennison is determined to make her mark in the mostly all-boys club of the British police force. Tennison inherits a baffling murder case and then comes across a connected second murder. The story ranks among the best police procedurals, and Tennison always fascinates. 240m. **DIR:** Chris Menaul. **CAST:** Helen Mirren, Tom Bell, John Benfield, John Bowe, Zoe Wanamaker. **1990 DVD**

PRIME SUSPECT 2 ★★★★ Detective Chief Inspector Jane Tennison, tries to integrate her squad with the team's first black inspector. The remains of a young girl are found beneath an apartment patio in a primarily Afro-Caribbean neighborhood, and race relations are strained past the breaking point by an opportunistic politician. While at times overly melodramatic, this miniseries, by most standards, is a corker. 240m. **DIR:** John Strickland. **CAST:** Helen Mirren, Colin Salmon, John Benfield, Jack Ellis, Claire Benedict, George Harris. **1992 DVD**

PRIME SUSPECT 3 ★★★★ Detective Chief Inspector Jane Tennison, having been demoted from homicide to Soho's Vice Squad, must again endure the sexist derision of a colleague she thought she had left behind (back in *Prime Suspect 1*). Personal antagonisms are shuttled aside, however, when the burned body of a 15-year-old male prostitute is found in the apartment of a cross-dressing cabaret entertainer. Creator Lynda La Plante weaves a complex mystery involving cover-ups, departmental spying, and homophobia. 240m. **DIR:** David Drury. **CAST:** Helen Mirren, Tom Bell, Peter Capaldi, David Thewlis, Michael J. Shannon, Mark Strong. **1993**

PRIME SUSPECT: SCENT OF DARKNESS ★★★★ Investigating a series of murders that strongly resembles an earlier case she had solved, detective Jane Tennison (Helen Mirren) begins to wonder if the first killer she arrested was the right man. Another intelligently plotted entry in the popular British series. Not rated; contains adult situations. 102m. **DIR:** Paul Marcus. **CAST:** Helen Mirren, Tim Woodward, Stephen Boxer. **1996**

PRIME TARGET 🦃 While a courier for the FBI, a hick lawman discovers that he and the handcuffed crime boss he's transporting are moving targets. A third-rate version of *Midnight Run*. Rated R for nudity, violence, and profanity. 87m. **DIR:** David Heavener. **CAST:** David Heavener, Isaac Hayes, Robert Reed, Andrew Robinson, Jenilee Harrison, Don Stroud, Tony Curtis. **1991**

PRIME TIME MURDER ★★1/2 Sleazy TV reporter hooks up with homeless ex-cop to stalk a slasher who only attacks defenseless street people. Tim Thomerson is intriguing as the eccentric former cop, but the script is much too typical. Rated R for violence and profanity. 95m. **DIR:** Gary Skeen Hall. **CAST:** Tim Thomerson, Anthony Finetti, Laura Reed, Sally Kirkland. **1992**

PRIMO BABY ★★★1/2 A ward of the state is forced to live with a widowed rancher who has a mean-spirited, wheelchair-bound son. Though a rip-off of *The Secret Garden*, this film is still fun to watch. Not rated. 97m. **DIR:** Eda Lever Lishman. **CAST:** Duncan Regehr, Janet Laine Green. **1988**

PRIMROSE PATH ★★★★ In one of her best dramatic roles, Ginger Rogers stars as a young woman from the wrong side of the tracks who cons Joel McCrea into marriage. A fine film with a literate script, deftly crafted characters, fine production values—and heart. B&W; 93m. **DIR:** Gregory La Cava. **CAST:** Ginger Rogers, Joel McCrea, Marjorie Rambeau, Henry Travers. **1940**

PRINCE AND THE PAUPER, THE (1937) ★★★1/2 Enjoyable story of the young Prince of England trading places with his identical look-alike, a street beggar. One of Errol Flynn's lesser-known films. Erich Wolfgang Korngold wrote the music. B&W; 120m. **DIR:** William Keighley. **CAST:** Errol Flynn, Claude Rains, Barton MacLane, Alan Hale Sr., Billy Mauch, Bobby Mauch. **1937**

PRINCE AND THE PAUPER, THE (1978) ★★★1/2 In Mark Twain's novel of mistaken identity in not-so-jolly old England, Edward, the only son of King Henry VIII, trades places with his double, a child from the London slums. The young prince has trouble even with the aid of a swashbuckling soldier-of-fortune. The costumed adventure should satisfy young and old. Rated PG. 113m. **DIR:** Richard Fleischer. **CAST:** Charlton Heston, Oliver Reed, George C. Scott, Rex Harrison, Mark Lester. **1978**

PRINCE AND THE SHOWGIRL, THE ★★1/2 Romantic comedy about the attraction of a nobleman for an American show girl. Marilyn Monroe and Laurence Olivier's acting talents are in full flower, and they are fun to watch; however, they are so dissimilar that they never click. 117m. **DIR:** Laurence Olivier. **CAST:** Laurence Olivier, Marilyn Monroe, Sybil Thorndike, Jeremy Spencer. **1957 DVD**

PRINCE BRAT AND THE WHIPPING BOY ★★★★ Everyone fears Prince Horace, a tiny terror next in line to the throne. Jemmy, an orphan, is recruited as the prince's whipping boy. The adventure begins when both boys are kidnapped. The kidnappers think Jemmy is the prince, so it's up to the real prince to rise above himself to help save the day. Fine family entertainment. Rated G. 96m. **DIR:** Syd Macartney. **CAST:** Truan Monro, Nic Knight, Karen Salt, George C. Scott, Kevin Conway, Vincent Schiavelli. **1994**

PRINCE OF BEL AIR ★★★ Ever-watchable Mark Harmon plays a pool cleaner who has his way with countless wealthy and beautiful women. Silly TV movie—but Kirstie Alley shines as Harmon's true love. 95m. **DIR:** Charles Braverman. **CAST:** Mark Harmon, Kirstie Alley, Robert Vaughn. **1985**

PRINCE OF CENTRAL PARK, THE ★★ Ruth Gordon is, as usual, a bright spot in this made-for-TV children's film about an orphaned brother and sister who flee their foster home for a tree house in Central Park. The script is a bit cynical for a story aimed at children, but Gordon's charm serves to turn that around to her benefit. 76m. **DIR:** Harvey Hart. **CAST:** T. J. Hargrave, Lisa Richards, Ruth Gordon, Marc Vahanian. **1976**

PRINCE OF DARKNESS Priest learns about a canister hidden below an unused church and suspects he's found Satan's resting place. Rated R for violence and language. 110m. **DIR:** John Carpenter. **CAST:** Donald Pleasence, Jameson Parker, Victor Wong, Lisa Blount, Dennis Dun, Alice Cooper. **1987 DVD**

PRINCE OF EGYPT ★★★★ This rendering of the biblical Exodus saga hits all the proper dramatic notes and tells its story without the artificially adorable frills one expects from a full-length animated feature. This is an ambitious film: There are moments of humor, even amid such great tragedy; more opera than musical, with nine primary songs superbly integrated into its script. The "money effects"—God's speaking to Moses from the burning bush, the parting of the Red Sea—are vivid and breathtaking. Further assisted by some splendid vocal talents (Patrick Stewart, Val Kilmer, and Ralph Fiennes), this emerges as the best *Classics Illustrated* Bible adaptation ever created. Rated PG for dramatic intensity. 99m. **DIR:** Brenda Chapman, Steve Hickner, Simon Wells. **1998 DVD**

PRINCE OF PENNSYLVANIA Keanu Reeves portrays a morbid, morose teenager in a small Pennsylvania mining town. Rated R for nudity, violence, and profanity. 93m. **DIR:** Ron Nyswander. **CAST:** Fred Ward, Bonnie Bedelia, Keanu Reeves, Amy Madigan. **1988**

PRINCE OF THE CITY ★★★★ Director Sidney Lumet has created one of the screen's most intense character studies out of the true story of a corrupt New York narcotics cop, played wonderfully by Treat Williams. In becoming a government agent, the cop destroys the lives of his closest friends. Rated R because of violence and strong profanity. 167m. **DIR:** Sidney Lumet. **CAST:** Treat Williams, Jerry Orbach, Richard Foronjy. **1981**

PRINCE OF TIDES, THE ★★★1/2 Strong themes are explored in Barbra Streisand's adaptation of Pat Conroy's novel. Streisand plays a psychiatrist attempting to delve into the deep psychological problems of the suicidal Melinda Dillon with the help of brother Nick Nolte. Rated R for profanity, violence, and simulated sex. 132m. **DIR:** Barbra Streisand. **CAST:** Barbra Streisand, Nick Nolte, Blythe Danner, Kate Nelligan, Jeroen Krabbé, Melinda Dillon, Jason Gould, George Carlin, Brad Sullivan. **1991 DVD**

PRINCE VALIANT (1954) ★★★1/2 Harold Foster's splendid saga of a young Scandinavian prince who enters the court of King Arthur and returns his family to their throne and restores his birthright. High adventure and great to look at. Fun for the whole family. 100m. **DIR:** Henry Hathaway. **CAST:** Robert Wagner, James Mason, Janet Leigh, Debra Paget, Sterling Hayden, Victor McLaglen, Donald Crisp, Brian Aherne, Tom Conway, Neville Brand. **1954**

PRINCE VALIANT (1997) ★★ This German–United Kingdom coproduction does a decent job of bringing the comic strip to life, but the film as a whole is rather lackluster. Director Anthony Hickox also does a decent job of evoking the time and the place, yet budget constraints and sloppy editing sabotage the film at every turn. Hickox even has the audacity to link the action together with cartoon panels as a tribute to the strip. Rated PG for violence. 92m. **DIR:** Anthony Hickox. **CAST:** Stephen Moyer, Katherine Heigl, Edward Fox, Ron Perlman. **1997**

PRINCES IN EXILE ★★★ A tough subject, teenagers with life-threatening diseases, is handled adroitly by a

cast of unknowns and director Giles Walker. The plot has vestiges of teen movies but the film never slips over the edge and loses its humor or intelligence. Rated PG-13. 103m. **DIR:** Giles Walker. **CAST:** Zachary Ansley, Nicholas Shields, Stacy Mistysyn. **1990**

PRINCESS ACADEMY, THE Another girls' school movie, in which the entire point is to cram in as many extraneous shower and bedroom scenes as possible. Rated R. 90m. **DIR:** Bruce Block. **CAST:** Eva Gabor, Lar Park Lincoln. **1987**

PRINCESS AND THE GOBLIN, THE ★★1/2 The title pretty much tells all in this passable piece of children's fare. There are a few high points in the storytelling, but these are hampered by crude, uninspired animation. That said, youngsters—especially girls under the age of eight—are likely to enjoy it. Rated G. 76m. **DIR:** Jozsef Gemes. **1994**

PRINCESS AND THE PIRATE, THE ★★★ A happy, hilarious Bob Hope howler. He and the beautiful Virginia Mayo are pursued by pirates and trapped by potentate Walter Slezak. Victor McLaglen is menacing as a buccaneer bent on their destruction. Walter Brennan is something else—a pirate? This one's lots of fun for all! 94m. **DIR:** David Butler. **CAST:** Bob Hope, Virginia Mayo, Victor McLaglen, Walter Brennan, Walter Slezak. **1944 DVD**

•PRINCESS AND THE WARRIOR, THE ★★★★ A psychiatric nurse becomes obsessed with a petty criminal who saved her life in a chance encounter, convinced that their destinies are somehow linked. Elements of romantic thriller, bank heist, and psychological drama blend into something quite original, with unexpected side trips that make the film fresh and fascinating. In German with English subtitles. Rated R for mature themes, profanity (in subtitles), and sexual scenes. 129m. **DIR:** Tom Tykwer. **CAST:** Franka Potente, Benno Fürmann, Joachim Król, Lars Rudolph. **2002 DVD**

PRINCESS BRIDE, THE ★★★★1/2 In this grand adaptation of William Goldman's cult novel, Cary Elwes battles horrible monsters and makes unusual friends while fighting to save his beloved Buttercup from the clutches of the smarmy Prince Humperdinck. The cast is uniformly excellent, with Mandy Patinkin a standout. A wonderful fantasy for all ages. Rated PG for modest violence and language. 98m. **DIR:** Rob Reiner. **CAST:** Cary Elwes, Robin Wright, Mandy Patinkin, Andre the Giant, Chris Sarandon, Wallace Shawn, Billy Crystal, Carol Kane, Peter Falk, Fred Savage. **1987 DVD**

PRINCESS CARABOO ★★★ Based on a true story, this mellow, romantic mystery plays like an adult fairy tale. A young woman traveling through the bandit-plagued countryside of nineteenth-century England is arrested as a vagrant. When she begins talking in an unidentifiable language, a socialite declares the stranger to be foreign royalty and takes her into her home while a sympathetic but determined journalist tries to verify her identity. Rated PG. 94m. **DIR:** Michael Austin. **CAST:** Phoebe Cates, Kevin Kline, John Lithgow, Jim Broadbent, Stephen Rea, Wendy Hughes. **1994 DVD**

PRINCESS COMES ACROSS, THE ★★★1/2 Fred MacMurray sings, Carole Lombard vamps, and together they solve a mystery on a transatlantic ocean liner while falling for one another. Not rated. B&W; 77m. **DIR:** William K. Howard. **CAST:** Carole Lombard, Fred MacMurray, Douglass Dumbrille, Alison Skipworth, William Frawley, Porter Hall. **1936**

PRINCESS DAISY ★★1/2 If you enjoy sleaze and glitter, then you should be tickled by this made-for-TV rendition of Judith Krantz's novel of a poor little rich girl. Stacy Keach and Claudia Cardinale give the best performances. 188m. **DIR:** Waris Hussein. **CAST:** Lindsay Wagner, Paul Michael Glaser, Robert Urich, Claudia Cardinale, Ringo Starr, Merete Van Kamp, Sada Thompson, Stacy Keach, Barbara Bach, Rupert Everett. **1983**

•PRINCESS DIARIES, THE ★★★1/2 Enchanting Disney transformation film challenges an awkward geek (brilliantly portrayed by Anne Hathaway) to become a poised princess. What would otherwise have been just another teen angst flick is elevated by Hathaway's self-assured mentors, Julie Andrews and Hector Elizondo. Andrews, as Queen Clarisse Renaldi, comes to San Francisco seeking her granddaughter, the heir to Genovia's throne. Her royal presence is good for a few chuckles as she deals with "common" situations. Rated G. 115m. **DIR:** Garry Marshall. **CAST:** Anne Hathaway, Julie Andrews, Hector Elizondo, Heather Matarazzo. **2001 DVD**

PRINCESS MONONOKE ★★★1/2 A medieval Japanese prince slays a monster, but not before it passes on a fatal infection to him; the prince spends his remaining time questing for the monster's origin. It's no wonder this animated epic was a huge hit in Japan, with its striking visuals, complex characters, and dense, evocative story. For American release, a first-rate voice cast was added, including Billy Crudup, Claire Danes, Billy Bob Thornton, and Minnie Driver. Rated PG-13 for images of violence and gore. 133m. **DIR:** Hayao Miyazaki. **1997 DVD**

PRINCESS TAM TAM ★★★1/2 The best of several movies featuring the legendary Josephine Baker. She plays an African girl brought to Paris by a writer who passes her off as an Indian princess. In French with English subtitles. B&W; 77m. **DIR:** Edmond Gréville. **CAST:** Josephine Baker, Albert Préjean. **1935**

PRINCESS WHO HAD NEVER LAUGHED, THE ★★★★ In this funny Grimm's fairy tale, laughter does prove to be the best medicine for the forlorn princess (Ellen Barkin). When she locks herself in her room, her father decrees a Royal Laugh-off to make his daughter happy. 51m. **DIR:** Mark Cullingham. **CAST:** Howie Mandel, Ellen Barkin, Howard Hesseman. **1984**

PRINCESS YANG KWEI FEI ★★★1/2 Color is used with great effect in this big-budget epic of eighth-century China. When the current empress dies, the emperor falls in love with and marries a servant girl. But her life is ruined by jealous members of the royal court. In Japanese with English subtitles. 91m. **DIR:** Kenji Mizoguchi. **CAST:** Masayuki Mori, Machiko Kyo. **1955**

PRINCIPAL, THE ★★ Unrealistic treatment and poor writing sabotage this story of a renegade teacher (James Belushi) who, as punishment, is made principal of a high school where all the hardship cases from the other schools are relegated. Belushi doesn't do justice to his role, but Louis Gossett Jr. is good as the school's security chief. Rated R for language and violence. 110m. **DIR:** Christopher Cain. **CAST:** James Belushi, Louis

Gossett Jr., Rae Dawn Chong, Michael Wright, Esai Morales. **1987**

PRISON 🦃 An old prison is haunted by the vengeful ghost of a man executed in 1964. Rated R for language and violence. 102m. **DIR:** Renny Harlin. **CAST:** Lane Smith, Chelsea Field, Andre de Shields, Lincoln Kilpatrick. **1988**

PRISON FOR CHILDREN ★★★ Depressing, fact-based story of young offenders beaten down by a brutal system that tosses abandonded kids in with delinquents. This made-for-TV story is told with sensitivity but is on the sappy side. Especially touching is Raphael Sbarge as a countrified teen warehoused in a vicious juvenile prison. Not rated; contains adult themes. 96m. **DIR:** Larry Peerce. **CAST:** Raphael Sbarge, Kenny Ransom, John Ritter, Betty Thomas, Jonathan Chapin, Josh Brolin. **1986**

PRISON ON FIRE ★★★★ Sent to prison for killing a man in self-defense, a white-collar worker learns how to survive with the aid of a more hardened prisoner (Asian superstar Chow Yun-Fat). Ringo Lam, one of Hong Kong's top directors, keeps everything moving in this entertaining thriller. In Cantonese with English subtitles. Not rated; contains strong violence. 98m. **DIR:** Ringo Lam. **CAST:** Chow Yun-Fat, Leung Ka Fai. **1987 DVD**

PRISON STORIES: WOMEN ON THE INSIDE ★★★ This three-segment made-for-cable anthology directed by and starring women attempts to draw attention to problems facing prison mothers. Because of its TV production values, a lot of the grit is missing. As a result, real-life drama has been downplayed as the main characters turn into disposable stereotypes. Partial nudity, profanity, and violence. 94m. **DIR:** Penelope Spheeris, Donna Deitch, Joan Micklin Silver. **CAST:** Lolita Davidovich, Rachel Ticotin, Rae Dawn Chong, Annabella Sciorra. **1991**

PRISONER, THE ★★★★ Gripping political drama with outstanding performances by Alec Guinness and Jack Hawkins. Guinness portrays a cardinal being held as a political prisoner in a communist country. Jack Hawkins is the head of the secret police in charge of breaking down and brainwashing Guinness. Not rated. 91m. **DIR:** Peter Glenville. **CAST:** Alec Guinness, Jack Hawkins. **1955**

PRISONER, THE (TV SERIES) ★★★★ This sci-fi series was the brainchild of star Patrick McGoohan, who intended it to be an oblique follow-up to his successful *Danger Man* and *Secret Agent* series. The main character (McGoohan), whose name never is given—although he is believed to be *Secret Agent*'s John Drake—abruptly resigns from a sensitive intelligence position without explanation. He is abducted and awakens one morning in a mysterious community known only as The Village where every resident is known only by a number. Superior episodes are "The Arrival," "The Chimes of Big Ben," "Schizoid Man," "Many Happy Returns," "Living in Harmony," an episode never shown on American television, and "Once upon a Time" and "Fallout," the two-parter that brings the story to a close. 52m. **DIR:** Patrick McGoohan, David Tomblin, Don Chaffey, Pat Jackson. **CAST:** Patrick McGoohan, Angelo Muscat, Leo McKern, Peter Bowles, Nigel Stock, Peter Wyngarde. **1968 DVD**

PRISONER OF HONOR ★★★★ Scripter Ron Hutchinson's fascinating account of 1895's Dreyfus Affair, which became a national scandal and an international embarrassment. Richard Dreyfuss, superbly proud and defiant as Colonel George Picquart, grows convinced that Captain Alfred Dreyfus was convicted of espionage simply because of being a Jew; the resulting investigation makes a public mockery of French justice. Compelling made-for-cable drama. 88m. **DIR:** Ken Russell. **CAST:** Richard Dreyfuss, Oliver Reed, Peter Firth, Jeremy Kemp, Brian Blessed, Lindsay Anderson. **1991**

PRISONER OF LOVE 🦃 Model Naomi Campbell stars as a woman who witnesses a mob hit and finds herself targeted by the killer. Billed as an erotic thriller, it is neither erotic nor thrilling. Rated R for violence, language, and adult situations. 94m. **DIR:** Steve DiMarco. **CAST:** Naomi Campbell, Eric Thal, Beau Starr, James Gallander. **1999 DVD**

PRISONER OF SECOND AVENUE, THE ★★★★ Neil Simon blends laughter with tears in this film about an executive (Jack Lemmon) who loses his job and has a nervous breakdown. Anne Bancroft plays Lemmon's wife. Rated PG. 105m. **DIR:** Melvin Frank. **CAST:** Jack Lemmon, Anne Bancroft, Gene Saks, Elizabeth Wilson, Florence Stanley. **1975**

PRISONER OF THE MOUNTAINS ★★★1/2 Two Russian soldiers are taken hostage in the ethnic strife that has accompanied the breakup of the Soviet Union; gradually they develop an awkward rapport with their captors, and with each other. This lyrical Russian film, loosely based on a children's story by Tolstoy, seems constantly on the verge of becoming predictable, then strikes off in new and surprising directions. It's a confident mix of comedy, tragedy, and magical realism, with excellent performances. In Russian with English subtitles. Rated R for violence. 99m. **DIR:** Sergei Bodrov. **CAST:** Oleg Menshikov, Sergei Bodrov Jr., Jemal Sikharulidze, Susanna Mekhralieva. **1996**

PRISONER OF ZENDA, THE (1937) ★★★1/2 An outstanding cast, lavish costuming and sets, and a wholesome derring-do plot combine to make this a highly entertaining film. Commoner Ronald Colman is forced to stand in for a "twin" cousin in a political plot to gain control of a small European kingdom. Of the five screen versions of Anthony Hope's famous 1894 novel, this is absolutely the best. B&W; 101m. **DIR:** John Cromwell. **CAST:** Ronald Colman, Madeleine Carroll, Mary Astor, Douglas Fairbanks Jr., C. Aubrey Smith, Raymond Massey, David Niven. **1937**

PRISONER OF ZENDA, THE (1952) ★★★ An innocent traveler in a small European country is the exact double of its king and gets involved in a murder plot. This is a flashy Technicolor remake of the famous 1937 Ronald Colman version. 101m. **DIR:** Richard Thorpe. **CAST:** Stewart Granger, Deborah Kerr, Jane Greer, Louis Calhern, James Mason, Lewis Stone. **1952**

PRISONER OF ZENDA, THE (1979) ★★★1/2 Zany rendition of the classic tale of a look-alike commoner who stands in for the endangered king of Ruritania. A warm and hilarious film despite the lack of critical acclaim. Rated PG for language. 108m. **DIR:** Richard Quine. **CAST:** Peter Sellers, Lionel Jeffries, Elke Sommer, Lynne Frederick. **1979**

PRISONER OF ZENDA, INC. ★★★1/2 William Shatner makes a delightfully hammy villain in this kid-oriented update of Anthony Hope's swashbuckling classic. Teenager Jonathan Jackson plays dual roles, as an introverted software genius whose company is coveted by the dastardly Shatner and as the baseball-loving "ordinary kid" who stands in when the computer nerd is abducted. Great fun for the entire family and suitable for all ages. Rated PG for mild mayhem. 100m. **DIR:** Stefan Scaini. **CAST:** Jonathan Jackson, William Shatner, Jay Brazeau, Richard Lee Jackson. **1996**

PRISONERS OF INERTIA ★★ Slow-paced comedy features newlyweds (Amanda Plummer and Christopher Rich) attempting to enjoy a Manhattan Sunday. *Inertia* describes the film's tempo. Rated R for nudity. 92m. **DIR:** J. Noyes Scher. **CAST:** Amanda Plummer, Christopher Rich, John C. McGinley. **1989**

PRISONERS OF THE LOST UNIVERSE ★★ A low-budget science-fantasy adventure about three people transported to a parallel universe. Once there, they must use modern technology and archaic weaponry to battle an evil warlord. Although riddled with poor special effects, the film is actually a lot of good-natured fun. Made for Showtime cable network; contains some profanity and mild violence. 94m. **DIR:** Terry Marcel. **CAST:** Richard Hatch, Kay Lenz, John Saxon. **1983**

PRISONERS OF THE SUN ★★★ This Australian drama offers a complex look at justice in the West versus the East, especially when it's clouded by political corruption. Bryan Brown plays an Australian military lawyer pressing war-crimes charges against Japanese officers and soldiers who killed hundreds of Australian POWs in a death camp during World War II. Rated R. 109m. **DIR:** Stephen Wallace. **CAST:** Bryan Brown, George Takei, Terry O'Quinn. **1991**

PRIVATE AFFAIRS OF BEL AMI, THE ★★★★ Nobody ever played a cad better than George Sanders, and this is his crowning achievement. He is the antihero in Guy de Maupassant's famous story of a charmer who loves the ladies and leaves them until it finally catches up with him. The ending is pure Hollywood. UCLA's Film Archive restored the original print for the video release. B&W; 112m. **DIR:** Albert Lewin. **CAST:** George Sanders, Angela Lansbury, Frances Dee, Ann Dvorak, Albert Basserman, John Carradine, Hugo Haas, Warren William, Marie Wilson. **1947**

PRIVATE BENJAMIN ★★★★ This comedy is at its best in the first half, when Goldie Hawn, as a spoiled Jewish princess, joins the army. The last part of the movie gets a little heavy on the message end, but Hawn's buoyant personality makes it easy to take. Rated R for profanity, nudity, and implicit sex. 110m. **DIR:** Howard Zieff. **CAST:** Goldie Hawn, Eileen Brennan, Armand Assante, Robert Webber, Sam Wanamaker. **1980 DVD**

PRIVATE BUCKAROO ★★ Showcase vehicle for Patty, LaVerne, and Maxene, the Andrews Sisters, who decide to put on a show for soldiers. The Donald O'Connor/Peggy Ryan duo stands out. B&W; 68m. **DIR:** Eddie Cline. **CAST:** The Andrews Sisters, Joe E. Lewis, Dick Foran, Jennifer Holt, Donald O'Connor, Peggy Ryan, Harry James. **1942 DVD**

PRIVATE EYES, THE 🦃 Holmes and Watson send-up. Rated PG. 91m. **DIR:** Lang Elliott. **CAST:** Tim Conway, Don Knotts, Trisha Noble, Bernard Fox. **1980**

PRIVATE FILES OF J. EDGAR HOOVER, THE ★★1/2 A soap-opera-style account of the life and times of J. Edgar Hoover, concentrating on the seamier side of the FBI man's investigations. James Wainwright plays the young protagonist with low-key (some would say boring) intensity, while Broderick Crawford growls his way through Hoover's elder years. Rated PG for language and gangster violence. 111m. **DIR:** Larry Cohen. **CAST:** Broderick Crawford, Michael Parks, José Ferrer, Celeste Holm, Rip Torn, Ronee Blakley, James Wainwright, Dan Dailey, Lloyd Nolan. **1977**

PRIVATE FUNCTION, A ★★★★ The Michael Palin/Maggie Smith team repeat the success of *The Missionary* with this hilarious film about a meek foot doctor and his socially aspiring wife who become involved with the black market during the food rationing days of post–World War II England when they acquire an unlicensed pig. The humor is open to those who like Monty Python, but is also accessible to audiences who do not find that brand of humor funny. Rated R. 96m. **DIR:** Malcolm Mowbray. **CAST:** Michael Palin, Maggie Smith, Denholm Elliott, Richard Griffiths. **1985**

PRIVATE HELL 36 ★★1/2 Tight, well-constructed story of two cops who skim money from a haul they have intercepted and have trouble living with it, is nicely acted by veteran performers. Ida Lupino, equally adept on either side of the camera, cowrote and produced this grim drama. B&W; 81m. **DIR:** Don Siegel. **CAST:** Ida Lupino, Steve Cochran, Howard Duff, Dean Jagger, Dorothy Malone. **1954**

PRIVATE INVESTIGATIONS 🦃 Los Angeles architect is chased around town by bad guys who think he knows something that could expose their schemes. Rated R for language and violence. 91m. **DIR:** Nigel Dick. **CAST:** Clayton Rohner, Ray Sharkey, Paul LeMat, Talia Balsam, Anthony Zerbe. **1987**

PRIVATE LIFE OF DON JUAN, THE ★★ A vehicle for the aging Douglas Fairbanks, his last picture is set in seventeenth-century Spain. A famous lover (Fairbanks) fakes a suicide in order to make a comeback in disguise. It is somewhat tragic that the first great hero of the screen should have ended up in this disappointment. B&W; 90m. **DIR:** Alexander Korda. **CAST:** Douglas Fairbanks Sr., Merle Oberon, Binnie Barnes, Benita Hume, Joan Gardner, Melville Cooper. **1934**

PRIVATE LIFE OF HENRY THE EIGHTH, THE ★★★★ This well-paced historical chronicle of England's bluebeard monarch and his six wives stars Charles Laughton as the notorious king. Laughton's real-life spouse, Elsa Lanchester, plays Anne, the fourth wife. She manages to keep her head off the chopping block by humoring the volatile king during a memorable game of cards. B&W; 87m. **DIR:** Alexander Korda. **CAST:** Charles Laughton, Robert Donat, Merle Oberon, Elsa Lanchester, Binnie Barnes. **1933**

PRIVATE LIFE OF SHERLOCK HOLMES, THE ★★★★1/2 Director Billy Wilder's affectionately satirical pastiche of the Conan Doyle stories reveals the "secrets" allegedly shared by Sherlock Holmes (Robert Stephens) and Dr. John H. Watson (Colin Blakely). It does so with wit, humor, taste, and even suspense. Rated PG. 125m. **DIR:** Billy Wilder. **CAST:** Robert Stephens, Colin Blakely, Genevieve Page, Christopher Lee, Irene Handl, Clive Revill, Stanley Holloway. **1970**

PRIVATE LIVES ★★★1/2 A divorced couple meet by accident on their second honeymoons; soon they've abandoned their new spouses and run off, endlessly bickering and making up. Noel Coward's sparkling play stylishly filmed; laughs multiply by the minute. B&W; 84m. **DIR:** Sidney Franklin. **CAST:** Norma Shearer, Robert Montgomery, Reginald Denny, Una Merkel. **1931**

PRIVATE LIVES OF ELIZABETH AND ESSEX, THE ★★★1/2 Bette Davis is Queen Elizabeth and Errol Flynn is her dashing suitor in this enjoyable costume drama. 106m. **DIR:** Michael Curtiz. **CAST:** Bette Davis, Errol Flynn, Olivia de Havilland, Vincent Price, Donald Crisp, Nanette Fabray, Henry Daniell, Alan Hale Sr., Robert Warwick, Henry Stephenson. **1939**

PRIVATE MATTER, A ★★★★★ The abortion movement's roots are traced in this unflinchingly forceful (and true) account. Sherri Finkbine, a host of the children's television show *Romper Room*, learns that her use of thalidomide-based tranquilizers has almost certainly harmed the baby she is carrying. Attempts to handle the situation go awry when a strong sense of moral outrage prompts her to spread the news, in the hopes of warning other women. Made for cable. 89m. **DIR:** Joan Micklin Silver. **CAST:** Sissy Spacek, Aidan Quinn, Estelle Parsons, Sheila McCarthy. **1992**

PRIVATE NAVY OF SGT. O'FARRELL, THE ★★ A tasteless comedy about a sergeant who recruits a group of nurses to improve the morale of the troops. Instead of beautiful women, he gets Phyllis Diller, the most unglamorous female of all. 92m. **DIR:** Frank Tashlin. **CAST:** Bob Hope, Phyllis Diller, Gina Lollobrigida, Mylene Demongeot, Jeffrey Hunter. **1968 DVD**

PRIVATE OBSESSION ★★ Erotic-thriller video-vixen Shannon Whirry stars as a fashion model who is abducted by an obsessed fan. Pedestrian plot just an excuse to get Whirry out of her clothes again. Rated R for nudity, strong language, and adult situations. 90m. **DIR:** Lee Frost. **CAST:** Shannon Whirry, Michael Christian, Bo Svenson, Rip Taylor. **1994 DVD**

PRIVATE PARTS (1972) ★★ When a teenage runaway seeks refuge at her aunt's San Francisco hotel, she finds that the residents can get downright deadly, as well as kinky. Mildly entertaining for fans of hack-and-slash erotic thrillers. Rated R for violence and nudity. 86m. **DIR:** Paul Bartel. **CAST:** Ann Ruymen, Lucille Benson, John Ventantonio. **1972**

PRIVATE PARTS (1997) ★★★ The story of Howard Stern, radio's notorious "shock jock," is carefully crafted to make him a movie star, and Stern does have a genial, breezy screen presence. Director Betty Thomas keeps the rags-to-riches story clipping along with zest. The pace flags, however, whenever Stern plops down in front of his microphone, and the film glosses over his more offensive on-air excesses. Rated R for profanity, nudity, and sexual humor. 108m. **DIR:** Betty Thomas. **CAST:** Howard Stern, Robin Quivers, Mary McCormack, Fred Norris. **1997 DVD**

PRIVATE RESORT ★★ This teen comedy features two young men (Rob Morrow and Johnny Depp) seeking romance and excitement at a luxurious resort. Few funny moments. Rated R for nudity, obscenities, and sexual situations. 82m. **DIR:** George Bowers. **CAST:** Rob Morrow, Johnny Depp, Tony Azito, Dody Goodman, Hector Elizondo. **1985**

PRIVATE SCHOOL 🦃 Enroll at your own risk. Rated R for nudity and profanity. 97m. **DIR:** Noel Black. **CAST:** Phoebe Cates, Martin Mull, Sylvia Kristel, Ray Walston, Julie Payne, Michael Zorek, Matthew Modine. **1983**

PRIVATE SNUFFY SMITH ★★ Cloned from the comic strip "Barney Google and Snuffy Smith," this grade B time passer has cantankerous hillbilly Snuffy being allowed to join up after saving the life of an army sergeant. Supporting player Jimmie Dodd went on to shepherd Disney's Mouseketeers. B&W; 67m. **DIR:** Eddie Cline. **CAST:** Bud Duncan, Edgar Kennedy, Doris Linden, Jimmie Dodd. **1942**

PRIVATE WAR ★★ Former war hero goes to Vietnam as a DI for an elite military unit. Members of his squad meet with mysterious accidents before one member figures out the psychotic DI is responsible. Familiar territory. Rated R for violence and profanity. 95m. **DIR:** Frank DePalma. **CAST:** Martin Hewitt, Joe Dallesandro, Kimberly Beck. **1988**

PRIVATE WARS ★★★ An alcoholic ex-cop helps intimidated inner-city residents to eradicate a violent street gang. In the villain's corner: a rapacious businessman who wants to raze the neighborhood for a new high rise. The only major flaw is an abrupt, dissatisfying conclusion. Rated R for profanity, violence, and suggested sex. 94m. **DIR:** John Weidner. **CAST:** Steve Railsback, Michael Champion, Dan Tullis Jr., Holly Floria, Stuart Whitman. **1993**

PRIVATES ON PARADE ★★★1/2 While this story of a gay USO-type unit in the British army is a comedy, it has its serious moments. These come when the unit accidentally runs into a gang of gunrunners. John Cleese is hilarious as the pathetic army major who's ignorant of the foul play that goes on under his nose. Rated PG-13 for adult situations and profanity. 107m. **DIR:** Michael Blakemore. **CAST:** John Cleese, Denis Quilley, Michael Elphick, Simon Jones, Joe Melia, John Standing, Nicola Pagett. **1983**

PRIX DE BEAUTE (BEAUTY PRIZE) ★★★★★ Directly after making *Pandora's Box* and *Diary of a Lost Girl*, Louise Brooks made one other memorable movie, this early French sound film. She plays an ambitious young beauty contestant who aspires to a movie career. Her actions, however, infuriate her jealous husband. In French with English subtitles. B&W; 97m. **DIR:** Augusto Genina. **CAST:** Louise Brooks. **1930**

PRIZE, THE ★★★★ A fast-moving thriller based on Irving Wallace's popular novel. Paul Newman plays a Nobel Prize winner in Stockholm who gets involved in espionage, a passionate affair, and politics. 136m. **DIR:** Mark Robson. **CAST:** Paul Newman, Edward G. Robinson, Elke Sommer, Anna Lee, Kevin McCarthy, Micheline Presle, Don Dubbins, Sergio Fantoni, Leo G. Carroll, Diane Baker, Virginia Christine, John Qualen. **1963**

PRIZE PULITZER, THE: THE ROXANNE PULITZER STORY ★★★ Uneven, but surprisingly sturdy telling of the divorce scandal of the 1980s. Made-for-TV bioshocker. 95m. **DIR:** Richard A. Colla. **CAST:** Perry King, Courteney Cox, Chynna Phillips. **1989**

PRIZEFIGHTER, THE ★★1/2 In addition to starring in this goofy comedy, Tim Conway wrote the story. In it, we get a glimpse of 1930s boxing, with Conway playing a stupid boxer who has Don Knotts for his manager. Children may find the corny gags amusing, but most adults will be disappointed. Rated PG. 99m. **DIR:** Michael Preece. **CAST:** Tim Conway, Don Knotts, David Wayne. **1979**

PRIZZI'S HONOR ★★★★★ This totally bent comedy is perhaps best described as *The Godfather* gone stark, raving mad. Jack Nicholson plays a Mafia hit man who falls in love with a mystery woman (Kathleen Turner), who turns out to be full of surprises. Perhaps the blackest black comedy ever made. It's a real find for fans of the genre. Rated R for nudity, suggested sex, profanity, and violence. 130m. **DIR:** John Huston. **CAST:** Jack Nicholson, Kathleen Turner, Robert Loggia, John Randolph, William Hickey, Anjelica Huston. **1985 DVD**

PROBABLE CAUSE ★★ Silly but strangely involving tale of a cop accused of sexism and his new female partner. Someone is killing cops one by one and it seems as though both partners know more than they're telling. The "surprise" ending is anything but. Rated R for profanity, violence, and sexuality. 90m. **DIR:** Paul Ziller. **CAST:** Michael Ironside, Kate Vernon, Craig T. Nelson, M. Emmet Walsh, Kirk Baltz. **1994**

PROBE ★★1/2 Pilot film for the TV series *Probe*. Hugh O'Brian stars as an agent with an electronic transmitter implanted in him, which allows him to relay and receive information from headquarters. 97m. **DIR:** Russ Mayberry. **CAST:** Hugh O'Brian, Elke Sommer, Lilia Skala, Burgess Meredith. **1972**

PROBLEM CHILD ★★ A bickering yuppie couple (John Ritter, Amy Yasbeck) decide to adopt a child so they can get invited to all the upscale kiddie birthday parties. They end up with a foul-mouthed, destructive youngster (Michael Oliver). Moronic combination of *Police Academy* and *The Exorcist*. Rated PG for vulgar language and violence. 81m. **DIR:** Dennis Dugan. **CAST:** John Ritter, Jack Warden, Michael Oliver, Gilbert Gottfried, Amy Yasbeck, Michael Richards. **1990 DVD**

PROBLEM CHILD 2 ★★ John Ritter and Michael Oliver return as Ben Healy and his devilish adopted son Junior in this sequel. Too bad the writers had to heap projectile vomiting and dog feces on the audience. Rated PG-13 for mild profanity and scatological humor. 91m. **DIR:** Brian Levant. **CAST:** John Ritter, Michael Oliver, Laraine Newman, Amy Yasbeck, Ivyann Schwan, Jack Warden. **1991**

PRODIGAL, THE ★★★ Sexy stuff with Lana as a high priestess in biblical days who seduces Edmund Purdom and makes him wish he never left home. Somewhat silly and contrived but highly enjoyable thanks to a good cast. 114m. **DIR:** Richard Thorpe. **CAST:** Lana Turner, Edmund Purdom, Taina Elg, Neville Brand, Louis Calhern, Joseph Wiseman, Cecil Kellaway, James Mitchell. **1955**

PRODUCERS, THE ★★★★ Mel Brooks's first film as a director remains a laugh-filled winner. Zero Mostel stars as a sleazy Broadway promoter who, with the help of a neurotic accountant (Gene Wilder), comes up with a scheme to produce an intentional flop titled *Springtime for Hitler* and bilk its backers. The plan backfires, and the disappointed duo ends up with a hit and more troubles than before. Rated PG. 88m. **DIR:** Mel Brooks. **CAST:** Zero Mostel, Gene Wilder, Kenneth Mars, Dick Shawn, Lee Meredith, Christopher Hewett. **1968**

PROFESSIONAL, THE ★★★★ A fusion of the character-driven drama of French cinema and the conventions of the American action film, this film is a true oddity in which a simple-minded Italian hit man becomes the only friend of an abused 12-year-old girl. While not for all tastes, it's strangely compelling. You'll either love it or hate it. Rated R for violence and profanity. 110m. **DIR:** Luc Besson. **CAST:** Jean Reno, Gary Oldman, Natalie Portman, Danny Aiello, Peter Appel, Michael Badalucco, Ellen Greene. **1994 DVD**

PROFESSIONALS, THE ★★★★1/2 A rip-snorting adventure film with Lee Marvin, Burt Lancaster, Robert Ryan, and Woody Strode as the title characters out to rescue the wife (Claudia Cardinale) of a wealthy industrialist (Ralph Bellamy) from the clutches of a Mexican bandit (Jack Palance) who allegedly kidnapped her. Directed with a fine eye for character and action by Richard Brooks. 117m. **DIR:** Richard Brooks. **CAST:** Lee Marvin, Burt Lancaster, Robert Ryan, Woody Strode, Claudia Cardinale, Ralph Bellamy. **1966 DVD**

PROFILE FOR MURDER ★★1/2 Typical thriller stars Joan Severance as a criminal psychologist who finds herself under the influence of a man suspected of being a serial killer. Lance Henriksen opens up his usual bag of tricks as the enigmatic suspect while Severance still finds time to take off her clothes when she's not playing games with her subject. Rated R for adult situations, language, nudity, and violence. 95m. **DIR:** David Winning. **CAST:** Joan Severance, Lance Henriksen, Jeff Wincott. **1997**

PROGENY Even though the talent behind the camera comes with a horror pedigree, what they deliver on the screen in this direct-to-video effort is a dog. A husband suspects that his wife has been impregnated by aliens. So what else is new? Lame special effects. Rated R for violence, language, and adult situations. 96m. **DIR:** Brian Yuzna. **CAST:** Arnold Vosloo, Jillian McWhirter, Wilford Brimley, Brad Dourif. **1998 DVD**

PROGRAM, THE ★★★★ Director David S. Ward's best-written work since *The Sting*. This ensemble piece features Craig Sheffer as the troubled quarterback for Eastern State University who believes he has to engage in life-threatening stunts to cement his position of leadership. About the enormous pressure on participants in college sports, *The Program* has many richly drawn characters and situations. Rated R for profanity, violence, and drug use. 114m. **DIR:** David S. Ward. **CAST:** James Caan, Halle Berry, Omar Epps, Craig Sheffer, Kristy Swanson, Abraham Benrubi, Duane Davis. **1993 DVD**

PROGRAMMED TO KILL ★★ Sandahl Bergman plays a terrorist who is killed only to be brought back to life as a computer-controlled antiterrorist weapon for the United States. The plan backfires. Acting is poor and so is the script. Rated R for violence, profanity, and nudity. 91m. **DIR:** Allan Holzman. **CAST:** Robert Ginty, Sandahl Bergman, James Booth. **1987**

PROJECT A-KO ★★★ Another of the more lighthearted entries in the Japanese animation wave, the story here revolves around a simple rivalry for the

friendship of a dopey kid named C-Ko as disputed by the two heroines, A-Ko and B-Ko, who both happen to possess superhuman powers. In Japanese with English subtitles. Not rated, with violence and illustrated nudity. 86m. **DIR:** Katsuhiko Nishijima. **1986 DVD**

PROJECT A (PART I) ★★★ Vintage Jackie Chan period comedy full of Buster Keaton–style slapstick and martial arts action. Chan plays a Marine cadet in turn-of-the-century Hong Kong, who battles smugglers and pirates operating on the South China Sea. Remarkable stunts, brilliantly choreographed. In Cantonese with English subtitles. Not rated. 95m. **DIR:** Jackie Chan. **CAST:** Jackie Chan, Sammo Hung. **1983 DVD**

PROJECT A (PART II) ★★★1/2 Jackie Chan returns as Dragon Ma, the only uncorrupt cop in turn-of-century Hong Kong, where he finds himself at odds with the Chinese syndicate. As usual, the brilliantly staged martial arts battles are laced with comedy. In Cantonese with English subtitles. Not rated. 101m. **DIR:** Jackie Chan. **CAST:** Jackie Chan, Maggie Cheung. **1987 DVD**

PROJECT MOON BASE ★★ Futuristic story (set in far-off 1970!) chronicles the fate of an expedition that leaves a space station orbiting Earth and heads for the Moon. Made by independent producer Robert Lippert, this dull space story was co-authored by the esteemed Robert E. Heinlein, but it doesn't reflect his touch. B&W; 53m. **DIR:** Richard Talmadge. **CAST:** Ross Ford, Donna Martell, James Craven. **1953**

PROJECT SHADOWCHASER 3000 ★★ *Alien* meets *The Terminator* in this so-so sequel. Frank Zagarino returns as the dead android purposely lost in space for the safety of all mankind. When a seemingly deserted mining vessel crashes into a space station, occupants have little time to plan before the android is up and running, wreaking havoc on the station. Rated R for violence and adult language. 99m. **DIR:** John Eyres. **CAST:** Frank Zagarino, Sam Bottoms, Musetta Vander, Christopher Atkins. **1995**

PROJECT X ★★ A misguided attempt to turn a serious issue—the abuse of research animals—into a mainstream comedy-drama. Matthew Broderick is an air force misfit who winds up assigned to a secret project involving chimpanzees and air-flight simulators. Rated PG for intensity of theme. 108m. **DIR:** Jonathan Kaplan. **CAST:** Matthew Broderick, Helen Hunt, Bill Sadler, Jonathan Stark, Robin Gammell, Stephen Lang. **1987**

PROJECT: ALIEN 🦃 Confusing sci-fi dud surrounds an explosion and shower of flaming objects over Norway. Rated R for language. 92m. **DIR:** Frank Shields. **CAST:** Michael Nouri, Darlanne Fluegel, Maxwell Caulfield, Charles Durning. **1992**

PROJECT: ELIMINATOR 🦃 Government agents track down terrorists who have kidnapped a special weapons specialist. A trying and tired film. Even David Carradine is powerless to add a little kick to the proceedings. Rated R for violence. 89m. **DIR:** H. Kaye Dyal. **CAST:** David Carradine, Frank Zagarino, Drew Snyder. **1989 DVD**

PROJECT: METALBEAST 🦃 Another sorry tale of a government project to build the perfect living weapon gone awry, with Barry Bostwick simply awful as the leader of the project. Rated R for gore. 92m. **DIR:** Alessandro de Gaetano. **CAST:** Kim Delaney, Barry Bostwick. **1994**

PROJECTIONIST, THE ★★ A projectionist in a New York movie palace escapes his drab life by creating fantasies, casting himself as the hero in various films. The movie intercuts new footage into old classics, a technique used later by Steve Martin in *Dead Men Don't Wear Plaid*. The film has surprisingly little entertainment value. Rated R for profanity and partial nudity. 85m. **DIR:** Harry Hurwitz. **CAST:** Chuck McCann, Ina Balin, Rodney Dangerfield. **1970 DVD**

PROM NIGHT ★★ This okay slasher flick has a group of high school students being systematically slaughtered as payment for the accidental death of one of their friends when they were all children. Rated R. 92m. **DIR:** Paul Lynch. **CAST:** Jamie Lee Curtis, Leslie Nielsen, Casey Stevens. **1980 DVD**

PROM NIGHT III—LAST KISS ★★1/2 Prom queen from hell Mary Lou Maloney returns to her old high school to knock 'em dead. Done with some style and humor. Watch for the jukebox from hell. Rated R for nudity, violence, and profanity. 97m. **DIR:** Ron Oliver, Peter Simpson. **CAST:** Tim Conlon, Cyndy Preston. **1989**

PROM NIGHT IV—DELIVER US FROM EVIL ★★1/2 A religious fanatic stalks four teens he feels have transgressed the law of God. Really no different from a zillion other recent horror movies, but it's moderately well-done of its type. (It has, however, nothing to do with the other three *Prom Night* entries.) Rated R for violence. 95m. **DIR:** Clay Borris. **CAST:** Nikki De Boer, Alden Kane. **1991**

PROMISE, THE (1978) ★★1/2 After a car accident, Kathleen Quinlan accepts money from her fiancé's mother to have extensive reconstructive surgery and never see him again. Destiny and true love override all obstacles in this obvious romance. Rated PG for mild profanity. 97m. **DIR:** Gilbert Cates. **CAST:** Kathleen Quinlan, Stephen Collins, Beatrice Straight. **1978**

PROMISE, THE (1995) ★★★★ Director and cowriter Margarethe von Trotta puts a face on politics by depicting a romance splintered by the Berlin Wall. Beautifully shot, this intelligently made love story is a touching study of the human spirit. Von Trotta wisely used two sets of actors for the maturing lovers and propelled the story through time without pandering to her audience. In German with English subtitles. Rated R for sexual situations, nudity, and profanity. 115m. **DIR:** Margarethe von Trotta. **CAST:** Meret Becker, Corinna Harfouch, Anian Zollner, August Zirner. **1995**

PROMISE HER ANYTHING ★★1/2 Single mom Leslie Caron must find a father for her precocious son. Dated romp is a direct precursor to *Look Who's Talking*. 97m. **DIR:** Arthur Hiller. **CAST:** Warren Beatty, Leslie Caron, Robert Cummings, Keenan Wynn. **1965**

PROMISED A MIRACLE ★★★ Although greater depth should have been brought to this TV movie, it remains a thought-provoking account of two Christian parents seeking a miracle from God—the faith healing of their diabetic son. Based on the book *We Let Our Son Die* by Larry Parker. 94m. **DIR:** Stephen Gyllenhaal. **CAST:** Rosanna Arquette, Judge Reinhold, Maria O'Brien. **1988**

PROMISED LAND ★★ A segment from the lives of four young people, three of whom have just graduated from high school. And the film is all exposition and not much insight. Kiefer Sutherland is convincing as an insecure,

misguided wanderer. Rated R for profanity. 101m. **DIR:** Michael Hoffman. **CAST:** Kiefer Sutherland, Meg Ryan, Jason Gedrick. **1988**

PROMISES IN THE DARK ★★★1/2 This film is about a young girl dying of cancer. Marsha Mason costars as her sympathetic doctor. Good movie, but very depressing! Rated PG. 115m. **DIR:** Jerome Hellman. **CAST:** Marsha Mason, Ned Beatty, Susan Clark, Michael Brandon, Kathleen Beller, Paul Clemens, Donald Moffat. **1979**

PROMISES, PROMISES 🦃 The only thing going for this film is the scenes of a next-to-totally-naked Jayne Mansfield. Silly and crude. 75m. **DIR:** King Donovan. **CAST:** Jayne Mansfield, Marie McDonald, Tommy Noonan, Mickey Hargitay, Fritz Feld. **1963**

PROMOTER, THE ★★★ Alec Guinness is clever, conniving, and all innocence in this comedy centering on a penniless young man who exploits every opportunity to get ahead in the world. Glynis Johns is delightful as the girl who believes in him. B&W; 88m. **DIR:** Ronald Neame. **CAST:** Alec Guinness, Glynis Johns, Valerie Hobson, Petula Clark. **1952**

PRONTO ★★★ Based on an Elmore Leonard novel, this strange crime comedy–drama can't decide what to be when it grows up. Career grifter Peter Falk gets set up for some action he didn't orchestrate, and wisely flees to remote parts . . . but his tendency to share the same stories with anybody who'll listen brings the bad guys hot on his heels. Rated R for violence, profanity, nudity, and simulated sex. 100m. **DIR:** Jim McBride. **CAST:** Peter Falk, Glenne Headly, James LeGros, Sergio Castellitto, Walter Olkewicz, Glenn Plummer. **1997**

PROOF ★★★★ Blind since birth, Martin is convinced that his mother hated him for being blind and deceived him with her descriptions of what she saw. Now Martin wants to trust someone to describe to him the countless photographs he takes—thereby giving him the proof of a long-dead mother's love. Add a psychosexual love triangle, intriguing cinematography, and original music, and we have the film that swept the 1991 Australian Film Institute Awards. Rated R for profanity and nudity. 90m. **DIR:** Jocelyn Moorhouse. **CAST:** Hugo Weaving, Genevieve Picot, Russell Crowe. **1991**

PROOF OF LIFE ★★★ In a mythical South American country, a kidnap-and-ransom negotiator (Russell Crowe) falls for a woman (Meg Ryan) whose husband he is working to free. The unusual premise, Crowe's smoldering intensity, and Taylor Hackford's efficient direction compensate for the film's length and the lack of screen chemistry between the two stars. Rated R for profanity and violence. 135m. **DIR:** Taylor Hackford. **CAST:** Meg Ryan, Russell Crowe, David Caruso, David Morse, Pamela Reed, Anthony Heald. **2000 DVD**

PROPHECY (1979) 🦃 Dull ecological horror film about a mutated beast that inhabits a northeastern American forest. Rated PG. 95m. **DIR:** John Frankenheimer. **CAST:** Talia Shire, Robert Foxworth, Armand Assante, Richard Dysart, Victoria Racimo. **1979 DVD**

PROPHECY, THE (1995) ★★★ Instead of the usual unexplained gorefest, this horror flick makes a real statement about good and evil, both of which are of biblical proportions. The story of angels battling over the future of heaven is too convoluted, and probably too introspective to appeal to mainstream tastes. Rated R for violence and profanity. 97m. **DIR:** Gregory Widen. **CAST:** Christopher Walken, Eric Stoltz, Virginia Madsen, Viggo Mortensen, Amanda Plummer, Elias Koteas, Adam Goldberg, Maria Snyder. **1995 DVD**

PROPHECY II, THE ★★★ This second in the horror series is a taut thriller with all of the trimmings. Christopher Walken returns as the fallen angel Gabriel, sent to Earth to make sure that pregnant Jennifer Beals doesn't give birth to the spirit that will destroy him. This direct-to-video sequel is an impressive collection of special effects, engaging characters, and sharp dialogue. Rated R for adult situations, language, nudity, and violence. 83m. **DIR:** Greg Spence. **CAST:** Christopher Walken, Jennifer Beals, Russell Wong, Brittany Murphy, Eric Roberts. **1997 DVD**

PROPHECY 3: THE ASCENT ★★ Christopher Walken reprises his role as the fallen angel Gabriel, now looking to return to seraphim status once again after having been made mortal at the end of the last movie. This series is going downhill fast, losing the story and intrigue established in the first movie—and Walken's hair is actually getting worse. Rated R for violence and language. 107m. **DIR:** Patrick Lussier. **CAST:** Christopher Walken, Vincent Spano, Brad Dourif. **1999 DVD**

PROPOSITION, THE ★★★1/2 Rather than be forced into marriage with a local lord, a widow decides to save her farm by driving her livestock to market herself. It sounds like a Western, but this drama is actually set in nineteenth-century Wales, and it's surprisingly good. Rated R for nudity and violence. 99m. **DIR:** Strathford Hamilton. **CAST:** Theresa Russell, Patrick Bergen, Richard Lynch. **1997**

PROPRIETOR, THE 🦃 Confusing and convoluted film follows a famous French novelist as she returns home in an attempt to attain closure with her long-dead mother. Even Jeanne Moreau—appropriately cast as the novelist—can't save this film. Rated R for brief sexuality. 103m. **DIR:** Ismail Merchant. **CAST:** Jeanne Moreau, Sean Young, Sam Waterston, Christopher Cazenove, Nell Carter, Jean-Pierre Aumont, Austin Pendleton. **1996**

PROSPERO'S BOOKS ★★★ In this dense, ornate, relentlessly lush version of *The Tempest*, director Peter Greenaway shocks with graphic exactness, yet charms with lavish sets and Renaissance costumes designed by someone seemingly on LSD. Sir John Gielgud speaking Shakespeare's magnificent lines makes the film occasionally soar. Rated R for nudity and violence. 126m. **DIR:** Peter Greenaway. **CAST:** John Gielgud, Michael Clark, Isabelle Pasco, Michel Blanc. **1991**

PROTECTOR, THE (1985) ★★1/2 Standard kung fu film distinguished by nicely photographed action sequences and a sense of humor. Story has Jackie Chan as an undercover New York cop traveling to Hong Kong to break up a big heroin ring. Rated R for violence, nudity, and language. 94m. **DIR:** James Glickenhaus. **CAST:** Jackie Chan, Danny Aiello, Roy Chiao. **1985**

PROTECTOR (1998) ★★ Mario Van Peebles heads up a strong cast in this mediocre crime-drama about an undercover cop given ten days to bring in the killers of a mob witness. His search is hindered when he is also saddled with keeping the slain witness's girlfriend alive. Utter nonsense delivered with a modicum of conviction and believability. Rated R for violence, language, nudity, and adult situations. 94m. **DIR:** B. D. Clark. **CAST:**

Mario Van Peebles, Randy Quaid, Zerha Leverman, Ben Gazzara, Rae Dawn Chong. **1998 DVD**

PROTEUS ★★1/2 Aren't people ever going to learn? When their boat goes down, six survivors are forced to take refuge on an abandoned oil rig. Or at least they think it's abandoned. Actually, it's the home of a nasty scientific experiment that's hungry for company. This direct-to-video effort has decent special effects, an eerie setting, and an OK cast. Rated R for violence and profanity. 97m. **DIR:** Bob Keen. **CAST:** Craig Fairbrass, William Marsh, Doug Bradley, Ricco Ross. **1996**

PROTOCOL ★★★1/2 In this film, directed by Herbert Ross, Goldie Hawn is a lovable airhead who goes through a startling metamorphosis to become a true individual. Sound a little like *Private Benjamin*? You bet your blond movie actress. It's no classic. However, viewers could do a lot worse. Rated PG for violence, partial nudity, and adult situations. 96m. **DIR:** Herbert Ross. **CAST:** Goldie Hawn, Chris Sarandon, Richard Romanus, Cliff De Young, Gail Strickland. **1984 DVD**

PROTOTYPE ★★★ Christopher Plummer heads a government research team that has perfected an android. Contrary to his wishes, the Pentagon reprograms the android for its own sinister reasons. Nothing original, but entertaining nonetheless. Made for TV. 97m. **DIR:** David Greene. **CAST:** Christopher Plummer, David Morse, Stephen Elliott, Frances Sternhagen, Arthur Hill. **1983**

PROTOTYPE X29A ★★1/2 In a postnuclear-war future, cyborg hunter killers seek out mutants. This is basically a cross between *Robocop* and *Terminator*, with none of the originality that made those two films smash hits. Rated R for violence, profanity, and nudity. 98m. **DIR:** Phillip Roth. **CAST:** Lane Lenhart. **1992**

PROUD MEN ★★1/2 Routine father-and-son conflicts are given conviction by a strong cast, led by Charlton Heston and Peter Strauss in this made-for-cable Western. 94m. **DIR:** William A. Graham. **CAST:** Charlton Heston, Peter Strauss, Belinda Balaski. **1987**

•PROUD ONES, THE ★★★1/2 Martin Scorsese championed the restoration of this largely forgotten French film set in a dingy Latin American resort town. After her husband suddenly dies in an outbreak of spinal meningitis, a Frenchwoman loses her bearings and takes up with the local doctor, an alcoholic who has also lost his connection to life. Surprisingly grim and seedy, it is nonetheless masterfully directed and quite compelling. Adapted from a story by Jean-Paul Sartre. Original title: *Les Orgueilleux*; also known as *The Proud and the Beautiful*. In French with English subtitles. Not rated; contains adult themes. 105m. **DIR:** Yves Allegret. **CAST:** Michèle Morgan, Gérard Philipe. **1953**

PROUD REBEL, THE ★★★1/2 A post–Civil War sentimental drama about a Confederate veteran searching for a doctor who can cure his mute son. The principals in this one are excellent, the chemistry great. Well worth the watching, this was the ill-fated Alan Ladd's last "class" film. 103m. **DIR:** Michael Curtiz. **CAST:** Alan Ladd, Olivia de Havilland, David Ladd, Dean Jagger, Henry Hull. **1958 DVD**

PROVIDENCE ★★★★ Director Alain Resnais's first English-language film includes the great cast of Dirk Bogarde, John Gielgud, Ellen Burstyn, and David Warner. An old and dying writer (Gielgud) completing his last novel invites his family up for the weekend. The fast cutting between the writer's imagined thoughts and real life makes this film difficult to follow for some. Rated R. 104m. **DIR:** Alain Resnais. **CAST:** Dirk Bogarde, John Gielgud, Ellen Burstyn, David Warner, Elaine Stritch. **1977**

PROVOCATEUR ★★★ A North Korean agent infiltrates a U. S. base masquerading as a nanny. Once there, however, she falls in love with her new "family" and her objectives become blurred. Rated R for nudity and profanity. 104m. **DIR:** Jim Donovan. **CAST:** Jane March, Nick Mancuso, Cary-Hiroyuki Tagawa, Stephen Mendel, Lillo Brancato. **1997**

PROWLER, THE ★★ Early slasher film features special effects by Tom Savini. They are the sole redeeming value to this nihilistic film. Rated R for violence, profanity, gore, and nudity. 88m. **DIR:** Joseph Zito. **CAST:** Farley Granger, Vicki Dawson, Lawrence Tierney. **1981**

•PROXIMITY ★★1/2 A convict discovers a plot to exact violent justice on prisoners via a fee paid by their victims' families and a conspiracy of prison guards and a corrupt victims' rights group. Intriguing idea doesn't get its due with this choppy film despite a first-rate cast. Rated R. 90m. **DIR:** Scott Ziehl. **CAST:** Rob Lowe, Jonathan Banks, Kelly Rowan, James Coburn. **2001 DVD**

PSYCH-OUT ★★1/2 The psychedelic Sixties couldn't have been more outrageous. A pretty, deaf runaway ends up in Haight-Ashbury while searching for her missing brother. She encounters a rock musician (Jack Nicholson) with whom she falls in love. Too self-important to be taken seriously. Rated PG. 82m. **DIR:** Richard Rush. **CAST:** Susan Strasberg, Jack Nicholson, Adam Roarke, Dean Stockwell, Bruce Dern. **1968**

PSYCHIC KILLER ★★ This is a completely ordinary thriller about a man who acquires psychic powers. *Psychic Killer* doesn't take itself seriously and that's a plus, but it's not sufficiently engrossing. Rated PG. 89m. **DIR:** Ray Danton. **CAST:** Jim Hutton, Paul Burke, Julie Adams, Nehemiah Persoff, Neville Brand, Aldo Ray, Della Reese. **1975 DVD**

PSYCHIC, THE (1977) ★★ Jennifer O'Neill gives a wonderful performance in this otherwise mundane Italian shocker. Some psychic visions are also worth a look, but overall Lucio Fulci's mad camera movements distract the viewer instead of adding suspense. Rated R for violence, profanity, and gore. 89m. **DIR:** Lucio Fulci. **CAST:** Jennifer O'Neill, Gabriele Ferzetti, Marc Porel. **1977**

PSYCHIC (1992) ★★ A serial killer is on the loose with a deadly belt buckle. A psychic (Zach Galligan) dreams the deaths of various females, including the professor (Catherine Mary Stewart) that he has fallen in love with. Poor writing and acting strangle this film. Made for cable. 91m. **DIR:** George Mihalka. **CAST:** Zach Galligan, Catherine Mary Stewart, Michael Nouri. **1992**

PSYCHO (1960) ★★★★★ The quintessential shocker, which started a whole genre of films about psychotic killers enacting mayhem on innocent victims, still holds up well today. Anthony Perkins's performance and the ease with which Hitchcock maneuvers your emotions make *Psycho* far superior to the numerous films that tried to duplicate it. B&W; 109m. **DIR:** Alfred Hitchcock. **CAST:** Anthony Perkins, Janet Leigh,

Vera Miles, John Gavin, John McIntire, Simon Oakland, John Anderson, Frank Albertson, Patricia Hitchcock, Martin Balsam. **1960 DVD**

PSYCHO (1998) ★★1/2 What you've heard is true: It's a remake of Hitchcock's 1960 classic in every sense of the word, and it's fair to say that Hitchcock himself directed this film, nearly 20 years removed from the grave. At best, Gus Van Sant might be termed a conductor of somebody else's symphony. Van Sant's biggest contribution is to make everything more vulgar. This is no more than a novelty: a bit of celluloid trickery that will blissfully fade from memory. Rated R for violence, nudity, and sexual candor. 106m. **DIR:** Gus Van Sant. **CAST:** Vince Vaughn, Julianne Moore, Anne Heche, Viggo Mortensen, William H. Macy. **1998 DVD**

PSYCHO II ★★★1/2 Picking up where Alfred Hitchcock's original left off, this sequel begins with Norman Bates (Anthony Perkins) being declared sane after twenty-two years in an asylum. Old Normie goes right back to the Bates Motel, and strange things begin to happen. Directed with exquisite taste and respect for the old master by Richard Franklin. It's suspenseful, scary, and funny. Rated R for profanity and violence. 113m. **DIR:** Richard Franklin. **CAST:** Anthony Perkins, Vera Miles, Meg Tilly, Robert Loggia, Dennis Franz, Hugh Gillin. **1983 DVD**

PSYCHO III ★★ Second follow-up to *Psycho* works mainly because actor-director Anthony Perkins understands poor Norman Bates inside and out. Although lensed beautifully by Bruce Surtees, the film fails in the most critical area: creating suspense. Rated R for gory violence. 93m. **DIR:** Anthony Perkins. **CAST:** Anthony Perkins, Diana Scarwid, Jeff Fahey, Hugh Gillin. **1986 DVD**

PSYCHO 4: THE BEGINNING ★★★ Once more into the Bates Motel, dear friends . . . Scripter Joseph Stefano, who adapted Robert Bloch's novel for Hitchcock's original *Psycho*, returns with this made-for-cable tale purporting to explain why poor Norman Bates (Anthony Perkins) became such a monster. Rated R for sex, nudity, and violence. 95m. **DIR:** Mick Garris. **CAST:** Anthony Perkins, Henry Thomas, Olivia Hussey, C.C.H. Pounder. **1990**

•PSYCHO BEACH PARTY ★★ Unlike *The Rocky Horror Picture Show*, which actually improved on its camp appeal after leaping from the stage to the screen, this spoof of 1960s beach musicals and haunted-house films falls flat on its face. There's hardly a reason to laugh in this misguided big-screen mess that fails to understand the play's appeal. The larger-than-life stage performances seem small and insignificant on screen, while the camp is so forced it is no longer funny. No one here seems to be having a beach ball. Not rated; contains adult situations, language, and violence. 94m. **DIR:** Robert Lee King. **CAST:** Lauren Ambrose, Thomas Gibson, Nicholas Brendon, Kimberley Davies, Matt Keeslar. **2000 DVD**

PSYCHO COP 2 Wacko cop decides to break up an illicit bachelor party by killing those who participate in illegal activity. But who's going to stop the filmmakers from making *Psycho Cop 3*? Rated R for extreme violence, nudity, and strong language. 80m. **DIR:** Rif Coogan. **CAST:** Bobby Ray Shafer, Barbara Lee Alexander. **1993**

PSYCHO GIRLS ★★★ Over-the-top horror parody will appeal most to avid horror fans, who will appreciate the black humor. A writer of mystery novels holds a dinner party that is disrupted by a psychotic woman. Rated R for violence and nudity. 90m. **DIR:** Gerard Ciccoritti. **CAST:** John Haslett Cuff, Darlene Wignacci. **1986**

PSYCHO SISTERS ★★★★ After her husband is killed, a woman goes to stay with her sister—her sister who has only recently emerged from an insane asylum and is still hearing their dead mother's voice. This film is a classic of the early 1970s horror/gore/exploitation cycle. Rated PG for mild violence. 76m. **DIR:** Reginald LeBorg. **CAST:** Susan Strasberg, Faith Domergue, Charles Knox Robinson. **1972**

PSYCHOMANIA ★★ This British-made film is about a motorcycle gang. They call themselves the Living Dead because they committed a group suicide and only came back to life through a pact with the devil. The film moves slowly and includes lots of violence. Rated R. 95m. **DIR:** Don Sharp. **CAST:** George Sanders, Nicky Henson, Mary Larkin, Patrick Holt, Beryl Reid. **1971**

PSYCHOPATH ★★★1/2 Courtroom drama starring Madchen Amick as a district attorney whose efforts to convict an accused serial killer are complicated by links he has to her past. An engrossing thriller with a surprising twist ending. Also released as *Twist of Fate*. Rated R for violence, profanity, and nudity. 95m. **DIR:** Max Fischer. **CAST:** Madchen Amick, Chris Mulkey, Bruce Dinsmore. **1997 DVD**

PSYCHOS IN LOVE ★★1/2 This film is an *Eating Raoul*–style horror comedy. Joe is a bar owner who has no trouble meeting women and getting dates. The problem is that he is a psychopath who ends up killing them—generally when he finds out they like grapes! This made-for-video movie has lots of gore and nudity. 88m. **DIR:** Gorman Bechard. **CAST:** Carmine Capobianco, Debi Thibeault, Frank Stewart. **1985**

PT 109 ★★1/2 Cliff Robertson is John F. Kennedy in this monument to the former president's war adventures on a World War II PT boat. Robertson is credible, but the story is only interesting because of the famous people and events it represents. 140m. **DIR:** Leslie Martinson. **CAST:** Cliff Robertson, Robert Culp, Ty Hardin, James Gregory, Robert Blake, Grant Williams. **1963**

PUBERTY BLUES ★★★1/2 This film takes a frank look at the coming-of-age of two teenagers as they grow up on the beaches of Australia. The two girls become temporary victims of peer group pressure that involves drugs, alcohol, and sex. Unlike many other teenage films, *Puberty Blues* offers interesting insights into the rite of passage as seen from a female point of view. Rated R. 86m. **DIR:** Bruce Beresford. **CAST:** Nell Schofield, Jad Capelja. **1981**

PUBLIC ACCESS ★★★1/2 A stranger stirs up the citizenry of a small town in this tense and incisive low-budget effort. Whiley Pritcher is a newcomer to the town of Brewster who starts up a local call-in program to discuss "what's wrong" with the community. Director Bryan Singer infuses the proceedings with a subtle menace that draws the viewer in; unfortunately, the movie's finale fizzles. Not rated; contains strong language, adult situations, and violence. 86m. **DIR:** Bryan Singer. **CAST:** Ron Marquette, Dina Brooks, Burt

Williams, Larry Maxwell, Charles Kavanaugh, Brandon Boyle. **1995 DVD**

PUBLIC COWBOY #1 ★★1/2 Singing cowboy Gene Autry battles modern-day rustlers who utilize airplanes. B&W; 59m. **DIR:** Joseph Kane. **CAST:** Gene Autry, Smiley Burnette, Ann Rutherford, William Farnum. **1937**

PUBLIC ENEMY ★★★★1/2 *Public Enemy*, with a snarling, unredeemable James Cagney in the title role, is still a highly watchable gangster film. William Wellman expertly directed this fast-paced and unpretentious portrait of the rise and fall of a vicious hoodlum. B&W; 84m. **DIR:** William Wellman. **CAST:** James Cagney, Jean Harlow, Mae Clarke, Edward Woods, Beryl Mercer. **1931**

PUBLIC ENEMY #1 ★★★ Theresa Russell brings considerable sass to her energized portrayal of the infamous Ma Barker, whose devotion to "her boys" now includes more than a faint whiff of incest, thanks to C. Courtney Joyner's revisionist script. The action is lively enough to overcome the often corny dialogue. Rated R for violence, profanity, nudity, simulated sex, and drug use. 91m. **DIR:** Mark L. Lester. **CAST:** Theresa Russell, Dan Cortese, Gavin Harrison, Joseph Lindsey, Joseph Dain, James Marsden, Frank Stallone, Eric Roberts. **1995**

PUBLIC EYE, THE ★★★1/2 Writer-director Howard Franklin's fascinating *film noir* homage concerns a scrappy 1940s tabloid photographer (Joe Pesci) whose reputation for quality makes him the shutterbug of choice when major criminals get booked. Our hero gets involved in a twisty case involving a nightclub owner. Rated R for violence and profanity. 98m. **DIR:** Howard Franklin. **CAST:** Joe Pesci, Barbara Hershey, Jared Harris, Stanley Tucci. **1992**

PUCKER UP AND BARK LIKE A DOG ★★★1/2 Cute romantic comedy about a reclusive and shy painter who searches for the girl of his dreams while trying to display his paintings in public. Wendy O. Williams gives the title its kinkiness as a biker who shows him how to live a little. Rated R for violence and nudity. 74m. **DIR:** Paul Salvatore Parco. **CAST:** Jonathan Gries, Lisa Zane, Barney Martin, Robert Culp, Wendy O. Williams, Paul Bartel, Phyllis Diller, Isabel Sanford. **1989**

PUDD'NHEAD WILSON ★★★1/2 Mark Twain's sometimes humorous but always entertaining tale of deceit is faithfully re-created in this American Playhouse production. When a rash of crimes are committed in a Midwest town, only Pudd'nhead Wilson and his newfangled fingerprinting theory can unearth the culprit. Fine slice of Americana! 90m. **DIR:** Alan Bridges. **CAST:** Ken Howard, Lise Hilboldt. **1984**

PULP ★★1/2 Sometimes funny, sometimes lame black comedy casts Michael Caine as a pulp mystery writer hired to pen the biography of retired film star and reputed mobster Mickey Rooney. Caine carries the film well enough, with his voice-over narration a nice Chandleresque touch, and Rooney is excellent in his few scenes, but the film never really catches fire. Rated PG for profanity and violence. 95m. **DIR:** Mike Hodges. **CAST:** Michael Caine, Mickey Rooney, Lionel Stander, Lizabeth Scott, Al Lettieri. **1972**

PULP FICTION ★★★★ Writer-director Quentin Tarantino spares the viewer little in this tale of the underbelly of Los Angeles, where philosophizing hit men and techno-druggies live on the thrill-packed edge. If nothing else, *Pulp Fiction* will be remembered as the movie that shot John Travolta's career full of adrenaline. It's quite a wild ride. Rated R for violence, profanity, nudity, and sex. 153m. **DIR:** Quentin Tarantino. **CAST:** John Travolta, Samuel L. Jackson, Uma Thurman, Harvey Keitel, Tim Roth, Amanda Plummer, Maria de Medeiros, Ving Rhames, Eric Stoltz, Rosanna Arquette, Christopher Walken, Bruce Willis. **1994 DVD**

PULSE 🦃 Cliff De Young against some incredibly vicious electrical pulses. Rated PG-13. 90m. **DIR:** Paul Golding. **CAST:** Cliff De Young, Roxanne Hart, Joey Lawrence, Matthew Lawrence, Charles Tyner, Dennis Redfield. **1988**

PUMP UP THE VOLUME ★★★ Unable to make friends at his new high school, teenager Christian Slater creates a charismatic alter ego with a pirate radio station set up in his bedroom. Director Alan Moyle's script is a little sketchy, but the film has a hip, youthful energy and the cast is uniformly strong. Rated R for language and nudity. 100m. **DIR:** Alan Moyle. **CAST:** Christian Slater, Scott Paulin, Samantha Mathis, Ellen Greene, James Hampton. **1990 DVD**

PUMPING IRON ★★★★ Very good documentary concerning professional bodybuilding. Arnold Schwarzenegger and Lou Ferrigno ("The Incredible Hulk") are at the forefront as they prepare for the Mr. Universe contest. Always interesting and at times fascinating. Rated PG for language. 85m. **DIR:** George Butler, Robert Fiore. **CAST:** Arnold Schwarzenegger, Lou Ferrigno, Matty and Victoria Ferrigno, Mike Katz. **1977**

PUMPING IRON II: THE WOMEN ★★★★1/2 This documentary on the 1983 Women's World Cup held at Caesar's Palace is more than just beauty and brawn. While it does seem to side with one contestant (and when you see Bev Francis's massive body, you'll know why), the film has all the passion and wit of a first-rate narrative. Not rated, but an equivalent of a PG. 107m. **DIR:** George Butler. **CAST:** Lori Bowen, Carla Dunlap, Bev Francis, Rachel McLish. **1985**

PUMPKINHEAD 🦃 A backwoods witch. Rated R for violence. 87m. **DIR:** Stan Winston. **CAST:** Lance Henriksen, Jeff East. **1989**

PUMPKINHEAD II: BLOODWINGS ★★1/2 Sequel lacks the raw edge of its predecessor, but provides enough creepy moments to satisfy. The creature is resurrected and immediately goes on a killing spree. Attempts to delve deeper into the legend, showing how the cruel hazing of a retarded boy led to his death, and the birth of the creature. Rated R for violence, language, and nudity. 88m. **DIR:** Jeff Burr. **CAST:** Ami Dolenz, Andrew Robinson, Steve Kanaly, Caren Kaye, Linnea Quigley, Soleil Moon Frye. **1994**

PUNCH THE CLOCK 🦃 A professional car thief and the law school grad who has the hots for her. A movie this bad is a crime. Rated R for violence. 88m. **DIR:** Eric L. Schlagman. **CAST:** Mike Rogen. **1990**

PUNCHLINE ★★★ An energetic performance from Tom Hanks can't quite compensate for the bewildering miscasting of Sally Field in this tribute to the hellishly difficult life of stand-up comics. Although Hanks superbly conveys the anguish of a failed med-school student with comedy in his blood, Field never convincingly

captures the conservative housewife who yearns for more. Inexplicably rated R for language. 128m. **DIR:** David Seltzer. **CAST:** Tom Hanks, Sally Field, John Goodman, Mark Rydell. **1988 DVD**

PUNISHER, THE ★★★ Lean and mean adaptation of the Marvel Comics publication has Dolph Lundgren (looking like a cross between Elvis Presley and Clint Walker in his *Cheyenne* days) as the Punisher, a police-officer-turned-vigilante. Solid entertainment in a comic-book vein. Rated R for violence and profanity. 92m. **DIR:** Mark Goldblatt. **CAST:** Dolph Lundgren, Louis Gossett Jr., Jeroen Krabbé, Kim Miyori. **1990 DVD**

P.U.N.K.S. ★★1/2 Kids will enjoy this engaging romp about a preteen named Drew who decides he's had enough of school bullies. Drew and his friends turn the table on their tormentors and an evil scientist (Henry Winkler) when they steal his invention that turns ninety-pound weaklings into the sort of guys who kick sand in the faces of ninety-pound weaklings. Rated PG. 99m. **DIR:** Sean McNamara. **CAST:** Henry Winkler, Randy Quaid, Cathy Moriarty, Patrick Renna, Ted Redwine. **1997**

PUPPET MASTER, THE ★★★1/2 Highly effective chiller about a puppet maker (William Hickey) who uses an ancient Egyptian power to breed life into his demonic dolls. After his untimely death by suicide, a group of psychics tries to locate these terrifying toys. Excellent animation and special effects by David Allen (*Willow, Batteries Not Included*). Rated R for nudity and graphic violence. 90m. **DIR:** David Schmoeller. **CAST:** Paul LeMat, Irene Miracle, William Hickey. **1989**

PUPPET MASTER II ★★1/2 The diabolically deadly dolls from the first film resurrect their dead creator and go on another rampage. Moderately scary. Rated R for violence, profanity, and mild gore. 90m. **DIR:** David Allen. **CAST:** Elizabeth MacLellan, Collin Bernsen, Gregory Webb, Charlie Spradling, Steve Welles, Nita Talbot. **1990**

PUPPET MASTER III: TOULON'S REVENGE ★★1/2 In this second sequel, we go back and watch how Toulon and his killer puppets murder Nazis and escape from World War II Germany. Rated R for violence and profanity. 95m. **DIR:** David DeCoteau. **CAST:** Guy Rolfe, Ian Abercrombie, Sarah Douglas, Richard Lynch. **1991**

PUPPET MASTER FOUR ★★ Excellent special effects and creative animation remain the highlights in this continuing series. In this chapter, a genius whiz kid and friends conduct experiments in the abandoned hotel where viewers were first introduced to the lifelike puppets. This one will remind viewers of the old Saturday afternoon matinee serial chapterplays, à la Flash Gordon and Commando Cody. Rated R for violence, nudity, and profanity. 80m. **DIR:** Jeff Burr. **CAST:** Gordon Currie, Chandra West, Jason Adams, Teresa Hill, Guy Rolfe. **1993**

PUPPET MASTER 5: THE FINAL CHAPTER ★★ It's hard to keep a good puppet down, as this direct-to-video series seems to suggest with each new entry. The deadly puppets must battle two foes: an evil doctor obsessed with learning the secret to their animation, and a demon from another dimension who plans to kill the Puppetmaster and steal the puppets' magic. Rated R for violence. 81m. **DIR:** Jeff Burr. **CAST:** Guy Rolfe, Gordon Currie, Chandra West, Nicholas Guest, Willard E. Pugh. **1994**

PUPPET MASTERS, THE ★★1/2 Aliens invade Earth by taking over the bodies of American citizens, with only Donald Sutherland and his crew of agents standing between them and ultimate conquest. Halfhearted adaptation of Robert Heinlein's 1951 novel wastes the potential of its cast and source material. Rated R for violence and profanity. 109m. **DIR:** Stuart Orme. **CAST:** Donald Sutherland, Eric Thal, Julie Warner, Keith David, Will Patton, Richard Belzer, Yaphet Kotto. **1994**

PUPPET ON A CHAIN ★★1/2 American agent battles a Dutch heroin ring in this lackluster Alistair MacLean thriller. There's an exciting speedboat chase through the canals of Amsterdam, but the rest of the film is a snoozer. Rated PG. 97m. **DIR:** Geoffrey Reeve. **CAST:** Sven-Bertil Taube, Barbara Parkins, Alexander Knox. **1972**

PUPPETOON MOVIE, THE ★★★★ Pioneering fantasy director-producer George Pal established his initial Hollywood credentials with a series of so-called "Puppetoon" shorts, all made with a rarely used technique known as replacement animation. Pal and staff constructed up to five *thousand* wooden figures for each cartoon; minor distinctions from one figure to the next, when filmed one frame at a time, thus conveyed the illusion of movement. This collection of shorts gathers the best of Pal's work. 80m. **DIR:** Arnold Leibovit. **1987**

PUPS ★★★1/2 A 13-year-old California boy takes a gun from his mother's bedroom and, with a female classmate, tries to rob a bank. When it goes awry, they take everyone inside hostage as police circle the building. Echoes of *Dog Day Afternoon*, among other films, are intentional in this sobering film about media-age children. Burt Reynolds gives a good performance as an FBI agent trying to negotiate the precarious situation. Rated R for profanity and violence. 100m. **DIR:** Ash. **CAST:** Mischa Barton, Cameron Van Hoy, Burt Reynolds, Adam Farrar, David Alan Graf, Kurt Loder. **1999 DVD**

PURCHASE PRICE, THE ★★★1/2 A good cast and skillful direction turn a predictable script into good entertainment. A torch singer trying to get away from her gangster boyfriend marries a perfect stranger. The stars make it believable. B&W; 74m. **DIR:** William Wellman. **CAST:** Barbara Stanwyck, George Brent, Lyle Talbot, David Landau. **1932**

PURE COUNTRY ★★★ Featuring nearly a dozen George Strait songs destined for extended jukebox play, this warmhearted story about a personable country singer is predictable but entertaining. Too bad Strait's down-home charm is buried under a pile of clichés. Rated PG for language. 112m. **DIR:** Christopher Cain. **CAST:** George Strait, Lesley Ann Warren, John Doe, Isabel Glasser, Rory Calhoun. **1992 DVD**

PURE DANGER ★★ A short-order cook and his waitress girlfriend find a bag of diamonds and think they've hit pay dirt. Then they meet the mobsters who will do anything to get the gems back. Rated R for violence, profanity, and nudity. 99m. **DIR:** C. Thomas Howell. **CAST:** C. Thomas Howell, Teri Ann Linn, Leon, Michael Russo. **1995**

PURE FORMALITY, A ★★ A famous writer, under arrest in an isolated police station, is interrogated by a

sinister official who professes to admire the writer, but pressures him to confess to some terrible unnamed crime. The two stars are excellent, but the film is sluggish; you'll probably guess the "surprise" ending long before it arrives. In French with English subtitles. Not rated; contains mature themes and brief nudity. 108m. **DIR:** Giuseppe Tornatore. **CAST:** Gérard Depardieu, Roman Polanski. **1994**

PURE LUCK ★★ In this Americanized version of Francis Veber's *Le Chevre*, Danny Glover plays a hapless detective assigned to work with a bumbling accountant in order to locate the world's most accident-prone heiress. The actors try hard, but it just ain't that funny, folks. Rated PG. 96m. **DIR:** Nadia Tass. **CAST:** Martin Short, Danny Glover, Sheila Kelley, Scott Wilson, Harry Shearer, Sam Wanamaker, Jorge Luke. **1991**

PURGATORY ★★★★ High marks to writer Gordon Dawson's marvelously clever Western allegory, which concerns a violent band of outlaws that stumbles into a strange little town—dubbed Refuge—where the sheriff doesn't carry a gun, and the oddly familiar citizens seem resigned to whatever Fate provides. Sam Shepard is perfect as the dignified yet powerful sheriff, while Eric Roberts is appropriately evil as the gang leader who unwisely decides to shear all these apparently sheeplike civilians. The results should please even those who don't normally care for conventional Westerns. Rated PG-13 for violence and profanity. 95m. **DIR:** Uli Edel. **CAST:** Sam Shepard, Eric Roberts, Peter Stormare, Brad Rowe, Donnie Wahlberg, Randy Quaid. **1999**

PURLIE VICTORIOUS ★★★1/2 Alan Alda made his film debut as a southern liberal in this good-humored comedy written by Ossie Davis. Davis and his wife, Ruby Dee, play an evangelist couple who try to convert an old barn into an integrated church. Their chief opposition comes from the bigot (Sorrel Booke) who owns the barn. Also known as *Gone Are the Days.* B&W; 93m. **DIR:** Nicholas Webster. **CAST:** Ossie Davis, Ruby Dee, Sorrell Booke, Alan Alda, Godfrey Cambridge, Beah Richards. **1963**

PURPLE HEART, THE ★★★★ Dana Andrews and Richard Conte are leaders of a group of American fliers who are captured by the Japanese after they bomb Tokyo and put on trial for war crimes. This fascinating film is a minor classic. B&W; 99m. **DIR:** Lewis Milestone. **CAST:** Dana Andrews, Richard Conte, Farley Granger, Sam Levene, Tala Birell, Nestor Paiva. **1944**

PURPLE HEARTS ★★ Anyone who can sit all the way through this Vietnam War–film romance deserves a medal. Ken Wahl stars as a surgeon in the United States Navy Medical Corps who falls in love with a nurse (Cheryl Ladd). There's an additional forty minutes of unnecessary and unoriginal story tacked on. Rated R for nudity, profanity, violence, and gore. 115m. **DIR:** Sidney J. Furie. **CAST:** Ken Wahl, Cheryl Ladd. **1984**

PURPLE MONSTER STRIKES, THE ★★★ The Purple Monster lands near Dr. Cyrus Layton's observatory and tricks him into revealing the plans for a new spaceship. Although the science is ridiculous and the effects unsophisticated by today's standards, this is one of Republic Studios' best-remembered serials of the mid-1940s and features master heavy Roy Barcroft in one of his finest roles. B&W; 15 chapters. **DIR:** Spencer Gordon Bennet, Fred Brannon. **CAST:** Dennis Moore, Linda Stirling, Roy Barcroft. **1945**

PURPLE NOON ★★★ An amoral wastrel (Alain Delon) is sent to the Mediterranean to bring an American playboy home but decides instead to murder him and assume his identity. Director René Clement builds an atmosphere of languid, decadent menace and draws a fascinating, reptilian performance from Delon, but the film is overlong and ambles through some false climaxes before the final, ironic twist. In French with English subtitles. Rated PG-13 for mature themes. 118m. **DIR:** René Clement. **CAST:** Alain Delon, Maurice Ronet, Marie Laforet. **1961 DVD**

PURPLE PEOPLE EATER ★★1/2 A sappy family flick about an alien (the title character) who comes to Earth to join a rock 'n' roll band. The fine cast, headed by Ned Beatty, is overshadowed by a sickeningly sweet alien puppet. Rated PG. 91m. **DIR:** Linda Shayne. **CAST:** Ned Beatty, Shelley Winters, Neil Patrick Harris, Peggy Lipton. **1988**

PURPLE RAIN ★★1/2 In his first movie, pop star Prince plays a struggling young musician searching for self-awareness and love while trying to break into the rock charts. The film unsuccessfully straddles the line between a concert release and a storytelling production. As it is, the music is great, but the plot leaves a lot to be desired. Rated R for nudity, suggested sex, and profanity. 113m. **DIR:** Albert Magnoli. **CAST:** Prince, Apollonia Kotero, Morris Day, Olga Karlatos. **1984 DVD**

PURPLE ROSE OF CAIRO, THE ★★★★ Mia Farrow is a Depression-era housewife who finds her dreary day-to-day existence enlivened when a dashing, romantic hero walks off the screen and sweeps her off her feet. Like Woody Allen's *Zelig* and *Broadway Danny Rose*, this mixes humor with very human situations. The result is a very satisfying work. Rated PG for violence. 85m. **DIR:** Woody Allen. **CAST:** Mia Farrow, Jeff Daniels, Danny Aiello, Edward Herrmann, John Wood. **1985 DVD**

PURPLE TAXI, THE ★★★ Fred Astaire, Edward Albert, and Philippe Noiret star in this exploration of angst, love, and friendship in Ireland, where a collection of expatriate characters impaled on memories and self-destructive compulsions work out their kinks before returning to various homelands. Fine backdrops in Ireland's "curtain of rain" and impressive acting. Rated R. 107m. **DIR:** Yves Boisset. **CAST:** Fred Astaire, Edward Albert, Philippe Noiret, Peter Ustinov, Charlotte Rampling, Agostina Belli. **1977**

PURSUED ★★★ A cowboy, Robert Mitchum, searches for the murderer of his father in this taut, atmospheric Western. The entire cast is very good, and famed action director Raoul Walsh keeps things moving along at a brisk pace. B&W; 101m. **DIR:** Raoul Walsh. **CAST:** Robert Mitchum, Teresa Wright, Judith Anderson, Dean Jagger, Harry Carey Jr., Alan Hale Sr. **1947**

PURSUIT ★★ So-so mercenary flick pits a purist against greedy cohorts in an attempt to recover the gold meant to stabilize an African nation's economy. Rated R for nudity, violence, and profanity. 94m. **DIR:** John H. Parr. **CAST:** James Ryan. **1990**

PURSUIT OF D. B. COOPER ★★1/2 The famous skyjacker is turned into a fun-loving good old boy in this

hit-and-miss comedy starring Treat Williams, Robert Duvall, and Kathryn Harrold. If you liked *Smokey and the Bandit*, you'll probably enjoy this. Rated PG because of minimal violence and sexuality. 100m. **DIR:** Roger Spottiswoode. **CAST:** Treat Williams, Robert Duvall, Kathryn Harrold, Ed Flanders, Paul Gleason, R. G. Armstrong. **1981**

PURSUIT OF HAPPINESS, THE ★★★1/2 Although it will seem dated to many, this heartfelt drama about a young man standing up for his ideals is still worth a look. Robert Mulligan's direction is excellent, and the cast features many now-familiar faces in small roles. Rated PG. 85m. **DIR:** Robert Mulligan. **CAST:** Michael Sarrazin, Barbara Hershey, Robert Klein, Arthur Hill, E. G. Marshall, David Doyle, Barnard Hughes, Sada Thompson, Rue McClanahan, William Devane, Charles Durning. **1971**

PURSUIT OF THE GRAF SPEE ★★★1/2 Highly enjoyable account of the World War II sea chase and eventual battle involving British naval forces and the German's super warship, the *Graf Spee*. Featuring a solid cast, the film benefits from attention to detail and a realistic building of tension. 106m. **DIR:** Michael Powell, Emeric Pressburger. **CAST:** John Gregson, Anthony Quayle, Peter Finch, Bernard Lee, Ian Hunter, Patrick Macnee, Christopher Lee. **1957**

PURSUIT TO ALGIERS ★★★ Basil Rathbone's Holmes and Nigel Bruce's Watson become bodyguards accompanying the young heir to a royal throne on a hazardous sea voyage. Their client disguises himself as Watson's nephew, which makes for some droll dialogue. One of the few Rathbone/Bruce films that borrows nothing from the canon. Not rated—suitable for family viewing. B&W; 65m. **DIR:** Roy William Neill. **CAST:** Basil Rathbone, Nigel Bruce, John Abbott, Marjorie Riordan, Martin Kosleck, Rosalind Ivan. **1945**

PUSHED TO THE LIMIT ★★ Vengefest features a young woman taking on a ruthless Asian drug dealer who has killed her brother. Not rated; contains seemingly endless violence. 96m. **DIR:** Michael Mileham. **CAST:** Mimi Lesseos, Henry Hayshi. **1992**

PUSHING HANDS ★★★1/2 Seriocomic account of the culture clash that occurs when an elderly T'ai chi master from mainland China comes to live with his son's suburban New York family. Director Ang Lee's understated first feature is slow going at first but then exhibits a charm that's infectious. The unfamiliar cast prove completely at home in their roles—including Lee's son Haan as the American grandson living between two cultures. In English and Mandarin with subtitles. Not rated. 108m. **DIR:** Ang Lee. **CAST:** Sihung Lung, Lai Wang, Bo Z. Wang, Deb Snyder, Haan Lee, Emily Liu. **1992 DVD**

PUSHING TIN ★★★ Two air traffic controllers develop an intense rivalry while their marriages fray in this *M*A*S*H* of the skyways. The acting, characters, and workplace details are engaging, but the story's underlying threat of professional and domestic mass hysteria is dulled by soap opera plotting and an unconvincing ending. Based on the article "Something's Got to Give" by Darcy Frey. Rated R for language, nudity, and sexual content. 110m. **DIR:** Mike Newell. **CAST:** John Cusack, Billy Bob Thornton, Cate Blanchett, Angelina Jolie. **1999 DVD**

PUTNEY SWOPE ★★★★ This wildly funny film concerns a black man who takes over a Madison Avenue advertising firm. Alan Abel, Mel Brooks, and Allen Garfield appear in this zany parody of American lifestyles. Rated R. 88m. **DIR:** Robert Downey. **CAST:** Alan Abel, Mel Brooks, Allen Garfield, Pepi Hermine, Ruth Hermine, Antonio Fargas. **1969 DVD**

PYGMALION ★★★★1/2 This is an impeccable adaptation of George Bernard Shaw's classic play. The comedy is deliciously sophisticated. The performances are exquisite, particularly that of Leslie Howard, who'll make you forget Rex Harrison's Henry Higgins in an instant. As the professor's feisty Cockney pupil, Wendy Hiller is a delight. B&W; 95m. **DIR:** Anthony Asquith, Leslie Howard. **CAST:** Leslie Howard, Wendy Hiller, Wilfrid Lawson, Marie Lohr, David Tree. **1938**

PYRATES Real-life husband-and-wife Kevin Bacon and Kyra Sedgwick play a couple who ignite sparks whenever they have sex, setting fires. Too bad they couldn't turn up the heat in this one-joke effort. Rated R for nudity. 98m. **DIR:** Noah Stern. **CAST:** Kevin Bacon, Kyra Sedgwick. **1991**

PYROMANIAC'S LOVE STORY, A ★★1/2 A bakery burns to the ground, igniting passionate fires in everyone connected to it, but the romantic entanglements are complicated and overdone. A few impressive performances, especially John Leguizamo as a well-meaning but muddled baker, but this romantic fable is too precious for its own good. Rated PG for profanity. 94m. **DIR:** Joshua Brand. **CAST:** William Baldwin, John Leguizamo, Sadie Frost, Erika Eleniak, Michael Lerner, Joan Plowright. **1995**

PYTHON ★★ Another *Anaconda* rip-off, this one about a giant killer snake on the loose, turning victims into bloody pulp. It's all supposed to be tongue-in-cheek but never reaches that level. The actors are dreadful, and you never once believe that the computer-generated snake appears in the same frame with them. Jenny McCarthy pops up briefly as the now standard guest victim. She's lucky—she gets dispatched early in this direct-to-video effort. Rated R for language, nudity, and violence. 99m. **DIR:** Richard Clabaugh. **CAST:** Casper Van Dien, Robert Englund, Jenny McCarthy, Wil Wheaton, Frayne Rosanoff. **2000 DVD**

PYX, THE A dead prostitute and the police investigation mounted to uncover her killer. Rated R for violence. 111m. **DIR:** Harvey Hart. **CAST:** Karen Black, Christopher Plummer, Donald Pilon. **1973**

Q

Q ★★★★ This is an old-fashioned giant monster film. The stop-motion animation is excellent, the acting (done tongue-in-cheek) is perfect. The story revolves around the arrival of a giant flying lizard in New York City. A series of ritualistic murders follow and point to the monster being Quetzelcoatl (the flying serpent god of the Aztecs). Rated R. 93m. **DIR:** Larry Cohen. **CAST:**

Michael Moriarty, David Carradine, Candy Clark, Richard Roundtree, James Dixon. **1982**

Q & A ★★★★ Nick Nolte gives a compelling performance as a much-decorated police detective whose brutal killing of a Puerto Rican drug dealer brings about an investigation, which novice assistant district attorney Timothy Hutton is drafted into conducting. Rated R for brutal violence, profanity, and nudity. 134m. **DIR:** Sidney Lumet. **CAST:** Nick Nolte, Timothy Hutton, Armand Assante, Patrick O'Neal. **1990 DVD**

QB VII ★★★★ Leon Uris's hefty bestseller is vividly brought to life in this five-hours-plus made-for-television drama about a Polish expatriate doctor living in England who sues an American writer for libel when the writer accuses him of carrying out criminal medical activities for the Nazis during World War II. Anthony Hopkins is brilliant as the physician, Ben Gazzara is outraged and tenacious as the writer. Expect a powerful, engrossing ending. 312m. **DIR:** Tom Gries. **CAST:** Anthony Hopkins, Ben Gazzara, Leslie Caron, Lee Remick, Anthony Quayle. **1974 DVD**

QUACKSER FORTUNE HAS A COUSIN IN THE BRONX ★★★★ This comedy-drama falls into the category of sleeper. Gene Wilder is delightful as an Irishman who marches to the beat of a different drummer. Margot Kidder is a rich American going to university in Dublin who meets and falls in love with him. Filmed in Ireland and rated R for nudity and language. 88m. **DIR:** Waris Hussein. **CAST:** Gene Wilder, Margot Kidder, Eileen Colgan. **1970 DVD**

QUADROPHENIA ★★★1/2 Based on The Who's rock opera, this is the story of a teenager growing up in the early 1960s and the decisions he is forced to make on the path to adulthood. Rated R because the language is rough and the violence graphic. 115m. **DIR:** Franc Roddam. **CAST:** Phil Daniels, Mark Wingett, Philip Davis, Sting. **1979**

QUAKE ★★ The good news is that lovely Erika Anderson has survived a ravaging San Francisco earthquake. The bad news is that Steve Railsback, obsessed with Anderson, kidnaps her amidst all the confusion. The psychological aftershocks between the two barely keep this slight effort from slipping into the cracks. Rated R for language and violence. 89m. **DIR:** Louis Morneau. **CAST:** Steve Railsback, Erika Anderson, Eb Lottimer, Burton Gilliam, Dick Miller. **1992**

QUALITY STREET ★★1/2 In early nineteeth-century England, a schoolteacher (Katharine Hepburn) worries about whether her youthful flame (Eric Blore) will return from war. A familiar story, but a fine cast elevates the proceedings. B&W; 84m. **DIR:** George Stevens. **CAST:** Katharine Hepburn, Joan Fontaine, Eric Blore, Franchot Tone. **1937**

QUANTUM LEAP (TV SERIES) ★★★★ When scientist Dr. Sam Beckett gets lost during a time-travel experiment, he's bounced from time to time, leaping into troubled individuals and helping them overcome their problems. His only companion is a holographic image of another scientist. Television series tackles important issues in a sensitive yet entertaining way. Available episodes include "The Pilot Episode," "The Color of Truth," "Camikazi Kid," "What Price Gloria?" and "Catch a Falling Star." Pilot episode 93m; 48m. **DIR:** David Hemmings, Mike Vejar, Alan J. Levi, Donald P. Bellisario. **CAST:** Scott Bakula, Dean Stockwell, Jennifer Runyon, Jason Priestley, John Cullum, Janine Turner. **1989 DVD**

QUARANTINE ★★ A sense that this film has no real conclusion hurts what could have been a top-notch sci-fi film. A Gestapo-like police force herds carriers of a disease into a quarantined area. Interesting commentary on the AIDS epidemic. Rated PG-13 for violence and profanity. 92m. **DIR:** Charles Wilkinson. **CAST:** Garwin Sanford, Jerry Wasserman, Tom McBeath. **1989**

QUARREL, THE ★★★1/2 Saul Rubinek and R. H. Thomson shine in this two-person exchange of ideas and faith. The men play Holocaust survivors who have lost their families to the death camps. Relocated in Montreal, the men meet in 1948. One has turned to his religion for strength; the other has turned his back on religion. As they discuss the past twenty years, their differences and similarities come to the surface. Not rated. 90m. **DIR:** Eli Cohen. **CAST:** Saul Rubinek, R. H. Thomson. **1990 DVD**

QUARTERBACK PRINCESS ★★1/2 True story of Tami Maida, the girl who came to a small Oregon town and managed to become a star on the football team as well as the homecoming queen. Helen Hunt is adequate as Tami; Don Murray is better as her supportive dad. Made for television. 96m. **DIR:** Noel Black. **CAST:** Helen Hunt, Don Murray, Barbara Babcock, Dana Elcar, John Stockwell. **1983**

QUARTET (1948) ★★★★ A dramatization of W. Somerset Maugham's favorite stories: "The Facts of Life," "The Alien Corn," "The Kite," and "The Colonel's Lady." All four are immensely watchable. B&W; 120m. **DIR:** Ken Annakin, Arthur Crabtree, Harold French, Ralph Smart. **CAST:** Dirk Bogarde, Hermione Baddeley, Mervyn Johns, Cecil Parker, Basil Badford, Françoise Rosay, Susan Shaw, Naunton Wayne, Mai Zetterling. **1948**

QUARTET (1981) ★★ In terms of acting, this is a first-rate film. Unfortunately, the pathetic characters that mope around in this period piece drag down any positive points. Isabelle Adjani plays the wife of a convicted criminal who ends up in a ménage à trois with a married couple, played by Alan Bates and Maggie Smith. Rated R for nudity. 101m. **DIR:** James Ivory. **CAST:** Isabelle Adjani, Alan Bates, Anthony Higgins, Maggie Smith. **1981**

QUATERMASS AND THE PIT ★★★ Nigel Kneale's inscrutable, indefatigable Prof. Quatermass—who launched rockets from Britain to deep space, locked horns with authority figures and became one of the most popular British TV heroes of the Fifties—is played here by Andre Morell in a full-length BBC telecast. It's technically primitive and rather talky, but as the talk is by top fantasy scripter Kneale, who's complaining? B&W; 180m. **DIR:** Rudolph Cartier. **CAST:** Andre Morell, Cec Linder, Anthony Bushell, Michael Ripper. **1958 DVD**

QUATERMASS CONCLUSION, THE ★★ It's sad to see a great premise destroyed by bad editing and sloppy script continuity. Of course, the fact that this film is an edited-down version of a British miniseries may be the cause. In the strange future world of the story, society seems to be suffering a terrible case of inertia. The

world's teen population is committing mass suicide, and only Dr. Quatermass (John Mills), genius scientist, can save them. 105m. **DIR:** Piers Haggard. **CAST:** John Mills, Simon MacCorkindale, Barbara Kellerman, Margaret Tyzack. **1979**

QUATERMASS EXPERIMENT, THE ★★★ The first Hammer Films horror film is a splendid, low-budget exercise in British suspense, science fiction, and futuristic horror. When an experimental spacecraft returns to Britain, its crew has mysteriously vanished—all save one member, who is comatose and covered in a thin layer of slime, which subtly begins to change him. This film launched the world horror and sci-fi revival that otherwise was dominated by dreadful teen horror flicks. Also titled (in U.S. only): *The Creeping Unknown*. B&W; 78m. **DIR:** Val Guest. **CAST:** Brian Donlevy, Jack Warner, Richard Wordsworth. **1956**

QUATORZE JULIET ★★★★ Paris had no better publicist than René Clair, whose early films were delightfully simple musical fantasies of living in that city. *Quatorze Juliet* follows two young lovers—a taxi driver and a flower peddler—as they come into contact with different citizens and neighborhoods of Paris. In French with English subtitles. B&W; 85m. **DIR:** René Clair. **CAST:** Annabella, George Rigaud. **1932**

QUEEN CHRISTINA ★★★★ This haunting romance might be laughable if anyone but Greta Garbo were in it. She plays the controversial Swedish queen who gave up her throne for the sake of love (according to the movie). The last scene—of Garbo looking wistfully into the camera—has become her trademark. B&W; 97m. **DIR:** Rouben Mamoulian. **CAST:** Greta Garbo, John Gilbert, Lewis Stone, C. Aubrey Smith, Reginald Owen. **1933**

QUEEN ELIZABETH ★★ Sarah Bernhardt stars as Queen Elizabeth I in this heavy-handed silent melodrama. The plot revolves around a love triangle involving the queen, the earl of Essex, and the countess of Nottingham. Silent. B&W; 46m. **DIR:** Henri Desfontanes. **CAST:** Sarah Bernhardt. **1927**

QUEEN KELLY ★★★ Gloria Swanson used her clout to keep Erich Von Stroheim's *Queen Kelly* buried for nearly sixty years. This reconstructed version is but a shadow of the five-hour epic Von Stroheim had intended to make. The sumptuously mounted melodrama is fascinating—and often hilarious—for its indulgences, decadence, and outright perversity. Swanson plays a rebellious schoolgirl who is kidnapped from a convent and introduced to the pleasures of life by a debauched prince. Silent. B&W; 95m. **DIR:** Erich Von Stroheim. **CAST:** Gloria Swanson. **1928**

QUEEN MARGOT ★★★★ The bloody Saint Bartholomew's Day Massacre of 1572, when thousands of French Protestants were slaughtered at the command of King Charles IX, provides the background for this sumptuous film of Alexandre Dumas's novel. The plot revolves around the marriage of Charles's sister Marguerite to the Protestant Henri Navarre and the intrigues of the French court. Florid, passionate, and enthralling. In French with English subtitles. Rated R for nudity, sex, and violence. 143m. **DIR:** Patrice Chereau. **CAST:** Isabelle Adjani, Daniel Auteuil, Jean-Hugues Anglade, Virna Lisi, Vincent Perez, Pascal Greggory. **1994**

QUEEN OF HEARTS ★★★★ A comedy-drama with dialogue primarily in English but a sensibility that is very Italian. By running away from her marriage to a wealthy Sicilian, the beautiful Rosa (Anita Zagaria) sets in motion a tragic and funny tale of revenge. Not rated, the film has profanity and violence. 112m. **DIR:** Jon Amiel. **CAST:** Anita Zagaria, Joseph Long, Eileen Way. **1989**

QUEEN OF OUTER SPACE ★★★ Earthmen venture to Venus to find an all-female civilization led by Zsa Zsa Gabor. So bad, it's hysterical. A must for all B-film fanatics. 80m. **DIR:** Edward L. Bernds. **CAST:** Zsa Zsa Gabor, Eric Fleming, Paul Birch. **1958**

•QUEEN OF THE DAMNED ★★ This adaptation of the third book from Anne Rice's *The Vampire Chronicles* probably would've been a waste of time anyway, but the film suffers further from the tragic mid-shoot death of its star, Aaliyah. She's the title character, an ultrasexy and equally vicious bloodsucker who hopes to make the conscience-ridden vampire Lestat (Stuart Townsend) her companion during a reign of terror against human and vampire alike. Only those who've read Rice's books will have the slightest idea what's going on, because it appears the filmmakers just went with what they'd already shot, in the hopes that nobody would notice the difference. (That would be wrong.) Rated R for violence, profanity, and gore. 101m. **DIR:** Michael Rymer. **CAST:** Stuart Townsend, Aaliyah, Marguerite Moreau, Vincent Perez, Lena Olin. **2002 DVD**

QUEEN OF THE STARDUST BALLROOM ★★★★ Touching love story about a lonely widow (Maureen Stapleton) who finally finds Mr. Right (Charles Durning). Stapleton is outstanding. 100m. **DIR:** Sam O'Steen. **CAST:** Maureen Stapleton, Charles Durning, Michael Brandon, Michael Strong. **1975 DVD**

QUEENIE ★★★ Lavish television production based on Michael Korda's novel, a fictionalized story of the youth and early movie career of his real-life aunt, Merle Oberon. The opening scenes, set in early 1930s India, are more interesting than her adult years. 235m. **DIR:** Larry Peerce. **CAST:** Mia Sara, Kirk Douglas, Claire Bloom, Joel Grey, Martin Balsam, Sarah Miles, Topol, Kate Emma Davies. **1987**

QUEENS LOGIC ★★★ Maturity and contentment can arrive at any age, assuming, of course, they arrive at all. That's the theme of this rambling, uneven, but amiable coming-of-age comedy-drama. It's *thirtysomething* crossed with *Diner*. Rated R for profanity. 116m. **DIR:** Steve Rash. **CAST:** Joe Mantegna, Kevin Bacon, John Malkovich, Ken Olin, Linda Fiorentino, Jamie Lee Curtis. **1991 DVD**

QUERELLE ★★1/2 In this depressing rendering of Jean Genet's story, Brad Davis stars in the title role as a young sailor whose good looks set off a chain reaction. This is a disturbing and depressing portrait of terminally unhappy people. In German with English subtitles. Rated R for nudity and obscenity. 120m. **DIR:** Rainer Werner Fassbinder. **CAST:** Rainer Werner Fassbinder, Brad Davis, Franco Nero, Jeanne Moreau. **1982 DVD**

QUEST, THE (1985) ★★ Henry Thomas plays a young boy living in Australia who has reason to believe that a monster lives in a small lake not far from his home. He sets out to prove the creature's existence—or to expose it as a fraud. Though slow, this film has decent acting.

Rated PG. 94m. **DIR:** Brian Trenchard-Smith. **CAST:** Henry Thomas, Tony Barry, John Ewart. **1985**

QUEST, THE (1996) ★★ The plot of Jean-Claude Van Damme's directorial debut (he is also credited with the original story) defies synopsis. Set in the 1920s, it has something to do with a gang of New York street urchins (led by Van Damme), South Sea pirates (who kidnap Van Damme), and a sort of international martial arts championship deep in the Himalayas (in which Van Damme competes). Not much sense or drama, but plenty of bone-crunching action for the director-star's fans. Rated PG-13 for martial arts violence. 95m. **DIR:** Jean-Claude Van Damme. **CAST:** Jean-Claude Van Damme, Roger Moore, James Remar. **1996 DVD**

QUEST FOR CAMELOT 🦃 A young girl and a blind hermit thwart an evil knight's uprising against King Arthur. A weak story, shoddy animation, poor voice work, (despite the talented cast), and atrocious songs make this one of the worst cartoon features ever made. Featuring the voices of Jessalyn Gilsig, Cary Elwes, Eric Idle, Don Rickles, Gary Oldman, Jane Seymour, and Pierce Brosnan. Rated G. 85m. **DIR:** Frederik Du Chau. **1998 DVD**

QUEST FOR FIRE ★★★★1/2 In this movie, about the attempt to learn the secret of making fire by a tribe of primitive men, director Jean-Jacques Annaud (*Black and White in Color*) and screenwriter Gerard Brach (*Tess*) have achieved what once seemed to be impossible: a first-rate, compelling film about the dawn of man. Rated R for violence, gore, nudity, and semi-explicit sex. 97m. **DIR:** Jean-Jacques Annaud. **CAST:** Everett McGill, Rae Dawn Chong, Ron Perlman. **1981**

QUEST FOR THE MIGHTY SWORD 🦃 Latest, and hopefully last, of the *Ator* sword-'n'-sorcery sagas. None of these films were any good, but this one's the pits. Rated PG-13 for violence. 94m. **DIR:** David Hills. **CAST:** Eric Allen Kramer, Margaret Lenzey, Donald O'Brien, Laura Gemser. **1989**

QUEST OF THE DELTA KNIGHTS ★★★ In this enchanting, funny medieval story about good and evil, a young slave finds he's the key to the treasures of Archimedes and ventures on a dangerous journey. Good fight scenes. Rated PG. 97m. **DIR:** James Dodson. **CAST:** David Warner, Olivia Hussey, Corbin Allred, Brigid Conley Walsh, David Kind, Sarah Douglas. **1993**

QUESTION OF FAITH ★★★1/2 Made-for-TV tear-jerker, originally aired under the title *Leap of Faith*. Superior cast, led by Anne Archer and Sam Neill, and literate script help this incurable disease movie to transcend the boundaries usually associated with such fare. 90m. **DIR:** Stephen Gyllenhaal. **CAST:** Anne Archer, Sam Neill, Frances Lee McCain, Louis Giambalvo, James Tolkan, Michael Constantine. **1993 DVD**

QUESTION OF HONOR, A ★★★★ Superior made-for-TV movie tells the true story of an honest New York narcotics officer who got caught in the middle of a federal drug scam and found himself accused of corruption. Based on a book by Sonny Grosso, the cop portrayed by Roy Scheider in *The French Connection*. Not rated. 134m. **DIR:** Jud Taylor. **CAST:** Ben Gazzara, Robert Vaughn, Paul Sorvino, Tony Roberts, Danny Aiello. **1982**

QUESTION OF SILENCE, A ★★★★1/2 After an unusual murder is committed, three women, all strangers to one another, stand trial for the same crime. A woman psychiatrist is appointed to the case after the three openly display their hostilities toward male-dominated society. Rated R for profanity. Available in original Dutch or dubbed. 92m. **DIR:** Marleen Gorris. **CAST:** Cox Habbema, Nelly Frijda. **1983**

QUICK ★★★1/2 Scripter Frederick Bailey's apparently routine crime thriller takes an intriguing turn when hit lady Teri Polo spares her latest target—a nerdish accountant, superbly played by Martin Donovan—and employs him as a bargaining chip to save her own skin. Their blossoming relationship sparkles in this low-budget saga. Rated R for nudity, simulated sex, profanity, and violence. 99m. **DIR:** Rick King. **CAST:** Jeff Fahey, Teri Polo, Robert Davi, Martin Donovan, Tia Carrere. **1993**

QUICK AND THE DEAD, THE (1987) ★★★★ Made-for-HBO Western is the third in a trilogy of high-class shoot-'em-ups adapted from the stories by Louis L'Amour for star Sam Elliott. He is marvelous as a grizzled frontiersman who comes to the aid of a family (headed by Tom Conti and Kate Capshaw) making its way across the American wilderness. 90m. **DIR:** Robert Day. **CAST:** Sam Elliott, Kate Capshaw, Tom Conti, Matt Clark, Kenny Morrison. **1987**

QUICK AND THE DEAD, THE (1995) ★★★1/2 Tribute to the spaghetti Western is a mixture of the good, the bad, and the sluggish. Sharon Stone convincingly plays a "lady" gunslinger on the revenge trail. Problem is, she has to wait her turn in a protracted quick-draw competition to get at villain Gene Hackman, and, as a result, the story moves in fits and starts. That said, it's generally enjoyable, especially for fans of this subgenre. Rated R for violence, gore, profanity, and nudity. 105m. **DIR:** Sam Raimi. **CAST:** Sharon Stone, Gene Hackman, Russell Crowe, Leonardo DiCaprio, Lance Henriksen, Keith David, Pat Hingle, Kevin Conway, Woody Strode. **1995 DVD**

QUICK CHANGE ★★★★1/2 Robbing a bank is easy for Bill Murray (who co-directed), Geena Davis, and Randy Quaid—three New Yorkers driven to desperate measures. It's the getaway that they find nearly impossible. Adapted from the 1981 novel by Jay Cronley, this fast-and-funny caper film benefits from Murray's off-the-cuff comedy style. Rated R. 98m. **DIR:** Bill Murray, Howard Franklin. **CAST:** Bill Murray, Geena Davis, Randy Quaid, Jason Robards Jr. **1990**

QUICK, LET'S GET MARRIED 🦃 Made in 1964 but not released for seven years, this feeble farce has Ginger Rogers as the madam of a bordello conspiring to pull off a hoax on a supposedly innocent prostitute. 96m. **DIR:** William Dieterle. **CAST:** Ginger Rogers, Ray Milland, Barbara Eden, Walter Abel, Michael Ansara, Elliott Gould. **1971**

QUICKER THAN THE EYE ★★ Magic is the gimmick in this story of a group of terrorists who plan to assassinate a foreign diplomat. Poorly dubbed Swiss-produced film. Rated PG for language and violence. 94m. **DIR:** Nicolas Gessner. **CAST:** Ben Gazzara, Mary Crosby. **1989**

QUICKSAND: NO ESCAPE ★★1/2 An honest family man (Tim Matheson) gets mixed up in deceit, bribery, and murder. Donald Sutherland is great at portraying the nemesis: a slimy private detective. The twists in this made-for-cable chiller seem interesting at first, but

then they just become unbelievable. 96m. **DIR:** Michael Pressman. **CAST:** Donald Sutherland, Tim Matheson, Jay Acovone, Timothy Carhart. **1991**

QUICKSILVER ★★ Wretched mess of a film. Kevin Bacon stars as a Wall Street wizard who blows it all one day and then puts his natural talents to work by becoming . . . a bicycle messenger! Rated PG for mild violence. 101m. **DIR:** Tom Donnelly. **CAST:** Kevin Bacon, Jami Gertz, Paul Rodriguez, Rudy Ramos, Laurence Fishburne. **1986**

QUICKSILVER HIGHWAY ★★★ Faithful but not particularly frightening adaptations of stories by Stephen King ("Chattery Teeth") and Clive Barker ("The Body Politic"). Fine score by Mark Mothersbaugh. Not rated; contains scenes of mild horror violence. 100m. **DIR:** Mick Garris. **CAST:** Christopher Lloyd, Matt Frewer, Raphael Sbarge, Missy Crider, Veronica Cartwright. **1998**

QUIET COOL 🦃 New York cop journeys to the Pacific Northwest to take on maniacal marijuana growers. Rated R. 80m. **DIR:** Clay Borris. **CAST:** James Remar, Adam Coleman Howard, Daphne Ashbrook, Jared Martin, Nick Cassavetes. **1986**

QUIET DAY IN BELFAST, A ★★★1/2 This fine Canadian message film reveals the hopelessness and insanity of Ireland's civil war. Margot Kidder plays Catholic twins, one in love with a British soldier. Not rated; contains profanity, nudity, and violence. 92m. **DIR:** Milad Bessada. **CAST:** Margot Kidder, Barry Foster. **1978**

QUIET DAYS IN HOLLYWOOD ★★ Sex is the factor that links the different characters in this episodic movie set in Los Angeles. The awful dialogue may be the result of a script that was written in German then translated into English; but for whatever reason, it wastes a good cast. Rated R for sex and nudity. 95m. **DIR:** Josef Rusnak. **CAST:** Hilary Swank, Peter Dobson, Daryl Mitchell, Meta Golding, Chad Lowe, Natasha Gregson Wagner, Jake Busey. **1997 DVD**

QUIET EARTH, THE ★★★★ First-rate science-fiction thriller from New Zealand. A scientific researcher (Bruno Lawrence) wakes one morning and discovers that all living beings—people and animals—have vanished. Fearful that the world-encircling energy grid on which he'd been working may have been responsible, he sets out to find other people. Intelligent and absorbing adaptation of the book by Craig Harrison. Rated R for nudity and sexual situations. 91m. **DIR:** Geoff Murphy. **CAST:** Bruno Lawrence, Alison Routledge. **1985**

QUIET FIRE ★★ Passable low-budget shoot-'em-up features Lawrence-Hilton Jacobs running for his life when a corrupt Senate candidate decides to eliminate anyone capable of exposing his past. Rated R for nudity, profanity, and violence. 90m. **DIR:** Lawrence Hilton-Jacobs. **CAST:** Lawrence Hilton-Jacobs, Robert Z'Dar, Karen Black. **1991**

QUIET MAN, THE ★★★★★ John Ford's easygoing and marvelously entertaining tribute to the people and the land of Ireland. The story centers around an American ex-boxer (John Wayne) who returns to his native land, his efforts to understand the culture and people of a rural village, and especially his interest in taming a spirited colleen (Maureen O'Hara) in spite of the disapproval of her brother (Victor McLaglen). 129m. **DIR:** John Ford. **CAST:** John Wayne, Maureen O'Hara, Victor McLaglen, Barry Fitzgerald, Mildred Natwick, Arthur Shields, Ward Bond, Jack MacGowran. **1952 DVD**

QUIET ROOM, THE ★★1/2 A young girl reacts to her parents' fighting by punishing them with silence, causing her to become lost in her own fantasies. This admirable effort to look into the mind of a troubled child eventually demands too much patience from viewers, who won't find anything or anyone here to sympathize with. Rated PG. 91m. **DIR:** Rolf De Heer. **CAST:** Celine O'Leary, Paul Blackwell, Chloe Ferguson, Phoebe Ferguson. **1996**

QUIET THUNDER 🦃 Inane cross between *Raiders of the Lost Ark* and *Crocodile Dundee*. No rating, but contains violence and brief nudity. 94m. **DIR:** David Rice. **CAST:** Wayne Crawford, June Chadwick. **1988**

QUIGLEY DOWN UNDER ★★★★ In this rip-snorting adventure movie, Tom Selleck plays a sharpshooting American cowboy who travels to Australia in the 1860s to work for British rancher Alan Rickman. Old-fashioned Western that just as easily might have starred John Wayne or, in one of his mellower moods, Clint Eastwood. Fans of the genre should love it. Rated PG for light violence and nudity. 106m. **DIR:** Simon Wincer. **CAST:** Tom Selleck, Laura San Giacomo, Alan Rickman. **1990 DVD**

QUILLER MEMORANDUM, THE ★★★1/2 First-rate espionage film abandons the gadgets and gimmickry that marked most of the spy movies of the 1960s and concentrates on Harold Pinter's intelligent script. An American secret agent (George Segal) goes undercover to shatter a neo-Nazi hate organization that is gaining strength in Berlin. 105m. **DIR:** Michael Anderson. **CAST:** George Segal, Alec Guinness, Max von Sydow, George Sanders, Senta Berger, Robert Helpmann. **1966**

QUILLS ★★★ It's 1794. French pornographer and felon Marquis de Sade is incarcerated in an insane asylum, but has several nasty tales to share. A laundry maid smuggles his literary spasms of lust, sexual fantasies, blasphemy, and overripe prose into public domain while men of science and men of the cloth try to curb the feverish scribe. This lush production explores hypocrisy, censorship, and the dark side of eroticism with only partial success. Rated R for language, nudity, sex, and violence. 123m. **DIR:** Philip Kaufman. **CAST:** Geoffrey Rush, Kate Winslet, Joaquin Phoenix, Michael Caine. **2000 DVD**

QUINTET ★★ This is about as pessimistic a view of the future as one is likely to see. Director Robert Altman has fashioned a murky, hard-to-follow film, concerning the ultimate game of death, set against the background of a frozen postnuclear wasteland. An intriguing idea, but Altman doesn't pull this one off. Rated R. 110m. **DIR:** Robert Altman. **CAST:** Paul Newman, Fernando Rey, Bibi Andersson. **1979**

QUIZ SHOW ★★★★★ This thoughtful examination of the TV scandal of the 1950s boasts a compelling tale of what can happen when decent people allow themselves to be corrupted. John Turturro is unforgettable as the quiz-show champ whose middle-class, Jewish background is considered to be a ratings threat by the show's producers. They force him out in order to install clean-cut, Ivy League college professor Ralph Fiennes as their

new champion—thus setting in motion a chain of events that leads to exposure of this and other questionable practices. Rated PG-13 for profanity. 130m. **DIR:** Robert Redford. **CAST:** John Turturro, Rob Morrow, Ralph Fiennes, Paul Scofield, David Paymer, Hank Azaria, Christopher McDonald, Johann Carlo, Elizabeth Wilson, Martin Scorsese, Barry Levinson. **1994 DVD**

QUO VADIS (1951) ★★★ Colossal! Roman soldier Robert Taylor loves and pursues Christian maiden Deborah Kerr. It's Christians versus Nero and the lions in the eternal fight between good and evil. 171m. **DIR:** Mervyn LeRoy. **CAST:** Robert Taylor, Deborah Kerr, Peter Ustinov, Leo Genn, Finlay Currie, Patricia Laffan, Abraham Sofaer, Felix Aylmer, Buddy Baer. **1951**

QUO VADIS? (1985) ★★★ Lavish adaptation of Henryk Sienkiewicz's novel set during the reign of Nero. Klaus Maria Brandauer gives a brilliant performance as Nero in this made-for-Italian-television production. 200m. **DIR:** Franco Rossi. **CAST:** Klaus Maria Brandauer, Frederic Forrest, Cristina Raines, Francesco Quinn. **1985**

R

RABBIT RUN ★★ John Updike's novel concerning an ex–high school athlete's trouble adjusting to life off the field is brought to the screen in a very dull fashion. James Caan has the title role as the lost ex-jock. Supporting cast is good, but the script sinks everyone involved. 74m. **DIR:** Jack Smight. **CAST:** James Caan, Carrie Snodgress, Jack Albertson, Henry Jones, Anjanette Comer. **1970**

RABBIT TEST The world's first pregnant man. Rated R—profanity. 84m. **DIR:** Joan Rivers. **CAST:** Billy Crystal, Roddy McDowall, Joan Prather. **1978**

RABID ★★ This horror flick has become a cult favorite despite many repulsive scenes. In it, porn queen Marilyn Chambers lives on human blood after a motorcycle accident operation. For fans of director David Cronenberg only. Rated R. 90m. **DIR:** David Cronenberg. **CAST:** Marilyn Chambers, Joe Silver, Patricia Gage. **1977**

RABID GRANNIES ★★★ A birthday party for two old ladies turns into a zombiefest thanks to a present sent by the family Satanist. Gruesome special effects are the name of the game in this over-the-top horror movie. Not rated, but not for kids or the squeamish. 83m. **DIR:** Emmanuel Kervyn. **CAST:** Catherine Aymerie, Caroline Braekman. **1989 DVD**

RACE ★★★ A Latino housepainter challenges a black ex-radical for a seat on the Los Angeles city council in a race that heats up as voters line up along ethnic lines. This low-budget film has excellent performances, though its simple-minded view of politics is irksome. Also released as *Melting Pot*. Rated R for profanity. 100m. **DIR:** Tom Musca. **CAST:** Paul Rodriguez, C.C.H. Pounder, Cliff Robertson, Una Damon. **1997 DVD**

•RACE AGAINST TIME ★★★ Futuristic thriller pits a desperate father (Eric Roberts) against a body-parts acquisition enterprise. Roberts sells his body to LIFECORPS in order to save his son before he realizes that they won't be waiting the customary year to collect. While on the run, he befriends a bounty hunter and discovers the sinister day-to-day business conducted behind the corporation's sterile facade. Suspense-filled sequences and a very convincing Roberts make this TNT original worth watching. Not rated; contains violence. 92m. **DIR:** Geoff Murphy. **CAST:** Eric Roberts, Cary Elwes, Sarah Wynter. **2000 DVD**

RACE FOR GLORY ★★ In his quest to be a "legend in my own time," a talented, young motorcyclist (Alex McArthur) abandons his friends for a chance to compete on the international racing circuit. This unrated mediocrity has profanity and violence. 105m. **DIR:** Rocky Lang. **CAST:** Alex McArthur, Peter Berg, Lane Smith. **1989**

RACE FOR YOUR LIFE, CHARLIE BROWN ★★★ Third entry in the "Peanuts" film series has moved further away from the poignant sophistication of *A Boy Named Charlie Brown* and closer to the mindless pap of Saturday-morning cartoon fare. Rated G. 75m. **DIR:** Bill Melendez. **1977**

RACE THE SUN ★★ Underdog Hawaiian high-school students design and race a solar-powered car inspired by the aerodynamics of a cockroach. This film has its heart in the right place but is just another mediocre teen-misfits-make-good movie. A real-life story of determination and courage turned into formulaic mush. Rated PG. 105m. **DIR:** Charles Kanganis. **CAST:** Halle Berry, James Belushi, Casey Affleck, Anthony Ruivivar, Bill Hunter, Eliza Dushku, Kevin Tighe, Steve Zahn, J. Moki Cho, Dion Basco. **1996**

RACE WITH THE DEVIL ★★ Good cast and exciting chase sequences can't save this muddled yarn. It's about two couples who accidentally intrude on a witches' sacrificial ceremony. Rated PG for violence. 88m. **DIR:** Jack Starrett. **CAST:** Warren Oates, Peter Fonda, Loretta Swit, Lara Parker. **1975**

RACERS, THE ★★★ A reworking of *Champion* set in the world of car racers, with Kirk Douglas as the idealist who becomes a racing champion and then an unethical competitor. The photography at the racetrack is unusually effective. 112m. **DIR:** Henry Hathaway. **CAST:** Kirk Douglas, Gilbert Roland, Bella Darvi, Cesar Romero, Katy Jurado, Lee J. Cobb. **1955**

RACHEL AND THE STRANGER ★★★1/2 This leisurely paced Western is made easier to watch by a fine cast. William Holden's love for his wife Loretta Young finally comes to full blossom only after she is wooed by stranger Robert Mitchum. A nice story done with charm and class. B&W; 93m. **DIR:** Norman Foster. **CAST:** William Holden, Loretta Young, Robert Mitchum. **1948**

RACHEL PAPERS ★★★1/2 Dexter Fletcher (who looks like a young Mick Jagger) plays an infatuated young man persistently pursuing the girl of his dreams (Ione Skye). When she finally acknowledges him, the film takes a decidedly serious and downhill turn. Rated R for profanity and nudity. 95m. **DIR:** Damian Harris. **CAST:** Dexter Fletcher, Ione Skye, Jonathan Pryce. **1989**

RACHEL, RACHEL ★★★1/2 Paul Newman's directorial debut focuses on a spinsterish schoolteacher

(Joanne Woodward) and her awakening to a world beyond her job and her elderly mother's influence. This bittersweet story is perfectly acted by Woodward, with strong support by James Olson as her short-term lover and Estelle Parsons as her friend. Rewarding on all levels. Rated R. 101m. **DIR:** Paul Newman. **CAST:** Joanne Woodward, James Olson, Kate Harrington, Estelle Parsons. **1968**

RACHEL RIVER ★★★ *American Playhouse* presentation boasts a screenplay by *Ordinary People* author Judith Guest and an excellent cast in this tale of a lonely small-town woman who falls for the one guy in town who makes her happy. Watching these two opposites attract is magnetic. 97m. **DIR:** Sandy Smolan. **CAST:** Pamela Reed, Craig T. Nelson, Viveca Lindfors, James Olson. **1988**

RACING WITH THE MOON ★★★1/2 Sean Penn and Elizabeth McGovern star in this thoroughly entertaining and touching comedy-romance set during World War II. He's just a regular town boy who discovers he's fallen in love with one of the area's rich girls. But that doesn't stop him from trying to win her heart. Rated PG for nudity, profanity, suggested sex, and brief violence. 108m. **DIR:** Richard Benjamin. **CAST:** Sean Penn, Elizabeth McGovern, Nicolas Cage, John Karlen, Rutanya Alda, Carol Kane. **1984**

RACKET, THE ★★★ This pessimistic look at political corruption focuses on the steps honest police captain Robert Mitchum takes in order to bring underworld figure Robert Ryan to justice. Mitchum is a man alone as he confronts seemingly insurmountable opposition from both police and political higher-ups who want to keep things just as crooked as they are. B&W; 88m. **DIR:** John Cromwell. **CAST:** Robert Mitchum, Robert Ryan, Lizabeth Scott, William Talman, Ray Collins, Robert Hutton. **1951**

RACKETEER ★★1/2 This early sound gangster film finds gang leader Robert Armstrong involved in the familiar eternal triangle as he falls for Carole Lombard. She, in turn, pines for an ailing concert violinist. This primitive talkie has some snappy dialogue and features lively performances. B&W; 68m. **DIR:** Howard Higgin. **CAST:** Robert Armstrong, Carole Lombard, John Loder, Paul Hurst, Hedda Hopper. **1930**

RAD ★★1/2 Staunch character players Talia Shire, Ray Walston, and Jack Weston support this film about a daredevil bicyclist (Bill Allen) who competes to win a thousand dollars. Fairly entertaining, thanks to the exciting race sequences. Rated PG. 95m. **DIR:** Hal Needham. **CAST:** Bill Allen, Lori Loughlin, Talia Shire, Ray Walston, Jack Weston. **1986**

RADAR MEN FROM THE MOON ★★ Commando Cody, Sky Marshal of the Universe and inventor of a flying suit and a rocket ship, uses all the means at his disposal to aid America in combating Retik, the ruler of the moon, who is bent on (what else?) invading the Earth. The bullet-headed hero chases villains on land, in the air, and all the way to the moon and back and gets his fair share of abuse along the way. Lots of fisticuffs and stock footage. B&W; 12 chapters. **DIR:** Fred Brannon. **CAST:** George Wallace, Aline Towne, Roy Barcroft. **1952**

RADIO DAYS ★★★ One of writer-director Woody Allen's gentler fables, a pleasant little fantasy about people whose lives revolved around the radio during the days prior to World War II. This affectionate overview does for radio what *The Purple Rose of Cairo* did for the movies; unfortunately, many of the characters in his large ensemble cast get lost, and too much time is spent with others. Rated PG. 85m. **DIR:** Woody Allen. **CAST:** Mia Farrow, Seth Green, Julie Kavner, Josh Mostel, Michael Tucker, Dianne Wiest. **1987 DVD**

RADIO FLYER ★★ Two youngsters attempt to escape the terrors inflicted on them by their violent stepfather by turning their Radio Flyer wagon into a flying machine. The horrors of child abuse are ineffectively wed with innocent childhood fantasies in this disturbing film. A misfire. Rated PG-13 for violence and profanity. 114m. **DIR:** Richard Donner. **CAST:** Lorraine Bracco, John Heard, Elijah Wood, Joseph Mazzello, Adam Baldwin, Tom Hanks, Ben Johnson. **1992**

RADIO INSIDE ★★★ A lackluster cast and unfocused plotting sabotage what might have been a nice little spin on Truffaut's *Jules and Jim*. Two brothers vie for the romantic affections of a pouty young woman, while the younger sibling struggles to overcome guilt feelings relating to their father's accidental death. Occasional witty touches do not compensate for long, empty scenes. Rated PG-13 for profanity and brief nudity. 95m. **DIR:** Jeffrey Bell. **CAST:** William McNamara, Elisabeth Shue, Dylan Walsh. **1994**

RADIO RANCH (MEN WITH STEEL FACES, PHANTOM EMPIRE) ★★1/2 Condensed version of popular science-fiction serial *Phantom Empire*, this sketchily tells the story of Gene Autry and his fight against scientists who want his Radio Ranch for the precious ore it contains, and his strange adventures in the underground city of Murania. The 12-chapter serial makes more sense. B&W; 80m. **DIR:** Otto Brewer, B. Reeves "Breezy" Eason. **CAST:** Gene Autry, Frankie Darro, Betsy King Ross, Dorothy Christy, Smiley Burnette. **1940**

RADIOACTIVE DREAMS ★★★ This one has a little bit of everything: action, adventure, science fiction, fantasy, and an excellent score. Essentially a spoof, the story begins in a post-apocalypse fallout shelter where two boys have lived most of their lives. They end up in the middle of a gang war with a mutant surfer, hippie cannibals, and biker women. Rated R for nudity and violence. 94m. **DIR:** Albert Pyun. **CAST:** John Stockwell, Michael Dudikoff, George Kennedy, Don Murray, Michelle Little, Norbert Weisser, Lisa Blount. **1984**

RADIOLAND MURDERS ★★ The behind-the-scenes happenings come so fast and furious in this confusing whodunit that most viewers are left scratching their heads. The only comprehensible plot line, the failed romance between Mary Stuart Masterson and Brian Benben, gets a much-needed shot in the arm when he becomes the prime suspect in a series of murders. Musical score is the only plus. Rated PG for violence and adult situations. 108m. **DIR:** Mel Smith. **CAST:** Mary Stuart Masterson, Brian Benben, Christopher Lloyd, Ned Beatty. **1994 DVD**

RAFFERTY AND THE GOLD DUST TWINS ★★1/2 Amusing and entertaining little film with Sally Kellerman and Mackenzie Phillips kidnapping a hapless Alan Arkin and forcing him to drive them to New Orleans from California. Good cast and pacing make up for simple plot. Rated PG for profanity. 92m. **DIR:** Dick

Richards. **CAST:** Sally Kellerman, Mackenzie Phillips, Alan Arkin, Alex Rocco, Charles Martin Smith, Harry Dean Stanton. **1975**

RAFFLE, THE ★★1/2 Harmless fluff about two men who run an international raffle in which the winner gets a date with the most beautiful woman in the world. Now they have to come up with the prize, and their search takes them on a global quest. If film didn't have its heart in the right place, it might seem sexist. Rated R for adult situations. 100m. **DIR:** Gavin Wilding. **CAST:** Nicholas Lea, Bobby Dawson, Jennifer Clement, Jay Underwood, Mark Hamill, Teri-Lynn Rutherford. **1994**

RAGDOLL ★★ After an extremely slow first hour, this revenge thriller set in an urban setting finally picks up. The problem is that you'll probably fall asleep way before then. The titular creature doesn't even show up to reek its mayhem until the hour mark and even then it is barely seen. Perhaps that is for the better since the effects are quite poor. Rated R for excessive profanity and violence. 90m. **DIR:** Ted Nicolaou. **CAST:** Russell Richardson, Jennia Watson. **1999**

RAGE (1972) ★★★ This pits a lone man against the impersonal Establishment (in this instance the U.S. Army). Not a happy film by any means, but an interesting one. Making his directorial debut, George C. Scott plays a peaceful sheep rancher whose son is the victim of military chemical testing. Seeking revenge, he sets out to nail those responsible. Rated PG. 104m. **DIR:** George C. Scott. **CAST:** George C. Scott, Martin Sheen, Richard Basehart, Barnard Hughes. **1972**

RAGE (1980) ★★★ David Soul travels through the agonies of intense therapy as a convicted rapist in this above-par TV-movie drama. Loaded with fine performances from an incredible cast. 100m. **DIR:** William A. Graham. **CAST:** David Soul, James Whitmore, Craig T. Nelson, Yaphet Kotto, Caroline McWilliams, Leo Gordon, Sharon Farrell, Vic Tayback. **1980**

RAGE (1995) ★★ Although this badly edited thriller makes no sense whatsoever, it boasts a few incredible action sequences. Nice guy Gary Daniels gets involved in some weird plot to make supersoldiers and winds up battling half the United States to win back his freedom. Rated R for violence, profanity, and deviant sexuality. 91m. **DIR:** Joseph Merhi. **CAST:** Gary Daniels, Kenneth Tigar, Fiona Hutchison. **1995**

RAGE AND HONOR ★★ Martial-arts greats Cynthia Rothrock and Richard Norton team up to expose drug-dealing cops. She tries to protect her video camera–wielding student while Norton attempts to clear his name after being framed for murder. If the gratuitous sleaze had been left out, this could have been an above-average kickfest. Rated R for profanity and violence. 93m. **DIR:** Terence H. Winkless. **CAST:** Cynthia Rothrock, Richard Norton, Terri Treas, Brian Thompson, Catherine Bach. **1992**

RAGE AND HONOR II: HOSTILE TAKEOVER ★★ Predictable martial-arts sequel finds CIA operative Cynthia Rothrock battling bad guys in Jakarta. Richard Norton, her former partner, helps her resolve a dispute between her employer and his greedy son. High kicks and little else. Rated R for violence and language. 98m. **DIR:** Guy Norris. **CAST:** Cynthia Rothrock, Richard Norton, Patrick Muldoon, Frans Tumbuan. **1992**

RAGE AT DAWN ★★★★ Solid Western has granite-jawed Randolph Scott as an undercover agent out to trap the infamous Reno brothers (played with zest by Forrest Tucker, J. Carrol Naish, and Myron Healey). Scott takes time out to romance their pretty sister (Mala Powers) before bringing the boys to justice. 87m. **DIR:** Tim Whelan. **CAST:** Randolph Scott, Forrest Tucker, Mala Powers, J. Carrol Naish, Myron Healey, Edgar Buchanan. **1955 DVD**

RAGE IN HARLEM, A ★★★ Adapted from the novel by Chester Himes, this movie can't make up its mind whether to be a comedy à la *The Sting* or a violent action film like *New Jack City*. Still, it's quite a roller-coaster ride as southern con-woman Robin Givens makes her way to Harlem with a load of stolen gold, seduces sweet-natured accountant Forest Whitaker, and tries to deal with gangster Danny Glover. Rated R for violence, nudity, and profanity. 115m. **DIR:** Bill Duke. **CAST:** Forest Whitaker, Gregory Hines, Danny Glover, Zakes Mokae, John Toles-Bey, Robin Givens. **1991**

RAGE OF PARIS, THE ★★★ Famed French star Danielle Darrieux made her U.S. film debut in this airy romantic comedy about mistaken identity and artful conniving. Deft direction steered the excellent cast through an engaging script. Good, clean fun all around. B&W; 78m. **DIR:** Henry Koster. **CAST:** Danielle Darrieux, Douglas Fairbanks Jr., Mischa Auer, Helen Broderick, Glenda Farrell, Louis Hayward, Harry Davenport, Samuel S. Hinds. **1938**

RAGE, THE: CARRIE 2 ★★1/2 This predictable little chiller, unimaginatively follows the sequence of events from Stephen King's career-making first novel, and the landmark 1976 film adapted from it. A tormented high-school girl, mostly unaware of her telekinetic abilities, attracts the attention of a sports jock with a bit more compassion than his grunting-pig friends, and thus sets into motion a nasty plot hatched by the local "power crowd" that climaxes when our heroine, tragically embarrassed and betrayed, orchestrates fearsome vengeance during a huge party. The only real change relates to the escalated level of acceptable carnage, climaxing in a "money shot" that represents a new low, even for this genre. Rated R for violence, profanity, nudity, gore, and sexual content. 104m. **DIR:** Katt Shea. **CAST:** Emily Bergl, Jason London, Dylan Bruno, J. Smith-Cameron, Zachery Ty Bryan, Amy Irving, Gordon Clapp. **1999 DVD**

RAGGEDY MAN ★★★1/2 Sissy Spacek gives another outstanding performance as a World War II divorcée trying to raise two sons and improve their lives in a small Texas Gulf Coast town. The film is a curious mixture of styles. It begins as a character study and ends like a horror film. But it works. Rated PG for violence. 94m. **DIR:** Jack Fisk. **CAST:** Sissy Spacek, Eric Roberts, William Sanderson, Tracey Walter, Sam Shepard, Henry Thomas. **1981**

RAGGEDY RAWNEY, THE ★★1/2 A quaint, modest effort most notable because its first-time writer-director is the superb Cockney actor, Bob Hoskins. He created this folk fable about Gypsies and a myth about a speechless madwoman with magical powers who follows the caravans about. 102m. **DIR:** Bob Hoskins. **CAST:** Bob Hoskins, Dexter Fletcher. **1988**

RAGING ANGELS ★★ The one decent performance in this lame supernatural adventure is a wildly exuberant turn by Diane Ladd as a spiritualist with the knack to see demons and angels. A bloated Michael Pare phones in his performance as an evangelistic singer whose positive appearance belies an evil intent. Rated R for violence, profanity, and sexual situations. 97m. **DIR:** Alan Smithee. **CAST:** Sean Patrick Flanery, Diane Ladd, Michael Paré, Monet Mazur, Shelley Winters. **1994**

RAGING BULL ★★★★1/2 This tough, compelling film is one movie you won't want to miss. In playing prizefighter Jake La Motta from his twenties through to middle age, Robert De Niro undergoes a transformation that takes him from his normal weight of 150 to 212 pounds. Startling, yes, but the performance he gives is even more so—see it. Rated R. B&W; 128m. **DIR:** Martin Scorsese. **CAST:** Robert De Niro, Cathy Moriarty, Joe Pesci, Frank Vincent, Nicholas Colasanto, Theresa Saldana. **1980 DVD**

RAGS TO RICHES ★★ Joseph Bologna plays millionaire Nick Foley, who tries to soften his ruthless-businessman image by adopting six girls. This was a pilot for the TV series of the same name. 96m. **DIR:** Bruce Seth Green. **CAST:** Joseph Bologna, Tisha Campbell. **1986**

RAGTIME ★★★★1/2 James Cagney returned to the screen after an absence of twenty years in this brilliant screen adaptation of E. L. Doctorow's bestselling novel about New York City at the turn of the century. It's a bountifully rewarding motion picture. Rated PG for violence and nudity. 155m. **DIR:** Milos Forman. **CAST:** James Cagney, Brad Dourif, Pat O'Brien, Donald O'Connor, Elizabeth McGovern, Mary Steenburgen. **1981**

RAID ON ENTEBBE ★★★ Second of three dramas filmed in 1976–1977 about the daring Israeli commando assault on the Entebbe airport in Uganda, this TV movie avoids the soap-opera tone of the earlier *Victory at Entebbe* (also made for TV) and focuses on the action and power struggle between the Israelis and Idi Amin. More effective when it was initially shown, but it's still worth a watch. 150m. **DIR:** Irvin Kershner. **CAST:** Peter Finch, Charles Bronson, Horst Buchholz, Martin Balsam, John Saxon, Jack Warden, Yaphet Kotto. **1977**

RAID ON ROMMEL 🦃 Substandard war film. Rated PG for violence. 98m. **DIR:** Henry Hathaway. **CAST:** Richard Burton, John Colicos, Clinton Greyn, Wolfgang Preiss. **1971 DVD**

RAIDERS OF THE LOST ARK ★★★★★ For sheer spirit-lifting entertainment, you can't do better than this film, by director Steven Spielberg and writer-producer George Lucas. Harrison Ford stars as Indiana Jones, the roughest, toughest, and most unpredictable hero to grace the silver screen, who risks life and limb against a set of the nastiest villains you've ever seen. It's all to save the world—what else? Rated PG for violence and gore. 115m. **DIR:** Steven Spielberg. **CAST:** Harrison Ford, Karen Allen, Wolf Kahler, Paul Freeman, Ronald Lacey, John Rhys-Davies, Denholm Elliott. **1981**

RAIDERS OF THE SUN ★★ Roger Corman produced this trite postnuclear-holocaust shoot-'em-up. Rated R for nudity, violence, and profanity. 80m. **DIR:** Cirio H. Santiago. **CAST:** Richard Norton. **1991**

RAILROADED ★★★ Future TV father Hugh Beaumont has his hands full as a police detective trying to run interference between gangster John Ireland and his intended victim Sheila Ryan. Tough, tight, and deadly, this early effort from director Anthony Mann oozes suspense and remains a fine example of American *film noir*, modestly budgeted and effectively conveyed. B&W; 71m. **DIR:** Anthony Mann. **CAST:** John Ireland, Sheila Ryan, Hugh Beaumont, Jane Randolph, Keefe Brasselle. **1947 DVD**

RAILWAY CHILDREN, THE ★★★★1/2 Wonderful family fare from Great Britain. Set in 1905, this tale focuses on a family whose idyllic life is shattered. Director Lionel Jeffries, a popular British comic actor, also wrote the screenplay based on the novel by E. Nesbit. Warmth, comedy, and adventure—a must-see. 104m. **DIR:** Lionel Jeffries. **CAST:** Dinah Sheridan, Bernard Cribbins, William Mervyn, Ian Cuthbertson, Jenny Agutter, Sally Thomsett, Gary Warren. **1970**

RAILWAY STATION MAN, THE ★★1/2 An offbeat love story set in Ireland involves painter Julie Christie with a red-haired, one-handed Donald Sutherland, who plays the title character. The two stars, working together twenty years after making *Don't Look Now*, make this TV movie watchable but cannot overcome a confusing subplot involving terrorists. 93m. **DIR:** Michael Whyte. **CAST:** Julie Christie, Donald Sutherland, John Lynch, Frank McCusker, Mark Tandy. **1993**

RAIN ★★★★ Joan Crawford plays island hussy Sadie Thompson in this depressing drama. Walter Huston is the preacher who wants to "save" her—for himself. B&W; 93m. **DIR:** Lewis Milestone. **CAST:** Joan Crawford, Walter Huston, William Gargan, Guy Kibbee, Walter Catlett, Beulah Bondi. **1932 DVD**

RAIN KILLER, THE ★★★ Good suspense film, in which the police try to track down a homicidal maniac, who only kills women during rainstorms. Many impressive plot twists, as well as interesting sets and lighting. Rated R for violence, nudity, and profanity. 94m. **DIR:** Ken Stein. **CAST:** Ray Sharkey, David Beecroft, Michael Chiklis, Tania Coleridge, Woody Brown. **1990**

RAIN MAN ★★★★★ Dustin Hoffman gives the performance of his career as the autistic older brother of Tom Cruise, who plays a thoughtless, self-centered hustler with room in his life only for money. Greed propels him to take a cross-country road trip with Hoffman, who inherited the bulk of Dad's vast estate. The blend of pathos with gentle humor allows us to laugh with, but never at, Hoffman's autistic savant. Inexplicably rated R for occasional profanity. 140m. **DIR:** Barry Levinson. **CAST:** Dustin Hoffman, Tom Cruise, Valeria Golino. **1988 DVD**

RAIN PEOPLE, THE ★★★★ James Caan plays a retired football star who is picked up by a bored pregnant woman (played by Shirley Knight). She felt trapped as a housewife and ran away from her husband to be free. Directed by Francis Ford Coppola, this is an interesting, well-acted character study. Rated R. 102m. **DIR:** Francis Ford Coppola. **CAST:** James Caan, Shirley Knight, Robert Duvall, Tom Aldredge. **1969**

RAIN WITHOUT THUNDER ★★★1/2 This often-intriguing abortion rights drama with a decided pro-choice agenda is set in a not-so-distant future when abortion is again illegal. It assumes a mock documen-

tary style to tell the story of a mother and daughter charged with traveling to Sweden to obtain an abortion. Rated PG-13, with profanity and adult issues. 87m. **DIR:** Gary Bennett. **CAST:** Jeff Daniels, Betty Buckley, Linda Hunt, Frederic Forrest, Graham Greene, Austin Pendleton. **1993**

RAINBOW, THE ★★★★ Director Ken Russell returns to D. H. Lawrence, the source of his great success, *Women in Love*. This time, he focuses on the companion novel, a prequel. Sammi Davis is wonderful as an adolescent English girl exposed to the ways of love at the hands of both a soldier and her teacher, and makes a decision to seek a more satisfying life for herself. Rated R. 102m. **DIR:** Ken Russell. **CAST:** Sammi Davis, Paul McGann, Glenda Jackson, Amanda Donohoe, David Hemmings, Christopher Gable. **1989**

RAINBOW DRIVE ★★1/2 Roderick Thorpe's suspense novel is not well served by this turgid made-for-cable police melodrama, which features Peter Weller as an honest cop embroiled in a cover-up. The cast tries to rise above the material. Not rated, but with violence and brief nudity. 96m. **DIR:** Bobby Roth. **CAST:** Peter Weller, Sela Ward, David Caruso, Bruce Weitz, Kathryn Harrold. **1990**

RAINBOW THIEF, THE ★★★1/2 Lunacy prevails when a rich, eccentric man succumbs to the pleasures of life, and his family fights over his estate. The good news is that Uncle Rudolph's dirt-poor nephew is the sole heir. The bad news is that he's totally nuts. When the family schemes to have him written out of the will, the crazy nephew and his best friend decide to take matters into their own hands. Peter O'Toole and Omar Sharif are delightful as the wacky nephew and his friend. Not rated. 88m. **DIR:** Alejandro Jodorowsky. **CAST:** Peter O'Toole, Omar Sharif, Christopher Lee. **1990**

RAINBOW VALLEY ★★★ A young John Wayne goes undercover to round up the outlaws who have been blocking the building of a road into the mining town of Rainbow Valley. In this breezy outing, Wayne works especially well with Gabby Hayes. B&W; 52m. **DIR:** Robert N. Bradbury. **CAST:** John Wayne, Lucille Brown, LeRoy Mason, George "Gabby" Hayes, Buffalo Bill Jr. **1935 DVD**

RAINBOW WARRIOR ★★1/2 Direct-to-video mystery is based on the real-life bombing of the Greenpeace vessel *Rainbow Warrior*, which resulted in the death of a crew member. Sam Neill and Jon Voight play men on opposite sides of the law who team up to solve the crime. Less preachy than one might expect, it makes a statement while remaining entertaining. Rated PG for violence. 93m. **DIR:** Michael Tuchner. **CAST:** Sam Neill, Jon Voight, Bruno Lawrence, Kerry Fox, John Callen. **1994**

RAINING STONES ★★★★ Director Ken Loach again cuts to the heart of human essence in this raw and quirky flick. Bruce Jones is an unemployed laborer determined to get his daughter an expensive outfit for her First Communion ceremony. As he scrambles through a series of jobs on both sides of the law, Jones depicts a comedy of errors that much of humanity enacts while searching for a better life. Not rated; contains profanity and nudity. 90m. **DIR:** Kenneth Loach. **CAST:** Bruce Jones, Julie Brown, Ricky Tomlinson, Tom Hickey, Gemma Phoenix. **1993 DVD**

RAINMAKER, THE (1956) ★★★1/2 Based on N. Richard Nash's play, the movie adaptation could easily have seemed confined, but the boundless intensity and energy of Burt Lancaster's performance as the smooth-talking con man gives the whole film an electric crackle. Katharine Hepburn has the magnetism to hold her own in the role of the spinster. 121m. **DIR:** Joseph Anthony. **CAST:** Burt Lancaster, Katharine Hepburn, Wendell Corey, Lloyd Bridges, Earl Holliman, Wallace Ford, Cameron Prud'homme. **1956**

RAINMAKER, THE (1997) ★★★★ Ah, what a fairy tale. This adaptation of John Grisham's bestseller is a tale ripped straight from modern headlines and our worst fears: on one side, represented by a team of one-grand-per-hour legal sharpies, a recalcitrant insurance company that refuses to honor what seems a legitimate claim for desperately needed medical technology; on the other side, the young Tennessee victim and his needy parents, represented by a kid fresh out of law school and one assistant who hasn't been able to pass the bar in six consecutive attempts. It's all wholly preposterous wish-fulfillment . . . and a delight, from start to finish. Rated PG-13 for violence, profanity, and dramatic intensity. 137m. **DIR:** Francis Ford Coppola. **CAST:** Matt Damon, Claire Danes, Jon Voight, Danny DeVito, Mary Kay Place, Mickey Rourke. **1997 DVD**

RAINS CAME, THE ★★★ Louis Bromfield's epic novel of India has been turned into a so-so drama of forbidden romance between a white woman and an Indian doctor. A spectacular earthquake and tidal wave, but little more. Remade in 1955 as *The Rains of Ranchipur*. B&W; 104m. **DIR:** Clarence Brown. **CAST:** Myrna Loy, Tyrone Power, George Brent, Brenda Joyce, Nigel Bruce, Maria Ouspenskaya, Joseph Schildkraut, Jane Darwell, Marjorie Rambeau, Henry Travers, H. B. Warner. **1939**

RAINTREE COUNTY ★★★ Civil War melodrama with Elizabeth Taylor as a southern belle is two and one-half hours of showy tedium that wastes a fine cast and miles of film. Bestselling novel comes to the screen as an extended soap opera with little promise and fewer results. 168m. **DIR:** Edward Dmytryk. **CAST:** Elizabeth Taylor, Montgomery Clift, Eva Marie Saint, Nigel Patrick, Lee Marvin, Rod Taylor, Agnes Moorehead, Walter Abel, Rhys Williams. **1957**

RAISE THE RED LANTERN ★★★★1/2 Chinese director Zhang Yimou's magnificent film chronicles the life of a 1920s maiden who, at her mother's urgings, agrees to marry a wealthy man. She becomes "Fourth Mistress" in a house where being the master's favorite means all. Based on a novel by Su Tong. In Mandarin with English subtitles. Not rated; the film has suggested sex and violence. 125m. **DIR:** Yimou Zhang. **CAST:** Gong Li. **1991**

RAISE THE TITANIC 🦃 Disastrously dull disaster flick. Rated PG. 112m. **DIR:** Jerry Jameson. **CAST:** Jason Robards Jr., David Selby, Richard Jordan, Anne Archer, Alec Guinness, J. D. Cannon. **1980**

RAISIN IN THE SUN, A (1961) ★★★★ A black family tries to escape from their crowded apartment life by moving to a house in an all-white neighborhood. Sidney Poitier delivers his usual outstanding performance in this film with a message about the limited opportunities open to blacks in the 1950s. B&W; 128m. **DIR:** Daniel Petrie. **CAST:** Sidney Poitier, Claudia McNeil, Ruby

Dee, Diana Sands, Ivan Dixon, John Fiedler, Louis Gossett Jr. **1961 DVD**

RAISIN IN THE SUN, A (1988) ★★★★ Gripping TV remake of the 1961 classic, with Danny Glover replacing Sidney Poitier as the angry young man who's ready to explode. Esther Rolle superbly struggles to reunite her family by buying a home that just happens to be in an all-white neighborhood. 171m. **DIR:** Bill Duke. **CAST:** Danny Glover, Esther Rolle, Starletta Dupois. **1988**

RAISING ARIZONA ★★★★ An almost indescribable lunatic comedy from the makers of *Blood Simple*. Nicolas Cage plays an ex-convict married to policewoman Holly Hunter. Both want children but cannot have any. So they decide to help themselves to one. What follows is a delightful, offbeat comedy that is extremely fast-paced, with eye-popping cinematography and decidedly different characters. Rated PG-13. 94m. **DIR:** Joel Coen. **CAST:** Nicolas Cage, Holly Hunter, Randall "Tex" Cobb, Trey Wilson, John Goodman, William Forsythe. **1987 DVD**

RAISING CAIN 🦃 Psychological thrillers don't come much sillier than this hopelessly muddled study of a demented child psychologist (John Lithgow, *way* over the top) who kidnaps small children. A real low for director Brian De Palma. Rated R for violence and profanity. 95m. **DIR:** Brian De Palma. **CAST:** John Lithgow, Lolita Davidovich, Steven Bauer, Frances Sternhagen. **1992 DVD**

RAISING HEROES ★★★ Unconventional action film stars Troy Sistillio and Henry White as a gay couple ready to adopt the baby of a late friend. Then White witnesses a mob hit, and their lives and the chances of adopting the child are in jeopardy. When the mob decides to silence them, the couple must rise to the occasion to clean up the mess. Low-budget affair tweaks conventional action films into a new hybrid. Not rated; contains adult situations, language, nudity, and violence. 85m. **DIR:** Douglas Langway. **CAST:** Troy Sistillio, Henry White, Edmond Sorel, Stewart Groves. **1996**

RAISING THE HEIGHTS ★★ Well-intended but incompetently made urban drama about a Brooklyn student trying to expose teachers who sell drugs to students. Rated R for profanity and violence. 86m. **DIR:** Max Gottlieb. **CAST:** Gilbert Brown Jr., Fia Perera. **1998**

RAMBLING ROSE ★★★★ Everything is just right in this film about a 13 year old boy who falls in love with his 19 year old nanny, a sexy ball of fire called Rose. Rose scorches everyone in her path in this uproariously funny, heart-tugging, and sexy release adapted from the semiautobiographical book by Calder Willingham. Rated R for profanity, nudity, and suggested sex. 112m. **DIR:** Martha Coolidge. **CAST:** Laura Dern, Robert Duvall, Diane Ladd, Lukas Haas, John Heard, Kevin Conway. **1991 DVD**

RAMBO III ★★ Sylvester Stallone's hammer-handed tendencies operate at overdrive in this second sequel to *First Blood*. As cowriter, Stallone is responsible for the jingoistic story that makes child-killing sadists of the Russians (led by Marc de Jonge's near-hysterical Soviet colonel) who control a particular sector of Afghanistan. This is button-pushing, lowest-common-denominator filmmaking all the way. Rated R for extreme violence. 101m. **DIR:** Peter MacDonald. **CAST:** Sylvester Stallone, Richard Crenna, Marc de Jonge, Kurtwood Smith. **1988 DVD**

RAMBO: FIRST BLOOD II ★★★ This sequel to *First Blood* is an old-fashioned war movie. Its hero is larger than life, and the villains are pure mule-mean. In other words, it's an action fan's delight. Sylvester Stallone goes back to Vietnam to rescue American prisoners of war. Rated R. 94m. **DIR:** George Pan Cosmatos. **CAST:** Sylvester Stallone, Richard Crenna, Charles Napier, Steven Berkoff, Julia Nickson, Martin Kove. **1985 DVD**

RAMPAGE ★★ Based on the "vampire killings" committed by Richard Trenton Chase in Sacramento, California, in the late 1970s, writer-director William Friedkin's film sat on the shelf for more than five years—and probably should have stayed there. Rated R for violence and profanity. 97m. **DIR:** William Friedkin. **CAST:** Michael Biehn, Alex McArthur, Nicholas Campbell, Deborah Van Valkenburgh, John Harkins, Art La Fleur. **1992**

RAMPARTS OF CLAY ★★★★ Terse but hauntingly beautiful documentary-style film set against the harsh background of a poor North African village. A young woman (Leila Schenna) struggles to free herself from the second-class role imposed on her by the village culture, much as the village tries to liberate itself from subservience to the corporate powers that control its salt mines. In Arabic with English subtitles. Rated PG. 87m. **DIR:** Jean-Louis Bertucelli. **CAST:** Leila Schenna and the villagers of Tehouda, Algeria. **1970**

RAMROD ★★1/2 It's sheep versus cattle again in the Old West. Joel McCrea fights off Preston Foster's murderous cowhands and the increasingly amorous Veronica Lake. B&W; 94m. **DIR:** André de Toth. **CAST:** Veronica Lake, Joel McCrea, Ian McDonald, Charlie Ruggles, Preston Foster, Arleen Whelan, Lloyd Bridges, Donald Crisp. **1947**

RAN ★★★★★ This superb Japanese historical epic tells the story of a sixteenth-century warlord's time of tragedy. Based on Shakespeare's *King Lear*, this is yet another masterwork from Akira Kurosawa. It is stunningly photographed and acted, and blessed with touches of glorious humor and hair-raising battle sequences. In Japanese with English subtitles. Rated R for violence and suggested sex. 160m. **DIR:** Akira Kurosawa. **CAST:** Tatsuya Nakadai, Akira Terao. **1985 DVD**

RANCHO DELUXE ★★★ Two small-time cattle rustlers (Jeff Bridges, Sam Waterston) run afoul of lawmen almost as incompetent as they are. Raunchy but good-natured Western-comedy with slow stretches; look for country singer Jimmy Buffett in a small role. Rated R for nudity and profanity. 93m. **DIR:** Frank Perry. **CAST:** Jeff Bridges, Sam Waterston, Elizabeth Ashley, Clifton James, Slim Pickens, Harry Dean Stanton, Patti D'Arbanville. **1975**

RANCHO NOTORIOUS ★★★1/2 Brooding revenge Western is a curio of the 1950s, one of those films that appears to mean something more than what the action implies. This film, while not a great Western, is fun to watch and a treat for Marlene Dietrich fans. 89m. **DIR:** Fritz Lang. **CAST:** Marlene Dietrich, Arthur Kennedy, Mel Ferrer, Lloyd Gough, William Frawley, Gloria Henry, Jack Elam, George Reeves. **1952**

RANDOM HARVEST ★★★★ Ronald Colman and Greer Garson are at their best in this touching, tearful

story. A shell-shocked World War I veteran is saved from oblivion by the compassion of a music-hall entertainer. A stellar cast supports. B&W; 124m. **DIR:** Mervyn LeRoy. **CAST:** Ronald Colman, Greer Garson, Philip Dorn, Henry Travers, Reginald Owen. **1942**

RANDOM HEARTS ★★★ This one moves like molasses, despite director Sydney Pollack's intention to make another glossy, theatrical, star-driven, romantic melodrama in the mold of his *Out of Africa*. All the elements are in place: an environment of entitlement; Philippe Rousselot's gorgeous cinematography, which makes Washington, D.C., look much prettier than it deserves; and Dave Grusin's melancholy, languidly jazzy soundtrack. Yes, it's all nice to look at—as are Harrison Ford and Kristin Scott Thomas—but the pregnant pauses and tortured dialogue wear thin. Similarly, the notion that an Internal Affairs cop and a congresswoman would become an item, after being thrown together following the tragic deaths of their respective spouses (who were, themselves, having an affair), is too contrived for words. Needlessly rated R for violence, tasteful sensuality, and brief, completely gratuitous profanity. 132m. **DIR:** Sydney Pollack. **CAST:** Harrison Ford, Kristin Scott Thomas, Charles Dutton, Bonnie Hunt, Dennis Haysbert, Richard Jenkins, Paul Guilfoyle. **1999**

RANDY RIDES ALONE ★★★ John Wayne stars in this enjoyable B Western as a lawman who goes undercover to catch a gang that has been robbing an express office. The opening is particularly good. B&W; 60m. **DIR:** Henry Frazer. **CAST:** John Wayne, Alberta Vaughan, George "Gabby" Hayes, Earl Dwire, Yakima Canutt. **1934 DVD**

RANGE DEFENDERS ★★★ Cattlemen try to rid the range of sheep at all costs. The Three Mesquiteers settle the feud. Certainly nothing new, but well-done. B&W; 54m. **DIR:** Mack V. Wright. **CAST:** Robert Livingston, Ray "Crash" Corrigan, Max Terhune, Eleanor Stewart, Harry Woods. **1937**

RANGE FEUD ★★★★ It's *Romeo and Juliet* on the range as lawman Buck Jones tries to keep the peace between two feuding ranchers whose offspring have fallen in love. A gangly John Wayne does just fine as the youthful hero in another better-than-B Western from the great Buck Jones. B&W; 64m. **DIR:** D. Ross Lederman. **CAST:** Buck Jones, John Wayne, Susan Fleming, Harry Woods, Glenn Strange. **1931**

RANGE WAR ★★1/2 Hopalong Cassidy (William Boyd) rounds up a gang that is trying to stop construction on the railroad. Lesser entry in the Cassidy series. Britt Wood is no replacement for George "Gabby" Hayes or Andy Clyde, who was yet to come. B&W; 64m. **DIR:** Lesley Selander. **CAST:** William Boyd, Russell Hayden, Britt Wood. **1939**

RANGER AND THE LADY, THE ★★1/2 Buckskin-clad Roy Rogers is a Texas Ranger trying to clear up some trouble on the old Santa Fe Trail in the days before the Civil War. Fetching Jacqueline Wells plays the lady leading a wagon train to Texas. B&W; 59m. **DIR:** Joseph Kane. **CAST:** Roy Rogers, George "Gabby" Hayes, Jacqueline Wells, Harry Woods, Henry Brandon, Noble Johnson, Yakima Canutt, Art Dillard. **1940**

•**RANGERS** A movie so bad and so cheap you wonder if they had a budget for anything more than film developing. Matt McCoy heads up a special unit to rescue a ranger being held captive by terrorists after a botched mission. He should head up a special mission to destroy this botched attempt at action-adventure. Rated R for violence. 112m. **DIR:** Jim Wynorski. **CAST:** Corbin Bernsen, Matt McCoy, Glenn Plummer, Bean Miller, Dartanyan Edmonds, Rene Rivera. **2000 DVD**

RANMA 1/2 (TV SERIES) ★★★1/2 Despite a dubbed English soundtrack, the episodes are still quite entertaining. Ranma and his father, Genma, both avid martial-arts students, have fallen afoul of ancient curses that periodically change one into a young girl and the other into a giant panda. Another quirky series from Rumiko Takahashi (*Rumik World, Urusei Yatsura*). Dubbed in English. Not rated; contains some brief nudity. 50m. **DIR:** Tsutomu Shibayama. **1985–1987 DVD**

RANSOM (1977) ★★1/2 When a psycho begins killing people in a small town and refuses to stop until he receives a $4 million ransom, Stuart Whitman (the richest man in town) hires a mercenary (Oliver Reed) to kill the extortionist. There are some slow moments, but worse than these are the unanswered questions about why the murderer dresses like an American Indian and what his motive really is. Rated PG for violence. 90m. **DIR:** Richard Compton. **CAST:** Oliver Reed, Stuart Whitman, Deborah Raffin, John Ireland, Jim Mitchum, Paul Koslo. **1977**

RANSOM (1996) ★★★★ Gripping thriller casts Mel Gibson as a millionaire businessman whose son is kidnapped. Rather than leave it to the police, Gibson takes matters into his own hands. Plot twists abound as our hero finds he must match wits with the bad guys and the authorities. Although it invites some comparisons to *Death Wish*, this remake of the 1956 Glenn Ford film has a high gloss and believability. René Russo is topnotch as Gibson's concerned wife, and Gary Sinise is brilliant as a detective involved in the case. Rated R for profanity and violence. 120m. **DIR:** Ron Howard. **CAST:** Mel Gibson, René Russo, Gary Sinise, Delroy Lindo, Lili Taylor, Liev Schreiber, Evan Handler, Brawley Nolte, Dan Hedaya, Paul Guilfoyle. **1996 DVD**

RAPA NUI ★★ This primitive, loincloth film is set in seventeenth-century Easter Island. Two young bucks from rival clans compete for the hand of a maiden and the blessing of their gods by swimming to a nearby isle and fetching a bird egg. The film's *National Geographic* splendor and provocative historical speculation is crippled by laughable accents and dialogue and limp pacing. But love those crazy statues. Rated R for violence, nudity, and suggested sex. 107m. **DIR:** Kevin Reynolds. **CAST:** Jason Scott Lee, Sandrine Holt, Esai Morales. **1994**

RAPE AND MARRIAGE: THE RIDEOUT CASE ★★ Despite the dramatic potential of its story line and a strong cast, this fact-based TV drama—about the infamous 1978 husband-wife rape case in Oregon—falls far short of answering any questions about the issues. 96m. **DIR:** Peter Levin. **CAST:** Mickey Rourke, Rip Torn, Linda Hamilton, Eugene Roche, Gail Strickland, Conchata Ferrell. **1980**

RAPE OF LOVE (L'AMOUR VIOLÉ) ★★★★ A graphic rape scene may scare some viewers away from this French export, but that would be unfortunate. It is a telling account of one woman's quest to come to terms

with her tragic experience. In French with English subtitles. Not rated, but has graphic violence, nudity, and profanity. 111m. **DIR:** Yannick Bellon. **CAST:** Nathalie Nell, Alain Foures. **1979**

RAPE OF THE SABINES 🦃 Roger Moore plays Romulus, founder of Rome, in this cheesy Italian-French coproduction. 100m. **DIR:** Richard Pottier. **CAST:** Mylene Demongeot, Roger Moore. **1961**

RAPID FIRE ★★★1/2 Compact action film casts Brandon Lee as a college student who runs afoul of the mob. Lee shows his father Bruce's talent for incorporating comedy into the fist-and-foot action. This is definitely better than the average kung fu flick. Rated R for violence, simulated sex, and profanity. 95m. **DIR:** Dwight H. Little. **CAST:** Brandon Lee, Powers Boothe, Nick Mancuso, Raymond J. Barry. **1992**

RAPPACCINI'S DAUGHTER ★★★★1/2 This Nathaniel Hawthorne tale concerns a university student who accepts new lodgings overlooking a beautiful and mysterious garden. What follows is a particularly spellbinding tale of love and tragedy. Introduced by Henry Fonda; unrated and suitable for family viewing. 57m. **DIR:** Dezso Magyar. **CAST:** Kristoffer Tabori, Kathleen Beller, Michael Egan, Leonardo Cimino. **1980**

RAPPIN' ★★ Rap songs get the *Breakin'* treatment in this uninspired formula musical. Once again, a street performer (Mario Van Peebles) takes on the baddies and still has time to make it in show biz. Rated PG for profanity. 92m. **DIR:** Joel Silberg. **CAST:** Mario Van Peebles, Tasia Valenza, Charles Flohe. **1985**

RAPTURE, THE ★★★★ Mimi Rogers is riveting as a Los Angeles telephone operator who tires of mate-swapping and turns to a religious sect for spiritual guidance. Writer-director Michael Tolkin's bold approach to religious themes makes this tragic drama both a demanding and unforgettable experience. It's an amazing, disturbing story of squandered life, rebirth, and tested faith. Rated R for nudity and language. 102m. **DIR:** Michael Tolkin. **CAST:** Mimi Rogers, Kimberly Cullum, Patrick Bauchau. **1991**

RARE BREED, THE ★★★ This is a generally rewarding Western. Jimmy Stewart is a Texas cattle rancher who grudgingly assists an Englishwoman's (Maureen O'Hara) attempts to introduce a new line of short-horned cattle to the Texan range. The story is quite original and holds one's interest throughout. 108m. **DIR:** Andrew V. McLaglen. **CAST:** James Stewart, Maureen O'Hara, Brian Keith, Juliet Mills, Jack Elam, Ben Johnson. **1966**

RASCALS, THE ★★★ Two kids (Bernard Brieux and Thomas Chabrol) go through school together trying to beat the system. Taking place in the German-occupied France of 1942, the film deals with the coming-of-age themes we have seen many times. But the film's nationalistic subtext, which results in a triumphant ending, is, perhaps, a new one. In French with English subtitles. Rated R for sex and nudity. 93m. **DIR:** Bernard Revon. **CAST:** Bernard Brieux, Thomas Chabrol, Pascale Rocard. **1979**

RASHOMON ★★★★★ After a violent murder and rape is committed by a bandit, four people tell their own different versions of what happened. Set in medieval Japan, this examination of truth and guilt is charged with action. The combination of brilliant photography, stellar acting, direction, and script won this Japanese classic the Oscar for best foreign film. B&W; 83m. **DIR:** Akira Kurosawa. **CAST:** Toshiro Mifune, Machiko Kyo, Masayuki Mori. **1951 DVD**

RASPUTIN (1985) ★★★★ Controversial film that was suppressed by the Soviet Union for nearly a decade. Director Elem Klimov brilliantly captures the rise of the illiterate "prophet" who sparked the Russian Revolution. In Russian with English subtitles. Not rated but contains nudity and violence. 107m. **DIR:** Elem Klimov. **CAST:** Alexei Petrenko. **1985**

RASPUTIN (1996) ★★★ Despite its lavish production and strong cast, this is a routine, superficial study of the mad Russian monk who brought down a dynasty. Alan Rickman is well cast as the title character, but he's given little to do; Peter Pruce's script scarcely examines the supposed mystic. Instead, we're left with yet another chronicle of Nicholas and Alexandra's final days. It's a gripping story, but better told elsewhere. Rated R for violence and simulated sex. 105m. **DIR:** Uli Edel. **CAST:** Alan Rickman, Greta Scacchi, Ian McKellen, David Warner, John Wood, James Frain. **1996**

RASPUTIN AND THE EMPRESS ★★1/2 Lionel Barrymore portrays the mad monk Rasputin (he's badly miscast), and siblings Ethel (in her sound-film debut) and John costar in this overlong historical melodrama of court intrigue during the troubled reign of Nicholas and Alexandra in czarist Russia. B&W; 123m. **DIR:** Richard Boleslawski. **CAST:** John Barrymore, Ethel Barrymore, Lionel Barrymore, Ralph Morgan. **1932**

RASPUTIN: THE MAD MONK ★★★ Hammer brought the famous Russian pseudopriest to life with Christopher Lee in the starring role in this effective if highly inaccurate telling of the story. Historical changes aside, the film presents Rasputin as a hypnotic and darkly sexy man who manages to insinuate himself into the last of the Russian monarchy, thereby increasing his stature. 92m. **DIR:** Don Sharp. **CAST:** Christopher Lee, Barbara Shelley. **1966 DVD**

RAT PACK, THE ★★★ Although you'll get a strong sense of late 1950s bedroom and back-room politics, this fantasy-laced "biography" of Frank Sinatra and his entertainer cronies plays fast and loose with known facts. Don Cheadle has one magnificent scene, playing Sammy Davis Jr. "striking back" at the racist boors who objected to his marriage to a Swedish actress, and Joe Mantegna makes a wonderfully dour Dean Martin . . . but the rest aren't even close. Rated R for profanity, nudity, and simulated sex. 120m. **DIR:** Rob Cohen. **CAST:** Ray Liotta, Joe Mantegna, Don Cheadle, Angus MacFadyen, Zeljko Ivanek, William L. Petersen, Dan O'Herlihy, Veronica Cartwright, Bobby Slayton. **1998 DVD**

RAT PFINK A BOO BOO 🦃 A loose parody of *Batman*, it has everything a bad-movie lover could ever want. 72m. **DIR:** Ray Dennis Steckler. **CAST:** Vin Saxon, Carolyn Brandt. **1965**

•RAT RACE ★★★1/2 Although a blatant imitation of *It's a Mad, Mad, Mad, Mad World*, this energetic comedy is funny in its own right. Hoping to entertain his wealthiest high rollers, a casino tycoon sends six ordinary people on a no-holds-barred race from Las Vegas to a deserted New Mexico train station, where a locker holds $2 million for the winner. The breakneck pace ensures that one weak sight gag is quickly eclipsed by the

next five. The film gets much of its oomph from the hilariously earnest performances of Cuba Gooding Jr. and Jon Lovitz, but the strong ensemble cast is uniformly delightful. Rated PG-13 for profanity, sexual content, and crude humor. 112m. **DIR:** Jerry Zucker. **CAST:** Rowan Atkinson, Lanai Chapman, John Cleese, Whoopi Goldberg, Cuba Gooding Jr., Seth Green, Wayne Knight, Jon Lovitz, Breckin Meyer, Kathy Najimy, Amy Smart, Dave Thomas, Vince Vieluf. **2001 DVD**

RATBOY ★★ Not a horror film but a satirical allegory directed by and starring Sondra Locke. Eugene, a boy with the face of a rat, is torn out of his peaceful existence in a dump by an unemployed window dresser (Locke). With her two brothers, she sets out to market the "ratboy" as a media star. Rated PG-13 for profanity and some violence. 104m. **DIR:** Sondra Locke. **CAST:** Sondra Locke, Robert Townsend, Louie Anderson, Gerrit Graham, Christopher Hewett. **1986**

RATCATCHER ★★★ This relentlessly grim yet occasionally lyrical story about the misery, alienation, survival, sexual awakening, and dreams of a 12 year old boy is set in early 1970s Glasgow slums during a sanitation workers' strike. The lad drowns a neighborhood boy in a canal behind their apartments, becomes immersed in guilt, strikes up a relationship with an older lass, and fantasizes about sharing a new suburban home with his dysfunctional family. In thick Scottish accents with English subtitles. Not rated; contains profanity, violence, sex, and nudity. 105m. **DIR:** Lynne Ramsay. **CAST:** William Eadie, Leanne Mullen, Tommy Flanagan, Mandy Matthews, Lynne Ramsay Jr., Michelle Stewart. **2001**

RATED X ★★★ This made-for-cable treatment of the Mitchell brothers' story suffers from too little plot. Sure, the Mitchells were called the kings of porn, and their descent into drugs and other sordid entertainment *sounds* interesting, but the movie just moves from one scene to another without any sense of cohesion. Then again, you can't beat the acting intensity between real-life brothers Charlie Sheen and Emilio Estevez. Rated R for profanity, violence, nudity, and simulated sex. 115m. **DIR:** Emilio Estevez. **CAST:** Charlie Sheen, Emilio Estevez, Tracy Hutson, Megan Ward, Danielle Brett. **2000 DVD**

RATINGS GAME, THE ★★★★ Danny DeVito directs and leads an amiable cast in this comedy about a millionaire trying to break into the Hollywood scene with his rotten screenplays. When he falls in love with an employee from the Computron company (Rhea Perlman), they fix the TV ratings. Not rated, has profanity. 102m. **DIR:** Danny DeVito. **CAST:** Danny DeVito, Rhea Perlman, Gerrit Graham, Louis Giambalvo, Ronny Graham, Huntz Hall, Kevin McCarthy, John Megna, Michael Richards, Mark L. Taylor. **1984**

RATS Italian-made gore-a-thon set in the future after The Bomb has destroyed civilization. Dubbed in English. Not rated, but loaded with violence. 97m. **DIR:** Vincent Dawn. **CAST:** Richard Raymond, Alex McBride. **1983**

RATS ARE COMING! THE WEREWOLVES ARE HERE!, THE England is besieged by a pack of werewolves in the 1800s. Rated R. 92m. **DIR:** Andy Milligan. **CAST:** Hope Stansbury, Jackie Skarvellis. **1972**

RATTLE OF A SIMPLE MAN ★★★ One of the realistic, kitchen-sink dramas that were in vogue in England at the time, this resembles a British version of *Marty*. Middle-aged Percy, a virgin who lives with his mother, is goaded by his friends into a bet that he can't pick up and spend the night with an attractive waitress. In his attempt to do so, he finds love for the first time. B&W; 96m. **DIR:** Muriel Box. **CAST:** Harry H. Corbett, Diane Cilento, Michael Medwin. **1964**

RATTLED ★★1/2 Not for the ophiophobic, this made-for-cable original features rattlesnakes running amok in a small town, mediocre acting (on the humans' part, that is), dull dialogue, and laughable scenes in snake-o-vision. Rated PG-13 for violence. 90m. **DIR:** Tony Randel. **CAST:** William Katt, Shanna Reed, Ed Lauter, Bibi Besch. **1996**

RATTLER KID An unjustly accused army officer escapes prison and turns to a life of crime. Believing his own press clippings, he thinks of himself as a legendary outlaw. An unbelievable story line makes this one of the worst of the spaghetti Westerns. Not rated; contains violence. 87m. **DIR:** Leon Klimovsky. **CAST:** Richard Wyler, Brad Harris, Femi Benussi, William Spolt. **1968**

RAVAGE ★★★1/2 There is more excitement and action per square inch in this ultralow-budget flick than in any ten recent big-budget blockbusters. Director Ronnie Sortor's tale of a criminal psychologist who witnesses the murder of his family and then goes on a violent rampage is a tight, white-knuckle suspenser that will leave the viewer addicted right up to the end. Not rated; contains violence, gore, and profanity. 85m. **DIR:** Ronnie Sortor. **CAST:** Mark Brazaele, Dan Rowland, Dina Harris. **1996**

RAVAGER ★★ Cheesy special effects and bargain-basement sets get a workout in this familiar tale of a spaceship crew who unleash a biological weapon that infects them one at a time. Ho hum. Rated R for language and violence. 92m. **DIR:** James D. Deck. **CAST:** Bruce Payne, Yancy Butler, Salvator Xuereb, Juliet Landau. **1997**

RAVE REVIEW ★★★1/2 Outrageous antics ensue as a headstrong theatrical director bullies an influential critic to give him a good review. Instead, the director goes too far, and the critic ends up dead. Insightful humor and madcap lunacy make this little independent comedy a big winner in the laughs department. Rated PG-13 for adult language. 91m. **DIR:** Jeff Seymour. **CAST:** Ed Begley Jr., Leo Rossi, Joe Spano, James Handy. **1994**

RAVEN, THE (1935) ★★★★ Solid Universal Pictures horror-thriller casts Bela Lugosi as a mad scientist who is obsessed with the writings of Edgar Allan Poe. Boris Karloff is the hapless fugitive Lugosi deforms in order to carry out his evil schemes. Unlike many of the 1930s horror classics, this one has retained its suspense and drama. Available on a double-feature videocassette with *Black Cat*. B&W; 62m. **DIR:** Louis Friedlander. **CAST:** Boris Karloff, Bela Lugosi, Irene Ware, Lester Matthews, Samuel S. Hinds. **1935**

RAVEN, THE (1963) ★★★★ The best of the Roger Corman–directed Edgar Allan Poe adaptations, this release benefits from a humorous screenplay by Richard Matheson and tongue-in-cheek portrayals by Boris Karloff, Vincent Price, and Peter Lorre. Look for Jack

Nicholson in an early role as Lorre's son. 86m. **DIR:** Roger Corman. **CAST:** Boris Karloff, Vincent Price, Peter Lorre, Jack Nicholson, Hazel Court. **1963**

RAVEN (1997) 🦃 An ex-mercenary is hunted down by his former team leader, played by Burt Reynolds in a film so bad that he looks embarrassed to be in it. Rated R for violence, sexual situations, and profanity. 93m. **DIR:** Russell Solberg. **CAST:** Burt Reynolds, Matt Battaglia, Krista Allen. **1997 DVD**

RAVEN HAWK ★★★ Here's a switch: a reasonably intelligent action-thriller blessed with a strong and credible female protagonist. If star Rachel McLish were a better actress, we'd be all set. She plays an American Indian, falsely accused of having killed her parents, who escapes from prison and pursues the men actually responsible for the heinous deed. While hardly in Tony Hillerman's league, scripter Kevin Elders successfully mixes this unfamiliar culture with standard heroics. Rated R for nudity, profanity, rape, and violence. 87m. **DIR:** Albert Pyun. **CAST:** Rachel McLish, John Enos, Ed Lauter, Matt Clark, William Atherton, John de Lancie. **1995**

RAVEN TENGU KABUTO ★★★1/2 High-tech gadgetry meets samurai sword in this animated video entry as Japanese mythology is blended skillfully with dark science fiction. Kabuto, the wandering swordsman, matches his sword and mystic arts against an evil sorceress. In Japanese with English subtitles. Not rated, with violence and nudity. 45m. **DIR:** Buichi Terasawa. **1992**

RAVENOUS ★★1/2 United States soldiers at a remote outpost in 1840s California are menaced by a madman who thrives on human flesh. Despite some pretentious speechifying about history and Manifest Destiny (about which writer Ted Griffin seems to know very little), this is really just a supernatural slasher movie dressed up with high-caliber actors who deserve better. Rated R for violence and gore. 100m. **DIR:** Antonia Bird. **CAST:** Guy Pearce, Robert Carlyle, Jeffrey Jones, Jeremy Davies, David Arquette. **1999 DVD**

RAVISHING IDIOT, THE 🦃 Thin plot concerns a spy out to steal NATO plans of ship movements. B&W; 110m. **DIR:** Edouard Molinaro. **CAST:** Anthony Perkins, Brigitte Bardot. **1965**

RAW COURAGE ★★★★ Three cross-country runners must fend for themselves when they run into a group of weekend warriors in the Colorado desert lands. Ronny Cox is excellent as one of the runners. However, Cox, who wrote the screenplay, has taken a few too many pages from James Dickey's *Deliverance*. Still, *Raw Courage* has enough white-knuckle moments to make you forget about the lack of originality. Rated R for violence and profanity. 90m. **DIR:** Robert L. Rosen. **CAST:** Ronny Cox, Tim Maier, Art Hindle, M. Emmet Walsh, William Russ, Lisa Sutton, Lois Chiles. **1983**

RAW DEAL ★★★1/2 Big Arnold Schwarzenegger stars in this fast-paced action film as a former FBI agent who is recruited by his former boss (Darren McGavin) to infiltrate the Chicago mob as an act of revenge. It's predictable, even formula. But the formula works. Rated R for profanity and violence. 107m. **DIR:** John Irvin. **CAST:** Arnold Schwarzenegger, Kathryn Harrold, Darren McGavin, Sam Wanamaker, Paul Shenar, Steven Hill, Joe Regalbuto, Ed Lauter, Robert Davi. **1986 DVD**

RAW JUSTICE ★★ Caught in the crossfire of a conspiracy, dogged bounty hunter David Keith teams up with a wrongfully accused man and a hapless prostitute. While entertaining, this one can't quite decide whether it's a spoof or just a tremendous waste of talent. Rated R for violence and nudity. 92m. **DIR:** David A. Prior. **CAST:** David Keith, Robert Hays, Pamela Anderson. **1993 DVD**

RAW MEAT ★★★ Stylish British horror film about a race of cannibals living under the subway system. An atmosphere of dread is maintained throughout as the underground dwellers make occasional trips to the surface for food and mates. Rated R for violence, profanity, and gore. 87m. **DIR:** Gary A. Sherman. **CAST:** Donald Pleasence, Christopher Lee, Clive Swift. **1973**

RAW NERVE ★★1/2 A race car driver suddenly finds himself psychically connected with a killer. Better-than-average thriller utilizes best elements of the exploitation genre to its advantage. Rated R for violence and nudity. 91m. **DIR:** David A. Prior. **CAST:** Glenn Ford, Traci Lords, Ted Prior, Sandahl Bergman, Jan-Michael Vincent. **1991**

RAW TARGET 🦃 Kick-boxing champion goes undercover for the police as a gang member and learns the leader was responsible for his brother's death. Obviously the filmmakers have never seen another kick-boxing movie before. Rated R for language and violence. 92m. **DIR:** Tim Spring. **CAST:** Dale "Apollo" Cook, Ron Hall, Mychelle Charters, Nicholas Hill. **1996**

RAWHEAD REX ★★1/2 A satanic demon is accidentally unearthed and begins to wreak havoc on a small village in Ireland. The acting and script are both low caliber, but worth watching if you like raunch. Rated R for profanity, nudity, and plenty-o'-gore. 89m. **DIR:** George Pavlou. **CAST:** David Dukes, Kelly Piper, Niall Toibin. **1986 DVD**

RAWHIDE (1938) ★★ Lou Gehrig in a Western? Yes, the Pride of the Yankees made one sagebrush adventure in support of former bandleader Smith Ballew. Gehrig plays a rancher at constant odds with the badmen and Ballew plays the two-fisted young lawyer who helps to organize the honest folk. Ballew is a rather bland lead, but the presence of Gehrig makes this one worth a watch. B&W; 58m. **DIR:** Ray Taylor. **CAST:** Smith Ballew, Lou Gehrig, Lafe McKee, Evalyn Knapp. **1938**

RAWHIDE (1951) ★★★ Sturdy Western concerns an outlaw gang holding hostages at a remote stagecoach station. Veteran director Henry Hathaway knows how to keep things clicking right along; the final shoot-out is electrifying. A good cast keeps this one on target. 86m. **DIR:** Henry Hathaway. **CAST:** Tyrone Power, Susan Hayward, Dean Jagger, Hugh Marlowe, Jack Elam, Edgar Buchanan, Jeff Corey, George Tobias. **1951**

RAWHIDE (TV SERIES) ★★★★ One of TV's best written and directed Western series. The theme of the show was the long cattle drive from Texas to Kansas, but it was the wide variety of people that trail boss Gil Favor and his drovers encountered along the way that gave the series its momentum. B&W; **DIR:** Charles Marquis Warren. **CAST:** Eric Fleming, Clint Eastwood, Sheb Wooley, Paul Brinegar. **1959–1966**

RAY BRADBURY'S CHRONICLES: THE MARTIAN EPISODES ★★★1/2 Although produced with minimal budgets, these five installments of TV's *Ray Bradbury*

Theater are infinitely superior to the network-television's miniseries versions. Credit Bradbury himself, whose adaptations retain the pathos and poetic impact that have made his tales classics. "Mars Is Heaven" remains the best known, but "The Martian" is by far the best piece, featuring an alien willing to kill itself to please the strangers who've settled its native planet. The tape also includes "The Concrete Mixer," "And the Moon Be Still as Bright," and "The Earthmen." 112m. **DIR:** Various. **CAST:** Hal Linden, Ben Cross, John Vernon, Sheila Moore, David Carradine, David Birney. **1989–1990**

RAY CHARLES: THE GENIUS OF SOUL ★★★★★ Superb made-for-TV documentary about Ray Charles's personal life and his music—which weds gospel, jazz, and blues to create soul music. Through narration and interviews writer-director Yvonne Smith gives viewers an uncompromising, in-depth and well-rounded look at a complex, brilliant man. David "Fathead" Newman, Dr. John, Hank Crawford, Billy Joel, Willie Nelson, and Billy Preston are among those interviewed. 60m. **DIR:** Yvonne Smith. **1991**

RAZOR BLADE SMILE ★★ Director-writer Jake West seems more concerned with style over substance in this anemic tale of a female vampire who works as a contract killer. The visual flourishes are exciting, but not enough to keep the story from drying up. Rated R for violence, language, and nudity. 101m. **DIR:** Jake West. **CAST:** Eileen Daly, Christopher Adamson, Jonathon Coote, Kevin Howarth. **1998 DVD**

RAZOR, THE: SWORD OF JUSTICE ★★★1/2 If you liked the Japanese *Lone Wolf and Cub* movies, be sure to check out this, the first film in a similar series. *The Razor* is a nineteenth-century Tokyo policeman who battles injustice on both sides of the law. Sort of a Samurai Dirty Harry but much meaner (and sexier, too). Not rated; the film contains strong violence, nudity, and sexual situations. In Japanese with English subtitles. 90m. **DIR:** Misumi Kenji. **CAST:** Katsu Shintaro, Asaoka Yukiji. **1972**

RAZORBACK ★★★1/2 This Australian film, concerning a giant pig that is terrorizing a small Aussie village, surprises the viewer by turning into a great little film. The special effects, photography, editing, and acting are great. Rated R. 95m. **DIR:** Russell Mulcahy. **CAST:** Gregory Harrison. **1983**

RAZOR'S EDGE, THE (1946) ★★★★1/2 A long but engrossing presentation of Somerset Maugham's philosophical novel about a young man seeking the goodness in life. Full of memorable characterizations and scenes. Herbert Marshall steers the plot, playing the author. B&W; 146m. **DIR:** Edmund Goulding. **CAST:** Tyrone Power, Gene Tierney, Clifton Webb, Herbert Marshall, Anne Baxter, John Payne, Elsa Lanchester. **1946**

RAZOR'S EDGE, THE (1984) ★★★1/2 Bill Murray gives a finely balanced comic and dramatic portrayal as a man searching for meaning after World War I in this adaptation of W. Somerset Maugham's novel. The result is a richly rewarding film, which survives the unevenness of John Byrum's direction. Rated PG-13 for suggested sex, violence, and profanity. 128m. **DIR:** John Byrum. **CAST:** Bill Murray, Theresa Russell, Catharine Hicks, James Keach, Brian Doyle-Murray. **1984**

RE-ANIMATOR ★★★★ Stylishly grotesque and gory filming of H. P. Lovecraft's "Herbert West, Reanimator" hits the mark. This is Grand Guignol in the classic sense as we follow brilliant young medical student Herbert West in his deranged efforts to bring the dead back to life. Some outrageous scenes highlight this terror entry and, although very well-done, it's not for the squeamish. 86m. **DIR:** Stuart Gordon. **CAST:** Bruce Abbott, Barbara Crampton, David Gale, Robert Sampson, Jeffrey Combs. **1985 DVD**

RE-BIRTH OF MOTHRA II ★★★ Mothra and three young humans must uncover a mysterious treasure in order to stop an evil woman from taking over Earth. Superior special effects and vivid cinematography set this chapter apart from the others, as does its even more kid-friendly tone. Not rated. 110m. **DIR:** Kunio Miyoshi. **CAST:** Megumi Kobayashi, Sayaka Yamaguchi, Aki Hano. **1997 DVD**

REACH THE ROCK ★★ The preposterous script by John Hughes is filled with clichéd characters and outrageous plot development in this tale of a tough kid squaring off against an equally tough cop. Rated R for language and violence. 100m. **DIR:** William Ryan. **CAST:** Bill Sadler, Alessandro Nivola, Bruce Norris, Karen Sillas, Norman Reedus. **1998**

REACHING FOR THE MOON (1917) ★★★ One of several products of the Douglas Fairbanks/Anita Loos/John Emerson triumvirate. Lots of brash, physical comedy and stunts in the early Fairbanks manner. Silent. B&W; 91m. **DIR:** John Emerson. **CAST:** Douglas Fairbanks Sr., Eileen Percy. **1917**

REACHING FOR THE MOON (1931) ★★★ Robust and energetic Douglas Fairbanks plays a financier on whom liquor has an interesting effect. Edward Everett Horton is his valet and Bebe Daniels is the girl. B&W; 62m. **DIR:** Edmund Goulding. **CAST:** Douglas Fairbanks Sr., Bebe Daniels, Edward Everett Horton. **1931**

READY TO RUMBLE ★★ Two dimwit fans of professional wrestling set out to save the career of their favorite wrestler. There is a smattering of cheap laughs here and there, but generally the film is just as doltish and dull as the two heroes. The best moments belong to a gleeful Martin Landau as a famous old wrestling coach. Rated PG-13 for mild profanity and wrestling violence. 100m. **DIR:** Brian Robbins. **CAST:** David Arquette, Oliver Platt, Scott Caan, Rose McGowan, Diamond Dallas Page, Joe Pantoliano, Martin Landau. **2000 DVD**

READY TO WEAR ★★★1/2 A murder-mystery plot loosely ties together the various goings-on in this irreverent and episodic study of the fashion scene. The results are not for all tastes. Indeed, the superficiality of the on-screen events seems to be a sort of commentary on the inflated self-importance of the players in the fashion world. Rated R for profanity, nudity, and scatological humor. 132m. **DIR:** Robert Altman. **CAST:** Sophia Loren, Marcello Mastroianni, Julia Roberts, Tim Robbins, Kim Basinger, Stephen Rea, Anouk Aimée, Lauren Bacall, Lili Taylor, Sally Kellerman, Linda Hunt, Tracey Ullman, Rupert Everett, Forest Whittaker, Richard E. Grant, Danny Aiello, Teri Garr, Lyle Lovett, Cher, Jean Rochefort, Michel Blanc, Jean-Pierre Cassel. **1994 DVD**

REAL AMERICAN HERO, THE ★★ Below-average TV movie does not do justice to slain sheriff Buford Pusser. Brian Dennehy plays Pusser, a frustrated law enforcer who will do anything—even risk his own life—to get the bad guys. Ken Howard plays a ruthless bar owner. *Walking Tall* says it all better. Not rated; contains profanity and violence. 94m. **DIR:** Lou Antonio. **CAST:** Brian Dennehy, Forrest Tucker, Brian Kerwin, Ken Howard, Sheree North. **1978 DVD**

REAL BLONDE, THE ★★★1/2 Image and appearance make the world go 'round in this lively satire of 1990s relationships and America's fixation with glamour. This clever adult comedy tracks the overlapping personal and professional lives of several stubbornly foolish characters who try to survive their own obsessions and mistakes in trendy Manhattan. Rated R for sexual content and language. 105m. **DIR:** Tom DiCillo. **CAST:** Matthew Modine, Catherine Keener, Maxwell Caulfield, Daryl Hannah, Elizabeth Berkeley, Marlo Thomas. **1998 DVD**

REAL GENIUS ★★★ This is a mildly amusing comedy about a group of science prodigies (led by Val Kilmer) who decide to thwart the plans of their egomaniacal mentor (William Atherton). Director Martha Coolidge does her best to keep things interesting, but she can't overcome the predictability of the climax. Rated PG for profanity. 105m. **DIR:** Martha Coolidge. **CAST:** Val Kilmer, Gabe Jarret, Michelle Meyrink, William Atherton, Ed Lauter. **1985**

REAL GLORY, THE ★★★★ After the American army pulls out of the Philippines in 1910, it's left to a small band of professional soldiers to equip and train the natives to fight off a pirate-like tribe of cutthroats. This lesser-known adventure film ranks alongside *Beau Geste* and *The Lives of a Bengal Lancer* as one of Gary Cooper's best in the genre. B&W; 109m. **DIR:** Henry Hathaway. **CAST:** Gary Cooper, Andrea Leeds, David Niven, Reginald Owen, Broderick Crawford. **1939**

REAL HOWARD SPRITZ, THE ★★★★ Delightful family tale about a detective novelist who can't find a publisher for his latest hard-boiled epic. With the help of a little girl, he develops a series of books for children that becomes the cat's meow. Quaint, charming picture with a delightful performance by Kelsey Grammer. Rated PG. 93m. **DIR:** Vadim Jean. **CAST:** Kelsey Grammer, Amanda Donohoe, Genevieve Tessier. **1998**

REAL LIFE ★★★ Albert Brooks's fans will eat up this tasty satire parodying an unrelenting PBS series that put the day-to-day life of an American family under the microscope. In Brooks's film the typical family comes hilariously unglued under the omnipresent eye of the camera. The script (written by Brooks) eventually falters, but not before a healthy number of intelligent laughs are produced. Rated PG. 99m. **DIR:** Albert Brooks. **CAST:** Albert Brooks, Charles Grodin, Frances Lee McCain, J. A. Preston. **1979**

REAL MCCOY, THE ★★ Kim Basinger plays an ace safecracker, trying to go straight, who is blackmailed into one last heist by her former boss. Except for the gender switch on the protagonist, the premise is old hat. Still, with the actors on hand, it could have been better if there had been a few surprises in the script or any suspense in the direction. Rated PG-13 for violence and profanity. 104m. **DIR:** Russell Mulcahy. **CAST:** Kim Basinger, Val Kilmer, Terence Stamp, Gailard Sartain. **1993 DVD**

REAL MEN ★★★ This action-filled comedy features James Belushi as an infallible Bond-like CIA agent. His latest mission is to protect his wimpish new partner (John Ritter) and make contact with powerful aliens. Rated PG-13 for profanity, violence, and brief nudity. 86m. **DIR:** Dennis Feldman. **CAST:** James Belushi, John Ritter, Bill Morey, Gail Barl, Barbara Barrie. **1987**

REAL THING, THE ★★★1/2 Riveting crime-drama about an ex-con who agrees to carry out his brother's plans to rob a popular nightclub in New York on New Year's Eve. He faces a big problem when another gang decides to hit the nightclub at the same time. Better-than-average results for this direct-to-video effort that features memorable characters and vicious violence. Rated R for language and violence. 89m. **DIR:** James Merendino. **CAST:** James Russo, Emily Lloyd, Gary Busey, Rod Steiger, Jeremy Piven, Max Perlich. **1996**

REALITY BITES ★★★1/2 This mordantly amusing, often tragic drama is the first to speak for the Generation X'ers. College valedictorian Winona Ryder vacillates between financially successful dropout Ben Stiller and philosophical Ethan Hawke, who coasts through life. The film's video verité cinematography is the perfect statement for the MTV generation. Rated PG-13 for profanity, drug use, and sexual frankness. 99m. **DIR:** Ben Stiller. **CAST:** Winona Ryder, Ethan Hawke, Ben Stiller, Janeane Garofalo, Steve Zahn. **1994 DVD**

REALLY WEIRD TALES ★★★ These three short stories produced for HBO have their moments. Martin Short plays a hack lounge singer at a playboy's swank party in "All's Well That Ends Strange." "Cursed with Charisma" features John Candy as a successful hustler. The last story, featuring Catherine O'Hara, is the best. "I'll Die Loving" is about a woman who is cursed with the odd power of loving people to death. Not rated, has profanity. 85m. **DIR:** Paul Lynch, Don McBrearty, John Blanchard. **CAST:** Joe Flaherty, John Candy, Catherine O'Hara, Martin Short, Dan Harron, Olivia D'Abo, Sheila McCarthy. **1986**

REAP THE WILD WIND ★★★1/2 Bawdy tale of the shipping and salvage business off the coast of Georgia during the early nineteenth century. John Wayne is a robust sea captain and Ray Milland is a well-to-do owner of a shipping company. Plenty of old-fashioned action and humor with the typical Cecil B. DeMille touches. Entire cast is first-rate, especially the villainous Raymond Massey. The final underwater action scenes are classics. 124m. **DIR:** Cecil B. DeMille. **CAST:** John Wayne, Ray Milland, Raymond Massey, Paulette Goddard, Robert Preston, Charles Bickford, Susan Hayward. **1942 DVD**

REAR WINDOW (1954) ★★★★★ James Stewart plays a magazine photographer who, confined to a wheelchair because of a broken leg, seeks diversion in watching his neighbors, often with a telephoto lens. He soon becomes convinced that one neighbor (Raymond Burr) has murdered his spouse and dismembered the body. One of the director's best. 112m. **DIR:** Alfred Hitchcock. **CAST:** James Stewart, Raymond Burr, Grace Kelly, Wendell Corey, Thelma Ritter, Judith Evelyn. **1954 DVD**

REAR WINDOW (1998)★★★ A man confined to a wheelchair spies on his neighbors and thinks he over-

hears a murder. This two-dimensional remake of Alfred Hitchcock's classic acts more as a showcase of Christopher Reeve's new life as a disabled person than as a character study. Reeve can still act reasonably well, and the story is suspenseful in its updated version, but it lacks the multitude of stories that made the original so compelling. Rated PG for mild violence. 89m. **DIR:** Jeff Bleckner. **CAST:** Christopher Reeve, Daryl Hannah, Ruben Santiago Hudson, Anne Twomey, Robert Forster. **1998**

REASON TO BELIEVE, A ★★★ Though somewhat simplistic, this unflinching tale of date rape paints a sadly accurate portrayal of college life. The assault of a popular young woman during a frat party brings out the worst in everyone around her. Friends don't believe her, strangers scream at her, and media-hungry feminists claim her as their poster child. Rated R for violence, sexual situations, and profanity. 108m. **DIR:** Douglas Tirola. **CAST:** Jay Underwood, Allison Smith, Daniel Quinn, Georgia Emelin, Kim Walker, Keith Coogan, Christopher Birt, Holly Marie Combs, Obba Babatundé. **1995**

REASON TO DIE ★★ A razor fiend is tracked by a bounty hunter, after a series of erotic slicings. Typical slasher, though at least high-voltage actor Wings Hauser is the protagonist. Not rated. 96m. **DIR:** Tim Spring. **CAST:** Wings Hauser. **1989**

REASONS OF THE HEART ★★★1/2 This sometimes predictable, sometimes surprising made-for-cable original is about a woman who visits a small town to woo a reclusive writer back into publishing, and to search for the secret of her own past. Solid, but not spectacular, performances by Terry Farrell and Jim Davidson; the story is what really keeps you watching. Not rated. 95m. **DIR:** Rick Jacobson. **CAST:** Terry Farrell, Jim Davidson. **1996**

REBECCA ★★★★★ *Rebecca* won an Oscar for best picture and nominations for its stars, Laurence Olivier and Joan Fontaine. The popular Daphne du Maurier novel was transferred to the screen without losing any of its gothic blend of romance and mystery. Judith Anderson as the sinister housekeeper is one of the most compelling figures in film history. B&W; 130m. **DIR:** Alfred Hitchcock. **CAST:** Laurence Olivier, Joan Fontaine, George Sanders, Nigel Bruce, Reginald Denny, Judith Anderson. **1940 DVD**

REBECCA OF SUNNYBROOK FARM (1917) ★★1/2 Once again, the adult Mary Pickford successfully portrays a saucy teenager who wins love, respect, and prosperity in this rags-to-riches tearjerker based on the famous Kate Douglas Wiggin bestseller. Shirley Temple starred in a talkie version in 1938. Silent. B&W; 77m. **DIR:** Marshall Neilan. **CAST:** Mary Pickford, Eugene O'Brien, Helen Jerome Eddy. **1917**

REBECCA OF SUNNYBROOK FARM (1938) ★★★1/2 Lightweight but engaging Shirley Temple vehicle has the 1930s superstar playing a child performer who wants to be on radio. While Temple hoofs with the likes of Jack Haley and Bill "Bojangles" Robinson, Randolph Scott, in one of his few screen appearances out of the saddle, romances Gloria Stuart. B&W; 80m. **DIR:** Allan Dwan. **CAST:** Shirley Temple, Randolph Scott, Jack Haley, Gloria Stuart, Phyllis Brooks, Helen Westley, Slim Summerville, Bill Robinson. **1938**

REBECCA'S SECRET 🦃 Awful rip-off of *Diabolique* in which the filmmakers were apparently so busy auditioning naked women they didn't take time to make sense of the plot. Rated R for nudity and sex. 84m. **DIR:** Ellyn Michaels. **CAST:** Amy Rochelle, Lauren Hays, Michael Baci. **1997 DVD**

REBEL (1973) ★★ This early Sylvester Stallone movie casts him as a student radical who begins to ponder his future. This low-budget production only proves that Stallone started out mumbling. It is unrated. 80m. **DIR:** Robert Schnitzer. **CAST:** Sylvester Stallone, Anthony Page, Henry G. Sanders. **1973**

REBEL (1985) 🦃 During World War II, a Marine sergeant in Australia goes AWOL and falls in love with a nightclub singer. Rated R for profanity. 93m. **DIR:** Michael Jenkins. **CAST:** Matt Dillon, Debbie Byrne, Bryan Brown, Bill Hunter, Ray Barrett. **1985**

REBEL LOVE 🦃 Yankee widow falls in love with a Confederate spy. Not rated; there is some mild sexual content. 84m. **DIR:** Milton Bagby Jr. **CAST:** Jamie Rose, Terence Knox, Fran Ryan, Charles Hill. **1986**

REBEL ROUSERS ★★ This drive-in biker film from the late 1960s would barely rate a second look if it weren't for a crop of future big-name stars and character performers who inhabit it. The ill-mannered-youth-on-motorcycles-versus-uptight-establishment-straights story takes a backseat to flamboyant characterizations in this one. 78m. **DIR:** Martin B. Cohen. **CAST:** Cameron Mitchell, Jack Nicholson, Bruce Dern, Diane Ladd, Harry Dean Stanton. **1967 DVD**

REBEL STORM ★★1/2 Mildly diverting futuristic thriller about a group of freedom fighters attempting to overthrow a suppressive government. 99m. **DIR:** Franky Schaeffer. **CAST:** Zach Galligan, Wayne Crawford, June Chadwick, John Rhys-Davies. **1990**

REBEL WITHOUT A CAUSE ★★★★★ This is the film that made James Dean a legend. Directed by Nicholas Ray, it is undoubtedly the classic film about juvenile delinquency. Featuring fine performances by Dean, Natalie Wood, and Sal Mineo as the teens in trouble, it has stood up surprisingly well over the years. 111m. **DIR:** Nicholas Ray. **CAST:** James Dean, Natalie Wood, Sal Mineo, Jim Backus, Ann Doran, Corey Allen, Edward Platt, Dennis Hopper, Nick Adams. **1955 DVD**

REBELS, THE ★★★ The second of John Jakes's bicentennial bestsellers to be converted into a TV miniseries, this is a step up from *The Bastard*. Much of the sleaze has been replaced with swashbuckling adventure thanks to Don Johnson and Doug McClure's contributions. Using America's history from 1775 to 1781 as a background, this allows us to experience the eventual triumph of our Continental army. 190m. **DIR:** Russ Mayberry. **CAST:** Andrew Stevens, Don Johnson, Doug McClure, Joan Blondell, Tanya Tucker. **1979**

REBOUND ★★★★ This is the true story of Earl "The Goat" Manigault, who was, according to such greats as Wilt Chamberlain and Kareem Abdul-Jabbar, the best basketball player who never made it to the NBA. A series of misfortunes, then a rapid descent into drug abuse, left "The Goat" without a future. This made-for-cable original is well acted and poignant. Not rated; contains profanity and violence. 111m. **DIR:** Eriq La Salle. **CAST:** Don Cheadle, James Earl Jones, Clarence Williams, III, Eriq La Salle, Forest Whitaker. **1996**

RECESS: SCHOOL'S OUT ★★★1/2 Finally: American animation with attitude and sophistication! This expan-

sion of the top-rated Saturday-morning show infuses fourth-grade melodrama with humor that adults can also appreciate. Here, TJ and his pals attempt to save the ultimate recess, summer vacation, from a renegade principal. Among the many celebrities giving voice to the characters are Dabney Coleman, Robert Stack, Robert Goulet, Melissa Joan Hart, and James Woods. Rated G. 83m. **DIR:** Chuck Sheetz. **2001 DVD**

RECKLESS (1935) ★★ Jean Harlow, terribly miscast as a Broadway musical star, marries troubled alcoholic playboy Franchot Tone, who feels she entrapped him and heads downhill toward suicide. William Powell stands by until needed. B&W; 97m. **DIR:** Victor Fleming. **CAST:** Jean Harlow, William Powell, Franchot Tone, May Robson, Rosalind Russell, Mickey Rooney. **1935**

RECKLESS (1984) ★★ A 1980s version of the standard 1950s "angry young man" movie, this features Aidan Quinn as a motorcycle-riding, mumbling (à la James Dean and Marlon Brando) outcast and Daryl Hannah as the "good girl." That should give you an idea of how original this movie is. Rated R for nudity, profanity, violence, and suggested sex. 90m. **DIR:** James Foley. **CAST:** Aidan Quinn, Daryl Hannah, Kenneth McMillan, Cliff De Young, Lois Smith, Adam Baldwin, Dan Hedaya. **1984**

RECKLESS (1995) ★★★1/2 A happily married housewife discovers on Christmas Eve that her husband has plotted her murder and the film chronicles her picaresque adventures as she flees from the hired killer. Offbeat and unpredictable, this has its own weird charm and plenty of surprises; the biggest surprise of all, ultimately, is how genuinely touching it is by the time it's over. Rated PG-13 for mild profanity and seriocomic violence. 92m. **DIR:** Norman René. **CAST:** Mia Farrow, Scott Glenn, Mary-Louise Parker, Tony Goldwyn, Eileen Brennan, Stephen Dorff. **1995**

RECKLESS KELLY ★★1/2 Australian comic Yahoo Serious returns in a spoof of the career of outlaw Ned Kelly, Australia's answer to Jesse James. Serious is an engaging performer, and the film is fast-paced, with bright, carnival-colored wide-screen photography (which will suffer on video). High-spirited and likable, it's just not funny. Rated PG. 80m. **DIR:** Yahoo Serious. **CAST:** Yahoo Serious, Melora Hardin, Alexei Sayle, Hugo Weaving, Kathleen Freeman. **1994**

RECORD OF LODOSS WAR ★★★★ Sprawling six-volume anime adapting a popular novel and comic-book series, *Record of Lodoss War* is an amazing achievement in animated fantasy. From the distinctive art style to the complex and epic plot, this film will have fantasy fans cheering. A young boy named Parn dreams of becoming a knight like his father and soon gets his chance as he is drawn into a struggle between kingdoms for control of the continent. Not rated; contains violence. 55m. **DIR:** Akinori Nagaoka, Shigeto Makino, Taiji Ryu, Kazunori Mizuno, Akio Sakai, Hiroshi Kawasaki. **1990–1991 DVD**

RECORD OF LODOSS WAR: CHRONICLES OF THE HEROIC KNIGHT ★★★★1/2 Five years after the events of the first film, the adventurers unite to save their homeland from invading forces. This time they are joined by new friends who must carve out their own place in history. Where the first *Record of Lodoss War* was a fine achievement, this is an awe-inspiring masterpiece of fantasy animation. Everything about the film—from the art to the story to the music—clicks. The only quibble one could have is the short child-oriented segment at the end of each volume, which detracts from the lush fantasy preceding. Not rated; contains violence and some scenes too scary for tots. 90m. **DIR:** Yoshihiro Takamoto. **1998 DVD**

RECRUITS A sheriff hires hookers, thieves, and bums as deputies. Rated R. 90m. **DIR:** Rafal Zielinski. **CAST:** Alan Deveau, Annie McAuley. **1987**

RECTOR'S WIFE, THE ★★★★★ A subtle tale of duty and domination, this four-episode British production is based on the novel by Joanna Trollope. A vicar's wife in a small English parish finds she is disappearing under her title. As she slowly steps out of the rector's shadow, this mousy facilitator finds herself on a path of liberation, romance, and intrigue. Not rated. 52m. **DIR:** Giles Foster. **CAST:** Lindsay Duncan, Ronald Pickup, Jonathan Coy, Prunella Scales, Stephen Dillane. **1993**

RED ★★★1/2 Polish filmmaker Krzysztof Kieslowski concludes his *Three Colors* trilogy by examining the wary friendship that develops between a young fashion model and a retired judge who has become a voyeur in his old age. The film is slow-moving but fascinating, and its beautiful images linger in the mind. In French with English subtitles. Rated R for nudity and simulated sex. 99m. **DIR:** Krzysztof Kieslowski. **CAST:** Irène Jacob, Jean-Louis Trintignant, Frederique Feder, Jean-Pierre Lorit. **1994**

RED ALERT ★★★1/2 This 1977 made-for-TV film about a nuclear power plant is just as timely today as when it first aired. An incident at the plant has killed fourteen workers. Was it an accident, sabotage, or computer fault? A fine cast lends an air of reality and immediacy to this gripping mystery. 95m. **DIR:** William Hale. **CAST:** William Devane, Michael Brandon, Ralph Waite, Adrienne Barbeau, David Hayward, M. Emmet Walsh, Don Wiseman. **1977**

RED AND THE WHITE, THE ★★★★ Hungarian director Miklos Jancso creates a bleak and startling film of the senseless slaughter and sheer absurdity of war. The film depicts the bloody encounters between Russia's Bolshevik Red Army and the counterrevolutionary forces in central Russia during the Civil War of 1918. In Russian with English subtitles. 92m. **DIR:** Miklos Jancso. **CAST:** Tibor Molnar, Andreas Kozak, Josef Madaras. **1968 DVD**

RED BADGE OF COURAGE, THE ★★★1/2 Natural performances mark this realistic treatment of Stephen Crane's famous Civil War novel of a young soldier's initiation to battle. A John Huston classic, and a major film achievement by any standard. B&W; 69m. **DIR:** John Huston. **CAST:** Audie Murphy, Bill Mauldin, Royal Dano, Arthur Hunnicutt, Douglas Dick. **1951**

RED BALLOON, THE ★★★★★ This fanciful, endearing tale of a giant balloon that befriends a small boy in Paris is a delight for children and adults alike. Outside of a catchable word or two here and there, the film is without dialogue. The story is crystal clear in the visual telling, punctuated by an engaging musical score. 34m. **DIR:** Albert Lamorisse. **CAST:** Pascal Lamorisse, Georges Sellier. **1956**

RED BARRY ★★1/2 Serial superstar Buster Crabbe plays comic-strip sleuth Red Barry in this decent chapterplay. It seems some scurrilous spies have stolen $2

million in negotiable bonds from a friendly ally, and the fate of the world hangs in the balance. B&W; 13 chapters. **DIR:** Ford Beebe, Alan James. **CAST:** Buster Crabbe, Frances Robinson, Edna Sedgewick. **1938**

RED BEARD ★★★★1/2 In the early nineteenth century, a newly graduated doctor hopes to become a society doctor. Instead, he is posted at an impoverished clinic run by Dr. Niide (Toshiro Mifune), whose destitute patients affectionately call him "Red Beard." Akira Kurosawa, at one of his directorial pinnacles, describes his film as a "monument to the goodness in man." In Japanese with English subtitles. B&W; 185m. **DIR:** Akira Kurosawa. **CAST:** Toshiro Mifune. **1965**

RED-BLOODED AMERICAN GIRL ★★1/2 A quirky story about a scientist (Andrew Stevens) who is called upon to reverse the effects of a new drug that causes vampirism. Rated R for language, violence, and nudity. 90m. **DIR:** David Blyth. **CAST:** Heather Thomas, Andrew Stevens, Lydie Denier, Christopher Plummer, Kim Coates. **1990**

RED CORNER ★★★ In this generally gripping drama, Richard Gere is an American businessman who becomes caught up in the Chinese legal system after being accused of a crime. Guilty until proven innocent, he must convince his defense advocate (Bai Ling) to use what are to her unorthodox methods in securing his freedom while he endures dehumanizing treatment on an almost daily basis. Gere successfully engages our sympathies as the innocent man caught up in almost impossible-to-overcome circumstances while Ling is even more impressive as the functionary who must rise to the occasion. Rated R for violence, profanity, and partial nudity. 119m. **DIR:** Jon Avnet. **CAST:** Richard Gere, Bai Ling, Bradley Whitford, Byron Mann, Peter Donat, James Hong. **1997 DVD**

RED DAWN ★★★1/2 Some viewers undoubtedly will feel that right-wing writer-director John Milius (*The Wind and the Lion* and *Conan the Barbarian*) has gone too far with this tale of the Russians invading a small American town. But we took this film as a simple "what if?" entertainment and really enjoyed it. Rated PG-13 for violence and profanity. 114m. **DIR:** John Milius. **CAST:** Patrick Swayze, C. Thomas Howell, Ron O'Neal, Lea Thompson, Ben Johnson, Harry Dean Stanton, William Smith, Powers Boothe, Charlie Sheen. **1984 DVD**

RED DESERT ★★★★ An acutely depressed married woman (Monica Vitti) finds her life with an industrial-engineer husband to be demanding. Photographed in the industrial wasteland of northern Italy by Carlo Di Palma, this film remains one of the most beautiful of director Michelangelo Antonioni's works. Italian with English subtitles. 116m. **DIR:** Michelangelo Antonioni. **CAST:** Monica Vitti, Richard Harris. **1964 DVD**

RED DUST ★★★★ *Red Dust* is one of those remarkable films where the performances of its stars propel a movie to classic status despite a rather uninspired story. A hackneyed story of a rubber plantation boss (Gable) who dallies with another man's wife only to return to the arms of a shady lady (Harlow) with the proverbial heart of gold. B&W; 83m. **DIR:** Victor Fleming. **CAST:** Clark Gable, Jean Harlow, Mary Astor, Donald Crisp, Gene Raymond, Tully Marshall. **1932**

RED DWARF, THE ★★★1/2 Jean-Yves Thual is excellent as Lucien in this fascinating, offbeat tale of a diminutive forger who composes incriminating letters for a law firm while dreaming of a better life. When an affair leads to tragedy, Lucien joins the circus to find redemption. Moody black-and-white images recall early David Lynch and Jean Cocteau. In French with English subtitles. Rated R for adult situations, language, nudity, and violence. 101m. **DIR:** Yvonne Le Moine. **CAST:** Jean-Yves Thual, Anita Ekberg, Dyna Gauzy, Arno Chevrier. **1998 DVD**

RED DWARF (TV SERIES) ★★★1/2 This wonderfully inventive British TV series is pure lunaey as the remnant crew of the *Red Dwarf*, a gigantic spaceship, hurtles through the universe millions of years in the future. Absolutely perfect casting, with Craig Charles as likable slob/hero Dave Lister and Chris Barrie as his obnoxious, repressed roommate. 84–90m. **DIR:** Ed Bye. **CAST:** Chris Barrie, Craig Charles, Danny John-Jules, Robert Llewellyn. **1988–1993 DVD**

RED FIRECRACKER, GREEN FIRECRACKER ★★ A forbidden romance blossoms between a young fireworks manufacturer and her new hired hand, while the factory foreman looks on with sour jealousy. Turgid and sluggish, soap opera's pace is leaden even when the skyrockets and firecrackers are going full blast. In Mandarin with English subtitles. Not rated; suitable for general audiences. 117m. **DIR:** He Ping. **CAST:** Ning Jing, Wu Gang, Zhao Xiao Rui, Gao Yang. **1994 DVD**

RED FLAG: THE ULTIMATE GAME ★★1/2 The air force has a jet-fighter combat course located near Las Vegas that over the years has fine-tuned thousands of the best pilots in the air force. The combat game is called Red Flag. It's an older and weaker version of *Top Gun* and suffers by comparison. 90m. **DIR:** Don Taylor. **CAST:** Barry Bostwick, Joan Van Ark, Fred McCarren, George Coe. **1981**

RED GARTERS ★★★1/2 A delightful and inventive spoof of Westerns with everything offbeat, from the casting to the stage-stylized sets and the original songs of Jay Livingston and Ray Evans. Oscar nomination for the truly surrealistic set decoration. 91m. **DIR:** George Marshall. **CAST:** Rosemary Clooney, Jack Carson, Guy Mitchell, Pat Crowley, Gene Barry, Cass Daley, Frank Faylen, Reginald Owen, Buddy Ebsen. **1954**

RED-HEADED STRANGER, THE ★★★ Willie Nelson's country "opera" served as the basis for this little-seen Western, which most fans of the genre will enjoy. Nelson plays a right-thinking preacher who takes on an evil family (headed by Royal Dano) that is terrorizing the townspeople of this new parish. Rated R for violence and profanity. 105m. **DIR:** William Witliff. **CAST:** Willie Nelson, R. G. Armstrong, Morgan Fairchild, Royal Dano, Katharine Ross. **1986**

RED-HEADED WOMAN ★★★1/2 Every female star on every major motion-picture lot wanted the plum role of the gal who followed her heart and her instincts to gain social prominence and a swell guy. Young Jean Harlow took the prize and made it her own in this pre-Code gem. B&W; 79m. **DIR:** Jack Conway. **CAST:** Jean Harlow, Chester Morris, Leila Hyams, Lewis Stone, Una Merkel, Henry Stephenson, May Robson. **1932**

RED HEAT (1985) ★★ Linda Blair is mistakenly arrested as a spy and sentenced to prison. Lurid and exces-

sively violent. 104m. **DIR:** Robert Collector. **CAST:** Linda Blair, Sylvia Kristel, William Ostrander, Sue Kiel. **1985**

RED HEAT (1988) ★★★★ Director Walter Hill has taken his biggest hit, *48 Hrs.*, and reworked it as a vehicle for Arnold Schwarzenegger and James Belushi. Big Arnold plays a Soviet police officer forced to team up with a wisecracking Chicago cop (Belushi) to track down a Russian drug dealer (Ed O'Ross). It's fast and exciting; a best bet for action buffs. Rated R for violence, profanity, and nudity. 107m. **DIR:** Walter Hill. **CAST:** Arnold Schwarzenegger, James Belushi, Peter Boyle, Ed O'Ross, Laurence Fishburne, Gina Gershon, Richard Bright. **1988 DVD**

RED HOT ★★★ Rock 'n' roll is called American propaganda and banned in the Soviet Union in 1959. One youth, Alexei, gets a taste of the music, refuses to give it up, and puts himself in jeopardy. Alexei risks everything to stay one step ahead of the KGB and satisfy his passion for rock 'n' roll. Interesting cast and a real sense of time and place make this enjoyable. Rated PG. 95m. **DIR:** Paul Haggis. **CAST:** Balthazar Getty, Carla Gugino, Jan Niklas, Hugh O'Connor, Donald Sutherland, Armin Mueller-Stahl. **1993**

RED HOUSE, THE ★★★1/2 A gripping suspense melodrama enhanced by a musical score by Miklos Rozsa. Edward G. Robinson employs Rory Calhoun to keep the curious away from a decaying old house deep in the woods. But his niece and a young hired hand *must* learn the secret. B&W; 100m. **DIR:** Delmer Daves. **CAST:** Edward G. Robinson, Lon McCallister, Allene Roberts, Julie London, Judith Anderson, Rory Calhoun, Ona Munson. **1947 DVD**

RED KIMONO, THE 🦃 A young lady is abandoned by her philandering husband and forced to become a scarlet woman. Silent. B&W; 95m. **DIR:** Walter Lang. **CAST:** Priscilla Bonner, Nellie Bly Baker, Mary Carr, Tyrone Power Sr. **1925**

RED KING, WHITE KNIGHT ★★1/2 Tom Skerritt's impeccable rendering of a retired and weary CIA agent brought back into the fold (initially as a dupe) enlivens Ron Hutchinson's dreary story about a rogue Soviet KGB official who plots against Gorbachev to retain the cold war status quo. Things also improve considerably when the brilliant Max von Sydow appears. Made for HBO; considerable violence and frank dialogue. 107m. **DIR:** Geoff Murphy. **CAST:** Tom Skerritt, Max von Sydow, Helen Mirren, Tom Bell, Barry Corbin. **1989**

RED KISS (ROUGE BAISER) ★★★1/2 In 1952 France, a teenage girl raised by leftist parents is caught between her upbringing and a romance with an apolitical news photographer. This autobiographical tale is reminiscent of the films of Diane Kurys, with an added political dimension. In French with English subtitles. Not rated; brief sexual situations. 110m. **DIR:** Vera Belmont. **CAST:** Charlotte Valandrey, Lambert Wilson, Marthe Keller, Gunter Lamprecht. **1985**

RED LETTERS ★★ A mixed bag of ideas that eventually goes nowhere. Peter Coyote is okay as a college professor whose involvement with a convicted murderess and the dean's daughter turns his life into a living nightmare. The film contains all of the elements of direct-to-video exploitation, but director Bradley Battersby can't make up his mind if the film is an erotic thriller or a goof on the genre. Rated R for adult situations, language, and nudity. 102m. **DIR:** Bradley Battersby. **CAST:** Peter Coyote, Nastassja Kinski, Fairuza Balk, Ernie Hudson, Jeremy Piven. **2000 DVD**

RED LIGHT STING, THE ★★ Pale TV film about a young district attorney (Beau Bridges) who is assigned to buy a whorehouse to bring out an elusive big-time crook (Harold Gould). Not rated, but the equivalent of a PG for adult subject matter. 96m. **DIR:** Rod Holcomb. **CAST:** Farrah Fawcett, Beau Bridges, Harold Gould, Paul Burke, Alex Henteloff, Conrad Janis, James Luisi, Philip Charles MacKenzie. **1984**

RED LINE ★★1/2 Spectacular car stunts and chase scenes highlight this otherwise unexceptional tale of a former professional race-car driver who finds himself enmeshed with a crime kingpin who wants him to steal cars. Rated R for profanity. 90m. **DIR:** John Sjorgen. **CAST:** Chad McQueen, Michael Madsen, Roxana Zal, Jan-Michael Vincent, Dom DeLuise, Corey Feldman, Chuck Zito. **1995 DVD**

RED LINE 7000 ★★1/2 Car-race melodrama about three drivers and the women in their lives bogs down when the story leaves the track. Veteran director Howard Hawks would make only two more films after this tired actioner. 110m. **DIR:** Howard Hawks. **CAST:** James Caan, Laura Devon, Charlene Holt, Marianna Hill, James Ward, Norman Alden, George Takei. **1965**

RED LION ★★★ Toshiro Mifune is well cast as a man who impersonates a military officer in order to return to his village in grand style. Once there, he must liberate his followers from an oppressive government. In Japanese with English subtitles. 115m. **DIR:** Kihachi Okamoto. **CAST:** Toshiro Mifune, Shima Iwashita. **1969**

RED MENACE, THE 🦃 A sloppily written movie made to capitalize on the McCarthy menace with onetime *Our Miss Brooks* hero Robert Rockwell menaced by Communist sympathizers in a very unconvincing way. B&W; 87m. **DIR:** R. G. Springsteen. **CAST:** Robert Rockwell, Betty Lou Gerson, Barbara Fuller, Hanne Axman. **1949**

RED NIGHTS 🦃 A New England youth with stars in his eyes heads out to Hollywood. Rated R. 89m. **DIR:** Izhak Hanooka. **CAST:** Christopher Parker, Brian Matthews, Jack Carter, William Smith. **1988**

RED PLANET 🦃 The year 2000 will be remembered as the year that saw the release of dreadful sci-fi entries set on Mars. Val Kilmer smirks his way through a stupid storyline that drags interminably and botches just about every scientific element in the laughable script. Rated PG-13 for profanity, brief nudity, violence, and gore. 116m. **DIR:** Antony Hoffman. **CAST:** Val Kilmer, Carrie-Anne Moss, Tom Sizemore, Benjamin Bratt, Simon Baker, Terence Stamp. **2000 DVD**

RED PLANET MARS 🦃 Anti-commie sci-fi from the 1950s, as mysterious coded transmissions from Mars turn out to be God telling Earth that communists can't be trusted! Talky, uneventful, and visually flat. B&W; 87m. **DIR:** Harry Horner. **CAST:** Peter Graves, Andrea King, Marvin Miller. **1952**

RED PONY, THE ★★ It is very hard to make a dull movie from a John Steinbeck novel. This rendition manages to. Myrna Loy and Robert Mitchum are wasted in this story of a young northern California boy who is given a colt, which runs away. 89m. **DIR:** Lewis Mile-

stone. **CAST:** Myrna Loy, Robert Mitchum, Peter Miles, Louis Calhern, Shepperd Strudwick, Margaret Hamilton. **1948**

RED RIVER ★★★★★ After seeing this Western, John Ford remarked, "I didn't know the big lug could act." The "big lug" he was referring to was the star, John Wayne, whom Ford had brought to stardom in 1939's *Stagecoach*. This shoot-'em-up adaptation of *Mutiny on the Bounty* features Wayne at his best in the role of a tough rancher making a historic cattle drive. B&W; 133m. **DIR:** Howard Hawks. **CAST:** John Wayne, Montgomery Clift, Walter Brennan, Joanne Dru, John Ireland, Noah Beery Jr., Paul Fix, Coleen Gray, Harry Carey, Harry Carey Jr. **1948 DVD**

RED RIVER RANGE ★★1/2 When entire herds of cattle begin disappearing from the Red River range, the Three Mesquiteers are called in to solve the mystery. John Wayne's presence makes it worth watching for fans. B&W; 59m. **DIR:** George Sherman. **CAST:** John Wayne, Ray "Crash" Corrigan, Max Terhune, Polly Moran, Kirby Grant. **1938**

RED RIVER RENEGADES ★★★1/2 Postal inspector Sunset Carson sets out to stop a series of mail robberies on the Red River stage line. He is helped and hindered by a female Pinkerton agent. B&W; 55m. **DIR:** Thomas Carr. **CAST:** Sunset Carson, Peggy Stewart, Tom London. **1946**

RED RIVER SHORE ★★★1/2 Marshall Rex Allen is forced to kill a crooked businessman but vows to keep the man's guilt a secret. When the man's son arrives, trouble develops over the dead man's bogus oil-drilling operation. B&W; 54m. **DIR:** Harry Keller. **CAST:** Rex Allen, Slim Pickens, Douglas Fowley, Bill Phipps. **1953**

RED ROCK WEST ★★★1/2 Try as he might, mostly honest drifter Nicolas Cage can't leave the small town of Red Rock West . . . and he gets in more trouble each time he returns. The plot involves a corrupt sheriff arranging the murder of his scheming wife, and the impertinent killer hired for the job. The seriocomic tone properly emphasizes Cage's plight in a story that will keep you guessing. Rated R for profanity and violence. 98m. **DIR:** John Dahl. **CAST:** Nicolas Cage, Dennis Hopper, Lara Flynn Boyle, Timothy Carhart, J. T. Walsh. **1993 DVD**

RED SCORPION 🦃 A Soviet agent is sent to infiltrate and kill the leader of a band of African rebels. Rated R for violence. 100m. **DIR:** Joseph Zito. **CAST:** Dolph Lundgren, M. Emmet Walsh. **1989 DVD**

RED SCORPION 2 ★★★ This sequel-in-name-only, a compact retread of *The Dirty Dozen*, is far better than its predecessor. Commando expert Matt McColm and plucky Jennifer Rubin lead a team of highly specialized assassins and technicians on a raid of a covert American hate group; the resulting action scenes are well-handled. Rated R for violence, torture, nudity, and simulated sex. 89m. **DIR:** Michael Kennedy. **CAST:** Matt McColm, John Savage, Jennifer Rubin, Paul Ben-Victor, Michael Ironside. **1994**

RED SHOES, THE ★★★★ Fascinating backstage look at the world of ballet manages to overcome its unoriginal, often trite, plot. A ballerina (Moira Shearer) is urged by her forceful and single-minded impresario (Anton Walbrook) to give up a romantic involvement in favor of her career, with tragic consequences. Good acting and fine camera work save this British film. 136m. **DIR:** Michael Powell, Emeric Pressburger. **CAST:** Moira Shearer, Anton Walbrook, Marius Goring. **1948 DVD**

RED SONJA 🦃 Dreadful sword-and-sorcery film. Rated PG-13 for violence. 89m. **DIR:** Richard Fleischer. **CAST:** Arnold Schwarzenegger, Brigitte Nielsen, Sandahl Bergman, Paul Smith, Ernie Reyes Jr. **1985**

RED SORGHUM ★★★★★ A superb pastoral epic from the People's Republic of China and the winner of the Golden Bear at the 1988 Berlin Film Festival. The story relates a passionate folk tale about village wine makers who fight against interloping Japanese invaders. Lyrical and affecting drama. In Chinese with English subtitles. 91m. **DIR:** Yimou Zhang. **CAST:** Gong Li, Jian Weng, Liu Ji. **1988**

RED SQUIRREL, THE ★★★ Style overcomes story in this Spanish drama about a rock singer who becomes involved with a woman who loses her memory after they are in an accident. At least she seems to have lost her memory—or is she just trying to escape her loony husband? In Spanish with English subtitles. Not rated; contains nudity, violence, profanity, and sexual situations. 104m. **DIR:** Julio Medem. **CAST:** Emma Suarez, Nacho Novo, Maria Barranco. **1993**

RED SUN ★★1/2 All-star, fitfully entertaining Western has an interesting premise—samurai vs. cowboys—but ultimately wastes the considerable talents of the great Japanese actor Toshiro Mifune. Charles Bronson has another of those offbeat-character parts that he underplays into a leading role. Rated PG. 112m. **DIR:** Terence Young. **CAST:** Charles Bronson, Alain Delon, Toshiro Mifune, Ursula Andress, Capucine. **1972 DVD**

RED SUN RISING ★★★ Entertaining players rise above pedestrian material in this modest martial arts saga, starring the always appealing Don "The Dragon" Wilson as a Japanese cop sent to the United States to extradite a criminal don and the hulking henchman who kills opponents with the legendary "death touch." Mystical elements are played too broadly, but the formula still works. Rated R for violence and profanity. 99m. **DIR:** Francis Megahy. **CAST:** Don "The Dragon" Wilson, Terry Farrell, Mako, Michael Ironside, Soon-Tek Oh, Edward Albert. **1993**

RED SURF ★★1/2 Two drug-dealing surf bums try for one last big score. Things begin falling apart when one of their friends turns informer. Rated R for violence, profanity, and nudity. 104m. **DIR:** H. Gordon Boos. **CAST:** George Clooney, Doug Savant, Dedee Pfeiffer, Gene Simmons, Philip McKeon. **1990 DVD**

RED TENT, THE ★★1/2 Sean Connery heads an international cast in this slow-moving reconstruction of a polar expedition that ended in tragedy in 1928. The scope of the film and the trials faced by the party in their struggles for survival are enthralling, but too much reliance on flashbacks works against this one. 121m. **DIR:** Mikhail K. Kalatozov. **CAST:** Sean Connery, Claudia Cardinale, Hardy Kruger, Peter Finch, Massimo Girotti. **1970**

RED VIOLIN, THE ★★★★1/2 While a rare old violin is being auctioned off in Paris, flashbacks tell the instrument's story through the centuries: its creation in Renaissance Italy, its travels from country to country over the years, and its final discovery in modern-day China. The stories are a bit uneven, but never less than en-

grossing, and sometimes quite moving. In English, French, German, Italian, and Mandarin, with subtitles where appropriate. Rated R for sexual scenes. 131m. **DIR:** Francois Girard. **CAST:** Samuel L. Jackson, Greta Scacchi, Jason Flemyng, Colm Feore, Don McKellar. **1998 DVD**

REDHEAD FROM WYOMING, THE ★★1/2 The title says it all in a Western about a colorful redhead who takes the rap for a scheming politician, then turns against him when she meets a more likable lawman. Very predictable but sprightly because of the personalities. 80m. **DIR:** Lee Sholem. **CAST:** Maureen O'Hara, Dennis Weaver, Alex Nicol, Alexander Scourby, William Bishop, Robert Strauss. **1952**

REDLINE 🦃 Poor Rutger Hauer. Once a major star, now relegated to direct-to-video trash such as this tale of a smuggler who is killed by his partner and brought back to life, exploiting every possible B-movie cliché known to man. Just dreadful. A.k.a. *Deathline* and *Armageddon.* Not rated; contains violence and language. 113m. **DIR:** Tibor Takacs. **CAST:** Rutger Hauer, Mark Dacascos, Yvonne Scio. **1997 DVD**

REDNECK 🦃 Vile crime story about two criminals who take a young boy hostage. Not rated. 89m. **DIR:** Silvio Narizzano. **CAST:** Telly Savalas, Franco Nero, Mark Lester. **1972**

REDNECK ZOMBIES 🦃 Rednecks consume a nasty beer that turns them into mindless creatures. And the difference is? Rated R for violence, profanity, and gore. 83m. **DIR:** Pericles Lewnes. **CAST:** Lisa DeHaven, William C. Benson, P. Floyd Piranha, Zoofoot. **1988 DVD**

REDS ★★★★★ Warren Beatty produced, directed, cowrote, and starred in this $33 million American film masterpiece. This three-hour-plus film biography of left-wing American journalist John Reed (Beatty) and Louise Bryant (Diane Keaton) also features brilliant bits from Jack Nicholson, Gene Hackman, and Maureen Stapleton. Rated PG because of profanity, silhouetted sex scenes, and war scenes. 200m. **DIR:** Warren Beatty. **CAST:** Warren Beatty, Diane Keaton, Jack Nicholson, Gene Hackman, Edward Herrmann, Maureen Stapleton, Jerzy Kosinski. **1981**

REDWOOD CURTAIN ★★★1/2 Rather convoluted plot for a *Hallmark Hall of Fame*, this focuses on the search of an Amerasian adoptee for her biological father. Her search takes her to the Redwoods and a homeless man who hides there. Startling ending is a satisfying reward for keeping up with multiple twists and turns. 95m. **DIR:** John Korty. **CAST:** Lea Salonga, John Lithgow, Jeff Daniels, Debra Monk, Catharine Hicks. **1995**

REEFER MADNESS ★★1/2 This 1930s anti-marijuana film is very silly, and sometimes funny. It's a cult film that really isn't as good as its reputation suggests. B&W; 67m. **DIR:** Louis J. Gasnier. **CAST:** Dave O'Brien, Dorothy Short, Warren McCollum, Lillian Miles, Carleton Young. **1936 DVD**

REET, PETITE AND GONE ★★★1/2 Louis Jordan, the overlooked hero of prerock days, is well captured (along with his hot backup band, the Tympany Five) in this farcical all-black musical. Jordan's sound is a blues-pop fusion known as jumpin' jive, and it gets slick film treatment in this little-known movie treasure. 67m. **DIR:** William Forest Crouch. **CAST:** Louis Jordan. **1946**

REF, THE ★★★ Jewel thief Denis Leary soon regrets taking perennially bickering married couple Judy Davis and Kevin Spacey hostage in a ritzy neighborhood. It's supposed to be a black comedy, but it's just bleak at times, and lacks appealing characters. There are some very funny moments, though. Rated R for profanity and frank sexual discussions. 92m. **DIR:** Ted Demme. **CAST:** Denis Leary, Judy Davis, Kevin Spacey, Robert J. Steinmiller, Glynis Johns, Christine Baranski, Richard Bright, Adam LeFevre, Raymond J. Barry. **1994**

REFLECTING SKIN, THE ★★★★ The innocence of a small boy is stripped away as he observes the strange and macabre characters that surround him. Life in a small town is magnified beyond reality into a surreal quasi-fantasy that brilliantly fuses the mind of the child and that of the adult, directly challenging our idealized notions of the innocence of childhood. A must for those who appreciate the work of David Lynch, and enjoy challenging alternative cinema. Rated R for violence and suggested sex. 98m. **DIR:** Philip Ridley. **CAST:** Viggo Mortensen, Lindsay Duncan, Jeremy Cooper. **1991**

REFLECTION OF FEAR ★★1/2 Confusing, uninspired story of a beautiful young girl who becomes the central figure in a cobweb of crime and murder. Should have been better, considering the cast. Rated R. 102m. **DIR:** William Fraker. **CAST:** Robert Shaw, Mary Ure, Sally Kellerman, Signe Hasso, Sondra Locke. **1973**

REFLECTIONS IN A GOLDEN EYE ★★1/2 Very bizarre film concerning a homosexual army officer (Marlon Brando) stationed in the South. This very strange film very rarely works—despite a high-powered cast. 108m. **DIR:** John Huston. **CAST:** Marlon Brando, Elizabeth Taylor, Brian Keith, Julie Harris, Robert Forster. **1967**

REFLECTIONS IN THE DARK ★★ Pampered housewife, stifled by a sensitive, perfect husband who dotes on her every move, relieves her anguish by killing the poor slob. She justifies this bewildering act during a tedious monologue prior to her execution. Boring. Rated R for profanity, violence, and nudity. 84m. **DIR:** Jon Purdy. **CAST:** Mimi Rogers, Billy Zane. **1995**

REFLECTIONS OF MURDER ★★★ A wife and a mistress set out to kill their abusive mate. They set up a foolproof trap to lure him to his death. The "accident" that kills him leads to more terror and horror than either woman expected. A TV-movie version of the French classic *Diabolique*. 98m. **DIR:** John Badham. **CAST:** Tuesday Weld, Joan Hackett, Sam Waterston. **1987**

REFORM SCHOOL GIRL ★★ Gloria Castillo, a long way from her supporting role in *Night of the Hunter*, is the innocent teen packed off to reform school. Standard late-Fifties American-International programmer. B&W; 71m. **DIR:** Edward L. Bernds. **CAST:** Gloria Castillo, Ross Ford, Edd Byrnes, Ralph Reed, Sally Kellerman. **1957**

REFORM SCHOOL GIRLS ★★ "So young. So bad. So what?" That was the promo line for this spoof of the women-in-prison genre. Writer-director Tom DeSimone manages to get in the usual exploitative ingredients—women taking showers, etc.—while simultaneously making fun of them. Rated R for violence, profanity, nudity, and simulated sex. 94m. **DIR:** Tom DeSimone. **CAST:** Wendy O. Williams, Sybil Danning, Pat Ast, Linda Carol. **1986**

REGARDING HENRY ★★★★ Harrison Ford gives one of his finest performances as Henry Turner, a successful, self-centered attorney who loses all memory of his past when a robber shoots him in the head with a small-caliber weapon. Annette Bening is equally fine as the wife who finds herself falling in love with the gentle, childlike man who emerges in her husband's body. Rated PG-13 for violence and profanity. 107m. **DIR:** Mike Nichols. **CAST:** Harrison Ford, Annette Bening, Bill Nunn, Donald Moffat, Nancy Marchand, Elizabeth Wilson. **1991**

REGENERATED MAN, THE 🦃 When a scientist is forced to drink the flesh-regenerating fluid he's invented, he becomes a horrible monster. Rated R for horror, violence, and language. 90m. **DIR:** Ted A. Bohus. **CAST:** Arthur Lindquist, Cheryl Hendricks, Chris Kidd. **1994**

REGENERATION ★★★1/2 One of the first full-length gangster films ever made, this morality play follows the life of a street kid who is turned around by a well-meaning social worker. Age has taken its toll, as a few scenes are so worn you can barely make out what is happening. Packaged with a 10-minute Thomas Edison production *The Police Force of New York City* that records the daily activities of Gotham's finest in 1910. Silent. Not rated; contains violence. B&W; 72m. **DIR:** Raoul Walsh. **CAST:** Rockcliffe Fellowes, Anna Q. Nilsson, William Sheer, H. McCoy. **1915**

REGGIE'S PRAYER 🦃 Well-intended but poorly made film starring football star Reggie White as a high-school coach trying to keep his players away from violent drug dealers. Not rated; contains mild violence. 94m. **DIR:** Paul McKellips. **CAST:** Reggie White, Noriyuki "Pat" Morita, Rosey Grier. **1997**

REGINA ★★★ This strange psychological drama features Ava Gardner as a nagging wife and mother who is obsessed with keeping her 36 year old son at home with her. Anthony Quinn is the much-put-upon husband. An Italian film, it is not rated but contains mature themes. 86m. **DIR:** Jean-Yves Prate. **CAST:** Anthony Quinn, Ava Gardner, Ray Sharkey, Anna Karina. **1983 DVD**

REHEARSAL FOR MURDER ★★★1/2 Richard Levinson and William Link, those clever fellows behind the creation of *Columbo*, occasionally stray into the realm of made-for-television movies; this is one of the best. Robert Preston leads his stage friends through the reading of a play designed to ferret out the killer of star Lynn Redgrave. Levinson and Link deliver another of their surprise conclusions. 100m. **DIR:** David Greene. **CAST:** Robert Preston, Lynn Redgrave, Jeff Goldblum, Patrick Macnee, William Daniels, Lawrence Pressman. **1982 DVD**

REI-REI ★★ Very sexually oriented, this is the animated tale of a goddess of love who comes down to Earth to help solve problems of the romantic variety. Some story cleverness nearly saves this one. In Japanese with English subtitles. Not rated; contains nudity, sexual situations, and violence. 60m. **DIR:** Yoshikio Yamamoto. **1993**

REILLY: THE ACE OF SPIES ★★ Sam Neill is wasted in this slow-moving, so-called thriller about the first James Bond–type spy employed by the British. In 1901 Russia he manages not only to smuggle secret maps out of the country but also to lure a surly minister's young wife into his bed. Not rated, this made-for-TV production contains violence and nudity. 80m. **DIR:** Jim Goddard. **CAST:** Sam Neill, Leo McKern, Norman Rodway, Peter Egan. **1984**

REINCARNATE, THE 🦃 A lawyer will live forever, as long as he can find a new body to inhabit when his present one dies. Rated PG. 89m. **DIR:** Don Haldane. **CAST:** Jack Creley, Jay Reynolds. **1971**

REINCARNATION OF GOLDEN LOTUS, THE ★★★★★ In this compelling and tastefully erotic Hong Kong production, a woman (Joey Wang) murdered by a powerful lord in ancient times uses reincarnation as a way of exacting revenge. In Chinese with English subtitles. Not rated, the film has violence and nudity. 99m. **DIR:** Clara Law. **CAST:** Joey Wang. **1989**

REINCARNATION OF PETER PROUD, THE 🦃 Turgid direction, contrived plot. Rated R for considerable nudity. 104m. **DIR:** J. Lee Thompson. **CAST:** Michael Sarrazin, Jennifer O'Neill, Margot Kidder, Cornelia Sharpe. **1975**

REINDEER GAMES ★★★ Ehren Kruger's screenplay is sabotaged by an opening flash-forward that completely ruins any suspense. Ben Affleck stars as a minor felon whose prison buddy is killed mere days before his release; when Ben subsequently gets his own walking papers, he poses as his former friend to score with his voluptous pen pal. Unfortunately, the gal has a crazy brother who wants assistance on a heist from the guy Ben is *supposed* to be. When we reach the caper itself, with its telegraphed outcome, it's little more than wham, bam, thank you, ma'am. Rated R for profanity, nudity, sexual content, and considerable violence. 105m. **DIR:** John Frankenheimer. **CAST:** Ben Affleck, Gary Sinise, Charlize Theron, Dennis Farina, James Frain, Donal Logue, Clarence Williams, III. **2000 DVD**

REIVERS, THE ★★★★ Grand adaptation of the William Faulkner tale concerning a young boy (Mitch Vogel) who, with the help of his mischievous older friends (Steve McQueen and Rupert Crosse), "borrows" an automobile and heads for fun and excitement in 1905 Mississippi. The charming vignettes include a stopover in a brothel and a climactic horse race that could spell doom for the adventurers. Rated PG. 107m. **DIR:** Mark Rydell. **CAST:** Steve McQueen, Rupert Crosse, Will Geer, Sharon Farrell, Mitch Vogel, Michael Constantine. **1969**

REJUVENATOR, THE ★★★ This flick begins by resembling *Re-Animator* in more than just name, but it soon takes on a life of its own. A rich woman funds a doctor's research into reversing the aging process in hopes he will discover a way to make her young again. Some very nasty side effects occur. Above-average special effects make this a must for horror-film fans. Rated R for extreme violence. 90m. **DIR:** Brian Thomas Jones. **CAST:** Vivian Lanko, John MacKay. **1988**

RELATIVE FEAR ★★ What happens when the baby of a psychotic couple is switched at birth with the baby of a perfectly sane couple? The fun comes from watching the normal parents respond when their son starts showing his true colors. Some suspense in this made-for-cable thriller. Rated R for violence. 94m. **DIR:** George Mihalka. **CAST:** Darlanne Fluegel, Martin Neufeld, James Brolin, Denise Crosby, M. Emmet Walsh. **1995**

RELATIVE VALUES ★★★1/2 Noel Coward's 1951 satire gets a good workout from a stellar cast. Julie Andrews shines as the Countess of Marshwood, who objects when she learns her son, Prince Nigel (Edward Atterton) plans to marry an American starlet (Jeanne Tripplehorn). The news also comes as a shock to the starlet's former lover (William Baldwin) and her long-lost sister, the Countess's maid. Coward's sharp and witty dialogue about class distinction remains intact. Rated PG-13. 90m. **DIR:** Eric Styles. **CAST:** Julie Andrews, Edward Atterton, William Baldwin, Colin Firth, Stephen Fry, Jeanne Tripplehorn. **2000 DVD**

RELAX . . . IT'S JUST SEX ★★★ Writer/director P.J. Castellaneta follows the romantic ups and downs of a circle of friends (mostly gays and lesbians) in this awkward, occasionally preachy, but well-acted film. Castellaneta has a good hand with witty dialogue and the film's shifts from comedy to drama and back, but let the title be a warning—his frank treatment of sexual intercourse will not be to all tastes. Rated R for nudity, sexual scenes, and discussions of sexual themes. 110m. **DIR:** P.J. Castellaneta. **CAST:** Jennifer Tilly, Mitchell Anderson, Cynda Williams, Serena Scott-Thomas, Lori Petty. **1998 DVD**

RELENTLESS ★★★ Catch this modest police procedural as the vehicle to boost minor player Leo Rossi's career. He's cast as a transplanted New York cop itching, in the wake of a string of murders committed by a so-called Sunset Killer, to show new Los Angeles partner Robert Loggia a thing or two. The deft and sympathetic screenplay, although credited to one Jack T. D. Robinson, is actually the work of Phil Alden Robinson. Rated R for violence and brief nudity. 92m. **DIR:** William Lustig. **CAST:** Judd Nelson, Robert Loggia, Leo Rossi, Meg Foster. **1989**

RELENTLESS II: DEAD ON ★★ Meg Foster and Leo Rossi reprise their roles from *Relentless*. A woman and her child were menaced by a serial killer at the end of that film. This one shows what effect it had on that child. Very bloody and violent, but also exciting and suspenseful. Rated R for violence, nudity, and tension. 93m. **DIR:** Michael Schroeder. **CAST:** Ray Sharkey, Meg Foster, Leo Rossi, Marc Poppel, Dale Dye, Miles O'Keeffe. **1991**

RELENTLESS 3 ★★ Ex–New York cop Sam Dietz, played by series-star Leo Rossi, finds himself drawn into the case of a Los Angeles serial killer who carves up his victims and mails the evidence to the police. His interest in the case is heightened when he learns that his past connection to the killer could endanger his girlfriend. Familiar territory for Rossi, but William Forsythe has some good, creepy moments as the killer. Rated R for nudity, violence, and language. 84m. **DIR:** James Lemmo. **CAST:** Leo Rossi, William Forsythe, Signy Coleman, Robert Costanzo. **1992**

RELIC, THE ★★1/2 A ghastly monster imported from the South American jungle stalks the halls of Chicago's Field Museum; only tough cop Tom Sizemore and leggy scientist Penelope Ann Miller stand between the human race and annihilation. Director Peter Hyams relies on loud noises for thrills, and darkness to build suspense (no light bulb seems to burn more than ten watts). The monster is startling but not really scary, and the film is comfortably predictable. Rated R for violence and profanity. 110m. **DIR:** Peter Hyams. **CAST:** Tom Sizemore, Penelope Ann Miller, James Whitmore. **1996 DVD**

RELUCTANT ASTRONAUT, THE ★★ In this typical Don Knotts vehicle, he plays a nervous sort who wants to be an astronaut but is afraid of heights. Rated G. 101m. **DIR:** Edward Montagne. **CAST:** Don Knotts, Arthur O'Connell, Leslie Nielsen, Joan Freeman, Jesse White. **1967**

RELUCTANT DEBUTANTE, THE ★★★ Kay Kendall steals the show as the new stepmother of Rex Harrison's American-bred daughter. Angela Lansbury is deliciously vicious, as always, as Kendall's snooty cousin. 94m. **DIR:** Vincente Minnelli. **CAST:** Rex Harrison, Kay Kendall, Angela Lansbury, Sandra Dee, John Saxon. **1958**

RELUCTANT DRAGON, THE ★★★★1/2 This delightful, though somewhat unorthodox, medieval dragon tale is a must-see for anyone! Director Charles Nichols orchestrates a fast-paced, hilarious romp—a droll encounter between a bard and a dragon. This is truly a Disney gem. Not rated. Suitable for the entire family. 28m. **DIR:** Hamilton Luske. **1957**

REMAINS OF THE DAY ★★★★★ Anthony Hopkins and Emma Thompson give remarkable performances in this heart-wrenching exploration of English reserve and unrequited love. Hopkins is a gentleman's gentleman whose private life and longings are subjugated to his professional responsibilities; this very dedication leads to personal tragedy in a seamless blend of period detail and drama. Exquisite. Rated PG-13 for brief profanity. 134m. **DIR:** James Ivory. **CAST:** Anthony Hopkins, Emma Thompson, James Fox, Christopher Reeve, Peter Vaughan, Hugh Grant, Michel Lonsdale, Tim Pigott-Smith. **1993 DVD**

REMBRANDT ★★★★ This is one of the few satisfying movie biographies of an artist. The depiction of the famous Dutch painter and his struggle to maintain his artistic integrity is related with respectful restraint and attention to factual detail. Charles Laughton, as Rembrandt, is brilliant in what was for him an atypically low-key performance. B&W; 90m. **DIR:** Alexander Korda. **CAST:** Charles Laughton, Gertrude Lawrence, Elsa Lanchester. **1936 DVD**

REMBRANDT—1669 ★★★ From his start at painting dead bodies for a surgeon, to his ultimate bankruptcy and death, this film portrays Rembrandt's life in a dark and almost voiceless story. Although the characters are well portrayed by all the actors, the plot moves along too slowly. In Dutch with English subtitles. Not rated; contains nudity. 114m. **DIR:** Jos Stelling. **CAST:** Frans Stelling, Ton de Koff, Aye Fil. **1977**

REMEDY FOR RICHES ★★1/2 When not dispensing country medicine to his patients, kindly Dr. Christian keeps an eye out for their financial well-being by alerting them to a con man's phony oil scheme. Modest series entry with a parade of eccentric characters. 67m. **DIR:** Erle C. Kenton. **CAST:** Jean Hersholt, Dorothy Lovett, Edgar Kennedy. **1941**

REMEMBER THE NIGHT ★★★★1/2 Preston Sturges wrote this excellent comedy-drama that deftly balances humor with sentimentality. A shoplifter awaiting trial (Barbara Stanwyck) sees the error of her ways when she spends Christmas with the family of the assistant

D.A. (Fred MacMurray) whose job it is to prosecute her. 86m. **DIR:** Mitchell Leisen. **CAST:** Barbara Stanwyck, Fred MacMurray, Beulah Bondi, Sterling Holloway. **1940**

REMEMBER THE TITANS ★★★★1/2 A feel-good movie with plenty of bite, this is the true story of a black football coach who is assigned to a newly integrated high school in Virginia. Denzel Washington shines in the lead role as he confronts hatred and ignorance with each step he takes toward placing his team in the championship play-offs. The film relies on a few sports-movie clichés to entertain the audience, but it also confronts the subject matter with refreshing honesty and insight. There's more to root for here than just the team. Rated PG. 113m. **DIR:** Boaz Yakin. **CAST:** Denzel Washington, Will Patton, Wood Harris, Ryan Hurst, Donald Adeosun Faison, Craig Kirkwood, Ethan Suplee, Kip Pardue, Hayden Panettiere, Nicole Ari Parker. **2000 DVD**

REMINGTON STEELE (TV SERIES) ★★★ Early episodes feature dashing Pierce Brosnan as a front man for Laura Holt's (Stephanie Zimbalist) savvy detective. Steele provides comic relief as he and another partner (played by James Read) vie for Holt's attentions. Very watchable, the first two volumes are entitled "Steele Crazy After All These Years" and "In the Steele of the Night." 50m. **DIR:** Don Weis, Burt Brinckerhoff. **CAST:** Stephanie Zimbalist, Pierce Brosnan, James Read. **1982–83**

REMO WILLIAMS: THE ADVENTURE BEGINS ★★★ This adaptation of the *Destroyer* novels is like a second-rate James Bond adventure. Fred Ward is fine as the hero of the title and Joel Grey is a kick as his Asian martial arts mentor, but the film takes too much time establishing the characters and too little giving us the adventure promised in the title. Rated PG-13 for violence and profanity. 121m. **DIR:** Guy Hamilton. **CAST:** Fred Ward, Joel Grey, Wilford Brimley, J. A. Preston, George Coe, Charles Cioffi, Kate Mulgrew. **1985**

REMOTE ★★★ This *Home Alone* wannabe stars Chris Carrara as a 13 year old whiz kid trapped in a model home with three bungling burglars. Draggy in parts but kids may find it diverting. Rated PG for cartoonish violence. 80m. **DIR:** Ted Nicolaou. **CAST:** Chris Carrara, Jessica Bowman, John Diehl, Derya Ruggles, Tony Longo, Stuart Fratkin. **1993**

REMOTE CONTROL (1987) ★★1/2 The manager of a video-rental outlet learns that many of his customers are being brutally murdered after watching a certain cassette. Rated R for violence and profanity. 88m. **DIR:** Jeff Lieberman. **CAST:** Kevin Dillon, Jennifer Tilly, Deborah Goodrich. **1987**

REMOTE CONTROL (1992) ★★★ Craziness from Iceland follows a timid auto mechanic as his life is turned upside down when he attempts to save a kidnapped woman. In Icelandic with English subtitles. Not rated. 85m. **DIR:** Oskar Jonasson. **CAST:** Bjorn Jorundur Fridbjornsson, Eggert Thorliefsson, Helgi Bjornsson, Soley Eliasdottir. **1992**

RENAISSANCE MAN ★★★1/2 After losing a cushy advertising job, Danny DeVito winds up teaching remedial studies to an octet of goof-ups at a nearby army post. When all else fails, he finally grabs their attention with Shakespeare. (Right.) Jim Burnstein's script too often feels like an English professor's underdeveloped dream come true. Rated PG-13 for mild profanity. 130m. **DIR:** Penny Marshall. **CAST:** Danny DeVito, Gregory Hines, James Remar, Cliff Robertson, Kadeem Hardison, Richard T. Jones, Mark Wahlberg, Stacey Dash. **1994**

RENDEZ-VOUS ★★★ Provocative French import paints a rather unsettling portrait of alienated youth. Juliette Binoche is captivating as a promiscuous young woman wandering the Paris nightlife scene. In French with English subtitles. Not rated; contains nudity, profanity, and violence. 82m. **DIR:** André Téchiné. **CAST:** Juliette Binoche, Lambert Wilson, Wadeck Stanczak, Jean-Louis Trintignant. **1985**

RENDEZVOUS IN PARIS ★★1/2 Veteran French filmmaker Eric Rohmer gives us three stories of romantic mishaps between lovers and would-be lovers. Unfortunately, Rohmer's penchant for uneventful conversation makes this one tough going. It doesn't help that the first story is easily the best; it's all downhill from there. In French with English subtitles. Not rated; suitable for adults and mature teenagers. 95m. **DIR:** Éric Rohmer. **CAST:** Clara Bellar, Antoine Basler, Aurore Rauscher, Serge Renko. **1996**

RENEGADE ★★ Pilot film for the syndicated television series stars Lorenzo Lamas as a street cop named Reno, who is framed for murder. He hops on his motorcycle and leaves town, becoming a bounty hunter along the way. Not rated; contains violence. 95m. **DIR:** Ralph Hemecker, R. Marvin. **CAST:** Lorenzo Lamas, Kathleen Kinmont, Branscombe Richmond, Martin Kove, Charles Napier. **1993**

RENEGADE GIRL ★★1/2 Ann Savage plays a free-thinking, vixen leader of a band of Confederate raiders. She tragically falls in love with the Union soldier stalking her. B&W; 65m. **DIR:** William Berke. **CAST:** Ann Savage, Alan Curtis, Russell Wade, Jack Holt, Ray "Crash" Corrigan, John King. **1946**

RENEGADE RANGER ★★★★ Star George O'Brien and director David Howard made some of the finest series Westerns in the Thirties and Forties. O'Brien, a member of director John Ford's stock company since starring in the classic *Iron Horse*, is in top form as a Texas Ranger who is assigned to bring in a female bandit (Rita Hayworth) accused of murder. B&W; 60m. **DIR:** David Howard. **CAST:** George O'Brien, Rita Hayworth, Tim Holt, Ray Whitley. **1938**

RENEGADE TRAIL ★★★ Hopalong Cassidy helps a woman and her son save the day when their cattle are the target of the woman's outlaw ex-husband and the boy's father whom he thinks died a hero. Bit slower than most of the Hoppy series. B&W; 61m. **DIR:** Lesley Selander. **CAST:** William Boyd, George "Gabby" Hayes, Russell Hayden, Roy Barcroft, Sonny Bupp. **1939**

RENEGADES 🦃 Disappointing, lackluster thriller from the director of *The Hidden*. Rated R for profanity and violence. 110m. **DIR:** Jack Sholder. **CAST:** Kiefer Sutherland, Lou Diamond Phillips, Jami Gertz. **1989 DVD**

RENO AND THE DOC ★★1/2 Though it has a slow start, this tale of two middle-aged men brought together by mental telepathy soon gains momentum. Ken Walsh plays Reno, a solitary mountain man who is induced by Doc (Henry Ramer) to enter the pro-ski tour. Mild nudity and obscenities. 88m. **DIR:** Charles Dennis.

CAST: Kenneth Walsh, Henry Ramer, Linda Griffiths. **1984**

RENT-A-COP 🦃 When a drug bust goes awry and both cops and crooks are killed, a police detective is accused of masterminding the hit. Rated R for violence and profanity. 95m. **DIR:** Jerry London. **CAST:** Burt Reynolds, Liza Minnelli, James Remar, Richard Masur, Bernie Casey, Robby Benson, John P. Ryan. **1988 DVD**

RENT-A-KID ★★★ Kids will enjoy this comedy about the joys and pains of parenthood. Leslie Nielsen plays Harry, a slick salesman who agrees to run his son's orphanage while he's away on vacation. Harry puts his marketing skills to good use when he rents out three of the kids to a couple who want a test-drive before they decide to have children. There's plenty of heart and havoc as the three kids give their new parents a run for their money. Rated G. 89m. **DIR:** Fred Gerber. **CAST:** Leslie Nielsen, Christopher Lloyd, Matt McCoy, Sherry Miller. **1992**

RENTED LIPS 🦃 Martin Mull and Dick Shawn play inept documentary filmmakers (*Aluminum, Our Friend,* etc.) who agree to complete a porno film called *Halloween in the Bunker.* Rated R for profanity, nudity, and violence. 85m. **DIR:** Robert Downey. **CAST:** Martin Mull, Dick Shawn, Jennifer Tilly, Robert Downey Jr., June Lockhart, Pat McCormick, Eileen Brennan. **1988**

REPENTANCE ★★★ Set in Georgia in the Soviet Union, this richly varied film presents a central character who personifies all European villains—a cross, most obviously, between Stalin and Hitler. The film is not only a brutally direct comment on evil in politics, but a marvelous study of Georgian life. No rating but there are violent scenes. In Russian with English subtitles. 151m. **DIR:** Tenghiz Abuladze. **CAST:** Avtandil Makharadze. **1987**

REPLACEMENT KILLERS, THE ★★★1/2 Hong Kong action star Chow Yun-Fat reprises his hit-man-with-a-conscience character in this American-made thriller. When he refuses to carry out an assignment—which would leave the son of a police officer fatherless—his contract is passed on to others, who are to eliminate him in the process. Mira Sorvino gets caught up in Yun-Fat's predicament and must shoot her way out of many a tight situation. It's fast-paced fun. Rated R for strong violence and language. 88m. **DIR:** Antoine Fuqua. **CAST:** Chow Yun-Fat, Mira Sorvino. **1998 DVD**

REPLACEMENTS, THE ★★★1/2 You can't beat an underdog sports fantasy, even one this familiar and predictable. A former quarterback is recruited for the Washington Sentinels, who go on strike mere days before the play-offs. Surrounded by misfits and second-stringers, he somehow pulls 'em all together while finding time to romance a cheerleader (who "never dates players," of course). The good-natured script has all the right moves; you'll have a good time with this one. Rated PG-13 for profanity and coarse sexual content. 118m. **DIR:** Howard Deutch. **CAST:** Keanu Reeves, Gene Hackman, Orlando Jones, Jon Favreau, Brooke Langton, Rhys Ifans, Faizon Love, Michael Taliferro, Ace Yonamine. **2000 DVD**

•REPLICANT ★★ Preposterous thriller stars Jean-Claude Van Damme not once but twice, playing a clone of himself. The original Van Damme is a vicious serial killer terrorizing Seattle. The second Van Damme is a clone of the killer, created with the hopes of being used to track down the original. It plays as silly as it sounds, a science-fiction rehash of several genres with as much flair and excitement as dead grass. The production values are higher, but the acting and script are just what you would expect from yet another Van Damme direct-to-video masterpiece. Rated R for language and violence. 100m. **DIR:** Ringo Lam. **CAST:** Jean-Claude Van Damme, Michael Rooker, Catherine Dent, Ian Robison. **2001 DVD**

REPLIKATOR: CLONED TO KILL ★★ Hodgepodge sci-fi film tries to create a chaotic world of the future and instead only confuses its viewers. Ned Beatty stars as a cop whose job it is to stop the supercriminal Replikator and his mechanical human beings. Above-average special effects and another great performance by Beatty don't overcome confusing atmosphere and pace. Rated R for violence. 96m. **DIR:** G. Philip Jackson. **CAST:** Michael St. Gerard, Brigitte Bako, Ned Beatty. **1994**

REPO MAN ★★★★ Wild, weird, and unpredictable, this film stars Emilio Estevez as a young man who gets into the repossession racket. Under the tutelage of Harry Dean Stanton (in a typically terrific performance), Estevez learns how to steal cars from people who haven't kept up their payments. Meanwhile, bizarre events lead them to an encounter with what may be beings from space. Those who occasionally like to watch something different will enjoy it. Rated R. 92m. **DIR:** Alex Cox. **CAST:** Emilio Estevez, Harry Dean Stanton, Vonetta McGee, Sy Richardson, Tracey Walter. **1984**

REPORT ON THE PARTY AND THE GUESTS, A ★★★★ Kafkaesque parable about a group of party guests who suffer a mean practical joke at the hands of their host. The cast is composed of prominent Prague artists and intellectuals, and many of the references will be lost on American viewers, but the overall allegory is clear. In Czech with English subtitles. Not rated. B&W; 71m. **DIR:** Jan Nemec. **CAST:** Ivan Vyskocil, Jan Klusak, Josef Skvorecky. **1966**

REPORT TO THE COMMISSIONER ★★★★ One of the best of the urban crime films to come out in the early Seventies. Michael Moriarty plays an innocent rookie in the New York Police Department. Not understanding the politics of the cop on the beat, he commits a series of errors that leads to his downfall. Look for Richard Gere in a small part as a pimp. Rated PG for violence, profanity, and nudity. 113m. **DIR:** Milton Katselas. **CAST:** Michael Moriarty, Yaphet Kotto, Susan Blakely, Hector Elizondo, Tony King, William Devane, Richard Gere. **1974**

REPOSSESSED ★★★1/2 Linda Blair gets to make fun of the genre she is most associated with in this uproarious parody of *Exorcist*-style flicks. Nielsen is great as a priest who relates the story of a possessed housewife (Blair) and his attempts to exorcise the devil from within her. Rated PG-13 for language. 89m. **DIR:** Bob Logan. **CAST:** Linda Blair, Ned Beatty, Leslie Nielsen. **1990**

REPTILE, THE ★★1/2 A young couple moves to a Cornish village where people die of a strange malady known as "the black death" caused by two puncture wounds on the victim's neck. Stylish, atmospheric but uneven Hammer Studios film. 90m. **DIR:** John Gilling. **CAST:**

Noel Willman, Jennifer Daniels, Ray Barrett, Jacqueline Pearce. **1966 DVD**

•**REPTILIAN** 🦃 Aliens resurrect a Godzilla-sized armored dinosaur named Yonggary that can walk upright, shoot laser beams, and longs to destroy the human race. *Reptilian* has some of the worst CGI special effects ever made, with the same scenes repeated over and over. Simply awful. Rated PG-13 for some violence. 99m. **DIR:** Hyung-rae Shim. **CAST:** Harrison Young, Donna Philipson, Richard B. Livingston. **1999 DVD**

REPTILICUS 🦃 Simply dreadful action-adventure about scientists growing a prehistoric beast from its recently discovered tail. Welcome to Jurassic Bark. 90m. **DIR:** Sidney Pink. **CAST:** Carl Ottoson, Marla Behrens, Mimi Heinrich. **1962 DVD**

REPULSION ★★★★1/2 This brilliant British production, the first English-language film directed by Roman Polanski, is a classic chiller. Catherine Deneuve plays a sexually repressed, mentally ill young girl who is terrified of men. Left alone at her sister's home for a weekend, she suffers a series of severe hallucinations that finally lead her to commit murder. B&W; 105m. **DIR:** Roman Polanski. **CAST:** Catherine Deneuve, Ian Hendry, Yvonne Furneaux, John Fraser, Patrick Wymark. **1965 DVD**

REQUIEM FOR A DREAM ★★1/2 A Jewish Coney Island widow is ravaged by an addiction to food, diet pills, and TV at the same time her son, his girlfriend, and his buddy get hooked on street drugs. Even though its split screens, microphotography, machine-gun editing, fisheye imagery, and fast-motion effects are intoxicating, the film ultimately becomes more exploitative than exhilarating. Rated R for language, violence, drug use, nudity, and sex. 102m. **DIR:** Darren Aronofsky. **CAST:** Jared Leto, Jennifer Connelly, Marlon Wayans, Ellen Burstyn, Christopher McDonald, Louise Lasser, Keith David. **2000 DVD**

REQUIEM FOR A HEAVYWEIGHT (1956) (TELEVISION) ★★★★ Superb drama written for *Playhouse 90* by Rod Serling, about a washed-up heavyweight boxer (Jack Palance) who is forced to find a life outside the ring. Keenan Wynn is magnificent as his gruff, self-centered manager, and Ed Wynn is perfect as the trainer. One of the best live dramas to come out of the Golden Age of Television. Hosted by Jack Klugman, with interviews with the stars and background information on the show. B&W; 89m. **DIR:** Ralph Nelson. **CAST:** Jack Palance, Keenan Wynn, Kim Hunter, Ed Wynn, Ned Glass. **1956**

REQUIEM FOR A HEAVYWEIGHT (1962) ★★★1/2 Anthony Quinn, Julie Harris, Jackie Gleason, Mickey Rooney, and Muhammad Ali (at that time Cassius Clay) give fine performances in this watchable film about boxing corruption. An over-the-hill boxer (Quinn) receives career counseling from a social worker (Harris). B&W; 100m. **DIR:** Ralph Nelson. **CAST:** Anthony Quinn, Julie Harris, Jackie Gleason, Mickey Rooney. **1962**

REQUIEM FOR DOMINIC ★★★ Torn from the headlines, a powerful and riveting true story of revolution and the inhumane treatment of prisoners. When a Romanian political exile looks into the disappearance of his childhood friend, he discovers that he is being held prisoner for the murder of eighty innocent workers. In German with English subtitles. Rated R for violence. 88m. **DIR:** Robert Dornhelm. **CAST:** Felix Mitterer. **1991**

RESCUE, THE ★★ Another dopey movie about a group of teens who set out to rescue their dads from a prisoner-of-war camp. Ferdinand Fairfax achieves some genuine excitement and suspense along the way, but the basic premise is preposterous. Rated PG for profanity and violence. 99m. **DIR:** Ferdinand Fairfax. **CAST:** Kevin Dillon, Kristina Harnos, Marc Price, Charles Haid, Edward Albert. **1988**

RESCUE FORCE ★★ The female CIA agents in this rescue force have names like Candy and Angel and run around half-dressed. You get the picture. Rated R for violence and nudity. 92m. **DIR:** Charles Nizet. **CAST:** Richard Harrison. **1980**

RESCUE ME 🦃 High-school loser bribes a Vietnam-vet drifter to rescue a cheerleader after she is kidnapped by two dim-witted hoods. Rated PG. 90m. **DIR:** Arthur Allan Seidelman. **CAST:** Stephen Dorff, Ami Dolenz, Michael Dudikoff, Peter DeLuise. **1993**

RESCUERS, THE ★★★★ The first adventure of Mouse Rescue Aid Society operatives Bernard (voiced by Bob Newhart) and Bianca (Eva Gabor) is a little gem that signaled the awakening of the Disney animation giant after a long slumber of mediocrity. Don Bluth was partly responsible for the studio's return to quality in this story, based on the writings of Margery Sharp. Rated G. 77m. **DIR:** Wolfgang Reitherman, John Lounsbery, Art Stevens. **1977**

RESCUERS DOWN UNDER ★★★ Disney's first sequel to an animated film doesn't match the charm of the original. Nevertheless, children will enjoy this feature about an Australian boy who takes on a ruthless trapper with the help of mouse heroes. Fine voice work by Bob Newhart, Eva Gabor, George C. Scott, and John Candy. Rated G. 74m. **DIR:** Hendel Butoy, Mike Gabriel. **1990 DVD**

RESCUERS, STORIES OF COURAGE, "TWO WOMEN" ★★★ Two stories about courageous women who stood up to the Nazis during World War II. Inspiring. Barbra Streisand was executive producer. Rated PG-13 for adult situations and violence. 107m. **DIR:** Peter Bogdanovich. **CAST:** Elizabeth Perkins, Sela Ward, Anne Jackson, Fritz Weaver, Al Waxman. **1997**

RESERVOIR DOGS ★★★★1/2 Writer-director Quentin Tarantino debuts with this story of a diamond heist gone awry. Strong ensemble acting and a brain-twisting array of unexpected plot turns make this one of the best crime-thrillers ever made. The brutal violence may be too much for some, but it is never glorified. Rated R for violence and profanity. 99m. **DIR:** Quentin Tarantino. **CAST:** Harvey Keitel, Tim Roth, Michael Madsen, Christopher Penn, Steve Buscemi, Lawrence Tierney, Randy Brooks, Quentin Tarantino. **1992 DVD**

•**RESIDENT EVIL** ★★★ Crack commando squad has three hours to invade the Umbrella Corp.'s subterranean laboratory complex (known as The Hive) and neutralize a supercomputer that has run amok. This cannibal-zombie thriller about genetics experimentation and corporations that think they are above the law blends high-tech conspiracy and low-tech flesh munching. The action borrows Cube's slice-and-dice laser while bloodied Dobermans from Hell and the rotting Living Dead hunt humans in a clammy, tense nightmare

adapted from the popular video game. Rated R for language, violence, sexual content, and nudity. 100m. **DIR:** Paul Anderson. **CAST:** Milla Jovovich, Michelle Rodriguez, Eric Mabius, James Purefoy, Martin Crewes. **2002**

REST IN PIECES 🦃 A young couple inherit an old Spanish estate occupied by murderous Satanists. Not rated; contains graphic violence and nudity. 90m. **DIR:** Joseph Braunsteen. **CAST:** Carrot Top (Scott Thompson), Lorin Jean, Dorothy Malone, Patty Shepard. **1987**

RESTAURANT ★★★ Employees of an upscale Hoboken bar and grill struggle to maintain peace in the workplace and find happiness as their multiethnic friendships, artistic pursuits, and love lives fray. This provocative drama focuses on an anguished, alcoholic bartender who tries to exorcise emotional wounds left by a bigoted father and broken interracial romance just as a semiautobiographical play he wrote is cast and opens. Rated R for language and violence. 108m. **DIR:** Eric Bross. **CAST:** Adrien Brody, Elsie Neal, Malcolm-Jamal Warner, Lauryan Hill. **2000 DVD**

RESTLESS ★★ This Greek movie with Raquel Welch, originally titled *The Beloved,* was unknown until it appeared on video, and if you watch it, you'll know why. There's a lot of pretty island scenery, but the plot about housewife Raquel having an affair with a childhood friend is a guaranteed sleep inducer. Not rated; the film contains sexual situations and violence. 75m. **DIR:** George Pan Cosmatos. **CAST:** Raquel Welch, Richard Johnson, Flora Robson. **1972 DVD**

RESTLESS BREED, THE 🦃 B Western murdered-father/son-takes-revenge plot. 86m. **DIR:** Allan Dwan. **CAST:** Scott Brady, Anne Bancroft, Jay C. Flippen, Jim Davis. **1957**

RESTLESS NATIVES ★★★1/2 Okay, so it's not perfect—the humor and the characterizations are broad and the thick, Scottish accents sometimes make the dialogue difficult to decipher. But that doesn't stop this film from being thoroughly entertaining. Two young Scots, disguised as a clown and a wolf-man, rob tourist buses and become national heroes in the process. Rated PG. 90m. **DIR:** Michael Hoffman. **CAST:** Vincent Friell, Joe Mulloney, Teri Lolly, Ned Beatty. **1986**

RESTORATION ★★★1/2 This bawdy, garish period piece is set in 1660s England, when years of somber Puritanical rule were replaced by a monarchy hot on exploring the arts and sciences. In this court climate, a disheveled, hedonistic, and latently heroic young physician squanders and then rekindles his own restorative talents, personifying both the lightness and darkness of an era engulfed in enlightenment, debauchery, natural disaster, and plagues. Rated PG. 113m. **DIR:** Michael Hoffman. **CAST:** Robert Downey Jr., Sam Neill, David Thewlis, Meg Ryan. **1996 DVD**

RESTRAINING ORDER ★★ Eric Roberts stars as an attorney who witnesses a client commit murder. He tries to secretly arrange the conviction of his client but ends up having to take things into his own hands. Rated R for profanity and violence. 95m. **DIR:** Lee H. Katzin. **CAST:** Eric Roberts, Hannes Jaenicke, Dean Stockwell, Kevin Dobson. **1999 DVD**

RESURRECTED, THE ★★★ An enjoyable tongue-in-cheek production of H. P. Lovecraft's *The Case of Charles Dexter Ward.* The wife of a reclusive doctor asks a detective to find out what her husband has been doing in the lab late at night. Planted firmly in the dark comic tradition of the other Lovecraft-based films: *The Re-animator* and *From Beyond.* Rated R for gore and profanity. 108m. **DIR:** Dan O'Bannon. **CAST:** Chris Sarandon, John Terry, Jane Sibbett. **1991**

RESURRECTION (1980) ★★★★1/2 After Ellen Burstyn loses her husband and the use of her legs in a freak automobile accident, she discovers she has the power to heal not only herself but anyone who is sick or crippled. Pulitzer Prize–winning playwright Sam Shepard is memorable as the young hell-raiser who begins to believe she is Jesus reborn. Rated PG. 103m. **DIR:** Daniel Petrie. **CAST:** Ellen Burstyn, Sam Shepard, Richard Farnsworth, Roberts Blossom, Clifford David, Pamela Payton-Wright, Eva LeGallienne. **1980**

RESURRECTION (1998) ★★ Fifteen minutes into the film, you get the idea that the filmmakers saw *Seven* and decided to rip it off. Christopher Lambert is a big city detective tracking down a serial killer who kills his victims with the precision of a doctor. You'll figure the plot out before the halfway mark in this made-for-cable thriller. Rated R for violence, language, and adult situations. 108m. **DIR:** Russell Mulcahy. **CAST:** Christopher Lambert, Robert Joy, Leland Orser, Barbara Tyson. **1998 DVD**

RESURRECTION MAN ★★★1/2 Chilling Irish thriller about a thug who makes his living collecting debts on soccer bets. Stuart Townsend is absolutely menacing as Victor, a man who prides himself on a job well done, even if it means breaking kneecaps. When Victor and his gang use local politics to spread their terror, their newfound fame attracts all sorts of attention, including a local journalist whose life becomes entwined with the killers. Tough and brutal at every turn, the film never flinches. Rated R for adult situations, language, and violence. 100m. **DIR:** Marc Evans. **CAST:** Stuart Townsend, Brenda Fricker, David Williamson, George Shane, Lee Mulrooney. **1998**

RESURRECTION OF ZACHARY WHEELER, THE ★★ Disappointing science-fiction–mystery has a well-known senator (Bradford Dillman) taken to a bizarre out-of-the-way treatment center in New Mexico after a serious car accident. Confusing movie. Rated G. 100m. **DIR:** Bob Wynn. **CAST:** Bradford Dillman, Angie Dickinson, Leslie Nielsen. **1971**

RETREAT HELL ★★1/2 In this predictable war film, an untested Marine Corps combat unit battles it out behind enemy lines near the Chosin Reservoir in North Korea. All the tried-and-true ingredients are here, including a wet-behind-the-ears private and a tough-talking platoon sergeant. B&W; 95m. **DIR:** Joseph H. Lewis. **CAST:** Frank Lovejoy, Richard Carlson, Russ Tamblyn. **1954**

RETRIBUTION (1988) ★★ In this supernatural thriller, a mild-mannered, down-and-out artist attempts suicide at the same moment a small-time hood is tortured to death. The artist becomes possessed by the soul of the hood and then proceeds to avenge his murder. Low-budget shocker with an inadequate script. Rated R for violence and profanity. 109m. **DIR:** Guy Magar. **CAST:** Dennis Lipscomb, Leslie Wing, Hoyt Axton. **1988**

RETRIBUTION (2000) ★★★★ Tough and gritty import about an investigative newspaper reporter whose latest story is knocking them dead. While covering a nu-

clear arms conspiracy, reporter Cameron Colley becomes alarmed when every subject of his article meets an untimely and occasionally grotesque death. The officials soon suspect Colley, forcing him to go underground to get the real story. Powerful performances, unflinching action, and lots of local Scottish color. Also released as *Complicity*. Rated R for adult situations, language, nudity, and violence. 100m. **DIR:** Gavin Millar. **CAST:** Jonny Lee Miller, Brian Cox, Keeley Hawes, Paul Higgins. **2000 DVD**

RETRO PUPPETMASTER ★★★ Seventh installment in the ongoing series relocates the action to pre–World War II and details how a young Andre Toulon first encounters the magic that brings the puppets to life. This time out the filmmakers took a more mystical bent, lending a fresh feeling to the series. Rated PG-13 for violence. 90m. **DIR:** Joseph Tennent. **CAST:** Greg Sisero, Brigitta Dau, Jack Donner, Guy Rolfe. **1999 DVD**

RETURN, THE (1980) Terminally boring flick about a close encounter. Rated PG. 91m. **DIR:** Greydon Clark. **CAST:** Jan-Michael Vincent, Cybill Shepherd, Martin Landau, Raymond Burr, Neville Brand. **1980**

RETURN (1984) ★★ Right before her father's bid for the Arkansas governorship, Diana (Karlene Crockett) decides to find out about her grandfather's mysterious death. She meets a young man who relives her grandfather's life through hypnosis. Below-par mystery. Rated R for profanity, violence, and partial nudity. 78m. **DIR:** Andrew Silver. **CAST:** Karlene Crockett, John Walcutt, Anne Francis, Frederic Forrest. **1984**

RETURN FROM WITCH MOUNTAIN ★★ Christopher Lee and Bette Davis capture Ike Eisenmann to use his supernatural powers to accomplish their own purposes. Sequel to *Escape to Witch Mountain*, in which Eisenmann and Kim Richards discover their powers and the effect they can have on humans. A good children's film, but weak Disney. Rated G. 93m. **DIR:** John Hough. **CAST:** Bette Davis, Christopher Lee, Kim Richards, Ike Eisenmann. **1978**

RETURN OF A MAN CALLED HORSE, THE ★★★ Every bit as good as its predecessor, *A Man Called Horse*. Both films present an honest, and sometimes shocking, glimpse at the culture of the American Indian. The new film picks up with a bored and unhappy Morgan deciding to return to America. Rated PG for violence. 129m. **DIR:** Irvin Kershner. **CAST:** Richard Harris, Gale Sondergaard, Geoffrey Lewis, Bill Lucking, Jorge Luke, Enrique Lucero. **1976 DVD**

RETURN OF CAPTAIN INVINCIBLE, THE ★★1/2 Camp send-up of old comic-book-hero serials of the Thirties and Forties. Arkin is Captain Invincible, fighting crime and Nazis and preserving the American way of life. During the communist witch-hunt of the Fifties, though, the captain is accused of being a Red and quickly becomes a national disgrace. Alan Arkin flies high as Captain Invincible. Songs, special effects, and corny melodrama all combine to get you through the occasional dull bits. Rated PG for profanity and violence. 101m. **DIR:** Philippe Mora. **CAST:** Alan Arkin, Christopher Lee. **1984 DVD**

RETURN OF CHANDU, THE (THE MAGICIAN) ★★1/2 Crackerjack fantasy-adventure serial has enough action, trickery, and plot twists for two chapterplays as Bela Lugosi plays Chandu, Master of White Magic, hot on the trail of evil Lemurians who have stolen his beloved Princess Nadji. Hokey but fun family fare. B&W; 12 chapters. **DIR:** Ray Taylor. **CAST:** Bela Lugosi, Maria Alba, Clara Kimball Young, Lucien Prival, Bryant Washburn. **1934**

RETURN OF DR. FU MANCHU ★★1/2 Evil genius Dr. Fu Manchu returns to England to fulfill his vow to kill John Petrie, last of the descendants of those responsible for the death of Fu's family. Aerial kidnappings, mind-sapping potions, and action-filled fights form the backdrop as the well-fed fiend chews up the scenery, leering, and gloatingly uttering things like, "The thought of inflicting two deaths on a victim delights my peculiar sense of humor." B&W; 73m. **DIR:** Rowland V. Lee. **CAST:** Warner Oland, O. P. Heggie, Neil Hamilton, Jean Arthur, William Austin. **1930**

RETURN OF DR. X ★★ Director Vincent Sherman's first motion picture is not, as one might assume, a sequel to *Dr. X*. Instead, it borrows from Boris Karloff's *The Walking Dead* in a tale of an executed man brought back to life. Worth watching for Humphrey Bogart's only appearance in a horror movie. B&W; 62m. **DIR:** Vincent Sherman. **CAST:** Dennis Morgan, Humphrey Bogart, Wayne Morris, Rosemary Lane, John Litel. **1939**

RETURN OF DRACULA ★★1/2 Until Hammer Films revived him, Count Dracula wasn't seen much in the 1950s, but this above-average outing is one of the exceptions. Francis Lederer takes the title role, assuming a European painter's identity in order to bleed modern California dry. Video release includes a color climax. B&W; 77m. **DIR:** Paul Landres. **CAST:** Francis Lederer, Norma Eberhardt, Ray Stricklyn. **1958**

RETURN OF ELIOT NESS, THE ★★1/2 Robert Stack suits up again as legendary crime fighter Eliot Ness in this made-for-television crime-drama. Now that Al Capone is out of the picture, the streets of Chicago are up for grabs. With every thug in town trying to make a name for himself, Ness comes out of retirement to clean up the streets. Stack is good as the resurrected Ness, but telefilm is more nostalgic than anything else. 94m. **DIR:** James A. Contner. **CAST:** Robert Stack, Jack Coleman, Philip Bosco, Charles Durning, Lisa Hartman. **1991**

RETURN OF FRANK CANNON, THE ★★1/2 When an ex-CIA agent is murdered, portly detective Frank Cannon (William Conrad) comes out of retirement. Made for television. 96m. **DIR:** Corey Allen. **CAST:** William Conrad, Arthur Hill, Diana Muldaur, Ed Nelson. **1980**

RETURN OF FRANK JAMES, THE ★★★ Gene Tierney made her film debut in this inevitable sequel to *Jesse James* (1939). Henry Fonda reprises his role as brother Frank and attempts to avenge Jesse's death at the hands of "dirty little coward" Bob Ford, played by John Carradine. Thanks to Fonda's fine acting and Fritz Lang's sensitive direction, what could have been a pale rip-off is an enjoyable Western. 92m. **DIR:** Fritz Lang. **CAST:** Henry Fonda, Gene Tierney, Donald Meek, John Carradine, Jackie Cooper, J. Edward Bromberg, Henry Hull. **1940**

RETURN OF JAFAR, THE ★★★ Somewhere between Saturday-morning cartoons and Disney theatrical releases lies this direct-to-video sequel of *Aladdin*. The kids will still enjoy it, but parents will probably snooze. The same characters (Aladdin, Jasmine, Genie, Iago,

and Abu) are confronted by the dastardly Jafar when a bandit releases the evil genie. Aladdin's friends must work together to set him free from Jafar's deadly lava pit. Not rated; contains plenty of comic-book violence. 66m. **DIR:** Toby Shelton, Tad Stones, Alan Zaslove. **1994**

RETURN OF JESSE JAMES, THE ★★1/2 In this low-budget oater, John Ireland portrays a small-time outlaw who bears a striking resemblance to Jesse James. Taking advantage of this rumor, he sets out to prove to everyone that Jesse James, shot and killed by fellow gang member Bob Ford, did not die and is still in business. Plodding, but fairly well acted. B&W; 75m. **DIR:** Arthur Hilton. **CAST:** John Ireland, Ann Dvorak, Hugh O'Brian, Henry Hull. **1950**

RETURN OF JOSEY WALES ★★ The name is the only similarity between Clint Eastwood's *The Outlaw Josey Wales* and this mediocre Western. Wanted man Wales stands up to a crooked Mexican sheriff. Rated R for a rape scene and violence. 90m. **DIR:** Michael Parks. **CAST:** Michael Parks. **1986**

RETURN OF MARTIN GUERRE, THE ★★★★1/2 Brilliantly absorbing account of an actual sixteenth-century court case in which a man returns to his family and village after years away at the wars, only to have his identity questioned. Gérard Depardieu and Nathalie Baye give outstanding, carefully restrained performances. In French with English subtitles. No MPAA rating. 111m. **DIR:** Daniel Vigne. **CAST:** Gérard Depardieu, Nathalie Baye, Roger Planchon. **1982 DVD**

RETURN OF OCTOBER, THE ★★★ A girl thinks her uncle is reincarnated as the horse, October. This fun movie set the stage, tone, and sense of humor for body-switch movies that came along a generation later. 87m. **DIR:** Joseph H. Lewis. **CAST:** Glenn Ford, Terry Moore, James Gleason, May Whitty, Albert Sharpe, Henry O'Neill, Samuel S. Hinds, Nana Bryant, Jackie Gleason. **1948**

RETURN OF PETER GRIMM, THE ★★★1/2 Enjoyable blend of *It's a Wonderful Life* and *A Christmas Carol* with the incomparable Lionel Barrymore as Peter Grimm, who dies and is given a second chance to return to Earth and reconcile his family and affairs. B&W; 82m. **DIR:** George Nicholls Jr. **CAST:** Lionel Barrymore, Helen Mack, Edward Ellis, Donald Meek. **1935**

RETURN OF SPINAL TAP, THE ★★★★ The world's most lovable heavy-metal band is back in this wonderful follow-up to Rob Reiner's cult 1984 "rockumentary," *This Is Spinal Tap*. This time the boys are in their native England where they blend excellent live-concert footage (including some new songs), interviews with old friends, and recollections of their formative years. Great music and great fun. Not rated. 110m. **DIR:** Jim DiBergi. **CAST:** Christopher Guest, Michael McKean, Harry Shearer. **1993**

RETURN OF SUPERFLY, THE ★★ Priest (Nathan Purdee) returns to the United States, only to be hunted by both the law and drug lords. The shaky plot and acting are marginally redeemed by the anti-drug message. Rated R for nudity, profanity, and violence. 94m. **DIR:** Sig Shore. **CAST:** Nathan Purdee, Margaret Avery, Christopher Curry, David Groh. **1990**

RETURN OF THE ALIEN'S DEADLY SPAWN, THE ★★ Blood-filled horror film about alien creatures from outer space who kill and destroy anyone and everything that gets in their way. Lots of gore, ripped flesh, and off-the-wall humor. For people who like sick movies. Rated R for profanity and gore. 90m. **DIR:** Douglas McKeown. **CAST:** Charles George Hildebrandt. **1984**

RETURN OF THE APE MAN ★★★ Scientists Bela Lugosi and John Carradine revive a Neanderthal man, who soon goes on a rampage. Above-average monogram poverty-row programmer, just fast-paced (and poker-faced) enough to be diverting. B&W; 68m. **DIR:** Phil Rosen. **CAST:** Bela Lugosi, John Carradine. **1944**

RETURN OF THE BAD MEN ★★★ Randolph Scott has his hands full in this routine Western. No sooner does he settle down in Oklahoma than he must slap leather with Billy the Kid, the Dalton gang, the Younger brothers, and the Sundance Kid. As the latter, Robert Ryan shore ain't the appealing gun hand who rode with Butch Cassidy. B&W; 90m. **DIR:** Ray Enright. **CAST:** Randolph Scott, Anne Jeffreys, Robert Ryan, George "Gabby" Hayes, Lex Barker. **1948**

RETURN OF THE DRAGON ★★★1/2 After seeing *Return of the Dragon*, we have no doubt that Bruce Lee, not Robert Clouse, directed *Enter the Dragon*. Lee was credited with staging the fight scenes, but our guess is that he was well aware of the latter film's possible impact and exercised control over the creative nonacting facets of the film whenever he could. *Return of the Dragon* was made before *Enter*, and it shows Lee's considerable directorial talent. A delightful film, brimful of comedy, action, and acrobatics. Rated R. 91m. **DIR:** Bruce Lee. **CAST:** Bruce Lee, Chuck Norris, Nora Miao. **1973 DVD**

RETURN OF THE EVIL DEAD ★★ This Spanish zombie shocker has nothing to do with Sam Raimi's *Evil Dead* films. It's one of the entries in de Ossorio's intermittently scary Blind Dead cycle (see also *Horror of the Zombies*), retitled for U.S. release. A few scenes of the rotting undead stalking their victims have a claustrophobic quality that foreshadows John Carpenter's *The Fog*. Rated R. 85m. **DIR:** Amando de Ossorio. **CAST:** Victor Petit. **1975**

RETURN OF THE FAMILY MAN 🦃 Low-budget rip-off of the far superior *The Stepfather* will leave you wondering why Hollywood can't come up with more than one or two ideas. Not rated; contains violence. 90m. **DIR:** John Murlowski. **CAST:** Ron Smerczak. **1990**

RETURN OF THE FLY, THE ★★★ In this fine sequel to *The Fly*, the son of the original insect makes the same mistake as his father . . . with identical results. Effective film benefits from stark black-and-white photography and solid effects. Watch out for the guinea-pig scene! B&W; 80m. **DIR:** Edward L. Bernds. **CAST:** Vincent Price, Brett Halsey, David Frankham. **1959**

RETURN OF THE JEDI ★★★★★ Third film in the *Star Wars* series centers on the all-out attempt by the Rebel forces—led by Luke Skywalker, Han Solo, Princess Leia, and Lando Calrissian—to turn back the tidal wave of interplanetary domination by the evil Galactic Empire and its forces, led by Darth Vader. Rated PG. 133m. **DIR:** Richard Marquand. **CAST:** Mark Hamill, Harrison Ford, Carrie Fisher, Billy Dee Williams, Dave Prowse, Peter Mayhew, Anthony Daniels, James Earl Jones. **1983**

RETURN OF THE KILLER TOMATOES ★★1/2 The mad scientist, whose experiments caused the first tomato war, perfects his process that creates intelligent vegetable life. Although it lacks the spontaneous humor the original exhibited, this *Return* has its moments. Language may not be suitable for a younger audience. Rated PG. 99m. **DIR:** John DeBello. **CAST:** Anthony Starke, George Clooney, John Astin. **1988 DVD**

RETURN OF THE LIVING DEAD, THE ★★★★ Extremely gory horror film produced with a great deal of style and ample amounts of comedy as well. The residents of a small Virginia cemetery are brought back to life after accidental exposure to a strange chemical, and they're hungry... for human brains. Rated R for violence, nudity, and language. 91m. **DIR:** Dan O'Bannon. **CAST:** Clu Gulager, James Karen, Don Calfa, Thom Mathews. **1985**

RETURN OF THE LIVING DEAD PART II ★★ The dead have once again risen from their long slumber and are hungry for human brains. A drum of special gas that seems to reanimate the dead has been discovered by a trio of children. They unwittingly loose the gas on the unsuspecting town. Definitely an R rating for the violence and language. 90m. **DIR:** Ken Wiederhorn. **CAST:** James Karen, Thom Mathews, Dana Ashbrook. **1988**

RETURN OF THE LIVING DEAD 3 ★★★ Love never dies, at least not in this sequel. When Curt's girlfriend Mindy dies, he drags her body to a top-secret government lab where his father works on reanimating the dead. Curt revives Mindy, but when she starts craving human flesh, their relationship becomes strained. Goofy humor, outrageous special effects, and a likable cast make this series worth reviving. Rated R for nudity, language, and extreme violence. 96m. **DIR:** Brian Yuzna. **CAST:** J. Trevor Edmond, Mindy Clarke, Sarah Douglas, Kent McCord. **1993 DVD**

RETURN OF THE MAN FROM U.N.C.L.E., THE ★★★ Secret agents Napoleon Solo (Robert Vaughn) and Illya Kuryakin (David McCallum) are called out of a fifteen-year retirement. Fans of the original series will find this lighthearted spy adventure especially entertaining. 109m. **DIR:** Ray Austin. **CAST:** Robert Vaughn, David McCallum, Patrick Macnee, Tom Mason, Gayle Hunnicutt, Geoffrey Lewis, Anthony Zerbe, Keenan Wynn, George Lazenby. **1983**

RETURN OF THE MUSKETEERS ★★★★ Filled with humor and swashbuckling high adventure, this adaptation of Alexandre Dumas's *Twenty Years After* finds D'Artagnan and Porthos pitted against Athos and Aramis when they mistakenly ally themselves with the queen and her power-crazed lover/cardinal. Dedicated to the memory of the marvelous Roy Kinnear, who died as the result of an accident during the filming. 100m. **DIR:** Richard Lester. **CAST:** Michael York, Oliver Reed, Richard Chamberlain, Frank Finlay, C. Thomas Howell, Kim Cattrall, Geraldine Chaplin, Christopher Lee, Philippe Noiret, Roy Kinnear, Jean-Pierre Cassel, Alan Howard, Bill Paterson. **1989**

RETURN OF THE NATIVE, THE ★★★★ Enchanting Catherine Zeta Jones plays Thomas Hardy's ill-fated heroine in this fine *Hallmark Hall of Fame* presentation. When Jones, as bewitching Eustacia Vye, joins her grandfather in a small, superstitious town, she has several of the young men falling in love with her. Her reckless actions stir gossip and tragedy. Costumes and fabulous English countryside are further complemented by the perfect score played by the Royal Philharmonic Orchestra. Not rated; contains mature themes. 98m. **DIR:** Jack Gold. **CAST:** Catherine Zeta Jones, Ray Stevenson, Clive Owen, Joan Plowright, Steven Mackintosh. **1994 DVD**

RETURN OF THE PINK PANTHER, THE ★★★★ Writer-director Blake Edwards and star Peter Sellers revived their Inspector Clouseau character for a new series of comic adventures beginning with this slapstick classic. There are many funny scenes as Sellers attempts to track down the Phantom (Christopher Plummer) while making life intolerable for the chief inspector (Herbert Lom). Rated PG. 113m. **DIR:** Blake Edwards. **CAST:** Peter Sellers, Christopher Plummer, Herbert Lom, Catherine Schell, Burt Kwouk, Peter Arne. **1975 DVD**

RETURN OF THE SAND FAIRY, THE ★★★1/2 Very cute, very British fairy tale set in the English countryside around 1910. Based on the story by children's writer Edith Nesbit, this revolves around the old adage, "careful for what you wish, it may come true." Four children, forced to visit a cranky great-aunt, discover a sand fairy who grants all their desires. This film has a witty intelligence and humor. Not rated. 139m. **DIR:** Marilyn Fox. **CAST:** Toby Uffindell-Phillips, Ellie Laura Clarke, Leonard Kirby, Vicci Avery. **1992**

RETURN OF THE SECAUCUS 7 ★★★★1/2 Here's a gem of a movie about the reunion of seven friends ten years after they were wrongfully busted in Secaucus, New Jersey, while on their way to the last demonstration against the Vietnam war in Washington, D.C. It is a delicious blend of characterization, humor, and insight. No MPAA rating, but *Secaucus 7* has nudity, profanity, and implicit sex. 100m. **DIR:** John Sayles. **CAST:** Mark Arnott, Gordon Clapp, Maggie Cousineau, Adam LeFevre, Bruce MacDonald, Jean Passanante, Maggie Renzi. **1980**

RETURN OF THE SEVEN ★★1/2 Drab, inferior sequel to *The Magnificent Seven* follows Yul Brynner doing what he does best, getting six Yankee gunfighters fool enough to take on scores of Mexican bandits for no pay at all. 96m. **DIR:** Burt Kennedy. **CAST:** Yul Brynner, Robert Fuller, Warren Oates, Claude Akins, Emilio Fernandez, Jordan Christopher. **1966**

RETURN OF THE SOLDIER, THE ★★★★★ During World War I, a soldier (Alan Bates) suffers shell shock and forgets the last twenty years of his life. His doctors must decide whether he should be allowed to enjoy what has resulted in a carefree second youth, or be brought back to real life and the responsibilities that go with it. Everyone in the cast is superb. Not rated; contains adult situations. 105m. **DIR:** Alan Bridges. **CAST:** Glenda Jackson, Julie Christie, Ann-Margret, Alan Bates, Ian Holm, Frank Finlay, Jeremy Kemp. **1985**

RETURN OF THE SWAMP THING ★★★ The big, green monster-hero comes out of the swamp to do battle once again with evil scientist Louis Jourdan, while Heather Locklear is the object of his affections. Unlike the first film, which was also based on the DC Comics character, you're not supposed to take this sequel seriously. Rated PG-13. 87m. **DIR:** Jim Wynorski. **CAST:** Louis Jourdan, Heather Locklear, Dick Durock. **1989**

RETURN OF THE TALL BLOND MAN WITH ONE BLACK SHOE, THE ★★1/2 This sequel to the original *Tall Blond Man* . . . is, unfortunately, inferior. But it's still a delight to watch Pierre Richard go through his comic paces. Once again his reactions to what he's faced with are the reason to see this. In French with English subtitles. No MPAA rating. 84m. **DIR:** Yves Robert. **CAST:** Pierre Richard, Mireille Darc, Jean Rochefort. **1974**

RETURN OF THE VAMPIRE, THE ★★★ Set during World War II, this surprisingly good vampire tale has the supposedly destroyed fiend, Armand Tesla (Bela Lugosi), unearthed by a German bombing raid on London. B&W; 69m. **DIR:** Lew Landers, Kurt Neumann. **CAST:** Bela Lugosi, Frieda Inescort, Nina Foch, Miles Mander, Matt Willis. **1943**

RETURN TO BOGGY CREEK A cheap and boring sequel about a mysterious creature that stalks the swamps of a small fishing community. Rated PG. 87m. **DIR:** Tom Moore. **CAST:** Dawn Wells. **1978**

RETURN TO EDEN ★★★ This four-and-one-half-hour miniseries, originally made for Australian television, is a bit much to watch at one sitting. Fans of soaps, however, will find it holds their interest. A wealthy woman discovers that her handsome husband only married her for her money when he feeds her to the crocodiles. Miraculously surviving, she alters her appearance and sets about gaining revenge. Not rated, but with brief nudity. 259m. **DIR:** Karen Arthur. **CAST:** Rebecca Gilling, James Reyne, Wendy Hughes. **1983**

RETURN TO FANTASY ISLAND ★★ If you liked the television series *Fantasy Island*, you'll like this made-for-TV movie. Ricardo Montalban is the suave operator of a wish-fulfillment island, assisted by his tiny friend Tattoo (Herve Villechaize). It's pure hokum, but it does offer a chance to watch some fine actors. 100m. **DIR:** George McCowan. **CAST:** Ricardo Montalban, Joseph Campanella, Joseph Cotten, Adrienne Barbeau, Laraine Day, Herve Villechaize, Cameron Mitchell, Karen Valentine, France Nuyen, George Chakiris, Horst Buchholz, George Maharis. **1977**

RETURN TO FROGTOWN Unbelievably bad sequel to *Hell Comes to Frogtown*. When a flying Texas ranger (Lou Ferrigno) is captured by a crazed amphibian, a sexy doctor and her reluctant partner try to rescue him. Grade-Z sets, story, and dialogue. Rated PG-13 for violence. 90m. **DIR:** Donald G. Jackson. **CAST:** Lou Ferrigno, Charles Napier, Robert Z'Dar, Denice Duff, Don Stroud. **1992 DVD**

RETURN TO LONESOME DOVE ★★★★ Sequel to the milestone miniseries lacks the quirky, bawdy qualities of its predecessor, but there is much for Western fans to enjoy in this sprawling epic. Captain Call and his son Newt become involved in a range war. Unrelated to author Larry McMurtry's continuation of the story, *Streets of Laredo*. 330m. **DIR:** Mike Robe. **CAST:** Jon Voight, Barbara Hershey, Rick Schroder, Louis Gossett Jr., William L. Petersen, Oliver Reed, Dennis Haysbert, Reese Witherspoon, Timothy Scott, Chris Cooper, C.C.H. Pounder, Nia Peeples, William Sanderson. **1993**

RETURN TO MACON COUNTY Two fun-loving boneheads run afoul of the law in the rural South. Rated PG. 104m. **DIR:** Richard Compton. **CAST:** Don Johnson, Nick Nolte, Robin Mattson. **1975**

RETURN TO MAYBERRY ★★1/2 Nostalgia time. Andy, Barney, and most of the gang are reunited in this TV-movie valentine to *The Andy Griffith Show.* The many plot lines include Opie's impending fatherhood, Barney's campaign for sheriff, and the appearance of a monster in the lake. 95m. **DIR:** Bob Sweeney. **CAST:** Andy Griffith, Don Knotts, Ron Howard, Jim Nabors, George Lindsey, Aneta Corseaut, Betty Lynn. **1986**

RETURN TO ME ★★★★ This captivating tale of love lost and found again concerns an architect (David Duchovny) who loses his wife unexpectedly; elsewhere, long-suffering Minnie Driver gets her life back with a heart transplant . . . taken from Duchovny's wife. Driver and Duchovny eventually meet and fall in love, neither aware of the medical miracle that bonds them; the point of the story is what will happen after they *do* find out. The result is a charming example of the kinder, gentler filmmaking that our parents often complain we "don't see enough of anymore." Rated PG for the mildest of expletives. 115m. **DIR:** Bonnie Hunt. **CAST:** David Duchovny, Minnie Driver, Carroll O'Connor, Robert Loggia, Bonnie Hunt, David Alan Grier, Joely Richardson, James Belushi. **2000 DVD**

•RETURN TO NEVER LAND ★★★ Defying their own straight-to-video tradition for sequels, Disney Studios took their capper to 1953's *Peter Pan* to the big screen. Much of its success must be attributed to their faithfulness to the original Pan character. This time he must rescue Jane, Wendy's daughter, from Captain Hook and his crew. A jaded WWII preteen, Jane has a liberated attitude and needs a great deal of convincing before she can believe in the magical powers surrounding her. The crocodile has been replaced by a less appealing octopus and the animation, overall, is just average. Not rated. 64m. **DIR:** Robin Budd, Donovan Cook. **2002 DVD**

RETURN TO OZ ★★★★ In this semisequel to *The Wizard of Oz*, viewers will hear no songs nor see any Munchkins. It is a very different, but equally enjoyable, trip down the Yellow Brick Road, with young star Fairuza Balk outstanding as Dorothy. It gets pretty scary at times and isn't all fluff and wonder like the Oz of yore. This is nevertheless a magical film for the child in everyone. Rated PG for scary stuff. 110m. **DIR:** Walter Murch. **CAST:** Fairuza Balk, Nicol Williamson, Jean Marsh, Piper Laurie, Matt Clark. **1985 DVD**

RETURN TO PARADISE (1953) ★★1/2 An American arrives on a remote South Seas island and locks horns with a religious fanatic who dominates the natives. *Very* loosely based on part of James Michener's *Tales of the South Pacific*. 88m. **DIR:** Mark Robson. **CAST:** Gary Cooper, Barry Jones, Roberta Haynes. **1953**

RETURN TO PARADISE (1998) ★★★1/2 A fascinating moral dilemma is at the heart of this captivating drama, which builds to an unexpectedly powerful climax. After a prologue showing that three vacationing guys in Malaysia just want to have fun, we flash-forward two years and discover that two of these young men have built lives for themselves. Enter passionate attorney Anne Heche, who explains that their friend has been in jail on a drug charge ever since they left him . . . and that he's soon to be executed, unless these two New Yorkers return to Malaysia and "share" a jail term. The perfor-

mances are uniformly strong, and the script is surprisingly pungent and heartfelt. Nothing here should be taken for granted. Rated R for profanity, drug use, and sexual content. 109m. **DIR:** Joseph Ruben. **CAST:** Vince Vaughn, Anne Heche, Joaquin Phoenix, David Conrad, Jada Pinkett Smith. **1998 DVD**

RETURN TO PEYTON PLACE ★★ A misfire that should have scored. The sequel to one of the most popular films of all time suffers from a bad case of miscasting. No one from the first film reappears in the sequel, and none of the players look or act at ease with their characters. 122m. **DIR:** José Ferrer. **CAST:** Eleanor Parker, Carol Lynley, Jeff Chandler, Robert Sterling, Tuesday Weld, Mary Astor, Bob Crane, Luciana Paluzzi, Brett Halsey, Gunnar Hellstrom. **1961**

RETURN TO SALEM'S LOT, A 🦃 A divorced father, recently reunited with his teenage son, goes back to the town of his birth to find that its inhabitants are vampires. Rated R for nudity and violence. 101m. **DIR:** Larry Cohen. **CAST:** Michael Moriarty, Samuel Fuller, Andrew Duggan, Evelyn Keyes. **1987**

RETURN TO SAVAGE BEACH 🦃 Filmmaker Andy Sidaris rehashes his triple-B formula (babes, bosoms, and bullets) in this tale of female agents after a stolen computer disk. Rated R for adult situations, language, nudity, and violence. 98m. **DIR:** Andy Sidaris. **CAST:** Julie Strain, Julie K. Smith, Shae Marks, Cristian Letelier. **1998**

RETURN TO SNOWY RIVER, PART II ★★★★1/2 In this spectacular sequel to *The Man from Snowy River*, Tom Burlinson returns to right wrongs and romance Sigrid Thornton in rugged, Old West–style Australia. Director Geoff Burrowes, who produced the first film, outdoes the original at every turn. A movie the whole family can love. Rated PG for some violence. 100m. **DIR:** Geoff Burrowes. **CAST:** Tom Burlinson, Sigrid Thornton, Brian Dennehy, Nicholas Eadie, Bryan Marshall. **1988**

RETURN TO THE BLUE LAGOON 🦃 The beautifully photographed scenes of a lush tropical island cannot salvage this lame sequel which basically rehashes the story of its 1980 predecessor. Rated PG-13 for nudity and brief violence. 101m. **DIR:** William A. Graham. **CAST:** Milla Jovovich, Brian Krause, Lisa Pelikan, Courtney Phillips, Garette Patrick Ratliff. **1991**

RETURN TO THE LOST WORLD ★★1/2 Continuation of British remake is actually more exciting than the first try, although the dinosaurs are still laughable. A group of scientists and tagalongs returns to the mysterious plateau, now threatened by a greedy oil prospector and a volcano. Modest but engaging. Rated PG for violence. 99m. **DIR:** Timothy Bond. **CAST:** John Rhys-Davies, David Warner, Eric McCormack, Tamara Gorski, Nathania Stanford. **1992**

RETURN TO TREASURE ISLAND ★★★1/2 This five-tape series was produced for the Disney Channel. It is a sequel to Disney's 1950 film *Treasure Island*, based on Robert Louis Stevenson's classic novel. The action here takes place ten years later with young Jim Hawkins (Christopher Guard), now an educated young man being reunited with the scheming Long John (Brian Blessed). 101m. **DIR:** Piers Haggard. **CAST:** Brian Blessed, Christopher Guard, Kenneth Colley. **1985 DVD**

RETURN TO TWO-MOON JUNCTION ★★★ This languid girl-meets-boy erotic drama fulfills the genre's requirements—attractive performers, idyllic setting, and playfully sensual lovemaking—and is quite superior to its predecessor. Rated R for nudity, simulated sex, and profanity. 96m. **DIR:** Farhad Mann. **CAST:** Melinda Clarke, John Clayton Schafer, Louise Fletcher. **1994**

RETURNING, THE 🦃 A woman copes with the death of her son and the apparent madness of her husband. 86m. **DIR:** Joel Bender. **CAST:** Gabriel Walsh, Susan Strasberg. **1990**

REUBEN, REUBEN ★★★★1/2 A funny, touching, and memorable character study about an irascible Scottish poet, this film, directed by Robert Ellis Miller (*The Heart Is a Lonely Hunter*) and written by Julius J. Epstein (*Casablanca*), ranges from romantic to ribald, and from low-key believability to blistering black comedy. In short, it's a rare cinematic treat. First and foremost among the picture's assets is a superb leading performance by Tom Conti. Rated R for profanity and suggested sex. 101m. **DIR:** Robert Ellis Miller. **CAST:** Tom Conti, Kelly McGillis, Roberts Blossom, Cynthia Harris, E. Katherine Kerr, Joel Fabiani, Lois Smith. **1983**

REUNION ★★★★ Jason Robards portrays an elderly Jew who returns to Germany fifty-five years after escaping the rise of Hitler in this touching film about letting go of the past by grasping the present. But Robards's scenes are just bookends to the central story of his character as a boy and the friendship that develops between him and a German aristocrat's son. Rated PG-13 for brief nudity. 110m. **DIR:** Jerry Schatzberg. **CAST:** Jason Robards Jr. **1991**

REUNION IN FRANCE ★★ A romantic melodrama that is badly dated, especially considering the fact that it top lines John Wayne and he doesn't get the girl in the last reel. Joan Crawford is a sophisticated Parisian who finds out her lover (Philip Dorn) is apparently collaborating with the Nazis. She switches her affections to an American flier (John Wayne) running from the Gestapo. B&W; 102m. **DIR:** Jules Dassin. **CAST:** Joan Crawford, John Wayne, Philip Dorn, Reginald Owen, John Carradine. **1942**

REVENGE (1971) (SHELLEY WINTERS) ★★ Made for television, this has Shelley Winters out for—you guessed it—revenge for her daughter's rape. Not as bad as it could have been. 78m. **DIR:** Jud Taylor. **CAST:** Shelley Winters, Stuart Whitman, Bradford Dillman, Roger Perry. **1971**

REVENGE (1971) (JOAN COLLINS) ★★ When a little girl is abducted and murdered, her family kidnaps the man they believe responsible, torturing and finally killing him. Interesting suspense film, but it lacks the intensity it should have. Not rated. 85m. **DIR:** Sidney Hayers. **CAST:** Joan Collins, James Booth, Sinead Cusack. **1971**

REVENGE (1990) ★★ Pilot Kevin Costner falls in love with the beautiful young wife (Madeleine Stowe) of a powerful Mexican gangster (Anthony Quinn), whose life Costner once saved. Poorly paced melodrama, rated R for nudity, profanity, simulated sex, and violence. 120m. **DIR:** Tony Scott. **CAST:** Kevin Costner, Anthony Quinn, Madeleine Stowe, Sally Kirkland. **1990 DVD**

REVENGE OF DR. X, THE ★★ Worth hunting down for bad-movie buffs. Not rated, but unobjectionable despite

a brief skinny-dipping scene. 88m. **DIR:** Not credited. **CAST:** James Craig. **1970**

REVENGE OF FRANKENSTEIN ★★★★ The best of the Hammer Studios Frankenstein movies, this sequel to *The Curse of Frankenstein* sets the pace for all the entries that followed, focusing on the continuing exploits of Dr. Victor Frankenstein (Peter Cushing) rather than the amblings of his first creation. Once again, the doctor's essentially well-meant experiments create havoc, and Cushing is in top form. 91m. **DIR:** Terence Fisher. **CAST:** Peter Cushing, Francis Matthews, Eunice Gayson, Michael Gwynn, Lionel Jeffries. **1958**

REVENGE OF THE CREATURE ★★ Even as sequels go, this follow-up to *Creature from the Black Lagoon* is disappointing. Scientists capture him and take him to Florida, he gets loose, and they kill him. Only the ferocity of some of the murders and Clint Eastwood's screen debut as a dim-witted lab assistant break the monotony. B&W; 82m. **DIR:** Jack Arnold. **CAST:** John Agar, Lori Nelson, John Bromfield, Clint Eastwood. **1955**

REVENGE OF THE MUSKETEERS ★★★ Sophie Marceau shines in this sexy version of the Dumas classic, playing the feisty daughter of D'Artagnan. When she learns of a plot against France, her father summons the musketeers for one last mission. There is much to relish in director Bertrand Tavernier's French production, including exquisite period detail and a wild sense of abandon. In French with English subtitles. Rated R for adult situations, language, nudity, and violence. 130m. **DIR:** Bertrand Tavernier. **CAST:** Sophie Marceau, Philippe Noiret, Claude Rich, Sami Frey, Jean-Luc Bideau, Raoul Billerey. **1994**

REVENGE OF THE NERDS ★★★ The title characters, Lewis (Robert Carradine) and Gilbert (Anthony Edwards), strike back at the jocks who torment them in this watchable, fitfully funny comedy. Rated R. 90m. **DIR:** Jeff Kanew. **CAST:** Robert Carradine, Anthony Edwards, Julie Montgomery, Curtis Armstrong, Ted McGinley, Michelle Meyrink, James Cromwell, Bernie Casey, Timothy Busfield, John Goodman. **1984 DVD**

REVENGE OF THE NERDS II: NERDS IN PARADISE 🦃 With this sequel, one assumes that the filmmakers were out for revenge against their audience. Rated PG-13 for profanity and tasteless humor. 95m. **DIR:** Joe Roth. **CAST:** Robert Carradine, Timothy Busfield, Curtis Armstrong, Larry B. Scott, Courtney Thorne-Smith, Anthony Edwards, Ed Lauter. **1987**

REVENGE OF THE NERDS III: THE NEXT GENERATION 🦃 The nerds take their act to television, giving new meaning to the term "boob tube." 93m. **DIR:** Roland Mesa. **CAST:** Robert Carradine, Ted McGinley, Curtis Armstrong, Morton Downey Jr. **1992**

REVENGE OF THE NERDS IV: NERDS IN LOVE ★★★ They're still lovable, but in this made-for-television comedy, the nerds have lost their edge. Most of the original cast returns, but their antics have been watered down for the small screen. Not rated. 90m. **DIR:** Steve Zacharias. **CAST:** Robert Carradine, Curtis Armstrong, Joseph Bologna, Ted McGinley, Larry B. Scott, Donald Gibb. **1994**

REVENGE OF THE NINJA 🦃 Japanese karate experts take on the mob in this kung fu flick. Rated R for violence and nudity. 88m. **DIR:** Sam Firstenberg. **CAST:** Sho Kosugi, Keith Vitali, Arthur Roberts, Mario Gallo. **1983**

REVENGE OF THE PINK PANTHER, THE ★★★★1/2 This is arguably the best of the slapstick series. It contains inspired bits penned by director Blake Edwards and played to perfection by Peter Sellers. Rated PG. 99m. **DIR:** Blake Edwards. **CAST:** Peter Sellers, Dyan Cannon, Robert Webber, Marc Lawrence, Herbert Lom, Burt Kwouk, Robert Loggia, Paul Stewart. **1978 DVD**

REVENGE OF THE RED BARON ★★ A modicum of suspense saves this hokey thriller about a veteran flying ace (Mickey Rooney) who shot down the infamous Red Baron. Now in a wheelchair, Rooney must fight to save his family from a model biplane possessed by the spirit of the dead pilot. The plane creates havoc, but the film mostly creates laughs. Rated PG-13 for violence. 90m. **DIR:** Robert Gordon. **CAST:** Mickey Rooney, Tobey Maguire, Cliff De Young, Laraine Newman, Ronnie Schell. **1994**

REVENGE OF THE STEPFORD WIVES 🦃 A TV sequel to the suspense classic. 95m. **DIR:** Robert Fuest. **CAST:** Arthur Hill, Don Johnson, Sharon Gless, Mason Adams, Audra Lindley. **1980**

REVENGE OF THE TEENAGE VIXENS FROM OUTERSPACE 🦃 This attempt to re-create the corny invader films of the 1950s nearly succeeds, but why bother? This time four hot chicks from outer space start hitting on high-school boys, so the boys' girlfriends decide to take the vixens on. Not rated. 83m. **DIR:** Jeff Ferrell. **CAST:** Lisa Schwedop, Howard Scott, Amy Crumpacker, Sterling Ramberg. **1985**

REVENGE OF THE ZOMBIES ★★1/2 As soon as the Hollywood back-lot native walks across the foggy bog in baggy underwear and begins to wail "Whoooooo," you know this is going to be one of those films. And it sure is, with mad scientist John Carradine, his zombie wife Veda Ann Borg (in her best role), do-gooders Gale Storm and Robert Lowery, and "feets do yo' stuff" Mantan Moreland aiding escaping zombies and Nazis in this low-budget howler. B&W; 61m. **DIR:** Steve Sekely. **CAST:** John Carradine, Robert Lowery, Gale Storm, Veda Ann Borg, Mantan Moreland, Bob Steele. **1943**

REVERSAL OF FORTUNE ★★★★ This absorbing drama is fueled by Ron Silver's portrayal of Alan Dershowitz, the fiercely driven Harvard law professor who accepted the challenge of defending the unloved and icily aristocratic Claus Von Bulow (rendered here with aloof arrogance by Oscar-winner Jeremy Irons). Glenn Close, as Sunny Von Bulow, contributes acerbic voice-over narration from her comatose state in a hospital bed. Rated R for language. 111m. **DIR:** Barbet Schroeder. **CAST:** Glenn Close, Jeremy Irons, Ron Silver, Annabella Sciorra, Uta Hagen. **1990**

REVOLT OF JOB, THE ★★★★ In this moving account of the Holocaust in rural Hungary, an old Jewish couple awaiting the inevitable Nazi takeover adopt a gentile orphan boy to survive them. Nominated for best foreign-language film in 1983's Academy Awards. In Hungarian with English subtitles. No rating. 97m. **DIR:** Imre Gyongyossy. **CAST:** Fereno Zenthe, Hedi Tenessy. **1983**

REVOLT OF THE ZOMBIES ★★ Following the unexpected success of their independently produced *White Zombie* in 1932, brothers Edward and Victor Halperin

found themselves making another zombie movie in 1936. Lacking the style and imagination of their earlier effort, this quasi-supernatural story involves the use of a stupor-inducing potion that turns Cambodian troops into dull-eyed slaves. For curiosity seekers only. B&W; 65m. **DIR:** Victor Halperin. **CAST:** Dean Jagger, Roy D'Arcy, Dorothy Stone, George Cleveland. **1936 DVD**

REVOLUTION ★★ Director Hugh Hudson must have had good intentions going into this project, examining what it might have been like to be involved in the American Revolution. Unfortunately, his actors are so miscast and the script so ragged that Hudson's project stalls almost before it gets started. Rated R. 125m. **DIR:** Hugh Hudson. **CAST:** Al Pacino, Nastassja Kinski, Donald Sutherland. **1986**

REVOLVER ★★1/2 Robert Urich is fine as a secret service agent who's felled by a bullet, paralyzed and must come to accept his new life in a wheelchair if he is to track down the gangster who put him there. Made-for-TV action entry is most involving during Urich's struggles to adapt. 93m. **DIR:** Gary Nelson. **CAST:** Robert Urich, Dakin Matthews, Steven Williams. **1992**

RHAPSODY ★★★ A soap opera with classical music background. Elizabeth Taylor plays a woman involved with a violinist and a pianist. They take out their frustration with flamboyant concerts. 115m. **DIR:** Charles Vidor. **CAST:** Elizabeth Taylor, Vittorio Gassman, John Ericson, Louis Calhern, Michael Chekhov. **1954**

RHAPSODY IN AUGUST ★★★ In another screen poem not unlike his *Dreams*, Japanese director Akira Kurosawa looks back on the bombing of Nagasaki during World War II through the eyes of four Japanese youngsters. Richard Gere has a brief but effective role. In Japanese with English subtitles. 98m. **DIR:** Akira Kurosawa. **CAST:** Sachiko Murase, Hisashi Igawa, Richard Gere. **1992**

RHAPSODY IN BLUE ★★★★ Don't for a minute think this is an accurate biography of George Gershwin (played by Robert Alda), but it's a lavish, colorful, and affectionate musical film. Of special interest are the appearances by Paul Whiteman (as himself) and the dubbed-in piano work of Gershwin's friend, Oscar Levant. The "Rhapsody in Blue" and "American in Paris" numbers are standouts. 139m. **DIR:** Irving Rapper. **CAST:** Robert Alda, Alexis Smith, Joan Leslie. **1945**

RHINESTONE 🦃 A country singer and a New York cabbie. Rated PG for profanity, sexual innuendo, and violence. 111m. **DIR:** Bob Clark. **CAST:** Sylvester Stallone, Dolly Parton, Richard Farnsworth, Ron Leibman. **1984**

RHODES ★★★1/2 Exquisite period detail and a fine performance from Martin Shaw elevate this historical saga mired in controversy. Shaw plays Cecil Rhodes, the nineteenth-century businessman who used his wealth and success from the African silver mines to help colonize South Africa. Film deftly explores Rhodes's achievements without endorsing them. Made for BBC Television. Not rated; contains violence. 336m. **DIR:** David Drury. **CAST:** Martin Shaw, Frances Barber, Joe Shaw, Patrick Shai. **1996**

RHODES OF AFRICA (RHODES) ★★★ The annexation and assimilation of a culture and people for material gain is not a plot that could sell a film today, but flagrant exploitation of the wealth of South Africa is still timely. Location photography, a good cast, and a standout performance by Walter Huston as the visionary opportunist whose dreams of empire are barely blunted by his philanthropic efforts make this film palatable to modern audiences. B&W; 89m. **DIR:** Berthold Viertel. **CAST:** Walter Huston, Oscar Homolka, Basil Sydney, Peggy Ashcroft, Bernard Lee. **1936**

RHYTHM ON THE RANGE ★★★1/2 Der Bingle's rendition of "I'm an Old Cowhand" and "Empty Saddles" are enough to make this musical Western work. Bing Crosby plays a dude-ranch owner who helps an heiress dodge the wedding her father engineered for her. B&W; 85m. **DIR:** Norman Taurog. **CAST:** Bing Crosby, Frances Farmer, Martha Raye, Bob Burns, Lucille Gleason. **1936**

RHYTHM ON THE RIVER ★★★1/2 Bing Crosby writes music, Mary Martin writes lyrics. Both are secret "ghost" partners of Basil Rathbone, who joins their works and reaps the profit and glory. Lots of fun in this easygoing musical comedy. The song "Only Forever" was Oscar nominated. B&W; 94m. **DIR:** Victor Schertzinger. **CAST:** Bing Crosby, Mary Martin, Basil Rathbone, Oscar Levant, Charley Grapewin, William Frawley, Jeanne Cagney. **1940**

RICH AND FAMOUS ★★★★ Jacqueline Bisset and Candice Bergen star in this warm, witty, and involving chronicle of the ups, downs, joys, and heartbreak experienced by two friends during a twenty-year relationship. Hollywood great George Cukor directed in his inimitable style. Rated R because of profanity and sex. 117m. **DIR:** George Cukor. **CAST:** Jacqueline Bisset, Candice Bergen, David Selby, Hart Bochner, Steven Hill, Meg Ryan, Matt Lattanzi, Michael Brandon. **1981**

RICH AND STRANGE ★★1/2 This quirky little drama from Alfred Hitchcock concerns a bickering couple (Henry Kendall and Joan Barry) who come into money, take a world cruise, and suffer through a few minor adventures. The domestic squabbling, which forms the story's only true conflict, is far from Hitchcock's forte; this probably will be of interest only to the director's devotees. Not rated; suitable for family viewing. B&W; 83m. **DIR:** Alfred Hitchcock. **CAST:** Henry Kendall, Joan Barry, Percy Marmont. **1932 DVD**

RICH GIRL ★★★ Jill Schoelen is the title character who strikes out on her own as a waitress in a nightclub. The best rich-girl-falls-in-love-with-a-guy-from-the-wrong-side-of-the-tracks film since *Dirty Dancing*. Rated R for profanity and mild violence. 96m. **DIR:** Joel Bender. **CAST:** Jill Schoelen, Don Michael Paul, Sean Kanan, Ron Karabatsos, Paul Gleason, Willie Dixon. **1991**

RICH IN LOVE ★★★★ Kathryn Erbe comes home from high school one day to find a note from her mother (Jill Clayburgh) to her father (Albert Finney) that says she has gone off "to start a second life." Skillful portrait of an American family crumbling from its core. Thought-provoking and insightful, it's a real gem. Rated PG-13 for profanity and nudity. 105m. **DIR:** Bruce Beresford. **CAST:** Albert Finney, Jill Clayburgh, Kathryn Erbe, Kyle MacLachlan, Piper Laurie, Ethan Hawke, Suzy Amis, Alfre Woodard. **1993**

RICH KIDS ★★ A poor screenplay plagues this movie about two kids going through puberty. A great cast helps. Also, there is an unforgettable heartfelt moment between mother and daughter (Kathryn Walker and

Trini Alvarado). Rated PG for language. 97m. **DIR:** Robert M. Young. **CAST:** Trini Alvarado, Jeremy Levy, John Lithgow, Kathryn Walker, Terry Kiser, Paul Dooley. **1979**

RICH LITTLE—ONE'S A CROWD ★★1/2 Rich Little is both host and entire cast in a sort of "Greatest Hits" video album. Little is, of course, very good at his craft, but his self-written material is not always the best, and his unique talent wears a little thin after an hour or so. Not rated, but with mild profanity. 86m. **DIR:** Thomas E. Engel. **CAST:** Rich Little. **1988**

RICH LITTLE'S LITTLE SCAMS ON GOLF ★★ Rich Little's talents are wasted in this compendium of ways to cheat at golf. Extremely boring. Not rated. 44m. **DIR:** Kimberlie Chambers. **CAST:** Rich Little. **1991**

RICH MAN'S WIFE, THE This trashy, cruel-humored thriller is about an unhappy woman who spills her guts to a squabbling detective duo after becoming the primary suspect in the murder of her unfaithful, alcoholic husband. Rated R for violence, language, and sex. 94m. **DIR:** Amy Holden Jones. **CAST:** Halle Berry, Christopher McDonald, Peter Greene, Clive Owen, Clea Lewis. **1996 DVD**

RICH, YOUNG AND PRETTY ★★ A slim excuse for a movie without glossy production numbers to back up the casting of Jane Powell and Vic Damone in the leading roles. Powell plays an American-raised daughter of French Danielle Darrieux. She goes to Paris to meet her mother and gets involved in romantic dalliances. 95m. **DIR:** Norman Taurog. **CAST:** Jane Powell, Vic Damone, Danielle Darrieux, Fernando Lamas, Wendell Corey, Una Merkel, Hans Conried, Richard Anderson. **1951**

RICHARD III (1955) ★★★★ Once again, as in *Henry V* and *Hamlet*, England's foremost player displays his near-matchless acting and directing skills in bringing Shakespeare to life on film. His royal crookback usurper is beautifully malevolent, a completely intriguing, smiling villain. The film fascinates from first to last. 161m. **DIR:** Laurence Olivier. **CAST:** Laurence Olivier, Ralph Richardson, John Gielgud, Claire Bloom. **1955**

RICHARD III (1995) ★★★ Shakespeare's melodrama of treachery and murder during the War of the Roses is transplanted to the 1930s, with evil King Richard portrayed as a jackbooted fascist. The concept is intriguing, but it takes over the production and shoves Shakespeare into the background. Acting is generally good. Rated R for violence. 107m. **DIR:** Richard Loncraine. **CAST:** Ian McKellen, Annette Bening, Kristin Scott Thomas, Maggie Smith, Robert Downey Jr., Jim Broadbent. **1995 DVD**

RICHARD'S THINGS ★★ Gloomy drama about a widow who gets seduced by her late husband's girlfriend. Liv Ullmann plays the patsy as if she were on depressants. 104m. **DIR:** Anthony Harvey. **CAST:** Liv Ullmann, Amanda Redman, David Markham. **1980**

RICHIE RICH ★★★ Surprisingly entertaining big-screen adaptation of the comic-book character dubbed "the richest boy in the world," who just wants to be like other kids. British actor Jonathan Hyde steals the film as the faithful and highly resourceful gentleman's gentleman. Rated PG. 94m. **DIR:** Donald Petrie. **CAST:** Macaulay Culkin, John Larroquette, Edward Herrmann, Jonathan Hyde, Christine Ebersole. **1994**

RICOCHET ★★★1/2 A rookie cop rises to the position of deputy district attorney after capturing a heartless killer. This is a taut, action-packed crime-drama that is elevated above others in its genre by the acting. Rated R for violence, profanity, and nudity. 105m. **DIR:** Russell Mulcahy. **CAST:** Denzel Washington, John Lithgow, Ice T, Kevin Pollak, Lindsay Wagner, Josh Evans. **1991**

RIDDLE OF THE SANDS ★★★★ Based on the spy novel by Erskine Childers, this is the story of two young Englishmen (Michael York, Simon MacCorkindale) who set sail on a holiday just prior to World War I and stumble upon political intrigue and adventure in the North Sea. The result is an absorbing adventure film. Rated PG for slight violence and profanity. 102m. **DIR:** Tony Maylam. **CAST:** Michael York, Jenny Agutter, Simon MacCorkindale. **1984**

RIDE A motley bunch of Harlem youths takes off in a decrepit bus for Florida, to appear in a rap star's music video. Sloppy, amateurish, and teeming with offensive racial stereotypes, the film is hopeless—even the beat of the hip-hop soundtrack is boring. Rated R for nonstop profanity. 90m. **DIR:** Millicent Shelton. **CAST:** Malik Yoba, Melissa DeSousa, Fredro Starr, John Witherspoon, Sticky Fingaz. **1998 DVD**

RIDE A WILD PONY ★★★ This entertaining Disney film is the tale of a horse and the two children who want to own him, a poor boy and a rich girl with polio. The setting is Australia. Rated G. 86m. **DIR:** Don Chaffey. **CAST:** Michael Craig, John Meillon. **1976**

RIDE BEYOND VENGEANCE ★★ A buffalo hunter, branded by three badmen, sets out for revenge. A great cast, savage brutality, and sexual innuendo aren't able to save this adult Western from being a waste of time. 100m. **DIR:** Bernard McEveety. **CAST:** Chuck Connors, Michael Rennie, Kathryn Hays, Gary Merrill, Claude Akins, Gloria Grahame, Bill Bixby, Joan Blondell, James MacArthur, Ruth Warrick, Arthur O'Connell. **1966**

RIDE 'EM COWBOY ★★★ Two hot-dog vendors find themselves in the wild West working on a dude ranch. Some funny bits, a good cast, and top musical numbers and talent (including Ella Fitzgerald) make this Abbott and Costello comedy one of the best in the series. B&W; 84m. **DIR:** Arthur Lubin. **CAST:** Bud Abbott, Lou Costello, Anne Gwynne, Dick Foran, Johnny Mack Brown, Samuel S. Hinds, Douglass Dumbrille. **1942**

RIDE 'EM COWGIRL ★★ Singing cowgirl Dorothy Page and her horse Snowy battle the bad guys who bilked her father out of $5,000. The concept seems designed to prove that a woman can rope, ride, and yodel as well as any cowboy. Well, in this case, they were wrong. 52m. **DIR:** Samuel Diege. **CAST:** Dorothy Page, Milton Frome, Vince Barnett. **1939**

RIDE HIM COWBOY ★★1/2 Thanks to the unfunny antics of would-be comic relief Harry Gribbon and the belief-stretching feats of Duke, the miracle horse, John Wayne's first B Western for Warner Bros. has much less to recommend it than his later outings. Even the plot, in which a town is terrorized by a masked rider and his gang, is more melodramatic and simplistic than usual. B&W; 56m. **DIR:** Fred Allen. **CAST:** John Wayne, Ruth Hall, Henry B. Walthall, Otis Harlan, Harry Gribbon, Frank Hagney, Lafe McKee. **1932**

RIDE IN THE WHIRLWIND Throwaway Western with good cast goes nowhere in the muddled story of

three riders wrongfully pursued by an unrelenting posse. 83m. **DIR:** Monte Hellman. **CAST:** Jack Nicholson, Cameron Mitchell, Millie Perkins, Harry Dean Stanton, Rupert Crosse. **1965**

RIDE LONESOME ★★★★1/2 Lawman Randolph Scott competes with two bounty hunters for possession of outlaw James Best. Well written by Burt Kennedy; superbly acted under the able direction of Budd Boetticher, who directed Scott in some of the best Westerns made in the 1950s. 73m. **DIR:** Budd Boetticher. **CAST:** Randolph Scott, Pernell Roberts, Karen Steele, Lee Van Cleef, James Coburn, James Best. **1959**

RIDE, RANGER, RIDE ★★1/2 Texas Ranger Gene Autry works undercover to stop Comanches from looting ammunition-laden wagon trains. Film debut of Max Terhune, who soon starred in Three Mesquiteer Westerns. B&W; 54m. **DIR:** Joseph Kane. **CAST:** Gene Autry, Smiley Burnette, Kay Hughes, Monte Blue, Max Terhune. **1936**

RIDE THE HIGH COUNTRY ★★★★1/2 Joel McCrea and Randolph Scott play two old-time gunslingers who team up to guard a gold shipment. McCrea just wants to do a good job, but Scott cares nothing for noble purpose and tries to steal the gold. From that point on, they are friends no longer. The result is a picture so good that McCrea and Scott decided to retire after making it—both wanted to go out with a winner. 94m. **DIR:** Sam Peckinpah. **CAST:** Joel McCrea, Randolph Scott, Warren Oates, R. G. Armstrong, Mariette Hartley, John Anderson, James Drury, L. Q. Jones, Edgar Buchanan. **1962**

RIDE THE MAN DOWN ★★ A Western shot in the traditional manner. A ranch manager fights to keep the property out of the greedy hands of land grabbers. 90m. **DIR:** Joseph Kane. **CAST:** Brian Donlevy, Rod Cameron, Ella Raines, Chill Wills, Jack LaRue. **1952**

RIDE THE WILD SURF ★★ Though shot in Hawaii, this teens-on-the-beach musical contains innumerable shots of Fabian and Tab Hunter perched in front of back-projection screens of surfing footage, while someone off-camera sprays a hose at them. Jan and Dean sing the title tune. Overall, pretty feeble. 101m. **DIR:** Don Taylor. **CAST:** Fabian, Tab Hunter, Barbara Eden, Shelley Fabares. **1964**

RIDE WITH THE DEVIL ★★ During the Civil War, two young men, friends from childhood, join a guerrilla faction of the Confederate Army. Director Ang Lee's least successful film often presents beautiful vistas but generally has nothing original to say about war. Buried under layers of hair and mud, the characters are often hard to distinguish, and the plot is equally hard to follow. Rated R for violence and sexual themes. 139m. **DIR:** Ang Lee. **CAST:** Skeet Ulrich, Tobey Maguire, Jewel, Jeffrey Wright. **1999 DVD**

RIDER FROM TUCSON ★★★ Tim Holt is a rodeo star who aids an old friend whose gold strike is the target of claim jumpers. B&W; 60m. **DIR:** Lesley Selander. **CAST:** Tim Holt, Richard Martin, Elaine Riley, Douglas Fowley, Veda Ann Borg, Robert Shayne. **1950**

RIDER ON THE RAIN ★★★★ Charles Bronson gives one of his finest screen performances in this gripping, Hitchcock-style thriller made in France. The story deals with the plight of a woman (Marlene Jobert) who kills an unhinged rapist and dumps his body into the sea. She is soon pursued by a mysterious American (Bronson). Thus begins a fascinating game of cat and mouse. Rated R for violence. 115m. **DIR:** René Clement. **CAST:** Charles Bronson, Marlene Jobert, Jill Ireland. **1970**

RIDERS FOR JUSTICE ★★★ Late-in-the-run Three Mesquiteers entry benefits from no-nonsense direction from John English, a relatively straightforward story, and the charisma of Western-film veterans Tom Tyler and Bob Steele. This time, our heroes are out to foil a gang of bank robbers who are implicating innocent men. Retitled from *Westward Ho* for release to television so as not to conflict with the John Wayne Western of the same name. B&W; 56m. **DIR:** John English. **CAST:** Tom Tyler, Bob Steele, Rufe Davis, Evelyn Brent, Donald Curtis, Kenne Duncan. **1942**

RIDERS OF DEATH VALLEY ★★★1/2 Dick Foran and his pals Buck Jones and Leo Carrillo head a group of men organized to police the mining districts and to fight it out with the thieves and murderers that flocked to the gold claims. A fine serial. B&W; 15 chapters. **DIR:** Ford Beebe, Ray Taylor. **CAST:** Dick Foran, Buck Jones, Leo Carrillo, Charles Bickford, Lon Chaney Jr., Noah Beery Jr., Guinn Williams, Monte Blue, Glenn Strange. **1941**

RIDERS OF DESTINY ★★★ The earliest low, low-budget John Wayne B Western available on tape, this casts an extremely young-looking Duke as Singin' Sandy, an undercover agent out to help ranchers regain their water rights. Fun for fans of the star. B&W; 50m. **DIR:** Robert N. Bradbury. **CAST:** John Wayne, Cecilia Parker, George "Gabby" Hayes, Forrest Taylor, Al St. John, Heinie Conklin, Earl Dwire. **1933 DVD**

RIDERS OF THE BLACK HILLS ★★★ Just before the richest horse race of the year, an illustrious Thoroughbred is kidnapped in a daring train robbery. The Three Mesquiteers ride to the rescue. B&W; 54m. **DIR:** George Sherman. **CAST:** Robert Livingston, Ray "Crash" Corrigan, Max Terhune. **1938**

RIDERS OF THE PURPLE SAGE ★★★1/2 When a female rancher and her two ranch hands are threatened by the man who intends to marry her, a mysterious stranger rides to the rescue. Unlike previous adaptations of Zane Grey's story, this TNT production is dark and brooding, with excellent performances by Ed Harris and Amy Madigan in a sometimes confusing story of justice, revenge, and dark secrets. Made for TV. 96m. **DIR:** Charles Haid. **CAST:** Ed Harris, Amy Madigan, Henry Thomas, G. D. Spradlin, Tom Bower, Robin Tunney, Norbert Weisser. **1996**

RIDERS OF THE RIO GRANDE ★★★★ The last in an eight-year string of Three Mesquiteers Westerns is one of the best. Involved plot line has the Mesquiteers mistaken for the Cherokee Boys, a trio of outlaws. Plenty of action and a tongue-in-cheek story that often spoofs the genre without belittling it. B&W; 55m. **DIR:** Howard Bretherton. **CAST:** Bob Steele, Tom Tyler, Jimmie Dodd, Edward Van Sloan, Rick Vallin, Roy Barcroft, Charles King. **1943**

RIDERS OF THE ROCKIES ★★1/2 Entertaining Tex Ritter Western finds the two-fisted singer joining a gang of rustlers in order to get the goods on them. Silent comedian Snub Pollard plays his comic sidekick. One of Ritter's best Westerns. B&W; 56m. **DIR:** Robert N. Brad-

bury. **CAST:** Tex Ritter, Louise Stanley, Charles King, Snub Pollard, Yakima Canutt. **1937**

RIDERS OF THE STORM Dennis Hopper as the captain of an ancient B-29 that has been circling the country for fifteen years to broadcast an illegal television network. Rated R for nudity. 92m. **DIR:** Maurice Phillips. **CAST:** Dennis Hopper, Michael J. Pollard, Eugene Lipinski. **1987**

RIDERS OF THE TIMBERLINE ★★1/2 Hopalong Cassidy and company head for the hills to help an old friend whose timber business is being sabotaged. Ropin' and ridin', fightin' and shootin'. B&W; 54m. **DIR:** Lesley Selander. **CAST:** William Boyd, Brad King, Andy Clyde, J. Farrell MacDonald, Eleanor Stewart, Tom Tyler, Victor Jory. **1941**

RIDERS OF THE WHISTLING PINES ★★★1/2 Framed as a timberland killer and cattle poisoner, Gene Autry fights to prove his innocence and save the woodlands for the Forestry Department. B&W; 70m. **DIR:** John English. **CAST:** Gene Autry, Patricia White, Jimmy Lloyd, Clayton Moore. **1949**

RIDERS OF THE WHISTLING SKULL ★★★ The Three Mesquiteers gallop into one of their best adventures. They brave Indians and ghostly goings-on to find a fabled lost city and its fabulous treasure. An eerie story, and the easy camaraderie of the three saddle pals makes this outdoor adventure one of the most popular in the series. B&W; 58m. **DIR:** Mack V. Wright. **CAST:** Robert Livingston, Ray "Crash" Corrigan, Max Terhune, Mary Russell, Yakima Canutt, C. Montague Shaw, Chief Thundercloud. **1937**

RIDICULE ★★★ A man in seventeenth-century France learns that a sharp wit and a quick tongue are perhaps his most important tools of survival in this daringly original (sometimes too much so) film. Rated R for nudity, sexual situations, and violence. 102m. **DIR:** Patrice Leconte. **CAST:** Fanny Ardant, Charles Berling, Bernard Guirardeau, Jean Rochefort. **1996**

RIDING BEAN ★★★★ Japanese animation. Highly amusing tale set in (of all places) Chicago and involving a special courier named Bean, who, with the aid of a supercar and female assistant, takes on bad guys and a bumbling police force. In Japanese with English subtitles. Not rated with violence, profanity, and illustrated nudity. 46m. **DIR:** Tanaka Masahiro, Kamijoo Osamu, Oohira Hiroya, Okuda Tadashi. **1989 DVD**

RIDING HIGH ★★1/2 A Bing Crosby musical with a plot, this film revolves around a racehorse whose owner risks his marriage on the horse and loses both. Pleasant Crosby tunes. A human-interest musical remake of the Depression-era classic, *Broadway Bill*. B&W; 112m. **DIR:** Frank Capra. **CAST:** Bing Crosby, Coleen Gray, Charles Bickford, Frances Gifford, Oliver Hardy, Ward Bond, Joe Frisco, Percy Kilbride, William Demarest. **1950**

•RIDING IN CARS WITH BOYS ★★ Daughter of a Connecticut cop and housewife gets pregnant at the age of fifteen and wallows in a low-rent marriage to a dumb junkie as her dreams of becoming a writer fade. The film is split between scenes of her past and those involving a road trip with her young-adult son whose life has been tainted by his mom's misery. This artificially sweetened, strained drama about parent-child relationships, self-absorption, young love, and shattered dreams injects a TV sit-com sensibility into nearly every crucial conflict and personal challenge. Rated PG-13 for language, drug use, and sexuality. 122m. **DIR:** Penny Marshall. **CAST:** Drew Barrymore, Steve Zahn, Brittany Murphy, Adam Garcia, Lorraine Bracco, James Woods. **2001 DVD**

RIDING ON AIR ★★★ Lots of thrills and laughs in this topically dated comedy adventure about two small-town newspaper correspondents vying for the same girl and the scoop on a story. Joe E. Brown is, as always, warm, winning, and wholesome. B&W; 58m. **DIR:** Edward Sedgwick. **CAST:** Joe E. Brown, Florence Rice, Vinton Haworth, Guy Kibbee. **1937**

RIDING THE EDGE ★★ Formulaic adventure flick set in the Middle East—a ground attempt at *Iron Eagle*. A man has been captured by terrorists, so who do you send in? A trained professional? Nonsense. Send in his teenage son. Rated PG-13. 100m. **DIR:** James Fargo. **CAST:** Peter Haskell, Raphael Sbarge, Catherine Mary Stewart. **1990**

RIDING TORNADO, THE ★★★ A strong series entry for Tim McCoy. He's a wandering cowboy hired by rancher Shirley Grey, whose cattle are being systematically stolen. Of course, our hero sets things right. B&W; 64m. **DIR:** D. Ross Lederman. **CAST:** Tim McCoy, Shirley Grey. **1932**

RIDING WITH DEATH ★★ Compilation of two hour-long shows from *The Gemini Man* television series, edited together by some mysterious and unconvincing process. Ben Murphy plays a man who, through a scientific accident, can render himself invisible for short bursts of time. Real comic-book stuff. 97m. **DIR:** Alan J. Levi, Don McDougall. **CAST:** Ben Murphy, Katherine Crawford, Richard Dysart, William Sylvester, Andrew Prine, Alan Oppenheimer, Don Galloway. **1976**

RIFF-RAFF (1990) ★★★★ The fringes of British society are explored in this documentary-like drama about homeless men doing laborer work at a construction site. *Riff-Raff* is an excellent example of independent filmmaking. Naturalistic humor offsets the inherent social commentary as director Ken Loach helps his cast create unforgettable characters. Not rated, the film has profanity, nudity, suggested sex, and violence. 96m. **DIR:** Kenneth Loach. **CAST:** Robert Carlyle, Emer McCourt, Richard Belgrave, Jimmy Coleman, George Moss, Ricky Tomlinson. **1990**

RIFFRAFF (1936) ★★ The give-and-take banter between Spencer Tracy and Jean Harlow is all that holds together this muddled melodrama about the relationship of two tough-as-nails waterfront workers. A confusing script and an over-abundance of characters who are never knit into the central story. B&W; 89m. **DIR:** J. Walter Ruben. **CAST:** Spencer Tracy, Jean Harlow, Una Merkel, Joseph Calleia. **1936**

RIFFRAFF (1947) ★★1/2 Two-fisted private eye Pat O'Brien is hired as a bodyguard by a man with a chart to some rich South American oil fields, but when O'Brien signs on, he doesn't know that his employer is a killer and some heavy competition is gunning for them. This race-for-riches programmer quickly bogs down and runs out of pep. B&W; 80m. **DIR:** Ted Tetzlaff. **CAST:** Pat O'Brien, Walter Slezak, Anne Jeffreys, Percy Kilbride, Jerome Cowan. **1947**

RIFIFI ★★★★ A milestone that begat a continuing breed of films hinging on the big, carefully planned rob-

bery that falls apart—usually just as the criminals and the audience are convinced of success. This one is sure to have you pumping adrenaline from start to finish, especially during the brilliant twenty-minute silent robbery sequence that is its selling point, and the falling out of thieves that follows. B&W; 115m. **DIR:** Jules Dassin. **CAST:** Jean Servais, Carl Mohner, Perlo Vita, Robert Manuel, Magali Noel. **1955 DVD**

RIFLEMAN, THE (TV SERIES) ★★★1/2 Created by Sam Peckinpah, this sometimes brutal, sometimes touching Western series starred brawny Chuck Connors as the rifle-toting rancher, Lucas McCain. A widower, McCain raises his young son, Mark (Johnny Crawford), as best he can, while frequently being called upon by Marshal Micah Torrance (Paul Fix) to help keep the peace in the town of Northfork, New Mexico. The early episodes are the best. B&W; 30m. **DIR:** Various. **CAST:** Chuck Connors, Johnny Crawford, Paul Fix, Joan Taylor, Patricia Blair. **1958–1963**

RIGHT HAND MAN, THE 🦃 A dying, disabled, nobleman's repressed love for his doctor's daughter. Rated R for nudity and suggested sex. 101m. **DIR:** Di Drew. **CAST:** Rupert Everett, Hugo Weaving, Arthur Dignam, Jennifer Claire. **1987**

RIGHT OF WAY ★★★★ This made-for-cable work deals with a rather unusual decision made by an old married couple (Bette Davis and James Stewart), who have decided to commit suicide. Thus begins a battle between daughter (Melinda Dillon) and parents. The result is a surprisingly gripping character study. 106m. **DIR:** George Schaefer. **CAST:** James Stewart, Bette Davis, Melinda Dillon, Priscilla Morrill, John Harkins. **1983**

RIGHT STUFF, THE ★★★★★ From Tom Wolfe's best-seller about the early years of the American space program, this epic screen tribute examines the men (both test pilots and astronauts) who "pushed the outside of the envelope," and the women who watched and waited while the world watched them. Rated PG for profanity. 193m. **DIR:** Phil Kaufman. **CAST:** Sam Shepard, Scott Glenn, Ed Harris, Dennis Quaid, Barbara Hershey, Fred Ward, Kim Stanley, Veronica Cartwright, Pamela Reed, Donald Moffat, Levon Helm, Scott Wilson, Jeff Goldblum, Harry Shearer, Lance Henriksen. **1983 DVD**

RIGHT TEMPTATION, THE ★★1/2 A businessman becomes embroiled in a sexual triangle that leads to murder. Typical story buoyed by fresh direction and strong performances. Rated R for violence, language, and sexuality. 93m. **DIR:** Lyndon Chubbuck. **CAST:** Kiefer Sutherland, Rebecca DeMornay, Dana Delaney. **2000 DVD**

RIGHT TO REMAIN SILENT, THE ★★★1/2 Mark Fauser and Brent Briscoe's clever stage play turns into an equally intriguing drama, focusing on a new police recruit surviving her first graveyard-shift encounters with a half-dozen villains and victims. Their compelling stories are related via flashback and some work better than others, but each tale is well told by the impressive ensemble cast. Rated R for profanity, violence, and rape. 96m. **DIR:** Hubert de la Bouillerie. **CAST:** Lea Thompson, Robert Loggia, LL Cool J, Patrick Dempsey, Amanda Plummer, Carl Reiner, Judge Reinhold, Colleen Camp, Fisher Stevens, Christopher Lloyd, Laura San Giacomo. **1995**

RIKISHA-MAN ★★★★ In turn-of-the-century Japan, an uneducated rickshaw puller looks out for a boy whose father has died. Rewarding human story with a typically strong performance by Toshiro Mifune. In Japanese with English subtitles. 105m. **DIR:** Hiroshi Inagaki. **CAST:** Toshiro Mifune. **1958**

RIKKI AND PETE ★★★ An offbeat comedy from Australia. A geologist and her crazy brother abandon the city for the Australian outback. This film is a great crash course in living your own life. Highly engaging! Rated R for nudity and language. 101m. **DIR:** Nadia Tass. **CAST:** Nina Landis, Stephen Kearny, Bruce Spence, Bruno Lawrence. **1988**

RIKYU ★★★★ This poignant film, which won a special jury award at the Cannes Film Festival, explores the struggle between art and power in sixteenth-century Japan. The central character, Sen-no Rikyu, refined the art of the tea ceremony, lifting it to aesthetic, spiritual heights. A beautifully crafted character study with fine ensemble acting. In Japanese with English subtitles. Not rated. 116m. **DIR:** Hiroshi Teshigahara. **CAST:** Rentaro Mikuni, Tsutomu Yamazaki. **1990 DVD**

RIM OF THE CANYON ★★★1/2 Gene Autry in a dual role as a marshal who corrals a gang of stagecoach bandits and as his son who faces the same gang twenty years later in a ghost town showdown. Supernatural overtones give this one a different twist. B&W; 70m. **DIR:** John English. **CAST:** Gene Autry, Nan Leslie, Jock Mahoney, Alan Hale Jr., Thurston Hall. **1949**

RIMFIRE ★★★ Better-than-average B Western has federal agent James Millican looking for stolen gold. He's aided in his search by the ghost of a gambler who was unjustly hanged for cheating! 64m. **DIR:** B. Reeves "Breezy" Eason. **CAST:** James Millican, Mary Beth Hughes, Reed Hadley, Henry Hull, Fuzzy Knight, Jason Robards Sr., Glenn Strange. **1949**

RING, THE ★★ Long before Sylvester Stallone turned boxing into a filmic event, Alfred Hitchcock toyed with the sports medium in this unremarkable melodrama. The story is little more than a love triangle between two boxing champions (Carl Brisson and Ian Hunter) and the woman loved by both (Lillian Hall-Davies). Not rated; suitable for family viewing. B&W; 73m. **DIR:** Alfred Hitchcock. **CAST:** Carl Brisson, Lillian Hall-Davies, Ian Hunter. **1927 DVD**

RING OF BRIGHT WATER ★★★★ The stars of *Born Free* return for this delightful story of a secluded writer and his pet otter. The story has some odd quirks that adults will appreciate, but this underrated film also has terrific production values and an utterly irresistible animal star. Not rated. 107m. **DIR:** Jack Couffer. **CAST:** Bill Travers, Virginia McKenna. **1969**

RING OF FIRE 3: LION STRIKE ★★★ Kick-boxing physician Johnny Wu (Don Wilson) is forced back into action when he comes into possession of a computer disk belonging to international gangsters. Rated R for violence and profanity. 90m. **DIR:** Rick Jacobson. **CAST:** Don "The Dragon" Wilson, Bobbie Phillips. **1995**

RING OF SCORPIO ★★1/2 Three women seek revenge on the drug smugglers who used them as pawns during their college days. The women's story is exciting, but the flashbacks are ineffective. Made for cable. 120m. **DIR:**

Ian Barry. **CAST:** Catherine Oxenberg, Jack Scalia, Caroline Goodall. **1991**

RING OF STEEL ★★★ An Olympic fencer accidently kills a man during a regional tournament. Expelled from the sport, he is hired by an illicit nightclub that stages duels for money. He soon learns that he either fights to the death or he and his girlfriend will be killed. Good swashbuckling action, fast-paced direction, humor, and style make for an entertaining film. Rated R for simulated sex, nudity, violence, and profanity. 94m. **DIR:** David Frost. **CAST:** Joe Don Baker, Carol Alt, Richard Chapin, Gary Kasper, Darlene Vogel. **1994**

RING OF THE MUSKETEER ★★1/2 In one of those "what must they have been thinking?" scenarios, David Hasselhoff, Alison Doody, Thomas Gottschalk, and Cheech Marin play great-great-great descendants of the original Musketeers, now fighting for decency in modern times. Their latest assignment: rescuing a boy from a mob figure. It may be more than they can handle, but they'll have fun trying. Rated PG-13 for language. 86m. **DIR:** John Paragon. **CAST:** David Hasselhoff, Richard "Cheech" Marin, Corbin Bernsen, Alison Doody, Thomas Gottschalk, John Rhys-Davies. **1993**

RINGMASTER 🦃 This fictional valentine to Jerry Springer's sleazy TV show creeps backstage to uncover— *ta duh*—more sleaze. Rated R for sexual content, profanity, and nudity. 90m. **DIR:** Neil Abramson. **CAST:** Jerry Springer, Jaime Pressly, Molly Hagan, William McNamara, Wendy Raquel Robinson, Michael Jai Wite, Michael Dudikoff, Dawn Maxey, Ashely Holbrook. **1998 DVD**

RIO BRAVO ★★★★1/2 A super-Western, with John Wayne, Walter Brennan, Ward Bond, Ricky Nelson (aping Montgomery Clift's performance in *Red River*), and the scene-stealing Dean Martin taking on cattle baron John Russell, who's out to get his kill-crazy brother (Claude Akins) out of jail. 141m. **DIR:** Howard Hawks. **CAST:** John Wayne, Walter Brennan, Ward Bond, Ricky Nelson, Dean Martin, John Russell, Claude Akins, Angie Dickinson, Bob Steele. **1959**

RIO CONCHOS ★★★ Rip-roaring Western action ignites this briskly paced yarn set in post–Civil War Texas. Richard Boone and his pals go undercover to get the goods on outlaws responsible for stealing a shipment of rifles. Boone gives a wry performance. 107m. **DIR:** Gordon Douglas. **CAST:** Richard Boone, Stuart Whitman, Anthony Franciosa, Edmond O'Brien, Jim Brown. **1964**

RIO DIABLO ★★1/2 Country singers ride the TV-movie West again in this middling tale of a hard-boiled bounty hunter reluctantly helping a young man track down the outlaws who kidnapped his bride. 97m. **DIR:** Rod Hardy. **CAST:** Kenny Rogers, Travis Tritt, Naomi Judd, Stacy Keach, Brian James, Bruce Greenwood, Laura Harring, Michael G. Hagerty. **1993**

RIO GRANDE ★★★★ The last entry in director John Ford's celebrated cavalry trilogy (which also includes *Fort Apache* and *She Wore a Yellow Ribbon*), this stars John Wayne as a company commander coping with renegade Indians and a willful wife (Maureen O'Hara), who wants to take their soldier son (Claude Jarman Jr.) home. B&W; 105m. **DIR:** John Ford. **CAST:** John Wayne, Maureen O'Hara, Claude Jarman Jr., Ben Johnson, Harry Carey Jr., Victor McLaglen, Chill Wills, J. Carrol Naish. **1950 DVD**

RIO LOBO ★★★ Neither star John Wayne nor director Howard Hawks was exactly at the peak of his powers when this second reworking of *Rio Bravo* (the first being *El Dorado*) was released. If one adjusts the normally high expectations he or she would have for a Western made by these two giants, *Rio Lobo* is a fun show. Jack Elam is terrific in a delightful supporting role. Rated G. 114m. **DIR:** Howard Hawks. **CAST:** John Wayne, Jack Elam, Jorge Rivero, Jennifer O'Neill, Chris Mitchum, Mike Henry. **1970**

RIO RITA ★★★ Vintage Bud Abbott and Lou Costello, with routines that somehow seem fresh and familiar at the same time. They stowaway in the trunk of a car thinking it is going to New York and end up at a Texas ranch infested with Nazi spies. B&W; 91m. **DIR:** S. Sylvan Simon. **CAST:** Bud Abbott, Lou Costello, Kathryn Grayson, John Carroll, Tom Conway, Barry Nelson. **1942**

RIOT (1969) ★★1/2 Familiar story of tough cons turning the tables on tough guards, taking over part of a prison in an escape attempt. Violence for violence's sake. Filmed at the Arizona State Prison. Rated R. 97m. **DIR:** Buzz Kulik. **CAST:** Jim Brown, Gene Hackman, Mike Kellin, Gerald S. O'Loughlin. **1969**

RIOT (1996) ★★★ When a British SAS officer (Gary Daniels) tries to rescue an ambassador's daughter taken hostage during a Florida race riot, he learns there's more to the explosive tensions than meets the eye. Solid vehicle for action star Daniels is aided by an odd but intriguing plot. Rated R for violence and profanity. 98m. **DIR:** Joseph Merhi. **CAST:** Gary Daniels, Sugar Ray Leonard, Paige Rowland, Charles Napier. **1996**

RIOT (1996) (TV MOVIE) ★★★1/2 Basically an arty examination of the 1991 L.A. riots, this made-for-cable original is composed of four separate but interlocking stories about everyday people. Good performances all around, but a sense of closure for any of these stories is lacking. Rated R for profanity and violence. 120m. **DIR:** David C. Johnson, Richard Dilello, Galen Yuen, Alex Muñoz. **CAST:** Mario Van Peebles, Cicely Tyson, Luke Perry, Dante Basco, Mako, Alexis Cruz, Yelba Osorio. **1996**

RIOT IN CELL BLOCK ELEVEN ★★★1/2 This taut prison drama with a message depicts an aborted prison escape that ends with the convicts barricaded and demanding to be heard. Made at the height of the "exposé" and true-crime wave in the mid-Fifties, this film avoids the sensational and documentary style of its contemporaries and focuses on the action and the characterizations of the convicts, the prison staff, and the media. B&W; 80m. **DIR:** Don Siegel. **CAST:** Neville Brand, Leo Gordon, Emile Meyer, Frank Faylen. **1954**

RIPE ★★★ It's hard to tell whether this drama about 14 year old twin girls who take up with a pair of army workers after their parents are killed is an honest attempt to explore adolescent trauma or merely exploitative. Either way, the film's sexual content is both surprising and shocking. Rated R for profanity and sexual situations. 93m. **DIR:** Mo Ogrodnik. **CAST:** Monica Keena, Daisy Eagan, Ron Brice. **1997**

RIPPER, THE (1985) 🦃 In this poorly filmed modernization of the Jack the Ripper legend, a college profes-

sor finds a ring, originally belonging to the nineteenth-century killer. 104m. **DIR:** Christopher Lewis. **CAST:** Tom Schreier, Wade Tower. **1985**

RIPPER, THE (1997) ★★★ Unremarkable telling of the Jack the Ripper story buoyed by excellent performances by its cast. Rated R for violence. 100m. **DIR:** Janet Meyers. **CAST:** Patrick Bergin, Gabrielle Anwar, Michael York. **1997**

•RIPPER: LETTER FROM HELL ★★ Uneven thriller about a 16-year-old survivor of a mass murderer who tries to put her past behind her and get on with her life. Eager to learn more about serial killers, Molly signs up for a forensics science class. When a class assignment targets a local campus murder, Molly begins to believe that the suspect is re-creating Jack the Ripper's killing spree. Or is Molly just having horrific flashbacks? There's not enough ambiguity in the script to make us care one way or the other. Rated R for adult situations, language, and violence. 113m. **DIR:** John Eyres. **CAST:** A. J. Cook, Bruce Payne, Ryan Northcott, Jurgen Prochnow. **2001 DVD**

RIPPER MAN 🦃 Ex-cop works in a nightclub as a hypnotist and when the bodies start piling up you know you've seen this all before. Rated R for violence, gore, nudity, and language. 89m. **DIR:** Phil Sears. **CAST:** Mike Norris, Timothy Bottoms. **1997**

RIPPING YARNS ★★★1/2 Wildly funny series featuring Michael Palin in different roles as he romps through six vignettes that comically parody the social structure and history of the British empire. Originally produced for British TV, this double cassette features "Tomkin's Schooldays," "Escape from Stalag Luft 112B," "Golden Gordon," "The Testing of Eric Olthwaite," "Whinfrey's Last Case," and "The Curse of the Claw." Not rated. 180m. **DIR:** Jim Franklin, Alan Bell, Terry Hughes. **CAST:** Michael Palin. **1978**

RIPTIDE ★★★ A soap opera about the failings of the rich that was obviously made to help a Depression-era audience feel superior to those who still had money. It holds up because of good acting and directing, not good writing. The bored rich heroine dallies with a former lover while her husband is away. B&W; 90m. **DIR:** Edmund Goulding. **CAST:** Norma Shearer, Robert Montgomery, Herbert Marshall, Mrs. Patrick Campbell, Lilyan Tashman, Skeets Gallagher, Arthur Treacher, Ralph Forbes. **1934**

RISE AND FALL OF LEGS DIAMOND, THE ★★★1/2 One of the best gangster films, punchily directed and heartily acted by Ray Danton as the self-centered, manipulative low-life who became a Prohibition-era bigshot. Dyan Cannon's debut. 101m. **DIR:** Budd Boetticher. **CAST:** Ray Danton, Karen Steele, Elaine Stewart, Jesse White, Warren Oates, Dyan Cannon. **1960**

RISE OF LOUIS XIV, THE ★★ Slow-paced docudrama chronicles King Louis XIV's acquisition of power over corrupt French noblemen. He is portrayed as a wise ruler despite his reputation. Lack of action, however, makes this import nearly impossible to sit through. In French with English subtitles. 100m. **DIR:** Roberto Rossellini. **CAST:** Jean-Marie Patte, Raymond Jourdan. **1966**

RISING SON ★★★1/2 Superb TV drama focuses on an auto-parts plant-manager's life after he is laid off. With a son not wanting to finish college and a wife going back to work against his will to help support the family, Brian Dennehy's character is forced to reevaluate his own life and beliefs. 96m. **DIR:** John David Coles. **CAST:** Brian Dennehy, Graham Beckel, Matt Damon, Ving Rhames, Piper Laurie. **1990**

RISING SUN ★★★1/2 In attempting to tone down the alleged Japan-bashing in Michael Crichton's novel, director Phil Kaufman delivers a somewhat confusing thriller that succeeds primarily because of the performances. Sean Connery and Wesley Snipes are terrific in what is best viewed as another in the long line of cop/buddy flicks. As such it's a cut above the competition. Rated R for violence, nudity, simulated sex, and profanity. 130m. **DIR:** Phil Kaufman. **CAST:** Sean Connery, Wesley Snipes, Harvey Keitel, Cary-Hiroyuki Tagawa, Kevin Anderson, Mako, Ray Wise, Stan Egi, Stan Shaw, Tia Carrere, Steve Buscemi. **1993 DVD**

•RISK ★★★ It's difficult to turn the life of a young insurance adjuster into a thriller, but that's exactly what the filmmakers have done in this fine-tuned Australian import. Ben Madigan, the new kid on the insurance block, is taken under the wing of jaded veteran John Kreisky, who sees Ben as the perfect patsy to help him defraud the company. With the help of his beautiful girlfriend Louise, John takes Ben on the ride of his life. It's fun to watch Ben fall into their tangled web and then struggle to get out. Rated R for adult situations, drugs, and language. 92m. **DIR:** Alan White. **CAST:** Bryan Brown, Tom Long, Claudia Karvan. **2000 DVD**

RISKY BUSINESS ★★★★ An ordinarily well-behaved boy (Tom Cruise) goes wild when his parents are on vacation. His troubles begin when a gorgeous hooker (Rebecca DeMornay) who doesn't exactly have a heart of gold makes a house call. It's stylish, funny, and sexy—everything, in fact, that most movies of this kind generally are not. Rated R for nudity, profanity, and suggested sex. 99m. **DIR:** Paul Brickman. **CAST:** Tom Cruise, Rebecca DeMornay, Curtis Armstrong, Bronson Pinchot, Raphael Sbarge, Joe Pantoliano, Nicholas Pryor, Richard Masur. **1983 DVD**

RITA HAYWORTH: THE LOVE GODDESS ★★1/2 This lifeless attempt to re-create pinup queen Rita Hayworth's exciting life falls short of its goal. Beautiful Lynda Carter as Hayworth, however, keeps the viewer's attention. Made for television. 100m. **DIR:** James Goldstone. **CAST:** Lynda Carter, Michael Lerner, John Considine, Alejandro Rey. **1983**

RITES OF PASSAGE ★★★ An aging father and his two sons meet up at the family's cabin in the woods. So do two escaped convicts. So-so storyline is rescued by sharp direction and sharper performances. Rated R for violence and profanity. 94m. **DIR:** Victor Salva. **CAST:** Dean Stockwell, Jason Behr, Robert Keith, Jaimz Woolvett, James Remar. **1999 DVD**

RITUALS ★★ Several middle-aged men head up to the wilds on a camping trip, only to be stalked by a relentless killer. This cheap rip-off of *Deliverance* offers little in the way of entertainment. Rated R for violence and profanity. 100m. **DIR:** Peter Carter. **CAST:** Hal Holbrook, Lawrence Dane, Robin Gammell. **1981**

RITZ, THE ★★★★ This film is brimful of belly laughs that will leave you exhausted. After the death of his father-in-law, Jack Weston (as Geatano Proclo) flees Cleveland. His brother-in-law has put out a contract on

him to prevent his inheriting any part of the family garbage business. His escape takes him to New York City and, by accident, a gay hotel called The Ritz. Rated R for profanity. 91m. **DIR:** Richard Lester. **CAST:** Jack Weston, Rita Moreno, Jerry Stiller, Kaye Ballard, F. Murray Abraham, Treat Williams. **1976**

RIVER, THE (1951) ★★★1/2 Beautiful locations enhance this lyrical drama about English children growing up in Bengal. This well-orchestrated character study is brilliantly directed by cinema master Jean Renoir and is equally blessed with rich color photography by his brother Claude. 99m. **DIR:** Jean Renoir. **CAST:** Nora Swinburne, Arthur Shields. **1951**

RIVER, THE (1984) ★★★1/2 Following as it does on the heels of two other first-rate farmer films, this work by director Mark Rydell often seems hopelessly unoriginal and, as a result, boring. As with *Country*, it deals with a farming family who must battle a severe storm and foreclosure proceedings. It simply has little new to say. Rated PG for nudity, violence, and profanity. 122m. **DIR:** Mark Rydell. **CAST:** Mel Gibson, Sissy Spacek, Scott Glenn. **1984 DVD**

RIVER OF DEATH 🦃 An adventurer wades his way through hostile Indians, cannibals, river pirates, and Nazis to rescue an archaeologist's daughter. Rated R for violence and profanity. 103m. **DIR:** Steve Carver. **CAST:** Michael Dudikoff, Robert Vaughn, Donald Pleasence, Herbert Lom, L. Q. Jones. **1990 DVD**

RIVER OF DIAMONDS 🦃 An adventurer braves villains to seek his fortune on a mysterious island. Rated PG-13 for violence and profanity. 88m. **DIR:** Robert J. Smawley. **CAST:** Dack Rambo, Angela O'Neill, Ferdinand Mayne. **1990**

RIVER OF NO RETURN ★★★ Rory Calhoun has deserted Marilyn Monroe, believe it or not. She hires Robert Mitchum to track him down. The story line is predictable and sometimes plodding, under Otto Preminger's heavy directorial hand. Nevertheless, Mitchum's quirky strength and the gorgeous color shots of Monroe and western vistas make the film sufficiently entertaining. 91m. **DIR:** Otto Preminger. **CAST:** Robert Mitchum, Marilyn Monroe, Rory Calhoun, Tommy Rettig. **1954 DVD**

RIVER OF UNREST ★★ Melodrama about the Sinn Fein rebellion in Ireland bears a strong resemblance to John Ford's classic *The Informer*, but there's more emphasis on the love story between Antoinette Cellier and the two men in her life. Good performances by a capable cast help this slow-moving story, which was based on a stage play. B&W; 69m. **DIR:** Brian Desmond, Walter Summers. **CAST:** John Lodge, John Loder, Antoinette Cellier, Niall MacGinnis, Clifford Evans. **1937**

RIVER PIRATES, THE ★★★ Young Ryan Francis stars as a 12 year old whose summer vacation in Mississippi during World War II provides the backdrop for a number of adventures. Familiar faces dot the landscape, but the focus is on Francis and his friends as they tackle everything from racial injustice to river pirates. Excellent production values and a genuine sense of adventure make this family film watchable. Rated PG. 108m. **DIR:** Tom G. Robertson. **CAST:** Ryan Francis, Richard Farnsworth, Gennie James, Doug Emerson, Anne Ramsey, Maureen O'Sullivan. **1988**

RIVER RAT, THE ★★★1/2 Although essentially the story of the growing love between a long-separated father (Tommy Lee Jones), who has been in prison for thirteen years, and daughter (newcomer Martha Plimpton), this release is much more than a simple tear-jerker. Writer-director Tom Rickman has invested his story with a grit and realism that set it apart from similar works. As a result, he's created a powerful, thought-provoking motion picture. Rated R for profanity and violence. 109m. **DIR:** Tom Rickman. **CAST:** Tommy Lee Jones, Martha Plimpton, Brian Dennehy. **1984**

RIVER RUNS THROUGH IT, A ★★★★ Robert Redford's elegiac coming-of-age story is based on the memoir by Norman Maclean. Brad Pitt is the young man who finds peace and comradeship in fly-fishing. Redford narrates the film, which compares favorably with his first directorial triumph, *Ordinary People*, in every way. Rated PG for profanity and nudity. 123m. **DIR:** Robert Redford. **CAST:** Brad Pitt, Craig Sheffer, Tom Skerritt, Brenda Blethyn, Emily Lloyd, Edie McClurg, Stephen Shellen. **1992 DVD**

RIVER WILD, THE ★★★1/2 Meryl Streep successfully invades Schwarzenegger and Stallone territory when her family is terrorized by a psychotic killer while on a white-water rafting vacation. Strong character development, top-flight performances, and effective commentary on the effect of modern-day stress on family relationships help make this more than just another by-the-numbers suspense thriller. Rated PG-13 for violence, nudity, and profanity. 111m. **DIR:** Curtis Hanson. **CAST:** Meryl Streep, Kevin Bacon, David Strathairn, Joseph Mazzello, John C. Reilly, Benjamin Bratt. **1994 DVD**

RIVER'S EDGE ★★★1/2 This is a deeply disturbing film based on a real-life 1980 murder case. The teenage murderer in *River's Edge* takes his friends to see the corpse of his classmate-victim. The death becomes a secret bond among them until two decent kids (Keanu Reeves, Ione Skye) decide to do something about it. Rated R for violence, profanity, nudity, and simulated sex. 99m. **DIR:** Tim Hunter. **CAST:** Dennis Hopper, Crispin Glover, Keanu Reeves, Ione Skye, Roxana Zal, Daniel Roebuck, Tom Bower, Leo Rossi. **1987**

RKO 281 ★★★★1/2 Any fan of *Citizen Kane* or Orson Welles has to see this award-winning made-for-cable movie, which dramatizes the events surrounding Welles's most famous film. The look of the film is lush and jazzy, perfect for setting the prewar mood, and Liev Schreiber puts in a superb performance as the "boy genius," who remains above all else obsessed with his art. While you can't claim it's a straight documentary, the film is certainly entertaining. Not rated; contains profanity and nudity. 83m. **DIR:** Benjamin Ross. **CAST:** Liev Schreiber, James Cromwell, Melanie Griffith, John Malkovich, Brenda Blethyn, Roy Scheider. **1999 DVD**

ROAD AGENT ★★★1/2 Tim Holt and his sidekick Chito pose as masked riders to overcome a tyrannical land boss. B&W; 60m. **DIR:** Lesley Selander. **CAST:** Tim Holt, Richard Martin, Dorothy Patrick, Tom Tyler. **1952**

ROAD ENDS ★★★★ Stylish thriller about a mysterious stranger who comes to a small town and seems to bring nothing but trouble with him—until the townfolk discover he may be just another innocent victim in the

bigger scheme of things. Excellent performances, a taut script, and fresh, stylish direction make this film much more than one might expect. Rated R for violence and profanity. 98m. **DIR:** Rick King. **CAST:** Dennis Hopper, Peter Coyote, Chris Sarandon, Joanna Gleason, Mariel Hemingway, Bert Remsen. **1997 DVD**

ROAD GAMES ★★ An elusive latter-day Jack the Ripper is loose in Australia. Even though director Richard Franklin (*Psycho II*) actually studied under Alfred Hitchcock, he doesn't show any of his mentor's ability here. Rated PG. 100m. **DIR:** Richard Franklin. **CAST:** Stacy Keach, Jamie Lee Curtis, Marion Howard, Grant Page. **1981**

ROAD HOME, THE (1995) ★★1/2 A sickly sweet continuation, of sorts, of *Boys' Town* with plot holes so huge even young kids won't miss them. Two orphaned brothers make their way across the country, with the help of some adorable hobos, to the famed Nebraska orphanage, now run by Mickey Rooney. Rated PG for a fiery explosion. 90m. **DIR:** Dean Hamilton. **CAST:** Charles Martin Smith, Kris Kristofferson, Danny Aiello, Dee Wallace, Mickey Rooney, Will Estes, Keegan MacIntosh. **1995**

•ROAD HOME, THE (1999) ★★1/2 This luminous, meditative drama about love in a land of arranged marriages, tradition, and respect for the dead begins as a city engineer learns that his schoolteacher father has died. He returns to the village where he was born, finds that his mother wants his father's body carried on foot from the hospital morgue back to the village, and contemplates his father's burial. The film then flashes back to the courtship of his parents, which is highlighted by striking Cinemascope images of the Chinese countryside. In Mandarin with English subtitles. Rated G. 100m. **DIR:** Zhang Yimou. **CAST:** Zhang Ziyi, Zheng Hao, Zhao Yuelin, Sun Honglei. **1999 DVD**

ROAD HOUSE (1948) ★★★1/2 Nifty little *film noir* about nightclub singer Ida Lupino and the two men competing for her. Gritty and well acted. B&W; 95m. **DIR:** Jean Negulesco. **CAST:** Ida Lupino, Cornel Wilde, Richard Widmark, Celeste Holm. **1948**

ROAD HOUSE (1989) ★★ Hot on the heels of *Dirty Dancing,* Patrick Swayze turns to a rowdy, rough-house movie about a bar bouncer who cleans out a Missouri saloon. A male action film with lots of fistfights, a high body count, and a disappointing level of sexist humor. Rated R. 108m. **DIR:** Rowdy Herrington. **CAST:** Patrick Swayze, Ben Gazzara, Sam Elliott. **1989**

ROAD KILLERS, THE ★★ Where have you seen this one before? Vacationing family is terrorized on a rural highway by a gang of crazy joyriders. They may be on the highway to hell, but they have a devil of a time coming up with anything original. Rated R for language and violence. 89m. **DIR:** Deran Sarafian. **CAST:** Christopher Lambert, Craig Sheffer. **1993**

ROAD LAWYERS AND OTHER BRIEFS ★★1/2 Three student-made films: "Road Lawyers," a *Mad Max* parody set in a future world where lawyers battle for clients; "Escape from Heaven," featuring an insufferable nun; and "Hairline," in which a man can't cope with losing his hair. Rounding out the package is a segment of the Fifties serial *Radar Men From the Moon* with new overdubbed (not very funny) dialogue. Not rated. 79m. **DIR:** Tim Doyle, James Desmarais, David Lipman, Robert Rhine. **1989**

•ROAD RAGE ★★1/2 Very silly but admittedly action-packed thriller about a limousine driver being chased by a madman he accidentally cut off. Lots of car chases and crashes. Rated R for language and violence. 96m. **DIR:** Sidney J. Furie. **CAST:** Casper Van Dien, Danielle Brett, Joseph Griffin. **2000 DVD**

ROAD TO BALI ★★★1/2 Excellent entry in the Bob Hope/Bing Crosby *Road* series. In this one the boys play a pair of vaudeville performers in competition for Dorothy Lamour, pursuing her to the South Seas island of Bali, where they must contend with all sorts of jungle dangers, from cannibalistic natives to various Hollywood stars who appear in hilarious (though very brief) cameos. The Humphrey Bogart scene is a classic. 90m. **DIR:** Hal Walker. **CAST:** Bob Hope, Bing Crosby, Dorothy Lamour, Murvyn Vye. **1952**

ROAD TO EL DORADO, THE ★★1/2 Lasting friendship and colonial conquest clash in this colorful, comic, animated adventure film, an uninspired recycling of Rudyard Kipling's *The Man Who Would Be King*. After two sixteenth-century con men win a treasure map to the legendary City of Gold in a crooked craps game, they travel to the New World and plot with a curvaceous native to steal a fortune in gold. Kevin Kline, Kenneth Branagh, Rosie Perez, Armand Assante, and Edward James Olmos supply the voices. Rated PG. 83m. **DIR:** Eric "Bibo" Bergeron, Don Paul. **2000 DVD**

ROAD TO FREEDOM: THE VERNON JOHNS STORY ★★★★ James Earl Jones delivers a stellar performance as the controversial reverend who incited his congregation to fight against injustice wherever they found it. His views weren't very popular back in Alabama in the early 1950s, even among his congregation, who replaced Rev. Johns with another young idealist, Martin Luther King Jr. This made-for-television drama is rich in period detail and excellent performances. Rated PG. 91m. **DIR:** Kenneth Fink. **CAST:** James Earl Jones, Mary Alice, Cissy Huston, Joe Seneca. **1994**

ROAD TO GALVESTON, THE ★★★ Cicely Tyson plays a recent widow who takes in Alzheimer's patients to pay the mortgage on her farm in this made-for-cable original. Not a very strong plot, but still viewable. Not rated, but suitable for all audiences. 95m. **DIR:** Michael Toshiyuki Uno. **CAST:** Cicely Tyson, Piper Laurie, Tess Harper, James McDaniel. **1996**

ROAD TO HONG KONG, THE ★★ Bob Hope and Bing Crosby play con men in this listless effort that involves international intrigue and space exploration. This was the last of the *Road* pictures, which means that Hope and Crosby made one *Road* picture too many. B&W; 91m. **DIR:** Norman Panama. **CAST:** Bing Crosby, Bob Hope, Joan Collins, Dorothy Lamour, Robert Morley, Peter Sellers. **1962**

ROAD TO MECCA, THE ★★★★ An eccentric widow living in a small South African town has a spiritual revelation to build a large sculpture garden in her yard, made to resemble Mecca. This unusual film is adapted by Athol Fugard from his play. Not rated. 106m. **DIR:** Athol Fugard, Peter Goldsmid. **CAST:** Kathy Bates, Yvonne Bryceland, Athol Fugard. **1991**

ROAD TO MOROCCO ★★★1/2 Fun in the sun as Bob Hope and Bing Crosby end up in sandy Morocco where

Crosby sells Hope as a slave to princess Dorothy Lamour. The real fun begins when both men attempt to win the heart of the princess. Enjoyable romp with pleasant songs and lots of laughs. 83m. **DIR:** David Butler. **CAST:** Bob Hope, Bing Crosby, Dorothy Lamour, Yvonne De Carlo, Anthony Quinn, Monte Blue. **1942 DVD**

ROAD TO RIO ★★★ More a straight comedy than madcap mayhem, this fifth *Road* show has Bob Hope and Bing Crosby hopping a boat to Rio de Janeiro. On board they meet and fall for Dorothy Lamour, who runs hot and cold because her wicked aunt (Gale Sondergaard) is hypnotizing her so she will accept an arranged marriage. Lots of laughs. B&W; 100m. **DIR:** Norman Z. McLeod. **CAST:** Bob Hope, Bing Crosby, Dorothy Lamour, Gale Sondergaard, Frank Faylen, Jerry Colonna, The Andrews Sisters. **1947**

ROAD TO RUIN, THE (1928) 🦃 A classic exploitation feature, this silent quickie is creaky and heavily moralistic. Silent. B&W; 45m. **DIR:** Norton S. Parker. **CAST:** Helen Foster, Grant Withers, Charles Miller. **1928**

ROAD TO RUIN (1991) ★★1/2 Decent romance features a playboy millionaire signing away his money in order to see if a beautiful model really loves him. Predictable time passer. Rated PG-13 for sexual situations. 94m. **DIR:** Charlotte Brandstrom. **CAST:** Peter Weller, Carey Lowell, Michel Duchaussoy. **1991**

ROAD TO SINGAPORE ★★★1/2 Two happy-go-lucky adventurers on the lam from responsibility end up in the tropics where they sing and perform with local lovely Dorothy Lamour, the object of their affection and rivalry. This breezy film was the first of seven pictures that cemented Bob Hope and Bing Crosby as a top comedy team and provided some of the easiest laughs of the 1940s. B&W; 85m. **DIR:** Victor Schertzinger. **CAST:** Bing Crosby, Bob Hope, Dorothy Lamour, Charles Coburn, Anthony Quinn, Jerry Colonna, Johnny Arthur, Miles Mander. **1940 DVD**

ROAD TO UTOPIA ★★★ The Klondike and a hunt for an Alaskan gold mine provide the background for this fourth of the seven *Roads* Bob Hope, Bing Crosby, and Dorothy Lamour traveled between 1940 and 1962. Rated the best of the bunch by fans, it's a mix of songs, sight gags, wisecracks, inside jokes, hoke, and the usual love triangle. B&W; 90m. **DIR:** Hal Walker. **CAST:** Bob Hope, Bing Crosby, Dorothy Lamour, Hillary Brooke, Douglass Dumbrille, Jack LaRue, Robert Benchley. **1945 DVD**

ROAD TO WELLVILLE, THE 🦃 Writer-director Alan Parker's treatment of the eccentric Dr. Kellogg's turn-of-the-century health sanatorium is moronic, embarrassing, and absolutely humorless. Rarely is such a talented cast so ill used. Rated R for nudity, simulated sex, and profanity. 120m. **DIR:** Alan Parker. **CAST:** Anthony Hopkins, Bridget Fonda, Matthew Broderick, John Cusack, Dana Carvey, Michael Lerner, Colm Meaney, Lara Flynn Boyle. **1994**

ROAD TO YESTERDAY, THE ★★★ This is Cecil B. DeMille's first independent film. The plot involves reincarnation and modern characters who flash back historically to seventeenth-century England and explain their actions and feelings years later. The action sequences make this a compelling mix of melodrama and spectacle. Silent with musical score. B&W; 136m. **DIR:** Cecil B. DeMille. **CAST:** Joseph Schildkraut, William Boyd, Vera Reynolds, Sally Rand. **1925**

ROAD TO ZANZIBAR ★★★★ Bob Hope and Bing Crosby play two fast-talking con men always just ahead of the authorities and ready to chuck everything for a sob story from a female. The story takes the adventurers to Africa in search of a diamond mine (and Dorothy Lamour!), but the funniest moments come as Fearless Frazier (Hope) is talked into one outlandishly dangerous stunt after another. B&W; 90m. **DIR:** Victor Schertzinger. **CAST:** Bing Crosby, Bob Hope, Dorothy Lamour, Una Merkel, Eric Blore, Iris Adrian, Douglass Dumbrille, Joan Marsh, Luis Alberni, Leo Gorcey. **1941 DVD**

ROAD TRIP ★★ New York college student Josh discovers in this raunchy, gross-out sex comedy that a videotape of his drunken infidelity has been mailed to his girlfriend in Texas. He and his buddies—a manic party animal, a virginal nerd, and a group intellectual—try to intercept the incriminating package amid misadventures involving a sperm bank deposit, a snake feeding, a desecrated order of French toast, and lots of gratuitous female nudity. Rated R for nudity, crude humor, sex, profanity, and drug use. 93m. **DIR:** Todd Phillips. **CAST:** Breckin Meyer, Rachel Blanchard, Amy Stuart, Seann William Scott, DJ Qualls, Paulo Costanzo, Tom Green. **2000 DVD**

ROAD WARRIOR, THE ★★★★ A sequel to *Mad Max*, this exciting adventure features Mel Gibson as a fast-driving, cynical Robin Hood in the desolate post-apocalypse world of the future. Good fun! Rated R for violence, nudity, and profanity. 94m. **DIR:** George Miller. **CAST:** Mel Gibson, Bruce Spence, Vernon Wells, Mike Preston. **1981 DVD**

ROADHOUSE 66 ★★★1/2 As teen exploitation films go, this one is pretty good. Judge Reinhold plays a yuppie stuck in a small New Mexico town with car trouble. Willem Dafoe is an ex-rock-and-roller and all-around tough guy. The film drags a bit and Dafoe overplays his role, but there are some good moments to be had. Rated R for sex, nudity, violence, and profanity. 94m. **DIR:** John Mark Robinson. **CAST:** Willem Dafoe, Judge Reinhold, Kaaren Lee, Kate Vernon, Stephen Elliott, Alan Autry. **1984**

ROADRACERS ★★ Ultrastylish but not quite whole film from *El Mariachi* director Robert Rodriguez stars David Arquette as a rebel named Dude who just wants to play guitar—but the bad guys in his life (read overbearing authorities) just won't let him. Violence ensues. Rated R for language and violence. 93m. **DIR:** Robert Rodriguez. **CAST:** David Arquette, John Hawkes, Salma Hayek, Jason Wiles, Bill Sadler. **1994**

ROADS TO THE SOUTH ★★★1/2 Sequel to *La Guerre Est Finie* reteams screenwriter Jorge Semprun and actor Yves Montand to give us an update on the antifascist exile (played to perfection by Montand) after he's joined the establishment enough to become a wealthy writer. In French with English subtitles. Not rated; contains profanity and violence. 100m. **DIR:** Joseph Losey. **CAST:** Yves Montand, Laurent Malet, Miou-Miou, Jose Luis Gomez. **1978**

ROADSIDE PROPHETS ★★★★ Entrusted with the cremated remains of a man he barely knows, John Doe (of the rock group X) searches for the mythical Nevada

town the man had once spoke of. Along the way he hooks up with a strange kid. A road movie with a difference. Rated R for profanity and nudity. 96m. **DIR:** Abbe Wool. **CAST:** John Doe, Adam Horovitz, John Cusack, David Carradine, Arlo Guthrie, Timothy Leary. **1992**

ROAMIN' WILD ★★★ Undercover marshal (Tom Tyler) goes after a gang of outlaws operating in the goldfields trying to take over a woman's stage line. Fast-moving, with plenty of excitement. B&W; 56m. **DIR:** Bernard B. Ray. **CAST:** Tom Tyler, Carol Wyndham, Al Ferguson, George Chesebro. **1936**

ROARING GUNS ★★★ A ruthless cattle baron attempts to drive out the independent ranchers. It's up to steely-eyed Tim McCoy to set things aright in this low-budget but enjoyable series Western. B&W; 66m. **DIR:** Sam Newfield. **CAST:** Tim McCoy, Rosalinda Price, Wheeler Oakman. **1936**

ROARING ROAD, THE ★★★ Car salesman Wallace Reid represents his company in a famous auto race. Lots of real racing footage. Silent. B&W; 57m. **DIR:** James Cruze. **CAST:** Wallace Reid. **1919**

ROARING TWENTIES, THE ★★★★1/2 James Cagney and Humphrey Bogart star in this superb Warner Bros. gangster entry. Produced by Mark Hellinger and directed by Raoul Walsh (*White Heat*), it's one of the best of its kind, with Cagney featured as a World War I veteran who comes back to no job and no future after fighting for his country. Embittered by all this, he turns to crime. B&W; 104m. **DIR:** Raoul Walsh. **CAST:** James Cagney, Humphrey Bogart, Priscilla Lane, Gladys George, Jeffrey Lynn, Frank McHugh, Joe Sawyer. **1939**

ROB ROY ★★★★ Stately but lusty tale of the Scottish hero's fight for justice and honor in the Highlands of 1713. Neeson and Lange are glorious together, but it is Roth, as the embodiment of pure evil, who most enlivens this uncommonly serious-minded swashbuckler. Rated R for violence and simulated sex. 139m. **DIR:** Michael Caton-Jones. **CAST:** Liam Neeson, Jessica Lange, John Hurt, Tim Roth, Eric Stoltz, Andrew Keir, Brian Cox. **1995 DVD**

ROB ROY, THE HIGHLAND ROGUE ★★ Slow-moving historical saga is not up to the usual Walt Disney adventure film and is perhaps the weakest of the three films made in England with sturdy Richard Todd as the heroic lead. The few battle scenes are enjoyable enough and the scenery is lovely, but the pace is erratic and there is just too much dead time. 85m. **DIR:** Harold French. **CAST:** Richard Todd, Glynis Johns, James Robertson Justice, Michael Gough, Finlay Currie. **1954**

ROBBERS OF THE SACRED MOUNTAIN ★★ This action-adventure film could have been another *Raiders of the Lost Ark*. Unfortunately, poor acting and choppy editing leave it in the mediocre range. Rated R for sex, nudity, and violence. 90m. **DIR:** Bob Schulz. **CAST:** John Marley, Simon MacCorkindale, Louise Vallance, George Touliatos. **1982**

ROBBERY ★★★1/2 Suspenseful crime-drama about the complex heist of the British Royal Mail. Solid direction and excellent performances surpass the predictable script. 114m. **DIR:** Peter Yates. **CAST:** Stanley Baker, Joanna Pettet, James Booth. **1967**

ROBE, THE ★★★★ Richard Burton is the Roman tribune charged with overseeing the execution of Christ in this story of his involvement with the followers of Christ and the effect the robe of Jesus has on all involved. It is a well-made film, and not heavy-handed in its approach. 135m. **DIR:** Henry Koster. **CAST:** Richard Burton, Victor Mature, Jean Simmons, Michael Rennie, Richard Boone, Dean Jagger, Dawn Addams, Jay Robinson. **1953 DVD**

ROBERT ET ROBERT ★★★★1/2 A brilliant French film about two lonely but very different men (Charles Denner and Jacques Villeret) who strike up a tenuous friendship while waiting for their respective computer dates. It is a bittersweet tale of loneliness and compassion. No MPAA rating. 105m. **DIR:** Claude Lelouch. **CAST:** Charles Denner, Jacques Villeret, Jean-Claude Brialy, Macha Meril, Regine. **1978**

ROBERTA ★★★1/2 This lighthearted story of a group of entertainers who find themselves operating a dress shop in Paris belongs to the second and third-billed Fred Astaire and Ginger Rogers. With the music of Jerome Kern and Otto Harbach, including those gems "Smoke Gets in Your Eyes" and "I Won't Dance," this carefree film is very enjoyable. Later remade as *Lovely to Look At*. B&W; 85m. **DIR:** William A. Seiter. **CAST:** Irene Dunne, Fred Astaire, Ginger Rogers, Randolph Scott, Helen Westley. **1935**

ROBIN AND MARIAN ★★★★1/2 Take the best director of swashbucklers, Richard Lester; add the foremost adventure film actor, Sean Connery; mix well with a fine actress with haunting presence, Audrey Hepburn; and finish off with some of the choicest character actors. You get *Robin and Marian*, a triumph for everyone involved. Rated PG. 112m. **DIR:** Richard Lester. **CAST:** Sean Connery, Audrey Hepburn, Richard Harris, Ian Holm, Robert Shaw, Nicol Williamson, Denholm Elliott, Kenneth Haigh. **1976**

ROBIN & THE SEVEN HOODS ★★★ Musical reworking of the Robin Hood legend set in Jazz Age, gangster-ruled Chicago. Frank Sinatra and Dean Martin, et al. are the Merry Men, with Bing Crosby the silver-tongued spokesman Alan A. Dale. Sometimes stretches a point to be too Runyonesque, but good tunes and actors make it pleasant. 123m. **DIR:** Gordon Douglas. **CAST:** Frank Sinatra, Dean Martin, Sammy Davis Jr., Bing Crosby, Peter Falk, Barbara Rush, Victor Buono, Edward G. Robinson. **1964 DVD**

ROBIN COOK'S INVASION ★★★1/2 Riveting science-fiction thriller finds a young couple living in Phoenix taking different paths during an alien invasion. When her boyfriend is infected by an alien virus, she teams up with a ragtag group of believers to combat the aliens and thwart their planned colonization of Earth. This made-for-television miniseries features engaging characters, creepy situations, and stunning special effects. Not rated; contains adult situations and violence. 179m. **DIR:** Armand Mastroianni. **CAST:** Luke Perry, Rebecca Gayheart, Kim Cattrall, Christopher Orr. **1997**

ROBIN HOOD (1923) ★★★★ A rousing, fast-moving silent movie that established the character as a devil-may-care adventurer with a passion for justice and the wistful Maid Marian—in that order. Fairbanks wrote the screenplay and financed the then astronomical $1.5 million film. B&W; 118m. **DIR:** Allan Dwan. **CAST:**

Douglas Fairbanks Sr., Enid Bennett, Wallace Beery, Alan Hale Sr. **1923 DVD**

ROBIN HOOD (1973) ★★★ A feature-length cartoon featuring Robin Hood and his gang, this is one of the lesser animated works from the Walt Disney Studios, but still good for the kiddies. Rated G. 83m. **DIR:** Wolfgang Reitherman. **1973 DVD**

ROBIN HOOD (1991) ★★★ In an adventure film whose style of storytelling and atmosphere are reminiscent of John Boorman's *Excalibur*, the legend of Robin Hood is played out with most of the well-known events staged with conviction and an occasional twist. This made-for-television production doesn't have the high spirits of Errol Flynn's *The Adventures of Robin Hood* or the spectacle of Kevin Costner's *Robin Hood: Prince of Thieves*, but it's enjoyable nonetheless. 116m. **DIR:** John Irvin. **CAST:** Patrick Bergin, Uma Thurman, Jurgen Prochnow, Edward Fox, Jeroen Krabbé. **1991**

ROBIN HOOD AND THE SORCERER ★★★★ While the telling of the Robin Hood legend in this film may be less straightforward than most, the added element of the mysticism enhances the all-too-familiar story and gives the dusty old characters new life. Michael Praed plays the legendary English outlaw with conviction. 115m. **DIR:** Ian Sharp. **CAST:** Michael Praed, Anthony Valentine, Nickolas Grace, Clive Mantle, Peter Williams. **1983**

ROBIN HOOD GANG, THE ★★ When two young boys find a suitcase filled with cash in their apartment building's attic, they use the cash to help out the needy in their town. Too bad the loot belongs to a bank robber who will do anything to get his stash back. No big deal, yet small children may not recognize the familiar story and antics of the young cast. Rated PG. 86m. **DIR:** Eric Hendershot. **CAST:** Clayton Taylor, Steven Losack, Dalin Christiansen, Brenda Price, Scott Christopher. **1997 DVD**

ROBIN HOOD OF TEXAS ★★★ More of a detective story than a formula Western, Gene Autry's last film for Republic Studios finds him accused of bank robbery and keeping one step ahead of the law in order to clear his name. Better than many of his films with a nicely turned story and more action and fisticuffs than most of Autry's productions, B&W; 71m. **DIR:** Lesley Selander. **CAST:** Gene Autry, Lynne Roberts, Sterling Holloway, Adele Mara. **1947**

ROBIN HOOD OF THE PECOS ★★★ Roy Rogers and Gabby Hayes fight for law, order, and honest government in this history-based post–Civil War Western-drama. B&W; 50m. **DIR:** Joseph Kane. **CAST:** Roy Rogers, George "Gabby" Hayes, Marjorie Reynolds, Jay Novello, Roscoe Ates. **1941**

ROBIN HOOD: HERNE'S SON ★★★ The third in this series from the BBC begins with the death of Robin of Locksley and the choosing of Robert of Huntingdon (Jason Connery) as his successor by Herne the Hunter. The refusal of the new Robin to serve leads to the breakup of the band, followed by the abduction of Maid Marion. The new Robin must then unite his followers and save his love. 101m. **DIR:** Robert Young. **CAST:** Jason Connery, Oliver Cotton, George Baker, Michael Craig, Nickolas Grace. **1986**

ROBIN HOOD: MEN IN TIGHTS ★★1/2 Director Mel Brooks's rude comic shtick seems pretty shopworn these days, although there are some genuine laughs. For more of the same, see *When Things Were Rotten*, Brooks's 1975 TV comedy featuring the same characters and ideas. Rated PG-13 for brief profanity, scatological humor, and sexual references. 104m. **DIR:** Mel Brooks. **CAST:** Cary Elwes, Richard Lewis, Roger Rees, Amy Yasbeck, Mark Blankfield, Dave Chappelle, Isaac Hayes, Megan Cavanaugh, Tracey Ullman, Patrick Stewart, Dom DeLuise, Dick Van Patten, Mel Brooks. **1993**

ROBIN HOOD: PRINCE OF THIEVES ★★★★ The Robin Hood legend gets a fresh, innovative telling in this action-packed, funny, and suspenseful adult-oriented adventure, which presents Kevin Costner as the title hero. Alan Rickman is delightfully sinister as the evil Sheriff of Nottingham, and Morgan Freeman plays a Moorish warrior who aids Robin in his robbing of the rich to give to the poor. Rated PG-13 for violence and profanity. 138m. **DIR:** Kevin Reynolds. **CAST:** Kevin Costner, Morgan Freeman, Mary Elizabeth Mastrantonio, Alan Rickman, Christian Slater, Sean Connery, Brian Blessed. **1991 DVD**

ROBIN HOOD: THE SWORDS OF WAYLAND ★★★★ The second of the *Robin Hood* series from the BBC is as good as the first, if not better. This adventure pits Robin against the forces of darkness represented by the sorceress Morgwyn of Ravenscar (Rula Lenska). The story twists and turns as the sorceress gathers the seven swords of Wayland, one of which is in Robin's hands. 105m. **DIR:** Robert Young. **CAST:** Michael Praed, Rula Lenska, Nickolas Grace. **1986**

ROBIN OF LOCKSLEY ★★★1/2 The *Robin Hood* saga goes high-tech in this engaging family drama that concerns a precocious computer hacker who raids large business accounts for funds needed by an injured school chum. Larry Sugar's script echoes the familiar classic while maintaining reasonably proper ethics; it's a tightwire act, but Devon Sawa—as the resourceful lad—is charming enough to make it work. Rated PG for mild violence. 97m. **DIR:** Michael Kennedy. **CAST:** Devon Sawa, Joshua Jackson, Sarah Chalke, Billy O'Sullivan, Tyler Labine. **1996**

ROBO C.H.I.C. 🦃 Female crime fighter made in a lab has all of the right parts as played by former *Playboy* Playmate Kathy Shower, but film is long in the tooth and light in the budget department. Send this one back to the factory unopened. Not rated; contains violence and nudity. 101m. **DIR:** Ed Hansen, Jeff Mandel. **CAST:** Kathy Shower, Jack Carter, Burt Ward, Philip Proctor. **1990**

ROBO VAMPIRE 🦃 Drug smugglers vs. Asian vampires in a movie that's almost—but not quite—so bad it's good. Not rated; contains violence and brief nudity. 90m. **DIR:** Joe Livingstone. **CAST:** Harry Myles, Joe Browne. **1993 DVD**

ROBOCOP ★★★★ *RoboCop* is the ultimate superhero movie. A stylish and stylized cop thriller set in the far future, it concerns a mortally wounded policeman (Peter Weller) who is melded with a machine to become the ultimate defender of justice, RoboCop. One word of warning: this is an extremely violent motion picture. Rated R. 103m. **DIR:** Paul Verhoeven. **CAST:** Peter Weller, Nancy Allen, Dan O'Herlihy, Ronny Cox, Kurtwood Smith, Miguel Ferrer. **1987 DVD**

ROBOCOP 2 ★★ Inferior, overly gory sequel pits RoboCop (Peter Weller) against a wily gang of drug dealers and the title creature, a supposedly improved version of himself that has gone berserk. Some interesting character angles but these are all too quickly abandoned in favor of mind-numbing violence. Rated R. 110m. **DIR:** Irvin Kershner. **CAST:** Peter Weller, Nancy Allen, Dan O'Herlihy, Felton Perry, Belinda Bauer. **1990 DVD**

ROBOCOP 3 ★★ Completed in 1991 and unreleased for two years, this second sequel to the 1987 hit was hardly worth waiting for, although it is a slight improvement over *RoboCop 2*. The mayhem is a little more under control, but the story is thin and the Japanese villains are straight off a World War II recruiting poster. Rated PG-13 for violence. 104m. **DIR:** Fred Dekker. **CAST:** Robert Burke, Nancy Allen, Rip Torn, Mako, C.C.H. Pounder. **1993 DVD**

ROBOT HOLOCAUST 🦃 Inept attempt at a sci-fi epic that features giant worms that look like sock puppets. Not rated; contains violence and profanity. 79m. **DIR:** Tim Kincaid. **CAST:** Norris Culf, Nadine Hart, Joel von Omsteiner, Jennifer Delora. **1987**

ROBOT IN THE FAMILY 🦃 This cheap, sophomoric comedy about an ambulatory robot is one of the worst films we've ever seen; the producers apparently felt they could get away with a $1.98 budget and that kids wouldn't know the difference. (Ours did.) Rated G. 85m. **DIR:** Jack Shaoul, Mark Richardson. **CAST:** Joe Pantoliano, Amy Wright, Peter Maloney, Danny Gerard, John Rhys-Davies. **1991**

ROBOT JOX ★★ Transformers-style gladiator adventure aimed at preteen boys, this futuristic tale of battles for world territorial possession will play better on home video than on the big screen. Rated PG for violence and mild profanity. 85m. **DIR:** Stuart Gordon. **CAST:** Gary Graham, Anne-Marie Johnson, Paul Koslo, Robert Sampson, Hilary Mason. **1990**

ROBOT MONSTER ★★ Take a desolate-looking canyon outside of Los Angeles, borrow Lawrence Welk's bubble machine, and add a typical family on an outing and a man dressed in a gorilla suit wearing a diving helmet, and you have a serious competitor for the worst movie of all time. This absurd drama of the last days of Earth and its conquest by robot gorillas has long been considered the most inept of all science-fiction films. A must-see for all fans of truly terrible films. B&W; 63m. **DIR:** Phil Tucker. **CAST:** George Nader, Gregory Moffett, Claudia Barrett. **1953**

ROBOT NINJA ★★ Robot Ninja is a superhero come to life in the form of its creator after he witnesses a brutal crime. With the help of an inventor, he builds armor to combat crime. Batman jokes abound with the character being hailed as the next Caped Crusader. Burt Ward makes an in-joke appearance. Not rated; contains violence, profanity, and gore. 82m. **DIR:** J. R. Bookwalter. **CAST:** Michael Todd, Bogdan Pecic, Burt Ward, Linnea Quigley, Scott Spiegel. **1989**

ROBOT WARS 🦃 Albert Band has a go at remaking his son Charles's film *Robot Jox*, about post-apocalyptic humanity battling it out in giant machines, and fails more miserably. Not rated, but with profanity and violence. Rated PG. 106m. **DIR:** Albert Band. **CAST:** Don Michael Paul, Barbara Crampton, James Staley, Yuji Okumoto, Danny Kamekona. **1993**

ROCCO & HIS BROTHERS ★★★★ Compelling drama about a mother and her five sons who leave their peasant home in the south of Italy for the big city. One of Luchino Visconti's strongest screen efforts. In Italian with English subtitles. B&W; 170m. **DIR:** Luchino Visconti. **CAST:** Alain Delon, Annie Girardot, Renato Salvatori, Claudia Cardinale. **1960 DVD**

ROCK, THE ★★★★ A group of Marines takes eighty-one tourists hostage on Alcatraz island and threatens to launch chemical warheads into the city of San Francisco unless the U.S. government accedes to their demands (a ransom of $100 million and proper military honors for comrades who have died in secret operations). Enter FBI lab scientist Nicolas Cage whose expertise on toxic weapons puts him at the head of a special task force that must break into the prison and neutralize the threat. It's suspenseful and occasionally beyond belief—but never boring. Rated R for violence, profanity, and simulated sex. 125m. **DIR:** Michael Bay. **CAST:** Sean Connery, Nicolas Cage, Ed Harris, David Morse, William Forsythe, John Spencer. **1996 DVD**

ROCK-A-DOODLE ★★★★ Former Disney animation director Don Bluth recovers nicely from the debacle of *All Dogs Go to Heaven* with this delightfully tuneful tale of a barnyard rooster who leaves his home for the big city. It's Elvis Presley as myth, with fine voice work by Glen Campbell, Christopher Plummer, Phil Harris, Sandy Duncan, Eddie Deezen, Charles Nelson Reilly, and Ellen Greene. Rated G. 74m. **DIR:** Don Bluth. **1992 DVD**

ROCK AND ROLL CIRCUS, THE ★★★★ This never-aired special made for British television by the Rolling Stones is a veritable buried treasure. All of the bands featured are in peak form, but highlights include the Who's "A Quick One While He's Away" and an all-star jam featuring John Lennon and Eric Clapton. Made for TV. 65m. **DIR:** Michael Lindsay-Hogg. **CAST:** The Rolling Stones, John Lennon, Yoko Ono, The Who, Jethro Tull, Marianne Faithfull, Taj Mahal. **1968**

ROCK AND RULE ★★1/2 Muddled fantasy of an aging rock star looking for the secret to immortality. The backgrounds are strong but the animation is static, and while the score boasts names like Lou Reed, Iggy Pop, Cheap Trick, and Blondie, the songs they contribute are mostly throwaways. Rated PG. 85m. **DIR:** Clive Smith. **1983**

ROCK, BABY, ROCK IT ★★ Filmed in Dallas, this obscure feature offers a threadbare let's-put-on-a-show plot as an excuse to showcase a lot of long-forgotten doo-wop and rockabilly acts. B&W; 77m. **DIR:** Murray Douglas Sporup. **CAST:** Johnny Carroll, Kay Wheeler. **1957**

ROCK HOUSE 🦃 When narcotics agent Joseph Jennings loses his wife to vicious drug dealers, he takes the law into his own hands. If this guy were a football player, he would have fumbled the ball. Not rated; contains violence. 98m. **DIR:** Jack Vacek. **CAST:** Joseph Jennings. **1988**

ROCK 'N' ROLL HIGH SCHOOL ★★★1/2 The stern new principal tries to turn a school into a concentration camp. The popular Riff (P. J. Soles) goes against the principal by playing loud Ramones music all the time. Meanwhile, boring Tom (Vincent Van Patten) has a crush on Riff. The film includes lots of laughs and good

rock 'n' roll music—a cult favorite. Rated PG. 93m. **DIR:** Allan Arkush. **CAST:** P. J. Soles, Vincent Van Patten, Clint Howard, Dey Young, The Ramones. **1979 DVD**

ROCK 'N' ROLL HIGH SCHOOL FOREVER 🦃 Super-lame sequel to the cult hit. Rated PG-13 for profanity. 94m. **DIR:** Deborah Brock. **CAST:** Corey Feldman, Mary Woronov, Larry Linville. **1990**

ROCK 'N' ROLL WRESTLING WOMEN VS. THE AZTEC APE ★★ As if your usual lady-wrestlers-battling-evil-monsters movie wasn't funny enough, this one features rockabilly songs newly dubbed in over the wrestling scenes! Sort of like *Wrestlemania* without Vince McMahon. B&W; 77m. **DIR:** René Cardona Sr. **CAST:** Elizabeth Campbell. **1962**

ROCK 'N' ROLL WRESTLING WOMEN VS. THE AZTEC MUMMY 🦃 Some folks found this old Mexican horror flick and attempted to turn it into a comedy by redubbing the dialogue, giving it a comical rock 'n' roll soundtrack, and retitling it. Not rated; has violence. B&W; 88m. **DIR:** René Cardona Sr., Manuel San Fernando. **CAST:** Lorena Velazquez, Armand Silvestre. **1986**

ROCK, PRETTY BABY ★★ John Saxon plays Jimmy Daley, 18 year old leader of a struggling rock 'n' roll combo whose life is complicated by his doctor father who wants him to go into the medical profession and a difficult first-love relationship with Luana Patten. So laughably awful in spots that it becomes enjoyable. B&W; 89m. **DIR:** Richard Bartlett. **CAST:** John Saxon, Sal Mineo, Rod McKuen, Luana Patten, Edward Platt, Fay Wray, Shelley Fabares. **1957**

ROCK, ROCK, ROCK ★★ If you love Tuesday Weld, Fifties rock, or entertainingly terrible movies, this nostalgic blast from the past is for you. The plot is so flimsy, Dobie Gillis would have rejected it. But watching a young Weld lip-synch to songs actually sung by Connie Francis is a wonderful treat. B&W; 83m. **DIR:** Will Price. **CAST:** Tuesday Weld, Teddy Randazzo, Alan Freed, Frankie Lymon and the Teenagers, Chuck Berry, The Flamingos, The Johnny Burnette Trio. **1956 DVD**

•**ROCK STAR** ★★★1/2 A few comic moments can't disguise the unsavory lifestyle of a heavy metal band in the 1980s. Wannabe Mark Wahlberg brings his innocence and idealism to the hardened group he idolizes. The message is clear: "Beware of your desires . . ." Jennifer Aniston, as Wahlberg's longtime love, can only take so much of his new life. Watchable, at times painfully so, and insightful. Rated R for drug use, sexual situations, nudity, profanity, and violence. 104m. **DIR:** Stephen Herek. **CAST:** Mark Wahlberg, Jennifer Aniston, Dominic West, Timothy Olyphant. **2001 DVD**

ROCKET ATTACK USA 🦃 American spies attempt to steal the plans for Sputnik from the Russians. B&W; 71m. **DIR:** Barry Mahon. **CAST:** John McKay. **1958**

ROCKET GIBRALTAR ★★★ A bittersweet comedy-drama about the reunion of an eccentric family in the Hamptons, drawn by the 77th birthday of the patriarch. Burt Lancaster plays the elder, giving this slight, sentimental film credibility. Rated PG. 100m. **DIR:** Daniel Petrie. **CAST:** Burt Lancaster, Suzy Amis, John Glover, Bill Pullman. **1988**

ROCKETEER, THE ★★★★1/2 Bill Campbell stars as a young pilot who is transformed into a jet-propelled hero when Nazi agents attempt to steal a top-secret invention and it lands in his lap. This is Commando Cody done right; a glorious adventure for the young and the young at heart. Rated PG for violence. 110m. **DIR:** Joe Johnston. **CAST:** Bill Campbell, Alan Arkin, Jennifer Connelly, Timothy Dalton, Paul Sorvino, Terry O'Quinn, Ed Lauter. **1991 DVD**

ROCKETMAN ★★1/2 Stand-up comic Harland Williams's big-screen starring debut is about a desk-bound computer geek who winds up on NASA's first manned mission to Mars. Although wonderful with impressions and owner of the coolest T-shirts in the universe, Williams emerges as yet another adolescent in a man's body, substituting cracks about bodily functions for genuine humor. Undiscriminating 8 year olds will love this, but all others are advised to steer clear. Rated PG for mildly disgusting humor. 94m. **DIR:** Stuart Gillard. **CAST:** Harland Williams, Jessica Lundy, Bill Sadler, Jeffrey DeMunn, Beau Bridges. **1997**

ROCKETSHIP X-M ★★1/2 A rocket heading for the moon is knocked off course by a meteor storm and is forced to land on Mars. The crewmen find Mars to be very inhospitable, as it has been devastated by atomic war and has mutated creatures inhabiting the planet. While the story is weak and the acting only passable, this is one of the first of the science-fiction films that dominated the 1950s. B&W; 77m. **DIR:** Kurt Neumann. **CAST:** Lloyd Bridges, Hugh O'Brian, Noah Beery Jr., Osa Massen, John Emery. **1950 DVD**

ROCKFORD FILES, THE (TV SERIES) ★★★★ As Jim Rockford, an ex-con turned private eye, James Garner finally breaks his typecasting as *Maverick*. In the pilot episode for this fine series, Lindsay Wagner comes to Rockford's beachside trailer with a question: was her father killed or did he commit suicide? Robert Donley was replaced in the role of Rockford's father by Noah Beery Jr. when the show began its run on NBC. Made for TV. 90m. **DIR:** Richard T. Heffron. **CAST:** James Garner, Lindsay Wagner, William Smith, Nita Talbot, Joe Santos, Robert Donley. **1974**

ROCKIN' RONNIE ★★★ Hilariously manic collage of Ronald Reagan's films, commercials, and political statements is irreverently blended. Slick, rapid-fire clips. 45m. **DIR:** Stuart Samuels. **CAST:** Ronald Reagan, Nancy Reagan. **1986**

ROCKING HORSE WINNER, THE ★★★1/2 Impressive screen adaptation of D. H. Lawrence's disturbing story about a sensitive little boy's uncanny ability to predict racehorse winners by riding his rocking horse. B&W; 91m. **DIR:** Anthony Pelissier. **CAST:** Valerie Hobson, John Howard Davies, John Mills. **1949**

ROCKTOBER BLOOD ★★ The ghost of a rock star, executed for murder, returns from the dead to avenge himself upon his former band members. The film starts off well and ends decently, but the middle wanders aimlessly. Non-horror fans will probably find this tedious. Rated R for violence, nudity, and profanity. 88m. **DIR:** Ferd Sebastian, Beverly Sebastian. **CAST:** Tray Loren. **1984**

ROCKULA ★★1/2 Entertaining but ultimately silly musical-comedy about a vampire who falls in love every twenty-two years. Shot with the look and feel of a music video, this flick has some good music and some funny lines. Rated PG-13. 90m. **DIR:** Luca Bercovici. **CAST:**

Dean Cameron, Susan Tyrrell, Bo Diddley, Thomas Dolby, Toni Basil. **1990**

ROCKWELL: A LEGEND OF THE WILD WEST ★★ Low-budget and exploitative, film gets saddle sore long before calling it quits. Not rated; contains violence. 100m. **DIR:** Richard Lloyd Dewey. **CAST:** Randy Cleave, Karl Malone, George Sullivan. **1993**

ROCKY ★★★★★ Those put to sleep by the endless sequels in this series probably have forgotten the gentleness and dignity of this initial entry about Rocky Balboa, the painfully shy boxer who only "wants to go the distance" with champ Apollo Creed. One of the ultimate feel-good films, and it works every time. Rated PG for violence. 119m. **DIR:** John G. Avildsen. **CAST:** Sylvester Stallone, Burgess Meredith, Talia Shire, Burt Young, Carl Weathers. **1976 DVD**

ROCKY II ★★ The weakest entry in Sylvester Stallone's boxing series, about a down-and-out fighter attempting to prove himself through a rematch with the champ (Carl Weathers). Talia Shire, Burgess Meredith, and Burt Young reprise their series roles in this soaper in the ring. Rated PG. 119m. **DIR:** Sylvester Stallone. **CAST:** Sylvester Stallone, Carl Weathers, Talia Shire, Burgess Meredith, Burt Young. **1979 DVD**

ROCKY III ★★★ Writer-director-star Sylvester Stallone's third entry in the Rocky Balboa series is surprisingly entertaining. Though we've seen it all before, Stallone manages to make it work. Rated PG for violence and mild profanity. 99m. **DIR:** Sylvester Stallone. **CAST:** Sylvester Stallone, Talia Shire, Burgess Meredith, Mr. T, Carl Weathers. **1982 DVD**

ROCKY IV ★★★ Sylvester Stallone's Everyman returns to take on a massive Russian fighter (Dolph Lundgren) trained via computer and programmed to kill. The result is deliciously corny, enjoyably predictable entertainment. Rated PG for violence and profanity. 90m. **DIR:** Sylvester Stallone. **CAST:** Sylvester Stallone, Talia Shire, Burt Young, Carl Weathers, Brigitte Nielsen, Tony Burton, Michael Pataki, Dolph Lundgren. **1985 DVD**

ROCKY V ★★★1/2 Rocky returns home from the Soviet Union to a hero's welcome but financial ruin, thanks to naïve business decisions by brother-in-law Paulie (Burt Young). The saga of Sylvester Stallone's Rocky Balboa concludes with a suitably subdued whisper. Rated PG-13. 104m. **DIR:** John G. Avildsen. **CAST:** Sylvester Stallone, Talia Shire, Burt Young, Burgess Meredith. **1990**

ROCKY HORROR PICTURE SHOW, THE ★★★1/2 Delicious send-up of science-fiction–horror flicks, set to rock 'n' roll beat. If you're not experiencing this scintillating spoof at a midnight showing, you're missing much of the fun. Audience participation is a key. Nevertheless, this madcap musical-comedy has plenty to offer, even for the solitary viewer hunched in front of a small screen. Rated R. 100m. **DIR:** Jim Sharman. **CAST:** Tim Curry, Susan Sarandon, Barry Bostwick, Richard O'Brien, Jonathan Adams, Patricia Quinn, Little Nell, Meat Loaf, Charles Gray. **1975**

ROCKY MARCIANO ★★★★ Outstanding made-for-cable bio-drama chronicles the life of championship boxer Marciano. Jon Favreau pulls no punches as Marciano, perfectly portraying the spirit of the heavyweight. The events and characters are compelling and engaging, and even though the fight scenes lack the emotional wallop of *Raging Bull*, they do convey the impact of the sport. Rated R for adult situations, language, and violence. 90m. **DIR:** Charles Winkler. **CAST:** Jon Favreau, Penelope Ann Miller, Judd Hirsch, Tony Lo Bianco, George C. Scott. **1999**

ROCKY MOUNTAIN RANGERS ★★★ The Three Mesquiteers impersonate outlaws in order to avenge the murder of a young Texas Ranger comrade. Then the real outlaws show up. Bob Livingston has a meaty dual role. B&W; 54m. **DIR:** George Sherman. **CAST:** Robert Livingston, Duncan Renaldo, Raymond Hatton, Sammy McKim, LeRoy Mason. **1940**

RODAN ★★★1/2 This minor classic was Japan's answer to the nuclear "big bug" films of the decade. Murderous insects are just a prelude to the main event featuring not one but *two* supersonic-speed giant pterodactyls. Released in the United States with a stock-footage preface concerning the danger of radioactive experiments, this well-constructed thriller boasts special effects by Eiji Tsuburaya that are superior to many of its American counterparts. 72m. **DIR:** Inoshiro Honda. **CAST:** Kenji Sahara. **1956**

RODEO GIRL ★★★★ Katharine Ross is Sammy, the wife of rodeo champ Will Garrett (Bo Hopkins). When she decides to try her hand at roping and bronco riding, she finds that she has the potential to be a rodeo champ. But complications arise when she discovers she is pregnant. Based on a true story. 92m. **DIR:** Jackie Cooper. **CAST:** Katharine Ross, Bo Hopkins, Candy Clark, Jacqueline Brooks, Wilford Brimley. **1980**

RODEO KING AND THE SENORITA ★★★ In this remake of Roy Rogers's *My Pal Trigger*, rodeo rider Rex Allen exposes the crook who's trying to bankrupt a traveling wild West show. B&W; 67m. **DIR:** Philip Ford. **CAST:** Rex Allen, Buddy Ebsen, Mary Ellen Kay, Roy Barcroft, Tristram Coffin. **1951**

RODGERS & HAMMERSTEIN'S CINDERELLA ★★★ This hip, multiracial version of the classic fairy tale features Whitney Houston as a fairy godmother (with attitude) to the moping Brandy Norwood in the title role. The real show stopper is Paolo Montalban as the prince. A part as the prince's valet was created for Jason Alexander. This lavish made-for-TV production employs elaborate and colorful sets and costumes. Not rated; contains no objectionable material. 90m. **DIR:** Robert Iscove. **CAST:** Brandy Norwood, Bernadette Peters, Paolo Montalban, Whoopi Goldberg, Whitney Houston, Jason Alexander, Victor Garber. **1997 DVD**

ROE VS. WADE ★★★★ Winner of two Emmy Awards—for outstanding drama special and outstanding lead actress—this fine telefilm shows the abortion issue from the point of a down-and-out, unmarried woman (Holly Hunter). Amy Madigan, as Hunter's determined attorney, delivers an electrifyingly intense statement before the court justices. Contains frank adult discussion. 92m. **DIR:** Gregory Hoblit. **CAST:** Holly Hunter, Amy Madigan, Kathy Bates, Chris Mulkey, James Gammon. **1989**

ROGER & ME ★★★★ Michael Moore's controversial documentary about the growing despair, homelessness, and crime in Flint, Michigan, where more than 30,000 autoworkers were left unemployed by the closing of General Motors plants. Scathingly funny and ultimately

sobering. Rated R for brief profanity. 106m. **DIR:** Michael Moore. **1989**

ROGUE TRADER ★★★ Ewan McGregor stars as Nick Leeson, the British futures trader whose risky dealings eventually caused the collapse of that country's oldest bank. Based on Leeson's autobiography, the film seems a bit too sympathetic to this character, but McGregor is nonetheless fascinating to watch as he digs himself in deeper and deeper. Rated R for profanity and brief nudity. 98m. **DIR:** James Dearden. **CAST:** Ewan McGregor, Anna Friel, Betsy Brantley. **1999 DVD**

ROLL OF THUNDER, HEAR MY CRY ★★★1/2 Heartwarming tale of a black family struggling to get by in Depression-era Mississippi. Made for television, this was meant to be shown in three parts, and it's best viewed that way—the pace is a little too leisurely (especially for kids) to watch this in one sitting. 150m. **DIR:** Jack Smight. **CAST:** Claudia McNeil, Janet MacLachlan, Robert Christian, Morgan Freeman. **1978**

ROLL ON TEXAS MOON ★★★1/2 Gabby Hayes's standout role in Roy Rogers's Westerns as the owner of a cattle ranch at odds with encroaching sheep herders led by Dale Evans. Outlaws play the two sides against each other. First of the "new era" William Witney–directed, less-songs-more-action Rogers B Westerns. B&W; 67m. **DIR:** William Witney. **CAST:** Roy Rogers, George "Gabby" Hayes, Dale Evans, Elisabeth Risdon, Bob Nolan and the Sons of the Pioneers. **1946**

ROLLERBALL (1975) ★★★★ Vastly underappreciated science-fiction film envisions a world controlled by business corporations; with no wars or other aggressive activities, the public gets its release in rollerball, a violent combination of basketball, ice hockey, and roller derby. James Caan is a top rollerball champ who refuses to quit the game in spite of threats from industrialist John Houseman, who fears that Caan may turn into a public folk hero. Rated R for violence. 128m. **DIR:** Norman Jewison. **CAST:** James Caan, John Houseman, Maud Adams, Ralph Richardson, John Beck. **1975 DVD**

•ROLLERBALL (2002) ★★ This new version of Norman Jewison's 1975 science-fiction film (from William Harrison's story) is a remake in name only. Gone is the futuristic plot; it's the present day and the title sport is big business in eastern Europe, dominated by the Russian Mafia. The plot makes little sense and the action is poorly photographed and clumsily edited. Rated PG-13 for profanity, sports violence, and one sexual scene. 98m. **DIR:** John McTiernan. **CAST:** Chris Klein, Jean Reno, LL Cool J, Rebecca Romijn-Stamos. **2002 DVD**

ROLLERBLADE 🦃 *Mad Max* meets *Kansas City Bomber* and *Red Sonja*. 88m. **DIR:** Donald G. Jackson. **CAST:** Suzanne Solari, Jeff Hutchinson. **1986**

ROLLERCOASTER ★★★★1/2 Fast-paced suspense film about an extortionist (Timothy Bottoms) blowing up rides in some of the nation's most famous amusement parks, and the efforts of a county safety inspector (George Segal) and an FBI agent (Richard Widmark) to nab him. Very well-done, this much-maligned film has great action, crisp dialogue, and a brilliant, nail-biting climax. Rated PG for language and violence. 119m. **DIR:** James Goldstone. **CAST:** George Segal, Richard Widmark, Timothy Bottoms, Susan Strasberg, Henry Fonda. **1977 DVD**

ROLLING THUNDER ★★★★ When a Vietnam POW returns home to Texas, he is honored with two thousand silver dollars by the local merchants for his courage and endurance under torture. (A dollar for every day served as a POW.) A gang of vicious killers attempts to rob him, but he will not tell them where the silver is, even when they begin to torture him. After some hospitalization, he recruits his Vietnam buddy and the hunt is violently and realistically played out. Rated R. 99m. **DIR:** John Flynn. **CAST:** William Devane, Tommy Lee Jones, Linda Haynes, James Best, Dabney Coleman, Lisa Richards, Luke Askew. **1977**

ROLLING VENGEANCE ★★1/2 A young trucker avenges the murder of his family and the rape of his girlfriend. A cross between a trucker movie and *Rambo*. Rated R for violence and language. 92m. **DIR:** Steven H. Stern. **CAST:** Don Michael Paul, Lawrence Dane, Ned Beatty, Lisa Howard. **1987**

ROLLOVER ★★★1/2 Jane Fonda plays an ex–film star who inherits a multimillion-dollar empire when her husband is mysteriously murdered in this gripping, but not great, film. Kris Kristofferson is the financial troubleshooter who joins forces with her to save the company. Soon both their lives are in danger. Rated R because of profanity. 118m. **DIR:** Alan J. Pakula. **CAST:** Jane Fonda, Kris Kristofferson, Hume Cronyn, Josef Sommer, Bob Gunton. **1981**

ROMAN HOLIDAY ★★★★★ Amid the beauty and mystique of Rome, an American newspaperman (Gregory Peck) is handed a news scoop on the proverbial silver platter. A princess (Audrey Hepburn) has slipped away from her stifling royal lifestyle. In her efforts to hide as one of Rome's common people, she encounters Peck. Their amiable adventures provide the basis for a charming fantasy-romance. B&W; 119m. **DIR:** William Wyler. **CAST:** Gregory Peck, Audrey Hepburn, Eddie Albert. **1953**

ROMAN SCANDALS ★★★ Old Banjo Eyes dreams himself back to ancient Rome. Busby Berkeley staged the requisite musical numbers, including one censor-baiting stanza featuring seminude chorus girls, Goldwyn Girl Lucille Ball among them. B&W; 92m. **DIR:** Frank Tuttle. **CAST:** Eddie Cantor, Ruth Etting, Alan Mowbray, Edward Arnold. **1933**

ROMAN SPRING OF MRS. STONE, THE ★★ A sensitive, elegant middle-aged actress (Vivien Leigh) has retreated to Rome to get a new focus. Warren Beatty plays a sleek, surly, wet-lipped Italian gigolo out for what he can get with the help of a crass, waspish procuress (Lotte Lenya). Banal. 104m. **DIR:** Jose Quintero. **CAST:** Vivien Leigh, Warren Beatty, Lotte Lenya, Jill St. John. **1961**

ROMANCE (1930) ★★★ Greta Garbo, even miscast as an Italian singer, brings interest to this tale of a woman of questionable character finding herself pursued by a young minister. At the 1929–30 Academy Awards Garbo and director Clarence Brown were each nominated for this movie and *Anna Christie*; both lost. B&W; 79m. **DIR:** Clarence Brown. **CAST:** Greta Garbo, Lewis Stone, Gavin Gordon, Elliott Nugent. **1930**

ROMANCE (1999) ★★ When a young woman is unable to arouse her boyfriend's sexual interest, she resorts to anonymous couplings with strangers and a sadomasochistic affair with her boss. Writer-director

Catherine Breillat's film gained some notoriety for its graphic sex and frontal nudity, but it's just so much puerile, self-consciously "shocking" Eurotrash. Much of the dialogue (at least in translation) is hilariously silly. In French with English subtitles. Rated R for graphic sexual scenes and profanity (in subtitles). 99m. **DIR:** Catherine Breillat. **CAST:** Caroline Ducey, Sagamore Stevenin, Francois Berleand, Rocco Siffredi. **1999 DVD**

ROMANCE IN MANHATTAN ★★★ Francis Lederer as a friendly, ebullient Czech immigrant deals bravely with an inhospitable New York City and wins the love of Ginger Rogers, who befriends him. She's good, but it's his picture. B&W; 78m. **DIR:** Stephen Roberts. **CAST:** Ginger Rogers, Francis Lederer, Donald Meek, Sidney Toler. **1935**

ROMANCE ON THE HIGH SEAS ★★★ A delightful musical that introduced Doris Day to the movies. The plot is a merry mix-up about glamor gals testing their husbands' faithfulness, and Day gets third billing. Her part was originally written for Judy Garland and scaled down when Garland was unavailable. 99m. **DIR:** Michael Curtiz. **CAST:** Jack Carson, Janis Paige, Doris Day, Don DeFore, Oscar Levant, S. Z. Sakall, Franklin Pangborn, Eric Blore, Fortunio Bonanova. **1948**

ROMANCE ON THE ORIENT EXPRESS 🦃 This British TV movie is ruined by insipid dialogue. 96m. **DIR:** Lawrence Gordon Clark. **CAST:** Cheryl Ladd, Stuart Wilson, John Gielgud. **1985**

ROMANCE ON THE RANGE ★★1/2 Roy Rogers's serial is marred by poor lighting and film quality. Such technical difficulties, however, can't dim his heroics in exposing a fur-trapping scam with his faithful sidekicks, Gabby Hayes and the Sons of the Pioneers. Not rated; contains violence. 53m. **DIR:** Joseph Kane. **CAST:** Roy Rogers, George "Gabby" Hayes, Sally Payne, Linda Hayes, Sons of the Pioneers. **1942**

ROMANCE WITH A DOUBLE BASS ★★★1/2 Monty Python madman John Cleese stars in this delightfully silly vignette about a double-bass player and a princess who are caught naked in a pond when a thief makes off with their clothes. The ensuing romance will tickle and charm most adult viewers with its refreshing subtlety, but a word of caution for parents: This short will not win any awards for costume design. 40m. **DIR:** Robert Young. **CAST:** John Cleese, Connie Booth, Graham Crowden, Desmond Jones, Freddie Jones, Andrew Sachs. **1974**

ROMANCING THE STONE ★★★★1/2 A rip-snorting adventure film that combines action, a love story, suspense, and plenty of laughs, this movie stars Kathleen Turner as a timid romance novelist who becomes involved in a situation more dangerous, exciting, and romantic than anything she could ever dream up. Michael Douglas plays the shotgun-wielding soldier of fortune who comes to her aid. Rated PG for violence, nudity, and profanity. 105m. **DIR:** Robert Zemeckis. **CAST:** Kathleen Turner, Michael Douglas, Danny DeVito, Alfonso Arau, Zack Norman. **1984 DVD**

ROMANTIC COMEDY ★★★ In this enjoyable comedy, based on the 1979 Broadway play, Dudley Moore and Mary Steenburgen star as two collaborating playwrights who, during their long association, suffer from "unsynchronized passion." Rated PG for profanity and suggested sex. 103m. **DIR:** Arthur Hiller. **CAST:** Dudley Moore, Mary Steenburgen, Frances Sternhagen, Janet Eilber, Robyn Douglass, Ron Leibman. **1983**

ROMANTIC ENGLISHWOMAN, THE ★★★★ Based on Thomas Wiseman's novel, this film features Michael Caine as a pulp novel writer who impels his discontented, but presumably faithful, wife into an affair with a gigolo. Rated R for language, adult situations. 115m. **DIR:** Joseph Losey. **CAST:** Glenda Jackson, Michael Caine, Helmut Berger. **1975**

ROME ADVENTURE ★★★1/2 A soap opera produced just as Hollywood was getting sexier and starring two of the sexiest women of the 1960s: Suzanne Pleshette and Angie Dickinson. The locale is romantic Rome where a visiting schoolteacher has an affair with an aging playboy, then meets a man closer to her own age she likes better. The performances are especially good. 120m. **DIR:** Delmer Daves. **CAST:** Angie Dickinson, Troy Donahue, Suzanne Pleshette, Rossano Brazzi, Chad Everett, Hampton Fancher, Al Hirt, Constance Ford. **1962**

ROMEO AND JULIET (1936) ★★★ An almost literal translation of Shakespeare's classic romance, and it would have been better with some streamlining. Both Norma Shearer and Leslie Howard were much too old to play the young lovers, but they deliver the poetic dialogue with sincerity as well as emotion. John Barrymore and Basil Rathbone take acting honors, especially Barrymore as the hapless Mercutio. B&W; 126m. **DIR:** George Cukor. **CAST:** Norma Shearer, Leslie Howard, Basil Rathbone, Edna May Oliver, Andy Devine, John Barrymore, Reginald Denny, C. Aubrey Smith. **1936**

ROMEO AND JULIET (1954) ★★★1/2 Though one of the lesser-known adaptations of Shakespeare's famous tragedy, this version is one of the more beautiful to look at, thanks to location shooting around Italy. This was the only film appearance for Susan Shentall, who plays Juliet. 140m. **DIR:** Renato Castellani. **CAST:** Laurence Harvey, Susan Shentall, Flora Robson, Bill Travers, Sebastian Cabot. **1954**

ROMEO AND JULIET (1968) ★★★★1/2 Franco Zeffirelli directed this excellent version of *Romeo and Juliet*. When it was filmed, Olivia Hussey was only 15 and Leonard Whiting was only 17, keeping their characters in tune with Shakespeare's hero and heroine. Rated PG. 138m. **DIR:** Franco Zeffirelli. **CAST:** Olivia Hussey, Leonard Whiting, John McEnery, Michael York, Milo O'Shea. **1968 DVD**

ROMEO AND JULIET (1983) ★★★1/2 A first-class stage production of Shakespeare's tale of the young "star-crossed" lovers, Romeo and Juliet. Esther Rolle is interesting, and quite good, as Juliet's nurse, but the acting honors go to Dan Hamilton as the spirited, fun-loving Mercutio. A Bard Productions Ltd. release. 165m. **DIR:** William Woodman. **CAST:** Alex Hyde-White, Blanche Baker, Esther Rolle, Dan Hamilton, Fredric Lehne, Alvah Stanley. **1983**

ROMEO AND JULIET (1988) ★★★1/2 Made for British television, this production of Shakespeare's timeless tale of star-crossed lovers is highly rewarding. Ann Hasson makes an especially sweet and beguiling Juliet. 360m. **DIR:** Joan Kemp-Welch. **CAST:** Christopher Neame, Ann Hasson, Peter Jeffrey, Peter Dyneley. **1988**

ROMEO IS BLEEDING ★★★★ In this bizarre thriller crooked cop Gary Oldman's avaricious plans come a cropper when he runs into maniacal hit woman Lena Olin. Some viewers are likely to be offended by the outrageous sex and violence, but folks who enjoyed *Reservoir Dogs* and *Bad Lieutenant* will find this nightmarish flick right up their dark alley. Rated R for violence, profanity, nudity, and simulated sex. 97m. **DIR:** Peter Medak. **CAST:** Gary Oldman, Lena Olin, Annabella Sciorra, Juliette Lewis, David Proval, Will Patton, Ron Perlman, Dennis Farina. **1994 DVD**

ROMEO MUST DIE ★★ It's a shame that a performer as engaging as Jet Li must tolerate overproduced and underscripted swill such as this low-rent *West Side Story* wannabe. Mitchell Kapner's all but illiterate script is the thinnest possible retread of *Romeo and Juliet*, an homage only barely distinguishable amid the mindless violence, jive-ass dialogue and shrieking soundtrack. Only Li's personality and winning smile save this from turkeydom. Rated R for violence and profanity. 118m. **DIR:** Andrzej Bartkowiak. **CAST:** Jet Li, Aaliyah, Isaiah Washington, Russell Wong, DMX, Delroy Lindo. **2000 DVD**

ROMERO ★★★1/2 An exquisitely understated and heartfelt performance by Raul Julia in the title role enlivens this somewhat heavy-handed political and religious message movie. It chronicles the struggle of Salvadoran Archbishop Oscar Romero, who was assassinated in 1980 by representatives of the repressive government the mild-mannered cleric had been forced to fight. Rated PG-13 for violence. 105m. **DIR:** John Duigan. **CAST:** Raul Julia, Richard Jordan, Ana Alicia, Eddie Velez, Tony Plana, Harold Gould. **1989**

ROMPER STOMPER ★★★ A group of skinheads terrorizes the Asian community in Melbourne, Australia, and a bizarre love story is mixed between countless acts of violence. At first this movie may disgust the viewer, but keep watching—you could end up enjoying it. Available in R-rated and unrated versions; contains violence, profanity, nudity, and graphic sex. 83m. **DIR:** Geoffrey Wright. **CAST:** Russell Crowe, Daniel Pollock, Jacqueline McKenzie, Alex Scott. **1992**

ROMY AND MICHELE'S HIGH SCHOOL REUNION ★★1/2 Stars Mira Sorvino and Lisa Kudrow are marvelous in this tale of ditzy best friends who adopt new identities in an effort to impress former tormentors at a ten-year high-school reunion, but Robin Schiff's screenplay is too incoherent to sustain this potentially amusing premise. A lengthy, midfilm dream sequence merely emphasizes the fact that this story can't fill more than a 30-minute television sitcom slot. Rated R for profanity. 91m. **DIR:** David Mirkin. **CAST:** Mira Sorvino, Lisa Kudrow, Janeane Garofalo, Alan Cumming. **1997 DVD**

RONIN ★★★★ This is a throwback to those wonderfully complex Cold War thrillers of the 1960s and early 1970s. Director John Frankenheimer knows the territory well, having helmed numerous intelligent thrillers; and credit coscripter David Mamet, hiding behind an alias after an unsatisfying Writers Guild arbitration. The title characters, a reference to an ancient Japanese samurai legend, are mercenaries hired to retrieve a mysterious briefcase. Things go awry, during which the briefcase becomes a classic Hitchcock McGuffin: far less important for what it contains, than for who has possession of it. Special mention must be made of Jean-Claude Lagniez, who coordinated the sensational car chases. Rated R for violence, profanity, and a particularly gruesome do-it-yourself surgery. 121m. **DIR:** John Frankenheimer. **CAST:** Robert De Niro, Jean Reno, Natascha McElhone, Stellan Skarsgard, Sean Bean, Jonathan Pryce, Michel Lonsdale. **1998 DVD**

RONNIE & JULIE ★★★ This family-oriented "Shakespeare Lite" concerns an ill-fated romance between the daughter of a political incumbent and the son of a hopeful challenger: two battling families with names derived from the Montagues and Capulets. The teens, of course, care not for their parents' rivalry; to lend further spice to this meeting of dissimilar minds, she's a figure-skater, while he's on the school hockey team. Rated PG; suitable for all ages. 99m. **DIR:** Philip Spink. **CAST:** Teri Garr, Joshua Jackson, Margot Finley, Tom Butler, Alexandra Purvis. **1996**

ROOFTOPS ★★ What a coincidence! *West Side Story* director Robert Wise returns to make a film about streetwise teenagers in New York who dance, rumble, and struggle to survive. This time, star-crossed lovers (Jason Gedrick and Troy Beyer) combine kung fu with dirty dancing. Rated R for rampant profanity, violence, and brief nudity. 95m. **DIR:** Robert Wise. **CAST:** Jason Gedrick, Troy Beyer, Eddie Velez. **1989**

ROOKIE, THE (1990) ★★1/2 Clint Eastwood is a maverick detective who is saddled with the rookie (Charlie Sheen) of the title while attempting to get the goods on a German criminal. Although it delivers the goods for the action crowd, this is an otherwise disappointing effort from star-director Eastwood. Rated R for violence and profanity. 121m. **DIR:** Clint Eastwood. **CAST:** Clint Eastwood, Charlie Sheen, Raul Julia, Sonia Braga, Tom Skerritt, Pepe Serna, Tony Plana. **1990**

•ROOKIE, THE (2002) ★★★★ Football may capture America's hearts and minds in the living room and on the bleachers, but baseball rules in Hollywood. The sport already has fielded its share of marvelous based-on-a-true-story heart-tuggers, and *The Rookie* is another one. The subject is pitcher Jim Morris, played with affable charm by Dennis Quaid, who had a shot at "the show" twelve years earlier, but now teaches high-school chemistry and coaches sports in a fly-speck Texas town. Ah, but he's never given up his dream, and destiny comes calling when his forever-in-last-place school baseball team makes a bargain: If they somehow take the district championship, then he'll agree to try out, one more time, with a major league ball club. What follows is pure magic. Rated G. 129m. **DIR:** John Lee Hancock. **CAST:** Dennis Quaid, Rachel Griffiths, Jay Hernandez, Beth Grant, Angus T. Jones, Brian Cox. **2002**

ROOKIE OF THE YEAR ★★★★ Sweet- natured family comedy is sure to be a hit with all ages. A 12 year old boy achieves the ultimate fantasy: his broken arm heals oddly, leaving Thomas Ian Nicholas with a powerful pitching arm that he uses to lead the Chicago Cubs to victory. Terrific supporting cast and deft comedy bits make Daniel Stern's directorial debut memorable. Rated PG for brief profanity. 103m. **DIR:** Daniel Stern. **CAST:** Thomas Ian Nicholas, Gary Busey, Albert Hall,

Amy Morton, Dan Hedaya, Bruce Altman, Eddie Bracken, Daniel Stern. **1993 DVD**

ROOM AT THE TOP ★★★★★ John Braine's powerful novel, adapted for the screen by Neil Patterson, is a smashing success. Laurence Harvey is an opportunist who will stop at nothing, including a dalliance with his boss's daughter, to get to the top in the business world. A great cast and superb direction. This is a must-see film. B&W; 115m. **DIR:** Jack Clayton. **CAST:** Laurence Harvey, Simone Signoret, Heather Sears, Hermione Baddeley. **1959 DVD**

ROOM SERVICE ★★★ After leaving his brothers (Groucho, Harpo, and Chico) to try movie producing, Zeppo Marx came up with this Broadway play about a foundering stage production and attempted to have it rewritten to suit his siblings' talents. He wasn't completely successful, but this romp does have its moments. Look for Lucille Ball and Ann Miller in early supporting roles. B&W; 78m. **DIR:** William A. Seiter. **CAST:** The Marx Brothers, Lucille Ball, Ann Miller. **1938**

ROOM WITH A VIEW, A ★★★★★ This is a triumph of tasteful, intelligent filmmaking. Director James Ivory painstakingly re-creates the milieu of 1908 Edwardian England as he explores the consequence of a tour of Florence, Italy, taken by an innocently curious young woman and her meddling aunt. Not rated, the film has one brief scene of violence and some male frontal nudity. 115m. **DIR:** James Ivory. **CAST:** Maggie Smith, Helena Bonham Carter, Denholm Elliott, Julian Sands, Daniel Day-Lewis, Simon Callow, Judi Dench, Rosemary Leach, Rupert Graves. **1986 DVD**

ROOMMATES ★★★★ Warmhearted and often humorous tearjerker about a cantankerous Polish-American baker, who raises his 5 year old grandson after the death of the boy's parents. Falk has a field day as the tough old patriarch. Rated PG. 108m. **DIR:** Peter Yates. **CAST:** Peter Falk, D. B. Sweeney, Julianne Moore, Jan Rubes, Ellen Burstyn, Frankie Faison, Noah Fleiss. **1995**

ROOSTER COGBURN ★★★1/2 Okay, so this sequel to *True Grit* is only *The African Queen* reworked, with John Wayne playing the Humphrey Bogart part opposite the incomparable Katharine Hepburn, but we like—no, love—it. Watching these two professionals playing off each other is what movie watching is all about. The plot? Well, it's not much, but the scenes with Wayne and Hepburn are, as indicated, priceless. Rated PG. 107m. **DIR:** Stuart Millar. **CAST:** John Wayne, Katharine Hepburn, Richard Jordan, Anthony Zerbe, Strother Martin, John McIntire. **1975 DVD**

ROOSTERS ★★1/2 An ex-con (Edward James Olmos) returns to his Arizona home to resume breeding fighting cocks and ruling his poverty-stricken family. Acting is earnest and efficient (especially by Maria Conchita Alonso as Olmos's sister), but hampered by the pretentiously poetic dialogue and obvious symbolism of the script. Robert M. Young's ponderous direction doesn't help. Rated R for mature themes. 93m. **DIR:** Robert M. Young. **CAST:** Edward James Olmos, Sonia Braga, Maria Conchita Alonso, Danny Nucci, Sarah Lassez, Valente Rodriguez. **1995**

ROOTS ★★★★★ Unique in television history is this six-volume chronicle of eighteenth and nineteenth century black life from African enslavement to and beyond Civil War emancipation. It is a triumph in every aspect—acting, writing, and production—and an illuminating look into a tragic side of American social history. Outstanding are Lou Gossett Jr., as the wise and diplomatic antebellum house servant Fiddler, and Ben Vereen as the ebullient, post–Civil War freeman Chicken George. 540m. **DIR:** Marvin J. Chomsky. **CAST:** LeVar Burton, Edward Asner, Lloyd Bridges, Cicely Tyson, Lorne Greene, Ben Vereen, Sandy Duncan, Leslie Uggams, Chuck Connors, Burl Ives, Louis Gossett Jr. **1977 DVD**

ROOTS SEARCH ★★ Japanese animation. A spaceship crew is stalked and killed by an alien presence in this often graphically violent thriller. In Japanese with English subtitles. Not rated; contains violence and nudity. 45m. **DIR:** Hisashi Sugai. **1986**

ROOTS—THE GIFT ★★1/2 This made-for-TV spinoff from *Roots* and *Roots: The Next Generation* brings back Lou Gossett Jr. and LeVar Burton as Fiddler and Kunte Kinte to lead fellow slaves to freedom on Christmas Eve. Nice, but contrived. 100m. **DIR:** Kevin Hooks. **CAST:** Louis Gossett Jr., LeVar Burton, Michael Learned, Avery Brooks, Kate Mulgrew, Shaun Cassidy. **1988**

ROOTS: THE NEXT GENERATION ★★★★★ A seven-cassette, Emmy-winning continuation of *Roots*, television's most highly acclaimed dramatic series. An outstanding cast re-enacts the mesmerizing saga of slave Kunte Kinte's descendants forward from 1882 to post–World War II days, when author Alex Haley began the ancestral search for his "old African," and the beginning of his family. Like its predecessor, a fine, rewarding production. 686m. **DIR:** John Erman, Charles S. Dubin, Georg Stanford Brown, Lloyd Richards. **CAST:** Olivia de Havilland, Henry Fonda, Marlon Brando, Richard Thomas, Georg Stanford Brown, Ossie Davis, Dorian Harewood, James Earl Jones. **1979**

ROPE ★★★★1/2 Recently resurrected Alfred Hitchcock film is based in part on the famous Leopold-Loeb thrill-murder case in Chicago in the 1920s. In it, the two killers divulge clues to their horrific escapade at a dinner party, to the growing suspicion of the other guests. It's one of Hitchcock's best. 80m. **DIR:** Alfred Hitchcock. **CAST:** James Stewart, John Dall, Farley Granger, Cedric Hardwicke. **1948**

RORRET ★★★ Movie buffs will enjoy this odd thriller about the murderous owner of a revival theater, if only to spot the various re-created scenes from classic suspense films. But it's a gimmick that never really leads anywhere. In Italian with English subtitles. 103m. **DIR:** Fulvio Wetzl. **CAST:** Lou Castel, Anna Galiena. **1988**

ROSALIE ★★1/2 From those thrilling days of yesteryear at MGM comes this gigantic musical about hero Nelson Eddy and his winning of a disguised Balkan princess (Eleanor Powell). It's big, colorful, and has a nice music score by Cole Porter. B&W; 122m. **DIR:** W. S. Van Dyke. **CAST:** Eleanor Powell, Nelson Eddy, Frank Morgan, Edna May Oliver, Ray Bolger, Ilona Massey. **1937**

ROSALIE GOES SHOPPING ★★★1/2 The *Bagdad Café* gang is back with another bit of quirky American-landscape comedy. German writer-director Percy Adlon

and his talented German star Marianne Sagebrecht tackle consumer greed, credit card debt, and true love in this offbeat tale of an eccentric Little Rock, Arkansas family. Rated PG. 94m. **DIR:** Percy Adlon. **CAST:** Marianne Sagebrecht, Brad Davis. **1990**

ROSARY MURDERS, THE ★★★ Donald Sutherland is a priest who hears the confession of a killer who is murdering nuns and priests. An interesting film, thanks to strong performances by Sutherland and Charles Durning as the bishop. Slow pacing by director Fred Walton and a needlessly murky denouement keep this murder mystery from being top rank. Rated R for violence and nudity. 107m. **DIR:** Fred Walton. **CAST:** Donald Sutherland, Charles Durning, Belinda Bauer, Josef Sommer, James Murtaugh. **1987**

ROSE, THE ★★★★ Bette Midler stars as a Janis Joplin–like rock singer who falls prey to the loneliness and temptations of superstardom. Mark Rydell directed this fine character study, which features memorable supporting performances by Alan Bates and Frederic Forrest, and a first-rate rock score. Rated R. 134m. **DIR:** Mark Rydell. **CAST:** Bette Midler, Alan Bates, Frederic Forrest, Harry Dean Stanton. **1979**

ROSE AND THE JACKAL, THE TV movie concerning the Secret Service's attempt to stop Confederate espionage in Washington, D.C., at the outbreak of the Civil War. 95m. **DIR:** Jack Gold. **CAST:** Christopher Reeve, Madolyn Smith, Carrie Snodgress, Kevin McCarthy, Jeff Corey. **1990**

ROSE GARDEN, THE ★★★1/2 In modern-day Germany, a Holocaust survivor (Maximilian Schell) is arrested for assaulting a successful elderly businessman. Defense attorney (Liv Ullmann) discovers that the businessman was a former S.S. officer who presided over a brutal Nazi death camp and was responsible for the murder of dozens of children. Engrossing psychological drama. Rated PG-13 for violence. 152m. **DIR:** Fons Rademakers. **CAST:** Liv Ullmann, Maximilian Schell, Peter Fonda. **1990**

ROSE HILL ★★★1/2 *Hallmark Hall of Fame* production features four New York street urchins circa 1866 who become law-abiding citizens after finding an abandoned baby girl. The boys head out west to start a new life and raise their new "sister." Oddly, despite their best intentions and greatest efforts, they raise a willful, spoiled brat. Overall, very watchable and entertaining. Not rated; contains violence. 91m. **DIR:** Christopher Cain. **CAST:** Jeffrey Sams, Jennifer Garner, Kristin Griffith, Justin Chambers, Zak Orth, Tristan Tait, Casey Siemaszko, David Newsom. **1997**

ROSE MARIE (1936) ★★1/2 If you enjoy MGM's perennial songbirds Nelson Eddy and Jeanette MacDonald, you might have fun with this musical romp into the Canadian Rockies. Unintentionally funny dialogue is created by the wooden way Eddy delivers it. B&W; 110m. **DIR:** W. S. Van Dyke. **CAST:** Nelson Eddy, Jeanette MacDonald, James Stewart, Alan Mowbray. **1936**

ROSE MARIE (1954) ★★ A remake that shouldn't have been. Without the chemistry of Nelson Eddy and Jeanette MacDonald, the plot is creaky and the music sounds too old-fashioned. The highlight is the subplot between raspy-voiced Marjorie Main and Bert Lahr as "The Mountie Who Never Got His Man." 115m. **DIR:** Mervyn LeRoy. **CAST:** Howard Keel, Ann Blyth, Fernando Lamas, Marjorie Main, Bert Lahr, Ray Collins, Joan Taylor. **1954**

ROSE OF WASHINGTON SQUARE ★★★1/2 Tyrone Power is a slick con artist who marries showgirl Alice Faye to cash in on her rising success. Al Jolson (performing many of his famous songs) is outstanding as Faye's mentor. Some cassettes open with an "added feature" of Faye singing "I'm Always Chasing Rainbows" and Jolson belting out both "Avalon" and "April Showers." These were deleted from the movie before its release. B&W; 86m. **DIR:** Gregory Ratoff. **CAST:** Alice Faye, Tyrone Power, Al Jolson, William Frawley, Joyce Compton, Hobart Cavanaugh. **1939**

ROSE TATTOO, THE ★★★★ Making her American film debut, volatile Italian star Anna Magnani handily won a best-actress Oscar playing the widow obsessed by the memory of her stud husband. She finally lets go when she finds truck driver Burt Lancaster has a rose tattoo, the symbol of sexual prowess that the departed sported. Tangy and torrid. B&W; 117m. **DIR:** Daniel Mann. **CAST:** Anna Magnani, Burt Lancaster, Marisa Pavan, Ben Cooper, Jo Van Fleet, Virginia Grey. **1955**

ROSEANNE: AN UNAUTHORIZED BIOGRAPHY Definitely one of those "What were they thinking?" excursions into tabloid-television trash. Not rated. 90m. **DIR:** Paul Schneider. **CAST:** Denny Dillon, David Graf, John Karlen. **1994**

ROSEBUD BEACH HOTEL, THE (NOSTELL HOTEL, THE) Colleen Camp and Peter Scolari take over her father's failing hotel and hire prostitutes as bellgirls to improve business. Rated R. 82m. **DIR:** Harry Hurwitz. **CAST:** Colleen Camp, Peter Scolari, Christopher Lee, Hamilton Camp, Eddie Deezen, Chuck McCann, Hank Garrett. **1985**

ROSELAND ★★1/2 A somewhat overly respectful triptych set in the famous, now-tattered, New York dance palace. The three stories are quietly compelling, but only Christopher Walken (certainly a good enough dancer) and Don DeNatale (who was an emcee at Roseland) give the film any vim. 103m. **DIR:** James Ivory. **CAST:** Christopher Walken, Geraldine Chaplin, Teresa Wright, Lou Jacobi, Don DeNatale, Lilia Skala. **1977**

ROSEMARY'S BABY ★★★★ Mia Farrow is a young woman forced by her husband (John Cassavetes) into an unholy arrangement with a group of devil worshipers. The suspense is sustained as she is made aware that people around her are not what they seem. Ruth Gordon is priceless in her Oscar-winning role as one of the seemingly normal neighbors. Rated R. 136m. **DIR:** Roman Polanski. **CAST:** Mia Farrow, John Cassavetes, Ruth Gordon, Ralph Bellamy, Elisha Cook Jr., Maurice Evans, Patsy Kelly. **1968**

ROSENCRANTZ AND GUILDENSTERN ARE DEAD ★★★1/2 Filmization of Tom Stoppard's immensely witty Shakespearean spin-off, which changes the tone of *Hamlet* from tragedy to comedy. The screen version marks the playwright's debut as a director. Rated PG. 118m. **DIR:** Tom Stoppard. **CAST:** Gary Oldman, Tim Roth, Richard Dreyfuss. **1991**

ROSEWOOD ★★★★ This compelling study of events that led to the destruction of a peaceful 1923 Florida

community begins when a promiscuous white woman in Sumner claims to have been beaten by a black man; her angry white-trash neighbors, jealous of the dignified black residents in neighboring Rosewood, seize this excuse to mount a massive lynching party. Oddly, director John Singleton blends this bleak slice of history with a bit of Kurosawa; Ving Rhames, cast as a heroic "man with no name," rides into Rosewood at just the right moment. The climax adopts the tone of an *Indiana Jones* adventure, but Singleton adroitly juggles these varying moods. Rated R for violence, profanity, nudity, and torture. 140m. **DIR:** John Singleton. **CAST:** Jon Voight, Ving Rhames, Don Cheadle, Bruce McGill, Loren Dean, Esther Rolle, Michael Rooker. **1997 DVD**

ROSIE ★★★ Rosemary Clooney sings behind Sondra Locke's acting in this vivid, no-holds-barred rendition of the famed singer's autobiography *This for Remembrance.* Always an upfront gal, Clooney let it all hang out in telling of her rise to stardom, mental breakdown, and successful uphill fight to regain star status. Made for TV. 100m. **DIR:** Jackie Cooper. **CAST:** Sondra Locke, Tony Orlando, Katherine Helmond, Penelope Milford, Kevin McCarthy, John Karlen. **1982**

ROSWELL ★★★ This purported docudrama concerns a 1947 UFO crash discovered—and subsequently buried—by army intelligence officers. Kyle MacLachlan and Martin Sheen lend stature to an otherwise pedestrian project that wallows in melodrama while taking itself far too seriously. Rated PG-13 for profanity. 91m. **DIR:** Jeremy Paul Kagan. **CAST:** Kyle MacLachlan, Martin Sheen, Dwight Yoakam, Xander Berkeley, Kim Greist, Charles Martin Smith. **1994**

ROSWELL: THE ALIENS ATTACK Pitiful made-for-TV movie about the crash of an alien spacecraft, a government cover-up, and aliens in human form, complete with glowing green eyes. Of all the films about the supposed Roswell incident, this has to be the absolute worst one. Rated PG for mild violence. 89m. **DIR:** Brad Turner. **CAST:** Steven Flynn. **1998**

R.O.T.O.R. Abysmal variation on the *Robocop* theme has a part-man, part-machine police officer going berserk. Rated R for violence and profanity. 91m. **DIR:** Cullen Blaine. **CAST:** Richard Gesswein. **1988**

ROUGH CUT ★★★ The screenplay, by Francis Burns, is a welcome return to the stylish romantic comedies of the 1930s and 1940s with the accent on witty dialogue, action, and suspense. Burt Reynolds and Lesley-Anne Down are a perfect screen combination. As two sophisticated jewel thieves who plot to steal $30 million in uncut diamonds, they exchange quips, become romantically entwined, and are delightful. Rated R. 112m. **DIR:** Don Siegel. **CAST:** Burt Reynolds, Lesley-Anne Down, David Niven, Patrick Magee. **1980**

ROUGH JUSTICE Spaghetti Western, with Klaus Kinski as a sex-crazed outlaw. Not rated; contains violence. 95m. **DIR:** Mario Costa. **CAST:** Klaus Kinski, Steven Tedd. **1987**

ROUGH MAGIC ★★★ This very strange brew of *film noir,* magic realism, and screwball adventure is an entertaining mess. Magician's assistant Myra flees to Mexico in the 1950s after her politically ambitious fiancé shoots her mentor. An American reporter hired to find Myra falls in love with her. Myra then shares an elixir with a Mayan sorceress, lays a blue egg, and transforms a menacing cantina owner into a large sausage. Rated PG-13 for language, violence, and sex between rabbits. 104m. **DIR:** Clare Peploe. **CAST:** Bridget Fonda, Russell Crowe, Jim Broadbent, D. W. Moffett, Paul Rodriguez. **1997**

ROUGH NIGHT IN JERICHO ★★1/2 Former marshal George Peppard doesn't want to get involved when Jean Simmons finds her stagecoach line threatened with a takeover. Power-hungry town boss Dean Martin's brutal tactics make Peppard change his mind. Violent Western has its moments, both good and not so good. 104m. **DIR:** Arnold Laven. **CAST:** Dean Martin, Jean Simmons, George Peppard, John McIntire, Slim Pickens, Don Galloway. **1967 DVD**

ROUGH RIDERS ★★★★ High production values set this TNT miniseries apart from typical TV fare. Based on Teddy Roosevelt's successful siege at San Juan Hill in Cuba circa 1898, Tom Berenger creates an annoying stereotype of our former president as an overeager military novice. Berenger is overshadowed by Sam Elliott's commanding presence and a scene-stealing Gary Busey. Brian Keith appears in his final role, as President McKinley. Epic battle scenes blend grit with glory. Not rated; contains violence and nudity. 175m. **DIR:** John Milius. **CAST:** Tom Berenger, Gary Busey, Sam Elliott, William Katt, Brad Johnson, Brian Keith, Illeana Douglas. **1997**

ROUGH RIDERS' ROUNDUP ★★1/2 The accent is more on action than music in this early Roy Rogers Western about the Rough Riders reuniting to rid the range of an outlaw gang. In all, it's better than most of the Rogers vehicles that followed. B&W; 58m. **DIR:** Joseph Kane. **CAST:** Roy Rogers, Lynne Roberts, Raymond Hatton, Eddie Acuff. **1939**

ROUGHNECKS ★★ This TV miniseries centers around a bunch of good old boys trying to drill a geothermal well in Texas. The old-timers resent the land being disrupted. Protracted would-be-actioner. 180m. **DIR:** Bernard McEveety. **CAST:** Sam Melville, Cathy Lee Crosby, Vera Miles, Harry Morgan, Steve Forrest. **1980**

ROUND MIDNIGHT ★★★★ French director Bertrand Tavernier's ode to American jazz is a long overdue celebration of that great American music and its brilliant exponents. It tells a semifictionalized story of a friendship between a self-destructive, be-bop tenor saxophonist (Dexter Gordon) and an avid French fan (François Cluzet). Rated R. 133m. **DIR:** Bertrand Tavernier. **CAST:** Dexter Gordon, François Cluzet, Lonette McKee, Christine Pascal, Herbie Hancock. **1986**

ROUND NUMBERS ★★ A dowdy woman suspects her husband is cheating. Uneven and frequently amateurish sex comedy. Rated R for profanity and nudity. 98m. **DIR:** Nancy Zala. **CAST:** Kate Mulgrew, Samantha Eggar. **1992**

ROUND TRIP TO HEAVEN ★★1/2 Corey Feldman drags cousin Zach Galligan along to Palm Springs in a stolen Rolls to meet a super model. Typical chase film. Rated R for violence, nudity, and language. 97m. **DIR:** Alan Roberts. **CAST:** Corey Feldman, Zach Galligan, Ray Sharkey, Julie McCullough. **1991**

ROUND-UP, THE ★★★★ In 1868, Hungarian police looking for the leaders of a political uprising subject a

group of suspects to psychological warfare. A powerful, austere work; one of the most influential films in Hungarian cinema. In Hungarian with English subtitles. Not rated. B&W; 94m. **DIR:** Miklos Jancso. **CAST:** Janos Gorbe, Tibor Molnar. **1965**

ROUNDERS, THE (1965) ★★1/2 Burt Kennedy, a solid scriptwriter of Fifties Westerns, turned director in the Sixties—with hit-and-miss results. He had one of his stronger casts in this comic saga of two reluctant ranch-hand cronies. 85m. **DIR:** Burt Kennedy. **CAST:** Glenn Ford, Henry Fonda, Sue Ane Langdon, Hope Holiday, Edgar Buchanan, Chill Wills, Kathleen Freeman. **1965**

ROUNDERS (1998) ★★★★ Director John Dahl's edgy film is a mesmerizing study of the high-stakes poker (under) world, and its impact on one young man (Matt Damon) who tries to remain honorable in the face of increasingly overwhelming odds. Damon plays a "recovered" high-stakes poker player trying to stay clean while working his way through law school. Plans are derailed by the arrival of his best friend "Worm" (Edward Norton), freshly out of prison and determined to settle some scores. And, much to our hero's horror, Worm cheats. What follows is a study of integrity among thieves. Rated R for profanity, nudity, and violence. 120m. **DIR:** John Dahl. **CAST:** Matt Damon, Edward Norton, John Turturro, Famke Janssen, Gretchen Mol, John Malkovich, Martin Landau. **1998 DVD**

ROUSTABOUT ★★1/2 Barbara Stanwyck, as the carnival owner, upgrades this typical Elvis Presley picture. In this release, Presley is a young wanderer who finds a home in the carnival as a singer. Naturally, Elvis combines romance with hard work on the midway. 101m. **DIR:** John Rich. **CAST:** Barbara Stanwyck, Elvis Presley, Leif Erickson, Sue Ane Langdon. **1964 DVD**

ROUSTERS, THE ★★★ TV pilot actioner features Chad Everett as a carnival bouncer named Wyatt Earp III. He cleverly deals with insurance fraud, domestic abuse, and an armed robbery. Fun blend of violence, humor, and crime resolution. Rated PG for violence. 72m. **DIR:** E. W. Swackhamer. **CAST:** Chad Everett, Jim Varney, Mimi Rogers. **1983**

ROUTE 9 ★★ Despite a decent cast and some genuinely suspenseful moments, this tale of two small-town deputies who stumble across a van full of dead people, drugs, and $1 million in cash fails to rise above the ordinary. Rated R for violence, language, and adult situations. 102m. **DIR:** David Mackay. **CAST:** Kyle MacLachlan, Peter Coyote, Amy Locane, Wade Andrew Williams, Roma Maffia, Miguel Sandoval. **1998 DVD**

•ROUTE 666 ★★ Dusty chiller about two special agents who find themselves trapped on a haunted stretch of highway in the desert while pursuing a suspect. Lou Diamond Phillips and Lori Petty play the agents who discover too late that they've become the hunted. The back story about a chain-gang murder spree is much more fascinating than what happens in the here and now as the two stars find themselves battling something worse than the supernatural: a bad script. Rated R for language and violence. 90m. **DIR:** William Wesley. **CAST:** Lou Diamond Phillips, Lori Petty, Steven Williams. **2001 DVD**

ROVER DANGERFIELD ★★★ Rodney Dangerfield takes the plunge as an animated character in this feature-length cartoon about a city dog who ends up on a farm. Some harder-edged elements—suggestions of violence and songs about dogs "doing their business" on a Christmas tree—may offend some parents. Otherwise, it's generally enjoyable. Rated G. 71m. **DIR:** Jim George, Bob Seely. **1991**

ROWING WITH THE WIND ★★★★ Moody, atmospheric Spanish production that stars Hugh Grant as Lord Byron, who spends a fateful summer with Percy and Mary Shelley, and Claire Clairmont. When Mary Shelley begins writing *Frankenstein*, she fears that her monster has risen from the pages to bring death to their small group. Nightmarish images, lush locales, a European feel, and performances with conviction distinguish this effort. Rated R for violence, adult themes, and nudity. 120m. **DIR:** Gonzalo Suarez. **CAST:** Hugh Grant, Elizabeth Hurley, Lizzy McInnerny, Valentine Pelka. **1987**

ROXANNE ★★★★1/2 Steve Martin's most effective and rewarding comedy, based on Rostand's *Cyrano de Bergerac*. Martin plays the big-nosed fire chief who befriends a professional firefighter who has come to train the inept local firemen. While there, he meets and falls in love with the title character and enlists Martin's aid in wooing her with words. Rated PG for profanity and suggested sex. 107m. **DIR:** Fred Schepisi. **CAST:** Steve Martin, Daryl Hannah, Shelley Duvall, Rick Rossovich, Michael J. Pollard, Fred Willard. **1987 DVD**

ROXIE HART ★★★★★ Ginger Rogers stars in one of Hollywood's funniest satires. She plays a conniver who looks for as much sympathetic publicity as possible at her own murder trial. It's played for laughs and set in the Roaring Twenties before real-life criminals started doing the same thing. B&W; 75m. **DIR:** William Wellman. **CAST:** Ginger Rogers, George Montgomery, Adolphe Menjou, Phil Silvers, Iris Adrian, Spring Byington. **1942**

ROY ROGERS SHOW, THE (TV SERIES) ★★★ These six tapes contain two episodes each of the 1954–56 TV series. All the memories come back as Roy, Dale, Pat, Trigger, Bulle, and Nellybelle keep the West a safe place to live. Good fun for all. B&W; 46m. **CAST:** Roy Rogers, Dale Evans, Pat Brady. **1954–56**

ROYAL DECEIT ★★★ *Hamlet* redux, as *Babette's Feast* director Gabriel Axel spins this lush tale of a young prince's fight for his father's throne. Gabriel Byrne stars as the bloodthirsty, usurping uncle, and Christian Bale as the prince in this handsome period piece set in sixth-century Denmark. Released in Europe as *Prince of Jutland*. Rated R for nudity and violence. 85m. **DIR:** Gabriel Axel. **CAST:** Gabriel Byrne, Christian Bale, Helen Mirren, Brian Cox, Kate Beckinsale. **1994**

ROYAL HUNT OF THE SUN ★★★1/2 There's lots of pomp and pageantry in director Irving Lerner's big screen adaptation of Peter Schaffer's stage play. An excellent cast, most notably Robert Shaw and Christopher Plummer, bring life to this tale of Spanish explorer Pizarro, and his search to find gold in South America. Rated G. 118m. **DIR:** Irving Lerner. **CAST:** Robert Shaw, Christopher Plummer, Nigel Davenport, Leonard Whiting, Michael Craig, James Donald. **1969 DVD**

•**ROYAL TENENBAUMS, THE** ★★★★ Members of the dysfunctional Tenenbaum family find it difficult to live both with and without each other in this comedy of fractured relationships. The three former child-genius Tenenbaum siblings and their long-estranged father Royal all return home for reasons running from depression and destitution to psychotic behavior just as Mrs. Tenenbaum is courted by the family's accountant. The clan sorts through family failures, disasters, and betrayals in a wacky story that is both funny and emotionally rewarding. Rated R for profanity, nudity, and sexual content. 106m. **DIR:** Wes Anderson. **CAST:** Gene Hackman, Anjelica Huston, Gwyneth Paltrow, Ben Stiller, Luke Wilson, Danny Glover. **2001 DVD**

ROYAL WEDDING ★★★ Brother and sister Fred Astaire and Jane Powell are performing in London when Princess Elizabeth marries Philip, and manage to find their own true loves while royalty ties the knot. 92m. **DIR:** Stanley Donen. **CAST:** Fred Astaire, Jane Powell, Sarah Churchill, Peter Lawford, Keenan Wynn. **1951 DVD**

ROYCE ★★★ Amiable spy foolishness, with James Belushi as a wisecracking agent operating for a covert U.S. organization—the Black Hand. Our hero goes into action after cutbacks disband the unit, and disgruntled members steal some nuclear warheads. Rated R for violence, profanity, and nudity. 100m. **DIR:** Rod Holcomb. **CAST:** James Belushi, Chelsea Field, Miguel Ferrer, Peter Boyle. **1994**

R.P.M. (REVOLUTIONS PER MINUTE) ★★ In this story set on a small-town college campus in the late 1960s, a liberal professor (Anthony Quinn) and his coed mistress (Ann-Margret) become involved in the efforts of a liberal student (Gary Lockwood) to have the professor made president of the university. Good intentions turn into campus unrest and violence. Rated R for violence. 92m. **DIR:** Stanley Kramer. **CAST:** Anthony Quinn, Ann-Margret, Gary Lockwood. **1970**

RSVP ★★★ This is an out-and-out sex comedy with lots of nudity and sexual situations. An author has written a novel that turns out to be based on fact. The people who inspired the "characters" have been invited to a Hollywood party to celebrate the making of a movie from the book. The writing is lively, and the puns and gags are funny. Rated R for sexual situations and language that will be offensive to some. 87m. **DIR:** John Almo, Lem Almo. **CAST:** Ray Colbert, Veronica Hart, Carey Hayes. **1984**

RUBBERFACE ★★ Comedian Jim Carrey made this Canadian story about an aspiring stand-up comedian in 1981. Carrey plays a cook at a local comedy club who yearns for the spotlight. He stinks, but with the help of a friend, he improves and gets his big chance. Slight effort plays like an after-school special on television. Rated PG. 41m. **DIR:** Glen Salzman, Rebecca Yates. **CAST:** Jim Carrey, Adah Glassbourg. **1981**

RUBIN & ED ★★ Wannabe salesman Howard Hesseman must bring someone—anyone—to his success seminar. The only one he can convince is a very weird Sixties throwback (Crispin Glover) who insists on burying his cat on the way. Plain strange. Rated PG-13 for profanity. 82m. **DIR:** Trent Harris. **CAST:** Crispin Glover, Howard Hesseman, Karen Black, Michael Greene. **1991**

RUBY (1977) ★★ A sleazy drive-in is the setting for this unexciting horror film about a young girl possessed by the homicidal ghost of a dead gangster. Rated R for gore. 84m. **DIR:** Curtis Harrington. **CAST:** Piper Laurie, Stuart Whitman, Roger Davis. **1977 DVD**

RUBY (1991) ★★★1/2 Superb performances help elevate this largely fictional account of the secret life of Dallas nightclub owner Jack Ruby, who became infamous for killing Lee Harvey Oswald. As with director John Mackenzie's classic British gangster film, *The Long Good Friday*, the characters and tense, realistic situations overcome the familiarity of certain key events. Rated R for violence and profanity. 100m. **DIR:** John Mackenzie. **CAST:** Danny Aiello, Sherilyn Fenn, Arliss Howard, Tobin Bell, David Duchovny, Richard Sarafian, Joe Cortese, Marc Lawrence. **1991**

RUBY BRIDGES ★★★★1/2 Chaz Monet delivers a powerhouse performance as 6 year old Ruby Bridges, an African-American girl who defied a nation when she helped integrate New Orleans schools in the early 1960s. Forced to attend an all-white school, Ruby shows up for class, only to find her white classmates' parents have pulled their children from school. Thanks to an understanding teacher and a strong-willed mother, Ruby excels while becoming a symbol of reason and patience. Outstanding cast and understanding direction and writing make this made-for-television film a must-see. Not rated. 88m. **DIR:** Euzhan Palcy. **CAST:** Michael Beach, Patrika Darbo, Gil Johnson, Kevin Pollak, Penelope Ann Miller, Chaz Monet, Lela Rochon. **1998**

RUBY GENTRY ★★★ An excellent cast and sensitive direction make this drama of a Carolina swamp girl's social progress better than might be expected. Its focus is the caste system and prejudice in a picturesque region of the great melting pot. B&W; 82m. **DIR:** King Vidor. **CAST:** Jennifer Jones, Charlton Heston, Karl Malden, Tom Tully. **1952**

RUBY IN PARADISE ★★★★ Engagingly offbeat character study about a young woman who leaves her husband and home in the Tennessee mountains for what she hopes will be a better life in Florida. The challenges faced by a young woman out on her own are thoughtfully presented in this well-made film, which benefits from an impressive big-screen debut by Ashley Judd. Rated R for brief profanity and simulated sex. 105m. **DIR:** Victor Nunez. **CAST:** Ashley Judd, Todd Field, Bentley Mitchum, Allison Dean, Dorothy Lyman, Betsy Douds, Felicia Hernandez. **1993**

RUBY JEAN AND JOE ★★★ Star–executive producer Tom Selleck obviously liked what he saw in James Lee Barrett's charming little script, and the resulting film is an engaging—if lightweight—character study. Selleck's an aging rodeo star with a fondness for classical music and an uncertain future; Rebekah Johnson is a precocious teenage hitchhiker who becomes a companion, then friend, then . . . ? Rated PG-13 for profanity and nudity. 100m. **DIR:** Geoffrey Sax. **CAST:** Tom Selleck, JoBeth Williams, Ben Johnson, Rebekah Johnson, Eileen Seeley, John Diehl. **1995**

RUCKUS ★★★1/2 This lighthearted adventure film is like *Rambo* without the killing. That's one of the appealing things about this tale of a Vietnam soldier, Dirk Benedict, who escapes from an army psycho ward in Mobile and ends up in a little southern town where he is

harassed by the locals—but not for long. PG for violence and language. 91m. **DIR:** Max Kleven. **CAST:** Dirk Benedict, Linda Blair, Ben Johnson, Richard Farnsworth, Matt Clark. **1984**

RUDE ★★★★ This extremely well-made look at urban life interweaves stories about a woman recovering from a failed relationship, a sexually confused athlete, and an ex-con who is finding it hard to go straight. A film-festival favorite that wasn't widely distributed, this is worth seeing. Rated R for profanity, sexual situations, and violence. 90m. **DIR:** Clement Virgo. **CAST:** Sharon M. Lewis, Richard Chevolleau, Rachel Crawford. **1996 DVD**

RUDE AWAKENING (1982) ★★1/2 In another of Elvira's "Thriller Video" series, and one of the best, a real-estate broker finds himself sucked into dreams that seem like reality; or is it the other way around? It sounds standard, but it's better than you would think. 60m. **DIR:** Peter Sasdy. **CAST:** Denholm Elliott, James Laurenson, Pat Heywood. **1982**

RUDE AWAKENING (1989) ★★★ In 1969 two draft dodgers (Cheech Marin and Eric Roberts) flee from the FBI and drop out to Central America until a twist of fate fans their liberal fires and propels them to New York City in 1989. Rated R for language. 100m. **DIR:** Aaron Russo. **CAST:** Richard "Cheech" Marin, Eric Roberts, Julie Hagerty, Robert Carradine, Buck Henry, Louise Lasser, Cindy Williams, Andrea Martin, Cliff De Young. **1989**

RUDE BOY ★★★1/2 Meandering, overlong docudrama about an unemployed British teen who gets a job as a roadie with The Clash. An interesting document of the punk era, but what makes it essential viewing for music fans are plentiful performances by The Clash. Not rated, but an R equivalent for profanity. 133m. **DIR:** Jack Hazan, David Mingay. **CAST:** Ray Gange. **1980**

RUDY ★★★★1/2 Based on the life of Daniel E. (Rudy) Ruettiger, this is an excellent family film about a young man who sets a goal for himself and pursues it with dogged determination. From the people who made the equally impressive *Hoosiers*, it's a down-to-earth story with spirit-lifting rewards. Like young Rudy, played with engaging sincerity by Sean Astin, the filmmakers have us cheering them all the way. Rated PG for brief profanity. 112m. **DIR:** David Anspaugh. **CAST:** Sean Astin, Ned Beatty, Charles Dutton, Robert Prosky, Jason Miller, Lili Taylor, Greta Lind, Chelcie Ross. **1993**

RUDYARD KIPLING'S THE JUNGLE BOOK (1994) ★★★★ Terrific family adventure about a boy, Mowgli, who is lost in the jungle at the age of five and raised by animals. Returning to civilization as a young adult, our pure-hearted hero falls in love and finds himself in conflict with a rival suitor. Both parents and their children should enjoy this lavish, smartly paced film. Rated PG for violence. 110m. **DIR:** Stephen Sommers. **CAST:** Jason Scott Lee, Cary Elwes, Lena Headey, Sam Neill, John Cleese, Jason Flemyng. **1994**

RUGGLES OF RED GAP ★★★★1/2 Charles Laughton is superb as Ruggles, the valet who is lost in a poker game by a continental gentleman (Roland Young) to Americans (Charlie Ruggles and Mary Boland). The latter take him from Paris to the wilds of 1908 Washington State. Hilarious. B&W; 92m. **DIR:** Leo McCarey. **CAST:** Charles Laughton, Mary Boland, Charlie Ruggles, ZaSu Pitts, Roland Young, Leila Hyams. **1935**

RUGRATS IN PARIS ★★ Nickelodeon's disappointing follow-up to *The Rugrats Movie* focuses on the willful babies who handle (and create!) their own problems. This time Chuckie sets out to get a new mom but his future stepmother is the Cruella De Vil of an amusement park in Paris. The kids wreak so much havoc with their surroundings that one can easily relate to her abhorrence of them. Rated G; contains excessive potty humor. 84m. **DIR:** Paul Demeyer, Stig Bergqvist. **2000 DVD**

RUGRATS MOVIE, THE ★★★1/2 This feature will be adored by those who enjoy the Nickelodeon television series on which it is based. These folks deserve high fives for their successful translation of this wacky tot's-eye view of life in the big, wide world. It's a charming adventure, presented in the inventive, squiggly line art that has become the Rugrats signature style; the artwork perfectly conveys the sloppy, sticky, and unfathomable universe as experienced by a gaggle of unusually perceptive toddlers. The story concerns the arrival of Tommy Pickles's new baby brother, a shrieking little bundle of joy named Dylan (shortened to Dil). All ages will have fun with what follows. Rated G; suitable for all ages. 87m. **DIR:** Norton Virgien, Igor Kovalyov. **1998 DVD**

RULE #3 ★★ If the acting weren't so atrocious, this would be a pretty slick little thriller. Alas, writer-star-director Mitchell Cox is wearing at least two hats too many; his twists on *The Sting* may keep folks guessing, but the stiff performances are strictly amateur night. Rated PG-13 for violence and profanity. 90m. **DIR:** Mitchell Cox. **CAST:** Mitchell Cox, Marcia Swayze, Jerry Rector. **1993**

RULES OF ENGAGEMENT ★★★★ Sent in to rescue the besieged American ambassador to Yemen, highly decorated Marine Col. Terry Childers orders his men to open fire on the crowd of seemingly peaceful demonstrators, causing the deaths of more than eighty men, women, and children, while ignoring the rooftop snipers openly firing on the embassy. An international incident results with Childers held responsible, so he asks Col. Hays Hodges, whose life he saved in Vietnam, to defend him. Director William Friedkin keeps the audience guessing along with the characters as to Childers's guilt or innocence in this gripping drama. Rated R for profanity and violence. 123m. **DIR:** William Friedkin. **CAST:** Tommy Lee Jones, Samuel L. Jackson, Guy Pearce, Bruce Greenwood, Ben Kingsley, Blair Underwood, Philip Baker Hall, Anne Archer, Mark Feuerstein. **2000 DVD**

RULES OF THE GAME, THE ★★★★★ This is Jean Renoir's masterful comedy-farce that deftly exposes the moral bankruptcy of the French upper classes. A manor house is the location for a party as the shallowness of each guest is brilliantly exposed. B&W; 110m. **DIR:** Jean Renoir. **CAST:** Marcel Dalio, Nora Gregor, Mila Parely. **1939**

RULING CLASS, THE ★★★★ Superbly irreverent satire about upper-crust British eccentricities. Peter O'Toole plays the heir to a peerage who proves problematic because of his insane belief that he is Jesus Christ. Rated PG. 154m. **DIR:** Peter Medak. **CAST:** Peter

O'Toole, Alastair Sim, Arthur Lowe, Harry Andrews, Coral Browne. **1972 DVD**

RUMBLE FISH ★★ Francis Ford Coppola's black-and-white screen portrait of S. E. Hinton's second-rate novel about a teenage boy (Matt Dillon) seeking to escape his hellish life is a disappointing misfire. Rated R. B&W; 94m. **DIR:** Francis Ford Coppola. **CAST:** Christopher Penn, Tom Waits, Matt Dillon, Dennis Hopper, Vincent Spano, Mickey Rourke, Diane Lane, Nicolas Cage. **1983 DVD**

RUMBLE IN THE BRONX ★★★★ You don't have to be a Jackie Chan fan to enjoy this action-packed comedy from the Hong Kong superstar. Chan plays an innocent abroad—and he's in New York City for a very short time before a grocery store run by a friend is under siege by a biker gang. Of course, it's up to the remarkable Chan, who does all of his own stunts, to save the day. This is topflight entertainment. Rated R for profanity and violence. 97m. **DIR:** Stanley Tong. **CAST:** Jackie Chan, Anita Mui, Francoise Yip. **1996 DVD**

RUMIK WORLD: FIRETRIPPER ★★ In this animated feature, a young girl with the unexplained ability to time travel lives in two worlds—feudal and modern-day Japan. Not as engrossing as others in the *Rumik World* series, but it does have a few points of interest. In Japanese with English subtitles. Not rated; contains brief nudity. 50m. **DIR:** Osamu Uemura. **1992**

RUMIK WORLD: LAUGHING TARGET ★★★ A suspenseful animated story of love and demonic possession (not a strange combination when compared to other Japanese animation) that moves along with the excellent pacing we expect from the *Rumik World* series. Most viewers will find this exploration of the Japanese occult world a refreshing change of pace. In Japanese with English subtitles. Not rated; contains violence and brief nudity. 50m. **DIR:** Tohru Matsuzono. **1992**

RUMIK WORLD: THE SUPERGAL ★★★ Japanese animation. One of four stories from Rumiko Takahashi's imaginative *Rumik World* universe. Maris, a young woman in the service of the Space Police, lives in perpetual debt because of the inadvertent destruction of property brought about by her incredible strength. When assigned to rescue the kidnapped son of a billionaire, Maris sees her chance to finally get out of hock. In Japanese with English subtitles. Not rated; contains nudity. 50m. **DIR:** Kazuyashi Katayama, Tomoko Konparu. **1992**

RUMOR MILL, THE ★★ Hokey soap opera played to the hilt by Elizabeth Taylor and Jane Alexander as rival gossip queens Louella Parsons and Hedda Hopper. Plenty of cat fights and eye-piercing high camp. Made-for-TV melodrama (that originally aired as *Malice in Wonderland*). 94m. **DIR:** Gus Trikonis. **CAST:** Elizabeth Taylor, Jane Alexander, Richard Dysart. **1988**

RUMOR OF WAR, A ★★★ A well-made television movie about a Marine combat unit in Vietnam. Brad Davis plays a young officer who bravely leads his men into combat. He eventually gets charged with murder. The video version is about an hour and a half shorter than the original television print. Too bad. 105m. **DIR:** Richard T. Heffron. **CAST:** Brad Davis, Keith Carradine, Stacy Keach, Michael O'Keefe. **1980**

RUMPELSTILTSKIN ★★ Inane, vicious thriller about the sadistic storybook character on the loose in modern-day Los Angeles. A young mother unleashes the devilish dwarf and then is forced into action when Rumpelstiltskin sets his sights on her son. Standard-issue horror entry brings nothing new to the genre. Rated R for violence, profanity, and adult situations. 91m. **DIR:** Mark Jones. **CAST:** Kim Johnston Ulrich, Tommy Blaze, Allyce Beasley, Max Grodenchik. **1995 DVD**

RUMPOLE OF THE BAILEY (TV SERIES) ★★★★★ John Mortimer's charming and witty *Rumpole of the Bailey* is faithfully adapted in this British TV mystery series concerning a lovable old barrister who defends his clients with originality and flamboyance. Leo McKern's Horace Rumpole brings the English criminal justice system to life with the help (or hindrance) of fellow Chambers members Claude Erskine-Brown (Julian Curry), Phyllida Trant (Patricia Hodge), and Guthrie Featherstone (Peter Bowles). Rumpole's wife, Hilda, is wonderfully portrayed by Marion Mathie. Although the entire series is superb, take particular note of "Rumpole and the Alternative Society" and "Rumpole and the Blind Tasting." 52m. **DIR:** Roger Bamford, Rodney Bennett, Martyn Friend. **CAST:** Leo McKern, Marion Mathie, Julian Curry, Patricia Hodge, Peter Bowles. **1979–1981**

RUN ★★★ Patrick Dempsey is a young law student who is wrongly accused of murdering the son of a mob boss, and must now avoid the vengeful father and the corrupt local police force. The action is nonstop and Dempsey's one-liners are always perfectly timed. Rated R for violence and profanity. 89m. **DIR:** Geoff Burrowes. **CAST:** Patrick Dempsey, Kelly Preston, Ken Pogue, Christopher Lawford. **1991**

RUN FOR THE DREAM ★★★ This serviceable account of Olympic champion Gail Devers, who struggled to master a disease that nearly crippled her, has its heart in the right place; it's simply too pat and superficial to really engage the viewer. Focusing on her deterioration, the film sheds little insight into her hell-on-wheels battle to walk and run again. Rated PG for medical intensity. 95m. **DIR:** Neema Barnette. **CAST:** Louis Gossett Jr., Charlayne Woodard, Jeffrey Sams, Tina Lifford, Paula Kelly, Robert Guillaume. **1996**

RUN FOR THE ROSES (THOROUGHBRED) ★★1/2 This is a *Rocky*-ish saga about a horse that eventually competes in the Kentucky Derby. A Puerto Rican boy devotes himself to making the nearly lame horse a winner. Rated PG. 93m. **DIR:** Henry Levin. **CAST:** Vera Miles, Stuart Whitman, Sam Groom, Panchito Gomez. **1978**

RUN FOR THE SUN ★★★1/2 There have been many adaptations of Richard Connell's masterful suspense tale, *The Most Dangerous Game*, but this crackling remake is the first one in color. Plane crash survivors Richard Widmark and Jane Greer are the quarry of fugitive Nazi Peter Van Eyck in the South American jungle. Ferocious, imaginative, and exciting. Filmed in Mexico. 99m. **DIR:** Roy Boulting. **CAST:** Richard Widmark, Jane Greer, Trevor Howard, Peter Van Eyck. **1956**

RUN FOR YOUR MONEY, A ★★★★ A pair of Welsh miners in London for a day get into more than their share of misadventures. One of the best of the Ealing Studios comedies—if you're a fan of British humor, this

one's a must-see. B&W; 83m. **DIR:** Charles Frend. **CAST:** Alec Guinness, Meredith Edwards, Moira Lister, Donald Houston, Hugh Griffith. **1949**

RUN IF YOU CAN An incomprehensible police thriller. Rated R for nudity and violence. 92m. **DIR:** Virginia Lively Stone. **CAST:** Martin Landau, Yvette Napir, Jerry Van Dyke. **1987**

RUN LOLA RUN ★★★1/2 You've got to love the manic energy at work here, even if the execution is rather strange. German writer-director Tom Tykwer's central gimmick in this 81-minute marvel concerns the differing paths that lives will take, as with *Sliding Doors* or *Groundhog Day*, on the basis of seemingly insignificant changes. The resulting series of varying loops will continue until a woman can get 100,000 marks to her boyfriend—in 20 minutes—and save him. If it's true that half the fun of any artistic medium is discovering those who eschew the same-old-same-old and deliver something fresh, then Tykwer clearly is a talent on the upswing. While not for all tastes—many will dismiss Tykwer as hopelessly bizarre and self-indulgent—this is an impressively vivid experience. Rated R for profanity, violence, nudity, and drug use. In German with English subtitles. 81m. **DIR:** Tom Tykwer. **CAST:** Franka Potente, Moritz Bleibtreu, Herbert Knaup, Armin Rohde. **1999 DVD**

RUN OF THE ARROW ★★★ One of the strangest of all adult Westerns of the 1950s, this film tells the story of a man who joins the Sioux tribe after the Civil War rather than accept the reality of the South's defeat. Rod Steiger does a good job in a difficult role. While not entirely successful, this thought-provoking film is worth watching. 85m. **DIR:** Samuel Fuller. **CAST:** Rod Steiger, Brian Keith, Ralph Meeker, Sarita Montiel, Tim McCoy, Jay C. Flippen, Charles Bronson. **1957**

RUN OF THE COUNTRY, THE ★★★★ Fabulous Irish film features Albert Finney as a crusty constable who must cope with his son, as well as his own failed dreams, after his wife's death. Superior acting, gorgeous scenery, and a fine musical score enhance the intriguing plot and add up to nonstop entertainment. Rated R for nudity, sex, violence, and profanity. 110m. **DIR:** Peter Yates. **CAST:** Albert Finney, Matt Kesslar, Anthony Brophy, Victoria Smurfit. **1995**

RUN, REBECCA, RUN ★★★★ This action-filled adventure finds a brave young girl captured by an illegal alien on an Australian island. Her fear of him soon dissolves as she helps him face the Australian authorities in order to be legally admitted to their country. 81m. **DIR:** Peter Maxwell. **CAST:** Henri Szeps, Simone Buchanan, John Stanton. **1983**

RUN SILENT, RUN DEEP ★★★★ Clark Gable becomes the captain of a submarine that Burt Lancaster was to command. Although he resents his new boss, Lancaster stays on. Tensions rise among Lancaster, Gable, and the crew as they set out from Pearl Harbor to destroy a Japanese cruiser. This film is noted as one of the finest World War II submarine movies. B&W; 93m. **DIR:** Robert Wise. **CAST:** Clark Gable, Burt Lancaster, Jack Warden, Don Rickles. **1958 DVD**

RUN STRANGER RUN ★★★1/2 Ron Howard plays a teenager searching for his biological parents in a seaside town. Once there, he discovers that some of the town inhabitants have been disappearing. Unfortunately, the disappearances are closely linked to his past. Overall, this film keeps viewer interest without dwelling on the slash-'em-up theme. Rated PG for gore. 92m. **DIR:** Darren McGavin. **CAST:** Patricia Neal, Cloris Leachman, Ron Howard, Bobby Darin. **1973**

RUNAWAY (1984) ★★★ Tom Selleck is a futuristic cop trying to track down a bunch of killer robots controlled by the evil villain (Gene Simmons, from the rock band KISS). It's a cinematic comic book and, although meant to be a thriller, never really gets the viewer involved in the story. Rated PG-13 for violence. 99m. **DIR:** Michael Crichton. **CAST:** Tom Selleck, Cynthia Rhodes, Gene Simmons, Kirstie Alley. **1984**

RUNAWAY, THE (2000) ★★★1/2 In a racist Georgia town in the 1940s, a progressive sheriff and two best friends—one black and one white—challenge the "good old boy" hatred which had run rampant until then. Heavy message is compounded by Maya Angelou's predictions throughout this *Hallmark Hall of Fame* production. Not rated; contains violence and mature themes. 98m. **DIR:** Arthur Allan Seidelman. **CAST:** Dean Cain, Duane McLaughlin, Cody Newton, Maya Angelou. **2000 DVD**

RUNAWAY BRIDE ★★★1/2 Julia Roberts surmounts this project's improbable script through sheer force of will, and the result—while absolutely preposterous—is reasonably entertaining. She plays a woman in rural Maryland with a habit of leaving eligible husbands at the altar; this intrigues a New York–based journalist (Richard Gere) who routinely lambastes women in a regular column intended to shed light on the battle of the sexes. He gets some facts wrong; she complains and gets him fired. And so, by way of revenge, he travels to her small community and falls in love with her. Or something like that. Not one remotely credible character inhabits this film, but Roberts is impossible to resist: a classic case of star power overwhelming pedestrian material. Rated PG for mild dramatic content. 106m. **DIR:** Garry Marshall. **CAST:** Julia Roberts, Richard Gere, Joan Cusack, Rita Wilson, Hector Elizondo, Paul Dooley. **1999 DVD**

RUNAWAY FATHER ★★ Made-for-TV true story stars Donna Mills as a wife out to prove that her missing husband faked his death in order to leave his family. Standard fare gets a boost from durable cast, including Jack Scalia as the scoundrel. Not rated. 94m. **DIR:** John Nicolella. **CAST:** Donna Mills, Jack Scalia, Chris Mulkey, Jenny Lewis, Priscilla Pointer. **1991**

RUNAWAY NIGHTMARE Two Nevada worm ranchers are kidnapped by a gang of beautiful women. 104m. **DIR:** Michael Cartel. **CAST:** Michael Cartel, Al Valletta. **1984**

RUNAWAY TRAIN ★★★★ In this riveting, pulse-pounding adventure movie, two convicts escape from prison and, accompanied by a hostage (Rebecca DeMornay), make the mistake of hopping a train speeding straight for disaster. While the story gets a bit too allegorical and philosophical on occasion, the unrelenting intensity more than makes up for it. Rated R for violence, gore, and profanity. 112m. **DIR:** Andrei Konchalovsky. **CAST:** Jon Voight, Eric Roberts, Rebecca DeMornay, John P. Ryan, Kenneth McMillan, Kyle T. Heffner, T. K. Carter. **1986 DVD**

RUNESTONE ★★★ An ancient Norse runestone that contains a mythical demon is unearthed and brought to New York City. When an archaeologist discovers its forbidden curse, not even the police can stop the carnage. Rated R for violence, profanity, and nudity. 105m. **DIR:** Willard Carroll. **CAST:** Peter Riegert, Joan Severance, William Hickey, Tim Ryan, Lawrence Tierney, Chris Young, Alexander Godunov. **1990**

RUNNER STUMBLES, THE ★★★ A good adaptation of Milan Stitt's play, which certainly did not deserve the scorching hatred generated during its brief box-office appearance. Dick Van Dyke plays a priest who falls in love with Kathleen Quinlan's appealing nun. The subject may make viewers uneasy, but the film is by no means tacky or exploitative. Rated PG for adult subject matter. 99m. **DIR:** Stanley Kramer. **CAST:** Dick Van Dyke, Kathleen Quinlan, Maureen Stapleton, Beau Bridges. **1979**

RUNNING AGAINST TIME ★★1/2 Historian Robert Hays employs physicist Sam Wanamaker's time-travel machine in an effort to prevent Kennedy's assassination but things go horribly awry. Those accustomed to the carefully plotted intricacies of *Back to the Future* will be dismayed by this sloppy made-for-cable time-travel tale, adapted rather freely from Stanley Shapiro's *A Time to Remember*. Rated PG. 93m. **DIR:** Bruce Seth Green. **CAST:** Robert Hays, Catharine Hicks, Sam Wanamaker. **1990**

RUNNING AWAY ★★ Pointless WWII film features Sophia Loren and Sydney Penny as an Italian mother and daughter team traveling from what seemed a comparatively safe Rome to the mountains. Rated PG-13 for violence. 101m. **DIR:** Dino Risi. **CAST:** Sophia Loren, Sydney Penny, Robert Loggia, Andrea Occhipinti. **1989**

RUNNING BRAVE ★★★★ Robby Benson stars as Billy Mills, whose winning the ten-thousand meter race in the 1964 Olympics was one of the biggest upsets in sports history. The direction is pedestrian at best. But Benson's fine performance and the true-life drama of Mills's determination to set a positive example of achievement for his people—the Sioux and all Native Americans—is affecting. Rated PG for profanity. 105m. **DIR:** Donald Shebib. **CAST:** Robby Benson, Pat Hingle, Jeff McCracken. **1983**

RUNNING COOL ★★★ Surprisingly decent biker story stars Andrew Divoff as a gallant cycle cowboy helping an old friend save wetlands from developers. Sexism mars the eco-friendly spirit, but it's fun to watch "outlaw" bikers save the day. Rated R for language and sexuality. 106m. **DIR:** Ferd Sebastian, Beverly Sebastian. **CAST:** Andrew Divoff, Dedee Pfeiffer, James Gammon, Paul Gleason. **1993**

RUNNING DELILAH ★★ Kim Cattrall stars as an undercover agent who is ambushed by a notorious international arms dealer. Her partner (Billy Zane) races her body to a secret government laboratory where they turn her into a cyborg. Lifeless rip-off of TV's *The Bionic Woman*. Rated PG-13 for violence. 85m. **DIR:** Richard Franklin. **CAST:** Kim Cattrall, Billy Zane, Francois Guetary, Yorgo Voyagis, Diana Rigg. **1993**

RUNNING FREE ★★★ The story of a young boy and his best friend—an abandoned young colt named Lucky. Solid entertainment for the entire family. Rated G. 85m. **DIR:** Sergei Bodrov. **CAST:** Chase Moore, Jan Decleir, Arie Verveen, Maria Geelbooi. **1999 DVD**

RUNNING HOT ★★★ Eric Stoltz gives a very good performance as a 17 year old sentenced to death row. The publicity of his case arouses the interest of 30 year old Monica Carrico, who sends him love letters in prison. His escape and bizarre affair with her have serious consequences in this fast-paced drama. Rated R for sex, violence, language, and nudity. 88m. **DIR:** Mark Griffiths. **CAST:** Eric Stoltz, Stuart Margolin, Monica Carrico, Virgil Frye. **1983**

RUNNING KIND, THE ★★★★ The straitlaced scion (David Packer) of an Akron, Ohio, family takes the summer off from dad's law firm to follow a sexy, free-thinking rock drummer (Brie Howard) into the bowels of Los Angeles's punk scene. A marvelously inventive comedy from writer-director Max Tash. Rated R for profanity and brief violence. 90m. **DIR:** Max Tash. **CAST:** David Packer, Brie Howard. **1989**

RUNNING MAN, THE ★★★1/2 In this silly but exciting outing, Arnold Schwarzenegger is an honest cop who is framed for a crime he didn't commit and forced to fight for his life on a bizarre twenty-first-century game show. Another successful variation on the big guy's standard film formula. Rated R for profanity and violence. 101m. **DIR:** Paul Michael Glaser. **CAST:** Arnold Schwarzenegger, Maria Conchita Alonso, Richard Dawson, Yaphet Kotto, Jim Brown. **1987 DVD**

RUNNING MATES (1985) ★★ Stereotyped characters populate this story of two teenagers who fall in love, only to be torn apart when their respective fathers run against each other in an election. Rated PG for adult situations. 90m. **DIR:** Thomas L. Neff. **CAST:** Gregg Webb, Barbara Howard. **1985**

RUNNING MATES (1992) ★★★ Political vulnerability is the topic of A. L. Appling's script, which concerns the fallout resulting from presidential candidate Ed Harris's growing involvement with children's book author Diane Keaton (whose condescending behavior wears thin *very* quickly). Alas, this made-for-cable romantic comedy concludes unsatisfyingly, without confronting this issue of privacy versus the public's right to know. 88m. **DIR:** Michael Lindsay-Hogg. **CAST:** Diane Keaton, Ed Harris, Ed Begley Jr., Ben Masters, Russ Tamblyn. **1992**

RUNNING MATES (2000) ★★★ Tom Selleck plays a likable Michigan governor and Democratic nominee for president who's feeling pressure from all sides about whom to choose for VP. Four of the women he's slept with—wife, campaign manager, Hollywood star, and a pushy senator's wife—form a strange sorority, but ultimately Selleck must decide whether to sell himself out to get elected. Made for TV. 90m. **DIR:** Ron Lagomarsino. **CAST:** Tom Selleck, Nancy Travis, Laura Linney, Faye Dunaway, Teri Hatcher. **2000 DVD**

RUNNING ON EMPTY ★★★★ Extremely well-made film looks at a fugitive family that has been on the lam from the FBI for years. Unable to establish roots anywhere because of the constant fear of detection, parents Christine Lahti and Judd Hirsch must decide what to do when their son, River Phoenix, is accepted to the Juilliard School of Music. Rated PG-13. 116m. **DIR:** Sidney Lumet. **CAST:** Christine Lahti, Judd Hirsch, River Phoenix, Martha Plimpton. **1988 DVD**

RUNNING SCARED (1980) ★★★ Ken Wahl and Judge Reinhold are servicemen returning home after two years in the Panama Canal Zone. Reinhold unknowingly filmed a secret base that is to be used in the Bay of Pigs operation. When their plane lands, authorities find negatives and the chase is on. Not rated. 82m. **DIR:** Paul Glicker. **CAST:** Ken Wahl, Judge Reinhold, Bradford Dillman, Pat Hingle, Lonny Chapman, John Saxon. **1980**

RUNNING SCARED (1986) ★★★★ Fast, funny, and exciting, this *Beverly Hills Cop*–style comedy-cop thriller features inspired on-screen teamwork from Gregory Hines and Billy Crystal as a pair of wisecracking detectives on the trail of a devious drug dealer. Rated R for violence, nudity, and profanity. 107m. **DIR:** Peter Hyams. **CAST:** Gregory Hines, Billy Crystal, Steven Bauer, Darlanne Fluegel, Joe Pantoliano, Dan Hedaya, Jimmy Smits, Jonathan Gries, Tracy Reed. **1986 DVD**

RUNNING TIME ★★★1/2 While other films have tried to tell a story set in real time, very few have successfully achieved such a concept. Until now. *Running Time* brings all of the elements together when "reformed" convict Bruce Campbell attempts to rob the prison that has just released him. A fine achievement. Not rated; contains violence, profanity, and simulated sex. B&W; 70m. **DIR:** Josh Becker. **CAST:** Bruce Campbell, Jeremy Roberts, Anita Barone. **1997 DVD**

RUNNING WILD (1927) ★★ W. C. Fields is miscast and overplays his role of a toady worm suddenly turned (by hypnotism) into a coarse, violent lion—mean to family, friends, and dog. Far from vintage Fields, this film is a disappointing outing for his comic genius. Silent with titles. B&W; 68m. **DIR:** Gregory La Cava. **CAST:** W. C. Fields, Mary Brian, Claude Buchanan. **1927**

RUNNING WILD (1955) ★★ Rookie cop William Campbell pretends to be a young tough to get the goods on an auto-theft gang headed by Keenan Wynn. Made to catch the teenage rock 'n' roll crowd. 81m. **DIR:** Abner Biberman. **CAST:** William Campbell, Mamie Van Doren, Keenan Wynn, Katherine Case, Jan Merlin, John Saxon. **1955**

RUNNING WILD (1994) ★★ Low-budget road movie features Jennifer Barker as a woman about to marry a man twice her age when she falls for his handsome son. Then they're off and headed for Mexico with a friend in a stolen car. Some local color and a couple of offbeat moments rally to make this more than it is. Rated R for nudity, language, and violence. 97m. **DIR:** Phillippe Blot. **CAST:** Jennifer Barker, Daniel DuPont, Daniel Spector, Eliot Kenner. **1994**

RUNNING WILD (1998) ★★★1/2 This charming little family film concerns a boy and a girl who join their father in Zimbabwe, befriend a baby elephant, and foil a bunch of nasty poachers. It's definitely Africa by way of Disneyland in the tradition of *Clarence, the Cross-Eyed Lion* and other similarly friendly wild-life adventures: films we don't see often enough these days. Rated PG for brief violence against animals. 90m. **DIR:** Timothy Bond. **CAST:** Gregory Harrison, Lori Hallier, Cody Jones, Brooke Nevin, Simon MacCorkindale, Themba Ndaba, Munyaradzi Kanaventi. **1998 DVD**

RUSH ★★★ For her directorial debut, Lili Fini Zanuck (wife of producer Richard) chose a hard-edged story about undercover narcotics officers who become heavy users while busting other addicts in a small Texas town. It's downright dreary much of the time, with the fine acting of Sam Elliott and Max Perlich adding several bright moments. Rated R for profanity, violence, and drug use. 120m. **DIR:** Lili Fini Zanuck. **CAST:** Jason Patric, Jennifer Jason Leigh, Sam Elliott, Max Perlich, Gregg Allman, Bill Sadler. **1991**

RUSH HOUR ★★★ Jackie Chan and Chris Tucker are the main attractions in this low-rent *48 Hrs.*: an oil-and-vinegar "buddy thriller" where two outcasts eventually put aside petty differences and Save the Day. The advertising signature line pretty much sums it up: "The fastest hands in the East versus the biggest mouth in the West." When a Chinese consul's daughter is kidnapped while in the United States, good friend Jackie Chan is summoned. The FBI, resenting this intrusion, co-opts a reprobate LAPD officer to play nursemaid. The rest involves considerable martial arts mayhem—in Chan's signature style—and the explosive destruction of ample real estate. It's all fun, if rather soulless. Rated PG-13 for profanity and martial arts mayhem. 97m. **DIR:** Brett Ratner. **CAST:** Jackie Chan, Chris Tucker, Tom Wilkinson, Philip Baker Hall, Elizabeth Peña. **1998 DVD**

•**RUSH HOUR 2** ★★★1/2 Although even less credible than its predecessor, and certainly sloppier from a scripting standpoint, this action-oriented sequel is non-stop fun, thanks to the contrasting styles and talents of stars Jackie Chan and Chris Tucker. The wafer-thin plot involves flawless counterfeit $100 bills that are being shipped from Hong Kong to the United States, and our heroes get involved despite their best efforts to enjoy a vacation. Tucker's runaway mouth and Chan's brilliantly choreographed martial arts moves remain the primary attraction, so just settle back and enjoy the ride. Rated PG-13 for action, violence, profanity, and mild sensuality. 90m. **DIR:** Brett Ratner. **CAST:** Jackie Chan, Chris Tucker, John Lone, Alan King, Zhang Ziyi, Roselyn Sanchez, Harris Yulin. **2001 DVD**

RUSH WEEK ★★ A reporter (Pamela Ludwig) gets a scoop on murdered models and gets herself in the most ridiculously suicidal situations to follow her leads. Rated R for nudity, violence, and gore. 96m. **DIR:** Bob Bralver. **CAST:** Dean Hamilton, Pamela Ludwig, Gregg Allman, Roy Thinnes. **1989 DVD**

RUSHMORE ★★★1/2 This parable concerns what might happen if a precocious 15 year old geek had the talent and resources to bring his every whim to life. Max Fischer is a tenth-grader at prestigious Rushmore Academy, a preppy private school where he excels at extracurricular activities—while neglecting his "real" studies. Things get more complicated when Max meets and develops a crush on a first-grade teacher, and one of the school's primary benefactors also falls in love with the same teacher. What follows is a small treasure: funny, poignant, raw, and at times as clumsy as its protagonist . . . but no less adorable. Rated R for profanity. 93m. **DIR:** Wes Anderson. **CAST:** Jason Schwartzman, Bill Murray, Olivia Williams, Brian Cox, Seymour Cassel, Mason Gamble, Sara Tanaka. **1998 DVD**

RUSSELL MULCAHY'S TALE OF THE MUMMY ★★ Russell Mulcahy's low-budget adventure was once headed for the big screen, but was relegated to video after Universal beat him to the punch. Good thing. Mulcahy's film is an okay diversion, but lacks the appeal and

thrills needed to make it grand entertainment. After a promising beginning, the film becomes a tired detective story set in London. The special effects are anything but special. Rated R for language and violence. 88m. **DIR:** Russell Mulcahy. **CAST:** Jason Scott Lee, Christopher Lee, Louise Lombard, Lysette Anthony, Shelley Duvall. **1999**

RUSSIA HOUSE, THE ★★★★ A British book publisher (Sean Connery) becomes involved in international espionage when a Russian woman (Michelle Pfeiffer) sends him an unsolicited manuscript. This first-rate adaptation of the John Le Carre novel is a thinking-person's spy movie. Rated R for profanity. 123m. **DIR:** Fred Schepisi. **CAST:** Sean Connery, Michelle Pfeiffer, Roy Scheider, Klaus Maria Brandauer, James Fox, John Mahoney, Michael Kitchen, J. T. Walsh, Ken Russell. **1990 DVD**

RUSSIAN ROULETTE ★★ George Segal plays a Royal Canadian Mountie sucked into a secret service plot to kidnap a Russian dissident prior to a visit from the Soviet premier. Good premise, but no action or thrills. Rated PG. 100m. **DIR:** Lou Lombardo. **CAST:** George Segal, Cristina Raines, Bo Brudin, Denholm Elliott, Richard Romanus, Gordon Jackson, Peter Donat, Nigel Stock, Louise Fletcher. **1975**

RUSSIANS ARE COMING, THE RUSSIANS ARE COMING, THE ★★★1/2 A Russian submarine runs aground off Nantucket Island, and the townspeople go gaga, not knowing what to do first, get guns or pour vodka. Cued by Alan Arkin's engaging portrayal of an out-of-his-depth Russian sailor, the cast delivers a solid comedy as cultures clash. With Jonathan Winters aboard, think wacky. 120m. **DIR:** Norman Jewison. **CAST:** Alan Arkin, Carl Reiner, Paul Ford, Theodore Bikel, Brian Keith, Jonathan Winters, Eva Marie Saint. **1966**

RUSSKIES ★★1/2 A sweet-natured Russian sailor (Whip Hubley) becomes stranded in Key West, Florida, when a raft capsizes and aborts a secret mission. He finds three youngsters who eventually agree to help him escape. The cast is appealing, but the laughs aren't frequent enough. Rated PG-13 for slight violence and profanity. 90m. **DIR:** Rick Rosenthal. **CAST:** Whip Hubley, Leaf Phoenix, Peter Billingsley, Charles Frank. **1987**

RUSTLERS, THE ★★★★ Clever, sprightly paced Western has Tim Holt and his saddle pal, the ever-amorous Richard "Chito" Martin, tracking down Steve Brodie and his gang of rustlers. A winner. B&W; 61m. **DIR:** Lesley Selander. **CAST:** Tim Holt, Martha Hyer, Richard Martin, Steve Brodie, Addison Richards. **1949**

RUSTLER'S RHAPSODY ★★★ In this fun spoof of the singing cowboy movies of the 1930s, 1940s, and 1950s, Tom Berenger plays the horseback crooner of them all, Rex O'Herlihan. Viewers need to be familiar with the old B Westerns to get the jokes. If you are, it's a hoot. Rated PG for mild violence and slight profanity. 88m. **DIR:** Hugh Wilson. **CAST:** Tom Berenger, G. W. Bailey, Marilu Henner, Andy Griffith, Fernando Rey, Patrick Wayne. **1985**

RUTANGA TAPES, THE ★★1/2 A frighteningly current movie dealing with the use of chemical weapons by a government on its own people. David Dukes is the spy–economic adviser sent to the African nation with the purpose of uncovering the details. Rated R for violence. 88m. **DIR:** David Lister. **CAST:** David Dukes, Susan Anspach. **1990**

RUTHERFORD COUNTY LINE ★★ Wooden acting dampens an otherwise decent script about real-life Rutherford County, North Carolina, Sheriff Damon Husky (Earl Owensby) and his efforts to police the rural Blue Ridge community. The actors appear to read their lines from cue cards. Not rated; the film contains episodes of profanity and graphic violence. 98m. **DIR:** Thom McIntyre. **CAST:** Earl Owensby, Terry Loughlin. **1985**

RUTHLESS FOUR, THE ★★ This spaghetti Western could have been a lot worse, but that's no reason to watch it. Van Heflin plays a prospector who strikes gold, only to have to split the fortune with three other men less honest than he. 96m. **DIR:** Giorgio Capitani. **CAST:** Van Heflin, Gilbert Roland, Klaus Kinski, George Hilton. **1969**

RUTHLESS PEOPLE ★★★★1/2 Danny DeVito decides to murder his obnoxious wife, played by Bette Midler. But when he arrives home to carry out the deed, he discovers she has been abducted. The kidnappers demand fifty thousand dollars "or else." Exactly what DeVito has in mind, so he refuses to pay a cent. A comedy classic. Rated R for nudity and profanity. 90m. **DIR:** Jim Abrahams, David Zucker, Jerry Zucker. **CAST:** Danny DeVito, Bette Midler, Judge Reinhold, Helen Slater, Anita Morris, Bill Pullman. **1986 DVD**

RUTLES, THE (ALL YOU NEED IS CASH) ★★★★ Superb spoof of the Beatles has Eric Idle in a dual role as a television reporter and one of the Rutles, whose songs include "Cheese and Onions" and "Doubleback Alley." It's great stuff for fans of the Fab Four—with cameos from rock stars (including Beatle George Harrison) and members of *Saturday Night Live*'s Not Ready for Prime-Time Players. 78m. **DIR:** Eric Idle, Gary Weis. **CAST:** Eric Idle, Neil Innes, Ricky Fataar, John Halsey, Mick Jagger, Paul Simon, George Harrison, John Belushi, Dan Aykroyd, Gilda Radner. **1978 DVD**

RYAN'S DAUGHTER ★★1/2 Acclaimed director David Lean took a critical beating with this release, about a spoiled woman (Sarah Miles) who shamelessly lusts after an officer (Christopher Jones). Robert Mitchum, as Miles's husband, is the best thing about this watchable misfire. Rated PG. 176m. **DIR:** David Lean. **CAST:** Sarah Miles, Christopher Jones, Robert Mitchum, Trevor Howard, John Mills, Leo McKern. **1970**

S

S*P*Y*S CIA agents assisting a Russian dancer wanting to defect to the West. 87m. **DIR:** Irvin Kershner. **CAST:** Donald Sutherland, Elliott Gould, Joss Ackland. **1974**

SABOTAGE ★★★ Despite the convoluted plot, Mark Dacascos and Carrie Anne Moss make a superb investigating team. He's a bodyguard trying to learn why his latest client was assassinated; she's an FBI agent trying

to balance professional duty with responsibility for her young daughter. Both are targeted by Tony Todd's sadistic villain, who brings new meaning to the phrase "big gun." Slick pacing and genuine suspense raise this several cuts above the usual genre dreck. Rated R for violence and profanity. 99m. **DIR:** Tibor Takacs. **CAST:** Mark Dacascos, Carrie-Anne Moss, Tony Todd, Graham Greene, John Neville. **1996**

SABOTAGE ★★★ One of the first of Alfred Hitchcock's characteristic thrillers. London's being terrorized by an unknown bomber, and movie theater cashier Sylvia Sidney begins to fear that her husband (Oscar Homolka) is behind it all. Hitch was still experimenting, and his use of shadows and sound effects betrays the influence of German silent films. B&W; 76m. **DIR:** Alfred Hitchcock. **CAST:** Sylvia Sidney, Oscar Homolka, John Loder. **1936 DVD**

SABOTEUR ★★★★1/2 Outstanding Alfred Hitchcock film about a World War II factory worker (Robert Cummings) turned fugitive after he's unjustly accused of sabotage. The briskly paced story follows his efforts to elude police while he tries to unmask the real culprit. A humdinger of a climax. B&W; 108m. **DIR:** Alfred Hitchcock. **CAST:** Robert Cummings, Priscilla Lane, Norman Lloyd, Otto Kruger. **1942**

SABRINA (1954) ★★★★ Elfin Audrey Hepburn shines in the title role. She's the simple chauffeur's daughter who is swept off her feet by wealthy rake William Holden. Humphrey Bogart, as Holden's business-minded brother, attempts to save her from the ne'er-do-well. Director Billy Wilder paces things with his usual deft touch. B&W; 113m. **DIR:** Billy Wilder. **CAST:** Audrey Hepburn, Humphrey Bogart, William Holden, John Williams. **1954 DVD**

SABRINA (1995) ★★★1/2 Samuel Taylor's delightful stage play, concerning the plain chauffeur's daughter who blossoms into a beauty and wins the heart of a millionaire, doesn't play quite as well in this remake. Julia Ormond properly updates her character to a woman of the 1990s, but it's a bit of a stretch to believe that Harrison Ford's Linus Larrabee is a "plain stiff" lacking any gentler social graces. Billy Wilder's original is the story of a mousy young woman's self-discovery, but this update is more about a rich guy's midlife crisis. Rated PG for mild sensuality. 127m. **DIR:** Sydney Pollack. **CAST:** Harrison Ford, Julia Ormond, Greg Kinnear, Nancy Marchand, John Wood. **1995 DVD**

SABRINA, THE TEENAGE WITCH ★★★ The *Archie Comics* costar gets her own live-action feature, with reasonable results. Perky Melissa Joan Hart learns of her spell-casting heritage during the first full moon after her sixteenth birthday and struggles with true love and bitchy rivals while learning how to control her new powers. The subject of witchcraft notwithstanding, the film delivers strong moral lessons. Suitable for all ages. 91m. **DIR:** Tibor Takacs. **CAST:** Melissa Joan Hart, Sherry Miller, Charlene Fernetz. **1996**

SACCO AND VANZETTI ★★★★ Excellent historical drama recounts the trial and eventual execution of Sacco and Vanzetti, the Italian immigrants who were convicted of murder in 1921. The case was a *cause célèbre* at the time, since many felt that they were condemned on the basis of their politics rather than on the weak evidence against them. Dubbed in English. Rated PG. 121m. **DIR:** Giuliano Montaldo. **CAST:** Gian Maria Volonté, Riccardo Cucciolla, Cyril Cusack, Milo O'Shea. **1971 DVD**

SACKETTS, THE ★★★★ Fine made-for-TV Western adapted from two novels by Louis L'Amour, *The Daybreakers* and *The Sacketts*. Sam Elliott, Tom Selleck, Glenn Ford, and Ben Johnson are terrific in the lead roles, and there's plenty of action. 200m. **DIR:** Robert Totten. **CAST:** Sam Elliott, Tom Selleck, Glenn Ford, Ben Johnson, Ruth Roman, Gilbert Roland, Slim Pickens, Jack Elam, Gene Evans. **1979**

SACRED CARGO ★★★ An ex-Marine (Chris Penn) must rescue his brother, a priest (Martin Sheen), after his plan to help an order of Franciscans escape from Russia goes awry. Shot on location in Russia, this thriller is more interesting for its scenery than its rather predictable plot. Not rated; contains gore, sexual situations, and profanity. 97m. **DIR:** Alexander Buravsky. **CAST:** Christopher Penn, J. T. Walsh, Anna Karina, Martin Sheen. **1995**

SACRED GROUND ★★★1/2 Interracial marriage between a white mountain man and an Apache woman is further complicated when they have their child on the burial grounds of another Indian tribe. The trials they endure should hold viewer interest. Rated PG. 100m. **DIR:** Charles B. Pierce. **CAST:** Tim McIntire, Jack Elam, Serene Hedin. **1983**

SACRIFICE, THE (1986) ★★★★ The actors here do most of the work that expensive special effects would accomplish in an American film with a similar theme. During an approaching world holocaust, we don't see devastation. Rather, the camera records the various emotional reactions of six people in a house in the secluded countryside. Actors' faces and unpredictable actions mirror horror, pathos, and even grim humor as the plot twists in a surprisingly supernatural direction. In Swedish with English subtitles. Not rated, the film has suggested sex. 145m. **DIR:** Andrei Tarkovsky. **CAST:** Erland Josephson, Susan Fleetwood, Valerie Mairesse, Allan Edwall. **1986 DVD**

•SACRIFICE (2000) ★★ A bank robber escapes from prison in order to track down a serial killer that murdered his daughter. As he searches for more clues about the killer, he also discovers some things that he never knew about his own daughter. Not a bad movie per se, just easily forgettable. Rated R for violence, language, and sexuality. 90m. **DIR:** Mark L. Lester. **CAST:** Michael Madsen, Bokeem Woodbine, Jamie Luner, Joshua Leonard. **2000 DVD**

SACRILEGE ★★ Controversial drama where sin and lust take place behind the walls of a convent. An illicit affair between a nun and a nobleman escalates to a dangerous climax. Lavishly produced erotica. In Italian with English subtitles. Not rated; contains nudity and violence and is recommended for adults. 104m. **DIR:** Luciano Odorisio. **CAST:** Myriem Roussel, Alessandro Gassman. **1990**

SAD SACK, THE ★★1/2 Jerry Lewis in the army. That's all the plot there is in this better-than-average Lewis vehicle which, as usual, will please his fans and annoy all others. 98m. **DIR:** George Marshall. **CAST:** Jerry Lewis, David Wayne, Phyllis Kirk, Peter Lorre. **1957**

SADAT ★★★1/2 Although much of the great Egyptian statesman's life is left out of this two-part TV movie,

what is seen is well-made and impressively acted, particularly by Lou Gossett Jr. as Sadat. 191m. **DIR:** Richard Michaels. **CAST:** Louis Gossett Jr., John Rhys-Davies, Madolyn Smith, Jeremy Kemp, Anne Heywood, Barry Morse, Nehemiah Persoff, Paul Smith, Jeffrey Tambor. **1983**

SADDLE MOUNTAIN ROUNDUP ★★★ The Range Busters set out to find the killer of a grouchy old rancher. B&W; 55m. **DIR:** S. Roy Luby. **CAST:** Ray "Crash" Corrigan, John King, Max Terhune, Jack Mulhall, George Chesebro. **1941**

SADDLE TRAMPS ★★ A Casanova named Coburn (Bud Spencer) seduces Mary, the sister of a gunfighter named Sonny (Jack Palance), and Sonny pursues Coburn all over the West. Good performance by Spencer, in a role where he's not his usual brutish clown, makes this a fine parody Western. Rated PG. 90m. **DIR:** Maurizio Lucidi. **CAST:** Bud Spencer, Jack Palance, Francisco Rabal, Renato Cestie. **1971**

SADIE MCKEE ★★ A dated character study about a working girl who moves to the other side of the tracks, dragging her boyfriends behind her. This is the kind of movie Joan Crawford specialized in, but it is way out of style today. B&W; 89m. **DIR:** Clarence Brown. **CAST:** Joan Crawford, Franchot Tone, Edward Arnold, Gene Raymond, Esther Ralston, Leo G. Carroll, Akim Tamiroff. **1934**

SADIE THOMPSON ★★★ Screen legend Gloria Swanson is Somerset Maugham's famous South Seas floozy in this silent predecessor of the better-known 1932 Joan Crawford sound remake. Director-writer-costar Raoul Walsh more than holds his own against her, as reformer Lionel Barrymore resists but eventually succumbs to the sins of the flesh. B&W; 97m. **DIR:** Raoul Walsh. **CAST:** Gloria Swanson, Raoul Walsh, Lionel Barrymore. **1928**

SADIST, THE 🦃 A serial killer and his girlfriend terrorize three teachers stranded in the middle of nowhere. Not rated; contains some violence. B&W; 90m. **DIR:** James Landis. **CAST:** Arch Hall Jr., Helen Hovey, Marilyn Manning. **1963 DVD**

SAFE ★★ San Fernando homemaker is a Stepford-like wife who is being polluted into a physical and mental meltdown by everything from car exhaust to insulting cocktail-hour jokes. She becomes a human Geiger counter to all that ails the world and seeks sanctuary at a New Age health ranch managed by an AIDS-infected motivational guru. The film is visually striking, provocative, and exasperating. Rated R for nudity, sex, and language. 119m. **DIR:** Todd Haynes. **CAST:** Julianne Moore, Xander Berkeley, Peter Friedman, Mary Carver, James LeGros, Jessica Harper. **1995 DVD**

SAFE HOUSE ★★★1/2 Just because you're paranoid doesn't mean they aren't *really* out to get you. Truer words were never spoken in this clever yarn, which concerns a senior citizen who keeps his wits sharpened with violent tactical exercises and has turned his home into a fortress. He claims it's for personal safety, because of something from his "former career"; his daughter, fearing senility, initiates a compromise in the form of a new housekeeper-companion whose efforts to gain her client's trust have unexpected results. Rated R for violence, profanity, and nudity. 112m. **DIR:** Eric Steven Stahl. **CAST:** Patrick Stewart, Kimberly Williams, Joy Kilpatrick, Craig Shoemaker, James Harlow, Hector Elizondo. **1997 DVD**

SAFE MEN ★★★1/2 Madcap comedy about two lousy lounge singers who are mistaken by the mob for a safecracking team. Steve Zahn and Sam Rockwell go from inept lounge singers to inept burglars, all in the name of comedy and a good time. There's a lot to admire about this quirky little exercise in mistaken identity. Rated R for language and adult situations. 89m. **DIR:** John Hamburg. **CAST:** Steve Zahn, Sam Rockwell, Harvey Fierstein, Paul Giamatti, Michael Lerner. **1998**

SAFE PASSAGE ★★★1/2 An overprotective mother is pushed to her emotional limits when she fears her son's death in a military explosion and must wait for official notice. Her care-giving eldest son tries to keep the family together while Mom is losing it. Her estranged husband just wants to return to their home and marriage. Thought-provoking look inside a family's pathos. Rated PG-13 for drug use and mature themes. 98m. **DIR:** Robert Allen Ackerman. **CAST:** Susan Sarandon, Sam Shepard, Robert Sean Leonard, Nick Stahl, Marcia Gay Harden. **1994**

SAFETY LAST ★★★★ Country bumpkin Harold Lloyd sets out to make his fortune in the big city, and eventually winds up—in one of the most famous images in movie history—dangling from a clock on the side of a tall building. Outstanding silent comedy is hilarious and exciting; Lloyd knows exactly how far to push the skyscraper derring-do before whisking his hero to safety. Not rated. B&W; 78m. **DIR:** Fred Newmeyer, Sam Taylor. **CAST:** Harold Lloyd, Mildred Davis, Bill Strothers, Noah Young. **1923**

SAGA OF DEATH VALLEY ★★1/2 Early Roy Rogers film finds him fighting a gang of outlaws led by a desperado who turns out to be his own brother! This well-produced Western isn't lacking in action and excitement. B&W; 56m. **DIR:** Joseph Kane. **CAST:** Roy Rogers, George "Gabby" Hayes, Don Barry. **1939**

SAGA OF THE VIKING WOMEN AND THEIR VOYAGE TO THE WATERS OF THE GREAT SEA SERPENT, THE (VIKING WOMEN AND THE SEA SERPENT, THE) 🦃 Even director Roger Corman called this Nordic snoozer, "One of the biggest mistakes of my life." B&W; 66m. **DIR:** Roger Corman. **CAST:** Abby Dalton, Susan Cabot. **1957**

SAGEBRUSH TRAIL ★★★ Big John Wayne, almost before he was shaving, is sent to prison for a murder he didn't commit. Naturally, our hero breaks out of the big house to clear his name. In a nice twist, he becomes friends—unknowingly—with the killer, who dies bravely in a climactic shoot-out. Good B Western. B&W; 58m. **DIR:** Armand Schaefer. **CAST:** John Wayne, Nancy Shubert, Lane Chandler, Yakima Canutt. **1933 DVD**

SAHARA ★★★1/2 One of the better war films, this production contains plenty of action, suspense, and characterization. Humphrey Bogart plays the head of a British-American unit stranded in the desert. The soldiers must keep the ever-present Nazi forces at bay while searching for the precious water they need to stay alive. It's a down-to-the-bone, exciting World War II drama. B&W; 97m. **DIR:** Zoltán Korda. **CAST:** Humphrey Bogart, Bruce Bennett, Lloyd Bridges, Dan Duryea, J. Carrol Naish. **1943 DVD**

SAHARA (1984) 🦃 A young heiress enters "the world's most treacherous auto race" (across the Sahara

Desert). Rated PG for violence and profanity. 104m. **DIR:** Andrew V. McLaglen. **CAST:** Brooke Shields, Lambert Wilson, Horst Buchholz, John Rhys-Davies, John Mills. **1984**

SAHARA (1995) ★★★1/2 James Belushi steps capably into Humphrey Bogart's shoes in this solid remake, assisted by a strong supporting cast. This old-style WWII drama pits our heroes and a temperamental tank dubbed Lulubelle against hundreds of German soldiers determined to take control of a prized desert well. Full of heroics, impossible odds, and noble deaths. Rated PG-13 for violence and profanity. 105m. **DIR:** Brian Trenchard-Smith. **CAST:** James Belushi, Alan David Lee, Simon Westaway, Mark Lee, Jerome Ehlers. **1995**

SAIGON COMMANDOS ★★1/2 In Vietnam, U.S. military cop Richard Young investigates the murders of local drug dealers. Okay action drama, with more than a passing resemblance to *Off Limits* (though this was made earlier). Rated R for strong violence and profanity. 91m. **DIR:** Clark Henderson. **CAST:** Richard Young, P. J. Soles, John Allen Nelson. **1987**

SAILOR WHO FELL FROM GRACE WITH THE SEA, THE ★★ Much of Japanese culture remains misunderstood, and this inept adaptation of Yukio Mishima's novel is a perfect example. Kris Kristofferson doesn't have to stretch his limited abilities as an amiable sailor who falls in love with Sarah Miles. Rated R for violence and sex. 104m. **DIR:** Lewis John Carlino. **CAST:** Sarah Miles, Kris Kristofferson, Margo Cunningham, Earl Rhodes. **1976**

SAINT, THE (TV SERIES) ★★ Roger Moore honed his suavity in the series *The Saint*, and sparkled as international adventurer Simon Templar, a connoisseur of fine wine and women. The devilishly daring troubleshooter continually aided the police, who considered him a foe. Made in England, the production provided intriguing mysteries, witty dialogue, and solid action. Two episodes per tape, 100m. **DIR:** Roy Ward Baker, Leslie Norman. **CAST:** Roger Moore, Winsley Pithey, Norman Pitt, Ivor Dean, Percy Herbert, Ronald Radd, Lois Maxwell. **1963–1969 DVD**

SAINT, THE (1997) ★★ Big budget and lofty pretensions aside, this misfired mess bears more of a resemblance to the equally bombastic, big-screen desecration of *Mission: Impossible,* than to the Leslie Charteris character who delighted readers for more than half a century. Val Kilmer is much too dour in the title role. Charteris must be spinning in his grave. Rated PG-13 for violence and profanity. 116m. **DIR:** Phillip Noyce. **CAST:** Val Kilmer, Elisabeth Shue, Rade Serbedzija, Valery Nikolaev. **1997 DVD**

ST. BENNY THE DIP ★★ A good cast is about all that recommends this time-worn story of con artists who disguise their larceny behind clerics' robes and find themselves thinking clearer and walking the straight and narrow as a result of their contact with religion. B&W; 79m. **DIR:** Edgar G. Ulmer. **CAST:** Dick Haymes, Nina Foch, Roland Young, Lionel Stander, Freddie Bartholomew. **1951**

ST. ELMO'S FIRE ★★★ This film would have us believe a group of college graduates are, at the age of 22, all suffering from mid-life crises. However, fine acting by some of the screen's hottest young stars helps us forgive this off-kilter premise. The movie succeeds almost in spite of itself. Rated R for suggested sex, violence, nudity, and profanity. 110m. **DIR:** Joel Schumacher. **CAST:** Emilio Estevez, Rob Lowe, Andrew McCarthy, Demi Moore, Judd Nelson, Ally Sheedy, Mare Winningham, Martin Balsam, Andie MacDowell, Joyce Van Patten. **1985 DVD**

ST. HELENS ★★1/2 Very shallow look at the Mount St. Helens volcanic eruption and the following disasters. Art Carney plays Harry, the old man who refuses to move from his home. Pretty bland stuff. Rated PG for no particular reason. 90m. **DIR:** Ernest Pintoff. **CAST:** Art Carney, David Huffman, Cassie Yates, Albert Salmi, Ron O'Neal. **1981**

•ST. FRANCISVILLE EXPERIMENT, THE 🦃 In this horrid rip-off of *The Blair Witch Project*, four video-camera-wielding students spend an evening in a haunted house, hoping to document actual ghost footage. Cheesy, fake effects, intentionally amateur camera work, and deplorable acting make for a hackneyed waste of time. Rated PG-13 for language and spookiness. 77m. **CAST:** Paul Palmer, Madison Charap, Ryan Larson, Tim Baldwin. **2000 DVD**

SAINT IN LONDON, THE ★★★ George Sanders as The Saint is up to his halo in spies, murder, and intrigue in this entertaining series entry, the second to star Sanders as Simon Templar. Entrusted to protect a foreign ambassador from hired killers, The Saint fails and feels honor-bound to track down the culprits. This handsome programmer is fun to watch. B&W; 72m. **DIR:** John Paddy Carstairs. **CAST:** George Sanders, Sally Gray, David Burns, Ralph Truman. **1939**

SAINT IN NEW YORK, THE ★★★ The first of Leslie Charteris's popular crime novels to hit the screen, this smooth adventure features Louis Hayward as The Saint, gentleman crime fighter, and his efforts to put an end to six gangsters who have been plaguing their metropolis. Hayward is fine in the title role. B&W; 71m. **DIR:** Ben Holmes. **CAST:** Louis Hayward, Kay Sutton, Jonathan Hale, Jack Carson, Sig Ruman. **1938**

ST. IVES ★★★1/2 This is a good Charles Bronson film about a former police reporter who becomes involved in a murder. Director J. Lee Thompson pulls an understated and believable performance out of the star. Rated PG. 93m. **DIR:** J. Lee Thompson. **CAST:** Charles Bronson, Jacqueline Bisset, John Houseman, Maximilian Schell, Harry Guardino, Dana Elcar, Dick O'Neill, Elisha Cook Jr. **1976 DVD**

SAINT JACK ★★★ Although an interesting film, it lacks power and a sense of wholeness. Ben Gazzara plays an oddly likable pimp plying his trade in Singapore in the 1970s who wants to become rich and powerful by running the classiest whorehouse in the Far East. Rated R. 112m. **DIR:** Peter Bogdanovich. **CAST:** Ben Gazzara, Denholm Elliott, James Villiers, Joss Ackland, Peter Bogdanovich, George Lazenby. **1979**

SAINT JOAN ★★ Even a screenplay by Graham Greene can't salvage Otto Preminger's dull screen version of George Bernard Shaw's intriguing play. Jean Seberg seems at a loss and the presence of such performers as Richard Widmark and John Gielgud just remind one what could have been. B&W; 110m. **DIR:** Otto Preminger. **CAST:** Jean Seberg, Richard Widmark, Richard Todd, John Gielgud, Anton Walbrook, Harry Andrews, Felix Aylmer. **1957**

SAINT MAYBE ★★★★ Whimsical *Hallmark Hall of Fame* special features Thomas McCarthy as a college student who blames himself for his brother's suicide. Suddenly feeling responsible for his brother's stepchildren, he begins a dramatic metamorphosis from self-centered teenager to loving parent. Although the plot is activated by the family's loss, there are a number of humorous scenes. Not rated; contains mature themes. 92m. **DIR:** Michael Pressman. **CAST:** Thomas McCarthy, Mary-Louise Parker, Blythe Danner, Edward Herrmann. **1998**

SAINT OF FORT WASHINGTON, THE ★★★1/2 Well-acted drama focuses on two homeless men struggling to survive both physically and spiritually on the mean streets of New York. Matt Dillon is an emotionally troubled photographer who finds himself protected by streetwise Danny Glover in a strong film that goes somewhat astray in the last half. Rated R for violence and profanity. 103m. **DIR:** Tim Hunter. **CAST:** Matt Dillon, Danny Glover, Rick Aviles, Nina Siemaszko, Ving Rhames, Joe Seneca, Harry Ellington. **1993**

SAINT STRIKES BACK, THE ★★★ A good cast, a good story, and a charming performance by George Sanders as Simon Templar, debonair crime fighter, make this one of the best of a very pleasant series. Sanders, in his first appearance as the suave adventurer, pulls out all the stops in his efforts to clear the name of a dead policeman and straighten out his wayward daughter. B&W; 67m. **DIR:** John Farrow. **CAST:** George Sanders, Wendy Barrie, Jonathan Hale, Jerome Cowan, Neil Hamilton, Barry Fitzgerald. **1939**

ST. VALENTINE'S DAY MASSACRE, THE ★★ Watching the leads ham it up provides sporadic fun, but this gaudy gangster picture is long on violence and short on dramatic impact. Where's Eliot Ness when you need him? 100m. **DIR:** Roger Corman. **CAST:** Jason Robards Jr., George Segal, Ralph Meeker, Jean Hale, Frank Silvera, Joseph Campanella, Bruce Dern. **1967**

SAINT-EX ★★★ Made for the BBC, this biography of the French pilot who wrote the children's classic *The Little Prince* has the usual pros and cons of British television productions—nice to look at and well acted, but occasionally slow and too dry. Not rated. 90m. **DIR:** Anand Tucker. **CAST:** Bruno Ganz, Miranda Richardson, Janet McTeer, Katrin Cartlidge, Eleanor Bron. **1997**

SAINTS & SINNERS ★★ Best friends wind up on different sides of the law in this crime-thriller. Pooch becomes a cop. His friend "Big Boy" Baynes becomes a drug dealer. When they both fall for the same woman, Pooch uses Baynes as bait in a sting operation. When it starts to fall apart, Pooch must choose between his loyalty to his friend or his badge. Rated R for violence, nudity, adult situations, and language. 99m. **DIR:** Paul Mones. **CAST:** Damian Chapa, Jennifer Rubin, Scott Plank, William Atherton. **1994**

SAINT'S VACATION, THE ★★ Simon Templar finds mystery and adventure instead of peace and quiet when he encounters intrigue on his vacation attempt. Hugh Sinclair plays the sophisticated Saint for the first time. Passable, but not up to the earlier entries in the series. B&W; 60m. **DIR:** Leslie Fenton. **CAST:** Hugh Sinclair, Sally Gray, Arthur Macrae, Cecil Parker, Gordon McLeod. **1941**

SAKHAROV ★★★★ Compassionate story of the nuclear physicist and designer of the H-bomb, Andrei Sakharov (Jason Robards), who won the Nobel Peace Prize after waking up to the global terror of the nuclear gambit and contributing to the budding human rights movement in the Soviet Union during the late 1960s. 118m. **DIR:** Jack Gold. **CAST:** Jason Robards Jr., Glenda Jackson, Michael Bryant, Paul Freeman, Anna Massey, Joe Melia, Jim Norton. **1984**

SALAAM BOMBAY! ★★★★1/2 In the most potent film about street children since Hector Babenco's *Pixote*, director Mira Nair takes us on a sobering, heartrending tour of the back alleys and gutters of India. It is there that young Krishna (Shafiq Syed) must struggle to survive among the drug dealers, pimps, and prostitutes. In Hindi with English subtitles. Not rated, the film has profanity, violence, and suggested sex. 113m. **DIR:** Mira Nair. **CAST:** Shafiq Syed, Sarfuddin Qurrassi. **1988**

SALAMANDER, THE 🦃 Abysmal political action-thriller. Rated R; contains violence and profanity. 101m. **DIR:** Peter Zinner. **CAST:** Franco Nero, Anthony Quinn, Martin Balsam, Sybil Danning, Christopher Lee, Cleavon Little, Paul Smith, Claudia Cardinale, Eli Wallach. **1981**

SALEM'S LOT ★★★★ This story of vampires in modern-day New England is one of the better adaptations of Stephen King's novels on film. Some real chills go along with an intelligent script in what was originally a two-part TV movie. 112m. **DIR:** Tobe Hooper. **CAST:** David Soul, James Mason, Reggie Nalder, Lance Kerwin, Elisha Cook Jr., Ed Flanders, Bonnie Bedelia. **1979 DVD**

SALLAH ★★★ Haym Topol, the future star of *Fiddler on the Roof*, is the main reason to see this comedy about a Jewish family who moves to Israel only to find that life still isn't a bed of roses. Though it was nominated for the Oscar for best foreign language film, it's primitively made and miscasts Topol as a man much older than he was at the time. In Hebrew with English subtitles. B&W; 105m. **DIR:** Ephraim Kishon. **CAST:** Topol, Geula Noni, Esther Greenberg. **1964**

SALLY OF THE SAWDUST ★★★★ W. C. Fields is at his brilliant best as the lovable con-man guardian of pretty Carol Dempster in this early film of his Broadway hit, *Poppy*. Knowing the identity of her wealthy grandparents, he works to restore her to her rightful place in society, does so after a variety of problems, and says farewell with the now-classic line—Fields's accepted credo—"Never give a sucker an even break." Silent. B&W; 91m. **DIR:** D. W. Griffith. **CAST:** Carol Dempster, W. C. Fields, Alfred Lunt. **1925 DVD**

SALO: 120 DAYS OF SODOM 🦃 A shocking, repulsive film set during World War II in Italy, where a group of bourgeois Fascists brutalize and sexually degrade teenagers. In Italian with English subtitles. Not rated; contains scenes of graphic sex and violence. 115m. **DIR:** Pier Paolo Pasolini. **CAST:** Paolo Bonacelli. **1975**

SALOME (1923) ★★ Campy silent version of Oscar Wilde's play. Rejected and cursed by John the Baptist, Salome plans her revenge. B&W; 48m. **DIR:** Charles Bryant. **CAST:** Anna Nazimova. **1923**

SALOME (1953) ★★ Biblical belly dancer Salome (Rita Hayworth) offers herself up as a sacrifice to save John the Baptist (Stewart Granger). Inane. 103m. **DIR:**

William Dieterle. **CAST:** Rita Hayworth, Stewart Granger, Judith Anderson, Charles Laughton, Cedric Hardwicke. **1953**

SALOME (1985) ★1/2 This is a strange mixture. It is the story of the famous temptress Salome, but in director Claude D'Anna's version the Roman soldiers are in World War II overcoats, there is an elevator in the palace, and the slaves are listening to portable radios. Whatever he had in mind, it doesn't make it. Rated R. 105m. **DIR:** Claude D'Anna. **CAST:** Jo Ciampa, Tomas Milian, Tim Woodward. **1985**

SALOME, WHERE SHE DANCED 🦃 Yvonne De Carlo plays an exotic dancer in the American West. 90m. **DIR:** Charles Lamont. **CAST:** Yvonne De Carlo, Rod Cameron, Walter Slezak, David Bruce, Albert Dekker, Marjorie Rambeau. **1945**

SALOME'S LAST DANCE ★★★★ Ken Russell pays homage to Oscar Wilde in this outrageous dark comedy that takes place in 1895 London. A group of eccentric actors enact Wilde's play *Salome* in the most bizarre setting imaginable: a brothel. Glenda Jackson is simply remarkable, and she's supported by an equally gifted cast in this brilliantly staged surreal fantasy. Rated R for nudity and profanity. 93m. **DIR:** Ken Russell. **CAST:** Glenda Jackson, Stratford Johns, Nickolas Grace, Douglas Hodge, Imogen Millais Scott. **1988 DVD**

SALT OF THE EARTH ★★★ Miners in New Mexico go on strike after a series of accidents and face a long, bitter battle. This once-controversial melodrama uses real mine workers in the cast and has a realistic feel. B&W; 94m. **DIR:** Herbert J. Biberman. **CAST:** Rosoura Revueltas, Will Geer. **1953 DVD**

SALT WATER MOOSE ★★★1/2 This charming family drama is set in Canada's rugged Nova Scotia, where baseball-loving city kid Johnny Morina encounters a pert local girl (Katharine Isobel) on a mission. Since a bull moose has trapped itself (during low tide) on one of the many small islands surrounding their cove, she plans to provide a mate by capturing a female moose and transporting it across the small stretch of ocean. Utterly delightful. Rated G. 100m. **DIR:** Stuart Margolin. **CAST:** Johnny Morina, Katharine Isobel, Timothy Dalton, Lolita Davidovich. **1995**

SALTMEN OF TIBET, THE ★★★ This meditative documentary chronicles a traditional spring trek to an isolated lake by Tibetan nomads. It explores the rituals, hardships, legends, and social etiquette of the journey as well as the personalities of tribesmen who perpetuate this vanishing lifestyle. Rural vistas encountered by the nomads and their yak caravan are stunning. Not rated. 110m. **DIR:** Ulrike Koch. **1998 DVD**

SALUT L'ARTISTE ★★★1/2 A struggling middle-aged actor, who works primarily in commercials, tries to reconcile with his ex-wife. Bittersweet comedy about the eternal appeal of show business, with Marcello Mastroianni perfectly cast as a man finally realizing that his dreams are unlikely to come true. In French with English subtitles. Not rated; contains brief nudity. 96m. **DIR:** Yves Robert. **CAST:** Marcello Mastroianni, Françoise Fabian, Jean Rochefort. **1973**

SALVADOR ★★★★ James Woods plays screenwriter-photojournalist Richard Boyle in the latter's semiautobiographical account of the events that occurred in El Salvador circa 1980–81. It is a fascinating movie despite its flaws and outrageousness. Rated R for profanity, nudity, suggested sex, drug use, and violence. 120m. **DIR:** Oliver Stone. **CAST:** James Woods, John Savage, James Belushi, Michael Murphy, Elpidia Carrillo, Tony Plana, Cynthia Gibb. **1986**

SALVATION ★★★1/2 A punk's wife sends the family cash to a televangelist. Angered, the punk has his teenage sister-in-law seduce the preacher and then blackmails him into sharing his religious revenues. Beth B., who directed and shares writing and production credits, has delivered a raw, insightful film. Rated R for nudity and profanity. 80m. **DIR:** Beth B. **CAST:** Stephen McHattie, Dominique Davalos, Exene Cervenka. **1986**

SALZBURG CONNECTION, THE ★★ This incredibly bad spy film set in Europe has Barry Newman playing an American lawyer on vacation who gets mixed up with Nazi spies. Rated PG for violence and language. 93m. **DIR:** Lee H. Katzin. **CAST:** Barry Newman, Anna Karina, Joe Maross, Wolfgang Preiss, Helmut Schmid, Udo Kier, Klaus Maria Brandauer. **1972**

SAMANTHA ★★★ Upon learning she was adopted, a 21-year-old eccentric sets about to discover her "real" self. Martha Plimpton's acerbic lead performance helps to balance a too-cute script. A pleasant diversion. Rated PG for profanity. 101m. **DIR:** Stephen La Rocque. **CAST:** Martha Plimpton, Dermot Mulroney, Hector Elizondo, Mary Kay Place, Ione Skye. **1992**

SAMARITAN: THE MITCH SNYDER STORY ★★★★ Martin Sheen portrays a nonviolent activist named Mitch Snyder, who successfully convinces city officials to deal with the problems of the homeless. Sensitive made-for-TV biography. 90m. **DIR:** Richard T. Heffron. **CAST:** Martin Sheen, Roxanne Hart, Cicely Tyson. **1986**

SAME TIME NEXT YEAR ★★★★ Funny, touching film begins with an accidental meeting in 1951 between two married strangers at a rural California inn. Doris (Ellen Burstyn) is a young housewife from California, and George (Alan Alda) an accountant from New Jersey. Their meetings become an annual event. And through them, we see the changes in America and its people as we return to the same cottage every five years until 1977. Rated PG. 117m. **DIR:** Robert Mulligan. **CAST:** Ellen Burstyn, Alan Alda. **1978**

SAMMY AND ROSIE GET LAID ★★★★ Excellent sexual farce set in riot-torn East London concerns a young married couple who receive an unexpected visit from Sammy's father, an arrogant politician who is fleeing from a Middle Eastern country. His world becomes shaken up by the couple's sexually liberated, anarchic friends. Outrageous comedy from the creators of *My Beautiful Laundrette*. Not rated; contains nudity and violence. 97m. **DIR:** Stephen Frears. **CAST:** Shashi Kapoor, Frances Barber, Claire Bloom, Ayub Khan Din. **1987**

SAMMY, THE WAY-OUT SEAL ★★1/2 Better than the title would imply. This series of misadventures involves two young brothers and the seal they attempt to keep as a pet. The film moves along briskly and features larger-than-life comic Jack Carson in one of his last performances. 89m. **DIR:** Norman Tokar. **CAST:** Jack Carson, Robert Culp, Patricia Barry, Billy Mumy, Ann Jillian, Michael McGreevey, Elisabeth Fraser. **1962**

SAM'S SON ★★★1/2 Written and directed by Michael Landon, this sweetly nostalgic semiautobiographical family film features Timothy Patrick Murphy as the young Eugene Orowitz (Landon's real name), whose parents, Sam (Eli Wallach) and Harriet (Anne Jackson), seem destined never to realize their fondest dreams until their son lends a hand. Rated PG for brief violence. 104m. **DIR:** Michael Landon. **CAST:** Timothy Patrick Murphy, Eli Wallach, Anne Jackson. **1984**

SAMSON Samson uses his strength to restore peace in his kingdom. This dubbed film is a yawner. 99m. **DIR:** Gianfranco Parolini. **CAST:** Brad Harris, Bridgette Corey. **1960**

SAMSON AND DELILAH (1949) ★★★★ This Cecil B. DeMille extravaganza still looks good today. Hedy Lamarr plays the beautiful vixen Delilah, who robs Samson (Victor Mature) of his incredible strength. Dumb but fun. 128m. **DIR:** Cecil B. DeMille. **CAST:** Hedy Lamarr, Victor Mature, George Sanders, Angela Lansbury. **1949**

SAMSON AND DELILAH (1984) ★★1/2 An okay TV remake of the DeMille classic that had Victor Mature in the lead. This time, Mature plays Samson's father. Mature and the other veteran actors (Max von Sydow and José Ferrer) help to save the movie. Lots of action—lions, chains, and crumbling masonry. 100m. **DIR:** Lee Philips. **CAST:** Antony Hamilton, Belinda Bauer, Max von Sydow, Stephen Macht, Maria Schell, José Ferrer, Victor Mature. **1984**

SAMSON AND DELILAH (1996) ★★ Disappointing biblical miniseries from the Turner Network suffers from a lack of believability on the part of the principal players. Eric Thal as Samson seems temperamental and immature rather than historically significant, and Dennis Hopper, as an enlightened Philistine, sleepwalks through his scenes. Not rated; contains sexual situations and violence. 175m. **DIR:** Nicolas Roeg. **CAST:** Eric Thal, Elizabeth Hurley, Dennis Hopper, Diana Rigg, Paul Freeman, Michael Gambon. **1996**

SAMURAI COWBOY ★★★ A workaholic Japanese businessman who longs for a home on the range bites the bullet and buys himself a dilapidated Wyoming ranch. Veterinarian Catherine Mary Stewart provides romance and Robert Conrad is around for some old-fashioned macho wrangling. Even if the goings get goofy, straight-faced Go is such a delight you'll find this more endearing than it has a right to be. Rated PG for mild profanity and violence. 101m. **DIR:** Michael Keusch. **CAST:** Hiromi Go, Matt McCoy, Catherine Mary Stewart, Robert Conrad, Conchata Ferrell. **1993**

SAMURAI REINCARNATION ★★ Weak adventure yarn about a shogunate warrior who rises from the dead. Gory Japanese metaphysical drama. In Japanese with English subtitles. Not rated; contains nudity and graphic violence. 122m. **DIR:** Kinji Fukasaku. **1981**

SAMURAI SAGA ★★★ Toshiro Mifune is in top form as a gallant samurai who challenges a powerful warrior clan in 1599 Japan while getting caught up in a love triangle involving a beautiful princess. Great action sequences. In Japanese with English subtitles. B&W; 112m. **DIR:** Hiroshi Inagaki. **CAST:** Toshiro Mifune. **1959**

SAMURAI TRILOGY, THE ★★★★★ This brilliant and cinematically beautiful three-deck epic tells the story of the legendary Japanese hero Musashi Miyamoto, a sixteenth-century samurai who righted wrongs in the fashion of Robin Hood and Zorro. The film follows Miyamoto from his wild youth through spiritual discovery to the final battle with his archenemy, Sasaki Kojiro. The samurai film for the uninitiated. In Japanese with English subtitles. B&W; 303m. **DIR:** Hiroshi Inagaki. **CAST:** Toshiro Mifune, Koji Tsuruta. **1954**

SAN ANTONIO ★★★ Sturdy Warner Bros. Western pits Errol Flynn against villain Victor Francen, with Alexis Smith in the middle. Nothing new, just solid action and production values. Final shoot-out at the Alamo is pretty good. 111m. **DIR:** David Butler. **CAST:** Errol Flynn, Alexis Smith, Victor Francen, S. Z. Sakall, Paul Kelly, Florence Bates. **1945**

SAN ANTONIO KID ★★★1/2 Outlaws use violence and vandalism to scare ranchers off oil-rich rangeland until Red Ryder and Little Beaver intervene with blazing guns. B&W; 59m. **DIR:** Howard Bretherton. **CAST:** William Elliot, Robert Blake, Alice Fleming, Linda Stirling, Glenn Strange, Duncan Renaldo. **1944**

SAN FERNANDO VALLEY ★★1/2 Cowgirls replace cowboys on a large cattle ranch. Nevertheless, Roy Rogers is brought in to rid the valley of the lawless element. Roy got his first screen kiss, from Jean Porter, in this leisurely paced oater, which was the year's number one box-office Western. B&W; 54m. **DIR:** John English. **CAST:** Roy Rogers, Dale Evans, Bob Nolan and the Sons of the Pioneers, Jean Porter. **1944**

SAN FRANCISCO ★★★★ In its heyday, MGM boasted it had more stars than were in the heavens, and it made some terrific star-studded movies as a result. Take this 1936 production, starring Clark Gable, Jeanette MacDonald, and Spencer Tracy, for example. It's entertainment of the first order, with special effects—of the San Francisco earthquake—that still stand up today. B&W; 115m. **DIR:** W. S. Van Dyke. **CAST:** Clark Gable, Jeanette MacDonald, Spencer Tracy. **1936**

SANCTUARY OF FEAR ★★ Barnard Hughes does a fine job of bringing G. K. Chesterton's crime-busting priest, Father Brown, to life. Unfortunately, the rest of the cast seems detached from the action. This TV movie contains violence. 98m. **DIR:** John Llewellyn Moxey. **CAST:** Barnard Hughes, Kay Lenz, Michael McGuire, George Hearn. **1979**

•SAND ★★ A good cast gets buried in the sand in this predictable revenge thriller. Michael Vartan stars as Tyler Briggs, a man on the run from his violent family, looking for a new start and a life free of brutality. He believes he's found paradise when he returns to his old childhood home in a small secluded beach town. Just as he hooks up with a new girlfriend and sees the light at the end of the tunnel, his brothers show up to teach him a lesson. Filled with nasty characters doing nasty things to each other, it's easy to stand behind Briggs and his mission to end the nightmare forever. Not rated; contains adult situations, language, and violence. 89m. **DIR:** Matt Palmieri. **CAST:** Michael Vartan, Kari Wuhrer, Denis Leary, Harry Dean Stanton, Julie Delpy, Jon Lovitz, Emilio Estevez. **2000 DVD**

SAND AND BLOOD ★★1/2 Brooding drama that explores the relationship between a young, gifted matador and a cultivated doctor-musician. Both leads give exceptional performances that get lost in this slow-moving drama. In French with English subtitles. Not rated;

contains nudity and violence. 101m. **DIR:** Jeanne Labrune. **CAST:** Patrick Catalifo, Sami Frey. **1987**

SAND PEBBLES, THE ★★★1/2 Steve McQueen is compelling as Hollman, an ordinary seaman on an American warship stationed off China in 1925. He prefers to remain below deck with his only love, the ship's engines. That way he avoids involvement or decisions. When he is forced to become involved with the world outside his engine room, the result is an enjoyable, sweeping epic with unforgettable characters. 179m. **DIR:** Robert Wise. **CAST:** Steve McQueen, Richard Crenna, Richard Attenborough, Candice Bergen, Mako, Simon Oakland, Gavin MacLeod. **1966 DVD**

SANDAKAN NO. 8 ★★★★ Penetrating drama about a female journalist who becomes friends with an old woman who had been sold into prostitution and sent to Borneo in the early 1900s. Winner at the Berlin Film Festival and nominated for an Academy Award. In Japanese with English subtitles. Not rated, but is recommended for adult viewers. 121m. **DIR:** Kei Kumai. **CAST:** Kinuyo Tanaka. **1974**

SANDERS OF THE RIVER ★★1/2 "Sandy the lawgiver" is the heavy right hand of the British Empire in this action-drama of colonialism in darkest Africa. Paul Robeson rises above demeaning circumstances and fills the screen with his commanding presence. Great footage of the people and terrain of Africa add to the mood of this adventure and give it an aura lacking in many jungle films. B&W; 98m. **DIR:** Zoltán Korda. **CAST:** Paul Robeson, Leslie Banks, Nina Mae McKinney, Robert Cochran. **1935**

SANDLOT, THE ★★★1/2 Youngsters will get a big kick out of this kids'-eye-view story of what happens when a shy boy moves to a new neighborhood and becomes involved with a ragtag baseball team. Wonderfully funny moments mix with a few ineffective ones for a show that will even keep Mom and Dad entertained. Rated PG for scary stuff. 100m. **DIR:** David Mickey Evans. **CAST:** Karen Allen, Denis Leary, James Earl Jones, Arliss Howard, Tom Guiry. **1993 DVD**

SANDMAN (1992) ★★ The director-star of this low-budget spooker died after principal photography, and we can only imagine that he might have made more sense of it in the editing stage. As it is, this story about a house that contains a door to its past has some effective moments but is too confused. Top-billed Robert Wuhl has only a cameo role, as do reunited *Dick Van Dyke Show* costars Morey Amsterdam and Rose Marie. Not rated; contains violence and profanity. 92m. **DIR:** Eric Woster. **CAST:** Eric Woster, Dedee Pfeiffer, Frank Rhodes, Stuart Whitman, Robert Wuhl. **1992**

SANDMAN, THE (1996) ★★★★ An insomniac writer discovers late one night that someone or something is murdering the residents of the trailer park while they sleep. The film emerges as a triumph of suspense and terror, proving that a good horror film doesn't need elaborate gore effects to be scary. Highly recommended for horror fans, this one will leave you checking under your bed and in the closet. Not rated; contains violence and profanity. 90m. **DIR:** J. R. Bookwalter. **CAST:** A. J. Richards, Rita Gutowski, Stan Fitzgerald. **1996**

SANDPIPER, THE Corny love triangle. 116m. **DIR:** Vincente Minnelli. **CAST:** Richard Burton, Elizabeth Taylor, Eva Marie Saint, Charles Bronson. **1965**

SANDS OF IWO JIMA ★★★★1/2 Superb war film. The Duke was never better than as the haunted Sergeant Stryker, a man hated by his men (with a few exceptions) for his unyielding toughness, but it is by that attitude that he hopes to keep them alive in combat. Watch it and see how good the Duke really was. B&W; 110m. **DIR:** Allan Dwan. **CAST:** John Wayne, John Agar, Forrest Tucker, Richard Jaeckel, Arthur Franz. **1949 DVD**

SANJURO ★★★★1/2 First-rate sequel to *Yojimbo* has the original "Man With No Name" (Toshiro Mifune) again stirring up trouble in feudal Japan. He is recruited by several young would-be samurai as their teacher and leader in exposing corruption in their clan. In his usual gentle manner, Mifune wreaks all sorts of havoc while occasionally warning, "Watch it, I'm in a bad mood." In Japanese with English subtitles. B&W; 96m. **DIR:** Akira Kurosawa. **CAST:** Toshiro Mifune, Tatsuya Nakadai, Takashi Shimura. **1962 DVD**

SANSHIRO SUGATA ★★★1/2 In this vintage film directed by Akira Kurosawa, Sanshiro Sugata (Susumu Fujita) is among the strongest practitioners of judo, but spiritually he is weak. Can he find inner strength and purity? This is an elegant film about spiritual triumph. In Japanese with English subtitles. B&W; 82m. **DIR:** Akira Kurosawa. **CAST:** Susumu Fujita, Takashi Shimura. **1943**

SANSHO THE BAILIFF ★★★ This beautifully photographed tale presents the suffering and heroism of a mother who is separated from her two children by a brutal man called Sansho. A poetic film that exhibits the humanism for which director Kenji Mizoguchi is well-known. In Japanese with English subtitles. B&W; 125m. **DIR:** Kenji Mizoguchi. **CAST:** Kinuyo Tanaka. **1954**

SANTA CLAUS CONQUERS THE MARTIANS About a bunch of aliens abducting St. Nick because they don't have one of their own. 80m. **DIR:** Nicholas Webster. **CAST:** John Call, Leonard Hicks. **1964**

SANTA CLAUS—THE MOVIE ★★★ In this enjoyable family film, one of Santa's helpers (Dudley Moore), visits Earth and innocently joins forces with an evil toy manufacturer (delightfully played by John Lithgow). It is up to Santa (David Huddleston) to save him—and the spirit of Christmas. Rated PG for light profanity and adult themes. 105m. **DIR:** Jeannot Szwarc. **CAST:** Dudley Moore, John Lithgow, David Huddleston, Burgess Meredith, Judy Cornwell. **1985**

SANTA CLAUSE, THE ★★★★ TV star–comedian Tim Allen crosses over to the big screen in this light-hearted, humorous tale. An advertising executive finds himself filling in for Santa Claus when the big guy tumbles to his death after being caught unawares on our hero's roof. Slight story works primarily because of Allen's wry wit and charm, and the result is a movie destined to be a holiday perennial. Rated PG. 97m. **DIR:** John Pasquin. **CAST:** Tim Allen, Judge Reinhold, Wendy Crewson, Eric Lloyd, David Krumholtz, Peter Boyle, Larry Brandenburg, Mary Gross, Paige Tamada. **1994 DVD**

SANTA CLAWS ★★ Not much of a shocker here with a nutcase in a Santa suit killing people. Fans of writer-director John Russo's *Night of the Living Dead* can look for Karl Hardman and Marilyn Eastman in cameos. Not rated; contains violence, nudity, and profanity. 85m. **DIR:** John Russo. **CAST:** Debbie Rochon. **1996 DVD**

SANTA FE MARSHAL ★★1/2 Hopalong Cassidy goes undercover with a medicine show. B&W; 54m. **DIR:** Lesley Selander. **CAST:** William Boyd, Russell Hayden. **1940**

SANTA FE SADDLEMATES ★★★★1/2 Government investigator Sunset Carson sets out to bust up a diamond-smuggling ring along the U.S.-Mexican border. Top-notch action makes this the best of Carson's fifteen Republic Westerns. B&W; 56m. **DIR:** Thomas Carr. **CAST:** Sunset Carson, Linda Stirling, Olin Howlin, Roy Barcroft. **1945**

SANTA FE STAMPEDE ★★1/2 The Three Mesquiteers (John Wayne, Ray Corrigan, and Max Terhune) ride to the rescue of an old friend (William Farnum) who strikes it rich with a gold mine. A villain (LeRoy Mason) is trying to steal his claim. Lightweight Western with plenty of action. B&W; 58m. **DIR:** George Sherman. **CAST:** John Wayne, Ray "Crash" Corrigan, Max Terhune, William Farnum, LeRoy Mason. **1938**

SANTA FE TRAIL ★★★1/2 Errol Flynn, Alan Hale, and Olivia de Havilland save this muddled Western, with Ronald Reagan as one of Flynn's soldier buddies who go after John Brown (Raymond Massey). B&W; 110m. **DIR:** Michael Curtiz. **CAST:** Errol Flynn, Alan Hale Sr., Olivia de Havilland, Ronald Reagan, Raymond Massey, Ward Bond, Van Heflin. **1940 DVD**

SANTA FE UPRISING ★★★★ Allan Lane takes over the role of Red Ryder for this first of seven films. Outlaws kidnap Little Beaver to stop the duchess from taking over a toll road she has inherited. B&W; 55m. **DIR:** R. G. Springsteen. **CAST:** Allan "Rocky" Lane, Robert Blake, Barton MacLane, Jack LaRue, Dick Curtis. **1946**

SANTA SANGRE ★★★1/2 A disturbed young man who kills at the behest of his armless mother. A weird and often wonderful surreal thriller that looks like a slasher film made by Federico Fellini with Salvador Dali as art director. Rated R for strong violence and sexual content. 124m. **DIR:** Alejandro Jodorowsky. **CAST:** Axel Jodorowsky, Guy Stockwell. **1990**

SANTA WITH MUSCLES ★★1/2 A health-food tycoon (Hulk Hogan) loses his memory in an accident and thinks he's Santa Claus. He then comes to the aid of an orphanage that is about to be shut down by a greedy real-estate developer. Silly holiday comedy is strictly for young kids. Rated PG for violence. 98m. **DIR:** John Murlowski. **CAST:** Hulk Hogan, Ed Begley Jr., Don Stack, Robin Curtis, Kevin West, Garrett Morris, Clint Howard. **1996**

SANTEE ★★1/2 Bounty hunter with a heart (Glenn Ford) loses his son and adopts the son of an outlaw he kills. A fine variety of old Western hands add zip to this otherwise average oater. As usual, Ford turns in a solid performance. PG. 93m. **DIR:** Gary Nelson. **CAST:** Glenn Ford, Dana Wynter, Michael Burns, Robert Donner, Jay Silverheels, Harry Townes, John Larch. **1973**

SAPPHIRE ★★★ This mystery about Scotland Yard detectives searching for the murderer of a young black woman was judged a failure at the time because of the reticent way it addressed then current racial tensions. Now it can be enjoyed as a solid police procedural. 92m. **DIR:** Basil Dearden. **CAST:** Nigel Patrick, Yvonne Mitchell, Michael Craig, Paul Massie, Bernard Miles. **1959**

SAPS AT SEA ★★★ Oliver Hardy contracts "hornophobia," and the only cure is rest and sea air. Comic timing is off and some of the jokes misfire, but enough of them work to make the movie enjoyable. B&W; 57m. **DIR:** Gordon Douglas. **CAST:** Oliver Hardy, Stan Laurel, Ben Turpin. **1940**

SARA DANE ★★ Headstrong eighteenth-century girl manages to raise her status through marriages as well as wise business decisions. This Australian film's premise is very similar to *A Woman of Substance*. 150m. **DIR:** Rod Hardy, Gary Conway. **CAST:** Harold Hopkins, Brenton Whittle. **1981**

SARAFINA! ★★★★1/2 Both rapturous and devastating, this antiapartheid musical rockets along, alternating song and dance with the horrors of life in a South African military state. It's a film about the irreversible decision one black schoolgirl is driven to make by forces of bigotry and oppression. Whoopi Goldberg's classy, moving performance as a Soweto schoolteacher is reason enough to snatch this movie up. Rated PG-13 for violence. 101m. **DIR:** Darrell Roodt. **CAST:** Whoopi Goldberg, Leleti Khumalo, Miriam Makeba. **1992**

SARAH, PLAIN AND TALL ★★★★ Heartwarming story of a headstrong New England spinster who answers an ad for a mail-order wife placed by a stoic Kansas widower with two children. Sarah says she's not looking for love, but love and special courage win the day just when it seems all is lost. First in a series of videotape releases of *Hallmark Hall of Fame* television presentations. Rated G. 98m. **DIR:** Glenn Jordan. **CAST:** Glenn Close, Christopher Walken, Lexi Randall, Margaret Sophie Stein, Jon De Vries, Christopher Bell. **1991 DVD**

SARATOGA ★★★ When Jean Harlow learns her late father lost control of their racehorse farm to bookie Clark Gable, she plots to win it back. Harlow died during production; many scenes were completed by her standin. B&W; 92m. **DIR:** Jack Conway. **CAST:** Clark Gable, Jean Harlow, Lionel Barrymore, Frank Morgan, Walter Pidgeon, Una Merkel, Hattie McDaniel. **1937**

SARDINE: KIDNAPPED ★★★ Intriguing adventure set on the Italian island of Sardinia. Peasants have traditionally obtained land by kidnapping members of wealthy families and ransoming them for land. One family has the courage to stand up to the bandits and informs the police. Directed by a former documentary filmmaker, this English-dubbed film benefits from a realistic look. 110m. **DIR:** Gianfranco Mingozzi. **CAST:** Franco Nero, Charlotte Rampling. **1968**

SATAN MET A LADY ★★ A pale shadow of *The Maltese Falcon*, using the same plot with different character names and a ram's horn instead of a statuette of a falcon. Bette Davis often ridiculed it as one of her worst pictures. B&W; 77m. **DIR:** William Dieterle. **CAST:** Bette Davis, Warren William, Alison Skipworth, Arthur Treacher, Marie Wilson, Winifred Shaw, Porter Hall. **1936**

SATANIC RITES OF DRACULA, THE ★★1/2 Substantially better than the previous year's appalling *Dracula A.D. 1972*, this is the final Hammer Films *Dracula* outing to star Christopher Lee and Peter Cushing as the count and his arch-foe, Professor Van Helsing. Actually it's Van Helsing's *grandson*, since this film is set in modern London. Rated R for nudity and gore. 88m. **DIR:**

Alan Gibson. **CAST:** Christopher Lee, Peter Cushing, Freddie Jones. **1973 DVD**

SATAN'S BED 🦃 An unfinished film starring Yoko Ono as a Japanese woman abandoned in Manhattan is padded out with unrelated footage of juvenile delinquents molesting Long Island housewives. It's a mess. Not rated; contains strong sexual content. B&W; 71m. **DIR:** Marshall Smith. **CAST:** Yoko Ono, Val Avery, Gene Nielson. **1965**

SATAN'S BREW ★★★ Wicked Rainer Werner Fassbinder comedy is dark and devious and will not sit easy with most, but for those willing to take a ride on the wild side, the trip is worth it. Fassbinder sets his sights on Artaud's Theater of Cruelty and depicts the crazy world of a hack poet who believes he is the reincarnation of a nineteenth-century German poet. His strange behavior incites family and friends. Not rated; contains adult situations. 112m. **DIR:** Rainer Werner Fassbinder. **CAST:** Kurt Raab, Helen Vita, Volker Spengler, Margit Carstensen. **1976**

SATAN'S CHEERLEADERS 🦃 Cheerleaders run afoul of a cult of Satanists. Rated PG. 92m. **DIR:** Greydon Clark. **CAST:** Kerry Sherman, John Ireland, Yvonne De Carlo, John Carradine, Jack Kruschen. **1977 DVD**

SATAN'S PRINCESS ★★ An ex-cop turned private detective takes on a missing-persons case that leads him straight to a centuries-old demoness, who kills people as often as she changes her wardrobe. Amateurish. Rated R for violence. 90m. **DIR:** Bert I. Gordon. **CAST:** Robert Forster, Lydie Denier, Caren Kaye. **1989**

SATAN'S SADISTS 🦃 Infamous biker film whose advertising campaign traded on the Manson murders is a vicious, sleazy orgy of death and gore disguised as social comment that makes you wonder how (and why) name actors ever got involved in this mess. Not rated; contains partial nudity and violence. 87m. **DIR:** Al Adamson. **CAST:** Russ Tamblyn, Scott Brady, Kent Taylor, John Cardos, Gary Kent, Graydon Clark, Regina Carrol, Jodie Taylor. **1969 DVD**

SATAN'S SCHOOL FOR GIRLS ★★1/2 Originally made as an ABC Movie of the Week, this decent shocker concerns a series of apparent suicides at a prominent girls' school, but we all know better. Good acting and some creepy atmosphere, but the typical TV ending falls flat. 74m. **DIR:** David Lowell Rich. **CAST:** Pamela Franklin, Kate Jackson, Roy Thinnes, Cheryl Ladd. **1973**

SATELLITE IN THE SKY ★★ The crew of a spaceship attempts to recover a runaway experimental bomb. Tedious sci-fi adventure memorable for a fun performance by Donald Wolfit as the bomb's eccentric inventor. B&W; 84m. **DIR:** Paul Dickson. **CAST:** Kieron Moore, Lois Maxwell, Donald Wolfit, Bryan Forbes, Shirley Lawrence. **1956**

SATISFACTION 🦃 Justine Bateman is the leader of a rock band. Rated PG-13 for profanity and suggested sex. 95m. **DIR:** Joan Freeman. **CAST:** Justine Bateman, Liam Neeson, Trini Alvarado, Julia Roberts, Deborah Harry, Chris Nash. **1988**

SATURDAY NIGHT AT THE PALACE ★★★ The fears and hatreds behind South Africa's policy of apartheid are explored in a microcosm in this intense South African film. It expands upon a real-life incident, a late-night confrontation between a white man and a black man at a suburban hamburger joint. Paul Slabolepszy, who plays the white antagonist, also wrote the screenplay. 87m. **DIR:** Robert Davies. **CAST:** Paul Slabolepszy, John Kani. **1988**

SATURDAY NIGHT FEVER ★★★★ From the first notes of "Stayin' Alive" by the Bee Gees over the opening credits, it is obvious that *Saturday Night Fever* is more than just another youth exploitation film. It is *Rebel Without a Cause* for the 1970s, with realistic dialogue and effective dramatic situations. Rated R for profanity, violence, partial nudity, and simulated sex. 119m. **DIR:** John Badham. **CAST:** John Travolta, Donna Pescow, Karen Lynn Gorney. **1977**

SATURDAY NIGHT KID, THE ★★★★ A clever comedy designed to showcase Clara Bow's perky personality. The plot involves two department-store clerks in love with the same man. The triangle gets tangled more than usual because the girls are sisters. B&W; 75m. **DIR:** Edward Sutherland. **CAST:** Clara Bow, Jean Arthur, Jean Harlow, James Hall, Edna May Oliver, Frank Ross, Ethel Wales. **1929**

SATURDAY NIGHT SHOCKERS ★★★ Each of these four tapes includes a pair of cheapo horror movies, cartoons, short subjects, and coming attractions, all from the thirties, forties, and fifties. Thus seen in their proper context, these trash classics are more entertaining than they would be if viewed alone. The titles are: Volume 1, *The Creeping Terror* and *Chained for Life*; Volume 2, *Man Beast* and *Human Gorilla*; Volume 3, *Murder in the Red Barn* and *A Face at the Window*; and Volume 4, *Mesa of Lost Women* and *The Monster of Piedras Blancas*. Not rated; no objectionable content. 150m. **DIR:** Various.

SATURDAY THE 14TH 🦃 Richard Benjamin and Paula Prentiss star in this low-budget horror comedy about a family that moves into a haunted house. Rated PG. 75m. **DIR:** Howard R. Cohen. **CAST:** Richard Benjamin, Paula Prentiss, Jeffrey Tambor, Rosemary DeCamp. **1981**

SATURN 3 ★★ Although this space shocker is endowed with a fair amount of chills and surprises, there's very little else to it. The story takes place in the distant future on the Eden-like space station Titan, which is happily inhabited by two chemists (Kirk Douglas and Farrah Fawcett). A strangely hostile newcomer (Harvey Keitel) unleashes a terror that threatens to destroy them all. Rated R. 88m. **DIR:** Stanley Donen. **CAST:** Kirk Douglas, Farrah Fawcett, Harvey Keitel. **1980 DVD**

SAVAGE ★★★ Martial arts star Olivier Gruner gets to strut his stuff as a man tracking down the scum responsible for the death of his wife and son. Aided by a policewoman, Savage (Gruner) find his prey, who deals in virtual reality and is planning the apocalypse. Exciting premise and creative computer-generated graphics. Rated R for language, nudity, and violence. 103m. **DIR:** Avi Nesher. **CAST:** Olivier Gruner, Jennifer Grant, Sam McMurray, Kario Salem, Kristin Minter. **1995**

SAVAGE ATTRACTION ★★★★ A psychotic German becomes sadistically obsessed with a lovely Australian girl in this bizarre but true tale. He uses both mental and physical cruelty to keep her with him. The suspense is never lacking. Rated R for sadism, nudity, and violence. 93m. **DIR:** Frank Shields. **CAST:** Kerry Mack, Ralph Schicha. **1983**

SAVAGE BEACH 🦃 In this sequel to *Picasso Trigger*, two female agents with the Drug Enforcement Division

uncover a plot to retrieve gold lost during World War II. Rated R. 95m. **DIR:** Andy Sidaris. **CAST:** Dona Speir, Hope Marie Carlton, Bruce Penhall, John Aprea. **1990 DVD**

SAVAGE BEES, THE ★★1/2 Above-average thriller about a plague of African killer bees wreaking havoc on New Orleans during Mardi Gras. Oscar-winner Ben Johnson gives dramatic punch to this made-for-TV chiller. Some good thrills. 99m. **DIR:** Bruce Geller. **CAST:** Ben Johnson, Michael Parks, Horst Buchholz. **1976**

SAVAGE DAWN 🦃 A motorcycle gang takes over a small town in the desert. Rated R for violence, nudity, and profanity. 102m. **DIR:** Simon Nuchtern. **CAST:** George Kennedy, Richard Lynch, Lance Henriksen, Karen Black, William Forsythe. **1984**

SAVAGE GUNS ★★ Revenge story has an outlaw destroy a saloon to prevent the owner from testifying against him. Only a gunfighter is wounded and his brother killed in the attack. The gunfighter recuperates and goes after the outlaw. Exciting action but weak story. Not rated; contains violence. 85m. **DIR:** Miles Deem. **CAST:** Robert Woods, Dean Stratford, Dennis Colt, Simone Blondell. **1971**

SAVAGE HEARTS ★★★ Offbeat thriller centers on mob assassin Maryam D'Abo, who has only six months to live. In order to enjoy her remaining days, D'Abo steals two million dollars of the mob's money. The theft enrages mob kingpin Richard Harris, who will stop at nothing to retrieve the stolen loot. Hiding out in a hotel, Baxter encounters two con artists whose fates are sealed when they attempt to help her. Rated R for violence, profanity, and adult situations. 90m. **DIR:** Mark Ezra. **CAST:** Jamie Harris, Maryam D'Abo, Richard Harris, Myriam Cir, Jerry Hall. **1995 DVD**

SAVAGE INSTINCT 🦃 When Debra Sweaney accidentally walks into the dark and seedy world of a drug dealer, she is beaten and left for dead. She survives and comes back with a vengeance. Charles Bronson did it with more conviction. Not rated; contains graphic violence. 88m. **DIR:** Patrick G. Donahue. **CAST:** Debra Sweaney. **1991**

SAVAGE INTRUDER, THE 🦃 An aging film star hires a male nurse who turns out to be a psycho. 90m. **DIR:** Donald Wolfe. **CAST:** Miriam Hopkins, John David Garfield, Gale Sondergaard. **1977**

SAVAGE IS LOOSE, THE 🦃 Tedious tale strands a young man and his parents on an island for many years. Rated R. 114m. **DIR:** George C. Scott. **CAST:** George C. Scott, Trish Van Devere, John David Carson, Lee Montgomery. **1974**

SAVAGE JUSTICE 🦃 The daughter of an American ambassador is caught up in a revolution in a foreign country. Not rated, the film has nudity and violence. 90m. **DIR:** Joey Romero. **CAST:** Julie Montgomery, Steve Memel. **1988**

SAVAGE LAND ★★★ A stagecoach on the way to Colorado is ambushed by fake Indians, and the occupants must go on the run. Mildly entertaining, with lots of lessons. Rated PG. 91m. **DIR:** Dean Hamilton. **CAST:** Corbin Bernsen, Corey Carrier, Brian James, Mercedes McNab, Charlotte Ross, Graham Greene, Vivian Schilling. **1994**

SAVAGE MESSIAH ★★1/2 This flamboyant love story dramatized in the Ken Russell tradition of excess only works in part. The story of a French sculptor's affair with a much older Polish woman symbolizes the generation gap as well as the culture clash. It would have worked better as a morality play without Russell's overworked and self-indulgent camera tricks. Rated R. 100m. **DIR:** Ken Russell. **CAST:** Dorothy Tutin, Scott Anthony, Helen Mirren, John Justin, Michael Gough, Lindsay Kemp. **1972**

SAVAGE NIGHTS ★★1/2 A young bisexual filmmaker with AIDS is torn between an unstable teenage girl and a shallow young boy. Despite some fine scenes and good acting, the story loses momentum and seems much longer than it is. In French with English subtitles. Rated R for mature themes and sexual scenes. 126m. **DIR:** Cyril Collard. **CAST:** Cyril Collard, Romane Bohringer, Carlos Lopez. **1992**

SAVAGE SAM ★★1/2 Officially a sequel to *Old Yeller*, the film has little in common with its predecessor, except for some of the character names. Captured by Indians, the only hope of rescue for three children lies with Savage Sam, Old Yeller's son. An entertaining action film, without the depth of its predecessor. 103m. **DIR:** Norman Tokar. **CAST:** Brian Keith, Tommy Kirk, Kevin Corcoran, Dewey Martin, Jeff York, Marta Kristen. **1963**

SAVAGE STREETS 🦃 Linda Blair is the tough leader of a street gang. Rated R for everything imaginable. 90m. **DIR:** Danny Steinmann. **CAST:** Linda Blair, Robert Dryer, Sal Landi, John Vernon. **1985**

SAVAGE WEEKEND ★★ Several couples head out from the big city into the backwoods to watch a boat being built, but they are killed off one by one. The only reason this movie earns any stars is for talented actor William Sanderson's performance as a demented lunatic who may or may not be the killer. Rated R for nudity, simulated sex, and violence. 88m. **DIR:** John Mason Kirby. **CAST:** Christopher Allport, James Doerr, Marilyn Hamlin, William Sanderson. **1979**

SAVAGES (1973) ★★★ James Ivory's offbeat look at society, in which a naked group of primitives find their sacrificial rites disrupted by a croquet ball. This discovery leads them to a deserted mansion where an odd cluster of events culminates in a transformation in which they are civilized. Not rated, contains nudity and violence. 108m. **DIR:** James Ivory. **CAST:** Lewis J. Stadlen, Anne Francine, Thayer David, Salome Jens. **1973**

SAVAGES (1974) ★★★ Man hunts man! Sam Bottoms is guiding Andy Griffith on a hunt in the desert when Griffith goes bananas and begins a savage, relentless pursuit of Bottoms. A sandy rendition of the famous short story, "The Most Dangerous Game." Thrilling, suspenseful, and intriguing to watch. Made for TV. 78m. **DIR:** Lee H. Katzin. **CAST:** Andy Griffith, Sam Bottoms, Noah Beery Jr., James Best. **1974**

SAVANNAH SMILES ★★★1/2 In this surprisingly good, independently made family film, a 6-year-old runaway named Savannah (Bridgette Anderson) accidentally hides in the backseat of a car operated by two small-time crooks, Alvie (Mark Miller) and Boots (Donovan Scott). It's love at first sight for the trio, who decide to try to be a real family. The authorities, however, have other ideas. Rated G. 107m. **DIR:** Pierre De-

Moro. **CAST:** Bridgette Anderson, Mark Miller, Donovan Scott, Peter Graves, Chris Robinson, Michael Parks. **1982**

SAVATE ★★1/2 Here's an oddity: a post–Civil War, kickboxing rip-off of *The Quick and the Dead*. An expatriate French soldier competes in a series of battles to help good citizens retain the rights to their two-bit town. Aside from the exotic fighting style, everything else about this film is borrowed—most notably the soundtrack, which should prompt a lawsuit from composer Ennio Morricone. Rated PG-13 for violence. 88m. **DIR:** Isaac Florentine. **CAST:** Olivier Gruner, Ian Ziering, Ashley Laurence, Marc Singer, James Brolin. **1994**

SAVE ME ★★1/2 Harry Hamlin strips down for some steamy sex with a mystery woman (Lysette Anthony). Hamlin finds plenty of diversion with Anthony, whom he believes he is saving from an abusive husband, but then someone tries to kill him. Thanks to his latest tryst, the list of suspects keeps growing. R-rated and unrated versions available; both contain sex, nudity, adult language, and violence. 90m. **DIR:** Alan Roberts. **CAST:** Harry Hamlin, Lysette Anthony, Steve Railsback, Olivia Hussey, Michael Ironside. **1993**

SAVE THE LADY ★★★ Four kids set out to fight City Hall after a bureaucrat orders the historic *Lady Hope* steam ferry to be destroyed. The kids rescue *Lady Hope*'s former skipper from a retirement home. Together with an expert engineer, the team valiantly repairs and repaints the boat. 76m. **DIR:** Leon Thau. **CAST:** Matthew Excell, Robert Clarkson, Miranda Cartledge, Kim Clifford. **1981**

SAVE THE LAST DANCE ★★★ Teen romance develops when a middle-class white girl (Julia Stiles) transfers into a tough inner-city high school. Befriended by an impressive Sean Patrick Thomas, she combines her ballet background with hip-hop moves. Racial conflicts are touched on too lightly to make much of a social statement. Rated PG-13 for violence, profanity, and sexual innuendo. 115m. **DIR:** Thomas Carter. **CAST:** Julia Stiles, Sean Patrick Thomas, Vince Green, Terry Kinney. **2001 DVD**

SAVE THE TIGER ★★★ Jack Lemmon won the Academy Award for best actor for his portrayal in this 1973 film as a garment manufacturer who is at the end of his professional and emotional rope. His excellent performance helps offset the fact that the picture is essentially a downer. Rated R. 101m. **DIR:** John G. Avildsen. **CAST:** Jack Lemmon, Jack Gilford, Thayer David. **1973**

SAVED BY THE LIGHT ★★★1/2 Inspirational tale of a real jerk whose life is changed for the better when he is hit by lightning and visits the afterlife. Terrific performance by Eric Roberts. Not rated; contains profanity. 95m. **DIR:** Lewis Teague. **CAST:** Eric Roberts, Lynette Walden, K. Callan, Don McManus. **1995**

SAVING GRACE (1986) ★★★★ The pope (Tom Conti), frustrated with his lack of freedom, finds himself in the small, depressed Italian village of Montepetra where he gets back to helping people on a one-on-one basis. *Saving Grace* is very good, showing moments of conflict with the human element exposed in all its emotions. Rated PG for violence and profanity. 112m. **DIR:** Robert M. Young. **CAST:** Tom Conti, Fernando Rey, Edward James Olmos, Giancarlo Giannini, Erland Josephson. **1986**

SAVING GRACE (2000) ★★★1/2 Small-town housewife Brenda Blethyn, recently widowed and just discovering the financial crisis into which her deceased husband has dumped her, turns her horticultural talents to an illegal—if highly profitable—crop, in this whimsical charmer. The chuckles are slow-building but consistent, and the characters are deliciously eccentric. Although the story falls apart in the final few scenes, getting there is a hoot. Rated R for profanity and drug content. 94m. **DIR:** Nigel Cole. **CAST:** Brenda Blethyn, Craig Ferguson, Martin Clunes, Tcheky Karyo, Jamie Foreman, Bill Bailey, Valerie Edmond. **2000 DVD**

SAVING PRIVATE RYAN ★★★★★ As he did with *Schindler's List*, Steven Spielberg has delivered what probably will remain a statement of record for decades to come. The opening twenty-minute depiction of the fateful D-Day assault is mesmerizing . . . and very, very hard to watch. And it's merely prologue to a tale of individual courage that sends eight men into German-occupied France to rescue a soldier whose brothers all have been killed in combat. Our ground-level guide is Captain John Miller (Tom Hanks), an honorable soldier who believes in just causes and the merit of chain of command. His men are stereotypes but no less real, and their subsequent adventures unfold against Spielberg's stated desire to portray dignity and decency in the charnel house of combat. The result is not a film to be embraced frivolously: it's raw, powerful, incredibly violent . . . and absolutely unforgettable. Rated R for violence, profanity, and war-related gore and carnage. 170m. **DIR:** Steven Spielberg. **CAST:** Tom Hanks, Tom Sizemore, Edward Burns, Barry Pepper, Adam Goldberg, Matt Damon, Vin Diesel, Giovanni Ribisi, Jeremy Davies. **1998 DVD**

SAVING SILVERMAN ★★ Tacky, sexist, and gross aptly describe the humor in this post-adolescent flick about the friendship of three devoted Neil Diamond fans. When a domineering young woman begins to take over Silverman's life, his pals take extreme measures to get him back. Don't be too surprised by an occasional sight gag or insane plot twist that evokes gut-splitting laughter. Rated PG-13 for language, sexual situations, and nudity. 91m. **DIR:** Dennis Dugan. **CAST:** Jason Biggs, Jack Black, Steve Zahn, Amanda Peet. **2001 DVD**

SAVIOR ★★★ Grim, convoluted story about an American who becomes a mercenary for the Serbs as an act of revenge for the murder of his wife and child. He rediscovers his humanity against the atrocities and horrors of the war through a young Serb woman and her newborn daughter. Dennis Quaid's performance is stellar. Rated R for brutal violence, profanity, and brief nudity. 104m. **DIR:** Peter Antonijevic. **CAST:** Dennis Quaid, Nastassja Kinski, Stellan Skarsgard, Natasa Ninkovic. **1997 DVD**

SAWBONES ★★★ What might have been a by-the-numbers goreflick is enlivened by Nina Siemaszko, as a plucky young woman trying to solve medical-related serial killings. More howdunnit than whodunnit, Sam Montgomery's script is much smarter than usual, and the blood is surprisingly restrained for such an obvious genre entry. Rated R for brief violence, brief nudity, and a single profanity. 85m. **DIR:** Catherine Cyran. **CAST:**

Adam Baldwin, Nina Siemaszko, Nicholas Sadler, Don Harvey, Don Stroud, Barbara Carrera. **1995**

SAWDUST AND TINSEL ★★★1/2 A traveling circus is the background for this study of love relationships between a circus manager, the woman he loves, and her lover. Director Ingmar Bergman scores some emotional bull's-eyes in this early effort. Love triangle leads to a powerful climax, somewhat reminiscent of *The Blue Angel*. B&W; 95m. **DIR:** Ingmar Bergman. **CAST:** Harriet Andersson, Anders Ek. **1953**

SAY AMEN, SOMEBODY ★★★★ This is a joyful documentary about gospel singers Thomas A. Dorsey and Willie Mae Ford Smith. Two dozen gospel songs make this modest film a treat for the ears as well as the eyes and soul. Rated G. 100m. **DIR:** George T. Nierenberg. **CAST:** Thomas A. Dorsey, Willie Mae Ford Smith, Sallie Martin. **1982**

SAY ANYTHING ★★★1/2 So many things are right with this comedy-drama about first love that one can't help wincing when it takes a wrong turn. Yet everything else is honest in its depiction of a well-meaning, unexceptional guy (John Cusack) who falls in love with a seemingly unattainable beauty with brains (Ione Skye). It's a minor gem from first-time director Cameron Crowe, who wrote *Fast Times at Ridgemont High*. Rated PG-13 for suggested sex and profanity. 100m. **DIR:** Cameron Crowe. **CAST:** John Cusack, Ione Skye, John Mahoney. **1989 DVD**

SAY GOODBYE, MAGGIE COLE ★★★ A retired doctor reopens her practice in a tough Chicago neighborhood after her husband dies. Standard TV movie elevated by star Susan Hayward in her final performance. 74m. **DIR:** Jud Taylor. **CAST:** Susan Hayward, Darren McGavin, Michael Constantine, Beverly Garland. **1972**

SAY IT ISN'T SO 🦃 This unfunny and cheerfully perverse romantic comedy is about a former orphan who loses an ear to, and falls madly in love with, a gorgeous female barber who may be his sister. Rated R for profanity and sexual situations. 98m. **DIR:** James B. Rogers. **CAST:** Chris Klein, Heather Graham, Orlando Jones, Richard Jenkins, Sally Fields. **2001 DVD**

SAY YES ★★1/2 A multimillionaire (Jonathan Winters) dies, leaving his estate to his son (Art Hindle) on the condition that he marry before his thirty-fifth birthday—only a day away. The comedy doesn't work most of the time, but the story is cute enough to tolerate. Rated PG-13 for sex, nudity, and profanity. 87m. **DIR:** Larry Yust. **CAST:** Art Hindle, Lissa Layng, Logan Ramsey, Jonathan Winters, Maryedith Burrell, Anne Ramsey. **1986**

SAYONARA ★★★★ Marlon Brando is an American airman who engages in a romance with a Japanese actress while stationed in Japan after World War II. His love is put to the test by each culture's misconceptions and prejudices. James A. Michener's thought-provoking tragedy-romance still holds up well. Red Buttons and Miyoshi Umeki deservedly won Oscars for their roles as star-crossed lovers "American Occupation"–style. 147m. **DIR:** Joshua Logan. **CAST:** Marlon Brando, Red Buttons, Miyoshi Umeki, Ricardo Montalban, James Garner. **1957 DVD**

SCALAWAG BUNCH, THE ★★ Italian-made adaptation of the Robin Hood story is cheaply made and poorly dubbed into English. But the story is still entertaining. Not rated. 103m. **DIR:** Giorgio Ferroni. **CAST:** Mark Damon. **1975**

SCALPEL 🦃 Plastic surgeon transforms a young accident victim into the spitting image of his missing daughter to pull an inheritance swindle. Rated R. 96m. **DIR:** John Grissmer. **CAST:** Robert Lansing, Judith Chapman, Arlen Dean Snyder, Sandy Martin. **1976**

SCALPHUNTERS, THE ★★★1/2 Fine, old-fashioned Western finds fur-trapper Burt Lancaster and runaway slave Ossie Davis pitted against Telly Savalas and his gang of cutthroats. Frequent bits of comedy make this a solid genre entry. 102m. **DIR:** Sydney Pollack. **CAST:** Burt Lancaster, Shelley Winters, Telly Savalas, Ossie Davis, Dabney Coleman, Nick Cravat. **1968**

SCALPS ★★ Early effort from Florida poverty-row director Fred Olen Ray shows him still imitating better-financed Hollywood filmmakers. Presence of experienced character actors lends novelty value to horror thriller about resurrected Indian ghost and its teenage prey. Rated R. 82m. **DIR:** Fred Olen Ray. **CAST:** Kirk Alyn, Carol Borland. **1983**

SCAM ★★1/2 Sultry Lorraine Bracco, who picks up rich men only to drug and rob them, reluctantly agrees to help FBI agent Christopher Walken execute a similar sting on a specific target. Sadly, Craig Smith's twisty mystery eventually gets too convoluted for its own good, resulting in a double-reverse climax which makes no sense in view of what has taken place earlier. Rated R for profanity and violence. 102m. **DIR:** John Flynn. **CAST:** Christopher Walken, Lorraine Bracco, Miguel Ferrer, Martin Donovan. **1993**

SCANDAL ★★★★1/2 A remarkable motion picture, this British production takes on the Profumo affair of the 1960s and emerges as an uncommonly satisfying adult-oriented drama, rich in character and insight. John Hurt is superb as Stephen Ward, the London osteopath who groomed teenage Christine Keeler (Joanne Whalley-Kilmer) into the femme fatale who brought down the British Conservative government. Rated R for nudity, simulated sex, violence, and profanity. 105m. **DIR:** Michael Caton-Jones. **CAST:** John Hurt, Joanne Whalley, Bridget Fonda, Ian McKellen. **1989**

SCANDAL IN A SMALL TOWN ★★ Predictable (and misleadingly titled) drama starring Raquel Welch as a waitress who opposes an anti-Semitic schoolteacher. Cardboard characters and situations are the real scandal in this made-for-TV movie. 90m. **DIR:** Anthony Page. **CAST:** Raquel Welch, Christa Denton, Frances Lee McCain, Ronny Cox. **1989**

SCANDALOUS (1983) ★★ Robert Hays plays an investigative reporter who gets mixed up with spies, con men, and murder in London. The cast includes Pamela Stephenson and John Gielgud, as a pair of con artists. Gielgud seems to be having a grand old time playing everything from an old Chinese man to the world's oldest punk rocker. Rated PG for profanity, nudity, and brief violence. 93m. **DIR:** Rob Byrum. **CAST:** Robert Hays, Pamela Stephenson, John Gielgud, Jim Dale, M. Emmet Walsh. **1983**

SCANDALOUS (1988) 🦃 A penniless playboy is hired to find a secretary who has witnessed the murder of a renowned author. 90m. **DIR:** Robert W. Young. **CAST:** Lauren Hutton, Albert Fortell, Capucine. **1988**

SCANDALOUS JOHN ★★★ Brian Keith stars as an eccentric ranch owner fighting to maintain his way of life. In his world, a cattle drive consists of one steer, and gunfights are practiced in the house with live ammunition. He must battle with the law, the world in general, and reality to keep his ranch and the life he loves. Laughs and poignancy are combined in this movie. Rated G. 113m. **DIR:** Robert Butler. **CAST:** Brian Keith, Alfonso Arau, Michele Carey, Rick Lenz, Harry Morgan, Simon Oakland. **1971**

SCANDALOUS ME: THE JACQUELINE SUSANN STORY ★★★ You would think the life of Jacqueline Susann (who wrote the bestselling book *Valley of the Dolls*) would make an interesting movie, and yet something's certainly missing. Such a short film can't do justice to her complex and troubling life, but the highlights are pretty well presented here. Susann contends with an adulterous father, drug abuse, a mentally deficient son, the high price of success, an on-off relationship with her husband, and finally, cancer. Michele Lee shines as the sassy and sensitive Susann. Not rated. 95m. **DIR:** Bruce McDonald. **CAST:** Michele Lee, Peter Riegert, James Farentino, Sherry Miller. **1998**

SCANNER COP ★★1/2 The filmmakers try a new tack to keep the series alive: the Scanner joins the police department. The young rookie, who has been silencing the voices in his head, is asked to uncork those feelings when members of the force are being killed, and all clues point to someone with scanning abilities. The special effects are more abstract this outing, hoping to pump some new life into the franchise. Rated R for strong violence. 94m. **DIR:** Pierre David. **CAST:** Daniel Quinn, Darlanne Fluegel, Richard Lynch, Brian James, Richard Grove. **1993**

SCANNERS ★★★1/2 From its first shocking scene—in which a character's head explodes, spewing blood, flesh, and bone all over—the film poses a challenge to its viewers: How much can you take? Shock specialist David Cronenberg wrote and directed this potent film, about a bloody war among people with formidable extrasensory powers. Rated R. 102m. **DIR:** David Cronenberg. **CAST:** Jennifer O'Neill, Patrick McGoohan, Stephen Lack, Lawrence Dane, Michael Ironside. **1981 DVD**

SCANNERS 2: THE NEW ORDER ★★1/2 Pretty much the same old thing, with a new breed of scanners roaming the streets, causing people to hemorrhage and explode. Good guy scanners David Hewlett and Deborah Raffin attempt to stop the bad guy scanners from controlling the city. Rated R for violence. 102m. **DIR:** Christian Duguay. **CAST:** David Hewlett, Deborah Raffin. **1991**

SCANNERS 3: THE TAKEOVER 🦃 This third installment is distant from David Cronenberg's original vision. Dull. Rated R for nudity and profanity. 101m. **DIR:** Christian Duguay. **CAST:** Liliana Komorowska, Valerie Valois, Steve Parrish. **1992**

SCANNERS 4: THE SHOWDOWN ★★1/2 A detective and a serial killer, both of whom are scanners, must scan to the death in this gory but passable film. Rated R for violence and profanity. 95m. **DIR:** Steve Barnett. **CAST:** Daniel Quinn, Patrick Kilpatrick, Khrystyne Haje. **1994**

SCAR, THE ★★★★ Fans of hardboiled *film noir* will want to look for this lesser-known but memorable example of the genre. Paul Henreid plays two parts: a gambler fleeing from the police and a psychiatrist who is his exact double. The gambler plans to escape the law by killing the doctor and assuming his identity. Look for Jack Webb in a small role. B&W; 83m. **DIR:** Steve Sekely. **CAST:** Paul Henreid, Joan Bennett, Eduard Franz, Leslie Brooks, John Qualen. **1948**

SCARAMOUCHE ★★★★ This big-screen adaptation of the Rafael Sabatini story is first-class entertainment for the whole family. Stewart Granger is perfectly cast as the swashbuckling Scaramouche, who sets out to avenge his brother's murder by a villainous master swordsman (Mel Ferrer). A wonderfully witty script, splendid cinematography, fine performances, and outstanding action scenes. 118m. **DIR:** George Sidney. **CAST:** Stewart Granger, Eleanor Parker, Mel Ferrer, Janet Leigh. **1952**

SCARECROW ★★★ A real downer about two losers (Al Pacino and Gene Hackman) trying to make something of themselves, this drama is made watchable by the performances. Rated R. 115m. **DIR:** Jerry Schatzberg. **CAST:** Al Pacino, Gene Hackman, Eileen Brennan, Richard Lynch. **1973 DVD**

SCARECROWS ★★★★ This is something rare—a truly frightening horror film, loaded with suspense, intelligent writing, and decent acting. The story involves a group of military deserters who have ripped off a federal money exchange and are flying south in a stolen cargo plane. They land in a secluded wilderness of cornfields filled with . . . scarecrows. Not recommended for the squeamish, but horror fans will find this to be a feast. Not rated; contains graphic violence. 88m. **DIR:** William Wesley. **CAST:** Ted Vernon, Michael Simms, Richard Vidan. **1988**

SCARED STIFF 🦃 A newly married couple move into an old house cursed by a voodoo priest. Rated R for violence. 85m. **DIR:** Richard Friedman. **CAST:** Andrew Stevens, Mary Page Keller. **1986**

SCARED TO DEATH (1946) ★★ Tepid thriller is noteworthy primarily because it is Bela Lugosi's only color film, not for the lukewarm story about a woman who dies without a traceable cause. Plenty of hocus-pocus, red herrings, and hypnosis. Directed by Christy Cabanne, a silent film pioneer. 65m. **DIR:** Christy Cabanne. **CAST:** Bela Lugosi, Douglas Fowley, Joyce Compton, George Zucco, Nat Pendleton. **1946 DVD**

SCARED TO DEATH (1980) ★★1/2 Although it's an unabashed rip-off of *Alien*, this film manages to build straight through to the harrowing ending. However, little compassion for the characters ruins what could have been terrific fright fare. Rated R for violence. 95m. **DIR:** William Malone. **CAST:** John Stinston, Diana Davidson. **1980**

SCARFACE (1932) ★★★★1/2 Subtitled "Shame of the Nation" when released in the 1930s, this thinly veiled account of the rise and fall (the latter being fictional) of Al Capone easily ranks as one of the very best films in the gangster genre. Paul Muni is first-rate as the Chicago gangster and receives excellent support from Ann Dvorak, George Raft, and, outstanding as a rival gangster, Boris Karloff. See it. B&W; 93m. **DIR:** Howard

Hawks. **CAST:** Paul Muni, Ann Dvorak, George Raft, Boris Karloff, Osgood Perkins. **1932**

SCARFACE (1983) ★★★★1/2 Onetime "Godfather" Al Pacino returns to his screen beginnings with a bravura performance in the title role of this updating of Howard Hawks's 1932 gangster classic. Rather than bootleg gin as Paul Muni did in the original, Pacino imports and sells cocaine. Directed by Brian De Palma, it's the most violent, thrilling, revolting, surprising, and gruesome gangster movie ever made. Rated R for nudity, violence, sex, and profanity. 170m. **DIR:** Brian De Palma. **CAST:** Al Pacino, Steven Bauer, Robert Loggia, Paul Shenar. **1983 DVD**

SCARLET AND THE BLACK, THE ★★1/2 The action in this film is centered around the Vatican during the time of the German occupation of Rome in 1943. Based on "The Scarlet Pimpernel of the Vatican," it chronicles the adventures of an Irish priest who manages to elude the German captors in true Pimpernel fashion. Moderately entertaining. 143m. **DIR:** Jerry London. **CAST:** Gregory Peck, Christopher Plummer, John Gielgud. **1983**

SCARLET CLAW, THE ★★★★ Stunningly atmospheric entry in the Universal series of Sherlock Holmes mysteries has the detective journeying to Canada to find the culprit in a bizarre series of murders. This is a true whodunit, which keeps you guessing right to the end. B&W; 74m. **DIR:** Roy William Neill. **CAST:** Basil Rathbone, Nigel Bruce, Gerald Hamer, Paul Cavanagh, Arthur Hohl, Miles Mander, Ian Wolfe. **1944**

SCARLET CLUE, THE ★★ Standard, workmanlike *Charlie Chan* entry in the latter-day Monogram Pictures cycle, from its most prolific hack director. A suspect is killed as Charlie investigates a plot to purloin government radar plans. Some atmosphere on a grade-C scale, but no tension. B&W; 64m. **DIR:** Phil Rosen. **CAST:** Sidney Toler, Benson Fong, Mantan Moreland, I. Stanford Jolley. **1945**

SCARLET DAWN ★★ The characters bounce between coping with the Russian Revolution and sex orgies in an uneven melodrama that is as heavy as the ornate sets and garish makeup on the faces of big-time stars who should have known better. More of a curiosity piece than a satisfying film. B&W; 80m. **DIR:** William Dieterle. **CAST:** Douglas Fairbanks Jr., Lilyan Tashman, Nancy Carroll, Earle Fox. **1932**

SCARLET EMPRESS, THE ★★★★1/2 This classic is a stunning cinematic achievement dominated by the seductive Marlene Dietrich. A naïve, shy girl becomes a worldly wise woman adept at court intrigue as she goes from being the unwilling bride of Czar Peter to the empress of all the Russias. Visually impressive and marvelously detailed, this is a must-see movie. B&W; 110m. **DIR:** Josef von Sternberg. **CAST:** Marlene Dietrich, Louise Dresser, Sam Jaffe, John Lodge, Maria Sieber, C. Aubrey Smith, Gavin Gordon, Olive Tell, Jane Darwell, Jameson Thomas. **1934 DVD**

SCARLET LETTER, THE (1926) ★★★ Hester Prynne wears the scarlet letter A for adultery. Only her sadistic husband Roger knows that minister Arthur Dimmesdale is the father of her daughter, Pearl. Roger taunts Arthur, who plans to flee with Hester and the child but finally confesses his sin publicly. Silent. B&W; 80m. **DIR:** Victor Sjöström. **CAST:** Lillian Gish, Henry B. Walthall, Karl Dane, Lars Hanson. **1926**

SCARLET LETTER, THE (1934) ★★★ Twenties-flapper star Colleen Moore proved she had acting skill in this second version (first sound) of Nathaniel Hawthorne's great classic of love, hate, jealousy, and emotional blackmail in Puritan New England. As in the 1926 silent version, D. W. Griffith star Henry B. Walthall portrays the heartless persecutor Roger Chillingworth. B&W; 69m. **DIR:** Robert Vignola. **CAST:** Colleen Moore, Hardie Albright, Henry B. Walthall. **1934**

SCARLET LETTER (1973) ★★★1/2 Wim Wenders's stunning psychological portrait of bigotry and isolation, this follows a story about the social sanctions imposed upon a woman suspected of adultery in seventeenth-century Salem, Massachusetts. Based on Nathaniel Hawthorne's classic novel, this film version is given some fine contemporary touches by Wenders. In German with English subtitles. 90m. **DIR:** Wim Wenders. **CAST:** Senta Berger, Lou Castel, Hans-Christian Blech, Yella Rottlander. **1973**

SCARLET LETTER, THE (1995) Little besides the title of Nathaniel Hawthorne's novel survives in this dreary, foolish film. Attempting to justify the many departures (including graphic sex, childbirth, an Indian war, and a happy ending), star Demi Moore once blurted, "Hardly anybody's read the book." Obviously, neither had she. Rated R for nudity and simulated sex. 135m. **DIR:** Roland Joffe. **CAST:** Demi Moore, Gary Oldman, Robert Duvall, Joan Plowright, Robert Prosky. **1995**

SCARLET PIMPERNEL, THE (1934) ★★★ Leslie Howard plays Sir Percy, an English aristocrat engaged in the underground effort to snatch out from under the blade of the guillotine Frenchmen caught in the Reign of Terror. His ruse may throw off the French authorities, as ably represented by a sinister Raymond Massey, but he is also turning off his beautiful wife, Merle Oberon. B&W; 95m. **DIR:** Harold Young. **CAST:** Leslie Howard, Raymond Massey, Merle Oberon, Nigel Bruce. **1934 DVD**

SCARLET PIMPERNEL, THE (1982) ★★★1/2 This is the made-for-TV version of the much-filmed (seven times) adventure classic. Anthony Andrews makes a dashing hero leading a double life aiding French revolutionaries while posing as a foppish member of British society. Jane Seymour is breathtakingly beautiful as his ladylove. This lavish production proves that remakes, even for television, can be worthwhile. 150m. **DIR:** Clive Donner. **CAST:** Anthony Andrews, Jane Seymour, Ian McKellen, James Villiers, Eleanor David. **1982**

SCARLET RIVER ★★★ Unique movie within a movie, as Western screen star Tom Keene comes to Scarlet River ranch to shoot his next movie and ends up in a series of real shoot-outs with bad men plotting to take over the ranch. Cameo appearances by Joel McCrea and Myrna Loy as themselves. B&W; 54m. **DIR:** Otto Brower. **CAST:** Tom Keene, Lon Chaney Jr., Edgar Kennedy. **1933**

SCARLET SPEAR, THE The son of an African chief undertakes a series of ritual tasks to prove his manhood. 78m. **DIR:** George Breakston, Ray Stahl. **CAST:** Ray Bentley, Martha Hyer. **1954**

SCARLET STREET ★★★1/2 The director (Fritz Lang) and stars (Edward G. Robinson, Joan Bennett, and Dan Duryea) of the excellent *Woman in the Window* reteamed with less spectacular results for this film about a mild-mannered fellow (Robinson) seduced into

a life of crime by a temptress (Bennett). B&W; 103m. **DIR:** Fritz Lang. **CAST:** Edward G. Robinson, Joan Bennett, Dan Duryea, Margaret Lindsay, Rosalind Ivan. **1945**

SCARLETT ★★1/2 Prime-time soap opera fare at its gaudiest. Timothy Dalton plays a Rhett Butler whose Southern drawl is by way of London, and Joanne Whalley is just a tad coarse and screechy as the Georgia peach who drags her troubles to Ireland. The $45-million budget is evident in carriages, houses, scenery, and costumes that will take your breath away. Rated PG for mild sexual situations and violence. 360m. **DIR:** John Erman. **CAST:** Joanne Whalley, Timothy Dalton, Stephen Collins, Annabeth Gish, Colm Meaney, Jean Smart, Sean Bean. **1994 DVD**

SCARS OF DRACULA ★★★ A young couple searching for the husband's brother follow the trail to Dracula's castle, and soon regret it. Compares well with other films in the series, thanks primarily to Christopher Lee's dynamite portrayal of the Count, and the first-rate direction of horror veteran Roy Ward Baker. Rated R. 94m. **DIR:** Roy Ward Baker. **CAST:** Christopher Lee, Dennis Waterman, Christopher Matthews. **1970 DVD**

SCARY MOVIE ★★ This overly raunchy parody of the *Scream* series and similar movies feels like a string of *In Living Color* sketches crammed with more drugs, penises, oral sex, shrubbery-size pubic hair, and female flatulence than ingenuity. The film has some monstrous laughs as the cast is stalked by a robed, ghost-faced killer, but is generally more gross than fun. Rated R for nudity, violence, sex, and language. 88m. **DIR:** Keenen Ivory Wayans. **CAST:** Anna Faris, Marlon Wayans, Shawn Wayans, Cheri Oteri, Shannon Elizabeth, Jon Abrahams, Carmen Electra, Dave Sheridan. **2000 DVD**

•SCARY MOVIE 2 🦃 College students who survived the original *Scary Movie* massacre are tricked into staying in a haunted house by an oily professor, and the night becomes a crass, tedious parade of penis gags, body-fluid eruptions, and pop-culture parodies. Rated R for language and sexual references. 80m. **DIR:** Keenen Ivory Wayans. **CAST:** Anna Faris, Shawn Wayans, Marlon Wayans, Tori Spelling, Christopher Masterson, Tim Curry, Kathleen Robertson, Regina Hall, David Cross, Chris Elliott. **2001 DVD**

SCAVENGER HUNT 🦃 *It's a Mad Mad Mad Mad World* writhes again as a bunch of wackos run hither, thither, and yawn. Rated PG. 117m. **DIR:** Michael Schultz. **CAST:** Richard Benjamin, James Coco, Scatman Crothers, Ruth Gordon, Cloris Leachman, Roddy McDowall, Cleavon Little, Robert Morley, Richard Mulligan, Tony Randall, Vincent Price. **1979**

SCAVENGERS 🦃 Miami University professor and his ex-girlfriend against the CIA, KGB, and a local African drug kingpin. Rated PG-13 for violence. 94m. **DIR:** Duncan McLachlan. **CAST:** Kenneth Gilman, Brenda Bakke, Ken Gampu. **1988**

SCENE OF THE CRIME (1985) ★★ A cross between a game show and a murder mystery, this film is cut into three episodes, narrated by Orson Welles, that ask the viewers to try to solve the murder at the end of each. Originally made for network TV. 74m. **DIR:** Walter Grauman, Harry Falk. **CAST:** Orson Welles, Markie Post, Alan Thicke, Ben Piazza. **1985**

SCENE OF THE CRIME (1987) ★★★ Romantic thriller with an Oedipal angle. A nightclub owner (Catherine Deneuve) and her son get caught up in an increasingly dangerous attempt to safeguard a criminal. This watchable movie could use fast pacing and less obvious camera pyrotechnics. In French with English subtitles. 90m. **DIR:** André Téchiné. **CAST:** Catherine Deneuve, Danielle Darrieux, Wadeck Stanczak, Victor Lanoux. **1987**

SCENES FROM A MALL ★★ It would be hard to imagine a drearier comedy than this uninspired tale of a married couple (Woody Allen, Bette Midler) breaking up and making up as they romp through a Beverly Hills shopping mall. Only the film's first twenty minutes—a sprightly introduction of the two main characters—make it worth watching. Rated R for profanity. 87m. **DIR:** Paul Mazursky. **CAST:** Bette Midler, Woody Allen, Bill Irwin. **1991**

SCENES FROM A MARRIAGE ★★★★★ Director Ingmar Bergman successfully captures the pain and emotions of a marriage that is disintegrating. Several scenes are extremely hard to watch because there is so much truth to what is being said. Originally a six-part film for Swedish television, the theatrical version was edited by Bergman. Believable throughout, this one packs a real punch. In Swedish. No rating (contains some strong language). 168m. **DIR:** Ingmar Bergman. **CAST:** Liv Ullmann, Erland Josephson, Bibi Andersson. **1973**

SCENES FROM A MURDER 🦃 Inept thriller about a killer who stalks an actress. Filmed in Italy. 90m. **DIR:** Alberto De Martino. **CAST:** Telly Savalas, Anne Heywood. **1972**

SCENES FROM THE CLASS STRUGGLE IN BEVERLY HILLS ★★★★ Director Paul Bartel helms this bizarre sexual romp through the lives of the glamorous Tinseltown set. Jacqueline Bisset is delicious as a neurotic ex-sitcom star whose television comeback is complicated by her dead husband (Paul Mazursky), who keeps materializing while pledging his infernal love to her. This offbeat adult comedy is rated R for nudity and profanity. 95m. **DIR:** Paul Bartel. **CAST:** Jacqueline Bisset, Ray Sharkey, Ed Begley Jr., Paul Mazursky, Wallace Shawn, Robert Beltran. **1989**

SCENES FROM THE GOLDMINE ★★1/2 Music industry exposé with Catherine Mary Stewart as a musician-composer who joins a rock band and falls in love with the lead singer. Even rock fans will find the band's performances somewhat synthetic. Rated R for sexual situations and profanity. 105m. **DIR:** Marc Rocco. **CAST:** Catherine Mary Stewart, Cameron Dye, Steve Railsback, Joe Pantoliano, Lee Ving, Lesley-Anne Down. **1987**

SCENT OF A WOMAN ★★★1/2 Al Pacino's over-the-top performance in this coming-of-age movie will delight some viewers and put off others. Pacino plays a foulmouthed ex-serviceman who takes high school–age companion Chris O'Donnell on a last hurrah in New York City, where the older man intends to wine, dine, and have sex before committing suicide. Rated R for profanity and suggested sex. 157m. **DIR:** Martin Brest. **CAST:** Al Pacino, Chris O'Donnell, James Rebhorn, Gabrielle Anwar, Richard Venture. **1992 DVD**

SCENT OF GREEN PAPAYA, THE ★★★ The first Vietnamese nominee for the Best Foreign Film Oscar tells

the story of a young serving girl in Saigon who grows up to be the servant, and later the lover, of a composer. The film is exquisitely photographed and graceful, but the elliptical, allusive style makes it a bit slow-moving and uneventful. In Vietnamese with English subtitles. Not rated, but suitable for mature general audiences. 103m. **DIR:** Tran Anh Hung. **CAST:** Tran Nu Yen-Khe, Lu Man San, Truong Thi Loc, Nguyen Anh Hoa. **1993 DVD**

SCHINDLER ★★★ A documentary of the man who helped save Jews from Hitler during World War II. The film combines actual footage from the war, testimonials from some of the Jews who were saved, and an interview with Amon Goeth's mistress. The real Oskar Schindler is revealed here: womanizer, boozer, black-market entrepreneur, and rescuer of 1,100 Jews. Not rated; contains graphic footage of concentration camps. 80m. **DIR:** Jon Blair. **1981**

SCHINDLER'S LIST ★★★★★ The story of one man's struggle to save the lives of one thousand Polish Jews during the Third Reich's implementation of Hitler's "final solution," this Oscar-winner for best picture may well be director Steven Spielberg's masterpiece. Skillfully shaded performances by Liam Neeson (whose Oskar Schindler evolves from a fast-living opportunist to a man of conscience) and Ben Kingsley bring humanity to this tale of real-life horror, one of the best films on the subject. Rated R for nudity and violence. 185m. **DIR:** Steven Spielberg. **CAST:** Liam Neeson, Ben Kingsley, Ralph Fiennes, Caroline Goodall, Jonathan Sagalle, Embeth Davidtz. **1993**

SCHIZO 🦃 A deranged night worker freaks out when his favorite figure skater announces her wedding plans. Rated R. 109m. **DIR:** Pete Walker. **CAST:** Jack Watson, Lynne Frederick, John Leyton. **1978 DVD**

SCHIZOID 🦃 This is an unimaginative slasher flick with typically gory special effects. Rated R. 91m. **DIR:** David Paulsen. **CAST:** Klaus Kinski, Marianna Hill, Craig Wasson, Christopher Lloyd. **1980**

SCHIZOPOLIS ★★★ One of those movies you either love or hate, *Schizopolis* is virtually a home movie made by Steven Soderbergh (*sex, lies, and videotape*). The loose plot features Soderbergh as a speechwriter for a double-talking spiritualist, but the film is more concerned with Kafkaesque examinations of the unknowable nature of modern life. There are many amusing bits but just as many that go nowhere, making this one for adventurous audiences. Not rated; contains nudity and profanity. 96m. **DIR:** Steven Soderbergh. **CAST:** Steven Soderbergh, Betsy Brantley, Mike Malone, David Jensen. **1997**

SCHLOCK ★★★ Directed by and starring John Landis, this film is a spoof of not only "missing link" monster movies but other types of horror and science-fiction films. This is Landis's first film, and while it doesn't have the laughs of his later effort, *Animal House*, it does include some chuckles of its own. Rated PG. 80m. **DIR:** John Landis. **CAST:** John Landis, Saul Kahan, Joseph Piantadosi. **1971 DVD**

SCHOOL DAZE ★★★1/2 Writer-director Spike Lee tries to get people to wake up not only to the conflict in South Africa but also to the problems that exist among different factions of the black community. Too much time is spent on a silly subplot involving a college fraternity; however, the film features some first-rate production numbers and a fine musical score by the filmmaker's father, Bill Lee. Rated R for profanity and nudity. 120m. **DIR:** Spike Lee. **CAST:** Laurence Fishburne, Giancarlo Esposito, Tisha Campbell, Spike Lee, Ossie Davis. **1988**

SCHOOL FOR SCANDAL ★★1/2 Richard Sheridan's eighteenth-century comedy about philandering and infidelity became a decent but basically crude and static film in this early adaptation. The limitations of early sound techniques are painfully obvious in this stage-bound presentation. B&W; 75m. **DIR:** Maurice Elvey. **CAST:** Madeleine Carroll, Basil Gill, Ian Fleming. **1930**

SCHOOL FOR SCOUNDRELS ★★★★1/2 A wry, witty British comedy about a training school for one-upmanship with some of England's most talented comics. They teach each other how to get the best of every and any situation. B&W; 94m. **DIR:** Robert Hamer. **CAST:** Alastair Sim, Terry-Thomas, Dennis Price, Ian Carmichael, Janette Scott. **1960**

SCHOOL OF FLESH ★★★1/2 Intense physical attraction keeps the age, class, and cultural differences of two lovers temporarily at bay in this superbly acted French drama. A wealthy, sophisticated career woman invites a younger, bisexual hustler to live with her and seeks out his former male lovers for insights into his shady past and guarded emotions. This intriguing story is loosely based on the novel by Yukio Mishima. In French with English subtitles. Rated R for language and strong sexuality. 101m. **DIR:** Benoit Jacquot. **CAST:** Isabelle Huppert, Vincent Martinez, Vincent Lindon, Marthe Keller. **1999 DVD**

SCHOOL SPIRIT 🦃 Stupid high school flick about an obnoxious libido case (Tom Nolan) who dies in an auto accident and returns as a ghost. Not rated, but an easy R for nudity and profanity. 90m. **DIR:** Alan Holleb. **CAST:** Tom Nolan, Elizabeth Foxx, Larry Linville. **1985**

SCHOOL TIES ★★★★ Dick Wolf's thoughtful study of persecution for the teenage set, with Brendan Fraser just right as a 1950s-era high school senior who conceals his Jewish heritage hoping to cash in on his football skills. A compelling little sleeper. Rated PG-13 for profanity. 107m. **DIR:** Robert Mandel. **CAST:** Brendan Fraser, Chris O'Donnell, Andrew Lowery, Amy Locane, Peter Donat, Zeljko Ivanek. **1992 DVD**

SCI-FIGHTERS ★★★1/2 In twenty-first century Boston, cop Roddy Piper battles a criminal who has escaped from a lunar prison and contracts a virus that transforms him into a fire-breathing mutant. Direct-to-video sci-fi action is well above average for the genre. Rated R for violence, sexual situations, and nudity. 90m. **DIR:** Peter Svatek. **CAST:** Roddy Piper, Billy Drago, Jayne Heitmeyer. **1996 DVD**

SCISSORS ★★1/2 Scissors are the weapon of choice in this intense psychological thriller. Sharon Stone believes she's going insane—or is someone driving her to the edge? Rated R for violence. 105m. **DIR:** Frank DeFelitta. **CAST:** Sharon Stone, Steve Railsback, Michelle Phillips, Ronny Cox. **1990**

SCORCHERS ★★ The lives of three women are tangled up in this poorly written and directed film. Not rated; contains profanity and simulated sex. 80m. **DIR:** David Beaird. **CAST:** Faye Dunaway, James Earl Jones,

Emily Lloyd, Jennifer Tilly, Denholm Elliott, James Wilder, Anthony Geary. **1991**

SCORCHY Connie Stevens is an undercover cop trying to bust a major drug ring. Rated R. 99m. **DIR:** Howard Avedis. **CAST:** Connie Stevens, Cesare Danova, William Smith, Marlene Schmidt, Normann Burton, Joyce Jameson. **1976**

•SCORE, THE ★★★★ Here's a rarity: an old-style caper thriller that gets its juice from strong characterizations and intricate plotting rather than dumb twists and mindless explosions. Career thief Robert DeNiro, despite his better instincts, is suckered into one last heist set up by impatient wannabe Edward Norton; the swag is a priceless scepter stored deep inside Montreal's Customs House. Marlon Brando does a marvelous job as a fey and eccentric fence, and you'll get a kick out of watching these three method actors upstage each other as the "impossible" crib is cracked. Rated R for profanity and violence. 123m. **DIR:** Frank Oz. **CAST:** Robert DeNiro, Edward Norton, Marlon Brando, Angela Bassett. **2001 DVD**

SCORNED ★★1/2 Better-than-average sex thriller about the wife of a businessman who kills himself when a business deal goes sour. Seeking out the man responsible—a family man—she insinuates her way into his life by posing as a tutor for his son and then methodically tears the family apart. The sex is mundane, but the setup is explosive. R-rated and unrated versions; both contain nudity, adult situations, language, and violence. 90m. **DIR:** Andrew Stevens. **CAST:** Shannon Tweed, Andrew Stevens. **1993**

SCORNED 2 ★★1/2 Tane McClure takes over for Shannon Tweed as the vengeance-seeking killer who at the outset of the film has lost her memory and entered into a happy marriage to a psychiatrist. But the past catches up with her. Much of the plot won't make sense if you haven't seen the original *Scorned*. Rated R for sex, violence, and profanity. 97m. **DIR:** Rodney McDonald. **CAST:** Tane McClure, Andrew Stevens, Myles O'Brien, Wendy Schumacher. **1997 DVD**

SCORPIO ONE This blatant rip-off of *2001: A Space Odyssey* is another tedious space-station thriller featuring lifeless performances and clumsy plotting and direction. Rated R for violence and language. 92m. **DIR:** Worth Keeter. **CAST:** Robert Carradine, Jeff Speakman, Robin Curtis, George Murdock, Steve Kanaly. **1997**

SCORPION Dim-witted martial arts film stars nonactor Tonny Tulleners, who takes on a band of terrorists. Grade Z gobbler. Rated R. 98m. **DIR:** William Riead. **CAST:** Tonny Tulleners, Don Murray. **1987 DVD**

•SCORPION KING, THE ★★★ Pro wrestler The Rock turns movie star with this sword-and-sandal swashbuckler, reprising the role he played (briefly) in *The Mummy Returns*. Then he was a villain; now he's a heroic warrior leading a revolt against wicked king Steven Brand, with the help of a beautiful soothsayer (Kelly Hu). It's all good tongue-in-cheek fun, and The Rock makes a likable action hero. Rated PG-13 for action violence and some sensuality. 94m. **DIR:** Chuck Russell. **CAST:** The Rock (Dwayne Johnson), Michael Clarke Duncan, Kelly Hu, Steven Brand. **2002 DVD**

SCORPION SPRING ★★★ A cross-country traveler makes the mistake of offering a ride to a couple of drug runners. One of the better Quentin Tarantino–inspired video thrillers. Rated R for nudity, violence and profanity. 89m. **DIR:** Brian Cox. **CAST:** Patrick McGaw, Esai Morales, Matthew McConaughey, Alfred Molina, Rubén Blades, John Doe. **1996**

SCORPION WOMAN, THE ★★★1/2 An interesting and intelligent May-December story with an ironic twist. A woman judge has an affair with a 23-year-old law trainee. Believable characters highlight what might have been soap-opera material. In German with English subtitles. Not rated. 101m. **DIR:** Susanne Zanke. **CAST:** Angelica Domrose, Fritz Hammel. **1989**

•SCOTLAND, PA ★★★1/2 Shakespeare's *Macbeth* turns into a mordant, blue-collar black comedy here by transplanting it to a fast-food restaurant in the 1970s, with fry cook Joe McBeth and his wife Pat scheming to take over the business. Thanks to good performances, some clever dialogue, and a great 1970s pop soundtrack, the joke never wears out. Rated R for profanity, violence, and drug use. 104m. **DIR:** Billy Morrissette. **CAST:** James LeGros, Maura Tierney, Christopher Walken, Kevin Corrigan, James Rebhorn. **2001**

SCOTT OF THE ANTARCTIC ★★★★ This impeccable re-creation of the race to the South Pole superbly captures the unrelenting frustration of explorer Robert Scott's ill-fated final expedition. Gorgeously lensed and orchestrated by director Charles Frend. 110m. **DIR:** Charles Frend. **CAST:** John Mills, Derek Bond, Kenneth More, Christopher Lee. **1948**

SCOUNDREL, THE ★★★1/2 After his untimely death, an arrogant writer (Noel Coward) is sent back to earth to make amends for the grief he caused. The combination of Coward and dialogue by Ben Hecht and Charles MacArthur is to die for, even if the plot is thin. B&W; 78m. **DIR:** Ben Hecht, Charles MacArthur. **CAST:** Noel Coward, Julie Haydon, Stanley Ridges, Alexander Woollcott, Lionel Stander. **1935**

SCOUT, THE ★★★★ Albert Brooks and Brendan Fraser are outstanding in this touching comedy about a down-on-his-luck major-league baseball scout and his unlikely discovery. In order to keep his job, Brooks needs to find a winner. His search ends in Mexico, where he discovers Steve Nebraska, a natural player with big emotional problems. Dianne Wiest is the psychiatrist desperate to unlock Nebraska's past. Rated PG-13 for adult situations and language. 101m. **DIR:** Michael Ritchie. **CAST:** Albert Brooks, Brendan Fraser, Dianne Wiest, Anne Twomey. **1994 DVD**

SCREAM (1982) A group of vacationing friends spend the night in a ghost town. Rated R. 86m. **DIR:** Byron Quisenberry. **CAST:** Woody Strode, John Ethan Wayne, Hank Worden, Alvy Moore, Gregg Palmer. **1982**

SCREAM (1996) ★★★1/2 This bloody, playful slice of offbeat horror-comedy alternately spoofs and chillingly mimics the slasher film genre. Here a stalker dresses as the Grim Reaper and butchers teens just "to see what your insides look like." It's a scary, often hilarious movie about kids who have picked up all the unwritten rules of Hollywood slasher films (don't answer the door, have sex, or abuse drugs or alcohol—or you die), but break them anyway. Rated R for gore, violence, and language. 111m. **DIR:** Wes Craven. **CAST:** Neve Campbell, David

Arquette, Courteney Cox, Skeet Ulrich, Matthew Lillard, Drew Barrymore, Rose McGowan. **1996 DVD**

SCREAM 2 ★★ When a tabloid TV reporter interviews survivors of the original Woodsboro massacre to promote a film based on the murders, a copycat killer renews the carnage. The self-parody here is that the latest killing spree, like this film, is a sequel and everyone knows how much sequels usually suck. The body and suspect counts go ballistic, but the wicked humor smacks more of formula than ghoulish inspiration. Rated R for gore, nudity, language, and violence. 96m. **DIR:** Wes Craven. **CAST:** Neve Campbell, Jerry O'Connell, Liev Schreiber, David Arquette, Sarah Michelle Gellar, Jamie Kennedy, Courteney Cox, Omar Epps, Jada Pinkett. **1997 DVD**

SCREAM 3 ★★ A serial killer plagues a movie set where the "true" events of *Scream* are being made into a movie. The second sequel to the surprise teen-slasher hit of 1996 hammers the premise even further into the ground; let's hope we can believe director Wes Craven when he promises this will be the last of the series. Carrie Fisher, Roger Corman, Jason Mewes, and Kevin Smith play uncredited cameos. Rated R for violence and profanity. 116m. **DIR:** Wes Craven. **CAST:** David Arquette, Neve Campbell, Courteney Cox Arquette, Patrick Dempsey, Parker Posey. **1999 DVD**

SCREAM AND SCREAM AGAIN ★★★1/2 A top-notch cast excels in this chilling, suspenseful story of a crazed scientist (Vincent Price) attempting to create a race of superbeings while a baffled police force copes with a series of brutal murders that may or may not be related. Complex film benefits from polished performances. Based on the novel *The Disoriented Man*, by Peter Saxon. Rated PG for violence, language, and brief nudity. 95m. **DIR:** Gordon Hessler. **CAST:** Vincent Price, Peter Cushing, Christopher Lee, Christopher Matthews, Michael Gothard. **1970**

SCREAM, BLACULA, SCREAM William Marshall returns as the black vampire, Blacula, in this unimpressive sequel. Rated R. 96m. **DIR:** Bob Kelljan. **CAST:** William Marshall, Pam Grier, Michael Conrad. **1973**

SCREAM DREAM Recently fired musician uses witchcraft to get revenge and sends her screaming fans to commit bloody murders. Not rated; contains gore, violence, and nudity. 69m. **DIR:** Donald Farmer. **CAST:** Melissa Moore. **1989**

SCREAM FOR HELP A suspense-thriller about a teenage girl whose stepfather is trying to kill her and her mother. Rated R for nudity, profanity, and violence. 95m. **DIR:** Michael Winner. **CAST:** Rachel Kelly, David Brooks. **1986**

SCREAM OF FEAR ★★★★ In this overlooked crackerjack thriller, Susan Strasberg plays an invalid who visits her father's Riviera mansion, only to be followed by the corpse of her away-on-business daddy. Well-crafted tale will have you second-guessing yourself to the very end. B&W; 81m. **DIR:** Seth Holt. **CAST:** Susan Strasberg, Ronald Lewis, Ann Todd, Christopher Lee. **1961**

SCREAMERS (1979) An uncharted island, a mad doctor, a crazy inventor, and a bunch of underpaid extras in native costumes. Rated R. 90m. **DIR:** Sergio Martino, Dan T. Miller. **CAST:** Claudio Cassinelli, Richard Johnson, Joseph Cotten. **1979**

SCREAMERS (1996) ★★1/2 So-so science-fiction film features Peter Weller as the commander of a small force attempting to surive the aftermath of a full-fledged war between corporate interests and workers on a far-flung mining planet in the year 2078. Slow-paced and predictable. Rated R for violence and profanity. 107m. **DIR:** Christian Duguay. **CAST:** Peter Weller, Roy Dupuis, Jennifer Rubin, Andrew Lauer, Ron White, Charles Powell. **1996 DVD**

SCREAMING FOR SANITY: TRUTH OR DARE 3 The copper-mask-faced killer returns for yet another go at it in the third film in this turgid series. Not rated; contains violence and gore. 80m. **DIR:** Tim Ritter. **CAST:** Joel Wynkoop. **1997**

SCREAMING MIMI ★★★ After she is nearly murdered, burlesque dancer Anita Ekberg goes for counseling to a psychiatrist, who becomes obsessed with her. Obscure but offbeat psychological thriller atmospherically directed by Gerd Oswald, who went on to TV's *The Outer Limits*. B&W; 79m. **DIR:** Gerd Oswald. **CAST:** Anita Ekberg, Philip Carey, Gypsy Rose Lee, Harry Townes, Linda Cherney, Red Norvo. **1958**

SCREAMING SKULL, THE The old saw about a greedy husband trying to drive his wife crazy. B&W; 68m. **DIR:** Alex Nicol. **CAST:** John Hudson, Peggy Webber, Alex Nicol. **1958 DVD**

SCREEN TEST Teenage boys pose as film producers in order to audition beautiful women nude. Rated R. 84m. **DIR:** Sam Auster. **CAST:** Michael Allan Bloom, Robert Bundy. **1986**

SCREWBALL ACADEMY When a production company tries to make a movie in a small beachfront town, assorted loonies come out of the closet. Reuben Rose is former *SCTV* director John Blanchard under a pseudonym. Rated R for profanity. 90m. **DIR:** Reuben Rose. **CAST:** Colleen Camp, Kenneth Welsh. **1987**

SCREWBALLS Teen-lust comedy takes place at Taft and Adams Educational Center, otherwise known as "T&A High." Rated R for nudity and profanity. 80m. **DIR:** Rafal Zielinski. **CAST:** Peter Keleghan, Linda Speciale, Linda Shayne. **1983**

SCREWED A mistreated chauffeur plots to kidnap and ransom the dog belonging to his miserly employer. The title is all too appropriate in this laughless, brainless, slovenly comedy. Rated PG-13 for profanity. 85m. **DIR:** Scott Alexander, Larry Karaszewski. **CAST:** Norm MacDonald, Elaine Stritch, Dave Chappelle, Daniel Benzali, Sherman Hemsley, Danny DeVito. **2000 DVD**

SCROOGE (1935) ★★★ This little-known British version of Charles Dickens's classic *A Christmas Carol* is faithful to the original story and boasts a standout performance by Seymour Hicks, who also cowrote the screenplay. A truly enjoyable film, unjustly overshadowed by Alistair Sim's bravura performance as Scrooge in the venerated 1951 version. B&W; 78m. **DIR:** Henry Edwards. **CAST:** Seymour Hicks, Donald Calthrop, Robert Cochran, Maurice Evans. **1935**

SCROOGE (1970) ★★★ Tuneful retelling of Charles Dickens's classic *A Christmas Carol* may not be the best acted, but it's certainly the liveliest. Albert Finney paints old curmudgeon Ebeneezer Scrooge with a broad brush, but he makes his character come alive. Rated G. 118m. **DIR:** Ronald Neame. **CAST:** Albert Finney, Alec Guinness, Edith Evans, Kenneth More, Michael Medwin, Laurence Naismith, Kay Walsh. **1970**

SCROOGED ★★1/2 The power of Charles Dickens's uncredited source material and an energetic turn by Carol Kane as the Ghost of Christmas Present save this bloated comedy from total disaster. Bill Murray waltzes through his role as a venal television executive. Rated PG-13 for language. 101m. **DIR:** Richard Donner. **CAST:** Bill Murray, Karen Allen, John Forsythe, John Glover, Bob Goldthwait, Carol Kane, Robert Mitchum, Alfre Woodard. **1988 DVD**

SCRUBBERS ★★★1/2 Realistic depiction of life inside a girls' reform school. With an eye toward inspiring reform, this British film suggests that the well-intentioned but misguided treatment of troubled children puts them on a road to becoming permanently institutionalized. Rated R. 94m. **DIR:** Mai Zetterling. **CAST:** Amanda York, Elizabeth Edmonds. **1982**

SCRUPLES ★★1/2 Bestseller from author Judith Krantz gets the glossy TV soap-opera treatment: an ordinary woman is thrown for a loop when she inherits a conglomerate. Edited down from the television miniseries into feature-length. 100m. **DIR:** Robert Day. **CAST:** Priscilla Barnes, Shelley Smith, Vonetta McGee, Dirk Benedict, James Darren, Jessica Walter, Roy Thinnes. **1981**

SCUM ★★1/2 Harrowing look inside a British reform school. Rated R for violence and profanity. 98m. **DIR:** Alan Clarke. **CAST:** Ray Winstone, Mick Ford, John Judd, Phil Daniels, John Blundell. **1980**

SEA CHASE, THE ★★ Weak and generally uninvolving World War II story finds German sea captain John Wayne attempting to elude capture by British naval forces. Film moves at a snail's pace. 117m. **DIR:** John Farrow. **CAST:** John Wayne, Lana Turner, James Arness, Tab Hunter, Lyle Bettger, Claude Akins, David Farrar. **1955**

SEA DEVILS ★★ Victor McLaglen and Ida Lupino play father and daughter in this soggy tale of Coast Guard trial and tribulation. McLaglen and Preston Foster are service rivals given to settling problems with their fists. Unfortunately, the audience can't fight back. B&W; 88m. **DIR:** Ben Stoloff. **CAST:** Victor McLaglen, Preston Foster, Ida Lupino, Donald Woods. **1937 DVD**

SEA GYPSIES, THE ★★★ Director Stewart Raffill wrote this adventure movie which tells of five castaways in the Pacific who end up on a remote Aleutian island. This Disney-style tale is climaxed by a race against the approaching Alaskan winter to build a makeshift escape craft. Rated G. 102m. **DIR:** Stewart Raffill. **CAST:** Robert Logan, Mikki Jamison-Olsen, Heather Rattray. **1978**

SEA HAWK, THE ★★★★ Errol Flynn was the best of the screen's costumed adventurers. *The Sea Hawk* shows him at his swashbuckling peak. He plays a buccaneer sea captain who is given tacit approval by Queen Elizabeth I (Flora Robson) to wreak havoc on the Spanish fleet and their cities in the New World. B&W; 109m. **DIR:** Michael Curtiz. **CAST:** Errol Flynn, Flora Robson, Claude Rains, Donald Crisp, Alan Hale Sr., Henry Daniell, Gilbert Roland. **1940**

SEA HOUND, THE ★★ Modern-day pirates searching for a buried Spanish treasure on an uncharted island find that they've bitten off more than they can chew when veteran action star Buster Crabbe shows up to spoil their plans. Every generation deserves its own pirate adventures, and with good-natured, dedicated Crabbe along, it's always an enjoyable ride. B&W. **DIR:** Walter B. Eason, Mack V. Wright. **CAST:** Buster Crabbe, Jimmy Lloyd, Pamela Blake, Ralph Hodges, Robert Barron, Hugh Prosser, Rick Vallin, Jack Ingram, Spencer Chan, Pierce Lyden. **1947**

SEA LION, THE ★★1/2 Stern sea story with hard-bitten Hobart Bosworth as a tyrannical ship's master who vents his pent-up hatred on the men in his charge. But romance rears its head and we find out that he's not all bad; he was just acting like a sadist because he had a broken heart. Silent. B&W; 50m. **DIR:** Rowland V. Lee. **CAST:** Hobart Bosworth, Bessie Love, Richard Morris. **1921**

SEA OF GRASS, THE ★★1/2 This is more soap than horse opera, where ruthless cattle baron Spencer Tracy drives his eastern-bred wife, Katharine Hepburn, into the arms of lawyer Melvyn Douglas. Disappointing. B&W; 123m. **DIR:** Elia Kazan. **CAST:** Spencer Tracy, Katharine Hepburn, Melvyn Douglas, Robert Walker, Harry Carey. **1946**

SEA OF LOVE ★★★★ Al Pacino made an explosive comeback in this sexy thriller as a New York police detective in the midst of a middle-age crisis. To forget his woes, Pacino throws himself into an investigation of some serial killings, which seems to have something to do with the lonely hearts listings in the newspaper personals columns. Rated R for violence, profanity, and simulated sex. 110m. **DIR:** Harold Becker. **CAST:** Al Pacino, Ellen Barkin, John Goodman. **1989 DVD**

SEA PEOPLE ★★★1/2 This amiable, family-oriented fable, scripted by Wendy Biller and Christopher Hawthorne, involves an adolescent girl and the two rather eccentric older folks she befriends; it seems these senior citizens have a propensity for sleeping while submerged in tanks of seawater. The story turns on the young heroine's efforts to help these oldsters "return home" when their land-based life proves unworkable; the result is both charming and bittersweet, without ever becoming unduly maudlin. Suitable for all ages. 92m. **DIR:** Vic Sarin. **CAST:** Hume Cronyn, Joan Gregson, Tegan Moss, Shawn Roberts. **1998 DVD**

SEA SHALL NOT HAVE THEM, THE ★★★ Nicely done World War II film about British air rescue operations. Main story follows an RAF bomber crew shot down over the North Sea and their rescue from the ocean. B&W; 92m. **DIR:** Lewis Gilbert. **CAST:** Michael Redgrave, Dirk Bogarde, John Mitchell. **1955**

SEA WOLF, THE (1941) ★★★★1/2 Rousing version of Jack London's dark seafaring adventure features a splendidly complex portrayal by Edward G. Robinson as the evil ship captain of the title. One of director Michael Curtiz's best films. B&W; 90m. **DIR:** Michael Curtiz. **CAST:** Edward G. Robinson, John Garfield, Ida Lupino, Alexander Knox, Gene Lockhart, Barry Fitzgerald, Stanley Ridges, David Bruce, Howard DaSilva. **1941**

SEA WOLF, THE (1993) 🦃 Boredom washes over the deck in waves in this painful-to-watch remake of the oft-filmed Jack London novel. A flat script and poor performances combine to sink this unworthy effort. Made for TV. 96m. **DIR:** Michael Anderson. **CAST:** Charles Bronson, Christopher Reeve, Catherine Mary Stewart, Marc Singer. **1993**

SEA WOLVES, THE ★★★ A World War II version of *The Over the Hill Gang*. Gregory Peck and Roger Moore play British officers who recruit a bunch of Boer War veter-

ans now in their autumn years to do some espionage along the coast of India. While the film relies too heavily on comedy that doesn't work, the last twenty minutes have enough spirit to redeem it. The film is based on a true story. Rated PG for violence and sex. 120m. **DIR:** Andrew V. McLaglen. **CAST:** Gregory Peck, Roger Moore, David Niven, Trevor Howard, Barbara Kellerman, Patrick Macnee. **1980 DVD**

•SEAFARERS, THE ★★ This propaganda film for the Seafarers International Union is completely unremarkable, except that the late, great Stanley Kubrick directed it. Kubrick took the contract for this work early in his career, and this was his first color feature. Lost for forty years, this video is now available for avid fans, but the average viewer will not find much of interest here. Not rated; contains brief nudity. 29m. **DIR:** Stanley Kubrick. **1952**

•SEAMLESS 🦃 The streets brought them together, their love of Rave parties threatens to tear them apart. There's nothing seamless about this ineptly made teen drama that jumps from one clumsy moment to the next, where characters make speeches rather than talk to each other, and then try to look cool. They're not. There's nothing here that would have warranted a release except costar Shannon Elizabeth's current popularity. Also released as *Seamless: Kidz Rule*. Rated R for adult situations, drug use, language, and violence. 91m. **DIR:** Debra LeMattre. **CAST:** Kentaro Seagal, Shannon Elizabeth, Peter Alexander. **1999 DVD**

SEANCE ON A WET AFTERNOON ★★★★1/2 This is an absolutely fabulous movie. An unbalanced medium (Kim Stanley) involves her meek husband (Richard Attenborough) in a kidnapping scheme that brings about their downfall. Brilliant acting by all, working from a superb script. No rating, but some intense sequences. B&W; 115m. **DIR:** Bryan Forbes. **CAST:** Kim Stanley, Richard Attenborough, Patrick Magee, Nanette Newman. **1964**

SEARCH, THE ★★★★★ Heart-tugging story of the plight of displaced children in post–World War II Europe. One mother (Jarmila Novotna) searches for her son (Ivan Jandl), taken from her in a concentration camp. Montgomery Clift is an American soldier who finds and cares for the boy while the mother's search continues. B&W; 105m. **DIR:** Fred Zinnemann. **CAST:** Montgomery Clift, Aline MacMahon, Wendell Corey, Jarmila Novotna, Ivan Jandl. **1948**

SEARCH AND DESTROY (1981) 🦃 Vietnam veteran is chased by a Vietnamese villain. Not rated, the film has violence and profanity. 93m. **DIR:** William Fruet. **CAST:** Perry King, Don Stroud, Tisa Farrow, George Kennedy, Park Jong Soo. **1981**

SEARCH AND DESTROY (1988) ★★ There's no shortage of action, but little else noteworthy in this science-fiction action yarn about the capturing of a secret biological warfare research station. Rated R, primarily for violence. 90m. **DIR:** J. Christian Ingvordsen. **CAST:** Stuart Garrison Day. **1988**

SEARCH AND DESTROY (1995) ★★ A dream team of terminally cool actors is wasted in this quirky, mostly unfunny satire about desperate hustling, pop philosophy, and big money. Rated R for language, drug use, and violence. 100m. **DIR:** David Salle. **CAST:** Griffin Dunne, Illeana Douglas, Christopher Walken, John Turturro, Ethan Hawke, Rosanna Arquette, Martin Scorsese, Dennis Hopper. **1995 DVD**

SEARCH FOR BRIDEY MURPHY, THE ★★ Made quickly and cheaply (it shows) to cash in on the then-popular and controversial book by Morey Bernstein. Story of a woman under hypnosis who was able to recall her previous existence as a small girl in Ireland in the early 1800s. Dull. B&W; 84m. **DIR:** Noel Langley. **CAST:** Teresa Wright, Louis Hayward. **1956**

SEARCH FOR ONE-EYE JIMMY, THE ★★★ Everyone in this Brooklyn neighborhood is too much of a character, but earthy humor and an unusual cast counteract the outrageousness. There are laugh-out-loud moments and the ending is a scream, despite the sorry budget. Worth renting just for John Turturro's debut as a disco dancer. Rated R for profanity and violence. 86m. **DIR:** Sam Henry Kass. **CAST:** Michael Badalucco, Holt McCallany, Samuel L. Jackson, John Turturro, Steve Buscemi, Jennifer Beals, Nicholas Turturro, Ray "Boom Boom" Mancini, Anne Meara. **1993**

SEARCH FOR SIGNS OF INTELLIGENT LIFE IN THE UNIVERSE, THE ★★★★ As Trudy says in this film, reality "is nothing but a collective hunch." But the hunch that evolves from the fertile imaginations of actress Lily Tomlin and writer Jane Wagner is funny, perceptive, and right on target. Trudy, a bag lady in touch with alien life-forms, is just one of a dozen diverse characters brought to life in a bravura performance by Tomlin, cleverly adapted from her one-woman play. Rated PG-13. 109m. **DIR:** John Bailey. **CAST:** Lily Tomlin. **1991**

SEARCH FOR THE GODS ★★ This fairly involving but failed TV-pilot about three adventurers in search of missing pieces to an ancient puzzle makes for an unfinished picture. 90m. **DIR:** Jud Taylor. **CAST:** Kurt Russell, Stephen McHattie, Victoria Racimo, Raymond St. Jacques, Albert Paulsen, Ralph Bellamy. **1975**

SEARCHERS, THE ★★★★★ John Ford is the most celebrated director of Westerns, and *The Searchers* is considered by many to be his masterpiece. This thoughtful film follows Ethan Edwards, an embittered Indian-hating, ex–Confederate soldier as he leads the search for his niece, who was kidnapped years earlier by Indians. As time goes on, we begin to wonder whether Edwards is out to save the girl or kill her. 119m. **DIR:** John Ford. **CAST:** John Wayne, Natalie Wood, Jeffrey Hunter, Ward Bond, Vera Miles, Harry Carey Jr., Ken Curtis, Lana Wood, Patrick Wayne. **1956 DVD**

SEARCHING FOR BOBBY FISCHER ★★★★1/2 This film is about prodigy Josh Waitzkin, a 7-year-old boy whose understanding of chess puts him in the running to be "the next Bobby Fischer." This praise could easily be a curse—Fischer devoted his life to the game and then became a recluse after becoming the world champion. Adapted from the book by Josh's father, Fred Waitzkin, this thought-provoking commentary explores how success in America is often emphasized over decency. Rated PG for brief profanity. 107m. **DIR:** Steven Zaillian. **CAST:** Joe Mantegna, Ben Kingsley, Laurence Fishburne, Joan Allen, Max Pomeranc, Robert Stephens, David Paymer, William H. Macy, Dan Hedaya. **1993 DVD**

SEASIDE SWINGERS ★★ Fans of the Sixties British invasion will want to see this comedy about a TV talent contest starring Freddie and the Dreamers. There are lots of songs by different groups. Trivia buffs may want

to see costar Michael Sarne, who went on to direct *Myra Breckenridge*. 94m. **DIR:** James Hill. **CAST:** John Leyton, Michael Sarne, Freddie and the Dreamers, Ron Moody, Liz Fraser. **1965**

SEASON OF FEAR ★★ Upon locating his estranged inventor father, a young man discovers Dad's latest wife to be the victim of extreme mental and physical cruelty at the homestead. Or is she? Fetid thriller has overtones of *Body Heat*. Rated R for nudity. 89m. **DIR:** Doug Campbell. **CAST:** Michael Bowen, Ray Wise, Clancy Brown, Clare Wren, Michael J. Pollard. **1989**

SEASON OF GIANTS, A ★★ Slow-moving, overly long TV bio of artist Michelangelo. With a running time of over three hours, this is rough going. 195m. **DIR:** Jerry London. **CAST:** F. Murray Abraham, Steven Berkoff, John Glover, Ian Holm, Raf Vallone, Mark Frankel. **1991**

SEASON OF THE WITCH 🦃 Also known as *Hungry Wives*. Rated R. 90m. **DIR:** George A. Romero. **CAST:** Jan White, Ray Lane. **1972**

SECOND BEST ★★★★ William Hurt plays an emotionally repressed, 42-year-old single man who decides to adopt a 10-year-old boy. The troubled new arrival doesn't mesh well with Hurt's ordered life, but before long each begins to view the other as a second shot at possible happiness. The only drawback is David Cook's script—adapted from his own novel—which concludes abruptly. Rated PG-13 for dramatic intensity. 105m. **DIR:** Chris Menges. **CAST:** William Hurt, Jane Horrocks, Prunella Scales, John Hurt, Chris Cleary Miles. **1994**

SECOND CHANCE ★★1/2 Robert Mitchum plays protector to a former gangster's girlfriend (Linda Darnell) as they are pursued through South America by hit man Jack Palance. This passable chase melodrama was Howard Hughes's first excursion into wide screen, and the often-imitated climax aboard the gondola cars suspended above a deep chasm is the centerpiece of the film. 82m. **DIR:** Rudolph Maté. **CAST:** Robert Mitchum, Linda Darnell, Jack Palance, Reginald Sheffield, Roy Roberts. **1953**

SECOND CHORUS ★★★ Rival trumpet players Fred Astaire and Burgess Meredith vie for the affections of Paulette Goddard, who works for Artie Shaw. The two want into Shaw's orchestra and make a comic mess of Goddard's attempts to help them. B&W; 83m. **DIR:** H. C. Potter. **CAST:** Paulette Goddard, Fred Astaire, Burgess Meredith, Charles Butterworth. **1940**

SECOND CIVIL WAR, THE ★★★ In a scenario of the near future, the United States has lost its unity; California is wholly Latino, and Rhode Island is filled with Asian immigrants. Idaho governor Beau Bridges takes a stand and closes his borders to refugee third-world children, which sets up a confrontation between his National Guard troops and the U.S. Army. The whole shooting match unfolds as witnessed by the producers and reporters of one television station, and tempers flare all around as the crisis escalates. While there are some genuinely hilarious moments, the whole eventually sags beneath the weight of its disparate parts. Rated R for profanity and violence. 100m. **DIR:** Joe Dante. **CAST:** Beau Bridges, Joanna Cassidy, James Coburn, Kevin Dunn, Phil Hartman, Dan Hedaya, James Earl Jones, Denis Leary, Elizabeth Peña, Ron Perlman. **1997**

SECOND FIDDLE ★★★1/2 Irving Berlin's original score makes this movie work today. It's a spoof of the search for the right actress to play Scarlett O'Hara. Talent scouts seeking "A Girl of the North" go to Minnesota to interview a pretty schoolteacher who ice skates like a dream. One of Sonja Henie's most popular films with one of her best supporting casts. B&W; 86m. **DIR:** Sidney Lanfield. **CAST:** Sonja Henie, Tyrone Power, Rudy Vallee, Edna May Oliver, Mary Healy, Lyle Talbot, Alan Dinehart, The King Sisters. **1939**

SECOND JUNGLE BOOK, THE: MOWGLI AND BALOO ★★★1/2 Satisfying addition to the *Jungle Book* series (this one didn't come from the Disney factory) stars young Jamie Williams as jungle boy Mowgli, who lives with his bear friend, Baloo, in the jungle. Their serene existence is interrupted by a scout representing P. T. Barnum. When Mowgli hides out deeper in the forest, he stumbles across a lost city whose only inhabitant is a deranged soldier. Rated PG. 89m. **DIR:** Duncan MacLachlan. **CAST:** Bill Campbell, Roddy McDowall, Jamie Williams, David Paul Francis. **1997**

SECOND SIGHT ★★ Silly rip-off of *Ghostbusters* stars John Larroquette as the head of a detective agency that solves its cases with the help of a mystic (Bronson Pinchot). TV-sitcom–style shtick. Rated PG for profanity and violence. 85m. **DIR:** Joel Zwick. **CAST:** John Larroquette, Bronson Pinchot, Bess Armstrong, Stuart Pankin, John Schuck, James Tolkan. **1989**

•SECOND SKIN ★★1/2 Decent stab at *film noir* bleeds more twist than plot, but the cast seems up to the challenge. Angus MacFadyen stars as a used bookshop owner haunted by his past. When the woman he has just hired as an assistant gets hit by a car and loses her memory, he decides to help her piece together her past. This act leads him to reconcile his bitterness, putting both characters on the path to recovery. Then bad guy Peter Fonda shows up, setting into motion a series of events that are less satisfying than the characters trapped in them. Plot twists help disguise the fact that we've seen most of this before. Rated R for adult situations, language, and violence. 95m. **DIR:** Darrell Roodt. **CAST:** Natasha Henstridge, Angus MacFadyen, Peter Fonda, Liam Waite. **2000 DVD**

SECOND WOMAN, THE ★★★ Is Robert Young paranoid, or is the whole world crazy? Strange and violent occurrences are plaguing the life of this talented architect. Betsy Drake, smitten with the confused fellow, is the only onlooker who doesn't doubt his sanity. This dark drama maintains a steady undercurrent of suspense. B&W; 91m. **DIR:** James V. Kern. **CAST:** Robert Young, Betsy Drake, John Sutton. **1951 DVD**

SECONDS ★★★★ Director John Frankenheimer's riveting thriller, originally released in 1966, makes its video debut with additional footage cut from the U.S. print. John Randolph costars as an older man who turns to a secret organization for a new lease on life. After extensive plastic surgery, he emerges as young and handsome Rock Hudson. Fascinating premise plays like a creepy episode of *The Twilight Zone*. Rated R for nudity. B&W; 107m. **DIR:** John Frankenheimer. **CAST:** Rock Hudson, John Randolph, Murray Hamilton, Salome Jens, Will Geer. **1996 DVD**

SECRET, THE ★★★1/2 When it is discovered that an otherwise bright and talented 9-year-old boy cannot

read, family ties begin to unravel in a small town on Cape Cod. Outstanding performances, assured direction, and insightful writing transform what could have been a typical "disease-of-the-week" TV movie about dyslexia into a touching human drama. Made for TV. 92m. **DIR:** Karen Arthur. **CAST:** Kirk Douglas, Bruce Boxleitner, Brock Peters, Linda Harrington, Jesse R. Tendler. **1992**

SECRET ADMIRER ★★1/2 A sweet-natured sex comedy that suffers from predictability, this stars C. Thomas Howell as a 16-year-old who, on the last day of school before summer vacation, receives an anonymous letter from a female who swears undying love. He hopes it's from the girl of his dreams (Kelly Preston) and decides to find out. Rated R for nudity, light violence, and profanity. 100m. **DIR:** David Greenwalt. **CAST:** C. Thomas Howell, Lori Loughlin, Kelly Preston, Dee Wallace, Cliff De Young, Fred Ward, Leigh Taylor-Young. **1985**

SECRET AGENT, THE (1936) ★★★ Offbeat espionage film by the master of suspense contains many typical Alfred Hitchcock touches, but lacks the pacing and characterizations that set his best efforts apart from those of his contemporaries. Alternately grim and humorous, this uneven film (based on a novel by Somerset Maugham) is still watchable and comparable with many of the best films in the genre. B&W; 93m. **DIR:** Alfred Hitchcock. **CAST:** John Gielgud, Madeleine Carroll, Robert Young, Peter Lorre, Percy Marmont, Lilli Palmer. **1936 DVD**

SECRET AGENT, THE (1996) ★★★1/2 Slow-moving but involving, this handsome adaptation retains the ironical humor and multilayered drama of Joseph Conrad's novel. A morally challenged anarchist lives in 1894 London with his wife and her brother. The story's truth is found in the wife's emotional performance as she offers up innocence at the altar of politics. Rated R for violence and profanity. 95m. **DIR:** Christopher Hampton. **CAST:** Bob Hoskins, Patricia Arquette, Gérard Depardieu, Christian Bale, Robin Williams. **1996**

SECRET AGENT (TV SERIES) ★★★1/2 The suave and resourceful John Drake turned out to have more than one life; after the limited success of his 1961 series, *Danger Man*, he returned in 1965 with the flamboyant and popular *Secret Agent*. The new show disappeared after forty-five episodes had been aired. (But Drake would appear again—in a sense—as *The Prisoner*.) In this format, Drake worked for the British agency known as M.I.9 and took orders from an "M"-like figure named Hobbs. The hour-length dramas were grittier and more realistic than their American counterparts. B&W; 53m. **DIR:** Don Chaffey, Peter Maxwell, Michael Truman. **CAST:** Patrick McGoohan, Peter Madden. **1965–1966 DVD**

SECRET AGENT CLUB 🦃 Professional wrestler Hulk Hogan softens up for this completely banal exercise in warped family values, playing a toy store owner by day, secret agent by night. Rated PG for violence. 90m. **DIR:** John Murlowski. **CAST:** Hulk Hogan, Lesley-Anne Down, Richard Moll, Barry Bostwick, James Hong. **1996**

SECRET BEYOND THE DOOR ★★1/2 Master craftsman Fritz Lang does the best he can with this melodramatic potboiler about a lonely woman (Joan Bennett) who marries a mysterious stranger (Michael Redgrave) after a whirlwind courtship. Slowly she begins to suspect that her husband may be a murderer. B&W; 99m. **DIR:** Fritz Lang. **CAST:** Joan Bennett, Michael Redgrave. **1948**

SECRET CEREMONY ★★1/2 Typical Joseph Losey psychodrama about a psychotic girl (Mia Farrow) semikidnapping an aging streetwalker (Elizabeth Taylor) who reminds her of her dead mother. Robert Mitchum plays Farrow's lecherous stepfather. With its strong sexual undertones, this film is not for kids (and probably not for some adults). 108m. **DIR:** Joseph Losey. **CAST:** Elizabeth Taylor, Mia Farrow, Robert Mitchum, Peggy Ashcroft, Pamela Brown. **1968**

SECRET CUTTING ★★★ Most films covering issues of abuse or addiction wind up no better than public-service announcements—but this made-for-cable original, about the pressures that drive one high-school girl to cut herself, is actually quite interesting. Decent acting pads out the somewhat thin plot, and several scenes of extremely bad parenting lighten up the sobering story. Not rated. 95m. **DIR:** Norma Bailey. **CAST:** Sean Young, Kimberlee Peterson, Robert Wisdom, Taylor Stanley, Rhea Perlman. **2000**

SECRET DIARY OF SIGMUND FREUD, THE ★★★1/2 A consistently humorous satire on the early life of Freud. Everyone in the cast looks to be having a swell time. Sexual and psychological jokes abound. That they are flamboyantly funny is no small feat. Rated PG. 129m. **DIR:** Danford B. Greene. **CAST:** Bud Cort, Carol Kane, Klaus Kinski, Marisa Berenson, Carroll Baker, Ferdinand Mayne, Dick Shawn. **1984**

SECRET FRIENDS ★★★1/2 Dennis Potter, creator of *The Singing Detective*, made his feature directorial debut with this strange, challenging mind-game film. Alan Bates stars as an artist obsessed with doing away with his wife. Rewarding, if difficult, film. Bates, as usual, is superb. Not rated. 97m. **DIR:** Dennis Potter. **CAST:** Alan Bates, Gina Bellman, Frances Barber, Tony Doyle. **1992**

SECRET GARDEN, THE (1949) ★★★★ A captivating adaptation of Frances Hodgson Burnett's classic. Margaret O'Brien dominates the story as the youngster who finds a beautiful garden in the midst of adult confusion in Victorian England. The story itself inspired a made-for-TV movie in 1987 and a grandiose Broadway musical in 1991. The final sequence is in Technicolor. B&W; 92m. **DIR:** Fred M. Wilcox. **CAST:** Margaret O'Brien, Dean Stockwell, Herbert Marshall, Gladys Cooper, Elsa Lanchester. **1949**

SECRET GARDEN, THE (1984) ★★1/2 Slow BBC production about a little girl uprooted from India and placed in the care of her cold, stern uncle in his manor house in England. Of course the girl thaws her uncle because of her resemblance to his dear, late wife. Pretty standard stuff, although it's well acted at least. Not rated; suitable for all. 107m. **DIR:** Katrina Murray. **CAST:** Sarah Hollis Andrews, David Patterson. **1984**

SECRET GARDEN, THE (1987) ★★★★ *Hallmark Hall of Fame*'s adaptation of the classic children's story. Gennie James is fantastic as Mary Lennox, the spoiled girl who must live with her mean-spirited uncle after her parents die of cholera. Good acting from the entire cast, a wonderful plot, and beautiful sets make this an enjoyable film for the whole family. 100m. **DIR:** Alan

Grint. **CAST:** Gennie James, Barret Oliver, Michael Hordern, Billie Whitelaw, Derek Jacobi. **1987 DVD**

SECRET GARDEN, THE (1993) ★★★★ Director Agnieszka Holland creates a truly gorgeous, remarkably subtle and stately version of the children's classic. After her self-indulgent, unloving parents are killed during an earthquake in India, a spoiled, headstrong little girl is sent to live with her uncle in a house full of mysterious secrets. Magical. Rated G. 106m. **DIR:** Agnieszka Holland. **CAST:** Kate Maberly, Heydon Prowse, Andrew Knott, Maggie Smith, Laura Crossley, John Lynch. **1993 DVD**

SECRET GARDEN, THE (1994) ★★★ Based on Frances Hodgson Burnett's book, this is the tale of a spoiled orphan who learns to help someone else (her bedridden cousin). She also discovers the joy of animals and the beauty to be found in an abandoned garden. Average animation is helped by riveting plot. Anndi McAffee provides the voice of Mary, the heroine. Of the five original songs written for the film, only the one about flowers blooming is a winner. Not rated, but the witch-like housekeeper/control freak may be too frightening for young viewers. 72m. **DIR:** Dave Edwards. **1994**

SECRET HONOR ★★★★ This one-man show features Philip Baker Hall as Richard Nixon—drinking, swearing, and going completely over the top in his ravings, on such subjects as Castro, Kennedy, and Henry Kissinger. Fascinating, with Hall's performance a wonder. A one-of-a-kind movie from Robert Altman. Rated PG. 90m. **DIR:** Robert Altman. **CAST:** Philip Baker Hall. **1984**

SECRET KINGDOM, THE ★★ A boy discovers a tiny kingdom hidden beneath the kitchen sink. He and his sister are drawn into the world where they find themselves battling for an evil king. So-so entertainment for the kids. Rated PG. **DIR:** David Schmoeller. **CAST:** Billie O., Jamieson K. Price, Tricia Dickson, Andrew Dicote. **1997**

SECRET LIFE OF AN AMERICAN WIFE, THE ★★ Bored wife Anne Jackson decides to moonlight as a call girl. Her first client is her husband's employer. Husband walks in on wife and employer, etc. Director and writer George Axelrod had a cute idea, but it really doesn't gel. 93m. **DIR:** George Axelrod. **CAST:** Walter Matthau, Anne Jackson, Patrick O'Neal, Edy Williams, Richard Bull. **1968**

SECRET LIFE OF JEFFREY DAHMER, THE ★★★ Fictional portrayal of the infamous serial killer is a low-budget effort that works despite its shortcomings. Carl Crew is magnetic as Dahmer, who invited unsuspecting men into his spider's web, took advantage of them, and then killed them. Most of the mayhem is offscreen but is effective nonetheless, giving us some insight about the loner who captivated the nation. Not rated; contains violence, adult language, and situations. 100m. **DIR:** David R. Bowen. **CAST:** Carl Crew. **1993 DVD**

SECRET LIFE OF WALTER MITTY, THE ★★★★ Based on James Thurber's story, this comedy presents Danny Kaye as a timid man who dreams of being a brave, glory-bound hero. This comedy provides plenty of laughs and enjoyable moments. 105m. **DIR:** Norman Z. McLeod. **CAST:** Danny Kaye, Virginia Mayo, Boris Karloff, Reginald Denny, Florence Bates, Ann Rutherford, Thurston Hall. **1947 DVD**

SECRET OBSESSIONS 🦃 Maudlin, morose, melodramatic yawner. Rated PG. 82m. **DIR:** Henri Vart. **CAST:** Julie Christie, Ben Gazzara, Patrick Bruel, Jean Carmet. **1988**

SECRET OF MY SUCCESS, THE ★★★1/2 The secret of this movie's success can be found in its ingredients: a witty script, vibrant direction, bouncy pop score, ingratiating star, and gifted supporting cast. Michael J. Fox is terrifically likable as a wildly ambitious Kansas lad who heads for New York City with plans to conquer the corporate world overnight. Rated PG-13. 110m. **DIR:** Herbert Ross. **CAST:** Michael J. Fox, Helen Slater, Margaret Whitton, Richard Jordan, Christopher Murney, John Pankow, Fred Gwynne. **1987 DVD**

SECRET OF NIMH, THE ★★★★★ Lovers of classic screen animation, rejoice! Don Bluth's *The Secret of Nimh* is the best feature-length cartoon to be released since the golden age of Walt Disney. This movie, about the adventures of a widow mouse, is more than just a children's tale. Adults will enjoy it, too. Dom DeLuise, Peter Strauss, John Carradine (voices). Rated G. 82m. **DIR:** Don Bluth. **1982 DVD**

SECRET OF ROAN INISH, THE ★★★★ When a 10-year-old girl is sent to live with her grandparents on Ireland's rugged west coast, she hears local legends of *selkies*—half-human, half-seal Celtic beings—and becomes convinced that these strange creatures may somehow have saved her infant brother, thought lost at sea years earlier. Haskell Wexler's rich cinematography lends a sumptuous aura to a story guaranteed to delight all ages. Not rated. 103m. **DIR:** John Sayles. **CAST:** Jeni Courtney, Mick Lallay, Eileen Colgan, Richard Sheridan. **1994**

SECRET OF THE BLUE ROOM, THE ★★ A woman challenges her three suitors to vie for her affections by spending the night at a castle in a room that has been sealed since three people were murdered there twenty years ago. Obviously inspired by *The Old Dark House,* but not nearly as good. B&W; 66m. **DIR:** Kurt Neumann. **CAST:** Lionel Atwill, Gloria Stuart, Paul Lukas, Edward Arnold, Onslow Stevens. **1933**

SECRET OF THE SWORD, THE 🦃 Characters from the television series *He-Man and the Masters of the Universe* are featured in this poorly animated, ineptly written feature-length cartoon. Rated G. 90m. **DIR:** Bill Reed, Gwen Wetzler, Ed Friedman, Lou Kachivas, Marsh Lamore. **1985**

SECRET PASSION OF ROBERT CLAYTON, THE ★★★ Who really killed the stripper? If you like good court scenes, you'll enjoy this twisted plot of love, death, family, and the law. Made for cable. 91m. **DIR:** E. W. Swackhamer. **CAST:** John Mahoney, Scott Valentine, Eve Gordon, Kevin Conroy. **1992**

SECRET RAPTURE, THE ★★★★ David Hare's stage play is the catalyst for this mesmerizing and haunting tale of two estranged sisters whose lives are thrown into chaos when their father dies. Not only must they contend with each other, they must also put up with their scheming, alcoholic stepmother, deliciously played by Joanne Whalley. Tensions mount as tragedy befalls the household, turning sister against sister. Rated R for adult situations. 96m. **DIR:** Howard Davies. **CAST:** Joanne Whalley, Juliet Stevenson, Penelope Wilton, Neil Pearson, Alan Howard. **1993**

SECRET WAR OF HARRY FRIGG, THE ★★ A group of Allied generals has been captured by the Italians. In

their vast wisdom, the high command chooses a disgruntled private (Paul Newman) to go behind the lines and free them. This is a very basic comedy, with few original laughs. Rated PG. 110m. **DIR:** Jack Smight. **CAST:** Paul Newman, Sylva Koscina, Andrew Duggan, James Gregory. **1968**

SECRET WEAPON ★★ A lab technician working on Israel's secret nuclear bomb capabilities decides to go public in order to stop the arms proliferation. Predictable and slowly paced TV movie. 95m. **DIR:** Ian Sharp. **CAST:** Karen Allen, Griffin Dunne, Jeroen Krabbé. **1990**

SECRET WEAPONS Sleazy made-for-TV potboiler about a Russian espionage training camp. 96m. **DIR:** Don Taylor. **CAST:** James Franciscus, Sally Kellerman, Linda Hamilton, Geena Davis. **1985**

SECRETARY, THE ★★★ Another in the you-just-can't-get-good-help-these-days series of suspense thrillers. Mel Harris stars as an executive whose newly assigned secretary wants not only her job but apparently her head as well. Rated R for profanity and violence. 94m. **DIR:** Andrew Lane. **CAST:** Mel Harris, Sheila Kelley, Barry Bostwick, James Russo. **1994**

SECRETS ★★ Jacqueline Bisset's torrid sex scene is about the only interesting thing in this turgid soap opera. Rated R for nudity, suggested sex, and profanity. 86m. **DIR:** Philip Saville. **CAST:** Jacqueline Bisset, Per Oscarsson, Shirley Knight, Robert Powell. **1971 DVD**

SECRETS AND LIES ★★★★★ This searing, hilarious examination of the human condition is packed with riveting dialogue as an extended working-class British family peers at the world through an enslaving veil of deceit, anxious hope, and broken dreams. A black optometrist initiates a fall of emotional dominoes when she seeks out her biological mum after the death of her adopted parents. The trail leads to the home of a frumpy white factory worker awash in self-pity, and a dark domestic storm erupts with painful but cleansing force. Rated R for language. 142m. **DIR:** Mike Leigh. **CAST:** Brenda Blethyn, Marianne Jean-Baptiste, Timothy Spall, Phyllis Logan, Claire Rushbrook, Ron Cook. **1996**

SECRETS IN THE ATTIC ★★★ Independent thriller about a 12-year-old girl named Amy, whose retreat to her aunt's house unlocks a murder mystery dating back thirty years involving her grandparents. While rummaging through the attic, Amy comes across dolls representing her grandparents which seem to communicate the killer's identity, and after doing some investigative work, she comes to a startling conclusion. Creepy moments involving the haunted dollhouse and eerie flashbacks recalling the murders give this thriller the right stuff to raise goose bumps. Rated PG-13 for violence. 89m. **DIR:** Diane Haak. **CAST:** Amanda Roese, Lindsay Jackson, Rebekah Baker. **1993**

SECRETS OF A MARRIED MAN TV-movie involves William Shatner's attempt at conquering the final frontier of infidelity. 100m. **DIR:** William A. Graham. **CAST:** William Shatner, Cybill Shepherd, Michelle Phillips, Glynn Turman. **1984**

SECRETS OF A SOUL ★★ A chemistry professor is troubled by dream images and premonitions of murder when he learns his wife's cousin is returning from India. This early attempt to convert psychoanalysis into cinematic entertainment was bound to suffer from heavy-handed and simplistic imagery (but then, was *Spellbound* any better twenty years later?). Germany. Silent. 94m. **DIR:** G. W. Pabst. **CAST:** Werner Krauss. **1926**

SECRETS OF THE WASTELAND ★★1/2 Hopalong Cassidy and his friends agree to help a group of archaeologists search some cliff dwellings but run into trouble with the local Chinese. Not as much action as some in the series but plenty of skulduggery and secret passages highlight this entry. B&W; 65m. **DIR:** Derwin Abrahams. **CAST:** William Boyd, Brad King, Andy Clyde, Barbara Britton, Douglas Fowley, Soo Young. **1941**

SECRETS OF WOMEN (WAITING WOMEN) ★★★1/2 Infidelity is the theme of this early Ingmar Bergman film. Three wives (Anita Bjork, May Britt, and Eva Dahlbeck) who are staying at a summer house recount adventures from their marriages. Clearly illustrates Bergman's talent for comedy and was his first commercial success. B&W; 107m. **DIR:** Ingmar Bergman. **CAST:** Anita Bjork, Jarl Kulle, Eva Dahlbeck, Gunnar Björnstrand, May Britt, Birger Malmsten. **1952**

SECT, THE ★★ The second collaboration between Dario Argento and Michele Soavi is not as good as its predecessor, *The Church*, but it still has moments. Rated R for profanity, violence, and brief nudity. 112m. **DIR:** Michele Soavi. **CAST:** Herbert Lom, Kelly Curtis. **1991**

SEDUCED ★★ The supporting cast attracts most of the attention in made-for-TV tale about an up-and-coming young politician who falls for the wife of an influential businessman. The wife gets murdered, and the politico is forced to become a sleuth. 100m. **DIR:** Jerrold Freedman. **CAST:** Gregory Harrison, Cybill Shepherd, Adrienne Barbeau, Mel Ferrer, José Ferrer. **1985**

SEDUCED AND ABANDONED ★★★1/2 This raucous Italian film takes wonderfully funny potshots at Italian life and codes of honor. It centers on a statute of Italian law that absolves a man for the crime of seducing and abandoning a girl if he marries her. This is one of the funniest movies exposing the stratagems of saving face. In Italian with English subtitles. B&W; 118m. **DIR:** Pietro Germi. **CAST:** Saro Urzi, Stefania Sandrelli. **1964**

SEDUCTION OF JOE TYNAN, THE ★★★ Alan Alda plays Senator Joe Tynan in this story of behind-the-scenes romance and political maneuvering in Washington, D.C. Tynan must face moral questions about himself and his job. It's familiar ground for Alda but still entertaining. Rated PG for language and brief nudity. 107m. **DIR:** Jerry Schatzberg. **CAST:** Alan Alda, Barbara Harris, Meryl Streep, Rip Torn, Charles Kimbrough, Melvyn Douglas. **1979**

SEDUCTION OF MIMI, THE ★★★★ Giancarlo Giannini gives an unforgettable performance as the sad-eyed Mimi, a Sicilian who migrates to the big city. He soon gets into trouble because of his obstinate character and his simple mind. Like all Wertmuller's films, sex and politics are at the heart of her dark humor. Includes one of the funniest love scenes ever filmed. Rated R for language and sex. 89m. **DIR:** Lina Wertmuller. **CAST:** Giancarlo Giannini, Mariangela Melato, Agostina Belli. **1974 DVD**

SEE NO EVIL ★★★1/2 Chilling yarn follows a young blind woman (Mia Farrow) as she tries to escape the

clutches of a ruthless killer who has done away with her entire family at their quiet country farm. Mia Farrow is very convincing as the maniac's next target. Rated PG for tense moments. 90m. **DIR:** Richard Fleischer. **CAST:** Mia Farrow, Dorothy Alison, Robin Bailey. **1971**

SEE NO EVIL, HEAR NO EVIL ★★★1/2 Richard Pryor and Gene Wilder play two handicapped buddies—one deaf, one blind—who find themselves running from cops and killers alike when they "witness" a murder. Forget the contrived, stale plot and enjoy the marvelous interplay between the stars. Rated R for profanity, nudity, and violence. 103m. **DIR:** Arthur Hiller. **CAST:** Gene Wilder, Richard Pryor, Joan Severance, Kevin Spacey. **1989**

SEE SPOT RUN A canine-phobic mailman reluctantly adopts an FBI dog who is being stalked by mob hit men. Sloppy, gross, and unfunny, the film is even more infantile than its title. Rated PG. 95m. **DIR:** John Whitesell. **CAST:** David Arquette, Leslie Bibb, Michael Clarke Duncan, Angus T. Jones, Paul Sorvino. **2001 DVD**

SEE YOU IN THE MORNING ★★★★ A touching character study. Jeff Bridges is a New York psychiatrist whose first marriage to model Farrah Fawcett crumbles, catching him off guard. A second marriage, to Alice Krige, seems more promising, but our hero has a number of obstacles to overcome. Rated PG-13 for profanity. 115m. **DIR:** Alan J. Pakula. **CAST:** Jeff Bridges, Alice Krige, Farrah Fawcett, Drew Barrymore, Lukas Haas, David Dukes, Frances Sternhagen, Linda Lavin. **1989**

SEEDPEOPLE ★★1/2 Obviously the creators have seen *Invasion of the Body Snatchers*, because they snatch the plot from that classic almost verbatim. Intergalactic pod-people invade a small community in a film that's so awful, it's actually quite entertaining on that level. Overall, fails to take root. Rated R for violence. 87m. **DIR:** Peter Manoogian. **CAST:** Sam Hennings. **1992**

SEEKERS, THE ★★ Most melodramatic and unbelievable TV production from the John Jakes's bicentennial series, this is part three of the Kent Family Chronicles. The original French immigrant is now a cynical man of wealth (Martin Milner) whose son (Randolph Mantooth) defies him by farming in Ohio. 189m. **DIR:** Sidney Hayers. **CAST:** Randolph Mantooth, Barbara Rush, Delta Burke, Edie Adams, Brian Keith, Martin Milner, George Hamilton, Hugh O'Brian, John Carradine, Gary Merrill, Ed Harris, Stuart Whitman. **1979**

SEEMS LIKE OLD TIMES ★★★ This slick, commercial package is much better than it deserves to be. It's another predictable Neil Simon sitcom packed with one-liners. But at least it's funny most of the time. Rated PG. 121m. **DIR:** Jay Sandrich. **CAST:** Goldie Hawn, Chevy Chase, Charles Grodin, Robert Guillaume, Harold Gould. **1980 DVD**

SEIZE THE DAY ★★★ Robin Williams is watchable in this drama, but like so many comedians who attempt serious acting, he is haunted by his madcap persona. This PBS *Great Performances* entry casts Williams as Wilhelm "Tommy" Adler, the Jewish ne'er-do-well son of wealthy, unsympathetic Joseph Wiseman. The story concerns the disintegration of Tommy's life. 87m. **DIR:** Fielder Cook. **CAST:** Robin Williams, Joseph Wiseman, Jerry Stiller, Glenne Headly, John Fiedler, Tom Aldredge, Tony Roberts. **1986**

SEIZURE ★★★ In Oliver Stone's directorial debut, an author of horror stories has a recurring dream about the murder of his houseguests by a trio of diabolical characters. Dream and reality intersect. Definitely a respectable chiller. Rated PG. 93m. **DIR:** Oliver Stone. **CAST:** Jonathan Frid, Martine Beswick, Herve Villechaize, Troy Donahue. **1974**

SELENA ★★1/2 This interminable, sugarcoated portrait of the *Tejano* singer whose life was tragically cut short couldn't be more sanitized if it were produced by her father—which, in fact, it was. Jennifer Lopez certainly mimics Selena's strut and sass to good effect, and she has the body for the midriff-baring outfits that became the performer's trademark. Only Edward James Olmos, as her father, brings any depth to his performance. Rated PG for mild profanity. 127m. **DIR:** Gregory Nava. **CAST:** Jennifer Lopez, Edward James Olmos, Jon Seda, Constance Marie, Jacob Vargas. **1997 DVD**

SELL-OUT, THE ★★1/2 Double agent Oliver Reed screws up and finds that both the Soviets and the Americans have put out contracts on him. Okay spy stuff, though a bit heavy on the shoot-outs and car chases toward the end. Filmed in Israel. Rated PG. 88m. **DIR:** Peter Collinson. **CAST:** Richard Widmark, Oliver Reed, Gayle Hunnicutt, Sam Wanamaker. **1976**

SELMA LORD SELMA ★★★★ This companion piece to *Ruby Bridges* features Jurnee Smollett, who plays a young girl so overcome by a Rev. Martin Luther King speech that she ends up marching with him from Selma to Montgomery. Smollett is riveting, while the rest of the cast lends uncommon depth to the proceedings. Not rated. 88m. **DIR:** Charles Burnett. **CAST:** Mackenzie Astin, Jurnee Smollett, Clifton Powell, Ella Joyce, Yolanda King. **1999**

SEMI-TOUGH ★★ Semihumorous love triangle set in a professional football background is just not as funny as it should be. Some inspired moments and very funny scenes make it a highly watchable film (especially Lotte Lenya's guest bit as an untemptable masseuse), and the character actors are fine, but much of the humor relies on profanity and cruel situations. Rated R. 108m. **DIR:** Michael Ritchie. **CAST:** Burt Reynolds, Jill Clayburgh, Kris Kristofferson, Robert Preston, Bert Convy, Lotte Lenya. **1977**

SENATOR WAS INDISCREET, THE ★★★ A staid and irreproachable U.S. senator's diary disclosures cause considerable embarrassment in this satire. Urbane and suave as always, William Powell is perfect in the title role. B&W; 81m. **DIR:** George S. Kaufman. **CAST:** William Powell, Ella Raines, Peter Lind Hayes, Arleen Whelan, Hans Conried. **1947**

SEND ME NO FLOWERS ★★★ Typically bright and bubbly Doris Day vehicle has Rock Hudson as her hypochondriacal hubby, who, believing he is dying, keeps trying to find a mate for his increasingly flustered wife. This is a light, frothy comedy that provokes some solid chuckles, thanks to the two leads and Tony Randall's supporting turn. 100m. **DIR:** Norman Jewison. **CAST:** Rock Hudson, Doris Day, Tony Randall, Paul Lynde, Clint Walker, Hal March, Edward Andrews. **1964**

SENDER, THE ★★★ Those who like their horror movies with a little subtlety should have a look at this low-key but effective yarn. A young man brought to a hospital after he attempts suicide is discovered to have telepathic powers. Because of his emotional disturbances, he is unable to control himself and unleashes his nightmares into the minds of doctors and patients. Rated R for violence. 91m. **DIR:** Roger Christian. **CAST:** Kathryn Harrold, Zeljko Ivanek, Shirley Knight, Paul Freeman. **1982**

SENIORS, THE 🦃 Sophomoric. 87m. **DIR:** Rod Amateau. **CAST:** Jeffrey Byron, Gary Imhoff, Dennis Quaid, Priscilla Barnes, Edward Andrews, Alan Reed. **1978 DVD**

SENSATION ★★★ Clever plot twists enliven this otherwise routine erotic thriller that finds college student Kari Wuhrer employing "psychometry" (second sight) to determine whether obsessed professor Eric Roberts actually killed a former lover. Watch this one with a date; Brian Grant's arty direction generates a fair amount of heat and passion. Rated R for nudity, simulated sex, profanity, and violence. 105m. **DIR:** Brian Grant. **CAST:** Eric Roberts, Kari Wuhrer, Ron Perlman, Paul LeMat, Claire Stansfield, Ed Begley Jr. **1994**

SENSATIONS 🦃 Odd-couple love story between a prostitute and a male stripper. Rated R for strong sexual situations. 91m. **DIR:** Chuck Vincent. **CAST:** Rebecca Lynn, Blake Bahner. **1988**

SENSATIONS OF 1945 ★★ Yet another one of those all-star jumbles so popular during the mid-1940s, this uninspired musical limps along, saddled with a stale story of a producer who wants to put on a show. The great W. C. Fields isn't in his best form here, but any chance to see him and Cab Calloway in action is worth something. B&W; 87m. **DIR:** Andrew L. Stone. **CAST:** Eleanor Powell, W. C. Fields, Sophie Tucker, Dennis O'Keefe, Cab Calloway, C. Aubrey Smith, Eugene Pallette. **1944**

SENSE AND SENSIBILITY ★★★★★ A superb adaptation of Jane Austen's comedy of manners involving the potentially dire fate awaiting the newly widowed Mrs. Dashwood and her three headstrong daughters, when their estate and fortune must (by law) pass to the deceased's male heir by a previous marriage. With their social status correspondingly reduced, sisters Elinor and Marianne find that their prospects for "making a good match" are similarly dashed. Star Emma Thompson collected an Oscar for her cunning screenplay adaptation, and the result is a rich costume romp that succeeds on all levels. Rated PG for the lusty pursuit of true love. 135m. **DIR:** Ang Lee. **CAST:** Emma Thompson, Alan Rickman, Kate Winslet, Hugh Grant, James Fleet, Harriet Walter, Gemma Jones, Elizabeth Spriggs, Robert Hardy. **1995 DVD**

SENSE OF FREEDOM, A ★★★ The true story of Jimmy Boyle, a violent Scottish criminal who refused to temper his viciousness during over a decade in various prisons. The film never attempts to make a hero out of Boyle, but neither does it offer any insight into his personality. A very well-made film from John Mackenzie, whose excellent *The Long Good Friday* featured a similar protagonist. Rated R. 81m. **DIR:** John Mackenzie. **CAST:** David Hayman, Alex Norton, Jake D'Arcy, Fulton MacKay. **1983**

SENSELESS ★★ A cash-strapped student takes desperate measures to ensure his future security in this crude, uneven comedy. Daryl Witherspoon supports his single mom and younger siblings by selling his body fluids to blood and sperm banks and holding down menial college jobs. Then he volunteers to test a drug that enhances his five senses—and his chances to land a lucrative position at one of Manhattan's top financial firms. Rated R for language, nudity, and sexual content. 88m. **DIR:** Penelope Spheeris. **CAST:** Marlon Wayans, David Spade, Matthew Lillard, Brad Dourif, Rip Torn. **1998 DVD**

SENSUAL MAN, THE ★★ Unengaging dubbed comedy about the sexual exploits of an aristocratic young man (Giancarlo Giannini). Good cast never rises above the mediocre sexist script. Rated R for nudity and profanity. 98m. **DIR:** Marco Vicario. **CAST:** Giancarlo Giannini, Rossana Podesta, Lionel Stander. **1983**

SENSUOUS NURSE, THE 🦃 A wealthy aristocrat has a heart attack and his two fortune-hunting, conniving nephews decide to help their lecherous uncle meet his maker. This dubbed Italian comedy is a dud. Rated R for nudity. 76m. **DIR:** Nello Rossati. **CAST:** Ursula Andress, Jack Palance, Duilio Del Prete, Luciana Paluzzi. **1978**

SENSUOUS WIFE, THE 🦃 Exploitation comedy about wife-swapping notable only for an appearance by Edward D. Wood Jr. as a transvestite. Originally titled *Mrs. Stone's Thing*. Not rated. 64m. **DIR:** Joseph F. Robertson. **CAST:** Victor Rich, Karen Johnson, Edward D. Wood Jr. **1969**

SENTINEL, THE 🦃 A woman unknowingly moves into an apartment building over the gates of hell. Rated R for nudity, profanity, and violence. 93m. **DIR:** Michael Winner. **CAST:** Chris Sarandon, Cristina Raines, Martin Balsam, John Carradine, José Ferrer, Ava Gardner, Arthur Kennedy, Burgess Meredith, Sylvia Miles, Deborah Raffin, Eli Wallach. **1977 DVD**

SEPARATE BUT EQUAL ★★★★ In one of his finest performances, Sidney Poitier stars as Thurgood Marshall, the NAACP lawyer who took the fight for racial equality to the Supreme Court via the Brown vs. Board of Education case in 1954. Richard Kiley is marvelous as Chief Justice Earl Warren, and Burt Lancaster is typically dignified and believable as the opposing counsel. Gripping drama that originally aired as a two-parter on television. 200m. **DIR:** George Stevens Jr. **CAST:** Sidney Poitier, Burt Lancaster, Richard Kiley, Cleavon Little, John McMartin. **1991**

SEPARATE LIVES ★★ A transparent and silly variation on the executive-by-day/hooker-by-night theme. James Belushi is an ex-cop studying psychology, Linda Hamilton's the professor who hires him to tail her, as she "may" have a multiple-personality disorder. The sad part is that someone actually cashed a check for penning this kibble. Rated R for violence, profanity, nudity, and sexual situations. 102m. **DIR:** David Madden. **CAST:** James Belushi, Linda Hamilton, Vera Miles. **1994**

SEPARATE PEACE, A ★★★ Based on John Knowles's bestselling novel, this involving story of a young man's first glimpse of adult emotions and motivations—some say homosexual frustration—is watchable for plot and performance. Gene and Finny are prep school roommates at the beginning of World War II. Jealous of

Finny's popularity, Gene betrays his roommate in a moment of anger and treachery, and is responsible for a crippling accident. Rated PG. 104m. **DIR:** Larry Peerce. **CAST:** John Heyl, Parker Stevenson, Peter Brush. **1972**

SEPARATE TABLES ★★★★★ This is a cable-television remake of the 1958 film with Burt Lancaster and Wendy Hiller. This time the work achieves a remarkable intimacy on tape with a top-notch British cast. Divided into two segments, this is a sort of British *Grand Hotel* room with Alan Bates and Julie Christie in dual roles. Richly engrossing adult entertainment. Rated PG for adult subject matter. 108m. **DIR:** John Schlesinger. **CAST:** Julie Christie, Alan Bates, Claire Bloom. **1983 DVD**

SEPARATE VACATIONS ★★★1/2 This comedy about Richard, a bored husband (David Naughton) suddenly seeking romance outside his marriage, has some hilarious, if contrived, moments. Rated R for nudity and sexual situations. 92m. **DIR:** Michael Anderson. **CAST:** David Naughton, Jennifer Dale, Mark Keyloun, Tony Rosato. **1985**

SEPTEMBER ★★★1/2 Woody Allen in his serious mode. Mia Farrow is superb as a troubled woman living in Vermont. Her houseguests are her hard-living mother (Elaine Stritch), her stepfather (Jack Warden), her best friend (Dianne Wiest), and an aspiring writer (Sam Waterston). What transpires are subtle yet intense love-hate relationships. Rated PG. 82m. **DIR:** Woody Allen. **CAST:** Mia Farrow, Dianne Wiest, Sam Waterston, Denholm Elliott, Elaine Stritch, Jack Warden. **1987 DVD**

SEPTEMBER AFFAIR ★★1/2 Superficial romantic tale about two married people who are reported dead after a plane crash. This gives them their chance to conduct a love affair. Bonuses: nice photography on the isle of Capri and the famous Walter Huston recording of the title song. B&W; 104m. **DIR:** William Dieterle. **CAST:** Joseph Cotten, Joan Fontaine, Françoise Rosay, Jessica Tandy, Robert Arthur, Jimmy Lydon. **1950**

SEPTEMBER GUN ★★ A good cast can't save this overly talky TV Western about an aged good-hearted gunfighter reluctantly becoming the protector of a nun and some orphaned Apache children. 100m. **DIR:** Don Taylor. **CAST:** Robert Preston, Patty Duke, Christopher Lloyd, Sally Kellerman. **1983**

SERENADE ★★1/2 A James M. Cain sordid story set to music to show off Mario Lanza, but it doesn't work too well. 121m. **DIR:** Anthony Mann. **CAST:** Mario Lanza, Joan Fontaine, Sarita Montiel, Vincent Price. **1956**

•SERENDIPITY ★★★1/2 Scripter Marc Klein sets up a chance encounter between John Cusack and Kate Beckinsale, who meet while Christmas shopping at Bloomingdale's. Although both are deeply involved with other people, they agree to meet again, *if* Fate is so inclined. What follows owes much to the sparkling cast and witty script, but since the other two people involved seem equally worthy, we can't help feeling that somebody's gonna wind up with the fuzzy end of the lollipop. Rated PG-13 for brief profanity and one brief sex scene. 90m. **DIR:** Peter Chelsom. **CAST:** John Cusack, Kate Beckinsale, Molly Shannon, John Corbett, Jeremy Piven, Bridget Moynahan. **2001 DVD**

SERENDIPITY, THE PINK DRAGON ★★1/2 "The fates had been kind," intones the narrator with unintended irony, as a shipwrecked young boy floats to the safety of Paradise Island. That's pretty glib, considering the poor lad moments earlier had lost both his parents. Once past this questionable introduction, we settle into the pleasant little tale of the boy, his massive pink friend, and their attempts to save Paradise Island from the greedy Captain Smudge. 90m. **DIR:** Yoshikuni Nishi, Toyo Ebishima. **1989**

SERGEANT RUTLEDGE ★★★1/2 Underrated and somewhat forgotten Western tells the story of a black cavalry officer on trial for rape and murder. The film's main focus is on the characters. Very good use of flashbacks to show events leading up to court-martial. B&W; 118m. **DIR:** John Ford. **CAST:** Woody Strode, Jeffrey Hunter, Constance Towers, Billie Burke. **1960**

SERGEANT RYKER ★★★ This film revolves around the court-martial of Sergeant Ryker (Lee Marvin), a Korean War soldier. Ryker, accused of treason, is valiantly defended by his attorney (Bradford Dillman in a superb performance). Originally shown on television as *The Case Against Sergeant Ryker,* then released theatrically under the shortened title. 86m. **DIR:** Buzz Kulik. **CAST:** Lee Marvin, Bradford Dillman, Vera Miles, Peter Graves, Lloyd Nolan, Murray Hamilton. **1968**

SERGEANT YORK ★★★ A World War II morale booster that is still good entertainment today. Gary Cooper got an Academy Award as the deeply religious young farmer from backwoods Tennessee who tries to avoid service in World War I because of his religious convictions only to become the war's most decorated American hero! B&W; 134m. **DIR:** Howard Hawks. **CAST:** Gary Cooper, Walter Brennan, George Tobias, Ward Bond, Noah Beery Jr., June Lockhart, Joan Leslie. **1941**

SERIAL ★★★1/2 Harvey Holroyd (Martin Mull) finds it difficult to go with the flow, especially when he finds out his wife, Kate (Tuesday Weld), is having an affair with a Cuban poodle-groomer while his daughter, Joan (Jennifer McAlister), has joined a religious cult. That's when the problems really begin. Rated R. 86m. **DIR:** Bill Persky. **CAST:** Martin Mull, Tuesday Weld, Jennifer McAlister, Bill Macy, Tom Smothers, Christopher Lee. **1980**

SERIAL BOMBER ★★ Direct-to-video thriller apes every mad serial-bomber movie that has blown across the screen during the past five years. Lori Petty is the FBI agent who has seventy-two hours to stop a serial bomber from toasting Seattle. Rated R for adult situations, language, and violence. 89m. **DIR:** Keoni Waxman. **CAST:** Lori Petty, Jason London, James LeGros. **1996 DVD**

SERIAL KILLER The one about the female cop who goes undercover to find out who is killing her friends. Rated R for violence, adult language, and nudity. 94m. **DIR:** Pierre David. **CAST:** Kim Delaney, Gary Hudson, Tobin Bell, Pam Grier, Andrew Prine. **1995**

SERIAL MOM ★★★★ Picture June Cleaver with a homicidal streak and you have Beverly Sutphin—a "perfect" mother driven to murder when her middle-class family life is even slightly jostled by outsiders. This warped social comedy skewers the media for turning killers into celebrities and turns a one-note joke into a

savagely funny romp that is definitely not for everyone. Rated R for simulated sex, language, violence, and gore. 97m. **DIR:** John Waters. **CAST:** Kathleen Turner, Sam Waterston, Ricki Lake, Matthew Lillard, Scott Wesley Morgan, Walt MacPherson. **1994 DVD**

•SERIES 7: THE CONTENDERS ★★ Six participants in a reality-based TV show are each given a handgun and must ambush each other until there is only one survivor. This graphic satire stops to smell the decaying humanity of All Things Tabloid and then takes the format of such shows as *Cops* and *Survivor* to new heights of shameless exploitation. Still, it's hard to skewer a genre in which actual people willingly spill their guts and wave their soiled underwear to the world. Rated R for language and violence. 91m. **DIR:** Daniel Minahan. **CAST:** Brooke Smith, Marylouise Burke, Michael Kaycheck, Richard Venture, Merrit Wever, Donna Hanover, Glenn Fitzgerald, Angelina Phillips. **2001 DVD**

SERPENT AND THE RAINBOW, THE ★★★1/2 Loosely based on the nonfiction book of the same name, this is about a sociologist who goes to Haiti to bring back a potion that reportedly resurrects the dead. Rated R for violence, language, and nudity. 98m. **DIR:** Wes Craven. **CAST:** Bill Pullman, Cathy Tyson, Zakes Mokae, Paul Winfield. **1988 DVD**

SERPENT'S EGG, THE ★★ Two trapeze artists are trapped in Berlin during pre-Nazi Germany where they discover a satanic plot. Director Ingmar Bergman's nightmare vision is disappointing. 120m. **DIR:** Ingmar Bergman. **CAST:** Liv Ullmann, David Carradine, Gert Fröbe, James Whitmore. **1977**

•SERPENT'S KISS, THE ★★ A dreary tale of love and betrayal set in eighteenth-century England, where world-famous architect Meneer Chrome has been hired to design and build an elaborate garden on an equally elaborate estate. As the work progresses, Chrome finds himself interrupted by a number of eccentric characters, all of whom have some special interest in his work. It doesn't take long before Chrome suspects that his garden is actually a ruse for something more sinister. In this period piece, the performances are dull, the dialogue thin, and the look of the film suspiciously flat. Rated R for adult situations and language. 104m. **DIR:** Philippe Rousselot. **CAST:** Ewan McGregor, Greta Scacchi, Pete Postlethwaite, Richard E. Grant. **1997 DVD**

SERPENT'S LAIR ★★ Nice guy Jeff Fahey is unfortunate enough to encounter a succubus, which slowly kills him via excessive lovemaking. Scripter Marc Rosenberg drags in everything up to Satan himself, before this tawdry little chiller crashes to a wholly unsatisfying halt. Rated R for violence, profanity, nudity, and simulated sex. 90m. **DIR:** Jeffrey Reiner. **CAST:** Jeff Fahey, Lisa B., Heather Medway, Anthony Palermo, Patrick Bauchau. **1995**

SERPICO ★★★★ Al Pacino is magnificent in this poignant story of an honest man who happens to be a cop. The fact that this is a true story of one man's fight against corruption adds even more punch. Rated R. 130m. **DIR:** Sidney Lumet. **CAST:** Al Pacino, Tony Roberts, John Randolph, Biff McGuire, Jack Kehoe. **1973**

SERVANT, THE ★★★★ A conniving manservant (Dirk Bogarde) gradually dominates the life of his spoiled master in this psychological horror story. By preying on his sexual weaknesses, he is able to easily maneuver him to his will. The taut, well-acted adult drama holds your interest throughout, mainly because the shock value is heightened for the audience because of its plausibility. B&W; 115m. **DIR:** Joseph Losey. **CAST:** Dirk Bogarde, Sarah Miles, James Fox. **1963 DVD**

SERVANTS OF TWILIGHT ★★★ Dean R. Koontz's *Twilight* is the source of this fast-paced, made-for-cable spin on *The Omen*, which features Bruce Greenwood as a dedicated private detective determined to save a little boy from a maniacal cult whose leader believes him to be the Antichrist. Violence and subdued sexual themes. 95m. **DIR:** Jeffrey Obrow. **CAST:** Bruce Greenwood, Belinda Bauer, Grace Zabriskie, Richard Bradford, Jack Kehoe. **1991 DVD**

SESAME STREET PRESENTS FOLLOW THAT BIRD ★★★★ Although this kiddie film has an impressive "guest cast," the real stars are *Sesame Street* TV show regulars Big Bird, the Cookie Monster, Oscar the Grouch, Count von Count, the Telly Monster, etc. Children will love this story about Big Bird being evicted from Sesame Street. Rated G. 88m. **DIR:** Ken Kwapis. **CAST:** Sandra Bernhard, Chevy Chase, John Candy, Dave Thomas, Joe Flaherty, Waylon Jennings. **1985**

•SESSION 9 ★★★★1/2 Honestly unnerving suspense thriller about five hazmat workers hired to clean out an old abandoned mental hospital. After being closed for fifteen years, the Danverse State Mental Hospital is about to get a face-lift, if the crew can stay alive long enough to finish the job. One by one the workers fall under the hospital's evil spell, or do they? That's the big question in this creepy thriller that constantly keeps us guessing and on the edge of our seats. As with *The Blair Witch Project*, we see only what the filmmaker wants us to see. A constant feeling of dread running through the film's undercurrent is unsettling and hard to shake. Rated R for language and violence. 100m. **DIR:** Brad Anderson. **CAST:** David Caruso, Stephen Gevedon, Peter Mullan, Brendan Sexton III, Joshua Lucas. **2001 DVD**

SESSIONS ★★★ Veronica Hamel poses as a career woman who also takes pleasure in being a high-priced call girl in the evening. Soap-opera drama? Yes, but that's what you expect in this made-for-TV movie. And it's done with class. 100m. **DIR:** Richard Pearce. **CAST:** Veronica Hamel, Jeffrey DeMunn, Jill Eikenberry. **1983**

SET IT OFF ★★ In this very violent, old-school revenge movie, four Los Angeles African American women begin robbing banks to supplement their meager janitorial paychecks. The film first focuses on the desperation of its main characters, but then wallows in sensationalism. When these women exhale, all hell breaks loose. Rated R for language, drug use, violence, and suggested sex. 105m. **DIR:** F. Gary Gray. **CAST:** Jada Pinkett, Queen Latifah, Vivica A. Fox, Kimberly Elise. **1996 DVD**

SET-UP, THE (1949) ★★★★ Taut *film noir* boxing flick takes the simple story of an over-the-hill boxer who refuses to disregard his principles and throw the big fight and elevates it to true tragedy. Robert Ryan as the has-been fighter gives another of the finely drawn and fiercely independent portrayals that marked his illustri-

ous career as one of Hollywood's finest character actors. B&W; 72m. **DIR:** Robert Wise. **CAST:** Robert Ryan, Audrey Totter, George Tobias, Alan Baxter, James Edwards, Wallace Ford. **1949**

SET-UP, THE (1995) ★★★1/2 Genius burglar and programmer Billy Zane goes straight, falls in love, and—after his new paramour is kidnapped—finds himself forced to sneak past his own security devices in a supposedly impregnable bank. This spiffy little caper flick is based loosely on British author James Hadley Chase's *My Laugh Comes Last*. Good fun, although our hero goes through all seven levels of hell before turning the tables on his tormentors. Rated R for violence, nudity, simulated sex, and profanity. 91m. **DIR:** Strathford Hamilton. **CAST:** Billy Zane, James Coburn, Mia Sara, James Russo, Louis Mandylor. **1995**

SEVEN ★★★★ Riveting thriller about a young detective (Brad Pitt) and an older, more experienced police officer (Morgan Freeman) attempting to track down a maniacal serial killer. The two leads are excellent, and the screenplay keeps you guessing right up to the nail-biting conclusion. Not for the faint of heart. Rated R for profanity, violence, and gruesome situations. 127m. **DIR:** David Fincher. **CAST:** Morgan Freeman, Brad Pitt, Gwyneth Paltrow, Kevin Spacey, R. Lee Ermey, Richard Roundtree. **1995 DVD**

SEVEN BEAUTIES ★★★★★ Winner of many international awards, this Italian film classic is not what the title might suggest. *Seven Beauties* is actually the street name for a small-time gangster, played by Giancarlo Giannini. We watch him struggle and survive on the streets and in a World War II German prisoner-of-war camp. Excellent! Rated R. 115m. **DIR:** Lina Wertmuller. **CAST:** Giancarlo Giannini, Fernando Rey, Shirley Stoler. **1976 DVD**

SEVEN BRIDES FOR SEVEN BROTHERS ★★★★★ Delightful musical. Howard Keel takes Jane Powell as his wife. The fun begins when his six younger brothers decide they want to get married, too . . . immediately! 103m. **DIR:** Stanley Donen. **CAST:** Howard Keel, Jane Powell, Russ Tamblyn, Julie Newmar, Marc Platt. **1954 DVD**

SEVEN BROTHERS MEET DRACULA, THE ★★1/2 Hammer Film's last Dracula movie was a coproduction with the Shaw Brothers of Hong Kong, known mainly for their kung fu films. A martial arts–horror-fantasy about Professor Van Helsing fighting a vampire cult in China. An interesting attempt, but unless you are a kung fu fan, this entry will seem all too silly. Rated R; this feature was originally titled *Legend of the Seven Golden Vampires*. 88m. **DIR:** Roy Ward Baker. **CAST:** Peter Cushing, David Chaing, Julie Ege. **1973**

SEVEN CHANCES ★★★★1/2 Buster Keaton has until 7 P.M. to get married or lose a huge inheritance; a misunderstanding estranges him from his true love, and he goes wife-hunting. One of Keaton's most enjoyable silent features, climaxed by an athletic chase and the famous rock-slide scene. A few racial gags may appear in questionable taste to today's audiences. Not rated. B&W (some video releases have the opening scene in color); 56m. **DIR:** Buster Keaton. **CAST:** Buster Keaton, T. Roy Barnes, Snitz Edwards, Ruth Dwyer. **1925 DVD**

SEVEN CITIES OF GOLD ★★★ Michael Rennie plays an incredibly pious Father Junípero Serra, struggling to set up his first mission in California. His love of the Indians contrasts sharply with the ruthless greed of the Spanish military leaders (played by Anthony Quinn and Richard Egan). Not rated, this contains violence. 103m. **DIR:** Robert D. Webb. **CAST:** Michael Rennie, Richard Egan, Anthony Quinn, Jeffrey Hunter, Rita Moreno. **1955**

SEVEN DAYS IN MAY ★★★★ A highly suspenseful account of an attempted military takeover of the U.S. government. After a slow buildup, the movie's tension snowballs toward a thrilling conclusion. This is one of those rare films that treat their audiences with respect. A working knowledge of the political process is helpful for optimum appreciation. B&W; 120m. **DIR:** John Frankenheimer. **CAST:** Burt Lancaster, Fredric March, Kirk Douglas, Ava Gardner, Edmond O'Brien, Martin Balsam. **1964 DVD**

SEVEN DAYS' LEAVE ★★ Lucille Ball and Victor Mature are paired up again in this light musical comedy about two sailors on leave who seek out romantic opportunities. Lucy's charisma is unfortunately undermined by a poor script and weak direction. Some good tunes are performed by the Freddy Martin and Les Brown bands. B&W; 87m. **DIR:** Tim Whelan. **CAST:** Lucille Ball, Victor Mature, Harold Peary. **1942**

SEVEN DEADLY SINS, THE ★★★ This collection of seven episodes illustrating the capital sins has its moments, but it should have been much better. Best is Jean-Luc Godard's segment on Laziness. In French with English subtitles. B&W; 113m. **DIR:** Sylvain Dhomme, Eugene Ionesco, Max Douy, Edouard Molinaro, Philippe de Broca, Jacques Demy, Jean-Luc Godard, Roger Vadim, Claude Chabrol. **CAST:** Claude Brasseur, Jean-Louis Trintignant, Eddie Constantine, Jean-Pierre Aumont, Sami Frey, Jean-Claude Brialy, Claude Berri. **1961**

SEVEN DIALS MYSTERY, THE ★★★★ This lighthearted Agatha Christie whodunit concerns a group of friends who spend the weekend at The Chimneys, the ancestral home of one Lady Eileen Brent (affectionately known as Bundle). A misfired practical joke leads to an unexpectedly tragic conclusion, which somehow involves a secret society known as the Seven Dials Club. Made for TV. 110m. **DIR:** Tony Wharmby. **CAST:** Cheryl Campbell, Harry Andrews, James Warwick, John Gielgud. **1981**

SEVEN DOORS OF DEATH ★★ This is the American release title (trimmed to obtain an R rating) of *The Beyond*, a stylishly gross Italian horror shocker about a Louisiana hotel situated on one of seven mythical gateways to hell. Even R-rated, this atmospheric shocker is incredibly gruesome. 86m. **DIR:** Lucio Fulci. **CAST:** Katherine MacColl, David Warbeck. **1981**

SEVEN DOORS TO DEATH ★★ When circumstances throw a down-on-his-luck fellow and a young heiress together, he involves himself in her troubles, which include murder. The title refers to the possible suspects in a killing that occurred in a courtyard owned by the girl's dead aunt—any of the business owners there could be the culprit. Hastily edited and definitely low-budget, but entertains with red herrings, odd characters, and clever dialogue. B&W; 61m. **DIR:** Elmer Clifton. **CAST:** Chick Chandler, June Clyde, George Meeker, Michael Raffetto. **1944**

7 FACES OF DR. LAO ★★★★ A first-rate fantasy taken from Charles Finney's classic story, "The Circus of

Dr. Lao." Tony Randall plays multiple roles as a mysterious Chinese gentleman and his many strange circus sideshow creatures. Fabulous makeup and special effects, surrounded by a heartwarming story. Perfect for all ages, one of the few films to capture the wonder and sinister overtones of a traveling circus. 100m. **DIR:** George Pal. **CAST:** Tony Randall, Barbara Eden, Arthur O'Connell. **1964 DVD**

SEVEN FOOTPRINTS TO SATAN ★★ Footloose young heir spends a sobering night in a house of horrors where he witnesses torture, murder, devil worship, and excess of all types—all orchestrated by the man's uncle and fiancée to bring him back to his senses and to provide the audience with violence and debauchery ordinarily denied by local censors. Based on a fantasy classic by A. Merritt, this comic thriller offers a rare viewing experience for film buffs because of its source material, fabled director, and position in fantasy film lore. Silent, with Italian subtitles and musical score. B&W; 60m. **DIR:** Benjamin Christensen. **CAST:** Creighton Hale, Thelma Todd, Sheldon Lewis, William V. Mong, DeWitt Jennings, Laska Winters. **1929**

SEVEN GIRLFRIENDS ★★★ Tim Daly hits the right notes as a thirty-something restaurateur going through a personal crisis. When Jesse (Daly) learns that his ex-girlfriend has died, he starts to question his life and relationships. To find the answers, he begins a quest to locate all of his past girlfriends. Although this ground was better covered in *High Fidelity*, director Paul Lazarus gets to make his point without embarrassing anyone. Daly makes a likable lead, while the film features the right mix of comedy and drama. Rated R for adult situations and language. 100m. **DIR:** Paul Lazarus. **CAST:** Timothy Daly, Olivia D'Abo, Mimi Rogers, Laura Leighton, Elizabeth Peña, Jami Gertz. **1999 DVD**

SEVEN HILLS OF ROME, THE ★★★ A TV star (Mario Lanza) goes to Rome to rest, finds a pretty girl, and sings his heart out. For Lanza fans, that's enough, but this isn't one of his better films. Beautiful scenery and his voice are the only selling points. 104m. **DIR:** Roy Rowland. **CAST:** Mario Lanza, Peggie Castle, Rosella Como, Marisa Allasio, Renato Rascel. **1958**

SEVEN HOURS TO JUDGMENT ★★ An action-thriller that loses much of its thrill due to its baby-faced star (and his jumpy direction). Bridges is a judge who, after letting a gang of thugs off on a technicality, must run a gauntlet through their territory. Ron Leibman steals the film as the distraught (and psychotic) husband of the gang's victim. Rated R for violence and profanity. 89m. **DIR:** Beau Bridges. **CAST:** Beau Bridges, Ron Leibman, Julianne Phillips, Reginald Vel Johnson, Al Freeman Jr. **1988**

SEVEN LITTLE FOYS, THE ★★★ Deftly tailored to Bob Hope, this biography of famed vaudevillian Eddie Foy and his performing offspring is gag-filled entertainment until death makes him a widower at odds with his talented brood. A classic scene with James Cagney as George M. Cohan has Hope dancing on a tabletop. All's well that ends well—in church! 95m. **DIR:** Melville Shavelson. **CAST:** Bob Hope, Milly Vitale, George Tobias, Billy Gray, James Cagney. **1955**

SEVEN MAGNIFICENT GLADIATORS, THE 🦃 Seven gladiators defend the people of a small village. Rated PG. 86m. **DIR:** Bruno Mattei. **CAST:** Lou Ferrigno, Sybil Danning, Brad Harris, Dan Vadis, Mandy Rice-Davies. **1983**

SEVEN MINUTES, THE 🦃 Pornography is put on trial when a man claims that he was driven to commit rape after reading a sexy novel. Look for Tom Selleck in a small role. Rated R. 115m. **DIR:** Russ Meyer. **CAST:** Wayne Maunder, Marianne McAndrew, Jay C. Flippen, Edy Williams, Yvonne De Carlo, John Carradine. **1971**

SEVEN MINUTES IN HEAVEN ★★1/2 When her only parent leaves town on business, 15 year old Natalie (Jennifer Connelly) allows classmate Jeff (Byron Thames) to move into her home. Their relationship is purely platonic, but no one will believe them. Average but well-meant teen comedy. Rated PG for tastefully suggested sex. 95m. **DIR:** Linda Feferman. **CAST:** Jennifer Connelly, Byron Thames, Maddie Corman, Michael Zaslow. **1986**

SEVEN-PER-CENT SOLUTION, THE ★★★★ Sherlock Holmes (Nicol Williamson) attempts to get rid of his cocaine addiction by getting treatment from Sigmund Freud (Alan Arkin). This is a fast-paced adventure with touches of humor. Robert Duvall's portrayal of Dr. Watson nearly steals the show. Great fun. Rated PG; okay for everyone. 113m. **DIR:** Herbert Ross. **CAST:** Nicol Williamson, Alan Arkin, Robert Duvall, Laurence Olivier, Vanessa Redgrave, Joel Grey. **1976 DVD**

SEVEN SAMURAI, THE ★★★★★ This Japanese release—about seven swordsmen coming to the aid of a besieged peasant village—is one of those rare screen wonders that seems to end much too soon. Its timeless and appealing story served as the basis for *The Magnificent Seven* and other American films. In Japanese with English subtitles. Not rated; the film has violence. B&W; 197m. **DIR:** Akira Kurosawa. **CAST:** Toshiro Mifune, Takashi Shimura. **1954 DVD**

SEVEN SINNERS ★★★ A brawling story of saloon life in the steamy tropics, as John Wayne and Albert Dekker vie for sultry Marlene Dietrich, who walks through this slight story with good humor as a heartbreaking "entertainer." A serviceable action tale. B&W; 87m. **DIR:** Tay Garnett. **CAST:** John Wayne, Marlene Dietrich, Albert Dekker, Broderick Crawford, Mischa Auer, Anna Lee. **1940**

SEVEN THIEVES ★★★ A rousing cops-and-robbers tale told from the robbers' viewpoint with Edward G. Robinson and Rod Steiger in top form. The setting is Monte Carlo, where thieves prosper and there is a lot of competition. B&W; 103m. **DIR:** Henry Hathaway. **CAST:** Edward G. Robinson, Rod Steiger, Eli Wallach, Joan Collins, Sebastian Cabot, Michael Dante, Alexander Scourby. **1960**

SEVEN-UPS, THE ★★ Hoping to cash in on the popularity of *The French Connection*, the producer of that film directs this slam-bang action flick in an intellectual vacuum. All that's missing are William Friedkin, Gene Hackman, and an intelligent story... but what the hey, we've got a better car chase! Roy Scheider is, as always, quite appealing, but he can't make something out of this nothing. Rated PG for violence. 103m. **DIR:** Philip D'Antoni. **CAST:** Roy Scheider, Tony Lo Bianco, Richard Lynch. **1973**

SEVEN YEAR ITCH, THE ★★★★ This movie is Marilyn Monroe's most enjoyable comedy. Marilyn lives upstairs from average American Tom Ewell. It seems his

wife has escaped the heat of their New York home by going on vacation. This leaves Tom alone and unprotected, and one visit from luscious neighbor Marilyn leads him on a Walter Mitty–style adventure that is a joy to behold. 105m. **DIR:** Billy Wilder. **CAST:** Tom Ewell, Marilyn Monroe, Oscar Homolka, Carolyn Jones. **1957 DVD**

SEVEN YEARS' BAD LUCK ★★★1/2 A welcome opportunity to sample the dapper comedic talents of the French master, Max Linder. He plays a bachelor who must endure all manner of misfortunes due (apparently) to the accidental smashing of a mirror. Plenty of slapstick comedy and screwball situations. Silent. B&W; 85m. **DIR:** Max Linder. **CAST:** Max Linder. **1920**

SEVEN YEARS IN TIBET ★★★1/2 This study of personal growth concerns Austrian mountaineer Heinrich Harrer, who was granted the role of outside observer in the 1940s during one of this century's greatest tragedies. Initially a member of the Nazi party and part of an Aryan team climbing a Himalayan peak in 1939, Harrer endured many adventures before winding up in Tibet and befriending the young Dalai Lama. Years passed, during which Harrer eventually grew to mistrust and subsequently despise the Communist Chinese invaders bent on subjugating Tibet. The only sour note comes from star Brad Pitt, excellent at conveying Harrer's early arrogance but less convincing as a man spiritually cleansed. Rated PG-13 for violence and mild profanity. 131m. **DIR:** Jean-Jacques Annaud. **CAST:** Brad Pitt, David Thewlis, B. D. Wong, Mako, Jamyang Jamtsho Wangchuk. **1997 DVD**

7TH CAVALRY ★★ Randolph Scott as a cavalry officer accused of cowardice for being on leave during the battle of the Little Big Horn. Talkie and slow-moving. 75m. **DIR:** Joseph H. Lewis. **CAST:** Randolph Scott, Barbara Hale, Donald Curtis, Jay C. Flippen. **1956**

SEVENTH COIN, THE ★★★1/2 Were it not for some brutality and a wholly pointless scene in a Turkish-style bath, this lively adventure would be acceptable for all ages. American Alexandra Powers and Arabian Navin Chowdhry flee through modern Jerusalem with the implacably villainous Peter O'Toole hot on their heels, all because of a rare coin. Rated PG-13 for violence, profanity, and brief nudity. 95m. **DIR:** Dror Soref. **CAST:** Alexandra Powers, Navin Chowdhry, Peter O'Toole, John Rhys-Davies, Ally Walker. **1993**

SEVENTH CROSS, THE ★★★★1/2 In 1936 Germany an anti-Nazi escapee from a concentration camp turns to friends for shelter and help in fleeing the country. Suspenseful, gripping drama. B&W; 111m. **DIR:** Fred Zinnemann. **CAST:** Spencer Tracy, Signe Hasso, Hume Cronyn, Jessica Tandy, Agnes Moorehead, Felix Bressart, George Macready, Ray Collins, Steven Geray, George Zucco. **1944**

SEVENTH FLOOR, THE ★★ Brooke Shields went Down Under for this routine thriller that finds her trapped in her high-tech apartment building by a madman. Even though the film is filled with plenty of action and close calls, it brings nothing new to the genre. It's hard to take Shields seriously as she stumbles over one victim after another. Rated R for violence. 99m. **DIR:** Ian Berry. **CAST:** Brooke Shields, Masaya Kato, Linda Cropper, Craig Pearce. **1993 DVD**

SEVENTH SEAL, THE ★★★★1/2 This is considered by many to be Ingmar Bergman's masterpiece. It tells the story of a knight coming back from the Crusades. He meets Death, who challenges him to a chess match, the stakes being his life. The knight is brilliantly played by Max von Sydow. In Swedish with English subtitles. B&W; 96m. **DIR:** Ingmar Bergman. **CAST:** Max von Sydow, Bibi Andersson, Gunnar Björnstrand. **1956 DVD**

SEVENTH SIGN, THE ★★★1/2 Finely crafted suspense film with Demi Moore portraying a woman whose unborn baby is threatened by the biblical curse of the Apocalypse. Moore is superb and Jurgen Prochnow is perfect as the avenging angel. Rated R for language and shock effects. 94m. **DIR:** Carl Schultz. **CAST:** Demi Moore, Michael Biehn, Jurgen Prochnow, John Heard. **1988 DVD**

•SEVENTH STREAM, THE ★★★ Scott Glenn stars as a lonely Irish widower who gets a second chance at love in this mystical *Hallmark Hall of Fame* presentation. Saffron Burrows, as a damsel in distress, is also a sea creature whose two-legged days are numbered. Slow start is compensated for by the development of both characters. Not rated; contains mature themes. 99m. **DIR:** John Gray. **CAST:** Scott Glenn, Saffron Burrows, John Lynch, Eamon Morrissey, Fiona Shaw. **2001**

SEVENTH VEIL, THE ★★★1/2 A young woman forsakes her family and chooses to become a musician, encountering many men along the way. Safe and satisfying, this middle-brow entertainment owes much of its success to a strong performance by James Mason and an Oscar-winning screenplay. Ann Todd is just right as the freethinking heroine. B&W; 94m. **DIR:** Compton Bennett. **CAST:** James Mason, Ann Todd, Herbert Lom, Hugh McDermott, Albert Lieven. **1945**

SEVENTH VICTIM, THE ★★★ Innocent Kim Hunter stumbles onto a New York City coven of devil worshipers in this eerie thriller-chiller ancestor of *Rosemary's Baby*. Leave the lights on. B&W; 71m. **DIR:** Mark Robson. **CAST:** Tom Conway, Kim Hunter, Jean Brooks, Evelyn Brent, Hugh Beaumont, Isabel Jewell, Barbara Hale. **1943**

7TH VOYAGE OF SINBAD, THE ★★★★ Sinbad battles an evil magician who has reduced the princess, who is also Sinbad's fiancée, to six inches in height. Our hero must battle a sword-wielding skeleton, a roc (giant bird), and other dangers to restore his bride-to-be to her normal size. This film contains some of the best stop-motion animation ever created by the master in that craft, Ray Harryhausen. 87m. **DIR:** Nathan Juran. **CAST:** Kerwin Mathews, Kathryn Grant, Torin Thatcher. **1958 DVD**

SEVERED ARM, THE ★★1/2 Before being rescued, a group of trapped mine explorers cut off the arm of one of the men as food for the others. Many years later, the survivors of the expedition are systematically slaughtered. This low-budget independent production is fairly suspenseful, though the acting is often listless and the gore a bit excessive. Rated R. 86m. **CAST:** Paul Carr, Deborah Walley, Marvin Kaplan. **1973**

SEVERED TIES ★★1/2 Outrageous special effects punctuate this campy horror film about a brilliant scientist who has found a way to regenerate limbs. He becomes the first recipient of his new discovery. Rated R for violence and language. 85m. **DIR:** Damon Santoste-

fano. **CAST:** Oliver Reed, Elke Sommer, Garrett Morris, Billy Morrissette. **1992**

SEX AND THE COLLEGE GIRL ★★ This low-budget version of *Sex and the Single Girl* has two things going for it: the witty and informative intro by Joe Bob Briggs and the fact that it didn't force a happy ending. Not rated, but implied sex and immorality abound. 100m. **DIR:** Joseph Adler. **CAST:** Julie Sommars, Charles Grodin, John Gabriel, Richard Arlen, Luana Anders. **1964**

SEX AND THE OTHER MAN ★★★ An impotent husband finds his interest renewed when he catches his wife in their bed with her boss, so to keep things hot he ties him up in the room for the weekend. This adaptation of a stage comedy betrays its origins in an abundance of talk, but the characters are strongly drawn. Rated R for profanity, nudity, and sex. 89m. **DIR:** Karl Slovin. **CAST:** Kari Wuhrer, Ron Eldard. **1996 DVD**

SEX AND THE SINGLE GIRL ★★★ A skin magazine editor makes a play for a lady psychologist by using all the ploys espoused in his magazine. A risqué premise handled in a tastefully entertaining way. 115m. **DIR:** Richard Quine. **CAST:** Tony Curtis, Natalie Wood, Lauren Bacall, Henry Fonda, Mel Ferrer, Larry Storch, Stubby Kaye, Edward Everett Horton. **1964**

SEX AND ZEN ★★★1/2 In this outrageously bawdy comedy based on an ancient Chinese story, a scholar (Lawrence Ng) bemoans his inability to satisfy his wife (Hong Kong sex star Amy Yip). A doctor cures his problem by—well, we can't describe it here, but you've never seen anything like it. The combination of high production values, directorial verve, and sheer uninhibitedness make this a one-of-a-kind film. In Cantonese with English subtitles. Not rated; absolutely not for kids. 94m. **DIR:** Michael Mak. **CAST:** Lawrence Ng, Amy Yip, Kent Chung, Elvis Tsui. **1991 DVD**

SEX APPEAL ★★ A nerdish accountant makes an all-out attempt to attract the opposite sex with humorously disastrous results. Gratuitous sleaze mars an otherwise cute story. Rated R for nudity and profanity. 81m. **DIR:** Chuck Vincent. **CAST:** Louie Bonanno. **1986**

SEX CRIMES ★★ After a female judge is raped, she collects the names of all known sex offenders and systematically kills them. Incredibly bad acting wrecks this revenge drama. Not rated; contains violence, profanity, and nudity. 90m. **DIR:** David Garcia. **CAST:** Jeff Osterhage, Maria Richwine. **1991 DVD**

SEX, DRUGS, ROCK & ROLL ★★★★ Eric Bogosian stars as a succession of ten different characters in this aggressive, thought-provoking, often astonishing film version of his one-man off-Broadway show. Writer-actor Bogosian (of *Talk Radio* fame) creates full-bodied minidramas and comedies with varying, believable characters. Rated R, with strong profanity. 100m. **DIR:** John McNaughton. **CAST:** Eric Bogosian. **1991 DVD**

SEX, LIES AND VIDEOTAPE ★★★★1/2 Deliciously offbeat winner of the 1989 Palme d'Or at the Cannes Film Festival revolves around a romantic triangle. Soft-spoken James Spader visits old college chum Peter Gallagher and ends up bringing to light Gallagher's affair with the sexy sister (Laura San Giacomo) of his slightly neurotic wife (Andie MacDowell). Rated R for simulated sex, profanity, and brief violence. 104m. **DIR:** Steven Soderbergh. **CAST:** James Spader, Andie MacDowell, Peter Gallagher, Laura San Giacomo. **1989 DVD**

SEX, LOVE, AND COLD HARD CASH ★★★1/2 High marks to this clever mystery from writer-director Harry S. Longstreet. Ex-con Anthony Denison teams up with call-girl JoBeth Williams to find a mob accountant who skipped with millions. Pleasant chemistry between the two leads, and Longstreet's tale moves in genuinely unexpected directions. Rated PG-13 for violence and mild sensuality. 86m. **DIR:** Harry S. Longstreet. **CAST:** JoBeth Williams, Anthony Denison, Robert Forster, Eric Pierpoint. **1993**

SEX MADNESS 🦃 "Educational" film about the dangers of syphilis. B&W; 50m. **DIR:** Dwain Esper. **1934**

SEX MONSTER, THE ★★ Be careful what you wish for, you just might get it. That's what happens to Marty, who convinces his meek wife to have a ménage à trois. Marty begins having second thoughts when his wife turns on to the experiment and starts inviting other women into her bed. What should have been a funny look at the pitfalls of male fantasy instead becomes nothing more than a titillating sex farce. Rated R for adult situations and language. 96m. **DIR:** Mike Binder. **CAST:** Mariel Hemingway, Mike Binder, Renee Humphrey, Taylor Nichols, Kevin Pollak, Stephen Baldwin. **1999 DVD**

SEX WITH A SMILE ★1/2 Silly, badly dubbed Italian film featuring five short stories on sexual misunderstandings. Marty Feldman's section produces some laughs. Rated R for nudity and sex. 100m. **DIR:** Sergio Martino. **CAST:** Marty Feldman, Edwige Fenech, Sydne Rome, Barbara Bouchet, Dayle Haddon. **1976**

SEXTETTE 🦃 A dreadful movie that documents the vulgar campiness of the nearly 80-year-old Mae West. Rated R. 91m. **DIR:** Ken Hughes, Irving Rapper. **CAST:** Mae West, Timothy Dalton, Dom DeLuise, Tony Curtis, Ringo Starr, George Hamilton, George Raft. **1978**

SEXTON BLAKE AND THE HOODED TERROR ★★1/2 One of a series of British mysteries featuring Sexton Blake, a detective in the Sherlock Holmes tradition. He's on the trail of an international gang known as the Hooded Terror, led by a millionaire (Tod Slaughter). Slaughter, Britain's king of Grand Guignol, is the best reason to see this, even though he's relatively restrained in a supporting role. B&W; 69m. **DIR:** George King. **CAST:** George Curzon, Tod Slaughter, Greta Gynt. **1938**

SEXUAL INTENT ★★ Libidinous lothario wines, dines, and rips off women for a living, but he's about to face a career crisis. Based on a true story, with Gary Hudson as the Sweetheart Scammer, who took over forty women for a ride. Now they're in the driver's seat, and what they've got planned for Mr. Romance is a vigilante feminist's dream come true. Rated R for nudity, language, and adult situations. 88m. **DIR:** Kurt Mac Carley. **CAST:** Gary Hudson, Michele Brin, Sarah Hill. **1993**

SEXUAL MALICE 🦃 Suspenseless erotic thriller centered around an unhappily married businesswoman who has a one-night stand with a male stripper. Rated R for sexual situations and strong language. (An "adult" version, not rated, also is available.) 93/96m. **DIR:** Jag Mundhra. **CAST:** Edward Albert, Chad McQueen, John Laughlin, Diana Barton, Samantha Phillips. **1993 DVD**

•SEXY BEAST ★★1/2 Two retired Cockney thugs and their wives (a former porn star and an orgy regular) are

enjoying retirement on the Costa del Sol when a crass, expletive-spewing, corrosive menace from their previous life of crime badgers one of the ex-cons into one last heist. This profane British crime story is more memorable for its intoxicating visuals and one blowtorch performance than character arcs, caper thrills, or revelatory surprises. Rated R for language and violence. 91m. **DIR:** Jonathan Glazer. **CAST:** Ray Winstone, Ben Kingsley, Ian McShane, Cavan Kendall, Amanda Redman, Julianne White, James Fox. **2001 DVD**

S.F.W. ★★★ The media take a much deserved skewering in this angry and offbeat love story. Writer/director Jefery Levy has a lot to say about the violence and madness perpetrated by media that reduce everything to a catchphrase. Rated R for excessive profanity, off-camera violence, sexual situations, and brief nudity. 94m. **DIR:** Jefery Levy. **CAST:** Stephen Dorff, Reese Witherspoon. **1994**

SGT. BILKO ★★1/2 Phil Silvers has nothing to worry about; long after this humdrum film adaptation has vanished, he'll still be remembered for having created the part on television. Steve Martin isn't bad in the role, but Andy Breckman's screenplay doesn't provide much material. "Wild 'n' Crazy" Steve can't generate laughs in a vacuum, and that's all he has to work with here. Rated PG for mild profanity and blue humor. 94m. **DIR:** Jonathan Lynn. **CAST:** Steve Martin, Dan Aykroyd, Phil Hartman, Glenne Headly, Daryl Mitchell. **1996 DVD**

SGT. BILKO (TV SERIES) ★★★★1/2 Master Sergeant Ernie Bilko was indeed a master of bilking. His job was to helm the motor pool. But his mission in life was to con anyone who could cough up a buck or two. For Phil Silvers, this was the role of a lifetime. A superb supporting cast added to the hilarity. The series, originally named *You'll Never Get Rich*, became *The Phil Silvers Show* and, finally, in syndication, *SGT. Bilko*. Two episodes are included per tape. B&W; 60m. **DIR:** Al DeCaprio. **CAST:** Phil Silvers, Harvey Lembeck, Paul Ford, Joe E. Ross, Allan Melvin, Herbie Faye, Maurice Gosfield, Billy Sands, Elisabeth Fraser. **1955–1959**

SGT. KABUKIMAN N.Y.P.D. ★★★ Wacky cop movie with a sci-fi twist. A New York detective inherits the superhuman powers of the Kabuki and changes into a colorfully dressed, if not totally competent, crime fighter. Some bad acting and a tongue-in-cheek attitude make this fun to watch with friends. Rated PG-13 for violence, profanity, and simulated sex. 99m. **DIR:** Lloyd Kaufman, Michael Herz. **CAST:** Rick Gianasi, Susan Byun, Bill Weeden, Thomas Crnkovich, Noble Lee Lester, Brick Bronsky, Larry Robinson, Pamela Alster, Shaler McClure, Fumio Furuya. **1991 DVD**

SGT. PEPPER'S LONELY HEARTS CLUB BAND Universally panned musical. Rated PG. 111m. **DIR:** Michael Schultz. **CAST:** The Bee Gees, Peter Frampton, Donald Pleasence, George Burns. **1978**

SHACK-OUT ON 101 ★★★1/2 This odd blend of character study and espionage thriller, which takes place at a highway hash house, involves some of the most colorful patrons you'll ever run across. Perky Terry Moore plays the waitress who helps the authorities close in on the men who have sabotage plans for a local chemical plant, and Lee Marvin is at his most audacious as Slob, a name he does his best to live up to. B&W; 80m. **DIR:** Edward Dein. **CAST:** Frank Lovejoy, Terry Moore, Lee Marvin, Keenan Wynn, Whit Bissell. **1955**

SHADES OF LOVE: CHAMPAGNE FOR TWO ★★★ Enjoyable romp features a likable chef who becomes the unlikely roommate of a harried architect. Made for Canadian TV, this *Shades of Love* romance has more general audience appeal than anything found in the Romance Theatre collection. Not rated; contains mild profanity, nudity, and sex. 82m. **DIR:** Lewis Furey. **CAST:** Nicholas Campbell, Kirsten Bishop, Carol Ann Francis, Terry Haig. **1987**

SHADES OF LOVE: LILAC DREAM ★★ Mystery and romance combine in this tale of a young woman left brokenhearted. Then a storm leaves a man with no memory on the shore of her island. She nurses him back to health. Gradually, his past comes back to haunt him. 83m. **DIR:** Marc Voizard. **CAST:** Dack Rambo, Susan Almgren. **1987**

SHADES OF LOVE: SINCERELY, VIOLET ★★ In this mediocre story of love and romance, a professor (Patricia Phillips) becomes a cat burglar named Violet. She is caught in the act by Mark Janson (Simon MacCorkindale) who tries to reform her. 86m. **DIR:** Mort Ransen. **CAST:** Simon MacCorkindale, Patricia Phillips. **1987**

SHADES OF LOVE: THE ROSE CAFE ★★ Dreams can sometimes hide the truth, and in the case of Courtney Fairchild (Linda Smith), her dream of opening a restaurant has hidden her feelings for the men in her life. 84m. **DIR:** Daniele J. Suissa. **CAST:** Parker Stevenson, Linda Smith. **1987**

SHADEY ★★1/2 Mildly entertaining British comedy about Shadey (Antony Sher), a man who has the ability to "think pictures onto film." These little movies turn out to be prophecies that are ultimately fulfilled. Plodding one moment, all-out bizarre the next. Rated PG-13 for violence and profanity. 90m. **DIR:** Philip Saville. **CAST:** Antony Sher, Billie Whitelaw, Patrick Macnee, Katherine Helmond. **1987**

SHADOW, THE ★★★ Enjoyable, well-mounted, but ultimately forgettable film resurrects 1930s pulp and radio hero, The Shadow. As the one "who knows what evil lurks in the hearts of men," Alec Baldwin is more effective in makeup than out. Here, The Shadow attempts to thwart the evil plans of a descendant of Genghis Khan. Rated PG-13 for violence. 107m. **DIR:** Russell Mulcahy. **CAST:** Alec Baldwin, John Lone, Penelope Ann Miller, Peter Boyle, Ian McKellen, Tim Curry, Jonathan Winters, Sab Shimono, Andre Gregory. **1994 DVD**

SHADOW BOX, THE ★★★ A fine cast and smooth direction highlight this powerful story of one day in the lives of three terminally ill patients at an experimental hospice in California. Adapted from the prize-winning Broadway stage play. 100m. **DIR:** Paul Newman. **CAST:** Joanne Woodward, Christopher Plummer, Valerie Harper, James Broderick, Melinda Dillon, Sylvia Sidney, John Considine. **1980**

SHADOW CONSPIRACY ★★ Presidential aide Charlie Sheen suddenly finds himself the inexplicable target of steely-eyed hit man Stephen Lang. Soon Sheen is running for his life while trying to unravel the mystery, and his only ally is chief of staff Donald Sutherland (sporting his best "trust me" leer). Far-fetched and silly, with a climactic attempt to assassinate the chief executive by means of a toy helicopter! Rated R for violence and

profanity. 103m. **DIR:** George Pan Cosmatos. **CAST:** Charlie Sheen, Donald Sutherland, Linda Hamilton, Sam Waterston, Ben Gazzara, Stephen Lang. **1996**

SHADOW CREATURE ★★1/2 Enjoyably hokey horror spoof in which Cleveland is terrorized by a half-man, half–zebra mussel mutant. Not rated; contains gore, sexual situations, substance abuse, and profanity. 93m. **DIR:** James Gribbins. **CAST:** Shane Minor, Tracy Godard, Dennis Keefe, Anthony Chrysostom. **1995 DVD**

SHADOW DANCING ★★★ Surprisingly entertaining suspense-thriller about an aspiring dancer who desperately wants to become a member of a dance ensemble. Her obsession is the perfect target for the resurrection of a former star, who died fifty years earlier in the same theater. Rated R for violence. 95m. **DIR:** Lewis Furey. **CAST:** Nadine Van Der Velde, John Colicos, Christopher Plummer. **1989**

SHADOW HUNTER ★★★ After a needlessly seamy prologue, writer-director J. S. Cardone's moody made-for-cable thriller settles comfortably into territory mined by mystery author Tony Hillerman. Burned-out big city cop Scott Glenn muffs an assignment to extradite a killer from a Navajo reservation, and then joins the forces tracking the escaped maniac . . . who can become a *skinwalker* and invade the dreams of his pursuers. Rated R for profanity, nudity, and violence. 98m. **DIR:** J. S. Cardone. **CAST:** Scott Glenn, Angela Alvarado, Robert Beltran. **1993**

•**SHADOW MAGIC** ★★★ In turn-of-the-century China, a photographer's assistant becomes fascinated with Western inventions, especially motion pictures, which only arouses the suspicion of his community. The slow-paced film is a bit too long, but performances are good and there are some marvelous scenes—notably the amazed reactions of rural villagers to seeing movies for the first time. Mostly in Mandarin with English subtitles; some scenes in English. Rated PG. 115m. **DIR:** Ann Hu. **CAST:** Jared Harris, Yu Xia, Yufei Xing, Peiqi Liu. **2000 DVD**

SHADOW OF A DOUBT ★★★★1/2 This disturbing suburban drama, Alfred Hitchcock's personal favorite among his films, probes the hidden facets of a family with a secret. Teenager Charlie adores the uncle after whom she was named and is delighted when he comes to stay for an indefinite period . . . until she begins to suspect that "dear Uncle Charlie" may be the killer wanted by the police for having sent several widows to their premature reward. Not rated; a bit intense for younger viewers. B&W; 108m. **DIR:** Alfred Hitchcock. **CAST:** Joseph Cotten, Teresa Wright, Macdonald Carey, Henry Travers, Hume Cronyn. **1943 DVD**

SHADOW OF A SCREAM ★★1/2 When a police detective goes undercover to trap a suspected sex killer, she not only becomes attracted to her prey but learns that she harbors a dark nature of her own. Filmed in Ireland (but set in Boston!), this is above average for the erotic thriller genre, though the weak conclusion hurts it. Rated R for gore, nudity, sexual situations, and profanity. 84m. **DIR:** Howard McCain. **CAST:** Athena Massey, David Chokachi, Timothy Busfield, Cyril O'Reilly. **1997**

SHADOW OF CHINA ★★★1/2 An idealistic Chinese revolutionary escapes to Hong Kong where he builds a financial empire. His dream of changing China through his business connections is threatened by the exposure of his early money-making schemes and his heritage. Rated PG-13 for violence. 100m. **DIR:** Mitsuo Yanagimachi. **CAST:** John Lone, Vivian Wu, Sammi Davis. **1991**

SHADOW OF THE EAGLE ★★1/2 John Wayne's second serial for Mascot Pictures is another one of those stolen inventions–kidnapped scientist affairs, this time masterminded by a mysterious criminal known as The Eagle, who likes to write his threats in the sky with an airplane. Although a bit creaky, this is fun to watch. B&W; 12 chapters. **DIR:** Ford Beebe. **CAST:** John Wayne, Dorothy Gulliver, Walter Miller, Kenneth Harlan, Yakima Canutt. **1932**

SHADOW OF THE THIN MAN ★★★★ Fourth in the series, with sleuths Nick and Nora Charles (William Powell and Myrna Loy) dividing their time between mysteries, Asta the wonder dog, and a stroller-bound Nick Jr. (who arrived in the previous film). Barry Nelson and Donna Reed are among the innocents this time around, and the story concerns dire deeds at the local race track. Another sumptuous serving of sophisticated fun. B&W; 97m. **DIR:** W. S. Van Dyke. **CAST:** William Powell, Myrna Loy, Sam Levene, Donna Reed, Barry Nelson. **1941**

SHADOW OF THE VAMPIRE ★★★ Willem Dafoe's Oscar-nominated portrayal of the title character is the only reason to see this unusual little film, which starts with a great premise but expires when the story falls apart. John Malkovich is too hammy by half as German silent-film director F. W. Murnau, who, wanting authenticity for his unauthorized adaptation of Bram Stoker's *Dracula*, hires an actual vampire for the part. Well-educated film buffs will be impressed by the fidelity with which Murnau's original *Nosferatu* is reproduced, but Dafoe's mischievous snacking on various crew members soon becomes an anemic running joke. Rated R for violence, profanity, gore, drug use, nudity, and sexual deviancy. 91m. **DIR:** E. Elias Merhige. **CAST:** John Malkovich, Willem Dafoe, Udo Kier, Cary Elwes, Catherine McCormack, Eddie Izzard, Aden Gillett, Ronan Vibert. **2000 DVD**

SHADOW OF THE WOLF ★★1/2 This gorgeously filmed Arctic adventure–soap about the encroachment of white men on Eskimo land and culture during the 1930s is also part mediocre crime-drama. Lou Diamond Phillips is physically convincing as an outcast Inuit hunter in a mediocre story heightened by enthralling anthropological detail and scenery. Rated PG-13 for violence and language. 108m. **DIR:** Jacques Dorfmann. **CAST:** Lou Diamond Phillips, Toshiro Mifune, Jennifer Tilly, Donald Sutherland. **1993**

SHADOW PLAY ★★ Dee Wallace Stone plays a Manhattan playwright who is obsessed by the tragic death of her fiancé seven years earlier. Indeed, she becomes possessed by his ghost, which inspires her to write awful poetry. Rated R for profanity and violence. 101m. **DIR:** Susan Shadburne. **CAST:** Dee Wallace, Cloris Leachman, Ron Kuhlman, Barry Laws. **1986**

SHADOW RIDERS, THE ★★★1/2 The stars of the superb made-for-television Western *The Sacketts* reunite for another adventure inspired by a Louis L'Amour tale. This time, brothers Tom Selleck, Sam Elliott, and Jeffrey Osterhage take on a white slaver. Good, old-fashioned cowboy fun. 96m. **DIR:** Andrew V. McLaglen.

CAST: Sam Elliott, Tom Selleck, Ben Johnson, Katharine Ross, Geoffrey Lewis, Jeff Osterhage, Gene Evans, Harry Carey Jr., Jane Greer. **1982 DVD**

SHADOW STRIKES, THE ★★ Loosely based on *The Ghost of the Manor*, one of hundreds of stories featuring the mysterious Shadow, this effort finds Rod La Rocque on the trail of a gang of crooks who have murdered his father, a prominent attorney. B&W; 61m. **DIR:** Lynn Shores. **CAST:** Rod La Rocque, Lynn Anders, Norman Ainsley. **1937**

SHADOW WARRIORS ★★ Because it was coproduced by Roger Corman and the Russian studio Mosfilm, this *Robocop* rip-off at least has some interesting Russian settings. The special effects are okay, but the story is forgettable nonsense. Rated R for violence and profanity. 80m. **DIR:** Rick Jacobson. **CAST:** Terry O'Quinn, Patrick Cavanaugh, Evan Lurie. **1995**

SHADOW ZONE: THE UNDEAD EXPRESS ★★ Juvenile horror movie features a teen who discovers vampires in the abandoned subway tunnels of New York City. No blood or violence in this made-for-cable original, so it is suitable for all audiences. But the acting is so stiff, it's hard to tell who is living and who is undead. Not rated. 95m. **DIR:** Stephen Williams. **CAST:** Ron Silver, Chauncey Leopardi, Natanya Ross, Tony T. Johnson, Ron White. **1996**

SHADOWLANDS ★★★★1/2 Based on screenwriter William Nicholson's play, this exquisite film chronicles the risqué (for its time) love affair between author and lecturer C. S. Lewis (Anthony Hopkins) and an American fan/writer, Joy Gresham (Debra Winger). An emotionally fulfilling and memorable motion picture. Rated PG for brief profanity. 130m. **DIR:** Richard Attenborough. **CAST:** Anthony Hopkins, Debra Winger, Edward Hardwicke, John Wood, Michael Denison, Peter Firth. **1993 DVD**

SHADOWS ★★★ A zealous young minister takes it upon himself to convert the local Chinese laundrymen. Lon Chaney as Yen Sin gives a moving performance as the man who must confront the self-righteous churchman, played by Harrison Ford (no relation to today's star). A colorful cast of good character actors help to make this a thought-provoking film. Silent. B&W; 70m. **DIR:** Tom Forman. **CAST:** Lon Chaney Sr., Harrison Ford, Marguerite de la Motte, Walter Long. **1922 DVD**

SHADOWS AND FOG ★★ Only the parade of familiar faces engages much interest in this all-star, brooding misfire from writer-director-star Woody Allen. Rated PG-13 for violence. B&W; 86m. **DIR:** Woody Allen. **CAST:** Woody Allen, Kathy Bates, John Cusack, Mia Farrow, Jodie Foster, Fred Gwynne, Julie Kavner, Madonna, John Malkovich, Kenneth Mars, Kate Nelligan, Donald Pleasence, Lily Tomlin, Philip Bosco, Robert Joy, Wallace Shawn, Kurtwood Smith, Josef Sommer. **1992 DVD**

SHADOWS IN THE STORM ★★ Umpteenth version of a daydreaming nebbish's fatal obsession for a young beauty. Ned Beatty stars as a corporate librarian who meets vixen Mia Sara and finds himself going totally out of control. Rated R for violence and profanity. 90m. **DIR:** Terrell Tannen. **CAST:** Ned Beatty, Mia Sara. **1989**

SHADOWS OF FORGOTTEN ANCESTORS ★★★★ A brilliant, epic story of star-crossed lovers set against the panoramic background of the Carpathian mountains. A visual masterpiece. In Ukrainian with English subtitles. 99m. **DIR:** Sergi Parajanov. **CAST:** Ivan Mikolaichuk, Larisa Kadochnikova. **1964**

SHADOWZONE ★★1/2 A NASA dream-research experiment goes awry, releasing beings from a different dimension. Good gore effects highlight this suspenseful tale. Rated R for violence and gore. 88m. **DIR:** J. S. Cardone. **CAST:** David Beecroft, James Hong, Shawn Weatherly, Louise Fletcher. **1989 DVD**

SHADRACH ★★★1/2 Notable debut for filmmaker Susanna Styron, who coadapts father William Styron's short story about an elderly black man who shows up at the Virginia plantation where he once worked as a slave hoping to be buried there. Even though the film never lacks sincerity, it does tend to skirt several important issues. Rated PG-13 for language and adult situations. 88m. **DIR:** Susanna Styron. **CAST:** Harvey Keitel, Andie MacDowell, John Franklin Sawyer, Daniel Treat, Scott Terra. **1998 DVD**

SHAFT (1971) ★★★ One of the best black films from the late 1960s and early 1970s. There is plenty of action and raw energy as private eye Shaft (Richard Roundtree) battles the bad guys in order to rescue a kidnapped woman. Great musical score by Isaac Hayes. Rated PG for violence. 100m. **DIR:** Gordon Parks Jr. **CAST:** Richard Roundtree, Charles Cioffi, Moses Gunn. **1971 DVD**

SHAFT (2000) ★★★★ Ernest Tidyman's sassy, street-smart private eye gets a fresh spin in this more politically astute remake, which Samuel L. Jackson dominates like a force of nature. He's a dedicated cop who, tired of a system that tolerates racism and seems hell-bent on putting the bad guys back on the street, hands in his badge and strikes out on his own. The case that drives this taut story concerns a pampered rich snot who kills a young man and then dares our hero to do anything about it; Shaft rises to the challenge with marvelous style. The cast is strong, Isaac Hayes's Oscar-winning theme gets things off to a proper start, and director/co-scripter John Singleton concludes his tale with an unexpected moment of cynicism. Even given all these dynamic elements, you'll not be able to take your eyes off Jackson. Rated R for violence, profanity, drug use, and sexual content. 99m. **DIR:** John Singleton. **CAST:** Samuel L. Jackson, Vanessa L. Williams, Jeffrey Wright, Christian Bale, Busta Rhymes, Dan Hedaya, Toni Collette, Richard Roundtree. **2000 DVD**

SHAFT'S BIG SCORE! ★★★ Obligatory first sequel to the original *Shaft* is one of the best blaxploitation action films of the Seventies. Topflight violence competes for screen time with pungent dialogue by *French Connection* scriptwriter Ernest Tidyman. Ball-of-twine plot has Shaft take on the mob. Rated R for profanity and mayhem. 104m. **DIR:** Gordon Parks Jr. **CAST:** Richard Roundtree, Moses Gunn, Joseph Mascolo. **1972 DVD**

SHAG, THE MOVIE ★★★1/2 This appealing film didn't get a fair shake on the big screen, which was surprising, considering the delightful cast and solid performances. It's set in Myrtle Beach, S.C., circa 1963, and chronicles a last fling by a covey of southern belles before their society debut takes them away from the realities of their age. The title, incidentally, connotes a popular dance style. Rated PG for brief nudity, the film is harmless enough for most age-groups. 96m. **DIR:** Zelda Barron. **CAST:** Phoebe Cates, Scott Coffey, Bridget

Fonda, Annabeth Gish, Page Hannah, Tyrone Power. **1989 DVD**

SHAGGY D.A., THE ★★ So-so sequel to Disney's far superior *The Shaggy Dog*, this retread stars Dean Jones as the victim of an ancient curse that turns him into a canine at the worst of moments. Rated G. 91m. **DIR:** Robert Stevenson. **CAST:** Dean Jones, Tim Conway, Suzanne Pleshette. **1976**

SHAGGY DOG, THE ★★★1/2 An ancient spell turns a boy into a sheepdog, and the fur flies in this slapstick Disney fantasy. Many of the gags are good, but the film sometimes drags. 104m. **DIR:** Charles Barton. **CAST:** Fred MacMurray, Jean Hagen, Tommy Kirk, Annette Funicello. **1959**

SHAKA ZULU ★★★1/2 Epic chronicling the rise of Shaka, king of the Zulus. Set against the emergence of British power in Africa during the early nineteenth century, this film provides some valuable insights into comparative cultures despite some poor editing and an overly dramatic, inappropriate musical score. Not rated, this release contains graphic violence and frequent nudity. 300m. **DIR:** William C. Faure. **CAST:** Edward Fox, Robert Powell, Trevor Howard, Fiona Fullerton, Christopher Lee, Henry Cole, Roy Dotrice, Gordon Jackson. **1986 DVD**

SHAKE HANDS WITH THE DEVIL ★★★★ In 1921 Dublin, an Irish-American student (Don Murray) innocently becomes involved in rebel activities and finds himself a fugitive. He joins an IRA cell led by James Cagney, whom he at first admires, but soon comes to realize is a murderous fanatic. Another spellbinding performance by the magnificent Cagney in this hard-hitting, action-filled drama. B&W; 110m. **DIR:** Michael Anderson. **CAST:** James Cagney, Don Murray, Dana Wynter, Glynis Johns, Cyril Cusack, Michael Redgrave, Sybil Thorndike, Richard Harris. **1959**

•SHAKE, RATTLE & ROCK ★★★ Nostalgic hoot is part of Showtime's *Rebel Highway* series, and stars a young Renee Zellweger as Susan Doyle, a hip teenager who rebels against her mother (Nora Dunn) by starting a rock and roll band. Set in the square 1950s, the film has a lot of fun with the clichés of the time. Filled with bad girls, bad boys, and lots of evil rock and roll music, a real kick for those looking for something mindless and fun. Rated PG-13 for adult situations. 83m. **DIR:** Allan Arkush. **CAST:** Renee Zellweger, Howie Mandel, Nora Dunn, Patricia Childress. **1994 DVD**

SHAKER RUN ★★ A New Zealand laboratory accidentally creates a deadly virus. Not rated, but the equivalent of a PG for violence and profanity. 91m. **DIR:** Bruce Morrison. **CAST:** Cliff Robertson, Leif Garrett, Lisa Harrow, Shane Briant. **1985**

SHAKES THE CLOWN ★★1/2 Stand-up comedian Bobcat Goldthwait makes his directorial debut with this clown-out-of-circus tale. Goldthwait is the clown who hits rock bottom. Former *Brady* mom Florence Henderson is downright hilarious as a clown groupie. Rated R for profanity. 88m. **DIR:** Bob Goldthwait. **CAST:** Bob Goldthwait, Julie Brown, Paul Dooley, Florence Henderson. **1991 DVD**

SHAKESPEARE IN LOVE ★★★★★ This ingenious pastiche is an erotic and enormously witty blend of history and fabrication. The setting is London in the summer of 1593, where young playwright Shakespeare has developed an acute case of writer's block which can be traced to his lack of captivating female companionship. Then the inconceivable happens: an impassioned actor reads for the role of Romeo and Shakespeare discovers that this talented thespian is actually Viola De Lesseps (Paltrow), a young woman of title and privilege unwilling to abide by the strictures of her era. Viola willingly throws herself into a double deception: tragedian in disguise by day, and clandestine lover, with Will, by night. What *fun*! Rated R for nudity and earthy sexual content. 113m. **DIR:** John Madden. **CAST:** Gwyneth Paltrow, Joseph Fiennes, Geoffrey Rush, Colin Firth, Ben Affleck, Judi Dench, Simon Callow. **1998 DVD**

SHAKESPEARE WALLAH ★★★★ A family troupe of Shakespearean players performs to disinterested, dwinding audiences in the new India (*wallah* is Hindustani for *peddler*). Frustrated sensuality, social humiliation, dedication to a dying cause, and familial devotion are rendered here with the sensitivity and delicacy that we have come to expect from director James Ivory. Madhur Jaffrey won the best actress award at the Berlin Festival for her satiric rendering of a Bombay musical star. B&W; 114m. **DIR:** James Ivory. **CAST:** Shashi Kapoor, Geoffrey Kendall, Laura Liddell, Felicity Kendal, Madhur Jaffrey. **1964**

SHAKIEST GUN IN THE WEST, THE ★★ This picture is a remake of *The Paleface* with Don Knotts in the Bob Hope role. A fun family film. 100m. **DIR:** Alan Rafkin. **CAST:** Don Knotts, Barbara Rhoades, Jackie Coogan, Don Barry. **1968**

SHAKING THE TREE ★★1/2 This bland male-bonding film will seem familiar to anyone who's seen *Diner*. A lot of similar ground is covered in telling the story of a group of pals entering into a new era of responsibility as adults. PG-13 for profanity. 97m. **DIR:** Duane Clark. **CAST:** Arye Gross, Doug Savant, Steven Wilde, Courteney Cox, Gale Hansen. **1992**

SHAKMA ★★ Probably the world's first slasher film with a baboon as the villain. Rated R for violence. 101m. **DIR:** Hugh Parks, Tom Logan. **CAST:** Christopher Atkins, Amanda Wyss, Ari Meyers, Roddy McDowall. **1990**

SHALAKO ★★ Odd British Western about European immigrants Sean Connery, Brigitte Bardot, Stephen Boyd, Jack Hawkins, and Honor Blackman menaced by Apaches in the Old West. 113m. **DIR:** Edward Dmytryk. **CAST:** Sean Connery, Brigitte Bardot, Stephen Boyd, Jack Hawkins, Honor Blackman, Woody Strode. **1968 DVD**

SHALL WE DANCE? (1937) ★★★★1/2 Fred Astaire and Ginger Rogers team up (as usual) as dance partners in this musical comedy. The only twist is they must pretend to be married in order to get the job. Great songs include "Let's Call the Whole Thing Off." B&W; 109m. **DIR:** Mark Sandrich. **CAST:** Fred Astaire, Ginger Rogers, Eric Blore, Edward Everett Horton. **1937**

SHALL WE DANCE? (1996) ★★★★ Writer-director Masayuki Suo's charming little drama concerns a repressed and weary businessman who secretly enrolls in a ballroom dance class and discovers that he actually enjoys the challenge and endless exercise. It's easy to see why this delightful film collected all thirteen Japanese Academy Awards. In Japanese with English subtitles. Rated PG for no particular reason. 118m. **DIR:**

Masayuki Suo. **CAST:** Koji Yakusho, Tamiyo Kusakari, Naoto Takenaka, Eriko Watanabe, Akira Emoto, Yu Tokui, Hiromasa Taguchi, Reiko Kusamura. **1996**

SHALLOW GRAVE (1987) 🦃 Four college girls witness a killing. Not rated; contains violence and nudity. 90m. **DIR:** Richard Styles. **CAST:** Tony March, Lisa Stahl, Tom Law. **1987**

SHALLOW GRAVE (1994) ★★1/2 Although it tries for the dark satire of *Blood Simple* or *Pulp Fiction*, this extremely gory Scottish thriller just isn't as shrewd or sophisticated. Three flatmates find a suitcase filled with cash after their new tenant dies of a drug overdose, and they elect to dispose of the body and keep the money, rather than alert the police. Greed then fuels hostility and suspicion. Rated R for profanity, violence, and brief nudity. 91m. **DIR:** Danny Boyle. **CAST:** Kerry Fox, Chris Eccleston, Ewan McGregor, Ken Scott, Keith Allen. **1994 DVD**

•SHALLOW HAL 🦃 The running gag in this lengthy comedy is that Hal (Jack Black) sees his very obese girlfriend as reed-slim Gwyneth Paltrow. We're not laughing and, no matter how many times Paltrow pouts sensing cruelty about her weight, we're not buying it. The only pluses are Joe Viterelli as her protective Irish dad and the cameo role of self-confidence guru Tony Robbins. Rated PG-13 for profanity and sexual dialogue. 113m. **DIR:** Bobby Farrelly, Peter Farrelly. **CAST:** Jack Black, Gwyneth Paltrow, Joe Viterelli, Jason Alexander. **2001 DVD**

SHAME (1987) ★★★★ While on a motorcycling vacation, a lawyer (Deborra-Lee Furness) ends up in an out-of-the-way Australian town where young women are terrorized and ritually raped by a gang of young toughs. So the two-fisted Furness decides to make them pay for their crimes. It sounds corny, but *Shame* is really quite effective. Rated R for violence and profanity. 90m. **DIR:** Steve Jodrell. **CAST:** Deborra-Lee Furness, Tony Barry, Simone Buchanan. **1987**

SHAME (1992) ★★1/2 Stranger in town Amanda Donohoe learns some hard lessons when she encourages a rape victim to fight back, and in return becomes the next victim of the vicious gang. This seedy little morality tale was made for cable and features a strong performance from Donohoe. Not rated; contains adult situations. 91m. **DIR:** Dan Lerner. **CAST:** Amanda Donohoe, Dean Stockwell. **1992**

SHAMELESS ★★ The culture of London drug abuse is seen from the points of view of a rich young addict (Elizabeth Hurley) and a cop on the breaking point (Joss Ackland)—two people headed for a collision. Competently made but uninvolving thriller. Rated R for nudity, sexual situations, drug use, and strong violence. 99m. **DIR:** Henry Cole. **CAST:** Elizabeth Hurley, C. Thomas Howell, Joss Ackland, Jeremy Brett, Claire Bloom. **1994 DVD**

SHAMELESS OLD LADY, THE ★★★★1/2 Bertolt Brecht's reminiscences of his grandmother provided the basis for this comedy about a 70-year-old woman, wonderfully played by the great character actress Sylvie. A joyous movie. In French with English subtitles. 95m. **DIR:** Rene Allio. **CAST:** Sylvie, Malka Ribovska, Victor Lanoux. **1965**

SHAMING, THE ★★ A spinster schoolteacher is raped by a janitor and continues to have sex with him until she is exposed and then ostracized by the school. This film is rated R for sex. 90m. **DIR:** Marvin J. Chomsky. **CAST:** Anne Heywood, Donald Pleasence, Robert Vaughn, Carolyn Jones, Dorothy Malone, Dana Elcar. **1975**

SHAMPOO ★★★★ Star Warren Beatty and Robert Towne cowrote this perceptive comedy of morals, most of them bad, which focuses on a hedonistic Beverly Hills hairdresser played by Beatty. Although portions come perilously close to slapstick, the balance is an insightful study of the pain caused by people who try for no-strings-attached relationships. Rated R—sexuality and adult themes. 112m. **DIR:** Hal Ashby. **CAST:** Warren Beatty, Julie Christie, Lee Grant, Jack Warden, Goldie Hawn, Carrie Fisher. **1975**

SHAMUS ★★1/2 An okay detective thriller, with Burt Reynolds playing Burt Reynolds. Nothing new, but lots of action keeps things moving along in this story of a private eye investigating a weapons-smuggling ring. Rated PG. 106m. **DIR:** Buzz Kulik. **CAST:** Burt Reynolds, Dyan Cannon, John P. Ryan. **1973**

SHANDRA, THE JUNGLE GIRL 🦃 Scientists hunt a jungle queen who kills men with her physical charms. Made-for-video soft-core erotica. Not rated; contains nudity and heavy sexual content. 80m. **DIR:** Cybil Richards. **CAST:** Lisa Throw, Venesa Talor. **1999**

SHANE ★★★★★ *Shane* is surely among the best Westerns ever made. Alan Ladd plays the title role, the mysterious stranger who helps a group of homesteaders in their struggle against the cattlemen. 118m. **DIR:** George Stevens. **CAST:** Alan Ladd, Jean Arthur, Jack Palance, Van Heflin, Ben Johnson, Elisha Cook Jr., Brandon de Wilde. **1953**

SHANGHAI COBRA, THE ★★ Routine poverty-row *Charlie Chan* programmer, from Monogram Pictures. A murderer stages his killings to make them resemble snake attacks. B&W; 64m. **DIR:** Phil Karlson. **CAST:** Sidney Toler, Benson Fong, Mantan Moreland, Joan Barclay. **1945**

SHANGHAI EXPRESS ★★★★ Marlene Dietrich's trademark role during the first stage of her Hollywood career has been copied but no one has ever equaled her sultry appeal. She plays a woman of dubious reputation who causes the downfall of a Chinese warlord to save the life and reputation of the man she really loves. B&W; 80m. **DIR:** Josef von Sternberg. **CAST:** Marlene Dietrich, Warner Oland, Anna May Wong, Clive Brook, Eugene Pallette, Louise Closser Hale, Gustav von Seyffertitz. **1932**

SHANGHAI GESTURE, THE ★★ Camp melodrama—an excursion into depravity in mysterious Shanghai. Walter Huston wants to close the gambling casino run by Ona Munson, who has a hold over his daughter Gene Tierney. Atmospheric idiocy. B&W; 106m. **DIR:** Josef von Sternberg. **CAST:** Gene Tierney, Ona Munson, Walter Huston, Albert Basserman, Eric Blore, Victor Mature, Maria Ouspenskaya, Mike Mazurki. **1942 DVD**

SHANGHAI JOE ★★ One of the last spaghetti Westerns to incorporate martial arts. A young Chinese laborer wants to become a cowboy, but he is faced with racial prejudice. He uses his brain and kung-fu skills to fight back, and in the meantime, uncovers an illegal-alien smuggling ring. Lots of kung-fu action. Rated R for vio-

lence. 97m. **DIR:** Mario Caiano. **CAST:** Chen Lee, Carla Romanelli, Klaus Kinski, Giacomo Rossi-Stuart, Gordon Mitchell. **1973**

SHANGHAI NOON ★★★ As a Chinese imperial guard, Jackie Chan teams up with a Sundance Kid–type bandit to rescue a Chinese princess. Set primarily in Nevada circa 1881, this East-meets-West actioner doesn't sweat the small stuff (such as historical accuracy), but focuses instead on a kaleidoscope of silly gags and corny showdowns. In a departure from the Chan-dominated film format, Wilson shares center stage as the action sequences take a backseat to the comic romp. Rated PG-13 for violence, profanity, and sexual innuendo. 105m. **DIR:** Tom Dey. **CAST:** Jackie Chan, Owen Wilson, Lucy Liu. **2000 DVD**

SHANGHAI SURPRISE 🦃 Madonna plays an uptight missionary in Shanghai, 1938. She recruits a con artist (Sean Penn) to help her recover eleven hundred pounds of opium. Rated PG. 93m. **DIR:** Jim Goddard. **CAST:** Sean Penn, Madonna, Paul Freeman, Richard Griffiths, Philip Sayer, Victor Wong. **1986**

SHANGHAI TRIAD ★★★1/2 A young country-bumpkin cousin to an elderly 1930s gang lord is called to Shanghai to wait on the mobster's girlfriend in this gorgeously shot crime-melodrama. The moll reluctantly takes the boy under wing until her mob sugar daddy is nearly killed in a violent power struggle. They all slip away to an isolated island hideout where the spoiled femme fatale is dogged by tragedy. In Mandarin with English subtitles. Rated R for simulated sex and violence. 107m. **DIR:** Yimou Zhang. **CAST:** Gong Li, Li Baotian, Shun Chun, Wang Xiao, Jiang Baoying. **1995**

SHANTY TRAMP ★★1/2 It's the sexy sharecropper's daughter versus the hypocritical evangelist in this drive-in classic. Not rated; contains nudity and simulated sex. B&W; 70m. **DIR:** Joseph Prieto. **CAST:** Lee Holland, Kenneth Douglas. **1966**

SHAOLIN TEMPLE ★★★★ The best kung fu film since *Enter the Dragon*, this period piece, set in seventh-century China, traces the history of the Shaolin Temple. It stars the country's top martial arts experts, yet characterization and plot are not slighted. In Chinese with English subtitles. Not rated, the film has violence. 111m. **DIR:** Chang Hsin Yen. **CAST:** Li Lin Jei. **1982**

SHAPESHIFTER ★★ Unimpressive teen fantasy has a boy with the power to morph into whatever he can see or touch. Rated PG for mild violence. 90m. **DIR:** Philip Browning. **CAST:** Paul Nolan. **1999**

SHARK ATTACK ★★ There's not much bite in this made-for-cable adventure-thriller. Casper Van Dien plays a marine biologist who suspects that the sharks offshore may be the byproduct of a sinister experiment. The film is one awful cliché after another. Rated R for language and violence. 95m. **DIR:** Bob Misiorowski. **CAST:** Casper Van Dien, Ernie Hudson, Bentley Mitchum, Jenny McShane. **1999 DVD**

SHARK ATTACK 2 ★★ Genetically altered sharks run amok in this waterlogged thriller that brings absolutely nothing new to the party. When the sharks start feasting on wind surfers off Australia, it's up to a noted shark hunter, the scientist, and a shark-attack survivor to save the day. Low budget robs the film of any thrills. Rated R for violence. 93m. **DIR:** David Worth. **CAST:** Thorsten Kaye, Nikita Ager, Daniel Alexander, Danny Keogh. **2000 DVD**

SHARK HUNTER, THE 🦃 A Caribbean island recluse beats up sharks and searches for buried treasure. Not rated, but the equivalent of a PG for violence and brief nudity. 92m. **DIR:** Enzo G. Castellari. **CAST:** Franco Nero, Jorge Luke, Mike Forrest. **1984**

SHARK! (MANEATERS!) 🦃 Waterlogged undersea adventure. Rated PG. 92m. **DIR:** Samuel Fuller. **CAST:** Burt Reynolds, Barry Sullivan, Arthur Kennedy, Silvia Pinal, Enrique Lucero. **1969**

SHARK'S TREASURE 🦃 Good guys and bad guys search for sunken treasure. Rated PG for violence. 95m. **DIR:** Cornel Wilde. **CAST:** Cornel Wilde, Yaphet Kotto, John Nellson, Cliff Osmond. **1975**

SHARKY'S MACHINE ★★★★1/2 This is one of the best cop thrillers ever made. It's exciting, suspenseful, funny, and intelligent, so good it joins *48 Hrs.*, *Dirty Harry*, and *Tightrope* as the best of the genre. Burt Reynolds stars under his own direction as an undercover cop who has a compulsion to crack down on a new wave of crime in his city. Rated R because of violence and profanity. 119m. **DIR:** Burt Reynolds. **CAST:** Burt Reynolds, Rachel Ward, Brian Keith, Bernie Casey, Vittorio Gassman, Charles Durning. **1981 DVD**

SHARON'S SECRET ★★★1/2 Taut thriller about a 16-year-old accused of slaughtering and mutilating her parents. The teen is almost catatonic and refuses to speak, but is she the real killer? The complex plot of this made-for-cable original will keep you guessing right to the end. Not rated; contains violence. 91m. **DIR:** Michael Scott. **CAST:** Mel Harris, Alex McArthur, Candace Cameron, Gregg Henry. **1995**

SHARPE (TV SERIES) ★★★★ Twelve volumes based on the British TV series starring Sean Bean as a gutsy British soldier during the campaign against Napoleon. Each volume (*Sharpe's Rifles*, *Sharpe's Enemy*, etc.) is an exciting adventure, spellbinding, with large-scale battle scenes and believable characters. Not rated; contains violence and sexual situations. 100m. **DIR:** Tom Clegg. **CAST:** Sean Bean, Assumpta Serna, Hugh Fraser, Brian Cox. **1995**

SHATTER ★★ Stuart Whitman stars as the title character, a hip man of action who finds himself being deceived and set up as a patsy. Of course, he doesn't take this sitting down. Can't hold up to the test of time. Not rated; contains nudity and violence. 90m. **DIR:** Michael Carreras. **CAST:** Stuart Whitman, Peter Cushing, Anton Duffring. **1974**

SHATTER DEAD ★★★ This zombie epic is definitely not for everyone. In this story, no one can die, so zombies walk among us. Director Scooter McCrae goes for the excess-is-good approach and in the case of the zombie stuff, this is some of the best since George Romero first woke the dead, but a sex scene goes too far. Not rated; contains violence, gore, profanity, and a graphic sex scene. 85m. **DIR:** Scooter McCrae. **CAST:** Stark Raven, Flora Fauna. **1994**

SHATTERED (1972) ★★ Peter Finch plays a mild-mannered, neurotic businessman who picks up a hitchhiker (Linda Hayden) only to have her attach herself to him. As a result, he slowly begins to lose his sanity. Shelley Winters plays Finch's obnoxious wife. Like a lot of British thrillers, this one has little action until it ex-

plodes in the final fifteen minutes. Rated R for profanity and violence. 100m. **DIR:** Alastair Reid. **CAST:** Peter Finch, Shelley Winters, Colin Blakely, John Stride, Linda Hayden. **1972**

SHATTERED (1991) ★★1/2 Director Wolfgang Petersen's adaptation of Richard Neely's novel is a well-acted and fairly suspenseful flick about a man who wakes up in a hospital remembering nothing of his past. Even though his wife has pictures of them together, our hero has a feeling that something isn't quite right. Rated R for violence, nudity, and profanity. 106m. **DIR:** Wolfgang Petersen. **CAST:** Tom Berenger, Bob Hoskins, Greta Scacchi, Joanne Whalley, Corbin Bernsen, Theodore Bikel. **1991**

SHATTERED DREAMS ★★ Lindsay Wagner and Michael Nouri are fine as a couple who resort to abuse when things get tough, but the script and direction are so melodramatic they dilute any chance the film has of garnering our sympathy. Based on a true story. Made-for-television. Not rated; contains violence. 94m. **DIR:** Robert Iscove. **CAST:** Lindsay Wagner, Michael Nouri. **1990**

SHATTERED IMAGE (1993) ★★ The FBI tries to locate the criminals who kidnapped the owner of a modeling agency. This made-for-cable movie is quite confusing and contains too many twists—it feels as if even the writer really didn't know what was going on. Not rated; contains violence and sex. 95m. **DIR:** Fritz Kiersch. **CAST:** Jack Scalia, Bo Derek, John Savage, Dorian Harewood, Ramon Franco, Michael Harris, Carol Lawrence. **1993**

SHATTERED IMAGE (1998) ★★ What could have been an involving thriller about a woman with split personalities becomes a trite exercise in overkill. Anne Parillaud is desperately shallow as a hired killer and her alter ego, a newlywed on the verge of killing herself. William Baldwin is equally uninvolved as her target and husband. The filmmakers had two opportunities to get it right and dropped the ball both times. Rated R for adult situations, language, nudity, and violence. 103m. **DIR:** Raúl Ruiz. **CAST:** Anne Parillaud, William Baldwin, Graham Greene. **1998 DVD**

SHATTERED SPIRITS ★★★ Hard-hitting, made-for-television drama focuses on a father whose casual drinking problem turns into substance abuse with tragic results. When his drinking escalates to an uncontrollable rage, his family is torn apart. 93m. **DIR:** Robert Greenwald. **CAST:** Martin Sheen, Melinda Dillon, Matthew Laborteaux, Lukas Haas, Roxana Zal. **1986**

SHATTERED VOWS ★★★1/2 Based on a true story, this explores a young girl's commitment to become a nun—and her later decision to leave the convent. Made for TV. 95m. **DIR:** Jack Bender. **CAST:** Valerie Bertinelli, David Morse, Patricia Neal, Tom Parsekian. **1984**

SHAWSHANK REDEMPTION, THE ★★★★ Uplifting tale of a man imprisoned for the murder of his wife and her lover, who must endure the horrors of prison life until he's befriended by Morgan Freeman. Based on the short novel by Stephen King, this is a thoroughly rewarding movie. Rated R for violence, profanity, nudity, and suggested sex. 142m. **DIR:** Frank Darabont. **CAST:** Tim Robbins, Morgan Freeman, Bob Gunton, Bill Sadler, Clancy Brown, Gil Bellows, James Whitmore, Mark Rolston, Jeffrey DeMunn. **1994 DVD**

SHE (1925) ★★1/2 Statuesque vamp Betty Blythe portrays the ageless Queen Ayesha (She) to perfection in this seventh and final silent version of adventure novelist H. Rider Haggard's fantasy about a lost tribe and a flame of eternal life in darkest Africa. Filmed in London and Berlin. Silent, with background music. B&W; 77m. **DIR:** G. B. Samuelson. **CAST:** Betty Blythe, Carlyle Blackwell, Mary Odette. **1925**

SHE (1935) ★★★ Adventurers brave frozen wastelands in their quest for the flame of eternal life and discover an ancient civilization ruled by a stern, long-lived lady. Fantasy-adventure classic falls flat despite splendid sets and a strong performance by Helen Gahagan as the title character. B&W; 101m. **DIR:** Irving Pichel, Lansing C. Holden. **CAST:** Helen Gahagan, Randolph Scott, Helen Mack, Nigel Bruce, Gustav von Seyffertitz, Samuel S. Hinds, Noble Johnson, Lumsden Hare. **1935 DVD**

SHE (1983) Sandahl Bergman is She, the leader of a post-apocalyptic nation that looks upon men as second-class citizens. Not rated, but would be an R for violence and nudity. 90m. **DIR:** Avi Nesher. **CAST:** Sandahl Bergman, Quin Kessler, Harrison Muller, Gordon Mitchell. **1983**

S.H.E. ★★★ This average made-for-TV spy-action thriller has one twist . . . a female James Bond. Beautiful Cornelia Sharpe is S.H.E. (Security Hazards Expert). She pursues Robert Lansing, the U.S. syndicate boss, throughout Europe. Omar Sharif makes an appearance as a wine baron. 105m. **DIR:** Robert Lewis. **CAST:** Omar Sharif, Cornelia Sharpe, Robert Lansing, Anita Ekberg. **1979**

SHE BEAST, THE ★★1/2 It's undeniably crude and extremely low-budget, but this Italian-Yugoslavian horror chiller about a reincarnated witch shouldn't be dismissed. 74m. **DIR:** Michael Reeves. **CAST:** Ian Ogilvy, Barbara Steele, Mel Welles. **1966**

SHE COULDN'T SAY NO ★★ An oil-rich woman (Jean Simmons) wishes to repay the citizens of her hometown of Progress, Arkansas for the kindnesses shown her in childhood. Her idea of showering the town with money is charitable, but disrupts the day-to-day life of the citizenry. Robert Mitchum, as the town doctor, seems out of place in this picture. B&W; 89m. **DIR:** Lloyd Bacon. **CAST:** Robert Mitchum, Jean Simmons, Arthur Hunnicutt, Edgar Buchanan. **1954**

SHE CREATURE, THE ★★1/2 American-International's answer to *Creature from the Black Lagoon* mixes Fifties reincarnation hocus-pocus with conventional monster lore. The eye-filling title beast is the finest creation of zero-budget makeup master Paul Blaisdell, who recycled the same suit for *Voodoo Woman* and *Ghost of Dragstrip Hollow*. B&W; 77m. **DIR:** Edward L. Cahn. **CAST:** Marla English, Tom Conway, Chester Morris. **1957**

SHE DEMONS A crazed Nazi scientist holds an uncharted island in a grip of terror. B&W; 80m. **DIR:** Richard Cunha. **CAST:** Irish McCalla, Tod Griffin, Victor Sen Yung, Gene Roth. **1958**

SHE-DEVIL ★★★ Meryl Streep is a hoot as a snooty romance novelist who takes Ed Begley Jr., away from frumpy Roseanne. The moments of mirth come as Roseanne methodically manages her wifely revenge. The story is predictable, and the pace is sometimes plodding and deliberate, but there are enough funny bits to make it worth watching. Rated PG-13 for profan-

ity and suggested sex. 94m. **DIR:** Susan Seidelman. **CAST:** Meryl Streep, Roseanne, Ed Begley Jr., Sylvia Miles, Linda Hunt. **1989 DVD**

SHE-DEVILS ON WHEELS 🦃 Atrocious Florida biker flick. Not rated. 83m. **DIR:** Herschell Gordon Lewis. **CAST:** Cristie Wagner. **1968**

SHE DONE HIM WRONG ★★★★ Mae West woos Cary Grant in this comedy classic. She is a lady saloon keeper in the Gay Nineties. He is the undercover cop assigned to bring her in. She says, "Come up and see me sometime." He does, and the result is movie magic. B&W; 66m. **DIR:** Lowell Sherman. **CAST:** Mae West, Cary Grant, Gilbert Roland, Noah Beery Sr., Rochelle Hudson, Louise Beavers. **1933**

SHE FREAK, THE 🦃 A remake of the classic *Freaks*. B&W; 87m. **DIR:** Byron Mabe. **CAST:** Claire Brennan, Lee Raymond. **1966 DVD**

SHE GOES TO WAR ★★ Farfetched comedy-drama about a spoiled woman who takes her fiancé's place at the front. Loaded with stereotypes, coincidences, stilted dialogue, and miserable songs. B&W; 87m. **DIR:** Henry King. **CAST:** Eleanor Boardman, John Holland, Edmund Burke. **1929**

SHE WAITS ★★ Producer-director Delbert Mann tries hard but cannot breathe any real thrills into this pedestrian tale of a young wife (Patty Duke) who becomes possessed by the spirit of her husband's first wife. Made-for-TV mediocrity. 74m. **DIR:** Delbert Mann. **CAST:** Patty Duke, David McCallum, Lew Ayres, Beulah Bondi, Dorothy McGuire. **1971**

SHE WORE A YELLOW RIBBON ★★★★★ Lest we forget, John Wayne was one of the screen's greatest actors. The Duke gave what was arguably his greatest performance in this gorgeous color Western made by John Ford. As the aging Captain Nathan Brittles, Wayne plays a man set to retire but unwilling to leave his command at a time of impending war with the Apaches. This is one of the great Westerns. 103m. **DIR:** John Ford. **CAST:** John Wayne, Ben Johnson, Victor McLaglen, Harry Carey Jr., George O'Brien. **1949**

SHEBA BABY ★★ One of Pam Grier's last blaxploitation opuses. This time, she's a private eye struggling to save the family business. Less raunchy than some entries in the series, but still mostly routine. Rated R. 90m. **DIR:** William Girdler. **CAST:** Pam Grier, Austin Stoker, D'Urville Martin. **1975**

SHEENA 🦃 Tanya Roberts as the Queen of the Jungle. Rated PG. 117m. **DIR:** John Guillermin. **CAST:** Tanya Roberts, Ted Wass, Donovan Scott. **1984 DVD**

SHEEP HAS FIVE LEGS ★★★★ The beloved French comedian Fernandel plays six roles in one of his funniest movies: five identical brothers and their father. The humor doesn't come from the plot but from watching Fernandel juggle six comic characters. Great for families, if your kids don't mind a few subtitles. B&W; 92m. **DIR:** Henri Verneuil. **CAST:** Fernandel. **1954**

SHEER MADNESS ★★★1/2 The growing friendship between two women threatens to overwhelm their respective marriages in this complex, intelligently made film. Somewhat slow, but worth the effort. In German with English subtitles. Not rated. 110m. **DIR:** Margarethe von Trotta. **CAST:** Hanna Schygulla, Angela Winkler. **1985**

SHEIK, THE ★★1/2 The story of an English lady abducted by a hot-blooded Arab promising illicit pleasure in the desert is tame today, but Rudolph Valentino made millions of female fans his love slaves. Predicted to flop by studio brass, this melodramatic blend of adventure and eroticism nonetheless catapulted the handsome Italian import to reigning stardom. Silent. B&W; 80m. **DIR:** George Melford. **CAST:** Rudolph Valentino, Agnes Ayres, Adolphe Menjou, Lucien Littlefield. **1921**

SHELTERING SKY, THE ★★1/2 So much is left unexplained, one cannot help but wonder if director Bernardo Bertolucci is trying to put something over on us. This tale of three aimless Americans becoming involved in an odd romantic triangle while enduring hardships in post–World War II North Africa mainly leaves one with the urge to read Paul Bowles's original novel and find out what the fuss was all about. Rated R for nudity, profanity, and simulated sex. 133m. **DIR:** Bernardo Bertolucci. **CAST:** Debra Winger, John Malkovich, Campbell Scott, Jill Bennett, Timothy Spall. **1990**

SHENANDOAH ★★★★ James Stewart gives a superb performance in this, director Andrew V. McLaglen's best Western. Stewart plays a patriarch determined to keep his family out of the Civil War. He ultimately fails and is forced into action to save his children from the ravages of war. It's an emotionally moving, powerful tale. 105m. **DIR:** Andrew V. McLaglen. **CAST:** James Stewart, Doug McClure, Glenn Corbett, Patrick Wayne, Katharine Ross, George Kennedy, Strother Martin. **1965**

SHEPHERD ★★ Heavily armed religious cults shoot it out in a post-apocalyptic wasteland. It's hard to make much sense out of this standard Roger Corman production, which is recommended only to fans of explosions and campy acting (at which former pro wrestler "Rowdy" Roddy Piper excels). Rated R for violence, profanity, and nudity. 86m. **DIR:** Peter Hayman. **CAST:** C. Thomas Howell, Roddy Piper, David Carradine, Heidi Von Palleske, Clarence Williams, III. **1998**

SHEPHERD OF THE HILLS, THE ★★★★ John Wayne's first color film has a better storyline than most of his movies. It's set in the Ozarks and tells the story of a fellow determined to kill the man who abandoned his mother. Beautiful scenery adds atmosphere and a superb cast puts life into the story. 98m. **DIR:** Henry Hathaway. **CAST:** John Wayne, Harry Carey, Betty Field, Marjorie Main, Ward Bond, Beulah Bondi, John Qualen. **1941**

SHERIFF OF LAS VEGAS ★★★ Red Ryder steps in to clear a young man framed for the murder of his father. B&W; 54m. **DIR:** Lesley Selander. **CAST:** William Elliott, Robert Blake, Peggy Stewart, Jay Kirby. **1944**

SHERLOCK HOLMES AND THE DEADLY NECKLACE ★★★ Director Terence Fisher made one of the best versions of Sir Conan Doyle's *Hound of the Baskervilles* for Hammer Films in 1959, yet only three years later he foundered with this loose, German-made (dubbed) adaptation of *The Valley of Fear*. Curt Siodmak's screenplay is sometimes silly and a bit too skewed to the tastes of German audiences. B&W; 85m. **DIR:** Terence Fisher, Frank Winterstein. **CAST:** Christopher Lee, Thorley Walters, Senta Berger. **1962**

SHERLOCK HOLMES AND THE INCIDENT AT VICTORIA FALLS ★★★1/2 A request from King George (Joss Ackland) to safeguard the Star of Africa diamond on its journey from South Africa to England brings Sherlock Holmes (Christopher Lee) and Dr. Watson (Patrick Macnee) out of retirement. First of a series. Not rated; the film has violence. 120m. **DIR:** Bill Corcoran. **CAST:** Christopher Lee, Patrick Macnee, Jenny Seagrove, Claude Akins, Richard Todd, Joss Ackland. **1991**

SHERLOCK HOLMES AND THE LEADING LADY ★★ Edited down from a miniseries that ran over three hours (sans commercials), this romantic mystery of Sherlock Holmes and Dr. Watson in retirement emerges as a fitfully coherent, highlights-only digest version. But Christopher Lee and Patrick Macnee are splendid as Holmes and Watson. 100m. **DIR:** Peter Sasdy. **CAST:** Christopher Lee, Patrick Macnee, Morgan Fairchild. **1992**

SHERLOCK HOLMES AND THE SECRET WEAPON ★★★ Although the contemporary (1940s) setting makes the Baker Street sleuth seem oddly out of place, Basil Rathbone remains one of the definitive Holmeses as he once again faces the ruthless Professor Moriarty. 68m. **DIR:** Roy William Neill. **CAST:** Basil Rathbone, Nigel Bruce, Lionel Atwill, Kaaren Verne, Dennis Hoey, Mary Gordon. **1942 DVD**

SHERLOCK HOLMES AND THE SPIDER WOMAN ★★★1/2 Originally released under the abridged title *Spider Woman*, this Sherlockian adventure is one of the better modernized versions of the Conan Doyle stories. In this one, the villain is a fiendishly evil woman who drives gambling men to suicide in order to increase her personal fortune. It's full of tension and fine performances. B&W; 62m. **DIR:** Roy William Neill. **CAST:** Basil Rathbone, Nigel Bruce, Gale Sondergaard, Dennis Hoey. **1944**

SHERLOCK HOLMES AND THE VOICE OF TERROR ★★★ This first entry in the Universal series is enjoyable. Set during World War II, it has our heroes going after spies who are using radio broadcasts to sabotage Allied efforts. B&W; 65m. **DIR:** John Rawlins. **CAST:** Basil Rathbone, Nigel Bruce, Evelyn Ankers, Henry Daniell, Montagu Love, Thomas Gomez, Hillary Brooke, Mary Gordon. **1942**

SHERLOCK HOLMES FACES DEATH ★★★ Holmes (Basil Rathbone) and Watson (Nigel Bruce) find themselves back in the shadows and fog—albeit in modern times—as they attempt to solve a murder. Based on Conan Doyle's "The Musgrave Ritual," this is a good entry in the series. B&W; 68m. **DIR:** Roy William Neill. **CAST:** Basil Rathbone, Nigel Bruce, Dennis Hoey, Hillary Brooke. **1943**

SHERLOCK HOLMES IN WASHINGTON ★★1/2 Cornball wartime propaganda has Sherlock Holmes (Basil Rathbone) and Dr. Watson (Nigel Bruce) chasing after spies in Washington, D.C. Strong villainy from George Zucco and Henry Daniell helps, and the stars are as watchable as ever. B&W; 71m. **DIR:** Roy William Neill. **CAST:** Basil Rathbone, Nigel Bruce, Marjorie Lord, Henry Daniell, George Zucco. **1943**

SHERLOCK HOLMES: HANDS OF A MURDERER ★★★ This reasonable facsimile of Sir Arthur Conan Doyle's work is somewhat unevenly paced, but the performances, set designs, and costumes capably capture the flavor of Victorian England. The complex story involves the dread Moriarty, critical national secrets, and a cult of Thugee murderers. Genre purists will appreciate the intelligent, self-assured Dr. Watson. Not rated; contains violent themes. 90m. **DIR:** Stuart Orme. **CAST:** Edward Woodward, John Hillerman, Anthony Andrews, Kim Thomson, Peter Jeffrey, Warren Clarke. **1990**

SHERLOCK JR. ★★★★ In this film about film, projectionist Buster Keaton dreams about being a detective and miraculously finds himself inside the film he is showing. The plot involves saving his beloved from the villain, but the real thrust and appeal of the film lies in brilliant camera tricks providing some of the greatest of silent comedy sight gags. Silent. B&W; 45m. **DIR:** Buster Keaton. **CAST:** Buster Keaton, Kathryn McGuire. **1924 DVD**

SHERLOCK: UNDERCOVER DOG ★★ Kids may toss this amateurish comedy a bone, but adults will find it cheap and silly. Two kids spending their summer vacation on Catalina Island find adventure when they're recruited by a talking police dog trying to save his master from kidnappers. Totally preposterous premise, executed with little flair. Rated PG. 80m. **DIR:** Richard Harding Gardner. **CAST:** Benjamin Eroen, Brynne Cameron, Anthony Simmons, Margy Moore. **1994**

SHERMAN'S MARCH ★★★★ In 1981 Boston-based documentary filmmaker Ross McElwee received a $9,000 grant to make a movie about the effects of General William Tecumseh Sherman's bloody march on the South. Then McElwee's girlfriend left him. He made the film, but *Sherman's March* is only tangentially about that historic figure. Subtitled "A Meditation on the Possibility of Romantic Love in an Era of Nuclear Weapons Proliferation," it mostly deals with the filmmaker's hilarious search for the meaning of life and someone to love. Not rated, the film has brief nudity. 150m. **DIR:** Ross McElwee. **1987**

SHE'S ALL THAT ★★★ Surprisingly watchable teen romance features adorable Freddie Prinze Jr. as the cool dude on campus who accepts a bet to play "Professor Higgins" to a cause-conscious but nerdy "Eliza Doolittle" (Rachel Leigh Cook). Despite the lesson about looks not defining a person, which gives this film a John Hughes feel, there are plenty of fun, silly moments that guarantee at least a wide grin. Rated PG-13 for language and sexual situations. 95m. **DIR:** Robert Iscove. **CAST:** Freddie Prinze Jr., Rachael Leigh Cook, Matthew Lillard, Jodi O'Keefe, Kieran Culkin. **1999 DVD**

SHE'S BACK ★★1/2 Black comedy finds Carrie Fisher returning from the dead, edging her meek husband to seek retribution against the street thugs who iced her. Rated R for violence. 88m. **DIR:** Tim Kincaid. **CAST:** Carrie Fisher, Robert Joy. **1989**

SHE'S DRESSED TO KILL ★★ Acceptable murder mystery concerning the deaths of high-fashion models. Eleanor Parker is excellent as a garish, once-renowned designer trying to stage a comeback. This made-for-TV movie was retitled *Someone's Killing the World's Greatest Models*. 100m. **DIR:** Gus Trikonis. **CAST:** Eleanor Parker, Jessica Walter, John Rubinstein, Jim McMullan, Corinne Calvet. **1979**

SHE'S GOTTA HAVE IT ★★★★ A movie about a randy young woman who's "gotta have it" might seem a bit iffy. But independent filmmaker Spike Lee—who wrote, directed, and edited this unique narrative-quasidocumentary—set up the challenge for himself and then set out to succeed *con gusto*. The beautiful lady in question, Nola Darling, is played by Tracy Camilla Johns. Rated R for language and nudity. B&W; 100m. **DIR:** Spike Lee. **CAST:** Tracy Camilla Johns, Redmond Hicks, John Terrell, Spike Lee. **1986**

SHE'S HAVING A BABY ★★ Director John Hughes, champion of the teenage set, advanced from the breakfast club to the breakfast table in this bland account of a young newlywed couple, played by Kevin Bacon and Elizabeth McGovern. A major (and deserved) failure. Rated PG-13 for profanity, suggested sex, and sexual themes. 110m. **DIR:** John Hughes. **CAST:** Kevin Bacon, Elizabeth McGovern, William Windom, James Ray, Holland Taylor. **1988**

SHE'S IN THE ARMY NOW ★★★ The distributor has labeled this made-for-TV film a comedy, but there is very little to laugh about in the story of seven weeks of basic training in a women's squadron. Kathleen Quinlan as the appointed squadron leader and Jamie Lee Curtis as the streetwise recruit with problems are both very good. 97m. **DIR:** Hy Averback. **CAST:** Kathleen Quinlan, Jamie Lee Curtis, Melanie Griffith, Janet MacLachlan. **1981**

SHE'S OUT OF CONTROL 🦃 Tony Danza overplays the father of a 15-year-old girl who suddenly blossoms into a sexy young woman. Rated PG. 97m. **DIR:** Stan Dragoti. **CAST:** Tony Danza, Catharine Hicks, Wallace Shawn, Ami Dolenz. **1989**

SHE'S SO LOVELY ★★1/2 The depth of characterization normally associated with a film by John Cassavetes is missing from this story of a pregnant woman who is beaten and nearly raped by her neighbor. Her husband shoots a police officer and lands in a mental institution. Ten years later, he is released to find his now-ex-wife remarried and his daughter raised by another man. In a messy resolution, the three main characters are forced to confront their emotions, loyalties, and lives. Rated R for violence, profanity, and suggested sex. 97m. **DIR:** Nick Cassavetes. **CAST:** Sean Penn, Robin Wright, John Travolta, Harry Dean Stanton, Debi Mazar, James Gandolfini, Gena Rowlands. **1997 DVD**

SHE'S THE ONE ★★★1/2 Writer-director-star Edward Burns's second big-screen effort essentially reprises much of *The Brothers McMullen*. He's a shy, artistic cabby still recovering from the shock of having been cuckolded by his ex-fiancée; what he doesn't know is that she cheated on him with his own brother! Rated PG-13 for profanity and sexual candor. 96m. **DIR:** Edward Burns. **CAST:** Edward Burns, Mike McGlone, John Mahoney, Cameron Diaz, Maxine Bahns, Jennifer Aniston. **1996 DVD**

SHILOH ★★★★ Top-notch family entertainment stars young Blake Heron as Marty, who befriends a mistreated beagle who has run away from his cruel owner. Marty's efforts to keep the dog are met with resistance from his father, who doesn't believe the dog is worth the trouble. With the help of a local shopkeeper, Marty follows his heart and fights for what he believes in. Solid family values and engaging performances are just the icing on this treat. Rated PG. 93m. **DIR:** Dale Rosenbloom. **CAST:** Blake Heron, Scott Wilson, Michael Moriarty, Rod Steiger. **1996 DVD**

SHILOH 2: SHILOH SEASON ★★ Misguided sequel fails to capture the sweetness and charm of the original. Some of the original cast is back, including Zachary Browne as Marty, the young boy who befriends Shiloh and saves him from his mean owner. The filmmakers lay it on thick and sweet, and sometimes it's too much to bear. Rated PG. 96m. **DIR:** Sandy Tung. **CAST:** Zachary Browne, Scott Wilson, Michael Moriarty, Ann Dowd, Rod Steiger. **1999 DVD**

SHIN HEINKE MONOGATARI ★★★ Fans of the great Kenji Mizoguchi may be disappointed to find that this film is a historical samurai adventure rather than a story of oppressed women, his usual subject. Not one of Mizoguchi's best, though his striking use of color is memorable. In Japanese with English subtitles. 113m. **DIR:** Kenji Mizoguchi. **CAST:** Raizo Ichikawa. **1955**

SHINE ★★★★ Geoffrey Rush collected a well-deserved Oscar for his galvanic portrayal of deeply troubled Australian piano prodigy David Helfgott, who suffered a crippling nervous breakdown on the verge of international fame. Anybody who has even seen Helfgott knows how superbly the actor caught his behavior and remarkable style of speaking. Rate PG-13 for nudity, sensuality, and strong dramatic content. 105m. **DIR:** Scott Hicks. **CAST:** Geoffrey Rush, Armin Mueller-Stahl, Noah Taylor, Lynn Redgrave, John Gielgud. **1996 DVD**

SHINING, THE ★★1/2 A struggling writer (Jack Nicholson) accepts a position as the caretaker of a large summer resort hotel during the winter season. The longer he and his family spend in the hotel, the more Nicholson becomes possessed by it. Considering the talent involved, this is a major disappointment. Director Stanley Kubrick keeps things at a snail's pace, and Nicholson's performance approaches high camp. Rated R for violence and language. 146m. **DIR:** Stanley Kubrick. **CAST:** Jack Nicholson, Shelley Duvall, Scatman Crothers. **1980 DVD**

SHINING HOUR, THE ★★★ Soap opera about a nightclub entertainer (Joan Crawford) who fights for acceptance from her husband's small-town family with small-town values. An energetic film with good acting and a predictable plot. B&W; 81m. **DIR:** Frank Borzage. **CAST:** Joan Crawford, Margaret Sullavan, Melvyn Douglas, Robert Young, Fay Bainter, Hattie McDaniel, Allyn Joslyn, Frank Albertson. **1938**

SHINING SEASON, A ★★★ Fact-based story of track star and Olympic hopeful John Baker (Timothy Bottoms) who, when stricken by cancer, devoted his final months to coaching a girls' track team. This is very familiar territory, but director Stuart Margolin keeps things above water most of the time. Bottoms is an engaging hero-victim. Made for television. 100m. **DIR:** Stuart Margolin. **CAST:** Timothy Bottoms, Allyn Ann McLerie, Ed Begley Jr., Rip Torn, Mason Adams. **1979**

SHINING THROUGH ★★★1/2 Working from the best-seller by Susan Isaacs, writer-director David Seltzer has come up with a clever and effective homage to the war films of the Forties. Melanie Griffith is a wisecracking dame who figures out that her boss (Michael Douglas) is an American spy from what she's seen in movies. In

no time, she's behind enemy lines in Nazi Germany attempting to gather information. Rated R for violence, profanity, and nudity. 125m. **DIR:** David Seltzer. **CAST:** Michael Douglas, Melanie Griffith, Liam Neeson, Joely Richardson, John Gielgud. **1992**

SHIP AHOY ★★★ Entertaining musical, thanks to Eleanor Powell's energetic tap dancing. The World War II plot is somewhat dated, but Powell and Red Skelton are excellent. The film showcases Tommy Dorsey's orchestra when Buddy Rich was his drummer and Sinatra his soloist. Enjoyable. B&W; 95m. **DIR:** Edward Buzzell. **CAST:** Eleanor Powell, Red Skelton, Bert Lahr, Virginia O'Brien, Tommy Dorsey, Jo Stafford, Frank Sinatra, Buddy Rich. **1942**

SHIP OF FOOLS ★★★★★ In 1933, a vast and varied group of characters take passage on a German liner sailing from Mexico to Germany amidst impending doom. The all-star cast features most memorable performances in this superb screen adaptation of the Katherine Anne Porter novel. B&W; 150m. **DIR:** Stanley Kramer. **CAST:** Vivien Leigh, Oskar Werner, Simone Signoret, José Ferrer, Lee Marvin, George Segal, Michael Dunn, Elizabeth Ashley, Lilia Skala, Charles Korvin. **1965**

•SHIPPING NEWS, THE ★★1/2 Newspaper print shop employee Quoyle is left to raise a daughter after the death of his wayward wife. He returns to the small Newfoundland fishing village where his family originated, uncovers a dark secret of an aunt, becomes a mediocre journalist, and meets a day-care supervisor who changes his life. This messy, overtly quirky, and pretentious adaptation of E. Annie Proulx's 1994 Pulitzer Prize–winning novel about the lingering effects of family history feels more like a self-conscious exercise in eccentricity than anything resembling real life. Rated R for language, sexuality, and violence. 120m. **DIR:** Lasse Hallstrom. **CAST:** Kevin Spacey, Judi Dench, Julianne Moore, Cate Blanchett. **2001 DVD**

SHIPS WITH WINGS ★★1/2 Typical patriotic British war movie, this one is set on an aircraft carrier preparing for battle. Some good character bits, but on the whole rather perfunctory. B&W; 103m. **DIR:** Sergei Nolbandov. **CAST:** John Clements, Ann Todd, Leslie Banks, Hugh Williams, Michael Wilding, Michael Rennie, Cecil Parker. **1941**

SHIPWRECKED ★★★★ A sort of *Home Alone* meets *Treasure Island*, this is a rousing adventure film based on the classic Norwegian novel *Haakon Haakonsen* by O.V. Falck-Ytter. About a young lad who goes to sea to help get his parents out of debt, and finds himself battling a bloodthirsty pirate (Gabriel Byrne) for buried treasure. This Disney release has plenty of action, thrills, and suspense. Rated PG for light violence. 93m. **DIR:** Nils Gaup. **CAST:** Stian Smestad, Gabriel Byrne, Bjorn Sundquist. **1991**

SHIRLEY VALENTINE ★★★★ Adult viewers will revel in this wise and witty movie. Pauline Collins is terrific as the title character, who one day decides to chuck it all and head for romance in the Greek Isles. Tom Conti is fun as the restaurant owner who woos the wacky but sympathetic heroine. Rated R for profanity and nudity. 160m. **DIR:** Lewis Gilbert. **CAST:** Pauline Collins, Tom Conti, Julia McKenzie, Joanna Lumley, Bernard Hill, Sylvia Syms. **1989**

SHIVERS, THE ★★ Plans to turn a haunted house into a dance club don't go quite as envisioned in this yawnfest from director Todd Sheets. As usual, subtlety seems to be a foreign concept to Sheets and the film would have done much better had it taken a few pointers from classier material like *The Haunting* or *The Shining*. Not rated; contains gore, violence, and profanity. 90m. **DIR:** Todd Sheets. **CAST:** Rico Love, Nick Stodden. **1999**

SHOCK, THE (1923) ★★★ The legendary Lon Chaney Sr. added yet another grotesque character to his growing closet of skeletons when he played Wilse Dilling. This decent crime melodrama, no different in plot than dozens of other films over the years, has the advantage of Chaney and an exciting climax consisting of a bang-up earthquake. Corny at times, this one is still a good bet if you're interested in silent films. B&W; 96m. **DIR:** Lambert Hillyer. **CAST:** Lon Chaney Sr., Christine Mayo. **1923 DVD**

SHOCK (1946) ★★★ Highly effective thriller features Vincent Price in an early performance as a murderer—in this case he's a psychiatrist who murders his wife and is then forced to silence a witness through drugs and hypnosis. This minor classic provided the framework for many subsequent suspense movies. B&W; 70m. **DIR:** Alfred Werker. **CAST:** Vincent Price, Lynn Bari, Reed Hadley, Pierre Watkin, Frank Latimore. **1946**

SHOCK CORRIDOR ★★1/2 Newspaper reporter Peter Breck poses as insane to learn who committed a murder inside a state asylum, and we watch as he goes bonkers himself. Brilliant action sequences interspersed with tedium. B&W; 101m. **DIR:** Samuel Fuller. **CAST:** Peter Breck, Constance Towers, Gene Evans. **1963 DVD**

SHOCK TO THE SYSTEM, A ★★★★ In this deliciously wicked black comedy, Michael Caine plays a middle-aged executive waiting impatiently for a big promotion, which goes instead to younger man Peter Riegert. So, Caine does what any man in that position would do: he plots murder. Screenwriter Andrew Klavan's loose adaptation of Simon Brett's novel makes an uncommonly satisfying thriller. Rated R for violence and profanity. 91m. **DIR:** Jan Egleson. **CAST:** Michael Caine, Peter Riegert, Elizabeth McGovern, Swoosie Kurtz, Will Patton, John McMartin. **1990**

SHOCK TREATMENT 🦃 Forgettable sequel to *The Rocky Horror Picture Show*. Janet and Brad go on a TV game show and end up trying to escape from it. Rated PG. 94m. **DIR:** Jim Sharman. **CAST:** Jessica Harper, Cliff De Young, Richard O'Brien. **1981**

SHOCK WAVES (DEATH CORPS) 🦃 Vacationers stumble upon a crazed army of underwater zombies. Rated PG. 86m. **DIR:** Ken Wiederhorn. **CAST:** Peter Cushing, Brooke Adams, John Carradine. **1977**

SHOCK'EM DEAD ★★ What starts out as an entirely lame scare flick ends as a completely lame scare flick. But in between are some truly frightening shocks as we see a wimp sell his soul to the devil in return for becoming the greatest rock star in the world. Rated R for violence, profanity, and gore. 94m. **DIR:** Mark Freed. **CAST:** Traci Lords, Aldo Ray, Troy Donahue. **1990**

SHOCKER ★★ Wes Craven introduces Horace Pinker, a maniacal TV repairman with a Freddy Krueger personality and special powers. He spends his evenings hacking up families. Rated R for violence, profanity, and

gore. 110m. **DIR:** Wes Craven. **CAST:** Mitch Pileggi, Michael Murphy. **1989 DVD**

SHOES OF THE FISHERMAN 🦃 A boring film about an enthusiastic pope who single-handedly attempts to stop nuclear war, starvation, and world strife. 157m. **DIR:** Michael Anderson. **CAST:** Anthony Quinn, Laurence Olivier, Oskar Werner, David Janssen, Vittorio De Sica, John Gielgud, Leo McKern, Barbara Jefford. **1968**

SHOESHINE ★★★★ Neorealist classic about two boys whose friendship gets them through hard times in Rome during the Nazi occupation. But in a harsh jail, their relationship falters. Winner of a special Academy Award. In Italian with English subtitles. 93m. **DIR:** Vittorio De Sica. **CAST:** Rinaldo Smerdoni, Franco Interlenghi. **1946**

SHOGUN (FULL-LENGTH VERSION) ★★★★ This ten-hour original is the only one that does justice to James Clavell's sweeping novel. Richard Chamberlain began his reign as king of the miniseries with his portrayal of Blackthorne, the English sailor shipwrecked among the feudal Japanese. It all works, from the breathtaking cinematography to the superb acting. 600m. **DIR:** Jerry London. **CAST:** Richard Chamberlain, Toshiro Mifune, Yoko Shimada, Damien Thomas. **1980**

SHOGUN ASSASSIN ★★★ Meticulously reedited, rescripted, rescored, and English-dubbed version of the original *Baby-Cart at the River Styx*: swords enter bodies at the most imaginative angles; a body count is impossible; all records are broken for bloodletting. Rated R for the violence, which really is fairly aesthetic. 90m. **DIR:** Kenji Misumi, David Weisman, Robert Hous. **CAST:** Tomisaburo Wakayama. **1980**

SHOOT (1976) ★★★1/2 A group of buddies spending a weekend hunting are attacked by another group of hunters who are after game more interesting than deer. When one of their party is wounded, the attacked hunters, led by Cliff Robertson and Ernest Borgnine, want revenge and mount a military-style campaign to get it. Rated R for violence and profanity. 98m. **DIR:** Harvey Hart. **CAST:** Cliff Robertson, Ernest Borgnine, Henry Silva. **1976**

SHOOT (1991) ★★1/2 Passable spoof of undercover greed features DeDee Pfeiffer as a ditzy photographer studying her crime boss's gambling operation. His real ace in the hole is a million-dollar pearl he plans to sell to the highest bidder. Surprise ending is too strange to be believed. Not rated; contains violence and criminial activity. 97m. **DIR:** Hugh Parks. **CAST:** Dedee Pfeiffer, Miles O'Keeffe, Christopher Atkins, Fred Ottaviano. **1991**

SHOOT LOUD, LOUDER . . . I DON'T UNDERSTAND 🦃 Antique dealer confronts inept gunmen. Not rated; contains violence. 100m. **DIR:** Eduardo De Filippo. **CAST:** Marcello Mastroianni, Raquel Welch, Leopoldo Trieste. **1966 DVD**

SHOOT THE MOON ★★ Why didn't they just call it *Ordinary People Go West*? Of course, this film isn't really a sequel to the 1980 Oscar winner. It's closer to a rip-off. None of the style, believability, or consistency of its predecessor. Rated R because of profanity, violence, and adult themes. 123m. **DIR:** Alan Parker. **CAST:** Albert Finney, Diane Keaton, Karen Allen, Dana Hill, Tracey Gold. **1982**

SHOOT THE PIANO PLAYER ★★★1/2 Singer Charles Aznavour plays to perfection the antihero of this minor masterpiece directed by François Truffaut. Don't look for plot, unity of theme, or understandable mood transitions. This one's a brilliantly offbeat mix of crime, melodrama, romance, and slapstick. In French with English subtitles. B&W; 85m. **DIR:** François Truffaut. **CAST:** Charles Aznavour, Marie Dubois, Nicole Berger, Michele Mercier. **1962 DVD**

SHOOT TO KILL ★★★1/2 Sidney Poitier returns to the screen after a ten-year absence to portray a streetwise FBI agent determined to track down a ruthless killer. The chase leads to the mountains of the Pacific Northwest, where Poitier teams with tracker Tom Berenger. A solid thriller. Rated R for language and violence. 110m. **DIR:** Roger Spottiswoode. **CAST:** Sidney Poitier, Tom Berenger, Kirstie Alley, Clancy Brown, Richard Masur, Andrew Robinson. **1988**

SHOOTFIGHTER ★★★ Two friends in the deadly world of shootfighting—a brutal, sometimes lethal sport—team up to stay alive. A workable cast, combined with some extremely brutal fight sequences, blend together for an action film that rises above the genre. Two versions available: one rated R for violence, and one unrated with more of the same. **DIR:** Pat Alan. **CAST:** Bolo Yeung, Maryam D'Abo, William Zabka, Martin Kove, Edward Albert. **1993**

SHOOTFIGHTER 2: KILL OR BE KILLED 🦃 For those who didn't get their fill of the original *Shootfighter*, more of the same. Rated R for violence. 90m. **DIR:** Paul Ziller. **CAST:** Bolo Yeung, William Zabka, Michael Bernardo, Jorge Gil. **1996**

SHOOTING, THE ★★★ This early Jack Nicholson vehicle, directed by cult figure Monte Hellman, is a moody Western about revenge and murder. An interesting entry into the genre, it may not be everyone's cup of tea. No rating; contains some violence. 82m. **DIR:** Monte Hellman. **CAST:** Warren Oates, Millie Perkins, Will Hutchins, Jack Nicholson. **1967**

SHOOTING ELIZABETH ★★1/2 A husband tells his friend that he is going to kill his wife during their second honeymoon. Mundane plot and acting. Not rated. 96m. **DIR:** Baz Taylor. **CAST:** Jeff Goldblum, Mimi Rogers, Burt Kwouk. **1992**

SHOOTING FISH ★★★ This breezy British comedy caper focuses on two likable swindlers who are nearly exposed by peddling bogus miracle computers. They then both develop a crush on their scrappy female assistant, run a risky attic insulation scam, and get involved with a racing-horse con that may turn them into urban Robin Hoods while also making them rich. The storyline stretches credibility, but the chemistry of the characters, and the film's fizzy 1960s feel are irresistible. Rated PG. 93m. **DIR:** Stefan Schwartz. **CAST:** Dan Futterman, Stuart Townsend, Kate Beckinsale. **1998 DVD**

SHOOTING PARTY, THE ★★★★ This meditation on the fading English aristocracy is an acting showcase. All main characters are played with verve, or at least the verve one would expect from English nobility in the years preceding World War I. While nothing much happens here, the rich texture of the characters, the highly stylized sets, and the incidental affairs in the plot are enough to sustain the viewer. Not rated, but equivalent to a PG for partial nudity. 97m. **DIR:** Alan Bridges.

CAST: James Mason, Edward Fox, Dorothy Tutin, John Gielgud, Gordon Jackson, Cheryl Campbell, Robert Hardy. **1985 DVD**

SHOOTIST, THE ★★★★1/2 John Wayne's final film is an intelligent tribute to the passing of the era known as the "wild West." Wayne's masterful performance is touching and bitterly ironic as well. He plays a famous gunfighter dying of cancer and seeking a place to die in peace, only to become a victim of his own reputation. Rated PG. 99m. **DIR:** Don Siegel. **CAST:** John Wayne, Lauren Bacall, James Stewart, Ron Howard, Richard Boone, Hugh O'Brian, John Carradine, Harry Morgan, Scatman Crothers. **1976 DVD**

SHOP AROUND THE CORNER, THE ★★★★ A charming period comedy dealing with the lives of two people who work in the same Budapest shop and become loving pen pals. MGM later remade this picture as *In the Good Old Summertime*, and it formed the basis of the stage musical *She Loves Me*. B&W; 98m. **DIR:** Ernst Lubitsch. **CAST:** James Stewart, Margaret Sullavan, Frank Morgan, Joseph Schildkraut. **1939**

SHOP ON MAIN STREET, THE ★★★★ This film finds a Jewish woman removed from her small business and portrays her growing relationship with the man who has been put in charge of her shop. Set among the turbulent days of the Nazi occupation of Czechoslovakia, this tender film depicts the instincts of survival among the innocent pawns of a brutal war. A moving film. B&W; 128m. **DIR:** Ján Kadár. **CAST:** Elmar Klos, Josef Kroner, Ida Kaminska. **1964**

SHOPPING ★★1/2 In the near future, the favorite sport of disaffected teens is "shopping"—stealing cars and driving them to malls, which they then loot. Early indications that this may be a comment on the future of a spiritually dead consumer society fade as *Shopping* becomes a stylish but familiar action flick. Rated R for violence and nudity. 87m. **DIR:** Paul Anderson. **CAST:** Sadie Frost, Jude Law, Sean Pertwee, Jonathan Pryce, Fraser James, Sean Bean, Marianne Faithfull. **1995 DVD**

SHOPWORN ANGEL, THE ★★★1/2 Margaret Sullavan plays a callous and selfish actress who toys with the affections of shy soldier James Stewart until she is won over by his sincerity. Predictable, but this team is always a joy to watch. B&W; 85m. **DIR:** H. C. Potter. **CAST:** Margaret Sullavan, James Stewart, Walter Pidgeon, Hattie McDaniel, Nat Pendleton, Alan Curtis, Sam Levene. **1938**

SHORT CIRCUIT ★★★★ In this enjoyable sci-fi comedy-adventure, a sophisticated robot, Number Five, is zapped by lightning during a storm and comes alive (à la Frankenstein's monster) to the shock of his creator (Steve Guttenberg). Created as the ultimate war weapon, the mechanical man learns the value of life from an animal lover (Ally Sheedy) and sets off on his own—with the military in hot pursuit. Rated PG for profanity and violence. 95m. **DIR:** John Badham. **CAST:** Ally Sheedy, Steve Guttenberg, Fisher Stevens, Austin Pendleton, G. W. Bailey. **1986**

SHORT CIRCUIT 2 ★★ If it weren't filled with profanity, this might have been a good film for the kiddies. Indian inventor Fisher Stevens goes into the toy business with streetwise hustler Michael McKean and that lovable robot, Number Five. Rated PG for profanity and violence. 110m. **DIR:** Kenneth Johnson. **CAST:** Fisher Stevens, Michael McKean, Cynthia Gibb, Jack Weston. **1988 DVD**

SHORT CUTS ★★★★★ Director Robert Altman scores again with this superb film that intertwines several of Raymond Carver's short stories into a fascinating, thought-provoking panorama of modern-day life. The performances by a huge, all-star cast are uniformly excellent. Rated R for profanity, nudity, and violence. 188m. **DIR:** Robert Altman. **CAST:** Andie MacDowell, Bruce Davison, Jack Lemmon, Julianne Moore, Matthew Modine, Anne Archer, Fred Ward, Jennifer Jason Leigh, Christopher Penn, Lili Taylor, Robert Downey Jr., Madeleine Stowe, Tim Robbins, Lily Tomlin, Tom Waits, Frances McDormand, Peter Gallagher, Annie Ross, Lori Singer, Lyle Lovett, Buck Henry, Huey Lewis. **1993 DVD**

SHORT EYES ★★★★ Film version of Miguel Pinero's hard-hitting play about a convicted child molester at the mercy of other prisoners. A brutal and frightening film. Excellent, but difficult to watch. Rated R for violence and profanity. 104m. **DIR:** Robert M. Young. **CAST:** Bruce Davison, Jose Perez. **1977**

SHORT FUSE 🦃 Racial tensions between the black community and the police. Rated R for violence and profanity. 91m. **DIR:** Blaine Novak. **CAST:** Art Garfunkel, Harris Yulin. **1989**

SHORT GRASS ★★★★ Returning home after several years, Rod Cameron is pushed off his land by larger ranchers. Intricate script, from his own novel, by Tom Blackburn. B&W; 82m. **DIR:** Lesley Selander. **CAST:** Rod Cameron, Johnny Mack Brown, Cathy Downs, Alan Hale Jr. **1950**

SHORT TIME ★★★1/2 In this sometimes hilarious action-comedy, Dabney Coleman is a soon-to-retire police officer who is incorrectly diagnosed as having a terminal disease. He spends the last few days on the force attempting to get killed to leave his wife (Teri Garr) and son a substantial insurance settlement. Rated PG-13 for violence and profanity. 102m. **DIR:** Gregg Champion. **CAST:** Dabney Coleman, Matt Frewer, Teri Garr, Barry Corbin, Joe Pantoliano. **1990**

SHOT IN THE DARK, A ★★★★ *A Shot in the Dark* is a one-man show, with Peter Sellers outdoing himself as the character he later reprised in *The Return of the Pink Panther*, *The Pink Panther Strikes Back*, and *The Revenge of the Pink Panther*. In this slapstick delight, Clouseau attempts to discover whether or not a woman (Elke Sommer) is guilty of murdering her lover. 101m. **DIR:** Blake Edwards. **CAST:** Peter Sellers, Elke Sommer, George Sanders, Burt Kwouk, Herbert Lom. **1964 DVD**

•SHOT IN THE HEART ★★★ Based on a true story from the 1970s, this made-for-cable movie follows Mikal Gilmore, the youngest brother of Gary Gilmore, as he comes to talk his brother out of seeking the death sentence. Gary wants the notoriety of being the first man executed after the federal government lifted its moratorium on death sentences, while Mikal is searching for answers that only Gary can give. In all, it's an interesting drama, if a bit slow at times. Rated R for profanity and violence. 98m. **DIR:** Agnieszka Holland. **CAST:** Giovanni Ribisi, Elias Koteas, Eric Bogosian, Lee Tergensen, Terry Beaver, Amy Madigan, Sam Shepard. **2001 DVD**

SHOT THROUGH THE HEART ★★★★ Searing tale based loosely on actual events and set during the atrocious, inhumane siege of Sarajevo, Bosnia. A pair of sharpshooters, best friends, hope to qualify for the Olympics. But when the situation in Bosnia explodes, their different backgrounds place them on opposite sides as snipers. This film conveys the terrible extremes to which former friends may be driven in the face of horrifying, all-out war. Rated R for violence, profanity, nudity, and simulated sex. 112m. **DIR:** David Attwood. **CAST:** Linus Roache, Vincent Perez, Lia Williams, Adam Kotz, Soo Garay, Lothaire Bluteau. **1998**

SHOTGUN ★★★ Violent melodramatic track-down story has Marshal Sterling Hayden pursuing the gunrunning shotgun killer of a town sheriff. Along the way he encounters a saloon girl and a bounty hunter. 80m. **DIR:** Lesley Selander. **CAST:** Sterling Hayden, Zachary Scott, Yvonne De Carlo. **1955**

SHOUT, THE (1979) ★★★ Enigmatic British chiller about a wanderer's chilling effect on an unsuspecting couple. He possesses the ancient power to kill people by screaming. Well made, with an excellent cast. The film may be too offbeat for some viewers. Rated R. 87m. **DIR:** Jerzy Skolimowski. **CAST:** Alan Bates, Susannah York, John Hurt, Robert Stephens, Tim Curry. **1979**

SHOUT (1991) 🦃 This rock 'n' roll fantasy, in which a delinquent is reformed by the love of a good woman, has its heart in the right place; but its brain is dead. Rated PG-13 for violence and profanity. 89m. **DIR:** Jeffrey Hornady. **CAST:** James Walters, Heather Graham, John Travolta, Richard Jordan, Linda Fiorentino, Scott Coffey. **1991 DVD**

SHOUT AT THE DEVIL ★★ Good action scenes elevate this otherwise distasteful and overly complicated film about a hard-drinking American adventurer (Lee Marvin) and an upper-crust Englishman (Roger Moore) who join forces to blow up a German battleship before the breakout of World War I. Rated PG. 119m. **DIR:** Peter R. Hunt. **CAST:** Lee Marvin, Roger Moore, Barbara Parkins, Ian Holm. **1976**

SHOUT: THE STORY OF JOHNNY O'KEEFE ★★★1/2 A slow start builds up to a satisfying send-up for the man who put Australian rock music on the international map. Terry Serio is brilliant as Johnny O'Keefe, the Boomerang Kid—a man who lets conceit and self-promotion stand in the way of his happiness and sanity. Not rated, contains profanity, violence, and drug use. 192m. **DIR:** Ted Robinson. **CAST:** Terry Serio. **1985**

SHOW, THE ★★ Billed as the first "rapumentary," this hip-hop documentary is long on unenlightening talking-head commentary by noted names in the field. Performance scenes, the heart and soul of any concert film, are too short, too grainy, and too scarce. Rated R for profanity. 97m. **DIR:** Brian Robbins. **CAST:** Craig Mack, Doctor Dre, Naughty by Nature, Run DMC, Slick Rick, Tha Dogg Pound, Warren G, Wu-Tang Clan. **1995**

SHOW BOAT (1936) ★★★★★ The definitive film version of America's best-loved musical, it marked the first full-sound version of the 1927 Broadway hit and featured many performers in roles they played onstage. Paul Robeson sings "Ol' Man River" the way it is *supposed* to be sung. 113m. **DIR:** James Whale. **CAST:** Irene Dunne, Allan Jones, Helen Morgan, Charles Winninger, Hattie McDaniel, Paul Robeson. **1936**

SHOW BOAT (1951) ★★★1/2 This watchable musical depicts life and love on a Mississippi showboat during the early 1900s. Kathryn Grayson, Howard Keel, and Ava Gardner try but can't get any real sparks flying. 115m. **DIR:** George Sidney. **CAST:** Kathryn Grayson, Howard Keel, Ava Gardner, Joe E. Brown, Agnes Moorehead, Marge Champion, Gower Champion. **1951 DVD**

SHOW BUSINESS ★★★ Based on incidents in Eddie Cantor's entertainment career, this slick, brassy, and nostalgic picture provides fun and good music. For Cantor and Joan Davis fans, this film is a peach. B&W; 92m. **DIR:** Edwin L. Marin. **CAST:** Eddie Cantor, George Murphy, Joan Davis, Nancy Kelly, Constance Moore. **1944**

SHOW OF FORCE, A ★★ This engaging but occasionally unconvincing conspiracy thriller is loosely based on an infamous Puerto Rican scandal involving the fatal shooting of two pro-independence activists. Amy Irving stars as a television journalist who finds that the incident may have been a politically motivated murder. Rated R for language and violence. 93m. **DIR:** Bruno Barreto. **CAST:** Amy Irving, Lou Diamond Phillips, Robert Duvall, Andy Garcia. **1990**

SHOW-OFF, THE (1926) ★★★ Self-centered title character does his best to ruin his life and those of his wife and her inventor brother before being taken to task by peppery Louise Brooks in an early starring role. The first of three film versions of the popular play, this is as much melodrama as comedy and is considered to be the best. B&W; 82m. **DIR:** Malcolm St. Clair. **CAST:** Ford Sterling, Lois Wilson, Louise Brooks, Gregory Kelly, Claire McDowell. **1926**

SHOW-OFF, THE (1946) ★★1/2 The third version of George Kelly's play is the weakest, but Red Skelton has the right personality for the leading role. He plays an office clerk who will do anything to impress a girlfriend and winds up getting in big trouble. Most of the laughs are supplied by the supporting cast because, strangely, Skelton has more straight lines than punch lines. B&W; 84m. **DIR:** Harry Beaumont. **CAST:** Red Skelton, Marilyn Maxwell, Marjorie Main, Eddie "Rochester" Anderson, Leon Ames, Marshall Thompson, Grady Sutton, Lila Leeds. **1946**

SHOW PEOPLE ★★★★ Loosely based on the career of Gloria Swanson, this was the justly fabled Marion Davies's last silent film. Davies is warm and genuinely touching as innocent Polly Pepper, a young actress whose ambitions are thwarted at nearly every turn. As a satire on the industry, this is a glittering gem, right on the money. Charlie Chaplin, John Gilbert, May Murray, and Norma Talmadge are among a coterie of stars appearing as themselves. Silent. B&W; 81m. **DIR:** King Vidor. **CAST:** Marion Davies, William Haines, Polly Moran. **1928**

SHOW THEM NO MERCY ★★★ Four gangsters snatch a child and are paid off in bills that can be traced. Nobody wins in this compelling drama about a kidnapping that goes sour. B&W; 76m. **DIR:** George Marshall. **CAST:** Rochelle Hudson, Bruce Cabot, Cesar Romero, Edward Norris, Edward Brophy. **1935**

SHOWDOWN (1973) ★★★★ Starting with the familiar tale of childhood friends who end up on opposite sides of the law, director George Seaton and his screen-

writers mix inventive plot twists and sharply drawn characterizations for a compelling tale that plays especially well on the small screen. Rated PG for violence. 100m. **DIR:** George Seaton. **CAST:** Rock Hudson, Dean Martin, Susan Clark, Donald Moffat, John McLiam, Ed Begley Jr. **1973**

SHOWDOWN, THE (1950) ★★★★ "Wild" Bill Elliott's last Western for Republic Pictures is one of his best, a revenge story enlivened by a top-flight cast and a powerful performance by its star. Elliott is a former lawman on the trail of the man who murdered his brother, a trail that leads to a cattle drive. B&W; 86m. **DIR:** Darrell McGowan, Stuart E. McGowan. **CAST:** William Elliott, Walter Brennan, Marie Windsor, Harry Morgan, Jim Davis, Rhys Williams, Leif Erickson, Yakima Canutt. **1950**

SHOWDOWN AT BOOT HILL ★★1/2 Stone-faced Charles Bronson does some impressive work as a lawman who finds that the criminal he has killed in the line of duty is actually a respected citizen in another community. B&W; 71m. **DIR:** Gene Fowler Jr. **CAST:** Charles Bronson, Robert Hutton, John Carradine. **1958**

SHOWDOWN AT WILLIAMS CREEK ★★★1/2 A British soldier, John Brown (Tom Burlinson), leaves Ireland for America in hopes of making his fortune and "coming back a gentleman." But the rugged, dangerous life in the frontier, with its treacherous schemers, teaches Brown what it means to be a survivor—and on trial for murder. Donnelly Rhodes gives a superb supporting turn. Fascinating, hard-edged Western was based on true events. Rated R for violence, nudity, and profanity. 97m. **DIR:** Allan Kroeker. **CAST:** Tom Burlinson, Donnelly Rhodes, Raymond Burr. **1991**

SHOWDOWN IN LITTLE TOKYO ★★ As martial arts films go, this one is only fair. Its appeal lies in the action sequences and with the stars Dolph Lundgren and Brandon Lee. Rated R for violence, profanity, and nudity. 77m. **DIR:** Mark L. Lester. **CAST:** Dolph Lundgren, Brandon Lee, Tia Carrere. **1991 DVD**

SHOWER ★★★ Ambition and ego wrestle with tradition in this modern return of the prodigal son. A Chinese yuppie returns to his hometown of Beijing after misinterpreting a postcard he received from his mentally challenged brother. He makes tentative peace with his estranged father and is reintroduced to the Old World community that thrives in his father's bathhouse. This low-key, bittersweet story about a vanishing lifestyle suggests a sort of group therapy *Rain Man*. In Mandarin with English subtitles. Rated PG-13 for language and nudity. 92m. **DIR:** Zhang Yang. **CAST:** Cun Xin, Jiang Wu, Xu Zhu, He Zheng. **2000 DVD**

SHOWGIRL MURDERS ★★ Despite its low-budget and low-rent cast, this erotic thriller is actually better than *Showgirls* in that it never strives to be anything more than it is. Maria Ford is Tamra, a stripper on the run from a violent past, who helps turn a dingy bar into a popular hot spot. Lots of flesh with no excuses. Not rated; contains nudity, adult situations, violence, and profanity. 85m. **DIR:** Gene Hertel. **CAST:** Maria Ford, Matt Preston, Samantha Carter, Bob McFarland. **1995**

SHOWGIRLS 🦃 This so-called insider's glance at the life of a Las Vegas lap dancer may well be the worst big-studio production ever filmed, thanks in equal part to superstar scripter Joe Eszterhas's odious screenplay, and neophyte star Elizabeth Berkeley's atrocious acting. Rarely has so much been spent to produce so little. Rated NC-17 for nudity, simulated sex, rape, profanity, and violence. 131m. **DIR:** Paul Verhoeven. **CAST:** Elizabeth Berkeley, Kyle MacLachlan, Gina Gershon, Glenn Plummer, Robert Davi, Alan Rachins. **1995 DVD**

SHREK ★★★★ A big green ogre (voice by Mike Myers) and a talking donkey (Eddie Murphy at his best) set off to rescue a beautiful princess (Cameron Diaz) from a dragon. This computer-animated feature pokes good-natured fun at fairy-tale conventions even as it revives them, building toward the inevitable happily-ever-after ending. The spirit of Looney Tunes is present in every scene, and laughs are loud and frequent. Rated PG. 89m. **DIR:** Andrew Adamson, Vicky Jenson. **CAST:** Mike Myers, Eddie Murphy, Cameron Diaz, John Lithgow. **2001**

SHRIEK IF YOU KNOW WHAT I DID LAST FRIDAY THE 13TH ★★ Low-rent *Scary Movie* clone is worth a look. Every scene is loaded with enough visual and verbal humor to choke a donkey in this film about yet another high school that is haunted by a serial killer. The characters and situations are all familiar, but some have a spin that makes them fresh. Rated R for adult situations, language, and violence. 86m. **DIR:** John Blanchard. **CAST:** Tiffani-Amber Thiessen, Tom Arnold, Coolio, Majandra Delfino, Shirley Jones, Simon Rex. **2000 DVD**

SHRIEK IN THE NIGHT, A ★★★ Ginger Rogers and Lyle Talbot play two fast-talking reporters competing for a juicy scoop on a murder case in this entertaining low-budget whodunit. This tidy thriller makes up for its lack of production quality by the spunky, enthusiastic performances by the two leads. B&W; 66m. **DIR:** Albert Ray. **CAST:** Ginger Rogers, Lyle Talbot, Arthur Hoyt, Purnell Pratt. **1933**

SHRIEKER ★★ Creaky dark-house horror-thriller about a group of six college students who meet their fate one by one when they encounter a nasty two-headed monster from another dimension. Director Victoria Sloan follows the formula that's been spoofed in *Scream* to the letter. Not much to scream about, but horror fans might be a little less demanding. Rated R for adult situations, language, nudity, and violence. 80m. **DIR:** Victoria Sloan. **CAST:** Tanya Dempsey, Jamie Gannon, Parry Allen, Alison Cuffe, Roger Crowe, Chris Boyd. **1997**

SHRIEKING, THE 🦃 Tedious wannabe horror-action flick about Indian witchcraft used on some good old boys on motorcycles. Rated PG for violence. 93m. **DIR:** Leo Garen. **CAST:** Keith Carradine, Gary Busey, Scott Glenn. **1974**

SHRIMP ON THE BARBIE ★★ The ordinarily watchable and funny Richard "Cheech" Marin is cast in this disappointing comedy as an unemployed Mexican-American who decides to try his luck in Australia. Rated PG-13 for profanity. 90m. **DIR:** Alan Smithee. **CAST:** Richard "Cheech" Marin, Emma Samms. **1990**

SHRUNKEN HEADS ★★★1/2 Off-the-wall comedy-thriller involving three teens who attempt to clean up their mean streets and wind up dead. Their heads are severed by a voodoo practitioner, reanimated, and given special powers to hunt down their killers. Outrageous special effects and great camp performances make this

direct-to-video effort a cut above the rest. Rated R for violence, language, and adult situations. 86m. **DIR:** Richard Elfman. **CAST:** Aeryk Egan, Becky Herbst, A. J. Damato, Bo Sharon, Julius W. Harris, Meg Foster. **1994**

SHUTTERED ROOM, THE 🦃 Unfaithful shocker is yet another in a long line of disappointments for fans of H. P. Lovecraft. 99m. **DIR:** David Greene. **CAST:** Gig Young, Carol Lynley, Oliver Reed. **1967**

SHY PEOPLE ★★★ Moody drama about a New York writer (Jill Clayburgh) who journeys to the Louisiana bayous to get family-background information from distant Cajun relatives. Barbara Hershey, in an offbeat role, plays a dominating Cajun mother. Clayburgh gives a strong performance, and Martha Plimpton as her troublemaking daughter is fine too. Rated R for language and sexual content. 118m. **DIR:** Andrei Konchalovsky. **CAST:** Barbara Hershey, Jill Clayburgh, Martha Plimpton, Merritt Butrick, John Philbin, Mare Winningham. **1987**

SIBERIADE ★★★★ Fabulous Russian epic follows two families from 1900 to 1960. Featuring two sexy female leads, this dispels the myths about passionless and unappealing Russian women. Spectacular scenery throughout and explosive special effects for the finale make this one of the most watchable Russian films to date. In Russian with English subtitles. Not rated; contains violence, gore, and sex. Interesting mix of B&W and color. 206m. **DIR:** Andrei Konchalovsky. **CAST:** Vladimir Samoilov, Vitaly Solomin, Nikita Mikhalkov, Lyudmilla Gurchenko, Sergei Shakurov. **1980**

SIBLING RIVALRY ★★★1/2 Kirstie Alley gives a hilarious performance as a woman whose first affair leads to disaster. By sheer force of combined will, director Carl Reiner and Alley turn a gimmicky, cutesy story into a genuinely amusing—albeit uneven—laughfest. Rated PG-13 for profanity. 89m. **DIR:** Carl Reiner. **CAST:** Kirstie Alley, Bill Pullman, Carrie Fisher, Jami Gertz, Sam Elliott, Scott Bakula, Frances Sternhagen, John Randolph, Ed O'Neill, Paul Benedict, Bill Macy. **1990**

SICILIAN, THE 🦃 This adaptation of Mario Puzo's novel becomes a tedious bore thanks to heavy-handed and pretentious direction. Rated R for violence and profanity. 105m. **DIR:** Michael Cimino. **CAST:** Christopher Lambert, Terence Stamp, Joss Ackland, John Turturro, Richard Bauer, Barbara Sukowa, Giula Boschi, Barry Miller, Andreas Katsulas, Ramon Bieri. **1987 DVD**

SICK: THE LIFE AND DEATH OF BOB FLANAGAN, SUPERMASOCHIST ★★★ Flanagan, afflicted from birth with cystic fibrosis, a lung disorder that usually kills its victims by age 30, died at 43 in 1994. The premise of this strange but fascinating documentary is that Flanagan's longevity may have been due to his embracing—rather than trying to escape—a life of constant agony. Much of it was recorded on home video by his dominatrix lover and incorporated into this film. Not rated; contains extremely graphic (and completely genuine) scenes of sadomasochism. 90m. **DIR:** Kirby Dick. **1997**

SID AND NANCY ★★★1/2 Leave it to Alex Cox, director of the suburban punk classic *Repo Man*, to try to make sense out of deceased punk rocker Sid Vicious and his girlfriend Nancy Spungen. Its compassionate portrait of the two famed nihilists is a powerful one, which nevertheless is not for everyone. Rated R for violence, sex, nudity, and adult subject matter. 111m. **DIR:** Alex Cox. **CAST:** Gary Oldman, Chloe Webb, Drew Schofield, David Hayman. **1986 DVD**

SIDE BY SIDE: THE TRUE STORY OF THE OSMOND FAMILY ★★ If the title alone hasn't scared you away, you'll probably enjoy this schmaltzy TV movie featuring Marie Osmond as her own mother, raising nine children. It was produced by the Osmond family's own company, and it's every bit as squeaky-clean as that would indicate. 98m. **DIR:** Russ Mayberry. **CAST:** Marie Osmond, Joseph Bottoms. **1982**

SIDE OUT ★★1/2 Peter Horton is a has-been volleyball pro with little going for him until he strikes up with C. Thomas Howell, who sparks his interest in a comeback. Some great contests with current pros Sinjin Smith and Randy Stoklos in this otherwise routine story. Rated PG-13. 103m. **DIR:** Peter Israelson. **CAST:** C. Thomas Howell, Peter Horton, Sinjin Smith, Randy Stoklos. **1990**

SIDE SHOW ★★1/2 A young boy runs away to join the circus and discovers alcoholism, sex, and racial prejudice. When he witnesses a murder, he has to stay one step ahead of the killer. Not rated, but may not be suited for younger audiences. 98m. **DIR:** William Conrad. **CAST:** Lance Kerwin, Anthony Franciosa, Red Buttons, Connie Stevens. **1986**

SIDEKICKS ★★★1/2 One of the best underdog fairy tales to emerge in years. Jonathan Brandis stars as an asthmatic high school kid who daydreams himself into elaborate, Walter Mitty–esque fantasies at the side of longtime hero Chuck Norris (who plays himself, and superbly spoofs many of his macho action hits). The supporting cast is excellent. Rated PG for fantasy-level violence. 100m. **DIR:** Aaron Norris. **CAST:** Beau Bridges, Mako, Jonathan Brandis, Chuck Norris, Julia Nickson, Richard Moll, Joe Piscopo. **1993**

SIDEWALKS OF LONDON ★★★★ Street entertainer Charles Laughton puts pretty petty thief Vivien Leigh in his song-and-dance act, then falls in love with her. Befriended by successful songwriter Rex Harrison, she puts the streets and old friends behind her and rises to stage stardom while her rejected and dejected mentor hits the skids. Vivien Leigh is entrancing, and Charles Laughton is compelling and touching, in this dramatic sojourn in London byways. B&W; 85m. **DIR:** Tim Whelan. **CAST:** Vivien Leigh, Charles Laughton, Rex Harrison, Tyrone Guthrie. **1940**

SIDEWALKS OF NEW YORK (1931) ★★ This Buster Keaton comedy would have made a very funny silent movie, but the actor gets bogged down with talk here. The camera lingers so long on his deadpan expression that the pace is irritatingly slow. The story of a rich playboy in love with a poor tenement girl turns into a sentimental cliché. B&W; 70m. **DIR:** Jules White, Zion Myers. **CAST:** Buster Keaton, Anita Page, Cliff Edwards, Syd Saylor, Clark Marshall, Frank Rowan, Frank La Rue. **1931**

•**SIDEWALKS OF NEW YORK (2001)** ★★★1/2 In this wry, romantic comedy, a handheld camera establishes intimacy, immediacy, and movement as an unseen interviewer questions several characters amid scenes from their lives. We meet a producer for TV's *Entertainment This Week* who is dumped by his girlfriend, his

womanizing show host, a female Italian–Puerto Rican schoolteacher, a doorman-songwriter, a waitress-student, and an adulterous dentist and his Realtor wife. Couples connect and disconnect and suspicions of infidelity escalate. Rated R for language and sexual content. 100m. **DIR:** Edward Burns. **CAST:** Edward Burns, Rosario Dawson, David Krumholtz, Stanley Tucci, Brittany Murphy, Heather Graham, Dennis Farina. **2001 DVD**

SIDEWINDER 1 ★★ Michael Parks is a quiet, reclusive motocross racer who becomes a partner in developing a new dirt bike. *Sidewinder 1* has good racing scenes—motocross fans will love them—but the story is studded with sexist remarks and attitudes. Rated PG. 97m. **DIR:** Earl Bellamy. **CAST:** Marjoe Gortner, Michael Parks, Susan Howard, Alex Cord. **1977**

SIEGE, THE ★★★1/2 An intriguing premise is undermined by ill-defined central characters and an absurdly abrupt conclusion in this frequently disturbing urban thriller. Following the "extraction" of a Middle Eastern sheik believed responsible for an overseas terrorist incident that claimed numerous American lives, the man's fanatically devoted followers embark on a series of increasingly heinous acts in New York City. The military eventually places the Big Apple under martial law. Is it provocative? Absolutely. Is it persuasive? Regrettably . . . no. Rated R for violence, profanity, and sexual content. 115m. **DIR:** Edward Zwick. **CAST:** Denzel Washington, Annette Bening, Bruce Willis, Tony Shalhoub, Sami Bouajila. **1998 DVD**

SIEGE OF FIREBASE GLORIA, THE ★★★ Outnumbered five to one, our Marines defended the hilltop outpost called Firebase Gloria during the Tet offensive in 1968. This is the dramatization of their seemingly hopeless struggle. Grisly scenes of death and destruction bring the Vietnam War close to home. Rated R. 95m. **DIR:** Brian Trenchard-Smith. **CAST:** Wings Hauser, R. Lee Ermey. **1988**

SIEGFRIED ★★★★ Vivid, spectacular story of young god Siegfried, whose conquests and eventual murder form an intrinsic part of Teutonic legend, this nationalistic triumph for German director Fritz Lang was the most ambitious attempt to transfer folklore to film and proved an international success. Moody sets and photography give the movie an otherworldly feeling and evoke just the right atmosphere. Silent. B&W; 100m. **DIR:** Fritz Lang. **CAST:** Paul Richter, Margarete Schon, Theodor Loos, Bernhard Goetzke. **1923**

SIESTA ★★★1/2 Oddly fascinating and sexually intense drama. Ellen Barkin plays a stuntwoman in love with a former trainer (Gabriel Byrne), a man who loved her but married someone else. The film plays with time, reality, and consciousness, turning them into something suspenseful. Rated R for language and sex. 90m. **DIR:** Mary Lambert. **CAST:** Ellen Barkin, Gabriel Byrne, Julian Sands, Jodie Foster, Martin Sheen, Isabella Rossellini, Grace Jones. **1987**

SIGN OF FOUR, THE ★★★1/2 Ian Richardson makes a fine Sherlock Holmes in this film produced for British television and fairly faithful adaptation from the story by Sir Arthur Conan Doyle. A cache of jewels brings nothing but avarice and danger to whoever possesses it, and it's up to Holmes and Dr. John H. Watson (well played by David Healy) to bring to justice a couple of creepy killers out to claim the treasure. 103m. **DIR:** Desmond Davis. **CAST:** Ian Richardson, David Healy, Cherie Lunghi, Terrence Rigby, Thorley Walters. **1983 DVD**

SIGN OF ZORRO, THE ★★1/2 Baby boomers, beware. If you have fond memories of this swashbuckling Disney television series about the Z-slashing Robin Hood of Old Mexico, skip this uneven feature compilation of original episodes. It's still fine for the kiddies, however. B&W; 91m. **DIR:** Norman Foster, Lewis R. Foster. **CAST:** Guy Williams, Henry Calvin, Gene Sheldon, Britt Lomond, George J. Lewis, Lisa Gaye. **1960**

SIGNAL 7 ★★★ Absorbing character study of two San Francisco cabbies features standout performances by Bill Ackridge and Dan Leegant. Entirely improvised, the film has a loose, almost documentary aproach. Not rated; contains a lot of profanity. 92m. **DIR:** Rob Nilsson. **CAST:** Bill Ackridge, Dan Leegant. **1983**

SIGNS OF LIFE ★★★ When a shipyard goes out of business, its employees and owner are forced to face the inevitability of change. Rated PG-13 for profanity and violence. 95m. **DIR:** John David Coles. **CAST:** Arthur Kennedy, Beau Bridges, Vincent D'Onofrio, Kate Reid. **1989**

SILAS MARNER ★★★★ Fate is the strongest character in this BBC-TV adaptation of George Eliot's novel, although Ben Kingsley gives an excellent performance as the cataleptic eighteenth-century English weaver. Betrayed by his closest friend and cast out of the church, Marner disappears into the English countryside and becomes a bitter miser, only to have his life wonderfully changed when fate brings an orphan girl to his hovel. 97m. **DIR:** Giles Foster. **CAST:** Ben Kingsley, Jenny Agutter, Patrick Ryecart, Patsy Kensit. **1985**

SILENCE, THE ★★ One of Ingmar Bergman's more pretentious and claustrophobic films. Two sisters who are traveling together stop for a time in a European hotel. The film is laden with heavy-handed symbolism and banal dialogue. In Swedish with English subtitles. 95m. **DIR:** Ingmar Bergman. **CAST:** Ingrid Thulin, Gunnel Lindblom, Birger Malmsten. **1963**

SILENCE LIKE GLASS 🦃 Disease-of-the-week movie about a ballet dancer afflicted with cancer, a giant ego, and a clichéd screenplay. Rated R for profanity. 103m. **DIR:** Carl Schenkel. **CAST:** Jami Gertz, Martha Plimpton, George Peppard, Bruce Payne, Rip Torn, Gayle Hunnicutt, James Remar. **1990**

SILENCE OF THE HAMS ★★ Half-baked attempt at spoofing *Psycho* and *Silence of the Lambs*. Director-writer-star Ezio Greggio strives to be the next Mel Brooks, but film is often uninspired and predictable. Some good jokes and an interesting cast are not enough to save this one from expiring before the big finale. Rated R for nudity, adult language, and comic violence. 85m. **DIR:** Ezio Greggio. **CAST:** Billy Zane, Dom DeLuise, Charlene Tilton, Ezio Greggio, Martin Balsam, John Astin, Phyllis Diller. **1993**

SILENCE OF THE HEART ★★★1/2 Powerful examination of teen suicide and the effects it has on the survivors. Mariette Hartley is exceptional as a mother and wife who is emotionally crippled but who still needs to be strong after the suicide of her son. Chad Lowe perfectly conveys the disillusionment of a teenager who feels like he's failing everyone and sees no way out. This

made-for-television movie handles a tough subject with respect. Not rated. 100m. **DIR:** Richard Michaels. **CAST:** Mariette Hartley, Dana Hill, Howard Hesseman, Chad Lowe, Elizabeth Berridge, Charlie Sheen. **1984 DVD**

SILENCE OF THE LAMBS ★★★★★ In this shock-filled powerhouse, an FBI cadet is assigned by her superior to interview an imprisoned, cannibalistic psychopath in the hopes of getting his help in capturing a crazed serial killer. Superb performances by Foster and Hopkins. From the novel by Thomas Harris. Rated R for violence, gore, nudity, and profanity. 118m. **DIR:** Jonathan Demme. **CAST:** Jodie Foster, Anthony Hopkins, Scott Glenn, Ted Levine, Tracey Walter, Charles Napier, Roger Corman. **1991 DVD**

SILENCE OF THE NORTH ★★ There are some of us at the *Video Movie Guide* who would follow Ellen Burstyn anywhere. But Burstyn's narration here is pure melodrama, and ninety minutes of one catastrophe after the next is more tiring than entertaining. Burstyn portrays a woman who falls in love with a fur trapper, played by Tom Skerritt, and moves into the Canadian wilderness. Rated PG for violence. 94m. **DIR:** Allan Winton King. **CAST:** Ellen Burstyn, Tom Skerritt, Gordon Pinsent. **1981**

SILENCER, THE ★★1/2 Newcomer Lynette Walden reaches the point of no return as a hit woman for a top-secret government agency. After she takes out the garbage, she drags in the trash, fulfilling her sexual desires by bedding down strangers off the street. She begins to suspect that she's on someone else's hit list. Decent action entry. Rated R for nudity, violence, and language. 85m. **DIR:** Amy Goldstein. **CAST:** Lynette Walden, Chris Mulkey, Paul Ganus, Jamie Gomez. **1992**

SILENT ASSASSINS 🦃 Stupid action flick about a CIA biggie gone bad. Not rated, but has violence and profanity. 91m. **DIR:** Lee Doo Young, Scott Thomas. **CAST:** Sam Jones, Linda Blair, Jun Chong, Phillip Rhee, Bill Erwin, Mako. **1987**

SILENT CONFLICT ★★ A traveling charlatan hypnotizes and drugs Lucky into stealing money and trying to kill Hoppy and California. A fair series Western. B&W; 61m. **DIR:** George Archainbaud. **CAST:** William Boyd, Andy Clyde, Rand Brooks, Virginia Belmond. **1948**

SILENT ENEMY, THE ★★1/2 World War II adventure has frogmen fighting it out in Gibraltar Harbor. Highlight: the underwater photography. B&W; 91m. **DIR:** William Fairchild. **CAST:** Laurence Harvey, Dawn Addams, John Clements. **1958**

SILENT FALL ★★★1/2 Watchable murder mystery has reclusive doctor Richard Dreyfuss coming out of a self-imposed exile to help an autistic 9-year-old witness to a bizarre double murder. Director Bruce Beresford brings his usual commitment to strong character development to the piece, but it is Dreyfuss's outstanding performance that holds the film together. Rated R for violence and profanity. 100m. **DIR:** Bruce Beresford. **CAST:** Richard Dreyfuss, Linda Hamilton, John Lithgow, J. T. Walsh, Ben Faulkner, Liv Tyler. **1994 DVD**

SILENT HUNTER ★★★ Retired Florida cop Miles O'Keeffe gets a second crack at the crooks who murdered his family when they pull a robbery near the mountain where he now lives. Rated R for violence, profanity, and nudity. 97m. **DIR:** Fred Williamson. **CAST:** Miles O'Keeffe, Fred Williamson. **1995**

SILENT MADNESS 🦃 Escaped maniac terrorizes a college campus. Rated R for nudity, violence, and profanity. 93m. **DIR:** Simon Nuchtern. **CAST:** Belinda Montgomery, Viveca Lindfors, Sidney Lassick. **1985**

SILENT MOBIUS ★★ This animated story of futuristic ghostbusters is almost interesting at times, but in the end it's only mediocre. In a twenty-first century metropolis, a group of psychic policewomen track down evil spirits that infest the city. Dubbed. Not rated; contains nudity and graphic violence. 50m. **DIR:** Michitaka Kikuchi. **1991**

SILENT MOTIVE ★★★ Scandalous screenwriter Patricia Wettig gets a taste of her own medicine when a copycat killer uses her scripts as a blueprint for murder. Detective Mike Farrell must prove she didn't do it, or did she? Right! Standard made-for-TV thriller gets a boost from familiar, durable cast. 90m. **DIR:** Lee Philips. **CAST:** Patricia Wettig, Edward Asner, Mike Farrell, Rick Springfield, David Packer. **1991**

SILENT MOUSE ★★★★ A mouse rescued by a young village boy determines to repay his kindness by becoming the church mouse. Filmed in the magic mountains of Austria and Czechoslovakia and featuring many of Europe's most famous ensembles, choirs, and orchestras, this playful made-for-TV story will delight viewers of all ages. 50m. **DIR:** Robin Crichton. **CAST:** Lynn Redgrave, Gregor Fisher, Jack McKenzie. **1990**

SILENT MOVIE ★★★1/2 Mel Brooks's *Silent Movie* is another kitchen-sink affair, with Brooks going from the ridiculous to the sublime with a beautiful idea that bears more exploring. Silent films were the best for comedy, and Brooks, along with costars Marty Feldman, Dom De Luise, and Sid Caesar, supplies numerous funny moments. Rated PG. 86m. **DIR:** Mel Brooks. **CAST:** Mel Brooks, Marty Feldman, Dom DeLuise, Bernadette Peters, Sid Caesar, James Caan, Burt Reynolds, Paul Newman, Liza Minnelli, Anne Bancroft, Marcel Marceau, Harry Ritz, Ron Carey. **1976**

SILENT NIGHT, BLOODY NIGHT ★★★ Give this one an extra star for originality, even if it's not that well produced. Lawyer Patrick O'Neal and girlfriend Mary Woronov spend a few nights in an old house that he is trying to sell. But the place used to be an insane asylum, and it has quite an interesting history. Rated R, it may be a bit too strong for kids. 88m. **DIR:** Theodore Gershuny. **CAST:** Patrick O'Neal, John Carradine, Mary Woronov. **1973**

SILENT NIGHT, DEADLY NIGHT 🦃 This is the one that caused such a commotion among parents' groups for its depiction of Santa Claus as a homicidal killer. No rating, but contains gobs of nudity and violent bloodshed. Rated R. 92m. **DIR:** Charles E. Sellier Jr. **CAST:** Lilyan Chauvin, Gilmer McCormick, Robert Brian Wilson, Toni Nero. **1984**

SILENT NIGHT, DEADLY NIGHT PART 2 🦃 The first half of this sequel is composed almost entirely of flashback scenes from the earlier movie. Rated R for nudity and gore. 88m. **DIR:** Lee Harry. **CAST:** Eric Freeman, James L. Newman, Elizabeth Cayton. **1987**

SILENT NIGHT, DEADLY NIGHT 3: BETTER WATCH OUT! ★★ Better than the first two in the slasher Santa series, but still nothing to get excited over. The Santa

slasher awakens from a coma with a psychic connection to a young woman. Rated R for violence, profanity, and nudity. 91m. **DIR:** Monte Hellman. **CAST:** Richard Beymer, Bill Moseley, Samantha Scully, Robert Culp. **1989**

SILENT NIGHT, DEADLY NIGHT 4—INITIATION ★★★ This fourth installment doesn't have any relation to the previous three films. Supernatural story that just happens to take place around Christmas. Rated R for violence and profanity. 90m. **DIR:** Brian Yuzna. **CAST:** Maud Adams, Tommy Hinkley, Allyce Beasley, Clint Howard. **1990**

SILENT NIGHT, DEADLY NIGHT 5: THE TOY MAKER An old toymaker named Joe Peto and his oddball son Pino make deadly toys designed to kill their child owners. A twisted but silly attempt at horror. Rated R for violence, profanity, and simulated sex. 90m. **DIR:** Martin Kitrosser. **CAST:** Mickey Rooney, Jane Higginson. **1991**

SILENT NIGHT, LONELY NIGHT ★★1/2 Slow-moving, but fairly interesting TV film about two lonely people (Lloyd Bridges and Shirley Jones) who share a few happy moments at Christmastime. Flashbacks to previous tragedies are distracting. Not rated. 98m. **DIR:** Daniel Petrie. **CAST:** Lloyd Bridges, Shirley Jones, Carrie Snodgress, Robert Lipton. **1969**

SILENT PARTNER, THE ★★★★1/2 This suspense-thriller is what they call a sleeper. It's an absolutely riveting tale about a bank teller (Elliott Gould) who, knowing of a robbery in advance, pulls a switch on a psychotic criminal (Christopher Plummer) and might not live to regret it. A real find for movie buffs, but be forewarned; it has a couple of truly unsettling scenes of violence. Rated R. 103m. **DIR:** Daryl Duke. **CAST:** Elliott Gould, Christopher Plummer, Susannah York, John Candy. **1978**

SILENT PREDATORS ★★ If you've seen one movie about snakes on the rampage, you've seen them all. Aggressive developing in a small town stirs up a den of deadly hybrid rattlesnakes, which then go out and kill people. Despite the best efforts of the cast, this made-for-cable original just can't struggle beyond its lame dialogue and insipid action. Not rated; contains violence. 95m. **DIR:** Noel Nosseck. **CAST:** Harry Hamlin, Shannon Sturges, David Spielberg, Patty McCormack, Jack Scalia. **1999**

SILENT PREY Incompetent action film made as a vehicle for Carol Shaya, a New York cop who was fired after she posed for *Playboy*. Not rated; contains nudity, violence, and profanity. 93m. **DIR:** Tom Avitabile. **CAST:** Carol Shaya, Frank Pelligrino, Neal Jones. **1998**

SILENT RAGE A Texas sheriff is pitted against a psychotic killer. Rated R for nudity, profanity, and violence. 105m. **DIR:** Michael Miller. **CAST:** Chuck Norris, Ron Silver, Stephen Furst. **1982 DVD**

SILENT REBELLION ★★ Telly Savalas plays a naturalized American who goes back to his hometown in Greece to visit. But the cross-cultural experience is not always pleasant. Some poignant moments, but lots of dull ones, too. Not rated. 90m. **DIR:** Charles S. Dubin. **CAST:** Telly Savalas, Michael Constantine, Keith Gordon. **1982**

SILENT RUNNING ★★★★ True science fiction is most entertaining when it is not just glittering special effects and is, instead, accompanied by a well-developed plot and worthwhile message. This is such a picture. Bruce Dern is in charge of a futuristic space station that is entrusted with the last living remnants of Earth's botanical heritage. His efforts to preserve those trees and plants in spite of an order to destroy them makes for thoughtful moviemaking. Rated G. 89m. **DIR:** Douglas Trumbull. **CAST:** Bruce Dern, Cliff Potts, Ron Rifkin. **1971 DVD**

SILENT SCREAM ★★1/2 This is a well-done shock film with a semi-coherent plot and enough thrills to satisfy the teens. Rated R. 87m. **DIR:** Denny Harris. **CAST:** Yvonne De Carlo, Barbara Steele, Avery Schreiber, Rebecca Balding. **1980**

SILENT TONGUE ★★★ Talbot grieves for his Indian wife, who died during childbirth. His father tracks down the man from whom he bought Talbot's first wife. This tidy little morality play gets pretty weird at moments, but the cast and Shepard's words keep us interested. Rated PG-13 for violence and language. 101m. **DIR:** Sam Shepard. **CAST:** Richard Harris, Alan Bates, River Phoenix, Dermot Mulroney, Tantoo Cardinal, Sheila Tousey. **1991**

SILENT TOUCH, THE ★★★★ Max von Sydow delivers a bravura performance as an aging world-famous composer who feels his career and life have come to an end. Enter a mysterious young man who sets out to heal his wounds and give him the strength to make music again. Rated PG-13 for strong language. 92m. **DIR:** Krzysztof Zanussi. **CAST:** Max von Sydow, Lothaire Bluteau, Sarah Miles. **1992**

SILENT TRIGGER ★★★ Weary contract killer Dolph Lundgren wants out of the assassination game, but his never-seen supervisor has other ideas. Rated R for violence, profanity, and brief nudity. 90m. **DIR:** Russell Mulcahy. **CAST:** Dolph Lundgren, Gina Bellman, Conrad Dunn, Christopher Heyerdahl. **1996 DVD**

SILENT VICTIM ★★★1/2 Compelling true story follows distraught, pregnant wife Michele Greene, whose suicide attempt kills her unborn child. Her husband then sues her for performing an illegal abortion. Interesting idea gets plenty of mileage in the courtroom, where the issues of responsibility and morality are examined in gripping fashion. Rated R for language. 116m. **DIR:** Menahem Golan. **CAST:** Michele Greene, Kyle Secor, Alex Hyde-White, Ely Pouget. **1992**

SILENT VICTORY: THE KITTY O'NEIL STORY ★★★ Better-than-average TV biography of ace stuntwoman Kitty O'Neil, who overcame the handicap of being deaf to excel in her profession. Proof positive is O'Neil doubling Channing in the stunt scenes. 100m. **DIR:** Lou Antonio. **CAST:** Stockard Channing, James Farentino, Colleen Dewhurst, Edward Albert, Brian Dennehy. **1979**

SILENT WITNESS ★★1/2 Dutch director Dick Maas can't decide whether he wants this film to be a dark comedy or a thriller. He wants it to be both, and that's where it falls apart. William Hurt is wasted as an American doctor who is in Amsterdam with his family on business. When his mute daughter witnesses a grisly crime and is spotted by the killers, she finds herself on the run. The result is a chase film filled with flat performances, familiar plotting, and awkward humor. Jennifer Tilly has some nice moments as the concerned

mother. Also released as *Do Not Disturb*. Rated R for language and violence. 94m. **DIR:** Dick Maas. **CAST:** William Hurt, Jennifer Tilly, Denis Leary, Michael Chiklis, Francesca Brown. **1999 DVD**

SILENT WITNESS: WHAT A CHILD SAW ★★★ An African-American boy witnesses the murder of three Koreans in this made-for-cable movie. It generates interest, thanks to the plight of the young boy. Not rated; contains violence. 93m. **DIR:** Bruce Pittman. **CAST:** Mia Korf, Clark Johnson, Bill Nunn, Richard Chevolleau, Richard Yearwood, Amir Williams, Ron White. **1993**

SILHOUETTE 🦃 Cosmopolitan Faye Dunaway witnesses a murder in this insipid made-for-cable whodunit. 95m. **DIR:** Carl Schenkel. **CAST:** Faye Dunaway, David Rasche, John Terry. **1990**

SILK DEGREES ★★ A TV star is being stalked by a terrorist, and it's up to two federal agents to keep him from discovering her whereabouts. Rated R for violence and sexual scenes. 90m. **DIR:** Armand Garabidian. **CAST:** Marc Singer, Deborah Shelton, Michael Des Barres, Mark Hamill, Adrienne Barbeau, Charles Napier, Gilbert Gottfried. **1994**

SILK ROAD, THE ★★★1/2 Boasting a cast of thousands, this is actually a romance set amid turbulent China of 1026 B.C. An educated young man, enslaved in military service, saves a princess but is forced to leave her. When he returns, she is betrothed to the fierce prince whose armies have overrun her land and killed her father. In Chinese with English subtitles. Rated PG-13 for violence and gore. 99m. **DIR:** Junya Sato. **CAST:** Gohei Kogure, Kazuo Haruna, Toshiyuki Nishida, Koichi Sato, Anna Nakagawa. **1988**

SILK STOCKINGS ★★★ In this remake, Greta Garbo's classic *Ninotchka* is given the Cole Porter musical treatment with a degree of success. Fred Astaire is a Hollywood producer who educates a Russian agent in the seductive allure of capitalism. Cyd Charisse plays the Garbo role. 117m. **DIR:** Rouben Mamoulian. **CAST:** Fred Astaire, Cyd Charisse, Janis Paige, Peter Lorre, Barrie Chase. **1957**

SILKWOOD ★★★★ At more than two hours, *Silkwood* is a shift-and-squirm movie that's worth it. The fine portrayals by Meryl Streep, Kurt Russell, and Cher keep the viewer's interest. Based on real events, the story focuses on 28-year-old nuclear worker and union activist Karen Silkwood, who died in a mysterious car crash while she was attempting to expose the alleged dangers in the Oklahoma plutonium plant where she was employed. Rated R for nudity, sex, and profanity. 128m. **DIR:** Mike Nichols. **CAST:** Meryl Streep, Kurt Russell, Cher, Craig T. Nelson, Fred Ward, Sudie Bond. **1984 DVD**

SILVER BEARS ★★ If *Silver Bears* was meant to be a comedy, it isn't funny. If it was meant to be a drama, it isn't gripping. It's boring. Michael Caine stars as a Mafia henchman sent to Switzerland to buy a bank. He's swindled and ends up buying two rooms over a pizza parlor. Rated PG. 113m. **DIR:** Ivan Passer. **CAST:** Michael Caine, Cybill Shepherd, Louis Jourdan, Martin Balsam, Stéphane Audran, Tom Smothers, David Warner. **1978**

SILVER BLAZE ★★★ Arthur Wontner starred as Holmes in five handsome but low-budget films; ironically, this movie was not released in America until after *Hound of the Baskervilles* introduced Basil Rathbone as the screen's most famous detective. So impressive was Rathbone's debut as Holmes, the American distributor retitled *Silver Blaze* as *Murder at the Baskervilles*. This is a loose adaptation of the original story about the disappearance of a prized racehorse. It may not be faithful, but *Silver Blaze* is fun for mystery fans. B&W; 60m. **DIR:** Thomas Bentley. **CAST:** Arthur Wontner, Ian Fleming, Lyn Harding, John Turnbull, Robert Horton, Arthur Goulet. **1937**

SILVER BULLET ★★★★ A superior Stephen King horror film, this release moves like the projectile after which it was named. From the opening scene, in which a railroad worker meets his gruesome demise at the claws of a werewolf, to the final confrontation between our heroes (Gary Busey and Corey Haim) and the hairy beast, it's an edge-of-your-seat winner. Rated R for violence and gore. 90m. **DIR:** Daniel Attias. **CAST:** Gary Busey, Everett McGill, Corey Haim, Megan Follows, James Gammon, Robin Groves. **1985**

SILVER CHALICE, THE ★★ Full of intrigue and togas, this film is notable only for two unnotable screen debuts by Paul Newman and Lorne Greene. 144m. **DIR:** Victor Saville. **CAST:** Jack Palance, Joseph Wiseman, Paul Newman, Virginia Mayo, Pier Angeli, E. G. Marshall, Alexander Scourby, Natalie Wood, Lorne Greene. **1954**

SILVER DREAM RACER ★★1/2 This so-so British drama features David Essex as a mechanic turned racer. He is determined to win not only the World Motorcycle Championship, but another man's girlfriend as well. Rated PG. 110m. **DIR:** David Wickes. **CAST:** David Essex, Beau Bridges, Cristina Raines, Clark Peters, Harry H. Corbett. **1980**

SILVER ON THE SAGE ★★1/2 Hopalong Cassidy discovers a crooked ranch foreman and a saloon owner are actually look-alike brothers bleeding the locals and anyone else who comes their way. The crooks pin Hoppy down with hot lead until his sidekicks show up with help. B&W; 68m. **DIR:** Lesley Selander. **CAST:** William Boyd, Russell Hayden, George "Gabby" Hayes, Stanley Ridges, Jack Rockwell. **1939**

SILVER QUEEN ★★ Young and devoted daughter Priscilla Lane is determined to uphold her family's honor and pay her father's debts by gambling in San Francisco, where she develops a reputation as a real sharpie. B&W; 81m. **DIR:** Lloyd Bacon. **CAST:** George Brent, Priscilla Lane, Bruce Cabot, Lynne Overman, Eugene Pallette, Guinn Williams. **1942**

SILVER RIVER ★★1/2 Promising Western starts out well enough but becomes bogged down. A good cast of veterans manages to make things interesting, but film could have been much better. B&W; 110m. **DIR:** Raoul Walsh. **CAST:** Errol Flynn, Ann Sheridan, Thomas Mitchell, Bruce Bennett, Barton MacLane. **1948**

SILVER SPURS ★★★1/2 Better-than-average cast and strong screenplay raise the routine plot to make this one of Roy Rogers's better middle-era Westerns. Nefarious John Carradine tries to fleece Rogers's boss out of oil-rich land. B&W; 54m. **DIR:** Joseph Kane. **CAST:** Roy Rogers, Smiley Burnette, John Carradine, Phyllis Brooks, Sons of the Pioneers, Jerome Cowan. **1943**

SILVER STALLION, THE ★★1/2 Although trying for the mythic qualities and superior horsemanship of *The*

Man from Snowy River, this Australian adaptation of Elyne Mitchell's *The Silver Brumby* moves at a snail's pace. Only avid horse lovers will sit still for the ponderous story-within-a-story that follows the author (played reasonably well by Caroline Goodall) as she writes of the wild stallion who roams the Australian bush. While it's nice to have wholesome family entertainment, must it be so dull? Rated G. 93m. **DIR:** John Tatoulis. **CAST:** Caroline Goodall, Russell Crowe, Ami Daemion. **1994**

SILVER STRAND ★★★ Scripter Douglas Day Stewart returns to the territory he mined so well in *An Officer and a Gentleman*, with this familiar study of a young officer finding his soul while surviving Navy SEAL training. Anjul Nigam truly shines as a jovial recruit from Bangladesh. You're likely to have trouble with the conclusion; Stewart may have intended it as triumphant, but we're not so sure. Rated R for profanity, violence, nudity, and simulated sex. 104m. **DIR:** George Miller. **CAST:** Nicollette Sheridan, Gil Bellows, Jay O. Sanders, Tony Plana, Jennifer O'Neill, Wolfgang Bodison, Anjul Nigam. **1995**

SILVER STREAK (1934) ★★ Interesting primarily for the vintage locomotives and the railway system as well as a good cast of unique personalities. B&W; 72m. **DIR:** Thomas Atkins. **CAST:** Charles Starrett, Sally Blane, Hardie Albright, William Farnum, Irving Pichel, Arthur Lake. **1934**

SILVER STREAK (1976) ★★★★1/2 Fast-paced action story laced with comedy and stars will have you cheering, laughing, and gasping. *Streak* pits neurotic Wilder, sexy Clayburgh, and shifty Pryor against a cool millionaire villain and his evil henchman in a wild high-speed chase. Rated PG. 113m. **DIR:** Arthur Hiller. **CAST:** Gene Wilder, Jill Clayburgh, Richard Pryor, Patrick McGoohan, Ray Walston, Ned Beatty, Richard Kiel. **1976**

SILVERADO ★★★★1/2 Scott Glenn, Kevin Kline, Kevin Costner, and Danny Glover ride side by side to clean up the town of Silverado. Excitement, laughs, thrills, and chills abound in this marvelous movie. Even those who don't ordinarily like Westerns are sure to enjoy it. Rated PG-13 for violence and profanity. 133m. **DIR:** Lawrence Kasdan. **CAST:** Kevin Kline, Scott Glenn, Kevin Costner, Danny Glover, Rosanna Arquette, John Cleese, Brian Dennehy, Linda Hunt, Jeff Goldblum. **1985 DVD**

SILVERLAKE LIFE: THE VIEW FROM HERE ★★★★ Brutal but mesmerizing, this uncompromising documentary follows Mark Massi, diagnosed with AIDS, and his longtime companion, AIDS patient Tom Joslin. A "video diary" chronicles their love, shortened life span, and Tom's death. One of the most personal, and political, films ever made. Not rated; contains profanity and adult themes. 99m. **DIR:** Tom Joslin, Peter Friedman. **CAST:** Mark Massi, Tom Joslin. **1993**

SIMBA ★★★★ In this hard-hitting drama, the ne'er-do-well brother (Dirk Bogarde) of a philanthropic doctor arrives in Kenya to find his brother has been murdered. Thought-provoking study of racial strife. 99m. **DIR:** Brian Desmond Hurst. **CAST:** Dirk Bogarde, Virginia McKenna, Basil Sydney. **1955**

SIMON ★★ Weird, weird comedy about an average guy (Alan Arkin) who is brainwashed into thinking he's a visitor from outer space. The film has some funny moments, but it just doesn't work as a whole. Rated PG. 97m. **DIR:** Marshall Brickman. **CAST:** Alan Arkin, Madeline Kahn, Austin Pendleton, William Finley, Fred Gwynne. **1980**

SIMON BIRCH ★★★★ In its own quiet way, Mark Steven Johnson's loose take on John Irving's *A Prayer for Owen Meany* will break your heart, yet leave you uplifted. The ugly-duckling title character is a little boy trying to fathom the reason for his presence on Earth. His one staunch friend knows only too well the stigma of being an outcast. This film is sentimental without becoming maudlin, upsetting without becoming intolerable, instructive without becoming didactic. Rated PG for dramatic intensity and mild profanity. 110m. **DIR:** Mark Steven Johnson. **CAST:** Joseph Mazzello, Oliver Platt, David Strathairn, Ian Michael Smith, Dana Ivey, Ashley Judd. **1998 DVD**

SIMON, KING OF THE WITCHES 🦃 Modern-day warlock lives in a Los Angeles sewer. Rated R. 90m. **DIR:** Bruce Kessler. **CAST:** Andrew Prine, Brenda Scott. **1971**

SIMON OF THE DESERT ★★★★1/2 Impossible to deny the sly pleasure we have with St. Simon Stylites, the desert anchorite who spent thirty-seven years atop a sixty-foot column (circa A.D. 400) preaching to Christian flocks and avoiding temptation. Good nasty fun for aficionados and novices alike. In Spanish with English subtitles. B&W; 40m. **DIR:** Luis Buñuel. **CAST:** Claudio Brook, Silvia Pinal. **1965**

SIMPATICO ★★1/2 Sam Shepard's snakelike 1994 play about festering souls and secret dirty laundry doesn't quite make the leap to the big screen. A Kentucky horse breeder plunges into the aftermath of a racing scam after a derelict buddy calls from California and makes murky references to a crime from the men's past. The all-star cast is excellent but this initially intriguing story about personal demons, corruption, lost love, and emotional vengeance slowly stagnates. Rated R for language and sexual content. 106m. **DIR:** Matthew Warchus. **CAST:** Jeff Bridges, Nick Nolte, Albert Finney, Sharon Stone, Catherine Keener. **2000 DVD**

SIMPLE JUSTICE ★★1/2 A team of madmen rob a bank, fatally shooting some and leaving a beautiful newlywed (Cady McClain) for dead. Her husband (Matthew Galle) and grandparents must cope with continued threats from the men who fear McClain will testify against them. Rated R for violence and profanity. 91m. **DIR:** Deborah Del Prete. **CAST:** Cesar Romero, Doris Roberts, Matthew Galle, Cady McClain. **1989**

SIMPLE MEN ★★★ Director Hal Hartley's offbeat road movie is short on plot but long on eccentric behavior. Brothers Robert Burke and William Sage go looking for their father and encounter a cast of characters more off kilter than they are. One brother and the father are wanted by the law, but when they team up with mystery women Karen Sillas and Elina Lowensohn, their lives really become complicated. Rated R for language and adult situations. 105m. **DIR:** Hal Hartley. **CAST:** Robert Burke, William Sage, Karen Sillas, Elina Lowensohn, Mary Mackenzie. **1992**

SIMPLE PLAN, A ★★★★ Blood bonds are strenuously tested as two midwestern brothers find over $4 million in a rural plane wreck. Their plan to split the loot with a beer-swilling chum trots us through a bleak moral landscape soon littered with bodies. This lean crime-drama

is a powder keg of surprises. Rated R for language and violence. 96m. **DIR:** Sam Raimi. **CAST:** Bill Paxton, Billy Bob Thornton, Brent Briscoe, Bridget Fonda. **1998 DVD**

SIMPLE STORY, A ★★★1/2 Marie (Romy Schneider) is pregnant and decides to have an abortion. At forty, she is forced to reevaluate her life and her relationships with men. Rewarding film is paced very slowly and plot is interwoven with subplots of other characters in distress. One of Romy Schneider's best performances. In French with English subtitles. No rating. 110m. **DIR:** Claude Sautet. **CAST:** Romy Schneider, Bruno Cremer, Claude Brasseur, Roger Pigaut. **1978**

SIMPLE TWIST OF FATE, A ★★★1/2 Star-writer Steve Martin updates George Eliot's *Silas Marner* for this effective tale of a man who all but cuts himself off from the world after he discovers that the child his wife is about to have is not his. Then, a baby is left on his doorstep. Rated PG-13 for profanity. 106m. **DIR:** Gillies MacKinnon. **CAST:** Steve Martin, Gabriel Byrne, Laura Linney, Catherine O'Hara, Stephen Baldwin, Bryon Jennings, Michael Des Barres, Amelia Campbell, Kellen Crosby. **1994**

SIMPLE WISH, A ★★1/2 Martin Short plays a bumbling fairy godmother (yes, godmother) who tries to grant a young girl's wish for success for her struggling actor father. There are some good things here: nice performances and a clever parody of Lord Andrew Lloyd Webber. But the film is a hodgepodge, and director Michael Ritchie can't quite bring all the good things together in one coherent piece, Rated PG. 89m. **DIR:** Michael Ritchie. **CAST:** Martin Short, Mara Wilson, Kathleen Turner, Robert Pastorelli, Amanda Plummer, Ruby Dee, Teri Garr. **1997 DVD**

SIN OF HAROLD DIDDLEBOCK (MAD WEDNESDAY) ★★★1/2 This is a much better film than popular Hollywood legend implies. It's a story about a middle-aged man fired from his job and set adrift with nothing but unfulfilled potential. Backer Howard Hughes rereleased it in 1950 as *Mad Wednesday* and edited it down to 79 minutes. B&W; 90m. **DIR:** Preston Sturges. **CAST:** Harold Lloyd, Frances Ramsden, Jimmy Conlin, Raymond Walburn, Edgar Kennedy, Arline Judge, Lionel Stander, Margaret Hamilton, Rudy Vallee. **1947**

SIN OF MADELON CLAUDET, THE ★★★★ The heroine's sin in this unabashed tearjerker is bearing a child out of wedlock. Her redemption lies in a lifetime of devotion and sacrifice. Helen Hayes's Oscar-winning performance is a distinct plus. B&W; 73m. **DIR:** Edgar Selwyn. **CAST:** Helen Hayes, Neil Hamilton, Lewis Stone, Marie Prevost, Karen Morley, Jean Hersholt, Robert Young. **1931**

SINBAD AND THE EYE OF THE TIGER ★★1/2 Sinbad seeks the hand of Princess Farah and permission from her brother, who has been turned into a baboon. Not a terrible movie (children will love it), but all the movie tricks in the world cannot disguise a bad story. Rated G. 113m. **DIR:** Sam Wanamaker. **CAST:** Patrick Wayne, Jane Seymour, Damien Thomas, Margaret Whiting, Patrick Troughton, Taryn Power. **1977 DVD**

SINBAD OF THE SEVEN SEAS ★★ Lou Ferrigno stars in this mediocre Italian adaptation of the familiar fairy tale. Ferrigno, as Sinbad, must take on an evil wizard and return his kingdom to its former bliss. Rated PG-13 for violence. 95m. **DIR:** Enzo G. Castellari. **CAST:** Lou Ferrigno, John Steiner. **1989**

SINBAD THE SAILOR ★★★ Aping his father, Douglas Fairbanks Jr., as Sinbad, sails forth in search of Alexander the Great's fabled treasure and hits a variety of reefs. Unfortunately, the plot not only thickens but gets murky, to boot. Some say it's all tongue-in-cheek, but it's really more foot-in-mouth. Nonetheless, it is fun. 117m. **DIR:** Richard Wallace. **CAST:** Douglas Fairbanks Jr., Walter Slezak, Maureen O'Hara, Jane Greer, Anthony Quinn, Sheldon Leonard. **1947**

SINCE YOU WENT AWAY ★★ This overlong, World War II soap opera doesn't hold together despite a great cast of stars and character actors, often in minor roles. Big-budget weeper tells of life on the home front. B&W; 152m. **DIR:** John Cromwell. **CAST:** Claudette Colbert, Joseph Cotten, Jennifer Jones, Shirley Temple, Monty Woolley, Lionel Barrymore, Robert Walker, Hattie McDaniel, Agnes Moorehead, Guy Madison. **1944**

SINCE YOU'VE BEEN GONE ★★1/2 *Friends* star David Schwimmer stars in and makes his directorial debut with this pedestrian comedy about a high-school reunion. The characters and situations are obvious in this made-for-cable film. Rated R for language. 96m. **DIR:** David Schwimmer. **CAST:** David Schwimmer, Lara Flynn Boyle, Teri Hatcher, Joey Slotnick, Marisa Tomei, Jennifer Grey, Jerry Springer. **1997**

SINCERELY CHARLOTTE ★★★ Caroline Huppert directs her sister Isabelle in this intriguing tale of a woman with a shady past. Isabelle finds herself in trouble with the law and seeks the help of her old lover, who's now married. It's the interaction among these three characters that is fun and enticing. In French with English subtitles. 92m. **DIR:** Caroline Huppert. **CAST:** Isabelle Huppert, Neils Arestrup, Christine Pascal, Luc Beraud. **1986**

SINCERELY YOURS Ridiculous, sincerely. 115m. **DIR:** Gordon Douglas. **CAST:** Liberace, Joanne Dru, Dorothy Malone, William Demarest, Lurene Tuttle, Richard Eyer. **1955**

SINFUL LIFE, A An aging chorus girl must find a husband before she is declared an unfit mother by her daughter's teacher. Based on the stage play *Just Like the Pom Pom Girls.* Rated R for profanity. 90m. **DIR:** William Schreiner. **CAST:** Anita Morris, Rick Overton, Dennis Christopher. **1989**

SING ★★★ A teen film with a commendable twist: no car chases! Actually, this is a cross between *Lady and the Tramp* and *Fame.* A tough Italian punk is forced to work with an innocent Jewish girl on the class musical. You guessed it! They fall for each other. Rated PG-13 for profanity. 99m. **DIR:** Richard Baskin. **CAST:** Peter Dobson, Jessica Steen, Lorraine Bracco, Patti LaBelle, Louise Lasser. **1989**

SING, COWBOY, SING ★★★★ Wagon-train raiders are thwarted by Tex Ritter and his pards masquerading as entertainers. They needn't masquerade—this one entertains with the best of the B Westerns. Look for ex–Mack Sennett clowns Snub Pollard, Chester Conklin, and Al St. John. B&W; 59m. **DIR:** Robert N. Bradbury. **CAST:** Tex Ritter, Louise Stanley, Al St. John, Karl Hackett, Charles King, Snub Pollard, Chester Conklin. **1937**

SINGAPORE ★★★1/2 Stylish *film noir* in which pearl smuggler Fred MacMurray returns to Singapore and the bittersweet memories of a lost love believed to have been killed during a Japanese bombing. Credibility is stretched a bit thin, but the cinematography alone provides substance. Remade in 1957 as *Istanbul*. Not rated. B&W; 80m. **DIR:** John Brahm. **CAST:** Fred MacMurray, Ava Gardner, Richard Haydn, Thomas Gomez, George Lloyd, Porter Hall, Spring Byington, Michael Van Leyden. **1947**

SINGIN' IN THE RAIN ★★★★★ In the history of movie musicals, no single scene is more fondly remembered than Gene Kelly's song-and-dance routine to the title song. This picture has more to it than Kelly's well-choreographed splash through a wet city street. It has an interesting plot based on the panic that overran Hollywood during its conversion to sound, and it has wonderful performances. 102m. **DIR:** Gene Kelly, Stanley Donen. **CAST:** Gene Kelly, Debbie Reynolds, Donald O'Connor, Jean Hagen, Cyd Charisse, Rita Moreno. **1952 DVD**

SINGING NUN, THE ★★ Unbearably cheerful little bio-pic about the Dominican nun who sang on Ed Sullivan's TV show and supposedly captured the hearts of the nation. Just as slim as you'd expect. 98m. **DIR:** Henry Koster. **CAST:** Debbie Reynolds, Ricardo Montalban, Greer Garson, Agnes Moorehead, Chad Everett, Katharine Ross, Ed Sullivan. **1966**

SINGING THE BLUES IN RED ★★★1/2 An oppressed East German protest singer is forced to defect and ply his trade in the West, only to discover new avenues of repression in the capitalist system. Exactingly scripted in English with German subtitles. Not rated. 110m. **DIR:** Kenneth Loach. **CAST:** Gerulf Pannach. **1989**

SINGLE GIRL ★★★1/2 Presumably inspired by Agnes Varda's nouvelle vague classic *Cleo from 5 to 7*, this French drama takes place in real time as a young woman spends her first day on a new job in a fancy hotel pondering her life and the news that she is pregnant. Like most real-time films, it's a bit contrived, but effective due to a strong performance by Virginie Ledoyen. In French with English subtitles. Not rated; contains nudity, sexual situations, and profanity. 90m. **DIR:** Benoit Jacquot. **CAST:** Virginie Ledoyen, Benoit Magimel. **1996 DVD**

SINGLE ROOM FURNISHED 🦃 Jayne Mansfield's last movie was this lurid overwrought melodrama. 93m. **DIR:** Matt Cimber. **CAST:** Jayne Mansfield, Dorothy Keller, Fabian Dean. **1968 DVD**

SINGLE STANDARD, THE ★★ Tepid Greta Garbo vehicle that, like most avowedly feminist dramas of its time, fails to deliver on its initial premise. Garbo is a woman who tosses aside her wealth and social position to seek equality with an ex–prize fighter. Of interest primarily to Garbo completists who must see *everything*. Silent. B&W; 88m. **DIR:** John S. Robertson. **CAST:** Greta Garbo, Nils Asther, Johnny Mack Brown. **1929**

SINGLE WHITE FEMALE ★★★ This entry in the stranger-from-hell subgenre gets a good start when cultivated career woman Bridget Fonda, recovering from the betrayal of an unfaithful boyfriend, accepts mousy Jennifer Jason Leigh as her new roommate. Alas, things go to pot in the third act. Rated R for language, violence, and nudity. 107m. **DIR:** Barbet Schroeder. **CAST:** Bridget Fonda, Jennifer Jason Leigh, Steven Weber, Peter Friedman. **1992 DVD**

SINGLES ★★★★ High marks to writer-director Cameron Crowe for this witty study of twentysomethings seeking romance and personal fulfillment in the Seattle rock scene. The central players often speak directly to the viewer while justifying their behavior. Crowe has a definite ear for the verbal byplay of young love, and his ensemble cast is superb. Rated PG-13 for profanity and suggested sex. 99m. **DIR:** Cameron Crowe. **CAST:** Bridget Fonda, Campbell Scott, Kyra Sedgwick, Matt Dillon, Sheila Kelley, Jim True, Bill Pullman. **1992 DVD**

SINGLETON'S PLUCK ★★★ In this gentle British comedy, a goose farmer, whose business has been shut down by a strike, decides to herd his gaggle to the slaughterhouse himself. Television reporters begin to cover his hundred-mile trip and he becomes a national figure. 93m. **DIR:** Richard Eyre. **CAST:** Ian Holm, Penelope Wilton. **1984**

SINISTER INVASION 🦃 Boris Karloff filmed scenes for this Mexican horror film just before his death. Also available in a truncated version, *Alien Terror*. 88m. **DIR:** Juan Ibanez, Jack Hill. **CAST:** Boris Karloff. **1968**

SINISTER URGE, THE ★★ Ed *(Plan 9 From Outer Space)* Wood's last film as a writer-director is one his fans won't want to miss. The police battle a ring of pornographers and a killer who gets so worked up by looking at these "dirty pictures" that he then goes to the park to kill innocent young women. In the best early-Sixties fashion, Wood got away with flashes of nudity by claiming social significance. Look for him in a brief appearance as a participant in a fistfight. B&W; 75m. **DIR:** Edward D. Wood Jr. **CAST:** Kenne Duncan, James Moore, Jean Fontaine. **1961**

SINK OR SWIM ★★ When a group of writers learns that one of their friends has been offered a job writing for a new television series, they stoop to new lows in friendship when they try to beat him to the punch. Rated R for language and adult situations. 93m. **DIR:** Gary Rosen. **CAST:** Stephen Rea, Illeana Douglas, John Ritter, David Foley, Robert Patrick, Tom Arnold. **1997 DVD**

SINK THE BISMARCK ★★★★ True story of the British Navy's relentless search for the German "super" battleship *Bismarck* is topflight war adventure. A standout production admired by both action fans and military historians. B&W; 97m. **DIR:** Lewis Gilbert. **CAST:** Kenneth More, Dana Wynter, Carl Mohner, Laurence Naismith, Geoffrey Keen, Karel Stepanek, Michael Hordern. **1960**

SINNERS IN PARADISE ★★1/2 Survivors of a plane crash find themselves on a tropical island, where they have plenty of time to reflect on their secrets and the things in their past that haunt them. An old idea is handled effectively. B&W; 65m. **DIR:** James Whale. **CAST:** Bruce Cabot, Madge Evans, Marion Martin, Gene Lockhart, John Boles, Milburn Stone, Don Barry. **1938**

SINS OF DORIAN GRAY, THE ★★ This modern-day version of Oscar Wilde's famous horror tale manages to disappoint at nearly every turn. Only the plot—about a beautiful woman who sells her soul for eternal youth and then watches a video screen test of herself age and decay—manages to fascinate. Made for television. 98m.

DIR: Tony Maylam. **CAST:** Anthony Perkins, Belinda Bauer, Joseph Bottoms, Olga Karlatos, Michael Ironside. **1983**

SINS OF THE MIND ★★ In this made-for-cable drama, a woman suffers from a loss of sexual inhibition after being in a car accident. Her family thinks she's now a bad girl, but her doting father believes something physical is wrong. The rest of the plot is as hard to believe as the premise. Rated R for suggested sex. 93m. **DIR:** James Frawley. **CAST:** Jill Clayburgh, Mike Farrell, Louise Fletcher. **1997**

SINYSTER ★★1/2 Imaginative haunted-house movie. First-time director Ronnie Sortor has created a tense, violent film about a killer being infected by an evil house, but poor sound quality lessens the viewing experience. Not rated; contains violence. 80m. **DIR:** Ronnie Sortor. **CAST:** Steve Kelly, Lei Renniks, Frank Alexander. **1994**

SIOUX CITY ★★ Adopted at an early age by rich Caucasian parents, a Native-American medical intern is haunted by visions of his biological mom. He returns to his birthplace—a Lakota reservation—to investigate her murder, is beaten by bad cops, and uses tribal rites to solve the crime. It's *Thunderheart* meets *Dr. Kildare* on a shoestring budget in this culturally sensitive but hollow search for ethnic roots and justice. Rated PG-13 for language, suggested sex, and violence. 102m. **DIR:** Lou Diamond Phillips. **CAST:** Lou Diamond Phillips, Salli Richardson, Ralph Waite, Melinda Dillon, Adam Roarke. **1994**

SIR ARTHUR CONAN DOYLE'S THE LOST WORLD ★★★ Not exactly *Jurassic Park*, this direct-to-video release features story elements and situations geared toward adults. Although some of the special effects are a little cheesy, the overall effort stays true to Doyle's vision. A heroic Patrick Bergin stars as zoologist George Challenger, who treks to Northern Mongolia with a scientific expedition to prove that dinosaurs still exist. There's lots of action, close calls, dinosaurs, and some gore in this worthy entry into the genre. Rated R for violence. 96m. **DIR:** Bob Keen. **CAST:** Patrick Bergin, Jayne Heitmeyer. **1998**

SIRENS (1993) ★★★★ Straitlaced young minister Hugh Grant and his wife (Tara Fitzgerald) have their eyes opened when they visit a bohemian artist (Sam Neill) at his secluded mountain estate. Writer-director John Duigan's study of art, religion, and sexual repression manages to be thoughtful, erotic, and charmingly funny all at the same time. Rated R for nudity and mature themes. 94m. **DIR:** John Duigan. **CAST:** Hugh Grant, Tara Fitzgerald, Sam Neill, Elle Macpherson, Portia de Rossi, Kate Fischer. **1993**

SIRENS (1999) ★★★1/2 Racial issues and police negligence are the subjects of this engaging made-for-cable original. The police accost a woman (Dana Delany) and her black ex-husband; misreading the situation, the cops shoot him. From then on, Delany pursues justice in any way she can, but she has a hard time convincing anyone that the police have erred. Delany and the rest put in good performances. Not rated; contains violence, profanity, and nudity. 105m. **DIR:** John Scaret Young. **CAST:** Dana Delany, Keith Carradine, Justin Theroux, Vondie Curtis-Hall, Brian Dennehy. **1999 DVD**

SIRINGO ★★★ Moderately entertaining film about a marshall who goes looking for stolen money but ends up finding love. Not rated; contains violence. 90m. **DIR:** Kevin G. Cremin. **CAST:** Brad Johnson, Chad Lowe, Stephen Macht, Crystal Bernard. **1994**

SIROCCO ★★★ Humphrey Bogart plays a successful crook operating in postwar Syria. He is forced to intercede in a terrorist-police situation and gets himself in trouble with both factions. One of Bogart's best later works and a representative sample of the darker side of romance and intrigue, poles apart from, but structurally related to, films like *Casablanca* and *Beat the Devil*. Give it a try. B&W; 98m. **DIR:** Curtis Bernhardt. **CAST:** Humphrey Bogart, Marta Toren, Lee J. Cobb, Everett Sloane, Zero Mostel. **1951 DVD**

SISTER ACT ★★★1/2 Fast-living nightclub singer Whoopi Goldberg has to hide out in a convent after she witnesses her gangster boyfriend (Harvey Keitel) preside over the killing of a police informant. Goldberg is a delight in this surprisingly funny and heartwarming romp. Rated PG for profanity. 100m. **DIR:** Emile Ardolino. **CAST:** Whoopi Goldberg, Maggie Smith, Kathy Najimy, Wendy Makkena, Mary Wickes, Harvey Keitel, Bill Nunn. **1992 DVD**

SISTER ACT 2: BACK IN THE HABIT ★★★1/2 Reacting to the surprise popularity of *Sister Act*, Disney made this family-oriented, toned-down sequel. Sister Mary Clarence goes undercover as a music teacher at an inner-city school in an attempt to reach rebellious students. Very tame—but charming. Rated PG for light profanity. 107m. **DIR:** Bill Duke. **CAST:** Whoopi Goldberg, Maggie Smith, Kathy Najimy, Mary Wickes, Wendy Makkena, Barnard Hughes, James Coburn, Michael Jeter, Robert Pastorelli, Brad Sullivan. **1993 DVD**

SISTER-IN-LAW, THE (1974) ★★1/2 A struggling young singer is lured into drug smuggling by his brother's adulterous wife. Downbeat but occasionally interesting, at least as an early effort in the career of John Savage (who also wrote and sings a few songs). Rated R for nudity. 80m. **DIR:** Joseph Ruben. **CAST:** John Savage. **1974**

SISTER-IN-LAW, THE (1995) ★★ A wealthy family is victimized by a woman posing as their long-lost relation. Not too many surprises in this made-for-cable original. Rated PG-13. 95m. **DIR:** Noel Nosseck. **CAST:** Kate Vernon, Shanna Reed, Craig Wasson, Kent Williams. **1995**

SISTER KENNY ★★ Rosalind Russell is noble and sincere in the title role of the Australian nurse who fought polio in the bush. But the telling of her life in this dull and slow box-office flop is tiresome. B&W; 116m. **DIR:** Dudley Nichols. **CAST:** Rosalind Russell, Alexander Knox, Dean Jagger, Charles Dingle, Philip Merivale, Beulah Bondi, John Litel. **1946**

•SISTER MARY EXPLAINS IT ALL ★★★1/2 Both comic and tragic, this made-for-cable film features Sister Mary Ignatius giving her annual lecture and Q&A session on Catholic doctrine. Her explanations of life and sin are quaint, funny, and sometimes outrageous, but Sister Mary really comes unglued when four of her former students (all horrendous sinners, in her eyes) return to relive the Christmas pageant they performed twenty-five years ago. The film is a disturbing look at fa-

naticism, and has some fine acting as well, but some might think it anti-Catholic. Not rated; contains profanity and violence. 77m. **DIR:** Marshall Brickman. **CAST:** Diane Keaton, Brian Benben, Wallace Langham, Laura San Giacomo, Jennifer Tilly, Martin Mull. **2001**

SISTER, MY SISTER ★★★ Two sisters (Joely Richardson, Jodhi May) are hired as chambermaids by a snobbish widow and her pampered daughter. Based on the real-life French case that inspired Jean Genet's play *The Maids*, the film is a chilly and fascinating study of sexual repression and class conflict, well acted by all. The ending is a bit over the top. Rated R for climactic violence and several lesbian love scenes. 89m. **DIR:** Nancy Meckler. **CAST:** Joely Richardson, Jodhi May, Julie Walters, Sophie Thursfield. **1995 DVD**

SISTER, SISTER ★★★ A gothic thriller set in the Louisiana bayou. Jennifer Jason Leigh is a frail lass who is haunted by a demon lover and taken care of by an overprotective older sister (Judith Ivey). Rated R for violence, nudity, simulated sex, and profanity. 91m. **DIR:** Bill Condon. **CAST:** Eric Stoltz, Jennifer Jason Leigh, Judith Ivey, Dennis Lipscomb, Anne Pitoniak. **1988 DVD**

SISTERHOOD, THE ★★1/2 Futuristic tale set in a post-apocalyptic society, where a secret society of female superwarriors battle the male establishment. Filipino-made movie is okay for fans of the genre. Rated R. 76m. **DIR:** Cirio H. Santiago. **CAST:** Rebecca Holden, Chuck Wagner, Lynn-Holly Johnson. **1988**

SISTERS, THE (1938) ★★★★ This film offered Errol Flynn, after becoming a star, his first opportunity to play something besides a hero. He portrays a writer who, unable to make a success of himself, turns to the bottle for escape, breaking wife Bette Davis's heart. B&W; 98m. **DIR:** Anatole Litvak. **CAST:** Errol Flynn, Bette Davis, Alan Hale Sr., Donald Crisp, Anita Louise, Jane Bryan, Beulah Bondi, Dick Foran. **1938**

SISTERS (1973) ★★★★1/2 A terrifying tale of twin sisters (Margot Kidder). One is normal; the other is a dangerous psychopath. It's an extremely effective thriller on all levels. Charles Durning and Jennifer Salt give the standout performances in this Brian De Palma release. Rated R for violence, nudity, and language. 93m. **DIR:** Brian De Palma. **CAST:** Margot Kidder, Charles Durning, Jennifer Salt, Barnard Hughes. **1973 DVD**

SISTERS OF THE GION ★★★★ In one of his first great successes, Japanese filmmaker Kenji Mizoguchi explores the conflict between old and modern values with a story of two sisters, both geisha. The elder sister is a traditionalist who believes in her work, while the younger one sees her clients only as stepping-stones to a better life. Exquisitely filmed, giving a profound sense of a time and place long gone. In Japanese with English subtitles. B&W; 66m. **DIR:** Kenji Mizoguchi. **CAST:** Isuzu Yamada, Yôko Umemura, Benkei Shiganoya, Eitarô Shindô. **1936**

SITCOM ★★★1/2 A normal suburban family is revealed to be anything but when Dad brings home a pet rat whose bite causes each member to reveal his or her inner self. Fans of John Waters may be the best audience for this outrageous but somewhat pointless black comedy that doesn't know when to stop. In French with English subtitles. Not rated; features nudity and sexual situations. 85m. **DIR:** François Ozun. **CAST:** Évelyne Dandry, François Marthouret, Marina de Van, Adrien de Van. **1998**

SITTING DUCKS 🦃 A Mafia accountant and his pal steal a day's payroll and hit the road. Rated R for nudity and language. 90m. **DIR:** Henry Jaglom. **CAST:** Michael Emil, Zack Norman, Patrice Townsend, Richard Romanus. **1980**

SIX DAYS, SEVEN NIGHTS ★★1/2 Star power doesn't keep this underimagined, South Seas romantic comedy-adventure buoyant. Harrison Ford and Anne Heche crash on an uncharted island, where they're chased by pirates and fall in opposites-attract love because the screenplay says they should. Rated PG-13 for violence, language, and suggested sex. 101m. **DIR:** Ivan Reitman. **CAST:** Harrison Ford, Anne Heche, David Schwimmer, Jacqueline Obradors. **1998 DVD**

SIX DEGREES OF SEPARATION ★★★1/2 Fine performances elevate this uneven comedy-drama about a young man (Will Smith) who passes himself off as Sidney Poitier's son in order to gain access to the privileged world of a wealthy couple. John Guare's screenplay gives us fascinating characters and a story with hard edges. Rated R for profanity, violence, and suggested sex. 111m. **DIR:** Fred Schepisi. **CAST:** Stockard Channing, Will Smith, Donald Sutherland, Mary Beth Hurt, Bruce Davison, Heather Graham, Anthony Michael Hall, Eric Thal, Richard Masur, Ian McKellen. **1993 DVD**

633 SQUADRON ★★★ A British squadron of bomber pilots prepare for a difficult but important mission against a Nazi rocket fuel factory in Norway. Not rated, but there is graphic action. 95m. **DIR:** Walter Grauman. **CAST:** Cliff Robertson, George Chakiris, Harry Andrews, Donald Houston. **1963**

SIX IN PARIS (PARIS VUE PAR . . .) ★★★ Six *nouvelle vague* directors contributed short 16mm films about a Paris neighborhood to this collection. The shorts by Eric Rohmer and Claude Chabrol foreshadow their more mature work, though the rest is thin (Jean-Luc Godard's effort is particularly trivial). In French with English subtitles. 98m. **DIR:** Jean Douchet, Jean Rouch, Jean-Daniel Pollet, Eric Rohmer, Jean-Luc Godard, Claude Chabrol. **CAST:** Barbet Schroeder, Joanna Shimkus, Stéphane Audran, Claude Chabrol. **1965**

SIX PACK 🦃 Kenny Rogers plays a footloose stock-car racer who is latched onto by six homeless, sticky-fingered kids. Rated PG for profanity. 110m. **DIR:** Daniel Petrie. **CAST:** Kenny Rogers, Diane Lane, Erin Gray, Barry Corbin. **1982**

SIX-STRING SAMURAI ★★ Visually impressive but annoyingly arch postapocalypse nonsense. After the Russians have conquered all of an alternative-universe America except for Las Vegas, vagabond warrior/musicians cross the desert to vie for the king's crown. This low-budget student film makes an artfully grungy virtue of its staging limitations; too bad all it stages are repetitive fight scenes and pop culture posings. Rated R for violence and language. 81m. **DIR:** Lance Mungia. **CAST:** Jeffrey Falcon, Justin McGuire, Stephane Gauger. **1998 DVD**

SIX WAYS TO SUNDAY ★★★ Ambitious dark comedy about a young man who gets tangled up with the mob.

Norman Reedus is excellent as the young man whose close relationship with his mother is tested when his mob duties escalate into violence and a higher position in the family. Unexpected moments distinguish this offbeat effort. Rated R for violence, language, and adult situations. 97m. **DIR:** Adam Bernstein. **CAST:** Norman Reedus, Deborah Harry, Adrien Brody, Isaac Hayes. **1999 DVD**

SIX WEEKS ★★★1/2 Dudley Moore and Mary Tyler Moore star as two adults trying to make the dreams of a young girl—who has a very short time to live—come true in this tearjerker. Directed by Tony Bill, it's enjoyable for viewers who like a good cry. Rated PG for strong content. 107m. **DIR:** Tony Bill. **CAST:** Dudley Moore, Mary Tyler Moore, Katherine Healy, Joe Regalbuto. **1982**

SIX WIVES OF HENRY VIII, THE (TV SERIES) ★★★★ One of the first BBC costume dramas to appear on PBS, and still one of the best. What's really special is Keith Michell's virtuosic and sympathetic portrayal of the last Henry. Almost before your eyes, Henry is transformed from a handsome, brilliant young monarch to a corpulent, pitiable old tyrant. 90m. **DIR:** Naomi Capon. **CAST:** Keith Michell, Annette Crosbie, Dorothy Tutin, Anne Stallybrass. **1972**

SIXTEEN CANDLES ★★★★ Molly Ringwald stars in this fast and funny teen comedy as a high school student who is crushed when the whole family forgets her sixteenth birthday. Things, it seems to her, go downhill from there—that is, until the boy of her dreams suddenly starts showing some interest. Rated PG for profanity. 93m. **DIR:** John Hughes. **CAST:** Molly Ringwald, Paul Dooley, Blanche Baker, Edward Andrews, Anthony Michael Hall, Billie Bird. **1984 DVD**

16 FATHOMS DEEP ★★ Sponge fisherman Creighton Chaney (Lon Chaney Jr.) borrows money to buy a boat so he and his girl can get married, but his efforts are sabotaged. Low-rent offering from Monogram uses a lot of stock underwater shots and original footage taken on Catalina Island. B&W; 59m. **DIR:** Armand Schaefer. **CAST:** Sally O'Neil, Lon Chaney Jr. **1934**

6TH DAY, THE ★★★1/2 This thinking man's sci-fi actioner focuses on the ethics of human cloning. When Arnold Schwarzenegger inadvertently becomes the target of a cloning ring, chase scenes and shoot-'em-ups abound, making the two-hour film time fly. Rated PG-13; contains nudity, violence, and profanity more typical of an R. 120m. **DIR:** Roger Spottiswoode. **CAST:** Arnold Schwarzenegger, Michael Rapaport, Tony Goldwyn, Robert Duvall, Sarah Wynter. **2000 DVD**

SIXTH MAN, THE ★★ March Madness gets its own movie salute with this supernatural basketball comedy. Hoop star Antoine dies midway during a college game and his brother is left to lead the team to the NCAA championship. Antoine returns for unearthly assists but the running joke grows tiresome. Rated PG-13 for language. 104m. **DIR:** Randall Miller. **CAST:** Marlon Wayans, Kadeem Hardison, Michael Michel, David Paymer. **1997**

SIXTH SENSE, THE ★★★★★ A child psychologist, who failed one of his young charges with disastrous results, attempts to redeem himself by helping a young boy (Oscar nominee Haley Joel Osment), who "sees dead people." Brilliantly written and directed by M. Night Shyamalan, this is the first film since Alfred Hitchcock's *Psycho* to be so respected by moviegoers that they refused to give away the ending. And so it should be; this motion picture contains a remarkably moving twist that will leave viewers with the irresistible urge to watch it again. Osment gives a terrific performance, as does an unusually subdued Willis. Rated PG-13 for profanity, violence, and gore. 107m. **DIR:** M. Night Shyamalan. **CAST:** Bruce Willis, Toni Collette, Olivia Williams, Haley Joel Osment, Donnie Wahlberg, Glenn Fitzgerald, Mischa Barton, Trevor Morgan, Bruce Norris. **1999 DVD**

'68 ★★ Hungarian immigrants settle in San Francisco, each with an idea of what America should be. While Dad tries to make it in the restaurant business, one son becomes an antiwar advocate as the other struggles with his homosexuality. This one redefines low budget. Rated R for nudity, violence, and profanity. 100m. **DIR:** Steven Kovacs. **CAST:** Eric Larson, Sandor Tecsi, Robert Locke, Terra Vandergaw, Neil Young. **1987 DVD**

•61* ★★★★ This made-for-cable film is a good character drama based on the Yankees' 1961 season, when Roger Maris and Mickey Mantle strived to break the home run record set by Babe Ruth. There's more to the story than the athletic challenge, though. While Mantle battles his own excesses, and Maris fights a long string of bad press and fan resentment, the baseball commissioners scheme to save the Babe's long-standing record. Excellent performances by the lead actors and a superb script bring this film to life. Not just for baseball fans. Rated R for profanity. 129m. **DIR:** Billy Crystal. **CAST:** Barry Pepper, Thomas Jane, Richard Masur, Bruce McGill, Chris Bauer, Jennifer Crystal Foley. **2001 DVD**

SIZZLE TV movie should be called *Fizzle*. 100m. **DIR:** Don Medford. **CAST:** Loni Anderson, John Forsythe, Michael Goodwin, Leslie Uggams, Roy Thinnes, Richard Lynch, Phyllis Davis. **1981**

SIZZLE BEACH, U.S.A. Drive-in fodder about three girls who head to L.A. notable only as the debut of Kevin Costner (whose appearance isn't as prominent as the video box would lead you to believe). Rated R for nudity and sexual situations. 93m. **DIR:** Richard Brander. **CAST:** Terry Congie, Leslie Brander, Roselyn Royce, Kevin Costner. **1976 DVD**

SKAG ★★★1/2 Home-ridden to recuperate after being felled by a stroke, veteran steelworker Pete Skagska must deal with family problems, his own poor health, and the chance his illness may leave him impotent. In the title role, Karl Malden gives a towering, hard-driving performance as a man determined to prevail, no matter what the emotional cost. TV movie. 152m. **DIR:** Frank Perry. **CAST:** Karl Malden, Piper Laurie, Craig Wasson, Peter Gallagher, George Voskovec. **1980**

SKATEBOARD KID, THE ★★ This imbecile spin on TV's *My Mother the Car* is the sort of moronic fluff that Mother warned would stunt your growth if watched indiscriminately. Concerns a young loner who discovers a skateboard with a conscience (and the voice of Dom DeLuise) and manages to work in hidden gold and a secret map before limping to an outrageously corny conclusion. Quite a few talented players waste their time. Rated PG for mild violence. 77m. **DIR:** Larry Swerdlove.

CAST: Timothy Busfield, Bess Armstrong, Rick Dean, Trevor Lissauer, Cliff De Young. **1993**

SKATEBOARD KID 2, THE ★★★ Children into the sport of skateboarding will enjoy this fantasy about a kid desperately attempting to fit in. Rated PG. 95m. **DIR:** Andrew Stevens. **CAST:** Trent Knight, Andrew Stevens, Dee Wallace, Andrew Keegan, Bruce Davison. **1994**

SKEETER 🦃 Mutant mosquitoes suck the life out of this low-rent nature-gone-awry thriller. Badly directed and poorly acted. Rated R for violence, language, and sexual situations. 95m. **DIR:** Clark Brandon. **CAST:** Tracy Griffith, Jim Youngs, Charles Napier, Michael J. Pollard. **1993**

SKEEZER ★★1/2 Made-for-TV movie about a lonely young woman and her friendship with a mutt named Skeezer. This dog eventually helps her to reach emotionally disturbed children in a group home where she is a volunteer. Good for family viewing. 100m. **DIR:** Peter H. Hunt. **CAST:** Karen Valentine, Dee Wallace, Tom Atkins, Mariclare Costello. **1982**

SKELETONS ★★★1/2 Ron Silver moves to a small town and learns the story of how a gay man was framed for the murder of his lover. He is quickly drawn in to the frame-up that the locals have contrived. Captivating and timely, director David DeCoteau makes the leap here from direct-to-video T&A to the big leagues and shows that he can play with the big boys and girls. Rated R for violence and profanity. 91m. **DIR:** David DeCoteau. **CAST:** Ron Silver, James Coburn, Christopher Plummer, Dee Wallace, Dennis Christopher. **1997**

•SKELETONS IN THE CLOSET ★★★ Will Reed (Treat Williams) worries that his son Seth (Joshua Jackson) may be up to some bad deeds, possibly even murder. The more he secretly investigates his son's doings, the more questions arise. Should a father try to turn in his own son based on suspicion alone? Either way, it could tear their family apart. Noble performances by Williams and Jackson, but a lackluster one by Linda Hamilton. Rated R for language and violence. 86m. **DIR:** Wayne Powers. **CAST:** Treat Williams, Joshua Jackson, Linda Hamilton, Schuyler Fisk. **2000 DVD**

SKETCH ARTIST ★★1/2 Sexy made-for-cable thriller benefits from writer Michael Angeli's intriguing premise. Jeff Fahey is a police sketch artist whose rendition of a murder suspect—concocted from a description given by a briefly seen Drew Barrymore—turns out to be the spitting image of his wife (Sean Young). Alas, he then turns total fool, and plot cohesion goes right out the window. 88m. **DIR:** Phedon Papamichael. **CAST:** Jeff Fahey, Sean Young, Frank McRae, Drew Barrymore. **1992**

SKETCH ARTIST II: HANDS THAT SEE ★★★1/2 Jeff Fahey, always a dynamic presence, returns for a second crack at the police-department artist with an uncanny knack for capturing faces. Scripter Michael Angeli's premise is quite intriguing: Rape victim Courteney Cox is blind, and therefore cannot evaluate the sketch in progress. As the culprit's identity is never in doubt, this evolves into a clever, *Columbo*-style courtroom drama. Rated R for nudity, rape, profanity, and violence. 95m. **DIR:** Jack Sholder. **CAST:** Jeff Fahey, Courteney Cox, Michael Beach, Brian James, James Tolkan, Jonathan Silverman. **1995**

SKETCHES OF A STRANGLER 🦃 Allen Garfield, in the days when he was billing himself as Allan Goorwitz, stars as a painter with a fixation on his dead mother. 91m. **DIR:** Paul Leder. **CAST:** Allen Garfield, Meredith MacRae. **1978**

SKI PATROL ★★ Comedy fluff about the antics of a group of misfit skiers who work for a popular resort. Never gets off the beginners' slope. Rated PG. 91m. **DIR:** Richard Correll. **CAST:** Roger Rose, Ray Walston, Martin Mull. **1990**

SKI SCHOOL ★★1/2 An obvious rip-off of *Animal House*, this teen comedy is nonetheless very funny thanks in part to Dean Cameron as the leader of a wacko class of ski bums. Not rated; contains nudity and profanity. 85m. **DIR:** Damien Lee. **CAST:** Dean Cameron, Tom Breznahan, Patrick Labyorteaux, Mark Thomas Miller. **1990**

SKIN ART ★★1/2 Tattoo artist Kirk Baltz makes a living branding Oriental prostitutes at a brothel in Manhattan. When he starts to fall for his latest masterpiece, she revives memories of his days as a Vietnam POW. His obsession to turn her into a living canvas reeks of *Tattoo*, starring Bruce Dern. Kinky but not erotic. Rated R for nudity, violence, and language. 90m. **DIR:** W. Blake Herron. **CAST:** Kirk Baltz, Ariane, Jake Webber, Nora Ariffin, Hil Cato. **1993**

SKIN DEEP ★★ Writer-director Blake Edwards tries for another sex farce in the *10* vein, but this one fails to rise to its potential. John Ritter's undeniable charm cannot compensate for the fact that his character—a womanizing alcoholic—is utterly lacking in redeeming social qualities. Viewers with raised consciousnesses are advised to stay away from this one. Rated R for nudity, profanity, and explicit sexual themes. 98m. **DIR:** Blake Edwards. **CAST:** John Ritter, Vincent Gardenia, Alyson Reed, Joel Brooks, Julianne Phillips, Don Gordon, Nina Foch. **1989**

SKIN GAME, THE (1931) ★★1/2 This early effort from Alfred Hitchcock, an adaptation of a play by John Galsworthy, is one of the last films he'd make in relative obscurity before 1935's *The Thirty-Nine Steps* shot him to fame. The story, which concerns a feud between an established landowner and an upstart newcomer, is talky and boring, despite the inclusion of a love story and a suicide. B&W; 85m. **DIR:** Alfred Hitchcock. **CAST:** C. V. France, Helen Hayes, Jill Esmond, Edmund Gwenn, John Longden, Phyllis Konstam. **1931 DVD**

SKIN GAME (1971) ★★★★ Perceptive social comedy-drama set during the slave era. James Garner and Louis Gossett Jr. are con artists; Garner "sells" Gossett to unsuspecting slave owners and later helps break him free. The fleecing continues until they meet up with evil Edward Asner, who catches on to the act . . . then the story takes a chilling turn toward realism. Excellent on all levels. Rated PG for light violence. 102m. **DIR:** Paul Bogart. **CAST:** James Garner, Louis Gossett Jr., Susan Clark, Edward Asner, Andrew Duggan. **1971**

SKINHEADS 🦃 Three college friends and two female backpackers encounter a gang of skinheads. Rated R for violence and partial nudity. 93m. **DIR:** Greydon Clark. **CAST:** Chuck Connors, Barbara Bain, Brian Brophy, Jason Culp. **1988**

SKINNED ALIVE ★★★ Similar to *Texas Chainsaw Massacre*, this film actually benefits from its ultralow budget. The story has a family selling fine leather out of the back of their van. Read the title again to see where they obtain their materials. Not rated; contains violence, gore, and profanity. 80m. **DIR:** Jon Killough. **CAST:** Mary Jackson, Scott Spiegel. **1990**

SKINNER 🦃 Just imagine Ted Raimi in a bloody "skin" suit and a disfigured Traci Lords limping after him for five years and you'll never have to watch this miserable movie. Rated R for profanity, violence, and nudity. 90m. **DIR:** Ivan Nagy. **CAST:** Theodore Raimi, Traci Lords, Ricki Lake. **1993 DVD**

•SKIPPED PARTS ★★★1/2 It's 1963, and Sam Callahan (Bug Hall) is a boy on the verge of sexual discovery. His open-minded mother Lydia (Jennifer Jason Leigh) is more than willing to let him and his girlfriend Maurey (Mischa Barton) experiment on their own. A little harmless fun becomes serious when Maurey finds herself pregnant before she ever has her first period. *Skipped Parts* brims with cute laughs and heartfelt emotions. Rated R for sex between minors and language. 93m. **DIR:** Tamra Davis. **CAST:** Bug Hall, Jennifer Jason Leigh, Mischa Barton, Drew Barrymore, Brad Renfro, R. Lee Ermey. **2000 DVD**

SKIRTS AHOY! ★★ Slow-moving story of three women from different backgrounds joining the WAVES, and their problems in training and the men in their lives. 109m. **DIR:** Sidney Lanfield. **CAST:** Esther Williams, Joan Evans, Vivian Blaine, Barry Sullivan. **1952**

SKOKIE ★★★ The threat of neo-Nazism comes to the small, predominantly Jewish town of Skokie, Illinois in the late 1970s. An all-star cast drives this well-written TV drama, which succeeds in portraying the two sides in unemotional terms. 121m. **DIR:** Herbert Wise. **CAST:** Danny Kaye, Brian Dennehy, Eli Wallach, Kim Hunter, Carl Reiner. **1981**

SKULL, THE ★★★★ A collector of occult memorabilia covets the death's-head of the infamous Marquis de Sade. Based on a fine Robert Bloch short story, this imaginative fantasy is the apex of the Amicus Productions horror cycle of the 1960s. The modern-day setting helps rather than hinders. 83m. **DIR:** Freddie Francis. **CAST:** Peter Cushing, Patrick Wymark, Christopher Lee, Jill Bennett, Nigel Green, Patrick Magee. **1965**

SKULL AND CROWN ★★1/2 A border patrolman and his faithful guard dog combine talents to break up a band of smugglers. Lassie fans will love this one. B&W; 55m. **DIR:** Elmer Clifton. **CAST:** Rin Tin Tin Jr., Regis Toomey, Jack Mulhall. **1935**

SKULLDUGGERY 🦃 A costume store employee inherits a Satanic curse that sends him on a killing rampage. Not rated, but would earn a PG for violence and profanity. 95m. **DIR:** Ota Richter. **CAST:** Thom Haverstock, Wendy Crewson. **1983**

SKULLS, THE ★★ When wannabe attorney Luke McNamara is recruited to join a secret university society styled after Yale's real-life Skull and Bones, his best friend warns, "If it's elite and secret, it's got to be bad." Luke joins anyway because the fraternity will pay his tuition and he is starstruck by former members that include judges and politicians. His commitment to this group soon jeopardizes his relationship with a female artist and his personal safety. Rated PG-13 for language, violence, and sexuality. 107m. **DIR:** Rob Cohen. **CAST:** Joshua Jackson, Hill Harper, Leslie Bibb, Paul Walker, Christopher McDonald, William L. Petersen, Craig T. Nelson. **2000 DVD**

SKY BANDITS 🦃 An uninspired mixing of *Butch Cassidy and the Sundance Kid* and *The Blue Max*. Rated PG for violence. 95m. **DIR:** Zoran Perisic. **CAST:** Scott McGinnis, Jeff Osterhage, Ronald Lacey. **1986**

SKY HEIST ★★ Frank Gorshin and Stefanie Powers hijack a police helicopter to help steal a fortune in gold bullion. Lots of familiar faces in this otherwise unmemorable TV movie. Not rated; contains no objectionable material. 96m. **DIR:** Lee H. Katzin. **CAST:** Don Meredith, Joseph Campanella, Larry Wilcox, Ken Swofford, Stefanie Powers, Frank Gorshin, Shelley Fabares, Steve Franken, Suzanne Somers, Richard Jordan. **1975**

SKY IS GRAY, THE ★★★ Generosity comes from unexpected quarters in this languid TV adaptation of Ernest J. Gaines's melancholy study of a young boy's first exposure to racism, poverty, and pride in 1940s Louisiana. James Bond III is the youth, dragged to town by his strong-willed mother (Olivia Cole) to have an infected tooth removed. Introduced by Henry Fonda; suitable for family viewing. 46m. **DIR:** Stan Lathan. **CAST:** Olivia Cole, James Bond, III, Margaret Avery, Cleavon Little, Clinton Derricks-Carroll. **1980**

SKY PILOT, THE ★★★ An idealistic young preacher hoping to spread the gospel in the Canadian Northwest must first win acceptance from the rough-and-tumble ranchers. Sincere, heartwarming, and well-acted, this lovely little film was based on a bestseller of the day. B&W; 63m. **DIR:** King Vidor. **CAST:** John Bowers, David Butler, Colleen Moore, James Corrigan, Kathleen Kirkham, Donald MacDonald. **1921**

SKYLARK ★★★1/2 *Hallmark Hall of Fame*'s sequel to *Sarah, Plain and Tall* combines high production values with wholesome entertainment. Glenn Close is terrific as the Maine-born, mail-order bride adapting to a difficult life on the Kansas plains. During a severe drought, she must comfort her husband (Christopher Walken) and stepchildren while coming to grips with her own ambiguous feelings about the land. Rated G. 98m. **DIR:** Joseph Sargent. **CAST:** Glenn Close, Christopher Walken, Lexi Randall, Christopher Bell. **1992 DVD**

SKYLINE ★★★ Antonio Resines plays a Spanish photographer named Gustavo who comes to New York seeking international fame. Once there, he struggles to learn English, find work, and pursue friendship and romance. In Spanish and English, with subtitles it would be excellent for bilingual viewers. The twist ending really gives one a jolt. We'd rate it PG for slight profanity. 84m. **DIR:** Fernando Colombo. **CAST:** Antonio Resines, Susana Ocana. **1984**

SKY'S THE LIMIT, THE ★★★★ This rare blend of comedy and drama is more than just another Fred Astaire musical. He plays a Flying Tiger ace on leave, who meets and falls in love with magazine photographer Joan Leslie, but nixes anything permanent. Both audiences and critics misjudged this film when it debuted, seeing it as light diversion rather than incisive comment on war and its effect on people. B&W; 89m. **DIR:** Edward H. Griffith. **CAST:** Fred Astaire, Joan Leslie,

Robert Benchley, Elizabeth Patterson, Clarence Kolb, Robert Ryan, Richard Davis, Peter Lawford, Eric Blore. **1943**

SKYSCRAPER 🦃 The seemingly inexhaustible *Die Hard* formula hits rock bottom with this made-for-video thriller that vainly tries to make bosomy Anna Nicole Smith into an action heroine. Rated R for profanity, violence, nudity, and sexual situations. 96m. **DIR:** Raymond Martino. **CAST:** Anna Nicole Smith, Richard Steinmetz, Branko Cikatic. **1996**

SKYSCRAPER SOULS ★★★1/2 A one hundred–story office building is the setting for this *Grand Hotel*–type mélange of stories. Warren William is outstanding as the industrialist who seeks to control the entire building. B&W; 99m. **DIR:** Edgar Selwyn. **CAST:** Warren William, Maureen O'Sullivan, Gregory Ratoff, Anita Page, Jean Hersholt, Hedda Hopper. **1932**

SLACKER ★★★★ Imagine if you will a movie that has ninety-seven roles of equal importance, yet never spends more than five minutes with any character. Meet *Slacker*. A rogue's gallery of deadbeats, pseudointellectuals and just-plain folks is presented in this semi-twisted examination of attitudes among college students in Austin, Texas. It's surprisingly entertaining. Rated R for profanity. 97m. **DIR:** Richard Linklater. **1991**

•SLACKERS 🦃 Three cheating college buddies get blackmailed by a creepy nerd who is stalking a campus beauty. This is supposed to be a comedy, but it's about as loathsome and repulsive as a movie can get. Rated R for profanity, gross sexual humor, and drug use. 87m. **DIR:** Dewey Nicks. **CAST:** Devon Sawa, James King, Jason Schwartzman, Jason Segel, Michael C. Maronna. **2002 DVD**

SLAM ★★★1/2 A nickel-and-dime weed dealer and street poet-rapper gets a nasty taste of the criminal-justice system when arrested. This preachy but potent drama about the redemptive powers of art says that true liberation lies ahead in prison rather than in the gang-haunted shadows of the nation's capital. Handheld-camera effects give the film a riveting rawness and urgency. Rated R for nudity, simulated sex, profanity, and violence. 100m. **DIR:** Marc Levin. **CAST:** Saul Williams, Sonja Sohn, Bonz Malone. **1998 DVD**

SLAM DANCE ★★1/2 An L.A. artist (Tom Hulce) becomes embroiled in two murders of high-priced call girls in this Hitchcockian thriller. The standard situations involving an innocent man trying to clear himself are given some fresh approaches, but there are several holes in the plot, and some events make little sense. Rated R. 99m. **DIR:** Wayne Wang. **CAST:** Tom Hulce, Mary Elizabeth Mastrantonio, Virginia Madsen, Harry Dean Stanton, Adam Ant, Don Opper. **1987**

SLAM DUNK ERNEST 🦃 The least funny of the Ernest movies, this one dealing with magic shoes that turn him into a basketball star. Not even close. Rated PG. 93m. **DIR:** John R. Cherry, III. **CAST:** Jim Varney, Cylk Cozart, Miguel A. Nunez Jr., Lester Barrie, Kareem Abdul-Jabbar. **1994**

SLAMMER GIRLS ★★ Spoof of women's prison films. A male reporter disguises himself as a woman to prove the heroine's innocence. A few funny bits, but many more that are plain stupid. Rated R for nudity and profanity. 82m. **DIR:** Chuck Vincent. **CAST:** Devon Jenkin, Jeff Eagle, Jane Hamilton. **1987**

SLAP SHOT ★★★★ When released in 1977, this comedy about a down-and-out hockey team was criticized for its liberal use of profanity. The controversy tended to obscure the fact that *Slap Shot* is a very funny, marvelously acted movie. Paul Newman, as an aging player-coach who's a loser in love and on the ice until he instructs the members of his team to behave like animals during their matches, has never been better. Rated R. 122m. **DIR:** George Roy Hill. **CAST:** Paul Newman, Strother Martin, Jennifer Warren, Lindsay Crouse, Melinda Dillon. **1977 DVD**

SLAPPY AND THE STINKERS ★★ This hybrid that mixes *Our Gang* with *Andre* will please small children, who will most enjoy the slapstick shenanigans of five youngsters who steal a seal from a local aquarium with plans to set him free. Their plan is complicated by a nasty animal broker who will stop at nothing to steal the seal. Childish chaos ensues. Rated PG. 79m. **DIR:** Barnet Kellman. **CAST:** B. D. Wong, Bronson Pinchot, Sam McMurray. **1997**

SLAPSTICK OF ANOTHER KIND 🦃 Jerry Lewis hasn't made a funny film in years, and this sci-fi spoof is no exception. Rated PG. 85m. **DIR:** Steven Paul. **CAST:** Jerry Lewis, Madeline Kahn, Marty Feldman. **1983**

SLASH DANCE 🦃 It's the slasher-stalking-the-dancer story yet again, this time set at Broadway auditions. Not rated; contains violence. 83m. **DIR:** James Shyman. **CAST:** Cindy Maranne, Joel von Omsteiner. **1989**

SLASHER ★★ This routine Italian police melodrama, with former Hitchcock leading man Farley Granger hunting a serial killer, has been released in the United States under three titles: *Slasher*, *The Slasher Is the Sex Maniac*, and, finally, in a hard-core version (for the mid-seventies porno chic audience, with unrelated sex scenes having nothing to do with Granger) called *Penetration*. You don't need to race out and track down any of them. Rated R. 100m. **DIR:** Roberto Montero. **CAST:** Farley Granger. **1974**

SLATE, WYN, AND ME 🦃 Two sociopaths kidnap a woman who witnessed a murder they committed. Rated R for endless profanities and violence. 90m. **DIR:** Don McLennan. **CAST:** Sigrid Thornton, Simon Burke, Martin Sacks. **1987**

SLAUGHTER ★★1/2 The first, and tightest (thanks to the direction of underrated action specialist Jack Starrett) of two blaxploitation sagas in which Jim Brown portrays a heroic Vietnam vet who returns home to avenge his family's murder. Augmented by a cast of upscale character actors, slumming in roles far beneath them. 92m. **DIR:** Jack Starrett. **CAST:** Jim Brown, Stella Stevens, Rip Torn, Don Gordon. **1972**

SLAUGHTER HIGH ★★ Ten years after disfiguring a schoolmate, several former high school friends attend a deadly reunion. The rest of the film is fairly predictable. The ending is a welcome change from the norm, though, and it's nice to see horror queen Caroline Munro still working. Not rated; contains graphic violence and adult situations. 91m. **DIR:** George Dugdale. **CAST:** Caroline Munro, Simon Scuddamore. **1986**

SLAUGHTER IN SAN FRANCISCO 🦃 Another abysmal martial arts chop-socky fest. Rated R for violence and

profanity. 87m. **DIR:** William Lowe. **CAST:** Chuck Norris, Robert Jones, Daniel Ivan. **1974**

SLAUGHTER OF THE INNOCENTS ★★★1/2 Thanks to a morbidly fascinating tone that is borrowed from *Silence of the Lambs*, you'll probably forgive writer-director James Glickenhaus's effort to make his grade-school son a star. An overly precocious boy shares insights overlooked by his father, an F.B.I. investigator. Rated R for graphic violence and profanity. 103m. **DIR:** James Glickenhaus. **CAST:** Scott Glenn, Jesse Cameron-Glickenhaus, Sheila Tousey, Zitto Kazann, Darlanne Fluegel, Zakes Mokae. **1993**

SLAUGHTER OF THE VAMPIRES 🦃 A hunted vampire bites the neck of a beautiful victim. Italian would-be thriller. B&W; 81m. **DIR:** Roberto Mauri. **CAST:** Walter Brandi. **1971**

SLAUGHTER TRAIL 🦃 Good actors trapped in a clichéd story with outlaws, Indians, and cavalry. One of the hokiest soundtrack songs ever recorded. 78m. **DIR:** Irving Allen. **CAST:** Brian Donlevy, Virginia Grey, Gig Young, Andy Devine. **1951**

SLAUGHTERHOUSE 🦃 A disturbed man butchers people as if they were farm animals. Rated R for violence and profanity. 85m. **DIR:** Rick Roessler. **CAST:** Joe Barton, Sherry Rendorf. **1987 DVD**

SLAUGHTERHOUSE FIVE ★★★★ Based on Kurt Vonnegut's novel, which centers around the activities of Billy Pilgrim, who has become unstuck in time. This enables, or forces, him to jump back and forth among different periods in his life and even experience two separate time-space incidents simultaneously. Well done. Rated R. 104m. **DIR:** George Roy Hill. **CAST:** Michael Sacks, Valerie Perrine, Eugene Roche, John Dehner, Holly Near. **1972 DVD**

SLAUGHTER'S BIG RIP-OFF ★★ The second, and less interesting, of Jim Brown's popular blaxploitation pair in which our indestructible one-man army takes on assorted sadistic criminals. Tepid entry in a waning action cycle. 93m. **DIR:** Gordon Douglas. **CAST:** Jim Brown, Ed McMahon, Brock Peters, Don Stroud. **1973**

SLAVE GIRLS FROM BEYOND INFINITY ★★ A pair of space bimbos in bikinis find themselves on a weird planet whose sole occupant hunts intergalactic visitors. Low budget, but with decent effects and lighting. Not nearly campy enough. Rated R for nudity. 80m. **DIR:** Ken Dixon. **CAST:** Elizabeth Cyton, Cindy Beal, Brinke Stevens. **1987 DVD**

SLAVE OF DREAMS ★★★1/2 The biblical story of Joseph gets restrained treatment in this acceptable drama, which concerns Joseph's rise from common desert slave to trusted second-in-command of the pharaoh's executioner. Rated PG-13 for nudity and simulated sex. 95m. **DIR:** Robert M. Young. **CAST:** Adrian Pasdar, Edward James Olmos, Sherilyn Fenn, Philip Newman. **1995**

SLAVE OF LOVE, A ★★★★1/2 Shortly after the Bolshevik revolution, a crew of silent filmmakers attempt to complete a melodrama while fighting the forces of the changing world around them. This examines the role of the bourgeois as Olga (Elena Soloyei) changes from matinee idol to revolutionary. Politically and emotionally charged. In Russian with English subtitles. Not rated. 94m. **DIR:** Nikita Mikhalkov. **CAST:** Elena Soloyei, Rodion Nakhapetov, Alexander Kalyagin. **1978**

SLAVE OF THE CANNIBAL GOD 🦃 A woman encounters a cult of flesh-eaters while attempting to find her missing husband in New Guinea. Rated R for violence and nudity. 87m. **DIR:** Sergio Martino. **CAST:** Stacy Keach, Ursula Andress. **1979**

SLAVERS ★★ Ray Milland plays an Arab slave trader in nineteenth-century Africa who treats his charges like cattle. Rated R for violence, nudity, and sexual situations. 102m. **DIR:** Jurgen Goslar. **CAST:** Trevor Howard, Ron Ely, Britt Ekland, Ray Milland, Cameron Mitchell. **1977**

SLAVES OF NEW YORK 🦃 Manhattan's downtown art scene. Rated R, with profanity and sexual situations. 125m. **DIR:** James Ivory. **CAST:** Bernadette Peters, Chris Sarandon, Mary Beth Hurt, Madeleine Potter. **1989**

SLAVES TO THE UNDERGROUND ★★1/2 Despite good intentions, this tale of a romantic triangle involving two girls and a guy lacks emotional drive. Director Kristine Peterson effectively captures the look and feel of the underground clubs and coffeehouses, but fails to capture the romantic entanglements with the same honesty and reality. The music is the main interest here. Rated R for adult situations, language, and nudity. 94m. **DIR:** Kristine Peterson. **CAST:** Molly Gross, Marisa Ryan, Jason Bortz. **1996 DVD**

SLAYGROUND ★★ Based on the hardboiled Parker series of crime novels, this will disappoint fans of the books. The character of Parker, a tough, no-nonsense professional criminal who shoots first and walks away, has been softened into a whiny thief named Stone (Peter Coyote). Rated R. 89m. **DIR:** Terry Bedford. **CAST:** Peter Coyote, Billie Whitelaw, Philip Sayer, Bill Luhr. **1984**

SLC PUNK ★★ Salt Lake City punk Stevo takes us on a rather senseless Reagan-era tour of his promiscuous, paranoid, druggie, and hardcore friends in this sometimes comic slice of life. The blue-haired anarchist wants to raze the local university instead of attending law school in the footsteps of his ex-hippie dad. Rated R for drug use, language, violence, and sexual content. 97m. **DIR:** James Marendino. **CAST:** Matthew Lillard, Michael A. Goorjian, Annabeth Gish, Jennifer Lien, Christopher McDonald. **1999 DVD**

SLEAZEMANIA STRIKES BACK ★★1/2 More fast-paced, bad-taste trailers from movies—e.g., *Suburban Roulette*—you'd never be seen buying a ticket for. B&W/color; 60m. **DIR:** Johnny Legend, Jeff Vilencia. **1987**

SLEAZY UNCLE, THE ★★★ Italian comedy features Vittorio Gassman as a lecherous old man. Although he is at times repulsive, there is something to be said for Gassman's obvious love of life. In Italian with English subtitles. Not rated; contains profanity and sexual innuendo. 104m. **DIR:** Franco Brusati. **CAST:** Vittorio Gassman, Giancarlo Giannini, Andrea Ferreol. **1991**

SLEEP WITH ME ★★1/2 Talky love triangle is marred by its wholly unsympathetic characters, who spend all their time smoking and drinking. The only genuinely amusing moment comes when partygoer Quentin Tarantino discourses on the homoerotic subtext of *Top Gun*. Rated R for profanity, simulated sex, and brief nu-

dity. 86m. **DIR:** Rory Kelly. **CAST:** Craig Sheffer, Eric Stoltz, Meg Tilly, Dean Cameron, June Lockhart, Quentin Tarantino. **1994**

SLEEPAWAY CAMP This bloody, disgusting film is one that will make you appreciate the fast-forward feature on your VCR. 88m. **DIR:** Robert Hiltzik. **CAST:** Mike Kellin, Paul DeAngelo. **1983**

SLEEPAWAY CAMP II: UNHAPPY CAMPERS ★★1/2 Gory and funny sequel about naughty kids being slaughtered by a puritanical camp counselor. Rated R for nudity, violence, and profanity. 81m. **DIR:** Michael A. Simpson. **CAST:** Pamela Springsteen, René Estevez, Brian Patrick Clarke. **1988**

SLEEPAWAY CAMP III Angela (Pamela Springsteen), the murderous happy camper, returns to Camp Happy Woods. Rated R for violence and nudity. 80m. **DIR:** Michael A. Simpson. **CAST:** Pamela Springsteen, Michael J. Pollard. **1988**

SLEEPER ★★★★ Writer-star-director Woody Allen finally exhibited some true filmmaking talent with this 1973 sci-fi spoof. The frenetic gag-a-minute comedy style of Allen's earlier films was replaced by nice bits of character comedy. The most enjoyable of Allen's pre–*Annie Hall* creations. Rated PG. 88m. **DIR:** Woody Allen. **CAST:** Woody Allen, Diane Keaton, John McLiam, John Beck. **1973 DVD**

SLEEPERS ★★★★ Thoughtful drama which concerns four Hell's Kitchen teenagers who ruin their lives with a single, senseless act of mischief. The four enter the juvenile-detention system and emerge as wholly different people. Two become psychopathic criminals, one becomes an attorney, one remains the group's collective conscience. These divergent elements collide when fate provides an opportunity for revenge against the sadistic guard who molested them during their childhood incarceration. Director Barry Levinson has a fine touch with ensemble casts, and this film contains many powerful moments. Rated R for violence, profanity, rape, and child abuse. 152m. **DIR:** Barry Levinson. **CAST:** Jason Patric, Brad Pitt, Robert De Niro, Dustin Hoffman, Kevin Bacon, Minnie Driver, Vittorio Gassman, Billy Crudup, Ron Eldard, Brad Renfro. **1996 DVD**

SLEEPING BEAUTY (1959) ★★★★1/2 This Disney adaptation of Charles Perrault's seventeenth-century version of the famous fairy tale features storybook-style animation that may surprise those accustomed to the softer style of the studio's other feature-length cartoons. Nevertheless, it is the last genre classic to be supervised by Walt Disney himself and belongs in any list of the best children's films (while having the added asset of being enjoyable for adults, as well). Rated G. 75m. **DIR:** Clyde Geronimi. **1959**

SLEEPING BEAUTY (1983) ★★★★ This is one of the funniest *Faerie Tale Theatre* episodes. Christopher Reeve is excellent as the handsome prince, and Bernadette Peters makes a sweet and pretty princess. Sally Kellerman is wonderful as the queen. 60m. **DIR:** Jeremy Paul Kagan. **CAST:** Beverly D'Angelo, Bernadette Peters, Christopher Reeve, Sally Kellerman. **1983**

SLEEPING CAR, THE ★★ Haunted railway car converted into a rental home just may be the death of a disenchanted journalist. Stale one-liners and cheapie special effects weaken this potentially fascinating horror-comedy. Rated R for violence, language, and nudity. 96m. **DIR:** Douglas Curtis. **CAST:** David Naughton, Kevin McCarthy, Jeff Conaway. **1990**

SLEEPING CAR MURDERS, THE ★★★★ An all-star French cast and crisp direction from Costa-Gavras (his first film) make this a first-rate thriller. Yves Montand stars as the detective investigating the case of a woman found dead in a sleeping compartment of a train when it pulls into Paris. Soon other occupants of the car are found murdered as well. In French with English subtitles. B&W; 92m. **DIR:** Constantin Costa-Gavras. **CAST:** Yves Montand, Simone Signoret, Pierre Mondy, Michel Piccoli, Jean-Louis Trintignant, Charles Denner. **1966**

SLEEPING DOGS ★★1/2 Here's a "what if?" film set in New Zealand during a time of economic crisis. Sam Neill discovers his wife is having an affair, so he goes off to live by himself for a while. Meanwhile, a group of government agents kill innocent bystanders during demonstrations and make it look like the work of the protesters. No rating. 107m. **DIR:** Roger Donaldson. **CAST:** Sam Neill, Warren Oates, Nevan Rowe, Ian Mune. **1977**

SLEEPING MURDER ★★★★ Two newlyweds fall in love with a strange old house in an English seaside town. Into this well-established mood of foreboding comes Miss Marple (Joan Hickson), who helps the young couple decipher the events behind an unsolved murder. Not rated, but suitable for family viewing. 102m. **DIR:** John Davies. **CAST:** Joan Hickson, Geraldine Alexander, John Moulder-Brown, Frederick Treves, Jack Watson. **1986**

SLEEPING TIGER, THE ★★★1/2 A woman finds herself caught up in a tense triangular love affair with her psychiatrist husband and a cunning crook out on parole and released in her husband's custody. Dirk Bogarde gives a stunning performance as the ex-con. B&W; 89m. **DIR:** Joseph Losey. **CAST:** Alexis Smith, Alexander Knox, Dirk Bogarde. **1954**

SLEEPING WITH STRANGERS ★★1/2 Quirky British bedroom farce offers some priceless complications: Rowdy rock star and his entourage check into a little out-of-the-way hotel for some peace and quiet, but instead encounter mistaken identities, curious neighbors and boarders, and the media. The actors seem game; it's the direction that lacks any spark. Rated R for adult situations. 103m. **DIR:** William T. Bolson. **CAST:** Adrienne Shelly, Kimberly Huffman, Neil Duncan, Shawn Thompson, Scott McNeil, Todd Warren. **1993**

SLEEPING WITH THE ENEMY ★★★1/2 Battered wife Julia Roberts manages to escape from her sadistic husband (Patrick Bergin) and create a new life—but only for a short time until hubby discovers the ruse and comes for revenge. Recalls director Joseph Rubin's *The Stepfather* so much that it might have been called *The Husband*. Rated R for violence and profanity. 99m. **DIR:** Joseph Ruben. **CAST:** Julia Roberts, Patrick Bergin, Kevin Anderson. **1991**

SLEEPLESS IN SEATTLE ★★★★ When recently widowed Tom Hanks's plight is described during a radio talk show by his well-meaning son, soon-to-be-wed reporter Meg Ryan becomes obsessed with the idea of meeting him. Witty, insightful romantic comedy. Rated PG for brief profanity. 101m. **DIR:** Nora Ephron. **CAST:** Tom Hanks, Meg Ryan, Bill Pullman, Ross Malinger,

Rosie O'Donnell, Gaby Hoffman, Victor Garber, Rita Wilson, Barbara Garrick, Carey Lowell, Dana Ivey, Rob Reiner. **1993 DVD**

SLEEPWALKER ★★★ Bilingual computer operator translates an ancient Chinese manuscript as a free-lance job, only to find the content manifesting itself in her daily existence. Offbeat low-budget suspenser has genuine intrigue and fine values. Rated R. 78m. **DIR:** Sara Driver. **CAST:** Suzanne Fletcher, Ann Magnuson, Dexter Lee. **1987**

SLEEPY HOLLOW ★★★★ Paying tribute to the beloved horror movies of Universal Studios and Hammer Films, director Tim Burton creates his most lavishly atmospheric and effective motion picture to date, although fans of Washington Irving's "Legend of Sleepy Hollow" will find little to remind them of that classic tale. Johnny Depp's Ichabod Crane is a crime investigator sent by the New York justice system, tired of his "advanced" methods and theories, to the hamlet of Sleepy Hollow, where a headless horseman is killing off its inhabitants. Scare-film fans will be delighted by the appearances of genre greats Christopher Lee and Michael Gough, while casual viewers will be equally caught up in this suspenseful, exquisitely crafted movie. Rated R for violence and sex. 105m. **DIR:** Tim Burton. **CAST:** Johnny Depp, Christina Ricci, Miranda Richardson, Michael Gambon, Casper Van Dien, Jeffrey Jones, Christopher Lee, Richard Griffiths, Ian McDiarmid, Michael Gough, Christopher Walken, Martin Landau. **1999 DVD**

SLENDER THREAD, THE ★★★1/2 Sidney Poitier is a psychology student working at a crisis clinic in Seattle. He fields a call from housewife Anne Bancroft, who has taken an overdose of barbiturates. Fine performances. B&W; 98m. **DIR:** Sydney Pollack. **CAST:** Sidney Poitier, Anne Bancroft, Telly Savalas, Steven Hill, Edward Asner, Dabney Coleman. **1965**

SLEUTH ★★★★★ Michael Caine and Laurence Olivier engage in a heavyweight acting *bataille royal* in this stimulating mystery. Both actors are brilliant as the characters engage in the struggle of one-upmanship and social game-playing. Without giving away the movie's twists and turns, we can let on that the ultimate game is being played on its audience. Rated PG. 138m. **DIR:** Joseph L. Mankiewicz. **CAST:** Michael Caine, Laurence Olivier. **1972**

SLIDING DOORS ★★★★1/2 A missed subway, and its impact on one woman's life, is the beguiling premise of writer-director Peter Howitt's absolutely delightful comedy-drama. You'll enjoy the story about perky London PR exec Gwyneth Paltrow and the characters involved with her two dissimilar lives, but you'll also admire the way it's all put together. Rated PG-13 for mild profanity and sensuality. 99m. **DIR:** Peter Howitt. **CAST:** Gwyneth Paltrow, John Hannah, John Lynch, Jeanne Tripplehorn. **1998 DVD**

SLIGHT CASE OF MURDER, A ★★★ This TNT original is a dark comedy featuring William H. Macy as a film critic caught up in the suspicious death of his girlfriend and subsequent blackmail attempts. Having a knack for making matters worse, he manages to compound his problems as he relies on old movie plots for guidance. Though the action is meant to be contemporary, there's a fortyish *film noir* feel to it. Not rated; contains violence and sexual situations. 89m. **DIR:** Steven Schachter. **CAST:** William H. Macy, Adam Arkin, Felicity Huffman, James Cromwell. **1999**

SLIGHTLY HONORABLE ★★★ Wisecracks and red herrings provide the drawing cards in this fast-paced comedy-thriller. The plot's muddy, but basically it concerns a lawyer, Pat O'Brien, who is set up for a murder by crooked politician Edward Arnold. B&W; 85m. **DIR:** Tay Garnett. **CAST:** Pat O'Brien, Edward Arnold, Broderick Crawford, Evelyn Keyes, Phyllis Brooks, Eve Arden. **1939**

SLIGHTLY PREGNANT MAN, A ★★ This French comedy features Marcello Mastroianni as the first pregnant man. The reversal of parenting roles provides a few laughs and the surprise ending is worth the wait in an otherwise ho-hum film. Not rated; contains adult subject matter. In French with subtitles. 92m. **DIR:** Jacques Demy. **CAST:** Catherine Deneuve, Marcello Mastroianni, Mireille Mathieu. **1973**

SLIGHTLY SCARLET ★★ Confused blend of romance, crime, and political corruption focuses on good girl falling for gang leader. Forget the story. Just watch the actors interplay. 99m. **DIR:** Allan Dwan. **CAST:** John Payne, Arlene Dahl, Rhonda Fleming, Kent Taylor. **1956 DVD**

SLIME PEOPLE, THE 🦃 Hideous monsters burrow up from deep inside Earth and invade Los Angeles. Grade Z. B&W; 76m. **DIR:** Robert Hutton. **CAST:** Robert Hutton, Les Tremayne, Susan Hart. **1962 DVD**

SLING BLADE ★★★★★ Star-writer-director Billy Bob Thornton collected a screenplay Oscar for this mesmerizing, southern Gothic study of a simpleminded killer who, after spending twenty-five years in an asylum, returns to his backwater hometown. The stage is set for further tragedy with Thornton wholly compelling in the lead role. This film is absolutely perfect in all respects. Rated R for violence, profanity, and gut-wrenching descriptions of violent behavior. 134m. **DIR:** Billy Bob Thornton. **CAST:** Billy Bob Thornton, Dwight Yoakam, John Ritter, Lucas Black, Natalie Canerday. **1996 DVD**

SLINGSHOT, THE ★★★ Making slingshots from contraband condoms is one of several misadventures for 10-year-old Roland in 1920s Sweden as he learns to cope with prejudice, harsh discipline, sex, and stinging rights to the nose from his aspiring pugilist brother. Comic, dramatic, and tragic, but misses the exhilaration of a slice-of-life classic. Adapted from Roland Schutt's autobiographical novel. In Swedish with English subtitles. Rated R for violence and language. 101m. **DIR:** Ake Sandgren. **CAST:** Jesper Salen, Stellan Skarsgard, Basia Frydman, Niclas Olund, Ernst-Hugo Jaregard, Frida Hallgren. **1994**

•SLIPPER & THE ROSE, THE ★★ For a fairy tale, this live-action musical is extremely dry. The songs stink, as does the lethargic direction of Bryan Forbes, who treats every musical number like a burden. Richard Chamberlain is oddly cast as Prince Charming, while newcomer Gemma Craven never really fills the shoes of Cinderella. There's very little magic in this epic disaster that seems to go on long after midnight. Rated G. 127m. **DIR:** Bryan Forbes. **CAST:** Richard Chamberlain, Gemma Craven, Margaret Lockwood, Annette Crosbie, Dame Edith Evans, Kenneth More. **1976 DVD**

SLIPPING INTO DARKNESS ★★ An ex–motorcycle gang member's brother is murdered. So the biker gets his former buddies together to find out whodunit. Rated R for violence, nudity, and profanity. 87m. **DIR:** Eleanor Gawer. **CAST:** Michelle Johnson, Neill Barry. **1988**

SLIPSTREAM ★★1/2 With its high production values and sweeping Elmer Bernstein score, this movie about a futuristic world raises high hopes. Unfortunately, the story becomes mired down in its sluggishness. Oscar-winners Ben Kingsley and F. Murray Abraham have far too brief cameos late in the film. Rated PG-13 for violence. 92m. **DIR:** Steven Lisberger. **CAST:** Bob Peck, Bill Paxton, Kitty Aldridge, Mark Hamill, Eleanor David, Ben Kingsley, F. Murray Abraham. **1989**

SLITHER ★★★ In this bizarre comedy the four leads are after a cache of stolen money, carrying them on a California odyssey with a house trailer in tow, pursued by two of the most ominous looking RVs ever built. Rated PG. 92m. **DIR:** Howard Zieff. **CAST:** James Caan, Sally Kellerman, Peter Boyle, Louise Lasser. **1973**

SLITHIS ★★ Okay horror tale of a gruesome monster, derived from garbage and radiation in southern California, and his reign of terror. While earnestly done, the film just can't overcome its budget restrictions. Actual on-screen title: *Spawn of the Slithis*. Rated PG. 92m. **DIR:** Stephen Traxler. **CAST:** Alan Blanchard, Judy Motulsky. **1978**

SLIVER ★★1/2 Sharon Stone moves into a high-rise, Manhattan apartment building—a sliver—and ends up becoming romantically involved with Tom Berenger and William Baldwin. After a while, Stone gets the feeling she's being watched, and that's when her new life becomes a nightmare. An involving but trashy movie. Rated R for nudity, simulated sex, profanity, and violence. 115m. **DIR:** Phillip Noyce. **CAST:** Sharon Stone, Tom Berenger, William Baldwin, Martin Landau, Colleen Camp, Polly Walker, C.C.H. Pounder, Nina Foch. **1993**

SLOW BULLET Vietnam veteran and his haunting memories of combat. Rated R for violence and nudity. 95m. **DIR:** Allen Wright. **CAST:** Jim Baskin. **1988**

SLOW BURN ★★ Newspaper reporter Eric Roberts is hired as a private investigator to find the son of a Palm Springs artist. Beverly D'Angelo plays the lost son's mother who may or may not know what happened to him. A muddled plot and apprentice-like direction. This made-for-cable movie is equivalent to a PG-13 for violence and profanity. 88m. **DIR:** Matthew Chapman. **CAST:** Eric Roberts, Beverly D'Angelo, Dennis Lipscomb. **1986**

SLUGGER'S WIFE, THE ★★ The most shallow of Neil Simon's works to date, this is bad television situation comedy blown up to big-screen size. Darryl Palmer (Michael O'Keefe) is a self-centered baseball player who bullies his way into the affections of Debby Palmer (Rebecca DeMornay), a would-be rock star. Rated PG-13 for nudity and profanity. 105m. **DIR:** Hal Ashby. **CAST:** Michael O'Keefe, Rebecca DeMornay, Martin Ritt, Randy Quaid, Cleavant Derricks. **1985**

SLUGS, THE MOVIE Mutated slugs infest a small town, devouring anyone they can crawl across. Rated R for violence and brief nudity. 90m. **DIR:** Juan Piquer Simon. **CAST:** Michael Garfield, Kim Terry, Patty Shepard. **1988**

SLUMBER PARTY 57 In this sleazy, smutty movie, six girls sit around a campfire and tell about the first time they "did it." Rated R. 89m. **DIR:** William A. Levey. **CAST:** Noelle North, Debra Winger, Rainbeaux Smith, Joe E. Ross. **1977**

SLUMBER PARTY MASSACRE A mass murderer has escaped from a mental hospital and is killing young girls with a power drill. Rated R for nudity and graphic violence. 77m. **DIR:** Amy Jones. **CAST:** Michele Michaels, Robin Stille, Michael Villella. **1982**

SLUMBER PARTY MASSACRE II ★★ The driller killer is back, but this time he appears as the ghost of a 1950s rock star. His weapon: a heavy-metal guitar with a high-powered drill extending from the neck. The producers tried to be original, but they didn't go far enough. Maybe next time. Rated R for violence, nudity, and profanity. 90m. **DIR:** Deborah Brock. **CAST:** Crystal Bernard. **1987 DVD**

SLUMBER PARTY MASSACRE 3 The driller killer is back yet again, boring holes into kicking and screaming scantily clad girls. Predictable gory schlock. Not rated; contains nudity, profanity, and violence. 80m. **DIR:** Sally Mattison. **CAST:** Keely Christian, M. K. Harris, David Greenlee. **1990**

SLUMS OF BEVERLY HILLS ★★★1/2 Writer-director Tamara Jenkins's study of dysfunctional family life presents a portrait of American youth that is so earthy and nakedly personal that parents probably shouldn't watch with their own children. Set in the early 1970s, the story concerns a blossoming teenage girl whose financially challenged father is always one short step ahead of eviction. This isn't a film for all tastes, but there are significant truths in Jenkins's perceptive script, which honors the disenfranchised fringe-dwellers. Rated R for profanity, nudity, drug use, and strong sexual content. 91m. **DIR:** Tamara Jenkins. **CAST:** Natasha Lyonne, Alan Arkin, Marisa Tomei, Eli Marienthal, David Krumholtz, Kevin Corrigan. **1998 DVD**

SMALL CHANGE ★★★★★ One of François Truffaut's best pictures, this is a charming and perceptive film viewing the joys and sorrows of young children's lives in a small French town. Wonderfully and naturally acted by a cast of children. French. 104m. **DIR:** François Truffaut. **CAST:** Geary Desmouceaux, Philippe Goldman. **1976**

SMALL CIRCLE OF FRIENDS, A ★1/2 Despite a solid cast, this story of campus unrest during the 1960s never comes together. As college students at Harvard, Karen Allen, Brad Davis, and Jameson Parker play three inseparable friends living and loving their way through protests and riots. Rated PG. 112m. **DIR:** Rob Cohen. **CAST:** Karen Allen, Brad Davis, Jameson Parker, Shelley Long, John Friedrich. **1980**

SMALL FACES ★★ Three adolescent brothers try to grow up in 1968 Glasgow. One is a rebellious youngster, another an aspiring artist, the oldest a stupid brute; all become embroiled in the war between teenage gangs running the city. Director Gillies MacKinnon's pseudo-realistic style can't disguise the melodramatic contrivances of the script or make the characters interesting, and the thick Scottish accents are all but unintelligible to American ears. Rated R for profanity

and violence. 102m. **DIR:** Gillies MacKinnon. **CAST:** Joseph McFadden, Iain Robertson, J. S. Duffy. **1996**

SMALL KILLING, A ★★★1/2 This above-average made-for-TV movie gains some of its appeal from the casting. Ed Asner is a cop going undercover as a wino and Jean Simmons is a professor posing as a bag lady. They're out to bust a hit man but manage to fall in love along the way. The supporting cast is equally wonderful. 100m. **DIR:** Steven H. Stern. **CAST:** Edward Asner, Jean Simmons, Sylvia Sidney, Andrew Prine. **1981**

SMALL SACRIFICES ★★★★ Farrah Fawcett delivers a fine but chilling performance as Diana Downs, the sociopathic mother who tried to kill her three children because her ex-boyfriend didn't like kids. John Shea brings intensity to the role of DA Frank Joziak who must protect the two surviving children while seeking a conviction of Downs. Absorbing made-for-TV movie. 159m. **DIR:** David Greene. **CAST:** Farrah Fawcett, John Shea, Ryan O'Neal, Gordon Clapp. **1989**

SMALL SOLDIERS ★★1/2 Destructive little soldier action figures are brought to lethal life by computer chips originally designed for military applications. A sequence involving malevolent Barbie dolls (voiced by Sarah Michelle Gellar and Christina Ricci) is a stroke of demented genius. Rated PG-13 for unexpectedly grim violence. 108m. **DIR:** Joe Dante. **CAST:** Kirsten Dunst, Gregory Smith, Jay Mohr, Phil Hartman, Kevin Dunn, David Cross, Ann Magnuson, Denis Leary. **1998 DVD**

SMALL TIME ★★★ Frightening look at a sociopathic young hood raised in Harlem by a mother who depends on the money he steals. Divided into five segments, this is clearly a moral play about a life of crime. Low-budget production manages to hammer home its message loudly and clearly. Not rated; contains violence and profanity. B&W; 88m. **DIR:** Norman Loftis. **CAST:** Richard Barboza, Carolyn Kinebrew, Scott Ferguson, Keith Allen, Jane Williams. **1990**

SMALL TIME CROOKS ★★1/2 Woody Allen's familiar character tics and directorial flourishes have grown tiresome, particularly with projects this threadbare. This film opens as a screwball heist comedy, with Allen fronting a band of hilariously inept bank robbers, and then loses its way—along with its initial roster of characters—and turns into a parable about the seductive dangers of wealth. The transition, abrupt and unsettling, feels as if Allen suddenly changed his mind about how he intended his script to proceed . . . and then let the first bit remain, because he'd already filmed it. When the first-act supporting players disappear, they take all the film's energy with them; what follows, frankly, is a yawn. Rated PG for mild vulgarity. 95m. **DIR:** Woody Allen. **CAST:** Woody Allen, Tracey Ullman, Elaine May, Jon Lovitz, Hugh Grant, Michael Rapaport. **2000 DVD**

SMALL TOWN GIRL ★★1/2 Farley Granger plays a rich playboy who speeds through a small town, gets a ticket, and promptly falls in love with the judge's daughter (Jane Powell), making his fiancée (Ann Miller) so jealous she dances up a storm. Not a memorable musical, but some interesting production numbers. 93m. **DIR:** Leslie Kardos, Busby Berkeley. **CAST:** Jane Powell, Farley Granger, Ann Miller, Bobby Van, S. Z. Sakall, Billie Burke, Fay Wray, Dean Miller, William Campbell, Nat King Cole. **1953**

SMALL TOWN IN TEXAS, A ★★ Fairly effective B picture pits a revenge-lusting Timothy Bottoms against the crooked sheriff (Bo Hopkins) who framed him in a drug bust and stole his wife (Susan George). Car crashes, fights, and even a little suspense. Rated R. 95m. **DIR:** Jack Starrett. **CAST:** Timothy Bottoms, Susan George, Bo Hopkins, Art Hindle, Morgan Woodward. **1976**

SMALLEST SHOW ON EARTH, THE ★★★1/2 Warm, often hilarious comedy about a couple who inherit a run-down movie theater and its wacky attendants. Excellent performances by Peter Sellers and Margaret Rutherford. B&W; 80m. **DIR:** Basil Dearden. **CAST:** Peter Sellers, Bill Travers, Margaret Rutherford. **1957**

SMASH PALACE ★★★★ A scrap yard of crumpled and rusting automobiles serves as a backdrop to the story of a marriage in an equally deteriorated condition in this well-made, exceptionally acted film from New Zealand. Explicit sex and nude scenes may shock some viewers. It's a *Kramer vs. Kramer*, *Ordinary People*–style of movie that builds to a scary, nail-chewing climax. No MPAA rating; this has sex, violence, nudity, and profanity. 100m. **DIR:** Roger Donaldson. **CAST:** Bruno Lawrence, Anna Jemison, Greer Robson, Desmond Kelly. **1981**

SMASH-UP: THE STORY OF A WOMAN ★★★ Nightclub songbird Susan Hayward puts her songwriter husband's (Lee Bowman) career first. As he succeeds, she slips. His subsequent neglect and indifference make her a scenery-shedding bottle baby until near tragedy restores her sobriety and his attention. B&W; 103m. **DIR:** Stuart Heisler. **CAST:** Susan Hayward, Lee Bowman, Marsha Hunt, Eddie Albert, Carleton Young, Carl Esmond. **1947**

SMASHING THE RACKETS ★★ Chester Morris plays an easily recognizable facsimile of racket-busting Thomas E. Dewey in this cardboard melodrama about an assistant district attorney who becomes a special prosecutor and the scourge of crooks everywhere. Strictly routine. B&W; 68m. **DIR:** Lew Landers. **CAST:** Chester Morris, Frances Mercer, Bruce Cabot, Rita Johnson. **1938**

•SMELL OF CAMPHOR, FRAGRANCE OF JASMINE ★★★ An Iranian filmmaker, whom the government has prohibited from making films for nearly twenty years, accepts an assignment for Japanese television to make a documentary on Iranian funeral rites, and begins to plan his own burial. This melancholy, vaguely comic meditation on tyranny and mortality is broken into three acts: A Bad Day, The Funeral Arrangements, and Throw a Stone in the Water. In Farsi with English subtitles. Not rated. 93m. **DIR:** Bahman Farmanara. **CAST:** Bahman Farmanara. **2001**

SMILE ★★★★ Don't miss this one; it's a true neglected classic. This backstage look at a teenage beauty pageant is great satirical fun every inch of the way, managing to be both tough-minded and soft-hearted. Rated PG. 113m. **DIR:** Michael Ritchie. **CAST:** Bruce Dern, Barbara Feldon, Michael Kidd, Geoffrey Lewis, Nicholas Pryor, Maria O'Brien, Colleen Camp, Joan Prather, Annette O'Toole, Melanie Griffith. **1975**

SMILE, JENNY, YOU'RE DEAD ★★★1/2 Neurotic obsession triggers murder and suspense in this exceptional pilot for *Harry O*, David Janssen's follow-up television series to *The Fugitive*. Definitely a keeper. 100m.

DIR: Jerry Thorpe. **CAST:** David Janssen, Jodie Foster, Andrea Marcovicci, Howard DaSilva, Clu Gulager, John Anderson, Martin Gabel, Zalman King. **1974**

SMILE LIKE YOURS, A ★★ This comedy suffers from an overdose of sex (in elevators, men's rooms, etc.) as a couple try to have a baby. Last half hour picks up a bit if you're willing to wade through the sludge. Rated R for profanity and sex. 97m. **DIR:** Keith Samples. **CAST:** Greg Kinnear, Lauren Holly, Joan Cusack, Jay Thomas, Jill Hennessy, Sheridan Samples. **1997**

SMILES OF A SUMMER NIGHT ★★★★★ Nowhere in Ingmar Bergman's amazing *oeuvre*, perhaps nowhere in cinema, is there such a classic of carnal comedy. An elegant roundelay that is, at heart, an enlightened boudoir farce. Used as the basis of Stephen Sondheim's *A Little Night Music*. In Swedish with English subtitles. B&W; 106m. **DIR:** Ingmar Bergman. **CAST:** Ulla Jacobsson, Gunnar Björnstrand, Eva Dahlbeck, Harriet Andersson, Jarl Kulle. **1955**

SMILIN' THROUGH (1932) ★★★1/2 The love of a soldier and an heiress is threatened by a crime his father committed against her family decades earlier. Satisfying fantasy-love story. Remade in 1941. B&W; 98m. **DIR:** Sidney Franklin. **CAST:** Norma Shearer, Fredric March, Leslie Howard, O. P. Heggie. **1932**

SMILIN' THROUGH (1941) ★★ If you can believe it, an orphaned and brave Jeanette MacDonald falls in love with the son of a murderer. Directed and played for tear value. Best thing to come out of the picture was Jeanette's marriage to Gene Raymond. 100m. **DIR:** Frank Borzage. **CAST:** Jeanette MacDonald, Gene Raymond, Brian Aherne, Ian Hunter. **1941**

•SMILING FISH & GOAT ON FIRE ★★★★ Director Kevin Jordan makes a splendid debut with this warm and funny tale of two opposite brothers looking for the same things in life. Real-life brothers Steven and Derick Martini play on-screen siblings Tony and Chris. Tony is an aspiring actor who has taken an interest in his mail lady. Chris is a starched-collar accountant also looking for love, and finding it with a movie wildlife wrangler. Filled with hilarious insights, soulful performances, and a general sense of whimsy, this latent coming-of-age tale is both smart and charming. Rated R for adult situations, drugs, and language. 93m. **DIR:** Kevin Jordan. **CAST:** Steven Martini, Derick Martini, Bill Henderson, Christa Miller, Rosemarie Addeo. **1999 DVD**

SMILING GHOST, THE ★★★ Good-natured young man just shy of oafdom takes a job posing as the prospective groom of a wealthy woman whose former fiancés are either dead or crippled. Accompanied by his "valet" and a nosy newswoman who has a crush on him, the slow-witted sucker moves into the mansion of his betrothed, risking the wrath of the "smiling ghost" who terminates all potential suitors. Creepy doings, weird relatives, and all the stock "haunted house" stuff make this horror-comedy click. Willie Best as the groom's hired man comes in for his share of racial slurs, which may contribute to this film's obscurity. B&W; 72m. **DIR:** Lewis Seiler. **CAST:** Wayne Morris, Brenda Marshall, Alexis Smith, Alan Hale Sr., David Bruce, Lee Patrick, Willie Best. **1941**

SMILLA'S SENSE OF SNOW ★★★ Scientist investigates the death of a young boy—who jumped to his death—by following the scent of a crime cover-up to secrets hidden below her homeland ice. Dreamy cinematography keeps the film riveting even as it melts into a flaky James Bond–like finale. Rated R for language, violence, and sex. 121m. **DIR:** Bille August. **CAST:** Julia Ormond, Gabriel Byrne, Richard Harris, Robert Loggia, Vanessa Redgrave, Clipper Miano. **1997 DVD**

SMITH! ★★★ A fine cast and sensitive screenplay distinguish this story of a strongman's efforts to secure a fair trial for an Indian accused of murder. Glenn Ford is believably rugged and righteous, and Chief Dan George is highly effective as the stoic focal point of the territory's rage. Good fare for the whole family. Rated G. 101m. **DIR:** Michael O'Herlihy. **CAST:** Glenn Ford, Nancy Olson, Dean Jagger, Keenan Wynn, Warren Oates, Chief Dan George. **1969**

SMITHEREENS ★★★ An independently made feature (its budget was only $100,000), this work by producer-director Susan Seidelman examines the life of an amoral and aimless young woman (Susan Berman) living in New York. Rated R. 90m. **DIR:** Susan Seidelman. **CAST:** Susan Berman, Brad Rinn, Richard Hell, Roger Jett. **1982**

SMOKE (1970) ★★★ Distraught over his father's death and his mother's remarriage, a farm boy gives his affection to an injured German shepherd instead. Well-acted, satisfying family drama from the Disney studios. 90m. **DIR:** Vincent McEveety. **CAST:** Ron Howard, Earl Holliman, Andy Devine. **1970**

SMOKE (1995) ★★★★ Novelist Paul Auster's 1990 Christmas fable has been transformed into a brilliant little ensemble piece, revolving around the idiosyncratic regulars at a Brooklyn cigar shop. The film unfolds like a skillfully staged play, and the characters are fascinating. Rated R for profanity and mild violence. 112m. **DIR:** Wayne Wang. **CAST:** Harvey Keitel, William Hurt, Forest Whitaker, Stockard Channing, Harold Perrineau Jr., Ashley Judd. **1995**

SMOKE SIGNALS ★★★1/2 Interesting but dramatically unfocused tale of two young Idaho Indians on a trip to Arizona. Despite fascinating cultural details and enchanting, unusual dialogue (by the fine writer Sherman Alexie, who adapted the screenplay from his short story collection *The Lone Ranger and Tonto Fistfight in Heaven*), the piece's finer points never really gel. Rated PG-13 for language. 89m. **DIR:** Chris Eyre. **CAST:** Adam Beach, Evan Adams, Gary Farmer, Irene Bedard. **1998 DVD**

•SMOKERS, THE ★★ A novel idea goes up in smoke in this black comedy about a trio of boarding-school girlfriends who decide to give men a taste of their own medicine. That means putting on silly masks, luring them into a barn, raping them at gunpoint, and then leaving them humiliated. The revenge fantasy might have been acceptable if the girls, nicknamed Smokers, had any redeemable qualities. They're a nasty bunch, so it's difficult to rally around their decision to get even with the men who treated them badly. The film wants to be *Heathers*, but it lacks the wit or bite. Rated R for adult situations, language, and violence. 97m. **DIR:** Christina Peters. **CAST:** Dominique Swain, Busy Philipps, Keri Lynn Pratt, Oliver Hudson, Thora Birch. **2000 DVD**

SMOKESCREEN ★★★ A fledgling ad executive, tired of being low man on the totem pole, becomes involved with a model who in turn involves him with a mob

leader. Well acted and fairly well written, the film's main fault lies in its contrived ending. Rated R. 91m. **DIR:** Martin Lavut. **CAST:** Kim Cattrall, Matt Craven, Kim Coates, Dean Stockwell. **1990**

SMOKEY AND THE BANDIT ★★★1/2 *Smokey and the Bandit* may strain credibility, but it never stops being fun. The Bandit (Burt Reynolds) is an infamous independent trucker who is hired to transport four hundred cases of Coors beer from Texarkana, Texas, where it is legal, to Atlanta, Georgia, where it is not. Hold on to your hat. Rated PG for profanity. 97m. **DIR:** Hal Needham. **CAST:** Burt Reynolds, Pat McCormick, Jerry Reed, Sally Field, Mike Henry, Jackie Gleason, Paul Williams. **1977 DVD**

SMOKEY AND THE BANDIT II ★★ *Smokey II* is just more proof that "sequels aren't equal." But it isn't a total loss. Don't turn it off until the credits roll (although you may want to fast-forward). Outtakes featuring the stars flubbing their lines are spliced together at the end, and they're hilarious. Rated PG. 101m. **DIR:** Hal Needham. **CAST:** Burt Reynolds, Jerry Reed, Pat McCormick, Paul Williams, Mike Henry, Jackie Gleason, Dom DeLuise. **1980**

SMOKEY AND THE BANDIT III 🦃 The Bandit may be back, but it ain't Burt. Rated PG for nudity, profanity, and scatological humor. 86m. **DIR:** Dick Lowry. **CAST:** Jerry Reed, Jackie Gleason, Paul Williams, Pat McCormick. **1983**

SMOKEY BITES THE DUST ★★1/2 Jimmy McNichol stars as a mischievous teenager who takes great delight in stealing cars and making buffoons out of the sheriff and his deputies. This is pretty standard car-chase action, but it does move along and there are some laughs along the way. Rated PG. 85m. **DIR:** Charles B. Griffith. **CAST:** Jimmy McNichol, Walter Barnes, John Blythe Barrymore, William Forsythe. **1981**

SMOKEY TRAILS ★★★ Once again Bob Steele is after the killer of his father—chasing him right into Lost Canyon, an outlaw den that he cleans out with plenty of fisticuffs and blazing six-shooters. Above average. B&W; 57m. **DIR:** Bernard B. Ray. **CAST:** Bob Steele, Jimmy Aubrey, Ted Adams, Carleton Young. **1939**

SMOKY MOUNTAIN CHRISTMAS ★★★ Typical made-for-TV seasonal heartwarmer, this features Dolly Parton as a burned-out singer-actress who takes to the hills of Tennessee for rest and seclusion. There she rediscovers the real meaning of Christmas. Suitable for family viewing. 100m. **DIR:** Henry Winkler. **CAST:** Dolly Parton, Lee Majors, Dan Hedaya, Bo Hopkins, John Ritter. **1986**

SMOOTH TALK ★★★★ Coltish Laura Dern owns this film, an uncompromising adaptation of the Joyce Carol Oates short story "Where Are You Going, Where Have You Been?" Dern hits every note as a sultry woman-child poised on the brink of adulthood and sexual maturity. Mary Kay Place does well as an exasperated mom, and Elizabeth Berridge is a sympathetic older sister. Rated PG-13 for language and sexual situations. 92m. **DIR:** Joyce Chopra. **CAST:** Laura Dern, Treat Williams, Mary Kay Place, Elizabeth Berridge, Levon Helm. **1985**

SMOOTH TALKER ★★1/2 Cop Joe Guzaldo is at the end of his rope: his attorney wife just walked out and unless he can come up with a lead on a killer of 976-Phone Girls, he's about to hit the pavement, sans badge. Things heat up when the only suspect in the case winds up being prosecuted by his ex-wife. Rated R for language and violence. 89m. **DIR:** Tom E. Milo. **CAST:** Joe Guzaldo, Burt Ward, Stuart Whitman. **1991**

SMURFS AND THE MAGIC FLUTE, THE ★★ Those little blue people from the popular television cartoon show are featured in their first movie. The kiddies will probably love it, but parents should read a book. Rated G. 80m. **DIR:** John Rust. **1983**

SNAKE EATER 🦃 Lorenzo Lamas is a lone wolf cop in pursuit of the hillbillies who killed his parents. This hybrid of *Rambo* and *The Hills Have Eyes* had us laughing at all the wrong moments. Rated R for profanity, violence, and nudity. 89m. **DIR:** George Erschbamer. **CAST:** Lorenzo Lamas. **1989**

SNAKE EATER III: HIS LAW ★★1/2 Renegade cop Lorenzo Lamas returns. This outing, he helps a family whose daughter was brutalized by a gang of bikers called Hell's Furies. Rated R for violence, simulated sex, and profanity. 109m. **DIR:** George Erschbamer. **CAST:** Lorenzo Lamas, Minor Mustain. **1992**

SNAKE EATER 2, THE DRUG BUSTER ★★ Mel Gibson's marketable character from the *Lethal Weapon* movies finds new merchandising life in this rip-off action flick. Lorenzo Lamas portrays Soldier, an unorthodox cop turned vigilante. Rated R for violence and profanity. 93m. **DIR:** George Erschbamer. **CAST:** Lorenzo Lamas, Michele Scarabelli, Larry B. Scott, Vittorio Rossi. **1989**

SNAKE EYES ★★★1/2 Nicolas Cage owns this energetic thriller. The plot, a slight nod to Kurosawa's *Rashomon*, finds Cage as an Atlantic City police detective on hand during a televised heavyweight boxing match, when the U.S. secretary of defense is gunned down. The story itself is a mildly clever conspiracy piece, in good company with De Palma's *Blow Out*. Rated R for violence and profanity. 98m. **DIR:** Brian De Palma. **CAST:** Nicolas Cage, Gary Sinise, John Heard, Carla Gugino, Stan Shaw, Kevin Dunn. **1998 DVD**

SNAKE PEOPLE 🦃 In this Mexican movie with scenes of Boris Karloff shot just before his death, the ailing actor plays a rich man whose niece is kidnapped by demon worshipers. 90m. **DIR:** Juan Ibanez, Jack Hill. **CAST:** Boris Karloff. **1968**

SNAKE PIT, THE ★★★★★ One of the first and best movies about mental illness and the treatment of patients in hospitals and asylums. Olivia de Havilland turns in an exceptional performance as a woman suffering from a nervous breakdown. Based on an autobiographical novel by Mary Jane Ward. B&W; 108m. **DIR:** Anatole Litvak. **CAST:** Olivia de Havilland, Mark Stevens, Leo Genn, Celeste Holm, Betsy Blair, Ruth Donnelly, Glenn Langan, Beulah Bondi, Leif Erickson. **1948**

SNAPDRAGON ★★ A detective (Chelsea Field), investigating a case involving serial murders, requests the assistance of a police psychologist (Steve Bauer). A young amnesic woman may know something about the murders or the identity of the killer. Predictable but watchable thriller. Rated R for nudity, profanity, and violence. 96m. **DIR:** Worth Keeter. **CAST:** Steven Bauer, Chelsea Field, Pamela Anderson. **1993**

SNAPPER, THE ★★★★1/2 The second film made from author Roddy Doyle's *Barrytown* trilogy (follow-

ing *The Commitments*) is a delightful character study. The strong-willed daughter in a working-class family becomes pregnant and refuses to divulge the name of the father. This is a gem! Rated R for frank discussions of sex and brief profanity. 95m. **DIR:** Stephen Frears. **CAST:** Colm Meaney, Ruth McCabe, Tina Kellegher, Colm O'Bryne, Pat Laffan. **1994 DVD**

SNATCH ★★★★ Guy Ritchie's marvelously amoral blend of guns and British gangsters will be adored by fans who saw the humor in *Pulp Fiction*, but mainstream viewers are advised to steer clear: No matter how impressive the delivery, this is tasteless stuff. It all starts with the heist of a whopping big diamond, which passes through numerous hands during a series of progressively complicated schemes involving bare-knuckle boxing, Irish gypsies, pawnshop owners, an overweight getaway driver, a nasty criminal kingpin who disposes of unwanted bodies by feeding them to his pet pigs, and a dog that likes to swallow things. This film has attitude and creativity to spare. Rated R for violence, profanity, and brief nudity. 102m. **DIR:** Guy Ritchie. **CAST:** Benicio Del Toro, Dennis Farina, Jason Flemyng, Vinnie Jones, Brad Pitt, Rade Sherbedgia, Jason Statham. **2000 DVD**

SNATCHED ★★1/2 In this mediocre made-for-television film, the wives of three rich men are kidnapped and held for ransom. The crime is complicated when one of the husbands refuses to pay his share of the ransom. 73m. **DIR:** Sutton Roley. **CAST:** Howard Duff, Leslie Nielsen, Sheree North, Barbara Parkins, Robert Reed, John Saxon, Tisha Sterling, Anthony Zerbe, Richard Davalos. **1973**

SNEAKERS ★★★★ In this slick, enjoyable piece of escapism, Robert Redford gives a star-quality performance as a computer trickster turned security expert—until government agents use his shady past to force him into a battle of wits with a former colleague. Fine acting and sly bits of humor add to the fun. Rated PG-13 for profanity and violence. 126m. **DIR:** Phil Alden Robinson. **CAST:** Robert Redford, Dan Aykroyd, Ben Kingsley, Mary McDonnell, River Phoenix, Sidney Poitier, David Strathairn, Timothy Busfield, George Hearn. **1992 DVD**

SNIPER ★★1/2 Male posturing reaches ludicrous heights in this tedious jungle drama, which finds Marine sniper Tom Berenger sent into the wilds of Panama to assassinate a Colombian drug baron. Rated R for violence and profanity. 98m. **DIR:** Luis Llosa. **CAST:** Tom Berenger, Billy Zane, J. T. Walsh. **1993 DVD**

SNO-LINE A Texas cocaine operation is threatened by the mob. Rated R for violence and language. 89m. **DIR:** Douglas F. O'Neans. **CAST:** Vince Edwards, Paul Smith, June Wilkinson. **1984**

SNOOPERS ★1/2 A group of youthful sleuths, known as the Knickerbockers, investigates what appears to be an evil phantom. Nonsensical; strictly for the younger set. Rated PG. 81m. **DIR:** Marian D. Vajda. **CAST:** Aled Roberts, Olivia Hallinan, Rebecca Keeling, Mathias Rothammer. **1999**

SNOOPY, COME HOME ★★★1/2 Charming second entry in the "Peanuts" film series doesn't contain the childhood *angst* of the first but maintains the irreverent view of life found in the best of Charles Schulz's comic strips. Snoopy decides life at home ain't all it's cracked up to be, so he and Woodstock set off to find America. Needless to say, there's no place like home. Rated G. 70m. **DIR:** Bill Melendez. **1972**

SNOOPY: THE MUSICAL ★★★ This is another unwieldy mix of animation and off-Broadway music, drawn from the second live-action play starring Charlie Brown and the Peanuts gang. The material was severely abridged for its original one-hour television time slot. While Larry Grossman and Hal Hackady's songs remain poignant and cute, the show feels rushed . . . and it's still odd to watch an animated Snoopy actually talk (and sing). Not rated. 50m. **DIR:** Sam Jaimes. **1988**

SNOOPY'S REUNION ★★1/2 The story of how Charlie Brown came to adopt Snoopy could have been told much better. Aside from the novelty of watching Snoopy and his doggie siblings perform in a jug band, there's little to recommend this weak Peanuts entry. Not rated. 25m. **DIR:** Sam Jaimes. **1991**

SNOW COUNTRY ★★★1/2 A painter's romance with a lovely geisha is complicated by various friends and acquaintances. Fine Japanese love story set amidst the snowbanks of an isolated village. In Japanese with English subtitles. B&W; 134m. **DIR:** Shiro Toyoda. **CAST:** Ryo Ikebe. **1957**

SNOW CREATURE, THE Abominable Snowman movie is one of the weakest of the batch that hit American theatres in the mid-1950s. B&W; 70m. **DIR:** W. Lee Wilder. **CAST:** Paul Langton, Leslie Denison. **1954**

SNOW DAY ★★1/2 Chevy Chase takes a backseat to his children in this family film. Most of the film is devoted to his daughter's crusade to rid the streets of a maniacal snow-plow dude, and his son's romantic endeavors. Passable entertainment but unmemorable. Rated PG for comic-book violence. 89m. **DIR:** Chris Koch. **CAST:** Chevy Chase, Chris Elliott, Jean Smart. **2000 DVD**

•SNOW DOGS ★★ Miami dentist Cuba Gooding Jr. inherits an Alaskan sled dog team and locks horns with a local sourdough (James Coburn) who wants the team for himself. Bad jokes and shameless mugging are the main features of this flat comedy. Rated PG. 99m. **DIR:** Brian Levant. **CAST:** Cuba Gooding Jr., James Coburn, Joanna Bacalso, Nichelle Nichols, M. Emmet Walsh. **2002 DVD**

SNOW FALLING ON CEDARS ★★1/2 In a small Pacific Northwest town shortly after World War II, the trial of a Japanese American for murder awakens slumbering racism and memories of the wartime internment camps. David Guterson's best-selling novel gets a sluggish filming by director Scott Hicks, with the characters taking a backseat to lingering shots of the scenery and weather. Some of the story's inherent drama manages to survive. Rated PG-13 for mature themes. 126m. **DIR:** Scott Hicks. **CAST:** Ethan Hawke, Youki Kudoh, Rick Yune, James Rebhorn, Max von Sydow, Sam Shepard. **1999 DVD**

•SNOW IN AUGUST ★★★ This made-for-cable original is definitely geared toward a younger audience, as it features only a little violence and a whole lot of fantasy. The time is the late 1940s, and the story involves a boy who witnesses the beating of a Jewish store owner. He struggles with the right thing to do, and in the end, only a miracle can fix the situation. Not rated; contains vio-

lence. 104m. **DIR:** Dick Friedenberg. **CAST:** Stephen Rea, Lolita Davidovich, Peter Anthony Tambakis. **2001**

SNOW KILL ★★★1/2 An executive's plan for a weekend survival trip on a mountain turns into trouble when three escaped convicts try to recover their cocaine stash. Good action with David Dukes shining as the villain. Not rated, but has violence. 94m. **DIR:** Thomas Wright. **CAST:** Terence Knox, Patti D'Arbanville, David Dukes. **1990**

SNOW QUEEN ★★ An exceedingly dull *Faerie Tale Theatre* tale, the Snow Queen (played by Lee Remick), teaches an unruly boy a lesson. The sets and special effects are second only to the actors' lines for their banality. 48m. **DIR:** Peter Medak. **CAST:** Melissa Gilbert, Lance Kerwin, Lee Remick, Lauren Hutton, Linda Manz, David Hemmings. **1983 DVD**

SNOW WHITE: A TALE OF TERROR ★★1/2 Returning to the Brothers Grimm no doubt was intended to remove the cloying taint of Disney and other sanitized adaptations, but this rendition of the wholesome young woman and her evil stepmother trades cute forest creatures and cheerful dwarfs for pointless gore and ill-conceived characters. Rated R for violence, gore, and simulated sex. 100m. **DIR:** Michael Cohn. **CAST:** Sigourney Weaver, Sam Neill, Monica Keena, Gil Bellows, Taryn Davis, David Conrad, Brian Glover. **1996 DVD**

SNOW WHITE AND THE SEVEN DWARFS (1938) ★★★★★ This first full-length animated film produced by Walt Disney was the culmination of a dream. *Snow White* is nothing short of breathtaking. The fairy tale, adapted from the works of the Brothers Grimm, has arrived with most of its power intact. Disney collected a special Academy Award for this film—one normal-sized statuette and seven little ones. Not rated; suitable for family viewing. 83m. **DIR:** David Hand. **1938**

SNOW WHITE AND THE SEVEN DWARFS (1983) ★★★★ Both Vincent Price and Vanessa Redgrave are wickedly wonderful in this splendid adaptation of the Grimm's tale. Price plays the evil queen's (Redgrave) advising mirror. Lovely Elizabeth McGovern plays a sweet Snow White. 51m. **DIR:** Peter Medak. **CAST:** Elizabeth McGovern, Vanessa Redgrave, Vincent Price, Rex Smith. **1983**

SNOW WHITE AND THE THREE STOOGES 🦃 Sad entry from what was left of the Three Stooges. 107m. **DIR:** Walter Lang. **CAST:** The Three Stooges, Patricia Medina, Carol Heiss, Guy Rolfe, Buddy Baer, Edgar Barrier. **1961**

SNOWBALL EXPRESS ★★ This formula comedy stars the Disney stable of players from the 1960s and 1970s. Dean Jones inherits a run-down hotel and attempts to turn it into a ski resort. Standard family viewing with a ski chase to help the pace. Rated G. 99m. **DIR:** Norman Tokar. **CAST:** Dean Jones, Nancy Olson, Harry Morgan, Keenan Wynn, Johnny Whitaker. **1972**

SNOWBEAST 🦃 Hokey white Sasquatch–Abominable Snowman makes life miserable on the slopes. 100m. **DIR:** Herb Wallerstein. **CAST:** Bo Svenson, Yvette Mimieux, Robert Logan, Clint Walker, Sylvia Sidney. **1977**

SNOWBOARD ACADEMY 🦃 Troublesome snowboarders, masquerading as hip rebels, go head-to-head with the moronic staff of a ski resort. As ridiculous as it sounds. Rated PG. 89m. **DIR:** John Shepphird. **CAST:** Corey Haim, Jim Varney, Brigitte Nielsen, Joe Flaherty. **1996**

SNOWS OF KILIMANJARO, THE ★★★★ A broad and colorful canvas of foreign adventure with author-hero (Gregory Peck) lying injured on the slope of Africa's famous mountain reflecting on his life. From Africa to Spain to the Riviera and back again. One of the better renderings of a Hemingway novel. 117m. **DIR:** Henry King. **CAST:** Gregory Peck, Susan Hayward, Ava Gardner, Leo G. Carroll, Hildegarde Neff, Torin Thatcher. **1952 DVD**

SO DEAR TO MY HEART ★★★★ Loving re-creation of small-town life in the early years of this century. Young Bobby Driscoll (one of the finest of all child actors) has taken a notion to enter his black lamb Danny in the county fair. A singing blacksmith (Burl Ives in his film debut) encourages him in his dreams. This gentle film is loaded with love, goodwill, and sentiment. 84m. **DIR:** Harold Schuster. **CAST:** Burl Ives, Beulah Bondi, Harry Carey, Luana Patten, Bobby Driscoll, Matt Willis. **1949 DVD**

SO ENDS OUR NIGHT ★★★★ Fredric March gives one of his best performances as a German trying to escape Nazi Germany but forced to return when he learns that his wife is terminally ill. The movie was produced before Pearl Harbor and was dismissed by critics and public alike. After the United States entered the war, it was reissued to acclaim and still has strong entertainment value. B&W; 118m. **DIR:** John Cromwell. **CAST:** Fredric March, Margaret Sullavan, Glenn Ford, Frances Dee, Erich Von Stroheim, Anna Sten. **1941**

SO FINE ★★ This so-called sex comedy—about a fashion house (run by Ryan O'Neal and Jack Warden) that introduces a new line of designer jeans with see-through plastic inserts in the seat—is little more than a television situation comedy with leers. Rated R because of nudity and profanity. 91m. **DIR:** Andrew Bergman. **CAST:** Ryan O'Neal, Jack Warden, Richard Kiel, Fred Gwynne, Mike Kellin, David Rounds. **1981**

SO I MARRIED AN AXE MURDERER ★★1/2 Mike Myers proves he can get some laughs outside of *Wayne's World* in this comedy about a modern-day beat poet's ill-fated marriage to a butcher's assistant. There are some good moments in this paper-thin whodunit. Rated PG-13 for violence, suggested sex, nudity, and vulgarity. 94m. **DIR:** Thomas Schlamme. **CAST:** Mike Myers, Nancy Travis, Anthony LaPaglia, Amanda Plummer, Brenda Fricker, Matt Doherty, Charles Grodin, Alan Arkin, Phil Hartman, Debi Mazar, Michael Richards, Steven Wright. **1993 DVD**

SO PROUDLY WE HAIL ★★★★ Hollywood's foremost actresses worked together to make this first tribute to women in World War II a morale-builder as well as a money-maker. Nurses at the siege of Bataan in an action-filled movie with the right touch of romance to keep both men and women involved. B&W; 126m. **DIR:** Mark Sandrich. **CAST:** Claudette Colbert, Paulette Goddard, Veronica Lake, Barbara Britton, Sonny Tufts, George Reeves, Bill Goodwin, Ann Doran, Walter Abel. **1943**

SO THIS IS WASHINGTON ★★1/2 From a park bench in Washington, D.C., Charles Lauck and Norris Goff, radio's cracker-barrel philosophers Lum and Abner, dispense common sense to senators and congressmen.

Third in a series, this product of wartime mentality is a simpleminded feature aimed at warming the heart. B&W; 65m. **DIR:** Ray McCarey. **CAST:** Charles Lauck, Norris Goff, Alan Mowbray, Minerva Urecal. **1943**

SOAPDISH ★★★1/2 Daytime soap operas get the raspberry in this often funny spoof, which features lively performances by the cast. Rated PG-13 for profanity. 97m. **DIR:** Michael Hoffman. **CAST:** Sally Field, Kevin Kline, Whoopi Goldberg, Robert Downey Jr., Cathy Moriarty, Elisabeth Shue, Teri Hatcher, Garry Marshall, Carrie Fisher. **1991**

S.O.B. ★★★ Director Blake Edwards vents his resentment over Hollywood's treatment of him in the early 1970s in this failed attempt at satire. There are some good moments, but too few. Self-indulgent. Rated R. 121m. **DIR:** Blake Edwards. **CAST:** Julie Andrews, William Holden, Robert Preston, Richard Mulligan, Robert Vaughn, Loretta Swit, Larry Hagman, Craig Stevens, Shelley Winters, Rosanna Arquette. **1981**

SOCCER DOG: THE MOVIE ★★1/2 Derivative rehash of *Air Bud* aimed squarely at the unassuming children's market. Young Jeremy is having a hard time fitting in with his new foster parents and at school. He turns to soccer for solace and becomes a school hero when his furry four-legged friend becomes the school's new soccer star. The usual complications follow. Rated PG. 98m. **DIR:** Tony Giglio. **CAST:** Jeremy Foley, James Marshall, Olivia D'Abo. **1998**

SOCIETY ★★1/2 Every child's worst nightmare comes true for a Beverly Hills teenager who is plunged into a nightmarish world of ritual sacrifice and monstrous cruelty. Rated R for violence, profanity, and nudity. 99m. **DIR:** Brian Yuzna. **CAST:** Billy Warlock, Devin DeVasquez, Evan Richards. **1992**

SODBUSTERS ★★1/2 This ponderous Western comedy isn't even fit to stand in the shadow of *Blazing Saddles*. Stone-faced Kris Kristofferson, playing a maimed gunfighter dubbed Destiny, rides into sleepy Marble Hat, Colorado, and joins local farmers hoping to thwart a greedy railroad tycoon. Only a few laughs accidentally emerge from this riff on *Shane* that wastes the talents of all involved. Rated PG-13 for profanity and a few surprisingly violent scenes. 97m. **DIR:** Eugene Levy. **CAST:** Kris Kristofferson, Fred Willard, John Vernon, Wendel Meldrum, Max Gail, Steve Landesberg. **1994**

SODOM AND GOMORRAH ★★★ Better-than-average biblical epic concerning the twin cities of sin. Extremely long film contains good production values and performances. No rating, but film does contain scenes of violence and gore. 154m. **DIR:** Robert Aldrich. **CAST:** Stewart Granger, Stanley Baker, Pier Angeli, Rossana Podesta. **1963**

SOFIE ★★★1/2 The great Norwegian actress Liv Ullmann directs her first film, a slow-moving but affecting family saga in turn-of-the-century Sweden. We follow the life of the title character, an enterprising and independent Jewish woman. Ullmann learned a lot from Ingmar Bergman, and layers in textures of family warmth, humor, and mystery, as well as a masterful performance by Bergman veteran Erland Josephson as Sofie's beloved father. In Swedish with English subtitles. 146m. **DIR:** Liv Ullmann. **CAST:** Karen-Lise Mynster, Erland Josephson, Ghita Norby. **1993 DVD**

SOFT DECEIT ★★★ Clever little thriller about an undercover cop (Kate Vernon) who falls in love with the criminal mastermind who stole the $6 million she's supposed to recover. Although plot holes abound and numerous side issues are left unresolved, Vernon brings far more depth to her character than this genre usually supplies; you'll genuinely care about what happens to her. Rated R for nudity, simulated sex, and profanity. 95m. **DIR:** Jorge Montesi. **CAST:** Patrick Bergin, Kate Vernon, John Wesley Shipp, Gwynyth Walsh. **1994**

SOFT FRUIT ★★1/2 Jeanie Drynan stars as the dying matriarch of a dysfunctional family that hasn't seen each other in years. When the children come to the aid of their soon-to-be-departed mother, they must put aside their petty differences in order to help make their mom's last wishes come true. Performances aren't bad, but the movie gets a little mushy around the edges. Rated R for adult situations, language, and drug use. 101m. **DIR:** Christina Andreef. **CAST:** Jeanie Drynan, Linal Haft, Genevieve Lemon, Sacha Horler. **1999**

SOFT KILL, THE ★★ When his girlfriend is found brutally murdered, a private eye discovers he's the main suspect. As the body count rises, he fights a desperate battle to prove his innocence. Another so-so crime-thriller that's predictable almost from frame one. Rated R for profanity and violence. 95m. **DIR:** Eli Cohen. **CAST:** Michael Harris, Brian James, Corbin Bernsen. **1994**

SOFT SKIN, THE ★★★1/2 For some critics, this ranks as one of the new-wave master's worst; for some it remains one of his best. As usual, the truth lies in between. What keeps it from being at least a minor classic is the less-than-fresh plot. In French with English subtitles. 118m. **DIR:** François Truffaut. **CAST:** Jean Desailly, Nelly Benedetti, Françoise Dorleac. **1964 DVD**

SOIS BELLE ET TAIS-TOI (JUST ANOTHER PRETTY FACE) ★★★ This French import tries to be a lighthearted, romantic adventure, but doesn't focus itself properly. Mylene Demongeot is Virginie, an 18-year-old orphan who runs away from a reformatory and falls in with a jewel-smuggling gang. Jean-Paul Belmondo and Alain Delon, both in their first film roles, are members of the teenage gang. In French with English subtitles. B&W; 110m. **DIR:** Marc Allegret. **CAST:** Mylene Demongeot, Henri Vidal, René Lefévre, Jean-Paul Belmondo, Alain Delon. **1958**

SOL BIANCA ★★★★ After the pirate ship *Sol Bianca* unknowingly takes on a passenger, the five-woman crew of freebooters set their sights on a new prize: the "Gnosis," a treasure beyond price. Unfortunately the obstacle in their path, a tyrannical emperor, is determined to keep the treasure. Japanese animation from the director of *Bubblegum Crisis*. In Japanese with English subtitles. Not rated, with violence and profanity. 60m. **DIR:** Akiyama Katsuhito. **1990**

SOLAR CRISIS ★★ The sun is the only thing that flares up in this minor effort. A solar flare-up threatens to destroy life on Earth unless a group of scientists can shoot an antimatter bomb into the sun. The direction reduces everything to bargain-basement clichés. Rated PG-13 for violence. 111m. **DIR:** Alan Smithee. **CAST:** Tim Matheson, Charlton Heston, Peter Boyle, Corin Nemec, Jack Palance, Annabel Schofield. **1992 DVD**

SOLAR FORCE In this cheesy representation of the twenty-first century, Michael Paré must stop colonists

from regenerating the Earth's environment, which should not be difficult, as bad guy Billy Drago has sucked up all the hot air. Rated R for violence and profanity. 91m. **DIR:** Boaz Davidson. **CAST:** Michael Paré, Billy Drago, Walker Brandt. **1994**

SOLARBABIES In the far future, a group of sports teens joins forces with a mystical force. Rated PG-13 for violence. 94m. **DIR:** Alan Johnson. **CAST:** Richard Jordan, Jami Gertz, Jason Patric, Charles Durning, Lukas Haas. **1986**

SOLARIS ★★★★ Based on a story by noted Polish author Stanislaw Lem, this motion picture explores the workings of a man's mind and how he deals with visions from his past. A space station situated over a water-covered planet has become almost deserted, and a scientist is sent to unravel the mysteries surrounding the death of a doctor on board the station. A milestone in the history of science-fiction cinema. In Russian with English subtitles. Not rated. 167m. **DIR:** Andrei Tarkovsky. **CAST:** Donatas Banionis, Natalya Bondarchuk. **1972**

SOLAS ★★★1/2 A rural Spanish wife stays with her embittered daughter in the big city while her abusive husband recovers from surgery in the hospital; the daughter's unwanted pregnancy and the mother's halting friendship with an elderly neighbor change all their lives in big and little ways. This slice-of-life drama is perceptive and well-acted. In Spanish with English subtitles. Not rated; suitable for mature audiences. 98m. **DIR:** Benito Zambrano. **CAST:** Maria Galiana, Ana Fernandez, Carlos Alvarez-Novoa, Paco De Osca. **1999**

SOLDIER, THE (1982) Russian agents steal enough plutonium for a large nuclear explosion. Rated R for violence and profanity. 96m. **DIR:** James Glickenhaus. **CAST:** Ken Wahl, Klaus Kinski, William Prince. **1982**

SOLDIER (1998) ★★★ Sci-fi fans will recognize this as one of the most basic plots: A supersoldier, designed to blindly follow orders without a twinge of conscience, is forced by circumstance to reevaluate his priorities and—having found his humanity—becomes the sole protector of a ragtag band of colonists facing overwhelming odds. It works because of star Kurt Russell, who is absolutely credible and wholly sympathetic in the title role. Rated R for violence. 95m. **DIR:** Paul Anderson. **CAST:** Kurt Russell, Jason Scott Lee, Connie Nielsen, Michael Chiklis, Gary Busey. **1998 DVD**

SOLDIER BLUE ★★1/2 An extremely violent film that looks at the mistreatment of Indians at the hands of the U.S. Cavalry. This familiar subject has fared much better in films such as *Little Big Man*. Final attack is an exercise in excessive gore and violence. Rated R. 112m. **DIR:** Ralph Nelson. **CAST:** Candice Bergen, Peter Strauss, John Anderson, Donald Pleasence. **1970**

SOLDIER BOYZ Yet another variant on *The Dirty Dozen* (and undoubtedly not the last) has ghetto punks released from prison to rescue a hostage in North Vietnam. Rated R for violence and profanity. 91m. **DIR:** Louis Mourneau. **CAST:** Michael Dudikoff, David Barry Gray, Cary-Hiroyuki Tagawa, Don Stroud. **1995**

SOLDIER IN THE RAIN ★★★ *My Bodyguard* director Tony Bill is among the featured performers in this fine combination of sweet drama and rollicking comedy starring Steve McQueen, Jackie Gleason, and Tuesday Weld. Gleason is great as a high-living, worldly master sergeant, and McQueen is equally good as his protégé. B&W; 88m. **DIR:** Ralph Nelson. **CAST:** Steve McQueen, Tony Bill, Jackie Gleason, Tuesday Weld, Tom Poston. **1963**

SOLDIER OF FORTUNE ★★1/2 Clark Gable helps Susan Hayward search for her husband, lost in Red China. Exotic Asian locations are the main reason to see this standard adventure-drama. Gable is virile, Hayward makes a good match for him, and Hong Kong never looked better. 96m. **DIR:** Edward Dmytryk. **CAST:** Clark Gable, Susan Hayward, Michael Rennie, Gene Barry, Tom Tully, Alex D'Arcy, Anna Sten. **1955 DVD**

SOLDIER OF ORANGE ★★★★★ Rutger Hauer became an international star as a result of his remarkable performance in this Dutch release, in which he plays one of four college buddies galvanized into action when the Nazis invade the Netherlands. This is an exceptional work; an exciting, suspenseful, and intelligent war adventure. In several languages and subtitled. Rated R for nudity, profanity, implied sex, and violence. 165m. **DIR:** Paul Verhoeven. **CAST:** Rutger Hauer, Peter Faber, Jeroen Krabbé. **1979 DVD**

SOLDIER OF THE NIGHT This Israeli movie about a man who kills soldiers by night while working in a toy store by day has some psychological thriller elements, but its plodding story line and poor dubbing make it almost impossible to watch. Not rated, has nudity, violence, and profanity. 89m. **DIR:** Dan Wolman. **CAST:** Iris Kaner, Hillel Neeman, Yftach Katzur. **1984**

SOLDIER'S DAUGHTER NEVER CRIES, A ★★★ The autobiographical novel by Kaylie Jones, daughter of writer James Jones (*From Here to Eternity*, *The Thin Red Line*) is adapted by writer Ruth Prawer Jhabvala and director James Ivory into a tasteful, well-acted film. It's refreshing to see a film about a functional family for once; Kris Kristofferson, as the father, has seldom been better. Rated R for profanity. 124m. **DIR:** James Ivory. **CAST:** Kris Kristofferson, Barbara Hershey, Leelee Sobieski, Anthony Roth Costanzo. **1998 DVD**

SOLDIER'S FORTUNE ★★1/2 When ex–Green Beret turned mercenary Gil Gerard finds out that his daughter has been kidnapped, he pulls together an elite fighting team in order to bring her back alive. Likable cast helps move things along. Rated R for violence. 92m. **DIR:** Arthur N. Mele. **CAST:** Gil Gerard, Charles Napier, Dan Haggerty. **1990**

SOLDIER'S HOME ★★★1/2 Melancholy adaptation of an Ernest Hemingway story. The war in question is World War I, "the war to end all wars," and young Harold Krebs (Richard Backus) learns, almost to his shame, that he'd prefer that the fighting continue; without it, he has no sense of purpose. Introduced by Henry Fonda; not rated and suitable for family viewing. 41m. **DIR:** Robert Young. **CAST:** Richard Backus, Nancy Marchand, Robert McIlwaine, Lisa Essary, Mark La Mura, Lane Binkley. **1976**

SOLDIER'S STORY, A ★★★★★ A murder mystery, a character study, and a deeply affecting drama rolled into one, based on Charles Fuller's 1981 Pulitzer Prize–winning play, this is an unforgettable viewing experience. This riveting movie examines man's inhumanity to man in one of its most venal forms: racial hatred. Rated PG for violence and profanity. 102m. **DIR:** Nor-

man Jewison. **CAST:** Howard Rollins Jr., Adolph Caesar. **1984 DVD**

SOLDIER'S SWEETHEART, A ★★★1/2 "Vietnam is full of strange stories," the narrator tells us, and few will be more unusual than this fascinating adaptation of Tim O'Brien's short story. When one of the doctors in a M.A.S.H. unit unwisely pulls strings to bring his girlfriend over from the States for a few weeks of companionship, he's horrified to discover, as the days pass, that she *likes* the dangerous environment. Rated R for profanity, violence, simulated sex, and hospital gore. 111m. **DIR:** Thomas Michael Donnelly. **CAST:** Kiefer Sutherland, Skeet Ulrich, Georgina Cates. **1998**

SOLDIER'S TALE, A ★★★ During World War II, romance develops between a British soldier (Gabriel Byrne) and a beautiful Frenchwoman (Marianne Basler) accused of collaborating with the Germans against the French Resistance. Ending is quite a surprise. Rated R for nudity, violence, and profanity. 95m. **DIR:** Larry Parr. **CAST:** Gabriel Byrne, Judge Reinhold, Marianne Basler. **1988 DVD**

SOLE SURVIVOR ★★ A gory remake of a fine English suspense thriller of the same title—about the lone survivor of an airplane crash, haunted by the ghosts of those who died in the tragedy. A psychic tries to help this haunted woman by keeping the ghosts from killing her. Although there are some chills, this version pales in comparison to its predecessor—with Robert Powell and Jenny Agutter. Rated R for sexual situations and violence. 85m. **DIR:** Thom Eberhardt. **CAST:** Anita Skinner, Kurt Johnson. **1985**

SOLITAIRE FOR 2 ★★★ When a playboy meets a woman who can read minds, it takes more than his come-on lines to win her over. Once he does, however, her mind-reading skills threaten to sabotage the relationship. In much the same vein as *Four Weddings and a Funeral* but not quite as charming. Rated R for profanity and a brief sex scene. 105m. **DIR:** Gary Sinyor. **CAST:** Mark Frankel, Amanda Pays, Roshan Seth, Jason Isaacs, Maryam D'Abo. **1995**

SOLO ★★ Hollywood's first African American android hero is a perfect fighting machine except for one thing—he's developing feelings. This angers military brass so much that they intend to mess with his microchips, so he flees into the South American jungle where he saves local peasants from armed rebels, battles an evil android, and learns to laugh. Rated PG-13 for violence and language. 93m. **DIR:** Norberto Barba. **CAST:** Mario Van Peebles, Bill Sadler, Adrien Brody, Barry Corbin, Seidy Lopez. **1996 DVD**

SOLOMON AND GAENOR ★★1/2 In 1911 Wales, a Jewish pawnbroker's son and a local miner's daughter fall in love, with dire consequences. This well-acted Romeo-and-Juliet tale would be more poignant if the young lovers had something to lose. But the film is doom-laden from the start, and happiness never seems possible; all they fall from is misery. Rated R for sexual scenes and brief violence. 102m. **DIR:** Paul Morrisson. **CAST:** Ioan Gruffudd, Nia Roberts, Sue Jones-Davis, William Thomas. **1999 DVD**

SOLOMON AND SHEBA (1959) ★★★ High times in biblical times as Sheba vamps Solomon. The emphasis is on lavish spectacle. Eyewash, not brain food. 139m. **DIR:** King Vidor. **CAST:** Yul Brynner, Gina Lollobrigida, George Sanders. **1959**

SOLOMON AND SHEBA (1995) ★★ Epic love story disappoints due to Jimmy Smits's and Halle Berry's failure to exude the larger-than-life personas of a legendary king and queen. Not rated; contains sex and violence. 95m. **DIR:** Robert M. Young. **CAST:** Halle Berry, Jimmy Smits, Nickolas Grace, Kenneth Colley, Ruben Santiago Hudson. **1995**

SOME CALL IT LOVING Jazz musician buys a "Sleeping Beauty" from a circus sideshow for his own perverse enjoyment. Rated R for nudity and language. 103m. **DIR:** James B. Harris. **CAST:** Zalman King, Carol White, Tisa Farrow, Richard Pryor, Logan Ramsey. **1974**

SOME CAME RUNNING ★★★1/2 Based on James Jones's novel of life in a midwestern town, this film offers an entertaining study of some rather complex characters. Shirley MacLaine gives a sparkling performance as the town's loose woman who's in love with Frank Sinatra. The story is not strong, but the performances are fine. 136m. **DIR:** Vincente Minnelli. **CAST:** Frank Sinatra, Dean Martin, Shirley MacLaine, Arthur Kennedy, Martha Hyer. **1958**

SOME GIRLS ★★★ European tale about a young man (Patrick Dempsey) invited to join a girl and her very strange family over the Christmas season. Concentrates more on character and dramatic depth than story development. Rated R for language, nudity, and simulated sex. 95m. **DIR:** Michael Hoffman. **CAST:** Patrick Dempsey, Jennifer Connelly, Lila Kedrova, Florinda Bolkan. **1988**

SOME KIND OF HERO ★★ This Richard Pryor movie can't decide whether to tell the story of a Vietnam prisoner of war returning to American society or be another comedy caper film. As a result, it's neither very funny nor worth thinking about. Rated R for profanity, nudity, and violence. 97m. **DIR:** Michael Pressman. **CAST:** Richard Pryor, Margot Kidder, Ronny Cox, Olivia Cole. **1982**

SOME KIND OF WONDERFUL ★★★★ Eric Stoltz stars as an affable lad who can't seem to make any headway with women. Unaware of the deep affection hurled in his direction by constant companion Mary Stuart Masterson (who all but steals the show), Stoltz sets his sights high on Lea Thompson. Perceptive, thoughtful viewing. Rated PG-13 for mature situations. 93m. **DIR:** Howard Deutch. **CAST:** Eric Stoltz, Mary Stuart Masterson, Lea Thompson, Craig Sheffer, John Ashton. **1987**

SOME LIKE IT HOT ★★★★★ Billy Wilder's *Some Like It Hot* is the outlandish story of two men (Jack Lemmon and Tony Curtis) who accidentally witness a gangland slaying. They pose as members of an all-girl band in order to avoid the gangsters, who are now trying to silence them permanently. Marilyn Monroe is at her sensual best as the band's singer. Joe E. Brown is also hilarious as a wealthy playboy who develops an attraction for an obviously bewildered Lemmon. B&W; 119m. **DIR:** Billy Wilder. **CAST:** Marilyn Monroe, Jack Lemmon, Tony Curtis, Joe E. Brown, George Raft, Pat O'Brien, Nehemiah Persoff, Mike Mazurki. **1959**

SOME MOTHER'S SON ★★★ Story of the 1981 hunger strike in Ireland is told from the point of view of

the strikers' mothers, giving it a fresh poignancy. Rated R for language and violence. 112m. **DIR:** Terry George. **CAST:** Helen Mirren, Fionnula Flanagan, Aiden Gillen. **1996**

SOMEBODY HAS TO SHOOT THE PICTURE ★★★★ Two mesmerizing performances fuel this gripping made-for-cable indictment of the cruel and unusual treatment that often precedes capital punishment. Roy Scheider stars as a burned-out, Pulitzer Prize–winning photojournalist who accepts convict Arliss Howard's last wish: that his final moments be captured by a photographer. Probably too intense for younger viewers. Rated R for language and intensity. 104m. **DIR:** Frank Pierson. **CAST:** Roy Scheider, Arliss Howard, Bonnie Bedelia, Robert Carradine. **1990 DVD**

SOMEBODY IS WAITING ★★★1/2 A strong cast and well-executed plot distinguish this tale of a prodigal son whose life is shattered by the death of his mother and the reappearance of his alcoholic father. Rated R for language and violence. 90m. **DIR:** Martin Donovan. **CAST:** Gabriel Byrne, Nastassja Kinski, Johnny Whitworth, Shirley Knight, Rebecca Gayheart, Valeria Golino. **1996**

SOMEBODY TO LOVE ★★1/2 The best aspect of this independent film is ball of fire Rosie Perez as a modern-day, dollar-a-dance girl trying to break into show biz. Harvey Keitel is her sleazy lover, a former child star competing with handsome illegal alien Michael DeLorenzo for her affections. Manic plot tangents and weak direction undermine some of the grittier and more humorous aspects. Rated R for violence, profanity, and sexual situations. 103m. **DIR:** Alexandre Rockwell. **CAST:** Rosie Perez, Harvey Keitel, Michael DeLorenzo, Steve Buscemi, Anthony Quinn, Stanley Tucci, Quentin Tarantino. **1994**

SOMEBODY UP THERE LIKES ME ★★★★1/2 This is a first-rate biography. Boxer Rocky Graziano's career is traced from the back streets of New York to the heights of fame in the ring. It's one of the very best fight films ever made and features a sterling performance by Paul Newman. B&W; 113m. **DIR:** Robert Wise. **CAST:** Paul Newman, Pier Angeli, Everett Sloane, Sal Mineo, Eileen Heckart, Robert Loggia, Steve McQueen. **1956**

SOMEONE BEHIND THE DOOR ★★1/2 A brain surgeon takes an amnesiac into his home and, during the course of his treatment, conditions him to murder his wife. Intense suspense-drama with a decent cast. The story contains too many plot twists though. Not rated; contains violence. 93m. **DIR:** Nicolas Gessner. **CAST:** Charles Bronson, Anthony Perkins, Jill Ireland, Henri Garcin. **1971**

SOMEONE ELSE'S AMERICA ★★1/2 Two European immigrants patch together tragicomic family lives while pursuing the American Dream from a corner Brooklyn bar and restaurant. The thin, meandering story has several funny and tender moments but lacks deep emotional resonance. In Spanish and English with English subtitles. Rated PG. 96m. **DIR:** Goran Paskaljevic. **CAST:** Tom Conti, Miki Manojlovic, Maria Casares, Andjela Stojkovic, Sergej Trifunovic, Lazar Kalmic, Zorka Manojlovic. **1995**

SOMEONE I TOUCHED ★★ The subject is VD as architect James Olson and pregnant wife Cloris Leachman trade accusations over who's to blame. The actors are far better than their material in this dated disease-of-the-week TV movie. 78m. **DIR:** Lou Antonio. **CAST:** Cloris Leachman, James Olson, Glynnis O'Connor, Andrew Robinson. **1975**

SOMEONE LIKE YOU ★★1/2 A single woman (Ashley Judd) pines over an on-again-off-again romance with her caddish boss (Greg Kinnear), never knowing that true love, in the person of her roommate (Hugh Jackman), is right under her nose. Appealing performances compensate somewhat for the film's excruciating predictability and the unsure direction of Tony Goldwyn. Rated PG-13 for mature themes and mild profanity. 100m. **DIR:** Tony Goldwyn. **CAST:** Ashley Judd, Hugh Jackman, Greg Kinnear, Marisa Tomei, Ellen Barkin. **2001 DVD**

SOMEONE TO DIE FOR ★★ Corbin Bernsen is the saving grace of this melodramatic thriller. He plays Jack Davis, a detective who blames three fellow officers for his daughter's death. When the three cops end up dead, Davis becomes the main suspect. Now Davis must find the real killer and prove his innocence. Been there, done that. Rated R for violence and adult language. 98m. **DIR:** Clay Borris. **CAST:** Corbin Bernsen, Ally Walker, Robert Stewart. **1995**

SOMEONE TO LOVE ★★ Danny (Henry Jaglom) decides to have a filmmaking–Valentine's Day party with single people explaining directly into the camera why they are alone. Orson Welles (in his last screen appearance) sits on the balcony, commenting. One small problem: This movie wallows in all there is to detest about the Los Angeles art scene. Rated R for language. 112m. **DIR:** Henry Jaglom. **CAST:** Henry Jaglom, Michael Emil, Andrea Marcovicci, Sally Kellerman, Orson Welles. **1986**

SOMEONE TO WATCH OVER ME ★★★★ This first-rate thriller benefits from director Ridley Scott's visual dynamics and an intelligent script. Ultrarich lady Mimi Rogers witnesses a horrible murder and barely escapes with her life; Tom Berenger is the down-home cop from the Bronx assigned to protect her. Rated R for language, nudity, and violence. 106m. **DIR:** Ridley Scott. **CAST:** Tom Berenger, Mimi Rogers, Lorraine Bracco, Andreas Katsulas. **1987 DVD**

SOMETHING ABOUT SEX ★★★1/2 Three L.A. couples are forced into discussions about what they want from marriage after a bachelor friend starts an argument about the impossibility of fidelity. This frank, funny comedy is not one to watch with someone you love unless you're ready for a heavy discussion afterwards. Also released as *Denial*. Rated R for sex, nudity, and profanity. 93m. **DIR:** Adam Rifkin. **CAST:** Jonathan Silverman, Jason Alexander, Patrick Dempsey, Amy Yasbeck, Christine Taylor. **1998 DVD**

SOMETHING FOR EVERYONE ★★★ This sleeper about a manipulative, amoral young man (Michael York) and the lengths he goes to in order to advance himself might not be to everyone's tastes. Angela Lansbury gives one of her best performances as the down-on-her-luck aristocrat who falls victim to York's charms. Mature themes and situations make this film more suitable for an older audience. 112m. **DIR:** Harold Prince. **CAST:** Michael York, Angela Lansbury, Anthony Corlan, Jane Carr. **1970**

•**SOMETHING MORE** ★★1/2 This is the story of an honest, hardworking guy, his mooch of a friend, other friends of theirs, and their relationships with each other. Each aspect of their lives—work, sex, or play—involves recurring themes, especially aggressive male competition. Rated R for language and adult situations. 97m. **DIR:** Rob King. **CAST:** Michael A. Goorjian, David Lovgren, Jennifer Beals, Chandra West. **1999 DVD**

SOMETHING OF VALUE ★★★ White settlers in Kenya are preyed upon by bloodthirsty Mau Mau tribesmen sick of oppression in this often too-graphic drama, which opens with a specially filmed foreword from Winston Churchill. B&W; 113m. **DIR:** Richard Brooks. **CAST:** Rock Hudson, Dana Wynter, Sidney Poitier, Wendy Hiller, Frederick O'Neal, Juano Hernandez, William Marshall, Michael Pate. **1957**

SOMETHING SHORT OF PARADISE ★★★ This romantic comedy is something short of perfect but still manages to entertain. Two New Yorkers (Susan Sarandon and David Steinberg) manage to find love and happiness together despite distractions from other conniving singles. Marilyn Sokol is great as one of the obstacles. Rated PG. 91m. **DIR:** David Helpern Jr. **CAST:** Susan Sarandon, David Steinberg, Marilyn Sokol, Jean-Pierre Aumont. **1979**

SOMETHING SPECIAL ★★★ Offbeat but surprisingly pleasant comedy about a 15-year-old girl named Milly (Pamela Segall) who is convinced that life would be easier if she were a boy. With the help of a magical potion and a solar eclipse, she manages to grow a penis. She changes her name to Willy to please her father and to satisfy her own curiosity. Rated PG-13. 90m. **DIR:** Paul Schneider. **CAST:** Patty Duke, Pamela Segall, Eric Gurry, Mary Tanner, John Glover, Seth Green. **1987**

SOMETHING TO SING ABOUT ★★ Even the great talents of James Cagney can't lift this low-budget musical above the level of mediocrity. In it, he plays a New York bandleader who tests his mettle in Hollywood. B&W; 93m. **DIR:** Victor Schertzinger. **CAST:** James Cagney, William Frawley, Evelyn Daw, Gene Lockhart. **1937 DVD**

SOMETHING TO TALK ABOUT ★★★1/2 Excellent characterizations elevate the familiar story of how Julia Roberts's life is thrown into turmoil when she discovers that husband Dennis Quaid has been cheating on her. Rated R for profanity and suggested sex. 106m. **DIR:** Lasse Hallstrom. **CAST:** Julia Roberts, Dennis Quaid, Robert Duvall, Gena Rowlands, Kyra Sedgwick, Brett Cullen, Haley Aull, Muse Watson, Anne Shropshire. **1995 DVD**

SOMETHING WEIRD Tedious and bloodless time waster about a burn victim who finds he has gained extrasensory powers. There's also a subplot about a witch who restores his looks. None of it makes sense. 83m. **DIR:** Herschell Gordon Lewis. **CAST:** Tony McCabe, Elizabeth Lee. **1967 DVD**

SOMETHING WICKED THIS WAY COMES ★★★ Ray Bradbury's classic fantasy novel has been fashioned into a good, but not great, movie by the Walt Disney Studios. Jason Robards Jr. stars as the town librarian whose task it is to save his family and friends from the evil temptations of Mr. Dark (Jonathan Pryce) and his Pandemonium Carnival. It's an old-fashioned, even gentle tale of the supernatural; a gothic *Wizard of Oz* that seems likely to be best appreciated by preteens. Rated PG. 94m. **DIR:** Jack Clayton. **CAST:** Jason Robards Jr., Jonathan Pryce, Pam Grier, Shawn Carson. **1983 DVD**

SOMETHING WILD ★★★★1/2 Jeff Daniels stars as a desk-bound investment type whose idea of yuppie rebellion is stiffing a local diner for the price of a lunch. This petty larceny is observed by a mysterious woman (Melanie Griffith) who, to Daniels's relief and surprise, takes him not to the local police but to a seedy motel, where they share an afternoon that justifies the film's R rating. This moves from hilarious beginnings to true edge-of-the-seat terror. Rated R. 113m. **DIR:** Jonathan Demme. **CAST:** Jeff Daniels, Melanie Griffith, Ray Liotta, Margaret Colin, Tracey Walter. **1986 DVD**

SOMETIMES A GREAT NOTION ★★★ Paul Newman plays the elder son of an Oregon logging family that refuses to go on strike with the other lumberjacks in the area. The family pays dearly for its unwillingness to go along. One scene in particular, which features Newman aiding Richard Jaeckel, who has been pinned in the water by a fallen tree, is unforgettable. Rated PG. 114m. **DIR:** Paul Newman. **CAST:** Paul Newman, Henry Fonda, Lee Remick, Michael Sarrazin, Richard Jaeckel. **1971**

SOMETIMES AUNT MARTHA DOES DREADFUL THINGS ★★ Weird obscurity about a killer hiding out from the police by holing up in a Miami beach house dressed as a woman. He has an indecisive young male lover whom he passes off as his nephew. There are a few touches of black comedy, but not enough. Rated R for nudity. 95m. **DIR:** Thomas Casey. **CAST:** Abe Zwick, Scott Lawrence, Robin Hughes. **1971**

SOMETIMES THEY COME BACK ★★★1/2 Chilling made-for-TV thriller gets good mileage from Stephen King's book. Tim Matheson is superb as the high school teacher who returns to his hometown thirty years after his brother died in a freak accident. The bullies responsible, who also died in the accident, come back one by one to seek revenge against Matheson. 97m. **DIR:** Tom McLoughlin. **CAST:** Tim Matheson, Brooke Adams, Robert Rusler. **1991 DVD**

SOMETIMES THEY COME BACK AGAIN ★★★1/2 Gripping sequel finds psychologist John Porter and his teenage daughter returning to his boyhood home when his mother dies. Porter is immediately haunted by the spirit of the vicious teen who was responsible for his sister's ritualistic death thirty years earlier. Father and daughter must stand up to the evil or be lost to it forever. Rated R for violence, profanity, and nudity. 98m. **DIR:** Adam Grossman. **CAST:** Michael Gross, Alexis Arquette, Hilary Swank, Jennifer Elise Cox. **1996 DVD**

SOMEWHERE I'LL FIND YOU ★★★★ A war picture that zeroes in on the dangerous lives and loves of war correspondents in the heat of battle, this movie also has the distinction of Lana Turner's sexy allure and Clark Gable's obvious appreciation of it. They play war correspondents coping with their passions. Strong dramatic scenes set the tone for this WWII drama. B&W; 108m. **DIR:** Wesley Ruggles. **CAST:** Clark Gable, Lana Turner, Robert Sterling, Keenan Wynn, Reginald Owen, Charles Dingle, Lee Patrick, Patricia Dane. **1942**

SOMEWHERE IN SONORA ★★★ John Wayne, wrongly accused of cheating during a rodeo race, redeems himself by joining an outlaw gang to foil their

plans. This was the first of many films to team Wayne with character actor Paul Fix, who wrote the screenplay for *Tall in the Saddle*, and played the wise old lawman on TV's *The Rifleman*. B&W; 57m. **DIR:** Mack V. Wright. **CAST:** John Wayne, Henry B. Walthall, Shirley Palmer, J. P. Macgowan, Ann Fay, Frank Rice, Paul Fix, Ralph Lewis, Billy Franey. **1933**

SOMEWHERE IN THE CITY ★★ The lives of the tenants in a building on New York's Lower East Side intertwine in a number of haphazard ways. The script has several witty moments and the acting is good throughout. But there is no dramatic momentum, and the film fizzles off into two halfhearted climaxes twenty minutes apart. Not rated; contains profanity and sexual scenes. 93m. **DIR:** Ramin Niami. **CAST:** Sandra Bernhard, Robert John Burke, Bai Ling, Ornella Muti, Peter Stormare, Bulle Ogier. **1997**

SOMEWHERE IN THE NIGHT ★★★1/2 An early film from Oscar-winner Joe Mankiewicz that set the stage for sinister, confusing mystery melodramas in the pre-TV era. An amnesiac tries to uncover his identity and finds out he might possibly be a murderer. B&W; 110m. **DIR:** Joseph L. Mankiewicz. **CAST:** Lloyd Nolan, John Hodiak, Richard Conte, Nancy Guild, Sheldon Leonard, Josephine Hutchinson. **1946**

SOMEWHERE IN TIME ★★★ This gentle, old-fashioned film directed by Jeannot Szwarc celebrates tender passions with great style and atmosphere. The story by Richard Matheson does have a bit of a twist to it—instead of the lovers having to overcome such mundane obstacles as dissenting parents, terminal illness, or other tragedies, they must overcome time itself. Rated PG. 103m. **DIR:** Jeannot Szwarc. **CAST:** Christopher Reeve, Jane Seymour, Christopher Plummer, Bill Erwin, Teresa Wright. **1980 DVD**

SOMEWHERE, TOMORROW ★★★ *The Ghost and Mrs. Muir* for a teen audience, this film is about a girl, played by Sarah Jessica Parker, who learns how to deal with her father's death by falling in love with the ghost of a teenage boy. The result is good family entertainment. 91m. **DIR:** Robert Wiemer. **CAST:** Sarah Jessica Parker, Nancy Addison, Tom Shea, Rick Weber. **1986**

SOMMERSBY ★★★★ French director Daniel Vigne's brilliant *The Return of Martin Guerre* is transferred to the post–Civil War South for this involving tale of redemption. Richard Gere is fine as the returning soldier who resumes his relationship with willing wife Jodie Foster and the running of his plantation while former acquaintances marvel at his new sense of honor and responsibility. *Sommersby* retains many of the outstanding qualities of the original. Rated PG-13 for nudity and violence. 120m. **DIR:** Jon Amiel. **CAST:** Richard Gere, Jodie Foster, Bill Pullman, James Earl Jones, William Windom. **1993 DVD**

SON-IN-LAW ★★★ Credit irrepressible Pauly Shore with keeping this hayseed comedy afloat, despite tired sight gags milked to death years ago on television's *Green Acres*. He plays a spaced-out valley guy who transforms the repressed and conservative parents of girlfriend Carla Gugino. Although terminally silly, the film delivers a solid, family-oriented moral. Rated PG-13 for sexual innuendo. 96m. **DIR:** Steve Rash. **CAST:** Pauly Shore, Carla Gugino, Lane Smith. **1993 DVD**

SON OF ALI BABA ★★1/2 Aged Ali Baba is kidnapped by an evil caliph. His son comes to the rescue and wins a beautiful princess to boot. Juvenile, but fun. Victor Jory again plays a great villain. 85m. **DIR:** Kurt Neumann. **CAST:** Tony Curtis, Piper Laurie, Susan Cabot, William Reynolds, Hugh O'Brian, Victor Jory, Gerald Mohr. **1952**

SON OF BLOB (BEWARE! THE BLOB) ★★ Larry Hagman made this sequel to *The Blob* in his low period between *I Dream of Jeannie* and *Dallas*. It looks like he just got some friends together and decided to have some fun. The result is rather lame. Rated PG. 88m. **DIR:** Larry Hagman. **CAST:** Robert Walker Jr., Godfrey Cambridge, Carol Lynley, Larry Hagman, Cindy Williams, Shelley Berman, Gerrit Graham, Dick Van Patten. **1972**

SON OF CAPTAIN BLOOD 🦃 Poorly produced, amateurishly acted pirate programmer. 88m. **DIR:** Tulio Demichell. **CAST:** Sean Flynn, Alessandra Panaro, Jose Nieto, Ann Todd. **1962**

SON OF DRACULA (1943) ★★★1/2 Moody horror film features Lon Chaney's only turn as the Count, this time stalking a southern mansion as Alucard (spell it backward). Compelling, highly original Universal chiller boasts several eye-catching effects, dazzling camera work by George Robinson. B&W; 80m. **DIR:** Robert Siodmak. **CAST:** Lon Chaney Jr., Louise Allbritton, Robert Paige, Evelyn Ankers, Frank Craven, J. Edward Bromberg. **1943**

SON OF DRACULA (1974) 🦃 Addle-brained vampire musical-comedy. 90m. **DIR:** Freddie Francis. **CAST:** Harry Nilsson, Ringo Starr, Freddie Jones. **1974**

SON OF FLUBBER ★★★1/2 This Disney sequel to *The Absent-Minded Professor* once again stars Fred MacMurray as the inventor of Flubber. Two new discoveries are featured: "dry rain" and "flubbergas." While not as good as the original, it does have some moments reminiscent of the original. B&W; 100m. **DIR:** Robert Stevenson. **CAST:** Fred MacMurray, Nancy Olson, Keenan Wynn, Tommy Kirk, William Demarest, Paul Lynde. **1963**

SON OF FRANKENSTEIN ★★★★1/2 A strong cast (including Boris Karloff in his last appearance as the monster) makes this second sequel to *Frankenstein* memorable. This time, Frankenstein's son Wolf revives the dormant monster with the help of insane shepherd Ygor (Bela Lugosi, in his most underrated performance). Impressive, intelligent production. B&W; 99m. **DIR:** Rowland V. Lee. **CAST:** Boris Karloff, Basil Rathbone, Bela Lugosi, Lionel Atwill, Josephine Hutchinson. **1939**

SON OF FURY ★★★★ Based on Edison Marshall's novel *Benjamin Blake*, this follows the life of a young man who's been robbed of his title and fortune by his cruel uncle. He seeks his fortune on the high seas, finds romance with a beautiful island girl, and plans revenge against his dastardly uncle. Fast-paced, filled with intrigue and adventure. B&W; 99m. **DIR:** John Cromwell. **CAST:** Tyrone Power, Roddy McDowall, Gene Tierney, George Sanders, Frances Farmer, John Carradine. **1941**

SON OF GODZILLA ★★ Juvenile production has the cute offspring of one of Japan's biggest fire-breathing stars taking on all sorts of crazy-looking monsters, with a little help from dear old Dad. Good special effects and

miniature sets make this at least watchable, but the story is just too goofy for its own good. Recommended viewing age: 2 and under. Rated PG. 86m. **DIR:** Jun Fukuda. **CAST:** Tadao Takashima, Kenji Sahara. **1969**

SON OF KONG, THE ★★★1/2 To cash in on the phenomenal success of *King Kong*, the producers hastily rushed this sequel into production using virtually the same cast and crew. Carl Denham (Robert Armstrong) returns to Skull Island only to find King Kong's easygoing son trapped in a pool of quicksand. Denham saves the twelve-foot albino gorilla, who becomes his protector. B&W; 70m. **DIR:** Ernest B. Schoedsack. **CAST:** Robert Armstrong, Helen Mack, Victor Wong, John Marston, Frank Reicher. **1933**

SON OF LASSIE ★★1/2 Lassie's son, Laddie, follows in his parent's pawprints by smuggling himself aboard master Peter Lawford's bomber on a mission over enemy territory. Mixture of sentiment and war action doesn't really jell. 100m. **DIR:** S. Sylvan Simon. **CAST:** Peter Lawford, Donald Crisp, June Lockhart, Nigel Bruce, Leon Ames, Nils Asther, Donald Curtis. **1945**

SON OF MONTE CRISTO, THE ★★★ True to established swashbuckler form, masked avenging hero Louis Hayward crosses wits, then swords, with would-be dictator George Sanders. Honoring tradition, he then frees imprisoned fair lady Joan Bennett from the villain's clutches. B&W; 102m. **DIR:** Rowland V. Lee. **CAST:** Louis Hayward, Joan Bennett, George Sanders, Florence Bates, Montagu Love, Ian Wolfe, Clayton Moore, Ralph Byrd. **1941**

SON OF PALEFACE ★★★1/2 Bob Hope is in top shape as he matches wits with smooth villain DouglasDumbrille and consistently loses, only to be aided by guntotin' Jane Russell and government agent Roy Rogers. 95m. **DIR:** Frank Tashlin. **CAST:** Bob Hope, Jane Russell, Roy Rogers, Douglass Dumbrille, Bill Williams, Harry Von Zell, Iron Eyes Cody. **1952**

SON OF THE MORNING STAR ★★★★1/2 Impressively mounted, acted, and directed TV miniseries was based on the bestseller by Evan S. Connell *(Mr. Bridge, Mrs. Bridge)* and chronicles the life and times of Gen. George Armstrong Custer (Gary Cole), culminating in the Battle of the Little Bighorn. Outstanding. 183m. **DIR:** Mike Robe. **CAST:** Gary Cole, Rosanna Arquette, Dean Stockwell, Rodney A. Grant, David Strathairn, Terry O'Quinn. **1990**

SON OF THE PINK PANTHER ★★ Writer-director Blake Edwards should quit while he's behind. Despite the usually funny Roberto Benigni (as Inspector Clouseau's illegitimate son), this leaden comedy loses its appeal after Bobby McFerrin's quirky rendition of Henry Mancini's "Pink Panther Theme." Rated PG for comic violence. 93m. **DIR:** Blake Edwards. **CAST:** Roberto Benigni, Herbert Lom, Claudia Cardinale, Jennifer Edwards, Robert Davi, Burt Kwouk. **1993**

SON OF THE SHEIK ★★1/2 This sequel to the 1921 adventure, *The Sheik*, proved to be bedroom-eyed, ex-gardener Rudolph Valentino's final film. It was released to coincide with his funeral and was an immediate hit. In the title role, the legendary Valentino acquitted himself with confidence and flair, foiling his enemies and winning the heart of nomadic dancer Vilma Banky. Silent. B&W; 62m. **DIR:** George Fitzmaurice. **CAST:** Rudolph Valentino, Vilma Banky, Bull Montana, Montagu Love, George Fawcett, Karl Dane. **1926 DVD**

SONATINE ★★★★ The survivors of a *yakuza* war hide out, assuming the worst is over. It isn't. An intriguing, stylish, well-acted drama. In Japanese with English subtitles. Rated R for violence and profanity. 94m. **DIR:** Takeshi Kitano. **CAST:** Takeshi Kitano, Aya Kikumai, Tetsu Watanabe, Masanobu Katsumura. **1993**

SONG IS BORN, A ★★ A remake of the classic comedy *Ball of Fire*, with more music and less personality. Danny Kaye heads a team of professors studying the origin of jazz. The music is sharp but the story is flat. 115m. **DIR:** Howard Hawks. **CAST:** Danny Kaye, Virginia Mayo, Steve Cochran, Benny Goodman, Louis Armstrong, Tommy Dorsey, Lionel Hampton, Hugh Herbert, Felix Bressart. **1948**

SONG OF BERNADETTE, THE ★★★★ Four Oscars, including one to Jennifer Jones for best actress, went to this beautifully filmed story of the simple nineteenth-century French peasant girl, Bernadette Soubirous, who saw a vision of the Virgin Mary in the town of Lourdes. B&W; 156m. **DIR:** Henry King. **CAST:** Jennifer Jones, Charles Bickford, William Eythe, Vincent Price, Lee J. Cobb, Gladys Cooper, Anne Revere. **1943**

SONG OF FREEDOM ★★★ A black laborer shucks his newfound fame as a singer when he discovers the medallion he has worn since babyhood entitles him to the throne of an African island. The singer and his wife return to their roots as potentates of the primitive island and find jealousy and superstition working against them. The decision to live in both worlds and "upgrade" the primitive quality of his native island smacks of colonialism and works against the positive points of the movie. Still a very interesting effort and one of Paul Robeson's favorite roles. B&W; 77m. **DIR:** J. Elder Wills. **CAST:** Paul Robeson, Elisabeth Welch, Esme Percy, Robert Adams, James Solomon, Ronald Simpson. **1936 DVD**

SONG OF LOVE ★★1/2 When the writers and producers acknowledge up front that they have taken "certain liberties," you can throw away all thoughts of a factual story of the marriage of Clara Wieck (Katharine Hepburn) to Robert Schumann (Paul Henreid) and their close friendship with young Johannes Brahms (Robert Walker). Close your eyes and listen to the piano interludes, dubbed, uncredited, by Arthur Rubinstein. B&W; 119m. **DIR:** Clarence Brown. **CAST:** Katharine Hepburn, Paul Henreid, Robert Walker, Henry Daniell, Henry Stephenson, Leo G. Carroll. **1947**

SONG OF NEVADA ★★1/2 Roy, Dale, and the boys at the ranch come to the aid of an innocent girl who has become prey of a crook and his henchmen. This tuneful, hard-riding horse opera is chock-full of former cowboys and familiar faces. It's typical of Roy's mid-1940s movies. B&W; 75m. **DIR:** Joseph Kane. **CAST:** Roy Rogers, Dale Evans, Mary Lee, Bob Nolan and the Sons of the Pioneers, Lloyd Corrigan, Thurston Hall, John Eldredge, Forrest Taylor, George Meeker, LeRoy Mason, Kenne Duncan. **1944**

SONG OF NORWAY If he were not dead, Norwegian composer Edvard Grieg would expire upon seeing this insult to his life and career. Rated G. 142m. **DIR:** Andrew L. Stone. **CAST:** Florence Henderson, Torval Maurstad, Edward G. Robinson, Robert Morley. **1970**

SONG OF TEXAS ★★1/2 Most of the action comes at the end of this songfest as Roy competes in a chuckwagon race in order to win back yet another stolen ranch. Roy and the boys squeeze ten songs into this programmer. B&W; 69m. **DIR:** Joseph Kane. **CAST:** Roy Rogers, Sheila Ryan, Barton MacLane, Harry Shannon, Pat Brady, Arline Judge, Eve March, Hal Taliaferro, Bob Nolan and the Sons of the Pioneers, Tom London. **1943**

SONG OF THE EXILE ★★★★ A recent graduate of a British university returns home to Hong Kong where she is reunited with her mother and a battle of wills begins. One of the most beautiful and astonishing motion pictures of the new Asian cinema, this is director Ann Hui's finest achievement to date. In Mandarin and Japanese with English subtitles. Not rated. 100m. **DIR:** Ann Hui. **CAST:** Shwu Sen Chang, Maggie Cheung. **1990**

SONG OF THE ISLANDS ★★ A Hawaiian cattle baron feuds with a planter over land while his son romances the planter's daughter. Everyone quarrels, but love wins. En route, Betty Grable sings and dances in the standard grass skirt. Mainly a slick travelogue with singing and dancing. 75m. **DIR:** Walter Lang. **CAST:** Betty Grable, Victor Mature, Jack Oakie, Thomas Mitchell. **1942**

SONG OF THE THIN MAN ★★★1/2 Sixth and final entry in the series, a cut above the previous one because of its involvement in jazz music circles. Nick and Nora Charles (William Powell and Myrna Loy) match wits with a murderer this time out, and the setting helps their dialogue regain its crisp sparkle. All in all, a worthy effort with which to conclude things. B&W; 86m. **DIR:** Edward Buzzell. **CAST:** William Powell, Myrna Loy, Keenan Wynn, Dean Stockwell, Gloria Grahame, Patricia Morison. **1947**

SONG REMAINS THE SAME, THE ★★★ If any band is truly responsible for the genre of "heavy-metal" music, it is Led Zeppelin. Although this movie is a must for Zeppelin fans, the untrained ear may find numbers such as the twenty-three-minute version of "Dazed and Confused" a bit tedious. Rated PG. 136m. **DIR:** Peter Clifton, Joe Massot. **CAST:** Led Zeppelin, Peter Grant. **1976**

SONG SPINNER ★★★★ Enchanting fable about a small, mythical kingdom called Shandrilan, where the king has outlawed noise. To this mythical kingdom comes Zantalalia, a mysterious woman who gives ten year old Aurora a "song-spinner," which makes a beautiful noise known as music. Once exposed to the wonderful music, Aurora does her best to dodge noise police and get to the king so she can convince him to change his tune. This made-for-cable fable is great family entertainment. Rated G. 95m. **DIR:** Randy Bradshaw. **CAST:** Patti LuPone, John Neville, Meredith Henderson. **1995**

SONG TO REMEMBER, A ★★★ The music is superb, but the plot of this Chopin biography is as frail as the composer's health is purported to have been. Cornel Wilde received an Oscar nomination as the ill-fated tubercular Chopin, and Merle Oberon is resolute but vulnerable in the role of his lover, French female novelist George Sand. 113m. **DIR:** Charles Vidor. **CAST:** Cornel Wilde, Merle Oberon, Paul Muni, George Coulouris, Nina Foch, Sig Arno. **1945**

SONG WITHOUT END ★★★ An Academy Award–winning score manages to save this bio-pic of composer Franz Lizst. As Lizst, Dirk Bogarde is not in his element, but perseveres. 141m. **DIR:** Charles Vidor, George Cukor. **CAST:** Dirk Bogarde, Capucine, Genevieve Page, Patricia Morison, Martita Hunt. **1960**

•SONGCATCHER ★★★★ Song as a powerful cultural tradition is at the heart of this engaging little drama, which stars Janet McTeer as a stiffly formal music scholar who, at the beginning of the twentieth century, flees big-city academia to visit her sister in a struggling rural school in Appalachia. Our heroine, forever laboring in the shadow of male colleagues, discovers a treasure trove of ancient Scot and Irish ballads, all handed down from one generation to the next. Hoping to establish her reputation beyond all doubt, McTeer sets about recording her new neighbors on wax cylinders . . . but then begins to wonder if she might be exploiting these trusting people. The script suffers from contemporary feminism, but on the whole this is a beautifully realized character study. Rated PG-13 for sensuality. 105m. **DIR:** Maggie Greenwald. **CAST:** Janet McTeer, Aidan Quinn, Pat Carroll, Jane Adams, Greg Cook, Emmy Rossum, Taj Mahal. **1999 DVD**

SONGWRITER ★★★★ Wonderfully wacky and entertaining wish-fulfillment by top country stars Willie Nelson and Kris Kristofferson, who play—what else?—top country stars who take on the recording industry and win. A delight. Rated R for profanity, nudity, and brief violence. 100m. **DIR:** Alan Rudolph. **CAST:** Willie Nelson, Kris Kristofferson, Lesley Ann Warren, Melinda Dillon, Rip Torn. **1984**

SONNY AND JED A naive young girl seeks adventure by following a noted outlaw hunted by a determined lawman. This Western approach to the Bonnie and Clyde story doesn't work. An irritating performance by Tomas Milian. Even an effective musical score by the master Ennio Morricone can't help this film. Rated PG. 85m. **DIR:** Sergio Corbucci. **CAST:** Tomas Milian, Susan George, Telly Savalas, Eduardo Fajardo, Rosanna Yanni. **1973**

SONNY BOY ★★1/2 If you've ever wanted to see David Carradine in drag, you're in luck. As Pearl, he's the mother of a monstrous family that terrorizes a small desert town. You decide whether this one is funny on purpose or just bad: either way, it's pretty bizarre. Rated R for violence and gore. 98m. **DIR:** Robert Martin Carroll. **CAST:** David Carradine, Paul Smith, Brad Dourif, Sidney Lassick. **1987**

SONS OF KATIE ELDER, THE ★★★ John Wayne stars in this entertaining film about four brothers reunited after the death of their mother and forced to fight to get back their land. Although this Western rarely goes beyond the predictable, there's plenty of action and roughhouse comedy. 122m. **DIR:** Henry Hathaway. **CAST:** John Wayne, Dean Martin, Earl Holliman, Michael Anderson Jr., James Gregory, George Kennedy, Martha Hyer, Jeremy Slate, Paul Fix. **1965 DVD**

SONS OF THE DESERT ★★★★★ Stan Laurel and Oliver Hardy scheme to get away from their wives and attend a lodge convention in Chicago. After persuading the wives that Ollie needs to sail to Honolulu for his health, they go to Chicago. The boat sinks on the way

back from Hawaii, and the boys end up having to explain how they got home a day earlier than the other survivors (they ship-hiked). B&W; 69m. **DIR:** William A. Seiter. **CAST:** Stan Laurel, Oliver Hardy, Charlie Chase. **1933**

SONS OF THE PIONEERS ★★★1/2 Roy Rogers plays a scientist who returns to his hometown after numerous ranches have been sabotaged. Using his scientific savvy and an occasional yodel, he saves the day. B&W; 53m. **DIR:** Joseph Kane. **CAST:** Roy Rogers, George "Gabby" Hayes, Maris Wrixon, Forrest Taylor, Pat Brady. **1942**

SONS OF THE SEA ★★1/2 Made and released in Great Britain as World War II began, this topical suspense-thriller drama involves the son of a naval commander with eyes-only clearance who unknowingly aids an enemy spy. Good show, but far better things were to come as the war progressed and England geared up its propaganda machine. B&W; 83m. **DIR:** Maurice Elvey. **CAST:** Leslie Banks, Kay Walsh, Mackenzie Ward, Cecil Parker. **1939**

SONS OF TRINITY, THE ★★ The offspring of the infamous Italian duo find themselves in hot water when they become the sheriff and deputy of a small town. More of the same with a different cast. Rated PG for adult situations, language, and violence. 90m. **DIR:** E. B. Clucher. **CAST:** Heath Kizzier, Keith Neubert, Yvonne De Bark, Ronald Nitschke. **1995**

SOONER OR LATER ★★ This made-for-TV romance may fascinate preteens. A 13-year-old girl (Denise Miller) sets her sights on a 17-year-old rock guitarist (Rex Smith). She pretends to be older and gets caught up in her lies. 100m. **DIR:** Bruce Hart. **CAST:** Denise Miller, Rex Smith, Morey Amsterdam, Judd Hirsch, Lynn Redgrave, Barbara Feldon. **1978**

SOPHIA LOREN: HER OWN STORY ★★1/2 Sophia Loren portrays herself in this television drama that chronicles her life from obscurity to international stardom. At times, it appears more like a self-parody. Interesting, but not compelling enough to justify its extreme length. 150m. **DIR:** Mel Stuart. **CAST:** Sophia Loren, John Gavin, Rip Torn. **1980**

SOPHIE'S CHOICE ★★★★★ A young, inexperienced southern writer named Stingo (Peter MacNicol) learns about love, life, and death in this absorbing, wonderfully acted, and heartbreaking movie. One summer, while observing the affair between Sophie (Meryl Streep), a victim of a concentration camp, and Nathan (Kevin Kline), a charming, but sometimes explosive biologist, Stingo falls in love with Sophie, a woman with deep, dark secrets. Rated R. 157m. **DIR:** Alan J. Pakula. **CAST:** Meryl Streep, Kevin Kline, Peter MacNicol. **1982 DVD**

SOPHISTICATED GENTS, THE ★★★1/2 Arguably one of the best TV movies ever made, this ensemble drama was based by Melvin Van Peebles on John A. Williams's book, *The Junior Bachelor Society*. A powerful production. 200m. **DIR:** Harry Falk. **CAST:** Bernie Casey, Rosey Grier, Robert Hooks, Ron O'Neal, Thalmus Rasulala, Raymond St. Jacques, Melvin Van Peebles, Dick Anthony Williams, Paul Winfield, Denise Nicholas. **1981**

SOPRANOS, THE (TV SERIES) ★★★★ Writer David Chase's fascinating series about the "folks next door" who just happen to be in the business of crime. Patriarch Tony Soprano, a New Jersey mobster, uses his waste-removal business as a cover for his illegal activities. Superbly acted and written, this groundbreaking cable series is an important addition to the gangster canon. Some viewers may think it too brutal and foul-mouthed at times or find the dark humor incongruous, yet it is a work of originality and startling creativity. Made for TV; contains profanity, violence, nudity, sex and drug use. 60m. **DIR:** Daniel Attias, Martin Bruestle. **CAST:** James Gandolfini, Lorraine Bracco, Edie Falco, Michael Imperioli, Nancy Marchand, Steve Van Zandt, Jamie Lynn Sigler, Tony Sirico, Vincent Pastore, Robert Iler, Dominic Chianese, Aida Turturro. **1999 DVD**

SORCERER ★★★★ Remake of Henri Couzot's classic, *Wages of Fear*, is a cult favorite. An American criminal flees to Latin America to escape prosecution but finds life there a living hell. A superb score enhances this atmospheric thriller. Rated R for violence and profanity. 122m. **DIR:** William Friedkin. **CAST:** Roy Scheider, Bruno Cremer, Francisco Rabal, Souad Amidou, Ramon Bieri. **1977 DVD**

SORCERESS, THE (1988) ★★★1/2 Visually rich, enthralling tale set in a small village in medieval France about a priest on a search for those still practicing pagan rituals. Unfortunately, the English-dubbed version kills some of the film's impact. 98m. **DIR:** Suzanne Schiffman. **CAST:** Tcheky Karyo, Christine Boisson, Jean Carmet. **1988**

SORCERESS (1994) ★★ Low-budget thriller is saved by novel plot twists. Julie Strain plays the wife of an up-and-coming executive who gets rid of her husband's competition. She makes a fatal mistake when she attempts to kill his main rival, not realizing the man's wife is a witch. It's nice to see a movie where people get exactly what they deserve. Edited and unedited versions available; both contain adult situations. 93m. **DIR:** Jim Wynorski. **CAST:** Julie Strain, Linda Blair, Edward Albert, Larry Poindexter. **1994 DVD**

SORE LOSERS ★★★ Tongue-in-cheek horror-comedy about an alien who resembles a 1950s greaser who comes to Earth to kill hippies. The stars are musicians from various psychobilly bands. Definitely not for all tastes, but better than average for this kind of no-budget cult movie. Not rated; contains gore, violence, nudity, and profanity. 90m. **DIR:** John Michael McCathy. **CAST:** Jack Oblilvian, Kerine Elkins, Mike Maker, Dave Friedman. **1997 DVD**

SORORITY BABES IN THE SLIMEBALL BOWL-O-RAMA 🦃 Two sorority pledges find themselves trapped in a bowling alley from hell when they are forced to steal a trophy as part of their pledge in this supposed horror-comedy. Rated R for violence, profanity, and nudity. 78m. **DIR:** David DeCoteau. **CAST:** Linnea Quigley, Robin Rochelle, Brinke Stevens. **1987 DVD**

•SORORITY BOYS 🦃 Three college morons get kicked out of their fraternity and go into drag to join a sorority noted for its homely membership. To enjoy this imbecilic farce you'd have to be as clueless as the characters in the film who don't wise up to the "girls." Rated R for profanity, nudity, and crude sexual humor. 94m. **DIR:** M. Wallace Wolodarsky. **CAST:** Barry Watson, Harland Williams, Michael Rosenbaum, Melissa Sagemiller, Heather Matarazzo. **2002**

SORORITY GIRL ★★ Susan Cabot is the bad girl who makes life difficult for new sorority pledge Barboura Morris. The ads promised spankings and even a hint of lesbianism, but the movie itself is tame enough for 1950s TV. B&W; 60m. **DIR:** Roger Corman. **CAST:** Susan Cabot, Dick Miller, Barboura Morris, June Kenney. **1957**

SORORITY GIRLS AND THE CREATURE FROM HELL 🦃 No relation to David DeCoteau's *Sorority Babes* series, this flick doesn't even have those films' sleazy charm. Not rated; contains violence and adult situations. 90m. **DIR:** John McBrearty. **CAST:** Deborah Dutch, Stacy Lynn. **1990**

SORORITY HOUSE MASSACRE 🦃 Features a vengeful killer slashing the sexy residents of a sorority house. Rated R for profanity, nudity, and violence. 74m. **DIR:** Carol Frank. **CAST:** Angela O'Neill, Wendy Martel. **1986**

SORORITY HOUSE MASSACRE 2 🦃 Lame hack-and-slash thriller about busty babes fighting off a bloodthirsty killer while in various states of undress. Typical shock horror, nearly plotless and badly acted. Not rated; contains nudity, profanity, and graphic violence. 80m. **DIR:** Jim Wynorski. **CAST:** Robin Harris, Melissa Moore. **1992**

SORORITY HOUSE PARTY 🦃 Lamebrained trash about a rock star who tries to escape inept hit men with the help of a pair of sorority girls. Not rated; contains nudity and sexual scenes. 95m. **DIR:** David Michael Latt. **CAST:** Attila, April Lerman, Kim Little, Mark Stulce. **1994**

SORRENTO BEACH ★★★★ In this involving, well-acted drama, one of three sisters is now a successful writer whose latest bestseller exposes family secrets. Rated R for language. 112m. **DIR:** Richard Franklin. **CAST:** Caroline Goodall, Joan Plowright, Tara Morice, Caroline Gillmer. **1995**

SORROW AND THE PITY, THE ★★★★★ Probably the most revealing work in any medium on the subject of collaboration in World War II. Marcel Ophuls carefully and intimately examines the residents of a French town that spent the war partly under Vichy rule and partly under the Nazis. Despite its great length, there is not a single wasted moment in this perfectly realized documentary. 270m. **DIR:** Marcel Ophuls. **1970**

SORROWFUL JONES ★★★ Bob Hope's first semiserious film, this is a remake of the 1934 Shirley Temple hit, *Little Miss Marker*. Bob, as a bookie, gets tangled up with nightclub singer Lucille Ball and an assortment of gangsters while baby-sitting a gambler's baby daughter. A good mix of wisecracks, fast action, and sentiment. B&W; 88m. **DIR:** Sidney Lanfield. **CAST:** Bob Hope, Lucille Ball, Mary Jane Saunders, Thomas Gomez, William Demarest, Bruce Cabot. **1949**

SORROWS OF SATAN, THE ★★★ Lavish surreal drama about a struggling literary critic whose engagement to an impoverished writer becomes complicated by Satan in the form of a cunning wealthy gentleman. Visually impressive. B&W; 90m. **DIR:** D. W. Griffith. **CAST:** Adolphe Menjou, Carol Dempster, Ricardo Cortez, Lya de Putti. **1926**

SORRY, WRONG NUMBER (1948) ★★★★ Slick cinema adaptation, by the author herself, of Lucille Fletcher's famed radio drama. Barbara Stanwyck is superb—and received an Oscar nomination—as an invalid who, due to those "crossed wires" so beloved in fiction, overhears two men plotting the murder of a woman. Gradually Stanwyck realizes that she is the target. B&W; 89m. **DIR:** Anatole Litvak. **CAST:** Barbara Stanwyck, Burt Lancaster, Wendell Corey, Ed Begley Sr., Ann Richards. **1948**

SORRY, WRONG NUMBER (1989) ★★ A made-for-TV update of the suspenseful story of an invalid who learns that her husband plans to have her killed. But it doesn't hold a candle to the Barbara Stanwyck version. Loni Anderson looks better than she acts, and that's not all bad in this case. 100m. **DIR:** Tony Wharmby. **CAST:** Loni Anderson, Patrick Macnee, Carl Weintraub, Hal Holbrook. **1989**

SOS COAST GUARD ★★1/2 All-American Coast Guard stalwart Terry Kent (Ralph Byrd) has his hands full as he battles crazed inventor Boroff (Bela Lugosi). There's so much going on in this serial that it's best just to forget about the story line and sit back and enjoy the action. B&W; 12 chapters. **DIR:** William Witney, Alan James. **CAST:** Ralph Byrd, Bela Lugosi. **1937 DVD**

S.O.S. TITANIC ★★★ The "unsinkable" once again goes to her watery grave in this made-for-television docudrama compounded of fiction and fact. 105m. **DIR:** William Hale. **CAST:** David Janssen, Cloris Leachman, Susan Saint James, David Warner. **1979 DVD**

SOTTO SOTTO ★★★ A sexy, raucous, hilarious farce about a woman who finds herself romantically drawn to her best friend's wife. This leads to comically disastrous results. Good entertainment, especially for hard-core fans of Lina Wertmuller. In Italian with English subtitles. 104m. **DIR:** Lina Wertmuller. **CAST:** Enrico Montesano, Veronica Lario. **1984**

SOUL FOOD ★★★1/2 This little film deserves your attention. It's a genuinely heartwarming study of the importance of tradition even during moments of strife and adversity. Sunday dinner is a noisy, tempestuous gathering in the massive old home of "Big Mama" Mother Joe, but in the eyes of a young grandson, they're all family. When it becomes clear that Big Mama has been ignoring her diabetes, everything crumbles . . . and putting matters right falls to one very scared, but nonetheless determined, little boy. Rated R for profanity, sexual content, and brief violence. 114m. **DIR:** George Tillman Jr. **CAST:** Vanessa L. Williams, Vivica A. Fox, Nia Long, Michael Beach, Mekhi Phifer, Brandon Hammon, Irma P. Hall. **1997 DVD**

SOUL HUSTLER 🦃 A drug-using wanderer swindles gullible hicks. Execrable. Rated PG for strong language. 81m. **DIR:** Burt Topper. **CAST:** Fabian, Nai Bonet, Tony Russell. **1986**

SOUL MAN ★★★ Los Angeles preppie Mark Watson (C. Thomas Howell) masquerades as a needy black to gain entrance to Harvard Law School. Director Steve Miner keeps things moving so fast one doesn't have time to consider how silly it all is. Rated PG-13 for profanity, suggested sex, and violence. 101m. **DIR:** Steve Miner. **CAST:** C. Thomas Howell, Rae Dawn Chong, James Earl Jones, Arye Gross, James B. Sikking, Leslie Nielsen. **1986 DVD**

SOUL OF THE GAME ★★★★ Strong account of the events that changed America's favorite pastime after World War II. The story involves three superstars, each

superbly portrayed: Satchel Paige, who single-handedly turned every personal appearance into a major event; the doomed Josh Gibson; and dignified, young Jackie Robinson, the man to break the color barrier. Great drama. Rated PG-13 for profanity and brief nudity. 95m. **DIR:** Kevin Rodney Sullivan. **CAST:** Delroy Lindo, Mykelti Williamson, Blair Underwood, Edward Herrmann, R. Lee Ermey, Salli Richardson, Gina Ravera. **1996 DVD**

•SOUL SURVIVORS ★★ College student Melissa Sagemiller has strange supernatural experiences after surviving an auto accident in which her boyfriend is killed. Director Stephen Carpenter trots out every horror-flick cliché in the book, to little effect. Even the "surprise" ending is a cop-out, and will only surprise those who aren't paying attention. Rated PG-13 for horror violence and sexual scenes. 84m. **DIR:** Stephen Carpenter. **CAST:** Melissa Sagemiller, Casey Affleck, Wes Bentley, Eliza Dushku, Luke Wilson. **2001 DVD**

SOUL VENGEANCE (WELCOME HOME BROTHER CHARLES) ★★★ Wildly over-the-top blaxploitation film about an ex-con seeking revenge on the men who sent him to prison. A must-see for sheer weirdness, including a strangulation scene we can't describe here. Rated R for nudity, sex, profanity, and strong violence. 91m. **DIR:** Jamaa Fanaka. **CAST:** Marlo Monte, Reatha Grey. **1975**

SOULER OPPOSITE, THE ★★ A low-rent riff on *Seinfeld* that concerns a condescending would-be stand-up comic who can't score with women... and, after a scant few moments in his company, you'll understand why. Dull, dull, dull. Rated R for profanity and sexual candor. 103m. **DIR:** Bill Kamelson. **CAST:** Christopher Meloni, Janel Moloney, Timothy Busfield. **1998 DVD**

•SOULKEEPER ★★★ Two small-time thieves find themselves working for a man who wants them to steal a rare artifact. Little do they know that this artifact is capable of releasing a demon with plans to conquer the world. Surprisingly amusing, cheapo horror film with a smart-aleck script that surpasses its low-budget special effects and sometimes slow direction. Rated R for horror violence, language, and nudity. 106m. **DIR:** Darin James Ferriola. **CAST:** Rodney Rowland, Kevin Patrick Walls, Robert Davi, Brad Dourif, Karen Black, Deborah Gibson, Tom "Tiny" Lister Jr. **2001 DVD**

SOUND AND FURY ★★★1/2 Documentarian Josh Aronson explores an extended family's reaction to a revolutionary surgical procedure that enables the deaf to hear. Hearing family members see the operation as a miracle, while the deaf family members see it as a threat to their own identity. Aronson's approach gives both sides their due, and the result is provocative and fascinating. Not rated; suitable for all audiences. 80m. **DIR:** Josh Aronson. **2000 DVD**

SOUND AND THE SILENCE,THE ★★★★ Superior miniseries explores the multifaceted genius of Alexander Graham Bell. Known as the inventor of the telephone, his life story has him dabbling in medicine, aeronautics, and more. John Bach plays Bell as self-absorbed and obsessive but ultimately successful at his many ventures. Exterior shots are especially breathtaking. Not rated; contains no objectionable material. 184m. **DIR:** John Kent Harrison. **CAST:** John Bach, Ian Bannen, Elizabeth Quinn, Vanessa Vaughan, Brenda Fricker. **1992**

SOUND OF MUSIC, THE ★★★★1/2 Winner of the Academy Award for best picture, this musical has it all: comedy, romance, suspense. Julie Andrews plays the spunky Maria, who doesn't fit in at the convent. When she is sent to live with a large family as their governess, she falls in love with and marries her handsome boss, Baron Von Trapp (Christopher Plummer). Problems arise when the Nazi invasion of Austria forces the family to flee. 172m. **DIR:** Robert Wise. **CAST:** Julie Andrews, Christopher Plummer, Eleanor Parker. **1965**

SOUNDER ★★★★★ Beautifully made film detailing the struggle of a black sharecropper and his family. Director Martin Ritt gets outstanding performances from Cicely Tyson and Paul Winfield. When her husband is sent to jail, Tyson must raise her family and run the farm by herself while trying to get the eldest son an education. A truly moving and thought-provoking film. Don't miss this one. Rated G. 105m. **DIR:** Martin Ritt. **CAST:** Cicely Tyson, Paul Winfield, Kevin Hooks, Carmen Mathews, Taj Mahal, James Best, Janet MacLachlan. **1972**

SOUNDSTAGE: BLUES SUMMIT IN CHICAGO ★★★★ Homage is paid to blues great Muddy Waters in this music-packed documentary. Willie Dixon, Koko Taylor, Dr. John, Mike Bloomfield, Junior Wells, Johnny Winter, Nick Gravenites, and Buddy Miles are among the students who sit in with the master of Chicago blues, who beams with pleasure at the high quality of the music. Good interview footage, too. Made for TV. 58m. **DIR:** Dave Erdman. **1974**

SOUP FOR ONE ★★★ Marcia Strassman (formerly the wife on *Welcome Back Kotter*) stars as the dream girl to an often disappointed lover. Although there are a few slow-moving parts, it is a generally enjoyable comedy. Rated R for sexual themes. 87m. **DIR:** Jonathan Kaufer. **CAST:** Saul Rubinek, Marcia Strassman, Teddy Pendergrass. **1982**

SOURCE, THE ★★★★ This fascinating documentary, from filmmaker Chuck Workman (famed for his Academy Award–clip retrospectives), traces the writers' revolution during the white-bread 1950s, and the impact this movement was to have on the social unrest of the 1960s. Workman's diary of the Beat Generation is seen mostly through the eyes, commentary, and work of the movement's Unholy Trinity: Jack Kerouac, Allen Ginsberg, and William Burroughs. Watching them should forever swear viewers off mind-altering substances; these guys clearly smoked, swallowed, sniffed, and shot every drug known to humanity. But what sounds like gibberish and drug-hazed ramblings during period footage—which admittedly captures these seminal figures in far less than their best light—becomes something entirely different when interpreted by guest artists such as John Turturro and Johnny Depp. Not rated; contains considerable profanity and unapologetic depictions of drug use. 90m. **DIR:** Chuck Workman. **CAST:** Johnny Depp, Dennis Hopper, John Turturro. **1999 DVD**

SOURDOUGH ★★1/2 Marvelously picturesque but dull family fare about the daily activities of a grizzled mountain man—works best as a travelogue depicting the wonders of the Northwestern wilderness. Rated G.

92m. **DIR:** Martin J. Spinelli. **CAST:** Gil Perry, Charles Brock, Slim Carlson, Carl Clark. **1975**

SOUTH BEACH 🦃 Has-been, ex–football players Gary Busey and Fred Williamson are wanna-be Miami private eyes, who become embroiled with mystery-woman Vanity. This slice of Miami could have used more vice. Rated R for violence and adult situations. 93m. **DIR:** Fred Williamson. **CAST:** Fred Williamson, Peter Fonda, Gary Busey, Vanity, Robert Forster. **1992**

SOUTH BEACH ACADEMY ★★ If he loses a bet with a competitor, the owner of South Beach Academy—a resort for half-naked party animals—will lose his business. A pair of brothers makes sure that doesn't happen. Simply an excuse to put as many naked women on film as possible. Rated R for profanity, nudity, and sexual situations. 91m. **DIR:** Joe Esposito. **CAST:** Corey Feldman, Al Lewis, James Hong, Keith Coulouris, Elizabeth Kaitan. **1995**

SOUTH CENTRAL ★★★★ Tough, uncompromising urban drama about a father's attempts to keep his son out of gangs hits home and hits hard. Explosive action coupled with hard-as-nails drama make this an exceptional film. Rated R for violence, language, and adult situations. 99m. **DIR:** Stephen Anderson. **CAST:** Glenn Plummer, Carl Lumbly, Byron Keith Minns, LaRita Shelby, Kevin Best. **1992 DVD**

•SOUTH OF HEAVEN, WEST OF HELL ★★★ Country-singer-turned-actor Dwight Yoakam steps behind the camera as director-cowriter of this traditional Western about a U.S. marshal trying to escape his violent past. When his old gang terrorizes his small Arizona town, Marshal Valentine Casey is forced to confront his past in order to reconcile his present. Yoakam isn't stoic enough to carry the load, so he wisely surrounds himself with strong actors who make him look good. Vaughn is especially nasty as the gang's brutal leader. Rated R for adult situations, language, nudity, and violence. 105m. **DIR:** Dwight Yoakam. **CAST:** Dwight Yoakam, Vince Vaughn, Bridget Fonda, Billy Bob Thornton, Peter Fonda, Paul Reubens, Bud Cort. **2000 DVD**

SOUTH OF PAGO PAGO ★★ A good title is wasted on this so-so action tale of pirates heisting native-harvested pearls and being pursued and engaged by the locals. Typical South Sea fare. B&W; 98m. **DIR:** Alfred E. Green. **CAST:** Victor McLaglen, Jon Hall, Frances Farmer, Olympe Bradna, Gene Lockhart. **1940**

SOUTH OF RENO ★★★ This surreal psychodrama offers a compelling look at one man's struggle with desperation in a broiling Nevada backroads community. When he learns that his wife is carrying on an extramarital affair, he goes over the edge. Rated R; contains nudity, profanity, and violence. 98m. **DIR:** Mark Rezyka. **CAST:** Jeff Osterhage, Lisa Blount, Lewis Van Bergen, Joe Phelan. **1987**

SOUTH OF ST. LOUIS ★★★★ Joel McCrea, Zachary Scott, and Douglas Kennedy seek revenge for the burning of their respective spreads. Dorothy Malone and Alexis Smith provide the love interest. If you like dusty, exciting ranch epics, this film should be high on your list. 88m. **DIR:** Ray Enright. **CAST:** Joel McCrea, Zachary Scott, Douglas Kennedy, Dorothy Malone, Alexis Smith. **1949**

SOUTH OF THE BORDER ★★1/2 Gene and Smiley mosey on down to Mexico as government operatives in order to quell a rebellion engineered by foreign powers who wish to control that country's oil resources. This patriotic film contains some good action scenes. B&W; 71m. **DIR:** George Sherman. **CAST:** Gene Autry, Smiley Burnette, Duncan Renaldo, June Storey. **1939**

SOUTH PACIFIC (1958) ★★★ This extremely long film, adapted from the famous Broadway play about sailors during World War II, seems dated and is slow-going for the most part. Fans of Rodgers and Hammerstein will no doubt appreciate this one more than others. 150m. **DIR:** Joshua Logan. **CAST:** Mitzi Gaynor, Rossano Brazzi, Ray Walston, John Kerr. **1958 DVD**

•SOUTH PACIFIC (2001) ★★★ The classic Richard Rodgers/Oscar Hammerstein stage musical leaps to the screen for the second time, and the results are better than expected. Glenn Close makes a wonderful Nelly Forbush, while the made-for-television movie forsakes the horrid color hues in the original film's musical numbers. Not nearly as epic in scope, the television movie makes up for it with winning performances, strong direction by Richard Pearce, who understands he's making a musical and not a war film, and gorgeous scenery. Not rated; contains adult situations, language, and violence. 135m. **DIR:** Richard Pearce. **CAST:** Glenn Close, Harry Connick Jr., Rade Sherbedgia, Jack Thompson, Lori Tan Chinn, Ilene Graff, Robert Pastorelli. **2001 DVD**

SOUTH PARK: BIGGER, LONGER & UNCUT ★★★★ Although it features cute animated characters, parents should be aware that *this is not a movie for youngsters.* In their first big-screen romp, Kyle, Stan, Cartman, and Kenny offer a scathing indictment of the hypocrisy of American morality groups. It has something to offend everybody—and is frequently hilarious. Rated R for profanity, photos of male sex organs, implied sex acts of all descriptions, scatological humor, and violence. 81m. **DIR:** Trey Parker. **1999 DVD**

SOUTHERN COMFORT ★★★★ Director Walter Hill's 1981 "war" film focuses on the plight of a National Guard unit lost in Cajun country while on routine training maneuvers. Armed only with M-16 rifles loaded with blanks, the soldiers (who include Keith Carradine and Powers Boothe) find themselves ill-equipped to deal with the hostile locals—and an edge-of-your-seat entertainment is the result. Rated R for violence. 106m. **DIR:** Walter Hill. **CAST:** Keith Carradine, Powers Boothe, Fred Ward, Brian James. **1981**

SOUTHERN YANKEE, A ★★★ Red Skelton captures an elusive Confederate spy, then assumes his identity, going behind rebel lines with fake Union war plans. Some very good sight gags, reportedly devised by Buster Keaton. B&W; 90m. **DIR:** Edward Sedgwick. **CAST:** Red Skelton, Brian Donlevy, Arlene Dahl, John Ireland. **1948**

SOUTHERNER, THE ★★★★ Stark life in the rural South before civil rights. Dirt-poor tenant farmer (Zachary Scott) struggles against insurmountable odds to provide for his family while maintaining his dignity. Visually a beautiful film, but uneven in dramatic continuity. Nonetheless, its high rating is deserved. B&W; 91m. **DIR:** Jean Renoir. **CAST:** Zachary Scott, Betty Field, J. Carrol Naish. **1945 DVD**

SOUTHIE ★★ Increasingly annoying film in which a son returns home to find his family up to its eyes in debt

with the local bookie. Edgy performances barely pierce the noisy atmosphere created by director John Shea. Rated R for violence and profanity. 96m. **DIR:** John Shea. **CAST:** Donnie Wahlberg, Rose McGowan, Lawrence Tierney. **1998 DVD**

SOUVENIR ★★ Former German soldier returns to France for the first time in forty years to visit his daughter and come to terms with the guilt he feels. Christopher Plummer is wasted in this talky, predictable drama. Rated R for brief nudity. 93m. **DIR:** Geoffrey Reeve. **CAST:** Christopher Plummer, Catharine Hicks, Michel Lonsdale. **1988**

SOYLENT GREEN ★★★ In this watchable science-fiction flick, the year is 2022, and New York City is grossly overcrowded. Food is so scarce the government creates a product, Soylent Green, for people to eat. Heston plays the policeman who discovers what it's made of. There is some violence. Rated PG. 97m. **DIR:** Richard Fleischer. **CAST:** Charlton Heston, Edward G. Robinson, Joseph Cotten, Chuck Connors. **1973**

SPACE COWBOYS ★★★1/2 A former test pilot gets a second chance at going into outer space when it's discovered that a mechanism only he understands has mysteriously found its way into a Russian satellite that is plummeting toward Earth. He insists on reteaming with the members of his "old" crew, much to the consternation of the top brass, and they all get a chance at a last hurrah. With its potent star power and resultant marvelous performances, *Space Cowboys* is proof that they still can "make 'em like they used to." Rated PG-13 for profanity and brief violence. 130m. **DIR:** Clint Eastwood. **CAST:** Clint Eastwood, Tommy Lee Jones, Donald Sutherland, James Garner, James Cromwell, Marcia Gay Harden, William Devane, Loren Dean, Courtney B. Vance, Barbara Babcock, Blair Brown, Jay Leno. **2000 DVD**

SPACE JAM ★★1/2 While it has its heart in the right place, casting Michael Jordan as a hero willing to save the cartoon world from intergalactic baddies, this is a harebrained mess. Little kids will love it, but fans of Warner Bros. toon stars are advised to steer clear. Rated PG. 81m. **DIR:** Joe Pytka. **CAST:** Michael Jordan, Wayne Knight, Theresa Randle, Bill Murray. **1996 DVD**

SPACE MARINES ★★★ Fans of old sci-fi serials should love this retro action epic, which sends futuristic cousins of "the few and the proud" up against an insane pirate determined to leave a rather explosive mark in galaxial history. Robert Moreland's script has the sense not to take itself too seriously, and Billy Wirth shines as the gleefully maniacal villain. Rated R for violence and profanity. 93m. **DIR:** John Weidner. **CAST:** Billy Wirth, John Pyper-Ferguson, Edward Albert, Cady Huffman, James Shigeta, Meg Foster, Blake Boyd. **1995**

SPACE 1999 (TV SERIES) ★★ An atomic explosion occurs on the Moon, throwing it out of orbit and forcing the occupants of Moon Base Alpha to wander the stars aimlessly. Low production values on this TV series hold back the occasionally original stories. This show still has a small cult following, and the producers have managed to compile some of the better episodes. Not rated. 92m. **DIR:** Ray Austin, Lee H. Katzin. **CAST:** Martin Landau, Barbara Bain, Barry Morse. **1974**

SPACE RAGE 🦃 Richard Farnsworth as a retired twenty-first-century cop living on a prison planet. Rated R for violence galore. 78m. **DIR:** Conrad E. Palmisano. **CAST:** Richard Farnsworth, Michael Paré, John Laughlin, Lee Purcell, William Windom. **1986**

SPACE RAIDERS ★★★1/2 In this low-budget sci-fi flick from B-movie king Roger Corman, a 10-year-old boy (David Mendenhall) is kidnapped by a group of space pirates led by Vince Edwards, who becomes his mentor. It's an entertaining adventure film which not-too-young youngsters will enjoy. Rated PG for profanity and violence. 82m. **DIR:** Howard R. Cohen. **CAST:** Vince Edwards, David Mendenhall. **1983**

SPACE RANGERS (TV SERIES) ★★★ Fast-paced hokum about a motley crew of outer-space good guys, whose job it is to put a stop to the activities of intergalactic smugglers, hustlers, killers, and thieves. Good special effects and action elevate unexceptionally scripted TV fare. Each tape features three episodes of the short-lived series. 100m. **DIR:** Ben Bolt. **CAST:** Jeff Kaake, Linda Hunt, Marjorie Monaghan, Cary-Hiroyuki Tagawa, Jack McGee, Clint Howard. **1993**

SPACE TRUCKERS ★★★1/2 Great, goofy fun awaits those looking for something offbeat as space truckers are called upon to save the world from an attack by evil robots. Everything is tongue-in-cheek in this made-for-cable feature. Rated PG-13 for language and violence. 97m. **DIR:** Stuart Gordon. **CAST:** Dennis Hopper, Stephen Dorff, Debi Mazar, Charles Dance. **1997 DVD**

SPACEBALLS ★★ The plot loosely concerns planet Spaceball's attempt to "steal" the atmosphere from neighbor Druidia by kidnapping and ransoming off the royally spoiled Princess Vespa. The wacky Dark Helmet (Rick Moranis) is responsible for this dastardly plot, and he is opposed by rogue trader Lone Starr (Bill Pullman). Rated PG for mild profanity. 96m. **DIR:** Mel Brooks. **CAST:** Mel Brooks, John Candy, Rick Moranis, Bill Pullman, Daphne Zuniga, Dick Van Patten, George Wyner, Michael Winslow, Lorene Yarnell. **1987 DVD**

SPACECAMP ★★★ Kate Capshaw is a reluctant instructor at the U.S. Space Camp in Alabama. She and her independent charges—four teens and a younger child—board a real space shuttle and are accidentally launched on a perilous journey. With an attractive cast, impressive special effects, and a noble heart, the movie should inspire the astronauts of the future. Rated PG for suspense. 104m. **DIR:** Harry Winer. **CAST:** Kate Capshaw, Lea Thompson, Tom Skerritt, Kelly Preston, Tate Donovan, Leaf Phoenix. **1986**

SPACED INVADERS ★★ There are some funny moments in this spoof about inept mini-Martians who mistake a fiftieth anniversary broadcast of Orson Welles's *War of the Worlds* radio show for the real thing. Too many hick jokes drag this one down. Rated PG for vulgarity and violence. 100m. **DIR:** Patrick Read Johnson. **CAST:** Douglas Barr, Royal Dano. **1990**

SPACED OUT ★★★ In this spoof of science-fiction films, the Earth is visited by an all-female crew on a broken-down spaceship. Three men and a woman are taken hostage and the discovery of the differences between men and women make for a watchable but raunchy comedy. This film is rated R for nudity and implied sex. 85m. **DIR:** Norman J. Warren. **CAST:** Barry Stokes, Tony Maiden, Glory Annen. **1985 DVD**

SPACEHUNTER: ADVENTURES IN THE FORBIDDEN-ZONE 🦃 A futuristic hero takes on an army of militant humanoids on a plague-infested planet. Rated PG for violence. 90m. **DIR:** Lamont Johnson. **CAST:** Peter Strauss, Molly Ringwald, Ernie Hudson, Andrea Marcovicci, Michael Ironside, Beeson Carroll. **1983 DVD**

SPACESHIP (NAKED SPACE) 🦃 This "comedy" is all about an unwanted alien tagging along on a rocket full of idiots. Original title: *The Creature Wasn't Nice*. Rated PG. 88m. **DIR:** Bruce Kimmel. **CAST:** Cindy Williams, Bruce Kimmel, Leslie Nielsen, Gerrit Graham. **1981 DVD**

SPAGHETTI HOUSE ★★ Five Italian restaurant employees are held hostage in a food storage room by three crooks. Most of the film is lighthearted, though—and, unfortunately, light-headed. In Italian with English subtitles. Not rated, contains violence and profanity. 103m. **DIR:** Giulio Paradisi. **CAST:** Nino Manfredi, Rita Tushingham. **1985**

SPAGHETTI WESTERN ★★★ Typical of the genre: some big-name American actors trek to Italy for large bucks to film the kind of grade-B Western that made Clint Eastwood a household word. It's hard to tell, at times, if this is a literal send-up of the genre, but it succeeds on several levels anyway. Not rated, with violence. 90m. **DIR:** Not credited. **CAST:** Franco Nero, Martin Balsam, Sterling Hayden. **1969**

SPALDING GRAY: TERRORS OF PLEASURE ★★★★ Spalding Gray, the master storyteller, relates the humorous adventure of finding the perfect retreat and piece of land to call his own. This HBO special was filmed in concert, but some terrific editing takes you to the scenes he describes. The star of *Swimming to Cambodia* also describes his brief encounter with Hollywood. 60m. **DIR:** Thomas Schlamme. **CAST:** Spalding Gray. **1988**

•**SPANISH JUDGES** ★★ Like *The Mexican*, this film deals with an unsavory group of players in search of a prized pistol, or in this case, two prized pistols—the Spanish Judges—which a con man hopes to obtain with the help of a couple of professional thieves. When the deal goes down, it's every man (or woman) for himself. Not nearly as exciting as it sounds. Rated R for drug use, language, nudity, and violence. 96m. **DIR:** Oz Scott. **CAST:** Vincent D'Onofrio, Matthew Lillard, Valeria Golino. **1999 DVD**

SPANISH PRISONER, THE ★★★ This effort from writer-director David Mamet is simultaneously fascinating and infuriating. Its twisty script involves a convoluted con game guaranteed to please fans, but the fun is undercut by performances that are stiff and mannered to the point of absurdity. The plot concerns a genius inventor with a super-secret "process" who falls in with the wrong crowd. Rated PG for implied violence. 112m. **DIR:** David Mamet. **CAST:** Campbell Scott, Rebecca Pidgeon, Steve Martin, Ben Gazzara, Ricky Jay. **1998 DVD**

SPANKING THE MONKEY ★★★1/2 A first-year college student resents having to spend his summer nursing his mother; his anger and her frustration lead to some unexpected developments. Writer-director David O. Russell's first film is a promising debut. Not rated; contains profanity and sexual situations, including incest. 100m. **DIR:** David O. Russell. **CAST:** Jeremy Davies, Alberta Watson, Carla Gallo, Benjamin Hendrickson. **1994**

SPARKLE ★★★1/2 Largely forgotten but appealing study of a Supremes-like girl group's rise to fame in the 1960s Motown era. Lots of good musical numbers from Curtis Mayfield and the luscious Lonette McKee. Rated PG for profanity and nudity. 100m. **DIR:** Sam O'Steen. **CAST:** Irene Cara, Dorian Harewood, Lonette McKee, Curtis Mayfield. **1976**

SPARROWS ★★★ The legendary Mary Pickford—"Our Mary" to millions during her reign as Queen of Hollywood when this film was made—plays the resolute, intrepid champion of a group of younger orphans besieged by an evil captor. Silent melodrama at its best, folks. B&W; 84m. **DIR:** William Beaudine. **CAST:** Mary Pickford, Gustav von Seyffertitz. **1926 DVD**

SPARTACUS ★★★★1/2 One of the more rewarding big-budget epics that marked the late 1950s and 1960s. Even though this fictional story of an actual slave revolt against the Roman Empire is large-scale in every detail, it never lets the human drama get lost in favor of spectacle. Rated PG-13. 196m. **DIR:** Stanley Kubrick. **CAST:** Kirk Douglas, Jean Simmons, Laurence Olivier, Peter Ustinov, Charles Laughton, Tony Curtis. **1960 DVD**

SPASMS ★★★ If it were not for the poor acting, this would be a top-notch horror film. Oliver Reed plays a millionaire trophy hunter who, on a hunting trip in a tropical jungle, becomes cursed by a giant monster-like snake. Peter Fonda plays the special psychologist who is hired to examine him. When the serpent is brought back to the hunter, the tension rises as the body count goes up. Not rated; contains profanity, nudity, and gore. 92m. **DIR:** William Fruet. **CAST:** Peter Fonda, Oliver Reed, Kerrie Keane, Al Waxman, Marilyn Lightstone. **1982**

SPAWN ★★ This live-action adaptation of Todd McFarlane's hugely popular comic-book antihero is a mess, a veritable triumph of style over substance. Covert agent is killed, winds up in Hell, and comes back with so many snazzy powers that he's basically unbeatable. The film's minimal charm comes from John Leguizamo's comedic role as a "guardian evil clown." Rated PG-13 for violence. 90m. **DIR:** Mark A. Z. Dippe. **CAST:** John Leguizamo, Michael Jai White, Martin Sheen, Theresa Randle, Melinda Clarke. **1997 DVD**

SPEAK EASILY ★★1/2 Naïve college professor Buster Keaton is falsely informed that he has inherited a large sum of money and sets out to see the world. Along the way he befriends an itinerant theater troupe, headed by Jimmy Durante. Tired and thin story. B&W; 82m. **DIR:** Edward Sedgwick. **CAST:** Buster Keaton, Jimmy Durante, Thelma Todd, Sidney Toler, Hedda Hopper, Edward Brophy, Henry Armetta. **1932**

SPEAK OF THE DEVIL ★★ Weak horror-comedy in which a phony evangelist and his nymphomaniac wife buy a haunted house and turn it into a church. Not rated; contains violence, profanity, gore, and nudity. 99m. **DIR:** Raphael Nussbaum. **CAST:** Robert Elarton, Jean Miller. **1991**

SPEAKING PARTS ★★★ Stylistically offbeat drama about an actor who supports himself by working as a housekeeper in a posh hotel. Canadian filmmaker Atom Egoyan combines the media of film and video technology to create a stunning visual display. Not rated; con-

tains nudity and profanity. 92m. **DIR:** Atom Egoyan. **CAST:** Michael McManus, Arsinée Khanjian, Gabrielle Rose. **1989 DVD**

SPECIAL BULLETIN ★★★ A group of antinuclear scientists on a tugboat in Charleston, South Carolina, take a TV crew hostage then demand network airtime. They have a nuclear bomb and threaten to detonate it. Realistically effective made-for-television movie. 103m. **DIR:** Edward Zwick. **CAST:** Ed Flanders, Kathryn Walker, Roxanne Hart, Christopher Allport, David Clennon, David Rasche, Rosalind Cash. **1983**

SPECIAL DAY, A ★★★★ Antonietta (Sophia Loren), a slovenly housewife, and Gabriele (Marcello Mastroianni), a depressed homosexual, meet in the spring of 1938—the same day Hitler arrives in Rome. Their experience together enriches but does not change the course of their lives. In Italian with English subtitles. No rating. 106m. **DIR:** Ettore Scola. **CAST:** Sophia Loren, Marcello Mastroianni. **1977**

SPECIAL EFFECTS Low-budget horror about a film director who murders a would-be actress. Not rated, but the film contains nudity and violence. 90m. **DIR:** Larry Cohen. **CAST:** Zoe Tamerlis, Eric Bogosian, Brad Rjin, Kevin O'Connor. **1984**

SPECIALIST, THE ★★ Only the action sequences and the larger-than-life supporting performance by James Woods save *The Specialist* from being an utter disaster. Sylvester Stallone and Sharon Stone are a woeful mismatch in this story of an explosives specialist hired by a woman seeking revenge against the Cuban-American gangsters who killed her parents. Rated R for violence, profanity, nudity, and simulated sex. 109m. **DIR:** Luis Llosa. **CAST:** Sylvester Stallone, Sharon Stone, James Woods, Rod Steiger, Eric Roberts. **1994 DVD**

•SPECIALS, THE ★★ Good intentions aren't enough to save this comedy about a group of ragtag superheroes who would rather hash out life's problems than solve them. These superheroes are all talk and no action, which would be fine if this were a Henry Jaglom comedy, but it's not. Second-rate all the way, including a rather peculiar lack of special effects. Rated R for adult language. 82m. **DIR:** Craig Mazin. **CAST:** Rob Lowe, Jamie Kennedy, Thomas Haden Church, Kelly Coffield. **2000 DVD**

SPECIES ★★★ Scientific researchers blend alien DNA with a human being, and wind up with a gorgeous woman who slaughters everyone interfering with her attempts to reproduce. Logical plotting and strong characterizations are sacrificed in favor of shock cuts and gory murders. Rated R for violence, nudity, simulated sex, and profanity. 108m. **DIR:** Roger Donaldson. **CAST:** Ben Kingsley, Michael Madsen, Alfred Molina, Forest Whitaker, Marg Helgenberger, Natasha Henstridge. **1995 DVD**

SPECIES II First man on Mars returns to Earth as a tentacle-sprouting sex machine that brutally copulates with human women before he crosses paths with a captive half-human, half-alien clone named Eve. Rated R for violence, gore, sex, nudity, and language. 93m. **DIR:** Peter Medak. **CAST:** Natasha Henstridge, Justin Lazard, Michael Madsen, Marg Helgenberger, James Cromwell, Mykelti Williamson. **1998 DVD**

SPECIMEN ★★1/2 A young man with strange powers learns he is only half human, part of a breeding experiment by an alien race that sends a bounty hunter to bring him back. Fairly well made as far as low-budget sci-fi goes, but the script is too lackluster to matter. Rated R for violence, nudity, sexual situations, and profanity. 85m. **DIR:** John Bradshaw. **CAST:** Mark Paul Gosselaar, Doug O'Keefe, Ingrid Kalevaars. **1997 DVD**

SPECKLED BAND, THE ★★★ In his motion-picture debut, Raymond Massey makes a sturdy Sherlock Holmes, who must bring to justice the evil villain, Dr. Grimesby Roylott (Lyn Harding). Harding, who later played Professor Moriarty in the Arthur Wontner series of Holmes mysteries, is a superb villain, and the sets are decidedly gothic. Time has not been kind to the overall production, but *The Speckled Band* has much to offer fans of the canon. B&W; 48m. **DIR:** Jack Raymond. **CAST:** Raymond Massey, Lyn Harding. **1931**

SPECTER OF THE ROSE, THE ★★★★ Surreal thriller written and directed by Ben Hecht about a young ballerina who discovers that her new husband is going insane. Unique, stylish filmmaking that is reminiscent of the work of Jean Cocteau. B&W; 90m. **DIR:** Ben Hecht. **CAST:** Judith Anderson, Michael Chekhov, Lionel Stander. **1946**

SPECTERS Archaeologists uncover an ancient tomb in Rome. Not rated; contains violence and brief nudity. 95m. **DIR:** Marcello Avallone. **CAST:** Donald Pleasence, John Pepper, Erna Schurer. **1987**

SPECTRE ★★ Creaky tale about a haunted manor in Ireland that won't give up the ghost. Greg Evigan plays the lucky soul who inherits the manor and immediately drags his family off to live there. Unfortunately, the spirit of a young girl who died in the house decides that she doesn't want or need the company. Typical dark-house thrills won't impress any but the clueless few. Rated R for language and violence. 87m. **DIR:** Scott Levy. **CAST:** Greg Evigan, Alexandra Paul, Briana Evigan. **1997**

SPEECHLESS ★★1/2 Insomnia drives political speech writers Geena Davis and Michael Keaton to "meet cute" while arguing over the last bottle of Nytol. They begin an affair, initially unaware that they're working for rival candidates in a New Mexico senate race; they fight, they make up, they fight, they make up . . . far too many times. Robert King's dialogue isn't nearly as clever as he'd like to believe, and he shamefully wastes a strong supporting cast. Rated PG-13 for profanity and suggested sex. 99m. **DIR:** Ron Underwood. **CAST:** Michael Keaton, Geena Davis, Christopher Reeve, Bonnie Bedelia, Ernie Hudson, Charles Martin Smith. **1994**

SPEED ★★★★★ Action-thriller more than lives up to its name, as LAPD SWAT cops Keanu Reeves and Jeff Daniels match wits with mad bomber Dennis Hopper. Sandra Bullock gives a standout performance as a take-charge bystander who ends up piloting a runaway bus (rigged to explode if it slows to less than 50 mph), but it is Reeves, in a highly effective switch to action hero, who dominates the film. Rated R for violence and profanity. 115m. **DIR:** Jan De Bont. **CAST:** Keanu Reeves, Dennis Hopper, Sandra Bullock, Joe Morton, Jeff Daniels, Alan Ruck. **1994 DVD**

SPEED 2: CRUISE CONTROL ★★ A disgruntled ex-employee of a cruise-ship line takes control of its most luxurious vessel, jeopardizing the heroine of the first film and her new SWAT-unit boyfriend. A big, loud, disappointing sequel that wastes the talent of everyone in-

volved. Rated PG-13 for language and violence. 121m. **DIR:** Jan De Bont. **CAST:** Sandra Bullock, Jason Patric, Willem Dafoe. **1997 DVD**

SPEED ZONE 🦃 Another yawner about the *Cannonball Run* cross-country road race. Rated PG. 87m. **DIR:** Jim Drake. **CAST:** John Candy, Donna Dixon, Joe Flaherty, Eugene Levy, Tom Smothers, Tim Matheson, Jamie Farr, Peter Boyle, Brooke Shields. **1989**

SPEEDWAY ★★ Elvis Presley plays a generous stock-car driver who confronts a seemingly heartless IRS agent (Nancy Sinatra). Not surprisingly, she melts in this unremarkable musical. Rated G. 94m. **DIR:** Norman Taurog. **CAST:** Elvis Presley, Nancy Sinatra, Bill Bixby, Gale Gordon. **1968 DVD**

SPELLBINDER 🦃 The obsession of a lawyer for a young woman who is a Satanist. Rated R for profanity, nudity, and violence. 99m. **DIR:** Janet Greek. **CAST:** Timothy Daly, Kelly Preston, Rick Rossovich, Audra Lindley. **1988**

SPELLBOUND ★★★★ Hitchcock said in his usual, understated manner that *Spellbound* "is just another manhunt story wrapped up in pseudo-psychoanalysis." The story is more than just another manhunt story; of that we can assure you. We can divulge that Ingrid Bergman plays the psychiatrist, Gregory Peck is the patient, and Salvador Dalí provides the nightmare sequences. B&W; 111m. **DIR:** Alfred Hitchcock. **CAST:** Ingrid Bergman, Gregory Peck, Leo G. Carroll, John Emery, Wallace Ford, Rhonda Fleming, Bill Goodwin. **1945 DVD**

SPELLBREAKER: SECRET OF THE LEPRECHAUNS ★★ An American boy visiting his grandfather in Ireland helps local leprechauns battle the evil Queen of the Dead. A sequel to *Leapin' Leprechauns*, this low-budget fantasy (it was filmed in Romania, not Ireland) may appeal to families with a liking for Irish culture. Rated G. 84m. **DIR:** Ted Nicolaou. **CAST:** Gregory Edward Smith, John Bluthal, Godfrey James, Madeleine Potter, Sylvester McCoy. **1996**

SPELLCASTER 🦃 Music television contest winners are brought to a castle to vie for a $1-million check. Tame little romp. Rated R for profanity. 83m. **DIR:** Rafal Zielinski. **CAST:** Richard Blade, Gail O'Grady, Adam Ant. **1991**

SPENCER'S MOUNTAIN ★★1/2 Henry Fonda is fine as the head of a poor Wyoming family determined that his oldest son must go to college, but the movie is strangely unmoving. From the novel by Earl Hammer Jr., this is the basis for TV's *The Waltons*, and comparisons are inevitable. 118m. **DIR:** Delmer Daves. **CAST:** Henry Fonda, Maureen O'Hara, James MacArthur, Donald Crisp, Wally Cox, Virginia Gregg, Whit Bissell. **1963**

SPENSER: CEREMONY ★★★★ Robert B. Parker's celebrated detective hero, Spenser, was not particularly well served by the network series bearing his name, except for the casting of Robert Urich in the lead role and Avery Brooks as the formidable Hawk. Characters get much better treatment in this made-for-TV movie in which our heroes find the runaway daughter of a powerful politician in an underworld of violence, prostitution, drugs, and blackmail—just the place where our heroes can get the job done best. 96m. **DIR:** Andrew Wild. **CAST:** Robert Urich, Avery Brooks, Barbara Williams, J. Winston Carroll, Dave Nichols. **1993**

SPENSER: PALE KINGS & PRINCES ★★★1/2 When a reporter friend of Dr. Susan Silverman (Barbara Williams) is killed while investigating a story on cocaine dealers in a picturesque New England hamlet, she asks her personal private eye, Spenser (Robert Urich), to mount his white horse and slay some drug-dealing dragons. Working from a script by Robert B. Parker (the celebrated detective-series's author) and Joan H. Parker, Urich and company take a giant step up from the original network TV series. Made for TV. 96m. **DIR:** Vic Sarin. **CAST:** Robert Urich, Avery Brooks, Barbara Williams, Sonja Smits, J. Winston Carroll. **1993**

SPETTERS ★★★★1/2 A study of the dreams, loves, discoveries, and tragedies of six young people in modern-day Holland, this is yet another tough, uncompromising motion picture from Paul Verhoeven. Though the sex scenes are more graphic than anything we've ever had in a major American movie, the film is never exploitative. MPAA-unrated, it contains violence, profanity, nudity. 115m. **DIR:** Paul Verhoeven. **CAST:** Hans Van Tongeren, Toon Agterberg, Renee Soutendijk. **1980**

SPHERE ★★ Despite the star power of Dustin Hoffman, Sharon Stone, and Samuel L. Jackson, the direction of Barry Levinson, and a screenplay adapted from Michael Crichton's bestseller, this movie is confusing, talky and ultimately disappointing. This chronicles an expedition to the bottom of the ocean to explore the discovery of what may be an extraterrestrial vehicle. Rated PG-13. 144m. **DIR:** Barry Levinson. **CAST:** Dustin Hoffman, Sharon Stone, Samuel L. Jackson. **1998 DVD**

SPHINX, THE (1933) ★★1/2 Horror-film great Lionel Atwill plays a dual role in this effective low-budget murder mystery with overtones of the supernatural. The Sphinx of the title refers to Atwill's twin brother, who is a deaf-mute. B&W; 63m. **DIR:** Phil Rosen. **CAST:** Lionel Atwill, Sheila Terry, Paul Fix. **1933**

SPHINX (1981) ★★ This is a watchable film . . . but not a good one. Taken from the tedious novel by Robin Cook (*Coma*), it concerns the plight of an Egyptologist (Lesley-Anne Down) who inadvertently runs afoul of the underworld. Rated PG. 117m. **DIR:** Franklin J. Schaffner. **CAST:** Lesley-Anne Down, Frank Langella, Maurice Ronet, John Gielgud. **1981**

SPICE WORLD ★★★ This overlong rock video is unrelentingly silly and pretty much bereft of plot, but in spite of all this, it's pure dumb fun: just like its five stars. This is classic British whimsy. Rated PG for brief nudity. 93m. **DIR:** Bob Spiers. **CAST:** Spice Girls, Richard E. Grant, Claire Rushbrook, Alan Cumming, Roger Moore, George Wendt, Meat Loaf. **1997 DVD**

SPICES ★★★1/2 This spirited, feminist fable from India stars Smita Patil (two-time winner of India's National Best Actress Award) in the role of an impoverished woman who struggles against oppression. Excellent direction and fine performances by some of India's top-name stars. In Hindi with English subtitles. Not rated. 98m. **DIR:** Ketan Mehta. **CAST:** Smita Patil. **1986**

•SPIDER-MAN ★★★★ Our friendly neighborhood wall-crawler is very well served by this energetic big-screen adaptation, which retains all the essential elements of the long-running Marvel comic-book series and has the added bonus of a wonderful performance by

Tobey Maguire, who's perfect as nerdy, downtrodden Peter Parker. Maguire's so good, in fact, that his scenes as Spidey's "normal" alter ego are far more interesting than the web-spinning, superheroics that are delivered with a tad too much computer-generated imagery. Director Sam Raimi moves the action scenes at such a ferocious pitch that it's sometimes hard to view them as anything but an expensive cartoon, but Maguire injects well-needed humanity every time the film threatens to become too unbelievable. Rated PG-13 for violence and mild sensuality. 121m. **DIR:** Sam Raimi. **CAST:** Tobey Maguire, Willem Dafoe, Kirsten Dunst, James Franco, Cliff Robertson, Rosemary Harris, J. K. Simmons. **2002 DVD**

SPIDER AND THE FLY, THE ★★★1/2 Two writers are suspected of a murder because of a prank they played in this well-scripted made-for-cable mystery. Good acting, and you won't know who did it until the end. Rated PG-13 for violence. 87m. **DIR:** Michael Katleman. **CAST:** Mel Harris, Ted Shackelford, Kim Coates, Colm Feore, Frankie Faison, Cynthia Belliveau, Peggy Lipton. **1994**

SPIDER BABY ★★1/2 Lon Chaney Jr. plays a chauffeur caring for a family of homicidal mental defectives. An odd little film, just quirky enough to interest fans of the weird. B&W; 81m. **DIR:** Jack Hill. **CAST:** Lon Chaney Jr., Carol Ohmart, Quinn Redeker. **1964 DVD**

SPIDERS, THE (1919) ★★★ Long considered a lost film, *The Spiders* (written and directed by Fritz Lang) is an adventure story about a gang of organized criminals. Although planned as a serial, only the first two parts were completed. Fritz Lang used exotic locations, combining a labyrinth of plots. The film had its first American showing in 1979. Tinted B&W; 137m. **DIR:** Fritz Lang. **CAST:** Carl de Vogy, Ressel Orla, Lil Dagover. **1919 DVD**

SPIDERS (2000) ★★ Every generation deserves its own giant spider movie, and this one isn't any better or worse than the rest. A scientist alters the DNA of a spider found inside the mummified remains of an alien, creating a giant, deadly breed that uses humans as hosts for its eggs. Some actual creepy moments as the spiders make their way through town. Most of the cast deserve what they get. Rated R for violence. 93m. **DIR:** Gary Jones. **CAST:** Lana Parrilla, Josh Green, Oliver Macready, Nick Swarts, Mark Phelan. **2000 DVD**

SPIDER'S STRATAGEM, THE ★★★★ Compelling mystery about a young man who returns to a small Italian town where his father was murdered thirty years earlier. One of director Bernardo Bertolucci's most stunning cinematic works. In Italian with English subtitles. Not rated. 97m. **DIR:** Bernardo Bertolucci. **CAST:** Giulio Brogi, Alida Valli, Tino Scotti. **1970**

SPIES ★★★★ Thrilling, imaginative drama of the underworld and the dark doings of espionage agents is one of the finest of all such films and remains a classic of the genre as well as a terrific adventure movie. The camera moves in and out among the shadowy doings of the spies and their pursuers like a silent spider weaving all the components together. The final chase provides a fitting climax to this topflight entertainment from Fritz Lang. Silent. B&W; 90m. **DIR:** Fritz Lang. **CAST:** Rudolf Klein-Rogge, Gerda Maurus, Willy Fritsch, Fritz Rasp. **1928 DVD**

SPIES, LIES, AND NAKED THIGHS ★★★1/2 If you laughed at *The In-Laws*, you should enjoy this similar made-for-TV movie. Harry Anderson plays an eccentric government agent who enlists skeptical interpreter Ed Begley Jr. in his quest to save the world from a maniac armed with... well, we won't spoil it. 100m. **DIR:** James Frawley. **CAST:** Harry Anderson, Ed Begley Jr., Linda Purl, Wendy Crewson. **1988**

SPIES LIKE US ★★1/2 Chevy Chase and Dan Aykroyd, who were co-stars on the original *Saturday Night Live* television show, appeared together on the big screen for the first time in this generally enjoyable comedy about two inept recruits in a U.S. intelligence organization's counterespionage mission. Rated PG for violence and profanity. 104m. **DIR:** John Landis. **CAST:** Chevy Chase, Dan Aykroyd, Bruce Davison, William Prince, Steve Forrest, Bernie Casey, Donna Dixon. **1985 DVD**

SPIKE & MIKE'S FESTIVAL OF ANIMATION ★★★★ Well-balanced compilation of animated short subjects that include two Academy Award–winning efforts: "Tango" and "Charade." Impressive representation of the medium includes everything from the hilarious "Snookles" and "Bambi Meets Godzilla" to the abstract "Primiti Too Taa." Not rated. 80m. **DIR:** Mike Gribble, Craig Decker. **1991**

SPIKE OF BENSONHURST ★★ Haphazard comedy-drama about life in a Mafia-run neighborhood in New York City. Sasha Mitchell stars as a young Italian boxer trying to get his big break. Rated R for nudity, violence, and profanity. 102m. **DIR:** Paul Morrissey. **CAST:** Sasha Mitchell, Ernest Borgnine, Sylvia Miles. **1989**

SPINOUT ★★ A lesser Elvis vehicle, this features a perky drummer (Deborah Walley), a spoiled heiress (Shelley Fabares), and a pushy sociologist (Diane McBain) trying to get the King to say "I do." Dated attitudes and styles don't age well. 93m. **DIR:** Norman Taurog. **CAST:** Elvis Presley, Shelley Fabares, Deborah Walley, Diane McBain, Carl Betz. **1966**

SPIRAL STAIRCASE, THE (1946) ★★★★ Dorothy McGuire gives what some call the performance of her career as a mute servant in a hackle-raising household harboring a killer. Watch this one late at night, but not alone. B&W; 83m. **DIR:** Robert Siodmak. **CAST:** George Brent, Dorothy McGuire, Ethel Barrymore, Kent Smith, Elsa Lanchester, Sara Allgood. **1946**

SPIRAL STAIRCASE, THE (1975) 🦃 Sad remake. Not rated; contains mild violence. 89m. **DIR:** Peter Collinson. **CAST:** Jacqueline Bisset, Christopher Plummer, Sam Wanamaker, Gayle Hunnicutt. **1975**

SPIRIT LOST ★★1/2 A heavy use of smoke and mirrors bogs down this sexy ghost story. An artist and his wife move into their dream house by the sea, only to find it inhabited by a two-hundred-year-old spirit desperate for sexual misadventure. There are some stylish segues and fades, but too much of this looks like soft porn and the ending is ridiculous. Rated R for nudity, profanity, and sexual situations. 90m. **DIR:** Neema Barnette. **CAST:** Leon, Regina Taylor, Cynda Williams. **1996**

SPIRIT OF '76, THE ★★ Spoof of the Seventies has three people traveling back in time to bring back the Constitution—and thereby revive their dying culture. We found this comedy a disco drag, but it has its admirers. Rated PG for profanity. 82m. **DIR:** Lucas Reiner. **CAST:** David Cassidy, Olivia D'Abo, Leif Garrett, Bar-

bara Bain, Julie Brown, Tommy Chong, Don Novello, Carl Reiner, Rob Reiner, Moon Zappa. **1991**

SPIRIT OF ST. LOUIS, THE ★★★★ Jimmy Stewart always wanted to portray Charles Lindbergh in a re-creation of his historic solo flight across the Atlantic. When he finally got his chance, at age 48, many critics felt he was too old to be believable. Stewart did just fine. The action does drag at times, but this remains a quality picture for the whole family. 138m. **DIR:** Billy Wilder. **CAST:** James Stewart, Patricia Smith, Murray Hamilton, Marc Connelly. **1957**

SPIRIT OF THE BEEHIVE, THE ★★★★ A disturbing cinematic study of the isolation of an individual. Ana Torrent gives an unforgettable performance as a lonely girl who enters the world of fantasy when she sees the 1931 *Frankenstein* and falls in love with the monster. By far one of the most haunting films ever made about children. In Spanish with English subtitles. Not rated. 95m. **DIR:** Victor Erice. **CAST:** Fernando Fernán Gómez, Ana Torrent. **1974**

SPIRIT OF THE DEAD ★★★1/2 Originally titled *The Asphyx*, slightly edited for videocassette. Interesting tale of a scientist who discovers the spirit of death possessed by all creatures. If the spirit is trapped, its owner becomes immortal. Well-made British film with sincere performances. Rated PG for mild violence. 82m. **DIR:** Peter Newbrook. **CAST:** Robert Stephens, Robert Powell, Jane Lapotaire. **1972**

SPIRIT OF THE EAGLE ★★ A widowed father takes his son into the wilderness to begin a new life, only to see the child kidnapped. This slow-moving adventure film may be rousing to youngsters, but most adults will probably nod off quickly. Not rated. 93m. **DIR:** Boon Collins. **CAST:** Dan Haggerty, William Smith. **1990 DVD**

SPIRIT OF THE WEST ★★ This entertaining but primitive Western employs a tired old gimmick that Hoot Gibson had used in previous films—that of a tough hombre who masquerades as a silly fool in order to help the gal in distress and bring the greedy, land-grabbing varmints to justice. B&W; 60m. **DIR:** Otto Brower. **CAST:** Hoot Gibson, Doris Hill, Lafe McKee, Hooper Atchley. **1932**

SPIRIT OF WEST POINT, THE ★★1/2 West Point football stars play themselves in this realistic saga of the Long Gray Line. B&W; 77m. **DIR:** Ralph Murphy. **CAST:** Felix "Doc" Blanchard, Anne Nagel, Alan Hale Sr., Tom Harmon. **1947**

SPIRIT: STALLION OF THE CIMARRON ★★★ A wild mustang in the Old West is stolen from his herd and pressed into service, first in the U.S. Cavalry, then on the transcontinental railroad, but he remains defiant and unbreakable. The simplistic, predictable story and numerous anachronisms are balanced by the truly stunning animation, a fine score by Hans Zimmer, and good songs from Bryan Adams. Rated G. 82m. **DIR:** Kelly Asbury, Lorna Cook. **2002 DVD**

SPIRITS ★★1/2 Group of psychic researchers investigate a supposedly haunted house where a series of murders took place ten years before. Erik Estrada plays a doubting priest who must face off against the evil. As usual, things go bump in the night. Rated R for violence and nudity. 94m. **DIR:** Fred Olen Ray. **CAST:** Erik Estrada, Robert Quarry, Brinke Stevens, Oliver Darrow, Carol Lynley. **1990**

SPITE MARRIAGE ★★★★ Buster Keaton is a pants presser who masquerades as a millionaire to impress actress Dorothy Sebastian. When she is spurned by her lover, she marries Keaton out of spite, and he seeks to win her true love. Silent. B&W; 77m. **DIR:** Edward Sedgwick. **CAST:** Buster Keaton, Dorothy Sebastian. **1929**

SPITFIRE (1934) ★★★1/2 A girl (Katharine Hepburn) believes herself to have healing powers and is cast out from her Ozark Mountain home as a result. It's an interesting premise, and well-acted. B&W; 88m. **DIR:** John Cromwell. **CAST:** Katharine Hepburn, Robert Young, Ralph Bellamy, Sara Haden, Sidney Toler. **1934**

SPITFIRE (1994) 🦃 Complicated mess about a champion gymnast globe-trotting in an effort to save her superspy father. Rated R for violence, language, and adult situations. 95m. **DIR:** Albert Pyun. **CAST:** Kristie Phillips, Tim Thomerson, Lance Henriksen, Sarah Douglas. **1994**

SPITFIRE GRILL, THE ★★★ Female-bonding drama that's always striving too hard for earthy sensitivity. Ex-con Alison Elliott tries to restart her life in a tiny Maine town, where she helps the women who run the local diner find themselves. From the creator of TV's *MacGyver*, which should give you some idea of how contrived this supposedly naturalistic drama plays, despite the best efforts of a fine cast. Rated PG-13. 111m. **DIR:** Lee David Zlotoff. **CAST:** Alison Elliott, Ellen Burstyn, Marcia Gay Harden, Will Patton. **1996 DVD**

SPLASH ★★★★★ An uproarious comedy about a young man (Tom Hanks) who unknowingly falls in love with a mermaid (Daryl Hannah). John Candy and Eugene Levy add some marvelous bits of comedy. Rated PG for profanity and brief nudity. 111m. **DIR:** Ron Howard. **CAST:** Tom Hanks, Daryl Hannah, John Candy, Eugene Levy, Dody Goodman, Richard B. Shull. **1984 DVD**

SPLATTER UNIVERSITY 🦃 Typical slasher film featuring students having sex and then getting hacked to pieces. Rated R for profanity, brief nudity, and violence. 78m. **DIR:** Richard W. Haines. **CAST:** Francine Forbes, Ric Randig. **1985**

SPLENDOR ★★★ Kathleen Robertson plays a woman without any romance in her life. In the course of one evening, all of that changes when she falls in love with two different men—and they with her. She introduces them to each other and much to her surprise, they all get along and soon find themselves living together. Then another man enters and their whole love triangle is jeopardized. Plenty of sex, including the obligatory ménage à trois. Rated R. 93m. **DIR:** Gregg Araki. **CAST:** Kathleen Robertson, Johnathon Schaech, Matt Keeslar. **1998 DVD**

SPLENDOR IN THE GRASS ★★★★ Warren Beatty made his film debut in this 1961 film, as a popular, rich high school boy. Natalie Wood plays his less-prosperous girlfriend who has a nervous breakdown when he dumps her. A few tears shed by the viewer make this romantic drama all the more intriguing. 124m. **DIR:** Elia Kazan. **CAST:** Warren Beatty, Natalie Wood, Pat Hingle, Audrey Christie. **1961 DVD**

SPLIT DECISIONS ★★ Gene Hackman might have been hoping for an audience-pleasing sports film on a par with *Hoosiers* when he agreed to do this fight picture, but the result is another failed takeoff on the

Rocky series. Pure melodrama: Hackman attempts to groom one son (Craig Sheffer) for the Olympics while fearing that he, like his older brother (Jeff Fahey), will opt for the easy money offered by sleazy fight promoters. Rated R for violence and profanity. 95m. **DIR:** David Drury. **CAST:** Gene Hackman, Craig Sheffer, Jeff Fahey, Jennifer Beals, John McLiam. **1988**

SPLIT IMAGE ★★★★ This is a very interesting, thought-provoking film about religious cults and those who become caught up in them. Michael O'Keefe plays a young man who is drawn into a pseudo-religious organization run by Peter Fonda. The entire cast is good, but Fonda stands out in one of his best roles. Rated R for language and nudity. 113m. **DIR:** Ted Kotcheff. **CAST:** Peter Fonda, James Woods, Karen Allen, Michael O'Keefe. **1982**

SPLIT SECOND (1953) ★★★ Tense film about an escaped convict who holds several people hostage in a deserted town has a lot working for it, including the fact that the place they're holed up in is a nuclear test site. B&W; 85m. **DIR:** Dick Powell. **CAST:** Stephen McNally, Alexis Smith, Jan Sterling, Paul Kelly, Richard Egan. **1953**

SPLIT SECOND (1992) This murky sci-fi thriller—about a cop searching for the inhuman killer of his partner in twenty-first-century London—is a poor rip-off of the visuals of *Blade Runner* and the story line of *Predator*. Rated R for violence, profanity, and nudity. 90m. **DIR:** Tony Maylam. **CAST:** Rutger Hauer, Kim Cattrall, Pete Postlethwaite, Michael J. Pollard. **1992 DVD**

SPLITTING HEIRS ★★★★ Wonderfully silly comedy about two babies switched at birth, resulting in the wrong man becoming the sixteenth Duke of Bournemouth. When the real heir discovers the truth about his heritage, he plots to murder the man who stole his title. Marvelous confection of comic situations and hilarious bits. Rated PG-13 for profanity, nudity, suggested sex, and violence. 88m. **DIR:** Robert Young. **CAST:** Eric Idle, Rick Moranis, John Cleese, Barbara Hershey, Catherine Zeta Jones, Sadie Frost, Stratford Johns. **1993**

SPOILERS, THE ★★★★ John Wayne is a miner who strikes gold in Nome, Alaska. An unscrupulous gold commissioner (Randolph Scott) and his cronies plot to steal the rich claim. But the Duke, his partner (Harry Carey), and their backer (Marlene Dietrich) have other ideas. This was the fourth of five screen versions of Rex Beach's novel. B&W; 87m. **DIR:** Ray Enright. **CAST:** Marlene Dietrich, Randolph Scott, John Wayne, Harry Carey, Russell Simpson, George Cleveland. **1942**

SPONTANEOUS COMBUSTION Government experiment turns Brad Dourif into a human flame thrower, but the film extinguishes itself long before any sparks ignite. Sorry effort from director Tobe Hooper. Rated R for violence. 97m. **DIR:** Tobe Hooper. **CAST:** Brad Dourif, Cynthia Bain, Melinda Dillon, Dick Butkus, Jon Cypher. **1990**

SPOOKIES Zombies of all varieties maim and kill people trapped in an old mansion. Rated R for violence and profanity. 85m. **DIR:** Eugine Joseph, Thomas Doran, Brenden Faulkner. **CAST:** Felix Ward, Dan Scott. **1985**

SPOOKS RUN WILD Bela Lugosi in another silly role that gives the aging East Side Kids a chance to humiliate him on-screen. B&W; 69m. **DIR:** Phil Rosen. **CAST:** Bela Lugosi, The East Side Kids, Dave O'Brien, Dennis Moore. **1941**

SPORTING CLUB, THE An allegory of America that takes place at an exclusive hunting club. Look for Linda Blair in a small role. 104m. **DIR:** Larry Peerce. **CAST:** Robert Fields, Nicolas Coster, Margaret Blye, Jack Warden, Richard Dysart. **1971**

SPRING FEVER Canadian production is an unbelievably dull story about a rising young tennis star (Carling Bassett). Rated PG. 100m. **DIR:** Joseph L. Scanlan. **CAST:** Jessica Walter, Susan Anton, Frank Converse, Carling Bassett, Stephen Young. **1983**

SPRING FORWARD ★★★★ Two New England Parks Department workers share philosophies in this modest, understated drama about second chances and friendship. The elder worker is on the verge of retirement, while his new partner is a hotheaded ex-convict struggling to reenter society. The episodic talkfest steadily grows in strength as these two very different and very ordinary men try to make sense out of life. Rated R for language and drug content. 110m. **DIR:** Tom Gilroy. **CAST:** Ned Beatty, Liev Schreiber, Campbell Scott, Peri Gilpin. **2001**

SPRING PARADE ★★★★ This lilting musical confection stars Deanna Durbin as a baker's assistant in love with an army drummer. Set in Austria. B&W; 89m. **DIR:** Henry Koster. **CAST:** Deanna Durbin, Robert Cummings, S. Z. Sakall, Henry Stephenson, Mischa Auer, Reginald Denny, Allyn Joslyn. **1940**

SPRING SYMPHONY ★★ A routine presentation of the lives of German composer Robert Schumann and celebrated pianist Clara Wieck. The film portrays emotion in fairy-tale fashion, simplistic and overstated. The music is the star of this show. Dubbed in English. Rated PG. 102m. **DIR:** Peter Schamoni. **CAST:** Nastassja Kinski, Herbert Gronemeyer, Bernhard Wicki. **1984 DVD**

•SPRINGFIELD RIFLE ★★★ Gary Cooper goes undercover to discover the brains behind a horse-rustling gang that threatens to destroy the U.S. Cavalry. Branded a coward by his military peers, he must also deal with an unhappy wife. Coop relies on his wits until the finale when the quick-loading rifle comes into play. Intrigue adds to an otherwise average Western. Not rated; contains violence. 93m. **DIR:** André de Toth. **CAST:** Gary Cooper, Phyllis Thaxter, Davis Brian, Paul Kelly. **1952**

SPRINGTIME IN THE ROCKIES (1937) ★★ Foreman Gene Autry has all he can handle as a young girl arrives at his cattle ranch with a herd of sheep. Pretty tame. B&W; 54m. **DIR:** Joseph Kane. **CAST:** Gene Autry, Smiley Burnette, Polly Rowles. **1937**

SPRINGTIME IN THE ROCKIES (1942) ★★★ Lake Louise and other breathtaking Canadian scenic wonders provide backgrounds for this near-plotless show-business musical. Jealous Broadway entertainers Betty Grable and John Payne fight and make up with the help of Carmen Miranda, Cesar Romero, and a bushel of songs and dances. 90m. **DIR:** Irving Cummings. **CAST:** Betty Grable, John Payne, Carmen Miranda, Cesar Romero, Edward Everett Horton, Charlotte Greenwood, Jackie Gleason, Harry James. **1942**

SPRINGTIME IN THE SIERRAS ★★ Beady-eyed Roy Rogers sets his sights on stopping evil Stephanie Bachelor and her hulking henchman Roy Barcroft from shooting game animals out of season. There's more action

than story in this fast-paced series entry. 75m. **DIR:** William Witney. **CAST:** Roy Rogers, Jane Frazee, Andy Devine, Stephanie Bachelor. **1947**

SPRUNG ★★ A romance between two young African Americans is broken up by their jealous best friends. Then, inexplicably, the friends try to get them back together. Everyone overacts shamelessly, and the film never makes psychological sense. Rated R for profanity and raunchy humor. 105m. **DIR:** Rusty Cundieff. **CAST:** Tisha Campbell, Rusty Cundieff, Paula Jai Parker, Joe Torry, John Witherspoon, Jennifer Lee, Clarence Williams, III. **1997 DVD**

SPUTNIK ★★★ The memorable character actor Mischa Auer (remember the artist who imitated a gorilla in *My Man Godfrey*?) costars in this French comedy about an animal lover trying to protect a dog and a mouse that escaped from a Russian satellite. Pleasant family comedy. B&W; 80m. **DIR:** Jean Dreville. **CAST:** Noel-Noel, Denise Grey, Mischa Auer. **1960**

SPY ★★1/2 A mediocre spy thriller involving a retired spy turned artist, who goes into hiding when his former colleagues decide he must die. Made for cable. 91m. **DIR:** Philip F. Messina. **CAST:** Bruce Greenwood, Jameson Parker, Tim Choate, Catharine Hicks, Ned Beatty, Michael Tucker. **1989**

•SPY GAME ★★★1/2 Taut action thriller acts as a bit of a history lesson on the Cold War and the outbreak of violence in Beirut. The pace is brisk as soon-to-retire CIA agent Robert Redford attempts to rescue longtime associate Brad Pitt from a Chinese prison. Concurrently, we learn about their relationship via flashbacks. Enjoyable, though the ending stretches the boundaries of reality. Rated R for violence, profanity, and brief sexuality. 126m. **DIR:** Tony Scott. **CAST:** Robert Redford, Brad Pitt, Catherine McCormack, Stephen Dillane, Larry Bryggman, Marianne Jean-Baptiste, Matthew March, Todd Boyce, Michael Paul Chan. **2001 DVD**

SPY GAMES ★★1/2 A comic look at the life of a spy in the post–Cold War era. More often witty than not, with a talented cast. Rated R for profanity and violence. 95m. **DIR:** Ilkka Jarvi-Laturi. **CAST:** Bill Pullman, Irène Jacob, Bruno Kirby, Udo Kier. **1999 DVD**

SPY HARD ★★ Once again, Leslie Nielsen gamely spoofs his own stalwart leading-man image; this time, he's Dick Steele, Secret Agent WD-40, on the trail of arch-villain General Rancor. Everyone tries hard to be zany, but the script is warmed-over *Get Smart*. Rated PG-13 for mild sexual humor. 85m. **DIR:** Rick Friedberg. **CAST:** Leslie Nielsen, Nicollette Sheridan, Charles Durning, Barry Bostwick, Andy Griffith, Marcia Gay Harden. **1996 DVD**

SPY IN BLACK, THE ★★★ Unusual espionage-cum-romance story of German agent Conrad Veidt and his love affair with British agent Valerie Hobson. British director Michael Powell brings just the right blend of duty and tragedy to this story, set in the turmoil of World War I. B&W; 82m. **DIR:** Michael Powell. **CAST:** Conrad Veidt, Valerie Hobson, Sebastian Shaw, June Duprez, Marius Goring. **1939**

SPY KIDS ★★★★ This delightful, family-oriented thriller concerns a pair of plucky adolescents forced to save the world when their secret agent parents are abducted by the nefarious Fegan Floop. Parents will appreciate the absence of guns and other conventional weapons in this spy spoof, which plays like a kid-oriented mix of James Bond and *Time Bandits*, and confines itself to colorful supervillains and wonderful gadgets such as electroshock bubble gum, crayon lasers, and a goldfish-shaped Super Guppy submarine pod. Rated PG for comic action. 88m. **DIR:** Robert Rodriguez. **CAST:** Antonio Banderas, Carla Gugino, Alan Cumming, Teri Hatcher, Alexa Vega, Daryl Sabara, Richard "Cheech" Marin, Danny Trejo, Tony Shalhoub, Robert Patrick. **2001 DVD**

SPY OF NAPOLEON ★★ Heavy-handed historical hokum finds Emperor Napoleon III using his illegitimate daughter to ferret out dissidents and enemies. Amusing enough and stars former silent-screen good guy Richard Barthelmess in a meaty role. B&W; 77m. **DIR:** Maurice Elvey. **CAST:** Richard Barthelmess, Dolly Hass. **1936**

SPY SMASHER ★★★ The costumed radio hero (Kane Richmond) takes on the Nazis in this fun-for-fans cliffhanger serial. B&W; 12 chapters. **DIR:** William Witney. **CAST:** Kane Richmond, Sam Flint, Marguerite Chapman, Hans Schumm, Tristram Coffin. **1942**

SPY WHO CAME IN FROM THE COLD, THE ★★★★ Realism and stark authenticity mark this sunless drama of the closing days in the career of a British cold-war spy in Berlin. Richard Burton is matchless as embittered, burned-out Alec Leamas, the sold-out agent. No 007 glamour and gimmicks here. 112m. **DIR:** Martin Ritt. **CAST:** Richard Burton, Claire Bloom, Oskar Werner, Bernard Lee, George Voskovec, Peter Van Eyck, Sam Wanamaker. **1965**

SPY WHO LOVED ME, THE ★★★★ This, the tenth James Bond epic, is Roger Moore's third, and he finally hits his stride. Directed with a blend of excitement and tongue-in-cheek humor, the film teams Bond with Russian agent XXX (Barbara Bach) in an effort to stop an industrialist (Curt Jurgens) from destroying the surface world so he can rule an undersea kingdom. Rated PG for violence and sexual situations. 125m. **DIR:** Lewis Gilbert. **CAST:** Roger Moore, Barbara Bach, Curt Jurgens, Richard Kiel, Bernard Lee, Lois Maxwell, Desmond Llewellyn, Caroline Munro. **1977 DVD**

SPY WITH A COLD NOSE, THE ★★★ This cute British spy spoof features Lionel Jeffries as an un-Bond-like counterintelligence agent. His plan to implant a microphone in the goodwill gift to the Soviets goes awry. The gift, a bulldog, may require an operation, and then the Soviets would be outraged. 113m. **DIR:** Daniel Petrie. **CAST:** Laurence Harvey, Daliah Lavi, Lionel Jeffries, Eric Sykes, Paul Ford. **1966**

SPY WITHIN, THE ★★★ Actor Steve Railsback makes his directorial debut with this effective spy thriller. Desperate agent Theresa Russell tries to escape the clandestine government organization she worked for that now wants her dead. Rated R for nudity, violence, and profanity. 92m. **DIR:** Steve Railsback. **CAST:** Scott Glenn, Theresa Russell, Lane Smith, Terence Knox, Katherine Helmond, Alex Rocco, Joe Pantoliano. **1994**

SPYMAKER: THE SECRET LIFE OF IAN FLEMING ★★★ Enjoyable fluff concentrates on writer Ian Fleming's exploits during World War II and his work with British intelligence. Jason Connery, Sean's son, is quite

good as Fleming, bringing the right amounts of humor and derring-do to the character. Made for TV. 77m. **DIR:** Ferdinand Fairfax. **CAST:** Jason Connery, Kristin Scott Thomas, Joss Ackland, Patricia Hodge, David Warner, Richard Johnson, Colin Welland. **1990**

SQUANTO: A WARRIOR'S TALE ★★★ A young Indian warrior (Adam Beach) is kidnapped by seventeenth-century English traders and exhibited as a wild man back in England. The story of how he escapes and returns home makes a farfetched but enjoyable Disney family adventure, in the tradition of *The Light in the Forest* and *Tonka*. Rated PG. 97m. **DIR:** Xavier Koller. **CAST:** Adam Beach, Eric Schweig, Michael Gambon, Nathaniel Parker, Alex Norton, Stuart Pankin, Donal Donnelly, Mandy Patinkin. **1994**

SQUARE DANCE ★★★★ A coming-of-age drama about a 13 year old Texas girl (Winona Ryder), *Square Dance* has so much atmosphere that you can almost smell the chicken-fried steaks. When the girl's loose-living mother (well played by Jane Alexander) takes her away from the comfort and care of her grandfather's (Jason Robards) ranch, the youngster's life goes from idyllic to hard-edged. Rated PG-13 for profanity and suggested sex. 110m. **DIR:** Daniel Petrie. **CAST:** Jason Robards Jr., Jane Alexander, Winona Ryder, Rob Lowe, Guich Koock. **1987**

SQUEEZE ★★1/2 Young friends try to survive the difficult life on the streets. Intense yet typical. Rated R for profanity and violence. 102m. **DIR:** Robert Patton-Spruill. **CAST:** Tyrone Burton, Eddie Cutanda, Phuong Duong, Geoffrey Rhue. **1996**

SQUEEZE, THE (1977) ★★1/2 Stacy Keach plays an alcoholic detective whose ex-wife is kidnapped for a large ransom. Good performances do not save this mediocre film. Rated R for nudity and language. 106m. **DIR:** Michael Apted. **CAST:** Stacy Keach, David Hemmings, Edward Fox, Stephen Boyd, Carol White. **1977**

SQUEEZE, THE (1987) 🦃 Michael Keaton can always be counted on for at least a few laughs, but a few laughs is about all you get in this dreary comedy-thriller. It's rated PG-13 for language and violence. 101m. **DIR:** Roger Young. **CAST:** Michael Keaton, Rae Dawn Chong, Meat Loaf. **1987**

SQUEEZE PLAY ★★ Another Troma trauma from the world's cheapest movie studio, a proudly dumb comedy that transfers the battle of the sexes to a softball field. Strictly for the couchbound whose remote controls are broken. Rated R for vulgarity and brief nudity. 92m. **DIR:** Samuel Weil. **CAST:** Jim Harris. **1980 DVD**

SQUIRM 🦃 Ugly film has hordes of killer worms attacking a small town. Rated PG. 92m. **DIR:** Jeff Lieberman. **CAST:** Don Scardino, Patricia Pearcy. **1976**

SQUIZZY TAYLOR ★★1/2 Fairly interesting film about the notorious Australian gangster of the 1920s. David Atkins gives a convincing performance. But the story begins to lose its edge after a while. Not rated. Has sex, nudity, and violence. 103m. **DIR:** Kevin James Dobson. **CAST:** David Atkins, Jacki Weaver, Alan Cassell, Michael Long. **1983**

S.S. HELL CAMP 🦃 Cheap, incredibly gross Eurotrash stomach-turner set in a Nazi compound. No rating, but sexually explicit and very sadistic. 88m. **DIR:** Ivan Katansky. **CAST:** Macha Magall, John Braun. **1975**

ST. ELSEWHERE (TV SERIES) ★★★ This 1980s medical drama began with a superb first season but quickly became an overly melodramatic parody of itself. The dedicated staff at St. Eligius hospital didn't always win against the Grim Reaper, which at the time was something of a novelty. With medical shows completely redefined by *ER* in the 1990s, this series hasn't dated all that well. 47m. **DIR:** Various. **CAST:** Ed Flanders, William Daniels, Norman Lloyd, David Birney, Ed Begley Jr., David Morse, Cynthia Sikes, Howie Mandel, Terence Knox, Christina Pickles, Denzel Washington, Mark Harmon. **1982–88**

STACKING ★★★1/2 A cut above the righteous save-the-farm films that abound these days, because it doesn't allow for an overblown triumphant outcome and the performances are exquisite. Frederic Forrest is wonderful as a hard-drinking hired hand, and Christine Lahti really gets under the skin of her restless character. Rated PG. 95m. **DIR:** Martin Rosen. **CAST:** Christine Lahti, Frederic Forrest, Megan Follows, Jason Gedrick, Ray Baker, Peter Coyote. **1988**

STACY'S KNIGHTS ★★ Kevin Costner's career has come a long way since this early snoozer, sort of a cross between *The Karate Kid* and *The Sting* set at the blackjack tables of Reno. Rated PG. 95m. **DIR:** Jim Wilson. **CAST:** Andra Millian, Kevin Costner. **1982**

STAG ★★★ Gripping morality play about a group of successful men who gather for a bachelor stag party and find their lives turned upside down when they accidentally kill a female stripper. As they decide what action to take, several members of the group panic, escalating the situation and tension. Made-for-cable. Rated R for adult situations, language, nudity, and violence. 92m. **DIR:** Gavin Wilding. **CAST:** Mario Van Peebles, Andrew McCarthy, Kevin Dillon, Taylor Dane, John Stockwell, William McNamara, John Henson, Ben Gazzara. **1997**

STAGE DOOR ★★★★ A funny and tender taste of New York theatrical life. Katharine Hepburn and Ginger Rogers are two aspiring actresses who undergo the stifling yet stimulating life of a lodging house that caters to a vast array of prospective actresses. Eve Arden, Lucille Ball, and Ann Miller also take residence in this overcrowded and active boardinghouse. B&W; 92m. **DIR:** Gregory La Cava. **CAST:** Katharine Hepburn, Ginger Rogers, Eve Arden, Lucille Ball, Ann Miller. **1937**

STAGE DOOR CANTEEN ★★ An all-star cast play themselves in this mildly amusing romance. Unless you enjoy looking at the many stage luminaries during their early years, you will find this entire film to be ordinary, predictable, and uninspired. B&W; 85m. **DIR:** Frank Borzage. **CAST:** William Terry, Cheryl Walkers, Katharine Hepburn, Harpo Marx, Helen Hayes, Count Basie, Edgar Bergen. **1943 DVD**

STAGE FRIGHT ★★★ Another winner from Alfred Hitchcock. Drama student Jane Wyman spies on actress Marlene Dietrich to prove she murdered her husband. Alastair Sim steals his moments as Wyman's protective parent, but most of the other moments go to the hypnotic Dietrich. B&W; 110m. **DIR:** Alfred Hitchcock. **CAST:** Marlene Dietrich, Jane Wyman, Michael Wilding, Alastair Sim, Richard Todd, Kay Walsh, Patricia Hitchcock. **1950 DVD**

STAGE STRUCK (1936) ★★ A no-talent singer-dancer, Joan Blondell, makes a bid for Broadway by financing a show for herself. She hires Dick Powell to direct. They clash, fall in love, clash, and depend on good old suave Warren William to smooth it all out. Not that anyone should care too much. Below par. B&W; 86m. **DIR:** Busby Berkeley. **CAST:** Joan Blondell, Dick Powell, Warren William, Frank McHugh, Jeanne Madden, Carol Hughes, Hobart Cavanaugh, Spring Byington. **1936**

STAGE STRUCK (1958) ★★ Despite a fine cast—Susan Strasberg excepted—this rehash of *Morning Glory* is flat and wearisome. You don't really care to pull for the young actress trying to make her mark. The late Joan Greenwood's throaty voice, however, is sheer delight. 95m. **DIR:** Sidney Lumet. **CAST:** Henry Fonda, Susan Strasberg, Joan Greenwood, Herbert Marshall, Christopher Plummer. **1958**

STAGE TO CHINO ★★★1/2 In this first-rate B Western, George O'Brien is a postal inspector who goes undercover to investigate a gold-shipping scam. The always reliable Roy Barcroft is the leader of the baddies, and Virginia Vale is the not-so-helpless principal victim. O'Brien's Westerns were always marked by fine acting, lots of action, and snappy dialogue, and this is a good example. B&W; 58m. **DIR:** Edward Killy. **CAST:** George O'Brien, Virginia Vale, Roy Barcroft, Hobart Cavanaugh, Carl Stockdale, William Haade, Glenn Strange. **1940**

STAGE TO MESA CITY ★★★ Lash LaRue and sidekick Fuzzy Q. Jones set out to nail bandits who are robbing stagecoaches. B&W; 56m. **DIR:** Ray Taylor. **CAST:** Lash LaRue, Al St. John, Jennifer Holt. **1947**

STAGE TO TUCSON ★★★★ After several stagecoaches are stolen, two government agents are sent to lead an investigation. Well scripted, action-packed. B&W; 82m. **DIR:** Ralph Moody. **CAST:** Rod Cameron, Wayne Morris, Kay Buckley, Carl Benton Reid. **1951**

STAGECOACH (1939) ★★★★★ John Ford utilized the *Grand Hotel* formula of placing a group of unrelated characters together. A stagecoach trip across the Old West provides the common setting and plenty of shared danger. Riding together with the mysterious Ringo Kid (John Wayne) is a grand assortment of some of Hollywood's best character actors. B&W; 99m. **DIR:** John Ford. **CAST:** John Wayne, Claire Trevor, Thomas Mitchell, John Carradine, Donald Meek, Andy Devine, George Bancroft, Tim Holt. **1939 DVD**

STAGECOACH (1986) ★★★ This made-for-television remake of John Ford's classic 1939 Western bears little resemblance to its predecessor, but the cast of country stars seems to be enjoying itself so much you can't help but join in. Certain conceits, such as Willie Nelson substituting the character of Doc Holliday for the less glamorous original character, seem out of place, but it's enjoyable. 98m. **DIR:** Ted Post. **CAST:** Willie Nelson, Kris Kristofferson, Johnny Cash, Waylon Jennings, John Schneider, Elizabeth Ashley, Anthony Franciosa, Anthony Newley, Mary Crosby, Lash LaRue. **1986**

STAGECOACH TO DENVER ★★★1/2 A supposedly good citizen resorts to murder and kidnapping in an all-out effort to get a woman's property. Red Ryder and Little Beaver put the owl hoots in their place. Action-packed. B&W; 54m. **DIR:** R. G. Springsteen. **CAST:** Allan "Rocky" Lane, Bobby Blake, Peggy Stewart, Roy Barcroft. **1946**

STAGECOACH WAR ★★★1/2 Hopalong Cassidy finds himself in the middle of a contract war between rival stage lines. B&W; 63m. **DIR:** Lesley Selander. **CAST:** William Boyd, Russell Hayden, J. Farrell MacDonald. **1940**

STAIRCASE ★★★ Although probably quite scandalous for its time, Charles Dyer's odd little British play-turned-film is interesting now only because of the novelty casting of Rex Harrison and Richard Burton as a couple of gay hairdressers who show their mutual affection by continuously sniping at each other. It's actually much tougher to watch Burton's character care for his invalid mother, whose confinement to bed is portrayed with graphic detail. Rated R for nudity, simulated sex, profanity, and sexual candor. 100m. **DIR:** Stanley Donen. **CAST:** Rex Harrison, Richard Burton, Cathleen Nesbitt, Beatrix Lehmann. **1969**

STAKEOUT ★★★★1/2 The fastest and funniest cop thriller since the original *Beverly Hills Cop*. A pair of detectives (Richard Dreyfuss and Emilio Estevez) strive to apprehend psychotic killer Aidan Quinn, who has escaped from prison. Rated R for profanity, nudity, and suggested sex, and violence. 116m. **DIR:** John Badham. **CAST:** Richard Dreyfuss, Emilio Estevez, Madeleine Stowe, Aidan Quinn, Dan Lauria, Forest Whitaker. **1987**

STALAG 17 ★★★★★ Many critics felt William Holden's Academy Award for *Stalag 17* was a gift for failing to give him proper recognition in *Sunset Boulevard*. Those critics should view this prison camp comedy-drama again. This film still holds up brilliantly today. Billy Wilder successfully alternated between suspense and comedy in this story of a World War II prison camp. Holden plays an opportunistic and cynical sergeant whose actions make him a natural suspect as the spy in the POWs'. midst. B&W; 120m. **DIR:** Billy Wilder. **CAST:** William Holden, Robert Strauss, Peter Graves, Otto Preminger. **1953 DVD**

STALIN ★★1/2 Robert Duvall's compelling portrayal of the infamous Soviet dictator is sabotaged by Paul Monash's haphazard script, which fails to provide the depth required to explain just how Stalin remained in power for so many years. Made for cable. 172m. **DIR:** Ivan Passer. **CAST:** Robert Duvall, Julia Ormond, Jeroen Krabbé, Joan Plowright, Maximilian Schell. **1992**

STALINGRAD ★★★1/2 This German antiwar film follows the WWII Stalingrad campaign through the eyes of six German soldiers, from early triumphs through crumbling fortunes and final catastrophe. The film follows exactly the structure of *All Quiet on the Western Front*, with the comrades one by one meeting horrible ends. The characters are two-dimensional archetypes, but the film is spectacularly well made, and the horrors of war are forcefully dramatized. In German with English subtitles. Not rated; contains graphic war violence. 135m. **DIR:** Joseph Vilsmaier. **CAST:** Thomas Kreischmann, Jochen Nickel, Sebastian Rudolph, Sylvester Groth. **1993 DVD**

STALKED ★★ Nothing new in this tale of an obsessed man and the lengths to which he's willing to go in order to be with the woman he loves. Rated R for violence and

language. 94m. **DIR:** Douglas Jackson. **CAST:** Maryam D'Abo, Tod Fennell, Jay Underwood, Lisa Blount, Karen Robinson. **1994**

STALKER ★★★★ In a decrepit future, a guide takes a scientist and a writer into the mysterious "Zone," site of a meteor crash, to find a source of great extraterrestrial knowledge. Definitely not for *Star Wars* fans, this adaptation of a Stanislaw Lem novel moves slowly but is filled with unforgettably beautiful images. In Russian with English subtitles. Not rated. 161m. **DIR:** Andrei Tarkovsky. **CAST:** Alexander Kaidanovsky, Anatoly Solanitsin. **1979 DVD**

STALKING MOON, THE ★★★ Gregory Peck is an army scout who takes in a white woman (Eva Marie Saint) and the child she bore while a captive of the Apaches. The Apache father kidnaps the child and starts a chase that lasts through most of the movie. Familiar, but captivating and with exceptional performances. 109m. **DIR:** Robert Mulligan. **CAST:** Gregory Peck, Eva Marie Saint, Robert Forster, Frank Silvera, Lou Frizell. **1969**

STAMPEDE ★★★★ Rod Cameron and his brother fight to hold on to their cattle empire against encroaching settlers. B&W; 78m. **DIR:** Lesley Selander. **CAST:** Rod Cameron, Don Castle, Gale Storm, Johnny Mack Brown. **1949**

STAND, THE ★★★1/2 Stephen King contemplated nothing less than the end of the world in his monumental novel, and it was reasonably well served by this television miniseries. After a "super-flu" virus decimates the United States, the few immune survivors gather into two camps: the forces of good and of evil. The strong ensemble cast works hard to sell the apocalyptic concept. Rated PG. 360m. **DIR:** Mick Garris. **CAST:** Gary Sinise, Molly Ringwald, Rob Lowe, Laura San Giacomo, Jamey Sheridan, Ruby Dee, Corin Nemec, Matt Frewer, Miguel Ferrer, Ossie Davis, Ray Walston, Adam Storke, Bill Faggerbakke. **1994 DVD**

STAND AND DELIVER ★★★★1/2 A *Rocky*esque interpretation of high school math teacher Jaime Escalante's true-life exploits. Edward James Olmos stars as Escalante, a man who gave up a high-paying job in electronics to make a contribution to society. Recognizing that his inner-city students need motivation to keep them from a lifetime of menial labor, he sets them a challenge: preparation for the state Advanced Placement Test . . . in calculus. Rated PG for language. 105m. **DIR:** Ramon Menendez. **CAST:** Edward James Olmos, Lou Diamond Phillips, Rosana De Soto, Andy Garcia. **1988 DVD**

STAND BY ME (1986) ★★★★1/2 Based on Stephen King's novella *The Body*, the story involves four young boys in the last days of summer and their search for the missing body of a young boy believed hit by a train. Morbid as it may sound, this is not a horror movie. Rather, it is a story of ascending to manhood. Sometimes sad and often funny. Rated R. 90m. **DIR:** Rob Reiner. **CAST:** Wil Wheaton, River Phoenix, Corey Feldman, Jerry O'Connell, Kiefer Sutherland, John Cusack, Richard Dreyfuss. **1986**

STAND BY ME (1988) ★★★ This spirited AIDS Day benefit was recorded at London's Wembley Arena April 1, 1987, and features three songs sung by George Michael, including "Everything She Wants," with his onetime Wham partner, Andrew Ridgeley. The show serves as a time capsule of the mid-'80s British music scene. Not rated. 60m. **DIR:** Mike Mansfield. **CAST:** George Michael, Boy George, Meat Loaf, Elton John, John Entwistle, Andy Summers, Herbie Hancock. **1988 DVD**

STAND-IN ★★★ This send-up of Hollywood rubbed more than one Tinsel Town mogul the wrong way by satirizing front office studio manipulators. Eastern financial genius Leslie Howard is sent west to "stand in" for stockholders and find out why Colossal Pictures is heading for skidsville. B&W; 91m. **DIR:** Tay Garnett. **CAST:** Leslie Howard, Humphrey Bogart, Joan Blondell, Jack Carson, Alan Mowbray. **1937**

STAND-INS ★★★ Fascinating character study about the women who served as stand-ins for some of Hollywood's golden-age leading ladies. Director Harvey Keith does an excellent job of evoking time and place, while his gifted actresses seem to envelop themselves in their roles. The hopes and dreams of these women who came to Hollywood to become stars but instead stand in the shadows are perfectly realized. Not rated; contains adult situations and language. 88m. **DIR:** Harvey Keith. **CAST:** Daphne Zuniga, Costas Mandylor, Charlotte Chatton, Jordan Ladd. **1997 DVD**

STAND OFF ★★ An ex-convict takes the Bahamian consul in Ottawa hostage, then has to negotiate with a reasonable police chief and a trigger-happy head of the Canadian Mounties. Some suspense, but there's nothing new here. Rated R for violence and profanity. 92m. **DIR:** Murray Battle. **CAST:** David Strathairn, Dejanet Sears, Stephen Shellen, Gordon Clapp. **1995**

STAND UP AND CHEER ★★★ Depression-plagued Americans need something to bring them out of their slump. Is it jobs, money, a chicken in every pot? No! The president says it's the curly-headed little dynamo he appoints as the Secretary of Amusement. Little Shirley manages to buoy spirits through her songs, dances, and sage advice. B&W; 80m. **DIR:** Hamilton MacFadden. **CAST:** Warner Baxter, Shirley Temple, Madge Evans, James Dunn, Stepin Fetchit. **1934**

STANDING TALL ★★1/2 During the Depression, the struggling owner of a small cattle ranch refuses to sell out to a competitor and finds himself under attack. The always-watchable Robert Forster is the only reason to see this standard made-for-TV Western. 100m. **DIR:** Harvey Hart. **CAST:** Robert Forster, Will Sampson, L. Q. Jones, Buck Taylor, Linda Evans, Chuck Connors. **1978**

STANDOFF ★★★ Topical issues are addressed in this action-thriller about a botched FBI raid on a Texas cult compound. Taut without being derivative. Rated R for adult situations, language, nudity, and violence. 105m. **DIR:** Andrew Chapman. **CAST:** Robert Sean Leonard, Keith Carradine, Dennis Haysbert, Natasha Henstridge. **1997**

STANLEY ★★ A crazy Vietnam vet (Chris Robinson) uses deadly snakes to destroy his enemies in this watchable, though rather grim, horror yarn. Rated PG for violence and unpleasant situations. 106m. **DIR:** William Grefe. **CAST:** Chris Robinson, Alex Rocco, Susan Carroll, Steve Alaimo. **1972**

STANLEY AND IRIS ★★★ Jane Fonda stars as a recently widowed bakery worker who teaches an illiterate coworker (Robert De Niro) how to read. A predictable but likable low-key romance derived from Pat Banker's

excellent novel, *Union Street*. Rated PG-13. 114m. **DIR:** Martin Ritt. **CAST:** Jane Fonda, Robert De Niro, Feodor Chaliapin, Martha Plimpton, Swoosie Kurtz, Harley Cross, Jamey Sheridan. **1990**

STANLEY AND LIVINGSTONE ★★★ When Spencer Tracy delivers the historic line, "Doctor Livingstone, I presume," to Sir Cedric Hardwicke in this production, you know why he was such a great screen actor. His performance, as a reporter who journeys to Africa in order to find a lost Victorian explorer, injects life and interest into what could have been just another stodgy prestige picture. B&W; 101m. **DIR:** Henry King. **CAST:** Spencer Tracy, Cedric Hardwicke, Richard Greene, Nancy Kelly. **1939**

STAR, THE (1952) ★★★ Bette Davis earned one of her ten Oscar nominations for her role of a has-been earnestly trying to make a comeback in show business. The story of a once-famous actress on the skids resembled her career at the time, and she makes more out of the role because of it. B&W; 89m. **DIR:** Stuart Heisler. **CAST:** Bette Davis, Sterling Hayden, Natalie Wood, Warner Anderson, Barbara Lawrence, June Travis, Minor Watson. **1952**

STAR! (1968) ★★★1/2 This 1968 biopic about fabled musical-comedy star Gertrude Lawrence has been remastered by director Robert Wise and restored to its original length. Though star Julie Andrews is in top form, the film is overly long and uneven. Not rated; contains mild profanity. 172m. **DIR:** Robert Wise. **CAST:** Julie Andrews, Richard Crenna, Daniel Massey, Michael Craig, Robert Reed. **1968**

STAR CHAMBER, THE ★★★★ A model group of superior court judges lose faith in the constitutional bylaws that they have sworn to uphold and decide to take the law into their own hands. Michael Douglas plays the idealistic young judge who uncovers the organization. Rated R for violence and profanity. 109m. **DIR:** Peter Hyams. **CAST:** Michael Douglas, Hal Holbrook, Yaphet Kotto, Sharon Gless, Jack Kehoe. **1983**

STAR CRASH 🦃 A vapid science-fiction space opera with but one redeeming quality: the scanty costumes worn by Caroline Munro as heroine Stella Star. Rated PG—some violence. 92m. **DIR:** Lewis Coates. **CAST:** Caroline Munro, Christopher Plummer, Joe Spinell, Marjoe Gortner, David Hasselhoff. **1979**

STAR CRYSTAL 🦃 Two astronauts encounter a rock containing a monster that feeds on and destroys humans. Rated R for nudity and violence. 93m. **DIR:** Lance Lindsay. **CAST:** Juston Campbell. **1986**

STAR 80 ★★★★ A depressing, uncompromising, but brilliantly filmed and acted portrait of a tragedy. Mariel Hemingway stars as Dorothy Stratten, the Playboy playmate of the year who was murdered in 1980 by the husband (an equally impressive portrayal by Eric Roberts) she had outgrown. The movie paints a bleak portrait of her life, times, and death. Rated R for nudity, violence, profanity, and sex. 102m. **DIR:** Bob Fosse. **CAST:** Mariel Hemingway, Eric Roberts, Cliff Robertson, Carroll Baker. **1983 DVD**

STAR HUNTER 🦃 High-school football players and cheerleaders become the prey of a group of vicious space monsters on a hunting trip. What you expect, only worse. Rated R for adult situations and violence. 84m. **DIR:** Cole McKay, Sam Newfield. **CAST:** Roddy McDowall, Stella Stevens, Rebecca Budig, Ken Stott, Zack Ward. **1995**

STAR IS BORN, A (1937) ★★★★ The first version of this thrice-filmed in-house Hollywood weeper, this is the story of an aging actor (Fredric March) whose career is beginning to go on the skids while his youthful bride's (Janet Gaynor) career is starting to blossom. Great acting and a tight script keep this poignant movie from falling into melodrama. 111m. **DIR:** William Wellman. **CAST:** Fredric March, Janet Gaynor, Adolphe Menjou, May Robson. **1937 DVD**

STAR IS BORN, A (1954) ★★★★1/2 Judy Garland's acting triumph is the highlight of this movie, which is considered to be the best version of this classic romantic tragedy. This one is well worth watching. James Mason is also memorable in the role originated by Fredric March. Be sure to get the full restored version. 154m. **DIR:** George Cukor. **CAST:** Judy Garland, James Mason, Charles Bickford, Jack Carson, Tommy Noonan. **1954 DVD**

STAR IS BORN, A (1976) ★★ The third and by far least watchable version of this venerable Hollywood war-horse has been sloppily crafted into a vehicle for star Barbra Streisand. The rocky romance between a declining star (Kris Kristofferson) and an up-and-coming new talent (Streisand) has been switched from the world of the stage to that of rock 'n' roll. Rated R. 140m. **DIR:** Frank Pierson. **CAST:** Barbra Streisand, Kris Kristofferson, Gary Busey, Oliver Clark. **1976**

STAR KID ★★★ Ignored by his dad, put down by his sister, beat up by the school bully: what's a 12-year-old to do? Save the world, of course! Costing a mere $10 million to make, this film relies on the wild imaginations of preteen viewers rather than sophisticated special effects to dazzle. This family film uses humor to teach little ones to confront their fears. Rated PG for violence. 101m. **DIR:** Manny Coto. **CAST:** Joseph Mazzello, Richard Gilliland, Corinne Bohrer, Joey Simmrin, Ashlee Levitch. **1997 DVD**

STAR KNIGHT 🦃 Medieval knights meet a visitor from outer space in a film that depicts the period with authenticity, but is pure hokum. Rated R for nudity and violence. 92m. **DIR:** Fernando Colombo. **CAST:** Klaus Kinski, Harvey Keitel, Fernando Rey. **1991**

STAR MAKER, THE ★★ A con man drives through Sicily with a truckload of motion-picture equipment, selling screen tests and promising fame and fortune to the gullible peasants he meets on his way. A grim companion piece to writer-director Giuseppe Tornatore's *Cinema Paradiso*, the film is overlong, ugly, and rather mean-spirited. In Italian with English subtitles. Rated R for (subtitled) profanity and simulated sex. 120m. **DIR:** Giuseppe Tornatore. **CAST:** Sergio Castellitto, Tiziana Lodato, Franco Scaldati, Leopoldo Trieste, Clelia Rondinella. **1995**

STAR MAPS ★★★ A young L.A. hustler harbors sweet dreams of being the next Antonio Banderas, but his pimp is also his father, and Dad is determined to keep the boy earning money on the streets. The acting is strong, especially by Douglas Spain as the hero—and Annette Murphy as the father's abused mistress. Rated R for strong sexuality, profanity, and brief violence. 86m. **DIR:** Miguel Arteta. **CAST:** Douglas Spain, Efrain

Figueroa, Annette Murphy, Kandeyce Jorden, Lysa Flores, Martha Velez. **1997**

STAR OF MIDNIGHT ★★1/2 William Powell, in a role cloned from his *Thin Man* series, is a debonair, urbane lawyer accused of murder. Abetted by Ginger Rogers, he sallies forth, repartee in mouth, to catch the real culprit. The police and gangsters alike make it difficult. Not bad. B&W; 90m. **DIR:** Stephen Roberts. **CAST:** William Powell, Ginger Rogers, Paul Kelly, Gene Lockhart, Ralph Morgan. **1935**

STAR PACKER, THE ★★★ The Shadow and his band of outlaws have a group of ranchers cowed until John Wayne rides into town and turns the tables on the baddies. A good B Western that will be best appreciated by Wayne fans. B&W; 60m. **DIR:** Robert N. Bradbury. **CAST:** John Wayne, Verna Hillie, George "Gabby" Hayes, Yakima Canutt. **1934 DVD**

STAR QUEST ★★★ Better-than-average remake of *Ten Little Indians* finds eight multinational astronauts who awaken from cybersleep only to find Earth has been destroyed by a nuclear holocaust. One by one the astronauts wind up dead, leading to a suspenseful climax. Emma Samms stands out as an android who literally goes to pieces. Rated R for nudity, violence, and language. 95m. **DIR:** Rick Jacobson. **CAST:** Steven Bauer, Brenda Bakke, Alan Rachins, Emma Samms, Cliff De Young, Ming-Na Wen. **1994**

STAR SLAMMER ★★ Here's an original idea: Take the standard mid-1970s women-in-prison movie and put it in outer space. Too bad the rest of the movie didn't live up to the premise. Rated R for violence, profanity, and adult situations. 88m. **DIR:** Fred Olen Ray. **CAST:** Ross Hagen, Aldo Ray, John Carradine, Bobbie Bresee, Sandy Brooke. **1986 DVD**

STAR SPANGLED RHYTHM ★★★1/2 Sailor Eddie Bracken thinks his gatekeeper father is in charge of Paramount Studios and shows up with shipmates for a deluxe tour. A good excuse to have cameos, skits, and specialty numbers by every Paramount star from William Bendix to Vera Zorina. B&W; 110m. **DIR:** George Marshall. **CAST:** Eddie Bracken, Betty Hutton, Victor Moore, Anne Revere, Walter Abel. **1942**

STAR TREK—THE MOTION PICTURE ★★1/2 Even though it reunites the cast of the popular television series and was directed by Robert Wise, who made one of the best science-fiction films of all time (*The Day the Earth Stood Still*), this $35 million film is a real hit-and-miss affair. Fans of the series may find much to love, but others will be bewildered—and sometimes bored—by the overemphasis on special effects and the underemphasis on characterization. Rated G. 132m. **DIR:** Robert Wise. **CAST:** William Shatner, Leonard Nimoy, DeForest Kelley, James Doohan, Nichelle Nichols, George Takei, Walter Koenig. **1979 DVD**

STAR TREK (TV SERIES) ★★★1/2 These are the voyages of the Starship *Enterprise*. Her original five-year mission was given short shrift by television executives who pulled the plug after a mere three years from late 1966 to mid-1969, and then watched in horror as fans turned it into the single most popular television series ever made. Paramount has reissued the original shows on tapes made from 35-mm masters, and the *Enterprise* and her crew never have looked lovelier. 50m. **DIR:** Marc Daniels, Joseph Pevney, James Goldstone, Gerd Oswald, Vincent McEveety. **CAST:** William Shatner, Leonard Nimoy, DeForest Kelley, George Takei, Walter Koenig, Nichelle Nichols, Majel Barrett, Grace Lee Whitney, James Doohan. **1966–1969 DVD**

STAR TREK II: THE WRATH OF KHAN ★★★★ James T. Kirk, Mr. Spock and the entire crew of the Starship *Enterprise* once more "boldly go where no man has gone before." It's no *Gone With the Wind*—or even *Raiders of the Lost Ark*. But it is fun to watch, and Trekkies are sure to love it. Rated PG for violence and gore. 113m. **DIR:** Nicholas Meyer. **CAST:** William Shatner, Leonard Nimoy, DeForest Kelley, Ricardo Montalban, James Doohan, George Takei, Nichelle Nichols, Walter Koenig, Kirstie Alley. **1982 DVD**

STAR TREK III: THE SEARCH FOR SPOCK ★★★★1/2 In this thrill-packed release, the crew of the U.S.S. *Enterprise* goes looking for Spock, who appeared to give his life to save his friends—at the end of *Star Trek II: The Wrath of Khan*. But is he dead? Finding out may be one of the most entertaining things you ever do in front of a TV set. Rated PG. 105m. **DIR:** Leonard Nimoy. **CAST:** Leonard Nimoy, William Shatner, DeForest Kelley, James Doohan, George Takei, Nichelle Nichols, Walter Koenig, Christopher Lloyd. **1984 DVD**

STAR TREK IV: THE VOYAGE HOME ★★★★1/2 Our stalwart heroes journey back to Earth in their "borrowed" enemy spacecraft just in time to witness a new tragedy in the making: an alien deep-space probe is disrupting our planet's atmosphere by broadcasting a message that nobody understands. When Spock identifies the "language" as that of the humpback whale, extinct in the twenty-third century, Kirk leads his crew back to the twentieth century in an attempt to locate two of the great mammals and utilize them for translation duty. Charming and lighthearted, though rated PG for somewhat intense themes. 119m. **DIR:** Leonard Nimoy. **CAST:** William Shatner, Leonard Nimoy, DeForest Kelley, James Doohan, George Takei, Walter Koenig, Nichelle Nichols, Catharine Hicks. **1986 DVD**

STAR TREK V: THE FINAL FRONTIER ★★1/2 In this entry of the big-screen series, a Vulcan (Laurence Luckinbill) takes control of the *Enterprise* to pursue his personal quest for spiritual enlightenment. Luckinbill delivers a strong performance, and the script features a number of witty exchanges between the stars. However, its ambitious, metaphysical premise is diluted by a weak, unsatisfying ending. Rated PG for profanity. 110m. **DIR:** William Shatner. **CAST:** William Shatner, Leonard Nimoy, DeForest Kelley, James Doohan, Walter Koenig, Nichelle Nichols, George Takei, David Warner, Laurence Luckinbill. **1989 DVD**

STAR TREK VI: THE UNDISCOVERED COUNTRY ★★★★ In this enjoyable piece of entertainment, Capt. Kirk and Dr. McCoy find themselves on trial for murder. Rated PG for violence. 101m. **DIR:** Nicholas Meyer. **CAST:** William Shatner, Leonard Nimoy, DeForest Kelley, George Takei, James Doohan, Nichelle Nichols, Walter Koenig, Kim Cattrall, David Warner, Christopher Plummer, Michael Dorn, Kurtwood Smith, Brock Peters, Iman. **1991 DVD**

STAR TREK: FIRST CONTACT ★★★★★ It's true. The even-numbered Star Trek entries are invariably the best, and this lean-and-mean face-off between the cast of *Star Trek: The Next Generation* and the Borg collec-

tive is no exception. Even if you don't know much about the Borg, a race of half-human, half-machine beings that absorb whole planet populations into their culture, it doesn't matter. The screenplay lays it all out quite clearly. Rated PG-13 for violence. 110m. **DIR:** Jonathan Frakes. **CAST:** Patrick Stewart, Jonathan Frakes, Brent Spiner, LeVar Burton, Michael Dorn, Gates McFadden, Marina Sirtis, Alfre Woodard, James Cromwell, Alice Krige, Robert Picardo, Dwight Schultz. **1996 DVD**

STAR TREK: GENERATIONS ★★★★ Fans of the two *Star Trek* TV series will be more than pleased by the big-screen teaming up of captains James T. Kirk (William Shatner) and Jean-Luc Picard (Patrick Stewart), despite the contrived circumstances under which they join forces to combat galactic evil. Rated PG for mild violence and light profanity. 118m. **DIR:** David Carson. **CAST:** Patrick Stewart, William Shatner, Malcolm McDowell, Jonathan Frakes, Brent Spiner, LeVar Burton, Michael Dorn, Gates McFadden, Marina Sirtis, James Doohan, Walter Koenig, Whoopi Goldberg, Alan Ruck. **1994 DVD**

STAR TREK: INSURRECTION ★★★★ This *Trek* adventure, while perhaps not among the best installments in this venerable series, delivers all the right moves and should keep fans quite happy. The story concerns an Eden-like planet populated by several hundred denizens who, unbeknownst to them, are being studied by a cloaked research team of Federation officers and the rather slimy and sinister Son'a. Great escapist fun. Rated PG for violence and rather ooky medical procedures. 103m. **DIR:** Jonathan Frakes. **CAST:** Patrick Stewart, Jonathan Frakes, Brent Spiner, LeVar Burton, Michael Dorn, F. Murray Abraham, Donna Murphy, Anthony Zerbe. **1998 DVD**

STAR TREK: THE CAGE ★★★★ The first pilot episode of the *Star Trek* television series, initially rejected by NBC for being "too cerebral" and "too good for TV." This is the only recorded story of Captain Christopher Pike (Jeffrey Hunter) and his quite different *Enterprise* crew. The plot concerns a planet of aliens who entrap various forms of animal life in their interplanetary "zoo." Not rated; suitable for family viewing. 65m. **DIR:** Robert Butler. **CAST:** Jeffrey Hunter, Leonard Nimoy, Majel Barrett, John Hoyt, Susan Oliver. **1964**

STAR TREK: THE MENAGERIE ★★★★ Combining the original *Star Trek* pilot, which starred Jeffrey Hunter as the captain, with footage featuring the show's eventual stars, it tells a fascinating story of how Spock brings comfort to his former commander on a planet capable of fulfilling any fantasy. It's science-fiction entertainment of the first order. 100m. **DIR:** Marc Daniels. **CAST:** William Shatner, Leonard Nimoy, Jeffrey Hunter, Susan Oliver, DeForest Kelley, James Doohan, Nichelle Nichols, George Takei. **1967**

STAR TREK: THE NEXT GENERATION (TV SERIES) ★★★★ The second crew of the Starship *Enterprise* "to boldly go" on a series of intergalactic adventures boasts an ensemble of fine actors. A lavishly produced, well-written program that, in our opinion, outclasses its predecessor. 96m. **DIR:** Paul Lynch. **CAST:** Patrick Stewart, Jonathan Frakes, Brent Spiner, Marina Sirtis, Gates McFadden, LeVar Burton, Denise Crosby, Michael Dorn, Wil Wheaton. **1987**

STAR WARS ★★★★★ May the Force be with you! Writer-director George Lucas blended the best of vintage pulp science fiction, old-fashioned cliff-hangers, comic books, and classic fantasy to come up with the ultimate adventure "a long time ago in a galaxy far, far away." Rated PG. 121m. **DIR:** George Lucas. **CAST:** Mark Hamill, Harrison Ford, Carrie Fisher, Alec Guinness, Peter Cushing, Anthony Daniels. **1977**

STAR WARS: EPISODE I THE PHANTOM MENACE ★★★★★ Jedi Knights are dispatched to planet Naboo to help in their battle with the Trade Federation, which is being manipulated by the dark side of the Force. This prequel to writer-director George Lucas's 1977 hit ranks high in the series, second only to the original. With its eye-popping special effects and fine performances, this all-ages entertainment actually lives up to its nearly overwhelming media hype. Rated PG for violence. 131m. **DIR:** George Lucas. **CAST:** Liam Neeson, Ewan McGregor, Natalie Portman, Jake Lloyd, Ian McDiarmid, Hugh Quarshie, Anthony Daniels, Kenny Baker, Terence Stamp, Samuel L. Jackson, Frank Oz, Ray Park. **1999**

•STAR WARS: EPISODE II ATTACK OF THE CLONES ★★★★★ In the ten years since *Phantom Menace*, Princess Padmé Amidala has become a senator. When her life is threatened, by "the dark side," Jedi apprentice Anakin Skywalker and his mentor, Obi-Wan Kenobi, are assigned to protect her, which leads to a "forbidden" romance between Padmé and Anakin, as well as the discovery of a plot by the Trade Federation to create an army of mindless warriors. Writer-director George Lucas nicely balances intimate moments with the large-scale action scenes, which are eye-poppingly spectacular. Rated PG for violence. 142m. **DIR:** George Lucas. **CAST:** Ewan McGregor, Natalie Portman, Hayden Christensen, Christopher Lee, Samuel L. Jackson, Frank Oz, Ian McDiarmid, Pernilla August, Temuera Morrison, Jimmy Smits, Jack Thompson. **2002 DVD**

STARBIRDS ★★ Refugees from a destroyed solar system plot to invade Earth in order to survive. The fact that these aliens look suspiciously like angels is somewhat disturbing. Mediocre. 75m. **DIR:** Michael Part, Tadao Nagahama. **1986**

STARDUST MEMORIES 🦃 Absolutely unwatchable Woody Allen film, his most chaotic and Bergmanesque attempt to claim that he can't stand his fans. Rated PG—profanity. B&W; 88m. **DIR:** Woody Allen. **CAST:** Woody Allen, Charlotte Rampling, Jessica Harper, Marie-Christine Barrault. **1980 DVD**

STARFLIGHT ONE 🦃 Airport '82? 115m. **DIR:** Jerry Jameson. **CAST:** Lee Majors, Hal Linden, Lauren Hutton, Ray Milland, Gail Strickland, George DiCenzo, Tess Harper, Terry Kiser, Robert Webber. **1982**

STARGATE ★★ A surprise hit at the box office, this sci-fi epic is long on special effects and short on sense. When it is discovered that a pyramid contains a portal to the universe, an Egyptologist accompanies a military force to the other side of the galaxy where they encounter human slaves forced to serve an all-powerful alien. Silly and often boring. Rated PG-13 for profanity and violence. 121m. **DIR:** Roland Emmerich. **CAST:** Kurt Russell, James Spader, Jaye Davidson, Viveca Lindfors, Alexis Cruz, Leon Rippy, John Diehl. **1994 DVD**

STARGATE SG-1 ★★★ Made-for-cable pilot led to a series whose plot picks up about a year after the theatrical film's ending. Earthlings reenter the portal to the universe, a shortcut to other stars and planets, to rescue those who've been kidnapped by aliens inhabiting their bodies. Film relies on *Star Trek*–type adventure formula rather than extraordinary special effects to hook viewers. Rated R for violence. 97m. **DIR:** Mario Azzopardi. **CAST:** Richard Dean Anderson, Michael Shanks, Amanda Tapping, Christopher Judge. **1997 DVD**

STARK ★★★1/2 Above-average TV movie about a Kansas cop butting heads against corrupt Las Vegas politicians and mobsters as he searches for the killers of his sister. Nicolas Surovy's sure performance and Ernest Tidyman's script make this a must for private eye buffs. 95m. **DIR:** Rod Holcomb. **CAST:** Nicolas Surovy, Marilu Henner, Dennis Hopper. **1985**

STARLIGHT HOTEL ★★ Familiar tale, although with a new setting: 1929 New Zealand. A 12-year-old runaway bound for Australia heads across the New Zealand countryside. Rated PG for profanity and violence. 91m. **DIR:** Sam Pillsbury. **CAST:** Peter Phelps. **1987**

STARMAN ★★★★ Jeff Bridges stars as an alien who falls in love with Earthling Karen Allen. *Starman* is best described as a fairy tale for adults, but the kiddies undoubtedly will enjoy it, too. Rated PG-13 for suggested sex, violence, and profanity. 115m. **DIR:** John Carpenter. **CAST:** Jeff Bridges, Karen Allen, Charles Martin Smith, Richard Jaeckel. **1984 DVD**

STARS AND BARS ★★ Inept comedy about a well-groomed British art expert who finds himself in a culture clash when he is sent to rural Georgia to acquire a priceless Renoir from an eccentric businessman. Pretty disappointing considering the fine cast. Rated R for nudity and profanity. 99m. **DIR:** Pat O'Connor. **CAST:** Daniel Day-Lewis, Harry Dean Stanton, Maury Chaykin, Joan Cusack, Keith David, Spalding Gray, Will Patton, Martha Plimpton, Steven Wright. **1988**

STARS AND STRIPES FOREVER ★★★ Don't expect an in-depth biography of John Philip Sousa, the March King, and you will probably enjoy this musical tribute. Loud and stirring. Turn up the sound and we can all march around the breakfast table. Good family viewing. 89m. **DIR:** Henry Koster. **CAST:** Clifton Webb, Ruth Hussey, Debra Paget, Robert Wagner. **1952**

STARS FELL ON HENRIETTA, THE ★★★★ Strong cast strikes oil in this Depression-era drama. Robert Duvall is wonderful as a prospector who discovers oil underneath the land of Aidan Quinn and family. Getting their permission to drill isn't as precarious as raising the necessary funds. Things heat up when Duvall steals the money from oil man Brian Dennehy. Rated PG for language. 110m. **DIR:** James Keach. **CAST:** Robert Duvall, Aidan Quinn, Frances Fisher, Brian Dennehy. **1995**

STARS IN MY CROWN ★★★★ Joel McCrea plays a frontier minister with quiet strength in a warm, gentle tale of pioneer families in the nineteenth century. A strong cast gives the story dignity as well as charm. B&W; 89m. **DIR:** Jacques Tourneur. **CAST:** Joel McCrea, Amanda Blake, James Arness, Ellen Drew, Ed Begley Sr., Alan Hale Sr., Dean Stockwell. **1950**

STARS LOOK DOWN, THE ★★★★ Classic film about a Welsh coal miner and his struggle to rise above his station and maintain his identity and the respect of his community is every bit as good today as it was when released. A coup for director Carol Reed and another great performance by Michael Redgrave as a man of quiet dignity and determination. Well worth the watching. B&W; 110m. **DIR:** Carol Reed. **CAST:** Michael Redgrave, Margaret Lockwood, Edward Rigby, Emlyn Williams, Cecil Parker. **1939**

STARSHIP 🦃 Rebels on a mining planet strive to overcome the evil rulers, who want to replace the workers with robots. Rated PG. 98m. **DIR:** Roger Christian. **CAST:** John Tarrant. **1985**

STARSHIP INVASIONS 🦃 How did these wily Canadians get such a top cast for such a dreadful movie? By lying to them about how cheesy it would be, assert Robert Vaughn and Chris Lee. Imagine an amalgam of the worst liabilities of Monogram's early Fifties sci-fi stiffs (e.g., *Flight to Mars*) and Sunn Classics's mid-Seventies UFO schlockumentaries. Rated PG. 87m. **DIR:** Edward Hunt. **CAST:** Robert Vaughn, Christopher Lee, Helen Shaver. **1977**

STARSHIP TROOPERS ★★ Some truly awesome special effects do not make up for the lack of dramatic punch in this sci-fi adventure about a group of cadets who graduate to find themselves thrust into an intergalactic war. The film only begins to get interesting at the end, where an abrupt ending seems to suggest that the filmmakers ran out of money. Rated R for violence and profanity. 129m. **DIR:** Paul Verhoeven. **CAST:** Casper Van Dien, Dina Meyer, Denise Richards, Jake Busey, Neil Patrick Harris, Clancy Brown, Michael Ironside. **1997 DVD**

STARSTRUCK ★★★1/2 A 17-year-old (Jo Kennedy) wants to be a star and goes after it at top speed. Director Gillian Armstrong has taken the let's-put-on-a-show! plot and turned it into an affable punk-rock movie. Rated PG for nudity and profanity. 95m. **DIR:** Gillian Armstrong. **CAST:** Jo Kennedy, Ross O'Donovan, Max Cullen. **1982 DVD**

START THE REVOLUTION WITHOUT ME ★★★★ Gene Wilder and Donald Sutherland star in this hilarious comedy as two sets of twins who meet just before the French Revolution. Cheech and Chong's *The Corsican Brothers* covered the same ground. If you want to see the story done right, check this one out. Rated PG. 98m. **DIR:** Bud Yorkin. **CAST:** Gene Wilder, Donald Sutherland, Hugh Griffith, Jack MacGowran. **1970**

STARTING OVER ★★★★ Burt Reynolds and Jill Clayburgh are delightful in this Alan Pakula film about two lonely hearts trying to find romance in a cynical world. Candice Bergen is superb as Reynolds's off-key singer/ex-wife, whom he has trouble trying to forget in this winner. Rated R. 106m. **DIR:** Alan J. Pakula. **CAST:** Burt Reynolds, Jill Clayburgh, Candice Bergen, Charles Durning, Frances Sternhagen. **1979**

•STARTUP.COM ★★★1/2 Chronicling the rise and fall of a multimillion-dollar Internet company, *Startup.com* is a sneak peek into the dangerous on-line world of the late 1990s—where an on-line company can be worth a fortune in fast-growing stocks, yet may not be a viable company in reality. Beginning with a handful of young entrepreneurs, we follow their journey from an original idea that turns into an on-line company worth millions to its subsequent descent into bankruptcy. *Startup.com*

holds no punches as we see all of the ups and even more of the downs of one particular ill-fated business. Rated R for language. 107m. **DIR:** Chris Hegedus, Jehane Noujaim. **CAST:** Kaleil Isaza Tuzman, Tom Herman. **2001 DVD**

STATE & MAIN ★★★★1/2 This delightfully wicked comedy features William H. Macy as a Hollywood director whose production crew descends on a small New England town to make a movie called *The Old Mill*. Never mind that the town's mill burned down years ago. This fish-out-of-water comedy is even funnier when the sharks realize they're out of their element. Great cast, including Alec Baldwin as the leading man with a thing for underage girls, and Sarah Jessica Parker as the leading lady who won't do her contractual nude scene. Funny, incisive, warm, and occasionally sweet. Rated R for adult situations, language, and nudity. 105m. **DIR:** David Mamet. **CAST:** William H. Macy, Alec Baldwin, Sarah Jessica Parker, Philip Seymour Hoffman, Rebecca Pidgeon, Julia Stiles, Charles Durning. **2000 DVD**

STATE FAIR (1945) ★★★ Wholesome atmosphere marks this nostalgic Middle America story of the adventures of a farm family—Pa's prize hog, Ma's spiked mincemeat, winsome daughter, and yearning son—at the Iowa State Fair. Rodgers and Hammerstein did a standout score for it, winning an Oscar with "It Might As Well Be Spring." Donald Meek's bit as a cooking judge is cameo-sharp comedy. 100m. **DIR:** Walter Lang. **CAST:** Dana Andrews, Jeanne Crain, Vivian Blaine, Dick Haymes, Fay Bainter, Charles Winninger, Donald Meek, Frank McHugh, Percy Kilbride, Harry Morgan. **1945 DVD**

STATE FAIR (1962) ★★ Lesser remake of the 1933 and 1945 films focusing on a very wholesome family's visit to the Iowa State Fair. A bit too hokey as predictable romantic situations develop. Only comic moment has Tom Ewell singing to a pig. 118m. **DIR:** José Ferrer. **CAST:** Pat Boone, Bobby Darin, Ann-Margret, Pamela Tiffin, Alice Faye, Tom Ewell. **1962**

STATE OF EMERGENCY ★★★★ Overcrowded inner-city emergency wards are the focus of this taut medical drama that emphasizes the impending disintegration of the U.S. hospital network. Performances are top-notch, but you won't be left with a good feeling. Rated R for profanity and graphic surgical procedures. 97m. **DIR:** Lesli Linka Glatter. **CAST:** Joe Mantegna, Lynn Whitfield, Melinda Dillon, Paul Dooley, Richard Beymer. **1994**

STATE OF GRACE ★★★ Intriguing first big-budget film from director Phil Joanou focuses on an undercover cop (Sean Penn) who comes back to his old neighborhood to bring down the Irish mob led by childhood friends Ed Harris and Gary Oldman. Oldman's performance is so over the top that he seems to have walked in from a John Waters or David Lynch movie. Rated R for violence, profanity, and nudity. 134m. **DIR:** Phil Joanou. **CAST:** Sean Penn, Ed Harris, Gary Oldman, Robin Wright, John Turturro, John C. Reilly, Burgess Meredith. **1990**

STATE OF SIEGE ★★★★ This is a highly controversial but brilliant film about the kidnapping of an American A.I.D. official by left-wing guerrillas in Uruguay. The film follows step-by-step how U.S. aid is sent to fascist countries through the pretext of helping the economy and strengthening democracy. No MPAA rating. 120m. **DIR:** Constantin Costa-Gavras. **CAST:** Yves Montand, O. E. Hasse, Renato Salvatori. **1973**

STATE OF THE UNION ★★★ This is a political fable about an American businessman who is encouraged by opportunities to run for the presidency, and leave his integrity behind in the process. Spencer Tracy and Katharine Hepburn are a joy to watch, as usual. B&W; 124m. **DIR:** Frank Capra. **CAST:** Spencer Tracy, Katharine Hepburn, Adolphe Menjou, Van Johnson, Angela Lansbury. **1948**

STATE OF THINGS, THE ★★★★1/2 Absorbing account of a film crew stranded on an island in Portugal during the production of a movie dealing with the aftermath of a nuclear holocaust. Running out of money and film stock, the German director, who is a parody of Wim Wenders, attempts to locate an American producer who is on the lam from loan sharks. In German and English. B&W; 120m. **DIR:** Wim Wenders. **CAST:** Allen Garfield, Samuel Fuller, Paul Getty, III, Viva, Roger Corman, Patrick Bauchau. **1983**

•STATE PROPERTY 🦃 Philadelphia thug gathers a crew of urban "soldiers" called the ABM (All Black Mafia) and forcefully takes over the city's drug trade in a pointless rap-punctuated stream of mayhem and female nudity. Rated R for profanity, violence, nudity, sexual content, and drug use. 85m. **DIR:** Abdul Malik Abbott. **CAST:** Beanie Sigel, Jay-Z, Damon Dash, Memphis Bleek, Omillio Sparks, Sundy Carter. **2002**

STATELINE MOTEL ★★ This Italian-made film involves a jewelry store robbery by a ruthless killer (Eli Wallach) and his handsome partner, Floyd (Fabio Testi). Not much to the film except the surprise ending featuring Barbara Bach. The film is dubbed and rated R for nudity, violence, sexual situations, and obscenities. 87m. **DIR:** Maurizio Lucidi. **CAST:** Ursula Andress, Eli Wallach, Barbara Bach, Fabio Testi, Massimo Girotti. **1975**

STATE'S ATTORNEY ★★1/2 John Barrymore is in good form in this barely believable story of a crooked lawyer who defends a prostitute as a lark and finds himself falling in love. Only in Hollywood, folks. B&W; 80m. **DIR:** George Archainbaud. **CAST:** John Barrymore, Helen Twelvetrees, William "Stage" Boyd. **1932**

STATIC ★★★ This highly offbeat drama explores isolation and alienation in human experience and the need to believe in something greater. The story centers around a would-be inventor (Keith Gordon) who attempts to enlighten people through a device that monitors images of Heaven. Surreal film falls somewhere between *Eraserhead* and *True Stories*. Rated R. 93m. **DIR:** Mark Romanek. **CAST:** Keith Gordon, Amanda Plummer, Bob Gunton. **1985**

STATION, THE ★★★ Adaptation of a popular Italian stage play takes place during one evening at a small railway station, as the manager meets a beautiful heiress on the run from her fiancé. Fresh, well-acted comic romance. In Italian with English subtitles. Not rated. 92m. **DIR:** Sergio Rubini. **CAST:** Sergio Rubini, Margherita Buy. **1990**

STATION WEST ★★★ An army undercover agent (Dick Powell) attempts to find out who is responsible for a rash of gold robberies, eventually falling in love with the ringleader (Jane Greer). This sturdy Western

boasts a fine supporting cast, good location cinematography, and nice action scenes. 92m. **DIR:** Sidney Lanfield. **CAST:** Dick Powell, Jane Greer, Tom Powers, Raymond Burr, Agnes Moorehead, Burl Ives, Regis Toomey, Steve Brodie, Guinn Williams. **1948**

STATUE, THE A Nobel Prize–winning linguist and a nude statue. Rated R for innuendos and nudity. 84m. **DIR:** Rod Amateau. **CAST:** David Niven, Virna Lisi, Robert Vaughn, John Cleese. **1971**

STAVISKY ★★★★ Complex drama about a crafty French swindler and a brilliant con man, whose financial exploits in the Thirties brought on riots that helped topple a government. With a superb musical score by Stephen Sondheim and dazzling cinematography by Sacha Vierny. In French with English subtitles. 117m. **DIR:** Alain Resnais. **CAST:** Jean-Paul Belmondo, Anny Duperey, Charles Boyer, Gérard Depardieu. **1974 DVD**

STAY AS YOU ARE ★★★★ This film begins conventionally but charmingly as the story of a romance between a 20 year old girl, Francesca (Nastassja Kinski), and Giulio (Marcello Mastroianni), a man old enough to be her father. It remains charming, but the charm becomes mingled with a controlled anguish when it becomes evident that Giulio may indeed be her father. No MPAA rating. 95m. **DIR:** Alberto Lattuada. **CAST:** Nastassja Kinski, Marcello Mastroianni, Francisco Rabal. **1978**

STAY AWAY JOE A lesser Elvis vehicle. Rated PG for countless sexual situations. 102m. **DIR:** Peter Tewksbury. **CAST:** Elvis Presley, Burgess Meredith, Joan Blondell. **1968**

STAY HUNGRY ★★★★1/2 An underrated film dealing with a young southern aristocrat's (Jeff Bridges) attempt to complete a real estate deal by purchasing a bodybuilding gym. Bridges begins to appreciate the gym as well as getting some insights into his own life. Rated R for violence, brief nudity, and language. 103m. **DIR:** Bob Rafelson. **CAST:** Jeff Bridges, Sally Field, R. G. Armstrong, Arnold Schwarzenegger. **1976**

STAY TUNED ★★★ A couch potato buys a devilish satellite dish from the prince of darkness himself. Before long, he and his wife are sucked into a nightmarish world of television where programs like "Meet the Mansons" and "Driving Over Miss Daisy" compete with game shows like "You Can't Win" and "Sadistic Hidden Videos." Dopey fun for the TV generation. Rated PG for mild violence. 98m. **DIR:** Peter Hyams. **CAST:** John Ritter, Pam Dawber, Jeffrey Jones, Eugene Levy, David Tom, Heather McComb. **1992 DVD**

STAYING ALIVE ★★ Sequel to the gutsy, effective *Saturday Night Fever* is a slick, commercial near rip-off. Six years have passed. Tony Manero (John Travolta) now attempts to break into the competitive life of Broadway dancing. Rated PG for language and suggested sex. 96m. **DIR:** Sylvester Stallone. **CAST:** John Travolta, Cynthia Rhodes, Finola Hughes, Steve Inwood. **1983**

STAYING TOGETHER ★★★★ Skillfully directed by Lee Grant, this splendid character study focuses on the McDermott family and the fried-chicken restaurant they run in Ridgeway, South Carolina. You'll be pleasantly surprised at how deeply you become involved with the characters. Rated R for profanity, nudity, and suggested sex. 91m. **DIR:** Lee Grant. **CAST:** Sean Astin, Stockard Channing, Melinda Dillon, Jim Haynie, Levon Helm, Dinah Manoff, Dermot Mulroney, Tim Quill, Keith Szarabajka, Daphne Zuniga. **1989**

STEAGLE, THE ★★★ Black comedy about how a daydreaming college professor (Richard Benjamin) deals with his mortality during the Cuban missile crisis. The week-long living spree he goes on has some hilarious consequences, but the screenplay is not handled very well despite the excellent cast. Rated PG for profanity and sex. 94m. **DIR:** Paul Sylbert. **CAST:** Richard Benjamin, Cloris Leachman, Chill Wills, Susan Tyrrell, Peter Hobbs. **1971**

STEAL BIG, STEAL LITTLE ★★ Adopted twin brothers—one a blue-collar hero full of brotherly love, the other a corporate shark driven by greed—struggle for control of a Santa Barbara lemon ranch owned by their deceased mother. This long, emotionally sluggish movie tries but fails to be a folksy comedy-drama. Rated PG-13 for language and violence. 134m. **DIR:** Andrew Davis. **CAST:** Andy Garcia, Rachel Ticotin, Alan Arkin, Holland Taylor, Joe Pantoliano, David Ogden Stiers, Kevin McCarthy. **1995**

STEAL THE SKY ★★ In this pretentious, melodramatic misfire, first telecast on HBO, Ben Cross is an Iraqi jet pilot who is targeted by Israeli intelligence for its own purposes. Mariel Hemingway is the agent assigned to seduce him into cooperating. Not rated. 110m. **DIR:** John Hancock. **CAST:** Ben Cross, Mariel Hemingway. **1988**

STEAL THIS MOVIE ★★★★ The life and times of antiwar activist Abbie Hoffman are effectively re-created in this wonderfully engaging film. It's obvious from the start that this is a valentine and not a poison pen letter, played out with romanticized idealism. Vincent D'Onofrio is perfect as Hoffman, whose past is recalled during a 1977 interview. Janeane Garofalo shines as his wife Anita, whose life experience with Hoffman and the media make her suspect. Rated R for adult situations, language, and nudity. 107m. **DIR:** Robert Greenwald. **CAST:** Vincent D'Onofrio, Janeane Garofalo, Jeanne Tripplehorn, Kevin Pollak, Donal Logue, Kevin Corrigan. **2000 DVD**

STEALING BEAUTY ★★★★ Tuscany's lush countryside and a gorgeous villa provide the idyllic setting for this slight but intoxicating tale of blossoming womanhood. A gawky late-teen virgin searches for love and answers to the mysteries of her mom's diary in Italy. Rated R for language, nudity, and sex. 102m. **DIR:** Bernardo Bertolucci. **CAST:** Liv Tyler, Jeremy Irons, Donal McCann, Sinead Cusack, Rachel Weisz, D. W. Moffett, Stefania Sandrelli, Jean Marais. **1996 DVD**

STEALING HEAVEN ★★ Middle Ages story of a forbidden love between a member of the clergy and a beautiful young aristocrat—Abelard and Heloise. Lots of lust and guilt but little else to sustain the film. Rated R for nudity. 108m. **DIR:** Clive Donner. **CAST:** Derek de Lint, Kim Thomson, Denholm Elliott. **1988**

STEALING HOME ★★★1/2 Enjoyable and sporadically disarming character study about a gifted athlete who renews his commitment to baseball after several years of aimless drifting. An ensemble cast does a fine job with this bittersweet tale. Rated PG-13 for profanity and suggested sex. 98m. **DIR:** Steven Kampmann, Will Aldis. **CAST:** Mark Harmon, Jodie Foster, Blair Brown, John Shea, Jonathan Silverman, Harold Ramis. **1988 DVD**

STEALTH FIGHTER Exceptionally bad terrorist thriller that suffers from weak direction, mundane act-

ing and writing, and a meager budget. Ice T, a former military pilot who fakes his death in order to steal a Stealth Fighter, now works with the bad guys, holding the United States up for ransom. Rated R for language and violence. 87m. **DIR:** Jim Wynorski. **CAST:** Ernie Hudson, Costas Mandylor, Ice T, Andrew Divoff, Erika Eleniak, John Enos III. **1999 DVD**

STEAM: THE TURKISH BATH ★★★★ Misleadingly promoted as a gay love story, this film can be enjoyed and even cherished by a wide audience. An Italian architect inherits his aunt's property, which includes a run-down public steam bath, in Istanbul. He travels there intending to dispose of the bath, but the change in atmosphere affects his outlook on life. A beautifully photographed, palpably sensual film. In Italian and Turkish with English subtitles. Not rated; contains adult situations and nudity. 94m. **DIR:** Ferzan Ozpetek. **CAST:** Alessandro Gassman, Francesca D'Aloja, Carlo Cecchi, Halil Ergün. **1997 DVD**

STEAMBOAT BILL JR. ★★★★1/2 Buster Keaton is at his comedic-genius best in this delightful silent film as an accident-prone college student who is forced to take over his father's old Mississippi steamboat. The climax features spectacular stunts by Keaton. It is truly something to behold—and to laugh with. Silent. B&W; 71m. **DIR:** Charles F. Reisner. **CAST:** Buster Keaton, Ernest Torrence, Marion Byron. **1928 DVD**

STEAMING ★★ Nell Dunn's play takes place in an English Turkish-style bathhouse where a group of women share their feelings about life. Vanessa Redgrave lends some needed reality to this sweaty gabfest. Rated R. 112m. **DIR:** Joseph Losey. **CAST:** Vanessa Redgrave, Sarah Miles, Diana Dors, Brenda Bruce, Felicity Dean. **1984**

STEEL (1980) ★★★ Plenty of action and stunts keep this minor film popping along surprisingly well. Lee Majors stars as the head of a construction crew struggling to complete a skyscraper on schedule. Majors is almost convincing, and a strong cast of character actors are great fun to watch. Rated R. 99m. **DIR:** Steve Carver. **CAST:** Lee Majors, Jennifer O'Neill, Art Carney, George Kennedy, Harris Yulin, Terry Kiser, Richard Lynch, Roger E. Mosley, Albert Salmi, R. G. Armstrong. **1980**

STEEL (1997) ★★1/2 Following DC Comics' temporary demise of Superman, new heroes were created to protect Metropolis. One of these newcomers was Steel, an idealistic army weapons engineer named John Henry Irons. Watchable with explosive special effects. Rated PG-13 for violence. 94m. **DIR:** Kenneth Johnson. **CAST:** Shaquille O'Neal, Judd Nelson, Annabeth Gish, Richard Roundtree, Gary Graham, Eric Pierpoint, Charles Napier. **1997**

STEEL AND LACE ★★ A rather depressingly brutal sci-fi thriller involving a classical pianist's brutal gang rape. Her brother, an ex-NASA scientist, plots to reap revenge on her attackers. Rated R for language and violence. 92m. **DIR:** Ernest Farino. **CAST:** Bruce Davison, David Naughton, Clare Wren, Stacy Naiduk, Michael Cerveris, David L. Lander, Brian Backer, John J. York. **1991**

STEEL DAWN Brainless bore set in the post-apocalyptic future has martial arts warrior joining in to help widow protect a colony of peaceful settlers. Rated R for violence. 100m. **DIR:** Lance Hool. **CAST:** Patrick Swayze, Lisa Niemi, Christopher Neame, Brian James, Anthony Zerbe. **1987**

STEEL FRONTIER ★★ Poor version of *The Road Warrior* in which a band of killers terrorizes a helpless town, and an unknown hero comes to save the day. Rated R for violence and profanity. 100m. **DIR:** Paul G. Volk, Jacobsen Hart. **CAST:** Joe Lara, Bo Svenson, Stacie Foster, Brian James. **1994**

STEEL HELMET, THE ★★★1/2 Director-writer Samuel Fuller's war movies actually improve with age. This one, shot (as usual) on a low budget and set in the Korean War, is packed with irony, lightning pace and vivid action. A war movie made with style and authority. B&W; 84m. **DIR:** Samuel Fuller. **CAST:** Gene Evans, Robert Hutton, Steve Brodie, James Edwards. **1951**

STEEL MAGNOLIAS ★★★★1/2 An all-star cast in a classy tearjerker about the enduring friendships among six women in a small southern town. Rated PG for brief profanity. 118m. **DIR:** Herbert Ross. **CAST:** Sally Field, Dolly Parton, Shirley MacLaine, Daryl Hannah, Olympia Dukakis, Julia Roberts, Sam Shepard, Tom Skerritt. **1989 DVD**

STEEL SHARKS ★★ The botched rescue attempt of an American scientist causes an elite commando squad to be captured and held hostage on an enemy submarine. It's up to Gary Busey and Billy Dee Williams to save the day. Derivative situations, stock characters, and unimaginative direction and special effects sabotage this murky thriller every step of the way. Rated R for language and violence. 94m. **DIR:** Rodney McDonald. **CAST:** Gary Busey, Billy Dee Williams, Billy Warlock, Shaun Toub, Barry Livingston. **1996**

STEELE JUSTICE One-man-army Martin Kove is hired to wipe out the Vietnamese Mafia in Los Angeles. Rated R for profanity and violence. 94m. **DIR:** Robert Boris. **CAST:** Martin Kove, Sela Ward, Ronny Cox, Bernie Casey, Joseph Campanella, Sarah Douglas, Soon-Tek Oh. **1987**

STEELE'S LAW ★★ Fred Williamson is Chicago's answer to *Dirty Harry* as he goes undercover in Texas. Williamson wears all hats—as director, producer, story-idea creator, and star—in this barely watchable actioner. Not rated, contains nudity, profanity, and violence. 90m. **DIR:** Fred Williamson. **CAST:** Fred Williamson, Bo Svenson. **1991 DVD**

STEELYARD BLUES ★★★1/2 This is a quirky little film about a group of social misfits who band together to help one of their own against his government-employed brother. Jane Fonda, Donald Sutherland, and Peter Boyle seem to have fun playing the misfits. Boyle's imitation of Marlon Brando is a highlight. Rated PG for language. 93m. **DIR:** Alan Myerson. **CAST:** Jane Fonda, Donald Sutherland, Peter Boyle, Alan Myerson, Garry Goodrow. **1973**

STELLA (1950) ★★ A family of screwballs and the suspicion of murder don't add up in this black comedy of errors. David Wayne believes he killed his uncle, buried the body, and forgot where. A moderately likable misfire. B&W; 83m. **DIR:** Claude Binyon. **CAST:** Ann Sheridan, Victor Mature, David Wayne, Leif Erickson, Frank Fontaine. **1950**

STELLA (1955) ★★★ Melina Mercouri made her screen debut in this melodrama as a free-spirited bar singer who leads two men to tragic ends. She's appeal-

ingly sexy, though the film (despite able work by director Michael Cacoyannis, who went on to make *Zorba the Greek*) is a bit dreary. In Greek with English subtitles. B&W; 94m. **DIR:** Michael Cacoyannis. **CAST:** Melina Mercouri, Yiorgo Fountas. **1955 DVD**

STELLA (1990) ★★ The Divine Miss M. takes a pratfall in this sudsy, airheaded remake of *Stella Dallas.* As in the original 1937 film, Bette Midler's Stella is a working-class gal who gives up her daughter to be raised by her wealthy father. Unfortunately for the film, the social conditions that existed during the Great Depression no longer prevail, and Stella's sacrifice seems stupid rather than noble. Rated PG-13 for profanity and frank sexual themes. 106m. **DIR:** John Erman. **CAST:** Bette Midler, John Goodman, Trini Alvarado, Stephen Collins, Marsha Mason. **1990**

STELLA DALLAS ★★★★ Barbara Stanwyck's title-role performance as the small-town vulgar innocent who sacrifices everything for her daughter got her a well-deserved Oscar nomination and set the standard for this type of screen character. John Boles is the elegant wealthy heel who does her wrong. Anne Shirley is Laurel, the object of her mother's completely selfeffacing conduct. B&W; 111m. **DIR:** King Vidor. **CAST:** Barbara Stanwyck, Anne Shirley, John Boles, Alan Hale Sr., Tim Holt, Marjorie Main. **1937 DVD**

STELLA MARIS ★★★★★ Arguably Mary Pickford's masterpiece, although it stands in stark contrast to the sweetness-and-light qualities of many other popular vehicles. Some amazing double-exposure photography allows her to play *two* roles, a beautiful invalid and an ugly drab who plays an important part in the invalid's life. Silent. B&W; 70m. **DIR:** Marshall Neilan. **CAST:** Mary Pickford, Conway Tearle. **1918 DVD**

STENDHAL SYNDROME, THE ★★★1/2 One of the most complex films ever from Italian director Dario Argento, this is also his most character-driven piece. The director's daughter Asia Argento stars as a detective engaged in a game of cat and mouse with a serial rapist/killer. This film marks Argento's return to the form of his earlier *giallos* with its complexities and a brutality that seems to become an art form of its own. Haunting. Not rated; contains violence, nudity, and simulated sex. 113m. **DIR:** Dario Argento. **CAST:** Asia Argento, Thomas Kretschmann, John Quentin. **1998 DVD**

STEP LIVELY ★★★1/2 As a jazzy, bright musical remake of the Marx Brothers film *Room Service*, this film is a very enjoyable story about George Murphy's attempt to get his show produced on Broadway. It's in this film that Frank Sinatra receives his first screen kisses (from Gloria DeHaven), which caused swoons from numerous female Sinatraphiles. As the hotel manager, Walter Slezak almost steals the show. 89m. **DIR:** Tim Whelan. **CAST:** Frank Sinatra, George Murphy, Walter Slezak, Adolphe Menjou. **1944**

STEPDAUGHTER, THE ★★ Poor Susan Miller. After years of abuse living in foster homes, she decides to go after the birth mother who gave her up. When Susan finds her, she takes a job at the ranch that her mother and her husband own, giving her time to contemplate her revenge. Lightweight and shy considering the genre. Rated R for adult situations, language, and violence. 92m. **DIR:** Peter Liapis. **CAST:** Andrea Roth, Lisa Dean Ryan, Cindy Pickett, Jaimz Woolvett, Gil Gerard. **1999 DVD**

STEPFATHER, THE ★★★★ Jerry Blake (Terry O'Quinn) is so relentlessly cheerful that his stepdaughter, Stephanie Maine (Jill Schoelen), complains to a friend, "It's just like living with Ward Cleaver." Little does she know that the accent should be on the cleaver. Jerry, you see, is a raving maniac. A thriller of a chiller. Rated R for violence, profanity, and brief nudity. 90m. **DIR:** Joseph Ruben. **CAST:** Terry O'Quinn, Shelley Hack, Jill Schoelen, Charles Lanyer, Stephen Shellen. **1987**

STEPFATHER II ★★ A misfire because it obviously tries to take advantage of its predecessor. The psychotic killer from the first film starts the same routine all over again by posing as a marriage counselor and preying on unsuspecting divorcées and widows. Rated R for gratuitous violence. 86m. **DIR:** Jeff Burr. **CAST:** Terry O'Quinn, Meg Foster, Henry Brown, Jonathan Brandis, Caroline Williams, Mitchell Laurance. **1989**

STEPFATHER III: FATHER'S DAY ★★ Make room for daddy once again, as the world's worst father returns after escaping from an insane asylum, having had his face surgically altered. Obviously the filmmaker hasn't heard of family values. Rated R for violence and language. 109m. **DIR:** Guy Magar. **CAST:** Robert Wrightman, Priscilla Barnes, Season Hubley. **1992**

STEPFORD HUSBANDS, THE ★★1/2 Once more back to Connecticut for a tale of programmable zombies. Donna Mills stars as a wife trying to free her husband, novelist Michael Ontkean, from the experiment. The script has a been-there-done-that feel to it. Not rated; contains mild violence. 120m. **DIR:** Fred Walton. **CAST:** Donna Mills, Michael Ontkean, Sarah Douglas, Louise Fletcher, Cindy Williams. **1996**

STEPFORD WIVES, THE ★★★ Ira Levin's "adult horror story" is a letdown after *Rosemary's Baby* and nowhere near as credible. Small-town newcomers can't quite figure out why all the other women in their community act so perpetually euphoric; the answer concerns a bit of misguided technology and the need to believe that all men are pigs. Rated PG for brief nudity. 115m. **DIR:** Bryan Forbes. **CAST:** Katharine Ross, Paula Prentiss, Peter Masterson, Patrick O'Neal. **1975 DVD**

•STEPHANIE, NATHALIE, CAROLINE AND VINCENT ★★ A man breaks off a stable relationship with one woman to pursue another, but his life falls to pieces soon after. This French-Canadian film attempts to be an existential sex farce, without the benefit of nudity, sex, or comedy. In French with English subtitles. Not rated; contains profanity. 74m. **DIR:** Carl Ulrich. **CAST:** Simon Boisvert, Natasha M. Leroux, Diana Lewis, Sylvain Latendresse. **2001**

STEPHEN KING'S GOLDEN YEARS (TV SERIES) ★★★ Seven-episode TV miniseries about an elderly janitor who is exposed to a mysterious form of radiation during a lab accident at a secret government research facility. Soon the old man finds himself slowly growing younger and developing unexplained powers, while being pursued by a shadowy intelligence organization. Quirky, funny, and suspenseful. Not rated; contains violence and adult situations. 232m. **DIR:** Stephen Tolkin, Michael Gornick, Allen Coulter, Kenneth Fink. **CAST:**

Keith Szarabajka, Felicity Huffman, Frances Sternhagen, Ed Lauter. **1991**

STEPHEN KING'S GRAVEYARD SHIFT ★★ Based on a short story from King's *Night Shift* collection, this is a disappointing film about workers who are menaced by a giant mutant rat-bat while cleaning a factory basement. Rated R for violence, profanity, and gore. 90m. **DIR:** Ralph S. Singleton. **CAST:** David Andrews, Kelly Wolf, Stephen Macht, Brad Dourif, Andrew Divoff. **1990**

STEPHEN KING'S SLEEPWALKERS ★★ An incestuous mother-son duo stalk virginal young women to feed their vampirelike hunger in this film of an original script from Stephen King. This film differs from his books in that it lacks all the things that make a Stephen King novel a Stephen King novel: fully fleshed out characters interacting in a cohesive plot. Rated R for violence, profanity, and gore. 91m. **DIR:** Mick Garris. **CAST:** Brian Krause, Madchen Amick, Alice Krige, Jim Haynie, Cindy Pickett, Ron Perlman. **1992**

STEPHEN KING'S THE SHINING ★★★1/2 King's disappointment over Stanley Kubrick's version of his best-selling novel resulted in this spooky made-for-television miniseries that's more true to King's vision. King wrote the screenplay himself, thus fleshing out the nightmare that awaits the Torrance family when they agree to act as caretakers for the Overlook Hotel. Not rated; contains violence. 270m. **DIR:** Mick Garris. **CAST:** Steven Weber, Rebecca DeMornay, Courtland Mead, Melvin Van Peebles. **1997**

STEPMOM ★★ Fluffy little tale concerns Julia Roberts's efforts to win the respect, if not actual affection, of her fiance's two children, who'd much rather stay with divorced mom Susan Sarandon. Unfortunately, Susan Sarandon's character is so cruel and abrasive that you'll quickly cease to care about her, even when the film plunges into its lamentable third act. Rated PG-13 for profanity and sexual candor. 124m. **DIR:** Chris Columbus. **CAST:** Julia Roberts, Susan Sarandon, Ed Harris, Jena Malone, Liam Aiken. **1998 DVD**

STEPMONSTER ★★★★ A Tropopkin, a comic-book monster who can assume a human form, becomes engaged to a man. His son, who's an avid comic-book reader, realizes what is happening, but no one believes him. Enjoyable for all ages, with good acting all around. Rated PG-13 for profanity and violence. 87m. **DIR:** Jeremy Stanford. **CAST:** Alan Thicke, Robin Riker, George Gaynes, Ami Dolenz, Edie McClurg, John Astin, Corey Feldman, Billy Corben, Molly Cheek. **1992**

STEPPENWOLF ★★1/2 In this United States–Switzerland coproduction, director Fred Haines gives us an almost literal adaptation of Hermann Hesse's most widely read novel. It's a good try, but the source really isn't filmable. Rated PG. 105m. **DIR:** Fred Haines. **CAST:** Max von Sydow, Dominique Sanda, Pierre Clementi. **1974**

STEPPING OUT ★★★1/2 Musical-comedy fans will delight in this sweet-natured, lightweight story of a struggling dance teacher (Liza Minnelli) who decides to coach her generally inept students into a crack dance troupe. A first-rate cast, and Minnelli sparkles with enthusiasm. Rated PG for profanity. 101m. **DIR:** Lewis Gilbert. **CAST:** Liza Minnelli, Shelley Winters, Bill Irwin, Ellen Greene, Julie Walters, Jane Krakowski, Sheila McCarthy, Andrea Martin. **1991**

STEPSISTER, THE ★★ A young woman's father remarries, and she gains a stepsister as well as a stepmother. From the start, the stepsisters don't get along, and things soon turn nasty. This made-for-cable thriller might have been a good movie if it had a better plot, better acting, and a better script. Rated PG-13 for violence. 95m. **DIR:** Charles Correll. **CAST:** Rena Sofer, Bridgette Wilson, Richard Joseph Paul, Alan Rachins, Linda Evans. **1997**

STERILE CUCKOO, THE ★★★★ Painfully poignant story about a dedicated young college lad (Wendell Burton) and the loopy young woman (Liza Minnelli) who, unable to handle people on their own terms, demands too much of those with whom she becomes involved. Minnelli's Pookie Adams won the actress a well-deserved Academy Award nomination. Rated PG for sexual situations. 107m. **DIR:** Alan J. Pakula. **CAST:** Liza Minnelli, Wendell Burton, Tim McIntire. **1969**

STEVIE ★★★★ Glenda Jackson gives a brilliant performance as reclusive poet Stevie Smith in this stagy, but still interesting, film. Mona Washbourne is the film's true delight as Smith's doting—and slightly dotty—aunt. Trevor Howard narrates and costars in this British release. Rated PG for brief profanity. 102m. **DIR:** Robert Enders. **CAST:** Glenda Jackson, Mona Washbourne, Trevor Howard, Alec McCowen. **1978**

STICK ★★★ *Stick* is an odd mixture of comedy and violence that more than once strains the viewer's suspension of disbelief. Fans of the original novel, by Elmore Leonard, will be shocked at how far Burt Reynolds's film strays from its source. What should have been a tough, lean, and mean movie contains a surprising amount of clowning by its stars. Despite all this, it has enough action and genuine laughs to please Reynolds's fans. Rated R for profanity and violence. 109m. **DIR:** Burt Reynolds. **CAST:** Burt Reynolds, Charles Durning, George Segal, Candice Bergen. **1985**

STICK TO YOUR GUNS ★★ The old Bar-20 crowd is summoned to fight a gang of slick rustlers, and Hopalong Cassidy and California get to the trouble first. Assuming false identities, the two are invited to join the outlaw gang and then alert the Bar-20 boys. A silly subplot, too many songs, and too much Andy Clyde attempting humor mar this otherwise gritty series entry, which is a who's who of veteran actors. B&W; 63m. **DIR:** Lesley Selander. **CAST:** William Boyd, Andy Clyde, Brad King, Dick Curtis, Jacqueline Holt, Charles Middleton, Kermit Maynard. **1941**

STICK-UP, THE The alternate title, *Mud,* seems more appropriate for this dreary romance-adventure set in 1935 England. 101m. **DIR:** Jeffrey Bloom. **CAST:** David Soul, Pamela McMyler. **1977**

STICKY FINGERS Two struggling female musicians are handed $900,000 in dirty money by a drug-dealing friend. Rated PG-13 for language and sexual allusions. 89m. **DIR:** Catlin Adams. **CAST:** Helen Slater, Melanie Mayron, Eileen Brennan, Christopher Guest, Stephen McHattie, Shirley Stoler, Gwen Welles, Danitra Vance, Carol Kane. **1988**

•STIFF UPPER LIPS ★★1/2 The Masterpiece Theater/Merchant Ivory genre of films like *A Room with a View* and *Howards End* are parodied in this lukewarm

comedy. It hits all the clichés on the nose with a tale of sexually repressed Edwardian Brits going to Italy to loosen up. Your enjoyment of it will depend on how much you have seen the films it's making fun of. Rated R for sexual humor. 94m. **DIR:** Gary Sinyor. **CAST:** Peter Ustinov, Prunella Scales, Georgina Cates, Samuel West, Robert Portal, Sean Pertwee. **1998 DVD**

STIGMA An ex–medical student just out of prison battles prejudice and an epidemic of VD in a sheltered island community. 93m. **DIR:** David E. Durston. **CAST:** Philip Michael Thomas. **1972**

STIGMATA ★★ Atheist Pittsburgh hairdresser receives rosary beads in the mail that were stolen from a dead South American priest and experiences seizures and bloody wounds associated with the crucifixion of Jesus. A priest-scientist investigates while a cardinal emphasizes public-relations spin control over The Truth. This pretentious, mind-numbing religious thriller is a sort of MTV version of *The Exorcist* sensationalized by a Vatican conspiracy. Rated R for violence, language, and sexual content. 102m. **DIR:** Rupert Wainwright. **CAST:** Patricia Arquette, Gabriel Byrne, Jonathan Pryce, Nia Long. **1999 DVD**

STILETTO A rich jet-setter also happens to be a professional killer. Rated R. 98m. **DIR:** Bernard Kowalski. **CAST:** Alex Cord, Britt Ekland, Patrick O'Neal, Barbara McNair. **1969**

STILL CRAZY ★★1/2 This lightly amusing comedy is a sort of *Full Monty* meets *Spinal Tap*. British rock dinosaurs from the 1970s attempt a reunion tour of their group Strange Fruit to tune up for the anniversary restaging of a legendary rock concert. Trouble brews as the middle-aged lads discover they are very rusty at rocking and are still nagged by past personality conflicts. Rated R for language, sexuality, and drug content. 94m. **DIR:** Brian Gibson. **CAST:** Stephen Rea, Timothy Spall, Jimmy Nail, Bill Nighy, Juliet Aubrey, Billy Connelly. **1998 DVD**

STILL NOT QUITE HUMAN ★★1/2 While still delivering family fun, this made-for-cable film is the weakest and most unbelievable in the Disney trilogy. Chip's scientist father (Alan Thicke) is cloned by an evil scientist. Chip must find his real dad who is being tortured to reveal his computer technology secrets. 90m. **DIR:** Eric Luke. **CAST:** Alan Thicke, Jay Underwood, Christopher Neame, Rosa Nevin, Betsy Palmer. **1992**

STILL OF THE NIGHT ★★★1/2 In this well-crafted thriller by writer-director Robert Benton a psychiatrist (Roy Scheider) falls in love with an art curator (Meryl Streep) who may have killed one of his patients and may be after him next. If you like being scared out of your wits, you won't want to miss it. Rated PG for violence and adult themes. 91m. **DIR:** Robert Benton. **CAST:** Roy Scheider, Meryl Streep, Jessica Tandy, Joe Grifasi, Sara Botsford. **1982**

STILL SMOKIN' Shambles about a film festival in Amsterdam. Rated R for nudity and scatological humor. 91m. **DIR:** Thomas Chong. **CAST:** Cheech and Chong, Hansman In't Veld, Carol Van Herwijnen. **1983**

STILTS, THE (LOS ZANCOS) ★★★1/2 This film, about an aged playwright and professor (Fernando Fernán Gomez) who falls in love with a young actress (Laura Del Sol), is occasionally melodramatic. Her unwillingness to commit herself to him gives the film its tension, and the acting is good enough to overcome most of the overwrought moments. In Spanish with English subtitles. Not rated; contains nudity. 95m. **DIR:** Carlos Saura. **CAST:** Laura Del Sol, Fernando Fernán Gómez, Francisco Rabal, Antonio Banderas. **1984**

STING, THE ★★★★1/2 Those *Butch Cassidy and the Sundance Kid* stars, Paul Newman and Robert Redford, were reunited for this fast-paced entertainment as two con men who outcon a con. Winner of seven Academy Awards—including best picture—this film, directed by George Roy Hill (*A Little Romance* and *Butch Cassidy*) revived Scott Joplin's music. For that, and the more obvious reasons, it is not to be missed. Rated PG. 129m. **DIR:** George Roy Hill. **CAST:** Paul Newman, Robert Redford, Robert Shaw, Charles Durning, Ray Walston, Eileen Brennan, Harold Gould, Dana Elcar. **1973 DVD**

STING II, THE ★★ You could hardly expect a sequel to such a joyously entertaining film as *The Sting* to measure up. True to those expectations, this film, starring Jackie Gleason, Mac Davis, Teri Garr, and Karl Malden, doesn't come close. Rated PG for violence. 102m. **DIR:** Jeremy Paul Kagan. **CAST:** Jackie Gleason, Mac Davis, Teri Garr, Karl Malden, Oliver Reed, Bert Remsen. **1983**

STINGRAY Two young men buy a Stingray, unaware that it's filled with stolen cash and drugs. Rated R for violence and profanity. 100m. **DIR:** Richard Taylor. **CAST:** Chris Mitchum, Sherry Jackson, Bill Watson. **1978**

STIR CRAZY ★★★1/2 Richard Pryor and Gene Wilder work something close to a miracle, making something out of nothing or, at least, close to nothing. It's a simple-minded spoof of crime and prison movies with, of all things, a little *Urban Cowboy* thrown in. But you have so much fun watching the stars, you don't mind. Rated R. 111m. **DIR:** Sidney Poitier. **CAST:** Richard Pryor, Gene Wilder, Georg Stanford Brown, JoBeth Williams. **1980 DVD**

STIR OF ECHOES ★★★1/2 Two films released during the summer of 1999 found characters trying to help the dead rest easy; everybody raved about *The Sixth Sense*, while this one quietly came and went. It deserved better; director-scripter David Koepp intelligently adapted Richard Matheson's 1958 novel, and star Kevin Bacon credibly plays a working-class guy who, after an experimentation with hypnosis, finds himself "open" to all sorts of phenomena. It turns out that his young son *also* possesses this "gift," and both find their talent utilized in an unsolved murder case that has remained a neighborhood dark secret. Koepp displays plenty of imagination as a visual stylist; the key murder, shown through the eyes of the victim rather than the killer, is nothing short of chilling, in terms of conveying the sheer, ghastly horror of the moment. Rated R for profanity, violence, and rape. 99m. **DIR:** David Koepp. **CAST:** Kevin Bacon, Kathryn Erbe, Illeana Douglas, Liza Weil, Kevin Dunn, Zachary David Cope. **1999 DVD**

STITCHES (1985) Med school students playing pranks. Rated R. 92m. **DIR:** Alan Smithee. **CAST:** Parker Stevenson, Geoffrey Lewis, Eddie Albert. **1985**

•STITCHES (2001) ★★ From the makers of *Dolls* and *Puppet Master*, a new film that treads familiar ground. Nice little old lady has a nasty secret: she turns people into little dolls. Rated R for violence and profanity. 85m. **DIR:** Neal Stevens. **CAST:** Elizabeth Ince, Debra Mayer.

2000

STOLEN FACE ★★★ Early Hammer Films sleeper from the British studio's greatest director, Terence Fisher. Imported American lead Paul Henreid plays a noted plastic surgeon who remakes a female convict's face into the image of a woman he loved and lost. Taut and imaginative low-budget item. B&W; 72m. **DIR:** Terence Fisher. **CAST:** Paul Henreid, Lizabeth Scott, Andre Morell, Mary Mackenzie. **1952**

STOLEN HEARTS 🦃 Even the strippers are dull in this erotic thriller about a club owner who hires a private detective to find the con man who robbed her. Rated R for nudity and sexual situations. 82m. **DIR:** Ralph Portillo. **CAST:** Landon Hall, Paula Aletonis, Vincent Dale. **1995**

STOLEN HOURS ★★1/2 A fair remake of the classic 1939 Bette Davis tearjerker, *Dark Victory*. Susan Hayward is a fun-loving playgirl who learns she has only months to live and tries to make her limited time meaningful. Okay . . . if you haven't seen the original. 97m. **DIR:** Daniel Petrie. **CAST:** Susan Hayward, Michael Craig, Diane Baker, Edward Judd. **1963**

STOLEN KISSES ★★★★★ This is François Truffaut's third film in the continuing story about Antoine Doinel (Jean-Pierre Léaud) that began with *400 Blows*. Like the other films in the series, this work resembles Truffaut's autobiography as he romantically captures the awkwardness of Doinel and his encounters with women. This delightful comedy is often considered one of Truffaut's best movies. In French with English subtitles. 90m. **DIR:** François Truffaut. **CAST:** Jean-Pierre Léaud, Delphine Seyrig, Michel Lonsdale, Claude Jade, Daniel Ceccaldi. **1968 DVD**

STOLEN LIFE, A ★★★ Bette Davis produced this film herself. It shows her histrionic talents off to good advantage because she plays twins—one good, the other bad. When one sister takes over the other's life, she also takes the boyfriend they both want. B&W; 109m. **DIR:** Curtis Bernhardt. **CAST:** Bette Davis, Glenn Ford, Dane Clark, Bruce Bennett, Charlie Ruggles, Walter Brennan. **1946**

STONE BOY, THE ★★★★★ A superb ensemble cast elevates this rural *Ordinary People*–style film about a boy who accidentally shoots the older brother he adores and begins losing touch with reality. It's a tough subject, exquisitely handled. For some reason, this fine film was never theatrically released on a wide scale. Rated PG for brief violence and some profanity. 93m. **DIR:** Christopher Cain. **CAST:** Robert Duvall, Frederic Forrest, Glenn Close, Wilford Brimley. **1984**

STONE COLD ★★★ Ex–football player Brian Bosworth's motion picture debut is better than might be expected. "The Boz" plays an undercover cop who infiltrates a sleazy group of motorcycle outlaws. Rated R for violence, nudity, and profanity. 90m. **DIR:** Craig R. Baxley. **CAST:** Brian Bosworth, Lance Henriksen, William Forsythe, Sam McMurray. **1991**

STONE COLD DEAD ★★ This fair film, based on the novel *Sin Sniper* by Hugh Garner, centers on the investigation by Sergeant Boyd (Richard Crenna) into a bizarre series of prostitute killings. Rated R. 97m. **DIR:** George Mendeluk. **CAST:** Richard Crenna, Belinda Montgomery, Paul Williams, Linda Sorenson. **1980**

STONE FOX, THE ★★★ A boy and his dog enter a sled race hoping to win enough money to save the family farm. Predictable, made-for-TV story with some memorable race sequences. Not rated; contains no objectionable scenes. 96m. **DIR:** Harvey Hart. **CAST:** Joey Cramer, Buddy Ebsen, Belinda Montgomery, Gordon Tootoosis. **1987**

STONE KILLER, THE ★★★1/2 A *Dirty Harry*–style cop thriller, this casts Charles Bronson as a no-nonsense New York cop who gets transferred to Los Angeles because of his direct way of dealing with gun-toting criminals . . . he shoots them. It packs a wallop. Rated R. 95m. **DIR:** Michael Winner. **CAST:** Charles Bronson, Martin Balsam, David Sheiner, Norman Fell, Ralph Waite. **1973**

STONE OF SILVER CREEK ★★★★ Another of producer-star Buck Jones's superior Westerns for Universal, this offbeat, often funny movie casts Jones as a straight-shooting saloon owner who fights off a pair of persistent baddies, gives the town preacher an education in manliness, and weighs in as an all-around champion of justice. B&W; 62m. **DIR:** Nick Grindé. **CAST:** Buck Jones, Noel Francis. **1935**

STONEBROOK ★★★ Two Stonebrook College students generate a few original ideas on how to produce enough capital to pay tuition by cheating people out of their money. Unfortunately, one of the people they swindle happens to be in the mob, and these two students are bound to learn lessons that they would have never learned in college. Rated PG-13 for some violence. 90m. **DIR:** Byron W. Thompson. **CAST:** Seth Green, Brad Rowe, Zoe McLellan. **1999 DVD**

STONED AGE, THE ★★1/2 Somewhat enjoyable teen romp about a couple of stoner dudes out looking for drugs, babes, and parties. They run into the usual complications, but also get to listen to a cool soundtrack featuring classic 1970s rock 'n' roll. Rated R for drug use, adult situations, and language. 90m. **DIR:** James Melkonian. **CAST:** Michael Kopelow, Bradford Tatum, China Kantner, Renee Ammann, David Groh, Frankie Avalon. **1993 DVD**

STONES OF DEATH 🦃 Nothing new here: teenagers getting knocked off one by one by supernatural forces. Rated R for nudity, profanity, and violence. 95m. **DIR:** James Bagle. **CAST:** Zoe Carides, Tom Jennings, Eric Oldfield. **1988**

STONEWALL ★★ Director Nigel Finch's film, originally produced for British TV, is set against the background of the 1969 riots that erupted when the New York Police Department raided the Stonewall Tavern, a popular gay hangout. The film's intentions are good, but it's a trite soap opera, not very well acted, and Finch's shoestring budget is all too obvious. Rated R for profanity. 99m. **DIR:** Nigel Finch. **CAST:** Guillermo Diaz, Frederick Weller, Brendan Corbalis, Bruce MacVittie, Duane Boutte. **1996 DVD**

STOOGEMANIA 🦃 It's the story of Howard F. Howard (Josh Mostel), a man whose life is controlled by watching Three Stooges films. Not rated. 83m. **DIR:** Chuck Workman. **CAST:** Josh Mostel, Melanie Chartoff, Sid Caesar, Moe Howard, Curly Howard, Larry Fine, Shemp Howard. **1985**

STOP MAKING SENSE ★★★★ This has been called a star-vehicle. Filmed over a three-night period in De-

cember 1983 at Hollywood's Pantages Theater, the movie is a straight recording of a Talking Heads concert that offers the movie audience front-row-center seats. It offers great fun for the band's fans. Rated PG for suggestive lyrics. 88m. **DIR:** Jonathan Demme. **CAST:** Talking Heads. **1984**

STOP! OR MY MOM WILL SHOOT ★★★ Silly farce about a cop attempting to survive a visit by his overbearing mother. Anyone who is disappointed by this piece of fluff should have known better than to rent it in the first place. Rated PG. 87m. **DIR:** Roger Spottiswoode. **CAST:** Sylvester Stallone, Estelle Getty, JoBeth Williams, Roger Rees, Martin Ferrero, Gailard Sartain, Dennis Burkley. **1992**

STOP THE WORLD I WANT TO GET OFF ★★★1/2 Filmed version of the Broadway musical, an allegory about a little fellow who wonders if he's a fool or not because of his romantic and political adventures. Good music, lively songs, and energetic dance numbers, but not mass-appeal material. 98m. **DIR:** Victor Saville. **CAST:** Tony Tanner, Millicent Martin. **1966**

STOPOVER TOKYO ★★ Based on a story by John P. Marquand, this ho-hum espionage tale has an American spy (Robert Wagner) chasing a communist undercover agent all over Tokyo. Wagner is earnest, as usual, but even the cast's enthusiasm can't put life into this one. Joan Collins is worth watching, as always. 100m. **DIR:** Richard L. Breen. **CAST:** Robert Wagner, Edmond O'Brien, Joan Collins, Ken Scott. **1957**

STORM ★★★ Thieves return years after the crime to dig up their buried cache. Suspenseful low-budget film. Rated PG-13 for violence. 100m. **DIR:** David Winning. **CAST:** David Palfy. **1987**

STORM AND SORROW ★★1/2 Lori Singer is the "Rocky Mountain Spider Woman" who joins a 1974 expedition to climb one of Russia's highest mountains. Gorgeous scenery, but s-l-o-w going as people trudge through snow, pant, rest, then trudge some more. Made for TV. 96m. **DIR:** Richard A. Colla. **CAST:** Lori Singer, Todd Allen. **1990**

STORM IN A TEACUP ★★★ The refusal of an old lady to pay for a dog license touches off this amusing farrago on love, politics, and life. Rex Harrison is, of course, smashing. The dialogue is the thing. B&W; 87m. **DIR:** Victor Saville, Ian Dalrymple. **CAST:** Vivien Leigh, Rex Harrison, Cecil Parker, Sara Allgood. **1937**

STORM OF THE CENTURY ★★★★ Quite possibly one of the best adaptations of the work of Stephen King to the screen, this TV miniseries captures the essence of what makes a King book scary: that evil can be anywhere, even in your own backyard. Colm Feore is subtly menacing as the demonic Andre Linoge, a stranger who comes to a small, isolated island during a devastating snowstorm and begins killing the populace until they agree to give him what he wants. The violence of Linoge and the loneliness and despair of the townsfolk is effectively mirrored in the raging of the storm. Rated PG-13 for violence and intense situations. 247m. **DIR:** Craig R. Baxley. **CAST:** Tim Daly, Colm Feore, Deborah Farentino. **1999 DVD**

STORM OVER ASIA ★★★★ Also known as *The Heir to Genghis Khan*, this masterpiece is from the great Russian director, Vsevolod Pudovkin. It tells the story of a young Mongol hunter who is discovered to be the heir of the great Khan. A superb example of the formal beauty of the silent film. Silent. B&W; 102m. **DIR:** V. I. Pudovkin. **CAST:** Valeri Inkizhinov. **1928 DVD**

STORM TRACKER ★★1/2 Luke Perry stars as a meteorologist who is developing a revolutionary new technology that can control the direction of storm fronts. Martin Sheen plays a renegade general who has commandeered this technology, and is threatening Los Angeles with a hurricane that would level the city. Cheesy special effects combined with halfhearted performances make for a long ninety minutes. Not rated; may be inappropriate for children. 90m. **DIR:** Harris Done. **CAST:** Luke Perry, Martin Sheen. **1999 DVD**

STORMQUEST Amazon women battling a band of renegade men from a neighboring tribe. Not rated. 90m. **DIR:** Alex Sessa. **CAST:** Brent Huff. **1987**

STORMY MONDAY ★★★★ In this stylish British thriller, Melanie Griffith and Sean Bean play unlikely lovers who attempt to stop ruthless American businessman Tommy Lee Jones from taking over a jazz nightclub owned by Sting. The generally strong performances, inventive filmmaking techniques, and offbeat sensibilities make the film worth watching. Rated R for violence. 93m. **DIR:** Mike Figgis. **CAST:** Melanie Griffith, Tommy Lee Jones, Sting, Sean Bean. **1988**

STORMY WATERS ★★★★ Tough rescue-ship captain Jean Gabin braves stormy waters to save hauntingly beautiful Michele Morgan. They then have a passionate love affair. This film is a fine example of French cinema at its pre–WWII zenith. 75m. **DIR:** Jean Gremillon. **CAST:** Jean Gabin, Michèle Morgan, Madeleine Renaud, Fernand Ledoux. **1941**

STORMY WEATHER ★★★★ A delightful kaleidoscope of musical numbers. Lena Horne performs the title number and Fats Waller interprets his own "Ain't Misbehavin'." Dooley Wilson of *Casablanca* fame and the Nicholas Brothers are also really great. This is an overlooked 20th Century Fox classic. B&W; 77m. **DIR:** Andrew L. Stone. **CAST:** Lena Horne, Bill Robinson, Cab Calloway, Fats Waller. **1943**

STORY LADY, THE ★★★ Jessica Tandy feels worthless after coming to live with her daughter, so she buys public-access time on cable TV to share her favorite fairy tales. When an advertising executive and part-time mom decides to market Tandy's spellbinding talents, she is forced to see the damage her all-encompassing career is having on her own daughter. Heartwarming as well as thought-provoking family viewing. Not rated; contains no objectionable material. 93m. **DIR:** Larry Elikann. **CAST:** Jessica Tandy, Stephanie Zimbalist, Tandy Cronyn, Lisa Jakub, Christopher Gartin. **1991 DVD**

STORY OF A LOVE STORY ★★ In this offbeat and increasingly off-putting adaptation by screenwriter Nicholas Mosely of his novel *Impossible Object*, Alan Bates stars as an English novelist who becomes involved in an affair with a married Frenchwoman (Dominique Sanda). In English and French with some subtitles. Rated R for nudity and brief violence. 110m. **DIR:** John Frankenheimer. **CAST:** Alan Bates, Dominique Sanda, Evans Evans, Lea Massari, Michel Auclair. **1973**

STORY OF A THREE DAY PASS, THE ★★★1/2 A black soldier falls in love with a white French girl while on

leave in Paris. First-time director Melvin Van Peebles makes the most of a shoestring budget on a project that contains only some of the rage that surfaced in his *Sweet Sweetback's Baadasssss Song*. 87m. **DIR:** Melvin Van Peebles. **CAST:** Harry Baird, Nicole Berger, Christian Marin. **1967**

STORY OF ADELE H, THE ★★★1/2 This basically simple story of author Victor Hugo's daughter, who loves a soldier in vain, is surprisingly textured and intriguing. Slow, exquisite unfolding of many-layered love story is arresting and pictorially beautiful. Nicely done. Some adult situations. In French with English subtitles. Rated PG. 97m. **DIR:** François Truffaut. **CAST:** Isabelle Adjani, Bruce Robinson. **1975 DVD**

STORY OF BOYS AND GIRLS ★★★★ Italian director Pupi Avati serves up a spicy, thought-provoking slice of life as thirty-plus participants in an engagement party indulge in a mouth-watering, eighteen-course meal. Set in pre–World War II Italy, this delicious import provides a feast of fascinating characters while examining the attitudes that led to the rise of fascism. In Italian with English subtitles. Not rated; the film has scenes of simulated sex. 92m. **DIR:** Pupi Avati. **CAST:** Felice Andreasi, Angiola Baggi. **1991**

STORY OF DAVID, THE ★★★1/2 The first half of this two-part TV movie tells the story of young David's defeat of the Philistine champion Goliath. The second half presents David as king, in love with the forbidden Bathsheba. Lavish, respectfully produced biblical epic. Not rated; contains no objectionable material. 192m. **DIR:** Alex Segal, David Lowell Rich. **CAST:** Timothy Bottoms, Anthony Quayle, Norman Rodway, Keith Michell, Jane Seymour, Brian Blessed, Barry Morse. **1976**

STORY OF DR. WASSELL, THE ★★1/2 Plodding biopic about a navy doctor who risks court-martial to save the lives of severely wounded soldiers on Java during World War II. Based on the book by James Hilton. Not rated. 137m. **DIR:** Cecil B. DeMille. **CAST:** Gary Cooper, Laraine Day, Signe Hasso, Dennis O'Keefe, Carol Thurston, Carl Esmond, Stanley Ridges. **1944**

STORY OF FAUSTA, THE ★★★ A Brazilian woman, sick of her lazy and abusive husband, seeks the easy way out by befriending a wealthy old man. The more she mistreats her rescuer, the more anxious he is to please her. The humor here is deeply black. In Portuguese with English subtitles. Not rated, contains violence, profanity, and nudity. 90m. **DIR:** Bruno Barreto. **CAST:** Betty Faria, Daniel Filho, Brandao Filho. **1988**

STORY OF G. I. JOE, THE ★★★★1/2 Mesmerizing film about Pulitzer Prize–winning WWII correspondent Ernie Pyle and the men of Company C of the 18th Infantry. Gritty, unblinking, and frank with a steely, Oscar-nominated performance by then-newcomer Robert Mitchum. Not rated; features gritty battle scenes. B&W; 108m. **DIR:** William Wellman. **CAST:** Robert Mitchum, Burgess Meredith. **1945 DVD**

STORY OF JACOB AND JOSEPH, THE ★★★1/2 Handsome adaptation of two Bible stories. First, Jacob battles his brother Esau over their birthright. Later, Jacob's favorite son, Joseph, has his own sibling problems when his jealous brothers sell him into slavery. Not rated; contains no objectionable material. 96m. **DIR:** Michael Cacoyannis. **CAST:** Keith Michell, Tony Lo Bianco, Colleen Dewhurst, Herschel Bernardi, Harry Andrews, Julian Glover. **1974**

STORY OF LOUIS PASTEUR, THE ★★★1/2 Master actor Paul Muni won an Oscar for his restrained portrayal of the famous French founder of bacteriology in this well-honed film biography. This is an honest, engrossing character study that avoids sentimentality. B&W; 85m. **DIR:** William Dieterle. **CAST:** Paul Muni, Josephine Hutchinson, Anita Louise, Donald Woods, Porter Hall, Akim Tamiroff. **1936**

STORY OF O, THE ★★ Adaptation of the French erotic novel. The filmmakers attempt to beautify what is basically a soft-core tale of bondage and sadomasochism. No matter how much Vaseline you apply to the camera lens, a nude whipping is still a nude whipping. Rated R (though it'd get an NC-17 today). 97m. **DIR:** Just Jaeckin. **CAST:** Udo Kier, Corinne Clery. **1975**

STORY OF QIU JU, THE ★★★★★ The masterful Yimou Zhang, the first Chinese director to acquire a western following, here makes his first film about contemporary Chinese life. Viewers can observe both the marvelous and mundane in modern Chinese life. Star Gong Li proves again that she's one of the world's greatest actresses. In Chinese with English subtitles. Rated PG. 100m. **DIR:** Yimou Zhang. **CAST:** Gong Li, Lei Lao Sheng, Liu Pei Qi. **1993 DVD**

STORY OF ROBIN HOOD, THE ★★★ Disney's live-action version of the Robin Hood legend has elements that give the movie its own identity. One nice touch is the use of a wandering minstrel, who draws the story together. Richard Todd is a most appealing Robin Hood, while James Robertson Justice, as Little John, and Peter Finch, as the Sheriff of Nottingham, are first-rate. 83m. **DIR:** Ken Annakin. **CAST:** Richard Todd, Joan Rice, Peter Finch, James Hayter, James Robertson Justice, Michael Hordern. **1952**

STORY OF RUTH, THE ★★★ Pagan priestess Ruth renounces her graven gods to embrace the true faith of Israel but finds acceptance rough going in this static retelling of the classic Bible story. 132m. **DIR:** Henry Koster. **CAST:** Elana Eden, Stuart Whitman, Tom Tryon, Peggy Wood, Viveca Lindfors, Jeff Marrow. **1960**

STORY OF SEABISCUIT, THE ★★1/2 A thoroughbred horse recovers from an injury to become a big prizewinner. Based on a true incident, this predictable family programmer gives Barry Fitzgerald as the trainer full throttle to ham and charm his way into the audience's heart. 92m. **DIR:** David Butler. **CAST:** Shirley Temple, Barry Fitzgerald, Lon McCallister, Rosemary DeCamp, Pierre Watkin, Donald MacBride. **1949**

STORY OF THE LATE CHRYSANTHEMUMS, THE ★★★★1/2 The adopted son of a family of great actors finds success only after he sets out on his own and marries the family maid, who tutors him in his craft. Director Kenji Mizoguchi's distinctive style, in which careful compositions, long takes, and a gently tracking camera impart a deep humanism, redeems this melodramatic, three-hankie story. In Japanese with English subtitles. B&W; 142m. **DIR:** Kenji Mizoguchi. **CAST:** Shotaro Hanayagi, Kakuro Mori. **1939**

STORY OF US, THE ★★1/2 Director Rob Reiner's somber study of the collapse of a fifteen-year marriage probably wasn't intended to be so depressing. In using a

continual flashback/flashforward style of storytelling, he ends up putting too much emphasis on the bickering between heartbroken mates and not enough on their early years of love and harmony. This lack of balance mars what might have been a touching, involving movie. Rated R for profanity, sex, and violence. 94m. **DIR:** Rob Reiner. **CAST:** Bruce Willis, Michelle Pfeiffer, Tim Matheson, Rob Reiner, Rita Wilson, Paul Reiser, Julie Hagerty, Tom Poston, Jayne Meadows, Betty White, Red Buttons. **1999 DVD**

STORY OF VERNON AND IRENE CASTLE, THE ★★★★ Another fine film with the flying footsies of Fred Astaire and the always lovely Ginger Rogers. B&W; 93m. **DIR:** H. C. Potter. **CAST:** Fred Astaire, Ginger Rogers, Edna May Oliver, Walter Brennan. **1939**

STORY OF WOMEN, THE ★★★★ Excellent political drama from director Claude Chabrol based on a true story about the last woman to be guillotined in France, at the onset of World War II. Isabelle Huppert delivers a powerful performance as an abortionist who becomes the victim of an indifferent society. This riveting performance won her the best-actress prize at the Venice Film Festival. In French with English subtitles. 112m. **DIR:** Claude Chabrol. **CAST:** Isabelle Huppert, François Cluzet. **1988**

STORY OF XINGHUA, THE ★★★1/2 Powerful tale of adultery finds an obedient wife looking outside her brutal marriage for love and compassion. Xinghua challenges hundreds of years of tradition as she seeks the strength to find true happiness. Engaging performances and picture-postcard scenery make this a satisfying experience. In Chinese with English subtitles. Not rated; contains adult situations. 89m. **DIR:** Cui Junde. **CAST:** Jiang Wenli, Zhang Guoli, Tian Shaoujun. **1993**

STORYBOOK ★★★1/2 Kids will love this romp through the pages of a magical storybook, brought to life when a boy named Brandon enters the book. Before he can get out, he must save the magical kingdom from an evil queen. Brandon is joined by some fanciful friends, including Woody the Woodsman, a kangaroo, and a wise old owl. Rated G. 88m. **DIR:** Lorenzo Doumani. **CAST:** William McNamara, Swoosie Kurtz, James Doohan, Richard Moll, Jack Scalia, Milton Berle. **1995**

•**STORYTELLING** ★★ This obscene, absurd drama features two separate narratives in which characters rub our faces in issues of sex, race, degradation, celebrity, and exploitation. In *Fiction*, a female coed has sex with a classmate who has cerebral palsy, as well as with their African American Pulitzer Prize–winning English professor. She then reads an account of one affair in class in a collision of denial and shame. In *Nonfiction*, a creepy filmmaker wiggles his way into the life of a rudderless high-school student and his family. Rated R for profanity, violence, sex, and nudity. 84m. **DIR:** Todd Solondz. **CAST:** Robert Wisdom, Selma Blair, Leo Fitzpatrick, Paul Giamatti, Mark Webber, John Goodman, Julie Hagerty. **2001**

•**STORYVILLE** ★★1/2 In this tepid look at old-fashioned New Orleans politics, James Spader stars as a young lawyer trying to find out why a conspiracy seeks to keep him from running for public office. Rated R for language, sensuality, and violence. 113m. **DIR:** Mark Frost. **CAST:** James Spader, Joanne Whalley, Jason Robards Jr., Charlotte Lewis, Piper Laurie, Michael Parks, Chuck McCann, Woody Strode. **1992**

STOWAWAY ★★★ Tale of missionary ward Shirley Temple lost in Shanghai and befriended by American Robert Young. She holds her own against such seasoned scene snitchers as Eugene Pallette, Arthur Treacher, and J. Edward Blomberg, while bringing playboy Young and Alice Faye together romantically, singing in Chinese, and imitating Fred Astaire, Al Jolson, and Eddie Cantor. B&W; 86m. **DIR:** William A. Seiter. **CAST:** Shirley Temple, Robert Young, Alice Faye, Allan "Rocky" Lane, Eugene Pallette, Helen Westley, Arthur Treacher, J. Edward Bromberg. **1936**

STRAIGHT FOR THE HEART ★★★ Covering Contra atrocities in Nicaragua, a Canadian photographer copes by repressing his emotional reactions. But when he returns home, he finds that detachment difficult to shake. A grim but involving drama, featuring splendid Montreal locations. In French with English subtitles. Not rated. 92m. **DIR:** Léa Pool. **CAST:** Matthias Habich, Johanne-Marie Tremblay. **1988**

STRAIGHT LINE ★★1/2 Laughable action film stars Mr. T as a private eye who gets the job of a lifetime: track down the man brainwashing kids into enforcing white supremacy by killing. Hokey, unbelievable, and quite entertaining in a goofy sort of way. 95m. **DIR:** George Mihalka. **CAST:** Mr. T, Kenneth Welsh. **1988**

STRAIGHT OUT OF BROOKLYN ★★★1/2 Nineteen year old writer-producer-director Matty Rich makes a solid filmmaking debut with this thought-provoking drama about a black teenager (Lawrence Gilliard Jr.) who decides that robbing a local drug dealer is the best and quickest way to get his family out of the poverty-stricken housing projects of Red Hook in Brooklyn. Rated R for profanity, violence, and suggested sex. 91m. **DIR:** Matty Rich. **CAST:** George T. Odom, Lawrence Gilliard Jr., Matty Rich. **1991**

STRAIGHT SHOOTING ★★★ John Ford's first major film holds up remarkably well today. Everything about it seems a prototype for his great Westerns to come: the authoritative presence of the solitary cowboy, Harry Carey; the striking location photography; and the rousing action scenes. Silent. B&W; 57m. **DIR:** John Ford. **CAST:** Harry Carey. **1917**

STRAIGHT STORY, THE ★★★★ When 73-year-old Alvin Straight (Richard Farnsworth) learns that he may have little time left, he decides to visit his estranged brother, with whom he has not spoken in ten years. The problem is Alvin can barely walk (having to use two canes) and his eyesight is poor (making a driver's license an impossibility), so the determined senior citizen hitches up a homemade, wooden trailer to his 1966 John Deere riding mower and embarks on his quest. A superb performance from Farnsworth (who was nominated for an Oscar as best actor) and uncommonly sensitive direction by David Lynch make this an unforgettable viewing experience. Rated G. 111m. **DIR:** David Lynch. **CAST:** Richard Farnsworth, Sissy Spacek, Everett McGill, Harry Dean Stanton, Jane Galloway Heitz, Jennifer Edwards, Barbara Robertson, John Farley. **1999 DVD**

STRAIGHT TALK ★★★1/2 An Arkansas country girl decides to try her luck in Chicago, where she finds her gift for gab the ticket to success as a radio talk-show

host. Dolly Parton and a superb supporting cast make every scene believable. Surprisingly good. Rated PG for profanity. 87m. **DIR:** Barnet Kellman. **CAST:** Dolly Parton, James Woods, Griffin Dunne, Michael Madsen, Philip Bosco, Jerry Orbach, John Sayles, Teri Hatcher, Spalding Gray, Charles Fleischer. **1992**

STRAIGHT TIME ★★★★ Well-told story of an ex-convict (Dustin Hoffman) attempting to make good on the outside only to return to crime after a run-in with his parole officer (M. Emmet Walsh). Hoffman's performance is truly chilling. A very grim and powerful film that was sadly overlooked on its initial release. Rated R for violence, nudity, and language. 114m. **DIR:** Ulu Grosbard. **CAST:** Dustin Hoffman, Harry Dean Stanton, Gary Busey, Theresa Russell, M. Emmet Walsh. **1978**

STRAIGHT TO HELL Self-indulgent Western spoof with bank robbers and thugs shooting at each other in a desert town. 86m. **DIR:** Alex Cox. **CAST:** Sy Richardson, Joe Strummer, Dennis Hopper, Elvis Costello. **1987 DVD**

STRAIT-JACKET ★★★1/2 Chilling vehicle for Joan Crawford as a convicted ax murderess returning home after twenty years in an insane asylum, where it appears she was restored to sanity. But was she? Genuinely frightening film features one of Joan's most powerful performances. George Kennedy is almost as good in an early role as a farmhand. B&W; 89m. **DIR:** William Castle. **CAST:** Joan Crawford, Diane Baker, Leif Erickson, George Kennedy. **1964 DVD**

STRANDED ★★★ A story of bigotry and intolerance centered around aliens escaping from another world and landing in a small town. Cameron Dye is the young man who tries to help them escape from the local sheriff, a gang of good ol' boys, and an assassin from outer space. More character development and pacing than usual for a science-fiction film. Rated PG-13 for profanity and violence. 80m. **DIR:** Tex Fuller. **CAST:** Ione Skye, Joe Morton, Cameron Dye, Brendan Hughes, Maureen O'Sullivan. **1987**

STRANGE AFFAIR OF UNCLE HARRY, THE ★★★★ George Sanders tried to get by the censors during the 1940s with several movies that bucked the system. This one cheats by changing the ending of Thomas Job's successful stage play about incest and murder. Hollywood kept the murder part, but you have to read between the lines to get the incest situation. The video print comes from a UCLA Archive restoration. B&W; 80m. **DIR:** Robert Siodmak. **CAST:** George Sanders, Geraldine Fitzgerald, Moyna McGill, Ella Raines, Sara Allgood, Samuel S. Hinds, Harry Von Zell. **1945**

STRANGE BEDFELLOWS ★★1/2 Straightlaced American Rock Hudson marries eccentric Italian liberal Gina Lollobrigida, leaves her, then woos her again seven years later. This cornball fluff offers up some laughs, even if the plot is wildly out of control. Not rated. 114m. **DIR:** Melvin Frank. **CAST:** Rock Hudson, Gina Lollobrigida, Gig Young, Nancy Kulp, Bernard Fox, Terry-Thomas. **1965**

STRANGE BEHAVIOR ★★★1/2 Michael Murphy stars as the police chief of Galesburg, Illinois, who suddenly finds himself inundated by unexplained knife murders. In all, this offbeat film is a true treat for horror-movie fans and other viewers with a yen for something spooky. Rated R. 98m. **DIR:** Michael Laughlin. **CAST:** Michael Murphy, Marc McClure, Dan Shor, Fiona Lewis, Louise Fletcher, Arthur Dignam. **1981**

STRANGE BREW ★★★1/2 Okay, all you hosers and hoseheads, here come those *SCTV* superstars from the Great White North, Bob and Doug McKenzie (Rick Moranis and Dave Thomas) in their first feature film. Beauty, eh? A mad scientist employed by a brewery controls a group of mental patients by feeding them beer laced with a mind-controlling drug. Rated PG. 90m. **DIR:** Dave Thomas, Rick Moranis. **CAST:** Rick Moranis, Dave Thomas, Max von Sydow, Paul Dooley, Lynne Griffin. **1983**

STRANGE CARGO ★★★ *Strange* is the best way to describe this one, but the forceful and compelling personalities make it worth watching. Clark Gable leads a group of convicts out of Devil's Island in a daring escape. 105m. **DIR:** Frank Borzage. **CAST:** Clark Gable, Joan Crawford, Ian Hunter, Albert Dekker, Peter Lorre, Paul Lukas, Eduardo Ciannelli, J. Edward Bromberg. **1940**

STRANGE CASE OF DR. JEKYLL AND MR. HYDE, THE (1968) ★★ The offbeat casting of Jack Palance in the title role(s) is the main attraction in this taped-for-television production. Charles Jarrott directs with the same ponderous hand he brought to *Anne of the Thousand Days* and *Mary, Queen of Scots*, but the distinguished supporting cast is a plus. Not rated. 96m. **DIR:** Charles Jarrott. **CAST:** Jack Palance, Denholm Elliott, Torin Thatcher, Oscar Homolka, Leo Genn, Billie Whitelaw. **1968 DVD**

STRANGE CASE OF DR. JEKYLL AND MR. HYDE, THE (1989) ★★★1/2 Surprisingly effective entry in Shelley Duvall's Nightmare Classics series, this does not rely on a Hulk-like transition of Dr. Jekyll (Anthony Andrews) to terrify viewers. Instead, Andrews brilliantly creates two personalities—one timid, the other frightfully uninhibited—that refuse to overlap. Not rated, contains violence. 55m. **DIR:** Michael Lindsay-Hogg. **CAST:** Anthony Andrews, George Murdock, Laura Dern, Nicholas Guest. **1989**

STRANGE CASE OF DR. RX, THE ★★ Private eye Patric Knowles tracks down a vigilante killer. The best thing about this average murder mystery (misleadingly advertised as a horror movie) is the comic relief. B&W; 66m. **DIR:** William Nigh. **CAST:** Lionel Atwill, Patric Knowles, Anne Gwynne, Samuel S. Hinds, Shemp Howard, Mantan Moreland. **1942**

STRANGE CASE OF THE COSMIC RAYS, THE ★★★1/2 This Bell Science educational film introduces the atom, ultraviolet radiation, and galactic phenomena. All this is explained by Dr. Frank Baxter with the help of the Bill and Cora Baird puppets and the animation of Shamus Culhane. 59m. **DIR:** Frank Capra. **CAST:** Dr. Frank Baxter. **1957**

STRANGE CONFESSION ★★ Chemist Lon Chaney Jr. seeks revenge on his employer (J. Carrol Naish) in this below-average entry in the *Inner Sanctum* series. B&W; 60m. **DIR:** John Hoffman. **CAST:** Lon Chaney Jr., Brenda Joyce, J. Carrol Naish, Milburn Stone, Lloyd Bridges. **1945**

STRANGE DAYS ★★ The drug of choice in 1999 is a virtual-reality setup that allows people to relive their own or someone else's experiences. During the last forty-eight hours of the twentieth century, a seedy former

vice cop gets involved with two such "wiretrips."—Virtual reality greased with sleaze. Rated R for graphic violence, sex, nudity, and language. 145m. **DIR:** Kathryn Bigelow. **CAST:** Ralph Fiennes, Angela Bassett, Tom Sizemore, Juliette Lewis, Michael Wincott, Vincent D'Onofrio. **1995 DVD**

STRANGE DOOR, THE ★★1/2 Charles Laughton turns up as the evil French nobleman Sire de Maletroit, who takes delight in punishing his brother, imprisoned in the dungeon after he wed the woman Maletroit loved. Not rated. B&W; 81m. **DIR:** Joseph Pevney. **CAST:** Charles Laughton, Boris Karloff, Sally Forrest, Richard Stapley, Michael Pate. **1951**

STRANGE ILLUSION ★★ Following the mysterious disappearance of his father, a teenager on a fishing holiday with the family physician is disturbed by a strange dream concerning his mother. Trite. B&W; 80m. **DIR:** Edgar G. Ulmer. **CAST:** Jimmy Lydon, Sally Eilers, Regis Toomey. **1945 DVD**

STRANGE INTERLUDE (1932) ★★1/2 Eugene O'Neill's plays make heavy-handed movies, and this is one of the heaviest. Clark Gable and Norma Shearer play lovers who grow old together while married to other people. B&W; 110m. **DIR:** Robert Z. Leonard. **CAST:** Clark Gable, Norma Shearer, Robert Young, Maureen O'Sullivan, May Robson, Henry B. Walthall, Ralph Morgan. **1932**

STRANGE INTERLUDE (1988) ★★★★ Eugene O'Neill's complex love story is not for viewers seeking mindless entertainment, but for those willing to endure the considerable length, it offers ample rewards. Glenda Jackson plays a neurotic woman who, in the course of twenty-five years, manages to control the lives of the three men who love her. High-class soap opera. Not rated, this PBS production contains adult themes. 190m. **DIR:** Herbert Wise. **CAST:** Glenda Jackson, José Ferrer, David Dukes, Ken Howard, Edward Petherbridge. **1988**

STRANGE INVADERS ★★★★ A splendid parody of 1950s science-fiction movies, this film opens in 1958, with bug-like aliens taking over a farm town called Centerville, Illinois. The story then jumps to New York City, twenty-five years later. Rated PG for violence. 94m. **DIR:** Michael Laughlin. **CAST:** Paul LeMat, Diana Scarwid, Nancy Allen, Louise Fletcher, Michael Lerner, Kenneth Tobey, June Lockhart. **1983 DVD**

STRANGE JUSTICE ★★★1/2 If you happened to miss the Judge Clarence Thomas Senate hearing in 1991, this made-for-cable dramatization of the event will nicely sum up the key points of the whole debacle for you. The film does a good job straddling the issue, presenting both sides as compelling and truthful. Emotional reenactment of the hearing spices up the otherwise dull-as-a-post testimony, and edgy visual effects add tension to the more staid scenes. Not rated; contains profanity. 95m. **DIR:** Ernest R. Dickerson. **CAST:** Delroy Lindo, Mandy Patinkin, Regina Taylor, Louis Gossett Jr. **1999**

STRANGE LOVE OF MARTHA IVERS, THE ★★★ Terrible title doesn't do this well-acted drama justice. Woman-with-a-past Barbara Stanwyck excels in this story of a secret that comes back to threaten her now-stable life and the lengths she must go to in order to ensure her security. Young Kirk Douglas in his film debut already charges the screen with electricity. B&W; 117m. **DIR:** Lewis Milestone. **CAST:** Barbara Stanwyck, Van Heflin, Kirk Douglas, Lizabeth Scott, Judith Anderson, Darryl Hickman. **1946**

STRANGE LOVE OF MOLLY LOUVAIN, THE ★★★1/2 A well-played melodrama with comic overtones and almost as much sexual innuendo as movies of the 1990s. An unwed mother dallies with gangsters of every stripe and color because she just plain likes men. B&W; 80m. **DIR:** Michael Curtiz. **CAST:** Ann Dvorak, Lee Tracy, Leslie Fenton, Richard Cromwell, Guy Kibbee, Mary Doran, Frank McHugh. **1932**

STRANGE NEW WORLD ★★1/2 After spending almost two centuries in suspended animation, three astronauts return to Earth to discover a *Strange New World* in this made-for-television entry. Through the miracle of cloning, Earth's inhabitants face eternal life, but with a price. 78m. **DIR:** Robert Butler. **CAST:** John Saxon, Keene Curtis, Martine Beswick, James Olson, Kathleen Miller. **1975**

STRANGE SHADOWS IN AN EMPTY ROOM 🦃 A cop investigates his sister's mysterious death. Not rated; contains violence. 97m. **DIR:** Martin Herbert. **CAST:** Stuart Whitman, John Saxon, Martin Landau, Tisa Farrow. **1976**

STRANGE TALES: RAY BRADBURY THEATER ★★★★ These three initial episodes from cable's *Ray Bradbury Theater* are noteworthy for strong casting and Bradbury's faithful adaptations of his own short stories. The most disturbing entry is "The Town Where No One Got Off," with Jeff Goldblum as a rail commuter who gets involved in a perfect murder scheme. Superior production values. 86m. **DIR:** Don McBrearty, Bruce Pittman, Douglas Jackson. **CAST:** Peter O'Toole, Charles Martin Smith, Drew Barrymore, Jeff Goldblum, Ed McNamara, Cec Linder. **1986**

STRANGE WOMAN, THE ★★ Lusty tale of a woman who conspires with her stepson to kill her husband. A strange adaptation of the Ben Ames Williams bestseller, mainly because Hedy Lamarr looks better than she acts. She bought the rights to the book, selected cast and director, and listed herself as an associate producer. B&W; 100m. **DIR:** Edgar G. Ulmer. **CAST:** Hedy Lamarr, George Sanders, Gene Lockhart, Louis Hayward, Hillary Brooke, Rhys Williams, June Storey, Ian Keith. **1946 DVD**

STRANGENESS, THE 🦃 The Gold Spike Mine is haunted by a creature from down deep inside the Earth. Not rated. 90m. **DIR:** David Michael Hillman. **CAST:** Dan Lunham, Terri Berland. **1985**

STRANGER, THE (1946) ★★★★ Nazi war criminal (Orson Welles) assumes a new identity in a small New England town following World War II, unaware that a government agent (Edward G. Robinson) is tailing him. Extremely well-done film, holds the viewer's interest from start to finish. B&W; 95m. **DIR:** Orson Welles. **CAST:** Orson Welles, Edward G. Robinson, Loretta Young, Richard Long. **1946 DVD**

STRANGER, THE (1986) ★★★★ Taut psychological thriller that keeps you on the edge of your seat. Bonnie Bedelia plays a woman with amnesia trying to put the pieces together after a car accident. She thinks she may or may not have witnessed a murder. Peter Riegert is her psychiatrist who may or may not be trying to help her. This unique sleeper is fast-paced and suspenseful.

Rated R for brief nudity and violence. 93m. **DIR:** Adolfo Aristarian. **CAST:** Bonnie Bedelia, Peter Riegert. **1986**

STRANGER, THE (1992) ★★★★1/2 A middle-class Calcutta husband and wife whose lives are disrupted when the wife's long-lost and unknown-to-them uncle arrives at the doorstep. The final film of the great Satyajit Ray, who died in 1992, is an entertaining, affecting modern-day fable, offering Ray's thoughtful views on families, cultural tradition, and the flaws in modern civilization. An apt reminder of Ray's place among the master filmmakers of the world. In Bengali with English subtitles. 120m. **DIR:** Satyajit Ray. **CAST:** Mamata Shankar, Deepankar De, Utpal Dutt. **1992**

STRANGER, THE (1994) ★★ Pouty Kathy Long makes a poor substitute for Clint Eastwood in this laughable biker variation on *High Plains Drifter* that mimics everything down to the mock Ennio Morricone score. Even worse, justice is hardly served by Gregory Poirier's trite script. Rated R for violence, profanity, nudity, and simulated sex. 98m. **DIR:** Fritz Kiersch. **CAST:** Kathy Long, Eric Pierpoint, Robin Lynn Heath. **1994**

STRANGER AMONG US, A ★★★1/2 Melanie Griffith becomes a tough-talkin' New York cop in this fish-out-of-water thriller. She penetrates New York's Hasidic Jewish community after a jeweler turns up dead and his sizable inventory is missing. Rated PG-13 for violence and profanity. 111m. **DIR:** Sidney Lumet. **CAST:** Melanie Griffith, Eric Thal, John Pankow, Tracy Pollan, Lee Richardson, Mia Sara, Jamey Sheridan. **1992**

STRANGER AND THE GUNFIGHTER, THE ★★1/2 The world may never be ready for this improbable mix, a tongue-in-cheek spaghetti Western by way of a standard kung-fu chop-chop flick. Lee Van Cleef, as another of his weary gunslingers, teams with martial arts master Lo Lieh. A classic this isn't, but the fast action and camp humor make it watchable. Rated PG for violence. 107m. **DIR:** Anthony M. Dawson. **CAST:** Lee Van Cleef, Lo Lieh, Patty Shepard. **1976**

STRANGER BY NIGHT ★★1/2 Proving once again that you can't trust a film that opens in a psychiatrist's office, Steven Bauer does little but look frustrated in this routine thriller about a cop who fears he may be murdering women during mental blackouts. The story deserves credit for an eleventh-hour twist, but the viewing experience is seriously marred by Ashley Irwin's god-awful music. Rated R for violence, profanity, nudity, and simulated sex. 91m. **DIR:** Gregory Brown. **CAST:** Steven Bauer, Jennifer Rubin, William Katt, Michael Parks, Luca Bercovici, Michele Greene. **1994 DVD**

STRANGER FROM VENUS 🦃 The same plot and the same star (Patricia Neal) as the classic *The Day the Earth Stood Still* does not guarantee the same quality. A visitor from Venus attempts to warn Earth of the dangers of nuclear weapons but meets with suspicion and hatred. B&W; 78m. **DIR:** Burt Balaban. **CAST:** Patricia Neal, Helmut Dantine, Derek Bond. **1954**

STRANGER IN THE HOUSE ★★ Fate plays a hand in this story of a man whose plans to murder his wife are interrupted by a mysterious stranger—with plans of his own. Mildly entertaining. Rated R for profanity and violence. 94m. **DIR:** Rodney Gibbons. **CAST:** Michele Greene, Kathleen Kinmont, Steve Railsback. **1997**

STRANGER IN THE KINGDOM, A ★★★ The picture-postcard town of Kingdom, Vermont, is one of those quaint places where everybody knows everyone else's name and business. Tossed into the mix are black reverend Walter Andrews and his teenage son. Set in 1952, director Jay Craven's film incorporates the themes of racism in a murder mystery that pits the town against the reverend when he is accused of killing a woman. Despite familiar themes, the film manages to carve out an identity all its own. Rated PG-13 for violence. 112m. **DIR:** Jay Craven. **CAST:** Ernie Hudson, Martin Sheen, Sean Nelson, David Lansbury, Carrie Snodgress. **1998 DVD**

STRANGER IS WATCHING, A ★★ A psychotic killer kidnaps two young ladies and keeps them prisoner in the catacombs beneath Grand Central Station. This commuter's nightmare is an ugly, dimly lit suspenser. Rated R. 92m. **DIR:** Sean S. Cunningham. **CAST:** Kate Mulgrew, Rip Torn, James Naughton. **1982**

STRANGER ON MY LAND ★★★1/2 Sparks fly when the government tries to entice and then force a family of ranchers off its land in order to expand a nearby military base. Thoughtful characters on all sides of the issue, an excellent cast, and fine pacing make this story unfold nicely. Not rated; contains some violence. 94m. **DIR:** Larry Elikann. **CAST:** Tommy Lee Jones, Dee Wallace, Ben Johnson, Barry Corbin. **1990**

STRANGER ON THE THIRD FLOOR ★★★★ Peter Lorre gives yet another singular performance as a disinterested murderer, a character truly alien yet strangely sympathetic. A great hallucination sequence and good performances all the way around make this a compelling treat. B&W; 64m. **DIR:** Boris Ingster. **CAST:** Peter Lorre, John McGuire, Elisha Cook Jr., Margaret Tallichet. **1940**

STRANGER THAN FICTION ★★1/2 A group of friends assembles in the middle of the night when one of them seeks help for having accidentally killed someone. A series of bad judgments follows while they try to cover up the killing, and more light is shed on what may have actually been a murder. The performances are decent, but the plot and characters are often frustratingly stupid. Rated R for language, sex, and violence. 90m. **DIR:** Eric Bross. **CAST:** Todd Field, Natasha Gregson Wagner, Mackenzie Astin, Dina Meyer. **1999 DVD**

STRANGER THAN PARADISE ★★★★1/2 In this superb independently made comedy, three oddball characters go on a spontaneous road trip through the United States, where they encounter boredom, routine problems, bad luck, and outrageous good fortune. The film, which won acclaim at the Cannes and New York film festivals, plays a lot like a Woody Allen comedy. It's a silly film for smart people. Rated R for profanity. B&W; 90m. **DIR:** Jim Jarmusch. **CAST:** John Lurie, Richard Edson, Eszter Balint. **1985**

STRANGER WITHIN, THE 🦃 A housewife is mysteriously impregnated, and her unborn child begins to have a strange effect on her personality. Typical TV tripe. Not rated. 74m. **DIR:** Lee Philips. **CAST:** Barbara Eden, George Grizzard, Joyce Van Patten, David Doyle. **1979**

STRANGER WORE A GUN, THE ★★1/2 Randolph Scott joins forces with evil George Macready in a plot to steal government gold shipments. Scott has a change of heart, and they end up as enemies. Initially released in 3-D; the action scenes were obviously devised for that medium. 83m. **DIR:** André de Toth. **CAST:** Randolph

Scott, Claire Trevor, George Macready, Lee Marvin, Ernest Borgnine. **1953**

STRANGERS ★★ Three mediocre vignettes. Too bad someone couldn't come up with just one good idea. Rated R for nudity and simulated sex. 90m. **DIR:** Daniel Vigne, Wayne Wang, Joan Tewkesbury. **CAST:** Linda Fiorentino, James Remar, François Montagut, Joan Chen, Lambert Wilson, Timothy Hutton. **1991**

STRANGERS IN GOOD COMPANY ★★★ Leisurely paced coming-of-age film of the geriatric set. A group of gray foxes are stuck in the wilderness when their tour bus breaks down. There they get to know each other while revealing their secret fears and desires. Enlightening Canadian film. Rated PG. 101m. **DIR:** Cynthia Scott. **CAST:** Alice Diabo, Constance Garneau. **1990**

STRANGERS IN THE CITY ★★★★ This forceful film set in a Manhattan slum paints a vivid picture of a Puerto Rican family struggling to adjust to life in a new country. When the proud father loses his job, other family members have to go to work to support themselves. The final third gives way to cheap melodrama, but the film is still well worth seeing. B&W; 83m. **DIR:** Rick Carrier. **CAST:** Robert Gentile, Camilo Delgado. **1961**

STRANGERS KISS ★★1/2 Offbeat film about the making of a low-budget movie, circa 1955. A strange romantic relationship between the male and female leads develops off-camera. A good script inspired by Stanley Kubrick's *Killer's Kiss* is quite absorbing despite some production flaws. Rated R for sexual situations. 94m. **DIR:** Matthew Chapman. **CAST:** Peter Coyote, Victoria Tennant, Blaine Novak, Dan Shor. **1984**

STRANGERS ON A TRAIN ★★★★★ One of the most discussed and analyzed of all of Alfred Hitchcock's films. *Strangers on a Train* was made during the height of Hitchcock's most creative period, the early 1950s. When you add a marvelous performance by Robert Walker as the stranger, you have one of the most satisfying thrillers ever. B&W; 101m. **DIR:** Alfred Hitchcock. **CAST:** Farley Granger, Robert Walker, Ruth Roman, Leo G. Carroll, Patricia Hitchcock, Marion Lorne. **1951**

STRANGERS: THE STORY OF A MOTHER AND A DAUGHTER ★★★1/2 Bette Davis won an Emmy Award in this taut, made-for-television drama about a long-estranged daughter's sudden reentry into the life and home of her bitter, resentful mother. Gena Rowlands, as the daughter, holds her own matching Davis scene for scene. 100m. **DIR:** Milton Katselas. **CAST:** Bette Davis, Gena Rowlands, Ford Rainey, Royal Dano. **1979**

STRANGERS WHEN WE MEET ★★1/2 An all-star cast fails to charge this overblown soap opera about an unhappily married architect who falls in love with his beautiful neighbor. Evan Hunter derived the screenplay from his novel of the same name. Not rated. 117m. **DIR:** Richard Quine. **CAST:** Kirk Douglas, Kim Novak, Ernie Kovacs, Barbara Rush, Walter Matthau, Virginia Bruce, Kent Smith, Helen Gallagher. **1960**

STRANGLEHOLD ★★ Often-told tale of terrorists who take over a chemical-weapons plant and hold a congresswoman hostage. Of course, there's only one man who can stop them, and he's world kick-boxing champion Jerry Trimble. So who's going to save us from Trimble's less-than-stellar acting abilities? Rated R for violence and adult language. 73m. **DIR:** Cirio H. Santiago. **CAST:** Jerry Trimble, Jillian McWhirter, Vernon Wells. **1994**

STRANGLER, THE ★★1/2 Victor Buono gives a good performance as corpulent, mother-fixated maniac who murders nurses and throws Chicago into a state of alarm. This low-budget thriller didn't get a lot of play dates as a result of the real-life horrors of Boston strangler Albert De Salvo and the senseless murder of eight nurses by Richard Speck. Not rated, but violent and gruesome. Also available at 80 minutes. B&W; 89m. **DIR:** Burt Topper. **CAST:** Victor Buono, David McLean, Ellen Corby, Jeanne Bates. **1964**

STRANGLER OF THE SWAMP ★★ Ghostly revenge story about a ferryman who was unjustly lynched and who hangs his murderers one by one is atmospheric and eerie but bogged down by a cheap budget and an unnecessary love story. Considered a minor classic among fantasy fans. B&W; 60m. **DIR:** Frank Wisbar. **CAST:** Rosemary La Planche, Robert Barrat, Blake Edwards, Charles Middleton. **1946 DVD**

STRAPLESS ★★★★ Deftly handled story of an American doctor in London who marries an enigmatic businessman in a moment of rapture, only to find him inscrutable and deceptive. Strong performances. Rated R. 99m. **DIR:** David Hare. **CAST:** Blair Brown, Bruno Ganz, Bridget Fonda. **1990**

STRAPPED ★★★ Although intelligently scripted and artily helmed by actor Forest Whitaker (in his directorial debut), this slice of inner-city life is no different from any film by John Singleton, Spike Lee, or countless imitators: a bludgeoning indictment of failed social systems. A young man tries to help his pregnant, drug-dealing girlfriend but is hampered by a cop and gun-dealer. Rated R for incessant profanity and violence. 102m. **DIR:** Forest Whitaker. **CAST:** Bokeem Woodbine, Kia Joy Goodwin, Fredro, Paul McCrane, Craig Wasson, Michael Biehn. **1993**

STRATEGIC AIR COMMAND ★★1/2 Aviation and sports come together as professional baseball player Jimmy Stewart is called back to active service and forced to leave his career, his teammates, and his wife (June Allyson). Air force veterans and baseball fans will enjoy, but, otherwise, this is just routine studio fare. 114m. **DIR:** Anthony Mann. **CAST:** James Stewart, June Allyson, Frank Lovejoy, Barry Sullivan, Bruce Bennett, Rosemary DeCamp. **1955**

STRATEGIC COMMAND ★★ Shameless rip-off of *Executive Decision* stars direct-to-video Kurt Russell wannabe Michael Dudikoff, who leads an elite commando squad aboard a hijacked airplane carrying terrorists, the vice president of the United States, and a deadly chemical. Rated R for language and violence. 95m. **DIR:** Rick Jacobson. **CAST:** Michael Dudikoff, Paul Winfield, Richard Norton. **1997**

STRATTON STORY, THE ★★★★ Heartwarming true-life story of Chicago White Sox pitcher Monte Stratton, who lost a leg in a hunting accident at the height of his career. Fine performances in a "feel-good" movie. B&W; 106m. **DIR:** Sam Wood. **CAST:** James Stewart, June Allyson, Frank Morgan, Agnes Moorehead, Bill Williams. **1949**

STRAW DOGS ★★★★ An American intellectual mathematician (played brilliantly by Dustin Hoffman) takes a wife (Susan George) and returns to her ancestral

village on the coast of England. She taunts her former boyfriends with her wealth and power, and soon she is viciously raped. This violent, controversial shocker by Sam Peckinpah is rated R. 113m. **DIR:** Sam Peckinpah. **CAST:** Dustin Hoffman, Susan George, Peter Vaughan, T. P. McKenna, Peter Arne, David Warner. **1971 DVD**

STRAWBERRY AND CHOCOLATE ★★★ This amiable sort of *Odd Couple*, set in 1979 Havana, focuses on the blossoming friendship between a flamboyant, art-minded gay and a determinedly straight political-science student who learns to place compassion above ideology. It's an entertaining, gingerly paced seriocomedy about tolerance. In Spanish with English subtitles. Rated R for language and suggested sex. 104m. **DIR:** Tomas Gutierrez Alea, Juan Carlos Tabio. **CAST:** Jorge Perugorria, Vladimir Cruz, Mirta Ibarra. **1994**

STRAWBERRY BLONDE, THE ★★★ Sentimental flashback story of young man's unrequited love for *The Strawberry Blonde* (Rita Hayworth) is a change of pace for dynamic James Cagney and one of the most evocative period pieces produced in America about the innocent "Gay Nineties." Winsome Olivia de Havilland and a great cast of characters (including Alan Hale as Cagney's father) breathe life into this tragicomic tale. B&W; 97m. **DIR:** Raoul Walsh. **CAST:** James Cagney, Olivia de Havilland, Rita Hayworth, Alan Hale Sr., Jack Carson, George Tobias, Una O'Connor, George Reeves. **1941**

STRAWBERRY STATEMENT, THE ★★ Inane message film attempts to make some sense (and money) out of student dissidents and rebellion. Some good performances in this hodgepodge of comedy, drama, and youth-authority confrontations. Rated R. 103m. **DIR:** Stuart Hagmann. **CAST:** Kim Darby, Bruce Davison, Bob Balaban, James Kunen. **1970**

STRAY DOG ★★★★ In a fascinatingly detailed portrait of postwar Tokyo, a young detective (Toshiro Mifune) desperately searches the underworld for his stolen service revolver. Akira Kurosawa has created a tense thriller in the tradition of early Forties crime-dramas. In Japanese with English subtitles. Not rated. B&W; 122m. **DIR:** Akira Kurosawa. **CAST:** Toshiro Mifune, Takashi Shimura. **1949**

STRAYS This bargain-basement critter entry attempts—and fails—to make deadly menaces of cuddly house cats. Supermom Kathleen Quinlan just looks foolish retreating in fear from a water-soaked tabby. Made for cable. Rated R for violence. 83m. **DIR:** John McPherson. **CAST:** Kathleen Quinlan, Timothy Busfield, Claudia Christian. **1991**

STREAMERS ★★★1/2 This tense film is about four recruits and two veterans awaiting orders that will send them to Vietnam. The six men are a microcosm of American life in the late 1960s and early 1970s. A powerful, violent drama, this film is not suitable for everyone. Rated R. 118m. **DIR:** Robert Altman. **CAST:** Matthew Modine, Michael Wright, Mitchell Lichtenstein. **1984**

STREET, THE ★★1/2 Lured by the fantasy and excitement of the street—a metaphor for elusive freedom—a husband leaves his monotonous home and is caught up in a life of gambling and murder. Classic German progenitor of a more realistic style. Silent. B&W; 87m. **DIR:** Karl Grune. **CAST:** Eugen Klopfer. **1923**

STREET ASYLUM Cops are implanted with a device that compels them to clean up the streets in the most violent fashion possible. Rated R for violence and profanity. 94m. **DIR:** Gregory Brown. **CAST:** Wings Hauser, G. Gordon Liddy, Sy Richardson, Brian James. **1987**

STREET CRIMES ★★1/2 Dennis Farina adds integrity to this tale of a police officer who creates a youth center so that gang kids can settle their differences with fists and feet in the ring. A drug lord takes exception and soon both cops and kids find themselves to be targets. It's *Rocky* with a not-so-new twist. Rated R for profanity and violence. 93m. **DIR:** Stephen Smoke. **CAST:** Dennis Farina, Max Gail, Michael Worth. **1992**

STREET FIGHTER (1975) ★★ Sonny Chiba first caught the attention of American audiences in this martial arts hit. But the extreme violence (so strong that the film was originally rated X) is missing from this video version: shorn of 10 minutes, what's left is often hard to follow. Rated R. 75m. **DIR:** S. Ozawa. **CAST:** Sonny Chiba. **1975 DVD**

STREET FIGHTER (1994) ★★★ This entertaining action-fu adventure, based on the popular video game, is wired for grins as well as drop-kicks and shoot-outs. Jean-Claude Van Damme plays a cynical Allied Nation commando leader who must stop a wannabe world ruler from exchanging hostages for a kazillion dollars. Stephen de Souza, who penned *48 Hrs.* and *Die Hard*, makes his directorial debut and tones down the splatter. Rated PG-13 for language and violence. 95m. **DIR:** Stephen de Souza. **CAST:** Jean-Claude Van Damme, Raul Julia, Wes Studi, Ming-Na Wen, Damian Chapa. **1994 DVD**

STREET HITZ (STREET STORY) Low-budget drama about two brothers caught up in the violent world of street gangs in South Bronx. Pretty cheesy. Not rated; contains violence. 90m. **DIR:** Joseph B. Vasquez. **CAST:** Angelo Lopez, Cookie, Lydia Ramirez, Melvin Muza. **1991**

STREET HUNTER Drugs and gang wars. Rated R for violence. 96m. **DIR:** John Gallagher. **CAST:** Steve Harris, Reb Brown. **1990**

STREET JUSTICE ★★ Ex-CIA agent returns home after thirteen years of captivity to find his wife has remarried a political reformer involved in a power struggle with a corrupt political machine. Rated R for violence and profanity. 93m. **DIR:** Richard C. Sarafian. **CAST:** Michael Ontkean, Joanna Kerns, Catherine Bach. **1987**

STREET KNIGHT ★★★ *Perfect Weapon*'s Jeff Speakman returns to clean up the streets of Los Angeles in this satisfying action thriller. He's a retired cop forced back into action when a mysterious group attempts to incite rival gangs into war. There's more plot than usual, so martial-artist Speakman has more to do than beat up the bad guys, led by Christopher Neame. Rated R for violence, language, and nudity. 91m. **DIR:** Albert Magnoli. **CAST:** Jeff Speakman, Christopher Neame. **1993**

STREET LAW A down-but-not-broken trial lawyer is lured into a life of crime by a childhood friend. Rated R for violence and language. 98m. **DIR:** Damien Lee. **CAST:** Jeff Wincott, Paco Christian Prieto, Christina Cox. **1994 DVD**

STREET MUSIC ★★★1/2 An aspiring singer and her boyfriend, a tour guide, try to save a building full of senior citizens from eviction. Likable comedy-drama benefits from a realistic script and magnificent performances by Elizabeth Daily and Larry Breeding. Not

rated; the film has sexual situations. 92m. **DIR:** Jenny Bowen. **CAST:** Elizabeth Daily, Larry Breeding, Ned Glass. **1981**

STREET OF FORGOTTEN WOMEN, THE ★★ Silent exploitation movie masquerading as an exposé of urban squalor and prostitution. Entertainingly absurd, with an appropriately melodramatic organ score: a must for bad-movie buffs. B&W; 55m. **DIR:** Unknown. **1927**

STREET OF SHAME ★★★★ A penetrating study of love and sex that honestly examines the dreams and problems of a group of prostitutes living in a Tokyo brothel. In his final film, Japan's master director Kenji Mizoguchi creates a stirring portrait of communal life among women trapped in a harsh and degrading existence. In Japanese with English subtitles. B&W; 88m. **DIR:** Kenji Mizoguchi. **CAST:** Machiko Kyo. **1956**

STREET PEOPLE 🦃 Roger Moore and Stacy Keach travel from Italy to San Francisco to rub out a mobster. Rated R for violence. 92m. **DIR:** Maurizio Lucidi. **CAST:** Roger Moore, Stacy Keach. **1976**

STREET SCENE ★★★1/2 Playwright Elmer Rice wrote the screenplay for this fine film version of his Pulitzer Prize–winning drama of life in the New York tenements and the yearning and anguish of the young and hopeful who are desperate to get out. The cast is excellent, the score classic Alfred Newman, the camera work outstanding. B&W; 80m. **DIR:** King Vidor. **CAST:** Sylvia Sidney, William Collier Jr., Beulah Bondi, David Landau, Estelle Taylor, Walter Miller. **1931**

STREET SMART ★★1/2 Christopher Reeve gives a listless performance as a magazine writer under pressure who fabricates the life story of a New York pimp. Problems arise when parallels with a real pimp under investigation by the DA surface. Morgan Freeman plays the pimp Fast Black with an electrifying mesh of elegance and sleaze. Rated R for language and theme. 97m. **DIR:** Jerry Schatzberg. **CAST:** Christopher Reeve, Kathy Baker, Mimi Rogers, Andre Gregory, Morgan Freeman. **1986**

STREET SOLDIERS ★★1/2 Better-than-average revenge flick has a group of high school students banding together to take out the hoodlums who killed one of their ranks. Slick production values and fast-paced action sequences add up to a rousing tale. Rated R for violence and language. 99m. **DIR:** Lee Harry. **CAST:** Jun Chong, Jeff Rector. **1990**

STREET TRASH 🦃 Filmed in New York's Lower East Side, it focuses on street transients who consume a new brew that's been spiked by the military and go on a gory killing spree. 90m. **DIR:** Jim Muro. **CAST:** Bill Chepil, Jane Arakawa. **1987**

STREET WARS 🦃 Good intentions are not enough to save this unusual twist on the pedestrian street-gang formula. Rated R for language, violence, and adult situations. 90m. **DIR:** Jamaa Fanaka. **CAST:** Alan Joseph, Bryan O'Dell, Clifford Shegog. **1994 DVD**

STREET WITH NO NAME ★★★1/2 Semidocumentary about the FBI's infiltration of a gang of young hoodlums is hard-hitting and grimly realistic. Richard Widmark is at his best as the gang leader who rules his young thugs with military precision, and Mark Stevens plays the agent who poses as a tough in order to get the goods on the hoods. B&W; 94m. **DIR:** William Keighley. **CAST:** Mark Stevens, Richard Widmark, Lloyd Nolan, Barbara Lawrence, Ed Begley Sr., John McIntire. **1948**

STREETCAR NAMED DESIRE, A (1951) ★★★★★ Virtuoso acting highlights this powerful and disturbing drama based on the Tennessee Williams play. Vivien Leigh once again is the southern belle. Unlike Scarlett O'Hara, however, her Blanche DuBois is no longer young. She is a sexually disturbed woman who lives in a world of illusion. Her world begins to crumble when she moves in with her sister and brutish brother-in-law (Marlon Brando). B&W; 122m. **DIR:** Elia Kazan. **CAST:** Vivien Leigh, Marlon Brando, Kim Hunter, Karl Malden. **1951 DVD**

STREETCAR NAMED DESIRE, A (1983) ★★ Some films should never be remade; watch the five-star original instead of this slow-moving, lackluster version. Not rated; contains violence. 119m. **DIR:** John Erman. **CAST:** Ann-Margret, Treat Williams, Beverly D'Angelo, Randy Quaid. **1983**

STREETCAR NAMED DESIRE, A (1995) ★★1/2 Made-for-television, this is little more than a photographed version of the Broadway revival of Tennessee Williams's play. Although it uses the complete text, it runs a poor second to the 1951 film, with Alec Baldwin miscast as the brutish Stanley and Jessica Lange unsympathetic as Blanche. Not rated; contains sexual situations. 156m. **DIR:** Glenn Jordan. **CAST:** Jessica Lange, Alec Baldwin, Diane Lane, John Goodman. **1995**

STREETFIGHT (COONSKIN) ★★ Originally released in 1975 as *Coonskin*, this mixture of animation and live action was labeled racist by many. The animation tells the tale in almost *Song of the South* characterizations of a young black country rabbit caught up in Harlem's drug world. Definitely a curiosity. Rated R. 89m. **DIR:** Ralph Bakshi. **CAST:** Barry White, Scatman Crothers, Philip Michael Thomas. **1987**

STREETHAWK ★★ Only kiddies—and fans of the short-lived television series, if there are any—will find much to enjoy in this story of a police officer (Rex Smith) left for dead by drug dealers. 60m. **DIR:** Virgil Vogel. **CAST:** Rex Smith, Jayne Modean, Christopher Lloyd, Joe Regalbuto, Lawrence Pressman, Robert Beltran. **1986**

STREETS 🦃 A prostitute is pursued by a psychotic cop. Rated R for violence, nudity, and depiction of drug use. 86m. **DIR:** Katt Shea Ruben. **CAST:** Christina Applegate, David Mendenhall. **1989**

STREETS OF FIRE ★★★ This comic book–style movie is a diverting compendium of nonstop action set to a rocking backbeat. In it a famous rock singer (Diane Lane) is captured by a motorcycle gang in Walter Hill's mythic world, which combines 1950s attitudes and styles with a futuristic feel. It's up to her two-fisted former boyfriend, Tom Cody (Michael Paré) to save her. Rated R for profanity and violence. 93m. **DIR:** Walter Hill. **CAST:** Diane Lane, Michael Paré, Rick Moranis, Amy Madigan, Willem Dafoe. **1984 DVD**

STREETS OF GOLD ★★★ This is a pleasant story about an ex-boxer (Klaus Maria Brandauer) who decides to regain his self-worth by passing on his skills to a pair of street boxers. Brandauer puts a lot of energy into his role, demonstrating shading and character depth far beyond what you'd expect from a routine story. Inexplicably rated R for mild language and violence. 95m.

DIR: Joe Roth. **CAST:** Klaus Maria Brandauer, Adrian Pasdar, Wesley Snipes, Angela Molina. **1986**

STREETS OF L.A., THE ★★★1/2 Joanne Woodward plays a struggling real estate saleswoman who gets her new tires slashed by a group of angry Hispanics and decides to pursue them in the hopes of getting reimbursed. The acting is quite good even if the film is a low-budget production. A sensitive, rather quiet drama. Not rated; contains violence. 94m. **DIR:** Jerrold Freedman. **CAST:** Joanne Woodward, Robert Webber, Michael C. Gwynne, Audrey Christie, Isela Vega, Pepe Serna, Miguel Pinero, Tony Plana. **1979**

STREETS OF LAREDO ★★★★★ In the official sequel to Larry McMurtry's *Lonesome Dove*, James Garner takes over the role of Capt. Woodrow Call and gives one of his greatest performances. This time, Call and his longtime deputy, Pea Eye (Sam Shepard), are on the trail of a bloodthirsty train robber—a youngster named Joey Garza—and a group of outlaws who burn their victims. A wonderful cast does memorable work, especially Sissy Spacek (as Lorena, Pea Eye's wife) and Randy Quaid (as John Wesley Hardin). Made for TV. 227m. **DIR:** Joseph Sargent. **CAST:** James Garner, Sissy Spacek, Sam Shepard, Sonia Braga, Ned Beatty, Randy Quaid, Wes Studi, Charles Martin Smith, George Carlin, Alexis Cruz, Kevin Conway, James Gammon, Anjanette Comer. **1996**

STREETWALKIN' 🦃 Incoherent. Rated R for simulated sex, profanity, and violence. 84m. **DIR:** Joan Freeman. **CAST:** Julie Newmar, Melissa Leo, Leon Robinson, Antonio Fargas. **1985**

STREETWISE ★★★★★ A powerful, emotionally compelling glimpse into the lives of displaced homeless youths surviving as pimps, prostitutes, muggers, panhandlers, and small-time drug dealers on the streets of Seattle. This Oscar nominee explores its disturbing theme with great sensitivity while creating a portrait of a teenage wasteland. Highly recommended. Not rated; contains violence and profanity. 92m. **DIR:** Martin Bell, Mary Ellen Mark, Cheryl McCall. **1985**

STRICTLY BALLROOM ★★★★ Australian director Baz Luhrmann takes the garish visual style of cult director John Waters and gives it heart, in this offbeat *Cinderella* tale of a male dancer who breaks with the rules of ballroom dancing, and the wallflower who dreams of being his partner. While not for all tastes, this off-kilter musical has remarkable warmth. Rated PG for profanity. 94m. **DIR:** Baz Luhrmann. **CAST:** Paul Mercurio, Tara Morice, Bill Hunter, Pat Thomson, Barry Otto. **1992 DVD**

STRICTLY BUSINESS ★★★ Frequent laughs, deft characterizations, and fine acting save what could have been little more than a paint-by-the-numbers movie about a streetwise office boy whose success in business is connected to the rise of a junior executive. Rated PG-13 for profanity and violence. 83m. **DIR:** Kevin Hooks. **CAST:** Tommy Davidson, Joseph C. Phillips, Halle Berry, Anne-Marie Johnson, David Marshall Grant, Jon Cypher. **1991**

STRIKE (1924) ★★★★ Shot in a documentarylike style, this drama about a labor dispute during the czarist era was Sergei Eisenstein's first feature film. Advanced for its time and using techniques Eisenstein would perfect in his later masterpieces, *Strike* remains a remarkable achievement and still holds one's interest today. Silent. B&W; 82m. **DIR:** Sergei Eisenstein. **CAST:** Grigori Alexandrov, Alexander Antonov. **1924 DVD**

STRIKE! (1998) ★★★★ An exciting young cast and a sense of nostalgia fuel this invigorating film. In a private girls' school, four protagonists form a club to be true to themselves and their school, which is in dire financial straits. Fun, funny, dramatic, and beautifully realized by a stellar cast, *Strike!* is first class. A.k.a. *The Hairy Bird.* Rated PG-13 for language and adult situations. 97m. **DIR:** Sarah Kernochan. **CAST:** Gaby Hoffman, Kirsten Dunst, Rachael Leigh Cook, Lynn Redgrave, Merrit Wever, Tom Guiry. **1998 DVD**

STRIKE A POSE 🦃 This so-called thriller is nothing more than thinly veiled soft-core junk, with inept performances and a laughable plot interrupted every seven minutes by sweaty love-making. Rated R for nudity, simulated sex, profanity, and violence. 87m. **DIR:** Dean Hamilton. **CAST:** Robert Eastwick, Michelle LaMothe, Margie Peterson. **1993 DVD**

STRIKE COMMANDO 🦃 A Vietnam vet goes behind enemy lines. Rated R for Refuse. 92m. **DIR:** Vincent Dawn. **CAST:** Reb Brown, Christopher Connelly. **1987**

STRIKE FORCE ★★ A *French Connection* rehash, this made-for-television movie stars Richard Gere as a cop out to make a big drug bust. Lots of action, not much story. 74m. **DIR:** Barry Shear. **CAST:** Richard Gere, Cliff Gorman, Donald Blakely, Edward Grover, Joe Spinell. **1975 DVD**

STRIKE IT RICH ★★ Whirlwind romance results in a honeymoon at Monte Carlo for a prudish British accountant (Robert Lindsay) and his young wife (Molly Ringwald). Bland romantic comedy derived from a Graham Greene novel. Rated PG. 90m. **DIR:** James Scott. **CAST:** Robert Lindsay, Molly Ringwald, John Gielgud, Simon de la Brosse. **1990**

STRIKE UP THE BAND ★★★ This encore to *Babes in Arms* has ever-exuberant Mickey Rooney leading a high school band that would shade Glenn Miller's. Second banana Judy Garland sings. "Come on, kids, let's put on a show" in a different setting. B&W; 120m. **DIR:** Busby Berkeley. **CAST:** Mickey Rooney, Judy Garland, June Preisser, Paul Whiteman. **1940**

STRIKER'S MOUNTAIN ★★ Predictable plot with suspenseless conflicts. A small-time resort owner alternately courts and repels the big corporate backing that Leslie Nielsen, as a ruthless millionaire, controls. The ski scenes are the best part of the film. Not rated. 99m. **DIR:** Allen Simmonds. **CAST:** Leslie Nielsen, August Schellengberg, Mimi Kuzyk, Bruce Greenwood. **1987**

STRIKING DISTANCE ★★★1/2 An honest cop finds himself on river patrol after testifying against another police officer who brutally beat a suspect to death. Then he picks up the trail of a serial killer. While not up to the high standards of the star's *Die Hard* movies, this is still enjoyable action fare. Rated R for profanity, violence, and simulated sex. 97m. **DIR:** Rowdy Harrington. **CAST:** Bruce Willis, Sarah Jessica Parker, Dennis Farina, Tom Sizemore, Robert Pastorelli, Timothy Busfield, John Mahoney, Andre Braugher, Tom Atkins. **1993 DVD**

STRIKING POINT ★★ The Cold War may be over, but ex-KGB agents are nurturing a war of their own by shipping deadly weapons into the United States and supply-

ing them to street gangs. Rated R for violence and adult language. 93m. **DIR:** Thomas Fenton. **CAST:** Chris Mitchum, Tracy Spaulding, Ivan Rogers, Stan Morse. **1994**

STRIKING POSES ★★1/2 A photographer who stalks celebrities for a tabloid finds the tables turned when someone starts stalking her. It's no *The Conversation*, but this straight-to-video suspense drama is better than the box (which makes it look like an erotic thriller) would suggest. Rated R for profanity and violence. 99m. **DIR:** Gail Harry. **CAST:** Shannen Doherty, Joseph Griffin, Tamara Gorski, Colm Feore. **1998**

STRIPES ★★★★ It's laughs aplenty when *Saturday Night Live* graduate Bill Murray enlists in the army. But hey, as Murray might say, after a guy loses his job, his car, and his girl all in the same day, what else is he supposed to do? Thanks to Murray, Harold Ramis, and John Candy, the U.S. Army may never be the same. Warren Oates also is in top form as the no-nonsense sergeant. Rated R. 105m. **DIR:** Ivan Reitman. **CAST:** Bill Murray, Harold Ramis, John Candy, Warren Oates, P. J. Soles, Sean Young, John Larroquette. **1981 DVD**

STRIPPER, THE ★★1/2 Somewhat engrossing account of an aging stripper (Joanne Woodward) falling in love with a teenager (Richard Beymer). Good performances by all, but the film tends to drag and become too stagy. Based on William Inge's play. 95m. **DIR:** Franklin J. Schaffner. **CAST:** Joanne Woodward, Richard Beymer, Claire Trevor, Carol Lynley, Robert Webber, Gypsy Rose Lee, Louis Nye. **1963**

STRIPTEASE ★★★1/2 Carl Hiaasen's provocative bestseller stars Demi Moore as a former FBI clerk forced to earn money as a stripper, while petitioning the court to regain her daughter from a low-life former husband. Rated R for nudity, profanity, violence, and strong sexual content. 115m. **DIR:** Andrew Bergman. **CAST:** Demi Moore, Armand Assante, Ving Rhames, Robert Patrick, Burt Reynolds, Stuart Pankin. **1996 DVD**

STROKE OF MIDNIGHT ★★1/2 Filmed in Paris, this features Jennifer Grey as a drab high-fashion dresser who makes a Cinderella-type transformation after a fairy godmother rewards her for a good deed. Cute fantasy is okay time-passer. Rated PG for profanity. 102m. **DIR:** Tom Clegg. **CAST:** Jennifer Grey, Rob Lowe, Andrea Ferreol. **1990**

STROKER ACE ★★★ Film critics all over the country jumped on this car-crash-and-corn-pone comedy. It's not all that bad. About an egotistical, woman-chasing race-car driver, it's the same old predictable nonsense. Yet it's certain to please the audience it was intended for. Rated PG for sexual innuendo and violence. 96m. **DIR:** Hal Needham. **CAST:** Burt Reynolds, Ned Beatty, Jim Nabors, Loni Anderson, Parker Stevenson. **1983 DVD**

STROMBOLI ★★ This potboiler from the director of *Open City* is a brooding, sometimes boring movie about an attractive woman who marries a fisherman and attempts to adjust. Even Ingrid Bergman (by this time married to Rossellini) couldn't salvage this film. Subtitled. B&W; 81m. **DIR:** Roberto Rossellini. **CAST:** Ingrid Bergman, Mario Vitale. **1950**

STRONG MAN, THE ★★★1/2 At one time silent comedy star Harry Langdon gave Charlie Chaplin, Buster Keaton, and Harold Lloyd a run for their money. *The Strong Man*, directed by a very young Frank Capra, is Langdon's best feature film. Langdon plays a young Belgian soldier who wistfully dreams of the American girl he has been corresponding with while bungling most of his assignments on the battlefield. Silent. B&W; 75m. **DIR:** Frank Capra. **CAST:** Harry Langdon, Priscilla Bonner, Robert McKim. **1926**

STROSZEK ★★★★ Werner Herzog's hilarious, poignant vision of three misfits—a drunk, a soulful prostitute, and an eccentric old man—who leave Berlin and follow the American dream to rural Wisconsin. This funny, richly perceptive look at the American experience through the eyes of three German outcasts won international critical acclaim. In German with English subtitles. Not rated. 108m. **DIR:** Werner Herzog. **CAST:** Bruno S., Eva Mattes, Clemens Scheitz. **1977 DVD**

STRYKER 🦃 A soldier of fortune attempting to wrest a group of warrior women from the clutches of an evil tribe. Rated R. 86m. **DIR:** Cirio H. Santiago. **CAST:** Steve Sandor, Andria Savio. **1983**

STUART LITTLE ★★★★ Magical, heartwarming family film based on E. B. White's children's book. A couple's adoption of a second son, oblivious to the fact that he's a mouse, leads to problems with their human son which pale in comparison to the family cat's resentment. High-quality computer-generated detail allows the mouse to appear real and permits the many featured cats to talk freely. Jonathan Lipnicki is adorable as the human son and the voices of Michael J. Fox as Stuart and Nathan Lane as his nemesis Snowbell perfectly fit the roles. Rated PG for *Road Runner*-ish violence toward the cats. 86m. **DIR:** Rob Minkoff. **CAST:** Geena Davis, Hugh Laurie, Jonathan Lipnicki. **1999 DVD**

STUART SAVES HIS FAMILY ★★★1/2 Al Franken recreates his *Saturday Night Live* role of Stuart Smalley, the soft-spoken host of *Daily Affirmation* and neurotic veteran of several twelve-step foundations. In exploring Stuart's rocky history with his world-class dysfunctional family, the film is not only warmly funny but also a sweet-tempered satire of modern hang-ups. Rated PG-13 for mature themes and mild profanity. 90m. **DIR:** Harold Ramis. **CAST:** Al Franken, Laura San Giacomo, Vincent D'Onofrio, Lesley Boone, Shirley Knight, Harris Yulin. **1995**

STUD, THE 🦃 Sordid soft-core porn film concerning a young man's various affairs. Rated R. 95m. **DIR:** Quentin Masters. **CAST:** Joan Collins, Oliver Tobias. **1978**

STUDENT BODIES ★★1/2 This comedy-horror release has something extra, because it is a parody of blood-and-guts films. Rated R. 86m. **DIR:** Mickey Rose. **CAST:** Kristin Ritter, Matthew Goldsby, Joe Flood. **1981**

STUDENT CONFIDENTIAL ★★1/2 A new school counselor helps some problem children with high IQs. *Student Confidential* does not speak to teens with the self-satisfaction of *The Breakfast Club* or the brutality of *River's Edge*, but it is far better than most teen films. Rated R for violence, profanity, and nudity. 92m. **DIR:** Richard Horian. **CAST:** Eric Douglas, Marlon Jackson, Ronee Blakley. **1987**

STUDENT NURSES, THE ★★★ In their last year of schooling, four young women begin to experience life in the real world of medicine and men. The first of Roger Corman's successful *Nurse* movies, this is a well-written

exploitation movie that you don't have to feel guilty about liking. Rated R for nudity. 85m. **DIR:** Stephanie Rothman. **CAST:** Elaine Giftos, Karen Carlson, Barbara Leigh. **1970**

STUDENT OF PRAGUE ★★★★ One of the most important films in silent German Expressionist cinema. The film is based on the myths of the Doppelgänger and Faust legends. Brilliantly photographed. Silent with English titles. B&W; 45m. **DIR:** Henrik Galeen. **CAST:** Conrad Veidt, Werner Krauss. **1926**

STUDENT PRINCE, THE ★★★★ A captivating, colorful, and charming rendition of Sigmund Romberg's famous operetta, and the only talkie version made from it. Mario Lanza recorded the soundtrack but was much too fat to play the Prince of Heidelberg who lives among the commoners and falls for a barmaid (Ann Blyth). Newcomer Edmund Purdom took his place. 107m. **DIR:** Richard Thorpe. **CAST:** Ann Blyth, Edmund Purdom, John Ericson, Louis Calhern, Edmund Gwenn. **1954**

STUDENT PRINCE IN OLD HEIDELBERG, THE ★★★★ The famous Lubitsch touch is in evidence in the story of a Bavarian prince eager to sow some wild oats. He enrolls at Heidelberg University, falls in love with a barmaid, and comes of age. Later versions with the famous Sigmund Romberg score turned the tale into a moodier romance. Silent. B&W; 105m. **DIR:** Ernst Lubitsch. **CAST:** Norma Shearer, Ramon Novarro, Jean Hersholt, Gustav von Seyffertitz. **1927**

STUDS LONIGAN ★★ Film version of James T. Farrell's landmark first novel is a major disappointment. Depressing tale of a young man's slide into drunkenness and debauchery pulls most of the punches that the book delivered and ends up drastically changing the ending to a more conventional Hollywood fade-out. B&W; 95m. **DIR:** Irving Lerner. **CAST:** Christopher Knight, Frank Gorshin, Jack Nicholson, Venetia Stevenson, Dick Foran, Jay C. Flippen, Carolyn Craig. **1960**

STUDY IN SCARLET, A ★★ Bearing absolutely no resemblance to the first of Arthur Conan Doyle's Sherlock Holmes stories, this low-budget entry is perhaps the most lackluster of all the sound Holmes films. B&W; 70m. **DIR:** Edwin L. Marin. **CAST:** Reginald Owen, Anna May Wong, Alan Dinehart, June Clyde, Alan Mowbray. **1933**

STUDY IN TERROR, A ★★★★ Superior Sherlock Holmes adventure pits "the original caped crusader," as the ads called him, against Jack the Ripper. John Neville is an excellent Holmes. And Donald Houston is perhaps the screen's finest Dr. John Watson. 94m. **DIR:** James Hill. **CAST:** John Neville, Donald Houston, Georgia Brown, John Fraser, Anthony Quayle, Barbara Windsor, Robert Morley, Cecil Parker. **1965**

STUFF, THE A scrumptious, creamy dessert devours from within all those who eat it. Rated R for gore and profanity. 93m. **DIR:** Larry Cohen. **CAST:** Michael Moriarty, Andrea Marcovicci, Garrett Morris, Paul Sorvino, Danny Aiello. **1985**

STUFF STEPHANIE IN THE INCINERATOR Excruciatingly bad stalk-and-hunt comedy that has nothing to do with an incinerator, but still deserves to get stuffed. Rated PG-13. 97m. **DIR:** Lloyd Kaufman. **CAST:** Catherine Dee. **1989**

STUNT MAN, THE ★★★★1/2 Nothing is ever quite what it seems in this fast-paced, superbly crafted film. It's a Chinese puzzle of a movie and, therefore, may not please all viewers. Nevertheless, this directorial tour de force by Richard Rush has ample thrills, chills, suspense, and surprises for those with a taste for something different. Rated R. 129m. **DIR:** Richard Rush. **CAST:** Peter O'Toole, Steve Railsback, Barbara Hershey, Chuck Bail, Allen Garfield, Adam Roarke, Alex Rocco. **1980 DVD**

STUPIDS, THE ★★ Dumb down the Brady Bunch a few notches and you have the Stupids, a family so out of it that they think they're on to it. While investigating the weekly theft of his garbage, Stanley Stupid (Tom Arnold) uncovers a plot to sell high-powered weapons to international tyrants. Meanwhile, his wife seeks her children, believed to have been kidnapped by the police. You'll laugh in spite of the fact that this film can only live up to its title. Rated PG for violence. 93m. **DIR:** John Landis. **CAST:** Tom Arnold, Jessica Lundy, Alex McKenna, Bug Hall, Mark Metcalf, Matt Keeslar. **1996**

SUB DOWN ★★1/2 Three scientists try to help out a disabled nuclear submarine stuck below the arctic ice cap. This made-for-cable original is not a bad little action-rescue movie, but several stupid story twists and a few bad lines sink the whole film, which is probably why director Gregg Champion decided to hide behind the Alan Smithee pseudonym. Not rated. 95m. **DIR:** Alan Smithee. **CAST:** Stephen Baldwin, Gabrielle Anwar, Tom Conti. **1997**

SUBJECT WAS ROSES, THE ★★★ A young soldier (Martin Sheen) returns home to his unhappily married parents (Patricia Neal, Jack Albertson). Well acted, especially by Neal in her first role after her near-fatal stroke. Vaudeville veteran Albertson won an Oscar. Rated G. 107m. **DIR:** Ulu Grosbard. **CAST:** Patricia Neal, Jack Albertson, Martin Sheen. **1968**

SUBMERGED ★1/2 A passenger jet is forced into the ocean by bad guys who want to steal a top-secret government device. Silly action-adventure movie asks the audience to suspend its disbelief far too often. Rated R for violence and language. 94m. **DIR:** Ed Raymond. **CAST:** Coolio, Nicole Eggert, Fred Williamson. **2000 DVD**

SUBSPECIES ★★★ Two vampire brothers—one good, one evil—fight for a bloodstone left by their father. This interesting twist on the vampire legend suffers from bad acting, but benefits by holding true to many aspects of vampire lore. Not rated; contains violence, profanity, and mild gore. 90m. **DIR:** Ted Nicolaou. **CAST:** Michael Watson, Laura Tate, Angus Scrimm. **1990**

SUBSPECIES 4: BLOODSTORM ★★★ Characters from *Subspecies* combine with characters from *Vampire Journals* to set in motion this fourth installment in the durable series. After being burnt to death by the sun, Radu somehow returns to stalk Michelle, enlisting the aid of Ash and his vampire coven in the search for Michelle. A lot of things don't make sense, but fans of the series will no doubt be overjoyed with a new episode. Rated R for violence and nudity. 90m. **DIR:** Ted Nicolaou. **CAST:** Denice Duff, Anders Hove, Jonathon Morris. **1998 DVD**

SUBSTANCE OF FIRE, THE ★★★★ Manhattan publishing magnate Isaac Geldhart is descending into madness, and his once-respected literary house is "hemorrhaging money." The bitter Holocaust survivor, unable to express love to his own children, is determined to

print very pricey volumes of Nazi medical atrocities that have been documented by an old friend. This compelling drama about an adult struggling with a traumatic past and an all-consuming commitment to moral and artistic excellence, blends lofty themes with fine performances. Rated R for language. 101m. **DIR:** Daniel Sullivan. **CAST:** Ron Rifkin, Sarah Jessica Parker, Tony Goldwyn, Timothy Hutton. **1996**

SUBSTITUTE, THE (1993) ★★★ In this made-for-cable original, a college professor kills her husband and his lover, then resurfaces as a substitute high-school teacher. She falls in love with the father of one of her students, but people are getting suspicious, so she must kill again. Pretty predictable story line, but the acting is good. Rated R for violence and suggested sex. 86m. **DIR:** Martin Donovan. **CAST:** Amanda Donohoe, Dalton James, Natasha Gregson Wagner, Eugene Glazer, Mark Wahlberg. **1993**

SUBSTITUTE, THE (1996) ★★1/2 This unintentionally wacky, reactionary urban thriller introduces the ultimate high-school disciplinarian—an unemployed mercenary soldier. Rated R for violence and language. 114m. **DIR:** Robert Mandel. **CAST:** Tom Berenger, Diane Venora, Ernie Hudson, Glenn Plummer, Raymond Cruz, William Forsythe. **1996 DVD**

SUBSTITUTE, THE: FAILURE IS NOT AN OPTION ★★ Treat Williams stars in the latest installment of the franchise, playing an undercover cop attempting to stop a group of neo-Nazi students from bringing down a military school. Class is in session, but logic is tossed out the door as cop Karl Thomasson tries to keep the peace. This made-for-cable thriller is exploitation at its most obvious. Rated R for adult situations, language, and violence. 91m. **DIR:** Robert Radler. **CAST:** Treat Williams, Angie Everhart, Patrick Kilpatrick, Bill Nunn. **2000**

SUBSTITUTE WIFE, THE ★★★★1/2 Keep the tissue handy when you watch this charming, tender story of love and unselfishness. Peter Weller and Lea Thompson lead a stellar cast in this made-for-television tearjerker about a couple trying to keep their children and Nebraska farm together despite the odds. Set in 1869, the film is rich in period detail and strong family values. Rated PG-13 for theme. 92m. **DIR:** Peter Werner. **CAST:** Farrah Fawcett, Lea Thompson, Peter Weller. **1994**

SUBURBAN COMMANDO ★★1/2 Wrestler Hulk Hogan is extremely likable as an outer-space bounty hunter in this humorous comedy. Christopher Lloyd is a nebbish architect who learns to handle his boss with the help of Hogan's commando tactics. Rated PG. 85m. **DIR:** Burt Kennedy. **CAST:** Hulk Hogan, Christopher Lloyd, Shelley Duvall, Larry Miller, Jack Elam. **1991**

SUBURBAN ROULETTE 🦃 Showcased by Joe Bob Briggs, this piece of trash about wife swapping is tame and boring by today's standards. Not rated. 91m. **DIR:** Herschell Gordon Lewis. **CAST:** Elizabeth Wilkinson. **1967**

SUBURBANS, THE ★★ If it weren't for the overused plot, weak acting, poor direction, and silly script, *The Suburbans* might have been a good movie. The premise—a record executive encourages a one-hit 1980s band to reunite—is ripe for satire, but everyone involved goes for the obvious instead, and good talent gets wasted. Rated R for adult situations and language. 81m. **DIR:** Donal Lardner Ward. **CAST:** Donal Lardner Ward, Craig Bierko, Will Ferrell, Tony Guma, Amy Brenneman, Bridgette Wilson. **1999 DVD**

SUBURBIA (1983) ★★★ Penelope Spheeris, who directed the punk-rock documentary *Decline of Western Civilization*, did this low-budget film of punk rockers versus local rednecks and townspeople in a small suburban area. Not for all tastes, but a good little film for people who are bored with releases like *Cannonball Run II*. Rated R. 96m. **DIR:** Penelope Spheeris. **CAST:** Chris Pederson, Bill Coyne, Jennifer Clay. **1983 DVD**

SUBURBIA (1997) ★★★1/2 Aimless 20-year-olds loiter around the parking lot of a convenience store, wondering what to do with the rest of their lives. When a former comrade, now successful rock singer, pays a visit, it sparks a night of partying spiked with outbursts of envy and hostility. Eric Bogosian's almost plotless play is smoothly transferred to the screen; the stage origins show through, but Richard Linklater's direction is sensitive and inconspicuous, with fine, well-balanced acting by the young ensemble cast. Rated R for profanity. 118m. **DIR:** Richard Linklater. **CAST:** Giovanni Ribisi, Nicky Katt, Steve Zahn, Amie Carey, Jayce Bartok, Parker Posey, Dina Spybey. **1997**

SUBWAY ★★ The stunning Isabelle Adjani plays a young wife who becomes involved with a streetwise rogue played by Christopher Lambert. The plot is not very clear and the bad jokes don't help. Fast-paced action scenes keep the film interesting, but they all lead nowhere. In French with English subtitles. Rated R for profanity and violence. 110m. **DIR:** Luc Besson. **CAST:** Isabelle Adjani, Christopher Lambert, Richard Bohringer. **1985 DVD**

SUBWAY STORIES ★★★ This HBO original derives from an intriguing contest that allowed "regular folks" to submit some of their more interesting experiences in the New York City subway system. The resulting ten vignettes are hit or miss, ranging from the quite funny to the provocative, to the completely pointless. Each episode comes from a different writer-director team; unfortunately, the combined whole never quite lives up to its desire to become a "subway symphony." Rated PG-13 for profanity. 83m. **DIR:** Jonathan Demme, Abel Ferrara. **CAST:** Gregory Hines, Bill Irwin, Christine Lahti, Denis Leary, Rosie Perez, Michael Rapaport, Mercedes Ruehl, Jerry Stiller. **1997**

SUBWAY TO THE STARS ★★★ A near triumph of style over substance by a gifted Brazilian filmmaker. A musician searching for his girlfriend is guided through a nightmarish, Dante's Inferno–like labyrinth of Rio de Janeiro nightlife. Fascinating but overlong. 103m. **DIR:** Carlos Diegues. **CAST:** Guilherme Fontes. **1987**

SUCCESS IS THE BEST REVENGE ★★★1/2 Polish exile hustles to make a film about his native country while ignoring his own family problems. Director Jerzy Skolimowski, who dazzled us with the 1982 film *Moonlighting* is in good form with this biting drama. Not rated; but has violence, profanity, and nudity. 95m. **DIR:** Jerzy Skolimowski. **CAST:** Michael York, Anouk Aimée, Michael Lyndon, John Hurt, Jane Asher, Michel Piccoli. **1984**

SUDAN ★★★1/2 Good formula escapism fare, but the formula for Montez's pictures was wearing thin by the time this came out. It was one of her last. 76m. **DIR:** John Rawlins. **CAST:** Maria Montez, Jon Hall, Turhan

Bey, Andy Devine, George Zucco, Robert Warwick. **1945**

SUDDEN DEATH (1986) 🦃 Cheaply made rehash of *Death Wish* and *Ms. .45*. Rated R. 93m. **DIR:** Sig Shore. **CAST:** Denise Coward, Frank Runyeon, Jaime Tinelli. **1986**

SUDDEN DEATH (1995) ★★1/2 *Die Hard* in a hockey arena. A fireman with a troubled past takes his kids to the Stanley Cup finals in Pittsburgh, where his daughter and the vice president of the United States are nabbed by terrorists. The film doesn't break any new ground but provides several big action thrills as the extortionists threaten to blow up the arena and parking lot. Rated R for language and violence. 110m. **DIR:** Peter Hyams. **CAST:** Jean-Claude Van Damme, Powers Boothe, Raymond J. Berry, Whittni Wright, Ross Malinger. **1995 DVD**

SUDDEN FEAR ★★★★ An eerie thriller about a playwright who finds out her husband plans to kill her. She works to turn the tables on him and get his girlfriend to take the blame. Moody film that capitalizes on Joan Crawford's wide-eyed looks of shock and frustration. Because it is so well-written, the rest of the cast gets a chance to shine as well. B&W; 110m. **DIR:** David Miller. **CAST:** Joan Crawford, Jack Palance, Gloria Grahame, Mike Connors. **1952 DVD**

SUDDEN IMPACT ★★★★ "Dirty Harry" Callahan (Clint Eastwood) is back, and he's meaner, nastier, and—surprise!—funnier than ever in this, his fourth screen adventure. Harry's job is to track down a female revenge killer but not until he's done away with a half-dozen villains and delivered twice as many quips including, "Go ahead, make my day." Rated R for violence and profanity. 117m. **DIR:** Clint Eastwood. **CAST:** Clint Eastwood, Sondra Locke, Pat Hingle, Bradford Dillman. **1983 DVD**

SUDDEN THUNDER 🦃 Umpteenth take on the female cop avenging her father's death by taking on the mob. The only thunder is this bomb going off. Not rated; contains violence. 90m. **DIR:** David Hunt. **CAST:** Andrea Lamatsch, Corwyn Sperry, James Paoleilei, Ernie Santana. **1990**

SUDDENLY ★★★★ Here's top-notch entertainment with Frank Sinatra perfectly cast as a leader of a gang of assassins out to kill the president of the United States. Film has gone largely unnoticed over the last few years, but thanks to home video, we can all enjoy this gem of a picture. B&W; 77m. **DIR:** Lewis Allen. **CAST:** Frank Sinatra, Sterling Hayden, James Gleason, Nancy Gates. **1954 DVD**

SUDDENLY, LAST SUMMER ★★★ Another one of those unpleasant but totally intriguing forays of Tennessee Williams. Elizabeth Taylor is a neurotic girl being prodded into madness by the memory of her gay cousin's bizarre death, a memory that Katharine Hepburn, his adoring mother, wants to remain vague if not submerged. She prevails upon Montgomery Clift to make sure it does. B&W; 114m. **DIR:** Joseph L. Mankiewicz. **CAST:** Elizabeth Taylor, Montgomery Clift, Katharine Hepburn. **1959 DVD**

SUDIE & SIMPSON ★★★1/2 This finely etched portrait of racial intolerance in a small 1940s Georgia town shows how the friendship between the kindly black Simpson and sprite Sudie teaches the locals a lesson about understanding and prejudice. Excellent performances from all in this made-for-TV movie. Not rated. 95m. **DIR:** Joan Tewkesbury. **CAST:** Louis Gossett Jr., Sara Gilbert, Frances Fisher, John Jackson. **1990 DVD**

SUGAR AND SPICE ★★★1/2 Finally, a teen flick that adults can enjoy! When the head cheerleader gets pregnant, the squad supports her plans to rob a bank. Each girl brings her own special hang-ups to the heist, adding laughs to what might, under less skillful direction, be just another what's-wrong-with-kids-today handwringer. At times dark and biting but never boring! Rated PG-13 for language and illegal activity. 85m. **DIR:** Francine McDougall. **CAST:** Marley Shelton, James Marsden, Mena Suvari, Marla Sokoloff. **2001 DVD**

SUGAR COOKIES 🦃 Two women are set up to be murdered by a porno filmmaker. Rated R for nudity, profanity, and violence. 89m. **DIR:** Michael Herz. **CAST:** Mary Woronov, Monique Van Vooren, Lynn Lowry. **1988**

SUGAR HILL ★★1/2 Despite fine performances by Wesley Snipes and Michael Wright, this story of two brothers involved in the Harlem drug trade does not have the punch of *New Jack City*. Director Leon Ichaso has a great eye for detail and settings, but he is unable to add excitement to the all-too-familiar story line that has Snipes attempting to leave his gangster ways behind. Rated R for violence, profanity, and nudity. 123m. **DIR:** Leon Ichaso. **CAST:** Wesley Snipes, Michael Wright, Theresa Randle, Clarence Williams, III, Abe Vigoda, Larry Joshua, Ernie Hudson, Leslie Uggams. **1994**

SUGAR TOWN ★★★1/2 Aging rockers seek a comeback record deal in this earthy, sweetly comic ensemble piece. Set in the fast, clogged lanes of Los Angeles's music and film scene, this sprawling stream of characters, moods, and melodrama says just as much about American culture and show business as it does individual dreams, conceits, and scruples. Its intersecting stories wheeze a bit but feel refreshingly honest. Rated R for drug content, language, and sexual content. 93m. **DIR:** Allison Anders, Kurt Voss. **CAST:** Jade Gordon, Ally Sheedy, Larry Klein, Michael Des Barres, John Taylor, Martin Kemp, John Doe. **1999**

SUGARBABY ★★★1/2 In this decidedly offbeat comedy-drama from German filmmaker Percy Adlon, an overweight morgue attendant (Marianne Sägebrecht) finds new meaning in her life when she falls in love with a subway driver. In German with English subtitles. Not rated; the film has nudity. 86m. **DIR:** Percy Adlon. **CAST:** Marianne Sagebrecht. **1986**

SUGARCANE ALLEY ★★★★★ Set in Martinique of the 1930s, this superb French import examines the lives led by black sugarcane plantation workers. Specifically, it focuses on the hopes and dreams of José (Garry Cadenat), an 11 year old orphan with a brilliant mind, which just may be the key to his breaking the bonds of slavery. In French with English subtitles. Not rated, the film has some scenes of violence. 100m. **DIR:** Euzhan Palcy. **CAST:** Garry Cadenat, Darling Legitimus. **1983**

SUGARLAND EXPRESS, THE ★★★★ A rewarding film in many respects, this was Steven Spielberg's first feature effort. Based on an actual incident in Texas during the late 1960s, a prison escapee and his wife try to regain custody of their infant child. Their desperation results in a madcap chase across the state with a kidnapped state trooper. Rated PG. 109m. **DIR:** Steven

Spielberg. **CAST:** Goldie Hawn, Ben Johnson, Michael Sacks, William Atherton. **1974**

SUGARTIME ★★★ Scripter Martyn Burke's based-on-truth gangster saga is pretty ordinary compared to contemporaries such as *Bugsy* or *Casino*, but there's nonetheless a certain fascination to this study of a Vegas shark's relationship with singing star Phyllis McGuire (leader of the popular 1950s group, the McGuire Sisters). John Turturro is acceptable as the gangster with a soft spot, but Mary-Louise Parker plays Phyllis as a little fool too naïve for words. Rated R for violence and profanity. 110m. **DIR:** John N. Smith. **CAST:** John Turturro, Mary-Louise Parker, Elias Koteas, Maury Chaykin, Louis Del Grande. **1995**

SUICIDE BATTALION The newsreel stock footage is more exciting than the movie itself in this stage-bound WWII programmer set at Pearl Harbor. B&W; 79m. **DIR:** Edward L. Cahn. **CAST:** Mike Connors, John Ashley, Russ Bender. **1958**

SUICIDE CLUB, THE ★★ Uneven, contrived shocker features Mariel Hemingway as a bored heiress involved with a group of self-indulgent aristocrats who engage in bizarre ritualistic games. Hemingway turns in a compelling performance in this otherwise disappointing thriller. Rated R; contains nudity and violence. 90m. **DIR:** James Bruce. **CAST:** Mariel Hemingway, Robert Joy, Madeleine Potter, Michael O'Donoghue. **1988**

SUICIDE KINGS ★★★ Four New York preppies kidnap a Mafia kingpin. The story is preposterous, and the telling of it is unnecessarily complicated, but it does hold your interest with dark, jittery energy, and the hypnotically menacing Christopher Walken as the mobster. Rated R for profanity and violence. 107m. **DIR:** Peter O'Fallon. **CAST:** Christopher Walken, Henry Thomas, Lara Harris, Jeremy Sisto, Sean Patrick Flanery, Jay Mohr, Denis Leary. **1998 DVD**

SUICIDE RIDE ★★ Barney decides to cash it in and hires a hit man to do the job. The hit man, who's on the verge of retiring, offers Barney his job instead of killing him. Now the suicidal Barney wants to live but realizes there's no job security in his new profession. Low-budget, independent effort makes good use of its limited resources. Not rated; contains adult situations, language, nudity, and violence. 86m. **DIR:** Samer Daboul, Trever Sands. **CAST:** Tim Quill, Matthias Hues, Frank Adonis. **1994**

SUITE 16 ★★★ A wealthy invalid (Peter Postlethwaite) gives refuge to a young criminal, as long as he participates in living out his host's increasingly dangerous erotic fantasies. Misleadingly marketed as a standard erotic thriller, this is a European psychodrama of a higher level that will keep even jaded viewers intrigued. Rated R for strong sexuality, language, violence, and drug use. 93m. **DIR:** Dominique Deruddere. **CAST:** Pete Postlethwaite, Antonie Kamerling, Geraldine Pailhas, Tom Jansen. **1994 DVD**

SULLIVAN'S TRAVELS ★★★★★ Pure genius produced this social comedy, witty and knowing spoof of Hollywood. A film director decides to find out what life outside the Tinseltown fantasyland is really like. This is a genuine Hollywood classic. B&W; 90m. **DIR:** Preston Sturges. **CAST:** Joel McCrea, Veronica Lake, Robert Warwick, William Demarest, Franklin Pangborn, Porter Hall, Eric Blore, Jimmy Conlin. **1941 DVD**

•SUM OF ALL FEARS, THE ★★★ CIA analyst Jack Ryan (Ben Affleck, taking over from Alec Baldwin and Harrison Ford) vies with terrorists using a stolen A-bomb to provoke war between the U.S. and Russia. It's hard to believe even super-spy Ryan could just shrug off a nuclear blast and whip out his cell phone to solve the mystery; still, the film is fast-paced and efficient, with a good cast to lend credibility. Rated PG-13 for violence and some profanity. 119m. **DIR:** Phil Alden Robinson. **CAST:** Ben Affleck, Morgan Freeman, James Cromwell, Bridget Moynahan, Liev Schreiber, Ciarán Hinds. **2002 DVD**

SUM OF US, THE ★★★1/2 A working-class Australian widower and his gay son live together in respectful harmony while they look for, respectively, Ms. and Mr. Right. Well acted and enjoyable, with a core of decency and right-mindedness that adds to its poignancy and charm. Not rated; contains mature themes, mild profanity, and one homosexual love scene. 100m. **DIR:** Kevin Dowling, Geoff Burton. **CAST:** Jack Thompson, Russell Crowe, John Polson, Deborah Kennedy. **1994**

SUMMER ★★★★ Eric Rohmer's fifth of his six-part *Comedies and Proverbs* is the slight but emotionally resonant tale of Delphine (Marie Riviere), a Paris secretary whose vacation plans are suddenly ruined. Like the previous films in the series, *Summer* requires a commitment on the part of the viewer. Ultimately, the story touches your heart. In French with English subtitles. Rated R for nudity and profanity. 98m. **DIR:** Eric Rohmer. **CAST:** Marie Riviere, Lisa Heredia, Beatrice Romand. **1986 DVD**

SUMMER AND SMOKE ★★1/2 Love-hungry spinster dominated by narrow-minded parents plays her cards wrong and can't turn a trick. Talky Tennessee Williams tale. Geraldine Page is fine, but one performance does not a hit make. 118m. **DIR:** Peter Glenville. **CAST:** Geraldine Page, Laurence Harvey, Una Merkel, Rita Moreno, John McIntire. **1961**

SUMMER CAMP The madcaps in this case are teens invited to a reunion of their old summer camp. Rated R. 85m. **DIR:** Chuck Vincent. **CAST:** Michael Abrams, Jake Barnes. **1979**

SUMMER CAMP NIGHTMARE ★★ Based on *The Butterfly Revolution* and misleadingly retitled to cash in on the teen-horror market, this is actually an antifascist parable similar to *Lord of the Flies*. A young counselor at a preteen summer camp stages a revolution, overthrowing the strict director and setting himself up in charge. The ambitious premise is never resolved satisfactorily, with a particularly anticlimactic ending. Rated PG-13 for violence and nudity. 88m. **DIR:** Bert L. Dragin. **CAST:** Chuck Connors, Charles Stratton. **1986**

•SUMMER CATCH ★★★ Class consciousness sustains the primary drama in this well-intentioned little tale. Freddie Prinze Jr. plays a blue-collar kid from Cape Cod who joins a roster of college hopefuls in an effort to get signed by a professional baseball team. That portion of the story plays out reasonably well; our hero's developing relationship with wealthy Vassar graduate Jessica Biel is less successful, because Biel can't act a *lick*. Every time she utters a line, the film grinds to a dead stop. The script's smarmy sexuality also doesn't help; all concerned would have been better off concentrating on baseball and male bonding. Rated PG-13 for profanity,

sexual content, and brief nudity. 113m. **DIR:** Mike Tollin. **CAST:** Freddie Prinze Jr., Jessica Biel, Matthew Lillard, Bruce Davison, Brittany Murphy, Jason Gedrick, Fred Ward, Brian Dennehy. **2001 DVD**

SUMMER CITY ★★ Mel Gibson stars in this Australian teen rebel flick that lacks a fresh approach to one of the oldest stories in film: four teens go on a surfing weekend at a sleepy little seaside community only to find trouble when one of the delinquents messes around with a local's daughter. A few intense moments, and the acting is not bad, but some of the dialogue is indistinguishable in the muddy audio. Not rated, but the equivalent of PG for some sex, partial nudity, and violence. 83m. **DIR:** Christopher Fraser. **CAST:** Mel Gibson, Phil Avalon, Steve Bisley. **1976**

SUMMER DREAMS ★★★ Unauthorized made-for-television biography of the rock 'n' roll group that defined the California sound: the Beach Boys. From their humble beginnings to the tumultuous years that broke up the band, this docudrama makes an honest attempt to give an overall picture of how fame and fortune can divide even the best of friends and make them crazy. Good cast, but songs were rerecorded by another group. Rated R for some additional scenes of nudity. 94m. **DIR:** Michael Switzer. **CAST:** Casey Sander, Greg Kean, Bruce Greenwood, Arlen Dean Snyder, Bo Foxworth. **1985**

SUMMER FLING ★★★ Enchanting, rich story about a young Irish boy coming of age amongst his wildly eccentric family. Excellent performances throughout. Cowritten by Gabriel Byrne and director David Keating. Also known as *Last of the High Kings*. Rated R for sexuality, profanity, and adult situations. 103m. **DIR:** David Keating. **CAST:** Catherine O'Hara, Jared Leto, Christina Ricci, Gabriel Byrne, Stephen Rea, Colm Meaney. **1996**

SUMMER HEAT (1983) 🦃 Bruce Davison stars as a young sheepherder who, upon being sentenced to prison, attempts to escape with his new love. Rated R for violence, profanity, and implied sex. 101m. **DIR:** Jack Starrett. **CAST:** Bruce Davison, Susan George, Anthony Franciosa. **1983**

SUMMER HEAT (1987) 🦃 This is a barely lukewarm sex-and-soap sizzler. Rated R. 95m. **DIR:** Michie Gleason. **CAST:** Lori Singer, Bruce Abbott, Anthony Edwards, Clu Gulager, Kathy Bates. **1987**

SUMMER HOLIDAY ★★1/2 A musical remake of Eugene O'Neill's *Ah, Wilderness*, and the music gets in the way. It just isn't hummable and takes up time the personalities could have used to flesh out this charming coming-of-age story set in the early twentieth-century in mid-America. Walter Huston is excellent as the wise head of the house. 92m. **DIR:** Rouben Mamoulian. **CAST:** Mickey Rooney, Walter Huston, Agnes Moorehead, Marilyn Maxwell, Gloria De Haven, Frank Morgan, "Butch" Jenkins, Anne Francis. **1948**

SUMMER HOUSE, THE ★★★1/2 Director Waris Hussein makes mincemeat of Alice Thomas Ellis's novel, *The Clothes in the Wardrobe.* We're never quite sure why sweet, hard-drinking Margaret agreed to marry the boorish Syl, but coconspirators derailing the upcoming nuptials, are so deliciously oddball that the movie succeeds almost in spite of itself. Not rated, the film has brief moments of profanity, violence, and suggested sex. 83m. **DIR:** Waris Hussein. **CAST:** Jeanne Moreau, Joan Plowright, Julie Walters, Lena Headey, David Threlfall, Maggie Steed, John Wood, Gwenyth Strong, Catherine Schell. **1993**

SUMMER INTERLUDE ★★★1/2 An aging ballerina recalls a lost love from her youth and she learns through her newly reawakened memories to cope successfully with her present life. Perhaps Ingmar Bergman's first major film, and one of his most beautifully lyric. In Swedish with English subtitles. B&W; 90m. **DIR:** Ingmar Bergman. **CAST:** May Britt. **1950**

SUMMER LOVERS 🦃 Study of a *ménage à trois* in Greece. Rated R for nudity, profanity, and implied sex. 98m. **DIR:** Randal Kleiser. **CAST:** Peter Gallagher, Daryl Hannah, Valerie Quennessen, Barbara Rush, Carole Cook. **1982**

SUMMER MAGIC ★★1/2 Dorothy McGuire is a recent widow who finds out she has no money available. She moves her family to Maine, where they live in a fixer-upper house but are charged no rent by Burl Ives. Deborah Walley, a snobbish cousin, comes to visit and causes trouble. Lightweight and enjoyable. Rated G. 100m. **DIR:** James Neilson. **CAST:** Hayley Mills, Burl Ives, Dorothy McGuire, Deborah Walley, Eddie Hodges, Peter Brown. **1963**

SUMMER NIGHT ★★★ The full title is *Summer Night, with Greek Profile, Almond Eyes and Scent of Basil*, and it's a semisequel-reprise of Wertmuller's *Swept Away . . .*, with Mariangela Melato in a similar role as a rich industrialist who captures a terrorist and holds him prisoner on a secluded island. Wertmuller fans will be disappointed; it covers nothing she hasn't done better before. In Italian with English subtitles. Rated R for nudity and sexual situations. 94m. **DIR:** Lina Wertmuller. **CAST:** Mariangela Melato, Michele Placido. **1987**

SUMMER OF BEN TYLER, THE ★★★★ Heartening tale of understanding and prejudice features a winning James Woods as small southern town lawyer Temple Rayburn, whose decision to take in the black son of his late housekeeper threatens his practice and life. This *Hallmark Hall of Fame* television production, set during World War II, manages to get its message across without appearing too preachy. Rated PG. 134m. **DIR:** Arthur Allan Seidelman. **CAST:** James Woods, Elizabeth McGovern, Len Cariou. **1996**

SUMMER OF FEAR ★★ Confine Wes Craven to television and his horrific abilities fly out the window. A set-upon Linda Blair is the tormented target. Originally telecast as *Stranger In Our House*. 100m. **DIR:** Wes Craven. **CAST:** Linda Blair, Macdonald Carey, Carol Lawrence, Jeff East, Lee Purcell, Jeremy Slate, Jeff McCracken. **1978**

SUMMER OF '42 ★★★★ Set against the backdrop of a vacationers' resort island off the New England coast during World War II. An inexperienced young man (Gary Grimes) has a crush on the 22-year-old bride (Jennifer O'Neill) of a serviceman. His stumbling attempts to acquire sexual knowledge are handled tenderly and thoughtfully. Rated PG. 102m. **DIR:** Robert Mulligan. **CAST:** Gary Grimes, Jennifer O'Neill, Jerry Houser, Oliver Conant, Christopher Norris, Lou Frizell. **1971 DVD**

SUMMER OF MY GERMAN SOLDIER ★★★★ Heartwarming tale of an open-minded girl's friendship with a German POW during World War II. Esther Rolle is superb as the family cook to whom the girl confides. Made for TV. 98m. **DIR:** Michael Tuchner. **CAST:** Kristy McNichol, Bruce Davison, Esther Rolle, Michael Constantine. **1978**

SUMMER OF SAM ★★★1/2 Spike Lee's ambitious ensemble drama is a fictionalized re-creation of New York City during the blistering summer of 1977, when the serial murderer dubbed "Son of Sam" erupted into full-blown homicidal fury. The resulting cauldron of suspicion and paranoia is tailor-made for Lee, who demonstrated a similar fascination with friendship under heat-induced stress in *Do the Right Thing*. The cynical director always expects people to revert to jungle savagery, and he structures the relationships in this film accordingly. The key story involves the deteriorating marriage between John Leguizamo and Mira Sorvino, and the latter's good-hearted spirit helps balance the film's often nasty tone; in a film littered with deplorable and repellent characters, Sorvino positively sparkles. Rated R for violence, profanity, drug use, nudity, and deviant sexual behavior. 136m. **DIR:** Spike Lee. **CAST:** John Leguizamo, Adrien Brody, Mira Sorvino, Jennifer Esposito, Michael Rispoli, Saverio Guerra, Brian Tarantino, Al Palagonia. **1999 DVD**

SUMMER OF THE MONKEYS ★★1/2 Wholesome yet ultimately staid family film set in turn-of-the-century Canada. It's there that young Jay dreams of owning his own horse. When a circus train crashes nearby and four chimpanzees escape, Jay decides to find them and collect the reward money to help his family. First he must beat a reclusive local and some cruel bullies to the punch. Slow and predictable, this effort is best left to the nondemanding viewer. Rated G. 101m. **DIR:** Michael Anderson. **CAST:** Corey Sevier, Michael Ontkean, Wilford Brimley. **1998**

SUMMER PLACE, A ★★1/2 Big box-office bonanza for 1959 is a comparatively tame story of extramarital love and teenage infatuation. This mixed-audience melodrama made Troy Donahue and Sandra Dee household names. 130m. **DIR:** Delmer Daves. **CAST:** Dorothy McGuire, Richard Egan, Sandra Dee, Troy Donahue, Arthur Kennedy, Beulah Bondi, Constance Ford. **1959**

SUMMER RENTAL ★★1/2 John Candy is watchable in his first film as star. Unfortunately, the film itself does not live up to his talents. It starts off well enough—with air traffic controller Candy exhibiting the kind of stress that causes his superiors to suggest a vacation—but after a fairly funny first hour, it sinks into the mire of plot resolution. Rated PG for profanity. 88m. **DIR:** Carl Reiner. **CAST:** John Candy, Richard Crenna, Karen Austin, Rip Torn, Kerri Green. **1985**

SUMMER SCHOOL ★★★★ This teen comedy does something almost unheard of for its genre—it bridges the generation gap and entertains young and old alike. Director Carl Reiner knows how to milk every scene for a laugh. Mark Harmon stars as a P.E. coach forced to teach remedial English in summer school. Rated PG-13 for obscenities and gore. 95m. **DIR:** Carl Reiner. **CAST:** Mark Harmon, Kirstie Alley, Nels Van Patten, Carl Reiner, Courtney Thorne-Smith, Lucy Lee Flippin, Shawnee Smith. **1987**

SUMMER SCHOOL TEACHERS ★★★ The usual Roger Corman *Nurse* movie formula: three young women of different backgrounds are devoted to their professions, but not so busy that they don't have time for a little love and lust. Director Barbara Peeters keeps it from being too exploitative, but never forgets who her true drive-in audience is. Rated R for nudity. 87m. **DIR:** Barbara Peeters. **CAST:** Candice Rialson, Pat Anderson, Dick Miller. **1975**

SUMMER STOCK ★★★ An echo of the Mickey Rooney–Judy Garland talented-kids/let's-give-a-show films, this likable musical is built around a troupe of ambitious performers, led by Gene Kelly, who invade farmer Judy Garland's barn. Love blooms. Judy's "Get Happy" number, filmed long after the movie was completed and spliced in to add needed flash, is inspired. 109m. **DIR:** Charles Walters. **CAST:** Judy Garland, Gene Kelly, Eddie Bracken, Gloria De Haven, Phil Silvers, Hans Conried, Marjorie Main. **1950**

SUMMER STORY, A ★★★1/2 A farm girl (Imogen Stubbs) falls for a young London barrister (James Wilby). Can their odd coupling endure class-conscious turn-of-the-century England? Strong performances draw the viewer firmly into the story. Rated PG-13 for partial nudity. 97m. **DIR:** Piers Haggard. **CAST:** James Wilby, Imogen Stubbs, Susannah York, Kenneth Colley, Sophie Ward. **1989**

SUMMER TO REMEMBER, A ★★★1/2 Heartwarming story about a deaf-mute boy. When the boy befriends an intelligent orangutan, he begins to see beyond his closed world. Rated PG for no apparent reason. 98m. **DIR:** Robert Lewis. **CAST:** James Farentino, Louise Fletcher, Burt Young. **1984 DVD**

SUMMER VACATION: 1999 🦃 Pubescent awakenings, hormones, homicide, and acting so inept there should be some kind of penalty to prevent it. In Japanese with English subtitles. Not rated. 90m. **DIR:** Shusuke Kaneko. **CAST:** Eri Miyagian. **1988**

SUMMER WISHES, WINTER DREAMS 🦃 Manhattan housewife's depression. Rated PG. 95m. **DIR:** Gilbert Cates. **CAST:** Joanne Woodward, Martin Balsam, Sylvia Sidney, Dori Brenner. **1973**

SUMMER'S END ★★★★ A young boy, still grieving over his father's death, befriends a retired doctor living on a lake, but the racial intolerance of the other locals starts to sour their happy relationship. This simple and solid character drama works because of the chemistry between the actors, and this made-for-cable original is certainly worthwhile. Rated PG for violence. 100m. **DIR:** Helen Shaver. **CAST:** James Earl Jones, Brendan Fletcher, Jake LeDoux, Al Waxman, Wendy Crewson. **1999 DVD**

SUMMERTIME ★★★★ Katharine Hepburn is a sensitive, vulnerable spinster on holiday in Venice. She falls in love with unhappily married shopkeeper Rossano Brazzi, and the romantic idyll is beautiful. David Lean's direction is superb, Jack Hildyard's cinematography excellent. 99m. **DIR:** David Lean. **CAST:** Katharine Hepburn, Rossano Brazzi, Edward Andrews, Darren McGavin, Isa Miranda. **1955 DVD**

SUMMERTIME KILLER, THE ★★1/2 A boy witnesses the beating and drowning of his father by a gang of hoods. Twenty years pass, and we follow the grownup son as he systematically pursues and kills these men in

New York, Rome, and Portugal. There are some exciting motorcycle pursuits along the way before the ending takes a slight twist. Rated R for violence and language. 100m. **DIR:** Antonio Isasi. **CAST:** Chris Mitchum, Karl Malden, Olivia Hussey, Raf Vallone, Claudine Auger, Gerard Tichy. **1972**

SUN BUNNIES 🦃 A female reporter and her friends track a reclusive movie star at a beach resort in this sex comedy written by Ed Wood. Not rated; contains strong sexual situations and nudity. 89m. **DIR:** A. C. Stephen. **CAST:** Brenda Fogerty, Mariwin Roberts. **1976**

SUN COMES UP, THE ★★★ A script custom designed for Jeanette MacDonald in her later years suits her personality and gives her a chance to sing some sentimental favorites. Her character, Helen Winter, is a bitter war widow who is taken aback when an orphan enters her life and endears himself to her. So does his dog, Lassie, in this tearjerker that probably wouldn't have worked with anyone else in the primary roles. 93m. **DIR:** Richard Thorpe. **CAST:** Jeanette MacDonald, Claude Jarman Jr., Lloyd Nolan, Percy Kilbride, Lewis Stone, Margaret Hamilton. **1949**

SUN SHINES BRIGHT, THE ★★★ Lovable old curly-locked Charles Winninger steals the show in John Ford's remake of *Judge Priest*, his touching 1934 slice of small-town Americana. B&W; 92m. **DIR:** John Ford. **CAST:** Charles Winninger, Arleen Whelan, John Russell, Milburn Stone. **1953**

SUN VALLEY SERENADE ★★★1/2 John Payne agrees to care for a child refugee, who turns out to be Sonja Henie. Take it from there, but enjoy the trip. Henie is truly endearing, both on and off skates. Glenn Miller and his orchestra are on hand to help move things along. B&W; 86m. **DIR:** H. Bruce Humberstone. **CAST:** Sonja Henie, John Payne, Lynn Bari, Milton Berle, Joan Davis. **1941**

SUNBURN 🦃 Farrah Fawcett pretends to be the wife of insurance investigator Charles Grodin to get the real scoop on a suicide case in Acapulco. Rated PG. 94m. **DIR:** Richard C. Sarafian. **CAST:** Farrah Fawcett, Charles Grodin, Art Carney, William Daniels, Joan Collins. **1979**

SUNCHASER ★★ When a teen gang member is diagnosed with cancer, he breaks out of prison, kidnaps a doctor, and forces him to drive to Arizona in search of a mystical lake he believes can cure him. The miscasting of Woody Harrelson as a cerebral physician is only the first mistake made by this inane combination of road thriller and male-bonding movie. Rated R for profanity and violence. 122m. **DIR:** Michael Cimino. **CAST:** Woody Harrelson, Jon Seda, Talisa Soto, Anne Bancroft. **1996**

SUNDAY ★★★★ Oliver is a dumpy IBM downsizing victim who wanders into a strange encounter with a washed-up acting beauty who thinks he is a famed art-film director. Is he or isn't he? This fascinating, disorienting character study is about loneliness, desperation, die-hard egos, and a possible case of mistaken identity. Not rated; contains profanity and frontal nudity of both sexes. 92m. **DIR:** Jonathan Nossiter. **CAST:** David Suchet, Lisa Harrow, Larry Pine. **1997**

SUNDAY, BLOODY SUNDAY ★★★ Brilliant performances by Peter Finch and Glenda Jackson are the major reason to watch this very British three-sided love story; the sides are a bit different, though . . . both love Murray Head. Difficult to watch at times, but intriguing from a historical standpoint. Rated R for sexual situations. 110m. **DIR:** John Schlesinger. **CAST:** Peter Finch, Glenda Jackson, Murray Head, Peggy Ashcroft, Maurice Denham. **1971**

SUNDAY IN THE COUNTRY, A ★★★★ Filmed like an Impressionist painting, this is a romantic look at family life in pre–World War II France. Bertrand Tavernier won the best-director prize at the 1984 Cannes Film Festival for this delightful drama. In French with English subtitles. Rated G. 94m. **DIR:** Bertrand Tavernier. **CAST:** Louis Ducreux, Michel Aumont, Sabine Azema. **1984 DVD**

SUNDAY IN THE PARK WITH GEORGE ★★★★★ This is a taped version of a performance of one of the most honored musicals of the 1980s. A Pulitzer Prize–winner, the entire play is a fabrication of plot and characters based on the Georges Seurat painting, "Sunday Afternoon on the Island of La Grande Jatte." The painting comes to life, and each of the figures has a story to tell. Seurat is played expertly by Mandy Patinkin. 147m. **DIR:** James Lapine. **CAST:** Mandy Patinkin, Bernadette Peters, Barbara Byrne, Charles Kimbrough. **1986 DVD**

SUNDAY TOO FAR AWAY ★★★1/2 An Australian film about the life and lot of a sheepshearer down under circa 1956. Jack Thompson stars as Foley, a champion shearer who finds his mantle challenged. Not rated; the film has profanity, nudity, and violence. 100m. **DIR:** Ken Hannam. **CAST:** Jack Thompson, Max Cullen, John Ewart, Reg Lye. **1983**

SUNDAYS AND CYBÈLE ★★★★ A shell-shocked soldier, who feels responsible for the death of a young girl in the war, seeks redemption through a friendship with a 12 year old orphan. But he fails to see the suspicion with which the authorities view their relationship. Superb acting and direction mark this Oscar winner for best foreign film. In French with English subtitles. B&W; 110m. **DIR:** Serge Bourguignon. **CAST:** Hardy Kruger, Patricia Gozzi. **1962**

SUNDAY'S CHILDREN ★★★★★ Though Ingmar Bergman retired from film directing, he's continued to write beautiful scripts. This is a gem, entrusted into the hands of his son, director Daniel Bergman, and tells of the summer of Ingmar's eighth year, when he came to know his minister father. The film is full of warmth, the mystical and the mysterious, and is a true "Bergman film" in every way. In Swedish with English subtitles. 117m. **DIR:** Daniel Bergman. **CAST:** Thommy Berggren, Lena Endre, Henrik Linnros. **1993**

SUNDOWN (1941) ★★1/2 Fairly entertaining British drama in Africa features Bruce Cabot as a Canadian and George Sanders as the army officer who replaces him. It seems that the local tribesmen are being armed by the Germans. Although there are some bursts of energy, this is still slow-going. B&W; 90m. **DIR:** Henry Hathaway. **CAST:** Gene Tierney, Bruce Cabot, George Sanders, Harry Carey, Cedric Hardwicke, Joseph Calleia, Reginald Gardiner, Marc Lawrence. **1941 DVD**

SUNDOWN (1990) ★★1/2 Purgatory is a small desert community established by a group of vampires fed up with the old ways. They manufacture their own blood and use sun block. A new generation of bloodsuckers decides enough is enough and declares war. Unique

slant on the vampire legend starts off promisingly, but then gets batty toward the end. Rated R for nudity and violence. 104m. **DIR:** Anthony Hickox. **CAST:** David Carradine, Maxwell Caulfield, Morgan Brittany, Bruce Campbell, John Ireland. **1990**

SUNDOWN RIDER, THE ★★★★ Solid, brooding Western has Buck Jones as an easygoing cowpoke who happens upon a band of rustlers. The baddies leave Jones to "guard" their camp, where he is caught and brutally branded by revenge-minded lawmen despite his protests of innocence. So Jones swears revenge. Rewarding shoot-'em-up. B&W; 66m. **DIR:** Lambert Hillyer. **CAST:** Buck Jones, Barbara Weeks, Wheeler Oakman, Ward Bond. **1933**

SUNDOWN RIDERS ★★★ First of a proposed trio series (Russell Wade, Jay Kirby, Andy Clyde) that never materialized. Too bad, because it has plenty of action. Good chance to see famed stuntman Henry Wills in an acting role. B&W; 56m. **DIR:** Lambert Hillyer. **CAST:** Russell Wade, Jay Kirby, Andy Clyde, Evelyn Finley, Jack Ingram, Marshall Reed. **1948**

SUNDOWNERS, THE (1950) ★★★ Robert Preston is the good brother and Robert Sterling is the bad one in this tolerable Western. The siblings face each other in a climactic showdown. 83m. **DIR:** George Templeton. **CAST:** Robert Preston, Cathy Downes, Robert Sterling, John Drew Barrymore, Jack Elam. **1950**

SUNDOWNERS, THE (1960) ★★★★ Robert Mitchum and Deborah Kerr were one of the great screen teams, and this is our choice as their best film together. The story of Australian sheepherders in the 1920s, it is a character study brought alive by Fred Zinnemann's sensitive direction, as well as by the fine acting of a superb cast. 113m. **DIR:** Fred Zinnemann. **CAST:** Robert Mitchum, Deborah Kerr, Peter Ustinov, Glynis Johns, Dina Merrill, Chips Rafferty. **1960**

SUNRISE ★★★★ Director F. W. Murnau's emotionally charged silent classic about a romantic triangle leading to attempted murder. Oscars went to star Janet Gaynor, cinematographers Karl Struss and Charles Rosher, and the film itself—which is stunning on a visual and narrative level. B&W; 110m. **DIR:** F. W. Murnau. **CAST:** George O'Brien, Janet Gaynor, Margaret Livingston, J. Farrell MacDonald. **1927**

SUNRISE AT CAMPOBELLO ★★★★★ Producer-writer Dore Schary's inspiring and heartwarming drama of Franklin Delano Roosevelt's public political battles and private fight against polio. Ralph Bellamy is FDR; Greer Garson is Eleanor. Both are superb. The acting is tops, the entire production sincere. Taken from Schary's impressive stage play, with all the fine qualities intact. 143m. **DIR:** Vincent J. Donehue. **CAST:** Ralph Bellamy, Greer Garson, Alan Bunce, Hume Cronyn. **1960**

SUNSET ★★★1/2 Writer-director Blake Edwards begins this charming little *soufflé* with an intriguing notion: what if legendary lawman Wyatt Earp (James Garner) had met silent-screen cowboy Tom Mix (Bruce Willis) and the two had become fast friends? The boys get involved in a seamy murder case. Rated R for language and violence. 107m. **DIR:** Blake Edwards. **CAST:** James Garner, Bruce Willis, Malcolm McDowell, Mariel Hemingway, Kathleen Quinlan, Jennifer Edwards, Patricia Hodge, M. Emmet Walsh, Joe Dallesandro. **1988 DVD**

SUNSET BOULEVARD ★★★★★ *Sunset Boulevard* is one of Hollywood's strongest indictments against its own excesses. It justly deserves its place among the best films ever made. William Holden plays an out-of-work gigolo-screenwriter who attaches himself to a faded screen star attempting a comeback. Gloria Swanson, in a stunning parody, is brilliant as the tragically deluded Norma Desmond. B&W; 110m. **DIR:** Billy Wilder. **CAST:** William Holden, Gloria Swanson, Erich Von Stroheim, Fred Clark, Jack Webb, Hedda Hopper, Buster Keaton. **1950**

SUNSET GRILL ★★1/2 Passable private-investigator mystery features Peter Weller as a down-and-out detective trying to find his wife's assassin. Weller elevates an otherwise low-budget effort by creating a quirky, mesmerizing character. Not rated; contains nudity, sex, violence, and profanity. 105m. **DIR:** Kevin Connor. **CAST:** Peter Weller, Lori Singer, Stacy Keach, Alexandra Paul, John Rhys-Davies. **1992**

SUNSET HEAT ★★1/2 Photojournalist Michael Paré finds his former life as a drug dealer intruding on his new career when he returns to Los Angeles. A reunion with his old buddy Adam Ant results in Paré being hunted by drug lord Dennis Hopper, his former partner. Sleazy, but well acted. Rated R for profanity, nudity, and violence. 94m. **DIR:** John Nicolella. **CAST:** Michael Paré, Dennis Hopper, Adam Ant, Little Richard, Charlie Schlatter, Daphne Ashbrook. **1992**

SUNSET LIMOUSINE John Ritter plays an out-of-work comic who must make something of himself before his girlfriend (Susan Dey) will take him back. Made for TV. 92m. **DIR:** Terry Hughes. **CAST:** John Ritter, Susan Dey, Martin Short, Paul Reiser, Audrie Neenan, Lainie Kazan. **1983**

SUNSET PARK ★★ Young, charismatic actors are trapped in a familiar underdog sports drama. A woman high-school gym teacher takes the job of boys' basketball coach. Her players sort through romantic, personality, and motivation challenges and teach their rookie coach about court warfare and inner-city survival. She teaches them the aesthetics of winning. Rated R for language and drug use. 100m. **DIR:** Steve Gomer. **CAST:** Rhea Perlman, Fredro Starr, Carol Kane, Terrence DaShon Howard, Camille Saviola, De'Aundre Bonds, James Harris, Anthony Hall. **1996**

SUNSET SERENADE ★★1/2 Beady-eyed Roy Rogers and his ornery sidekick Gabby Hayes thwart the plans of a couple of no-goods who aim to murder the heir to a ranch and take it over for themselves. Enjoyable enough and not too demanding. B&W; 58m. **DIR:** Joseph Kane. **CAST:** Roy Rogers, George "Gabby" Hayes, Helen Parrish, Onslow Stevens, Joan Woodbury. **1942**

SUNSET STRIP And strip they do in this shabby tale of a young woman who has an affair with a club owner in L.A.'s exotic dance scene. Rated R for nudity and sex. 93m. **DIR:** Paul G. Volk. **CAST:** Jeff Conaway, Michelle Foreman. **1991**

SUNSHINE BOYS, THE ★★★★ The story of two feuding ex-vaudeville stars who make a TV special. Walter Matthau, Richard Benjamin, and (especially) George Burns give memorable performances. Director Herbert Ross turns this adaptation of the successful Broadway

play by Neil Simon into a celluloid winner. Rated PG. 111m. **DIR:** Herbert Ross. **CAST:** Walter Matthau, Richard Benjamin, George Burns, Lee Meredith, Carol Arthur, Howard Hesseman, Ron Rifkin. **1975**

SUNSTROKE 🦃 Bad accents, poor acting, and a horrible plot ruin this tale about a woman trying to locate her daughter. Rated R for violence and profanity. 91m. **DIR:** James Keach. **CAST:** Jane Seymour, Stephen Meadows, Steve Railsback, Ray Wise, Don Ameche. **1992**

SUPER, THE ★★★ Star Joe Pesci, as a slumlord sentenced to live in his dilapidated New York tenement building, makes this thin comedy easy to take. Without him, the silly, predictable story would be painful to watch. Rated R for profanity. 98m. **DIR:** Rod Daniel. **CAST:** Joe Pesci, Vincent Gardenia, Madolyn Smith, Rubén Blades. **1991**

SUPER FORCE 🦃 Despite an engaging early cameo by Patrick Macnee, this TV pilot is far from super; Ken Olandt is terminally bland as an astronaut-turned-cop who dons an ersatz RoboCop suit to battle crime in the year 2020. Although not rated, the squeaky-clean material could pass for G. 92m. **DIR:** Richard Compton. **CAST:** Ken Olandt, Larry B. Scott, Patrick Macnee, G. Gordon Liddy. **1993**

SUPER FUZZ ★★1/2 For adults, this is a silly, mindless film . . . but it's great fun for the kids. Terence Hill stars as Dave Speed, a police officer with supernatural powers. Rated PG. 94m. **DIR:** Sergio Corbucci. **CAST:** Terence Hill, Ernest Borgnine, Joanne Dru, Marc Lawrence. **1981**

SUPER MARIO BROTHERS, THE ★★★ A big-screen version of a popular Nintendo game, this movie is aimed at indiscriminating kids and young adults. When the dirty near-human dinos kidnap Princess Daisy, a couple of plumbers from Brooklyn save the day. Fast-moving action/comedy could have used a bit more sense. Rated PG. 118m. **DIR:** Rocky Morton, Annabel Jankel. **CAST:** Bob Hoskins, John Leguizamo, Dennis Hopper, Samantha Mathis, Fisher Stevens, Fiona Shaw, Richard Edson. **1993**

SUPER SOUL BROTHER 🦃 A wino (raunchy comic Wildman Steve) is given superpowers in this lame spoof of TV's *Six Million Dollar Man*. Not rated; contains strong profanity and nudity. 80m. **DIR:** Rene Martinez. **CAST:** Steve Wildman, Joycelyn Norris, Peter Conrad. **1978**

•SUPER TROOPERS ★★ The comedy troupe Broken Lizard updates the old Keystone Kops/*Police Academy* formula in this farce about the Vermont Highway Patrol. The cast is goofy and game for anything, but laughs are few and far between. Brian Cox as their commander and Marisa Coughlan as a friendly city cop add a touch of class—but only a touch. Rated R for profanity, drug use, and brief nudity. 103m. **DIR:** Jay Chandrasekhar. **CAST:** Jay Chandrasekhar, Brian Cox, Marisa Coughlan, Kevin Heffernan, Paul Soter, Steve Lemme, Erik Stolhanske. **2002 DVD**

SUPERCARRIER ★★★ This is the TV-movie premiere of the short-lived series of the same name. The action takes Top Gun graduates on a mission aboard a supercarrier. The Russians have a plane in U.S. air space and two pilots are assigned to escort it out. The flight and action scenes are engrossing, but on the ground *Supercarrier* is pretty routine. 90m. **DIR:** William A. Graham. **CAST:** Robert Hooks, Paul Gleason, Ken Olandt, Richard Jaeckel. **1988**

SUPERCOP ★★★ Following the box-office success of *Rumble in the Bronx*, this Hong Kong actioner was dubbed for American release. Part of a police-story trilogy, this has Jackie Chan teaming up with Michelle Khan, who, like himself, does her own stunt work and is an extraordinary martial artist. The two pose as brother and sister to infiltrate a vicious drug ring. Frequent comic moments, the trademark of Chan films, elevate this a notch above the kung fu flicks of the 1970s. Rated R for violence. 90m. **DIR:** Stanley Tong. **CAST:** Jackie Chan, Michelle Khan, Maggie Cheung, Yuen Wah. **1992 DVD**

SUPERDAD ★★1/2 Bob Crane doesn't approve of his daughter's boyfriend (Kurt Russell) or the crowd she runs with. She claims that he just doesn't understand them. He decides to find out about the kids first-hand. Rated G. 94m. **DIR:** Vincent McEveety. **CAST:** Bob Crane, Barbara Rush, Kurt Russell, Joe Flynn. **1973**

SUPERFLY ★★★ This exciting film follows a Harlem drug dealer's last big sale before he attempts to leave the drug world for a normal life. Rated R. 96m. **DIR:** Gordon Parks Jr. **CAST:** Ron O'Neal, Carl Lee, Sheila Frazier, Julius W. Harris. **1972**

SUPERFLY T.N.T. 🦃 The first mistake connected with this sequel to *Superfly* was allowing its star, Ron O'Neal, to direct it. The second mistake was removing the title character from the tense, urban setting of the first movie. Here, the ex-drug dealer is living in exile in Europe when he decides to become involved in the plight of an African nationalist. 87m. **DIR:** Ron O'Neal. **CAST:** Ron O'Neal, Roscoe Lee Browne, Sheila Frazier, Robert Guillaume. **1973**

SUPERGIRL ★★1/2 Helen Slater makes a respectable film debut as Superman's cousin in this screen comic book, which should delight the kiddies and occasionally tickle the adults. The stellar supporting cast doesn't seem to take it seriously, so why should we? Rated PG. 105m. **DIR:** Jeannot Szwarc. **CAST:** Faye Dunaway, Peter O'Toole, Helen Slater, Mia Farrow, Brenda Vaccaro, Simon Ward, Peter Cook, Hart Bochner. **1984**

SUPERGRASS, THE ★★ The reluctant hero (Adrian Edmondson) of this English farce pretends to be an important drug dealer in order to impress his girlfriend. Ultimately, the bloke is in way over his head. So-so comedy. 96m. **DIR:** Peter Richardson. **CAST:** Adrian Edmondson, Jennifer Saunders, Peter Richardson. **1987**

SUPERMAN ★★★1/2 After a somewhat overblown introduction, which encompasses the end of Krypton and Clark Kent's adolescence in Smallville, this film takes off to provide some great moments as Superman swings into action. The action is complemented by fine tongue-in-cheek comedy. Rated PG. 143m. **DIR:** Richard Donner. **CAST:** Christopher Reeve, Margot Kidder, Jackie Cooper, Marc McClure, Marlon Brando, Glenn Ford, Gene Hackman. **1978 DVD**

SUPERMAN II ★★★★ Even better than the original, this terrific adventure of the Man of Steel includes a full-fledged—and beautifully handled—romance between Lois Lane (Margot Kidder) and Superman (Christopher Reeve) and a spectacular battle that pits our hero against three supervillains (during which the city of Metropolis is almost completely destroyed).

Rated PG. 127m. **DIR:** Richard Lester. **CAST:** Margot Kidder, Christopher Reeve, Gene Hackman, Ned Beatty, Jackie Cooper, Terence Stamp. **1980 DVD**

SUPERMAN III ★★1/2 If it weren't for Christopher Reeve's excellent performance in the title role, *Superman III* would be a total disappointment. The story features a subdued Richard Pryor as a computer whiz who is hired by bad guy Robert Vaughn to do dastardly deeds with his magic programming. Rated PG. 125m. **DIR:** Richard Lester. **CAST:** Christopher Reeve, Richard Pryor, Robert Vaughn, Annette O'Toole, Jackie Cooper, Marc McClure, Pamela Stephenson. **1983 DVD**

SUPERMAN IV: THE QUEST FOR PEACE ★★ A well-intentioned plot about Superman (Christopher Reeve) attempting to rid the Earth of nuclear weapons cannot save this overlong, overwrought, confusing, and sometimes downright dull third sequel. Rated PG for violence. 90m. **DIR:** Sidney J. Furie. **CAST:** Christopher Reeve, Gene Hackman, Margot Kidder, Jackie Cooper, Mariel Hemingway, Jon Cryer, Marc McClure, Sam Wanamaker. **1987 DVD**

SUPERMAN AND THE MOLE MEN ★★1/2 George Reeves dons the tights and cape that he was to be identified with for the rest of his life. This story concerns a huge oil well that drills too far and yields fuzzy midgets from inside the Earth. This film led to the famous television series and was subsequently shown as a two-part episode. B&W; 67m. **DIR:** Lee Sholem. **CAST:** George Reeves, Phyllis Coates, Jeff Corey, Walter Reed. **1951**

SUPERMAN CARTOONS ★★★★ All other superhero cartoons pale in comparison to this collection of excellent "Man of Steel" shorts from the Max Fleischer Studios. Made between 1941 and 1943, these actually constitute the company's finest work, its Popeye cartoons notwithstanding. There are several tapes available with a selection of seven or eight shorts (approximately 75 minutes) made from 16mm prints of varying quality. One company (Video Rarities) offers a 150-minute tape with all seventeen Superman shorts taken from mint-condition 35mm Technicolor prints, and the difference is amazing. 75m. **DIR:** Dave Fleischer, Seymour Kneitel, Isadore Sparber. **1940 DVD**

SUPERMAN—THE SERIAL ★★1/2 The first live-action Superman serial was one of the highest grossing of all chapterplays ever made, as well as Columbia's most prestigious effort in that field. The film relies on inept flying sequences and the by-now classic relationship between Clark Kent and Lois Lane for the bulk of its action. B&W; **DIR:** Spencer Gordon Bennet, Thomas Carr. **CAST:** Kirk Alyn, Noel Neill, Tommy Bond, Carol Forman, Pierre Watkin, George Meeker, Charles King, Charles Quigley, Herbert Rawlinson. **1948**

SUPERNATURAL ★★★1/2 The spirit of an executed murderess takes charge of a beautiful young socialite's body and bides its time until it can take revenge. Eerie opening credits set the tone for this somber excursion into the unknown, and decent special effects and a certain respect for the subject matter help make this one of the few Hollywood films about the occult that doesn't cheat at the end and invalidate the production. B&W; 64m. **DIR:** Victor Halperin. **CAST:** Carole Lombard, Randolph Scott, Vivienne Osborne, Alan Dinehart, H. B. Warner, Beryl Mercer, William Farnum. **1933**

SUPERNATURALS, THE ★★★1/2 A group of modern-day soldiers face off against Civil War Confederate zombies. The commanding officer (Nichelle Nichols) must find the secret to exorcise these evil spirits before they kill her and her men. Good scary entertainment. Rated R for graphic violence. 91m. **DIR:** Armand Mastroianni. **CAST:** Nichelle Nichols, Maxwell Caulfield, Talia Balsam, LeVar Burton. **1988**

SUPERNOVA ★★ When a medical-rescue starship responds to a distress call from a supposedly abandoned planet, the crew find themselves faced with an evil force they can't understand. You may not understand it either, with the movie's gaping plot holes, clichés, and signs of last-minute tampering. Director Thomas Lee is actually Walter Hill, who had his name removed from the film. Rated PG-13 for violence. 91m. **DIR:** Thomas Lee. **CAST:** James Spader, Angela Bassett, Peter Facinelli, Lou Diamond Phillips, Robin Tunney, Robert Forster. **2000 DVD**

SUPERSTAR: DARE TO DREAM ★★ Only diehard fans of the *Saturday Night Live* character Mary Katherine Gallagher, the Catholic-school girl, will appreciate the expansion of Molly Shannon's sketch persona into a feature-length film. Here she lives with her eccentric grandmother and drools over the most popular boy at school (Will Ferrell). Some laughs and guffaws. Rated PG-13 for sexual situations and profanity. 88m. **DIR:** Bruce McCulloch. **CAST:** Molly Shannon, Will Ferrell, Glynis Johns. **1999 DVD**

SUPPORT YOUR LOCAL GUNFIGHTER ★★★1/2 Although not quite as fresh or genuinely rib tickling as predecessor *Support Your Local Sheriff*, this charming Western spoof nonetheless gives James Garner another chance to modify the charming hustler honed to perfection during all those years on television's *Maverick*. This time out he's a con artist "selling" drifter Jack Elam as a professional gunfighter. Rated PG for minimal violence. 92m. **DIR:** Burt Kennedy. **CAST:** James Garner, Suzanne Pleshette, Jack Elam, Harry Morgan, John Dehner, Joan Blondell, Chuck Connors. **1971**

SUPPORT YOUR LOCAL SHERIFF! ★★★★1/2 The time-honored backbone of the industry, the Western, takes a real ribbing in this all-stops-out send-up. If it can be parodied, it is—in spades. James Garner is great as a gambler "just passing through" who gets roped into being sheriff and tames a lawless mining town against all odds, including an inept deputy, a fem-lib mayor's daughter, and a snide gunman. A very funny picture. Rated G. 93m. **DIR:** Burt Kennedy. **CAST:** James Garner, Joan Hackett, Walter Brennan, Harry Morgan, Jack Elam, Bruce Dern, Henry Jones. **1969 DVD**

SUPPOSE THEY GAVE A WAR AND NOBODY CAME? ★★ In this comedy involving a confrontation between a rural town and a nearby military base, Brian Keith, Tony Curtis, and Ivan Dixon play three army buddies who take it upon themselves to stop the fighting. Some funny moments. Rated PG for adult themes. 113m. **DIR:** Hy Averback. **CAST:** Brian Keith, Ernest Borgnine, Suzanne Pleshette, Tom Ewell, Tony Curtis, Bradford Dillman, Ivan Dixon, Arthur O'Connell, Don Ameche. **1970**

SUPREME SANCTION ★★1/2 Silly but serviceable thriller about a female assassin who breaks away from her employers only to become a target. Rated R for vio-

lence, sexuality, and profanity. 93m. **DIR:** John Terlesky. **CAST:** Kristy Swanson, Michael Madsen, Tom "Tiny" Lister Jr., Donald Faison, David Dukes. **1999 DVD**

SURE FIRE 🦃 Heavy-handed message film moves at a snail's pace. Two men choose different paths in life—one seeks material wealth while the other is content with his modest farm. Obvious cuts are a major distraction. Not rated; contains profanity and violence. 83m. **DIR:** Jon Jost. **CAST:** Tom Blair, Kristi Hager, Robert Ernst, Kate Dezina. **1990 DVD**

SURE THING, THE ★★★1/2 This enjoyable romantic comedy, about two college freshmen who discover themselves and each other through a series of misadventures on the road, is more or less director Rob Reiner's updating of Frank Capra's *It Happened One Night*. John Cusack and Daphne Zuniga star as the unlikely protagonists. Rated PG-13 for profanity and suggested sex. 100m. **DIR:** Rob Reiner. **CAST:** John Cusack, Daphne Zuniga, Anthony Edwards, Boyd Gaines, Lisa Jane Persky. **1985**

SURF NAZIS MUST DIE ★★1/2 The Surf Nazis are a gang of weirdos who rule the Los Angeles beaches. Vile, stupid, and pointless, but there's something about this film . . . Rated R for violence, language, sex, and nudity. 83m. **DIR:** Peter George. **CAST:** Barry Brenner, Gail Neely, Dawn Wildsmith. **1987 DVD**

SURF NINJAS ★★★ Ninja nonsense. Two California-surf dudes discover that they're actually heirs to a small South Seas kingdom. That's the good news. The bad news is that evil warlord Leslie Nielsen will stop at nothing to keep them off the throne. This mix of several different genres loses focus, but kids will get a big kick out of it. Rated PG for make-believe violence. 87m. **DIR:** Neal Israel. **CAST:** Ernie Reyes Jr., Rob Schneider, Tone Loc, Leslie Nielsen, Nicolas Cowan. **1993**

SURF 2 ★★ Combination spoof of beach party and horror movies, with lunatic Eddie Deezen out for revenge on a group of surfers. Fitfully funny, with the best joke in the title: there is no *Surf 1*. Rated R for the obligatory topless beach bunnies. 91m. **DIR:** Randall Badat. **CAST:** Eddie Deezen, Linda Kerridge, Cleavon Little, Lyle Waggoner, Eric Stoltz, Corinne Bohrer, Ruth Buzzi. **1984**

SURFACE TO AIR 🦃 Lots of military hardware and not an ounce of common sense highlight this tale of two brothers on the same aircraft carrier fighting in the Persian Gulf. First off, the military doesn't allow family to share the same duty station. Logic goes downhill from there. Rated R for language and violence. 93m. **DIR:** Rodney McDonald. **CAST:** Matthew R. Anderson, Michael Madsen, Chad McQueen. **1997**

SURFACING 🦃 *Deliverance* stirred with psychological mumbo jumbo and kinky sex. Rated R. 90m. **DIR:** Claude Jutra. **CAST:** Joseph Bottoms, Kathleen Beller, R. H. Thomson. **1984**

SURGEON, THE ★★★1/2 A disgruntled ex-surgeon returns to the scene of the crime in order to complete his sinister experiments. Gruesome special effects, high production values, likable cast, and taut direction make this a must-see for fans of the genre. Rated R for violence, nudity, profanity, and adult situations. 90m. **DIR:** Carl Schenkel. **CAST:** Isabel Glasser, James Remar, Charles Dance, Peter Boyle, Malcolm McDowell. **1994 DVD**

SURPRISE PACKAGE ★★1/2 A change of pace for Yul Brynner as a high-living gambler deported to Greece, where he meets and decides to rob an exiled king (Noel Coward, who also sings the title song). So-so comedy, based on a novel by Art Buchwald. B&W; 100m. **DIR:** Stanley Donen. **CAST:** Yul Brynner, Mitzi Gaynor, George Coulouris, Noel Coward, Eric Pohlmann. **1960**

SURRENDER ★★★ Sally Field gives a sparkling performance as a confused woman in love with Michael Caine, Steve Guttenberg, and money, not necessarily in that order. Caine and Guttenberg are superb. At times contrived and a bit forced, overall, this is an enjoyable light comedy. Rated PG-13 for language and sex. 105m. **DIR:** Jerry Belson. **CAST:** Sally Field, Michael Caine, Steve Guttenberg, Peter Boyle, Julie Kavner, Jackie Cooper. **1987**

SURVIVAL GAME 🦃 Mike Norris, Chuck's son, fails to fill his father's boots. R rating for mild profanity. 89m. **DIR:** Herb Freed. **CAST:** Mike Norris, Deborah Goodrich, Seymour Cassel, Arlene Golonka. **1987**

SURVIVAL QUEST ★★★1/2 Survival course students encounter a paramilitary group on maneuvers. Their adventure then turns into a genuine and compelling fight for survival. Rated R for violence. 91m. **DIR:** Don Coscarelli. **CAST:** Lance Henriksen, Dermot Mulroney. **1989**

SURVIVAL ZONE 🦃 Nuclear-holocaust survivors battling evil. Not rated, contains violence and nudity. 90m. **DIR:** Percival Rubens. **CAST:** Gary Lockwood, Morgan Stevens, Camilla Sparv. **1983**

SURVIVALIST, THE 🦃 A tepid action-thriller that purports to dramatize the confusion that mounts before the bombs are dropped. The real bomb is this hokey doomsday entry that literally goes up in smoke. Rated R for violence and profanity. 96m. **DIR:** Sig Shore. **CAST:** Steve Railsback, Susan Blakely, Cliff De Young, Marjoe Gortner, David Wayne. **1987**

SURVIVE THE NIGHT ★★★1/2 Surprisingly believable film in which three women end up fighting for their lives in a part of New York where the police don't like to go. Stefanie Powers does a fine job portraying the mother who will do anything to protect her daughter. Not rated, made for cable, but contains violence. 95m. **DIR:** Bill Corcoran. **CAST:** Stefanie Powers, Helen Shaver, Kathleen Robertson, Lawrence Gilliard Jr., Currie Graham. **1992**

SURVIVING DESIRE ★★★ Kooky made-for-TV romance based on literary ideas rather than passion ignites between an untalented college professor (Martin Donovan) and his only attentive student (Mary Ward). Ward is a comic gem especially as she halfheartedly offers to help customers in a bookstore. Also included on the tape are two other Hal Hartley shorts *Theory of Achievement* and *Ambition*. 86m. **DIR:** Hal Hartley. **CAST:** Martin Donovan, Mary Ward, Matt Malloy, Rebecca Nelson. **1991 DVD**

SURVIVING PICASSO ★★★ Another portrait of the artist as a selfish pig, this one based on Françoise Gilot's memoir of her ten-year-plus affair with Pablo Picasso. Anthony Hopkins hits all the right notes of roaring egotism, but his performance is strangely passionless and uncharismatic, and the same is true of the film as a

whole. Rated R for profanity and nudity. 129m. **DIR:** James Ivory. **CAST:** Anthony Hopkins, Natascha McElhone, Jane Lapotaire, Diane Venora, Julianne Moore. **1996**

SURVIVING THE GAME ❤ Homeless African-American is hunted for perverse sport by a group of men in the Pacific Northwest wilderness. Rated R for language and violence. 93m. **DIR:** Ernest R. Dickerson. **CAST:** Ice T, Rutger Hauer, Charles Dutton, John C. McGinley, Gary Busey, William McNamara, F. Murray Abraham. **1994 DVD**

SURVIVOR ★★ While on a space mission, an astronaut witnesses a full-scale nuclear war. Upon return to Earth, he finds total destruction. Richard Moll plays a fine villain in this otherwise routine and violent science-fiction story. 92m. **DIR:** Michael Shackleton. **CAST:** Chris Mayer, Richard Moll, Sue Kiel, Richard Haines. **1987**

SURVIVORS, THE ★★★1/2 This is an often funny movie about a goofy "survivalist" (Robin Williams), who is "adopted" by a service station owner (Walter Matthau) and pursued by a friendly but determined hit man (Jerry Reed). Generally a black comedy, this movie features a variety of comedic styles, and they all work. Rated R for vulgar language and violence. 102m. **DIR:** Michael Ritchie. **CAST:** Robin Williams, Walter Matthau, Jerry Reed, James Wainwright. **1983 DVD**

SURVIVORS OF THE HOLOCAUST ★★★★ A TBS documentary capturing the heartbreaking testimonials of Nazi concentration camp survivors, this is artistically presented by producer Steven Spielberg. It works on several levels, but the emotional impact and final message of hope are what will stay with you. Also included are Spielberg and Ben Kingsley presenting a 10-minute description of the Survivors of the Shoah Visual History Foundation, a cutting-edge preservation group. Not rated; contains brief nudity and adult themes. B&W/color; 70m. **DIR:** Allan Holzman. **CAST:** Ben Kingsley, Steven Spielberg. **1995**

SUSAN AND GOD ★★★ A strong cast bolsters this story of a woman who devotes herself to a new religious movement, pushing her newly adopted standards and beliefs on her family and friends. Fredric March is fine as her weak, alcoholic husband. B&W; 115m. **DIR:** George Cukor. **CAST:** Joan Crawford, Fredric March, Ruth Hussey, John Carroll, Rita Hayworth, Nigel Bruce, Marjorie Main, Gloria De Haven. **1940**

SUSAN LENOX: HER FALL AND RISE ★★★ Greta Garbo flees a brutish father eager to marry her off and takes refuge with Clark Gable. The melodramatic plot's tired, but Garbo and Gable give charged performances. B&W; 76m. **DIR:** Robert Z. Leonard. **CAST:** Greta Garbo, Clark Gable, Alan Hale Sr., Jean Hersholt. **1931**

SUSAN SLEPT HERE ★★1/2 Screenwriter Dick Powell must keep a tight leash on the ultrahigh-spirited vagrant teenager he protects and falls for in the course of researching a script on juvenile delinquency. Amusing dialogue and lots of innuendo mark this otherwise pedestrian sex comedy. 98m. **DIR:** Frank Tashlin. **CAST:** Dick Powell, Debbie Reynolds, Anne Francis, Glenda Farrell. **1954**

SUSANNA ★★ This lurid soap opera from Luis Buñuel concerns a voluptuous young girl who escapes from a reformatory and hides out with a plantation family. Unfortunately, the movie lacks Buñuel's comic surreal touch in exploiting his characters' obsessions. In Spanish with English subtitles. Not rated. B&W; 82m. **DIR:** Luis Buñuel. **CAST:** Rosita Quintana, Fernando Soler. **1951**

SUSANNAH OF THE MOUNTIES ★★★ After her parents are killed in an Indian attack, curly Shirley is raised by a kind Canadian Mountie (Randolph Scott). Not one to hold a grudge, Shirley decides to play peacemaker for the whites and Indians by befriending the chief's son. B&W; 78m. **DIR:** William A. Seiter. **CAST:** Shirley Temple, Randolph Scott, Margaret Lockwood. **1939**

SUSPECT ★★★1/2 Cher is just fine as a public defender assigned to prove a deaf and mute street bum (Liam Neeson) innocent of the murder of a Washington, D.C., secretary. One of the jurors, lobbyist Dennis Quaid, takes a liking to Cher and begins helping her with the seemingly impossible case, thus putting her career and their lives in danger. Rated R for violence and profanity. 128m. **DIR:** Peter Yates. **CAST:** Cher, Dennis Quaid, Joe Mantegna, Liam Neeson, Philip Bosco, John Mahoney, Fred Melamed. **1987**

SUSPECT DEVICE ★★★1/2 Producer Roger Corman's clever thriller doesn't always make sense, but it sure moves. An analyst is the lone survivor of a hit on his espionage section and his entire life becomes a fading memory. Great, mindless fun. Rated R for violence, nudity, profanity, and drug use. 90m. **DIR:** Rick Jacobson. **CAST:** C. Thomas Howell, Stacey Travis, Jed Allan, Jonathan Fuller, John Beck. **1995**

SUSPENDED ★★★1/2 Falsely accused and sentenced to death in Stalinist Poland, an ex-army officer escapes from prison and is hidden by a woman he met during the war. Their underground relationship becomes a metaphor for political repression in this provocative drama. In Polish with English subtitles. Not rated. 92m. **DIR:** Waldemar Kyzystek. **CAST:** Krystyna Janda, Jerzy Radziwilowicz. **1986**

SUSPICION (1941) ★★★★ A timid woman is gradually unnerved by apprehension. Bits of evidence lead her to believe that her charming husband is a killer and that she is the intended victim. Joan Fontaine played a similar role in *Rebecca* and eventually won a best-actress Oscar for her performance in *Suspicion*. Cary Grant is excellent, too. B&W; 99m. **DIR:** Alfred Hitchcock. **CAST:** Joan Fontaine, Cary Grant, Cedric Hardwicke, Nigel Bruce, May Whitty, Isabel Jeans. **1941**

SUSPICION (1987) ★★ A plain country Jane (Curtin) grows suspicious of her hubby's intentions after piecing together the plot for a murder that would benefit her penniless mate. This Alfred Hitchcock remake lacks the subtle suspense of the original. Rated PG. 97m. **DIR:** Andrew Grieve. **CAST:** Jane Curtin, Anthony Andrews, Betsy Blair, Michael Hordern, Vivian Pickles, Jonathan Lynn. **1987**

SUSPICIOUS AGENDA ★★ The only thing suspicious about this crime-thriller is its resemblance to a million others like it. It helps to have Richard Grieco along as the streetwise cop tracking down a serial killer. Rated R for violence, nudity and language. 97m. **DIR:** Clay Borris. **CAST:** Richard Grieco, Nick Mancuso, Jim Byrnes. **1994**

SUSPICIOUS MINDS ★★ A detective falls in love with the woman whose husband hired him to spy on her. This by-the-numbers pseudo *noir* understands the conven-

tions of the genre but can't do anything interesting with them. Rated R for violence and sex. 97m. **DIR:** Alain Zaloum. **CAST:** Patrick Bergin, Jayne Heitmeyer, Gary Busey. **1997**

SUSPIRIA ★★★★ Now classic art-horror chiller is even more fearsome in the uncut version. A timid American girl enrolls in a prudish European ballet academy, only to discover it's staffed by a coven of witches who trim the roster with frightening regularity. Malevolent atmosphere steers clear of the usual camp and is genuinely apprehensive. Not rated. 97m. **DIR:** Dario Argento. **CAST:** Jessica Harper, Stefania Casini, Joan Bennett, Alida Valli, Flavio Bucci, Udo Kier. **1977 DVD**

SUTURE ★★ An innocent man is unwittingly drawn into his half-brother's scheme of arson and attempted murder. A promising idea is sunk by pretentious, sophomoric filmmaking, pompous psycho-babble, and deliberately unbelievable situations and plot developments. Not rated; contains mild violence. B&W; 102m. **DIR:** David Siegel, Scott McGehee. **CAST:** Dennis Haysbert, Mel Harris, Sab Shimono, Dina Merrill, Michael Harris, Fran Ryan, David Graf, John Ingle. **1994**

SUZY ★★ Cary Grant plays a WWI pilot who falls for American show girl Jean Harlow. A spy story with charismatic performers who don't seem to connect. Not up to expectations. B&W; 99m. **DIR:** George Fitzmaurice. **CAST:** Jean Harlow, Cary Grant, Franchot Tone, Lewis Stone, Benita Hume, Una O'Connor. **1936**

SVENGALI (1931) ★★★★ Adapted from the George Du Maurier novel that put Svengali into the language as one who controls another. John Barrymore plays Svengali, a demonic artist obsessed with Trilby, a young artist's model. Under his hypnotic influence, she becomes a singer who obeys his every command. Bizarre sets and arresting visual effects make this a surrealistic delight. B&W; 76m. **DIR:** Archie Mayo. **CAST:** John Barrymore, Marian Marsh, Donald Crisp, Carmel Myers, Bramwell Fletcher. **1931**

SVENGALI (1983) ★★ Even stars like Peter O'Toole and Jodie Foster can't help this poorly scripted remake of the classic tale. Made for cable. 96m. **DIR:** Anthony Harvey. **CAST:** Peter O'Toole, Jodie Foster, Elizabeth Ashley, Larry Joshua, Holly Hunter. **1983**

SWAMP THING ★★ Kids will love this movie, about a monster-hero—part plant, part scientist—who takes on a supervillain (Louis Jourdan) and saves heroine Adrienne Barbeau. But adults may find it corny. Based on the popular 1972 comic book of the same name. Rated PG, it has some tomato-paste violence and brief nudity. 91m. **DIR:** Wes Craven. **CAST:** Louis Jourdan, Adrienne Barbeau, Ray Wise, David Hess. **1982**

SWAMP WOMEN ★★ Female undercover cop infiltrates a trio of tough-talking tomatoes, engineers a prison break, and accompanies them to a danger-infested swamp to retrieve the jewels they've stashed there. Low-budget drive-in fare was shot on location in Louisiana and features "B" queens Beverly Garland and Marie Windsor in classic hardboiled roles. Cheap but fun. 70m. **DIR:** Roger Corman. **CAST:** Carole Matthews, Beverly Garland, Marie Windsor, Jill Jarmyn, Mike Connors. **1955**

SWAN, THE (1925) ★★1/2 While adored by a commoner, a princess is pursued by a playboy prince in this classic comedy-drama of manners drawn from the Ferenc Molnàr play. Silent. B&W; 112m. **DIR:** Dimitri Buchowetzki. **CAST:** Frances Howard, Adolphe Menjou, Ricardo Cortez. **1925**

SWAN, THE (1956) ★★★ First filmed with Frances Howard in 1925, then in 1930 with Lillian Gish, this Ferenc Molnar comedy, about a princess courted by a commoner while promised to a prince, gave Hollywood princess Grace Kelly ample time to act in reel life what she shortly became in real life. 112m. **DIR:** Charles Vidor. **CAST:** Grace Kelly, Louis Jourdan, Alec Guinness, Agnes Moorehead, Brian Aherne, Jessie Royce Landis, Estelle Winwood, Leo G. Carroll, Robert Coote. **1956**

SWAN PRINCESS, THE ★★★1/2 This gorgeous, animated musical-romance, based on the German *Swan Lake* legend, is about a princess who is turned into a swan by a banished magician. The charming story includes messages about how relationships between boys and girls change as they grow up and the inability of males to verbally express their emotions. Voices are provided by Sandy Duncan, Steven Wright, Jack Palance, and John Cleese. Rated G. 90m. **DIR:** Richard Rich. **1994**

SWANN IN LOVE ★★★★ Slow-moving but fascinating film portrait of a Jewish aristocrat (Jeremy Irons) totally consumed by his romantic and sexual obsession with an ambitious French courtesan (Ornella Muti). It's definitely not for all tastes. However, those who can remember the overwhelming ache of first love may find it worth watching. In French with English subtitles. Rated R for nudity and suggested sex. 110m. **DIR:** Volker Schlöndorff. **CAST:** Jeremy Irons, Ornella Muti, Alain Delon, Fanny Ardant, Marie-Christine Barrault. **1985**

SWAP, THE (SAM'S SONG) 🦃 Robert De Niro fans, don't waste your time. This hodgepodge uses a few minutes of film from an unreleased movie De Niro made in 1969 called *Sam's Song* to pad out a story about an excon looking for his brother's murderer. Rated R. 87m. **DIR:** John Shade, John Broderick, Jordon Leondopoulos. **CAST:** Robert De Niro, Jennifer Warren, Lisa Blount, Sybil Danning. **1980 DVD**

SWARM, THE 🦃 Inept. Rated PG. 116m. **DIR:** Irwin Allen. **CAST:** Michael Caine, Katharine Ross, Richard Widmark, Henry Fonda, Olivia de Havilland, Richard Chamberlain, Fred MacMurray. **1978**

SWASHBUCKLER (1976) ★★ Only a strong cast saves this pirate movie from being a total swashbungler. Even so, it's a stylistic nightmare as a sword-wielding hero (Robert Shaw) who comes to the aid of a damsel (Genevieve Bujold) in distress. Rated PG for violence and nudity. 101m. **DIR:** James Goldstone. **CAST:** Robert Shaw, James Earl Jones, Peter Boyle, Genevieve Bujold, Beau Bridges, Geoffrey Holder, Avery Schreiber, Anjelica Huston. **1976 DVD**

SWASHBUCKLER, THE (1984) 🦃 Stupid story about a naturalized American who gets caught up in the French Revolution while delivering grain and seeking a divorce from his wife. 100m. **DIR:** Jean-Paul Rappeneau. **CAST:** Jean-Paul Belmondo, Marlene Jobert, Laura Antonelli, Michel Auclair, Julien Guiomar. **1984**

SWEATER GIRLS 🦃 Teen sexcapade. Rated R for sex and language. 84m. **DIR:** Don Jones. **CAST:** Harry

Moses, Meegan King, Noelle North, Kate Sarchet, Charlene Tilton. **1984**

SWEENEY TODD ★★★★★ This is not a film, but rather an eight-camera video of a Broadway musical taped during a performance before an audience. And what a musical it is, this 1979 Tony Award winner! George Hearn is terrifying as Sweeney Todd, the barber who seeks revenge on the English judicial system by slashing the throats of the unfortunate who wind up in his tonsorial chair. Angela Lansbury is spooky as Mrs. Lovett, who finds a use for Todd's leftovers by baking them into meat pies. 150m. **DIR:** Harold Prince. **CAST:** Angela Lansbury, George Hearn, Sara Woods. **1982**

SWEEPER, THE ★★1/2 Star C. Thomas Howell fares well in this derivative crime-thriller. Howell plays L.A. cop Mark Goddard, whose suspects have a habit of dying. Goddard's tortured past (he witnessed his family's execution) comes into play when he's asked to join a secret police society that breaks the law in order to enforce it. When Goddard suspects the society may have been behind his family's death, havoc ensues. Rated R for violence and profanity. 101m. **DIR:** Joseph Merhi. **CAST:** C. Thomas Howell, Jeff Fahey, Ed Lauter, Cynda Williams. **1995**

SWEEPERS ★★ That noise you hear isn't the numerous on-screen explosions but action star Dolph Lundgren's career hitting rock bottom. Lundgren plays a former mine-sweeping expert who is called back into duty to help stop terrorists from exporting a new deadly mine to the United States. The only bombs here are the functional script, thoughtless direction, and paper-thin performances. Rated R for violence and language. 96m. **DIR:** Darby Black. **CAST:** Dolph Lundgren, Claire Stansfield, Bruce Payne. **1997 DVD**

SWEET ADELINE ★★★★ One of the first Broadway musicals transferred to the screen with most of its original score intact, this is also the first of five Jerome Kern musicals to star Irene Dunne. She gives her all to such songs as "Why Was I Born?" The story of spies and singers may be hokey, but the music is marvelous. B&W; 87m. **DIR:** Mervyn LeRoy. **CAST:** Irene Dunne, Donald Woods, Louis Calhern, Winifred Shaw, Nydia Westman, Hugh Herbert, Ned Sparks, Phil Regan, Noah Beery Sr. **1935**

SWEET AND LOWDOWN ★★★1/2 Bittersweet tale of a Depression-era jazz genius infatuated with himself, whose arrogant behavior and mistreatment of women become palatable only because he is, as it happens, a jazz guitarist almost without compare. (It's not hard to imagine Woody Allen lecturing us about the need to separate art from the artist.) When Samantha Morton is on camera, as a mute laundress who falls in love with Emmet, the film becomes magical and moves into Charlie Chaplin territory, specifically 1931's *City Lights*. While lacking the snap of Allen's best work, this film is nonetheless entertaining and playfully poignant. Rated PG-13 for brief profanity and sexual candor. 95m. **DIR:** Woody Allen. **CAST:** Sean Penn, Samantha Morton, Uma Thurman, Anthony LaPaglia. **1999 DVD**

SWEET BIRD OF YOUTH (1962) ★★★★ Crowds lined up to see this near-perfect big screen translation of Tennessee Williams's steamy Broadway hit about a has-been film star and her lusty, fame-hungry young lover. Director and scripter Richard Brooks got the best out of everyone in a fine cast. Definitely not for the kiddies. 120m. **DIR:** Richard Brooks. **CAST:** Geraldine Page, Paul Newman, Shirley Knight, Rip Torn, Madeleine Sherwood, Ed Begley Sr., Mildred Dunnock. **1962**

SWEET BIRD OF YOUTH (1989) ★★★1/2 Gritty adaptation of Tennessee Williams's play features Elizabeth Taylor as a fading film star often in a drunken stupor. Hitting rock bottom she takes up with a handsome gigolo (Mark Harmon). She seeks a companion, but all he wants is her connections. Harmon's performance is powerful. Made for TV, but contains nudity, violence, and adult themes. 95m. **DIR:** Nicolas Roeg. **CAST:** Mark Harmon, Elizabeth Taylor, Cheryl Paris, Valerie Perrine. **1989**

SWEET CHARITY ★★★★ This was a Broadway smash hit, and it lost nothing in transfer to the screen. Neil Simon adapted the story from Federico Fellini's *Nights of Cabiria*. Shirley MacLaine is a prostitute who falls in love with a naïve young man who is unaware of her profession. The musical numbers by Dorothy Fields and Cy Coleman are terrific. Bob Fosse, in his directorial debut, does an admirable job. Rated G. 133m. **DIR:** Bob Fosse. **CAST:** Shirley MacLaine, Chita Rivera, Paula Kelly, Ricardo Montalban, Sammy Davis Jr. **1969**

SWEET COUNTRY 🦃 Chile under military rule after the murder of Allende. Rated R for violence and nudity. 105m. **DIR:** Michael Cacoyannis. **CAST:** Jane Alexander, John Cullum, Jean-Pierre Aumont, Irene Papas, Franco Nero, Carole Laure, Joanna Pettet, Randy Quaid. **1985**

SWEET DREAMS ★★★★1/2 Jessica Lange is Patsy Cline, one of the greatest country-and-western singers of all time, in this film that is much more than a response to the popularity of *Coal Miner's Daughter*. Lange's performance is flawless right down to the singing, where she perfectly mouths Cline's voice. Rated PG for profanity and sex. 115m. **DIR:** Karel Reisz. **CAST:** Jessica Lange, Ed Harris, Ann Wedgeworth, David Clennon, Gary Basaraba. **1985 DVD**

SWEET EVIL ★★ Overly familiar tale of a young couple desperate to have children. Their plan to invite a surrogate mom into their home turns deadly when the stranger unveils her own secret agenda. Adoption would have been easier and less predictable. Rated R for adult situations, language, nudity, and violence. 92m. **DIR:** Rene Eram. **CAST:** Bridgette Wilson, Peter Boyle, Scott Cohen, Seiko Matsuda. **1995 DVD**

SWEET 15 ★★★1/2 Marta's dream of a huge birthday celebration is shattered when her father fears he will be deported to Mexico in this fine family film first aired on PBS. Recommended. 110m. **DIR:** Victoria Hochberg. **CAST:** Karla Montana, Tony Plana. **1989**

SWEET HEREAFTER, THE ★★★★ Five minutes into this film and you just know it's the sort of work that would have prompted the Cannes voters to award it the 1997 grand prize. This is a story of people seeking redemption and peace in the aftermath of a great tragedy and of the purgatory that awaits those who channel their anger and frustration in unwise directions. Based on the novel by Russell Banks. Although meticulously crafted and impeccably performed, this film lacks compelling fascination and the aftermath is unsatisfying. Rated R for nudity, profanity, and strong sexual content. 110m. **DIR:** Atom Egoyan. **CAST:** Ian Holm, Sarah Pol-

ley, Bruce Greenwood, Tom McCamus, Gabrielle Rose. **1997 DVD**

SWEET HOME CHICAGO ★★★★★ The story of Chicago's Chess Records and its timeless blues recordings is told with admirable attention to detail by filmmakers Alan and Susan Raymond. Rare footage of performances by the label's pacesetters—Muddy Waters, Howlin' Wolf, Sonny Boy Williamson, John Lee Hooker, Otis Spann, Buddy Guy, Chuck Berry, and Willie Dixon, among others—is integrated with anecdote-packed interviews for a one-of-a-kind viewing experience. Blues fans will want to own it. Made for video. 64m. **DIR:** Alan Raymond, Susan Raymond. **1993**

SWEET HOSTAGE ★★ Congenial kidnapper Martin Sheen espouses poetry and simple common sense in trying to convince captive Linda Blair that a world awaits her away from the confines of the farm. Not rated. 93m. **DIR:** Lee Philips. **CAST:** Linda Blair, Martin Sheen. **1976**

SWEET JUSTICE ★★ Women vigilantes battle small-town gangsters. Not to be taken seriously—the cast certainly didn't. Rated R for violence and nudity. 92m. **DIR:** Allen Plone. **CAST:** Finn Carter, Kathleen Kinmont, Marc Singer, Frank Gorshin, Mickey Rooney. **1991 DVD**

SWEET KILLING 🦃 A strong cast is wasted in this imbecilic mess. A bored husband kills his wife and concocts a fictitious murderer, then meets a man claiming to be that very murderer. Rated R for profanity, nudity, and simulated sex. 87m. **DIR:** Eddy Matalon. **CAST:** Anthony Higgins, F. Murray Abraham, Leslie Hope, Andrea Ferreol, Michael Ironside. **1993**

SWEET LIBERTY ★★★★ Writer-director-star Alan Alda strikes again, this time with the story of a small-town historian (Alda) whose prize-winning saga of the Revolutionary War is optioned by Hollywood and turned into a movie. When the film crew descends on Alda's hometown for location shooting, predictable chaos erupts. Quite entertaining. Rated PG for mild sexual situations. 107m. **DIR:** Alan Alda. **CAST:** Alan Alda, Michael Caine, Michelle Pfeiffer, Bob Hoskins, Lise Hilboldt, Lillian Gish, Saul Rubinek, Lois Chiles, Linda Thorson. **1986**

SWEET LIES ★★ This so-called comedy contains little to laugh at, as Treat Williams plays an insurance investigator out to prove that a wheelchair-bound litigant is faking his injury. Ho-hum. Rated R for nudity and sexual situations. 96m. **DIR:** Nathalie Delon. **CAST:** Treat Williams, Joanna Pacula, Julianne Phillips. **1987**

SWEET LORRAINE ★★★★ There's a lot to like in this nostalgic stay at The Lorraine, a hotel in the Catskills. Maureen Stapleton is the owner of the 80 year old landmark that may be seeing its last summer. It needs extensive repairs and developers are offering a tempting price. A perfect cast makes this small-scale film a huge success. Rated PG-13. 91m. **DIR:** Steve Gomer. **CAST:** Maureen Stapleton, Trini Alvarado, Lee Richardson, John Bedford Lloyd, Giancarlo Esposito. **1987**

SWEET LOVE, BITTER ★★ This film, adapted from the book *Night Song*, is loosely based on the life of Charlie Parker. Sax player (Dick Gregory) befriends a down-and-out college professor (Don Murray). Great jazz score (with Charles McPherson ghosting for Gregory on sax) and one hilarious pot-smoking scene are the only recommendations for this otherwise dated and cliché-ridden relic. Not rated; contains some violence. B&W; 92m. **DIR:** Herbert Danska. **CAST:** Dick Gregory, Don Murray, Diane Varsi, Robert Hooks. **1966**

SWEET MOVIE 🦃 Incoherent, surreal comedy centers around a wealthy South African mining tycoon who purchases a virgin bride, then continues to exploit her sexually. In English and French with English subtitles. Not rated; contains sexually explicit material. 97m. **DIR:** Dusan Makavejev. **CAST:** Carole Laure, Pierre Clementi, Sami Frey. **1974**

SWEET MURDER 🦃 Attractive Helene Udy allows Embeth Davidtz to move into her apartment, although Davidtz looks amazingly like the ax murderer she is. Could become infamous as the worst impersonation plot on film. Rated R for violence, profanity, and nudity. 101m. **DIR:** Percival Rubens. **CAST:** Helene Udy, Embeth Davidtz, Russell Todd. **1993**

SWEET NOTHING ★★★★ The tense realism and jangling emotional honesty add up to cinema verité disguised as drama. A Wall Street exec begins a downward spiral by sampling too much of the crack he deals on the side. Watching the relentless destruction of a family is tough going, but we're left with a sliver of hope and the lingering effect of two extremely powerful performances. Rated R for violence, profanity, sexual situations, and drug use. 89m. **DIR:** Gary Winick. **CAST:** Michael Imperioli, Mira Sorvino, Paul Calderon. **1994**

SWEET NOVEMBER ★★★ Charlize Theron sparkles as a free-spirited "gal with a secret" in this updated remake of the 1968 charmer, but costar Keanu Reeves hasn't a romantic bone in his body; he plays every scene—happy, sad, angry—with the same stern expression and flat delivery. As a result, it's difficult to embrace the fairy-tale story of an emotionally withdrawn guy whose better qualities are brought out by Theron's vivacious Earth sprite. The whole concept seems too much a part of the 1960s, which perhaps explains why the original was more successful. Rated PG-13 for sexual candor and mild profanity. 114m. **DIR:** Pat O'Connor. **CAST:** Keanu Reeves, Charlize Theron, Jason Isaacs, Greg Germann, Liam Aiken. **2001 DVD**

SWEET POISON ★★ This psychological thriller, which explores how far a decent man can be pushed, might play better if the dialogue weren't so weak and the performances so overblown. Rated R for language, sexual situations, and violence. 101m. **DIR:** Brian Grant. **CAST:** Steven Bauer, Edward Herrmann, Patricia Healy, Noble Willingham. **1991**

SWEET REVENGE (1987) ★★ Nancy Allen plays a Los Angeles newswoman investigating the disappearance of several young women. She gets her story the hard way when she is kidnapped and taken to a slave market in Southeast Asia. Average action tale is marred by a disappointing ending and the miscasting of Allen. Rated R for violence, nudity, and sexual situations. 99m. **DIR:** Mark Sobel. **CAST:** Nancy Allen, Ted Shackelford, Martin Landau. **1987**

SWEET REVENGE (1990) ★★★★ A newly divorced couple wrangle nonstop in this romantic comedy, originally telecast on cable. Lighthearted and pleasant, with some colorful European backgrounds. 89m. **DIR:** Charlotte Brandstrom. **CAST:** Carrie Fisher, John Sessions, Rosanna Arquette. **1990**

SWEET REVENGE (1998) ★★★ Two strangers meet on a bridge, where each is attempting suicide. They discuss their woes, and agree to seek revenge on each other's enemy. While this made-for-cable movie has good acting and interesting characters, a much better version is Alfred Hitchcock's *Strangers on a Train*. Also released as *The Revengers' Comedies*. Rated PG-13 for profanity and violence. 91m. **DIR:** Malcolm Mowbray. **CAST:** Sam Neill, Helena Bonham Carter, Kristin Scott Thomas, Rupert Graves, Martin Clunes, Steve Coogan. **1998 DVD**

SWEET SIXTEEN ★★ In this static mystery, a young woman (Aliesa Shirley) from the big city reluctantly spends her summer—and her sixteenth birthday—in a small Texas town and becomes the chief suspect in a series of murders. Rated R for profanity and partial nudity. 96m. **DIR:** Jim Sotos. **CAST:** Aliesa Shirley, Bo Hopkins, Patrick Macnee, Susan Strasberg, Don Stroud. **1984**

SWEET SMELL OF SUCCESS ★★★1/2 Burt Lancaster is superb as a ruthless newspaper columnist. Tony Curtis is equally great as the seedy press agent who will stop at nothing to please him. Outstanding performances by a great cast and brilliant cinematography by James Wong Howe perfectly capture the nightlife in Manhattan. Screenplay by Clifford Odets and Ernest Lehman. B&W; 96m. **DIR:** Alexander Mackendrick. **CAST:** Burt Lancaster, Tony Curtis, Martin Milner, Sam Levene, Barbara Nichols, Susan Harrison. **1957 DVD**

SWEET SWEETBACK'S BAADASSSSS SONG ★★★1/2 Minor cult black film about a man running from racist white police forces. Melvin Van Peebles plays the title character, who will do anything to stay free. Very controversial when released in 1971. Lots of sex and violence gave this an X rating at the time. Probably the best of the black-produced and -directed films of the early 1970s. Rated R. 97m. **DIR:** Melvin Van Peebles. **CAST:** Melvin Van Peebles, Rhetta Hughes, Simon Chuckster, John Amos. **1971**

SWEET TALKER ★★★ Ex-convict Harry Reynolds (Bryan Brown) dupes the residents of an Australian village into investing in the excavation of a bogus sunken ship filled with gold. Harry befriends the local hotel owner's son, only to have the boy see him as a surrogate father. Charming story and good acting. Rated PG. 91m. **DIR:** Michael Jenkins. **CAST:** Bryan Brown, Karen Allen, Chris Haywood, Bill Kerr. **1990 DVD**

SWEET WILLIAM ★★★1/2 Sam Waterston and Jenny Agutter shine in this low-key adult comedy, which, while concerned with sex, doesn't feel the need to display any of it. She is attracted to his frenetic romanticism but slowly realizes that that same trait gets him into bed with every woman in sight. The women get the last laugh in this gentle British farce. Rated R for talk, not action. 92m. **DIR:** Claude Whatham. **CAST:** Sam Waterston, Jenny Agutter, Anna Massey, Tim Pigott-Smith. **1980**

•SWEETEST THING, THE ★★★1/2 This ribald sex farce, belying its name, is a tawdry little flick lacking anything in the way of redeeming social values, which panders to crude and smarmy sexuality, demeans the very nature of love, and turns the battle of the sexes into a sparring ground of smut. And we had a *great* time with it. Scripter Nancy M. Pimental's West Coast answer to the HBO TV series *Sex in the City* follows best friends and career singles Cameron Diaz and Christina Applegate, as they undertake a road trip in an effort to locate a specific guy who initiated more than a few sparks during a brief nightclub chat. The coarse and profane result is delivered with irrepressible, revved-up glee. Rated R for profanity, nudity, and strong sexual content. 84m. **DIR:** Roger Kumble. **CAST:** Cameron Diaz, Christina Applegate, Thomas Jane, Selma Blair, Jason Bateman, Parker Posey. **2002 DVD**

SWEETHEARTS (1938) ★★★1/2 Good acting, splendid singing, and a bright updated script make this version of the ancient Victor Herbert operetta a winning comedy about a temperamental stage duo on a collision course set by jealousy. The Technicolor cinematography won an Oscar. 120m. **DIR:** W. S. Van Dyke. **CAST:** Jeanette MacDonald, Nelson Eddy, Frank Morgan, Ray Bolger, Mischa Auer. **1938**

SWEETHEARTS (1996) ★★★ Director Aleks Horvat's frothy romantic comedy about four people looking for love in all the wrong places is filled with funny performances and equally funny dialogue. The focus is on Janeane Garofalo and Mitch Rouse, who meet as a blind date and end up spending the evening spilling their guts. Lucky for us, the script is filled with delicious slams and insights. The director manages to make this little chamber piece into an actual slice of life. Rated R for adult situations and language. 83m. **DIR:** Aleks Horvat. **CAST:** Janeane Garofalo, Mitch Rouse, Margaret Cho, Bob Goldthwait. **1996**

SWEETHEARTS' DANCE ★★★ From Ernest (*On Golden Pond*) Thompson, a delightful little movie about love and relationships. High school sweethearts Don Johnson and Susan Sarandon are a married couple whose marriage has stagnated. There are subplots about male bonding, best friends, and father-son relationships. Rated R for profanity. 101m. **DIR:** Robert Greenwald. **CAST:** Don Johnson, Susan Sarandon, Jeff Daniels, Elizabeth Perkins, Justin Henry. **1988**

SWEETHEARTS ON PARADE ★★ Country girl and city girl go hunting jobs and husbands. A marine and a sailor take a shine to the pair and join forces to save the country girl when she is taken in by a wealthy married man. Easygoing comedy may be sexist, but it touches on other stereotypes, too, and handles them all with good nature. One of the last silent feature films released. B&W; 66m. **DIR:** Marshall Neilan. **CAST:** Alice White, Lloyd Hughes, Marie Prevost, Kenneth Thompson, Ray Cooke, Wilbur Mack. **1930**

SWEETIE ★★★1/2 Surrealistic first film by Australian writer-director Jane Campion recalls David Lynch's *Eraserhead* and *Blue Velvet* in its odd camera angles and bizarre characters. The title character (Genevieve Lemon) is a grotesque version of the spoiled daddy's girl. Rated R for profanity, nudity, and violence. 100m. **DIR:** Jane Campion. **CAST:** Genevieve Lemon, Karen Colston. **1990**

•SWEETWATER ★★★1/2 Dramatization of the true story of the rock band Sweetwater, the very first opening act for the original Woodstock Festival. Intriguing, behind-the-scenes story of a band that could have been really big and the tragedies that kept them from being so. Rated PG-13 for drug and alcohol abuse. 95m. **DIR:** Lorraine Senna Ferrara. **CAST:** Amy Jo Johnson,

Michelle Phillips, Kelli Williams, Adam Ant, Frederic Forrest. **1999**

SWEPT AWAY ★★★1/2 The full title is *Swept Away by an Unusual Destiny in the Blue Sea in August*, and what this Italian import addresses is a condescending, chic goddess who gets hers on a deserted island. In Italian with English subtitles. Rated R. 116m. **DIR:** Lina Wertmuller. **CAST:** Giancarlo Giannini, Mariangela Melato. **1975 DVD**

SWEPT FROM THE SEA ★★★★ A shipwreck victim washes ashore and falls in love with the local "crazy lady." Effective period romance featuring a very appealing cast and a sweeping score by the legendary John Barry. Rated PG-13. 114m. **DIR:** Beeban Kidron. **CAST:** Vincent Perez, Rachel Weisz, Ian McKellen, Joss Ackland, Kathy Bates. **1997 DVD**

SWIMMER, THE ★★★★ A middle-aged man in a gray flannel suit who has never achieved his potential swims from neighbor's pool to neighbor's pool on his way home on a hot afternoon in social Connecticut. Each stop brings back memories of what was and what might have been. Burt Lancaster is excellent in the title role. Rated PG. 94m. **DIR:** Frank Perry. **CAST:** Burt Lancaster, Janet Landgard, Janice Rule, Joan Rivers, Tony Bickley, Marge Champion, Kim Hunter. **1968**

SWIMMING POOL, THE 🦃 This slow-moving French film features Alain Delon, Romy Schneider, and Maurice Ronet in a love triangle that leads to homicide. Dubbed into English. Not rated; contains nudity. 85m. **DIR:** Jacques Deray. **CAST:** Alain Delon, Romy Schneider, Maurice Ronet, Jane Birkin. **1970**

SWIMMING TO CAMBODIA ★★★★ This low-budget movie consists of nothing more than actor-monologist Spalding Gray sitting at a desk while he tells about his experiences as a supporting actor in *The Killing Fields*. But seldom has so much come from so little. Gray is an excellent storyteller and his extended anecdotes—covering the political history of Cambodia, the filming of the movie, the sex and drugs available in Southeast Asia, and life in New York City—are often hilarious. Not rated. 87m. **DIR:** Jonathan Demme. **CAST:** Spalding Gray. **1987**

SWIMMING WITH SHARKS ★★★★ Sort of a personalized *The Player* in which a misanthropic Hollywood studio executive's long- suffering assistant takes his boss hostage and tortures back. Rated R for language, violence, and sex. 93m. **DIR:** George Huang. **CAST:** Kevin Spacey, Frank Whaley, Michelle Forbes. **1995**

SWIMSUIT 🦃 Lousy made-for-TV movie about the search for a model for a new swimsuit line. 95m. **DIR:** Chris Thomson. **CAST:** William Katt, Catherine Oxenberg, Nia Peeples, Tom Villard, Jack Wagner, Billy Warlock, Cyd Charisse. **1989 DVD**

SWINDLE, THE ★★★1/2 Con artists lure conventioneers into sharing a few cocktails, then drug them and steal their IDs and money. One mark turns out to be a bag man for the mob and the story thickens. This satirical caper about shifting and shiftless human relationships includes gorgeous globe-trotting, cheeky characterizations, and slick twists. In French with English subtitles. Not rated. 104m. **DIR:** Claude Chabrol. **CAST:** Isabelle Huppert, Michel Serrault, François Cluzet, Jean-François Balmer. **1999 DVD**

SWING ★★1/2 Occasionally enjoyable musical drama features Hugo Speer as Martin, a likable chap whose financial indiscretions find him behind bars, where he befriends a musician who teaches him the saxophone. Upon his release, Martin puts together a band, which includes his ex-girlfriend. Speer and his cronies bring local color to the film, but leading lady Lisa Stansfield lacks the presence to be anything more than a vocalist. Rated R for language. 97m. **DIR:** Nick Mead. **CAST:** Hugo Speer, Lisa Stansfield, Paul Usher, Tom Bell, Rita Tushingham, Clarence Clemons. **1999**

SWING HIGH, SWING LOW ★★1/2 Entertainers Carole Lombard and Fred MacMurray, stranded in Panama, get married, split, and fight ennui and a variety of troubles. This is a slanted-for-comedy remake of 1929's highly successful tearjerking backstage drama, *The Dance of Life*. B&W; 95m. **DIR:** Mitchell Leisen. **CAST:** Carole Lombard, Fred MacMurray, Dorothy Lamour, Charles Butterworth, Franklin Pangborn, Anthony Quinn. **1937**

SWING IT, SAILOR ★★ Envision two gobs after one gal, or make it two swabs after one skirt, and you've got this film figured out. Broad, roughhouse humor is the order of the day. The story is stale, but moves along at a decent clip. B&W; 61m. **DIR:** Raymond Connon. **CAST:** Wallace Ford, Isabel Jewell, Ray Mayer. **1937**

SWING KIDS ★★1/2 The premise is certainly fascinating: young German "bop" fans resisted induction of the Hitler youth. Kenneth Branagh's ominously chilling SS officer is undercut by *Hogan's Heroes*–style cartoon Nazis (reflecting the film's Disney origins). Rated PG-13 for violence and profanity. 112m. **DIR:** Thomas Carter. **CAST:** Robert Sean Leonard, Christian Bale, Frank Whaley, Barbara Hershey, Kenneth Branagh. **1993**

SWING SHIFT ★★ Goldie Hawn stars in this disappointing 1940s-era romance as Kay Walsh, the girl who's left behind when her husband, Jack (Ed Harris), goes off to fight in World War II. Rated PG for profanity and suggested sex. 100m. **DIR:** Jonathan Demme. **CAST:** Goldie Hawn, Kurt Russell, Ed Harris, Fred Ward, Christine Lahti, Sudie Bond. **1984**

SWING TIME ★★★★1/2 Fred Astaire is a gambler trying to save up enough money to marry the girl he left behind (Betty Furness). By the time he's saved the money, he and Ginger Rogers are madly in love with each other. B&W; 105m. **DIR:** George Stevens. **CAST:** Ginger Rogers, Fred Astaire, Betty Furness, Victor Moore, Helen Broderick. **1936**

SWINGERS ★★★★ The male title characters in this Cocktail Nation comedy all look "money, baby"—at least to each other if not to the "beautiful babies" they romantically stalk and covet in the retro-swing lounges of Los Angeles. This crash course in 1990s dating protocol is a hilarious ensemble piece that paints men as both desperate lechers and shell-shock victims of the singles wars. Rated R for language. 96m. **DIR:** Doug Liman. **CAST:** Jon Favreau, Vince Vaughn, Ron Livingston, Patrick Van Horn, Alex Desert, Deena Martin, Heather Graham. **1996 DVD**

SWINGIN' SUMMER, A ★★ This is one of those swingin' Sixties flicks where three swingin' teens move to a swingin' summer resort for a swingin' vacation. They start up their own swingin' dance concert schedule and book big-name acts like Gary and the Playboys,

the Rip Tides, and the Righteous Brothers. Raquel Welch debuts here and also sings. 82m. **DIR:** Robert Sparr. **CAST:** Raquel Welch, James Stacy, William Wellman Jr., Quinn O'Hara, Martin West. **1965**

SWISS CONSPIRACY, THE ★★1/2 Swiss banker Ray Milland hires ex-Fed David Janssen to thwart a sophisticated blackmail scheme involving supposedly secret numbered accounts. Sexy Senta Berger and John Saxon, as a Chicago gangster double-crossing his friends, are among those being threatened with exposure and death. Rated PG. 92m. **DIR:** Jack Arnold. **CAST:** David Janssen, Senta Berger, Ray Milland, Elke Sommer, John Ireland, John Saxon. **1977 DVD**

SWISS FAMILY ROBINSON, THE ★★★1/2 Walt Disney's comedy-adventure film, adapted from the classic children's story by Johann Wyss about a family shipwrecked on a lush South Seas island. 128m. **DIR:** Ken Annakin. **CAST:** John Mills, Dorothy McGuire, James MacArthur, Tommy Kirk, Sessue Hayakawa. **1960 DVD**

SWISS MISS ★★★ Here we have Stan Laurel and Oliver Hardy in the Swiss Alps. A weak and uneven script is overcome by the stars, who seize several opportunities for brilliant comedy. For the most part, however, the film is mediocre. B&W; 72m. **DIR:** John G. Blystone. **CAST:** Stan Laurel, Oliver Hardy, Della Lind, Walter Woolf King, Eric Blore. **1938**

SWITCH ★★★ Writer-director Blake Edwards continues his exploration of the sexes with this story of a sleazy womanizer (Perry King) who is killed by his jilted ex-lovers only to come back as a woman. Ellen Barkin is wonderful as a male in a female body. Rated R for profanity and brief nudity. 104m. **DIR:** Blake Edwards. **CAST:** Ellen Barkin, Jimmy Smits, JoBeth Williams, Lorraine Bracco, Tony Roberts, Perry King, Bruce Payne. **1991**

SWITCHBACK ★★★★ Intricate plotting amplifies this tricky murder mystery, and writer-director Jeb Stuart scores points for credible characters, provocative storytelling, and an underlying puzzle that'll keep everybody guessing right up to the exciting conclusion. The title reflects the film's cross-cutting style of alternating between two apparently separate narratives that we know must be related . . . but how? Rated R for violence, profanity, and several close-ups of nude pinups. 121m. **DIR:** Jeb Stuart. **CAST:** Dennis Quaid, Danny Glover, Jared Leto, Ted Levine, R. Lee Ermey. **1997 DVD**

SWITCHBLADE SISTERS ★★★ Deserving of kudos for its drive-in entertainment value, this 1975 cheapie has been delivered to video by Quentin Tarantino. Doesn't matter if this cast of hot-pants-clad nobodies boasts minimal acting talent, there's more than enough campy dialogue, action, and blue eye shadow to go around. Rated R for violence, profanity, sexual situations, and brief nudity. 91m. **DIR:** Jack Hill. **CAST:** Robbie Lee, Joanne Nail, Monica Gayle, Janice Karman, Kitty Bruce, Marlene Clark. **1975 DVD**

SWITCHED AT BIRTH ★★★1/2 Above-average made-for-TV miniseries chronicles the controversial true story of two baby girls swapped at birth. When tragedy strikes and one of the girls dies, it is discovered that her blood type doesn't match that of her parents, and the search for the truth begins. Long in the tooth, but entertaining nonetheless. 200m. **DIR:** Waris Hussein. **CAST:** Bonnie Bedelia, Brian Kerwin, Ariana Richards, Edward Asner, Eve Gordon. **1991**

SWITCHING CHANNELS ★★★ Effective performances by Kathleen Turner, Burt Reynolds, and Christopher Reeve enliven this fourth big-screen version of Ben Hecht and Charles MacArthur's *The Front Page*. More specifically a remake of Howard Hawks's 1940 comedy classic, *His Girl Friday*, *Switching Channels* switches from newspapers to television but keeps many of the elements of the original's plot. Rated PG for profanity. 113m. **DIR:** Ted Kotcheff. **CAST:** Kathleen Turner, Burt Reynolds, Christopher Reeve, Ned Beatty, Henry Gibson, Joe Silver. **1988**

SWITCHING GOALS ★★1/2 The Olsen twins, Mary-Kate and Ashley, mine *The Parent Trap* formula, playing identical twins who decide to switch identities. Mary-Kate is Sam, the tomboy of the two, while Ashley is Emma, rotten on the playing field but an ace at home and in school. When they wind up on opposing soccer teams, the girls are unhappy with their teammates and coach. In order not to rock the boat, they decide to impersonate each other, which means keeping up the charade both on and off the field. Rated G. 85m. **DIR:** David Steinberg. **CAST:** Mary-Kate Olsen, Ashley Olsen, Eric Lutes, Kathryn Greenwood, Joe Grifasi. **1999**

SWOON ★★★★ *Swoon* follows in the footsteps of *Rope* and *Compulsion* as films inspired by the real-life exploits of 1920s Chicago college-boy killers, Nathan Leopold Jr. and Richard Loeb. The changing climate in America, though, allows Kalin to explore a heretofore ignored aspect of the story—that Leopold and Loeb were homosexual lovers. It's stylish, original, and exciting. Rated R, with profanity and sexual content. B&W; 90m. **DIR:** Tom Kalin. **CAST:** Daniel Schlachet, Craig Chester, Ron Vawter, Michael Kirby. **1992**

SWORD AND THE ROSE, THE (1953) ★★1/2 Romance, intrigue, and heroic acts of derring-do are the order of the day in this colorful Walt Disney adaptation of *When Knighthood Was in Flower*. Richard Todd makes an ideal lead and Michael Gough is a truly malevolent heavy. 93m. **DIR:** Ken Annakin. **CAST:** Richard Todd, Glynis Johns, James Robertson Justice, Michael Gough. **1953**

SWORD AND THE SORCERER, THE ★★ But for the derring-do and bits of comedy provided by star Lee Horsley, this film would be a complete waste of time and talent. A soldier of fortune (Horsley) rescues a damsel in distress (Kathleen Beller) and her brother (Simon MacCorkindale) from an evil king and his powerful wizard. Rated R because of nudity, violence, gore, and sexual references. 100m. **DIR:** Albert Pyun. **CAST:** Lee Horsley, Kathleen Beller, Simon MacCorkindale, George Maharis, Richard Lynch, Richard Moll. **1982 DVD**

SWORD IN THE STONE, THE ★★★1/2 The legend of King Arthur provided the story line for this animated feature film from the Walt Disney studios. Although not up to the film company's highest standards, it still provides fine entertainment for the young and the young at heart. Rated G. 80m. **DIR:** Wolfgang Reitherman. **1963**

SWORD OF DOOM ★★★ Tatsuya Nakadai gives a fascinating performance as a brutal samurai, whose need to kill alienates even his once-devoted father. Several

stories are interwoven in this film, but, surprisingly, at least two are left unresolved. This will make it disappointing—and confusing—for all but the most devoted fans of Japanese action movies. In Japanese with English subtitles. 122m. **DIR:** Kihachi Okamoto. **CAST:** Tatsuya Nakadai, Toshiro Mifune. **1967**

SWORD OF GIDEON ★★★1/2 To avenge the 1972 murders of Israeli Olympic-team members in Munich, five commandos are sent on a globe-hopping mission to destroy selected leaders of the terrorist Black September movement. Location filming is a plus in this suspenseful and action-packed TV movie. Colleen Dewhurst has a touching cameo as Prime Minister Golda Meir. 150m. **DIR:** Michael Anderson. **CAST:** Steven Bauer, Michael York, Rod Steiger, Robert Joy, Leslie Hope, Laurent Malet, Linda Griffiths, Lino Ventura, Cyrielle Claire, Colleen Dewhurst. **1986**

SWORD OF HONOR ★★1/2 This kung fu action flick's earnest cast tries hard but cannot overcome lackluster direction and idiotic camera tricks (notably accelerated frame speed). Dedicated Las Vegas cop Steven Vincent Leigh sets out to avenge his best friend's death and recover the prized titular object. Rated R for violence, profanity, nudity, and simulated sex. 95m. **DIR:** Robert Tiffe. **CAST:** Steven Vincent Leigh, Angelo Tiffe, Sophia Crawford, Jerry Tiffe. **1994**

SWORD OF LANCELOT ★★★ Colorful production and location photography highlight this pre- *Camelot* version of life at the court of King Arthur and the forbidden love between Lancelot and Queen Guinevere (Mr. and Mrs. Cornel Wilde in real life). Long on pageantry, action, and chivalrous acts of derring-do, this is a "fun" film in the same vein as *Ivanhoe* and *The Vikings*. 116m. **DIR:** Cornel Wilde. **CAST:** Cornel Wilde, Jean Wallace, Brian Aherne, George Baker. **1963**

SWORD OF THE VALIANT ★★★1/2 The Old English tale of Sir Gawain and the Green Knight is brought to the screen with an appealing blend of action-adventure and tongue-in-cheek humor. Rated PG. 162m. **DIR:** Stephen Weeks. **CAST:** Miles O'Keeffe, Sean Connery, Trevor Howard. **1984**

•SWORDFISH ★★★1/2 Criminal mastermind John Travolta lures recently paroled computer hacker Hugh Jackman into taking part in the theft of an all-but-forgotten DEA bank account that has swelled from its original amount of $400 million to $9.5 billion after fifteen years. Jackman, who only wants money to pay court costs in his fight to reunite with his young daughter, finds himself involved in a ruthless gambit that costs innocent lives. In the wake of the events of September 11th, what was originally a straightforward piece of entertainment now has darker overtones. Still, its fast pace and atypical characters will enthrall those viewers who can ignore some disturbing parallels. Rated R for violence, profanity, nudity, and sex. 99m. **DIR:** Dominic Sena. **CAST:** John Travolta, Hugh Jackman, Halle Berry, Don Cheadle, Sam Shepard, Vinnie Jones, Drea de Matteo, Rudolf Martin, Zach Grenier, Camryn Grimes. **2001 DVD**

SWORDSMAN, THE 🦃 A psychic police detective sword-battles his way through a case involving stolen antiquities and mass murder, eventually discovering that he is the reincarnation of Alexander the Great. Rated R for violence and profanity. 98m. **DIR:** Michael Kennedy. **CAST:** Lorenzo Lamas, Claire Stansfield, Michael Champion. **1992**

SWORN ENEMIES ★★★ Michael Paré and Peter Greene stand out in this tale of best friends and partners turned mortal enemies. Greene is hungry for power, and he's killing those who stand in his way. Paré is the local sheriff of their quiet, backwater town and will do anything to put an end to the killing spree. Rated R for adult situations, language, and violence. 101m. **DIR:** Shimon Dotan. **CAST:** Michael Paré, Peter Greene, Macha Grenon. **1996 DVD**

SYBIL ★★★★ Sally Field is outstanding in this deeply disturbing but utterly fascinating made-for-TV drama of a young woman whose intense psychological childhood trauma has given her seventeen distinct personalities. Joanne Woodward is the patient, dedicated psychiatrist who sorts it all out. 116m. **DIR:** Daniel Petrie. **CAST:** Joanne Woodward, Sally Field, William Prince. **1976**

SYLVESTER ★★★★ Director Tim Hunter does an admirable job with this hard-edged *National Velvet*–style drama about a tomboy (Melissa Gilbert) who rides her horse, Sylvester, to victory in the Olympics' Three-Day Event in Lexington, Kentucky. Gilbert is first-rate as the aspiring horsewoman, and Richard Farnsworth is his reliable, watchable self as her cantankerous mentor. Rated PG-13 for profanity and violence. 109m. **DIR:** Tim Hunter. **CAST:** Melissa Gilbert, Richard Farnsworth, Michael Schoeffling, Constance Towers. **1985**

SYLVIA ★★ About as underwhelming as a film can get and still have some redeeming qualities. Were it not for the fine performance by Eleanor David in the title role, this film about seminal educator Sylvia Ashton-Warner would be a muddled bore. It jumps from one event to another with little or no buildup or continuity. Rated PG for graphic descriptions of violence. 97m. **DIR:** Michael Firth. **CAST:** Eleanor David, Nigel Terry, Tom Wilkinson, Mary Regan. **1985**

SYLVIA AND THE PHANTOM ★★★★ A delightful story concerning ghosts and the fantasies of a young lady living with her family in a castle. As the story begins, we meet Sylvia on the eve of her sixteenth birthday and find that she fantasizes about the portrait of her grandmother's lover and the rumors that he haunts the castle. In French with English subtitles. 97m. **DIR:** Claude Autant-Lara. **CAST:** Odette Joyeux, François Perier, Julien Carette. **1950**

SYLVIA SCARLETT ★★★1/2 The first screen teaming of Katharine Hepburn and Cary Grant lacks the sprightly pace and memorable humor of *Holiday* and *The Philadelphia Story*, which also were directed by George Cukor, but it's still a real find for fans of the stars. When Hepburn's con-man father (Edmund Gwenn) runs afoul of the law, they must quickly leave France while she masquerades as a boy to avert suspicion. B&W; 94m. **DIR:** George Cukor. **CAST:** Katharine Hepburn, Cary Grant, Brian Aherne, Edmund Gwenn. **1936**

SYNAPSE ★★ The quest for eternal youth is still on in the future. A company known as Life Corp. has found a way of transferring someone's mind to another body. Their first experiment, a betrayed coworker whose brain is transferred into that of a beautiful woman, backfires. The woman escapes and brings back an army of renegades anxious to put an end to Life Corp. Okay at

moments, but nothing new here. Rated R for violence, nudity, and adult language. 89m. **DIR:** Allan A. Goldstein. **CAST:** Karen Duffy, Chris Makepeace, Saul Rubinek, Matt McCoy. **1994**

SYNGENOR ★★1/2 Syngenor stands for synthetic genetic organism. Starr Andreeff plays a woman fighting for her life when the beast gets loose. This slight film is fun in a no-brainer sort of way. Rated R for violence, profanity, and nudity. 98m. **DIR:** George Elanjian Jr. **CAST:** Starr Andreeff, David Gale. **1990**

SYNTHETIC PLEASURES ★★★ Occasionally intriguing documentary about virtual reality and other artifical modes of pleasure attainment (drugs not included, unless you count the "smart drinks" imbibed by some young club goers). Like the *Mondo* movies of the 1960s, all that is here passes without comment, and the film tends to stray from its theme (particularly in the case of a performance artist obsessed with plastic surgery). Not rated; contains sexual themes. 83m. **DIR:** Iara Lee. **1996**

T-FORCE ★★★1/2 When a squad of robotic crime fighters becomes more of a problem than the bad guys they're supposed to be fighting, detective Jack Scalia is hired to rein them in. Rated R for profanity and violence. 101m. **DIR:** Richard Pepin. **CAST:** Jack Scalia, Erin Gray, Evan Lurie. **1995**

T-MEN ★★1/2 Two undercover operatives for the Treasury Department infiltrate a master counterfeiting ring and find themselves on opposite sides when the lead starts to fly. Unable to save the life of his partner without exposing himself, agent Dennis O'Keefe courageously continues the work of both men. B&W; 92m. **DIR:** Anthony Mann. **CAST:** Dennis O'Keefe, Alfred Ryder, Mary Meade, Wallace Ford, June Lockhart, Charles McGraw, Jane Randolph. **1948**

TABLE FOR FIVE ★★★ Had it up to here with *Kramer vs. Kramer* clones about single parents coping with their kids? If you have, you'll probably decide to skip this movie—and that would be a shame, because it's a good one. Jon Voight stars as J. P. Tannen, a divorcé who takes his three youngsters on a Mediterranean cruise in hopes of getting back into their lives full-time. Rated PG for mature situations. 122m. **DIR:** Robert Lieberman. **CAST:** Jon Voight, Richard Crenna, Millie Perkins. **1983**

TABU ★★★1/2 Begun as a collaboration between F. W. Murnau and documentarian Robert Flaherty, this is an unusual but unique South Seas romance filmed with a combination of naturalistic settings and an expressionistic technique. A native girl falls in love with a young man despite the fact that she has been promised to the gods. Silent. 81m. **DIR:** F. W. Murnau. **CAST:** Anna Chevalier, Matahi. **1931**

TACTICAL ASSAULT ★★★ Dazzling midair combat and lots of high-impact energy keep this direct-to-video action-thriller off the ground. Rutger Hauer is perfectly cast as an air force pilot serving in the Gulf War. When he snaps during a mission and tries to down an airliner, he comes under attack from a fellow pilot and enters a deadly game of cat-and-mouse. Rated R for language and violence. 89m. **DIR:** Mark Griffiths. **CAST:** Rutger Hauer, Robert Patrick, Isabel Glasser. **1998 DVD**

TAFFIN ★★★ The ever-watchable Pierce Brosnan plays a surprisingly tough "collector" in this fun-to-watch Irish film. The city folks approach Brosnan to get rough with the chemical plant thugs who are bulldozing their fair countryside. Rated R for violence, profanity, and nudity. 96m. **DIR:** Francis Megahy. **CAST:** Pierce Brosnan, Ray McAnally, Alison Doody. **1987 DVD**

TAG—THE ASSASSINATION GAME ★★★1/2 The short-lived fad for campus war games, in which students stalked each other with rubber darts, is the basis for this comic thriller. Student reporter Robert Carradine, smitten with star player Linda Hamilton, follows her on her hunt. Neither realizes that one player has started using a real gun. Rated PG. 92m. **DIR:** Nick Castle. **CAST:** Robert Carradine, Linda Hamilton, Bruce Abbott, Michael Winslow. **1982**

TAGGET ★★★1/2 A smooth and sympathetic lead performance from Daniel J. Travanti highlights this intriguing tale of a disabled Vietnam veteran plagued by disturbing flashbacks. His efforts to decipher the dreams reveal traces of a decade-old CIA dirty tricks cover-up. Slick, violent made-for-cable thriller. 89m. **DIR:** Richard T. Heffron. **CAST:** Daniel J. Travanti, Roxanne Hart, Peter Michael Goetz, Bill Sadler. **1991**

TAI-PAN ★★ Pretentious, overblown adaptation of James Clavell's bestseller, this disjointed mess plays like a television miniseries chopped from eight hours to two. Bryan Brown is properly stoic as the "Tai-Pan," chief trader, who dreams of establishing a colony to be named Hong Kong. Joan Chen is ludicrous as his concubine. Rated R for brief nudity and violence. 127m. **DIR:** Daryl Duke. **CAST:** Bryan Brown, John Stanton, Joan Chen, Tim Guinee. **1986**

TAIL LIGHTS FADE ★★ The young, attractive cast of this road movie is the only reason to take this trip. Tanya Allen, as Angie, recruits her boyfriend and another couple to accompany her on a Canadian cross-country trip to help her brother, a drug dealer who has just been busted. The film is dialogue heavy, and while the actors are fine, they struggle through some inane speeches. What could have been an insightful journey turns out to be a wrong turn. Rated R for adult situations, language, and nudity. 87m. **DIR:** Malcolm Ingram. **CAST:** Tanya Allen, Jake Busey, Breckin Meyer, Denise Richards, Elizabeth Berkley. **1999 DVD**

•TAILOR OF PANAMA, THE ★★★★ Dissolute British spy Pierce Brosnan is banished to Panama, where he sets about rehabilitating himself with the reluctant help of a local tailor (Geoffrey Rush) with a shady past. This adaptation of the John Le Carré novel is a wickedly intelligent black comedy, fast-paced and well-acted, especially by Rush and Brosnan, who plays a kind of evil twin to James Bond. Rated R for profanity, sexual scenes, and brief violence. 109m. **DIR:** John Boorman. **CAST:** Pierce Brosnan, Geoffrey Rush, Jamie Lee Curtis, Leonor Varela, Catherine McCormack, Harold Pinter. **2001 DVD**

TAILS YOU LIVE, HEADS YOU'RE DEAD ★★★ Suspenseful made-for-cable original about a stranger who picks his murder victims at random and plays mind games with them. Corbin Bernsen is excellent as the killer and Ted McGinley does a good job as his next victim. Rated R for violence and profanity. 95m. **DIR:** Tim Matheson. **CAST:** Corbin Bernsen, Ted McGinley, Tim Matheson. **1995**

TAILSPIN ★★★ Docu-style drama concerning the Soviet Union's tragic shooting down of Korean Airline's flight 007 over the Sea of Japan. A tactical error or an act of aggression? Made for TV. 82m. **DIR:** David Durlow. **CAST:** Michael Moriarty, Michael Murphy, Chris Sarandon, Harris Yulin. **1989**

TAINTED BLOOD ★★★1/2 A nationally known writer is doing research on children who inherit killer tendencies. She goes in search of a girl whose mother killed her parents and whose twin brother killed his adoptive parents. The viewer meets two families who each have an adopted daughter. At every turn, the very twisted plot keeps the viewer unsure which girl has the tainted blood. Not rated, made for cable, but contains violence. 95m. **DIR:** Matthew Patrick. **CAST:** Raquel Welch, Alley Mills, Kerri Green, Natasha Gregson Wagner, Joan Van Ark. **1993**

TAKE, THE ★★ This lurid, by-the-numbers cop thriller features Ray Sharkey as a Miami police officer who does jail time for attempting to cut himself into a drug deal, and then—surprise, surprise—faces exactly the same temptation after being released. Not rated, but with considerable violence. 95m. **DIR:** Leon Ichaso. **CAST:** Ray Sharkey, R. Lee Ermey, Larry Manetti, Lisa Hartman. **1990**

TAKE A HARD RIDE ★★1/2 When his friend and partner (Dana Andrews) dies, big Jim Brown is charged with taking the proceeds from a cattle sale to their homestead in Sonora, Mexico. On the way, a ruthless bounty hunter (Lee Van Cleef) attempts to take the money. A good cast falls prey to the shortcomings of this spaghetti Western, but there is some enjoyable action and humor. Rated R. 103m. **DIR:** Anthony M. Dawson. **CAST:** Jim Brown, Lee Van Cleef, Fred Williamson, Catherine Spaak, Dana Andrews, Barry Sullivan, Jim Kelly, Harry Carey Jr. **1975**

TAKE DOWN ★★1/2 Earnest comedy-drama set in the arena of high school wrestling. It centers on two initially reluctant participants: an intellectual teacher-turned-coach and a fiery student. The movie has enough heart to carry it to victory. Rated PG. 107m. **DIR:** Kieth Merrill. **CAST:** Edward Herrmann, Kathleen Lloyd, Lorenzo Lamas, Maureen McCormick, Kevin Hooks, Stephen Furst. **1978 DVD**

TAKE IT BIG ★★ In the early 1940s at Paramount Pictures, a B-movie unit was formed by William H. Pine and William C. Thomas. With a good track record, they tried to produce more elaborate films. This so-so musical is one of those bigger productions. Jack Haley is at the wrong end in a horse act that inherits a dude ranch. Ozzie Nelson and his band supply the musical numbers. B&W; 75m. **DIR:** Frank McDonald. **CAST:** Jack Haley, Ozzie Nelson, Harriet Nelson. **1944**

TAKE ME BACK TO OKLAHOMA ★★★★★ Top 50 B Western stars Tex Ritter who comes to the aid of a female owner of a stage line being harassed by unscrupulous competitors. This is the first Western to feature Bob Wills's fabulous Western swing music as well as a terrific rendition of Jimmy Davis's "You Are My Sunshine." B&W; 67m. **DIR:** Albert Herman. **CAST:** Tex Ritter, Bob Wills and the Texas Playboys, Arkansas Slim Andrews, Terry Walker, Karl Hackett. **1940**

TAKE ME OUT TO THE BALL GAME ★★★ Don't expect to see the usual Berkeley extravaganza in this one; this is just a run-of-the-mill musical. It does contain some entertaining musical numbers, such as "O'Brien to Ryan to Goldberg." 93m. **DIR:** Busby Berkeley. **CAST:** Gene Kelly, Frank Sinatra, Esther Williams, Betty Garrett, Jules Munshin. **1949**

TAKE THE MONEY AND RUN ★★★★ Woody Allen's first original feature is still a laugh-filled delight as the star-director plays an inept criminal in a story told in pseudo-documentary-style (à la *Zelig*). It's hilarious. Rated PG. 85m. **DIR:** Woody Allen. **CAST:** Woody Allen, Janet Margolin, Marcel Hillaire. **1969 DVD**

TAKE THIS JOB AND SHOVE IT ★★★1/2 Robert Hays stars as a rising corporate executive who returns, after a ten-year absence, to his hometown to take charge of a brewery where he once worked, and winds up organizing a revolt among his fellow employees. This contemporary comedy-drama is out to raise one's spirits, and it does just that. Rated PG. 100m. **DIR:** Gus Trikonis. **CAST:** Robert Hays, Art Carney, Barbara Hershey, Martin Mull, Eddie Albert. **1981**

TAKEN AWAY ★★ Valerie Bertinelli is a waitress/student who leaves her daughter alone one night and finds the child has become a ward of the state. Extremely manipulative, as the system set up to protect children rakes Bertinelli over the legal coals. Made as a movie of the week, and it shows. Not rated. 94m. **DIR:** John Patterson. **CAST:** Valerie Bertinelli, Kevin Dunn, Juliet Sorcey. **1989**

TAKEOVER, THE ★★ Lackluster crime-drama stars Billy Drago as an East Coast crime lord looking to take over the West Coast from Nick Mancuso. Everyone involved seems to wish they were somewhere else and the low-budget, low-power gun battles don't help. Rated R for violence, nudity, and profanity. 91m. **DIR:** Troy Cook. **CAST:** Billy Drago, John Savage, Nick Mancuso, Eric DaRe, David Ramos, Cali Timmins, Gene Mitchell. **1994**

TAKING CARE OF BUSINESS ★★★ Small-time crook James Belushi finds the Filofax of high-powered businessman Charles Grodin and takes over his business dealings, with predictable results. Wastes the talents of the two stars, mainly by not giving them enough scenes together. A harmless time killer. Rated R for profanity and sexual themes. 108m. **DIR:** Arthur Hiller. **CAST:** Charles Grodin, James Belushi. **1990 DVD**

TAKING MY TURN ★★ This is a videotape of an off-Broadway musical. Unfortunately, you had to be there to really enjoy it. Sort of *A Chorus Line* for the Geritol generation, this features aging actors lamenting the way times have changed. Their song-and-dance routines are good, but for the most part this is pretty depressing. 90m. **DIR:** Robert H. Livingston. **CAST:** Margaret Whiting, Marni Nixon, Sheila Smith, Cissy Houston. **1984**

TAKING OF BEVERLY HILLS, THE ★★★ Fans of nonstop action will cheer this *Die Hard*-esque movie about a quarterback who teams up with a crooked cop to stop

the looting of Beverly Hills by a clever crime boss. Rated R for violence and profanity. 102m. **DIR:** Sidney J. Furie. **CAST:** Ken Wahl, Matt Frewer, Harley Jane Kozak, Robert Davis, Lee Ving, Lyman Ward, Michael Bowen, William Prince. **1991**

TAKING OF PELHAM ONE TWO THREE, THE ★★★★ Walter Matthau is at his growling, grumbling, gum-chewing best in this edge-of-your-seat movie. He plays the chief detective of security on the New York subway who must deal with the unthinkable: the hijacking of a train by four men (with a fine Robert Shaw as their leader) and a demand by them for a $1 million ransom to prevent their killing the passengers one by one. Rated R for violence and profanity. 104m. **DIR:** Joseph Sargent. **CAST:** Walter Matthau, Robert Shaw, Martin Balsam, Tony Roberts. **1974 DVD**

TAKING THE HEAT ★★★1/2 Gutsy cop Lynn Whitfield has her hands full in this entertaining thriller, when she's assigned to escort reluctant witness Tony Goldwyn to a court appointment. A routine trip across New York City becomes a nightmare thanks to a heat wave, a power blackout, and pursuing goons ordered by crime-lord Alan Arkin to eliminate Goldwyn. Rated R for profanity, violence, nudity, and suggested sex. 90m. **DIR:** Tom Mankiewicz. **CAST:** Tony Goldwyn, Lynn Whitfield, George Segal, Peter Boyle, Will Patton, Alan Arkin. **1993**

TALE OF A VAMPIRE ★★★★ Julian Sands plays a scholarly vampire who thinks he's found love again in Suzanna Hamilton, a woman similar to his long-dead paramour. Archenemy Kenneth Cranham arrives and casts a pall of tragic romanticism over the lovers. Slow but effectively moody in a gothic, gory manner. Rated R for violence and gore. 93m. **DIR:** Shimako Sato. **CAST:** Julian Sands, Suzanna Hamilton, Kenneth Cranham. **1993**

TALE OF RUBY ROSE, THE ★★★ Rousing frontier adventure about a woman named Ruby Rose, who has lived her entire life in the backwoods of Tasmania. Then she takes a courageous journey in search of her grandmother, a trip that causes her to look to her inner self to survive a world she never knew existed. Exhilarating. Rated PG. 101m. **DIR:** Roger Scholes. **CAST:** Melita Jurisic, Chris Haywood. **1987**

TALE OF SPRINGTIME, A ★★★ A French schoolteacher is befriended by a young woman. She then becomes entangled in touchy family affairs when she's romantically paired with the girl's father. Eric Rohmer's passion for intelligent, witty discourse and subtle tension continues in a story he says "deals less with what people do than with what is going on in their minds while they are doing it." This is the third installment in his sophisticated *Tales of the Four Seasons* film series. In French with English subtitles. Rated PG. 107m. **DIR:** Eric Rohmer. **CAST:** Anne Teyssedre, Florence Darel, Hugues Quester. **1992 DVD**

TALE OF TWO CITIES, A (1935) ★★★★★ A satisfactory rendition of Charles Dickens's novel. It is richly acted, with true Dickens flavor. Ronald Colman was ideally cast in the role of Sydney Carton, the English no-account who finds purpose in life amid the turmoil of the French Revolution. The photography in this film is one of its most outstanding features. The dark shadows are in keeping with the spirit of this somber Dickens story. B&W; 121m. **DIR:** Jack Conway. **CAST:** Ronald Colman, Basil Rathbone, Edna May Oliver, Elizabeth Allan. **1935**

TALE OF TWO CITIES, A (1967) ★★★1/2 Impressive detailed adaptation of the Charles Dickens novel that chronicles the turmoil of the French Revolution and features some good performances by a top-notch cast. 117m. **DIR:** Ralph Thomas. **CAST:** Dirk Bogarde, Donald Pleasence, Christopher Lee, Dorothy Tutin. **1967**

TALE OF TWO CITIES, A (1980) ★★★ Acceptable version of the Dickens classic, though the other versions available on video are better. There's a topflight cast, but Chris Sarandon is a bit wan for Sydney Carton. Not rated. 216m. **DIR:** Jim Goddard. **CAST:** Chris Sarandon, Peter Cushing, Kenneth More, Barry Morse, Flora Robson, Billie Whitelaw, Alice Krige. **1980**

TALE OF TWO CITIES, A (1991) ★★★★ This magnificent PBS production of Charles Dickens's classic lavishly re-creates the costumes and setting of France from 1767 to 1790. A self-imposed exile of French nobility (Xavier Deluc) finds himself helplessly drawn into the revolutionary madness of mob rule. 240m. **DIR:** Philippe Monnier. **CAST:** James Wilby, Xavier Deluc, Serena Gordon, Jean-Pierre Aumont. **1991**

TALENT FOR THE GAME ★★★1/2 Little-known film is a treasure trove of wonderful performances and memorable moments. The marvelous Edward James Olmos stars as a talent scout for the California Angels. An examination of life in modern America as compared with the values inherent in the game of baseball. Rated PG for profanity. 91m. **DIR:** Robert M. Young. **CAST:** Edward James Olmos, Lorraine Bracco, Jamey Sheridan, Terry Kinney, Jeff Corbett, Tom Bower, Janet Carroll, Felton Perry, Thomas Ryan. **1991**

TALENTED MR. RIPLEY, THE ★★★★1/2 Matt Damon shines in the title role of this meticulously crafted character drama, adapted by scripter-director Anthony Minghella from a particularly unsettling Patricia Highsmith novel. The result is an intriguing analysis of the extremes to which one man will go to be accepted by an arrogant, class-based social strata in which he feels out of place. The setting is *La Dolce Vita* of the late 1950s, with Damon's Tom Ripley hired to "spy" on a rich American's wayward son, who's throwing his life away on jazz and expatriate girlfriend Gwyneth Paltrow. Minghella's style is strikingly Hitchcockian, but it's Damon's show: Present in absolutely every scene, he is nothing short of mesmerizing. Rated R for violence and profanity. 140m. **DIR:** Anthony Minghella. **CAST:** Matt Damon, Gwyneth Paltrow, Jude Law, Cate Blanchett, Philip Seymour Hoffman, Jack Davenport, James Rebhorn. **1999 DVD**

TALES FROM A PARALLEL UNIVERSE ★★ Hokum about a group of space rebels who hijack a spaceship to find a lost planet in order to revive their leader. Their quest is jeopardized when they encounter a holographic prankster who doesn't realize the spaceship is also a deadly weapon that can destroy the universe, and will self-destruct if the occupants are killed. Made-for-cable series. Rated R for adult situations, language, and violence. 93m. **DIR:** Ron Oliver. **CAST:** Brian Downey, Eva Habermann, Michael McManus, Tim Curry. **1996**

TALES FROM THE CRYPT ★★★1/2 Excellent anthology has five people gathered in a mysterious cave where the keeper (Ralph Richardson) foretells their futures, one by one, in gruesome fashion. Director Freddie Fran-

cis keeps things moving at a brisk pace, and the performances are uniformly fine, most notably Peter Cushing's in one of the better segments—"Poetic Justice." Don't miss it. Rated PG. 92m. **DIR:** Freddie Francis. **CAST:** Peter Cushing, Joan Collins, Ralph Richardson. **1972 DVD**

TALES FROM THE CRYPT PRESENTS BORDELLO OF BLOOD A private eye searches for the missing brother of a televangelist in a mortuary staffed by half-naked, undead silicone transplantees. Bare breasts and exploding bodies are all the rage in this dull gorefest. Rated R for gore, violence, nudity, and sex. 87m. **DIR:** Gilbert Adler. **CAST:** Dennis Miller, Erika Eleniak, Angie Everhart, Chris Sarandon, Corey Feldman. **1996 DVD**

TALES FROM THE CRYPT (TV SERIES) ★★★1/2 Three creepy tales told with tongue firmly in cheek just as the original comic books were. Not rated; contains violence. 90m. **DIR:** Walter Hill, Robert Zemeckis, Richard Donner. **CAST:** Bill Sadler, Mary Ellen Trainor, Larry Drake, Joe Pantoliano, Robert Wuhl. **1989 DVD**

TALES FROM THE CRYPT: DEMON KNIGHT ★★1/2 On par with the TV series, this theatrical release focuses on a likable collector who has come for the key that will allow evil to take over completely. Unlike many horror films that take themselves too seriously, this pokes fun at both itself and the genre. Rated R for nudity, profanity, violence, gore, and sexual situations. 85m. **DIR:** Ernest R. Dickerson. **CAST:** Billy Zane, Bill Sadler, Jada Pinkett, Brenda Bakke. **1994 DVD**

TALES FROM THE DARKSIDE, THE MOVIE ★★★ This horror anthology (inspired by the hit TV series) features a few exceptional moments and a lot of more mundane horror-film conventions. Rated R for violence and profanity. 90m. **DIR:** John Harrison. **CAST:** Deborah Harry, Christian Slater, David Johansen, William Hickey. **1990**

TALES FROM THE DARKSIDE, VOL. I ★★ The first installment in this ongoing series of TV-episode compilations is the only one worth bothering with, largely because of the three stories adapted: Stephen King's "Word Processor of the Gods," and Harlan Ellison's "D'Jinn, No Chaser," and "Slippage." The penny-ante budget doesn't help, though. 70m. **DIR:** Michael Gornick. **1985**

TALES FROM THE GIMLI HOSPITAL ★★★★ Blend of Scandinavian folktales, the severe look of German-expressionist silents, and a slightly skewed and surreal sense of humor. The bizarre plot line centers around a tortured character who is admitted to the primitive-looking title institution during an outbreak of plague. Singularly deadpan brand of avant-garde humor. Not rated. 68m. **DIR:** Guy Maddin. **CAST:** Kyle McCulloch, Michael Gottli, Angela Heck, Margaret Anne MacLeod, Heather Neale, David Neale. **1988**

TALES FROM THE HOOD ★★ This violent horror anthology features a mortician who spooks three gangstas searching for a missing drug stash by telling them four grisly stories. Rated R for language, violence, and gore. 97m. **DIR:** Rusty Cundieff. **CAST:** David Alan Grier, Wings Hauser, Corbin Bernsen, Joe Torry, De'Aundre Bonds, Sam Monroe. **1995 DVD**

TALES OF EROTICA ★★1/2 Four famous directors take a stab at erotic filmmaking in this uneven quartet of passionate stories. Mira Sorvino stands out as a woman who enters a painting in order to fulfill her sexual desires. Rated R for nudity, profanity, and adult situations. 103m. **DIR:** Ken Russell, Susan Seidelman, Bob Rafelson, Gus Van Sant. **CAST:** Mira Sorvino, Aida Turturro, Hetty Baynes, Simon Shepherd, Richard Barboza, Cynda Williams, Arliss Howard, Kathleen Wilhoite. **1994 DVD**

TALES OF HOFFMAN ★★★★1/2 A beautifully photographed blend of opera, ballet, and cinematic effects with Jacques Offenbach's familiar score for a backdrop. Robert Rounseville stars as the tale-spinner who recalls various romantic interludes in his life. The film was a follow-up to *The Red Shoes* with the same directors, stars, and color consultants. 120m. **DIR:** Michael Powell, Emeric Pressburger. **CAST:** Moira Shearer, Robert Rounseville, Robert Helpmann, Leonide Massine, Pamela Brown. **1951**

TALES OF MANHATTAN ★★★★1/2 One of the best of the many episodic films produced during the 1940s, this one uses a man's tailcoat as the link between episodes. Every new owner has an adventure associated with the coat, and they range from romance to melodrama with a little comedy thrown in. B&W; 118m. **DIR:** Julien Duvivier. **CAST:** Ginger Rogers, Henry Fonda, Edward G. Robinson, Rita Hayworth, Ethel Waters, Paul Robeson, Eddie "Rochester" Anderson, Charles Laughton, Cesar Romero, George Sanders. **1942**

TALES OF ORDINARY MADNESS Ben Gazzara in the role of infamous drunken poet Charles Bukowski, who interacts with a strange assortment of women. Rated R for profanity and nudity. 107m. **DIR:** Marco Ferreri. **CAST:** Ben Gazzara, Ornella Muti, Susan Tyrrell, Tanya Lopert. **1983 DVD**

TALES OF PARIS ★★1/2 Lightweight omnibus film featuring four stories of young women and their romantic escapades in Paris. The last segment is the most memorable, if only for a chance to see 19 year old Catherine Deneuve in one of her first films. B&W; 85m. **DIR:** Marc Allegret, Jacques Poitrenaud, Michel Boisrone, Claude Barma. **CAST:** Dany Saval, Dany Robin, Jean Poiret, Catherine Deneuve, Johnny Hallyday. **1962**

TALES OF TERROR ★★★ An uneven anthology of horror stories adapted from the works of Edgar Allan Poe. Directed by Roger Corman, it does have a few moments. 90m. **DIR:** Roger Corman. **CAST:** Vincent Price, Basil Rathbone, Peter Lorre, Debra Paget. **1962**

TALES OF THE UNEXPECTED ★★1/2 Four half-hour made-for-television shows are included in this compilation. 101m. **DIR:** Gordon Hessler, Norman Lloyd, Paul Annett, Ray Danton. **CAST:** Don Johnson, Arthur Hill, Samantha Eggar, Sharon Gless, Dick Smothers, James Carroll Jordan, Charles Dance, Zoe Wanamaker, Sondra Locke, Frank Converse, Charles Hallahan. **1981–1987**

TALES THAT WITNESS MADNESS ★★★ Black-comic horror anthology featuring four stories told by an asylum keeper to a new psychiatrist. Most memorable is the third, in which Joan Collins fights for her husband's affections against his new lover: a possessed tree! Rated R for minor grossness. 90m. **DIR:** Freddie Francis. **CAST:** Donald Pleasence, Jack Hawkins, Suzy Kendall, Joan Collins, Kim Novak. **1973**

TALES TILL THE END If you've seen every other ultralow-budget horror flick on the planet, then this one's

for you. Not rated, but contains profanity, violence, nudity, and gore. 88m. **DIR:** Barry Gaines, Philip Herman, Ben Stanski. **CAST:** Barry Gaines, Philip Herman, Ben Stanski. **1995**

TALION ★★ Two bounty hunters (Robert Lansing and Patrick Wayne) go on the vengeance trail against a turncoat (Slim Pickens). The twist is that in an early gun battle, Wayne is blinded and Lansing's gun hand is crippled. Lansing looks vaguely uncomfortable in a cowboy hat, and the writing is sometimes ridiculous. 92m. **DIR:** Michael Moore. **CAST:** Robert Lansing, Patrick Wayne, Slim Pickens, Gloria Talbott, Paul Fix, Strother Martin, Clint Howard. **1966**

TALK OF ANGELS ★★★ An intimate romance between a governess and her employer's son is set against an epic, sprawling civil war in this uneven yet handsome production. Polly Walker rises to the occasion as Mary Lavelle, an Irish governess who falls for the married son of her employer. Set in Spain in 1936 just before the civil war, the film's smaller moments are constantly engulfed by the grandeur of the film. Rated PG-13 for adult situations. 97m. **DIR:** Nick Hamm. **CAST:** Polly Walker, Vincent Perez, Franco Nero, Frances McDormand. **1997**

TALK OF THE TOWN, THE ★★★★ Falsely accused of arson and murder, parlor radical Cary Grant escapes jail and holes up in a country house Jean Arthur is readying for law professor Ronald Colman. The radical and the egghead take to one another. Gifted direction and a brilliant cast make this topflight entertainment. B&W; 118m. **DIR:** George Stevens. **CAST:** Ronald Colman, Jean Arthur, Cary Grant, Edgar Buchanan, Glenda Farrell, Emma Dunn, Charles Dingle, Tom Tyler, Don Beddoe, Rex Ingram. **1942**

TALK RADIO ★★★★ Powerful story centers on a controversial Dallas radio talk-show host's rise to notoriety—and the ultimate price he pays for it. Eric Bogosian repeats his acclaimed Broadway stage performance as the radio host who badgers and belittles callers and listeners alike. A highly cinematic, fascinating film. Director Oliver Stone keeps his camera moving and the pace rapid throughout. Rated R. 110m. **DIR:** Oliver Stone. **CAST:** Eric Bogosian, Alec Baldwin, Ellen Greene, John Pankow, John C. McGinley. **1989**

TALKIN' DIRTY AFTER DARK ★★1/2 Black comedy stars Martin Lawrence as a comedian who will do anything to land a spot at the infamous Dukie's nightclub, and that includes sleeping with the main man's main squeeze. Too much jive and not enough laughs. Rated R for language and nudity. 86m. **DIR:** Topper Carew. **CAST:** Martin Lawrence, John Witherspoon. **1991**

TALKING ABOUT SEX ★★1/2 At a party to promote publication of a manual to help couples nurture sexual intimacy, the guests learn more than they had anticipated about each other. Apparently designed to be similarly nurturing to viewers, this uninvolving drama tries to pack too many issues into one film. Not rated; contains nudity, sexual situations, and profanity. 87m. **DIR:** Aaron Speiser. **CAST:** Kim Wayans, Daniel Beer, Daria Lynn, Randy Powell, Kerry Ruff. **1993**

TALKING WALLS ★★ Offbeat, mildly interesting comedy-drama about a student who decides to do his thesis on sexual relationships by videotaping unwitting guests as they cavort in a sleazy Hollywood motel. Not rated, contains nudity, sex, and vulgar language. 85m. **DIR:** Stephen F. Verona. **CAST:** Stephen Shellen, Marie Laurin, Sybil Danning, Sally Kirkland, Barry Primus. **1987**

TALL BLOND MAN WITH ONE BLACK SHOE, THE ★★★★ If you're looking for an entertaining, easy-to-watch comedy, this is one of the best. Pierre Richard plays the bumbling blond man to hilarious perfection, especially when it comes to physical comedy. The story involves spies, murder, a mysterious sexy woman, and plenty of action. Highly recommended, but try to see the original version, with subtitles, not the dubbed version. Rated PG. 90m. **DIR:** Yves Robert. **CAST:** Pierre Richard, Bernard Blier, Mireille Darc. **1972**

TALL, DARK AND DEADLY ★★ Slightly suspenseful tale about a woman stalked by a psychotic, mysterious man. Not rated; contains violence and sexual situations. 88m. **DIR:** Kenneth Fink. **CAST:** Jack Scalia, Kim Delaney, Todd Allen, Gina Mastrogiacomo. **1994**

TALL GUY, THE ★★★1/2 Delightfullly whacked-out comedy about an American actor (Jeff Goldblum) stuck in a dead-end London gig as a foil for a loud, obnoxious, and egotistical comedian (Rowan Atkinson). This all changes when he falls in love with a no-nonsense nurse (Emma Thompson). Rated R for profanity and nudity. 90m. **DIR:** Mel Smith. **CAST:** Jeff Goldblum, Emma Thompson, Rowan Atkinson, Geraldine Jones. **1990 DVD**

TALL IN THE SADDLE ★★★★ A first-rate B Western that combines mystery with shoot-'em-up action. John Wayne is wrongly accused of murder and must find the real culprit. Helping him is Gabby Hayes, and hindering is Ward Bond. B&W; 87m. **DIR:** Edwin L. Marin. **CAST:** John Wayne, George "Gabby" Hayes, Ward Bond, Ella Raines. **1944**

TALL MEN, THE ★★ Confederate army veterans Clark Gable and Cameron Mitchell join cattle baron Robert Ryan to drive his herd to market through Indian country. All three fancy Jane Russell. 122m. **DIR:** Raoul Walsh. **CAST:** Clark Gable, Jane Russell, Robert Ryan, Cameron Mitchell, Mae Marsh. **1955**

TALL STORY ★★★ Jane Fonda makes a delightful college student who falls for a basketball player. This is Fonda's first movie and shows her flair for comedy. B&W; 90m. **DIR:** Joshua Logan. **CAST:** Jane Fonda, Anthony Perkins, Elizabeth Patterson, Ray Walston, Anne Jackson, Murray Hamilton, Gary Lockwood, Marc Connelly, Tom Laughlin. **1960**

TALL T, THE ★★★★★ Rancher Randolph Scott and several stagecoach passengers are captured and held by outlaws. Top-notch Burt Kennedy script from an Elmore Leonard story. Fine performances from all concerned. This is a little-known classic. 78m. **DIR:** Budd Boetticher. **CAST:** Randolph Scott, Richard Boone, Maureen O'Sullivan, Henry Silva, Skip Homeier. **1957**

TALL TALE: THE UNBELIEVABLE ADVENTURES OF PECOS BILL ★★★1/2 Youngsters will be charmed by this story of how three legendary figures—Pecos Bill (Patrick Swayze), Paul Bunyan (Oliver Platt), and John Henry (Roger Aaron Brown)—help a young boy save his family's farm from the clutches of the evil, land-grabbing J. P. Stiles. Rated PG for violence. 96m. **DIR:** Jeremiah S. Chechik. **CAST:** Patrick Swayze, Oliver Platt, Roger Aaron Brown, Nick Stahl, Scott Glenn, Stephen Lang, Jared Harris, Catherine O'Hara. **1995**

TALONS OF THE EAGLE ★★ Nothing special. Two DEA agents go undercover to bust a notorious crime lord. Once they gain his trust, they take him down in one of those extended martial-arts sequences that cap such affairs. Rated R for violence, language, and adult situations. 96m. **DIR:** Michael Kennedy. **CAST:** Billy Blanks, Jalal Merhi, James Hong, Priscilla Barnes. **1992**

TAMARIND SEED, THE ★★★ A sudsy melodrama in the old tradition, but still a lot of fun. Julie Andrews falls in love with a foreign emissary played by Omar Sharif, only to be told (by her own State Department) to stay away from him. The cold war intrigue seems pretty absurd these days, but Andrews and Sharif generate a playful chemistry that overlooks many sins. Rated PG. 123m. **DIR:** Blake Edwards. **CAST:** Omar Sharif, Julie Andrews, Anthony Quayle. **1974**

TAMING OF THE SHREW, THE (1929) ★★★ The first royal couple of Hollywood costarred in this film while under the duress of a failing marriage. Mary Pickford is properly shrewish as Katharine; Douglas Fairbanks is smug, commanding, and virile as Petruchio. Critics liked it and the public flocked to see the famous duo have at the Bard. Director Sam Taylor gave Hollywood one of its enduring anecdotes by taking screen credit for additional dialogue. B&W; 66m. **DIR:** Sam Taylor. **CAST:** Mary Pickford, Douglas Fairbanks Sr., Dorothy Jordan. **1929**

TAMING OF THE SHREW, THE (1966) ★★★★1/2 This is a beautifully mounted comedy of the battle of the sexes. Petruchio (Richard Burton), a spirited minor nobleman of the Italian Renaissance, pits his wits against the man-hating Kate (Elizabeth Taylor) in order to win her hand. The zest with which this famous play is transferred to the screen can be enjoyed even by those who feel intimidated by Shakespeare. 126m. **DIR:** Franco Zeffirelli. **CAST:** Richard Burton, Elizabeth Taylor, Cyril Cusack, Michael York. **1966 DVD**

TAMING OF THE SHREW (1982) ★★★★ Inventive and laugh-filled, a stage production of Shakespeare's best-loved comedy as the ambitious Petruchio (Franklyn Seales) comes to wed himself well in Padua, choosing the fiery, mean-spirited Kate (Karen Austin) as his reluctant bride. Catch the running visual joke concerning Pisa. Released by Bard Productions Ltd. 115m. **DIR:** John Allison. **CAST:** Franklyn Seales, Karen Austin, Larry Drake, Kathryn Johnson, Bruce Davison, David Chemel. **1982 DVD**

TAMMY AND THE BACHELOR ★★★ Like Debbie Reynolds's number-one hit song *Tammy*, the movie is corny but irresistible. Ingenuous country girl Reynolds falls in love with injured pilot Leslie Nielsen and nurses him back to health. The romance and humor are sweet and charming. The movie's success led to sequels and a TV series. 89m. **DIR:** Joseph Pevney. **CAST:** Debbie Reynolds, Leslie Nielsen, Walter Brennan, Mala Powers, Fay Wray, Sidney Blackmer, Mildred Natwick, Louise Beavers. **1957**

TAMMY AND THE DOCTOR ★★ Cutesy romance between country gal Sandra Dee and young Peter Fonda is relatively harmless, but this is definitely a film with a limited audience. No muss, no fuss—in fact, not much of anything at all. 88m. **DIR:** Harry Keller. **CAST:** Sandra Dee, Peter Fonda, Macdonald Carey, Beulah Bondi, Margaret Lindsay, Reginald Owen, Adam West. **1963**

TAMMY & THE T-REX Nonsense about a man who is turned into a T-Rex in order to impress a girl he wants to date. Didn't he ever hear of flowers? Not rated. 82m. **DIR:** Stewart Raffill. **CAST:** Terry Kiser, Ellen Dubin, Denise Richards, Paul Walker. **1993**

TAMPOPO ★★★★ This Japanese spoof of the Italian spaghetti Western (which was, in turn, a spin-off of the samurai movie) shows a female diner owner (Nobuko Miyamoto) learning how to make perfect noodles. As silly as it sounds, this is a wonderful movie full of surprises. In Japanese with English subtitles. Not rated, with nudity and brief violence. 95m. **DIR:** Juzo Itami. **CAST:** Nobuko Miyamoto. **1987 DVD**

TANGO ★★1/2 Hard-core dance fans may enjoy this melancholy but rather monotonous story about an Argentine choreographer who tries to make a socially vital film about the sensuous tango. His project gradually becomes a reflection of his own midlife crisis, relationships with women, and political repression. In Spanish with English subtitles. Rated PG-13 for language, sexual themes, and violent images. 112m. **DIR:** Carlos Saura. **CAST:** Miguel Angel Sola, Cecilia Narova, Mia Maestro. **1998 DVD**

TANGO AND CASH ★★ Sylvester Stallone and Kurt Russell play rival L.A. detectives who find themselves framed by a powerful drug lord (Jack Palance) and must join forces to clear their names. *Tango and Cash* starts off well, with plenty of action and great comic quips, and then descends into a near parody of itself. Rated R for profanity, nudity, and violence. 98m. **DIR:** Andrei Konchalovsky. **CAST:** Sylvester Stallone, Kurt Russell, Jack Palance, Michael J. Pollard, Brian James, James Hong, Geoffrey Lewis. **1989 DVD**

TANGO BAR ★★★ Part musical, part documentary, part romantic-triangle love story, this film employs all those elements to detail the historical and cultural importance of the tango. Raul Julia and Ruben Juarez play two tango performers who are reunited. In Spanish with English subtitles. 90m. **DIR:** Marcos Zurinaga. **CAST:** Raul Julia, Valeria Lynch, Ruben Juarez. **1988**

TANGO LESSON, THE ★★★★1/2 An English filmmaker (writer-director Sally Potter, playing a fictional version of herself) takes a break from writing her latest screenplay to attend a tango exhibition and becomes fascinated by the sensuous rhythms of the Argentine dance. Film is sensuous and fascinating, with fluidly hypnotic tango sequences and marvelous screen chemistry between Potter and tango master Pablo Veron. In English, French, and Spanish with English subtitles where needed. Rated PG. B&W/color; 100m. **DIR:** Sally Potter. **CAST:** Sally Potter, Pablo Veron, Carolina Lotti, Heathcote Williams, Gustavo Naveira, Fabian Salas. **1997**

TANK ★★1/2 The always likable James Garner plays Sgt. Maj. Zack Carey, an army career soldier who has to use his privately owned Sherman tank to rescue his family (Shirley Jones and C. Thomas Howell) from the clutches of a mean country sheriff (G. D. Spradlin). It's all a bunch of hokum, but a sure audience pleaser. Rated PG. 113m. **DIR:** Marvin J. Chomsky. **CAST:** James Garner, Shirley Jones, C. Thomas Howell, G. D. Spradlin. **1984 DVD**

TANK GIRL ★★★1/2 Alan Martin and Jamie Hewlett's savagely punk comic-book heroine gets a first-class adaptation. Although definitely not for all tastes, this should delight the midnight crowd that embraced *Rocky Horror Picture Show*. Rated R for profanity and violence. 104m. **DIR:** Rachel Talalay. **CAST:** Lori Petty, Malcolm McDowell, Ice T, Naomi Watts, Don Harvey, Jeff Kober. **1995**

TANKS ARE COMING, THE ★★★ A hard-line war movie about the Third Amored Division's efforts to overturn Nazi onslaughts in Europe. Produced long after World War II ended so it did not have a lot of exposure. It has since become a cult favorite. B&W; 90m. **DIR:** Lewis Seiler. **CAST:** Steve Cochran, Philip Carey, Paul Picerni, Harry Bellaver, James Dobson, Mari Aldon. **1951**

TANNER '88 ★★★1/2 *Doonesbury* creator Garry Trudeau wrote this insightful tale of a dark-horse presidential candidate (played to perfection by Michael Murphy). Along the way Tanner runs into Bob Dole, Gary Hart, and Pat Robertson. Originally aired on HBO. 120m. **DIR:** Robert Altman. **CAST:** Michael Murphy, Pamela Reed, Cynthia Nixon, Kevin J. O'Connor, Daniel H. Jenkins. **1988**

TANYA'S ISLAND ★★★ This little cult oddity is one that you'll either love or hate. A woman escapes her abusive husband to a fantasy island where she spends her time with a sentient ape named Blue. Rob Bottin contributes some nifty makeup special effects. Rated R for violence, nudity, profanity, and simulated sex. 93m. **DIR:** Alfred Sole. **CAST:** D.D. Winters, Richard Sargent, Vanity. **1980**

TAO OF STEVE, THE ★★★ Jenniphr Goodman's little romantic comedy made a minor splash at the Sundance Film Festival, but its initial charms are overcome by a talky script and static execution. The central character, Dex, is an arrested adolescent who believes he has women figured out to an exact science. When newcomer Greer Goodman enters the picture, the equation naturally changes . . . but we're not convinced that Dex deserves true happiness. Rated R for profanity and drug content. 87m. **DIR:** Jenniphr Goodman. **CAST:** Donal Logue, Greer Goodman, James "Kimo" Wills, Ayelet Kaznelson, David Aaron Baker. **2000 DVD**

TAP ★★★★ This *Flashdance*-style musical-drama about a gifted tap dancer (Gregory Hines) is so good, you'll want to watch it a second time—not for the silly jewel-heist story, but for the marvelous dance sequences. See it for the eye-popping choreography and a *cut* contest—featuring old pros Sammy Davis Jr., Harold Nicholas, Bunny Briggs, Sandman Sims, Steve Condos, Rico, and Arthur Duncan—that will make your jaw drop. Rated PG-13 for profanity and violence. 111m. **DIR:** Nick Castle. **CAST:** Gregory Hines, Sammy Davis Jr., Joe Morton, Dick Anthony Williams. **1989**

TAP DOGS ★★★ Six Australian construction-worker hunks put their feet down in this rhythmic collection of dance and noise. Decked out in hard hats, flannel shirts, and jeans, the talented cast members tap-dance through several spectacular numbers while performing live at London's Lyric Theatre. Not rated. 75m. **DIR:** Nigel Triffitt, Aubrey Powell. **1996 DVD**

TAPEHEADS ★★★ In this off-the-wall *Night Shift*, John Cusack plays a pretentious and obnoxious con man who convinces Tim Robbins, a video genius, to make music videos. Weird and funny viewing, and the chemistry between the two leads is perfect. Not rated; contains offensive language and sexual situations. 94m. **DIR:** Bill Fishman. **CAST:** John Cusack, Tim Robbins, Mary Crosby, Connie Stevens, Doug McClure, Lyle Alzado. **1988**

TAPS ★★★1/2 George C. Scott is an iron-jawed commander of a military academy and Timothy Hutton a gung ho cadet who leads a student revolt in this often exciting but mostly unbelievable and unnecessarily violent drama. Rated R. 118m. **DIR:** Harold Becker. **CAST:** George C. Scott, Timothy Hutton, Ronny Cox, Tom Cruise. **1981 DVD**

TAR ★★ A Harlem cop falls in love with a petty thief who is being recruited to join a terrorist gang. Although attractively filmed, this low-budget effort changes directions so often that it ends up nowhere. Not rated; contains violence, nudity, sexual situations, substance abuse, and profanity. 91m. **DIR:** Goetz Grossman. **CAST:** Kevin Thigpen, Nicole Prescott, Seth Gilliam. **1997**

TARANTELLA ★★★ A young woman rediscovers her Italian heritage while going through her mother's things shortly after her mother's death. Mira Sorvino's performance is compelling but the story moves a trifle slowly. Not rated; contains profanity. 84m. **DIR:** Helen DeMichel. **CAST:** Mira Sorvino, Rose Gregorio, Matthew Lillard, Frank Pellegrino, Antonia Rey. **1995 DVD**

TARANTULA ★★★ Pretty good entry in the giant-bug subgenre of 1950s horror and science-fiction films. Heroic John Agar must deal with a mountain-sized arachnid created by well-meaning Leo G. Carroll's supergrowth formula. Don't blink during the final scenes—Clint Eastwood has a *very* brief bit as the fighter pilot who brings the beastie down. B&W; 80m. **DIR:** Jack Arnold. **CAST:** John Agar, Mara Corday, Leo G. Carroll, Eddie Parker, Clint Eastwood. **1955**

TARANTULAS—THE DEADLY CARGO ★★ A small town is terrorized by a bumper crop of spiders in this TV movie that wastes too much time setting the viewer up for scare scenes which, when they finally arrive, aren't especially scary. 100m. **DIR:** Stuart Hagmann. **CAST:** Claude Akins, Charles Frank, Deborah Winters, Howard Hesseman. **1977**

TARAS BULBA ★★★ Tony Curtis and Yul Brynner give top-notch performances in this action-packed adventure centering on Cossack life during the sixteenth century in the Ukraine. Great location photography in Argentina by Joe MacDonald, and a fine musical score by Franz Waxman. Solid entertainment. 122m. **DIR:** J. Lee Thompson. **CAST:** Tony Curtis, Yul Brynner. **1962**

TARGET ★★★ In this fast-paced, entertaining suspense-thriller directed by Arthur Penn (*Bonnie and Clyde*), a father (Gene Hackman) and son (Matt Dillon) put aside their differences when they become the targets of an international spy ring. *Target* is a tad predictable, but it is the kind of predictability that adds to the viewer's enjoyment. Rated R for violence, profanity, and nudity. 117m. **DIR:** Arthur Penn. **CAST:** Gene Hackman, Matt Dillon, Gayle Hunnicutt, Josef Sommer, Victoria Fyodora, Herbert Berghof. **1985**

TARGET EAGLE 🦃 A mercenary is hired by a Spanish police department to infiltrate a drug-smuggling ring.

Not rated, has violence. 101m. **DIR:** J. Anthony Loma. **CAST:** Jorge Rivero, Maud Adams, George Peppard, Max von Sydow, Chuck Connors. **1982**

TARGET OF SUSPICION 🦃 An extremely boring and badly acted made-for-cable movie about an American who is set up while on a business trip to Paris. One to avoid. Not rated; contains violence. 95m. **DIR:** Bob Swaim. **CAST:** Tim Matheson, Lysette Anthony, Agnes Soral. **1994**

TARGET: FAVORITE SON ★★★ Television miniseries *Favorite Son* edited down to feature-length still packs quite a wallop for those into soap-opera politics. The usual collection of love, sex, politics, espionage, and assassination make this dramatic thriller as much fun as the real thing. 115m. **DIR:** Jeff Bleckner. **CAST:** Harry Hamlin, Linda Kozlowski, Robert Loggia, John Mahoney, Ronny Cox. **1988**

TARGETS ★★★★★ The stunning filmmaking debut of critic-turned-director Peter Bogdanovich juxtaposes real-life terror, in the form of an unhinged mass murderer (Tim O'Kelly), with its comparatively subdued and safe screen counterpart, as represented by the scare films of Byron Orlock (Boris Karloff in a brilliant final bow). Rated PG. 90m. **DIR:** Peter Bogdanovich. **CAST:** Tim O'Kelly, Boris Karloff, Nancy Hsueh, Peter Bogdanovich. **1968**

TARNISHED ANGELS, THE ★★★1/2 William Faulkner's novel *Pylon* was the basis for this assured melodrama starring Robert Stack as a WWI flying ace who becomes a daredevil stunt pilot. Rock Hudson is a reporter who gradually comes under the spell of Stack and his traveling family. 91m. **DIR:** Douglas Sirk. **CAST:** Robert Stack, Rock Hudson, Dorothy Malone. **1958**

TARO, THE DRAGON BOY ★★★★ Distinctive animation, reminiscent of Japanese silkscreens, provides an engaging forum for introducing young viewers to Japanese mythology and culture. Here, young Taro makes a pilgrimage to a faraway lake to rescue his mother, who has been turned into a dragon. 75m. **DIR:** K. Urayama. **1985**

•TART ★★1/2 *Tart* primarily focuses on teenager Cat Storm (Dominique Swain) and the relationships that she has with her friends and rivals, some of which switch places in the course of the film. Staying on top of the social in crowd involves Cat in drug use, sex, and other situations that she wouldn't have dreamed of participating in without the influence of those she considers her friends. The acting is not bad, but the story is slow and treads on tired ground. Rated R for strong drug use, language, some sexual content, and a scene of violence—all involving teens. 94m. **DIR:** Christina Wayne. **CAST:** Dominique Swain, Brad Renfro, Bijou Phillips, Mischa Barton, Lacey Chabert, Melanie Griffith. **2001**

TARTUFFE ★★★ Let's be upfront about this one: It's a sophisticated version of Molière's play about religious hypocrisy. The satire is funny and biting, but this Royal Shakespeare Company production is not for everyone. The performances, especially Antony Sher's interpretation of Tartuffe, are brilliant, but very subtle. 110m. **DIR:** Bill Alexander. **CAST:** Antony Sher, Nigel Hawthorne, Alison Steadman. **1984**

TARZAN ★★★★★ Superb animation and clever storytelling make this one of Disney's true, timeless classics. While Edgar Rice Burroughs's original tale is shunted aside once again by the filmmakers, the joys of this all-ages entertainment are many. Rated G. 88m. **DIR:** Kevin Lima, Chris Buck. **1999 DVD**

TARZAN AND HIS MATE ★★★★★ Tarzan against ivory hunters. The best MGM Tarzan movie is a bona fide film classic, one of the few sequels to surpass the original. A marvelously entertaining motion picture. B&W; 105m. **DIR:** Cedric Gibbons. **CAST:** Johnny Weissmuller, Maureen O'Sullivan, Neil Hamilton, Paul Cavanagh. **1934**

TARZAN AND THE GOLDEN LION ★★1/2 In this last silent Tarzan feature, the Lord of the Jungle tracks a look-alike who has ransacked his estate and absconded with his friend's fiancée. Then a lost race of diamond hoarders seizes her and plans to sacrifice her to their sun god. This long-lost minor epic is the only one of four full-length presound movies about the twentieth century's best-known noble savage that exists in anything near its original form. Silent, with musical score. B&W; 58m. **DIR:** J. P. McGowan. **CAST:** James Pierce, Dorothy Dunbar, Edna Murphy, Harold Goodwin, Fred Peters, Boris Karloff. **1927**

TARZAN AND THE GREEN GODDESS ★★ Olympic champion Herman Brix (a.k.a. Bruce Bennett) makes one of the best-looking of all movie Tarzans as he journeys to South America to help secure a priceless stone image known as the "Green Goddess." Primitive filming conditions and a horrible soundtrack hinder the jungle nonsense. B&W; 72m. **DIR:** Edward Kull. **CAST:** Bruce Bennett, Ula Holt, Frank Baker. **1938**

TARZAN AND THE LEOPARD WOMAN ★★1/2 Above-average Tarzan entry pits him against legendary bad actress Acquanetta (*Captive Wild Woman*) as the titular villainess, leader of a murderous jungle cult. B&W; 72m. **DIR:** Kurt Neumann. **CAST:** Johnny Weissmuller, Johnny Sheffield, Brenda Joyce, Acquanetta, Dennis Hoey. **1946**

TARZAN AND THE LOST CITY ★★1/2 Compared to most of the other Tarzan films that Hollywood has butchered from Edgar Rice Burroughs's original classics, this one is generally tolerable. But the vine swinging and annoying yell are still here so as not to leave out those raised on the Johnny Weissmuller films. Poor acting by the leads, however, brings down what could have been an enjoyable romp. Rated PG for violence. 84m. **DIR:** Carl Schenkel. **CAST:** Casper Van Dien, Jane March. **1998 DVD**

TARZAN AND THE TRAPPERS ★★ This oddity is actually three television pilots that producer Sol Lesser was unable to sell to networks back in 1958. This is pretty ordinary, uninspired stuff, but it's a one-of-a-kind Tarzan film, unavailable for years. B&W; 74m. **DIR:** H. Bruce Humberstone. **CAST:** Gordon Scott, Evelyn Brent, Rickie Sorenson, Maurice Marsac. **1958 DVD**

TARZAN ESCAPES ★★★ Once again greed spurs an expedition but instead of ivory, Tarzan is the prize. This troubled production took two years and three directors before it reached the screen due to negative audience reaction to the grim nature of many scenes as well as the inevitable pressure brought on all productions by the Breen Office and the Legion of Decency. B&W; 95m. **DIR:** Richard Thorpe. **CAST:** Johnny Weissmuller, Maureen O'Sullivan, Benita Hume, William Henry, E. E. Clive. **1936**

TARZAN FINDS A SON ★★★1/2 Tarzan and Jane find an infant, the only survivor of a plane crash, and raise him as their "Boy." Five years later, relatives of his rich parents arrive and attempt to return him to civilization. Plenty of jungle action. B&W; 82m. **DIR:** Richard Thorpe. **CAST:** Johnny Weissmuller, Maureen O'Sullivan, Johnny Sheffield, Ian Hunter, Henry Stephenson, Frieda Inescort, Henry Wilcoxon, Laraine Day. **1939**

TARZAN OF THE APES ★★★1/2 The first filmed version of Edgar Rice Burroughs's classic tells the story of the Greystokes. Their child is raised by a she-ape and becomes Tarzan of the Apes. Barrel-chested Elmo Lincoln portrayed Tarzan and actually killed the lion he fights in one of the film's more exciting moments. This silent extravaganza is well worth the watch. Silent. B&W; 130m. **DIR:** Scott Sidney. **CAST:** Elmo Lincoln, Enid Markey, George French. **1918**

TARZAN THE APE MAN (1932) ★★★1/2 *Tarzan the Ape Man* is the film that made Johnny Weissmuller a star and Tarzan an idiot. That classic "Me Tarzan, you Jane" blasphemy is here in its original splendor. Maureen O'Sullivan seduces the dumb beast, and it's all great fun. Hollywood at its peak . . . but no relation to Edgar Rice Burroughs's hero. B&W; 99m. **DIR:** W. S. Van Dyke. **CAST:** Johnny Weissmuller, Maureen O'Sullivan, Neil Hamilton. **1932**

TARZAN THE APE MAN (1981) Even counting the lowest of the Tarzan flicks, this remake is the absolute worst. Rated R for profanity and nudity. 112m. **DIR:** John Derek. **CAST:** Bo Derek, Richard Harris, Miles O'Keeffe, John Phillip Law. **1981**

TARZAN THE FEARLESS Leave this one on the vine. B&W; 85m. **DIR:** Robert Hill. **CAST:** Buster Crabbe, Jacqueline Wells, E. Alyn Warren, Edward Woods. **1933 DVD**

TARZAN THE MIGHTY ★★1/2 Tarzan number five Frank Merrill once earned the title of "World's Most Perfect Man" and his jungle heroics made this Universal serial the hit of 1928. It was expanded from twelve to fifteen episodes by astute executives who correctly gauged a receptive audience. Merrill pioneered many of the stunts associated with the series, especially the vine swinging and aerial acrobatics. Silent. B&W; 15 chapters. **DIR:** Jack Nelson. **CAST:** Frank Merrill, Natalie Kingston, Al Ferguson. **1928**

TARZAN THE TIGER ★★ Based loosely on Edgar Rice Burroughs's *Tarzan and the Jewels of Opar*, this serial was shot as a silent but released with sychronized musical score and sound effects. Frank Merrill as Tarzan inaugurated the popular vine swing used by later ape-men and was the first to give his rendition of the famous cry of the bull ape—sans mixer and dubbers. This sequel to *Tarzan the Mighty* was long considered a lost film. B&W; 15 chapters. **DIR:** Henry McRae. **CAST:** Frank Merrill, Natalie Kingston, Lillian Worth, Al Ferguson. **1929**

TARZAN TRIUMPHS Just like Sherlock Holmes, Tarzan was called on to do his part for the war effort by battling Nazis in this, one of the worst of the Johnny Weissmuller series. B&W; 78m. **DIR:** William Thiele. **CAST:** Johnny Weissmuller, Johnny Sheffield, Frances Gifford, Stanley Ridges, Sig Ruman. **1943**

TARZAN'S NEW YORK ADVENTURE ★★★1/2 Boy is kidnapped by a circus owner and taken to New York to be put on display. Tarzan and Jane follow. Lots of fun with the jungle man out of his element, then scaling skyscrapers, swinging on flagpole lines until chased atop the Brooklyn Bridge. Maureen O'Sullivan's sixth and last appearance as Jane. B&W; 72m. **DIR:** Richard Thorpe. **CAST:** Johnny Weissmuller, Maureen O'Sullivan, Johnny Sheffield, Virginia Grey, Charles Bickford, Paul Kelly, Chill Wills. **1942**

TARZAN'S REVENGE Back-lot nonsense. B&W; 70m. **DIR:** D. Ross Lederman. **CAST:** Glenn Morris, Eleanor Holm, George Barbier, C. Henry Gordon, Hedda Hopper, George Meeker. **1938**

TARZAN'S SECRET TREASURE ★★★ Members of a scientific expedition are corrupted by gold found in Tarzan's paradise. By this fifth teaming of Johnny Weissmuller and Maureen O'Sullivan as Tarzan and Jane, the situations were becoming predictable. Yet, there is lots of terrific action. B&W; 81m. **DIR:** Richard Thorpe. **CAST:** Johnny Weissmuller, Maureen O'Sullivan, Johnny Sheffield, Barry Fitzgerald, Reginald Owen, Tom Conway, Philip Dorn. **1941**

TASK FORCE ★★1/2 Standard military soap opera tracing the development of the aircraft carrier. Predictable script, with all the usual heroics, but the stalwart cast holds it up. B&W; 116m. **DIR:** Delmer Daves. **CAST:** Gary Cooper, Jane Wyatt, Wayne Morris, Walter Brennan, Julie London, Jack Holt. **1949 DVD**

TASTE FOR KILLING, A ★★1/2 Two rich boys spend their summer vacation on an offshore oil rig only to become involved in a murder. Of course it looks like they did the killing. A boring premise, but nicely acted made-for-cable thriller. 96m. **DIR:** Lou Antonio. **CAST:** Michael Biehn, Jason Bateman, Henry Thomas, Helen Cates, Blue Deckert. **1992**

TASTE OF BLOOD, A The most ambitious film by Herschell Gordon Lewis, "The Godfather of Gore." The plot involves an American descendant of Dracula. 120m. **DIR:** Herschell Gordon Lewis. **CAST:** Bill Rogers. **1967**

TASTE OF CHERRY ★★ An Iranian businessman, determined to commit suicide, tries to find someone who will help him end it all. The film won the Palme d'Or at Cannes, but the prize must have been a political statement (the film was banned in Iran, where the subject of suicide is taboo), because the film is a windy, interminable bore. In Farsi with English subtitles. Not rated; suitable for general audiences. 95m. **DIR:** Abbas Kiarostami. **CAST:** Homayon Ershadi, Abdolrahman Bagheri, Afshin Khorshid Bakhtiari, Safar Ali Moradi. **1997 DVD**

TASTE OF HONEY, A ★★★1/2 Offbeat comedy-drama memorably tells the story of a lower-class teenager (Rita Tushingham) made pregnant by a black sailor. Tough but tender, this piece of attempted social realism by new-wave British director Tony Richardson is based on a successful stage play. B&W; 100m. **DIR:** Tony Richardson. **CAST:** Rita Tushingham, Dora Bryan, Murray Melvin, Robert Stephens. **1961**

•TASTE OF OTHERS, THE ★★★★ Opposites attract and relationships crumble in this suburban, rather serene French comedy. An affluent, disconnected couple seems headed for divorce. She is a neurotic who cares more for her dog than people. He is a crass industrialist who throws himself into the arts after becoming

infatuated with a theater actress and hiring her as his English tutor. Other players in this fresh, casual game of cultural bumper cars include the industrialist's chauffer and a bodyguard who both date the same bar waitress. In French with English subtitles. Not rated. 112m. **DIR:** Agnès Jaoui. **CAST:** Jean-Pierre Bacri, Christiane Millet, Anne Alvaro, Agnès Jaoui, Gerard Lanvin. **1999**

TASTE THE BLOOD OF DRACULA ★★★ This fourth entry in Hammer Films's *Dracula* cycle is a big improvement after *Dracula Has Risen from the Grave*, but there's a problem: where's Dracula? We're almost half an hour into the movie before three Victorian family men revive the Count (unwittingly, natch). Stylish and creepy, but with more for the indefatigable Chris Lee to do, this might've been a four-star film. Rated PG. 95m. **DIR:** Peter Sasdy. **CAST:** Christopher Lee, Linda Hayden, Geoffrey Keen, Anthony Higgins, Roy Kinnear, Ralph Bates, Gwen Watford, John Carson, Isla Blair. **1970**

TATIE DANIELLE ★★★1/2 While in the process of destroying the lives and home of her great-nephew and his sweet-natured wife, a cranky old lady manages to make them look like the culprits. This black comedy is exceedingly dark, and, therefore, not for all tastes. In French with English subtitles. Not rated; the film has profanity and nudity. 107m. **DIR:** Étienne Chatiliez. **CAST:** Tsilla Chelton, Catherine Jacob, Isabelle Nanty, Neige Dolsky, Eric Prat. **1991**

TATTLE TALE ★★1/2 C. Thomas Howell is a struggling actor whose ex-wife writes a "kiss and tell" book. Ally Sheedy is fabulous as the bitchy, egocentric hack, but Howell is lost amid silly disguises and a thin plot. Some clever moments but too unbelievable overall. Rated PG for profanity. 93m. **DIR:** Baz Taylor. **CAST:** C. Thomas Howell, Ally Sheedy. **1993**

TATTOO 🦃 Simply the most vile, reprehensible, sexist, and misogynistic piece of tripe ever released under the guise of a mainstream film. Bruce Dern is a demented tattoo artist who kidnaps Maud Adams to use as a "living tableau." Rated R for gross violence and kinky sex. 103m. **DIR:** Bob Brooks. **CAST:** Bruce Dern, Maud Adams, John Getz. **1981**

TATTOO CONNECTION 🦃 Typical chop-phooey fare. Rated R for violence, profanity, and nudity. 95m. **DIR:** Lee Tso-Nan. **CAST:** Jim Kelly. **1978**

TAXI BLUES ★★★★1/2 This Russian film details the volatile love-hate relationship between a fiercely independent, undisciplined Jewish jazz artist and a stern, muscular, narrow-minded cabdriver. It's as aggressive and stimulating as the hard-driving sax solos that permeate the soundtrack. In Russian with English subtitles. Not rated. 100m. **DIR:** Pavel Lounguine. **CAST:** Piotr Zaitchenko, Piotr Mamonov. **1991**

TAXI DANCERS 🦃 Small-town girl must turn to dancing in a seedy club when her Hollywood dreams fail to materialize. Not rated; contains adult situations, language, and violence. 97m. **DIR:** Norman Thaddeus Vane. **CAST:** Sonny Ladham, Robert Miano, Brittany McCrena, Michelle Hess. **1993**

TAXI DRIVER ★★★★★ Robert De Niro plays an alienated Vietnam-era vet thrust into the nighttime urban sprawl of New York City. In his despair after a romantic rejection by an attractive political campaign aide, he focuses on "freeing" a 12 year old prostitute by unleashing violent retribution on her pimp. It's unnerving and realistic. Rated R for violence and profanity. 113m. **DIR:** Martin Scorsese. **CAST:** Robert De Niro, Harvey Keitel, Cybill Shepherd, Jodie Foster, Peter Boyle. **1976 DVD**

TAXI ZUM KLO (TAXI TO THE TOILET) ★★★1/2 Sexually explicit film by and about Frank Ripploh, a restless and promiscuous gay elementary-school teacher in Berlin. Ripploh pulls absolutely no punches in his portrait of his sexual encounters, and that should be a fair warning. Get through the sex, however, and the humor will seem refreshing compared to a lot of other films that try to capture gay life. In German with English subtitles. Not rated; contains profanity and frank sexual content. 92m. **DIR:** Frank Ripploh. **CAST:** Frank Ripploh, Bernd Broaderup. **1981**

TAXING WOMAN, A ★★★ After exposing the world to the inner workings of the noodle business in *Tampopo*, director Juzo Itami focused on Japan's nasty Internal Revenue Service. Nobuko Miyamoto plays a hard-line tax inspector. Nicely offbeat. In Japanese with English subtitles. Not rated, with adult themes. 118m. **DIR:** Juzo Itami. **CAST:** Nobuko Miyamoto, Tsutomu Yamazaki. **1988 DVD**

TAXING WOMAN'S RETURN, A ★★★ In this follow-up to his 1987 hit, director Juzo Itami scores another high. This time the diligent heroine, tax inspector Nobuko Miyamoto, tackles a corrupt fundamentalist religious order. In Japanese with English subtitles. Rated R for nudity and violence. 127m. **DIR:** Juzo Itami. **CAST:** Nobuko Miyamoto. **1988**

TBONE N WEASEL ★★ Lame story follows the misadventures of two not-so-smart criminals. The film is played for laughs that never really come off. Stars try hard, but to no avail. 105m. **DIR:** Lewis Teague. **CAST:** Gregory Hines, Christopher Lloyd, Ned Beatty, Larry Hankin, Graham Jarvis. **1992**

TC 2000 🦃 In the year 2020, the atmosphere is gone, so the worthy inhabitants of the Earth live underground. A female cop is killed, turned into a powerful evil android, and sent to destroy all the surface people. Extremely bad acting. Rated R for violence and profanity. 92m. **DIR:** T.J. Scott. **CAST:** Bolo Yeung, Jalal Merhi, Billy Banks, Bobbie Phillips, Matthias Hues. **1993**

TCHAO PANTIN ★★★★1/2 Violent *film noir* about an ex-cop suffering from alienation as a result of the tragic death of his son from narcotics. He befriends a young stranger who deals heroin. The two form an odd relationship that eventually leads to disaster. This movie swept the French Oscars. In French with English subtitles. 94m. **DIR:** Claude Berri. **CAST:** Coluche, Richard Anconina, Philippe Léotard. **1985**

TEA AND SYMPATHY ★★★★ Well-crafted story (from the Broadway play) of an introverted student who finds understanding and love with the wife of the school's headmaster. Sensitively directed and with convincing acting, this is a must-see film. 123m. **DIR:** Vincente Minnelli. **CAST:** Deborah Kerr, John Kerr, Leif Erickson, Edward Andrews, Darryl Hickman, Dean Jones. **1959**

TEA FOR TWO ★★★ Doris Day planning to back and star in a musical play, finds she has lost her wealth in the stock market crash. To win a $25,000 bet, she must say "No" to every question for forty-eight hours, even those asked by amorous Gordon MacRae. Loosely based

on *No, No, Nanette*. 98m. **DIR:** David Butler. **CAST:** Doris Day, Gordon MacRae, Gene Nelson, Eve Arden, Billy DeWolfe, S. Z. Sakall. **1950**

TEA WITH MUSSOLINI ★★★ Odd assortment of English and American women in 1935 Florence, Italy, take illegitimate 7-year-old Luca into their fold after his mother dies. Tender if somewhat uneven piece of time travel as Mussolini's Fascists rise to power in the 1940s and Luca joins the Resistance. Rated PG. 116m. **DIR:** Franco Zeffirelli. **CAST:** Joan Plowright, Cher, Judi Dench, Maggie Smith, Lily Tomlin, Charlie Lucas. **1999 DVD**

TEACH ME TONIGHT ★★ The plot of this erotic thriller, about a woman's attempt to find the killer of her philandering boyfriend, is only there to space out the endless sex scenes (they're even more endless in the 93-minute unrated version). Rated R for profanity, nudity, and sexual situations. 74m. **DIR:** Rick Blaine. **CAST:** Judy Thompson, Kim Yates, Jack Becker. **1998 DVD**

TEACHERS ★★ This satirical look at a contemporary urban high school flunks as a film. Teachers will hate it because it's not serious enough; students will hate it because it's just terrible. It's no more interesting than a dull day in high school. Rated R for sexual innuendo, violence, and profanity. 106m. **DIR:** Arthur Hiller. **CAST:** Nick Nolte, JoBeth Williams, Judd Hirsch, Richard Mulligan, Ralph Macchio. **1984**

TEACHER'S PET ★★★ Winsome journalism instructor Doris Day fascinates and charms hardboiled city editor Clark Gable in this near plotless but most diverting comedy of incidents. The two are terrific, but Gig Young, as the teacher's erudite but liquor-logged boyfriend, is the one to watch. B&W; 120m. **DIR:** George Seaton. **CAST:** Clark Gable, Doris Day, Gig Young, Mamie Van Doren, Nick Adams, Jack Albertson, Marion Ross. **1958 DVD**

TEACHING MRS. TINGLE ★★ Three high-school students hold their meanest teacher hostage to teach her some humanity. This film panders shamelessly to the whining of spoiled mall rats (parents are clueless, teachers are evil, teenagers are pure, decent, and loyal). Helen Mirren easily outacts her callow costars, literally with her hands tied. Rated PG-13 for profanity and brief violence. 96m. **DIR:** Kevin Williamson. **CAST:** Helen Mirren, Katie Holmes, Marisa Coughlan, Barry Watson, Michael McKean. **1999 DVD**

TEAHOUSE OF THE AUGUST MOON, THE ★★★1/2 The post–World War II Americanizing of Okinawa gets sent up in faultless style in this screen version of the 1952 Broadway stage comedy hit. Marlon Brando is amusing as the clever Okinawan interpreter who binds it all together, but it is blustering Paul Ford, from the stage production, who comes knife-edge close to stealing this memorable film. 123m. **DIR:** Daniel Mann. **CAST:** Marlon Brando, Glenn Ford, Eddie Albert, Machiko Kyo, Paul Ford. **1956**

TEAMSTER BOSS: THE JACKIE PRESSER STORY ★★★1/2 Brian Dennehy's larger-than-life performance as self-made Teamster president Jackie Presser fuels this strawberry-lensed TV adaptation of James Neff's *Mobbed Up*. Abby Mann's script works far too hard at glossing over the controversial figure's unpleasant qualities. Rated R for violence, suggested sex, and profanity. 110m. **DIR:** Alastair Reid. **CAST:** Brian Dennehy, Jeff Daniels, Maria Conchita Alonso, Eli Wallach, Robert Prosky, Donald Moffat. **1992**

TEARAWAY ★★ In this film from Australia, the young streetwise son of an alcoholic father rescues a rich girl from a gang of lecherous toughs. Regrettably, tragic but predictable events cause this otherwise gritty study to degenerate into another ordinary tale of revenge. Rated R for violence and strong language. 100m. **DIR:** Bruce Morrison. **CAST:** Matthew Hunter, Mark Pilisi. **1987**

TED & VENUS ★★ Quirky, offbeat love story from director Bud Cort, who knows the territory well (he was Harold in *Harold & Maude*). This time he plays a poet whose fascination with the girl of his dreams forces him to go to extremes in order to get her attention. Some funny moments, but it's just too cordial to be crazy. Rated R for nudity and adult language. 100m. **DIR:** Bud Cort. **CAST:** Bud Cort, Carol Kane, James Brolin, Rhea Perlman, Andrea Martin, Martin Mull, Woody Harrelson. **1990**

TEEN ALIEN 🦃 A group of kids put on a Halloween spook show in an abandoned mining mill. Rated PG for mild violence. 88m. **DIR:** Peter Senelka. **CAST:** Vern Adix. **1988**

TEEN SORCERY 🦃 Full Moon Entertainment brings us this modern-day tale of *Sleeping Beauty* complete with Prince Charming and evil cheerleaders. Possibly good for those people with only half a brain. Rated PG for cheesy violence. 90m. **DIR:** Victoria Muspratt. **CAST:** A. J. Cook, Craig Olejnik, Lexa Doig. **1999**

TEEN VAMP 🦃 High school nerd is transformed into a vampire by a bloodsucking prostitute. Rated R for violence and profanity. 87m. **DIR:** Samuel Bradford. **CAST:** Clu Gulager, Karen Carlson. **1988**

TEEN WITCH ★★ Robyn Lively plays Louise, a high school wallflower who discovers on her sixteenth birthday that she has the powers of witchcraft. Some blandly catchy songs (by Larry Weir) are patched in for the music-video market. Rated PG-13 for mild profanity. 90m. **DIR:** Dorian Walker. **CAST:** Robyn Lively, Zelda Rubinstein, Dick Sargent, Shelley Berman. **1989**

TEEN WOLF 🦃 Pitifully bad film about a teenager who discovers he has the ability to change into a werewolf. Rated PG. 95m. **DIR:** Rod Daniel. **CAST:** Michael J. Fox, James Hampton, Scott Paulin. **1985**

TEEN WOLF, TOO 🦃 In this painfully dull sequel, the original Teen Wolf's cousin goes to college on a sports scholarship. Rated PG. 95m. **DIR:** Christopher Leitch. **CAST:** Jason Bateman, Kim Darby, John Astin, James Hampton. **1987**

TEENAGE BONNIE AND KLEPTO CLYDE ★★1/2 Minor hoods Scott Wolf and Maureen Flannigan chuck their comfortable lives for a little excitement. What starts off as teen rebellion quickly turns deadly as the pair rob and kill their way to mythic status. Rated R for violence, nudity, language, and adult situations. 90m. **DIR:** John Shepphird. **CAST:** Scott Wolf, Maureen Flannigan, Bentley Mitchum, Don Novello. **1993**

TEENAGE CONFIDENTIAL 🦃 A rip-off, advertised as "an in-depth study," wherein Mamie Van Doren introduces a couple of short, juvenile delinquency documentaries from the 1940s, followed by "Previews of Coming Attractions" of rock 'n' roll, high school, and biker movies that packed the drive-ins during the 1950s.

B&W/color; 60m. **DIR:** Various!. **1987**

TEENAGE EXORCIST ★★ When a reserved young woman (Brinke Stevens, who also wrote the screenplay) moves into a haunted house, a lustier side of her personality comes to the fore. Not rated; contains nudity, violence, and adult situations. 90m. **DIR:** Grant Austin Waldman. **CAST:** Brinke Stevens, Eddie Deezen, Oliver Darrow, Jay Richardson, Elena Sahagun, Robert Quarry, Michael Berryman. **1991**

TEENAGE MUTANT NINJA TURTLES ★★★★ Cowabunga, dude, the movie debut of the *Teenage Mutant Ninja Turtles* is a fun- and action-packed comic book for the screen. Leonardo, Raphael, Michelangelo, and Donatello come to the aid of a female newscaster (Judith Hoag) when her life is threatened by the minions of the evil Shredder. Rated PG for comic-book-style violence and vulgarity. 93m. **DIR:** Steve Barron. **CAST:** Judith Hoag, Elias Koteas. **1990 DVD**

TEENAGE MUTANT NINJA TURTLES II: THE SECRET OF THE OOZE ★★★1/2 The lean, green teens return to face their archenemy Shredder, and find the secret to their origins in the sewers of New York. David Warner costars as the professor who developed the toxic green ooze responsible for the Turtles' large size and superpowers. Rated PG for mild violence. 88m. **DIR:** Michael Pressman. **CAST:** Paige Turco, David Warner, Ernie Reyes Jr. **1991**

TEENAGE MUTANT NINJA TURTLES III ★★ This franchise has been taken to the well once too often. Although writer-director Stuart Gillard gets off to a good start by sending our youthful ninjas-on-the-half-shell back in time to feudal Japan, the setting is wasted on wafer-thin foes who don't even prompt our heroes to work up a sweat. Rated PG for comic-book violence. 95m. **DIR:** Stuart Gillard. **CAST:** Elias Koteas, Paige Turco, Stuart Wilson, Sab Shimono, Vivian Wu. **1993**

TEKWAR: THE ORIGINAL MOVIE ★★★ Telefilm was the springboard for syndicated series about an ex-cop, falsely accused of murder, who was sentenced to a cryogenic prison. Not rated; contains some violence. 92m. **DIR:** William Shatner. **CAST:** Greg Evigan, William Shatner, Sheena Easton, Eugene Clark. **1993**

TELEFON ★★★ In this good suspense film, Charles Bronson is a KGB agent who, with the help of the CIA's Lee Remick, is out to stop some preprogrammed Soviet spies from blowing up the United States. Rated PG. 102m. **DIR:** Don Siegel. **CAST:** Charles Bronson, Lee Remick, Donald Pleasence, John Mitchum, Patrick Magee. **1977**

TELEGRAPH TRAIL, THE ★★★1/2 Before moving on, John Wayne made a series of quality B Westerns for Warner Bros.—this film about the stringing of telegraph lines is one of the best. The scenes featuring Wayne's "miracle horse," Duke, do strain credibility, however. B&W; 54m. **DIR:** Tenny Wright. **CAST:** John Wayne, Marceline Day, Frank McHugh, Otis Harlan, Albert J. Smith, Yakima Canutt, Lafe McKee. **1933**

TELEPHONE, THE ★★ It's hard to like, but even harder to walk away from, this uneven comedy-drama. Whoopi Goldberg stars as an out-of-work actress who is more than a little nuts. Definitely for the midnight-movie junkie who will enjoy the bizarre ending. Rated R for profanity. 96m. **DIR:** Rip Torn. **CAST:** Whoopi Goldberg, Elliott Gould, Amy Wright, John Heard, Severn Darden. **1987**

TELEVISION PARTS HOME COMPANION ★★★ This is more of Mike Nesmith's *Elephant Parts* style of variety-show entertainment. Again, he has hilarious skits and mock commercials, as well as choreographed stories to accompany his songs. 40m. **DIR:** William Dear, Alan Myerson. **CAST:** Mike Nesmith, Joe Allain, Bill Martin. **1984**

TELL IT TO THE JUDGE ★★★ Robert Cummings tries to talk ex-wife Rosalind Russell into remarrying him, not Gig Young. Amiable comedy coasts on star power. B&W; 87m. **DIR:** Norman Foster. **CAST:** Rosalind Russell, Robert Cummings, Gig Young, Marie McDonald, Louise Beavers. **1949**

TELL IT TO THE MARINES ★★★ Lon Chaney Sr. is good in a rare nonhorror role as a marine sergeant training new recruits in the Philippines. Silent. B&W; 75m. **DIR:** George Hill. **CAST:** Lon Chaney Sr., William Haines, Warner Oland. **1926**

TELL ME A RIDDLE ★★★1/2 Melvyn Douglas and Lila Kedrova give memorable performances as an elderly married couple whose relationship has grown bitter. Their love for each other is rekindled when they take a cross-country trip. This poignant drama marked the directorial debut of actress Lee Grant. Rated PG. 94m. **DIR:** Lee Grant. **CAST:** Melvyn Douglas, Lila Kedrova, Brooke Adams, Dolores Dorn, Zalman King. **1980**

TELL-TALE HEART, THE ★★1/2 Fascinating, if extremely low-budget, study in sexual obsession and murder. A shy recluse, lured out of his dismal lifestyle by the new woman in his Victorian neighborhood, goes murderously mad when he spies her bedding down (shades of *Rear Window*!) with his best pal. B&W; 81m. **DIR:** Ernest Morris. **CAST:** Laurence Payne, Adrienne Corri, Dermot Walsh. **1961**

TELL THEM WILLIE BOY IS HERE ★★★ Robert Redford is a southwestern sheriff in the early days of this country. He is pursuing an Indian (Robert Blake) who is fleeing to avoid arrest. The story is elevated from a standard Western chase by the dignity and concern shown to the Indian's viewpoint. Rated PG. 96m. **DIR:** Abraham Polonsky. **CAST:** Robert Redford, Robert Blake, Katharine Ross. **1969**

TELLING LIES IN AMERICA ★★★★1/2 This is a gently sentimental coming-of-age saga set in 1961 at an expensive private Catholic high school where Hungarian-born Karchy comes under the spell of a slick radio deejay (Kevin Bacon, absolutely perfect), the nearest thing to an honest-to-God celebrity Cleveland kids might reasonably expect to meet. What follows is one young man's encounter with questionable ethics and the dawning awareness that ultimately compels him to do the right thing. Rated PG-13 for profanity and sexual content. 102m. **DIR:** Guy Ferland. **CAST:** Brad Renfro, Kevin Bacon, Calista Flockhart, Maximilian Schell, Paul Dooley. **1997 DVD**

TELLING YOU ★★ Dreadful tale of two college graduates who stand behind the counter of a pizzeria while their friends all go on to bigger and better things. Rated R for profanity and sexuality. 90m. **DIR:** Robert DeFranco. **CAST:** Jennifer Love Hewitt, Peter Facinelli, Richard Libertini, Rick Rossovich. **1998 DVD**

TEMP, THE ★★ There's been kids from hell. Cops from hell. Dates from hell. And nannies from hell. Now comes the temporary office assistant from you know where—a femme fatale way beyond bitch who is just as efficient and sexy as she may be ruthless and insane. More of a slick crowd teaser than an actual thriller. Rated R for language and violence. 100m. **DIR:** Tom Holland. **CAST:** Lara Flynn Boyle, Timothy Hutton, Dwight Schultz, Oliver Platt, Faye Dunaway. **1993 DVD**

TEMPEST (1928) ★★1/2 Set during the 1914 Bolshevik uprising in Russia, this richly romantic drama has army officer John Barrymore stepping out of place to court his aristocratic commandant's daughter. As a result, both are undone and must flee for their lives and love. Silent, with music track. B&W; 105m. **DIR:** Sam Taylor. **CAST:** John Barrymore, Camilla Horn, Louis Wolheim, George Fawcett. **1928**

TEMPEST (1982) 🦃 An architect has prophetic dreams. Rated PG; the film has nudity and profanity. 140m. **DIR:** Paul Mazursky. **CAST:** John Cassavetes, Gena Rowlands, Vittorio Gassman, Molly Ringwald, Susan Sarandon. **1982**

TEMPEST, THE (1983) ★★1/2 A slow-moving stage production of Shakespeare's tale of sorcery and revenge on a desolate island controlled by the mystical Prospero (Efrem Zimbalist Jr.). Zimbalist is interesting but very wooden in the role. A Bard Productions Ltd. release. 126m. **DIR:** William Woodman. **CAST:** Efrem Zimbalist Jr., William H. Bassett, Ted Sorel, Kay E. Kuter, Edward Edwards, Nicholas Hammond. **1983**

TEMPTATION ★★★ An ex-con (Jeff Fahey) gets his chance for revenge when the partner who left him for the cops ten years ago inadvertently hires him to captain his pleasure yacht. Loads of action and a couple of steamy love scenes make it fairly easy to overlook the film's Swiss-cheese plot. David Keith gives an exceptional performance as Fahey's Australian buddy. Rated R for violence, profanity, nudity, and sexual situations. 91m. **DIR:** Strathford Hamilton. **CAST:** Jeff Fahey, David Keith, Alison Doody, Philip Casnoff. **1994**

TEMPTATION OF A MONK ★★★★ An elaborate epic set in seventh-century China in which a pair of generals battle to the death and a beautiful princess (Joan Chen) becomes a destructive temptress. Grandly visual, stunningly powerful filmmaking. In Mandarin with English subtitles. Not rated, but features many bloody battle scenes. 118m. **DIR:** Clara Law. **CAST:** Joan Chen, Hsin Kuo Wu, Zhang Fengyi, Michael Lee, Lisa Lu. **1993 DVD**

TEMPTER, THE 🦃 Lurid Italian demonic-possession flick about a crippled woman who is the reincarnation of a witch. Rated R for profanity and violence. 96m. **DIR:** Alberto De Martino. **CAST:** Carla Gravina, Mel Ferrer, Arthur Kennedy. **1978**

TEMPTRESS ★★ The spirit of a mythical goddess invades the body of a sexy female photographer and all hell breaks loose. Not nearly as suspenseful, erotic, or entertaining as it should be. Rated R for profanity and sexuality. 93m. **DIR:** Lawrence Lanoff. **CAST:** Kim Delaney, Chris Sarandon, Corbin Bernsen, Ben Cross. **1995**

TEMPTRESS MOON ★★★1/2 Hardened gigolo in 1920s Shanghai specializes in blackmailing rich women. The ravishing-looking film needs more momentum and a few strategically placed emotional depth charges. In Mandarin with English subtitles. Rated R for drug use and intense sexual content. 115m. **DIR:** Chen Kaige. **CAST:** Leslie Cheung, Gong Li, Kevin Lin, Saifei He, Zhang Shi. **1997**

10 ★★★1/2 Ravel's "Bolero" enjoyed a renewed popularity, and Bo Derek rocketed to stardom because of this uneven but generally entertaining sex comedy, directed by Blake Edwards (*The Pink Panther*). Most of the film's funny moments come from the deftly timed physical antics of Dudley Moore, who plays a just-turned-40 songwriter who at long last meets the girl (Bo Derek) of his dreams—on her wedding day. Rated R. 122m. **DIR:** Blake Edwards. **CAST:** Dudley Moore, Bo Derek, Julie Andrews, Robert Webber. **1979 DVD**

TEN BENNY ★★1/2 Standard-issue drama about a young New Jersey salesman whose hopes of turning a tip on a racehorse into a nest egg for his future go awry when he loses. Too bad he borrowed the seed money from a hood. Rated R for language, violence, adult situations, and nudity. 98m. **DIR:** Eric Bross. **CAST:** Adrien Brody, Sybil Temchen, Tony Gillian, Michael Gallagher, Frank Vincent. **1996 DVD**

TEN COMMANDMENTS, THE (1923) ★★★ Master showman Cecil B. DeMille's monumental two-phase silent version of the Book of Exodus and the application of the Ten Commandments in modern life. Part One, set in ancient times, is in early color; Part Two, set in the modern (1923) period, is in black and white. Impressive special effects, including the parting of the Red Sea. In scope, this is the film that foreshadows DeMille's great spectacles of the sound era. B&W; 140m. **DIR:** Cecil B. DeMille. **CAST:** Theodore Roberts, Charles de Roche, Estelle Taylor, James Neill, Noble Johnson, Richard Dix, Rod La Rocque, Leatrice Joy, Nita Naldi. **1923**

TEN COMMANDMENTS, THE (1956) ★★★1/2 A stylish, visually stunning, epic-scale biblical study as only Cecil B. DeMille could make 'em (until William Wyler came along three years later with *Ben Hur*). Charlton Heston, as Moses, in charge of "God's people," holds the lengthy film together. Not rated; suitable for family viewing. 219m. **DIR:** Cecil B. DeMille. **CAST:** Charlton Heston, Yul Brynner, Edward G. Robinson, Cedric Hardwicke, John Derek, Anne Baxter, Debra Paget. **1956 DVD**

TEN DAYS WONDER ★★★★ One of Claude Chabrol's superb *hommages* to the American detective thriller. Originally titled *La Decade Prodigieuse*, it is based on one of Ellery Queen's finest psychological studies of a serial murderer. Typically, Chabrol is more interested in characterization and mood than in pacing and graphic violence. 100m. **DIR:** Claude Chabrol. **CAST:** Orson Welles, Marlene Jobert, Anthony Perkins, Michel Piccoli. **1972**

10 FROM YOUR SHOW OF SHOWS ★★★★ Ten skits from the early 1950s television program that set the pace for all variety shows. Granted, the style is dated and far from subtle, but as a joyful look at television's formative years, it can't be beat. Not rated. B&W; 92m. **DIR:** Max Liebman. **CAST:** Sid Caesar, Imogene Coca, Carl Reiner, Howard Morris, Louis Nye. **1973**

TEN LITTLE GALL FORCE/SCRAMBLE WARS ★★★ This animated double feature is a sound spoof of the genre in a "superdeformed" format (caricatures of animated characters). The first feature includes animated

"outtakes" of *Gall Force* and a live-action short about the story's creator Shonora Kenichi. In the second, characters from three different animation stories compete in a contest reminiscent of *Cannonball Run*. In Japanese with English subtitles. Not rated; contains nudity and violence. 67m. **DIR:** Yatagai Kenichi, Fukushima Hiroyuki. **1988**

TEN LITTLE INDIANS (1966) ★★★1/2 A good retelling of the Agatha Christie classic with ten complete strangers trapped in an Alpine chateau, one among them having murder in mind. B&W; 92m. **DIR:** George Pollock. **CAST:** Hugh O'Brian, Shirley Eaton, Fabian, Leo Genn, Stanley Holloway, Marianne Hoppe, Wilfrid Hyde-White, Daliah Lavi, Dennis Price, Mario Adorf. **1966**

TEN LITTLE INDIANS (1975) Absolutely dismal third version of the Agatha Christie classic. This one completely mucks up the plot, switching from an isolated island mansion to a hotel deep in the Iranian desert(!). Rated PG—mild violence. 98m. **DIR:** Peter Collinson. **CAST:** Oliver Reed, Richard Attenborough, Elke Sommer, Herbert Lom, Gert Fröbe. **1975**

TEN LITTLE INDIANS (1989) ★★ Agatha Christie's suspenseful whodunit loses much of its flair in this slow-moving, poorly acted rendition. A group of ten is systematically picked off at an isolated African campsite. Rated PG. 99m. **DIR:** Alan Birkinshaw. **CAST:** Donald Pleasence, Frank Stallone, Brenda Vaccaro. **1989**

10 MILLION DOLLAR GETAWAY, THE ★★★1/2 Doug Feiden's published account of the infamous Lufthansa robbery is transformed by scripter Christopher Canaan into a slick (made-for-cable) character study that unequivocally proves that crime does not pay. The excellent cast is led by John Mahoney. Rated PG-13. 93m. **DIR:** James A. Contner. **CAST:** John Mahoney, Joseph Carberry, Terrence Mann, Karen Young, Tony Lo Bianco. **1991**

10 RILLINGTON PLACE ★★★★ This bleak true-crime drama is based on one of England's most famous murder cases and was actually shot in the house and the neighborhood where the crimes took place. The seamy squalor of the surroundings perfectly mirrors the poverty of mind and soul that allowed John Christy to murder and remain undetected for over ten years. 111m. **DIR:** Richard Fleischer. **CAST:** Richard Attenborough, Judy Geeson, John Hurt, Andre Morell. **1971**

10 THINGS I HATE ABOUT YOU ★★★1/2 This engaging little film, which borrows heavily from Shakespeare's *Taming of the Shrew*, starts off like a slapstick teen comedy, but eventually becomes genuinely funny, compelling, and charming. Bianca has been told by their single-parent father that she cannot date until older sister Kat does... and no one expects that to happen until hell freezes over. Bianca and her new beau orchestrate a scheme whereby another school outcast is paid to squire Kat about town. What follows plays out with deft wit—and strong sexual chemistry—against a zesty collection of pop tunes. Rated PG-13 for profanity and crude sexual commentary. 94m. **DIR:** Gil Junger. **CAST:** Heath Ledger, Julia Stiles, Joseph Gordon Levitt, Larisa Oleynik, David Krumholtz, Andrew Keegan, Larry Miller, Susan May Pratt, Gabrielle Union. **1999 DVD**

TEN TO MIDNIGHT Old "Death Wish" himself goes up against a *Friday the 13th*–type killer. Rated R for nudity, profanity, and violence. 101m. **DIR:** J. Lee Thompson. **CAST:** Charles Bronson, Andrew Stevens, Lisa Eilbacher, Cosie Costa. **1983**

10 VIOLENT WOMEN Female coal miners land in jail after a jewel robbery and a cocaine deal go bad. Rated R for violence and a little nudity. 95m. **DIR:** Ted V. Mikels. **CAST:** Sherri Vernon, Dixie Lauren, Georgia Morgan. **1982 DVD**

TEN WANTED MEN ★★★1/2 Small Arizona landowner Richard Boone attempts to wrest control of the territory by framing cattle baron Randolph Scott's nephew. 80m. **DIR:** H. Bruce Humberstone. **CAST:** Randolph Scott, Richard Boone, Dennis Weaver, Lee Van Cleef, Skip Homeier, Leo Gordon. **1955**

TEN WHO DARED In 1869, Major John Wesley Powell and nine other explorers set out to explore the wild Colorado River. 92m. **DIR:** William Beaudine. **CAST:** Brian Keith, John Beal, James Drury, David Stollery. **1960**

TENANT, THE ★★★ Roman Polanski is superb in this cryptic thriller about a bumbling Polish expatriate in France who leases an apartment owned previously by a young woman who committed suicide. Increasingly, Polanski believes the apartment's tenants conspired demonically to destroy the woman and are attempting to do the same to him. Rated R. 125m. **DIR:** Roman Polanski. **CAST:** Roman Polanski, Melvyn Douglas, Shelley Winters. **1976**

TENDER COMRADE ★★★ This sentimental melodrama, in which Ginger Rogers ably portrays one of several wives left at home while their men are fighting in World War II, demonstrates that she was underrated as a dramatic actress. The film later attracted unwarranted controversy after its writer, Dalton Trumbo, and director, Edward Dmytryk, fell victim to the anticommunist blacklist. 102m. **DIR:** Edward Dmytryk. **CAST:** Ginger Rogers, Robert Ryan, Ruth Hussey. **1943**

TENDER MERCIES ★★★★★ Robert Duvall more than deserved his best-actor Oscar for this superb character study about a down-and-out country singer trying for a comeback. His Mac Sledge is a man who still has songs to sing, but barely the heart to sing them. That is, until he meets up with a sweet-natured widow (Tess Harper) who gives him back the will to live. Rated PG. 89m. **DIR:** Bruce Beresford. **CAST:** Robert Duvall, Tess Harper, Ellen Barkin. **1983 DVD**

TENDER TRAP, THE ★★★ Swinging bachelor Frank Sinatra takes aim at a young actress (Debbie Reynolds) who turns out less naïve (and more marriage-minded) than she seems. Sprightly stage-derived romantic comedy has clever dialogue, attractive stars, and a solid supporting cast. 111m. **DIR:** Charles Walters. **CAST:** Frank Sinatra, Debbie Reynolds, Celeste Holm, David Wayne, Carolyn Jones, Lola Albright. **1955**

TENDER YEARS, THE ★★1/2 The fight against cruelty to animals is at the heart of this sentimental film about a small-town minister who steals the dog his son loves, to save it from being used in illicit dogfighting. B&W; 81m. **DIR:** Harold Schuster. **CAST:** Joe E. Brown, Josephine Hutchinson, Charles Drake. **1948**

TENDRES COUSINES ★★ Okay soft-core sex comedy about two pubescent cousins. Directed by renowned photographer, David Hamilton. In French with English

subtitles. Rated R. 90m. **DIR:** David Hamilton. **CAST:** Thierry Tevini, Anja Shute. **1980**

TENNESSEE STALLION ★★★ Interesting background, beautiful photography, and more than competent acting save this otherwise ordinary action-adventure film set in the world of the Tennessee walking-horse show circuit. Jimmy Van Patten is excellent as a man who makes it to the big time with his outstanding horse and the help of the woman who loves him. 87m. **DIR:** Don Hulette. **CAST:** Audrey Landers, Judy Landers, James Van Patten. **1978**

TENNESSEE'S PARTNER ★★1/2 Allan Dwan directed this minor Western featuring Ronald Reagan as a stranger who steps into the middle of a fight between gamblers and ends up befriending one (John Payne). This is one of Payne's better roles. Good little drama; better than the title suggests. 87m. **DIR:** Allan Dwan. **CAST:** John Payne, Ronald Reagan, Rhonda Fleming, Coleen Gray. **1955 DVD**

TENTACLES 🦃 Rotten monster movie from Italy about a phony-looking octopus attacking and devouring some famous Hollywood stars. Rated PG. 90m. **DIR:** Ovidio Assonitis (Oliver Hellman). **CAST:** John Huston, Shelley Winters, Henry Fonda, Bo Hopkins, Cesare Danova. **1977**

10TH KINGDOM, THE ★★★ Sprawling TV miniseries attempts to incorporate traditional fantasy, fairy tales, and realism into one new whole and, for the most part, succeeds. Thanks in large part to offbeat casting (Camryn Manheim as a grown-up Snow White) and some dead-on casting (Ed O'Neill as the Troll King), this film captures a sense of wonder. The literate script lends a distinguished air to the proceedings as a young daughter and her father are whisked away into the world of the kingdoms (of which Earth is the tenth) and must find their way back. Recommended for fans of fantasy. Rated PG for violence, but suitable for the young. 480m. **DIR:** David Carson, Herbert Wise. **CAST:** Kimberly Williams, John Larroquette, Dianne Wiest, Ed O'Neill, Warwick Davis, Camryn Manheim, Rutger Hauer, Ann-Margret. **2000 DVD**

TENTH MAN, THE ★★★★ Superb made-for-TV adaptation of Graham Greene's novel starring Anthony Hopkins as a wealthy French attorney taken hostage by the Nazis during the occupation of France. When the French Resistance kills some Nazi officers, the Nazis order every tenth man held in prison executed in retaliation. Hopkins strikes a bargain when he becomes the tenth man. 87m. **DIR:** Jack Gold. **CAST:** Anthony Hopkins, Kristin Scott Thomas, Derek Jacobi, Cyril Cusack. **1992**

TENTH MONTH, THE ★★1/2 Tiresome overlong drama about a middle-aged divorcée who has an affair with a married man and becomes pregnant. Good performances by Carol Burnett and Keith Michell are the only bright spots in this made-for-TV film. 130m. **DIR:** Joan Tewkesbury. **CAST:** Carol Burnett, Keith Michell, Dina Merrill. **1979**

TENTH VICTIM, THE ★★★1/2 A weird little science-fiction film that has achieved minor cult status, thanks to droll performances and an intriguing plot taken from the novel by Robert Sheckley. The setting is the near future, and pop culture has embraced an assassination/hunt game with only one winner. Not rated, contains sexual situations. 92m. **DIR:** Elio Petri. **CAST:** Marcello Mastroianni, Ursula Andress, Elsa Martinelli, Massimo Serato. **1965 DVD**

TEOREMA ★★★ The title translates as *Theorem*, which indicates the mathematical style of this attack on bourgeois values. A handsome young man enters the home of a middle-class family, whose members are unable to cope with life after he leaves. In Italian with English subtitles. Not rated; contains strong sexual content. 93m. **DIR:** Pier Paolo Pasolini. **CAST:** Terence Stamp, Silvana Mangano, Massimo Girotti. **1968**

•TEQUILA BODY SHOTS ★★ While on a trip to Mexico, three friends find themselves caught between the realms of Earth and the afterlife, brought on by an old mystery and some magical alcohol. Maybe a few drinks could make watching this one a little more entertaining, but that's not very likely. Rated R for language, violence, and some substance abuse. 92m. **DIR:** Tony Shyu. **CAST:** Joey Lawrence, Dru Mouser, Nathan Anderson. **1999 DVD**

TEQUILA SUNRISE ★★★★1/2 Screenwriter Robert Towne *(Chinatown, The Last Detail)* takes an oft-used plot and makes it new. Childhood friends end up on opposite sides of the law with a beautiful woman the object of their affections. A fascinating and often surprising movie. Rated R for profanity, violence, suggested sex, and drug use. 116m. **DIR:** Robert Towne. **CAST:** Mel Gibson, Kurt Russell, Michelle Pfeiffer, Raul Julia. **1988 DVD**

TERESA'S TATTOO ★★★ Likable, familiar cast fleshes out this dark comedy about a kidnapping that goes haywire. When an accident kills their hostage, three goofball kidnappers must come up with a replacement or face the wrath of her gangster brother. The kidnappers find a dead ringer in college student Adrienne Shelly, with just one exception. The woman needs a tattoo in order to pull off the charade. The comic complications that ensue are moderately funny. Rated R for adult situations. 95m. **DIR:** Julie Cypher. **CAST:** C. Thomas Howell, Nancy McKeon, Adrienne Shelly, Lou Diamond Phillips, Jonathan Silverman, Casey Siemaszko. **1992**

TERMINAL BLISS ★★1/2 A slow-moving and utterly depressing story of a group of rich teenagers who overindulge in drugs and angst. Despite its deep undercurrent of despair, this is a watchable film that will have you worried about the future of our youth. Rated R for violence, profanity, and drug use. 93m. **DIR:** Jordan Alan. **CAST:** Luke Perry, Timothy Owen. **1990**

TERMINAL CHOICE ★★ If it's blood you want, you'll get your money's worth with this one—by the gallons! There's some real tension in this film about a hospital staff that secretly bets on the mortality of its patients—not exactly family entertainment. Rated R for nudity, language, and plenty of gore. 98m. **DIR:** Sheldon Larry. **CAST:** Joe Spano, Diane Venora, David McCallum, Robert Joy, Don Francks, Nicholas Campbell, Ellen Barkin. **1984**

•TERMINAL COUNTDOWN ★★ Somewhere in the jungles of South America, a secret U.S. nuclear missile has started countdown on its own. Only an elite commando has the skills and power to stop it, but can he get there in time? Once again Louis Gossett Jr. shines in a role that is far beneath him while Malcolm McDowell

chews scenery so thoroughly you may want to check for holes in your TV screen afterwards. Rated R for violence, language, and sexuality. 104m. **DIR:** Richard Pepin. **CAST:** Louis Gossett Jr., Jaimz Woolvett, Ed O'Ross, Sarah Chalke, Malcolm McDowell. **1999 DVD**

TERMINAL ENTRY ★★ This *War Games* clone is only moderately entertaining. Three teenage couples tap into a computer game called Terminal Entry. It turns out that the game is real and they're caught in the middle of a U.S. antiterrorist strike force and foreign invaders. Rated R for nudity and violence. 95m. **DIR:** John Kincade. **CAST:** Edward Albert, Paul Smith, Yaphet Kotto, Patrick Labyorteaux. **1986**

TERMINAL IMPACT ★★ A pair of federal marshals find themselves battling a group of genetically-engineered and computer-enhanced superwarriors when they try to find a missing news reporter. Bad performances, sloppy direction, and corny writing overwhelm the dazzling fire effects and stunts that save this film from getting a turkey. Rated R for violence and profanity. 94m. **DIR:** Yossi Wein. **CAST:** Frank Zagarino, Bryan Genesse, Jennifer Miller, Ian Roberts, Justin Illusion, Michael Brunner. **1995**

TERMINAL ISLAND 🦃 Trite piece of exploitation. Rated R. 88m. **DIR:** Stephanie Rothman. **CAST:** Phyllis Davis, Tom Selleck, Don Marshall, Marta Kristen. **1977**

TERMINAL JUSTICE ★★★ Clever plotting lifts this futuristic action saga above its genre cousins. Loner cop Lorenzo Lamas tracks a particularly nasty criminal fronting a new black-market sensation: cloned lovers who won't care how they're abused. The emphasis is on high-tech gadgetry rather than graphic violence, and that's a nice switch. Rated R for profanity, nudity, simulated sex, and violence. 95m. **DIR:** Rick King. **CAST:** Lorenzo Lamas, Chris Sarandon, Kari Wuhrer, Peter Coyote. **1995**

TERMINAL JUSTICE, CYBERTECH P.D. ★★ In the future, a special division of police is formed to prevent the misuse of virtual reality. Dull and just plain silly. Rated R for profanity, nudity, and violence. 94m. **DIR:** Rick King. **CAST:** Lorenzo Lamas, Peter Coyote, Chris Sarandon. **1995**

TERMINAL MAN, THE ★★ A dreary adaptation of the crackling novel by Michael Crichton, although George Segal tries hard to improve the film's quality. He stars as a paranoid psychotic who undergoes experimental surgery designed to quell his violent impulses; unfortunately (and quite predictably), he becomes even worse. Rated R for violence. 104m. **DIR:** Mike Hodges. **CAST:** George Segal, Joan Hackett, Jill Clayburgh. **1974**

TERMINAL VELOCITY ★★★1/2 A spectacular stunt in which a daredevil sky diver attempts a midair rescue—by opening the trunk of a plummeting automobile—is one of the key elements that help save this big, dumb but enjoyable espionage thriller. Entertaining for those willing to turn off their logic centers and go with the flow. Rated PG-13 for violence and profanity. 100m. **DIR:** Deran Sarafian. **CAST:** Charlie Sheen, Nastassja Kinski, James Gandolfini, Christopher McDonald, Gary Bullock, Hans R. Howes, Mario Van Peebles, Richard Sarafian. **1994 DVD**

TERMINAL VIRUS 🦃 This poverty-row quickie, about a post-apocalyptic virus that has rendered sexual contact between men and women fatal to both, is just another dumb excuse for women to shed clothes and men to shoot guns. Rated R for nudity, rape, violence, profanity, and simulated sex. 81m. **DIR:** Dan Golden. **CAST:** James Brolin, Bryan Genesse, Kehli O'Byrne, Elena Sahagun, Richard Lynch. **1995**

TERMINATOR, THE ★★★1/2 In this science-fiction–time-travel adventure, Arnold Schwarzenegger stars as a cyborg (part man, part machine) sent from the future to present-day Los Angeles to murder a woman (Linda Hamilton). Her offspring will play an important part in the world from which the killer came. Michael Biehn is the rebel soldier sent to thwart Schwarzenegger's plans. Rated R for nudity, simulated sex, violence, and profanity. 108m. **DIR:** James Cameron. **CAST:** Arnold Schwarzenegger, Linda Hamilton, Michael Biehn. **1984 DVD**

TERMINATOR 2: JUDGMENT DAY ★★★★★ A rip-roaring juggernaut of a thriller that far surpasses the original *Terminator*. What elevates this one are elements you may not expect: a fascinating continuation of the original time-travel plot and an engrossing human story about the conflict between man and machine. Rated R, with strong violence and profanity. 135m. **DIR:** James Cameron. **CAST:** Arnold Schwarzenegger, Linda Hamilton, Robert Patrick, Joe Morton, Edward Furlong. **1991 DVD**

TERMINI STATION ★★★1/2 Mom's a drunk, her daughter can't sustain relationships, and her son will sacrifice anything to get a promotion. Probing into this dysfunctional family's past reveals the root of everyone's problems. Colleen Dewhurst is terrific as the formerly passionate woman drowning her loneliness in a bottle. Not rated; this Canadian film contains profanity and violence. 105m. **DIR:** Allan Winton King. **CAST:** Colleen Dewhurst, Megan Follows, Gordon Clapp. **1989**

TERMS OF ENDEARMENT ★★★★ This stylish soap opera, written, produced, and directed by James L. Brooks, covers thirty years in the lives of a Houston matron, played by Shirley MacLaine, and her daughter, played by Debra Winger, who marries an English teacher with a wandering eye. Jack Nicholson is also on hand, to play MacLaine's neighbor, an astronaut with the wrong stuff. Rated PG for profanity and suggested sex. 132m. **DIR:** James L. Brooks. **CAST:** Shirley MacLaine, Debra Winger, Jack Nicholson, Danny DeVito, Jeff Daniels. **1983**

TERRIFIED ★★1/2 A young woman is stalked by an assailant she can never quite see. Kudos to the makers of this thriller for having the sense to emulate such classic intelligent shockers as *Repulsion* and *Carnival of Souls*. Too bad the film never lives up to its potential. Rated R for profanity, violence, and sexual situations. 95m. **DIR:** James Merendino. **CAST:** Heather Graham, Lisa Zane, Rustam Branaman, Tom Breznahan, Max Perlich, Richard Lynch. **1996 DVD**

TERROR, THE 🦃 This is an incomprehensible sludge of mismatched horror scenes even Boris Karloff can't save. 81m. **DIR:** Roger Corman. **CAST:** Boris Karloff, Jack Nicholson, Sandra Knight. **1963 DVD**

TERROR ABOARD ★★★ The grim events on a derelict yacht boarded by salvagers reveal a man willing to kill his passengers and crew to escape the justice awaiting him at the end of his voyage. The cold-blooded killer al-

most does away with all the witnesses and escapes his fate. Almost. Sometimes gruesome, precode independent is a mystery-horror-thriller with running humor that works well on all levels. B&W; 67m. **DIR:** Paul Sloane. **CAST:** John Halliday, Charlie Ruggles, Shirley Grey, Neil Hamilton, Verree Teasdale, Jack LaRue, Stanley Fields, Eila Bennett. **1933**

TERROR AT LONDON BRIDGE ★★ Jack the Ripper is mystically resurrected in contemporary Arizona and goes on a killing spree in the British-style tourist trap. Only one man suspects that this is more than the work of a serial killer, and he must convince someone before it's too late. Predictable made-for-TV movie with some schlock gore effects. 96m. **DIR:** E. W. Swackhamer. **CAST:** David Hasselhoff, Stepfanie Kramer, Randolph Mantooth, Adrienne Barbeau. **1985**

TERROR AT THE OPERA ★★1/2 In this stylish and suspenseful Italian production, a beautiful young diva is terrorized by a hooded maniac who makes her watch him murder the members of her opera company. An intense musical score, realistic effects, and the killer's brutality make this a disturbing experience. The movie fizzles out with a senseless conclusion. Not rated, but with extreme violence and some nudity. 107m. **DIR:** Dario Argento. **CAST:** Cristina Marsillach, Ian Charleson, Daria Nicolodi. **1991**

TERROR AT THE RED WOLF INN (TERROR HOUSE) ★★★ This is a sometimes ghoulishly funny horror-comedy about a college student who is chosen as the winner of a free vacation at an inn owned by a sweet old couple. Not all of the scenes work, but we guarantee it will give you the willies and the sillies. Rated R. (Also known as *The Folks at the Red Wolf Inn* and *Terror House*.) 98m. **DIR:** Bud Townsend. **CAST:** Linda Gillin, Arthur Space, John Neilson, Mary Jackson. **1972**

TERROR BY NIGHT ★★★ Penultimate entry in the Rathbone/Bruce Sherlock Holmes series, with the master sleuth and his loyal companion up against a series of murders on a train bound from London to Edinburgh. The culprit ultimately turns out to be Col. Sebastian Moran, but you'll have to watch the film to discover which of the passengers he impersonates! B&W; 69m. **DIR:** Roy William Neill. **CAST:** Basil Rathbone, Nigel Bruce, Alan Mowbray, Renee Godfrey, Billy Bevan, Dennis Hoey. **1946 DVD**

TERROR CREATURES FROM THE GRAVE ★★1/2 Grade-Z title tacked onto what is actually a fairly stately, decorous Barbara Steele vehicle from Italy. She plays the wife of an occult scientist who summons zombies from the grounds of their Gothic estate. Atmospheric and fun. B&W; 83m. **DIR:** Ralph Zucker (Massimo Pupillo). **CAST:** Barbara Steele, Walter Brandi. **1966**

TERROR FROM THE YEAR 5,000 ★★ Not-bad cheapjack sci-fi about contemporary scientists who bring a woman from A.D. 5,000 to their own time and soon regret it. Fast-paced. B&W; 74m. **DIR:** Robert Gurney Jr. **CAST:** Ward Costello, Joyce Holden, Salome Jens. **1958**

TERROR IN PARADISE Grade-Z thriller finds an American couple battling terrorists on a small island getaway. Paradise lost! Rated R for nudity and violence. 81m. **DIR:** Peer J. Oppenheimer. **CAST:** Gary Lockwood, Joanna Pettet, David Anthony Smith, Leslie Ryan, David McKnight. **1992**

TERROR IN THE HAUNTED HOUSE ★★★ Although the title of this movie makes it sound as if it's a horror film, it is actually a psychological thriller along the Hitchcock line. It is the story of a young newlywed woman who has a recurring nightmare about a house she has never seen. She fears that something in the attic will kill her. The terror starts when her new husband takes her from Switzerland, where she has been since childhood, to the United States and . . . the house in her horrid dream. 90m. **DIR:** Harold Daniels. **CAST:** Gerald Mohr, Cathy O'Donnell. **1958 DVD**

TERROR IN THE SWAMP A Sasquatch-like creature is stalking the swamp. Rated PG for violence. 87m. **DIR:** Joe Catalanotto. **CAST:** Billie Holiday. **1984**

TERROR IN THE WAX MUSEUM ★★ The all-star cast from yesteryear looks like a sort of Hollywood wax museum. Their fans will suffer through this unsuspenseful murder mystery. Rated PG. 93m. **DIR:** Georg Fenady. **CAST:** Ray Milland, Broderick Crawford, Elsa Lanchester, Maurice Evans, Shani Wallis, John Carradine, Louis Hayward, Patric Knowles. **1973**

TERROR OF MECHAGODZILLA ★★ Another outlandish Godzilla epic from the 1970s with the big guy battling his own robot double, Mechagodzilla. Nothing special, but a lot of flashy effects and explosions. As always, the kids will love it. Rated G. 89m. **DIR:** Inoshiro Honda. **CAST:** Katsuhiko Sasaki. **1978 DVD**

TERROR OF THE TONGS, THE ★★★ In 1910 Hong Kong, sea captain Geoffrey Toone's daughter is killed by Christopher Lee's Red Dragon Tong. Competent, atmospheric revenge adventure. Not rated; contains violence. 80m. **DIR:** Anthony Bushell. **CAST:** Christopher Lee, Geoffrey Toone, Yvonne Monlaur, Marne Maitland. **1961**

TERROR OF TINY TOWN, THE The definitive all-midget Western, with action, gunplay, romance, and a happy ending to boot. B&W; 63m. **DIR:** Sam Newfield. **CAST:** Billy Curtis, Yvonne Moray, Little Billy. **1938**

TERROR ON ALCATRAZ A group of teenagers split off from a tour of a former prison and end up locked in overnight. Not rated; contains violence. 96m. **DIR:** Philip Marcus. **CAST:** Aldo Ray. **1987**

TERROR ON THE 40TH FLOOR ★★ A typical disaster film, this deals with a skyscraper fire. Not rated. 100m. **DIR:** Jerry Jameson. **CAST:** John Forsythe, Joseph Campanella, Don Meredith. **1974 DVD**

TERROR OUT OF THE SKY ★★ This made-for-television film is a sequel to *The Savage Bees* (1976). Here two bee experts and a gung ho pilot try everything to stop another infestation of the flying killers in the United States. Stick with the original. 100m. **DIR:** Lee H. Katzin. **CAST:** Efrem Zimbalist Jr., Dan Haggerty, Tovah Feldshuh, Lonny Chapman, Ike Eisenmann, Steve Franken. **1978**

TERROR SQUAD ★★★ Better-than-average action movie about small-town Indiana police chief Chuck Connors battling Libyan terrorists. This offers some thrills and style despite the obvious low budget. Not rated. 92m. **DIR:** Peter Maris. **CAST:** Chuck Connors, Kerry Brennan. **1987**

TERROR STALKS THE CLASS REUNION ★★ The closing of a school on a German army base attracts a

couple of psychos, one of whom still has a deadly crush on a former teacher. Geraint Wyn Davies captures Kate Nelligan, chains her to his wall, and plans their wedding. This Mary Higgins Clark story is clichéd, but Nelligan's performance is interesting. Rated PG for violence. 95m. **DIR:** Clive Donner. **CAST:** Jennifer Beals, Kate Nelligan, Geraint Wyn Davies. **1992**

TERROR TRACT ★★1/2 This omnibus of three horror stories stars John Ritter as a real estate agent trying to unload a trio of houses with blood-soaked pasts. A young newlywed couple looking for their first home together sets the stage for the vignettes. The cast is fun to watch, especially Bryan Cranston squaring off against his daughter's pet monkey. Ritter rises to the occasion, delivering a maniacal performance. Rated R for violence. 97m. **DIR:** Lance W. Dreesen, Clint Hutchison. **CAST:** John Ritter, Bryan Cranston, Marcus Bagwell, Will Estes, Rachel York. **2000 DVD**

TERROR TRAIN ★★★★ This is perhaps the best slasher film made in the eighties. The story involves a New Year's Eve frat party taking place on a moving train, with everyone having a great time until students start showing up murdered. This film relies on true suspense and good performances for its thrills. Rated R for violence. 97m. **DIR:** Roger Spottiswoode. **CAST:** Ben Johnson, Jamie Lee Curtis, Hart Bochner, David Copperfield. **1980**

TERROR VISION ★★★ An imaginative spoof of sci-fi films, with a hip slant. A family of swinging yuppies accidentally beam down a hostile alien through their satellite dish. Horror fans will be delighted. Rated R for violence and adult situations. 84m. **DIR:** Ted Nicolaou. **CAST:** Diane Franklin, Gerrit Graham, Mary Woronov, Chad Allen. **1986**

TERROR WITHIN, THE ★★1/2 A moderately scary terror film in the *Alien* mold. A group of scientists deep underground are the only people left after a plague wipes out mankind. Rated R for violence and profanity. 89m. **DIR:** Thierry Notz. **CAST:** George Kennedy, Andrew Stevens. **1988 DVD**

TERROR WITHIN 2, THE It's sort of *Alien* meets *Mad Max Beyond Thunderdome* this time around as scientists battle superhuman mutants and a killer virus. Dopey. Rated R for nudity, profanity, and violence. 89m. **DIR:** Andrew Stevens. **CAST:** Andrew Stevens, Stella Stevens, Chick Vennera, R. Lee Ermey, Burton Gilliam. **1990**

TERRORIST, THE ★★★★1/2 A young guerrilla fighter in some unnamed struggle for independence volunteers for a suicide mission to assassinate an important politician, but as the appointed day draws near she begins to doubt her dedication for the cause. Writer-director Santosh Sivan uses his well-constructed story, evocative photography, and the expressive face of Ayesha Dharkar in the title role to draw us into the thoughts of this young woman as she prepares herself for a martyr's death. In Hindi with English subtitles. Not rated; contains brief violence. 95m. **DIR:** Santosh Sivan. **CAST:** Ayesha Dharkar, Vinshwa, Bhanu Prakash, Sonu Sisupal, Vishnu Vardhan. **1998 DVD**

TERRORISTS, THE ★★★★ Solid suspense-thriller has Sean Connery as the bullheaded commander of Norway's national security force, which is galvanized into action when a group of English terrorists takes over the British embassy. Rated PG for violence. 100m. **DIR:** Caspar Wrede. **CAST:** Sean Connery, Ian McShane, James Maxwell, Isabel Dean, Jeffrey Wickham, John Quentin, Robert Harris. **1975**

TERRORNAUTS, THE ★★ A British scientist succeeds in contacting an alien civilization. They beam the entire building in which he works to their galaxy. British science fiction tends to be talky, and this is no exception. 75m. **DIR:** Montgomery Tully. **CAST:** Simon Oates, Zena Marshall, Charles Hawtrey, Max Adrian. **1967**

TERRY FOX STORY, THE ★★★ This made-for-HBO film chronicles the "Marathon of Hope" undertaken by amputee Terry Fox (Eric Fryer), who jogged 3,000 miles across Canada before collapsing in Ontario. Based on a true story, this uplifting film is helped by solid performances, direction, and writing. 96m. **DIR:** Ralph L. Thomas. **CAST:** Eric Fryer, Robert Duvall, Chris Makepeace, Rosalind Chao, Michael Zelniker. **1983**

TESS ★★★★1/2 A hypothetically beautiful adaptation of Thomas Hardy's late-nineteenth-century novel *Tess of the D'Urbervilles*, this is director Roman Polanski's finest artistic achievement. Nastassja Kinski is stunning as the country girl who is "wronged" by a suave aristocrat and the man she marries. The story unfolds at the pace of a lazy afternoon stroll, but Polanski's technical skills and the cinematography are spellbinding. Rated PG. 170m. **DIR:** Roman Polanski. **CAST:** Nastassja Kinski, Peter Firth, John Bett. **1979**

TEST OF LOVE, A ★★ This tearjerker, taken from the Australian bestselling novel *Annie's Coming Out*, vividly displays the love and determination a therapist (Angela Punch McGregor) has in fighting for the rights of Anne O'Farrell, a severely disabled teenager who was misdiagnosed as being retarded. Yet the makers of this movie lack the finesse it takes to make the antagonists of this story more than one-dimensional. Rated PG for profanity. 93m. **DIR:** Gil Brealey. **CAST:** Angela Punch McGregor, Drew Forsythe, Tina Arhondis. **1984**

TEST PILOT ★★★1/2 A top-notch cast playing believable characters made this drama of daredevils who try out new aircraft a big winner with critics and at the box office as World War II loomed. Cinematographer Ray June's aerial sequences are stunning. One of the biggest hits in MGM history. B&W; 118m. **DIR:** Victor Fleming. **CAST:** Clark Gable, Spencer Tracy, Myrna Loy, Marjorie Main, Lionel Barrymore, Louis Jean Heydt. **1938**

TESTAMENT ★★★★★ In its own quiet, unspectacular way, this film tells a simple story about what happens to one family when World War III begins and ends in a matter of minutes. Jane Alexander is superb as the mother attempting to cope with the unthinkable, and this fine movie is one you won't soon forget. Rated PG. 90m. **DIR:** Lynne Littman. **CAST:** Jane Alexander, William Devane, Ross Harris, Roxana Zal, Lukas Haas, Lila Kedrova, Leon Ames, Kevin Costner, Rebecca DeMornay. **1983**

TESTAMENT OF DR. CORDELIER, THE ★★★1/2 This is the great Jean Renoir's exploration of the Jekyll/Hyde theme, and of interest primarily for that unique departure. Made for French TV but released to theaters, it has a certain flatness that belies its director's talent. The transformation scenes, however, have an almost transcendent energy. B&W; 74m. **DIR:** Jean Renoir. **CAST:** Jean-Louis Barrault. **1959**

TESTAMENT OF DR. MABUSE ★★★1/2 In this sequel to *Dr. Mabuse the Gambler* by Thea Von Harboll and the director Fritz Lang, the infamous criminal mastermind dies in an asylum, and his assistant takes over his identity. It's a fast-moving picture, said by Lang to be a diatribe against Adolf Hitler. Whatever it is, it rates as slick entertainment. B&W; 122m. **DIR:** Fritz Lang. **CAST:** Rudolf Klein-Rogge, Otto Wernicke. **1933**

TESTAMENT OF ORPHEUS, THE ★★★ Jean Cocteau's last film, it marks the final installment of an Orpheus Trilogy, began with *The Blood of the Poet* (1930) and continued with *Orpheus* (1949). While its nonlinear sequence of events is quite incomprehensible, the fifteen episodes are generally concerned with an eighteenth-century poet (Jean Cocteau) who dies and is reborn into modern times. In French with English subtitles. 80m. **DIR:** Jean Cocteau. **CAST:** Jean Cocteau, Jean Marais. **1959 DVD**

TETSUO: THE IRON MAN ★★★ There's hardly any story in this hyperkinetic cult hit about an office worker mutating into a part-human, part-metal being. Grotesque makeup, stop-action animation, and time-lapse photography make this the perfect visual equivalent of the industrial-music soundtrack. In Japanese with English subtitles. B&W; 67m. **DIR:** Shinya Tsukamoto. **CAST:** Tomoroh Taguchi, Kei Fujiwara. **1989 DVD**

TETSUO II: BODY HAMMER ★★1/2 Less a sequel than a variant on the same film, *Tetsuo II* has more of a plot as a frustrated "salary man" is driven by the pressures of Tokyo life to mutate into a half-metal being. As in the first film, the imagery is wildly bizarre, but a little of this goes a long, long way. Not rated; contains strong violence, nudity, and sexual situations. In Japanese with English subtitles. 90m. **DIR:** Shinya Tsukamoto. **CAST:** Tomoroh Taguchi, Nodu Kanaoka, Shinya Tsukamoto. **1991 DVD**

TEVYE ★★★1/2 The stories of writer Sholem Aleichem that were later adapted for the stage and film hit *Fiddler on the Roof* also inspired this feature made for the once-flourishing Yiddish film industry that operated out of New York. Despite some technical limitations and hammy acting, it's worth seeing as a peek into the past, with nineteenth-century Russia re-created by people who came to America from there. In Yiddish with English subtitles. B&W; 93m. **DIR:** Maurice Schwartz. **CAST:** Maurice Schwartz, Miriam Riselle. **1939**

TEX ★★★★1/2 Matt Dillon, Jim Metzler, and Ben Johnson star in this superb coming-of-age adventure about the struggles and conflicts of two teenage brothers growing up in the Southwest without parental guidance. Rated PG for violence and mature situations. 103m. **DIR:** Tim Hunter. **CAST:** Matt Dillon, Jim Metzler, Ben Johnson, Emilio Estevez, Meg Tilly. **1982 DVD**

TEX AND THE LORD OF THE DEEP ★★ Based on the Italian cartoon-character Tex Willer. Tex fights an Indian uprising spurred on by a medicine man who has discovered a glowing green rock that turns people into instant mummies. Good performances by spaghetti Western veterans Giuliano Gemma and William Berger are not enough to overcome the concept. Not rated, contains violence. 90m. **DIR:** Duccio Tessari. **CAST:** Giuliano Gemma, William Berger, Carlo Mucari, Isabel Russinova, Aldo Sambrell. **1985**

TEXAS (1941) ★★★ Friends William Holden and Glenn Ford are rivals for the affections of Claire Trevor in this lively, action-jammed Western pitting cattleman against cattle rustler. It might have been an epic, but a cost-conscious producer kept a tight rein. Good, though! B&W; 93m. **DIR:** George Marshall. **CAST:** William Holden, Glenn Ford, Claire Trevor, George Bancroft, Edgar Buchanan, Raymond Hatton. **1941**

TEXAS (1994) ★★1/2 In an interesting twist, this two-part James A. Michener miniseries about the founding of our twenty-eighth state debuted on video before going to television. A $12 million historical soap opera, it's chock-full of romance, politics, and adventure, but never feels gritty enough. Perhaps it's those nudie shots intercut with the battle scenes. Not rated; contains profanity, violence, and nudity. 90m. **DIR:** Richard Lang. **CAST:** Maria Conchita Alonso, Benjamin Bratt, Patrick Duffy, Chelsea Field, Anthony Michael Hall, Stacy Keach, David Keith, John Schneider, Grant Show, Randy Travis, Rick Schroder. **1994 DVD**

TEXAS ACROSS THE RIVER ★★1/2 Low-brow Western comedy has the dubious distinction of being the only movie to feature Joey Bishop as an Indian. That said, the film was a sizable hit and has its fans, despite inept postproduction work that is glaringly obvious on the small screen. A Spanish nobleman, officer Peter Graves, and a con-man save a small Texas settlement from an inept Comanche tribe. 101m. **DIR:** Michael Gordon. **CAST:** Dean Martin, Alain Delon, Rosemary Forsyth, Joey Bishop, Tina Marquand, Peter Graves, Michael Ansara, Andrew Prine, Roy Barcroft. **1966**

TEXAS CARNIVAL ★★★ When down-and-out carnival workers, Red Skelton and Esther Williams are mistaken for brother and sister cattle millionaires, they go along with the mix-up. 77m. **DIR:** Charles Walters. **CAST:** Esther Williams, Red Skelton, Howard Keel, Ann Miller, Keenan Wynn. **1951**

TEXAS CHAINSAW MASSACRE, THE ★★★ This, the first film about a cannibalistic maniac by horror specialist Tobe Hooper, went pretty much unnoticed in its original release. That's probably because it sounds like the run-of-the-mill drive-in exploitation fare. While it was made on a very low budget, it nevertheless has been hailed as a ground-breaking genre work by critics and film buffs and became a cult classic. Rated R for extreme violence. 83m. **DIR:** Tobe Hooper. **CAST:** Marilyn Burns, Gunnar Hansen, Edwin Neal. **1974 DVD**

TEXAS CHAINSAW MASSACRE 2, THE ★★1/2 Leatherface is back! In fact, so is most of the family in this maniacal sequel. Dennis Hopper stars as a retired lawman out to avenge the gruesome murder of his nephew, and Caroline Williams plays the disc jockey who helps him locate the butchers. Not rated, but loaded with repulsive gore. 95m. **DIR:** Tobe Hooper. **CAST:** Dennis Hopper, Caroline Williams. **1986 DVD**

TEXAS CHAINSAW MASSACRE: THE NEXT GENERATION ★★ Virtual remake of Tobe Hooper's trend-setting horror–thriller is most notable as the springboard from which current hot stars Matthew McConaughey and Renee Zellweger made their first leap into film. Instead of bringing anything new to the party, writer-director Kim Henkel completely apes Hooper's film, this time in color. Rated R for language and violence. 93m.

DIR: Kim Henkel. **CAST:** Matthew McConaughey, Renee Zellweger, Robert Jacks. **1994 DVD**

TEXAS CYCLONE ★★★★ An easygoing cowpoke (Tim McCoy) is mistaken for a straight-shooting rancher and sticks around to help the rancher's wife (Shirley Grey) fight off cattle rustlers. A top-notch McCoy gets some solid support from a couple of newcomers, John Wayne and Walter Brennan. B&W; 63m. **DIR:** D. Ross Lederman. **CAST:** Tim McCoy, Shirley Grey, John Wayne, Walter Brennan, Wheeler Oakman, Mary Gordon. **1932**

TEXAS GUNS ★★★ Enjoyable romp from veteran Western helmer Burt Kennedy, who lassos a bevy of old stable hands to tell the tale of a group of aging train robbers whose efforts are thwarted by a senior citizen posse and a young upstart played by Shaun Cassidy. Made-for-television film also known as *Once Upon a Texas Train*. 100m. **DIR:** Burt Kennedy. **CAST:** Willie Nelson, Richard Widmark, Shaun Cassidy, Angie Dickinson, Chuck Connors, Stuart Whitman. **1988**

TEXAS JOHN SLAUGHTER: STAMPEDE AT BITTERCREEK ★★1/2 Former Texas Ranger John Slaughter is falsely accused of rustling as he attempts to drive his cattle into New Mexico despite threats from a rival rancher and his hired gun. Tom Tryon is ruggedly heroic in this Disney adventure Western culled from episodes originally featured on *Walt Disney Presents* from 1958 to 1962. 52m. **DIR:** Harry Keller. **CAST:** Tom Tryon, Harry Carey Jr., Adeline Harris, Annette Gorman, Betty Lynn. **1962**

TEXAS LADY ★★ An out-of-her-element Claudette Colbert is a crusading newspaper editor in the Old West. If you're a Western fan, you'll like it. 86m. **DIR:** Tim Whelan. **CAST:** Claudette Colbert, Barry Sullivan, John Litel. **1955**

TEXAS MASQUERADE ★★★★ Hopalong Cassidy masquerades as an eastern Milquetoast to get the goods on badmen in this slam-bang Western that is one of the best of the series. B&W; 59m. **DIR:** George Archainbaud. **CAST:** William Boyd, Andy Clyde, Jimmy Rogers, Don Costello. **1944**

TEXAS PAYBACK ★★ Familiar faces flesh out this pedestrian action-thriller about an escaped convict out to even the score with the Texas Ranger who put him away. Rated R for nudity, violence, and profanity. 96m. **DIR:** Richard W. Munchkin. **CAST:** Sam Jones, Gary Hudson, Bo Hopkins, Kathleen Kinmont. **1994**

TEXAS RANGERS (1936) ★★★1/2 Outlaw buddies Fred MacMurray, Jack Oakie, and Lloyd Nolan rob trains and then part ways when MacMurray and Oakie join the Texas Rangers. A few years go by and the two rangers are assigned to track down the most notorious outlaw of the day: their old buddy, Nolan. If the plot sounds familiar, it's been used several times, most notably in the official remake, *Streets of Laredo*. But this is the original, and fans of shoot-'em-ups will enjoy it despite some uneven moments. B&W; 95m. **DIR:** King Vidor. **CAST:** Fred MacMurray, Jack Oakie, Jean Parker, Lloyd Nolan, George "Gabby" Hayes, Fred Kohler Sr. **1936 DVD**

TEXAS RANGERS, THE (1951) ★★★★ George Montgomery and the Texas Rangers vs. Sam Bass, the Sundance Kid and their band of outlaws. Superior B filmmaking. 74m. **DIR:** Phil Karlson. **CAST:** George Montgomery, Gale Storm, Jerome Courtland, William Bishop, John Dehner, Douglas Kennedy, Noah Beery Jr. **1951**

•TEXAS RANGERS (2001) ★★★★ After the American Civil War, it becomes necessary for the Texas Rangers to be formed to bring law and order to the West, which is being ravaged by gangs of rustlers, murderers, and thieves. We were unprepared for the skill and savvy brought to this often-neglected film genre by director Steve Miner, who creates a shoot-'em-up that stands with the best of its kind. The movie's only shortcoming is an occasionally too moody and "method"-esque performance by top-billed Dylan McDermott. Rated PG-13 for violence. 90m. **DIR:** Steve Miner. **CAST:** Dylan McDermott, Robert Patrick, Alfred Molina, Randy Travis, Tom Skerritt, Vincent Spano, James van der Beek, Matt Keeslar, Rachael Leigh Cook, Jon Abrahams, Usher Raymond. **2001 DVD**

TEXAS TERROR ★★1/2 John Wayne hangs up his guns (for a while) in this Lone Star Western about a lawman falsely accused of the death of his friend. Wayne finds the real culprits and gets a chance to do some hard ridin' and fancy sluggin'. B&W; 58m. **DIR:** Robert N. Bradbury. **CAST:** John Wayne, Lucille Brown, LeRoy Mason, George "Gabby" Hayes, Yakima Canutt. **1935**

TEXAS TRAIL ★★1/2 It's 1898 and Hopalong Cassidy and the boys are chomping at the bit to get into the fight in Cuba, but the government needs horses more than fighting men. They round up the required horses but crooks rustle the herd. With the help of the U.S. Cavalry, Hoppy and his "rough riders" settle things with the bad guys, get into their uniforms, and sail for the fray with Spain. B&W; 59m. **DIR:** David Selman. **CAST:** William Boyd, George "Gabby" Hayes, Russell Hayden, Judith Allen. **1937**

TEXASVILLE ★★★★ This much-maligned sequel to *The Last Picture Show* is surprisingly good—an absorbing tale of people facing the truth about themselves. The naïveté, manipulation, and hope that propelled the characters' lives in the original film (when they were decades younger) have given way to wisdom and sober truth. An uncommonly rich motion picture. Rated R for profanity. 125m. **DIR:** Peter Bogdanovich. **CAST:** Jeff Bridges, Cybill Shepherd, Annie Potts, Timothy Bottoms, Cloris Leachman, Randy Quaid, Eileen Brennan. **1990**

THA EASTSIDAZ 🦃 You'd have to be a really hard-core fan of Snoop Dogg to make it all the way through this amateurish gangsta drama in which the rapper seeks revenge on the rival gang members who have sent him to prison in order to take over his operation. Rated R for violence, profanity, and drug use. 90m. **DIR:** Michael Martin. **CAST:** Snoop Dogg, Goldie Loc, Tray Deee. **2000 DVD**

THANK GOD IT'S FRIDAY ★★ This film is episodic and light in mood and features a cast primarily of newcomers. Donna Summer plays an aspiring singer who pesters a disc jockey, Bobby Speed (Ray Vitte), to let her sing. Rated PG. 90m. **DIR:** Robert Klane. **CAST:** Donna Summer, The Commodores, Ray Vitte, Debra Winger, Jeff Goldblum. **1978**

THANK YOU, MR. MOTO ★★★ The Japanese detective races with villains in search of Chinese scrolls that reveal the location of the treasure-laden tomb of

Genghis Khan. The second and best of the Mr. Moto movies, with Peter Lorre in peak form as the wily sleuth. B&W; 66m. **DIR:** Norman Foster. **CAST:** Peter Lorre, Thomas Beck, Pauline Frederick, John Carradine. **1937**

THANK YOUR LUCKY STARS ★★★1/2 Practically nonexistent plot—involving banjo-eyed Eddie Cantor as a cabdriver and the organizer of this gala affair—takes a backseat to the wonderful array of Warner Bros. talent gathered together for the first and only time in one film. Lots of fun for film buffs. B&W; 127m. **DIR:** David Butler. **CAST:** Eddie Cantor, Dennis Morgan, Joan Leslie, Bette Davis, Olivia de Havilland, Ida Lupino, Ann Sheridan, Humphrey Bogart, Errol Flynn, John Garfield. **1943**

THANKSGIVING STORY, THE ★★1/2 Originally a TV holiday special, this features the wholesome Walton family. John-boy (Richard Thomas) tries to impress the girl of his dreams while applying for a college scholarship. An accident causing brain damage threatens his future. A bit slow-paced and overly sweet. 95m. **DIR:** Philip Leacock. **CAST:** Richard Thomas, Ralph Waite, Michael Learned, Ellen Corby, Will Geer. **1973**

THAT BRENNAN GIRL ★★★1/2 A forerunner of the juvenile-delinquency movies of the 1950s and 1960s, this film tells the story of a young woman who learns that money isn't everything, and she learns it the hard way. Dated in style but not content. B&W; 95m. **DIR:** William Nigh. **CAST:** Mona Freeman, James Dunn, William Marshall. **1946**

THAT CERTAIN THING ★★★ When a poor working-class girl (Viola Dana) marries a wealthy idler (Ralph Graves), they are cut off from his inheritance. Fairy-tale romance with more than a touch of the screwball comedies to come from director Frank Capra. Silent. B&W; 70m. **DIR:** Frank Capra. **CAST:** Viola Dana, Ralph Graves. **1928**

THAT CERTAIN WOMAN ★★1/2 A gangster's widow marries a weak alcoholic playboy, and his father forces an annulment. When they learn she has a child, they try to take him from her. Enough self-sacrifice by lovely Bette Davis to fill four movies. B&W; 96m. **DIR:** Edmund Goulding. **CAST:** Bette Davis, Henry Fonda, Ian Hunter, Donald Crisp, Anita Louise. **1937**

THAT CHAMPIONSHIP SEASON (1982) ★★1/2 Former high school basketball stars (Bruce Dern, Stacy Keach, Martin Sheen, and Paul Sorvino) and their coach (Robert Mitchum) get together for the twenty-fourth annual celebration of their championship season. While there's nothing wrong with a sobering look at broken dreams and the pain of mid-life crisis, we've seen it all on screen before. Rated R for profanity, racial epithets, violence, and adult content. 110m. **DIR:** Jason Miller. **CAST:** Bruce Dern, Stacy Keach, Martin Sheen, Paul Sorvino, Robert Mitchum. **1982**

THAT CHAMPIONSHIP SEASON (1999) ★★★ Jason Miller's Pulitzer-winning play made a disappointing transition to the big screen in 1982; this interminable new adaptation isn't any better . . . possibly because it's directed by and stars Paul Sorvino, who also appeared in the original. His tunnel-visioned handling of the material merely amplifies its flaws, resulting in yet another tedious tale of male bonding that goes awry when too much alcohol loosens tongues and inhibitions. The setting is the twenty-fourth annual reunion of a small-town high-school basketball coach and the now-grown students he motivated toward success; the predictable climax, long in coming, is that these men haven't done anything significant with their lives ever since. Their so-called camaraderie is quick to evaporate amid increasingly spiteful bickering, leaving us to wonder how they ever functioned as a team in the first place. While the savage and brittle dialogue might fuel formidable performances on a live stage, it becomes only so much sniping in the confines of a screen. Rated R for profanity, racial epithets, and sexual candor. 127m. **DIR:** Paul Sorvino. **CAST:** Vincent D'Onofrio, Terry Kinney, Tony Shalhoub, Gary Sinise, Paul Sorvino. **1999**

THAT COLD DAY IN THE PARK ★★ This claustrophobic study of an emotionally disturbed woman and her obsessive interest in a young man is just about as strange as they come. It nonetheless gives gifted Sandy Dennis one of her most memorable roles. This film focuses on repressed sexuality, but also hints at incest and other subjects considered taboo when this Canadian-made movie was released. 113m. **DIR:** Robert Altman. **CAST:** Sandy Dennis, Michael Burns, Suzanne Benton, John Garfield Jr., Luana Anders, Michael Murphy. **1969**

THAT DARN CAT (1965) ★★1/2 Trust Disney to take a great book— *Undercover Cat*, by Gordon and Mildred Gordon—and turn it into a moronic slapstick farce. A fulsome feline returns from his nightly rounds with a watch belonging to a woman taken hostage in a recent bank robbery. Enter an ailurophobic FBI agent. 116m. **DIR:** Robert Stevenson. **CAST:** Dean Jones, Hayley Mills, Dorothy Provine, Roddy McDowall, Elsa Lanchester, Neville Brand, William Demarest, Ed Wynn, Frank Gorshin. **1965**

THAT DARN CAT (1997) 🦃 Even this comedy's star feline looks indignant and bored as its teen owner teams up with an inept rookie FBI agent to crack a kidnapping case. Rated PG. 89m. **DIR:** Bob Spiers. **CAST:** Christina Ricci, Doug E. Doug, Dyan Cannon, Michael McKean, Dean Jones, Peter Boyle. **1997**

•THAT DARN PUNK ★★1/2 This ultralow-budget ($21,000!) independent feature plays like a parody of a Quentin Tarantino film. The story follows a punk rocker who is kidnapped by hit men, meets a woman with a human head in the trunk of her car, is abducted by flying saucers, framed by a conspiracy theorist, and, oh, yeah, his girlfriend has left him. Often bizarre, sometimes hilarious film also features music by bands like the Vandals, Rancid, Pennywise, and more. Not rated; contains profanity and violence. 97m. **DIR:** Jeff Richardson. **CAST:** Joe Escalante, Katalina, Mia Crowe, Kandis Scalise, Lisa Hannon, Zander Schloss, Warren Fitzgerald. **2001**

THAT FORSYTE WOMAN ★★ Greer Garson has the central role of a woman trapped in a marriage of convenience. She flouts the rigid social taboos of nineteenth-century England. Based on the first book of John Galsworthy's epic *Forsyte Saga*. A dull movie with little conviction. B&W; 114m. **DIR:** Compton Bennett. **CAST:** Greer Garson, Errol Flynn, Janet Leigh, Walter Pidgeon, Robert Young, Harry Davenport. **1949**

THAT HAMILTON WOMAN ★★★1/2 The legendary acting duo of Mr. and Mrs. Laurence Olivier re-creates

one of England's legendary romantic scandals: the love of naval hero Horatio Nelson for the alluring Lady Emma Hamilton. B&W; 128m. **DIR:** Alexander Korda. **CAST:** Vivien Leigh, Laurence Olivier. **1941**

THAT LUCKY TOUCH ★★★ This romantic comedy features unlikely neighbors falling in love. Roger Moore plays Michael Scott, a weapons merchant. Susannah York, on the other hand, is an antimilitary writer. Shelley Winters provides a few laughs as the airhead wife of a NATO general (Lee J. Cobb). Comparable to a PG, but basically pretty tame. 93m. **DIR:** Christopher Miles. **CAST:** Roger Moore, Susannah York, Shelley Winters, Lee J. Cobb, Sydne Rome. **1975**

THAT MAN FROM RIO ★★★★ This fast-moving comedy-action-thriller about a stolen artifact—with Jean-Paul Belmondo as a cross between James Bond and Indiana Jones—never lets up. In French with English subtitles. 115m. **DIR:** Philippe de Broca. **CAST:** Jean-Paul Belmondo, Françoise Dorleac, Simone Renant, Adolfo Celi. **1964**

THAT MIDNIGHT KISS ★★★ Mario Lanza makes his film debut as an ex-GI making it as a truck driver when he gets involved with an heiress who wants to be an opera star. Slight plot, but it's the music that counts. A fine rendition of "They Won't Believe Me." 96m. **DIR:** Norman Taurog. **CAST:** Mario Lanza, Kathryn Grayson, José Iturbi, Ethel Barrymore, Keenan Wynn, J. Carrol Naish, Thomas Gomez, Marjorie Reynolds, Arthur Treacher. **1949**

THAT NIGHT ★★★ Nostalgic slice of life finds young Eliza Dushku acting as a go-between for popular Juliette Lewis and tough guy C. Thomas Howell. The year is 1961, and when Lewis becomes pregnant, it's up to Dushku to keep them together. Period soundtrack, an eye for detail, and sensitive, likable characters. Rated PG-13 for adult situations. 89m. **DIR:** Craig Bolotin. **CAST:** C. Thomas Howell, Juliette Lewis, Eliza Dushku. **1993**

THAT OBSCURE OBJECT OF DESIRE ★★★★1/2 Luis Buñuel's last film cunningly combines erotic teasing, wit, and social comment. Mathieu (Fernando Rey) is a 50 year old man who falls hopelessly in love with a young woman. Buñuel, a master of surrealism, tantalizes the viewer by casting two actresses to play the heroine and a third actress to do the voice of both. Rated R for profanity and nudity. 100m. **DIR:** Luis Buñuel. **CAST:** Fernando Rey, Carole Bouquet, Angela Molina. **1977 DVD**

THAT OLD FEELING ★★★★ Bette Midler and Dennis Farina, divorced for years and unable to speak a civil word to each other, suddenly relight the old torch at their daughter's wedding. Leslie Dixon's sly script is equal parts farce, romantic comedy, and satire, and is directed with madcap grace by Carl Reiner. Rated PG-13 for profanity. 107m. **DIR:** Carl Reiner. **CAST:** Bette Midler, Dennis Fariña, Paula Marshall, Gail O'Grady, David Rasche, Danny Nucci, Jamie Denton. **1997 DVD**

THAT SINKING FEELING ★★★★ Following Scottish director Bill Forsyth's box-office success with *Gregory's Girl* and *Local Hero,* his first feature was resurrected for release in America. It's a typically wry and dry comic affair about a group of unemployed young men deciding on a life of crime. The result is engaging silliness. Rated PG. 92m. **DIR:** Bill Forsyth. **CAST:** Robert Buchanan, John Hughes, Billy Greenlees, Gordon John Sinclair. **1979**

THAT SUMMER OF WHITE ROSES ★★★ Guests at an isolated Yugoslavian summer resort clash with Nazis during WWII. A well-seasoned drama that simmers at the start, but eventually comes to a full boil. Rated R for profanity and violence. 98m. **DIR:** Rajko Grlic. **CAST:** Tom Conti, Susan George, Rod Steiger. **1990**

THAT THING YOU DO! ★★★★★ It seems one of the hardest things to do is make a fully convincing and entertaining movie about rock 'n' roll, but that's exactly what first-time director Tom Hanks has done with this light, fluffy but knowing tale of the one-hit "Wonders." Every detail, from the player's attitudes to the bottom line of the record companies, is right on the mark. Hanks himself is on board to add his distinctive brand of humor. It's a hoot. Rated PG. 110m. **DIR:** Tom Hanks. **CAST:** Tom Everett Scott, Liv Tyler, Johnathon Schaech, Steve Zahn, Ethan Embry, Tom Hanks, Alex Rocco, Bill Cobbs, Rita Wilson, Chris Isaak, Kevin Pollak. **1996 DVD**

THAT TOUCH OF MINK ★★★1/2 This 1962 romantic comedy is enjoyable, but only as escapist fare. Doris Day stars as an unemployed girl pursued by a wealthy businessman (Cary Grant). 99m. **DIR:** Delbert Mann. **CAST:** Doris Day, Cary Grant, Gig Young, Audrey Meadows, John Astin. **1962 DVD**

THAT UNCERTAIN FEELING ★★1/2 This is an amusing film about marital unrest until the midpoint, when the time-tried romantic triangle plot thins rather than thickens. Burgess Meredith all but filches the film in a supporting role. Merle Oberon is devastatingly beautiful, even when she has the hiccups—an important plot device. B&W; 86m. **DIR:** Ernst Lubitsch. **CAST:** Merle Oberon, Melvyn Douglas, Alan Mowbray, Burgess Meredith, Eve Arden, Sig Ruman. **1941 DVD**

THAT WAS ROCK ★★★★★ Compilation of two previous films, *The T.A.M.I. Show* and *The Big T.N.T. Show*, which were originally shot in the mid-1960s in black and white. The video is muddy, the simulated stereo is annoying, and the audience nearly drowns out the performers, but it's one of the best collections of rock 'n' roll and R&B talent you will ever see. Not rated. 92m. **DIR:** Steve Binder, Larry Peerce. **CAST:** The Rolling Stones, Chuck Berry, Tina Turner, Marvin Gaye, The Supremes, Smokey Robinson and the Miracles, James Brown, Ray Charles, Gerry and the Pacemakers, The Ronettes. **1984**

THAT WAS THEN . . . THIS IS NOW ★★★★ Adapted from a novel by S. E. Hinton (*The Outsiders*; *Rumble Fish*). The cuteness and condescension that mar most coming-of-age films are laudably absent in its tale of two working-class teenagers (Emilio Estevez and Craig Sheffer) coming to grips with adulthood. A work that teens and adults alike can appreciate. Rated R for violence and profanity. 103m. **DIR:** Christopher Cain. **CAST:** Emilio Estevez, Craig Sheffer, Kim Delaney, Morgan Freeman, Larry B. Scott, Barbara Babcock. **1985**

THAT'LL BE THE DAY ★★★★ A provocative character study. Charismatic David Essex stars as a British working-class youth whose adolescent restlessness points him toward rock music. Ringo Starr contributes an engaging performance as a rough-hewn lad who eventu-

ally proves to be less morally suspect than the protagonist. The film's sequel *Stardust* offers some of filmdom's most fascinating glimpses into the rock 'n' roll world. 90m. **DIR:** Claude Whatham. **CAST:** David Essex, Ringo Starr, Rosemary Leach, James Booth, Billy Fury, Keith Moon. **1974 DVD**

THAT'S ADEQUATE ★★ This mock documentary rapidly exhausts its welcome. The sixty-year examination of the Adequate Pictures Studio includes glimpses of its many exploitation fiascos, such as *Singing in the Synagogue* and *Sigmund Freud in Sherwood Forest*. Rated R for raunchy language and brief nudity. 80m. **DIR:** Harry Hurwitz. **CAST:** Tony Randall, James Coco, Jerry Stiller, Anne Meara, Bruce Willis, Richard Lewis. **1989**

THAT'S ENTERTAINMENT ★★★★★ A feast of screen highlights. Culled from twenty-nine years of MGM classics, this release truly has something for everybody. Taken from Metro-Goldwyn-Mayer's glory days when it boasted "more stars than there are in heaven," nearly every sequence is a showstopper. Rated G. 135m. **DIR:** Jack Haley Jr. **CAST:** Judy Garland, Fred Astaire, Frank Sinatra, Gene Kelly, Esther Williams. **1974**

THAT'S ENTERTAINMENT! III ★★★★1/2 This fourth compilation of old MGM musical routines feels a bit repetitious, but it's gussied up with a treasury of outtakes, previously unseen production numbers, and behind-the-scenes footage. It's proof positive why MTV will never be MGM. Rated G. 113m. **DIR:** Bud Friedgen, Michael J. Sheridan. **CAST:** June Allyson, Cyd Charisse, Lena Horne, Howard Keel, Gene Kelly, Ann Miller, Debbie Reynolds, Mickey Rooney, Esther Williams. **1994**

THAT'S ENTERTAINMENT PART II ★★★★ More wonderful scenes from the history of MGM highlight this compilation, hosted by director Gene Kelly and Fred Astaire. It's a real treat for film buffs. Rated G. 132m. **DIR:** Gene Kelly. **CAST:** Gene Kelly, Fred Astaire. **1976**

THAT'S LIFE ★★★ Jack Lemmon and Julie Andrews play a married couple enduring a torrent of crises during one fateful weekend. The film is a mixture of good and bad, funny and sad, tasteful and tasteless. That it ends up on the plus side is to the credit of its lead players. Rated PG-13 for profanity and scatological humor. 102m. **DIR:** Blake Edwards. **CAST:** Julie Andrews, Jack Lemmon, Sally Kellerman, Robert Loggia, Jennifer Edwards, Chris Lemmon. **1986 DVD**

THAT'S MY BABY 🦃 Unemployed man wants his career-oriented girlfriend to have his baby. Rated PG-13 for nudity. 97m. **DIR:** Edie Yolles, John Bradshaw. **CAST:** Timothy Webber, Sonja Smits. **1989**

THAT'S SINGING: THE BEST OF BROADWAY ★★1/2 You'll find this on the shelf with *That's Dancing* and *That's Entertainment*. It should be with *The Adventures of Ozzie and Harriet*. This is a television show where stars present an offering from Broadway musicals in which they appeared. The highlight is Jerry Orbach, singing "Try To Remember" from *The Fantasticks*. The star rating is for Broadway diehards only. 117m. **DIR:** Robert Iscove. **CAST:** Tom Bosley, Diahann Carroll, Glynis Johns, Ethel Merman, Jerry Orbach, Robert Morse, Debbie Reynolds. **1982**

THAT'S THE WAY I LIKE IT ★★★1/2 Delightful Singapore comedy about a young man who idolizes the film *Saturday Night Fever* and enters a disco-dance contest in order to buy a Triumph motorcycle. Fans of the John Travolta film and early Woody Allen comedies will appreciate the irony and similarities in the story, while the likable cast will win over everyone else. Totally charming and funny. Rated PG for language and violence. 95m. **DIR:** Glen Goei. **CAST:** Adrian Pang, Madeline Tan, Pierre Png, Anna Belle Francis, Steven Lim. **1998 DVD**

THEATRE OF BLOOD ★★★★ Deliciously morbid horror-comedy about a Shakespearean actor (Vincent Price) who, angered by the thrashing he receives from a series of critics, decides to kill them in uniquely outlandish ways. He turns to the Bard for inspiration, and each perceived foe is eliminated in a manner drawn from one of Shakespeare's plays. Rated R for violence. 104m. **DIR:** Douglas Hickox. **CAST:** Vincent Price, Diana Rigg, Robert Morley. **1973 DVD**

THEATRE OF DEATH ★★1/2 Mildly interesting mystery succeeds mainly due to Christopher Lee's assured performance and some well-timed scares as a series of gruesome murders is committed in Paris with an apparent connection to the local theater company. Good title sequence deserves mention. 90m. **DIR:** Samuel Gallu. **CAST:** Christopher Lee, Julian Glover, Lelia Goldoni. **1967 DVD**

THEIR ONLY CHANCE ★★ True-life adventure film about a young man (Steve Hoddy) who has a way with wild animals. Former Tarzan Jock Mahoney has a dual role as a rancher and a mountain man. A nice, quiet wildlife film suitable for the entire family. 84m. **DIR:** David Siddon. **CAST:** Jock Mahoney, Steve Hoddy. **1975**

THELMA & LOUISE ★★★★ Director Ridley Scott and screenwriter Callie Khouri skillfully interweave suspense and comedy in this distaff *Easy Rider*, in which two buddies set off on a vacation and end up running from the law after one of them shoots a would-be rapist. Entertaining action-movie/road-picture. Rated R for violence, profanity, and suggested sex. 128m. **DIR:** Ridley Scott. **CAST:** Susan Sarandon, Geena Davis, Harvey Keitel, Michael Madsen, Christopher McDonald, Brad Pitt. **1991 DVD**

THEM! ★★★★ Classic 1950s sci-fi about colossal mutant ants, at large in a New Mexico desert, threatening to take over the world. Frightening special effects and lightning pace make this a supercharged entertainment, with Edmund Gwenn delivering a standout performance as the scientist who foretells the danger. Great. B&W; 94m. **DIR:** Gordon Douglas. **CAST:** Edmund Gwenn, James Arness, James Whitmore, Fess Parker. **1954**

THEODORA GOES WILD ★★★ The usually serious Irene Dunne tries her hand at screwball comedy and plays a small-town writer who visits New York after her *Peyton Place*-ish novel becomes a bestseller. Melvyn Douglas is a good foil as the big city sophisticate who becomes her guide. B&W; 94m. **DIR:** Richard Boleslawski. **CAST:** Irene Dunne, Melvyn Douglas, Thomas Mitchell, Thurston Hall. **1936**

THEODORE REX 🦃 Whoopi Goldberg proves what a good actress she is by making it through this science-fiction comedy with a straight face. Goldberg plays futuristic police officer Katie Coltrane, who exists in a future where dinosaurs have been reanimated and live

among humans. When a dinosaur is found murdered, Coltrane is paired with a Tyrannosaurus Rex named Teddy, and together they set out to solve the case. A disaster. Rated PG. 92m. **DIR:** Jonathan Betuel. **CAST:** Whoopi Goldberg, Armin Mueller-Stahl, Juliet Landau, Richard Roundtree. **1996**

THEORY OF FLIGHT, THE ★★★ Kenneth Branagh and Helena Bonham Carter are outstanding in this tale of true friendship. Branagh is the disillusioned man who doesn't mind risking his life for a thrill. Bonham Carter is the woman suffering from Lou Gehrig's disease who turns to him for one last favor. Even though the film attempts to deal with serious subject matters, a clunky script and direction almost detract from the marvelous performances. Rated R for language and adult situations. 98m. **DIR:** Paul Greengrass. **CAST:** Kenneth Branagh, Helena Bonham Carter, Gemma Jones, Holly Aird. **1998**

THERE GOES MY BABY ★★★ Although trying for the youthful angst of *American Graffiti*, writer-director Floyd Mutrux's farewell glimpse of the 1965 Westwood High senior class is a bit overwrought. The B-level ensemble cast tries hard, but never rises above the facile stereotypes: surfer, draft dodger, flower girl, earnest valedictorian, etc. Rated R for profanity and violence. 99m. **DIR:** Floyd Mutrux. **CAST:** Dermot Mulroney, Rick Schroder, Kelli Williams, Noah Wyle, Jill Schoelen, Kristin Minter, Lucy Deakins. **1994**

THERE GOES THE NEIGHBORHOOD ★★★★ Prison shrink Jeff Daniels learns of $8.5 million of Mafia loot buried in the suburbs. Catherine O'Hara is the woman living over said loot. Quirky and cute, this breezy comedy is unpredictable and sweetly enjoyable. Rated PG-13 for profanity. 88m. **DIR:** Bill Phillips. **CAST:** Jeff Daniels, Catherine O'Hara, Dabney Coleman, Hector Elizondo, Judith Ivey, Rhea Perlman. **1992**

THERE WAS A CROOKED MAN ★★★1/2 Crooked-as-they-come Kirk Douglas bides and does his time harried by holier-than-thou Arizona prison warden Henry Fonda, who has more than redemption on his mind. A good plot and clever casting make this oater well worth the watching. And, yes, rattlesnakes do make good watchdogs. Rated R. 123m. **DIR:** Joseph L. Mankiewicz. **CAST:** Kirk Douglas, Henry Fonda, Hume Cronyn, Warren Oates, Burgess Meredith, Arthur O'Connell. **1970**

THEREMIN: AN ELECTRONIC ODYSSEY ★★★★★ Russian scientist who virtually created the field of electronic music in the 1920s and later was devastatingly suppressed by the U.S.S.R. Just as fascinating is the story of Clara Rockmore, the woman who loved Theremin and helped popularize his musical instruments. Highly unusual and intriguing on several levels. B&W/color; 85m. **DIR:** Steven M. Martin. **CAST:** Leon Theremin, Clara Rockmore, Robert Moog, Brian Wilson. **1994 DVD**

THERE'S A GIRL IN MY SOUP ★★1/2 Goldie Hawn hadn't completely shed her *Laugh-In* image when this British sex farce came out, and it didn't do her career any good. Quite a letdown, after her Oscar-winning performance in *Cactus Flower*. Peter Sellers is a middle-aged boob who falls in lust with flower child Hawn. A low point for all concerned. Rated R. 95m. **DIR:** Roy Boulting. **CAST:** Peter Sellers, Goldie Hawn, Diana Dors, Tony Britton. **1970**

THERE'S NO BUSINESS LIKE SHOW BUSINESS ★★ Even the strength of the cast can't save this marginally entertaining musical comedy about a show-biz family. Irving Berlin's tunes and Monroe's scenes are the only redeeming qualities in this one. 117m. **DIR:** Walter Lang. **CAST:** Ethel Merman, Dan Dailey, Marilyn Monroe, Donald O'Connor, Johnnie Ray, Mitzi Gaynor, Hugh O'Brian, Frank McHugh. **1954 DVD**

THERE'S NOTHING OUT THERE ★★★ Independent filmmaker Rolf Kanefsky sends up haunted house, hockey-mask groaners. His teens visiting a cabin in the middle of nowhere are in for a surprise. Sure, there's the alien creature patroling the woods, but there's also plenty of humor. One low-budget entry that defies its origins. Not rated; contains nudity and adult language. 91m. **DIR:** Rolf Kanefsky. **CAST:** Craig Peck, Wendy Bednarz, John Carhart, III. **1990 DVD**

THERE'S SOMETHING ABOUT MARY ★★★ The late 1990s resurgence in "moron comedy" probably saw its finest hour with this effort, which blends low humor, bad taste, and slapstick silliness with an unexpectedly touching love story. Geeky Ben Stiller, madly in love since high school with Cameron Diaz, eventually wonders what has become of her, now that both have reached adulthood. He hires a private detective who decides to court the fair lady himself; as the story progresses, it seems that everybody who ever encountered Mary now wants to become a permanent part of her life. Some of the bits are hilarious, others forced and unfunny, but it's great fun for an undemanding Friday evening. Rated R for profanity and strong sexual content. 119m. **DIR:** Bobby Farrelly, Peter Farrelly. **CAST:** Cameron Diaz, Matt Dillon, Ben Stiller, Lee Evans, Chris Elliott, Jeffrey Tambor. **1998 DVD**

THERESE ★★★★1/2 French director Alain Cavalier's breathtakingly beautiful film is the story of St. Theresa of Lisieux, who entered a Carmelite nunnery in the late nineteenth century at the age of 15 and lived there for eight years until she died of tuberculosis. She was declared a saint by Pope Pius XI in 1925, twenty-eight years after her death. In French with English subtitles. 90m. **DIR:** Alain Cavalier. **CAST:** Catherine Mouchet, Helene Alexandridis. **1986**

THERESE AND ISABELLE ★★★ Tender, gorgeously filmed tale of young love in a French private school. As the new girl in school, Therese finds herself an outsider. When she meets Isabelle, she finds a friend and then a lover as she explores her sexual desires. One of the first films to deal openly with lesbian relationships, this blast from the past is both titillating and honest in its portrayal of the subject matter. Not rated; contains nudity. B&W; 118m. **DIR:** Radley Metzger. **CAST:** Essy Presson, Anna Gael, Barbara Laage, Anne Vernon. **1967**

THESE GIRLS WON'T TALK ★★ As a series of three silent short stories, this Mack Sennett–produced series is short of inspiration. The shorts are called *Her Bridal Nightmare*, *Campus Carmen*, and *As Luck Would Have It*. The most interesting thing about this compilation is seeing Carole Lombard long before she was a star. B&W; 50m. **DIR:** Mack Sennett. **CAST:** Colleen Moore, Carole Lombard, Betty Compson. **1920**

THESE THREE ★★★★ A superb cast brings alive this story of two upright and decent schoolteachers victimized by the lies of a malicious student. Miriam Hopkins and Merle Oberon are the pair brutally slandered; Bonita Granville is the evil liar. Script by Lillian Hellman, loosely based on her play *The Children's Hour*, under which title the film was remade in 1961. B&W; 93m. **DIR:** William Wyler. **CAST:** Miriam Hopkins, Merle Oberon, Joel McCrea, Bonita Granville, Marcia Mae Jones. **1936**

THESIS ★★★★ A young university student searches for extreme examples of violence in the media—the subject of her thesis. She gets more than she asks for when she comes across a snuff film in which the murder of a young woman is actually captured on video. The tension escalates when she realizes that the victim was just one of many female students missing from her university, and some of the faculty must be involved. In Spanish with English subtitles. Rated R for violence. 121m. **DIR:** Alejandro Amenabar. **CAST:** Ana Torrent, Fele Martinez, Eduardo Noriega, Nieves Herranz. **1996 DVD**

THEY ALL LAUGHED ★★★★ This is director Peter Bogdanovich at his best. A very offbeat comedy that looks at four New York private eyes' adventures and love lives. Final film of ex–Playboy bunny Dorothy Stratten. Worth a look. Rated PG. 115m. **DIR:** Peter Bogdanovich. **CAST:** Audrey Hepburn, Ben Gazzara, John Ritter, Dorothy Stratten. **1981**

THEY BITE ★★ Cheesy low-budget chiller echoes *Horror of Party Beach* with its tale of scaly sea creatures that are really from outer space. The effects are cheap and the acting passable, but it is all in good fun. Rated R for gore, violence, and nudity. 96m. **DIR:** Brett Piper. **CAST:** Donna Frotscher, Charlie Barnett, Ron Jeremy, Susie Owens. **1995**

THEY CALL IT SIN ★★1/2 A four-sided romance that uses top character stars to play stereotypes. The heroine is engaged to a womanizer, fights off an aging playboy, and cries on the shoulder of an uptight doctor in her search for lasting romance. Good but not great. B&W; 75m. **DIR:** Thornton Freeland. **CAST:** Loretta Young, George Brent, David Manners, Louis Calhern, Una Merkel, Helen Vinson, Nella Walker. **1932**

THEY CALL ME BRUCE? ★★ In this unsophisticated kung fu comedy, Johnny Yune portrays an Asian immigrant who, because of his "resemblance" to Bruce Lee and an accidental exhibition of craziness (misinterpreted as martial arts expertise), gets a reputation as a mean man with fists and feet. But it is Ralph Mauro, playing Bruce's chauffeur, who steals the show. Rated PG. 88m. **DIR:** Elliot Hong. **CAST:** Johnny Yune, Ralph Mauro, Margaux Hemingway. **1982**

THEY CALL ME MISTER TIBBS ★★★ An inferior follow-up, this contains the further adventures of the character Sidney Poitier created for the film *In the Heat of the Night*. Detective Virgil Tibbs is again investigating a murder and trying to clear his friend, as well. Rated PG—contains strong language and some violence. 108m. **DIR:** Gordon Douglas. **CAST:** Sidney Poitier, Barbara McNair, Martin Landau. **1970**

THEY CALL ME TRINITY ★★1/2 This Western-comedy can be best described as an Italian *Blazing Saddles*. Terence Hill and Bud Spencer team up as half brothers trying to protect a colony from cattle rustlers and a shady sheriff. Rated G. 109m. **DIR:** E. B. Clucher. **CAST:** Terence Hill, Bud Spencer, Farley Granger. **1971 DVD**

THEY CAME FROM BEYOND SPACE ★★★ Enjoyable tale of formless aliens landing in Cornwall and taking over the minds and bodies of a group of scientists in an effort to preserve their dissipating race. Robert Hutton plays the one man who can't be controlled because of a metal plate in his skull. Based on *The Gods Hate Kansas* by Joseph Millard. 86m. **DIR:** Freddie Francis. **CAST:** Robert Hutton, Jennifer Jayne, Zia Mohyeddin, Bernard Kay, Michael Gough. **1967**

THEY CAME FROM WITHIN ★★★ This is David Cronenberg's commercial feature-film debut. Even at this early stage in his career, his preoccupation with violence and biological rebellion is very much in evidence. Slimy, disgusting parasites invade the sterile orderliness of a high-rise apartment complex, turning the inhabitants into raving sex maniacs. Rated R. 87m. **DIR:** David Cronenberg. **CAST:** Paul Hampton, Joe Silver, Lynn Lowry, Barbara Steele. **1975**

THEY CAME TO CORDURA ★★ This film, which examines the true character of the war hero, is not one of Gary Cooper's best. The story has Cooper in Mexico during World War I as one of six military men returning to base. The hardships they encounter on the way create the drama. The movie has a nice look, but just not enough action. 123m. **DIR:** Robert Rossen. **CAST:** Gary Cooper, Rita Hayworth, Van Heflin, Tab Hunter, Richard Conte. **1959**

THEY DIED WITH THEIR BOOTS ON ★★★★ Errol Flynn gives a first-rate performance as General George Custer in this Warner Bros. classic directed by Raoul Walsh. The superb supporting cast adds to this Western epic. B&W; 138m. **DIR:** Raoul Walsh. **CAST:** Errol Flynn, Olivia de Havilland, Arthur Kennedy, Gene Lockhart, Anthony Quinn, Sydney Greenstreet. **1941**

THEY DO IT WITH MIRRORS ★★★ When told there is something very strange going on at a childhood friend's country estate (which serves as a reform institution for young criminals), Miss Marple promptly pays a visit. Numerous scene shifts and a large cast make this BBC Agatha Christie adaptation unnecessarily convoluted and confusing. Not rated; suitable for family viewing. 100m. **DIR:** Norman Stone. **CAST:** Joan Hickson, Jean Simmons, Joss Ackland, Faith Brook, Gillian Barge, David Horovitch. **1991**

THEY DRIVE BY NIGHT ★★★★ Here's a Warner Bros. gem! George Raft and Humphrey Bogart star as truck-driving brothers who cope with crooked bosses while wooing Ann Sheridan and Ida Lupino. The dialogue is terrific, and the direction by Raoul Walsh is crisp. B&W; 93m. **DIR:** Raoul Walsh. **CAST:** George Raft, Humphrey Bogart, Ann Sheridan, Ida Lupino. **1940**

THEY GOT ME COVERED ★★1/2 Typical Bob Hope vehicle of the 1940s is full of gals, gags, goofy situations, snappy dialogue, and one-line zingers, and boasts an incredible supporting cast of great character actors and actresses. Thin story about spy nonsense in Washington, D.C., is secondary to the zany antics of Paramount's ski-nosed comedian. B&W; 95m. **DIR:** David Butler. **CAST:** Bob Hope, Dorothy Lamour, Lenore Aubert, Otto Preminger, Eduardo Ciannelli, Marion Martin, Donald MacBride, Donald Meek, Philip Ahn. **1943 DVD**

THEY KNEW WHAT THEY WANTED ★★★ This film is a fine example of offbeat casting that somehow succeeds. Charles Laughton and Carole Lombard were required to submerge their usual histrionics in order to bring off a low-key little tragedy. The story is of the unrequited love of an Italian wine grower for the opportunistic hash house waitress that he marries. B&W; 96m. **DIR:** Garson Kanin. **CAST:** Charles Laughton, Carole Lombard, William Gargan, Harry Carey. **1940**

THEY LIVE ★★ The first two-thirds of this science-fiction–horror hybrid is such harebrained fun that one is truly disappointed when it falls apart at the end. Roddy Piper is a drifter in the not-so-distant future who discovers that the human population of Earth is being hypnotized into subservience by alien-created television signals. Rated R for nudity and violence. 95m. **DIR:** John Carpenter. **CAST:** Roddy Piper, Keith David, Meg Foster. **1988 DVD**

THEY LIVE BY NIGHT ★★★1/2 A seminal film dealing with youth, alienation, and the concept of the loner who operates outside the confines of conventional behavior and morality. This postwar crime drama gave American youth a minor cultural folk hero in Farley Granger and began the directing career of young Nicholas Ray, who would in turn provide the world with the ultimate image of teenage alienation: *Rebel Without a Cause*. B&W; 95m. **DIR:** Nicholas Ray. **CAST:** Farley Granger, Cathy O'Donnell, Howard DaSilva, Jay C. Flippen. **1949**

THEY MADE ME A CRIMINAL ★★1/2 John Garfield's film persona is a direct result of this Warner Bros. story about the redemption of a loner on the lam from the law for a crime he didn't commit. A great cast still doesn't change the fact that this remake of 1933's *The Life of Jimmy Dolan* is muddled and not too solidly constructed. B&W; 92m. **DIR:** Busby Berkeley. **CAST:** John Garfield, Claude Rains, Ann Sheridan, Gloria Dickson, The Dead End Kids, Ward Bond. **1939 DVD**

THEY MEET AGAIN ★★ In this film, the last in the popular Dr. Christian series about a snoopy small-town doctor, genial Jean Hersholt is upset because a man he feels is innocent is serving time. The good doctor finds out who embezzled the missing money. B&W; 69m. **DIR:** Erle C. Kenton. **CAST:** Jean Hersholt, Robert Baldwin, Neil Hamilton, Dorothy Lovett, Arthur Hoyt. **1941**

THEY MET IN BOMBAY ★★★ Clark Gable and Rosalind Russell are jewel thieves pursued from Bombay to Hong Kong. He is mistaken for a British officer and becomes a reluctant war hero in this odd mixture of light comedy and action-drama. The stars are fun to watch. B&W; 93m. **DIR:** Clarence Brown. **CAST:** Clark Gable, Rosalind Russell, Peter Lorre, Jessie Ralph, Reginald Owen, Eduardo Ciannelli. **1941**

THEY MIGHT BE GIANTS ★★★★ Stylish and engaging study of a retired judge (George C. Scott) who imagines himself to be Sherlock Holmes. With visions of dollar signs floating before his eyes, the judge's brother hopes to have this ersatz detective committed; to this end, the brother brings in a female psychiatrist whose name happens to be—you guessed it—Watson. Rated PG. 88m. **DIR:** Anthony Harvey. **CAST:** George C. Scott, Joanne Woodward, Jack Gilford. **1971 DVD**

THEY NEST Bug, bugs, and more bugs in this made-for-cable original—with predictable results. To be avoided at all costs. Not rated; contains violence. 90m. **DIR:** Ellory Elkayem. **CAST:** Thomas Calabro, Dean Stockwell, Kristen Dalton, John Savage. **2000**

THEY ONLY KILL THEIR MASTERS ★★★ Pretty solid whodunit (if a bit TV-ish), with James Garner terrific as always, playing a small-town California sheriff. He solves a pregnant woman's murder. The title refers to a deadly Doberman pinscher. Rated PG. 97m. **DIR:** James Goldstone. **CAST:** James Garner, Katharine Ross, Hal Holbrook, Harry Guardino, June Allyson, Peter Lawford, Edmond O'Brien, Arthur O'Connell, Christopher Connelly, Tom Ewell, Ann Rutherford. **1972**

THEY SAVED HITLER'S BRAIN This bargain-basement bomb is actually a used movie since a major portion of it was lifted from an entirely different film made ten years earlier. B&W; 74m. **DIR:** David Bradley. **CAST:** Walter Stocker, Audrey Caire, Carlos Rivas, John Holland, Marshall Reed, Nestor Paiva. **1963 DVD**

THEY SHALL HAVE MUSIC ★★★ Good cast and great music increase the appeal of this attempt to make concert violinist Jascha Heifetz a film star. Simple plot has a group of poor kids convincing him to play a benefit and save Walter Brennan's music school in the slums. B&W; 101m. **DIR:** Archie Mayo. **CAST:** Jascha Heifetz, Joel McCrea, Andrea Leeds, Walter Brennan, Marjorie Main, Porter Hall. **1939**

THEY SHOOT HORSES, DON'T THEY? ★★★★★ The desperation and hopelessness of the Great Depression are graphically shown in this powerful drama, through a pitiful collection of marathon dancers. Some of the group will endure this physical and mental assault on their human spirit; some will not. Jane Fonda, as a cynical casualty of the Depression, and Gig Young, as the uncaring master of ceremonies, give stunning performances. Rated PG. 121m. **DIR:** Sydney Pollack. **CAST:** Jane Fonda, Gig Young, Michael Sarrazin. **1969 DVD**

THEY STILL CALL ME BRUCE Perhaps one of the least-anticipated sequels ever, this attempt by Korean comic Johnny Yune to follow up his 1982 nonhit *They Call Me Bruce?* is completely hopeless. It's rated PG for Yune's occasionally off-color humor. 91m. **DIR:** Johnny Yune, James Orr. **CAST:** Johnny Yune, David Mendenhall, Joey Travolta. **1987**

THEY (THEY WATCH) ★★★ Rudyard Kipling's eerie short story gets stretched too far in this study of a distraught father (Patrick Bergin) who can't stop grieving for his dead daughter. He's got good reason, since the girl's spirit seems to be trapped in a house owned by weird southern mystic Vanessa Redgrave. Although everybody tries hard, there's just not enough plot to keep this feature going. Rated PG. 100m. **DIR:** John Korty. **CAST:** Patrick Bergin, Vanessa Redgrave, Valerie Mahaffey. **1993**

THEY WENT THAT-A-WAY AND THAT-A-WAY ★★ Tim Conway wrote and stars in this comedy. He plays a small-town deputy who follows the governor's orders by being secretly placed in a maximum-security prison as an undercover agent. Fellow deputy (Chuck McCann) is his partner. When the governor suddenly dies, the two must escape from the prison. There are some silly gags, but this film does provide a few laughs and no deep plots. Rated PG. 106m. **DIR:** Edward Montagne, Stuart E. McGowan. **CAST:** Tim Conway, Chuck McCann, Reni Santoni, Richard Kiel, Dub Taylor. **1978**

THEY WERE EXPENDABLE ★★★★1/2 First-rate action-drama about American PT boat crews fighting a losing battle against advancing Japanese forces in the Philippines. Director John Ford based this film, his most personal, on his war experiences and the people he knew in the conflict. No phony heroics or glory here, but a realistic, bleak, and ultimately inspiring picture of men in war. B&W; 136m. **DIR:** John Ford. **CAST:** John Wayne, Robert Montgomery, Donna Reed, Jack Holt, Ward Bond, Marshall Thompson, Louis Jean Heydt. **1945 DVD**

THEY WON'T BELIEVE ME ★★★1/2 Robert Young is a grade-A stinker in this classic *film noir* of deceit, mistaken murder, suicide, and doomed romance. Rita Johnson is especially fine as the wronged wife. B&W; 95m. **DIR:** Irving Pichel. **CAST:** Robert Young, Susan Hayward, Jane Greer, Rita Johnson, Tom Powers, Don Beddoe, Frank Ferguson. **1947**

THICKER THAN BLOOD ★★ Earnest attempt at addressing complex issues falls victim to formulaic writing and direction. Griffin Byrne is a New York City Catholic-school teacher who believes that he can save all of the school's at-risk youth. His biggest test is a student with artistic skills whose future is clouded by a bad home life. The priest who runs the school realizes that setting one's goal too high can lead to more than failure. Despite strong direction, the film suffers from being too simplistic in its approach. Not rated. 90m. **DIR:** Richard Pearce. **CAST:** Mickey Rourke, Dan Futterman, Carlo Alban. **1998**

THICKER THAN WATER ★★★1/2 An intriguing use of vignettes, combined with the talents of Jonathan Pryce and Theresa Russell, rescue this BBC thriller from narrative hell. She plays telepathic twins, one of whom is happily married. The other twin is, naturally, rather naughty. The film is too long and is weakened by a switch in the focus from one of the twins to Pryce. Honest, well-written dialogue and bold editing ease some of the narrative flaws. Not rated; contains profanity and violence. 150m. **DIR:** Marc Evans. **CAST:** Theresa Russell, Jonathan Pryce. **1993 DVD**

THIEF, THE (1952) ★★1/2 A scientist for the Atomic Energy Commission tries to flee the country when the FBI discovers he's been selling information to enemy spies. Filmed entirely without dialogue, this *noir* thriller has strong visuals and an intense performance by Ray Milland, but the silence becomes a burdensome gimmick before long. B&W; 87m. **DIR:** Russell Rouse. **CAST:** Ray Milland, Martin Gabel, Rita Gam. **1952 DVD**

THIEF (1981) ★★★★ James Caan stars in this superb study of a jewel thief. Caan's character tries desperately to create the life he visualized while in prison—one complete with a car, money, house, wife, and kids. But as soon as he manages to acquire these things, they start slipping away. It's an interesting plot, and Michael Mann's direction gives it a sense of realism. Visually stunning, with a great score by Tangerine Dream. Rated R for violence, language, and brief nudity. 122m. **DIR:** Michael Mann. **CAST:** James Caan, Tuesday Weld, James Belushi, Willie Nelson. **1981 DVD**

THIEF, THE (1997) ★★★★ Homeless woman with a young son meets a soldier on a train in Stalin's Russia and falls in love. Then a dark side seeps through his air of respectability that threatens to destory them all. This entrancing story uses domestic dynamics as a metaphor for a political system that cannibalizes its own people. In Russian with English subtitles. Rated R for violence, language, and sexual content. 93m. **DIR:** Pavel Chukhrai. **CAST:** Yehaterina Rednikova, Vladimir Mashkov, Misha Philipchuk. **1997 DVD**

THIEF OF BAGDAD, THE (1924) ★★★1/2 The first of four spectacular versions of this classic Arabian Nights–ish fantasy-adventure of derring-do with magically flying carpets, giant genies, and crafty evil sorcery. The now-fabled Douglas Fairbanks Sr. is the thief, Julanne Johnson the beautiful princess he carries away on an airborne rug. Of all silent epics, this one is rated the most imaginative. The sets rival everything filmed before and since. Silent. B&W; 140m. **DIR:** Raoul Walsh. **CAST:** Douglas Fairbanks Sr., Julanne Johnson, Anna May Wong, Sojin. **1924 DVD**

THIEF OF BAGDAD, THE (1940) ★★★★★ With its flying carpets, giant genies, magic spells, and evil wizards, this film ranks as one of the finest fantasy films of all time. John Justin plays a young king, Ahmad, who is duped by his Grand Vizier, Jaffar, and loses his throne. With the aid of a colossal genie (excellently played by Rex Ingram) and other magical devices, Ahmad must do battle with Jaffar in a rousing fairy tale of good versus evil. 106m. **DIR:** Ludwig Berger, Tim Whelan, Michael Powell. **CAST:** Sabu, John Justin, June Duprez, Rex Ingram, Conrad Veidt. **1940**

THIEF OF BAGHDAD (1978) ★★ A passable television version of the Arabian Nights fable made bland by low-budget special effects but offset, if marginally, by an excellent cast. Not rated, it's certainly suitable for family viewing. 100m. **DIR:** Clive Donner. **CAST:** Peter Ustinov, Terence Stamp, Roddy McDowall, Ian Holm, Pavla Ustinov. **1978**

THIEF OF HEARTS ★★★ A young, upwardly mobile married woman loses her intimate diary of sexual fantasies to a thief who has broken into her home. In an interesting premise, the woman becomes a willing participant in the thief's sexual manipulations without knowing that he is the man who stole her secrets. Rated R. 100m. **DIR:** Douglas Day Stewart. **CAST:** Steven Bauer, Barbara Williams. **1984 DVD**

THIEF WHO CAME TO DINNER, THE ★★★ Silly stuff about Ryan O'Neal leading a double life: as a bookish computer programmer by day and a jewel thief by night. The film's most interesting performance comes from Jill Clayburgh in an early screen role. It's mindless fluff and inoffensive. Rated PG. 102m. **DIR:** Bud Yorkin. **CAST:** Ryan O'Neal, Jacqueline Bisset, Warren Oates, Jill Clayburgh, Charles Cioffi, Ned Beatty. **1973**

THIEVES (LES VOLEURS) ★★★1/2 Catherine Deneuve and Daniel Auteuil are scintillating in this erotic crime caper. An intelligent professor and police detective both fall under the spell of a young car thief who leads them into her world of crime and murder. Nothing is what it seems in this tale of a lovers' triangle. In French with English subtitles. Rated R for adult situations, language, nudity, and violence. 116m. **DIR:** André Téchiné. **CAST:** Catherine Deneuve, Daniel Auteuil, Laurence Cote, Benoit Magimel, Julien Riviere. **1996**

THIEVES LIKE US ★★★★ A classic melodrama about gangsters that relies more on story and characters than gunfire and bloodshed. Robert Altman turns the story of

survivors during the Depression into a heartfelt love story with sensitive acting and exceptional production values. It plays like a documentary and looks like a movie because of Altman's unique storytelling style. Rated R. 123m. **DIR:** Robert Altman. **CAST:** Keith Carradine, Shelley Duvall, Louise Fletcher, Bert Remsen, Tom Skerritt, John Schuck. **1974**

THIEVES OF FORTUNE ★★1/2 Shawn Weatherly attempts to win a $28 million bet that involves outrageous cliff-hanging stunts. Rated R for language and violence. 100m. **DIR:** Michael McCarthy. **CAST:** Michael Nouri, Shawn Weatherly, Lee Van Cleef, Liz Torres. **1989**

THIN BLUE LINE, THE ★★★★ Fascinating look into the 1976 murder of a Dallas policeman that led to a highly debated conviction of a drifter. Filmmaker Errol Morris's terrifying account of this incident raises some serious questions about the misuse of our current justice system. Not rated. 90m. **DIR:** Errol Morris. **1988**

THIN ICE ★★★★ One of Sonja Henie's most successful films. She stars as an ice-skating teacher who meets a European prince traveling in her country incognito. Naturally, they fall in love and she helps him solve his political problems. Of course, she also skates well. One of the movie's highlights is the performance of comedienne Joan Davis as an orchestra leader. B&W; 78m. **DIR:** Sidney Lanfield. **CAST:** Sonja Henie, Tyrone Power, Joan Davis, Arthur Treacher, Raymond Walburn, Alan Hale Sr., Sig Ruman, Leah Ray. **1937**

THIN LINE BETWEEN LOVE AND HATE, A ★★ Never say "I love you" to a lady—no matter what the circumstance—is the rule that a slick womanizer makes, breaks, and then pays for heavily in this sporadically comic, crude *Fatal Attraction*. The film tries to be both a hip, bawdy sitcom and a film with real heart as two partners in crimes of the heart use their jobs as nightclub promoters to score dates. Rated R for language and violence. 97m. **DIR:** Martin Lawrence. **CAST:** Martin Lawrence, Bobby Brown, Lynn Whitfield, Regina King, Della Reese. **1996 DVD**

THIN MAN, THE ★★★★1/2 Viewers and critics alike were captivated by William Powell and Myrna Loy in this first (and best) of a series based on Dashiell Hammett's mystery novel about his "other" detective and wife, Nick and Nora Charles. The thin man is a murder victim. But never mind. The delight of this fun film is the banter between its stars. You'll like their little dog, too. B&W; 89m. **DIR:** W. S. Van Dyke. **CAST:** William Powell, Myrna Loy, Edward Brophy, Porter Hall, Maureen O'Sullivan. **1934**

THIN MAN GOES HOME, THE ★★1/2 Fifth and weakest entry in the series. Nick Charles (William Powell) returns to his old hometown, accompanied by Nora (Myrna Loy) and young Nick Jr. Still entertaining, but a lesser effort. B&W; 101m. **DIR:** Richard Thorpe. **CAST:** William Powell, Myrna Loy, Lucile Watson, Gloria De Haven, Anne Revere, Helen Vinson, Harry Davenport, Leon Ames, Donald Meek, Edward Brophy. **1944**

THIN RED LINE, THE ★★★ Eclectic director-scripter Terence Malick's ponderous style destroys any dramatic impact in this dull WWII-based drama, adapted from James Jones's novel. It's wrapped in artificially symbolic narration, needlessly melancholy cinematography, and far too much time wasted on atmosphere-establishing shots. You're left with a film that apparently *knows* that it's pretentious. Rated R for violence, profanity, and the charnel-house atrocities of war. 170m. **DIR:** Terence Malick. **CAST:** Sean Penn, Nick Nolte, Adrien Brody, Jim Caviezel, Ben Chaplin, Arie Verveen, Dash Mihok. **1998 DVD**

THING (FROM ANOTHER WORLD), THE (1951) ★★★★★ A highly entertaining film, this was based on a John W. Campbell's story about a hostile visitor from space at large at an army radar station in the Arctic. Considered by many to be a classic, this relies on the unseen rather than the seen for its power, and as such it is almost unbearably suspenseful. James Arness, in an early role, plays the monster. B&W; 87m. **DIR:** Christian Nyby. **CAST:** Kenneth Tobey, Margaret Sheridan, James Arness. **1951**

THING, THE (1982) ★★★★ The modern master of fright, John Carpenter, has created a movie so terrifying, it'll crawl right up your leg. Rather than a remake, this updated version of Howard Hawks's 1951 science-fiction–horror classic is closer to a sequel, with Kurt Russell and his crew arriving at the Antarctic encampment after the chameleon-like creature from outer space has finished off its inhabitants. It's good ol' "tell me a scary story" fun. Rated R for profanity and gore. 108m. **DIR:** John Carpenter. **CAST:** Kurt Russell, Wilford Brimley, Richard Dysart. **1982 DVD**

THING CALLED LOVE, THE ★★★1/2 River Phoenix, in his last role, is well cast as a frustrated singer trying to make it in Nashville. Director Peter Bogdanovich's film follows four young aspiring stars, and the exciting cast, fleshed out by real country stars, turns up the heat on and off the stage. Rated PG-13 for adult language and situations. 116m. **DIR:** Peter Bogdanovich. **CAST:** River Phoenix, Samantha Mathis, Sandra Bullock, Dermot Mulroney. **1993**

THING THAT COULDN'T DIE, THE Severed head of a devil worshiper takes over the minds of those who dig it up from its ancient tomb. B&W; 69m. **DIR:** Will Cowan. **CAST:** William Reynolds, Andra Martin, Carolyn Kearney. **1958**

THINGS ARE TOUGH ALL OVER Richard "Cheech" Marin and Tommy Chong up to no good. Rated R for profanity. 92m. **DIR:** Tom Avildsen. **CAST:** Cheech and Chong, Rikki Marin, Rip Taylor. **1982 DVD**

•THINGS BEHIND THE SUN ★★★1/2 This made-for-cable original is an interesting character drama about a rising rock star who was raped when she was twelve. Things get more complicated when a journalist comes to interview her for a music magazine, and he says he knows who her rapist was. Decent acting somewhat makes up for a mostly predictable story. Rated R for profanity, violence, nudity, and simulated sex. 119m. **DIR:** Allison Anders. **CAST:** Kim Dickens, Gabriel Mann, Eric Stoltz, Rosanna Arquette, Don Cheadle. **2001**

THINGS CHANGE ★★★★ Director David Mamet and his coscreenwriter, Shel Silverstein, have fashioned a marvelously subtle and witty comedy about an inept, low-level gangster (Joe Mantegna). He goes against orders to take an old shoe-shine "boy" (Don Ameche) on one last fling before the latter goes to prison for a crime he didn't commit. Rated PG for profanity and violence. 100m. **DIR:** David Mamet. **CAST:** Don Ameche, Joe Mantegna, Robert Prosky. **1988 DVD**

THINGS TO COME ★★★★ The world of the future as viewed from the perspective of the 1930s, this is an interesting screen curio based on the book by H. G. Wells. Special effects have come a long way since then, but sci-fi fans will still enjoy the spectacular sets in this honorable, thoughtful production. B&W; 92m. **DIR:** William Cameron Menzies. **CAST:** Raymond Massey, Cedric Hardwicke, Ralph Richardson. **1936 DVD**

THINGS TO DO IN DENVER WHEN YOU'RE DEAD ★★★1/2 Although this slick entry in the wiseguy-noir subgenre is an obvious imitation of *Pulp Fiction*, scripter Scott Rosenberg has a lot of fun with the hard-luck gangsters populating his story. When smooth-talking Jimmy the Saint and his gang muff an easy assignment, there's hell to pay... but at least they go out with style. Rated R for violence and profanity. 117m. **DIR:** Gary Fleder. **CAST:** Andy Garcia, Christopher Walken, William Forsythe, Christopher Lloyd, Bill Nunn, Treat Williams, Gabrielle Anwar. **1995 DVD**

THINGS WE DID LAST SUMMER ★★1/2 A mixed bag used to supplement *Saturday Night Live* episodes in the show's first golden era, this features some of The Not Ready For Prime Time Players in skits of varying quality. The highlights are provided by John Belushi and Dan Aykroyd performing live in concert as the Blues Brothers. 50m. **DIR:** Gary Weis. **CAST:** John Belushi, Dan Aykroyd, Bill Murray, Gilda Radner, Garrett Morris, Laraine Newman. **1977**

•THINGS YOU CAN TELL JUST BY LOOKING AT HER ★★★★ Absolutely charming, witty, and absorbing film features a stellar cast, a sense of sisterhood that is contagious, and smart writing that says a lot without standing on a soapbox. Believable characters come to life with their wants and desires. The entire cast gives fine-tuned performances, especially Glenn Close as a physician whose love life is in need of a checkup, and Cameron Diaz as the blind sister of police officer Amy Brenneman. You'll walk away from this film feeling satisfied and emotionally fulfilled. Rated PG-13 for adult situations and language. 109m. **DIR:** Rodrigo Garcia. **CAST:** Glenn Close, Cameron Diaz, Calista Flockhart, Kathy Baker, Amy Brenneman, Holly Hunter. **2000 DVD**

THINK BIG ★★1/2 The perpetually late Barbarian Brothers (Peter and David Paul) are sent to L.A. to deliver a truckload of toxic waste, and a stowaway throws a wrench into their gears. Surprisingly good-natured in the dubious tradition of the all-star *Gumball Rally/Cannonball Run* films. PG-13. 86m. **DIR:** Jon Turteltaub. **CAST:** Martin Mull, Richard Moll, Michael Winslow, David Carradine, Richard Kiel, Ari Meyers, Claudia Christian, Peter Paul, David Paul. **1988**

THINK FAST, MR. MOTO ★★★ German actor Peter Lorre may have seemed an odd choice to play a Japanese detective, but he was so popular in this film that seven sequels were made in two years, and Mr. Moto nearly eclipsed Charlie Chan. Here he's on the trail of jewel smugglers on a ship to Shanghai. B&W; 66m. **DIR:** Norman Foster. **CAST:** Peter Lorre, Virginia Field, Sig Ruman, J. Carrol Naish. **1937**

THINKIN' BIG ★★ Soft-core beach romp with the usual horny teens heading for spring-break fun in the sun. Rated R for nudity. 94m. **DIR:** S. F. Brownrigg. **CAST:** Bruce Anderson, Nancy Buechler. **1986**

THINNER ★★ Stephen King's skinny horror novel (under the pen name Richard Bachman) was funnier and scarier as a quick midnight read. Chubby Maine attorney Billy Halleck is getting oral sex from his wife while driving in a rainstorm when he runs over an elderly gypsy woman. Billy's judge and cop buddies keep him out of jail, but the woman's ancient father puts a curse on him that makes him lose weight no matter how much he eats. Rated R for violence, gore, language, and sexual references. 92m. **DIR:** Tom Holland. **CAST:** Robert Burke, Joe Mantegna, Lucinda Jenney, Joy Lenz, Michael Constantine. **1996 DVD**

THIRD DEGREE BURN ★★★ Debt-ridden ex-cop reluctantly accepts a domestic investigation, only to fall headlong for the blonde subject. (Virginia Madsen is the perfect Monroe-like sex bomb.) Steamy mystery twists like a snake. Made for HBO. 97m. **DIR:** Roger Spottiswoode. **CAST:** Treat Williams, Virginia Madsen, C.C.H. Pounder, Richard Masur. **1989**

THIRD MAN, THE ★★★★★ Considered by many to be the greatest suspense film of all time, this classic inevitably turns up on every best-film list. It rivals any Hitchcock thriller as being the ultimate masterpiece of film suspense. A writer (Joseph Cotten) discovers an old friend he thought dead to be the head of a vicious European black market organization. Unfortunately for him, that information makes him a marked man. B&W; 104m. **DIR:** Carol Reed. **CAST:** Joseph Cotten, Orson Welles, Alida Valli, Trevor Howard. **1949 DVD**

THIRD MAN ON THE MOUNTAIN ★★★ James MacArthur stars as a young man whose father was killed in a climbing accident. The Citadel (actually the Matterhorn) has never been scaled. Miraculously, he finds the secret passage his father had been seeking. Breathtaking scenery and an excellent script make this an excellent adventure story for the family. Not rated. 106m. **DIR:** Ken Annakin. **CAST:** Michael Rennie, James MacArthur, Janet Munro, Herbert Lom. **1959**

THIRD MIRACLE, THE ★★★★ A priest investigates a candidate for sainthood while grappling with his own crisis of faith; meanwhile, he is strongly attracted to the candidate's daughter, who has her own doubts about her late mother's saintliness. This strong, subtle drama deals intelligently with issues of faith and cynicism, with fine acting throughout. Rated R for mature themes, brief profanity, and violence. 119m. **DIR:** Agnieszka Holland. **CAST:** Ed Harris, Anne Heche, Barbara Sukowa, Armin Mueller-Stahl. **1999 DVD**

THIRD SOLUTION, THE 🦃 Don't let the (usually) talented cast sucker you into sampling this laughably convoluted, poorly dubbed Italian political melodrama. Rated R for violence and brief nudity. 113m. **DIR:** Pasquale Squiteri. **CAST:** F. Murray Abraham, Treat Williams, Danny Aiello, Rita Rusic. **1989**

•THIR13EN GHOSTS ★★ Sean Hargreaves's gorgeous production design notwithstanding, this in-name-only update of the 1960 William Castle horror quickie is a laughable contest to see whether Tony Shalhoub or Matthew Lillard can chew up more of the scenery. The story makes no sense whatsoever, and you'll soon hope that the gory spectres in this upscale haunted house kill *all* its human inhabitants. Rated R for profanity, nudity, violence, and gore. 90m. **DIR:** Steve Beck. **CAST:** Tony

Shalhoub, Embeth Davidtz, Matthew Lillard, Shannon Elizabeth, F. Murray Abraham. **2001 DVD**

THIRST 🦃 An innocent young woman is kidnapped by a Satanic brotherhood and subjected to diabolical torture. Rated R for nudity and violence. 96m. **DIR:** Rod Hardy. **CAST:** Chantal Contouri, David Hemmings, Henry Silva, Rod Mullinar. **1988**

THIRSTY DEAD, THE 🦃 Charles Mansonesque figure lives in the jungle and sacrifices young women in bloody rituals. Rated PG. 90m. **DIR:** Terry Becker. **CAST:** John Considine, Jennifer Billingsley. **1975**

13 AT DINNER ★★★1/2 Above-average made-for-TV Agatha Christie mystery, with Peter Ustinov reprising his big-screen role as fastidious Belgian sleuth Hercule Poirot. This time out, the dapper detective contends with a murdered British lord and his thespian widow (Faye Dunaway). Notable for the presence of David Suchet as Scotland Yard's Inspector Japp, a few years before Suchet took over the role of Poirot himself. 100m. **DIR:** Lou Antonio. **CAST:** Peter Ustinov, Faye Dunaway, David Suchet, Lee Horsley, Amanda Pays. **1985**

THIRTEEN DAYS ★★★1/2 Although historical liberties have been taken here, you'll still be amazed that we and the Soviets *didn't* ignite World War III during the fortnight-long Cuban Missile Crisis. And while the drama is compelling, the problem lies with the way presidential special assistant Kenneth O'Donnell's role has been amplified to suit star Kevin Costner. One comes to believe that only O'Donnell stood between us and nuclear annihilation, and, of course, that's just rubbish. Costner's overwrought theatrics also overshadow the much finer work by Bruce Greenwood and Steven Culp as, respectively, JFK and RFK. Rated PG-13 for brief profanity. 145m. **DIR:** Roger Donaldson. **CAST:** Kevin Costner, Bruce Greenwood, Steven Culp, Dylan Baker, Michael Fairman, Henry Strozier, Frank Wood, Kevin Conway, Tim Kelleher, Len Cariou. **2000 DVD**

13 GHOSTS ★★★ Lighthearted horror tale of an average family inheriting a haunted house complete with a creepy old housekeeper (Margaret Hamilton) who may also be a witch, and a secret fortune hidden somewhere in the place. William Castle directs with his customary style and flair. Pretty neat. B&W; 88m. **DIR:** William Castle. **CAST:** Charles Herbert, Donald Woods, Martin Milner, Rosemary DeCamp, Jo Morrow, Margaret Hamilton. **1960 DVD**

13 RUE MADELEINE ★★★ Espionage thriller, inspired by the *March of Time* series, shot in semidocumentary style. James Cagney is an OSS chief who goes to France to complete a mission when one of his men is killed. B&W; 95m. **DIR:** Henry Hathaway. **CAST:** James Cagney, Annabella, Walter Abel, Frank Latimore, Melville Cooper, E. G. Marshall, Karl Malden, Sam Jaffe, Richard Conte. **1946**

THIRTEENTH FLOOR, THE (1990) ★★ A young girl watches as her ruthless politician father has a man and his son executed. Years later, on the run from her father, she takes refuge in the same building where the killing took place. She soon discovers it's haunted by the spirit of the murdered boy. Rated R for violence and profanity. 86m. **DIR:** Chris Roach. **CAST:** Lisa Hensley, Tim McKenzie. **1990**

THIRTEENTH FLOOR, THE (1999) ★★★ Yet another of the many cyberspace/virtual reality scenarios released by Hollywood in the spring of 1999, and among the least interesting. A wealthy software programmer, investigating the murder of his mentor, begins to suspect that his world isn't quite all it seems. A B effort at best. Rated R—rather unfairly—for brief profanity and fairly mild violence. 120m. **DIR:** Josef Rusnak. **CAST:** Craig Bierko, Gretchen Mol, Vincent D'Onofrio, Dennis Haysbert, Armin Mueller-Stahl. **1999 DVD**

THIRTEENTH GUEST, THE ★★★ A gathering of relatives in a spooky old mansion invites murder in this superior thriller. While a storm rages outside, the reading of a strange will is interrupted by a mysterious figure, and when the lights come on there's a corpse. B&W; 65m. **DIR:** Albert Ray. **CAST:** Ginger Rogers, Lyle Talbot, J. Farrell MacDonald. **1932**

13TH WARRIOR, THE ★★★★ Taken from Michael Crichton's fact-based, 1976 novel, *Eaters of the Dead*, this is the epic tale of an Arabian prince and poet (Antonio Banderas) who finds himself conscripted by a band of Vikings off to battle supernatural monsters. Although this film was shelved for two years and allegedly underwent some editorial changes against the wishes of director John McTiernan, it nevertheless emerges as a blood-stirring epic. Rated R for nudity, violence, and gore. 103m. **DIR:** John McTiernan. **CAST:** Antonio Banderas, Diane Venora, Dennis Storhoi, Vladmir Kulich, Omar Sharif, Anders T. Anderson, Richard Bremmer, Tony Curran. **1999 DVD**

38 VIENNA BEFORE THE FALL ★★★ The romance between a Jewish theatrical producer and a beautiful Aryan woman becomes threatened by the prejudicial climate of Nazi Germany. In German with English subtitles. Rated R for nudity, profanity, and violence. 97m. **DIR:** Wolfgang Gluck. **CAST:** Tobias Engel, Sunnyi Melles. **1989**

35 UP ★★★★1/2 When he's not working on mainstream films, English director Michael Apted returns to the brilliant, ongoing documentary with which he first made his reputation. The filming of the lives and times of a select group of fourteen English men and women. They've been interviewed and depicted on film at seven-year intervals, starting when they were seven, in 1963. You don't have to be familiar with earlier segments to gain a lot from *35 Up*. Not rated. 127m. **DIR:** Michael Apted. **1991**

30-FOOT BRIDE OF CANDY ROCK, THE ★★ A nebbish inventor turns his girlfriend into a giant. A mild comedy with a certain amount of charm, this was the last film made by Columbia's B-picture unit, and Lou Costello's only feature film after breaking up with Bud Abbott. He died before the film was released. B&W; 75m. **DIR:** Sidney Miller. **CAST:** Lou Costello, Dorothy Provine, Gale Gordon, Charles Lane, Doodles Weaver. **1959**

30 IS A DANGEROUS AGE, CYNTHIA ★★ Dated British comedy features Dudley Moore as a pianist-composer who intends to find a bride and write a musical before he turns 30. 83m. **DIR:** Joseph McGrath. **CAST:** Dudley Moore, Suzy Kendall, Eddie Foy Jr., John Bird, Patricia Routledge. **1967**

THIRTY-NINE STEPS, THE (1935) ★★★★★ Alfred Hitchcock was assigned to direct what was intended to

be a simple, low-budget spy-chase thriller. Using the style and technique that were to make him famous, he gained immediate audience sympathy for the plight of his central character, an innocent Canadian (Robert Donat) who while visiting England is implicated in the theft of national secrets and murder. The result was a big hit. B&W; 87m. **DIR:** Alfred Hitchcock. **CAST:** Robert Donat, Madeleine Carroll, Lucie Mannheim. **1935 DVD**

THIRTY-NINE STEPS, THE (1959) ★★1/2 Inferior remake of Alfred Hitchcock's suspense classic has Kenneth More as the hapless fellow who innocently becomes involved in a spy plot. The 1978 version with Robert Powell also has it beat. 93m. **DIR:** Ralph Thomas. **CAST:** Kenneth More, Taina Elg, Brenda de Banzie, Barry Jones, Sidney James. **1959**

THIRTY-NINE STEPS, THE (1978) ★★★1/2 An innocent man stumbles onto a spy plot in pre–World War I London with nowhere to turn. The best of several Hitchcock remakes in the 1970s. It can't compete with the original, of course. Rated PG. 102m. **DIR:** Don Sharp. **CAST:** Robert Powell, David Warner, Eric Porter, Karen Dotrice, John Mills. **1978**

THIRTY SECONDS OVER TOKYO ★★★★ Spencer Tracy is in top form as General Doolittle, who led the first bombing attack on Tokyo during World War II. A true-life adventure that, despite its length, never bogs down. B&W; 138m. **DIR:** Mervyn LeRoy. **CAST:** Spencer Tracy, Van Johnson, Robert Walker, Phyllis Thaxter, Scott McKay, Robert Mitchum, Stephen McNally. **1944**

30-SEP-55 ★★★1/2 Affecting, sentimental portrait of a group of young adults and how the death of movie star James Dean changes their lives. Richard Thomas gathers up his friends for a wake and then for a celebration of Dean's spirit that ends tragically before the evening is out. Rated PG for language and violence. 107m. **DIR:** James Bridges. **CAST:** Richard Thomas, Lisa Blount, Dennis Quaid, Tom Hulce, Dennis Christopher, Deborah Benson. **1977**

36 FILLETTE ★★★ A sexually charged comedy-drama from France, about a 14 year old girl and her frustrated efforts to cast off her virginity. Delphine Zentout is most impressive as the girl. The title is a reference to a French adolescent dress size. In French with English subtitles. 92m. **DIR:** Catherine Brellat. **CAST:** Delphine Zentout, Etienne Chicot. **1988 DVD**

36 HOURS ★★★1/2 An intriguing psychological war-drama. James Garner, a designer of the secret Allied invasion plans, is kidnapped by Nazis and brainwashed into believing the war is long over. Rod Taylor is so likable as the doctor leading the ruse that you almost hope his plan succeeds. Remade for cable as *Breaking Point*. 115m. **DIR:** George Seaton. **CAST:** James Garner, Eva Marie Saint, Rod Taylor, Werner Peters, Alan Napier. **1964**

36 HOURS TO DIE ★★★1/2 Tense drama unfolds when mobsters make a high-tech takeover attempt of a family-owned brewery. Treat Williams is terrific in this TNT original as he is forced to outsmart vicious Saul Rubinek. Unrated, contains violence and nudity. 89m. **DIR:** Yves Simoneau. **CAST:** Treat Williams, Kim Cattrall, Saul Rubinek, Carroll O'Connor. **1999**

THIRTY-TWO SHORT FILMS ABOUT GLENN GOULD ★★★★★ This innovative portrayal of the eccentric, controversial Canadian pianist—one of the greatest musicians of the twentieth century—won four Genie Awards (Canadian Oscars) including best picture and best director. As refreshing and visionary as the man himself. Not rated. 90m. **DIR:** Francois Girard. **CAST:** Colm Feore. **1994 DVD**

THIS BOY'S LIFE ★★★ Young Tobias Wolff is trapped when his mother tries to do the right thing by marrying "a good provider." The boy's life slowly becomes a nightmare. Screenwriter Robert Getchell's adaptation of Wolff's autobiographical book skimps on character depth, leaving us a good—but not great—film. Rated R for profanity, violence, nudity, and simulated sex. 114m. **DIR:** Michael Caton-Jones. **CAST:** Robert De Niro, Ellen Barkin, Leonardo DiCaprio, Chris Cooper. **1993**

THIS COULD BE THE NIGHT ★★★ A timid schoolteacher becomes a secretary to two nightclub owners and finds herself pursued by one of them. A fair try at a Damon Runyon atmosphere. Joan Blondell and J. Carrol Naish steal the movie. B&W; 103m. **DIR:** Robert Wise. **CAST:** Jean Simmons, Paul Douglas, Anthony Franciosa, Julie Wilson, Joan Blondell, J. Carrol Naish, ZaSu Pitts. **1957**

THIS GUN FOR HIRE (1942) ★★★★ Alan Ladd made his first big impression in this 1942 gangster film as a bad guy who turns good guy in the end. Robert Preston and Veronica Lake costar in this still enjoyable revenge film. B&W; 80m. **DIR:** Frank Tuttle. **CAST:** Alan Ladd, Robert Preston, Veronica Lake. **1942**

THIS GUN FOR HIRE (1991) ★★★ Graham Greene's moody thriller gets another go-around, this time with Robert Wagner reprising the role that made Alan Ladd a star. Wagner's an implacable hired gunman who finds his soul at the wrong moment. Greene's cynical view of humanity remains seductive. Made for cable TV. Rated R for violence and sexual themes. 89m. **DIR:** Lou Antonio. **CAST:** Robert Wagner, Nancy Everhard, Fredric Lehne, John Harkins. **1991**

THIS HAPPY BREED ★★★★ Slice of British nostalgia chronicles the lives of a working-class family from 1919 to 1939. Adapted from a Noel Coward play, this is an extraordinary film of collector caliber. 114m. **DIR:** David Lean. **CAST:** Robert Newton, Celia Johnson, John Mills, Kay Walsh, Stanley Holloway. **1944**

THIS HAPPY FEELING ★★ Curt Jurgens is an aging actor, Debbie Reynolds is the young girl who develops a crush on him, and John Saxon is Jurgens's handsome young neighbor who falls hard for Reynolds. The film is truly reflective of the 1950s, with its unreal colors and a musical score inundating every scene. Alexis Smith as "the other woman" is enjoyable. 92m. **DIR:** Blake Edwards. **CAST:** Debbie Reynolds, Curt Jurgens, John Saxon, Alexis Smith, Mary Astor, Estelle Winwood, Troy Donahue. **1958**

THIS IS AMERICA, CHARLIE BROWN ★★★1/2 This eight-part miniseries employs the Peanuts gang to teach viewers about seminal moments in American history, from the Mayflower voyages and signing of the Constitution, to a NASA space station and an overview of American music. The soundtracks are superbly scored by jazz greats such as Dave Brubeck, Wynton Marsalis, George Winston, and David Benoit. Sadly, the uneven

animation occasionally spoils the package. Not rated. 25m. **DIR:** Evert Brown, Sam Jaimes, Bill Melendez, Sam Nicholson. **1988**

THIS IS ELVIS ★★★★ A blend of film footage of the "real" Elvis with other portions, played by convincing stand-ins. The result is a warm, nostalgic portrait of a man who touched the hearts of young and old throughout the world. Rated PG because of slight profanity. 101m. **DIR:** Malcolm Leo, Andrew Solt. **CAST:** Elvis Presley, David Scott, Paul Boensh, III. **1981**

THIS IS MY AFFAIR ★★1/2 A turn-of-the-century melodrama produced to take advantage of the real-life romantic pairing of Robert Taylor and Barbara Stanwyck in Hollywood. He is the navy man accused of a crime. She is the saloon singer who appeals directly to President McKinley for help. B&W; 100m. **DIR:** William A. Seiter. **CAST:** Robert Taylor, Barbara Stanwyck, Brian Donlevy, Victor McLaglen, John Carradine, Sidney Blackmer. **1937**

THIS IS MY FATHER ★★1/2 A middle-aged schoolteacher travels to Ireland to learn about the star-crossed courtship between his parents (Aidan Quinn, Moya Farrelly) during the 1930s. The film is a sincere, well-intentioned labor of love for the Quinn brothers (star Aidan, cinematographer Declan, and writer-director Paul) and well-acted by all, but it's also clumsy and plodding. The modern-day "framing" story is less interesting than the flashbacks. Rated R for sexual scenes and mature themes. 120m. **DIR:** Paul Quinn. **CAST:** James Caan, Aidan Quinn, Moya Farrelly, John Cusack, Jacob Tierney, Stephen Rea. **1998 DVD**

THIS IS MY LIFE ★★★ Sparkling dialogue and memorable characters help elevate this comedy about conflicting mother-daughter perspectives. The low spots involve onstage comedy routines by Mom (Julie Kavner). As with most movies about stand-up comics, these bits aren't really funny. Rated PG-13 for profanity. 94m. **DIR:** Nora Ephron. **CAST:** Julie Kavner, Samantha Mathis, Gaby Hoffman, Carrie Fisher, Dan Aykroyd. **1992**

THIS IS SPINAL TAP ★★★★1/2 This is one of the funniest movies ever made about rock 'n' roll. This is a satire of rock documentaries that tells the story of Spinal Tap, an over-the-hill British heavy-metal rock group that's fast rocketing to the bottom of the charts. *This Is Spinal Tap* isn't consistently funny, but does it ever have its moments. Some of the song lyrics are hysterical, and the performances are perfect. Rated R for profanity. 82m. **DIR:** Rob Reiner. **CAST:** Michael McKean, Christopher Guest, Harry Shearer, Rob Reiner. **1984**

THIS IS THE ARMY ★★★ Hoofer (later U.S. senator) George Murphy portrays Ronald Reagan's father in this musical mélange penned by Irving Berlin to raise funds for Army Emergency Relief during World War II. It's a star-studded, rousing show of songs and skits from start to finish, but practically plotless. 121m. **DIR:** Michael Curtiz. **CAST:** George Murphy, Joan Leslie, Ronald Reagan, George Tobias, Alan Hale Sr., Joe Louis, Kate Smith, Irving Berlin, Frances Langford, Charles Butterworth. **1943**

THIS IS THE SEA ★★★ This film about star-crossed lovers on opposite sides of the Irish conflict arrives too late to make an impact. Writer-director Mary McGuckian's efforts to transplant *Romeo and Juliet* in the middle of war-torn Northern Ireland fall considerably short of other recent efforts like *Some Mother's Son.* Ross McDade and Samantha Morton are the ill-fated lovers, one a Catholic, the other a Protestant, whose love affair brings about tragic consequences. Decent supporting cast includes Richard Harris and Gabriel Byrne. Rated R for language. 104m. **DIR:** Mary McGuckian. **CAST:** Gabriel Byrne, Richard Harris, John Lynch, Samantha Morton, Ross McDade. **1998**

THIS ISLAND EARTH ★★★ A fine 1950s sci-fi flick about scientists kidnapped by aliens to help them save their planet, this has good makeup and effects for the era. 86m. **DIR:** Joseph M. Newman. **CAST:** Jeff Morrow, Rex Reason, Faith Domergue, Russell Johnson. **1955 DVD**

THIS LAND IS MINE ★★★ Charles Laughton performs another fine characterization, this time as a timid French teacher who blossoms as a hero when he is incited to vigorous action by the Nazi occupation. Time has dulled this wartime film, but the artistry of the director and players remains sharp. B&W; 103m. **DIR:** Jean Renoir. **CAST:** Charles Laughton, Maureen O'Hara, George Sanders, Walter Slezak. **1943**

THIS MAN CAN'T DIE ★★★ Yet another "revenge for a slaughtered family" sadistic spaghetti Western with Guy Madison as a government agent avenger on the trail of an outlaw who murdered his parents. 90m. **DIR:** Gianfranco Baldanello. **CAST:** Guy Madison, Lucienne Bridou, Rik Battaglia. **1968**

THIS MAN MUST DIE ★★★★ Claude Chabrol pays homage to Alfred Hitchcock with this outstanding thriller about a man who sets out to find the hit-and-run driver responsible for the death of his son. Complications ensue as the father encounters the murderer's sister, whom he seduces. A riveting shocker with a startling climax. French, dubbed into English. 112m. **DIR:** Claude Chabrol. **CAST:** Michel Duchaussoy, Jean Yanne, Caroline Cellier. **1970**

THIS PROPERTY IS CONDEMNED ★★1/2 Marginal film interpretation of Tennessee Williams's play. Owen Legate (Robert Redford) is a stranger in town, there for the purpose of laying off local railroaders. Alva (Natalie Wood) is a flirtatious southern girl who casts her spell of romance on the stranger. 109m. **DIR:** Sydney Pollack. **CAST:** Natalie Wood, Robert Redford, Charles Bronson, Kate Reid, Robert Blake. **1966**

THIS SPECIAL FRIENDSHIP ★★1/2 At a boys' boarding school, a relationship between an older student and a younger, innocent boy is broken up by teachers. Once-controversial story of homoeroticism now seems merely sentimental and self-consciously sensitive. In French with English subtitles. B&W; 105m. **DIR:** Jean Delannoy. **CAST:** Francis Lacombrade, Didier Haudepin, Michel Bouquet. **1964**

THIS SPORTING LIFE ★★★1/2 Richard Harris and Rachel Roberts shine in this stark, powerful look into the life and dreams of a Yorkshire coal miner who seeks to become a professional rugby player. The squeamish will not like all the game scenes. 129m. **DIR:** Lindsay Anderson. **CAST:** Rachel Roberts, Richard Harris, Colin Blakely. **1963 DVD**

•THIS SWEET SICKNESS ★★★ A lonely man (Gérard Depardieu), obsessed with a married woman, builds an elaborate mountain house in an attempt to seduce her.

The effect of his obsession on both himself and the woman (Miou-Miou), whose love he spurns, form the basis of this unsettling psychological drama. In French with English subtitles. Not rated; sexual themes make it inappropriate for young children. 101m. **DIR:** Claude Miller. **CAST:** Gérard Depardieu, Miou-Miou, Dominique Laffin, Josiane Balasko. **1977**

THIS TIME FOR KEEPS ★★★ A typical Esther Williams swimming event with more musical variety than usual pits her allure against the comedy of Jimmy Durante and the sophistication of opera-star Lauritz Melchior. On Mackinac Island Melchior's son promptly falls in love with Williams, and the movie dissolves into a series of musical numbers. More padding than plot, but the padding is classy stuff. 105m. **DIR:** Richard Thorpe. **CAST:** Esther Williams, Lauritz Melchior, Jimmy Durante, May Whitty, Johnnie Johnston, Sharon MacManus, Kenneth Tobey, Esther Dale, Ludwig Stossel, Xavier Cugat. **1947**

THIS WORLD, THEN THE FIREWORKS ★★★ Decent stab at *film noir* stars Billy Zane as an investigative reporter in Chicago in the 1950s whose latest story is too hot for the local law. Filled with unsavory characters doing unsavory things to each other and a voice-over narration that pulls it all together, this film is at times dark and depressing, but never boring. Rated R for violence, language, nudity, and adult situations. 99m. **DIR:** Michael Oblowitz. **CAST:** Billy Zane, Gina Gershon, Sheryl Lee, Rue McClanahan. **1996**

THOMAS AND THE MAGIC RAILROAD ★★1/2 Alec Baldwin is adorable as the magical little conductor of Shining Time Station who must get more gold dust to protect the steam engines from a wicked diesel. All of Baldwin's perky enthusiasm, however, can't make this watchable for anyone beyond preschoolers. Even they will be disappointed by the limited animation of the heroic Thomas the Tank Engine and his pals. Rated G. 86m. **DIR:** Britt Allcroft. **CAST:** Alec Baldwin, Peter Fonda, Mara Wilson, Michael Rodgers. **2000 DVD**

THOMAS CROWN AFFAIR, THE (1968) ★★★★ Combine an engrossing bank-heist caper with an offbeat romance and you have the ingredients for a fun-filled movie. Steve McQueen and Faye Dunaway are at their best as the sophisticated bank robber and unscrupulous insurance investigator. The emotional tricks and verbal sparring between these two are a joy. This is one of the few films where the split-screen technique really moves the story along. 102m. **DIR:** Norman Jewison. **CAST:** Steve McQueen, Faye Dunaway, Paul Burke. **1968**

THOMAS CROWN AFFAIR, THE (1999) ★★★★ This striking, stylish remake succeeds on its own merits, in great part because of the playful chemistry between Pierce Brosnan and René Russo. The material is updated and reworked—and considerably more erotic—but the central premise remains intact: that of a successful corporate playboy who moonlights as an art thief, and draws the attention of a vibrantly sophisticated insurance investigator determined to nail him. The resulting capers, crosses, and double crosses are a joy: sleek and loaded with charm and savoir faire. Brosnan and Russo are perfectly suited to these characters: dueling titans who must appear icily superficial and above common worldly concerns. Director John McTiernan has crafted a delicious bit of cat-and-mouse whimsy: a worthy successor to *To Catch a Thief*, *How to Steal a Million*, and *The Thief Who Came to Dinner*. Rated R for nudity, strong sexual content, and profanity. 113m. **DIR:** John McTiernan. **CAST:** Pierce Brosnan, René Russo, Denis Leary, Ben Gazzara, Frankie Faison, Fritz Weaver, Faye Dunaway. **1999 DVD**

THOMAS GRAAL'S BEST CHILD ★★★★ The best of the Thomas Graal films. Newlyweds Victor Sjöström and Karin Molander bicker about the best ways to rear their child. Among the many subjects satirized is the so-called liberated woman of contemporary Sweden. Silent. B&W; 94m. **DIR:** Mauritz Stiller. **CAST:** Victor Sjöström, Karin Molander. **1918**

THOMAS GRAAL'S BEST FILM ★★★★ One of a popular series of Thomas Graal films, all starring Victor Sjöström and his wife. They all presented satiric jabs at contemporary life, much in the same way as today's television sitcoms do. In this one Graal is a screenwriter distracted by a romance with a rich man's daughter. Sweden. Silent. B&W; 67m. **DIR:** Mauritz Stiller. **CAST:** Victor Sjöström, Karin Molander. **1917**

THOMAS JEFFERSON ★★★1/2 The first in a projected series of films on great Americans by Ken Burns, this two-tape documentary is similar in style to his past projects, relying on famous voices, narrated letters, and careful research. However, there are not enough interviews, the reenactments are limited to two repetitive scenes and far too many of the shots are stagnant. Burns tackles the enigma that was Jefferson, and there is much here of quality, but the overall production is not up to his usually high standards. Narrated by Ossie Davis. Not rated. 180m. **DIR:** Ken Burns. **1997 DVD**

THOMPSON'S LAST RUN ★★★1/2 Robert Mitchum plays a criminal who is being transferred to a new prison by a school friend who chose the right side of the law and is ready to retire. Bittersweet story with solid performances by all. 95m. **DIR:** Jerrold Freedman. **CAST:** Robert Mitchum, Wilford Brimley, Kathleen York. **1986 DVD**

THORNBIRDS, THE ★★★ Originally a ten-hour TV miniseries, this much-edited film is still worth a watch. Richard Chamberlain plays an ambitious priest who falls in love with an innocent, trusting young woman (Rachel Ward). It's all played out against shifting backgrounds of outback Australia, Vatican Rome, and idyllic Greece. This has been released for a limited time and copies may be hard to locate. 150m. **DIR:** Daryl Duke. **CAST:** Richard Chamberlain, Rachel Ward, Christopher Plummer, Bryan Brown, Barbara Stanwyck, Richard Kiley, Jean Simmons, John Friedrich, Philip Anglim. **1983**

THOROUGHBREDS DON'T CRY ★★★ In this first teaming of Mickey Rooney and Judy Garland, he is a discredited jockey (sound familiar?), and they help a young English boy win a big race with his horse, The Pookah. Garland does get to sing, but Sophie Tucker, as her aunt, is wasted in a nonsinging role. B&W; 80m. **DIR:** Alfred E. Green. **CAST:** Judy Garland, Mickey Rooney, Sophie Tucker, C. Aubrey Smith. **1937**

THOROUGHLY MODERN MILLIE ★★★ First-rate music characterizing America's Jazz Age dominates this harebrained-plotted, slapstick-punctuated spoof of the 1920s, complete with villains, a bordello, and a cooing flapper so smitten with her stuffed-shirt boss that she

can't see her boyfriend for beans. It's toe-tapping entertainment, but a tad too long. 138m. **DIR:** George Roy Hill. **CAST:** Julie Andrews, Mary Tyler Moore, Carol Channing, James Fox, Beatrice Lillie, John Gavin, Noriyuki "Pat" Morita, Jack Soo. **1967**

THOSE CALLOWAYS ★★★★ Sensitive, sentimental film about a family in New England. Man battles townspeople and nature to preserve a safe haven for geese. Marvelous scenes of life in a small town and the love between individuals. Rated G. 131m. **DIR:** Norman Tokar. **CAST:** Brian Keith, Vera Miles, Brandon de Wilde, Linda Evans. **1965**

THOSE DARING YOUNG MEN IN THEIR JAUNTY JALOPIES ★★★ Director Ken Annakin's follow up to *Those Magnificent Men In Their Flying Machines* lacks that certain spark it takes to make a classic, but there are some hilarious moments in this tale of a European road rally in the 1920s. Peter Cook and Dudley Moore as two very, very British officers are the best of the international cast. Rated G. 125m. **DIR:** Ken Annakin. **CAST:** Tony Curtis, Susan Hampshire, Peter Cook, Gert Fröbe, Dudley Moore, Terry-Thomas. **1969**

THOSE ENDEARING YOUNG CHARMS ★★★ Heroine Laraine Day brings smoothie Robert Young to bay and then to heel in this cliché-plotted, but sprightly played, romantic comedy. Public hunger for wholesome laughter and sentimental tears as World War II wound down made this a box-office bonanza. Ann Harding is perfect as the wise mother. B&W; 82m. **DIR:** Lewis Allen. **CAST:** Robert Young, Laraine Day, Bill Williams, Ann Harding, Anne Jeffreys, Lawrence Tierney. **1945**

THOSE GLORY GLORY DAYS ★★ A group of young girls idolize the members of their school's soccer team. Tired nostalgia from the British television anthology *First Love*. 77m. **DIR:** Philip Saville. **CAST:** Julia McKenzie, Elizabeth Spriggs. **1984**

THOSE LIPS, THOSE EYES ★★ So-so "let's put on a show" musical features Frank Langella as a would-be stage star forced to play to small towns, though he longs to appear on Broadway. Rated R for profanity and brief nudity. 106m. **DIR:** Michael Pressman. **CAST:** Frank Langella, Glynnis O'Connor, Tom Hulce, Jerry Stiller, Kevin McCarthy. **1980**

THOSE MAGNIFICENT MEN IN THEIR FLYING MACHINES ★★★★ An air race between London and Paris in the early days of flight is this comedy's centerpiece. Around it hang an enjoyable number of rib-tickling vignettes. A large international cast, each get their chance to shine as the contest's zany participants. Terry-Thomas stands out as the hapless villain. 132m. **DIR:** Ken Annakin. **CAST:** Terry-Thomas, Stuart Whitman, Sarah Miles, Gert Fröbe. **1965**

THOU SHALT NOT KILL . . . EXCEPT 🦃 A violent cult (complete with a Charles Manson look-alike) goes on a killing spree. Not rated, but has violence, profanity, and comic-book gore. 84m. **DIR:** Josh Becker. **CAST:** Brian Schulz, Tim Quill, Sam Raimi. **1987**

THOUSAND ACRES, A ★★1/2 Jane Smiley's Pulitzer-winning novel descends into relentless male-bashing. Jessica Lange and Michelle Pfeiffer are sensational as the dissimilar sisters drawn together by a land dispute involving their cruel and bellicose father. Rated R for profanity and strong sexual content. 104m. **DIR:** Jocelyn Moorhouse. **CAST:** Michelle Pfeiffer, Jessica Lange, Jason Robards Jr., Jennifer Jason Leigh, Colin Firth, Keith Carradine, Kevin Anderson, Pat Hingle. **1997 DVD**

THOUSAND CLOWNS, A ★★★★ Famous Broadway play comes to the screen with memorable performances by all the principals and standout jobs by Jason Robards as a talented nonconformist and Barry Gordon as his precocious ward. They struggle against welfare bureaucracy in order to stay together. Very funny in spots and equally poignant in others. B&W; 118m. **DIR:** Fred Coe. **CAST:** Jason Robards Jr., Barry Gordon, Barbara Harris, Martin Balsam, Gene Saks, William Daniels. **1965**

THOUSAND EYES OF DR. MABUSE, THE ★★1/2 Famed suspense *auteur* Fritz Lang's return to Germany and his attempt to revive Dr. Mabuse, his notorious master criminal, is a middling success. But a Lang near miss is better than a triumph by almost anyone else, so this intricately plotted mystery should delight film buffs. Ignore the dopey romantic subplot. Also titled: *Eyes of Evil, The Secret of Dr. Mabuse* and *The Diabolical Dr. Mabuse*. B&W; 103m. **DIR:** Fritz Lang. **CAST:** Dawn Addams, Peter Van Eyck, Gert Fröbe, Wolfgang Preiss. **1960**

THOUSAND HEROES, A ★★★ Exciting docudrama about the events leading up to the United Airlines flight that lost its hydraulics over Iowa on July 19, 1989, and was forced to make a crash landing. How nearly two hundred passengers lived through this horrendous event was credited to the ground crew, who had prepared for such an emergency. While Charlton Heston attempts to stabilize the plane in the air, Richard Thomas and James Coburn play members of the ground team. Rated PG. 95m. **DIR:** Lamont Johnson. **CAST:** Charlton Heston, Richard Thomas, James Coburn. **1992**

THOUSAND PIECES OF GOLD ★★★★ Ah, the joys of independent cinema: no formulas, no studio-policy compromises, no catering to star's images—just solid storytelling and committed filmmaking. Encompassing a story that begins in China and settles in Idaho's gold country in 1880, this wonderful movie about a woman who goes from slavery to fierce independence, offers a fresh perspective on the Old West. Not rated, the film has profanity and suggested sex. 105m. **DIR:** Nancy Kelly. **CAST:** Rosalind Chao, Chris Cooper, Dennis Dun. **1991**

THOUSANDS CHEER ★★★ The typical story about someone putting together a talent show for some good cause who gets a major shot in the arm by the appearances of top MGM performers. 126m. **DIR:** George Sidney. **CAST:** John Boles, Kathryn Grayson, Mickey Rooney, Judy Garland, Gene Kelly, Red Skelton, Lucille Ball, Ann Sothern, Eleanor Powell, Frank Morgan, Lena Horne, Virginia O'Brien. **1943**

THRASHIN' 🦃 Hotshot skateboarder comes to L.A. and gets on the bad side of a gang of street skaters. Rated PG-13 for sexual situations. 92m. **DIR:** David Winters. **CAST:** Josh Brolin, Robert Rusler, Chuck McCann. **1986**

THREADS ★★★★ Unforgettable British TV depiction of the effects of nuclear war on two small-town families makes *The Day After* look like a Hollywood musical. It doesn't indulge in shock or false sentimentality, rendering a chillingly plausible account of life after the end.

110m. **DIR:** Mick Jackson. **CAST:** Karen Meagher, Reece Dinsdale. **1984**

THREAT, THE ★★★1/2 Underrated suspense feature packs every minute with tension as vengeance-minded Charles McGraw escapes from jail and kidnaps the police detective and district attorney as well as snatches a singer he thinks may have told on him for good measure. The police put the pressure on the kidnapper, and he puts the squeeze on his captives. B&W; 65m. **DIR:** Felix Feist. **CAST:** Charles McGraw, Michael O'Shea, Frank Conroy, Virginia Grey, Julie Bishop, Robert Shayne, Anthony Caruso, Don McGuire. **1949**

THREE AGES, THE ★★★1/2 Frozen-faced Buster Keaton coproduced and codirected this parody on the films of that master of excessiveness, Cecil B. DeMille. A funny and very enjoyable silent film. Not Keaton's best, but far from mundane. B&W; 89m. **DIR:** Buster Keaton, Eddie Cline. **CAST:** Buster Keaton, Wallace Beery, Oliver Hardy. **1923 DVD**

•3 A.M. ★★★★ This offbeat suspense film about a series of cabby murders in New York City mixes in a torrent of other stories about the people driving New York cabs. What's really fascinating here is how the story elements weave in and out of each part of the plot—something introduced early on fits in perfectly with events that happen later. Excellent acting and a surprise ending for each of the story lines cap off this made-for-cable original. Not rated; contains profanity and violence. 92m. **DIR:** Lee Davis. **CAST:** Danny Glover, Pam Grier, Michelle Rodriguez, Sergej Trifunovic, Sarita Choudhury. **2001 DVD**

THREE AMIGOS ★★1/2 In this send-up of *The Cowboy Star*, Steve Martin, Chevy Chase, and Martin Short play three silent-screen cowboys who attempt to save a Mexican village from bloodthirsty banditos. Steve Martin, in particular, has some very funny moments. Overall, it's pleasant—even amusing—but nothing more. Rated PG. 105m. **DIR:** John Landis. **CAST:** Steve Martin, Chevy Chase, Martin Short, Alfonso Arau, Patrice Martinez, Joe Mantegna, Jon Lovitz. **1986 DVD**

THREE BROADWAY GIRLS ★★★ Three streetwise gold diggers stalk their prey among New York's socially prominent in this comedy adapted from Zoe Atkins's 1930 Broadway hit. Also titled *The Greeks Had a Word for Them.* B&W; 78m. **DIR:** Lowell Sherman. **CAST:** Joan Blondell, Ina Claire, Madge Evans, David Manners, Betty Grable. **1932**

THREE BROTHERS ★★★★★ Francesco Rosi directed this thoughtful, emotionally powerful movie that details the effect of a mother's recent death on her family. A drama with great insight and compassion. In Italian with English subtitles. Not rated; the film has a few scenes of violence. 113m. **DIR:** Francesco Rosi. **CAST:** Philippe Noiret, Michele Placido, Vittorio Mezzogiorno. **1980**

THREE CABALLEROS, THE ★★★ In Walt Disney's first attempt at combining animation and live action, Donald Duck is joined by two Latin feathered friends. Originally designed as a World War II propaganda piece promoting inter-American unity, it still holds up well today and remains a timeless learning experience for the kids. 72m. **DIR:** Walt Disney. **1942 DVD**

THREE CAME HOME ★★★ During World War II, British families residing in Borneo are forced into prison camps by Japanese troops. The courage and suffering of the confined women make for compelling drama. Claudette Colbert delivers one of her finest performances. 106m. **DIR:** Jean Negulesco. **CAST:** Claudette Colbert, Patric Knowles, Sessue Hayakawa. **1950**

THREE CASES OF MURDER ★★★★ Presented in a letter-box format, these three eerie stories are a wonderfully written collection of the macabre. Most effective is the opening tale in which we see a museum painting from the other side of the canvas. The final episode is by W. Somerset Maugham and stars Orson Welles as a brilliant but cold foreign minister who learns a harsh lesson about heartlessness. Not rated; contains implied violence. B&W; 99m. **DIR:** Wendy Toye, David Eady, George More O'Ferrall. **CAST:** Orson Welles, Alan Badel, John Gregson, Elizabeth Sellars. **1954**

THREE CHARLIES AND A PHONEY! ★★★ Two early Keystone comedies, "Recreation" and "His Musical Career," a special World War I bond sales promotion, "The Bond," and "His Day Out" make up this slapstick anthology. Silent. 1914–1918 with organ music; B&W; 69m. **DIR:** Charles Chaplin. **CAST:** Charlie Chaplin, Mack Swain, Edna Purviance, Sydney Chaplin.

THREE COMRADES ★★★1/2 Three friends in Germany have romantic designs on the same woman, and she has an incurable disease. A real weeper, but the acting is terrific. F. Scott Fitzgerald cowrote the screenplay with E. E. Paramore and got screen credit. It was Fitzgerald's only credit during his entire Hollywood stay. B&W; 98m. **DIR:** Frank Borzage. **CAST:** Robert Taylor, Margaret Sullavan, Robert Young, Franchot Tone, Monty Woolley, Lionel Atwill, Charley Grapewin, Guy Kibbee. **1938**

THREE DARING DAUGHTERS ★★★ Divorcée Jeanette MacDonald meets and weds pianist Jose Iturbi—her daughters object until they learn he can play boogie-woogie. Slight plot but wonderful music. A joke is that Iturbi plays himself. 115m. **DIR:** Fred M. Wilcox. **CAST:** Jeanette MacDonald, José Iturbi, Jane Powell, Edward Arnold, Harry Davenport, Elinor Donahue. **1948**

THREE DAYS OF THE CONDOR ★★★★ Robert Redford is a CIA information researcher who is forced to flee for his life when his New York cover operation is blown and all of his coworkers brutally murdered. What seems at first to be a standard man-on-the-run drama gradually deepens into an engrossing mystery as to who is chasing him and why. Faye Dunaway expertly handles a vignette as the stranger Redford uses to avoid capture. Rated R. 117m. **DIR:** Sydney Pollack. **CAST:** Robert Redford, Cliff Robertson, Max von Sydow, Faye Dunaway, John Houseman. **1975 DVD**

THREE DAYS TO A KILL ★★ Serviceable macho heroics from some old (and we do mean old) familiar faces. Seasoned mercenaries Fred Williamson and Bo Svenson rescue a U.S. diplomat from sneering drug lord Henry Silva. Rated R for violence. 90m. **DIR:** Fred Williamson. **CAST:** Fred Williamson, Bo Svenson, Henry Silva, Chuck Connors, Van Johnson, Sonny Landham. **1991**

THREE FACES OF EVE, THE ★★★★★ This distinguished movie boasts Joanne Woodward's Oscar-winning performance as a woman with multiple personali-

ties. Woodward progresses through all three personalities in one amazing scene. Based on a true-life case. 91m. **DIR:** Nunnally Johnson. **CAST:** Joanne Woodward, Lee J. Cobb, David Wayne, Vince Edwards. **1957**

THREE FACES WEST ★★★ John Wayne is the leader of a group of Dust Bowl farmers attempting to survive in this surprisingly watchable Republic release. Sigrid Gurie and Charles Coburn co-star as the European immigrants who show them what courage means. B&W; 79m. **DIR:** Bernard Vorhaus. **CAST:** John Wayne, Charles Coburn, Sigrid Gurie, Spencer Charters. **1940**

THREE FOR BEDROOM C ★★★ Adequate farce that was the first film made by Gloria Swanson after her stunning comeback in *Sunset Boulevard.* She portrays a movie star who books a compartment on a train that is also occupied by a Harvard scientist. Predictable. 74m. **DIR:** Milton H. Bren. **CAST:** Gloria Swanson, James Warren, Fred Clark, Hans Conried, Margaret Dumont. **1952**

THREE FOR THE ROAD ★★ Dull comedy about a senator's aide (Charlie Sheen) who is assigned to take his employer's difficult daughter (Kerri Green) to a reform school. Rated PG. 95m. **DIR:** B.W.L. Norton. **CAST:** Charlie Sheen, Kerri Green, Alan Ruck, Sally Kellerman. **1987**

THREE FUGITIVES ★★★ France's current master of film comedy, Francois Veber, made his American debut with this overly sentimental but often hilarious comedy about a hardened criminal (Nick Nolte) thrown together with a mute girl (Sarah Rowland Doroff) and her down-and-out dad (Martin Short) when the latter robs a bank and takes Nolte hostage. Rated PG-13 for profanity and violence. 90m. **DIR:** Francis Veber. **CAST:** Nick Nolte, Martin Short, James Earl Jones, Kenneth McMillan, Sarah Rowland Doroff. **1989 DVD**

THREE GODFATHERS, THE ★★★1/2 Director John Ford's second version of Peter B. Kyne's biblically oriented Western features John Wayne, Harry Carey Jr., and Pedro Armendariz as three good-hearted outlaws who discover a baby in the desert and dedicate themselves to saving its life. The three leads work well together, and Ford's stock company—Ward Bond in particular—adds grit to the sentimental story. 103m. **DIR:** John Ford. **CAST:** John Wayne, Harry Carey Jr., Pedro Armendariz, Ward Bond, Mae Marsh, Jane Darwell, Ben Johnson. **1949**

301/302 ★★★ A pair of neighbors—one a cook, the other a writer—share a strange relationship that ends in wild culinary exploration. Fascinating character study with a bizarre story to boot. Not rated; contains nudity, violence, and profanity. 98m. **DIR:** Chui-Soo Park. **CAST:** Eun-Jin Bang, Sin-Hye Hwang, Chu-Ryun Kim. **1996**

317TH PLATOON, THE ★★★ Near the end of the French involvement in Vietnam, a group of soldiers tries to make its way back to its squadron after a failed offensive. Filmed in Cambodia, this is an eerie precursor to recent American films about Vietnam. In French with English subtitles. 100m. **DIR:** Pierre Schoendoerffer. **CAST:** Jacques Perrin, Bruno Cremer. **1965**

365 NIGHTS IN HOLLYWOOD ★★1/2 Washed-up movie director gets a chance to make a comeback picture and defies crooks who want to plunder the budget. A young Alice Faye plays a Jean Harlow look-alike who carhops by day and sings and acts her way into this slightly goofy movie about moviemaking. Interesting musical productions and Faye's sparkling performance compensate for some low-level comedy that slows the film. B&W; 74m. **DIR:** George Marshall. **CAST:** James Dunn, Alice Faye, Frank Mitchell, John Bradford, Grant Mitchell, John Qualen. **1934**

3:10 TO YUMA ★★★★ This first-rate adult Western draws its riveting drama and power from the interaction of well-drawn characters rather than gun-blazing action. A farmer (Van Heflin) captures a notorious gunman (Glenn Ford) and, while waiting for the train to take them to Yuma prison, must hole up in a hotel and overcome the killer's numerous ploys to gain his freedom. B&W; 92m. **DIR:** Delmer Daves. **CAST:** Glenn Ford, Van Heflin, Felicia Farr, Leora Dana, Henry Jones, Richard Jaeckel, Robert Emhardt. **1957 DVD**

THREE IN THE ATTIC ★★ Three women kidnap the college Lothario and get revenge by making him their sex slave. The titillating premise of this curio soon gives way to tired debates about relationships. Rated R. 91m. **DIR:** Richard Wilson. **CAST:** Christopher Jones, Yvette Mimieux, Judy Pace. **1968**

THREE IN THE CELLAR 🦃 Wes Stern as a college student who has just lost his scholarship. Not rated, this low-budget yawner contains nudity and sexual situations. 93m. **DIR:** Theodore J. Flicker. **CAST:** Wes Stern, Joan Collins, Larry Hagman, David Arkin, Judy Pace. **1970**

THREE KINGS ★★★★ What appears at first to be a cynical take on *Kelly's Heroes* set during the 1991 Gulf War is actually an intelligent, thought-provoking study of America's role as police force to the world and the evils it fosters. That said, there's action, horror, and humor aplenty as George Clooney leads a band of renegade soldiers on a quest for Sadam Hussein's hidden cache of Kuwaiti gold. The twist comes when our antiheroes decide to help the innocent people being victimized by Iraq's Republican Guard, thus adding a dash of adrenaline-pumping heroism to the mix. It's a thrilling war picture—with a conscience. Rated R for violence, profanity, and sex. 115m. **DIR:** David O. Russell. **CAST:** George Clooney, Mark Wahlberg, Ice Cube, Spike Jonze, Nora Dunn, Jamie Kennedy, Mykelti Williamson, Clifford Curtis. **1999 DVD**

THREE LITTLE WORDS ★★1/2 That this is supposedly Fred Astaire's favorite among his numerous films says little for his taste. He and Red Skelton thoroughly enjoyed playing ace songwriters Bert Kalmar and Harry Ruby in this semiaccurate bio-pic, but, overall, the film lacks luster. 102m. **DIR:** Richard Thorpe. **CAST:** Fred Astaire, Red Skelton, Vera-Ellen, Gloria De Haven, Arlene Dahl, Debbie Reynolds, Keenan Wynn. **1950**

THREE LIVES AND ONLY ONE DEATH ★★★★ Marcello Mastroianni gives one of his best performances in this comedy as three very different people who may in fact be the same person. The first relatively mainstream work by veteran filmmaker Raoul Ruiz shows that he is perfectly able to adapt the structural playfulness of his avant-garde work in order to entertain (but not condescend to) a general audience. in French with English subtitles. Not rated; contains no objectionable material. 125m. **DIR:** Raúl Ruiz. **CAST:** Marcello Mastroianni,

Arielle Dombasle, Chiara Mastroianni, Lou Castel. **1996**

THREE LIVES OF KAREN, THE ★★★ A woman about to be married gets the shock of her life when the husband and daughter she doesn't remember come back into her life. Amnesia is suspected, but how many other lives is this woman suppressing? This made-for-cable drama is moving, despite the trite plotline. Rated PG-13. 95m. **DIR:** David Burton Morris. **CAST:** Gail O'Grady, Dennis Boutsikaris, Tim Guinee. **1997**

THREE LIVES OF THOMASINA, THE ★★★★ An excellent cast and innovative ways of telling the story highlight this tale of love and caring. A young girl's cat is brought back to life by a woman who also teaches the girl's father to let others into his life. The cat's trip to cat heaven is outstandingly executed. 97m. **DIR:** Don Chaffey. **CAST:** Patrick McGoohan, Susan Hampshire, Karen Dotrice, Vincent Winter. **1964**

THREE MEN AND A BABY ★★★1/2 Tom Selleck, Steve Guttenberg, and Ted Danson are three carefree bachelors in this energetic remake of the French *Three Men and a Cradle*. The trio find an unexpected bundle at the door of their impeccably furnished apartment. The conclusion (changed from the French original) is hopelessly hokey, but getting there's a lot of fun. Rated PG for language. 102m. **DIR:** Leonard Nimoy. **CAST:** Tom Selleck, Steve Guttenberg, Ted Danson, Nancy Travis, Margaret Colin. **1987 DVD**

THREE MEN AND A CRADLE ★★★★ In this sweet-natured character study from France, three high-living bachelors become the guardians of a baby girl. In addition to turning their life-styles inside out, she forces them to confront their values—with heartwarming results. Rated PG for profanity and nudity. In French with English subtitles. 105m. **DIR:** Coline Serreau. **CAST:** Roland Giraud, Michel Boujenah, André Dussolier. **1985**

THREE MEN AND A LITTLE LADY ★★★ Amiable, lightweight sequel to *Three Men and a Baby*, in which the title trio (Tom Selleck, Steve Guttenberg, and Ted Danson) must confront the possibility of losing their ward when her mother (Nancy Travis) decides to marry. Rated PG for brief profanity. 106m. **DIR:** Emile Ardolino. **CAST:** Tom Selleck, Steve Guttenberg, Ted Danson, Nancy Travis, Robin Weisman, Christopher Cazenove. **1990 DVD**

THREE MEN FROM TEXAS ★★★★★ A likely contender for the best Hopalong Cassidy film made. This one breaks every rule in the book as the romantic interest is killed off. Sidekick Andy Clyde is a reformed outlaw as he and Hoppy bust up Morris Ankrum's plot to gain control of the Mexican border territory. B&W; 75m. **DIR:** Lesley Selander. **CAST:** William Boyd, Russell Hayden, Andy Clyde, Morris Ankrum, Dick Curtis. **1940**

THREE MEN IN A BOAT ★★★ A male-bonding comedy that shows how men on a boat trip down the Thames River are quick to desert their buddies when a pretty girl enters the scene. 84m. **DIR:** Ken Annakin. **CAST:** Laurence Harvey, David Tomlinson, Jimmy Edwards, Martita Hunt, Jill Ireland, Shirley Eaton, Adrienne Corri. **1956**

THREE MEN ON A HORSE ★★★1/2 Frank McHugh, a timid greeting-card writer, handicaps winning horses as a hobby. Some small-time gamblers, led by Sam Levene, learn of his talent and turn it to their advantage. Stagy, but fun to watch. B&W; 87m. **DIR:** Mervyn LeRoy. **CAST:** Frank McHugh, Joan Blondell, Sam Levene, Guy Kibbee, Carol Hughes, Allen Jenkins, Edgar Kennedy, Eddie "Rochester" Anderson. **1936**

THREE MUSKETEERS, THE (1921) ★★★★1/2 Lavish silent adaptation of the classic tale with Douglas Fairbanks as the character he was born to play—D'Artagnan, the fledgling musketeer who proves his skills with a sword and foils the nefarious efforts of the dastardly Cardinal Richelieu. B&W; 119m. **DIR:** Fred Niblo. **CAST:** Douglas Fairbanks Sr., Leon Barry, Marguerite de la Motte, Eugene Pallette, Adolphe Menjou. **1921 DVD**

THREE MUSKETEERS, THE (1933) ★★ The weakest and least-seen of John Wayne's three serials for Mascot Studios. This desert-bound story presents four friends who fight against a harsh environment and the evil Devil of the Desert. Standard Foreign Legion stuff. B&W; 12 chapters. **DIR:** Armand Schaefer, Colbert Clark. **CAST:** John Wayne, Ruth Hall, Jack Mulhall, Raymond Hatton, Francis X. Bushman, Noah Beery Jr. **1933 DVD**

THREE MUSKETEERS, THE (1935) ★★★ With middle-aged actors in the swashbuckling roles, this is the most sedate of the many versions of the story. They don't swash as many buckles as those who followed, but they do tell a good story and keep it on a very serious level. Author Alexandre Dumas would be pleased with the attention paid to the details of his story. B&W; 90m. **DIR:** Rowland V. Lee. **CAST:** Walter Abel, Paul Lukas, Moroni Olsen, Onslow Stevens, Heather Angel, Margot Grahame, Ian Keith, Ralph Forbes, Rosamond Pinchot, John Qualen, Nigel de Brulier. **1935**

THREE MUSKETEERS, THE (1939) ★★★ The Ritz Brothers as Dumas's famous trio? Yes, it's true. As a comedy-musical, this picture rides a moderate course, sticking closely to the original story but never taking anything too seriously. Don Ameche is very sharp as D'Artagnan and Binnie Barnes is charming as Lady DeWinter. B&W; 73m. **DIR:** Allan Dwan. **CAST:** Don Ameche, The Ritz Brothers, Lionel Atwill, Binnie Barnes. **1939**

THREE MUSKETEERS, THE (1948) ★★ MGM's all-star version of the classic swashbuckler by Alexandre Dumas gets its swords crossed up, primarily due to some blatant miscasting. Gene Kelly as D'Artagnan and June Allyson playing the queen's seamstress are never convincing as French citizens during the reign of Louis XIII. Fans of Lana Turner may find the movie worthwhile, because hidden in this fluff is one of her finest performances as the villainous Lady DeWinter. B&W; 128m. **DIR:** George Sidney. **CAST:** Gene Kelly, Lana Turner, June Allyson, Van Heflin, Vincent Price, Gig Young, Angela Lansbury, Keenan Wynn. **1948**

THREE MUSKETEERS, THE (1973) ★★★★★ Alexandre Dumas's oft-filmed swashbuckler classic—there may have been as many as ten previous versions—finally came to full life with this 1973 release. It is a superb adventure romp with scrumptious moments of comedy, character, and action. Rated PG. 105m. **DIR:** Richard Lester. **CAST:** Michael York, Oliver Reed, Raquel Welch, Richard Chamberlain, Faye Dunaway, Charlton Heston. **1973 DVD**

THREE MUSKETEERS, THE (1993) ★★★1/2 The Brat Pack tackles Dumas's swashbuckling classic with gen-

erally pleasing results. We still prefer the Richard Lester triptych, but every generation needs a cast of its own to proclaim, "All for one, one for all." Rated PG for light violence. 105m. **DIR:** Stephen Herek. **CAST:** Charlie Sheen, Kiefer Sutherland, Chris O'Donnell, Oliver Platt, Tim Curry, Rebecca DeMornay, Gabrielle Anwar, Paul McGann, Julie Delpy, Hugh O'Connor. **1993 DVD**

THREE NINJAS ★★★1/2 Kids will love this *Karate Kid* knockoff about youngsters who help their mentor-grandfather take on a criminal and his army of evil ninjas. Rated PG for light violence. 85m. **DIR:** Jon Turteltaub. **CAST:** Victor Wong, Michael Treanor, Max Elliott Slade, Chad Power. **1992**

THREE NINJAS KICK BACK ★★★1/2 More kid-pleasing entertainment has our three youthful heroes forced to choose between playing in a championship baseball game and accompanying their all-wise grandfather to Japan for a martial arts tournament. It's *The Karate Kid*, *The Three Stooges*, *The Bad News Bears*, and *Indiana Jones* all crammed into one fast-paced movie that works surprisingly well. Rated PG for goofy violence. 99m. **DIR:** Mark Saltzman. **CAST:** Victor Wong, Sab Shimono, Max Elliott Slade, Evan Bonifant, Caroline Junko King, Alan McRae, Margarita Franco. **1994 DVD**

THREE NINJAS KNUCKLE UP ★★ More of the same as the three brothers team up to take on a toxic-waste dumper. Younger kids will enjoy this third entry in the series, but older kids will be bored. Rated PG-13 for violence. 93m. **DIR:** Simon S. Sheen. **CAST:** Victor Wong, Charles Napier, Michael Treanor, Max Elliott Slade, Chad Power. **1995 DVD**

THREE NUTS IN SEARCH OF A BOLT 🦃 Three loonies, too poor to see a psychiatrist on their own, hire an out-of-work actor to pretend he has each of their symptoms. Not rated, but equal to PG-13 for nudity and adult situations. 78m. **DIR:** Tommy Noonan. **CAST:** Mamie Van Doren, Tommy Noonan, Paul Gilbert, Ziva Rodann. **1964**

THREE O'CLOCK HIGH ★★1/2 Director Phil Joanou leaves no doubt of his technical skill in his first film. Too bad his story is just a teen variation on *High Noon*. Jerry Mitchell (Casey Siemaszko) is an average high schooler who ends up having the worst day of his life. Rated PG-13 for profanity and violence. 95m. **DIR:** Phil Joanou. **CAST:** Casey Siemaszko, Anne Ryan, Richard Tyson, Jeffrey Tambor, Philip Baker Hall, John P. Ryan. **1987**

THREE OF HEARTS ★★★ A lesbian hires a male escort to break the heart of her former lover, but this film handles the premise with sensitivity, warmth, and humor. William Baldwin is endearing and Kelly Lynch is a revelation as the stereotype-busting lesbian. The buddy relationship the two develop makes the movie memorable. Rated R for language and suggested sex. 93m. **DIR:** Yurek Bogayevicz. **CAST:** William Baldwin, Kelly Lynch, Sherilyn Fenn, Joe Pantoliano, Gail Strickland. **1993**

THREE ON A MATCH ★★★ Tough direction, a nifty script, and snappy editing make a winner of this tale of the reunion of three slum girls who ignore superstition to tempt fate and court tragedy by lighting their cigarettes from the same match. Ann Dvorak lights up last, and is outstanding in an outstanding cast. B&W; 68m. **DIR:** Mervyn LeRoy. **CAST:** Joan Blondell, Bette Davis, Ann Dvorak, Humphrey Bogart, Glenda Farrell, Edward Arnold. **1932**

THREE ON THE TRAIL ★★★ A crooked sheriff and the local vice lord fool a British rancher into taking sides against Hopalong Cassidy. Pleasant musical interludes, good interplay among the friends, and lots of action and gunplay place this early entry on the list of best of series. B&W; 67m. **DIR:** Howard Bretherton. **CAST:** William Boyd, James Ellison, Onslow Stevens, Muriel Evans, George "Gabby" Hayes, Claude King, William Duncan. **1936**

THREE SEASONS ★★★ Several characters briefly cross paths in Saigon as their lives change and the city's past rubs shoulders with the present in this delicately woven drama. A bicycle taxi driver becomes emotionally attached to a hooker; an American who fought in the Vietnam War searches for a daughter he has never met; a street kid tries to find his stolen case of tourist trinkets; a woman flower vendor sings her way into the home of a hermitlike Buddhist master. In Vietnamese with English subtitles. Rated PG-13 for adult themes. 113m. **DIR:** Tony Bui. **CAST:** Don Duong, Nguyen Ngoc Hiep, Tran Manh, Harvey Keitel. **1999**

THREE SECRETS ★★★ Three women, each with her own reason for believing she is his mother, anxiously await the rescue of a five year old boy, the sole survivor of a plane crash in rugged mountains. B&W; 98m. **DIR:** Robert Wise. **CAST:** Eleanor Parker, Patricia Neal, Ruth Roman, Frank Lovejoy, Leif Erickson, Ted de Corsia. **1950**

THREE SMART GIRLS ★★★★ Starring debut of fourteen year old Deanna Durbin as Penny Craig, who with her two sisters, saves their easygoing father from the clutches of a gold digger. Fast-moving musical, with some fine comedy touches, particularly by Mischa Auer. B&W; 84m. **DIR:** Henry Koster. **CAST:** Deanna Durbin, Binnie Barnes, Alice Brady, Ray Milland, Charles Winninger, Mischa Auer, Nan Gray, Barbara Read, Lucile Watson. **1937**

THREE SMART GIRLS GROW UP ★★★1/2 Deanna Durbin returns in this sequel, this time acting as matchmaker for her two sisters and their assorted beaux. Nice mixture of light comedy and song. B&W; 90m. **DIR:** Henry Koster. **CAST:** Deanna Durbin, Charles Winninger, Nan Gray, Helen Parrish, Robert Cummings, William Lundigan. **1939**

THREE SOVEREIGNS FOR SARAH 🦃 Salem witch trials. Supposedly a true story about the real motivations that led to this dark spot in American history. 171m. **DIR:** Philip Leacock. **CAST:** Vanessa Redgrave, Ronald Hunter, Patrick McGoohan, Will Lyman, Kim Hunter. **1987**

THREE STOOGES, THE (VOLUMES 1–10) ★★★★ The Three Stooges made 190 two-reel short subjects between 1934 and 1959. For over fifty years, people have either loved them or hated them. If you are a fan, you'll find these collections the answer to a knucklehead's dream. Each cassette features three shorts of impeccable quality, transferred from brand-new, complete 35-mm prints. All of the films are from the classic "Curly" period, when the team was at the peak of its energy and originality. B&W; 60m. **DIR:** Various!. **CAST:** Moe Howard, Curly Howard, Larry Fine. **1934**

THREE STRANGE LOVES ★★1/2 Three former ballerinas struggle to find happiness in their private lives. Ingmar Bergman's gloomy style is the perfect backdrop for the disappointment and heartache the women face. In Swedish with subtitles that flicker by at a pace suitable only for a speed reader. B&W; 84m. **DIR:** Ingmar Bergman. **CAST:** Eva Henning, Birger Malmsten. **1949**

3 STRIKES 🦃 This tedious, vulgar crime comedy is about a two-time loser who, immediately upon release from prison, is chased by police and thugs throughout South Central Los Angeles. Rated R for drug use, profanity, nudity, suggested sex, and sexual references. 82m. **DIR:** D. J. Pooh. **CAST:** Brian Hooks, Starletta Dupois, George Wallace, N'Bushe Wright, David Alan Grier. **2000 DVD**

THREE TEXAS STEERS ★★★ The Three Mesquiteers ride to the rescue of Carole Landis when bad guys try to force her to sell her ranch. Their solution is to enter her horse into a trotting race, which produces some amusing footage of John Wayne spitting the horse's tail out of his mouth while being pursued by the baddies. Max Terhune's last appearance as a Mesquiteer. B&W; 59m. **DIR:** George Sherman. **CAST:** John Wayne, Ray "Crash" Corrigan, Max Terhune, Carole Landis, Ralph Graves, Roscoe Ates, Billy Curtis, David Sharpe. **1939**

THREE THE HARD WAY ★★★ A white supremacist (Jay Robinson) attempts to wipe out the black race by putting a deadly serum in the country's water supply. Fred Williamson, Jim Brown and Jim Kelly team up to stop him in this action-packed movie. Rated PG for violence. 93m. **DIR:** Gordon Parks Jr. **CAST:** Fred Williamson, Jim Brown, Jim Kelly, Sheila Frazier, Jay Robinson. **1974**

3,000 MILES TO GRACELAND ★★ This is the sort of swill that we'd expect to find in a store's direct-to-video, two-for-a-buck rental bin . . . but it achieved big-screen release thanks to the involvement of Kurt Russell and Kevin Costner. It's another ludicrously violent, testosterone-fueled entry in the boys-with-guns subgenre of modern Hollywood thrillers: a tiresome kill-or-be-killed saga. The story concerns some Elvis impersonators who knock off a casino before squabbling and knocking off each other. Been there, done that. Rated R for profanity, sexual candor, and considerable violence. 125m. **DIR:** Demian Lichtenstein. **CAST:** Kurt Russell, Kevin Costner, Courteney Cox, Christian Slater, Kevin Pollak, David Arquette, Howie Long. **2001 DVD**

THREE TO TANGO ★★★1/2 This utterly delightful, gender-bending screwball romp proves that the romantic comedy is far from dead. Credit scripters Rodney Vaccaro and Aline Brosh McKenna, and Neve Campbell, displaying the spunky personality and deft comic timing of, say, Irene Dunne or Jean Arthur. Although impossible to condense, the complicated plot involves a Chicago architect (Matthew Perry) who gets a chance to design a cultural center for a pretentious tycoon, who has the mistaken impression that our hero is gay . . . and thus selects the guy to spy on his mistress (Campbell). What follows is fun-fun-fun. If the conclusion seems a bit rushed and trite, well . . . some things are inevitable. Rated PG-13 for sensuality and brief profanity. 98m. **DIR:** Damon Santostefano. **CAST:** Matthew Perry, Neve Campbell, Dylan McDermott, Oliver Platt, John C. McGinley, Bob Balaban. **1999 DVD**

THREE VIOLENT PEOPLE ★★★ Charlton Heston returns to Texas after the Civil War with his bride and finds himself fighting land grabbers. Should have been better but Elaine Stritch is colorful as a saloon hostess. 100m. **DIR:** Rudolph Maté. **CAST:** Charlton Heston, Anne Baxter, Gilbert Roland, Tom Tryon, Forrest Tucker, Bruce Bennett, Elaine Stritch, Barton MacLane. **1956**

THREE WISHES ★★1/2 A minor but cute fairy tale that tries to enchant, but travels down territory everyone but kids will find too familiar. A mysterious drifter enters the life of a widow and her two sons at a time when they really could use a helping hand. This does make a good case for listening to your own heart, as the story is set in 1955, when conformity was a way of life. Rated PG for brief nudity and suggested sex. 115m. **DIR:** Martha Coolidge. **CAST:** Patrick Swayze, Mary Elizabeth Mastrantonio, Joseph Mazzello, Seth Mumy. **1995 DVD**

THREE-WORD BRAND, THE ★★★ Indians murder a homesteader, thus orphaning his twin sons. The brothers become separated—going their own ways—until circumstances reunite them many years later. William S. Hart deftly portrays the father and the sons in this silent sagebrush drama. B&W; 75m. **DIR:** Lambert Hillyer. **CAST:** William S. Hart, Jane Novak. **1921**

THREE WORLDS OF GULLIVER, THE ★★★ Following a violent storm at sea, Dr. Lemuel Gulliver (Kerwin Mathews) finds himself ashore on Lilliput, an island with miniature people. A biting satire on human nature, featuring seamless special effects by Ray Harryhausen and an ear-filling Bernard Herrmann score. Based on the classic by Jonathan Swift. Great fun. 100m. **DIR:** Jack Sher. **CAST:** Kerwin Mathews, June Thorburn, Jo Morrow, Gregoire Aslan. **1960 DVD**

3 X 3 EYES, VOLS. 1–4 ★★★ Japanese animation. Bizarre but intriguing horror series. Pai, the last surviving member of her mythic three-eyed race, goes in search of the artifact that will at last transform her into a human being. Violent but entertaining. 30m. **DIR:** Daisuke Nishio. **1991 DVD**

3:15—THE MOMENT OF TRUTH ★★1/2 *High Noon* in high school, as Adam Baldwin prepares for a showdown. Director Larry Gross, a Walter Hill protégé, doesn't have Hill's ability to rise above the too-plentiful action clichés. Rated R for violence. 85m. **DIR:** Larry Gross. **CAST:** Adam Baldwin, Deborah Foreman, René Auberjonois, Ed Lauter, Mario Van Peebles, Wings Hauser. **1985**

THREEPENNY OPERA, THE ★★★★ Based on John Gay's *The Beggar's Opera*. Classic gangster musical features mob leader Mack the Knife, his moll, and the hordes of the underworld. This Bertolt Brecht satire (with music by Kurt Weill), although not too popular with the Nazis or their predecessors, is always a favorite with the audience. B&W; 113m. **DIR:** G. W. Pabst. **CAST:** Rudolph Forster, Lotte Lenya, Reinhold Schunzel, Carola Neher. **1931**

THREE'S TROUBLE ★★★1/2 Screenwriter David Williamson often hits the bull's-eye with this warm, witty *Mr. Mom* Australian style. When a much put upon housewife hires a baby-sitter (handsome Steven Vidler), her know-it-all husband is forced to reassess his contributions to the family. Not rated, contains profan-

ity. 93m. **DIR:** Chris Thomson. **CAST:** Jacki Weaver, John Waters, Steven Vidler. **1985**

THREESOME ★★ A woman (Lara Flynn Boyle) is assigned two male roommates in a college dorm. This clumsy film tries to mix leering sex farce with soulful sensitivity[emdash] *Porky's* meets *A Separate Peace*. The muttered dialogue is often inaudible. Rated R for profanity and simulated sex. 93m. **DIR:** Andrew Fleming. **CAST:** Lara Flynn Boyle, Stephen Baldwin, Josh Charles. **1994 DVD**

THRESHOLD ★★ Donald Sutherland stars in this film about the first artificial-heart transplant. Rated PG. 106m. **DIR:** Richard Pearce. **CAST:** Donald Sutherland, John Marley, Jeff Goldblum, Michael Lerner. **1981**

THRILL KILLERS, THE 🦃 Psycho killer Cash Flagg (a.k.a. writer-director Ray Dennis Steckler) and three escaped mental patients meet up at a diner, where they terrorize the patrons. Pretty dull. B&W; 69m. **DIR:** Ray Dennis Steckler. **CAST:** Cash Flagg, Liz Renay, Carolyn Brandt, Atlas King. **1965**

THRILL OF A ROMANCE ★★ Esther Williams's groom deserts her on their wedding night to close a business deal. Opera star Lauritz Melchior feels she could do better with war hero Van Johnson, so he acts as cupid. 104m. **DIR:** Richard Thorpe. **CAST:** Van Johnson, Esther Williams, Lauritz Melchior, Spring Byington. **1946**

THRILL OF IT ALL, THE ★★★ Married life is perfect for housewife and mother Doris Day and doctor James Garner until she accepts a high-paying television commercial job in this witty observation of television, advertising, and domestic bliss, as scripted by Carl Reiner. 103m. **DIR:** Norman Jewison. **CAST:** Doris Day, James Garner, Arlene Francis, Edward Andrews, ZaSu Pitts, Elliott Reid, Reginald Owen, Alice Pearce. **1963**

THRILLED TO DEATH ★★ An unsuspecting couple is framed for murder and drug running. The dupes are so incredibly naïve that you'll find yourself yelling at them to wake up. Rated R for nudity and violence. 93m. **DIR:** Chuck Vincent. **CAST:** Blake Bahner. **1988**

THRILLER (TV SERIES) ★★★1/2 As was true of this television anthology series during its brief network run in the early 1960s, host and sometimes star Boris Karloff is the main draw. Fortunately, three of the first six episodes released on tape feature the venerated horror actor and are recommended. Made for TV. B&W; 58m. **DIR:** Robert Florey, John Brahm, Douglas Heyes. **CAST:** Boris Karloff, John Carradine, Hazel Court, William Shatner, Sidney Blackmer, Patricia Medina, Elizabeth Montgomery, Tom Poston, Dick York, Guy Rolfe, Audrey Dalton. **1960–62**

THRILLKILL 🦃 Woman has a falling-out with her partners after stealing $3 million via computer. Not rated; contains some violence and frank language. 88m. **DIR:** Anthony Kramreither, Anthony D'Andrea. **CAST:** Robin Ward, Gina Massey. **1986**

THRONE OF BLOOD ★★★★★ Japanese director Akira Kurosawa's retelling of *Macbeth* may be the best film adaptation of Shakespeare ever made. Kurosawa uses the medium to present Shakespeare's themes in visual images. When Birnam Wood literally comes to Dunsinane, it is a truly great moment you would have believed could only happen in the limitless landscapes of a dream. In Japanese with English subtitles. B&W; 105m. **DIR:** Akira Kurosawa. **CAST:** Toshiro Mifune, Minoru Chiaki, Takashi Shimura. **1957**

THROUGH A GLASS DARKLY ★★ Two siblings compete for their father's love. The father, who happens to be a famous writer, sits back and observes. Ingmar Bergman goes overboard this time with endless monologues on God and love. In Swedish with English subtitles, this film is unrated but contains mature themes. B&W; 90m. **DIR:** Ingmar Bergman. **CAST:** Harriet Andersson, Gunnar Björnstrand, Max von Sydow. **1961**

THROUGH NAKED EYES ★★★ A pretty good made-for-TV mystery thriller with voyeurism in high-rise apartments as the pivotal plot line. David Soul is watching Pam Dawber across the way, but she's also been watching him. When a series of murders occurs in their buildings, it appears someone else is watching, too. Not rated. 91m. **DIR:** John Llewellyn Moxey. **CAST:** David Soul, Pam Dawber, Rod McCary. **1983**

THROUGH THE LOOKING GLASS ★★1/2 A likable adaptation of the adventures of Alice after her trip to Wonderland. This production loses some of its charm due to a more contemporary telling, but voice characterizations by Phyllis Diller, Mr. T, and Jonathan Winters help. No rating. 70m. **DIR:** Andrea Bresciani, Richard Slapczynski. **1987**

THROW MOMMA FROM THE TRAIN ★★★ Gravel-voiced Anne Ramsey, as the titular Momma, is by far the best element of this comedy, which marks the directing debut of star Danny DeVito. He's a would-be writer in novelist Billy Crystal's class, and the two concoct a scheme to trade murders *à la* Hitchcock's *Strangers on a Train*. The finished film just doesn't provide the manic delight promised by its two stars. Rated PG-13 for language. 88m. **DIR:** Danny DeVito. **CAST:** Danny DeVito, Billy Crystal, Anne Ramsey, Kim Greist, Kate Mulgrew. **1987**

THUGS 🦃 If this movie were any more of a dog, it would have a tail. Uninspired low-budget effort about a street punk anxious to impress the local syndicate. Been there, done that. Rated R for adult situations, language, nudity, and violence. 93m. **DIR:** Travis Milloy. **CAST:** Justin Pagel, Scott Cooke, Michael Egan. **1998**

THUMBELINA (1983) ★★★★ This is an *Alice in Wonderland*–type tale of a thumb-size girl (Carrie Fisher) and her adventures as she tries to find her way home. The creatures she meets along the way are well characterized. This is one of the more rewarding *Faerie Tale Theatre* productions. David Hemmings, Carrie Fisher, William Katt, Burgess Meredith (voices). 48m. **DIR:** Michael Lindsay-Hogg. **1983**

THUMBELINA (1989) ★★★★ David Johnson's exquisitely delicate illustrations are the primary appeal here. The Hans Christian Andersen tale concerns a little girl—no larger than the tip of one's thumb. Kelly McGillis narrates the story, and background music is provided by Mark Isham. 30m. **DIR:** Tim Raglin. **1989**

THUNDER AND LIGHTNING ★★ Weak "action film" about moonshiners. Stars David Carradine and Kate Jackson are watchable enough, but a few touches of originality wouldn't have hurt. Rated PG for profanity and violence. 95m. **DIR:** Corey Allen. **CAST:** David Carradine, Kate Jackson, Roger C. Carmel, Sterling Holloway. **1977**

THUNDER BAY ★★★1/2 James Stewart plays an oil driller forced to take on a nasty group of Louisiana shrimp fishermen. The story is full of action and fine characterizations from a talented cast. 102m. **DIR:** Anthony Mann. **CAST:** James Stewart, Dan Duryea, Joanne Dru, Jay C. Flippen, Gilbert Roland. **1953**

THUNDER IN PARADISE ★★★ A hotel owner must marry within two days or she will lose her hotel to her greedy uncle. A nice mix of kidnapping and treasure hunting, plus an amazing high-speed boat race make for an enjoyable film. Even Hulk Hogan manages to perform well in a likable role. Rated PG. 104m. **DIR:** Douglas Schwartz. **CAST:** Hulk Hogan, Felicity Waterman, Carol Alt, Robin Weisman, Chris Lemmon, Patrick Macnee, Sam Jones, Charlotte Rae. **1993**

THUNDER IN PARADISE II 🦃 Inane full-length version of the syndicated TV show featuring Hulk Hogan and Chris Lemmon as soldiers of fortune. Real star is their high-tech super boat. Unbelievable, uninteresting, and unwatchable. Rated PG for comic book violence. 89m. **DIR:** Douglas Schwartz. **CAST:** Hulk Hogan, Chris Lemmon, Carol Alt, Ashley Correll, Patrick Macnee. **1994**

THUNDER IN THE CITY ★★ Time severely dates this comedy-drama about a brash, fast-talking American promotor (Edward G. Robinson) who goes to staid London to promote modern U.S. advertising methods. Nigel Bruce fared far better as Holmes's Dr. Watson. B&W; 85m. **DIR:** Marion Gering. **CAST:** Edward G. Robinson, Nigel Bruce, Ralph Richardson. **1937**

THUNDER PASS ★★ A good cast wasted as cavalry captain Dane Clark leads settlers out of Indian Territory. B&W; 80m. **DIR:** Frank McDonald. **CAST:** Dane Clark, Dorothy Patrick, Raymond Burr, Andy Devine, John Carradine, Mary Ellen Kay. **1954**

THUNDER POINT ★★★ Lackluster telling of an intriguing Jack Higgins story stars Kyle MacLachlan as a former IRA terrorist pressed into duty by the British government to find a potentially world-shattering secret document. Rated R for violence, nudity, and profanity. 95m. **DIR:** George Mihalka. **CAST:** Kyle MacLachlan, Alan Thicke, Michael Sarrazin. **1996**

THUNDER ROAD ★★★★ Robert Mitchum wrote the original story and hit theme song for this fast-paced, colorful tale of a bootlegger (Mitchum) who attempts to outwit revenuer Gene Barry. It's one of Mitchum's few all-around, big-screen successes and a tribute to his talents in front of and behind the camera. The star's son, Jim Mitchum, made his film debut as Robert's younger brother. B&W; 92m. **DIR:** Arthur Ripley. **CAST:** Robert Mitchum, Gene Barry, Keely Smith, Jim Mitchum. **1958 DVD**

THUNDER RUN 🦃 Grade Z action flick. Rated R for nudity, profanity, suggested sex, and violence. 89m. **DIR:** Gary Hudson. **CAST:** Forrest Tucker, John Ireland, John Shepherd, Jill Whitlow, Cheryl M. Lynn. **1986**

THUNDER TRAIL ★★1/2 Gilbert Roland and James Craig, two brothers, are separated as youngsters by outlaws. Years later they are on opposite sides of the law. An A cast fails to lift this Zane Grey story out of a B-movie mold. B&W; 58m. **DIR:** Charles Barton. **CAST:** Gilbert Roland, Charles Bickford, Marsha Hunt, J. Carrol Naish, James Craig. **1937**

THUNDER WARRIOR 🦃 In this shameless rip-off of the action scenes in *First Blood*, a tough Indian goes on a one-man rampage. Rated R for profanity, violence, and nudity. 84m. **DIR:** Larry Ludman. **CAST:** Mark Gregory, Bo Svenson. **1983**

THUNDER WARRIOR II 🦃 Sleazy, Italian-made action flick. Rated R. 84m. **DIR:** Larry Ludman. **CAST:** Mark Gregory, Bo Svenson. **1985**

THUNDERBALL ★★★ When originally released in 1965, this fourth entry in the James Bond series suffered from comparison to its two admittedly superior predecessors, *From Russia with Love* and *Goldfinger*. However, time has proved it to be one of the more watchable movies based on the books by Ian Fleming, with Sean Connery in top form as 007 and assured direction by Terence Young. 129m. **DIR:** Terence Young. **CAST:** Sean Connery, Claudine Auger, Adolfo Celi. **1965 DVD**

THUNDERBOLT AND LIGHTFOOT ★★★★ Clint Eastwood's right-on-target performance is equaled by those of his costars in this decidedly offbeat caper picture. *Thunderbolt and Lightfoot* proved a little too offbeat when originally released in 1974. However, movie buffs have since proclaimed it a cinematic gem, a reputation it deserves. Rated R. 114m. **DIR:** Michael Cimino. **CAST:** Clint Eastwood, Jeff Bridges, George Kennedy, Geoffrey Lewis, Gary Busey. **1974 DVD**

THUNDERHEART ★★★★1/2 FBI agent Val Kilmer is assigned to help veteran agent Sam Shepard investigate the murder of an Oglala Sioux on a reservation in the badlands of South Dakota. Michael Apted's richest and most compelling movie since *Coal Miner's Daughter*. Rated R for violence and profanity. 127m. **DIR:** Michael Apted. **CAST:** Val Kilmer, Sam Shepard, Graham Greene, Fred Ward, Fred Dalton Thompson. **1992 DVD**

THUNDERING HOOFS ★★1/2 A rancher's son wins a horse and a beautiful señorita. Chock-full of daring stunts, winning performances, and unbridled enthusiasm, this early Fred Thomson series entry shows why he was one of the highest regarded of all cowboy stars before his untimely death. Stunt legend Yakima Canutt doubled Thomson in a daring horse-to-stagecoach transfer that predates Canutt's similar stunts in bigger-budgeted films a dozen years later. B&W; 53m. **DIR:** Albert S. Rogell. **CAST:** Fred Thomson, Fred Huntley, Charles Mailes, Ann May. **1924**

THURSDAY'S GAME ★★★ Engaging made-for-television film about two ordinary guys (Gene Wilder and Bob Newhart) who continue to get together on Thursday nights after their weekly poker game collapses. Both make the most of this small rebellion. The supporting cast is excellent. Not rated; adult themes. 74m. **DIR:** Robert Moore. **CAST:** Gene Wilder, Bob Newhart, Ellen Burstyn, Cloris Leachman, Rob Reiner, Nancy Walker, Valerie Harper. **1974**

THX 1138 ★★★1/2 Science-fiction and movie buffs may want to rent this moody, atmospheric picture, starring Robert Duvall and Donald Pleasence, to see an example of the type of work director George Lucas was doing pre–*Star Wars*. It was the fabulously successful filmmaker's first. Interesting. Rated PG. 88m. **DIR:** George Lucas. **CAST:** Robert Duvall, Donald Pleasence, Maggie McOmie. **1971**

•TIC CODE, THE ★★1/2 Tourette's syndrome and jazz take center stage in this well-intentioned but by-the-numbers drama. A single mother raises her musical

prodigy son who has Tourette's. When she falls for a jazz saxophonist who also suffers from the syndrome, she sees him as just what the doctor ordered to help her son live with his condition. While the film suffers from a script that is convenient, lacking the courage to tackle the subject matter with honesty, the cast rises above the material, creating characters we can believe in. Rated R for adult language. 91m. **DIR:** Gary Winick. **CAST:** Gregory Hines, Polly Draper, Chris Marquette, Tony Shalhoub, Bill Nunn. **1998 DVD**

TICK, THE (TV SERIES) ★★★ Based on the underground comic book of the same name, this entertaining animated series unmercifully parodies the typical superhero fare with irreverent glee as clueless Tick and his pal Arthur save the world from an assortment of oddball villains. Not rated. 50m. **DIR:** Richard Bowman. **1994–1995**

TICK . . . TICK . . . TICK . . . ★★★ Newly elected sheriff Jim Brown struggles against racism, ignorance, and some good-ole-boys to keep a rural southern community from exploding. Dated but still entertaining. Rated PG for violence. 100m. **DIR:** Ralph Nelson. **CAST:** Jim Brown, George Kennedy, Fredric March, Don Stroud, Clifton James, Lynn Carlin, Janet MacLachlan. **1970**

•TICK TOCK ★★1/2 *Tick Tock* is a tale of murder and betrayal, centering around two women bent on either ripping someone off, getting someone killed, or backstabbing each other. Each scene is shown more than once, where what we know from one person's perspective is often completely changed when we learn additional details from another's view of the same situation. Credit is due to the screenwriter for a neat idea, but the acting and the cohesiveness of the movie are not up to par. Rated R for violence, sex, and language. 95m. **DIR:** Kevin S. Tenney. **CAST:** Megan Ward, Kristin Minter, John Ratzenberger. **2000 DVD**

•TICKER ★★ Not horrible but not very good action-thriller about a mad bomber making life miserable for an elite San Francisco bomb squad led by Zen master Steven Seagal. Dennis Hopper is true to form as the mad bomber who plans on blowing up the city unless his girlfriend is released from custody. Tom Sizemore plays the cop on the edge who has lost his family and partner and now has a score to settle. Low-rent rip-off of *Speed*, which also starred Hopper as a mad bomber. Rated R for language and violence. 92m. **DIR:** Albert Pyun. **CAST:** Steven Seagal, Tom Sizemore, Dennis Hopper, Jaime Pressly, Nas, Ice T. **2001 DVD**

TICKET, THE ★★1/2 A family on the verge of poverty wins the lottery but must fly across snow-packed mountains to claim the prize. Their plane is sabotaged, and the bad guys start chasing them to steal the winning ticket. It's a fairly moronic plot in this made-for-cable original, but there are one or two adequately acted scenes sprinkled through the action. Rated PG-13 for violence. 95m. **DIR:** Stuart Cooper. **CAST:** Shannen Doherty, James Marshall, Heidi Swedberg, Al Mancini. **1997**

TICKET OF LEAVE MAN, THE ★★ British horror star Tod Slaughter gleefully plays a maniacal killer who swindles rich philanthropists with a phony charity organization he has established. Slaughter single-handedly presided as Great Britain's unofficial hobgoblin during the 1930s and early 1940s. The majority of his films have been unavailable for years in America. B&W; 71m. **DIR:** George King. **CAST:** Tod Slaughter, John Warwick, Marjorie Taylor. **1937**

TICKET TO HEAVEN ★★★ This Canadian film presents a lacerating look at the frightening phenomenon of contemporary religious cults. Nick Mancuso is riveting as the brainwashed victim. Saul Rubinek and Meg Foster are splendid in support. But R. H. Thomson almost steals the show as a painfully pragmatic deprogrammer. Nice touches of humor give the movie balance. Rated PG. 107m. **DIR:** Ralph L. Thomas. **CAST:** Nick Mancuso, Saul Rubinek, Meg Foster, Kim Cattrall, R. H. Thomson. **1981 DVD**

TICKLE ME ★★ The plot falls below that found in a standard Elvis vehicle in this unfunny comedy-musical, which has Elvis working and singing at an all-female health ranch. Mindless fluff. 90m. **DIR:** Norman Taurog. **CAST:** Elvis Presley, Jocelyn Lane, Julie Adams, Jack Mullaney, Merry Anders. **1965**

•TIDAL WAVE: NO ESCAPE 🦃 Preposterous made-for-television disaster film about a madman generating killer tidal waves and the burnt-out scientist brought out of retirement to stop him. Bad special effects, bad acting, bad writing, and bad directing. Bad. Not rated. 91m. **DIR:** George Miller. **CAST:** Corbin Bernsen, Julianne Phillips, Gregg Henry, Lawrence Hilton-Jacobs, Harve Presnell. **1997**

TIDES OF WAR ★★1/2 Clichéd wartime intrigue concerning a German naval officer who lands on a Caribbean island to secure it as a Nazi missile site and gradually discovers he sympathizes with the Allied cause. Rated PG-13 for violence and brief nudity. 91m. **DIR:** Nello Rossati. **CAST:** David Soul, Yvette Heyden, Rod Obregon, Ernest Borgnine, Stephen Luotto, Bo Svenson. **1990**

TIDY ENDINGS ★★★★ Tender, touching AIDS drama deals with the confrontation between the victim's wife, wonderfully played by Stockard Channing, and the man's gay lover, sensitively played by Harvey Fierstein. Both wife and lover must come to grips with each other, and what each other meant to the deceased. Insightful and human. 54m. **DIR:** Gavin Millar. **CAST:** Stockard Channing, Harvey Fierstein, Nathaniel Moreau, Jean De Baer. **1989**

TIE-DIED: ROCK 'N' ROLL'S MOST DEDICATED FANS ★★1/2 An almost entertaining intro into the land of the Dead, where Jerry Garcia was king and the 1960s never ended. It really is about the fans and not the group, and director Andrew Behar does reveal the downside to life's longest road trip. Rated R for profanity and drug use. 88m. **DIR:** Andrew Behar. **1995 DVD**

TIE ME UP! TIE ME DOWN! ★★★1/2 From Spain's hot cult director Pedro Almodóvar, concerning the unorthodox romance between a soft-core porno star named Marina (Victoria Abril) and a recently released psychiatric patient named Ricky (Antonio Banderas). This film exists in both R and unrated versions, due to profanity and explicit sexual content. In Spanish with English subtitles. 105m. **DIR:** Pedro Almodóvar. **CAST:** Victoria Abril, Antonio Banderas. **1990**

TIE THAT BINDS, THE ★★ Two psycho serial killers set out to retrieve their 6 year old daughter from the decent couple who have adopted her. This wildly implausible melodrama has only its middle-class-nightmare

premise to recommend it; not even the performances of the usually reliable cast can redeem the film's tawdry excesses. Rated R for extreme violence (even the little girl winds up with blood on her hands). 98m. **DIR:** Wesley Strick. **CAST:** Daryl Hannah, Keith Carradine, Moira Kelly, Vincent Spano, Julia Devin. **1995 DVD**

TIEFLAND ★★★1/2 A shepherd and a marquis vie for the affections of a Spanish dancer in this atmospheric, visually poetic melodrama featuring gorgeous black-and-white photography. Leni Riefenstahl did most of the filming in 1935 but was unable to complete it for nineteen years because of the war and later problems with the French government. B&W; 98m. **DIR:** Leni Riefenstahl. **CAST:** Leni Riefenstahl, Franz Eichberger. **1954**

TIGER AND THE PUSSYCAT, THE ★★1/2 Male menopause comedy-drama of middle-aged Vittorio Gassman entranced with Ann-Margret, an American student living and loving in Italy. Pretty dated; the stars make it bearable. In English. Not rated, with some innocuous sex talk. 105m. **DIR:** Dino Risi. **CAST:** Ann-Margret, Vittorio Gassman, Eleanor Parker. **1967 DVD**

TIGER BAY ★★★1/2 Young Hayley Mills began her film career—in a part originally written for a boy—as an imaginative girl who witnesses a murder and then befriends the killer. Since the child is a known liar, nobody believes her until events escalate to the point of desperation. Horst Buchholz is excellent as the remorseful murderer. A thoughtful drama for all ages. Not rated; suitable for family viewing. B&W; 105m. **DIR:** J. Lee Thompson. **CAST:** John Mills, Horst Buchholz, Hayley Mills, Yvonne Mitchell, Anthony Dawson. **1959 DVD**

TIGER HEART ★★ Sort of a grittier take on *The Karate Kid*, with T. J. Roberts as a teenage martial arts champion who helps protect his girlfriend's uncle from thugs trying to make him sell his supermarket. Designed for teen viewers who are too old for cartoons but too young for most action films. Rated PG-13 for mild profanity and violence. 90m. **DIR:** Georges Chamchoum. **CAST:** Ted Jan Roberts, Robert LaSardo, Jennifer Lyons. **1996**

TIGER TOWN ★★1/2 In this passable movie, made for the Disney Channel, Roy Scheider stars as a legendary baseball player whose final year with the Detroit Tigers looks dismal until a young boy (Justin Henry) "wishes" him to success. At least, that's what the boy believes. Both Scheider and Henry give good performances, but the overall effect is not as impressive as it could have been. Rated G. 76m. **DIR:** Alan Shapiro. **CAST:** Roy Scheider, Justin Henry. **1984**

TIGER WALKS, A ★★1/2 This Disney drama about an escaped circus tiger and the impact his fate has on a small town boasts a good cast of veteran film personalities as well as a jaundiced view of politics and mass hysteria. 88m. **DIR:** Norman Tokar. **CAST:** Brian Keith, Vera Miles, Pamela Franklin, Sabu, Kevin Corcoran, Peter Brown, Una Merkel, Frank McHugh. **1964**

TIGER WARSAW ★★ Members of a family torn apart by a tragic incident struggle through their lives—all the while unable to forgive and forget. Patrick Swayze is Tiger Warsaw, a man haunted by the memory of shooting his father. Vague film lacking in substance and direction. Rated R for violence and profanity. 92m. **DIR:** Amin Q. Chaudhri. **CAST:** Patrick Swayze, Barbara Williams, Lee Richardson, Piper Laurie. **1987**

TIGER'S TALE, A 🦃 Grievously unfunny comedy about a not-so-bright teenage stud from Texas. Rated R for nudity. 97m. **DIR:** Peter Douglas. **CAST:** Ann-Margret, C. Thomas Howell, Charles Durning, Kelly Preston, William Zabka, Ann Wedgeworth, Tim Thomerson. **1988**

TIGGER MOVIE, THE ★★★ Don't expect the latest dazzling animation in this sweet, mild adaptation of author A. A. Milne's *Hundred Acre Woods* characters. The background scenery is flat, giving the film a booklike feel. What isn't flat is Tigger's over-the-top personality as he seeks companionship and receives help from Winnie the Pooh and pals. Adorable Roo steals every scene. Rated G. 85m. **DIR:** Jun Falkenstein. **2000 DVD**

TIGHT LITTLE ISLAND ★★★★ A World War II transport laden with whiskey founders just off the shore of a Scottish island. Hilarious hell breaks loose as delirious lads and lassies seek to salvage the water of life before authorities can claim it. One of the great comedies that revived the British film industry after the war. B&W; 82m. **DIR:** Alexander Mackendrick. **CAST:** Basil Radford, Joan Greenwood, James Robertson Justice, Gordon Jackson. **1949**

TIGHTROPE ★★★★★ A terrific, taut suspense-thriller, this ranks with the best films in the genre. Written and directed by Richard Tuggle, it casts Clint Eastwood as Wes Block, homicide inspector for the New Orleans Police Department. His latest assignment is to track down a Jack the Ripper–style sex murderer. This case hits disturbingly close to home in more ways than one. Rated R for violence. 115m. **DIR:** Richard Tuggle. **CAST:** Clint Eastwood, Genevieve Bujold, Dan Hedaya, Alison Eastwood. **1984**

TIGRERO: A FILM THAT WAS NEVER MADE ★★★★ In 1954, maverick director Sam Fuller went to the jungles of Brazil to scout locations for a film he was going to make, *Tigrero*, starring John Wayne, Ava Gardner, and Tyrone Power. For insurance reasons the studio canceled the project. Forty years later Fuller, accompanied by fellow filmmaker Jim Jarmusch, returns to visit the members of the Karaja tribe he met on his original trip and shows them the films he took of them and their now-dead relatives. A fascinating cultural document. Not rated; contains no objectionable material. 75m. **DIR:** Mika Kaurismaki. **CAST:** Samuel Fuller, Jim Jarmusch. **1995**

TIGRESS, THE ★★ Tired blood makes this kitty roll over and play dead. Sultry Valentina Vargas gets involved with con man James Remar. Available in two versions: unrated for less-than-titillating sex scenes, and rated R for less of the same. **DIR:** Karin Howard. **CAST:** James Remar, Valentina Vargas, George Peppard, Hannes Jaenicke. **1992 DVD**

'TIL THERE WAS YOU ★★1/2 Searching for Mr. Right is a test of stamina for audiences and leading ladies alike, in this sugary romantic comedy. The tease here is that it takes twenty years for two strangers to cross paths several times and then sort of fall in love at first sight. The story bulges with group-hug humanity, but is rather uninvolving. Rated PG-13 for profanity and mature themes. 114m. **DIR:** Scott Winant. **CAST:** Jeanne Tripplehorn, Dylan McDermott, Sarah Jessica Parker,

Jennifer Aniston, Craig Bierko, Michael Tucker, Karen Allen. **1997 DVD**

TILL DEATH DO US PART ★★★1/2 Made-for-TV film based on Los Angeles DA Vincent Bugliosi's brilliant case against spouse killer Alan Palliko in 1966. All the evidence against Palliko and his gal pal was circumstantial. Suspenseful and spellbinding moments. Not rated; contains violence and nudity. 93m. **DIR:** Yves Simoneau. **CAST:** Treat Williams, Arliss Howard, Rebecca Jenkins. **1991**

TILL MARRIAGE DO US PART ★★ Although a slight Italian sex comedy, its star, Laura Antonelli, is as delicious as ever. It's a treat for her fans only. Rated R. 97m. **DIR:** Luigi Comencini. **CAST:** Laura Antonelli. **1974**

TILL MURDER DO US PART ★★★ Meredith Baxter-Birney is good as convicted murderess Betty Broderick in this made-for-television docudrama. When a devoted wife's husband leaves her for another woman, she goes off the deep end and begins a campaign of terror that culminates in murder. Stephen Collins and Michelle Johnson costar as the unfaithful husband and mistress whose affair is the catalyst for Broderick's breakdown. Not rated. 82m. **DIR:** Dick Lowry. **CAST:** Meredith Baxter-Birney, Stephen Collins, Michelle Johnson, Kelli Williams. **1992**

TILL THE CLOUDS ROLL BY ★★1/2 Biography of songwriter Jerome Kern is a barrage of MGM talent that includes Judy Garland, Frank Sinatra, Lena Horne, Dinah Shore, Kathryn Grayson, and many more in short, tuneful vignettes that tie this all-out effort together. Not too bad as musical bio-pics go, but singing talent is definitely the star in this production. 137m. **DIR:** Richard Whorf. **CAST:** Robert Walker, Van Heflin, Judy Garland, Lucille Bremer. **1946 DVD**

TILL THE END OF THE NIGHT ★★★ Scott Valentine gives an effective performance as a man who discovers that his wife's past includes a marriage to a hardened criminal. Of course, he discovers this when that hardened criminal is released from prison and begins to harass his family. Sure, it's silly at times but performances throughout are solid and the film does offer some suspense and action. Rated R for profanity and violence. 90m. **DIR:** Larry Brand. **CAST:** Scott Valentine, Katherine Kelly Lang, Roger Clinton. **1994**

TILL THE END OF TIME ★★★ Three veterans of World War II come home to find life, in general and how it was when they left, considerably changed. Readjustment is tough, and the love they left has soured. A good drama. B&W; 105m. **DIR:** Edward Dmytryk. **CAST:** Dorothy McGuire, Guy Madison, Robert Mitchum, Jean Porter. **1946**

TILL THERE WAS YOU ★★ A lackluster film about an American saxophonist (Mark Harmon) who goes to the island nation of Vanuatu. An almost plotless mystery. Rated PG-13 for violence and nudity. 94m. **DIR:** John Seale. **CAST:** Mark Harmon, Deborah Unger, Jeroen Krabbé, Briant Shane. **1991**

TILT 🦃 Brooke Shields's third movie (after *Alice, Sweet Alice* and *Pretty Baby*) is a mess. Rated PG. 104m. **DIR:** Rudy Durand. **CAST:** Brooke Shields, Ken Marshall, Charles Durning, Geoffrey Lewis. **1978**

TIM ★★★★1/2 An unforgettable character study from down under, this features Mel Gibson in his film debut as a simpleminded young adult and Piper Laurie as the older woman who finds herself falling in love with him. Superb supporting performances by the Australian cast—especially Alwyn Kurts and Pat Evison, as Tim's parents. Rated PG for suggested sex. 108m. **DIR:** Michael Pate. **CAST:** Mel Gibson, Piper Laurie, Alwyn Kurts. **1979**

TIME AFTER TIME ★★★★ H. G. Wells (Malcolm McDowell) pursues Jack the Ripper (David Warner) into modern-day San Francisco via a time machine. It's an enjoyable pastiche that has quite a few nice moments. Rated PG. 112m. **DIR:** Nicholas Meyer. **CAST:** Malcolm McDowell, David Warner, Mary Steenburgen. **1979**

•TIME AND TIDE ★★★1/2 Hong Kong filmmaker Tsui Hark returns to the high-octane action genre he helped define with films such as *Peking Opera Blues* and *A Chinese Ghost Story*, and the result is long on visual flash and short on linear storytelling. The broad strokes concern a callow young man who becomes a bodyguard for quick cash, and befriends a disillusioned mercenary. The two wind up on opposite sides of a complex drug war, which is further complicated by the mercenary's desire to protect his pregnant wife who eventually figures in one of the most preposterous scenes ever delivered by the action genre. Hark's films are for fans who prefer style over substance, and this one has style to burn. Rated R for strong violence and drug use. 113m. **DIR:** Tsui Hark. **CAST:** Nicholas Tse, Wu Bai, Candy Lo, Cathy Tsui, Anthony Wong Chau-Sang. **2000 DVD**

TIME BANDITS ★★★★ Anyone with a sense of adventure will find a lot to like about this delightful tale of a boy and six dwarves—no, this isn't *Snow White*—who travel back in time through holes in the fabric of the universe. Rated PG for violence and adult themes. 110m. **DIR:** Terry Gilliam. **CAST:** Sean Connery, Shelley Duvall, Ralph Richardson, Ian Holm, David Warner, John Cleese, Michael Palin. **1981 DVD**

TIME BOMB ★★ Michael Biehn plays an amnesiac who suddenly finds himself a target for assassination. Patsy Kensit costars as a psychiatrist who Biehn first abducts and persuades to restore his memory. Rated R for violence, profanity, and simulated sex. 96m. **DIR:** Avi Nesher. **CAST:** Michael Biehn, Patsy Kensit, Tracy Scoggins, Robert Culp, Richard Jordan. **1991**

TIME CHASERS ★★★1/2 After the time machine he invented destroys the future of mankind, a physics teacher tries to go back in time to undo the damage. Clever low-budget sci-fi tale proves you don't need a $100 million budget if you have imagination and a good story. Not rated; contains nothing objectionable. 90m. **DIR:** David Giancola. **CAST:** Matthew Burch, Bonnie Pritchard, Peter Harrington. **1995**

TIME FLIES WHEN YOU'RE ALIVE ★★★★ Actor Paul Linke's monologue chronicling his wife's battle with cancer and how it affected his family is a wonderful mix of humor and sorrow. Linke takes the audience on a roller coaster ride of emotions from heartbreaking tales of death and loss to amusing anecdotes celebrating life. Not rated; contains profanity. 80m. **DIR:** Roger Spottiswoode. **CAST:** Paul Linke. **1990**

TIME FOR DRUNKEN HORSES, A ★★★★1/2 Powerful images and performances fuel this haunting film about the harsh realities Kurds face living on the Iran-Iraq border where men, women, and children smuggle contraband in exchange for money. The film focuses on

the plight of one family and the amazing strength and courage they show as they make ends meet. Real people from the village add an extraordinary degree of realism to the proceedings. The performances are authentic and ultimately heartbreaking. In Kurdish with English subtitles. Not rated. 77m. **DIR:** Bahman Ghobadi. **CAST:** Ayoub Ahmadi, Rojin Younessi, Ameneh Ekhtiar-Dini, Madi Ekhtiar-Dini. **2000**

TIME GUARDIAN, THE 🦃 Enemies of the future—man and metallic man—go back in time to prepare to do battle. Rated PG for violence. 80m. **DIR:** Brian Hannant. **CAST:** Carrie Fisher, Tom Burlinson, Dean Stockwell. **1987**

TIME MACHINE, THE (1960) ★★★★ Rod Taylor plays a scientist in the early 1900s who invents a device that can transport him within the dimensions of time. He goes forward past three world wars and into the year 802,701, where he encounters a world very different from the one he left. This movie has all the elements that make up a classic in science fiction. 103m. **DIR:** George Pal. **CAST:** Rod Taylor, Yvette Mimieux, Alan Young, Sebastian Cabot. **1960 DVD**

•TIME MACHINE, THE (2002) ★★ H. G. Wells's cautionary novel about science versus humanity and the clash of castes is reduced to a brisk but toothless monster movie. A nerdy mathematics professor whose fiancée is murdered during a Central Park robbery becomes obsessed with building a machine that allows him to travel through time and control fate. He careens 800,000 years into the future where mankind has evolved into two species: an underground horde of cannibals ruled by an albino Morlock and cliff-side, pod-dwelling pacifists called the Eloi. Rated PG-13 for mature themes and violence. 95m. **DIR:** Simon Wells. **CAST:** Guy Pearce, Sienna Guillory, Jeremy Irons, Samantha Mumba, Phyllida Law, Mark Addy, Orlando Jones, Omero Mumba. **2002 DVD**

TIME OF DESTINY, A ★★1/2 Old-fashioned tale of love, hate, and revenge set against the backdrop of World War II. William Hurt is the guilt-ridden son of a Basque family in San Diego out to avenge the accidental death of his father. Timothy Hutton is the subject of Hurt's revenge. Beautiful photography, terrific editing and pacing help keep you from noticing the weak spots in the familiar plot. Rated PG-13 for violence and profanity. 118m. **DIR:** Gregory Nava. **CAST:** William Hurt, Timothy Hutton, Melissa Leo, Stockard Channing. **1988**

TIME OF THE GYPSIES ★★★★ A young psychic gypsy boy learns the meaning of life the hard way. Absorbing character study, brilliantly photographed. The film weaves magical realism, visual humor, and pathos. A must-see! In Yugoslavian with English subtitles. Rated R. 136m. **DIR:** Emir Kusturica. **CAST:** Davor Dujmovic, Bora Todorovic. **1989**

TIME OF THEIR LIVES, THE ★★1/2 Bearing more than a passing resemblance to *The Canterville Ghost* and *I Married a Witch*, this story of ghostly goings-on is one of Abbott and Costello's most unusual features. Costello plays a man mistakenly shot as a traitor during the Revolutionary War and doomed to haunt a Colonial mansion until proved innocent. B&W; 82m. **DIR:** Charles Barton. **CAST:** Bud Abbott, Lou Costello, Marjorie Reynolds, Binnie Barnes, John Shelton, Gale Sondergaard, Robert Barrat, Donald MacBride. **1946**

TIME OF YOUR LIFE, THE ★★★1/2 Originally a prize-winning play by the brilliant William Saroyan. Director H. C. Potter and a talented group of actors have created a pleasing film about the diverse characters who are regulars at Nick's Saloon, Restaurant and Entertainment Palace on San Francisco's Barbary Coast. A charmer, this picture grows on you. B&W; 109m. **DIR:** H. C. Potter. **CAST:** James Cagney, Wayne Morris, Broderick Crawford, Jeanne Cagney, Ward Bond, Jimmy Lydon, Gale Page. **1948 DVD**

TIME OUT FOR LOVE ★★ Romantic roundelay with Jean Seberg as an American girl who gets caught in the middle of a failed love affair between a race-car driver and a suicidal fashion designer. In French with English subtitles. 93m. **DIR:** Jean Valère. **CAST:** Jean Seberg, Micheline Presle. **1961**

TIME REGAINED ★★★★ This adaption of the last book of Marcel Proust's series of novels *Remembrance of Things Past* is set in the latter part of the nineteenth century in France. The film doesn't have a plot, but consists of randomly shifting glimpses that slowly form a pattern. Watching it can be difficult, at least initially, but the effort is rewarded. In French with English subtitles. 165m. **DIR:** Raúl Ruiz. **CAST:** Catherine Deneuve, Emmanuelle Beart, Vincent Perez, John Malkovich, Marie-France Pisier, Chiara Mastroianni, Arielle Dombasle. **1999 DVD**

TIME RUNNER ★★ Story alternates between the year 2022, when Earth is at war with aliens, and 1992, when a man from 2022 has arrived on Earth. Of course his actions during 1992 will determine the outcome of the future war. Predictable. Rated R for profanity and violence. 90m. **DIR:** Michael Mazo. **CAST:** Mark Hamill, Brian James, Marc Baur, Gordon Tipple, Rae Dawn Chong. **1992**

TIME SERVED 🦃 A woman sent to prison agrees to participate in a work-release program so that she can dance topless at the club frequented by the psychotic judge who sentenced her. No one here gets time off for good behavior. Rated R for adult situations, language, nudity, and violence. 94m. **DIR:** Glen Pitre. **CAST:** Catherine Oxenberg, Jeff Fahey, Bo Hopkins, Larry Manetti, Louise Fletcher. **1999**

TIME SHIFTERS, THE ★★★ Watchable sci-fi feature focuses on a tabloid journalist's discovery that futuristic tourists are visiting historic disaster sites. After the journalist prevents a plane crash, the Thrill Seeker "tour company" must stop him from further altering their time line. Not rated; contains violence and language. 91m. **DIR:** Mario Azzopardi. **CAST:** Casper Van Dien, Catherine Bell, Theresa Saldana, Peter Outerbridge. **1999**

TIME STALKERS ★★★ A mildly entertaining made-for-TV movie about a modern-day Old West buff who helps a scientist from the future track a villain into the past. An exciting conclusion. Not rated; contains mild violence. 96m. **DIR:** Michael Schultz. **CAST:** William Devane, Lauren Hutton, John Ratzenberger, Forrest Tucker, Klaus Kinski. **1986**

TIME STANDS STILL ★★1/2 This Hungarian export dwells so much on the "art for art's sake" credo that it nearly destroys some of the life the film tries to depict.

It's about restless youths at the threshold of adulthood in Hungary. The film is presented in the original language with subtitles. Not rated, but the equivalent of an R for nudity and language. 99m. **DIR:** Peter Gothar. **CAST:** Ben Barenholtz, Albert Schwartz. **1982**

TIME TO DIE, A (1983) ★★ Despite the name actors and source material by Mario Puzo, this vengeance flick has a story as dog-eared as they come. An American spy returns to Europe after World War II to hunt the Nazis who killed his French wife. The twists unravel too easily to make for a thrilling affair. Rated R for nudity and violence. 89m. **DIR:** Matt Cimber. **CAST:** Rex Harrison, Rod Taylor, Edward Albert, Raf Vallone. **1983**

TIME TO DIE, A (1991) 🦃 The only mystery in this tale of a female photographer (former porn star Traci Lords) who catches a cop in a compromising position, is why anyone would want to watch it in the first place. Rated R for violence and profanity. 90m. **DIR:** Charles Kanganis. **CAST:** Traci Lords, Richard Roundtree, Jeff Conaway. **1991**

TIME TO KILL (1990) ★★ Nicolas Cage stars as Enrico, an Italian officer stationed in Africa who accidentally kills a woman. Rated R for violence and nudity. 100m. **DIR:** Giuliano Montaldo. **CAST:** Nicolas Cage. **1990 DVD**

TIME TO KILL, A (1996) ★★1/2 John Grisham's overwrought first novel gets equally melodramatic treatment in this *too*-faithful adaptation. Mississippi attorney defends a factory worker who killed the two racist thugs guilty of raping his 10 year old daughter; the subsequent case becomes a media sensation involving the KKK, the National Guard, and several kitchen sinks. Rated R for violence, profanity, and rape. 145m. **DIR:** Joel Schumacher. **CAST:** Sandra Bullock, Samuel L. Jackson, Matthew McConaughey, Kevin Spacey, Brenda Fricker, Oliver Platt, Charles Dutton, Ashley Judd, Patrick McGoohan, Donald Sutherland, Kiefer Sutherland. **1996 DVD**

TIME TO LOVE AND A TIME TO DIE, A ★★1/2 A well-intentioned but preachy and largely unsatisfying antiwar film adapted from the novel by Erich Maria Remarque who also portrays the professor. John Gavin is a German soldier who receives a furlough from the Russian front in 1944. He returns home to find his town a bombed-out shell and his parents missing. 133m. **DIR:** Douglas Sirk. **CAST:** John Gavin, Lilo Pulver, Jock Mahoney, Don DeFore, Keenan Wynn, Erich Maria Remarque, Jim Hutton, Klaus Kinski. **1958**

TIME TRACKERS ★★ Scientists from the future chase one of their own through time in an effort to stop him from changing the course of history. Great medieval costumes, but the production is too amateurish to soar very high. Rated PG. 86m. **DIR:** Howard R. Cohen. **CAST:** Wil Shriner, Ned Beatty, Kathleen Beller, Bridget Hoffman, Lee Bergere, Alex Hyde-White. **1989**

TIME TRAVELERS, THE ★★★1/2 Imaginative story of scientists who plunge into a time corridor to rescue a colleague and find themselves stuck in the wreckage of the Earth of the future. Similar in many respects to other survival-after-nuclear-holocaust films, this entertaining film boasts vicious mutants, intelligent survivors who live under the surface of Earth, and a trick ending that is unique and intriguing. 82m. **DIR:** Ib Melchior. **CAST:** Preston Foster, Philip Carey, Merry Anders, Steve Franken, John Hoyt, Joan Woodbury. **1964**

TIME WALKER 🦃 Egyptologist accidentally brings an ancient mummy back to life. Avoid it. Rated PG. 83m. **DIR:** Tom Kennedy. **CAST:** Ben Murphy, Nina Axelrod, Kevin Brophy, Shari Belafonte. **1982**

TIME WITHOUT PITY ★★★★ Suspenseful British thriller with a clear anti-capital-punishment message. An alcoholic just out of the hospital has twenty-four hours to save his son from the gallows. It all gets a bit overwrought by the end. Not rated; contains violence. B&W; 88m. **DIR:** Joseph Losey. **CAST:** Michael Redgrave, Ann Todd, Leo McKern, Peter Cushing, Alec McCowen, Renee Houston, Joan Plowright, Lois Maxwell. **1957**

TIMECODE ★★★ Director Mike Figgis experiments with this film by following a large cast of characters from four points of view as they interact in and around the offices of a small-time Hollywood production company. Filming with four cameras in a single 93-minute "real time" take, he shows all four simultaneously for the entire length of the film. It's not as chaotic as you might think, but the experiment is more interesting than the story, and the film is sure to suffer on home video. Rated R for profanity, drug use, sexual scenes, and brief violence. 97m. **DIR:** Mike Figgis. **CAST:** Stellan Skarsgard, Saffron Burrows, Salma Hayek, Jeanne Tripplehorn, Holly Hunter, Steven Weber. **2000 DVD**

TIMECOP ★★★1/2 Jean-Claude Van Damme is the Timecop, a law-enforcement officer whose job it is to prevent crooks from using a new time-travel technology to get rich. Some plot twists lead to lapses in logic; however, an affecting subplot concerning the death of Van Damme's wife works well enough to redeem the whole affair. Rated R for violence, profanity, nudity, and simulated sex. 98m. **DIR:** Peter Hyams. **CAST:** Jean-Claude Van Damme, Mia Sara, Ron Silver, Bruce McGill, Gloria Reuben, Scott Bellis, Jason Schombing. **1994 DVD**

TIMEMASTER ★★ Another vanity production from director James Glickenhaus, starring his son Jesse as an orphan who believes his parents are alive but are being held prisoner in another galaxy. He enlists the aid of a wise, old inventor to help him defeat the evil dictator, free his parents, and save the world from an evil virtual-reality game. Rated PG-13 for violence. 110m. **DIR:** James Glickenhaus. **CAST:** Noriyuki "Pat" Morita, Jesse Cameron-Glickenhaus, Joanna Pacula, Michael Dorn, Michelle Williams. **1995**

TIMERIDER 🦃 A motorcycle rider and his motorcycle break the time barrier and end up being chased by cowboys in the Old West. Rated PG. 94m. **DIR:** William Dear. **CAST:** Fred Ward, Belinda Bauer, Peter Coyote, L. Q. Jones, Ed Lauter. **1983 DVD**

TIMES SQUARE 🦃 A totally unbelievable story involving two New York teens who hang out in Times Square. Rated R for profanity. 111m. **DIR:** Alan Moyle. **CAST:** Tim Curry, Robin Johnson, Trini Alvarado, Peter Coffield. **1980**

TIMES TO COME ★★★ When an innocent man is accidentally shot during a demonstration, this act hurls him into a nightmarish world where he must struggle to survive. A futuristic city plagued with political unrest and violence provides the backdrop for this baffling science-fiction thriller. In Spanish with English subtitles. Not

rated; the film has profanity, nudity, and violence. 98m. **DIR:** Gustavo Mosquera. **CAST:** Hugo Soto, Juan Leyrado. **1988**

TIN CUP ★★★★1/2 Director Ron Shelton touches all the bases in this look at the game of golf and the personalities drawn to it. Kevin Costner is terrific as the burned-out pro, now a golf instructor in the middle of nowhere, whose attraction to René Russo revives an old rivalry with circuit champ Don Johnson. A thought-provoking drama with real insight and romance. Rated R for profanity and brief nudity. 135m. **DIR:** Ron Shelton. **CAST:** Kevin Costner, René Russo, Don Johnson, Richard "Cheech" Marin, Linda Hart, Dennis Burkley, Rex Linn. **1996 DVD**

TIN DRUM, THE ★★★★1/2 Günter Grass's bizarre tale of 3 year old Oskar, who stops growing as the Nazis rise to power in Germany. Oskar expresses his outrage by banging on a tin drum. This unique film has a disturbing dreamlike quality, while its visuals are alternately startling and haunting. Received the Academy Award for best foreign film. In German with English subtitles. Rated R for nudity and gore. 142m. **DIR:** Volker Schlöndorff. **CAST:** David Bennent, Mario Adorf, Angela Winkler, Daniel Olbrychski. **1979 DVD**

TIN MAN ★★★ For the most part, this is an intriguing drama about a deaf auto mechanic who invents a computer with which he can hear and speak. When he attempts to get the device manufactured, the computer company sets out to exploit him. Timothy Bottoms is extraordinary, and the story holds your attention, but the film is hurt by cardboard villains and a pat ending. Not rated. 95m. **DIR:** John G. Thomas. **CAST:** Timothy Bottoms, Deana Jurgens, John Phillip Law, Troy Donahue. **1983**

TIN MEN ★★★★ Writer-director Barry Levinson takes a simple subject—the vendetta between two aluminum-siding salesmen in the 1950s—and fashions it into an insightful, witty comedy. The tone is similar to Levinson's earlier *Diner*. He has elicited top-notch performances from his trio of stars. Barbara Hershey is convincing as she transforms her character from mousy pawn to attractive, assertive woman. Rated R. 110m. **DIR:** Barry Levinson. **CAST:** Richard Dreyfuss, Danny DeVito, Barbara Hershey. **1987 DVD**

TIN PAN ALLEY ★★★1/2 Showgirl sisters Alice Faye and Betty Grable cross romantic paths with song pluggers John Payne and Jack Oakie from the turn of the century until World War I. Many wonderful songs from that era and an Oscar for Alfred Newman's score. Some cassettes open with an "added feature" of Faye singing "Get Out and Get Under." This was deleted from the movie before its release. B&W; 94m. **DIR:** Walter Lang. **CAST:** Alice Faye, Betty Grable, Jack Oakie, John Payne, Allen Jenkins, Billy Gilbert, Elisha Cook Jr., John Loder. **1940**

TIN SOLDIER, THE ★★1/2 This inane update of Hans Christian Andersen's fairy tale was one of the silliest results of 1995's Voices Against Violence Week. Rated PG for mild violence. 100m. **DIR:** Jon Voight. **CAST:** Jon Voight, Ally Sheedy, Dom DeLuise, Trent Knight. **1995**

TIN STAR, THE ★★★★ Solid Anthony Mann–directed adult Western has Anthony Perkins as the inexperienced sheriff of a wild-and-woolly town seeking the help of hardened gunfighter Henry Fonda. Although it contains some unconvincing moments, it succeeds overall thanks to the skilled playing of its cast. B&W; 93m. **DIR:** Anthony Mann. **CAST:** Henry Fonda, Anthony Perkins, Betsy Palmer, John McIntire, Michel Ray, Neville Brand, Lee Van Cleef. **1957**

TINGLER, THE ★★★ Director William Castle's stylish thriller is probably best known for its theatrical gimmick—joy buzzers installed in seats. The jolt was to create hysteria in theaters to match the panic on the screen. On video, the film is a campy treat, thanks to Vincent Price's coroner, who discovers that fear creates a creepy parasite on the spinal cord. The terror comes when the parasites break free. Fun blast from the past. 82m. **DIR:** William Castle. **CAST:** Vincent Price, Judith Evelyn, Darryl Hickman, Philip Coolidge. **1959 DVD**

TINTORERA 🦃 Interminable *Jaws* rip-off. Rated R for gore and T&A. 91m. **DIR:** René Cardona Jr. **CAST:** Susan George, Hugo Stiglitz, Fiona Lewis. **1977**

TINY TOON ADVENTURES ★★★★ Downsized classic cartoon characters have not always been successful—*The Flintstone Kids* being a nauseous example—but the pint-sized inhabitants of Warner Bros. Tiny Toons universe are wisecracking strokes of genius. Elmyra, a shrill little girl who *looooves* her "fuzzy-wuzzy buddies," is a wholly original character clearly shaped by executive producer Steven Spielberg. Certain parodies may be too scary for small fry. Each collection includes a mix of shorter and longer stories. 40m. **DIR:** Various!. **1993**

TINY TOONS ADVENTURES: HOW I SPENT MY VACATION ★★★★ The Warner Bros. cartoon legacy lives on, thanks to producer Steven Spielberg's lovingly crafted pint-sized renditions of the classic animated superstars. This made-for-video feature concerns the various members of ACME Acres, as school lets out for summer. Babs and Buster Bunny take a river journey through the deep South; Plucky Duck and Hampton Pig share the family car-trip from hell; holy terror Elmira (who "wuvs kitties") has a close encounter with the big cats of a safari park. 80m. **DIR:** Steven Spielberg. **1992**

TITAN A.E. ★★★1/2 This ambitious space saga, something of an animated riff on *Star Wars*, delivers solid characters and dramatic conflict in a package that feels like an American take on traditional Japanese *anime*. The year is 3028, and Earth has been destroyed by a race of energy beings bent on eradicating humans from the universe; one of the few survivors, a young man whose father invented a massive spaceship rumored to be mankind's only hope, is sucked into a series of dangerous adventures while trying to find this near-mythical craft. Although the characters here (thankfully) never break into song, the score is laced with cutting-edge rock from bands such as Powerman 5000, Electrasy, Bliss, The Urge, and Fun Lovin' Criminals; at times you'll wonder if the sound track album was deemed more important than the film itself. Rated PG for dramatic content. 94m. **DIR:** Don Bluth, Gary Goldman. **2000 DVD**

TITANIC (1953) ★★★1/2 The sinking of the "unsinkable" 1912 luxury liner on its maiden voyage dramatically solves the domestic problems of a rich but unhappy couple, Barbara Stanwyck and Clifton Webb, in this powerful fiction and fact re-creation of the most famous peacetime sea tragedy of this century. Superb acting, special effects, and a first-rate story make this film

a classic. 97m. **DIR:** Jean Negulesco. **CAST:** Barbara Stanwyck, Clifton Webb, Robert Wagner, Audrey Dalton, Thelma Ritter, Allyn Joslyn, Brian Aherne. **1953**

TITANIC (1995) ★★★★★ The fascinating story of the dream that became a nightmare is vividly told through interviews with survivors, diary excerpts, still photos, and newsreels. Narrated by David McCallum. Not rated. 200m. **DIR:** Melissa Peltier. **1995**

TITANIC (1996) ★★★ Once again the greatest steamship in the world sails majestically to her tragic end in the deep Atlantic. This account, a blend of fiction and fact, adds little to the legend, but should please fans of the ship and her sad history. 173m. **DIR:** Robert Lieberman. **CAST:** Peter Gallagher, George C. Scott, Eva Marie Saint, Tim Curry, Marilu Henner. **1996 DVD**

TITANIC (1997) ★★★★★ Writer-director James Cameron has, against all odds, come up with an old-fashioned-style classic in the oft-told tale of the sinking of the luxury liner. Leonardo DiCaprio and Kate Winslet are perfectly cast as the vulnerable young lovers from opposite ends of the social strata who find true passion before the ship inevitably collides with an iceberg. As are *Gone with the Wind* and *Casablanca*, *Titanic* is a touching story against a cataclysmic backdrop with universal emotions and timeless grace. Rated PG-13 for violence, nudity, and language. 194m. **DIR:** James Cameron. **CAST:** Leonardo DiCaprio, Kate Winslet, Billy Zane, Kathy Bates, Frances Fisher, Gloria Stuart, Bill Paxton, Bernard Hill, Jonathan Hyde, Victor Garber, David Warner, Suzy Amis, Bernard Fox. **1997 DVD**

TITANIC: A QUESTION OF MURDER ★★★ The greatest sea disaster of the twentieth century is again scrutinized. This time the focus is on new evidence about the *Titanic* and how the hundreds of lives lost when she went down in April 1912 might have been saved. Produced for television and reported by Peter Williams; footage includes interviews with survivors vividly recalling the tragedy. 53m. **DIR:** Alan Ravenscroft. **1983**

TITANIC: THE NIGHTMARE AND THE DREAM ★★★ The nightmare is the tragic sinking of the *Titanic*, on her maiden voyage from England to New York. The dream, realized more than seventy years later, is that of undersea geologist Dr. Robert D. Ballard, who sought and found the grave of the great steamship lost more than two miles beneath the Atlantic Ocean off Newfoundland. 56m. **DIR:** Graham Hurley. **1986**

TITANICA ★★★ This fascinating documentary tells the story of the greatest of all modern sea disasters, the cruel sinking of the unsinkable *Titanic* on her 1912 maiden voyage, through the eyes of survivor Eva Hart and deep-sea photography exploring the ship where she lies, two-and-a-half miles below the surface of the icy Atlantic. B&W/color; 95m. **DIR:** Stephen Low. **1991**

TITO AND ME ★★★★ In 1954 Yugoslavia, Zoran, a 10 year old underachiever tries to impress a girl and finds himself on a state-sponsored hike through the homeland of President Tito. Political satire shares the screen with broad comedy, as Zoran's extended family lives in an apartment that's far too small for them. In Croatian with English subtitles. Not rated; contains no objectionable material. 104m. **DIR:** Goran Markovic. **CAST:** Dimitrie Vojnov, Lazar Ristovski. **1992 DVD**

TITUS ★★★★ A Roman general becomes embroiled in a spiraling web of vengeance with a malevolent queen. Shakespeare's first and bloodiest tragedy, *Titus Andronicus*, is also one of his least produced, mainly because it offers a parade of horrors—rape, murder, mutilation, cannibalism—in place of the poetry, power, and insight that would be the hallmark of the mature Bard. Even so, it gets a stylish, energetic filming from director Julie Taymor and a first-rate cast. Rated R for violence, nudity, and sexual scenes. 162m. **DIR:** Julie Taymor. **CAST:** Anthony Hopkins, Jessica Lange, Alan Cumming, Colm Feore, Angus MacFadyen, Laura Fraser, James Frain. **1999 DVD**

TNT JACKSON A sexy kung fu expert who comes to Hong Kong to exact revenge on her brother's killer. Rated R for nudity, profanity, and violence. 73m. **DIR:** Cirio H. Santiago. **CAST:** Jeanne Bell, Stan Shaw, Pat Anderson. **1975 DVD**

TO ALL A GOOD NIGHT ★★ In this typical slasher film, a group of young teenage girls gets away from supervision, and the mad killer shows up with a sharp weapon. A slightly above-average film of its genre. Rated R; has nudity, violence, and profanity. 90m. **DIR:** David Hess. **CAST:** Jennifer Runyon, Forrest Swenson. **1983**

TO ALL MY FRIENDS ON SHORE ★★★★ The dreams of two working-class parents to move their family out of the city fade when they learn that their son has sickle-cell anemia. Much better than the usual disease-of-the-week TV movie, with strong performances and a heartfelt script. 75m. **DIR:** Gilbert Cates. **CAST:** Bill Cosby, Gloria Foster, Dennis Hines. **1972**

TO BE OR NOT TO BE (1942) ★★★★1/2 After gaining early stardom in *Twentieth Century*, Carole Lombard returned to another black comedy and another role as an oddball theater performer, for the last film of her life. One of Hollywood's premier comedy directors, Ernst Lubitsch, coached excellent performances from Carole Lombard and costar Jack Benny in this hilarious farce about a theater couple who outwit the Nazis. B&W; 99m. **DIR:** Ernst Lubitsch. **CAST:** Carole Lombard, Jack Benny, Robert Stack. **1942**

TO BE OR NOT TO BE (1983) ★★★★ In this hilarious remake of the Jack Benny–Carole Lombard classic from 1942, Mel Brooks and Anne Bancroft are Polish actors who foil the Nazis at the outbreak of World War II. It's producer-star Brooks's best film since *Young Frankenstein* and was directed by Alan Johnson, who choreographed *Springtime for Hitler* for Brooks's first film, *The Producers*. Rated PG. 108m. **DIR:** Alan Johnson. **CAST:** Mel Brooks, Anne Bancroft, Charles Durning, Tim Matheson. **1983**

TO CATCH A KILLER ★★★ Much-edited, former miniseries chronicles the mounting evidence against—and eventual arrest of—serial killer John Wayne Gacy. Brian Dennehy is truly frightening as Gacy, the man responsible for the deaths of thirty-two teenage boys. Michael Riley is also convincing as the dedicated lieutenant who would stop at nothing to halt Gacy's reign of terror. 95m. **DIR:** Eric Till. **CAST:** Brian Dennehy, Michael Riley, Margot Kidder, David Eisner. **1991 DVD**

TO CATCH A KING ★★ Made-for-cable spy thriller that fails to live up to its promising premise. In 1940, cunning Nazis plot to kidnap the Duke and Duchess of Windsor during the romantic couple's respite in Lisbon. Robert Wagner plays a café owner, a more debonair ver-

sion of *Casablanca*'s Rick. Teri Garr is a nightclub singer. The film is neither convincing nor exciting. 113m. **DIR:** Clive Donner. **CAST:** Robert Wagner, Teri Garr, Horst Janson, Barbara Parkins. **1984**

TO CATCH A THIEF ★★★★ John Robie (Cary Grant) is a retired cat burglar living in France in peaceful seclusion. When a sudden rash of jewel thefts hits the Riviera, he is naturally blamed. He sets out to clear himself, and the fun begins. This is certainly one of director Alfred Hitchcock's most amusing films. 103m. **DIR:** Alfred Hitchcock. **CAST:** Cary Grant, Grace Kelly, John Williams, Jessie Royce Landis. **1955**

TO CATCH A YETI ★★1/2 Made-for-cable children's movie about the search for the Himalayan yeti. Meat Loaf plays the hunter looking for the creature, who turns out to be a cuddly pet of a millionaire's spoiled son. It's up to a little girl to save the yeti and release him back into the wild. Cute creature, cute kids, cute endings. You get the idea. Rated PG. 87m. **DIR:** Bob Keen. **CAST:** Meat Loaf, Chantellese Kent, Jeff Moser, Rick Howland, Jim Gordon, Leigh Lewis. **1993**

TO DANCE WITH THE WHITE DOG ★★★★ Hume Cronyn delivers the performance of a lifetime in this moving *Hallmark Hall of Fame* special. When his wife dies, he befriends a white dog only seen by him, and his daughters fear that he's losing his mind. Exceptional acting and superior production values do justice to Terry Kay's novel about eternal love. 95m. **DIR:** Glenn Jordon. **CAST:** Hume Cronyn, Jessica Tandy, Esther Rolle, Christine Baranski. **1993**

TO DIE FOR (1989) ★★ Tooth-and-neck story stays fairly close to traditional vampire values, as warring brothers resolve a 500 year old family feud in downtown L.A. Rated R for nudity and profanity. 94m. **DIR:** Deran Sarafian. **CAST:** Steve Bond, Sydney Walsh, Amanda Wyss, Duane Jones, Scott Jacoby, Brendan Hughes. **1989**

TO DIE FOR (1995) ★★★★ Vapid, would-be media celebrity marries a nice guy and, after discovering his family values cramp her style, seduces a stoned teenager into killing him. Joyce Maynard's wonderfully nasty novel has been turned by veteran scribe Buck Henry into an equally dark and funny movie. Rated R for profanity, violence, simulated sex, and drug use. 103m. **DIR:** Gus Van Sant. **CAST:** Nicole Kidman, Matt Dillon, Joaquin Phoenix, Casey Affleck, Illeana Douglas, Alison Foland, Dan Hedaya. **1995 DVD**

TO DIE FOR 2: SON OF DARKNESS ★★ The 500 year old bloodsuckers are back, and it's up to the hero from the first film to put an end to their horror once and for all. Rated R for violence, profanity, and nudity. 95m. **DIR:** David F. Price. **CAST:** Rosalind Allen, Steve Bond, Scott Jacoby, Michael Praed, Amanda Wyss. **1991**

TO DIE STANDING ★★★ Easily irritated FBI agent Cliff De Young goes to Peru to extradite a drug boss. Thrilling, intertwined tale of love and power. Rated R for violence and profanity. 87m. **DIR:** Louis Morneau. **CAST:** Cliff De Young, Robert Beltran, Jamie Rose, Gerald Anthony. **1990**

TO FORGET VENICE ★★★★ Character-driven drama puts two pairs of gay lovers (one male, one female) in a quiet country house for a weekend. Prompted by the death of the woman who raised three of them, they are forced to come to grips with their lives. Beautifully acted. Dubbed in English. 110m. **DIR:** Franco Brusati. **CAST:** Erland Josephson, Mariangela Melato, Eleonora Giorgi, David Pontremoli. **1979**

TO GILLIAN ON HER 37TH BIRTHDAY ★★1/2 A thirtysomething widower (Peter Gallagher) can't let go of his dead wife (Michelle Pfeiffer), even as his teenage daughter starves for affection. The film entirely misses the point of Michael Brady's original play (the dead wife wasn't the flawless saint the husband remembers), no doubt because Pfeiffer's husband, David E. Kelley, produced and wrote the screenplay. All that's left is the play's blubbery sentimentality, and it gets old in a hurry. Rated PG-13 for mild profanity. 92m. **DIR:** Michael Pressman. **CAST:** Peter Gallagher, Michelle Pfeiffer, Claire Danes, Kathy Baker, Wendy Crewson, Bruce Altman. **1996**

TO HAVE AND HAVE NOT ★★★★1/2 Director Howard Hawks once bet Ernest Hemingway he could make a good film from one of the author's worst books. Needless to say, he won the bet with this exquisite entertainment, which teamed Humphrey Bogart and Lauren Bacall for the first time. B&W; 100m. **DIR:** Howard Hawks. **CAST:** Humphrey Bogart, Lauren Bacall, Walter Brennan. **1944**

TO HEAL A NATION ★★★ Touching TV drama about the attempts of three Vietnam veterans to have the memorial wall built recounts the opposition and the enthusiasm. 100m. **DIR:** Michael Pressman. **CAST:** Eric Roberts, Glynnis O'Connor, Marshall Colt, Scott Paulin, Lee Purcell, Laurence Luckinbill. **1988**

TO HELL AND BACK ★★1/2 Real-life war hero Audie Murphy plays himself in this sprawling World War II action film. Murphy received twenty-four medals, including the Congressional Medal of Honor, which made him the most decorated soldier in World War II. Good performances and true-life drama make up for a static script. 106m. **DIR:** Jesse Hibbs. **CAST:** Audie Murphy, Marshall Thompson, Charles Drake, Gregg Palmer, Jack Kelly, Paul Picerni, Susan Kohner, David Janssen. **1955**

TO KILL A CLOWN A husband and wife move from the big city to a remote island in an effort to save their marriage. Rated R for violence. 82m. **DIR:** George Bloomfield. **CAST:** Alan Alda, Blythe Danner. **1983**

TO KILL A MOCKINGBIRD ★★★★★ *To Kill a Mockingbird* is a leisurely paced, flavorful filming of Harper Lee's bestselling novel. Gregory Peck earned an Oscar as a small-town southern lawyer who defends a black man accused of rape. Mary Badham, Philip Alford, and John Megna are superb as Peck's children and a visiting friend who are trying to understand life in a small town. B&W; 129m. **DIR:** Robert Mulligan. **CAST:** Gregory Peck, Mary Badham, Philip Alford, John Megna. **1962 DVD**

TO KILL A PRIEST ★★ Set in Warsaw, Poland, in 1984, this story tells of a secret police officer (Ed Harris) obsessed with a Catholic priest (Christopher Lambert) who is aiding the Solidarity movement. An interesting story is hampered by a mishmash of French, American, and British accents. Rated R for violence and profanity. 117m. **DIR:** Agnieszka Holland. **CAST:** Christopher Lambert, Ed Harris, David Suchet, Joanne Whalley, Joss Ackland. **1990**

TO LIVE ★★★★ Spanning thirty years of Chinese history beginning in the 1940s, this intimate, compassion-

ate, sometimes humorous epic of survival focuses on the common folk who were emotionally and physically bloodied by civil war, Mao's Great Leap Forward, and the Cultural Revolution. Their resiliency becomes the heart of the film. In Mandarin with English subtitles. Not rated; contains violence. 135m. **DIR:** Yimou Zhang. **CAST:** Ge You, Gong Li. **1994**

TO LIVE AND DIE IN L.A. Overly violent account of lone wolf William L. Petersen's attempt to shut down counterfeiter Willem Dafoe. Rated R for nudity and excessive violence. 114m. **DIR:** William Friedkin. **CAST:** William L. Petersen, Willem Dafoe, John Pankow, Dean Stockwell, Debra Feuer, John Turturro, Darlanne Fluegel. **1985**

TO PARIS WITH LOVE ★★1/2 Alec Guinness stands out like a pumpkin in a pea patch in this average comedy about a rich and indulgent father who takes his son to gay Paree to learn the facts of life. 78m. **DIR:** Robert Hamer. **CAST:** Alec Guinness, Odile Versois, Austin Trevor, Vernon Gray. **1955**

TO PLEASE A LADY ★★★ Racing film designed to sustain Clark Gable's macho image didn't win at the box office but looks pretty good today. The star-powered love/hate relationship between Gable's devil-may-care driver and Barbara Stanwyck's tough newspaper columnist is more exciting than the speedway scenes. B&W; 91m. **DIR:** Clarence Brown. **CAST:** Clark Gable, Barbara Stanwyck, Adolphe Menjou, Will Geer, Roland Winters. **1950**

TO PROTECT AND SERVE ★★★ C. Thomas Howell is quite effective in this hard-hitting, gritty thriller about a renegade group of killer cops who are being picked off themselves by someone who's in on their scheme. The cast is both attractive and believable. Rated R for nudity, violence, and language. 93m. **DIR:** Eric Weston. **CAST:** C. Thomas Howell, Lezlie Deane, Richard Romanus, Joe Cortese. **1992**

TO SEE SUCH FUN ★★ This is a compilation of a vast number of comedy film clips from 1930 to 1970. Many of the clips illustrate the British love of puns, rhymes, and slapstick. Viewers hoping to see a lot of Peter Sellers, Benny Hill, and Marty Feldman clips will be disappointed because most of the footage comes from films of the 1930s and 1940s. 90m. **DIR:** Jon Scoffield. **CAST:** Peter Sellers, Marty Feldman, Benny Hill, Eric Idle, Margaret Rutherford, Alec Guinness, Dirk Bogarde, Spike Milligan, Norman Wisdom. **1977**

TO SIR WITH LOVE ★★★★ A moving, gentle portrait of the influence of a black teacher upon a classroom of poverty-ridden teenagers in London's East End, this stars Sidney Poitier, in one of his finest performances, as the teacher. He instills in his pupils a belief in themselves and respect for one another. 105m. **DIR:** James Clavell. **CAST:** Sidney Poitier, Judy Geeson, Christian Roberts, Suzy Kendall, Lulu. **1967 DVD**

TO SLEEP WITH A VAMPIRE ★★★ Better-than-average slant on the vampire legend finds lonely bloodsucker Scott Valentine longing for the pleasures of daylight. When he meets lonely stripper Charlie Spradling, he finds a willing tutor. As the night comes to a close, the two have a difficult decision to make. Stylish thriller with fangs. Rated R for nudity, violence, and adult situations. 81m. **DIR:** Adam Friedman. **CAST:** Scott Valentine, Charlie Spradling, Richard Zobel, Ingrid Vold. **1993**

TO SLEEP WITH ANGER ★★★★1/2 Writer-director Charles Burnett based much of this superb, offbeat film on the southern folktales told to him by his grandmother. Its most unusual character, Harry (Danny Glover), is what she called a trickster, "a man who comes to town to steal your soul, and you have to trick him out of it." Rated PG for profanity. 101m. **DIR:** Charles Burnett. **CAST:** Danny Glover, Paul Butler, Mary Alice, Carl Lumbly, Vonetta McGee, Richard Brooks, Sheryl Lee Ralph, Julius W. Harris. **1990**

TO THE DEVIL, A DAUGHTER ★★★1/2 Based on Dennis Wheatley's book this above-average thriller is about occult novelist John Verney, who finds himself pitted against Satanists. Rated R for nudity, profanity, and violence in small quantities. 95m. **DIR:** Peter Sykes. **CAST:** Richard Widmark, Christopher Lee, Honor Blackman, Denholm Elliott, Nastassja Kinski. **1976**

TO THE LAST MAN ★★★★ Feudin' and fussin' in the Old West, Zane Grey style. Based on an actual clan clash that took place in Arizona during the 1880s, this is a top-quality oater from Paramount Pictures' series of films based on Grey's novels. Randolph Scott was directed in several of these by Henry Hathaway, and they made a potent team. Look for Shirley Temple in one of her earliest roles. B&W; 61m. **DIR:** Henry Hathaway. **CAST:** Randolph Scott, Richard Dix, Esther Ralston, Noah Beery Sr., Buster Crabbe, Jack LaRue. **1933**

TO THE LIGHTHOUSE ★★★ Virginia Woolf's experimental novel about a family and their hidden troubles makes for a rather dry film. Director Colin Gregg (*We Think the World of You*) is unable to make the talky script very interesting, though he does get uniformly strong performances from his cast. Not rated; contains nothing offensive. 115m. **DIR:** Colin Gregg. **CAST:** Rosemary Harris, Michael Gough, Kenneth Branagh, T. P. McKenna. **1983**

TO THE LIMIT ★★1/2 Supermodel Anna Nicole Smith had her first starring vehicle with this improbable crime-drama about a no-nonsense CIA agent (Smith) who becomes allied with a Mafia chieftain to oppose a renegade agency operative. Delivers plenty of shoot-'em-up action, but somehow the true focus seems to be Smith's hygienic habits, as evidenced in numerous shower scenes. Rated R for adult situations, nudity, violence, and strong language. 96m. **DIR:** Raymond Martino. **CAST:** Anna Nicole Smith, Joey Travolta, John Aprea, David Proval, Branscombe Richmond, Michael Nouri. **1995**

TO THE SHORES OF TRIPOLI ★★★ This wartime tribute to the Marines has smart-aleck recruit John Payne earning the love of navy nurse Maureen O'Hara after learning some humility and respect for the Corps. 87m. **DIR:** H. Bruce Humberstone. **CAST:** Maureen O'Hara, John Payne, Randolph Scott, Nancy Kelly, Maxie Rosenbloom, Alan Hale Jr. **1942**

TO WONG FOO, THANKS FOR EVERYTHING, JULIE NEWMAR ★★★1/2 Don't let the documentary-type intro to transvestites prevent you from enjoying what becomes a delightful comedy. When three fairy godbrothers—Patrick Swayze, Wesley Snipes, and John Leguizamo—descend on a sleepy Nebraska town, they manage to turn lives around for the better. Surprisingly

uplifting. Watch for cameos by RuPaul, Robin Williams, and Julie Newmar. Rated PG-13 for language, alternate lifestyles, and violence. 109m. **DIR:** Beeban Kidron. **CAST:** Wesley Snipes, Patrick Swayze, John Leguizamo, Stockard Channing, Blythe Danner, Arliss Howard, Christopher Penn. **1995**

TOAST OF NEW ORLEANS ★★1/2 Don't look for too much plot in this colorful showcase for the considerable vocal talent of the late Mario Lanza. Aided and abetted by the engaging soprano of Kathryn Grayson, Lanza sings up a storm. "Be My Love" was the film's and record stores' big number. 97m. **DIR:** Norman Taurog. **CAST:** Kathryn Grayson, Mario Lanza, Thomas Mitchell, David Niven, J. Carrol Naish, Rita Moreno. **1950**

TOAST OF NEW YORK, THE ★★★ Semiaccurate biography of legendary post–Civil War Wall Street wheeler-dealer James Fisk. But, even so, it is a good film. Edward Arnold superbly plays Fisk. Jack Oakie does a fine turn. Don't expect the Cary Grant you know and love, however. B&W; 109m. **DIR:** Rowland V. Lee. **CAST:** Edward Arnold, Cary Grant, Frances Farmer, Jack Oakie, Donald Meek, Clarence Kolb, Billy Gilbert. **1937**

TOBE HOOPER'S NIGHT TERRORS ★★ The infamous Marquis de Sade is back, and he has his sights set on a young woman living in New York. Except for the creative set design, which provides an impressive backdrop for the madness and mayhem, this film really doesn't have much to recommend it. Rated R for nudity, violence, and language. 98m. **DIR:** Tobe Hooper. **CAST:** Robert Englund, Zoe Trilling, William Finley. **1993**

TOBOR THE GREAT ★★ Kids foil commie plot to steal secret robot plans. Terrific-looking robot is only saving grace. B&W; 77m. **DIR:** Lee Sholem. **CAST:** Charles Drake, Karin Booth, Billy Chapin. **1954**

TOBRUK ★★★ Rock Hudson, Nigel Green, and George Peppard lead a ragtag group of British soldiers and homeless Jews against the Nazi and Italian armies in the North African desert during World War II. An exciting climax, beautiful photography, and good performances help offset a farfetched script. 110m. **DIR:** Arthur Hiller. **CAST:** Rock Hudson, George Peppard, Guy Stockwell, Nigel Green. **1966**

TOBY AND THE KOALA BEAR ★★ Adventure tale from Australia in which cartoon characters are placed in real-life settings. Toby is a youngster living in the Australia of yesteryear, in a camp for convicts. After he adopts an adorable pet koala bear, he sets off on a walkabout. 76m. **DIR:** Yoram Gross. **CAST:** Rolf Harris. **1981**

TOBY MCTEAGUE ★★★ Solid children's story about Canadian teenager Toby McTeague, who has to take over the reins of his father's dog-racing team for the big race. Some profane language, but otherwise suitable for almost everyone. 94m. **DIR:** Jean-Claude Lord. **CAST:** Winston Rekert, Yannick Bisson, Timothy Webber. **1987**

TOBY TYLER ★★★1/2 Disney version of the popular juvenile book about a young runaway and his adventures with the circus is breezy entertainment and a showcase for young Kevin Corcoran (Moochie of many Disney television shows and the *Mickey Mouse Club*). 96m. **DIR:** Charles Barton. **CAST:** Kevin Corcoran, Henry Calvin, Gene Sheldon, Bob Sweeney, James Drury. **1960**

TODAY WE LIVE ★★ A typical Joan Crawford movie of the 1930s, this film has all the right ingredients but doesn't come off well. It's set during World War I with Gary Cooper, Robert Young, and Franchot Tone competing for Crawford's affections between wartime exploits. The battle scenes are better than the love scenes and include some daredevil air sequences and a very exciting torpedo run. B&W; 113m. **DIR:** Howard Hawks. **CAST:** Gary Cooper, Joan Crawford, Robert Young, Franchot Tone, Roscoe Karns, Louise Closser Hale. **1933**

TODD KILLINGS, THE ★★1/2 Harrowing fact-based drama about a rebellious young murderer (Robert F. Lyons) and the alienated kids who protect him. This film offers a penetrating look into the pathological mind of a 23 year old killer who seeks out teenage girls. Shocking, disturbing portrait of a thrill-seeking psychopath. Rated R, contains nudity and violence. 93m. **DIR:** Barry Shear. **CAST:** Robert F. Lyons, Richard Thomas, Belinda Montgomery, James Broderick, Gloria Grahame, Holly Near, Edward Asner, Barbara Bel Geddes. **1971**

•TOGETHER ★★★ A commune in 1970s Stockholm sees some changes when the sister of one resident leaves her abusive husband and moves in, bringing her adolescent son and daughter along. Laid-back and cozy, the film pokes affectionate fun at its characters and profits from appealing performances, especially by Emma Samuelsson as the daughter and Gustav Hammarsten as her easygoing uncle. In Swedish with English subtitles. Rated R for nudity, profanity (in subtitles), and sexual scenes. 106m. **DIR:** Lukas Moodysson. **CAST:** Lisa Lindgren, Michael Nyqvist, Emma Samuelsson, Sam Kessel, Gustav Hammarsten. **2000**

TOKYO DECADENCE ★★★1/2 Decadent study of a 22 year old Tokyo call girl who longs for a better life but must perform kinky sex in order to survive. Ali (Miho Nikhaido) sees her life as a steady stream of deviate johns. Then she meets a dominatrix who opens the door to her dreams. The degradation Ali is forced to endure makes for kinky viewing. In Japanese with English subtitles. Rated NC-17 for strong sexual content. 92m. **DIR:** Ryu Murakami. **CAST:** Miho Nikhaido, Sayoko Amano, Chie Sema. **1991 DVD**

TOKYO-GA ★★★ German filmmaker Wim Wenders presents an absorbing film diary of his visit to Japan, where he attempts to define his relationship to a culture and city he knows only through the cinematic work of Yasujiro Ozu, the director of *Tokyo Story*. A great introspective account of Ozu's career is much of the film's focus. In Japanese with English subtitles. 92m. **DIR:** Wim Wenders. **CAST:** Chishu Ryu, Yuharu Atsuta, Werner Herzog. **1983**

TOKYO JOE ★★ Sinister intrigue in postwar Japan has Humphrey Bogart dealing with a blackmailing Sessue Hayakawa. Definitely not vintage Bogie. B&W; 88m. **DIR:** Stuart Heisler. **CAST:** Humphrey Bogart, Alexander Knox, Sessue Hayakawa. **1949**

TOKYO POP ★★ If you want a gander at modern-day Japan and its pop-music world, this is just the ticket. When Wendy (Carrie Hamilton) leaves her punk band in New York and flies to Tokyo, she finds herself pursued by a would-be rocker who has decided his group needs a

Western girl. Despite a maudlin love story, the film is worth watching for its revealing depictions of Tokyo street life and Japanese traditions. Rated R. 101m. **DIR:** Fran Rubel Kuzui. **CAST:** Carrie Hamilton, Yutaka Tadokoro. **1988**

•TOKYO RAIDERS ★★1/2 Director Jingle Ma incorporates John Woo–style action and Jackie Chan–style slapstick comedy in this tale of a trio of strangers on the run from a powerful crime lord and his henchmen. Hong Kong perennial Tony Leung stars as the private detective who winds up baby-sitting a bride-to-be and an interior decorator as they take to the streets of Tokyo in an effort to stay one step ahead of their pursuers. Ma feels compelled to use cinematic gimmicks when straightforward storytelling would suffice. The film was a big hit in Hong Kong, but it loses some of its kick in the translation. Rated PG-13 for martial arts violence. 100m. **DIR:** Jingle Ma. **CAST:** Tony Leung Chiu Wai, Ekin Cheng, Kelly Chen. **2000 DVD**

TOKYO STORY ★★★★★ Yasujiro Ozu's overpowering masterpiece is a deeply felt human drama about an elderly couple who travel to Tokyo, where they are unenthusiastically received by their grown-up children. Outstanding black-and-white cinematography brilliantly captures the landscape of Tokyo. In Japanese with English subtitles. B&W; 139m. **DIR:** Yasujiro Ozu. **CAST:** Chishu Ryu, Chiyeko Higashiyama. **1953**

TOL'ABLE DAVID ★★1/2 Though it creaks a bit with age, this stalwart tale of good besting evil deserves attention and rewards it. Silent. B&W; 80m. **DIR:** King Vidor. **CAST:** Richard Barthelmess, Gladys Hulette, Ernest Torrence, Warner Richmond. **1921 DVD**

TOLLBOOTH ★★★1/2 Quirky, offbeat comedy about a tollbooth operator named Jack (Lenny Van Dohlen), who's in love with a gas-station attendant named Doris (Fairuza Balk). Unfortunately, Doris won't marry Jack and leave their Florida Keys stomping grounds until her long-lost daddy finally returns home. Get a clue, Doris. Daddy's been gone for ten years, and his departure has left Doris and her mom a wreck. Outrageously novel dark comedy features wonderful performances and tight direction. Rated R for profanity, nudity, and violence. 108m. **DIR:** Salome Breziner. **CAST:** Lenny von Dohlen, Fairuza Balk, Will Patton, Seymour Cassel, Louise Fletcher. **1994**

TOM AND HUCK ★★★ Mark Twain's classic story about friendship and loyalty is revived with all its familiar characters and misadventures intact. Rated PG. 92m. **DIR:** Peter Hewitt. **CAST:** Jonathan Taylor Thomas, Brad Renfro, Amy Wright, Charles Rocket, Eric Schweig, Rachael Leigh Cook. **1995**

TOM & JERRY: THE MOVIE ★★ This full-length animated feature begins with the manic intensity expected of the dueling cat and mouse, but everything goes awry about ten minutes in when our hitherto mute heroes begin to *talk*. It's bad enough that Tom and Jerry suddenly lose their Buster Keaton–style charm—then they become another tediously smarmy couple of chums determined to reunite a girl with her missing father. Rated G. 84m. **DIR:** Phil Roman. **1993 DVD**

TOM & VIV ★★★ At first glance, this appears to be nothing but a talkfest aimed at the menstrual problems suffered by T. S. Eliot's wife, Vivien Haigh-Wood. As the story unfolds, you realize it is an astute, even maddening commentary on the treatment of women. Miranda Richardson is dead-on as the clever but imbalanced woman who finds herself trampled under the ego of her poetic, uptight husband. Rated PG-13 for profanity and adult themes. 115m. **DIR:** Brian Gilbert. **CAST:** Willem Dafoe, Miranda Richardson, Rosemary Harris, Tim Dutton, Nickolas Grace. **1995**

TOM BROWN'S SCHOOL DAYS (1940) ★★1/2 "Old school tie" story mixes top Hollywood production values and minor classic of British secondary schools into an enjoyable froth filled with all the clichés. Better than one would think and not the creaky old groaner it could have been. B&W; 86m. **DIR:** Robert Stevenson. **CAST:** Cedric Hardwicke, Freddie Bartholomew, Gale Storm, Jimmy Lydon, Josephine Hutchinson, Polly Moran, Billy Halop. **1940**

TOM BROWN'S SCHOOLDAYS (1950) ★★★1/2 Tom, played by John Howard Davies, brings a civilizing influence to his peers in this engaging account of life in a Victorian England boys' school. Robert Newton, of course, is superb. An excellent cast, under good direction, makes this a particularly fine film. B&W; 93m. **DIR:** Gordon Parry. **CAST:** Robert Newton, John Howard Davies, James Hayter, Hermione Baddeley. **1950**

TOM, DICK AND HARRY ★★★1/2 An energetic comic delight has Ginger Rogers trying to decide which very eligible bachelor to have for her beau. The entire cast comes through with solid performances, but Phil Silvers almost walks off with the show in his role as an obnoxious ice-cream man. Garson Kanin's direction is sharp. B&W; 86m. **DIR:** Garson Kanin. **CAST:** Ginger Rogers, George Murphy, Burgess Meredith, Alan Marshal, Phil Silvers. **1941**

TOM HORN ★★1/2 Steve McQueen doesn't give a great performance in his next-to-last motion picture, about the last days of a real-life Wyoming bounty hunter, nor does director William Wiard craft a memorable Western. Rated R. 98m. **DIR:** William Wiard. **CAST:** Steve McQueen, Richard Farnsworth, Billy Green Bush, Slim Pickens, Elisha Cook Jr. **1980**

TOM JONES ★★★★★ Rarely has a movie captured the spirit and flavor of its times or the novel on which it was based. This is a rambunctious, witty, and often bawdy tale of a youth's misadventures in eighteenth-century England. Albert Finney is a perfect rascal as Tom. We joyously follow him through all levels of British society as he tries to make his fortune and win the lovely Sophie (Susannah York). The entire cast is brilliant. 129m. **DIR:** Tony Richardson. **CAST:** Albert Finney, Susannah York, Hugh Griffith, Edith Evans. **1963 DVD**

TOM SAWYER (1917) ★★★1/2 This faithful adaptation of Mark Twain's nineteenth-century American classic includes most of his familiar vignettes of small-town life and boyish behavior, but the film ends partway into the novel and omits the famous section of Injun' Joe's cave. This title is one of the few available that William Desmond Taylor directed. Silent, with musical score. B&W; 59m. **DIR:** William Desmond Taylor. **CAST:** Jack Pickford, Helen Gilmore, Clara Horton, Antrum Short, Robert Gordon, Carl Goetz. **1917**

TOM SAWYER (1930) ★★1/2 Adequate version of the famous Mark Twain novel. It's worth seeing for child star Jackie Coogan in the title role, but parents beware: kids

will find this dull. B&W; 85m. **DIR:** John Cromwell. **CAST:** Jackie Coogan, Junior Durkin, Jane Darwell. **1930**

TOM SAWYER (1973) ★★★ This musical version of Mark Twain's classic has a few contrived moments here and there, but it is, on the whole, enjoyable. Rated G. 102m. **DIR:** Don Taylor. **CAST:** Johnny Whitaker, Celeste Holm, Jeff East, Jodie Foster, Warren Oates. **1973**

TOM SAWYER (1973) ★★ Mark Twain's classic story loses its satirical edge in this homogenized made-for-television production about the adventures of Tom Sawyer (Josh Albee) and Huckleberry Finn (Jeff Tyler). The kids may enjoy it, but adults will want to reread the book. Better yet, read the book to your kids. Rated G. 78m. **DIR:** James Nielson. **CAST:** Josh Albee, Jeff Tyler, Jane Wyatt, Buddy Ebsen, Vic Morrow, John McGiver. **1973**

TOM THUMB ★★★1/2 This underrated George Pal fantasy is a treat for young and old viewers. Good effects, pleasant tunes, and a distinguished cast of veteran British performers combine with Russ Tamblyn's infectious lead to make this a surefire choice for the kids. 98m. **DIR:** George Pal. **CAST:** Russ Tamblyn, June Thorburn, Peter Sellers, Terry-Thomas, Alan Young, Jessie Matthews, Bernard Miles. **1958**

TOMB, THE ★★ Typical high-energy (and low-budget) Fred Olen Ray production, with the veteran stars on hand for B-movie marquee value, while a largely unknown young cast handles the strenuous mayhem. The plot centers on a curse that follows the desecrators of an Egyptian tomb. Rated R. 84m. **DIR:** Fred Olen Ray. **CAST:** Cameron Mitchell, John Carradine, Fred Olen. **1985**

TOMB OF LIGEIA ★★★ A grieving widower is driven to madness by the curse of his dead wife. This was Roger Corman's final Poe-inspired movie. The most subtle and atmospheric entry in the series, it was photographed by Nicolas Roeg on sets left over from *Becket*. The screenplay was by Robert Towne, who went on to write *Chinatown*. 81m. **DIR:** Roger Corman. **CAST:** Vincent Price, Elizabeth Shepherd. **1964**

TOMBOY AND THE CHAMP 🦃 The kids will hate this overwrought story of a young Texas tomboy and her pet heifer. But adults who cherish really bad movies are sure to love its inane melodramatics, with tunes from cowboy singer Rex Allen. Not rated. 92m. **DIR:** Francis D. Lyon. **CAST:** Candy Moore, Ben Johnson, Rex Allen, Jesse White. **1961**

TOMBS OF THE BLIND DEAD ★★★ First entry in an entertaining exploitation-horror series, centering on the periodic resurrection of thirteenth-century Knights Templar and their quest for victims. Visually breathtaking—and one of the few examples of a Spanish horror film that has appeal for U.S. viewers. Rated R. 86m. **DIR:** Amando de Ossorio. **CAST:** Oscar Burner. **1971 DVD**

TOMBSTONE ★★★★ After cleaning up Dodge City, the Earp brothers attempt to settle down in Tombstone, but a marauding outlaw gang forces them to put their guns back on. Val Kilmer may well be the screen's best Doc Holliday. Rated R for violence and profanity. 130m. **DIR:** George Pan Cosmatos. **CAST:** Kurt Russell, Val Kilmer, Michael Biehn, Powers Boothe, Robert Burke, Dana Delany, Sam Elliott, Stephen Lang, Terry O'Quinn, Jason Priestley, Joanna Pacula, Dana Wheeler-Nicholson, Harry Carey Jr., Billy Zane, Charlton Heston, Michael Rooker, Bill Paxton. **1993 DVD**

TOMCAT: DANGEROUS DESIRES ★★ Richard Grieco is purr-fectly cast as a handsome loner whose rare blood disease leads him to scientist Maryam D'Ado. After being injected with a new serum, he develops unusual catlike tendencies. The good news is that he's an animal in bed. The bad news is that he uses people who discover his secret as a scratching post. Made-for-cable erotic sci-fi thriller just manages to keep its paws out of the litter box. Rated R for nudity and violence. 96m. **DIR:** Paul Donovan. **CAST:** Richard Grieco, Maryam D'Abo, Natalie Radford. **1993**

•TOMCATS 🦃 Several pals pool their money in a trust fund that will go to whichever one resists marriage longest—as if any woman would stoop to marrying any of the morons in this drooling, stupid, Neanderthal noncomedy. Rated R for profanity and crude sexual humor. 95m. **DIR:** Gregory Poirier. **CAST:** Jerry O'Connell, Shannon Elizabeth, Jake Busey, David Ogden Stiers. **2001 DVD**

TOMMY ★★1/2 In bringing The Who's ground-breaking rock opera to the screen, director Ken Russell let his penchant for bad taste and garishness run wild. The result is an outrageous movie about a deaf, dumb, and blind boy who rises to prominence as a "Pinball Wizard" and then becomes the new Messiah. Rated PG. 111m. **DIR:** Ken Russell. **CAST:** Roger Daltrey, Ann-Margret, Jack Nicholson, Oliver Reed, Elton John, Tina Turner. **1975 DVD**

TOMMY BOY ★★★1/2 Basically a takeoff of *Planes, Trains and Automobiles*, this buddy and coming-of-age film features Chris Farley as the unlikely proprietor of an auto-parts factory. *Saturday Night Live* creator Lorne Michaels's production offers some incredibly funny scenes. Rated PG-13 for profanity, brief nudity, and comic-book violence. 98m. **DIR:** Peter Segal. **CAST:** Chris Farley, David Spade, Bo Derek, Brian Dennehy, Julie Warner, Rob Lowe, Dan Aykroyd. **1995 DVD**

TOMMYKNOCKERS, THE ★★1/2 This network-television miniseries about a town taken over by long-dormant aliens suffers from the same flaws that plagued Stephen King's novel: second-rate characters and a slow, rambling narrative. King fans are destined to howl over the altered conclusion. Rated R for violence, profanity, and sensuality. 120m. **DIR:** John Power. **CAST:** Jimmy Smits, Marg Helgenberger, John Ashton, Allyce Beasley, Robert Carradine, Joanna Cassidy, Traci Lords, E. G. Marshall. **1993 DVD**

TOMORROW ★★★★★ Robert Duvall gives yet another sensitive, powerful, and completely convincing performance in this superb black-and-white character study about a caretaker who finds himself caring for—in both senses—a pregnant woman (Olga Bellin) who turns up one day at the lumber mill where he works. Rated PG for violence. B&W; 103m. **DIR:** Joseph Anthony. **CAST:** Robert Duvall, Olga Bellin, Sudie Bond. **1972**

TOMORROW AT SEVEN ★★ Obscure murder drama pits crime novelist Chester Morris and bumbling policemen Allen Jenkins and Frank McHugh against the mysterious Ace, who sends his victims a calling card and tells them where to go to die, which they inevitably do. This routine whodunit has little to offer. B&W; 62m. **DIR:** Ray Enright. **CAST:** Chester Morris, Vivienne Os-

borne, Allen Jenkins, Frank McHugh, Henry Stephenson, Grant Mitchell, Charles Middleton. **1933**

TOMORROW IS FOREVER ★★★★ Orson Welles is tempermentally suited for the role of the man who has disappeared for twenty years. When he returns, he finds out his wife (Claudette Colbert) has remarried and has children by her second husband (George Brent). Weepy (but wonderful) melodrama. B&W; 105m. **DIR:** Irving Pichel. **CAST:** Claudette Colbert, Orson Welles, George Brent, Natalie Wood, Lucile Watson, Richard Long. **1946**

TOMORROW NEVER COMES 🦃 Absolutely brainless movie about a weirdo who goes on a rampage. Not rated; the film has violence. 109m. **DIR:** Peter Collinson. **CAST:** Oliver Reed, Susan George, Stephen McHattie, Raymond Burr, John Ireland, Donald Pleasence, Paul Koslo. **1977**

TOMORROW NEVER DIES ★★★★ Pierce Brosnan demonstrates more of the right stuff in his second outing as not-so-secret agent James Bond, this time opposed by a media mogul hoping to goose his satellite network's ratings by starting a world war. Better still, though, is Asian action costar Michelle Yeoh as Bond's true equal: a tough-talking, tougher-fighting agent from the People's Republic of China who matches him stunt for stunt. Further good news is the properly 007-flavored soundtrack. Rated PG-13 for violence and sensuality. 119m. **DIR:** Roger Spottiswoode. **CAST:** Pierce Brosnan, Jonathan Pryce, Michelle Yeoh, Teri Hatcher, Judi Dench, Joe Don Baker, Gotz Otto, Ricky Jay. **1997 DVD**

TOMORROW'S CHILD ★★ Made during television's cause-of-the-week period, this saga deals with the topics of in vitro fertilization and surrogate motherhood. *Remington Steele* charmer Stephanie Zimbalist is acceptably overwrought, as is most of the cast of familiar TV faces. 100m. **DIR:** Joseph Sargent. **CAST:** Stephanie Zimbalist, Arthur Hill, William Atherton, Bruce Davison, James Shigeta, Susan Oliver, Ed Flanders, Salome Jens. **1982**

TONGS ★★★ Set in Manhattan's teeming Chinatown, this variation on *Scarface* stars current Hong Kong superstar Simon Yam as an immigrant who schemes and kills his way to the top of a drug empire. Not rated; contains strong violence. 89m. **DIR:** Philip Chan. **CAST:** Simon Yam, Tony Leung Chiu Wai. **1988**

TONI ★★★★ In story, style, and mood, *Toni* anticipates the methods of the future master postwar directors. A love quadrangle, a murder, a trial, an execution, a confession—these are the everyday elements director Jean Renoir chose to show as objectively as possible. Renoir was proud of his film, and it holds up well. In French with English subtitles. B&W; 90m. **DIR:** Jean Renoir. **CAST:** Charles Blavette, Max Dalban. **1934**

TONIGHT AND EVERY NIGHT ★★★ Another Forties song-and-dance extravaganza—this time in war-torn London. In spite of bomb raids and uncertainty in their private lives, a determined troupe keeps their show alive. Seems a bit dated now, but Rita Hayworth is worth watching. 92m. **DIR:** Victor Saville. **CAST:** Rita Hayworth, Lee Bowman, Janet Blair, Leslie Brooks, Marc Platt. **1945**

TONIO KROGER ★★ This adaptation of Thomas Mann's semiautobiographical novel, about a young writer wandering Europe while trying to choose between bourgeois comfort and the excitement of the unchained life, never comes alive on screen. In German with English subtitles. 92m. **DIR:** Rolf Thiele. **CAST:** Jean-Claude Brialy, Nadja Tiller, Werner Heinz, Gert Fröbe. **1965**

TONKA ★★★ Sal Mineo is White Bull, a Sioux Indian who captures and tames a wild stallion and names it Tonka Wakan—The Great One. Tribal law requires him to give the horse to his older Indian cousin, a bully who would mistreat the animal. Rather than do so, Mineo frees the horse. Thus begins an enjoyable adventure story for the family. 97m. **DIR:** Lewis R. Foster. **CAST:** Sal Mineo, Philip Carey, Jerome Courtland. **1958**

TONS OF TROUBLE ★★ Four children find a wounded elephant and try to hide it from an obsessed hunter. Substandard family fair. Rated PG. 92m. **DIR:** Marina Martins. **CAST:** Karen Black, Lee Purcell, John Laughlin. **1998**

TONY ROME ★★★ Pretty good private eye film has detective Frank Sinatra looking for clues into the disappearance of a wealthy man's daughter. Good atmosphere and a fine cast lend support as well. 110m. **DIR:** Gordon Douglas. **CAST:** Frank Sinatra, Jill St. John, Sue Lyons, Richard Conte, Simon Oakland, Gena Rowlands. **1967**

TOO BEAUTIFUL FOR YOU ★★★★1/2 Bertrand Blier's subtle, surprising French comedy about an offbeat romantic triangle. Gérard Depardieu stars as a married automobile dealer who falls for the rather dowdy secretary who works in his office. In French with English subtitles. Rated R for profanity. 91m. **DIR:** Bertrand Blier. **CAST:** Gérard Depardieu, Carole Bouquet, Josiane Balasko. **1990**

TOO FAST TOO YOUNG ★★ A teen is forced by the cousin who raised him to help out with an armored-car robbery. Nothing here you haven't seen before, and probably done much better. Rated R for violence, strong profanity, nudity, and sexual situations. 92m. **DIR:** Tim Everitt. **CAST:** Michael Ironside, Kasia Figura, James Wellington, Patrick Tiller, Marshall Bell, Richard Riehle. **1996**

TOO HOT TO HANDLE ★★★ Daredevil newsreel photographer Clark Gable and spunky pilot Myrna Loy team up in this fast-paced comedy-adventure that bounces from China to Borneo. Gable and Loy, the "king and queen" of Hollywood that year, make this screwy adventure click. B&W; 105m. **DIR:** Jack Conway. **CAST:** Clark Gable, Myrna Loy, Walter Pidgeon, Leo Carrillo, Virginia Weidler, Marjorie Main. **1938**

TOO LATE THE HERO ★★★1/2 Great World War II action-drama about two reluctant soldiers who are sent on a suicide mission to an island in the Pacific. Shown on network TV as *Suicide Run*. Rated PG. 133m. **DIR:** Robert Aldrich. **CAST:** Michael Caine, Cliff Robertson, Henry Fonda. **1970 DVD**

TOO MANY GIRLS ★★★1/2 Four young men are hired by prestigious Pottawatomie College in Stopgap, New Mexico, to keep an eye on carefree student Lucille Ball. This marked the debut of Eddie Bracken, Desi Arnaz, *and*, in the chorus, Van Johnson. A trivia lover's delight, this is pure fun to watch. B&W; 85m. **DIR:** George Abbott. **CAST:** Lucille Ball, Richard Carlson, Eddie Bracken, Ann Miller, Desi Arnaz Sr. **1940**

TOO MUCH SUN 🦃 Utterly tasteless comedy about the gay son and lesbian daughter of a multimillionaire

(Howard Duff) whose will decrees that one or the other of his offspring must produce a son. Rated R for profanity and simulated sex. 97m. **DIR:** Robert Downey. **CAST:** Robert Downey Jr., Laura Ernst, Jim Haynie, Eric Idle, Ralph Macchio, Andrea Martin, Leo Rossi, Howard Duff. **1991**

TOO OUTRAGEOUS ★★ In this disappointing sequel to 1977's surprise hit *Outrageous*, Craig Russell reprises his role as the gay hairdresser, now having realized his dreams of becoming a successful female impersonator. Hollis McLaren is his schizophrenic friend. Rated R for language and sexual content. 100m. **DIR:** Richard Benner. **CAST:** Craig Russell, Hollis McLaren, David McIlwraith. **1987**

TOO SHY TO TRY ★★★ Director Pierre Richard stars in this romantic comedy about a man who takes a crash course in romance after meeting the girl of his dreams. Some genuinely funny moments. In French with English subtitles. Not rated; contains nudity. 89m. **DIR:** Pierre Richard. **CAST:** Pierre Richard, Aldo Maccioni, Jacques François. **1982**

•TOO SMOOTH ★★ A romantic comedy that is so formulaic and lifeless it arrives DOA. Boy meets girl, boy falls in love with girl, boy loses girl because he's male, boy spends the rest of the film trying to win the girl back. Not only been there, done that, but done that so long ago. Also known as *Hairshirt*. Rated R for adult situations and language. 91m. **DIR:** Dean Paras. **CAST:** Dean Paras, Chris Hogan, Neve Campbell, Rebecca Gayheart, Evan Glenn. **1998 DVD**

TOO YOUNG TO DIE ★★ Brad Pitt and Juliette Lewis dismally reprise their roles from the film *Kalifornia*. Rated R for violence, nudity, and profanity. 92m. **DIR:** Robert Markowitz. **CAST:** Brad Pitt, Juliette Lewis, Michael Tucker, Michael O'Keefe. **1994**

TOOTSIE ★★★★★ Dustin Hoffman is Michael Dorsey, an out-of-work actor who disguises himself as a woman—Dorothy Michaels—to get a job and becomes a big star on a popular television soap opera. An absolute delight, *Tootsie* is hilarious, touching, and marvelously acted. Rated PG for adult content. 119m. **DIR:** Sydney Pollack. **CAST:** Dustin Hoffman, Bill Murray, Jessica Lange, Teri Garr, Dabney Coleman, Sydney Pollack, George Gaynes, Charles Durning. **1982 DVD**

TOP DOG ★★ Chuck Norris teams up with a canine partner to bring down a white supremacist group. A derivative buddy film that's long on violence and short on charm. Rated PG-13 for violence. 93m. **DIR:** Aaron Norris. **CAST:** Chuck Norris, Timothy Bottoms, Michele Lamar Richards. **1994 DVD**

TOP GUN ★★★1/2 Tom Cruise stars as a student at the navy's Fighter Weapons School, where fliers are turned into crack fighter pilots. While competing for the title of Top Gun there, he falls in love with an instructor (Kelly McGillis of *Witness*). Rated PG for light profanity, suggested sex, and violence. 110m. **DIR:** Tony Scott. **CAST:** Tom Cruise, Kelly McGillis, Val Kilmer, Anthony Edwards, Tom Skerritt, Michael Ironside, John Stockwell, Rick Rossovich, Barry Tubb, Whip Hubley. **1986 DVD**

TOP HAT ★★★★★ The most delightful and enduring of the Fred Astaire–Ginger Rogers musicals of the 1930s. This movie has an agreeable wisp of a plot and amusing, if dated, comedy dialogue. B&W; 99m. **DIR:** Mark Sandrich. **CAST:** Fred Astaire, Ginger Rogers, Edward Everett Horton, Eric Blore, Helen Broderick. **1935**

TOP SECRET ★★1/2 By the makers of *Airplane!*, this film makes up for its flimsy plot with one gag after another. Nick Rivers (Val Kilmer), a rock 'n' roll star, visits East Germany. There he falls in love with Hilary and becomes involved in the plot to free her scientist father. Lots of lively old Beach Boys and Elvis Presley tunes. Rated PG for some profanity and sexually oriented gags. 90m. **DIR:** Jim Abrahams, David Zucker, Jerry Zucker. **CAST:** Val Kilmer, Omar Sharif, Peter Cushing, Lucy Gutteridge. **1984**

TOPAZ ★★★ Medium-to-rare Hitchcock suspense-thriller about cloak-and-dagger intrigue concerning Russian involvement in Cuba and infiltration of the French government. Constant shift of scene keeps viewers on their toes. Rated PG. 127m. **DIR:** Alfred Hitchcock. **CAST:** John Forsythe, Frederick Stafford, Dany Robin, John Vernon. **1969**

TOPAZE (1933) ★★★1/2 John Barrymore gives one of his finest comic performances in this engaging film about a college professor who is innocently inveigled into a swindle and ends up turning the tables on the crooks. Witty and often moving. B&W; 80m. **DIR:** Harry D'Arrast. **CAST:** John Barrymore, Myrna Loy. **1933**

TOPAZE (1951) ★★★★ Another version of Marcel Pagnol's perennially popular satirical play (it was also adapted as a vehicle for John Barrymore and Peter Sellers) about a lowly schoolteacher who is dismissed from his job but finds success in the business world. The best and most faithful adaptation of the play makes a fine showcase for French-comedian Fernandel. In French with English subtitles. Not rated. B&W; 135m. **DIR:** Marcel Pagnol. **CAST:** Fernandel, Marcel Vallee, Jacqueline Pagnol. **1951**

TOPKAPI ★★★★★ This is one of the finest and funniest of the "big heist" genre. Director Jules Dassin assembled a highly talented international cast. They are members of a charming group of jewel thieves whose target is a priceless jeweled dagger in a Turkish museum. The execution of their clever plan is both humorous and exciting. 120m. **DIR:** Jules Dassin. **CAST:** Peter Ustinov, Melina Mercouri, Maximilian Schell. **1964 DVD**

TOPPER ★★★★ This is the original feature of what became a delightful fantasy movie series and television series. Cary Grant and Constance Bennett are the Kirbys, a duo of social high livers who, due to an unfortunate auto accident, become ghosts. They now want to transfer their spirit of living the good life to a rather stodgy banker, the fellow they are now haunting, one Cosmo Topper (Roland Young). Good fun all around. B&W; 97m. **DIR:** Norman Z. McLeod. **CAST:** Cary Grant, Constance Bennett, Roland Young, Billie Burke. **1937**

TOPPER RETURNS ★★★ Cary Grant and Constance Bennett have gone on to their heavenly rewards, but Roland Young, as Cosmo Topper, is still seeing ghosts. This time the spooky personage is that of Joan Blondell, who helps our hero solve a murder in this entertaining comedy. B&W; 87m. **DIR:** Roy Del Ruth. **CAST:** Roland Young, Joan Blondell, Eddie "Rochester" Anderson, Carole Landis, Dennis O'Keefe, H. B. Warner. **1941**

TOPPER TAKES A TRIP ★★★ Second film in the original series finds Cosmo and Henrietta Topper on the French Riviera accompanied by their ghostly friend Marion Kirby, portrayed by the star of the original film, Constance Bennett. Topper and Marion pool forces to stop Mrs. Topper from being victimized by a smooth-talking confidence man. Cary Grant makes a brief appearance in a flashback sequence. Harmless fun. B&W; 85m. **DIR:** Norman Z. McLeod. **CAST:** Constance Bennett, Roland Young, Billie Burke, Alan Mowbray, Franklin Pangborn. **1939**

TOPSY TURVY (1984) ★★ A conservative young man finds his world turned topsy-turvy when a swinging neighbor girl takes him on vacation. This European sex comedy, dubbed into English is mediocre. 90m. **DIR:** Edward Fleming. **CAST:** Lisbet Dahl, Ebbe Rode. **1984**

TOPSY-TURVY (1999) ★★★★1/2 Writer-director Mike Leigh's film deals with the touchy partnership of Gilbert and Sullivan and the creation of their most popular work, *The Mikado*. It's a loving, minutely detailed examination of the creative process and one of the best movies ever made about the theater. It's also an incisive portrait of life in London at the zenith of the British Empire, with every detail so convincing that it feels like a trip in a time machine. The icing on the cake is the marvelous rendition of several of Gilbert and Sullivan's songs. Rated R for brief nudity. 161m. **DIR:** Mike Leigh. **CAST:** Jim Broadbent, Allan Corduner, Timothy Spall, Lesley Manville, Ron Cook, Wendy Nottingham. **1999 DVD**

TORA! TORA! TORA! ★★★★ An American-Japanese cooperative venture reenacts the events up to and including the December 7 attack on Pearl Harbor. Although many well-known actors contribute their skills, they are overshadowed by the technical brilliance of the realistic re-creation of the climactic attack. Rated G. 143m. **DIR:** Richard Fleischer, Toshio Masuda, Kinji Fakasaku. **CAST:** Jason Robards Jr., Martin Balsam, James Whitmore, Joseph Cotten. **1970 DVD**

TORCH SONG ★★ A muddled melodrama made to show off Joan Crawford's form and figure when she was approaching fifty. She plays a tough chorus-girl-turned-Broadway-dancer. 90m. **DIR:** Charles Walters. **CAST:** Joan Crawford, Michael Wilding, Gig Young, Marjorie Rambeau, Harry Morgan. **1953**

TORCH SONG TRILOGY ★★★ Harvey Fierstein's prize-winning play of the same title couldn't be better suited to film, but this comedy-drama is not for everyone. Fierstein plays Arnold Beckoff, an insecure female impersonator looking for that one, all-encompassing relationship. Anne Bancroft is his unbending Jewish mama. The musical numbers in the gay nightclub are classy and clever. Rated R. 120m. **DIR:** Paul Bogart. **CAST:** Harvey Fierstein, Anne Bancroft, Matthew Broderick, Brian Kerwin. **1988**

TORMENT ★★ Low-budget slasher film starts off slow and, if it weren't for one interesting plot twist halfway through, would be an exercise in boredom. The story revolves around a man who becomes a psychotic killer when he is rejected by a younger woman. R for violence and gore. 90m. **DIR:** Samson Aslanian, John Hopkins. **CAST:** Taylor Gilbert. **1986**

TORN APART ★★1/2 An Israeli soldier and an Arab girl incur the wrath of their friends and families when they fall in love. Based on Chayym Zeldis's novel *A Forbidden Love*. A tolerable time-waster. Rated R for violence. 120m. **DIR:** Jack Fisher. **CAST:** Adrian Pasdar, Cecilia Peck. **1987**

TORN BETWEEN TWO LOVERS ★★★1/2 This made-for-TV romantic triangle features a married Lee Remick who finds herself having an affair with a divorced architect. She must finally tell her husband the truth and choose between the two. Nothing boring about this soap! 100m. **DIR:** Delbert Mann. **CAST:** Lee Remick, Joseph Bologna, George Peppard, Giorgio Tozzi. **1979**

TORN CURTAIN ★★★ Just-okay film was directed by Alfred Hitchcock in 1966. Paul Newman plays an American scientist posing as a defector, with Julie Andrews as his secretary-lover. Somehow we aren't moved by the action or the characters. 128m. **DIR:** Alfred Hitchcock. **CAST:** Paul Newman, Julie Andrews, Lila Kedrova, David Opatoshu. **1966**

TORNADO! 🦃 The very reason some directors keep their projects under wraps. This rip-off of *Twister* features the same plot and identical characters, but is poorly executed and the special effects are a real joke. Television may have beaten *Twister* to the punch, but it's a sucker punch at best. Rated PG. 89m. **DIR:** Noel Nosseck. **CAST:** Bruce Campbell, Shannon Sturges, Ernie Hudson, L. Q. Jones. **1996 DVD**

TORPEDO ALLEY ★★ World War II pilot Bob Bingham (Mark Stevens) is haunted by guilt after the deaths of his flight crew. He gets a second chance to prove himself when he applies for submarine duty during the Korean War. B&W; 84m. **DIR:** Lew Landers. **CAST:** Mark Stevens, Dorothy Malone, Charles Winninger, Bill Williams. **1953**

TORPEDO RUN ★★★1/2 A driving pace marks this tautly exciting World War II mouse-chases-cat story about a navy submarine tracking, catching, and destroying a Japanese aircraft carrier in Kiska Harbor. 98m. **DIR:** Joseph Pevney. **CAST:** Glenn Ford, Ernest Borgnine, Dean Jones, Diane Brewster. **1958**

TORRENTS OF SPRING 🦃 Beautifully photographed but uninvolving costume drama set in Europe during the 1840s. Rated R. 97m. **DIR:** Jerzy Skolimowski. **CAST:** Timothy Hutton, Nastassja Kinski, Valeria Golino, William Forsythe, Urbano Barberini. **1990**

TORSO ★★1/2 Who's bumping off (and hacking apart) the pretty coeds at an Italian university? It takes forever to find out in this mechanical stalk-and-slash melodrama. However, the film springs to life for a climactic battle to the death between hero and masked villain. Rated R. 86m. **DIR:** Sergio Martino. **CAST:** Suzy Kendall, John Richardson, Tina Aumont, Luc Merenda. **1973 DVD**

TORTILLA FLAT ★★★1/2 A watered-down (understandable for the times) adaptation of John Steinbeck's lusty novel of a group of *paisanos* on the California coast, led by Spencer Tracy, whose main purpose in life is to avoid any form of work or responsibility. One, John Garfield, inherits two run-down houses and his outlook changes, much to the concern of his friends. B&W; 105m. **DIR:** Victor Fleming. **CAST:** Spencer Tracy, Hedy Lamarr, John Garfield, Frank Morgan, Akim Tamiroff, Sheldon Leonard. **1942**

•TORTILLA SOUP ★★★★1/2 A semiretired master chef and his three daughters face a number of domestic

and romantic complications. Ang Lee's Taiwanese charmer *Eat Drink Man Woman* is transplanted from Taipei to Latino Los Angeles, becoming even more delightful in the process. Performances are fine (especially Hector Elizondo as the father and Elizabeth Peña as his oldest daughter) and the food is mouthwatering. Rated PG-13 for some sexual content. 102m. **DIR:** Maria Ripoll. **CAST:** Hector Elizondo, Elizabeth Peña, Jacqueline Obradors, Tamara Mello, Paul Rodriguez, Raquel Welch. **2001 DVD**

TORTURE CHAMBER OF BARON BLOOD, THE ★★ Boring Italian production is basically nonsense as a long-dead nobleman (Joseph Cotten) is inadvertently restored to life, only to (naturally) embark on a horrendous killing spree. Worth watching for Mario Bava's unique directorial style. Originally titled *Baron Blood*. Rated R. 90m. **DIR:** Mario Bava. **CAST:** Joseph Cotten, Elke Sommer, Massimo Girotti. **1972 DVD**

TORTURE CHAMBER OF DR. SADISM, THE ★★ Based on Poe's "The Pit and the Pendulum," this German production has Christopher Lee as a count who lures Lex Barker and Karin Dor to his foreboding castle. Although containing some good shock scenes, *Torture Chamber* doesn't live up to its source material or title. Not rated; contains violence and torture. 90m. **DIR:** Harald Reinl. **CAST:** Christopher Lee, Lex Barker, Karin Dor. **1967**

TORTURE GARDEN ★★★1/2 A group of patrons at a carnival sideshow has their possible futures exposed to them by a screwball barker (Burgess Meredith) who exclaims, "I've promised you horror . . . and I intend to keep that promise." He does more than this in this frightening film laced with plenty of shock, plot twists, and intense situations. Rated PG. 93m. **DIR:** Freddie Francis. **CAST:** Burgess Meredith, Jack Palance, Beverly Adams, Peter Cushing, Maurice Denham, Robert Hutton. **1968**

TOTAL ECLIPSE ★★★ Writer Christopher Hampton (adapting one of his early plays) dramatizes the sadomasochistic, destructive relationship between nineteenth-century French poets Arthur Rimbaud and Paul Verlaine. Acting is excellent; unfortunately, the central characters are such cruel, selfish boors that many viewers will be turned off. Rated R for profanity, nudity, and simulated sex. 110m. **DIR:** Agnieszka Holland. **CAST:** Leonardo DiCaprio, David Thewlis, Romane Bohringer, Dominique Blanc. **1995 DVD**

TOTAL EXPOSURE ★★★ When fashion photographer Season Hubley is framed for murdering a model, she turns to private eye Michael Nouri to clear her name. Nouri begins to suspect that his client might actually be guilty. Watch this one to see what develops. Rated R for nudity, strong language, and violence. 96m. **DIR:** John Quinn. **CAST:** Michael Nouri, Season Hubley, Christian Bocher, Jeff Conaway, Robert Prentiss. **1990**

TOTAL RECALL ★★★★1/2 Arnold Schwarzenegger flexes plenty of action-movie muscle in this terrific sci-fi adventure. The film has impressive bloodlines: it's adapted from a short story by Philip K. Dick (who also inspired *Blade Runner*), with a screenplay from the *Alien* creators, and direction by the creator of *RoboCop*. A thrill-a-minute futuristic tale. Rated R, with strong violence and profanity. 109m. **DIR:** Paul Verhoeven. **CAST:** Arnold Schwarzenegger, Rachel Ticotin, Sharon Stone, Ronny Cox, Michael Ironside. **1990 DVD**

TOTEM ★★1/2 Six teenagers find themselves drawn to a cabin in the woods with no recollection as to why. One by one they begin to fall prey to the evil forces in the woods. Average film is bolstered by fine production values and the cast is attractive, but one can't help feeling as if he's seen this all before. Rated R for violence and profanity. 80m. **DIR:** Martin Tate. **CAST:** Marissa Tait, Jason Faunt. **1999**

TOTO THE HERO ★★★★ In Belgian director Jaco Van Dormael's inventive black comedy, a cranky old man's reveries are made to seem the universal story of modern man. Toto's reminiscences are colored by his perspective, which, as the story unfolds, is proven to be somewhat askew. Rated PG-13 for nudity and violence. 90m. **DIR:** Jaco Van Dormael. **CAST:** Michel Bouquet, Mireille Perrier. **1991**

TOUCH ★★★1/2 Skeet Ulrich works miracles in this dark comedy about the exploitation of religion. He plays Juvenal, a miracle healer who catches the attention of a former evangelist who sees Juvenal as his ticket to the big time. His plan backfires when the woman he sends to lure Juvenal into his fold falls in love with him. Sharp, witty dialogue. Rated R for adult situations, language, and nudity. 96m. **DIR:** Paul Schrader. **CAST:** Skeet Ulrich, Bridget Fonda, Christopher Walken, Tom Arnold. **1997**

TOUCH AND DIE 🦃 Martin Sheen stars as an American journalist in Rome assigned to cover the murders of three people. His investigation reveals a conspiracy. Warning: title tells it all. Rated R for violence, profanity, and nudity. 108m. **DIR:** Piernico Solinas. **CAST:** Martin Sheen, René Estevez, David Birney, Franco Nero. **1991**

TOUCH AND GO ★★1/2 A comedy that sat on the shelf for two years. Chicago hockey player falls in love with the mother of a young delinquent who mugged him. Michael Keaton is appealing, Maria Conchita Alonso is fiery, and the script contains sharp dialogue, a few good laughs, and a number of sweet moments. Rated R for profanity and violence. 101m. **DIR:** Robert Mandel. **CAST:** Michael Keaton, Maria Conchita Alonso, Ajay Naidu. **1984**

TOUCH OF CLASS, A ★★★★★ In one of the best romantic comedies of recent years, George Segal and Glenda Jackson are marvelously paired as a sometimes loving—sometimes bickering—couple who struggle through an extramarital affair. They begin their oddball romance when he runs over one of her children while chasing a fly ball in a baseball game. Fine acting and witty dialogue. Rated PG. 105m. **DIR:** Melvin Frank. **CAST:** George Segal, Glenda Jackson, Paul Sorvino, Hildegard Neil. **1972 DVD**

TOUCH OF EVIL ★★★★1/2 In 1958, director-actor Orson Welles proved that he was still a filmmaking genius, with this dark and disturbing masterpiece about crime and corruption in a border town. B&W; 108m. **DIR:** Orson Welles. **CAST:** Orson Welles, Charlton Heston, Marlene Dietrich, Janet Leigh, Zsa Zsa Gabor. **1958**

TOUCH OF FROST, A (TV SERIES) ★★★★ A gripping series based upon British author Rodney Wingfield's Detective Frost novels. The disorganized and disheveled (yet amazingly perceptive) Detective Inspector solves relentlessly complicated crimes, uncon-

cerned with bad publicity or suspects with bruised feelings. The witty scripts, and occasional spark of humor make this a superior series. Not rated; contains violent themes. 95m. **DIR:** Don Leaver, Ross Devenish. **CAST:** David Jason, Bruce Alexander, Sally Dexter. **1995**

TOUCHED ★★★ This sensitive drama involves the struggle of two young psychiatric patients who try to make it outside the hospital walls. Robert Hays and Kathleen Beller are terrific as the frightened couple who must deal with numerous unforeseen obstacles. Rated R for mature topic. 89m. **DIR:** John Flynn. **CAST:** Robert Hays, Kathleen Beller, Gilbert Lewis, Ned Beatty. **1982**

TOUCHED BY LOVE ★★★ Strong performances make this affecting sentimental drama about a teenage cerebral palsy victim given hope through correspondence with singer Elvis Presley. Deborah Raffin is excellent as the nurse who nurtures patient Diane Lane from cripple to functioning teenager. Originally titled *From Elvis with Love*. Rated PG. 95m. **DIR:** Gus Trikonis. **CAST:** Deborah Raffin, Diane Lane, Michael Learned, Cristina Raines, Mary Wickes, Clu Gulager, John Amos. **1980**

TOUGH AND DEADLY ★★★ Action heroes Roddy Piper and Billy Blanks team up again, the former as a seedy private investigator and the latter as a rogue CIA agent with amnesia. Naturally, both must punch and kick all sorts of nefarious folks, although the predictable action is kept palatable thanks to tongue-in-cheek performances and lighthearted direction. Rated R for violence and profanity. 92m. **DIR:** Steve Cohen. **CAST:** Billy Blanks, Roddy Piper, Richard Norton, James Karen. **1994**

TOUGH ENOUGH ★★1/2 Dennis Quaid plays the "Country-and-Western Warrior," a singer-fighter who slugs his way through taxing "Toughman" contests from Fort Worth to Detroit in a quest for fame and fortune. It's *Rocky* meets *Honeysuckle Rose*, yet still mildly enjoyable. Rated PG for profanity and violence. 106m. **DIR:** Richard Fleischer. **CAST:** Dennis Quaid, Warren Oates, Stan Shaw, Pam Grier, Wilford Brimley. **1983**

TOUGH GUYS ★★★ This enjoyable movie features Burt Lancaster and Kirk Douglas as two flamboyant train robbers who are released from prison after thirty years to find they have no place in society. They decide to strike back by doing what they do best. It's featherweight, but the stars make it fun. Rated PG for light profanity, suggested sex, and mild violence. 103m. **DIR:** Jeff Kanew. **CAST:** Burt Lancaster, Kirk Douglas, Charles Durning, Alexis Smith, Dana Carvey, Darlanne Fluegel, Eli Wallach. **1986**

TOUGH GUYS DON'T DANCE ★★ Interesting but uneven attempt at *film noir*. Strenuous dialogue and bizarre acting make this excursion into experimental filmmaking confusing. Ryan O'Neal is an ex-con who wants to be a writer. Newcomer Debra Sundland is stunning as an obnoxious southern belle. Rated R for nudity, language, and violence. 110m. **DIR:** Norman Mailer. **CAST:** Ryan O'Neal, Isabella Rossellini, Wings Hauser, Debra Sundland, Frances Fisher. **1987**

TOUR OF DUTY ★★★ Pilot for the TV series of the same name, *Tour of Duty* is like a 90-minute course in Vietnam War history with prime-time cleanliness. And while the cleanliness hinders the film's credibility, the action scenes make it worth watching. Not rated, has violence. 93m. **DIR:** B.W.L. Norton. **CAST:** Terence Knox, Stephen Caffrey, Joshua Maurer, Kevin Conroy. **1987**

TOURNAMENT TEMPO ★★ Professional hockey player catches the eye of a beautiful talent scout who signs him up to make films. When his team's chances at the championship are jeopardized the star has to choose which career to concentrate on. B&W; 67m. **DIR:** George Blair. **CAST:** Allan "Rocky" Lane, Jean Rogers, Edward Ashley, Frank Albertson, Robert Armstrong, Paul Harvey. **1946**

TOUS LES MATINS DU MONDE ★★★ Music for its own sake is the prevailing metaphor in this sumptuously photographed biography of little-known seventeenth-century viol player and composer Monsieur de Sainte Colombe. Music lovers will be awed by the richly textured soundtrack, but mainstream viewers are apt to nod off. Not rated, with brief nudity and simulated sex. 114m. **DIR:** Alain Corneau. **CAST:** Jean-Pierre Marielle, Gérard Depardieu, Anne Brochet, Guillaume Depardieu, Caroline Sihol, Carole Richert. **1993**

TOUTE UNE NUIT ★★ Overly fragmented movie about the various stages and states of relationships. The end product is ultimately creatively arid. Not one of Akerman's finer efforts. In French with English subtitles. Rated R for nudity. 90m. **DIR:** Chantal Akerman. **CAST:** Aurore Clement, Tcheky Karyo. **1983**

TOVARITCH ★★★1/2 A Russian duchess and her consort flee the revolution to Paris while entrusted with the tzar's fortune of forty billion francs. Too honest to spend any of it, they hire themselves out as domestics. Good farce. B&W; 98m. **DIR:** Anatole Litvak. **CAST:** Claudette Colbert, Charles Boyer, Basil Rathbone, Anita Louise, Melville Cooper, Isabel Jeans, Montagu Love, Curt Bois. **1937**

TOWARD THE TERRA ★★ In the far future a group of telepaths are driven from society and forced to fight the computer-controlled human majority for their inheritance. Although entertaining to a point, this animated feature loses what impact the story should have by simply taking too long. In Japanese with English subtitles. Not rated; contains violence and brief nudity. 112m. **DIR:** Hideo Onchi. **1980**

TOWER OF LONDON (1939) ★★★1/2 Basil Rathbone really sinks his teeth into the role of Richard III (and some of the scenery) in this historical drama about the evil prince's bloody rise to power. Despite a weak ending, this is an enjoyable movie of terror. In one of his all-too-rare leading roles, Rathbone is wonderful to watch, as are Boris Karloff (properly menacing as the executioner, Mord) and Vincent Price (as the conniving but ineffectual Duke of Clarence). B&W; 92m. **DIR:** Rowland V. Lee. **CAST:** Basil Rathbone, Boris Karloff, Vincent Price, Barbara O'Neil, Ian Hunter, Nan Grey, Leo G. Carroll, Miles Mander. **1939**

TOWER OF LONDON (1962) ★★★ A bloody update of the 1939 classic. Vincent Price plays Richard III, who systematically murders everyone who stands in his way to the throne of England. One can feel the chills crawling up the spine. Roger Corman's melodramatic style works well in this gothic setting. Not rated. B&W; 79m. **DIR:** Roger Corman. **CAST:** Vincent Price, Michael Pate, Joan Freeman. **1962**

TOWER OF SCREAMING VIRGINS, THE ★★ Lush, stately, sex-filled, and often sadistic medieval horror—

supposedly based on an Alexander Dumas novel—set in and around a Gothic castle and its chamber of tortures. Despite the ad copy and lurid box art, the virgins are a bunch of young *men*, who fall prey to a sinister group of femmes fatales. Rated R. 89m. **DIR:** François Legrand. **CAST:** Terry Torday, Jean Piat, Uschi Glas. **1971**

TOWERING INFERNO, THE ★★★★ This is the undisputed king of the disaster movies of the 1970s. An all-star cast came together for this big-budget thriller about a newly constructed San Francisco high-rise hotel and office building that is set ablaze due to substandard materials. Rated PG. 165m. **DIR:** John Guillermin, Irwin Allen. **CAST:** Steve McQueen, Paul Newman, William Holden, Faye Dunaway, Fred Astaire, Richard Chamberlain. **1974 DVD**

•TOWN & COUNTRY ★★ Goodness, what a train wreck. Long in the making and deservedly trashed when finally released, this attempt to drag a 1940s-style screwball comedy into the present day is sabotaged by a cast that's too bloody old to make the material palatable. Warren Beatty and Diane Keaton are successful New York architects, wealthier than God, who entertain a number of eccentric houseguests at any given moment. Beatty's an unapologetic womanizer whose philandering ways are about to catch up with him, but you're unlikely to care. This film also deserves an award for the most humiliating cameo appearances ever conceived, played by Charlton Heston and Marian Seldes. Rated R for profanity and sexual content. 104m. **DIR:** Peter Chelsom. **CAST:** Warren Beatty, Diane Keaton, Andie MacDowell, Garry Shandling, Jenna Elfman, Nastassja Kinski, Goldie Hawn, Charlton Heston, Marian Seldes. **2001 DVD**

TOWN CALLED HELL, A 🦃 Confusing action yarn about a manhunt for a Mexican revolutionary. Rated R. 95m. **DIR:** Robert Parrish. **CAST:** Robert Shaw, Telly Savalas, Stella Stevens. **1971**

TOWN LIKE ALICE, A ★★★★1/2 This outstanding PBS series is even more enjoyable to watch in one viewing than during a six-week period. It is the story of female British POWs in Malaysia and their incredible struggle. Helen Morse is wonderful as the one who takes charge to help maintain the sanity and welfare of the group. Bryan Brown is the soldier who risks his life to help the women and falls in love with Morse. 301m. **DIR:** David Stevens. **CAST:** Helen Morse, Bryan Brown, Gordon Jackson. **1980**

TOWN THAT DREADED SUNDOWN, THE ★★★1/2 The fact that this is based on actual events makes this effective little film all the more chilling. The story takes place in the year 1946 in the small border town of Texarkana. It begins in documentary style, with a narrator describing the post–World War II atmosphere, but soon gets to the unsettling business of the Phantom, a killer who terrorized the locals. Rated R for violence. 90m. **DIR:** Charles B. Pierce. **CAST:** Ben Johnson, Andrew Prine, Dawn Wells. **1977**

TOXIC AVENGER, THE ★★★ Just another "nerdy pool attendant tossed into a tub of toxic waste becomes mutant crime-fighter" picture. Actually, this low-budget horror spoof has a number of inspired moments. If you are looking for sick humor and creative bloodshed. Enjoy. Rated R for violence. 100m. **DIR:** Michael Herz, Samuel Weil. **CAST:** Mitchell Cohen. **1985 DVD**

TOXIC AVENGER PART II, THE ★★1/2 The makers of the original are back with another tongue-in-cheek bloodfest. Toxie goes to Japan in search of the man who might be his father. Not as bad as it sounds but just as weird. Rated R for violence and nudity. 96m. **DIR:** Michael Herz, Lloyd Kaufman. **CAST:** Ron Fazio, Lisa Gaye. **1989 DVD**

TOXIC AVENGER PART III, THE: THE LAST TEMPTATION OF TOXIE ★★★1/2 With nothing to do after ridding the town of Tromaville of all the bad guys, the Toxic Avenger unknowingly gets a job promoting a corporation bent on polluting the world. It's all in good fun. An unrated version runs a minute longer. Rated R for violence, profanity, and nudity. 102m. **DIR:** Michael Herz, Lloyd Kaufman. **CAST:** Ron Fazio, Lisa Gaye. **1989**

TOY, THE ★★ You would think any comedy that combines the talents of Richard Pryor and Jackie Gleason would have to be exceptionally good, to say nothing of funny. But that's simply not true of this movie, about a spoiled rich kid (Scott Schwartz) whose father (Gleason) allows him to buy the ultimate toy (Pryor). Rated PG for profanity and adult themes. 99m. **DIR:** Richard Donner. **CAST:** Richard Pryor, Jackie Gleason, Scott Schwartz, Ned Beatty. **1982 DVD**

TOY SOLDIERS (1983) 🦃 Inept film about a group of vacationing college students in Latin America. Rated R. 85m. **DIR:** David Fisher. **CAST:** Jason Miller, Cleavon Little, Rodolfo DeAnda. **1983**

TOY SOLDIERS (1991) ★★★1/2 In what might be called *The Godfather Meets Taps*, a group of rich-kid rejects take on a band of terrorists who are holding them hostage to force the release of a South American drug lord. The preposterous story line benefits from assured performances by Denholm Elliott and young leads Sean Astin, Keith Coogan, Wil Wheaton, and George Perez. Rated R for violence and profanity. 112m. **DIR:** Daniel Petrie Jr. **CAST:** Sean Astin, Wil Wheaton, Keith Coogan, Louis Gossett Jr., Denholm Elliott, R. Lee Ermey, Jerry Orbach, George Perez. **1991**

TOY STORY ★★★★★ Ground-breaking, state-of-the-art moviemaking meets a delightful, all-ages story in this instant classic from Disney. Whenever humans aren't around, the toys in Andy's room spring to life. A birthday present of spaceman Buzz Lightyear creates more than a few problems for cowboy Woody, who, up to that point, was king of the toy shelf. Excellent voice work by Tom Hanks and Tim Allen, Don Rickles, Jim Varney, Annie Potts, Wallace Shawn, John Ratzenberger, and R. Lee Ermey. Rated G. 80m. **DIR:** John Lasseter. **1995 DVD**

TOY STORY 2 ★★★★★ The folks at Pixar and Disney do the impossible—by coming up with a computer-animated sequel that's even better than the original. This time, cowboy Woody (voiced by Tom Hanks) is sold during a garage sale to a toy collector, thus sending Buzz Lightyear (Tim Allen) and the other toys on a quest to save their buddy. It's delightful, with so many memorable bits that there's not enough room to call attention to them here. Suffice to say, you won't want to miss the ending credits, where the filmmakers send up the outtake "blooper" clips made popular by director Hal Need-

ham in his *Smokey and the Bandit* days. Rated G. 92m. **DIR:** John Lasseter. **1999 DVD**

TOYS 🦃 Idiotic waste of Robin Williams's talents. He's a toy manufacturer's whimsical, spacey son. Dad Donald O'Connor's death results in a battle between Williams and militaristic uncle Michael Gambon, who is bent on making lethal war toys. A rare misfire from director Barry Levinson. Rated PG-13 for violence. 121m. **DIR:** Barry Levinson. **CAST:** Robin Williams, Michael Gambon, Joan Cusack, Robin Wright, Donald O'Connor, Arthur Malet, Jack Warden. **1992 DVD**

TOYS IN THE ATTIC ★★ A man brings his baby doll bride home to confront his two overly protective spinster sisters in this watered-down screen version of the Lillian Hellman stage play. As the sisters, Geraldine Page and Wendy Hiller are superb, as always. B&W; 90m. **DIR:** George Roy Hill. **CAST:** Dean Martin, Geraldine Page, Wendy Hiller, Yvette Mimieux, Gene Tierney, Nan Martin, Larry Gates. **1963**

TRACES OF RED ★★ Half-baked erotic thriller—narrated by the fresh corpse of a homicide detective—features a Palm Beach serial killer who slashes women with a letter opener, smears their faces with Yves Saint Laurent lipstick, steals their clothes, and mails out lousy poetry that warns of further mayhem. Rated R for language, nudity, simulated sex, and violence. 104m. **DIR:** Andy Wolk. **CAST:** James Belushi, Lorraine Bracco, Tony Goldwyn, William Russ. **1993**

TRACK OF THE MOON BEAST 🦃 A mineralogist comes into contact with a fragment of a meteor. 90m. **DIR:** Richard Ashe. **CAST:** Chase Cordell. **1976**

•TRACK 16 ★★ An interesting idea, but this valiant attempt at independent filmmaking ultimately suffers due to budget constraints and a cast that seems more anxious than talented. After reviewing his late-night recording session, a musician hears what sounds like a muffled scream on one of the tracks. When he discovers a dead body outside the studio, he becomes the main suspect in the murder. Even as the plot gets weighed down by rudimentary dialogue and heavy-handed acting, director Mick McCleery shows potential behind the camera. Not rated; contains adult situations, language, and violence. 90m. **DIR:** Mick McCleery. **CAST:** Billy Franks, Bobby Ashton, C. Fox, Alan Pratt, Renee Nocito. **2001**

TRACK 29 ★★ British director Nicolas Roeg continues his downhill creative slide with this psycho-silly story of a bored, alcoholic housewife (Theresa Russell) who takes up with a strange hitchhiker (Gary Oldman) who may or may not be her son. Rated R for violence and gore. 90m. **DIR:** Nicolas Roeg. **CAST:** Theresa Russell, Gary Oldman, Christopher Lloyd, Colleen Camp, Sandra Bernhard, Seymour Cassel. **1988**

TRACKED ★★ Made-for-cable action-drama about a prisoner who is punished by becoming a "dog boy," human bait for the prison's attack dogs. While Bryan Brown is efficient as a scrupulous guard, Tia Carrere is totally miscast as an assistant district attorney. Some exciting moments early on, but the film becomes one long chase at the end. A.k.a. *Dogboys.* Rated PG-13 for language and violence. 92m. **DIR:** Ken Russell. **CAST:** Dean Cain, Bryan Brown, Tia Carrere, Ken James, Sean McCann. **1998**

TRACKER, THE ★★★ In this generally effective made-for-HBO Western, Kris Kristofferson stars as famed tracker Noble Adams. He hunts down a bloodthirsty religious zealot–turned-outlaw (Scott Wilson) wanted for multiple murders and the kidnapping of a teenage girl. The film is sometimes slow and a bit too talky, but it's sporadically inventive. 90m. **DIR:** John Guillermin. **CAST:** Kris Kristofferson, Scott Wilson, Mark Moses, David Huddleston, Karen Kopins. **1988**

TRACKERS, THE ★★ Ernest Borgnine plays a vengeful rancher out to get the men who killed his son and kidnapped his daughter. He reluctantly enlists the aid of a black professional tracker (Sammy Davis Jr.). It's a mildly entertaining Western made for TV. 73m. **DIR:** Earl Bellamy. **CAST:** Sammy Davis Jr., Ernest Borgnine. **1971**

TRACKS 🦃 A Vietnam War veteran escorts his dead buddy on a train cross-country and goes crazy in the process. Rated R. 90m. **DIR:** Henry Jaglom. **CAST:** Dennis Hopper, Taryn Power, Dean Stockwell, Topo Swope, Michael Emil. **1977**

TRACKS OF A KILLER ★★ A high-powered executive invites his protégé to his wilderness retreat to see if the young man has the right stuff to take over the company. He finds out the hard way that his replacement has the killer instinct—in spades. So-so suspense thriller. Rated R for violence and profanity. 100m. **DIR:** Harvey Frost. **CAST:** Kelly LeBrock, Wolf Larson, James Brolin, Courtney Taylor, George Touliatos. **1995**

TRADE OFF ★★ Theresa Russell "accidentally" bumps into Adam Baldwin at a trade show and suggests they knock off each other's spouses. Baldwin's character is an idiotic bungler and the jazz score is annoying. Feels like a setup from the opening credits and then spins completely out of control. Rated R for profanity, violence, nudity, and sexual situations. 92m. **DIR:** Andrew Lane. **CAST:** Theresa Russell, Adam Baldwin, Barry Primus, Megan Gallagher. **1994**

TRADE SECRETS ★★ Picture-postcard locations set the tone for this sophisticated but uninvolving French whodunit, as ex-Interpol policeman Sam Waterston probes the suspicious demise of a Bordeaux-wine heiress. Rated R for nudity and adult situations. 91m. **DIR:** Claude Feraldo. **CAST:** Sam Waterston, Marisa Berenson, Bernard Pierre Donnadieu, Lauren Hutton, Arielle Dombasle. **1986**

TRADING FAVORS ★★ Tired tale of young college jock who gets involved with a wild woman. She ends up stealing his car and taking him on a crime-laden road trip. It was a match made in heaven, which gets real hot toward the end when the woman's volatile ex-boyfriend enters the picture. Rated R for adult situations, language, nudity, and violence. 103m. **DIR:** Sondra Locke. **CAST:** Rosanna Arquette, Devon Gummersal, Peter Greene, George Dzundza. **1997**

TRADING HEARTS ★★★ A period charmer written by Frank Deford casts Raul Julia as a washed-up baseball player who's lured into the sedate Florida family life of a single mother and her precocious child. Predictable and occasionally schmaltzy, but entertaining. Rated PG. 88m. **DIR:** Neil Leifer. **CAST:** Raul Julia, Beverly D'Angelo, Nina Axelrod, Jenny Lewis. **1987**

TRADING MOM ★★★1/2 Delightful family movie, based on the short story "The Mommy Market," finds

Sissy Spacek playing four different roles. She plays the mother of three who decide they want another mommy. They go to the Mommy market, where they are given the chance to test-drive three candidates, also played by Spacek. Children will enjoy the whimsical situations, while parents will appreciate the life lessons. Rated PG. 83m. **DIR:** Tia Brelis. **CAST:** Sissy Spacek, Anna Chlumsky, Maureen Stapleton, Aaron Michael Metchik, Asher Metchik. **1993**

TRADING PLACES ★★★★ Here's an uproarious comedy about what happens when uptight Philadelphia broker (Dan Aykroyd) and dynamic black street hustler (Eddie Murphy) change places. Rated R for nudity and profanity. 117m. **DIR:** John Landis. **CAST:** Dan Aykroyd, Eddie Murphy, Ralph Bellamy, Don Ameche, Jamie Lee Curtis, Denholm Elliott. **1983**

TRAFFIC (1971) ★★★ Mr. Hulot is back, and this time his escapades revolve around an international auto show. The sight and sound gags are quite amusing. Multilingual with some English dubbed in, but the spoken word is not needed to enjoy the film. Not rated. 89m. **DIR:** Jacques Tati. **CAST:** Jacques Tati, Marla Kimberly. **1971**

TRAFFIC (2000) ★★★★★ This superbly visualized, densely layered, and damning indictment of America's drug problem recasts the "war" as an endless chess game, complete with aggressive kings, too few knights, and far too many pawns. But while Stephen Gaghan's screenplay—adapted from the 1989 British miniseries—clearly displays this cynical viewpoint, the film is remarkably free of partisan bias and it makes fascinating viewing. Cast standouts include Benicio Del Toro as a shrewd and unexpectedly romantic Mexican police officer, and Erika Christensen as the drug-addicted daughter of new American "drug czar" Michael Douglas. Rated R for violence, profanity, drug use, nudity, and strong sexual content. 147m. **DIR:** Steven Soderbergh. **CAST:** Michael Douglas, Don Cheadle, Benicio Del Toro, Luis Guzman, Dennis Quaid, Catherine Zeta-Jones, Steven Bauer, Erika Christensen, Miguel Ferrer. **2000 DVD**

TRAFFIC IN SOULS ★★★1/2 One of the first exploitation films ever made, this makes great use of New York City locations and natives as it uncovers the "true crime" horrors of forced prostitution. The documentarylike realism is still gripping, but the film is so cropped that telegrams and newspapers are illegible. Somewhat overblown by today's standards, but the timeless social commentary never undermines the plot. Silent. Not rated; contains adult themes. B&W; 88m. **DIR:** George Loane Tucker. **CAST:** Matt Moore, Jane Gail, Ethel Grandin. **1913**

TRAFFIC JAM ★★★ A road trip slowly turns into a disaster when a hard-working Japanese man decides to take his family to visit his parents. The humor isn't as broad as in the *National Lampoon Vacation* series and an undercurrent of strong affection among the characters makes this enjoyable viewing. Original title: *Jutai*. In Japanese with English subtitles. Not rated; contains no objectionable material. 108m. **DIR:** Mitsuo Kurotsuchi. **CAST:** Junko Takarada, Shingo Yuzawa, Eiji Okada. **1992**

TRAGEDY OF A RIDICULOUS MAN ★★★1/2 A wealthy businessman struggles with the most difficult decision of his life: Should he sell his beloved cheese factory to raise the ransom money for his kidnapped son, or should he assume that his son has already been murdered? Ugo Tognazzi won the Cannes best-actor award for his role as the distraught father. In Italian with English subtitles. Not rated; contains nudity and profanity. 117m. **DIR:** Bernardo Bertolucci. **CAST:** Ugo Tognazzi, Anouk Aimée, Laura Morante, Victor Cavallo. **1981**

TRAGEDY OF FLIGHT 103, THE: THE INSIDE STORY ★★★★ A tragic and riveting account of the events leading up to the destruction of Pan Am Flight 103, resulting in the deaths at Christmastime in 1988 of 270 people over Lockerbie, Scotland. This dramatized reconstruction exposes the inner workings of international terrorists, ineffectual cosmetic airport security, and how communication failures between intelligence agencies and airport officials have led to the loss of innocent lives. Made for TV. 89m. **DIR:** Leslie Woodhead. **CAST:** Peter Boyle, Ned Beatty, Vincent Gardenia. **1990**

TRAIL BEYOND, THE ★★1/2 Once again, John Wayne rides to the rescue in a low-budget Western from the 1930s. It's pretty typical stuff as the Duke fights outlaws who are attempting to steal a gold mine. But this B Western has lots of action and a rare appearance of father and son actors Noah Beery Sr. and Noah Beery Jr. B&W; 55m. **DIR:** Robert N. Bradbury. **CAST:** John Wayne, Verna Hillie, Noah Beery Sr., Noah Beery Jr. **1934 DVD**

TRAIL BLAZERS ★★★ The Three Mesquiteers stop a bandit gang run by a newspaper editor trying to halt the westward development of the telegraph. B&W; 54m. **DIR:** George Sherman. **CAST:** Robert Livingston, Bob Steele, Rufe Davis, Pauline Moore. **1940**

TRAIL DRIVE ★★★★ Cattleman Ken Maynard brings to justice an unscrupulous rancher on a thrill packed cattle drive. B&W; 60m. **DIR:** Alan James. **CAST:** Ken Maynard, Cecilia Parker, Bob Kortman. **1933**

TRAIL DUST ★★★ People up north are crying for beef, but a group of unscrupulous cattlemen are ignoring the crisis and holding out for top dollar. Hopalong Cassidy and some of the smaller ranchers combine herds and make a cattle drive marked by murder and sabotage by the rogue cowboys. There's plenty of action, a few songs, some funny business between Hoppy and Windy, and a great ending. B&W; 77m. **DIR:** Nate Watt. **CAST:** William Boyd, James Ellison, George "Gabby" Hayes, Morris Ankrum, Gwynne Shipman. **1936**

TRAIL OF ROBIN HOOD ★★★ This star-studded oddity finds Roy Rogers and a handful of contemporary Western heroes aiding screen great Jack Holt (playing himself) in his effort to provide Christmas trees to needy families in time for the holidays. Enjoyable film for all ages and a special treat for fans of the genre. 67m. **DIR:** William Witney. **CAST:** Roy Rogers, Penny Edwards, Gordon Jones, Jack Holt, Emory Parnell, Clifton Young, Rex Allen, Allan "Rocky" Lane, Monte Hale, Kermit Maynard, Tom Keene, Ray "Crash" Corrigan, William Farnum. **1950**

TRAIL OF THE LONESOME PINE, THE ★★★1/2 Railroad builder gets caught in the crossfire between feuding families in Virginia's Blue Ridge Mountains. Based on John Fox Jr.'s popular turn-of-the-century novel this

is old-fashioned but powerful, and it put young Henry Fonda on the map. Noteworthy as the first outdoor film shot in full Technicolor. Not rated; suitable for general audiences. 102m. **DIR:** Henry Hathaway. **CAST:** Sylvia Sidney, Fred MacMurray, Henry Fonda, Fred Stone, Beulah Bondi, Spanky McFarland, Nigel Bruce, Fuzzy Knight. **1936**

TRAIL OF THE PINK PANTHER, THE ★★1/2 Through the magic of editing, the late Peter Sellers "stars" as the bumbling Inspector Clouseau. Writer-director Blake Edwards uses outtakes of Sellers from previous films and combines them with new footage featuring David Niven, Herbert Lom, and Capucine. Disappointing. Rated PG for nudity and scatological humor. 97m. **DIR:** Blake Edwards. **CAST:** Peter Sellers, David Niven, Herbert Lom, Capucine, Robert Wagner. **1982**

TRAIL OF THE SILVER SPURS ★★★ The Range Busters investigate hidden passages, salted mines, and a mysterious ghost-town killer known as the Jingler. B&W; 58m. **DIR:** S. Roy Luby. **CAST:** Ray "Crash" Corrigan, John King, Max Terhune, Dorothy Short, I. Stanford Jolley. **1941**

TRAIL STREET ★★★ Randolph Scott plays Bat Masterson in this well-acted story of conflicting western philosophies as Robert Ryan defends the farmers against gambler Steve Brodie and the cattle-rancher faction. Gabby Hayes lends some levity to this otherwise dramatic adult Western. Skillful repackaging of a familiar story. B&W; 84m. **DIR:** Ray Enright. **CAST:** Randolph Scott, Robert Ryan, Anne Jeffreys, George "Gabby" Hayes, Steve Brodie. **1947**

TRAILIN' NORTH ★★ Texas Ranger Bob Steele heads to Canada where he works with the Mounties to bring back a prisoner. Every B-Western cliché in the book. B&W; 57m. **DIR:** John P. McCarthy. **CAST:** Bob Steele, Doris Hill, George "Gabby" Hayes. **1933**

TRAIN, THE ★★★★ A suspenseful World War II adventure about the French Resistance's attempt to stop a train loaded with fine art, seized from French museums, from reaching its destination in Nazi Germany. Burt Lancaster is fine as the head of the French railway system, but he is far outclassed by the performance of Paul Scofield as the unrelenting German commander. B&W; 133m. **DIR:** John Frankenheimer. **CAST:** Burt Lancaster, Paul Scofield, Michel Simon, Jeanne Moreau. **1965 DVD**

TRAIN KILLER, THE ★★ The true story of Sylvester Matushka, the Hungarian businessman who was responsible for a number of train wrecks in 1931. What is frustrating about this film is that it prepares the viewer for political intrigue that is never fully explained by the end of the film. Towje Kleiner is superb as Dr. Epstein, investigator of the train wrecks. Not rated; contains sex, nudity, and violence. 90m. **DIR:** Sandor Simo. **CAST:** Michael Sarrazin, Towje Kleiner. **1983**

TRAIN OF LIFE ★★1/2 The inhabitants of a Jewish village in Nazi-occupied Europe try to smuggle themselves to Palestine disguised as a deportation train, with some of them dressed in German uniforms to complete the ruse. This bizarre mixture of *Fiddler on the Roof* and *Von Ryan's Express* is energetic and pretty to look at, but there's a spurious implication behind the premise: that the Holocaust was no big deal if you could just keep a cheerful attitude. In French with English subtitles. Rated R for nudity. 102m. **DIR:** Radu Mihaileanu. **CAST:** Lionel Abelanski, Rufus, Clement Harari, Marie-Jose Nat. **1998**

TRAIN ROBBERS, THE ★★1/2 John Wayne and Ben Johnson join Ann-Margret in a search for a lost train and gold. Some nice moments but generally unsatisfying. For hard-core Wayne fans only. Rated PG for violence, but nothing extreme. 92m. **DIR:** Burt Kennedy. **CAST:** John Wayne, Ben Johnson, Ann-Margret, Rod Taylor, Ricardo Montalban. **1973**

TRAINED TO FIGHT ★★ Average martial arts actioner features a college freshman pursuing his interest in kung fu. He must win the $25,000 tournament money to help underprivileged kids. His master tries to explain why his moves are meant to promote nonviolence, but that's stretching it. Not rated; contains violence. 95m. **DIR:** Eric Sherman. **CAST:** Ken McLeod, Tang Tak Wing, Matthew Roy Cohen, Mark Williams. **1991**

•TRAINING DAY ★★★ A renegade LAPD narcotics detective wears a large crucifix and black leather jacket, and embraces the corruption and eat-or-be-eaten philosophy of the streets with quasireligious fervor. He is partnered with an idealistic narcotics squad rookie, a family man who must prove his mettle to his morally bankrupt, self-delusional superior. This crisp, gripping crime story slithers into a contrived, multiclimax third act. Rated R for language, violence, nudity, and drug use. 122m. **DIR:** Antoine Fuqua. **CAST:** Denzel Washington, Ethan Hawke, Scott Glenn, Tom Berenger, Cliff Curtis, Doctor Dre, Snoop Dogg. **2001 DVD**

TRAINSPOTTING ★★★★ Exuberant movie about the rigors and rushes of Scottish-junkie life. Working from Irvine Welsh's novel, director Danny Boyle doesn't flinch from depicting the horrid consequences of heroin use, but he never lets you forget that most people do it because it feels better than anything else. Surrealistic and speedy in a glib, rock-video kind of way, the film doesn't cover any new ground, but it does approach the dead-end scene with an irrepressible style and audacious visual wit. Rated R. 90m. **DIR:** Danny Boyle. **CAST:** Ewan McGregor, Ewen Bremner, Jonny Lee Miller, Kevin McKidd, Robert Carlyle. **1996 DVD**

TRAITOR, THE ★★1/2 Marshal Tim McCoy goes undercover to catch a gang of cutthroats. He succeeds in his plan of joining the outlaws, but his life is in constant danger. A game performance by McCoy, but the story is too typical and the direction is plodding. B&W; 56m. **DIR:** Sam Newfield. **CAST:** Tim McCoy, Frances Grant, Wally Wales, Karl Hackett. **1936**

TRAMP AT THE DOOR ★★★★ Poignant story of a transient who poses as a distant relative of a family to gain shelter and food from them. The script is solid, especially the stories that the tramp (played brilliantly by Ed McNamara) weaves for the astonished family. Not rated; for all ages. 81m. **DIR:** Allan Kroeker. **CAST:** Ed McNamara, August Schellengberg, Monique Mercure. **1985**

TRAMPLERS, THE ★★ Gordon Scott returns from the Civil War to find his father (Joseph Cotten) trying to preserve the prewar South by burning out settlers and starting mass lynchings. Scott and his younger brother (Jim Mitchum) join up with their father's enemies. 105m. **DIR:** Albert Band. **CAST:** Gordon Scott, Joseph Cotten, Jim Mitchum, Franco Nero. **1966**

TRANCERS ★★ Tim Thomerson is Jack Deth, a police officer in the 2280s who is sent to bring back a violent cult leader who escaped into the twentieth century. Rated PG-13 for profanity and lots of violence. 76m. **DIR:** Charles Band. **CAST:** Tim Thomerson, Helen Hunt, Michael Stefani, Art Le Fleur, Telma Hopkins, Richard Herd, Anne Seymour. **1985 DVD**

TRANCERS II (THE RETURN OF JACK DETH) 🦃 Jack Deth returns to Los Angeles to battle zombielike creatures in this technically abysmal production. Rated R for nudity and violence. 86m. **DIR:** Charles Band. **CAST:** Tim Thomerson, Helen Hunt. **1991**

TRANCERS III: DETH LIVES ★★★ In this third installment, Trancer tracker Jack Deth, played with aplomb by Tim Thomerson, is back to hunt down some new Trancers in town, and this time they're rougher and tougher. This series from Full Moon Productions is one of their highlights and is entertaining in a brutal, self-mocking sort of way. Rated R for violence and language. 83m. **DIR:** C. Courtney Joyner. **CAST:** Tim Thomerson, Melanie Smith, Andrew Robinson, Helen Hunt, Megan Ward. **1992**

TRANCERS 4: JACK OF SWORDS ★★1/2 In his fourth outing as Trancer hunter Jack Deth, Tim Thomerson is transported to another dimension where the locals are being bred as food. Trapped in a medieval world, Deth must utilize knowledge from his time to end the Trancers' reign of terror. New setting and swordplay breathe life into the series. Rated R for violence, nudity, and adult situations. 74m. **DIR:** David Nutter. **CAST:** Tim Thomerson, Stacie Randall, Ty Miller, Stephen Macht, Alan Oppenheimer. **1993**

TRANCERS 5: SUDDEN DETH ★★★ This (supposedly) closes out the Jack Deth flicks with a final battle with the life-sucking Trancers. A quick rundown of past installments shows us that time-traveler Deth has been stuck in a sword-and-sorcery universe in which everyone is named after a Shakespearean character. This is hardly art, but Deth's unflappability and cynical humor, combined with a fast pace, make for an enjoyable romp. Rated R for profanity and violence. 73m. **DIR:** David Nutter. **CAST:** Tim Thomerson, Stacie Randall, Ty Miller, Terri Ivens, Mark Arnold, Stephen Macht. **1994**

TRANSATLANTIC MERRY-GO-ROUND ★★ Jack Benny is the emcee of this transatlantic showboat, the S.S. *Progress*, en route from New York to Paris. This tub is loaded with romance, blackmail, chicanery, and murder. But it's rather lightweight overall. B&W; 90m. **DIR:** Ben Stoloff. **CAST:** Gene Raymond, Nancy Carroll, Jack Benny, Mitzi Green, Boswell Sisters. **1934**

TRANSATLANTIC TUNNEL ★★1/2 A truly splendid cast still manages to get bogged down a bit in this heavy-handed account of the building of a passageway under the Atlantic Ocean. Richard Dix plays the stalwart engineer who can get the job done and Walter Huston plays the president of the United States. B&W; 90m. **DIR:** Maurice Elvey. **CAST:** Richard Dix, Leslie Banks, Madge Evans, C. Aubrey Smith, George Arliss, Walter Huston, Helen Vinson. **1935**

TRANSFORMATIONS 🦃 An AIDS subtext runs through this sci-fi film, but the similarities to David Cronenberg's remake of *The Fly* overpower any good intentions. Rated R for violence, profanity, nudity, gore, and simulated sex. 84m. **DIR:** Jay Kamen. **CAST:** Rex Smith, Patrick Macnee, Lisa Langlois, Christopher Neame. **1988**

TRANSFORMERS, THE MOVIE 🦃 Animated vehicle for violence and destruction. Rated PG for violence and occasional obscenities. 80m. **DIR:** Nelson Shin. **1986**

TRANSMUTATIONS ★★ Much-lauded horror writer Clive Barker disowned this, the first of his stories to be filmed. A retired London mobster, searching for his missing girlfriend, discovers an underground society of mutants, the victims of drug experiments. The strong cast has little to do, and the story is more mystery than horror. Rated R. 103m. **DIR:** George Pavlou. **CAST:** Larry Lamb, Denholm Elliott, Nicola Cowper, Steven Berkoff, Miranda Richardson, Ingrid Pitt. **1985**

TRANSYLVANIA 6-5000 ★★ Sometimes amusing but ultimately silly horror spoof focusing on an inept pair of tabloid reporters (Jeff Goldblum and Ed Begley Jr.) sent to Transylvania to investigate the Frankenstein monster. Rated PG for mild profanity. 93m. **DIR:** Rudy DeLuca. **CAST:** Jeff Goldblum, Ed Begley Jr., Joseph Bologna, Carol Kane, Jeffrey Jones, John Byner, Michael Richards. **1985 DVD**

TRANSYLVANIA TWIST ★★1/2 No horror movie is safe in this lampoon from producer Roger Corman. Scenes from classics like *Frankenstein* and *Dracula*, along with more recent entries in the genre (*Friday the 13th* and *Nightmare on Elm Street*) are parodied in this tale of the search for a book that will raise the "evil one." Rated PG-13. 82m. **DIR:** Jim Wynorski. **CAST:** Robert Vaughn, Teri Copley, Steve Altman, Angus Scrimm, Jay Robinson, Howard Morris, Steve Franken. **1990**

TRAP, THE ★★★1/2 Fast pace and taut suspense mark this thriller about as fine a gaggle of fleeing gangsters as ever menaced the innocent inhabitants of a small California desert town. This is edge-of-chair stuff. It was in films such as this that Richard Widmark made his name praisingly hissable. 84m. **DIR:** Norman Panama. **CAST:** Richard Widmark, Lee J. Cobb, Earl Holliman, Tina Louise, Lorne Greene. **1958**

TRAP THEM AND KILL THEM 🦃 Originally titled *Emmanuelle and the Last Cannibals*, this gross out extravaganza merges the sexploitation *Emmanuelle* series of porn pictures with the Italian cannibal horror genre. Not rated, but sexually explicit and very gruesome. 85m. **DIR:** Joe D'Amato (Aristide Massaccesi). **CAST:** Laura Gemser, Gabriele Tinti, Susan Scott. **1977**

TRAPEZE ★★1/2 Overly familiar tale of professional (Burt Lancaster) who takes young protégé (Tony Curtis) under his wing only to have scheming opportunist Gina Lollobrigida come between them is okay but nothing out of the ordinary. Solid performances and competent stunts performed by the stars. 105m. **DIR:** Carol Reed. **CAST:** Burt Lancaster, Tony Curtis, Gina Lollobrigida, Katy Jurado, Thomas Gomez. **1956**

TRAPPED ★★1/2 Kathleen Quinlan's resourceful businesswoman saves this low-rent stuck-in-a-deserted-building-with-a-maniac programmer from complete turkeydom, but there's little to admire in Fred Walton's inane script or hackneyed direction. Made for cable. 88m. **DIR:** Fred Walton. **CAST:** Kathleen Quinlan, Bruce Abbott, Katy Boyer. **1989**

TRAPPED BY TELEVISION ★★1/2 Collection agent hooks up with a penniless inventor who is just about to complete a "televisor" that can transmit action to a re-

ceiver miles away! Our heroes battle the crooks who want to destroy the machine and corner the market with their own device. A low-budget treat. B&W; 64m. **DIR:** Del Lord. **CAST:** Lyle Talbot, Mary Astor, Nat Pendleton, Joyce Compton, Thurston Hall, Robert Strange. **1936**

TRAPPED IN PARADISE ★★ Three bumbling brothers (Nicolas Cage, Dana Carvey, Jon Lovitz) rob a small-town bank on Christmas Eve, then botch their getaway and wind up spending the holiday with the bank president and his wonderful family. Aimless, leaden farce wastes the talents of its three stars, then shamelessly and ineptly fumbles at your heartstrings. Rated PG-13 for comic violence and mild profanity. 111m. **DIR:** George Gallo. **CAST:** Nicolas Cage, Dana Carvey, Jon Lovitz, Donald Moffat, Madchen Amick, Florence Stanley, John Ashton. **1994**

TRAPPED IN SPACE ★★★ Entertaining, involving sci-fi drama about a group of space travelers who discover that—due to the unexpected rupture of their oxygen tanks—they've only got enough air left for one of them to return home. Who will it be? The cast is very good, displaying their various levels of paranoia and panic with precision. Based on the short story "Breaking Strain" by Arthur C. Clarke. Rated PG for violence. 87m. **DIR:** Arthur Allan Seidelman. **CAST:** Jack Wagner, Jack Coleman, Kay Lenz, Kevin Colson, Craig Wasson, Sigrid Thornton. **1994**

TRAPPER COUNTY WAR ★★ Two city boys trigger a blood feud when one of them falls for a country girl who's already spoken for. An oft-told tale of backwoods romance and revenge. Rated R for violence and profanity. 98m. **DIR:** Worth Keeter. **CAST:** Rob Estes, Betsy Russell, Bo Hopkins, Ernie Hudson. **1989 DVD**

TRASH ★★1/2 Favorite Andy Warhol actor Joe Dallesandro faces the squalor of New York once again. This is one of Warhol's more palatable productions. It contains some truly amusing scenes and insightful dialogue, as well as good performances by Dallesandro and Holly Woodlawn, whose relationship is the highlight of the film. Nudity, language, and open drug use fill the frames of this freewheeling life study. 110m. **DIR:** Paul Morrissey. **CAST:** Joe Dallesandro, Holly Woodlawn, Jane Forth. **1970 DVD**

TRAUMA ★★ American cast gets lost in this weak effort from noted Italian horror-director Dario Argento. A woman is traumatized when she sees her parents decapitated by a serial killer. Argento keeps things creepy, but the film is slow and the characters are uninteresting. Not rated and R-rated versions available; unrated contains more gore. 106m. **DIR:** Dario Argento. **CAST:** James Russo, Frederic Forrest, Brad Dourif, Piper Laurie, Christopher Rydell, Asia Argento. **1992**

TRAVELING MAN ★★★1/2 John Lithgow puts heart and soul into this engaging portrayal of a congenial road-bound salesman pushing foam insulation. Lithgow winds up chaperoning a wet-behind-the-ears trainee (Jonathan Silverman)—who then makes a grab for his mentor's route. Originally made for cable, it is unrated, but contains nudity. 105m. **DIR:** Irvin Kershner. **CAST:** John Lithgow, Jonathan Silverman, John Glover, Margaret Colin. **1989**

TRAVELLER ★★★★ Star-producer Bill Paxton shepherded this clever little drama to the screen, and it's easy to see why he cared so much. He's one of a roving band of modern-day Celtic gypsies, whose life grows complicated when he takes a surly young man under his wing, and falls in love with a spirited barmaid who's "outside the clan." Rich characterization and an excellent use of music are just a few of this film's many charms. Rated R for profanity and violence. 101m. **DIR:** Jack Green. **CAST:** Bill Paxton, Mark Wahlberg, Julianna Margulies, James Gammon, Luke Askew. **1996 DVD**

TRAVELLING NORTH ★★★1/2 Fine Australian romance focuses on the love of two senior citizens. Touching, delightful, and definitely worth watching. Rated PG-13 for profanity and adult themes. 97m. **DIR:** Carl Schultz. **CAST:** Leo McKern, Julia Blake. **1988**

TRAVELS WITH MY AUNT ★★1/2 Director George Cukor's screen version of Graham Greene's comic novel is only slightly above average. Maggie Smith's overbearing and overplayed aunt knocks what could have been a delightful *Auntie Mame*–style farce completely off-kilter. Alec McCowen gives an affecting performance as the bank executive who finds his tidy world disrupted. Rated PG. 109m. **DIR:** George Cukor. **CAST:** Maggie Smith, Alec McCowen, Louis Gossett Jr., Robert Stephens, Cindy Williams. **1972**

TRAXX ★★★ Wacky, often funny tale about a mercenary turned cookie maker who cleans the criminal element out of Hadleyville, Texas. Shadoe Stevens is Traxx, a man who derives simple pleasure from shooting people, causing mayhem—and baking the oddest-flavored cookies he can imagine. Rated R for cartoon violence and slight nudity. 85m. **DIR:** Jerome Gray. **CAST:** Shadoe Stevens, Priscilla Barnes, Robert Davi, John Hancock. **1988**

TREACHEROUS ★★ Tired thriller about a couple who find passion and intrigue while on vacation at a paradise resort. Rated R for violence, language, and sensuality. 90m. **DIR:** Kevin Brodie. **CAST:** C. Thomas Howell, Tia Carrere, Adam Baldwin, Kevin Bernhardt. **1993**

TREACHEROUS CROSSING ★★★1/2 Lindsay Wagner is a newlywed who goes on a honeymoon cruise with her new husband, only to have him disappear right after boarding. Wagner portrays the unstable character quite convincingly, and the story is twisted enough, so that one does not know who to believe. Made for cable. 95m. **DIR:** Tony Wharmby. **CAST:** Lindsay Wagner, Angie Dickinson, Grant Show, Joseph Bottoms, Karen Medak, Charles Napier, Jeffrey DeMunn. **1992**

TREASURE ISLAND (1934) ★★★★ This is an MGM all-star presentation of Robert Louis Stevenson's classic of a young boy's adventure with pirates, buried treasure, and that delightful rogue of fiction Long John Silver. It seems all the great character actors of the 1930s put in an appearance, including Wallace Beery, as Silver, and Lionel Barrymore, as Billy Bones. B&W; 105m. **DIR:** Victor Fleming. **CAST:** Wallace Beery, Lionel Barrymore, Jackie Cooper, Lewis Stone. **1934**

TREASURE ISLAND (1950) ★★★★ Disney remake of the Robert Louis Stevenson pirate adventure is powered by a memorable Robert Newton as Long John Silver. 87m. **DIR:** Byron Haskin. **CAST:** Robert Newton, Bobby Driscoll, Basil Sydney. **1950**

TREASURE ISLAND (1990) ★★★★1/2 Robert Louis Stevenson's classic adventure yarn receives its best

treatment in this rousing made-for-cable adaptation. The location photography is gorgeous, the sailing ship *Hispaniola* is a beauty, and the pirates look like N. C. Wyeth and Howard Pyle illustrations come to life. 132m. **DIR:** Fraser Heston. **CAST:** Charlton Heston, Christian Bale, Oliver Reed, Julian Glover, Richard Johnson, Clive Wood, Christopher Lee. **1990**

TREASURE OF ARNE ★★ Swedish master Mauritz Stiller forsook his flair for comedy and wrought this grim tale of crime, guilt, and sacrifice—famous in its day but unrelievedly tedious today. Based on Selma Lagerlöf's tale about escaped prisoners who steal a treasure with a curse on it. Silent. B&W; 100m. **DIR:** Mauritz Stiller. **CAST:** Richard Lund, Mary Johnson, Hjalmar Selander. **1919**

TREASURE OF PANCHO VILLA, THE ★★1/2 Rory Calhoun and Gilbert Roland pull off a gold robbery with the intention of giving the loot to the Mexican revolutionary forces. However, Calhoun begins to think the money would be better in his pocket. Complications ensue. Calhoun carries a great machine gun in this watchable Western, and Roland is fascinating as always. Good action scenes. 96m. **DIR:** George Sherman. **CAST:** Rory Calhoun, Shelley Winters, Gilbert Roland, Joseph Calleia. **1955**

TREASURE OF PIRATE'S POINT ★★ Nondiscerning children might enjoy this harmless but halfhearted family romp about a group of kids who suspect that a pirate's treasure is buried in their small town. They're *Goonies* wannabes. Rated PG. 88m. **DIR:** Richard Stanley. **CAST:** Asher Metchik, Brittany Alyse Smith, Sam Gifaldi, William Sheppard. **1998**

TREASURE OF THE AMAZON 🦃 Mexican-made action flick about a fortune in diamonds. Not rated; contains some violence. 105m. **DIR:** René Cardona Jr. **CAST:** Stuart Whitman, Bradford Dillman, Donald Pleasence, John Ireland. **1983**

TREASURE OF THE FOUR CROWNS 🦃 Logic is the victim of this steal from *Raiders of the Lost Ark*. Rated PG for violence. 97m. **DIR:** Ferdinando Baldi. **CAST:** Tony Anthony, Gene Quintano. **1983**

TREASURE OF THE SIERRA MADRE ★★★★★ Humphrey Bogart gives a brilliant performance in this study of greed. The setting is rugged mountains in Mexico where Bogart, with Tim Holt and a grizzled prospector, played marvelously by Walter Huston, set out to make a fortune in gold prospecting. They do, with their troubles getting worse. Seamless script and magnificent performances add up to a classic. B&W; 126m. **DIR:** John Huston. **CAST:** Humphrey Bogart, Tim Holt, Walter Huston, Bruce Bennett. **1948**

TREASURE OF THE YANKEE ZEPHYR ★★1/2 When an old trapper (Donald Pleasence) discovers a sunken treasure of military medals and liquor, he enlists the aid of his partner (Ken Wahl) and his daughter (Lesley Ann Warren) to bring in the haul. A ruthless claim jumper (George Peppard) and his henchmen follow. Rated PG for violence. 97m. **DIR:** David Hemmings. **CAST:** Ken Wahl, Lesley Ann Warren, Donald Pleasence, George Peppard, Bruno Lawrence. **1981**

TREASURES OF THE TITANIC ★★★ Two miles beneath the Atlantic Ocean lie the remains of RMS *Titanic*, lost April 14, 1912. This film of the 1987 French-American exploration of the famous wreck and retrieval of a variety of artifacts, such as a ship's safe, a bell, navigation equipment, and china, brings the haunting tragedy into greater and sharper focus. Included in the film is an interview with a survivor. Doug Llewelyn narrates. 60m. **DIR:** Steve Kroopnick. **1988**

TREE GROWS IN BROOKLYN, A ★★★★ A richly detailed and sentimental evocation of working-class Brooklyn at the turn of the century. The story focuses on the happiness and tragedies of a poor family ruled by a kindly but alcoholic father and a strong-willed mother. B&W; 128m. **DIR:** Elia Kazan. **CAST:** Dorothy McGuire, James Dunn, Joan Blondell, Peggy Ann Garner, Lloyd Nolan, James Gleason. **1945**

TREE OF THE WOODEN CLOGS, THE ★★★★★ Stunning, epic masterpiece about the hardships in the life of a community of peasants in northern Italy, just before the turn of the century. In Italian with English subtitles. Not rated. 185m. **DIR:** Ermanno Olmi. **CAST:** Luigi Ornaghi, Francesca Moriggi, Omar Brignoli. **1978**

TREEHOUSE HOSTAGE ★★ Jim Varney is the main attraction here, playing an escaped con who ends up being held hostage in a treehouse by a kid who plans to use him as a class project. The idea is totally inane, yet young children may find some of this entertaining. Rated PG. 90m. **DIR:** Sean McNamara. **CAST:** Jim Varney, Joey Zimmerman, Todd Bosley, Mark Moses, Debby Boone. **1999 DVD**

•**TREES** 🦃 You can see the *Trees* from the forest in this *Jaws* spoof. Unfortunately. Not rated. 90m. **DIR:** Michael Pleckaitis. **CAST:** Kevin McCauley, Peter Randazzo, Philip Gardiner. **2001**

TREES LOUNGE ★★★★ This seriocomic movie is the best road map to an alcoholic lifestyle since 1987's *Barfly*. Tommy has been fired, lost his pregnant girlfriend, and heads for disaster when he gets mixed up with a 17 year old girl. Rated R for drug use, language, and suggested sex. 96m. **DIR:** Steve Buscemi. **CAST:** Steve Buscemi, Anthony LaPaglia, Chloe Sevigny, Elizabeth Bracco, Michael Buscemi, Daniel Baldwin, Mark Boone Jr. **1996 DVD**

TREKKIES ★★★1/2 Documentarian Roger Nygard takes a bemused look at the *Star Trek* fan phenomenon, loosely tracing its development from the first convention in the early 1970s to the present. On the whole this is one of affection rather than disdain. With guest appearances from most of the cast of all four *Star Trek* series. Rated PG. 86m. **DIR:** Roger Nygard. **1998 DVD**

TREMORS ★★★★1/2 Here's a terrific, old-fashioned monster movie with great performances, a witty and suspenseful screenplay, and masterful direction. Kevin Bacon and Fred Ward are hilarious as a couple of independent cusses. One day our heroes discover a decapitated sheep rancher and his gruesomely devoured flock, and are forced to fight for their lives against a pack of flesh-eating, giant worms. Rated PG-13 for light profanity and remarkably limited violence. 90m. **DIR:** Ron Underwood. **CAST:** Kevin Bacon, Fred Ward, Finn Carter, Michael Gross, Reba McEntire, Victor Wong. **1990 DVD**

TREMORS 2: AFTERSHOCKS ★★★1/2 Although not quite as much fun as its predecessor, this engaging sequel doesn't miss by much. Monster-worm hunter Fred Ward returns and accepts an assignment to rid a Mexican oil refinery of the earth-burrowing "graboids" that

munch everything in their path. Survivalist Michael Gross also reappears, but Christopher Gartin is a weak replacement for Kevin Bacon. While our heroes get off to a good start, the worms turn clever and adapt into even more lethal forms. Very entertaining, particularly for folks who like monster flicks without the gore. Rated PG-13 for violence and profanity. 100m. **DIR:** S. S. Wilson. **CAST:** Fred Ward, Christopher Gartin, Helen Shaver, Michael Gross, Marcelo Tubert. **1995 DVD**

•TREMORS 3: BACK TO PERFECTION ★★★ Burt Gummer (Michael Gross) returns to where it all started—Perfection, Nevada. Those darn earth-tunneling "graboids" are back, as well as the "shrieker" form that they had evolved to in the second film. Now there's a brand-new option that these things can turn into, one that can fly and shoot a flame out its rear end, lovingly called "assblasters." If you didn't like the first two incarnations, then don't bother with this one, for it's the silliest one of the bunch. Rated PG for monster killing and mild language. 104m. **DIR:** Brent Maddock. **CAST:** Michael Gross. **2001 DVD**

TRENCHCOAT ★★ No one is what he appears to be in this inept spoof of the detective genre. While there are moments that evoke some chuckles, *Trenchcoat* rarely hits the mark. Rated PG. 91m. **DIR:** Michael Tuchner. **CAST:** Margot Kidder, Robert Hays, Daniel Faraldo. **1983**

TRESPASS ★★★★ Nobody directs action better than Walter Hill, and, by working from a tight script by Bob Gale and Robert Zemeckis, this rough-and-tumble, modern-day shoot-'em-up ranks as one of his best films. Two Arkansas firemen's search for lost treasure leads them to a taut battle of wits, fists, and flying bullets that will have fans of the genre cheering. Rated R for profanity and violence. 101m. **DIR:** Walter Hill. **CAST:** Bill Paxton, Ice T, Bill Sadler, Ice Cube, Art Evans. **1992 DVD**

TRESPASSES A beautiful woman is raped by two degenerate transients while her banker husband watches. Rated R for nudity and violence. 90m. **DIR:** Adam Roarke, Loren Bivens. **CAST:** Ben Johnson, Robert Kuhn, Mary Pillot, Van Brooks, Adam Roarke. **1986**

TRIAL, THE (1963) ★★★1/2 A man in an unnamed country is arrested for an unexplained crime he is never told about. It is never made too clear to the audience, either. Orson Welles's unique staging and direction nevertheless make it all fascinating, if disturbing, entertainment. B&W; 118m. **DIR:** Orson Welles. **CAST:** Anthony Perkins, Jeanne Moreau, Romy Schneider, Orson Welles, Elsa Martinelli, Akim Tamiroff. **1963 DVD**

TRIAL, THE (1992) ★★★★ Powerful story of persecution and paranoia as written by Harold Pinter and based on Franz Kafka's novel, this film is more effective than Orson Welles's 1963 version. Set in an unnamed country in some past time, a hapless bank clerk is accused of an unspecified crime, set for an unrevealed trial date. Rife with sexual tension and shadows of police states past and present. Not rated; contains profanity. 120m. **DIR:** David Jones. **CAST:** Kyle MacLachlan, Anthony Hopkins, Jason Robards Jr., Juliet Stevenson, Polly Walker, Alfred Molina. **1992 DVD**

TRIAL & ERROR (1992) ★★★ A prosecutor who sent a man to death row starts to have doubts about the man's guilt right before his execution. Tim Matheson does a fine job portraying the prosecutor. Not rated, made for cable, but contains violence. 95m. **DIR:** Mark Sobel. **CAST:** Tim Matheson, Helen Shaver, Sean McCann, Page Fletcher, Michael J. Reynolds, Ian D. Clark, Eugene A. Clark. **1992**

TRIAL AND ERROR (1997) ★★★1/2 Director Jonathan Lynn makes another courtroom delight, following the success of *My Cousin Vinny.* This time he features Michael Richards as an actor who fills in for his hungover attorney buddy (Jeff Daniels). Richards delivers the expected Kramer-esque slapstick he became famous for on *Seinfeld,* but then allows his character a more serious and rational side. Rated PG-13 for profanity and sexual situations. 98m. **DIR:** Jonathan Lynn. **CAST:** Michael Richards, Jeff Daniels, Charlize Theron, Jessica Steen, Austin Pendleton, Rip Torn. **1997 DVD**

TRIAL BY JURY ★★ Manhattan antiques dealer does her civic duty on a jury considering the fate of powerful, crazed mob boss who turns out to be the embodiment of pure evil. Soon becomes so contrived that it's difficult to watch. Rated R for violence, profanity, and suggested sex. 92m. **DIR:** Heywood Gould. **CAST:** Joanne Whalley, Armand Assante, Gabriel Byrne, William Hurt, Kathleen Quinlan, Margaret Whitton, Ed Lauter, Richard Ortnow, Joe Santos, Stuart Whitman. **1994 DVD**

TRIAL OF THE CATONSVILLE NINE, THE ★★ This film is a claustrophobic adaptation of a play about nine Baltimore antiwar protesters (two are priests), who faced trial in 1968. It's high-minded and self-righteous. 85m. **DIR:** Gordon Davidson. **CAST:** Ed Flanders, Douglas Watson, William Schallert, Peter Strauss, Richard Jordan, Barton Heyman. **1972**

TRIAL OF THE INCREDIBLE HULK ★★★ The green goliath hits New York City, only to be jailed on murder charges. Defending him is blind attorney Matt Murdock, whose alter ego is the swashbuckling superhero Daredevil. Together they team up to bring down the city's biggest crime lord, The Kingpin. Made for TV. 93m. **DIR:** Bill Bixby. **CAST:** Bill Bixby, Lou Ferrigno, Rex Smith. **1989**

•TRIANGLE, THE ★★★1/2 This TBS Superstation original is a good old-fashioned ghost story that takes place aboard a phantom cruise liner in the Bermuda Triangle. Luke Perry, as a show-off living far beyond his means, is possessed by a murderer from days gone by. A touch of voodoo is thrown in for good measure. Adequate special effects are capped off by a spectacular ending. Not rated; contains violence, gore, and profanity. 92m. **DIR:** Lewis Teague. **CAST:** Luke Perry, Dan Cortese, Olivia D'Abo, Dorian Harewood. **2001 DVD**

TRIBES ★★★1/2 Long-haired peacenik Jan-Michael Vincent is drafted into the Marines and faces a tough time from drill instructor Darren McGavin. TV movie is far above the usual television schlock, with insightful script and solid acting. One of Vincent's best performances. Seems a bit dated by today's standards, but still worth a look. 74m. **DIR:** Joseph Sargent. **CAST:** Jan-Michael Vincent, Darren McGavin, Earl Holliman. **1970**

•TRIBULATION The Antichrist (Nick Mancuso) is still trying to take over the Earth in this sequel to *Apocalypse* and *Revelation*. Gary Busey plays an atheist cop who joins the fight against Satan. This may have higher production values than previous Christian-themed thrillers, but poor scripting and laughable special ef-

fects aren't likely to win over nonbelievers. Rated PG-13 for violence. 95m. **DIR:** Andre Van Heerden. **CAST:** Gary Busey, Phillip Jarrett, Margot Kidder, Nick Mancuso, Howie Mandel. **2000 DVD**

TRIBUTE ★★★1/2 A moving portrait of a man in crisis, *Tribute* bestows a unique gift to its audience: the feeling that they have come to know a very special man. Jack Lemmon stars as a Broadway press agent who has contracted a terminal blood disease and is feted by his friends in show business. Though adjusted to his fate, Lemmon finds that he has some unfinished business: to make peace with his son, Robby Benson. Rated PG. 121m. **DIR:** Bob Clark. **CAST:** Jack Lemmon, Robby Benson, Lee Remick, Colleen Dewhurst, John Marley. **1980**

TRIBUTE TO A BAD MAN ★★★★ A mean-spirited Western that works because of the personalities. James Cagney chews the scenery as a ruthless land baron who defies everyone to take advantage of him and his holdings. Cagney treats the role as if it were written for him, even though it was meant for Spencer Tracy, who passed on the project. 95m. **DIR:** Robert Wise. **CAST:** James Cagney, Irene Papas, Lee Van Cleef, Vic Morrow, Don Dubbins, Royal Dano, Stephen McNally. **1956**

TRICK ★★1/2 Two young gay men looking for a place to have a one-night stand, find themselves genuinely falling in love. The script takes some amusing turns, but Jim Fall's direction is flat. Rated R for sexual themes and profanity. 89m. **DIR:** Jim Fall. **CAST:** Christian Campbell, John Paul Pitoc, Tori Spelling, Steve Hays, Clinton Leupp. **1999 DVD**

TRICK OR TREAT (1982) 🦃 A slow-moving mess about a baby-sitter and a spoiled brat on Halloween. Not rated; contains violence and profanity. 90m. **DIR:** Gary Graver. **CAST:** Peter Jason, Chris Graver, David Carradine, Carrie Snodgress, Steve Railsback. **1982**

TRICK OR TREAT (1986) ★★1/2 Perhaps it was inevitable that someone would make a horror film about the supposed Satanic messages found in heavy-metal rock music. While not a classic of the genre, *Trick or Treat* is both clever and funny. Marc Price's performance is one of the film's pluses. Rated R for profanity, nudity, suggested sex, and violence. 97m. **DIR:** Charles Martin Smith. **CAST:** Marc Price, Doug Savant, Elaine Joyce, Gene Simmons, Ozzy Osbourne. **1986**

TRICKS ★★★ Mimi Rogers stars as a former Reno showgirl who has to resort to prostitution in order to stay alive. Excellent performances help buoy an otherwise unoriginal script. Rated R for sexuality, nudity, violence, and profanity. 96m. **DIR:** Kenneth Fink. **CAST:** Mimi Rogers, Tyne Daly, Ray Walston. **1997**

TRICKS OF THE TRADE ★★ Short-on-laughs comedy features Cindy Williams as a well-to-do housewife involved with a Hollywood prostitute (Markie Post) after her husband is murdered in Post's apartment. Made for TV. 94m. **DIR:** Jack Bender. **CAST:** Cindy Williams, Markie Post, Scott Paulin, John Ritter. **1988**

TRIGGER EFFECT, THE ★★★ A suburban neighborhood falls apart during a massive power failure. The simplistic civics-lesson premise isn't terribly original (a Baby Boomer rehash of *Lord of the Flies*), and performances are constricted into stereotypes to make specific dramatic points. Still, writer-director David Koepp manages some passable suspense. Rated R for profanity and violence. 93m. **DIR:** David Koepp. **CAST:** Kyle MacLachlan, Elisabeth Shue, Dermot Mulroney, Richard T. Jones. **1996 DVD**

TRIGGER FAST ★★ Low-budget Civil War–era action film aims high but fails. Martin Sheen plays Confederate Gen. Jackson Baines Hardin, assigned by the president to head down to Mexico to pardon some Southern soldiers. Rated R for violence. 96m. **DIR:** David Lister. **CAST:** Martin Sheen, Jurgen Prochnow, Christopher Atkins, Corbin Bernsen. **1993**

TRIGGER HAPPY (MAD DOG TIME) ★★★1/2 Off-beat gangster comedy about a mob boss whose outrageous behavior lands him in a mental hospital and when released he systematically begins rubbing out the competition and trusted friends. All-star cast breathes life into this quirky effort that's more talk than action. Rated R for violence, language, and sexuality. 92m. **DIR:** Larry Bishop. **CAST:** Richard Dreyfuss, Jeff Goldblum, Ellen Barkin, Gabriel Byrne, Diane Lane, Gregory Hines, Kyle MacLachlan, Burt Reynolds. **1996**

TRIGGER, JR. ★★★ Trucolor Roy Rogers film has everything going for it in the form of plot, songs, character actors, and hard ridin'. Roy, Dale, and the gang battle an unscrupulous gang of blackmailers as well as teach a young boy to overcome his fear of horses. 68m. **DIR:** William Witney. **CAST:** Roy Rogers, Dale Evans, Pat Brady, Gordon Jones, Grant Withers. **1950**

TRILOGY OF TERROR ★★★ Karen Black stars in this trio of horror stories, the best of which is the final episode, about an ancient Indian doll coming to life and stalking Black. It's often very frightening, and well worth wading through the first two tales. Originally made as an ABC Movie of the Week. 78m. **DIR:** Dan Curtis. **CAST:** Karen Black, Robert Burton, John Karlen. **1974 DVD**

TRILOGY OF TERROR II ★★★ Director Dan Curtis returns to a familiar format, with Lysette Anthony starring—as different characters—in three deliciously grim little shockers. Rated PG-13 for violence, gore, and profanity. 95m. **DIR:** Dan Curtis. **CAST:** Lysette Anthony, Geraint Wyn Davies, Geoffrey Lewis, Matt Clark, Blake Heron, Richard Fitzpatrick, Thomas Mitchell. **1996**

TRINITY IS STILL MY NAME ★★ In this comedy sequel to *They Call Me Trinity*, Bud Spencer and Terence Hill again team up as the unlikely heroes of an Italian Western. Rated G. 117m. **DIR:** E. B. Clucher. **CAST:** Bud Spencer, Terence Hill, Harry Carey Jr. **1972 DVD**

TRIO ★★★★ Wonderful collection of Somerset Maugham's short stories, introduced by Maugham. Each has a nice twist ending. "The Verger" centers on a man's decisions after being fired for his illiteracy. "Mr. Know-All" is an obnoxious bore who is shunned by the others on his cruise. Finally, Michael Rennie and Jean Simmons co-star as TB patients who fall in love while they live in the sanitorium. B&W; 88m. **DIR:** Ken Annakin, Harold French. **CAST:** Jean Simmons, Michael Rennie, Nigel Patrick, Wilfrid Hyde-White. **1950 DVD**

TRIP, THE ★★ Peter Fonda plays a director of TV commercials who discovers the kaleidoscopic pleasures of LSD. This features outdated special effects and sensibilities. Screenplay by Jack Nicholson. 85m. **DIR:** Roger Corman. **CAST:** Peter Fonda, Susan Strasberg, Bruce

Dern, Dennis Hopper, Dick Miller, Luana Anders, Peter Bogdanovich. **1967**

TRIP TO BOUNTIFUL, THE ★★★★1/2 In 1947, an elderly widow (wonderfully played by Oscar-winner Geraldine Page) leaves the cramped apartment where she lives with her loving but weak son and his demanding wife to return to the small town where she had spent her happy youth . . . unaware that it no longer exists. A joyous celebration of life. Rated PG. 105m. **DIR:** Peter Masterson. **CAST:** Geraldine Page, John Heard, Carlin Glynn, Richard Bradford, Rebecca DeMornay. **1986**

TRIPLE IMPACT 🦃 Tedious entry in kick-fighting series has three world champions battling the usual array of bad guys. Even three stars can't kick start this mess. Not rated; contains violence. 97m. **DIR:** David Hunt. **CAST:** Ron Hall, Dale "Apollo" Cook, Bridget "Baby Doll" Riley, Robert Marius. **1992**

TRIPLE JUSTICE ★★★1/2 Once again, star George O'Brien and director David Howard take a standard B Western plot and infuse it with intelligence, character, and excitement. O'Brien is a peaceable cowpoke who innocently joins a gang of bank robbers. Silly, but surprisingly effective. B&W; 65m. **DIR:** David Howard. **CAST:** George O'Brien, Virginia Vale, Paul Fix, Glenn Strange. **1940**

TRIPLECROSS (1985) ★★★ Harmless made-for-TV comedy about a trio of former police detectives who, after being left sizable fortunes by a grateful crime victim, now battle each other as to who can solve the crime *du jour*. 97m. **DIR:** David Greene. **CAST:** Ted Wass, Markie Post, Gary Swanson, Shannon Wilcox, Barbara Horan, Robert Costanzo, Ric Mancini, Mike Genovese, Dennis Farina. **1985**

TRIPLECROSS (1995) ★★★ Ambitious convict Michael Paré is released to set up former partner Patrick Bergin on a phony diamond heist, all so obsessed FBI agent Billy Dee Williams can finally lay his fixation to rest. J. A. Rosen's twisty script tries for too many surprises during its final act. Rated R for profanity, violence, nudity, and simulated sex. 95m. **DIR:** Jeno Hodi. **CAST:** Michael Paré, Billy Dee Williams, Ashley Laurence, Patrick Bergin, James Hong. **1995 DVD**

TRIPODS ★★1/2 Though a bit hard to follow because it is a compilation of episodes from the middle of a BBC science-fiction TV series, this is an interesting release about a young man's attempts to escape alien conquerors of Earth in the far future. Once free, our hero decides to join the rebel forces. 150m. **DIR:** Graham Theakston, Christopher Barry. **CAST:** John Shackley, Jim Baker, Ceri Seel, Richard Wordsworth. **1984**

TRIPPIN' ★★1/2 Procrastinating high school senior "G" Reed spends more time daydreaming than filling out college applications in this swirl of social messages, sexual fantasies, and street profanity. G's hilarious scenes with his mom, dad, and grandfather highlight this hip-hop comedy. Rated R for language and sexual content. 92m. **DIR:** David Raynr. **CAST:** Dean Richmond, Donald Faison, Maia Campbell, Aloma Wright, Harold Sylvester, Bill Henderson. **1999 DVD**

TRIPWIRE ★★★ During a gun exchange, a terrorist leader's son is killed by a special agent. Fast-paced and well-acted adventure that allows for character development as well. Rated R for violence. 92m. **DIR:** James Lemmo. **CAST:** Terence Knox, David Warner, Isabella Hoffman, Yaphet Kotto. **1989**

TRISTANA ★★★★ Luis Buñuel's hilarious, surreal drama about a young woman who becomes a victim of her own captivating beauty as she becomes the object of desire between two men. The film is a brilliant examination of moral decay through the dispassionate eye of Luis Buuel. In Spanish with English subtitles. Not rated. 98m. **DIR:** Luis Buñuel. **CAST:** Catherine Deneuve, Fernando Rey, Franco Nero. **1970**

TRIUMPH OF SHERLOCK HOLMES, THE ★★★1/2 A candle is the clue that unlocks the secret of a murder in this superior Sherlock Holmes film featuring Arthur Wontner and Ian Fleming as the infallible consulting detective and his friend and assistant Dr. John Watson. Made by an independent production company on a limited budget, this rendering of Conan Doyle's *Valley of Fear* retains much of the story's original dialogue. B&W; 75m. **DIR:** Leslie S. Hiscott. **CAST:** Arthur Wontner, Ian Fleming, Lyn Harding, Leslie Perrins. **1935**

TRIUMPH OF THE SPIRIT ★★★1/2 Willem Dafoe plays a Greek Jew imprisoned at Auschwitz who boxes for the entertainment of the Nazi officers. Dafoe's limp performance makes the film soft in the center, but the innate drama of the story, fine performances by Edward James Olmos and Robert Loggia, and Robert M. Young's firmly understated direction make it compelling. Rated R. 120m. **DIR:** Robert M. Young. **CAST:** Willem Dafoe, Edward James Olmos, Robert Loggia. **1990 DVD**

TRIUMPH OF THE WILL ★★★★1/2 World-renowned German documentary of the rise of Hitler's Third Reich is a masterpiece of propaganda and remains a chilling testament to the insanity that can lurk in great art. Director Leni Riefenstahl created a powerful and noble image of a German empire that was already threatening Europe and would eventually engulf the world in a devastating war. B&W; 110m. **DIR:** Leni Riefenstahl. **1935**

TRIUMPHS OF A MAN CALLED HORSE 🦃 Richard Harris only makes a brief appearance in the title role as John Morgan, an English nobleman who was captured by the Sioux in 1825. Instead, the story focuses on his bland warrior son. Rated PG for violence and implied sex. 86m. **DIR:** John Hough. **CAST:** Richard Harris, Michael Beck, Ana De Sade. **1983**

TRIXIE ★★ Emily Watson plays an aspiring private eye who speaks in hardboiled malapropisms ("Senator, I'm still green behind the ears") investigating a sinister plot involving a shady politician. The plot is halfhearted, the characters irritating. Director-writer Alan Rudolph attempts a combination of *film noir* and screwball comedy, but his filmmaking skills lack the rigorous discipline to bring off either genre. Rated R for profanity and some violence. 117m. **DIR:** Alan Rudolph. **CAST:** Emily Watson, Nick Nolte, Nathan Lane, Dermot Mulroney, Lesley Ann Warren. **2000 DVD**

TROJAN WAR ★★ A high-school nerd spends an eventful night when he sets out in search of a condom after the cheerleader of his dreams makes him a one-night-only offer. Strained comedy isn't as offensive as it sounds, but (aside from a brief appearance by Anthony Michael Hall as a cranky bus driver) it isn't very funny, either. Rated PG-13 for sexual themes and profanity. 84m. **DIR:** George Huang. **CAST:** Will Friedle, Jennifer

Love Hewitt, Marley Shelton, Anthony Michael Hall, Lee Majors. **1997**

TROJAN WOMEN, THE ★★ This Greek-American film is worth seeing for the four female leads. Unfortunately, the plot (revolving around the Trojan War and their defeat) is lost. Rated PG. 105m. **DIR:** Michael Cacoyannis. **CAST:** Katharine Hepburn, Vanessa Redgrave, Genevieve Bujold, Irene Papas. **1972**

TROLL 🦃 A family besieged by evil little creatures. Rated PG-13 for profanity, violence, and gore. 95m. **DIR:** John Carl Buechler. **CAST:** Noah Hathaway, Michael Moriarty, Shelley Hack, Jenny Beck, June Lockhart, Anne Lockhart, Sonny Bono, Brad Hall. **1986**

TROLL II 🦃 Flat sequel-of-sorts to producer Charles Band's original spoof. Family unleashes malevolent specter who wreaks havoc before being banished to late-night cable outlets everywhere. Rated PG-13 for violence. 95m. **DIR:** Drago Floyd. **CAST:** Michael Stephenson, Connie McFarland. **1992**

TROLL IN CENTRAL PARK, A ★★ Brightly animated but uninvolving story of a pair of city kids who find a wealth of wonder in Stanley, the troll with a green thumb. Like some of producer-director Don Bluth's previous work, the story can't hold a candle to the animation. Featuring songs from the songwriters of *An American Tail*. Voices of Dom DeLuise, Cloris Leachman, Charles Nelson Reilly. Rated G. 69m. **DIR:** Don Bluth, Gary Goldman. **1994 DVD**

TROMA'S WAR ★★1/2 A shoot-'em-up about a group of air-crash survivors stranded on a deserted island. This ragtag bunch soon find themselves fighting terrorists bent on taking over the United States with the AIDS virus. Made by the people responsible for *The Toxic Avenger*, this frequently tasteless flick combines violent action with totally deadpan comedy. Not rated. 105m. **DIR:** Michael Herz, Samuel Weil. **CAST:** Carolyn Beauchamp, Sean Bowen. **1988 DVD**

TRON ★★★ An enjoyable, if somewhat light-headed, piece of escapism, this science-fiction adventure concerns a computer genius (Jeff Bridges) who suspects evil doings by a corporate executive (David Warner). During his investigation, Bridges is zapped into another dimension and finds himself a player in a gladiatorial video game. Rated PG. 96m. **DIR:** Steven Lisberger. **CAST:** Jeff Bridges, David Warner, Bruce Boxleitner, Cindy Morgan, Barnard Hughes. **1982 DVD**

TROOP BEVERLY HILLS 🦃 Shelley Long as a ditsy Beverly Hills mom who agrees to act as the troop leader for her daughter's Wilderness Girls group. Rated PG. 105m. **DIR:** Jeff Kanew. **CAST:** Shelley Long, Craig T. Nelson, Betty Thomas, Mary Gross. **1989**

TROPIC OF CANCER ★★ Want to see what an X-rated movie looked like when major stars would appear in one and it wasn't box-office poison? Here you are. Henry Miller's account of a hedonistic American in Paris finds an eager interpreter in Rip Torn. Pretentious and dated. X-rated for profanity, full nudity, and simulated sex. 87m. **DIR:** Joseph Strick. **CAST:** Rip Torn, James Callahan, Ellen Burstyn. **1970**

TROPICAL HEAT ★★1/2 Exotic locales enhance this sultry mystery, as insurance-investigator Rick Rossovich travels to India to track down the widow of a maharaja killed on a hunting safari. What starts off as a job becomes an infatuation as dangerous as the woman he has fallen for. Sexual content in unrated version really turns up the *Tropical Heat*. Rated R for sex, nudity, adult situations, and violence; unrated version contains more of the same. 86/88. **DIR:** Jag Mundhra. **CAST:** Rick Rossovich, Maryam D'Abo, Lee Anne Beaman, Asha Siewkumar. **1993**

TROPICAL SNOW ★★★★ Realistic story about two lovers from South America whose dream is to get to America and make enough money to support their families. Suspenseful and harrowing. Rated R for nudity. 87m. **DIR:** Ciro Duran. **CAST:** Nick Corri, Madeleine Stowe, David Carradine. **1988**

TROUBLE ALONG THE WAY ★★★ Disillusioned, divorced ex–football coach John Wayne cares about only one thing: his young daughter. So when the Probation Bureau decides that he's an unfit father, Duke decides to fight back—by coaching a ragtag team for a rundown Catholic college. Sentimental Hollywood stuff played and directed with no-nonsense expertise. B&W; 110m. **DIR:** Michael Curtiz. **CAST:** John Wayne, Donna Reed, Charles Coburn, Sherry Jackson, Marie Windsor, Tom Tully, Leif Erickson, Chuck Connors. **1953**

TROUBLE BOUND ★★ Michael Madsen is a luckless gambler who wins a car with a body in the trunk. Then he hooks up with sexy waitress Patricia Arquette, who turns out to be the granddaughter of a Mafia kingpin. Decent performances, but a thriller should never be wacky. Rated R for profanity and violence. 90m. **DIR:** Jeffrey Reiner. **CAST:** Michael Madsen, Patricia Arquette. **1992**

TROUBLE IN MIND ★★★★ An ex-cop, Kris Kristofferson, is paroled from prison and returns to Rain City, hoping to rekindle his romance with café owner Genevieve Bujold. Once there, he falls in love with the wife (Lori Singer) of a thief (Keith Carradine). Director Alan Rudolph's ultrabizarre, semifuturistic tale is an unusual screen experience that almost defies description. Rated R. 111m. **DIR:** Alan Rudolph. **CAST:** Kris Kristofferson, Keith Carradine, Genevieve Bujold, Lori Singer, Joe Morton, Divine. **1986**

TROUBLE IN PARADISE ★★ Made for TV, a reworking of *Swept Away*, with a diplomat's widow and a roughneck Australian sailor castaway on a tropical island. When opposites begin to attract, drug smugglers intrude. A joy only for Raquel Welch watchers. 100m. **DIR:** Di Drew. **CAST:** Raquel Welch, Jack Thompson, Nicholas Hammond. **1988**

TROUBLE IN TEXAS ★★1/2 Two-fisted singing rodeo cowboy Tex Ritter investigates crooked rodeo contests and seeks the men responsible for the death of his brother. Future glamour girl Rita Hayworth appears onscreen for the last time under her real name (Cansino). This enjoyable oater boasts a wild chase on a dynamite-laden wagon for a finale. B&W; 53m. **DIR:** Robert N. Bradbury. **CAST:** Tex Ritter, Rita Hayworth, Earl Dwire, Yakima Canutt. **1937**

TROUBLE IN THE GLEN ★★ A white-haired, cigar-chomping Orson Welles in Scots kilts is farfetched, to say the least. The film turns on a feud over a closed road. Thoroughly scotched by poor pacing and a script that misses the mark. Deep-dyed Welles fans will like it. 91m. **DIR:** Herbert Wilcox. **CAST:** Orson Welles, Margaret Lockwood, Victor McLaglen, Forrest Tucker. **1953**

TROUBLE ON THE CORNER ★★★1/2 This smartly made indie takes us into the mind of a psychiatrist who is starting to lose his grip after years of listening to his patients' problems. A strong cast of familiar faces and intelligent direction by newcomer Alan Madison make this a good bet for film buffs with a taste for the unusual. Not rated; contains nudity, sexual situations, profanity, and violence. 104m. **DIR:** Alan Madison. **CAST:** Tony Goldwyn, Edie Falco, Debi Mazar, Tammy Grimes, Charles Busch, Giancarlo Esposito, Joe Morton, Roger Rees, Daniel Von Bargen. **1997**

TROUBLE WITH ANGELS, THE ★★★ Rosalind Russell stars as the Mother Superior at the St. Francis Academy for Girls. Her serenity and the educational pursuits of the institution are coming apart at the seams due to the pranks of two rambunctious teenagers, Hayley Mills and June Harding. This comedy's humor is uninspired, but the warmth and humanity of the entire production make it worthwhile family viewing. 112m. **DIR:** Ida Lupino. **CAST:** Rosalind Russell, Hayley Mills, June Harding. **1966**

TROUBLE WITH DICK, THE 🦃 Study of frustrated author's peculiar work habits becomes self-consciously banal after the first five minutes. 86m. **DIR:** Gary Walkow. **CAST:** Tom Villard, Susan Dey, Elaine Giftos, Elizabeth Gorcey. **1986**

TROUBLE WITH GIRLS, THE ★★★1/2 First of all, forget the stupid title, which has nothing to do with this charming tale of the Chautauqua Players of 1927. It's sort of a *Music Man*–ish tale about a troupe of entertainers. Elvis is the manager of the troupe. Sheree North is the tainted woman who is ruthlessly pursued by her lecherous boss (Dabney Coleman). Refreshingly above Elvis's inane girly films. Rated G. 105m. **DIR:** Peter Tewksbury. **CAST:** Elvis Presley, Sheree North, Vincent Price, Dabney Coleman. **1969**

TROUBLE WITH HARRY, THE ★★★★ Shirley MacLaine made her film debut in this wickedly funny black comedy, directed by Alfred Hitchcock. This is the last of long-unseen screen works by the master of suspense to be rereleased, and the most unusual, because the accent is on humor instead of tension-filled drama. In it, a murdered man causes no end of problems for his neighbors in a peaceful New England community. Rated PG when it was rereleased. 100m. **DIR:** Alfred Hitchcock. **CAST:** John Forsythe, Edmund Gwenn, Shirley MacLaine, Mildred Natwick, Jerry Mathers. **1955**

TROUBLE WITH SPIES, THE ★★ Even Donald Sutherland's amiable charm can't save this inept secret-agent spoof, which makes no sense at all. Producer-director Burt Kennedy, who also adapted the script from Marc Lovell's *Apple Spy in the Sky*, lacks the simplest knowledge of pacing, shading, or tonal consistency. Rated PG-13 for partial nudity. 91m. **DIR:** Burt Kennedy. **CAST:** Donald Sutherland, Ned Beatty, Ruth Gordon, Lucy Gutteridge, Michael Hordern, Robert Morley. **1984**

TROUBLEMAKERS ★★ Italian Western-comedy looks like it has been plucked from the 1970s, when stars Terence Hill and Bud Spencer teamed up for several *Trinity* films. Hill directs himself as a famous gunfighter forced to reunite with his bounty-hunter brother for Christmas. Some serviceable laughs, but the presence of Ruth Buzzi makes this film seem even more dated. Rated PG. 98m. **DIR:** Terence Hill. **CAST:** Terence Hill, Bud Spencer, Ruth Buzzi. **1994 DVD**

TRUCE, THE ★★★1/2 Based on the memoir of Italian writer Primo Levi, who spent ten months in Auschwitz during World War II and, after being liberated by the Red Army, joined the millions of displaced persons trying to make their way home in the chaos of peace. The episodic film is slow-paced but compelling, and the acting is fine. Rated R for mature themes and frank portrayal of the Holocaust. 116m. **DIR:** Francesco Rosi. **CAST:** John Turturro, Massimo Ghini, Rade Serbedzija, Agnieszka Wagner, Stefano Dionisi. **1996**

TRUCK TURNER ★★ Singer Isaac Hayes traded in his gold chains for guns in this disappointing action-thriller. He and Alan Weeks play bounty hunters on the run from vengeful gangster Yaphet Kotto. Rated R for violence, profanity, and sexual situations. 91m. **DIR:** Jonathan Kaplan. **CAST:** Isaac Hayes, Yaphet Kotto, Alan Weeks, Scatman Crothers, Stan Shaw. **1974**

TRUCKS ★★ Trucks come to life and start killing people in this made-for-cable thriller. Based on a Stephen King story, this version is not as intelligent or scary as the original tale. Poor acting and a silly plot are only partly redeemed by a chilling ending. Not rated; contains violence. 95m. **DIR:** Chris Thomson. **CAST:** Timothy Busfield, Brenda Bakke. **1997 DVD**

TRUCKSTOP WOMEN 🦃 A truck-stop prostitution racket. Rated R. 82m. **DIR:** Mark L. Lester. **CAST:** Claudia Jennings, Lieux Dressler, John Martino. **1974**

TRUE BELIEVER ★★★★ James Woods gives a powerhouse performance in this gripping thriller, tautly directed by Joseph Ruben. Woods plays a maverick lawyer who takes on the case of a convicted killer, only to find himself bucking the powers-that-be in New York City. Robert Downey Jr. gives an effective performance as Woods's assistant. Rated R for violence and profanity. 103m. **DIR:** Joseph Ruben. **CAST:** James Woods, Robert Downey Jr., Margaret Colin, Kurtwood Smith. **1989**

•TRUE BLUE ★★ By the book detective thriller starring Tom Berenger as a veteran NYPD officer whose latest case hits home when he lets a murder victim's roommate stay at his place, and then begins to fall in love with her. The city may be full of suspects, but the real crime is the predictable way the script telegraphs every plot point. Rated R for adult situations, language, and violence. 96m. **DIR:** J. S. Cardone. **CAST:** Tom Berenger, Pamela Gidley, Barry Newman, Lori Heuring. **2001 DVD**

TRUE COLORS ★★★1/2 John Cusack and James Spader give impressive performances in this thought-provoking drama about how the desire for power corrupts a political hopeful. Strong support from Richard Widmark, as a hard-nosed senator, and Mandy Patinkin, as a sleazy developer, adds to this morality tale. Rated R for violence and profanity. 111m. **DIR:** Herbert Ross. **CAST:** John Cusack, James Spader, Richard Widmark, Imogen Stubbs, Mandy Patinkin. **1991**

TRUE CONFESSIONS ★★★★1/2 This is the thoughtful, powerful story of two brothers (Robert De Niro and Robert Duvall)—one a priest, the other a jaded detective—caught in the sordid world of power politics in post–World War II Los Angeles. It's a brilliant and disturbing film. Rated R. 108m. **DIR:** Ulu Grosbard. **CAST:**

Robert De Niro, Robert Duvall, Charles Durning, Burgess Meredith. **1981**

TRUE CRIME (1995) ★★★ Alicia Silverstone plays an amateur teen sleuth, looking for leads in the death of a classmate. With the help of police cadet Kevin Dillon, she uncovers the trail of a serial killer. As she digs deeper, she learns that the truth lies close to home, and she can't trust anyone, including the cadet. Rated R for violence and language. 94m. **DIR:** Pat Verducci. **CAST:** Alicia Silverstone, Kevin Dillon, Bill Nunn. **1995 DVD**

TRUE CRIME (1999) ★★1/2 It's unfortunate that this film's lethargic style and pacing make it seem as slow and tired as leading man Clint Eastwood. Self-indulgent behavior distracts the audience right out of a tidy little thriller about a gung-ho reporter who realizes he has less than a day to prevent an innocent man from being executed. Rated R for profanity, coarse dialogue, and dramatic impact. 127m. **DIR:** Clint Eastwood. **CAST:** Clint Eastwood, Isaiah Washington, Denis Leary, Lisa Gay Hamilton, James Woods, Diane Venora, Bernard Hill, Michael McKean, Michael Jeter. **1999 DVD**

TRUE GRIT ★★★★ John Wayne finally won his best-actor Oscar for his 1969 portrayal of a boozy marshal helping a tough-minded girl (Kim Darby) track down her father's killers. Well-directed by Henry Hathaway, it's still not one of the Duke's classics—although it does have many good scenes, the best of which is the final shoot-out between Wayne's Rooster Cogburn and chief baddie, Ned Pepper (Robert Duvall). Rated G. 128m. **DIR:** Henry Hathaway. **CAST:** John Wayne, Kim Darby, Robert Duvall, Glen Campbell. **1969 DVD**

TRUE HEART ★★★1/2 Enjoyable story about a pair of siblings, plane-wrecked in Canada, and the forest-dwelling native who helps them survive. Perfect for family viewing. Rated PG. 92m. **DIR:** Catherine Cyran. **CAST:** Kirsten Dunst, Zachery Ty Bryan, August Schellengberg, Dey Young, Michael Gross. **1997**

TRUE HEART SUSIE ★★★ Lillian Gish and Robert Herron are sweethearts in a small, rural, bedrock-solid American town in this sentimental silent film account of a young girl's transition from scatterbrained, uninhibited adolescent to dignified, self-assured woman. Sensitive acting and directing make what could have been cloying mush a touching, charming excursion back to what are nostalgically recalled as "the good old days." B&W; 62m. **DIR:** D. W. Griffith. **CAST:** Lillian Gish, Robert Herron, Wilbur Higby, George Fawcett, Carol Dempster. **1919**

TRUE IDENTITY ★★★ British comedian Lenny Henry makes his film debut in this generally enjoyable entry about an aspiring black actor who must masquerade as a white hit man. It's the little insights provided by director Charles Lane and the occasional big laughs from Henry's clowning that make this movie worth watching. Rated R for violence and profanity. 106m. **DIR:** Charles Lane. **CAST:** Lenny Henry, Frank Langella, Charles Lane, J. T. Walsh, Anne-Marie Johnson, Andreas Katsulas, Michael McKean, Peggy Lipton. **1991**

TRUE LIES ★★★★ Secret agent Arnold Schwarzenegger is content to pose as a dull computer salesman until he's forced to give his wife a taste of the real thing when he attempts to stop an Arab terrorist. Thrill-packed, special effects–laden, and little touches make it work. Rated R for violence, profanity, and suggested sex. 141m. **DIR:** James Cameron. **CAST:** Arnold Schwarzenegger, Jamie Lee Curtis, Tom Arnold, Bill Paxton, Tia Carrere, Art Malik, Charlton Heston. **1994 DVD**

TRUE LOVE ★★★★ A very funny yet sometimes painful look at the preparations for a New York wedding. From the engagement party to the wedding day, director Nancy Savoca finds all the comedy and drama involved between two people who probably shouldn't get married—and the family and friends around them. Rated R for profanity. 100m. **DIR:** Nancy Savoca. **CAST:** Annabella Sciorra, Ron Eldard. **1990**

TRUE ROMANCE ★★★★ Quentin Tarantino supplied the screenplay for this outrageously violent black comedy about a modern-day Bonnie and Clyde (albeit of the naïve and innocent variety) who get chased across the United States by the police and the mob. Wild performances by an all-star cast are certainly something to see and the story constantly surprises. Rated R for violence, profanity, simulated sex, and drug use. 120m. **DIR:** Tony Scott. **CAST:** Christian Slater, Patricia Arquette, Dennis Hopper, Christopher Walken, Val Kilmer, Gary Oldman, Brad Pitt, Bronson Pinchot, Conchata Ferrell, Saul Rubinek, Samuel L. Jackson, Michael Rapaport, Tom Sizemore, Christopher Penn. **1993 DVD**

TRUE STORIES ★★1/2 *True Stories* is Talking Heads leader David Byrne's satirical look at the imaginary town of Virgil, Texas. It's a mixture of *The National Enquirer* and deadpan cinematic humor. Some of the bits are truly funny, but the lethargic tone becomes an aggravating artistic conceit. Rated PG. 89m. **DIR:** David Byrne. **CAST:** David Byrne, John Goodman, Annie McEnroe, Swoosie Kurtz, Spalding Gray. **1986 DVD**

TRUE STORY OF FRANKENSTEIN, THE ★★★1/2 Well-written and -executed documentary surveys public fascination with Mary Shelley's unique gothic horror story through interviews with scholars and cinema personalities connected with the story over the years. Mel Brooks, Gene Wilder, Kenneth Branagh, John Cleese, and Robert De Niro are among film luminaries interviewed along with a coterie of English literature professors. A must for horror fans. 100m. **DIR:** Richard Brown. **1995**

TRUE WEST ★★★★ Sam Shepard's powerful play about sibling rivalry and responsibility is masterfully performed by members of the Steppenwolf Theater Company for public television. John Malkovich stars as a reclusive drifter who returns home to make his brother, a Hollywood screenwriter, sit up and take notice. Not rated. 110m. **DIR:** Gary Sinise. **CAST:** John Malkovich, Gary Sinise. **1983**

TRUE WOMEN ★★★★ Soaring Hallmark Productions presentation depicts the heartaches and struggles that faced pioneer women when their husbands were off winning independence from Mexico. Dana Delany and Annabeth Gish are superb as sisters Sarah and Euphemia, who are forced to summon up all of the courage within themselves and each other in order to fend off intruders and death. Both heroic and somber, this handsome period piece was originally broadcast as a television miniseries. Rated PG for violence. 170m. **DIR:** Karen Arthur. **CAST:** Dana Delany, Annabeth Gish, Angelina Jolie, Powers Boothe, Michael York, Charles Dutton. **1997**

TRUEBLOOD ★★1/2 Writer-director Frank Kerr gives a 1980s spin to urban underworld dramas of the 1940s like *The Naked City* and *Kiss of Death*. Jeff Fahey and Chad Lowe are brothers, estranged for ten years, who try to rebuild their relationship on the mean streets of Brooklyn. Rated R for profanity and graphic violence. 100m. **DIR:** Frank Kerr. **CAST:** Jeff Fahey, Chad Lowe. **1989**

TRULY, MADLY, DEEPLY ★★★★1/2 British writer-director Anthony Minghella's directorial debut is a truly, madly, deeply wonderful motion picture. Juliet Stevenson gives a remarkable performance as a young woman whose overpowering grief over the death of her lover turns to joy and maturity when he returns to help her back to the world of the living. Not rated, the film has brief profanity. 107m. **DIR:** Anthony Minghella. **CAST:** Juliet Stevenson, Alan Rickman, Bill Paterson, Michael Maloney. **1991 DVD**

TRUMAN ★★★★ Gary Sinise dominates this stylish adaptation of David McCullough's presidential biography, as a resolutely moral and dignified gentleman who can give 'em hell. More than anything, this made-for-HBO film evokes nostalgia for simpler times, and for the accidental ascension of a president. Rated PG-13 for profanity. 130m. **DIR:** Frank Pierson. **CAST:** Gary Sinise, Diana Scarwid, Richard Dysart, Colm Feore, James Gammon, Tony Goldwyn, Pat Hingle, Harris Yulin. **1995 DVD**

TRUMAN SHOW, THE ★★★★★ Profound and wildly outrageous bit of "theater of the absurd" boasts a cleverly crafted script, a frankly astonishing performance from Jim Carrey, and shrewd direction by Aussie Peter Weir. Carrey's Truman Burbank lives the American dream in a postcard-perfect small town, little realizing that he's the "star" of his own life, being broadcast twenty-four hours a day to an engrossed world. He's the only one who doesn't know it . . . although his suspicions are mounting. Rated PG for mild profanity. 104m. **DIR:** Peter Weir. **CAST:** Jim Carrey, Laura Linney, Ed Harris, Noah Emmerich. **1998 DVD**

•TRUMPET OF THE SWAN, THE ★★ Colorful but flat adaptation of the children's story about a Canadian trumpeter swan named Louie who cannot speak but desperately wants to voice his feelings to another swan named Serena. After several failed attempts at finding his own voice, Louie's father buys him a trumpet as a substitute. Louie becomes so good on the trumpet that he gains the attention of a shady street entrepreneur who promises him fame and fortune. Okay animation but insufficient magic and whimsy to entertain more than the wee small ones. Rated G. 75m. **DIR:** Richard Rich, Terry L. Noss. **CAST:** Jason Alexander, Mary Steenburgen, Reese Witherspoon, Carol Burnett, Seth Green. **2001 DVD**

TRUST ★★★★ Surprisingly touching tale of a pregnant high school dropout (whose father keels over dead with the baby news) and a somewhat older nihilistic electronics whiz (whose mother died giving birth to him). Surreal, but somehow believable. Rated R for language. 90m. **DIR:** Hal Hartley. **CAST:** Adrienne Shelly, Martin Donovan. **1991**

TRUST ME ★★★ Ex-rocker Adam Ant is an L.A. art dealer who loves the high life, but is on the verge of bankruptcy. Observing that dead artists' works seem to sell better than live ones, he starts looking for some talent that might be suicidal or terminal. Interesting black comedy. Rated R for language. 94m. **DIR:** Bobby Houston. **CAST:** Adam Ant, Talia Balsam, Barbara Bain. **1989**

TRUTH ABOUT CATS AND DOGS, THE ★★★★ Janeane Garofalo's starring debut is a delightful romantic comedy with echoes of *Cyrano de Bergerac*. She's a plain-Jane radio veterinarian who fears her reality won't live up to expectations. All sorts of entanglements ensue when she sends a blonde friend on a date in her place. The human performers receive able assistance from one of the greatest dogs in the world. Rated PG-13 for profanity and strong sexual content. 97m. **DIR:** Michael Lehmann. **CAST:** Janeane Garofalo, Uma Thurman, Ben Chaplin, Jamie Foxx, James McCaffrey. **1996 DVD**

TRUTH ABOUT WOMEN, THE ★★1/2 Playboy Laurence Harvey flirts with every woman in sight in this comedy-drama. This British production has a fine cast, especially Julie Harris, and the production design is also quite good, but it's sooo slow. 98m. **DIR:** Muriel Box. **CAST:** Laurence Harvey, Julie Harris, Eva Gabor, Diane Cilento, Mai Zetterling, Wilfrid Hyde-White. **1958**

TRUTH OR CONSEQUENCES, N.M. ★★★★ A group of petty criminals steals a shipment of drugs and finds themselves fleeing not only the cops but the mob as well. Kiefer Sutherland's directing debut is a stylish, edgy thriller with taut performances by all. Rated R for violence and language. 101m. **DIR:** Kiefer Sutherland. **CAST:** Vincent Gallo, Mykelti Williamson, Kiefer Sutherland, Kevin Pollak, Kim Dickens, Grace Phillips. **1997 DVD**

TRUTH OR DARE ★★★★ Pop superstar Madonna allowed first-time filmmaker Alek Keshishian complete access—both onstage and backstage—to her 1990 Blond Ambition tour. The result is a fascinating, not-so-flattering look at one of contemporary music's true phenomena. Rated R for nudity and profanity. 118m. **DIR:** Alek Keshishian. **CAST:** Madonna, Warren Beatty, Sandra Bernhard, Kevin Costner. **1991 DVD**

TRUTH OR DARE? A CRITICAL MADNESS The old grade-school game turns deadly in this unrelentingly bad movie credited to director Yale Wilson, although the culprit is really Tim Ritter. Not rated; contains violence, profanity, and gore. 87m. **DIR:** Yale Wilson. **CAST:** John Brace, Mary Fanaro. **1987**

TRUTH OR DIE ★★★1/2 Tony Danza delivers a powerful performance as convicted killer Jerry Rosenberg, sentenced to the electric chair, who turns his life around while on death row. Made-for-TV film, also known as *Doing Life*. 100m. **DIR:** Gene Reynolds. **CAST:** Tony Danza, Lisa Langlois, Alvin Epstein, Jon De Vries. **1986**

TRY AND GET ME ★★★1/2 A desperate, unemployed husband and father (Frank Lovejoy) teams up with a ruthless thief and murderer (Lloyd Bridges) but can't live with his guilt after their crime spree. Interesting analysis of criminality, yellow journalism, and mob rule. Not rated; contains violence. 91m. **DIR:** Cy Endfield. **CAST:** Frank Lovejoy, Lloyd Bridges, Kathleen Ryan, Richard Carlson. **1950**

TRYST Ludicrous and laughable tale about a rich woman (Barbara Carrera), her jealous husband (David

Warner), and their housemaid's son (Steve Bond). Completely unsuccessful attempt to take a new angle on the *Double Indemnity* and *Body Heat* types of filmmaking. Rated R for profanity, nudity, sexual situations, and violence. 101m. **DIR:** Peter Foldy. **CAST:** Barbara Carrera, Louise Fletcher, David Warner, Steve Bond. **1994**

TUCK EVERLASTING ★★★1/2 Entertaining family film about a 12 year old girl who discovers a family of immortals living in the woods on her father's property. She becomes involved in their lives and is eventually entrusted with their secret. Rated G. 100m. **DIR:** Frederick King Keller. **CAST:** Margaret Chamberlain, Fred A. Keller, James McGuire, Sonia Raimi. **1980**

TUCKER: A MAN AND HIS DREAM ★★★1/2 Francis Ford Coppola has always admired Preston Tucker, entrepreneurial genius and designer of a Forties automobile built to challenge the big three automakers. This movie catches the spirit of postwar times when everything seemed possible. Rated PG for language. 130m. **DIR:** Francis Ford Coppola. **CAST:** Jeff Bridges, Frederic Forrest, Joan Allen, Dean Stockwell, Martin Landau, Mako, Lloyd Bridges, Christian Slater. **1988**

TUFF TURF ★★ A forgettable movie about young love as the new kid in town falls for a streetwise young woman with a dangerous lover. Rated R for violence, profanity, and suggested sex. 112m. **DIR:** Fritz Kiersch. **CAST:** James Spader, Kim Richards, Paul Mones. **1984**

TULIPS 🦃 Canadian-made comedy casts Gabe Kaplan and Bernadette Peters as would-be suicides. Rated PG. 91m. **DIR:** Stan Ferris. **CAST:** Gabe Kaplan, Bernadette Peters, Henry Gibson, Al Waxman. **1981**

TULSA ★★1/2 Typical potboiler has feisty Susan Hayward as a strong-willed woman intent on drilling oil wells on her property no matter who tries to interfere. Standard stock situations made more palatable by fine cast of character actors. 90m. **DIR:** Stuart Heisler. **CAST:** Susan Hayward, Robert Preston, Pedro Armendariz, Chill Wills, Ed Begley Sr. **1949**

TULSA KID ★★★1/2 Don Barry deserts his gunfighter heritage to aid defenseless pioneers threatened by a ruthless racketeer and his hired gunman—who turns out to be Barry's foster father. B&W; 57m. **DIR:** George Sherman. **CAST:** Don Barry, Noah Beery Sr., Luana Walters. **1940**

TUMBLEWEEDS (1925) ★★★1/2 One of silent films' greatest action sequences, the Oklahoma Land Rush along the Cherokee Strip, highlights this prestigious Western, famed cowboy star William S. Hart's final film. He retired to write novels. This version, which was introduced with a prologue spoken by Hart—his only venture into sound film—was released in 1939. Silent, with musical score. B&W; 114m. **DIR:** William S. Hart, King Baggott. **CAST:** William S. Hart, Barbara Bedford, Lucien Littlefield, Lillian Leighton. **1925**

TUMBLEWEEDS (1999) ★★★★1/2 Janet McTeer turns in a fantastic performance as a single mother who, on a whim, packs up her daughter and herself and travels across the country, leaving behind whichever man she was living with at the time. When her current attack of wanderlust brings them to San Diego, her daughter wants to ensure that they cease the endless moving and plant their roots there. The remarkable mother-daughter relationship between McTeer and newcomer Kimberly J. Brown is the underlying strength that makes this a very good movie. Rated PG-13 for language and mild adult situations. 100m. **DIR:** Gavin O'Connor. **CAST:** Janet McTeer, Kimberly J. Brown, Jay O. Sanders. **1999 DVD**

TUNE, THE ★★★ Animator Bill Plympton's first feature is a whimsical endeavor. He uses his trademark style to tell the tale of a songwriter at a creative crossroads, who gets swept into the imaginary world of Flooby Nooby. Plympton experiments with various musical styles, each one complimented by his strange, surreal animation. Most unusual. Not rated. 72m. **DIR:** Bill Plympton. **1993 DVD**

TUNE IN TOMORROW ★★★ Thoroughly enjoyable romp has young, impressionable Keanu Reeves falling for spinster aunt Barbara Hershey, while assisting writer Peter Falk on a radio serial. Free-wheeling adaptation of Mario Vargas Llosa's *Aunt Julia and the Scriptwriter*—worth turning the dial for. Rated PG-13 for profanity. 102m. **DIR:** Jon Amiel. **CAST:** Peter Falk, Keanu Reeves, Barbara Hershey, Bill McCutcheon. **1990**

TUNES OF GLORY ★★★★ Gripping drama of rivalry between embittered older soldier Alec Guinness and his younger replacement John Mills is a classic study of cruelty as Guinness loses no opportunity to bully and belittle the competent but less aggressive Mills. Superb acting highlights this tragic story. 107m. **DIR:** Ronald Neame. **CAST:** Alec Guinness, John Mills, Susannah York, Dennis Price, Duncan Macrae, Kay Walsh, Gordon Jackson, John Fraser, Allan Cuthbertson. **1960**

TUNNEL, THE 🦃 Married woman and her obsessive lover. Rated R for nudity, simulated sex, and violence. 99m. **DIR:** Antonio Drove. **CAST:** Jane Seymour, Peter Weller, Fernando Rey. **1987**

TUNNEL OF LOVE, THE ★★★1/2 A mild sex farce, with Doris Day and Richard Widmark tied up in the adoption process. He considers adopting his own child as a result of his fling with social worker Gia Scala. B&W; 98m. **DIR:** Gene Kelly. **CAST:** Doris Day, Richard Widmark, Gig Young, Gia Scala. **1958**

TUNNEL VISION (1994) ★★★ Australian thriller focuses on a team of police officers (Patsy Kensit and Robert Reynolds) as they pursue a serial killer. Their relationship to each other takes center stage with a very surprising twist at the end. Gratuitous nudity and gore cheapen the film a bit, but edge-of-your-seat suspense keeps you watching. Not rated; contains nudity, violence, profanity, and gore. 100m. **DIR:** Clive Fleury. **CAST:** Patsy Kensit, Robert Reynolds, Rebecca Rigg, Gary Day, Shane Briant. **1994**

TUNNELVISION (1976) ★★1/2 Here is a lightweight spoof of television. Sometimes it is funny, and other times it is just gross. The "stars," like Chevy Chase, have small bits. Still, there are some funny moments. *Tunnelvision* is like *The Groove Tube* in most respects, the good equally in proportion to the bad. Rated R. 67m. **DIR:** Neal Israel, Brad Swirnoff. **CAST:** Chevy Chase, Howard Hesseman, Betty Thomas, Laraine Newman. **1976 DVD**

TURBO: A POWER RANGERS ADVENTURE 🦃 Abundantly cleavaged space pirate Divatox is pursued by the Rangers as she kidnaps a cuddly wizard (a cross between Yoda and a Troll doll) and tries to release a mon-

ster from an island lava pit in this fantasy adventure ripe with cheesy special effects, bad acting, and lame pseudorock music. Morph me outta here. Rated PG. 90m. **DIR:** David Winning, Shuki Levy. **CAST:** Jason David Frank, Steve Cardenas, Johnny Yong Bosch, Catherine Sutherland, Nakia Burrise, Blake Foster, Hilary Shepard Turner. **1997 DVD**

TURBULENCE ★★1/2 Ray Liotta riffs wickedly on the cunning psycho groove he developed in *Unlawful Entry* in this implausible but tense thriller. A convicted serial killer shoots his cop escorts and takes over a 747 en route from New York to Los Angeles on Christmas Eve. A feisty flight attendant locks herself in the cockpit (while the twisted felon and a level-six thunderstorm stalk her), then tries to get home safely. Rated R for suspense, violence, and language. 103m. **DIR:** Robert Butler. **CAST:** Ray Liotta, Lauren Holly, Ben Cross, Rachel Ticotin, Hector Elizondo, Brendan Gleeson. **1997 DVD**

•**TURBULENCE 2** ★★1/2 A group of people, fearful of flying, must take a short flight in order to pass a phobia-curing course. All of them stress and struggle to do this relatively simple task, and once all passengers have calmed down and the plane takes off, the commercial flight is summarily hijacked. Other than being predictable and having no stars from the first film, *Turbulence 2* is a decent airborne thriller. Rated R for language and violence. 104m. **DIR:** David Mackay. **CAST:** Craig Sheffer, Jennifer Beals, Tom Berenger. **2000 DVD**

•**TURBULENCE 3: HEAVY METAL** ★★ Glam rock sensation Slade Craven holds a concert at 30,000 feet, simultaneously broadcasted worldwide on the Internet. A crazed impostor takes control of the show and the lives of everyone on board are in jeopardy. The only one that can help is an Internet hacker (Craig Sheffer) who gets in contact with the real Slade Craven trapped on the plane. The Marilyn Manson parody is entertaining, but it can't hold the whole movie together. Rated R for violence. 98m. **DIR:** Jorge Montesi. **CAST:** Craig Sheffer, Gabrielle Anwar, Joe Mantegna, Rutger Hauer. **2001 DVD**

TURK 182 ★★ Timothy Hutton stars as a young man who embarks on a personal crusade against injustice. His older brother (Robert Urich), a fireman, has been denied his pension after being injured while saving a child from a burning building when he was off-duty. This is one of those manipulative movies thought by their makers to be a surefire hit. It's anything but. Rated PG-13 for violence, profanity, and suggested sex. 102m. **DIR:** Bob Clark. **CAST:** Timothy Hutton, Robert Urich, Kim Cattrall, Robert Culp, Darren McGavin, Peter Boyle. **1985**

TURKISH BATH, THE ★★★1/2 When an Italian goes to Istanbul to sell the Turkish bath he inherited from his expatriate aunt, he finds himself irresistibly drawn to the people and culture of Turkey. Released in America as *Steam: The Turkish Bath* and promoted as a gay romance, this film is actually about the contrast of cultures on several levels, including sexuality. In Italian and Turkish with English subtitles. Not rated; contains mature themes and brief scenes of homosexuality. 98m. **DIR:** Ferzan Ozpetek. **CAST:** Alessandro Gassman, Francesca D'Aloja, Carlo Cecchi, Halil Ergün. **1997**

TURKISH DELIGHT ★★★1/2 Those already familiar with the work of Dutch director Paul Verhoeven (*Spetters, The 4th Man*) will be the most appreciative audience for this drama about a bohemian artist and his wife. Others may be put off by the graphic sexuality and crude behavior. Dubbed in English. 96m. **DIR:** Paul Verhoeven. **CAST:** Rutger Hauer, Monique van de Ven. **1974 DVD**

TURN IT UP ★★ An aspiring hip-hop artist tries to make it big, dragged down by his best friend, a doomed loser. In fact, they're both losers—repellent, unlikable, murdering thugs. The story has an urban toughness, but it's riddled with the clichés of countless show-biz movies. Rated R for profanity and violence. 86m. **DIR:** Robert Adetuyi. **CAST:** Pras, Ja Rule, Jason Statham, Vondie Curtis Hall, Tamala Jones. **2000 DVD**

TURN OF THE SCREW, THE (1989) ★★★ This chilling entry in Shelley Duvall's *Nightmare Classics* features Amy Irving as the heroine of Henry James's novel. As a new governess, she tries to instill her two new charges with morality. In the process she must take on the evil spirit that possesses them. Not rated; contains nudity and violence. 55m. **DIR:** Graeme Clifford. **CAST:** Amy Irving, David Hemmings, Balthazar Getty, Micole Mercurio. **1989**

TURN OF THE SCREW (1992) ★★★★ Updated to the 1960s, this is an intense and intelligent adaptation of Henry James's moody masterpiece. Julian Sands hires Patsy Kensit to tutor his odd niece and nephew, without revealing the secrets of his country house. Heavy doses of eroticism help build the tension to a creepy, albeit overly symbolic conclusion. Rated R for brief nudity and simulated sex. 95m. **DIR:** Rusty Lemorande. **CAST:** Patsy Kensit, Stéphane Audran, Julian Sands, Marianne Faithfull. **1992**

TURNER AND HOOCH ★★★ *K-9* redux! Tom Hanks is a fussy police detective who finds himself stuck with a mean junkyard dog who is the only witness to a murder. Once again the Hanks magic elevates a predictable story into a fun film. Rated PG. 110m. **DIR:** Roger Spottiswoode. **CAST:** Tom Hanks, Mare Winningham. **1989 DVD**

TURNING POINT, THE ★★★★1/2 Well-crafted drama about a pair of dancers both blessed and cursed with the aftermaths of their own personal turning points. Blended with the story is a series of beautifully rendered ballet sequences featuring Mikhail Baryshnikov, in his film debut. Rated PG for intensity of theme. 119m. **DIR:** Herbert Ross. **CAST:** Anne Bancroft, Shirley MacLaine, Mikhail Baryshnikov, Leslie Browne, Tom Skerritt. **1977**

TURTLE BEACH (KILLING BEACH) ★★★ Shocking images propel this sobering, thought-provoking movie about the plight of the Vietnamese boat people. Set on the east Malaysian coast, it depicts an ongoing human tragedy, which two women, a journalist and a courtesan attempt to stop. Rated R for violence, suggested sex, and nudity. 88m. **DIR:** Stephen Wallace. **CAST:** Greta Scacchi, Joan Chen, Jack Thompson, Art Malik, Norman Kaye. **1992**

TURTLE DIARY ★★★★1/2 Deliciously offbeat bit of British whimsy about people living side by side but rarely touching. An author of children's books and a bookstore assistant share an obsession for turtles and

devise a plan to free creatures from a nearby zoo. Rated PG for nudity. 97m. **DIR:** John Irvin. **CAST:** Glenda Jackson, Ben Kingsley, Richard Johnson, Michael Gambon, Rosemary Leach, Eleanor Bron, Harriet Walter, Jeroen Krabbé. **1986**

TUSKEGEE AIRMEN, THE ★★★★ Inspirational docudrama about the first all-black WWII pilot squadron to actually face aerial combat. The flying footage is impressive, as are the facts revealed just prior to the closing credits. Rated PG-13 for profanity and wartime violence. 107m. **DIR:** Robert Markowitz. **CAST:** Laurence Fishburne, Allen Payne, Malcolm-Jamal Warner, Courtney B. Vance, Andre Braugher, Christopher McDonald, Daniel Hugh Kelly, John Lithgow, Cuba Gooding Jr. **1995 DVD**

TUSKS ★★1/2 Shot in the African wilderness, this tale of a conservationist kidnapped by a poacher to act as bait for the game warden is sometimes bogged down by bad writing and uneven pacing. When it is in stride, though, it is a tense and vicious look at man against animal. Rated R for nudity and profanity. 99m. **DIR:** Tara Moore. **CAST:** Lucy Gutteridge, Andrew Stevens, John Rhys-Davies, Julian Glover. **1990**

TUTTLES OF TAHITI, THE ★★★ Captain Bligh goes native in this comedy of arch indolence and planned sloth in beautiful, bountiful Tahiti. Impoverished Charles Laughton and Florence Bates are rivals whose son Jon Hall and daughter Peggy Drake respectively fall in love. A good-natured, congenial film of leisure life. B&W; 91m. **DIR:** Charles Vidor. **CAST:** Charles Laughton, Jon Hall, Peggy Drake, Mala, Florence Bates, Alma Ross, Victor Francen, Curt Bois, Gene Reynolds. **1942**

TUXEDO WARRIOR ★★ Trite story about a bar owner/soldier of fortune (John Wyman) who becomes embroiled with diamond thieves in South Africa. Two stars for the British accents and some decent action. Not rated; contains violence and profanity. 93m. **DIR:** Andrew Sinclair. **CAST:** John Wyman, Carol Royle, Holly Palance, James Coburn Jr. **1982**

TV'S BEST ADVENTURES OF SUPERMAN ★★★1/2 Excellent series of tapes combines two episodes of the TV series from the 1950s, one color and one black-and-white, with a Superman cartoon from the Max Fleischer Studios. This series is highly collectible for fans. B&W; 60m. **DIR:** Thomas Carr, George Reeves, Harry Gerstad, Dave Fleischer. **CAST:** George Reeves, Noel Neill, Phyllis Coates, Jack Larson, John Hamilton. **1950**

TWELFTH NIGHT ★★★★ Shakespeare's gender comedy gets a delightful spin in scripter-director Trevor Nunn's lavish adaptation, with sensational Imogen Stubbs as the bereft young woman who disguises herself as a man in order to make her way in a country at war with her homeland. Rated PG for mild sensuality. 134m. **DIR:** Trevor Nunn. **CAST:** Imogen Stubbs, Helena Bonham Carter, Richard E. Grant, Nigel Hawthorne, Ben Kingsley, Mel Smith, Toby Stephens, Nicolas Farrell. **1996**

12 ANGRY MEN (1957) ★★★★★ A superb cast under inspired direction makes this film brilliant in every aspect. Henry Fonda is the holdout on a jury who desperately seeks to convince his eleven peers to reconsider their hasty conviction of a boy accused of murdering his father. The struggle behind closed doors is taut, charged, and fascinating. B&W; 95m. **DIR:** Sidney Lumet. **CAST:** Henry Fonda, Lee J. Cobb, Ed Begley Sr., E. G. Marshall, Jack Klugman, Jack Warden, Martin Balsam, John Fiedler, Robert Webber, George Voskovec, Edward Binns, Joseph Sweeney. **1957 DVD**

12 ANGRY MEN (1997) ★★★★★ Reginald Rose's compelling story hasn't lost any of its power and this sizzling remake retains the clever premise and all the piquant dialogue while updating the concept with an integrated cast . . . and what a cast! A lone juror isn't necessarily convinced that a young man is guilty of killing his father; the other eleven men react with varying degrees of curiosity, disbelief, and outrage. As time passes in the hot, non-air-conditioned room the holdout gradually wears away at his companions' resolve, setting in motion what turns into a murder mystery by proxy. Absolutely sensational. Rated PG-13 for profanity. 116m. **DIR:** William Friedkin. **CAST:** Jack Lemmon, Courtney B. Vance, Ossie Davis, George C. Scott, Armin Mueller-Stahl, Dorian Harewood. **1997**

TWELVE CHAIRS, THE ★★★ Based on a Russian comedy fable about an impoverished nobleman seeking jewels secreted in one of a dozen fancy dining room chairs. Ron Moody is the anguished Russian, Dom DeLuise his chief rival in the hunt. Mel Brooks's direction keeps things moving with laughs. Rated G. 94m. **DIR:** Mel Brooks. **CAST:** Mel Brooks, Dom DeLuise, Frank Langella, Ron Moody. **1970 DVD**

TWELVE MILES OUT ★★1/2 Rumrunners on the lam break into a house and kidnap a man and his bored young fiancée. Just as rogue John Gilbert and captive Joan Crawford are warming up to each other, Gilbert's outlaw pal shows up and wants part of the action—and *all* of Joan. The two outlaws shoot it out, and when the law finally does arrives, it's too late. Originally released at 85 minutes, this version is all that is currently available. B&W; 60m. **DIR:** Jack Conway. **CAST:** John Gilbert, Joan Crawford, Ernest Torrence, Edward Earle. **1927**

12 MONKEYS ★★★★1/2 Bruce Willis gives a terrific performance as a time traveler from the future sent to the past to save mankind from extinction. You don't dare miss a single minute of Terry Gilliam's masterpiece, a work on a par with the best in the genre. Rated R for violence, profanity, and nudity. 130m. **DIR:** Terry Gilliam. **CAST:** Bruce Willis, Madeleine Stowe, Brad Pitt, Christopher Plummer, Jon Seda, Joseph Melito. **1995 DVD**

TWELVE MONTHS ★★1/2 A good-hearted waif is rewarded for her kindness by the incarnations of each month of the year when she is sent on an impossible errand by her evil stepmother. What might have been an entertaining tale is marred by a dragging pace. 90m. **DIR:** Kimio Yabuki. **1985**

TWELVE O'CLOCK HIGH ★★★★ Gregory Peck is the flight commander who takes over an England-based bomber squadron during World War II. He begins to feel the strain of leadership and becomes too involved with the men in his command. This is a well-produced and well-acted film. Dean Jagger won an Oscar for supporting actor for his fine performance. B&W; 132m. **DIR:** Henry King. **CAST:** Gregory Peck, Dean Jagger, Gary Merrill, Hugh Marlowe. **1950 DVD**

12:01 ★★★★ Surprisingly effective science-fiction thriller has accountant Jonathan Silverman trapped in time when an electrical shock "saves" him as the Earth is destroyed by a controversial experiment. Like Bill Murray in *Groundhog Day*, Silverman is fated to live the same day over and over again—unless he can change the course of history. Made for TV. 96m. **DIR:** Jack Sholder. **CAST:** Jonathan Silverman, Helen Slater, Martin Landau, Nicolas Surovy, Robin Bartlett, Jeremy Piven. **1993**

TWENTIETH CENTURY ★★★★ A screwball-comedy masterpiece, scripted from the hit play by Ben Hecht and Charles MacArthur. Egocentric Broadway producer, John Barrymore, turns shop girl Carole Lombard into a star, gets dumped, and pulls out all stops to win her back during a cross-country train trip. The fun is fast and furious as the miles fly by. Barrymore and Lombard couldn't be funnier. B&W; 91m. **DIR:** Howard Hawks. **CAST:** Carole Lombard, John Barrymore, Roscoe Karns, Walter Connolly, Edgar Kennedy. **1934**

TWENTY BUCKS ★★1/2 Money—what it does to people and what people do with it—is the subject of this low-budget comedy-drama. A single twenty-dollar bill gets lost, found, stolen, lent, spent, and ironically shuffled about by a bag lady, teen skateboarder, emigrant chewing-gum magnate, bride and groom, stripper, crooks, and aspiring writer in a series of quirky, uneven vignettes. Not consistently memorable. Rated R for nudity, violence, and language. 91m. **DIR:** Keva Rosenfeld. **CAST:** Brendan Fraser, Christopher Lloyd, Steve Buscemi, Linda Hunt, Elisabeth Shue. **1994**

20 DATES ★★ Sometimes funny, sometimes just plain annoying "documentary" in which director Myles Berkowitz goes on twenty dates in search of his perfect woman. Rated R for profanity. 92m. **DIR:** Myles Berkowitz. **CAST:** Myles Berkowitz, Tia Carrere. **1998**

28 DAYS ★★ Sandra Bullock tries gamely, but she's no match for this clumsy, ill-advised "comedy." Director Betty Thomas betrays a serious subject—one woman's struggle to overcome her addictions to alcohol and pills—by turning it into wincingly uncomfortable burlesque. Every time Susannah Grant's script threatens to become serious, every time a cast member struggles to deliver a poignant moment of genuine emotion, Thomas yanks the rug out and buries all concerned beneath a cheap giggle. Rated PG-13 for brief profanity and drug use. 103m. **DIR:** Betty Thomas. **CAST:** Sandra Bullock, Viggo Mortensen, Dominic West, Diane Ladd, Elizabeth Perkins, Steve Buscemi, Alan Tudyk. **2000 DVD**

28 UP ★★★★★ A riveting and innovative British documentary that follows the woes and wonders of fourteen young people, reuniting them for new interviews every seven years. The result is a movie that exposes human vulnerability, while exposing the ludicrous and pompous British class system. Not rated. 120m. **DIR:** Michael Apted. **1985**

25, FIREMEN'S STREET ★★★★ The troubled history of post–World War II Hungary is recounted in the memories of people living in an old house slated for demolition. Political upheavals take on personal resonance in this innovative, fascinating film. In Hungarian with English subtitles. Not rated. 93m. **DIR:** István Szabó. **CAST:** Rita Bekes. **1973**

25 X 5: THE CONTINUING HISTORY OF THE ROLLING STONES ★★★★★ The definitive history lesson on the Rolling Stones. Using extensive interviews and rare never-before-seen video footage, director Nigel Finch chronicles twenty-five years of the band—beginning in the early Sixties and ending with the Steel Wheels Tour. Not rated. Contains adult language and brief nudity. 130m. **DIR:** Nigel Finch. **1989**

TWENTY-FOUR EYES ★★★1/2 Beauty and innocence are lost as war and progress intrude upon a rural village in this poignant, touching drama. The story concerns a progressive schoolteacher from Tokyo who changes the lives of students in an elementary school on a remote island off Japan in the late 1920s. In Japanese with English subtitles. B&W; 158m. **DIR:** Keisuke Kinosita. **CAST:** Keisuke Kinosita, Chishu Ryu. **1954**

24-HOUR WOMAN ★★1/2 What begins as a smart comedy-drama about a harried television producer trying to juggle pregnancy and her job turns into melodrama with obvious results. Rosie Perez is fine as the producer, whose pregnancy becomes a ratings bonanza for her news program. Once the baby arrives, director Nancy Savoca loses focus and the film becomes a wasteland of clichés. Rated R for language and adult situations. 93m. **DIR:** Nancy Savoca. **CAST:** Rosie Perez, Marianne Jean-Baptiste, Karen Duffy, Patti LuPone, Diego Serrano. **1998**

20 MILLION MILES TO EARTH ★★★★ An egg from outer space grows into a giant monster that terrorizes Rome. Ray Harryhausen's stop-motion special effects are still impressive as the gargantuan Ymir battles an elephant and meets its fate in the ruins of the Colosseum. B&W; 84m. **DIR:** Nathan Juran. **CAST:** William Hopper, Joan Taylor. **1957**

29TH STREET ★★★★ Imagine winning the first New York state lottery of $6.2 million and being unhappy about it—that's what happens to Frank Pesce (Anthony LaPaglia) in this warmhearted, often hilarious movie. Frank has always been lucky, and now it seems his luck may destroy his family. The real Pesce plays older brother Vito. Rated R for profanity and violence. 105m. **DIR:** George Gallo. **CAST:** Danny Aiello, Anthony LaPaglia, Lainie Kazan, Robert Forster. **1991**

TWENTY-ONE ★★★ Irreverent glimpse inside the life of an adventurous young woman (Patsy Kensit). Kensit carries on a monologue chronicling her simultaneous affairs with a drug addict and a married man. Rated R for nudity, violence, profanity, and drug use. 92m. **DIR:** Don Boyd. **CAST:** Patsy Kensit, Jack Shepherd, Patrick Ryecart. **1990**

27TH DAY, THE 🦃 Anticommunist propaganda disguised as science fiction, in the less-than-capable hands of the director who created the TV show *Bewitched*. B&W; 75m. **DIR:** William Asher. **CAST:** Gene Barry, Valerie French, George Voskovec. **1957**

20,000 LEAGUES UNDER THE SEA (1916) ★★1/2 Confusing blend of three tales (Jules Verne's *Mysterious Island* and *20,000 Leagues Under the Sea* as well as the creation of an original past for Captain Nemo) forces viewers to jump back and forth trying to get a handle on what's actually happening. Further, the director's fascination with underwater photography reduces this to a lesser entry of a Jacques Cousteau docu-

mentary. Silent. B&W; 105m. **DIR:** Stuart Paton. **CAST:** Allan Holubar. **1916 DVD**

20,000 LEAGUES UNDER THE SEA (1954) ★★★★ In this Disney version of the famous Jules Verne adventure-fantasy, a sailor (Kirk Douglas) and a scientist (Paul Lukas) get thoroughly involved with Captain Nemo, played by James Mason, and his fascinating submarine of the future. The cast is great, the action sequences ditto. 127m. **DIR:** Richard Fleischer. **CAST:** Kirk Douglas, James Mason, Paul Lukas, Peter Lorre. **1954**

TWENTY THOUSAND LEAGUES UNDER THE SEA (1972) ★★ Less than thrilling adaptation of the Jules Verne classic. Here, Captain Nemo and his amazing submarine, the *Nautilus*, are the centerpiece of a number of deep-sea adventures. 60m. **DIR:** Arthur Rankin Jr., Jules Bass. **1972**

20,000 LEAGUES UNDER THE SEA (1996) ★★★ Michael Caine makes a stalwart Captain Nemo in this sporadically engaging television miniseries that goes back to the source material to tell the story of the obsessed sea captain and his dream of conquering the ocean. Not rated; contains violence. 180m. **DIR:** Rod Hardy. **CAST:** Michael Caine, Patrick Dempsey, Bryan Brown, Mia Sara, Adewale Akinnuoye-Agbaje. **1996**

TWENTYFOURSEVEN ★★★ The title of this familiar but richly textured drama reflects the daily rut of small-town English teens in the 1980s. A loner resurrects a boxing club he hopes will replace the anger and despair of local youth with dignity, discipline, and fitness. Rated R for language, violence, and drug use. B&W; 96m. **DIR:** Shane Meadows. **CAST:** Bob Hoskins, Frank Harper, Pamela Cundell, Danny Nussbaum, James Hooton, Darren Campbell, Justin Brady. **1998**

TWICE A JUDAS 🦃 Another case of amnesia on the prairie. Luke, suffering from amnesia, is set upon by a local swindler who, after murdering Luke's family, passes himself off as Luke's brother. An unbelievable story and lack of action make this a dull film, even with Klaus Kinski in a leading role. Not rated; contains violence. 96m. **DIR:** Nando Cicero. **CAST:** Klaus Kinski, Antonio Sabato, Cristina Galbo, Pepe Calvo. **1968**

TWICE DEAD ★★★ An all-American family moves into an old mansion inhabited by a street gang. The gang, furious about losing their clubhouse, starts terrorizing the family. This movie is highlighted by good performances, above-average effects, and a sharp wit. Rated R for violence and nudity. 90m. **DIR:** Bert L. Dragin. **CAST:** Tom Breznahan, Jill Whitlow, Todd Bridges. **1988**

TWICE IN A LIFETIME ★★★★★ Superior slice-of-life drama about a Washington mill worker who reaches a mid-life crisis. The cast is uniformly fine, the story poignant without being sugary. Rated R for adult situations. 111m. **DIR:** Bud Yorkin. **CAST:** Gene Hackman, Ann-Margret, Ellen Burstyn, Amy Madigan, Ally Sheedy, Brian Dennehy. **1985**

TWICE-TOLD TALES ★★ With all his usual feeling, Vincent Price lurks, leers, and hams his nefarious way through a trilogy of nineteenth-century novelist Nathaniel Hawthorne's most vivid horror stories, including *The House of the Seven Gables*. 119m. **DIR:** Sidney Salkow. **CAST:** Vincent Price, Sebastian Cabot, Joyce Taylor, Brett Halsey, Beverly Garland, Mari Blanchard. **1963 DVD**

TWICE UPON A TIME ★★★★ Sardonic wit is laced throughout this wild and wacky animated fairy tale from producer George Lucas. Filmmakers utilize a cut-and-paste animation process called Lumage to present intrepid heroes attempting to stop the evil Murkworks from blanketing the world in nightmares. Rated PG. 75m. **DIR:** John Korty, Charles Swenson. **1983**

TWICE UPON A YESTERDAY ★★1/2 Familiar themes are woven through this British romantic drama about a man who finds a way to turn back time and win back his girlfriend, who left him after he cheated. The film succumbs to the traditions of the genre, but with a little tweaking, it could have been something special. Rated R for adult situations and language. 94m. **DIR:** Maria Ripoll. **CAST:** Lena Headey, Douglas Henshall, Penelope Cruz, Elizabeth McGovern. **1998 DVD**

TWILIGHT ★★★ Mannered, updated *film noir* detective thriller. Paul Newman's weary private investigator and all the supporting players' every action is so calculated and slow that they seem to exist in a different universe. Rated R for profanity, violence, nudity, and sexual content. 94m. **DIR:** Robert Benton. **CAST:** Paul Newman, Susan Sarandon, Gene Hackman, James Garner, Stockard Channing, Reese Witherspoon, Giancarlo Esposito. **1998 DVD**

TWILIGHT MAN ★★★ Pretty good thriller about a university professor whose life is thrown into a shambles when a mysterious stranger begins futzing with his computer records—and killing his friends. Rated R for profanity and violence. 99m. **DIR:** Craig R. Baxley. **CAST:** Tim Matheson, Dean Stockwell, L. Scott Caldwell, Joel Polis, Yvette Nipar, Georgann Johnson. **1996**

TWILIGHT OF THE GOLDS, THE ★★1/2 Jonathan Tolin's stage play should have been a thoughtful drama but is a shrill polemic. Thanks to an experimental scientific procedure, a newly pregnant woman learns that her child will be born gay; the resulting '"crisis"' draws battle lines within her marriage and family. The shrieking tone isn't helped by the film's wretched soundtrack. Rated PG-13 for profanity. 95m. **DIR:** Ross Marks. **CAST:** Jennifer Beals, Faye Dunaway, Brendan Fraser, Garry Marshall, Sean O'Bryan, Jon Tenney. **1996 DVD**

TWILIGHT ON THE TRAIL ★★ An old friend needs a hand so Hopalong Cassidy and his pals impersonate British detectives to throw a curve to the cattle rustlers they're seeking. B&W; 58m. **DIR:** Howard Bretherton. **CAST:** William Boyd, Brad King, Andy Clyde, Jack Rockwell, Wanda McKay, Tom London. **1941**

TWILIGHT PEOPLE 🦃 Mad scientist on remote island dabbles with things better left unfilmed. Rated R for violence. 84m. **DIR:** Eddie Romero. **CAST:** John Ashley, Jan Merlin, Pam Grier. **1972**

TWILIGHT ZONE—THE MOVIE ★★★ A generally enjoyable tribute to the 1960s television series created by Rod Serling, this film, directed by Steven Spielberg, John Landis, Joe Dante, and George Miller, is broken into four parts. Miller brings us the best: a tale about a white-knuckled air traveler (John Lithgow) who sees a gremlin doing strange things on the wing of a jet. Rated PG. 102m. **DIR:** Steven Spielberg, John Landis, Joe Dante, George Miller. **CAST:** Vic Morrow, Scatman Crothers, Kathleen Quinlan, John Lithgow, Dan Aykroyd, Albert Brooks. **1983**

TWILIGHT ZONE, THE (TV SERIES) ★★★★1/2 Writer-producer Rod Serling's precedent-shattering anthology series, which ruled television during the early 1960s, earned its place in history thanks to a deft blend of credible human emotions amid incredible situations. Each video includes two episodes; Volume One is by far the strongest. 55m. **DIR:** Richard Donner, Douglas Heyes, Lamont Johnson, Buzz Kulik. **CAST:** Robert Redford, Agnes Moorehead, Lee Marvin, Burgess Meredith, Jack Klugman, Gladys Cooper, William Shatner. **1959 DVD**

TWILIGHT'S LAST GLEAMING ★★★ Although this is another maniac-at-the-button doomsday chronicle, it is so convincing that it makes the well-worn premise seem new. From the moment a group of ex-cons (Burt Lancaster, Paul Winfield, Burt Young, and William Smith) seize control of an air force pickup truck, it becomes obvious the audience is in the front seat of a nonstop roller coaster. Rated R for violence and profanity. 146m. **DIR:** Robert Aldrich. **CAST:** Burt Lancaster, Paul Winfield, Burt Young, William Smith, Charles Durning, Richard Widmark, Melvyn Douglas, Joseph Cotten. **1977**

TWIN DRAGONS ★★ This one's a stinker. And small wonder: It's merely the American rerelease of a lesser 1992 effort originally called *Shuang Long Hui*, and has been trimmed which explains why so little makes sense. Identical brothers are separated at birth and grow up to become radically different people. The obligatory mistaken-identity gags are rendered as clumsily as the often poor split-screen effects. Even the fight scenes are less imaginative than usual. Rated PG-13 for comic mayhem and grade-school sexual content. 89m. **DIR:** Tsui Hark, Ringo Lam. **CAST:** Jackie Chan, Maggie Cheung, Teddie Robin, Nina Li Chi. **1999 DVD**

TWIN FALLS IDAHO ★★★ When a good-hearted hooker befriends a pair of conjoined twins, she causes the first stirrings of conflict in the brothers' intimate relationship. The film is a real oddity, cowritten by brothers Michael and Mark Polish, who are identical twins (though not conjoined) in real life. Slow-paced and a bit overcontrolled, it's nevertheless compelling, offering a glimpse into a world where it's the so-called normal people who are the outsiders. Rated R for profanity and mature themes. 110m. **DIR:** Michael Polish. **CAST:** Michael Polish, Mark Polish, Michele Hicks, Garrett Morris, William Katt, Lesley Ann Warren. **1999 DVD**

TWIN PEAKS (MOVIE) ★★★ The television pilot for the mystery–soap opera thinking fan. The series went off in too many directions, but this still is a fascinating opening, where the logging town of Twin Peaks is stunned when a teenage girl is kidnapped, tortured, raped, and murdered. Contains added footage to wrap up the crime. 113m. **DIR:** David Lynch. **CAST:** Kyle MacLachlan, Michael Ontkean, Joan Chen, Richard Beymer, Peggy Lipton, Jack Nance, Piper Laurie, Russ Tamblyn. **1989**

TWIN PEAKS (TV SERIES) ★★ These seven episodes, following one of the most talked-about television pilot movies in years, became the shaggiest of all dogs when writers David Lynch and Mark Frost tried to attack our senses from too many directions, losing focus on an intriguing mystery. Those not familiar with the pilot will find these episodes valueless; those initially hooked may want to reflect on what might have been. 48m. **DIR:** Various!. **CAST:** Kyle MacLachlan, Michael Ontkean, Joan Chen, Richard Beymer, Peggy Lipton, Jack Nance, Piper Laurie, Russ Tamblyn. **1990 DVD**

TWIN PEAKS: FIRE WALK WITH ME ★★★ Fans of David Lynch's self-indulgent television series will no doubt be thrilled with this prequel; the rest of America is advised to steer clear. Angelo Badalamenti's main theme still brings a chill. Rated R for nudity and language. 135m. **DIR:** David Lynch. **CAST:** Kyle MacLachlan, Sheryl Lee, Moira Kelly, David Bowie, Chris Isaak, Harry Dean Stanton, Ray Wise, Kiefer Sutherland, Peggy Lipton. **1992 DVD**

TWIN SITTERS ★★★ A couple of muscle-bound morons are hired to watch over the nephews of a rich, former mob member. The brats-from-hell almost prove too much for the Barbarian Brothers who eventually turn the tables. Innocent family fare that offers laughs, action, and a message. Rated PG-13 for violence and mild profanity. 93m. **DIR:** John Paragon. **CAST:** Peter Paul, David Paul, Christian Cousins, Joseph Cousins, Rena Sofer, Jared Martin, Barry Dennen, George Lazenby. **1994**

TWIN TOWN ★★★ Fans of *Trainspotting* will enjoy this Welsh comedy about unemployed twin brothers out for revenge against their father's crooked boss, whom they blame for the injuries he suffered on the job. The broad, crude humor will appeal to an audience that doesn't normally go in for "foreign films." Not rated, but an R equivalent for profanity, nudity, violence, and adult situations. 98m. **DIR:** Kevin Allen. **CAST:** Llyr Evan, Rhys Hans, Huw Ceredig. **1997**

TWIN WARRIORS ★★★1/2 Jet Li's *The Tai Chi Masters* has been reedited and dubbed to become *Twin Warriors*. Fortunately, much of the action and pageantry remain intact. Li and Chi Sui Hou star as best friends who grow up together in a monastery. When they are expelled for fighting, the two go their separate ways. Their inevitable reunion years later—one sides with political rebels, the other with a desperate and ruthless ruler—is filled with lots of action and emotion. Rated R. 91m. **DIR:** Yuen Woo-Ping. **CAST:** Jet Li, Michelle Yeoh, Chi Sui Hou. **1993 DVD**

TWINS ★★★★ Arnold Schwarzenegger and Danny DeVito play the title roles in this marvelously silly movie, which has the far-from-identical twins—products of a supersecret scientific experiment—meeting as adults after being separated at birth. This could easily have been a one-joke movie, but director Ivan Reitman and the stars keep it warm, funny, and fast-paced right up to the nicely satisfying conclusion. Rated PG for profanity and violence. 105m. **DIR:** Ivan Reitman. **CAST:** Arnold Schwarzenegger, Danny DeVito, Kelly Preston, Chloe Webb. **1988 DVD**

TWINS OF EVIL ★★★ *Playboy* magazine's first twin Playmates, Madeleine and Mary Collinson, were tapped for this British Hammer Films horror entry about a good girl and her evil, blood-sucking sister. Peter Cushing adds class to what should in theory have been a forgettable exploitation film but provides surprisingly enjoyable entertainment for genre buffs. Rated R for nudity, violence, and gore. 85m. **DIR:** John Hough. **CAST:** Peter Cushing, Madeleine Collinson, Mary Collinson, Dennis Price. **1972**

TWINSANITY ★★★ Twins (Judy Geeson and Martin Potter) who still play games together are lured into London's underbelly. Sleazy sexual encounters lead the twins to concoct a game of murder. Though dated by its music and costuming, this film (originally released as *Goodbye Gemini*) does include some fine acting and a complex story line. Rated R for violence. 91m. **DIR:** Alan Gibson. **CAST:** Judy Geeson, Martin Potter, Alexis Kanner, Michael Redgrave, Mike Pratt, Freddie Jones, Peter Jeffrey. **1970**

TWIST AND SHOUT ★★★★1/2 An exceptional coming-of-age story about two friends, a drummer with a pseudo-Beatles group, and a quiet sort with severe problems at home, circa 1964. It is a true-to-life movie that will leave no viewer unmoved. In Danish with English subtitles. Not rated; contains profanity, nudity, and suggested sex. 99m. **DIR:** Bille August. **CAST:** Adam Tonsberg, Lars Simonsen. **1986**

TWIST AROUND THE CLOCK ★★1/2 The plot, about a concert promoter trying to cash in on the Twist dance craze, is just here to fill time between musical performances. The best are from Dion, who sings "Runaround Sue" and "The Wanderer." Give it an extra star if you're a big fan of the post-Elvis, pre-Beatles era. B&W; 86m. **DIR:** Oscar Rudolph. **CAST:** Chubby Checker, Dion, The Marcels. **1961**

TWISTED ★★1/2 Early Christian Slater thriller has the budding star playing a troubled teen who torments the new baby-sitter. Not rated, contains strong language and violence. 87m. **DIR:** Adam Holender. **CAST:** Christian Slater, Lois Smith, Tandy Cronyn, Dina Merrill, Noelle Parker. **1985 DVD**

TWISTED LOVE ★★ Former television teen stars can't breathe any life into this derivative story about a teen crush that goes too far. Rated R for violence. 80m. **DIR:** Eb Lottimer. **CAST:** Lisa Dean Ryan, Mark Paul Gosselaar, Soleil Moon Frye, Sasha Jenson. **1995**

TWISTED NIGHTMARE 🦃 A group of young people at a camp near a lake are menaced by a mysterious homicidal maniac. Sound familiar? Rated R for violence. 95m. **DIR:** Paul Hunt. **CAST:** Rhonda Gray, Cleve Hall. **1982**

TWISTED OBSESSION ★★ A screenwriter becomes infatuated with a film director's sister in this very offbeat tale of obsession and brother-sister domination. Not rated, but with nudity, profanity, and violence. 109m. **DIR:** Fernando Trueba. **CAST:** Jeff Goldblum, Miranda Richardson, Dexter Fletcher. **1990**

TWISTED TALES 🦃 Anthology of tales that wouldn't scare a 5 year old. Not rated; contains violence and profanity. 90m. **DIR:** Mick McCleery, Kevin J. Lindenmuth, Rita Klus. **CAST:** Mick McCleery, Laura McLaughlin, Theresa Oliver. **1993**

TWISTER (1988) ★★ Patriarch Harry Dean Stanton presides over a mansion filled with the spoiled, eccentric, and just plain lunatic members of his extended family. This adaptation of Mary Robison's *Oh* lacks the central point of view needed to make it palatable. Rated PG-13 for profanity. 95m. **DIR:** Michael Almereyda. **CAST:** Harry Dean Stanton, Suzy Amis, Crispin Glover, Dylan McDermott, Jenny Wright, Lois Chiles. **1988**

TWISTER (1996) ★★★1/2 This undeniably exciting drama, which gets most of its juice from awesome tornado sequences, won't play nearly as well on a small screen . . . and more's the pity. Absent that raw fury, Michael Crichton and Anne-Marie Martin's superficial script will be exposed as an anemic reworking of *His Girl Friday*. Rated PG-13 for wind-driven violence. 117m. **DIR:** Jan De Bont. **CAST:** Helen Hunt, Bill Paxton, Jami Gertz, Cary Elwes, Lois Smith. **1996 DVD**

TWISTS OF TERROR ★★1/2 This 1996 made-for-television omnibus takes its cue from the original *Trilogy of Terror*. Joseph Ziegler is the creepy host who introduces three tales of terror, including a wicked little story about a man on the run from a vicious dog who finds himself trapped in a hospital where you can't check out. As with all short-story collections, some stories are better than others, but all suffer from the restrictions of broadcast television standards. Not rated; contains violence. 90m. **DIR:** Douglas Jackson. **CAST:** Jennifer Rubin, Nick Mancuso, Carl Marotte, Andrew Jackson, Joseph Ziegler. **1996**

TWITCH OF THE DEATH NERVE ★★★ Also known as *Bay of Blood*, *Carnage*, and *Last House on the Left, Part II*, this is the ultimate splatter film, and it comes from an unexpected source: Mario Bava. The director was Italy's pioneer horror stylist, blending elegant visuals with gothic gore. In contrast, this *Ten Little Indians* clone is jarringly contemporary and features the most bloodletting ever in a non–X-rated shocker. Rated R. 87m. **DIR:** Mario Bava. **CAST:** Claudine Auger, Chris Avran, Laura Betti. **1970**

TWO BITS ★★★1/2 Newcomer Jerry Barone is excellent as a Depression-era 12 year old who desperately wants to attend the opening of a South Philadelphia movie house. In order to raise the two bits he needs for admission, he embarks on a number of schemes. Al Pacino shines as the boy's dying grandfather who dispenses words of wisdom. Rated PG-13 for adult situations. 83m. **DIR:** James Foley. **CAST:** Jerry Barone, Al Pacino, Mary Elizabeth Mastrantonio, Andy Romano. **1995**

TWO BITS & PEPPER ★★ In an odd bit of casting, Joe Piscopo plays a duo of bumbling kidnappers who abduct two girls and hold them for ransom. The girls outwit the pair with the help of two talking horses. Honest. And they say there's nothing new coming out of Hollywood. Rated PG. 90m. **DIR:** Corey Michael Eubanks. **CAST:** Joe Piscopo, Dennis Weaver, Lauren Eckstrom, Rachel Crane, Perry Stephens. **1995**

TWO BY SCORSESE ★★★ Interesting duet of early works by Martin Scorsese, one of the most prolific American film directors. *Italianamerican*, made in 1974, is a penetrating look at the filmmakers' parents. *The Big Shave*, made in 1968, is a black comedy musical about a man having a bloody shave to the tune of Bunny Berigan's "I Can't Get Started." Not rated; contains mild violence. 54m. **DIR:** Martin Scorsese. **1991**

•TWO CAN PLAY THAT GAME ★★ Advertising executive Shante catches her man on the town with another woman and invokes a ten-day strategy to both win him back and teach him a lesson. Shante spends quite a bit of time talking directly into the camera about her theories on today's mating game and lust. The script is mostly mildly amusing and occasionally funny as love is reduced to a game plan and timetable. Rated R for language and sexual references. 90m. **DIR:** Mark Brown. **CAST:** Vivica A. Fox, Morris Chestnut, Mo'Nique Imes-

Jackson, Wendy Raquel Robinson, Tamala Jones, Anthony Anderson, Bobby Brown. **2001 DVD**

TWO DAUGHTERS ★★★★ Satyajit Ray's beautiful two-part film is based on tales by Nobel Prize–winning author Rabindranath Tagore. With Chekhovian delicacy and pathos, Ray explores the hopes and disappointments of two young women experiencing first love. Ray's stories transcend the surface of Indian culture while creating a universally felt character study. In Bengali with English subtitles. B&W; 114m. **DIR:** Satyajit Ray. **CAST:** Anil Chatterjee, Chandana Bannerjee, Soumitra Chatterjee. **1961**

TWO DAYS IN THE VALLEY ★★1/2 Writer-director John Herzfeld attempts a Quentin Tarantino with this gory comedy-drama, but one *Pulp Fiction* was enough. Danny Aiello is the standout as a hit man left for dead by his partner. Rated R for violence, profanity, nudity, and simulated sex. 107m. **DIR:** John Herzfeld. **CAST:** Danny Aiello, James Spader, Teri Hatcher, Jeff Daniels, Greg Cruttwell, Glenne Headly, Peter Horton, Marsha Mason, Paul Mazursky, Charlize Theron, Eric Stoltz, Keith Carradine, Louise Fletcher, Austin Pendleton, Lawrence Tierney. **1996**

TWO DEATHS ★★★ In 1989 Romania, as civil war rages outside the door, four men gather for their yearly reunion. They reveal shocking secrets, but none more shocking than that of their host, who tells the story of why his beautiful housekeeper endures his abuse. Typically murky (but impeccably acted and filmed) psychodrama from Nicolas Roeg. Rated R for nudity, violence, and sexual situations. 102m. **DIR:** Nicolas Roeg. **CAST:** Michael Gambon, Sonia Braga, Patrick Malahide. **1994 DVD**

TWO ENGLISH GIRLS ★★★★1/2 Twenty-two minutes were later added to this very civilized and rewarding film. Set in pre–World War I Europe and based on the Henri-Pierre Roché novel (his only other being *Jules et Jim*, the modern flip side of the arrangement here), Truffaut's work has Frenchman Léaud the object of two English sisters' desire. In French with English subtitles. 130m. **DIR:** François Truffaut. **CAST:** Jean-Pierre Léaud, Kiki Markham, Stacey Tendeter. **1972 DVD**

TWO EVIL EYES ★★ A two-part Edgar Allan Poe film shot in Pittsburgh. The first story, George Romero's version of "The Facts in the Case of M. Valdemar," is a total washout—shrill, derivative, and boring. The second, Dario Argento's adaptation of "The Black Cat," has some narrative shortcomings (principally its ending), but contains a powerful performance by Harvey Keitel and offers a scary study in obsession. 121m. **DIR:** Dario Argento, George A. Romero. **CAST:** Harvey Keitel, Adrienne Barbeau, E. G. Marshall, John Amos. **1990**

TWO-FACED WOMAN ★★★ Garbo's last film is better than its reputation. She has an infectious sense of humor as the woman who tests her husband's faithfulness by posing as her own seductive twin sister. Fast-moving, full of clever dialogue, and professionally acted by the entire cast. 94m. **DIR:** George Cukor. **CAST:** Greta Garbo, Melvyn Douglas, Constance Bennett, Roland Young, Robert Sterling, Ruth Gordon. **1941**

TWO-FISTED LAW ★★★★ A couple of young whippersnappers, John Wayne and Walter Brennan, add zest to this tale of a rancher (Tim McCoy in top form) out to get the goods on the crooks who cheated him out of his ranch. The screenplay by Three Mesquiteers creator William Colt MacDonald makes this one of McCoy's best; an outstanding B-plus Western. B&W; 64m. **DIR:** D. Ross Lederman. **CAST:** Tim McCoy, Wheeler Oakman, Tully Marshall, John Wayne, Walter Brennan. **1932**

TWO FOR THE ROAD ★★★★ Clever editing and Frederic Raphael's inventive script highlight this delightful study of a marriage on the rocks, illuminated by deftly inserted flashbacks that occur each time the vacationing couple passes another car on the road. Albert Finney and Audrey Hepburn are the tempestuous lovers; the sweetly romantic score comes from Henry Mancini. 112m. **DIR:** Stanley Donen. **CAST:** Audrey Hepburn, Albert Finney, Jacqueline Bisset. **1967**

TWO FOR THE SEESAW ★★1/2 While reevaluating his life and previous marriage, a Nebraska attorney moves to New York City and has an affair with a quirky modern dancer. Candid dialogue and touching humor but a little too long to be fully recommended. B&W; 120m. **DIR:** Robert Wise. **CAST:** Robert Mitchum, Shirley MacLaine, Edmon Ryan, Elisabeth Fraser. **1962**

TWO FRIENDS ★★1/2 Jane Campion fans will be disappointed by this early effort, produced for Australian TV. The lives of two high-school girls unfold from the present to the past as we witness the small shifts in circumstance that alter their paths. A weird blend of styles and an awkward presentation make this feel like an experiment instead of a finished film. Letterboxed. Not rated; contains profanity. 76m. **DIR:** Jane Campion. **CAST:** Emma Coles, Kris Bidenko, Kris McQuade. **1986 DVD**

TWO GIRLS AND A SAILOR ★★★ June Allyson and Gloria De Haven run a canteen for servicemen, and both fall for sailor Van Johnson. Their romantic triangle is resolved, but not before guest stars perform specialty numbers to give the movie its entertainment value. The personalities are potent enough to keep the film entertaining beyond its era. 124m. **DIR:** Richard Thorpe. **CAST:** Van Johnson, June Allyson, Gloria De Haven, Tom Drake, Jimmy Durante, José Iturbi, Gracie Allen, Harry James, Xavier Cugat, Ben Blue. **1944**

TWO-GUN MAN FROM HARLEM ★★1/2 Framed for murder, a cowboy leaves town and heads to the big city to lose himself. One year later a two-fisted deacon arrives to bring the real culprit to justice. Lensed on weekends at a dude ranch, this was the first in a series of "all-colored" Westerns featuring Herbert Jeffrey as singing cowboy Bob Blake. B&W; 65m. **DIR:** Richard C. Kahn. **CAST:** Herbert Jeffrey, Clarence Brooks, Margaret Whitten, Mantan Moreland, Spencer Williams, Stymie Beard, Mae Turner. **1938**

200 CIGARETTES ★★ There's a lot of hot, young Hollywood talent on display in this drama-comedy, but they're saddled with a talkative script and pedestrian direction. It's a labored concept about a group of people trying to make the best of New Year's Eve in 1981. Rated R for language. 97m. **DIR:** Risa Bramon Garcia. **CAST:** Ben Affleck, Janeane Garofalo, Courtney Love, Christina Ricci, Gaby Hoffman. **1999 DVD**

200 MOTELS ★★1/2 Weird blend of comedy and music written and performed by Frank Zappa and the Mothers of Invention. This bizarre opera set against an even

stranger backdrop of completely berserk gags. The film never really finds its center. Rated R for nudity and profanity. 98m. **DIR:** Frank Zappa, Tony Palmer. **CAST:** Frank Zappa, Theodore Bikel, Ringo Starr, Keith Moon. **1971**

TWO IF BY SEA ★★ A small-time thief (Denis Leary) steals a valuable painting, then he and his put-upon girlfriend (Sandra Bullock) hide out in a Cape Cod mansion waiting to sell the art to a mysterious buyer. Bullock is charming once again, but her forced Brooklyn accent is a distraction and her surroundings are unworthy of her—the plot is farfetched, the supporting characters are unlikable, and the jokes aren't funny. Rated R for profanity. 96m. **DIR:** Bill Bennett. **CAST:** Sandra Bullock, Denis Leary, Yaphet Kotto. **1996 DVD**

TWO JAKES, THE ★★★1/2 Okay, so this sequel is not as good as its predecessor, *Chinatown*, but how many movies are? We loved the performances in this detective thriller set in 1948, when private eye Jake Gittes (Jack Nicholson, who also directed) is hired by another Jake (Harvey Keitel) to follow his wife. A convoluted, but noble effort. Rated R for violence and profanity. 133m. **DIR:** Jack Nicholson. **CAST:** Jack Nicholson, Harvey Keitel, Meg Tilly, Madeleine Stowe, Eli Wallach, Rubén Blades, Frederic Forrest, David Keith, Richard Farnsworth, Perry Lopez. **1990 DVD**

TWO-LANE BLACKTOP ★★★ Long unavailable on video, this feature is the definition of a cult movie: you'll either love it or hate it. Rock stars James Taylor and Dennis Wilson play a pair of guys who drive their '55 Chevy across the country, occasionally participating in illegal drag races. Neither can act, nor are they required to in this exercise in American ennui circa 1971. Warren Oates adds what life there is as a rival driver. Rated R for profanity and nudity. 102m. **DIR:** Monte Hellman. **CAST:** James Taylor, Warren Oates, Laurie Bird, Dennis Wilson, Harry Dean Stanton. **1971 DVD**

TWO LOST WORLDS 🦃 Pointless story involving pirates and kidnapping. B&W; 61m. **DIR:** Norman Dawn. **CAST:** James Arness, Laura Elliot, Bill Kennedy, Gloria Petroff, Tom Hubbard, Pierre Watkin, James Guilfoyle. **1950 DVD**

TWO MEN AND A WARDROBE ★★★1/2 Roman Polanski's award-winning short made while he was a student at the Polish Film Institute is a bitter parable blending slapstick and the absurd. Two men emerge from the sea sporting a single wardrobe. Also included in the package is a second short, *The Fat and the Lean*, an outrageously funny attack on governmental tyranny. Silent. B&W; 35m. **DIR:** Roman Polanski. **CAST:** Henlyk Kluga, Jakub Goldberg. **1958**

TWO-MINUTE WARNING ★★★ An all-star disaster film about a sniper loose in a crowded football stadium that is more exciting on video than it was on the big screen. The main reason is the lingering close-ups of the crowd and individual reactions are more impressive on a smaller screen. Rated R for violence, but the violence is tame by today's movie standards. 112m. **DIR:** Larry Peerce. **CAST:** John Cassavetes, Charlton Heston, Beau Bridges, Gena Rowlands, Marilyn Hassett, Martin Balsam, David Janssen, Walter Pidgeon, Jack Klugman, Brock Peters, Merv Griffin. **1976 DVD**

TWO MOON JULY ★★ The Kitchen, a New York City center for visual and performing arts, pays homage to the avant-garde with a diverse but uneven program of music, theater, dance, and film. An adventurous but uneven endeavor. 60m. **DIR:** Tom Bowes. **CAST:** Laurie Anderson, David Byrne. **1985**

TWO MOON JUNCTION ★★ Two weeks before her marriage, a young, well-to-do southern woman falls for a muscular carnival worker. A pattern in their relationship soon develops. They argue, they make love, and then she cries. Rated R for nudity, profanity, and violence. 104m. **DIR:** Zalman King. **CAST:** Sherilyn Fenn, Richard Tyson, Louise Fletcher, Burl Ives, Kristy McNichol. **1988 DVD**

TWO MRS. CARROLLS, THE ★★1/2 It won't take you as long as it takes Barbara Stanwyck to realize that the moody artist she has married is a self-made repeat widower. No real suspense, just hysteria galore. B&W; 99m. **DIR:** Peter Godfrey. **CAST:** Humphrey Bogart, Barbara Stanwyck, Alexis Smith, Nigel Bruce. **1947**

TWO MUCH ★★1/2 Donald E. Westlake's hilarious and inventive novel gets ho-hum treatment. Conniving South Florida art dealer gets swept away by a daffy socialite and then must inhabit the role of a fictitious twin brother when he falls genuinely in love with her sister. Sounds funny; plays dumb. Rated PG-13 for profanity, mild violence, and adult themes. 118m. **DIR:** Fernando Trueba. **CAST:** Antonio Banderas, Melanie Griffith, Daryl Hannah, Danny Aiello, Joan Cusack, Eli Wallach, Gambino Diego, Austin Pendleton. **1995**

TWO MULES FOR SISTER SARA ★★★ Clint Eastwood returns in his role of the "Man With No Name" (originated in Sergio Leone's Italian spaghetti Westerns) and Shirley MacLaine is an unlikely nun in this entertaining comedy-Western. Rated PG. 105m. **DIR:** Don Siegel. **CAST:** Clint Eastwood, Shirley MacLaine. **1970**

TWO OF A KIND (1951) ★★ Average suspense-drama concerning a con-artist team who attempt to steal the inheritance of two elderly people. Both the cast and script are okay, but that's just the problem. B&W; 75m. **DIR:** Henry Levin. **CAST:** Edmond O'Brien, Lizabeth Scott, Terry Moore, Alexander Knox. **1951**

TWO OF A KIND (1982) ★★★★ This heartwarming TV film features George Burns as a discarded senior citizen and Robby Benson as his retarded grandson. The two come together when the boy decides to help his seemingly disabled grandpa play golf again. Cliff Robertson and Barbara Barrie play Benson's parents. All in all, this is a fine film with a positive message about family unity. 102m. **DIR:** Roger Young. **CAST:** George Burns, Robby Benson, Cliff Robertson, Barbara Barrie, Ronny Cox. **1982**

TWO OF A KIND (1983) ★★ John Travolta and Olivia Newton-John, who first teamed on-screen in the box-office smash *Grease*, are reunited in this 1980s-style screwball comedy, which mixes clever ideas with incredibly stupid ones. Young viewers probably won't rave, but neither will they be too disappointed. Others, however, should stay away. Rated PG for profanity and violence. 87m. **DIR:** John Herzfeld. **CAST:** John Travolta, Olivia Newton-John, Charles Durning. **1983**

TWO OF US, THE ★★★1/2 This story of generational and religious differences joins an 8 year old Jewish boy (Alain Cohen) and an irascible Catholic grandpa (Michel Simon). The boy is fleeing Nazi-occupied

France in 1944 and comes to live with the anti-Semitic old man who is a family friend's relative. Beautifully acted, this is a different kind of movie for parents to enjoy with their older children. In French with English subtitles. 86m. **DIR:** Claude Berri. **CAST:** Alain Cohen, Michel Simon. **1968**

TWO ON A GUILLOTINE ★★ A woman has to spend the night in the spooky house of her father, a magician who claimed he would return from the dead, in order to inherit his estate. About as scary as one might expect for a film starring Connie Stevens and Dean Jones. B&W; 107m. **DIR:** William Conrad. **CAST:** Connie Stevens, Dean Jones, Cesar Romero, Parley Baer. **1964**

TWO OR THREE THINGS I KNOW ABOUT HER ★★★★ French director Jean-Luc Godard all but abandoned the conventions of narrative film with this "film essay" about both the city of Paris (the "Her" of the title) and his filmmaking process. Godard's musings on anything and everything (he narrates the film) are held together by the story of a housewife who works one day a week as a prostitute in order to support her shopping habit. A good introduction to this challenging but often difficult filmmaker. In French with English subtitles. Not rated; contains sexual themes. 90m. **DIR:** Jean-Luc Godard. **CAST:** Marina Vlady, Anny Duperey. **1977**

TWO RODE TOGETHER ★★★ In this variation of *The Searchers*, director John Ford explores the anguish of settlers over the children they have lost to Indian raiding parties and the racial prejudice that arises when one boy, now a full-blown warrior, is returned to his "people." It is not a fully effective film, but it does have its moments. 109m. **DIR:** John Ford. **CAST:** James Stewart, Richard Widmark, Shirley Jones, John McIntire, Woody Strode, Linda Cristal, Andy Devine. **1961**

TWO SISTERS FROM BOSTON ★★★1/2 Turn-of-the-century fun. Kathryn Grayson comes to New York to seek an operatic career, but she and sister June Allyson end up working at a Bowery honky-tonk owned by Jimmy Durante. The whole cast shines and Durante really shows the talent that endeared him to millions. B&W; 112m. **DIR:** Henry Koster. **CAST:** Kathryn Grayson, June Allyson, Lauritz Melchior, Jimmy Durante, Peter Lawford, Ben Blue. **1946**

TWO SMALL BODIES ★★★1/2 A cop thinks that a single mother/strip-bar hostess may have murdered her children. As he investigates, he finds himself being further and inexplicably drawn to her, despite the mounting evidence. Based on the play by Neal Bell. Not rated; contains violence, profanity, and sexual situations. 85m. **DIR:** Beth B. **CAST:** Fred Ward, Suzy Amis. **1993**

2,000 MANIACS 🦃 Full of cruel tortures and mutilation, this drive-in hit was the prototype of today's sick-humor slasher films. 84m. **DIR:** Herschell Gordon Lewis. **CAST:** Thomas Wood, Jeffrey Allen. **1964 DVD**

•2001: A SPACE TRAVESTY 🦃 Poor Leslie Nielsen. His brand of slapstick humor falls flat on its face in this horrible film that attempts to ape the *Airplane* genre of comedy but ends up crashing and burning on takeoff. Nielsen plays an International Security Force agent assigned to save the president, who has been kidnapped by aliens and replaced with a clone. Aw, now everything is starting to make sense. Rated R for adult situations and language. 108m. **DIR:** Allan A. Goldstein. **CAST:** Leslie Nielsen, Ophelie Winter, Peter Egan, Alexandra Kamp-Groenveld, Pierre, Damien Masson, Ezio Greggio. **2001 DVD**

2001: A SPACE ODYSSEY ★★★★★ There's no denying the visual magnificence of Stanley Kubrick's science-fiction epic. Ponderous, ambiguous, and arty, it's nevertheless considered a classic of the genre by many film buffs. The set design, costumes, cinematography, and Oscar-winning special effects combine to create unforgettable imagery. Rated G. 139m. **DIR:** Stanley Kubrick. **CAST:** Keir Dullea, William Sylvester, Gary Lockwood. **1968 DVD**

2010 ★★★★ The exciting sequel stars Roy Scheider, John Lithgow, Helen Mirren, and Bob Balaban as participants in a joint American-Russian space mission. We finally find out what really happened to astronaut Dave Bowman (Keir Dullea); the computer, HAL 9000; and the spaceship, *Discovery*, near the planet Jupiter. Rated PG. 116m. **DIR:** Peter Hyams. **CAST:** Roy Scheider, John Lithgow, Helen Mirren, Bob Balaban, Keir Dullea. **1984 DVD**

2020 TEXAS GLADIATORS 🦃 Alternately hilarious and just plain boring *Road Warrior* clone. Rated R for sex and gore, but turns up in censored version on Saturday-afternoon TV. 91m. **DIR:** Kevin Mancuso (Joe d'Amato). **CAST:** Harrison Muller. **1984**

TWO TICKETS TO BROADWAY ★★ Clichéd let's-put-on-a-show film features Janet Leigh as a small-town ingenue who heads for New York. Ann Miller's dance routines and Tony Martin's songs are highlights. 106m. **DIR:** James V. Kern. **CAST:** Tony Martin, Janet Leigh, Gloria De Haven, Ann Miller. **1951**

TWO TO TANGO ★★1/2 Satisfying little thriller starring Don Stroud as a burned-out hit man for an ominous organization called the Company. He's terminated one too many targets and bargains with his superior to do one last hit in Buenos Aires, Argentina; then he'll retire to Nepal. Rated R for violence and nudity. 87m. **DIR:** Hector Olivera. **CAST:** Don Stroud, Adrienne Sachs, Michael Cavanaugh, Dulio Marzio. **1988**

TWO-WAY STRETCH ★★★★ Delightful British caper comedy about a group of thieves plotting to break out of their lenient prison just long enough to pull a huge robbery and then return to their cells, leaving them with the perfect alibi. First-rate. 84m. **DIR:** Robert Day. **CAST:** Peter Sellers, Wilfrid Hyde-White, David Lodge, Bernard Cribbins, Lionel Jeffries. **1961**

TWO WEEKS IN ANOTHER TOWN ★★1/2 Kirk Douglas is uptight as a former movie actor who had a bout with the bottle and is trying for a comeback. A downer based on an Irwin Shaw novel. 107m. **DIR:** Vincente Minnelli. **CAST:** Kirk Douglas, Edward G. Robinson, Cyd Charisse, Claire Trevor, George Hamilton, Daliah Lavi, Rosanna Schiaffino, George Macready, James Gregory, Leslie Uggams. **1962**

TWO WEEKS WITH LOVE ★★ An old-fashioned musical set in a bygone age when corsets and long bathing suits were the norm. Debbie Reynolds and Carleton Carpenter sing "Abba Dabba Honeymoon," the novelty song that catapulted them to fame. Songs like "On Moonlight Bay" add to the romantic atmosphere. 92m. **DIR:** Roy Rowland. **CAST:** Jane Powell, Debbie Reynolds, Ricardo Montalban, Ann Harding, Louis Calhern, Carleton Carpenter. **1950**

TWO WOMEN ★★★★ In the performance that won her an Oscar, Sophia Loren is a widow who, with her 13 year old daughter, escapes war-torn Rome, eventually finding solace in her native village. This uncompromising drama was a Grand Prize winner at the Cannes Film Festival. In Italian with English subtitles. Not rated. 99m. **DIR:** Vittorio De Sica. **CAST:** Sophia Loren, Eleanora Brown, Jean-Paul Belmondo, Raf Vallone. **1960 DVD**

TWO WORLDS OF JENNIE LOGAN, THE 🦃 A young woman is magically transported one hundred years into the past. Made for TV. 99m. **DIR:** Frank DeFelitta. **CAST:** Lindsay Wagner, Marc Singer, Linda Gray, Alan Feinstein, Irene Tedrow, Henry Wilcoxon. **1979**

TWOGETHER ★★★ A lustful couple deals with a pregnancy. Though neither wants marriage, they agree to move in together and their unique lifestyles begin to clash. Complex, ambiguous tale is long on plot and short on characterization despite a hardworking cast. A feisty soundtrack contains songs from Duran Duran, Pat Benatar, Camouflage, and Primal Scream. Not rated; contains profanity, nudity, and strong sexual content. 123m. **DIR:** Andrew Chiaramonte. **CAST:** Nick Cassavetes, Brenda Bakke, Jeremy Piven, Jim Beaver. **1992**

TWONKY, THE ★★1/2 A television set literally takes over the life of a philosophy professor (Hans Conreid)—it walks, does chores, and even tells him what books to read! Bizarre, but not as much fun as it sounds—writer-director Arch Oboler (*Five*) truly hated television, and the film is a humorless harangue about the evils of the "magic box." B&W; 72m. **DIR:** Arch Oboler. **CAST:** Hans Conried, Billy Lynn, Gloria Blondell, Janet Warren. **1953**

TYCOON 🦃 A would-be epic about the building of a railroad through the Andes. 128m. **DIR:** Richard Wallace. **CAST:** John Wayne, Laraine Day, Cedric Hardwicke, Judith Anderson, Anthony Quinn, James Gleason. **1947**

TYCUS 🦃 Another comet-is-coming-to-destroy-the-Earth movie, this one about an engineer determined to complete his underground city before the comet destroys the Earth's surface. Unfortunately, terrible performances, a boring script, cheap and/or "borrowed" special effects doom this one way before the comet arrives. Rated R for violence and profanity. 94m. **DIR:** John Putch. **CAST:** Dennis Hopper, Peter Onorati, Finola Hughes, Chick Vennera. **2000 DVD**

TYSON ★★★ Scripter Robert Johnson's adaptation of José Torres's *Fire and Fear* presents a sanitized biography of championship boxer Mike Tyson, and this made-for-cable drama earns most of its respect from the strong supporting cast. Paul Winfield is a hoot as flamboyant promoter Don King, and George C. Scott is amiably irascible as Tyson's trainer and surrogate father, Cus D'Amato. Rated R for profanity, violence, and simulated sex. 105m. **DIR:** Uli Edel. **CAST:** George C. Scott, Paul Winfield, Michael Jai White, James B. Sikking, Malcolm-Jamal Warner, Tony Lo Bianco. **1995**

U

U-571 ★★★1/2 This claustrophobic WWII sub thriller is an old-fashioned, high-testosterone epic, where cast members "do the right thing" at the right moment, and address each other with nicknames such as Rabbit and Tank. In April 1942, with Hitler's U-boats pounding the hell out of Allied supply lines in the Atlantic, word comes down that the crew of an American sub will pull a "Trojan Horse" ploy and impersonate Germans during a rendezvous with a stranded U-boat, the goal being to snag the coding device that is standard equipment on all Nazi subs. The resulting mission is laden with melodrama and nail-biting tension. Rated PG-13 for war-related violence. 115m. **DIR:** Jonathan Mostow. **CAST:** Matthew McConaughey, Bill Paxton, Harvey Keitel, Jon Bon Jovi, Jake Webber, Matthew Settle, Erik Palladino, David Keith. **2000 DVD**

U-TURN ★★ Oliver Stone's adaptation of John Ridley's novel—with the author contributing his own script—is a parade of degenerate freaks given sham mythic status. This tale quickly becomes intolerable, since "victim" Sean Penn is every bit as amoral and deranged as the absurd residents of the tiny Arizona town where his 1964-1/2 Mustang breaks down. Rated R for profanity, violence, nudity, gore, and extremely strong sexual content. 125m. **DIR:** Oliver Stone. **CAST:** Sean Penn, Jennifer Lopez, Nick Nolte, Powers Boothe, Claire Danes, Joaquin Phoenix, Billy Bob Thornton, Jon Voight. **1997 DVD**

UBU AND THE GREAT GIDOUILLE ★★★1/2 Impressive animation feature by world-renowned animator Jan Lenica, loosely based on Alfred Jarry's bizarre play that recounts the grotesque adventures of Pére Ubu, who with his ignorance and greed seizes the throne of Poland and tyrannizes the people. A masterpiece of animation and black humor. In French with English subtitles. Not rated. 80m. **DIR:** Jan Lenica. **1979**

UFORIA ★★★★ Like *Repo Man* and *Stranger Than Paradise,* this low-budget American film deserved better treatment than it was given. Cindy Williams is hilarious as a born-again Christian who believes that salvation will come to Earth in the form of a flying saucer. Harry Dean Stanton plays a crooked evangelist who exploits the Jesus-in-a-spaceship concept for every penny he can get. Rated PG for profanity. 100m. **DIR:** John Binder. **CAST:** Cindy Williams, Harry Dean Stanton, Fred Ward, Harry Carey Jr., Darrell Larson. **1984**

UGETSU ★★★★1/2 Set in sixteenth-century Japan, this film follows the lives of two Japanese peasants as their greed and ambition brings disaster upon their families. There is a fine blending of action and comedy in this ghostly tale. In Japanese with English subtitles. 94m. **DIR:** Kenji Mizoguchi. **CAST:** Machiko Kyo, Masayuki Mori. **1953**

UGLY, THE ★★★ Writer-director Scott Reynolds has created a familiar yet ultimately chilling tale of a court-appointed psychiatrist whose interview with a con-

victed serial killer opens up a Pandora's box of evil. Paolo Rotundo is mesmerizing as the tormented killer who claims that demons called "The Ugly" are responsible for his reprehensible behavior. Not rated; contains graphic violence, language, and adult situations. 94m. **DIR:** Scott Reynolds. **CAST:** Paolo Rotundo, Rebecca Hobbs, Jennifer Ward-Lealand, Roy Ward. **1996 DVD**

UGLY AMERICAN, THE ★★1/2 With Marlon Brando playing an American ambassador newly arrived at his Asian post, more is expected of this film than just a routine potboiler. However, the film attempts to focus on the political interworkings of Brando's struggle with rising communist elements, but fails to generate any excitement. 120m. **DIR:** George Englund. **CAST:** Marlon Brando, Pat Hingle, Sandra Church, Arthur Hill, Eiji Okada, Jocelyn Brando. **1963**

UGLY DACHSHUND, THE ★★ In this Disney movie, Dean Jones and Suzanne Pleshette are husband and wife; she loves dachshunds and owns a number of puppies. Charlie Ruggles convinces Jones to take a Great Dane puppy to raise. Since all of its peers are dachshunds, the Great Dane tries to act like them. Somewhat entertaining along the lines of a made-for-TV-movie. Not rated. 93m. **DIR:** Norman Tokar. **CAST:** Dean Jones, Suzanne Pleshette, Charlie Ruggles, Parley Baer, Kelly Thordsen. **1966**

UHF ★★★1/2 A daydreamer finally lands in the right habitat: Channel 62, a UHF station with the lowest ratings in the country. Tastelessly innocent and funny. Rated PG-13 for profanity and violence. 95m. **DIR:** Jay Levey. **CAST:** "Weird Al" Yankovic, Victoria Jackson, Kevin McCarthy, Michael Richards, David Bowe, Anthony Geary, Billy Barty. **1989**

ULEE'S GOLD ★★★★1/2 Outstanding character study about an aging Florida beekeeper who comes out of his self-imposed emotional shell when his dysfunctional family reaches a crisis point. Peter Fonda gives the performance of his career as the taciturn Ulee (short, significantly, for Ulysses), a decent guy damaged almost beyond repair by the irresponsibility of his imprisoned son and drug-addicted daughter-in-law. Rated R. 113m. **DIR:** Victor Nunez. **CAST:** Peter Fonda, Patricia Richardson, Christine Dunford. **1997 DVD**

ULTERIOR MOTIVES ★★ A reporter pursuing a story about a research scientist stumbles onto a complex espionage plot involving the Japanese and the *yakuza*. Rated R for nudity, violence, and profanity. 95m. **DIR:** Terry Becker. **CAST:** Thomas Ian Griffith, Mary Page Keller, Joe Yamanaka, Ellen Crawford, M. C. Gainey, Ken Howard. **1992**

ULTIMATE DECEPTION ★★★ In this made-for-cable original, a woman wants a baby more than anything, and her husband is all too willing to oblige, but he commits a terrible crime to fulfill her wish. After a slow start, the story (inspired by true events) picks up momentum and builds tension to the end. Richard Grieco does a good job as the seemingly great guy who hides a dark side. Not rated, but contains violence. 95m. **DIR:** Richard A. Colla. **CAST:** Yasmine Bleeth, Richard Grieco. **1998**

ULTIMATE DESIRES A public defender poses as a prostitute to solve a murder mystery. Low-budget time waster with an overdose of sleaze. Rated R for drug use, violence, nudity, and profanity. 90m. **DIR:** Lloyd A. Simandl. **CAST:** Tracy Scoggins, Marc Singer, Brian James. **1991**

ULTIMATE WARRIOR, THE ★★1/2 The payoff doesn't match the promise of the premise in this less-than-thrilling science-fiction thriller. In the not-so-distant future, ragged residents of devastated New York City battle vicious gangs. Initially intriguing, the film stumbles to a ludicrous conclusion. Rated R. 94m. **DIR:** Robert Clouse. **CAST:** Yul Brynner, Max von Sydow, Joanna Miles, William Smith, Stephen McHattie. **1975**

ULTRAVIOLET ★★ A reconciling couple is forcibly separated by a sadistic madman in the vast expanse of Death Valley. A *Dead Calm* variation. Rated R for nudity and profanity. 80m. **DIR:** Mark Griffiths. **CAST:** Esai Morales, Patricia Healy, Stephen Meadows. **1992 DVD**

ULTRAWARRIOR Another patchwork film from Roger Corman that has scenes stolen from other films to pad the slight story. Rated R for profanity, violence, and nudity. 75m. **DIR:** Augusto Tamayo, Kevin Tent. **CAST:** Meshach Taylor, Clare Beresford. **1992**

ULYSSES ★★ One of Kirk Douglas's least successful independent productions, this heavily dubbed Italian epic emphasizes dialogue over thrills. Kirk Douglas does his best, but he gets mired down in this slow retelling of Ulysses's long voyage home after the Trojan War. 104m. **DIR:** Mario Camerini. **CAST:** Kirk Douglas, Silvana Mangano, Anthony Quinn, Rossana Podesta, Sylvie. **1955 DVD**

ULYSSES' GAZE ★★★1/2 The first of Theo Angelopoulos's films to be seen widely in the United States, *Ulysses' Gaze* is not the best introduction to the work of the renowned Greek filmmaker. This story of a historian (Harvey Keitel) searching the war-torn Balkans for three reels of film shot there in 1904 is, at three hours, rather slow-going. But it offers much of great beauty for those with the patience to stick with it. In English and Greek with English subtitles. Not rated; contains nudity, sexual situations, violence, and profanity. 178m. **DIR:** Theo Angelopoulos. **CAST:** Harvey Keitel, Maia Morgenstern, Erland Josephson. **1995 DVD**

ULZANA'S RAID ★★★★ A tense and absorbing film. Burt Lancaster and an expert cast and director take a fine screenplay penned by Alan Sharp and create a cavalry-Indians tale that is far from ordinary. Burt Lancaster plays an Indian scout who helps an inexperienced cavalry officer try to roust renegade Apache Ulzana and his tribe. Rated R. 103m. **DIR:** Robert Aldrich. **CAST:** Burt Lancaster, Bruce Davison, Jorge Luke, Richard Jaeckel, Lloyd Bochner. **1972 DVD**

UMBERTO D ★★★★★ Seems as poignant now as when it was initially released. Quite simply, the plot centers upon a retired civil servant trying to maintain some sort of dignity and life for himself and his dog on his meager government pension. The film is agonizingly candid. A Vittorio De Sica masterpiece. In Italian with English subtitles. B&W; 89m. **DIR:** Vittorio De Sica. **CAST:** Carlo Battisti, Maria Pia Casilio. **1955**

UMBRELLAS OF CHERBOURG, THE ★★★★ Simply the most romantic film to come from France in the 1960s. Catherine Deneuve made her first popular appearance, and we've been madly in love with her ever since. Simple story—boy meets girl—but played against a luxuriously photographed backdrop. Exquisite score from Michel Legrand. Watch this with some-

body you love. 91m. **DIR:** Jacques Demy. **CAST:** Catherine Deneuve, Nino Castelnuovo, Marc Michel. **1964 DVD**

UN CHIEN ANDALOU ★★★★★ Possibly the only film ever made completely according to surrealist principles, this famous short consists of a series of shocking and humorous images. Luis Buñuel and Salvador Dali wrote down some of their dreams and then photographed them. Sixty years later this seventeen-minute film retains the power to startle. The videotape includes four other avant-garde shorts. Of interest to the serious cinema student. B&W; 74m. **DIR:** Luis Buñuel, Salvador Dali. **1928**

UN COEUR EN HIVER ★★★★1/2 The delicacy and detail with which the French view romantic relationships often make for intoxicating viewing, as amply evidenced by this superb study of heartbreak. Enhanced by the glorious music of Ravel's sonatas and trios. In French with English subtitles. Not rated, the film has profanity, suggested sex, and light violence. **DIR:** Claude Sautet. **CAST:** Daniel Auteuil, Emmanuelle Beart, André Dussolier, Elisabeth Bourgnine, Brigitte Catillon, Maurice Garrel, Myriam Boyer. **1993**

UN SINGE EN HIVER (A MONKEY IN WINTER) ★★1/2 Alcoholic Jean Gabin vows to swear off if he and his wife survive the bombing of their village during World War II. They do, and he does. Years pass. A young version of Gabin arrives and rekindles the older man's memories of drink and dreams. In French with English subtitles. Originally released in the U.S. as *A Monkey in Winter*. Marred by murky photography. B&W; 105m. **DIR:** Henri Verneuil. **CAST:** Jean Gabin, Jean-Paul Belmondo, Suzanne Flon, Paul Frankeur, Noel Roquevert. **1962**

UNAPPROACHABLE, THE 🦃 A completely unwatchable film about a young man obsessed with a reclusive aging starlet. Not rated; contains profanity. 100m. **DIR:** Krzysztof Zanussi. **CAST:** Leslie Caron, Daniel Webb, Leslie Magon. **1982**

UNBEARABLE LIGHTNESS OF BEING, THE ★★★★★ One of the most playfully alive films ever made. Philip Kaufman calls his film a "variation" of Milan Kundera's novel about a womanizing neurosurgeon from Prague. What results is something poetic, erotic, funny, and exuberant. Rated R for sexual content. 164m. **DIR:** Phil Kaufman. **CAST:** Daniel Day-Lewis, Juliette Binoche, Lena Olin, Derek de Lint, Erland Josephson. **1988 DVD**

UNBELIEVABLE TRUTH, THE ★★1/2 When Robert Burke returns home after an extended vacation in prison, his presense gets the whole town talking. Offbeat film with an edge. Rated R for its profanity. 90m. **DIR:** Hal Hartley. **CAST:** Adrienne Shelly, Robert Burke, Christopher Cooke, Gary Sauer, Julia McNeal, Mark Bailey. **1990 DVD**

UNBORN, THE 🦃 Title says it all: another ferocious fetus movie that's unfortunately not stillborn. Rated R for nudity, violence, and profanity. 84m. **DIR:** Rodman Flender. **CAST:** Brooke Adams, Jeff Hayenga, James Karen, K. Callan, Jane Cameron. **1991 DVD**

UNBORN II, THE 🦃 Ferocious fetus returns for more mayhem, as Mom and a friend try to stop a fanatic from destroying the offspring. Just as bad as the first one. Rated R for violence and language. 84m. **DIR:** Rick Jacobson. **CAST:** Michele Greene, Scott Valentine, Robin Curtis, Michael James McDonald. **1994**

UNBREAKABLE ★★★1/2 Although the premise and setup are intriguing, you're bound to be unhappy with the conclusion: the final twist seems a contrived effort to top the surprise at the end of *The Sixth Sense*. Bruce Willis is too dour as the woebegone hero who gradually realizes that he possesses extraordinary talents. Samuel L. Jackson, as a gallery owner and comic-book historian, is a far more galvanic character. Still, it's interesting to watch them interact... the first time. Rated PG-13 for violence and dramatic intensity. 107m. **DIR:** M. Night Shyamalan. **CAST:** Bruce Willis, Samuel L. Jackson, Robin Wright, Spencer Treat Clark. **2000 DVD**

UNCANNY, THE 🦃 A paranoid writer tells three tales of cat-related horror. Rated R. 88m. **DIR:** Denis Heroux. **CAST:** Peter Cushing, Ray Milland, Susan Penhaligon, Joan Greenwood, Donald Pleasence, Samantha Eggar, John Vernon. **1977**

UNCERTAIN GLORY ★★ A curiosity piece from World War II days and a pale imitation of previous war melodramas. The movie has the advantage of Errol Flynn as its roguish leading man who turns himself into a hero. But it takes him much too long to do it. B&W; 102m. **DIR:** Raoul Walsh. **CAST:** Errol Flynn, Paul Lukas, Jean Sullivan, Lucile Watson, Faye Emerson. **1944**

UNCLE BUCK ★★★★ If you enjoyed John Candy in *Planes, Trains and Automobiles*, you'll love him here as the slobbish Uncle Buck who is called upon to take care of his brother's three kids when their mother's father has a heart attack. The results are hilarious and heartwarming. Rated PG for profanity. 106m. **DIR:** John Hughes. **CAST:** John Candy, Amy Madigan, Jean Kelly, Gaby Hoffman, Macaulay Culkin. **1989 DVD**

UNCLE SAM ★★★ Those *Maniac Cop* guys, director William Lustig and writer Larry Cohen, strike again. This time out an abusive marine shot down in Desert Storm returns from the grave to mete out vengeance in fine slasher style on draft dodgers, flag burners, and his ex-wife. Cohen and Lustig plant tongue firmly in cheek as our antihero dons an Uncle Sam outfit and begins his bloody redemption. Highly amusing entertainment for fans of this genre. Rated R for violence, profanity, and gore. 90m. **DIR:** William Lustig. **CAST:** Bo Hopkins, Timothy Bottoms, Robert Forster, P. J. Soles, Isaac Hayes. **1996 DVD**

UNCOMMON VALOR ★★★★ In this action-packed adventure film, retired Marine Gene Hackman learns that his son may still be alive in a Vietnamese prison camp ten years after being listed as missing in action. He decides to go in after him. Rated R for profanity and violence. 105m. **DIR:** Ted Kotcheff. **CAST:** Gene Hackman, Fred Ward, Reb Brown, Randall "Tex" Cobb, Harold Sylvester, Robert Stack. **1983 DVD**

UNCONQUERED ★★★★1/2 A colorful adventure set in colonial times with a sizzling romance between a soldier and the woman he rescues from slavery. Well-staged battle scenes and lush Technicolor landscapes give the film authenticity. Personable performers make it fun to watch in spite of its length. 146m. **DIR:** Cecil B. DeMille. **CAST:** Gary Cooper, Paulette Goddard, Boris Karloff, Howard DaSilva, Ward Bond, Mike Mazurki, C. Aubrey Smith. **1947**

UNDEAD, THE ★★★ Psychiatrist delving into the past lives of a prostitute gets taken for a ride back to the Mid-

dle Ages, where he tries to thwart his patient's impending execution but discovers that you can't alter history. A thinking fan's drive-in movie—a moody, offbeat melodrama—this is absolutely the best horror film with a trick ending ever shot in an abandoned grocery store. B&W; 71m. **DIR:** Roger Corman. **CAST:** Pamela Duncan, Richard Garland, Allison Hayes, Val Dufour, Dorothy Neuman, Billy Barty, Richard Devon. **1957**

UNDEFEATABLE 🦃 Kung fu queen Cynthia Rothrock is at it again. She's out to avenge the murder of her sister by a serial killer, who's also a martial arts expert. Rated R for nudity, violence, and profanity. 95m. **DIR:** Godfrey Hall. **CAST:** Cynthia Rothrock, Don Niam, John Miller, Donna Jason, Emilie Davazac, Hang Yip Kim, Gerald Klein. **1993**

UNDEFEATED, THE ★★ Lumbering large-scale Western has Yankee colonel John Wayne forming an uneasy alliance with Confederate colonel Rock Hudson to sell wild horses in Mexico. This film has little to recommend it—even to die-hard Wayne fans. Even the action is minimal. Rated PG. 119m. **DIR:** Andrew V. McLaglen. **CAST:** John Wayne, Rock Hudson, Bruce Cabot, Ben Johnson, Antonio Aguilar, Harry Carey Jr., Lee Meriwether, Jan-Michael Vincent. **1969**

UNDER CALIFORNIA STARS ★★1/2 Trigger, the "Smartest Horse in the Movies," is the victim of a horsenapping plot in this enjoyable Roy Rogers oater. 71m. **DIR:** William Witney. **CAST:** Roy Rogers, Jane Frazee, Andy Devine, Michael Chapin. **1948**

UNDER CAPRICORN ★★★ This film is about a nineteenth-century Australian household that is hiding some dark secrets. Michael Wilding is drawn into solving the family's mystery because of his attraction to the lady of the house, Ingrid Bergman. This is not a typical Alfred Hitchcock movie. It lacks his customary suspense, and its pace could be called leisurely at best. 117m. **DIR:** Alfred Hitchcock. **CAST:** Michael Wilding, Ingrid Bergman, Joseph Cotten. **1949**

UNDER FIRE ★★1/2 Nick Nolte, Gene Hackman, and Joanna Cassidy are journalists covering political upheaval in Central America circa 1979. While *Under Fire* has its moments (found primarily in the superb supporting performances of Ed Harris and French actor Jean-Louis Trintignant), you have to wade through a bit of sludge to get to them. Rated R for profanity, violence, and gore. 128m. **DIR:** Roger Spottiswoode. **CAST:** Nick Nolte, Gene Hackman, Joanna Cassidy, Ed Harris, Jean-Louis Trintignant. **1983 DVD**

UNDER INVESTIGATION ★★ Harry Hamlin stars as a grungy L.A. detective in this sordid murder mystery. His main suspect is the wife of a famous murdered artist who stands to inherit a small fortune. Lustful looks, heavy breathing, and panting are substituted for plot and dialogue. Rated R for nudity, simulated sex, violence, and profanity. 99m. **DIR:** Kevin Meyer. **CAST:** Harry Hamlin, Joanna Pacula, Ed Lauter, Richard Beymer, John Mese, Lydie Denier. **1993**

UNDER LOCK AND KEY ★★ To get the goods on a powerful drug lord, an FBI agent goes undercover in a women's prison. Rated R for sexual scenes, violence, and strong language. 90m. **DIR:** Henri Charr. **CAST:** Wendi Westbrook, Barbara Niven, Taylor Leigh, Stephanie Ann Smith, Sai Tyler. **1995**

UNDER MEXICALI STARS ★★★ Modern-day Western involves counterfeiters and gold smugglers using helicopters to transport their contraband. B&W; 67m. **DIR:** George Blair. **CAST:** Rex Allen, Buddy Ebsen, Dorothy Patrick, Roy Barcroft. **1950**

UNDER MILK WOOD ★★ Welsh poet Dylan Thomas's play loses its vitality in this slow, stuffy, dry, image-burdened film version. All the queen's men plus the beautiful Elizabeth Taylor, cannot infuse it with life. 90m. **DIR:** Andrew Sinclair. **CAST:** Elizabeth Taylor, Richard Burton, Peter O'Toole, Glynis Johns, Vivien Merchant, Sian Phillips. **1973**

UNDER OATH ★★★1/2 Two cops decide to solve their financial problems by shaking down a gunrunner. But the plan goes awry, leaving them desperately trying to cover up an accidental murder. Snappy, low-budget thriller, also released as *Blood Money* and *Unborn Justice*. Rated R for profanity, violence, and brief nudity. 89m. **DIR:** Dave Payne. **CAST:** Jack Scalia, James Russo, Richard Lynch. **1997 DVD**

UNDER PRESSURE ★★1/2 Mostly ludicrous thriller is buoyed by Charlie Sheen's portrayal of a psycho neighbor who's on the edge of exploding into violence. Also known as *Bad Day on the Block*. Rated R for profanity and violence. 88m. **DIR:** Craig R. Baxley. **CAST:** Charlie Sheen, Mare Winningham, David Andrews, Dawnn Lewis, John Ratzenberger. **1997**

UNDER SIEGE ★★★★1/2 Reuniting with director Andrew Davis, Steven Seagal comes up with another winner. A gang of terrorists take over a naval ship with nuclear capabilities only to discover that one-man-army Seagal is on board to give 'em hell. Rip-roaring entertainment. Rated R for profanity, nudity, and violence. 103m. **DIR:** Andrew Davis. **CAST:** Steven Seagal, Tommy Lee Jones, Gary Busey, Nick Mancuso, Erika Eleniak, Patrick O'Neal, Colm Meaney. **1992 DVD**

UNDER SIEGE 2: DARK TERRITORY ★★★1/2 While not as good as the original entry in the series, this sequel still has much to offer fans of Steven Seagal and action movies. This time, series hero Casey Ryback (Seagal) is escorting his niece by rail from her father's funeral when a group of terrorists take over the train. It's up to the ultimate one-man army to save the day. Rated R for violence and profanity. 100m. **DIR:** Geoff Murphy. **CAST:** Steven Seagal, Eric Bogosian, Katherine Heigl, Everett McGill, Morris Chestnut, Kurtwood Smith, Nick Mancuso. **1995 DVD**

UNDER SUSPICION (1991) ★★★ Womanizing private investigator Liam Neeson's wife and client are murdered, he becomes the prime suspect. Multiple plot twists and an edge-of-your-seat climax that border on the unbelievable. Rated R for nudity, violence, and profanity. 100m. **DIR:** Simon Moore. **CAST:** Liam Neeson, Laura San Giacomo, Kenneth Cranham, Maggie O'Neill. **1991**

•UNDER SUSPICION (2000) ★★★★ Riveting battle of wills played out in a Puerto Rico police station stars Gene Hackman as Henry B. Hearst, an American expatriate lawyer suspected of a series of brutal murders involving children. Morgan Freeman plays police captain Victor Benezet, who is in charge of the interrogation. As the evening wears on, both men wrestle for dominance in this intense chamber piece that constantly catches

you by surprise. You become so immersed in the drama you forget what you're watching is basically a two-character play. Rated R for adult situations, language, and violence. 110m. **DIR:** Stephen Hopkins. **CAST:** Gene Hackman, Morgan Freeman, Thomas Jane, Monica Bellucci. **2000 DVD**

UNDER TEXAS SKIES ★★★ Bob Steele's first with the Three Mesquiteers finds him suspected of killing a sheriff. B&W; 54m. **DIR:** George Sherman. **CAST:** Robert Livingston, Bob Steele, Rufe Davis, Henry Brandon. **1940**

UNDER THE BILTMORE CLOCK ★★★ This acceptable TV adaptation of F. Scott Fitzgerald's "Myra Meets His Family" presents Sean Young as a young woman who decides to marry for wealth; she then has the task of meeting fiancé Lenny Von Dohlen's eccentric family. 70m. **DIR:** Neal Miller. **CAST:** Sean Young, Lenny von Dohlen, Barnard Hughes. **1985**

UNDER THE BOARDWALK 🦃 In this *West Side Story* update, the *lowks* (local dudes) take on the *vals* to see who will rule the local waves and babes. Rated R for violence and profanity. 102m. **DIR:** Fritz Kiersch. **CAST:** Danielle von Zerneck, Keith Coogan, Richard Joseph Paul, Sonny Bono. **1988**

UNDER THE CHERRY MOON ★★ Prince plays a gigolo-type singer who pursues a debutante, Mary (Kristin Scott Thomas). Rated PG-13 for language and mature theme. B&W; 100m. **DIR:** Prince. **CAST:** Prince, Jerome Benton, Steven Berkoff, Alexandra Stewart, Kristin Scott Thomas, Francesca Annis. **1986**

UNDER THE DOMIM TREE ★★★ Slow-moving, loosely structured movie set in 1950s Israel, at a village for children whose parents died in Nazi death camps. Despite the unusual setting, it's not much different from many other coming-of-age movies, though obviously deeply felt. Not rated; no objectionable material. 102m. **DIR:** Eli Cohen. **CAST:** Kaipo Cohen, Juliano Mer. **1996**

UNDER THE GUN 🦃 A hotheaded St. Louis cop comes to Los Angeles to investigate the murder of his brother. Rated R for language, violence, and nudity. 90m. **DIR:** James Sbardellati. **CAST:** Vanessa L. Williams, Sam Jones, John Russell. **1988**

UNDER THE HULA MOON ★★★1/2 Offbeat romance about a luckless couple living in a trailer park in Arizona who dream of something better. Interesting characters and outrageous situations make this little slice of white-trash humor worth a look. Rated R for violence, adult situations, and language. 96m. **DIR:** Jeff Celentano. **CAST:** Stephen Baldwin, Emily Lloyd, Christopher Penn. **1995**

UNDER THE RAINBOW ★★1/2 While this comedy is not quite jam-packed with laughs, it certainly keeps your interest. Set in 1938, the improbable story centers around the making of *The Wizard of Oz*, assassination attempts on a duke and duchess, the nefarious doings of Nazi and Japanese spies prior to World War II, and the life span of a dog named Streudel. Rated PG because of slight nudity and suggestive dialogue. 98m. **DIR:** Steve Rash. **CAST:** Chevy Chase, Carrie Fisher, Eve Arden, Joseph Maher. **1981**

UNDER THE ROOFS OF PARIS ★★★★ This simple Parisian love story of a street singer and a young girl is less important for its plot than for its style: at a time when most movies were overdosing on dialogue, director René Clair used music and other types of sound to advance his story. It is also, like most of Clair's films, a charming depiction of his home city. In French with English subtitles. B&W; 92m. **DIR:** René Clair. **CAST:** Albert Préjean, Pola Illery. **1929**

•**UNDER THE SAND** ★★★★ Marie and Jean Drillon settle uneventfully into their French vacation house. During a trip to the beach, Jean goes off for a swim and never returns. Marie enlists the aid of local officials whose searches by lifeguards and a helicopter are futile. But when Marie returns home in a state of emotional limbo, Jean returns, too, making us wonder if he is an apparition or a figment of Marie's overtaxed imagination. In French with English subtitles. Not rated; contains nudity, sex, and profanity. 90m. **DIR:** François Ozon. **CAST:** Charlotte Rampling, Bruno Cremer, Jacques Nolot. **2001 DVD**

UNDER THE SKIN ★★★ Two sisters grow apart when their mother's death sends their sibling rivalry spinning out of control. The film's chief asset is a riveting performance by Samantha Morton as the younger, more unstable sister. Not rated; contains profanity and graphic sexual scenes. 85m. **DIR:** Carine Adler. **CAST:** Samantha Morton, Claire Rushbrook, Rita Tushingham, Stuart Townsend. **1997 DVD**

UNDER THE SUN OF SATAN ★★ Though well-acted and emotionally complex, this drama about a wavering French priest will only reach viewers willing to wade through the film's murky, slow-moving style. In French with English subtitles. Not rated. 97m. **DIR:** Maurice Pialat. **CAST:** Gérard Depardieu, Sandrine Bonnaire, Maurice Pialat. **1987**

UNDER THE VOLCANO ★★★★ Brilliant, but disturbing, adaptation of the Malcolm Lowry novel about a suicidal, alcoholic British consul in Mexico on the eve of World War II. Rated R for suggested sex, violence, and profanity. 109m. **DIR:** John Huston. **CAST:** Albert Finney, Jacqueline Bisset, Anthony Andrews. **1984**

UNDER WESTERN STARS ★★★1/2 Roy Rogers, in his first feature, plays a young congressman trying to obtain waterpower for the Dust Bowl area. Academy Award nomination for the song "Dust." B&W; 54m. **DIR:** Joseph Kane. **CAST:** Roy Rogers, Smiley Burnette, Carol Hughes. **1938**

UNDERCOVER (1987) ★★ Cliché-ridden cop story. David Neidorf is a policeman who goes undercover in a South Carolina high school. Rated R for language and nudity. 92m. **DIR:** John Stockwell. **CAST:** David Neidorf, Jennifer Jason Leigh, Barry Corbin, David Harris, Kathleen Wilhoite. **1987**

UNDERCOVER (1995) 🦃 Half-baked crime and sexploitation hybrid about a police detective who poses as a hooker. Rated R for sexual scenes and nudity. An "adult" version, not rated, is also available. 93/101. **DIR:** Alexander Gregory Hippolyte. **CAST:** Athena Massey, Tom Tayback, Anthony Guidera, Meg Foster. **1995 DVD**

UNDERCOVER ANGEL ★★★1/2 A struggling writer's bachelor life is interrupted when he's forced to take care of the six year old daughter of an ex-girlfriend. The moppet soon wins over the writer, and begins playing matchmaker for him. Likable cast makes this an engaging romantic comedy. Rated PG-13 for adult situations. 93m. **DIR:** Bryan Michael Stoller. **CAST:** Yasmine

Bleeth, Dean Winters, Emily Mae Young, Casey Kasem, James Earl Jones. **2000 DVD**

UNDERCOVER BLUES ★★★ Sometimes stupid films are so charming that you can't help enjoying them—Ian Abrams's terminally silly update of *The Thin Man* is a perfect example. Superspies Jane and Jeff Blue are called out of retirement and child-rearing to save the world from a master villainess. Stanley Tucci steals the show. Rated PG-13 for cartoon violence and sensuality. 89m. **DIR:** Herbert Ross. **CAST:** Kathleen Turner, Dennis Quaid, Fiona Shaw, Stanley Tucci, Larry Miller, Obba Babatundé. **1993**

UNDERCURRENT ★★ A bride (Katharine Hepburn) comes to realize her husband (Robert Taylor) is a scoundrel. Considering the talent involved, this is a peculiarly dull drama. B&W; 116m. **DIR:** Vincente Minnelli. **CAST:** Katharine Hepburn, Robert Taylor, Robert Mitchum, Edmund Gwenn, Jayne Meadows, Marjorie Main. **1946 DVD**

UNDERGRADS, THE ★★★1/2 This made-for-cable Disney film has only sporadic funny moments. Art Carney plays a spunky senior citizen whose son would like to put him into a rest home. Chris Makepeace (Carney's movie grandson) refuses to allow this. Instead, he and his grandfather become college roommates. A good film with some heavy moments. 102m. **DIR:** Steven H. Stern. **CAST:** Art Carney, Chris Makepeace, Jackie Burroughs, Len Birman, Alfie Scopp. **1984**

UNDERGROUND (1990) 🦃 A young woman takes a job as a waitress in a sleazy strip joint where she falls in love with a disc jockey searching for his missing sister, last seen in the bar. Not rated, with violence and nudity. 87m. **DIR:** Bret Carr. **CAST:** Rachel Carr, Clement von Franckenstein, Sean Rankin. **1990 DVD**

UNDERGROUND (1995) ★★★★ A manufacturer of black-market arms in World War II keeps his business going after the war by tricking his workers—all political refugees—into remaining in their underground factory by telling them that the war is still going on. Winner of the Palme d'Or at the 1995 Cannes Film Festival, *Underground* is a lively blend of absurd humor and political allegory. Not rated; contains nudity, strong violence, and sexual situations. 169m. **DIR:** Emir Kusturica. **CAST:** Miki Manojlovic, Mirjana Jokovic. **1995**

UNDERGROUND ACES 🦃 Big-city hotel parking attendants run amok. Rated PG for profanity and nudity. 93m. **DIR:** Robert Butler. **CAST:** Dirk Benedict, Melanie Griffith, Kario Salem, Robert Hegyes, Audrey Landers, Frank Gorshin. **1980**

UNDERNEATH, THE ★★★ Director Steven Soderbergh's tale of an ex-con who reverts to his old ways in order to be with the woman he loves. Uneven but often intriguing film isn't a complete success but is entertaining for the most part. Sadly, Elisabeth Shue is all but wasted as a local girl. Rated R for profanity. 100m. **DIR:** Steven Soderbergh. **CAST:** Peter Gallagher, Alison Elliott, Elisabeth Shue, Joe Don Baker, Paul Dooley. **1994 DVD**

UNDERSEA KINGDOM ★★1/2 "Crash" Corrigan plays himself in this science-fiction serial of the 1930s as he attempts to thwart the evil plans of Unga Khan and his followers, who live under the ocean in the ancient city of Atlantis. Filled with gadgetry, robots, and futuristic machines, this cliff-hanger was extremely popular with young audiences, and it's still a lot of fun today. B&W; 12 chapters. **DIR:** B. Reeves "Breezy" Eason, Joseph Kane. **CAST:** Ray "Crash" Corrigan, Lois Wilde, Monte Blue, William Farnum, Lee Van Atta, Smiley Burnette, Lon Chaney Jr. **1936 DVD**

UNDERSTUDY, THE: GRAVEYARD SHIFT II ★★ Silvio Oliviero returns in this sequel, playing an actor who gets the lead role in a vampire film without the rest of the cast knowing he really *is* a vampire. Rated R for nudity and gore. 88m. **DIR:** Gerard Ciccoritti. **CAST:** Wendy Gazelle, Mark Soper, Silvio Oliviero. **1988**

UNDERTAKER AND HIS PALS, THE 🦃 A mortician and two diner owners team up in a money-making venture, using human legs, breasts, etc., as the daily specials. Not rated. 70m. **DIR:** David C. Graham. **CAST:** Ray Dannis. **1967**

UNDERTAKER'S WEDDING, THE ★★★ Unexpectedly offbeat dark comedy about a young mortician working for the mob. Thanks to a long-standing rivalry, business is booming. Adrien Brody is deliciously wry as the young man who gets more than he bargained for when he's involved in a double cross. Kari Wuhrer shows maturity as an actress, playing the fiancée who is as understanding as she is good looking. Rated R for adult situations, language, and violence. 90m. **DIR:** John Bradshaw. **CAST:** Adrien Brody, Jeff Wincott, Kari Wuhrer, Burt Young. **1996**

UNDERTOW ★★1/2 Personable drifter Lou Diamond Phillips gets stranded during a hellish rainstorm with a wacko survivalist and his fearful wife. The cabin is crammed with guns and bear traps; you can work out the rest. The already sluggish film is made even more tedious by countless shots of both men bellowing in slow-motion frustration. Rated R for profanity, violence, nudity, and simulated sex. 93m. **DIR:** Eric Red. **CAST:** Lou Diamond Phillips, Mia Sara, Charles Dance. **1995**

UNDERWATER! ★★ The best stories about this sopping-wet adventure center around the elaborate publicity launched by reclusive millionaire Howard Hughes to sell it to the public. Hughes's original idea of supplying the press with Aqualungs and screening the film in an underwater theater didn't help the reviews and only made this costly, overblown story of sea scavengers more of a hoot than it already was. 99m. **DIR:** John Sturges. **CAST:** Jane Russell, Gilbert Roland, Richard Egan, Jayne Mansfield, Lori Nelson. **1955**

UNDERWORLD (1927) ★★★ After being rescued from prison by his moll and right-hand man, a gangster soon realizes that the two are having an affair. One of the first movies to look at crime through the gangster's point of view. Silent. B&W; 82m. **DIR:** Josef von Sternberg. **CAST:** George Bancroft, Evelyn Brent. **1927**

UNDERWORLD (1996) ★★★ Therapeutic revenge thriller about an ex-con trying to clear his thoughts by killing everyone responsible for taking out his old man. Denis Leary stars as Johnny Crown, fresh out of prison, who puts his future on hold in order to hunt down the responsible parties. Rated R for adult situations, language, and violence. 95m. **DIR:** Roger Christian. **CAST:** Denis Leary, Joe Mantegna, Annabella Sciorra, Traci Lords, Abe Vigoda. **1996 DVD**

UNDERWORLD STORY ★★1/2 Hardboiled story of a mercenary reporter who exposes a ruthless publisher who is attempting to frame an innocent man for murder.

The story is full of holes, and the portrait of journalism is about as sordid as anything done on the subject before or since. B&W; 90m. **DIR:** Cy Endfield. **CAST:** Dan Duryea, Herbert Marshall, Gale Storm, Howard DaSilva, Michael O'Shea, Mary Anderson, Melville Cooper, Gar Moore, Frieda Inescort, Art Baker. **1950**

UNDERWORLD U.S.A. ★★★1/2 Impressive crime-drama from writer-director Sam Fuller about a man (Cliff Robertson) who, after witnessing his father's death at the hands of mobsters, develops a lifetime obsession to get even with the murderers. Great cinematography and exceptional performances rise above the weak script. B&W; 99m. **DIR:** Samuel Fuller. **CAST:** Cliff Robertson, Dolores Dorn. **1961**

UNDYING MONSTER, THE ★★★1/2 A criminologist employs modern techniques to rid the moors of a murderous monster and free the local gentry from a centuries-old curse. Atmospheric thriller gives the impression of a British film shot on location. Actually, it's an intelligent, supernatural film that dignifies its subject. Little known to the general public, this beauty is one of the best werewolf movies and the only good horror film to come from Twentieth Century Fox in the 1940s. B&W; 64m. **DIR:** John Brahm. **CAST:** James Ellison, Heather Angel, John Howard, Bramwell Fletcher, Heather Thatcher, Aubrey Mather, Halliwell Hobbes. **1942**

UNE PARTIE DE PLAISIR (PIECE OF PLEASURE) ★★★ Life and art uncomfortably commingle in this loosely fictionalized look at the troubled marriage of Paul Gegauff, director Claude Chabrol's usual scriptwriter. Gegauff plays himself (opposite his real ex-wife)—one can only hope that the brutal behavior he displays here was exaggerated. (A few years later, he was murdered by his second wife.) Occasionally fascinating, it may leave the viewer feeling voyeuristic. In French with English subtitles. Not rated. 100m. **DIR:** Claude Chabrol. **CAST:** Paul Gegauff, Danielle Gegauff. **1975**

UNEARTHING, THE 🦃 Young, unwed pregnant girl accepts offer of a young heir to a wealthy estate to be his bride so his ailing mother can die happy. The girl's there for the money; the rest of the family wants to sacrifice her baby. Rated R for violence and language. 83m. **DIR:** Wrye Martin, Barry Poltermann. **CAST:** Norman Moses, Tina Ona Paukstelis. **1993**

UNEARTHLY, THE 🦃 Mad scientist goes back into the lab to torture more innocent victims. 73m. **DIR:** Brooke L. Peters. **CAST:** John Carradine, Allison Hayes, Myron Healey. **1957**

UNEXPECTED ENCOUNTERS 🦃 This couples-only, after-hours rental is little more than a tease. Not rated (however there's partial nudity). 60m. **DIR:** Mannie Marshall. **CAST:** Giselle Wilder, Justin Dylan. **1988**

UNEXPECTED FAMILY, AN ★★1/2 An unmarried woman inherits two children from her sister, who abandons them to pursue a love interest in London. Predictably, the woman and the kids don't get along, then slowly work things out. This made-for-cable original may have sounded like a good idea, but simply ends up boring. Not rated. 95m. **DIR:** Larry Elikann. **CAST:** Stockard Channing, Stephen Collins, Christine Ebersole, Noah Fleiss. **1996**

UNEXPECTED LIFE, AN ★★1/2 This overbearing drama is about a woman and her makeshift family—her boyfriend and her sister's two kids—and how they adjust to a new baby in the family. Everyone has issues in this made-for-cable original, and predictably, everything is patched up by the end. Not rated. 95m. **DIR:** David Jones. **CAST:** Stockard Channing, Stephen Collins, Christine Ebersole, Noah Fleiss, Elaine Stritch. **1997**

•UNFAITHFUL ★★★ Those who've followed director Adrian Lyne's career will expect this picture to be another smoldering erotic romp highlighted by gorgeous cinematography, seductive music, artful nudity, and passionate, drawn-out glances between attractive leads. To a degree, that expectation is met when philandering wife Diane Lane gets hot 'n' heavy with charismatic Frenchman Olivier Martinez. But the film takes an unexpected turn after its long first act, and settles into a dramatic mode that stone-faced costar Richard Gere (as Lane's husband) can't make credible. The central notion—that actions have consequences which will overwhelm ordinary people—was handled much better in 2001's *In the Bedroom*. Rated R for profanity, nudity, brief violence, and strong sexual content. 121m. **DIR:** Adrian Lyne. **CAST:** Richard Gere, Diane Lane, Olivier Martinez, Erik Per Sullivan. **2002 DVD**

UNFAITHFULLY YOURS (1948) ★★★ Symphony conductor Rex Harrison suspects his wife of infidelity and contemplates several solutions to his "problem." This film follows all the prerequisites of screwball comedies—mistaken identities, misinterpreted remarks. Harrison has fun, but his energy cannot sustain a film that runs about fifteen minutes too long. Not rated—family fare. B&W; 105m. **DIR:** Preston Sturges. **CAST:** Rex Harrison, Linda Darnell, Kurt Kreuger, Barbara Lawrence, Rudy Vallee, Lionel Stander. **1948**

UNFAITHFULLY YOURS (1984) ★★★ In this entertaining and sometimes hilarious remake of Preston Sturges's 1948 comedy, Dudley Moore plays a symphony orchestra conductor who suspects his wife (Nastassja Kinski) of fooling around with a violinist (Armand Assante) and decides to get revenge. Rated PG for nudity and profanity. 96m. **DIR:** Howard Zieff. **CAST:** Dudley Moore, Nastassja Kinski, Armand Assante, Albert Brooks. **1984**

UNFINISHED PIECE FOR THE PLAYER PIANO, AN (UNFINISHED PIECE FOR A MECHANICAL PIANO, AN) ★★★★ Based on the writing of Anton Chekhov, this film is alive with intimate character portraits. A group of aristocrats gather for an annual family reunion where they find their traditional values and way of life are slipping away, poisoned by their own excesses. In Russian with English subtitles. 100m. **DIR:** Nikita Mikhalkov. **CAST:** Alexander Kalyagin, Elena Soloyei, Yevgenta Clushenko, Oleg Tabakov. **1977**

UNFORGETTABLE ★★ This chilling, crackpot thriller involves several transfers of brain fluid between dead and living people but no credible smarts of its own. A Seattle forensic pathologist steals an experimental memory-retrieval potion and injects himself with his dead wife's cerebral juices in hopes of finding his wife's killer. The warped story unravels. Rated R for nudity and violence. 111m. **DIR:** John Dahl. **CAST:** Ray Liotta, Linda Fiorentino, Peter Coyote, Kim Cattrall, David Paymer, Christopher McDonald. **1996**

UNFORGETTABLE SUMMER, AN ★★★ In 1925, a Bulgarian officer and his wife are assigned to an un-

tamed outpost on the Bulgarian/Romanian border, where tribal hatreds seem impossible to overcome. While it is an effective history lesson, it is hurt by thin characterizations. In Swedish and Romanian with English subtitles. Not rated; contains nudity, violence, and adult themes. 81m. **DIR:** Lucian Pintilie. **CAST:** Claudiu Bleont, George Constantin, Kristin Scott Thomas, Marcel Iures. **1992**

UNFORGIVEN, THE (1960) ★★★1/2 This tough Texas saga is filled with pride, prejudice, and passion. Audrey Hepburn, as a troubled Indian girl raised by whites, is at the center of the turmoil. In addition to some intriguing relationships, the movie provides plenty of thrills with intense cowboy-versus-Indian action scenes. The cast is uniformly excellent. 125m. **DIR:** John Huston. **CAST:** Burt Lancaster, Audrey Hepburn, Audie Murphy, John Saxon, Charles Bickford, Lillian Gish, Doug McClure, Joseph Wiseman, Albert Salmi. **1960**

UNFORGIVEN (1992) ★★★★ A former outlaw returns to violence in order to bring down a corrupt sheriff in the troubled town of Big Whiskey. Actor-director Clint Eastwood returns to the Western genre in high style by going up against a strong adversary in the always reliable Gene Hackman. Rated R for violence and profanity. 127m. **DIR:** Clint Eastwood. **CAST:** Clint Eastwood, Gene Hackman, Morgan Freeman, Richard Harris. **1992 DVD**

UNHOLY, THE A priest attempts to battle a demon that prolongs its existence by killing sinners in the act of sinning. Rated R for gore, nudity, and profanity. 99m. **DIR:** Camilo Vila. **CAST:** Ben Cross, Hal Holbrook, Ned Beatty, Trevor Howard, William Russ. **1988**

UNHOLY THREE ★★★1/2 With his last film and first talkie, Lon Chaney became the man of a thousand voices. If he hadn't, in an ironic twist, died of cancer of the throat, Chaney would have starred in *Dracula* and maybe even *Frankenstein*. As it is, we have this early sound remake of Tod Browning's 1925 silent thriller, in which Chaney's carnival ventriloquist teams up with a midget and a strong man to commit crimes. B&W; 73m. **DIR:** Jack Conway. **CAST:** Lon Chaney Sr., Lila Lee, Elliott Nugent, Harry Earles. **1930**

UNHOOK THE STARS ★★★1/2 Class struggle, family conflict, and personal responsibility are the core of this well-acted dramatic comedy. Marisa Tomei, desperate for a baby-sitter for her young son, is a wild woman who crashes into the dignified and lonely life of neighbor Gena Rowlands. Directed by Rowland's son Nick Cassavetes with both sympathy and humor, this is a fascinating character study, though it sometimes lacks credibility. Rated R for profanity. 105m. **DIR:** Nick Cassavetes. **CAST:** Gena Rowlands, Marisa Tomei, Gérard Depardieu, Jake Lloyd. **1996**

UNICORN, THE ★★★ An innocent boy learns that even the magical powers of the Unicorn's horn can't change the world. Sadly, he learns this by buying a one-horned goat instead of the mythical beast. 29m. **DIR:** Carol Reed. **CAST:** Celia Johnson, Diana Dors, David Kossoff. **1983**

UNIDENTIFIED FLYING ODDBALL ★★1/2 Inept astronaut is transported to the court of King Arthur in his spacecraft. Once there, he discovers that Merlin and a knight are plotting against the king and sets out to expose them. Uneven script with situations not fully developed or explored hampers this Disney trifle. Rated G. 92m. **DIR:** Russ Mayberry. **CAST:** Dennis Dugan, Jim Dale, Ron Moody, Kenneth More. **1979 DVD**

UNINVITED, THE (1944) ★★★★★ Probably the greatest ghost-haunted house film ever made, all the terror being in the unseen, with a particularly satisfying and logical conclusion to the mystery. When brother and sister Ray Milland and Ruth Hussey buy a house on the English coast, a moody girl from the nearby village finds herself being drawn to it, although she has not lived there since she was a small child. Don't see this alone. B&W; 98m. **DIR:** Lewis Allen. **CAST:** Ray Milland, Ruth Hussey, Gail Russell, Donald Crisp, Cornelia Otis Skinner, Alan Napier. **1944**

UNINVITED, THE (1987) A group of college kids take staff jobs on a yacht and spend their spring break cruising to the Caribbean. Rated R for violence and nudity. 92m. **DIR:** Greydon Clark. **CAST:** George Kennedy, Alex Cord, Clu Gulager, Toni Hudson. **1987**

UNINVITED, THE (1993) Embarrassingly bad Western finds a ragtag group of prospectors looking for gold on sacred Indian burial ground. Top-billed Jack Elam disappears before the opening credits are over. Not rated; contains violence and adult situations. 90m. **DIR:** Michael Bohusz. **CAST:** Jack Elam, Christopher Boyer, Erin Noble. **1993**

UNINVITED GUEST ★★ This tried-and-true thriller manages to squeeze a modicum of suspense out of what happens when you let strangers into your home. The stranger here interrupts a husband and wife's anniversary dinner, asking to use the phone. Now he won't leave, and as the evening progresses, truths are revealed. We've seen it all before. Rated R for adult situations, language, and violence. 103m. **DIR:** Timothy Wayne Folsome. **CAST:** Mekhi Phifer, Kim Fields, Mari Morrow, Malinda Williams, Mel Jackson. **2000 DVD**

UNION CITY ★★★ Called the "punk rock *film noir*," *Union City* is a quietly disturbing tale of murder and paranoia circa 1953. Deborah Harry (of the rock group Blondie) stars as a bored housewife; Dennis Lipscomb is her high-strung, paranoid husband. The mood, tone, and feel of the film are spooky, though it may be too oblique for some. Rated PG for adult themes and violence. 87m. **DIR:** Mark Reichert. **CAST:** Deborah Harry, Dennis Lipscomb, Pat Benatar. **1980 DVD**

UNION PACIFIC ★★★1/2 Lots of action in this fast-moving tale of the building of the transcontinental railroad, with a stellar cast playing the heroes and villains. With Cecil B. DeMille at the helm, you know it is an epic, in every sense, for the entire family. B&W; 135m. **DIR:** Cecil B. DeMille. **CAST:** Barbara Stanwyck, Joel McCrea, Brian Donlevy, Robert Preston, Akim Tamiroff, Anthony Quinn. **1939**

UNION STATION ★★★ A big, bustling railroad terminal is the backdrop of this suspense-thriller centering on the manhunt that ensues following the kidnapping of a blind girl for ransom. William Holden is the hero, Lyle Bettger is the villain, Allene Roberts is the victim. The plot's tired, but ace cinematographer-turned-director Rudolph Maté keeps everything moving fast and frantic. B&W; 80m. **DIR:** Rudolph Maté. **CAST:** William Holden, Nancy Olson, Allene Roberts, Barry Fitzgerald, Lyle Bettger, Jan Sterling. **1950**

UNIVERSAL SOLDIER ★★1/2 Jean-Claude Van Damme and Dolph Lundgren are part of a top-secret, scientific project to create perfect human fighting machines from dead soldiers. The program goes awry when Van Damme begins remembering his past, and a personal war develops between him and Lundgren. Average. Rated R for violence and profanity. 98m. **DIR:** Roland Emmerich. **CAST:** Jean-Claude Van Damme, Dolph Lundgren, Ally Walker, Ed O'Ross, Jerry Orbach. **1992 DVD**

UNIVERSAL SOLDIER II: BROTHERS IN ARMS ★★ Mediocre by-the-numbers action-thriller picks up where the Dolph Lundgren/Jean Claude Van Damme original left off. Only things missing are Lundgren and Van Damme, which leaves precious little. Rated R for violence. 93m. **DIR:** Jeff Woolnough. **CAST:** Matt Battaglia, Chandra West, Jeff Wincott, Gary Busey. **1998**

UNKISSED BRIDE Tom Kirk plays the groom who passes out every time he and his wife (Anne Helm) contemplate lovemaking. 82m. **DIR:** Jack H. Harris. **CAST:** Tommy Kirk, Danica D'Hondt, Anne Helm, Jacques Bergerac, Joe Pyne. **1966**

UNKNOWN, THE ★★★1/2 Armless knife thrower (Lon Chaney Sr.) falls in love with another performer at his circus, a Gypsy horse rider (Joan Crawford) who despises being touched. Sounds like a perfect match, except that the circus strong man has eyes for her as well. Typically bizarre collaboration between director Tod Browning and the amazing Chaney, who throws knives and plays guitar with his feet! Silent. B&W; 61m. **DIR:** Tod Browning. **CAST:** Lon Chaney Sr., Joan Crawford, Norman Kerry. **1927**

UNKNOWN CHAPLIN ★★★★ In three parts—"My Happiest Years," "The Great Director," and "Hidden Treasures"—this is a fascinating excursion into the creative techniques and art of Charlie Chaplin. James Mason narrates. B&W; 60m. **DIR:** Kevin Brownlow, David Gill. **1983**

UNKNOWN ORIGIN ★★★ Lots of fun 10,000 feet under the sea as deep-sea miners encounter an alien life force in the year 2050. Good cast, decent special effects, and a quaint 1960s drive-in feel give this made-for-cable thriller its appeal. Rated R for violence. 95m. **DIR:** Scott Levy. **CAST:** Roddy McDowall, Alex Hyde-White, Melanie Shatner, Don Stroud, Roger Halston. **1995**

UNKNOWN TERROR, THE Scientist turns tropical natives into fungus men. Appropriately titled film in which terror is indeed unknown. B&W; 76m. **DIR:** Charles Marquis Warren. **CAST:** John Howard, Mala Powers, Paul Richards, Charles Gray. **1957**

UNKNOWN WORLD ★★ Low-budget science-fiction story about an inventor who builds a drill capable of exploring inner Earth seems to borrow from Edgar Rice Burroughs's *Pellucidar* series, but it is actually closer to the nuclear-holocaust films of the postwar period. Short on thrills, this effort uses extensive footage of Carlsbad Caverns to simulate the interior of our planet. B&W; 74m. **DIR:** Terrel O. Morse. **CAST:** Victor Kilian, Bruce Kellogg, Marilyn Nash. **1950**

UNLAWFUL ENTRY ★★★1/2 After finding an intruder in their home, upscale L.A. suburbanites Kurt Russell and Madeleine Stowe are grateful for the arrival of police officers Ray Liotta and Roger E. Mosley. But when Liotta becomes fixated on Stowe being his "perfect woman," he turns into the cop from hell. Suspense-flick fans will get a good fix from this formula thriller. Rated R for violence, profanity, and nudity. 111m. **DIR:** Jonathan Kaplan. **CAST:** Kurt Russell, Ray Liotta, Madeleine Stowe, Roger E. Mosley. **1992**

UNLIKELY ANGEL ★★1/2 Dolly Parton and the late Roddy McDowall are the main attractions of the heavenly made-for-television family film about a country-and-western singer (guess who) who dies in a car crash. Before she can be granted her wings she must heal a family's wounds back on Earth. Not rated. 90m. **DIR:** Michael Switzer. **CAST:** Dolly Parton, Roddy McDowall, Brian Kerwin, Allison Mack, Eli Marienthal, Gary Sandy. **1996 DVD**

UNMADE BEDS ★★★ This mixture of documentary and fiction was concocted from interviews with New Yorkers who had tried and failed to find mates through the personal ads. The four people featured play themselves, re-creating incidents from their experiences. Odd but often compelling, it's a refreshingly open view of modern romance. Not rated; contains strong adult situations, nudity, and profanity. 95m. **DIR:** Nicholas Barker. **CAST:** Aimee Copp, Michael DeStefano, Brenda Monte, Michael Russo. **1997 DVD**

UNMARRIED WOMAN, AN ★★★★★ Jill Clayburgh's Erica has settled into a comfortable rut and barely notices it when things begin to go wrong. One day, after lunch with her husband, Martin (Michael Murphy), she is shocked by his sobbing admission that he is in love with another woman. Her world is shattered. This first-rate film concerns itself with her attempts to cope with the situation. Rated R for sex, nudity, and profanity. 124m. **DIR:** Paul Mazursky. **CAST:** Jill Clayburgh, Michael Murphy, Alan Bates, Pat Quinn. **1978**

UNNAMABLE, THE ★★★ College students spend the night in a haunted house in this adaptation of an H. P. Lovecraft short story. While there, the promiscuous teens must contend with a family curse and a monstrous she-beast that delights in tearing humans limb from limb. There's a fair amount of good humor and some genuine chills. Horror fans should have a good time. Not rated; contains nudity and graphic violence. 87m. **DIR:** Jean Paul Ouellette. **CAST:** Charles King, Mark Kinsey Stephenson, Alexandra Durrell. **1988**

UNNAMABLE II, THE ★★ Sequels are usually worse than the originals, and this is no exception. A 300 year old winged demon is separated from the body and soul of the young, beautiful woman. So, of course, a bloody chase ensues. Not rated; contains violence and nudity. 95m. **DIR:** Jean Paul Ouellette. **CAST:** John Rhys-Davies, Mark Kinsey Stephenson, Julie Strain, Peter Breck, David Warner. **1992**

UNNATURAL ★★1/2 Gothic fantasy about a scientist who creates a beautiful femme fatale through artificial insemination. This German production is laced with impressive cinematography, giving the film an impressionistic look reminiscent of the early silent-film period. Unfortunately, it suffers from a weak script. B&W; 90m. **DIR:** Arthur Maria Rabenalt. **CAST:** Erich Von Stroheim, Hildegarde Neff, Carl Boehm. **1952**

UNNATURAL CAUSES ★★★★ Alfre Woodard stars in this made-for-TV movie about a Veterans Administration counselor who takes up the cause of linking Agent

Orange to stricken vets under her care. John Ritter gives a sensitive performance as one of the Vietnam vets. This fact-based story is given maximum impact thanks to the intelligent script of John Sayles. 100m. **DIR:** Lamont Johnson. **CAST:** John Ritter, Alfre Woodard, Patti LaBelle, John Sayles. **1986**

UNNATURAL PURSUITS ★★★1/2 This BBC production sends up artists, particularly writers, and America in general. Alan Bates is excellent as a talented but drunken playwright who breaks into song when the going gets tough. Bates pursues his play through several transformations on both sides of the Atlantic before finding tragedy and renewal. Bizarre, black, terribly clever, and far too long. Not rated; contains profanity and nudity. 143m. **DIR:** Christopher Morahan. **CAST:** Alan Bates, Bob Balaban, John Mahoney. **1994**

UNREMARKABLE LIFE, AN ★★★ Two elderly sisters who still live together in their family home find themselves at odds when one of them starts dating. Polished performances highlight what is an otherwise overwrought melodrama. Rated PG for racial epithets. 95m. **DIR:** Amin Q. Chaudhri. **CAST:** Patricia Neal, Shelley Winters, Mako. **1989**

UNSANE ★★★1/2 American fans of stylish Italian director Dario Argento had been awaiting his 1984 film *Tenebrae* for years. Although it never played theatrically in the U.S., it snuck onto video with a new title, *Unsane*. A mystery novelist discovers that a series of killings seems to be based on those in his latest book. Argento's trademarks—violent murders, a complex plot, and a pulsing synthesizer score—are all here in abundance. Not rated; the film contains nudity and violence. 92m. **DIR:** Dario Argento. **CAST:** Anthony Franciosa, Daria Nicolodi, John Saxon, Giuliano Gemma, John Steiner. **1984 DVD**

UNSEEN, THE A cellar-dwelling invisible critter that does what you'd expect. Rated R. 89m. **DIR:** Peter Foleg. **CAST:** Barbara Bach, Sidney Lassick, Stephen Furst. **1981**

UNSETTLED LAND Israeli-made production concerning a commune of young Jews from Europe establishing a settlement in the Sinai Desert after World War I. Overblown saga. Rated PG for violence. 109m. **DIR:** Uri Barbash. **CAST:** Kelly McGillis, John Shea. **1987**

UNSINKABLE MOLLY BROWN, THE ★★★ Noisy, big-budget version of hit Broadway musical has Debbie Reynolds at her spunkiest as the tuneful gal from Colorado who survives the sinking of the *Titanic* and lives to sing about it. High-stepping dance numbers and the performances by Reynolds and Harve Presnell make this a favorite with musicals fans, but it does drag a bit for the casual viewer. 128m. **DIR:** Charles Walters. **CAST:** Debbie Reynolds, Harve Presnell, Ed Begley Sr., Hermione Baddeley, Jack Kruschen. **1964**

UNSPEAKABLE, THE ★★1/2 Scripter Christopher Wood's police thriller gets a few points for keeping us guessing, but the central plot remains pretty silly. Cute cop Athena Massey goes deep undercover to entrap a suspected serial rapist/ killer, then falls in love with him. Only in the movies. Rated R for nudity, violence, gore, profanity, and simulated sex. 90m. **DIR:** Howard McCain. **CAST:** David Chokachi, Cyril O'Reilly, Athena Massey, Timothy Busfield. **1996**

UNSPEAKABLE ACTS ★★★1/2 This TV dramatization of the landmark day-care sexual-abuse case in 1984 Miami features Jill Clayburgh and Brad Davis as the child psychologists who interviewed the abused children. Though disturbing, the film is a must-see for everyone seeking qualified child care. Contains mature themes. 94m. **DIR:** Linda Otto. **CAST:** Jill Clayburgh, Brad Davis, Season Hubley, Gregory Sierra. **1989**

UNSTRUNG HEROES ★★★★ Franz Lidz's poignant book becomes a compelling little comedy-drama in director Diane Keaton's hands. Andie MacDowell is the one sane member of a family of misfits, but when she turns up with cancer, it's the screwball men who show their young nephew the values of faith, heritage, and family ties. A genuine tearjerker. Rated PG for dramatic intensity. 93m. **DIR:** Diane Keaton. **CAST:** Andie MacDowell, John Turturro, Michael Richards, Maury Chaykin, Nathan Watt, Kendra Krull. **1995**

UNTAMED HEART ★★★★ Tom Sierchio's poignant urban love story becomes a career-making vehicle for Marisa Tomei, in her first starring role. She's a perky Minneapolis twentysomething working as a waitress. She eventually connects with the diner's introverted busboy (Christian Slater, very good in a part completely unlike his usual work). Rated PG-13 for profanity. 102m. **DIR:** Tony Bill. **CAST:** Christian Slater, Marisa Tomei, Rosie Perez, Kyle Secor. **1993**

UNTIL SEPTEMBER ★★ A midwestern divorcée (Karen Allen) falls in love with a married Parisian banker (Thierry Lhermitte) during the summer vacation in this unabashed soap opera. Rated R. 95m. **DIR:** Richard Marquand. **CAST:** Karen Allen, Thierry Lhermitte, Christopher Cazenove. **1984**

UNTIL THE END OF THE WORLD ★★ Futuristic folly follows a good-time girl as she pursues a fugitive (William Hurt). Bounty hunters, bank robbers, her boyfriend, and a private eye become entangled in her cross-continental chase. New wave soundtrack and directionless plot make this nearly impossible to enjoy. Rated R for violence, nudity, and profanity. 158m. **DIR:** Wim Wenders. **CAST:** William Hurt, Solveig Dommartin, Sam Neill, Max von Sydow, Jeanne Moreau. **1991**

UNTIL THEY SAIL ★★★1/2 Romantic drama about a quartet of sisters and the men they meet during World War II in New Zealand. Based on a James Michener novel, so there's plenty of meat to the story, including a murder and some mismatched lovers. B&W; 96m. **DIR:** Robert Wise. **CAST:** Paul Newman, Jean Simmons, Joan Fontaine, Sandra Dee, Piper Laurie, Dean Jones, Charles Drake, Patrick Macnee. **1957**

UNTOLD STORY, THE ★★★ Like *Silence of the Lambs*, this Hong Kong tale of a gruesome serial killer won that country's equivalent of the Oscar for best actor (Anthony Wong) and best film. But it is a much more graphic film, with injections of comedy that are as shocking as they are tasteless. Not rated, but absolutely not for kids, or anyone with a weak stomach! In Cantonese with English subtitles. 95m. **DIR:** Herman Yau. **CAST:** Anthony Wong, Danny Lee. **1993 DVD**

UNTOUCHABLES, THE ★★★★1/2 An absolutely superb retelling of the beloved television series, with director Brian De Palma working his stylish magic in tandem with a deft script from Pulitzer-winning playwright

David Mamet. Prohibition-era Chicago has been beautifully re-created to emphasize big-city decadence. Al Capone was the populist hero for providing alcohol for the masses; Eliot Ness was the arrow-straight federal agent who rose to the challenge. (Look for Sean Connery in the performance of his career as a beat cop who assists Ness.) Rated R for language and extreme violence. 119m. **DIR:** Brian De Palma. **CAST:** Kevin Costner, Sean Connery, Robert De Niro, Charles Martin Smith, Andy Garcia, Billy Drago, Richard Bradford. **1987 DVD**

UNTOUCHABLES, THE: SCARFACE MOB ★★★ This violence-ridden film was released theatrically in 1962 but was actually the original two-part pilot for the popular TV series. Steely-eyed Robert Stack as Eliot Ness gets the government's go-ahead to form his own special team of incorruptible agents. B&W; 90m. **DIR:** Phil Karlson. **CAST:** Robert Stack, Keenan Wynn, Barbara Nichols, Pat Crowley, Neville Brand, Bruce Gordon, Anthony George, Abel Fernandez, Nick Giorgiade. **1962**

UNVEILED ★★1/2 While on vacation in Marrakech, a young woman learns that her childhood friend has been murdered. With the assistance of a handsome government official, she uses her feminine wiles to draw out the killer. Things get complicated when she begins to fall for the suspect. Rated R for nudity, adult situations, and violence. 103m. **DIR:** William Cole. **CAST:** Lisa Zane, Nick Chinlund, Whip Hubley, Martha Gehman, Amidou. **1993**

UNZIPPED ★★★ Fashion designer Isaac Mizrahi develops his fall 1994 collection in a film that is less documentary than infomercial and it's frankly adoring. Fortunately, Mizrahi has the dynamic presence of a born star. Rated R for profanity and brief nudity. 76m. **DIR:** Douglas Keeve. **CAST:** Isaac Mizrahi, Sarah Mizrahi, Sandra Bernhard, Cindy Crawford, Naomi Campbell, Eartha Kitt. **1995**

UP AGAINST THE WALL ★★ Black teenager has his moral code challenged when he moves from his mother's modest home to his brother's house in the affluent suburbs in this well-meaning but amateurish drama. Rated PG-13 for language and violence. 103m. **DIR:** Ron O'Neal. **CAST:** Marla Gibbs, Ron O'Neal, Stoney Jackson. **1991**

UP AT THE VILLA ★★1/2 This stuffy adaptation of W. Somerset Maugham's 1941 novel is about a widowed and soon-to-be penniless British socialite in pre–World War II Florence who snags a marriage proposal from a British diplomat, the heart of a poor refugee, and the attention of a brash, married American. She also learns that another wealthy widow knows where the local dirty political laundry is buried while Mussolini's Fascists begin to intimidate all foreigners. Rated PG-13 for language, violence, and sexual content. 115m. **DIR:** Philip Haas. **CAST:** Kristin Scott Thomas, Sean Penn, James Fox, Anne Bancroft. **2000 DVD**

UP CLOSE AND PERSONAL ★★★★ Old-fashioned Hollywood movies are hard to come by these days, and that is what makes this big-screen love story such a treasure. Writers Joan Didion and John Gregory Dunne, who based the screenplay on Alanna Nash's biography of ill-fated TV newswoman Jessica Savitch, have gone with a largely fictional tale, and this works very much in the film's favor. Rated PG-13 for profanity, violence, and suggested sex. 124m. **DIR:** Jon Avnet. **CAST:** Robert Redford, Michelle Pfeiffer, Stockard Channing, Joe Mantegna, Kate Nelligan, Glenn Plummer, Dedee Pfeiffer, Noble Willingham. **1996 DVD**

UP FROM THE DEPTHS 🦃 Perfunctory remake of *Creature from the Haunted Sea*. Rated R. 80m. **DIR:** Charles B. Griffith. **CAST:** Sam Bottoms, Susanne Reed, Virgil Frye. **1979**

UP IN ARMS ★★1/2 Danny Kaye's first film will not disappoint his fans, as he sings and mugs his way through the war. Dinah Shore loves the hypochondriac Kaye; the war takes a backseat to entertainment. 105m. **DIR:** Elliott Nugent. **CAST:** Danny Kaye, Dinah Shore, Dana Andrews, Constance Dowling. **1944**

UP IN SMOKE ★★★★ This is Cheech and Chong's first, and best, film. Forget about any plot as Cheech and Chong go on the hunt for good weed, rock 'n' roll, and good times. Several truly hysterical moments, with Stacy Keach's spaced-out cop almost stealing the show. Rated R for language, nudity, and general raunchiness. 87m. **DIR:** Lou Adler. **CAST:** Cheech and Chong, Strother Martin, Stacy Keach, Edie Adams, Tom Skerritt. **1978**

UP PERISCOPE ★★1/2 Edmond O'Brien is a by-the-book sub commander who risks his command and men on a dangerous mission. Well-done, but too familiar. 111m. **DIR:** Gordon Douglas. **CAST:** James Garner, Edmond O'Brien, Alan Hale Sr., Carleton Carpenter. **1959**

UP THE ACADEMY 🦃 This was *Mad* magazine's first and only attempt to emulate *National Lampoon*'s film success. Rated R for profanity and general disgustingness. 88m. **DIR:** Robert Downey. **CAST:** Ron Leibman, Wendell Brown, Ralph Macchio, Tom Citera, Tom Poston, Stacey Nelkin, Barbara Bach. **1980**

UP THE CREEK (1958) ★★★★ Left in charge of an unimportant naval base without a commanding officer, junior officer Peter Sellers turns it into a fountain for personal money-making schemes. Dryly funny British farce with a plethora of amusing supporting players. 86m. **DIR:** Val Guest. **CAST:** Peter Sellers, David Tomlinson, Wilfrid Hyde-White, Vera Day, Lionel Jeffries. **1958**

UP THE CREEK (1984) ★★★ Two stars from *Animal House*, Tim Matheson ("Otter") and Stephen Furst ("Flounder"), are reunited in this mostly entertaining raft-race comedy. It doesn't beg you to laugh at it the way *Police Academy* does. Matheson is charismatic enough to carry the film. Rated R for nudity, profanity, scatological humor, and violence. 95m. **DIR:** Robert Butler. **CAST:** Tim Matheson, Stephen Furst, Dan Monahan, John Hillerman, James B. Sikking, Tom Nolan. **1984**

UP THE DOWN STAIRCASE ★★★1/2 Sandy Dennis perfectly captures the flighty teacher of Bel Kaufman's hilarious novel about the New York City high school scene, but the students and minor plot crises do not wear as well as her performance. Although Dennis smoothly enacts the teacher we'd all like to have, Tad Mosel's script never quite catches the book's inspired lunacy. 124m. **DIR:** Robert Mulligan. **CAST:** Sandy Dennis, Eileen Heckart, Jean Stapleton. **1967**

UP THE SANDBOX ★★ A weird, uneven comedy about a neglected housewife (Barbra Streisand). Its fantasy sequences are among the strangest ever put on film.

Rated R. 97m. **DIR:** Irvin Kershner. **CAST:** Barbra Streisand, David Selby, Jane Hoffman. **1972**

UP TO A CERTAIN POINT ★★★1/2 It's one thing to talk about sexual and social liberation, but quite another to live up to it. So discovers a writer as he does research among working-class Cubans for a film on Latino machismo. A pointed satire from Cuba's best-known filmmaker. Not rated; contains no objectionable material. 68m. **DIR:** Tomas Gutierrez Alea. **CAST:** Oscar Alvarez, Mirta Ibarra. **1983**

UP YOUR ALLEY 🦃 L.A. street dwellers. Rated R for profanity. 90m. **DIR:** Bob Logan. **CAST:** Linda Blair, Murray Langston, Ruth Buzzi. **1988**

UP YOUR ANCHOR 🦃 Ever wonder what one of the beach films of the 1960s or *Love Boat* would be like with nudity and rampant sexual encounters? 89m. **DIR:** Dan Wolman. **CAST:** Yftach Katzur, Zachi Nay. **1985**

UP/DOWN/FRAGILE ★★★1/2 This musical about three young women in modern-day Paris is a tribute to the spirit of classic Hollywood musicals that aims to take out much of the starch by making the singing and dancing more ordinary. In French with English subtitles. Not rated; contains adult themes. 169m. **DIR:** Jacques Rivette. **CAST:** Marianne Denicourt, Nathalie Richard, Laurence Cote. **1995**

UPHILL ALL THE WAY 🦃 Ridiculous film concerns two down-and-outers mistaken for bank robbers. Rated PG. 86m. **DIR:** Frank Q. Dobbs. **CAST:** Roy Clark, Mel Tillis, Glen Campbell. **1985**

UPSTAIRS, DOWNSTAIRS ★★★★★ Life in a fashionable London town house between 1904 and 1930 is depicted with insight, wit, and charm through the activities and thoughts of the patrician family upstairs and the servants downstairs in this superb *Masterpiece Theater* series. The late Gordon Jackson is perfect as the unflappable butler Hudson, closely rivaled by Jean Marsh as the unpredictable maid Rose. 900m. **DIR:** Simon Langton. **CAST:** Gordon Jackson, Jean Marsh, Pauline Collins, Rachel Gurney, Ian Ogilvy, Raymond Huntley, Lesley-Anne Down. **1971**

UPTOWN NEW YORK ★★ Sobby melodrama about a doctor whose family forces him to jilt the girl he loves and marry for money. B&W; 80m. **DIR:** Victor Schertzinger. **CAST:** Jack Oakie, Shirley Grey. **1932**

UPTOWN SATURDAY NIGHT ★★★1/2 Sidney Poitier (who also directed), Bill Cosby, Harry Belafonte, Richard Pryor, and Flip Wilson head an all-star cast in this enjoyable comedy about a couple of buddies (Poitier and Cosby) who get into all sorts of trouble. Rated PG. 104m. **DIR:** Sidney Poitier. **CAST:** Sidney Poitier, Bill Cosby, Harry Belafonte, Richard Pryor, Flip Wilson. **1974**

URANUS ★★★★ Sumptuous character study of a group of villagers immediately following the Nazi occupation of France. The town has been torn into three camps: those who joined the Nazis, those who joined the resistance, and those who just minded their own business. In French with English subtitles. Not rated; contains nudity and violence. 100m. **DIR:** Claude Berri. **CAST:** Gérard Depardieu, Michel Blanc, Jean-Pierre Marielle, Philippe Noiret, Michel Galabru. **1992**

URBAN COWBOY ★★★ The film is a slice-of-life *Saturday Night Fever*–like look at the after-hours life of blue-collar cowboys. Overall, the film works because of excellent directing by James Bridges and the fine acting of John Travolta, Debra Winger, and Scott Glenn. Rated PG. 132m. **DIR:** James Bridges. **CAST:** John Travolta, Debra Winger, Scott Glenn, Madolyn Smith, Charlie Daniels Band. **1980**

URBAN CROSSFIRE ★★1/2 Gritty crime-drama about a cop whose partner is killed by a vicious drug dealer, and whose desire to apprehend the killer shoves him over the edge. If the film wasn't so exploitative, it would be a good reminder of the high wire that cops are forced to walk. Rated R for violence and language. 95m. **DIR:** Dick Lowry. **CAST:** Mario Van Peebles, Ray Sharkey, Peter Boyle, Courtney B. Vance, Michael Patrick Boatman. **1994**

URBAN JUNGLE ★★ Although the performances are uneven, viewers may enjoy some of the characters in this story about a young man trying to escape a life of crime in the inner city. Not rated; contains violence. 76m. **DIR:** Daniel Matmor. **CAST:** Brian Paul, McKinley Winston. **1990**

URBAN LEGEND ★★★1/2 First-time filmmakers Jamie Blanks and screenwriter Silvio Horta have quickly established their names with this thrilling chiller that takes the slasher film in its own new direction. As the anniversary of a university massacre—which may or may not have occurred—draws near, students find themselves caught up in a series of murders. Dark comedy abounds and you'll be guessing right up until the climactic moment as to who the killer is. Rated R for violence, profanity, sexual dialogue, and simulated sex. 108m. **DIR:** Jamie Blanks. **CAST:** Alicia Witt, Jared Leto, Rebecca Gayheart, Joshua Jackson, Tara Reid, Robert Englund, Danielle Harris, Natasha Gregson Wagner, Brad Dourif. **1998 DVD**

URBAN LEGENDS: FINAL CUT 🦃 Film students at a New England university compete for a prestigious Hitchcock Award given to best thesis film in a nonsequel (only one character has returned) that is as dull as it is grisly. Rated R for language, violence, gore, drug use, and sexuality. 94m. **DIR:** John Ottman. **CAST:** Jennifer Morrison, Matthew Davis, Hart Bochner, Loretta Devine, Joey Lawrence, Anson Mount. **2000 DVD**

URBAN MENACE ★★ After his family is killed and his church burned to the ground, a preacher seeks revenge on those who wronged him—with bad direction and godawful acting, both of which are plentiful in this film. Rated R for violence and profanity. 97m. **DIR:** Albert Pyun. **CAST:** Snoop Dog, Ice T, Big Pun, Fat Joe. **1999 DVD**

URBAN WARRIORS 🦃 A group of scientists survive a nuclear holocaust. Rated R for violence. 90m. **DIR:** Joseph Warren. **CAST:** Karl Landgren. **1989**

URBANIA ★★1/2 Charlie is a gay New Yorker who is reeling from an abruptly ended relationship. As he listens to the stories of, and plays ruthless mind games with, random strangers, he nurtures a dark, violent fantasy. This gritty, surreal Manhattan nightmare is a harrowing, homoerotic tale of personal loss, urban legends, narcissism, rage, and revenge that ultimately feels more exploitative than cathartic. Rated R for language, sex, violence, and drug use. 103m. **DIR:** Jon Shear. **CAST:** Dan Futterman, Alan Cumming, Matt Keeslar, Josh Hamilton, Lothaire Bluteau, William Sage, Barbara Sukowa. **2000 DVD**

URGE TO KILL ★★★★ A top-notch cast shines in this drama about a convicted killer who, upon release from a mental institution, comes home to face prejudice and violent recriminations. Well written and acted, the film's focus is on the quality of justice versus the quality of mercy and what people will do to subvert both. Holly Hunter is outstanding as the sister of the murder victim. Not rated; contains mature themes. 96m. **DIR:** Mike Robe. **CAST:** Karl Malden, Holly Hunter, Alex McArthur, Paul Sorvino, Catherine Mary Stewart, William Devane. **1984**

URINAL ★★★1/2 Structurally imaginative semidocumentary in which the ghosts of gay artists (including Sergey Eisenstein, Frida Kahlo, and Yukio Mishima) return to Canada to help combat police harassment of gays who meet in public washrooms. Not rated; contains nudity and strong sexual themes. 100m. **DIR:** John Greyson. **CAST:** Pauline Carey, Paul Bettis. **1988**

UROTSUKIDOJI: LEGEND OF THE OVERFIEND ★★★ An unbelievably violent and perverse animated Japanese feature based on *The Wandering Kid* comics and representative of the violent/erotic subgenre. Every 3,000 years the Overfiend returns to unite the three separate worlds of man, demon, and animal-man—but is the creature a healer or a destroyer? Dubbed in English. Rated NC-17; contains explicit sexual scenes and violence. 108m. An uncut, subtitled version in three parts also is available and runs 40 minutes longer. **DIR:** Hideki Takayama. **1989 DVD**

UROTSUKIDOJI II: LEGEND OF THE DEMON WOMB ★★ Less interesting than the original, this animated sequel has the Overfiend dealing with his beloved cousin, who has become the Evil King and is being manipulated by the crazed son of a Nazi scientist. Sound ridiculous? It is. Dubbed in English. Not rated; contains gratuitous violence and explicit sexual scenes. 88m. A director's cut of this film combines this with *Urotsukidoji: Legend of the Overfiend* and runs 40 extra minutes. **DIR:** Hideki Takayama. **1991 DVD**

URUSEI YATSURA: ONLY YOU ★★★★ Japanese animation. How long has our hero Ataru had his obsession with girls? Find out as his associates plan to attend a reunion with his first flirtation. The fast-paced story line is reminiscent of Blake Edwards's early Pink Panther films. In Japanese with English subtitles. 101m. **DIR:** Mamoru Oshii. **1983**

URUSEI YATSURA (TV SERIES) VOLS. 1–45 ★★★1/2 Japanese animation. Entertaining mixture of love triangles, humor, and science fiction. The main characters include teenage Romeo, Ataru Morobishi, his main girlfriend, Shinobu, and Lum, the alien princess who lives in Ataru's closet. In Japanese with English subtitles. 80m. **DIR:** Kazuo Yamazaki, Yuuji Moriyama. **1980–1982**

URUSEI YATSURA: BEAUTIFUL DREAMER ★★★★ Japanese animation. This is the second movie from the *Urusei Yatsura* collection. Strong, constantly developing characterizations make these feature films consistently enjoyable and a delightful change from the giant robots that transform into everything but the kitchen sink. In Japanese with English subtitles. Not rated. 90m. **DIR:** Mamoru Oshii. **1984**

URUSEI YATSURA: INABA THE DREAMMAKER ★★★1/2 Japanese animation. The further adventures of Ataru, Shinobu, and Lum as they are presented with several of their possible futures, not all of which are desirable. Holds to the high standards of comedy found in the original series episodes and movies. In Japanese with English subtitles. 57m. **DIR:** Dezuki Tetsu. **1987**

URUSEI YATSURA: REMEMBER LOVE ★★★★ Japanese animation. Once again, Ataru's twisted charm enmeshes him in extraterrestrial difficulties and involves his associates in situations that stretch the imagination. The vocal characterizations, expressive artwork, and excellent subtitling allow the viewer to easily follow the story. In Japanese with English subtitles. 93m. **DIR:** Kazuo Yamazaki. **1985**

U.S. MARSHALS ★★★1/2 Action-packed follow-up to *The Fugitive* brings back main character Chief Deputy Marshal Sam Gerard (Tommy Lee Jones) and pits him against a crafty, well-trained government operative accused of murdering two of his fellow agents. Full of surprises, suspense, and elaborate set pieces. Rated R for violence and profanity. 127m. **DIR:** Stuart Baird. **CAST:** Tommy Lee Jones, Wesley Snipes, Robert Downey Jr., Kate Nelligan, Joe Pantoliano, Irène Jacob. **1998 DVD**

USED CARS ★★★★ This is a riotous account of two feuding used-car businesses. Jack Warden and Kurt Russell are both excellent in this overlooked comedy. Fine support is offered by Frank McRae, Gerrit Graham, and Deborah Harmon. Rated R for language, nudity, and some violence. 111m. **DIR:** Robert Zemeckis. **CAST:** Jack Warden, Kurt Russell, Frank McRae, Gerrit Graham, Deborah Harmon. **1980 DVD**

USED PEOPLE ★★★1/2 Shirley MacLaine and Marcello Mastroianni are up to their tried-and-true tricks in this story of an Italian ne'er-do-well whose love for a Jewish woman is given full flower when her husband dies. The old pros manage to carry if off. Rated PG-13 for profanity and suggested sex. 116m. **DIR:** Beeban Kidron. **CAST:** Shirley MacLaine, Marcello Mastroianni, Jessica Tandy, Kathy Bates, Marcia Gay Harden, Sylvia Sidney, Bob Dishy, Joe Pantoliano. **1992**

USERS, THE ★★ Another bloated TV movie boasts a fine cast and little else. Jaclyn Smith stars as a beautiful girl who plays a major role in the resurgence of a down-and-out movie star's career. Standard "television" production values and "television" dialogue do this one in. 125m. **DIR:** Joseph Hardy. **CAST:** Jaclyn Smith, Tony Curtis, Joan Fontaine, Red Buttons. **1978**

USUAL SUSPECTS, THE ★★★★★ When five career criminals are picked up by the New York City police for a lineup, they decide to make use of their chance meeting and pull off a big job. Wild, crazy, gripping movie with terrific performances, assured direction, and brilliant writing. Bet you can't watch it just once. Rated R for profanity and violence. 105m. **DIR:** Bryan Singer. **CAST:** Gabriel Byrne, Kevin Spacey, Kevin Pollak, Stephen Baldwin, Chazz Palminteri, Benicio Del Toro, Suzy Amis, Dan Hedaya, Giancarlo Esposito. **1995 DVD**

UTAH ★★★ Roy Rogers tries to prevent show girl Dale Evans from selling her ranch to raise money to back a Broadway musical. B&W; 78m. **DIR:** John English.

CAST: Roy Rogers, George "Gabby" Hayes, Dale Evans, Peggy Stewart, Grant Withers. **1945**

UTILITIES ★★★1/2 Despite some rather crude humor once in a while, this modest comedy has a lot of charm and the heart of a Frank Capra film. Robert Hays plays a fed-up social worker who turns vigilante against the public utility companies. Rated PG for profanity and sex. 94m. **DIR:** Harvey Hart. **CAST:** Robert Hays, Brooke Adams, John Marley. **1983**

UTU ★★★★★ This stunner from New Zealand contains all the action of the great American Westerns, but with a moral message that leaves most of that genre's best in the dust. A Maori corporal in the nineteenth-century British army finds his family slaughtered by his own army and vows "utu" (Maori for revenge) to rid his land of white people. Rated R for violence. 100m. **DIR:** Geoff Murphy. **CAST:** Anzac Wallace, Bruno Lawrence, Kelly Johnson, Tim Elliot. **1985 DVD**

U2: RATTLE AND HUM ★★★★1/2 More than just a concert movie. It's an eloquent cry for change. The Irish rock quartet and 26 year old director Phil Joanou have combined forces to create a remarkably moving screen work. Filmed in black and white and color during the group's American tour in support of its ground-breaking *Joshua Tree* album, it captures the excitement of the live shows while underlining U2's timely message. Rated PG-13 for profanity. 99m. **DIR:** Phil Joanou. **CAST:** U2. **1988 DVD**

UTZ ★★★1/2 The director of *The Vanishing* here attempts a more subtle, complex film. Armin Mueller-Stahl stars as an obsessive collector of fine porcelain figures living in Prague. The Communist Czech government decides the collection belongs to the state. Peter Riegert costars as an American collector who unravels Utz's story in flashbacks, and the masterful Paul Scofield contributes a tasty bit as Utz's closest old friend. 101m. **DIR:** George Sluizer. **CAST:** Armin Mueller-Stahl, Brenda Fricker, Peter Riegert, Paul Scofield. **1992**

V

V ★★★1/2 Exciting science-fiction thriller began as a television miniseries and then evolved into a full-fledged series. The action begins immediately as several large saucers hover over all of the Earth's major cities, their occupants promising peace, but planning to use humans as food. A series of massive battles between freedom fighters and aliens ensues. Features outstanding special effects, extensive character development, and enough subplots to fuel several movies. 205m. **DIR:** Kenneth Johnson. **CAST:** Marc Singer, Jane Badler, Faye Grant, Michael Durrell, Andrew Prine, Richard Herd, Robert Englund. **1983**

V. I. WARSHAWSKI ★★★1/2 The mystery novels by Sara Paretsky are better, but we enjoyed this *Thin Man*-ish movie romp with Kathleen Turner as the wisecracking, two-fisted female detective of the title. In what, sadly, may be her only on-screen adventure because of a poor showing at the box office, V. I. Warshawski is hired by the daughter of a murdered pro hockey player to find his killer. Rated R for violence and profanity. 95m. **DIR:** Jeff Kanew. **CAST:** Kathleen Turner, Jay O. Sanders, Charles Durning, Angela Goethals, Frederick Coffin. **1991**

•VA SAVOIR ★★★★ Romance and mating are dissected as the affairs of the heart and loin of six men and women intertwine, fray, and unravel. French actress Camille returns to the Paris stage in Pirandello's *As You Desire Me* after three years in Italy. Her romance with a costar feels empty so she reconnects with her former lover, a scholar now married to a ballet teacher. The convoluted, comic story also involves a missing, unpublished manuscript of playwright Goldoni, multiple seductions, and thievery. It is delicately structured and drenched in the parallels of performance art and life. In French with English subtitles. Rated PG-13 for brief nudity. 150m. **DIR:** Jacques Rivette. **CAST:** Jeanne Balibar, Sergio Castellitto, Jacques Bonanaffé, Marianne Basler, Hélène de Fougerolles, Bruno Todeschini. **2001**

VAGABOND ★★★1/2 French new wave writer-director Agnes Varda's dispassionate but beautifully photographed "investigation"—via flashbacks—of a young misfit's meandering trek through the French countryside features a superb performance by Sandrine Bonnaire. Her *Vagabond* is presented as rude, lazy, ungrateful. Yet in some subliminal way the film draws one into the alienation that fuels this outsider's journey into death. In French with English subtitles. Rated R for profanity and suggested sex. 105m. **DIR:** Agnes Varda. **CAST:** Sandrine Bonnaire, Macha Meril. **1986 DVD**

VAGABOND LOVER, THE ★★★ Rudy Vallee portrays an orchestra conductor who has fallen deeply in love with the daughter (Sally Blane) of a dotty dowager (Marie Dressler). Conventional but entertaining. B&W; 69m. **DIR:** Marshall Neilan. **CAST:** Rudy Vallee, Sally Blane, Marie Dressler. **1929**

VAGRANT, THE ★★1/2 Bill Paxton is a Yuppie homeowner driven out of his mind by an intrusive, repulsive derelict. This weird, low-budget flick is riddled with a black humor that turns eerie as Paxton unravels. Not for everyone. Rated R for profanity and violence. 91m. **DIR:** Chris Walas. **CAST:** Bill Paxton, Michael Ironside. **1992**

VALDEZ IS COMING ★★★1/2 Burt Lancaster is superb as Valdez, an aging town constable who takes it upon himself to collect $100 from a ruthless rancher after the senseless killing of an innocent black man. Rated R for violence, profanity, and simulated sex. 90m. **DIR:** Edwin Sherin. **CAST:** Burt Lancaster, Susan Clark, Richard Jordan, Jon Cypher, Barton Heyman, Frank Silvera, Maria Montez, Nick Cravat, Hector Elizondo. **1971 DVD**

VALENTINA ★★★ Subtle drama based on a novel by Ramon Sender about Jose Garce's love for Valentina that lasted from childhood until his death. Produced by Anthony Quinn. In Spanish with English subtitles. 90m. **DIR:** Antonio J. Betancor. **CAST:** Jorge Sanz, Paloma Gomez. **1984**

VALENTINE Four attractive young women are being stalked and murdered, apparently by a geek they all tormented in junior high school. The slasher-movie formula that's been done to death gets no new lease on life

from this tiresome, predictable retread. Rated R for violence and profanity. 96m. **DIR:** Jamie Blanks. **CAST:** Denise Richards, Marley Shelton, David Boreanaz, Jessica Capshaw. **2001 DVD**

VALENTINO ★★1/2 This outrageous biography of one of the screen's greatest legends uses selective facts and historical settings in an attempt to isolate the real nature of the adulation of Rudolph Valentino. Director Ken Russell freely mixes truth and wild hallucinations. Rudolf Nureyev is somehow an apt choice to play Valentino, and the rest of the cast and production seems to fit. 132m. **DIR:** Ken Russell. **CAST:** Rudolf Nureyev, Leslie Caron, Michelle Phillips, Carol Kane, Felicity Kendal, Seymour Cassel, Huntz Hall, Alfred Marks, David de Keyser. **1977**

VALENTINO RETURNS ★★1/2 Small Town, U.S.A., 1955, proves too confining for Wayne Gibbs (Barry Tubb). He takes off in his new pink Cadillac and manages to take on a biker gang, ruin his car, and find love (lust) in short order. Rated R for violence, profanity, and nudity. 97m. **DIR:** Peter Hoffman. **CAST:** Frederic Forrest, Veronica Cartwright, Barry Tubb, Jenny Wright. **1988**

VALLEY, THE ★★1/2 The plot of this dated movie—hip young people travel to New Guinea—is forgettable. But the exquisite Nestor Almendros photography and the Pink Floyd score make it a pleasant viewing experience. In French with English subtitles. Not rated; contains nudity and sexual situations. 114m. **DIR:** Barbet Schroeder. **CAST:** Bulle Ogier, Jean-Pierre Kalfon, Michael Gothard. **1972**

VALLEY GIRL ★★★1/2 The story of a romance between a San Fernando Valley girl and a Hollywood punker, *Valley Girl* claims the distinction of being one of the few teen movies directed by a woman: Martha Coolidge. And, perhaps for that reason, it's a little treasure: a funny, sexy, appealing story that contains something for nearly everyone. Rated R. 95m. **DIR:** Martha Coolidge. **CAST:** Nicolas Cage, Deborah Foreman, Colleen Camp, Frederic Forrest, Lee Purcell. **1983**

VALLEY OF GWANGI ★★★ Prehistoric reptiles are found in Mexico in the early 1900s; attempts are made to capture them alive to be put on display. A cross between *King Kong* and *Hatari!*, with a Western flavor. Fine special effects by Ray Harryhausen. Rated PG. 95m. **DIR:** Jim O'Connolly. **CAST:** James Franciscus, Richard Carlson, Gila Golan. **1969**

VALLEY OF THE DOLLS 🦃 Trash film of Jacqueline Susann's trashy bestseller about the effect of drugs (the *dolls* of the title) on ladies from show business and society. John Williams was Oscar-nominated for his score. 123m. **DIR:** Mark Robson. **CAST:** Barbara Parkins, Patty Duke, Sharon Tate, Susan Hayward, Paul Burke, Martin Milner, Lee Grant. **1967**

VALLEY OF THE SUN ★★★ A discredited army scout runs into conflict with an unscrupulous government agent responsible for the maltreatment of Indians in the Arizona Territory in the 1800s. A Western that mixes in comedy. B&W; 84m. **DIR:** George Marshall. **CAST:** Lucille Ball, Cedric Hardwicke, Dean Jagger, James Craig. **1942**

VALLEY OF THE ZOMBIES ★★ A former mental patient with a craving for blood leaves cadavers everywhere in this low-budget comedy-thriller. Gallows humor, grim doings, and a spooky old house spice up this little oddity with head creep Ian Keith a standout. B&W; 57m. **DIR:** Philip Ford. **CAST:** Ian Keith, Robert Livingston, Adrian Booth, Thomas Jackson, Charles Trowbridge. **1946**

VALMONT ★★★★ Milos Forman took a great artistic risk in directing what amounts to a one-year-later remake of Stephen Frears's Oscar-winning *Dangerous Liaisons*, but the result is captivating, with a young cast bringing poignance and innocence to its tale of seduction and deceit. Rated R for nudity and violence. 137m. **DIR:** Milos Forman. **CAST:** Colin Firth, Annette Bening, Meg Tilly, Sian Phillips, Jeffrey Jones, Henry Thomas, Fabia Drake, Fairuza Balk. **1989**

VALS, THE ★★ Not as totally grody as one would expect, this teen flick features bored valley girls who transform from shop-aholics into charitable drug busters. Rated R for profanity. 96m. **DIR:** James Polakof. **CAST:** Jill Carroll, Elena Stratheros. **1982**

VAMP ★★★ Effective comedy shocker concerns a pair of college kids (Chris Makepeace and Robert Rusler) who must find a stripper for a big party being thrown that night. Upon arriving at the After Dark Club, the duo quickly decide on the outrageous Katrina (Grace Jones), little realizing that she is a vicious, bloodthirsty vampire in disguise. Rated R for gore and brief nudity. 93m. **DIR:** Richard Wenk. **CAST:** Chris Makepeace, Grace Jones, Robert Rusler, Sandy Baron, Gedde Watanabe, Dedee Pfeiffer. **1986 DVD**

VAMPING ★★ Dreary attempt to update *film noir*, with Patrick Duffy as a down-and-out musician persuaded to break into the home of a dead man. Once there, he falls in love with a photo of the man's widow. Overlong. Rated R for profanity. 110m. **DIR:** Frederick King Keller. **CAST:** Patrick Duffy, Catherine Hyland, Rod Arrants. **1984**

VAMPIRE, THE ★★1/2 Here it is, the first in a long line of late-Fifties/early-Sixties Mexican monster movies—all of them variously atmospheric, technically primitive, culturally eccentric . . . , and often compulsively watchable. German Robles was Mexico's Christopher Lee, although this first of his many vampire movies was shot a full year before Lee's *Horror of Dracula* debut. B&W; 84m. **DIR:** Fernando Mendez. **CAST:** German Robles, Abel Salazar. **1957**

VAMPIRE AT MIDNIGHT ★★ A young woman becomes the object of adoration of a brutal vampire posing as a motivational psychologist. This tries hard to be a character study rather than a horror movie, but it misses the mark. Rated R for violence and nudity. 94m. **DIR:** Greggor McClatchy. **CAST:** Jason Williams, Gustav Vintas, Leslie Milne, Jenie Moore, Robert Random. **1988**

VAMPIRE BAT, THE ★★★ Prolific director Frank Strayer gave low-rent Majestic Studios their biggest hit with this eerie thriller reminiscent of the great horror films. Lionel Atwill and Fay Wray reunite to share the screen with distinguished Melvyn Douglas as a skeptical magistrate out to solve several mysterious deaths. It seems the victims have all been drained of blood and great hordes of bats have been hovering about. . . . B&W; 63m. **DIR:** Frank Strayer. **CAST:** Lionel Atwill, Fay Wray, Melvyn Douglas, Dwight Frye, Maude Eburne. **1933 DVD**

VAMPIRE COP ★★ Low-budget direct-to-video tale of a vampire who becomes a cop and uses his position to evoke red from the criminals. They'll let just about anyone be a cop these days. Rated PG for violence. 86m. **DIR:** Donald Farmer. **CAST:** William Lucas, Melissa Moore, Donald Farmer. **1990**

VAMPIRE HAPPENING A Hollywood sexpot vacations in Europe and learns her grandmother was a vampire. Not rated. 97m. **DIR:** Freddie Francis. **CAST:** Pia Dagermark, Ferdinand Mayne, Thomas Hunter. **1971**

VAMPIRE HOLOCAUST Uneven, poorly paced production from schlockmeister Todd Sheets. Rated R for violence and gore. 72m. **DIR:** Shane Hatfield. **CAST:** Nick Stodden, Rico Love. **1997**

VAMPIRE HOOKERS (SENSUOUS VAMPIRES) Aging vampire lords over a bevy of beauteous bloodsuckers. (Also known as *Sensuous Vampires*.) Rated R for violence and nudity. 82m. **DIR:** Cirio H. Santiago. **CAST:** John Carradine. **1979**

VAMPIRE IN BROOKLYN ★★ This anemic vampire comedy is yet another misfire by star Eddie Murphy, apparently more concerned with playing multiple roles than with delivering a coherent film. His riff on the classic Dracula myth is neither funny nor scary; it's all pretty familiar as Murphy's faux-sophisticated fangster travels to New York City to find his "perfect mate." Ho hum. Rated R for profanity, violence, and gore. 100m. **DIR:** Wes Craven. **CAST:** Eddie Murphy, Angela Bassett, Allen Payne, Kadeem Hardison, John Witherspoon. **1995 DVD**

VAMPIRE JOURNALS ★★1/2 Anne Rice fans are the target audience for this overwrought tale of a junior vampire, the older bloodsucker who took his life, and the woman they both desire. Like many Full Moon productions, authentic European locations help provide plenty of atmosphere. Rated R for nudity, violence and sex. 92m. **DIR:** Ted Nicolaou. **CAST:** Jonathon Morris, David Gunn, Starr Andreeff. **1997 DVD**

VAMPIRE LOVERS, THE ★★★ Hammer Films of England revitalized the Frankenstein and Dracula horror series in the late 1950s. But by 1971, when this film was released, Hammer's horrors had become passé. Even adding sex to the mix, as the studio did in this faithful screen version of Sheridan LeFanu's *Camilla*, didn't help much. Nonetheless, sexy Ingrid Pitt makes a voluptuous vampire. Rated R for violence, nudity, suggested sex, and gore. 88m. **DIR:** Roy Ward Baker. **CAST:** Ingrid Pitt, Peter Cushing, Pippa Steele, Madeleine Smith, George Cole, Dawn Addams, Kate O'Mara. **1971**

VAMPIRE OVER LONDON This is one of many titles appended to Bela Lugosi's last British film, shot as *Old Mother Riley Meets the Vampire*, and starring Arthur Lucan as the washerwoman character he designed decades earlier for a drag act on the music hall circuit. Finally released in the United States in the Sixties as *My Son, the Vampire*. B&W; 74m. **DIR:** John Gilling. **CAST:** Bela Lugosi, Arthur Lucan. **1952**

VAMPIRE PRINCESS MIYU ★★ Spiritual investigator Himiko encounters strange happenings in two melodramatic, animated tales of the occult, Japanese style. In Japanese with English subtitles. 60m. **DIR:** Toshihiro Hirano. **1988**

VAMPIRE VIXENS FROM VENUS Totally lame horror-sex comedy noteworthy only for a cameo by comic Charlie Callas. Not rated; contains nudity and gore. 85m. **DIR:** Ted A. Bohus. **CAST:** Leon Head, Michelle Bauer, Charlie Callas. **1994**

VAMPIRELLA ★★ Talisa Soto makes a woefully anemic Vampirella in this laughable adaptation of the long-running comic-book series. Soto doesn't convey any of the character's innate menace or sensuality, and her costume's all wrong! Roger Daltrey is much better as the scenery-chewing villain; too bad he couldn't have played the hero. Rated R for violence, profanity, and nudity. 80m. **DIR:** Jim Wynorski. **CAST:** Talisa Soto, Roger Daltrey, Richard Joseph Paul, Brian Bloom. **1996**

VAMPIRES & OTHER STEREOTYPES ★★ When in doubt, take a small group of people, put them in a confined place, and besiege them with something. That's the road taken here in this film, which tries hard but never quite succeeds. Not rated; contains violence, gore, and profanity. 88m. **DIR:** Kevin J. Lindenmuth. **CAST:** Bill White, Ed Hubbard. **1995**

VAMPIRES FROM OUTER SPACE An undead bride from the planet Cirrus takes her unwitting groom to a strange island in this entirely amateurish shot-on-video production. Not rated. 114m. **DIR:** Steve Postal. **CAST:** Alan Ramey, Angela Shepard, Jennifer Tuck. **1990**

VAMPIRE'S KISS A ranting, obnoxious literary agent becomes convinced that he is a vampire. Rated R for violence, profanity, and brief nudity. 103m. **DIR:** Robert Bierman. **CAST:** Nicolas Cage, Maria Conchita Alonso, Jennifer Beals, Elizabeth Ashley. **1989**

VAMPIRES, THE (1915) (LES VAMPIRES) ★★★★ Generally considered the crowning achievement of Louis Feuillade, who took the form of the movie serial to its peak. The Vampires are a gang of costumed criminals led by the beautiful Musidora. Accused of glorifying crime, Feuillade and cast actually improvised much of the action in this ten-part silent serial. Still impressive today. B&W; 420m. **DIR:** Louis Feuillade. **CAST:** Musidora, Edouard Mathé. **1915–1916 DVD**

VAMPS: DEADLY DREAM GIRLS ★★1/2 A priest frequents a strip club (!) in an attempt to save the souls of the dancers. Instead he gets mixed up in a struggle with vampires for one girl's soul. An enjoyable, though underbudgeted film. Not rated; contains violence, profanity, and nudity. 90m. **DIR:** Mark Burchett, Michael D. Fox. **CAST:** Jennifer Huss, Paul Morris, Lorissa McComas. **1996 DVD**

VAMPYR (1931) ★★★★★ Director Carl Dreyer believed that horror is best implied. By relying on the viewer's imagination, he created a classic. A young man at a very bizarre inn discovers an unconscious woman, who had been attacked by a vampire in the form of an old woman. This outstanding film is one of the few serious films of the macabre. B&W; 68m. **DIR:** Carl Dreyer. **CAST:** Julian West, Sybille Schmitz. **1931 DVD**

VAMPYRE (1990) ★★1/2 Director Bruce G. Hallenbeck remakes Carl Dreyer's silent classic with only so-so results. Here a village is plagued by vampirism and a mysterious slayer arrives to confront the bloodsuckers. Not rated; contains violence. 90m. **DIR:** Bruce G. Hallenbeck. **CAST:** Cathy Seyler, John Brant, John McCarty. **1990**

VAMPYR, THE (1992) ★★ An operetta based on a nineteenth-century score, this misogynistic witches'

brew of gore, sex, and surrealism features a vampire released from an icy grave beneath London's skyscrapers. He must renew his pact with Satan by slaying three women within three days, all the while singing of his troubles. Difficult to sit through, very little narrative, and the structure is too stagy for the format. Not rated; contains violence, nudity, gore, sexual situations, and profanity. 115m. **DIR:** Nigel Finch. **CAST:** Omar Ebrahim, Richard van Allan, Fiona O'Neill, Philip Salmon, Colenton Freeman. **1992**

VAMPYRES ★★1/2 This tale of two beautiful female vampires living in an old mansion and sharing their male victims sexually before drinking their blood was considered pornographic in its time. It's pretty tame by current standards, and also easier to appreciate as a piece of serious, if low-budget, erotica. There are two versions available on video; the longer, unrated one has elongated sexual situations, though both feature abundant nudity. 87m. **DIR:** Joseph Larraz. **CAST:** Marianne Morris, Anulka, Murray Brown, Brian Deacon, Bessie Love. **1974**

VAN, THE (1976) 🦃 Inept teenager uses his impressive new van to seduce bimbos. Rated PG. 92m. **DIR:** Sam Grossman. **CAST:** Stuart Getz, Danny DeVito. **1976 DVD**

VAN, THE (1997) ★★★1/2 The final entry in Irish novelist Roddy Doyle's *Barrytown* trilogy is no less entertaining as it follows the ups and downs of two best friends and pubmates who unwisely go into business together. Rated R for profanity and sexual candor. 100m. **DIR:** Stephen Frears. **CAST:** Colm Meaney, Donal O'Kelly, Ger Ryan, Carolyn Rothwell, Brendan O'Carroll. **1997**

VAN GOGH ★★ If they keep telling the story of Vincent van Gogh, perhaps somebody will finally get it right. Maurice Pialat did not get it right in this long, dull exercise. Pialat's point with the story of the famous painter is to emphasize the mundane. It's a noble idea, but how do you make the mundane interesting for observers? Especially for nearly three hours? In French with English subtitles. 158m. **DIR:** Maurice Pialat. **CAST:** Jacques Dutronc, Bernard Le Coq, Gérard Séty, Alexandra London. **1991**

•VANILLA SKY ★★1/2 Manhattan publishing heir David Aames is bedding an emotionally unstable socialite when he lusts after the acquaintance of his best client and friend. The double betrayal leads to the disfigurement of Aames's face, a storyline that interweaves reality and nightmare, and a science-fiction ending that makes all that went before it feel both pretentious and preposterous. This surrealistic, overly long exercise in twisted illusions is a remake of the 1997 Spanish psychological thriller *Open Your Eyes*. Rated R for profanity, nudity, sex, and violence. 130m. **DIR:** Cameron Crowe. **CAST:** Tom Cruise, Penelope Cruz, Cameron Diaz, Jason Lee, Kurt Russell. **2001 DVD**

VANINA VANINI ★★1/2 Set in Italy in the 1800s, this film mixes politics and romance when a princess falls in love with a revolutionary on a mission to kill a traitor. One of director Roberto Rossellini's least memorable films: at the very least, it's difficult to understand fully unless you're a student of Italian history. Originally released in America as *The Betrayer*. In Italian with English subtitles. B&W; 125m. **DIR:** Roberto Rossellini. **CAST:** Martine Carol, Olimpia Cava, Sandra Milo, Laurent Terzieff. **1961**

VANISHING, THE (1988) ★★★★★ Superb thriller as well as an insightful portrait of a sociopath. The mysterious disappearance of his girlfriend leads Rex on an obsessive quest that results in a confrontation with her killer. The violence (including an unforgettable ending) is understated. Donnadieu's portrayal of the villain quietly freezes the blood. In Dutch and French with English subtitles. Rated R for adult content. 107m. **DIR:** George Sluizer. **CAST:** Bernard Pierre Donnadieu, Gene Bervoets, Johanna ter Steege. **1988 DVD**

VANISHING, THE (1993) ★★★1/2 Director George Sluizer's Americanized remake of his superb, 1988 Dutch thriller suffers from an imbalance caused by an overemphasis on the sociopathic killer. Rated R for profanity and violence. 120m. **DIR:** George Sluizer. **CAST:** Jeff Bridges, Kiefer Sutherland, Nancy Travis, Sandra Bullock, Park Overall, Maggie Linderman, Lisa Eichhorn. **1993**

VANISHING ACT ★★★1/2 A tense psychological drama with a knockout ending. Mike Farrell's wife of one week is missing. He routinely reports this to town cop Elliot Gould. Before the investigation begins, the wife reappears. But Farrell says she's not his wife. Rated PG. 95m. **DIR:** David Greene. **CAST:** Mike Farrell, Margot Kidder, Elliott Gould, Fred Gwynne, Graham Jarvis. **1987**

VANISHING AMERICAN, THE ★★★1/2 One of the few major studio releases of the silent era to treat the American Indian with compassion and dignity, this is a beautifully photographed silent gem from Paramount. Based on Zane Grey's popular melodramatic adventure, this landmark film is still historically important as well as being a fine job by director George Seitz. Silent. B&W; 114m. **DIR:** George B. Seitz. **CAST:** Richard Dix, Lois Wilson, Noah Beery Sr., Charles Stevens. **1925**

VANISHING POINT ★★1/2 Interesting story of a marathon car chase through Colorado and California. Cleavon Little gives a standout performance as the disc jockey who helps a driver (Barry Newman) elude the police. Richard Sarafian's direction is competent, but the story eventually runs out of gas before the film ends. Rated PG. 107m. **DIR:** Richard C. Sarafian. **CAST:** Cleavon Little, Barry Newman, Dean Jagger. **1971**

VANISHING PRAIRIE, THE ★★★1/2 Award-winning true-life adventure from Walt Disney ranks with *The Living Desert* as the finest (and certainly most widely seen) nature film of the 1950s. Beautifully photographed, this is a fun but sobering movie the whole family can enjoy. 75m. **DIR:** James Algar. **1954**

VANITY FAIR 🦃 In updating Thackeray's classic *Vanity Fair*, screenwriter F. Hugh Herbert and director Chester M. Franklin have created a disaster. B&W; 78m. **DIR:** Chester M. Franklin. **CAST:** Myrna Loy, Conway Tearle, Barbara Kent, Anthony Bushell. **1938**

VANYA ON 42ND STREET ★★★★★ A workshop production of Anton Chekhov's *Uncle Vanya*, performed in an abandoned Manhattan theater by actors in modern dress. Without the distraction of period sets and costumes, the splendid ensemble cast cuts right to the heart of Chekhov's great (and surprisingly modern) play. A filmed experiment in which everything goes marvelously right. Rated PG. 119m. **DIR:** Louis Malle. **CAST:** Wallace Shawn, Julianne Moore, Larry Pine, Brooke Smith, George Gaynes. **1994**

VARAN, THE UNBELIEVABLE ★★1/2 Another Godzilla rip-off with better-than-average effects. B&W; 70m. **DIR:** Inoshiro Honda. **CAST:** Jerry Baerwitz, Myron Healey, Tsuruko Kobayashi. **1962**

•VARIAN'S WAR ★★★1/2 Although it depicts a fascinating turn of events, this made-for-cable original about Varian Fry lacks the cinematic punch that made *Schindler's List* so powerful. Fry, like Schindler, rescued Jews from the clutches of Nazi Germany, but he focused his efforts on refugee intellectuals, artists, and writers. William Hurt does a fine job portraying the sensitive, somewhat naïve American filled with the sense of humanitarian courage necessary to accomplish this feat. Rated PG. 120m. **DIR:** Lionel Chetwynd. **CAST:** William Hurt, Julia Ormond, Matt Craven, Maury Chaykin, Alan Arkin, Lynn Redgrave. **2000**

VARIETY ★★★★★ A milestone of cinema art. It tells a simple, tragic tale of a famous and conceited vaudeville acrobat whose character flaw is cowardice; a clever and entirely unscrupulous girl; and a trusting waterfront circus boss—made a fool of by love—who murders because of that hollow love. The cast is incredible, the cinematography superb. Silent. B&W; 104m. **DIR:** E. A. Dupont. **CAST:** Emil Jannings, Lya de Putti. **1926**

VARIETY LIGHTS ★★★★ This is Federico Fellini's first film, though it's not entirely his. (It's codirected by Alberto Lattuada.) Still, Fellini fans will recognize themes of fantasy and illusion and the pursuit of impossible-to-capture dreams, as well as the presence of the sublime Giulietta Masina. In Italian with English subtitles. 93m. **DIR:** Federico Fellini, Alberto Lattuada. **CAST:** Peppino De Filippo, Carla Del Poggio, Giulietta Masina. **1950**

VARSITY BLUES ★★★1/2 This raucous high-school fantasy rises above stereotypes, thanks to W. Peter Iliff's thoughtful script about restless young men—and women—desperately trying to escape their dead-end, small-town environments. In West Canaan, Texas, the best hope is football, and the players are elevated to the status of local gods. The tale may be wholly predictable, but it's told with honesty, conviction, and a sound moral foundation. Rated R for profanity, nudity, and sexual content. 106m. **DIR:** Brian Robbins. **CAST:** James van der Beek, Jon Voight, Paul Walker, Ron Lester, Scott Caan, Richard Lineback, Tiffany C. Love, Amy Smart. **1999 DVD**

VASECTOMY ★★1/2 A bank vice president (Paul Sorvino) is having plenty of family problems. After bearing their eighth child, his wife urges him to have a vasectomy while other family members are stealing from his bank. This comedy is rated R for nudity and obscenities. 92m. **DIR:** Robert Burge. **CAST:** Paul Sorvino, Abe Vigoda, Cassandra Edwards, Lorne Greene. **1986**

VAULT OF HORROR ★★ British sequel to *Tales from the Crypt* boasts a fine cast and five short stories borrowed from the classic EC comics line of the early 1950s, but delivers very little in the way of true chills and atmosphere. Not nearly as effective as the earlier five-story thriller *Dr. Terror's House of Horrors* and not as much fun as the most recent homage to the EC horror story, *Creepshow*. Rated R. 87m. **DIR:** Roy Ward Baker. **CAST:** Daniel Massey, Anna Massey, Terry-Thomas, Glynis Johns, Curt Jurgens, Dawn Addams, Tom Baker, Denholm Elliott, Michael Craig, Edward Judd. **1973**

VEGA$ ★★1/2 A few days in the life of a high-flying, T-Bird-driving private eye whose beat is highways, byways, and gambling casinos of Las Vegas. Robert Urich, an ex-cop, is hired to find a runaway teenage girl who's gotten in too deep with the sleazy side of Fortune Town. 104m. **DIR:** Richard Lang. **CAST:** Robert Urich, Judy Landers, Tony Curtis, Will Sampson, Greg Morris. **1978**

VEGAS IN SPACE 🦃 Bad acting, bad sets, bad costumes, and bad dialogue are the high points of this outer space dragfest. Not rated; contains profanity, nudity, and adult situations. 85m. **DIR:** Philip Ford. **CAST:** Doris Fish, Miss X, Ginger Quest, Ramona Fisher. **1995**

VEGAS VACATION ★★★ The Griswolds arrive in Las Vegas: Dad becomes a gambling addict, Mom is courted by Wayne Newton, their son hooks up with hood-type high rollers, and their daughter goes out with a stripper. All this is fun but pales in comparison to Randy Quaid's performance as their unbalanced cousin. Rated PG for sexual situations. 90m. **DIR:** Stephen Kessler. **CAST:** Chevy Chase, Beverly D'Angelo, Randy Quaid, Wayne Newton, Ethan Embry, Wallace Shawn. **1997 DVD**

VELOCITY OF GARY, THE ★★1/2 Vincent D'Onofrio is the main reason to watch this conventional drama revolving around a love triangle between two men and a woman. He plays a porno star who attracts a telephone sex operator and a waitress, who can't stand each other, but are forced to reconcile their differences when D'Onofrio becomes ill. Director Dan Ireland creates lots of pretty pictures but not much heat or heart. Rated R for adult situations, language, and violence. 110m. **DIR:** Dan Ireland. **CAST:** Vincent D'Onofrio, Thomas Jane, Salma Hayek. **1998**

VELOCITY TRAP 🦃 In this very bad sci-fi movie, Olivier Gruner plays a man framed for murder, who must come to the rescue of a multibillion dollar starship that is threatened by space pirates and asteroids. Rated R for violence, language, and sexual situations. 89m. **DIR:** Phillip Roth. **CAST:** Olivier Gruner, Alicia Coppola, Bruce Weitz. **1998 DVD**

VELVET GOLDMINE ★★ This lurid fantasy revisits the world of 1970s glam rock associated with David Bowie, Marc Bolan, and Iggy Pop. It is awash in sultry leers of androgynous male rockers and star power, nostalgia, decadence, self-identity, and obsession. Fascinating only in spurts. Rated R for sex, nudity, profanity, and drug use. 117m. **DIR:** Todd Haynes. **CAST:** Christian Bale, Jonathan Rhys-Meyers, Ewan McGregor, Toni Collette, Eddie Izzard. **1998 DVD**

VELVET TOUCH, THE ★★★★1/2 This is a marvelous suspense-drama featuring Rosalind Russell as a stage actress. In a fit of rage, she kills her jealous producer, a blackmailer. Leo Rosten's screenplay crackles with spirit and polish. B&W; 97m. **DIR:** John Gage. **CAST:** Rosalind Russell, Leo Genn, Claire Trevor, Leon Ames, Sydney Greenstreet, Frank McHugh, Lex Barker. **1948**

VELVET VAMPIRE, THE ★★ Marginally unconventional low-budget horror about a young married couple vampirized by a sultry femme fatale. A few scenes are effective, but overall film is so slackly paced that it never generates any suspense. Rated R. 79m. **DIR:**

Stephanie Rothman. **CAST:** Sherry Miles, Michael Blodgett, Celeste Yarnall. **1971**

VENDETTA (1985) 🦃 A laughably bad women's prison flick. Rated R. 89m. **DIR:** Bruce Logan. **CAST:** Karen Chase, Sandy Martin, Roberta Collins, Kin Shriner. **1985**

VENDETTA (1999) ★★★1/2 Italian immigrants run afoul of racism and entrenched backroom politics in this sprawling, fact-based account of the largest lynching in U.S. history, which took place in New Orleans in 1890, when businessmen decided that they wanted to take over the docks controlled—mostly peacefully—by hard-working Italians. The story is seen through the eyes of a newly arrived young man who further compounds his plight by falling in love with an Irish girl. It all boils into a full-blown riot and racial bloodbath on par with the worst deep-South lynchings. Director Nicholas Meyer, always intrigued by little-known historical events, deserves credit for helping bring this atrocity to light; scripter Timothy Prager commendably condenses the events of Richard Gambino's far more ambitious book, which no doubt will be embraced by viewers wanting to learn more after seeing this film. Rated R for violence and torture. 117m. **DIR:** Nicholas Meyer. **CAST:** Luke Askew, Clancy Brown, Andrew Connolly, Bruce Davison, Joaquim de Almeida, Andrea di Stefano, Edward Herrmann, Richard Libertini, Christopher Walken. **1999 DVD**

VENGEANCE 🦃 Dull account of an escape from a Latin American prison camp. Not rated, the film has graphic violence and sex. 114m. **DIR:** Antonio Isasi. **CAST:** Jason Miller, Lea Massari, Marisa Peredes. **1987**

VENGEANCE IS MINE (1976) ★★ A stark and brutal story of backcountry justice. Murderous bank robbers run into Ernest Borgnine, who matches brutality with brutality. A bleak and stilted movie. Not rated; contains violence and profanity. 90m. **DIR:** John Trent. **CAST:** Ernest Borgnine, Michael J. Pollard, Hollis McLaren. **1976**

VENGEANCE IS MINE (1979) ★★★★ Terrifying, complex portrait of a mass murderer, played with chilling detachment by Ken Ogata. Shohei Imamura, Japan's most controversial director, has created a nightmarish film that is both poignant and disturbing in its depiction of a psychopathic mind at work. In Japanese with English subtitles. Not rated but contains scenes of graphic violence and nudity. 129m. **DIR:** Shohei Imamura. **CAST:** Ken Ogata. **1979**

VENGEANCE OF SHE, THE ★★★ Loose sequel to the Ursula Andress film version of H. Rider Haggard's *She* is an enjoyable romp with all the prerequisites for a fun adventure movie. Sexy Olinka Berova doesn't remember who she is. All she knows is that she is drawn to a lost city in the mountains where an evil priest is trying to lure her to her death. Rated G. 100m. **DIR:** Cliff Owen. **CAST:** Olinka Berova, Edward Judd, John Richardson, Andre Morell, George Sewell. **1968 DVD**

VENGEANCE VALLEY ★★ Slow-moving story of no-good cattle heir Robert Walker and his protective foster brother Burt Lancaster lacks suspense and doesn't have enough action. 83m. **DIR:** Richard Thorpe. **CAST:** Burt Lancaster, Robert Walker, Joanne Dru, Ray Collins, John Ireland, Sally Forrest. **1951 DVD**

VENICE/VENICE ★★★★ Henry Jaglom portrays a filmmaker at the Venice Film Festival doing the usual rounds of publicity until he's introduced to a female journalist from France. Their mutual interest continues through the festival and back at the filmmaker's home in Venice, California. (Hence, *Venice/Venice*). Highly enjoyable. Rated PG. 108m. **DIR:** Henry Jaglom. **CAST:** Henry Jaglom, Nelly Alard, Suzanne Bertish, Daphna Kastner, David Duchovny. **1992**

VENOM 🦃 This combination horror film and police thriller doesn't really work as either. Rated R for nudity and violence. 98m. **DIR:** Piers Haggard. **CAST:** Nicol Williamson, Klaus Kinski, Susan George, Oliver Reed, Sterling Hayden, Sarah Miles. **1982**

•VENOMOUS ★★ Prolific schlock director Fred Olen Ray, working under the pseudonym Ed Raymond, recruits new stock player Treat Williams to play a Mohave Desert physician trying to save his small town from virus-infected rattlesnakes and a government cover-up. Unless snakes make you coil up, this B-movie hybrid doesn't have much bite. Rated PG-13 for language and violence. 97m. **DIR:** Fred Olen Ray. **CAST:** Treat Williams, Mary Page Keller, Andrew Stevens, Anthony Azizi. **2001 DVD**

VENUS BEAUTY INSTITUTE ★★ Four women at a Parisian beauty boutique chat, date, mate, and give numerous facials in this tenderness-challenged romantic comedy about aging and beauty being only skin-deep. The main character is a fortyish beautician who accidentally disfigured her former boyfriend and now hides from love among a series of sexual flings. In French with English subtitles. Not rated. 105m. **DIR:** Tonie Marshall. **CAST:** Nathalie Baye, Bulle Ogier, Samuel Le Bihan, Jacques Bonnaffe, Audrey Tautou, Mathilde Seigner. **2000 DVD**

•VENUS DE MILO ★★ This French-Canadian film explores the familiar ground of a rising rock-and-roll band. When a dead-end group of musicians finally acquires a singer, things start to look up for them. Uninspired dialogue and a predictable plot follow, along with a surprising lack of actual music (i.e., practice sessions, recording sets) from the band. In French with English subtitles. Not rated; contains profanity. 88m. **DIR:** Diana Lewis. **CAST:** Simon Biosvert, Diana Lewis. **2001**

VENUS IN FURS 🦃 Poor mystery involving a musician and a mutilated woman who washes ashore. Rated R. 86m. **DIR:** Jess (Jesus) Franco. **CAST:** James Darren, Barbara McNair, Klaus Kinski, Dennis Price. **1970**

VENUS RISING ★★ When a man and woman escape from a brutal, futuristic prison, they travel back to civilization where they discover a world controlled by drugs and virtual reality. Maybe prison was better. Rated R for profanity, violence, and nudity. 91m. **DIR:** Leora Barish. **CAST:** Billy Wirth, Audie England, Costas Mandylor, Meredith Salenger, Morgan Fairchild, Joel Grey. **1995**

VENUS WARS, THE ★★★★ Outstanding example of the art of Japanese animation, certainly one of the finest available in America. Set on barren Venus in the twenty-first century, the story follows young Hiro and his friends, members of a racing team. All the excitement of *Akira*, with a better (and more coherent) story. In Japanese with English subtitles. Not rated; contains violence. 104m. **DIR:** Yoshikazu Yasuhiko. **1989 DVD**

VERA CRUZ ★★★ Two American soldiers of fortune find themselves in different camps during one of the many Mexican revolutions of the 1800s. Gary Cooper is the good guy, but Burt Lancaster steals every scene as

the smiling, black-dressed baddie. The plot is pretty basic but holds your interest until the traditional climactic gunfight. 94m. **DIR:** Robert Aldrich. **CAST:** Gary Cooper, Burt Lancaster, Denise Darcel, Ernest Borgnine. **1954**

VERDICT, THE ★★★★1/2 In this first-rate drama, Paul Newman brilliantly plays an alcoholic Boston lawyer who redeems himself by taking on slick James Mason in a medical malpractice suit. Rated R for profanity and adult situations. 129m. **DIR:** Sidney Lumet. **CAST:** Paul Newman, James Mason, Charlotte Rampling, Jack Warden. **1982**

VERMONT IS FOR LOVERS ★★ A couple of New York yuppies decide to tie the knot at a Vermont farm, but nearly talk us to death before the ceremony. Writer-director John O'Brien's casual, improvisational style is interesting enough to make you wonder what he could do with real actors and a viable budget. Not rated. 88m. **DIR:** John O'Brien. **CAST:** George Thrush, Marya Cohn, Ann O'Brien, Euclid Farnham. **1993**

VERNE MILLER ★★ Scott Glenn stars as the infamous gunman who masterminded and executed the violent Kansas City massacre at the insistence of crime czar Al Capone. Too many dull gunfights and too little story line or character development. Rated R for nudity and violence. 95m. **DIR:** Rod Hewitt. **CAST:** Scott Glenn, Barbara Stock, Thomas Waites, Lucinda Jenney, Sonny Carl Davis, Andrew Robinson. **1988**

VERNON, FLORIDA ★★★ Weirdos of the world seem to have united and set up housekeeping in Vernon, Florida. This unique and off-the-wall film comes from the strange vision of director Errol Morris. In this slice of life, the viewers become acquainted with (and amused by) the citizens of this slightly off-center small town. Not rated. 60m. **DIR:** Errol Morris. **1988**

VERONIKA VOSS ★★ A famous German actress tries to revive her flagging career with alcohol and drugs in this final addition to Rainer Werner Fassbinder's trilogy about the collapse of the West German postwar dream. While technically a well-made movie, Fassbinder's point is lost amid the bleak shadow life of the losers he so skillfully captures. In German with English subtitles. Rated R. 105m. **DIR:** Rainer Werner Fassbinder. **CAST:** Rosel Zech, Hilmar Thate. **1982**

VERTICAL LIMIT ★★★ Great stunts and breathtaking cinematography can't overcome the increasingly silly plot contrivances in this mountaineering thriller, which sends a group of veteran climbers up the face of K2 (the world's second highest peak) on a rescue mission. The results are exciting enough, but the purple dialogue and *Perils of Pauline*–style melodrama become pretty foolish, even for those who know nothing about mountain climbing. Rated PG-13 for violence, profanity, and dramatic intensity. 126m. **DIR:** Martin Campbell. **CAST:** Chris O'Donnell, Bill Paxton, Robin Tunney, Scott Glenn, Izabella Scorupco, Temuera Morrison, Stuart Wilson, Alexander Siddig. **2000 DVD**

•VERTICAL RAY OF THE SUN, THE ★★1/2 Infidelity and sexual awakening involving three Hanoi sisters are at the heart of this sensual, languidly paced, sometimes confusing Chekovian melodrama. The youngest sibling, who lives and flirts with her brother in their spacious apartment, works as a waitress in a Hanoi café owned by her married oldest sister. The middle sister is married to a writer. Amidst the bustle and lushness of modern Vietnam, these females share intimate secrets, make discoveries about their men, and learn about the vulnerability of all relationships. In Vietnamese with English subtitles. Rated PG-13 for sexual references and situations. 112m. **DIR:** Tran Anh Hung. **CAST:** Tran Nu Yen-Khe, Nguyen Nhu Quynh, Le Khanh, Chu Ngoc Hung, Tran Manh Cuong, Ngo Quang Hai. **2000 DVD**

VERTIGO ★★★★1/2 The first hour of this production is slow, gimmicky, and artificial. However, the rest of this suspense picture takes off at high speed. James Stewart stars as a San Francisco detective who has a fear of heights and is hired to shadow an old friend's wife (Kim Novak). He finds himself falling in love with her—then tragedy strikes. 128m. **DIR:** Alfred Hitchcock. **CAST:** James Stewart, Kim Novak, Barbara Bel Geddes. **1958 DVD**

VERY BAD THINGS ★★ The accidental killing of a hooker at a bachelor party snowballs into a nightmare of murder and mutilation. Writer-director Peter Berg clearly means this to be an outrageous black comedy, but there's not a laugh to be had from beginning to end; Berg shows little flair for even conventional comedy, let alone the kind that hinges on death and dismemberment. Rated R for profanity, sexual scenes, and several gruesome deaths. 101m. **DIR:** Peter Berg. **CAST:** Christian Slater, Jon Favreau, Cameron Diaz, Daniel Stern, Jeremy Piven, Jeanne Tripplehorn, Leland Orser. **1998 DVD**

VERY BRADY CHRISTMAS, A ★★★★ One of television's most revered families decides to get together for Christmas. All of the kids have grown up, and all but one of the original stars return to help. A little sappy, a little corny, but part of the American culture. 94m. **DIR:** Peter Baldwin. **CAST:** Robert Reed, Florence Henderson, Ann B. Davis. **1988**

VERY BRADY SEQUEL, A ★★★ While *The Brady Bunch Movie* drew guffaws, the sequel elicits genuine belly laughs. While Marcia and Greg have the hots for each other, a handsome stranger appears claiming to be Carol's first husband. Comic highlights include the teens' angst and the entire family's outdated trust and good cheer. Rated PG-13 for mild profanity and sexual innuendo. 90m. **DIR:** Arlene Sanford. **CAST:** Shelley Long, Gary Cole, Tim Matheson, Christine Taylor, Christopher Daniel Barnes. **1996**

VERY BRITISH COUP, A ★★★1/2 A very confusing tale about a socialist prime minister who succeeds at maintaining his ideals against the established British government. Ray McAnally does a wonderful job portraying the prime minister, and the editing is excellent, but the plot needs some work. Not rated. 180m. **DIR:** Mick Jackson. **CAST:** Ray McAnally, Alan MacNaughton, Keith Allen, Geoffrey Beevers, Jim Carter, Philip Madoc, Tim McInnerny, Marjorie Yates. **1988**

VERY CURIOUS GIRL, A ★★★ A village girl who has been sexually exploited by the town fathers gets revenge by charging for her "services." Broad (sometimes too broad) social satire. In French with English subtitles. Rated R for sexual content. 105m. **DIR:** Nelly Kaplan. **CAST:** Bernadette Lafont, Georges Geret, Michel Constantin. **1970**

VERY EDGE, THE ★★★ An ex-model loses the child she is carrying after she is raped. Her trauma puts a

strain on her marriage, while her attacker is still on the loose. Effective psychological suspense, marred slightly by a contrived ending. B&W; 82m. **DIR:** Cyril Frankel. **CAST:** Anne Heywood, Richard Todd, Jack Hedley, Maurice Denham, Patrick Magee. **1963**

VERY NATURAL THING, A ★★1/2 A blast from the past, this 1973 drama was one of the first gay films to be released into the mainstream. Robert Joel stars as Jason, a 26 year old gay man who leaves the priesthood and moves to New York in search of true love. What may have been daring more than twenty years ago now appears tame and campy. Film's depiction of uninhibited behavior in the pre-AIDS era may make some nostalgic. Not rated; contains nudity and adult situations. 85m. **DIR:** Christopher Larkin. **CAST:** Robert Joel, Curt Gareth, Bo White. **1973 DVD**

VERY OLD MAN WITH ENORMOUS WINGS, A ★★★★ A winged man lands inexplicably in a tiny Colombian village. People flock in droves to the new attraction, and a huge carnival is born, spewed forth from the womb of human superstition and curiosity. A frenetically frenzied furor full of fantastic, colorful absurdity. In Spanish with English subtitles. Rated R for nudity and simulated sex. 90m. **DIR:** Fernando Birri. **CAST:** Daisy Granados, Asdrubal Melendez. **1988**

VERY PRIVATE AFFAIR, A ★★★ Bardot fan, or just never had a chance to see her? In this romantic drama she plays a famous movie star who can no longer cope with notoriety, so she retreats from public scrutiny. Marcello Mastroianni is equally appealing as a director coming to her aid. In French with English subtitles. 95m. **DIR:** Louis Malle. **CAST:** Brigitte Bardot, Marcello Mastroianni. **1962**

VIBES ★★ This sad misfire should have been much better, given the track record of scripters Lowell Ganz and Babaloo Mandel, but the talented parts simply don't make an impressive whole. Cyndi Lauper and Jeff Goldblum play psychic hotshots hired by shifty Peter Falk, but everything plods along to a foolish finale. Rated PG. 99m. **DIR:** Ken Kwapis. **CAST:** Cyndi Lauper, Jeff Goldblum, Julian Sands, Peter Falk. **1988**

VIBRATIONS A recently crippled rock 'n' roller finds a friend in a metaphysical good Samaritan who unwittingly helps him come to terms with his new condition. Contrived, overplayed, and loaded with clichés. Rated R for language. 103m. **DIR:** Michael Paseornek. **CAST:** James Marshall, Christina Applegate, Faye Grant, Paige Turco. **1994**

VICE SQUAD ★★★1/2 Slick, fast-paced thriller set in the seamy world of pimps and prostitutes. Season Hubley is an adorable mom by day and a smart-mouthed hooker by night forced to help cop Gary Swanson capture a sicko killer, played with frightening intensity by Wings Hauser. A total fairy tale, but it moves quickly enough to mask improbabilities. Not for the squeamish. Rated R. 97m. **DIR:** Gary A. Sherman. **CAST:** Season Hubley, Wings Hauser, Gary Swanson, Beverly Todd. **1982**

VICE VERSA ★★★1/2 Young Fred Savage nearly steals the show from Judge Reinhold in this surprisingly entertaining comedy about a father who changes bodies with his son. We've seen it all many times before in lesser films such as *Freaky Friday* and *Like Father, Like Son*. However, the writing of Dick Clement and Ian De Frenais and the chemistry of the players make it seem almost fresh. Rated PG for profanity. 98m. **DIR:** Brian Gilbert. **CAST:** Judge Reinhold, Fred Savage, Swoosie Kurtz, Jane Kaczmarek, David Proval, William Prince. **1988**

VICIOUS ★★ In this bland Australian film a young man is unwittingly the provocateur of a sadistic attack on his wealthy girlfriend and her parents by a trio of thugs. The ensuing revenge is predictable. Rated R for graphic violence. 90m. **DIR:** Karl Zwicky. **CAST:** Tamblyn Lord, Craig Pearce. **1988**

VICIOUS CIRCLES ★★★ Kinky tale of an American woman who is forced to work as a prostitute for a mysterious gentleman in order to raise money to free her brother, who is in jail on drug-possession charges. Available in R-rated and not-rated versions; both contain adult situations, language, nudity, and violence. 90m. **DIR:** Alexander Whitelaw. **CAST:** Carolyn Lowery, Ben Gazzara, Paul Hipp, Jerome Davis. **1997**

VICIOUS SWEET, THE ★★★ Scream queen Sasha Graham finds herself kidnapped by an obsessed fan. The powerplay that goes on between these two never lets the momentum lag. Not rated; contains profanity and violence. 93m. **DIR:** Ron Bonk. **CAST:** Sasha Graham, Robert Licata. **1997**

VICTIM ★★★ One of the first films to deal with homosexuality, this well-made British effort has Dirk Bogarde as a lawyer confronting blackmailers who killed his lover. It was daring then, but not now. The story, though, is still interesting. B&W; 100m. **DIR:** Basil Dearden. **CAST:** Dirk Bogarde, Sylvia Syms, Dennis Price, John Barrie. **1961**

VICTIM OF LOVE ★★1/2 Psychologist JoBeth Williams finds herself in a quandary when she falls for professor Pierce Brosnan, who is having an affair with her patient Virginia Madsen. Director Jerry London keeps this made-for-television thriller on its toes, and additional footage added to the video adds just the right risqué touch. 92m. **DIR:** Jerry London. **CAST:** Pierce Brosnan, JoBeth Williams, Virginia Madsen. **1991 DVD**

VICTIMLESS CRIMES ★★1/2 Conspiracy and betrayal in the art world. Everyone from the gallery owner to the insurance company are making a buck off stolen paintings, until the artist decides that he's about to make a killing, too! Rated R for violence. 85m. **DIR:** Peter Hawley. **CAST:** Debra Sandlund, Craig Bierko. **1990**

•VICTORIA AND ALBERT ★★★★ Sumptuous British television production examines the rise to power in 1837 of the then 18-year-old Queen Victoria and her troubled but love-filled marriage to Prince Albert. As Victoria faces political intrigue, Albert must cope with being little more than a figurehead—but their mutual deep feelings help them surmount all obstacles until tragedy strikes. Although not always historically accurate, this valentine from England is thoroughly enjoyable—touching but not sugarcoated, filled with intrigue without unnecessary dramatic exaggeration, and wonderfully acted. Made for TV. Not rated. 240m. **DIR:** John Erman. **CAST:** Victoria Hamilton, Jonathan Firth, James Callis, David Suchet, Diana Rigg, Patrick Malahide, Roger Hammond, Penelope Wilton, Peter Ustinov, Delena Kidd, Timothy Carlton, John Wood, Nigel Hawthorne. **2001 DVD**

VICTOR/VICTORIA ★★★★ Director Blake Edwards takes us on a funny, off-the-wall romp through 1930s Paris. Julie Andrews plays a down-on-her-luck singer who poses as a gay Polish count to make ends meet. Rated PG because of adult situations. 133m. **DIR:** Blake Edwards. **CAST:** Julie Andrews, James Garner, Robert Preston, Lesley Ann Warren. **1982 DVD**

VICTORY (1919) ★★★ Man who lives a life of solitude on an island surrounded by books and ideas faces change when romance and danger invade his privacy. Silent version of Joseph Conrad's oft-filmed story is a mature drama with some very heavyweight scoundrels sleazing up the tropics. Lon Chaney as a knife-wielding sadist is outstanding. B&W; 51m. **DIR:** Maurice Tourneu. **CAST:** Jack Holt, Seena Owen, Ben Deely, Wallace Beery, Lon Chaney Sr., Bull Montana. **1919**

VICTORY (1981) ★★★ Sylvester Stallone and Michael Caine star in this entertaining but predictable World War II drama about a soccer game between Allied prisoners of war and the Nazis. With a title like *Victory*, guess who wins. Rated PG. 110m. **DIR:** John Huston. **CAST:** Sylvester Stallone, Michael Caine, Pelé, Max von Sydow. **1981 DVD**

VICTORY AT ENTEBBE ★★ All-star cast helps made-for-television film about the raid by Israeli commandos to free Jewish hostages being held by Arab terrorists in Uganda. Docudrama fails to capture the truth of the moment and instead relies on cardboard characters to tell the story. 150m. **DIR:** Marvin J. Chomsky. **CAST:** Kirk Douglas, Burt Lancaster, Helen Hayes, Helmut Berger, Theodore Bikel, Elizabeth Taylor, Linda Blair, Anthony Hopkins, Jessica Walter. **1976**

VIDEODROME ★★1/2 Director David Cronenberg strikes again with a clever, gory nightmare set in the world of television broadcasting. James Woods and Deborah Harry (of the rock group Blondie) star in this eerie, occasionally sickening horror film about the boss (Woods) of a cable TV station. Rated R for profanity, nudity, violence, gore, and pure nausea. 88m. **DIR:** David Cronenberg. **CAST:** James Woods, Deborah Harry, Sonja Smits. **1983 DVD**

VIETNAM, TEXAS ★★1/2 A Texas priest, haunted by guilt over the pregnant woman he abandoned when he was a soldier in Vietnam, tracks her down in Houston. He determines to save her from the drug-running mobster she has married. Shoot-'em-up with a social conscience. Rated R for violence. 92m. **DIR:** Robert Ginty. **CAST:** Robert Ginty, Haing S. Ngor, Tim Thomerson. **1990**

VIETNAM WAR STORY ★★★★ This is a collection of three outstanding episodes from HBO's short-term series. *The Pass* dramatizes one soldier's reluctance to return to duty. *The Mine* is about an independent soldier's reliance on others when he is trapped on a land mine. *Home* concerns disabled veterans in a hospital. All are heart-wrenching. There are no stars in the cast, but all performances are top-rate. Not rated, but for mature audiences. 90m. **DIR:** Kevin Hooks, Georg Stanford Brown, Ray Danton. **CAST:** Eriq La Salle, Nicholas Cascone, Tony Becker. **1988**

VIETNAM WAR STORY—PART TWO ★★★★ Three more segments of the HBO series: *An Old Ghost Walks the Earth*; *R&R* and *The Flagging*. Not rated, but for mature audiences. 90m. **DIR:** Michael Toshiyuki Uno, David Morris, Jack Sholder. **CAST:** Tim Guinee, Cynthia Bain. **1988**

VIEW TO A KILL, A ★★★ Despite a spectacular opening sequence, the James Bond series is starting to look a little old and tired—just like Roger Moore. Christopher Walken costars as the maniacal villain who plans to corner the world's microchip market by flooding the San Andreas Fault. For fans only. Rated PG for violence and suggested sex. 131m. **DIR:** John Glen. **CAST:** Roger Moore, Tanya Roberts, Christopher Walken, Grace Jones. **1985**

VIGIL ★★★ After the death of her father, a New Zealand farm girl observes the positive changes in her family brought on by the arrival of a young drifter. Compelling film is rich in visual imagery and texture. 90m. **DIR:** Vincent Ward. **CAST:** Penelope Stewart, Fiona Kay, Frank Whitten, Bill Kerr. **1984 DVD**

VIGILANTE ★★ After the death of his son, a cop joins a vigilante group to clean up the streets. It's all been done before, but the cast is game and the direction crisp. Rated R for violence and profanity. 91m. **DIR:** William Lustig. **CAST:** Fred Williamson, Carol Lynley, Robert Forster, Joe Spinell, Rutanya Alda. **1982 DVD**

VIGILANTES ARE COMING! ★★1/2 This early Republic serial features Robert Livingston in a story suspiciously similar to the Zorro legend: A young man returns to 1840s California and finds that an evil despot has taken his family's lands so he dons a mask and robe and finds the oppressor under the name of The Eagle. Action-packed and with impressive stunts. B&W; 12 chapters. **DIR:** Mack V. Wright, Ray Taylor. **CAST:** Robert Livingston, Kay Hughes, Guinn Williams, Raymond Hatton, Fred Kohler Sr., William Farnum, Bob Kortman, Ray "Crash" Corrigan, Yakima Canutt. **1936**

VIGILANTES OF BOOMTOWN ★★★1/2 Factions oppose the sanctioning of the heavyweight boxing bout between James Corbett and Bob Fitzsimmons in 1897 Carson City, Nevada. It takes Red Ryder to keep peace between the two pugilists as well as rout bank robbers and foil a kidnapping. B&W; 54m. **DIR:** R. G. Springsteen. **CAST:** Allan "Rocky" Lane, Bobby Blake, Peggy Stewart, Roy Barcroft, George Chesebro. **1947**

VIKING SAGAS, THE ★★1/2 Gorgeously filmed but rather pedestrian tale of revenge and redemption. Cinematographer Michael Chapman (*Raging Bull*) directed this familiar tale of one man's quest for revenge after his father has been killed and his people are run off their land. Lots of swordplay enhances the action scenes, but the performances are pretty dull. Rated R for violence and nudity. 83m. **DIR:** Michael Chapman. **CAST:** Ralph Moeller, Ingibjorg Stefansdottir, Sven-Ole Thorsen. **1995**

VIKINGS, THE ★★★1/2 Well-done action film following the exploits of a group of Vikings (led by Tony Curtis and Kirk Douglas). Many good battle scenes and beautiful photography and locations make the picture a standout. Ernest Borgnine gives a great performance. Don't miss it. 114m. **DIR:** Richard Fleischer. **CAST:** Kirk Douglas, Tony Curtis, Ernest Borgnine, Janet Leigh. **1958 DVD**

VILLA RIDES ★★ Uneven rehash of the Pancho Villa legend ignores the wealth of the real story and becomes yet another comic-book adventure. Good cast, but this ill-fated production doesn't deliver what it should.

125m. **DIR:** Buzz Kulik. **CAST:** Yul Brynner, Robert Mitchum, Charles Bronson, Herbert Lom, Jill Ireland, Alexander Knox, Fernando Rey. **1968**

VILLAGE OF THE DAMNED (1960) ★★★★ A science-fiction thriller about twelve strangely emotionless children all born at the same time in a small village in England. George Sanders plays their teacher, who tries to stop their plans for conquest. This excellent low-budget film provides chills. B&W; 78m. **DIR:** Wolf Rilla. **CAST:** George Sanders, Barbara Shelley, Michael C. Gwynne. **1960**

VILLAGE OF THE DAMNED (1995) ★★1/2 Although reasonably faithful to its predecessor and John Wyndham's original novel (*The Midwich Cuckoos*), this updated remake is remarkably lifeless. Rather than radiating menace, the malevolent "children from space" evoke laughter. Inexplicably rated R for restrained violence. 98m. **DIR:** John Carpenter. **CAST:** Christopher Reeve, Kirstie Alley, Linda Kozlowski, Mark Hamill, Meredith Salenger, Michael Paré. **1995 DVD**

VILLAGE OF THE GIANTS ★★ Utterly ridiculous story of a gang of teenage misfits taking over a small town after they ingest a bizarre substance and grow to gigantic heights. What makes this worth watching, though, are the famous faces of the many young stars-to-be. 80m. **DIR:** Bert I. Gordon. **CAST:** Tommy Kirk, Beau Bridges, Ron Howard, Johnny Crawford. **1965 DVD**

VILLAIN, THE ★★★ Live action *Road Runner* spoof features Kirk Douglas as the much abused Coyote figure and Arnold Schwarzenegger as the clever Road Runner type. There is a noticeable lack of lines for Schwarzenegger, whose English was not yet refined. Ann-Margret plays sort of a damsel in distress. Cameos by Paul Lynde, Ruth Buzzi, Strother Martin, and more add a number of sight gags and one-liners giving this a *Laugh In* feel. This should tickle your funny bone if silliness doesn't turn you off. Rated PG for cartoonish violence. 89m. **DIR:** Hal Needham. **CAST:** Kirk Douglas, Arnold Schwarzenegger, Ann-Margret. **1979**

VILLAIN STILL PURSUED HER, THE 🦃 Dull, old-fashioned melodrama. B&W; 66m. **DIR:** Eddie Cline. **CAST:** Anita Louise, Richard Cromwell, Hugh Herbert, Alan Mowbray, Buster Keaton, Billy Gilbert, Margaret Hamilton. **1940**

VINCENT AND THEO ★★★★ Based on letters written by the celebrated painter Vincent van Gogh (Tim Roth) to his art-dealer brother, Theo (Paul Rhys), this is a first-rate cinematic biography; perhaps the best ever to be made about the life of a painter. Rated PG-13 for profanity and nudity. 138m. **DIR:** Robert Altman. **CAST:** Tim Roth, Paul Rhys, Johanna ter Steege. **1990**

VINCENT, FRANÇOIS, PAUL AND THE OTHERS ★★★★★ A deeply moving film about friendship as a band of buddies survive marriage, affairs, and career challenges. Claude Sautet, one of France's most respected directors, gets superb performances from leading and supporting roles. Don't miss this one! In French with English subtitles. Not rated. 118m. **DIR:** Claude Sautet. **CAST:** Yves Montand, Michel Piccoli, Serge Reggiani, Gérard Depardieu, Stéphane Audran, Marie Dubois. **1974**

VINDICATOR, THE ★★ A comic-bookish story about a scientist who is blown up by his evil employers and put back together using cybernetic systems and a nearly indestructible futuristic space suit. Overall, it's a pretty typical story with some thrills and a fair amount of action and graphic violence. Rated R for violence, adult language, and brief nudity. 92m. **DIR:** Jean-Claude Lord. **CAST:** Teri Austin, Richard Cox, Pam Grier, Maury Chaykin. **1984**

VIOLATED 🦃 Soap-opera starlets are invited to Mafia parties, where they are brutally raped. Rated R for violence and nudity. 90m. **DIR:** Richard Cannistraro. **CAST:** J. C. Quinn, John Heard. **1984**

VIOLENCE AT NOON ★★★1/2 Complex drama about two rape victims and their rapist set against the socialist movement in postwar Japan. Director Nagisa Oshima explores the pathology of a society in which the criminal and victim reside. In Japanese with English subtitles. B&W; 100m. **DIR:** Nagisa Oshima. **CAST:** Saeda Kawaguchi, Akiko Koyama, Kei Sato. **1966**

VIOLENT BREED, THE 🦃 The CIA goes into Vietnam to stop a guerrilla gang. Gratuitous nudity and violence galore. 91m. **DIR:** Fernando Di Leo. **CAST:** Henry Silva, Harrison Muller, Woody Strode, Carole André. **1983**

VIOLENT COP ★★★1/2 For his debut as a film director, "Beat" Takeshi Kitano, a popular comedian on Japanese television, plays a *Dirty Harry*–like cop out to uncover a narcotics dealer with links to the police department. This film is better than the average *Dirty Harry* entry, with Kitano fascinating as a man of unshakable ideals. In Japanese with English subtitles. Not rated; but an R equivalent for violence, rape, and drug use. 103m. **DIR:** Takeshi Kitano. **CAST:** Takeshi Kitano, Maiko Kawakami, Shiro Sano. **1989 DVD**

VIOLENT MEN, THE ★★★ Edward G. Robinson is a crippled cattle baron, manipulated by his greedy wife and brother into a range war with a peace-loving rancher and valley settlers. Good action sequences. 96m. **DIR:** Rudolph Maté. **CAST:** Glenn Ford, Barbara Stanwyck, Edward G. Robinson, Brian Keith, Richard Jaeckel. **1954**

VIOLENT NEW BREED 🦃 Vile, repulsive film from goremeister Todd Sheets as a group of demons tries to bring about the birth of the Antichrist in the form of a little girl. Not rated; contains gore, violence, nudity, and profanity. 121m. **DIR:** Todd Sheets. **CAST:** Mark Glover, Nick Stodden, Jennifer Geigel, Rudy Ray Moore. **1996**

VIOLENT YEARS, THE ★★ The screenwriter of this camp classic was Edward D. Wood Jr., and it bears his unmistakable touch. A gang of rich girls don men's clothing and rob gas stations. In their spare time, they pet heavily at a combination pajama-cocktail party, rape a lover's-lane Lothario, and even get involved in an international communist conspiracy! Their response to every query is a sneered "So what?" A must-see for buffs of bad movies! 65m. **DIR:** Franz Eichorn. **CAST:** Jean Moorehead, Barbara Weeks, Glenn Corbett, I. Stanford Jolley. **1956**

VIOLETS ARE BLUE ★★★1/2 In this watchable screen soap opera, former sweethearts Sissy Spacek and Kevin Kline are reunited when she, a successful photojournalist, returns to her hometown. Their romance is rekindled although he is now married (to Bonnie Bedelia, who is terrific in her all-too-brief on-screen bits). Rated PG for suggested sex and light profanity. 89m. **DIR:** Jack Fisk. **CAST:** Sissy Spacek, Kevin Kline, Bonnie Bedelia, Augusta Dabney. **1986**

VIOLETTE ★★★★ Based on a true story that scandalized Paris in the 1930s, Isabelle Huppert plays a promiscuous young woman who tried to murder her parents in order to get their money. Her performance (for which she was awarded Best Actress at Cannes) is the best thing about this well-crafted but somewhat chilly movie. In French with English subtitles. Not rated, but an R equivalent for violence and sexual themes. 123m. **DIR:** Claude Chabrol. **CAST:** Isabelle Huppert, Stéphane Audran, Jean Carmet. **1997**

VIPER 🦃 A CIA operation breaks into a university and kills the members of the administration. Rated R for language and violence. 96m. **DIR:** Peter Maris. **CAST:** Linda Purl, James Tolkan, Jeff Kober, Chris Robinson. **1988**

V.I.P.S, THE ★★★ The problems of an assortment of passengers stranded at a London airport get glossy treatment in this drama thrown together to cash in on the real-life romance of Elizabeth Taylor and Richard Burton. The stars are easily upstaged by the solid supporting cast, especially Maggie Smith and Oscar-winner Margaret Rutherford. Not rated. 119m. **DIR:** Anthony Asquith. **CAST:** Elizabeth Taylor, Richard Burton, Margaret Rutherford, Maggie Smith, Rod Taylor, Louis Jourdan, Orson Welles. **1963**

VIRGIN AMONG THE LIVING DEAD, A 🦃 Available only in a severely cut version, this sub-gothic, damsel-in-distress snoozer is an atypical entry from its director's most prolific period—although the undead attack footage was shot eight years later by Jean Rollin during the making of *Zombie Lake*, and spliced in to make this English-language print releasable! 90m. **DIR:** Jess (Jesus) Franco. **CAST:** Christina von Blanc, Anne Libert, Howard Vernon. **1971**

VIRGIN AND THE GYPSY, THE ★★★1/2 The title tells the tale in this stylish, effective screen adaptation of the D. H. Lawrence novella. Franco Nero and Joanna Shimkus exude sexual tension as the gypsy and his love, a minister's daughter. Rated R for nudity. 95m. **DIR:** Christopher Miles. **CAST:** Franco Nero, Joanna Shimkus, Honor Blackman, Mark Burns, Maurice Denham. **1970**

VIRGIN HIGH 🦃 Inane tale of a girl sent to a Catholic boarding school in order to protect her virginity. Her boyfriend pursues her, disguising himself as a priest. Gratuitous sleaze downgrades an extremely mediocre teen romance. Rated R for nudity, sex, and profanity. 90m. **DIR:** Richard Gabai. **CAST:** Chris Dempsey, Burt Ward, Linnea Quigley, Tracy Dali. **1990**

VIRGIN OF NUREMBERG (HORROR CASTLE) 🦃 A hooded killer lurking in an ancient German castle. (Alternate title: *Horror Castle*.) 82m. **DIR:** Anthony M. Dawson. **CAST:** Rossana Podesta, George Riviere, Christopher Lee. **1963**

VIRGIN QUEEN, THE ★★★ Bette Davis reprises her memorable 1939 *Elizabeth and Essex* portrayal of Elizabeth I of England in this rehashing of majestic might and young love. This time around the queen dotes on Sir Walter Raleigh, who crosses her up, but survives to sail away to happiness. A fine example of Hollywood film history. 92m. **DIR:** Henry Koster. **CAST:** Bette Davis, Richard Todd, Joan Collins, Herbert Marshall. **1955**

VIRGIN QUEEN OF ST. FRANCIS HIGH, THE ★★★ This teen market release has more depth and interest than most in its genre. There's nothing much new in the first half hour, but the two leads, Joseph R. Straface and Stacy Christensen, have winning personalities. The ending is too pat and saccharine, though. Rated PG for profanity. 89m. **DIR:** Francesco Lucente. **CAST:** Joseph R. Straface, Stacy Christensen. **1988**

VIRGIN SOLDIERS, THE ★★★★ This outstanding drama of young British recruits in 1950 Singapore has some great performances. Hywel Bennett is one of the recruits who is as green with his first sexual encounter as he is on the battlefield. 96m. **DIR:** John Dexter. **CAST:** Hywel Bennett, Nigel Patrick, Lynn Redgrave, Nigel Davenport. **1969**

VIRGIN SPRING, THE ★★★★★ Ingmar Bergman's scenario is based on a fourteenth-century Swedish legend. Accompanied by her jealous older stepsister, a young girl is raped and killed while on a journey to her church—and the three killers make the mistake of seeking shelter with the parents. Won an Oscar for best foreign language film. In Swedish with English subtitles. B&W; 87m. **DIR:** Ingmar Bergman. **CAST:** Max von Sydow, Birgitta Pettersson, Gunnel Lindblom. **1960**

VIRGIN SUICIDES, THE ★★★1/2 This sweet, sad, dreamlike adaptation of Jeffery Eugenides's novel tackles the issues of budding sexual attraction and teen suicide. The film begins as the youngest of five sisters in an upscale 1970s Michigan suburb kills herself. A former neighborhood boy guides us through a whisper of a mystery propelled by raging hormones, overprotective parents, and the ache of puppy love. Rated R for mature themes. 97m. **DIR:** Sofia Coppola. **CAST:** Kirsten Dunst, Josh Hartnett, Hanna Hall, Kathleen Turner, James Woods, Chelse Sain, A. J. Cook, Leslie Hayman, Jonathan Tucker, Anthony DeSimone. **2000 DVD**

VIRGINIA CITY ★★★1/2 Errol Flynn's second big-budget Western for Warner Bros. is a hit-and-miss affair about three groups vying for a shipment of gold during the Civil War. B&W; 121m. **DIR:** Michael Curtiz. **CAST:** Errol Flynn, Miriam Hopkins, Randolph Scott, Humphrey Bogart, Alan Hale Sr., Guinn Williams, Frank McHugh, Douglass Dumbrille, John Litel, Ward Bond, Charles Middleton, Paul Fix, Russell Simpson. **1940**

VIRGINIAN, THE (1923) ★★ Lackluster version of Owen Wister's classic Western play and novel features good photography and some nice panoramas of the wide-open spaces, but the leads are stiff and the action is lacking. Kenneth Harlan doesn't cut it as the Virginian, and he brings the film down with him. Silent. B&W; 73m. **DIR:** Tom Forman. **CAST:** Kenneth Harlan, Florence Vidor, Russell Simpson, Pat O'Malley, Raymond Hatton. **1923**

VIRGINIAN, THE (1929) ★★★★ Although a bit slow in parts, this early Western still impresses today. Gary Cooper is terrific in the title role as a fun-loving but tough ranch foreman who has to face the worst task of his life when a friend falls in with an outlaw. B&W; 90m. **DIR:** Victor Fleming. **CAST:** Gary Cooper, Walter Huston, Mary Brian, Richard Arlen, Eugene Pallette, Chester Conklin. **1929**

VIRGINIAN, THE (1946) ★★★ OK remake of the Gary Cooper classic with Joel McCrea in the title role and Brian Donlevy properly menacing as the villain. Even as creaky as it may seem to some viewers, the 1929 version is by far

the superior film. 90m. **DIR:** Stuart Gilmore. **CAST:** Joel McCrea, Brian Donlevy, Barbara Britton, Sonny Tufts, Tom Tully, William Frawley, Fay Bainter, Henry O'Neill, Paul Guilfoyle, Marc Lawrence, Minor Watson. **1946**

VIRGINIAN, THE (1999) ★★★ Based on Owen Wister's novel, this TNT original allows the cowboy to become a crime-stopping hero. Director Bill Pullman also stars in the title role playing a cowpuncher working a Wyoming ranch in the late 1800s. When he's not struggling with cattle rustlers, he's pursuing the new schoolmarm (Diane Lane) who can't relate to the vigilante justice practiced in the territory. A cameo appearance by TV series *Virginian* James Drury adds a nice touch to a decent time passer. Not rated; contains violence. 95m. **DIR:** Bill Pullman. **CAST:** Bill Pullman, Diane Lane, Dennis Weaver, John Savage, Colm Feore. **1999**

VIRIDIANA ★★★★★ Angelic Viridiana (Silvia Pinal) visits her sex-obsessed uncle (Fernando Rey) prior to taking her religious vows. The film was an amazing *cause célèbre* at the time. Much to Spain's and the Catholic Church's consternation, it won the Palme d'Or at Cannes. In Spanish with English subtitles. B&W; 90m. **DIR:** Luis Buñuel. **CAST:** Silvia Pinal, Fernando Rey, Francisco Rabal, Margarita Lozano. **1961**

VIRTUAL ASSASSIN ★★ Michael Dudikoff jumps on the information superhighway to come to the aid of a father-daughter team of scientists whose new virus has attracted the interest of a madman who wants to control the world. Rated R for violence, language, and nudity. 99m. **DIR:** Robert Lee. **CAST:** Michael Dudikoff, Suki Kaiser, Brian James, James Thom, Jon Cuthbert. **1995**

VIRTUAL COMBAT 🦃 Pitiful cyber-thriller about a virtual-reality villain who becomes flesh and blood and challenges the gatekeeper of the grid to a fight to the death. Please! Rated R for violence, nudity, and adult language. 91m. **DIR:** Andrew Stevens. **CAST:** Don "The Dragon" Wilson, Athena Massey, Stella Stevens, Loreen Avedon. **1994 DVD**

VIRTUAL ENCOUNTERS 🦃 A woman vicariously lives out her sexual fantasies using the latest in virtual-reality technology. It's a thin excuse for a series of soft-core couplings. Available in R and unrated versions, both featuring nonstop nudity and sex. 86m. **DIR:** Cybil Richards. **CAST:** Elizabeth Kaitan, Taylore St. Claire, Rob Lee. **1996 DVD**

VIRTUAL SEDUCTION ★★★1/2 Until derailed by its bewildering climax, this intriguing little science-fiction drama deftly illustrates the addictive perils of too much virtual reality. Test subject Jeff Fahey finds he prefers the VR simulation of his deceased girlfriend to the real-life charms of his current paramour. Fortunately, the latter's not willing to give up quite that easily. Rated R for nudity, simulated sex, and violence. 90m. **DIR:** Paul Ziller. **CAST:** Jeff Fahey, Ami Dolenz, Carrie Genzel, Meshach Taylor. **1995**

VIRTUAL SEXUALITY ★★ This British import plays like a female version of *Weird Science*, without the sense of fun. Tired of losing every guy to her rival, 17 year old Justine attends a techno fair to find a date, but ends up instead creating the perfect man in a virtual-reality booth. The situation becomes preposterous when a freak explosion turns Justine into her dream date. Rated R for adult situations, language, and nudity. 92m. **DIR:** Nick Hurran. **CAST:** Laura Fraser, Rupert Penry-Jones, Luke De Lacey, Kieran O'Brien. **1999 DVD**

VIRTUOSITY ★★ Computer-generated killer Russell Crowe breaks free of his cyberspace boundaries and wreaks all sorts of havoc in this futuristic thriller, and only one man—jailed cop Denzel Washington—will be able to stop him. This obnoxiously noisy actionfest is long on violence and short on common sense, and you'll wonder what an actor of Washington's stature is doing in such a mess. Rated R for violence, profanity, and nudity. 105m. **DIR:** Brett Leonard. **CAST:** Denzel Washington, Kelly Lynch, Russell Crowe, Stephen Spinella, William Forsythe, Louise Fletcher. **1995 DVD**

VIRUS (1980) ★★★ Japan goes Hollywood. Film provides some moments of high drama and decent special effects, not to mention panoramic location shots in Antarctica. The story concerns a polar expedition that becomes the last vestige of humanity when a plague and nuclear war decimate the population. Rated PG. 155m. **DIR:** Kinji Fukasaku. **CAST:** George Kennedy, Chuck Connors, Glenn Ford, Sonny Chiba, Olivia Hussey, Henry Silva. **1980**

VIRUS (1996) ★★ Secret service agent Brian Bosworth tries to keep the president out of a national park where biological warfare chemicals have leaked. Of a long line of action heroes clogging video racks these days, Bosworth may be the dullest. Rated PG-13 for violence and profanity. 90m. **DIR:** Allan A. Goldstein. **CAST:** Brian Bosworth, Leah Pinsent. **1996**

VIRUS (1999) ★★ This bland, big-budget gorefest is about as stupid as horror thrillers can get. The story concerns the crew of a salvage tug who board a deserted Russian science ship and discover that an outer-space whatsis has "infected" all the on-board computers and machinery. Rated R for violence, profanity, and gobs o'gore. **DIR:** John Bruno. **CAST:** Jamie Lee Curtis, William Baldwin, Donald Sutherland, Joanna Pacula. **1999**

VIRUS KNOWS NO MORALS, A ★★★1/2 A comedy about AIDS may sound like the ultimate in tastelessness, but gay filmmaker Rosa von Praunheim's aim is to educate audiences while making them laugh. This loosely structured film, featuring a nonprofessional cast, makes fun of the public misconceptions and hysteria surrounding the disease. In German with English subtitles. Not rated. 82m. **DIR:** Rosa von Praunheim. **CAST:** Rosa von Praunheim, Dieter Dicken, Eva Kurz. **1985**

VISION QUEST ★★★1/2 A young athlete makes good against all odds. If you can get past the familiarity of the plot, it isn't bad. It benefits particularly from a charismatic lead performance by Matthew Modine. Rated R for nudity, suggested sex, violence, and profanity. 96m. **DIR:** Harold Becker. **CAST:** Matthew Modine, Linda Fiorentino, Michael Schoeffling, Ronny Cox, Harold Sylvester. **1985 DVD**

VISIT, THE ★★★1/2 Hill Harper delivers a powerful performance as a convict who has alienated everyone in his life. Sentenced to twenty-five years in prison for a rape he denies, Alex Waters (Harper) wants to make peace with his family when he learns he is dying from AIDS. Flashbacks and fantasies move us beyond the prison, while Harper's vital performance fills in the rest of the gaps. Rae Dawn Chong shines as a friend who has turned her life around. Rated R for language. 107m.

DIR: Jordan Walker Pearlman. **CAST:** Hill Harper, Obba Babatundé, Rae Dawn Chong, Marla Gibbs, Phylicia Rashad, Billy Dee Williams, Talia Shire. **2000 DVD**

VISITANTS, THE 🦃 Two aliens move into a house in an American suburb. Not rated. 93m. **DIR:** Rick Sloane. **CAST:** Marcus Vaughter, Johanna Grika, Nicole Rio. **1987**

VISITING HOURS 🦃 Here's a Canadian production that actually forces the viewer to wallow in the degradation, humiliation, and mutilation of women. Rated R for blood, gore, violence, and general unrelenting ugliness. 103m. **DIR:** Jean-Claude Lord. **CAST:** Lee Grant, William Shatner, Linda Purl, Michael Ironside. **1982**

VISITOR, THE ★★ An 8 year old girl, gifted with incredible powers, uses her abilities maliciously. As she formulates a plan that could lead the world toward destruction, an ancient alien mystic comes to Earth to stop her evil scheme. Great premise, flawed execution. Rated R for violence. 96m. **DIR:** Michael J. Paradise. **CAST:** Mel Ferrer, John Huston, Glenn Ford, Shelley Winters. **1979**

VISITORS, THE ★★ An American family moves to Sweden, and strange things begin to happen in their new home. While the climax of this standard possessed-house movie is above par, it's too bad the rest is so boring. Rated R for violence and profanity. 102m. **DIR:** Joakim Ersgard. **CAST:** Keith Berkeley, Lena Endre, John Force, John Olsen, Joanna Berg, Brent Landiss, Patrick Ersgard. **1989 DVD**

VISITORS OF THE NIGHT ★★ A mother believes that her daughter may have been abducted by a UFO. Sometimes engrossing, sometimes ludicrous. Rated PG-13 for profanity and intense moments. 90m. **DIR:** Jorge Montesi. **CAST:** Markie Post, Dale Midkiff, Candace Cameron. **1995 DVD**

VITAL SIGNS 🦃 Third-year med students struggling through hospital training. Rated R for sexual situations and profanity. 102m. **DIR:** Marisa Silver. **CAST:** Jimmy Smits, Adrian Pasdar, Diane Lane. **1990**

VIVA KNIEVEL 🦃 Evel Knievel (playing himself) is duped by a former buddy into doing a stunt tour of Mexico. Rated PG. 106m. **DIR:** Gordon Douglas. **CAST:** Evel Knievel, Marjoe Gortner, Leslie Nielsen, Gene Kelly, Lauren Hutton. **1977**

VIVA LAS VEGAS ★★ In this romantic musical, Elvis Presley plays a race-car driver who also sings. Ann-Margret is a casino dancer. Eventually Elvis and Ann-Margret get together, which is no surprise to any viewer who is awake. 86m. **DIR:** George Sidney. **CAST:** Elvis Presley, Ann-Margret, Cesare Danova, William Demarest, Jack Carter. **1964 DVD**

VIVA MARIA! ★★★★ Great slapstick and hilarious situations abound as two song-and-dance girls traveling with a carnival become involved with Mexican revolutionaries during the time of Pancho Villa. A fast-moving comedy gem. In French with English subtitles. 125m. **DIR:** Louis Malle. **CAST:** Jeanne Moreau, Brigitte Bardot, George Hamilton, Paulette Dubost. **1965**

VIVA MAX! ★★★ Skip credibility and enjoy. Peter Ustinov is a contemporary Mexican general who leads his men across the border to reclaim the Alamo as a tourist attraction. Jonathan Winters all but steals this romp, playing a bumbling, confused National Guard officer in the face of an audacious "enemy." Rated G. 92m. **DIR:** Jerry Paris. **CAST:** Peter Ustinov, Jonathan Winters, Keenan Wynn, Pamela Tiffin. **1969**

VIVA VILLA! ★★★★ Even though he left the project before completion, director Howard Hawks's breezy style is still in evidence throughout this, Wallace Beery's best starring vehicle. A whitewashed account of Pancho Villa's activities from 1910 to 1916, it allows Beery to do some hard riding, fast shooting, and a whole lot of mugging as he leads his *bandido* revolutionaries against the Federales. B&W; 115m. **DIR:** Jack Conway, Howard Hawks. **CAST:** Wallace Beery, Leo Carrillo, Fay Wray, Donald Cook, Stu Erwin, George E. Stone, Joseph Schildkraut, Katherine DeMille, Henry B. Walthall, Arthur Treacher. **1934**

VIVA ZAPATA! ★★★★1/2 This film chonicles Mexican revolutionary leader Emiliano Zapata from his peasant upbringing until his death as a weary, disillusioned political liability. Marlon Brando won an Oscar nomination for his insightful portrayal of Zapata. Anthony Quinn, as Zapata's brother, did manage to hold his own against the powerful Brando characterization and was rewarded with a supporting actor Oscar. B&W; 113m. **DIR:** Elia Kazan. **CAST:** Marlon Brando, Anthony Quinn, Jean Peters, Joseph Wiseman. **1952**

VIVACIOUS LADY ★★★ Cultures clash when small-town professor James Stewart impulsively weds New York nightclub singer Ginger Rogers, brings her back to the campus, and cannot tell his father, upright and stuffy college president Charles Coburn, who the new lady is. B&W; 90m. **DIR:** George Stevens. **CAST:** Ginger Rogers, James Stewart, Charles Coburn, Frances Mercer, James Ellison, Beulah Bondi, Franklin Pangborn, Grady Sutton, Jack Carson, Willie Best. **1938**

VIVE L'AMOUR ★★★ An empty apartment in bustling Taiwan becomes a microcosm of urban life for three people whose lives intersect there—a real-estate agent, the street vendor she sleeps with, and the homeless gay man who spies on them. The title is ironic in this elegant but chilly look at modern alienation. In Chinese with English subtitles. Not rated; contains nudity and sexual situations. **DIR:** Ming-liang Tsai. **CAST:** Kuei-Mei Yang, Chao-jung Chen, Kang-sheng Lee. **1996 DVD**

VOICES ★★★ A sentimental love story that manages to maintain a sensitive tone that ultimately proves infectious. Amy Irving stars as a deaf young woman who wants to become a dancer; Michael Ontkean is a young man who would rather be a singer. They meet, fall in love. The material is sugary, but Irving and Ontkean make it work. Rated PG for language and adult themes. 107m. **DIR:** Robert Markowitz. **CAST:** Amy Irving, Michael Ontkean, Herbert Berghof, Viveca Lindfors. **1979**

VOICES FROM A LOCKED ROOM ★★ In this true story, about composer Peter Warlock—the toast of London, circa 1930s—Warlock's work is music to everyone's ear except notorious music critic Philip Heseltine, who constantly rides Warlock. The verbal war escalates when Warlock threatens Heseltine. His new lover, chanteuse Lily Buxton, steps in and discovers a dark secret that threatens her existence. Nice period touches and exquisite score, but not much else. Rated R for

adult situations and language. 92m. **DIR:** Malcolm Clarke. **CAST:** Jeremy Northam, Tushka Bergen. **1995**

VOLCANO ★★1/2 The La Brea Tar Pits in Los Angeles suddenly begin spouting molten lava, and it's up to iron-jawed disaster-agency manager Tommy Lee Jones and spunky seismologist Anne Heche to save the day. Director Mick Jackson stages the cataclysm with headlong efficiency; the film hits the ground running almost before the opening credits are over. It's painfully predictable, with suspicious traces of last-minute editing, but it's briskly paced and easy to take. Rated PG-13 for profanity and violence. 104m. **DIR:** Mick Jackson. **CAST:** Tommy Lee Jones, Anne Heche, Don Cheadle, John Corbett, Keith David, Gaby Hoffman, Jacqueline Kim, John Carroll Lynch, Michael Rispoli. **1997 DVD**

VOLCANO: FIRE ON THE MOUNTAIN ★★ Television tries to cash in on the volcano craze with this molten mess about a ski resort threatened by an active volcano. Clichéd characters and situations, low-budget special effects, and leisurely direction do little to help the cause. Rated PG-13 for violence. 98m. **DIR:** Graeme Campbell. **CAST:** Dan Cortese, Cynthia Gibb, Brian Kerwin. **1997**

VOLERE VOLARE ★★★1/2 A sexy woman who makes her living fulfilling fantasies falls in love with a nerdy cartoon sound man in this delightful romp. Like *Who Framed Roger Rabbit*, this hilarious comedy skillfully mixes live action and animation. Maurizio Nichetti writes, directs, and stars as the sound genius. In Italian with English subtitles. Rated R for nudity and sexual situations. 92m. **DIR:** Guido Manuli, Maurizio Nichetti. **CAST:** Maurizio Nichetti, Angela Finocciaro, Mariella Valentini, Patrizio Roversi. **1991**

VOLPONE ★★★★ Filmed in 1939, this superb screen version of Shakespeare contemporary Ben Jonson's classic play of greed was not released until after World War II, by which time star Harry Baur, a titan of French cinema, was mysteriously dead, having probably been killed by the Nazis. Aided by his avaricious and parasitic servant, Mosca, Volpone, an old Venetian, pretends he is dying and convinces his greedy friends that each of them is his heir. In French with English subtitles. B&W; 80m. **DIR:** Maurice Tourneur. **CAST:** Harry Baur, Louis Jouvet. **1939**

VOLUNTEERS ★★ This comedy reunites Tom Hanks and John Candy, who were so marvelously funny together in Ron Howard's *Splash*. However, this film about high jinks in the Peace Corps in Thailand circa 1962 has very little going for it. Hanks and Candy do their best, but the laughs are few and far between. Rated R for profanity, violence, and sexual innuendo. 105m. **DIR:** Nicholas Meyer. **CAST:** Tom Hanks, John Candy, Rita Wilson, Tim Thomerson, Gedde Watanabe. **1985 DVD**

VON RYAN'S EXPRESS ★★★★ This is a first-rate World War II tale of escape from a prisoner-of-war camp aboard a German train to neutral Switzerland. Trevor Howard is the officer in charge until a feisty Frank Sinatra takes over the escape plan. This is a great action story, with Sinatra playing the hero's role perfectly. 117m. **DIR:** Mark Robson. **CAST:** Frank Sinatra, Trevor Howard, Edward Mulhare, James Brolin, Luther Adler. **1965**

VOODOO ★★ Pledging a fraternity can be murder. That's what student Corey Feldman learns when he takes the pledge, only to discover that he's joined a cult dedicated to the black arts. Making matters worse is that the cult has decided to use Feldman's girlfriend as its next human sacrifice. It's amazing what you have to do to get a good education today. Rated R for nudity, violence, and adult language. 91m. **DIR:** Rene Eram. **CAST:** Corey Feldman, Sarah Douglas, Jack Nance. **1995 DVD**

VOODOO DAWN ★★ The old story of good versus evil played out in a small town in the South. Two college buddies take a road trip to visit a friend, who unfortunately is in the process of being transformed into a zombie. Rated R for violence and nudity. 83m. **DIR:** Steven Fierberg. **CAST:** Raymond St. Jacques, Theresa Merritt, Gina Gershon. **1990 DVD**

VOODOO DOLLS Tender, young schoolgirls are seduced by the spirit residents of their old private academy. Rated R for profanity, nudity, suggested sex, and violence. 90m. **DIR:** Andre Pelletier. **CAST:** Maria Stanton. **1990**

VOODOO ISLAND In what is probably his dullest movie, Boris Karloff plays a scientist investigating claims of supernatural occurrences on a tropical island. B&W; 76m. **DIR:** Reginald LeBorg. **CAST:** Boris Karloff, Beverly Tyler, Murvyn Vye, Elisha Cook Jr., Rhodes Reason. **1957**

VOODOO MAN ★★1/2 So low-budget and corny it's unintentionally funny, this Monogram cheapie features Bela Lugosi as a doctor attempting to revive his wife from a twenty-year zombie state by stealing the "life force" from a group of young women. A remake of *The Corpse Vanishes*. B&W; 62m. **DIR:** William Beaudine. **CAST:** Bela Lugosi, John Carradine, George Zucco, Wanda McKay, Louise Currie, Ellen Hall. **1945**

VOODOO WOMAN ★★ Typical—if irresistible—American-International mixture of phony sets, too much talk, and an occasional outburst of mayhem as a jungle monster (AIP's *She Creature* suit, slightly reworked) is summoned by mad scientist Tom Conway. B&W; 77m. **DIR:** Edward L. Cahn. **CAST:** Marla English, Tom Conway, Mike Connors. **1957**

VOULEZ VOUS DANSER AVEC MOI? (WILL YOU DANCE WITH ME?) This is another interminable Brigitte Bardot film, one in which a marital squabble lands her in the center of a murder investigation. In French with English subtitles. 89m. **DIR:** Michel Boisrone. **CAST:** Brigitte Bardot, Henri Vidal, Dawn Addams, Noel Roquevert. **1959**

VOW TO KILL, A ★★ The daughter of a media mogul marries a poor photographer and goes on the honeymoon from hell. Not rated; contains violence and sexual situations. 93m. **DIR:** Harry S. Longstreet. **CAST:** Richard Grieco, Julianne Phillips, Gordon Pinsent, Peter MacNeill. **1994**

VOYAGE ★★★ A middle-aged couple, trying to find the love they once felt, takes a world trip on their yacht in this made-for-cable original. They pick up another couple along the way. Now starts the voyage from hell. Good acting all around, but the story doesn't move quickly enough. Not rated; contains implied sex. 95m. **DIR:** John Mackenzie. **CAST:** Rutger Hauer, Eric Roberts, Karen Allen, Connie Nielsen. **1993**

VOYAGE EN BALLON (STOWAWAY TO THE STARS) ★★★ This endearing French film is somewhat of a follow-up to *The Red Balloon* (also directed by Albert Lamorisse and starring son Pascal, this time allowing that boy to ascend into the clouds—in the basket of a hot-air balloon). Unfortunately, Lamorisse *père* is a far better director than writer, and this film lacks the drama needed to sustain its greater length. Not rated, suitable for family viewing. 82m. **DIR:** Albert Lamorisse. **CAST:** André Gille, Maurice Baquet, Pascal Lamorisse. **1959**

VOYAGE EN DOUCE ★★★★ A look into the hearts and minds of two lifelong friends, this involving French import is a character study in which plot plays little part. This is intentional, and all is eventually revealed and explained. In other words, *Voyage en Douce* offers exactly what fans of foreign films expect. In French with English subtitles. Not rated. 95m. **DIR:** Michel Deville. **CAST:** Dominique Sanda, Geraldine Chaplin, Jacques Zabor, Valerie Masterson. **1981**

VOYAGE IN ITALY ★★★ A married couple drives through Italy to inspect a property they have inherited. Removed from their usual routine, they begin to inspect their life together. Much admired by fans of director Roberto Rossellini, this slow neorealist drama is recommended only for the most patient viewers. In English. B&W; 97m. **DIR:** Roberto Rossellini. **CAST:** Ingrid Bergman, George Sanders. **1953**

VOYAGE OF TERROR: THE ACHILLE LAURO AFFAIR ★★ Beware of falling asleep during this telefilm based on the true story of the hijacking of a cruise ship. The viewer views most of the ordeal through an older American couple. 95m. **DIR:** Alberto Negrin. **CAST:** Burt Lancaster, Eva Marie Saint, Rebecca Schaeffer, Bernard Fresson, Robert Culp. **1990**

VOYAGE OF THE DAMNED ★★★★ This fine drama takes place in 1939 as a shipload of Jewish refugees are refused refuge in Havana and are forced to return to Germany for certain imprisonment or death. Rated PG. 134m. **DIR:** Stuart Rosenberg. **CAST:** Oskar Werner, Faye Dunaway, Max von Sydow, Orson Welles, Malcolm McDowell, James Mason, Julie Harris, Lee Grant. **1976 DVD**

VOYAGE 'ROUND MY FATHER, A ★★★★ Writer John Mortimer, famed for creating British barrister Horace Rumpole, composed this play to honor his rather idiosyncratic father. Laurence Olivier, who essays the lead, turns eccentricity into an art form. The younger Mortimer is played by Alan Bates. Originally made for British television and suitable for family viewing. 85m. **DIR:** Alvin Rakoff. **CAST:** Laurence Olivier, Alan Bates, Jane Asher, Elizabeth Sellars. **1983**

VOYAGE TO THE BOTTOM OF THE SEA ★★★ An atomic submarine rushes to save Earth from destruction by a burning radiation belt. Intrigue, adventure, and hokey fun, with a low-level all-star cast. Much better than the subsequent television show. Not rated, the film has mild violence. 105m. **DIR:** Irwin Allen. **CAST:** Walter Pidgeon, Joan Fontaine, Robert Sterling, Barbara Eden, Michael Ansara, Peter Lorre, Frankie Avalon, Henry Daniell. **1961**

VOYAGE TO THE PREHISTORIC PLANET Wisely hiding behind a pseudonym, director Curtis Harrington cobbled together this deadly dull space opera by mixing footage from a Soviet sci-fi movie (*Planet of Storms*) with a few talky scenes involving Basil Rathbone and Faith Domergue. Released directly to TV. 80m. **DIR:** Jonathan Sebastian. **CAST:** Basil Rathbone, Faith Domergue. **1965**

VOYAGER ★★ Slow-moving tale of a man, the woman he loves, and the forbidden secret they share. Although well acted, this is a dull and soapy nostalgia piece. Rated PG-13 for adult themes. 113m. **DIR:** Volker Schlöndorff. **CAST:** Sam Shepard, Julie Delpy, Barbara Sukowa. **1991**

VUKOVAR ★★★★ By turns gentle and horrifying, the film adopts a decidedly Shakespearean manner while revealing how even the purest love—between a Croatian man and a Serbian woman—can be tainted, battered, and finally eradicated by the horrors of war. It's a searing, unforgettable portrait of a country devouring itself. In Serbian with English subtitles. Rated R for violence, profanity, and brief nudity. 96m. **DIR:** Boro Draskovic. **CAST:** Boris Isakovic, Monika Romic, Nebojsa Glogovac, Predrag Ejdus, Mira Banjac. **1994**

VULTURES ★★ A murder mystery with slasher undertones. Poorly written and acted, but has some suspense. Not rated; contains graphic violence and adult situations. 101m. **DIR:** Paul Leder. **CAST:** Stuart Whitman, Greg Mullavey, Carmen Zapata, Yvonne De Carlo, Maria Perschy. **1983**

W

W ★★★1/2 Someone is trying to kill the Lewises, Katy (Twiggy) and Ben (Michael Witney). Each gets into a car and finds too late that it has been tampered with and nearly is killed in a headlong, high-speed crash. On each vehicle, the letter *W* is scrawled in the dust. Who could be after them? This is a highly involving, Hitchcockian thriller that will keep mystery lovers captivated. Rated PG. 95m. **DIR:** Richard Quine. **CAST:** Twiggy, Michael Witney, Eugene Roche, John Vernon, Dirk Benedict. **1974**

WABASH AVENUE ★★★★ A delightful musical that pokes fun at show-business stereotypes and uses romance, glamour, and colorful production numbers to keep them in perspective. 92m. **DIR:** Henry Koster. **CAST:** Betty Grable, Victor Mature, Phil Harris, Margaret Hamilton, Reginald Gardiner, Henry Kulky. **1950**

WACKIEST SHIP IN THE ARMY, THE ★★★ A battered ship becomes an unlikely implement for World War II heroism. The situation is played mostly for laughs, but dramatic moments are smoothly included. Jack Lemmon sets his performance at just the right pitch. Ricky Nelson is amiable and amusing. 99m. **DIR:** Richard Murphy. **CAST:** Jack Lemmon, Ricky Nelson, John Lund, Chips Rafferty, Tom Tully, Joby Baker, Warren Berlinger. **1960**

WACKO Excruciating parody of *Halloween*. Rated PG. 90m. **DIR:** Greydon Clark. **CAST:** Joe Don Baker, Stella Stevens, George Kennedy, Jeff Altman. **1981**

WACKY WORLD OF WILLS AND BURKE, THE ★★1/2 Incongruously lighthearted parody of the true story of the explorers who set out to cross Australia by camel in 1860. (A straight version of the ill-fated expedition, *Burke and Wills*, was made at the same time as this.) Some funny Monty Python-ish satire will be lost on those unfamiliar with Australian history. Not rated. 97m. **DIR:** Bob Weis. **CAST:** Garry McDonald, Kim Gyngell, Nicole Kidman, Colin Hay. **1985**

WAG THE DOG ★★★★★ Deliciously clever story of how the public's attention is diverted from an incident involving the president molesting a young girl in the White House. Political consultant invents a phony war with Armenia and, despite snafu after snafu, keeps the ruse going long enough to accomplish his goal. This is a wry, hilarious satire on just about everything in American culture. From the novel *American Hero* by Larry Beinhart. Woody Harrelson is especially effective in a cameo as an American hero unlike any you've ever seen before. Rated R for language. 97m. **DIR:** Barry Levinson. **CAST:** Dustin Hoffman, Robert De Niro, Anne Heche, Woody Harrelson, Denis Leary, Willie Nelson, Andrea Martin, Michael Belson, Craig T. Nelson, James Belushi, Suzanne Cryer, Kirsten Dunst, William H. Macy. **1997 DVD**

WAGES OF FEAR, THE ★★★★★ This masterpiece of suspense pits four seedy and destitute men against the challenge of driving two nitroglycerin-laden trucks over crude and treacherous Central American mountain roads to quell a monstrous oil-well fire. Incredible risk and numbing fear ride along as the drivers, goaded by high wages, cope with dilemma after dilemma. In French with English subtitles. B&W; 128m. **DIR:** Henri-Georges Clouzot. **CAST:** Yves Montand, Charles Vanel, Peter Van Eyck, Vera Clouzot. **1953 DVD**

WAGNER ★★★ This five-hour film gives you an idea of what the greatest opera composer may have been like, but the legendary supporting cast, although credible, is not up to his reputation. Not rated, but equal to an R for violence, profanity, and nudity. 300m. **DIR:** Tony Palmer. **CAST:** Richard Burton, Vanessa Redgrave, Gemma Craven, John Gielgud, Ralph Richardson, Laurence Olivier, Marthe Keller, Ronald Pickup. **1982**

WAGON TRAIN (TV SERIES) ★★★1/2 John Ford's *Wagonmaster* inspired the creation of this Western series, which starred Ward Bond as Major Seth Adams, the no-nonsense leader of a wagon train headed West, and Robert Horton, as scout Flint McCullough. In the premiere episode of this anthology-oriented show, Ernest Borgnine plays a former soldier from Adams's command. B&W; 60m. **DIR:** Herschel Daugherty. **CAST:** Ward Bond, Robert Horton, Ernest Borgnine, Marjorie Lord, Andrew Duggan, Beverly Washburn, Frank McGrath, Terry Wilson. **1957**

WAGON WHEELS ★★★ Scout Randolph Scott guides a wagon train to Oregon against all the Westward trek odds—the worst of which is a half-breed inciting the Indians into an uprising. Remake of *Fighting Caravans* (with Gary Cooper), including much stock footage. B&W; 56m. **DIR:** Charles Barton. **CAST:** Randolph Scott, Gail Patrick, Raymond Hatton, Monte Blue. **1934**

WAGON WHEELS WESTWARD ★★★ Red Ryder leads a wagon train of settlers into a seemingly deserted town, only to find it is inhabited by a gang of vicious outlaws. B&W; 56m. **DIR:** R. G. Springsteen. **CAST:** William Elliott, Robert Blake, Linda Stirling, Roy Barcroft. **1945**

WAGONMASTER ★★★★1/2 John Ford was unquestionably the greatest director of Westerns. This release ranks with the best of Ford's work. Ward Bond, who plays the elder in this story of a Mormon congregation migrating west, became a star, thanks to the popular television series it inspired: *Wagon Train*. And Ben Johnson, who won the best-supporting-actor Oscar in 1971 for *The Last Picture Show*, is excellent in his first starring role. B&W; 86m. **DIR:** John Ford. **CAST:** Ben Johnson, Ward Bond, Harry Carey Jr., Joanne Dru, James Arness. **1950**

WAGONS EAST 🦃 John Candy died on the set of this lame Western-comedy in which he plays a melancholy wagon-train master who gets a chance to recover his sobriety and self-respect by leading a group of disgruntled frontier settlers back east. Rated PG-13 for language. 101m. **DIR:** Peter Markle. **CAST:** John Candy, Richard Lewis, John C. McGinley, Robert Picardo, Ellen Greene, William Sanderson. **1994**

WAGONS ROLL AT NIGHT, THE ★★ Circus owner promotes an untried young man as his prize lion tamer but goes off the deep end when his kid sister falls for his new star. Humphrey Bogart was on the verge of greatness after several false starts, and tired rewrites of old films like this fueled his disputes with studio boss Jack Warner. B&W; 84m. **DIR:** Ray Enright. **CAST:** Humphrey Bogart, Eddie Albert, Sylvia Sidney, Joan Leslie, Sig Ruman, Cliff Clark, Charley Foy. **1941**

WAIKIKI WEDDING ★★★ This typical Bing Crosby musical, which produced the Oscar-winning song "Sweet Leilani," has all the ingredients of Depression-era escapist fare. It works, thanks to the personable talented combo of Bing Crosby, Martha Raye, and Bob Burns. B&W; 89m. **DIR:** Frank Tuttle. **CAST:** Bing Crosby, Shirley Ross, Martha Raye, Bob Burns, Anthony Quinn, Grady Sutton. **1937**

WAIT UNTIL DARK ★★★★ Suspense abounds in this chiller about a blind housewife (Audrey Hepburn) who is being pursued by a gang of criminals. She has inadvertently gotten hold of a doll filled with heroin. Alan Arkin is especially frightening as the psychotic gang's mastermind who alternates between moments of deceptive charm and sudden violence in his attempt to separate Hepburn from the doll. 108m. **DIR:** Terence Young. **CAST:** Audrey Hepburn, Alan Arkin, Richard Crenna, Efrem Zimbalist Jr. **1967**

WAIT UNTIL SPRING, BANDINI ★★★ Author John Fante's fond remembrance of his youth is lovingly brought to the screen in this nostalgic look at an immigrant family beating the odds in Colorado, circa 1920. Handsome production benefits from a warm cast, especially Joe Mantegna as the clan head. Rated PG for language. 102m. **DIR:** Dominique Deruddere. **CAST:** Joe Mantegna, Ornella Muti, Faye Dunaway, Burt Young, Daniel Wilson. **1989**

WAITING ★★★1/2 Imagine an Australian *Big Chill*, as told from a woman's perspective. Writer-director Jackie McKimmie has fashioned a charming tale of diverse female friends who come from around the world to help their friend with the forthcoming birth of her child. An

entertaining film. 90m. **DIR:** Jackie McKimmie. **CAST:** Noni Hezelhurst, Deborra-Lee Furness. **1992 DVD**

WAITING FOR GUFFMAN ★★★★ This deadpan mockumentary spoofs amateur theater productions, Middle America values, and small-town boosterism—and celebrates tackiness. The result is hilarious. Rated R for language and sex talk. 84m. **DIR:** Christopher Guest. **CAST:** Christopher Guest, Fred Willard, Catherine O'Hara, Eugene Levy, Parker Posey, Bob Balaban. **1997 DVD**

WAITING FOR THE LIGHT ★★★1/2 A single mother of two children inherits and reopens a run-down roadside café. When her aunt, an ex–circus magician, pulls a nighttime prank on their mean-spirited neighbor, he mistakes it for a heavenly visit. Set during the uneasy time of the Cuban missile crisis, the troubled and the faithful flock to the scene of the "miracle," and business booms. Rated PG for profanity. 94m. **DIR:** Christopher Monger. **CAST:** Shirley MacLaine, Teri Garr, Vincent Schiavelli, Clancy Brown, John Bedford Lloyd. **1991**

WAITING FOR THE MOON ★★ Linda Hunt is Alice B. Toklas and Linda Bassett is Gertrude Stein in this idiosyncratic, self-indulgent, and frustrating film. The stars' performances are fine, but the impressionistic style of cowriter-director Jill Godmilow tends to be more irritating than artistic. Rated PG-13 for profanity and adult themes. 88m. **DIR:** Jill Godmilow. **CAST:** Linda Hunt, Linda Bassett, Bruce McGill, Andrew McCarthy, Bernadette Lafont. **1987**

WAITING TO EXHALE ★★1/2 Four African American women support and comfort each other through a year of romantic ups and downs. This glossy, expensive-looking soap opera is self-conscious and affected, and awkwardly directed by actor Forest Whitaker. Rated R for profanity and simulated sex. 123m. **DIR:** Forest Whitaker. **CAST:** Whitney Houston, Angela Bassett, Lela Rochon, Loretta Devine, Dennis Haysbert, Gregory Hines, Mykelti Williamson. **1995 DVD**

WAKE ISLAND ★★★★ Hard-hitting tale of a small gallant detachment of U.S. Marines holding out against attack after attack by the Japanese army, navy, and air force. A true story from the early dark days of World War II. Brian Donlevy commands the troops, and William Bendix and Robert Preston fight each other as much as the Japanese. *Wake Island* received four Academy Award nominations and was the first realistic American film made about World War II. B&W; 88m. **DIR:** John Farrow. **CAST:** Brian Donlevy, Macdonald Carey, Robert Preston, Albert Dekker, William Bendix, Walter Abel. **1942**

WAKE OF THE RED WITCH ★★★★ Good, seafaring adventure tale with John Wayne outstanding as a wronged ship's captain seeking justice and battling an octopus for sunken treasure. B&W; 106m. **DIR:** Edward Ludwig. **CAST:** John Wayne, Gail Russell, Gig Young, Luther Adler. **1948 DVD**

•WAKING LIFE ★★1/2 Writer-director Richard Linklater tried an interesting experiment for this dream-within-dreams fantasy: shooting live-action footage of characters talking about their dreams, then computer-processing the images into colorful, free-form animation. But it's only an experiment, and the novelty doesn't outlast the endless, excruciating blather on the sound track. Rated R for profanity and some violent images. 99m. **DIR:** Richard Linklater. **2001 DVD**

WAKING NED DEVINE ★★★★ A national-lottery win transforms a small town in writer-director Kirk Jones's droll and charming British comedy, which is every bit as earthy and enchanting as the rugged Irish seacoast where it takes place. Study of an isolated group of people confronted by an event that could change their lives forever . . . and the somewhat unorthodox manner in which they react to it. Rated PG for mild sensuality and geezer nudity. 91m. **DIR:** Kirk Jones. **CAST:** Ian Bannen, David Kelly, Fionnula Flanagan, Susan Lynch, James Nesbitt. **1998 DVD**

WALK, DON'T RUN ★★★ During the summer Olympics in Tokyo, Samantha Eggar agrees to share her apartment in the crowded city with businessman Cary Grant and athlete Jim Hutton. Happy, wholesome havoc results. Cary Grant's last film, a remake of 1943's *The More the Merrier*. 114m. **DIR:** Charles Walters. **CAST:** Cary Grant, Samantha Eggar, Miiko Taka, Jim Hutton, John Standing, George Takei. **1966**

WALK IN THE CLOUDS, A ★★★ Keanu Reeves returns home after World War II and finds himself participating in a gallant lie: pretending to be the husband of a fellow bus traveler who cannot otherwise admit her pregnancy (by a departed lover) to old-fashioned father Giancarlo Giannini. Although the Napa Valley wine-country setting provides a suitably sensuous palate, the overly contrived story ultimately overwhelms the budding romance. Rated PG-13 for sexual content. 103m. **DIR:** Alfonso Arau. **CAST:** Keanu Reeves, Aitana Sanchez-Gijon, Anthony Quinn, Giancarlo Giannini, Angelica Aragon, Debra Messing. **1995 DVD**

WALK IN THE SPRING RAIN, A ★★1/2 Two well-into-middle-age people find romance while on vacation in the country. Their problem is that both are married to other people. From such a fine cast you expect more. Rated PG. 100m. **DIR:** Guy Green. **CAST:** Anthony Quinn, Ingrid Bergman, Fritz Weaver, Katherine Crawford. **1970**

WALK IN THE SUN, A ★★★★1/2 Based on Harry Brown's novel, this picture really gets to the heart of the human reaction to war. The story of an American army unit's attack on a German stronghold in World War II Italy is a first-rate character study. B&W; 117m. **DIR:** Lewis Milestone. **CAST:** Dana Andrews, Richard Conte, Sterling Holloway, John Ireland. **1945 DVD**

WALK INTO HELL ★★★ Popular Australian star Chips Rafferty is something of a precursor to "Crocodile" Dundee in this outback adventure. He plays a bush explorer who helps a businessman find oil in New Guinea. Of course, the aborigines aren't all too happy about this. Plenty of *National Geographic*–type footage pads out this okay adventure. 93m. **DIR:** Les Robinson. **CAST:** Chips Rafferty, Françoise Christophe, Reg Lye. **1957**

WALK LIKE A MAN Unfunny, forced attempt at a comic version of *The Jungle Book*. Rated PG-13 for language. 86m. **DIR:** Melvin Frank. **CAST:** Howie Mandel, Christopher Lloyd, Cloris Leachman, Amy Steel. **1987**

WALK ON THE MOON, A ★★★ In the summer of 1969, between the Apollo 11 moon landing and the Woodstock festival, a bored young housewife has an affair with a footloose hippie. This understated slice-of-life soap opera profits from intelligent writing and honest acting.

Rated R for nudity and sexual scenes. 106m. **DIR:** Tony Goldwyn. **CAST:** Diane Lane, Viggo Mortensen, Liev Schreiber, Anna Paquin, Tovah Feldshuh. **1999 DVD**

WALK ON THE WILD SIDE ★★ Trashy tale of a young man's attempt to find his girlfriend, only to discover she's working in a New Orleans brothel. Extremely slow-paced film wastes a first-rate cast and a great musical score by Elmer Bernstein. For lovers of soap operas only. B&W; 114m. **DIR:** Edward Dmytryk. **CAST:** Laurence Harvey, Jane Fonda, Capucine, Barbara Stanwyck, Anne Baxter. **1962**

WALK SOFTLY, STRANGER ★★1/2 Joseph Cotten plays a calculating predator who falls for crippled victim Alida Valli and decides to call the swindle off. The plot thickens when a tough gambler Cotten had robbed in the past shows up to cut himself in and put our hero out—permanently. B&W; 81m. **DIR:** Robert Stevenson. **CAST:** Joseph Cotten, Alida Valli, Spring Byington, Paul Stewart, Jack Paar, Jeff Donnell, John McIntire. **1950**

•**WALK TO REMEMBER, A** ★★★1/2 Although seemingly no more than an average drama of teenage opposites falling in love, this engaging little drama includes a story element which, in popular entertainment, is quite rare: a sympathetic and intelligent character who draws strength from her religious conviction and faith in God. Pop star Mandy Moore makes a capable starring debut as this young woman who, despite her unpopularity with the high-school in crowd, nonetheless catches the eye of local ne'er-do-well Shane West. The subsequent relationship, which blossoms in fits and starts, is the best part of this adaptation of the Nicholas Sparks novel; the third act, alas, becomes too sloppily melodramatic. Rated PG for mild vulgarity. 100m. **DIR:** Adam Shankman. **CAST:** Shane West, Mandy Moore, Peter Coyote, Daryl Hannah. **2002 DVD**

WALKABOUT ★★★★1/2 Mesmerizing, haunting tale of paradise lost and found. When their crazed father drives them to the middle of the Australian outback and then commits suicide, a teenage girl and her young brother must struggle to survive and find civilization. They are escorted on their journey by a young Aborigine man on a quest to prove his manhood. Explores the sexual awakening of young people without making it seem exploitative. Not rated; contains nudity, violence, and adult situations. 100m. **DIR:** Nicolas Roeg. **CAST:** Jenny Agutter, David Gulpilil, Lucien John, John Meillon. **1971 DVD**

WALKER ★★★ True story of William Walker and his takeover of Nicaragua in 1855 by director Alex Cox. Ed Harris has a great time with the broad character of Walker and makes clear that power corrupts. For those with a taste for something out of the ordinary, *Walker* is worth viewing. Rated R for language, nudity, and simulated sex. 98m. **DIR:** Alex Cox. **CAST:** Ed Harris, Richard Masur, René Auberjonois, Marlee Matlin, Sy Richardson, Peter Boyle. **1988**

WALKER: TEXAS RANGER ★★★ Chuck Norris stars as the title character, a rough-and-tumble Texas Ranger, complete with holster and cowboy hat. When he's assigned to protect a U.S. senator, he and a retired buddy unwittingly uncover an assassination plot. Not rated. 96m. **DIR:** Michael Preece. **CAST:** Chuck Norris, Clarence Gilyard Jr., Stuart Whitman, Sheree Wilson. **1994**

WALKING AND TALKING ★★★★ Two lifelong pals (Catherine Keener, Anne Heche) feel the strain in their friendship when one decides to marry. After a slow, talky start, writer-director Nicole Holofcener begins playfully and patiently fleshing out her characters, and the film grows stronger with every scene. Acting is excellent, especially Keener as the friend staying single, and Kevin Corrigan as a nerdy video-store clerk. Michael Spiller's cheerful cinematography is another plus. Rated R for profanity and mature themes. 90m. **DIR:** Nicole Holofcener. **CAST:** Catherine Keener, Anne Heche, Liev Schreiber, Todd Field, Kevin Corrigan. **1996**

WALKING DEAD, THE ★★1/2 A squad of marines in Vietnam, ambushed and stranded, hack their way through the jungle to rendezvous with another unit and escape to safety. Standard "lost patrol" heroics, interspersed with trite flashbacks to the home front. Rated R for violence and profanity. 90m. **DIR:** Preston A. Whitmore, II. **CAST:** Allen Payne, Eddie Griffin, Joe Morton. **1995**

WALKING ON AIR ★★★★ Uplifting Ray Bradbury tale about a paralyzed boy who refuses to submit to the law of gravity. Inspired by his zany science teacher (played to perfection by Lynn Redgrave), he petitions NASA for a chance to float in space. This WonderWorks production is suitable for the entire family. 58m. **DIR:** Ed Kaplan. **CAST:** Lynn Redgrave, Jordan Marder. **1986**

WALKING TALL ★★1/2 Poor Joe Don Baker never outran his one-note performance as Buford Pusser, the baseball bat–toting southern sheriff who decided to take the law into his own hands in his fight against the cancerous scum of society. Unpleasantly brutal and difficult to enjoy for any reason. Talented Elizabeth Hartman is completely wasted. Not a family picture. Rated R. 125m. **DIR:** Phil Karlson. **CAST:** Joe Don Baker, Elizabeth Hartman, Noah Beery Jr., Rosemary Murphy. **1973 DVD**

WALKING TALL PART II ★★ This follow-up to the successful *Walking Tall* proves that sequels are better off not being made at all. This story line gives Bo Svenson a chance to look mean, but that's about it. Rated R for violence and language. 109m. **DIR:** Earl Bellamy. **CAST:** Bo Svenson, Luke Askew, Richard Jaeckel, Noah Beery Jr. **1975**

WALL STREET ★★★★ The same energy and insight that propelled writer-director Oliver Stone's Oscar-winning *Platoon* helps make this look at double-dealing in the stock market much more entertaining than one would expect. Chief among its pleasures is Michael Douglas's deliciously evil character of Gordon Gekko, a hotshot financier who takes novice Bud Fox (Charlie Sheen) under his wing. Rated R for profanity, nudity, and violence. 120m. **DIR:** Oliver Stone. **CAST:** Michael Douglas, Charlie Sheen, Daryl Hannah, Martin Sheen, Terence Stamp, Sean Young, Hal Holbrook, James Spader. **1987**

WALL STREET COWBOY ★★★ Roy Rogers takes to the concrete canyons when a trial requires his presence in New York in his first contemporary Western of many to come. Often good-naturedly pokes fun at Roy's image. B&W; 54m. **DIR:** Joseph Kane. **CAST:** Roy Rogers,

George "Gabby" Hayes, Raymond Hatton, Ann Baldwin. **1939**

WALL, THE (1983) ★★★★ Based-on-fact story of life in a brutal Turkish prison where prisoners of all ages, genders, and types (political and criminal) are incarcerated together. Director Yilmaz Guney spent much of his life in such prisons before escaping in 1981. Not rated, but too brutal for children. 117m. **DIR:** Yilmaz Guney. **CAST:** Tuncel Kurtiz. **1983**

WALL, THE (1998) (U.S.) ★★★ The gimmick in this trilogy of stories might make a good TV series if viewers could get beyond the depressing concept. Each tale concerns one of the mementos left at the base of the Vietnam War memorial and how it relates to the characters whose fates we follow. Sadly, the premise is better than the execution; each story is underscripted, each character lamentably underdeveloped. Rated R for profanity and violence. 95m. **DIR:** Joseph Sargent. **CAST:** Edward James Olmos, Savion Glover, Ruby Dee, Frank Whaley, Michael DeLorenzo. **1998 DVD**

WALLACE & GROMIT: A CLOSE SHAVE ★★★★★ Nick Park's third clay animation Wallace and Gromit adventure is every bit as entertaining as its predecessors, and quite worthy of its Academy Award. Not to be missed. Not rated, but acceptable for all ages. 30m. **DIR:** Nick Park. **1995 DVD**

WALLACE & GROMIT: A GRAND DAY OUT ★★★★ Claymation animator Nick Park clearly was perfecting his skills during this, the first saga to star fussy, cheese-loving Wallace, and his wise but quiet canine companion, Gromit. The figure animation is a bit uneven, reflecting the years Park required to complete his first short feature, but the character interaction is already wonderful. Not rated. 25m. **DIR:** Nick Park. **1990 DVD**

WALLACE & GROMIT: THE WRONG TROUSERS ★★★★★ This Oscar-winning short subject may be one of the most perfect little films ever made, blending inventive clay animation with deliciously droll scripting and a simply astonishing climax. This wildly amusing short captures the very essence of dry British humor. Not rated. 30m. **DIR:** Nick Park. **1993 DVD**

WALLS OF GLASS ★★★1/2 A New York cabdriver who aspires to be an actor exposes us to the many characters of his life: his gambling family, his troubled youth, and the colorful customers in his cab. A truly warm and insightful drama with a bravura performance by Philip Bosco. Rated R for language. 85m. **DIR:** Scott Goldstein. **CAST:** Philip Bosco, Geraldine Page, Olympia Dukakis, William Hickey. **1988**

WALPURGIS NIGHT ★★★ This sudsy romance features a secretary in love with her married boss. In Swedish with English subtitles that are not grammatically correct in translation. B&W; 75m. **DIR:** Gustaf Edgren. **CAST:** Ingrid Bergman, Victor Sjöström, Lars Hanson. **1935**

•WALTER AND HENRY ★★★ A boy who lives alone with his father must learn to adapt when his father has a mental breakdown. The 12-year-old must live with relatives he's never met, must go to school for the first time in his life, and must consider what might happen if his father doesn't get better. This made-for-cable drama has interesting characters, played well by all the actors involved, but the story is a little slow and predictable. Not rated; contains profanity. 90m. **DIR:** Daniel Petrie. **CAST:** John Larroquette, Kate Nelligan, Nicholas Braun, Dorian Harewood, James Coburn. **2001**

WALTZ KING, THE ★★★1/2 The wonderful music of Johann Strauss Jr. is the real star of this Walt Disney biography filmed on location in Vienna. A treat to the eyes and ears, this is a good family film. 94m. **DIR:** Steve Previn. **CAST:** Kerwin Mathews, Brian Aherne, Senta Berger, Peter Kraus, Fritz Eckhardt. **1963**

WALTZ OF THE TOREADORS ★★★★ The unique Peter Sellers is superb as a retired military officer who can't subdue his roving eye. Margaret Leighton is fine, as always. Dany Robin is adorable. It's saucy and sexshot, but intellectually stimulating nonetheless. A charming film, and not just for Sellers's fans. 105m. **DIR:** John Guillermin. **CAST:** Peter Sellers, Margaret Leighton, Dany Robin. **1962 DVD**

WALTZ THROUGH THE HILLS ★★★1/2 Two Australian orphans, fearing separation, set off for a ship to take them to their grandparents in England. They are helped by an outback native (Ernie Dingo) who is both frightening and endearing. A WonderWorks production, this is fine family fare. 116m. **DIR:** Frank Arnold. **CAST:** Tina Kemp, Andre Jansen, Ernie Dingo, Dan O'Herlihy. **1988**

WALTZES FROM VIENNA ★★ Alfred Hitchcock . . . directing a musical? Not really. This biopic of the Strauss family is more of a romantic comedy. By any category, it's a misfire. Not rated; suitable for family viewing. B&W; 80m. **DIR:** Alfred Hitchcock. **CAST:** Jessie Matthews, Esmond Knight, Edmund Gwenn. **1933**

WANDA NEVADA ★★1/2 Interesting little film with Peter Fonda as a shifty, amoral gambler who wins Brooke Shields in a poker game. They come into the possession of a map that marks a gold strike. If you watch carefully, you'll see Henry Fonda as a gold prospector. It's the only film that father and son ever did together. Rated PG for violence and mature situations. 105m. **DIR:** Peter Fonda. **CAST:** Peter Fonda, Brooke Shields, Fiona Lewis. **1979**

WANDERER, THE ★★1/2 An exciting newcomer turns a girl's life upside down, but her loyalty to him is a mystery since a more worthwhile man loves her. Marvelous music and imaginative surreal sequences cannot completely compensate for the slow pace and confusion that permeate this arty film. In French with English subtitles. 107m. **DIR:** Jean Gabriel Albicocco. **CAST:** Brigitte Fossey, Jean Blaise, Alain Noury. **1967**

WANDERERS, THE ★★★★ This enjoyable film is set in the early 1960s and focuses on the world of teenagers. Though it has ample amounts of comedy and excitement, because it deals with life on the streets of the Bronx there is an atmosphere of ever-present danger and fear. The Wanderers are a gang of Italian-American youths who have banded together for safety and good times. Rated R. 113m. **DIR:** Phil Kaufman. **CAST:** Ken Wahl, John Friedrich, Karen Allen, Tony Ganios. **1979**

WANNABES ★★1/2 Japanese animation. This one does have a certain charm. The *Wannabes* are a duo of determined women wrestlers that become the unknowing test subjects of genetic research. Sounds like a stretch (and it is), but it has the flavor of a Fifties drive-in classic. In Japanese with English subtitles. Not rated. 45m. **DIR:** Masuzumi Matsumiya. **1986**

WANNSEE CONFERENCE, THE ★★★★ This is a fascinating historical drama about a meeting held on January 20, 1942, with the fourteen members of Hitler's hierarchy. Wannsee is the Berlin suburb where they met to decide "the final solution" to the Jewish problem. Chillingly told from the actual minutes taken at the conference. A must-see film. In German with subtitles. 87m. **DIR:** Keinz Schirk. **CAST:** Dietrich Mattausch. **1984**

WANTED: DEAD OR ALIVE ★★★ In this lean action thriller, Rutger Hauer stars as Nick Randall, the great-grandson of Old West bounty hunter Josh Randall (played by Steve McQueen in the *Wanted: Dead or Alive* television series). Nick is a former CIA agent who is brought out of retirement when an international terrorist (Gene Simmons) begins leaving a bloody trail across Los Angeles. Rated R for profanity and violence. 104m. **DIR:** Gary A. Sherman. **CAST:** Rutger Hauer, Gene Simmons, Robert Guillaume, Mel Harris, William Russ. **1987 DVD**

WANTED: DEAD OR ALIVE (TV SERIES) ★★★1/2 The public was first captivated by Steve McQueen's cool, tough, intense persona with this top-notch Western series. McQueen plays dedicated bounty hunter Josh Randall, who travels the country searching for outlaws. The first video releases feature "Reunion for Revenge" with James Coburn and Ralph Meeker and "Medicine Man" with J. Pat O'Malley and Cloris Leachman. 30m. **DIR:** Thomas Carr, Richard Donner. **CAST:** Steve McQueen, Wright King. **1958–1961**

WANTON CONTESSA, THE ★★★★1/2 Luchino Visconti—aristocrat by birth, Marxist by conviction—offers one of the lushest and most expressive Italian films ever made (known there as *Senso*). The large-budget spectacular is operatic in scope and look. Venice, 1866. A countess (the alluring Alida Valli) finds herself passionately in love with a young Austrian officer (Farley Granger). Dubbed in English (with dialogue by Tennessee Williams and Paul Bowles). 120m. **DIR:** Luchino Visconti. **CAST:** Alida Valli, Farley Granger, Massimo Girotti. **1954**

WAR, THE ★★★ This early 1970s lesson in tolerance is also a coming-of-age story that bogs down in syrupy sincerity. A Vietnam vet tortured by war memories has as much trouble keeping his son out of fistfights in a rural Mississippi town as he does keeping a job. Rated PG-13 for violence and language. 127m. **DIR:** Jon Avnet. **CAST:** Kevin Costner, Elijah Wood, Mare Winningham, Lexi Randall, Christine Baranski, Raynor Scheine. **1994 DVD**

WAR AND PEACE ★★1/2 Mammoth international effort to film this classic novel results in an overlong, unevenly constructed melodrama. The massive battle scenes and outdoor panoramas are truly impressive, as are the performers on occasion. But the whole production seems to swallow up the principals and the action, leaving a rather lifeless film. 208m. **DIR:** King Vidor. **CAST:** Henry Fonda, Audrey Hepburn, Mel Ferrer, John Mills. **1956**

WAR AND PEACE ★★★★★ Many film versions of great books take liberties that change important plot situations, and more. This Academy Award–winning Soviet production stays as close to the book as possible, making it terribly long, but one of the greatest re-creations of great literature ever done. It took five years to make at enormous cost; it is a cinematic treasure. Poorly dubbed. 373m. **DIR:** Sergei Bondarchuk. **CAST:** Lyudmila Savelyeva, Sergei Bondarchuk. **1968**

WAR AND REMEMBRANCE ★★★ Drawn-out sudsy TV docudrama is Herman Wouk's sequel to *Winds of War*. Action begins with Pearl Harbor and eventual battles with Hitler. 96–146. **DIR:** Dan Curtis. **CAST:** Robert Mitchum, Jane Seymour, Polly Bergen, Hart Bochner, Victoria Tennant. **1988 DVD**

WAR ARROW ★★ Pure cowboy-and-Indian pulp, this movie is more of an excuse to show that good guys always end up with good girls—even when the good guy bucks authority and tries to pit one tribe of Indians against another. OK, but not very original. 78m. **DIR:** George Sherman. **CAST:** Maureen O'Hara, Jeff Chandler, Suzan Ball, Charles McIntire, Jay Silverheels, Charles Drake. **1953**

WAR AT HOME, THE ★★★1/2 Father and son Emilio Estevez and Martin Sheen, shine in this film about the effects of the Vietnam War on an American family. Rated R for profanity. 119m. **DIR:** Emilio Estevez. **CAST:** Emilio Estevez, Kathy Bates, Martin Sheen, Kimberly Williams, Corin Nemec. **1996**

WAR BOY, THE ★★★1/2 A 12 year old boy (Jason Hopely) living in World War II Germany suffers the experiences of growing up amid the brutalities of conflict. Hopely's performance is terrific. The story and production are nowhere near as ambitious as *Hope and Glory* or *Empire of the Sun*, but *The War Boy* is a good film in its own right. Rated PG for violence and some sex. 96m. **DIR:** Allan Eastman. **CAST:** Helen Shaver, Kenneth Welsh, Jason Hopely. **1985**

WAR GAME, THE ★★★★★ Pseudo-documentary depicts the events preceding and following a nuclear attack. Originally made for the BBC, which never ran it because it was thought to be too unsettling for viewers. Not rated. 47m. **DIR:** Peter Watkins. **1965**

WAR LORD, THE ★★★1/2 In the eleventh century, the warlord (Charlton Heston) of the Duke of Normandy moves to secure the coastline against invaders and to claim a maiden. The battle scenes are great and Richard Boone, as the title character's right hand, turns in a fine performance. 120m. **DIR:** Franklin J. Schaffner. **CAST:** Charlton Heston, Richard Boone, Rosemary Forsyth, Maurice Evans, Guy Stockwell, Henry Wilcoxon, James Farentino. **1965 DVD**

WAR LOVER, THE ★★1/2 This is a very slow-moving account of pilots (Steve McQueen and Robert Wagner) in England during World War II. Both pilots are seeking the affections of the same woman. Nothing in the film raises it above the level of mediocrity. B&W; 105m. **DIR:** Philip Leacock. **CAST:** Steve McQueen, Robert Wagner, Shirley Ann Field. **1962**

WAR OF THE BUTTONS ★★★★ Engaging family film about the children of two Irish villages, who begin feuding for no particular reason and allow matters to escalate into a full-scale war. The children use buttons as the prize and set into motion an increasingly violent series of skirmishes that leave their parents completely mystified. The kids are wonderful, the scenery to die for, and the message heartfelt. Rated PG for mild language and nudity. 95m. **DIR:** John Roberts. **CAST:** Greg Fitzgerald, Gerard Kearney, Darag Naughton, Brendan McNamara, John Coffey, Paul Batt, Karl Byrne. **1995**

WAR OF THE COLOSSAL BEAST ★★1/2 This sequel to *The Amazing Colossal Man* actually restores the long missing color ending, in which our oversize friend (now looking like the title character of *The Cyclops*, after being mutilated in the climax to the previous film) stumbles into high-tension electrical wires. That lends this American-International cheapie some stature as a video keeper. B&W/color; 68m. **DIR:** Bert I. Gordon. **CAST:** Sally Fraser, Roger Pace, Russ Bender. **1958**

WAR OF THE GARGANTUAS ★★ Giant, furry monsters—one good, one evil—slug it out in mountainous and eventually urban Japan. Eye-filling, brain-dead Toho Films sci fi. 93m. **DIR:** Inoshiro Honda. **CAST:** Russ Tamblyn, Kumi Mizuno, Kipp Hamilton. **1966**

WAR OF THE ROSES, THE ★★★★★ A brilliant black comedy from director Danny DeVito, this frightening and funny film stars Michael Douglas and Kathleen Turner as a couple whose marriage collapses into a vicious divorce battle over material possessions. The acting is superb, and the direction is stunning. Rated R for profanity, seminudity, and violence. 100m. **DIR:** Danny DeVito. **CAST:** Michael Douglas, Kathleen Turner, Danny DeVito, Marianne Sagebrecht, Sean Astin, G. D. Spradlin, Peter Donat. **1989 DVD**

WAR OF THE SATELLITES 🦃 Confusing and boring Roger Corman sci-fi thriller of note only for having been conceived and produced in eight weeks in order to cash in on the launching of the first American space satellite. B&W; 66m. **DIR:** Roger Corman. **CAST:** Dick Miller, Susan Cabot, Richard Devon, Robert Shayne, Bruno Ve Sota. **1958**

WAR OF THE WILDCATS ★★★ Big John Wayne takes on bad guy Albert Dekker in this story of oil drillers at the turn of the century. Gabby Hayes adds a vintage touch to this standard-formula Republic feature. B&W; 102m. **DIR:** Albert S. Rogell. **CAST:** John Wayne, Martha Scott, Albert Dekker, George "Gabby" Hayes, Sidney Blackmer, Dale Evans. **1943**

WAR OF THE WORLDS, THE ★★★★ Gene Barry stars as a scientist who is among the first Earthlings to witness the Martian invasion of Earth. The film is an updated version of H. G. Wells's classic story, with the action heightened by excellent special effects. 85m. **DIR:** Byron Haskin. **CAST:** Gene Barry, Les Tremayne, Ann Robinson. **1953 DVD**

WAR PARTY ★★ An interesting idea, but not suitably developed, this film details what happens when a group of disgruntled, modern-day native Americans go on the warpath. They disrupt a summer festival by taking the cowboy-and-Indian war games seriously—and use real ammunition. Rated R, with strong violence. 100m. **DIR:** Franc Roddam. **CAST:** Kevin Dillon, Billy Wirth, Tim Sampson, M. Emmet Walsh. **1988**

WAR REQUIEM ★★★ Arty, at times surrealistic view of war as seen through the eyes of World War II soldiers, nurses, and children. All action is without dialogue using Wilfred Owen's poetry and Benjamin Britten's music with emotional and thought-provoking results. Not rated; contains violence. 92m. **DIR:** Derek Jarman. **CAST:** Laurence Olivier, Tilda Swinton, Owen Teale, Nathaniel Parker. **1988**

WAR ROOM, THE ★★★★ Nominated for an Oscar for best documentary in 1993, this film follows Bill Clinton's 1992 presidential campaign staff (including James Carville and George Stephanopoulos) from the first primary to the acceptance speech. The viewer gets a firsthand look at the inner workings of a campaign, including mudslinging. Very well done and quite fascinating. Rated PG for profanity. 96m. **DIR:** Chris Hegedus, D. A. Pennebaker. **1993 DVD**

WAR WAGON, THE ★★★ While not John Wayne at his best, this Western, costarring Kirk Douglas and directed by Burt Kennedy, does have plenty of laughs and action. It's guaranteed to keep fans of the Duke pleasantly entertained. 101m. **DIR:** Burt Kennedy. **CAST:** John Wayne, Kirk Douglas, Howard Keel, Keenan Wynn. **1967 DVD**

WAR ZONE, THE ★★1/2 A teenage boy (Freddie Cunliffe) suspects his father (Ray Winstone) is sexually abusing his sister (Lara Belmont). The theme of the film, from Alexander Stuart's novel, is the destruction of a family. But in director Tim Roth's relentlessly bleak and sullen film, the family is miserable and joyless even before the boy's suspicions are confirmed, so there seems no great loss. Rated R for profanity and graphic scenes of incest. 98m. **DIR:** Tim Roth. **CAST:** Ray Winstone, Tilda Swinton, Lara Belmont, Freddie Cunliffe. **1999 DVD**

WARBIRDS 🦃 Inept action flick concerns American intervention in a Middle Eastern revolution. Rated R for violence and profanity. 88m. **DIR:** Ulli Lommel. **CAST:** Jim Eldbert. **1988**

WARBUS ★★ A Vietnam adventure about a motley crew fleeing a mission in a school bus, heading south during the closing days of the war. Hardly realistic, but the characters are likable and the action is tightly paced. Rated R for violence and profanity. 90m. **DIR:** Ted Kaplan. **CAST:** Daniel Stephen, Rom Kristoff, Urs Althaus, Gwendoline Cook, Ernie Zarte, Don Gordon. **1985**

WARDEN, THE ★★★ An ambitious correctional administrator (Ally Sheedy) is blinded to the personal costs and dangers in accepting the wardenship at a tough men's prison. Production values at the start are uneven but if you can wade through the first hour of this TNT Original, the pace and intrigue pick up for a satisfying conclusion. Not rated; contains violence, profanity, and sexual situations. 94m. **DIR:** Stephen Gyllenhaal. **CAST:** Ally Sheedy, Lindsay Crouse, Sam Robards, Ron Rifkin. **2000**

WARDEN OF RED ROCK ★★★ Written by the late James Lee Barrett, this is the familiar tale of two friends who end up on opposite sides of the law. James Caan is the straitlaced title character, who is surprised to welcome one-time saddle pal David Carradine as one of his inmates. The two actors play well off each other, but it is Caan's relationship with the widow of an executed inmate that gives the film its emotional depth. Rated PG-13 for violence. 90m. **DIR:** Stephen Gyllenhaal. **CAST:** James Caan, David Carradine, Rachel Ticotin, Brian Dennehy, Jim Beaver, Billy Rieck, Lloyd Lowe Jr., Kirk Baltz. **2001**

WARGAMES ★★★★1/2 A young computer whiz (Matthew Broderick) who thinks he's hooking into a game manufacturer's computer accidentally starts World War III when he decides to "play" a selection titled "Global Thermonuclear Warfare." Though the movie contains almost no violence or any other sensa-

tionalistic content (apart from a wee bit of vulgar language), it still grips the viewer. Rated PG. 114m. **DIR:** John Badham. **CAST:** Matthew Broderick, Dabney Coleman, Ally Sheedy, John Wood, Barry Corbin. **1983 DVD**

WARHEAD ★★★ Special forces ranger tries to stop a white supremacist who has stolen a nuclear warhead and pointed it at Washington, D.C. Obviously inspired by *Broken Arrow*, this is weak on plot but features two extended action sequences that make it worthwhile for genre fans. Rated R for violence and profanity. 97m. **DIR:** Mark Roper. **CAST:** Frank Zagarino, Joe Lara, Elizabeth Giordano. **1996**

WARLOCK (1959) ★★★ Even a high-voltage cast cannot energize this slow-paced "adult" Western. Lack of action hurts this film, which concentrates on psychological homosexual aspects of the relationship between gunfighter Henry Fonda and gambler Anthony Quinn. Richard Widmark is all but lost in the background as the town sheriff. 121m. **DIR:** Edward Dmytryk. **CAST:** Henry Fonda, Richard Widmark, Anthony Quinn, Dorothy Malone. **1959**

WARLOCK (1988) ★★★ An ancient witch-hunter follows an evil warlock to the streets of contemporary Los Angeles. Some great one-liners and a streamlined story help this entry. Rated R for violence, profanity, and gore. 102m. **DIR:** Steve Miner. **CAST:** Julian Sands, Lori Singer, Richard E. Grant, Mary Woronov, Allan Miller, Anna Levine, David Carpenter. **1988 DVD**

WARLOCK: THE ARMAGEDDON The son of Satan returns for the final battle between good and evil in this rock-bottom stinker. Rated R for extreme violence and gore. 93m. **DIR:** Anthony Hickox. **CAST:** Julian Sands, Joanna Pacula. **1993 DVD**

WARLOCK III: THE END OF INNOCENCE Tedious sequel brings nothing new to the party and finds itself falling back on the old haunted house theme with lackluster results. Not nearly as exciting or terrifying as the original. Rated R for adult situations, language, and violence. 94m. **DIR:** Eric Freiser. **CAST:** Bruce Payne, Ashley Laurence, Angel Boris. **1999 DVD**

WARLORDS Genetic engineering goes awry in a post-nuclear holocaust world. Rated R for graphic violence and profanity. 87m. **DIR:** Fred Olen Ray. **CAST:** David Carradine, Sid Haig, Ross Hagen, Robert Quarry. **1988**

WARLORDS OF HELL Two dirt bike–riding brothers wander into a marijuana plantation south of the border. Rated R for nudity, violence, and profanity. 76m. **DIR:** Clark Henderson. **CAST:** Brad Henson, Jeffrey D. Rice. **1987**

WARLORDS OF THE 21ST CENTURY A cold-blooded killer leads his band of roving outlaws in a siege against a peaceful community. Rated R for violence. 91m. **DIR:** Harley Cokliss. **CAST:** James Wainwright, Annie McEnroe, Michael Beck. **1982**

WARM NIGHTS ON A SLOW MOVING TRAIN ★★1/2 In this offbeat drama, Wendy Hughes portrays a schoolteacher who spends many of her nights as a prostitute on a passenger train in order to support her ailing, morphine-dependent brother. Rated R for simulated sex. 91m. **DIR:** Bob Ellis. **CAST:** Wendy Hughes, Colin Friels, Norman Kaye. **1989**

WARM SUMMER RAIN Self-destructive woman botches a suicide attempt, flees to a roadside bar, purchases a five-legged iguana, uses it to belt a persistent fellow trying to pick her up, and then spends the rest of the film having her way with the same guy. Rated R for nudity. 96m. **DIR:** Joe Gayton. **CAST:** Kelly Lynch, Barry Tubb. **1989**

WARNING, THE Convoluted dirty-cop flick from Italy. Not rated, but probably equal to an R for violence, profanity, and nudity. 101m. **DIR:** Damiano Damiani. **CAST:** Martin Balsam, Giuliano Gemma, Giancarlo Zanetti. **1985**

WARNING SHADOWS ★★ Bela Lugosi hams it to the hilt as the curator of the House of Mystery. He's the tainted genius behind the lifelike wax figures that move and speak like human creatures. But is he the mysterious Whispering Shadow who jams the airwaves and can eavesdrop and even murder people by remote-control radio and television? This Mascot serial, though stilted and creaky, is worth a watch. B&W; 12 chapters. **DIR:** Albert Herman, Colbert Clark. **CAST:** Bela Lugosi, Henry B. Walthall, Karl Dane, Roy D'Arcy, Bob Kortman, Tom London, Lafe McKee, Ethel Clayton. **1933**

WARNING SHADOWS ★★★★ An insane husband's jealousy of his wife's lover comes to a head when a hypnotist performs a shadow play mirroring the trio's emotions and passions. A classic post–World War I German cinema drama laced with mystery, fantasy, romance, and psychological terror. Silent with English and German titles. B&W; 93m. **DIR:** Arthur Robison. **CAST:** Fritz Kortner, Ruth Weyher. **1923**

WARNING SIGN ★★★ This is a passable science-fiction thriller about what happens when an accident occurs at a plant, producing a particularly virulent microbe for germ warfare. Rated R for violence and gore. 99m. **DIR:** Hal Barwood. **CAST:** Sam Waterston, Kathleen Quinlan, Yaphet Kotto, Jeffrey DeMunn, Richard Dysart, G. W. Bailey, Rick Rossovich. **1985**

WARRIOR AND THE SORCERESS, THE Sword-and-sorcery version of *A Fistful of Dollars*. Rated R for gore and nudity. 81m. **DIR:** John Broderick. **CAST:** David Carradine, Luke Askew, Maria Socas. **1984**

WARRIOR OF THE LOST WORLD A lone warrior is convinced to help find a woman's father who has been kidnapped by their enemy in a post-apocalyptic world. Not rated; contains violence. 90m. **DIR:** David Worth. **CAST:** Robert Ginty, Persis Khambatta, Donald Pleasence, Fred Williamson. **1988**

WARRIOR QUEEN This stinker robs footage from an Italian epic about the eruption of Mount Vesuvius and pads it out with a nonstory about an emissary from Rome inspecting the city of Pompeii. There are two different versions, an R-rated one with nudity and violence and an unrated one with more nudity. 69–79. **DIR:** Chuck Vincent. **CAST:** Sybil Danning, Donald Pleasence, Richard Hill, Josephine Jacqueline Jones. **1987**

WARRIOR SPIRIT ★★★ Two boys become friends in a school for boys. Their differing races (one's white, one's Indian) make their friendship a difficult but ultimately rewarding one. Rated PG. 82m. **DIR:** Rene Manzor. **CAST:** Lukas Haas, Allan Musy, Jimmy Herman, Jean-Pierre Matte. **1994**

WARRIORS, THE (1955) ★★★ In this, his last swashbuckling role, Errol Flynn looks older than his 46 years.

Cast as a British prince, he seems more qualified to battle the bulge and the bottle than the murderous hordes of nasty Peter Finch. Nevertheless, even in his decline, Flynn was more adept with a sword and a leer than anyone else in Hollywood. Though the movie is predictable, it's also quite entertaining. 85m. **DIR:** Henry Levin. **CAST:** Errol Flynn, Joanne Dru, Peter Finch, Yvonne Furneaux, Michael Hordern. **1955**

WARRIORS, THE (1979) ★★★★ Comic book–style violence and sensibilities made this Walter Hill film an unworthy target for those worried about its prompting real-life gang wars. It's just meant for fun, and mostly it is, as a group of kids try to make their way home through the territories of other, less understanding gangs in a surrealistic New York. Rated R. 94m. **DIR:** Walter Hill. **CAST:** Michael Beck, James Remar, Thomas Waites, Deborah Van Valkenburgh. **1979 DVD**

WARRIORS (1994) ★★ Routine action entry about a highly trained government antiterrorist squad so volatile it's kept behind lock and key and its existence is denied. When the squad's leader escapes, only one man, his protégé, can track him down and defuse him. Gary Busey and Michael Paré walk through this one as hunted and hunter. Rated R for violence and adult language. 100m. **DIR:** Shimon Dotan. **CAST:** Gary Busey, Michael Paré, Wendi Fulford. **1994**

WARRIORS FROM HELL 🦃 When ruthless rebels take over a small African country, a ragtag group of commandos save the day. War truly is hell. Rated R for violence and language. 90m. **DIR:** Ronnie Isaacs. **CAST:** Deon Stewardson, Glen Gabela, Shayne Leith, Adrian Pearce. **1990**

WARRIORS OF THE APOCALYPSE ★★ Another low-rent post-apocalyptic adventure. Fifty years after war has killed most of the Earth's population, a band of nomads search for a mountain that is said to hold the secret of survival. Rated R for violence and brief nudity. 96m. **DIR:** Bobby A. Suarez. **CAST:** Michael James, Deborah Moore. **1985**

WARRIORS OF THE WASTELAND 🦃 Cheap Italian copy of *Road Warrior*, with nuclear-holocaust survivors battling the evil Templars. Not rated, contains violence and slight nudity. 92m. **DIR:** Enzo G. Castellari. **CAST:** Fred Williamson, Timothy Brent, George Eastman, Anna Kanakis, Thomas Moore. **1983**

WARRIORS OF VIRTUE ★★ Fantasy world struggle between good and evil. The heroes have sort of a Barney persona until they punch, swat, and join forces to overcome their drug-ingesting, youth-corrupting, ultraviolent adversary. This wouldn't interest adults, and who'd want kids to see it? Rated PG for violence. 95m. **DIR:** Ronny Yu. **CAST:** Angus MacFadyen, Mario Yedidia, Marley Shelton. **1997 DVD**

WASH, THE ★★★ A straightforward story of a fading marriage and the rekindling of love, unusual for the advanced age of its characters and the film's offbeat setting among Asian-Americans in California. The talented Mako is memorable as a gruff, seemingly unaffectionate retiree who can't understand why his wife (Nobu McCarthy) wants a separation. Rated PG. 100m. **DIR:** Michael Toshiyuki Uno. **CAST:** Mako, Nobu McCarthy. **1988**

•WASH, THE (2001) ★★1/2 Intermittently entertaining quasiremake of *Car Wash* stars hip-hop's Snoop Dogg and Dr. Dre in a tale about two losers who go to work at the local car wash to raise some much needed funds. While the film lacks the charm of the original, it allows the stars to do what they do best without straining their credibility. The result is an urban comedy with occasional crossover appeal. Rated R for adult situations and language. 93m. **DIR:** D. J. Pooh. **CAST:** Snoop Dogg, Doctor Dre, George Wallace, Angell Conwell. **2001 DVD**

WASHINGTON AFFAIR, THE ★★★ Jim Hawley (Tom Selleck) is an incorruptible federal agent who must award a government contract. Walter Nicholson (Barry Sullivan) tries to blackmail Hawley. There are enough surprises in this film to keep most viewers on the edge of their couch. Rated R for simulated sex. 104m. **DIR:** Victor Stoloff. **CAST:** Tom Selleck, Barry Sullivan, Carol Lynley. **1977**

WASHINGTON SQUARE ★★★ Henry James's novel was filmed before by William Wyler as *The Heiress*. This version follows the book more closely (except for a bizarre ending that reeks of the 1990s). Wyler's 1949 classic remains unsurpassed. Rated PG. 115m. **DIR:** Agnieszka Holland. **CAST:** Jennifer Jason Leigh, Albert Finney, Ben Chaplin, Maggie Smith, Judith Ivey. **1997**

WASP WOMAN (1960) 🦃 Laughable cult favorite centers around a cosmetics magnate who turns into a wasp-monster. B&W; 66m. **DIR:** Roger Corman. **CAST:** Susan Cabot, Anthony Eisley, Barboura Morris. **1960**

WASP WOMAN, THE (1995) 🦃 An aging model and businesswoman takes a dose of wasp venom to regain her youth, but instead turns into a you-know-what in this poorly acted, low-budget horror movie. Rated R for profanity, violence, nudity, and simulated sex. 90m. **DIR:** Jim Wynorski. **CAST:** Jennifer Rubin, Doug Wert, Maria Ford, Melissa Brasselle, Daniel J. Travanti. **1995**

WATCH IT ★★★ Peter Gallagher stars in this bittersweet drama about a young man who returns to his hometown to attempt a reconciliation with his male cousin. Moving in with the embittered relative and his roommates, Gallagher falls in love with his cousin's girlfriend. Rated R for nudity and profanity. 105m. **DIR:** Tom Flynn. **CAST:** Peter Gallagher, Suzy Amis, John C. McGinley, Jon Tenney, Cynthia Stevenson, Lili Taylor, Tom Sizemore. **1992**

WATCH ME WHEN I KILL 🦃 Sylvia Kramer plays a woman who is witness to a murder and is now in danger of becoming one of the killer's next victims. Dubbed in English. Not rated; has violence and profanity. 94m. **DIR:** Anthony Bido. **CAST:** Richard Stewart, Sylvia Kramer. **1981**

WATCH ON THE RHINE ★★★★ Lillian Hellman's exposé of Nazi terrorism was brought from Broadway to the screen in first-rate form. Paul Lukas won a best-actor Oscar for his role of an underground leader who fled Germany for the United States, only to be hunted down by Nazi agents. Bette Davis is wonderful in what was one of her few small supporting roles. B&W; 114m. **DIR:** Herman Shumlin. **CAST:** Paul Lukas, Bette Davis, Geraldine Fitzgerald. **1943**

WATCH THE BIRDIE ★★1/2 Red Skelton runs a photo shop and, with a borrowed newsreel camera, unknowingly films crooks. Passable family fodder. B&W; 71m.

DIR: Jack Donohue. **CAST:** Red Skelton, Arlene Dahl, Ann Miller. **1950**

WATCHED! 🦃 A former U.S. attorney suffers a drug-related mental breakdown and kills a narcotics agent. Not rated. 95m. **DIR:** John Parsons. **CAST:** Stacy Keach, Harris Yulin, Brigid Polk, Tony Serra. **1973**

WATCHER, THE ★★★ FBI detective James Spader moves from Los Angeles to Chicago after a serial killer (Keanu Reeves) causes the death of the woman he loves. Suffering from migraines, nightmares, and sleeplessness, he's on the verge of a nervous breakdown when the killer makes the 2,000-mile trip to resume their "game." Familiar material is worth watching for the performances and suspenseful atmosphere. Rated R for violence and profanity. 96m. **DIR:** Joe Charbanic, Jeff Jensen. **CAST:** James Spader, Keanu Reeves, Marisa Tomei, Ernie Hudson, Chris Ellis, Robert Cicchini, Yvonne Niami, Jenny McShane. **2000 DVD**

WATCHER IN THE WOODS, THE ★★ This typical teenage gothic plot (family moves into old mansion and strange things begin to happen) is completely obscure and ends by defiantly refusing to explain itself. Rated PG because of minor violence. 84m. **DIR:** John Hough. **CAST:** Bette Davis, Lynn-Holly Johnson, Carroll Baker, David McCallum. **1980 DVD**

WATCHERS ★★★1/2 Based on the novel by Dean R. Koontz, this is a refreshing sci-fi–horror film. About a boy (Corey Haim) who finds a superintelligent dog and becomes the target of a scientifically created monster, it plays fair with the viewer throughout. Director Jon Hess even leaves quite a bit to the imagination, building the kind of suspense so seldom seen in this age of gore-infested hack-'em-ups. Rated R for violence and profanity. 91m. **DIR:** Jon Hess. **CAST:** Corey Haim, Barbara Williams, Michael Ironside. **1988**

WATCHERS II ★★★ Huge fun for animal lovers, as a computer-literate dog aids a hapless couple in thwarting the activities of a murderous runaway biological experiment, reminiscent of Ridley Scott's *Alien*. Littered with classic horror homage, including a climax under L.A.'s storm drains. Rated R. 101m. **DIR:** Thierry Notz. **CAST:** Marc Singer, Tracy Scoggins, Irene Miracle, Mary Woronov. **1989**

WATER ★★★ In this delightful British comedy, Michael Caine is the governor of the small English colony located on the island of Cascara. The governor's wife (Brenda Vaccaro) is bored until an oil company sends out a famous actor to film a commercial. Pleasant craziness accompanied by a great soundtrack featuring the music of Eddy Grant, and a jam session with Ringo Starr, George Harrison, and Eric Clapton. Rated PG-13. 91m. **DIR:** Dick Clement. **CAST:** Michael Caine, Brenda Vaccaro, Valerie Perrine, Fred Gwynne. **1986**

WATER BABIES, THE ★★★ Big fans of *Mary Poppins* should enjoy this. In Victorian England a chimney sweep's apprentice has a series of adventures with animated characters who live underwater. Designed more for kids than for families, though adults can enjoy the cast of fine British character actors. Rated G. 93m. **DIR:** Lionel Jeffries. **CAST:** James Mason, Billie Whitelaw, Bernard Cribbins, Joan Greenwood, David Tomlinson. **1979**

WATER ENGINE, THE ★★★1/2 What happens when an assembly-line worker invents an engine that runs on water for its only fuel is the main thrust of this fine drama written by David Mamet. Greed, back-stabbing, and other selfish motives come into play as word of the engine begins to circulate. Set in Chicago during the 1930s, the film boasts several very good performances and fine production values. 108m. **DIR:** Steven Schachter. **CAST:** Charles Durning, Patti LuPone, John Mahoney, Joe Mantegna, Treat Williams, William H. Macy, Joanna Miles. **1992**

WATERBOY, THE ★★★1/2 Adam Sandler is at his comedic best as the product of a deranged mother (Kathy Bates) and the back bayous of Louisiana. While serving as a much-abused waterboy, he's discovered for his inner rage by a desperate football coach (Henry Winkler). Hilarious scenes as both the coach and Sandler's sexy girlfriend take on momma. Rated PG-13 for language and sexual innuendo. 88m. **DIR:** Frank Coraci. **CAST:** Adam Sandler, Henry Winkler, Kathy Bates, Fairuza Balk. **1998 DVD**

WATERDANCE, THE ★★★★ Eric Stoltz, Wesley Snipes, and William Forsythe are superb in writer-codirector Neal Jimenez's fictionalized retelling of the aftermath of a hiking accident that left him permanently paralyzed from the waist down. An absorbing, emotional, and often suprisingly humorous story of confronting the unthinkable. Rated R for profanity and violence. 106m. **DIR:** Neal Jimenez, Michael Steinberg. **CAST:** Eric Stoltz, Wesley Snipes, William Forsythe, Helen Hunt, Elizabeth Peña. **1992 DVD**

WATERFRONT ★★ Classic film villains John Carradine and J. Carrol Naish are properly menacing as Nazi spies who try to convert German-Americans to their cause in this low-budget wartime espionage drama. Uninspired. B&W; 68m. **DIR:** Steve Sekely. **CAST:** John Carradine, J. Carrol Naish, Terry Frost. **1944**

WATERHOLE #3 ★★★ Amusing Western-comedy follows the misadventures of three outlaws, led by James Coburn, who rob the Union Army of a fortune in gold. 95m. **DIR:** William A. Graham. **CAST:** James Coburn, Carroll O'Connor, Margaret Blye, Bruce Dern, Claude Akins, Joan Blondell, James Whitmore. **1967**

WATERLAND ★★★★ Jeremy Irons gives a superb performance as an Englishman suffering a nervous breakdown while teaching history at an American high school. At a loss to reach his disaffected students, let alone his increasingly manic-depressive wife, Irons turns to his past in an effort to explain the present. Rated R for nudity and profanity. 95m. **DIR:** Stephen Gyllenhaal. **CAST:** Jeremy Irons, Ethan Hawke, John Heard, Sinead Cusack, Grant Warnock, Lena Headey, David Morrissey. **1992**

WATERLOO ★★ Spectacular action and a confusing plot make a muddled movie. The story of Napoleon's defeat is staged in detail with the deft touch of Russia's Sergei Bondarchuk making it look larger than life. But the characters are cardboard and the dialogue lifeless. 123m. **DIR:** Sergei Bondarchuk. **CAST:** Rod Steiger, Orson Welles, Christopher Plummer, Jack Hawkins, Dan O'Herlihy, Virginia McKenna, Michael Wilding. **1971**

WATERLOO BRIDGE ★★★★ A five-hanky romance about the lives of two people caught up in the turmoil of World War II. This is a poignant tale of a beautiful ballerina (Vivien Leigh) who falls in love with a British offi-

cer (Robert Taylor) and how her life is altered when he leaves for the battlefields of Europe. This is one of Leigh's best performances, although she rarely gave a bad one. B&W; 103m. **DIR:** Mervyn LeRoy. **CAST:** Vivien Leigh, Robert Taylor, Lucile Watson. **1941**

WATERMELON MAN ★★ A bigoted white man wakes up one morning and finds himself black. Using the late, great black comedian Godfrey Cambridge in the title role shows that someone in production had his head on right. The film makes a statement. Trouble is, it makes it over and over and over again. Rated R. 97m. **DIR:** Melvin Van Peebles. **CAST:** Godfrey Cambridge, Estelle Parsons. **1970**

WATERSHIP DOWN ★★★★ Although it's a full-length cartoon about the adventures of a group of rabbits, you'll find no cutesy, Disney-styled Thumpers à la *Bambi*. About the odyssey that a small group of rabbits undertakes after one of them has a vision of evil things coming to destroy their homes. Their arduous journey is full of surprises and rewards. Rated PG. 92m. **DIR:** Martin Rosen. **1978 DVD**

WATERWORLD ★★★1/2 This futuristic adventure tale is better than its reputation would suggest. Costner stars as a "fish man" in the far future fighting for survival on an Earth that is almost completely covered by water. Although the story is a bit too reminiscent of George Miller's *Mad Max* trilogy there are still enough memorable moments in this science-fiction–adventure movie to make it well worth watching. Rated PG-13 for violence, nudity, and profanity. 135m. **DIR:** Kevin Reynolds. **CAST:** Kevin Costner, Dennis Hopper, Jeanne Tripplehorn, Tina Majorino, Michael Jeter, Gerard Murphy, R. D. Call, Kim Coates, Robert Joy, John Toles-Bey. **1995 DVD**

WAVELENGTH (1983) ★★★★ You've seen it all many times before in science-fiction movies of wide-ranging quality: the innocent visitors from outer space, the callous government officials who see them as guinea pigs instead of guests, the handful of compassionate Earthlings, even the race to the mother ship. But rarely has the plot been used so effectively. Rated PG. 87m. **DIR:** Mike Gray. **CAST:** Robert Carradine, Cherie Currie, Keenan Wynn. **1983**

WAVELENGTH (1995) ★★★ Romantic comedy stars Jeremy Piven as an Oxford professor desperately trying to unlock the mysteries of the universe. Too bad he can't unlock the mysteries of love, having both a wonderful wife (Kelli Williams) and a girlfriend (Liza Walker). Under pressure at work and in bed, Piven has only one person he can turn to—"The Visitor," played by Richard Attenborough. Nice little slice-of-life comedy. Rated R for profanity and adult situations. 94m. **DIR:** Benjamin Fry. **CAST:** Jeremy Piven, Kelli Williams, Liza Walker, Richard Attenborough. **1995**

WAX ★★1/2 Bizarre, hallucinatory film about a NASA weapons-guidance programmer and beekeeper. He enters an alternative reality after his bees drill a hole in his head and install a mirrored crystal that sends strange images to his brain. Shot on videotape, with film spliced in, plus some nifty computer simulated graphics. This film can either fascinate or disconcert, depending on the viewer's taste. Not rated. 85m. **DIR:** David Blair. **CAST:** David Blair, Meg Savlov, William S. Burroughs. **1993**

WAXWORK ★★★ In this thrilling tongue-in-cheek horror film, six college students are invited to a midnight show at a mysterious wax museum. The sets of wax figures, famous monsters and killers, are missing one ingredient that can bring them all back to life: a dead victim. Rated R. 100m. **DIR:** Anthony Hickox. **CAST:** Zach Galligan, Deborah Foreman, Michelle Johnson, Miles O'Keeffe, Patrick Macnee, David Warner. **1988**

WAXWORK II: LOST IN TIME ★★ The two survivors of the previous film embark on a journey through time and meet various famous movie monsters. Fairly entertaining, especially to fans of classic horror films. Not rated; contains violence. 104m. **DIR:** Anthony Hickox. **CAST:** Zach Galligan, Alexander Godunov, Bruce Campbell. **1991**

WAXWORKS ★★★ A young poet dreams about the wax figures he sees in a fair booth: an Oriental sultan (Harun-al-Rashid), Ivan the Terrible, and Jack the Ripper. Outstanding example of the German Expressionist cinema in the 1920s. Silent. B&W; 63m. **DIR:** Paul Leni. **CAST:** William Dieterle, Emil Jannings, Conrad Veidt, Werner Krauss. **1924**

WAY BACK HOME 🦃 Whatever cornball charm this folksy little radio-related oddity can claim relies on rural amusements, songs, hymns, and a plot line old as the hills. Bette Davis was originally billed seventh. B&W; 81m. **DIR:** William A. Seiter. **CAST:** Bette Davis, Phillips Lord, Frankie Darro. **1932**

WAY DOWN EAST ★★★ Classic story of a young woman ostracized by her family and community was an audience favorite of the early part of this century but old hat even by 1920, when this melodrama was released. Justly famous for the exciting and dangerous flight of the beautiful Lillian Gish across the ice floes, pursued and eventually rescued by stalwart yet sensitive Richard Barthelmess, this was one of classic director D. W. Griffith's last solid critical and commercial blockbusters. Silent. B&W; 119m. **DIR:** D. W. Griffith. **CAST:** Lillian Gish, Richard Barthelmess, Lowell Sherman. **1920 DVD**

WAY OF THE GUN, THE 🦃 A boring, ludicrously violent mess about two deadbeats who kidnap a surrogate mother and hold her for ransom, only to watch as the scheme escalates out of control. The birthing scene scales new heights of tastelessness. Rated R for profanity, sensuality, strong violence, and gore. 119m. **DIR:** Christopher McQuarrie. **CAST:** Ryan Phillippe, Benicio Del Toro, James Caan, Juliette Lewis, Taye Diggs, Nicky Katt, Geoffrey Lewis. **2000 DVD**

WAY OUT WEST ★★★★★ Stan Laurel and Oliver Hardy travel west to deliver a gold mine map to the daughter of a friend. The map is given to an imposter, and the boys have to retrieve it and ensure correct delivery. A delightful, marvelous film that demonstrates the team's mastery of timing and characterization. B&W; 65m. **DIR:** James W. Horne. **CAST:** Stan Laurel, Oliver Hardy, Sharon Lynn. **1937**

WAY WE WERE, THE ★★★1/2 The popular theme song somewhat obscures the fact that this is a rather slow-moving romance about a Jewish girl (Barbra Streisand) who marries a WASPish writer (Robert Redford). The film has its moments, but a portion dealing with the McCarthy Communist witch-hunt falls flat.

Rated PG. 118m. **DIR:** Sydney Pollack. **CAST:** Barbra Streisand, Robert Redford, Patrick O'Neal, Viveca Lindfors, Bradford Dillman, Lois Chiles. **1973 DVD**

WAY WEST, THE ★★ A strong cast cannot buoy this bloated Western about a wagon train inching its way along the Oregon Trail in 1843. Director Andrew McLaglen is obviously trying to make an epic in the style of his mentor, John Ford, but he fails miserably. 122m. **DIR:** Andrew V. McLaglen. **CAST:** Robert Mitchum, Kirk Douglas, Richard Widmark, Sally Field, Lola Albright, Stubby Kaye, John Mitchum. **1967**

WAY WEST, THE ★★★★ This four-part PBS miniseries is a detailed and informative look at an era that shaped our nation's character, the westward movement and the devastation of the Native Americans. Hosted by Russell Baker. Not rated. 360m. **DIR:** Ric Burns. **1995**

WAYNE'S WORLD ★★★1/2 Mike Myers and Dana Carvey re-create and flesh out their characters from the recurring *Saturday Night Live* sketch in this comedy that will appeal primarily to the show's fans. The familiar story has our heroes fighting a sleazy promoter to maintain the integrity of their cable show when it is moved to commercial television. Rated PG-13 for profanity and sexual humor. 95m. **DIR:** Penelope Spheeris. **CAST:** Mike Myers, Dana Carvey, Rob Lowe, Tia Carrere, Brian Doyle-Murray, Lara Flynn Boyle, Ed O'Neill, Colleen Camp, Donna Dixon, Alice Cooper, Meat Loaf. **1992 DVD**

WAYNE'S WORLD 2 ★★ More idiocy from the goofy head-banger hosts of cable-access TV—but not as infectiously funny. *Saturday Night Live* characters Wayne Campbell and Garth Algar return to stage a massive rock concert (Waynestock) amid misadventures filled with more movie spoofs than memorable laughs. Rated PG-13 for language and suggested sex. 91m. **DIR:** Stephen Surjik. **CAST:** Mike Myers, Dana Carvey, Tia Carrere, Olivia D'Abo, Aerosmith, Christopher Walken, Chris Farley, Kim Basinger, James Hong. **1993 DVD**

WE ALL LOVED EACH OTHER SO MUCH ★★★★ Exceptional high-spirited comedy about three friends and their lives and loves over the course of three decades. A wonderful homage to Fellini, De Sica, and postwar neorealism. In Italian with English subtitles. 124m. **DIR:** Ettore Scola. **CAST:** Nino Manfredi, Vittorio Gassman, Stefania Sandrelli. **1977**

WE ARE NO ANGELS ★★ Another *Trinity* wannabe. In 1910 a race is set to determine which company will obtain a transport concession. Of course the villains try to stop our heroes Rafael and Angel, but they invent hanggliders and win the race. A good cast makes this enjoyable. Rated PG. 90m. **DIR:** Frank Kramer. **CAST:** John Ireland, Woody Strode, Michael Coby, Paul Smith. **1976**

WE ARE THE CHILDREN ★★★ This made-for-television story—about an American doctor (Ally Sheedy) who goes to famine-torn Ethiopia and meets up with a globe-trotting television reporter (Ted Danson)—suffers from preachiness. Despite that, Sheedy and Danson, along with Judith Ivey as a nun, give credible performances that make this a film worth watching. 92m. **DIR:** Robert M. Young. **CAST:** Ted Danson, Ally Sheedy, Judith Ivey, Zia Mohyeddin. **1987**

WE DIVE AT DAWN ★★★1/2 Tense story about a British submarine's duel with a German battleship during World War II is top-notch entertainment with a documentary feel. A fine cast and sensitive direction by Anthony Asquith lend this film dignity. B&W; 93m. **DIR:** Anthony Asquith. **CAST:** John Mills, Eric Portman. **1943**

WE OF THE NEVER NEVER ★★★★1/2 The compelling story of a woman's year in the Australian outback, where she learns about aborigines and they learn about her, is based on a true-life account written by Jeannie Gunn and published in 1908. Rated G. 132m. **DIR:** Igor Auzins. **CAST:** Angela Punch McGregor, Arthur Dignam, Tony Barry. **1983**

WE THE JURY ★★★★ This excellent court drama focuses on the perspective of the jury in a murder trial involving a media icon. Emotions rage in this made-for-cable original, as very different people try to hash out the facts of the murder and reach a consensus. This conflict, with a little mystery thrown in, compels you to watch to the very end. Not rated. 95m. **DIR:** Sturla Gunnarsson. **CAST:** Kelly McGillis, Lauren Hutton, Nicholas Campbell, Christopher Plummer. **1996**

WE THE LIVING ★★1/2 Weak adaptation of Ayn Rand's compelling novel about a headstrong young Soviet woman who becomes romantically involved with a counterrevolutionary. In Italian with English subtitles. Not rated. B&W; 174m. **DIR:** Goffredo Alessandrini. **CAST:** Fosco Giachetti, Alida Valli, Rossano Brazzi. **1942**

WE THINK THE WORLD OF YOU ★★★1/2 A bittersweet British comedy, set in the 1950s, and based on the autobiographical novel by Joseph R. Ackerley. Alan Bates plays a frustrated and emotionally abused homosexual who can't seem to reconcile his relationship with an ex-sailor/ex-con (Gary Oldman). This is a quirky, gentle, offbeat film, elevated by strong performances. Rated PG. 100m. **DIR:** Colin Gregg. **CAST:** Alan Bates, Gary Oldman, Frances Barber, Max Wall. **1988**

•WE WERE SOLDIERS ★★★★1/2 Stirring drama depicts, in graphic and heart-wrenching detail, what became the first major encounter between the soldiers of North Vietnam and the United States. The men are led by Lt. Col. Harold G. Moore (Mel Gibson), an old-school soldier who makes a point of being the first man to set foot on any new battleground, and the last one to depart. Gibson credibly conveys the tortured nobility of a leader who recognizes the heavy responsibility of charisma. The storytelling here is powerful and unforgettable, the tone Shakespearean. Rated R for profanity, war violence, and considerable gore. 138m. **DIR:** Randall Wallace. **CAST:** Mel Gibson, Madeleine Stowe, Greg Kinnear, Sam Elliott, Chris Klein, Keri Russell, Barry Pepper. **2002**

WEAPONS OF MASS DISTRACTION ★★★ Scripter Larry Gelbart tries for the same darkly savage tone he nailed so effectively in *Barbarians at the Gate,* but this study of rival media tycoons is simply too nasty to be all that amusing. Rated R for profanity, violence, and brief nudity. 95m. **DIR:** Stephen Surjik. **CAST:** Gabriel Byrne, Ben Kingsley, Mimi Rogers, Jeffrey Tambor, Illeana Douglas, Chris Mulkey. **1997**

WEB OF DECEIT ★★1/2 West Coast lawyer Linda Purl gets summoned back to the aristocratic Atlanta of her youth, to defend a young man (Paul de Souza) accused of rape and murder. Writer-director Sandor Stern's by-

the-numbers mystery is redeemed by the performances. Rated PG-13 for violence. 93m. **DIR:** Sandor Stern. **CAST:** Linda Purl, James Read, Paul de Souza, Larry Black, Barbara Rush. **1990**

WEBBER'S WORLD (AT HOME WITH THE WEBBERS) ★★★1/2 Desperately in need of cash, a dysfunctional family agrees to turn their everyday lives into a twenty-four-hour-a-day cable show. Some moments are downright hilarious. Not rated; contains nudity, adult situations, and strong language. 109m. **DIR:** Brad Marlowe. **CAST:** Jeffrey Tambor, Rita Taggart, Jennifer Tilly, David Arquette, Brian Bloom, Caroline Goodall, Robby Benson. **1993**

WEBMASTER ★★ A computer hacker is drawn further into the cyberworld when another mysterious hacker starts interfering in his online presence. Even computer experts probably won't understand this confusing sci-fi film, notable mostly for its special effects. Rated R for profanity and violence. 102m. **DIR:** Thomas Birch Nielsen. **CAST:** Lars Bom, Lars Borch Nielsen, Jorgen Kiil, Dorthe Westh Lerhmann, Mads Parsum. **1998 DVD**

WEDDING, THE (1972) ★★★★ A wedding between a farm girl and a poet works as an allegory of the internal problems that have troubled Poland for centuries. One of director Andrzej Wajda's most cinematic films, its atmospheric virtuosity will be appreciated even by those who find its themes too obscure. In Polish with English subtitles. Not rated. B&W; 103m. **DIR:** Andrzej Wajda. **CAST:** Eva Zietek, Daniel Olbrychski, Wojiech Pszoniak. **1972**

WEDDING, A (1978) ★★★ The story deals with a wedding between two relatively wealthy families and the comic implications that follow. Fine acting keeps things afloat. Rated PG. 125m. **DIR:** Robert Altman. **CAST:** Carol Burnett, Desi Arnaz Jr., Geraldine Chaplin, Vittorio Gassman, Lillian Gish, Lauren Hutton, Paul Dooley, Howard Duff, Pam Dawber, Dina Merrill, John Considine. **1978**

WEDDING BANQUET, THE ★★★1/2 Gentle comedy about a New York real estate dealer who agrees to marry one of his tenants to help her get a green card and put an end to his parents' attempts to find him "the perfect Chinese wife." This is all done with the knowledge and consent of his male lover. Not rated, the film has brief profanity and suggested sex. 112m. **DIR:** Ang Lee. **CAST:** Winston Chao, May Chin, Mitchell Lichtenstein. **1993**

WEDDING BELL BLUES ★★★ On the verge of age 30, three female friends impulsively decide to head to Las Vegas, find husbands, and divorce them in the same day, just to stop their friends and families from badgering them about being unhitched. This implausible plot serves as a framework for a sharply observed buddy comedy that is well acted by its stars. Rated R for profanity and sexual situations. 101m. **DIR:** Dana Lustig. **CAST:** Illeana Douglas, Julie Warner, Paulina Porizkova, Charles Martin Smith, Richard Edson, Stephanie Beacham. **1996 DVD**

WEDDING GIFT, THE ★★★ A middle-class English couple (Jim Broadbent, Julie Walters) tries to cope with the wife's mysterious, debilitating illness. The film is a pretty standard disease-of-the-week drama, but worth watching for its fine acting, especially by Walters as the wife and Thora Hird as the dotty old mother-in-law. Rated PG-13 for adult themes and mild profanity. 87m. **DIR:** Richard Loncraine. **CAST:** Julie Walters, Jim Broadbent, Thora Hird, Sian Thomas. **1993**

WEDDING IN BLOOD ★★★★ As in the best of Hitchcock, no one can be trusted in this elegantly perverse murder mystery. Two unhappily married people having an affair plan to rid themselves of their spouses. The spouses, however, have their own plans. In French with English subtitles. 98m. **DIR:** Claude Chabrol. **CAST:** Michel Piccoli, Stéphane Audran, Claude Pieplu. **1973**

WEDDING IN GALILEE, A ★★★★★ A Palestinian village elder is determined to give his son a grand traditional wedding, but to do so he must agree to invite the occupying Israeli leaders as guests of honor. Exceptional drama works on many levels. Filmed on location in the occupied West Bank. In Arabic and Hebrew with English subtitles. Not rated; contains nudity. 113m. **DIR:** Michel Khleifi. **CAST:** Ali Mohammed El Akili. **1987**

WEDDING IN WHITE ★★ It's World War II and Carol Kane is the young naïve daughter of an authoritative father who only shows affection for his son. The film succeeds in making you feel outrage, but is bleak from beginning to end. Rated R. 103m. **DIR:** William Fruet. **CAST:** Donald Pleasence, Carol Kane, Doris Petrie. **1972**

WEDDING MARCH, THE ★★★1/2 The story is simple: the corrupt, money-hungry family of an Austrian prince forces him to forsake his true love, a penniless musician, and marry a dull, crippled heiress. The telling is incredibly overblown. Critics and big-city audiences acclaimed this film, but it laid eggs by the gross in the hinterlands. Silent. B&W; 140m. **DIR:** Erich Von Stroheim. **CAST:** Erich Von Stroheim, Fay Wray, ZaSu Pitts, George Fawcett. **1928**

WEDDING PARTY, THE 🦃 Plodding and irksome, this is about a groom who develops cold feet. Filmed in 1963, but not released until 1969; B&W; 92m. **DIR:** Cynthia Munroe, Wilford Leach, Brian De Palma. **CAST:** Robert De Niro, Jill Clayburgh, Jennifer Salt. **1969 DVD**

WEDDING PLANNER, THE ★★ San Francisco nuptial planner gets her high heel stuck in a manhole cover and a passing pediatrician saves her from being flattened by a runaway Dumpster. Cupid strikes but she is pressured to marry a family friend and he is the fiancé of one of her clients. This sometimes-funny affair about the basics and fallacies of love is crippled by dumb progressions in both plot and subplots. Rated PG-13 for language and mature themes. 107m. **DIR:** Adam Shankman. **CAST:** Jennifer Lopez, Matthew McConaughey, Justin Chambers, Bridgette Wilson-Sampras, Judy Greer. **2001 DVD**

WEDDING REHEARSAL ★★ There's not much magic or comedy in this shaky farce. Director Alexander Korda shows poor directorial technique in this story of an officer whose grandmother plans to get him married. You can catch the whole thing with one eye closed and your favorite radio station on. B&W; 84m. **DIR:** Alexander Korda. **CAST:** Roland Young, George Grossmith, John Loder, Lady Tree, Wendy Barrie, Maurice Evans, Merle Oberon. **1932**

WEDDING SINGER, THE ★★★1/2 This delightful little love story admirably displays the skills of Adam Sandler and Drew Barrymore. The setting is 1985, and San-

dler plays a musician making ends meet by performing as a host/singer at suburban weddings. Barrymore is the perky waitress who catches his eye. Rated PG-13 for profanity and sexual content. 96m. **DIR:** Frank Coraci. **CAST:** Adam Sandler, Drew Barrymore, Christine Taylor, Allen Covert, Angela Featherstone. **1998 DVD**

WEE WILLIE WINKIE ★★★★ The best of Shirley Temple's features from her star period is this adaptation of a Rudyard Kipling tale. Temple and her screen mother Constance Collier go to live with her disapproving grandfather C. Aubrey Smith in India. It's a real charmer and a fine adventure film to boot. B&W; 100m. **DIR:** John Ford. **CAST:** Shirley Temple, Victor McLaglen, C. Aubrey Smith, Cesar Romero, Constance Collier. **1937**

WEEDS ★★★ Nick Nolte gives one of his finest performances in this uneven but generally rewarding film as a San Quentin inmate doing "life without possibility" until he secures his release by writing a play that impresses a reporter. Rated R for profanity, nudity, and violence. 115m. **DIR:** John Hancock. **CAST:** Nick Nolte, Lane Smith, William Forsythe, Joe Mantegna, Ernie Hudson. **1987**

WEEKEND ★★★ Jean-Luc Godard's apocalyptic film can best be described as a dark comic vision of the decline and fall of consumer society through the eyes of a young perverted bourgeois couple. Recommended only for hard-core fans of Godard. Others may find this movie too disgusting and very confusing. In French with English subtitles. Not rated; contains sexual situations and violence. 105m. **DIR:** Jean-Luc Godard. **CAST:** Mireille Darc, Jean-Pierre Léaud, Jean Yanne. **1967**

WEEKEND AT BERNIE'S ★★1/2 In this tolerable comedy with some hilarious moments, Andrew McCarthy and Jonathan Silverman play upwardly mobile young executives all set to have a wild, wild weekend at their boss's swank beach house—until they find the murdered body of said boss. Terry Kiser steals the show as the dead man, which gives you an idea of how silly it all is. Rated PG-13 for profanity and tasteless humor. 110m. **DIR:** Ted Kotcheff. **CAST:** Andrew McCarthy, Jonathan Silverman, Catherine Mary Stewart, Terry Kiser. **1989 DVD**

WEEKEND AT BERNIE'S II ★★1/2 More of the same as yuppie junior executives Andrew McCarthy and Jonathan Silverman resurrect their dead boss (Terry Kiser) for another adventure. The plot is pretty lame, but Kiser is hilarious. He shows more life as a corpse—made more animate this time by a voodoo spell—than his supposedly livelier costars. Rated PG for light profanity and silly violence. 89m. **DIR:** Robert Klane. **CAST:** Andrew McCarthy, Jonathan Silverman, Terry Kiser, Barry Bostwick, Tom Wright, Steve James, Troy Beyer. **1993 DVD**

WEEKEND AT THE WALDORF ★★★ 1932's *Grand Hotel* updated to World War II and transplanted to New York's classiest hotel. Can't touch the original, of course, but well made and polished to a fine gloss. B&W; 130m. **DIR:** Robert Z. Leonard. **CAST:** Ginger Rogers, Lana Turner, Walter Pidgeon, Van Johnson, Edward Arnold, Keenan Wynn, Robert Benchley. **1945**

WEEKEND IN HAVANA ★★★ To keep salesgirl Alice Faye from suing over a mishap, a luxury-liner company sends executive John Payne to Havana to see she has a good vacation. Lots of songs and some good laughs, particularly from Cesar Romero as a two-bit lothario. Some cassettes open with an "added feature" of Faye singing "I'll See You in My Dreams." This was deleted from the movie before its release. 80m. **DIR:** Walter Lang. **CAST:** Alice Faye, Carmen Miranda, John Payne, Cesar Romero, Cobina Wright Jr., George Barbier, Sheldon Leonard, Leonid Kinskey, Crispin Martin, Billy Gilbert. **1941**

WEEKEND IN THE COUNTRY, A ★★★ Assorted neurotic characters converge in California's Napa Valley wine country in this West Coast cousin of Woody Allen's ensemble comedies. Although written and directed by the team responsible for *Peter's Friends,* the various elements here don't mesh quite as well. Rated PG for profanity and sexual candor. 95m. **DIR:** Martin Bergman. **CAST:** Jennifer Elise Cox, Faith Ford, Christine Lahti, Jack Lemmon, Richard Lewis, Dudley Moore, Rita Rudner, John Shea, Betty White. **1995**

WEEKEND WAR ★★ A group of National Guardsmen are assigned to repair a bridge in Honduras near the Nicaraguan border. Effective but bland antiwar drama. 100m. **DIR:** Steven H. Stern. **CAST:** Stephen Collins, Daniel Stern, Michael Beach, James Tolkan, Charles Haid. **1988**

WEEKEND WARRIORS ★★ Mildly amusing, excessively wacky tale of Hollywood actors, writers, and singers circa 1961—avoiding combat by enlisting in the reserves. Rated R for profanity and sexual innuendo. 90m. **DIR:** Bert Convy. **CAST:** Chris Lemmon, Lloyd Bridges, Vic Tayback, Graham Jarvis, Tom Villard. **1986**

WEEP NO MORE MY LADY ★★1/2 Agreeable adaptation of Mary Higgins Clark's bestselling mystery about the murder of a popular actress, with a French chateau full of suspects. Made-for-Canadian-cable effort maintains its level of suspense thanks to a tight script and a strong leading performance by Daniel J. Travanti. Rated PG-13 for violence and drug content. 92m. **DIR:** Michel Andrieu. **CAST:** Daniel J. Travanti, Shelley Winters, Kristin Scott Thomas, Francesca Annis. **1992**

WEIRD SCIENCE ★★★ In this wacky comedy by writer-director John Hughes, two put-upon nerds (Anthony Michael Hall and Ilan Mitchell-Smith), desperate for a date, cop an idea from James Whale's *Frankenstein* and create a sexy woman via computer. Thus begins a roller-coaster ride of hit-and-miss humor as the nerds get class fast. Rated PG-13 for slight violence, partial nudity, and profanity. 94m. **DIR:** John Hughes. **CAST:** Anthony Michael Hall, Kelly LeBrock, Ilan Mitchell-Smith, Bill Paxton. **1985 DVD**

WEIRD WOMAN ★★★ Second and best of the *Inner Sanctum* movies has Lon Chaney Jr. as a college professor who suspects that his new wife (Anne Gwynne) is using voodoo to advance his career. Later remade as *Burn Witch Burn!* and *Witches' Brew.* B&W; 62m. **DIR:** Reginald LeBorg. **CAST:** Lon Chaney Jr., Anne Gwynne, Evelyn Ankers, Ralph Morgan. **1944**

WELCOME HOME ★★★1/2 This unjustly neglected drama makes ample use of Kris Kristofferson (in perhaps his best performance ever) as a Vietnam soldier presumed killed in action, who fourteen years later turns up in Thailand needing medical assistance. Once back stateside, he learns his wife has remarried. Rated

R for language and brief nudity. 90m. **DIR:** Franklin J. Schaffner. **CAST:** Kris Kristofferson, JoBeth Williams, Sam Waterston, Brian Keith. **1990**

WELCOME HOME, ROXY CARMICHAEL ★★★★ Although shunned at the box office, Karen Leigh Hopkins's perceptive and poignant little tale says a great deal about friendship, love, and the dangers of idol worship. Winona Ryder stars as Dinky Bossetti, a small-town girl attaching special significance to the return of Roxy Carmichael, a local legend who achieved fame and fortune on the West Coast. Rated PG-13 for language. 98m. **DIR:** Jim Abrahams. **CAST:** Winona Ryder, Jeff Daniels, Laila Robins, Dinah Manoff. **1990**

WELCOME, STRANGER ★★★ Made to cash in on the popularity of Bing Crosby's successful teamwork with Barry Fitzgerald after both won Oscars for *Going My Way,* this movie casts them as doctors instead of priests. B&W; 107m. **DIR:** Elliott Nugent. **CAST:** Bing Crosby, Barry Fitzgerald, Joan Caulfield, Percy Kilbride, Charles Dingle, Elizabeth Patterson. **1947**

WELCOME TO 18 This low-budget film's only point of interest is that it marks the big-screen debut of Mariska Hargitay, the daughter of Jayne Mansfield. Rated PG-13 for profanity and nudity. 91m. **DIR:** Terry Carr. **CAST:** Mariska Hargitay, Courtney Thorne-Smith, Jo Ann Willette. **1986**

•WELCOME TO HOLLYWOOD ★★1/2 A "mockumentary" in which a Hollywood director (Adam Rifkin, playing himself) takes an ordinary guy and tries to turn him into a movie star. Egocentric Hollywood is a great source of cheap jokes, but Rifkin avoids them; unfortunately, the gentler humor he opts for isn't terribly funny. Rated R for profanity. 89m. **DIR:** Tony Markes, Adam Rifkin. **CAST:** Adam Rifkin, Tony Markes, Jane Jenkins, Scott Wolf, Angie Everhart, Peter Facinelli. **1998 DVD**

WELCOME TO L.A. ★★★1/2 Extremely well-made film concerning the disjointed love lives of several of Los Angeles's nouveaux riches. The film's focal point is songwriter Keith Carradine, whose romantic interludes set the wheels in motion. Entire cast is first-rate, with Richard Baskin's musical score the only drawback. Rated R. 106m. **DIR:** Alan Rudolph. **CAST:** Keith Carradine, Geraldine Chaplin, Harvey Keitel, Sally Kellerman, Sissy Spacek, Lauren Hutton. **1977**

•WELCOME TO PLANET EARTH ★★★ George Wendt stars as the father of a family of aliens that come to Earth for their vacation. They look like a normal middle-class family until they start to practice their hobby, extreme violence, which is not permitted on their planet. Fortunately, they confine their practice to criminals in a ghetto area. Funny, if you have a cult-movie sensibility. Also known as *Alien Avengers*. Rated R for violence, comic gore, profanity, and sexual situations. 81m. **DIR:** Lev J. Spiro. **CAST:** George Wendt, Shanna Reed, Christopher M. Brown, Anastasia Sakelaris. **1996**

WELCOME TO SARAJEVO ★★★★1/2 Using a seamless blend of graphic news footage and impassioned drama, this scathing drama crawls under the skin of the international press corps and inhabitants of battle-ravaged Sarajevo in the summer of 1992. A television newsman smuggles a young girl out of the country to reawaken his numb humanity. Inspired by the true story of British journalist Michael Nicholson. Rated R for violence, war atrocities, and language. 101m. **DIR:** Michael Winterbottom. **CAST:** Stephen Dillane, Woody Harrelson, Marisa Tomei, Emira Nusevic, Kerry Fox. **1997**

WELCOME TO SPRING BREAK ★★ Two of the least reputable movie genres—beach party and slasher—meet as an executed biker returns from the dead to wreak vengeance. *Where the Boys Are* it ain't. Rated R for violence and nudity. 92m. **DIR:** Harry Kirkpatrick. **CAST:** Nicolas de Toth, Sarah Buxton, Michael Parks, John Saxon. **1989**

WELCOME TO THE DOLLHOUSE ★★★★★ An awkward, unattractive New Jersey 11 year old is degraded at school and dismissed at home by parents who like her siblings better. Writer-director Todd Solondz finds scathing humor in nasty, heartbreaking behavior, and his cast of mostly unknowns creates a superbly observed tapestry of tacky self-absorption. A scream in every sense of the word. Rated R. 87m. **DIR:** Todd Solondz. **CAST:** Heather Matarazzo, Brendan Sexton Jr., Daria Kalinina, Matthew Faber, Eric Mabius. **1996 DVD**

WELCOME TO WOOP WOOP ★★★ Madcap whimsy in the small Australian outback town of Woop Woop, where everyone is welcome, but no one is allowed to leave. Woop Woop is a destination filled with laughs and heart. Rated R for language and adult situations. 97m. **DIR:** Stephan Elliott. **CAST:** Johnathon Schaech, Rod Taylor, Susie Porter, Paul Mercurio, Rachel Griffiths, Dee Smart. **1997**

WELL, THE ★★★ When a small black child becomes trapped in the bottom of a well, the gathering crowd's reactions say a lot about the small town in which they live. Powerful stuff. B&W; 85m. **DIR:** Leo Popkin, Russell Rouse. **CAST:** Harry Morgan, Barry Kelley, Ernest Anderson, Christine Larson. **1951 DVD**

WELL-DIGGER'S DAUGHTER, THE ★★★1/2 A well digger disowns his daughter when she is seduced and abandoned, but they are reunited by his assistant. As in all of the films of Marcel Pagnol, a melodramatic story becomes something greater. In French with English subtitles. B&W; 142m. **DIR:** Marcel Pagnol. **CAST:** Raimu, Fernandel, Charpin. **1940**

WE'RE BACK! A DINOSAUR'S STORY ★★1/2 Jumbled animated adaptation of the popular book by Hudson Talbott. A quartet of dinosaurs are fed intelligence-increasing Brain Grain by an intergalactic traveler and brought forward in time to fulfill the wishes of modern-day kids. The animation is first-rate, but the screenplay by John Patrick Shanley will confuse even adults. In addition, scenes set in a scary circus may be too frightening for the small fry. Rated G. 72m. **DIR:** Dick Zondag, Ralph Zondag, Phil Nibbelink, Simon Wells. **1993**

WE'RE GOING TO EAT YOU! ★★ A gross, stylish horror-comedy about an island inhabited by cannibals and the predictably grisly fate that awaits those who stray into their clutches. If you thought there was nothing new in the cannibal subgenre, see this wild low-budget item. Not rated, but with plenty of gore on an NC-17 level. 90m. **DIR:** Tsui Hark. **1980**

WE'RE NO ANGELS ★★1/2 The *New York Times* dubbed this "a slow, talky reprise of the delightful stage comedy" and was right. Three Devil's Island convicts "adopt" an island family and protect it against an uncle it can do without. There is a roguishness about the trio that almost makes them endearing, but the film does

drag. 106m. **DIR:** Michael Curtiz. **CAST:** Humphrey Bogart, Peter Ustinov, Aldo Ray, Basil Rathbone, Joan Bennett, Leo G. Carroll. **1955**

WE'RE NO ANGELS ★★★1/2 The screenplay by David Mamet is a goofy send-up of the old Warner Bros. gangster melodramas, with Robert De Niro and Sean Penn mugging it up as a couple of escaped convicts mistaken for priests, who find themselves involved in a miracle. Director Neil Jordan couldn't decide whether he was making a crime-drama or a comedy. Rated PG-13 for nudity, profanity, and violence. 106m. **DIR:** Neil Jordan. **CAST:** Robert De Niro, Sean Penn, Demi Moore, James Russo, Ray McAnally, Hoyt Axton, Wallace Shawn, Bruno Kirby. **1989**

WE'RE NOT DRESSING ★★★1/2 A shipwreck strands an heiress and her snob friends on an island. They are taught how to survive by an easygoing sailor (Bing Crosby). Short, fast-moving musical comedy based on James Barrie's classic, *The Admirable Crichton*. Barrie is not credited, but his play is mentioned. B&W; 74m. **DIR:** Norman Taurog. **CAST:** Bing Crosby, Carole Lombard, George Burns, Gracie Allen, Ethel Merman, Leon Errol, Ray Milland. **1934**

WE'RE NOT MARRIED ★★★1/2 Assorted couples learn their marriages were performed illegally, so now they have certain options. Great episodic comedy. B&W; 85m. **DIR:** Edmund Goulding. **CAST:** Fred Allen, Eve Arden, Eddie Bracken, Louis Calhern, Paul Douglas, Zsa Zsa Gabor, Mitzi Gaynor, Marilyn Monroe, Victor Moore, Ginger Rogers, David Wayne. **1952**

WE'RE TALKING SERIOUS MONEY ★★ Two con artists cheat a mob boss in New York and end up running to California. Unbelievable characters and bad acting make this a disappointing film. Rated PG-13 for profanity and violence. 92m. **DIR:** James Lemmo. **CAST:** Dennis Farina, Leo Rossi, Fran Drescher. **1991**

WEREWOLF 🦃 Archaeological team in the Mexican desert digs up the bones of an ancient werewolf, starting the predictable results. Rated R for nudity, violence, and profanity. 99m. **DIR:** Tony Zarindast. **CAST:** Jorge Rivero, Fred Cavalli, Adrianna Miles, Joe Estevez, Jules Desjarlais, Richard Lynch. **1996 DVD**

WEREWOLF OF LONDON ★★★ Universal's first attempt at a werewolf film is full of fog, atmosphere, and laboratory shots but short on chills and horror. Henry Hull just doesn't make the grade when his fangs grow. B&W; 75m. **DIR:** Stuart Walker. **CAST:** Henry Hull, Warner Oland, Valerie Hobson, Lester Matthews, Spring Byington. **1935**

WEREWOLF OF WASHINGTON ★★ Dean Stockwell plays the president's press secretary, who becomes a werewolf after a visit to eastern Europe. Although it was made at the height of the Watergate scandal, this satire is surprisingly lacking in bite. Stockwell gives a game performance, but the script doesn't give him much to work with. Rated PG. 90m. **DIR:** Milton Moses Ginsberg. **CAST:** Dean Stockwell, Biff McGuire, Clifton James, Michael Dunn. **1973**

WEREWOLF REBORN! ★★ Second in the *Filmonsters* series is a shadow of its predecessor. While technically well made, the film lacks plausible situations and sensible characters. Here, a young girl travels to Romania to visit her uncle, who has become a werewolf. Rated PG for violence. 70m. **DIR:** Jeff Burr. **CAST:** Ashley Lyn Cafagna, Robin Downes, Len Lesser. **1998**

WEREWOLVES ON WHEELS 🦃 Cursed bikers become werewolves. The worst of two genres. Rated R for nudity and violence. 85m. **DIR:** Michel Levesque. **CAST:** Steven Oliver, Barry McGuire, Billy Gray. **1971**

WES CRAVEN'S NEW NIGHTMARE ★★★ Director Wes Craven and his cast star as themselves in this wicked spin on the horror genre. Key players from earlier *Nightmare on Elm Street* installments are terrorized by Freddy Krueger and his razor-fingered glove as he crosses over into their offscreen lives. It's a life-imitating-art twist that's ghoulishly fun. Rated R for language, violence, and gore. 109m. **DIR:** Wes Craven. **CAST:** Robert Englund, Heather Langenkamp, Miko Hughes, Matt Winston, Rob LaBelle, David Newsom, Wes Craven. **1994 DVD**

WES CRAVEN'S WISHMASTER 🦃 Genies don't get much nastier than the Djinn who is released from an ancient Persian opal and tricks people into making requests that he can twist into hideous punishments. Rated R for gore, violence, and language. 96m. **DIR:** Robert Kurtzman. **CAST:** Tammy Lauren, Andrew Divoff, Wendy Benson, Kane Hodder, Robert Englund, Tony Todd. **1997 DVD**

WEST BEIRUT ★★★★ This autobiographical coming-of-age story of a teen Lebanese boy vividly paints human faces on the victims of the 1975 Beirut bloodshed and anarchy. News footage and splashes of humor provide both a chilling edge to, and affectionate taste of, what it's like to be young and reckless in a war zone. The film takes us into an Arab family under siege as Beirut divides into warring Muslim and Christian camps and a brothel becomes the city's only demilitarized zone. In Arabic with English subtitles. Not rated. 105m. **DIR:** Ziad Doueiri. **CAST:** Rami Doueiri, Mohamad Chamas, Rola Al Amin, Carmen Lebbos, Joseph Bou Nassar. **1999**

WEST OF THE DIVIDE ★★★ John Wayne is on the trail of his father's murderer (again) in this standard B Western, which has the slight twist of having the Duke also searching for his younger brother, who has been missing since dear old Dad took the fatal bullet. Looks as if it was made in a day—and probably was. Good stunt work, though. B&W; 54m. **DIR:** Robert N. Bradbury. **CAST:** John Wayne, Virginia Brown Faire, George "Gabby" Hayes, Yakima Canutt, Earl Dwire. **1934**

WEST OF THE LAW ★★★ The last of the Rough Riders Westerns, this entry takes the series out in style. The heroes help the townspeople defeat a band of rustlers. Buck Jones handles most of the horseback heroics while Tim McCoy instills fear in the bad guys with his steely-eyed stare. B&W; 60m. **DIR:** Howard Bretherton. **CAST:** Buck Jones, Tim McCoy, Raymond Hatton, Evelyn Cooke, Harry Woods, Jack Daley, Roy Barcroft. **1942**

WEST OF ZANZIBAR ★★★ Over-the-top melodrama casts Lon Chaney Sr. as a crippled magician in a jungle village plotting revenge against the man who caused his injuries. The plot is corny, but thanks to Chaney and director Tod Browning (*Freaks*) this is one intense film. Silent. B&W; 63m. **DIR:** Tod Browning. **CAST:** Lon Chaney Sr., Lionel Barrymore, Warner Baxter. **1928**

WEST POINT STORY, THE ★★★ James Cagney is an athletic Broadway hoofer reluctantly becoming involved in the West Point annual cadet review, even trying out dorm life. Oscar nomination for the score by Ray Heindorf. B&W; 107m. **DIR:** Roy Del Ruth. **CAST:** James Cagney, Virginia Mayo, Doris Day, Gordon MacRae, Gene Nelson, Roland Winters, Jerome Cowan, Alan Hale Jr. **1950**

WEST SIDE STORY ★★★★★ The Romeo-and-Juliet theme is updated to 1950s New York and given an endearing music score. The story of rival white and Puerto Rican youth gangs first appeared as a hit Broadway musical and none of the brilliance of the play was lost in its transformation to the screen. It received the Oscar for best picture. (Wood's vocals were dubbed by Marni Nixon.) 151m. **DIR:** Robert Wise, Jerome Robbins. **CAST:** Natalie Wood, Richard Beymer, Rita Moreno, George Chakiris, Russ Tamblyn. **1961 DVD**

WESTERN UNION ★★★1/2 Randolph Scott's strong performance as an outlaw trying to go straight elevates this somewhat predictable Western epic about the coming of telegraph lines to the Wild West. 94m. **DIR:** Fritz Lang. **CAST:** Randolph Scott, Robert Young, Dean Jagger, Virginia Gilmore, John Carradine, Slim Summerville, Chill Wills, Barton MacLane. **1941**

WESTERNER, THE ★★★★ The plot revolves around earnest settlers being run off their land. But the heart of this classic yarn rests in the complex relationship that entwines Judge Roy Bean (Walter Brennan) and a lanky stranger (Gary Cooper). Bean is a fascinating character, burdened with a strange sense of morality and an obsession for actress Lily Langtry. Brennan won an Oscar for his portrayal. Cooper is at his laconic best. B&W; 100m. **DIR:** William Wyler. **CAST:** Gary Cooper, Walter Brennan, Forrest Tucker, Chill Wills, Dana Andrews, Tom Tyler, Fred Stone. **1940 DVD**

WESTFRONT 1918 ★★★★ G. W. Pabst's first sound film chronicles the agonies suffered by four German soldiers sent to the French front during the last months of World War I. Brilliant use of mobile camera gives the battle scenes a shocking look of realism. In German with English subtitles. B&W; 98m. **DIR:** G. W. Pabst. **CAST:** Gustav Diessl. **1930**

WESTING GAME, THE ★★★ Ellen Raskin's delightful children's book becomes one of those equally darling little films made from the viewpoint of a child. Residents in an apartment complex become involved in a most unusual treasure hunt: one involving lots of money and secrets about the neighbors. Suitable for all ages. 95m. **DIR:** Terence H. Winkless. **CAST:** Ray Walston, Ashley Peldon, Sally Kirkland, Cliff De Young, Diane Lane. **1997**

WESTWARD HO ★★★ Better production values in this John Wayne B Western, an enjoyable outing in which the star is once again seeking revenge on the outlaws who killed his parents and (in an extra twist) kidnapped his brother. B&W; 60m. **DIR:** Robert N. Bradbury. **CAST:** John Wayne, Sheila Manners, Frank McGlynn Jr., Jack Curtis, Yakima Canutt, Dickie Jones. **1935 DVD**

WESTWARD HO, THE WAGONS ★★1/2 Episodic film about a wagon train traveling west. The basic appeal is seeing Fess Parker in another Davy Crockett–type role and four of the Mouseketeers as children in the train. Devoid of a real beginning or end, this movie just rambles along. Not rated. 90m. **DIR:** William Beaudine. **CAST:** Fess Parker, Kathleen Crowley, Jeff York, David Stollery, Sebastian Cabot, George Reeves. **1956**

WESTWARD THE WOMEN ★★★★1/2 A rousing Western that emphasizes the problems of women on the frontier. Indian attacks, cat fights among the women, and accidental deaths can't keep these strong women from finding lonesome cowpokes and populating the frontier. 118m. **DIR:** William Wellman. **CAST:** Robert Taylor, Denise Darcel, Hope Emerson, Julie Bishop, John McIntire, Marilyn Erskine. **1951**

WESTWORLD ★★★★ This is another science-fiction yarn from the author Michael Crichton. The film concerns an expensive world for well-to-do vacationers. They can live out their fantasies in the Old West or King Arthur's Court with the aid of programmed robots repaired nightly by scientists so they can be "killed" the next day by tourists. Richard Benjamin and James Brolin are tourists who come up against a rebellious robot (Yul Brynner). Rated PG. 88m. **DIR:** Michael Crichton. **CAST:** Yul Brynner, Richard Benjamin, James Brolin. **1973 DVD**

WET AND WILD SUMMER 🦃 Vulgar Aussie version of Frankie-and-Annette beach movies is sexist, badly acted, and buffoonish. Rated R for nudity, profanity, and general bad taste. 95m. **DIR:** Maurice Murphy, Martin McGrath. **CAST:** Christopher Atkins, Elliott Gould, Julian McMahon, Rebecca Cross. **1993**

WET GOLD 🦃 A waitress who follows an old alcoholic's lead to sunken gold. Substandard made-for-TV film. 95m. **DIR:** Dick Lowry. **CAST:** Brooke Shields, Burgess Meredith, Tom Byrd, Brian Kerwin. **1984**

•WET HOT AMERICAN SUMMER ★★★1/2 Frequently hilarious spoof of such summer camp comedies as *Meatballs* and *Little Darlings*. Welcome to Camp Firewood, 1981, where the counselors and campers will cram a whole summer's worth of activities into the last day of camp. Janeane Garofalo is the camp director looking to score with local astrophysicist David Hyde Pierce, who has his eye on the falling Skylab. Every conceivable cliché gets a new spin, creating many unexpected moments. Lots of fun for anyone who has been to summer camp, or at least seen a film about summer camp. Rated R for adult situations, drugs, and language. 97m. **DIR:** David Wain. **CAST:** Janeane Garofalo, David Hyde Pierce, Molly Shannon, Paul Rudd, Christopher Meloni, Michael Ian Black, Michael Showalter. **2001 DVD**

WETHERBY ★★1/2 Buried under *Wetherby*'s dismally portentous attitudes about England and loneliness is a pretty interesting story. The film unfolds like a thriller, but it doesn't satisfy in the end. Vanessa Redgrave in the lead is characteristically excellent. Rated R. 104m. **DIR:** David Hare. **CAST:** Vanessa Redgrave, Ian Holm, Judi Dench, Marjorie Yates, Joely Richardson, Tom Wilkinson, Stuart Wilson. **1985**

WHALE FOR THE KILLING, A ★★★ Peter Strauss's dramatic, powerful personal statement against the slaughter of whales off the rugged coast of Newfoundland. Based on Canadian environmentalist–nature writer Farley Mowat's noted book indicting the practice. Overlong, but engrossing, TV movie. 150m. **DIR:** Richard T. Heffron. **CAST:** Peter Strauss, Richard Wid-

mark, Dee Wallace, Kathryn Walker, Bruce McGill. **1981**

WHALES OF AUGUST, THE ★★★ The joy of seeing two screen legends, Bette Davis and Lillian Gish, together in a film tailor-made for them is considerably muted by the uneventfulness of playwright David Barry's story. Essentially, we watch Davis and Gish play two elderly sisters who cope, bicker, and reminisce at their summer home on an island off the coast of Maine. Rated PG for profanity. 90m. **DIR:** Lindsay Anderson. **CAST:** Bette Davis, Lillian Gish, Vincent Price, Ann Sothern, Harry Carey Jr., Mary Steenburgen. **1987**

WHARF RAT, THE ★★★1/2 Although it starts out slow, keep watching this film about two brothers—one a cop and one a criminal—and you'll be pleasantly surprised. Good acting all around and entertaining action. Rated R for profanity and violence. 90m. **DIR:** Jimmy Huston. **CAST:** Lou Diamond Phillips, Judge Reinhold, Rachel Ticotin. **1995**

WHAT ABOUT BOB? ★★★1/2 Fitfully hilarious tale of a deranged but lovable neurotic (Bill Murray) who attaches himself to the family of a high-profile psychiatrist (Richard Dreyfuss) while they're on vacation. Murray is typically goofy, but Dreyfuss gives a masterfully comic performance. Rated PG for brief profanity. 97m. **DIR:** Frank Oz. **CAST:** Bill Murray, Richard Dreyfuss, Julie Hagerty, Charlie Korsmo. **1991 DVD**

WHAT COMES AROUND ★★ Jerry Reed stars as a world-famous country-western singer who is strung out on booze and pills. Bo Hopkins plays the younger brother who kidnaps Reed to save him from his own self-destruction. This all-American action-comedy-drama features the country music of Jerry Reed. A must-see for his fans. Rated PG. 92m. **DIR:** Jerry Reed. **CAST:** Jerry Reed, Bo Hopkins, Barry Corbin, Arte Johnson. **1985**

WHAT DREAMS MAY COME ★★★1/2 A physician (Robin Williams) marries the woman of his dreams and starts a family, only to have both children taken away in a tragic accident. Williams dies shortly thereafter, leaving behind a widow who cannot begin to cope. Our hero's adventures in an afterlife of his own design—apparently we create our own visions of heaven—are interrupted when his Earth-bound wife commits an understandable but selfish act, which threatens to place her beyond reach through all eternity. What follows is a spiritual journey to the borders of heaven and hell. Not everybody will embrace this film: The story—adapted from Richard Matheson's novel—is slow, at times ponderously so, but it will appeal to those who celebrate the preeminent power of devotion. Rated PG-13 for dramatic intensity and brief nudity. 113m. **DIR:** Vincent Ward. **CAST:** Robin Williams, Cuba Gooding Jr., Annabella Sciorra, Max von Sydow. **1998 DVD**

WHAT EVER HAPPENED TO . . . ? ★★1/2 Wholly unnecessary TV-movie remake of the 1962 shocker *What Ever Happened to Baby Jane?* The Redgrave sisters earnestly incarnate the Hudson sisters, but Vanessa remains far too passive in the role of the victimized Blanche, while Lynn goes strictly over the top as the grotesquely looney Jane. 100m. **DIR:** David Greene. **CAST:** Lynn Redgrave, Vanessa Redgrave, John Glover, Bruce A. Young, Amy Steel, John Scott Clough, Samantha Jordon, Erinn Canavan. **1991**

WHAT EVER HAPPENED TO BABY JANE? ★★★1/2 One of the last hurrahs of screen giants Bette Davis and Joan Crawford in a chillingly unpleasant tale of two aged sisters. Davis plays a former child movie star who spends her declining years dreaming of lost fame and tormenting her sister (Crawford). Victor Buono deserves special notice in a meaty supporting role. B&W; 132m. **DIR:** Robert Aldrich. **CAST:** Bette Davis, Joan Crawford, Victor Buono. **1962 DVD**

•**WHAT GIRLS LEARN** ★★1/2 A woman and her two teenage daughters uproot and move across country to live with a man the mother just recently met. Then tragedy strikes in this made-for-cable original, and the newly formed, fragile family is put to the test. Decent acting all around, but lack of plot renders the film a tepid character drama. Not rated. 114m. **DIR:** Lee Rose. **CAST:** Elizabeth Perkins, Scott Bakula, Alison Pill, Margo Martindale, Tamara Hope. **2001**

WHAT HAPPENED WAS . . . ★★★1/2 There are a million stories in the naked city, but few so effectively capture the loneliness accompanying them, even if the execution is a little self-conscious. Writer-director Tommy Noonan shares the screen with Karen Sillas as a couple of colleagues hoping to connect on another level. The script explores and then transcends first-date awkwardness as it strips away the protective layers these two don like clothing. Not rated; contains profanity. 90m. **DIR:** Tommy Noonan. **CAST:** Karen Sillas, Tommy Noonan. **1993**

WHAT HAVE I DONE TO DESERVE THIS? ★★★★ Outrageously funny black comedy about a working-class housewife who struggles to maintain her sanity while keeping her crazy family afloat. This perverse fable on contemporary life is superbly directed by Pedro Almodóvar and features a brilliant performance by Carmen Maura. In Spanish with English subtitles. Not rated; contains nudity and profanity. 100m. **DIR:** Pedro Almodóvar. **CAST:** Carmen Maura. **1984**

WHAT LIES BENEATH ★★★★ Director Robert Zemeckis pays homage to Alfred Hitchcock in this spellbinding tale of a grieving woman who believes the spirit of a murdered woman is contacting her. Her behavior becomes increasingly bizarre, much to the consternation of her conservative, professor husband. Nothing is quite what it seems in this first-rate thriller, which features outstanding performances by its stars. The film relies on subtlety and suggestion, a rarity in this age of over-the-top shocks and special effects. Rated PG-13 for violence, suggested sex, and brief profanity. 129m. **DIR:** Robert Zemeckis. **CAST:** Harrison Ford, Michelle Pfeiffer, Diana Scarwid, Joe Morton, James Remar, Miranda Otto, Amber Valleta, Katherine Towne, Ray Baker, Wendy Crewson. **2000 DVD**

WHAT! NO BEER? ★★1/2 Then topical, now dated comedy, with Jimmy Durante pulling his friend, taxidermist Buster Keaton, and his money, into a plan to brew beer and have it ready for sale upon the end of Prohibition. Not enough deadpan Keaton antics. B&W; 66m. **DIR:** Edward Sedgwick. **CAST:** Buster Keaton, Jimmy Durante, Roscoe Ates, Edward Brophy, John Miljan. **1933**

WHAT PLANET ARE YOU FROM? ★★★★ This crisply written, science-fiction comedy about the Mars-Venus aspect of human relationships is hilarious. An all-male

race of aliens on a distant planet tries to save itself from extinction by sending a "chosen one" called Harold to mate with an Earth woman. Harold is an ET sperm bank who is outfitted with a male reproductive organ that hums when stimulated. He poses as a Phoenix loan officer and tries to connect with several females while befriending a promiscuous married man. Rated R for sexuality and language. 100m. **DIR:** Mike Nichols. **CAST:** Garry Shandling, Annette Bening, Greg Kinnear, Ben Kingsley, Linda Fiorentino, John Goodman. **2000 DVD**

WHAT PRICE GLORY? (1926) ★★★1/2 Two rough-edged fighting men compete for women all over the world and get down to serious business in France during World War I. A masterly blend of sex, humor, and action set against the carnage of war makes this one of the first and most effective pacifist statements from the American cinema. One of the great silent films. B&W; 116m. **DIR:** Raoul Walsh. **CAST:** Victor McLaglen, Edmund Lowe, Dolores Del Rio, William V. Mong, Phyllis Haver, Leslie Fenton, Barry Norton, Sammy Cohen, Ted McNamara. **1926**

WHAT PRICE GLORY (1952) ★★★ James Cagney is Captain Flagg, Dan Dailey is Sergeant Quirt in this rough-and-tumble tale of rivalry in romance set against the sobering background of World War I in France. The feisty pair of Marines vies for the affections of adorable Charmaine (Corinne Calvet). Between quarrels, they fight in the trenches. 109m. **DIR:** John Ford. **CAST:** James Cagney, Dan Dailey, Corinne Calvet, William Demarest, Robert Wagner, Marisa Pavan, James Gleason. **1952**

WHAT PRICE HOLLYWOOD? ★★★★ This first production of *A Star Is Born* packs the same punch as the two more famous versions and showcases Constance Bennett as a tough but tender girl who wants to reach the top. Bennett seems somehow less martyred and long-suffering than either Janet Gaynor or Judy Garland, and that gives this version an edge that the others lack. B&W; 88m. **DIR:** George Cukor. **CAST:** Constance Bennett, Lowell Sherman, Neil Hamilton, Gregory Ratoff. **1932**

WHAT THE DEAF MAN HEARD ★★★1/2 This *Hallmark Hall of Fame* made-for-TV film is a delightful survival tale of a suddenly orphaned boy who must make a life for himself in a new town. His decision to say nothing about himself leads people to believe that he is deaf and mute. Twenty years later he exacts his revenge on the town bully. Unbelievable plot is nonetheless too much fun to turn off. Not rated; contains adult themes. 90m. **DIR:** John Kent Harrison. **CAST:** Matthew Modine, Tom Skerritt, Judith Ivey, Jake Webber, Jerry O'-Connell, James Earl Jones. **1997 DVD**

WHAT WAITS BELOW 🦃 A group of military and scientific researchers explore a cave and find a race of mutants. Rated PG. 88m. **DIR:** Don Sharp. **CAST:** Robert Powell, Lisa Blount, Richard Johnson, Anne Heywood, Timothy Bottoms. **1983**

WHAT WOMEN WANT ★★★1/2 Chauvinistic ad man (Mel Gibson) doesn't have a clue about women until a freak accident allows him to hear women's thoughts. With his newly acquired skill, he sets out to undermine his new boss. Gibson's magnetic smile captivates throughout this warm, romantic funfest while Frank Sinatra tunes allow him to show off a graceful bad-boy shuffle. Rated PG-13 for profanity and sex. 125m. **DIR:** Nancy Meyers. **CAST:** Mel Gibson, Helen Hunt, Marisa Tomei, Alan Alda. **2000 DVD**

WHATEVER ★★1/2 A smart but confused high-school senior goes through the standard movie growing pains. Director Susan Skoog's script lacks originality—it's essentially a gender-switching update of *The Catcher in the Rye*—but the acting is strong. Rated R for profanity and sexual scenes. 112m. **DIR:** Susan Skoog. **CAST:** Liza Weil, Chad Morgan, Frederic Forrest, Kathryn Rossetter. **1998**

WHATEVER HAPPENED TO AUNT ALICE? ★★★1/2 Entertaining black comedy about an eccentric woman (impeccably performed by Geraldine Page) who stays wealthy by killing off her housekeepers and stealing their savings. Ruth Gordon is equally impressive as an amateur sleuth trying to solve the missing-persons mystery. Rated PG. 101m. **DIR:** Lee H. Katzin. **CAST:** Geraldine Page, Ruth Gordon, Rosemary Forsyth, Robert Fuller, Mildred Dunnock. **1969**

WHATEVER IT TAKES 🦃 This lame modernization of *Cyrano de Bergerac* is another teen comedy in which messy affairs of the heart and loins are all resolved on prom night. Rated PG-13 for language and sexual references. 92m. **DIR:** David Raynr. **CAST:** Shane West, James Franco, Marla Sokoloff, Jodi Lyn O'Keefe, Julia Sweeney. **2000 DVD**

WHAT'S COOKING? ★★★1/2 This Rainbow Coalition version of *Home for the Holidays* introduces four extended Los Angeles families (African American, Vietnamese, Jewish, Latino) as they meet for Thanksgiving. This volatile melting pot of vividly portrayed characters threatens to boil over as traditions are both embraced and compromised, tolerance is tested by same-sex and multiracial couplings, generation gaps widen and shrink, and two bloodlines cope with the fallout of adultery. Rated PG-13 for language and sexuality. 106m. **DIR:** Gurinder Chadha. **CAST:** Dennis Haysbert, Alfre Woodard, Joan Chen, Mercedes Ruehl, Lainie Kazan, Maury Chaykin, Kyra Sedgwick, Julianna Margulies. **2000 DVD**

WHAT'S EATING GILBERT GRAPE? ★★★1/2 Small-town grocery clerk—the passive anchor of an odd Iowa family—cares for his 500-pound recluse mom and mentally challenged brother but gets an emotional jump start from a free-spirited, vacationing lass. It's a strange, sad, melancholy story about how personal happiness can take a backseat to family responsibility, that is also sometimes very funny. Rated PG-13 for suggested sex and language. 118m. **DIR:** Lasse Hallstrom. **CAST:** Johnny Depp, Leonardo DiCaprio, Juliette Lewis, Mary Steenburgen, Kevin Tighe, John C. Reilly, Crispin Glover. **1994**

WHAT'S LOVE GOT TO DO WITH IT? ★★★★ The story of Ike and Tina Turner is based on Tina Turner's autobiography and stars two of Hollywood's most respected black performers. Even though biographical films can't rely on surprise elements, they can use strong personalities to advantage. Angela Bassett stars as Tina Turner from her teen years to the present. Rated R. 120m. **DIR:** Brian Gibson. **CAST:** Angela Bassett, Laurence Fishburne. **1993 DVD**

WHAT'S NEW, PUSSYCAT? ★★★ Peter O'Toole is a fashion editor who can't stop becoming romantically involved with his models. In spite of a strong supporting

cast, this dated 1960s "hip" comedy has few genuine laughs. Mostly, it's just silly. 108m. **DIR:** Clive Donner. **CAST:** Peter Sellers, Peter O'Toole, Woody Allen, Ursula Andress, Romy Schneider, Capucine, Paula Prentiss. **1965**

WHAT'S THE MATTER WITH HELEN? ★★★1/2 Circa 1930, Debbie Reynolds and Shelley Winters flee to Hollywood to escape public hounding after their sons are involved in a brutal murder. They soon begin to fear they may have been followed by someone with revenge in mind. Good suspense and a fine feel for the era. Rated PG. 101m. **DIR:** Curtis Harrington. **CAST:** Debbie Reynolds, Shelley Winters, Dennis Weaver, Agnes Moorehead. **1971**

•WHAT'S THE WORST THAT COULD HAPPEN? ★★ A confrontation between honest burglar Martin Lawrence and crooked businessman Danny DeVito escalates into an elaborately nasty game of one-upmanship. It's tempting to dismiss this clumsy comedy as a movie that answers its own question; the script goes nowhere and builds no comic momentum, wasting the talented cast. Rated PG-13 for profanity and sexual humor. 97m. **DIR:** Sam Weisman. **CAST:** Martin Lawrence, Danny De Vito, John Leguizamo, Glenne Headly, Carmen Ejogo, William Fichtner. **2001 DVD**

WHAT'S UP, DOC? ★★★★ A virtual remake of Howard Hawks's classic *Bringing Up Baby*, this manages to recapture much of the madcap charm and nonstop action of the original story. The zany final chase through the streets of San Francisco is one of filmdom's best. Rated G. 94m. **DIR:** Peter Bogdanovich. **CAST:** Ryan O'Neal, Barbra Streisand, Kenneth Mars, Austin Pendleton. **1972**

WHAT'S UP, TIGER LILY? ★★★ A dreadful Japanese spy movie has been given a zany English-language soundtrack by Woody Allen in one of his earliest movie productions. You are left with an offbeat spoof of the whole genre of spy films. The results are often amusing, but its one-joke premise gets rather tedious before it's over. 80m. **DIR:** Woody Allen. **CAST:** Tatsuya Mihashi, Miya Hana, Woody Allen. **1966**

WHEEL OF FORTUNE ★★1/2 John Wayne in a screwball comedy? Yep. Also titled *A Man Betrayed*, the surprise is that this low-budget production is watchable. B&W; 83m. **DIR:** John H. Auer. **CAST:** John Wayne, Frances Dee, Ward Bond. **1941**

WHEELER DEALERS, THE ★★★1/2 Texas millionaires risk huge sums without getting their grins or ten-gallon hats out of place. James Garner is at his delightfully devious best in this briskly paced romp. Lee Remick is a treat for the eyes. A gang of talented character actors lends strong support. 106m. **DIR:** Arthur Hiller. **CAST:** Lee Remick, James Garner, Jim Backus, Phil Harris, Chill Wills, John Astin, Louis Nye. **1963**

WHEELS OF FIRE Shameless rip-off of *The Road Warrior*. Rated R for nudity, violence, and profanity. 81m. **DIR:** Cirio H. Santiago. **CAST:** Gary Watkins, Laura Banks, Lynda Wiesmeiser, Linda Grovenor. **1984**

WHEELS OF TERROR Interminable trash that pits spunky school-bus driver Joanna Cassidy against an unseen child molester who uses his dirty black sedan as a weapon, clearly having seen Steven Spielberg's *Duel* a few too many times. Unwatchable made-for-cable junk. 85m. **DIR:** Christopher Cain. **CAST:** Joanna Cassidy, Marcie Leeds, Arlen Dean Snyder. **1990**

WHEELS: AN INLINE STORY ★★ A collection of so-so in-line skating stunts linked together with inane narration that's supposed to be a story. Remarkable only in that it is the product of three teenage brothers. Features music by Hanson. Not rated, but suitable for all ages. 30m. **DIR:** The Klein Brothers. **CAST:** Andrew Flack, Mathew Alexander, Merideth Ward, Spencer Rauum, Nic Klein. **1998**

WHEN A MAN LOVES A WOMAN ★★★★ A weeper with a cast of pros who make it work. Meg Ryan plays Andy Garcia's alcoholic wife. She gets help, but it takes its toll on their marriage. They try to pick up the pieces, but it's tough on both of them. Rated PG-13 for mature themes. 122m. **DIR:** Luis Mandoki. **CAST:** Meg Ryan, Andy Garcia, C.C.H. Pounder, Tina Majorino, Mae Whitman. **1994 DVD**

WHEN A MAN SEES RED ★★★★ Writer-director Alan James gives producer-star Buck Jones a marvelous story line, and Jones gives a breezy, authoritative performance. Peggy Campbell plays the spoiled rich girl who is heir to the California ranch that Jones oversees, and he is charged with looking after her interests. B&W; 60m. **DIR:** Alan James. **CAST:** Buck Jones, Peggy Campbell, LeRoy Mason. **1934**

WHEN A STRANGER CALLS ★★★ A *Psycho II*-style atmosphere pervades this film when the murderer of two children returns after seven years to complete his crime. Rated R. 97m. **DIR:** Fred Walton. **CAST:** Carol Kane, Charles Durning, Colleen Dewhurst, Tony Beckley, Rachel Roberts, Ron O'Neal. **1979 DVD**

WHEN A STRANGER CALLS BACK ★★★ Writer-director Fred Walton's sequel to the 1979 chiller begins superbly, with Jill Schoelen just right as a cautious baby-sitter being taunted by someone. Sadly, the momentum flags once the girl makes contact with psychologist Jill Johnson (Carol Kane) and investigator John Clifford (Charles Durning), who see parallels to the events they survived years earlier. Rated R for violence and nudity. 94m. **DIR:** Fred Walton. **CAST:** Carol Kane, Charles Durning, Jill Schoelen, Gene Lythgow. **1993**

WHEN A WOMAN ASCENDS THE STAIRS ★★★★1/2 As in many of his films, Mikio Naruse examines a woman trying to make her own way in the world, in this case a bar hostess struggling with debt and loneliness. Clearly influenced by Hollywood melodramas of the 1950s, he adapts their conventions (including the wide-screen format, preserved in this letter-boxed video transfer) to good effect. In Japanese with English subtitles. B&W; 110m. **DIR:** Mikio Naruse. **CAST:** Hideko Takamine. **1960**

WHEN BRENDAN MET TRUDY ★★★★ Extremely funny and affectionate comedy features a stellar performance from Peter McDonald, playing Irish teacher Brendan, who lives his life like a movie. A human doormat to his students, fellow teachers, and family, Brendan's life takes a major turnaround when he meets and falls in love with professional thief Trudy (Flora Montgomery). Mixing real life and fantasy, this homage to the movies is filled with many unexpected moments. Not rated; contains adult situations, language, and nudity. 90m. **DIR:** Kieron J. Walsh. **CAST:** Peter McDonald,

Flora Montgomery, Marie Mullen, Pauline McLynn, Don Wycherley. **2000**

WHEN COMEDY WAS KING ★★★★ A nostalgic, sidesplitting look back to the screen comedy days of yesteryear when absurdity and the sight gag reigned supreme. This clutch of classic comedy scenes from silent days is outstanding. B&W; 81m. **DIR:** Robert Youngson. **CAST:** Charlie Chaplin, Buster Keaton, Gloria Swanson, Mabel Normand, Oliver Hardy, Stan Laurel. **1960**

WHEN DANGER FOLLOWS YOU HOME ★★★ A psychology intern meddles a little too much in the life of a mentally unbalanced criminal, and the man follows her home. She befriends him, disaster strikes, and she's accused of murder. This made-for-cable thriller is well written, and has a solid plot, but doesn't rise much above the average. Not rated; contains violence. 95m. **DIR:** David Peckinpah. **CAST:** JoBeth Williams, William Russ, Michael Manasseri, Nicolas Surovy. **1997**

WHEN DINOSAURS RULED THE EARTH ★★★ British novelist and fantasy author J. G. Ballard (*Empire of the Sun*) wrote the treatment for this unusually ambitious Hammer Films epic, shot in the Canary Islands. Director Val Guest (one of Hammer's top talents) and effects wizard Jim Danforth succeed, possibly for the first time, in integrating the stop-motion dinosaur sequences seamlessly into the narrative—they aren't mere "stop-the-show" set pieces. Rated G. 96m. **DIR:** Val Guest. **CAST:** Victoria Vetri, Robin Hawdon, Patrick Allen. **1969**

WHEN FATHER WAS AWAY ON BUSINESS ★★★ Seen through the eyes of a young boy, the film deals with the sudden disappearance of a father from a family. Tension mounts when it becomes clear that it is the father's brother-in-law who turned him in and had him sent to a work camp. The film received the Palm D'Or at the 1985 Cannes Film Festival. Rated R for sex and nudity. In Slavic with English subtitles. 144m. **DIR:** Emir Kusturica. **CAST:** Moreno De Bartolli, Miki Manojlovic. **1985**

WHEN GANGLAND STRIKES ★★ Stale story of a lawman who has to knuckle under to hoodlums who have some dirt on him is adequate but nothing dynamic. B&W; 70m. **DIR:** R. G. Springsteen. **CAST:** Raymond Greenleaf, Marjie Millar, John Hudson, Anthony Caruso. **1956**

•WHEN GOOD GHOULS GO BAD ★★★ Christopher Lloyd is true to form as the wacky dead uncle of young Danny Walker (Joe Pichler), who helps his nephew rid their small town of a curse that prevents it from celebrating Halloween. When his beloved uncle dies, Danny must stop town legend and ghoul Curtis Danko, who has summoned his dead friends to wreak havoc on their Minnesota town. But being dead doesn't keep Uncle Fred down; he meets and greets Danko on his own ground. This made-for-television suspense comedy was based on a story by R. L. Stine. Rated PG for violence. 93m. **DIR:** Patrick Read Johnson. **CAST:** Christopher Lloyd, Joe Pichler, Tom Amandes, Brittany Byrnes. **2001 DVD**

WHEN HARRY MET SALLY ★★★★1/2 Wonderful character comedy stars Billy Crystal and Meg Ryan as longtime acquaintances who drift from mild animosity to friendship to love. Director Rob Reiner skillfully tickles our funny bones and touches our hearts with this semiautobiographical tale, which was scripted by Nora Ephron. Rated R for profanity and suggested sex. 110m. **DIR:** Rob Reiner. **CAST:** Billy Crystal, Meg Ryan, Carrie Fisher, Bruno Kirby. **1989 DVD**

WHEN HE'S NOT A STRANGER ★★★1/2 Date rape is sensitively handled in this made-for-TV drama. College freshman Annabeth Gish accepts an offer from popular John Terlesky to come up to his room and get acquainted, but what starts off innocently leads to a harrowing act. Gish must come to grips with the incident and seek the courage to fight back. Kevin Dillon is the friend who lends support. Not rated; contains adult situations. 90m. **DIR:** John Gray. **CAST:** Annabeth Gish, Kevin Dillon, John Terlesky. **1989**

WHEN LADIES MEET ★★★1/2 A spasmodically delightful high-society romantic romp. A writer falls in love with her married publisher, much to the dismay of her jealous suitor, who befriends the publisher's wife and invites her to the writer's home for the weekend. B&W; 105m. **DIR:** Robert Z. Leonard. **CAST:** Joan Crawford, Robert Taylor, Greer Garson, Herbert Marshall, Spring Byington. **1941**

WHEN NIGHT IS FALLING ★★★★ Provocative romantic triangle exists when a prim religious college teacher can't decide between her reserved minister boyfriend and a passionate and unpredictable female circus performer. Sensual, erotic, handsomely mounted production. R-rated and unrated versions; both contain nudity and adult situations. 94m. **DIR:** Patricia Rozema. **CAST:** Pascale Bussières, Rachel Crawford, Don McKellar, Tracy Wright, Henry Czerny. **1995**

WHEN THE BOUGH BREAKS ★★★ Competent thriller stars Martin Sheen as a Houston police chief who's on the trail of a serial killer. His only hope lies with a forensic expert played by Ally Walker, and a mentally disturbed child who is psychically connected to the killer. Decent performances and plenty of dark, twisted turns. Rated R for violence and adult language. 103m. **DIR:** Michael Cohn. **CAST:** Martin Sheen, Ally Walker, Ron Perlman. **1993**

WHEN THE BULLET HITS THE BONE ★★ When emergency-room doctor Jack Davies decides he's seen enough human carnage, he does something about it. Davies goes after the drug dealers causing the human misery, and in doing so, stumbles across a coverup that goes straight to the top of the United States government. Star Jeff Wincott has done so many of these lone-avenger films it's almost hard to tell one from the other. Rated R for violence, profanity, and adult situations. 92m. **DIR:** Damien Lee. **CAST:** Jeff Wincott, Michelle Johnson, Doug O'Keefe. **1995**

WHEN THE CAT'S AWAY ★★★★ Timid Parisian model makeup artist Chloe leaves her cat with an elderly neighborhood lady while she vacations at the seaside. The feline is missing when Chloe returns, and her attempts to find it slowly nudge her out of a hollow singles funk. The story, which is about the many shades of loneliness, is spare but rich in atmosphere. In French with English subtitles. Rated R for simulated sex and language. 95m. **DIR:** Cedric Klapisch. **CAST:** Garance Clavel, Renee Le Calm, Zinedine Soualem, Olivier Py, Romain Duris. **1996**

WHEN THE CLOUDS ROLL BY ★★★★ If you have to choose *the* outstanding example of the precostume Douglas Fairbanks comedies, surely this is it. It's a satire on hypochondriacs. The highlight is a chase in a revolving room and a subsequent scuffle in slow-motion photography. Silent. B&W; 77m. **DIR:** Victor Fleming. **CAST:** Douglas Fairbanks Sr. **1919**

WHEN THE DARK MAN CALLS ★★1/2 This slightly suspenseful made-for-cable original is about a woman who is haunted by suppressed memories of the murder of her parents. Not rated; contains violence. 89m. **DIR:** Nathaniel Gutman. **CAST:** Joan Van Ark, Chris Sarandon, James Read, Geoffrey Lewis. **1995**

WHEN THE LEGENDS DIE ★★★1/2 A young Ute Indian is taken from his home in the Colorado Rockies after his parents die. In the modern white world he is taught the "new ways." His extraordinary riding abilities make him a target for exploitation as Red Dillon (Richard Widmark) trains him as a rodeo bronco rider, then proceeds to cash in on his protégé's success. A touching story that finds Widmark in one of his better roles and introduces a young Frederic Forrest. Rated PG for some mild profanity. 105m. **DIR:** Stuart Millar. **CAST:** Richard Widmark, Frederic Forrest. **1972**

WHEN THE PARTY'S OVER ★★★★ Twenty-somethings share a house and some life lessons in this comedy-drama. At the center is Rae Dawn Chong, a successful businesswoman with a disastrous personal life. Though there are several intriguing characters, Fisher Stevens is especially good as a charismatic performance artist. Engrossing, but a bit rough around the edges. Rated R for profanity and sexual situations. 114m. **DIR:** Matthew Irmas. **CAST:** Rae Dawn Chong, Fisher Stevens, Elizabeth Berridge, Sandra Bullock, Kris Kamm, Brian McNamara. **1993**

WHEN THE SCREAMING STOPS ★★★ A woman who lives under the Rhine must turn into a monster and eat people's hearts to remain the ruler of a magnificent underwater kingdom. Cheap monster effects and amateur gore do not detract from the wild story. Rated R for violence and nudity. 86m. **DIR:** Amando de Ossorio. **CAST:** Tony Kendall, Helga Line. **1974**

WHEN THE TIME COMES ★★★ A 34 year old woman dying from cancer decides to take her own life, much to the dismay of her friends and family. Better-than-average made-for-TV suds, thanks to a strong performance by Bonnie Bedelia. 94m. **DIR:** John Erman. **CAST:** Bonnie Bedelia, Brad Davis, Terry O'Quinn, Karen Austin. **1987**

WHEN THE WHALES CAME ★★★1/2 Paul Scofield plays a deaf islander known as the birdman because of his fine carvings. Befriended by two village children, the three must save a beached whale that the villagers are hungrily eyeing. Rated PG. 100m. **DIR:** Clive Rees. **CAST:** Helen Mirren, Paul Scofield, David Suchet, Jeremy Kemp. **1989**

WHEN THE WIND BLOWS ★★★ Ironic full-length British cartoon that chronicles the preparations of a retired English couple for the coming nuclear holocaust. Their ignorance of the facts and innocent faith in the "powers that be" make this a touching and moving statement about the nuclear Armageddon. 80m. **DIR:** Jimmy T. Murakami. **1988**

WHEN THINGS WERE ROTTEN (TV SERIES) ★★★ This compilation of three episodes from the short-lived television series of the same name is sure to please fans of *Blazing Saddles*–style humor. Dick Gautier's nearly serious portrayal of Robin Hood is a perfect foil for the slapstick antics of the rest of the cast. 78m. **DIR:** Coby Ruskin, Marty Feldman, Peter Bonerz. **CAST:** Dick Gautier, Dick Van Patten, Bernie Kopell, Richard Dimitri, Henry Polic, II, Misty Rowe, David Sabin. **1975**

WHEN TIME EXPIRES ★★★ Engaging if somewhat convoluted sci-fi tale about a man from the future who must intervene in the past in order to prevent an impending nuclear war. Rated R for violence and sensuality. 93m. **DIR:** David Bourla. **CAST:** Richard Grieco, Cynthia Geary, Mark Hamill, Tim Thomerson, Chad Everett. **1997**

WHEN TIME RAN OUT! 🦃 Time never seems to run out as we wait and wait for a volcano to erupt and put the all-star cast out of its misery. Rated PG. 121m. **DIR:** James Goldstone. **CAST:** Paul Newman, Jacqueline Bisset, William Holden, James Franciscus, Edward Albert, Red Buttons, Ernest Borgnine, Burgess Meredith, Valentina Cortese, Alex Karras, Barbara Carrera. **1980**

WHEN TRUMPETS FADE ★★★★ *Saving Private Ryan* got all the attention during the summer of 1998, but this more intimate WWII drama—originally cablecast on HBO—is nearly as compelling. It concerns the little-known Battle of the Hurtgen Forest, and demonstrated a level of Allied stupidity perhaps matched only by the events depicted in *Gallipoli*. A grunt is the sole survivor when his squad is decimated by Germans; whether this results from luck or cowardice is very much the point, as he keeps climbing in rank after his superiors are killed. A searing indictment of war's senseless brutality. Rated R for violence, gore, profanity, and nudity. 92m. **DIR:** John Irvin. **CAST:** Ron Eldard, Frank Whaley, Zak Orth, Dylan Bruno, Martin Donovan, Timothy Olyphant, Dan Futterman, Dwight Yoakam. **1998 DVD**

WHEN WE WERE KINGS ★★★1/2 Muhammad Ali and George Foreman's Rumble in the Jungle, the 1974 heavyweight championship fight that spotlighted Zaire, is revisited in this provocative documentary. A melting pot of history, sports drama, music, and culture. Rated PG. 87m. **DIR:** Leon Gast. **1996 DVD**

WHEN WOLVES CRY 🦃 A 10 year old boy is diagnosed as being terminally ill. Originally titled *The Christmas Tree*. Rated G. 108m. **DIR:** Terence Young. **CAST:** William Holden, Virna Lisi, Brook Fuller, Bourvil. **1983**

WHEN WOMEN HAD TAILS ★★ Italian comedy about five cavemen discovering the delightful difference of the sexes when pretty Senta Berger suddenly appears in their midst. Despite plenty of potential, this farce falls flat. Rated R for language and nudity. 99m. **DIR:** Pasquale Festa Campanile. **CAST:** Senta Berger, Frank Wolff, Giuliano Gemma, Lando Buzzanca. **1970**

WHEN WOMEN LOST THEIR TAILS ★★1/2 Most of the cast of *When Women Had Tails* returns in a much more sophisticated sex comedy set in prehistoric times. This slapstick sequel takes a broader view, poking fun at the earliest manifestations of civilization. The Stone Age jabs are still silly, but many of the observations are surprisingly enlightening. Rated R. 94m. **DIR:** Pasquale

Festa Campanile. **CAST:** Senta Berger, Frank Wolff, Lando Buzzanca, Francesco Mule. **1971**

WHEN WORLDS COLLIDE ★★ Interesting end-of-the-world sci-fi fable from George Pal has dated badly since its original release in 1951. Final scene of Earth pilgrims landing on the planet and walking into an obvious superimposed painting is laughable today, but many of the other Oscar-winning effects are still quite convincing. 81m. **DIR:** Rudolph Maté. **CAST:** Richard Derr, Barbara Rush, Peter Hanson, Larry Keating, John Hoyt. **1951 DVD**

WHEN YOUR LOVER LEAVES Valerie Perrine plays the other woman who's just lost out to her lover's wife. Hideous TV movie. 96m. **DIR:** Jeff Bleckner. **CAST:** Valerie Perrine, Betty Thomas, David Ackroyd, Ed O'Neill, Dwight Schultz. **1983**

WHEN'S YOUR BIRTHDAY? ★★★ Joe E. Brown stars as a student of astrology who doubles as a boxer. The stars tell him when he'll win in the ring. Unfortunately, a gangster gets wind of his abilities and tries to turn them to his own ends. It's all a showcase for Brown, though Edgar Kennedy steals his scenes with his hilarious slow burn. B&W; 76m. **DIR:** Harry Beaumont. **CAST:** Joe E. Brown, Marian Marsh, Edgar Kennedy, Margaret Hamilton. **1937**

WHERE ANGELS FEAR TO TREAD ★★★ Adapted from E. M. Forster's less mature first novel, British director Charles Sturridge fails to find the central core of the story and weave the comic and tragic elements into a seamless whole. However, this story of English arrogance and class attitude in Italy offers well-crafted performances. Not rated. 112m. **DIR:** Charles Sturridge. **CAST:** Helena Bonham Carter, Judy Davis, Helen Mirren, Rupert Graves. **1991**

WHERE ARE THE CHILDREN? ★★★ On the ninth anniversary of the murder of her previous children, a mother's children from her new marriage disappear. Jill Clayburgh is very good as the mother attempting to piece together the reason for this second occurrence. This film has a crackerjack surprise ending. Rated R. 97m. **DIR:** Bruce Malmuth. **CAST:** Jill Clayburgh, Max Gail, Clifton James, Elizabeth Wilson, Barnard Hughes, Frederic Forrest. **1988**

WHERE EAGLES DARE ★★★ Clint Eastwood and Richard Burton portray Allied commandos in this World War II adventure film which is short on realism. Instead we have farfetched but exciting shoot-outs, explosions, and mass slaughter. Our heroes must break out an American general being held captive in a heavily fortified German castle. 158m. **DIR:** Brian G. Hutton. **CAST:** Richard Burton, Clint Eastwood, Mary Ure, Michael Hordern, Patrick Wymark, Anton Diffring, Robert Beatty, Donald Houston, Ingrid Pitt. **1969**

WHERE EAST IS EAST ★★★ Despite the presence of director Tod Browning and silent star Lon Chaney, this isn't a horror movie. It's an Oriental revenge melodrama, set in Indochina. Full of kinky sexual peccadilloes that would have had a rough time getting by the censors had it been made a decade later. B&W; 68m. **DIR:** Tod Browning. **CAST:** Lon Chaney Sr., Lupe Velez, Lloyd Hughes. **1925**

WHERE EVIL LIES A strip club turns out to be the headquarters of a white-slavery ring in this lurid women-in-jeopardy opus. Not rated; contains adult situations and violence. 83m. **DIR:** Kevin Alber. **CAST:** Nikki Fritz, Emile Levisetti, Melissa Park, Mark Kinsey Stephenson, Roma Court. **1995**

WHERE LOVE HAS GONE ★★ Hilariously anachronistic throwback to late-1940s "women's picture" histrionics, but the sleaze and vulgarity are vintage 1960s, as Joey Heatherton murders the lover of her mother, Susan Hayward. Adapted from Harold Robbins's novel, which echoed the Lana Turner–Johnny Stompanato killing, and anything else he could think of. Low camp. 114m. **DIR:** Edward Dmytryk. **CAST:** Bette Davis, Susan Hayward, Joey Heatherton, Michael Connors, Jane Greer. **1964**

WHERE SLEEPING DOGS LIE ★★★ Investigating a brutal murder, writer Dylan McDermott moves into the house where it took place. He gets more than he bargained for when a mysterious stranger, chillingly played by Tom Sizemore, arrives, offering information that only the killer could know. Respectful attempt at *film noir* costars Sharon Stone as McDermott's sultry editor. Rated R for violence, language, and adult situations. 92m. **DIR:** Charles Finch. **CAST:** Dylan McDermott, Tom Sizemore, Sharon Stone. **1991**

WHERE THE BOYS ARE ★★★ Connie Francis warbled the title tune and made her movie debut in this frothy, mildly entertaining film about teenagers doing what's natural during Easter vacation in Fort Lauderdale. It's miles ahead of the idiotic remake. 99m. **DIR:** Henry Levin. **CAST:** Dolores Hart, George Hamilton, Yvette Mimieux, Jim Hutton, Barbara Nichols, Connie Francis. **1960**

WHERE THE BOYS ARE '84 Poor remake. Rated R. 96m. **DIR:** Hy Averback. **CAST:** Lisa Hartman, Russell Todd, Lorna Luft, Lynn-Holly Johnson, Wendy Schaal, Howard McGillin, Louise Sorel. **1984**

WHERE THE BUFFALO ROAM Horrendous film about the exploits of gonzo journalist Hunter S. Thompson. Rated R. 96m. **DIR:** Art Linson. **CAST:** Bill Murray, Peter Boyle, Bruno Kirby, René Auberjonois, R. G. Armstrong, Rafael Campos, Leonard Frey. **1980 DVD**

WHERE THE DAY TAKES YOU ★★ This film switches between recorded interviews with a parolee and his life on the streets of Los Angeles. The viewer comes away feeling nothing for the characters in the film. Rated R for violence, profanity, and suggested sex. 107m. **DIR:** Marc Rocco. **CAST:** Sean Astin, Lara Flynn Boyle, Dermot Mulroney, Peter Dobson, Balthazar Getty, Kyle MacLachlan, Adam Baldwin, Nancy McKeon, Alyssa Milano, Leo Rossi, Rachel Ticotin, Laura San Giacomo, Christian Slater. **1992**

WHERE THE GREEN ANTS DREAM ★★★★ Another stark, yet captivating vision from perhaps the most popular director of modern German cinema. The film, set in Australia, is basically an ecological tug of war between progress and tradition, namely uranium mining interests against aborigines and their practices. Rated R. 100m. **DIR:** Werner Herzog. **CAST:** Bruce Spence, Ray Barrett, Norman Kaye. **1984**

WHERE THE HEART IS (1990) Mindless drivel about a successful demolition expert's fall from wealth. Rated R for profanity and adult situations. 111m. **DIR:** John Boorman. **CAST:** Dabney Coleman, Joanna Cassidy, Uma Thurman, Christopher Plummer. **1990**

WHERE THE HEART IS (2000) ★★1/2 For a while, this film overcomes its melodramatic trappings and becomes an engaging if unlikely account of a young woman, seventeen and pregnant, who is abandoned by her boyfriend at an Oklahoma Wal-Mart; once her baby is born, she befriends a series of colorful and eccentric characters who become the surrogate family she never had. Unfortunately, contrivance and heavy dollops of bathos eventually turn this adaptation of Billie Letts's novel into soap-opera swill. Rated PG-13 for profanity, sexual candor, and dramatic intensity. 120m. **DIR:** Matt Williams. **CAST:** Natalie Portman, Ashley Judd, Stockard Channing, Joan Cusack, James Frain, Dylan Bruno, Keith David. **2000 DVD**

WHERE THE LILIES BLOOM ★★★1/2 Heartwarming melodrama about four orphaned children in rural America who pretend their father is still alive in order to keep the authorities from separating them. The settings are beautiful, and the actors are all fine, especially Harry Dean Stanton. Background score by bluegrass legend Earl Scruggs. Rated G. 96m. **DIR:** William A. Graham. **CAST:** Julie Gholson, Jan Smithers, Harry Dean Stanton, Sudie Bond. **1974**

WHERE THE MONEY IS ★★★ For all its charm, this mildly comic heist film is an oddly unsatisfying experience, as if we've just watched a picture that was heavily truncated for television broadcast. The setup is clever, with Paul Newman as a career bank robber who feigns a stroke to get into a lesser-security nursing home; attendant Linda Fiorentino, smelling a rat, penetrates the façade and then announces that the price for her silence is involvement in a new caper. The subsequent character dynamics are intriguing, but the film fades away instead of delivering a proper third act. Rated PG-13 for brief nudity, brief violence, and sexual candor. 89m. **DIR:** Marek Kanievska. **CAST:** Paul Newman, Linda Fiorentino, Dermot Mulroney. **2000 DVD**

WHERE THE RED FERN GROWS ★★★★ Fine family fare about a boy's love for two hunting dogs and his coming of age in Oklahoma in the 1930s. Rated G. 90m. **DIR:** Norman Tokar. **CAST:** James Whitmore, Beverly Garland, Jack Ging, Lonny Chapman, Stewart Peterson. **1974 DVD**

WHERE THE RIVER RUNS BLACK ★★★1/2 A primitive child is snatched from his home in the Amazon rain forest and brought into the modern world of corruption and violence. Sumptuous images, courtesy of Juan Ruiz-Anchia's superb cinematography, fill the screen as its eerie, fanciful, and finally suspenseful tale is told. Rated PG for violence and suggested sex. 105m. **DIR:** Christopher Cain. **CAST:** Charles Durning, Peter Horton, Ajay Naidu, Conchata Ferrell. **1986**

WHERE THE RIVERS FLOW NORTH ★★★ Despite generous offers and promises, a stubborn timber man refuses to sell his land so that a new dam can be built. This circa-1920s drama boasts excellent performances and scenery as well as a usually engrossing storyline. Rated PG-13. 105m. **DIR:** Jay Craven. **CAST:** Rip Torn, Tantoo Cardinal, Bill Raymond, Michael J. Fox, John Griesemer, Mark Margolis. **1993 DVD**

WHERE THE SPIRIT LIVES ★★★ Stirring reenactment of Indian children in Canada being kidnapped and forced to live in terrifying residential schools in which physical, emotional, and sexual abuse were the order of the day. Michelle St. John stars as a defiant newcomer who decides that the only way to survive is to escape. Rated PG. 97m. **DIR:** Bruce Pittman. **CAST:** Michelle St. John, Anne-Marie Macdonald. **1989**

WHERE TRAILS END ★★1/2 World War II is in full swing. Aided by his wonder horse Prince, U.S. Marshal Tom Keene, in glaring white from hat to boots, protects ranchers from ruthless outlaws working for Nazis. B&W; 58m. **DIR:** Robert Emmett Tansey. **CAST:** Tom Keene, Joan Curtis, Charles King. **1942**

WHERE WERE YOU WHEN THE LIGHTS WENT OUT? 🦃 Bad attempt at farce and sexual mix-ups and misunderstandings. Backfires all the way. Rated PG. 94m. **DIR:** Hy Averback. **CAST:** Doris Day, Robert Morse, Terry-Thomas, Patrick O'Neal, Lola Albright, Steve Allen, Jim Backus, Ben Blue, Pat Paulsen. **1968**

WHERE'S PICCONE? ★★★★ Highly entertaining comedy starring Giancarlo Giannini as a small-time hustler searching for a respectable Italian businessman who inexplicably vanished in an ambulance on the way to the hospital. In Italian with English subtitles. Not rated; contains nudity, violence, and profanity. 110m. **DIR:** Nanni Loy. **CAST:** Giancarlo Giannini. **1984**

WHERE'S POPPA? ★★★★ One of George Segal's best comic performances is found in this cult favorite. Ruth Gordon co-stars as the senile mother whom Segal tries to scare into having a cardiac arrest. Director Carl Reiner's son, Rob, makes a short appearance as a fervent draft resister. Rated R. 82m. **DIR:** Carl Reiner. **CAST:** George Segal, Ruth Gordon, Trish Van Devere, Ron Leibman, Rae Allen, Vincent Gardenia, Barnard Hughes, Rob Reiner, Garrett Morris. **1970**

WHERE'S THE MONEY, NOREEN? ★★1/2 Just when you think this made-for-cable original might get interesting, it doesn't. Julianne Phillips portrays a recently paroled convict looking for the man who set her up. Rated PG-13 for violence and suggested sex. 93m. **DIR:** Artie Mandelberg. **CAST:** Julianne Phillips, A Martinez, Nigel Bennett, Nancy Warren. **1995**

WHICH WAY HOME ★★1/2 In 1979, a Red Cross nurse flees to Thailand and Australia with a small group of Cambodian and Vietnamese orphans. Often implausible, overlong cable-TV production. 141m. **DIR:** Carl Schultz. **CAST:** Cybill Shepherd, John Waters. **1991**

WHICH WAY IS UP? ★★★★ This irreverent, ribald farce reunites the talented comedy team of director Michael Shultz and star Richard Pryor (*Greased Lightning*) for one of the funnier movies of the 1970s. Pryor plays three major roles. His ability to create totally separate and distinctive characters contributes greatly to the success of this oft-tried but rarely believable gimmick. Rated R. 94m. **DIR:** Michael Schultz. **CAST:** Richard Pryor, Lonette McKee, Margaret Avery, Dolph Sweet, Morgan Woodward. **1977**

WHICH WAY TO THE FRONT? 🦃 Jerry Lewis directs and stars in this pathetic story about a rich 4-F American who enlists other such unfortunates into a military unit to combat Nazi Germany. Rated G. 96m. **DIR:** Jerry Lewis. **CAST:** Jerry Lewis, John Wood, Jan Murray, Kaye Ballard, Robert Middleton, Paul Winchell, Gary Crosby. **1970**

WHIFFS 🦃 Army private is a human guinea pig suffering annoying side effects from biological and chemical-weapons testing. Not rated. 92m. **DIR:** Ted Post. **CAST:**

Elliott Gould, Eddie Albert, Jennifer O'Neill, Harry Guardino. **1975**

WHILE THE CITY SLEEPS ★★1/2 An impressive cast and the talents of director Fritz Lang can't transform this standard newspaper-crime story into a great film. Rival newspaper executives compete with each other and the police in an effort to come up with the identity of a mad killer. Convoluted gabfest quickly bogs down. B&W; 100m. **DIR:** Fritz Lang. **CAST:** Dana Andrews, Ida Lupino, Rhonda Fleming, George Sanders, Vincent Price, John Drew Barrymore, Thomas Mitchell, Howard Duff, Mae Marsh. **1956**

WHILE YOU WERE SLEEPING ★★★★1/2 A series of misunderstandings leaves a coma victim's family believing a Good Samaritan to be his fiancée, only she's falling for someone else. The plot may be predictable, but this extremely entertaining romance owes all to Sandra Bullock's subtle, heartfelt performance. Rated PG for mild profanity. 100m. **DIR:** Jon Turteltaub. **CAST:** Sandra Bullock, Bill Pullman, Peter Gallagher, Peter Boyle, Glynis Johns, Jack Warden, Micole Mercurio, Michael Rispoli. **1995 DVD**

WHIPPED Amanda Peet degrades herself by stooping to the level of three misogynistic babe hounds in this thoroughly reprehensible mainstream romantic comedy that plays more like filmed segments from the *Penthouse* letters pages. Utter trash. Rated R for profanity, nudity, strong sexual content, and coarse behavior. 82m. **DIR:** Peter M. Cohen. **CAST:** Amanda Peet, Brian Van Holt, Judah Domke, Zorie Barber, Jonathan Abrahams. **1999 DVD**

WHISKERS ★★★1/2 Winsome family fun ensues as a 10-year-old boy turns to an Egyptian cat goddess for help when his parents want to get rid of his furry friend Whiskers. The cat is turned into a 30 year old man who helps teach young Jed some important lesssons about life. This tale of friendship and fun stars an enjoyable Brent Carver as the feline-turned-man. Made for cable. Rated G. 94m. **DIR:** James Kaufman. **CAST:** Brent Carver, Michael Caloz. **1996**

WHISPER KILLS, A Weak made-for-TV slasher film about a killer who warns the potential victim by phone before the inevitable murder. 96m. **DIR:** Christian I. Nyby, II. **CAST:** Loni Anderson, Joe Penny, June Lockhart. **1988 DVD**

WHISPERING, THE An insurance investigator learns that a demon is responsible for a recent series of suicides. Rated R for adult situations, language, and violence. 88m. **DIR:** Gregory Gieras. **CAST:** Cedrick Terrell, Mette Holt, Scott Johnson, Leslie Danon. **1996**

WHISPERS ★★ A woman is repeatedly attacked by a man with the perfect alibi, prompting the police to disbelieve her. Mediocre. Rated R for violence and nudity. 96m. **DIR:** Douglas Jackson. **CAST:** Victoria Tennant, Jean Leclerc, Chris Sarandon. **1990**

WHISPERS IN THE DARK ★★ Psychiatrist Annabella Sciorra finds herself drawn into a murder investigation, during which she enlists the aid of mentors Jill Clayburgh and Alan Alda. Over-the-top, campy, contrived suspense. Rated R for violence and profanity. 112m. **DIR:** Christopher Crowe. **CAST:** Annabella Sciorra, Jamey Sheridan, Anthony LaPaglia, Jill Clayburgh, Alan Alda, John Leguizamo, Deborah Unger. **1992**

WHISTLE BLOWER, THE ★★★★ Taut suspense-thriller from England combines the elements of a murder mystery with real-life human drama. Michael Caine, in one of his finest performances, stars as a stoic British subject whose tidy life is disrupted when his son (Nigel Havers) discovers what he believes are immoral acts on the part of the government. Rated PG for suspense. 100m. **DIR:** Simon Langton. **CAST:** Michael Caine, Nigel Havers, James Fox, Felicity Dean, John Gielgud, Kenneth Colley, Gordon Jackson, Barry Foster. **1987**

WHISTLE DOWN THE WIND ★★★1/2 Bryan Forbes's first film is a thoughtful, allegorical tale about three children who encounter an accused murderer hiding in a barn and take him to be a Christ figure fleeing from his persecutors. Based on Mary Hayley Bell's popular novel, this is one of the best films ever made dealing with the fragile nature of childhood trust and beliefs. B&W; 99m. **DIR:** Bryan Forbes. **CAST:** Hayley Mills, Alan Bates, Bernard Lee, Norman Bird, Elsie Wagstaff. **1961**

WHISTLE STOP Small-town girl returns from the big city. Tripe. B&W; 85m. **DIR:** Leonide Moguy. **CAST:** George Raft, Ava Gardner, Tom Conway, Victor McLaglen, Charles Drake, Jimmy Conlin. **1946**

WHISTLING IN BROOKLYN ★★★ Red Skelton returns as the radio sleuth, The Fox, this time pursued by the police from one Brooklyn landmark to another, and ending up at Ebbets Field pitching against the Dodgers. More slapstick than usual. B&W; 87m. **DIR:** S. Sylvan Simon. **CAST:** Red Skelton, Ann Rutherford, Rags Ragland, Jean Rogers, Ray Collins, Henry O'Neill, William Frawley, Sam Levene. **1943**

WHISTLING IN DIXIE ★★★1/2 Red Skelton's second outing as the radio detective, The Fox, plunges him and his bride into mysterious doings at an old southern mansion. Some good chills mixed in with lots of laughs. B&W; 74m. **DIR:** S. Sylvan Simon. **CAST:** Red Skelton, Ann Rutherford, George Bancroft, Guy Kibbee. **1942**

WHISTLING IN THE DARK ★★★1/2 Red Skelton is a radio criminologist, The Fox, noted for devising and solving ingenious crimes. He's pursued and kidnapped by Conrad Veidt, who wants him to construct a perfect murder. Lots of laughs in Skelton's first starring role, aided and abetted by the hilariously sinister Veidt. B&W; 77m. **DIR:** S. Sylvan Simon. **CAST:** Red Skelton, Conrad Veidt, Ann Rutherford, Virginia Grey, Rags Ragland, Eve Arden, Henry O'Neill, Reed Hadley. **1941**

WHITE ★★1/2 The second part of director Krzysztof Kieslowski's *Three Colors* trilogy. This one takes a hapless Pole from rags to riches, as he rebuilds his life after being dumped by his French wife. Interesting, but the progress of the story isn't always clear, and the ending is confusing and unsatisfying. In Polish and French with English subtitles. Rated R for simulated sex. 92m. **DIR:** Krzysztof Kieslowski. **CAST:** Zbigniew Zamachowski, Julie Delpy. **1994**

WHITE BALLOON, THE ★★★1/2 This Iranian import is short on plot—a little girl keeps losing her money on the way to market to buy a goldfish—but long on charm and sweet, gentle comedy. Given the simplicity of the story, it's also surprisingly suspenseful. Seven-year-old Aida Mohammadkhani gives an amazingly natural performance, by turns adorable and exasperating—just like a real little girl. In Farsi with English subtitles. Not rated; suitable for general audiences. 85m. **DIR:** Jafar

Panahi. **CAST:** Aida Mohammadkhani, Mohsen Kalifi, Fereshteh Sadr Orfani. **1995**

WHITE BUFFALO 🦃 All-star cast wallows in weird *Jaws*-inspired Western, which has Wild Bill Hickok (Charles Bronson) on the trail of a mythical beast. Myth thith one. Rated R for violence. 97m. **DIR:** J. Lee Thompson. **CAST:** Charles Bronson, Kim Novak, Clint Walker, Jack Warden, Will Sampson, Stuart Whitman, Slim Pickens, John Carradine. **1977**

WHITE CARGO ★★1/2 Hedy Lamarr is Tondelayo, a sultry African native girl who sets about seducing a group of British plantation managers. Considered daring when released, the movie is pretty corny today. Lamarr has never been lovelier, reason enough to give this one a look. B&W; 90m. **DIR:** Richard Thorpe. **CAST:** Hedy Lamarr, Walter Pidgeon, Frank Morgan, Richard Carlson, Reginald Owen, Henry O'Neill. **1942**

WHITE CHRISTMAS ★★★ This attempt to capitalize on the title tune is an inferior remake of 1942's *Holiday Inn* (in which the song "White Christmas" first appeared). It's another in that long line of let's-put-on-a-show stories, with the last several reels showcasing the singing, dancing, and mugging talents of the cast. 120m. **DIR:** Michael Curtiz. **CAST:** Bing Crosby, Danny Kaye, Vera-Ellen, Rosemary Clooney. **1954**

WHITE CLIFFS OF DOVER, THE ★★★★ Taking advantage of the patriotic pro-British sentiment of World War II, MGM successfully crafted an all-star, big-budget tearjerker very similar in content and texture to their popular *Mrs. Miniver*. The movie follows Irene Dunne as an American woman who marries into English aristocracy. She and her family are forced to endure the hardships of two world wars. B&W; 126m. **DIR:** Clarence Brown. **CAST:** Irene Dunne, Alan Marshal, Roddy McDowall, Frank Morgan, C. Aubrey Smith, May Whitty, Van Johnson. **1943**

WHITE COMANCHE ★★ Twin sons of an Indian mother and a white settler fight amongst themselves. One, Notah, leads a band of renegade Comanches while the other, Johnny Moon, lives among the whites. William Shatner plays dual roles and is aided by Joseph Cotten as the sheriff. Not rated; contains violence. 90m. **DIR:** Gilbert Kay. **CAST:** William Shatner, Joseph Cotten, Rossana Yani, Perla Cristal. **1967 DVD**

WHITE DAWN, THE ★★★★ This is a gripping and thought-provoking adventure film. Three whalers (Warren Oates, Lou Gossett Jr., and Timothy Bottoms) get lost in the Arctic and are rescued by Eskimos, whom they end up exploiting. Rated PG. 109m. **DIR:** Phil Kaufman. **CAST:** Warren Oates, Louis Gossett Jr., Timothy Bottoms. **1974**

WHITE DOG ★★★ In this adaptation of the Romain Gary novel, Kristy McNichol finds a dog and decides to keep it—unaware that it has been trained by white supremacists to attack black people. An intriguing premise, although not entirely successful in the telling. Rated R for profanity and violence. 89m. **DIR:** Samuel Fuller. **CAST:** Kristy McNichol, Paul Winfield, Burl Ives, Jameson Parker, Lynne Moody, Marshall Thompson, Paul Bartel, Dick Miller, Parley Baer. **1982**

WHITE DWARF ★★1/2 Almost-good futristic fantasy was a TV-pilot film for a proposed series. Circa A.D. 3040 a young doctor is stationed on a planet in the White Dwarf star system and he soon discovers the violent division between the light and dark sides of his new world. The problem with this film is its uneven pacing: bursts of action followed by long boring segments and an unsatisfactory ending. The plus is the decent special-effects work. Not rated; contains violence and gore. 91m. **DIR:** Peter Markle. **CAST:** Paul Winfield, Neal McDonough, C.C.H. Pounder, Ele Keats. **1995**

WHITE FANG ★★★★ A young man travels to Alaska in search of his father's lost gold mine and meets up with an old miner, an evil dogfight promoter, and a wolf. A wonderful Disney adventure film. Rated PG for violence. 104m. **DIR:** Randal Kleiser. **CAST:** Klaus Maria Brandauer, Ethan Hawke, Seymour Cassel, James Remar, Susan Hogan. **1991 DVD**

WHITE FANG AND THE HUNTER ★★ A dog, White Fang, and his master, Daniel (Robert Wood), are attacked by wolves. They are taken in by a young widow who is being forced to marry. So Daniel and the dog come to her aid. Poor acting and directing hamper this familiar story. Rated G. 87m. **DIR:** Alfonso Brescia. **CAST:** Robert Wood, Pedro Sanchez. **1985**

WHITE FANG 2: MYTH OF THE WHITE WOLF ★★1/2 This disappointing sequel banishes former star Ethan Hawke to cameo status and replaces him with overly wholesome Scott Bairstow. The insufferably politically correct story finds our hero and his loyal pooch battling greedy miners and helping Alaskan Native Americans. The stupid story line will annoy adults, and kids will be put off by the film's length and lack of action. Rated PG for mild violence. 105m. **DIR:** Ken Olin. **CAST:** Scott Bairstow, Charmaine Craig, Al Harrington, Alfred Molina, Geoffrey Lewis, Ethan Hawke. **1994 DVD**

WHITE GHOST 🦃 William Katt does an embarrassing Rambo imitation in this miserable rip-off. Rated R for violence and profanity. 93m. **DIR:** B. J. Davis. **CAST:** William Katt, Rosalind Chao, Martin Hewitt, Wayne Crawford, Reb Brown. **1988**

WHITE GOLD ★★★★ Remarkable drama about a woman condemned to a boring life on a sheep ranch. She is caught between a resentful father-in-law and a timid husband; and when she commits murder to fend off a would-be rapist, everyone can only believe the worst of her. Silent. B&W; 70m. **DIR:** William K. Howard. **CAST:** Jetta Goudal, Kenneth Thompson, George Bancroft. **1927**

WHITE HEAT ★★★★1/2 James Cagney gives one of his greatest screen performances as a totally insane mama's boy and gangster, Cody Jarrett. Margaret Wycherly is chillingly effective as the evil mom, and Virginia Mayo is uncommonly outstanding as the bad man's moll. But it is Cagney's picture pure and simple as he ironically makes it to "the top of the world, Ma!" B&W; 114m. **DIR:** Raoul Walsh. **CAST:** James Cagney, Margaret Wycherly, Virginia Mayo, Edmond O'Brien, Steve Cochran. **1949**

WHITE HOT ★★1/2 A quick-paced drama about a yuppie couple's fall from grace. Robby Benson (in his directorial debut) and Tawny Kitaen take over a drug lord's trade and become hopelessly immersed in the high life. Rated R for violence and drug use. 95m. **DIR:** Robby Benson. **CAST:** Robby Benson, Tawny Kitaen, Danny Aiello. **1989**

WHITE HOT: THE MYSTERIOUS MURDER OF THELMA TODD ★★ Melodramatic staging and dialogue mar what could have been compelling in this made-for-TV speculation on the death of Thirties starlet Thelma Todd. Loni Anderson is ever so glamorous in the title role of the siren who captivated men even after her death. 90m. **DIR:** Paul Wendkos. **CAST:** Loni Anderson, Robert Davi, Scott Paulin, Robin Strasser, Paul Dooley. **1991**

WHITE HUNTER, BLACK HEART ★★★★ Director-star Clint Eastwood boldly impersonates flamboyant director John Huston (renamed John Wilson) in Peter Vietel's fictionalized account of the filming of *The African Queen*—during which Huston/Wilson is more interested in shooting an elephant than shooting his movie. Fascinating. Rated PG for profanity and violence. 112m. **DIR:** Clint Eastwood. **CAST:** Clint Eastwood, Jeff Fahey, George Dzundza, Marisa Berenson. **1990**

WHITE LEGION ★★ The White Legion were doctors who fought to find a cure for the yellow fever that plagued workers building the Panama Canal. Unfortunately, their story doesn't make for much of a movie; it's artificially padded with melodramatic situations. B&W; 81m. **DIR:** Karl Brown. **CAST:** Ian Keith, Tala Birell, Snub Pollard. **1936**

WHITE LIE ★★★★ Samuel Charters's *Louisiana Black* gets first-cabin treatment from director Bill Condon and scripter Nevin Schreiner, who send New York mayoral press adviser Gregory Hines to the Deep South to investigate the events that led to his father's lynching thirty years earlier. Hines finds sympathetic pediatrician Annette O'Toole . . . who may have her own reasons for getting involved. Made for cable, with highly unsettling images and attitudes. Rated PG-13 for mild profanity and mild violence. 93m. **DIR:** Bill Condon. **CAST:** Gregory Hines, Annette O'Toole, Bill Nunn, Gregg Henry. **1991**

WHITE LIGHT ★★1/2 When cop Martin Kove bites the bullet, he meets the woman of his dreams on the other side. Weird fantasy directed by Kove's *Cagney and Lacey* costar, Al Waxman. Rated R for profanity and violence. 96m. **DIR:** Al Waxman. **CAST:** Martin Kove, Martha Henry. **1990**

WHITE LIGHTNING ★★ Good old boy Burt Reynolds as a speed-loving moonshiner fights the inevitable mean and inept cops and revenue agents in this comic-book chase and retribution film. A good cast of character actors makes this stock drive-in movie entertaining, although it is just like the majority of Burt Reynolds's car films—gimmicky and predictable. Rated PG. 101m. **DIR:** Joseph Sargent. **CAST:** Burt Reynolds, Jennifer Billingsley, Ned Beatty, Bo Hopkins, Matt Clark, Louise Latham, Diane Ladd. **1973**

WHITE LINE FEVER ★★★ Jan-Michael Vincent plays an incorruptible young trucker in this film. He is angered when forced to smuggle goods in his truck. He fights back after he and his pregnant wife (Kay Lenz) are attacked. Rated PG. 92m. **DIR:** Jonathan Kaplan. **CAST:** Jan-Michael Vincent, Kay Lenz, Slim Pickens, L. Q. Jones, Leigh French, Don Porter. **1975**

WHITE MAMA ★★★ Aging widow Bette Davis, living on a shoestring in a condemned tenement, is befriended by a streetwise black youth (Ernest Harden) and becomes the mother he can't remember when she provides him with a home in return for protection. A good story, touchingly told. Made for TV. 105m. **DIR:** Jackie Cooper. **CAST:** Bette Davis, Ernest Harden, Eileen Heckart, Lurene Tuttle, Virginia Capers. **1980**

WHITE MAN'S BURDEN ★★1/2 In an alternate-world Los Angeles, a white underclass struggles in the squalid inner city while wealthy blacks live in secure, gated mansions. In this atmosphere, a frustrated, out-of-work John Travolta kidnaps rich Harry Belafonte to show him how the other half lives. Writer-director Desmond Nakano sets up that gimmicky premise, then does nothing with it; the film wanders aimlessly with only the performances of the two stars to hold our interest. Rated R for profanity and violence. 90m. **DIR:** Desmond Nakano. **CAST:** John Travolta, Harry Belafonte, Tom Bower, Margaret Avery, Kelly Lynch. **1995 DVD**

WHITE MEN CAN'T JUMP ★★★★ As with writer-director Ron Shelton's *Bull Durham*, this movie about a pair of hoop hustlers (Wesley Snipes, Woody Harrelson) is smart, sassy, sexy, and rich in characterization. Deceptively adept at basketball, Harrelson arrives in Venice, California, to hook up with local hotshot Snipes for a big score. The dialogue is lightning fast, and the performances are just as electric. Rated R for profanity, nudity, and brief violence. 115m. **DIR:** Ron Shelton. **CAST:** Wesley Snipes, Woody Harrelson, Rosie Perez, Tyra Ferrell. **1992**

WHITE MILE ★★★★ Rapacious executive Alan Alda bullies staff and clients into a disastrous white-water rafting expedition, and then attempts to evade personal responsibility for the inevitable tragedy. After years of playing amiable good guys, this film casts Alda in an entirely new light . . . and he's positively chilling. Rated R for profanity and dramatic intensity. 96m. **DIR:** Robert Butler. **CAST:** Alan Alda, Peter Gallagher, Bruce Altman, Robert Loggia, Fionnula Flanagan. **1994**

WHITE MISCHIEF ★★1/2 In the early Forties while Britain was being pounded to rubble by German bombs, a group of wealthy colonials carried on with alcohol, drugs, and spouse swapping in Kenya. A stunning backdrop—complete with giraffes roaming in the backyards of opulent mansions—is the film's greatest asset. But James Fox's script is flat. Rated R for language and explicit sex scenes. 100m. **DIR:** Michael Radford. **CAST:** Charles Dance, Sarah Miles, Greta Scacchi, John Hurt, Joss Ackland. **1987**

WHITE NIGHTS (1957) ★★★★ In this stylish melodrama, a shy young man encounters a mysterious girl whose lover has not returned from a journey across the sea. Based on a story by Dostoyevski. In Italian with English subtitles. B&W; 107m. **DIR:** Luchino Visconti. **CAST:** Marcello Mastroianni, Maria Schell, Jean Marais. **1957**

WHITE NIGHTS (1985) ★★★1/2 Russian defector and ballet star Mikhail Baryshnikov, finding himself back in the U.S.S.R., joins forces with American defector Gregory Hines to escape to freedom in this soap opera–styled thriller. The plot is contrived, but the dance sequences are spectacular. Rated PG-13 for violence and profanity. 135m. **DIR:** Taylor Hackford. **CAST:** Mikhail Baryshnikov, Gregory Hines, Geraldine Page, Jerzy Skolimowski, Isabella Rossellini. **1985**

WHITE OF THE EYE ★★1/2 Tense film deals with a serial killer on the loose in Arizona. David Keith plays a commercial-stereo whiz who becomes a suspect in a se-

ries of bizarre and brutal murders of affluent women. Director Donald Cammell avoids the usual slasher pitfalls, although this one is saddled with a truly abysmal finale. Rated R. 113m. **DIR:** Donald Cammell. **CAST:** David Keith, Cathy Moriarty, Art Evans. **1988**

WHITE PALACE ★★★ Twitchy, blank-eyed James Spader is a widowed yuppie who slowly falls for burger-slingin' country gal Susan Sarandon. It's one of those movies that is terrific in the early-to-middle scenes and just so-so in the conclusion. Rated R for nudity and profanity. 106m. **DIR:** Luis Mandoki. **CAST:** Susan Sarandon, James Spader, Jason Alexander, Kathy Bates, Eileen Brennan, Steven Hill, Renee Taylor. **1990 DVD**

WHITE PHANTOM ★★ A Ninja gang attempts to deliver a plutonium weapon to terrorists. Bo Svenson is out to break up the plan and blackmails a dancer into infiltrating the gang. Not rated, but with the usual genre violence. 89m. **DIR:** Dusty Nelson. **CAST:** Jay Roberts Jr., Page Leong, Bo Svenson. **1987**

WHITE PONGO (BLOND GORILLA) 🦃 Reverently referred to by fans of genre films as the worst of all crazed-gorilla–missing link jungle movies. B&W; 74m. **DIR:** Sam Newfield. **CAST:** Richard Fraser, Lionel Royce, Al Ebon, Gordon Richards. **1945**

•WHITE RIVER ★★ Sad waste of good talent starring Bob Hoskins and Antonio Banderas as two con men sweeping through Arkansas, pretending to be men of the cloth, on a mission to fleece the common folks. The two men don't have a prayer when they find themselves taken hostage by a young serial killer (Wes Bentley) and his white-trash waitress fiancée (Kim Dickens). Colorful, eccentric characters, including a blind prostitute (Ellen Barkin) and a singing sheriff (Randy Travis), fill the film, but it's not enough to salvage a lackluster script that wants to be more clever than it really is. Rated R for language and violence. 99m. **DIR:** Arne Glimcher. **CAST:** Bob Hoskins, Antonio Banderas, Ellen Barkin, Wes Bentley, Kim Dickens, Beau Bridges, Randy Travis. **1999 DVD**

WHITE ROSE, THE (1923) ★★★ Bessie Williams (Mae Marsh) is seduced and abandoned by an aristocratic Southerner (Ivor Novello). Sheer melodrama, although the production is salvaged by the soft-focus photography of Billy Bitzer and Hendrik Sartov. Not one of the major Griffith efforts, its appeal is limited to Griffith purists and silent-film specialists. Silent. B&W; 100m. **DIR:** D. W. Griffith. **CAST:** Mae Marsh, Carol Dempster, Ivor Novello. **1923**

WHITE ROSE, THE (1983) ★★★ Based on a true story about a group of youths in wartime Germany who revolted against Hitler by printing and distributing subversive leaflets to the public. All of the young actors are good, especially Lena Stolze, who plays the protagonist. In German. Not rated. 108m. **DIR:** Michael Verhoeven. **CAST:** Lena Stolze, Wulf Kessler, Martin Benrath. **1983**

WHITE SANDS ★★★1/2 Willem Dafoe is a small-town sheriff whose investigation of a murder leads him deep inside an FBI sting. Lots of plot twists and turns will keep viewers interested, although the middle of this film drags a bit. Rated R for violence, profanity, and nudity. 105m. **DIR:** Roger Donaldson. **CAST:** Willem Dafoe, Samuel L. Jackson, Mickey Rourke, Mary Elizabeth Mastrantonio, M. Emmet Walsh, Mimi Rogers. **1992 DVD**

WHITE SHADOWS IN THE SOUTH SEAS ★★1/2 Documentary director Robert Flaherty worked on this South Seas romance (ultimately without credit), which in certain ways is a more conventional dry run for his later *Tabu*. The location cinematography is this turgid soap opera's main strength. B&W; 88m. **DIR:** W. S. Van Dyke. **CAST:** Monte Blue, Raquel Torres. **1927**

WHITE SHEIK, THE ★★★ A warm salute to romantic movie heroes. When a recently wed couple go to Rome, the bride sneaks off to a movie set where her idol, the White Sheik, is making a film. Federico Fellini manages to create an original cinematic piece with great satirical precision. In Italian with English subtitles. B&W; 86m. **DIR:** Federico Fellini. **CAST:** Brunella Bovo, Leopoldo Trieste, Alberto Sordi, Giulietta Masina. **1952**

WHITE SISTER, THE ★★★ Cheated out of an inheritance, Italian aristocrat Lillian Gish falls in love with an army officer. When he is reported dead, she joins a convent, only to be faced with renouncing her vows when he returns. Only about half of the original film remains, but that's more than enough. Silent. B&W; 68m. **DIR:** Henry King. **CAST:** Lillian Gish, Ronald Colman, Charles Lane, Juliette la Violette. **1923**

WHITE SQUALL ★★★ This oceanbound *Dead Poets Society*, set in the early 1960s, concerns a group of young men who forgo their senior year at a conventional high school in favor of a season in the Ocean Academy: crewing and studying on a square-rigged brigantine sailing the oceans. The titular disaster is suspensefully staged, but the film remains oddly uninvolving. Rated PG-13 for violence, profanity, and brief nudity. 127m. **DIR:** Ridley Scott. **CAST:** Jeff Bridges, Caroline Goodall, John Savage, Scott Wolf, Jeremy Sisto, Ryan Philippe, David Lascher. **1996 DVD**

WHITE TIGER ★★★ Brother and sister separated since childhood are reunited fifteen years later as thieves. Teaming up with the man responsible for their father's death, the three steal a fortune in jewels and hide out in a remote cabin where secrets long hidden are revealed. B&W; 81m. **DIR:** Tod Browning. **CAST:** Priscilla Dean, Raymond Griffith, Wallace Beery, Matt Moore. **1923**

WHITE TOWER, THE ★★1/2 Symbolic melodrama of a weird group of people who attempt the ascension of an Alpine mountain. The action scenes are good, but the actors seem to walk through their parts. 98m. **DIR:** Ted Tetzlaff. **CAST:** Glenn Ford, Claude Rains, Alida Valli, Oscar Homolka, Cedric Hardwicke, Lloyd Bridges. **1950**

WHITE WATER SUMMER ★★★ Kevin Bacon plays a ruthless wilderness guide who intends to transform four boys into men. Sean Astin is the boy most abused by Bacon and he must decide what to do when Bacon is seriously injured. Interesting coming-of-age adventure. Rated PG for profanity. 87m. **DIR:** Jeff Bleckner. **CAST:** Kevin Bacon, Sean Astin, Jonathan Ward, Matt Adler. **1987 DVD**

WHITE WOLVES: A CRY IN THE WILD II ★★1/2 During a camping trip a teacher falls over a cliff and his students must find and save him. Very predictable film about teenagers learning to understand and like each other. The young cast needs acting lessons. Rated PG. 74m. **DIR:** Catherine Cyran. **CAST:** Ami Dolenz, Mark

Paul Gosselaar, David Moscow, Amy O'Neill, Marc Riffon, Matt McCoy. **1993 DVD**

•WHITE WOLVES II: LEGEND OF THE WILD ★★1/2 The theme of young people struggling to survive in an Arctic wilderness is all this film has in common with other *White Wolves* entries. Bland but inoffensive family entertainment. Rated PG. 85m. **DIR:** Terence H. Winkless. **CAST:** Jeremy London, Elizabeth Berkley, Lucky Hayes, Corin Nemec. **1995 DVD**

WHITE ZOMBIE ★★★★ This eerie little thriller is the consummate zombie film, with hordes of the walking dead doing the bidding of evil Bela Lugosi as their overseer and master. A damsel-in-distress story with a new twist, this independently produced gem features sets and production standards usually found in films by the major studios. A minor classic, with a standout role by Lugosi. B&W; 73m. **DIR:** Victor Halperin. **CAST:** Bela Lugosi, Madge Bellamy, Robert Frazer. **1932 DVD**

WHITEBOYZ ★★★ In the rolling cornfields of Iowa, the only gangster rapper to be found is a stark white teenager named Flip Dogg. When he takes his posse on a road trip to Chicago in order to experience a real hood and get connections with some drug pushers, Flip Dogg gets himself into more trouble than he can deal with. Often funny, this movie has many cameo appearances by popular rap stars that also add to the soundtrack. Rated R for profanity, violence, and simulated sex. 88m. **DIR:** Marc Levin. **CAST:** Danny Hoch, Dash Mihok, Mark Webber. **1999**

WHITEWATER SAM ★★1/2 Keith Larsen wrote, directed, coproduced, and stars in this wilderness adventure. He plays the legendary Whitewater Sam, the first white man to survive the harsh Rocky Mountain winters. The real star, however, seems to be his dog, Sybar. The beautiful scenery makes this film more than watchable. Rated PG for violence. 85m. **DIR:** Keith Larsen. **CAST:** Keith Larsen. **1978**

WHO AM I? ★★★ This Jackie Chan entry went straight to cable, which is odd. This time our hero's a mercenary-for-hire who loses his memory following an assignment in South Africa and is unable to trust anybody. As usual, the action is played for laughs, and Chan finds plenty of outlets for his signature fight scenes with everyday objects . . . not to mention the climactic stunt, which is a real heart-stopper. Rated PG-13 for violence. 108m. **DIR:** Benny Chan, Jackie Chan. **CAST:** Jackie Chan, Michelle Ferre, Mirai Yamamoto. **1998 DVD**

WHO AM I THIS TIME? ★★★1/2 The new girl in town, Helene Shaw (Susan Sarandon), gets a part in the local theater group production of *A Streetcar Named Desire* opposite Harry Nash (Christopher Walken). Dreadfully shy, Harry only comes to life in every part he plays on the stage. Helene sets out to win him. This is a pleasing Kurt Vonnegut Jr. story played by a capable cast. 60m. **DIR:** Jonathan Demme. **CAST:** Susan Sarandon, Christopher Walken, Robert Ridgely. **1982**

WHO ARE THE DEBOLTS AND WHERE DID THEY GET 19 KIDS? ★★★★★ This Academy Award–winning documentary features Dorothy and Bob Debolt and their nineteen children—some natural, most adopted. Their family is unique not only for its great size but for the multiple physical disabilities their adopted children have, the positive way these problems are dealt with, and the fantastic organizational system under which their daily lives are run. This is an excellent and inspirational film. Rated G. 73m. **DIR:** John Korty. **1978**

WHO DONE IT? ★★1/2 Standard Abbott and Costello programmer about a pair of soda jerks who witness an on-the-air murder during a radio broadcast and pose as detectives. B&W; 75m. **DIR:** Erle C. Kenton. **CAST:** Bud Abbott, Lou Costello, Patric Knowles, William Gargan, Louise Allbritton, William Bendix, Thomas Gomez, Jerome Cowan. **1942**

WHO FRAMED ROGER RABBIT ★★★★1/2 In this innovative and vastly entertaining motion picture, which seamlessly blends animated characters with live action, cartoon character Roger Rabbit (voice by Charles Fleischer) is accused of murder and turns to a hard-boiled private detective (Bob Hoskins) for help. As with his *Back to the Future* and *Romancing the Stone*, director Robert Zemeckis has come up with a wonderful movie for all ages. Rated PG for vulgar language. 103m. **DIR:** Robert Zemeckis. **CAST:** Bob Hoskins, Christopher Lloyd, Joanna Cassidy, Stubby Kaye. **1988 DVD**

WHO IS KILLING THE GREAT CHEFS OF EUROPE? ★★★★ Scripter Peter Stone, working from Nan and Ivan Lyons's deliciously funny novel, whips up a droll entrée in that most difficult of genres: the comic mystery. Internationally renowned dessert chef Jacqueline Bisset wins a commission as the final course in the meal of the century, while fending off the boorish advances of her ex-husband, a fast-food mogul. Rated PG for imaginative violence. 112m. **DIR:** Ted Kotcheff. **CAST:** George Segal, Jacqueline Bisset, Robert Morley, Jean-Pierre Cassel, Madge Ryan. **1978**

WHO IS THE BLACK DAHLIA? ★★★★ An above-average semidocumentary crime-drama based on one of the Los Angeles Police Department's most famous unsolved cases: the 1947 murder and gruesome dissection of a mysterious young woman whose lifestyle and mode of dress earned her the nickname of Black Dahlia. An excellent cast performs a first-rate script in this gripping telemovie. 100m. **DIR:** Joseph Pevney. **CAST:** Lucie Arnaz, Efrem Zimbalist Jr., Ronny Cox, Macdonald Carey, Gloria De Haven, Tom Bosley, Mercedes McCambridge, Donna Mills, June Lockhart. **1975**

WHO KILLED BABY AZARIA? ★★★★ Made-for-Australian-TV version of the true story, told in the American *A Cry in the Dark*, about a woman accused of murdering a baby that she claims was dragged away by a wild dog in the outback. Less polished than the remake, but still compelling. Not rated. 96m. **DIR:** Judy Rymer. **CAST:** Elain Hudson, John Hamblin. **1983**

WHO KILLED MARY WHAT'S 'ER NAME? ★★1/2 Gritty detective melodrama about an ex-boxer who solves the murder of a prostitute when no one else seems to care. Above-average low-budget thriller. Rated PG. 90m. **DIR:** Ernest Pintoff. **CAST:** Red Buttons, Sylvia Miles, Conrad Bain, David Doyle, Ron Carey, Alice Playten, Sam Waterston. **1971**

WHO KILLED PASOLINI? ★★★1/2 Riveting docudrama about the 1975 murder of the infamous Italian director/poet. The film suggests that Pasolini, who made enemies with his homosexual lifestyle and attacks on political decadence, was the victim of an unholy conspiracy. The case's circumstances and shoddy investigation are teasingly open-ended. In Italian with

English subtitles. Not rated; contains adult themes. 100m. **DIR:** Marco Tuillo Giordana. **CAST:** Carlo De Filippi, Nicoletta Braschi, Toni Bertorelli, Guilio Scarpati. **1995**

WHO SHOT PAT? 🦃 A plotless, nostalgic return to the narrator's last year at vocational school and the harsh realities of growing up in Brooklyn. Not rated; contains profanity and violence. 111m. **DIR:** Robert Brooks. **CAST:** David Knight, Sandra Bullock. **1991 DVD**

WHO SLEW AUNTIE ROO? ★★ Ghoulish horror version of *Hansel and Gretel*, with Shelley Winters as the madwoman who lures two children (Mark Lester and Chloe Franks) into her evil clutches. Rated R for violence. 89m. **DIR:** Curtis Harrington. **CAST:** Shelley Winters, Mark Lester, Chloe Franks, Ralph Richardson, Lionel Jeffries, Hugh Griffith. **1971**

WHODUNIT? 🦃 Low-budget murder mystery in which characters are being systematically eliminated at a place called Creep Island. Rated R for violence and profanity. 82m. **DIR:** Bill Naud. **CAST:** Rick Bean, Gary Phillips. **1982**

WHOLE NINE YARDS, THE ★★★1/2 Canadian dentist Matthew Perry's already miserable life takes a turn for the worse when a well-known, mob hit man (Bruce Willis) moves in next door. Suddenly, Perry finds himself involved in all sorts of intrigue, thanks primarily to his scheming, money-hungry wife who talks him into betraying Willis in the hopes of getting her husband killed so she can collect a $1 million insurance policy. Several intertwining plots feature some fine bits of physical comedy by Perry and a dry, understated turn from Willis. Rated R for profanity, violence, and simulated sex. 97m. **DIR:** Jonathan Lynn. **CAST:** Bruce Willis, Matthew Perry, Rosanna Arquette, Michael Clarke Duncan, Natasha Henstridge, Amanda Peet, Kevin Pollak. **1999 DVD**

WHOLE WIDE WORLD, THE ★★★1/2 Writer Robert E. Howard (creator of *Conan the Barbarian*) who committed suicide in 1936, had a turbulent, unconsummated romance with schoolteacher Novalyne Price, which she chronicled in a 1988 memoir. This film, based on her book, takes an uncritical view of Howard's writing and features fine performances. Rated PG-13 for mild profanity and mature themes. 113m. **DIR:** Dan Ireland. **CAST:** Vincent D'Onofrio, Renee Zellweger, Ann Wedgeworth, Harve Presnell. **1996**

WHO'LL STOP THE RAIN ★★★★1/2 In this brilliant film, Nick Nolte gives one of his finest performances as a hardened vet who agrees to smuggle drugs for a buddy (the always effective Michael Moriarty). What neither of them knows is that it's a setup, so Nolte and Moriarty's neurotic wife, played to perfection by Tuesday Weld, have to hide out from the baddies (Anthony Zerbe, Richard Masur, and Ray Sharkey). Rated R. 126m. **DIR:** Karel Reisz. **CAST:** Nick Nolte, Michael Moriarty, Tuesday Weld, Anthony Zerbe, Richard Masur, Ray Sharkey, David Opatoshu, Gail Strickland. **1978 DVD**

WHOLLY MOSES! ★★1/2 *Wholly Moses!* pokes fun at Hollywood biblical epics in a rapid-fire fashion. While the film is sometimes very funny, it is also loaded with a fair share of predictable, flat, and corny moments. It's so-so viewing fare. Rated R. 109m. **DIR:** Gary Weis. **CAST:** Dudley Moore, Richard Pryor, Laraine Newman, James Coco, Paul Sand, Jack Gilford, Dom DeLuise, John Houseman, Madeline Kahn, David L. Lander, John Ritter. **1980**

WHOOPEE ★★1/2 The first of six Eddie Cantor musical films of the 1930s, this one's a two-color draft of his 1928 Broadway hit of the same name. The big-eyed comic plays a superhypochondriac on an Arizona dude ranch. Cowpokes and chorines abound. Busby Berkeley production numbers make it palatable. B&W; 93m. **DIR:** Thornton Freeland. **CAST:** Eddie Cantor, Eleanor Hunt, Paul Gregory, Ethel Shutta. **1930**

WHOOPEE BOYS, THE 🦃 A pair of obnoxious—and supposedly lovable—misfits attempt to save a school for needy children. Rated R for profanity. 94m. **DIR:** John Byrum. **CAST:** Michael O'Keefe, Paul Rodriguez, Lucinda Jenney, Denholm Elliott, Eddie Deezen. **1986**

WHOOPS APOCALYPSE ★★1/2 This overlong but sometimes rewarding British comedy consists of a news coverage spoof on events leading up to World War III. The plot centers around the theft of a U.S. nuclear bomb. Many viewers may get fidgety during the second, less successful half. Not rated, it contains nudity and obscene language. 137m. **DIR:** John Reardon. **CAST:** John Barron, John Cleese, Richard Griffiths, Peter Jones, Barry Morse. **1981**

WHORE ★★ This lurid walk on the wild side is just as harsh, brash, and uncompromising as the title implies. Sensationalism runs rampant as a streetwalker (Theresa Russell) talks directly into the camera between tricks about the intricacies of her profession, and hides out from her knife-wielding pimp. This film exists in both R and NC-17 versions, both due to profanity and explicit sexual content. 92m. **DIR:** Ken Russell. **CAST:** Theresa Russell, Benjamin Mouton, Antonio Fargas. **1991**

WHORE 2 ★★★★ Though it has little (read: nothing) to do with Ken Russell's 1991 *Whore*, this is a surprisingly engrossing drama about an author (Amos Kollek) who spends a couple of months in a red-light district to do research on prostitution. There he discovers a startling subculture whose existence seems impossible until the film's final moments reveal the majority of the cast are real hookers. Engrossing, enlightening, and disturbing. Not rated; contains profanity, violence, and sexual situations. 85m. **DIR:** Amos Kollek. **CAST:** Amos Kollek, Marla Sucharetza, Mari Nelson. **1993**

WHO'S AFRAID OF VIRGINIA WOOLF? ★★★★★ Edward Albee's powerful play about the love-hate relationship of a college professor and his bitchy wife was brilliantly transferred to the screen. Elizabeth Taylor gives one of her best acting performances and Richard Burton is equally stunning. B&W; 129m. **DIR:** Mike Nichols. **CAST:** Elizabeth Taylor, Richard Burton, Sandy Dennis, George Segal. **1966 DVD**

WHO'S GOT THE ACTION? ★★ One of Lana Turner's less glamorous roles teams her with Dean Martin in a spoof of gambling movies. The twist is that they are married, and she tries to keep his gambling losses in the family by being his bookie—incognito, of course. When he starts winning, she has to sell her assets to pay him. The comic twists are diluted by the posturing of the stars. 93m. **DIR:** Daniel Mann. **CAST:** Lana Turner, Dean Martin, Walter Matthau, Eddie Albert, Margo, Nita Talbot, Paul Ford. **1962**

WHO'S HARRY CRUMB? 🦃 Inept private eye Harry Crumb bumbles his way through the case of a kid-

napped heiress. Rated PG-13 for profanity and suggested sex. 87m. **DIR:** Paul Flaherty. **CAST:** John Candy, Jeffrey Jones, Annie Potts, Tim Thomerson, Barry Corbin. **1989 DVD**

WHO'S MINDING THE MINT? ★★★1/2 When a U.S. Mint employee (Jim Hutton) accidentally destroys thousands of newly printed bills, a group of misfits bands together to help him out. This film is often hilarious and always enjoyable. 97m. **DIR:** Howard Morris. **CAST:** Milton Berle, Jim Hutton, Dorothy Provine, Joey Bishop, Walter Brennan, Jamie Farr, Victor Buono. **1967**

WHO'S THAT GIRL 🦃 A warped, pseudoremake of the 1938 comedy classic *Bringing Up Baby*. Rated PG for profanity. 95m. **DIR:** James Foley. **CAST:** Madonna, Griffin Dunne, Haviland Morris, John McMartin, John Mills. **1987**

WHO'S THAT KNOCKING AT MY DOOR? ★★★ All the trademark obsessional concerns—women, money, peer pressure—of better-known Martin Scorsese melodramas are evident in this first feature by the distinctive director. Harvey Keitel fumbles violently through his stormy relationship with a free-thinking, elusive young woman while shedding the shackles of strict Catholicism. B&W; 90m. **DIR:** Martin Scorsese. **CAST:** Zina Bethune, Harvey Keitel. **1968**

WHO'S THE MAN? ★★★ Two inept Harlem haircutters reluctantly become inept Harlem cops and investigate the murder of their former barbershop boss in this funny, sassy, streetwise comedy but MTV rap hosts Dr. Dre and Ed Lover bring to the party the most rhythmic and natural comic chemistry since Cheech and Chong. Rated R for language. 100m. **DIR:** Ted Demme. **CAST:** Doctor Dre, Ed Lover, Jim Moody, Denis Leary, Colin Quinn, Badja Djola, Cheryl James, Andre Blake, Rozwill Young. **1993**

WHO'S WHO ★★★★★ This brilliant, ascerbic comedy deals with the violent differences in lifestyle and attitude that exist within the British class system. A pathetic, vacuous clerk in a stockbroker's office is obsessed with the aristocracy, who regard his social advances with facial expressions similar to the expressions of those who have just discovered fresh canine excrement on their shoes. Brilliant. Not rated. 75m. **DIR:** Mike Leigh. **CAST:** Bridget Kane, Sam Kelly, Simon Chandler, Adam Norton, Philip Davis. **1978**

WHOSE CHILD AM I? 🦃 Artificial insemination is the pitiful excuse for this ridiculously sordid film. 90m. **DIR:** Lawrence Britten. **CAST:** Kate O'Mara, Paul Freeman, Edward Judd. **1974**

WHOSE LIFE IS IT, ANYWAY? ★★★★ Richard Dreyfuss is superb as a witty and intellectually dynamic sculptor who is paralyzed after an auto accident and fights for his right to be left alone to die. John Cassavetes and Christine Lahti costar as doctors in this surprisingly upbeat movie. Rated R. 118m. **DIR:** John Badham. **CAST:** Richard Dreyfuss, John Cassavetes, Christine Lahti, Bob Balaban, Kenneth McMillan, Kaki Hunter, Janet Eilber. **1981**

WHY, CHARLIE BROWN, WHY? ★★★★ The Peanuts kids perform a superb public service in this poignant tale when one of Linus's best friends—a little girl named Janice—is hospitalized with leukemia. Aside from its sugar-coated conclusion, the instructive script doesn't pull any punches. Not rated. 25m. **DIR:** Sam Jaimes. **1990**

WHY DIDN'T THEY ASK EVANS? ★★★★ A famous explorer's dying question sends amateur sleuths Lady Derwent and Bobby Jones (Francesca Annis and James Warwick, who later teamed up for the popular *Partners in Crime* series) on the trail in this entertaining Agatha Christie TV yarn. That cryptic query, an attempt on Bobby's life, and an apparent suicide are just a few of the mysteries tackled by the energetic duo. The 1930s setting is re-created faithfully, and the costume design is excellent. Suitable for family viewing. 180m. **DIR:** John Davies. **CAST:** Francesca Annis, James Warwick, Eric Porter, John Gielgud, Joan Hickson. **1980**

WHY DO FOOLS FALL IN LOVE ★★★★ Three faces of rock legend Frankie Lymon are revealed during a heated courtroom battle over his estate. The marrying kind, with three wives before he overdosed at twenty-five, Lymon never divorced any of them. In this film, at least, Lymon played second fiddle to the strong-willed women who claimed separate aspects of the man. Heavy doses of humor are sprinkled with heartbreak. Rated R for violence, drug use, sex, nudity, language, and animal cruelty. 115m. **DIR:** Gregory Nava. **CAST:** Larenz Tate, Halle Berry, Vivica A. Fox, Lela Rochon, Paul Mazursky. **1998 DVD**

WHY DOES HERR R. RUN AMOK? ★★★ With an unmoving camera lending a sense of emotional claustrophobia, this film depicts the dreary life of a middle-class German family, culminating in murder and suicide. It's an experimental film that imparts the misery of the characters to the viewer, though that doesn't make it much fun to watch. In German with English subtitles. Not rated. 88m. **DIR:** Rainer Werner Fassbinder, Michael Fengler. **CAST:** Kurt Raab, Lilith Ungerer, Hanna Schygulla. **1970**

WHY HAS BHODI DHARMA LEFT FOR THE EAST? ★★★★ Essentially plotless, this South Korean film attempts to guide the viewer through the central tenets of Buddhism via a series of incidents in the lives of an adult and a child. You don't have to be interested in religion, however, to enjoy this beautifully photographed and elegantly paced movie, which was filmed over a period of seven years by an art professor with no previous filmmaking experience. In Korean with English subtitles. Not rated; contains no objectionable material. 137m. **DIR:** Yong-Kyun Bae. **CAST:** Hae-Jin Huang, Su-Myong Ko, Yi Pan-Yong, Sin Won-Sop. **1989 DVD**

WHY ME? 🦃 Two career burglars steal a cursed ruby. Badly acted, poorly written adventure. Rated R for profanity. 87m. **DIR:** Gene Quintano. **CAST:** Christopher Lambert, Kim Greist, Christopher Lloyd. **1989**

WHY SHOOT THE TEACHER? ★★★ Bud Cort stars in this intimate and simple film about a young instructor whose first teaching position lands him in the barren plains of Canada. Lean realism and bright dashes of humor give the picture some memorable moments, but this story develops with a disengaging slowness. Rated PG. 101m. **DIR:** Silvio Narizzano. **CAST:** Bud Cort, Samantha Eggar, Chris Wiggins, Gary Reineke. **1977**

WICKED, THE ★★1/2 The Terminus family are bloodsuckers who are more than thrilled when strangers visit their quaint small town. Okay shocker. Rated R for nudity and violence. 87m. **DIR:** Colin Eggleston. **CAST:**

Brett Cumo, Richard Morgan, Angela Kennedy, John Doyle. **1987 DVD**

WICKED CITY, THE (1992) ★★★ The imagery is dazzling, but the plot is nearly impossible to follow in this over-the-top live-action fantasy based on a Japanese cartoon. The story line seems to revolve around a race of shape-shifting creatures intent on taking over the Earth. The film races along at a fast clip, and features an array of eye-catching FX. Dubbed. Not rated; contains violence and nudity. 88m. **DIR:** Mak Tai-Kit. **CAST:** Jacky Cheung, Leon Lai, Michelle Reis, Tatsuya Nakadai. **1992 DVD**

WICKED CITY (1995) ★★★ Exciting Japanese animated film about a race of shape shifters and their ties to Earth, which is presently at risk unless a treaty is signed. Creatures have a style reminiscent of Rob Bottin's work on John Carpenter's remake of *The Thing*, but some viewers may be shocked by the sexuality expressed in the film. Not rated; contains violence, profanity, nudity, and simulated sex. 90m. **DIR:** Yoshiaki Kawajiri. **1995 DVD**

WICKED GAMES 🦃 The copper-masked serial killer from *Truth or Dare?* returns in this sleazy sequel coproduced by the local Shakespearean company (?!). Not rated; contains gore and violence. 80m. **DIR:** Tim Ritter. **CAST:** Joel Wynkoop, Kermit Christman. **1994**

WICKED LADY, THE (1945) ★★ Margaret Lockwood's scruples dip as low as her neckline in this somewhat tedious period piece about a vixen who masquerades as an outlaw. James Mason is appropriately evil as her companion in crime. B&W; 104m. **DIR:** Leslie Arliss. **CAST:** Margaret Lockwood, James Mason, Patricia Roc, Michael Rennie, Martita Hunt. **1945**

WICKED LADY, THE (1983) 🦃 An absolutely awful swashbuckler. Rated R. 98m. **DIR:** Michael Winner. **CAST:** Faye Dunaway, Alan Bates, John Gielgud, Denholm Elliott, Prunella Scales, Oliver Tobias, Glynis Barber. **1983**

WICKED STEPMOTHER, THE 🦃 A lame horror-comedy about an old woman who moves in with a family and turns their lives upside down with her evil powers. Rated PG-13 for profanity. 95m. **DIR:** Larry Cohen. **CAST:** Bette Davis, Barbara Carrera, Richard Moll, Tom Bosley. **1989**

WICKER MAN, THE ★★★★1/2 An anonymous letter that implies a missing girl has been murdered brings Sergeant Howie of Scotland Yard, to Summerisle, an island off the coast of England. Lord Summerisle, the ruler and religious leader of the island, seems to take it all as a joke, so Howie swears to find the truth. Rated R. 95m. **DIR:** Robin Hardy. **CAST:** Edward Woodward, Christopher Lee, Britt Ekland, Diane Cilento, Ingrid Pitt. **1973 DVD**

WIDE AWAKE ★★ Fifth-grader is on a spritual quest and questions his faith in God after the death of his widowed grandfather. The most intriguing rub of the film—that the boy's search for enlightenment is frustrated rather than simplified by his attendance at a boys-only Catholic school—is sapped of its potency by a rather saccharine script. Rated PG. 90m. **DIR:** M. Night Shyamalan. **CAST:** Joseph Cross, Robert Loggia, Timothy Reifsnyder, Dana Delany, Denis Leary, Julia Stiles, Rosie O'Donnell. **1998 DVD**

WIDE-OPEN TOWN ★★★ A saloon-based gang run by a beautiful woman and her cold-blooded henchman steals Hopalong Cassidy's cattle and kills an old prospector. Hopalong and ace villain Victor Jory duke it out in a no-holds-barred finale that puts a satisfying end to this superior series entry. B&W; 79m. **DIR:** Lesley Selander. **CAST:** William Boyd, Russell Hayden, Andy Clyde, Evelyn Brent, Victor Jory, Morris Ankrum, Roy Barcroft, Glenn Strange. **1941**

WIDE SARGASSO SEA ★★★1/2 Lush, gothic romance, based on Jean Rhys's celebrated novel, acts as a prequel to Charlotte Brontë's *Jane Eyre*. Englishman sets sail to Jamaica for an arranged marriage to a mysterious and sensual woman that leads him on an erotic journey that crosses all boundaries and eventually leads to betrayal. One hot film. Rated R and unrated versions available; both contain nudity and adult situations. 100m. **DIR:** John Duigan. **CAST:** Karina Lombard, Nathaniel Parker, Claudia Robinson, Michael York, Rachel Ward. **1993**

WIDOW COUDERC ★★★ Tense, well-acted thriller about a small-town woman's affair with an escaped killer. From a novel by Georges Simenon. In French with English subtitles. Not rated; contains no objectionable material. 92m. **DIR:** Pierre Granier-Deferre. **CAST:** Simone Signoret, Alain Delon. **1974**

•WIDOW OF ST. PIERRE, THE ★★★ On an island just off the coast of Newfoundland, the wife of the military commandant causes a scandal by befriending a fisherman convicted of murder. She makes the man her protégé while awaiting the arrival of a guillotine and an executioner from France. The condemned man's good deeds endear him to the community but local bureaucrats are determined to punish both him and his supporters in a provocative romantic drama about redemption, unconditional love, and uncompromised principles. In French with English subtitles. Rated R for violence, sex, and adult themes. 107m. **DIR:** Patrice Leconte. **CAST:** Juliette Binoche, Daniel Auteuil, Emir Kusturica. **2000 DVD**

WIDOW'S KISS ★★★ Beverly D'Angelo plays the black widow who beds, weds, and then disposes of her husbands. Unfortunately, her latest victim (Bruce Davison) has a son (MacKenzie Astin) who will stop at nothing to prove dear old stepmom is really a killer. That means having to get close to the woman who put Dad in the grave. Decent acting saves this formula thriller from falling through the cracks. Rated R for violence, profanity, and nudity. 103m. **DIR:** Peter Foldy. **CAST:** Beverly D'Angelo, Mackenzie Astin, Dennis Haysbert, Bruce Davison, Barbara Rush. **1996**

WIDOW'S PEAK ★★★★ Fabulous Irish film perfectly showcases Mia Farrow's talents. She plays the village oddball who is provided for by the upper-crust ladies. Joan Plowright also excels as the queen bee and manipulator extraordinaire. A number of plot twists and turns lead to a satisfying, surprise ending, rich in irony. Lush Irish countryside is a bonus. Rated PG for adult situations. 105m. **DIR:** John Irvin. **CAST:** Mia Farrow, Joan Plowright, Natasha Richardson, Adrian Dunbar. **1994**

WIFE, THE ★★★ A New Age version of *Who's Afraid of Virginia Woolf?* that is a vicious and darkly funny exploration of marriage and psychotherapy. Therapist couple find their remote Vermont home disturbed by the unex-

pected appearance of a patient and his trashy, outspoken wife. The performances and dialogue are delectably spiky and unexpectedly creepy. Letterboxed. Not rated; contains profanity and nudity. 101m. **DIR:** Tommy Noonan. **CAST:** Julie Hagerty, Tommy Noonan, Wallace Shawn, Karen Young. **1994 DVD**

WIFE! BE LIKE A ROSE! ★★★★ A young woman travels from Tokyo to rural Japan in search of her father, hoping to persuade him to abandon his mistress and return home to his wife. Gentle comedy–drama. In Japanese with English subtitles. B&W; 73m. **DIR:** Mikio Naruse. **CAST:** Sachiko Chiba. **1935**

WIFE VS. SECRETARY ★★ Jean Harlow is a super secretary to publisher Clark Gable. Friends and family of his wife (Myrna Loy) convince her that Harlow is kept around for more than efficiency, so she files for divorce. B&W; 88m. **DIR:** Clarence Brown. **CAST:** Clark Gable, Jean Harlow, Myrna Loy, May Robson, James Stewart. **1936**

WIFEMISTRESS ★★★1/2 Marcello Mastroianni stars as a husband in hiding, and Laura Antonelli as his repressed wife. When Mastroianni is falsely accused of murder, he hides out in a building across the street from his own home. His wife, not knowing where he is, begins to relive his sexual escapades. There are some comic moments as the former philandering husband must deal with his wife's new sexual freedom. Rated R. 110m. **DIR:** Marco Vicario. **CAST:** Marcello Mastroianni, Laura Antonelli, Leonard Mann. **1977**

WIGSTOCK: THE MOVIE ★★1/2 A hoot to watch, just don't expect any substance. Wigstock is an annual drag festival that's a combination concert, revue, and gay-pride forum. The movie, however, is little more than a home-video rendition of the festival. Rated R for profanity and adult themes. 82m. **DIR:** Barry Shils. **CAST:** Alexis Arquette, RuPaul, Lypsinka, Crystal Waters, Deee-Lite, Jackie Beat, John Kelly. **1995**

WILBY CONSPIRACY, THE ★★★1/2 This underappreciated political thriller tackled the issue of apartheid years before its worldwide recognition as a serious problem. Michael Caine stars as an apolitical Brit who gains social consciousness after encountering an idealistic revolutionary (Sidney Poitier). Somewhat implausible, but entertaining nonetheless. Rated PG. 104m. **DIR:** Ralph Nelson. **CAST:** Michael Caine, Sidney Poitier, Nicol Williamson. **1975**

WILD AMERICA ★★★ Three teen Stouffer brothers—armed with a 16mm camera—leave their rural Arkansas home in the summer of 1967 for the wilds. This lightweight, fact-based story is a rather sloppy outdoor adventure that says more about American myth building than it does about the animal kingdom. Rated PG. 106m. **DIR:** William Dear. **CAST:** Scott Bairstow, Devon Sawa, Jonathan Taylor Thomas, Jamey Sheridan, Frances Fisher. **1997 DVD**

WILD AND WOOLLY ★★★★ It's always fun to watch a performer spoof himself, and Douglas Fairbanks Sr. was especially good at it. He plays an easterner fascinated with the Old West and fantasies of adventure. When he gets the chance to go west, it's not what he imagined. Very entertaining. B&W; 90m. **DIR:** John Emerson. **CAST:** Douglas Fairbanks Sr., Eileen Percy, Sam de Grasse. **1917**

WILD ANGELS, THE ★★ It's 1960s hip, low-budget Hollywood style. If they gave Oscars for cool, Peter Fonda—in shades, three-day growth of beard, and leather—would win for sure. This cool motorcycle gang leader needs a hot mama. Unfortunately, he has to make do with Nancy ("These Boots Are Made for Walkin' ") Sinatra. But the movie's greatest asset is "Blue's Theme," which revs up the proceedings with wonderfully tacky fuzz-tone guitar. 93m. **DIR:** Roger Corman. **CAST:** Peter Fonda, Nancy Sinatra, Bruce Dern, Michael J. Pollard, Diane Ladd, Gayle Hunnicutt. **1966**

WILD AT HEART ★★★ One's gag reflex gets a real workout in this off-the-edge movie about a pair of young lovers (Nicolas Cage, Laura Dern) on the run. Director David Lynch explores the dark side of the American dream in a road picture that often seems to have been written and acted by the inmates of an insane asylum. Rated R for nudity, simulated sex, profanity, gore, and violence. 125m. **DIR:** David Lynch. **CAST:** Nicolas Cage, Laura Dern, Diane Ladd, Willem Dafoe, Isabella Rossellini, Harry Dean Stanton, Crispin Glover. **1990**

WILD BEASTS, THE ★★1/2 After PCP infects their water supply, animals and children go on a rampage killing anyone in sight. Made in Europe, where they must not have any animal-rights laws. Not rated; contains violence and nudity. 92m. **DIR:** Franco Prosperi. **CAST:** John Aldrich. **1985**

WILD BILL ★★★★ Episodic but engaging biopic on the lawman years of Old West legend Wild Bill Hickok features a marvelously twitchy performance by Jeff Bridges in the title role and the idiosyncratic filmmaking style of director Walter Hill. It's never boring. Rated R for violence, profanity, and simulated sex. 97m. **DIR:** Walter Hill. **CAST:** Jeff Bridges, Ellen Barkin, John Hurt, Diane Lane, David Arquette, Christina Applegate, Bruce Dern, James Gammon, Marjoe Gortner, James Remar, Keith Carradine, Steve Reevis. **1995 DVD**

WILD BUNCH, THE ★★★★1/2 A classic Western brilliantly directed by Sam Peckinpah. He created a whole new approach to violence in this landmark film about men making a last stand. It is without a doubt Peckinpah's greatest film and is bursting with action, vibrant characters, and memorable dialogue. Good acting, too, by a first-rate cast. Rated R. 145m. **DIR:** Sam Peckinpah. **CAST:** William Holden, Ernest Borgnine, Robert Ryan, Ben Johnson, Edmond O'Brien, Warren Oates, Strother Martin, L. Q. Jones, Emilio Fernandez. **1969 DVD**

WILD CACTUS ★★ Desert-bound thriller features many erotic encounters in a sordid plot line about a young wife held hostage by a murderous ex-con and his girlfriend. Available in R and unrated versions; both feature sex, violence, and profanity. **DIR:** Jag Mundhra. **CAST:** David Naughton, India Allen, Gary Hudson, Michelle Moffett, Kathy Shower, Robert Z'Dar. **1993**

WILD CARD ★★★ A former preacher is asked to investigate the mysterious death of a Texas landowner. Made for cable. 95m. **DIR:** Mel Damski. **CAST:** Powers Boothe, Cindy Pickett, Terry O'Quinn, René Auberjonois, M. Emmet Walsh. **1992**

WILD CHILD, THE (L'ENFANT SAUVAGE) ★★★★ Based on fact. In 1798 a boy, believed to be about 12, is

found running wild in the French woods, apparently abandoned there when little more than an infant. A doctor–teacher of deaf mutes, sensitively played by director François Truffaut, takes over the task of domesticating the snarling, bewildered youth. Completely absorbing from start to finish. In French with English subtitles. Not rated, but suitable for all. B&W; 86m. **DIR:** François Truffaut. **CAST:** François Truffaut, Jean-Pierre Cargol. **1970 DVD**

WILD DUCK, THE ★★1/2 Despite the cast, or maybe because of it, this poignant story of love and tragedy falls short of its ambitious mark. Jeremy Irons and Liv Ullmann are struggling parents whose child (Lucinda Jones) is slowly going blind. An idealistic friend (Arthur Dignam) complicates matters by unearthing truths that were better off buried. Derived from the classic Henrik Ibsen stage play. Rated PG for profanity. 96m. **DIR:** Henri Safran. **CAST:** Liv Ullmann, Jeremy Irons, Lucinda Jones, Arthur Dignam, John Meillon, Michael Pate. **1983**

WILD FLOWER (1991) ★★ A backwoods family tries to bring a mentally disabled girl (Patricia Arquette) out of her shell to join the rest of humanity. Although somewhat touching, this TV film tries to be all things and ends up never being compelling. 94m. **DIR:** Diane Keaton. **CAST:** Beau Bridges, Patricia Arquette, Susan Blakely, William McNamara. **1991**

WILD FLOWER (1993) (FIORILE) ★★★★ Directors Paolo and Vittorio Taviani once again have woven a colorful tapestry of several generations of an Italian family, as told from the point of view of grandfather Luigi. Funny, touching, and at times heartbreaking. Rated PG-13 for adult situations. 118m. **DIR:** Paolo Taviani, Vittorio Taviani. **CAST:** Claudio Bigagli, Michael Vartan, Lino Capolicchio, Constanze Englebrecht. **1993**

WILD FRONTIER ★★★★ Sheriff Rocky Lane goes after the outlaws responsible for his father's death, led by the town's dishonest saddle shop owner. First in the Rocky Lane series. B&W; 59m. **DIR:** Philip Ford. **CAST:** Allan "Rocky" Lane, Jack Holt, Eddy Waller, Roy Barcroft. **1947**

WILD GEESE, THE ★★★ Features the unlikely combination of Richard Burton, Roger Moore, and Richard Harris as three mercenaries hired by a rich British industrialist (Stewart Granger) to go into Rhodesia and free a captured humanist leader. Better than you would expect. Rated R. 134m. **DIR:** Andrew V. McLaglen. **CAST:** Richard Burton, Roger Moore, Richard Harris, Stewart Granger, Hardy Kruger, Jack Watson, Frank Finlay. **1978**

WILD GEESE II 🦃 A new group of mercenaries attempts to break into a Berlin prison to free Nazi war criminal Rudolf Hess. Rated R for violence and language. 118m. **DIR:** Peter R. Hunt. **CAST:** Scott Glenn, Barbara Carrera, Edward Fox, Laurence Olivier, Stratford Johns. **1985**

WILD GUITAR 🦃 An exploitative record company gets its comeuppance from hell-raising Arch Hall Jr., a motorcycle-riding rock 'n' roller who couldn't act if his life depended on it. Incredibly bad. 87m. **DIR:** Ray Dennis Steckler. **CAST:** Arch Hall Jr., Nancy Czar, William Watters, Cash Flagg. **1962**

WILD HEARTS CAN'T BE BROKEN ★★★★ A rebellious teenager (Gabrielle Anwar) in the 1920s runs away to join a traveling show, where she learns how to leap on horseback into a water tank from a forty-foot-high platform. Sparkling family film from the folks at Disney. Rated G. 90m. **DIR:** Steve Miner. **CAST:** Gabrielle Anwar, Michael Schoeffling, Cliff Robertson. **1991**

WILD HORSE HANK ★★1/2 Linda Blair is a horse lover pitted against a family that is stampeding wild horses. Richard Crenna plays her father. This Canadian feature is not rated. 94m. **DIR:** Eric Till. **CAST:** Linda Blair, Richard Crenna, Al Waxman, Michael Wincott. **1978**

WILD IN THE COUNTRY ★★★ Elvis Presley is encouraged to pursue a literary career when counseled during his wayward youth. Most viewers will find it interesting to see Elvis in such a serious role. The supporting cast also—Hope Lange, Millie Perkins, John Ireland, and (especially) Tuesday Weld—add to the okay script. 114m. **DIR:** Philip Dunne. **CAST:** Elvis Presley, Hope Lange, Tuesday Weld, Millie Perkins, John Ireland. **1961**

WILD IN THE STREETS ★★ Ridiculous what-if? film about future America when youth runs the show, the voting age is lowered to 14, and a rock singer involved in drug selling sits as president in the White House. This dated daydream of the 1960s was considered lame at the time of its release, but has gathered a following over the years. Rated PG. 97m. **DIR:** Barry Shear. **CAST:** Christopher Jones, Shelley Winters, Hal Holbrook, Diane Varsi, Ed Begley Sr., Millie Perkins, Richard Pryor, Bert Freed. **1968**

•**WILD IRIS** ★★1/2 This character drama revolves around a boy, his alcoholic mother, and his domineering grandmother. While it *sounds* like a charged situation, the story just circles and circles, never building up enough tension to satisfy the viewer with the conclusion. The mediocre acting in this made-for-cable original cannot overcome the stilted dialogue and lost plot. Not rated; contains profanity and violence. 93m. **DIR:** Daniel Petrie. **CAST:** Gena Rowlands, Laura Linney, Emile Hirsch, Lee Tergensen, Miguel Sandoval, Fred Ward. **2001**

WILD LIFE, THE ★★ From some of the same people who brought you *Fast Times at Ridgemont High* comes a film set in a world where your "cool" is measured by how many cigarettes you can smoke (and eat) and how many girls you can bed. Christopher Penn offers a believable performance as the leader of a pack of teens trying to grow up too fast. Rated R for suggested sex and language. 96m. **DIR:** Art Linson. **CAST:** Christopher Penn, Lea Thompson, Rick Moranis, Randy Quaid, Ilan Mitchell-Smith. **1984**

WILD MAN 🦃 An ex-CIA agent, Eric Wild, is pressured to take on one more assignment. Rated R for nudity, profanity, and violence. 105m. **DIR:** F. J. Lincoln. **CAST:** Don Scribner. **1989**

WILD MAN BLUES ★★★ Two-time Academy Award winner Barbara Kopple presents a record of Woody Allen's European tour with his New Orleans jazz band. It's more a concert film than a documentary about Allen, with several good performances by the band (Allen's talent as a clarinetist is modest but real) interspersed with scenes of the celebrated filmmaker generally carrying on like a character in one of his movies.

Rated PG. 106m. **DIR:** Barbara Kopple. **CAST:** Woody Allen, Soon-Yi Previn, Eddy Davis. **1998**

WILD ONE, THE ★★★1/2 This classic film (based loosely on a real event in Hollister, California) about rival motorcycle gangs taking over a small town is pretty tame stuff these days and provides more laughs than thrills. Marlon Brando and his brooding Johnny are at the heart of this film's popularity; that coupled with the theme of motorcycle nomads have assured the film a cult following. B&W; 79m. **DIR:** Laslo Benedek. **CAST:** Marlon Brando, Mary Murphy, Robert Keith, Lee Marvin, Jay C. Flippen, Jerry Paris, Alvy Moore. **1953 DVD**

WILD ORCHID ★★1/2 Mickey Rourke does Rio de Janeiro in this sexual adventure that's as short on provocative eroticism as it is on plot. Screenplay by Patricia Louisianna Knap and director Zalman King. Rated R for language and nudity. 105m. **DIR:** Zalman King. **CAST:** Mickey Rourke, Carré Otis, Jacqueline Bisset. **1990 DVD**

WILD ORCHID 2: TWO SHADES OF BLUE ★★ Not a sequel, but another exploration into the sexual awakening of a young woman. Nina Siemaszko stars as Blue, a teenage beauty sent off to live in a house of ill repute. How she redeems herself nicely offsets the decadence she must endure. Rated R for nudity, violence, and strong language. Unrated version contains more sexual content. The original *Wild Orchid* seems like a timeless classic by comparison. 111m. **DIR:** Zalman King. **CAST:** Wendy Hughes, Tom Skerritt, Robert Davi, Nina Siemaszko. **1992**

WILD ORCHIDS ★★★ A beautiful, young Greta Garbo is the highlight of this familiar story of tropic love. Plantation owner Lewis Stone busies himself with overseeing his property in Java, but local prince Nils Asther finds himself overseeing the owner's wife and the usual complications ensue. Silent. B&W; 103m. **DIR:** Sidney Franklin. **CAST:** Greta Garbo, Lewis Stone, Nils Asther. **1928**

WILD PAIR, THE ★★ Beau Bridges, a yuppie FBI agent, and Bubba Smith, a streetwise city cop, are assigned to investigate a drug-related murder. The two clash as they find surprises around each corner. Bridges's acting, even as Smith's, is fine, but his directing is wanting. Rated R for profanity, violence, and nudity. 89m. **DIR:** Beau Bridges. **CAST:** Beau Bridges, Bubba Smith, Lloyd Bridges, Raymond St. Jacques, Gary Lockwood, Danny De La Paz. **1987**

WILD PALMS ★★★1/2 James Belushi is a lawyer-turned-television-executive whose life becomes a nightmarish power struggle involving mind control. Twenty-five years in the future, a pseudoreligious government tries to alter reality through drugs and television. Eerie because it is so plausible, this made-for-TV miniseries looks great, but it's too dense and too slow. Not rated; contains violence. 150m. **DIR:** Paul Hewitt, Keith Gordon, Kathryn Bigelow, Phil Joanou. **CAST:** James Belushi, Dana Delany, Robert Loggia, Kim Cattrall, Angie Dickinson. **1993**

WILD PARTY, THE ★★★ Legendary silent star Clara Bow, the "It" girl, made her talkie debut in this fast-paced story of a sexy, uninhibited college coed. Critics panned the film, but the public loved it, finding Bow's Brooklyn accent perfectly suited to her vivacious personality. B&W; 76m. **DIR:** Dorothy Arzner. **CAST:** Clara Bow, Fredric March, Jack Oakie. **1929**

WILD PARTY, THE ★★★1/2 This is a very grim look at how Hollywood treats its fading stars. James Coco plays a one-time comedy star trying to come back with a hit film. Raquel Welch plays Coco's girlfriend who plans a party for Hollywood's elite in order to push his film. The film is based on the career of Fatty Arbuckle. Rated R. 107m. **DIR:** James Ivory. **CAST:** James Coco, Raquel Welch, Perry King, David Dukes. **1975**

WILD REEDS ★★★★ Involving coming-of-age story in which three young men and a young woman find their sexuality, their love, and their lives. Enlightening feature is well written and performed. In French with English subtitles. Not rated; contains profanity and sexual situations. 110m. **DIR:** André Téchiné. **CAST:** Elodie Bouchez, Gael Morel, Stéphane Rideau, Frederic Gorny. **1995 DVD**

WILD RIDE, THE 🦃 Early Jack Nicholson. Here he appears as a hedonistic hot-rodder who casually kills people. B&W; 63m. **DIR:** Harvey Berman. **CAST:** Jack Nicholson, Robert Bean. **1960**

WILD ROSE ★★ This low-budget film, shot in and around the Minnesota iron ore fields, floats between being a love story and a social commentary on mining conditions. By trying to cover all the bases, writer-director John Hanson fails to cover even one satisfactorily. 96m. **DIR:** John Hanson. **CAST:** Lisa Eichhorn, Tom Bower. **1984**

WILD ROVERS, THE ★★★★ Sadly overlooked Western tells the story of two cowboys running from the law after robbing a bank. Holden is perfect as the older and not so wiser of the two, and O'Neal gives one of his best performances as the young partner. Rich in texture and smoothly directed by Blake Edwards. Rated PG. 109m. **DIR:** Blake Edwards. **CAST:** William Holden, Ryan O'Neal, Karl Malden, Tom Skerritt, Lynn Carlin, Joe Don Baker, Moses Gunn. **1971**

WILD SIDE 🦃 Amazingly chintzy, dialogue-heavy bomb about a nympho who works in a bank by day and turns tricks at night; the whole dreary mess is filmed in a handful of cheap sets and motel rooms. Rated R for nudity, profanity, rape, simulated sex, and violence. 85m. **DIR:** Franklin Brauner. **CAST:** Anne Heche, Christopher Walken, Joan Chen, Steven Bauer. **1995 DVD**

WILD STRAWBERRIES ★★★★ This film is probably Ingmar Bergman's least ambiguous. Superbly photographed and acted, the film tells the story of an elderly professor facing old age and reviewing his life's disappointments. The use of flashbacks is very effective. B&W; 90m. **DIR:** Ingmar Bergman. **CAST:** Victor Sjöström, Ingrid Thulin, Bibi Andersson, Gunnar Björnstrand. **1957**

WILD THING ★★★1/2 Screenwriter (and sometimes director) John Sayles creates another wonderfully offbeat tale: A young boy witnesses the murder of his parents and escapes to grow up in the streets of New York as kind of an urban Tarzan. Lots of fun. Rated PG-13 for violence. 92m. **DIR:** Max Reid. **CAST:** Rob Knepper, Kathleen Quinlan, Robert Davi, Betty Buckley. **1987**

WILD THINGS ★★1/2 Mainstream taboos (male frontal nudity, bisexuality) abound in this kinky trash *noir* about a high-school counselor accused of raping a wealthy student. Testimony sends yacht-club society

into a snit as detectives poke at the case until it oozes dark secrets. The top-notch cast has fun but the script is so enamored with its cleverness that several flashbacks during the closing credits are needed to explain its twists. Rated R for nudity, sex, and violence. 106m. **DIR:** John McNaughton. **CAST:** Matt Dillon, Denise Richards, Neve Campbell, Kevin Bacon, Daphne Rubin-Vega, Theresa Russell, Carrie Snodgress, Robert Wagner. **1998 DVD**

WILD TIMES ★★★ A two-cassette Western originally made for television. Sam Elliott plays sharpshooter Hugh Cardiff, whose life is anything but easy as he makes his way across the Old West. This could have been helped by some trimming. 200m. **DIR:** Richard Compton. **CAST:** Sam Elliott, Ben Johnson, Timothy Scott, Harry Carey Jr., Bruce Boxleitner, Penny Peyser, Dennis Hopper. **1980**

WILD WEST ★★★★1/2 Eddie Dean and his pals string the Western telegraph against all odds including Indians and outlaws. The absolute best of Eddie Dean's Westerns with plenty of great action and good songs. 70m. **DIR:** Robert Emmett Tansey. **CAST:** Eddie Dean, Lash LaRue, Roscoe Ates, Buzz Henry, Louise Currie. **1946**

WILD WEST ★★1/2 Offbeat comedy about a group of Pakistani country-and-western musicians eking out a living in West London while hoping to travel to Nashville and make it big. Perhaps this British style of outrageous comedy doesn't travel well, but there is something in this film to offend nearly everyone. Not rated, the film has profanity, violence, and suggested sex. 85m. **DIR:** David Attwood. **CAST:** Naveen Andrews, Sarita Choudhury. **1993**

WILD WILD WEST (1999) 🦃 Hollywood never learns. This overblown re-creation of the famed Robert Conrad/Ross Martin TV series is a miserable failure in all respects: a slipshod, incoherent mess that bears all the hallmarks of a doomed picture consigned to heavy eleventh-hour editing in an attempt to salvage something from the carnage . . . an effort that failed. Rated PG-13 for violence and brief nudity. 107m. **DIR:** Barry Sonnenfeld. **CAST:** Will Smith, Kevin Kline, Kenneth Branagh, Salma Hayek, Ted Levine. **1999 DVD**

WILD WILD WEST REVISITED, THE ★★★ That diminutive genius, Miguelito Loveless, has a new plan for world domination. He's cloning heads of state. It's worked in England, Spain, and Russia. The United States and President Cleveland could be next. Those legendary agents James West and Artemus Gordon are called out of retirement to save the day. This revival of the Sixties series is breezily entertaining. 95m. **DIR:** Burt Kennedy. **CAST:** Robert Conrad, Ross Martin, Paul Williams, Harry Morgan, René Auberjonois, Robert Shields, Lorene Yarnell. **1979**

WILD WILD WEST, THE (TV SERIES) ★★★★ The mid-60s spy craze produced a lot of TV shows, none more inventive than this Civil War–era adventure series starring Robert Conrad as James T. West, an undercover agent for President Ulysses Grant. Operating out of a gadget-laden railroad car and paired with Ross Martin's often-disguised Artemus Gordon, West tackled numerous foes bent on creating havoc or fomenting rebellion in the still-youthful United States. Look for the black-and-white first-season episodes, vastly superior to those that followed during the full-color remainder of the show's five-year run. 52m. **DIR:** Various!. **CAST:** Robert Conrad, Ross Martin, Michael Dunn. **1965–1970**

WILD WOMEN OF WONGO 🦃 This early sex-exploitation adventure pits two primitive tribes against each other. 72m. **DIR:** James L. Wolcott. **CAST:** Jean Hawkshaw, Johnny Walsh, Ed Fury, Pat Crowley. **1958**

WILD WORLD OF BATWOMAN, THE (SHE WAS A HAPPY VAMPIRE) 🦃 Execrable James Bond spoof. B&W; 70m. **DIR:** Jerry Warren. **CAST:** Katherine Victor, George Andre, Steve Brodie. **1966**

WILDCATS ★★ Standard Goldie Hawn vehicle, with her playing high school football coach to a rowdy group of inner-city kids who need to prove their worth as much as she needs to raise her self-esteem and prove her skill to chauvinistic athletic directors. Director Michael Ritchie shows little of the tension he brought to *The Bad News Bears*. Rated R for nudity and language. 107m. **DIR:** Michael Ritchie. **CAST:** Goldie Hawn, Swoosie Kurtz, James Keach, Nipsey Russell, Woody Harrelson, M. Emmet Walsh. **1986**

WILDE ★★1/2 Irish-born writer, social satirist, and notorious public personality Oscar Wilde was convicted in late 1890s London of "gross indecency" (engaging in sodomy) after recklessly pursuing a defamation suit against his male lover's father. This rather stuffy drama covers Wilde's preceding adult years and the trial's crushing impact on his wife, private life, public acceptance, and creativity. It is excellently acted but still far from gripping. Rated R for simulated sex, nudity, and language. 115m. **DIR:** Brian Gilbert. **CAST:** Stephen Fry, Jude Law, Vanessa Redgrave, Jennifer Ehle, Michael Sheen, Gemma Jones, Tom Wilkinson. **1998 DVD**

WILDER NAPALM ★★★ Everything works in this quirky comedy except the show-offy script, which wants to be screwball but is merely screwed up. Two feuding brothers, both in love with the same woman, share the power to start fires at will. Eventually everything in this movie turns out to be window dressing covering a brick wall. Rated PG-13 for sexual situations. 110m. **DIR:** Glenn Gordon Caron. **CAST:** Debra Winger, Dennis Quaid, Arliss Howard, Jim Varney, M. Emmet Walsh, Glenn Gordon Caron. **1993**

WILDERNESS FAMILY, PART 2, THE ★★★ Taken on its own terms, *The Wilderness Family, Part 2* isn't a bad motion picture. Film fans who want thrills and chills or something challenging to the mind should skip it. Rated G. 105m. **DIR:** Frank Zuniga. **CAST:** Robert Logan, Susan D. Shaw, Heather Rattray, Ham Larsen, George "Buck" Flower, Brian Cutler. **1978**

WILDFIRE (1945) ★★★ Bob Steele—in color—protecting the rights of wild horses. 57m. **DIR:** Robert Emmett Tansey. **CAST:** Bob Steele, Sterling Holloway, William Farnum, Eddie Dean. **1945**

WILDFIRE (1988) ★★1/2 When a bank robbery goes wrong, a teen groom is imprisoned for eight years. In his absence his pregnant bride remarries a wealthy man. The imprisoned man returns for his woman with predictably disastrous results. Rated PG for profanity. 98m. **DIR:** Zalman King. **CAST:** Steven Bauer, Linda Fiorentino, Will Patton, Marshall Bell. **1988**

WILDING, THE CHILDREN OF VIOLENCE 🦃 Taking its name from the highly publicized rape in New York City's Central Park, this film trivializes the case. By as-

sociating itself with that factual incident with its opening scene, the film hints at condemning that crime while depicting an unrelated series of fictional beatings by a band of suburbanite youths on a rampage against L.A.'s police and residents. Not rated, though there is partial nudity, violence, and profanity. 92m. **DIR:** Eric Louzil. **CAST:** Wings Hauser, Joey Travolta. **1990**

WILL, G. GORDON LIDDY ★★★1/2 Robert Conrad is transformed into the fanatic, strong-willed Watergate mastermind Liddy. The first half lacks excitement or revelation. Liddy's stay in prison, however, is a fascinating study. 100m. **DIR:** Robert Leiberman. **CAST:** Robert Conrad, Katherine Cannon, Gary Bayer, James Rebhorn. **1982**

WILL PENNY ★★★★1/2 Charlton Heston gives the finest performance of his distinguished career in this gritty, unsentimental look at the life of an illiterate cowboy in the American West. Equivalent to a PG-13. 108m. **DIR:** Tom Gries. **CAST:** Charlton Heston, Joan Hackett, Donald Pleasence, Lee Majors, Bruce Dern, Anthony Zerbe, Clifton James, Ben Johnson, Slim Pickens. **1968**

WILL SUCCESS SPOIL ROCK HUNTER? ★★★★ A comedy about the early days of TV that isn't as dated as you might think. Jayne Mansfield created the part on Broadway and no one else has done it as well as she. 95m. **DIR:** Frank Tashlin. **CAST:** Jayne Mansfield, Tony Randall, Mickey Hargitay, Joan Blondell, Betsy Drake, John Williams, Henry Jones, Lili Gentle. **1957**

WILLA ★★1/2 Made-for-TV movie has something of a cult reputation for feminist themes, but it's a pretty standard drama about a waitress who wants to become a trucker. 95m. **DIR:** Joan Darling, Claudio Guzman. **CAST:** Deborah Raffin, Clu Gulager, Cloris Leachman, Diane Ladd, Nancy Marchand, John Amos, Hank Williams Jr., Corey Feldman. **1979**

WILLARD ★★1/2 This worked far better as a novel. Bruce Davison plays a put-upon wimp who identifies more with rodents than people. When nasty Ernest Borgnine becomes too unpleasant, Davison decides to make him the bait in a better rattrap. It was destined to get worse in the sequel, entitled *Ben*. Rated PG—mild violence. 95m. **DIR:** Daniel Mann. **CAST:** Bruce Davison, Ernest Borgnine, Sondra Locke. **1971**

WILLIAM SHAKESPEARE'S A MIDSUMMER NIGHT'S DREAM ★★★1/2 Director-scripter Michael Hoffman has made his rendition of the Bard's bawdy comedy into an earthy and erotic tale. The tale is transposed to northern Italy, toward the end of the 19th century and turns on two young lovers who flee into a nearby forest. Havoc is wreaked when the king and queen of the fairies misuse magic spells. It's all rather inconsequential when all is said and done. Rated PG-13 for considerable nudity, although it remains most discreet. 110m. **DIR:** Michael Hoffman. **CAST:** Kevin Kline, Michelle Pfeiffer, Rupert Everett, Stanley Tucci, Calista Flockhart, Anna Friel, Christian Bale, Dominic West, David Strathairn, Sophie Marceau. **1999 DVD**

WILLIAM SHAKESPEARE'S ROMEO AND JULIET ★★1/2 This latest take on Shakespeare's ill-starred lovers has raucous MTV-style editing, frantic gun battles, a kitschy vision of urban apocalypse, and hot teen actors in the title roles. But director Baz Luhrmann gets mainly floundering high-school performances from his talented cast. Rated PG-13 for violence. 121m. **DIR:** Baz Luhrmann. **CAST:** Leonardo DiCaprio, Claire Danes, Pete Postlethwaite, John Leguizamo, Harold Perrineau Jr., Paul Sorvino, Brian Dennehy, Miriam Margolyes. **1996 DVD**

WILLIE AND PHIL ★★1/2 Director Paul Mazursky's "hip" take on Truffaut's *Jules and Jim*, this story of a love triangle now seems quite dated. Margot Kidder is the love interest of two best friends who share her affections for nine years. Kidder's character is generally unsympathetic and, as a result, much of the film seems artificial. Rated R for nudity and profanity. 116m. **DIR:** Paul Mazursky. **CAST:** Michael Ontkean, Margot Kidder, Ray Sharkey, Jan Miner. **1980**

WILLIE MCBEAN AND HIS MAGIC MACHINE ★★ Saddled with a slow story line in which the hero must thwart the efforts of a mad scientist to change history, *Willie* lacks the charm and style of better animated characters and has little to offer compared to more sophisticated contemporary productions. 94m. **DIR:** Arthur Rankin Jr. **1959**

WILLIES, THE ★★1/2 Lies, tall tales, and boyish machismo abound in this silly yet watchable movie as three kids try to out-gross each other with wild stories. Rated PG-13. 92m. **DIR:** Brian Peck. **CAST:** James Karen, Sean Astin, Kathleen Freeman, Jeremy Miller. **1990**

WILLOW ★★★ A formulaic but entertaining fantasy epic, this focuses on the quest of an apprentice sorcerer, Willow (Warwick Davis), to keep a magical child safe from the minions of the wicked queen (Jean Marsh) she is destined to destroy. The first half tends to drag as the characters and situations are somewhat laboriously introduced. However, things pick up midway. Rated PG for violence. 120m. **DIR:** Ron Howard. **CAST:** Val Kilmer, Joanne Whalley, Jean Marsh, Warwick Davis, Patricia Hayes, Billy Barty. **1988 DVD**

WILLY WONKA AND THE CHOCOLATE FACTORY ★★★ Gene Wilder plays a candy company owner who allows some lucky kids to tour the facility. However, a few of his guests get sticky fingers (pun intended) and suffer the consequences. This essentially entertaining movie has its memorable moments—as well as bad. Rated G. 98m. **DIR:** Mel Stuart. **CAST:** Gene Wilder, Jack Albertson, Peter Ostrum, Roy Kinnear. **1971 DVD**

WILMA ★★1/2 This made-for-TV film chronicles the early years of Olympic star Wilma Rudolph (Cicely Tyson) and follows her career up to her winning the gold. Film fails to do justice to its subject matter. Lackluster production. 100m. **DIR:** Bud Greenspan. **CAST:** Cicely Tyson, Shirley Jo Finney, Joe Seneca, Jason Bernard. **1977**

WILSON ★★★★1/2 Outstanding film biography of the adult years of Woodrow Wilson (Alexander Knox) as dean of Princeton, governor of New Jersey, and president of the United States, with emphasis on World War I and his later determination to join the League of Nations. Winner of five Oscars, including Lamar Trotti's screenplay, with nominations for best picture, Knox's portrayal, and Henry King's direction. 154m. **DIR:** Henry King. **CAST:** Alexander Knox, Charles Coburn, Geraldine Fitzgerald, Thomas Mitchell, Ruth Nelson, Cedric Hardwicke, Vincent Price, William Eythe. **1944**

WIMPS 🦃 *Animal House* meets *Cyrano de Bergerac*. Rated R for language, nudity, and sexual situations.

94m. **DIR:** Chuck Vincent. **CAST:** Louie Bonanno, Deborah Blaisdell, Jim Abele, Jane Hamilton. **1986**

WIN, PLACE OR STEAL 🦃 Slow, boring comedy about three aging adolescents who prefer playing the ponies to working. Not rated. 88m. **DIR:** Richard Bailey. **CAST:** Dean Stockwell, Russ Tamblyn, Alex Karras, McLean Stevenson. **1972**

WINCHELL ★★★ Biography of Walter Winchell, the great newspaper and radio journalist, is mostly gloss without much dirt. The film paints Winchell as an egotistical hothead and genius with a well-deserved reputation, but leaves out much of the controversy of his life. Fine performances all around, and this made-for-cable production looks slick, but entertainment-wise, some crucial dimension is missing. Rated R for violence, profanity, and simulated sex. 105m. **DIR:** Paul Mazursky. **CAST:** Stanley Tucci, Glenne Headly, Paul Giamatti, Xander Berkeley, Kevin Tighe, Christopher Plummer. **1998**

WINCHESTER '73 ★★★ Cowboy James Stewart acquires the latest iron from the East, a Winchester '73 rifle, loses it to a thief, and pursues the prized weapon as it passes from hand to hand. Simple, brisk-paced, direct, action-packed, tongue-in-cheek, mean, sweaty, suspenseful, and entirely entertaining. B&W; 82m. **DIR:** Anthony Mann. **CAST:** James Stewart, Shelley Winters, Dan Duryea, Stephen McNally, Will Geer, Rock Hudson, Tony Curtis, John McIntire. **1950**

WIND, THE ★★★★ A gentle girl marries a brutish farmhand in order to escape from relatives who do not understand her sensitive nature. She finds no peace. As the girl, Lillian Gish joined Victor Seastrom (né Sjöström) in scoring an artistic triumph. An incredible film. Silent. B&W; 82m. **DIR:** Victor Sjöström. **CAST:** Lillian Gish, Lars Hanson, Montagu Love. **1928**

WIND, THE ★★1/2 There's some solid suspense in this tale of a mystery novelist on a secluded Mediterranean island who is terrorized by a psychopath. Director Nico Mastorakis makes good use of the Greek locations. Unfortunately, he lets his two stars overact. 92m. **DIR:** Nico Mastorakis. **CAST:** Meg Foster, Wings Hauser, Robert Morley. **1986 DVD**

WIND (1992) ★★★ This gorgeously photographed and highly romanticized *Rocky* of the seven seas stars Matthew Modine as a sailing enthusiast who pursues the America's Cup and an ex-girlfriend. The story has the feel of an ancient John Wayne action-comedy, but manages to stay rather dreamily afloat. Rated PG-13 for language. 123m. **DIR:** Carroll Ballard. **CAST:** Matthew Modine, Stellan Skarsgard, Rebecca Miller, Cliff Robertson, Jack Thompson, Jennifer Grey. **1992**

WIND AND THE LION, THE ★★★★ In the 1970s, Sean Connery made a trio of memorable adventure movies, one being this release, impressively directed by John Milius. As in the other two films—*The Man Who Would Be King* and *Robin and Marian*— *The Wind and the Lion*, in which Connery plays a dashing Arab chieftain, is a thoroughly satisfying motion picture. Rated PG. 119m. **DIR:** John Milius. **CAST:** Sean Connery, Brian Keith, Candice Bergen, John Huston, Geoffrey Lewis, Steve Kanaly, Vladek Sheybal. **1975**

WIND IN THE WILLOWS, THE ★★★★★ One of Disney's finest. This adaptation of Kenneth Grahame's classic deals with the adventures of J. Thaddeus Toad and his friends Cyril, Mole, Rat, and Mac Badger. Basil Rathbone narrates this classic short. 75m. **DIR:** Wolfgang Reitherman. **1949**

WIND IN THE WILLOWS, THE ★★★★1/2 Based on the famous Kenneth Grahame book, this collection of three separate stories is a delight of stop-motion animation. The much-loved characters of Mole, Ratty, and of course, Toad, are brought beautifully to life in miniature Edwardian settings. 60m. **DIR:** Mark Hall. **1983**

WIND WILL CARRY US, THE ★★1/2 A group of men arrives in an Iranian village on some unexplained mission; over the next few days their leader engages in a number of social activities, shaves several times, and drives repeatedly up a nearby hill for cell-phone conversations. This Iranian shaggy-dog story is interesting for a while but ultimately a whopping bore. In Farsi with English subtitles. Not rated; suitable for general audiences. 118m. **DIR:** Abbas Kiarostami. **CAST:** Behzad Dourani, Noghre Asadi, Roushan Karam Elmi. **1999**

WINDHORSE ★★★ This amateurish but engrossing melodrama begins as a young Tibetan girl's life is shattered by the murder of her Buddhist grandfather after he protests against the country's occupation by Chinese communists. The girl grows up to reassess her assimilation into repressive foreign rule after another family tragedy. The film was shot clandestinely on location in Tibet. In Tibetan and Mandarin with English subtitles. Not rated. 98m. **DIR:** Paul Wagner. **CAST:** Dadon, Hampa Kelsang, Richard Chang, Lu Yu. **1998**

WINDJAMMER ★★★1/2 Western hero George O'Brien trades the wide open spaces of the range for vast wastes of the Pacific Ocean in this story of high-seas smuggling. Solid adventure. B&W; 58m. **DIR:** Ewing Scott. **CAST:** George O'Brien, Constance Worth. **1937**

WINDMILLS OF THE GODS ★★★ Author Sidney Sheldon's bestselling novel gets the small-screen treatment, with mixed results. There's plenty to look at, from exotic locales to Jaclyn Smith as a lady professor assigned as Ambassador to Romania. Cast is likable, locations are great, but film suffers from melodrama-itis. 95m. **DIR:** Lee Philips. **CAST:** Jaclyn Smith, Robert Wagner, Franco Nero, Ruby Dee, Ian McKellen. **1987**

WINDOM'S WAY ★★★ In this British drama set on an island in the Far East, a struggle ensues between the natives and plantation owners over civil rights. A doctor (Peter Finch) is enlisted as the spokesperson for the natives. Set against the backdrop of World War II, it is enjoyable entertainment. 104m. **DIR:** Ronald Neame. **CAST:** Peter Finch, Mary Ure, Natasha Parry, Robert Flemyng, Michael Hordern, Marne Maitland, Gregoire Aslan. **1957**

WINDOW, THE ★★★1/2 This chilling drama about a young boy who witnesses a murder and finds himself unable to convince any authority figures of what he has seen is one of the classic nightmare films of the postwar period. Bobby Driscoll (who earned a special Academy Award for this film) is kidnapped by the murderers and the film becomes one taut encounter after another. B&W; 73m. **DIR:** Ted Tetzlaff. **CAST:** Bobby Driscoll, Arthur Kennedy, Barbara Hale, Paul Stewart, Ruth Roman. **1949**

WINDOW SHOPPING ★★★ With tongue firmly entrenched in cheek, this French musical-comedy of ro-

mantic error concerns Lilli, the belle of the shopping mall. Somewhat like a cross between *Romeo and Juliet* and *Grease*, this buoyant movie is a cinematographic curiosity piece. In French with English subtitles. Rated R for nudity. 96m. **DIR:** Chantal Akerman. **CAST:** Delphine Seyrig, Myriam Boyer, Fanny Cottençon, Charles Denner, John Berry. **1986**

WINDOW TO PARIS ★★★★1/2 East meets West with hilarious results in this delightful fantasy that skewers human nature and post–cold war nationalism. A young Russian music teacher moves into an apartment house where he and his landlord discover a magic window that opens onto a Paris rooftop. A riotous culture clash ensues as the Russians explore their new backyard. In Russian and French with English subtitles. Rated PG-13 for violence and language. 87m. **DIR:** Yuri Mamin. **CAST:** Sergei Dontsov, Viktor Mikhailov, Agnes Soral. **1995**

WINDRIDER 🦃 A self-centered windsurfer becomes obsessed with his quest to perform a 360-degree flip on his sailboard. Rated R for profanity and simulated sex. 83m. **DIR:** Vincent Morton. **CAST:** Tom Burlinson. **1986**

WINDRUNNER ★★★1/2 Warm, inspirational tale of high-school student fighting personal demons and a new low when he's cut from the football team. Then he encounters an Indian in the desert who agrees to help him. The boy learns many lessons from the wise stranger, and in exchange, tracks down and captures a white stallion for him. Revelations about who the Indian is, and why he is here, make for captivating entertainment. Rousing finale will leave viewers cheering. Rated PG. 110m. **DIR:** William Clark. **CAST:** Russell Means, Jason Wiles, Margot Kidder, Amanda Peterson, Bruce Weitz. **1994**

WINDS OF JARRAH, THE ★★ At the close of World War II, an Englishwoman on the rebound from a bad love affair takes a position in Australia as a nanny. Her employer is a bitter, lonely man who hates women. Readers of paperback romances will guess what happens within the first two minutes, and the rest of the audience won't be far behind. Not rated. 78m. **DIR:** Mark Egerton. **CAST:** Terence Donovan, Harold Hopkins, Susan Lyons. **1983**

WINDS OF KITTY HAWK, THE ★★★★ This made-for-TV movie is beautifully photographed, quietly acted, and gives a wonderful insight into the lives of the Wright brothers and the period in which they lived. A treat for the entire family. 100m. **DIR:** E. W. Swackhamer. **CAST:** Michael Moriarty, David Huffman, Kathryn Walker. **1978**

WINDS OF THE WASTELAND ★★★ Big John Wayne is the head of a stagecoach company that competes for a government mail contract in the days after the pony express. Better than most B Westerns made by the Duke, because he was beginning to show more polish and confidence, but still no classic. B&W; 57m. **DIR:** Mack V. Wright. **CAST:** John Wayne, Phyllis Fraser, Yakima Canutt, Lane Chandler. **1936 DVD**

WINDS OF WAR, THE ★★★1/2 Mega WWII epic follows the lives of a naval officer turned ambassador to Germany (Robert Mitchum) and his family from 1939 to 1941 with Hitler's conquests as a backdrop. Originally a TV miniseries, this adaptation of Herman Wouk's novel spared no expense in production and features dozens of well-known stars. 880m. **DIR:** Dan Curtis. **CAST:** Robert Mitchum, Polly Bergen, Jan-Michael Vincent, Ali MacGraw, John Houseman. **1983**

WINDSOR PROTOCOL, THE ★★★ A former IRA terrorist teams up with the British government to thwart a plan to revive the Third Reich. Interesting to see Alan Thicke play a bad guy. Rated R for violence, profanity, and nudity. 96m. **DIR:** George Mihalka. **CAST:** Kyle MacLachlan, Macha Grenon, Alan Thicke. **1996**

WINDWALKER ★★★★ Trevor Howard plays the title role in this superb film which spans three generations of a Cheyenne Indian family. It refutes the unwritten rule that family entertainment has to be bland and predictable and is proof that films don't need to include sensationalism to hold the attention of modern filmgoers. Rated PG. 108m. **DIR:** Kieth Merrill. **CAST:** Trevor Howard, Nick Ramus, James Remar, Serene Hedin. **1980**

WINDY CITY ★★ Very uneven, very frustrating attempt to chronicle the story of a group of young adults who have known one another since they were kids. It has the feel of being based on real-life experiences but is embarrassingly true to rude and off-putting behavior most people would rather have private memories of. Rated R. 103m. **DIR:** Armyan Bernstein. **CAST:** John Shea, Kate Capshaw, Josh Mostel, Jeffrey DeMunn, Lewis J. Stadlen, James Sutorius. **1984**

WING AND A PRAYER, A ★★★★ An all-male cast in an excellent film about the war in the South Pacific. A combination of actual wartime action photography and soundstage settings give the film an unusual look. One of the most successful propaganda films to be released during World War II. B&W; 98m. **DIR:** Henry Hathaway. **CAST:** Don Ameche, William Eythe, Dana Andrews, Charles Bickford, Cedric Hardwicke, Richard Jaeckel, Harry Morgan, Glenn Langan, Richard Crane. **1944**

WING AND A PRAYER, A ★★★1/2 This tense disaster thriller follows a burned-out air-traffic controller on his return flight to Salt Lake City. His wife is the head controller at Salt Lake, and she deals with all sorts of catastrophes when the computer goes down, but the worst is trying to get her husband's plane landed without radio or transponder. Not rated. 95m. **DIR:** Paul Wendkos. **CAST:** Claudia Christian, Jeff Yagher, Jessica Tuck, Christopher Cousins, Leon Russom. **1997**

WING CHUN ★★★★ Top-notch vehicle for Hong Kong action star Michelle Yeoh (AKA Michelle Khan, star of Jackie Chan's *Police Story III—Super Cop*). As Wing Chun, Yeoh uses her brains as well as her fighting skills to deal with the bandits making trouble in her village. Engaging comedy sequences and fight scenes that are more clever than violent make this one of the best of the Hong Kong action films. Not rated. Available dubbed or in Chinese with English subtitles. 93m. **DIR:** Yuen Wo Ping. **CAST:** Michelle Khan, Donnie Yen, Waise Lee. **1994 DVD**

WING COMMANDER 🦃 In the year 2564, two brash rookie pilots and their female military girlfriends blast aliens into space debris. Based on the popular computer game. Rated PG-13 for language, sexual references, and violence. 100m. **DIR:** Chris Roberts. **CAST:** Freddie Prinze Jr., Matthew Lillard, Jurgen Prochnow,

Saffron Burrows, Ginny Holder, David Suchet, David Warner. **1999 DVD**

WINGS ★★★★ First recipient of the Academy Award for best picture. The story concerns two buddies who join the Air Corps in World War I and go to France to battle the Germans. War scenes are excellent, even by today's standards. B&W; 139m. **DIR:** William Wellman. **CAST:** Clara Bow, Charles "Buddy" Rogers, Richard Arlen, Jobyna Ralston, Gary Cooper, Arlette Marchal, El Brendel. **1927**

WINGS OF DESIRE ★★★★ Angels see in black-and-white; mortals see in color. Wim Wenders's follow-up to *Paris, Texas* is a stark and moving story set in Berlin about two angels (Bruno Ganz and Otto Sander) who travel through the city listening to people's thoughts. Ganz grows weary of comforting others and decides to reenter the world as a human. Rated PG-13 for adult subject matter. In German and French with English subtitles. 130m. **DIR:** Wim Wenders. **CAST:** Bruno Ganz, Solveig Dommartin, Curt Bois, Peter Falk, Otto Sander. **1988**

WINGS OF EAGLES, THE ★★★★ An often moving bio-pic about navy-flier-turned-screenwriter Frank "Spig" Wead *(They Were Expendable)*, this film features fine dramatic performances from John Wayne and Maureen O'Hara. Features the usual John Ford elements of sentimentality and brawling slapstick, but there's also an underlying poignance that makes this a treat. 107m. **DIR:** John Ford. **CAST:** John Wayne, Maureen O'Hara, Dan Dailey, Ward Bond, Ken Curtis, Edmund Lowe, Kenneth Tobey. **1957**

WINGS OF FAME ★★★ Peter O'Toole delivers a deliciously droll performance as Cesar Valetin, an actor who's being stalked by Brian Smith, a young fan played by Colin Firth. When Brian kills Valetin during a film festival, he finds Valetin and himself trapped in a spiritual hotel where the famous and near-famous go after they die. The film takes great delight in exposing pretentions and how they relate to those we put on a pedestal. Insightful, imaginative, and very funny. Rated R for adult language and situations. 109m. **DIR:** Otakar Votocek. **CAST:** Peter O'Toole, Colin Firth, Marie Trintignant. **1990**

WINGS OF THE DOVE, THE ★★1/2 Two penniless English lovers conspire for the man to woo and wed a dying American heiress, expecting to live on her money after she's gone, but their scheme is undone by his conscience, her jealousy, and the heiress's genuine goodness. Henry James's novel of thwarted passion gets a strangely dispassionate filming. Rated R for nudity and sexual scenes. 101m. **DIR:** Iain Softley. **CAST:** Helena Bonham Carter, Linus Roache, Allison Elliot, Charlotte Rampling, Elizabeth McGovern, Michael Gambon. **1997 DVD**

WINNER, THE ★★★ This fresh, sassy, and unusual drama, based on the play *A Darker Purpose* by Wendy Riss, is the story of a Las Vegas man who can't lose and all the real losers around him. Great cast propels the strange story along nicely. Rated R for language and violence. 89m. **DIR:** Alex Cox. **CAST:** Rebecca DeMornay, Vincent D'Onofrio, Delroy Lindo, Michael Madsen, Billy Bob Thornton. **1996**

WINNERS OF THE WEST ★★★ The white hats of the railroad fight it out with the black hats of the unscrupulous land baron in this classic thirteen-part oater jammed with gunplay, burning work trains, dynamited bridges, and a kidnapped heroine. B&W; 234m. **DIR:** Ford Beebe, Ray Taylor. **CAST:** Dick Foran, James Craig, Anne Nagel, Harry Woods. **1940**

WINNERS TAKE ALL ★★1/2 A California teen decides to compete in a Texas regional motocross competition. All of the usual sports-movie clichés are present and accounted for, though the final grudge race is full of high-spirited stunts that even nonracing fans should enjoy. Rated PG-13. 103m. **DIR:** Fritz Kiersch. **CAST:** Don Michael Paul, Kathleen York, Robert Krantz. **1986**

WINNING ★★★1/2 Paul Newman is very good as a race car driver who puts winning above all else, including his family. Some very good racing sequences and fine support from Joanne Woodward and Richard Thomas. Rated PG. 123m. **DIR:** James Goldstone. **CAST:** Paul Newman, Joanne Woodward, Robert Wagner, Richard Thomas. **1969 DVD**

WINNING OF THE WEST ★★ Same old stuff about a brave newspaper publisher who enlists the aid of no-nonsense Gene Autry and all-nonsense Smiley Burnette. B&W; 57m. **DIR:** George Archainbaud. **CAST:** Gene Autry, Smiley Burnette, Gail Davis, Robert Livingston. **1953**

WINNING TEAM, THE ★★ This film biography of baseball pitcher Grover Cleveland Alexander would have worked better with a different cast. Ronald Reagan's inept acting is a distraction. B&W; 99m. **DIR:** Lewis Seiler. **CAST:** Doris Day, Ronald Reagan, Frank Lovejoy, Russ Tamblyn, Eve Miller, James Millican. **1952**

WINSLOW BOY, THE ★★★★ A proper British barrister defends a young naval cadet, wrongly accused of theft, against the overbearing pomp and indifferent might of the Crown. At stake is the long-cherished democratic right to be regarded as innocent until proven guilty by a fair trial. Based on an actual 1912 case, this is a superb courtroom melodrama. B&W; 118m. **DIR:** Anthony Asquith. **CAST:** Robert Donat, Margaret Leighton, Cedric Hardwicke, Basil Radford, Frank Lawton, Wilfrid Hyde-White, Neil North. **1950**

WINSLOW BOY, THE ★★★ American playwright David Mamet wrote and directed this adaptation of Terence Rattigan's play about a British youth falsely accused of petty theft. Edwardian England is a real change of pace for Mamet, and stiff upper lips may not be his style. The film is meticulously produced and generally well acted. Rated G. 104m. **DIR:** David Mamet. **CAST:** Nigel Hawthorne, Jeremy Northam, Rebecca Pidgeon, Gemma Jones, Guy Edwards. **1999 DVD**

WINTER GUEST, THE ★★1/2 Actor Alan Rickman's first directorial effort, adapted from Sharman Macdonald's play, concerns a day in the life of a recently widowed photographer, her strong-willed mother, son, and his new girlfriend, with barely relevant sidebars. The actors all do their best, but the film is uneventful and monumentally dull. Rated R for profanity and brief nudity. 110m. **DIR:** Alan Rickman. **CAST:** Phyllida Law, Emma Thompson, Gary Hollywood, Arlene Cockburn, Sheila Reid, Sandra Voe. **1997**

WINTER KILLS ★★★★ An all-star cast is featured in this sometimes melodramatic, but often wry, account of a presidential assassination. Rated R. 97m. **DIR:** William Richert. **CAST:** Jeff Bridges, John Huston, Be-

linda Bauer, Richard Boone, Anthony Perkins, Toshiro Mifune, Sterling Hayden, Eli Wallach, Ralph Meeker, Dorothy Malone, Tomas Milian, Elizabeth Taylor. **1979**

WINTER LIGHT ★★★ Second film in director Ingmar Bergman's "faith" trilogy (it follows *Through a Glass Darkly* and precedes *The Silence*) centers on a disillusioned priest who attempts to come to grips with his religion and his position in the inner workings of the church. This effort to explore the psyche of a cleric is a thoughtful, incisive drama with great performances. In Swedish with English subtitles. B&W; 80m. **DIR:** Ingmar Bergman. **CAST:** Ingrid Thulin, Gunnar Björnstrand, Max von Sydow, Gunnel Lindblom. **1962**

WINTER MEETING ★★1/2 Talky, slow-moving story of a spinsterish writer falling for a war hero, learning he plans to join the priesthood. Jim Davis's debut. B&W; 115m. **DIR:** Bretaigne Windust. **CAST:** Bette Davis, Jim Davis, Janis Paige, John Hoyt, Florence Bates. **1948**

WINTER OF OUR DREAMS ★★ An all-too-typical soaper about a married man (Bryan Brown) who tries to help a lost soul (Judy Davis). This downbeat film has good acting but less-than-adequate direction. Rated R. 90m. **DIR:** John Duigan. **CAST:** Judy Davis, Bryan Brown, Cathy Downes. **1981**

WINTER PEOPLE ★★★1/2 Kelly McGillis's outstanding performance in this drama elevates what is essentially a Hatfields-and-McCoys rehash. Kurt Russell stars as a clock maker in the Depression who ends up in the Blue Ridge Mountains, where unwed mother McGillis is about to stir up the feudin' locals. Somehow, director Ted Kotcheff and his cast help us forget how silly the film is for most of its running time. Rated PG-13 for violence. 110m. **DIR:** Ted Kotcheff. **CAST:** Kurt Russell, Kelly McGillis, Lloyd Bridges, Mitchell Ryan. **1989**

WINTER SLEEPERS ★★1/2 The film's title refers metaphorically to the six characters whose lives intersect in this technically brilliant but impotent drama about fate, chance encounters, and tragedy. In German with English subtitles. Not rated; contains nudity, simulated sex, profanity, and adult themes. 124m. **DIR:** Tom Tykwer. **CAST:** Floriane Daniel, Heino Ferch, Ulrich Matthes, Marie-Lou Sellem, Josef Bierbichler, Laura Maori Tonke. **2000 DVD**

WINTERBEAST ★★ Shot-on-video thriller concerns a winter resort built on ancient Indian burial grounds. Predictably enough, folks start to disappear. Not rated; contains violence and profanity. 80m. **DIR:** Christopher Thies. **CAST:** Tim R. Morgan, Mike Magri, Dori May Kelly. **1993**

WINTER'S END ★★★1/2 Final entry in the *Sarah, Plain and Tall* trilogy presented by *Hallmark Hall of Fame* features Glenn Close in a battle to survive both a blizzard and the sudden reappearance of her husband's father (Jack Palance). The winter of 1918 falls particularly hard on the Wittings and their Kansas farm but they rely on their Walton-ish bond to empower them. Close and Palance play well off each other in this memorable film. Not rated; contains mature themes. 95m. **DIR:** Glenn Jordan. **CAST:** Glenn Close, Christopher Walken, Jack Palance. **1999 DVD**

WINTERSET ★★1/2 Heavy-duty drama of a bitter young man's efforts to clear his father's name boasts a great cast of distinguished character actors and marks the screen debut of the versatile Burgess Meredith. Long on moralizing and short on action. B&W; 78m. **DIR:** Alfred Santell. **CAST:** Burgess Meredith, Margo, Eduardo Ciannelli, John Carradine, Paul Guilfoyle, Stanley Ridges, Mischa Auer. **1936**

WINTERTIME ★★ Sonja Henie's weakest movie and her last for a major studio. Her showy routines attract people to an old run-down hotel so the owners can afford to turn it into a profitable resort. The musical numbers are better than the dialogue and almost as good as the skating scenes. B&W; 82m. **DIR:** John Brahm. **CAST:** Sonja Henie, Cornel Wilde, Jack Oakie, Cesar Romero, Carole Landis, S. Z. Sakall, Helene Reynolds, Geary Steffen, Woody Herman. **1943**

WIRED 🦃 John Belushi (Michael Chiklis) clambers from a body bag in the morgue after his fatal drug overdose and is escorted through his past by a Puerto Rican angel/cabbie (Ray Sharkey). Rated R. 112m. **DIR:** Larry Peerce. **CAST:** Michael Chiklis, J. T. Walsh, Patti D'Arbanville, Alex Rocco, Ray Sharkey. **1989**

WIRED TO KILL 🦃 The year is 1998, and 120 million Americans are dead from a killer plague. Rated R for violence and raw language. 90m. **DIR:** Franky Schaeffer. **CAST:** Emily Longstreth, Deven Holescher, Merritt Buttrick. **1986**

•WIREY SPINDELL 🦃 Unwatchably self-indulgent and pretentious comedy-drama about a bisexual man reflecting on his romantic life on the eve of his marriage to a woman he can't bring himself to make love to. Not rated; an R equivalent for sexual situations, profanity, and drug use. 101m. **DIR:** Eric Schaeffer. **CAST:** Eric Schaeffer, Eric Mabius, Devon Matthews, Callie Thorne, Jennifer Wiltsie, John Doman, Caroline Strong. **1999 DVD**

WISDOM 🦃 Writer-director Emilio Estevez plays a modern-day Robin Hood who comes to the aid of farmers. Rated R for violence. 109m. **DIR:** Emilio Estevez. **CAST:** Emilio Estevez, Demi Moore, Tom Skerritt, Veronica Cartwright, William Allen Young. **1986**

WISE BLOOD ★★★★ While there are many laughs in this fascinating black comedy about a slow-witted country boy (Brad Dourif) who decides to become a man of the world, they tend to stick in your throat. This searing satire on southern do-it-yourself religion comes so close to the truth, it is almost painful to watch at times. Rated PG. 108m. **DIR:** John Huston. **CAST:** Brad Dourif, Harry Dean Stanton, Ned Beatty, Amy Wright, Dan Shor. **1979**

WISE GUYS ★★★1/2 Director Brian De Palma, apparently tired of derivative Hitchcockian thrillers, returned to his roots with this send-up of gangster movies. Danny DeVito and Joe Piscopo play Harry and Moe, a couple of goofball syndicate gofers. When they muck up a bet on the ponies, as punishment, the boss secretly instructs each to kill the other. Inexplicably rated R for language. 91m. **DIR:** Brian De Palma. **CAST:** Danny DeVito, Joe Piscopo, Harvey Keitel, Ray Sharkey, Dan Hedaya. **1986**

WISH ME LUCK 🦃 A genie tries to help a schlemiel lose his virginity. Not rated; contains nudity and adult situations. 91m. **DIR:** Philip J. Jones. **CAST:** Avalon Anders, Zen Gesner, Christine Harte, Raymond Storti, Stephanie Champlin, David Sobel. **1995**

WISH YOU WERE HERE ★★★★ The heroine of this British production is a foulmouthed, promiscuous 16

year old (superbly played by Emily Lloyd), who raises hackles in the straitlaced world of 1940s England. Her story is shocking, funny, and ultimately touching. Writer-director David Leland has created a hilarious comedy. Rated R for profanity, nudity, and simulated sex. 92m. **DIR:** David Leland. **CAST:** Emily Lloyd, Tom Bell, Jesse Birdsall, Geoffrey Durham, Pat Heywood. **1987**

WISHFUL THINKING ★★ A recluse receives a magical notebook. With it, he can have anything he wants, and he wants a beautiful woman. Sight gags are overdone. Not rated; contains nudity and violence. 94m. **DIR:** Murray Langston. **CAST:** Murray Langston, Michelle Johnson, Ruth Buzzi, Billy Barty, Ray "Boom Boom" Mancini. **1992**

WISHFUL THINKING ★★ Tepid love story told from the viewpoints of three of its main characters. Excellent performances throughout can't shake the dull out of this one. Rated R for profanity. 91m. **DIR:** Adam Park. **CAST:** Drew Barrymore, Jennifer Beals, Jon Stewart, James LeGros. **1997 DVD**

WISHMASTER 2: EVIL NEVER DIES ★★ Sloppy made-for-video sequel delivers more of the same, but with less style and logic. Andrew Divoff returns as the evil Djinn, and seems to have a ball as he grants unsuspecting victims their wishes. Unfortunately, writer-director Jack Sholder fails to realize any real suspense or terror, even though the prison setting is ripe for both. A low budget keeps the filmmakers from fulfilling their vision. Rated R for violence, language, and nudity. 96m. **DIR:** Jack Sholder. **CAST:** Andrew Divoff, Holly Fields, Paul Johansson, Bokeem Woodbine. **1999 DVD**

WISTFUL WIDOW OF WAGON GAP, THE ★★★ Back in the old West a salesman accidentally kills a man and finds that legally he must support the widow and her six children. This doesn't sound like a comedy, but when the salesman is Lou Costello and the widow is Marjorie Main laughs come easily. B&W; 77m. **DIR:** Charles Barton. **CAST:** Bud Abbott, Lou Costello, Marjorie Main, Audrey Young, George Cleveland, Gordon Jones, William Ching. **1947**

•WIT ★★★★1/2 When a professor of English Literature contracts ovarian cancer, her scholarly intellect cannot prepare her for the horrors of an experimental treatment and the very real possibility of her own death. Emma Thompson gives a touching performance, both in portraying the pain and suffering and in delivering witty commentary on the entire process to the viewer. Layered with meaning, emotional and inspiring, this made-for-cable film should not be missed. Rated PG-13 for profanity and brief nudity. 98m. **DIR:** Mike Nichols. **CAST:** Emma Thompson, Christopher Lloyd, Audra McDonald, Jonathon M. Woodward. **2001 DVD**

WITCH HUNT ★★★1/2 This entertaining sequel to *Cast a Deadly Spell* finds Dennis Hopper playing world-weary investigator H. Phillip Lovecraft, the only "regular guy" in a universe where everybody practices magic. Good sight gags and clever dialogue. Rated R for profanity and brief nudity. 100m. **DIR:** Paul Schrader. **CAST:** Dennis Hopper, Penelope Ann Miller, Eric Bogosian, Sheryl Lee Ralph, Julian Sands. **1994**

WITCHBLADE ★★ Destiny targets a tough New York cop to inherit the power of the witchblade, a hand weapon that opens her eyes to evil. Special effects are decent but concept and acting are mediocre. Not rated; contains violence. 90m. **DIR:** Ralph Hemecker. **CAST:** Yancy Butler, David Chokachi, Eric Etebari, Anthony Cistaro. **2000**

WITCHBOARD ★★ Some good moments buoy this horror film about a group of people who play with a Ouija board at a party and find themselves haunted into becoming murderers and victims. Rated R for profanity and violence. 100m. **DIR:** Kevin S. Tenney. **CAST:** Todd Allen, Tawny Kitaen, Stephen Nicholas, Kathleen Wilhoite, Rose Marie. **1987 DVD**

WITCHBOARD 2 🦃 Wannnabe artist moves into a new apartment, toys with an abandoned Ouija board, and unleashes the spirit of a murdered former tenant. A sequel "which bored, too." Rated R for nudity, violence, and profanity. 96m. **DIR:** Kevin S. Tenney. **CAST:** Ami Dolenz, Timothy Gibbs, Laraine Newman. **1993**

WITCHCRAFT 🦃 A new mother can't understand the strange nightmares she begins to have after she moves in with her mother-in-law. R rating. 90m. **DIR:** Robert Spera. **CAST:** Anat Topol-Barzilai. **1988 DVD**

WITCHCRAFT II: THE TEMPTRESS 🦃 This sequel to the original *Witchcraft* is as lame and ridiculous as its predecessor. Rated R for violence, profanity, and simulated sex. 88m. **DIR:** Mark Woods. **CAST:** Charles Solomon. **1990 DVD**

WITCHCRAFT III, THE KISS OF DEATH ★★ Two forces of evil confront each other over the love of a woman in this extremely sexy plot thinly disguised as a horror movie. Offers great-looking young men, sex kittens with breast implants, and mediocre-to-bad acting. Rated R for language. 85m. **DIR:** R. L. Tillmans. **CAST:** Charles Solomon. **1991**

WITCHCRAFT IV 🦃 A lawyer is lured into the world of witchcraft and devil worship, and seeks the help of a stripper. As banal as it sounds. Rated R for nudity. 92m. **DIR:** Kevin Morrissey. **CAST:** Charles Solomon, Julie Strain. **1992**

WITCHCRAFT 7: JUDGMENT HOUR 🦃 Bad-as-they-get sequel about an attorney who is drawn to the dark world of vampires. Rated R for nudity, violence, and language. 89m. **DIR:** Michael Paul Girard. **CAST:** David Byrnes, April Breneman, Alisa Christensen. **1995**

WITCHCRAFT THROUGH THE AGES (HAXAN) ★★★1/2 After seventy years of notoriety, this controversial film is still unique as one of the most outrageous movies of all time. Envisioned by director Benjamin Christensen as a study of black magic, witchcraft, and demonology from the Middle Ages to the present, this silent Scandinavian epic fluctuates between lecture material and incredibly vivid footage that gave the censors ulcers in the 1920s. B&W; 82m. **DIR:** Benjamin Christensen. **CAST:** Maren Pedersen. **1921**

WITCHCRAFT V: DANCE WITH THE DEVIL ★★ Caine (David Huffman), chief cook and bottle washer for Satan, uses unwilling warlock William (Marklen Kennedy) to bring about the release of his evil master. You find yourself wishing that Caine could open the gates of Hell so something interesting would happen. Rated R for violence, nudity, and sexual situations. 94m. **DIR:** Talun Hsu. **CAST:** Marklen Kennedy, Carolyn Taye-Loren, Nicole Sassaman, David Huffman. **1993**

WITCHCRAFT VI: THE DEVIL'S MISTRESS 🦃 More supernatural shenanigans with lawyer/warlock Will

Spanner. Rated R for violence, nudity, simulated sex, and profanity. 86m. **DIR:** Julie Davis. **CAST:** Jerry Spicer, Bryan Nutter, Debra Beatty. **1994**

WITCHCRAFT XI: SISTERS IN BLOOD 🦃 An evil Satanist tries to resurrect three ancient witches by utilizing the bodies of three topless drama students that star in his sacrilegious rendition of *Macbeth*. As terrible a movie as this is, it actually has better production values than *Witchcraft X*. Not rated; not for children. 90m. **DIR:** Ron Ford. **CAST:** Miranda Odell, Don Donason, Lauren Ian Richards. **2000**

WITCHERY ★★ A fairly typical, somewhat suspenseful, demonic-possessions flick about a group of real-estate speculators trapped in a haunted hotel. Not rated. 96m. **DIR:** Martin Newlin. **CAST:** David Hasselhoff, Linda Blair, Catherine Hickland. **1988**

WITCHES, THE (1967) ★★★ Decent chiller from Hammer concerning witchcraft at a private school. While the plot is a fairly well-used subgenre, the wonderful work by the cast really brings the film to life. Joan Fontaine plays the headmistress of the school. 90m. **DIR:** Cyril Frankel. **CAST:** Joan Fontaine, Kay Walsh, Alec McCowen. **1967 DVD**

WITCHES, THE (1990) ★★★★ Everyone over the age of eight will be fascinated by this spooky tale of a 9 year old boy who attempts to thwart the evil designs of the Grand High Witch (Anjelica Huston in top form) as she embarks on a campaign to turn all children into mice. The special effects and makeup are marvelous in this wonderfully spooky adaptation of a Roald Dahl story. Rated PG for scary stuff. 90m. **DIR:** Nicolas Roeg. **CAST:** Anjelica Huston, Mai Zetterling, Jasen Fisher. **1990 DVD**

WITCHES' BREW ★★ Margret (Teri Garr) and her two girlfriends have been dabbling in witchcraft to help their university professor husbands to succeed. It's supposed to be a horror spoof but turns out to be more of a horror rip-off of *Burn Witch Burn*! Lana Turner has a small role as the witchcraft mentor to the three young women. Rated PG. 98m. **DIR:** Richard Shoor, Herbert L. Strock. **CAST:** Richard Benjamin, Teri Garr, Lana Turner, Kathryn Leigh Scott. **1980**

WITCHES OF EASTWICK, THE ★★★★1/2 In this wickedly funny comedy, Jack Nicholson gives one of his finest–and funniest–performances as a self-described "horny little devil" who comes to a tiny hamlet at the behest of three women (Cher, Susan Sarandon, and Michelle Pfeiffer). Only trouble is, these "witches" have no idea of what they've done until it is very nearly too late. Rated R for profanity and suggested sex. 121m. **DIR:** George Miller. **CAST:** Jack Nicholson, Cher, Susan Sarandon, Michelle Pfeiffer, Veronica Cartwright, Richard Jenkins. **1987 DVD**

WITCHING, THE (NECROMANCY) (1972) 🦃 An embarrassment. Rated PG. 82m. **DIR:** Bert I. Gordon. **CAST:** Orson Welles, Pamela Franklin, Michael Ontkean, Lee Purcell. **1972**

WITCHING, THE (1994) ★★ A teen discovers he is the descendant of a witch hunter and is the only one who can stop the queen of the witches. Highly silly, but watchable. Not rated; contains violence and profanity. 70m. **DIR:** Eric Black. **CAST:** Auggi Alvarez, Mike Hellman, Veronica Orr, Frank Dunlay. **1994**

WITCHING OF BEN WAGNER, THE ★★★ Magical tale of 13-year-old Ben's encounter with Regina, a young girl who lives with her kind grandmother. Ben doesn't believe the town's rumors that Regina and her grandmother are witches, but when Ben's father falls under a spell that leads to disaster, he doesn't know what to believe. How Ben copes with the town's prejudices and his father set the scene for a magical encounter. Rated G. 96m. **DIR:** Paul Annett. **CAST:** Sam Bottoms, Justin Gocke, Harriet Hall, Bettina Rae, Sylvia Sydney. **1995**

WITCHING TIME ★★ Another entry from "Thriller Video," hosted by TV's Elvira, "Mistress of the Dark." The owner of an English farmhouse is visited by a previous occupant, a seventeenth-century witch. Unfortunately for him, after three hundred years, the old gal is hot to trot. Originally filmed for the British television series *Hammer House of Horror*. Not rated; nudity edited out of the print used for this cassette. 60m. **DIR:** Don Leaver. **CAST:** Jon Finch, Patricia Quinn, Prunella Gee, Ian McCulloch. **1985**

WITCHOUSE ★★1/2 It's a case of been-there-done-that as this tale of teens in a haunted house unfolds. Nothing new here as one teen resurrects the spirit of a witch and the others begin to fall prey to her. Still, the production values are good and the cast obviously had fun making the film. Rated R for violence, nudity, and gore. 90m. **DIR:** David DeCoteau. **CAST:** Matt Raftery, Ariauna Albright. **1999 DVD**

WITCH'S MIRROR, THE ★★ One of the better entries in the early-Sixties rash of low-budget Mexican horror movies that will bore the pants off some viewers, while entertaining the devotees. In the nineteenth century, the mirror of the title curses an unscrupulous surgeon. Weird and atmospheric, but unevenly dubbed into English. B&W; 75m. **DIR:** Chano Urveta. **CAST:** Rosita Arenas, Armando Calvo. **1960**

WITCHTRAP ★★ Takes place in a mansion haunted by its former owner, who practiced Satanic rituals in the attic. When the new owner hires a team of expert psychics to rid the mansion of its evil, a horrifying chain of events occurs. Rated R for nudity and profanity. 92m. **DIR:** Kevin S. Tenney. **CAST:** James W. Quinn, Kathleen Bailey, Linnea Quigley. **1989**

•WITH A FRIEND LIKE HARRY ★★★★ Independently wealthy Harry crosses paths in a roadside restroom with a former college classmate who is traveling to his country home with his wife and three young girls. Although the man barely remembers him, Harry, who has harbored an odd infatuation with his long-lost chum, worms his way into his life and begins a crusade to upgrade his pal's happiness and rekindle his literary passion. This sly, creepy thriller is an unforgettable personification of deranged obsession. In French with English subtitles. Rated R for language, violence, and nudity. 117m. **DIR:** Dominik Moll. **CAST:** Sergi Lopez, Laurent Lucas, Mathilde Seigner, Sophie Guillemin. **2001 DVD**

WITH HONORS ★★★ Joe Pesci plays a homeless philosopher who teaches blue-blooded Harvard student Brendan Fraser about life and compassion. The story is predictable, even when it takes a tearjerking turn, but Pesci's cocky charm and the remarkably attractive supporting ensemble keep things interesting. Rated PG-13 for profanity and mild nudity. 96m. **DIR:** Alek Keshishian. **CAST:** Joe Pesci, Brendan Fraser, Moira Kelly, Patrick Dempsey, Josh Hamilton, Gore Vidal. **1994 DVD**

WITH SIX YOU GET EGGROLL ★★ Widow Doris Day has three kids; widower Brian Keith has a daughter. They get together. Awwwww! *Bachelor Father* meets *Mother Knows Best*. The two stars refer to Doris and Brian, neither of whom helped their cause with this turkey. Strictly a picture for the 1960s. Not rated. 99m. **DIR:** Howard Morris. **CAST:** Doris Day, Brian Keith, Barbara Hershey. **1968**

WITHIN THE ROCK ★★★ A team of miners is sent to intercept a meteor and push it off its course with Earth by planting charges at its core. What they find at the center is a nasty alien just awakened from a million-year slumber. What could have been a cheesy *Alien* rip-off instead turns out to be an enjoyable romp thanks in large part to a decent script, atmospheric direction, and a great creature. Rated R for violence and profanity. 91m. **DIR:** Gary J. Tunnicliffe. **CAST:** Xander Berkeley, Caroline Barclay, Bradford Tatum, Brian Krause, Barbara Patrick, Duane Whitaker, Earl Boen. **1996 DVD**

WITHNAIL AND I ★★★★ A funny but sometimes grim comedy set in the Great Britain of the late 1960s. Two friends, whose decadent lifestyle of booze and drugs has hit bottom, try to make a new start by taking a holiday in the country. The performances are excellent, period details are perfect, and the movie is well made. Rated R for profanity and adult themes. 110m. **DIR:** Bruce Robinson. **CAST:** Richard E. Grant, Paul McGann, Richard Griffiths. **1987 DVD**

WITHOUT A CLUE ★★★★ In this delightful send-up of Conan Doyle's mysteries, it is revealed that Holmes was nothing more than a fictional creation of the real crime-fighting genius, Dr. John H. Watson (Ben Kingsley). The Great Detective was actually an inept, clumsy, and often inebriated actor, Reginald Kincaid (Michael Caine), hired by Watson. An overlooked gem of a comedy. Rated PG for violence. 106m. **DIR:** Thom Eberhardt. **CAST:** Michael Caine, Ben Kingsley, Jeffrey Jones, Lysette Anthony, Paul Freeman, Nigel Davenport, Peter Cook. **1988**

WITHOUT A TRACE ★★★ A drama about a boy who vanishes and his mother's unrelenting faith that he will return, this is yet another entry in the family-in-trouble movie genre. Well-acted but sometimes overwrought and predictable. Rated PG for mature content. 120m. **DIR:** Stanley Jaffe. **CAST:** Kate Nelligan, Judd Hirsch, David Dukes, Stockard Channing, Jacqueline Brooks, Kathleen Widdoes. **1983**

WITHOUT LOVE ★★★★ Widow Katharine Hepburn enters into a marriage of convenience with scientist Spencer Tracy. Great fun, with this wonderful team being matched every step of the way by wisecracking Lucille Ball and likable lush Keenan Wynn. B&W; 111m. **DIR:** Harold S. Bucquet. **CAST:** Spencer Tracy, Katharine Hepburn, Lucille Ball, Keenan Wynn, Patricia Morison, Felix Bressart. **1945**

WITHOUT MERCY ★★ Tedious actioner tells the story of a former Marine who—after seeing his fellow Marines murdered in an ambush—leaves the military and hits the streets of Somalia. There he winds up enmeshed with a brutal drug kingpin and the kingpin's girlfriend. Nothing new or unique to recommend this shabby direct-to-video release. Rated R for violence, profanity, and sexual situations. 88m. **DIR:** Robert Anthony. **CAST:** Frank Zagarino, Ayu Azhari, Frans Tumbuan, Martin Kove. **1995**

WITHOUT RESERVATIONS ★★★ Wartime comedy about an author and her plan to turn a soldier into the leading man of her filmed novel is light and enjoyable and sprinkled with guest appearances by Hollywood celebrities. B&W; 107m. **DIR:** Mervyn LeRoy. **CAST:** John Wayne, Claudette Colbert, Don DeFore, Phil Brown, Thurston Hall, Louella Parsons. **1946**

WITHOUT WARNING 🦃 Hollywood veterans battle with an intergalactic alien hunter (a rubber-faced leftover from the *Outer Limits* television series) and his hungry pets. Rated R. 89m. **DIR:** Greydon Clark. **CAST:** Jack Palance, Martin Landau, Cameron Mitchell, Larry Storch, Sue Ane Langdon. **1980**

WITHOUT WARNING: THE JAMES BRADY STORY ★★★★ Scripter Robert Bolt, drawing from Mollie Dickenson's book *Thumbs Up*, provides Beau Bridges with a plum role. He's absolutely splendid as press secretary James Brady in this TV-movie re-creation of John Hinckley's assassination attempt on Ronald Reagan, which left the president wounded and Brady crippled for life. 120m. **DIR:** Michael Toshiyuki Uno. **CAST:** Beau Bridges, Joan Allen, Bryan Clark, Steven Flynn, David Strathairn. **1991**

WITHOUT YOU I'M NOTHING ★★★★ Comedian and social satirist Sandra Bernhard stars in an adaptation (cowritten with director John Boskovich) of her celebrated one-woman show. Not for the prudish or easily offended, but there are many thought-provoking laughs as Bernhard pokes wicked fun at middle-class life, love, and sexual politics. Rated R for profanity. 89m. **DIR:** John Boskovich. **CAST:** Sandra Bernhard. **1990**

WITNESS ★★★★1/2 This is three terrific movies in one: an exciting cop thriller, a touching romance, and a fascinating screen study of a modern-day clash of cultures. Harrison Ford is superb as a detective who must protect an 8 year old Amish boy, the only witness to a drug-related murder. Rated R for violence, profanity, and nudity. 112m. **DIR:** Peter Weir. **CAST:** Harrison Ford, Kelly McGillis, Josef Sommer, Lukas Haas, Alexander Godunov, Danny Glover. **1985 DVD**

WITNESS FOR THE PROSECUTION (1957) ★★★★★ Superb performances help make this gripping courtroom drama an enduring favorite of film buffs. The screenplay was adapted from a play by Agatha Christie and features Charles Laughton as an aging lawyer called upon to defend an alleged murderer (Tyrone Power). It is Dietrich, in one of her greatest screen performances, who nearly steals the show. B&W; 114m. **DIR:** Billy Wilder. **CAST:** Tyrone Power, Charles Laughton, Marlene Dietrich, Elsa Lanchester, John Williams, Henry Daniell, Una O'Connor. **1957 DVD**

WITNESS FOR THE PROSECUTION (1982) ★★★ An enjoyable made-for-television remake of Agatha Christie's courtroom drama. Ralph Richardson and Deborah Kerr are adequate as the wily yet ailing barrister and his continually frustrated nurse. Unfortunately, they lack the rich humor brought to the roles by Charles Laughton and Elsa Lanchester in the original. Beau Bridges is particularly outstanding as the defendant. 100m. **DIR:** Alan Gibson. **CAST:** Ralph Richardson, Beau Bridges, Diana Rigg, Deborah Kerr. **1982**

WITNESS PROTECTION ★★★★ Taut, intense drama about a family forced into the government's witness protection program and the havoc it wreaks upon their lives. Excellent performances throughout. Rated R for violence and profanity. 105m. **DIR:** Richard Pearce. **CAST:** Tom Sizemore, Mary Elizabeth Mastrantonio, Shawn Hatosy, Sky McCole Bartusiak, Forest Whitaker, William Sandler. **1999 DVD**

WITNESS TO THE EXECUTION ★★★1/2 Enthralling made-for-television thriller about a TV executive who hits upon the next big thing: broadcasting an execution. The executive needs the perfect star, and she finds one in a handsome and personable death row inmate. There's just one problem: he may not be guilty. Rated PG-13 for some intense situations. 92m. **DIR:** Tommy Lee Wallace. **CAST:** Sean Young, Timothy Daly, Len Cariou, George Newbern, Alan Fudge, Dee Wallace. **1993**

WIVES UNDER SUSPICION ★★★ Fanatical district attorney whose sole purpose in life is executing murderers is slapped into reality when a case he is prosecuting bears an uneasy similarity to his own situation at home. Warren William is fine as the zealous avenger, and Gail Patrick shines as his ignored and restless wife. B&W; 68m. **DIR:** James Whale. **CAST:** Warren William, Gail Patrick, William Lundigan, Constance Moore, Ralph Morgan, Samuel S. Hinds. **1938**

WIZ, THE ★★ Ineffective updating of *The Wizard of Oz* with an all-black cast, including Diana Ross (who is too old for the part), Richard Pryor, and Michael Jackson. Adapted from a successful Broadway play, this picture should have been better. Rated G. 133m. **DIR:** Sidney Lumet. **CAST:** Diana Ross, Richard Pryor, Michael Jackson, Nipsey Russell, Ted Ross, Mabel King, Theresa Merritt, Thelma Carpenter, Lena Horne. **1978 DVD**

WIZ KID, THE ★★ Teenage high jinks find young computer whiz Martin Forbes cloning himself so his hipper alter self can make out with the prettiest girl in school. Predictable problems don't help this obviously dubbed foreign import. Rated PG for adult situations. 90m. **DIR:** Gloria Behrens. **CAST:** Martin Forbes, Gary Forbes, Heiner Lauterbach. **1993**

WIZARD, THE ★★ It's *Rain Man* meets the *Pinball Wizard* as Fred Savage takes his emotionally disturbed half brother (Luke Edwards) to the national video game championship. Little more than a cleverly disguised advertisement for Nintendo games and the Universal Studios Tour. Rated PG for light violence and profanity. 100m. **DIR:** Todd Holland. **CAST:** Fred Savage, Beau Bridges, Christian Slater, Luke Edwards, Jenny Lewis. **1989**

WIZARD OF GORE, THE 🦃 Blood and guts galore as a sideshow magician takes the old "saw the girl in half" trick a bit too far. Rated R. 80m. **DIR:** Herschell Gordon Lewis. **CAST:** Ray Sager. **1970 DVD**

WIZARD OF LONELINESS, THE ★★★1/2 After his mom dies and his dad goes off to war (World War II), young Wendall Oler (Lukas Haas) is forced to live with his grandparents, aunt, uncle, and cousin. Good acting and excellent Forties sets and costumes add to John Nichols's thought-provoking novel. Rated PG-13 for violence and profanity. 110m. **DIR:** Jenny Bowen. **CAST:** Lukas Haas, Lea Thompson, John Randolph, Anne Pitoniak. **1988**

WIZARD OF MARS, THE ★★ Low-budget interplanetary version of *The Wizard of Oz* finds a rocketship full of Earthlings on the planet Mars where magic and fantasy are the prevalent forces. Written, directed, and produced by David Hewitt, with technical assistance from famed science-fiction–fantasy expert Forrest J. Ackerman, this doesn't really compare to major science-fiction or fantasy films. 81m. **DIR:** David L. Hewitt. **CAST:** John Carradine, Vic McGee, Roger Gentry. **1964**

WIZARD OF OZ, THE ★★★★★ Fifty years old and still going strong—on a fresh, bright Technicolor print with special rare footage additions—this all-time classic continues to charm audiences of all ages. In this case, for watching great movies, "there is no place like home." Right, Toto? 119m. **DIR:** Victor Fleming. **CAST:** Judy Garland, Ray Bolger, Bert Lahr, Jack Haley, Frank Morgan, Billie Burke, Margaret Hamilton, Charley Grapewin, Clara Blandick. **1939 DVD**

WIZARD OF SPEED AND TIME, THE ★★★ Based on Mike Jittlov's own difficulties in breaking into show business, this tongue-in-cheek success story features him producing a special-effects masterpiece on a shoestring budget. Silly gags and slapstick surround five stop-motion shorts. Rated PG for language. 92m. **DIR:** Mike Jittlov. **CAST:** Mike Jittlov, Paige Moore, Richard Kaye, Philip Michael Thomas. **1986**

WIZARD OF THE LOST KINGDOM 🦃 Bo Svenson as a master swordsman who comes to the aid of a sorcerer's son. Rated PG for violence. 76m. **DIR:** Hector Olivera. **CAST:** Bo Svenson, Vidal Peterson, Thom Christopher. **1985**

WIZARD OF THE LOST KINGDOM II 🦃 In medieval times, a boy wizard is sent on a quest to bring freedom to three kingdoms. Rated PG. 80m. **DIR:** Charles B. Griffith. **CAST:** David Carradine, Bobby Jacoby, Mel Wells. **1989**

WIZARDS ★★★ Director-animator Ralph Bakshi's cost-cutting corners, which had not been that evident in his *Fritz the Cat* films, become a bit too noticeable in this charming little tale of ultimate good versus ultimate evil. Our hero is an aged wizard who relies on magic; his evil doppelgänger resorts to the horrors of technology. The conflict builds well until its climax, which (sadly) negates the premise of the entire battle. Rated PG for occasionally graphic violence. 81m. **DIR:** Ralph Bakshi. **1977**

•**WIZARDS OF THE DEMON SWORD** 🦃 Sword and sorcery nonsense that can't decide whether it wants to parody the genre or emulate it. Rated R for violence and nudity. 81m. **DIR:** Fred Olen Ray. **CAST:** Heidi Paine, Jay Richardson, Russ Tamblyn, Lawrence Tierney, Lyle Waggoner, Dawn Wildsmith, Michael Berryman. **1991**

WOLF ★★★★ A clever combination of horror film, social comment, and character study as publishing-house editor Jack Nicholson finds himself trapped as his company changes hands and a smarmy protégé co-opts his job. An accidental encounter with a wolf gives Nicholson a new edge. It's genre fun for smart people, with first-rate performances. Rated R for profanity, violence, and suggested sex. 125m. **DIR:** Mike Nichols. **CAST:** Jack Nicholson, Michelle Pfeiffer, James Spader, Kate

Nelligan, Richard Jenkins, Christopher Plummer, Om Puri, Ron Rifkin, Prunella Scales. **1994 DVD**

WOLF AT THE DOOR ★★ Pompous and heavy-handed, this film gnaws away at painter Paul Gauguin's life in a rather self-conscious fashion, despite some beautiful photography. Predictable and ponderous, and Gauguin's love life with 13-year-old girls is downright depressing. English-dubbed. Rated R. 94m. **DIR:** Henning Carlsen. **CAST:** Donald Sutherland, Fanny Bastien. **1987**

WOLF CALL ★★ Jack London's story of a dog brought from the city to join a wolf pack somehow evolves into a musical-adventure-drama in this curious film. Playboy John Carroll falls in love with Indian maiden Movita while investigating his father's radium mine. B&W; 61m. **DIR:** George Waggner. **CAST:** John Carroll, Movita. **1939**

WOLF MAN, THE ★★★★★ Classic horror film featuring a star-making performance by Lon Chaney Jr. as Lawrence Talbot (a role he would go on to play five times). Upon attempting to save a young woman from a wolf's vicious attack, Talbot is bitten by a werewolf. Now he too will become a bloodthirsty creature of the night whenever the full moon rises. B&W; 70m. **DIR:** George Waggner. **CAST:** Lon Chaney Jr., Evelyn Ankers, Claude Rains, Patric Knowles, Ralph Bellamy, Bela Lugosi, Maria Ouspenskaya, Warren William. **1941 DVD**

WOLFEN ★★ The best features of this sluggish horror film are its innovative visual work and actors who make the most of an uneven script. Directed by Michael Wadleigh, it follows a sequence of mysterious murders that are sometimes disturbingly bloody. This explains the R rating. 115m. **DIR:** Michael Wadleigh. **CAST:** Albert Finney, Diane Venora, Gregory Hines, Tommy Noonan, Edward James Olmos, Dick O'Neill. **1981**

WOLFHEART'S REVENGE ★★1/2 Wolfheart, a Rin-Tin-Tin look-alike, helps Guinn "Big Boy" Williams bring a killer to justice and win the girl in this silent oater. B&W; 64m. **DIR:** Fritz Lang. **CAST:** Guinn Williams, Helen Walton. **1925**

WOLFMAN 🦃 A young man inherits his ancestral home, only to be transformed into a wolfman by a cult of Satanists. Not rated; contains violence. 91m. **DIR:** Worth Keeter. **CAST:** Earl Owensby. **1978**

WOLVES, THE ★★1/2 Gorgeous scenery outshines this simplistic story about a brother and sister's plans to thwart a developer who seeks to turn the untamed wilderness into a toxic-dump site. The children are aided by a Native American, who wants to protect a pack of wolves that inhabit the area. Rated PG-13 for violence. 87m. **DIR:** Steve Carver. **CAST:** Darren Dalton, Raimund Harmstorf, Ben Cardinal, John Furey, Kristen Hocking. **1994**

WOLVES, THE ★★★ Three gangsters fight for survival in this stylish but slightly overlong *yakuza* story set in pre–World War II Japan, when the old samurai-based ways were beginning to collapse. In Japanese with English subtitles. Not rated. 132m. **DIR:** Hideo Gosha. **CAST:** Tatsuya Nakadai. **1981**

WOMAN AT HER WINDOW, A ★★★ A wealthy woman is drawn into political intrigue when she aids a revolutionary in his escape from Greece. Focus is primarily on her relationships with her philandering husband, an adoring fan, and the handsome man on the run. Suspense and romance make for a winning formula and Romy Schneider, as passion's plaything, is absolutely mesmerizing. In French with English subtitles. Not rated. 110m. **DIR:** Pierre Granier-Deferre. **CAST:** Romy Schneider, Philippe Noiret, Victor Lanoux, Umberto Orsini. **1977**

WOMAN AT WAR, A ★★★★ Well-conceived, taut drama about a young woman whose parents are arrested by the Gestapo in war-torn Brussels. Determined to survive, she goes undercover and infiltrates Gestapo headquarters, a move that could cost her life. Martha Plimpton and Eric Stoltz shine in this made-for-British-television drama. Not rated. 115m. **DIR:** Edward Bennett. **CAST:** Martha Plimpton, Eric Stoltz. **1991**

WOMAN CALLED GOLDA, A ★★★1/2 Ingrid Bergman won an Emmy for her outstanding performance as Israeli Prime Minister Golda Meir. Leonard Nimoy costars in this highly watchable film, which was originally made for TV. 200m. **DIR:** Alan Gibson. **CAST:** Ingrid Bergman, Judy Davis, Leonard Nimoy. **1982**

WOMAN CALLED MOSES, A ★★★ Cicely Tyson plays Harriet Tubman to perfection in this made-for-TV dramatization of her life. Unfortunately, this TV movie is soured by unnecessary narration by Orson Welles. 200m. **DIR:** Paul Wendkos. **CAST:** Cicely Tyson, Will Geer, Robert Hooks, James Wainwright, Hari Rhodes. **1978**

WOMAN CHASER, THE ★★★ A slick L.A. used-car salesman, convinced he was cut out for greater things, decides to break into the movie business. Director Robinson Devor cleverly follows the style of the grade-B *films noir* of the 1950s (when the story takes place). There's more style than depth, but the effort is interesting. Rated R for profanity and some sexual scenes. B&W; 87m. **DIR:** Robinson Devor. **CAST:** Patrick Warburton, Emily Newman, Eugene Roche, Lynette Bennett. **1999**

WOMAN, HER MEN AND HER FUTON, A 🦃 Pointless film about a shallow woman who uses men for sex, money, and her career. She's so insipid and unsympathetic that it's painful to watch. Rated R for nudity, suggested sex, and profanity. 92m. **DIR:** Mussef Sibay. **CAST:** Jennifer Rubin, Lance Edwards, Grant Show, Robert Lipton. **1991 DVD**

WOMAN IN FLAMES, A ★★★★ A male and a female prostitute fall in love and decide to set up shop in the same household, insisting that their business trysts will not interfere with their personal relationship. If erotic drama and bizarre twists are your fancy, this should be your film. Rated R for sexual situations and language. 104m. **DIR:** Robert Van Ackeren. **CAST:** Gudrun Landgrebe, Mathieu Carriere. **1984**

WOMAN IN GREEN, THE ★★★ This is a grisly little entry in the Rathbone/Bruce Sherlock Holmes series, with the master sleuth investigating a series of severed fingers sent to Scotland Yard. The culprit is, once again, Professor Moriarty (Henry Daniell). Careful viewers will detect moments from *The Adventure of the Empty House*. B&W; 68m. **DIR:** Roy William Neill. **CAST:** Basil Rathbone, Nigel Bruce, Hillary Brooke, Henry Daniell, Paul Cavanagh. **1945 DVD**

WOMAN IN QUESTION ★★★1/2 When a fortune-teller is murdered, the police detective who investigates tries to decide what to believe from conflicting testimony offered by five people who knew her. This structurally com-

plex drama has aged well and will be appreciated by Quentin Tarantino fans as well as English-mystery buffs. B&W; 84m. **DIR:** Anthony Asquith. **CAST:** Jean Kent, Dirk Bogarde, Hermione Baddeley. **1949**

WOMAN IN RED, THE ★★★★ Gene Wilder's funniest film in years, this is best described as a bittersweet romantic comedy. Wilder, who also adapted the screenplay and directed, plays an advertising executive and heretofore happily married man who becomes obsessed with a beautiful woman. The results are hilarious. Rated PG-13 for partial nudity, brief violence, and profanity. 87m. **DIR:** Gene Wilder. **CAST:** Gene Wilder, Charles Grodin, Joseph Bologna, Gilda Radner, Judith Ivey, Michael Huddleston, Kelly LeBrock. **1984 DVD**

WOMAN IN THE DUNES ★★★★★ An entomologist collecting beetles on the dunes misses his bus back to the city. Some locals offer him assistance, and he is lowered by a ladder down into a sand pit where he finds a woman willing to provide food and lodging in her shack. The ladder is removed, however, and he is trapped. A classic thriller. In Japanese with English subtitles. B&W; 123m. **DIR:** Hiroshi Teshigahara. **CAST:** Eiji Okada. **1964 DVD**

WOMAN IN THE MOON (GIRL IN THE MOON; BY ROCKET TO THE MOON) ★★★ Fritz Lang's last silent film is actually a futuristic melodrama written by his wife and collaborator, Thea von Harbou. Admired by science-fiction aficionados for Lang's imaginative visual sense, not the content of the story. German, silent. B&W; 115m. **DIR:** Fritz Lang. **CAST:** Gerda Maurus, Willy Fritsch, Fritz Rasp, Gustav von Waggenheim. **1929**

WOMAN IN THE WINDOW ★★★★1/2 A mild-mannered college professor (Edward G. Robinson) who would never dream of cheating on his wife indulges in an innocent conversation with a beautiful woman (Joan Bennett). Before he knows it, he's sucked into a spiral of murder and blackmail. One of the best from the classic period of Hollywood *film noir*, this is grippingly directed by Fritz Lang. Its only weakness is the ending, which many viewers may see as a Hollywood cop-out, even though it was planned by Lang. B&W; 99m. **DIR:** Fritz Lang. **CAST:** Edward G. Robinson, Joan Bennett, Raymond Massey, Dan Duryea. **1945**

WOMAN IS A WOMAN, A ★★★★ One of Jean-Luc Godard's most accessible movies is built around a love triangle involving a stripper (Anna Karina, whom Godard married after filming), her lover, and his best friend. Unlike much of Godard's later work, this tribute cum parody of Hollywood musicals keeps your attention even when the literal meaning is unclear. In French with English subtitles. 85m. **DIR:** Jean-Luc Godard. **CAST:** Anna Karina, Jean-Paul Belmondo, Jean-Claude Brialy, Jeanne Moreau. **1961 DVD**

WOMAN NAMED JACKIE, A ★★★ Made-for-television miniseries based on the best-selling biography by C. David Heymann, features a winning Roma Downey as the First Lady whose life was plagued by heartbreak. While Downey shines, the rest of the docudrama plays like a prime-time soap opera. Handsome production values and period detail. 289m. **DIR:** Larry Peerce. **CAST:** Roma Downey, William Devane, Stephen Collins, Joss Ackland, Wendy Hughes. **1993**

WOMAN NEXT DOOR, THE ★★★★1/2 François Truffaut is on record as one of the greatest admirers of Alfred Hitchcock, and the influence shows in this gripping, well-made film about guilt, passion, and the influence of a small sin that grows. In French with English subtitles. MPAA not rated, but contains nudity and violence. 106m. **DIR:** François Truffaut. **CAST:** Gérard Depardieu, Fanny Ardant, Henri Garcin. **1981 DVD**

WOMAN OBSESSED, A ★★ When a mentally unstable woman who had been forced to give up her son for adoption meets him as an adult, she goes crazy and kidnaps him, thinking he is her dead husband. Lurid melodrama takes too long to get going, though the later scenes are suspenseful. Rated R for violence and sexual situations. 103m. **DIR:** Chuck Vincent. **CAST:** Ruth Raymond, Gregory Patrick, Troy Donahue, Linda Blair. **1989**

WOMAN OF AFFAIRS, A ★★★ Young woman with wild tendencies loses her true love and enters into a disastrous marriage. Watered-down version of Michael Arelen's *The Green Hat*. Greta Garbo steals the show. Silent with synchronized score and effects. B&W; 90m. **DIR:** Clarence Brown. **CAST:** Greta Garbo, John Gilbert, Lewis Stone, Johnny Mack Brown, Douglas Fairbanks Jr., Hobart Bosworth. **1928**

WOMAN OF DESIRE ★★ The South African scenery and Robert Mitchum's shrewd defense attorney are the sole attractions in this relentlessly silly erotic thriller. It's impossible to determine who did what to whom, except that Bo Derek—who still acts with her fingers in her mouth—does it with nearly everybody. Rated R for profanity, nudity, and simulated sex. 97m. **DIR:** Robert Ginty. **CAST:** Jeff Fahey, Bo Derek, Steven Bauer, Robert Mitchum. **1993 DVD**

WOMAN OF DISTINCTION, A ★★★1/2 Though minor, this is really a quite enjoyable film. Rosalind Russell portrays a college dean who must face a tough decision involving a professor (Ray Milland). Familiar but fun. B&W; 85m. **DIR:** Edward Buzzell. **CAST:** Rosalind Russell, Ray Milland, Edmund Gwenn, Janis Carter, Francis Lederer. **1950**

WOMAN OF INDEPENDENT MEANS, A ★★★1/2 Disappointing conclusion mars an otherwise spellbinding adaptation of Elizabeth Forsythe Hailey's novel. Always terrific Sally Field plays Bess Alcott, a plucky southern belle. Having her own money, she challenges female norms from the time of her marriage in 1907 until 1963. Conflicts with her daughter are more annoying than plot enriching. A TV miniseries, this is unrated but contains adult themes. 270m. **DIR:** Robert Greenwald. **CAST:** Sally Field, Ron Silver, Charles Durning, Brenda Fricker, Tony Goldwyn, Jack Thompson. **1995**

WOMAN OF PARIS, A ★★★★ In this now-classic silent, a simple country girl (Edna Purviance) goes to Paris and becomes the mistress of a wealthy philanderer (Adolphe Menjou). In her wake follow her artist sweetheart and his mother. Director Charles Chaplin surprised everyone with this film by suddenly forsaking, if only momentarily, his Little Tramp comedy for serious caustic drama. B&W; 112m. **DIR:** Charles Chaplin. **CAST:** Edna Purviance, Adolphe Menjou, Henry Bergman. **1923 DVD**

WOMAN OF SUBSTANCE, A ★★★1/2 This TV miniseries retells Barbara Taylor Bradford's bestselling novel of love and revenge. Multimillionairess Emma Hart re-

calls her humble beginnings as a poor servant girl, her struggle to survive, and finding the love of her life. Fine entertainment. Three tapes. 300m. **DIR:** Don Sharp. **CAST:** Jenny Seagrove, Deborah Kerr, Barry Bostwick, John Mills, Barry Morse. **1984 DVD**

WOMAN OF THE TOWN ★★1/2 Albert Dekker, as famed sheriff Bat Masterson, is forced to choose between his job and his love for saloon girl Claire Trevor. Good supporting cast can't save the slow pace of this Western soap opera. B&W; 87m. **DIR:** George Archainbaud. **CAST:** Albert Dekker, Claire Trevor, Barry Sullivan, Henry Hull. **1943**

WOMAN OF THE YEAR ★★★★★ This is the film that first teamed Spencer Tracy and Katharine Hepburn, and it's impossible to imagine anybody else doing a better job. He's a sports reporter; she's a famed political journalist who needs to be reminded of life's simple pleasures. Like baseball . . . and her attempts to learn the game are priceless. The witty script garnered an Oscar for Ring Lardner Jr. and Michael Kanin. Not rated—family fare. B&W; 112m. **DIR:** George Stevens. **CAST:** Spencer Tracy, Katharine Hepburn, Fay Bainter, Reginald Owen, William Bendix. **1942**

WOMAN ON TOP ★★1/2 Leaving her homeland and cheating husband for a new life in San Francisco, Brazilian beauty Isabella moves into an apartment with a transvestite friend, becomes the star of a TV cooking show, and learns to take charge of her own future. This comic tale of self-empowerment is entertaining but has trouble sustaining its sense of magic realism. The title refers to her favorite sex position as well as her newfound state of mind. Rated R for language, nudity, and sexuality. 83m. **DIR:** Fina Torres. **CAST:** Penelope Cruz, Murilo Benicio, Harold Perrineau Jr., Mark Feuerstein. **2000 DVD**

WOMAN REBELS, A ★★★★ Surprisingly valid today despite its 1936 vintage. Katharine Hepburn plays a rebellious woman of Victorian England who flouts convention and becomes a fighter for women's rights. Van Heflin makes his film debut. B&W; 88m. **DIR:** Mark Sandrich. **CAST:** Katharine Hepburn, Herbert Marshall, Donald Crisp, Elizabeth Allan, Van Heflin. **1936**

WOMAN TIMES SEVEN ★★ Shirley MacLaine assays seven different roles in this episodic stew and is not as good as she could have been in any of them. There are some funny moments, but they do not a film make. 99m. **DIR:** Vittorio De Sica. **CAST:** Shirley MacLaine, Peter Sellers, Alan Arkin, Rossano Brazzi, Robert Morley, Michael Caine, Vittorio Gassman, Anita Ekberg. **1967**

WOMAN UNDER THE INFLUENCE, A ★★★★ Gena Rowlands is fascinating as a housewife mother swinging back and forth over the edge of insanity, with mood changes from vamp to childlike innocence. Peter Falk is her husband, trying to cope and be understanding, but often lashing out in utter frustration. The movie has been designated a "National Treasure" by the National Film Registry of the Library of Congress. Rated R for adult situations. 147m. **DIR:** John Cassavetes. **CAST:** Gena Rowlands, Peter Falk. **1974 DVD**

WOMAN UNDONE ★★1/2 Mary McDonnell provides more talent than this project deserves, as a philandering wife whose husband dies under very mysterious circumstances. It's absolutely impossible to identify with this self-centered sufferer, although McDonnell tries to make her sympathetic. Rated R for profanity, violence, and simulated sex. 92m. **DIR:** Evelyn Purcell. **CAST:** Mary McDonnell, Randy Quaid, Sam Elliott, Benjamin Bratt. **1995**

WOMAN WITH A PAST ★★★1/2 Forced to flee an abusive marriage with her two children, Pamela Reed (in a stellar performance) takes some drastic measures and becomes a fugitive of the law. After she establishes another identity, federal agents come knocking at her door and her perfect world begins to crumble. Torn from today's headlines, this film is a tour de force for Reed. Rated R for violence, language, and adult situations. 95m. **DIR:** Mimi Leder. **CAST:** Pamela Reed, Dwight Schultz, Richard Lineback, Carrie Snodgress, Paul LeMat. **1994**

WOMAN WITHOUT LOVE, A ★★★ Absorbing melodrama about a neglected housewife who indulges in an affair with an engineer only to return to her wealthy old husband. Twenty years later, the husband leaves a fortune to her son's lover, causing a family castastrophe. In Spanish with English subtitles. Not rated. B&W; 91m. **DIR:** Luis Buñuel. **CAST:** Rosario Granados, Julio Villarreal. **1952**

WOMAN'S FACE, A ★★★1/2 Joan Crawford is the heroine accused of villain Conrad Veidt's murder. Her personality undergoes an amazing transformation following plastic surgery in this taut, strongly plotted melodrama. B&W; 105m. **DIR:** George Cukor. **CAST:** Joan Crawford, Conrad Veidt, Melvyn Douglas, Osa Massen, Reginald Owen, Albert Basserman, Marjorie Main, Charles Quigley, Henry Daniell, George Zucco, Robert Warwick. **1941**

WOMAN'S SECRET, A ★★ Confusing story about a once-popular singer who confesses to the shooting of her protégé; done with flashbacks and testimonials. Second-rate whodunit. B&W; 85m. **DIR:** Nicholas Ray. **CAST:** Maureen O'Hara, Melvyn Douglas, Gloria Grahame, Victor Jory, Bill Williams, Jay C. Flippen, Ellen Corby. **1949**

WOMAN'S TALE, A ★★★★★ A superb film from the highly individual Australian director, Paul Cox. It focuses on Martha, a modern, young-at-heart, fiercely independent woman, trapped in an 80 year old body. This sensitive, humane, and gently profound film portrays Martha as she approaches the end of her life, refusing to give in to cynicism. Not rated. 94m. **DIR:** Paul Cox. **CAST:** Sheila Florance, Norman Kaye. **1992**

WOMAN'S WORLD ★★★★ A movie that paints a pretty picture of business and businessmen, this one is a curiosity piece as well as an entertaining film. Clever comedy about businesses and office politics. 94m. **DIR:** Jean Negulesco. **CAST:** June Allyson, Clifton Webb, Lauren Bacall, Fred MacMurray, Cornel Wilde, Arlene Dahl, Elliott Reid, Margalo Gilmore. **1954**

WOMEN, THE ★★★★1/2 Director George Cukor and some of Hollywood's finest female stars combine for a winning screen version of Clare Boothe's stage hit. This look at the state of matrimony is great entertainment. The script is full of witty, stinging dialogue. B&W; 132m. **DIR:** George Cukor. **CAST:** Norma Shearer, Joan Crawford, Rosalind Russell, Joan Fontaine, Paulette Goddard. **1939 DVD**

WOMEN & MEN: STORIES OF SEDUCTION ★★★★ Three short vignettes, adapted for HBO from noted

American short stories, are given first-class treatment. 90m. **DIR:** Ken Russell, Frederic Raphael, Tony Richardson. **CAST:** Elizabeth McGovern, Beau Bridges, Peter Weller, Molly Ringwald, James Woods, Melanie Griffith. **1990**

WOMEN & MEN 2 ★★★★ The second entry in HBO's American short story anthology series follows a theme that finds well-meaning men at a crossroads. Another class act by cast and crew. 90m. **DIR:** Walter Bernstein, Mike Figgis, Kristi Zea. **CAST:** Matt Dillon, Kyra Sedgwick, Ray Liotta, Andie MacDowell, Scott Glenn, Juliette Binoche. **1991**

WOMEN FROM DOWN UNDER ★★★1/2 Female sexuality is the subject of four short films by directors from Australia and New Zealand (hence the title). The best of the four, *Just Desserts,* is a humorous look at a girl who discovers the joys of Italian food and sex at just about the same time. Not rated; contains profanity and sexual situations. 52m. **DIR:** Christine Parker, Monica Pellizzari, Christina Andreef, Jane Schneider. **CAST:** Lucy Lawless, Tania Simon, Joel Tobeck. **1994**

WOMEN FROM THE LAKE OF THE SCENTED SOULS ★★★1/2 One woman's business savvy and success can't make up for a lifetime of abuse by her drunken husband. Ironically, she seals a similar fate for a poor village girl by buying her as a bride for her demented son. Eerily peaceful scenes contrast sharply with the women's despair. In Mandarin with English subtitles. Not rated; contains violence, sex, adult themes, and profanity. 106m. **DIR:** Xie Fei. **CAST:** Sigin Gaowa, Wu Yujuan, Lei Lao Sheng, Chen Baoguo. **1993**

WOMEN IN CELL BLOCK 9 🦃 Sleazy women's prison melodrama. Filmed in Spain; poorly dubbed into English. No rating, but packed with nudity and gore. 78m. **DIR:** Jess (Jesus) Franco. **CAST:** Susan Hemingway, Howard Vernon. **1977**

WOMEN IN LOVE ★★★★1/2 Glenda Jackson won an Oscar for her performance in this British film. Two love affairs are followed simultaneously in this excellent adaptation of D. H. Lawrence's novel. Rated R. B&W; 129m. **DIR:** Ken Russell. **CAST:** Glenda Jackson, Oliver Reed, Alan Bates, Eleanor Bron, Jennie Linden, Alan Webb. **1970**

WOMEN OF BREWSTER PLACE, THE ★★★1/2 Marvelous made-for-TV soap about black women sharing a tenement and endless problems. Producer Oprah Winfrey comes across as a near saint both in raising her son and helping out the women around her. 195m. **DIR:** Donna Deitch. **CAST:** Oprah Winfrey, Jackée, Robin Givens, Cicely Tyson. **1989**

WOMEN OF THE PREHISTORIC PLANET 🦃 Not only is this outer-space saga incredibly cheap, it's also misleadingly titled. There is only one woman, and she's not from the prehistoric planet. 92m. **DIR:** Arthur C. Pierce. **CAST:** Wendell Corey, John Agar, Keith Larsen, Merry Anders, Paul Gilbert, Adam Roarke, Stuart Margolin, Gavin MacLeod, Lyle Waggoner. **1966**

WOMEN OF VALOR ★★1/2 This made-for-TV feature about a group of army nurses who are captured by the invading Japanese in the Philippines of early World War II is merely average, but the stars raise it up a notch. 100m. **DIR:** Buzz Kulik. **CAST:** Susan Sarandon, Kristy McNichol, Alberta Watson, Valerie Mahaffey. **1986**

WOMEN ON THE ROOF, THE ★★1/2 Early in the twentieth century, a shy young woman learns about life when she is befriended by bohemians. Director Carl-Gustav Nykvist shows little eye for imagery or color and the film is adequately played but surprisingly unerotic. In Swedish with English subtitles. Not rated; contains nudity and sexual situations. 86m. **DIR:** Carl-Gustav Nykvist. **CAST:** Helena Bergstrom, Stellan Skarsgard, Amanda Ooms. **1997**

WOMEN ON THE VERGE OF A NERVOUS BREAKDOWN ★★★★ Delightful Spanish comedy features Carmen Maura as a pregnant soap-opera star who has just been dumped by her longtime lover. A madcap farce. In Spanish with bright yellow English subtitles. Rated R for profanity. 88m. **DIR:** Pedro Almodóvar. **CAST:** Carmen Maura, Fernando Guillen, Antonio Banderas. **1988**

WOMEN'S CLUB, THE 🦃 Rated R for profanity, brief nudity, and excessive sexual situations. 89m. **DIR:** Sandra Weintraub. **CAST:** Michael Paré, Maud Adams, Eddie Velez. **1986**

WONDER BAR ★★ All the ingredients for a great Warner Bros.–Busby Berkeley musical, but the mixture falls flat this time. Berkeley's musical numbers are as spectacular as ever, but one, "Goin' to Heaven on a Mule" (with Al Jolson in blackface), is perhaps the most colossally tasteless number in movie history. B&W; 84m. **DIR:** Lloyd Bacon. **CAST:** Al Jolson, Kay Francis, Dolores Del Rio, Ricardo Cortez, Guy Kibbee. **1934**

WONDER BOYS ★★★★ Among the wittiest and most benevolently caustic indictments of writers and writing ever captured on screen, Steve Kloves's script—adapted from Michael Chabon's novel—is certain to be enjoyed and embraced by book people . . . and particularly by anybody who ever withered beneath a barrage of superficial "criticism" from a creative writing classroom filled with no-talent hacks who wouldn't know parallel structure from parallel parking. Michael Douglas is marvelous as the rumpled Grady Tripp, a disheveled and eccentric university professor whose latest novel passed the 2,000-page mark several months back. During a single tumultuous weekend, he will deal with a pregnant (and married) lover; an impatient editor; a forlorn and slightly warped young man; and a cutesy-pie coed with a serious crush. Although the film sags a bit in the third act, its rarefied collegiate atmosphere remains palatable to all viewers. Rated R for profanity. 112m. **DIR:** Curtis Hanson. **CAST:** Michael Douglas, Tobey Maguire, Frances McDormand, Robert Downey Jr., Katie Holmes. **2000 DVD**

WONDER MAN ★★★ Deftly doubling, Danny Kaye plays identical twins with personalities as far apart as the polar regions. One, Buzzy Bellew, is a brash, irrepressible nightclub comic; his mirror, Edwin Dingle, is a mousy double-dome full of tongue-twisting erudition. Identities are switched, of course. Thin on plot, this is mostly a tailored showcase for Kaye's brilliant talents. 98m. **DIR:** H. Bruce Humberstone. **CAST:** Danny Kaye, Vera-Ellen, Virginia Mayo, Donald Woods, S. Z. Sakall, Allen Jenkins, Edward Brophy. **1945 DVD**

WONDERFUL HORRIBLE LIFE OF LENI RIEFENSTAHL ★★★★1/2 Leni Riefenstahl, probably one of the greatest filmmakers of all time, is also the most controversial. Among her works are some appalling, though

brilliant, propaganda films for the Nazis. After World War II her life was in ruins. She makes a fascinating subject for this long, engrossing documentary. In German with English subtitles. Not rated; suitable for general audiences. 181m. **DIR:** Ray Müller. **1993 DVD**

WONDERFUL ICE CREAM SUIT, THE ★★★★ Ray Bradbury's celebrated short story was the basis for this wonderfully engaging tale of five Hispanic gentlemen who pool their resources in order to buy a white suit that seems to have magical powers. A change of pace for director Stuart Gordon, who proves equally adept at comedy-drama as he does horror. The cast couldn't be better in this made-for-cable, culturally rich film. Rated PG. 77m. **DIR:** Stuart Gordon. **CAST:** Edward James Olmos, Joe Mantegna, Esai Morales, Gregory Sierra, Clifton González González, Sid Caesar. **1998**

WONDERFUL WORLD OF THE BROTHERS GRIMM, THE ★★★★ Excellent adaptations of the Grimm tales, featuring brilliant animation by Puppetoon master George Pal and Oscar-winning costumes by Mary Willis. One of the standout sequences has Buddy Hackett battling a fire-breathing dragon in a toy shop. Originally shown in Cinerama. 129m. **DIR:** Henry Levin, George Pal. **CAST:** Laurence Harvey, Claire Bloom, Karlheinz Böhm, Oscar Homolka, Barbara Eden, Russ Tamblyn, Buddy Hackett, Terry-Thomas. **1962**

WONDERLAND ★★★1/2 Meandering comedy-drama starts out as a romance between two gay teens, but turns into a thriller after they witness a gangland murder. Too overstuffed to be completely satisfying, though there are many nice bits. Originally known as *The Fruit Machine*. Rated R for sexual discussions. 103m. **DIR:** Philip Saville. **CAST:** Emile Charles, Tony Forsyth, Robert Stephens, Robbie Coltrane. **1988**

•WONDERLAND (1999) ★★★1/2 A dysfunctional family and their separate lives collide one balmy autumn weekend and they try to make sense of their relationships and each other. Gina McKee is a standout as Nadia, one of three sisters who is looking for love in all the wrong places, including the local personal ads. Molly (Molly Parker) is ready to have a baby but must contend with her husband's quest to pursue his dreams. Debbie (Shirley Henderson) is a single mother whose son takes a backseat to her many one-night stands. You may not like some of the characters, but that's the nature of the beast. Rated R for adult situations and language. 108m. **DIR:** Michael Winterbottom. **CAST:** Shirley Henderson, Gina McKee, Molly Parker, Ian Hart, Kika Markham, Jack Shepherd. **1999 DVD**

WONDERWALL ★★1/2 Experimental curiosity piece depicts the fantasies of an entomologist as he spies on the woman in the apartment next to his. Electronic music score by George Harrison. Not rated, the film includes some nudity. 93m. **DIR:** Joe Massot. **CAST:** Jack MacGowran, Jane Birkin, Irene Handl. **1968**

WOO ★★ A blind date between two young, urban Brooklynites (Jada Pinkett, Tommy Davidson) begins in misunderstanding but finally blossoms into romance. The script is repetitive, the direction is plodding, the jokes are stale; the film's only real assets are the appealing performances of Pinkett and Davidson and handsome photography by Jean Lapine. Rated R for profanity. 84m. **DIR:** Daisy von Scherler Mayer. **CAST:** Jada Pinkett, Tommy Davidson, Duane Martin, Michael Ralph, LL Cool J. **1998**

WOOD, THE ★★★ Three male friends reminisce about their formative years in Inglewood, California, in this meandering, clumsy, but entertaining comedy-drama. When one buddy is missing in action on his wedding day, his two pals have two hours to fetch him from the home of a former flame, sober him up, and cure his case of cold feet. The film then flashes back to the trio's 1980s school days where they shared their first brushes with crime, sex, and love. Rated R for language and sexual content. 106m. **DIR:** Rick Famuyiwa. **CAST:** Taye Diggs, Omar Epps, Richard T. Jones, Trent Cameron, Sean Nelson, Duane Finley. **1999 DVD**

WOODEN HORSE, THE ★★★ Good casting and taut direction make this tale of British POWs tunneling out of a Nazi prison camp well worth watching. Made when memories were fresh, the film glows with reality as English cunning, grit, and timing vie with Nazi suspicion, assumed superiority, and complacency. B&W; 101m. **DIR:** Jack Lee. **CAST:** Leo Genn, David Tomlinson, Anthony Steel, Peter Finch. **1950**

WOODEN MAN'S BRIDE, THE ★★★★ Gorgeously filmed, epic tale of forbidden love finds a young bride forced to marry a wooden effigy of her fiancé when he is killed in an accident. Tradition and a stern mother-in-law force the bride into the union, but she finds solace and love in the arms of the young peasant Kui. Exquisite period detail, mesmerizing performances, and intense subject matter make this foreign import a real treat. In Chinese with English subtitles. Not rated; contains violence and adult situations. 114m. **DIR:** Huang Jianxin. **CAST:** Chang Shih, Wang Lan, Ku Paoming, Wang Yumei. **1995**

WOODSTOCK ★★★1/2 Woodstock is probably, along with *Gimme Shelter*, the most important film documentation of the late 1960s counterculture in the United States. The bulk of the film consists of footage of the bands and various other performers who played at the festival. There are some great split-screen sequences and some imaginative interviews. Well worth viewing. Rated R. 184m. **DIR:** Michael Wadleigh. **CAST:** Country Joe and the Fish, Jimi Hendrix, Jefferson Airplane. **1970 DVD**

WOODY GUTHRIE—HARD TRAVELIN' ★★★1/2 Woody Guthrie's musical presence will be felt for many years. This tribute traces his brilliant songwriting career from the dust bowl of the Midwest to California in the early 1940s. Many performers, including Joan Baez and Arlo Guthrie, Woody's son, sing and discuss the Guthrie influence on their own music. 74m. **DIR:** Jim Brown. **CAST:** Hoyt Axton, Joan Baez, Judy Collins, Pete Seeger, Arlo Guthrie. **1984**

WORD, THE ★★★ In a catacomb beneath Ostia, Italy, an archaeologist discovers an ancient manuscript that could cause chaos in the Christian world. The manuscript is said to contain the writings of Christ's younger brother, James the Just. A good story, with wonderful actors. Not rated. 188m. **DIR:** Richard Lang. **CAST:** David Janssen, John Huston, James Whitmore. **1978**

WORDS AND MUSIC ★★1/2 Fictionalized biography of the song-writing team of Richard Rogers and Lorenz Hart, dwelling mostly on the short and tormented life of the latter. As long as there's music, song, and dance,

everything is great. The rest should have been silence. 119m. **DIR:** Norman Taurog. **CAST:** Mickey Rooney, Tom Drake, June Allyson, Betty Garrett, Judy Garland, Gene Kelly, Ann Sothern, Vera-Ellen, Cyd Charisse, Allyn Ann McLerie, Mel Torme, Janet Leigh, Perry Como. **1948**

WORKING GIRL ★★★★ Clever, sophisticated comedy makes up for a lack of all-out belly laughs with the ring of truth. Melanie Griffith is terrific as the good-hearted gal attempting to work her way up but is thwarted by her scheming boss. A high-powered deal maker rides to the rescue. Rated R for nudity and profanity. 120m. **DIR:** Mike Nichols. **CAST:** Harrison Ford, Sigourney Weaver, Melanie Griffith, Alec Baldwin, Joan Cusack. **1988 DVD**

WORKING GIRLS ★★★★ The sex in this feminist docudrama about prostitution is about as appealing as the smell of dirty socks. The story, on the other hand, is compelling, thought-provoking, oddly touching, and often funny. The main character, Molly (Louise Smith), is a Yale graduate who lives with a female lover and is working toward becoming a professional photographer. Not rated, the film has simulated sex, profanity, nudity, and violence. 90m. **DIR:** Lizzie Borden. **CAST:** Louise Smith, Ellen McElduff. **1987 DVD**

WORKING STIFFS ★★★ This video is composed of the first three episodes of the 1979 TV series about two brothers working as janitors. Good scripts and great timing between the two leads make you wonder why it was canceled. Not rated. 75m. **DIR:** Penny Marshall, Norman Abbott. **CAST:** James Belushi, Michael Keaton. **1979**

WORLD ACCORDING TO GARP, THE ★★★★1/2 Director George Roy Hill and screenwriter Steven Tesich have captured the quirky blend of humor and pathos of John Irving's bestseller. The acting is impressive, with first-rate turns by Robin Williams (in the title role), Glenn Close as his mother, Jenny Fields, and John Lithgow as a kindly transsexual. Rated R for nudity, profanity, sexual situations, and violence. 136m. **DIR:** George Roy Hill. **CAST:** Robin Williams, Glenn Close, John Lithgow, Mary Beth Hurt, Hume Cronyn, Jessica Tandy, Swoosie Kurtz, Amanda Plummer. **1982**

WORLD APART, A ★★★1/2 Based on a true story, this is an emotionally charged drama about an anti-apartheid South African journalist (Barbara Hershey) who becomes the first white woman to be held under that country's infamous ninety-day detention law. Seen largely through the half-understanding eyes of the woman's daughter. The musical score enhances the searing brutality of this "world apart." Rated PG. 135m. **DIR:** Chris Menges. **CAST:** Barbara Hershey, Jodhi May. **1988**

WORLD GONE MAD, THE ★★ This features Wall Street types of questionable character versus a district attorney and his investigators during the Prohibition era. A great cast, but the viewer loses interest. B&W; 73m. **DIR:** Christy Cabanne. **CAST:** Pat O'Brien, Evelyn Brent, Neil Hamilton, Mary Brian, Louis Calhern, J. Carrol Naish. **1933**

WORLD GONE WILD On Earth after the nuclear holocaust, a group of flower children live in Lost Wells, a desert oasis. Rated R for violence, profanity, and nudity. 84m. **DIR:** Lee H. Katzin. **CAST:** Bruce Dern, Michael Paré, Catherine Mary Stewart, Adam Ant. **1988**

WORLD IS FULL OF MARRIED MEN, THE ★★ Neglected wife Carroll Baker sets out for revenge on her womanizing husband (Anthony Franciosa) in this pseudofeminist soap opera, written by Jackie Collins at her trashiest. Fun for those who don't take it too seriously. Rated R for sexual situations. 107m. **DIR:** Robert Young. **CAST:** Anthony Franciosa, Carroll Baker. **1979**

WORLD IS NOT ENOUGH, THE ★★★1/2 Pierce Brosnan continues to fit the role of 007 with aplomb, and his work here—his third outing as Ian Fleming's "Bond . . . James Bond"—is smooth and assured. The film's production values are superb as always, the locales properly exotic, the action sequences smartly staged, and Sophie Marceau's supporting role intriguingly layered. But Denise Richards's clumsy and wholly unbelievable performance as nuclear weapons expert (!) Christmas Jones ranks at the bottom of the barrel, alongside brain-dead bimbettes Britt Ekland (*The Man with the Golden Gun*) and Tanya Roberts (*A View to a Kill*). Similarly, the story's pacing is uneven. Call this one a midlevel Bond, with Brosnan, Marceau, and composer David Arnold overcoming many of the film's shortcomings through sheer energy. Rated PG-13 for violence, and Bondian mayhem and sensuality. 128m. **DIR:** Michael Apted. **CAST:** Pierce Brosnan, Sophie Marceau, Robert Carlyle, Denise Richards, Robbie Coltrane, Judi Dench, Desmond Llewellyn, Samantha Bond. **1999 DVD**

WORLD OF ANDY PANDA, THE ★★1/2 The black-and-white Mickey Mouse look-alike, Andy Panda, went through a number of changes in appearance, and these cartoons from 1941 to 1946 reflect this. Many of his animated adventures often feature other, less bland critters. That said, "Apple Andy" is a near-classic, and the rest aren't bad. 62m. **DIR:** Walter Lantz.

WORLD OF APU, THE ★★★★ The concluding part of director Satyajit Ray's famed *Apu* trilogy covering the life and growth of a young man in India. In this last film, Apu marries and helps bring life into the world himself, completing the cycle amid realizations about himself and his limitations in this world. This movie and its predecessors form a beautiful tapestry of existence in a different culture and were among the most influential of all Indian films for many years. In Bengali with English subtitles. B&W; 103m. **DIR:** Satyajit Ray. **CAST:** Soumitra Chatterjee, Sharmila Tagore, Alok Charkravarty, Swapan Mukherji. **1959**

WORLD OF HENRY ORIENT, THE ★★★★ A quirky comedy for the whole family. Peter Sellers is a woman-crazy New York pianist who finds himself being followed by two teenage girls who have come to idolize him. Loads of fun, with a great performance by Angela Lansbury. 106m. **DIR:** George Roy Hill. **CAST:** Peter Sellers, Paula Prentiss, Angela Lansbury, Phyllis Thaxter. **1964**

WORLD OF STRANGERS, A ★★★ When a London publisher is transferred to South Africa, he finds new friends among both the black and white communities, gradually becoming aware of the tensions and inequities around him. An intelligent and often disturbing treatment from the novel by Nadine Gordimer. B&W; 89m. **DIR:** Henning Carlsen. **CAST:** Zakes

Mokae, Gideon Nxomalo, Evelyn Frank, Ivan Jackson. **1962**

WORLD OF SUZIE WONG, THE ★★ William Holden is an artist living a bohemian life in Hong Kong. He falls in love with Nancy Kwan, a prostitute. Tepid and without much action. Nancy Kwan is very good, but she can't save the slow romantic melodrama. 129m. **DIR:** Richard Quine. **CAST:** William Holden, Nancy Kwan, Sylvia Syms, Michael Wilding, Laurence Naismith, Jaqui Chan. **1960**

WORLD OF THE VAMPIRES ★★ One of the weaker Mexican-monster movies imported and dubbed into English by K. Gordon Murray, this convoluted melodrama *looks* marvelously atmospheric, but collapses midway along. Unintentionally funny. B&W; 85m. **DIR:** Alfonso Corona. **CAST:** Guillermo Murray. **1960**

WORLD WAR III ★★★1/2 In this made-for-TV thriller, Rock Hudson, as a U.S. president, must send a crack military unit to Alaska to stop the Russians from capturing the Alaska pipeline. The battle scenes are tense and effective, and Brian Keith, as the Russian secretary-general, is terrific. It's long but certainly worth a view. 200m. **DIR:** David Greene. **CAST:** Rock Hudson, David Soul, Brian Keith, Cathy Lee Crosby, Katherine Helmond, Jeroen Krabbé. **1982**

WORLD WITHOUT END ★★1/2 First manned spaceflight to Mars goes awry and the crew is propelled five centuries into the future. They find themselves on an Earth slowly recovering from nuclear holocaust and inhabited by things dear to such films: giant spiders, primitive mutants, and beautiful women in high heels. Optimistic, decently acted, and well-produced, this is one of the better efforts of its decade and solid second-tier science fiction. 81m. **DIR:** Edward L. Bernds. **CAST:** Hugh Marlowe, Nancy Gates, Rod Taylor, Nelson Leigh, Shawn Smith, Lisa Montell. **1956**

WORLD'S GREATEST ATHLETE, THE ★★★ John Amos is the athletics instructor at Merrivale College. He and his assistant, Tim Conway, travel to Africa to get away from their troubles and come across Nanu (Jan-Michael Vincent), the greatest natural athlete in the world. One of the better Disney college films. Rated G. 89m. **DIR:** Robert Scheerer. **CAST:** Jan-Michael Vincent, John Amos, Tim Conway, Roscoe Lee Browne. **1973**

WORLD'S GREATEST LOVER, THE ★★1/2 Gene Wilder plays a would-be silent-movie star who tests for the part of the "new Valentino" while his wife (Carol Kane) runs off with the real Rudolph. Dom DeLuise is around to brighten things up, but writer-director Wilder's ideas of what's funny aren't quite right. Rated PG. 89m. **DIR:** Gene Wilder. **CAST:** Gene Wilder, Carol Kane, Dom DeLuise, Fritz Feld, Carl Ballantine, Michael Huddleston, Matt Collins, Ronny Graham. **1977**

WORM EATERS, THE 🦃 Stomach-turning flick about southern town infested with night crawlers. Not rated. 75m. **DIR:** Herb Robins. **1977 DVD**

WORST WITCH, THE ★★★★ Jill Murphy's charming children's book gets first-cabin treatment in this delightful made-for-cable adaptation that features Fairuza Balk as hapless young Mildred Hubble, the only student at Miss Cackle's International Academy for Witches who cannot properly perform her spells. Screenwriter Mary Pleshette Willis retains the book's whimsical tone, and Diana Rigg is deliciously spooky as the imperious head mistress. 70m. **DIR:** Robert Young. **CAST:** Diana Rigg, Charlotte Rae, Tim Curry, Fairuza Balk, Sabina Franklyn. **1986**

WORTH WINNING 🦃 TV weatherman thinks he's the ultimate ladies' man. Rated PG-13 for profanity and suggested sex. 104m. **DIR:** Will Mackenzie. **CAST:** Mark Harmon, Madeleine Stowe, Lesley Ann Warren, Maria Holvoe, Mark Blum, Andrea Martin, David Brenner. **1989**

WOUNDED ★★1/2 A forest ranger hunts down the man who killed her fiancé in this routine chase-through-the-woods film. Rated R for violence and profanity. 91m. **DIR:** Richard Martin. **CAST:** Madchen Amick, Graham Greene, Adrian Pasdar. **1996**

WOUNDED HEART ★★1/2 A ruthless businesswoman goes to Texas to secure her inheritance, but instead ends up falling in love in this made-for-cable original. Simplistic and hackneyed storyline. Not rated; contains violence. 95m. **DIR:** Vic Sarin. **CAST:** Paula DeVicq, Jon Hensley, Stuart Whitman. **1995**

•WOUNDS, THE ★★★1/2 Dark, satirical comedy about two teenage friends who become gangsters in the chaos of Yugoslavian life in the early 1990s. Like his countryman Emir Kusturica, filmmaker Srdjan Dragojevic *(Pretty Village, Pretty Flame)* crafts a rowdy and violent depiction of life in a land where society is falling apart. In Serbo-Croatian with English subtitles. Not rated; an R equivalent for strong violence and profanity. 103m. **DIR:** Srdjan Dragojevic. **CAST:** Dusan Pekic, Milan Maric, Dragan Bjelogrlic, Branka Katic. **1998 DVD**

WOYZECK ★★★1/2 Powerful yet uneven adaptation of Georg Büchner's haunting, absurd play. Klaus Kinski plays a man who plunges into madness and murder. In German with English subtitles. Not rated; contains nudity and violence. 82m. **DIR:** Werner Herzog. **CAST:** Klaus Kinski, Eva Mattes. **1978**

WR: MYSTERIES OF THE ORGANISM ★★★★ Once-controversial film still has an anarchic kick, with too many ideas flying around to catch them all in one viewing. Writer-director Dusan Makavejev mixes documentary and fictional elements to explore the theories of sexologist Wilhelm Reich, with a number of amusing detours along the way. In Serbian with English subtitles. Not rated. 84m. **DIR:** Dusan Makavejev. **CAST:** Milena Dravic, Jagoda Kaloper. **1971**

WRAITH, THE ★★ A small town in Arizona is visited by a spirit taking revenge on a gang of road pirates. Some nice car wrecks and explosions. Car buffs will like the Wraith Mobile. A typical shallow revenge picture without style, substance, or surprises. Rated PG. 93m. **DIR:** Mike Marvin. **CAST:** Charlie Sheen, Randy Quaid, Clint Howard, Griffin O'Neal. **1986**

WRANGLER ★★1/2 Set in the Aussie outback, B-movie hunkster Jeff Fahey is the dashing businessman out to save Tushka Bergen from an evil rancher and a dangerous drover. The plot could have been lifted from a dime novel, but very pretty fluff. 93m. **DIR:** Ian Barry. **CAST:** Jeff Fahey, Tushka Bergen, Steven Vidler. **1993**

WRECK OF THE MARY DEARE, THE ★★★ Sea captain Gary Cooper, in attempting to prove the crew and owners of his ship were involved in an insurance scam, is himself accused of dereliction. After a suspenseful start, this bogs down and becomes predictable. 100m.

DIR: Michael Anderson. **CAST:** Gary Cooper, Charlton Heston, Michael Redgrave, Emlyn Williams, Cecil Parker, Alexander Knox, Virginia McKenna, Richard Harris. **1959**

WRECKING CREW, THE 🦃 Don't be confused. This isn't a remake of the 1969 Dean Martin–Matt Helm comedy-adventure, but a thoroughly awful gang film. Lots of bullets fly when warring gangs meet in an abandoned warehouse, only to be betrayed by those among their ranks. Tired and predictable. Rated R for language and violence. 78m. **DIR:** Albert Pyun. **CAST:** Ice T, Snoop Dog, Ernie Hudson Jr. **1999 DVD**

WRESTLING ERNEST HEMINGWAY ★★★1/2 Robert Duvall and Richard Harris show excellent teamwork in this easygoing drama about a Cuban barber and an Irish sea captain retired to a small Florida town. Director Randa Haines smooths out the aimless spots in Steve Conrad's episodic script, and the acting is first-rate. Sandra Bullock as a kindly waitress all but steals the show. Rated PG-13 for mild profanity. 122m. **DIR:** Randa Haines. **CAST:** Robert Duvall, Richard Harris, Sandra Bullock, Shirley MacLaine, Piper Laurie. **1993**

WRITE TO KILL ★★1/2 Routine vendetta thriller has writer Scott Valentine tracking down the gang of counterfeiters who killed his brother. Rated R for violence and profanity. 94m. **DIR:** Reuben Preuss. **CAST:** Scott Valentine, Joan Severance, Chris Mulkey, G. W. Bailey. **1990**

WRITTEN ON THE WIND ★★★1/2 Tame by today's standards, this film still provides quite a few good moments and an Academy Award–winning performance by Dorothy Malone. Rock Hudson and Robert Stack play good friends who meet, respectively, Dorothy Malone who has a problem just saying no and Lauren Bacall who is nice and loves Stack but loves his oil-dipped money even more. High-quality Hollywood soap opera. 99m. **DIR:** Douglas Sirk. **CAST:** Rock Hudson, Lauren Bacall, Robert Stack, Dorothy Malone, Robert Keith. **1956 DVD**

WRONG ARM OF THE LAW, THE ★★★★ Peter Sellers is hilarious as Pearly Gates, the Cockney leader of a group of bandits. Sellers and his gang join forces with police inspector Parker (Lionel Jeffries) after a group of Australians pose as police and capture Sellers's stolen goods. This British comedy contains enough to keep most viewers in stitches. B&W; 94m. **DIR:** Cliff Owen. **CAST:** Peter Sellers, Lionel Jeffries, Bernard Cribbins, Davy Kaye, Nanette Newman. **1962**

WRONG BOX, THE ★★★★ Some of Britain's best-known comics appear in this screwball farce about two zany families who battle over an inheritance in Victorian England. The film borders on black humor and is a delightful comedy. 105m. **DIR:** Bryan Forbes. **CAST:** John Mills, Ralph Richardson, Dudley Moore, Peter Sellers, Peter Cook, Michael Caine, Nanette Newman, Wilfrid Lawson, Tony Hancock. **1966**

WRONG GUYS, THE ★★ Low-energy farce about the camping-trip reunion of a 1962 Cub Scout Troop. The troop is mistaken for FBI agents by a crazed convict, and therein lies the comedy. Rated PG for language and comic-book violence. 86m. **DIR:** Danny Bilson. **CAST:** Louie Anderson, Richard Lewis, Richard Belzer, Franklin Ajaye, Tim Thomerson, John Goodman, Brian James, Ernie Hudson, Alice Ghostley, Kathleen Freeman. **1988 DVD**

WRONG IS RIGHT ★★★★ Sean Connery, as a globe-trotting television reporter, gives what may be the best performance of his career, in this outrageous, thoroughly entertaining end-of-the-world black comedy, written, produced, and directed by Richard Brooks. It's an updated combination of *Network* and *Dr. Strangelove*, and wickedly funny. Rated R because of profanity and violence. 117m. **DIR:** Richard Brooks. **CAST:** Sean Connery, Robert Conrad, George Grizzard, Katharine Ross, G. D. Spradlin, John Saxon, Henry Silva, Leslie Nielsen, Robert Webber, Rosalind Cash, Hardy Kruger, Dean Stockwell, Ron Moody. **1982**

WRONG MAN, THE ★★★★ In this frightening true-life tale, Henry Fonda plays a man falsely accused of robbery. Vera Miles is his wife, who can't handle the changes wrought in their lives by this gross injustice. Fonda is excellent. B&W; 105m. **DIR:** Alfred Hitchcock. **CAST:** Henry Fonda, Vera Miles, Anthony Quayle, Harold J. Stone, Nehemiah Persoff. **1956**

WRONG MAN, THE ★★★★ Raymond Chandler's *film noir* sensibilities blend with Tennessee Williams's earthy sensuality in this delicious drama that finds a ship-hand on the run for a murder he didn't commit. Includes a wonderfully eerie Los Lobos soundtrack. 98m. **DIR:** Jim McBride. **CAST:** Rosanna Arquette, Kevin Anderson, John Lithgow, Jorge Cervera Jr. **1993**

WRONG MOVE, THE ★★ Rudiger Vogler is cast as a would-be writer in this slow-moving character drama. It concerns a soul-searching odyssey across Germany by a diverse group of misfits. Initially absorbing, yet too disconcerting to recommend. German with English subtitles. 103m. **DIR:** Wim Wenders. **CAST:** Rudiger Vogler, Hanna Schygulla, Nastassja Kinski. **1978**

WRONGFULLY ACCUSED 🦃 Leslie Nielsen finds himself wrongfully accused of murder in this parody of *The Fugitive*. Endless sight gags and toilet humor fail to measure up to Nielsen's successful spoofs (*Airplane*, *Naked Gun*). Rated PG-13 for sexual situations. 85m. **DIR:** Pat Proft. **CAST:** Leslie Nielsen, Kelly LeBrock, Melinda McGraw, Richard Crenna. **1998 DVD**

WUTHERING HEIGHTS (1939) ★★★★ Taken from the Emily Brontë novel, this is a haunting, mesmerizing film. Set on the murky, isolated moors, it tells the tale of Heathcliff, a foundling Gypsy boy who loves Cathy, the spoiled daughter of the house. Their affair, born in childhood, is doomed. As the star-crossed lovers, Laurence Olivier and Merle Oberon are impressive. B&W; 103m. **DIR:** William Wyler. **CAST:** Merle Oberon, Laurence Olivier, Flora Robson, David Niven. **1939 DVD**

WUTHERING HEIGHTS (1953) ★★1/2 Luis Buñuel's film of the Emily Brontë classic. This Spanish version in no way measures up to the 1939 original. The Richard Wagner music, however, is perfect for the melodramatic performances. 90m. **DIR:** Luis Buñuel. **CAST:** Iraseme Dilian, Jorge Mistral. **1953**

WUTHERING HEIGHTS (1971) ★★★1/2 Inventive but not great rendition of Emily Brontë's classic about the star-crossed lovers, Heathcliff (Timothy Dalton) and Cathy (Anna Calder-Marshall). Dalton is especially good as Cathy's smoldering, abused, and later vengeful love. The 1939 version is still the best. Rated G. 105m. **DIR:** Robert Fuest. **CAST:** Timothy Dalton, Anna

Calder-Marshall, Harry Andrews, Hugh Griffith. **1971 DVD**

WYATT EARP ★★★1/2 Perhaps if this hadn't followed the energetic *Tombstone* into release, *Wyatt Earp* might have seemed fresher. The film moves in fits and starts as it covers more of Earp's life than we've previously seen. That said, it is most definitely a good film, though not the great one its makers had intended. Rated PG-13 for violence, profanity, and suggested sex. 189m. **DIR:** Lawrence Kasdan. **CAST:** Kevin Costner, Dennis Quaid, Gene Hackman, Jeff Fahey, Mark Harmon, Michael Madsen, Catherine O'Hara, Bill Pullman, Isabella Rossellini, Tom Sizemore, JoBeth Williams, Mare Winningham, David Andrews, Linden Ashby, James Gammon, Adam Baldwin, Annabeth Gish, Betty Buckley. **1994**

WYATT EARP: RETURN TO TOMBSTONE ★★★1/2 An aging Wyatt Earp (Hugh O'Brian) looks back on the highlights of his life as a frontier lawman. Made-for-TV production is a surprisingly effective combination of new footage and colorized sequences from O'Brian's classic TV series, *The Life and Legend of Wyatt Earp*. A timely tribute. 96m. **DIR:** Frank McDonald, Paul Landres. **CAST:** Hugh O'Brian, Bruce Boxleitner, Harry Carey Jr., Paul Brinegar, Bo Hopkins, Alex Hyde-White, Martin Kove, Don Meredith, Jay Underwood, Douglas Fowley, Rayford Barnes, Trevor Bardette, Morgan Woodward, Lloyd Corrigan, John Anderson, Dirk London, Nancy Hale, Bob Steele, Steve Brodie, Norm Alden, William Phipps, Ralph Reed, Stacy Harris. **1994**

WYOMING OUTLAW ★★★1/2 One of the best episodes in the popular "Three Mesquiteers" cowboy series. Silent-era *Tarzan* Elmo Lincoln, in a rare return to the screen, appears as a marshal. B&W; 62m. **DIR:** George Sherman. **CAST:** John Wayne, Ray "Crash" Corrigan, Raymond Hatton, Pamela Blake, Don Barry, LeRoy Mason, Yakima Canutt, Charles Middleton, Elmo Lincoln, David Sharpe. **1939**

X

X ★★ A teenage boy finds himself a reluctant warrior in the final battle between the Dragon of the Earth and the Dragon of Heaven, with the fate of humanity hanging in the balance. This Japanese sci-fi film may be a feature-length cartoon, but with its nonstop, bloody violence, it's not for small children. Adults too may be put off, because the film uses violence to conceal a lack of plot and character. The jerky, unimaginative animation, combined with the humdrum English-language voices, makes this one strictly for devotees of the Japanese "anime" genre. Rated R for animated violence, gore, and nudity. 97m. **DIR:** Taro Rin. **1996 DVD**

X-FILES, THE (1998) ★★★1/2 Based on the popular TV series, this feature film is both a culmination of and an expansion on many of the themes of the show's first five seasons. This ambitious science-fiction tale generates a few seat-jumping moments even for the uninitiated. Oh yes: Scully and Mulder discover the real intentions of alien visitors throughout history. Rated PG-13 for violence and creepy images. 117m. **DIR:** Rob Bowman. **CAST:** David Duchovny, Gillian Anderson, Martin Landau, Blythe Danner, Armin Mueller-Stahl, Mitch Pilleggi, William B. Davis, John Neville. **1998 DVD**

X-FILES, THE (TV SERIES) ★★★1/2 FBI agents Fox Mulder (David Duchovny) and Dana Scully (Gillian Anderson) investigate bizarre occurrences around the globe in this cult favorite from the Fox television network. Created by Chris Carter, the series covers all aspects of the outré, from voodoo to alien abductions. Made for TV. 90m. **DIR:** Various. **CAST:** David Duchovny, Gillian Anderson, Mitch Pileggi, Jerry Hardin, William B. Davis, Nicholas Lea, John Neville, Bruce Harwood, Steven Williams. **1993**

X FROM OUTER SPACE, THE ★★1/2 A mission to Mars returns with an alien spore that grows into Guilala, a huge, energy-absorbing monster that looks like a giant chicken with scales. Abundant destruction of model cities and planes highlights this none-too-professional entry in the Japanese big-rubber-monster movie category. Rated PG. 88m. **DIR:** Kazui Nihonmatzu. **CAST:** Toshiya Wazaki, Peggy Neal. **1967**

X-MEN ★★★★ At long last, the Marvel Comics Group has a top-quality film featuring its quirky superheroes: in this case, a group of mutants who work for the betterment of mankind in opposition to a gang of their brethren who want to rule the world. Hugh Jackman is the talon-sporting Wolverine who wants no part of Professor X and his crew of "do-gooders" until the gifted Rogue is kidnapped by the nefarious Magnus as part of his maniacal plot. Great fun; superb special effects. Rated PG-13 for comic-book violence. 104m. **DIR:** Bryan Singer. **CAST:** Hugh Jackman, Patrick Stewart, Ian McKellen, Famke Janssen, Halle Berry, Anna Paquin. **2000 DVD**

X (THE MAN WITH THE X-RAY EYES) ★★★ Intriguing, offbeat tale of a scientist (Ray Milland) who discovers a drug that gives him the power to see through objects. He has a great time at first, but soon becomes addicted and begins seeing more and more, until. . . . This production is highly enjoyable, with a surprisingly effective role by comedian Don Rickles as a carnival barker. 80m. **DIR:** Roger Corman. **CAST:** Ray Milland, Diana Van Der Vlis, Harold J. Stone, John Hoyt, Don Rickles. **1963 DVD**

X—THE UNKNOWN ★★★★ Scientist Dean Jagger, in one of his best performances, battles a deadly substance from the center of the earth in this outstanding Hammer Studios production. While not officially an entry in the similar *Quatermass* series, it is very much on a par—productionwise and in first-rate storytelling—with *The Creeping Unknown*, *Enemy from Space*, and *Five Million Years to Earth*. It was Hammer stalwart Jimmy Sangster's first produced screenplay. B&W; 80m. **DIR:** Leslie Norman. **CAST:** Dean Jagger, Leo McKern, Edward Judd, Anthony Newley, Edward Chapman, William Lucas, Peter Hammond. **1956 DVD**

X, Y AND ZEE 🦃 Pointless tale of sexual relationships. Rated R. 110m. **DIR:** Brian G. Hutton. **CAST:** Elizabeth Taylor, Michael Caine, Susannah York, Margaret Leighton, John Standing. **1972**

XANADU ★★1/2 This musical lacks inspiration and story line. It is basically a full-length video that includes some good numbers by Olivia Newton-John and Gene Kelly. See it for the musical entertainment, not for the story. Rated PG. 88m. **DIR:** Robert Greenwald. **CAST:** Olivia Newton-John, Gene Kelly, Michael Beck, James Sloyan, Sandahl Bergman. **1980 DVD**

XCHANGE ★★ Moderately entertaining but extremely silly futuristic thriller about an investigator whose latest case is a major headache. Scientific advancements allow people to transport their minds into other bodies. When Stefan Toffler discovers that his mind has been transferred into the body of a terrorist, he has 48 hours to switch back or else remain trapped in a killer's body. Good idea, so-so movie. Rated R for adult situations, language, and violence. 109m. **DIR:** Alan Moyle. **CAST:** Stephen Baldwin, Kyle MacLachlan, Pascale Bussières, Kim Coates, Tom Rack. **2000 DVD**

XIU XIU: THE SENT DOWN GIRL ★★★ During Mao Zedong's Cultural Revolution, a city girl is sent to the country to learn horse wrangling; homesickness and hardship eventually break her spirit. Director Joan Chen draws a sharp contrast between the utopian myth of Maoist propaganda and the grim reality of the young girl's life. Acting by Lu Lu as the heroine and Lopsang as her grizzled mentor is excellent. In Mandarin with English subtitles. Rated R for sexual scenes. 99m. **DIR:** Joan Chen. **CAST:** Lulu, Lopsang, Jie Gao, Wengqiang Wang. **1998 DVD**

XTRO 🦃 Grotesquely slimy sci-fi horror flick with an idiotic plot that revolves around a series of repulsive bladder effects. Rated R. 84m. **DIR:** Harry Davenport. **CAST:** Philip Sayer, Bernice Stegers, Maryam D'Abo. **1982 DVD**

XTRO II ★★★ If you saw the original *Xtro*, forget all about it. *Xtro II* has a whole new exciting plot that doesn't even follow the original. The Nexus computer program transports three scientists to a parallel universe, only to have one return with a hideous creature inside of it. The few remaining scientists inside the project attempt to kill off the beast. Rated R for violence. 92m. **DIR:** Harry Davenport. **CAST:** Jan-Michael Vincent, Paul Koslo, Tara Buckman. **1991**

XTRO: WATCH THE SKIES (XTRO 3) 🦃 Familiar UFO-conspiracy story about a misfit band of Marines who journey to an uncharted island on a top-secret mission only to encounter a bloodthirsty alien. Rated R. 97m. **DIR:** Harry Davenport. **CAST:** Sal Landi, Andrew Divoff, Karen Moncrieff, David M. Parker, Jim Hanks, Andrea Lauren-Herz. **1995**

Y

YAKUZA, THE ★★★★★ In this superb blending of the American gangster and Japanese samurai genres, Robert Mitchum plays Harry Kilmer, an ex-G.I. who returns to Japan when a friend's daughter has been kidnapped and is held for ransom. This forces Kilmer to call on a onetime enemy who owes him a debt. Thus begins a clash of cultures and a web of intrigue that keep the viewers on the edge of their seats. Rated R. 112m. **DIR:** Sydney Pollack. **CAST:** Robert Mitchum, Brian Keith, Ken Takakura, Herb Edelman, Richard Jordan. **1975**

YANK IN THE RAF, A ★★1/2 Title is misleading in this story of an American pilot, Tyrone Power, enlisting in the British air force and falling in love with Betty Grable. Standard plot lines and lack of any real action do not help matters in this slow-moving, generally uninteresting film. 98m. **DIR:** Henry King. **CAST:** Tyrone Power, Betty Grable, Reginald Gardiner, John Sutton. **1941**

YANKEE DOODLE DANDY ★★★★★ Magnetic James Cagney, stepping out of his gangster roles, gives a magnificent performance in the life story of dancing vaudevillian George M. Cohan. An outstanding show-business story with unassuming but effective production. B&W; 126m. **DIR:** Michael Curtiz. **CAST:** James Cagney, Joan Leslie, Walter Huston, Irene Manning, Rosemary DeCamp, Richard Whorf, Jeanne Cagney. **1942**

YANKS ★★★1/2 Director John Schlesinger re-created classic Hollywood, when smiling men went bravely off to battle while dedicated women stayed behind, in this World War II saga of England's reaction to young American GIs. Richard Gere (who cemented his pretty-boy image with this role) and Lisa Eichhorn handle the primary boy-meets-girl subplot, while William Devane and Vanessa Redgrave embark on a more subdued relationship. Rated R for nudity. 140m. **DIR:** John Schlesinger. **CAST:** Richard Gere, Vanessa Redgrave, William Devane, Lisa Eichhorn. **1979**

YARDS, THE ★★★ An ex-con's efforts to go straight are thwarted when he comes under the sinister influence of his best friend and his subway-contractor uncle. Fine performances and a gritty urban atmosphere compensate for the overfamiliarity of the story. Rated R for profanity and violence. 115m. **DIR:** James Gray. **CAST:** Mark Wahlberg, Joaquin Phoenix, Charlize Theron, James Caan, Ellen Burstyn, Faye Dunaway. **2000 DVD**

YARN PRINCESS, THE ★★★1/2 Jean Smart delivers a triumphant performance in this made-for-television drama about a mentally challenged mother who is forced to become the main care provider of her home and family when her husband becomes seriously ill. Dalene Young's screenplay allows her to grow as a person and maintain her dignity without resorting to melodrama. Not rated. 92m. **DIR:** Tom McLoughlin. **CAST:** Jean Smart, Robert Pastorelli, Dennis Boutsikaris, Shirley Knight, Jared Rushton. **1993**

YEAR IN PROVENCE, A ★★★★1/2 Based on Peter Mayle's delightful book, this four-part TV series is a visual, breezy delight. John Thaw and Lindsay Duncan are the British escapees who set up house in the south of France and chronicle their first year. Humorous and full of élan, but it presents a caricatured British view of the French villagers. Not rated. Four 90-minute episodes. **DIR:** David Tucker. **CAST:** John Thaw, Lindsay Duncan. **1992 DVD**

YEAR MY VOICE BROKE, THE ★★★★ A likable Australian coming-of-age drama with echoes of *The Last Picture Show* and the novels of S. E. Hinton. Though the film market has been saturated with adolescent dramas circa 1962, this movie's refreshing honesty makes it a

welcome addition to the genre. Rated PG-13, with profanity and some mild sexual situations. 103m. **DIR:** John Duigan. **CAST:** Noah Taylor. **1988 DVD**

YEAR OF LIVING DANGEROUSLY, THE ★★★★1/2 Set in 1965 Indonesia when the Sukarno regime was toppling from pressures left and right. Mel Gibson and Sigourney Weaver star as an Australian journalist and a British diplomatic attaché, respectively. The film, however, belongs to Linda Hunt, in her Academy Award–winning role as free-lance photographer Billy Kwan. Rated R for profanity, nudity, and violence. 115m. **DIR:** Peter Weir. **CAST:** Mel Gibson, Sigourney Weaver, Linda Hunt, Michael Murphy, Bill Kerr, Noel Ferrier. **1983 DVD**

YEAR OF THE COMET ★★1/2 In this slightly silly romantic adventure-comedy, Penelope Ann Miller finds a huge bottle of the world's finest and rarest wine—Lafitte 1811—only to have to rely on a boorish troubleshooter (Timothy Daly) to keep it out of the hands of thieves. This determinedly lightweight film was written by William Goldman. Rated PG-13 for profanity and violence. 91m. **DIR:** Peter Yates. **CAST:** Penelope Ann Miller, Timothy Daly, Louis Jourdan, Art Malik, Ian Richardson. **1992**

YEAR OF THE DRAGON 🦃 Youth gangs in New York's Chinatown. Rated R for violence, profanity, gore, simulated sex, and nudity. 136m. **DIR:** Michael Cimino. **CAST:** Mickey Rourke, John Lone, Ariane, Leonard Termo. **1985**

YEAR OF THE GUN ★★★ An American novelist (Andrew McCarthy) returns to terrorist-plagued Italy in 1978, hoping to free a married woman (Valeria Golino) from her abusive, politically powerful husband. A chance meeting with a photojournalist (Sharon Stone) puts our hero's life in danger, and a series of crosses and double crosses leads him to the truth. Rated R for violence, nudity, and profanity. 111m. **DIR:** John Frankenheimer. **CAST:** Andrew McCarthy, Valeria Golino, Sharon Stone, John Pankow. **1991 DVD**

YEAR OF THE QUIET SUN ★★★★ A beautifully orchestrated meditation on the nature of love, this import is about a Polish widow after World War II who becomes romantically involved with an American soldier during a war-crimes investigation. In Polish with English subtitles. Rated PG. 106m. **DIR:** Krzysztof Zanussi. **CAST:** Scott Wilson, Maja Komorowska. **1985**

YEARLING, THE ★★★★1/2 A beautiful film version of Marjorie Kinnan Rawlings's sensitive story of a young boy's love for a pet fawn that his father must destroy. Simply told, this emotionally charged drama has been rated one of the finest films ever made. 134m. **DIR:** Clarence Brown. **CAST:** Gregory Peck, Jane Wyman, Claude Jarman Jr., Chill Wills. **1946**

YELLOW ★★★★ Refreshingly insightful take on the teen comedy genre, and not just because they're all Korean Americans here. Writer-director Lee balances typical graduation-night high jinks with serious character drama, a little mystery, and a marvelous agenda about building bridges across age, racial, cultural, and gender divides. A little rough in places, but by and large an outstanding first feature. Not rated; contains language and mild violence. 101m. **DIR:** Chris Chan Lee. **CAST:** Michael Daeho Chung, Burt Bulos, Angie Suh, Mia Suh, Soon-Tek Oh. **1998 DVD**

YELLOW CAB MAN, THE ★★★1/2 Red Skelton is a bumbling cabdriver who develops a process for a new unbreakable safety glass. Crooks see the potential and come after it. Good sight gags. B&W; 85m. **DIR:** Jack Donohue. **CAST:** Red Skelton, Gloria De Haven, Walter Slezak, Edward Arnold, James Gleason, Jay C. Flippen. **1950**

YELLOW EARTH ★★★★ In 1939, a communist soldier is sent to a remote province to collect folk songs and learn about rural life. The first film from director Chen Kaige (*Farewell My Concubine*) is a small work of beautiful simplicity, in which the faces of characters communicate to the viewer feelings they cannot share with each other. In Chinese with English subtitles. Not rated, contains no objectionable material. 89m. **DIR:** Chen Kaige. **CAST:** Xue Bai, Wang Xueqi. **1984**

YELLOW HAIR AND THE FORTRESS OF GOLD ★★ Made to look like a 1940s serial, this film is more like a female *Indiana Jones*. Yellow Hair is a famed female Indian warrior, who is sent to find a lost treasure. Along the way she fights arrows, avalanches, and greedy gringos. Cameo appearances by spaghetti Western character actors make this a fun film. Rated R for violence. 102m. **DIR:** Matt Cimber. **CAST:** Laurene Landon, Ken Roberson, Luis Lorenzo, Aldo Sambrell, Claudia Gravy, Frank Brana, Eduardo Fajardo. **1984**

YELLOW SUBMARINE ★★★★ Clever cartoon versions of John, Paul, George, and Ringo journey into Pepperland to save it from the Blue Meanies in this delightful blend of psychedelic animation and topflight Beatles music. "All You Need Is Love," "When I'm 64," "Lucy in the Sky with Diamonds," and "Yellow Submarine" provide the background and power the action in a film that epitomized the flower generation. Rated G. 85m. **DIR:** George Dunning. **1968 DVD**

YELLOWBEARD ★★1/2 This pirate comedy barely contains a boatload of laughs under the directorship of first-timer Mel Damski. Rated PG for profanity, nudity, violence, gore, and scatological humor. 101m. **DIR:** Mel Damski. **CAST:** Graham Chapman, Eric Idle, John Cleese, Peter Cook, Cheech and Chong, Peter Boyle, Madeline Kahn, Marty Feldman, Kenneth Mars. **1983**

YENTL ★★1/2 Barbra Streisand, who also produced, coscripted, and directed, stars as a woman who must disguise herself as a man in order to pursue an education among Orthodox Jews in turn-of-the-century eastern Europe. The story is fine, but the songs all sound the same. Still, *Yentl* is, overall, a watchable work. Rated PG for brief nudity. 134m. **DIR:** Barbra Streisand. **CAST:** Barbra Streisand, Mandy Patinkin, Amy Irving, Nehemiah Persoff, Steven Hill. **1983**

YES, GIORGIO ★★ In this old-fashioned star vehicle, Luciano Pavarotti makes a less-than-memorable screen debut as Giorgio Fini, a macho Italian tenor who meets a pretty Boston throat specialist (Kathryn Harrold) when his voice suddenly fails him. They fall in love and the viewer falls asleep. Rated PG for adult themes. 110m. **DIR:** Franklin J. Schaffner. **CAST:** Luciano Pavarotti, Kathryn Harrold, Eddie Albert, James Hong. **1982**

YES, PRIME MINISTER ★★★ British sitcom manages to lampoon not only its own government but the world at large. Paul Eddington stars as the novice prime minister who works more on his photo opportunities than

his governing policies. He falls easy prey to his ever crafty, power-hungry Cabinet secretary, played to perfection by Nigel Hawthorne. Not rated, its aim is to offend all. Each tape contains three to four episodes. 90m. **DIR:** Sydney Lotterby. **CAST:** Paul Eddington, Nigel Hawthorne, Derek Fowlds. **1987**

YESTERDAY MACHINE, THE 🦃 Nazi scientist has invented a time machine that can move people to the past and the future. 85m. **DIR:** Russ Marker. **CAST:** Tim Holt, Jack Herman. **1962**

YESTERDAY, TODAY AND TOMORROW ★★★1/2 Hilarious three-vignette romp teaming Sophia Loren and Marcello Mastroianni. The first (and best) story features Loren as an impoverished woman who continues to have babies in order to avoid a jail sentence, with Mastroianni as her husband who gives in to the scheme. Italian dubbed into English. 119m. **DIR:** Vittorio De Sica. **CAST:** Sophia Loren, Marcello Mastroianni, Tina Pica. **1964**

YESTERDAY'S HERO ★★★ Ian McShane plays a washed-up alcoholic ex-soccer star who wants to make a comeback. He gets assistance from his old flame (Suzanne Somers), a pop star, and her singing partner (Paul Nicolas). Not rated. 95m. **DIR:** Neil Leifer. **CAST:** Ian McShane, Adam Faith, Paul Nicolas, Suzanne Somers. **1979**

YESTERDAY'S TARGET ★★ David Bourla's confused and rambling time-travel script plays like the pilot of an unsold series, which failed for obvious reasons. Four future metahumans with psi talents travel back to our present in an effort to change their past. Been there, done that. Rated R for violence and profanity. 84m. **DIR:** Barry Samson. **CAST:** Daniel Baldwin, Stacy Haiduk, T. K. Carter, LeVar Burton, Malcolm McDowell. **1996**

YI YI ★★★★ Several complex themes seep from a Taipei couple's midlife reassessment of their relationship and own self-worth, and from the emotional growing pains of their children. This compassionate, character-driven story begins with the stroke of an elderly family member and then gnaws for nearly three hours on such issues as first love, second chances, regret, spiritual emptiness, and moral confusion. In Taiwanese, Mandarin, and Japanese with English subtitles. Not rated; suitable for mature audiences. 173m. **DIR:** Edward Yang. **CAST:** Nien-Jen Wu, Elaine Jin, Issey Ogata, Kelly Lee, Jonathan Chang. **2000 DVD**

YIN AND YANG OF MR. GO, THE ★★ Jeff Bridges would probably like to forget that he made his debut in this confusing comic thriller about a Hong Kong weapons dealer who becomes a good guy due to the intervention of Buddha. Rated PG; contains brief nudity and violence. 89m. **DIR:** Burgess Meredith. **CAST:** James Mason, Jeff Bridges, Peter Lind Hayes, Burgess Meredith, Broderick Crawford. **1970**

YO-YO MAN ★★★★ This is ostensibly an instruction video on the development of yo-yo skills, but it is much more. The actual instruction consists of the basic tricks, tips on using the yo-yo, plus advanced skills that are great fun to watch and can be accomplished with practice. There are clips from *The Smothers Brothers Comedy Hour* series and new footage with Tommy Smothers and yo-yo expert Daniel Volk. Dick Smothers adds narrative and humor, and there is a catchy soundtrack. 38m. **DIR:** David Grossman. **CAST:** Tom Smothers, Dick Smothers, Daniel Volk. **1988**

YODELIN' KID FROM PINE RIDGE ★★★ Plot is reminiscent of his first film, *Tumbling Tumbleweeds*, as Gene Autry is banished by his father only to return to his Georgia hometown with a Wild West show five years later to find his father murdered. B&W; 54m. **DIR:** Joseph Kane. **CAST:** Gene Autry, Smiley Burnette, Betty Bronson, Charles Middleton. **1937**

YOJIMBO ★★★★1/2 Viewed from different perspectives this can be the most devastating comedy ever made; Kurosawa's parody of the American Western; or his satire on the United States and Soviet Union's achieving peace through nuclear proliferation. The plot: an unemployed samurai in nineteenth-century Japan sells his services to two rival merchants, each with killer gangs that are tearing the town apart. The film is boisterous and exuberant. (Remade by Sergio Leone as *A Fistful of Dollars*.) No rating, but very violent. B&W; 110m. **DIR:** Akira Kurosawa. **CAST:** Toshiro Mifune, Eijiro Tono. **1961 DVD**

YOL ★★★1/2 Winner of the Grand Prix at the Cannes Film Festival, this work written by Turkish filmmaker and political prisoner Yilmaz Guney follows several inmates of a minimum-security prison who are granted a few days' leave, telling their stories in parallel scenes. Guney—who smuggled instructions out of prison to his trusted assistants, then escaped from prison and edited the film—was hailed at Cannes for creating an eloquent protest against suppression and totalitarian government. Not rated, but the film has violence and suggested sex. 111m. **DIR:** Serif Goren. **CAST:** Tarik Akan, Serif Sezer. **1982**

YOLANDA AND THE THIEF ★★ An exotic fantasy, staged with near-cloying opulence, and now a cult favorite. Down on his luck con man Fred Astaire finds beautiful, rich, convent-bred Lucille Bremer praying to her guardian angel. His eye on her money, he claims to be the angel. 108m. **DIR:** Vincente Minnelli. **CAST:** Fred Astaire, Lucille Bremer, Frank Morgan, Mildred Natwick, Ludwig Stossel, Leon Ames, Gigi Perreau. **1945**

YONGARY—MONSTER FROM THE DEEP ★★ A Korean entry in the big-rubber-monster movie genre. An earthquake-causing monster (a dead ringer for Godzilla) rises to wage a destructive path across the country. Bad miniatures and a poor script make this more funny than scary. Rated PG. 79m. **DIR:** Kim Kiduk. **CAST:** Oh Young, Il. **1969**

YOU BET YOUR LIFE (TV SERIES) ★★★1/2 Over the years, two different game formats were devised for this show, but it was the interview segment that made the program a winner. In grilling the contestants, who ranged from average folks to celebrities to bizarre characters, Groucho Marx invariably got off a number of clever quips. B&W; 30m. **DIR:** Robert Dwan, Bernie Smith. **CAST:** Groucho Marx, George Fenneman. **1950–1961**

YOU CAN COUNT ON ME ★★★★1/2 Orphaned siblings in Upstate New York reunite as adults and rekindle their close but volatile relationship. Sammy is a single mom who attends church and still lives in their childhood home. Terry is a self-destructive drifter who visits his sister to borrow money for his girlfriend's abortion

and bonds with his precocious eight year old nephew. The excellent acting, understated script, and near-melodic direction provide a domestic drama of refreshing depth. Rated R for language, drug use, violence, and sexual content. 109m. **DIR:** Kenneth Lonergan. **CAST:** Laura Linney, Mark Ruffalo, Rory Culkin, Matthew Broderick. **2000 DVD**

YOU CAN'T CHEAT AN HONEST MAN ★★★1/2 Nearly plotless, this is, star W. C. Fields admitted, "a jumble of vaudeville skits"—which, nonetheless, brings together, with hilarious results, a cast of exquisite comedians. Fields fans will relish it all, of course. B&W; 76m. **DIR:** George Marshall. **CAST:** W. C. Fields, Edgar Bergen, Constance Moore, Mary Forbes, Thurston Hall, Eddie "Rochester" Anderson. **1939**

YOU CAN'T FOOL YOUR WIFE ★★★ A disillusioned Lucille Ball leaves her husband (James Ellison) and then tries to patch things up at a costume party. This is an average comedy with Ball playing two parts. B&W; 68m. **DIR:** Ray McCarey. **CAST:** Lucille Ball, Robert Coote, James Ellison. **1940**

YOU CAN'T HURRY LOVE ★★ A young man leaves Ohio to live with his hip cousin in Los Angeles. There he meets assorted women through a video dating service. Rated R for nudity and profanity. 92m. **DIR:** Richard Martini. **CAST:** David Leisure, Scott McGinnis, Anthony Geary, Bridget Fonda, Frank Bonner, Kristy McNichol. **1987**

YOU CAN'T TAKE IT WITH YOU ★★★★★ Frank Capra's adaptation of the beloved Kaufman and Hart stage classic continues to charm audiences. The fun starts when James Stewart and Jean Arthur fall in love and announce their desire to wed. This zany romp won 1938's Oscar for best picture. B&W; 126m. **DIR:** Frank Capra. **CAST:** James Stewart, Lionel Barrymore, Jean Arthur, Edward Arnold, Spring Byington, Mischa Auer, Ann Miller. **1938**

YOU CAN'T TAKE IT WITH YOU ★★★★1/2 Filmed on one set before a live audience, this Pulitzer Prize–winning Kaufman and Hart play features Jason Robards as the head of a very eccentric family. Now they must be on their best behavior to meet the parents of their daughter's beau. 116m. **DIR:** Kirk Browning. **CAST:** Jason Robards Jr., George Rose, Elizabeth Wilson, Colleen Dewhurst. **1984**

YOU KNOW MY NAME ★★★1/2 TNT original pays tribute to lawman Bill Tilghman (played by Sam Elliott), the famed marshal called out of retirement to become a small Oklahoma town's police chief in 1924. Elliott takes on a Gary Cooper-ish persona as the quiet, relentless good guy. Showdown is riveting. Not rated; contains profanity and violence. 91m. **DIR:** John Kent Harrison. **CAST:** Sam Elliott, Arliss Howard, Carolyn McCormick, Walter Olkewicz. **1999**

YOU LIGHT UP MY LIFE ★★1/2 Pretty weak story concerning a young girl, Didi Conn, trying to make it in show business. Notable for the title song, film proves it's tough to make a hit song stretch into a feature film. Rated PG. 90m. **DIR:** Joseph Brooks. **CAST:** Didi Conn, Michael Zaslow, Joe Silver, Stephen Nathan. **1977 DVD**

YOU MUST REMEMBER THIS ★★1/2 Heavy-handed message film exposes the shameful portrayals of black actors in early films. Robert Guillaume delivers a wooden performance as a former film director who could not exploit his black actors. Though not overly entertaining, this—being a Wonderworks Production—is worthy of family viewing and discussion. Not rated; contains no objectionable material. 102m. **DIR:** Helaine Head. **CAST:** Robert Guillaume, Tim Reid, Maria Celedonio, Vonte Sweet, Vonetta McGee. **1992**

YOU ONLY LIVE ONCE ★★ About a three-time loser (Henry Fonda) who can't even be saved by the love of a good woman (Sylvia Sidney) because society won't allow him to go straight. This film is a real downer—recommended for Fonda fans only. B&W; 86m. **DIR:** Fritz Lang. **CAST:** Henry Fonda, Sylvia Sidney, William Gargan, Barton MacLane, Jerome Cowan, Margaret Hamilton, Ward Bond, Guinn Williams. **1937**

YOU ONLY LIVE TWICE ★★★ Sean Connery as James Bond—who could expect more? Well, a better plot and more believable cliff-hanger situations come to mind. Still, this entry isn't a bad 007, and it does star the best Bond. 116m. **DIR:** Lewis Gilbert. **CAST:** Sean Connery, Akiko Wakabayashi, Tetsuro Tamba, Mie Hama, Karin Dor, Bernard Lee, Lois Maxwell, Desmond Llewellyn, Donald Pleasence. **1967**

YOU SO CRAZY ★★ Martin Lawrence's crude, lewd, sometimes very funny stand-up comedy is not as daring or as fresh as he may want us to think. Act includes riffs on Caucasians reacting to African Americans who talk at movies, racism, crack, the Rodney King beating, male and female genitalia, yeast infections, and the inner strength of his mother. Filmed at the Brooklyn Academy of Music's Majestic Theatre. Not rated by the MPAA. 86m. **DIR:** Thomas Schlamme. **CAST:** Martin Lawrence. **1994**

YOU TALKIN' TO ME ★★★ A struggling young New York actor whose idol is Robert De Niro (particularly De Niro's performance in *Taxi Driver*) moves to Los Angeles seeking his big break. Quirky offbeat film that eventually succeeds despite weak direction and clumsy dialogue. Rated R for violence and profanity. 97m. **DIR:** Charles Winkler. **CAST:** Jim Youngs, Faith Ford, Mykelti Williamson, James Noble. **1987**

YOU WERE NEVER LOVELIER ★★★★ In this interesting story, Fred Astaire goes stepping about with the most glamorous of all the stars—Rita Hayworth. This film's worth seeing twice. B&W; 97m. **DIR:** William A. Seiter. **CAST:** Fred Astaire, Rita Hayworth, Adolphe Menjou, Leslie Brooks, Adele Mara. **1942**

YOU'LL FIND OUT ★★★ Three titans of terror—Boris Karloff, Peter Lorre, and Bela Lugosi—menace bandleader Kay Kyser and heiress Helen Parrish in this silly but amiable comedy. Kyser isn't much of a screen personality, but director David Butler keeps the comedy, music, and suspense nicely balanced. B&W; 97m. **DIR:** David Butler. **CAST:** Kay Kyser, Peter Lorre, Boris Karloff, Bela Lugosi, Dennis O'Keefe, Helen Parrish. **1940**

YOU'LL NEVER GET RICH ★★★1/2 Musical comedy has play producer Fred Astaire getting drafted right before his big show. Somehow he manages to serve his country and put the show on while romancing Rita Hayworth. B&W; 88m. **DIR:** Sidney Lanfield. **CAST:** Fred Astaire, Rita Hayworth, John Hubbard, Robert Benchley, Osa Massen, Frieda Inescort, Guinn Williams. **1941**

YOUNG AMERICANS, THE ★★★1/2 Hard-hitting crime-drama about a Los Angeles narcotics cop who's loaned to Scotland Yard in an attempt to put an end to the reign of terror of an American drug dealer intent on taking over the drug trade in London. Rated R for extreme violence, language, and adult situations. 108m. **DIR:** Danny Cannon. **CAST:** Harvey Keitel, Viggo Mortensen, John Wood. **1993 DVD**

YOUNG AND INNOCENT ★★★ Reputedly director Alfred Hitchcock's favorite of the films he made in Great Britain, this film employs one of his favorite devices, that of an innocent man avoiding the police while attempting to catch the real criminal and prove his innocence. Not as well-known as many of his other films, this seldom-seen movie is vintage Hitchcock and on a par with much of his best work. B&W; 80m. **DIR:** Alfred Hitchcock. **CAST:** Derrek de Marney, Nova Pilbeam, Percy Marmont, Edward Rigby, Mary Clare, Basil Radford. **1937 DVD**

YOUNG AND WILLING ★★1/2 Hope springs eternal in the hearts of a gaggle of show business neophytes living and loving in a New York theatrical boardinghouse. Cute and entertaining, but formula. B&W; 82m. **DIR:** Edward H. Griffith. **CAST:** William Holden, Susan Hayward, Eddie Bracken, Barbara Britton, Robert Benchley. **1943**

YOUNG AT HEART ★★★1/2 A glossy remake of the Warner Bros. 1938 success *Four Daughters*. The plot presents Doris Day as a refined New England lass from a respected family who marries a down-on-his-luck musician (Frank Sinatra). 117m. **DIR:** Gordon Douglas. **CAST:** Doris Day, Frank Sinatra, Gig Young, Ethel Barrymore, Dorothy Malone. **1955 DVD**

YOUNG AT HEART COMEDIANS, THE ★★ Some of America's most famous comedians join together for this cable special. Moderately funny but dated material marks their routines. Not rated. 77m. **DIR:** Joe Hostettler. **CAST:** Carl Ballantine, Shelley Berman, Norm Crosby, Jackie Gayle, George Gobel, Jackie Vernon, Henny Youngman, David Brenner. **1984**

YOUNG BESS ★★★★1/2 Lavish, colorful, beautifully acted historical tale about England's Henry VIII and his tempestuous young daughter, Elizabeth. Charles Laughton repeats his Oscar-winning turn as the egotistical king. Good action and fiery performances. 112m. **DIR:** George Sidney. **CAST:** Charles Laughton, Jean Simmons, Stewart Granger, Deborah Kerr, Leo G. Carroll. **1953**

YOUNG BILL HICKOK ★★1/2 Highly fictionalized tale of Wild Bill Hickok takes place after the Civil War when Roy Rogers (as Hickok) goes after foreign agents trying to gain control of California land. Muddled. B&W; 54m. **DIR:** Joseph Kane. **CAST:** Roy Rogers, George "Gabby" Hayes, Julie Bishop, Sally Payne. **1940**

YOUNG CATHERINE ★★★ Lavish cable-TV costume drama focuses on the early life of Russia's Catherine the Great and her ascent to the throne. Political intrigue and romance take center stage in this rather lengthy but always interesting film. 165m. **DIR:** Michael Anderson. **CAST:** Julia Ormond, Vanessa Redgrave, Christopher Plummer, Franco Nero, Marthe Keller, Maximilian Schell, Mark Frankel, Reece Dinsdale. **1991**

YOUNG DOCTORS IN LOVE ★★★ This comedy attempts to do for medical soap operas what *Airplane!* did for disaster movies—and doesn't quite make it. Director Garry Marshall has nevertheless created an enjoyable movie for open-minded adults. The R-rated film is a bit too raunchy and suggestive for the younger set. 95m. **DIR:** Garry Marshall. **CAST:** Michael McKean, Sean Young, Harry Dean Stanton, Patrick Macnee, Hector Elizondo, Dabney Coleman, Pamela Reed, Michael Richards, Taylor Negron, Saul Rubinek, Titos Vandis. **1982**

YOUNG EINSTEIN 🦃 Einstein discovers how to split the atom and thus puts the bubbles into beer. Rated PG. 91m. **DIR:** Yahoo Serious. **CAST:** Yahoo Serious. **1989**

YOUNG FRANKENSTEIN ★★★★1/2 This is one of Mel Brooks's best. *Young Frankenstein* is the story of Dr. Frankenstein's college professor descendant who abhors his family history. This spoof of the old Universal horror films is hilarious from start to finish. Rated PG. B&W; 105m. **DIR:** Mel Brooks. **CAST:** Gene Wilder, Marty Feldman, Peter Boyle, Teri Garr, Madeline Kahn, Cloris Leachman, Kenneth Mars, Richard Haydn, Gene Hackman. **1974 DVD**

YOUNG GRADUATES 🦃 Misadventures of a high school girl who falls in love with her teacher. Rated PG. 99m. **DIR:** Robert Anderson. **CAST:** Patricia Wymer, Tom Stewart, Dennis Christopher. **1971**

YOUNG GUNS ★★ The Brat Pack attempts to ape the Wild Bunch in this disappointing Western. Emilio Estevez seems to be having a great time playing Billy the Kid, while his brother Charlie Sheen makes a more convincing cowboy. But it's all for naught because the story lacks any authenticity. The only bright moments are provided by genre veterans Jack Palance, Brian Keith, and Patrick Wayne in all-too-brief supporting roles. Rated R for violence and profanity. 102m. **DIR:** Christopher Cain. **CAST:** Emilio Estevez, Kiefer Sutherland, Charlie Sheen, Lou Diamond Phillips, Dermot Mulroney, Casey Siemaszko, Jack Palance, Brian Keith, Patrick Wayne. **1988 DVD**

YOUNG GUNS II ★★ More pop Western nonsense. This time Billy the Kid and his gang find themselves pursued by an old saddle pal, Pat Garrett. *Lonesome Dove* it ain't. Rated PG-13 for violence and profanity. 109m. **DIR:** Geoff Murphy. **CAST:** Emilio Estevez, Kiefer Sutherland, Lou Diamond Phillips, William L. Petersen, Christian Slater, James Coburn, Alan Ruck, Balthazar Getty. **1990 DVD**

YOUNG HERCULES ★★★★ The creators of the popular *Hercules* television series take a look at the strongest man in his younger days. Fans of the series won't be disappointed in this feature film that may not star Kevin Sorbo but is obviously of the same stuff. Rated PG-13. 93m. **DIR:** T.J. Scott. **CAST:** Ian Bohen, Dean O'Gorman, Chris Conrad, Johna Stewart, Kevin Smith. **1997 DVD**

YOUNG IN HEART, THE ★★★1/2 This delightful romp has a fortune-hunting family finding a change of heart when they meet a nice old lady, appropriately named Miss Fortune. The entire cast is wonderful in this lavish production. 91m. **DIR:** Richard Wallace. **CAST:** Janet Gaynor, Douglas Fairbanks Jr., Paulette Goddard, Roland Young, Billie Burke. **1938**

YOUNG LIONS, THE ★★★1/2 The impact of love and war on young lives is the focus of this gripping drama of World War II told from the German and American points of view. Marlon Brando is superb as the Aryan soldier

who comes to question his Nazi beliefs. Recommended. 167m. **DIR:** Edward Dmytryk. **CAST:** Marlon Brando, Montgomery Clift, Dean Martin, Hope Lange, Barbara Rush, May Britt, Maximilian Schell, Arthur Franz. **1958 DVD**

YOUNG LOVE, FIRST LOVE ★★ Boy loves girl, girl loves boy. Does girl love boy enough to go all the way? Nothing better to do? Then watch and find out. Valerie Bertinelli is supercute as the girl. Timothy Hutton is wasted as the boy with the sweats. Not rated. 100m. **DIR:** Steven H. Stern. **CAST:** Valerie Bertinelli, Timothy Hutton. **1979**

YOUNG MAGICIAN, THE ★★ Trite tale of a young man (Rusty Jedwab) who discovers he has magical powers and has a run-in with society. Special effects are good, but the dubbing in this Polish-Canadian production detracts a lot from the story. Not rated; suitable for the entire family. 99m. **DIR:** Waldemar Dziki. **CAST:** Rusty Jedwab. **1986**

YOUNG MAN WITH A HORN ★★★1/2 Interesting dramatic portrayal of a young horn player who fights to fill his need for music. Story becomes too melodramatic as Kirk Douglas becomes trapped in a romantic web between Lauren Bacall and Doris Day. Horn work by Harry James. B&W; 112m. **DIR:** Michael Curtiz. **CAST:** Kirk Douglas, Lauren Bacall, Doris Day, Hoagy Carmichael, Juano Hernandez. **1950**

YOUNG MR. LINCOLN ★★★★1/2 Director John Ford's tribute to the Great Emancipator is splendidly acted by Henry Fonda in the title role, with typically strong support from a handpicked supporting cast. This homespun character study develops into a suspenseful courtroom drama for a rousing conclusion. B&W; 100m. **DIR:** John Ford. **CAST:** Henry Fonda, Alice Brady, Marjorie Weaver, Donald Meek, Richard Cromwell, Eddie Quillan, Milburn Stone, Ward Bond. **1939**

YOUNG NURSES, THE ★★ There's more sex than plot in the next-to-last of producer Roger Corman's *Nurse* movies. Look for director Sam Fuller in a cameo as a villainous doctor. Rated R for nudity. 77m. **DIR:** Clinton Kimbrough. **CAST:** Jean Manson, Ashley Porter, Dick Miller, Sally Kirkland, Mantan Moreland. **1973**

YOUNG NURSES IN LOVE 🦃 A foreign spy poses as a nurse to steal the sperm from the sperm bank that was donated by world leaders, celebrities, and geniuses. Rated R for nudity. 82m. **DIR:** Chuck Vincent. **CAST:** Jeanne Marie. **1989**

YOUNG ONES, THE ★★★ Three episodes of the inventive, anarchic British TV series (you may have seen it on MTV) about a quartet of impoverished college students. Raucous, obnoxious, shrill—and often very funny. 96m. **DIR:** Geoffrey Posner. **CAST:** Rik Mayall, Adrian Edmondson, Nigel Planer, Alexei Sayle. **1982**

YOUNG PHILADELPHIANS, THE ★★★★ In this excellent film, Robert Vaughn stars as a rich young man accused of murder. Paul Newman, a young lawyer, defends Vaughn while pursuing society girl Barbara Rush. B&W; 136m. **DIR:** Vincent Sherman. **CAST:** Robert Vaughn, Paul Newman, Barbara Rush, Alexis Smith, Brian Keith, Adam West, Billie Burke, John Williams, Otto Kruger. **1959**

YOUNG POISONER'S HANDBOOK, THE ★★ British amateur chemist Graham Young spices up his stale teen life by spiking the tea of his family and fellow Londoners with lethal powders. This black comedy about a remorseless psychopath who charts the health of his victims in a diary begins with a wicked wallop but becomes monotonous about halfway through its dark, sick route. Rated R for language and the macabre. 105m. **DIR:** Benjamin Ross. **CAST:** Hugh O'Connor, Roger Lloyd Pack, Ruth Sheen, Samantha Edmonds, Antony Sher, Charlotte Coleman. **1996**

YOUNG SAVAGES, THE ★★★1/2 Members of an Italian-American gang are charged with the murder of a seemingly innocent blind Puerto Rican boy, and DA Burt Lancaster begins to wonder if everything is as it seems. Good adaptation of Evan Hunter's novel, *A Matter of Conviction*. B&W; 110m. **DIR:** John Frankenheimer. **CAST:** Burt Lancaster, Shelley Winters, Edward Andrews, Vivian Nathan, Larry Gates, Telly Savalas. **1961**

YOUNG SHERLOCK HOLMES ★★1/2 This disappointingly derivative Steven Spielberg production speculates on what might have happened if Sherlock Holmes and Dr. Watson had met during their student days in 1870 England. A better name for it might be *Sherlock Holmes and the Temple of Doom*. Youngsters are likely to enjoy it. Rated PG-13 for violence and scary stuff. 115m. **DIR:** Barry Levinson. **CAST:** Nicholas Rowe, Alan Cox, Sophie Ward, Anthony Higgins, Freddie Jones. **1985**

YOUNG SOUL REBELS ★★★★ Two black English soul DJ's attempt to break into mainstream radio stardom during the 1977 British punk explosion. This film accurately depicts the hazy sexual boundaries of the era. Rated R for nudity and profanity. 95m. **DIR:** Isaac Julien. **CAST:** Valentine Nonyela, Mo Sesau, Dorian Healy. **1991**

YOUNG TOM EDISON ★★★1/2 The first half of MGM's two-part tribute to Thomas Alva Edison (followed in months by *Edison, the Man*), geared to a subdued Mickey Rooney as the inquisitive teenage inventor. Mixture of fact and myth presented with respect. B&W; 86m. **DIR:** Norman Taurog. **CAST:** Mickey Rooney, Fay Bainter, George Bancroft, Virginia Weidler, Eugene Pallette, Clem Bevans. **1940**

YOUNG WARRIORS, THE ★★ Revenge exploitation with James Van Patten leading his college-frat brothers on a hunt for the psychos who raped and killed his sister. Rated R for violence. 105m. **DIR:** Lawrence D. Foldes. **CAST:** Ernest Borgnine, Richard Roundtree, Lynda Day George, James Van Patten, Anne Lockhart, Mike Norris, Dick Shawn, Linnea Quigley. **1983**

YOUNG WINSTON ★★★ Rousing and thoroughly entertaining account of this century's man for all seasons, England's indomitable Winston Churchill. The film takes him from his often wretched school days to his beginnings as a journalist of resource and daring in South Africa during the Boer War, up to his first election to Parliament. Simon Ward is excellent in the title role. Rated PG. 145m. **DIR:** Richard Attenborough. **CAST:** Simon Ward, Anne Bancroft, Robert Shaw, John Mills, Jack Hawkins, Robert Flemyng, Patrick Magee, Laurence Naismith. **1972**

YOUNGER AND YOUNGER ★★1/2 Percy Adlon's love story desperately wants to be enchantingly quirky but is more strained than sweet. A wife drops dead listening to her husband's latest infidelity. She begins to haunt

him, looking increasingly beautiful, growing ever younger, until she exacts a fitting revenge. Rated R for profanity, sexual situations, and brief nudity. 97m. **DIR:** Percy Adlon. **CAST:** Donald Sutherland, Lolita Davidovich, Brendan Fraser, Sally Kellerman, Julie Delpy, Linda Hunt. **1993**

YOUR FRIENDS & NEIGHBORS ★★ The coupling of a married woman and a weaselly drama teacher compounds the misery of six grating characters in this ugly black comedy. The film is a springboard for social commentary, savage satire, and introspection that has us wallow in—rather than squirm at—the current state of the human condition. Rated R for graphic sexual dialogue and profanity. 97m. **DIR:** Neil LaBute. **CAST:** Jason Patric, Aaron Eckhart, Amy Brenneman, Ben Stiller, Catherine Keener, Nastassja Kinski. **1998 DVD**

YOU'RE A BIG BOY NOW ★★★★1/2 Francis Ford Coppola not only directed this (his first) film but also wrote the screenplay. Peter Kastner, the product of overprotective parents, learns about life from streetwise go-go dancer Elizabeth Hartman. Fast-paced and very entertaining. 96m. **DIR:** Francis Ford Coppola. **CAST:** Peter Kastner, Elizabeth Hartman, Geraldine Page, Julie Harris, Rip Torn, Michael Dunn, Tony Bill, Karen Black. **1966**

YOU'RE JINXED FRIEND, YOU JUST MET SACRAMENTO ★★ A peaceful cowboy and his children are forced into a showdown with a spiteful town boss. Unimaginative, mindless spaghetti oater with Ty Hardin, made after his successful Warner Bros. *Bronco* TV series ended. 90m. **DIR:** Giorgio Cristallini. **CAST:** Ty Hardin, Christian Hay, Jenny Atkins. **1970**

YOU'RE NOT ELECTED, CHARLIE BROWN ★★★★ This school-themed special includes some classic material, from Sally's troubles with her locker (she can't reach it), to Linus's bid for class president . . . which seems a guaranteed success until the candidate extols the virtues of the Great Pumpkin. Listen for one of Vince Guaraldi's jazziest soundtracks. Not rated. 25m. **DIR:** Bill Melendez. **1972 DVD**

YOURS, MINE AND OURS ★★★ A widow with eight children marries a widower with ten of his own. This works as a harbinger of *The Brady Bunch.* Wholesome but never sterile or overly sentimental, this comedy-drama is probably Lucille Ball's best post–*I Love Lucy* vehicle. Rated G. 111m. **DIR:** Melville Shavelson. **CAST:** Lucille Ball, Henry Fonda, Van Johnson, Tom Bosley. **1968**

YOU'VE GOT MAIL ★★★★ Meg Ryan rules the screen in this mostly delightful update of Ernst Lubitsch's *The Shop Around the Corner*. She's the owner-proprietor of a much beloved children's bookstore tucked away in New York's Upper West Side while Tom Hanks—the apparent villain—owns a monolithic book superstore poised to open its newest branch across the street. But the slash-and-burn campaign soon to erupt is only half the story: our two heroes have been maintaining a strictly anonymous e-mail correspondence with each other despite other romatic ties and the certain knowledge that they'd hate each other on sight should the truth emerge. Rated PG for no particular reason. 119m. **DIR:** Nora Ephron. **CAST:** Tom Hanks, Meg Ryan, Parker Posey, Jean Stapleton, Greg Kinnear, Dave Chappelle, Steve Zahn. **1998 DVD**

YUMA ★★1/2 Big Clint Walker fights most of the rowdy elements of a tough town and has to expose a plan to undermine his authority as a lawman in this enjoyable made-for-television Western. 73m. **DIR:** Ted Post. **CAST:** Clint Walker, Barry Sullivan, Edgar Buchanan, Kathryn Hays, Peter Mark Richman, Morgan Woodward. **1970**

YURI NOSENKO, KGB ★★★1/2 This ably directed spy drama is based on the transcripts of public hearings, interviews, and published sources relating to the defection of KGB agent Yuri Nosenko in 1964. The filmmakers have filled in the gaps where direct evidence was unavailable. Tommy Lee Jones gives a tremendous performance as CIA agent Steve Daley. Oleg Rudnik is also good as Nosenko. 89m. **DIR:** Mick Jackson. **CAST:** Tommy Lee Jones, Josef Sommer, Ed Lauter, Oleg Rudnik. **1986**

Z

Z ★★★★ Director Costa-Gavras first explored political corruption in this taut French thriller. Yves Montand plays a political leader who is assassinated. Based on a true story. Academy Award for best foreign film. Well worth a try. No rating, with some violence and coarse language. 127m. **DIR:** Constantin Costa-Gavras. **CAST:** Yves Montand, Irene Papas, Jean-Louis Trintignant, Charles Denner. **1969 DVD**

ZABRISKIE POINT ★★1/2 An interesting but confusing story of a young college radical who shoots a policeman during a campus demonstration in the late 1960s. This film does not really say too much. Rated R. 112m. **DIR:** Michelangelo Antonioni. **CAST:** Mark Frechette, Daria Halprin, Rod Taylor. **1970**

ZACHARIAH ★★1/2 Forget the story line in this midnight movie Western and sit back and enjoy the music and the images. Television performers, a variety of musicians and actors, (including a youthful Don Johnson), populate this minor cult favorite and take every opportunity to be cool and break into song. There are tunes for most tastes and the fast-moving nature of the film makes it a good choice for company or a party. Rated PG. 93m. **DIR:** George Englund. **CAST:** John Rubinstein, Pat Quinn, Don Johnson, Country Joe and the Fish, Doug Kershaw. **1971 DVD**

ZANDALEE ★★ A sexually frustrated wife starts an affair with her husband's old friend. Unfortunately, writer Mari Kornhauser did a lousy job with an interesting idea. If you like graphic sex, you will love this film. Available in both R and unrated versions. 100m. **DIR:** Sam Pillsbury. **CAST:** Nicolas Cage, Judge Reinhold, Erika Anderson, Viveca Lindfors, Aaron Neville, Joe Pantoliano. **1990 DVD**

ZANDY'S BRIDE ★★1/2 Gene Hackman takes Liv Ullmann as a mail-order bride, uses (and abuses) her as chattel until shared hardships bring about respect and devotion. Also released as *For Better, For Worse*. Rated PG. 116m. **DIR:** Jan Troell. **CAST:** Gene Hackman, Liv

Ullmann, Eileen Heckart, Harry Dean Stanton, Susan Tyrrell, Sam Bottoms, Joe Santos. **1974**

ZANY ADVENTURES OF ROBIN HOOD, THE ★★ Made-for-TV spoof of the legendary hero of Sherwood Forest. George Segal is likable as Robin Hood. Okay time passer but nothing more. 90m. **DIR:** Ray Austin. **CAST:** George Segal, Morgan Fairchild, Roddy McDowall, Janet Suzman. **1984**

ZAPPED! ★★ A campy takeoff on high school movies that doesn't work. *Zapped* is a bore. Rated R for nudity and sexual situations. 96m. **DIR:** Robert J. Rosenthal. **CAST:** Scott Baio, Willie Aames, Felice Schachter, Heather Thomas, Scatman Crothers, Robert Mandan, Greg Bradford. **1982**

ZAPPED AGAIN ★★1/2 A new student inspires the science club to take on the jocks. His secret potion allows him to defy the law of gravity and manipulate people and things around him. As teen comedies go, this is not too bad. Rated R for nudity, profanity, and violence. 93m. **DIR:** Doug Campbell. **CAST:** Todd Eric Andrews, Kelli Williams, Linda Blair, Lyle Alzado. **1989**

ZARDOZ ★★1/2 Cult sci-fi about a strange society of the future and Sean Connery's attempts to free the people from the evil rulers. Murky plot is hard to follow, but it is amusing to watch Connery running around in a diaper for two hours. Rated R. 105m. **DIR:** John Boorman. **CAST:** Sean Connery, Charlotte Rampling. **1974**

ZARKORR! THE INVADER ♥ Inspired by Japanese monster flicks and presuperhero comic legends, the man in the monster suit thrashing about among the miniature cities looks pretty good. Unfortunately, he appears in very few scenes and, in the end, we're still unsure about Zarkorr's mission—and we no longer care. Rated PG for violence and profanity. 81m. **DIR:** Aaron Osborne. **CAST:** Rees Christian Pugh, DePrise Grossman, Mark Hamilton, Eileen Wesson, Charles Schneider. **1996**

ZATOICHI: MASSEUR ICHI AND A CHEST OF GOLD ★★★ Popular samurai series from Japan features a blind swordsman-masseur on an endless quest through the Japanese countryside. Zatoichi travels to pay his respects at the grave of a gambler he killed years ago. He is framed for robbery and murder. Zatoichi's character requires the viewer to suspend disbelief for enjoyment, but it's well worth it. In Japanese with English subtitles. Not rated; contains violence. 83m. **DIR:** Kazuo Ikehiro. **CAST:** Shintaro Katsu, Mikiko Tsubouchi, Machiko Hasgawa, Kenzaburo Joh, Shogo Shimada. **1964**

ZATOICHI: THE BLIND SWORDSMAN AND THE CHESS EXPERT ★★★★ The ragged, endearing character of the long-running Japanese series returns. This time he's on a gambling junket to Mt. Fuji. and incurs the wrath of gangsters when he wins all their money. In Japanese with English subtitles. Not rated; contains violence. 87m. **DIR:** Kenji Misumi. **CAST:** Shintaro Katsu, Mikio Narita, Chizu Hayashi, Kaneko Iwasaski, Gayo Kamamoto. **1965**

ZATOICHI: THE BLIND SWORDSMAN'S VENGEANCE ★★★★ Wandering blind swordsman-masseur Zatoichi chances upon a dying man who entrusts to him a bag of money to be delivered to someone named Taichi. When Zatoichi finally locates the mysterious Taichi, he finds more than he bargained for. Unique blend of action, comedy, and drama gives these films a Zen-like quality. In Japanese with English subtitles. Not rated; contains violence. 83m. **DIR:** Tokuzo Tanaka. **CAST:** Shintaro Katsu, Shigero Amachi, Mayumi Ogawa, Kei Sato, Jun Hamamura. **1966**

ZATOICHI VS. YOJIMBO ★★★1/2 Two of the giants of the Japanese samurai genre square off in this comic entry in the long-running blind-swordsman series. Shintaro Katsu is Zatoichi, an almost superhuman hero. The story is a send-up of Akira Kurosawa's *Yojimbo*, with Toshiro Mifune doing a comedic turn on his most famous character. It's fun for fans, but far from classic. In Japanese with English subtitles. 116m. **DIR:** Kihachi Okamoto. **CAST:** Shintaro Katsu, Toshiro Mifune. **1970**

ZAZIE DANS LE METRO ★★★★ Hilarious, offbeat tale of a foulmouthed 11 year old who comes to Paris to visit her drag-queen uncle (Philippe Noiret). Freewheeling fun. In French with English subtitles. 92m. **DIR:** Louis Malle. **CAST:** Catherine Demongeot, Philippe Noiret. **1960**

ZEBRA IN THE KITCHEN ★★ When a family moves to the city, their tame pet wildcat must go to an overcrowded zoo to comply with local regulations. Feeling a little mischievous, young star Jay North lets the animals loose. One-dimensional. 92m. **DIR:** Ivan Tors. **CAST:** Jay North, Martin Milner, Andy Devine, Joyce Meadows, Jim Davis. **1965**

•ZEBRA LOUNGE ★★ Tawdry little thriller about a bored married couple whose pursuit for excitement in their lovemaking leads them to a swingers club, where they meet an adventurous couple willing to spice up their bed. What begins as an experiment escalates into passion and then obsession. Will the married couple be able to get out alive or become victims of their own lust? Since this is the kind of movie you rent for the flesh, who really cares. Rated R for adult situations, drug use, language, and violence. 93m. **DIR:** Kari Skogland. **CAST:** Stephen Baldwin, Kristy Swanson, Brandy Ledford, Cameron Daddo. **2001 DVD**

ZEBRAHEAD ★★★★1/2 Michael Rapaport is a white, Jewish kid who is preoccupied with black culture. This low-budget but well-made examination offers a truthful, often funny peek at teenagers in the 1990s and pulsates with a taut undercurrent of anger. Rated R for profanity, violence, and sexual situations. 102m. **DIR:** Anthony Drazan. **CAST:** Michael Rapaport, Ray Sharkey, DeShonn Castle, N'Bushe Wright. **1992**

ZED AND TWO NOUGHTS, A ★★ Bizarre, unpleasant, but beautifully photographed (by Sacha Vierny) oddity about a woman who loses her leg in an auto accident, then becomes involved with the husbands of two women killed in the same wreck. A good deal of frontal nudity earned the film its R rating. 115m. **DIR:** Peter Greenaway. **CAST:** Andrea Ferreol, Brian Deacon, Eric Deacon, Frances Barber, Joss Ackland. **1985 DVD**

ZELDA ★★ Silly, contrived drama of F. Scott Fitzgerald's romance and marriage to Zelda. Zelda descends into mental illness while attempting to steer Fitzgerald toward his writing and away from his drinking. Natasha Richardson gives it her all in the title role, but she can't save this drivel. Made for cable TV. 94m. **DIR:** Pat O'Connor. **CAST:** Timothy Hutton, Natasha Richardson, Jon De Vries, Spalding Gray, Rob Knepper. **1993**

ZELIG ★★★★★ Woody Allen plays Leonard Zelig, a remarkable man who can fit anywhere in society because he can change his appearance at will. The laughs come fast and furious in this account of his adventures in the 1920s, when he became all the rage and hung out with the likes of F. Scott Fitzgerald, Jack Dempsey, and Babe Ruth. Allen seamlessly weds black-and-white newsreel footage with his humorous tale, allowing Zelig to be right in the thick of history. Rated PG. B&W; 79m. **DIR:** Woody Allen. **CAST:** Woody Allen, Mia Farrow. **1984 DVD**

ZELLY AND ME ★★ In this drama, we witness the turbulent life of a rich orphan played by Alexandra Johnes. She is overprotected and minus the knowledge of the ways of the real world. Isabella Rossellini and Glynis Johns are outstanding in secondary leads. The basic problem with this film, though, is that we never learn what happens to our orphan. Rated PG. 87m. **DIR:** Tina Rathborne. **CAST:** Isabella Rossellini, Alexandra Johnes, Glynis Johns, Kaiulani Lee. **1988**

ZENOBIA ★★★★ A cute comedy about a doctor called to treat an elephant. He treats the animal so well it refuses to leave him. One of Oliver Hardy's few appearances without Stan Laurel, and he's good enough to keep the elephant from upstaging him. B&W; 93m. **DIR:** Gordon Douglas. **CAST:** Oliver Hardy, Harry Langdon, Billie Burke, James Ellison, Jean Parker, Hattie McDaniel, Stepin Fetchit. **1939**

ZENTROPA ★★★ This surreal odyssey, whose chief attribute is style, follows a young man into a new job as a railway conductor in Germany immediately after the end of World War II. Often enigmatic, this Danish film uses the railway as a complex metaphor for the emerging of Europe after the war. Stunning photography and startling imagery abound. In Danish with English subtitles. 114m. **DIR:** Lars von Trier. **CAST:** Jean-Marc Barr, Barbara Sukowa, Lawrence Hartman, Udo Kier, Eddie Constantine. **1991**

ZEPPELIN ★★★ An emotionally wrought Michael York must choose between homeland and duty in this story of a German-born British aviator during World War I. Cast, design, and special effects blend to make this fine fare. Rated G. 101m. **DIR:** Etienne Perier. **CAST:** Michael York, Elke Sommer, Marius Goring, Peter Carsten, Anton Diffring. **1971**

ZERAM ★★ A female bounty hunter with a powerful computer must go into another universe to capture an evil alien being. Two stooges from the power company are accidently transported with her and must help her battle the alien. Dubbed in English. Not rated; contains excessive violence and gore. 92m. **DIR:** Keita Amamiya. **CAST:** Yuko Moriyama, Kunihiko Ida, Yukijiro Hotaru. **1991 DVD**

ZERO EFFECT ★★★ Daryl Zero is the world's greatest living private detective, and he's hired to end an ongoing extortion. The eccentric investigator uses his "deeply nuanced understanding of human nature" in this goofy, fragile spin on the private eye genre. Rated R for language. 115m. **DIR:** Jake Kasdan. **CAST:** Bill Pullman, Kim Dickens, Ben Stiller, Ryan O'Neal, Angela Featherstone. **1998 DVD**

ZERO FOR CONDUCT ★★★★1/2 Unique fantasy about the rebellion of boys in a French boarding school is told from the point of view of the students and provides perhaps the purest picture in the history of cinema of what authority appears to be to young minds. This all-too-short gem was sadly one of only four films made by terminally ill director Jean Vigo, at the age of 29. Banned across the Continent when first released, this film provided much of the story line for Lindsay Anderson's 1969 update *If*… In French with English subtitles. B&W; 44m. **DIR:** Jean Vigo. **CAST:** Jean Dasté. **1933**

ZERO KELVIN ★★★1/2 Unusual psychological drama set in 1925 Norway. A young writer accepts an assignment to write about fur trappers in the Arctic. Anticipating a rich adventure à la Jack London, he gets something rather different at a bleak tundra outpost where his only companions are a brooding scientist and a crude, bullying sailor. In Norwegian with English subtitles. Not rated; contains profanity, violence, nudity, and sexual situations. 113m. **DIR:** Hans Petter Moland. **CAST:** Stellan Skarsgard, Gard B. Eidsvold, Camilla Martins. **1995 DVD**

ZERO TOLERANCE ★★★ Although an early scene is needlessly sadistic, this explosive revenge saga certainly provides high-octane action and good, mindless fun. Robert Patrick delivers considerable tormented anguish as an FBI man who vows to terminate the so-called White Hand drug cartel: five mainstream businessmen who ordered his family's execution. The results are much better than this genre usually provides. Rated R for violence and profanity. 92m. **DIR:** Joseph Merhi. **CAST:** Robert Patrick, Titus Welliver, Kristen Meadows, Mick Fleetwood, Miles O'Keeffe. **1994**

ZEUS AND ROXANNE ★★ This bland and blatantly cute family film features single parents—a rock composer and a marine-biologist researcher—who get tricked into falling in love by their precocious kids while interspecies communication blossoms between the title's dog and dolphin. Rated PG. 98m. **DIR:** George Miller. **CAST:** Steve Guttenberg, Kathleen Quinlan, Arnold Vosloo, Dawn McMillan, Miko Hughes, Majandra Delfino, Jessica Howell. **1996 DVD**

ZIEGFELD FOLLIES ★★★ MGM tries to imitate a Ziegfeld-style stage show. Don't get confused; this is not the Oscar-winning *The Great Ziegfeld* (with William Powell). 110m. **DIR:** Vincente Minnelli. **CAST:** Fred Astaire, Lucille Ball, William Powell, Judy Garland, Fanny Brice, Lena Horne, Red Skelton, Victor Moore, Virginia O'Brien, Cyd Charisse, Gene Kelly, Edward Arnold, Esther Williams. **1946**

ZIEGFELD GIRL ★★★ Judy Garland becomes a star, Hedy Lamarr weds rich, and poor Lana Turner hits the bottle. This all-stops-out musical-drama is jammed with show girls, lavish sets and costumes, and songs no one but trivia buffs recall. B&W; 131m. **DIR:** Robert Z. Leonard. **CAST:** Judy Garland, Hedy Lamarr, Lana Turner, Edward Everett Horton, Eve Arden, James Stewart, Jackie Cooper, Dan Dailey. **1941**

ZIPPERFACE 🦃 Beautiful cop must go undercover to catch a serial killer who preys on prostitutes. Been there, done that. Not rated; contains nudity, violence, and language. 90m. **DIR:** Mansour Pourmand. **CAST:** Dona Adams, David Clover, Jonathan Mandell. **1992**

ZOLTAN—HOUND OF DRACULA 🦃 Dracula's faithful servant journeys to Los Angeles in search of the last surviving member of the Dracula clan. Rated R for vio-

lence. 85m. **DIR:** Albert Band. **CAST:** Michael Pataki, Reggie Nalder, José Ferrer. **1977**

ZOMBIE Gruesome, gory, and ghastly unauthorized entry in George Romero's zombie series. Rated X for gore and nudity. 91m. **DIR:** Lucio Fulci. **CAST:** Tisa Farrow, Ian McCulloch, Richard Johnson. **1979 DVD**

ZOMBIE ARMY Disgusting film has soldiers turned into the shuffling dead. Not rated; contains violence, gore, nudity, and profanity. 72m. **DIR:** Betty Stapleford. **CAST:** Eileen Saddow. **1993**

ZOMBIE BLOODBATH No one makes a zombie movie like George Romero and this woefully inept film proves that point. Not rated; contains graphic violence and gore. 98m. **DIR:** Todd Sheets. **CAST:** Auggi Alvarez, Frank Dunlay, Tonia Monahan. **1993**

ZOMBIE BLOODBATH 2 ★★ While Todd Sheets has come a long way as a filmmaker, he still has to learn that a story is more important than elaborate gore effects. This time around, teens return home to find it overrun by criminals and the living dead. Not rated; contains graphic violence, gore, and profanity. 90m. **DIR:** Todd Sheets. **CAST:** Kathleen McSweeney, Matthew Jason Walsh. **1995**

ZOMBIE COP ★★ After being turned into a zombie by a Haitian voodoo doctor, a cop teams up with his partner to hunt down the man responsible. Fails to generate any real thrills. The director is actually a pseudonym for cult fave J. R. Bookwalter. Not rated; contains violence, profanity, and gore. 75m. **DIR:** Lance Randas. **CAST:** Michael Kemper, Bill Morrison, James L. Edwards, Bogdan Pecic. **1991**

ZOMBIE HIGH Low-rent horror movie set at a prep school where the administration consists of 100 year old men who have kept their youth through a potion made with live brain tissue obtained from their students. Rated R. 93m. **DIR:** Ron Link. **CAST:** Virginia Madsen, Richard Cox, James Wilder. **1987**

ZOMBIE ISLAND MASSACRE Tourists in the Caribbean run into a pack of natives practicing voodoo. Rated R for violence, profanity, and nudity. 89m. **DIR:** John Carter. **CAST:** David Broadnax, Rita Jenrette. **1984**

ZOMBIE LAKE Third Reich storm troopers return from their watery graves in this cheesy Eurotrash gorefest. Rated R. 90m. **DIR:** Jean Rollin. **CAST:** Howard Vernon. **1982**

ZOMBIE NIGHTMARE ★★ This film—about an innocent boy who is killed by some "savage suburban teens" only to rise again as a zombie to avenge his murder—tries to be more mystical than gory. But it never becomes atmospheric enough to be interesting. Rated R for violence and profanity. 89m. **DIR:** Jack Brauman. **CAST:** Adam West, Tia Carrere, Linda Singer. **1986**

ZOMBIES OF MORA TAV ★★ Laughable, low-budget time waster about zombies and sunken treasure. Shows how dull zombies were before *Night of the Living Dead*. Not rated, but timid enough for your aunt Sally. B&W; 70m. **DIR:** Edward L. Cahn. **CAST:** Gregg Palmer, Allison Hayes. **1957**

ZOMBIES OF THE STRATOSPHERE (SATAN'S SATELLITES) (SERIAL) ★★ The Inter-Planetary Patrol tracks down part-human zombies and a renegade scientist who plan to blow Earth off its orbit. Balsa wood rocket ships and stock footage from the other "Rocket Man" serials make this one of the more ludicrous entries. B&W; 12 chapters. **DIR:** Fred Brannon. **CAST:** Judd Holdren, Aline Towne, Wilson Wood, Lane Bradford. **1952**

ZOMBIES ON BROADWAY ★★ Near–poverty row comedy starring Wally Brown and Alan Carney. The dimwitted duo portray press agents trying to book a zombie—a scheme that drops them into Bela Lugosi's clutches. B&W; 68m. **DIR:** Gordon Douglas. **CAST:** Wally Brown, Alan Carney, Bela Lugosi, Anne Jeffreys. **1945**

ZONE TROOPERS ★★ This is a dumb comic-book tale about an American troop in World War II lost behind German lines. Eventually, soldiers encounter space aliens who have crash-landed in the woods. Rated PG for mild violence. 86m. **DIR:** Danny Bilson. **CAST:** Tim Thomerson, Timothy Van Patten. **1985**

ZOO GANG, THE ★★ An oddball gang of crooks sets out to discover whether crime pays and winds up with more than it bargained for. Distinguished by Ben Vereen's excellent performance. Rated PG-13 for violence. 96m. **DIR:** John Watson, Pen Densham. **CAST:** Ben Vereen, Jason Gedrick, Eric Gurry. **1985**

ZOO RADIO ★★ This sophomoric comedy deals with dueling Los Angeles radio stations. A continuous stream of one-line jokes and sight gags—some work, some don't. Rated R for strong language. 88m. **DIR:** M. Ray Roach. **CAST:** Peter Feig, Ron Dickinson, David Pires, Terra Mays. **1990**

•ZOOLANDER ★★★ Wacky Ben Stiller spoof on male models is truly all his—as star in the title role, producer, director, and cowriter. Stiller is drawn into a plot to assassinate a benevolent prime minister determined to put an end to sweatshops and child labor. Stiller's wife, Christine Taylor, plays a reporter trying to clue him in before it's too late. Owen Wilson rivals Stiller as a model and in IQ points. Endless parade of celebrities adds to the fun. Rated PG-13 for drugs, sexual situations, and violence. 85m. **DIR:** Ben Stiller. **CAST:** Ben Stiller, Owen Wilson, Jerry Stiller, Christine Taylor. **2001 DVD**

ZOOMAN ★★★1/2 Potent adaptation of Charles Fuller's play about an inner-city gangbanger who accidentally kills a little girl. The grieving father, angered by scared neighbors who saw the murder but refuse to identify the killer, hangs a sign that collectively indicts the neighborhood . . . and then things *really* get interesting. Rated R for violence and incessant profanity. 95m. **DIR:** Leon Ichaso. **CAST:** Louis Gossett Jr., Cynthia Martellis, C.C.H. Pounder, Charles Dutton, Khalil Kain, Hill Harper. **1995**

ZOOT SUIT ★★★★ Adapted from his stage drama–musical by writer-director Luis Valdez, this innovative film presents a fictionalized version of the Sleepy Lagoon murder case that took place in 1942. Rated R for profanity and violence. 104m. **DIR:** Luis Valdez. **CAST:** Edward James Olmos, Charles Aidman, John Anderson, Tyne Daly, Daniel Valdez. **1981**

ZORBA THE GREEK ★★★★ A tiny Greek village in Crete is the home of Zorba, a zesty, uncomplicated man whose love of life is a joy to his friends and an eye-opener to a visiting stranger. Anthony Quinn is a delight as Zorba. Lila Kedrova was to win an Oscar for her poignant role as an aging courtesan in this drama. B&W;

146m. **DIR:** Michael Cacoyannis. **CAST:** Anthony Quinn, Alan Bates, Irene Papas, Lila Kedrova. **1963**

ZORRO ★★★ The dashing swordsman with the black mask and the flashing rapier rides against injustice, though in this version he rides in South America instead of California. Suitably swashbuckling, if a notch below the 1940 *Mark of Zorro*. Rated G. 88m. **DIR:** Duccio Tessari. **CAST:** Alain Delon, Stanley Baker, Enzo Cerusico, Ottavia Piccolo, Adriana Asti. **1975 DVD**

ZORRO RIDES AGAIN ★★★ A modern-day Zorro, played by John Carroll, lends his hand to a railway under siege by ruthless Noah Beery Sr., one of the cinema's greatest heavies. Constant harassment keeps Zorro on his toes. A great cast keeps this serial moving at a rapid clip. B&W; 12 chapters. **DIR:** William Witney, John English. **CAST:** John Carroll, Helen Christian, Reed Howes, Duncan Renaldo, Noah Beery Sr., Nigel de Brulier, Bob Kortman, Tom London. **1937**

ZORRO, THE GAY BLADE ★★★★ Here's another delight from (and starring) actor-producer George Hamilton. As with *Love at First Bite*, in which Hamilton played a slightly bent Count Dracula to great effect, the accent in *Zorro, the Gay Blade* is on belly-wrenching laughs . . . and there are plenty of them. Rated PG because of sexual innuendo. 93m. **DIR:** Peter Medak. **CAST:** George Hamilton, Lauren Hutton, Brenda Vaccaro, Ron Leibman, Donovan Scott. **1981 DVD**

ZORRO'S FIGHTING LEGION ★★★ Quality serial places Reed Hadley (as Zorro) at the helm of a determined band of patriotic ranchers eager to ensure safe passage of the gold shipments needed to continue Juarez's rule. B&W; 12 chapters. **DIR:** William Witney, John English. **CAST:** Reed Hadley, Sheila Darcy, C. Montague Shaw, Budd Buster, Carleton Young, Charles King. **1939**

ZOTZ! ★★★1/2 Charming, underrated little fantasy about a college professor (Tom Poston) who finds a magical coin blessed with three bizarre powers: sudden pain, slow motion, and explosive destruction. An excellent opportunity for Poston to control a film in one of his rare leading parts. Give this a try; you won't be disappointed. B&W; 87m. **DIR:** William Castle. **CAST:** Tom Poston, Jim Backus, Julia Meade. **1962**

ZOU ZOU ★★★ Josephine Baker's debut in talkies and a huge success in France. Baker's rendition of "Haiti" is the highlight. In French with English subtitles. B&W; 92m. **DIR:** Marc Allegret. **CAST:** Josephine Baker, Jean Gabin. **1934**

Z.P.G. (ZERO POPULATION GROWTH) In the pre–*Star Wars* 1970s, science fiction languished, and dreary films like this were a dime a dozen. Overpopulation imposes severe restrictions on life in the future. We guarantee no moviegoer will want to suffer through it. Rated PG. 95m. **DIR:** Michael Campus. **CAST:** Oliver Reed, Geraldine Chaplin, Don Gordon, Diane Cilento. **1972**

ZU: WARRIORS FROM THE MAGIC MOUNTAIN ★★★★ A must-see for all fans of action and fantasy films. The plot can be hard to follow as a young swordsman and a monk battle a demon queen intent on taking over the world. A wild, wonderfully imaginative movie. Available dubbed or in Cantonese with English subtitles. Not rated; contains no objectionable material. 98m. **DIR:** Tsui Hark. **CAST:** Yuen Biao, Adam Cheng, Brigitte Lin, Moon Lee, Sammo Hung. **1983 DVD**

ZULU ★★★★1/2 Several films have been made about the British army and its exploits in Africa during the nineteenth century. *Zulu* ranks with the finest. A stellar cast headed by Stanley Baker and Michael Caine who charge through this story of an outmanned British garrison laid to siege by several thousand Zulu warriors. Based on fact, this one delivers the goods for action and tension. 138m. **DIR:** Cy Endfield. **CAST:** Stanley Baker, Michael Caine, Jack Hawkins, Nigel Green. **1964 DVD**

ZULU DAWN ★★★ This prequel to the film *Zulu*, which was made fifteen years earlier, seems quite pale when compared with the first. Based on the crushing defeat of the British army at the hands of the Zulu warriors, *Zulu Dawn* depicts the events leading up to the confrontation portrayed in *Zulu*. Considering all involved, this is a disappointment. Rated PG for violence. 121m. **DIR:** Douglas Hickox. **CAST:** Burt Lancaster, Peter O'Toole, Simon Ward, John Mills, Nigel Davenport. **1979**

ZVENIGORA ★★★★ Prompted by their grandfather's stories, two young peasants dream of the legendary treasure buried in the hills of Zvenigora. Alexander Dovzhenko was the cinema's great epic poet, and in this, his first feature, he seamlessly blends mythology and his own personal beliefs with the history of the Ukraine. Silent. B&W; 73m. **DIR:** Alexander Dovzhenko. **1928**

CAST INDEX

Aadland, Beverly: Assault of the Rebel Girls (Cuban Rebel Girls)
Aaker, Lee: Hondo
Aaliyah: Queen of the Damned; Romeo Must Die
Aames, Angela: Lost Empire, The
Aames, Willie: Cut and Run; Frankenstein; Paradise; Zapped!
Aaron, Caroline: Modern Affair, A
Aaron, Hank: Hank Aaron: Chasing the Dream
Aaron, Tom: Body Puzzle
Abatantuono, Diego: Best Man, The; Mediterraneo
Abbott, Bruce: Bad Dreams; Black Scorpion; Bride of Re-Animator; Demolitionist, The; Dillinger; Interzone; Re-Animator; Summer Heat; Tag—The Assassination Game; Trapped
Abbott, Bud: Abbott and Costello Go to Mars; Abbott and Costello in Hollywood; Abbott and Costello in the Foreign Legion; Abbott and Costello Meet Captain Kidd; Abbott and Costello Meet Dr. Jekyll and Mr. Hyde; Abbott and Costello Meet Frankenstein; Abbott and Costello Meet the Invisible Man; Abbott and Costello Meet the Keystone Kops; Abbott and Costello Meet the Killer, Boris Karloff; Abbott and Costello Meet the Mummy; Abbott and Costello Show, The (TV Series); Africa Screams; Buck Privates; Buck Privates Come Home; Comin' Round the Mountain; Here Come the Co-Eds; Hey Abbott!; Hit the Ice; Hold That Ghost; In Society; Little Giant; Lost in a Harem; Lost in Alaska; Mexican Hayride; MGM's The Big Parade of Comedy; Naughty Nineties, The; Noose Hangs High, The; One Night in the Tropics; Pardon My Sarong; Ride 'em Cowboy; Rio Rita; Time of Their Lives, The; Who Done It?; Wistful Widow of Wagon Gap, The
Abbott, Diahnne: Jo Jo Dancer, Your Life Is Calling; Love Streams
Abbott, John: Pursuit to Algiers
Abbott, Philip: Invisible Boy, The
Abdul-Jabbar, Kareem: Airplane!; Game of Death; Jake Spanner Private Eye; Slam Dunk Ernest
Abdykalykov, Mirlan: Beshkempir, The Adopted Son
Abe, Hiroshi: Godzilla 2000
Abecassis, Yael: Kadosh
Abel, Alan: Putney Swope
Abel, Alfred: Metropolis (1926); Metropolis (1984 Musical Version)
Abel, Walter: Fury (1936); Island in the Sky; Mirage; Mr. Skeffington; Quick, Let's Get Married; Raintree County; So Proudly We Hail; Star Spangled Rhythm; 13 Rue Madeleine; Three Musketeers, The; Wake Island
Abelanski, Lionel: Train of Life
Abele, Jim: Wimps
Abell, Tim: Base, The
Abella, Helena: Final Justice
Abercrombie, Ian: Army of Darkness; Curse IV: The Ultimate Sacrifice; Johnny Mysto; Puppet Master III: Toulon's Revenge
Abercrombie, Jabee: Fugitive Girls
Aberle, Elke: I Only Want You to Love Me
Abilkassimov, Adir: Beshkempir, The Adopted Son
Abraham, F. Murray: Amadeus; Baby Face Nelson; Beyond the Stars; By the Sword; Children of the Revolution; Color of Justice; Dead Man's Walk; Dillinger & Capone; Eruption; Excellent Cadavers; Finding Forrester; Innocent Man, An; Intimate Power; Last Action Hero, The; Mighty Aphrodite; Mimic; Mobsters; Money; Muppets From Space; Name of the Rose, The; Nostradamus; Ritz, The; Season of Giants, A; Slipstream; Star Trek: Insurrection; Surviving the Game; Sweet Killing; Third Solution, The; Thir13en Ghosts
Abraham, Ken: Creepozoids; Deadly Embrace
Abrahams, Jon: Scary Movie; Texas Rangers (2001)
Abrahams, Jonathan: Whipped
Abrams, Michael: Summer Camp
Abreu, Claudia: Four Days in September
Abril, Victoria: After Darkness; Baton Rouge; Caged Heart, The (L'Addition); French Twist; High Heels; Jimmy Hollywood; Kika; Lovers (1992); Max Mon Amour; Moon in the Gutter, The; On the Line; Tie Me Up! Tie Me Down!
Abu-Warda, Yussuf: Kadosh
Acheson, James: Kazaam
Ackerman, Forrest J.: Ceremony; Curse of the Queerwolf; Hard to Die; Nudist Colony of the Dead
Ackerman, Leslie: Blame It on the Night
Ackland, Joss: Bill and Ted's Bogus Journey; Citizen X; Codename: Kyril; Daisies in December; Deadly Voyage; D3: The Mighty Ducks; Ghost Ship; Hunt for Red October, The; Jekyll & Hyde; Kid in King Arthur's Court, A; Lethal Weapon 2; Mighty Ducks, The; Mind Snatchers, The; Mother's Boys; Nowhere to Run; Palermo Connection, The; S*P*Y*S; Saint Jack; Shameless; Sherlock Holmes and the Incident at Victoria Falls; Sicilian, The; Spymaker: The Secret Life of Ian Fleming; Swept from the Sea; They Do It with Mirrors; To Kill a Priest; White Mischief; Woman Named Jackie, A; Zed and Two Noughts, A
Ackridge, Bill: Signal 7
Ackroyd, David: And I Alone Survived; Children of Times Square, The; Cocaine: One Man's Seduction; Dark Secret of Harvest Home, The; Dead On; Gun in the House, A; Love, Cheat & Steal; When Your Lover Leaves
Acosta, Rodolfo: Littlest Outlaw, The
Acovone, Jay: Beauty and the Beast (TV Series); Born to Run; Crash Dive; Crosscut; Doctor Mordrid; Opposite Corners; Quicksand: No Escape
Acquanetta: Captive Wild Woman; Dead Man's Eyes; Jungle Woman; Lost Continent, The; Tarzan and the Leopard Woman
Acuff, Eddie: Helldorado; Rough Riders' Roundup
Adair, Deborah: Endless Descent
Adair, Dick: Blind Rage
Adair, Jean: Arsenic and Old Lace
Adam, John: Chameleon
Adames, John: Gloria
Adams, Amy: Cruel Intentions 2
Adams, Ashby: Human Desires
Adams, Beverly: Ambushers, The; Torture Garden
Adams, Brandon: People Under the Stairs, The
Adams, Brooke: Almost You; Cuba; Days of Heaven; Dead Zone, The; Gas, Food, Lodging; Invasion of the Body Snatchers; James Dean—A Legend in His Own Time; Key Exchange; Last Hit, The; Lion of Africa, The; Man, a Woman and a Bank, A; Man on Fire; Murder on Flight 502; Picture Windows; Shock Waves (Death Corps); Sometimes They Come Back; Tell Me a Riddle; Unborn, The; Utilities
Adams, Buck: Major Rock
Adams, Carol: Bad Man of Deadwood
Adams, Casey: Bus Stop; Indestructible Man
Adams, Don: Get Smart Again; Nude Bomb, The (Return of Maxwell Smart,The)
Adams, Dona: Zipperface
Adams, Edie: Adventures Beyond Belief; Apartment, The; Best Man, The; Boxoffice; Call Me Bwana; Cry for Love, A; Ernie Kovacs: Television's Original Genius; Evil Roy Slade; Happy Hooker Goes Hollywood, The; Honey Pot, The; It's a Mad Mad Mad Mad World; Jake Spanner Private Eye; Love with the Proper Stranger; Lover Come Back; Seekers, The; Up in Smoke
Adams, Ernie: Arizona Gunfighter
Adams, Evan: Smoke Signals
Adams, Jane: Anniversary Party, The; Batman and Robin (Adventures of Batmanand Robin); Brute Man, The; Day at the Beach; Father of the Bride Part II; Happiness; House of Dracula; Light Sleeper; Mumford; Songcatcher
Adams, Jason: Ollie Hopnoodle's Haven of Bliss; Puppet Master Four
Adams, Jeb: Flowers in the Attic
Adams, Jill: Brothers In Law
Adams, Joey Lauren: Beautiful; Big Daddy; Chasing Amy; Cool, Dry Place, A

Adams, JoJo: Ice Cream Man
Adams, Jonathan: Rocky Horror Picture Show, The
Adams, Julie: Away All Boats; Bend of the River; Creature from the Black Lagoon; Francis Joins the Wacs; Last Movie, The (Chinchero); Man from the Alamo, The; Psychic Killer; Tickle Me
Adams, Kathryn: Fifth Avenue Girl
Adams, Lynne: Blood Relations; Carpenter, The
Adams, Marla: Gotcha!
Adams, Mason: Assault at West Point; Final Conflict, The; F/X; Kid with the Broken Halo, The; Night They Saved Christmas, The; Revenge of the Stepford Wives; Shining Season, A
Adams, Maud: Deadly Intent; Girl in Blue, The; Hostage Tower, The; Intimate Power; Jane and the Lost City; Killer Force; Man of Passion, A; Man with the Golden Gun, The; Nairobi Affair; Octopussy; Playing for Time; Rollerball; Silent Night, Deadly Night 4—Initiation; Target Eagle; Tattoo; Women's Club, The
Adams, Nick: Die, Monster, Die!; FBI Story, The; Godzilla vs. Monster Zero; Hell Is for Heroes; Interns, The; Mission Mars; No Time for Sergeants; Picnic; Rebel Without a Cause; Teacher's Pet
Adams, Robert: Song of Freedom
Adams, Ted: Arizona Gunfighter; Desert Phantom; Smokey Trails
Adams, Tom: Fighting Prince of Donegal, The
Adams, Wendy: Fool and His Money, A
Adamson, Amy: Last Stop
Adamson, Christopher: Razor Blade Smile
Adamson, Dave: City in Panic
Adamson, George: Christian the Lion
Aday, Meat Loaf: Crazy in Alabama
Addabbo, Tony: Crazy in Alabama
Addams, Dawn: King in New York, A; Liars, The; Moon Is Blue, The; Robe, The; Silent Enemy, The; Thousand Eyes of Dr. Mabuse, The; Vampire Lovers, The; Vault of Horror; Voulez Vous Danser avec Moi? (Will You Dance with Me?)
Addeo, Rosemarie: Smiling Fish & Goat on Fire
Addison, Nancy: Somewhere, Tomorrow
Addy, Mark: Flintstones in Viva Rock Vegas, The; Full Monty, The; Jack Frost; Knight's Tale, A; Time Machine, The (2002)
Addy, Wesley: Bostonians, The; Europeans, The; Hiroshima
Adebimpe, Tunde: Jump Tomorrow
Adele, Jan: High Tide
Adell, Traci: Life 101
Adelstein, Paul: Bedazzled
Adix, Vern: Teen Alien
Adjani, Isabelle: Camille Claudel; Diabolique; Driver, The; Ishtar; Next Year If All Goes Well; One Deadly Summer; Quartet; Queen Margot; Story of Adele H, The; Subway
Adkins, Seth: … First Do No Harm
Adler, Jerry: Manhattan Murder Mystery
Adler, Kim: Edgar Allan Poe's Madhouse
Adler, Luther: Brotherhood, The; Cornered; Crashout; Desert Fox, The; D.O.A.; Hoodlum Empire; House of Strangers; Kiss Tomorrow Goodbye; Last Angry Man, The; Loves of Carmen, The; Man in the Glass Booth; Murph the Surf; Von Ryan's Express; Wake of the Red Witch
Adler, Matt: Diving In; Flight of the Navigator; North Shore; White Water Summer
Adler, Stella: My Girl Tisa
Admire, Jenny: Dominion; Edgar Allan Poe's Madhouse; Goblin; Prehistoric Bimbos in Armageddon City
Adolphson, Edvin: Only One Night
Adonis, Frank: Suicide Ride
Adorée, Renée: Big Parade, The; Blackbird, The; Buster Keaton Festival Vol. 1–3
Adorf, Mario: Holcroft Covenant, The; Invitation au Voyage; King, Queen and Knave; Lola; Manhunt (1973) (The Italian Connection); Ten Little Indians; Tin Drum, The
Adrian, Iris: Blue Hawaii; Bluebeard; Horror Island; Lady of Burlesque; Road to Zanzibar; Roxie Hart
Adrian, Max: Boy Friend, The; Devils, The; Music Lovers, The; Terrornauts, The
Adrian, Patricia: I'm the One You're Looking For
Adu, Robinson Frank: Heart
Adu, Sade: Absolute Beginners
Aernouts, Kenny: Innocence
Aerosmith: Wayne's World 2
Affleck, Ben: Armageddon; Boiler Room; Bounce; Changing Lanes; Chasing Amy; Dogma; Forces of Nature; Going All the Way; Good Will Hunting; No Looking Back; Pearl Harbor; Phantoms; Reindeer Games; Shakespeare in Love; Sum of All Fears, The; 200 Cigarettes
Affleck, Casey: Attention Shoppers; Drowning Mona; Good Will Hunting; Ocean's Eleven (2001); Race the Sun; Soul Survivors; To Die For
Affleck, Neil: My Bloody Valentine
Agar, John: Along the Great Divide; Attack of the Puppet People; Brain from Planet Arous, The; Daughter of Dr. Jekyll; Fort Apache; Invisible Invaders; Jet Attack; Johnny Reno; Miracle Mile; Mole People, The; Perfect Bride, The; Revenge of the Creature; Sands of Iwo Jima; Tarantula; Women of the Prehistoric Planet
Agbayani, Tetchie: Deathfight; Gymkata
Agee, Arthur: Hoop Dreams
Ager, Nikita: Shark Attack 2
Agren, Janet: Aladdin; Emerald Jungle; Hands of Steel; Lobster for Breakfast
Agterberg, Toon: Spetters
Aguilar, Antonio: Undefeated, The
Agutter, Jenny: American Werewolf in London, An; Amy; Child's Play 2; Dark Tower; Dominique Is Dead; Equus; Gunfire; King of the Wind; Logan's Run; Man in the Iron Mask, The; Not a Penny More, Not a Penny Less; Othello; Railway Children, The; Riddle of the Sands; Silas Marner; Sweet William; Walkabout
Aherne, Brian: Beloved Enemy; Forever and a Day; I Confess; I Live My Life; Juarez; Lady in Question; Night to Remember, A; Prince Valiant; Smilin' Through; Swan, The; Sword of Lancelot; Sylvia Scarlett; Titanic; Waltz King, The
Aherne, Michael: Commitments, The
Ahlstedt, Borje: Emma's Shadow; I Am Curious Blue; I Am Curious Yellow
Ahmadi, Ayoub: Time for Drunken Horses, A
Ahmed, Lalita: Bhaji on the Beach
Ahn, Philip: Battle Circus; Betrayal from the East; Buck Rogers: Destination Saturn (PlanetOutlaws); Halls of Montezuma; His Majesty O'Keefe; Kung Fu (1971); They Got Me Covered
Aidman, Charles: Countdown; Hour of the Gun, The; King Lear; Kotch; Menace on the Mountain; Prime Suspect (1982) (Feature); Zoot Suit
Aiello, Danny: Alone in the Neon Jungle; Anything for Love; Brooklyn State of Mind, A; Cemetery Club, The; City Hall; Closer, The; Defiance; Do the Right Thing; Harlem Nights; Hudson Hawk; Jacob's Ladder; January Man, The; Key Exchange; Last Don, The; Mambo Café; Man on Fire; Me and the Kid; Mistress; Mojave Moon; Moonstruck; Old Enough; Once Around; Pickle, The; Power of Attorney; Preppie Murder, The; Professional, The; Protector, The (1985); Purple Rose of Cairo, The; Question of Honor, A; Ready to Wear; Road Home, The (1995); Ruby; Stuff, The; Third Solution, The; 29th Street; Two Days in the Valley; Two Much; White Hot
Aiello, Rick: Brooklyn State of Mind, A; Hollywood Confidential; Me and the Kid
Aiken, Liam: I Dreamed of Africa; Stepmom; Sweet November (2001)
Aimée, Anouk: Dr. Bethune; 8 1/2; Head Against the Wall; Justine; La Dolce Vita; Lola; Man and a Woman, A; Man and a Woman, A: 20 Years Later; Paris Express, The; Ready to Wear; Success Is the Best Revenge; Tragedy of a Ridiculous Man
Aimone, Gene: Freakshow
Ainsley, Norman: Shadow Strikes, The
Aird, Holly: Overindulgence; Theory of Flight, The
Airlie, Andrew: Common Ground; Hard Evidence
Aitchison, Suzy: Bloody New Year
Aitken, Spottiswoode: Eagle, The; Home, Sweet Home (1914)
Ajaye, Franklin: American Yakuza; Car Wash; Get Crazy; Wrong Guys, The

Akan, Tarik: Yol
Akili, Ali Mohammed El: Wedding in Galilee, A
Akinnuoye-Agbaje, Adewale: Legionnaire; 20,000 Leagues Under the Sea
Akins, Claude: Battle for the Planet of the Apes; Burning Hills, The; Curse, The; Death Squad, The; Devil's Brigade, The; Eric; Falling from Grace; Gambler Returns, The: Luck of the Draw; Inherit the Wind; Manhunt for Claude Dallas; Monster in the Closet; Night Stalker, The; Onionhead; Return of the Seven; Ride Beyond Vengeance; Rio Bravo; Sea Chase, The; Sherlock Holmes and the Incident at Victoria Falls; Tarantulas—The Deadly Cargo; Waterhole #3
Akiyama, Denis: Johnny Mnemonic
Akutagawa, Hiroshi: Mistress, The (1953)
Alaimo, Marc: Arena; Avenging Force; Fence, The
Alaimo, Steve: Stanley
Alajar, Gina: Debut, The
Alan, Craig: Game, The
Alan-Lee, Jeff: Beniker Gang, The
Alansu, John: Love Serenade
Alard, Nelly: Eating; Venice/Venice
Alaskey, Joe: Gross Jokes; Lucky Stiff
Alba, Jessica: Idle Hands
Alba, Maria: Mr. Robinson Crusoe; Return of Chandu (Magician, The)
Alban, Carlo: Thicker Than Blood
Albano, Lou: Body Slam
Albasiny, John: Kipperbang
Albee, Josh: Tom Sawyer
Alber, Kevin: Bram Stoker's Burial of the Rats
Alberghetti, Anna Maria: Cinderfella; Last Command, The
Alberni, Luis: Big Stampede, The; Madame X; Man from Monterey, The; Road to Zanzibar
Alberoni, Sherry: Nightmare Circus (Barn of the Living Dead) (Terror Circus)
Albers, Hans: Baron Münchhausen (1943)
Albert, Eddie: Act, The; Actors and Sin; Airport '79: The Concorde; Attack!; Beulah Land; Birch Interval, The; Bombardier; Captain Newman, M.D.; Carrie; Crash of Flight 401; Devil's Rain, The; Dreamscape; Dress Gray; Escape to Witch Mountain; Foolin' Around; Fuller Brush Girl, The; Goliath Awaits; Head Office; Heartbreak Kid, The; Hustle; I'll Cry Tomorrow; Longest Yard, The; McQ; Miracle of the White Stallions; Moving Violation; Oklahoma!; Perfect Marriage; Roman Holiday; Smash-Up: The Story of a Woman; Stitches; Take This Job and Shove It; Teahouse of the August Moon, The; Wagons Roll at Night, The; Whiffs; Who's Got the Action?; Yes, Giorgio
Albert, Edward: Body Language; Butterflies Are Free; Demon Keeper; Distortions; Exiled in America; Fist Fighter; Fool Killer, The; Forty Carats; Galaxy of Terror; Greek Tycoon, The; Guarding Tess; Hard Drive; House Where Evil Dwells, The; Ice Runner; Midway; Mindgames; Out of Sight Out of Mind; Purple Taxi, The; Red Sun Rising; Rescue, The; Sexual Malice; Shootfighter; Silent Victory: The Kitty O'Neil Story; Sorceress; Space Marines; Terminal Entry; Time to Die, A; When Time Ran Out!
Albert, Laura: Blood Games
Albert, Maxine: Home Remedy
Albert, Robert: Clean Shaven
Albertazzi, Giorgio: Last Year at Marienbad
Alberti, Lima: Clowns, The
Albertson, Frank: Ah, Wilderness; Alice Adams; Bachelor Mother; Connecticut Yankee, A; Dr. Christian Meets the Women; Doubting Thomas; Enemy Below, The; Hucksters, The; Louisiana Purchase; Man Made Monster (The Atomic Monster); Navy Blue and Gold; Psycho; Shining Hour, The; Tournament Tempo
Albertson, Jack: Big Business Girl; Dead and Buried; Don't Go Near the Water; Flim-Flam Man, The; How to Murder Your Wife; Justine; Kissin' Cousins; Lover Come Back; Period of Adjustment; Rabbit Run; Subject Was Roses, The; Teacher's Pet; Willy Wonka and the Chocolate Factory
Albright, Ariauna: Bloodletting; Horrorvision; Polymorph; Witchouse
Albright, Brad: Don't Let Your Meat Loaf
Albright, Hardie: Mom and Dad; Scarlet Letter, The; Silver Streak
Albright, Lola: Impossible Years, The; Joy House; Kid Galahad; Lord Love a Duck; Monolith Monsters, The; Peter Gunn (TV Series); Tender Trap, The; Way West, The; Where Were You When the Lights Went Out?
Alcaide, Chris: Gunslinger
Alcazar, Damian: Men with Guns
Alcroft, Jamie: Million Dollar Mystery
Alda, Alan: And the Band Played On; Betsy's Wedding; California Suite; Canadian Bacon; Crimes and Misdemeanors; Everyone Says I Love You; Flirting with Disaster; Four Seasons, The; Glass House, The; Killing Yard, The; Mad City; Manhattan Murder Mystery; M*A*S*H (TV Series); Mephisto Waltz, The; Murder at 1600; New Life, A; Object of My Affection, The; Paper Lion; Playmates; Purlie Victorious; Same Time Next Year; Seduction of Joe Tynan, The; Sweet Liberty; To Kill a Clown; What Women Want; Whispers in the Dark; White Mile
Alda, Beatrice: New Life, A
Alda, Robert: Beast with Five Fingers, The; Bittersweet Love; Cloak and Dagger; Devil in the House of Exorcism, The; House of Exorcism, The; I Will, I Will ... for Now; Imitation of Life; Man I Love, The; Rhapsody in Blue
Alda, Rutanya: Amityville II: The Possession; Apprentice to Murder; Dark Half, The; Racing with the Moon; Vigilante
Alden, Matt: Doin' Time on Planet Earth
Alden, Norm: Wyatt Earp: Return to Tombstone
Alden, Norman: Red Line 7000
Alden, Priscilla: Criminally Insane
Alden, Terry: Last Game, The
Alderman, John: Pink Angels
Aldon, Mari: Distant Drums; Tanks Are Coming, The
Aldredge, Tom: Man That Corrupted Hadleyburg, The; O Pioneers!; Rain People, The; Seize the Day
Aldrich, John: Wild Beasts, The
Aldrich, Matthew: My Sweet Suicide
Aldridge, Kitty: African Dream, An; American Roulette; Slipstream
Aldridge, Michael: Bullshot (Bullshot Crummond)
Aldrin, Buzz: Boy in the Plastic Bubble, The
Aleandro, Norma: Cousins; Gaby, a True Story; Official Story, The; One Man's War
Aleman, Julio: Green Wall, The
Alentova, Vera: Moscow Does Not Believe in Tears
Aleong, Aki: Braddock: Missing in Action III; Out for Blood
Alerme, Andre: Carnival in Flanders
Ales, John: Nutty Professor, The; Nutty Professor II: The Klumps
Aless, Jean: Homicidal
Aletonis, Paula: Stolen Hearts
Alexander, Alphonso: Bustin' Loose
Alexander, Barbara Lee: Psycho Cop 2
Alexander, Ben: Dragnet; Hearts of the World
Alexander, Bruce: Touch of Frost, A (TV Series)
Alexander, Daniel: Shark Attack 2
Alexander, Denise: Lindbergh Kidnapping Case, The
Alexander, Frank: Gladiator Cop II: The Swordsman; Sinyster
Alexander, Geraldine: Sleeping Murder
Alexander, Jane: All the President's Men; Betsy, The; Brubaker; Calamity Jane; City Heat; Friendship in Vienna, A; Great White Hope, The; Gunfight, A; In Love and War; Kramer vs. Kramer; Love and War; New Centurions, The; Night Crossing; Playing for Time; Rumor Mill, The; Square Dance; Sweet Country; Testament
Alexander, Jason: Adventures of Rocky and Bullwinkle, The; Coneheads; Dunston Checks In; For Better or Worse; I Don't Buy Kisses Anymore; Jacob's Ladder; Love! Valour! Compassion!; Paper, The; Rodgers & Hammerstein's Cinderella; Shallow Hal; Something About Sex; Trumpet of the Swan, The; White Palace
Alexander, John: Alien P.I.; Horn Blows at Midnight, The
Alexander, Katharine: Great Man Votes, The; Operator 13
Alexander, Khandi: House Party 3
Alexander, Laura: Knight Chills

Almgren, Susan: Deadly Surveillance; Shades of Love: Lilac Dream
Alonso, Chelo: Goliath and the Barbarians
Alonso, Ernesto: Criminal Life of Archibaldo de la Cruz,The
Alonso, Maria Conchita: Acts of Betrayal; Blackheart; Caught; Chain of Command; Colors; Extreme Prejudice; Fine Mess, A; High Noon; House of the Spirits, The; Knockout; McBain; Moscow on the Hudson; Predator 2; Roosters; Running Man, The; Teamster Boss: The Jackie Presser Story; Texas; Touch and Go; Vampire's Kiss
Alonso, Rafael: Mr. Superinvisible
Alosio, Ryan: Hi-line, The
Alphin, Patricia: Ma and Pa Kettle (The Further Adventures of Ma and Pa Kettle)
Alric, Catherine: Associate, The
Alster, Pamela: Sgt. Kabukiman N.Y.P.D.
Alt, Carol: Beyond Justice; Body Armor; Bye Bye, Baby; Deadly Past; Family Matter, A; Hostage Train; Millions; Ring of Steel; Thunder in Paradise; Thunder in Paradise II
Alterio, Hector: Basileus Quartet; Camila (1984); Nest, The; Official Story, The
Althaus, Urs: Warbus
Altman, Bruce: L.I.E.; Rookie of the Year; To Gillian on Her 37th Birthday; White Mile
Altman, Jeff: American Hot Wax; Doin' Time; In Love with an Older Woman; Wacko
Altman, Steve: Transylvania Twist
Alvarado, Angela: Nobody's Girls; Shadow Hunter
Alvarado, Trini: American Blue Note; American Friends; Babe, The (1992); Chair, The; Frighteners, The; Little Women; Mrs. Soffel; Nitti: The Enforcer; Rich Kids; Satisfaction; Stella; Sweet Lorraine; Times Square
Alvarez, Auggi: Dominion; Moonchild; Witching, The (1994); Zombie Bloodbath
Alvarez, Jesus M.: Apostate, The
Alvarez, Oscar: Up to a Certain Point
Alvarez-Novoa, Carlos: Solas
Alvaro, Anne: Taste of Others, The
Alyn, Kirk: Atom Man vs. Superman; Scalps; Superman—The Serial
Alyse-Smith, Brittany: Pinocchio's Revenge
Alzado, Lyle: Club Fed; Comrades in Arms; Double McGuffin, The; Ernest Goes to Camp; Neon City; Oceans of Fire; Tapeheads; Zapped Again
Amachi, Shigero: Zatoichi: The Blind Swordsman's Vengeance
Amalric, Mathieu: Alice & Martin
Amandes, Tom: When Good Ghouls Go Bad
Amano, Sayoko: Tokyo Decadence
Amar, Leonora: Captain Scarlett
Amastutz, Roland: Eyes of the Birds
Ambrose, Lauren: Can't Hardly Wait; Psycho Beach Party
Ambrosini, Philippe: Bye-Bye
Ameche, Don: Alexander's Ragtime Band; Cocoon; Cocoon: The Return; Corrina, Corrina; Down Argentine Way; Folks; Guest Wife; Happy Landing; Harry and the Hendersons; Heaven Can Wait; Hollywood Cavalcade; In Old Chicago; It's in the Bag; Midnight; Moon over Miami; Oddball Hall; One in a Million; Oscar (1991); Pals; Picture Mommy Dead; Sunstroke; Suppose They Gave a War and Nobody Came?; Things Change; Three Musketeers, The; Trading Places; Wing and a Prayer, A
Amendola, Claudio: Forever Mary; La Scorta
America, Paul: Ciao! Manhattan
Ames, Adrienne: Death Kiss, The; Harmony Lane
Ames, Leon: Any Number Can Play; Big Hangover, The; By the Light of the Silvery Moon; Date with Judy, A; Deadly Encounter; From the Terrace; Iron Major, The; Jake Speed; Lady in the Lake; Marshal of Mesa City; Merton of the Movies; Misadventures of Merlin Jones, The; Monkey's Uncle, The; Mr. Moto in Danger Island; Murders in the Rue Morgue; Mysterious Mr. Moto; On Moonlight Bay; Peggy Sue Got Married; Peyton Place; Show-Off, The; Son of Lassie; Testament; Thin Man Goes Home, The; Velvet Touch, The; Yolanda and the Thief
Ames, Ramsay: Mummy's Ghost, The
Ames, Rosemary: Our Little Girl
Amick, Madchen: Bombshell; Courtyard, The; Don't Tell Her It's Me; Dream Lover; French Exit; Heartless; Hunted (1997); I'm Dangerous Tonight; Love, Cheat & Steal; Psychopath (1997); Stephen King's Sleepwalkers; Trapped in Paradise; Wounded
Amidou: Unveiled
Amidou, Souad: Sorcerer
Amin, Rola Al: West Beirut
Amis, Suzy: Ballad of Little Jo, The; Beneficiary, The; Big Town, The; Blown Away; Cadillac Ranch; Ex, The; Firestorm; Judgment Day; Last Stand at Saber River; Nadja; One Good Turn; Plain Clothes; Rich in Love; Rocket Gibraltar; Titanic; Twister; Two Small Bodies; Usual Suspects, The; Watch It
Ammann, Renee: Number One Fan; Stoned Age, The
Amos, David: Flipping
Amos, John: American Flyers; Beastmaster, The; Coming to America; Die Hard 2: Die Harder; Jungle Heat; Let's Do It Again; Lock Up; Mac; Mardi Gras for the Devil; Sweet Sweetback's Baadasssss Song; Touched by Love; Two Evil Eyes; Willa; World's Greatest Athlete, The
Amos, Keith: Breach of Conduct
Amphlett, Christina: Monkey Grip
Amplas, John: Martin; Midnight
Amrani, Gabi: Lupo; Madron
Amsterdam, Morey: Beach Party; Dick Van Dyke Show, The (TV Series); Gay Purr-ee; Machine-Gun Kelly; Muscle Beach Party; Sooner or Later
Anbeh, Susan: French Kiss
Anchoriz, Leo: Bullet for Sandoval, A; Finger on the Trigger
Anconina, Richard: Love Songs (Paroles et Musique); Police; Tchao Pantin
Anders, Avalon: Wish Me Luck
Anders, Donna: Count Yorga, Vampire
Anders, Glenn: Lady from Shanghai
Anders, Luana: Border Radio; Dementia 13; Easy Rider; Greaser's Palace; Manipulator, The; One from the Heart; Pit and the Pendulum, The; Sex and the College Girl; That Cold Day in the Park; Trip, The
Anders, Lynn: Shadow Strikes, The
Anders, Merry: Farmer Takes a Wife, The; Hypnotic Eye, The; Tickle Me; Time Travelers, The; Women of the Prehistoric Planet
Andersen, Dana: Ginger Ale Afternoon
Andersen, Elga: Global Affair, A; Le Mans
Andersen, Isa: Night Angel
Andersen, Suzy: Black Sabbath
Anderson, Adisa: Daughters of the Dust
Anderson, Anders T.: 13th Warrior, The
Anderson, Anthony: Exit Wounds; Life; Two Can Play That Game
Anderson, Bridgette: Fever Pitch; Savannah Smiles
Anderson, Bruce: Thinkin' Big
Anderson, Carl: Jesus Christ, Superstar
Anderson, Daniel: Body of Influence 2
Anderson, Daphne: Hobson's Choice
Anderson, Dave: No Dead Heroes
Anderson, Eddie "Rochester": Birth of the Blues; Brewster's Millions; Buck Benny Rides Again; Cabin in the Sky; Green Pastures; Honolulu; It Happened in New Orleans; Jack Benny Program, The (TV Series); Meanest Man in the World, The; Show-Off, The; Tales of Manhattan; Three Men on a Horse; Topper Returns; You Can't Cheat an Honest Man
Anderson, Erich: Love Kills
Anderson, Erika: Object of Obsession; Quake; Zandalee
Anderson, Ernest: Well, The
Anderson, Erville: Haunted Gold
Anderson, Gabrych: Edge of Seventeen
Anderson, Gillian: Hellcab; House of Mirth, The; Mighty, The; Playing by Heart; X-Files, The (1998); X-Files, The (TV Series)
Anderson, Harry: It; Spies, Lies, and Naked Thighs
Anderson, Haskell V.: Brotherhood of Death
Anderson, Herbert: Benny Goodman Story, The; I Bury the Living
Anderson, James: Hunt the Man Down

Anderson, Jean: Back Home
Anderson, Jeff: Clerks
Anderson, Jill: Omaha (The Movie)
Anderson, John: Deerslayer, The (1978); Donner Pass: The Road to Survival; Executive Action; Firehouse; In Search of Historic Jesus; Man and Boy; Medicine Hat Stallion, The; Namu, the Killer Whale; Psycho; Ride the High Country; Smile, Jenny, You're Dead; Soldier Blue; Wyatt Earp: Return to Tombstone; Zoot Suit
Anderson, Judith: All Through the Night; And Then There Were None; Blood Money; Edge of Darkness; King's Row; Lady Scarface; Laura; Macbeth; Man Called Horse, A; Pursued; Rebecca; Red House, The; Salome; Specter of the Rose, The; Strange Love of Martha Ivers, The; Tycoon
Anderson, Kenneth: Feast of July
Anderson, Kevin: Hoffa; In Country; Liebestraum; Miles from Home; Monday Night Mayhem; Night We Never Met, The; Orphans; Orpheus Descending; Pink Nights; Rising Sun; Sleeping with the Enemy; Thousand Acres, A; Wrong Man, The
Anderson, Laurie: Two Moon July
Anderson, Lindsay: O Lucky Man!; Prisoner of Honor
Anderson, Loni: Jayne Mansfield Story, The; Munchie; My Mother's Secret Life; Night at the Roxbury, A; Sizzle; Sorry, Wrong Number; Stroker Ace; Whisper Kills, A; White Hot: The Mysterious Murder of Thelma Todd
Anderson, Louie: Ratboy; Wrong Guys, The
Anderson, Mary: Hunt the Man Down; Underworld Story
Anderson, Matthew R.: Surface to Air
Anderson, Melissa Sue: Chattanooga Choo Choo; Dead Men Don't Die; Equalizer, The: "Memories of Manon"; First Affair; Happy Birthday to Me; Little House on the Prairie (TV Series)
Anderson, Melody: Dead and Buried; Elvis—The Movie; Final Notice; Firewalker; Flash Gordon; Hitler's Daughter; Landslide; Marilyn & Bobby: Her Final Affair
Anderson, Michael J.: Dead and Buried; Elvis—The Movie; Final Notice; Firewalker; Flash Gordon; Hitler's Daughter; Landslide; Marilyn & Bobby: Her Final Affair
Anderson, Nathan: Tequila Body Shots
Anderson, Pamela: Baywatch: The Movie; Raw Justice; Snapdragon
Anderson, Pat: Summer School Teachers; TNT Jackson
Anderson, Richard: Bionic Woman, The; Escape from Fort Bravo; Gettysburg; Glass Shield, The; I Love Melvin; It's a Dog's Life; Magnificent Yankee, The; Night Strangler, The; Rich, Young and Pretty
Anderson, Richard Dean: Ordinary Heroes; Past the Bleachers; Stargate SG-1
Anderson, Warner: Armored Command; Destination Moon; Destination Tokyo; Drum Beat; Go for Broke!; Lawless Street, A; Objective, Burma!; Star, The (1952)
Anderson, Whitney: Prehysteria! 3
Anderson Jr., Michael: Dear Heart; In Search of the Castaways; Legacy for Leonette; Sons of Katie Elder, The
Andersson, Bibi: All These Women; Babette's Feast; Brink of Life; Devil's Eye, The; Duel at Diablo; I Never Promised You a Rose Garden; Magician, The; Passion of Anna, The; Persona; Quintet; Scenes from a Marriage; Seventh Seal, The; Wild Strawberries
Andersson, Harriet: Cries and Whispers; Dreams; Lesson in Love, A; Monika; Sawdust and Tinsel; Smiles of a Summer Night; Through a Glass Darkly
Andes, Keith: Away All Boats; Blackbeard the Pirate; Clash by Night; Farmer's Daughter, The
Andley, Eleanor: Hazel Christmas Show, The (TV Series)
Ando: Paper Tiger
Ando, Eiko: Barbarian and the Geisha, The
Andre, George: Wild World of Batwoman, The (She Was a Happy Vampire)
André, Carole: One Russian Summer; Violent Breed, The
André, Gaby: Cosmic Monsters, The; East of Kilimanjaro; Goliath and the Dragon
Andre the Giant: Princess Bride, The
Andreasi, Felice: Story of Boys and Girls
Andreeff, Starr: Amityville Dollhouse; Club Vampire; Dance of the Damned; Syngenor; Vampire Journals
Andrei, Damir: Caveman's Valentine, The
Andrei, Frederic: Diva
Andreichenko, Natasha: Operation Intercept
Andress, Ursula: Blue Max, The; Casino Royale; Chinatown Murders, The: Man Against the Mob; Dr. No; Fifth Musketeer, The; Four for Texas; Fun in Acapulco; Loves and Times of Scaramouche, The; Red Sun; Sensuous Nurse, The; Slave of the Cannibal God; Stateline Motel; Tenth Victim, The; What's New, Pussycat?
Andreu, Simon: Blood Spattered Bride, The
Andrews, Anthony: Brideshead Revisited; David Copperfield; Hanna's War; Haunted; Holcroft Covenant, The; Ivanhoe; Scarlet Pimpernel, The; Sherlock Holmes: Hands of a Murderer; Strange Case of Dr. Jekyll and Mr. Hyde,The (1989); Suspicion; Under the Volcano
Andrews, Arkansas Slim: Take Me Back to Oklahoma
Andrews, Barry: Dracula Has Risen from the Grave
Andrews, Carl: Lion of Africa, The
Andrews, Carol: Bullfighters, The
Andrews, Christian: Deceit
Andrews, Dana: Ball of Fire; Battle of the Bulge; Best Years of Our Lives, The; Beyond a Reasonable Doubt (1956); Boomerang; Born Again; Cobra, The (1967); Curse of the Demon; Devil's Brigade, The; Elephant Walk; Enchanted Island; Good Guys Wear Black; In Harm's Way; Johnny Reno; Kit Carson; Last Tycoon, The; Laura; My Foolish Heart; North Star, The (1943); Ox-Bow Incident, The; Pilot, The; Purple Heart, The; State Fair; Take a Hard Ride; Up in Arms; Walk in the Sun, A; Westerner, The; While the City Sleeps; Wing and a Prayer, A
Andrews, David: Apollo 13; Cherry 2000; Stephen King's Graveyard Shift (1990); Under Pressure; Wyatt Earp
Andrews, Edward: Avanti!; How to Frame a Figg; Kisses for My President; Send Me No Flowers; Seniors, The; Sixteen Candles; Summertime; Tea and Sympathy; Thrill of It All, The; Young Savages, The
Andrews, Giuseppe: Detroit Rock City
Andrews, Harry: Agony and the Ecstasy, The; Battle of Britain; Charge of the Light Brigade, The; Curse of King Tut's Tomb, The; Dandy in Aspic, A; Devil's Disciple, The; Entertaining Mr. Sloane; Equus; Four Feathers, The; Hill, The; I Want What I Want; Internecine Project, The; Jack the Ripper; Man of La Mancha; Medusa Touch, The; Nice Girl Like Me, A; Nightcomers, The; Ruling Class, The; Saint Joan; Seven Dials Mystery, The; 633 Squadron; Story of Jacob and Joseph, The; Wuthering Heights
Andrews, Jason: Federal Hill
Andrews, Julie: Americanization of Emily, The; Darling Lili; Duet for One; Fine Romance, A; Hawaii; Little Miss Marker; Man Who Loved Women, The; Mary Poppins; Our Sons; Princess Diaries, The; Relative Values; S.O.B.; Sound of Music, The; Star! (1968); Tamarind Seed, The; 10; That's Life; Thoroughly Modern Millie; Torn Curtain; Victor/Victoria
Andrews, Naveen: Buddha of Suburbia, The; Chippendales Murder, The; English Patient, The; Kama Sutra: A Tale of Love; Mighty Joe Young; My Own Country; Wild West
Andrews, Sarah Hollis: Secret Garden, The
Andrews, Stanley: Hi-Yo Silver; In Old Colorado
Andrews, Susan: Angel of Death
Andrews, Tige: Gypsy Angels; Mod Squad, The (TV Series)
Andrews, Tod: From Hell It Came
Andrews, Todd Eric: Zapped Again
Andrews Sisters, The: Follow the Boys; Private Buckaroo; Road to Rio
Andrex: Circonstances Attenuantes
Andriel, Lenore: Eyes of the Serpent; In the Time of Barbarians II
Andronica, James: Mirage; November Men, The
Andros, Spiro: Matter of Time, A
Anemone: Le Grand Chemin (The Grand Highway); Peril
Angarano, Michael: Almost Famous
Angel, Heather: Arrest Bulldog Drummond; Bold Caballero, The; Bulldog Drummond Escapes; Bulldog Drummond in

Africa; Bulldog Drummond's Bride; Bulldog Drummond's Secret Police; Daniel Boone; Informer, The; Last of the Mohicans, The; Lifeboat; Mystery of Edwin Drood, The; Premature Burial, The; Three Musketeers, The; Undying Monster, The

Angel, Vanessa: Camouflage; Cover Girl Murders, The; Homicidal Impulse; Kingpin; Partners (2000)

Angeli, Pier: Octaman; One Step to Hell; Silver Chalice, The; Sodom and Gomorrah; Somebody Up There Likes Me

Angelis, Michael: No Surrender

Angelou, Maya: How to Make an American Quilt; Poetic Justice; Runaway, The (2000)

Angelus, Muriel: Great McGinty, The

Angers, Avril: Brass Monkey, The

Anglade, Jean-Hugues: Betty Blue; Killing Zoe; La Femme Nikita; L'Homme Blessé (The Wounded Man); Maximum Risk; Nelly and Monsieur Arnaud; Queen Margot

Anglim, Philip: Deadly Currents; Elephant Man, The; Haunted Summer; Thornbirds, The

Angus, David: Hours and Times

Angustain, Ira: Can You Hear the Laughter? The Story of Freddie Prinze

Anholt, Christien: Class of '61

Animals, The: Monterey Pop

Animated: Heavy Traffic

Aniston, Jennifer: Leprechaun; Object of My Affection, The; Office Space; Picture Perfect; Rock Star; She's the One; 'Til There Was You

Anka, Paul: Captain Ron; Girls Town; Ordinary Magic

Ankers, Evelyn: Black Beauty; Captive Wild Woman; Frozen Ghost, The; His Butler's Sister; Invisible Man's Revenge, The; Jungle Woman; Last of the Redmen; Mad Ghoul, The; Pearl of Death, The; Sherlock Holmes and the Voice of Terror; Son of Dracula; Weird Woman; Wolf Man, The

Ankrum, Morris: Beginning of the End; Border Vigilantes; Chain Lightning; Doomed Caravan; Earth vs. the Flying Saucers; Flight to Mars; Fort Osage; Giant Claw, The; Giant from the Unknown; Half Human; Hills of Old Wyoming; I Dood It; In Old Colorado; Pirates on Horseback; Three Men from Texas; Trail Dust; Wide-Open Town

Ann, Melissa: Dinosaur Babes

Ann McLerie, Allyn: Jeremiah Johnson

Annabella: Dinner at the Ritz; Le Million; Quatorze Juliet; 13 Rue Madeleine

Annabi, Amina: Advocate, The

Annen, Glory: Spaced Out

Annese, Frank: House of the Rising Sun

Anniballi, Francesco: Down and Dirty

Annis, Francesca: Coming Out of the Ice; Doomsday Gun; Dune; Flipper's New Adventure; Lillie; Macbeth; Murder Most Foul; Onassis: The Richest Man in the World; Partners in Crime (Secret Adversary) (TV Series); Under the Cherry Moon; Weep No More My Lady; Why Didn't They Ask Evans?

Ann-Margret: Any Given Sunday; Bye Bye Birdie; Carnal Knowledge; C.C. & Company; Cheap Detective, The; Cincinnati Kid, The; 52 Pick-Up; Grumpier Old Men; Grumpy Old Men; I Ought to Be in Pictures; Joseph Andrews; Last Remake of Beau Geste, The; Lookin' to Get Out; Magic; Middle-Age Crazy; Murderers' Row; New Life, A; Newsies; Nobody's Children; Our Sons; Pocketful of Miracles; Return of the Soldier, The; R.P.M. (Revolutions per Minute); State Fair; Streetcar Named Desire, A; 10th Kingdom, The; Tiger and The Pussycat, The; Tiger's Tale, A; Tommy; Train Robbers, The; Twice in a Lifetime; Villain, The; Viva Las Vegas

Ansara, Michael: Access Code; Action in Arabia; Assassination; Border Shootout; Daring Game; Day of the Animals; Dear Dead Delilah; Guns of the Magnificent Seven; Harum Scarum; It's Alive!; Johnny Mysto; Knights of the City; Manitou, The; Message, The (Mohammad, Messenger of God); Mission to Glory; Powderkeg; Quick, Let's Get Married; Texas Across the River; Voyage to the Bottom of the Sea

Ansley, Zachary: Princes in Exile

Anspach, Susan: Back to Back; Big Fix, The; Blue Monkey; Blume in Love; Deadly Encounter; Devil and Max Devlin, The; Five Easy Pieces; Gas; Gone Are the Days; Hitchhiker, The (Series); Into the Fire; Mad Bull; Montenegro; Play It Again, Sam; Rutanga Tapes, The

Ant, Adam: Acting on Impulse; Cold Steel; Cyber Bandits; Face Down; Jubilee; Nomads; Slam Dance; Spellcaster; Sunset Heat; Sweetwater; Trust Me; World Gone Wild

Anthony, Gerald: To Die Standing

Anthony, Jay: Freedom Strike

Anthony, Lysette: Brilliant Disguise, A; Dead Cold; Dr. Jekyll and Ms. Hyde; Dracula: Dead and Loving It; Face the Music; Fiancé, The; Ghost in Monte Carlo, A; Hard Truth; Krull; Oliver Twist; Russell Mulcahy's Tale of the Mummy; Save Me; Target of Suspicion; Trilogy of Terror II; Without a Clue

Anthony, Ray: Five Pennies, The; Girl Can't Help It, The; Girls Town

Anthony, Scott: Savage Messiah

Anthony, Tony: Treasure of the Four Crowns

Antin, Steve: Accused, The; Inside Monkey Zetterland; Penitentiary III

Anton, Susan: Goldengirl; Spring Fever

Antonelli, Laura: Collector's Item; Divine Nymph, The; Dr. Goldfoot and the Girl Bombs; High Heels; How Funny Can Sex Be?; Innocent, The; Malicious; Passion of Love; Swashbuckler, The (1984); Till Marriage Do Us Part; Wifemistress

Antonio, Jim: Annihilators, The; Pigs (Daddy's Deadly Darling)

Antonio, Lou: Cool Hand Luke

Antonov, Alexander: Battleship Potemkin, The; Strike (1924)

Antonutti, Omero: Basileus Quartet; Kaos; Night of the Shooting Stars; Padre Padrone

Anulka: Vampyres

Anwar, Gabrielle: Body Snatchers, The (1993); For Love or Money; Grave, The; Guilty, The; In Pursuit of Honor; Innocent Lies; Nevada; Ripper, The; Scent of a Woman; Sub Down; Things to Do in Denver When You're Dead; Three Musketeers, The; Turbulence 3: Heavy Metal; Wild Hearts Can't Be Broken

Anzaldo, Jon: Little Ninjas

Apicella, Tina: Bellissima

Appel, Peter: Professional, The

Appleby, Noel: Lord of the Rings, The: Fellowship of the Ring

Appleby, Shiri: Perfect Family

Applegate, Christina: Across the Moon; Big Hit, The; Brutal Truth, The; Dance 'Til Dawn; Don't Tell Mom the Babysitter's Dead; Jane Austen's Mafia; Just Visiting; Kiss of Fire; Nowhere; Out in Fifty; Streets; Sweetest Thing, The; Vibrations; Wild Bill

Applegate, Royce D.: Million Dollar Mystery

Aprea, John: Savage Beach; To the Limit

Aquino, Amy: Alan and Naomi; Danielle Steel's Once in a Lifetime

Aragon, Angelica: Walk in the Clouds, A

Aragon, Frank: Angel Town

Arahanga, Julian: Broken English; Once Were Warriors

Arakawa, Jane: Street Trash

Arana, Tomas: Church, The

Aranda, Angel: Hellbenders, The; Last Days of Pompeii (1960); Planet of the Vampires

Aranguiz, Manuel: Paper Wedding

Arata: After Life

Aratama, Michiyo: Human Condition, The, Part One: No Greater Love; Kwaidan

Arau, Alfonso: Posse; Romancing the Stone; Scandalous John; Three Amigos

Araya, Zenda: Hearts and Armour

Arbatt, Alexandre: Dangerous Moves

Arbuckle, Roscoe "Fatty": Art of Buster Keaton, The; Buster and Fatty; Keystone Comedies: Vol. 1–5

Arbus, Allan: Coffy; Greaser's Palace

Arcand, Denys: Jesus of Montreal

Arcand, Gabriel: Blood of the Hunter

Arcand, Nathaniel: American Outlaws; Grey Owl

Archer, Anne: Anything for Love; Art of War, The; Body of Evidence; Cancel My Reservation; Check Is in the Mail, The; Clear and Present Danger; Eminent Domain; Family Prayers; Fatal Attraction; Good Guys Wear Black; Green Ice; Hero at Large; Last of His Tribe, The; Lifeguard; Love at Large; Man in the Attic, The; Mojave Moon; Nails; Naked Face, The; Narrow Margin

(1990); Patriot Games; Question of Faith; Raise the Titanic; Rules of Engagement; Short Cuts
Archer, John: Big Trees, The; Bowery at Midnight; Destination Moon; Gangs, Inc. (Paper Bullets); King of the Zombies
Ardant, Fanny: Afraid of the Dark; Confidentially Yours; Family, The; Francois Truffaut: Stolen Moments; Melo; Next Summer; Ridicule; Swann in Love; Woman Next Door, The
Arden, Eve: Anatomy of a Murder; At the Circus; Cinderella; Comrade X; Cover Girl; Doughgirls, The; Eternally Yours; Grease; Guide for the Married Woman, A; Having a Wonderful Time; Kid from Brooklyn, The; Letter of Introduction; Mildred Pierce; My Dream Is Yours; No, No Nanette; Our Miss Brooks (TV Series); Slightly Honorable; Stage Door; Tea for Two; That Uncertain Feeling; Under the Rainbow; We're Not Married; Whistling in the Dark; Ziegfeld Girl
Arditi, Pierre: Melo
Arenas, Rosita: Curse of the Crying Woman, The; Witch's Mirror, The
Aresco, Joey: Circle of Fear; Primary Target
Arestrup, Neils: Meeting Venus; Sincerely Charlotte
Argento, Asia: B. Monkey; Palombella Rossa; Phantom of the Opera; Stendhal Syndrome, The; Trauma
Argenziano, Carmen: Burning Season, The
Argo, Victor: Bad Lieutenant; Condition Red; Florida Straits; King of New York; Monkey Trouble
Argue, David: Backlash; BMX Bandits; Gallipoli
Arhondis, Tina: Test of Love, A
Ariane: Skin Art; Year of the Dragon
Arias, Imanol: Camila (1984); Demons in the Garden; Flower of My Secret, The; Labyrinth of Passion
Arias, Joey: Camila (1984); Demons in the Garden; Flower of My Secret, The; Labyrinth of Passion
Ariffin, Nora: Skin Art
Arkin, Adam: Doctor, The; Fourth Wise Man, The; Halloween: H20; Hanging Up; Necessary Parties; Not in This Town; Slight Case of Murder, A
Arkin, Alan: America's Sweethearts; Bad Medicine; Big Trouble (1985); Blood Money (1999); Catch-22; Chu Chu and the Philly Flash; Cooperstown; Coupe De Ville; Doomsday Gun; Edward Scissorhands; Escape from Sobibor; Four Days in September; Fourth Wise Man, The; Freebie and the Bean; Gattaca; Glengarry Glen Ross; Grosse Pointe Blank; Havana; Heart Is a Lonely Hunter, The; Hearts of the West; Heck's Way Home; Improper Channels; In-Laws, The; Indian Summer; Jakob the Liar; Joshua Then and Now; Last of the Red Hot Lovers; Little Murders; Magician of Lublin, The; Matter of Principle, A; Mother Night; Necessary Parties; Picture Windows; Popi; Rafferty and the Gold Dust Twins; Return of Captain Invincible, The; Rocketeer, The; Russians Are Coming, the Russians Are Coming, The; Seven-Per-cent Solution, The; Simon; Slums of Beverly Hills; So I Married an Axe Murderer; Steal Big, Steal Little; Taking the Heat; Varian's War; Wait Until Dark; Woman Times Seven
Arkin, David: Long Goodbye, The; Three in the Cellar
Arkin, Tony: Matter of Principle, A
Arkins, Robert: Commitments, The
Arklie, Thomas: Heaven's a Drag
Arlen, Elizabeth: In the Company of Spies
Arlen, Harold: In the Company of Spies
Arlen, Richard: Beggars of Life; Feel My Pulse; Flying Blind; Helldorado; Hostile Guns; Human Duplicators, The; Island of Lost Souls; Johnny Reno; Mountain, The; Sex and the College Girl; Virginian, The; Wings
Arletty: Children of Paradise, The; Circonstances Attenuantes; Le Jour Se Leve (Daybreak (1939)); Les Visiteurs Du Soir; Pearls of the Crown, The
Arliss, Florence: Disraeli
Arliss, George: Disraeli; Dr. Syn; Iron Duke, The; Transatlantic Tunnel
Armendariz, Pedro: Captain Sinbad; Conqueror, The; El Bruto (The Brute); Flor Sylvestre; Fugitive, The; Littlest Outlaw, The; Pearl, The; Three Godfathers, The; Tulsa
Armendariz Jr., Pedro: Bandits; Don't Be Afraid of the Dark; Le Chêvre (The Goat)
Armetta, Henry: Devil's Brother, The; Everybody Sing; Make a Wish; Manhattan Merry-Go-Round; Poor Little Rich Girl (1936); Speak Easily
Arms, Russell: By the Light of the Silvery Moon; Loaded Pistols
Armstrong, Alun: Awfully Big Adventure, An
Armstrong, Bess: Diamond Men; Dream Lover; Forever Love; High Road to China; Jaws 3; Jekyll & Hyde—Together Again; Nothing in Common; Perfect Daughter, The; Second Sight; Skateboard Kid, The
Armstrong, Curtis: Adventures of Huck Finn, The (1993); Bad Medicine; Elvis Meets Nixon; Gale Force; One Crazy Summer; Revenge of the Nerds; Revenge of the Nerds II: Nerds in Paradise; Revenge of the Nerds III: The Next Generation; Revenge of the Nerds IV: Nerds in Love; Risky Business
Armstrong, Jack: Guyver, The
Armstrong, Kerry: Hunting; Lantana
Armstrong, Lee: Leprechaun 3
Armstrong, Louis: Cabin in the Sky; Every Day's a Holiday; Five Pennies, The; Glenn Miller Story, The; High Society; Man Called Adam, A; Paris Blues; Song Is Born, A
Armstrong, Neil: Killing Time (1996)
Armstrong, R. G.: Angels Die Hard; Best of Times, The; Boss; Bulletproof; Children of the Corn; Dick Tracy; Dixie Dynamite; El Dorado; Evilspeak; Ghetto Blaster; Great Northfield Minnesota Raid, The; Hammett; Invasion of Privacy; Lone Wolf McQuade; Pack, The; Pat Garrett and Billy the Kid; Payback; Predator; Pursuit of D. B. Cooper; Red-Headed Stranger, The; Ride the High Country; Stay Hungry; Steel; Where the Buffalo Roam
Armstrong, Robert: Action in Arabia; Be Yourself; Big News; Blood on the Sun; Danger Lights; Dive Bomber; Ex-Mrs. Bradford, The; Fugitive, The; Girl in Every Port, A; Hold 'em Jail; Kansan, The; King Kong; Lost Squadron; Mighty Joe Young; Most Dangerous Game, The; Mr. Winkle Goes to War; Paleface, The; Palooka; Racketeer; Son of Kong, The; Tournament Tempo
Armstrong, Ronald K.: Bugged!
Armstrong, Todd: Jason and the Argonauts
Arnaz, Lucie: Jazz Singer, The; Lucy and Desi: A Home Movie; Mating Season, The; Who Is the Black Dahlia?
Arnaz Jr., Desi: Fakeout; House of the Long Shadows; Joyride; Lucy and Desi: A Home Movie; Mambo Kings, The; Wedding, A (1978)
Arnaz Sr., Desi: Bataan; Escape Artist, The; Forever Darling; Four Jacks and a Jill; I Love Lucy (TV Series); Long, Long Trailer, The; Lucy and Desi: A Home Movie; Too Many Girls
Arndt, Denis: Amelia Earhart: The Final Flight
Arndt, Jurgen: Celeste
Arne, Peter: Return of the Pink Panther, The; Straw Dogs
Arness, James: Alamo, The: Thirteen Days to Glory; Big Jim McLain; Farmer's Daughter, The; Gunsmoke (TV Series); Gunsmoke: Return to Dodge; Hondo; Island in the Sky; Sea Chase, The; Stars in My Crown; Them!; Thing (From Another World), The (1951); Two Lost Worlds; Wagonmaster
Arnez, Eva: Ferocious Female Freedom Fighters
Arngrim, Stephan: Fear No Evil
Arno, Alice: Erotikill
Arno, Sig: Melody Master (The Great Awakening) (NewWine); Palm Beach Story, The; Song to Remember, A
Arnold, Edward: Ambassador's Daughter, The; Annie Get Your Gun; Broken Trust; City That Never Sleeps; Come and Get It; Command Decision; Crime and Punishment; Dear Wife; Devil and Daniel Webster, The; Hucksters, The; Idiot's Delight; I'm No Angel; Johnny Apollo; Johnny Eager; Kismet; Let Freedom Ring; Mrs. Parkington; Roman Scandals; Sadie McKee; Secret of the Blue Room, The; Slightly Honorable; Three Daring Daughters; Three on a Match; Toast of New York, The; Weekend at the Waldorf; Yellow Cab Man, The; You Can't Take It with You; Ziegfeld Follies
Arnold, Jesse: Hard Hombre
Arnold, Mark: Trancers 5: Sudden Deth
Arnold, Steve: Apart from Hugh
Arnold, Tom: Animal Factory; Backfield in Motion; Big Bully; Carpool; Exit Wounds; Hero (1992); McHale's Navy; National

Lampoon's Golf Punks; Nine Months; Shriek If You Know What I Did Last Friday the 13th; Sink or Swim; Stupids, The; Touch; True Lies

Arnott, David: Crisscross (1992)

Arnott, Mark: Return of the Secaucus 7

Arnoul, Françoise: Forbidden Fruit; Little Theatre of Jean Renoir, The

Aronson, Judie: American Ninja; Desert Kickboxer

Arp, Philip: Last Five Days, The

Arquette, Alexis: Children of the Corn V: Fields of Terror; Clubland; Dead Weekend; Don't Do It; Grief; I Think I Do; Jack Be Nimble; Jumpin' at the Boneyard; Sometimes They Come Back Again; Wigstock: The Movie

Arquette, David: Alarmist, The; Dead Man's Walk; Dream with the Fishes; Fall Time; Free Money; Johns; Never Been Kissed; Ravenous; Ready to Rumble; Roadracers; Scream; Scream 3; Scream 2; See Spot Run; 3,000 Miles to Graceland; Webber's World (At Home with the Webbers); Wild Bill

Arquette, Patricia: Beyond Rangoon; Bringing Out the Dead; Dillinger; Ed Wood; Ethan Frome; Far North; Flirting with Disaster; Goodbye Lover; Hi-Lo Country, The; Holy Matrimony; Human Nature; Indian Runner, The; Infinity; Inside Monkey Zetterland; Little Nicky; Lost Highway; Nightmare on Elm Street 3, A: The DreamWarriors; Nightwatch; Prayer of the Rollerboys; Secret Agent, The; Stigmata; Trouble Bound; True Romance; Wild Flower (1991)

Arquette, Rosanna: After Hours; … Almost; Amazon Women on the Moon; Aviator, The; Baby, It's You; Big Blue, The; Black Rainbow; Crash (1996); Dark Secret of Harvest Home, The; Desperately Seeking Susan; Don't Hang Up; 8 Million Ways to Die; Executioner's Song, The; Fathers & Sons; Flight of the Intruder, The; Floating Away; Gone Fishin'; Gorp; I'm Losing You; In the Deep Woods; Linguini Incident, The; More American Graffiti; New York Stories; Nobody's Fool; Nowhere to Run; Off the Wall; One Cooks, the Other Doesn't; Promised a Miracle; Pulp Fiction; Search and Destroy; Silverado; S.O.B.; Son of the Morning Star; Sweet Revenge; Things Behind the Sun; Trading Favors; Whole Nine Yards, The; Wrong Man, The

Arrants, Rod: Vamping

Arrindell, Lisa: Livin' Large

Arroyave, Karina: 187

Artaud, Antonin: Napoleon; Passion of Joan of Arc, The

Arthur, Anna: Alley Cats, The

Arthur, Bea: Lovers and Other Strangers; Mame

Arthur, Carol: Sunshine Boys, The

Arthur, Jean: Arizona; Danger Lights; Devil and Miss Jones, The; Ex-Mrs. Bradford, The; History Is Made at Night; Lady Takes a Chance, A; More the Merrier, The; Mr. Deeds Goes to Town; Mr. Smith Goes to Washington; Mysterious Dr. Fu Manchu; Only Angels Have Wings; Plainsman, The; Return of Dr. Fu Manchu; Saturday Night Kid, The; Shane; Talk of the Town, The; You Can't Take It with You

Arthur, Johnny: Ghost Walks, The; Masked Marvel, The; Road to Singapore

Arthur, Maureen: How to Succeed in Business without Really Trying; Love God?, The

Arthur, Robert: Mother Wore Tights; September Affair

Artura, Michael: Mother Wore Tights; September Affair

Asadi, Noghre: Wind Will Carry Us, The

Asensi, Neus: Arachnid

Ash, William: MAD About Mambo

Ashbrook, Dana: Girlfriend from Hell; Return of the Living Dead Part II

Ashbrook, Daphne: Automatic; Deadman's Revenge; Intruders; Love Letter, The; Quiet Cool; Sunset Heat

Ashby, Linden: Beneficiary, The; Blast; Cadillac Ranch; Mortal Kombat; Murder She Purred; Night Angel; Perfect Bride, The; Wyatt Earp

Ashcroft, Peggy: Hullabaloo over George and Bonnie's Pictures; Jewel in the Crown, The; Joseph Andrews; Madame Sousatzka; Nun's Story, The; Passage to India, A; Rhodes of Africa (Rhodes); Secret Ceremony; Sunday, Bloody Sunday

Asher, Jane: Deep End; Dreamchild; Masque of the Red Death, The (1964); Success Is the Best Revenge; Voyage 'Round My Father, A

Asher, Joel: Merry Wives of Windsor, The

Asherson, Renée: Grey Owl; Henry V; Murder Is Announced, A

Asheton, Ron: Legion of the Night; Mosquito

Ashley, Edward: Dick Tracy Meets Gruesome; Tournament Tempo

Ashley, Elizabeth: Coma; Dragnet; Great Scout and Cathouse Thursday, The; Happiness; Just the Ticket; Man of Passion, A; 92 in the Shade; Paternity; Rancho Deluxe; Ship of Fools; Stagecoach; Svengali; Vampire's Kiss

Ashley, John: Beach Blanket Bingo; Beach Party; Beast of the Yellow Night; Beyond Atlantis; Brides of the Beast; Frankenstein's Daughter; High School Caesar; Motorcycle Gang; Muscle Beach Party; Suicide Battalion; Twilight People

Ashley, Karan: Mighty Morphin Power Rangers: The Movie

Ashmore, Jonathan: Kid for Two Farthings, A

Asholt, Jesper: Mifune

Ashton, Bobby: Track 16

Ashton, John: Beverly Hills Cop; Beverly Hills Cop II; Deliberate Stranger, The; Dirty Work; Fast Money; Hidden Assassin; Instinct; King Kong Lives; Last Resort; Little Big League; Love, Lies and Murder; Meet the Deedles; Midnight Run; Some Kind of Wonderful; Tommyknockers, The; Trapped in Paradise

Ashton, Joseph: Education of Little Tree, The

Ashton, Laura: America

Askew, Desmond: Go

Askew, Luke: Bulletproof; Culpepper Cattle Co., The; Dune Warriors; Great Northfield Minnesota Raid, The; Kung Fu—The Movie (1986); Night Games; Pat Garrett and Billy the Kid; Posse; Rolling Thunder; Traveller; Vendetta; Walking Tall Part II; Warrior and the Sorceress, The

Askonas, Paul: Hands of Orlac

Askwith, Robin: Hans Brinker; Horror Hospital

Aslan, Gregoire: Concrete Jungle, (1962) The (Criminal, The); Golden Voyage of Sinbad, The; Paris When It Sizzles; Three Worlds of Gulliver, The; Windom's Way

Asner, Ed: Animal, The; Our Friend, Martin

Asner, Edward: Bachelor, The; Case of Libel, A; Change of Habit; Common Ground; Daniel; El Dorado; Fort Apache—The Bronx; Friendship in Vienna, A; Gathering, The; Gus; Gypsy; Haunts of the Very Rich; Heads; Hey, I'm Alive!; JFK; Life and Assassination of the Kingfish,The; Not a Penny More, Not a Penny Less; O'Hara's Wife; Roots; Silent Motive; Skin Game (1971); Slender Thread, The; Small Killing, A; Switched at Birth; Todd Killings, The

Aso, Kumiko: Dr. Akagi

Aspen, Giles: I, Zombie

Assa, Rene: 976-EVIL II: The Astral Factor

Assante, Armand: After the Storm; Animal Behavior; Belizaire the Cajun; Blind Justice; Eternity; Fatal Instinct; Fever; Gotti; Hoffa; Hunley, The; I, the Jury; Jack the Ripper; Judge Dredd; Lady of the House; Little Darlings; Mambo Kings, The; Marrying Man, The; Napoleon and Josephine: A Love Story; Odyssey, The; On the Beach; 1492: The Conquest of Paradise; Paradise Alley; Penitent, The; Private Benjamin; Prophecy (1979); Q & A; Striptease; Trial by Jury; Unfaithfully Yours

Ast, Pat: Heat; Reform School Girls

Astaire, Fred: Amazing Dobermans; Band Wagon, The; Barkleys of Broadway, The; Belle of New York, The; Blue Skies; Broadway Melody of 1940; Carefree; Daddy Long Legs; Damsel in Distress, A; Dancing Lady; Easter Parade; Family Upside Down, A; Finian's Rainbow; Flying Down to Rio; Follow the Fleet; Funny Face; Gay Divorcée, The; Ghost Story; Holiday Inn; It Takes a Thief (TV Series); Let's Dance; Man in the Santa Claus Suit, The; On the Beach; Purple Taxi, The; Roberta; Royal Wedding; Second Chorus; Shall We Dance?; Silk Stockings; Sky's the Limit, The; Story of Vernon and Irene Castle, The; Swing Time; That's Entertainment; That's Entertainment Part II; Three Little Words; Top Hat; Towering Inferno, The; Yolanda and the Thief; You Were Never Lovelier; You'll Never Get Rich; Ziegfeld Follies

Austin, Lois: Mom and Dad
Austin, Teri: Vindicator, The
Austin, William: Fig Leaves; It; Mysterious Dr. Fu Manchu; Return of Dr. Fu Manchu
Auteuil, Daniel: Closet, The; Eighth Day, The; Elegant Criminal, The; Girl on the Bridge; Jean De Florette; La Separation; Les Voleurs; Ma Saison Preferée; Mama, There's a Man in Your Bed; Manon of the Spring; Queen Margot; Thieves (Les Voleurs); Un Coeur en Hiver; Widow of St. Pierre, The
Autry, Alan: Great Los Angeles Earthquake, The; Roadhouse 66
Autry, Gene: Beyond the Purple Hills; Big Sombrero, The; Blue Montana Skies; Colorado Sunset; Cow Town; Git Along, Little Dogies; Hills of Utah, The; In Old Santa Fe; Last of the Pony Riders; Last Round-Up; Loaded Pistols; Man from Music Mountain; Man of the Frontier (Red River Valley); Manhattan Merry-Go-Round; Melody Ranch; Melody Trail; Mexicali Rose; Mule Train; Oh! Susanna!; Old Corral; Phantom Empire (1935); Public Cowboy #1; Radio Ranch (Men with Steel Faces, Phantom Empire); Ride, Ranger, Ride; Riders of the Whistling Pines; Rim of the Canyon; Robin Hood of Texas; South of the Border; Springtime in the Rockies; Winning of the West; Yodelin' Kid from Pine Ridge
Avalon, Frankie: Alamo, The; Back to the Beach; Beach Blanket Bingo; Beach Party; Bikini Beach; Dr. Goldfoot and the Bikini Machine; How to Stuff a Wild Bikini; I'll Take Sweden; Muscle Beach Party; Panic in the Year Zero; Stoned Age, The; Voyage to the Bottom of the Sea
Avalon, Phil: Summer City
Avalos, Luis: Fires Within; Ghost Fever; Lone Justice; Lone Justice 2
Avedon, Loreen: No Retreat, No Surrender II; No Retreat, No Surrender 3: Blood Brothers; Operation Golden Phoenix; Virtual Combat
Avellana, José Mari: Deathfight
Avery, Linda: Hitchhikers
Avery, Margaret: Blueberry Hill; Color Purple, The; For Us the Living: The Medgar Evers Story; Heat Wave; Hell Up in Harlem; Jacksons, The: An American Dream; Mardi Gras for the Devil; Return of Superfly, The; Sky Is Gray, The; Which Way Is Up?; White Man's Burden
Avery, Val: Black Caesar; Dream of Kings, A; Firehouse; Heroes; Satan's Bed
Avery, Vicci: Return of the Sand Fairy, The
Aviles, Angel: Mi Vida Loca
Aviles, Rick: Saint of Fort Washington, The
Avital, Mili: After the Storm; Invasion of Privacy; Kissing a Fool
Avran, Chris: Twitch of the Death Nerve
Awashima, Chikage: Human Condition, The, Part One: No Greater Love
Axelrod, Nina: Cross Country; Motel Hell; Time Walker; Trading Hearts
Axman, Hanne: Red Menace, The
Axton, Hoyt: Act of Vengeance; Black Stallion, The; Buried Alive; Disorganized Crime; Dixie Lanes; Endangered Species; Gremlins; Heart Like a Wheel; King Cobra; Liar's Moon; Number One Fan; Retribution; We're No Angels; Woody Guthrie—Hard Travelin'
Ayashi, Sachiko: 8Man
Aykroyd, Dan: BluesBrothers, The; Blues Brothers 2000; Caddyshack II; Canadian Bacon; Celtic Pride; Chaplin; Coneheads; Couch Trip, The; Crossroads (2002); Curse of the Jade Scorpion, The; Doctor Detroit; Dragnet; Driving Miss Daisy; Dying to Get Rich; Evolution; Exit to Eden; Feeling Minnesota; Getting Away with Murder; Ghostbusters; Ghostbusters II; Great Outdoors, The; Grosse Pointe Blank; House of Mirth, The; Into the Night; Loose Cannons; Loser; Love at First Sight; My Fellow Americans; My Girl; My Girl 2; My Stepmother Is an Alien; Neighbors; Nothing But Trouble; 1941; Pearl Harbor; Rutles, The (All You Need Is Cash); Sgt. Bilko; Sneakers; Spies Like Us; Things We Did Last Summer; This Is My Life; Tommy Boy; Trading Places; Twilight Zone—The Movie
Aykroyd, Peter: Gas
Aylmer, Felix: As You Like It; Citadel, The; From the Terrace; Ghosts of Berkeley Square; Hamlet; Henry V; Iron Duke, The; Knights of the Round Table; Nine Days a Queen; Quo Vadis (1951); Saint Joan
Ayme, Jean: As You Like It; Citadel, The; From the Terrace; Ghosts of Berkeley Square; Hamlet; Henry V; Iron Duke, The; Knights of the Round Table; Nine Days a Queen; Quo Vadis (1951); Saint Joan
Aymerie, Catherine: Rabid Grannies
Ayres, Agnes: Sheik, The
Ayres, Jo Ann: In the Time of Barbarians
Ayres, Leah: Bloodsport; Burning, The; Eddie Macon's Run
Ayres, Lew: Advise and Consent; All Quiet on the Western Front; Battlestar Galactica; Broadway Serenade; Carpetbaggers, The; Cast the First Stone; Damien: Omen II; Dark Mirror, The; Dr. Kildare's Strange Case; Donovan's Brain; End of the World; Fingers at the Window; Francis Gary Powers: The True Story of the U-2 Spy Incident; Holiday; Johnny Belinda; Of Mice and Men; She Waits
Ayres, Robert: Battle Beneath the Earth
Ayres, Rosalind: Beautiful People
Azaria, Hank: America's Sweethearts; Birdcage, The; Cradle Will Rock; Godzilla (1998); Great Expectations; Grosse Pointe Blank; Homegrown; Mystery, Alaska; Mystery Men; Quiz Show
Azema, Sabine: Life and Nothing But; Melo; Sunday in the Country, A
Azhari, Ayu: Without Mercy
Azito, Tony: Private Resort
Azizi, Anthony: Venomous
Aznavour, Charles: Blockhouse, The; Head Against the Wall; Shoot the Piano Player
Azorín, Eloy: All About My Mother
Azzara, Candy: Doin' Time on Planet Earth; Easy Money; Fatso; Pandemonium
B., Lisa: Serpent's Lair
Baal, Karin: Dead Eyes of London
Babatundé, Obba: How High; Introducing Dorothy Dandridge; Life; Miss Evers' Boys; Reason to Believe, A; Undercover Blues; Visit, The
Babb, Sean: Pig's Tale, A
Babcock, Barbara: Christmas Coal Mine Miracle, The; Far and Away; News at Eleven; Quarterback Princess; Space Cowboys; That Was Then ... This Is Now
Bacall, Lauren: All I Want for Christmas; Appointment with Death; Big Sleep, The; Blood Alley; Dark Passage; Designing Woman; Dinner at Eight; Fan, The; Flame over India; Foreign Field, A; From the Mixed-Up Files of Mrs. Basil E. Frankweiler; Harper; How to Marry a Millionaire; Innocent Victim; Key Largo; Mirror Has Two Faces, The; Misery; Mr. North; Murder on the Orient Express; My Fellow Americans; Portrait, The; Ready to Wear; Sex and the Single Girl; Shootist, The; To Have and Have Not; Woman's World; Written on the Wind; Young Man with a Horn
Bacalso, Joanna: Snow Dogs
Baccaloni: Fanny
Bach, Barbara: Caveman; Force Ten from Navarone; Give My Regards to Broad Street; Princess Daisy; Spy Who Loved Me, The; Stateline Motel; Unseen, The; Up the Academy
Bach, Catherine: Masters of Menace; Rage and Honor; Street Justice
Bach, John: Crimebroker; Georgia; Sound and the Silence,The
Bachar, Dian: Orgazmo
Bachchan, Amitabh: God Is My Witness
Bachelor, Stephanie: I've Always Loved You; Springtime in the Sierras
Bachmann, Hans: Beyond the Rising Moon (Star Quest); Invader (1993)
Baci, Michael: Rebecca's Secret
Backer, Brian: Burning, The; Fast Times at Ridgemont High; Steel and Lace
Backus, Jim: Above and Beyond; Androcles and the Lion; Ask Any Girl; Billie; C.H.O.M.P.S.; Crazy Mama; Critic's Choice; Francis in the Navy; Good Guys Wear Black; Great Lover, The; His Kind of Woman; Horizontal Lieutenant, The; I Love Melvin; I Married Joan (TV Series); Ice Palace; I'll See You in My Dreams; Ma and Pa Kettle Go to Town; Man of a Thousand Faces; Meet

Me in Las Vegas; Now You See Him, Now You Don't; Opposite Sex, The (1956); Pete's Dragon; Rebel Without a Cause; Wheeler Dealers, The; Where Were You When the Lights Went Out?; Zotz!
Backus, Richard: Deathdream; Soldier's Home
Baclanova, Olga: Docks of New York, The; Freaks; Man Who Laughs, The
Bacon, Irving: Blondie Has Servant Trouble; Blondie Takes a Vacation; Caught in the Draft; Dreaming Out Loud; Guest Wife; Howards of Virginia, The; Interns Can't Take Money; It's a Great Life
Bacon, Kevin: Air Up There, The; Apollo 13; Balto; Big Picture, The; Criminal Law; Digging to China; Diner; End of the Line; Few Good Men, A; Flatliners; Footloose; Friday the 13th; He Said, She Said; Hollow Man; JFK; Murder in the First; My Dog Skip; Picture Perfect; Pyrates; Queens Logic; Quicksilver; River Wild, The; She's Having a Baby; Sleepers; Stir of Echoes; Telling Lies in America; Tremors; White Water Summer; Wild Things
Bacon, Lloyd: Charlie Chaplin ... Our Hero; Charlie Chaplin Carnival; Charlie Chaplin Cavalcade; Charlie Chaplin—The Early Years Vol. 1–4
Bacri, Jean-Pierre: Place Vendome; Taste of Others, The
Bad, Steven: Evil Laugh
Badal, Tom: Out on Bail
Badalucco, Michael: Mac; Man Who Wasn't There, The (2001); Professional, The; Search for One-Eye Jimmy, The
Baddeley, Hermione: Adventures of Bullwhip Griffin, The; Belles of St. Trinian's, The; Mary Poppins; Passport to Pimlico; Pickwick Papers, The; Quartet; Room at the Top; Tom Brown's Schooldays (1950); Unsinkable Molly Brown, The; Woman in Question
Badel, Alan: Arabesque; Children of the Damned; Day of the Jackal, The; Three Cases of Murder
Badel, Sarah: Cotton Mary
Badema: Close to Eden
Bader, Diedrich: Beverly Hillbillies, The (1993)
Bader, John: J. Lyle
Badford, Basil: Quartet
Badham, Mary: To Kill a Mockingbird
Badia, Nuria: Barcelona
Badie, Mina: Anniversary Party, The
Badland, Annette: Angels and Insects; Little Voice
Badler, Jane: V
Baer, Buddy: Giant from the Unknown; Jubilee Trail; Quo Vadis (1951); Snow White and the Three Stooges
Baer, Harry: Fox and His Friends
Baer, Max: Africa Screams; Beverly Hillbillies, The (TV Series); Beverly Hillbillies Go Hollywood, The; Harder They Fall, The
Baer, Meredith: Chicken Chronicles, The
Baer, Parley: Two on a Guillotine; Ugly Dachshund, The; White Dog
Baer Jr., Max: Macon County Line
Baerwitz, Jerry: Varan, the Unbelievable
Baez, Joan: Don't Look Back; Woody Guthrie—Hard Travelin'
Baeza, Paloma: Kid in King Arthur's Court, A
Baff, Regina: Below the Belt
Bagdasarian, Carol: Aurora Encounter
Baggett, Lynne: D.O.A.
Baggetta, Vincent: Man Who Wasn't There, The
Baggi, Angiola: Story of Boys and Girls
Bagheri, Abdolrahman: Taste of Cherry
Bagley, Ross Elliot: Little Rascals, The
Bagwell, Marcus: Terror Tract
Bahner, Blake: Blackbelt 2: Fatal Force; Sensations; Thrilled to Death
Bahns, Maxine: Brothers McMullen, The; She's the One
Bai, Wu: Time and Tide
Bai, Xue: Yellow Earth
Bail, Chuck: Stunt Man, The
Bailey, Bill: On the Edge; Saving Grace
Bailey, Blake: Killer Eye, The; Lurking Fear
Bailey, G. W.: Burglar (U.S.); Capture of Grizzly Adams, The; Doublecrossed; Mannequin; Police Academy 4: Citizens on Patrol; Police Academy 6: City Under Siege; Rustler's Rhapsody; Short Circuit; Warning Sign; Write to Kill
Bailey, Jim: Penitentiary III
Bailey, Kathleen: Witchtrap
Bailey, Marion: Meantime
Bailey, Mark: Unbelievable Truth, The
Bailey, Pearl: Carmen Jones; Norman ... Is That You?
Bailey, Raymond: Beverly Hillbillies, The (TV Series); Beverly Hillbillies Go Hollywood, The
Bailey, Robin: See No Evil
Baily, Joel: King Lear
Baily, Matt: Blood Thirsty
Bain, Barbara: Panic; Skinheads; Space 1999 (TV Series); Spirit of '76, The; Trust Me
Bain, Conrad: Child Bride of Short Creek; C.H.O.M.P.S.; Last Summer; Postcards from the Edge; Who Killed Mary What's 'Er Name?
Bain, Cynthia: Spontaneous Combustion; Vietnam War Story—Part Two
Bain, Ron: Experience Preferred ... But Not Essential
Bainter, Fay: Babes on Broadway; Children's Hour, The; Dark Waters; Human Comedy, The; Journey for Margaret; June Bride; Our Town; Presenting Lily Mars; Shining Hour, The; State Fair; Virginian, The; Woman of the Year; Young Tom Edison
Baio, Jimmy: Brass; Playing for Keeps
Baio, Scott: Alice in Wonderland; Bugsy Malone; Foxes; I Love N.Y.; Zapped!
Baird, Harry: Story of a Three Day Pass, The
Baird, Roxanne: Blackbelt 2: Fatal Force
Bairstow, Scott: Black Circle Boys; Killing Mr. Griffin; White Fang 2: Myth of the White Wolf; Wild America
Baisho, Mitsuko: Eijanaika (Why Not?)
Baitz, Jon Robin: Last Summer in the Hamptons
Bajpai, Maoj: Bandit Queen
Bakalyan, Dick: Blame It on the Night; Paratroop Command
Baker, Annie: Halloween Tree, The
Baker, Art: Underworld Story
Baker, Blanche: Cold Feet; French Postcards; Livin' Large; Mary and Joseph: A Story of Faith; Romeo and Juliet; Sixteen Candles
Baker, Carroll: Andy Warhol's Bad; Baby Doll; Big Country, The; But Not for Me; Captain Apache; Carpetbaggers, The; Cheyenne Autumn; Easy to Love; Game, The; Giant; Greatest Story Ever Told, The; Harlow; How the West Was Won; Ironweed; Just Your Luck; Kindergarten Cop; Miracle, The; Native Son; North Shore Fish; Paranoia; Secret Diary of Sigmund Freud, The; Star 80; Watcher in the Woods, The; World Is Full of Married Men, The
Baker, Colin: Dr. Who (TV series)
Baker, David Aaron: Tao of Steve, The
Baker, Diane: Baker's Hawk; Best of Everything, The; Closer, The; Horse in the Gray Flannel Suit, The; Journey to the Center of the Earth; Marnie; Mirage; Net, The; Pilot, The; Prize, The; Stolen Hours; Strait-Jacket
Baker, Dylan: Cell, The; Changing Lanes; Delirious; Disclosure; Happiness; Long Walk Home, The; Oxygen; Thirteen Days
Baker, Fay: Chain Lightning; Double Deal
Baker, Frank: New Adventures of Tarzan; Tarzan and the Green Goddess
Baker, George: At Bertram's Hotel; Curse of the Fly; For Queen and Country; Goodbye, Mr. Chips; Robin Hood: Herne's Son; Sword of Lancelot
Baker, Gregg: Kleptomania
Baker, James: Ferngully 2: The Magical Rescue
Baker, Jay: April Fool's Day
Baker, Jim: Tripods
Baker, Joby: Last Angry Man, The; Wackiest Ship in the Army, The
Baker, Joe Don: Adam at 6 A.M.; Cape Fear; Charley Varrick; Citizen Cohn; Congo; Criminal Law; Distinguished Gentleman, The; Edge of Darkness; Felony; Final Justice; Fletch; Framed; George Wallace; Goldeneye; Guns of the Magnificent Seven; Joy Sticks; Junior Bonner; Killing Time, The (1987); Leonard Part 6; Living Daylights, The; Natural, The; Pack, The; Panther; Poo-

dle Springs; Ring of Steel; Tomorrow Never Dies; Underneath, The; Wacko; Walking Tall; Wild Rovers, The
Baker, Josephine: French Way, The; Princess Tam Tam; Zou Zou
Baker, Kathy: Article 99; Clean and Sober; Dad; Edward Scissorhands; Image, The; Inventing the Abbotts; Jackknife; Jennifer 8; Killing Affair, A; Lush Life; Mad Dog and Glory; Mr. Frost; Not in This Town; Street Smart; Things You Can Tell Just by Looking at Her; To Gillian on Her 37th Birthday
Baker, Kenny: At the Circus; Goldwyn Follies, The; Harvey Girls, The; Mikado, The; Star Wars: Episode I The Phantom Menace
Baker, Lee Anne: At the Circus; Goldwyn Follies, The; Harvey Girls, The; Mikado, The; Star Wars: Episode I The Phantom Menace
Baker, Lenny: Next Stop, Greenwich Village
Baker, Nellie Bly: Red Kimono, The
Baker, Pamela: Bloody Wednesday
Baker, Phil: Gang's All Here, The
Baker, Ray: Anywhere But Here; Disaster at Silo 7; Final Cut, The; Hard Truth; Hexed; Masters of Menace; Stacking; What Lies Beneath
Baker, Rebekah: Secrets in the Attic
Baker, Renee: Delirious
Baker, Sala: Lord of the Rings, The: Fellowship of the Ring
Baker, Simon: Red Planet
Baker, Stanley: Accident; Concrete Jungle, (1962) The (Criminal, The); Cruel Sea, The; Dingaka; Guns of Navarone, The; Helen of Troy; Knights of the Round Table; Robbery; Sodom and Gomorrah; Zorro; Zulu
Baker, Tom: Angels Die Hard; Canterbury Tales, The; Curse of King Tut's Tomb, The; Dr. Who: Revenge of the Cybermen; Dr. Who (TV series); Freakmaker; Golden Voyage of Sinbad, The; Nicholas and Alexandra; Vault of Horror
Bakewell, Gary: BackBeat
Bakhtiari, Afshin Khorshid: Taste of Cherry
Bakke, Brenda: Death Spa; Fixer, The; Hot Shots Part Deux; Lone Justice 2; Scavengers; Star Quest; Tales from the Crypt: Demon Knight; Trucks; Twogether
Bakker, Jim: Eyes of Tammy Faye, The
Bako, Brigitte: Dark Tide; Double Take; Escape, The; Man in Uniform, A; Paranoia; Replikator: Cloned to Kill
Bakri, Muhamad: Beyond the Walls; Double Edge
Bakula, Scott: Color of Night; Invaders, The; Last Fling, The; Life as a House; Lord of Illusions; Luminarias; Major League: Back to the Minors; Mean Streak; Mercy Mission (The Rescue of Flight 711); Necessary Roughness; Passion to Kill, A; Quantum Leap (TV Series); Sibling Rivalry; What Girls Learn
Balaban, Bob: Absence of Malice; Altered States; Best in Show; City Slickers II; Dead-Bang; Deconstructing Harry; End of the Line; For Love or Money; Greedy; Jakob the Liar; Late Shift, The; Mexican, The; Strawberry Statement, The; Three to Tango; 2010; Unnatural Pursuits; Waiting for Guffman; Whose Life Is It, Anyway?
Balagtas, Bernadette: Debut, The
Balan, Ovidiu: Mondo
Balaski, Belinda: Bobbie Jo and the Outlaw; Cannonball; Proud Men
Balasko, Josiane: French Twist; This Sweet Sickness; Too Beautiful for You
Balasz, Samu: Cat's Play
Balding, Rebecca: Boogens, The; Gathering, Part II, The; Silent Scream
Baldwin, Adam: Bad Guys; Bitter Harvest; Blind Justice; Chocolate War, The; Cohen and Tate; Cold Sweat; D.C. Cab; Deadbolt; Digital Man; 800 Leagues Down the Amazon; Full Metal Jacket; Hadley's Rebellion; Lover's Knot; My Bodyguard; Next of Kin; Poison Ivy; Predator 2; Radio Flyer; Reckless; Sawbones; 3:15—The Moment of Truth; Trade Off; Treacherous; Where the Day Takes You; Wyatt Earp
Baldwin, Alec: Alamo, The: Thirteen Days to Glory; Alice; Beetlejuice; Confession, The; Dress Gray; Edge, The; Forever Lulu; Getaway, The; Ghosts of Mississippi; Glengarry Glen Ross; Great Balls of Fire; Heaven's Prisoners; Hunt for Red October, The; Juror, The; Looking for Richard; Malice; Marrying Man, The; Mercury Rising; Miami Blues; Nuremberg; Outside Providence; Pearl Harbor; Prelude to a Kiss; Shadow, The; State & Main; Streetcar Named Desire, A; Talk Radio; Thomas and the Magic Railroad; Working Girl
Baldwin, Ann: Wall Street Cowboy
Baldwin, Daniel: Active Stealth; Attack of the 50-Foot Woman; Car 54, Where Are You? (1991); Dead on Sight; Family of Cops; Harley Davidson and the Marlboro Man; Heroes of Desert Storm; In Pursuit; Invader, The (1996); John Carpenter's Vampires; Knight Moves; Lone Justice; Love Kills; Mulholland Falls; Pandora Project, The; Phoenix; Trees Lounge; Yesterday's Target
Baldwin, Dick: Mr. Moto's Gamble
Baldwin, Michael: Phantasm; Phantasm III: Lord of the Dead; Phantasm IV: Oblivion
Baldwin, Peter: Ghost, The (1963)
Baldwin, Robert: Courageous Dr. Christian, The; Meet Dr. Christian; They Meet Again
Baldwin, Stephen: Bio-Dome; Bitter Harvest; Crimetime; Crossing the Bridge; Cutaway; Dead Awake; Dead Weekend; 8 Seconds; Fall Time; Fled; Flintstones in Viva Rock Vegas, The; Friends and Lovers; Great American Sex Scandal, The; Mr. Murder; Mrs. Parker and the Vicious Circle; New Eden; One Tough Cop; Posse; Sex Monster, The; Simple Twist of Fate, A; Sub Down; Threesome; Under the Hula Moon; Usual Suspects, The; Xchange; Zebra Lounge
Baldwin, Tim: St. Francisville Experiment, The
Baldwin, William: Backdraft; Curdled; Fair Game; Flatliners; Internal Affairs; Preppie Murder, The; Pyromaniac's Love Story, A; Relative Values; Shattered Image; Sliver; Three of Hearts; Virus
Bale, Christian: American Psycho; Captain Corelli's Mandolin; Empire of the Sun; Little Women; Metroland; Newsies; Royal Deceit; Secret Agent, The; Shaft; Swing Kids; Treasure Island; Velvet Goldmine; William Shakespeare's A Midsummer Night's Dream
Balenda, Carla: Hunt the Man Down
Balfour, Betty: Champagne
Balibar, Jeanne: Va Savoir
Balin, Ina: Black Orchid, The; Charro!; Children of An Lac, The; Comancheros, The; From the Terrace; Patsy, The; Projectionist, The
Balin, Mireille: Pepe Le Moko
Balint, Andras: Father
Balint, Eszter: Bail Jumper; Linguini Incident, The; Stranger Than Paradise
Balk, Fairuza: Almost Famous; American History X; Craft, The; Danger of Love; Gas, Food, Lodging; Imaginary Crimes; Island of Dr. Moreau, The; Outside Chance of Maximilian Glick, The; Red Letters; Return to Oz; Tollbooth; Valmont; Waterboy, The; Worst Witch, The
Balkan, Florinda: Lizard In A Woman's Skin, A
Balkin, Karen: Lizard In A Woman's Skin, A
Ball, Angeline: Brothers in Trouble; Commitments, The; General, The
Ball, Bob: Invasion of the Star Creatures
Ball, Lucille: Affairs of Annabel, The; Annabel Takes a Tour; Beauty for the Asking; Best Foot Forward; Big Street, The; Broadway Bill; Critic's Choice; Dance, Girl, Dance; Dark Corner, The; Du Barry Was a Lady; Easy Living; Facts of Life; Fancy Pants; Five Came Back; Forever Darling; Fuller Brush Girl, The; Girl, a Guy and a Gob, A; Guide for the Married Man, A; Having a Wonderful Time; I Dream Too Much; I Love Lucy (TV Series); Joy of Living; Long, Long Trailer, The; Look Who's Laughing; Lucy and Desi: A Home Movie; Mame; Miss Grant Takes Richmond; Next Time I Marry; Panama Lady; Room Service; Seven Day's Leave; Sorrowful Jones; Stage Door; Thousands Cheer; Too Many Girls; Valley of the Sun; Without Love; You Can't Fool Your Wife; Yours, Mine and Ours; Ziegfeld Follies
Ball, Nicholas: Claudia; House That Bled to Death, The
Ball, Samuel: Last Castle, The
Ball, Suzan: War Arrow
Ball, Vincent: Blood of the Vampire

Barcroft, Roy: Arizona Cowboy; Bandits of Dark Canyon; Below the Border; Carson City Cyclone; Cherokee Flash; Down Dakota Way; Eyes of Texas; Far Frontier; Hidden Gold; Hidden Valley Outlaws; In Old Amarillo; Land of the Open Range; Marshal of Cedar Rock; Missourians, The; Pirates of the Prairie; Purple Monster Strikes, The; Radar Men from the Moon; Renegade Trail; Riders of the Rio Grande; Rodeo King and the Senorita; Santa Fe Saddlemates; Stage to Chino; Stagecoach to Denver; Texas Across the River; Under Mexicali Stars; Vigilantes of Boomtown; Wagon Wheels Westward; West of the Law; Wide-Open Town; Wild Frontier
Barda, Meital: Kadosh
Bardem, Javier: Before Night Falls; Farinelli Il Castrato; Jamon, Jamon; Live Flesh
Bardette, Trevor: Marshal of Cripple Creek; Wyatt Earp: Return to Tombstone
Bardot, Brigitte: A Coeur Joie (Head over Heels); And God Created Woman; Contempt; Crazy for Love; Dear Brigitte; Doctor at Sea; Le Repos du Guerrier (Warrior's Rest); Legend of Frenchie King, The; Mademoiselle Striptease; Ravishing Idiot, The; Shalako; Very Private Affair, A; Viva Maria!; Voulez Vous Danser avec Moi? (Will You Dance with Me?)
Bareikis, Arija: Deuce Bigalow: Male Gigolo; Myth of Fingerprints, The
Barenholtz, Ben: Time Stands Still
Barge, Gillian: They Do It with Mirrors
Barger, Sonny: Hell's Angels '69
Bari, Lynn: Abbott and Costello Meet the Keystone Kops; Amazing Mr. X; Bridge of San Luis Rey, The; Charlie Chan in City in Darkness; Elfego Baca: Six Gun Law; Falcon Takes Over, The; Francis Joins the Wacs; Hello, Frisco, Hello; Kit Carson; Nocturne; Orchestra Wives; Shock (1946); Sun Valley Serenade
Barilli, Francesco: Before the Revolution
Baring, Norah: Murder
Barjac, Sophie: Alice; Holiday Hotel
Barkan, Yuda: Lupo
Barker, Clive: Clive Barker's Salome and The Forbidden
Barker, Eric: Blue Murder at St. Trinian's
Barker, Jennifer: Running Wild
Barker, Judith: Daisies in December
Barker, Lex: Away All Boats; Farmer's Daughter, The; Girl in Black Stockings, The; Mission in Morocco; Return of the Bad Men; Torture Chamber of Dr. Sadism, The; Velvet Touch, The
Barkett, Steve: Empire of the Dark
Barkin, Ellen: Act of Vengeance; Adventures of Buckaroo Banzai, The; Bad Company; Big Easy, The; Clinton and Nadine; Crime & Punishment in Suburbia; Desert Bloom; Diner; Down by Law; Drop Dead Gorgeous; Eddie and the Cruisers; Fan, The; Fear and Loathing in Las Vegas; Harry and Son; Into the West; Johnny Handsome; Mac; Made in Heaven; Man Trouble; Mercy; Princess Who Had Never Laughed, The; Sea of Love; Siesta; Someone Like You; Switch; Tender Mercies; Terminal Choice; This Boy's Life; Trigger Happy (Mad Dog Time); White River; Wild Bill
Bark-Jones, David: Pride and Prejudice
Barkley, Janet: Harder They Come, The
Barkworth, Peter: Littlest Horse Thieves, The
Barl, Gail: Real Men
Barlow, Reginald: His Private Secretary
Barnes, Binnie: Adventures of Marco Polo, The; Broadway Melody of 1938; Call Out the Marines; Decameron Nights; Divorce of Lady X, The; Holiday; I Married an Angel; In Old California; It's in the Bag; Last of the Mohicans, The; Melody Master (The Great Awakening) (NewWine); Private Life of Don Juan, The; Private Life of Henry the Eighth, The; Three Musketeers, The; Three Smart Girls; Time of Their Lives, The
Barnes, Christopher Daniel: Angel of Fury; Murder Without Motive; Very Brady Sequel, A
Barnes, Ernie: Don't Look Back: The Story of Leroy "Satchel" Paige
Barnes, Jake: Drive-In Massacre; Summer Camp
Barnes, Joanna: Parent Trap, The
Barnes, Priscilla: Delta Fox; Erotique; Implicated; Last Married Couple in America, The; Lords of the Deep; National Lampoon's Attack of the 5' 2" Women; Scruples; Seniors, The; Stepfather III: Father's Day; Talons of the Eagle; Traxx
Barnes, Rayford: Wyatt Earp: Return to Tombstone
Barnes, Roosevelt: Mississippi Blues
Barnes, Suzanne: Clubhouse Detectives
Barnes, T. Roy: Seven Chances
Barnes, Walter: Escape from the KGB; Smokey Bites the Dust
Barnett, Charlie: They Bite
Barnett, Cindy: Ginger
Barnett, Vince: Death Kiss, The; Gangs, Inc. (Paper Bullets); Ride 'em Cowgirl
Barnwell, Jean Marie: Blue River; From the Mixed-Up Files of Mrs. Basil E. Frankweiler
Baron, Carina: Living Dead Girl
Baron, Joanne: Pet Shop
Baron, Lita: Jungle Jim
Baron, Sandy: Birdy; Broadway Danny Rose; If It's Tuesday, This Must Be Belgium; Out of Towners, The (1970); Vamp
Barondes, Elizabeth: Adrenalin: Fear the Rush; Love to Kill; Night of the Scarecrow; Not of This Earth; Oscar (1991)
Barone, Anita: Running Time
Barone, Jerry: Two Bits
Barouh, Pierre: Man and a Woman, A
Barr, Douglas: Spaced Invaders
Barr, Jean-Marc: Big Blue, The; Breaking the Waves; Hope and Glory; Lifeline; Plague, The; Zentropa
Barranco, Maria: Red Squirrel, The
Barrat, Robert: Bad Lands (1939); Baron of Arizona, The; Captain Caution; Distant Drums; Last of the Mohicans, The; Strangler of the Swamp; Time of Their Lives, The
Barrault, Jean-Louis: Children of Paradise, The; La Nuit de Varennes; Testament of Dr. Cordelier, The
Barrault, Marie-Christine: Cousin, Cousine; Daydreamer, The (1970) (Le Distrait); L'Etat Sauvage (The Savage State); Love in Germany, A; My Night at Maud's; Stardust Memories; Swann in Love
Barré, Chantal: Human Resources
Barrese, Katherine: Jezebel's Kiss
Barrett, Adrienne: Daughter of Horror
Barrett, Brendon Ryan: Casper: A Spirited Beginning
Barrett, Claudia: Robot Monster
Barrett, Jamie: House of the Rising Sun
Barrett, John: American Kickboxer
Barrett, Laurinda: Heart Is a Lonely Hunter, The
Barrett, Louise: Final Defeat, The
Barrett, Majel: Mommy; Star Trek (TV Series); Star Trek: The Cage
Barrett, Nitchie: Preppies
Barrett, Raina: Oh! Calcutta!
Barrett, Ray: Brilliant Lies; Frenchman's Farm; Heaven's Burning; Rebel; Reptile, The; Where the Green Ants Dream
Barrett, Tony: Impact
Barrette, Michelle: Boys, The (1997)
Barrie, Amanda: Carry on Cleo; Koroshi
Barrie, Barbara: Bell Jar, The; Breaking Away; Child of Glass; End of the Line; Execution, The; Judy Berlin; Real Men; Two of a Kind
Barrie, Chris: Red Dwarf (TV Series)
Barrie, John: Victim
Barrie, Lester: Slam Dunk Ernest
Barrie, Mona: Dawn on the Great Divide; Here Comes Trouble
Barrie, Wendy: Five Came Back; I Am the Law; If I Were Rich; Saint Strikes Back, The; Wedding Rehearsal
Barrier, Edgar: Arabian Nights; Cobra Woman; Journey into Fear; Macbeth; Phantom of the Opera; Snow White and the Three Stooges
Barrile, Anthony: Hamburger Hill; Kiss Me Guido
Barringer, Pat: Orgy of the Dead
Barrington, Rebecca: Dance or Die
Barris, Chuck: Hugo Pool
Barrish, Seth: Home Remedy
Barron, Bob: Ballad of a Gunfighter
Barron, Dana: Death Wish IV: The Crackdown; Magic Kid 2; National Lampoon's Vacation

Barron, John: Whoops Apocalypse
Barron, Robert: Sea Hound, The
Barry, Don: Adventures of Red Ryder; Bells of Rosarita; Carson City Cyclone; Days of Old Cheyenne; Dead Man's Gulch; Frankenstein 1970; Hostile Guns; Kansas Cyclone; Saga of Death Valley; Shakiest Gun in the West, The; Sinners in Paradise; Tulsa Kid; Wyoming Outlaw
Barry, Eric M.: cecil b. Demented
Barry, Gene: Adventures of Nellie Bly, The; China Gate; Cry for Love, A; Gambler Returns, The: Luck of the Draw; Maroc 7; Red Garters; Soldier of Fortune; Thunder Road; 27th Day, The; War of the Worlds, The
Barry, Glen: Beautiful Thing
Barry, Joan: Rich and Strange
Barry, Leon: Three Musketeers, The
Barry, Neill: Heat; O.C. & Stiggs; Old Enough; Slipping into Darkness
Barry, Patricia: Bogie; Sammy, the Way-Out Seal
Barry, Raymond J.: Born on the Fourth of July; Chamber, The; Cop; Dead Man Walking; Deep End, The; Headless Body in Topless Bar; K2; Out of Bounds; Rapid Fire; Ref, The
Barry, Sarah: Evil Dead 2
Barry, Tony: Archer's Adventure; Quest, The; Shame; We of the Never Never
Barry, Wendy: Knights of the City
Barrymore, Drew: Altered States; Amy Fisher Story, The; Babes in Toyland; Bad Girls; Best Men; Boys on the Side; Cat's Eye; Charlie's Angels; Donnie Darko; Doppelganger: The Evil Within; E.T.—The Extra-Terrestrial; Ever After; Everyone Says I Love You; Far from Home; Firestarter; Freddy Got Fingered; Guncrazy (1950); Home Fries; Irreconcilable Differences; Mad Love; Motorama; Never Been Kissed; No Place to Hide; Poison Ivy; Riding in Cars with Boys; Scream; See You in the Morning; Sketch Artist; Skipped Parts; Strange Tales: Ray Bradbury Theater; Wedding Singer, The; Wishful Thinking
Barrymore, Ethel: Deadline USA; Farmer's Daughter, The; It's a Big Country; Moonrise; None But the Lonely Heart; Paradine Case, The; Pinky; Portrait of Jennie; Rasputin and the Empress; Spiral Staircase, The; That Midnight Kiss; Young at Heart
Barrymore, John: Beau Brummell; Beloved Rogue; Bill of Divorcement, A; Bulldog Drummond Comes Back; Bulldog Drummond's Peril; Bulldog Drummond's Revenge; Dinner at Eight; Dr. Jekyll and Mr. Hyde; Don Juan; Grand Hotel; Great Man Votes, The; Invisible Woman, The; Marie Antoinette; Maytime; Midnight; Rasputin and the Empress; Romeo and Juliet; State's Attorney; Svengali; Tempest; Topaze; Twentieth Century
Barrymore, John Blythe: Americana; Smokey Bites the Dust
Barrymore, John Drew: Clones, The; High School Confidential!; Never Love a Stranger; Sundowners, The; While the City Sleeps
Barrymore, Lionel: Ah, Wilderness; Camille; Captains Courageous; David Copperfield; Devil Doll, The (1936); Dr. Kildare's Strange Case; Duel in the Sun; Free Soul, A; Girl from Missouri, The; Gorgeous Hussy, The; Grand Hotel; Guy Named Joe, A; It's a Wonderful Life; Key Largo; Lady Be Good; Let Freedom Ring; Little Colonel, The; Lone Star; Mark of the Vampire; Mata Hari; Navy Blue and Gold; On Borrowed Time; Rasputin and the Empress; Return of Peter Grimm, The; Sadie Thompson; Saratoga; Since You Went Away; Test Pilot; Treasure Island; West of Zanzibar; You Can't Take It with You
Barsky, Jared: Cutting Moments
Barsky, Vladimir: Battleship Potemkin, The
Barta, Carol: Dominion
Bartel, Paul: Acting on Impulse; Billy's Hollywood Screen Kiss; Desire and Hell at Sunset Motel; Eating Raoul; Hollywood Boulevard; Out of the Dark; Pope Must Diet, The; Pucker Up and Bark Like a Dog; White Dog
Barth, Eddie: Fame
Barthelmess, Richard: Broken Blossoms; Cabin in the Cotton; Heroes for Sale; Idol Dancer, The; Only Angels Have Wings; Spy of Napoleon; Tol'able David; Way Down East
Bartholomew, Freddie: Anna Karenina; Captains Courageous; David Copperfield; Listen, Darling; Little Lord Fauntleroy; Lloyd's of London; St. Benny the Dip; Tom Brown's School Days (1940)
Bartilson, Lynsey: Mrs. Santa Claus
Bartlett, Bonnie: Courtyard, The
Bartlett, Cal: Cyberzone
Bartlett, Jamie: Ernest Goes to Africa
Bartlett, Robin: Dangerous Minds; Deceived; Honey, We Shrunk Ourselves; If Looks Could Kill; 12:01
Barto, Robyn: Blue Skies Again
Bartok, Eva: Blood and Black Lace; Crimson Pirate, The; Gamma People, The; Operation Amsterdam
Bartok, Jayce: SubUrbia
Barton, Diana: Sexual Malice
Barton, Gregg: Mule Train
Barton, Joe: Slaughterhouse
Barton, Mischa: Lawn Dogs; Lost and Delirious; Pups; Sixth Sense, The; Skipped Parts; Tart
Barton, Peter: Friday the 13th—The Final Chapter; Hell Night
Bartusiak, Sky McCole: Witness Protection
Barty, Billy: Harum Scarum; Legend; Lobster Man from Mars; Night Patrol; UHF; Undead, The; Willow; Wishful Thinking
Baryshnikov, Mikhail: Company Business; Dancers; Turning Point, The; White Nights
Basaraba, Gary: Horse for Danny, A; Midnight Murders; No Mercy; One Magic Christmas; Sweet Dreams
Basco, Dante: Debut, The; Extreme Days; Riot (1996) (TV Movie)
Basco, Darion: Debut, The
Basco, Dion: Race the Sun
Basehart, Richard: Andersonville Trial, The; Bounty Man, The; Brothers Karamazov, The; Chato's Land; Cry Wolf; Flood!; Great Bank Hoax, The; Hans Brinker; He Walked by Night; Hitler; Il Bidone; Island of Dr. Moreau, The; La Strada; Mansion of the Doomed; Moby Dick; Rage
Basham, Tom: Pink Angels
Basie, Count: Stage Door Canteen
Basil, Toni: Rockula
Basinger, Kim: Batman; Bless the Child; Blind Date; Cool World; Final Analysis; Fool for Love; From Here to Eternity; Getaway, The; Hard Country; I Dreamed of Africa; L.A. Confidential; Man Who Loved Women, The; Marrying Man, The; Mother Lode; My Stepmother Is an Alien; Nadine; Natural, The; Never Say Never Again; 9 1/2 Weeks; No Mercy; Ready to Wear; Real McCoy, The; Wayne's World 2
Baskin, Elya: Name of the Rose, The
Baskin, Jim: Slow Bullet
Basler, Antoine: Rendezvous in Paris
Basler, Marianne: Overseas; Soldier's Tale, A; Va Savoir
Basque, Priscilla K.: Bugged!
Basquette, Lina: Hard Hombre; Heroes of the Heart
Bass, Alfie: Carry on Admiral; Fearless Vampire Killers, or, Pardon Me, But Your Teeth Are in My Neck, The; Lavender Hill Mob, The
Bass, Balduin: Orchestra Rehearsal
Bass, James Lance: On the Line (2001)
Bass, Tamara: Baby Boy
Basserman, Albert: Escape Me Never; Madame Curie; Melody Master (The Great Awakening) (NewWine); Moon and Sixpence, The; Once Upon a Honeymoon; Private Affairs of Bel Ami, The; Shanghai Gesture, The; Woman's Face, A
Bassett, Angela: City of Hope; Contact; Critters 4; Heroes of Desert Storm; How Stella Got Her Groove Back; Jacksons, The: An American Dream; Malcolm X; Music of the Heart; Our Friend, Martin; Passion Fish; Score, The; Strange Days; Supernova; Vampire in Brooklyn; Waiting to Exhale; What's Love Got to Do with It?
Bassett, Carling: Spring Fever
Bassett, Linda: East Is East; Waiting for the Moon
Bassett, Peter: Desolation Angels
Bassett, William H.: Tempest, The (1983)
Bassis, Paul: Ganjasaurus Rex
Bastedo, Alexandra: Blood Spattered Bride, The; Find the Lady
Bastien, Fanny: Wolf at the Door

Bataille, Sylvia: Day in the Country, A
Batalov, Alexei: Cranes Are Flying, The; Lady and the Dog, The
Batalov, Nikolai: Bed and Sofa
Bate, Anthony: Philby, Burgess and Maclean: Spy Scandalof the Century
Bateman, Charles: Brotherhood of Satan
Bateman, Jason: Breaking the Rules; Love Stinks; Necessary Roughness; Poison Ivy; Sweetest Thing, The; Taste for Killing, A; Teen Wolf, Too
Bateman, Justine: Closer, The; Deadbolt; Death Artist; Fatal Image, The; Night We Never Met, The; Primary Motive; Satisfaction
Bates, Alan: Club Extinction; Collection, The; Day in the Death of Joe Egg, A; Duet for One; Englishman Abroad, An; Entertainer, The; Far from the Madding Crowd; Georgy Girl; Go-Between, The; Gosford Park; Grave Indiscretion; Hamlet; Kind of Loving, A; King of Hearts; Mothman Prophecies, The; Mr. Frost; Nijinsky; Prayer for the Dying, A; Quartet; Return of the Soldier, The; Rose, The; Secret Friends; Separate Tables; Shout, The (1979); Silent Tongue; Story of a Love Story; Unmarried Woman, An; Unnatural Pursuits; Voyage 'Round My Father, A; We Think the World of You; Whistle Down the Wind; Wicked Lady, The; Women in Love; Zorba the Greek
Bates, Florence: Chocolate Soldier, The; Heaven Can Wait; Judge Steps Out, The; Kismet; Love Crazy; Lullaby of Broadway; Moon and Sixpence, The; San Antonio; Secret Life of Walter Mitty, The; Son of Monte Cristo, The; Tuttles of Tahiti, The; Winter Meeting
Bates, Jeanne: Eraserhead; Mom; Strangler, The
Bates, John: Animal Instincts: The Seductress
Bates, Kathy: American Outlaws; Angus; At Play in the Fields of the Lord; Come Back to the Five and Dime, Jimmy Dean, Jimmy Dean; Curse of the Starving Class; Diabolique; Dolores Claiborne; Dragonfly; Fried Green Tomatoes; Home of Our Own, A; Hostages; Late Shift, The; Men Don't Leave; Misery; Prelude to a Kiss; Primary Colors; Road to Mecca, The; Roe vs. Wade; Shadows and Fog; Summer Heat; Swept from the Sea; Titanic; Used People; War at Home, The; Waterboy, The; White Palace
Bates, Larry: Horrible Doctor Bones, The
Bates, Ralph: Devil Within Her, The; Dr. Jekyll and Sister Hyde; Fear in the Night (Dynasty of Fear); Horror of Frankenstein; Lust for a Vampire; Persecution; Taste the Blood of Dracula
Bates, William: Orgy of the Dead
Batinkoff, Randall: Dead Man's Curve; For Keeps
Batista, Lloyd: Last Plane Out
Batt, Bryan: Jeffrey
Batt, Paul: War of the Buttons
Battaglia, Matt: Raven (1997); Universal Soldier II: Brothers in Arms
Battaglia, Rik: Call of the Wild; This Man Can't Die
Battisti, Carlo: Umberto D
Battiston, Giuseppe: Bread and Tulips
Battle, Hinton: Foreign Student
Bauchau, Patrick: Blood Ties; Every Breath; Lisbon Story; Rapture, The; Serpent's Lair; State of Things, The
Bauche, Vanessa: Amores Perros
Bauer, Belinda: Act of Piracy; Case for Murder, A; Game of Love, The; H. P. Lovecraft's Necronomicon: Book of the Dead; RoboCop 2; Rosary Murders, The; Samson and Delilah; Servants of Twilight; Sins of Dorian Gray, The; Timerider; Winter Kills
Bauer, Cathleen: Music School, The
Bauer, Charlita: Cradle Will Fall, The
Bauer, Chris: 8MM; 61*
Bauer, Michelle: Attack of the 60-Ft. Centerfold; Blonde Heaven; Lady Avenger; Vampire Vixens from Venus
Bauer, Richard: Sicilian, The
Bauer, Steven: Along for the Ride; Beast, The; Climate for Killing, A; Drive Like Lightning; False Arrest; Gleaming the Cube; Navajo Blues; Raising Cain; Running Scared; Scarface; Snapdragon; Star Quest; Stranger by Night; Sweet Poison; Sword of Gideon; Thief of Hearts; Traffic; Wild Side; Wildfire; Woman of Desire
Baur, Harry: Abel Gance's Beethoven; Crime and Punishment; Golgotha; I Stand Condemned; Volpone
Baur, Marc: Time Runner
Bautista, Perla: Midnight Dancer
Bavier, Frances: Andy Griffith Show, The (TV Series); Benji
Baxley, Barbara: Come Along with Me
Baxter, Alan: Set-Up, The
Baxter, Amy Lynn: Bikini Bistro
Baxter, Anne: All About Eve; Angel on My Shoulder; Blue Gardenia, The; Carnival Story; Cimarron; East of Eden; Fighting Sullivans, The (Sullivans, The); Five Graves to Cairo; Guest in the House; Homecoming; I Confess; Jane Austen in Manhattan; Masks of Death; North Star, The (1943); Razor's Edge, The; Ten Commandments, The; Three Violent People; Walk on the Wild Side
Baxter, Dr. Frank: Gateway to the Mind; Strange Case of the Cosmic Rays, The
Baxter, Keith: Ash Wednesday; Chimes at Midnight (Falstaff)
Baxter, Lynsey: Cold Light of Day, The
Baxter, Warner: Adam Had Four Sons; Broadway Bill; 42nd Street; In Old Arizona; Stand Up and Cheer; West of Zanzibar
Baxter-Birney, Meredith: Beulah Land; Bittersweet Love; Jezebel's Kiss; Kissing Place, The; Till Murder Do Us Part
Bay, Frances: Changing Habits; Happy Gilmore; Paperboy, The
Bay, Sara: Devil's Wedding Night, The
Bayaertu: Close to Eden
Baye, Nathalie: Affair of Love, An; Beethoven's Nephew; Every Other Weekend; Francois Truffaut: Stolen Moments; Green Room, The; Honeymoon; La Balance; La Machine; Man Inside, The; Man Who Loved Women, The; Return of Martin Guerre, The; Venus Beauty Institute
Bayer, Gary: Will, G. Gordon Liddy
Baylor, Hal: Island in the Sky
Baynes, Hetty: Tales of Erotica
Bazinet, Brenda: Goosebumps: The Haunted Mask
Bazlen, Brigid: Honeymoon Machine, The
Beach, Adam: Boy Called Hate, A; Dance Me Outside; Last Stop; Smoke Signals; Squanto: A Warrior's Tale
Beach, Michael: Bad Company; Cadence; Casualties; Family Thing, A; Hit List, The (1992); In a Shallow Grave; Late for Dinner; Ms. Scrooge; One False Move; Ruby Bridges; Sketch Artist II: Hands That See; Soul Food; Weekend War
Beach, Scott: Out
Beacham, Stephanie: And Now the Screaming Starts; Confessional, The; Dracula A.D. 1972; Foreign Affairs; Napoleon and Josephine: A Love Story; Nightcomers, The; Wedding Bell Blues
Beachwood, Kermit: Ferngully 2: The Magical Rescue
Beaham, Kate: Chopper
Beal, Cindy: Slave Girls from Beyond Infinity
Beal, John: Break of Hearts; Cat and the Canary, The; Double Wedding; Edge of Darkness; I Am the Law; Little Minister, The; Madame X; Ten Who Dared
Beall, Aaron: Habit
Beals, Jennifer: Anniversary Party, The; Blood and Concrete, A Love Story; Bride, The; Caro Diario; Cinderella; Club Extinction; Day of Atonement; Dead on Sight; Devil in a Blue Dress; Flashdance; Four Rooms; Gamble, The; House Divided, A; In the Soup; Indecency; Out of Line; Prophecy II, The; Search for One-Eye Jimmy, The; Something More; Split Decisions; Terror Stalks the Class Reunion; Turbulence 2; Twilight of the Golds, The; Vampire's Kiss; Wishful Thinking
Beaman, Lee Anne: Other Woman, The; Tropical Heat
Bean, Katherine: All the Vermeers in New York
Bean, Orson: Anatomy of a Murder; Being John Malkovich; Final Judgment
Bean, Rick: Whodunit?
Bean, Robert: Wild Ride, The
Bean, Sean: Black Beauty; Caravaggio; Don't Say a Word; Essex Boys; Field, The; Goldeneye; Leo Tolstoy's Anna Karenina (1997); Lorna Doone; Patriot Games; Ronin; Scarlett; Sharpe (TV Series); Shopping; Stormy Monday
Beard, David: Last Broadcast, The
Beard, Glynn: Crier, The
Beard, Stymie: Two-Gun Man from Harlem
Bearse, Amanda: First Affair; Fright Night

Beart, Emmanuelle: Date with an Angel; La Belle Noiseuse; L'Enfer; Manon of the Spring; Mission: Impossible; Nelly and Monsieur Arnaud; Time Regained; Un Coeur en Hiver
Beasley, Allyce: Entertaining Angels; Moonlighting (1985) (TV Pilot); Rumpelstiltskin; Silent Night, Deadly Night 4—Initiation; Tommyknockers, The
Beasley, John: Apostle, The
Beat, Jackie: Grief; Wigstock: The Movie
Beatles, The: Compleat Beatles, The; Hard Day's Night, A; Help!; Let It Be; Magical Mystery Tour
Beatty, Clyde: Africa Screams
Beatty, Debra: Witchcraft VI: The Devil's Mistress
Beatty, Ned: Affair, The; All God's Children; Back to Hannibal: The Return of Tom Sawyer and Huckleberry Finn; Back to School; Big Bad John; Big Bus, The; Big Easy, The; Black Water; Blind Vision; Captain America; Chattahoochee; Cookie's Fortune; Cry in the Wild, A; Curse of Inferno, The; Deliverance; Ed & His Dead Mother; Execution of Private Slovik, The; Fourth Protocol, The; Friendly Fire; Going Under; Gray Lady Down; Great Bank Hoax, The; Gulliver's Travels (1996) (Television); Guyana Tragedy, The: The Story of Jim Jones; Hear My Song; Hopscotch; Illusions; Incredible Shrinking Woman, The; Just Cause; Last American Hero, The; Last Train Home; Midnight Crossing; Mikey and Nicky; Ministry of Vengeance; Nashville; Network; 1941; Our Town; Physical Evidence; Pray TV; Prelude to a Kiss; Promises in the Dark; Purple People Eater; Radioland Murders; Replikator: Cloned to Kill; Repossessed; Restless Natives; Rolling Vengeance; Rudy; Shadows in the Storm; Silver Streak; Spring Forward; Spy; Streets of Laredo; Stroker Ace; Superman II; Switching Channels; TBone N Weasel; Thief Who Came to Dinner, The; Time Trackers; Touched; Toy, The; Tragedy of Flight 103, The: The Inside Story; Trouble with Spies, The; Unholy, The; White Lightning; Wise Blood
Beatty, Robert: Captain Horatio Hornblower; Where Eagles Dare
Beatty, Warren: All Fall Down; Bonnie and Clyde; Bugsy; Bulworth; Dick Tracy; $ (Dollars); Fortune, The; Heaven Can Wait; Ishtar; Lilith; Love Affair; McCabe and Mrs. Miller; Parallax View, The; Promise Her Anything; Reds; Roman Spring of Mrs. Stone, The; Shampoo; Splendor in the Grass; Town & Country; Truth or Dare
Beauchamp, Carolyn: Troma's War
Beaulieu, Trace: Mystery Science Theatre 3000: The Movie
Beaumont, Hugh: Blue Dahlia, The; Human Duplicators, The; Lost Continent, The; Mole People, The; Objective, Burma!; Phone Call from a Stranger; Railroaded; Seventh Victim, The
Beaumont, Richard: Can It Be Love
Beaver, Jim: Divided by Hate; Twogether; Warden of Red Rock
Beaver, Terry: Impure Thoughts; Shot in the Heart
Beavers, Louise: Big Street, The; Coquette; Du Barry Was a Lady; General Spanky; Goodbye, My Lady; It Happened in New Orleans; Jackie Robinson Story, The; Never Wave at a WAC (Private Wore Skirts, The); She Done Him Wrong; Tammy and the Bachelor; Tell It to the Judge
Beccaria, Mario: Le Boucher (The Butcher)
Becher, John C.: Below the Belt
Beck, Dixie: Body Strokes (Siren's Call)
Beck, Jenny: Troll
Beck, John: Audrey Rose; Big Bus, The; Climate for Killing, A; Other Side of Midnight, The; Pat Garrett and Billy the Kid; Rollerball; Sleeper; Suspect Device
Beck, Julian: Oedipus Rex
Beck, Kimberly: Friday the 13th—The Final Chapter; Massacre at Central High; Private War
Beck, Michael: Blackout; Celebrity; Chiller; Deadly Game; Fade to Black; Forest Warrior; Gone to Texas; Megaforce; Triumphs of a Man Called Horse; Warlords of the 21st Century; Warriors, The; Xanadu
Beck, Rufus: Maybe, Maybe Not
Beck, Thomas: Charlie Chan at the Opera; Charlie Chan at the Racetrack; Charlie Chan in Egypt; Charlie Chan in Paris; Thank You, Mr. Moto
Beckel, Graham: Hardball; Jennifer 8; L.A. Confidential; Lost Angels; Lost in the Bermuda Triangle; Rising Son
Becker, Ben: Brother of Sleep; Harmonists, The
Becker, Gerry: Mickey Blue Eyes
Becker, Gretchen: Huck and the King of Hearts; Maniac Cop 3: Badge of Silence
Becker, Jack: Teach Me Tonight
Becker, Meret: Harmonists, The; Promise, The
Becker, Randy: Love! Valour! Compassion!
Becker, Tony: Vietnam War Story
Beckett, Scotty: Ali Baba and the Forty Thieves; Date with Judy, A; Listen, Darling
Beckinsale, Kate: Brokedown Palace; Cold Comfort Farm; Emma; Golden Bowl, The; Haunted; Last Days of Disco, The; Much Ado About Nothing; Pearl Harbor; Royal Deceit; Serendipity; Shooting Fish
Beckley, Tony: When a Stranger Calls
Beckman, Henry: Man Upstairs, The
Beckwith, Reginald: Men of Sherwood Forest
Beckwith, William: Prime Evil
Bedard, Irene: Crazy Horse; Lakota Woman: Siege at Wounded Knee; Lost Child, The; Navajo Blues; Smoke Signals
Beddoe, Don: Beyond the Purple Hills; Buck Privates Come Home; Bullwhip; Face Behind the Mask, The; Impossible Years, The; Talk of the Town, The; They Won't Believe Me
Bedelia, Bonnie: Big Fix, The; Boy Who Could Fly, The; Die Hard; Die Hard 2: Die Harder; Fallen Angels; Fat Man and Little Boy; Fire Next Time, The; Heart Like a Wheel; Homecoming; Judicial Consent; Lady from Yesterday, The; Locked in Silence; Lovers and Other Strangers; Memorial Day; Needful Things; Presumed Innocent; Prince of Pennsylvania; Salem's Lot; Somebody Has to Shoot the Picture; Speechless; Stranger, The; Switched at Birth; Violets Are Blue; When the Time Comes
Bedell, Rodney: Just for the Hell of It
Bedford, Barbara: Last of the Mohicans, The; Mockery; Tumbleweeds
Bedford, Brian: Grand Prix
Bedi, Kabir: Beyond Justice
Bednarz, Wendy: There's Nothing Out There
Bedos, Guy: Pardon Mon Affaire; Pardon Mon Affaire, Too!
Bee, Molly: Hillbillys in a Haunted House
Bee Gees, The: Sgt. Pepper's Lonely Hearts Club Band
Beecroft, David: Kidnapped in Paradise; Rain Killer, The; Shadowzone
Beene, Dan: Patriot, The
Beer, Daniel: Talking About Sex
Beery, Wallace: Ah, Wilderness; Art of Buster Keaton, The; Beggars of Life; Big House, The; Champ, The; China Seas; Date with Judy, A; Dinner at Eight; Grand Hotel; Last of the Mohicans, The; Lost World, The; Min and Bill; Old Ironsides; Robin Hood; Three Ages, The; Treasure Island; Victory; Viva Villa!; White Tiger
Beery Jr., Noah: Ace Drummond; Bad Lands (1939); Capture of Grizzly Adams, The; Carson City Kid; Decision at Sundown; Doolins of Oklahoma; Fastest Gun Alive, The; Francis Gary Powers: The True Story of the U-2 Spy Incident; Gung Ho! (1943); Hondo and the Apaches; Jubal; Only Angels Have Wings; Red River; Riders of Death Valley; Rocketship X-M; Savages; Sergeant York; Texas Rangers, The (1951); Three Musketeers, The; Trail Beyond, The; Walking Tall; Walking Tall Part II
Beery Sr., Noah: Adventures of Red Ryder; Big Stampede, The; Buffalo Stampede; Carson City Cyclone; Cockeyed Cavaliers; Devil Horse, The; Flesh and Blood (1922); Man of the Forest; Mark of Zorro, The; Mexicali Rose; Noah's Ark; She Done Him Wrong; Sweet Adeline; To the Last Man; Trail Beyond, The; Tulsa Kid; Vanishing American, The; Zorro Rides Again
Beesley, Max: Glitter; Kill Me Later
Beeson, Joel: Ballistic
Beetem, Chris: Grace and Glorie
Beevers, Geoffrey: Very British Coup, A
Beghe, Jason: Baby Monitor: Sound of Fear; Full Eclipse; G.I. Jane; Monkey Shines: An Experiment in Fear
Begley Jr., Ed: Accidental Tourist, The; Addams Family Reunion; Amazon Women on the Moon; Cat People; Children of Fury; Citizen's Band; Cooperstown; Crazysitter, The; Dark Horse; Dead of Night; Elvis—The Movie; Even Cowgirls Get the

Blues; Get Crazy; Great Los Angeles Earthquake, The; Greedy; Hourglass; Incident at Deception Ridge; Joey; Late Shift, The; Meet the Applegates; Ms. Bear; Murder She Purred; Not a Penny More, Not a Penny Less; Not in This Town; Rave Review; Running Mates; Santa with Muscles; Scenes from the Class Struggle in Beverly Hills; Sensation; She-Devil; Shining Season, A; Showdown; Spies, Lies, and Naked Thighs; St. Elsewhere (TV Series); Transylvania 6-5000

Begley Sr., Ed: Boomerang; Boots Malone; Dunwich Horror, The; Firecreek; Hang 'em High; It Happens Every Spring; Lone Star; On Dangerous Ground; Patterns; Sorry, Wrong Number; Stars in My Crown; Street with No Name; Sweet Bird of Youth; Tulsa; 12 Angry Men; Unsinkable Molly Brown, The; Wild in the Streets

Behar, Joy: Manhattan Murder Mystery

Behets, Briony: Long Weekend

Behling, Robert: Northern Lights

Behr, Jason: Rites of Passage

Behr, Melissa: Dollman vs. Demonic Toys; Landlady, The; Perfect Tenant, The

Behrens, Marla: Reptilicus

Behrens, Sam: Murder by Numbers (1989)

Behrozi, Soghra: Apple, The

Bekassy, Stephen: Interrupted Melody

Bekes, Rita: 25, Firemen's Street

Bekins, Richard: George Washington: The Forging of a Nation

Bel, Roger Le: Night Zoo

Bel Geddes, Barbara: Alfred Hitchcock Presents (TV Series); Blood on the Moon; By Love Possessed; Caught; Five Pennies, The; I Remember Mama; Panic in the Streets; Todd Killings, The; Vertigo

Belack, Doris: Hearst and Davies Affair, The

Belafonte, Harry: Buck and the Preacher; Carmen Jones; Kansas City; Uptown Saturday Night; White Man's Burden

Belafonte, Shari: Fire, Ice & Dynamite; French Silk; If You Could See What I Hear; Midnight Hour; Murder by Numbers (1989); Time Walker

Belcher, James: Man with the Perfect Swing, The

Belcher, Patricia: Jeepers Creepers

Belcourt, Dominique: Firelight

Belford, Christine: Christine; Gambler, The; Groundstar Conspiracy, The; Ladies Club; Pocket Money

Belgrave, Richard: Riff-Raff (1990)

Belita: Gangster, The; Never Let Me Go

Bell, Catherine: Time Shifters, The

Bell, Christopher: Sarah, Plain and Tall; Skylark

Bell, E. E.: 800 Leagues Down the Amazon

Bell, James: My Friend Flicka

Bell, Jamie: Billy Elliot

Bell, Jeanne: TNT Jackson

Bell, Marie: Phedre

Bell, Marshall: Heroes of Desert Storm; Payback; Too Fast Too Young; Wildfire

Bell, Monica: Everything Relative

Bell, Rex: Broadway to Cheyenne; Dawn on the Great Divide

Bell, Tobin: Brown's Requiem; Deadman's Revenge; Deep Red; New Eden; Ruby; Serial Killer

Bell, Tom: Feast of July; Holocaust; Prime Suspect 1; Prime Suspect 3; Red King, White Knight; Swing; Wish You Were Here

Belladonna, Joey: Pledge Night

Bellamy, Bill: Brothers, The; Love Jones; Love Stinks

Bellamy, Madge: White Zombie

Bellamy, Ned: Antitrust

Bellamy, Ralph: Ace of Aces; Amazon Women on the Moon; Awful Truth, The; Boy in the Plastic Bubble, The; Boy Meets Girl; Brother Orchid; Cancel My Reservation; Carefree; Court-martial of Billy Mitchell, The; Disorderlies; Dive Bomber; Footsteps in the Dark; Fourth Wise Man, The; Ghost of Frankenstein; Good Mother, The; Guest in the House; Hands Across the Table; Helldorado; His Girl Friday; Lady on a Train; Missiles of October, The; Murder on Flight 502; Oh, God!; Pretty Woman; Professionals, The; Rosemary's Baby; Search for the Gods; Spitfire; Sunrise at Campobello; Trading Places; Wolf Man, The

Bellar, Clara: First 9 1/2 Weeks, The; Rendezvous in Paris

Bellaver, Harry: House on 92nd Street, The; Old Man and the Sea, The; Tanks Are Coming, The

Belle, Camilla: Patriot, The

Beller, Kathleen: Are You in the House Alone?; Cloud Waltzing; Fort Apache—The Bronx; Movie Movie; Promises in the Dark; Rappaccini's Daughter; Surfacing; Sword and the Sorcerer, The; Time Trackers; Touched

Belli, Agostina: Blood Castle; Blood in the Streets; Holocaust 2000; Night of the Devils; Purple Taxi, The; Seduction of Mimi, The

Belli, Melvin: Gimme Shelter

Bellin, Olga: Tomorrow

Bellis, Scott: Timecop

Belliveau, Cynthia: Dark, The; Spider and the Fly, The

Bellman, Gina: Secret Friends; Silent Trigger

Bello, Jaime: Apostate, The

Bello, Maria: Coyote Ugly; Duets; Payback; Permanent Midnight

Bellomo, Sarah: Beach Babes from Beyond; Beach Babes 2: Cave Girl Island

Bellows, Gil: Black Day Blue Night; Judas Kiss; Love & a .45; Miami Rhapsody; Shawshank Redemption, The; Silver Strand; Snow White: A Tale of Terror

Bellucci, Monica: Brotherhood of the Wolf; Malena; Under Suspicion (2000)

Bellwood, Pamela: Cocaine: One Man's Seduction; Deadman's Curve; Double Standard; Heartless; Incredible Shrinking Woman, The

Belmond, Virginia: Dangers of the Canadian Mounted; Silent Conflict

Belmondo, Jean-Paul: Borsalino; Breathless; Cartouche; Casino Royale; High Heels; Is Paris Burning?; Le Doulos; Le Magnifique; Les Misérables; Love and the Frenchwoman; Mississippi Mermaid; Pierrot Le Fou; Sois Belle Et Tais-Toi (Just Another Pretty Face); Stavisky; Swashbuckler, The (1984); That Man from Rio; Two Women; Un Singe en Hiver (A Monkey in Winter); Woman Is a Woman, A

Belmont, Lara: War Zone, The

Belmore, Lionel: Madame Behave

Belson, Michael: Wag the Dog

Beltran, Robert: Eating Raoul; El Diablo; Gaby, a True Story; Kiss Me a Killer; Latino; Luminarias; Managua; Scenes from the Class Struggle in Beverly Hills; Shadow Hunter; Streethawk; To Die Standing

Belushi, James: About Last Night …; Angel's Dance; Backlash; Best Legs in the 8th Grade, The; Birthday Boy, The; Curly Sue; Destiny Turns on the Radio; Diary of a Hitman; Florentine, The; Gang Related; Homer and Eddie; Jingle All the Way; Joe Somebody; Jumpin' Jack Flash; K-9; Little Shop of Horrors (1986); Living in Peril; Man with One Red Shoe, The; Mr. Destiny; Once Upon a Crime; Only the Lonely; Palermo Connection, The; Parallel Lives; Pinocchio; Principal, The; Race the Sun; Real Men; Red Heat; Return to Me; Royce; Sahara; Salvador; Separate Lives; Taking Care of Business; Thief (1981); Traces of Red; Wag the Dog; Wild Palms; Working Stiffs

Belushi, John: Animal House; BluesBrothers, The; Continental Divide; Goin' South; Neighbors; Old Boyfriends; 1941; Rutles, The (All You Need Is Cash); Things We Did Last Summer

Belvaux, Rémy: Man Bites Dog

Belzer, Richard: America; Freeway; Get on the Bus; Groove Tube, The; Invaders, The; Missing Pieces; Not of This Earth; Off and Running; Puppet Masters, The; Wrong Guys, The

Ben Salem, El Hedi: Ali: Fear Eats the Soul

Benaderet, Bea: George Burns and Gracie Allen Show, The (TV Series)

Benatar, Pat: Union City

Benben, Brian: Flamingo Rising, The; Gangster Wars; I Come in Peace; Mortal Sins (1990) (Dangerous Obsession); Radioland Murders; Sister Mary Explains It All

Benchley, Robert: I Married a Witch; It's in the Bag; Road to Utopia; Sky's the Limit, The; Weekend at the Waldorf; You'll Never Get Rich; Young and Willing

Bender, Russ: Suicide Battalion; War of the Colossal Beast

Bendetti, Michael: Amanda and the Alien; Netherworld

Bendix, William: Babe Ruth Story, The; Big Steal, The; Blackbeard the Pirate; Blue Dahlia, The; Boys' Night Out; Crashout; Dangerous Mission; Dark Corner, The; Deep Six, The; Girl in Every Port, A; Glass Key, The; Guadalcanal Diary; Hairy Ape, The; It's in the Bag; Lifeboat; Macao; Wake Island; Who Done It?; Woman of the Year
Bendova, Jitka: Closely Watched Trains
Bendsen, Rikke: Memories of a Marriage
Benedetti, Nelly: Soft Skin, The
Benedict, Claire: Prime Suspect 2
Benedict, Dirk: Adventures of Young Brave, The; Alaska; Battlestar Galactica; Blue Tornado; Body Slam; Cruise into Terror; Demon Keeper; Georgia, Georgia; Mission Galactica: The Cylon Attack; November Conspiracy, The; Official Denial; Ruckus; Scruples; Underground Aces; W
Benedict, Nick: Pistol, The: The Birth of a Legend
Benedict, Paul: Arthur 2: On the Rocks; Chair, The; Desperate Moves; Man with Two Brains, The; Sibling Rivalry
Benedict, William: Adventures of Captain Marvel, The; Bowery Boys, The (Series)
Beneyton, Yves: By the Blood of Others; Lacemaker, The; Letters to an Unknown Lover
Benfield, John: Prime Suspect 1; Prime Suspect 2
Bengell, Norma: Hellbenders, The; Planet of the Vampires
Benichou, Maurice: A La Mode
Benicio, Murilo: Woman on Top
Benigni, Roberto: Down by Law; Johnny Stecchino; Life Is Beautiful; Monster, The; Night on Earth; Son of the Pink Panther
Bening, Annette: American Beauty; American President, The; Bugsy; Grifters, The; Guilty by Suspicion; In Dreams; Love Affair; Mars Attacks!; Postcards from the Edge; Regarding Henry; Richard III; Siege, The; Valmont; What Planet Are You From?
Benjamin, Paul: Education of Sonny Carson, The; Fence, The; Mr. Inside/Mr. Outside
Benjamin, Richard: Catch-22; Diary of a Mad Housewife; First Family; Goodbye Columbus; House Calls; How to Beat the High Co$t of Living; Last of Sheila, The; Love at First Bite; Packin' It In; Pentagon Wars, The; Portnoy's Complaint; Saturday the 14th; Scavenger Hunt; Steagle, The; Sunshine Boys, The; Westworld; Witches' Brew
Benji: Benji; Benji the Hunted; For the Love of Benji; Oh, Heavenly Dog!
Bennent, David: Legend; Tin Drum, The
Bennent, Heinz: From the Lives of the Marionettes
Bennett, Bruce: Alligator People, The; Before I Hang; Clones, The; Cosmic Man, The; Daniel Boone, Trail Blazer; Dark Passage; Lone Ranger, The; Man I Love, The; Mildred Pierce; New Adventures of Tarzan; Sahara; Silver River; Stolen Life, A; Strategic Air Command; Tarzan and the Green Goddess; Three Violent People; Treasure of the Sierra Madre
Bennett, Constance: Common Law, The; Goose Woman, The; Madame X; Topper; Topper Takes a Trip; Two-Faced Woman; What Price Hollywood?
Bennett, Eila: Terror Aboard
Bennett, Enid: Robin Hood
Bennett, Fran: King of the Carnival
Bennett, Hywel: Deadline; Endless Night; Loot; Murder Elite; Virgin Soldiers, The
Bennett, Jill: Charge of the Light Brigade, The; Concrete Jungle, (1962) The (Criminal, The); I Want What I Want; Lady Jane; Nanny, The; Old Curiosity Shop, The; Sheltering Sky, The; Skull, The
Bennett, Joan: Best of Dark Shadows, The; Bulldog Drummond; Colonel Effingham's Raid; Dark Shadows (TV Series); Disraeli; Father of the Bride; Father's Little Dividend; House Across the Bay, The; House of Dark Shadows; Little Women; Man Hunt (1941); Man in the Iron Mask, The; Mississippi; Scar, The; Scarlet Street; Secret Beyond the Door; Son of Monte Cristo, The; Suspiria; We're No Angels; Woman in the Window
Bennett, Leila: Emma
Bennett, Lynette: Woman Chaser, The
Bennett, Marion: Lantern Hill
Bennett, Nigel: Where's the Money, Noreen?
Bennett, Ray: Lovers' Lovers
Bennett, Richard: Arrowsmith; If I Had a Million
Bennett, Tony: Oscar, The (1966)
Bennett, Zachary: By Way of the Stars; Looking for Miracles
Benny, Jack: Broadway Melody of 1936; Buck Benny Rides Again; George Washington Slept Here; Guide for the Married Man, A; Hollywood Canteen; Horn Blows at Midnight, The; It's in the Bag; Jack Benny Program, The (TV Series); Meanest Man in the World, The; To Be or Not to Be; Transatlantic Merry-Go-Round
Benrath, Martin: White Rose, The
Benrubi, Abraham: Program, The
Benson, Deborah: Danger of Love; Just Before Dawn; Mutant on the Bounty; 30-Sep-55
Benson, Lucille: Private Parts
Benson, Martin: Battle Beneath the Earth; Gorgo; Hitchhiker's Guide to the Galaxy, The; Istanbul
Benson, Robby: All the Kind Strangers; Chosen, The; City Limits; Die Laughing; End, The; Harry and Son; Homewrecker; Ice Castles; Invasion of Privacy; Jory; Last of Mrs. Lincoln, The; Modern Love; Ode to Billy Joe; One on One; Our Town; Rent-a-Cop; Running Brave; Tribute; Two of a Kind; Webber's World (At Home with the Webbers); White Hot
Benson, Wendy: Wes Craven's Wishmaster
Benson, William C.: Redneck Zombies
Bentine, Michael: Down Among the "Z" Men
Bentley, James: Others, The
Bentley, John: Chair, The; Flight from Vienna; Istanbul
Bentley, Ray: Scarlet Spear, The
Bentley, Wes: American Beauty; Claim, The; Soul Survivors; White River
Benton, Barbi: Deathstalker; For the Love of It; Hospital Massacre
Benton, Eddie: Dr. Strange
Benton, Helen: Bloodbeat
Benton, Jerome: Graffiti Bridge; Under the Cherry Moon
Benton, Kevin: No Escape, No Return
Benton, Mark: Career Girls
Benton, Suzanne: Boy and His Dog, A; That Cold Day in the Park
Benussi, Femi: Rattler Kid
Ben-Victor, Paul: Corruptor, The; Evil Lives; Red Scorpion 2
Benz, Donna Kei: Pray for Death
Benz, Julie: Jawbreaker
Benzali, Daniel: Murder at 1600; Screwed
Beradino, John: Moon of the Wolf
Beraud, Luc: Sincerely Charlotte
Bercovici, Luca: Drop Zone; Frightmare; K2; Mission of Justice; Mortal Passions; Pacific Heights; Parasite; Stranger by Night
Berenger, Eric: Monsieur Hire
Berenger, Tom: At Play in the Fields of the Lord; Avenging Angel, The (1995); Betrayed; Beyond Obsession; Big Chill, The; Body Language; Born on the Fourth of July; Butch and Sundance: The Early Days; Chasers; Cutaway; Diplomatic Siege; Dogs of War, The; Eddie and the Cruisers; Fear City; Field, The; Gettysburg; Gingerbread Man, The; In Praise of Older Women; In the Company of Spies; Last of the Dogmen; Last Rites; Looking for Mr. Goodbar; Love at Large; Major League; Major League II; Murder of Crows, A; Occasional Hell, An; One Man's Hero; Platoon; Rough Riders; Rustler's Rhapsody; Shattered; Shoot to Kill; Sliver; Sniper; Someone to Watch Over Me; Substitute, The; Training Day; True Blue; Turbulence 2
Berenson, Marisa: Barry Lyndon; Death in Venice; Killer Fish; Night of the Cyclone; Secret Diary of Sigmund Freud, The; Trade Secrets; White Hunter Black Heart
Beresford, Clare: Ultrawarrior
Berfield, Justin: Kid with X-Ray Eyes, The
Berfield, Lorne: Double Blast
Berg, Joanna: Visitors, The
Berg, Peter: Across the Moon; Aspen Extreme; Case for Murder, A; Copland; Corky Romano; Crooked Hearts; Fire in the Sky; Girl 6; Great White Hype, The; Last Ride, The; Last Seduction,

The; Late for Dinner; Midnight Clear, A; Never on Tuesday; Race for Glory
Berge, Colette: Les Abysses
Berge, Francine: Judex; Les Abysses; Mr. Klein
Bergen, Candice: Bite the Bullet; Carnal Knowledge; Domino Principle, The; 11 Harrowhouse; Gandhi; Getting Straight; Mayflower Madam; Merlin & the Sword; Miss Congeniality; Night Full of Rain, A; Oliver's Story; Rich and Famous; Sand Pebbles, The; Soldier Blue; Starting Over; Stick; Wind and the Lion, The
Bergen, Edgar: Fun and Fancy Free; Goldwyn Follies, The; Letter of Introduction; Look Who's Laughing; Muppet Movie, The; Stage Door Canteen; You Can't Cheat an Honest Man
Bergen, Frances: Eating
Bergen, Patrick: Proposition, The
Bergen, Polly: Across the Rio Grande; At War with the Army; Cape Fear; Cry-Baby; Escape from Fort Bravo; Haunting of Sarah Hardy, The; Kisses for My President; Lightning Incident, The; Making Mr. Right; Murder on Flight 502; My Brother's Wife; Once Upon a Time `When We Were Colored; War and Remembrance; Winds of War, The
Bergen, Tushka: Barcelona; Voices From a Locked Room; Wrangler
Berger, Helmut: Ash Wednesday; Battle Force; Code Name: Emerald; Conversation Piece; Damned, The; Dorian Gray; Garden of the Finzi-Continis, The; Godfather, Part III, The; Romantic Englishwoman, The; Victory at Entebbe
Berger, Nicole: Shoot the Piano Player; Story of a Three Day Pass, The
Berger, Sarah: Green Man, The
Berger, Senta: Ambushers, The; Cast a Giant Shadow; Diabolically Yours; Full Hearts and Empty Pockets; Killing Cars; Quiller Memorandum, The; Scarlet Letter (1973); Sherlock Holmes and the Deadly Necklace; Swiss Conspiracy, The; Waltz King, The; When Women Had Tails; When Women Lost Their Tails
Berger, Sidney: Carnival of Souls
Berger, William: Dial: Help; Tex and the Lord of the Deep
Bergerac, Jacques: Gigi; Hypnotic Eye, The; Les Girls; Unkissed Bride
Bergere, Lee: Time Trackers
Bergeron, Philippe: Mangler 2, The
Berggren, Thommy: Elvira Madigan; Sunday's Children
Berghof, Herbert: Belarus File, The; Target; Voices
Bergin, Patrick: Amazons and Gladiators; Deadline; Devil's Prey; Double Cross; Durango; Eye of the Beholder; Frankenstein; Highway to Hell; Lawnmower Man 2: Jobe's War (Lawnmower Man: Beyond Cyberspace); Love Crimes; Map of the Human Heart; Mountains of the Moon; Patriot Games; Ripper, The; Robin Hood; Sir Arthur Conan Doyle's The Lost World; Sleeping with the Enemy; Soft Deceit; Suspicious Minds; They (They Watch); Triplecross
Bergl, Emily: Rage, The: Carrie 2
Bergman, Henry: Charlie Chaplin Cavalcade; Charlie Chaplin Festival; Charlie Chaplin—The Early Years Vol. 1–4; Circus, The/A Day's Pleasure; Woman of Paris, A
Bergman, Ingrid: Adam Had Four Sons; Anastasia; Arch of Triumph; Autumn Sonata; Bells of St. Mary's, The; Cactus Flower; Casablanca; Dr. Jekyll and Mr. Hyde; Dollar; Elena and Her Men; Fear; For Whom the Bell Tolls; Gaslight; Goodbye Again; Hideaways, The; Indiscreet; Inn of the Sixth Happiness, The; Intermezzo; Joan of Arc; June Night; Matter of Time, A; Murder on the Orient Express; Notorious; Only One Night; Spellbound; Stromboli; Under Capricorn; Voyage in Italy; Walk in the Spring Rain, A; Walpurgis Night; Woman Called Golda, A
Bergman, Jaime: Daybreak (2000)
Bergman, Peter: Phantom of the Ritz
Bergman, Sandahl: Body of Influence; Conan the Barbarian; Getting Physical; Hell Comes to Frogtown; Inner Sanctum 2; Kandyland; Lipstick Camera; Possessed by the Night; Programmed to Kill; Raw Nerve; Red Sonja; She; Xanadu
Bergmann, Erik: Ferngully 2: The Magical Rescue
Bergner, Elisabeth: As You Like It; Catherine the Great; Cry of the Banshee
Bergryd, Ulla: Bible, The
Bergstrom, Helena: House of Angels; Women on the Roof, The
Bergstrom, Linda: Children of Noisy Village, The
Berkeley, Elizabeth: First Wives Club, The; Real Blonde, The; Showgirls
Berkeley, Keith: Visitors, The
Berkeley, Xander: Air Force One; Candyman; Dead to Rights; If These Walls Could Talk; Persons Unknown; Poison Ivy 2: Lily; Roswell; Safe; Winchell; Within the Rock
Berkley, Elizabeth: Curse of the Jade Scorpion, The; Tail Lights Fade; White Wolves II: Legend of the Wild
Berkoff, Steven: Another 9 1/2 Weeks; Attila; Barry Lyndon; Fair Game; Legionnaire; Rambo: First Blood II; Season of Giants, A; Transmutations; Under the Cherry Moon
Berkowitz, Myles: 20 Dates
Berland, Terri: Pink Motel; Strangeness, The
Berle, Milton: Broadway Danny Rose; Cracking Up; Evil Roy Slade; It's a Mad Mad Mad Mad World; Legend of Valentino; Lepke; Loved One, The; Muppet Movie, The; Storybook; Sun Valley Serenade; Who's Minding the Mint?
Berleand, Francois: Romance
Berlin, Irving: This Is the Army
Berlin, Jeannie: Baby Maker, The; Heartbreak Kid, The; Housewife; In the Spirit; Portnoy's Complaint
Berlin Comic Opera Ballet: Cinderella
Berling, Charles: Dry Cleaning; Ridicule
Berlingame, Tiffany: Miami Hot Talk
Berlinger, Warren: Billie; Four Deuces, The; Free Ride; I Will, I Will … for Now; Lepke; Long Goodbye, The; Magician of Lublin, The; Outlaw Force; Wackiest Ship in the Army, The
Berman, Shelley: Best Man, The; Son of Blob (Beware! The Blob); Teen Witch; Young at Heart Comedians, The
Berman, Susan: Smithereens
Bern, Thomas: Dreamaniac
Bernal, Gael Garcia: Amores Perros
Bernard, Crystal: As Good as Dead; Face to Kill For, A; Siringo; Slumber Party Massacre II
Bernard, Jason: Liar, Liar; Wilma
Bernard, Maurice: Lucy and Desi: Before the Laughter
Bernard, Paul: Pattes Blanches (White Paws)
Bernard, Thelonious: Little Romance, A
Bernardi, Herschel: Irma La Douce; Love with the Proper Stranger; No Deposit, No Return; Peter Gunn (TV Series); Story of Jacob and Joseph, The
Bernardo, Michael: Shootfighter 2: Kill or Be Killed
Bernhard, Joachim: Last Five Days, The
Bernhard, Sandra: Anything for Love; Apocalypse, The; Hudson Hawk; Inside Monkey Zetterland; King of Comedy, The; Sesame Street Presents Follow That Bird; Somewhere in the City; Track 29; Truth or Dare; Unzipped; Without You I'm Nothing
Bernhardt, Daniel: Bloodsport II; Bloodsport III; Bloodsport IV: The Dark Kumite
Bernhardt, Kevin: Beauty School; Hellraiser 3: Hell on Earth; Kick or Die; Treacherous
Bernhardt, Sarah: Queen Elizabeth
Bernsen, Collin: Puppet Master II
Bernsen, Corbin: Baja; Bert Rigby, You're a Fool; Bloodhounds; Bloodhounds II; Breaking Point; Brilliant Disguise, A; Cover Me; Dead on the Money; Dentist, The; Dentist 2, The: Brace Yourself; Disorganized Crime; Final Mission; Frozen Assets; Ghost Brigade; Hello Again; Inhumanoid; Kounterfeit; L.A. Law; Major League; Major League II; Major League: Back to the Minors; Rangers; Ring of the Musketeer; Savage Land; Shattered; Soft Kill, The; Someone to Die For; Tails You Live, Heads You're Dead; Tales from the Hood; Temptress; Tidal Wave: No Escape; Trigger Fast
Bernstein, Caron: Business for Pleasure
Bernstein, Sheryl: Gross Jokes
Beron, David: Honor Thy Father & Mother: The Menendez Killings
Berova, Olinka: Vengeance of She, The
Berri, Claude: Le Sex Shop; Seven Deadly Sins, The
Berridge, Elizabeth: Amadeus; Funhouse, The; Montana; Silence of the Heart; Smooth Talk; When the Party's Over

Berry, Amanda: Palm Beach
Berry, Bill: High Country, The
Berry, Chuck: American Hot Wax; Chuck Berry Hail! Hail! Rock 'n' Roll; Go, Johnny, Go!; Rock, Rock, Rock; That Was Rock
Berry, Halle: B.A.P.S; Boomerang; Bulworth; Executive Decision; Father Hood; Flintstones, The; Introducing Dorothy Dandridge; Losing Isaiah; Monster's Ball; Program, The; Race the Sun; Rich Man's Wife, The; Solomon and Sheba; Strictly Business; Swordfish; Why Do Fools Fall in Love; X-Men
Berry, John: Man in Love, A; Window Shopping
Berry, Jules: Crime of Monsieur Lange, The; Le Jour Se Leve (Daybreak (1939)); Les Visiteurs Du Soir
Berry, Ken: Cat from Outer Space, The; Herbie Rides Again
Berry, Raymond J.: Sudden Death
Berry, Richard: Caged Heart, The (L'Addition); Day of Atonement; Honeymoon; La Balance; Man and a Woman, A: 20 Years Later
Berry, Vincent: Amnesia; Free Willy 3: The Rescue; Fury Within, The
Berryman, Dorothee: Decline of the American Empire, The; Paper Wedding
Berryman, Michael: Auntie Lee's Meat Pies; Barbarians, The; Cut and Run; Guyver, The; Hills Have Eyes, The: Part Two; Teenage Exorcist; Wizards of the Demon Sword
Berteloot, Jean-Yves: Deep Trouble
Berthelsen, Anders W.: Italian for Beginners; Mifune
Berti, Aldo: Big Rip-off, The
Bertin, Roland: Hairdresser's Husband, The; L'Homme Blessé (The Wounded Man)
Bertinelli, Valerie: C.H.O.M.P.S.; Number One with a Bullet; Ordinary Heroes; Pancho Barnes; Shattered Vows; Taken Away; Young Love, First Love
Bertish, Suzanne: Venice/Venice
Berto, Juliet: Celine and Julie Go Boating; Le Gai Savoir (The Joy of Knowledge); Le Sex Shop; Mr. Klein
Bertorelli, Toni: Who Killed Pasolini?
Bertrand, Janette: Big Red
Bervoets, Gene: Vanishing, The
Berz, Michael: Hot Resort
Besch, Bibi: Beast Within, The; Betrayal; Kill Me Again; Lonely Lady, The; Medicine Hat Stallion, The; Rattled
Besnehard, Dominique: A Nos Amours
Besse, Ariel: Beau Pere
Bessell, Ted: Billie; Breaking Up Is Hard to Do; Don't Drink the Water
Besser, Joe: Abbott and Costello Show, The (TV Series); Hey Abbott!
Best, Alyson: Dark Forces; Man of Flowers
Best, Edna: Ghost and Mrs. Muir, The; Man Who Knew Too Much, The
Best, James: Comanche Territory; Firecreek; Grey Matter; Killer Shrews, The; Left Handed Gun, The; Ma and Pa Kettle at the Fair; Ride Lonesome; Rolling Thunder; Savages; Sounder
Best, Kevin: South Central
Best, Willie: Face of Marble, The; Littlest Rebel, The; Monster Walks, The; Mr. Moto Takes a Vacation; Smiling Ghost, The; Vivacious Lady
Beswick, Martine: Bullet for the General, A; Cyclone; Dr. Jekyll and Sister Hyde; Happy Hooker Goes Hollywood, The; Prehistoric Women; Seizure; Strange New World
Bethune, Zina: Who's That Knocking at My Door?
Betsworth, Gary: Cutting Moments
Bett, John: Gregory's Girl; Tess
Bettany, Paul: Beautiful Mind, A; Mood Swingers
Bettger, Lyle: All I Desire; Gundown at Sandoval; Johnny Reno; Lone Ranger, The; Sea Chase, The; Union Station
Betti, Laura: Canterbury Tales, The; Lovers and Liars; Twitch of the Death Nerve
Bettina: Journey to Spirit Island
Bettis, Angela: Bless the Child
Bettis, Paul: Urinal
Bettles, Robert: Fourth Wish, The
Bettoia, Franca: Last Man on Earth, The
Betz, Carl: Deadly Encounter; Spinout
Bevan, Billy: Cavalcade; High Voltage; Li'l Abner; Lost Patrol, The; Terror by Night
Bevans, Clem: Of Human Hearts; Young Tom Edison
Bevis, Leslie: November Men, The
Bey, Turhan: Ali Baba and the Forty Thieves; Amazing Mr. X; Arabian Nights; Background to Danger; Climax, The; Dragon Seed; Mad Ghoul, The; Mummy's Tomb, The; Out of the Blue; Sudan
Beyer, Brad: Monday Night Mayhem
Beyer, Troy: Rooftops; Weekend at Bernie's II
Beymer, Richard: Blackbelt; Cross Country; Elvis Meets Nixon; Indiscretion of an American Wife; Johnny Tremain; Little Death, The; Presence, The; Silent Night, Deadly Night III: BetterWatch Out!; State of Emergency; Stripper, The; Twin Peaks (Movie); Twin Peaks (TV Series); Under Investigation; West Side Story
Bezace, Didier: Little Thief, The
Bezer, Amber: Appointment with Death
Bhaskar: Dragon Chow; I Drink Your Blood
Bhat, Rishi: Indian in the Cupboard, The
Biagli, Claudio: Mediterraneo
Bianca, Raquel: Abducted II
Bianchi, Daniela: From Russia with Love
Biao, Yuen: Eastern Condors; Millionaire's Express (Shanghai Express); Mr. Vampire (Vol. 1–4); Once Upon a Time in China; Zu: Warriors from the Magic Mountain
Bibb, Leslie: See Spot Run; Skulls, The
Bibby, Charles K.: Order of the Black Eagle
Biberman, Abner: Betrayal from the East; Panama Lady
Bickford, Charles: Anna Christie; Babe Ruth Story, The; Big Country, The; Big Hand for the Little Lady, A; Branded; Brute Force; Command Decision; Court-martial of Billy Mitchell, The; Days of Wine and Roses (1962); East of Borneo; Farmer's Daughter, The; Four Faces West; Jim Thorpe—All American; Johnny Belinda; Little Miss Marker; Not as a Stranger; Plainsman, The; Reap the Wild Wind; Riders of Death Valley; Riding High; Song of Bernadette, The; Star Is Born, A; Tarzan's New York Adventure; Thunder Trail; Unforgiven, The (1960); Wing and a Prayer, A
Bickley, Tony: Swimmer, The
Bicknell, Andrew: Buffalo Girls; Moving Finger, The
Bicknell, Gene: Gypsy Angels
Bideau, Jean-Luc: Jonah Who Will Be 25 in the Year 2000; Revenge of the Musketeers
Bidenko, Kris: Two Friends
Bidonde, Hector: Funny Dirty Little War (No Habra Mas Penas ni Olvido)
Biehn, Michael: Abyss, The; Aliens; Art of War, The; Blood of the Hunter; Breach of Trust; Chain of Command; Cherry Falls; Clockstoppers; Conundrum; Dead Men Can't Dance; Deadfall; Deep Red; Dying to Get Rich; Fan, The; Frame by Frame; In a Shallow Grave; Jade; K2; Magnificent Seven, The (TV Series); Mojave Moon; Navy Seals; Rampage; Seventh Sign, The; Strapped; Taste for Killing, A; Terminator, The; Time Bomb; Tombstone
Biel, Jessica: I'll Be Home for Christmas; Summer Catch
Bierbichler, Josef: Heart of Glass; Winter Sleepers
Bieri, Ramon: Badlands (1973); Christmas without Snow, A; Frisco Kid, The; Grandview, U.S.A.; It's Good to Be Alive; Sicilian, The; Sorcerer
Bierko, Craig: Long Kiss Goodnight, The; Suburbans, The; Thirteenth Floor, The; 'Til There Was You; Victimless Crimes
Big Pun: Urban Menace
Bigagli, Claudio: Wild Flower (1993) (Fiorile)
Biggs, Jason: American Pie; American Pie 2; Boys and Girls; Loser; Saving Silverman
Biggs, Roxann: Broken Angel; Darkman III: Die, Darkman, Die; Mortal Sins (1992)
Bignamini, Nino: All Screwed Up
Bihan, Samuel Le: Venus Beauty Institute
Bikel, Theodore: African Queen, The; Assassination Game, The; Colditz Story, The; Dark Tower; Defiant Ones, The; Dog of Flanders, A; Enemy Below, The; Final Days, The; Flight from Vienna; I Bury the Living; I Want to Live!; Murder on Flight 502;

My Side of the Mountain; Never Let Me Go; Pride and the Passion, The; Russians Are Coming, the Russians Are Coming, The; Shattered; 200 Motels; Victory at Entebbe
Bilderback, Nicole: Bring It On
Bill, Tony: Are You in the House Alone?; Come Blow Your Horn; Haunts of the Very Rich; Ice Station Zebra; Initiation of Sarah, The; Killing Mind, The; Less Than Zero; None But the Brave; Soldier in the Rain; You're a Big Boy Now
Billerey, Raoul: Revenge of the Musketeers
Billings, Dawn Ann: Human Desires
Billingsley, Barbara: Eye of the Demon
Billingsley, Jennifer: C.C. & Company; Thirsty Dead, The; White Lightning
Billingsley, Peter: Arcade; Beverly Hills Brats; Christmas Story, A; Dirt Bike Kid, The; Russkies
Billington, Francis: Blind Husbands
Billington, Michael: Invasion UFO
Binder, Mike: Contender, The; Sex Monster, The
Bindon, John: Man in the Wilderness
Bing, Herman: Bitter Sweet (1940); Bluebeard's Eighth Wife; Guardsman, The
Binkley, Lane: Bernice Bobs Her Hair; Soldier's Home
Binns, Edward: Hunter (1971); Oliver's Story; Pilot, The; 12 Angry Men
Binoche, Juliette: Alice & Martin; Blue; Chocolat; Couch in New York, A; Damage; Emily Bronte's Wuthering Heights; English Patient, The; Horseman on the Roof, The; Lovers on the Bridge; Rendez-Vous; Unbearable Lightness of Being, The; Widow of St. Pierre, The; Women & Men 2
Biosvert, Simon: Venus de Milo
Birch, Paul: Apache Woman; Queen of Outer Space
Birch, Thora: Alaska; All I Want for Christmas; American Beauty; Dungeons & Dragons; Ghost World; Hocus Pocus; Monkey Trouble; Night Ride Home; Now and Then; Paradise; Smokers, The
Birchall, Jeremy: Heaven
Bird, Billie: End of Innocence, The; Ernest Saves Christmas; Sixteen Candles
Bird, John: 30 Is a Dangerous Age, Cynthia
Bird, Laurie: Two-Lane Blacktop
Bird, Norman: Whistle Down the Wind
Birdsall, Jesse: Getting It Right; Wish You Were Here
Birdsong, Lori: Blood Salvage
Birell, Tala: Purple Heart, The; White Legion
Birkin, Jane: Beethoven's Nephew; Catherine & Co.; Daddy Nostalgia; Dark Places; Dust; Evil Under the Sun; La Belle Noiseuse; Last September, The; Le Petit Amour; Make Room for Tomorrow; Swimming Pool, The; Wonderwall
Birkin, Ned: Cement Garden, The
Birman, Len: Captain America; Captain America II: Death Too Soon; Lies My Father Told Me; Man Inside, The; Undergrads, The
Birman, Matt: Back in Action
Birney, David: Caravan to Vaccares; King Richard II; Night of the Fox; Nightfall; Oh, God! Book II; Only with Married Men; Pretty Kill; Ray Bradbury's Chronicles: The MartianEpisodes; St. Elsewhere (TV Series); Touch and Die
Birney, Reed: Greatest Man in the World, The
Birt, Christopher: Reason to Believe, A
Birve, Ullie: Alien Visitor
Bisco, Joy: Debut, The
Bishop, Debby: Blue Money
Bishop, Ed: Invasion UFO
Bishop, Jennifer: Jaws of Death, The
Bishop, Joey: Betsy's Wedding; Deep Six, The; Delta Force, The; Guide for the Married Man, A; Naked and the Dead, The; Onionhead; Texas Across the River; Who's Minding the Mint?
Bishop, Julie: Action in the North Atlantic; Hard Way, The; High and the Mighty, The; Last of the Redmen; Northern Pursuit; Threat, The; Westward the Women; Young Bill Hickok
Bishop, Kevin: Muppet Treasure Island
Bishop, Kirsten: Shades of Love: Champagne for Two
Bishop, Pat: Don's Party
Bishop, William: Redhead from Wyoming, The; Texas Rangers, The (1951)
Bishopric, Thor: Breaking All the Rules
Bisio, Claudio: Mediterraneo
Bisley, Steve: Chain Reaction; Fast Talking; Summer City
Bissell, Whit: Atomic Kid, The; Boots Malone; Brute Force; Creature from the Black Lagoon; He Walked by Night; I Was a Teenage Frankenstein; I Was a Teenage Werewolf; Lost Continent, The; Shack-Out on 101; Spencer's Mountain
Bisset, Jacqueline: Airport; Anna Karenina; Bullitt; Class; Crimebroker; Cul-de-Sac; Dangerous Beauty; Day for Night; Deep, The; Detective, The; End of Summer; Forbidden; Grasshopper, The; Greek Tycoon, The; High Season; Joan of Arc (1999); La Cérémonie; Le Magnifique; Life and Times of Judge Roy Bean, The; Maid, The; Mephisto Waltz, The; Murder on the Orient Express; Napoleon and Josephine: A Love Story; Rich and Famous; St. Ives; Scenes from the Class Struggle in Beverly Hills; Secrets; Spiral Staircase, The; Thief Who Came to Dinner, The; Two for the Road; Under the Volcano; When Time Ran Out!; Who Is Killing the Great Chefs of Europe?; Wild Orchid
Bissett, Josie: All-American Murder; Baby Monitor: Sound of Fear; Mikey
Bisson, Yannick: Toby McTeague
Bissonnette, Joel: Picture Windows
Biswas, Chhabi: Devi (The Goddess)
Biswas, Seema: Bandit Queen
Bitorajac, Rene: No Man's Land (2001)
Bixby, Bill: Apple Dumpling Gang, The; Clambake; Death of the Incredible Hulk, The; Fantasy Island; Incredible Hulk, The; Incredible Hulk Returns, The; Kentucky Fried Movie; Ride Beyond Vengeance; Speedway; Trial of the Incredible Hulk
Bixler, Denise: Assassination Game, The
Bizot, Philippe: Marquis
Bjelogrlic, Dragan: Wounds, The
Bjork, Anita: Miss Julie; Secrets of Women (Waiting Women)
Björk: Dancer in the Dark
Bjornsson, Helgi: Remote Control
Björnstrand, Gunnar: Devil's Eye, The; Dreams; Lesson in Love, A; Magician, The; Persona; Secrets of Women (Waiting Women); Seventh Seal, The; Smiles of a Summer Night; Through a Glass Darkly; Wild Strawberries; Winter Light
Black, Claudia: Farscape (TV series); Pitch Black
Black, Jack: Bongwater; High Fidelity; Jesus' Son; Neverending Story III, The: Escape toFantasia; Orange County; Saving Silverman; Shallow Hal
Black, James: Man with the Perfect Swing, The; Maximum Impact; Ozone
Black, Jennifer: Gospel According to Vic, The
Black, Karen: Airport 1975; Auntie Lee's Meat Pies; Bad Manners; Born to Win; Bound and Gagged: A Love Story; Burnt Offerings; Caged Fear; Can She Bake a Cherry Pie?; Capricorn One; Chanel Solitaire; Children of the Corn IV: The Gathering; Children of the Night; Cisco Pike; Club Fed; Come Back to the Five and Dime, Jimmy Dean, Jimmy Dean; Conceiving Ada; Cries of Silence; Crime & Passion; Crimetime; Cut and Run; Day of the Locust, The; Dinosaur Valley Girls; Dixie Lanes; Double-O Kid, The; Easy Rider; Eternal Evil; Evil Spirits; Family Plot; Final Judgment; Five Easy Pieces; Great Gatsby, The; Gunfight, A; Hitchhiker, The (Series); Homer and Eddie; Hostage; In Praise of Older Women; Invaders from Mars; Invisible Dad; Invisible Kid, The; It's Alive III: Island of the Alive; Killer Fish; Killing Heat; Last Word, The; Martin's Day; Men; Mirror Mirror; Miss Right; Mr. Horn; Nashville; Night Angel; Out of the Dark; Overexposed; Plan 10 from Outer Space; Portnoy's Complaint; Pyx, The; Quiet Fire; Rubin & Ed; Savage Dawn; Soulkeeper; Tons of Trouble; Trilogy of Terror; You're a Big Boy Now
Black, Larry: Web of Deceit
Black, Lucas: All the Pretty Horses; Crazy in Alabama; Flash (1998); Our Friend, Martin; Sling Blade
Black, Michael Ian: Wet Hot American Summer
Black, Pauline: Funnyman
Black, Ryan: Dance Me Outside
Blackburn, Diana: French Lessons

Blackman, Honor: Cat and the Canary, The; Conspirator; Goldfinger; Jason and the Argonauts; Night to Remember, A; Shalako; To the Devil, a Daughter; Virgin and the Gypsy, The
Blackman, Jeremy: Magnolia
Blackman, Joan: Blue Hawaii; Career; Daring Game; Kid Galahad
Blackmer, Sidney: Beyond a Reasonable Doubt (1956); Charlie Chan at Monte Carlo; Cheers for Miss Bishop; Count of Monte Cristo, The; Deluge (1993); High and the Mighty, The; How to Murder Your Wife; In Old Chicago; Law of the Pampas; Little Colonel, The; Love Crazy; People Will Talk; Tammy and the Bachelor; This Is My Affair; Thriller (TV Series); War of the Wildcats
Blackwell, Carlyle: She
Blackwell, Paul: Quiet Room, The
Blackwood, Nina: Number One Fan
Blacque, Taurean: Deepstar Six; Hill Street Blues (TV Series)
Blade, Richard: Spellcaster
Blades, Rubén: All the Pretty Horses; Chinese Box; Color of Night; Cradle Will Rock; Crazy from the Heart; Critical Condition; Crossover Dreams; Dead Man Out; Devil's Own, The; Disorganized Crime; Fatal Beauty; Josephine Baker Story, The; Lemon Sisters, The; Milagro Beanfield War, The; Million to Juan, A; Mo' Better Blues; One Man's War; Predator 2; Scorpion Spring; Super, The; Two Jakes, The
Blain, Gerard: American Friend, The; Le Beau Serge; Les Cousins
Blaine, Vivian: Cracker Factory; Dark, The; Doll Face; Guys and Dolls; Parasite; Skirts Ahoy!; State Fair
Blair, Betsy: Betrayed; Il Grido (Outcry, The); Marty (1955); Snake Pit, The; Suspicion
Blair, Bre: Baby-Sitters Club, The
Blair, David: Wax
Blair, Isla: Taste the Blood of Dracula
Blair, Janet: Black Arrow, The (1948); Boys' Night Out; Burn, Witch, Burn; Fabulous Dorseys, The; Fuller Brush Man, The; Tonight and Every Night
Blair, Kevin: Bloodlust: Subspecies III
Blair, Linda: Bad Blood; Bail Out; Bedroom Eyes II; Born Innocent; Chained Heat; Chilling, The; Dead Sleep; Double Blast; Exorcist, The; Exorcist II: The Heretic; Fatal Bond; Grotesque; Hell Night; Moving Target; Night Patrol; Nightforce; Red Heat; Repossessed; Ruckus; Savage Streets; Silent Assassins; Sorceress; Summer of Fear; Sweet Hostage; Up Your Alley; Victory at Entebbe; Wild Horse Hank; Witchery; Woman Obsessed, A; Zapped Again
Blair, Patricia: Rifleman, The (TV Series)
Blair, Selma: Brown's Requiem; Cruel Intentions; Down to You; Highway; Kill Me Later; Legally Blonde; No Laughing Matter; Storytelling; Sweetest Thing, The
Blair, Tom: Sure Fire
Blair, Venessa: L.I.P. Service (1999)
Blaisdell, Deborah: Wimps
Blaise, Jean: Wanderer, The
Blake, Amanda: Glass Slipper, The; Gunsmoke (TV Series); Gunsmoke: Return to Dodge; Stars in My Crown
Blake, Andre: Who's the Man?
Blake, Bobby: Last Round-Up; Stagecoach to Denver; Vigilantes of Boomtown
Blake, Geoffrey: Fatal Exposure; Getting Personal; Heaven or Vegas; Marilyn & Bobby: Her Final Affair
Blake, Jeremy: McVicar
Blake, Jon: Lighthorsemen, The
Blake, Julia: Father; Georgia; Innocence; Lonely Hearts; Travelling North
Blake, Julie: Clive Barker's Salome and The Forbidden
Blake, Noah: Base, The
Blake, Pamela: Hatbox Mystery, The; Sea Hound, The; Wyoming Outlaw
Blake, Peter: Murder on Line One
Blake, Rachael: Lantana
Blake, Robert: Coast to Coast; Electra Glide in Blue; Heart of a Champion: The Ray Mancini Story; In Cold Blood; Lost Highway; Marshal of Cripple Creek; Money Train; Of Mice and Men; Out California Way; Phantom of the Plains; PT 109; San Antonio Kid; Santa Fe Uprising; Sheriff of Las Vegas; Tell Them Willie Boy Is Here; This Property Is Condemned; Wagon Wheels Westward
Blake, Stephen: Mad at the Moon
Blake, Teresa: Payback
Blake, Valerie: Blastfighter
Blake, Whitney: Hazel Christmas Show, The (TV Series)
Blakely, Colin: Dogs of War, The; Equus; Evil Under the Sun; Little Lord Fauntleroy; Loophole; Pink Panther Strikes Again, The; Private Life of Sherlock Holmes, The; Shattered; This Sporting Life
Blakely, Donald: Strike Force
Blakely, Susan: Airport '79: The Concorde; Blackmail; Broken Angel; Bunker, The; Cry for Love, A; Dead Reckoning; Dreamer; Incident, The; Intruders; Lady Killers; Lords of Flatbush, The; Make Me an Offer; My Mom's a Werewolf; Out of Sight Out of Mind; Over the Top; Report to the Commissioner; Survivalist, The; Wild Flower (1991)
Blakemore, Michael: Country Life
Blakiston, Caroline: At Bertram's Hotel
Blakley, Ronee: Baltimore Bullet, The; Desperate Women; Driver, The; Murder by Numbers (1989); Nashville; Nightmare on Elm Street, A; Private Files of J. Edgar Hoover, The; Student Confidential
Blanc, Dominique: Total Eclipse
Blanc, Erica: Django Shoots First; Longest Hunt, The; Mark of the Devil, Part 2
Blanc, Manuel: Beaumarchais the Scoundrel
Blanc, Mel: Gay Purr-ee; Jack Benny Program, The (TV Series); Neptune's Daughter
Blanc, Michel: Dead Tired (Grosse Fatigue); Favor, the Watch and the Very Big Fish,The; Ménage; Merci La Vie; Monsieur Hire; Monster, The; Prospero's Books; Ready to Wear; Uranus
Blanchar, Pierre: Crime and Punishment; Man from Nowhere, The
Blanchard, Alan: Slithis
Blanchard, Felix "Doc": Spirit of West Point, The
Blanchard, Francoise: Living Dead Girl
Blanchard, Mari: Abbott and Costello Go to Mars; Twice-Told Tales
Blanchard, Rachel: Road Trip
Blanchett, Cate: Bandits (2001); Charlotte Gray; Elizabeth; Gift, The; Ideal Husband, An; Lord of the Rings, The: Fellowship of the Ring; Man Who Cried, The; Oscar & Lucinda; Paradise Road; Pushing Tin; Shipping News, The; Talented Mr. Ripley, The
Blanco, Roberto: Hell Hounds of Alaska
Blanco, Uxia: Butterfly
Bland, Peter: Came a Hot Friday
Blandick, Clara: Can't Help Singing; Drums of Jeopardy; Girl from Missouri, The; Wizard of Oz, The
Blane, Sally: Silver Streak; Vagabond Lover, The
Blankfield, Mark: Dracula: Dead and Loving It; Frankenstein General Hospital; Incredible Shrinking Woman, The; Jekyll & Hyde—Together Again; Robin Hood: Men in Tights
Blanks, Billy: Back in Action; Balance of Power; Expect No Mercy; Talons of the Eagle; Tough and Deadly
Blatchford, Ed: Birthday Boy, The
Blavette, Charles: Toni
Blaze, Tommy: Rumpelstiltskin
Bleachman, Jonah: Fall Time
Blech, Hans-Christian: Scarlet Letter (1973)
Bledsoe, Tempestt: Dance 'Til Dawn; Dream Date
Bledsoe, Will: Dark Side of the Moon, The
Blee, Debra: Beach Girls, The; Malibu Bikini Shop, The
Bleek, Memphis: State Property
Bleeth, Yasmine: Babe; Baseketball; Baywatch: The Movie; Heaven or Vegas; It Came from the Sky; Ultimate Deception; Undercover Angel
Bleibtreu, Moritz: Run Lola Run
Bleont, Claudiu: Unforgettable Summer, An
Blessed, Brian: Hamlet; High Road to China; Hound of the Baskervilles, The; I, Claudius; King Arthur, The Young Warlord;

Much Ado About Nothing; Prisoner of Honor; Return to Treasure Island; Robin Hood: Prince of Thieves; Story of David, The
Blessing, Jack: Game of Love, The; Last of His Tribe, The
Blethyn, Brenda: Buddha of Suburbia, The; Little Voice; Music from Another Room; River Runs Through It, A; RKO 281; Saving Grace; Secrets and Lies
Blier, Bernard: Buffet Froid (Cold Cuts); By the Blood of Others; Daydreamer, The (1970) (Le Distrait); Dedee D'Anvers; Jenny Lamour; L'Ecole Buissonniere; Les Misérables; Organizer, The; Passion for Life; Passion of Love; Tall Blond Man with One Black Shoe, The
Bloch, Debora: Bossa Nova
Block, Larry: Dead Man Out
Blocker, Dan: Bonanza (TV Series); Come Blow Your Horn; Lady in Cement
Blocker, Dirk: Night of the Scarecrow
Blodgett, Michael: Velvet Vampire, The
Blom, Dan: Mind Ripper
Blondell, Gloria: Twonky, The
Blondell, Joan: Adventure; Battered; Big Business Girl; Blonde Crazy; Bullets or Ballots; Dames; Dead Don't Die, The; Death at Love House; Desk Set; Footlight Parade; Gold Diggers of 1933; Illicit; Lady for a Night; Night Nurse; Opening Night; Opposite Sex, The (1956); Rebels, The; Ride Beyond Vengeance; Stage Struck; Stand-In; Stay Away Joe; Support Your Local Gunfighter; This Could Be the Night; Three Broadway Girls; Three Men on a Horse; Three on a Match; Topper Returns; Tree Grows in Brooklyn, A; Waterhole #3; Will Success Spoil Rock Hunter?
Blondell, Simone: Savage Guns
Bloom, Anne: Dirt Bike Kid, The
Bloom, Brian: Blood Money (1999); Confessions of a Sorority Girl; Escape from Atlantis; Knocking on Death's Door; Vampirella; Webber's World (At Home with the Webbers)
Bloom, Claire: Alexander the Great; Brainwashed; Brideshead Revisited; Brothers Karamazov, The; Buccaneer, The; Charly; Daylight; Déjà Vu; Doll's House, A; Haunting, The; Illustrated Man, The; Intimate Contact; Islands in the Stream; Limelight; Look Back in Anger; Mighty Aphrodite; Mirror Crack'd from Side to Side, The; Queenie; Richard III; Sammy and Rosie Get Laid; Separate Tables; Shameless; Spy Who Came in from the Cold, The; Wonderful World of the Brothers Grimm, The
Bloom, John: Brain of Blood; Casino
Bloom, Michael Allan: Screen Test
Bloom, Orlando: Lord of the Rings, The: Fellowship of the Ring
Bloom, Verna: After Hours; Badge 373; Blue Knight, The; High Plains Drifter; Hired Hand, The; Last Temptation of Christ, The; Medium Cool
Bloomfield, Don: Lost Angels
Bloomfield, George: And Then You Die
Blore, Eric: Ex-Mrs. Bradford, The; Gay Divorcée, The; I Dream Too Much; Lady Scarface; Moon and Sixpence, The; Quality Street; Road to Zanzibar; Romance on the High Seas; Shall We Dance?; Shanghai Gesture, The; Sky's the Limit, The; Sullivan's Travels; Swiss Miss; Top Hat
Blossom, Roberts: American Clock, The; Christine; Citizen's Band; Deranged; Escape from Alcatraz; Home Alone; Resurrection; Reuben, Reuben
Blount, Lisa: Blind Fury; Box of Moonlight; Cease Fire; Cut and Run; Judicial Consent; Nightflyers; Prince of Darkness; Radioactive Dreams; South of Reno; Stalked; Swap, The (Sam's Song); 30-Sep-55; What Waits Below
Blow, Kurtis: Krush Groove
Blue, Ben: Big Broadcast of 1938, The; Broadway Rhythm; College Swing; Two Girls and a Sailor; Two Sisters from Boston; Where Were You When the Lights Went Out?
Blue, Callum: In Love and War (2001)
Blue, Edgar Washington: Beggars of Life
Blue, Monte: Apache; Hawk of the Wilderness; Hell Town; Intolerance; Lives of a Bengal Lancer, The; Marriage Circle, The; Orphans of the Storm; Ride, Ranger, Ride; Riders of Death Valley; Road to Morocco; Undersea Kingdom; Wagon Wheels; White Shadows in the South Seas
Bluestone, Abby: Night of the Juggler
Bluhm, Brady: Alone in the Woods; Crazysitter, The
Blum, Mark: Blind Date; "Crocodile" Dundee; Defenders, The; Desperately Seeking Susan; Just Between Friends; Presidio, The; Worth Winning
Blum, Steven: Bram Stoker's Shadowbuilder
Blumenfeld, Alan: Dark Side of the Moon, The; Instant Karma; Night Life
Blundell, John: Scum
Bluteau, Lothaire: Bent; Black Robe; Jesus of Montreal; Shot Through the Heart; Silent Touch, The; Urbania
Bluthal, John: Leapin' Leprechauns; Spellbreaker: Secret of the Leprechauns
Blyden, Larry: On a Clear Day, You Can See Forever
Blye, Margaret: Ash Wednesday; Final Chapter—Walking Tall; Melvin Purvis: G-Man; Sporting Club, The; Waterhole #3
Blystone, Stanley: Ivory-Handled Gun, The
Blyth, Ann: All the Brothers Were Valiant; Great Caruso, The; Helen Morgan Story, The; Kismet; Mildred Pierce; Mr. Peabody and the Mermaid; One Minute to Zero; Rose Marie; Student Prince, The
Blythe, Benedick: Little Riders, The
Blythe, Betty: Gangster's Boy; Nomads of the North; She
Blythe, Catherine: Hawk's Vengeance
Blythe, John: Alfred Hitchcock's Bon Voyage and Aventure Malgache
Blythe, Robert: Experience Preferred ... But Not Essential
Boa, Bruce: Murder Story
Boardman, Eleanor: Crowd, The; She Goes to War
Boatman, Michael Patrick: China Beach (TV Series); Fourth Story; Glass Shield, The; Hamburger Hill; Urban Crossfire
Bob Wills and the Texas Playboys: Take Me Back to Oklahoma
Bobochkin, Boris: Chapayev
Bobulova, Barbora: In Love and War (2001)
Boccardo, Delia: Assisi Underground, The
Bocher, Christian: Total Exposure
Bochner, Hart: Apartment Zero; Break Up; Die Hard; Fellow Traveler; Having It All; Islands in the Stream; Mad at the Moon; Making Mr. Right; Mr. Destiny; Rich and Famous; Supergirl; Terror Train; Urban Legends: Final Cut; War and Remembrance
Bochner, Lloyd: Good Idea; Horse in the Gray Flannel Suit, The; Landslide; Lonely Lady, The; Man in the Glass Booth; Mary and Joseph: A Story of Faith; Mazes and Monsters; Morning Glory; Night Walker, The; Point Blank; Ulzana's Raid
Bodison, Wolfgang: Criminal Passion; Few Good Men, A; Freeway; Silver Strand
Bodner, Jenna: Huntress: Spirit of the Night
Bodrov Jr., Sergei: East-West; Prisoner of the Mountains
Boehm, Carl: Peeping Tom; Unnatural
Boen, Earl: Dentist, The; Within the Rock
Boensh, III, Paul: This Is Elvis
Bogarde, Dirk: Accident; Bridge Too Far, A; Daddy Nostalgia; Damn the Defiant!; Damned, The; Darling; Death in Venice; Despair; Doctor at Large; Doctor at Sea; Doctor in Distress; Doctor in the House; I Could Go On Singing; Ill Met by Moonlight; Justine; Night Ambush; Night Flight from Moscow; Night Porter, The; Permission to Kill; Providence; Quartet; Sea Shall Not Have Them, The; Servant, The; Simba; Sleeping Tiger, The; Song Without End; Tale of Two Cities, A; To See Such Fun; Victim; Woman in Question
Bogardus, Stephen: Love! Valour! Compassion!
Bogart, Humphrey: Across the Pacific; Action in the North Atlantic; African Queen, The; All Through the Night; Amazing Dr. Clitterhouse, The; Angels with Dirty Faces; Barefoot Contessa, The; Battle Circus; Beat the Devil; Big Sleep, The; Black Legion; Brother Orchid; Bullets or Ballots; Caine Mutiny, The; Casablanca; Chain Lightning; Conflict; Dark Passage; Dark Victory; Dead End; Dead Reckoning; Deadline USA; Desperate Hours, The (1955); Enforcer, The; Harder They Fall, The; High Sierra; In a Lonely Place; Key Largo; Kid Galahad; Knock on Any Door; Left Hand of God, The; Maltese Falcon, The; Marked Woman; Midnight; Oklahoma Kid, The; Passage to Marseilles; Petrified Forest, The; Return of Dr. X; Roaring Twenties, The; Sabrina; Sahara; Sirocco; Stand-In; Thank Your Lucky Stars; They Drive by Night; Three on a Match; To Have and Have Not;

Tokyo Joe; Treasure of the Sierra Madre; Two Mrs. Carrolls, The; Virginia City; Wagons Roll at Night, The; We're No Angels
Bogdanova, Elena: Adam's Rib
Bogdanovich, Peter: Independent, The; Saint Jack; Targets; Trip, The
Bogmaz, Dmitri: Forbidden Zone: Alien Abduction
Bogosian, Eric: Bright Shining Lie, A; Caine Mutiny Court Martial, The; Dolores Claiborne; Gossip; Sex, Drugs, Rock & Roll; Shot in the Heart; Special Effects; Talk Radio; Under Siege 2: Dark Territory; Witch Hunt
Bogush, Elizabeth: Eastside
Bohannon, Kelly: Idaho Transfer
Bohen, Ian: Frankenstein Sings; Young Hercules
Böhm, Karlheinz: Fox and His Friends; Wonderful World of the Brothers Grimm, The
Bohnen, Roman: Hard Way, The
Bohnet, Foiker: Bridge, The
Bohrer, Corinne: Dead Solid Perfect; Operation Intercept; Star Kid; Surf 2
Bohringer, Richard: Accompanist, The; Barjo; Bolero; Caged Heart, The (L'Addition); Cook, the Thief, His Wife & Her Lover, The; Le Grand Chemin (The Grand Highway); Peril; Subway
Bohringer, Romane: Accompanist, The; Chambermaid on the Titanic, The; Mina Tannenbaum; Savage Nights; Total Eclipse
Bois, Curt: Caught; Gypsy Wildcat; Tovaritch; Tuttles of Tahiti, The; Wings of Desire
Bois, Elaine: Legacy of Horror
Boisson, Christine: Sorceress, The (1988)
Boisvert, Simon: Stephanie, Nathalie, Caroline and Vincent
Bok, Sarel: Far Off Place, A
Bolam, James: End of the Affair, The
Boland, Mary: If I Had a Million; Julia Misbehaves; New Moon; Nothing But Trouble; Ruggles of Red Gap
Bolder, Cal: Jesse James Meets Frankenstein's Daughter
Boles, John: Craig's Wife; Curly Top; Frankenstein; King of Jazz, The; Last Warning, The; Littlest Rebel, The; Sinners in Paradise; Stella Dallas; Thousands Cheer
Bolger, John: Parting Glances
Bolger, Ray: April in Paris; Babes in Toyland; Daydreamer, The (1966); Four Jacks and a Jill; Harvey Girls, The; Just You and Me, Kid; Look for the Silver Lining; Rosalie; Sweethearts; Wizard of Oz, The
Bolkan, Florinda: Collector's Item; Day that Shook the World, The; Some Girls
Bolling, Tiffany: Bonnie's Kids; Centerfold Girls; Kingdom of the Spiders; Open House
Bologna, Joseph: Alligator II; Big Bus, The; Blame It on Rio; Chapter Two; Citizen Cohn; Cops and Robbers; Danger of Love; Deadly Rivals; Don's Analyst, The; Honor Thy Father; Jersey Girl; Love Is All There Is; My Favorite Year; Not Quite Human; One Cooks, the Other Doesn't; Rags to Riches; Revenge of the Nerds IV: Nerds in Love; Torn Between Two Lovers; Transylvania 6-5000; Woman in Red, The
Bolshoi Ballet: Anna Karenina
Bolt, David: Killing Man, The
Bom, Lars: Webmaster
Bon Jovi, Jon: Homegrown; Leading Man, The; Little City; Moonlight and Valentino; No Looking Back; Pay It Forward; U-571
Bonacelli, Paolo: Johnny Stecchino; Mille Bolle Blu; Salo: 120 Days of Sodom
Bonaduce, Danny: America's Deadliest Home Video; H.O.T.S.
Bonanaffé, Jacques: Va Savoir
Bonanno, Louie: Sex Appeal; Wimps
Bonanova, Fortunio: Ali Baba and the Forty Thieves; Fiesta; Romance on the High Seas
Bond, Derek: Nicholas Nickleby; Scott of the Antarctic; Stranger from Venus
Bond, Graham: Fast Lane Fever
Bond, Lilian: Old Dark House, The
Bond, Raymond: Man from Planet X, The
Bond, Rene: Fugitive Girls
Bond, Samantha: World Is Not Enough, The
Bond, Steve: Magdalene; Prey, The; To Die For; To Die For 2: Son of Darkness; Tryst
Bond, Sudie: Come Back to the Five and Dime, Jimmy Dean, Jimmy Dean; Greatest Man in the World, The; Silkwood; Swing Shift; Tomorrow; Where the Lilies Bloom
Bond, Tommy: Atom Man vs. Superman; Superman—The Serial
Bond, Ward: Blowing Wild; Bride Walks Out, The; Broadway Bill; Dakota; Devil Dogs of the Air; Dodge City; Drums Along the Mohawk; Falcon Takes Over, The; Fighting Code; Fighting Ranger, The; Fighting Shadows; Fighting Sullivans, The (Sullivans, The); Fort Apache; Fugitive, The; Gentleman Jim; Great Missouri Raid, The; Guy Named Joe, A; Gypsy Colt; Hello, Frisco, Hello; Hitler—Dead or Alive; Hondo; It Happened One Night; It's a Wonderful Life; Joan of Arc; Johnny Guitar; Kiss Tomorrow Goodbye; Law West of Tombstone; Long Gray Line, The; Maltese Falcon, The; Man Alone, A; Mister Roberts; Mortal Storm, The; Mr. Moto's Gamble; My Darling Clementine; Oklahoma Kid, The; On Dangerous Ground; Only the Valiant; Operation Pacific; Quiet Man, The; Riding High; Rio Bravo; Santa Fe Trail; Searchers, The; Sergeant York; Shepherd of the Hills, The; Sundown Rider, The; Tall in the Saddle; They Made Me a Criminal; They Were Expendable; Three Godfathers, The; Time of Your Life, The; Unconquered; Virginia City; Wagon Train (TV Series); Wagonmaster; Wheel of Fortune; Wings of Eagles, The; You Only Live Once; Young Mr. Lincoln
Bond, III, James: Def by Temptation; Sky Is Gray, The
Bondarchuk, Natalya: Solaris
Bondarchuk, Sergei: War and Peace
Bondi, Beulah: Arrowsmith; Back to Bataan; Baron of Arizona, The; Breakfast in Hollywood; Latin Lovers; Lone Star; Of Human Hearts; On Borrowed Time; Painted Veil, The; Rain; Remember the Night; She Waits; Shepherd of the Hills, The; Sister Kenny; Sisters, The (1938); Snake Pit, The; So Dear to My Heart; Street Scene; Summer Place, A; Tammy and the Doctor; Trail of the Lonesome Pine, The; Vivacious Lady
Bonds, De'Aundre: Sunset Park; Tales from the Hood
Bondy, Christopher: Deadly Surveillance
Bone, Tommy: Outside Providence
Bonerz, Peter: Medium Cool
Bones, Ken: Bellman and True; Jack the Ripper
Bonet, Lisa: Angel Heart; Bank Robber; Dead Connection; High Fidelity; New Eden
Bonet, Nai: Nocturna; Soul Hustler
Boni, Gabrille: Daddy's Girl
Bonifant, Evan: Breakout; Three Ninjas Kick Back
Bonilla, Hector: Mary My Dearest
Bonnaffe, Jacques: First Name: Carmen; Venus Beauty Institute
Bonnaire, Sandrine: A Nos Amours; Circle of Passion; East-West; La Cérémonie; La Puritaine; Monsieur Hire; Plague, The; Police; Under the Sun of Satan; Vagabond
Bonner, Frank: You Can't Hurry Love
Bonner, Priscilla: Red Kimono, The; Strong Man, The
Bonner, Tony: Creatures the World Forgot; Dead Sleep; Hurricane Smith; Lighthorsemen, The
Bonnevie, Maria: Jerusalem; Polar Bear King, The
Bonneville, Hugh: Notting Hill
Bonnucci, Emilio: In Love and War
Bono, Sonny: Dirty Laundry; Escape to Athena; Hairspray; Murder on Flight 502; Troll; Under the Boardwalk
Bonsall, Brian: Blank Check; Father & Scout; Father Hood; Mikey
Bonvoisin, Berangere: Dr. Petiot
Bonzo Dog Band: Magical Mystery Tour
Booke, Sorrell: Amazing Howard Hughes, The; Black Like Me; Joy House; Purlie Victorious
Booker T. and the MGs: Monterey Pop
Bookwalter, DeVeren: Othello
Boone, Debby: Hollywood Safari; Treehouse Hostage
Boone, Lesley: Stuart Saves His Family
Boone, Libby: Final Chapter—Walking Tall
Boone, Pat: Journey to the Center of the Earth; State Fair

Boone, Richard: Against a Crooked Sky; Alamo, The; Arrangement, The; Away All Boats; Beneath the 12-Mile Reef; Big Jake; Bushido Blade; Dragnet; Have Gun, Will Travel (TV Series); Hombre; I Bury the Living; Madron; Man without a Star; Night of the Following Day, The; Rio Conchos; Robe, The; Shootist, The; Tall T, The; Ten Wanted Men; War Lord, The; Winter Kills
Boone Jr., Mark: Trees Lounge
Boorem, Mika: Education of Little Tree, The; Hearts in Atlantis
Boorman, Charley: Emerald Forest, The
Booth, Adrian: Brimstone; Out California Way; Valley of the Zombies
Booth, Andrew: Dead Sleep
Booth, Bronwen: Call of the Wild: The Dog of the Yukon
Booth, Connie: American Friends; Fawlty Towers (TV Series); How to Irritate People; Leon the Pig Farmer; Little Lord Fauntleroy; Romance with a Double Bass
Booth, James: American Ninja IV: The Annihilation; Avenging Force; Bliss of Mrs. Blossom, The; Macho Callahan; Man Who Had Power over Women, The; Ninety Degrees in the Shade; Pray for Death; Programmed to Kill; Revenge (1971) (Joan Collins); Robbery; That'll Be the Day
Booth, Karin: Tobor the Great
Booth, Shirley: Come Back, Little Sheba; Hazel Christmas Show, The (TV Series); Hot Spell; Matchmaker, The
Boothe, Powers: Attila; Blue Sky; Breed Apart, A; By Dawn's Early Light; Cry for Love, A; Emerald Forest, The; Extreme Prejudice; Frailty; Guyana Tragedy, The: The Story of Jim Jones; Into the Homeland; Joan of Arc (1999); Mutant Species; Nixon; Rapid Fire; Red Dawn; Southern Comfort; Sudden Death; Tombstone; True Women; U-Turn; Wild Card
Borchers, Cornell: Big Lift, The; Istanbul
Bordeaux, Joe: Buster and Fatty; Keystone Comedies: Vol. 1–5
Borden, Olive: Chloe: Love is Calling You; Fig Leaves
Boreanaz, David: Valentine
Borelli, Carla: Asylum of Satan
Borg, Veda Ann: Big Jim McLain; Bitter Sweet (1940); Dr. Christian Meets the Women; Fog Island; Guys and Dolls; Honky Tonk; Julia Misbehaves; Kid Galahad; Revenge of the Zombies; Rider from Tucson
Borgard, Christopher: 84 Charlie Mopic
Borge, Victor: Daydreamer, The (1966); Higher and Higher
Borges, Alexandre: Bossa Nova
Borgese, Sal: Flight of the Innocent
Borgnine, Ernest: Alice Through the Looking Glass; All Quiet on the Western Front; Any Man's Death; Bad Day at Black Rock; Badlanders, The; Barabbas; Baseketball; Black Hole, The; Bullet for Sandoval, A; Catered Affair, The; Chuka; Code Name: Wild Geese; Convoy; Deadly Blessing; Demetrius and the Gladiators; Devil's Rain, The; Dirty Dozen, The; Dirty Dozen, The: The Deadly Mission; Dirty Dozen, The: The Fatal Mission; Dirty Dozen, The: The Next Mission; Double McGuffin, The; Escape from New York; Fire!; Flight of the Phoenix, The; From Here to Eternity; Greatest, The; Hannie Caulder; High Risk; Hustle; Ice Station Zebra; Jake Spanner Private Eye; Johnny Guitar; Jubal; Laser Mission; Last Command, The; Marty (1955); Merlin's Shop of Mystical Wonders; Mistress; Moving Target; Neptune Factor, The; Opponent, The; Oscar, The (1966); Pay or Die; Poseidon Adventure, The; Shoot; Spike of Bensonhurst; Stranger Wore a Gun, The; Super Fuzz; Suppose They Gave a War and Nobody Came?; Tides of War; Torpedo Run; Trackers, The; Vengeance Is Mine; Vera Cruz; Vikings, The; Wagon Train (TV Series); When Time Ran Out!; Wild Bunch, The; Willard; Young Warriors, The
Boris, Angel: Warlock III: The End of Innocence
Boris, Nicoletta: Mille Bolle Blu
Borisou, Oleg: Luna Park
Borizans, Pierre: Blue Jeans
Borland, Carol: Mark of the Vampire; Scalps
Borland, Scott: Heroes Die Young
Borlenghi, Matt: Blood Surf
Borlin, Jean: Le Voyage Imaginaire
Born, Roscoe: Haunting of Sarah Hardy, The; Lady Mobster
Borowitz, Katherine: Illuminata; Mac; Men of Respect
Borrego, Jesse: Bound by Honor; Mi Vida Loca
Borris, Clay: Alligator Shoes
Borrows, Anthony: Liam
Bortz, Jason: Slaves to the Underground
Bory, Jean-Marc: Le Repos du Guerrier (Warrior's Rest); Lovers, The (1958)
Bosch, Johnny Yong: Mighty Morphin Power Rangers: The Movie; Turbo: A Power Rangers Adventure
Boschi, Giula: Sicilian, The
Bosco, Philip: Angie; Children of a Lesser God; Cupid and Cate; F/X 2: The Deadly Art of Illusion; It Takes Two; Money Pit, The; Moon Over Broadway; Nobody's Fool; Return of Eliot Ness, The; Shadows and Fog; Straight Talk; Suspect; Walls of Glass
Bose, Lucia: Blood Castle; Lumiere
Bosé, Miguel: High Heels
Bosic, Andrea: Days of Wrath
Bosley, Todd: Treehouse Hostage
Bosley, Tom: Bang Bang Kid, The; Bastard, The; Divorce American Style; For the Love of It; Jesse Owens Story, The; Love with the Proper Stranger; Million Dollar Mystery; O'Hara's Wife; That's Singing: The Best of Broadway; Who Is the Black Dahlia?; Wicked Stepmother, The; Yours, Mine and Ours
Bossell, Simon: Aberration; Hotel de Love
Bossley, Caitlin: Crush (1994)
Bosson, Barbara: Great American Sex Scandal, The; Last Starfighter, The; Little Sweetheart
Bostwick, Barry: Danielle Steel's Once in a Lifetime; 800 Leagues Down the Amazon; George Washington; George Washington: The Forging of a Nation; Hitchhiker, The (Series); I Worship His Shadow; In the Heat of Passion II: Unfaithful; Megaforce; Movie Movie; Praying Mantis; Project: Metalbeast; Red Flag: The Ultimate Game; Rocky Horror Picture Show, The; Secret Agent Club; Secretary, The; Spy Hard; Weekend at Bernie's II; Woman of Substance, A
Boswell, Charles: Kiss Me a Killer
Boswell Sisters: Transatlantic Merry-Go-Round
Bosworth, Brian: Back in Business; Blackout; Mach 2; One Man's Justice; Operative, The; Stone Cold; Virus
Bosworth, Hobart: Abraham Lincoln; Big Parade, The; General Spanky; Just Imagine; Sea Lion, The; Woman of Affairs, A
Botes, Costa: Forgotten Silver
Botsford, Sara: By Design; Deadly Eyes; Gunrunner, The; Still of the Night
Bottoms, John: Blue Hotel
Bottoms, Joseph: Black Hole, The; Blind Date; Celebrity; Cloud Dancer; Crime & Passion; Inner Sanctum; Intruder Within, The; King of the Mountain; Open House; Side by Side: The True Story of the Osmond Family; Sins of Dorian Gray, The; Surfacing; Treacherous Crossing
Bottoms, Sam: Bronco Billy; Dolly Dearest; Gardens of Stone; Hunter's Blood; Prime Risk; Project Shadowchaser 3000; Savages; Up from the Depths; Witching of Ben Wagner, The; Zandy's Bride
Bottoms, Timothy: Ava's Magical Adventure; Deathgame; Diamondbacks; Digger; Drifter, The; East of Eden; Fantasist, The; Gift of Love, The; Hambone and Hillie; High Country, The; Hourglass; In the Shadow of Kilimanjaro; Invaders from Mars; Istanbul: Keep Your Eyes Open; Johnny Got His Gun; Land of Faraway, The; Last Picture Show, The; Lone Tiger; Love Leads the Way; Other Side of the Mountain, Part II, The; Paper Chase, The; Ripper Man; Rollercoaster; Shining Season, A; Small Town in Texas, A; Story of David, The; Texasville; Tin Man; Top Dog; Uncle Sam; What Waits Below; White Dawn, The
Bottone, Bonaventura: Mikado, The
Bouajila, Sami: Bye-Bye; Siege, The
Bouchet, Barbara: Sex with a Smile
Bouchey, Willis: Bridges at Toko-Ri, The
Bouchez, Elodie: Dreamlife of Angels, The; Wild Reeds
Bouchitey, Patrick: Great, My Parents Are Divorcing
Bouise, Jean: Final Combat, The; I Am Cuba; Mr. Klein
Bouix, Evelyne: Edith and Marcel
Boujenah, Michel: Les Misérables; Three Men and a Cradle
Boulanger, Jamieson: Frankenstein and Me
Bould, Sam: End of the Affair, The; Hollow Reed

Briant, Shane: Captain Kronos: Vampire Hunter; Frankenstein and the Monster from Hell; Grievous Bodily Harm; Shaker Run; Tunnel Vision (1994)
Brice, Fanny: Be Yourself; Everybody Sing; Great Ziegfeld, The; Ziegfeld Follies
Brice, Pierre: Mill of the Stone Women
Brice, Ron: Fly by Night; Horse for Danny, A; Ripe
Bridge, Alan: Badmen of the Hills; Forty-Niners
Bridges, Al: Call of the Prairie
Bridges, Beau: Alice Through the Looking Glass; Daddy's Dyin' and Who's Got the Will; Dangerous Company; Defenders, The; Defenders, The: Taking the First; Fabulous Baker Boys, The; Fifth Musketeer, The; For Love of Ivy; Four Feathers, The; Greased Lightning; Hammersmith Is Out; Heart Like a Wheel; Hidden in America; Honky Tonk Freeway; Hotel New Hampshire, The; Incident, The; Inherit the Wind; Iron Triangle, The; Killing Time, The (1987); Kissinger and Nixon; Losing Chase; Love Child; Married to It; Night Crossing; Nightjohn; Norma Rae; Other Side of the Mountain, The; Outer Limits: Sandkings; Outrage!; Positively True Adventures of the Alleged Texas Cheerleader-Murdering Mom, The; Red Light Sting, The; Rocketman; Runner Stumbles, The; Second Civil War, The; Seven Hours to Judgment; Sidekicks; Signs of Life; Silver Dream Racer; Swashbuckler (1976); Two-Minute Warning; Village of the Giants; White River; Wild Flower (1991); Wild Pair, The; Without Warning: The James Brady Story; Witness for the Prosecution; Wizard, The; Women & Men: Stories of Seduction
Bridges, Dylan: Outer Limits: Sandkings
Bridges, Jeff: Against All Odds (1984); American Heart; Arlington Road; Bad Company; Big Lebowski, The; Blown Away; Contender, The; Cutter's Way; 8 Million Ways to Die; Fabulous Baker Boys, The; Fat City; Fearless; Fisher King, The; Hearts of the West; Heaven's Gate; Hidden in America; Jagged Edge; K-Pax; King Kong; Kiss Me Goodbye; Last American Hero, The; Last Picture Show, The; Mirror Has Two Faces, The; Morning After, The; Muse, The; Nadine; Rancho Deluxe; See You in the Morning; Simpatico; Starman; Stay Hungry; Texasville; Thunderbolt and Lightfoot; Tron; Tucker: A Man and His Dream; Vanishing, The; White Squall; Wild Bill; Winter Kills; Yin and Yang of Mr. Go, The
Bridges, Krista: Bloodknot
Bridges, Lloyd: Abilene Town; Airplane!; Alice Through the Looking Glass; Apache Woman; Around the World Under the Sea; Bear Island; Blown Away; Blue and the Gray, The; Cousins; Daring Game; Devlin; Dress Gray; East of Eden; Fifth Musketeer, The; George Washington; Goddess, The; Great Wallendas, The; Haunts of the Very Rich; Heat's On, The; High Noon; Honey, I Blew Up the Kid; Hot Shots; Hot Shots Part Deux; Jane Austen's Mafia; Joe Versus the Volcano; Last of the Comanches; Little Big Horn; Master Race, The; Moonrise; Outer Limits: Sandkings; Rainmaker, The; Ramrod; Rocketship X-M; Roots; Sahara; Silent Night, Lonely Night; Strange Confession; Try and Get Me; Tucker: A Man and His Dream; Weekend Warriors; White Tower, The; Wild Pair, The; Winter People
Bridges, Todd: Homeboys; Twice Dead
Bridou, Lucienne: This Man Can't Die
Briers, Richard: Midwinter's Tale, A; Norman Conquests, The, Episode 1: Table Manners; Norman Conquests, The, Episode 3: Roundand Round the Garden; Norman Conquests, The, Episode 2: LivingTogether
Brieux, Bernard: Rascals, The
Briggs, Donald: Panama Lady
Bright, Richard: Cut and Run; Godfather, Part III, The; On the Yard; Panic in Needle Park; Pat Garrett and Billy the Kid; Red Heat; Ref, The
Brignoli, Omar: Tree of the Wooden Clogs, The
Brill, Fran: Look Back in Anger
Brill, Jason: Hell High
Brill, Robert: Look Back in Anger
Brilli, Nancy: Demons 2
Brimble, Nick: Calling, The; Gone Fishin'
Brimhall, Cynthia: Fit to Kill
Brimley, Wilford: Absence of Malice; Act of Vengeance; American Justice; Borderline; Brigham City; Cocoon; Cocoon: The Return; Country; Death Valley; Electric Horseman, The; End of the Line; Eternity; Ewoks: The Battle for Endor; Firm, The; Good Old Boys, The; Gore Vidal's Billy the Kid; Hard Target; Harry and Son; High Road to China; In & Out; Louis L'Amour's Crossfire Trail; Murder in Space; Mutant Species; My Fellow Americans; Natural, The; Progeny; Remo Williams: The Adventure Begins; Rodeo Girl; Stone Boy, The; Summer of the Monkeys; Thing, The (1982); Thompson's Last Run; Tough Enough
Brin, Michele: Sexual Intent
Brinegar, Paul: Gambler Returns, The: Luck of the Draw; How to Make a Monster; Rawhide (TV Series); Wyatt Earp: Return to Tombstone
Brink, Irvin: On Deadly Ground
Brinkley, Christie: National Lampoon's Vacation
Brinkley, Ritch: Cabin Boy
Brion, Françoise: French Lessons
Brisbane, Syd: Alien Visitor
Brisco, Gwen: Getting Over
Briscoe, Brent: Simple Plan, A
Brisebois, Danielle: Big Bad Mama II; Premonition, The (1975)
Brisson, Carl: Manxman, The; Murder at the Vanities; Ring, The
Bristow, Michael: Karate Cop
Britt, May: Secrets of Women (Waiting Women); Summer Interlude; Young Lions, The
Brittain, Charlotte: Get Real
Brittany, Morgan: Body Armor; In Search of Historic Jesus; Initiation of Sarah, The; LBJ: The Early Years; Legend of the Spirit Dog; Sundown
Britton, Barbara: Captain Kidd; Champagne for Caesar; Loaded Pistols; Secrets of the Wasteland; So Proudly We Hail; Virginian, The; Young and Willing
Britton, Connie: Brothers McMullen, The; Escape Clause
Britton, Pamela: D.O.A.; If It's Tuesday, This Must Be Belgium; Key to the City
Britton, Tony: Day of the Jackal, The; Dr. Syn, Alias the Scarecrow; Horsemasters; Night Watch; Operation Amsterdam; There's a Girl in My Soup
Brix, Herman: Hawk of the Wilderness; Hi-Yo Silver
Broadbent, Jim: Avengers, The; Borrowers, The; Bridget Jones's Diary; Bullets over Broadway; Crying Game, The; Enchanted April; Good Father, The; Life Is Sweet; Moulin Rouge (2001); Princess Caraboo; Richard III; Rough Magic; Topsy-Turvy (1999); Wedding Gift, The
Broaderup, Bernd: Taxi Zum Klo (Taxi to the Toilet)
Broadhurst, Kent: Dark Half, The
Broadnax, David: Zombie Island Massacre
Broche, Mario Gonzales: I Am Cuba
Brochet, Anne: Barjo; Cyrano De Bergerac; Tous les Matins du Monde
Brock, Charles: Sourdough
Brock, Phil: Dollman vs. Demonic Toys
Brockius, Lawrence: Deadmate
Brockman, Jay: Penpal Murders
Brocksmith, Roy: Kull the Conqueror
Brockwell, Gladys: Oliver Twist
Broderick, Beth: Are You Lonesome Tonight; In the Deep Woods; Maternal Instincts
Broderick, Chris: Legacy of Horror
Broderick, Helen: Bride Walks Out, The; My Love for Yours (Honeymoon in Bali); No, No Nanette; Rage of Paris, The; Swing Time; Top Hat
Broderick, James: Alice's Restaurant; Group, The; Shadow Box, The; Todd Killings, The
Broderick, Jocelyn: My Daughter's Keeper
Broderick, Matthew: Addicted to Love; Biloxi Blues; Cable Guy, The; Cinderella; Election; Family Business; Ferris Bueller's Day Off; Freshman, The; Glory; Godzilla (1998); Infamous Dorothy Parker, The; Infinity; Inspector Gadget; Ladyhawke; Life in the Theater, A; Master Harold and the Boys; Mrs. Parker and the Vicious Circle; Night We Never Met, The; On Valentine's Day; 1918; Out on a Limb; Project X; Road to

Wellville, The; Torch Song Trilogy; Wargames; You Can Count on Me
Brodie, Steve: Arizona Ranger; Brothers in the Saddle; Crossfire; Desperate; Donovan's Brain; Far Country, The; Frankenstein Island; Guns of Hate; Home of the Brave; Kiss Tomorrow Goodbye; Out of the Past; Rustlers, The; Station West; Steel Helmet, The; Trail Street; Wild World of Batwoman, The (She Was aHappy Vampire); Wyatt Earp: Return to Tombstone
Brodie, V. S.: Go Fish
Brody, Adrien: Bread and Roses; Harrison's Flowers; Last Time I Committed Suicide, The; Liberty Heights; Oxygen; Restaurant; Six Ways to Sunday; Solo; Summer of Sam; Ten Benny; Thin Red Line, The; Undertaker's Wedding, The
Brogi, Giulio: Spider's Stratagem, The
Brokop, Lisa: Harmony Cats
Brolin, James: Ambush Murders, The; Amityville Horror, The; Backstab; Bad Jim; Capricorn One; Car, The; Cheatin' Hearts; Expert, The; Final Justice; Finish Line; Gas, Food, Lodging; Haunted Sea, The; High Risk; Hold the Dream; Mae West; Night of the Juggler; Nightmare on the 13th Floor; Parallel Lives; Relative Fear; Savate; Ted & Venus; Terminal Virus; Tracks of a Killer; Von Ryan's Express; Westworld
Brolin, Josh: Bed of Roses; Finish Line; Gang in Blue; Goonies, The; Hollow Man; Mimic; Mod Squad, The; Nightwatch; Prison for Children; Thrashin'
Bromberg, J. Edward: Charlie Chan on Broadway; Cloak and Dagger; Jesse James; Lady of Burlesque; Mark of Zorro, The; Mr. Moto Takes a Chance; Pillow of Death; Return of Frank James, The; Son of Dracula; Stowaway; Strange Cargo
Bromfield, John: Big Bluff, The; Easy to Love; Manfish; Revenge of the Creature
Bromfield, Valri: Home Is Where the Hart Is
Bron, Eleanor: Attic: The Hiding of Anne Frank; Bedazzled; Help!; Hound of the Baskervilles, The; Little Princess, A; Saint-Ex; Turtle Diary; Women in Love
Bronsky, Brick: Class of Nuke 'em High 2: Subhumanoid Meltdown; Class of Nuke 'em High III; Sgt. Kabukiman N.Y.P.D.
Bronson, Betty: Are Parents People?; Ben-Hur; Naked Kiss, The; Peter Pan; Yodelin' Kid from Pine Ridge
Bronson, Charles: Act of Vengeance; Apache; Assassination; Battle of the Bulge; Borderline; Breakheart Pass; Breakout; Cabo Blanco; Chato's Land; Chino; Cold Sweat; Dead to Rights; Death Hunt; Death Wish; Death Wish II; Death Wish III; Death Wish IV: The Crackdown; Death Wish V: The Face of Death; Dirty Dozen, The; Drum Beat; Evil That Men Do, The; Family, The; Family of Cops; Four for Texas; Great Escape, The; Guns of Diablo; Hard Times; Honor Among Thieves; Indian Runner, The; Jubal; Kinjite (Forbidden Subjects); Love and Bullets; Machine-Gun Kelly; Magnificent Seven, The; Master of the World; Mechanic, The; Messenger of Death; Mr. Majestyk; Murphy's Law; Never So Few; Once Upon a Time in the West; Raid on Entebbe; Red Sun; Rider on the Rain; Run of the Arrow; St. Ives; Sandpiper, The; Sea Wolf, The; Showdown at Boot Hill; Someone Behind the Door; Stone Killer, The; Telefon; Ten to Midnight; This Property Is Condemned; Villa Rides; White Buffalo
Brook, Claudio: Cronos; Dr. Tarr's Torture Dungeon; Foxtrot; Interval; La Grande Vadrouille; Simon of the Desert
Brook, Clive: Cavalcade; Convoy; Hula; List of Adrian Messenger, The; On Approval; Shanghai Express
Brook, Faith: They Do It with Mirrors
Brook, Irina: Captive; Girl in the Picture, The
Brook, Jayne: Ed
Brooke, Hillary: Abbott and Costello Meet Captain Kidd; Abbott and Costello Show, The (TV Series); Africa Screams; Enchanted Cottage, The; Lost Continent, The; Monsieur Beaucaire; Road to Utopia; Sherlock Holmes and the Voice of Terror; Sherlock Holmes Faces Death; Strange Woman, The; Woman in Green, The
Brooke, Sandy: Star Slammer
Brooke, Tyler: Bluebeard's Eighth Wife; Hallelujah, I'm A Bum
Brooke, Walter: Green Hornet, The (TV Series)
Brooke-Taylor, Tim: How to Irritate People
Brooks, Albert: Broadcast News; Critical Care; Defending Your Life; Dr. Dolittle (1998); I'll Do Anything; Lost in America; Modern Romance; Mother; Muse, The; My First Mister; Out of Sight; Real Life; Scout, The; Twilight Zone—The Movie; Unfaithfully Yours
Brooks, Avery: Big Hit, The; Ernest Green Story, The; 15 Minutes; Roots—The Gift; Spenser: Ceremony; Spenser: Pale Kings & Princes
Brooks, Christopher: Almos' a Man
Brooks, Clarence: Bronze Buckaroo; Two-Gun Man from Harlem
Brooks, Claude: Hiding Out
Brooks, Conrad: Curse of the Queerwolf
Brooks, David: Magic in the Mirror; Scream for Help
Brooks, David Allen: Kindred, The
Brooks, Dina: Public Access
Brooks, Foster: Oddballs
Brooks, Geraldine: Challenge to Lassie; Cry Wolf; Johnny Tiger; Possessed
Brooks, Hazel: Body and Soul
Brooks, J. Cynthia: Live Wire: Human Timebomb
Brooks, Jacqueline: Entity, The; Gambler, The; Rodeo Girl; Without a Trace
Brooks, Jason: Darwin Conspiracy, The
Brooks, Jay: Laurel Avenue
Brooks, Jean: Boothill Bandits; Seventh Victim, The
Brooks, Joe: If Ever I See You Again
Brooks, Joel: Are You Lonesome Tonight; Dinner at Eight; Man Who Captured Eichmann, The; Mating Season, The; Skin Deep
Brooks, Leslie: Blonde Ice; Scar, The; Tonight and Every Night; You Were Never Lovelier
Brooks, Louise: Beggars of Life; Diary of a Lost Girl; Girl in Every Port, A; Overland Stage Raiders; Pandora's Box; Prix De Beaute (Beauty Prize); Show-Off, The
Brooks, Lucius: Bronze Buckaroo; Harlem Rides the Range
Brooks, Mel: Blazing Saddles; Dracula: Dead and Loving It; High Anxiety; History of the World, Part One, The; Life Stinks; Little Rascals, The; Muppet Movie, The; Putney Swope; Robin Hood: Men in Tights; Silent Movie; Spaceballs; To Be or Not to Be; Twelve Chairs, The
Brooks, Phyllis: Charlie Chan in Honolulu; Charlie Chan in Reno; Dangerous Passage; In Old Chicago; Rebecca of Sunnybrook Farm; Silver Spurs; Slightly Honorable
Brooks, Rand: Dangerous Venture; Ladies of the Chorus; Silent Conflict
Brooks, Randi: Cop; Hamburger—The Motion Picture
Brooks, Randy: Assassination; Colors; Reservoir Dogs
Brooks, Ray: Daleks—Invasion Earth 2150 A.D.; Knack ... and How to Get It, The; Office Romances
Brooks, Richard: Black Rose of Harlem; Chameleon; Crow: City of Angels, The; 84 Charlie Mopic; Memphis; To Sleep with Anger
Brooks, Rodney: Fast, Cheap and Out of Control
Brooks, Ursula: Daybreak (2000)
Brooks, Van: Trespasses
Broome, Jimmy: Angel of Destruction
Brophy, Anthony: Informant, The; Run of the Country, The
Brophy, Brian: Skinheads
Brophy, Edward: All Through the Night; Cameraman, The; Doughboys; Evelyn Prentice; Great Guy; Last Hurrah, The; Mad Love; Parlor, Bedroom and Bath; Show Them No Mercy; Speak Easily; Thin Man, The; Thin Man Goes Home, The; What! No Beer?; Wonder Man
Brophy, Kevin: Time Walker
Brosnan, Pierce: Around the World in 80 Days; Broken Chain, The; Dante's Peak; Death Train; Deceivers, The; Detonator II: Night Watch; Don't Talk to Strangers; Entangled; Fourth Protocol, The; Goldeneye; Grey Owl; Heist, The; Lawnmower Man, The; Live Wire; Long Good Friday, The; Love Affair; Manions of America, The; Mars Attacks!; Mirror Has Two Faces, The; Mister Johnson; Mrs. Doubtfire; Murder 101; Nomads; Remington Steele (TV series); Taffin; Tailor of Panama, The; Thomas Crown Affair, The; Tomorrow Never Dies; Victim of Love; World Is Not Enough, The
Brosset, Collette: La Grande Vadrouille
Brothers, Dr. Joyce: Lonely Guy, The; More Wild Wild West

Brousek, Otakar: Lies & Whispers
Brousse, Liliane: Paranoiac
Browder, Ben: Farscape (TV series)
Brower, Jordan: Forest Warrior
Brown, Andre: Bronx War, The
Brown, Barbara: Ma and Pa Kettle Back on the Farm
Brown, Barry: Bad Company; Daisy Miller
Brown, Billie: Oscar & Lucinda
Brown, Blair: Altered States; And I Alone Survived; Choirboys, The; Continental Divide; Day My Parents Ran Away, The; Flash of Green, A; Follow the Stars Home; In His Life: The John Lennon Story; Kennedy (TV Miniseries); One Trick Pony; Passed Away; Space Cowboys; Stealing Home; Strapless
Brown, Bobby: Thin Line Between Love and Hate, A; Two Can Play That Game
Brown, Brianna: Mysterious Museum
Brown, Bryan: Blame It on the Bellboy; Breaker Morant; Cocktail; Dead Heart; Dead in the Water; Devlin; Full Body Massage; F/X; F/X 2: The Deadly Art of Illusion; Good Wife, The; Gorillas in the Mist; Grizzly Falls; Last Hit, The; Odd Angry Shot, The; On the Beach; Palm Beach; Prisoners of the Sun; Rebel; Risk; Sweet Talker; Tai-Pan; Thornbirds, The; Town Like Alice, A; Tracked; 20,000 Leagues Under the Sea; Winter of Our Dreams
Brown, Caitlin: Babylon 5 (TV Series)
Brown, Carlos: Dangerous Company
Brown, Charles: Old Swimmin' Hole, The
Brown, Christopher M.: Aliens Among Us; Welcome to Planet Earth
Brown, Clancy: Ambition; Blue Steel; Bride, The; Cast a Deadly Spell; Donor Unknown; Extreme Prejudice; Female Perversions; Flubber; Highlander; In the Company of Spies; Last Light; Love, Lies and Murder; Past Midnight; Pet Sematary Two; Season of Fear; Shawshank Redemption, The; Shoot to Kill; Starship Troopers; Vendetta; Waiting for the Light
Brown, D. W.: Mischief
Brown, David: Chasing Dreams; Deadly Harvest
Brown, Dwier: Cutting Edge, The; Field of Dreams; Galaxies Are Colliding; Guardian, The; Intimate Betrayal
Brown, Dyann: Lone Wolf
Brown, Eleanora: Two Women
Brown, Francesca: Silent Witness
Brown, Georg Stanford: Ava's Magical Adventure; Dayton's Devils; House Party 2; Jesse Owens Story, The; Kid with the Broken Halo, The; Night the City Screamed, The; Roots: The Next Generation; Stir Crazy
Brown, Georgia: Bawdy Adventures of Tom Jones, The; Devil's Undead, The; Long Ago Tomorrow; Study in Terror, A
Brown, Gibran: Marvin and Tige
Brown, Henry: Stepfather II
Brown, James: Adios Amigo; Chain Lightning; Objective, Burma!; That Was Rock
Brown, Jim: Crack House; Dark of the Sun (Mercenaries) (1968); Dirty Dozen, The; El Condor; Fingers; Grasshopper, The; Ice Station Zebra; I'm Gonna Git You Sucka!; One Down, Two to Go; 100 Rifles; Original Gangstas; Pacific Inferno; Rio Conchos; Riot; Running Man, The; Slaughter; Slaughter's Big Rip-Off; Take a Hard Ride; Three the Hard Way; Tick … Tick … Tick …
Brown, Joe E.: Beware of Spooks; Comedy of Terrors; Daring Young Man, The; Earthworm Tractors; Pin-Up Girl; Riding on Air; Show Boat; Some Like It Hot; Tender Years, The; When's Your Birthday?
Brown, Johnny Mack: Belle of the Nineties; Between Men; Coquette; Deep in the Heart of Texas; Desert Phantom; Female; Hell Town; Lawman Is Born, A; Lone Star Trail; Our Dancing Daughters; Ride 'em Cowboy; Short Grass; Single Standard, The; Stampede; Woman of Affairs, A
Brown, Juanita: Caged Heat
Brown, Julie: Aliens Among Us; Earth Girls Are Easy; National Lampoon's Attack of the 5' 2" Women; Nervous Ticks; Opposite Sex (And How to Live with Them), The (1993); Raining Stones; Shakes the Clown; Spirit of '76, The
Brown, Katie: Bloodfist IV—Die Trying; Last Way Out, The
Brown, Ken: Palm Beach
Brown, Kimberly J.: Tumbleweeds
Brown, Lawrence: Big Fella
Brown, Lou: Alison's Birthday; Irishman, The
Brown, Lowell: High School Caesar
Brown, Lucille: Mystery Squadron; Rainbow Valley; Texas Terror
Brown, Matthew: God's Army
Brown, Matthew A.: Brigham City
Brown, Murray: Vampyres
Brown, Olivia: Memories of Murder; Miami Vice; Miami Vice: "The Prodigal Son"
Brown, Pamela: Becket; Cleopatra; Dracula; Half a Sixpence; Lust for Life; One of Our Aircraft Is Missing; Secret Ceremony; Tales of Hoffman
Brown, Peter: Asylum; Aurora Encounter; Concrete Jungle, The (1982); Foxy Brown; Summer Magic; Tiger Walks, A
Brown, Phil: Jungle Captive; Without Reservations
Brown, Ralph: Crying Game, The; Ivanhoe
Brown, Reb: Cage; Cage II: Arena of Death, The; Captain America; Captain America II: Death Too Soon; Death of a Soldier; Fast Break; Firing Line, The; Howling II … Your Sister Is a Werewolf; Last Flight to Hell; Mercenary Fighters; Street Hunter; Strike Commando; Uncommon Valor; White Ghost
Brown, Ritza: McGuffin, The
Brown, Rob: Finding Forrester
Brown, Roger: Paper Lion
Brown, Roger Aaron: China Moon; Miracle in Lane 2; Tall Tale: The Unbelievable Adventures of Pecos Bill
Brown, Ron: Charlie, the Lonesome Cougar
Brown, Terry: Bloodbeat
Brown, Tim: Pacific Inferno
Brown, Timothy: Girls Are for Loving
Brown, Tom: Anne of Green Gables; Buck Privates Come Home; In Old Chicago; Judge Priest; Navy Blue and Gold
Brown, Vanessa: Bless the Beasts and Children; Heiress, The; I've Always Loved You
Brown, Violet: Firehouse
Brown, W. Earl: Meat Loaf: To Hell and Back
Brown, Wally: Girl Rush; High and the Mighty, The; Zombies on Broadway
Brown, Wendell: Up the Academy
Brown, Woody: Accused, The; Animal Instincts 2; Rain Killer, The
Brown Jr., Gilbert: Raising the Heights
Brown Jr., Oscar: Original Gangstas
Browne, Coral: Auntie Mame; Courtney Affair, The; Dreamchild; Eleanor: First Lady of the World; Englishman Abroad, An; Killing of Sister George, The; Ruling Class, The
Browne, Joe: Robo Vampire
Browne, Kathie: Hondo and the Apaches
Browne, Leslie: Dancers; Nijinsky; Turning Point, The
Browne, Roscoe Lee: Black Like Me; Cisco Pike; Connection, The (1961); Cowboys, The; Dear God; For Us the Living: The Medgar Evers Story; Forest Warrior; Jumpin' Jack Flash; King; Legal Eagles; Liberation of L. B. Jones, The; Moon 44; Nothing Personal; Superfly T.N.T.; World's Greatest Athlete, The
Browne, Suzanne: Bikini Carwash Company 2
Browne, Zachary: Shiloh 2: Shiloh Season
Browning, Emily Jane: Echo of Thunder, The
Browning, Rod: Double McGuffin, The
Browning, Ryan: Extreme Days
Browning, Tod: Intolerance
Bruce, Brenda: Back Home; Nightmare; Steaming
Bruce, Cheryl Lynn: Daughters of the Dust
Bruce, David: Calling Dr. Death; Can't Help Singing; Gung Ho! (1943); Lady on a Train; Mad Ghoul, The; Salome, Where She Danced; Sea Wolf, The; Smiling Ghost, The
Bruce, Ed: Fire Down Below
Bruce, Kitty: Switchblade Sisters
Bruce, Lenny: Dance Hall Racket; Lenny Bruce Performance Film, The
Bruce, Nigel: Adventures of Sherlock Holmes, The; Becky Sharp; Blue Bird, The; Chocolate Soldier, The; Corn Is Green, The; Dressed to Kill; Follow the Boys; Gypsy Wildcat; Hound of the Baskervilles, The; House of Fear; Journey for Margaret; Ju-

lia Misbehaves; Lassie Come Home; Last of Mrs. Cheney, The; Limelight; Pearl of Death, The; Pursuit to Algiers; Rains Came, The; Rebecca; Scarlet Claw, The; Scarlet Pimpernel, The; She; Sherlock Holmes and the Secret Weapon; Sherlock Holmes and the Spider Woman; Sherlock Holmes and the Voice of Terror; Sherlock Holmes Faces Death; Sherlock Holmes in Washington; Son of Lassie; Susan and God; Suspicion; Terror by Night; Thunder in the City; Trail of the Lonesome Pine, The; Two Mrs. Carrolls, The; Woman in Green, The
Bruce, Virginia: Action in Arabia; Born to Dance; Great Ziegfeld, The; Invisible Woman, The; Jane Eyre; Let Freedom Ring; Pardon My Sarong; Strangers When We Meet
Bruckner, Agnes: Murder by Numbers (2002)
Brudin, Bo: Russian Roulette
Bruel, Patrick: Bandits; Lost & Found (1999); Secret Obsessions
Bruhl, Heidi: Captain Sinbad
Bruneau, Linda: Little Ghost
Bruni-Tedeschi, Valeria: Little Ghost
Brunkhorst, Natja: Christiane F.
Brunner, Michael: Terminal Impact
Brunning, Lorraine: Home Sweet Home (1982)
Bruno, Dylan: Rage, The: Carrie 2; When Trumpets Fade; Where the Heart Is
Bruno, Nando: Pardon My Trunk (Hello Elephant!)
Bruns, Phil: Mr. Inside/Mr. Outside; Opposite Sex (And How to Live with Them), The (1993)
Brush, Peter: Separate Peace, A
Bryan, Dora: Great St. Trinian's Train Robbery, The; No Highway in the Sky; Taste of Honey, A
Bryan, Jane: Case of the Black Cat, The; Each Dawn I Die; Kid Galahad; Sisters, The (1938)
Bryan, Zachery Ty: Bigfoot: The Unforgettable Encounter; First Kid; Rage, The: Carrie 2; True Heart
Bryant, Lee: Deathmask
Bryant, Michael: Sakharov
Bryant, Nana: Bathing Beauty; Eyes of Texas; Return of October, The
Bryant, Pamela: Lunch Wagon
Bryant, William: Hell Squad
Bryceland, Yvonne: Road to Mecca, The
Bryggman, Larry: Spy Game
Bryne, Michael: Overindulgence
Brynner, Yul: Anastasia; Brothers Karamazov, The; Buccaneer, The; Catlow; Futureworld; Fuzz; Invitation to a Gunfighter; King and I, The; Light at the End of the World, The; Madwoman of Chaillot, The; Magic Christian, The; Magnificent Seven, The; Morituri; Night Flight from Moscow; Poppy Is Also a Flower, The; Port of New York; Return of the Seven; Solomon and Sheba; Surprise Package; Taras Bulba; Ten Commandments, The; Ultimate Warrior, The; Villa Rides; Westworld
Brynolfsson, Reine: Les Misérables
Bucatinsky, Dan: All Over the Guy
Bucci, Flavio: Suspiria
Bucci, Joe: Exit
Buchanan, Barry: Loch Ness Horror, The
Buchanan, Claude: Running Wild
Buchanan, Edgar: Abilene Town; Any Number Can Play; Arizona; Benji; Big Hangover, The; Big Trees, The; Black Arrow, The (1948); Buffalo Bill; Cimarron; Coroner Creek; Human Desire; It Started With a Kiss; Lust for Gold; Make Haste to Live; Man from Colorado, The; Maverick (TV Series); McLintock!; Penny Serenade; Rage at Dawn; Rawhide; Ride the High Country; Rounders, The; She Couldn't Say No; Talk of the Town, The; Texas; Yuma
Buchanan, Erin: Cries of Silence
Buchanan, Ian: Blue Flame; Cool Surface, The; Double Exposure; Marilyn & Bobby: Her Final Affair
Buchanan, Jack: Band Wagon, The
Buchanan, Miles: Dangerous Game (1990)
Buchanan, Robert: That Sinking Feeling
Buchanan, Simone: Run, Rebecca, Run; Shame
Buchegger, Christine: From the Lives of the Marionettes
Buchholz, Christopher: Covert Assassin
Buchholz, Horst: Aces: Iron Eagle III; Aphrodite; Berlin Tunnel 21; Catamount Killing, The; Code Name: Emerald; Empty Canvas, The; Fanny; Faraway, So Close; From Hell to Victory; Life Is Beautiful; One, Two, Three; Raid on Entebbe; Return to Fantasy Island; Sahara; Savage Bees, The; Tiger Bay
Buck, David: Mummy's Shroud, The
Buck, Frank: Africa Screams
Buckley, A. J.: Extreme Days
Buckley, Betty: Baby Cakes; Critical Choices; Frantic; Rain Without Thunder; Wild Thing; Wyatt Earp
Buckley, Kay: Stage to Tucson
Buckman, Phil: American Werewolf in Paris, An
Buckman, Tara: Xtro II
Buckner, Susan: Deadly Blessing
Budac, Radoslav: Elementary School, The
Buday, Helen: Dingo; For Love Alone; Mad Max Beyond Thunderdome
Budig, Rebecca: Star Hunter
Budin, Gilles: Blue Jeans
Buechler, Nancy: Thinkin' Big
Buetel, Jack: Best of the Badmen; Half-Breed, The; Outlaw, The
Buff, David D.: Cop-Out
Buffalo Bill Jr.: Rainbow Valley
Bugner, Joe: Fatal Bond
Buhagiar, Valerie: HIghway 61
Buick, Denise: Angel Fist
Buie, Michael: Hard Time; Mystery, Alaska
Bujold, Genevieve: Adventures of Pinocchio, The; Anne of the Thousand Days; Another Man, Another Chance; Choose Me; Coma; Dead Ringers; Earthquake; Eye of the Beholder; False Identity; House of Yes, The; King of Hearts; Last Flight of Noah's Ark; Last Night; Moderns, The; Monsignor; Murder by Decree; Obsession; Oh, What a Night; Paper Wedding; Swashbuckler (1976); Tightrope; Trojan Women, The; Trouble in Mind
Buktenica, Raymond: Adventures of Nellie Bly, The
Bull, Peter: African Queen, The; Beau Brummell; Goodbye Again
Bull, Richard: Secret Life of an American Wife, The
Bullet, Stray: Leprechaun in the Hood
Bullock, Burl: Bus Is Coming, The
Bullock, Gary: Terminal Velocity
Bullock, Sandra: Demolition Man; Fool and His Money, A; Forces of Nature; Gun Shy; Hope Floats; In Love and War; Love Potion #9; Me and the Mob; Miss Congeniality; Murder by Numbers (2002); Net, The; Practical Magic; Speed; Speed 2: Cruise Control; Thing Called Love, The; Time to Kill, A (1996); 28 Days; Two If By Sea; Vanishing, The; When the Party's Over; While You Were Sleeping; Who Shot Pat?; Wrestling Ernest Hemingway
Bulos, Burt: Yellow
Bumiller, William: Death Spa
Bumpass, Rodger: National Lampoon's Class of '86
Bunce, Alan: Sunrise at Campobello
Bunce, Stuart: Behind the Lines
Bundy, Brooke: Firecreek; Francis Gary Powers: The True Story of the U-2 Spy Incident
Bundy, Robert: Screen Test
Bunnage, Avis: Loneliness of the Long Distance Runner,The; No Surrender
Bunster, Carmen: Alsino and the Condor
Bunting, Lisa: Crackerjack
Buntrock, Bobby: Hazel Christmas Show, The (TV Series)
Buono, Cara: Attention Shoppers; Cowboy Way, The
Buono, Victor: Arnold; Better Late than Never; Boot Hill; Evil, The; Four for Texas; Man from Atlantis, The; Man with Bogart's Face, The; More Wild Wild West; Northeast of Seoul; Robin & the Seven Hoods; Strangler, The; What Ever Happened to Baby Jane?; Who's Minding the Mint?
Bupp, Sonny: Renegade Trail
Buquet, Maud: Deep in the Woods
Burch, Matthew: Time Chasers
Burchill, Andrea: Housekeeping
Burdon, Eric: Comeback
Buress, Hedy: Foxfire

Burfield, Kim: Hero, The (1971)
Burgers, Michele: Friends
Burgess, Barbara: Grey Matter
Burgess, Dorothy: Hold Your Man; In Old Arizona
Burgess, Scott: Dead Easy
Burghoff, Gary: Casino; Man in the Santa Claus Suit, The; M*A*S*H; M*A*S*H (TV Series)
Burgi, Richard: I Married a Monster
Burke, Alfred: Children of the Damned; Glory Boys, The; Night Caller from Outer Space; One Day in the Life of Ivan Denisovich
Burke, Billie: Becky Sharp; Bill of Divorcement, A; Bride Wore Red, The; Christopher Strong; Craig's Wife; Dinner at Eight; Doubting Thomas; Eternally Yours; Everybody Sing; Father of the Bride; Father's Little Dividend; Finishing School; Forsaking All Others; In This Our Life; Man Who Came to Dinner, The; Navy Blue and Gold; Sergeant Rutledge; Small Town Girl; Topper; Topper Takes a Trip; Wizard of Oz, The; Young in Heart, The; Young Philadelphians, The; Zenobia
Burke, Billy: Jane Austen's Mafia; Komodo
Burke, Bryan: Forever Together
Burke, Charlotte: Paperhouse
Burke, David: Adventures of Sherlock Holmes, The (Series)
Burke, Delta: Bunny's Tale, A; Dynamite and Gold; First and Ten; Maternal Instincts; Seekers, The
Burke, Edmund: She Goes to War
Burke, Joe Michael: Last Warrior, The (2000)
Burke, Kaitlyn: Ms. Bear
Burke, Kathleen: Fighting Westerner, The; Island of Lost Souls; Lives of a Bengal Lancer, The; Murders in the Zoo
Burke, Kathy: Dancing at Lughnasa; Nil by Mouth
Burke, Marylouise: Series 7: The Contenders
Burke, Matt: Anna Christie
Burke, Michelle: Coneheads; Dazed and Confused; Last Word, The
Burke, Mildred: Below the Belt
Burke, Paul: Daddy's Gone A-Hunting; Disembodied, The; Francis in the Navy; Killing at Hell's Gate; Little Ladies of the Night; Psychic Killer; Red Light Sting, The; Thomas Crown Affair, The; Valley of the Dolls
Burke, Robert: Dust Devil; Fled; RoboCop 3; Simple Men; Thinner; Tombstone; Unbelievable Truth, The
Burke, Robert John: Somewhere in the City
Burke, Robert Karl: Basket, The
Burke, Simon: Irishman, The; Slate, Wyn, and Me
Burkett, Laura: Daddy's Boys
Burkholder, Scott: House IV
Burkley, Dennis: Doors, The; Four Eyes and Six Guns; Lambada; Pass the Ammo; Stop! Or My Mom Will Shoot; Tin Cup
Burks, Rick: Blood Diner
Burlaiev, Kolya: My Name Is Ivan
Burlinson, Tom: Flesh and Blood (Sword and the Rose, the (1985)); Landslide; Man from Snowy River, The; Phar Lap; Return to Snowy River, Part II; Showdown at Williams Creek; Time Guardian, The; Windrider
Burmester, Leo: Fly by Night; Mistrial; Old Man
Burner, Oscar: Tombs of the Blind Dead
Burnett, Anthony: Color of Friendship, The
Burnett, Carol: Annie; Between Friends; Chu Chu and the Philly Flash; Four Seasons, The; Friendly Fire; Front Page, The; Grass Is Always Greener over the Septic Tank, The; Moon Over Broadway; Noises Off; Pete 'n' Tillie; Tenth Month, The; Trumpet of the Swan, The; Wedding, A (1978)
Burnette, Justin: Escape from Atlantis
Burnette, Olivia: Final Verdict
Burnette, Smiley: Adventures of Rex and Rinty; Billy the Kid Returns; Blue Montana Skies; Colorado Sunset; Dick Tracy; Git Along, Little Dogies; Heart of the Golden West; In Old Santa Fe; King of the Cowboys; Last of the Pony Riders; Man from Music Mountain; Man of the Frontier (Red River Valley); Manhattan Merry-Go-Round; Melody Trail; Mexicali Rose; Oh! Susanna!; Old Corral; Phantom Empire (1935); Public Cowboy #1; Radio Ranch (Men with Steel Faces, Phantom Empire); Ride, Ranger, Ride; Silver Spurs; South of the Border; Springtime in the Rockies; Under Western Stars; Undersea Kingdom; Winning of the West; Yodelin' Kid from Pine Ridge
Burnquist, Bob: MVP2: Most Vertical Primate
Burns, Bob: Rhythm on the Range; Waikiki Wedding
Burns, Carol: Dusty
Burns, Cathy: Last Summer
Burns, David: It's Always Fair Weather; Saint in London, The
Burns, Edward: Brothers McMullen, The; 15 Minutes; Life or Something Like It; No Looking Back; Saving Private Ryan; She's the One; Sidewalks of New York (2001)
Burns, George: College Swing; Damsel in Distress, A; 18 Again; George Burns and Gracie Allen Show, The (TV Series); Going in Style; Honolulu; International House; Just You and Me, Kid; Oh, God!; Oh, God! Book II; Oh, God, You Devil!; Sgt. Pepper's Lonely Hearts Club Band; Sunshine Boys, The; Two of a Kind; We're Not Dressing
Burns, Jennifer: Blood Song (Haunted Symphony); Josh Kirby, Time Warrior (Series)
Burns, Jere: Greedy
Burns, Marilyn: Eaten Alive; Helter Skelter; Kiss Daddy Goodbye; Texas Chainsaw Massacre, The
Burns, Marion: Dawn Rider
Burns, Mark: Death in Venice; Virgin and the Gypsy, The
Burns, Megan: Liam
Burns, Michael: Santee; That Cold Day in the Park
Burns, Paul E.: Double Deal
Burns, Robert A.: Confessions of a Serial Killer
Burns, Ronnie: George Burns and Gracie Allen Show, The (TV Series)
Burns, Stephan W.: Herbie Goes Bananas
Burns, Tim: Mad Max
Burr, Raymond: Black Magic; Blue Gardenia, The; Bride of the Gorilla; Casanova's Big Night; Crime of Passion; Curse of King Tut's Tomb, The; Delirious; Desperate; Godzilla, King of the Monsters; Godzilla 1985; Gorilla at Large; His Kind of Woman; Key to the City; Love Happy; Love's Savage Fury; Man Alone, A; Meet Danny Wilson; Night the City Screamed, The; Passion; Pitfall; Place in the Sun, A; Rear Window; Return, The (1980); Showdown at Williams Creek; Station West; Thunder Pass; Tomorrow Never Comes
Burrell, Maryedith: Say Yes
Burrell, Sheila: Cold Comfort Farm; Paranoiac
Burrell, Terri: Eubie!
Burress, Hedy: Cabin by the Lake; Getting Personal
Burrise, Nakia: Turbo: A Power Rangers Adventure
Burroughs, Jackie: Bleeders; Final Notice; Grey Fox, The; Housekeeper, The; John and the Missus; Lost and Delirious; Undergrads, The
Burroughs, William S.: Drugstore Cowboy; Kerouac; Wax
Burrows, Darren E.: Northern Exposure (TV Series)
Burrows, Saffron: Circle of Friends; Deep Blue Sea; Hotel de Love; Loss of Sexual Innocence, The; Lovelife; Miss Julie; Nevada; Seventh Stream, The; Timecode; Wing Commander
Burstyn, Ellen: Act of Vengeance; Alex in Wonderland; Alice Doesn't Live Here Anymore; Ambassador, The; Cemetery Club, The; Deceiver; Dream of Passion, A; Dying Young; Exorcist, The; Flash (1998); Getting Gotti; Getting Out; Grand Isle; Hanna's War; Harry and Tonto; How to Make an American Quilt; King of Marvin Gardens, The; Night Ride Home; People vs. Jean Harris; Primal Secrets; Providence; Requiem for a Dream; Resurrection; Roommates; Same Time Next Year; Silence of the North; Spitfire Grill, The; Thursday's Game; Tropic of Cancer; Twice in a Lifetime; Yards, The
Bursztein, David: La Belle Noiseuse
Burt, Andrew: Gulliver in Lilliput
Burt, Clarissa: NeverEnding Story II, The
Burton, Haven: Frankenstein Reborn!
Burton, Kate: August; Big Trouble in Little China; Ellen Foster; Love Matters
Burton, LeVar: Almos' a Man; Battered; Guyana Tragedy, The: The Story of Jim Jones; Hunter, The (1980); Jesse Owens Story, The; Midnight Hour; Our Friend, Martin; Parallel Lives; Roots; Roots—The Gift; Star Trek: First Contact; Star Trek: Genera-

tions; Star Trek: Insurrection; Star Trek: The Next Generation (TV Series); Supernaturals, The; Yesterday's Target
Burton, Mark: Apprentice to Murder
Burton, Normann: Bloodsport; Gumball Rally, The; Pray for Death; Scorchy
Burton, Richard: Absolution; Alexander the Great; Anne of the Thousand Days; Assassination of Trotsky, The; Becket; Bluebeard; Bramble Bush, The; Breakthrough; Brief Encounter; Circle of Two; Cleopatra; Comedians, The; Desert Rats, The; Divorce His: Divorce Hers; Dr. Faustus; Ellis Island; Equus; Exorcist II: The Heretic; Gathering Storm; Hammersmith Is Out; Ice Palace; Klansman, The; Longest Day, The; Look Back in Anger; Love Spell; Massacre in Rome; Medusa Touch, The; Night of the Iguana, The; 1984; Raid on Rommel; Robe, The; Sandpiper, The; Spy Who Came in from the Cold, The; Staircase; Taming of the Shrew, The; Under Milk Wood; V.I.P.s, The; Wagner; Where Eagles Dare; Who's Afraid of Virginia Woolf?; Wild Geese, The
Burton, Robert: I Was a Teenage Frankenstein; Invasion of the Animal People; Trilogy of Terror
Burton, Steve: Cyber Tracker; Cyber Tracker 2; Last Castle, The
Burton, Tony: Assault on Precinct 13; Cyber Tracker 2; Flipping; Inside Moves; Magnificent Seven, The (TV Series); Oceans of Fire; Rocky IV
Burton, Tyrone: Squeeze
Burton, Wendell: Fortune and Men's Eyes; Sterile Cuckoo, The
Buscemi, Michael: Trees Lounge
Buscemi, Steve: Airheads; Armageddon; Big Lebowski, The; Billy Bathgate; Call Me; Con Air; Crisscross (1992); Desperado; Domestic Disturbance; Ed & His Dead Mother; Fargo; Floundering; Ghost World; Heart; Impostors, The; In the Soup; John Carpenter's Escape from L.A.; Kansas City; Living in Oblivion; Parting Glances; Reservoir Dogs; Rising Sun; Search for One-Eye Jimmy, The; Somebody to Love; Trees Lounge; Twenty Bucks; 28 Days
Busch, Charles: Trouble on the Corner
Busch, Ernest: Kameradschaft
Busch, Mae: Foolish Wives; Keystone Comedies: Vol. 1–5; Laurel and Hardy Classics: Vol. 1–9
Busey, Gary: Act of Piracy; Angels Hard as They Come; Barbarosa; Big Wednesday; Black Sheep; Breaking Point; Buddy Holly Story, The; Bulletproof; Canvas; Carny; Carried Away; Chain, The; Chasers; Chrome Soldiers; Dangerous Life, A; D.C. Cab; Detour; Diary of a Serial Killer; Drop Zone; Execution of Private Slovik, The; Eye of the Tiger; Fallen Angels; Fear and Loathing in Las Vegas; Firm, The; Foolin' Around; Gumball Rally, The; Hider in the House; Hitchhiker, The (Series); Insignificance; Last American Hero, The; Lethal Tender; Lethal Weapon; Let's Get Harry; Man with a Gun; My Heroes Have Always Been Cowboys; Neon Empire, The; Point Break; Predator 2; Real Thing, The; Rookie of the Year; Rough Riders; Shrieking, The; Silver Bullet; Soldier; South Beach; Star Is Born, A; Steel Sharks; Straight Time; Surviving the Game; Suspicious Minds; Thunderbolt and Lightfoot; Tribulation; Under Siege; Universal Soldier II: Brothers in Arms; Warriors (1994)
Busey, Jake: Black Cat Run; Enemy of the State; Fast Sofa; Frighteners, The; Home Fries; Quiet Days in Hollywood; Starship Troopers; Tail Lights Fade; Tomcats
Busfield, Timothy: Dead in a Heartbeat; Dream House; Erasable You; Fade to Black; Field of Dreams; First Kid; Little Big League; Revenge of the Nerds; Revenge of the Nerds II: Nerds in Paradise; Shadow of a Scream; Skateboard Kid, The; Sneakers; Souler Opposite, The; Strays; Striking Distance; Trucks; Unspeakable, The
Bush, Chuck: Fandango
Bush, Owen: Prehysteria 2
Bush, Rebeccah: Hunk
Bush, Sam: Hunk
Bushell, Anthony: Dark Journey; Disraeli; Quatermass and the Pit; Vanity Fair
Bushey, Trent: American Shaolin: King of the Kickboxers II
Bushman, Francis X.: Ben-Hur; Dick Tracy; Three Musketeers, The
Bushman, Ralph: Our Hospitality
Busia, Akosua: Color Purple, The; George McKenna Story, The; Low Blow; Native Son
Busia, Marion: Gone in 60 Seconds
Busker, Ricky: Big Shots
Bussières, Pascale: Five Senses, The; When Night is Falling; Xchange
Buster, Budd: Arizona Days; Zorro's Fighting Legion
Buster, Michael: God's Army
Bustric, Sergio: Life Is Beautiful
Butkus, Dick: Cracking Up; Deadly Games; Hamburger—The Motion Picture; Spontaneous Combustion
Butler, Calvin: Drying Up the Streets
Butler, Cindy: Boggy Creek II
Butler, David: Sky Pilot, The
Butler, Dean: Desert Hearts; Kid with the 200 I.Q., The; Little House on the Prairie (TV Series)
Butler, Gerard: Attila; Dracula 2000
Butler, Holly: Looking for Trouble
Butler, Jean: Brylcreem Boys, The
Butler, Kent: Curse of the Queerwolf
Butler, Paul: To Sleep with Anger
Butler, Tom: Ronnie & Julie
Butler, William: Inner Sanctum; Leatherface—the Texas Chainsaw Massacre III
Butler, Yancy: Drop Zone; Ex, The; Fast Money; Hard Target; Hit List, The (1992); Ravager; Witchblade
Butrick, Merritt: Death Spa; Head Office; Shy People
Butterworth, Charles: Cat and the Fiddle, The; Dixie Jamboree; Every Day's a Holiday; Forsaking All Others; Illicit; It Happened in New Orleans; Let Freedom Ring; Love Me Tonight; Second Chorus; Swing High, Swing Low; This Is the Army
Butterworth, Donna: Family Jewels, The
Butterworth, Peter: Carry on Doctor; Carry on Emmanuelle; Follow That Camel
Butterworth, Tyler: Consuming Passions
Buttle, Stephanie: Couch in New York, A
Buttons, Red: Alice in Wonderland; Alice Through the Looking Glass; C.H.O.M.P.S.; 18 Again; Five Weeks in a Balloon; Gay Purr-ee; Harlow; Hatari!; It Could Happen to You; Leave 'em Laughing; Movie Movie; One, Two, Three; Pete's Dragon; Poseidon Adventure, The; Sayonara; Side Show; Story of Us, The; Users, The; When Time Ran Out!; Who Killed Mary What's 'Er Name?
Buttram, Pat: Beyond the Purple Hills; Hills of Utah, The; Mule Train
Buttrick, Merritt: Wired to Kill
Buxton, Sarah: Listen; Welcome to Spring Break
Buy, Margherita: Station, The
Buzby, Zane: Americathon; Cracking Up; National Lampoon's Class Reunion
Buzzanca, Lando: When Women Had Tails; When Women Lost Their Tails
Buzzard, Eddie: Bulldog Courage
Buzzi, Ruth: Apple Dumpling Gang Rides Again, The; Bad Guys; Being, The; Boys Will Be Boys; Chu Chu and the Philly Flash; Dixie Lanes; Freaky Friday; My Mom's a Werewolf; Surf 2; Troublemakers; Up Your Alley; Wishful Thinking
Byers, Kate: Career Girls
Byington, Spring: Big Wheel, The; Blue Bird, The; Devil and Miss Jones, The; Dodsworth; Enchanted Cottage, The; Heaven Can Wait; In the Good Old Summertime; Jezebel; Little Women; Living in a Big Way; Lucky Partners; Meet John Doe; Please Don't Eat the Daisies; Presenting Lily Mars; Roxie Hart; Singapore; Stage Struck; Thrill of a Romance; Walk Softly, Stranger; Werewolf of London; When Ladies Meet; You Can't Take It with You
Bykov, Rolan: Overcoat, The
Byner, John: Great Smokey Roadblock, The; Man in the Santa Claus Suit, The; My 5 Wives; Transylvania 6-5000
Bynes, Amanda: Big Fat Liar
Byrd, Ralph: Dick Tracy; Dick Tracy Meets Gruesome; Dick Tracy Returns; Dick Tracy vs. Crime Inc.; Dick Tracy's Dilemma; Dick Tracy's G-Men; Son of Monte Cristo, The; SOS Coast Guard
Byrd, Tom: Wet Gold

Byrd-Nethery, Miriam: Civil War Diary
Byrne, Barbara: Sunday in the Park with George
Byrne, Catherine: Eat the Peach
Byrne, David: True Stories; Two Moon July
Byrne, Debbie: Rebel
Byrne, Eddie: Jack the Ripper
Byrne, Gabriel: Buffalo Girls; Christopher Columbus (1985); Cool World; Dangerous Woman, A; Dark Obsession; Dead Man; Defense of the Realm; End of Days; End of Violence, The; Frankie Starlight; Gothic; Hanna K.; Hello Again; Into the West; Julia and Julia; Lionheart; Little Women; Miller's Crossing; Point of No Return; Polish Wedding; Royal Deceit; Shipwrecked; Siesta; Simple Twist of Fate, A; Smilla's Sense of Snow; Soldier's Tale, A; Somebody Is Waiting; Stigmata; Summer Fling; This Is the Sea; Trial by Jury; Trigger Happy (Mad Dog Time); Usual Suspects, The; Weapons of Mass Distraction
Byrne, Karl: War of the Buttons
Byrne, Martha: Anna to the Infinite Power; Eyes of the Amaryllis
Byrne, Michael: Battlefield Earth; Infiltrator, The
Byrne, Niall: Miracle, The
Byrnes, Brittany: When Good Ghouls Go Bad
Byrnes, David: Witchcraft 7: Judgment Hour
Byrnes, Edd: Final Defeat, The; Go Kill and Come Back; Mankillers; Reform School Girl
Byrnes, Jim: Bloodhounds II; Dirty Work; Dream Man; Harmony Cats; Highlander: Endgame; Suspicious Agenda
Byrnes, Josephine: Brides of Christ; Frauds
Byron, Bruce: Brides of Christ; Frauds
Byron, David: Based on an Untrue Story; Fade to Black
Byron, Jean: Invisible Invaders; Magnetic Monster, The
Byron, Jeffrey: Dungeonmaster, The; Metalstorm: The Destruction of Jared-Syn; Seniors, The
Byron, Marion: Steamboat Bill Jr.
Byrska, Irene: Man of Iron
Byun, Susan: Sgt. Kabukiman N.Y.P.D.
Caan, James: Alien Nation; Another Man, Another Chance; Bolero; Bottle Rocket; Boy Called Hate, A; Brian's Song; Bridge Too Far, A; Bulletproof; Chapter Two; Cinderella Liberty; Comes a Horseman; Countdown; Dark Backward, The; Dead Simple; Dick Tracy; El Dorado; Eraser; Flesh and Bone; For the Boys; Freebie and the Bean; Funny Lady; Gambler, The; Gardens of Stone; Glimpse of Hell, A; Godfather, The; Godfather Epic, The; Gone with the West; Harry and Walter Go to New York; Hide in Plain Sight; Honeymoon in Vegas; Killer Elite, The; Kiss Me Goodbye; Lady in a Cage; Little Moon & Jud McGraw; Luckytown Blues; Mickey Blue Eyes; Misery; North Star (1996); Poodle Springs; Program, The; Rabbit Run; Rain People, The; Red Line 7000; Rollerball; Silent Movie; Slither; Thief (1981); This Is My Father; Warden of Red Rock; Way of the Gun, The; Yards, The
Caan, Scott: American Outlaws; Bongwater; Boy Called Hate, A; Novocaine; Ocean's Eleven (2001); Ready to Rumble; Varsity Blues
Cabezas, Oyanka: Carla's Song
Cabot, Bruce: Angel and the Badman; Ann Vickers; Best of the Badmen; Big Jake; Captain Caution; Chisum; Comancheros, The; Diamonds Are Forever; Dodge City; Fancy Pants; Finishing School; Fury (1936); Goliath and the Barbarians; Green Berets, The; Hellfighters; John Paul Jones; King Kong; Last of the Mohicans, The; McLintock!; Show Them No Mercy; Silver Queen; Sinners in Paradise; Smashing the Rackets; Sorrowful Jones; Sundown; Undefeated, The
Cabot, Sebastian: Family Jewels, The; Ivanhoe; Johnny Tremain; Omar Khayyam; Romeo and Juliet; Seven Thieves; Time Machine, The; Twice-Told Tales; Westward Ho, the Wagons
Cabot, Susan: Carnival Rock; Machine-Gun Kelly; Saga of the Viking Women and Their Voyage to the Waters of the Great Sea Serpent, The (Viking Women and the Sea Serpent, The); Son of Ali Baba; Sorority Girl; War of the Satellites; Wasp Woman (1960)
Cadell, Jean: Love from a Stranger
Cadell, Simon: Cold Light of Day, The
Cadenat, Garry: Sugarcane Alley
Cadieux, Jason: Iron Eagle IV; Lilies
Cadillacs, The: Go, Johnny, Go!
Caesar, Adolph: Club Paradise; Color Purple, The; Fortune Dane; Soldier's Story, A
Caesar, Shirley: Gospel
Caesar, Sid: Airport 1975; Alice in Wonderland; Barnaby and Me; Cheap Detective, The; Fiendish Plot of Dr. Fu Manchu, The; Grease; Guide for the Married Man, A; It's a Mad Mad Mad Mad World; Munsters' Revenge, The; Over the Brooklyn Bridge; Silent Movie; Stoogemania; 10 from Your Show of Shows; Wonderful Ice Cream Suit, The
Cafagna, Ashley Lyn: Midas Touch, The; Mystery Monsters; Werewolf Reborn!
Caffaro, Cheri: Ginger; Girls Are for Loving; Place Called Today, A
Caffrey, Peter: I Went Down
Caffrey, Stephen: Blowback; Buried Alive II; Tour of Duty
Cage, Nicolas: Amos & Andrew; Birdy; Boy in Blue, The; Bringing Out the Dead; Captain Corelli's Mandolin; City of Angels; Con Air; Deadfall; Face/Off; Family Man, The; Fast Times at Ridgemont High; Fire Birds; Gone in 60 Seconds; Guarding Tess; Honeymoon in Vegas; Industrial Symphony No. 1 The Dream of the Broken Hearted; It Could Happen to You; Kiss of Death; Leaving Las Vegas; 8MM; Moonstruck; Peggy Sue Got Married; Racing with the Moon; Raising Arizona; Red Rock West; Rock, The; Rumble Fish; Snake Eyes; Time to Kill (1990); Trapped in Paradise; Valley Girl; Vampire's Kiss; Wild at Heart; Zandalee
Cagen, Andrea: Hot Box, The
Cagney, James: Angels with Dirty Faces; Blonde Crazy; Blood on the Sun; Boy Meets Girl; Bride Came C.O.D., The; Captains of the Clouds; Ceiling Zero; City for Conquest; Devil Dogs of the Air; Each Dawn I Die; Fighting 69th, The; Footlight Parade; Gallant Hours, The; Great Guy; Johnny Come Lately; Kiss Tomorrow Goodbye; Lady Killer; Lion Is in the Streets, A; Love Me or Leave Me; Man of a Thousand Faces; Midsummer Night's Dream, A; Mister Roberts; Never Steal Anything Small; Oklahoma Kid, The; One, Two, Three; Public Enemy; Ragtime; Roaring Twenties, The; Seven Little Foys, The; Shake Hands with the Devil; Something to Sing About; Strawberry Blonde, The; 13 Rue Madeleine; Time of Your Life, The; Tribute to a Bad Man; West Point Story, The; What Price Glory; White Heat; Yankee Doodle Dandy
Cagney, Jeanne: Kentucky Rifle; Lion Is in the Streets, A; Man of a Thousand Faces; Rhythm on the River; Time of Your Life, The; Yankee Doodle Dandy
Cagney, William: Palooka
Cain, Dean: Best Men; Broken Hearts Club, The; Firetrap; Futuresport; No Alibi; Runaway, The (2000); Tracked
Caine, Michael: Alfie; Ashanti; Battle of Britain; Beyond the Limit; Beyond the Poseidon Adventure; Black Windmill, The; Blame It on Rio; Blood and Wine; Blue Ice; Bridge Too Far, A; Bullet to Beijing; Bullseye; Cider House Rules, The; Curtain Call; Deathtrap; Destructors, The; Dirty Rotten Scoundrels; Dressed to Kill; Eagle Has Landed, The; Educating Rita; Fourth Protocol, The; Funeral in Berlin; Gambit; Get Carter; Get Carter; Half-Moon Street; Hand, The; Hannah and Her Sisters; Harry and Walter Go to New York; Holcroft Covenant, The; Ipcress File, The; Island, The; Italian Job, The; Jack the Ripper; Jaws: The Revenge; Jekyll & Hyde; Jigsaw Man, The; Last Orders; Last Valley, The; Little Voice; Man Who Would Be King, The; Mandela and De Klerk; Miss Congeniality; Mona Lisa; Mr. Destiny; Muppet Christmas Carol, The; Noises Off; On Deadly Ground; Pulp; Quills; Romantic Englishwoman, The; Shock to the System, A; Silver Bears; Sleuth; Surrender; Swarm, The; Sweet Liberty; Too Late the Hero; 20,000 Leagues Under the Sea; Victory; Water; Whistle Blower, The; Wilby Conspiracy, The; Without a Clue; Woman Times Seven; Wrong Box, The; X, Y and Zee; Zulu
Caire, Audrey: They Saved Hitler's Brain
Cairns, Jason: Eye of the Snake
Calabro, Thomas: Lady Killers; They Nest
Calamai, Clara: Ossessione
Calder-Marshall, Anna: King Lear; Wuthering Heights
Calderon, Paul: Bad Lieutenant; Condition Red; Girlfight; Last Castle, The; Once in the Life; Sweet Nothing

Caldwell, Janette Allyson: Mandroid
Caldwell, L. Scott: Twilight Man
Caldwell, Zoe: Lantern Hill
Cale, Paula: Milo
Calegory, Jade: Mac and Me
Calfa, Don: Bank Shot; Chopper Chicks in Zombietown; Greaser's Palace; Me, Myself & I; Return of the Living Dead, The
Calfan, Nicole: Permission to Kill
Calhern, Louis: Annie Get Your Gun; Arch of Triumph; Asphalt Jungle, The; Athena; Betrayed; Blonde Crazy; Bridge of San Luis Rey, The; Count of Monte Cristo, The; Diplomaniacs; Duck Soup; Executive Suite; Forever Darling; Heaven Can Wait; Julius Caesar; Last Days of Pompeii, The (1935); Latin Lovers; Life of Emile Zola, The; Life of Her Own, A; Magnificent Yankee, The; Men of the Fighting Lady; Nancy Goes to Rio; Night after Night; Notorious; Prisoner of Zenda, The; Prodigal, The; Red Pony, The; Rhapsody; Student Prince, The; Sweet Adeline; They Call It Sin; Two Weeks with Love; We're Not Married; World Gone Mad, The
Calhoun, Coronji: Monster's Ball
Calhoun, Monica: Best Man, The; Players Club, The
Calhoun, Rory: Avenging Angel (1985); Bad Jim; Blue and the Gray, The; Dayton's Devils; Finger on the Trigger; Flatbed Annie and Sweetie Pie: Lady Truckers; Hell Comes to Frogtown; How to Marry a Millionaire; Mission to Glory; Motel Hell; Pure Country; Red House, The; River of No Return; Treasure of Pancho Villa, The
Call, Brandon: Blind Fury
Call, John: Santa Claus Conquers the Martians
Call, R. D.: Last Man Standing; Murder by Numbers (2002); Waterworld
Callahan, James: Outlaw Blues; Tropic of Cancer
Callan, K.: Saved by the Light; Unborn, The
Callan, Michael: Bon Voyage!; Cat and the Canary, The; Cat Ballou; Donner Pass: The Road to Survival; Double Exposure; Frasier the Lovable Lion (Frasier the Sensuous Lion); Freeway; Gidget Goes Hawaiian; Interns, The; Lepke; Mysterious Island
Callard, Rebecca: Borrowers, The
Callas, Charlie: Vampire Vixens from Venus
Callas, Maria: Medea
Calleia, Joseph: After the Thin Man; Branded; Five Came Back; For Whom the Bell Tolls; Four Faces West; Gilda; Jungle Book (1942); Littlest Outlaw, The; My Little Chickadee; Noose Hangs High, The; RiffRaff; Sundown; Treasure of Pancho Villa, The
Callen, John: Rainbow Warrior
Callie, Dayton: Boss of Bosses; Executive Target; Last Days of Frankie the Fly, The
Callis, James: Victoria and Albert
Callow, Simon: Ace Ventura: When Nature Calls; Bedrooms and Hallways; Crucifer of Blood; Four Weddings and a Funeral; Good Father, The; Jefferson in Paris; Manifesto; Mr. and Mrs. Bridge; No Man's Land (2001); Room with a View, A; Shakespeare in Love
Calloway, Cab: International House; Manhattan Merry-Go-Round; Sensations of 1945; Stormy Weather
Caloz, Michael: Little Men; Whiskers
Caltagirone, Daniel: Legionnaire
Caltett, Walter: Look for the Silver Lining
Calthrop, Donald: Blackmail; Number 17; Scrooge
Calton, Darren: Montana
Calvert, Bill: Montana
Calvert, Phyllis: Magic Bow, The; Man in Grey, The
Calvert, Steve: Bride and the Beast, The
Calvet, Corinne: Dr. Heckyl and Mr. Hype; Far Country, The; She's Dressed to Kill; What Price Glory
Calvin, Henry: Sign of Zorro, The; Toby Tyler
Calvin, John: Dragonworld; Foolin' Around; Ghost Warrior; Primary Target
Calvo, Armando: Witch's Mirror, The
Calvo, Pepe: Twice a Judas
Camardiel, Roberto: Adios, Hombre; Badlands Drifter (Challenge of McKenna); Machine Gun Killers
Cambridge, Godfrey: Cotton Comes to Harlem; Friday Foster; President's Analyst, The; Purlie Victorious; Son of Blob (Beware! The Blob); Watermelon Man
Cameron, Brynne: Sherlock: Undercover Dog
Cameron, Candace: Frankenstein Sings; Sharon's Secret; Visitors of the Night
Cameron, Dean: Men at Work; Miracle Beach; Rockula; Ski School; Sleep with Me
Cameron, James: Muse, The
Cameron, Jane: Pair of Aces; Unborn, The
Cameron, Kirk: Left Behind; Like Father, Like Son; Listen to Me
Cameron, Marjorie: Left Behind; Like Father, Like Son; Listen to Me
Cameron, Nadia: Merlin
Cameron, Rod: Brimstone; Evel Knievel; Fort Osage; G-Men vs. The Black Dragon; Mrs. Parkington; Ride the Man Down; Salome, Where She Danced; Short Grass; Stage to Tucson; Stampede
Cameron, Trent: Kid Who Loved Christmas, The; Wood, The
Cameron-Glickenhaus, Jesse: Slaughter of the Innocents; Timemaster
Camilleri, Terry: Cars That Eat People (The Cars That Ate Paris)
Camilo, Michel: Calle 54
Camp, Colleen: Backfield in Motion; Cloud Dancer; Deadly Games; Die Hard with a Vengeance; Doin' Time; Game of Death; Greedy; Illegally Yours; Love Stinks; Police Academy II: Their First Assignment; Right to Remain Silent, The; Rosebud Beach Hotel, The (Nostell Hotel,The); Screwball Academy; Sliver; Smile; Track 29; Valley Girl; Wayne's World
Camp, Hamilton: Arena; It Came Upon a Midnight Clear; Rosebud Beach Hotel, The (Nostell Hotel,The)
Campa, Jo: Beretta's Island
Campanella, Frank: Free Ride
Campanella, Joseph: Club Fed; Down the Drain; Game, The; Glass Cage, The; Hangar 18; Hit Lady; Last Call; Magic Kid; No Retreat, No Surrender 3: Blood Brothers; Return to Fantasy Island; Sky Heist; St. Valentine's Day Massacre, The; Steele Justice; Terror on the 40th Floor
Campbell, Amelia: Simple Twist of Fate, A
Campbell, Beatrice: Last Holiday; Master of Ballantrae, The
Campbell, Bill: Brylcreem Boys, The; Checkered Flag; Lover's Knot; Out There; Rocketeer, The; Second Jungle Book, The: Mowgli and Baloo
Campbell, Bruce: Army of Darkness; Crimewave; Evil Dead, The; Evil Dead 2; Hudsucker Proxy, The; John Carpenter's Escape from L.A.; Love Bug, The; Lunatics: A Love Story; Maniac Cop; Maniac Cop 2; McHale's Navy; Mindwarp; Moon Trap; Running Time; Sundown; Tornado!; Waxwork II: Lost in Time
Campbell, Cheryl: Chariots of Fire; Greystoke: The Legend of Tarzan, Lord of the Apes; Murder at the Vicarage; Seven Dials Mystery, The; Shooting Party, The
Campbell, Christian: I've Been Waiting for You; Trick
Campbell, Colin: Leather Boys, The
Campbell, Darren: Twentyfourseven
Campbell, Douglas: If You Could See What I Hear; Oedipus Rex
Campbell, Elizabeth: Rock 'n' Roll Wrestling Women vs. the Aztec Ape
Campbell, Eric: Charlie Chaplin Carnival; Charlie Chaplin Cavalcade; Charlie Chaplin Festival; Charlie Chaplin—The Early Years Vol. 1–4
Campbell, Glen: True Grit; Uphill All the Way
Campbell, Graeme: And Then You Die
Campbell, Jennifer: Blood Warriors
Campbell, Jo-Ann: Go, Johnny, Go!
Campbell, Judy: Convoy
Campbell, Julia: Diary of a Serial Killer; Livin' Large; Lone Justice; Opportunity Knocks; Poodle Springs
Campbell, Juston: Star Crystal
Campbell, K. Kenneth: Operation Delta Force 2
Campbell, Kate: Come on Tarzan

Campbell, Louise: Bulldog Drummond Comes Back; Bulldog Drummond's Peril; Bulldog Drummond's Revenge
Campbell, Maia: Trippin'
Campbell, Mrs. Patrick: Crime and Punishment; Riptide
Campbell, Naomi: Invasion of Privacy; Prisoner of Love; Unzipped
Campbell, Neve: Craft, The; Drowning Mona; 54; Northern Passage; Panic; Scream; Scream 3; Scream 2; Three to Tango; Too Smooth; Wild Things
Campbell, Nicholas: Big Slice, The; Certain Fury; Dirty Tricks; Knights of the City; No Contest; Rampage; Shades of Love: Champagne for Two; Terminal Choice; We the Jury
Campbell, Paul: Lunatic, The
Campbell, Peggy: When a Man Sees Red
Campbell, Rob: Hostile Waters; Lone Justice 2
Campbell, Stuart: Gallagher's Travels
Campbell, Tisha: House Party 2; Rags to Riches; School Daze; Sprung
Campbell, Torquil: Golden Seal, The
Campbell, William: Battle Circus; Dementia 13; Escape from Fort Bravo; Operation Pacific; Running Wild; Small Town Girl
Campeau, Frank: Man from Painted Post, The
Campell, Bill: Bram Stoker's Dracula
Campion, Cris: Beyond Therapy; Field of Honor; Pirates
Campisi, Tony: Home of Our Own, A
Campitelli, Tom: Gates of Hell Part II: Dead Awakening
Campos, Bruno: Mimic 2
Campos, Rafael: Astro-Zombies; Where the Buffalo Roam
Canada, Robert: Danger Zone, The (1986)
Canada, Ron: Lost in the Bermuda Triangle
Canale, Gianna Maria: Devil's Commandment, The; Goliath and the Vampires
Canalito, Lee: Paradise Alley
Canary, David: Posse
Canavan, Erinn: What Ever Happened To … ?
Cancelier, Urbain: Amélie
Candy, John: Armed and Dangerous; BluesBrothers, The; Brewster's Millions; Canadian Bacon; Career Opportunities; Cool Runnings; Delirious; Find the Lady; Going Berserk; Good Idea; Great Outdoors, The; Home Alone; Hostage for a Day; JFK; Last Polka, The; Little Shop of Horrors (1986); National Lampoon's Vacation; Nothing But Trouble; Once Upon a Crime; 1941; Only the Lonely; Planes, Trains and Automobiles; Really Weird Tales; Sesame Street Presents Follow That Bird; Silent Partner, The; Spaceballs; Speed Zone; Splash; Stripes; Summer Rental; Uncle Buck; Volunteers; Wagons East; Who's Harry Crumb?
Cane, Charles: Dead Reckoning
Cane, Susan: Colony (1996)
Canerday, Natalie: October Sky; Sling Blade
Canet, Guillaume: Beach, The
Cann, Sheila: Mark of the Beast, The
Canning, James: Boys in Company C, The
Cannon, Dyan: Anderson Tapes, The; Author! Author!; Based on an Untrue Story; Bob & Carol & Ted & Alice; Caddyshack II; Christmas in Connecticut; Coast to Coast; Deathtrap; Doctors' Wives; 8 Heads in a Duffel Bag; End of Innocence, The; Having It All; Heaven Can Wait; Honeysuckle Rose; Jenny's War; Lady of the House; Last of Sheila, The; Love Machine, The; Merlin & the Sword; Out to Sea; Pickle, The; Revenge of the Pink Panther, The; Rise and Fall of Legs Diamond, The; Shamus; That Darn Cat
Cannon, J. D.: Adventures of Nellie Bly, The; Cool Hand Luke; Death Wish II; Ike: The War Years; Lawman; Pleasure Palace; Raise the Titanic
Cannon, Katherine: Will, G. Gordon Liddy
Cannon, Wanda: For the Moment
Canova, Diana: First Nudie Musical, The
Canova, Judy: Adventures of Huckleberry Finn, The; Oklahoma Annie
Cantafora, Antonio: Gabriela
Cantarelli, Dario: Best Man, The
Cantarini, Giorgio: Life Is Beautiful
Cantinflas: Around the World in 80 Days
Cantó, Toni: All About My Mother
Cantor, Eddie: Glorifying the American Girl; Hollywood Canteen; If You Knew Susie; Kid Millions; Roman Scandals; Show Business; Thank Your Lucky Stars; Whoopee
Canutt, Yakima: Blue Steel; Cyclone in the Saddle; Dawn Rider; Devil Horse, The; Heart of the Rockies; King of the Pecos; Lonely Trail, The; Man from Utah, The; 'Neath Arizona Skies; Painted Stallion, The; Randy Rides Alone; Ranger and the Lady, The; Riders of the Rockies; Riders of the Whistling Skull; Sagebrush Trail; Shadow of the Eagle; Showdown, The (1950); Star Packer, The; Telegraph Trail, The; Texas Terror; Trouble in Texas; Vigilantes Are Coming!; West of the Divide; Westward Ho; Winds of the Wasteland; Wyoming Outlaw
Capaldi, Peter: Captives; John & Yoko: A Love Story; Lair of the White Worm; Prime Suspect 3
Capanna, Omero: Animal Called Man, An
Capelja, Jad: Puberty Blues
Capers, Hedge: Legend of Hillbilly John, The
Capers, Virginia: North Avenue Irregulars, The; Off the Mark; White Mama
Capobianco, Carmine: Galactic Gigolo; Psychos in Love
Capodice, John: Fatally Yours
Capolicchio, Lino: Garden of the Finzi-Continis, The; Wild Flower (1993) (Fiorile)
Capotoro, Carl: Mac
Capra, Francis: Bronx Tale, A; Free Willy 2: The Adventure Home; Kazaam
Caprari, Tony: Kickboxer 5: Redemption
Capri, Ahna: Brotherhood of Satan; Enter the Dragon; Payday
Capshaw, Jessica: Valentine
Capshaw, Kate: Alarmist, The; Best Defense; Black Rain; Code Name: Dancer; Dreamscape; How to Make an American Quilt; Indiana Jones and the Temple of Doom; Just Cause; Little Sex, A; Locusts, The; Love Affair; Love at Large; Love Letter, The; My Heroes Have Always Been Cowboys; Next Door; Power (1986); Quick and the Dead, The; SpaceCamp; Windy City
Capucine: Aphrodite; Con Artists, The; Fellini Satyricon; From Hell to Victory; Honey Pot, The; North to Alaska; Pink Panther, The; Red Sun; Scandalous; Song Without End; Trail of the Pink Panther, The; Walk on the Wild Side; What's New, Pussycat?
Cara, Irene: Aaron Loves Angela; Busted Up; Certain Fury; City Heat; Fame; For Us the Living: The Medgar Evers Story; Guyana Tragedy, The: The Story of Jim Jones; Killing 'Em Softly; Sparkle
Carafotes, Paul: Journey to the Center of the Earth
Carberry, Joseph: 10 Million Dollar Getaway, The
Carbone, Anthony: Bucket of Blood, A; Creature from the Haunted Sea, The; Pit and the Pendulum, The
Carbonell, Nestor: Attention Shoppers
Carbonell, Raul: Nueba Yol
Cardella, Richard: Crater Lake Monster, The
Cardellini, Linda: Dee Snider's Strangeland
Cardenas, Elsa: Brave One, The; Fun in Acapulco
Cardenas, Steve: Mighty Morphin Power Rangers: The Movie; Turbo: A Power Rangers Adventure
Cardille, Lori: Day of the Dead
Cardin, Ann: Buried Alive
Cardinal, Ben: How the West Was Fun; Wolves, The
Cardinal, Lorne: Crazy Horse
Cardinal, Tantoo: By Way of the Stars; Education of Little Tree, The; Hi-line, The; Lakota Woman: Siege at Wounded Knee; Lightning Incident, The; Lost Child, The; Loyalties; Nobody's Girls; Silent Tongue; Where the Rivers Flow North
Cardinale, Claudia: Battle of Austerlitz, The; Big Deal on Madonna Street; Burden of Dreams; Cartouche; Circus World; Conversation Piece; Corleone; 8 1/2; Escape to Athena; Fitzcarraldo; Gift, The; Girl with a Suitcase; Henry IV; Immortal Bachelor, The; Legend of Frenchie King, The; Leopard, The; Lost Command; Man in Love, A; Next Summer; Once Upon a Time in the West; One Russian Summer; Pink Panther, The; Princess Daisy; Professionals, The; Red Tent, The; Rocco & His Brothers; Salamander, The; Son of the Pink Panther
Cardona, Annette: Latino
Cardone, Natalie: L'Enfer
Cardos, John: Satan's Sadists
Cardoso, Pedro: Four Days in September

Carell, Lianella: Bicycle Thief, The
Carette, Bruno: May Fools
Carette, Julien: Grand Illusion; La Bête Humaine; La Marseillaise; Sylvia and the Phantom
Carey, Amie: SubUrbia
Carey, Clare: SubUrbia
Carey, Harry: Air Force; Among the Living; Angel and the Badman; Beyond Tomorrow; Buffalo Stampede; Devil Horse, The; Duel in the Sun; Great Moment, The; Kid Galahad; Last Outlaw, The; Law and Order; Law West of Tombstone; Man of the Forest; Powdersmoke Range; Red River; Sea of Grass, The; Shepherd of the Hills, The; So Dear to My Heart; Spoilers, The; Straight Shooting; Sundown; They Knew What They Wanted
Carey, Joyce: Brief Encounter; Cry, the Beloved Country
Carey, Macdonald: Access Code; Comanche Territory; Copper Canyon; End of the World; Great Missouri Raid, The; John Paul Jones; Let's Make It Legal; Shadow of a Doubt; Summer of Fear; Tammy and the Doctor; Wake Island; Who Is the Black Dahlia?
Carey, Mariah: Glitter
Carey, Michele: El Dorado; In the Shadow of Kilimanjaro; Live a Little, Love a Little; Scandalous John
Carey, Olive: On Dangerous Ground
Carey, Pauline: Urinal
Carey, Philip: Calamity Jane; Fighting Mad; Gun Fury; Operation Pacific; Screaming Mimi; Tanks Are Coming, The; Time Travelers, The; Tonka
Carey, Ron: Fatso; High Anxiety; Silent Movie; Who Killed Mary What's 'Er Name?
Carey, Timothy: Finger Man; Head (1968); Killing, The; Killing of a Chinese Bookie; Paths of Glory; Poor White Trash
Carey Jr., Harry: Billy the Kid vs. Dracula; Breaking In; Challenge to White Fang; Cherry 2000; Copper Canyon; Crossroads; Gundown at Sandoval; Island in the Sky; Last Stand at Saber River; Pursued; Red River; Rio Grande; Searchers, The; Shadow Riders, The; She Wore a Yellow Ribbon; Take a Hard Ride; Texas John Slaughter: Stampede at BitterCreek; Three Godfathers, The; Tombstone; Trinity Is Still My Name; Uforia; Undefeated, The; Wagonmaster; Whales of August, The; Wild Times; Wyatt Earp: Return to Tombstone
Cargill, Patrick: Countess from Hong Kong, A
Cargol, Jean-Pierre: Wild Child, The (L'Enfant Sauvage)
Carhart, Timothy: Beverly Hills Cop 3; Candyman: Farewell to the Flesh; Quicksand: No Escape; Red Rock West
Carhart, III, John: There's Nothing Out There
Carides, Gia: Backlash; Bad Company; Brilliant Lies; Last Breath; Maze; Paperback Romance
Carides, Zoe: Brilliant Lies; Death in Brunswick; Stones of Death
Cariou, Len: Drying Up the Streets; Executive Decision; Four Seasons, The; Kurt Vonnegut's Monkey House; Lady in White; Man in the Attic, The; Never Talk to Strangers; Summer of Ben Tyler, The; Thirteen Days; Witness to the Execution
Carl, George: Funnybones
Carle, Richard: Ghost Walks, The
Carlin, George: Bill and Ted's Bogus Journey; Bill and Ted's Excellent Adventure; George Carlin: Jammin' in New York; Outrageous Fortune; Prince of Tides, The; Streets of Laredo
Carlin, Leka: Night Stalker, The
Carlin, Lynn: Baxter; Deathdream; Tick ... Tick ... Tick ...; Wild Rovers, The
Carlin, Nancy: Jon Jost's Frameup
Carlisle, Anne: Liquid Sky; Perfect Strangers
Carlisle, Kitty: Murder at the Vanities; Night at the Opera, A
Carlisle, Mary: Beware of Spooks; Dead Men Walk; Kentucky Kernels; One Frightened Night; Palooka
Carlo, Johann: Quiz Show
Carloni, Ester: Ciao Professore
Carlson, June: Delinquent Daughters; Mom and Dad
Carlson, Karen: Brotherly Love; Dangerous Company; Fleshburn; In Love with an Older Woman; Octagon, The; Student Nurses, The; Teen Vamp
Carlson, Leslie: Deranged
Carlson, Richard: All I Desire; Beyond Tomorrow; Creature from the Black Lagoon; Flat Top; Ghost Breakers; Helen Morgan Story, The; Hold That Ghost; Howards of Virginia, The; It Came from Outer Space; Last Command, The; Little Foxes, The; Magnetic Monster, The; No, No Nanette; Presenting Lily Mars; Retreat Hell; Too Many Girls; Try and Get Me; Valley of Gwangi; White Cargo
Carlson, Slim: Sourdough
Carlson, Veronica: Dracula Has Risen from the Grave; Horror of Frankenstein
Carlton, Hope Marie: Hard Ticket to Hawaii; Savage Beach
Carlton, Rebekah: Leprechaun 4 in Space
Carlton, Timothy: Victoria and Albert
Carlucci, Milly: Adventures of Hercules, The
Carlyle, Robert: Angela's Ashes; Beach, The; Carla's Song; Full Monty, The; Go Now; Plunkett & Macleane; Priest; Ravenous; Riff-Raff (1990); Trainspotting; World Is Not Enough, The
Carmel, Roger C.: Hardly Working; Thunder and Lightning
Carmen, Jean: Arizona Gunfighter
Carmen, Jewel: American Aristocracy, An
Carmen, Julie: Can You Hear the Laughter? The Story of Freddie Prinze; Deadly Currents; Fright Night II; Gloria; In the Mouth of Madness; Kiss Me a Killer; Last Plane Out; Milagro Beanfield War, The; Neon Empire, The; Paint It Black; Penitent, The
Carmet, Jean: Black and White in Color; Buffet Froid (Cold Cuts); Circle of Deceit; Dog Day; Investigation; Little Theatre of Jean Renoir, The; Secret Obsessions; Sorceress, The (1988); Violette
Carmichael, Hoagy: Johnny Angel; Las Vegas Story, The; Young Man with a Horn
Carmichael, Ian: Betrayed; Brothers In Law; Colditz Story, The; Dark Obsession; I'm All Right Jack; Lady Vanishes, The; Lucky Jim; School for Scoundrels
Carmichael, Katy: Mood Swingers
Carminati, Tullio: London Melody
Carmine, Michael: Band of the Hand
Carnahan, Joe: Blood, Guts, Bullets & Octane
Carne, Judy: Americanization of Emily, The; Only with Married Men
Carnera, Primo: Hercules Unchained
Carney, Alan: Zombies on Broadway
Carney, Art: Bitter Harvest; Blue Yonder, The; Defiance; Going in Style; Guide for the Married Man, A; Harry and Tonto; Honeymooners, The: Lost Episodes (TV Series); Honeymooners, The (TV Series); House Calls; Izzy & Moe; Katherine; Last Action Hero, The; Late Show, The; Miracle of the Heart; Movie Movie; Muppets Take Manhattan, The; Naked Face, The; Night Friend; Night They Saved Christmas, The; St. Helens; Steel; Sunburn; Take This Job and Shove It; Undergrads, The
Carney, Zane: My Giant
Carnon, Angela: Pleasure Unlimited
Carnovsky, Morris: Cornered; Dead Reckoning; Edge of Darkness; Gambler, The; Gun Crazy
Carol, Cindy: Dear Brigitte; Gidget Goes to Rome
Carol, Linda: Reform School Girls
Carol, Martine: Beauties of the Night; Lola Montes; Nana; Vanina Vanini
Carol, Sue: Check and Double Check
Caron, Glenn Gordon: Wilder Napalm
Caron, Leslie: American in Paris, An; Battle of Austerlitz, The; Contract; Courage Mountain; Daddy Long Legs; Damage; Dangerous Moves; Fanny; Father Goose; Funnybones; Gigi; Glass Slipper, The; Goldengirl; Is Paris Burning?; Last of the Blonde Bombshells, The; Lili; Madron; Man Who Loved Women, The; Promise Her Anything; QB VII; Unapproachable, The; Valentino
Carpendale, Howard: No One Cries Forever
Carpenter, Carleton: Two Weeks with Love; Up Periscope
Carpenter, David: Crimes of the Heart; Warlock
Carpenter, Fred: Murdered Innocence
Carpenter, Gabriel: Drive Me Crazy
Carpenter, Horace: Maniac
Carpenter, John: First Works, Volumes 1 & 2
Carpenter, Thelma: Wiz, The
Carr, Bret: Girl with the Hungry Eyes, The
Carr, Carol: Down Among the "Z" Men

Carr, Darleen: Piranha
Carr, Hayley: Back Home; Mood Swingers
Carr, Jane: Something for Everyone
Carr, Marian: Indestructible Man
Carr, Mary: Forbidden Trail; Red Kimono, The
Carr, Paul: Severed Arm, The
Carr, Rachel: Underground
Carradine, Bruce: Americana
Carradine, David: Americana; Animal Instincts; Armed Response; Bird on a Wire; Bound for Glory; Boxcar Bertha; Cannonball; Capital Punishment; Children of the Corn V: Fields of Terror; Circle of Iron; Cloud Dancer; Code Name Jaguar; Crime Zone; Deadly Surveillance; Death Race 2000; Deathsport; Distant Justice; Dune Warriors; Evil Toons; Field of Fire; Future Zone; Gambler Returns, The: Luck of the Draw; Good Guys and the Bad Guys, The; Gray Lady Down; High Noon, Part Two; Karate Cop; Kill Zone; Knocking on Death's Door; Kung Fu (1971); Kung Fu—The Movie (1986); Last Stand at Saber River; Lone Wolf McQuade; Long Goodbye, The; Long Riders, The; Macho Callahan; Macon County Jail; Martial Law; Mean Streets; Misfit Brigade, The; Mr. Horn; North and South; Nowhere to Run; Oceans of Fire; On the Line; P.O.W.: The Escape; Project: Eliminator; Q; Ray Bradbury's Chronicles: The MartianEpisodes; Roadside Prophets; Serpent's Egg, The; Shepherd; Sonny Boy; Sundown; Think Big; Thunder and Lightning; Trick or Treat; Tropical Snow; Warden of Red Rock; Warlords; Warrior and the Sorceress, The; Wizard of the Lost Kingdom II
Carradine, John: Adventures of Huckleberry Finn, The; Adventures of Mark Twain, The; Antony and Cleopatra; Astro-Zombies; Bees, The; Big Foot; Billy the Kid vs. Dracula; Blood and Sand; Blood of Dracula's Castle; Bloodsuckers, The; Bluebeard; Boogeyman, The; Boxcar Bertha; Captain Kidd; Captive Wild Woman; Casanova's Big Night; Christmas Coal Mine Miracle, The; Cosmic Man, The; Crash! (1977); Daniel Boone; Death at Love House; Dimples; Drums Along the Mohawk; Everything You Always Wanted to Know About Sex but Were Afraid to Ask; Evil Spawn; Evils of the Night; Face of Marble, The; Female Jungle; Five Bloody Graves; Five Came Back; Frankenstein Island; Garden of Allah, The; Goliath Awaits; Good Guys and the Bad Guys, The; Grapes of Wrath, The; Gun Riders, The; Half Human; Hell Ship Mutiny; Hillbillys in a Haunted House; Horror of the Blood Monsters; Hound of the Baskervilles, The; House of Dracula; House of Frankenstein; House of Seven Corpses, The; House of the Long Shadows; Howling, The; Ice Pirates; Incredible Petrified World, The; Invisible Invaders; Invisible Man's Revenge, The; Jack-O; Jesse James; Johnny Guitar; Kentuckian, The; Killer Inside Me, The; Last Hurrah, The; Last Tycoon, The; Mary, Mary, Bloody Mary; Mary of Scotland; Monster Club, The; Monster in the Closet; Mr. Moto's Last Warning; Mummy and the Curse of the Jackals, The; Mummy's Ghost, The; Myra Breckenridge; Nesting, The; Night Strangler, The; Nocturna; Of Human Hearts; Patsy, The; Peggy Sue Got Married; Private Affairs of Bel Ami, The; Return of Frank James, The; Return of the Ape Man; Reunion in France; Revenge of the Zombies; Satan's Cheerleaders; Seekers, The; Sentinel, The; Seven Minutes, The; Shock Waves (Death Corps); Shootist, The; Showdown at Boot Hill; Silent Night, Bloody Night; Silver Spurs; Son of Fury; Stagecoach; Star Slammer; Terror in the Wax Museum; Thank You, Mr. Moto; This Is My Affair; Thriller (TV Series); Thunder Pass; Tomb, The; Unearthly, The; Vampire Hookers (Sensuous Vampires); Voodoo Man; Waterfront; Western Union; White Buffalo; Winterset; Wizard of Mars, The
Carradine, Keith: All Quiet on the Western Front; Almost Perfect Affair, An; Andre; Baby (2000); Bachelor, The; Backfire; Ballad of the Sad Cafe, The; Blackout; Capone; Chiefs; Choose Me; Cold Feet; Crisscross (1992); Daddy's Dyin' and Who's Got the Will; Dead Man's Walk; Diamond of Jeru, The; Duellists, The; Eye on the Sparrow; Forgotten, The; Hostage Hotel; Hunter's Moon; Idaho Transfer; Inquiry, The; Judgment; Kung Fu (1971); Last Stand at Saber River; Long Riders, The; Lumiere; Man on a String; Maria's Lovers; McCabe and Mrs. Miller; Moderns, The; Nashville; Night Ride Home; Old Boyfriends; Out of the Cold; Payoff; Pretty Baby; Rumor of War, A; Shrieking, The; Sirens; Southern Comfort; Standoff; Thieves Like Us; Thousand Acres, A; Tie That Binds, The; Trouble in Mind; Two Days in the Valley; Welcome to L.A.; Wild Bill
Carradine, Robert: All's Fair; As Is; Big Red One, The; Bird of Prey; Blackout; Breakout; Buy and Cell; Cannonball; Clarence; Coming Home; Conspiracy: The Trial of the Chicago 8; Disappearance of Christina, The; Doublecrossed; Gunfighter (1997); Heartaches; Humanoids from the Deep; Illusions; Incident, The; Jackson County Jail; John Carpenter Presents: Body Bags; Joyride; Kid with X-Ray Eyes, The; Long Riders, The; Massacre at Central High; Max Keeble's Big Move; Mean Streets; Number One with a Bullet; Orca; Revenge of the Nerds; Revenge of the Nerds II: Nerds in Paradise; Revenge of the Nerds III: The Next Generation; Revenge of the Nerds IV: Nerds in Love; Rude Awakening; Scorpio One; Somebody Has to Shoot the Picture; Tag—The Assassination Game; Tommyknockers, The; Wavelength
Carradine (narrator), John: Invasion of the Animal People
Carrara, Chris: Remote
Carrera, Barbara: Adventures of Young Brave, The; Condorman; Embryo; I, the Jury; Island of Dr. Moreau, The; Lone Wolf McQuade; Love at Stake; Love Is All There Is; Loverboy; Masada; Never Say Never Again; Point of Impact; Sawbones; Tryst; When Time Ran Out!; Wicked Stepmother, The; Wild Geese II
Carrere, Tia: Aloha Summer; Fatal Mission; High School High; Hollow Point; Hostile Intentions; Immortals, The; Jury Duty; Kull the Conqueror; My Teacher's Wife; Natural Enemy; Quick; Rising Sun; Showdown in Little Tokyo; Tracked; Treacherous; True Lies; 20 Dates; Wayne's World; Wayne's World 2; Zombie Nightmare
Carrey, Jim: Ace Ventura: Pet Detective; Ace Ventura: When Nature Calls; Batman Forever; Cable Guy, The; Dumb and Dumber; Earth Girls Are Easy; High Strung; How the Grinch Stole Christmas; Liar, Liar; Majestic, The; Man on the Moon; Mask, The; Me, Myself & Irene; Once Bitten; Rubberface; Truman Show, The
Carrico, Monica: Running Hot
Carrier, Corey: Savage Land
Carriere, Mathieu: Beethoven's Nephew; Bilitis; Coup De Grace; Woman in Flames, A
Carrillo, Elpidia: Beyond the Limit; Border, The; Bread and Roses; Lightning Incident, The; My Family; Predator; Salvador
Carrillo, Leo: American Empire; Captain Caution; Cisco Kid (TV Series); Fugitive, The; Ghost Catchers, The; Girl of the Golden West, The; Gypsy Wildcat; History Is Made at Night; Horror Island; Manhattan Melodrama; Manhattan Merry-Go-Round; One Night in the Tropics; Riders of Death Valley; Too Hot to Handle; Viva Villa!
Carrol, Regina: Satan's Sadists
Carroll, Barbara: Last Days of Pompeii (1960)
Carroll, Beeson: Spacehunter: Adventures in the Forbidden-Zone
Carroll, Diahann: Carmen Jones; Eve's Bayou; Five Heartbeats, The; From the Dead of Night; Goodbye Again; I Know Why the Caged Bird Sings; Paris Blues; That's Singing: The Best of Broadway
Carroll, Helena: Man Upstairs, The
Carroll, J. Winston: Spenser: Ceremony; Spenser: Pale Kings & Princes
Carroll, Janet: Talent for the Game
Carroll, Jill: Vals, The
Carroll, John: Decision at Sundown; Fabulous Texan, The; Farmer Takes a Wife, The; Fiesta; Flying Tigers, The; Go West; Only Angels Have Wings; Rio Rita; Susan and God; Wolf Call; Zorro Rides Again
Carroll, Johnny: Rock, Baby, Rock It
Carroll, Justin: Dark Secrets
Carroll, Kevin: Ed's Next Move
Carroll, Lane: Crazies, The
Carroll, Leo G.: Adventures of Topper, The; Bulldog Drummond's Secret Police; Charlie Chan in City in Darkness; Charlie Chan's Murder Cruise; Christmas Carol, A; Enchantment; Father of the Bride; Forever Amber; House on 92nd Street, The; Man from U.N.C.L.E., The (TV Series); Paradine Case, The;

Cassavetes, Nick: Assault of the Killer Bimbos; Astronaut's Wife, The; Backstreet Dreams; Black Rose of Harlem; Body of Influence; Broken Trust; Class of 1999 II: The Substitute; Delta Force 3; Life; Quiet Cool; Twogether
Cassel, Jean-Pierre: Alice; Baxter; Candide; Crimson Rivers, The; Discreet Charm of the Bourgeoisie, The; Elusive Corporal, The; Favor, the Watch and the Very Big Fish,The; Is Paris Burning?; La Cérémonie; La Vie Continue; Les Rendez-Vous D'Anna; Maid, The; Ready to Wear; Return of the Musketeers; Who Is Killing the Great Chefs of Europe?
Cassel, Sandra: Last House on the Left
Cassel, Seymour: Adventures in Spying; Animal Factory; Bad Love; Boiling Point; California Dreaming; Crew, The; Double Exposure; Eye of the Tiger; Fast Sofa; Hand Gun; Imaginary Crimes; In the Soup; Indecent Proposal; It Could Happen to You; Johnny Be Good; Killing of a Chinese Bookie; Love Streams; Plain Clothes; Rushmore; Survival Game; Tollbooth; Track 29; Valentino; White Fang
Cassel, Vincent: Birthday Girl; Brotherhood of the Wolf; Crimson Rivers, The; Hate
Cassell, Alan: Squizzy Taylor
Casseus, Gabriel: Black Dog; New Jersey Drive
Cassidy, David: Instant Karma; Night the City Screamed, The; Spirit of '76, The
Cassidy, Elaine: Felicia's Journey; Others, The
Cassidy, Jack: Andersonville Trial, The; Columbo: Murder by the Book; Eiger Sanction, The
Cassidy, Joanna: All-American Murder; Bank Shot; Barbarians at the Gate; Blade Runner; Chain Reaction; Children of Times Square, The; Club Paradise; Don't Tell Mom the Babysitter's Dead; Executive Power; Father's Revenge, A; Fourth Protocol, The; Ghosts of Mars; Invitation to Hell; Landslide; Live! From Death Row; Lonely Hearts; May Wine; Nightmare at Bittercreek; 1969; Package, The; Perfect Family; Second Civil War, The; Tommyknockers, The; Under Fire; Wheels of Terror; Where the Heart Is; Who Framed Roger Rabbit
Cassidy, Patrick: Fiancé, The; Hitler's Daughter; How the West Was Fun; Longtime Companion; Love at Stake; Off the Wall
Cassidy, Shaun: Roots—The Gift; Texas Guns
Cassidy, Ted: Addams Family, The (TV Series); Planet Earth
Cassie, Kyle: Children of the Corn: Revelation
Cassinelli, Claudio: Hands of Steel; Screamers
Cassisi, John: Bugsy Malone
Castaldi, Jean-Pierre: French Connection II, The
Castel, Lou: Beware of a Holy Whore; Bullet for the General, A; Irma Vep; Paranoia; Rorret; Scarlet Letter (1973); Three Lives and Only One Death
Castellaneta, Dan: Laughter on the 23rd Floor
Castellano, Richard: Godfather, The; Lovers and Other Strangers; Night of the Juggler
Castelli, Paulo: Happily Ever After
Castellitto, Sergio: Alberto Express; Pronto; Star Maker, The; Va Savoir
Castelloe, John: Me and the Mob
Castelloe, Molly: Clean Shaven
Castelnuovo, Nino: Escapade in Florence; Umbrellas of Cherbourg, The
Castille, Christopher: Beethoven's 2nd
Castillo, Gloria: Invasion of the Saucer Men; Meteor Monster (Teenage Monster); Reform School Girl
Castle, DeShonn: Zebrahead
Castle, Don: Stampede
Castle, John: Antony and Cleopatra; Crucifer of Blood; Lion in Winter, The; Mirror Crack'd from Side to Side, The; Murder Is Announced, A
Castle, Peggie: Beginning of the End; Finger Man; Invasion USA (1952); Seven Hills of Rome, The
Castle, Roy: Alice Through the Looking Glass; Dr. Terror's House of Horrors; Dr. Who and the Daleks
Castro, Analia: Official Story, The
Castrodad, Eddie: Night Train to Katmandu
Cataldo, Giusi: Flight of the Innocent
Catalifo, Patrick: Sand and Blood
Cates, Georgina: Awfully Big Adventure, An; Clay Pigeons; Frankie Starlight; Soldier's Sweetheart, A; Stiff Upper Lips
Cates, Helen: Taste for Killing, A
Cates, Phoebe: Anniversary Party, The; Bodies, Rest & Motion; Bright Lights, Big City; Date with an Angel; Drop Dead Fred; Fast Times at Ridgemont High; Gremlins; Gremlins 2: The New Batch; Heart of Dixie, The; Paradise; Princess Caraboo; Private School; Shag, the Movie
Catillon, Brigitte: Un Coeur en Hiver
Catlett, Walter: Every Day's a Holiday; On the Avenue; Rain
Cato, Hil: Skin Art
Caton, Juliette: Courage Mountain
Caton, Matiaz Bureau: Ponette
Caton, Michael: Animal, The; Castle, The
Cattand, Gabriel: Blue Jeans
Cattel, Christine: Bedroom Eyes
Cattrall, Kim: Above Suspicion; Baby Geniuses; Bastard, The; Big Trouble in Little China; Breaking Point; City Limits; Crossroads (2002); Deadly Harvest; Double Vision; Heidi Chronicles, The; Honeymoon Academy; Live Nude Girls; Mannequin; Masquerade; Midnight Crossing; Miracle in the Wilderness; Palais Royale; Police Academy; Porky's; Return of the Musketeers; Robin Cook's Invasion; Running Delilah; Smokescreen; Split Second; Star Trek VI: The Undiscovered Country; 36 Hours to Die; Ticket to Heaven; Turk 182; Unforgettable; Wild Palms
Caubère, Philippe: My Father's Glory; My Mother's Castle
Cauchy, Daniel: Bob le Flambeur
Caudell, Lane: Hanging on a Star
Caudell, Toran: Johnny Mysto; Max Is Missing
Caulfield, Joan: Blue Skies; Buckskin; Daring Dobermans, The; Dear Wife; Hatfields and the McCoys, The; Monsieur Beaucaire; Pony Express Rider; Welcome, Stranger
Caulfield, Maxwell: Alien Intruder; Animal Instincts; Beverly Hills 90210; Boys Next Door, The; Dance with Death; Empire Records; Exiled in America; Gettysburg; Grease 2; Midnight Witness; Mindgames; No Escape, No Return; Perfect Tenant, The; Project: Alien; Real Blonde, The; Sundown; Supernaturals, The
Cava, Olimpia: Vanina Vanini
Cavagnaro, Gary: Drive-In
Cavalli, Fred: Werewolf
Cavallo, Victor: Tragedy of a Ridiculous Man
Cavanagh, Paul: Bill of Divorcement, A; Bride of the Gorilla; Francis in the Haunted House; Goin' to Town; Scarlet Claw, The; Tarzan and His Mate; Woman in Green, The
Cavanaugh, Hobart: Kismet; Rose of Washington Square; Stage Struck; Stage to Chino
Cavanaugh, Megan: League of Their Own, A; Robin Hood: Men in Tights
Cavanaugh, Michael: Forced Vengeance; Full Fathom Five; Two to Tango
Cavanaugh, Patrick: Shadow Warriors
Cavazos, Lumi: Bottle Rocket; Like Water for Chocolate; Manhattan Merengue
Cave, Des: Paddy
Cave, Nick: Johnny Suede
Caven, Ingrid: In a Year of 13 Moons; Malou; Mother Kusters Goes to Heaven
Cavender, Glen: General, The; Keystone Comedies: Vol. 1–5
Cavett, Dick: Jimi Hendrix
Caviezel, James: Angel Eyes; High Crimes
Caviezel, Jim: Count of Monte Cristo, The (2002); Frequency; Thin Red Line, The
Cawthorn, Joseph: Dixiana
Cayton, Elizabeth: Necromancer; Silent Night, Deadly Night Part 2
Cazale, John: Conversation, The; Deer Hunter, The; Dog Day Afternoon; Godfather, The; Godfather Epic, The; Godfather, Part II, The
Cazenove, Christopher: Aces: Iron Eagle III; Children of the Full Moon; Eye of the Needle; Fantasist, The; Heat and Dust; Jenny's War; Mata Hari; Proprietor, The; Three Men and a Little Lady; Until September
Ceccaldi, Daniel: Holiday Hotel; Stolen Kisses

The; Grease; Heartburn; Life or Something Like It; Lily Dale; Married to It; Meet the Applegates; Men's Club, The; Moll Flanders; Not My Kid; Perfect Witness; Practical Magic; Silent Victory: The Kitty O'Neil Story; Six Degrees of Separation; Smoke; Staying Together; Tidy Endings; Time of Destiny, A; To Wong Foo, Thanks for Everything, Julie Newmar; Twilight; Unexpected Family, An; Unexpected Life, An; Up Close and Personal; Where the Heart Is; Without a Trace
Chao, Rosalind: Joy Luck Club, The; Terry Fox Story, The; Thousand Pieces of Gold; White Ghost
Chao, Winston: Wedding Banquet, The
Chapa, Damian: Bound by Honor; Saints & Sinners; Street Fighter
Chapel, Loyita: Legacy for Leonette
Chapin, Billy: Tobor the Great
Chapin, Jonathan: Prison for Children
Chapin, Michael: Under California Stars
Chapin, Miles: Bless the Beasts and Children; French Postcards; Funhouse, The; Get Crazy; Pandemonium
Chapin, Richard: Ring of Steel
Chapin, Tom: Lord of the Flies
Chaplin, Ben: Birthday Girl; Feast of July; Lost Souls; Murder by Numbers (2002); Thin Red Line, The; Truth About Cats and Dogs, The; Washington Square
Chaplin, Carmen: All About the Benjamins; Ma Saison Preferée
Chaplin, Charlie: Chaplin Revue, The; Charlie Chaplin ... Our Hero; Charlie Chaplin Carnival; Charlie Chaplin Cavalcade; Charlie Chaplin Festival; Charlie Chaplin—The Early Years Vol. 1–4; Circus, The/A Day's Pleasure; City Lights; Countess from Hong Kong, A; Days of Thrills and Laughter; Gold Rush, The; Great Dictator, The; Kid, The (1921)/The Idle Class; King in New York, A; Limelight; Modern Times; Monsieur Verdoux; Three Charlies and a Phoney!; When Comedy Was King
Chaplin, Geraldine: Age of Innocence, The; Bolero; Buffalo Bill and the Indians; Chaplin; Countess from Hong Kong, A; ¡Cria!; Crimetime; Dr. Zhivago; Duel of Hearts; Foreign Field, A; Gulliver's Travels (1996) (Television); Home for the Holidays (1995); Jane Eyre; Mama Turns 100; Moderns, The; Return of the Musketeers; Roseland; Voyage en Douce; Wedding, A (1978); Welcome to L.A.; Z.P.G. (Zero Population Growth)
Chaplin, Josephine: Canterbury Tales, The; Escape to the Sun; Jack the Ripper
Chaplin, Michael: King in New York, A
Chaplin, Sydney: Chaplin Revue, The; Countess from Hong Kong, A; Land of the Pharaohs; Limelight; Three Charlies and a Phoney!
Chapman, Edward: Convoy; Juno and the Paycock; X—The Unknown
Chapman, Graham: And Now for Something Completely Different; How to Irritate People; Life of Brian; Monty Python and the Holy Grail; Monty Python Live at the Hollywood Bowl; Monty Python's Flying Circus (TV Series); Monty Python's the Meaning of Life; Odd Job, The; Yellowbeard
Chapman, Judith: Dead Space; Scalpel
Chapman, Keri Jo: It's in the Water
Chapman, Lanai: Rat Race
Chapman, Lonny: Baby Doll; Bad News Bears Go to Japan, The; King; Moving Violation; Running Scared; Terror Out of the Sky; Where the Red Fern Grows
Chapman, Marguerite: Amazing Transparent Man, The; Charlie Chan at the Wax Museum; Coroner Creek; Daring Young Man, The; Flight to Mars; Green Promise, The; Spy Smasher
Chapman, Mark Lindsay: Langoliers, The
Chappell, Crystal: Bigfoot: The Unforgettable Encounter
Chappell, Lisa: Desperate Remedies
Chappelle, Dave: Getting In; Half Baked; Nutty Professor, The; Robin Hood: Men in Tights; Screwed; You've Got Mail
Charap, Madison: St. Francisville Experiment, The
Charbonneau, Patricia: Call Me; Desert Hearts; Disaster at Silo 7; Kiss the Sky; K2
Charisse, Cyd: Band Wagon, The; Black Tights; Brigadoon; East Side, West Side; Fiesta; Five Golden Hours; Harvey Girls, The; It's Always Fair Weather; Kissing Bandit, The; Maroc 7; Meet Me in Las Vegas; On an Island with You; Party Girl; Silk Stockings; Singin' in the Rain; Swimsuit; That's Entertainment! III; Two Weeks in Another Town; Words and Music; Ziegfeld Follies
Charkravarty, Alok: World of Apu, The
Charles, Craig: Red Dwarf (TV Series)
Charles, David: Julia Has Two Lovers
Charles, Emile: Wonderland
Charles, Josh: Cooperstown; Crossing the Bridge; Crossworlds; Don't Tell Mom the Babysitter's Dead; Grave, The; Little City; Norma Jean and Marilyn; Pie in the Sky; Threesome
Charles, Leon: Merry Wives of Windsor, The
Charles, Ray: That Was Rock
Charleson, Ian: Chariots of Fire; Codename: Kyril; Louisiana; Terror at the Opera
Charleson, Leslie: Most Wanted
Charlie Daniels Band: Urban Cowboy
Charney, Jordan: Imposter, The
Charney, Suzanne: Night Stalker, The: Two Tales of Terror (TV Series)
Charon, Jacques: Le Bourgeois Gentilhomme
Charpin: Le Schpountz; Well-Digger's Daughter, The
Charters, Mychelle: Raw Target
Charters, Spencer: Bat Whispers, The; Three Faces West
Chartoff, Melanie: Doin' Time; Gambler, Part III—The Legend Continues, The; Having It All; Stoogemania
Charvet, David: Baywatch: The Movie
Chase, Barrie: Silk Stockings
Chase, Charlie: Sons of the Desert
Chase, Chevy: Caddyshack; Caddyshack II; Cops and Robbersons; Deal of the Century; Ernie Kovacs: Television's Original Genius; Fletch; Fletch Lives; Foul Play; Funny Farm; Groove Tube, The; Hero (1992); Man of the House; Memoirs of an Invisible Man; Modern Problems; National Lampoon's Christmas Vacation; National Lampoon's European Vacation; National Lampoon's Vacation; Nothing But Trouble; Oh, Heavenly Dog!; Seems Like Old Times; Sesame Street Presents Follow That Bird; Snow Day; Spies Like Us; Three Amigos; Tunnelvision (1976); Under the Rainbow; Vegas Vacation
Chase, Courtney: Nick of Time
Chase, Ilka: Animal Kingdom, The
Chase, Karen: Vendetta
Chase, Steve: Eden (TV Series)
Chatel, Peter: Fox and His Friends
Chatman, Gregory Allen: Beyond the Doors
Chatterjee, Anil: Two Daughters
Chatterjee, Dhritiman: Adversary, The
Chatterjee, Soumitra: Days and Nights in the Forest; Devi (The Goddess); Distant Thunder; Home and the World; Two Daughters; World of Apu, The
Chatterton, Ruth: Dodsworth; Female
Chatterton, Tom: Drums of Fu Manchu
Chatton, Charlotte: Stand-Ins
Chaulet, Emmanuelle: All the Vermeers in New York; Boyfriends and Girlfriends
Chau-Sang, Anthony Wong: Time and Tide
Chauvin, Lilyan: Silent Night, Deadly Night
Chaveau, Zoe: Longshot (1981)
Chaves, Richard: Cease Fire; Predator
Chavez, Alonso: Bread and Roses
Chavez, Ingrid: Graffiti Bridge
Chavez, Oscar: Break of Dawn
Chayanne: Dance with Me
Chaykin, Maury: Adjuster, The; Art of War, The; Camilla (1994); Cold Comfort; Cutthroat Island; Def-Con 4; Devil in a Blue Dress; Entrapment; George's Island; Jerry and Tom; Love and Death on Long Island; Money for Nothing; My Cousin Vinny; Mystery, Alaska; Stars and Bars; Sugartime; Unstrung Heroes; Varian's War; Vindicator, The; What's Cooking?
Cheadle, Don: Boogie Nights; Bulworth; Colors; Devil in a Blue Dress; Family Man, The; Hamburger Hill; Mission to Mars; Out of Sight; Rat Pack, The; Rebound; Rosewood; Swordfish; Things Behind the Sun; Traffic; Volcano
Checchi, Carlo: La Scorta

Checci, Andrea: Black Sunday
Checker, Chubby: Twist Around the Clock
Cheech and Chong: Cheech and Chong's Next Movie; Corsican Brothers, The; Nice Dreams; Still Smokin'; Things Are Tough All Over; Up in Smoke; Yellowbeard
Cheek, Molly: Stepmonster
Cheirel, Micheline: Carnival in Flanders; Cornered
Chekhov, Michael: Rhapsody; Specter of the Rose, The
Chelton, Tsilla: Tatie Danielle
Chemel, David: Taming of the Shrew (1982)
Chen, Chang: Crouching Tiger, Hidden Dragon
Chen, Chao-jung: Vive L'Amour
Chen, Joan: Blood of Heroes; Deadlock; Golden Gate; Heaven and Earth; Hunted, The (1995); Judge Dredd; Last Emperor, The; On Deadly Ground; Precious Find; Strangers; Tai-Pan; Temptation of a Monk; Turtle Beach (Killing Beach); Twin Peaks (Movie); Twin Peaks (TV Series); What's Cooking?; Wild Side
Chen, Kelly: Tokyo Raiders
Chen, Sung Young: Legend of the Red Dragon
Chen, Tina: Alice's Restaurant; Devlin Connection III, The; Lady from Yesterday, The
Chenault, Lawrence: Body and Soul
Cheng, Adam: Zu: Warriors from the Magic Mountain
Cheng, Carol: Operation Condor (Jackie Chan)
Cheng, Ekin: Tokyo Raiders
Chepil, Bill: Street Trash
Cher: Come Back to the Five and Dime, Jimmy Dean, Jimmy Dean; Faithful; If These Walls Could Talk; Mask (1985); Mermaids; Moonstruck; Ready to Wear; Silkwood; Suspect; Tea with Mussolini; Witches of Eastwick, The
Chereau, Patrice: Danton; Last of the Mohicans, The
Cherkassov, Nikolai: Alexander Nevsky; Ivan the Terrible—Part I & Part II
Cherney, Linda: Screaming Mimi
Cherot, Christopher Scott: Hav Plenty
Cherrill, Virginia: City Lights
Cherry, Helen: Adam and Evalyn; Nemesis
Cheryl, Karen: Here Comes Santa Claus
Chesebro, George: Roamin' Wild; Saddle Mountain Roundup; Vigilantes of Boomtown
Chesnais, Patrick: La Lectrice (The Reader); Post Coitum
Chester, Craig: Grief; Swoon
Chester, Vanessa Lee: Harriet the Spy; Little Princess, A; Lost World, The: Jurassic Park
Chestnut, Morris: Best Man, The; Boyz N the Hood;Brothers, The; Ernest Green Story, The; Killing Yard, The; Two Can Play That Game; Under Siege 2: Dark Territory
Cheung, Daphne: On Dangerous Ground
Cheung, George: High Voltage
Cheung, Jacky: Bullet in the Head; Wicked City, The (1992)
Cheung, Leslie: Better Tomorrow, A; Better Tomorrow 2, A; Bride with White Hair, The; Chinese Ghost Story, A; Farewell My Concubine; Once a Thief; Temptress Moon
Cheung, Maggie: Chinese Box; In the Mood for Love; Irma Vep; Paper Marriage; Police Story III—Super Cop; Project A (Part II); Song of the Exile; Supercop; Twin Dragons
Chevalia, Kevin: Homeward Bound: The Incredible Journey; Homeward Bound II: Lost in San Francisco
Chevalier, Anna: Tabu
Chevalier, Maurice: Breath of Scandal, A; Can-Can; Fanny; Gigi; In Search of the Castaways; Love in the Afternoon; Love Me Tonight; Merry Widow, The; Monkeys Go Home; New Kind of Love, A; Panic Button
Chevolleau, Richard: Rude; Silent Witness: What a Child Saw
Chevrier, Arno: Red Dwarf, The
Chew, Kim: Dim Sum: A Little Bit of Heart
Cheyne, Hank: Bad Blood
Chi, Cheun-Hua: Legend of the Red Dragon
Chi, Nina Li: Twin Dragons
Chiaki, Minoru: Hidden Fortress, The; Throne of Blood
Chianese, Dominic: Gotti; Sopranos, The (TV series)
Chiang, David: Once Upon a Time in China II
Chiao, Roy: Protector, The (1985)
Chiari, Walter: Bellissima; Chimes at Midnight (Falstaff)
Chiaureli, Sofico: Color of Pomegranates, The
Chiba, Sachiko: Wife! Be Like a Rose!
Chiba, Sonny: Aces: Iron Eagle III; Immortal Combat; Legend of the Eight Samurai; Street Fighter; Virus
Chibas, Marissa: Cold Feet
Chicot, Etienne: 36 Fillette
Chief Big Tree: Hills of Old Wyoming
Chiklis, Michael: Rain Killer, The; Silent Witness; Soldier; Wired
Childress, Alvin: Amos and Andy (TV Series)
Childress, Patricia: Dead Man's Walk; Shake, Rattle & Rock
Childs, Jeremy: Last Castle, The
Chiles, Linden: Forbidden World
Chiles, Lois: Babysitter, The; Creepshow 2; Diary of a Hitman; Eye of the Snake; Lush Life; Moonraker; Raw Courage; Sweet Liberty; Twister; Way We Were, The
Chin, Joey: China Girl
Chin, May: Wedding Banquet, The
Chin, Tsai: Joy Luck Club, The
Ching, William: Pat and Mike; Wistful Widow of Wagon Gap, The
Ching-wan, Lau: Black Mask
Chinh, Kieu: Joy Luck Club, The; Operation C.I.A.
Chinlund, Nick: Letter to My Killer; Mr. Magoo; Unveiled
Chinn, Jade: Girl Who Spelled Freedom, The
Chinn, Lori Tan: South Pacific (2001)
Chin-Wai, Tony Leung: In the Mood for Love
Chi-Vy, Sam: China, My Sorrow
Chlumsky, Anna: Gold Diggers: The Secret of Bear Mountain; My Girl; My Girl 2; Trading Mom
Cho, J. Moki: Race the Sun
Cho, Margaret: Ground Control; I'm the One That I Want; It's My Party; Sweethearts
Cho, Seung-woo: Chunhyang
Choate, Tim: Def-Con 4; Europeans, The; First Time, The; Jane Austen in Manhattan; Spy
Chokachi, David: Shadow of a Scream; Unspeakable, The; Witchblade
Chokling, Neten: Cup, The
Chong, Jun: Silent Assassins; Street Soldiers
Chong, Marcus: Panther
Chong, Rae Dawn: Amazon; American Flyers; Beat Street; Boca; Borrower, The; Boulevard; Break, The; City Limits; Color Purple, The; Commando; Common Bonds; Curiosity Kills; Dangerous Relations; Denial; Far Out Man; Fear City; Hideaway; Mask of Death; Power of Attorney; Principal, The; Prison Stories: Women on the Inside; Protector (1998); Quest for Fire; Soul Man; Squeeze, The; Time Runner; Visit, The; When the Party's Over
Chong, Robbi: Poltergeist: The Legacy
Chong, Tommy: After Hours; Far Out Man; National Lampoon's Senior Trip; Spirit of '76, The
Chonjor, Lama: Cup, The
Choudhury, Sarita: Down Came a Blackbird; Gloria; House of the Spirits, The; Kama Sutra: A Tale of Love; Mississippi Masala; 3 A.M.; Wild West
Chow, China: Big Hit, The; Head Over Heels
Chow, Valerie: Chungking Express
Chowdhry, Navin: King of the Wind; Madame Sousatzka; Seventh Coin, The
Chowdhry, Ranjit: Lonely in America
Chriqui, Emmanuelle: On the Line (2001); 100 Girls
Christ, Chad: No Laughing Matter
Christensen, Alisa: Witchcraft 7: Judgment Hour
Christensen, Erika: Traffic
Christensen, Hayden: Life as a House; Star Wars: Attack of the Clones
Christensen, Stacy: Virgin Queen of St. Francis High, The
Christensen, Ute: Berlin Tunnel 21
Christian, Claudia: Adventures of a Gnome Named Gnorm, The; Arena; Babylon 5 (TV Series); Danielle Steel's Kaleidoscope; Final Voyage; Hexed; Hidden, The; Mad About You; Ma-

niac Cop 2; Mercenary 2: Thick and Thin; Never on Tuesday; Strays; Think Big; Wing and a Prayer, A
Christian, Helen: Zorro Rides Again
Christian, John: Little Patriot, The
Christian, Keely: Slumber Party Massacre 3
Christian, Leigh: Beyond Atlantis
Christian, Linda: Athena; Casino Royale; Full Hearts and Empty Pockets; Holiday in Mexico
Christian, Michael: Private Obsession
Christian, Paul: Beast from 20,000 Fathoms, The
Christian, Robert: Bustin' Loose; Roll of Thunder, Hear My Cry
Christians, Mady: All My Sons; Letter from an Unknown Woman
Christians, Rudolph: Foolish Wives
Christiansen, Dalin: Robin Hood Gang, The
Christie, Audrey: Frankie and Johnny; Splendor in the Grass; Streets of L.A., The
Christie, Julie: Afterglow; Billy Liar; Darling; Demon Seed; Dr. Zhivago; Don't Look Now; Dragonheart; Fahrenheit 451; Far from the Madding Crowd; Fools of Fortune; Go-Between, The; Hamlet; Heat and Dust; Heaven Can Wait; McCabe and Mrs. Miller; Miss Mary; Petulia; Power (1986); Railway Station Man, The; Return of the Soldier, The; Secret Obsessions; Separate Tables; Shampoo
Christine, Virginia: Billy the Kid vs. Dracula; Guess Who's Coming to Dinner; Mummy's Curse, The; Not as a Stranger; One Man's Way; Phantom of the Plains; Prize, The
Christman, Kermit: Wicked Games
Christmas, Eric: Air Bud; Challengers, The; Home Is Where the Hart Is; Philadelphia Experiment, The
Christophe, Françoise: Walk into Hell
Christopher, Dennis: Alien Predators; Bernice Bobs Her Hair; Breaking Away; California Dreaming; Chariots of Fire; Circuitry Man; Circuitry Man II: Plughead Rewired; Don't Cry, It's Only Thunder; Fade to Black; It; Jake Speed; Last Word, The; Sinful Life, A; Skeletons; 30-Sep-55; Young Graduates
Christopher, Jordan: Return of the Seven
Christopher, Kay: Dick Tracy's Dilemma
Christopher, Scott: Robin Hood Gang, The
Christopher, Thom: Deathstalker III—The Warriors from Hell; Wizard of the Lost Kingdom
Christopherson, Kathy: Executive Target; Guyver 2: Dark Hero
Christy, Dorothy: Big Business Girl; Parlor, Bedroom and Bath; Radio Ranch (Men with Steel Faces, Phantom Empire)
Christy, Vic: Challenge to Be Free
Chrysostom, Anthony: Shadow Creature
Chu, Emily: Heart of Dragon
Chuck D: Alan Smithee Film, An—Burn Hollywood Burn
Chuckles, The: Girl Can't Help It, The
Chuckster, Simon: Sweet Sweetback's Baadasssss Song
Chun, Shun: Shanghai Triad
Chung, Cherie: Once a Thief; Peking Opera Blues
Chung, David: Ballad of Little Jo, The
Chung, Kent: Sex and Zen
Chung, Michael Daeho: Yellow
Chung, Mok Siu: Once Upon a Time in China III
Church, Sandra: Ugly American, The
Church, Thomas Haden: Free Money; Mr. Murder; Specials, The
Churchill, Berton: Big Stampede, The
Churchill, Donald: Hound of the Baskervilles, The
Churchill, Marguerite: Ambassador Bill; Big Trail, The; Dracula's Daughter
Churchill, Sarah: Royal Wedding
Churikova, Inna: Adam's Rib
Chuvelov, Ivan: End of St. Petersburg, The
Ciampa, Jo: Salome
Ciannelli, Eduardo: Bulldog Drummond's Bride; Creeper, The; Dillinger; Gunga Din; Kitty Foyle; Lost Moment, The; Marked Woman; Monster from Green Hell; Mummy's Hand, The; Mysterious Dr. Satan; Strange Cargo; They Got Me Covered; They Met in Bombay; Winterset
Ciardi, Francesca: Cannibal Holocaust
Cicchini, Robert: Watcher, The
Ciepielewska, Anna: Passenger, The
Ciesar, Jennifer: Lovers' Lovers
Cikatic, Branko: Skyscraper
Cilento, Diane: Admirable Crichton, The; Agony and the Ecstasy, The; Hitler, the Last Ten Days; Hombre; Naked Edge, The; Rattle of a Simple Man; Truth About Women, The; Wicker Man, The; Z.P.G. (Zero Population Growth)
Cimino, Leonardo: Rappaccini's Daughter
Cinkozoev, Mirlan: Beshkempir, The Adopted Son
Cinnante, Kelly: Christmas in Connecticut
Cintra, Luis Miguel: Convent, The
Cioffi, Charles: Don Is Dead, The; Lucky Luciano; Remo Williams: The Adventure Begins; Shaft; Thief Who Came to Dinner, The
Cir, Myriam: Savage Hearts
Cistaro, Anthony: Witchblade
Citera, Tom: Up the Academy
Citrinti, Michael: Hideous
Citti, Franco: Accattone; Arabian Nights; Decameron, The; Mamma Roma; Oedipus Rex; Pigsty
Clabbers, Rein: Last Broadcast, The
Claire, Cyrielle: Code Name: Emerald; Sword of Gideon
Claire, Ina: Three Broadway Girls
Claire, Jennifer: Right Hand Man, The
Claire, Marion: Make a Wish
Clairiond, Aimée: Monsieur Vincent
Clancey, Bo: Easier Said
Clanton, Jimmy: Go, Johnny, Go!
Clanton, Rony: Education of Sonny Carson, The
Clapp, Gordon: Kurt Vonnegut's Monkey House; Morrison Murders, The; Rage, The: Carrie 2; Return of the Secaucus 7; Small Sacrifices; Stand Off; Termini Station
Clapton, Eric: Chuck Berry Hail! Hail! Rock 'n' Roll; Jimi Hendrix; Last Waltz, The
Clare, Diane: Plague of the Zombies
Clare, Mary: Citadel, The; Evil Mind, The (The Clairvoyant); Young and Innocent
Clark, Alexander: No Time for Sergeants (Television)
Clark, Andrew: Anzacs
Clark, Anthony: Dogfight; Hourglass; Murder She Purred
Clark, Brett: Alien Warrior; Deathstalker IV: Match of the Titans; Inner Sanctum
Clark, Bryan: Without Warning: The James Brady Story
Clark, Candy: American Graffiti; Amityville III: The Demon; Big Sleep, The; Blob, The; Blue Thunder; Cat's Eye; Cherry Falls; Citizen's Band; Cool As Ice; Fat City; Hambone and Hillie; James Dean—A Legend in His Own Time; Man Who Fell to Earth, The; More American Graffiti; Original Intent; Q; Rodeo Girl
Clark, Carl: Sourdough
Clark, Carol Higgins: Cry in the Night, A
Clark, Carolyn Ann: Cradle Will Fall, The; Mutator
Clark, Cliff: Wagons Roll at Night, The
Clark, Dane: Action in the North Atlantic; Destination Tokyo; Hollywood Canteen; Moonrise; Murder on Flight 502; Stolen Life, A; Thunder Pass
Clark, Dick: Deadman's Curve
Clark, Doran: Black Eagle
Clark, Eugene: Tekwar: The Original Movie
Clark, Eugene A.: Trial & Error (1992)
Clark, Fred: Auntie Mame; Bells Are Ringing; Boys' Night Out; Caddy, The; Curse of the Mummy's Tomb, The; Dr. Goldfoot and the Bikini Machine; Don't Go Near the Water; George Burns and Gracie Allen Show, The (TV Series); Here Come the Girls; Horse in the Gray Flannel Suit, The; It Started With a Kiss; Laugh for Joy (Passionate Thief) (1954); Lemon Drop Kid, The; Mating Game, The; Passionate Thief, The (1961); Sunset Boulevard; Three for Bedroom C
Clark, Graydon: Satan's Sadists
Clark, Harry: No Time for Sergeants (Television)
Clark, Harvey: Law for Tombstone
Clark, Ian D.: Lilies; Trial & Error (1992)
Clark, Jameson: Battle of the Sexes, The
Clark, Ken: Attack of the Giant Leeches

Clark, Kerrie: Angel 4: Undercover
Clark, Liddy: Blue Fin; Kitty and the Bagman
Clark, Marlene: Night of the Cobra Woman; Switchblade Sisters
Clark, Matt: Back to the Future III; Class Action; Country; Driver, The; Gambler, Part III—The Legend Continues, The; Great Northfield Minnesota Raid, The; Kiss of Fire; Mother; Out of the Darkness; Pat Garrett and Billy the Kid; Quick and the Dead, The; Raven Hawk; Return to Oz; Ruckus; Trilogy of Terror II; White Lightning
Clark, Michael: Prospero's Books
Clark, Mystro: Chairman of the Board
Clark, Oliver: Ernest Saves Christmas; One Cooks, the Other Doesn't; Star Is Born, A
Clark, Petula: Finian's Rainbow; Goodbye, Mr. Chips; Made in Heaven; Promoter, The
Clark, Robin: Boxoffice; Cyberzone
Clark, Roy: Matilda; Uphill All the Way
Clark, Spencer Treat: Arlington Road; Unbreakable
Clark, Susan: Apple Dumpling Gang, The; Choice, The; Colossus: The Forbin Project; Coogan's Bluff; Deadly Companion; Murder by Decree; Night Moves; Nobody's Perfekt; North Avenue Irregulars, The; Promises in the Dark; Showdown; Skin Game (1971); Valdez Is Coming
Clark Sisters: Gospel
Clarke, Alex: Learning Tree, The
Clarke, Bernadette L.: Love Jones
Clarke, Brian Patrick: Sleepaway Camp II: Unhappy Campers
Clarke, Caitlin: Dragonslayer; Penn & Teller Get Killed
Clarke, David: Great St. Louis Bank Robbery, The
Clarke, Ellie Laura: Return of the Sand Fairy, The
Clarke, Gary: How to Make a Monster; Missile to the Moon
Clarke, J. Jerome: Luther, The Geek
Clarke, John: Death in Brunswick
Clarke, Mae: Flying Tigers, The; Frankenstein; Great Guy; King of the Rocketmen; Lady Killer; Public Enemy
Clarke, Margi: Letter to Brezhnev
Clarke, Melinda: Killer Tongue; Return to Two-Moon Junction; Spawn
Clarke, Mindy: Return of the Living Dead 3
Clarke, Richard: Charlie Chan in City in Darkness
Clarke, Robert: Frankenstein Island; Hideous Sun Demon, The; Man from Planet X, The; Midnight Movie Massacre
Clarke, Warren: Cold Room, The; Firefox; From a Far Country; Great Riviera Bank Robbery, The; Greenfingers; Mandela; Sherlock Holmes: Hands of a Murderer
Clarke, Zelah: Jane Eyre
Clarke-Duncan, Michael: Planet of the Apes (2001)
Clarkin, Richard: Five Senses, The
Clarkson, Helene: Blood & Donuts
Clarkson, Lana: Barbarian Queen; Barbarian Queen II: Empress Strikes Back; Deathstalker
Clarkson, Patricia: Blindman's Bluff; Caught in the Act; Dead Pool, The; Four Eyes and Six Guns; High Art; Joe Gould's Secret; Jumanji; Legacy of Lies; Old Man and the Sea, The; Pharaoh's Army
Clarkson, Robert: Save the Lady
Clary, Robert: Hogan's Heroes (TV Series); New Faces
Clavel, Garance: When the Cat's Away
Clavier, Christian: Just Visiting
Clawson, Eric: Dead Hate the Living, The
Clay, Andrew: Adventures of Ford Fairlane, The; Brain Smasher … A Love Story; Casual Sex?; Foolish; National Lampoon's Favorite Deadly Sins; No Contest
Clay, Andrew Dice: My 5 Wives
Clay, Jennifer: Suburbia
Clay, Nicholas: Evil Under the Sun; Excalibur; Lady Chatterley's Lover; Love Spell
Clayburgh, Jill: Day of Atonement; First Monday in October; Fools Rush In; Griffin and Phoenix: A Love Story; Hanna K.; Honor Thy Father & Mother: The Menendez Killings; Hustling; I'm Dancing As Fast As I Can; It's My Turn; Miles to Go; Naked in New York; Portnoy's Complaint; Rich in Love; Semi-Tough; Shy People; Silver Streak; Sins of the Mind; Starting Over; Terminal Man, The; Thief Who Came to Dinner, The; Unmarried Woman, An; Unspeakable Acts; Wedding Party, The; Where Are the Children?; Whispers in the Dark
Claypool, Les: Adventures of the Kung Fu Rascals, The
Clayton, Ethel: Warning Shadows
Clayton, Jan: In Old Mexico
Clayworth, June: Dick Tracy Meets Gruesome
Cleave, Randy: Rockwell: A Legend of the Wild West
Cleese, John: And Now for Something Completely Different; Clockwise; Erik the Viking; Fawlty Towers (TV Series); Fierce Creatures; Fish Called Wanda, A; How to Irritate People; Life of Brian; Mary Shelley's Frankenstein; Monty Python and the Holy Grail; Monty Python Live at the Hollywood Bowl; Monty Python's Flying Circus (TV Series); Monty Python's the Meaning of Life; Out-of-Towners, The (1999); Privates on Parade; Rat Race; Romance with a Double Bass; Rudyard Kipling's The Jungle Book (1994); Silverado; Splitting Heirs; Statue, The; Time Bandits; Whoops Apocalypse; Yellowbeard
Clemens, Paul: Beast Within, The; Promises in the Dark
Clement, Aurore: Invitation au Voyage; Les Rendez-Vous D'Anna; Paris, Texas; Toute Une Nuit
Clement, Jennifer: Raffle, The
Clementi, Pierre: Belle de Jour; Conformist, The; Partner; Pigsty; Steppenwolf; Sweet Movie
Clemento, Steve: Hills of Old Wyoming
Clements, Edward: Metropolitan
Clements, John: Convoy; Four Feathers, The; Ships with Wings; Silent Enemy, The
Clements, Stanley: Babe Ruth Story, The; Bowery Boys, The (Series)
Clemmons, Clarence: Fatal Instinct
Clemons, Clarence: Swing
Clennon, David: Couch Trip, The; Hanna K.; Light Sleeper; Man Trouble; Missing; Special Bulletin; Sweet Dreams
Clery, Corinne: Dangerous Obsession; Story of O, The
Cleveland, George: Angel on My Shoulder; Blue Steel; Courage of Lassie; Drums of Fu Manchu; Lone Ranger, The; Man from Utah, The; Revolt of the Zombies; Spoilers, The; Wistful Widow of Wagon Gap, The
Cleveland, Rev. James: Gospel
Clevot, Philippe: Eyes of the Birds
Cliff, Jimmy: Club Paradise; Harder They Come, The; Jimmy Cliff—Bongo Man
Clifford, Cheryl: Original Sins
Clifford, Jack: King of the Pecos
Clifford, Kim: Save the Lady
Clift, Montgomery: Big Lift, The; From Here to Eternity; Heiress, The; I Confess; Indiscretion of an American Wife; Judgment at Nuremberg; Lonelyhearts; Misfits, The; Place in the Sun, A; Raintree County; Red River; Search, The; Suddenly, Last Summer; Young Lions, The
Climo, Brett: Archer's Adventure; Blackwater Trail
Cline, Eddie: Buster Keaton Festival Vol. 1–3
Clinger, Debra: Midnight Madness
Clinton, George: Cosmic Slop
Clinton, Roger: Till the End of the Night
Clive, Colin: Bride of Frankenstein; Christopher Strong; Frankenstein; History Is Made at Night; Jane Eyre; Mad Love
Clive, E. E.: Arrest Bulldog Drummond; Bulldog Drummond Comes Back; Bulldog Drummond Escapes; Bulldog Drummond's Revenge; Charlie Chan in London; Hound of the Baskervilles, The; Invisible Man, The; Night Must Fall; Personal Property; Tarzan Escapes
Cloke, Kristen: Final Destination
Clooney, George: Batman & Robin; ER: The Series Premiere; From Dusk Till Dawn; Ocean's Eleven (2001); One Fine Day; Out of Sight; Peacemaker, The (1997); Perfect Storm, The; Red Surf; Return of the Killer Tomatoes; Three Kings
Clooney, Rosemary: Here Come the Girls; Red Garters; White Christmas
Cloos, Hans Peter: Germany In Autumn
Close, Eric: Follow the Stars Home; Hercules and the Lost Kingdom; Magnificent Seven, The (TV Series)

Close, Glenn: Air Force One; Big Chill, The; Cookie's Fortune; Dangerous Liaisons; Fatal Attraction; Hamlet; Hook; House of the Spirits, The; Immediate Family; In the Gloaming; Jagged Edge; Mars Attacks!; Mary Reilly; Maxie; Meeting Venus; Natural, The; 101 Dalmatians (1996); 102 Dalmatians; Orphan Train; Paper, The; Paradise Road; Reversal of Fortune; Sarah, Plain and Tall; Skylark; South Pacific (2001); Stone Boy, The; Things You Can Tell Just by Looking at Her; Winter's End; World According to Garp, The
Clough, John Scott: Dog Trouble; Fast Forward; What Ever Happened To ... ?
Cloutier, Suzanne: Othello
Clouzot, Vera: Diabolique; Wages of Fear, The
Clover, David: Zipperface
Clunes, Martin: Saving Grace; Sweet Revenge
Clushenko, Yevgenta: Unfinished Piece for the Player Piano, An (Unfinished Piece for a Mechanical Piano, An)
Clute, Sidney: Cry of Battle
Clutsei, George: Legend of Walks Far Woman, The
Cluzet, François: French Kiss; Horse of Pride, The; L'Enfer; One Deadly Summer; Round Midnight; Story of Women, The; Swindle, The
Clyde, Andy: Bad Lands (1939); Border Patrol; Border Vigilantes; Dangerous Venture; Doomed Caravan; False Colors; Forty Thieves; Hoppy Serves a Writ; In Old Colorado; Leather Burners, The; Little Minister, The; Mystery Man; Outlaws of the Desert; Pirates on Horseback; Riders of the Timberline; Secrets of the Wasteland; Silent Conflict; Stick to Your Guns; Sundown Riders; Texas Masquerade; Three Men from Texas; Twilight on the Trail; Wide-Open Town
Clyde, June: Seven Doors to Death; Study in Scarlet, A
Clyde (the ape): Every Which Way But Loose
Coates, Kim: Amityville Curse, The; Battlefield Earth; Beyond Suspicion; Breach of Trust; Club, The; Cold Front; Dead Silence; Full Disclosure; Harmony Cats; Lethal Tender; Model by Day; Red-Blooded American Girl; Smokescreen; Spider and the Fly, The; Waterworld; Xchange
Coates, Phyllis: I Was a Teenage Frankenstein; Incredible Petrified World, The; Invasion USA (1952); Longhorn; Marshal of Cedar Rock; Superman and the Mole Men; TV's Best Adventures of Superman
Cobanoglu, Necmettin: Journey of Hope
Cobb, Lee J.: Anna and the King of Siam; Boomerang; Brothers Karamazov, The; Buckskin Frontier; But Not for Me; Call Northside 777; Come Blow Your Horn; Coogan's Bluff; Dark Past, The; Exodus; Exorcist, The; Four Horsemen of the Apocalypse; Golden Boy; Gorilla at Large; Green Mansions; In Like Flint; Lawman; Left Hand of God, The; Liberation of L. B. Jones, The; Macho Callahan; Mackenna's Gold; Man in the Gray Flannel Suit, The; Man of the West; Man Who Cheated Himself, The; Man Who Loved Cat Dancing, The; Men of Boys Town; Miracle of the Bells, The; North of the Rio Grande; On the Waterfront; Our Man Flint; Party Girl; Racers, The; Sirocco; Song of Bernadette, The; That Lucky Touch; Three Faces of Eve, The; Trap, The; 12 Angry Men
Cobb, Randall "Tex": Blind Fury; Buy and Cell; Collision Course; Critical Condition; Diggstown; Dirty Dozen, The: The Deadly Mission; Ernest Goes to Jail; Fletch Lives; Golden Child, The; Liar, Liar; Raising Arizona; Uncommon Valor
Cobbs, Bill: Air Bud; Always Outnumbered; Bodyguard, The; Decoration Day; Ed; Hudsucker Proxy, The; I Still Know What You Did Last Summer; Nightjohn; Out There; That Thing You Do!
Cobo, Roberto: Los Olvidados
Cobo De Garcia, Eva: Operation Condor (Jackie Chan)
Coburn, Charles: Bachelor Mother; Colonel Effingham's Raid; Devil and Miss Jones, The; Edison, The Man; Gentlemen Prefer Blondes; George Washington Slept Here; Heaven Can Wait; Idiot's Delight; Impact; In Name Only; In This Our Life; John Paul Jones; King's Row; Knickerbocker Holiday; Lady Eve, The; Made for Each Other; Monkey Business; More the Merrier, The; Mr. Music; Of Human Hearts; Paradine Case, The; Road to Singapore; Three Faces West; Trouble Along the Way; Vivacious Lady; Wilson
Coburn, David: Born American
Coburn, James: Affliction; Americanization of Emily, The; Avenging Angel, The (1995); Baltimore Bullet, The; Bite the Bullet; Bronco (TV Series); Bruce Lee: Curse of the Dragon; Charade; Cherokee Kid, The; Christmas Reunion, A; Cross of Iron; Dain Curse, The; Dead Heat on a Merry-Go-Round; Deadfall; Death of a Soldier; Draw; Eraser; Firepower; Fistful of Dynamite, A; Goldengirl; Great Escape, The; Hard Times; Hell Is for Heroes; High Risk; Hit List, The (1992); Hudson Hawk; In Like Flint; Internecine Project, The; Keys to Tulsa; Last of Sheila, The; Looker; Loved One, The; Loving Couples; Magnificent Seven, The; Major Dundee; Martin's Day; Massacre at Fort Holman (Reason to Live ... A Reason to Die, A); Maverick; Missing Pieces; Mr. Murder; Muppet Movie, The; Nutty Professor, The; Our Man Flint; Pat Garrett and Billy the Kid; Pinocchio; President's Analyst, The; Proximity; Ride Lonesome; Second Civil War, The; Set-Up, The; Sister Act 2: Back in the Habit; Skeletons; Snow Dogs; Thousand Heroes, A; Walter and Henry; Waterhole #3; Young Guns II
Coburn Jr., James: Tuxedo Warrior
Coby, Michael: Bitch, The; We Are No Angels
Coca, Imogene: Alice in Wonderland; 10 from Your Show of Shows
Coca, Richard: Hitz; Only the Strong
Cochran, Eddie: Girl Can't Help It, The; Go, Johnny, Go!
Cochran, Robert: I Stand Condemned; Sanders of the River; Scrooge
Cochran, Steve: Carnival Story; Chase, The; Copacabana; Deadly Companions, The; I, Mobster; Il Grido (Outcry, The); Jim Thorpe—All American; Kid from Brooklyn, The; Private Hell 36; Song Is Born, A; Tanks Are Coming, The; White Heat
Cochrane, Rory: Adventures of Sebastian Cole, The; Dazed and Confused; Empire Records; Fathers & Sons; Love & a .45; Low Life, The; Prime Gig, The
Cockburn, Arlene: Winter Guest, The
Cockburn, Serge: Crocodile Dundee in Los Angeles
Cocker, Joe: Mad Dogs and Englishmen
Coco, James: Chair, The; Cheap Detective, The; Generation (1969); Hunk; Littlest Angel, The; Man of La Mancha; Murder by Death; New Leaf, A; Only When I Laugh; Scavenger Hunt; That's Adequate; Wholly Moses!; Wild Party, The
Cocteau, Jean: Testament of Orpheus, The
Cody, Iron Eyes: Ernest Goes to Camp; Grayeagle; Son of Paleface
Cody, Kyle: Life 101
Cody, Lew: Dishonored
Coe, Barry: But Not for Me; Cat, The (1966); Dr. Death: Seeker of Souls; Peyton Place
Coe, George: Blind Date; End of Innocence, The; Flash of Green, A; Hollywood Detective, The; Listen to Your Heart; My Name Is Bill W; Red Flag: The Ultimate Game; Remo Williams: The Adventure Begins
Coe, Peter: Mummy's Curse, The; Okefenokee
Coffey, John: War of the Buttons
Coffey, Scott: Amazing Stories (TV Series); Montana; Shag, the Movie; Shout (1991)
Coffield, Kelly: Specials, The
Coffield, Peter: Times Square
Coffin, Frederick: V. I. Warshawski
Coffin, Tristram: Corpse Vanishes, The; Forbidden Trails; King of the Rocketmen; Ma Barker's Killer Brood; Pirates of the High Seas; Rodeo King and the Senorita; Spy Smasher
Coggio, Roger: Immortal Story
Coghill, Nikki: Dark Age
Coghlan Jr., Frank: Adventures of Captain Marvel, The; Drum Taps; Hell's House
Cohen, Alain: Two of Us, The
Cohen, Emma: Horror Rises from the Tomb
Cohen, Jeff: Goonies, The
Cohen, Kaipo: Under the Domim Tree
Cohen, Matthew Roy: Trained to Fight
Cohen, Mitchell: Toxic Avenger, The
Cohen, Sammy: What Price Glory? (1926)
Cohen, Scott: Sweet Evil
Cohn, Marya: Vermont Is for Lovers

Cohn, Mindy: Boy Who Could Fly, The
Colagrande, Stefano: Misunderstood
Colantoni, Enrico: Galaxy Quest; James Dean (2001); Member of the Wedding, The
Colao, Manuel: Flight of the Innocent
Colasanto, Nicholas: Fat City; Mad Bull; Raging Bull
Colbert, Claudette: Bluebeard's Eighth Wife; Boom Town; Cleopatra; Drums Along the Mohawk; Egg and I, The; Guest Wife; I Cover the Waterfront; It Happened One Night; Let's Make It Legal; Midnight; Palm Beach Story, The; Parrish; Since You Went Away; So Proudly We Hail; Texas Lady; Three Came Home; Tomorrow Is Forever; Tovaritch; Without Reservations
Colbert, Ray: RSVP
Colbourne, Maurice: Littlest Horse Thieves, The
Cole, Alexandra: Dr. Butcher, M.D. (Medical Deviate)
Cole, Dennis: Connection (1973); Death House; Powderkeg
Cole, Gary: Brady Bunch Movie, The; Echoes in the Darkness; Fall from Grace; Fatal Vision; I'll Be Home for Christmas; In the Line of Fire; Kiss the Sky; Office Space; Son of the Morning Star; Very Brady Sequel, A
Cole, George: Adventures of Sadie; Belles of St. Trinian's, The; Blue Murder at St. Trinian's; Dr. Syn, Alias the Scarecrow; Gone in 60 Seconds; Mary Reilly; Vampire Lovers, The
Cole, Henry: Shaka Zulu
Cole, Michael: Mod Squad, The (TV Series)
Cole, Nat King: China Gate; Istanbul; Small Town Girl
Cole, Natalie: Always Outnumbered; Freak City
Cole, Olivia: Sky Is Gray, The; Some Kind of Hero
Cole, Skyler: Adventures Beyond Belief
Cole, Stephanie: Grey Owl
Coleby, Robert: Archer's Adventure; Great Expectations—The Untold Story; Now and Forever; Plumber, The
Coleman, Charlotte: Beautiful People; Four Weddings and a Funeral; Oranges Are Not the Only Fruit; Young Poisoner's Handbook, The
Coleman, Dabney: Amos & Andrew; Bad Ronald; Beverly Hillbillies, The (1993); Bite the Bullet; Callie and Son; Clifford; Cloak and Dagger; Dragnet; Hot to Trot; How to Beat the High Co$t of Living; I Love My Wife; Inspector Gadget; Judicial Consent; Man with One Red Shoe, The; Meet the Applegates; Muppets Take Manhattan, The; Murrow; My Date with the President's Daughter; Never Forget; Nine to Five; Nothing Personal; Pray TV; President's Plane Is Missing, The; Rolling Thunder; Scalphunters, The; Short Time; Slender Thread, The; There Goes the Neighborhood; Tootsie; Trouble with Girls, The; Wargames; Where the Heart Is; Young Doctors in Love
Coleman, Frank J.: Charlie Chaplin Cavalcade
Coleman, Gary: Jimmy the Kid; Kid from Left Field, The; Kid with the Broken Halo, The; Kid with the 200 I.Q., The; On the Right Track
Coleman, Jack: Beneath the Bermuda Triangle; Daughter of Darkness; Foreign Student; Landlady, The; Return of Eliot Ness, The; Trapped in Space
Coleman, Jimmy: Riff-Raff (1990)
Coleman, Nancy: Edge of Darkness
Coleman, Patricia: Habit
Coleman, Signy: Relentless 3
Colen, Beatrice: Night Stalker, The: Two Tales of Terror (TV Series)
Coleridge, Tania: Rain Killer, The
Coles, Emma: Two Friends
Coles, Michael: Dracula A.D. 1972; I Want What I Want
Coley, Thomas: Dr. Cyclops
Colgan, Eileen: Quackser Fortune Has a Cousin in the Bronx; Secret of Roan Inish, The
Colicos, John: Drum; King Solomon's Treasure; No Contest; Nowhere to Hide; Phobia; Postman Always Rings Twice, The; Raid on Rommel; Shadow Dancing
Colin, Gregoire: Before the Rain; Dreamlife of Angels, The; Olivier, Olivier
Colin, Jean: Mikado, The
Colin, Margaret: Adventures of Sebastian Cole, The; Amos & Andrew; Butcher's Wife, The; Devil's Own, The; Independence Day; Like Father, Like Son; Martians Go Home; Something Wild; Three Men and a Baby; Traveling Man; True Believer
Colin Jr., David: Beyond the Door; Beyond the Door 2
Collard, Cyril: Savage Nights
Collazo, Damon: Patriot, The
Collazo, Luz Maria: I Am Cuba
Collet, Christopher: Langoliers, The; Manhattan Project, The; Prayer of the Rollerboys
Collette, Toni: Changing Lanes; Clockwatchers; Cosi; Dinner with Friends; Efficiency Expert, The (Spotswood); 8 1/2 Women; Emma; Muriel's Wedding; Pallbearer, The; Shaft; Sixth Sense, The; Velvet Goldmine
Colley, Kenneth: And Nothing But the Truth; Music Lovers, The; Plot to Kill Hitler, The; Return to Treasure Island; Solomon and Sheba; Summer Story, A; Whistle Blower, The
Collier, Constance: Damsel in Distress, A; Monsieur Beaucaire; Perils of Pauline, The; Wee Willie Winkie
Collier, Lois: Naughty Nineties, The; Night in Casablanca, A
Collier Jr., William: Cimarron; Street Scene
Collin, Maxime: Leolo
Collins, Alan: Exterminators of the Year 3000
Collins, Gary: Hangar 18; Kid from Left Field, The
Collins, Joan: Adventures of Sadie; Annie, a Royal Adventure!; Bawdy Adventures of Tom Jones, The; Bitch, The; Bravados, The; Cartier Affair, The; Dark Places; Decameron Nights; Devil Within Her, The; Empire of the Ants; Executioner, The; Fear in the Night (Dynasty of Fear); Fearless; Game for Vultures; Great Adventure, The; Homework; Land of the Pharaohs; Midwinter's Tale, A; Monte Carlo; Oh, Alfie; Opposite Sex, The (1956); Revenge (1971) (Joan Collins); Road to Hong Kong, The; Seven Thieves; Stopover Tokyo; Stud, The; Sunburn; Tales from the Crypt; Tales that Witness Madness; Three in the Cellar; Virgin Queen, The
Collins, Judy: Junior; Woody Guthrie—Hard Travelin'
Collins, Kevin: Garden, The
Collins, Lewis: Code Name: Wild Geese; Final Option, The; Jack the Ripper
Collins, Lisa: Danger Zone; Deep Red; Going Overboard
Collins, Matt: World's Greatest Lover, The
Collins, Patricia: Phobia
Collins, Patrick: Dirt Bike Kid, The
Collins, Pauline: City of Joy; Paradise Road; Shirley Valentine; Upstairs, Downstairs
Collins, Phil: And the Band Played On; Balto; Buster; Frauds; Hook
Collins, Ray: Badman's Territory; Big Street, The; Can't Help Singing; Citizen Kane; Commandos Strike at Dawn; Double Life, A; Francis, the Talking Mule; Heiress, The; Homecoming; Human Comedy, The; It Happens Every Spring; Ma and Pa Kettle Back on the Farm; Ma and Pa Kettle on Vacation; Man from Colorado, The; Racket, The; Rose Marie; Seventh Cross, The; Vengeance Valley; Whistling in Brooklyn
Collins, Roberta: Arousers, The; Vendetta
Collins, Russell: Enemy Below, The; Matchmaker, The
Collins, Ruth: Doom Asylum; Galactic Gigolo
Collins, Stephen: Between the Lines; Brewster's Millions; Chiefs; Choke Canyon; First Wives Club, The; Hold the Dream; Jumpin' Jack Flash; Loving Couples; My New Gun; Promise, The; Scarlett; Stella; Till Murder Do Us Part; Unexpected Family, An; Unexpected Life, An; Weekend War; Woman Named Jackie, A
Collins, Steve: Hitchhiker, The (Series)
Collins Jr., Clifton: Light It Up; Price of Glory
Collinson, Madeleine: Twins of Evil
Collyer, June: Drums of Jeopardy; Ghost Walks, The; Murder by Television
Colman, Renee: Pentathlon
Colman, Ronald: Arrowsmith; Bulldog Drummond; Champagne for Caesar; Double Life, A; If I Were King; Kismet; Lady Windermere's Fan; Lost Horizon; Lucky Partners; Prisoner of Zenda, The; Random Harvest; Tale of Two Cities, A; Talk of the Town, The; White Sister, The
Colodner, Joel: Plants Are Watching, The

Colomby, Scott: Porky's; Porky's II: The Next Day; Porky's Revenge
Colonna, Jerry: College Swing; Road to Rio; Road to Singapore
Colosimo, Clara: Orchestra Rehearsal
Colosimo, Vince: Chopper
Colson, Kevin: Trapped in Space
Colston, Karen: Sweetie
Colt, Beth: Chuck & Buck
Colt, Dennis: Savage Guns
Colt, Marshall: Beverly Hills Madam; To Heal a Nation
Coltrane, Robbie: Adventures of Huck Finn, The (1993); Alice in Wonderland; Bert Rigby, You're a Fool; Buddy; Chinese Boxes; Cracker (TV Series); Danny, The Champion of the World; Frogs for Snakes; From Hell; Goldeneye; Harry Potter and the Sorcerer's Stone; Message in a Bottle; Montana; Nuns on the Run; Oh, What a Night; Perfectly Normal; Pope Must Diet, The; Wonderland; World Is Not Enough, The
Coluche: My Best Friend's Girl; Tchao Pantin
Columbu, Franco: Beretta's Island; Last Man Standing
Colvin, Jack: Incredible Hulk, The
Colyar, Michael: Jugular Wine
Comacho, Felipe: Drive By
Combes, Norman: Kill or Be Killed
Combs, Holly Marie: Dr. Giggles; Our Mother's Murder; Reason to Believe, A
Combs, Jeffrey: Bride of Re-Animator; Castle Freak; Cyclone; Dead Man Walking; Doctor Mordrid; Felony; Frighteners, The; From Beyond; H. P. Lovecraft's Necronomicon: Book of the Dead; I Still Know What You Did Last Summer; Lurking Fear; Phantom Empire, The (1986); Pit and the Pendulum, The; Re-Animator
Combs, Sean "Puffy": Made; Monster's Ball
Comeau, Andy: 8 Heads in a Duffel Bag
Comen, Joshua D.: Night That Never Happened, The
Comer, Anjanette: Appaloosa, The; Baby, The; Lepke; Loved One, The; Netherworld; Rabbit Run; Streets of Laredo
Comingore, Dorothy: Citizen Kane
Commodores, The: Thank God It's Friday
Como, Perry: Doll Face; Words and Music
Como, Rosella: Seven Hills of Rome, The
Comont, Mathilde: Hard Hombre
Compson, Betty: Docks of New York, The; Great Gabbo, The; Invisible Ghost; These Girls Won't Talk
Compton, Fay: Haunting, The; Othello
Compton, Joyce: Balalaika; Country Gentlemen; Rose of Washington Square; Scared to Death; Trapped by Television
Compton, O'Neal: Kill Me Later
Comyn, Charles: Place of Weeping
Conant, Oliver: Summer of '42
Conaway, Cristi: Any Place But Home; Attack of the 50-Foot Woman; Nina Takes a Lover
Conaway, Jeff: Alien Intruder; Almost Pregnant; Breaking Up Is Hard to Do; Dirty Dozen, The: The Fatal Mission; Elvira, Mistress of the Dark; For the Love of It; Ghost Writer; Grease; L.A. Goddess; Patriot (1986); Sleeping Car, The; Sunset Strip; Time to Die, A; Total Exposure
Condominas, Laura Duke: Lancelot of the Lake
Condou, Charlie: Mood Swingers
Conelle, Patricia: Naked Venus
Conesa, Carmen: How to Be a Woman and Not Die in the Attempt
Congdon, James: 4D Man
Congie, Terry: Sizzle Beach, U.S.A.
Conklin, Chester: Apache Woman; Call of the Prairie; Charlie Chaplin ... Our Hero; Every Day's a Holiday; Hollywood Cavalcade; Knickerbocker Holiday; Li'l Abner; Sing, Cowboy, Sing; Virginian, The
Conklin, Heinie: Abbott and Costello Meet the Keystone Kops; Fig Leaves; Riders of Destiny
Conley, Jack: Brown's Requiem
Conlin, Jimmy: Great Moment, The; Mad Wednesday (see also Sin of Harold Diddlebock); Miracle of Morgan's Creek, The; Palm Beach Story, The; Sin of Harold Diddlebock (Mad Wednesday); Sullivan's Travels; Whistle Stop
Conlon, Tim: Prom Night III—Last Kiss
Conn, Didi: Grease; Grease 2; You Light Up My Life
Conn, Jack: Crippled Masters, The
Connell, Edward: Equinox (The Beast) (1971)
Connell, Jane: Mame
Connell, Maureen: Abominable Snowman of the Himalayas, The
Connelly, Billy: Still Crazy
Connelly, Christopher: Foxtrap; Hawmps!; Incredible Rocky Mountain Race, The; Jungle Raiders; Liar's Moon; Manhattan Baby; Mines of Kilimanjaro; Night of the Sharks; 1990: The Bronx Warriors; Operation 'Nam; Strike Commando; They Only Kill Their Masters
Connelly, Jennifer: Beautiful Mind, A; Career Opportunities; Creepers; Dark City; Heart of Justice; Higher Learning; Hot Spot; Inventing the Abbotts; Labyrinth; Mulholland Falls; Of Love and Shadows; Pollock; Requiem for a Dream; Rocketeer, The; Seven Minutes in Heaven; Some Girls
Connelly, Marc: Spirit of St. Louis, The; Tall Story
Conners, Kevin: Phantasm III: Lord of the Dead
Connery, Jason: Bullet to Beijing; Bye Bye, Baby; Robin Hood: Herne's Son; Spymaker: The Secret Life of Ian Fleming
Connery, Sean: Anderson Tapes, The; Another Time, Another Place; Avengers, The; Bridge Too Far, A; Cuba; Darby O'Gill and the Little People; Diamonds Are Forever; Dr. No; Dragonheart; Entrapment; Family Business; Finding Forrester; Fine Madness, A; First Knight; Five Days One Summer; From Russia with Love; Goldfinger; Good Man in Africa, A; Great Train Robbery, The; Highlander; Highlander 2: The Quickening; Hill, The; Hunt for Red October, The; Indiana Jones and the Last Crusade; Just Cause; Longest Day, The; Man Who Would Be King, The; Marnie; Medicine Man; Meteor; Molly Maguires, The; Murder on the Orient Express; Name of the Rose, The; Never Say Never Again; Offence, The; Outland; Playing by Heart; Presidio, The; Red Tent, The; Rising Sun; Robin and Marian; Robin Hood: Prince of Thieves; Rock, The; Russia House, The; Shalako; Sword of the Valiant; Terrorists, The; Thunderball; Time Bandits; Untouchables, The; Wind and the Lion, The; Wrong Is Right; You Only Live Twice; Zardoz
Connick Jr., Harry: Copycat; Excess Baggage; Hope Floats; Life Without Dick; Little Man Tate; Memphis Belle; South Pacific (2001)
Connolly, Andrew: Vendetta
Connolly, Billy: Absolution; Big Man; Blue Money; Everlasting Piece, An; Impostors, The; Mrs. Brown; Muppet Treasure Island
Connolly, Kevin: Alan and Naomi
Connolly, Walter: Adventures of Huckleberry Finn, The; Bitter Tea of General Yen, The; Broadway Bill; Fifth Avenue Girl; Good Earth, The; Lady by Choice; Lady for a Day; Nothing Sacred; Twentieth Century
Connor, Edgar: Hallelujah, I'm A Bum
Connor, Kenneth: Carry on Cleo; Carry on Cruising; Carry on Emmanuelle; Carry on Nurse
Connors, Chuck: Balboa; Blade Rider; Capture of Grizzly Adams, The; Day of the Assassin; Deserter, The; Designing Woman; Flipper; Gambler Returns, The: Luck of the Draw; High Desert Kill; Last Flight to Hell; Mad Bomber, The; 99 and 44/100 Percent Dead; Old Yeller; One Last Run; Pancho Villa; Ride Beyond Vengeance; Rifleman, The (TV Series); Roots; Skinheads; Soylent Green; Standing Tall; Summer Camp Nightmare; Support Your Local Gunfighter; Target Eagle; Terror Squad; Texas Guns; Three Days to a Kill; Trouble Along the Way; Virus
Connors, Kevin R.: Prehysteria 2
Connors, Michael: Where Love Has Gone
Connors, Mike: Casino; Day the World Ended, The; Fist Fighter; Harlow; Island in the Sky; Panic Button; Sudden Fear; Suicide Battalion; Swamp Women; Voodoo Woman
Conrad, Chris: Airborne; Next Karate Kid, The; Young Hercules
Conrad, David: Return to Paradise; Snow White: A Tale of Terror
Conrad, Jess: Konga
Conrad, Michael: Gone with the West; Hill Street Blues (TV Series); Longest Yard, The; Scream, Blacula, Scream
Conrad, Peter: Super Soul Brother

Conrad, Robert: Assassin; Bandits; Breaking Up Is Hard to Do; Crossfire; Jingle All the Way; Lady in Red; More Wild Wild West; Murph the Surf; Palm Springs Weekend; Samurai Cowboy; Wild Wild West Revisited, The; Wild Wild West, The (TV series); Will, G. Gordon Liddy; Wrong Is Right
Conrad, William: Any Number Can Play; Body and Soul; Cry Danger; Desert Song, The; Killing Cars; Moonshine County Express; Naked Jungle, The; Return of Frank Cannon, The
Conried, Hans: Affairs of Dobie Gillis, The; Behave Yourself!; Big Jim McLain; Big Street, The; Blondie's Blessed Event; Davy Crockett, King of the Wild Frontier; Falcon Takes Over, The; Five Thousand Fingers of Dr. T, The; Journey into Fear; Lady Takes a Chance, A; Monster That Challenged the World, The; My Friend Irma; Rich, Young and Pretty; Senator Was Indiscreet, The; Summer Stock; Three for Bedroom C; Twonky, The
Conroy, Frank: Ox-Bow Incident, The; Threat, The
Conroy, Kevin: Secret Passion of Robert Clayton, The; Tour of Duty
Conroy, Rory: Into the West
Conroy, Ruaidhri: Moondance
Considine, John: Dixie Changing Habits; Dr. Death: Seeker of Souls; Late Show, The; Opposing Force; Rita Hayworth: The Love Goddess; Shadow Box, The; Thirsty Dead, The; Wedding, A (1978)
Considine, Paddy: Last Resort
Considine, Tim: Clown, The; Daring Dobermans, The; Patton
Constable, Barbara Anne: Lady Terminator
Constantin, George: Unforgettable Summer, An
Constantin, Michel: Very Curious Girl, A
Constantine, Eddie: Alphaville; Beware of a Holy Whore; Box-office; Seven Deadly Sins, The; Zentropa
Constantine, Michael: Beyond Fear; Cold Sweat; Don't Drink the Water; Family, The; If It's Tuesday, This Must Be Belgium; In the Mood; Justine; My Life; North Avenue Irregulars, The; Prancer; Question of Faith; Reivers, The; Say Goodbye, Maggie Cole; Silent Rebellion; Summer of My German Soldier; Thinner
Conte, Richard: Assault on a Queen; Big Combo, The; Blue Gardenia, The; Call Northside 777; Circus World; Godfather, The; Guadalcanal Diary; Hotel; House of Strangers; I'll Cry Tomorrow; Lady in Cement; Purple Heart, The; Somewhere in the Night; They Came to Cordura; 13 Rue Madeleine; Tony Rome; Walk in the Sun, A
Conti, Tom: American Dreamer; Beyond Therapy; Deep Cover; Duellists, The; Dumb Waiter, The; Gospel According to Vic, The; Haunting of Julia, The; Merry Christmas, Mr. Lawrence; Miracles; Norman Conquests, The, Episode 1: Table Manners; Norman Conquests, The, Episode 3: Roundand Round the Garden; Norman Conquests, The, Episode 2: Living Together; Quick and the Dead, The; Reuben, Reuben; Saving Grace; Shirley Valentine; Someone Else's America; Sub Down; That Summer of White Roses
Contouri, Chantal: Goodbye, Miss 4th of July; Thirst
Converse, Frank: Bushido Blade; Cruise into Terror; Hour of the Gun, The; Pilot, The; Spring Fever; Tales of the Unexpected
Converse-Roberts, William: Courtship; Kiss the Girls; On Valentine's Day; 1918
Convy, Bert: Hero at Large; Jennifer; Man in the Santa Claus Suit, The; Semi-Tough
Conway, Deborah: Fast Lane Fever
Conway, Gary: American Ninja II; How to Make a Monster; I Was a Teenage Frankenstein
Conway, Kevin: Calm at Sunset; Elephant Man, The; Flashpoint; Gettysburg; Homeboy; Jennifer 8; Lawnmower Man 2: Jobe's War (Lawnmower Man: Beyond Cyberspace); One Good Cop; Prince Brat and the Whipping Boy; Quick and the Dead, The; Rambling Rose; Streets of Laredo; Thirteen Days
Conway, Morgan: Brother Orchid; Dick Tracy versus Cueball
Conway, Pat: Brighty of the Grand Canyon
Conway, Russ: Interval
Conway, Tim: Apple Dumpling Gang, The; Apple Dumpling Gang Rides Again, The; Billion Dollar Hobo, The; Dear God; Longshot, The (1985); Private Eyes, The; Prizefighter, The; Shaggy D.A., The; They Went That-A-Way and That-A-Way; World's Greatest Athlete, The
Conway, Tom: Atomic Submarine, The; Bride of the Gorilla; Cat People; Death of a Scoundrel; Falcon in Mexico, The; Falcon's Brother, The; I Walked with a Zombie; Prince Valiant; Rio Rita; Seventh Victim, The; She Creature, The; Tarzan's Secret Treasure; Voodoo Woman; Whistle Stop
Conway Jr., Tim: Beverly Hills Vamp
Conwell, Angell: Wash, The (2001)
Cooder, Joachim: Buena Vista Social Club, The
Coogan, Jackie: Addams Family, The (TV Series); Dr. Heckyl and Mr. Hype; Kid, The (1921)/The Idle Class; Lonelyhearts; Marlowe; Oliver Twist; Peck's Bad Boy; Prey, The; Shakiest Gun in the West, The; Tom Sawyer
Coogan, Keith: Adventures in Babysitting; Book of Love; Cheetah; Cousins; Don't Tell Mom the Babysitter's Dead; Downhill Willie; Forever; Hiding Out; Life 101; Power Within, The; Reason to Believe, A; Toy Soldiers; Under the Boardwalk
Coogan, Steve: Indian in the Cupboard, The; Sweet Revenge
Cook, A. J.: Out Cold (2001); Ripper: Letter from Hell; Teen Sorcery; Virgin Suicides, The
Cook, Barbara: Killing 'Em Softly
Cook, Ben: Little Men
Cook, Carole: Grandview, U.S.A.; Incredible Mr. Limpet, The; Summer Lovers
Cook, Dale "Apollo": Double Blast; Fist of Steel; Raw Target; Triple Impact
Cook, Donald: Baby Face; Viva Villa!
Cook, Greg: Songcatcher
Cook, Greg Russell: American Astronaut, The
Cook, Gwendoline: Warbus
Cook, Paul: Filth and the Fury, The; Great Rock and Roll Swindle, The
Cook, Penny: Deadly Possession
Cook, Peter: Bedazzled; Find the Lady; Getting It Right; Hound of the Baskervilles, The; Supergirl; Those Daring Young Men in Their Jaunty Jalopies; Without a Clue; Wrong Box, The; Yellowbeard
Cook, Rachael Leigh: Antitrust; Baby-Sitters Club, The; Blow Dry; Bumblebee Flies Anyway, The; Carpool; Eighteenth Angel, The; Get Carter; Hi-line, The; Josie and the Pussycats; Naked Man, The; She's All That; Strike! (1998); Texas Rangers (2001); Tom and Huck
Cook, Roger: Garden, The
Cook, Ron: Secrets and Lies; Topsy-Turvy (1999)
Cook, Tommy: Adventures of Red Ryder; Missile to the Moon
Cook Jr., Elisha: Big Sleep, The; Born to Kill; Dark Waters; Dillinger; Don't Bother to Knock; Drum Beat; Electra Glide in Blue; Gangster, The; Great Northfield Minnesota Raid, The; Hammett; Harry's War; Haunted Palace, The; Hellzapoppin; House on Haunted Hill; Killing, The; Leave 'em Laughing; Lonely Man, The; Mad Bull; Maltese Falcon, The; One-Eyed Jacks; Papa's Delicate Condition; Pat Garrett and Billy the Kid; Rosemary's Baby; St. Ives; Salem's Lot; Shane; Stranger on the Third Floor; Tin Pan Alley; Tom Horn; Voodoo Island
Cooke, Christopher: Unbelievable Truth, The
Cooke, Evelyn: West of the Law
Cooke, Gregory: Gore Vidal's Lincoln
Cooke, Jennifer: Friday the 13th, Part VI: Jason Lives
Cooke, John: Invader (1993)
Cooke, Keith: Heatseeker
Cooke, Ray: Sweethearts on Parade
Cooke, Scott: Thugs
Cookie: Street Hitz (Street Story)
Coolidge, Jennifer: Best in Show; Down to Earth; Pootie Tang
Coolidge, Philip: Tingler, The
Coolidge, Rita: Mad Dogs and Englishmen
Coolio: Alan Smithee Film, An—Burn Hollywood Burn; In Pursuit; Judgment Day; Leprechaun in the Hood; Phat Beach; Shriek If You Know What I Did Last Friday the 13th; Submerged
Coombs, Jeffrey: House on Haunted Hill
Cooney, Kevin: Arctic Blue; Full Moon in Blue Water
Cooper, Adam: Billy Elliot
Cooper, Alice: Monster Dog; Prince of Darkness; Wayne's World
Cooper, Barrett: Buford's Beach Bunnies
Cooper, Ben: Arizona Raiders; Rose Tattoo, The

Cooper, Chris: American Beauty; Great Expectations; Horse Whisperer, The; Lone Justice; Lone Star; Lonesome Dove; Matewan; Me, Myself & Irene; Money Train; October Sky; Patriot, The; Pharaoh's Army; Return to Lonesome Dove; This Boy's Life; Thousand Pieces of Gold
Cooper, Clancy: Distant Drums
Cooper, Gary: Adventures of Marco Polo, The; Along Came Jones; Ball of Fire; Beau Geste; Blowing Wild; Bluebeard's Eighth Wife; Casanova Brown; Cloak and Dagger; Court-martial of Billy Mitchell, The; Cowboy and the Lady, The; Distant Drums; Farewell to Arms, A; Fighting Caravans; For Whom the Bell Tolls; Fountainhead, The; Friendly Persuasion; General Died at Dawn, The; Good Sam; Hanging Tree, The; High Noon; If I Had a Million; It; It's a Big Country; Lives of a Bengal Lancer, The; Love in the Afternoon; Man of the West; Meet John Doe; Morocco; Mr. Deeds Goes to Town; Naked Edge, The; Northwest Mounted Police; Operator 13; Plainsman, The; Pride of the Yankees, The; Real Glory, The; Return to Paradise; Sergeant York; Springfield Rifle; Story of Dr. Wassell, The; Task Force; They Came to Cordura; Today We Live; Unconquered; Vera Cruz; Virginian, The; Westerner, The; Wings; Wreck of the Mary Deare, The
Cooper, Gladys: At Sword's Point; Happiest Millionaire, The; Homecoming; Iron Duke, The; Kitty Foyle; Mrs. Parkington; Nice Girl Like Me, A; Pirate, The; Secret Garden, The; Song of Bernadette, The; Twilight Zone, The (TV Series)
Cooper, Jackie: Champ, The; Gangster's Boy; Love Machine, The; Return of Frank James, The; Superman; Superman II; Superman III; Superman IV: The Quest for Peace; Surrender; Treasure Island; Ziegfeld Girl
Cooper, Jeanne: Intruder, The (1961); Plunder Road
Cooper, Jeff: Circle of Iron; Impossible Years, The
Cooper, Jeremy: Reflecting Skin, The
Cooper, Joe: Mississippi Blues
Cooper, Justin: Liar, Liar
Cooper, Kenn: Pre-Madonnas (Social Suicide)
Cooper, Maggie: And Baby Makes Six; Eye for an Eye
Cooper, Melville: Dawn Patrol, The; Immortal Sergeant, The; Murder over New York; Private Life of Don Juan, The; 13 Rue Madeleine; Tovaritch; Underworld Story
Cooper, Miriam: Birth of a Nation, The; Home, Sweet Home (1914)
Cooper, Terence: Fatal Past; Heart of the Stag
Coote, Jonathon: Razor Blade Smile
Coote, Robert: Alice Through the Looking Glass; Bad Lands (1939); Berlin Express; Nurse Edith Cavell; Othello; Swan, The; You Can't Fool Your Wife
Cope, Zachary David: Stir of Echoes
Copeland, Joan: Middle of the Night
Copeman, Michael: His Bodyguard
Copley, Peter: Knack … and How to Get It, The
Copley, Teri: Down the Drain; I Married a Centerfold; Masters of Menace; Transylvania Twist
Coplin, Linda: Love Feast, The
Copp, Aimee: Unmade Beds
Copperfield, David: Terror Train
Coppola, Alicia: Blood Money (1999); Velocity Trap
Coppola, Scott: Night That Never Happened, The
Coppola, Sofia: Godfather, Part III, The; Inside Monkey Zetterland
Coral, Matilde: Flamenco
Corbalis, Brendan: Stonewall
Corben, Billy: Stepmonster
Corbett, Glenn: Chisum; Homicidal; Shenandoah; Violent Years, The
Corbett, Harry H.: Adventures of a Private Eye; Crooks and Coronets (Sophie's Place); Rattle of a Simple Man; Silver Dream Racer
Corbett, Jeff: Talent for the Game
Corbett, John: Don't Look Back; Morrison Murders, The; Northern Exposure (TV Series); On Hostile Ground; Serendipity; Volcano
Corbett, Leonora: Heart's Desire
Corbett, Ronnie: Fierce Creatures
Corbin, Barry: Ballad of Gregorio Cortez, The; Career Opportunities; Conagher; Critters 2: The Main Course; Curdled; Face to Kill For, A; Hard Traveling; Held Up; Hot Spot; Lonesome Dove; Man Who Loved Women, The; Northern Exposure (TV Series); Nothing in Common; Off the Mark; Prime Suspect (1982) (Feature); Red King, White Knight; Short Time; Six Pack; Solo; Stranger on My Land; Undercover; Wargames; What Comes Around; Who's Harry Crumb?
Corbin, Ed: Flash (1998)
Corby, Ellen: Angels in the Outfield; I Remember Mama; Monsoon; On Moonlight Bay; Strangler, The; Thanksgiving Story, The; Woman's Secret, A
Corby, Jennifer: J. Lyle
Corcoran, Donna: Angels in the Outfield; Gypsy Colt
Corcoran, Kevin: Bon Voyage!; Johnny Shiloh; Mooncussers; Savage Sam; Tiger Walks, A; Toby Tyler
Corcoran, Noreen: I Love Melvin
Cord, Alex: Brotherhood, The; CIA Codename Alexa; Dirty Dozen, The: The Fatal Mission; Fire!; Grayeagle; Jungle Warriors; Minute to Pray, A Second to Die, A; Sidewinder 1; Stiletto; Uninvited, The
Corday, Mara: Giant Claw, The; Man without a Star; Tarantula
Corday, Paula: Because You're Mine; Black Castle, The
Corday, Rita: Dick Tracy versus Cueball
Cordell, Chase: Track of the Moon Beast
Cording, Harry: Dressed to Kill
Corduner, Allan: Topsy-Turvy (1999)
Cordy, Raymond: A Nous la Liberte
Corey, Bridgette: Fury of Hercules, The; Samson
Corey, Isabel: Bob le Flambeur
Corey, Jeff: Boston Strangler, The; Butch and Sundance: The Early Days; Catlow; Follow Me Quietly; Getting Straight; Home of the Brave; In Cold Blood; Judas Project, The; Little Big Man; Messenger of Death; My Friend Flicka; Next Voice You Hear, The; Premonition, The (1975); Rawhide; Rose and the Jackal, The; Superman and the Mole Men
Corey, Wendell: Any Number Can Play; Astro-Zombies; Buckskin; Great Missouri Raid, The; Holiday Affair; Light in the Forest, The; Loving You; Rainmaker, The; Rear Window; Rich, Young and Pretty; Search, The; Sorry, Wrong Number; Women of the Prehistoric Planet
Corff, Robert: Gas-s-s-s
Corlan, Anthony: Something for Everyone
Corley, Annie: Bridges of Madison County, The; Free Willy 3: The Rescue; Here on Earth
Corley, Sharron: New Jersey Drive
Cormack, Danielle: Price of Milk, The
Corman, Chip: Big Rip-off, The
Corman, Maddie: Mickey Blue Eyes; Seven Minutes in Heaven
Corman, Roger: First Works, Volumes 1 & 2; Independent, The; Silence of the Lambs; State of Things, The
Cornaly, Anne: Occurrence at Owl Creek Bridge, An
Cornell, Ellie: Chips, the War Dog; Halloween IV: The Return of Michael Myers; Halloween V: The Revenge of Michael Myers
Corniello, Jeff: Dinosaur Babes
Cornthwaite, Robert: Matinee
Cornu, Aurora: Claire's Knee
Cornwall, Anne: College
Cornwell, Judy: Mirror Crack'd from Side to Side, The; Santa Claus—The Movie
Coronado, José: Goya in Bordeaux
Corraface, Georges: Christopher Columbus: The Discovery (1992); John Carpenter's Escape from L.A.; Legends of the North
Correll, Ashley: Thunder in Paradise II
Correll, Charles: Check and Double Check
Corri, Adrienne: Clockwork Orange, A; Corridors of Blood; Hellfire Club, The; Madhouse; Tell-Tale Heart, The; Three Men in a Boat
Corri, Nick: Candyman 3: Day of the Dead; Gotcha!; In the Heat of Passion; Tropical Snow
Corrieri, Sergio: I Am Cuba; Memories of Underdevelopment
Corrigan, James: Sky Pilot, The

Corrigan, Kevin: Brown's Requiem; Henry Fool; Illtown; Kicked in the Head; Scotland, PA; Slums of Beverly Hills; Steal This Movie; Walking and Talking
Corrigan, Lloyd: Blondie Hits the Jackpot; Great Man's Lady, The; It; Lady in Question; Lights of Old Santa Fe; Song of Nevada; Wyatt Earp: Return to Tombstone
Corrigan, Ray "Crash": Arizona Stagecoach; Black Market Rustlers; Boothill Bandits; Frontier Horizon; Fugitive Valley; Heart of the Rockies; Hit the Saddle; Night Riders, The; Outlaws of Sonora; Overland Stage Raiders; Painted Stallion, The; Pals of the Saddle; Range Defenders; Red River Range; Renegade Girl; Riders of the Black Hills; Riders of the Whistling Skull; Saddle Mountain Roundup; Santa Fe Stampede; Three Texas Steers; Trail of Robin Hood; Trail of the Silver Spurs; Undersea Kingdom; Vigilantes Are Coming!; Wyoming Outlaw
Corseaut, Aneta: Blob, The; Return to Mayberry
Cort, Bud: Bernice Bobs Her Hair; Brain Dead; Brewster McCloud; But I'm a Cheerleader; Chocolate War, The; Die Laughing; Gas-s-s-s; Girl in the Cadillac; Going Under; Harold and Maude; Hysterical; Invaders from Mars; Love at Stake; Love Letters; Maria's Lovers; M*A*S*H; Out of the Dark; Pollock; Secret Diary of Sigmund Freud, The; South of Heaven, West of Hell; Ted & Venus; Why Shoot the Teacher?
Cort (voice), Bud: Electric Dreams
Cortese, Dan: At First Sight; Public Enemy #1; Triangle, The; Volcano: Fire on the Mountain
Cortese, Joe: Born to Run; Closer, The; Evilspeak; Malevolence; Ruby; To Protect and Serve
Cortese, Valentina: Juliet of the Spirits; Kidnap Syndicate, The; When Time Ran Out!
Cortez, Rez: Chain, The
Cortez, Ricardo: Big Business Girl; Case of the Black Cat, The; Charlie Chan in Reno; Gentleman from California; Illicit; Mockery; Mr. Moto's Last Warning; Murder over New York; Postal Inspector; Sorrows of Satan, The; Swan, The; Wonder Bar
Cortne, Carole: Boxoffice
Corwin, Linda: Nymphoid Barbarian in Dinosaur Hell, A
Cosby, Bill: California Suite; Devil and Max Devlin, The; Ghost Dad; I Spy (TV Series); Jack; Leonard Part 6; Let's Do It Again; Man and Boy; Meteor Man; Mother, Jugs, and Speed; Piece of the Action, A; To All My Friends on Shore; Uptown Saturday Night
Cosell, Howard: Bananas
Cosmo, James: Braveheart
Cossart, Ernest: Kitty Foyle; Letter of Introduction; Love from a Stranger
Cossins, James: At Bertram's Hotel
Costa, Cosie: Missing in Action 2: The Beginning; Ten to Midnight
Costa, James: L.I.E.
Costa, Marina: Final Executioner, The; Jungle Raiders
Costallos, Suzanne: Lotto Land
Costanzo, Anthony Roth: Soldier's Daughter Never Cries, A
Costanzo, Paulo: 40 Days and 40 Nights; Road Trip
Costanzo, Robert: Delusion; Relentless 3; Triplecross
Coste, Pierre: L'Ecole Buissonniere
Costello, Carol: Abbott and Costello Meet the Keystone Kops
Costello, Dolores: Breaking the Ice; Little Lord Fauntleroy; Noah's Ark
Costello, Don: Texas Masquerade
Costello, Elvis: No Surrender; Straight to Hell
Costello, Lou: Abbott and Costello Go to Mars; Abbott and Costello in Hollywood; Abbott and Costello in the Foreign Legion; Abbott and Costello Meet Captain Kidd; Abbott and Costello Meet Dr. Jekyll and Mr. Hyde; Abbott and Costello Meet Frankenstein; Abbott and Costello Meet the Invisible Man; Abbott and Costello Meet the Keystone Kops; Abbott and Costello Meet the Killer, Boris Karloff; Abbott and Costello Meet the Mummy; Abbott and Costello Show, The (TV Series); Africa Screams; Buck Privates; Buck Privates Come Home; Comin' Round the Mountain; Here Come the Co-Eds; Hey Abbott!; Hit the Ice; Hold That Ghost; In Society; Little Giant; Lost in a Harem; Lost in Alaska; Mexican Hayride; MGM's The Big Parade of Comedy; Naughty Nineties, The; Noose Hangs High, The; One Night in the Tropics; Pardon My Sarong; Ride 'em Cowboy; Rio Rita; 30-Foot Bride of Candy Rock, The; Time of Their Lives, The; Who Done It?; Wistful Widow of Wagon Gap, The
Costello, Mariclare: Coward of the County; Execution of Private Slovik, The; Heart of a Champion: The Ray Mancini Story; Skeezer
Costello, Ward: Gallant Hours, The; Terror from the Year 5,000
Coster, Nicolas: Big Business; Electric Horseman, The; Freedom Strike; Hearts Adrift; M.A.D.D.: Mothers Against Drunk Driving; Sporting Club, The
Costigan, George: Hawk, The
Costner, Kevin: Amazing Stories (TV Series); American Flyers; Bodyguard, The; Bull Durham; Chasing Dreams; Dances with Wolves; Dragonfly; Fandango; Field of Dreams; For Love of the Game; Gunrunner, The; JFK; Message in a Bottle; No Way Out; Perfect World, A; Postman, The; Revenge (1990); Robin Hood: Prince of Thieves; Silverado; Sizzle Beach, U.S.A.; Stacy's Knights; Testament; Thirteen Days; 3,000 Miles to Graceland; Tin Cup; Truth or Dare; Untouchables, The; War, The; Waterworld; Wyatt Earp
Cote, Laurence: Les Voleurs; Thieves (Les Voleurs); Up/Down/Fragile
Cote, Tina: Blast; Nemesis 2; Omega Doom
Coteas, Elias: Full Moon in Blue Water
Cotten, Joseph: Abominable Dr. Phibes, The; Beyond the Forest; Brighty of the Grand Canyon; Caravans; Casino; Citizen Kane; Delusion; Duel in the Sun; Farmer's Daughter, The; From the Earth to the Moon; Gaslight; Grasshopper, The; Hearse, The; Heaven's Gate; Hellbenders, The; Hush … Hush, Sweet Charlotte; Journey into Fear; Lady Frankenstein; Latitude Zero; Lindbergh Kidnapping Case, The; Lydia; Magnificent Ambersons, The; Niagara; Oscar, The (1966); Petulia; Portrait of Jennie; Return to Fantasy Island; Screamers; September Affair; Shadow of a Doubt; Since You Went Away; Soylent Green; Third Man, The; Tora! Tora! Tora!; Torture Chamber of Baron Blood, The; Tramplers, The; Twilight's Last Gleaming; Under Capricorn; Walk Softly, Stranger; White Comanche
Cottençon, Fanny: Window Shopping
Cotton, Oliver: Beowulf; Hiding Out; Robin Hood: Herne's Son
Cotton, III, Curtis: George Washington
Coufos, Paul: Busted Up; City of Shadows; Food of the Gods Part II; Lost Empire, The
Coughlan, Marisa: Freddy Got Fingered; Super Troopers; Teaching Mrs. Tingle
Coulouris, George: Arabesque; Citizen Kane; King of Kings (1961); Lady in Question; Lady on a Train; Master Race, The; Mr. Skeffington; Song to Remember, A; Surprise Package
Coulouris, Keith: Beastmaster III: The Eye of Braxus; Deadman's Revenge; South Beach Academy
Coulson, Bernie: Accused, The; Adventures in Spying; Eddie and the Cruisers II: Eddie Lives!
Coulter, Bridgid: Mean Streak
Coulter, Jack: Kerouac
Coulthard, Alice: Cement Garden, The
Coulthard, Raymond: Emma
Country Joe and the Fish: Gas-s-s-s; Monterey Pop; Woodstock; Zachariah
Courau, Clotilde: Deep in the Woods
Courcel, Nicole: Le Cas du Dr. Laurent
Courdi, Camille: King Ralph
Court, Hazel: Devil Girl from Mars; Ghost Ship; Masque of the Red Death, The (1964); Premature Burial, The; Raven, The; Thriller (TV Series)
Court, Roma: Where Evil Lies
Courtenay, Tom: Billy Liar; Dandy in Aspic, A; Dr. Zhivago; Dresser, The; Happy New Year (1987); I Heard the Owl Call My Name; King Rat; Last Butterfly, The; Last Orders; Leonard Part 6; Let Him Have It; Loneliness of the Long Distance Runner,The; Night of the Generals; Old Curiosity Shop, The; One Day in the Life of Ivan Denisovich; Operation Crossbow
Courtland, Jerome: Man from Colorado, The; Texas Rangers, The (1951); Tonka
Courtney, Alex: Enter the Ninja
Courtney, Bob: Dingaka

Il Bidone; Last of the Comanches; Little Romance, A; Lone Star; Not as a Stranger; Private Files of J. Edgar Hoover, The; Real Glory, The; Seven Sinners; Slightly Honorable; Terror in the Wax Museum; Time of Your Life, The; Yin and Yang of Mr. Go, The
Crawford, Cindy: Fair Game; Unzipped
Crawford, Ellen: Ulterior Motives
Crawford, H. Marion: Adventures of Sherlock Holmes, The (TV Series)
Crawford, Joan: Above Suspicion; Autumn Leaves; Berserk; Best of Everything, The; Bride Wore Red, The; Chained; Dance, Fools, Dance; Dancing Lady; Flamingo Road; Forsaking All Others; Gorgeous Hussy, The; Grand Hotel; Hollywood Canteen; Humoresque; I Live My Life; Johnny Guitar; Last of Mrs. Cheney, The; Laughing Sinners; Love on the Run; Mannequin; Mildred Pierce; Night Gallery; Our Dancing Daughters; Our Modern Maidens; Possessed; Possessed; Rain; Reunion in France; Sadie McKee; Shining Hour, The; Strait-Jacket; Strange Cargo; Sudden Fear; Susan and God; Today We Live; Torch Song; Twelve Miles Out; Unknown, The; What Ever Happened to Baby Jane?; When Ladies Meet; Woman's Face, A; Women, The
Crawford, John: Devil's Messenger, The; Grave Secrets
Crawford, Johnny: El Dorado; Gambler, Part II—The Adventure Continues, The; Gambler Returns, The: Luck of the Draw; Great Texas Dynamite Chase, The; Macbeth; Rifleman, The (TV Series); Village of the Giants
Crawford, Katherine: Riding with Death; Walk in the Spring Rain, A
Crawford, Michael: Barnum; Condorman; Funny Thing Happened on the Way to the Forum, A; Hello, Dolly!; How I Won the War; Knack ... and How to Get It, The
Crawford, Rachel: In His Father's Shoes; Rude; When Night is Falling
Crawford, Sophia: Sword of Honor
Crawford, Wayne: Crime Lords; Jake Speed; Quiet Thunder; Rebel Storm; White Ghost
Craze, Galaxy: Nadja
Creed-Miles, Charlie: Essex Boys; Nil by Mouth
Creer, Erica: Circle of Iron
Cregar, Laird: Black Swan, The; Hangover Square; Heaven Can Wait; Hello, Frisco, Hello; I Wake Up Screaming; Joan of Paris
Creley, Jack: Reincarnate, The
Cremer, Bruno: Josepha; Ménage; Simple Story, A; Sorcerer; 317th Platoon, The; Under the Sand
Crenna, Richard: Body Heat; Breakheart Pass; Case of Deadly Force, A; Catlow; Deathship; Deserter, The; Devil Dog: The Hound of Hell; Doctors' Wives; Evil, The; First Blood; Flamingo Kid, The; Hillside Stranglers, The; Hot Shots Part Deux; Intruders; Jade; Leviathan; Man Called Noon, The; Marooned; Montana; On Wings of Eagles; Our Miss Brooks (TV Series); Pride of St. Louis, The; Rambo III; Rambo: First Blood II; Sand Pebbles, The; Star! (1968); Stone Cold Dead; Summer Rental; Table for Five; Wait Until Dark; Wild Horse Hank; Wrongfully Accused
Crespo, Tara: La Cucaracha
Crew, Carl: Blood Diner; Secret Life of Jeffrey Dahmer, The
Crew, Robin: Mark of Cain
Crewes, Martin: Resident Evil
Crews, Laura Hope: Camille; Idiot's Delight
Crewson, Wendy: Air Force One; Better Than Chocolate; Bicentennial Man; Buffalo Jump; Corrina, Corrina; Doctor, The; Folks; Good Son, The; Mark of Cain; Mazes and Monsters; Mercy; Santa Clause, The; Skullduggery; Spies, Lies, and Naked Thighs; Summer's End; To Gillian on Her 37th Birthday; What Lies Beneath
Cribbins, Bernard: Adventures of Picasso, The; Daleks—Invasion Earth 2150 A.D.; Don't Raise the Bridge, Lower the River; Railway Children, The; Two-Way Stretch; Water Babies, The; Wrong Arm of the Law, The
Crick, Ed: Adventures of Picasso, The; Daleks—Invasion Earth 2150 A.D.; Don't Raise the Bridge, Lower the River; Railway Children, The; Two-Way Stretch; Water Babies, The; Wrong Arm of the Law, The
Crider, Missy: Beast, The; Boy Called Hate, A; Girls in Prison; Powder; Quicksilver Highway
Crisa, Erno: Lady Chatterley's Lover
Crisp, Donald: Adventures of Mark Twain, The; Amazing Dr. Clitterhouse, The; Black Pirate, The; Broken Blossoms; Brother Orchid; Challenge to Lassie; Charge of the Light Brigade, The; City for Conquest; Dawn Patrol, The; Dr. Jekyll and Mr. Hyde; Dog of Flanders, A; Don Q, Son of Zorro; Greyfriars Bobby; Hills of Home; Home, Sweet Home (1914); How Green Was My Valley; Knute Rockne—All American; Lassie Come Home; Last Hurrah, The; Life of Emile Zola, The; Little Minister, The; Long Gray Line, The; Man from Laramie, The; Mutiny on the Bounty; National Velvet; Oklahoma Kid, The; Old Maid, The; Prince Valiant; Private Lives of Elizabeth and Essex, The; Ramrod; Red Dust; Sea Hawk, The; Sisters, The (1938); Son of Lassie; Spencer's Mountain; Svengali; That Certain Woman; Uninvited, The; Woman Rebels, A
Crisp, Quentin: Orlando
Crisp, Sofie: Mumford
Criss, Peter: Kiss Meets the Phantom of the Park
Cristal, Linda: Dead Don't Die, The; Mr. Majestyk; Perfect Furlough; Two Rode Together
Cristal, Perla: Awful Dr. Orloff, The; Christmas Kid, The; White Comanche
Cristiani, Antoinette: Mudhoney
Cristofer, Michael: Last of Mrs. Lincoln, The
Criswell: Night of the Ghouls; Orgy of the Dead
Crnkovich, Thomas: Sgt. Kabukiman N.Y.P.D.
Croce, Gerard: Blue Jeans
Crocker, Barry: Barry McKenzie Holds His Own
Crocker, Harry: Circus, The/A Day's Pleasure
Crockett, Karlene: Massive Retaliation; Return (1984)
Crohem, Daniel: Paris Belongs to Us
Crombie, Jonathan: Bullies; Cafe Romeo
Cromwell, James: Babe; Babe: Pig in the City; Bachelor, The; Christmas without Snow, A; Education of Little Tree, The; General's Daughter, The; Green Mile, The; L.A. Confidential; People vs. Larry Flynt, The; Revenge of the Nerds; RKO 281; Slight Case of Murder, A; Space Cowboys; Species II; Star Trek: First Contact; Sum of All Fears, The
Cromwell, Richard: Emma; Lives of a Bengal Lancer, The; Strange Love of Molly Louvain, The; Villain Still Pursued Her, The; Young Mr. Lincoln
Cron, Claudia: Hit and Run
Cronenberg, David: Blood & Donuts; Last Night; Night Breed
Cronyn, Hume: Age-Old Friends; Batteries Not Included; Brewster's Millions; Brute Force; Camilla (1994); Cocoon; Cocoon: The Return; Conrack; FoxFire; Gin Game, The; Impulse; Lifeboat; Marvin's Room; Pelican Brief, The; People Will Talk; Phantom of the Opera; Postman Always Rings Twice, The; Rollover; Sea People; Seventh Cross, The; Shadow of a Doubt; Sunrise at Campobello; There Was a Crooked Man; To Dance with the White Dog; World According to Garp, The
Cronyn, Tandy: Age-Old Friends; Story Lady, The; Twisted
Cropper, Anna: Nemesis
Cropper, Linda: Seventh Floor, The
Crosbie, Annette: Chernobyl: The Final Warning; Six Wives of Henry VIII, The (TV Series); Slipper & the Rose, The
Crosby, Bing: Bells of St. Mary's, The; Birth of the Blues; Blue Skies; Country Girl, The; Emperor Waltz, The; Going Hollywood; Going My Way; Here Come the Waves; Here Comes the Groom; High Society; Holiday Inn; King of Jazz, The; Little Boy Lost; Mississippi; Mr. Music; Rhythm on the Range; Rhythm on the River; Riding High; Road to Bali; Road to Hong Kong, The; Road to Morocco; Road to Rio; Road to Singapore; Road to Utopia; Road to Zanzibar; Robin & the Seven Hoods; Waikiki Wedding; Welcome, Stranger; We're Not Dressing; White Christmas
Crosby, Bob: Five Pennies, The; Presenting Lily Mars
Crosby, Cathy: Girls Town
Crosby, Cathy Lee: Dark, The; Laughing Policeman, The; Roughnecks; World War III
Crosby, David: Hook
Crosby, Denise: Arizona Heat; Black Water; Dolly Dearest; Dream Man; Eliminators, The; Executive Power; High Strung; Mutant Species; Pet Sematary; Relative Fear; Star Trek: The Next Generation (TV Series)

Crosby, Gary: Justin Morgan Had a Horse; Which Way to the Front?
Crosby, Harry: Friday the 13th
Crosby, Kathryn: Initiation of Sarah, The
Crosby, Kellen: Simple Twist of Fate, A
Crosby, Mary: Berlin Conspiracy, The; Corporate Affairs; Cupid; Eating; Ice Pirates; Quicker Than the Eye; Stagecoach; Tapeheads
Crosby, Norm: Young at Heart Comedians, The
Cross, Alexander: Law for Tombstone
Cross, Ben: Ascent, The; Assisi Underground, The; Blood Song (Haunted Symphony); Chariots of Fire; Cold Sweat; Coming Out of the Ice; Corporate Ladder; Criminal Mind, The; Deep Trouble; Diamond Fleece, The; Far Pavilions, The; First Knight; House That Mary Bought, The; Invader, The (1996); Live Wire; Nightlife; Order, The; Paperhouse; Ray Bradbury's Chronicles: The MartianEpisodes; Steal the Sky; Temptress; Turbulence; Unholy, The
Cross, David: Scary Movie 2; Small Soldiers
Cross, Harley: Cohen and Tate; Stanley and Iris
Cross, Joseph: Jack Frost; Wide Awake
Cross, Rebecca: Last Warrior, The (2000); Wet and Wild Summer
Cross, Roger R.: Limbic Region, The
Crosse, Rupert: Reivers, The; Ride in the Whirlwind
Crossley, Laura: Secret Garden, The
Crothers, Scatman: Between Heaven and Hell; Black Belt Jones; Bronco Billy; Deadly Eyes; Detroit 9000 (Detroit Heat); Journey of Natty Gann, The; King of Marvin Gardens, The; One Flew over the Cuckoo's Nest; Scavenger Hunt; Shining, The; Shootist, The; Streetfight (Coonskin); Truck Turner; Twilight Zone—The Movie; Zapped!
Crouse, Lindsay: Arrival, The; Being Human; Between the Lines; Chantilly Lace; Communion; Daniel; Desperate Hours (1990); House of Games; Iceman; Indian in the Cupboard, The; Insider, The; Juror, The; Norma Jean and Marilyn; Parallel Lives; Paul's Case; Places in the Heart; Slap Shot; Warden, The
Crouse (voices), Lindsay: Halloween Tree, The
Crouther, Lance: Pootie Tang
Crovato, Luciano: Evil Clutch
Crow, Ashley: Final Verdict; Little Big League
Crow, Emilia: Grand Tour: Disaster in Time; Hitz
Crow, Sheryl: Minus Man, The
Crowden, Graham: Britannia Hospital; Romance with a Double Bass
Crowder, Jessie: Blind Rage
Crowe, Ian: Daisies in December
Crowe, Mia: That Darn Punk
Crowe, Roger: Shrieker
Crowe, Russell: Beautiful Mind, A; Breaking Up; Crossing, The; For the Moment; Gladiator; Heaven's Burning; Insider, The; L.A. Confidential; Mystery, Alaska; No Way Back; Proof; Proof of Life; Quick and the Dead, The; Romper Stomper; Rough Magic; Silver Stallion, The; Sum of Us, The; Virtuosity
Crowe, Tonya: Dark Night of the Scarecrow
Crowell, Frank: Attack of the Swamp Creature
Crowley, Kathleen: Curse of the Undead; Female Jungle; Westward Ho, the Wagons
Crowley, Pat: Hollywood or Bust; Menace on the Mountain; Red Garters; Untouchables, The: Scarface Mob; Wild Women of Wongo
Crowley, Suzan: Born of Fire
Crudup, Billy: Almost Famous; Charlotte Gray; Grind; Hi-Lo Country, The; Inventing the Abbotts; Jesus' Son; Monument Ave.; Sleepers
Cruickshank, Andrew: Body in the Library, The
Cruickshank, Laura: Buying Time
Cruise, Julee: Industrial Symphony No. 1 The Dream of the Broken Hearted
Cruise, Tom: All the Right Moves; Born on the Fourth of July; Cocktail; Color of Money, The; Days of Thunder; Eyes Wide Shut; Far and Away; Few Good Men, A; Firm, The; Interview with the Vampire; Jerry Maguire; Legend; Losin' It; Magnolia; Mission: Impossible; Mission: Impossible 2; Outsiders, The; Rain Man; Risky Business; Taps; Top Gun; Vanilla Sky
Crumb, Robert: Crumb
Crumpacker, Amy: Revenge of the Teenage Vixens from Outer-Space
Crutchley, Jeremy: Mangler, The
Cruttwell, Greg: Naked; Two Days in the Valley
Cruz, Alexis: Old Man and the Sea, The; Riot (1996) (TV Movie); Stargate; Streets of Laredo
Cruz, Carlos: Guantanamera!
Cruz, Charmain: Bronx War, The
Cruz, Penelope: All About My Mother; All the Pretty Horses; Belle Epoque; Blow; Captain Corelli's Mandolin; Hi-Lo Country, The; Jamon, Jamon; Open Your Eyes; Twice Upon A Yesterday; Vanilla Sky; Woman on Top
Cruz, Raymond: Alien Resurrection; Dragstrip Girl; Substitute, The
Cruz, Tania: Men with Guns
Cruz, Vladimir: Strawberry and Chocolate
Cruz, Wilson: All over Me; Joyride
Cruz III, Tirso: Debut, The
Cryer, Jon: Dudes; Heads; Hiding Out; Holy Man; Hot Shots; Morgan Stewart's Coming Home; No Small Affair; Noon Wine; O.C. & Stiggs; Plan B; Pompatus of Love, The; Pretty in Pink; Superman IV: The Quest for Peace
Cryer, Suzanne: Friends and Lovers; Wag the Dog
Crystal, Billy: America's Sweethearts; Analyze This; Breaking Up Is Hard to Do; City Slickers; City Slickers II; Deconstructing Harry; Enola Gay: The Men, the Mission, the Atomic Bomb; Father's Day; Forget Paris; Hamlet; Memories of Me; Mr. Saturday Night; My Giant; Princess Bride, The; Rabbit Test; Running Scared; Throw Momma from the Train; When Harry Met Sally
Cube, Ice: All About the Benjamins; Ghosts of Mars; Next Friday; Three Kings
Cubitt, David: I Shot a Man in Vegas
Cucciolla, Riccardo: Sacco and Vanzetti
Cucinotta, Maria Grazia: Picking up the Pieces; Postman, The (Il Postino)
Cudutz, Michael: Liars' Club, The
Cuervo, Frank: Indio 2: The Revolt
Cuevas, Ricardo: La Ciudad
Cuff, John Haslett: Psycho Girls
Cuffe, Alison: Shrieker
Cugat, Xavier: Date with Judy, A; Heat's On, The; Holiday in Mexico; Luxury Liner; Neptune's Daughter; This Time For Keeps; Two Girls and a Sailor
Cuka, Frances: Attic: The Hiding of Anne Frank
Culf, Norris: Robot Holocaust
Culkin, Christian: My Summer Story
Culkin, Kieran: Mighty, The; My Summer Story; Nowhere to Run; She's All That
Culkin, Macaulay: George Balanchine's The Nutcracker; Getting Even with Dad; Good Son, The; Home Alone; Home Alone 2: Lost in New York; Jacob's Ladder; My Girl; Only the Lonely; Pagemaster, The; Richie Rich; Uncle Buck
Culkin, Michael: Candyman
Culkin, Quinn: Good Son, The
Culkin, Rory: You Can Count on Me
Cullen, Brett: In a Stranger's Hands; Killing Jar, The; Prehysteria; Something to Talk About
Cullen, Max: Fast Lane Fever; Starstruck; Sunday Too Far Away
Culliver, Katheryn: Biohazard: The Alien Force
Cullum, John: Day After, The; Held Up; Inherit the Wind; Northern Exposure (TV Series); Quantum Leap (TV Series); Sweet Country
Cullum, Kimberly: Grave Secrets: The Legacy of Hilltop Drive; Rapture, The
Culp, Jason: Skinheads
Culp, Joseph: Arrival, The
Culp, Nancy: Beverly Hillbillies Go Hollywood, The
Culp, Robert: Big Bad Mama II; Blue Lighting, The; Bob & Carol & Ted & Alice; Castaway Cowboy, The; Flood!; Gladiator, The (1986) (Television); Goldengirl; Great Scout and Cathouse

Thursday, The; Hannie Caulder; I Spy (TV Series); Inside Out; Key to Rebecca, The; Mercenary; Murderous Vision; Newsbreak; Night the City Screamed, The; Outer Limits, The (TV Series); Pelican Brief, The; PT 109; Pucker Up and Bark Like a Dog; Sammy, the Way-Out Seal; Silent Night, Deadly Night III: Better Watch Out!; Time Bomb; Turk 182; Voyage of Terror: The Achille Lauro Affair
Culp, Steven: Gore Vidal's Lincoln; Jason Goes to Hell: The Final Friday; Thirteen Days
Culver, Michael: Moving Finger, The; Philby, Burgess and Maclean: Spy Scandalof the Century
Culver, Roland: Betrayed; Emperor Waltz, The; Encore; Great Lover, The; On Approval
Cumbuka, Ji-Tu: Bound for Glory
Cumming, Alan: Anniversary Party, The; Buddy; Circle of Friends; Company Man; Eyes Wide Shut; Get Carter; Josie and the Pussycats; Romy and Michele's High School Reunion; Spice World; Spy Kids; Titus; Urbania
Cumming, Dorothy: Dancing Mothers
Cummings, Burton: Melanie
Cummings, Constance: Battle of the Sexes, The; Behind the Mask; Blithe Spirit; Night after Night
Cummings, Quinn: Babysitter, The; Goodbye Girl, The
Cummings, Robert: Beach Party; Carpetbaggers, The; Chase, The; College Swing; Devil and Miss Jones, The; Dial M for Murder; Everything Happens at Night; Five Golden Dragons; Forever and a Day; It Started with Eve; King's Row; Lost Moment, The; Lucky Me; Moon over Miami; My Geisha; One Night in the Tropics; Promise Her Anything; Saboteur; Spring Parade; Tell It to the Judge; Three Smart Girls Grow Up
Cummings (voices), Jim: Balto
Cummings Jr., Richard: Beverly Hills 90210
Cummins, Gregory: Blood Games
Cummins, Martin: Love Come Down; Poltergeist: The Legacy
Cummins, Peggy: Captain's Table; Carry on Admiral; Curse of the Demon; Gun Crazy
Cummins, Peter: Blue Fire Lady
Cumo, Brett: Wicked, The
Cundell, Pamela: Twentyfourseven
Cundieff, Rusty: Fear of a Black Hat; Sprung
Cunliffe, Freddie: War Zone, The
Cunningham, Beryl: Exterminators of the Year 3000
Cunningham, Liam: Attila; Little Princess, A
Cunningham, Margo: Sailor Who Fell from Grace with the Sea,The
Cunninghame, June: Horrors of the Black Museum
Cuny, Alain: Camille Claudel; Christ Stopped at Eboli; Emmanuelle; Les Visiteurs Du Soir; Lovers, The (1958); Milky Way, The
Cuong, Tran Manh: Vertical Ray of the Sun, The
Curcio, E. J.: Hard Rock Zombies
Curnow, Graham: Horrors of the Black Museum
Curran, Lynette: Bliss
Curran, Pamela: Mutiny in Outer Space
Curran, Tony: 13th Warrior, The
Curreri, Lee: Fame
Currie, Cherie: Foxes; Wavelength
Currie, Finlay: Billy Liar; Bonnie Prince Charlie; 49th Parallel, The; Great Expectations; People Will Talk; Quo Vadis (1951); Rob Roy, the Highland Rogue
Currie, Gordon: Blood & Donuts; Fear, The: Halloween Night; Laserhawk; Listen; Puppet Master 5: The Final Chapter; Puppet Master Four
Currie, Louise: Adventures of Captain Marvel, The; Ape Man, The; Forty Thieves; Masked Marvel, The; Voodoo Man; Wild West
Curry, Christopher: C.H.U.D.; Return of Superfly, The
Curry, Don (DC): Next Friday
Curry, Julian: Rumpole of the Bailey (TV Series)
Curry, Stephen: Castle, The
Curry, Steven: Glen and Randa
Curry, Tim: Addams Family Reunion; Annie; Attila; Blue Money; Charlie's Angels; Clue; Congo; Home Alone 2: Lost in New York; Hunt for Red October, The; It; Legend; Lover's Knot; McHale's Navy; Muppet Treasure Island; National Lampoon's Loaded Weapon 1; Oliver Twist; Oscar (1991); Pass the Ammo; Passed Away; Ploughman's Lunch, The; Rocky Horror Picture Show, The; Scary Movie 2; Shadow, The; Shout, The (1979); Tales from a Parallel Universe; Three Musketeers, The; Times Square; Titanic; Worst Witch, The
Curtin, Jane: Coneheads; How to Beat the High Co$t of Living; O.C. & Stiggs; Suspicion
Curtin, Valerie: Big Trouble (1985); Christmas without Snow, A; Different Story, A; Maxie
Curtis, Alan: Buck Privates; Gung Ho! (1943); High Sierra; Hollywood Cavalcade; Invisible Man's Revenge, The; Mannequin; Melody Master (The Great Awakening) (NewWine); Naughty Nineties, The; Renegade Girl; Shopworn Angel, The
Curtis, Billy: Hellzapoppin; Terror of Tiny Town, The; Three Texas Steers
Curtis, Cliff: Training Day
Curtis, Clifford: Collateral Damage; Desperate Remedies; Three Kings
Curtis, Dick: Santa Fe Uprising; Stick to Your Guns; Three Men from Texas
Curtis, Donald: Earth vs. the Flying Saucers; It Came from Beneath the Sea; Riders for Justice; 7th Cavalry; Son of Lassie
Curtis, Jack: Westward Ho
Curtis, Jamie Lee: Amazing Grace and Chuck; As Summers Die; Blue Steel; Death of a Centerfold; Dominick and Eugene; Drowning Mona; Fierce Creatures; Fish Called Wanda, A; Fog, The; Forever Young; Grandview, U.S.A.; Halloween; Halloween II; Halloween: H20; Heidi Chronicles, The; Homegrown; House Arrest; Love Letters; Man in Love, A; Mother's Boys; My Girl; My Girl 2; Perfect; Prom Night; Queens Logic; Road Games; She's in the Army Now; Tailor of Panama, The; Terror Train; Trading Places; True Lies; Virus
Curtis, Joan: Where Trails End
Curtis, Keene: Blade; Strange New World
Curtis, Kelly: Sect, The
Curtis, Ken: California Gold Rush; Conagher; Gunsmoke (TV Series); Killer Shrews, The; Pony Express Rider; Searchers, The; Wings of Eagles, The
Curtis, Liane: Critters 2: The Main Course; Girlfriend from Hell
Curtis, Robin: Bloodfist VI: Ground Zero; Dark Breed; Santa with Muscles; Scorpio One; Unborn II, The
Curtis, Sonia: Evil Lives
Curtis, Susan: Octavia
Curtis, Todd: Chain of Command; Out for Blood
Curtis, Tony: Bad News Bears Go to Japan, The; Balboa; Boeing, Boeing; Boston Strangler, The; Brainwaves; Captain Newman, M.D.; Center of the Web; Chamber of Horrors; Christmas in Connecticut; Club Life; Count of Monte Cristo, The; Defiant Ones, The; Forty Pounds of Trouble; Francis, the Talking Mule; Great Impostor, The; Great Race, The; Houdini; Immortals, The; Insignificance; It Rained All Night the Day I Left; Kings Go Forth; Last of Philip Banter, The; Last Tycoon, The; Lepke; Little Miss Marker; Lobster Man from Mars; Mafia Princess; Manitou, The; Midnight; Mirror Crack'd, The; Operation Petticoat; Perfect Furlough; Persuaders, The (TV Series); Portrait of a Showgirl; Prime Target; Sex and the Single Girl; Sextette; Some Like It Hot; Son of Ali Baba; Spartacus; Suppose They Gave a War and Nobody Came?; Sweet Smell of Success; Taras Bulba; Those Daring Young Men in Their Jaunty Jalopies; Trapeze; Users, The; Vega$; Vikings, The; Winchester '73
Curtis-Hall, Vondie: Deadman's Revenge; Don King: Only in America; Drop Squad, The; Freedom Song; Passion Fish; Sirens
Curzi, Pierre: Blind Trust (Pouvoir Intime)
Curzon, George: Sexton Blake and the Hooded Terror
Cusack, Anne: Multiplicity
Cusack, Cyril: Children of Rage; Cry of the Innocent; Danny, The Champion of the World; Day of the Jackal, The; Elusive Pimpernel, The; Fahrenheit 451; Harold and Maude; Homecoming, The (1973); Ill Met by Moonlight; King Lear; Les Misérables; Love Spell; Manhunt (1973) (The Italian Connection); My Left Foot; Night Ambush; 1984; Sacco and Vanzetti; Shake Hands with the Devil; Taming of the Shrew, The; Tenth Man, The
Cusack, Joan: Addams Family Values; Allnighter, The; Arlington Road; Broadcast News; Corrina, Corrina; Cradle Will Rock;

Grosse Pointe Blank; Hero (1992); High Fidelity; In & Out; Men Don't Leave; Mr. Wrong; My Blue Heaven; Nine Months; Runaway Bride; Smile Like Yours, A; Stars and Bars; Toys; Two Much; Where the Heart Is; Working Girl

Cusack, John: America's Sweethearts; Anastasia; Being John Malkovich; Better Off Dead; Bullets over Broadway; City Hall; Con Air; Cradle Will Rock; Eight Men Out; Fat Man and Little Boy; Floundering; Grifters, The; Grosse Pointe Blank; Hellcab; High Fidelity; Hot Pursuit; Jack Bull, The; Journey of Natty Gann, The; Map of the Human Heart; Midnight in the Garden of Good and Evil; Money for Nothing; One Crazy Summer; Pushing Tin; Road to Wellville, The; Roadside Prophets; Say Anything; Serendipity; Shadows and Fog; Stand by Me; Sure Thing, The; Tapeheads; This Is My Father; True Colors

Cusack, Niamh: Closer You Get, The

Cusack, Sinead: Bad Behaviour; Cement Garden, The; Passion of Mind; Revenge (1971) (Joan Collins); Stealing Beauty; Waterland

Cutanda, Eddie: Squeeze

Cuthbert, Elisha: Believe

Cuthbert, Jon: Virtual Assassin

Cuthbertson, Allan: Tunes of Glory

Cuthbertson, Ian: Railway Children, The

Cutler, Allen: Halfback of Notre Dame, The

Cutler, Brian: Wilderness Family, Part 2, The

Cutt, Michael: Night of the Demon

Cutter, Lise: Fleshtone

Cutts, Dale: Cyborg Soldier

Cwiklinska, M.: Border Street

Cybulski, Zbigniew: Ashes and Diamonds

Cypher, Jon: Blade; Off the Mark; Spontaneous Combustion; Strictly Business; Valdez Is Coming

Cyphers, Charles: Halloween; Halloween II

Cyton, Elizabeth: Slave Girls from Beyond Infinity

Czar, Nancy: Wild Guitar

Czerny, Harry: Mission: Impossible

Czerny, Henry: Boys of St. Vincent; Clear and Present Danger; When Night is Falling

Czyzewska, Elzbieta: Misplaced

D., Chris: Border Radio

D'Onofrio, Vincent: Adventures in Babysitting; Being Human; Cell, The; Claire Dolan; Crooked Hearts; Desire; Dying Young; Ed Wood; Feeling Minnesota; Fires Within; Full Metal Jacket; Good Luck; Happy Accidents; Household Saints; Imaginary Crimes; Impostor; Men in Black; Mr. Wonderful; Mystic Pizza; Naked Tango; Newton Boys, The; Player, The; Signs of Life; Steal This Movie; Strange Days; Stuart Saves His Family; That Championship Season; Thirteenth Floor, The; Velocity of Gary, The; Whole Wide World, The; Winner, The

D'Rivera, Pacquito: Calle 54

Da Silva, Eric: Delta of Venus

Da Silva, Fernando Ramos: Pixote

Daans, Lara: Pixote

Dabas, Parvin: Monsoon Wedding

Dabney, Augusta: Violets Are Blue

D'Abo, Maryam: Double Obsession; Leon the Pig Farmer; Living Daylights, The; Money; Nightlife; Not a Penny More, Not a Penny Less; Savage Hearts; Shootfighter; Solitaire for 2; Stalked; Tomcat: Dangerous Desires; Tropical Heat; Xtro

D'Abo, Olivia: Bank Robber; Beyond the Stars; Big Green, The; Bolero; Bullies; Dream to Believe; Greedy; Into the Fire; Kicking and Screaming; Last Good Time, The; Live Nude Girls; Midnight's Child; Point of No Return; Really Weird Tales; Seven Girlfriends; Soccer Dog: The Movie; Spirit of '76, The; Triangle, The; Wayne's World 2

Dacascos, Mark: Base, The; Boogie Boy; Brotherhood of the Wolf; Deadly Past; DNA; Double Dragon; Dragstrip Girl; Kickboxer 5: Redemption; No Code of Conduct; Only the Strong; Redline; Sabotage

Dacqumine, Jacques: Phedre

Daddo, Andrew: Phedre

Daddo, Cameron: Zebra Lounge

Dade, Frances: Daughter of the Dragon; Phantom Thunderbolt

Dadon: Windhorse

Daemion, Ami: Silver Stallion, The

Dafoe, Willem: Affliction; American Psycho; Animal Factory; Body of Evidence; Born on the Fourth of July; Clear and Present Danger; Cry-Baby; English Patient, The; eXistenZ; Faraway, So Close; Flight of the Intruder, The; Hitchhiker, The (Series); Last Temptation of Christ, The; Light Sleeper; Loveless, The; Lulu on the Bridge; Mississippi Burning; New Rose Hotel; Night and the Moment, The; Off Limits; Platoon; Roadhouse 66; Shadow of the Vampire; Speed 2: Cruise Control; Spider-Man; Streets of Fire; To Live and Die in L.A.; Tom & Viv; Triumph of the Spirit; White Sands; Wild at Heart

Dagermark, Pia: Vampire Happening

Daggett, Jensen: Friday the 13th, Part VIII: Jason Takes Manhattan; Major League: Back to the Minors

Dagher, Laila: Angel in Training

D'Agostino, Liza: Bar Girls

Dagover, Lil: Cabinet of Doctor Caligari, The; Destiny; Spiders, The (1919)

Dahl, Arlene: Here Come the Girls; Journey to the Center of the Earth; Kisses for My President; Land Raiders; Night of the Warrior; Slightly Scarlet; Southern Yankee, A; Three Little Words; Watch the Birdie; Woman's World

Dahl, Lisbet: Topsy Turvy (1984)

Dahlbeck, Eva: Brink of Life; Counterfeit Traitor, The; Dreams; Lesson in Love, A; Secrets of Women (Waiting Women); Smiles of a Summer Night

Daichi, Yasuo: Minbo, or The Gentle Art of Japanese Extortion

Dailey, Dan: It's Always Fair Weather; Lady Be Good; Meet Me in Las Vegas; Mortal Storm, The; Mother Wore Tights; Pride of St. Louis, The; Private Files of J. Edgar Hoover, The; There's No Business Like Show Business; What Price Glory; Wings of Eagles, The; Ziegfeld Girl

Dailey, Irene: Grissom Gang, The

Daily, Elizabeth: One Dark Night; Pee-Wee's Big Adventure; Street Music

Daimon, Masaaki: Godzilla vs. Mechagodzilla

Dain, Joseph: Public Enemy #1

Dajani, Nadia: Breathing Room; Happy Accidents

Dalban, Max: Boudu Saved from Drowning; Toni

Dale, Colin: Diamond's Edge

Dale, Cynthia: Boy in Blue, The

Dale, Esther: Blondie Has Servant Trouble; Ma and Pa Kettle (The Further Adventures of Ma and Pa Kettle); Ma and Pa Kettle at the Fair; Ma and Pa Kettle Back on the Farm; This Time For Keeps

Dale, Jennifer: Dream House; John Woo's Once a Thief; Love Come Down; Of Unknown Origin; Separate Vacations

Dale, Jim: American Clock, The; Carry on Cleo; Carry on Cowboy; Carry on Doctor; Follow That Camel; Hot Lead and Cold Feet; Joseph Andrews; Pete's Dragon; Scandalous; Unidentified Flying Oddball

Dale, Vincent: Stolen Hearts

Dale, Virginia: Buck Benny Rides Again; Dragnet; Holiday Inn

Daley, Cass: Red Garters

Daley, Jack: West of the Law

Dali, Tracy: Virgin High

Dalio, Marcel: Black Jack; Cartouche; Grand Illusion; Lady L; Pepe Le Moko; Rules of the Game, The

Dall, John: Corn Is Green, The; Gun Crazy; Man Who Cheated Himself, The; Rope

Dalle, Beatrice: Betty Blue

Dallesandro, Joe: Andy Warhol's Dracula; Andy Warhol's Frankenstein; Bad Love; Critical Condition; Cry-Baby; Double Revenge; Flesh; Guncrazy (1950); Heat; Hollywood Detective, The; Limey, The; Private War; Sunset; Trash

Dallimore, Helen: Mr. Accident

Dallimore, Maurice: Collector, The

D'Aloja, Francesca: Steam: The Turkish Bath; Turkish Bath, The

Dalton, Abby: Cyber Tracker; Maverick (TV Series); Saga of the Viking Women and Their Voyage to the Waters of the Great Sea Serpent, The (Viking Women and the Sea Serpent, The)

Dalton, Audrey: Casanova's Big Night; Drum Beat; Elfego Baca: Six Gun Law; Monster That Challenged the World, The; Thriller (TV Series); Titanic
Dalton, Darren: Wolves, The
Dalton, Kristen: Digital Man; They Nest
Dalton, Timothy: American Outlaws; Antony and Cleopatra; Beautician and the Beast, The; Brenda Starr; Chanel Solitaire; Cromwell; Doctor and the Devils, The; Flash Gordon; Hawks; Informant, The; Jane Eyre; King's Whore, The; License to Kill; Lion in Winter, The; Living Daylights, The; Mistral's Daughter; Permission to Kill; Rocketeer, The; Salt Water Moose; Scarlett; Sextette; Wuthering Heights
Daltrey, Roger: Buddy's Song; Cold Justice; Dracula: The Dark Prince; Forgotten Prisoners; If Looks Could Kill; Legacy, The; Lisztomania; Mack the Knife; McVicar; Tommy; Vampirella
Daly, Eileen: Razor Blade Smile
Daly, Tim: Storm of the Century
Daly, Timothy: Associate, The; Caroline at Midnight; Dangerous Heart; Denise Calls Up; Dr. Jekyll and Ms. Hyde; House Divided, A; I Married a Centerfold; In the Line of Duty: Ambush in Waco; Love or Money?; Mirrors; Seven Girlfriends; Spellbinder; Witness to the Execution; Year of the Comet
Daly, Tyne: Aviator, The; Better Late than Never; Enforcer, The; Intimate Strangers; Money Kings; Movers and Shakers; Tricks; Zoot Suit
Damato, A. J.: Shrunken Heads
d'Amboise, Charlotte: American Blue Note
d'Amboise, Jacques: Carousel
Damevsky, Mony: 5 Dead on the Crimson Canvas
Damian, Leo: Ghosts Can't Do It; Hard Drive
Damita, Lily: Fighting Caravans
Damon, Mark: Anzio; Black Sabbath; Crypt of the Living Dead; Devil's Wedding Night, The; Fall of the House of Usher, The; Scalawag Bunch, The
Damon, Matt: All the Pretty Horses; Courage Under Fire; Dogma; Geronimo: An American Legend; Good Old Boys, The; Good Will Hunting; Legend of Bagger Vance, The; Mystic Pizza; Ocean's Eleven (2001); Rainmaker, The (1997); Rising Son; Rounders; Saving Private Ryan; Talented Mr. Ripley, The
Damon, Stuart: Cinderella
Damon, Una: Race
Damone, Vic: Athena; Hell to Eternity; Hit the Deck; Kismet; Rich, Young and Pretty
Damus, Mike: Pig's Tale, A
Dana, Barbara: Matter of Principle, A; Necessary Parties
Dana, Bill: Murder in Texas
Dana, Leora: Kings Go Forth; 3:10 to Yuma
Dana, Viola: That Certain Thing
Dance, Charles: Alien 3; Century; China Moon; Dark Blue World; Golden Child, The; Good Morning, Babylon; Gosford Park; Hilary and Jackie; In the Presence of Mine Enemies; Jewel in the Crown, The; Last Action Hero, The; McGuffin, The; Out on a Limb; Pascali's Island; Plenty; Space Truckers; Surgeon, The; Tales of the Unexpected; Undertow; White Mischief
Dancy, Hugh: David Copperfield
Dando, Evan: Heavy
Dandridge, Dorothy: Carmen Jones
Dandry, Evelyne: Sitcom
Dane, Karl: Scarlet Letter, The; Son of the Sheik; Warning Shadows
Dane, Lawrence: Case of Libel, A; Fatal Attraction; Find the Lady; Good Fight, The; Good Idea; Nothing Personal; Of Unknown Origin; Rituals; Rolling Vengeance; Scanners
Dane, Patricia: Johnny Eager; Somewhere I'll Find You
Dane, Shelton: Hidden in America
Dane, Taylor: Stag
Danes, Claire: Brokedown Palace; Home for the Holidays (1995); How to Make an American Quilt; Les Misérables; Little Women; Mod Squad, The; Polish Wedding; Rainmaker, The (1997); To Gillian on Her 37th Birthday; U-Turn; William Shakespeare's Romeo and Juliet
D'Angelo, Beverly: American History X; Big Trouble (1985); Coal Miner's Daughter; Cold Front; Crazysitter, The; Daddy's Dyin' and Who's Got the Will; First Love; Hair; High Spirits; Highpoint; Honky Tonk Freeway; Illuminata; In the Mood; Lansky; Lightning Jack; Lonely Hearts; Maid to Order; Man Trouble; Miracle, The; National Lampoon's Christmas Vacation; National Lampoon's European Vacation; National Lampoon's Vacation; Pacific Heights; Paternity; Pope Must Diet, The; Sleeping Beauty; Slow Burn; Streetcar Named Desire, A; Trading Hearts; Vegas Vacation; Widow's Kiss
Dangerfield, Rodney: Back to School; Caddyshack; Casper: A Spirited Beginning; Easy Money; Godson, The; Ladybugs; Meet Wally Sparks; Moving; My 5 Wives; Natural Born Killers; Projectionist, The
Daniel, Brittany: Joe Dirt; On Hostile Ground
Daniel, Floriane: Winter Sleepers
Daniel, Jennifer: Kiss of the Vampire
Daniel, Trudik: Castle, The
Danieli, Emma: Last Man on Earth, The
Danieli, Isa: Ciao Professore
Daniell, Henry: All This and Heaven Too; Body Snatcher, The (1945); Camille; Castle in the Desert; Diane; Dressed to Kill; Firefly, The; Five Weeks in a Balloon; Four Jacks and a Jill; Four Skulls of Jonathan Drake, The; Holiday; Jane Eyre; Madame X; Private Lives of Elizabeth and Essex, The; Sea Hawk, The; Sherlock Holmes and the Voice of Terror; Sherlock Holmes in Washington; Song of Love; Voyage to the Bottom of the Sea; Witness for the Prosecution; Woman in Green, The; Woman's Face, A
Danielle, Suzanne: Carpathian Eagle; Carry on Emmanuelle
Daniels, Alex: Meridian (Kiss of the Beast)
Daniels, Anthony: Empire Strikes Back, The; Return of the Jedi; Star Wars; Star Wars: Episode I The Phantom Menace
Daniels, Bebe: Dixiana; Feel My Pulse; Harold Lloyd's Comedy Classics; Reaching for the Moon
Daniels, Ben: Beautiful Thing; Passion in the Desert
Daniels, Danny D.: Beautiful Thing; Passion in the Desert
Daniels, Gary: Bloodmoon; Capital Punishment; Deadly Target; Epicenter; Firepower; Fist of the North Star; Hawk's Vengeance; Heatseeker; Rage; Riot
Daniels, J. D.: Beanstalk
Daniels, Jeff: Arachnophobia; Butcher's Wife, The; Caine Mutiny Court Martial, The; Cheaters; Checking Out; Dumb and Dumber; Fly Away Home; Gettysburg; Grand Tour: Disaster in Time; Heartburn; House on Carroll Street, The; Love Hurts; Marie; My Favorite Martian; 101 Dalmatians (1996); Pleasantville; Purple Rose of Cairo, The; Rain Without Thunder; Redwood Curtain; Something Wild; Speed; Sweethearts' Dance; Teamster Boss: The Jackie Presser Story; Terms of Endearment; There Goes the Neighborhood; Trial and Error (1997); Two Days in the Valley; Welcome Home, Roxy Carmichael
Daniels, Jennifer: Reptile, The
Daniels, John: Bare Knuckles; Getting Over
Daniels, Lisa: Glass Slipper, The
Daniels, Phil: Bad Behaviour; Breaking Glass; Meantime; Quadrophenia; Scum
Daniels, William: Blind Date; Blue Lagoon, The; City in Fear; Francis Gary Powers: The True Story of the U-2 Spy Incident; Her Alibi; Marlowe; Night Stalker, The: Two Tales of Terror (TV Series); One and Only, The; 1776; Parallax View, The; Rehearsal for Murder; St. Elsewhere (TV Series); Sunburn; Thousand Clowns, A
Danielson, Lynn: Mortuary Academy
Danner, Blythe: Alice; Another Woman; Are You in the House Alone?; Brighton Beach Memoirs; Call to Remember, A; Forces of Nature; Futureworld; Great Santini, The; Hearts of the West; Homage; Inside the Third Reich; Judgment; Mad City; Man, Woman and Child; Meet the Parents; Mr. and Mrs. Bridge; Murder She Purred; Myth of Fingerprints, The; Never Forget; No Looking Back; 1776; Prince of Tides, The; Saint Maybe; To Kill a Clown; To Wong Foo, Thanks for Everything, Julie Newmar; X-Files, The (1998)
Danning, Sybil: Albino; Amazon Women on the Moon; Chained Heat; Hercules; Hitchhiker, The (Series); Howling II ... Your Sister Is a Werewolf; Jungle Warriors; Kill Castro (Cuba Crossing, Mercenaries , Sweet Violent Tony); L.A. Bounty; Man with Bogart's Face, The; Phantom Empire, The (1986); Reform

School Girls; Salamander, The; Seven Magnificent Gladiators, The; Swap, The (Sam's Song); Talking Walls; Warrior Queen
Dannis, Ray: Undertaker and His Pals, The
Dano, Paul Franklin: L.I.E.
Dano, Royal: Cimarron; Cocaine Wars; Crime of Passion; Culpepper Cattle Co., The; Electra Glide in Blue; Ghoulies II; House II: The Second Story; Huckleberry Finn; Killer Inside Me, The; Killer Klowns from Outer Space; King of Kings (1961); Never Steal Anything Small; Red Badge of Courage, The; Red-Headed Stranger, The; Spaced Invaders; Strangers: The Story of a Mother and a Daughter; Tribute to a Bad Man
Danon, Leslie: Blood Thirsty; Whispering, The
Danova, Cesare: Chamber of Horrors; Scorchy; Tentacles; Viva Las Vegas
Danson, Ted: Body Heat; Chinese Web, The; Cousins; Dad; Fine Mess, A; Getting Even with Dad; Gulliver's Travels (1996) (Television); Homegrown; Jerry and Tom; Just Between Friends; Little Treasure; Loch Ness; Made in America; Mumford; Onion Field, The; Our Family Business; Pontiac Moon; Three Men and a Baby; Three Men and a Little Lady; We Are the Children
Dante, Michael: Beyond Evil; Big Score, The; Cage; Naked Kiss, The; Seven Thieves
Dantes, Roland: Pacific Connection, The
Dantine, Helmut: Bring Me the Head of Alfredo Garcia; Edge of Darkness; Operation Crossbow; Stranger from Venus
Danton, Ray: Centerfold Girls; I'll Cry Tomorrow; Majority of One, A; Onionhead; Rise and Fall of Legs Diamond, The
Danza, Tony: Angels in the Outfield; Brooklyn State of Mind, A; Going Ape!; Hollywood Knights, The; Illtown; Love to Kill; Mob Justice; Noah; North Shore Fish; She's Out of Control; Truth or Die
Dao, Catherine: Femme Fontaine: Killer Babe for the CIA
Dao-Lin, Sun: Go-Masters, The
Dapkounaite, Ingeborga: Burnt by the Sun; On Dangerous Ground
D'Arbanville, Patti: Big Wednesday; Bilitis; Boys Next Door, The; Call Me; Fan, The; Fifth Floor, The; Flesh; Fresh Horses; Modern Problems; Rancho Deluxe; Snow Kill; Wired
Darbo, Patrika: Fast Money; Ruby Bridges
Darby, Kim: Better Off Dead; Capture of Grizzly Adams, The; Don't Be Afraid of the Dark; Enola Gay: The Men, the Mission, the Atomic Bomb; Flatbed Annie and Sweetie Pie: Lady Truckers; Generation (1969); Grissom Gang, The; One and Only, The; People, The; Strawberry Statement, The; Teen Wolf, Too; True Grit
Darc, Mireille: Icy Breasts; Return of the Tall Blond Man with One Black Shoe, The; Tall Blond Man with One Black Shoe, The; Weekend
Darcel, Denise: Battleground; Dangerous When Wet; Vera Cruz; Westward the Women
Darcy, Sheila: Zorro's Fighting Legion
D'Arcy, Alex: Blood of Dracula's Castle; Soldier of Fortune
D'Arcy, Jake: Gregory's Girl; Sense of Freedom, A
D'Arcy, Roy: Last Warning, The; Merry Widow, The; Revolt of the Zombies; Warning Shadows
Darden, Severn: Back to School; Battle for the Planet of the Apes; Conquest of the Planet of the Apes; Dead Heat on a Merry-Go-Round; Disappearance of Aimee, The; Hired Hand, The; Justine; Legend of Hillbilly John, The; Luv; Playmates; Telephone, The
Dare, Debra: Hard to Die
DaRe, Eric: Takeover, The
Darel, Florence: A La Mode; Tale of Springtime, A
Darie, Frederic: Deep Trouble
Darin, Bobby: Captain Newman, M.D.; Come September; Hell Is for Heroes; Pressure Point; Run Stranger Run; State Fair
Darlene, Gigi: Bad Girls Go to Hell
Darling, Candy: Flesh
Darmon, Gerard: Obsession: A Taste for Fear
Darnell, Linda: Anna and the King of Siam; Blackbeard the Pirate; Blood and Sand; Buffalo Bill; City Without Men; Dakota Incident; Forever Amber; Hangover Square; Island of Desire; Letter to Three Wives, A; Mark of Zorro, The; My Darling Clementine; Second Chance; Unfaithfully Yours
Darnoux, George: Day in the Country, A
Darr, Lisa: Plan B
Darren, James: Boss' Son, The; Diamond Head; Gene Krupa Story, The; Gidget; Gidget Goes Hawaiian; Gidget Goes to Rome; Guns of Navarone, The; Scruples; Venus in Furs
Darrieux, Danielle: Alexander the Great; Bluebeard; Club des Femmes; Earrings of Madame De …, The; Five Fingers; La Ronde; Lady Chatterley's Lover; Le Plaisir; Le Rouge et le Noir; Mauvaise Graine (Bad Seed); Mayerling; Rage of Paris, The; Rich, Young and Pretty; Scene of the Crime
Darro, Frankie: Broadway Bill; Devil Horse, The; Little Men; Phantom Empire (1935); Radio Ranch (Men with Steel Faces, Phantom Empire); Way Back Home
Darrow, Henry: Attica; Badge 373; Criminal Passion; In Dangerous Company; L.A. Bounty; Last of the Finest, The
Darrow, Oliver: Bad Girls from Mars; Spirits; Teenage Exorcist
Darrow, Paul: Blake's 7 (TV Series)
Darrow, Tony: Me and the Mob; Mickey Blue Eyes
Dartez, Gail: Out
Darvas, Lili: Love; Meet Me in Las Vegas
Darvi, Bella: Racers, The
Darwell, Jane: Aggie Appleby, Maker of Men; All Through the Night; Bigamist, The; Captain January; Craig's Wife; Curly Top; Devil and Daniel Webster, The; Grapes of Wrath, The; Jesse James; Last Hurrah, The; Lemon Drop Kid, The; Little Miss Broadway; Mary Poppins; Ox-Bow Incident, The; Poor Little Rich Girl (1936); Rains Came, The; Scarlet Empress, The; Three Godfathers, The; Tom Sawyer
Dary, Rene: Grisbi
Das, Nandita: Earth
Das, Vasundhara: Monsoon Wedding
Dash, Damon: State Property
Dash, Stacey: Black Water; Clueless; Cold Around the Heart; Illegal in Blue; Mo' Money; Renaissance Man
DaSilva, Howard: Blue Dahlia, The; David and Lisa; Garbo Talks; Greatest Man in the World, The; Keeper of the Flame; Lost Weekend, The; Missiles of October, The; Nevada Smith; 1776; Sea Wolf, The; Smile, Jenny, You're Dead; They Live By Night; Unconquered; Underworld Story
Dassin, Jules: Never on Sunday
Dasté, Jean: Boudu Saved from Drowning; Green Room, The; Zero for Conduct
Datcher, Alex: Expert, The
Dau, Brigitta: Retro Puppetmaster
Dauden, Marlene: Combat Killers
Daughton, James: Blind Date; Girlfriend from Hell; House of the Rising Sun
Daugirda, Jerry: Gone in 60 Seconds
Dauphin, Claude: April in Paris; Is Paris Burning?; Lady L; Les Misérables; Little Boy Lost; Madame Rosa
Davalos, Dominique: Salvation
Davalos, Elyssa: House in the Hills, A; Jericho Fever
Davalos, Richard: Snatched
Davao, Charlie: Blind Rage
Davazac, Emilie: Undefeatable
Davenport, Alice: Keystone Comedies: Vol. 1–5
Davenport, Harry: Adventure; All This and Heaven Too; Courage of Lassie; Cowboy and the Lady, The; December 7th: The Movie; Enchanted Forest, The; Jack London; Kismet; Lucky Partners; Made for Each Other; Ox-Bow Incident, The; Rage of Paris, The; That Forsyte Woman; Thin Man Goes Home, The; Three Daring Daughters
Davenport, Jack: Talented Mr. Ripley, The
Davenport, Mark: Criminal Mind, The
Davenport, Nigel: Chariots of Fire; Cry of the Innocent; Dracula; Living Free; Phase IV; Royal Hunt of the Sun; Virgin Soldiers, The; Without a Clue; Zulu Dawn
Davi, Robert: Amazon; Beneficiary, The; Blind Justice; Center of the Web; Christopher Columbus: The Discovery (1992); Cops and Robbersons; Dangerous, The (1984); Dogfighters, The; Illicit Behavior; License to Kill; Maniac Cop 2; Maniac Cop 3: Badge of Silence; Mardi Gras for the Devil; No Contest; November Men, The; Occasional Hell, An; Peacemaker (1990); Predator 2; Quick; Raw Deal; Showgirls; Son of the Pink Panther;

Soulkeeper; Traxx; White Hot: The Mysterious Murder of Thelma Todd; Wild Orchid 2: Two Shades of Blue; Wild Thing
David, Angel: Mixed Blood
David, Clifford: Agent on Ice; Resurrection
David, Eleanor: Comfort and Joy; King's Whore, The; Scarlet Pimpernel, The; Slipstream; Sylvia
David, Elizabeth: Gruesome Twosome
David, Jody: Merlin of the Crystal Cave
David, Keith: Armageddon; Bird; Clockers; Dead Presidents; Executive Target; Final Analysis; Flipping; Grave, The; Johns; Marked for Death; Men at Work; Nails; Pitch Black; Puppet Masters, The; Quick and the Dead, The; Requiem for a Dream; Stars and Bars; They Live; Volcano; Where the Heart Is
David, Lawrence: Midnight Dancer
David, Thayer: Duchess and the Dirtwater Fox, The; Eiger Sanction, The; Savages; Save the Tiger
Davidovich, Lolita: Blaze; Boiling Point; Cobb; Dead Silence; For Better or Worse; 4 Days; Harvest of Fire; Indictment: The McMartin Trial; Inner Circle, The; Intersection; Jungle 2 Jungle; Keep the Change; Leap of Faith; Mystery, Alaska; Play It to the Bone; Prison Stories: Women on the Inside; Raising Cain; Salt Water Moose; Snow in August; Younger and Younger
Davidson, Diana: Scared to Death
Davidson, Doug: Mr. Write
Davidson, Eileen: Easy Wheels; Eternity
Davidson, Jaye: Crying Game, The; Stargate
Davidson, Jim: Reasons of the Heart
Davidson, John: Captain America; Dick Tracy vs. Crime Inc.; Happiest Millionaire, The; One and Only, Genuine, Original Family Band, The; Perils of Pauline, The
Davidson, Tommy: Bamboozled; Booty Call; Strictly Business; Woo
Davidtz, Embeth: Army of Darkness; Bicentennial Man; Fallen; Feast of July; Garden of Redemption, The; Gingerbread Man, The; Last Rites; Mansfield Park; Matilda; Murder in the First; Schindler's List; Sweet Murder; Thir13en Ghosts
Davies, Ann: Midwinter's Tale, A
Davies, Freddie: Funnybones
Davies, Geraint Wyn: Conspiracy of Fear, The; Hush Little Baby; Terror Stalks the Class Reunion; Trilogy of Terror II
Davies, Glynis: Child's Christmas in Wales, A (1986)
Davies, Jeremy: Going All the Way; Locusts, The; Ravenous; Saving Private Ryan; Spanking the Monkey
Davies, John: Positive I.D.
Davies, John Howard: Oliver Twist; Rocking Horse Winner, The; Tom Brown's Schooldays (1950)
Davies, Kate Emma: Queenie
Davies, Kimberley: Psycho Beach Party
Davies, Lane: Funland; Impure Thoughts; Magic of Lassie, The
Davies, Lindy: Malcolm
Davies, Marion: Going Hollywood; MGM's The Big Parade of Comedy; Operator 13; Show People
Davies, Ray: Absolute Beginners
Davies, Rudi: Object of Beauty, The
Davies, Rupert: Dracula Has Risen from the Grave; Five Golden Dragons; Night Visitor, The (1970); Oblong Box, The
Davies, Sian Leisa: Heaven on Earth
Davies, Stephen: Berlin Conspiracy, The; Ladykiller; Nest, The
Davion, Alexander: Paranoiac
Davis, Amy: All-American Murder
Davis, Ann B.: Brady Bunch, The (TV series); Lover Come Back; Very Brady Christmas, A
Davis, Bette: All About Eve; All This and Heaven Too; As Summers Die; Beyond the Forest; Bride Came C.O.D., The; Bureau of Missing Persons; Burnt Offerings; Cabin in the Cotton; Catered Affair, The; Corn Is Green, The; Dangerous (1935); Dark Secret of Harvest Home, The; Dark Victory; Dead Ringer; Death on the Nile; Deception; Disappearance of Aimee, The; Empty Canvas, The; Ex-Lady; Great Lie, The; Hell's House; Hollywood Canteen; Hush … Hush, Sweet Charlotte; In This Our Life; Jezebel; John Paul Jones; Juarez; June Bride; Kid Galahad; Letter, The; Little Foxes, The; Little Gloria, Happy at Last; Madame Sin; Man Who Came to Dinner, The; Marked Woman; Mr. Skeffington; Murder with Mirrors; Nanny, The; Now, Voyager; Of Human Bondage; Old Maid, The; Petrified Forest, The; Phone Call from a Stranger; Piano for Mrs. Cimino, A; Pocketful of Miracles; Private Lives of Elizabeth and Essex, The; Return from Witch Mountain; Right of Way; Satan Met a Lady; Sisters, The (1938); Star, The (1952); Stolen Life, A; Strangers: The Story of a Mother and a Daughter; Thank Your Lucky Stars; That Certain Woman; Three on a Match; Virgin Queen, The; Watch on the Rhine; Watcher in the Woods, The; Way Back Home; Whales of August, The; What Ever Happened to Baby Jane?; Where Love Has Gone; White Mama; Wicked Stepmother, The; Winter Meeting
Davis, Brad: Blood Ties; Caine Mutiny Court Martial, The; Chariots of Fire; Chiefs; Child of Darkness, Child of Light; Cold Steel; Greatest Man in the World, The; Habitation of Dragons, The; Heart; Midnight Express; Plot to Kill Hitler, The; Querelle; Rosalie Goes Shopping; Rumor of War, A; Small Circle of Friends, A; Unspeakable Acts; When the Time Comes
Davis, Chuck: How High
Davis, Clifton: Don't Look Back: The Story of Leroy "Satchel" Paige; Dream Date; Night the City Screamed, The
Davis, Cynthia: Cooley High
Davis, Daniel: Glen or Glenda
Davis, Donald: Man Inside, The; Memories of Murder
Davis, Drew: Man Inside, The; Memories of Murder
Davis, Duane: Program, The
Davis, Eddy: Wild Man Blues
Davis, Frances: Devil's Wedding Night, The
Davis, Gail: Annie Oakley (TV Series); Cow Town; Far Frontier; Winning of the West
Davis, Geena: Accidental Tourist, The; Angie; Beetlejuice; Cutthroat Island; Earth Girls Are Easy; Fly, The; Hero (1992); League of Their Own, A; Long Kiss Goodnight, The; Quick Change; Secret Weapons; Speechless; Stuart Little; Thelma & Louise
Davis, George: Circus, The/A Day's Pleasure
Davis, Guy: Beat Street
Davis, Hope: Arlington Road; Daytrippers, The; Hearts in Atlantis; Impostors, The; Joe Gould's Secret; Myth of Fingerprints, The; Next Stop Wonderland
Davis, Ilah: Hardcore
Davis, Jerome: Vicious Circles
Davis, Jim: Bad Company; Brimstone; Cariboo Trail; Comes a Horseman; Day Time Ended, The; Don't Look Back: The Story of Leroy "Satchel" Paige; Dracula vs. Frankenstein; El Dorado; Fabulous Texan, The; Five Bloody Graves; Gun Riders, The; Hellfire; Jesse James Meets Frankenstein's Daughter; Jubilee Trail; Last Command, The; Little Big Horn; Monster from Green Hell; Monte Walsh; Outcast, The; Restless Breed, The; Showdown, The (1950); Winter Meeting; Zebra in the Kitchen
Davis, Joan: Around the World; George White's Scandals; Hold That Ghost; I Married Joan (TV Series); If You Knew Susie; Just Around the Corner; On the Avenue; Show Business; Sun Valley Serenade; Thin Ice
Davis, Judy: Absolute Power; Alice; Barton Fink; Blood and Wine; Celebrity; Children of the Revolution; Cooler Climate, A; Deconstructing Harry; Echo of Thunder, The; Final Option, The; Georgia; Heatwave (1983); High Tide; Husbands and Wives; Impromptu; Kangaroo; My Brilliant Career; Naked Lunch; New Age, The; One Against the Wind; Passage to India, A; Ref, The; Where Angels Fear to Tread; Winter of Our Dreams; Woman Called Golda, A
Davis, Mac: Angel's Dance; Blackmail; Cheaper to Keep Her; North Dallas Forty; Possums; Sting II, The
Davis, Matthew: Legally Blonde; Urban Legends: Final Cut
Davis, Mildred: Grandma's Boy; Safety Last
Davis, Miles: Dingo
Davis, Nancy: Donovan's Brain; East Side, West Side; Hellcats of the Navy; It's a Big Country; Next Voice You Hear, The
Davis, Nathan: Code of Silence
Davis, Ossie: All God's Children; Android Affair, The; Avenging Angel (1985); Client, The; Do the Right Thing; Dr. Dolittle (1998); Don't Look Back: The Story of Leroy "Satchel" Paige; Get on the Bus; Gladiator; Grumpy Old Men; Harry and Son; Hill, The; Hot Stuff; I'm Not Rappaport; Joe Versus the Volcano; Jun-

gle Fever; King; Man Called Adam, A; Miss Evers' Boys; Purlie Victorious; Roots: The Next Generation; Scalphunters, The; School Daze; Stand, The; 12 Angry Men

Davis, Philip: High Hopes; Howling V—The Rebirth; Photographing Fairies; Quadrophenia; Who's Who

Davis, Phyllis: Sizzle; Terminal Island

Davis, Richard: Sky's the Limit, The

Davis, Robert: Taking of Beverly Hills, The

Davis, Roger: Ruby

Davis, Rudi: Frankie Starlight

Davis, Rufe: Gangs of Sonora; Lone Star Raiders; Riders for Justice; Trail Blazers; Under Texas Skies

Davis, Sammi: Chernobyl: The Final Warning; Consuming Passions; Hope and Glory; Horseplayer; Indecency; Lair of the White Worm; Perfect Bride, The; Prayer for the Dying, A; Rainbow, The; Shadow of China

Davis, Sonny: Last Night at the Alamo

Davis, Sonny Carl: Verne Miller

Davis, Stringer: Murder Ahoy; Murder at the Gallop; Murder Most Foul

Davis, Taryn: Snow White: A Tale of Terror

Davis, Tom: One More Saturday Night

Davis, Tracy: Beyond the Rising Moon (Star Quest)

Davis, Viola: Pentagon Wars, The

Davis, Viveka: Dangerous Woman, A; End of Innocence, The; Man Trouble; Morgan Stewart's Coming Home

Davis, Warwick: Ewok Adventure, The; Ewoks: The Battle for Endor; Leprechaun; Leprechaun 2; Leprechaun 4 in Space; Leprechaun in the Hood; Leprechaun 3; 10th Kingdom, The; Willow

Davis, William B.: Out of Line; X-Files, The (1998); X-Files, The (TV Series)

Davis Jr., Milton: Angels in the Outfield

Davis Jr., Sammy: Alice in Wonderland; Cannonball Run; Cannonball Run II; Gone with the West; Kid Who Loved Christmas, The; Little Moon & Jud McGraw; Man Called Adam, A; Ocean's Eleven; Robin & the Seven Hoods; Sweet Charity; Tap; Trackers, The

Davison, Bruce: Affair, The; Apt Pupil; At First Sight; Baby-Sitters Club, The; Brass Target; Color of Justice; Crazy/Beautiful; Crucible, The; Cure, The; Deadman's Curve; Down, Out & Dangerous; Far From Home: The Adventures of YellowDog; French Quarter; Grace of My Heart; Hidden in America; High Risk; Homage; Last Summer; Lies; Live! From Death Row; Locked in Silence; Longtime Companion; Lovelife; Misfit Brigade, The; Paulie; Poor Little Rich Girl: The Barbara Hutton Story; Short Cuts; Short Eyes; Six Degrees of Separation; Skateboard Kid 2, The; Spies Like Us; Steel and Lace; Strawberry Statement, The; Summer Catch; Summer Heat; Summer of My German Soldier; Taming of the Shrew (1982); Tomorrow's Child; Ulzana's Raid; Vendetta; Widow's Kiss; Willard

Davison, Peter: All Creatures Great and Small; Dr. Who (TV series); Pocketful of Rye, A

Davy, Maude: Only the Brave

Davys, Dolly: Le Voyage Imaginaire

Daw, Evelyn: Something to Sing About

Daw, Joseph: Bloodletting; Polymorph

Dawber, Pam: Mork & Mindy (TV Series); Stay Tuned; Through Naked Eyes; Wedding, A (1978)

Dawn, Marpessa: Black Orpheus

Dawson, Anthony: Curse of the Werewolf, The; Death Rides a Horse; Haunted Strangler, The; Tiger Bay

Dawson, Bob: Operative, The

Dawson, Bobby: Raffle, The

Dawson, Kamala: Lightning Jack

Dawson, Richard: Hogan's Heroes (TV Series); Running Man, The

Dawson, Rosario: Down to You; He Got Game; Josie and the Pussycats; Light It Up; Sidewalks of New York (2001)

Dawson, Vicki: Prowler, The

Day, Annette: Double Trouble

Day, Cora Lee: Daughters of the Dust

Day, Dennis: Buck Benny Rides Again; Jack Benny Program, The (TV Series)

Day, Doris: April in Paris; By the Light of the Silvery Moon; Calamity Jane; Glass Bottom Boat, The; I'll See You in My Dreams; It's a Great Feeling; Julie; Jumbo; Love Me or Leave Me; Lover Come Back; Lucky Me; Lullaby of Broadway; Man Who Knew Too Much, The; Midnight Lace; My Dream Is Yours; On Moonlight Bay; Pajama Game, The; Pillow Talk; Please Don't Eat the Daisies; Romance on the High Seas; Send Me No Flowers; Tea for Two; Teacher's Pet; That Touch of Mink; Thrill of It All, The; Tunnel of Love, The; West Point Story, The; Where Were You When the Lights Went Out?; Winning Team, The; With Six You Get Eggroll; Young at Heart; Young Man with a Horn

Day, Gary: Crimebroker; Tunnel Vision (1994)

Day, Josette: Beauty and the Beast

Day, Laraine: Arizona Legion; Dr. Kildare's Strange Case; Fingers at the Window; Foreign Correspondent; High and the Mighty, The; Journey for Margaret; Mr. Lucky; Murder on Flight 502; My Dear Secretary; Return to Fantasy Island; Story of Dr. Wassell, The; Tarzan Finds a Son; Those Endearing Young Charms; Tycoon

Day, Marceline: Broadway to Cheyenne; Cameraman, The; Telegraph Trail, The

Day, Matt: Kiss or Kill; Love and Other Catastrophes; Muriel's Wedding

Day, Morris: Graffiti Bridge; Purple Rain

Day, Stuart Garrison: Search and Destroy

Day, Vera: Up the Creek

Dayan, Assaf: Operation Thunderbolt

Dayka, Margit: Cat's Play

Day-Lewis, Daniel: Age of Innocence, The; Bounty, The; Boxer, The; Crucible, The; Eversmile New Jersey; In the Name of the Father; Last of the Mohicans, The; My Beautiful Laundrette; My Left Foot; Room with a View, A; Stars and Bars; Unbearable Lightness of Being, The

Dayrit, Dina: Infested (Ticks)

Dayton, Danny: Mad Bull

De, Deepankar: Stranger, The

de Almeida, Joaquim: Clear and Present Danger; Desperado; Good Morning, Babylon; La Cucaracha; Only You

De Baer, Jean: Tidy Endings

de Bankole, Isaach: Ghost Dog: The Way of the Samurai

de Banzie, Brenda: Doctor at Sea; Entertainer, The; Hobson's Choice; Thirty-Nine Steps, The

De Bark, Yvonne: Sons of Trinity, The

De Bartolli, Moreno: When Father Was Away on Business

de Beranger, Andre: Fig Leaves

De Boeck, Antje: Daens

De Boer, Nikki: Cube; Prom Night IV—Deliver Us from Evil

De Borg, Beatrice: Dangerous Prey

de Bray, Yvonne: Les Parents Terribles

de Brulier, Nigel: Iron Mask, The; Three Musketeers, The; Zorro Rides Again

De Cadanet, Amanda: Fall

De Carlo, Yvonne: American Gothic; Arizona Bushwhackers; Band of Angels; Captain's Paradise, The; Casbah; Cellar Dweller; Criss Cross (1948); Death of a Scoundrel; Global Affair, A; Good Idea; Hostile Guns; Liar's Moon; McLintock!; Mirror Mirror; Munsters' Revenge, The; Nocturna; Oscar (1991); Passion; Road to Morocco; Salome, Where She Danced; Satan's Cheerleaders; Seven Minutes, The; Shotgun; Silent Scream; Vultures

De Coff, Linda: Hurry Up or I'll Be 30

De Cordoba, Pedro: Before I Hang; Law of the Pampas; Mexican Hayride

De Cordova, Arturo: El (This Strange Passion); For Whom the Bell Tolls

de Corsia, Ted: Buccaneer, The; Enforcer, The; It Happens Every Spring; Lady from Shanghai; Mohawk; Naked City, The; Neptune's Daughter; Three Secrets

De Filippi, Carlo: Who Killed Pasolini?

De Filippo, Peppino: Variety Lights

de Fougerolles, Hélène: Va Savoir

de Funes, Louis: Candide; Delusions of Grandeur; Four Bags Full; La Grande Vadrouille

de Graaf, Marina: Antonia's Line

de Grasse, Sam: Blind Husbands; Man Who Laughs, The; Wild and Woolly
De Haven, Gloria: Best Foot Forward; Bog; Broadway Rhythm; Out to Sea; Summer Holiday; Summer Stock; Susan and God; Thin Man Goes Home, The; Three Little Words; Two Girls and a Sailor; Two Tickets to Broadway; Who Is the Black Dahlia?; Yellow Cab Man, The
de Havilland, Olivia: Adventures of Robin Hood, The; Ambassador's Daughter, The; Anastasia: The Mystery of Anna; Anthony Adverse; Captain Blood; Charge of the Light Brigade, The; Dark Mirror, The; Dodge City; Fifth Musketeer, The; Gone with the Wind; Heiress, The; Hollywood Canteen; Hush ... Hush, Sweet Charlotte; In This Our Life; Lady in a Cage; Midsummer Night's Dream, A; Not as a Stranger; Private Lives of Elizabeth and Essex, The; Proud Rebel, The; Roots: The Next Generation; Santa Fe Trail; Snake Pit, The; Strawberry Blonde, The; Swarm, The; Thank Your Lucky Stars; They Died with Their Boots On
de Hory, Elmyr: F for Fake
de Hoyos, Jaime: El Mariachi
de Jesus, Wanda: Gold Coast
de Jonge, Marc: Rambo III
de Keyser, David: Designated Mourner, The; Leon the Pig Farmer; Valentino
de Koff, Ton: Rembrandt—1669
De La Boulaye, Agathe: Girl, The (1999)
De La Bretonere, Esmee: Johnsons, The
de la Brosse, Simon: Strike It Rich
De La Croix, Raven: Lost Empire, The
de la Motte, Marguerite: Final Extra, The; Iron Mask, The; Mark of Zorro, The; Nut, The; Shadows; Three Musketeers, The
De La Paz, Danny: American Me; Barbarosa; Boulevard Nights; Wild Pair, The
de la Pena, George: Brain Donors; Nijinsky
De Lacey, Luke: Virtual Sexuality
de Lancie, John: Arcade; Deep Red; Evolver; Hand That Rocks the Cradle, The; Journey's End: The Saga of Star Trek:The Next Generation; Multiplicity; Raven Hawk
De Lano, Michael: Out for Blood
de Lint, Derek: Assault, The; Diary of a Mad Old Man; Little Riders, The; Mascara; Poltergeist: The Legacy; Stealing Heaven; Unbearable Lightness of Being, The
De Longis, Anthony: Assault, The; Diary of a Mad Old Man; Little Riders, The; Mascara; Poltergeist: The Legacy; Stealing Heaven; Unbearable Lightness of Being, The
de Marney, Derrek: Dangerous Moonlight (Suicide Squadron); Young and Innocent
de Matteo, Drea: Swordfish
de Medeiros, Maria: Henry & June; Pulp Fiction
De Mendoza, Alberto: Bullet for Sandoval, A
De Niro, Robert: Adventures of Rocky and Bullwinkle, The; Analyze This; Angel Heart; Awakenings; Backdraft; Bang the Drum Slowly; Bloody Mama; Born to Win; Brazil; Bronx Tale, A; Cape Fear; Casino; Copland; Deer Hunter, The; Falling in Love; Fan, The; 15 Minutes; Flawless; Godfather Epic, The; Godfather, Part II, The; Goodfellas; Great Expectations; Greetings; Guilty by Suspicion; Heat; Hi Mom; Jackie Brown; Jackknife; King of Comedy, The; Last Tycoon, The; Mad Dog and Glory; Marvin's Room; Mary Shelley's Frankenstein; Mean Streets; Meet the Parents; Men of Honor; Midnight Run; Mission, The; Mistress; New York, New York; Night and the City; Once Upon a Time in America (Long Version); 1900; Raging Bull; Ronin; Sleepers; Stanley and Iris; Swap, The (Sam's Song); Taxi Driver; This Boy's Life; True Confessions; Untouchables, The; Wag the Dog; Wedding Party, The; We're No Angels
de Oliveira, Lourdes: Black Orpheus
de Oliveira, Vincius: Central Station
De Osca, Paco: Solas
De Palma, Rossy: Flower of My Secret, The; Kika
de Pencier, Miranda: Harrison Bergeron
de Penguern, Artus: Amélie
de Putti, Lya: Othello; Sorrows of Satan, The; Variety
De Rienzo, Libero: Fat Girl
de Roche, Charles: Ten Commandments, The
de Rossi, Barbara: Blood Ties; Hearts and Armour; Mussolini and I
de Rossi, Portia: Sirens
De Sade, Ana: Triumphs of a Man Called Horse
De Salvo, Anne: Bad Manners; Compromising Positions; Dead in the Water
De Sando, Anthony: Kiss Me Guido
De Santis, Joe: Dino; Last Hunt, The
de Shields, Andre: Prison
De Sica, Christian: Detective School Dropouts
De Sica, Vittorio: Andy Warhol's Dracula; Battle of Austerlitz, The; Earrings of Madame De ... , The; General Della Rovere; Gold of Naples, The; It Started in Naples; Pardon My Trunk (Hello Elephant!); Shoes of the Fisherman
De Soto, Rosana: La Bamba; Picture Windows; Stand and Deliver
de Souza, Paul: Web of Deceit
de Toth, Nicolas: Welcome to Spring Break
de Van, Adrien: Sitcom
de Veaux, Nathaniel: Bad Attitude
de Villalonga, Jose Luis: Darling
De Vito, Danny: What's the Worst That Could Happen?
de Vogy, Carl: Spiders, The (1919)
De Vos, Ingrid: Istanbul
De Vries, Jon: Act of Passion; Lianna; Sarah, Plain and Tall; Truth or Die; Zelda
de Wilde, Brandon: All Fall Down; Deserter, The; Goodbye, My Lady; Hud; In Harm's Way; Member of the Wedding, The; Shane; Those Calloways
De Young, Cliff: Carnosaur 2; Code Name: Dancer; Dr. Giggles; Fear; Flashback; Flight of the Navigator; Forbidden Sun; Fourth Story; F/X; Hunger, The (1983); In Dangerous Company; Independence Day; King; Lindbergh Kidnapping Case, The; Nails; Protocol; Pulse; Reckless; Revenge of the Red Baron; Rude Awakening; Secret Admirer; Shock Treatment; Skateboard Kid, The; Star Quest; Survivalist, The; To Die Standing; Westing Game, The
Dea, Marie: Les Visiteurs Du Soir
Deacon, Brian: Jesus; Vampyres; Zed and Two Noughts, A
Deacon, Eric: Zed and Two Noughts, A
Deacon, Richard: Abbott and Costello Meet the Mummy; Dick Van Dyke Show, The (TV Series); Happy Hooker Goes Hollywood, The; My Sister Eileen
Dead End Kids, The: They Made Me a Criminal
Deakins, Lucy: Boy Who Could Fly, The; Cheetah; Little Nikita; There Goes My Baby
Dean, Allison: Ruby in Paradise
Dean, Bill: Family Life
Dean, Billy: Face to Kill For, A
Dean, Eddie: Caravan Trail; Colorado Serenade; Wild West; Wildfire
Dean, Fabian: Single Room Furnished
Dean, Felicity: Steaming; Whistle Blower, The
Dean, Isabel: Terrorists, The
Dean, Ivor: Saint, The (TV Series)
Dean, James: East of Eden; Giant; Rebel Without a Cause
Dean, Jimmy: Big Bad John
Dean, Laura: Fame
Dean, Loren: American Clock, The; Billy Bathgate; End of Violence, The; Enemy of the State; Gattaca; JFK: Reckless Youth; Mrs. Winterbourne; Mumford; 1492: The Conquest of Paradise; Passion of Darkly Noon, The; Rosewood; Space Cowboys
Dean, Priscilla: Outside the Law; White Tiger
Dean, Rick: Carnosaur 2; Carnosaur 3: Primal Species; Cheyenne Warrior; Max Is Missing; Naked Obsession; New Crime City: Los Angeles 2020; One Man Army; Skateboard Kid, The
Dean, Ron: Birthday Boy, The; Cold Justice
DeAnda, Rodolfo: Toy Soldiers
Deane, Lezlie: To Protect and Serve
DeAngelo, Paul: Sleepaway Camp
Deas, Justin: Dream Lover; Montana
DeBell, Kristine: Big Brawl, The
DeBello, James: Detroit Rock City

DeBenning, Burr: Incredible Melting Man, The

DeBoe, Alex: Chippendales Murder, The

Debucourt, Jean: La Chute de la Maison Usher; Monsieur Vincent

DeCamp, Rosemary: Big Hangover, The; By the Light of the Silvery Moon; Look for the Silver Lining; Main Street to Broadway; On Moonlight Bay; Saturday the 14th; Story of Seabiscuit, The; Strategic Air Command; 13 Ghosts; Yankee Doodle Dandy

DeCarlo, Mark: Angel 4: Undercover

Deckert, Blue: Taste for Killing, A

Decleir, Jan: Antonia's Line; Character (Karakter); Daens; Running Free

Declie, Xavier: Nemesis 3: Time Lapse

Decomble, Guy: Jour de Fête

Dee, Catherine: Stuff Stephanie in the Incinerator

Dee, Frances: Becky Sharp; Blood Money; Finishing School; Four Faces West; Gypsy Colt; I Walked with a Zombie; If I Had a Million; If I Were King; Little Women; Of Human Bondage; Private Affairs of Bel Ami, The; So Ends Our Night; Wheel of Fortune

Dee, Ruby: All God's Children; Baby Geniuses; Buck and the Preacher; Cat People; Cop and a Half; Court-martial of Jackie Robinson, The; Decoration Day; Do the Right Thing; Ernest Green Story, The; Gore Vidal's Lincoln; I Know Why the Caged Bird Sings; Incident, The; It's Good to Be Alive; Jackie Robinson Story, The; Jungle Fever; Just Cause; Mr. and Mrs. Loving; Passing Glory; Purlie Victorious; Raisin in the Sun, A; Simple Wish, A; Stand, The; Wall, The (1998) (U.S.); Windmills of the Gods

Dee, Sandra: Come September; Dunwich Horror, The; Fantasy Island; Gidget; Imitation of Life; Reluctant Debutante, The; Summer Place, A; Tammy and the Doctor; Until They Sail

Deee, Tray: Tha Eastsidaz

Deee-Lite: Wigstock: The Movie

Deely, Ben: Victory

Deering, Olive: Danger

Dees, Kevin: Jet Benny Show, The

Deezen, Eddie: Beverly Hills Vamp; Desperate Moves; Hollywood Boulevard II; I Wanna Hold Your Hand; Midnight Madness; Million Dollar Mystery; Mob Boss; Mugsy's Girls; Polish Vampire in Burbank, A; Rosebud Beach Hotel, The (Nostell Hotel,The); Surf 2; Teenage Exorcist; Whoopee Boys, The

Deezer D: CB4

DeFoe, Diane: Deceit

DeFore, Don: Adventures of Ozzie and Harriet, The (TV Series); Battle Hymn; Facts of Life; Girl in Every Port, A; Hazel Christmas Show, The (TV Series); Jumping Jacks; My Friend Irma; Romance on the High Seas; Time to Love and a Time to Die, A; Without Reservations

DeGeneres, Ellen: Dr. Dolittle (1998); EDtv; Goodbye Lover; Love Letter, The; Mr. Wrong

Degermark, Pia: Elvira Madigan; Looking Glass War, The

Deguy, Marie-Armelle: Elegant Criminal, The

DeHaven, Lisa: Redneck Zombies

Dehner, John: Apache; California Gold Rush; Creator; Dynamite Pass; Girl in Black Stockings, The; Golden Earrings; Hot Lead; Killer Inside Me, The; Left Handed Gun, The; Man of the West; Maverick (TV Series); Nothing Personal; Out California Way; Slaughterhouse Five; Support Your Local Gunfighter; Texas Rangers, The (1951)

Dekker, Albert: Among the Living; Beau Geste; Buckskin Frontier; Cass Timberlane; Dr. Cyclops; Fabulous Texan, The; Gamera the Invincible; Gentlemen's Agreement; Honky Tonk; In Old California; Kansan, The; Kiss Me Deadly; Once Upon a Honeymoon; Salome, Where She Danced; Seven Sinners; Strange Cargo; Wake Island; War of the Wildcats; Woman of the Town

Del Grande, Louis: Sugartime

Del Mar, Maria: Moonshine Highway; Price of Glory

Del Poggio, Carla: Variety Lights

Del Prete, Duilio: Sensuous Nurse, The

Del Rio, Dolores: Bird of Paradise; Children of Sanchez, The; Flaming Star; Flor Sylvestre; Flying Down to Rio; Fugitive, The; Journey into Fear; What Price Glory? (1926); Wonder Bar

Del Sol, Laura: Crew, The; El Amor Brujo; Hit, The (1984); Stilts, The (Los Zancos)

Del Toro, Benicio: Basquiat; China Moon; Excess Baggage; Fan, The; Fearless; Funeral, The; Usual Suspects, The; Fear and Loathing in Las Vegas; Joyride; Pledge, The; Snatch; Traffic; Way of the Gun, The

Del Toro, Guadalupe: Donna Herlinda and Her Son

Del Trecco, Caesar: Escape to White Mountain

deLacey, Philippe: Peter Pan

Delair, Suzy: Fernandel the Dressmaker; Gervaise; Jenny Lamour; Pattes Blanches (White Paws)

Delamare, Lise: Baxter

Delamere, Matthew: 8 1/2 Women

Delaney, Joan: Don't Drink the Water

Delaney, Kim: Body Parts; Campus Man; Darkman II: The Return of Durant; Disappearance of Christina, The; Drifter, The; First Affair; Force, The; Hunter's Blood; Project: Metalbeast; Serial Killer; Tall, Dark and Deadly; Temptress; That Was Then ... This Is Now

Delany, Dana: China Beach (TV Series); Dead Man's Curve; Dead to Rights; Enemy Within, The; Exit to Eden; Fly Away Home; Housesitter; Light Sleeper; Masquerade; Right Temptation, The; Sirens; Tombstone; True Women; Wide Awake; Wild Palms

DeLaria, Lea: Edge of Seventeen

Delfino, Majandra: Shriek If You Know What I Did Last Friday the 13th; Zeus and Roxanne

Delgado, Camilo: Strangers in the City

Delgado, Damian: Men with Guns

Delger, Jeff: On the Line

Dell, Claudia: Ghost Patrol

Dell, Dorothy: Little Miss Marker

Dell, Gabriel: Bowery Boys, The (Series); Framed

Dell, Howard: Mean Streak; Mean Streak

Dell, Myrna: Guns of Hate

DellaFemina, Michael: Mandroid

Delmar, Kenny: It's a Joke, Son!

Delon, Alain: Airport '79: The Concorde; Assassination of Trotsky, The; Borsalino; Diabolically Yours; Eclipse, The; Honor Among Thieves; Icy Breasts; Is Paris Burning?; Joy House; Le Samourai; Leopard, The; Lost Command; Melodie en Sous-Sol (The Big Grab) (AnyNumber Can Win); Mr. Klein; Purple Noon; Red Sun; Rocco & His Brothers; Sois Belle Et Tais-Toi (Just Another Pretty Face); Swann in Love; Swimming Pool, The; Texas Across the River; Widow Couderc; Zorro

Delon, Nathalie: Eyes Behind the Stars; Game of Seduction; Le Samourai

DeLongis, Anthony: Cyber Tracker 2; Final Round

Delora, Jennifer: Breeders; Robot Holocaust

DeLorenzo, Michael: Judgment Night; Somebody to Love; Wall, The (1998) (U.S.)

Delorme, Daniele: Les Misérables; Pardon Mon Affaire, Too!

Delpy, Julie: American Werewolf in Paris, An; Beatrice; Before Sunrise; Crime and Punishment; Killing Zoe; Passion of Ayn Rand, The; Sand; Three Musketeers, The; Voyager; White; Younger and Younger

Deluc, Xavier: Tale of Two Cities, A

DeLuise, Dom: Adventure of Sherlock Holmes' Smarter Brother, The; Almost Pregnant; American Tail, An; Baby Geniuses; Best Little Whorehouse in Texas, The; Cannonball Run; Cannonball Run II; Cheap Detective, The; Driving Me Crazy; End, The; Evil Roy Slade; Fail-Safe; Fatso; Glass Bottom Boat, The; Godson, The; Going Bananas; Haunted Honeymoon; History of the World, Part One, The; Hot Stuff; Last Married Couple in America, The; Loose Cannons; Muppet Movie, The; Only with Married Men; Red Line; Robin Hood: Men in Tights; Sextette; Silence of the Hams; Silent Movie; Smokey and the Bandit II; Tin Soldier, The; Twelve Chairs, The; Wholly Moses!; World's Greatest Lover, The

DeLuise, Michael: Boys Will Be Boys; Encino Man; Man without a Face, The; Midnight Edition

DeLuise, Peter: Children of the Night; Free Ride; Rescue Me

Demara, Ferdinand: Hypnotic Eye, The

Demarest, William: All Through the Night; Behave Yourself!; Charlie Chan at the Opera; Christmas in July; Devil and Miss Jones, The; Don't Be Afraid of the Dark; Dressed to Kill; Escape

from Fort Bravo; Great Moment, The; Hail the Conquering Hero; Hands Across the Table; Hell on Frisco Bay; Here Come the Girls; It's a Mad Mad Mad Mad World; Jazz Singer, The; Jolson Sings Again; Jolson Story, The; Lady Eve, The; Little Men; Love on the Run; Miracle of Morgan's Creek, The; Mountain, The; Palm Beach Story, The; Pardon My Sarong; Perils of Pauline, The; Riding High; Sincerely Yours; Son of Flubber; Sorrowful Jones; Sullivan's Travels; That Darn Cat; Viva Las Vegas; What Price Glory

Demazis, Orane: Angele; César; Fanny; Harvest (1937); Le Schpountz; Marius

Demercus, Ellem: Children of Noisy Village, The

Demetral, Chris: Blank Check

DeMille, Katherine: Black Room, The; Charlie Chan at the Olympics; Gentleman from California; In Old Caliente; Viva Villa!

Demiss, Darcy: Living to Die

Demongeot, Catherine: Zazie dans le Metro

Demongeot, Mylene: Bonjour Tristesse; Private Navy of Sgt. O'Farrell, The; Rape of the Sabines; Sois Belle Et Tais-Toi (Just Another Pretty Face)

DeMornay, Rebecca: And God Created Woman; Backdraft; Blind Side; By Dawn's Early Light; Con, The; Dealers; Feds; Getting Out; Guilty as Sin; Hand That Rocks the Cradle, The; Inconvenient Woman, An; Murders in the Rue Morgue; Never Talk to Strangers; Night Ride Home; Right Temptation, The; Risky Business; Runaway Train; Slugger's Wife, The; Stephen King's The Shining; Testament; Three Musketeers, The; Trip to Bountiful, The; Winner, The

DeMoss, Darcy: Eden (TV Series)

Dempsey, Chris: Virgin High

Dempsey, Donna: Begotten

Dempsey, Mark: Oh! Calcutta!

Dempsey, Patrick: Ava's Magical Adventure; Bank Robber; Bloodknot; Can't Buy Me Love; Coupe De Ville; Crime and Punishment; Escape, The; Face the Music; For Better and for Worse; Happy Together; Hugo Pool; In a Shallow Grave; In the Mood; JFK: Reckless Youth; Loverboy; Meatballs III; Mobsters; Outbreak; Right to Remain Silent, The; Run; Scream 3; Some Girls; Something About Sex; 20,000 Leagues Under the Sea; With Honors

Dempsey, Tanya: Shrieker

Dempster, Carol: Dream Street; Sally of the Sawdust; Sorrows of Satan, The; True Heart Susie; White Rose, The

DeMunn, Jeffrey: Blob, The; By Dawn's Early Light; Cash Crop; Christmas Evil; Citizen X; Frances; Hiroshima; Hitcher, The; Path to Paradise; Rocketman; Sessions; Shawshank Redemption, The; Treacherous Crossing; Warning Sign; Windy City

Demy, Mathieu: Le Petit Amour

DeNatale, Don: Roseland

Denberg, Susan: Frankenstein Created Woman

Dench, Judi: Chocolat; 84 Charing Cross Road; Goldeneye; Henry V; Jack and Sarah; Last of the Blonde Bombshells, The; Luther; Midsummer Night's Dream, A; Mrs. Brown; Room with a View, A; Shakespeare in Love; Shipping News, The; Tea with Mussolini; Tomorrow Never Dies; Wetherby; World Is Not Enough, The

Deneuve, Catherine: Act of Aggression; April Fools, The; Belle de Jour; Choice of Arms, A; Convent, The; Dancer in the Dark; Donkey Skin (Peau D'Àne); East-West; Fort Saganne; Genealogies of a Crime; Hunger, The (1983); Hustle; Indochine; Je Vous Aime (I Love You All); La Grande Bourgeoise; Last Metro, The; Les Voleurs; Love Songs (Paroles et Musique); Ma Saison Preferée; March or Die; Mississippi Mermaid; Musketeer, The; Place Vendome; Repulsion; Scene of the Crime; Slightly Pregnant Man, A; Tales of Paris; Thieves (Les Voleurs); Time Regained; Tristana; Umbrellas of Cherbourg, The

Dengel, Jake: Bloodsucking Pharaohs in Pittsburgh

Denham, Maurice: Carrington, V. C.; Curse of the Demon; Damn the Defiant!; 84 Charing Cross Road; 4:50 From Paddington; Hysteria; Luther; Mr. Love; Nanny, The; Night Caller from Outer Space; Paranoiac; Sunday, Bloody Sunday; Torture Garden; Very Edge, The; Virgin and the Gypsy, The

Denicourt, Marianne: La Belle Noiseuse; Up/Down/Fragile

Denier, Lydie: Guardian Angel; Mardi Gras for the Devil; Red-Blooded American Girl; Satan's Princess; Under Investigation

DeNiro, Robert: Score, The

Denis, Jacques: Jonah Who Will Be 25 in the Year 2000

Denison, Anthony: Amy Fisher Story, The; Brilliant Disguise, A; Child of Darkness, Child of Light; City of Hope; Criminal Passion; Full Eclipse; Full Exposure; Getting Gotti; Harvest, The (1992); Little Vegas; Men of War; Sex, Love, and Cold Hard Cash

Denison, Anthony John: Corporate Ladder

Denison, Leslie: Snow Creature, The

Denison, Michael: Importance of Being Earnest, The; Shadowlands

Dennehy, Brian: Acceptable Risks; Ants!; Belly of an Architect, The; Best Seller; Butch and Sundance: The Early Days; Check Is in the Mail, The; Cocoon; Cocoon: The Return; Day One; Dead Man's Walk; Diamond Fleece, The; Dish Dogs; Father's Revenge, A; Final Appeal; First Blood; Foreign Affairs; F/X; F/X 2: The Deadly Art of Illusion; Gladiator; Gorky Park; Indio; Jericho Mile, The; Killing in a Small Town; Last of the Finest, The; Legal Eagles; Lion of Africa, The; Never Cry Wolf; Out of the Cold; Perfect Witness; Presumed Innocent; Real American Hero, The; Return to Snowy River, Part II; Rising Son; River Rat, The; Silent Victory: The Kitty O'Neil Story; Silverado; Sirens; Skokie; Stars Fell on Henrietta, The; Summer Catch; Teamster Boss: The Jackie Presser Story; To Catch a Killer; Tommy Boy; Twice in a Lifetime; Warden of Red Rock; William Shakespeare's Romeo and Juliet

Dennen, Barry: Twin Sitters

Denner, Charles: And Now, My Love; Assassins de L'Ordre, Les (Law Breakers); Bluebeard; Bride Wore Black, The; Holes, The; Mado; Man Who Loved Women, The; Robert et Robert; Sleeping Car Murders, The; Window Shopping; Z

Denner, Joyce: Behind Locked Doors

Denning, Richard: Affair to Remember, An; Alice Through the Looking Glass; Black Beauty; Creature from the Black Lagoon; Day the World Ended, The; Double Deal; Hangman's Knot

Dennis, Michael: Mystery Monsters

Dennis, Sandy: Another Woman; Come Back to the Five and Dime, Jimmy Dean, Jimmy Dean; Demon (God Told Me To); Execution, The; Four Seasons, The; Indian Runner, The; Mr. Sycamore; Nasty Habits; 976-EVIL; Out of Towners, The (1970); Parents; That Cold Day in the Park; Up the Down Staircase; Who's Afraid of Virginia Woolf?

Dennison, Anthony: Opposite Corners

Denniston, Paul: Butch Camp

Denny, Reginald: Anna Karenina; Arrest Bulldog Drummond; Bulldog Drummond Comes Back; Bulldog Drummond Escapes; Bulldog Drummond's Bride; Bulldog Drummond's Peril; Bulldog Drummond's Revenge; Bulldog Drummond's Secret Police; Escape Me Never; Lost Patrol, The; Madame Satan; Parlor, Bedroom and Bath; Private Lives; Rebecca; Romeo and Juliet; Secret Life of Walter Mitty, The; Spring Parade

Dent, Catherine: Replicant

Denton, Chris: Bound and Gagged: A Love Story

Denton, Christa: Scandal in a Small Town

Denton, Crahan: Great St. Louis Bank Robbery, The

Denton, Jamie: That Old Feeling

Denton, Lucas: Losing Chase

Denver, John: FoxFire; Oh, God!

Denzongpa, Danny: God Is My Witness

Depardieu, Elisabeth: Manon of the Spring

Depardieu, Gérard: Bogus; Buffet Froid (Cold Cuts); Camille Claudel; Choice of Arms, A; Closet, The; Cyrano De Bergerac; Danton; Fort Saganne; Francois Truffaut: Stolen Moments; Get Out Your Handkerchiefs; Going Places; Green Card; Hamlet; Holes, The; Je Vous Aime (I Love You All); Jean De Florette; La Machine; Last Metro, The; Le Chêvre (The Goat); Les Comperes; Loulou; Maitresse; Man in the Iron Mask, The; Ménage; Merci La Vie; Mon Oncle d'Amerique; Moon in the Gutter, The; My Father, the Hero; 102 Dalmatians; 1492: The Conquest of Paradise; 1900; One Woman or Two; Police; Pure Formality, A; Return of Martin Guerre, The; Secret Agent, The; Stavisky; This Sweet Sickness; Too Beautiful for You; Tous les Matins du

Diamantidou, Despo: Dream of Passion, A
Diamond, Barry: Gross Jokes
Diamond, Neil: Jazz Singer, The; Last Waltz, The
Diamond, Reed: High Noon
Diamond, Reed Edward: Blind Spot; Ironclads
Diamont, Don: Marco Polo
Diaz, Cameron: Any Given Sunday; Being John Malkovich; Charlie's Angels; Fear and Loathing in Las Vegas; Feeling Minnesota; Last Supper, The; Life Less Ordinary, A; Mask, The; My Best Friend's Wedding; She's the One; Shrek; Sweetest Thing, The; There's Something About Mary; Things You Can Tell Just by Looking at Her; Vanilla Sky; Very Bad Things
Diaz, Guillermo: Half Baked; Just One Time; Party Girl; Stonewall
Diaz, Justino: Otello
Diaz, Vic: Pacific Inferno
DiBenedetto, Tony: Exterminator, The
Diberti, Luigi: All Screwed Up
DiCaprio, Leonardo: Basketball Diaries, The; Beach, The; Celebrity; Man in the Iron Mask, The; Marvin's Room; Quick and the Dead, The; This Boy's Life; Titanic; Total Eclipse; What's Eating Gilbert Grape?; William Shakespeare's Romeo and Juliet
DiCenzo, George: About Last Night …; Helter Skelter; Killing at Hell's Gate; Las Vegas Lady; Ninth Configuration, The; Omega Syndrome; Starflight One
DiCicco, Bobby: Big Red One, The; Frame Up; Ghoulies IV; I Wanna Hold Your Hand; Last Hour, The; Philadelphia Experiment, The
Dick, Andy: Best Men; Bongwater; In the Army Now; Inspector Gadget
Dick, Douglas: Casbah; Home of the Brave; Oklahoman, The; Red Badge of Courage, The
Dicken, Dieter: Virus Knows No Morals, A
Dickens, Kim: Hollow Man; Mercury Rising; Palookaville; Things Behind the Sun; Truth or Consequences, N.M.; White River; Zero Effect
Dickerson, George: Death Warrant; Death Wish IV: The Crackdown
Dickerson, Lori Lynn: Bloodsport II
Dickerson, Pamela: Overkill
Dickey, James: Deliverance
Dickey, Lucinda: Breakin'; Breakin' 2 Electric Boogaloo
Dickinson, Angie: Big Bad Mama; Big Bad Mama II; Bramble Bush, The; Captain Newman, M.D.; Cast a Giant Shadow; Charlie Chan and the Curse of the Dragon Queen; Chase, The; China Gate; Death Hunt; Dial M for Murder; Don's Analyst, The; Dressed to Kill; Duets; Even Cowgirls Get the Blues; Killers, The; Lucky Me; Maddening, The; Ocean's Eleven; One Shoe Makes It Murder; Point Blank; Poppy Is Also a Flower, The; Pray for the Wildcats; Resurrection of Zachary Wheeler, The; Rio Bravo; Rome Adventure; Texas Guns; Treacherous Crossing; Wild Palms
Dickinson, Ron: Zoo Radio
Dickson, Gloria: They Made Me a Criminal
Dickson, Neil: Biggles—Adventures in Time; Murders in the Rue Morgue
Dickson, Tricia: Secret Kingdom, The
Diddley, Bo: Chuck Berry Hail! Hail! Rock 'n' Roll; Rockula
Didi, Evelyne: Celestial Clockwork
Diebold, Steven R.: Ceremony
Diego, Gambino: Two Much
Diego, Juan: Cabeza de Vaca
Diehl, John: Amanda and the Alien; Anywhere But Here; Buffalo Girls; Climate for Killing, A; Dark Side of the Moon, The; Gettysburg; Glitz; Kickboxer 2: The Road Back; Madhouse; Managua; Miami Vice; Mikey; Mind Ripper; Mo' Money; New Age, The; Remote; Ruby Jean and Joe; Stargate
Dienstag, Christopher: Moneytree, The
Dierkes, John: Daughter of Dr. Jekyll; Hanging Tree, The
Dierkop, Charles: Angels Hard as They Come; Grotesque; Hot Box, The; Invisible Dad
Diesel, Vin: Fast and the Furious, The; Pitch Black; Saving Private Ryan
Diessl, Gustav: Westfront 1918
Dieterle, William: Backstairs; Waxworks
Dietrich, Marlene: Blonde Venus; Blue Angel, The; Destry Rides Again; Dishonored; Follow the Boys; Garden of Allah, The; Golden Earrings; Judgment at Nuremberg; Just a Gigolo; Kismet; Knight Without Armour; Lady Is Willing, The; Marlene; Morocco; No Highway in the Sky; Paris When It Sizzles; Pittsburgh; Rancho Notorious; Scarlet Empress, The; Seven Sinners; Shanghai Express; Spoilers, The; Stage Fright; Touch of Evil; Witness for the Prosecution
Dietz, Eileen: David Holzman's Diary
Dieudonné, Albert: Napoleon
Diffring, Anton: Beast Must Die, The; Circus of Horrors; Colditz Story, The; Fahrenheit 451; Mark of the Devil, Part 2; Where Eagles Dare; Zeppelin
Digges, Dudley: Emperor Jones, The; General Died at Dawn, The; Mutiny on the Bounty
Diggs, Taye: Best Man, The; Go; House on Haunted Hill; How Stella Got Her Groove Back; Way of the Gun, The; Wood, The
Dignam, Arthur: Everlasting Secret Family, The; Right Hand Man, The; Strange Behavior; We of the Never Never; Wild Duck, The
Dignam, Mark: Hamlet
Dilian, Iraseme: Wuthering Heights
Dillane, Stephen: Déjà Vu; Firelight; Rector's Wife, The; Spy Game; Welcome to Sarajevo
Dillard, Art: Ranger and the Lady, The
Dillard, Victoria: Deep Cover; Out of Sync
Diller, Phyllis: Boneyard, The; Boy, Did I Get a Wrong Number!; Mad Monster Party; Pink Motel; Private Navy of Sgt. O'Farrell, The; Pucker Up and Bark Like a Dog; Silence of the Hams
Dillinger, Brian: I Shot a Man in Vegas
Dillman, Bradford: Amsterdam Kill, The; Bridge at Remagen, The; Brother John; Bug; Compulsion; Enforcer, The; Escape from the Planet of the Apes; Force Five; Heart of Justice; Heroes Stand Alone; Legend of Walks Far Woman, The; Lords of the Deep; Love and Bullets; Mastermind; Moon of the Wolf; 99 and 44/100 Percent Dead; Piranha; Resurrection of Zachary Wheeler, The; Revenge (1971) (Shelley Winters); Running Scared; Sergeant Ryker; Sudden Impact; Suppose They Gave a War and Nobody Came?; Treasure of the Amazon; Way We Were, The
Dillon, Denny: Roseanne: An Unauthorized Biography
Dillon, Hugh: Hard Core Logo
Dillon, Kevin: Blob, The; Criminal Hearts; Doors, The; Heaven Help Us; Hidden Agenda (1998); Immediate Family; Midnight Clear, A; No Big Deal; No Escape; Pathfinder, The; Remote Control; Rescue, The; Stag; True Crime; War Party; When He's Not a Stranger
Dillon, Matt: Albino Alligator; Beautiful Girls; Big Town, The; Bloodhounds of Broadway; Drugstore Cowboy; Flamingo Kid, The; Frankie Starlight; Golden Gate; Grace of My Heart; In & Out; Kansas; Kiss Before Dying, A; Liar's Moon; Little Darlings; Mr. Wonderful; My Bodyguard; Native Son; One Night at McCool's; Outsiders, The; Over the Edge; Rebel; Rumble Fish; Saint of Fort Washington, The; Singles; Target; Tex; There's Something About Mary; To Die For; Wild Things; Women & Men 2
Dillon, Melinda: Absence of Malice; Bound for Glory; Captain America; Christmas Story, A; Close Encounters of the Third Kind; Entertaining Angels; Fallen Angel; F.I.S.T.; Harry and the Hendersons; How to Make an American Quilt; Prince of Tides, The; Right of Way; Shadow Box, The; Shattered Spirits; Sioux City; Slap Shot; Songwriter; Spontaneous Combustion; State of Emergency; Staying Together
Dillon, Mia: Lots of Luck
Dillon, Paul: Blink; Hellcab; Kiss Daddy Good Night
DiMaggio, Joe: Manhattan Merry-Go-Round
DiMaggio, John: Pirates of Silicon Valley
Dimambro, Joseph: Concrete Angels; Fatal Combat
DiMattia, Victor: Dennis the Menace: Dinosaur Hunter
Dimitri, Richard: When Things Were Rotten (TV Series)
Dimitrijevic, Mikica: Meetings with Remarkable Men
Din, Ayub Khan: Sammy and Rosie Get Laid

Dinehart, Alan: Everything Happens at Night; It's a Great Life; Second Fiddle; Study in Scarlet, A; Supernatural
Dingham, Arthur: Between Wars; Nostradamus Kid, The
Dingle, Charles: Guest Wife; Sister Kenny; Somewhere I'll Find You; Talk of the Town, The; Welcome, Stranger
Dingo, Ernie: Dead Heart; Waltz Through the Hills
Dingwall, Kelly: Custodian, The
Dinsdale, Reece: Partners in Crime (Secret Adversary) (TV Series); Threads; Young Catherine
Dinsmore, Bruce: Psychopath (1997)
Dion: Twist Around the Clock
Dionisi, Stefano: Farinelli Il Castrato; Kiss of Fire; Mille Bolle Blu; Truce, The
Director, Kim: Book of Shadows: Blair Witch 2
Dishy, Bob: Brighton Beach Memoirs; Critical Condition; Don Juan DeMarco; First Family; Judy Berlin; Jungle 2 Jungle; Last Married Couple in America, The; Used People
DiSue, Joe: Blackenstein
Ditchburn, Anne: Coming Out Alive; Curtains
Divine: Divine; Female Trouble; Hairspray; Lust in the Dust; Mondo Trasho; Multiple Maniacs; Out of the Dark; Pink Flamingos; Polyester; Trouble in Mind
Divoff, Andrew: Back in the U.S.S.R.; Blast; Deadly Voyage; Interceptor; Killers in the House; Low Down Dirty Shame, A; Nemesis 4; Oblivion 2: Backlash; Running Cool; Stealth Fighter; Stephen King's Graveyard Shift (1990); Wes Craven's Wishmaster; Wishmaster 2: Evil Never Dies; Xtro: Watch the Skies (Xtro 3)
Dix, Richard: Ace of Aces; American Empire; Buckskin Frontier; Cimarron; Kansan, The; Lost Squadron; Ten Commandments, The; To the Last Man; Transatlantic Tunnel; Vanishing American, The
Dix, Robert: Blood of Dracula's Castle; Five Bloody Graves; Gun Riders, The; Horror of the Blood Monsters
Dix, Tommy: Best Foot Forward
Dix, William: Nanny, The
Dixon, David: Hitchhiker's Guide to the Galaxy, The
Dixon, Donna: Beverly Hills Madam; Bosom Buddies (TV Series); Couch Trip, The; Lucky Stiff; Speed Zone; Spies Like Us; Wayne's World
Dixon, Ivan: Car Wash; Fer-de-Lance; Hogan's Heroes (TV Series); Nothing But a Man; Patch of Blue, A; Raisin in the Sun, A; Suppose They Gave a War and Nobody Came?
Dixon, James: It's Alive III: Island of the Alive; Q
Dixon, Jill: Night to Remember, A
Dixon, Joan: Hot Lead
Dixon, MacIntyre: Funny Farm
Dixon, Pamela: CIA II: Target: Alexa; L.A. Crackdown; L.A. Crackdown II
Dixon, Steve: Mosquito
Dixon, Willie: Rich Girl
Djola, Badja: Deterrence; Who's the Man?
Djuric, Branko: No Man's Land (2001)
DMX: Belly; Exit Wounds; Romeo Must Die
D'Obici, Valeria: Passion of Love
Dobrowolska, Gosia: Careful; Custodian, The
Dobson, James: Tanks Are Coming, The
Dobson, Kevin: Dirty Work; Hardhat and Legs; Orphan Train; Restraining Order
Dobson, Peter: Big Squeeze, The; Dead Cold; Drowning Mona; Frighteners, The; Last Exit to Brooklyn; Marrying Man, The; Norma Jean and Marilyn; Nowhere Land; Quiet Days in Hollywood; Sing; Where the Day Takes You
Dobson, Tamara: Chained Heat; Cleopatra Jones; Cleopatra Jones and the Casino of Gold
Dobtcheff, Vernon: House That Mary Bought, The
Dockery, Leslie: Eubie!
Documentary: Elvis '56
Dodd, Brian: Boys of St. Vincent
Dodd, Claire: Case of the Curious Bride, The; Case of the Velvet Claws, The; Mad Doctor of Market Street, The
Dodd, Jimmie: Private Snuffy Smith; Riders of the Rio Grande
Dodd, Molly: Hazel Christmas Show, The (TV Series)
Doe, John: Georgia; Knocking on Death's Door; Pure Country; Roadside Prophets; Scorpion Spring; Sugar Town
Doerr, James: Savage Weekend
Dogg, Snoop: Baby Boy; Bones; Tha Eastsidaz; Training Day; Urban Menace; Wash, The (2001)
Dogileva, Tatyana: Forgotten Tune for the Flute, A
Doherty, Matt: So I Married an Axe Murderer
Doherty, Shannen: Beverly Hills 90210; Blindfold: Acts of Obsession; Freeze Frame; Mall Rats; Nowhere; Striking Poses; Ticket, The
Doig, Lexa: No Alibi; Teen Sorcery
Dolan, Andrew: Partners in Crime
Dolan, Michael: Hamburger Hill
Dolan, Rainbow: In the Aftermath: Angels Never Sleep
Dolbey, Max: David Copperfield
Dolby, Thomas: Rockula
Doleman, Guy: Funeral in Berlin; Ipcress File, The
Dolenz, Ami: Can't Buy Me Love; Children of the Night; Infested (Ticks); Life 101; Miracle Beach; Pumpkinhead II: Bloodwings; Rescue Me; She's Out of Control; Stepmonster; Virtual Seduction; White Wolves: A Cry in the Wild II; Witchboard 2
Dolenz, Mickey: Head (1968); Love Bug, The
Doles, Gary: Jack-O
Doll, Dora: Black and White in Color; Grisbi
Dollaghan, Patrick: Circle of Fear
Dollarhide, Jessica: Castle Freak
Dolsky, Neige: Tatie Danielle
Doman, John: Wirey Spindell
Domasin, Larry: Island of the Blue Dolphins
Dombasle, Arielle: Boss' Wife, The; Celestial Clockwork; Le Beau Mariage; Little Indian, Big City; Pauline at the Beach; Three Lives and Only One Death; Time Regained; Trade Secrets
Domergue, Faith: Cult of the Cobra; House of Seven Corpses, The; It Came from Beneath the Sea; Psycho Sisters; This Island Earth; Voyage to the Prehistoric Planet
Dominczyk, Dagmara: Count of Monte Cristo, The (2002)
Domingo, Placido: Bizet's Carmen; La Traviata; Otello
Dominguez, Chano: Calle 54
Dominguez, Wade: City of Industry
Domino, Fats: Girl Can't Help It, The
Domke, Judah: Whipped
Dommartin, Solveig: Faraway, So Close; Until the End of the World; Wings of Desire
Domrose, Angelica: Scorpion Woman, The
Dona, Linda: Delta Heat; Final Embrace
Donadoni, Maurizio: In Love and War (2001)
Donahue, Elinor: Girls Town; Three Daring Daughters
Donahue, Heather: Blair Witch Project, The; Boys and Girls
Donahue, Troy: Chilling, The; Cockfighter; Cry-Baby; Cyclone; Deadly Prey; Deadly Spygames; Grandview, U.S.A.; Hard Rock Nightmare; Hollywood Cop; Imitation of Life; Low Blow; Monster on the Campus; Omega Cop; Palm Springs Weekend; Parrish; Perfect Furlough; Rome Adventure; Seizure; Shock'em Dead; Summer Place, A; This Happy Feeling; Tin Man; Woman Obsessed, A
Donald, James: Beau Brummell; Bridge on the River Kwai, The; Five Million Years to Earth; Glory at Sea; Immortal Battalion, The (The Way Ahead); Lust for Life; Pickwick Papers, The; Royal Hunt of the Sun
Donason, Don: Witchcraft XI: Sisters in Blood
Donat, Peter: Babe, The (1992); Deep End, The; Different Story, A; Game, The; Highpoint; Honeymoon; Lindbergh Kidnapping Case, The; Massive Retaliation; Mazes and Monsters; Red Corner; Russian Roulette; School Ties; War of the Roses, The
Donat, Richard: My American Cousin
Donat, Robert: Adventures of Tartu; Citadel, The; Count of Monte Cristo, The; Ghost Goes West, The; Goodbye, Mr. Chips; If I Were Rich; Inn of the Sixth Happiness, The; Knight Without Armour; Private Life of Henry the Eighth, The; Thirty-Nine Steps, The; Winslow Boy, The
Donath, Ludwig: Jolson Sings Again; Jolson Story, The
Donato, Marc: Locked in Silence
Donella, Chad E.: Final Destination

Donlevy, Brian: Allegheny Uprising; Arizona Bushwhackers; Barbary Coast, The; Beau Geste; Billy the Kid; Birth of the Blues; Command Decision; Curse of the Fly; Destry Rides Again; Enemy from Space; Errand Boy, The; Five Golden Dragons; Gamera the Invincible; Glass Key, The; Great Man's Lady, The; Great McGinty, The; Hangmen Also Die; Hoodlum Empire; Hostile Guns; Impact; In Old Chicago; Jesse James; Kiss of Death; Miracle of Morgan's Creek, The; Never So Few; Quatermass Experiment, The; Ride the Man Down; Slaughter Trail; Southern Yankee, A; This Is My Affair; Union Pacific; Virginian, The; Wake Island
Donley, Robert: Rockford Files, The (TV Series)
Donnadieu, Bernard Pierre: Beatrice; Trade Secrets; Vanishing, The
Donnell, Jeff: Because You're Mine; Blue Gardenia, The; Gidget Goes to Rome; Guns of Fort Petticoat; My Man Godfrey; Night to Remember, A; Walk Softly, Stranger
Donnellan, Jill: Order of the Black Eagle
Donnelly, Donal: Dead, The; Knack ... and How to Get It, The; Squanto: A Warrior's Tale
Donnelly, Patrice: Personal Best
Donnelly, Ruth: Affairs of Annabel, The; Annabel Takes a Tour; Bells of St. Mary's, The; Female; Hands Across the Table; Snake Pit, The
Donnelly, Tim: Clonus Horror, The
Donner, Jack: Retro Puppetmaster
Donner, Richard: First Works, Volumes 1 & 2
Donner, Robert: Allan Quartermain and the Lost City of Gold; Hysterical; Santee
D'Onofrio, Vincent: Spanish Judges
Donohoe, Amanda: Castaway; Dark Obsession; Foreign Body; I'm Losing You; Lair of the White Worm; Liar, Liar; Madness of King George, The; Paper Mask; Rainbow, The; Real Howard Spritz, The; Shame; Substitute, The
Donovan: Don't Look Back
Donovan, Jeffrey: Book of Shadows: Blair Witch 2
Donovan, King: Hanging Tree, The; Invasion of the Body Snatchers; Magnetic Monster, The
Donovan, Martin: Amateur (1995); Flirt; Hard Choices; Heaven; Hollow Reed; Living Out Loud; Nadja; Onegin; Opposite of Sex, The; Quick; Scam; Surviving Desire; Trust; When Trumpets Fade
Donovan, Robert: Don't Sleep Alone
Donovan, Tate: Case of Deadly Force, A; Dangerous Curves; Holy Matrimony; Inside Monkey Zetterland; Little Noises; Love Potion #9; Memphis Belle; Not My Kid; SpaceCamp
Donovan, Terence: Winds of Jarrah, The
Dontsov, Sergei: Window to Paris
DoobieBrothers, The: Window to Paris
Doody, Alison: Duel of Hearts; Ring of the Musketeer; Taffin; Temptation
Doohan, James: Bug Buster; Star Trek II: The Wrath of Khan; Star Trek III: The Search for Spock; Star Trek IV: The Voyage Home; Star Trek—The Motion Picture; Star Trek (TV Series); Star Trek V: The Final Frontier; Star Trek VI: The Undiscovered Country; Star Trek: Generations; Star Trek: The Menagerie; Storybook
Dooley, Brian: Boys of St. Vincent
Dooley, Paul: Big Trouble (1985); Breaking Away; Court-martial of Jackie Robinson, The; Dangerous Woman, A; Endangered Species; Evolver; Flashback; Guinevere; Last Rites; Lip Service (1988); Murder of Mary Phagan, The; My Boyfriend's Back; O.C. & Stiggs; Out There; Popeye; Rich Kids; Runaway Bride; Shakes the Clown; Sixteen Candles; State of Emergency; Strange Brew; Telling Lies in America; Underneath, The; Wedding, A (1978); White Hot: The Mysterious Murder of Thelma Todd
DoQui, Robert: Almos' a Man; Coffy; Mercenary Fighters; Original Intent
Dor, Karin: Torture Chamber of Dr. Sadism, The; You Only Live Twice
Doran, Ann: Blondie; High and the Mighty, The; It! The Terror from Beyond Space; Love Is Better Than Ever; Painted Hills, The; Perfect Marriage; Pitfall; Rebel Without a Cause; So Proudly We Hail
Doran, Jesse: Heart
Doran, Johnny: Hideaways, The
Doran, Mary: Strange Love of Molly Louvain, The
Dore, Charlie: Ploughman's Lunch, The
Dore, Edna: Nil by Mouth
Dorelli, Johnny: Bread and Chocolate
Dorff, Stephen: BackBeat; Blade; Blood and Wine; cecil b. Demented; City of Industry; Earthly Possessions; Entropy; Gate, The; I Shot Andy Warhol; Innocent Lies; Judgment Night; Power of One, The; Reckless; Rescue Me; S.F.W.; Space Truckers
Dorkin, Cody: Colony, The (1995)
Dorleac, Françoise: Cul-de-Sac; Soft Skin, The; That Man from Rio
Dorn, Dolores: Tell Me a Riddle; Underworld U.S.A.
Dorn, Michael: Amanda and the Alien; Mach 2; Star Trek VI: The Undiscovered Country; Star Trek: First Contact; Star Trek: Generations; Star Trek: Insurrection; Star Trek: The Next Generation (TV Series); Timemaster
Dorn, Philip: Fighting Kentuckian, The; I Remember Mama; I've Always Loved You; Random Harvest; Reunion in France; Tarzan's Secret Treasure
Dorne, Sandra: Eat the Rich
Doroff, Sarah Rowland: Three Fugitives
Dors, Diana: Adventures of a Private Eye; Amazing Mr. Blunden, The; Berserk; Children of the Full Moon; Deep End; Devil's Undead, The; From Beyond the Grave; I Married a Woman; Kid for Two Farthings, A; King of the Roaring Twenties; Long Haul; Steaming; There's a Girl in My Soup; Unicorn, The
D'Orsay, Fifi: Delinquent Daughters; Dixie Jamboree; Going Hollywood
Dorsett, Tony: Kill Zone
Dorsey, Jimmy: Fabulous Dorseys, The; Four Jills in a Jeep
Dorsey, Thomas A.: Say Amen, Somebody
Dorsey, Tommy: Broadway Rhythm; Du Barry Was a Lady; Fabulous Dorseys, The; Presenting Lily Mars; Ship Ahoy; Song Is Born, A
Dorville: Circonstances Attenuantes
Dorziat, Gabrielle: Les Parents Terribles
Dossett, John: Longtime Companion
Dotrice, Karen: Gnome-Mobile, The; Mary Poppins; Thirty-Nine Steps, The; Three Lives of Thomasina, The
Dotrice, Michele: And Soon the Darkness
Dotrice, Roy: Beauty and the Beast (TV Series); Carmilla; CorsicanBrothers, The; Cutting Edge, The; Eliminators, The; Shaka Zulu
Dottermans, Els: Antonia's Line
Doucette, John: Fighting Mad
Douds, Betsy: Ruby in Paradise
Doueiri, Rami: West Beirut
Doug, Doug E.: Class Act; Cool Runnings; Hangin' with the Homeboys; Operation Dumbo Drop; That Darn Cat
Dougherty, Suzi: Chameleon III: Dark Angel
Doughty, Kenny: Crush
Douglas, Angela: Carry on Cowboy
Douglas, Ann: Lone Wolf
Douglas, Brandon: Chips, the War Dog; Journey to Spirit Island
Douglas, Diana: Monsoon
Douglas, Don: Great Gabbo, The
Douglas, Donna: Beverly Hillbillies, The (TV Series); Beverly Hillbillies Go Hollywood, The; Frankie and Johnny
Douglas, Eric: Delta Force 3; Student Confidential
Douglas, Illeana: Cape Fear; Flypaper; Ghost World; Grace of My Heart; Grief; Happy, Texas; Message in a Bottle; Picture Perfect; Rough Riders; Search and Destroy; Sink or Swim; Stir of Echoes; To Die For; Weapons of Mass Distraction; Wedding Bell Blues
Douglas, John: Hell's Brigade
Douglas, Kenneth: Shanty Tramp
Douglas, Kirk: Along the Great Divide; Arrangement, The; Bad and the Beautiful, The; Big Sky, The; Big Trees, The; Brotherhood, The; Cast a Giant Shadow; Catch Me a Spy; Champion; Devil's Disciple, The; Dr. Jekyll and Mr. Hyde; Draw; Eddie Macon's Run; Final Countdown, The; Fury, The (1978); Greedy;

Gunfight, A; Gunfight at the O.K. Corral; Holocaust 2000; Home Movies; In Harm's Way; Is Paris Burning?; Last Train from Gun Hill; Letter to Three Wives, A; Light at the End of the World, The; Lonely Are the Brave; Lust for Life; Man from Snowy River, The; Man without a Star; My Dear Secretary; Once Is Not Enough; Oscar (1991); Out of the Past; Paths of Glory; Posse; Queenie; Racers, The; Saturn 3; Secret, The; Seven Days in May; Spartacus; Strange Love of Martha Ivers, The; Strangers When We Meet; There Was a Crooked Man; Tough Guys; 20,000 Leagues Under the Sea; Two Weeks in Another Town; Ulysses; Victory at Entebbe; Vikings, The; Villain, The; War Wagon, The; Way West, The; Young Man with a Horn

Douglas, Melvyn: Americanization of Emily, The; As You Desire Me; Being There; Captains Courageous; Changeling, The; Death Squad, The; Ghost Story; Gorgeous Hussy, The; Hotel; Hud; I Never Sang for My Father; Intimate Strangers; Mr. Blandings Builds His Dream House; My Forbidden Past; Ninotchka; Old Dark House, The; Sea of Grass, The; Seduction of Joe Tynan, The; Shining Hour, The; Tell Me a Riddle; Tenant, The; That Uncertain Feeling; Theodora Goes Wild; Twilight's Last Gleaming; Two-Faced Woman; Vampire Bat, The; Woman's Face, A; Woman's Secret, A

Douglas, Michael: Adam at 6 A.M.; American President, The; Basic Instinct; Black Rain; China Syndrome, The; Chorus Line, A; Coma; Disclosure; Don't Say a Word; Falling Down; Fatal Attraction; Game, The; Ghost and the Darkness, The; Hail, Hero!; It's My Turn; Jewel of the Nile, The; Napoleon and Samantha; One Night at McCool's; Perfect Murder, A; Romancing the Stone; Shining Through; Star Chamber, The; Traffic; Wall Street; War of the Roses, The; Wonder Boys

Douglas, Mike: Gator; Incredible Shrinking Woman, The

Douglas, Paul: Angels in the Outfield; Big Lift, The; Clash by Night; Executive Suite; Gamma People, The; It Happens Every Spring; Letter to Three Wives, A; Mating Game, The; Never Wave at a WAC (Private Wore Skirts, The); Panic in the Streets; This Could Be the Night; We're Not Married

Douglas, Robert: Adventures of Don Juan, The; At Sword's Point; Fountainhead, The

Douglas, Santiago: Girlfight

Douglas, Sarah: Art of Dying, The; Asylum; Beastmaster 2: Through the Portal of Time; Frankenstein Sings; Meatballs 4; Mirror, Mirror 2: Raven Dance; Nightfall; People That Time Forgot, The; Puppet Master III: Toulon's Revenge; Quest of the Delta Knights; Return of the Living Dead 3; Spitfire; Steele Justice; Stepford Husbands, The; Voodoo

Douglas, Shirley: Barney's Great Adventure

Douglas, Suzzanne: How Stella Got Her Groove Back; Inkwell, The; Jason's Lyric

Douglass, Gregg: Fist of Steel

Douglass, Robyn: Freeze Frame; Lonely Guy, The; Romantic Comedy

Dougnac, France: Hot Head

Dougnac, Marie-Laure: Delicatessen

Dourani, Behzad: Wind Will Carry Us, The

Dourif, Brad: Alien Resurrection; Amos & Andrew; Blackout; Body Parts; Brown's Requiem; Child's Play; Child's Play 2; Child's Play 3; Color of Night; Common Bonds; Critters 4; Dead Certain; Death Machine; Dune; Exorcist III: Legion; Eyes of Laura Mars, The; Fatal Beauty; Final Judgment; Grim Prairie Tales; Guyana Tragedy, The: The Story of Jim Jones; Heaven's Gate; Hidden Agenda; Horseplayer; Impure Thoughts; Istanbul; Jungle Fever; London Kills Me; Mississippi Burning; Murder in the First; Nightwatch; One Flew over the Cuckoo's Nest; Progeny; Prophecy 3: The Ascent; Ragtime; Senseless; Sonny Boy; Soulkeeper; Spontaneous Combustion; Stephen King's Graveyard Shift (1990); Trauma; Urban Legend; Wise Blood

Dove, Billie: Black Pirate, The

Dow, Peggy: Harvey

Dowd, Ann: Kingfish: A Story of Huey P. Long; Shiloh 2: Shiloh Season

Dowhen, Garrick: Appointment with Fear

Dowie, Freda: Distant Voices/Still Lives

Dowling, Constance: Knickerbocker Holiday; Up in Arms

Dowling, Doris: Bitter Rice; Blue Dahlia, The

Down, Lesley-Anne: Beastmaster III: The Eye of Braxus; Betsy, The; Death Wish V: The Face of Death; From Beyond the Grave; Great Train Robbery, The; Hanover Street; Hunchback (1982); In the Heat of Passion II: Unfaithful; Lady Killers; Little Night Music, A; Mardi Gras for the Devil; Munchie Strikes Back; Nomads; North and South; Over the Line; Pink Panther Strikes Again, The; Rough Cut; Scenes from the Goldmine; Secret Agent Club; Sphinx (1981); Upstairs, Downstairs

Downes, Cathy: Kentucky Rifle; Missile to the Moon; Noose Hangs High, The; Sundowners, The; Winter of Our Dreams

Downes, Robin: Werewolf Reborn!

Downey, Brian: Eating Pattern; Gigashadow; I Worship His Shadow; Tales from a Parallel Universe

Downey, Roma: Devlin; Hercules and the Amazon Women; Woman Named Jackie, A

Downey Jr., Morton: Predator 2; Revenge of the Nerds III: The Next Generation

Downey Jr., Robert: Air America; Back to School; Black and White (2000); Bowfinger; Chances Are; Chaplin; Danger Zone; Friends and Lovers; Gingerbread Man, The; Hail Caesar; Heart and Souls; Home for the Holidays (1995); Hugo Pool; In Dreams; Johnny Be Good; Less Than Zero; Natural Born Killers; One Night Stand; 1969; Only You; Pick-Up Artist, The; Rented Lips; Restoration; Richard III; Short Cuts; Soapdish; Too Much Sun; True Believer; U.S. Marshals; Wonder Boys

Downey Sr., Robert: Johnny Be Good

Downing, David: Gordon's War

Downs, Cathy: Amazing Colossal Man, The; Short Grass

Downs, Johnny: Mad Monster

Doyle, David: Love or Money?; My Boys Are Good Boys; Paper Lion; Pursuit of Happiness, The; Stranger Within, The; Who Killed Mary What's 'Er Name?

Doyle, Jerry: Babylon 5 (TV Series)

Doyle, John: Wicked, The

Doyle, Maria: Commitments, The

Doyle, Shannon: Kingdom of the Vampire

Doyle, Tony: I Went Down; Secret Friends

Doyle-Murray, Brian: Cabin Boy; Dr. Dolittle (1998); JFK; Jury Duty; Multiplicity; Razor's Edge, The; Wayne's World

D'Pella, Pamela: Caged Heat 2: Stripped of Freedom

Dr. John: Candy Mountain

Drach, Michel: Les Violons du Bal

Drago, Billy: China White; Cyborg 2; Deadly Heroes; Delta Force 2; Diplomatic Immunity; Doll in the Dark, A; In Self Defense; Lady Dragon 2; Martial Law Two—Undercover; Outfit, The; Sci-Fighters; Solar Force; Takeover, The; Untouchables, The

Drainie, John: Incredible Journey, The

Drake, Betsy: Clarence, the Cross-Eyed Lion; Every Girl Should Be Married; Second Woman, The; Will Success Spoil Rock Hunter?

Drake, Charles: Air Force; Comanche Territory; Conflict; Glenn Miller Story, The; Harvey; It Came from Outer Space; Night in Casablanca, A; Tender Years, The; To Hell and Back; Tobor the Great; Until They Sail; War Arrow; Whistle Stop

Drake, Claudia: Detour; Face of Marble, The; False Colors

Drake, Dennis: Preppies

Drake, Dona: Louisiana Purchase

Drake, Fabia: Pocketful of Rye, A; Valmont

Drake, Frances: Invisible Ray, The; Mad Love

Drake, Larry: Beast, The; Dark Asylum; Darkman; Darkman II: The Return of Durant; Desert Heat; Dr. Giggles; Journey of August King, The; Murder in New Hampshire; Paranoia; Tales from the Crypt (TV Series); Taming of the Shrew (1982)

Drake, Paul: Midnight Cabaret

Drake, Peggy: Tuttles of Tahiti, The

Drake, Tom: Bramble Bush, The; Cass Timberlane; Courage of Lassie; Hills of Home; Johnny Reno; Meet Me in St. Louis; Mortal Storm, The; Mrs. Parkington; Two Girls and a Sailor; Words and Music

Draper, Polly: Gold Diggers: The Secret of Bear Mountain; Million to Juan, A; Tic Code, The

Draven, Jamie: Billy Elliot

Dravic, Milena: Man Is Not A Bird; WR: Mysteries of the Organism
Dre, Doctor: Show, The; Training Day; Wash, The (2001); Who's the Man?
Drescher, Fran: American Hot Wax; Beautician and the Beast, The; Cadillac Man; Car 54, Where Are You? (1991); Hollywood Knights, The; Jack; We're Talking Serious Money
Dresdel, Sonia: Clouded Yellow, The
Dresden, John: No Dead Heroes
Dresser, Louise: Eagle, The; Goose Woman, The; Scarlet Empress, The
Dressler, Lieux: Truckstop Women
Dressler, Marie: Anna Christie; Dinner at Eight; Emma; Min and Bill; Vagabond Lover, The
Drew, Ellen: Baron of Arizona, The; Buck Benny Rides Again; China Sky; Christmas in July; Great Missouri Raid, The; If I Were King; Isle of the Dead; Man from Colorado, The; Man in the Saddle; Monster and the Girl, The; Stars in My Crown
Drew, Griffin: Dinosaur Valley Girls; Phantom Love
Dreyfus, Jean Claude: Delicatessen
Dreyfuss, James: Notting Hill
Dreyfuss, Lorin: Detective School Dropouts
Dreyfuss, Richard: Always; American Graffiti; Another Stakeout; Apprenticeship of Duddy Kravitz, The; Big Fix, The; Buddy System, The; Close Encounters of the Third Kind; Competition, The; Crew, The; Dillinger; Down and Out in Beverly Hills; Goodbye Girl, The; Inserts; Jaws; Krippendorf's Tribe; Lansky; Last Word, The; Let It Ride; Lost in Yonkers; Moon over Parador; Mr. Holland's Opus; Night Falls on Manhattan; Nuts; Oliver Twist; Once Around; Postcards from the Edge; Prisoner of Honor; Rosencrantz and Guildenstern Are Dead; Silent Fall; Stakeout; Stand by Me; Tin Men; Trigger Happy (Mad Dog Time); What About Bob?; Whose Life Is It, Anyway?
Drillinger, Brian: Brighton Beach Memoirs
Drinkwater, Carol: Father
Driscoll, Bobby: Fighting Sullivans, The (Sullivans, The); So Dear to My Heart; Treasure Island; Window, The
Driscoll, Mark: Concealed Weapon
Driscoll, Martha: Li'l Abner
Driscoll, Robin: Mr. Bean
Drivas, Robert: Cool Hand Luke; Illustrated Man, The
Driver, Minnie: Beautiful; Big Night; Circle of Friends; Good Will Hunting; Governess, The; Grosse Pointe Blank; Hard Rain; Ideal Husband, An; Return to Me; Sleepers
Dru, Joanne: All the King's Men; Hell on Frisco Bay; Light in the Forest, The; Pride of St. Louis, The; Red River; Sincerely Yours; Super Fuzz; Thunder Bay; Vengeance Valley; Wagonmaster; Warriors, The
Drummond, Alice: Daybreak (1993)
Druou, Claire: Le Bonheur
Druou, Jean-Claude: Le Bonheur; Light at the End of the World, The
Drury, James: Elfego Baca: Six Gun Law; Gambler Returns, The: Luck of the Draw; Ride the High Country; Ten Who Dared; Toby Tyler
Dryden, Darren: Lie Down with Dogs
Dryden, Mack: Million Dollar Mystery
Drye, Jenny: Man Bites Dog
Dryer, Fred: Death Before Dishonor
Dryer, Robert: Savage Streets
Dryhurst, Nia: Hedd Wyn
Drynan, Jeanie: Muriel's Wedding; Soft Fruit
Du Fresne, Georges: Ma Vie En Rose
Du Maurier, Gerald: Catherine the Great
Duane, Michael: City Without Men
Duarte, Lima: Me You Them
Duarte, Regina: Happily Ever After
Dubarry, Denise: Monster in the Closet
Dubbins, Don: D.I., The; Enchanted Island; From the Earth to the Moon; Prize, The; Tribute to a Bad Man
Dubin, Ellen: Tammy & the T-Rex
Dubois, Marie: Les Grandes Gueules (Jailbirds' Vacation); Shoot the Piano Player; Vincent, François, Paul and the Others
DuBois, Marta: Blackout; Boulevard Nights; Luminarias
Dubost, Paulette: May Fools; Viva Maria!
Dubov, Paul: Ma Barker's Killer Brood
Ducasse, Cecile: Chocolat
Ducati, Kristi: Bikini Carwash Company 2
Ducaux, Annie: Abel Gance's Beethoven
Duce, Sharon: Buddy's Song
Ducey, Caroline: Romance
Duchamp, Marcel: Avant Garde Program #2
Duchaussoy, Michel: May Fools; Road to Ruin (1991); This Man Must Die
Duchesne, Roger: Bob le Flambeur
Duchovny, David: Beethoven; Evolution; Julia Has Two Lovers; Kalifornia; Playing God; Return to Me; Ruby; Venice/Venice; X-Files, The (1998); X-Files, The (TV Series)
Ducommun, Rick: Blank Check; 'Burbs, The; Final Voyage
Ducreux, Louis: Sunday in the Country, A
Dudgeon, Neil: Different for Girls
Dudikoff, Michael: American Ninja; American Ninja II; American Ninja IV: The Annihilation; Avenging Force; Bounty Hunters; Chain of Command; Crash Dive; Freedom Strike; Gale Force; Human Shield, The; Midnight Ride; Moving Target; Platoon Leader; Radioactive Dreams; Rescue Me; Ringmaster; River of Death; Soldier Boyz; Strategic Command; Virtual Assassin
Dudley, Doris: Moon and Sixpence, The
Duel, Peter: Generation (1969)
Duering, Carl: Arabesque
Duez, Sophie: Eye of the Wolf
Duff, Amanda: Devil Commands, The; Mr. Moto in Danger Island
Duff, Debbie: Helter-Skelter Murders, The
Duff, Denice: Bloodfist V: Human Target; Bloodlust: Subspecies III; Bloodstone: Subspecies II; Return to Frogtown; Subspecies 4: Bloodstorm
Duff, Howard: All My Sons; Battered; Boys' Night Out; Brute Force; Deadly Companion; East of Eden; Kramer vs. Kramer; Late Show, The; Naked City, The; No Way Out; Oh, God! Book II; Private Hell 36; Snatched; Too Much Sun; Wedding, A (1978); While the City Sleeps
Duffey, Todd: Civil War Diary
Duffring, Anton: Shatter
Duffy, Dee: Shatter
Duffy, J. S.: Small Faces
Duffy, Jack: Madame Behave
Duffy, Karen: Blank Check; Dumb and Dumber; Synapse; 24-Hour Woman
Duffy, Patrick: Alice Through the Looking Glass; Danielle Steel's Daddy; Enola Gay: The Men, the Mission, the Atomic Bomb; Last of Mrs. Lincoln, The; Man from Atlantis, The; Texas; Vamping
Dufilho, Jacques: Black and White in Color; Horse of Pride, The
Dufour, Val: Undead, The
Dufresne, Annie: Deadline
Dugan, Dennis: Can't Buy Me Love; Howling, The; New Adventures of Pippi Longstocking, The; Norman … Is That You?; Unidentified Flying Oddball
Duggan, Andrew: Firehouse; Frankenstein Island; Housewife; In Like Flint; Incredible Journey of Dr. Meg Laurel,The; Incredible Mr. Limpet, The; It Lives Again; It's Alive!; Palm Springs Weekend; Return to Salem's Lot, A; Secret War of Harry Frigg, The; Skin Game (1971); Wagon Train (TV Series)
Duggan, Tom: Frankenstein 1970
Dujmovic, Davor: Time of the Gypsies
Dukakis, John: Delusion
Dukakis, Olympia: Cemetery Club, The; Dad; Dead Badge; Digger; I Love Trouble; In the Spirit; Jane Austen's Mafia; Jeffrey; Jerusalem; Joan of Arc (1999); Last of the Blonde Bombshells, The; Look Who's Talking; Look Who's Talking Too; Mighty Aphrodite; Moonstruck; Mother; Mr. Holland's Opus; Over the Hill; Pentagon Wars, The; Picture Perfect; Steel Magnolias; Walls of Glass
Duke, Bill: Action Jackson; Always Outnumbered; Bird on a Wire; Limey, The; Menace II Society; No Man's Land; Predator

Duke, Patty: Amityville 4: The Evil Escapes; Babysitter, The; Best Kept Secrets; Billie; By Design; Curse of the Black Widow; Daydreamer, The (1966); Family Upside Down, A; 4D Man; George Washington; George Washington: The Forging of a Nation; Grave Secrets: The Legacy of Hilltop Drive; Harvest of Fire; Miracle Worker, The; Miracle Worker, The; My Sweet Charlie; Prelude to a Kiss; September Gun; She Waits; Something Special; Valley of the Dolls
Duke, Robin: Blue Monkey; Hostage for a Day
Dukes, David: Cat on a Hot Tin Roof; Catch the Heat; Date with an Angel; First Deadly Sin, The; Fled; George Washington; Josephine Baker Story, The; Little Romance, A; Love Letter, The; Me and the Kid; Men's Club, The; Norma Jean and Marilyn; Rawhead Rex; Rutanga Tapes, The; See You in the Morning; Snow Kill; Strange Interlude; Supreme Sanction; Wild Party, The; Without a Trace
Dulany, Caitlin: Class of 1999 II: The Substitute; Maniac Cop 3: Badge of Silence
Dullea, Keir: Black Christmas; Blind Date; Brainwaves; David and Lisa; Haunting of Julia, The; Hoodlum Priest, The; Leopard in the Snow; Next One, The; Oh, What a Night; 2001: A Space Odyssey; 2010
Dumbrille, Douglass: Abbott and Costello in the Foreign Legion; Baby Face; Big Store, The; Broadway Bill; Buccaneer, The; Castle in the Desert; Dragnet; False Colors; Female; Firefly, The; Gypsy Wildcat; It's a Joke, Son!; Lady Killer; Lost in a Harem; Mr. Deeds Goes to Town; Naughty Marietta; Operator 13; Princess Comes Across, The; Ride 'em Cowboy; Road to Utopia; Road to Zanzibar; Son of Paleface; Virginia City
DuMond, Hayley: Hunter's Moon
Dumont, Margaret: Animal Crackers; At the Circus; Bathing Beauty; Big Store, The; Cocoanuts; Day at the Races, A; Duck Soup; Horn Blows at Midnight, The; Night at the Opera, A; Three for Bedroom C
Dun, Dennis: Big Trouble in Little China; Last Emperor, The; Prince of Darkness; Thousand Pieces of Gold
Dunarie, Malcolm: Heaven Help Us
Dunaway, Faye: Albino Alligator; Arizona Dreams; Arrangement, The; Barfly; Beverly Hills Madam; Bonnie and Clyde; Burning Secret; Casanova; Chamber, The; Champ, The; Chinatown; Christopher Columbus (1985); Cold Sassy Tree; Country Girl, The; Disappearance of Aimee, The; Don Juan DeMarco; Double Edge; Drunks; Dunston Checks In; Ellis Island; Eyes of Laura Mars, The; First Deadly Sin, The; Four Musketeers, The; Gamble, The; Handmaid's Tale, The; Little Big Man; Messenger: The Story of Joan of Arc, The; Midnight Crossing; Mommie Dearest; Network; Ordeal by Innocence; Running Mates; Scorchers; Silhouette; Supergirl; Temp, The; 13 at Dinner; Thomas Crown Affair, The; Thomas Crown Affair, The; Three Days of the Condor; Three Musketeers, The; Towering Inferno, The; Twilight of the Golds, The; Voyage of the Damned; Wait Until Spring, Bandini; Wicked Lady, The; Yards, The
Dunbar, Adrian: Crying Game, The; General, The; Hear My Song; Innocent Lies; Widow's Peak
Dunbar, Dixie: Alexander's Ragtime Band; One in a Million
Dunbar, Dorothy: Tarzan and the Golden Lion
Duncan, Andrew: Gig, The
Duncan, Archie: Adventures of Sherlock Holmes, The (TV Series)
Duncan, Bob: Adventures of Sherlock Holmes, The (TV Series)
Duncan, Bud: Private Snuffy Smith
Duncan, Carmen: Dark Forces; Escape 2000; Now and Forever
Duncan, Jayson: Mystery Island
Duncan, John: Batman and Robin (Adventures of Batmanand Robin)
Duncan, Julie: Fugitive Valley
Duncan, Kenne: Dynamite Canyon; Night of the Ghouls; Riders for Justice; Sinister Urge, The; Song of Nevada
Duncan, Lindsay: Body Parts; Ideal Husband, An; Loose Connections; Manifesto; Rector's Wife, The; Reflecting Skin, The; Year in Provence, A
Duncan, Mary: City Girl
Duncan, Michael Clarke: Green Mile, The; Scorpion King, The; See Spot Run; Whole Nine Yards, The
Duncan, Neil: Sleeping with Strangers
Duncan, Pamela: Attack of the Crab Monsters; Undead, The
Duncan, Rachel: Crazysitter, The
Duncan, Sandy: Cat from Outer Space, The; Million Dollar Duck, The; Roots
Duncan, William: Hopalong Rides Again; Three on the Trail
Dundas, Jennie: Beniker Gang, The; First Wives Club, The; Legal Eagles
Dunford, Christine: Ulee's Gold
Dungan, Sebastian: Man, Woman and Child
Dunlap, Carla: Pumping Iron II: The Women
Dunlap, Dawn: Barbarian Queen; Forbidden World
Dunlay, Frank: Dominion; Witching, The (1994); Zombie Bloodbath
Dunlop, Donn: Down Under
Dunn, Carolyn: Breaking All the Rules
Dunn, Conrad: Mask of Death; Silent Trigger
Dunn, Corey: Member of the Wedding, The
Dunn, Emma: Dr. Kildare's Strange Case; Hell's House; Madame X; Talk of the Town, The
Dunn, James: Baby Take a Bow; Bramble Bush, The; Bright Eyes; Elfego Baca: Six Gun Law; Stand Up and Cheer; That Brennan Girl; 365 Nights in Hollywood; Tree Grows in Brooklyn, A
Dunn, Kevin: Almost Heroes; Beethoven's 2nd; Chain Reaction; Chaplin; Dave; Godzilla (1998); Hit Woman: The Double Edge; Hot Shots; Little Big League; 1492: The Conquest of Paradise; Only the Lonely; Picture Perfect; Second Civil War, The; Small Soldiers; Snake Eyes; Stir of Echoes; Taken Away
Dunn, Michael: Dr. Frankenstein's Castle of Freaks; Freakmaker; Madigan; Murders in the Rue Morgue; No Way to Treat a Lady; Ship of Fools; Werewolf of Washington; Wild Wild West, The (TV series); You're a Big Boy Now
Dunn, Nora: Air Bud: Golden Receiver; Born Yesterday; Max Keeble's Big Move; Miami Blues; Shake, Rattle & Rock; Three Kings
Dunne, Dominique: Diary of a Teenage Hitchhiker; Poltergeist
Dunne, Elizabeth: Blondie Takes a Vacation
Dunne, Griffin: After Hours; Almost You; Amazon Women on the Moon; American Werewolf in London, An; Android Affair, The; Big Blue, The; Big Girls Don't Cry—They Get Even; Cold Feet; Hotel Room; I Like It Like That; Lip Service (1988); Lisa Picard is Famous; Love Matters; Me and Him; My Girl; Search and Destroy; Secret Weapon; Straight Talk; Who's That Girl
Dunne, Irene: Ann Vickers; Anna and the King of Siam; Awful Truth, The; Bachelor Apartment; Cimarron; Consolation Marriage; Guy Named Joe, A; I Remember Mama; Joy of Living; Life with Father; Love Affair; My Favorite Wife; Penny Serenade; Roberta; Show Boat; Sweet Adeline; Theodora Goes Wild; White Cliffs of Dover, The
Dunne, Murphy: Bad Manners
Dunne, Robin: Cruel Intentions 2
Dunne, Stephen: Big Sombrero, The
Dunning, Debbe: Leprechaun 4 in Space
Dunning, Judd: Night That Never Happened, The
Dunnock, Mildred: And Baby Makes Six; Baby Doll; Butterfield 8; Corn Is Green, The; Jazz Singer, The; Nun's Story, The; Peyton Place; Sweet Bird of Youth; Whatever Happened to Aunt Alice?
Dunoyer, François: Fatal Image, The
Dunsmore, Rosemary: Blades of Courage; Breaking the Surface: The Greg Louganis Story; Dancing in the Dark
Dunst, Kirsten: Anastasia; Bring It On; Cat's Meow, The; Crazy/Beautiful; Devil's Arithmetic, The; Dick; Drop Dead Gorgeous; Get Over It; Interview with the Vampire; Jumanji; Little Women; Lover's Prayer; Luckytown Blues; Mother Night; Small Soldiers; Spider-Man; Strike! (1998); True Heart; Virgin Suicides, The; Wag the Dog
Duong, Don: Three Seasons
Duong, Phuong: Squeeze
Duperey, Anny: Blood Rose; Pardon Mon Affaire; Stavisky; Two or Three Things I Know About Her
Dupois, Starletta: Hollywood Shuffle; Raisin in the Sun, A; 3 Strikes
DuPont, Daniel: Running Wild

Duport, Catherine Isabelle: Le Départ; Masculine Feminine
Duprez, June: And Then There Were None; Brighton Strangler, The; Four Feathers, The; None But the Lonely Heart; Spy in Black, The; Thief of Bagdad, The
Dupuis, Roy: Being at Home with Claude; Bleeders; Screamers
Duquenne, Pascal: Eighth Day, The
Durand, Kevin: Mystery, Alaska
Durano, Giustino: Life Is Beautiful
Durante, Jimmy: Alice Through the Looking Glass; Hollywood Party; It Happened in Brooklyn; It's a Mad Mad Mad Mad World; Jumbo; Little Miss Broadway; Man Who Came to Dinner, The; Melody Ranch; On an Island with You; Palooka; Speak Easily; This Time For Keeps; Two Girls and a Sailor; Two Sisters from Boston; What! No Beer?
Durbin, Deanna: Can't Help Singing; First Love; His Butler's Sister; It Started with Eve; It's a Date; Lady on a Train; Mad About Music; One Hundred Men and a Girl; Spring Parade; Three Smart Girls; Three Smart Girls Grow Up
Durfee, Minta: Keystone Comedies: Vol. 1–5
Durham, Geoffrey: Wish You Were Here
Durham, Steve: Born American
Duris, Romain: Gadjo Dilo; When the Cat's Away
Durkin, James: Perils of Pauline, The
Durkin, Junior: Hell's House; Little Men; Tom Sawyer
Durkin, Shevonne: Leprechaun 2
Durning, Charles: Attica; Backlash; Best Little Girl in the World, The; Best Little Whorehouse in Texas, The; Big Trouble (1985); Breakheart Pass; Cat Chaser; Choirboys, The; Connection (1973); Cop; Crisis at Central High; Dark Night of the Scarecrow; Death of a Salesman; Dick Tracy; Die Laughing; Dinner at Eight; Dog Day Afternoon; Far North; Front Page, The; Fury, The (1978); Gambler, Part III—The Legend Continues, The; Grass Harp, The; Greek Tycoon, The; Hadley's Rebellion; Happy New Year (1987); Hard Time; Harry and Walter Go to New York; Hi Life; Hindenburg, The; Home for the Holidays (1995); Hostage Hotel; Hudsucker Proxy, The; I.Q.; Jerry and Tom; Man Who Broke 1000 Chains, The; Man with One Red Shoe, The; Mass Appeal; Mrs. Santa Claus; Music of Chance, The; One Fine Day; Project: Alien; Pursuit of Happiness, The; Queen of the Stardust Ballroom; Return of Eliot Ness, The; Rosary Murders, The; Sharky's Machine; Sisters (1973); Solarbabies; Spy Hard; Starting Over; State & Main; Stick; Sting, The; Tiger's Tale, A; Tilt; To Be or Not to Be; Tootsie; Tough Guys; True Confessions; Twilight's Last Gleaming; Two of a Kind; V. I. Warshawski; Water Engine, The; When a Stranger Calls; When a Stranger Calls Back; Where the River Runs Black; Woman of Independent Means, A
Durock, Dick: Return of the Swamp Thing
Durr, Jason: Killer Tongue
Durrell, Alexandra: Unnamable, The
Durrell, Lawrence: Henry Miller Odyssey
Durrell, Michael: V
Dury, Ian: Different for Girls
Duryea, Dan: Along Came Jones; Bamboo Saucer (Collision Course); Battle Hymn; Criss Cross (1948); Five Golden Dragons; Flight of the Phoenix, The; Great Flamarion, The; Gundown at Sandoval; Lady on a Train; Little Foxes, The; Mrs. Parkington; None But the Lonely Heart; Platinum High School; Pride of the Yankees, The; Sahara; Scarlet Street; Thunder Bay; Underworld Story; Winchester '73; Woman in the Window
Dusek, Jaroslav: Divided We Fall
Dusenberry, Ann: Cutter's Way; Desperate Women; Heart Beat; Lies; Possessed, The (1977)
Dushku, Eliza: Bring It On; Journey; Race the Sun; Soul Survivors; That Night
Dusic, Joe: Bikini Carwash Company, The
Dussault, Nancy: Nurse, The
Dussolier, André: And Now, My Love; Le Beau Mariage; Melo; Three Men and a Cradle; Un Coeur en Hiver
Dutch, Deborah: Sorority Girls and the Creature from Hell
Dutcher, Richard: Brigham City; God's Army
Dutronc, Jacques: Les Tricheurs; L'Etat Sauvage (The Savage State); Place Vendome; Van Gogh
Dutt, Utpal: Stranger, The
Dutton, Charles: Alien 3; Black Dog; Blind Faith; Cookie's Fortune; "Crocodile" Dundee II; Deadlocked; Distinguished Gentleman, The; Foreign Student; Get on the Bus; Low Down Dirty Shame, A; Menace II Society; Mimic; Mississippi Masala; Nick of Time; Piano Lesson, The; Random Hearts; Rudy; Surviving the Game; Time to Kill, A (1996); True Women; Zooman
Dutton, Simon: Lion and the Hawk, The
Dutton, Tim: Tom & Viv
Duval, James: Clown at Midnight, The; Doom Generation, The; Nowhere
DuVall, Clea: Faculty, The; Ghosts of Mars; Girl, Interrupted
Duvall, Robert: Apocalypse Now; Apostle, The; Badge 373; Betsy, The; Breakout; Chase, The; Civil Action, A; Colors; Countdown; Days of Thunder; Deep Impact; Detective, The; Eagle Has Landed, The; Falling Down; Family Thing, A; Geronimo: An American Legend; Gingerbread Man, The; Godfather, The; Godfather Epic, The; Godfather, Part II, The; Gone in 60 Seconds; Great Northfield Minnesota Raid, The; Great Santini, The; Greatest, The; Handmaid's Tale, The; Hotel Colonial; Ike: The War Years; Joe Kidd; John Q; Killer Elite, The; Lady Ice; Lawman; Let's Get Harry; Lightship, The; Lonesome Dove; Man Who Captured Eichmann, The; M*A*S*H; Natural, The; Network; Newsies; Outer Limits, The (TV Series); Paper, The; Phenomenon; Plague, The; Pursuit of D. B. Cooper; Rain People, The; Rambling Rose; Scarlet Letter, The; Seven-Per-cent Solution, The; Show of Force, A; 6th Day, The; Something to Talk About; Stalin; Stars Fell on Henrietta, The; Stone Boy, The; Tender Mercies; Terry Fox Story, The; THX 1138; Tomorrow; True Confessions; True Grit; Wrestling Ernest Hemingway
Duvall, Shelley: Annie Hall; Bernice Bobs Her Hair; Changing Habits; 4th Floor, The; Frankenweenie; Home Fries; McCabe and Mrs. Miller; Popeye; Portrait of a Lady, The; Roxanne; Russell Mulcahy's Tale of the Mummy; Shining, The; Suburban Commando; Thieves Like Us; Time Bandits
Dux, Pierre: La Vie Continue
Dvorak, Ann: Abilene Town; Case of the Stuttering Bishop, The; Flame of the Barbary Coast; Life of Her Own, A; Manhattan Merry-Go-Round; Out of the Blue; Private Affairs of Bel Ami, The; Return of Jesse James, The; Scarface; Strange Love of Molly Louvain, The; Three on a Match
Dwire, Earl: Arizona Days; Assassin of Youth (Marijuana); Lawless Frontier; Man from Music Mountain; Mystery of the Hooded Horsemen; New Frontier; Randy Rides Alone; Riders of Destiny; Trouble in Texas; West of the Divide
Dwyer, Hilary: Conqueror Worm, The
Dwyer, Karyn: Better Than Chocolate
Dwyer, Ruth: Seven Chances
Dyall, Franklyn: Easy Virtue
Dyall, Valentine: Body in the Library, The
Dye, Cameron: Apocalypse, The; Body Rock; Fraternity Vacation; Heated Vengeance; Joy of Sex, The; Out of the Dark; Scenes from the Goldmine; Stranded
Dye, Dale: Operation Delta Force 2; Relentless II: Dead On
Dye, John: Campus Man
Dyer, Danny: Human Traffic
Dyktynski, Matthew: Love and Other Catastrophes
Dylan, Bob: Backtrack; Don't Look Back; Hearts of Fire; Last Waltz, The; Pat Garrett and Billy the Kid
Dylan, Justin: Unexpected Encounters
Dyneley, Peter: Manster, The; Romeo and Juliet
Dysart, Richard: Autobiography of Miss Jane Pittman, The; Back to the Future III; Bitter Harvest; Day One; Falcon and the Snowman, The; L.A. Law; Last Days of Patton, The; Marilyn & Bobby: Her Final Affair; Ordeal of Dr. Mudd, The; Pale Rider; People vs. Jean Harris; Prophecy (1979); Riding with Death; Rumor Mill, The; Sporting Club, The; Thing, The (1982); Truman; Warning Sign
Dytri, Mike: Living End, The
Dzandzanovic, Edin: Beautiful People
Dzhylkychiev, Bakit: Beshkempir, The Adopted Son
Dzundza, George: Act of Passion; Basic Instinct; Beast, The; Best Defense; Brotherly Love; Butcher's Wife, The; Crimson Tide; Dangerous Minds; Enemy Within, The; Glory Years; Im-

pulse; Instinct; Limbic Region, The; No Mercy; Trading Favors; White Hunter Black Heart
Eadie, Nicholas: Return to Snowy River, Part II
Eadie, William: Ratcatcher
Eagan, Daisy: Ripe
Eagle, Jeff: Slammer Girls
Earl, Elizabeth: Fairy Tale: A True Story
Earle, Edward: Twelve Miles Out
Earles, Harry: Unholy Three
Easley, Richert: Outrageous
East, Jeff: Deadly Blessing; Huckleberry Finn; Mary and Joseph: A Story of Faith; Pumpkinhead; Summer of Fear; Tom Sawyer
East Side Kids, The: Ghosts on the Loose; Spooks Run Wild
Easterbrook, Leslie: Police Academy 5: Assignment: Miami Beach; Police Academy III: Back in Training
Eastin, Steve: Last Man Standing
Eastland, Todd: Pledge Night
Eastman, George: Blastfighter; Detective School Dropouts; Hands of Steel; Warriors of the Wasteland
Easton, Michael: Coldfire
Easton, Robert: Comin' Round the Mountain
Easton, Rodney: Deadly Weapon
Easton, Sheena: John Carpenter Presents: Body Bags; Tekwar: The Original Movie
Eastwick, Robert: Strike a Pose
Eastwood, Alison: Black & White (1998); Friends and Lovers; Midnight in the Garden of Good and Evil; Tightrope
Eastwood, Clint: Absolute Power; Any Which Way You Can; Beguiled, The; Bridges of Madison County, The; Bronco Billy; City Heat; Coogan's Bluff; Dead Pool, The; Dirty Harry; Eiger Sanction, The; Enforcer, The; Escape from Alcatraz; Every Which Way But Loose; Firefox; Fistful of Dollars, A; For a Few Dollars More; Francis in the Navy; Gauntlet, The; Good the Bad and the Ugly, The; Hang 'em High; Heartbreak Ridge; High Plains Drifter; Honkytonk Man; In the Line of Fire; Joe Kidd; Kelly's Heroes; Magnum Force; Maverick (TV Series); Outlaw Josey Wales, The; Paint Your Wagon; Pale Rider; Perfect World, A; Pink Cadillac; Play Misty for Me; Rawhide (TV Series); Revenge of the Creature; Rookie, The (1990); Space Cowboys; Sudden Impact; Tarantula; Thunderbolt and Lightfoot; Tightrope; True Crime; Two Mules for Sister Sara; Unforgiven (1992); Where Eagles Dare; White Hunter Black Heart
Eastwood, Jayne: Hostile Take Over
Eastwood, Kyle: Honkytonk Man
Eaton, Mary: Glorifying the American Girl
Eaton, Shirley: Against All Odds (1968) (Kiss and Kill, Blood of Fu Manchu); Around the World Under the Sea; Doctor at Large; Girl Hunters, The; Naked Truth (Your Past Is Showing); Ten Little Indians; Three Men in a Boat
Eberhardt, Norma: Return of Dracula
Eberly, Bob: I Dood It
Ebersole, Christine: Acceptable Risks; Folks; Mac and Me; Pie in the Sky; Richie Rich; Unexpected Family, An; Unexpected Life, An
Ebon, Al: White Pongo (Blond Gorilla)
Ebouaney, Eriq: Lumumba
Ebrahim, Omar: Vampyr, The (1992)
Ebsen, Buddy: Andersonville Trial, The; Attack!; Between Heaven and Hell; Beverly Hillbillies, The (TV Series); Beverly Hillbillies Go Hollywood, The; Beverly Hillbillies, The (1993); Born to Dance; Breakfast at Tiffany's; Broadway Melody of 1938; Broadway Melody of 1936; Captain January; Davy Crockett and the River Pirates; Davy Crockett, King of the Wild Frontier; Girl of the Golden West, The; Interns, The; My Lucky Star; One and Only, Genuine, Original Family Band, The; President's Plane Is Missing, The; Red Garters; Rodeo King and the Senorita; Stone Fox, The; Tom Sawyer; Under Mexicali Stars
Eburne, Maude: Among the Living; Guardsman, The; Vampire Bat, The
Eccles, Aimee: Humanoid Defender
Eccles, Teddy: My Side of the Mountain
Eccleston, Chris: Elizabeth; Heart (1999); Jude; Let Him Have It; Others, The; Price Above Rubies, A; Shallow Grave
Echanove, Juan: Flower of My Secret, The
Echevarria, Emilio: Amores Perros
Eckart, Aaron: In the Company of Men
Eckhardt, Fritz: Almost Angels; Waltz King, The
Eckhart, Aaron: Erin Brockovich; Molly; Nurse Betty; Pledge, The; Your Friends & Neighbors
Eckhouse, James: Junior
Eckstine, Billy: Jo Jo Dancer, Your Life Is Calling
Eckstrom, Lauren: Two Bits & Pepper
Ecoffey, Jean-Philippe: Ma Vie En Rose
Ed Kemmer: Giant from the Unknown
Eddington, Paul: Murder at the Vicarage; Yes, Prime Minister
Eddy, Helen Jerome: Helldorado; Klondike Annie; Rebecca of Sunnybrook Farm
Eddy, Nelson: Balalaika; Bitter Sweet (1940); Chocolate Soldier, The; Girl of the Golden West, The; I Married an Angel; Knickerbocker Holiday; Let Freedom Ring; Maytime; Naughty Marietta; New Moon; Northwest Outpost; Phantom of the Opera; Rosalie; Rose Marie; Sweethearts
Edel, Alfred: My Father Is Coming
Edelman, Herb: Barefoot in the Park; Cracking Up; Front Page, The; Marathon; Odd Couple, The; Yakuza, The
Eden, Barbara: Amazing Dobermans; Chattanooga Choo Choo; Five Weeks in a Balloon; Flaming Star; From the Terrace; Harper Valley P.T.A.; How to Break Up a Happy Divorce; Lethal Charm; Quick, Let's Get Married; Ride the Wild Surf; 7 Faces of Dr. Lao; Stranger Within, The; Voyage to the Bottom of the Sea; Wonderful World of the Brothers Grimm, The
Eden, Elana: Story of Ruth, The
Edgerton, Earle: Carnival of Blood
Edmond, J. Trevor: Return of the Living Dead 3
Edmond, Valerie: Saving Grace
Edmonds, Dartanyan: Rangers
Edmonds, Elizabeth: Experience Preferred ... But Not Essential; Scrubbers
Edmonds, Samantha: Young Poisoner's Handbook, The
Edmondson, Adrian: Supergrass, The; Young Ones, The
Edney, Beatie: Diary of a Mad Old Man
Edson, Richard: Crossing the Bridge; Do the Right Thing; Intimate Betrayal; Joey Breaker; Love, Cheat & Steal; Platoon; Stranger Than Paradise; Super MarioBrothers, The; Wedding Bell Blues
Edwall, Allan: Brothers Lionheart, The; Emigrants, The; Sacrifice, The
Edwards, Anthony: Charlie's Ghost; Client, The; Delta Heat; Downtown; El Diablo; ER: The Series Premiere; Gotcha!; Hawks; Hometown Boy Makes Good; How I Got into College; Landslide; Miracle Mile; Mr. North; Pet Sematary Two; Revenge of the Nerds; Revenge of the Nerds II: Nerds in Paradise; Summer Heat; Sure Thing, The; Top Gun
Edwards, Blake: Strangler of the Swamp
Edwards, Cassandra: Vasectomy
Edwards, Cliff: Badmen of the Hills; Dance, Fools, Dance; Doughboys; Laughing Sinners; Parlor, Bedroom and Bath; Pirates of the Prairie; Sidewalks of New York
Edwards, Danny: Heaven
Edwards, Darryl: Brother from Another Planet, The
Edwards, Edward: Tempest, The (1983)
Edwards, Guy: Winslow Boy, The
Edwards, Hilton: Half a Sixpence
Edwards, Hugh: Lord of the Flies
Edwards, James: Home of the Brave; Joe Louis Story, The; Pork Chop Hill; Set-Up, The; Steel Helmet, The
Edwards, James L.: Bloodletting; Ozone; Polymorph; Zombie Cop
Edwards, Jennifer: All's Fair; Fine Mess, A; Overexposed; Perfect Match, The; Son of the Pink Panther; Straight Story, The; Sunset; That's Life
Edwards, Jimmy: Three Men in a Boat
Edwards, Lance: Peacemaker (1990); Woman, Her Men and Her Futon, A
Edwards, Luke: Cheaters; Little Big League; Little Riders, The; Newsies; Wizard, The
Edwards, Mark: Boldest Job in the West, The

Edwards, Megan: Poison Ivy: The New Seduction
Edwards, Meredith: Christmas Reunion, A; Run for Your Money, A
Edwards, Paul: Combat Killers
Edwards, Penny: In Old Amarillo; Pony Soldier; Trail of Robin Hood
Edwards, Rick: Hearts and Armour
Edwards, Sam: Gang Busters
Edwards, Sebastian Rice: Hope and Glory
Edwards, Snitz: Seven Chances
Edwards, Stacy: Dinner at Eight; Driven; Houdini; In the Company of Men
Edwards, Vince: Cellar Dweller; Deal of the Century; Desperados, The; Devil's Brigade, The; Dillinger; Dirty Dozen, The: The Deadly Mission; Fear, The (1994); Firehouse; Gumshoe Kid, The; Killing, The; Mad Bomber, The; Original Intent; Sno-Line; Space Raiders; Three Faces of Eve, The
Efron, Marshall: Blade
Egan, Aeryk: Shrunken Heads
Egan, Eddie: Badge 373; French Connection, The
Egan, Michael: Rappaccini's Daughter; Thugs
Egan, Peter: Lillie; Reilly: The Ace of Spies; 2001: A Space Travesty
Egan, Richard: Amsterdam Kill, The; Demetrius and the Gladiators; Love Me Tender; Mission to Glory; One Minute to Zero; Seven Cities of Gold; Split Second; Summer Place, A; Underwater!
Ege, Julie: Creatures the World Forgot; Seven Brothers Meet Dracula, The
Eggar, Samantha: All the Kind Strangers; Battle Force; Brood, The; Collector, The; Curtains; Dark Horse; Demonoid; Doctor Dolittle; Doctor in Distress; Exterminator, The; Ghost in Monte Carlo, A; Light at the End of the World, The; Molly Maguires, The; Phantom, The; Round Numbers; Tales of the Unexpected; Uncanny, The; Walk, Don't Run; Why Shoot the Teacher?
Eggert, Nicole: Amanda and the Alien; Blown Away; Demolitionist, The; Double-O Kid, The; Haunting of Morella, The; Just One of the Girls; Submerged
Eggerth, Marta: Presenting Lily Mars
Eggleton, Matthew: Loaded
Egi, Stan: Rising Sun
Egorova, Natalie: Luna Park
Eguren, Raul: Guantanamera!
Ehle, Jennifer: BackBeat; Bedrooms and Hallways; Paradise Road; Pride and Prejudice; Wilde
Ehlers, Jerome: Sahara
Eichberger, Franz: Tiefland
Eichhorn, Lisa: Cutter's Way; Devlin; Europeans, The; Grim Prairie Tales; King of the Hill; Modern Affair, A; Moon 44; Opposing Force; Vanishing, The; Wild Rose; Yanks
Eiding, Paul: Personals, The
Eidsvold, Gard B.: Zero Kelvin
Eigeman, Christopher: Barcelona; Kicking and Screaming; Last Days of Disco, The; Metropolitan; Mr. Jealousy
Eikenberry, Jill: Assault & Matrimony; Between the Lines; Cast the First Stone; Chantilly Lace; Hide in Plain Sight; Inconvenient Woman, An; L.A. Law; Manhattan Project, The; Night Full of Rain, A; Orphan Train; Parallel Lives; Sessions
Eilbacher, Lisa: Amazing Spiderman, The; Beverly Hills Cop; Blindman's Bluff; Deadly Intent; Hunt for the Night Stalker; Leviathan; Live Wire; Ten to Midnight
Eilber, Janet: Hard to Hold; Romantic Comedy; Whose Life Is It, Anyway?
Eilers, Sally: Black Camel, The; Long Long Trail; Parlor, Bedroom and Bath; Strange Illusion
Eisenberg, Aron: Playroom
Eisenberg, Avner: Jewel of the Nile, The
Eisenberg, Hallie Kate: Beautiful; Bicentennial Man
Eisenberg, Ned: Hiding Out; Path to Paradise
Eisenmann, Ike: Escape to Witch Mountain; Return from Witch Mountain; Terror Out of the Sky
Eisenstadt, Debra: Oleanna
Eisermann, Andre: Brother of Sleep
Eisley, Anthony: Journey to the Center of Time (Time Warp); Mummy and the Curse of the Jackals, The; Naked Kiss, The; Navy vs. the Night Monsters, The; Wasp Woman (1960)
Eisner, David: To Catch a Killer
Ejdus, Predrag: Vukovar
Ejogo, Carmen: Boycott; Metro; What's the Worst That Could Happen?
Ek, Anders: Sawdust and Tinsel
Ekberg, Anita: Abbott and Costello Go to Mars; Alphabet Murders, The; Artists and Models; Back from Eternity; Boccaccio 70; Call Me Bwana; Cobra, The (1967); Four for Texas; Hollywood or Bust; La Dolce Vita; Northeast of Seoul; Paris Holiday; Red Dwarf, The; Screaming Mimi; S.H.E.; Woman Times Seven
Ekhtiar-Dini, Ameneh: Time for Drunken Horses, A
Ekland, Britt: After the Fox; Baxter; Beverly Hills Vamp; Bobo, The; Endless Night; Get Carter; Great Wallendas, The; High Velocity; King Solomon's Treasure; Man with the Golden Gun, The; Monster Club, The; Night They Raided Minsky's, The; Slavers; Stiletto; Wicker Man, The
Eklund, Bengt: Port of Call
Ekman, Gosta: Adventures of Picasso, The; Faust; Inside Man, The; Intermezzo
El Sawy, Khaled: Legend of the Lost Tomb
Elam, Jack: Apple Dumpling Gang Rides Again, The; Appointment in Honduras; Aurora Encounter; Big Bad John; Cattle Queen of Montana; Creature from Black Lake; Dynamite and Gold; Firecreek; Grayeagle; Hannie Caulder; Hawmps!; Hot Lead and Cold Feet; Huckleberry Finn; Jubilee Trail; Kansas City Confidential; Man from Laramie, The; Man without a Star; Night of the Grizzly, The; Once Upon a Time in the West; Pat Garrett and Billy the Kid; Pocketful of Miracles; Pony Express Rider; Rancho Notorious; Rare Breed, The (1966); Rawhide; Rio Lobo; Sacketts, The; Sacred Ground; Suburban Commando; Sundowners, The; Support Your Local Gunfighter; Support Your Local Sheriff!; Uninvited, The
Elarton, Robert: Speak of the Devil
Elcar, Dana: Blue Skies Again; Fool Killer, The; Great Northfield Minnesota Raid, The; Inside Out; Jungle Warriors; Learning Tree, The; Nude Bomb, The (Return of Maxwell Smart,The); Quarterback Princess; St. Ives; Shaming, The; Sting, The
Eldard, Ron: Bastard Out of Carolina; Drop Dead Fred; Last Supper, The; Mystery, Alaska; Sex and the Other Man; Sleepers; True Love; When Trumpets Fade
Eldbert, Jim: Warbirds
Eldor, Gabi: Boy Takes Girl
Eldredge, John: Dangerous (1935); Flirtation Walk; Song of Nevada
Eldridge, Florence: Divorcee, The; Les Misérables
Electra, Carmen: Mating Habits of the Earthbound Human,The; Scary Movie
Eleniak, Erika: Beverly Hillbillies, The (1993); Chasers; Final Voyage; Girl in the Cadillac; Pandora Project, The; Pyromaniac's Love Story, A; Stealth Fighter; Tales from the Crypt Presents Bordello of Blood; Under Siege
Eles, Sandor: And Soon the Darkness
Elfman, Jenna: Can't Hardly Wait; EDtv; Keeping the Faith; Krippendorf's Tribe; Town & Country
Elfman, Marie-Pascale: Forbidden Zone
Elg, Taina: Diane; Great Wallendas, The; Les Girls; Prodigal, The; Thirty-Nine Steps, The
Elhers, Jerome: Fatal Bond
Elian, Yona: Last Winter, The
Elias, Alix: Citizen's Band; Munchies
Elias, Elaine: Calle 54
Eliasdottir, Soley: Remote Control
Elise, Christine: Body Snatchers, The (1993); Boiling Point; Child's Play 2; Escape from Mars
Elise, Kimberly: Beloved; Bojangles; John Q; Set It Off
Elizabeth, Monet: Island Fury
Elizabeth, Shannon: American Pie 2; Dish Dogs; Scary Movie; Seamless; Thir13en Ghosts; Tomcats
Elizondo, Hector: American Gigolo; Backstreet Justice; Being Human; Beverly Hills Cop 3; Born to Win; Chains of Gold; Cuba; Dain Curse, The; Dear God; Entropy; Exit to Eden; Final Ap-

proach; Flamingo Kid, The; Forgotten Prisoners; Frankie and Johnny; Getting Even with Dad; Honeyboy; Leviathan; Necessary Roughness; Nothing in Common; Out of the Darkness; Perfect Alibi; Power, Passion, and Murder; Princess Diaries, The; Private Resort; Report to the Commissioner; Runaway Bride; Safe House; Samantha; There Goes the Neighborhood; Tortilla Soup; Turbulence; Valdez Is Coming; Young Doctors in Love
Elkaïm, Jérémie: Come Undone
Elkins, Kerine: Sore Losers
Elle, Daniella: Facade
Ellerbe, Harry: Magnetic Monster, The
Ellers, Sally: Doughboys
Elliman, Yvonne: Jesus Christ, Superstar
Ellington, Duke: Belle of the Nineties; Murder at the Vanities
Ellington, Harry: Saint of Fort Washington, The
Elliot, Allison: Wings of the Dove, The
Elliot, Jane: Change of Habit
Elliot, John: Heart of Arizona
Elliot, Laura: Two Lost Worlds
Elliot, Shawn: Crossover Dreams
Elliot, Tim: Utu
Elliot, William: San Antonio Kid
Elliott, Alison: Buccaneers, The; Eternal, The; Monkey Trouble; Spitfire Grill, The; Underneath, The
Elliott, Chris: Cabin Boy; CB4; Groundhog Day; Kingpin; Osmosis Jones; Scary Movie 2; Snow Day; There's Something About Mary
Elliott, David James: Holiday Affair
Elliott, Denholm: Apprenticeship of Duddy Kravitz, The; Bleak House; Bourne Identity, The; Brimstone and Treacle; Child's Christmas in Wales, A (1986); Child's Christmas in Wales, A (1987); Codename: Kyril; Cuba; Deep Cover; Defense of the Realm; Doll's House, A; Hound of the Baskervilles, The; Hound of the Baskervilles, The; House That Dripped Blood, The; Indiana Jones and the Last Crusade; Madame Sin; Maurice; Missionary, The; Noises Off; Overindulgence; Private Function, A; Raiders of the Lost Ark; Robin and Marian; Room with a View, A; Rude Awakening; Russian Roulette; Saint Jack; Scorchers; September; Stealing Heaven; Strange Case of Dr. Jekyll and Mr. Hyde, The (1968); To the Devil, a Daughter; Toy Soldiers; Trading Places; Transmutations; Vault of Horror; Whoopee Boys, The; Wicked Lady, The
Elliott, Patricia: Natural Enemies
Elliott, Peter: Missing Link
Elliott, Peter Anthony: Pre-Madonnas (Social Suicide)
Elliott, Ross: Dynamite Pass; Hot Lead; Indestructible Man
Elliott, Sam: Blue Knight, The; Blue Lighting, The; Blue River; Buffalo Girls; Conagher; Contender, The; Desperate Trail; Fatal Beauty; Final Cut, The; Frogs; Gettysburg; Gone to Texas; Hi-Lo Country, The; I Will Fight No More Forever; Legacy, The; Lifeguard; Mask (1985); Murder in Texas; Prancer; Quick and the Dead, The; Road House; Rough Riders; Rush; Sacketts, The; Shadow Riders, The; Sibling Rivalry; Tombstone; We Were Soldiers; Wild Times; Woman Undone; You Know My Name
Elliott, Shawn: Hurricane Streets
Elliott, Stephen: Arthur; Arthur 2: On the Rocks; Assassination; Golden Honeymoon, The; Prototype; Roadhouse 66
Elliott, William: Bells of Rosarita; Calling Wild Bill Elliott; Death Valley Manhunt; Fabulous Texan, The; Hellfire; Hidden Valley Outlaws; In Early Arizona; Longhorn; Mojave Firebrand; Phantom of the Plains; Sheriff of Las Vegas; Showdown, The (1950); Wagon Wheels Westward
Ellis, Aunjanue: Caveman's Valentine, The; Girls Town; Men of Honor
Ellis, Chris: Watcher, The
Ellis, Diane: High Voltage
Ellis, Edward: Fury (1936); Return of Peter Grimm, The
Ellis, Jack: Prime Suspect 2
Ellis, James: Leapin' Leprechauns; No Surrender
Ellis, Patricia: Block-Heads; Case of the Lucky Legs, The; Postal Inspector
Ellis, Paul R.: In the Name of Justice
Ellis, Robin: Curse of King Tut's Tomb, The; Elizabeth R; Europeans, The
Ellison, Gwen: Curse of King Tut's Tomb, The; Elizabeth R; Europeans, The
Ellison, James: Bar-20 Rides Again; Borderland; Call of the Prairie; Eagle's Brood; Fifth Avenue Girl; Gang's All Here, The; I Walked with a Zombie; Next Time I Marry; Three on the Trail; Trail Dust; Undying Monster, The; Vivacious Lady; You Can't Fool Your Wife; Zenobia
Elmaloglou, Rebekah: Back of Beyond
Elmendorf, Raymond: Bloody Wednesday
Elmi, Roushan Karam: Wind Will Carry Us, The
Elphick, Michael: Arthur's Hallowed Ground; Buddy's Song; Element of Crime, The; Lion and the Hawk, The; Privates on Parade
Elsom, Isobel: Desirée; Escape Me Never; Love from a Stranger; Love Is a Many-Splendored Thing; Monsieur Verdoux
Eltinge, Julian: Madame Behave
Elvin, Justin: Happiness
Elvira: Elvira, Mistress of the Dark
Elwes, Cary: Another Country; Bram Stoker's Dracula; Cat's Meow, The; Chase, The; Cradle Will Rock; Crush, The (1993); Days of Thunder; Glory; Hot Shots; Informant, The; Kiss the Girls; Lady Jane; Leather Jackets; Liar, Liar; Pentagon Wars, The; Princess Bride, The; Race Against Time; Robin Hood: Men in Tights; Rudyard Kipling's The Jungle Book (1994); Shadow of the Vampire; Twister
Ely, Ron: Doc Savage ..., The Man of Bronze; Night of the Grizzly, The; Slavers
Embarek, Ouassini: Bye-Bye
Embry, Ethan: Can't Hardly Wait; Dancer, Texas: Pop. 81; That Thing You Do!; Vegas Vacation
Emelin, Georgia: Reason to Believe, A
Emerson, Doug: River Pirates, The
Emerson, Faye: Hard Way, The; Uncertain Glory
Emerson, Hope: All Mine to Give; Casanova's Big Night; Copper Canyon; Guns of Fort Petticoat; Peter Gunn (TV Series); Westward the Women
Emerson, Karrie: Evils of the Night
Emerton, Roy: Big Fella; Dr. Syn
Emery, Jesse: Chillers
Emery, John: Lawless Street, A; Mademoiselle Fifi; Rocketship X-M; Spellbound
Emge, David: Dawn of the Dead; Hellmaster
Emhardt, Robert: Mooncussers; No Time for Sergeants (Television); 3:10 to Yuma
Emil, Michael: Adventures in Spying; Can She Bake a Cherry Pie?; Insignificance; Sitting Ducks; Someone to Love; Tracks
Emile, Taungaroa: Once Were Warriors
Emilfork, Daniel: City of Lost Children, The
Eminem: Hip-Hop Witch Movie, Da
Emmanuel, Alphonsia: Peter's Friends
Emmanuel, Takis: Caddie; Kostas
Emmerich, Noah: Frequency; Love & Sex; Truman Show, The
Emmett, Fern: Forty-Niners
Emney, Fred: Adventures of a Private Eye
Emo, Maria: Hitler
Emoto, Akira: Dr. Akagi; Shall We Dance?
Empson, Tameka: Beautiful Thing
Emrick, Jarrod: Andersonville
Endre, Lena: Faithless; Jerusalem; Sunday's Children; Visitors, The
Endresz-Banlaki, Kelly: American Rhapsody, An
Engel, Georgia: Care Bears Movie, The
Engel, Tina: Boat Is Full, The
Engel, Tobias: 38 Vienna Before the Fall
England, Audie: Delta of Venus; Free Enterprise; Miami Hustle; Venus Rising
Englebrecht, Constanze: Wild Flower (1993) (Fiorile)
Engler, Lori-Nan: Head Office
English, Alex: Amazing Grace and Chuck
English, Marla: She Creature, The; Voodoo Woman
Englund, Morgan: Carnosaur 3: Primal Species; Not Like Us
Englund, Robert: Adventures of Ford Fairlane, The; Danse Macabre; Eaten Alive; Freddy's Dead: The Final Nightmare; Hobson's Choice; Killer Tongue; Mangler, The; Nightmare on

Elm Street, A; Nightmare on Elm Street 5, A: The Dream Child; Nightmare on Elm Street 4, A: The DreamMaster; Nightmare on Elm Street 3, A: The DreamWarriors; Paper Brigade, The; Phantom of the Opera; Python; Tobe Hooper's Night Terrors; Urban Legend; V; Wes Craven's New Nightmare; Wes Craven's Wishmaster
Enman, Gao: Not One Less
Ennis, Ethel: Mad Monster Party
Enoki, Takaaki: Heaven and Earth
Enos, John: Miami Hustle; Over the Line; Raven Hawk
Enos III, John: Stealth Fighter
Enriquez, Rene: Bulletproof; Hill Street Blues (TV Series)
Ensign, Michael: Children of the Corn III: Urban Harvest
Entertainer, Cedric the: Kingdom Come; Original Kings Of Comedy, The
Entwisle, Julie: Night Flier, The
Entwistle, John: Stand by Me
Eperjes, Karoly: Good Evening Mr. Wallenberg
Epperson, Brenda: Amore! (1993)
Epps, Mike: All About the Benjamins; Bait; Next Friday
Epps, Omar: Big Trouble (2002); Breakfast of Champions; Brother; Daybreak (1993); Deadly Voyage; First Time Felon; Higher Learning; In Too Deep; Juice; Love and Basketball; Major League II; Mod Squad, The; Program, The; Scream 2; Wood, The
Epstein, Alvin: Truth or Die
Erbe, Kathryn: Dream with the Fishes; D2: The Mighty Ducks; Kiss of Death; Rich in Love; Stir of Echoes
Erdman, Richard: Blue Gardenia, The; Cry Danger; Namu, the Killer Whale; Objective, Burma!
Ergün, Halil: Steam: The Turkish Bath; Turkish Bath, The
Erickson, Krista: First Time, The; Jekyll & Hyde—Together Again; Killer Image; Mortal Passions
Erickson, Leif: Abbott and Costello Meet Captain Kidd; Abduction; Arabian Nights; Big Broadcast of 1938, The; Conquest; Fastest Gun Alive, The; Gangster, The; Invaders from Mars; Istanbul; Man and Boy; Mirage; Night Monster; Roustabout; Showdown, The (1950); Snake Pit, The; Stella; Strait-Jacket; Tea and Sympathy; Three Secrets; Trouble Along the Way
Erickson, Lisa: Power, The (1980)
Ericson, Devon: Gone to Texas
Ericson, John: Bamboo Saucer (Collision Course); Bounty Man, The; Rhapsody; Student Prince, The
Eriksen, Kaj-Erik: Captains Courageous
Erin, Tami: New Adventures of Pippi Longstocking, The
Erin-Easley, Margaret: Crier, The
Erkal, Genco: Horse, The
Ermey, R. Lee: Body Snatchers, The (1993); Chain of Command; Dead Man Walking; Dead Men Can't Dance; Demonstone; Endless Descent; Frighteners, The; Full Metal Jacket; I'm Dangerous Tonight; Kid (1990); Love Is a Gun; Mississippi Burning; Murder in the First; On Deadly Ground; Prefontaine; Seven; Siege of Firebase Gloria, The; Skipped Parts; Soul of the Game; Switchback; Take, The; Terror Within 2, The; Toy Soldiers
Ernest, Harry: New Adventures of Tarzan
Ernsberger, Duke: Ernest Rides Again
Ernst, Laura: Too Much Sun
Ernst, Max: Age of Gold
Ernst, Robert: Sure Fire
Eroen, Benjamin: Sherlock: Undercover Dog
Errico, Melissa: Life or Something Like It
Errol, Leon: Flustered Comedy of Leon Errol, The; Higher and Higher; Invisible Man's Revenge, The; Make a Wish; Mexican Spitfire; Never Give a Sucker an Even Break; Noose Hangs High, The; We're Not Dressing
Ersgard, Patrick: Mandroid; Visitors, The
Ershadi, Homayon: Taste of Cherry
Erskine, Eileen: Hills of Home
Erskine, Marilyn: Westward the Women
Ertmanis, Victor: Paris France
Erving, Julius: Fish That Saved Pittsburgh, The
Erwin, Bill: Just Your Luck; Silent Assassins; Somewhere in Time
Erwin, Stu: Backdoor to Heaven; Ceiling Zero; Chained; Going Hollywood; Hold Your Man; International House; Misadventures of Merlin Jones, The; Palooka; Viva Villa!
Escalante, Joe: That Darn Punk
Escourrou, Emmanuelle: Evil Within, The
Esmond, Carl: Smash-Up: The Story of a Woman; Story of Dr. Wassell, The
Esmond, Jill: Casanova Brown; Skin Game, The (1931)
Espinoza, Mark: Eastside
Espiritu, Johnnie Saiko: Adventures of the Kung Fu Rascals, The
Esposito, Giancarlo: Ali; Amos & Andrew; Blue in the Face; Bob Roberts; Do the Right Thing; Fresh; Harley Davidson and the Marlboro Man; Mo' Better Blues; Monkeybone; Night on Earth; Nothing to Lose; Pinero; School Daze; Sweet Lorraine; Trouble on the Corner; Twilight; Usual Suspects, The
Esposito, Gianni: Les Misérables
Esposito, Jennifer: Brooklyn State of Mind, A; Don't Say a Word; I Still Know What You Did Last Summer; Just One Time; Summer of Sam
Esposito, Nick: Devil Dog: The Hound of Hell
Esposti, Piera Degli: Joke of Destiny
Esquivel, Alan: Alsino and the Condor
Essary, Lisa: Soldier's Home
Essex, David: Silver Dream Racer; That'll Be the Day
Estefan, Gloria: Music of the Heart
Estelita: Jesse James Meets Frankenstein's Daughter
Ester, Natalie: Excalibur Kid, The
Esterbrook, Leslie: Police Academy: Mission to Moscow
Esterman, Floyd Red Crow: Buffalo Girls
Estes, Rob: Checkered Flag; Phantom of the Mall—Eric's Revenge; Trapper County War
Estes, Will: Mimic 2; Road Home, The (1995); Terror Tract
Estevez, Emilio: Another Stakeout; Breakfast Club, The; D3: The Mighty Ducks; D2: The Mighty Ducks; Freejack; Judgment Night; Late Last Night; Maximum Overdrive; Men at Work; Mighty Ducks, The; Mission: Impossible; National Lampoon's Loaded Weapon 1; Nightbreaker; Nightmares; Outsiders, The; Rated X; Repo Man; St. Elmo's Fire; Sand; Stakeout; Tex; That Was Then ... This Is Now; War at Home, The; Wisdom; Young Guns; Young Guns II
Estevez, Joe: Acts of Betrayal; Beach Babes from Beyond; Blonde Heaven; Blood on the Badge; Breakaway; Dark Rider; Dark Secrets; Double Blast; L.A. Goddess; Lola's Game; Money to Burn; Werewolf
Estevez, Ramon: Cadence
Estevez, René: Forbidden Sun; Intruder (1988); Sleepaway Camp II: Unhappy Campers; Touch and Die
Estrada, Erik: Dirty Dozen, The: The Fatal Mission; Fire!; Honeyboy; Hour of the Assassin; Longest Drive, The; New Centurions, The; Spirits
Estrinn, Patricia: Dennis the Menace: Dinosaur Hunter
Etebari, Eric: Witchblade
Etting, Ruth: Hips, Hips, Hooray; Roman Scandals
Ettinger, Cynthia: Down, Out & Dangerous
Eubanks, Corey Michael: Payback
Eure, Wesley: C.H.O.M.P.S.; Jennifer
Evan, Llyr: Twin Town
Evanofski, Candace: George Washington
Evans, Alice: 102 Dalmatians
Evans, Angelo: Angelo, My Love
Evans, Art: CB4; Die Hard 2: Die Harder; Finishing Touch, The; Jo Jo Dancer, Your Life Is Calling; Mom; Native Son; Trespass; White of the Eye
Evans, Barry: Die Screaming, Marianne
Evans, Chris: Not Another Teen Movie
Evans, Clifford: Courageous Mr. Penn; Curse of the Werewolf, The; Kiss of the Vampire; Love on the Dole; River of Unrest
Evans, Dale: Along the Navajo Trail; Apache Rose; Bells of Coronado; Bells of Rosarita; Bells of San Angelo; Don't Fence Me In; Down Dakota Way; Golden Stallion, The; Helldorado; Lights of Old Santa Fe; My Pal Trigger; Roll on Texas Moon; Roy Rogers Show, The (TV Series); San Fernando Valley; Song of Nevada; Trigger Jr.; Utah; War of the Wildcats

Faison, Frankie: Down to Earth; Exterminator 2, The; Hannibal; Roommates; Spider and the Fly, The; Thomas Crown Affair, The
Faith, Adam: Beat Girl; McVicar; Yesterday's Hero
Faith, Dolores: Mutiny in Outer Space
Faithfull, Marianne: Assault on Agathon; Hamlet; Moondance; Rock and Roll Circus, The; Shopping; Turn of the Screw (1992)
Fajardo, Eduardo: Adios, Hombre; Long Live Your Death; Sonny and Jed; Yellow Hair and the Fortress of Gold
Falana, Lola: Klansman, The; Liberation of L. B. Jones, The; Man Called Adam, A
Falcao, Luzia: Luzia
Falco, Edie: Hurricane Streets; Judy Berlin; Sopranos, The (TV series); Trouble on the Corner
Falcon, Jeffrey: Six-String Samurai
Falconetti, Maria: Passion of Joan of Arc, The
Faldaas, Morten: Heart of Darkness
Falk, Peter: All the Marbles; Anzio; Balcony, The; Big Trouble (1985); Brinks Job, The; Cheap Detective, The; Columbo: Murder by the Book; Cookie; Corky Romano; Faraway, So Close; Great Muppet Caper, The; Great Race, The; Griffin and Phoenix: A Love Story; Happy New Year (1987); In-Laws, The; In the Spirit; It's a Mad Mad Mad Mad World; Luv; Made; Mikey and Nicky; Money Kings; Murder by Death; Pocketful of Miracles; Pressure Point; Princess Bride, The; Pronto; Robin & the Seven Hoods; Roommates; Tune in Tomorrow; Vibes; Wings of Desire; Woman Under the Influence, A
Fallender, Deborah: Jabberwocky
Fan, Jing-Ma: Madame Butterfly
Fanaro, Mary: Truth or Dare? A Critical Madness
Fancher, Hampton: Rome Adventure
Fancy, Richard: Nick Knight
Fanfan, Li: Not One Less
Fanning, Dakota: I Am Sam
Fantoni, Sergio: Prize, The
Faracy, Stephanie: Great Outdoors, The
Faraldo, Daniel: Above the Law; Trenchcoat
Farber, Arlene: All the Kind Strangers
Farentino, Debrah: Capone; Dead Air; Mortal Sins (1990) (Dangerous Obsession); Storm of the Century
Farentino, James: Bulletproof; Cop for the Killing, A; Cradle Will Fall, The; Dead and Buried; Honor Thy Father & Mother: The Menendez Killings; Possessed, The (1977); Scandalous Me: The Jacqueline Susann Story; Silent Victory: The Kitty O'Neil Story; Summer to Remember, A; War Lord, The
Farès, Nadia: Crimson Rivers, The
Fargas, Antonio: Ambush Murders, The; Borrower, The; Cisco Pike; Florida Straits; Howling VI: The Freaks; Huckleberry Finn; I'm Gonna Git You Sucka!; Milo; Night of the Sharks; Pretty Baby; Putney Swope; Streetwalkin'; Whore
Faria, Betty: Bye Bye Brazil; Story of Fausta, The
Faridany, Franchesca: Conceiving Ada
Farina, Carolyn: Age of Innocence, The; Metropolitan
Farina, Dennis: Another Stakeout; Bella Mafia; Big Trouble (2002); Birthday Boy, The; Code of Silence; Eddie; Get Shorty; Hillside Stranglers, The; Little Big League; Manhunter; Men of Respect; Midnight Run; Mod Squad, The; Out of Annie's Past; Out of Sight; Reindeer Games; Romeo Is Bleeding; Sidewalks of New York (2001); Snatch; Street Crimes; Striking Distance; That Old Feeling; Triplecross; We're Talking Serious Money
Faris, Anna: Scary Movie; Scary Movie 2
Farley, Chris: Almost Heroes; Beverly Hills Ninja; Black Sheep; Coneheads; Tommy Boy; Wayne's World 2
Farley, Jim: General, The
Farley, John: Straight Story, The
Farley, Teresa: Breeders
Farmanara, Bahman: Smell of Camphor, Fragrance of Jasmine
Farmer, Donald: No Justice; Vampire Cop
Farmer, Frances: Among the Living; Come and Get It; Rhythm on the Range; Son of Fury; South of Pago Pago; Toast of New York, The
Farmer, Gary: Blown Away; Dark Wind; Dead Man; Moonshine Highway; Powwow Highway; Smoke Signals
Farmer, Mark: Mr. Corbett's Ghost
Farmer, Mimsy: Allonsonfan; Autopsy; Black Cat, The; Code Name: Wild Geese; More
Farmer, Suzan: Die, Monster, Die!; Dracula—Prince of Darkness
Farmiga, Vera: Autumn in New York; Opportunists, The
Farnham, Euclid: Vermont Is for Lovers
Farnsworth, Richard: Anne of Green Gables; Comes a Horseman; Fire Next Time, The; Getaway, The; Grey Fox, The; Highway to Hell; Independence Day; Into the Night; Lassie; Misery; Natural, The; Resurrection; Rhinestone; River Pirates, The; Ruckus; Space Rage; Straight Story, The; Sylvester; Tom Horn; Two Jakes, The
Farnum, William: Between Men; Connecticut Yankee, A; Eagle's Brood; Git Along, Little Dogies; Kid Ranger; Law of the Sea; Lone Ranger, The; Mexicali Rose; Mr. Robinson Crusoe; Painted Desert, The; Powdersmoke Range; Public Cowboy #1; Santa Fe Stampede; Silver Streak; Supernatural; Trail of Robin Hood; Undersea Kingdom; Vigilantes Are Coming!; Wildfire
Farr, Felicia: Charley Varrick; Jubal; Kiss Me, Stupid; Kotch; Onionhead; 3:10 to Yuma
Farr, Jamie: Blue Knight, The; Curse II—The Bite; Fearless Tiger; Happy Hour; Speed Zone; Who's Minding the Mint?
Farrar, Adam: Pups
Farrar, David: Beat Girl; Black Narcissus; Escape to Burma; John Paul Jones; Lilacs in the Spring (Let's Make Up); Pearl of the South Pacific; Sea Chase, The
Farrell, Charles: Aggie Appleby, Maker of Men; City Girl; Convoy; Just Around the Corner; Old Ironsides
Farrell, Colin: Hart's War
Farrell, Glenda: Bureau of Missing Persons; City Without Men; Disorderly Orderly, The; Go into Your Dance; Gold Diggers of 1935; Hollywood Hotel; I Am a Fugitive from a Chain Gang; Johnny Eager; Lady for a Day; Middle of the Night; Mystery of the Wax Museum; Rage of Paris, The; Susan Slept Here; Talk of the Town, The; Three on a Match
Farrell, Kenneth: It's a Joke, Son!
Farrell, Mike: Battered; Dark River: A Father's Revenge; Incident at Dark River; Memorial Day; Prime Suspect (1982) (Feature); Silent Motive; Sins of the Mind; Vanishing Act
Farrell, Nicolas: Beautiful People; Berlin Tunnel 21; Chariots of Fire; Legionnaire; Midwinter's Tale, A; Twelfth Night
Farrell, Sharon: Arcade; Can't Buy Me Love; Fifth Floor, The; It's Alive!; Marlowe; Premonition, The (1975); Rage; Reivers, The
Farrell, Terry: Beverly Hills Madam; Deep Core; Off the Mark; Reasons of the Heart; Red Sun Rising
Farrell, Timothy: Glen or Glenda; Jail Bait (1954)
Farrell, Tommy: Pirates of the High Seas
Farrelly, Moya: This Is My Father
Farrington, Debbie: Black Panther, The
Farrington, Hugh: Arizona Heat
Farrow, Mia: Alice; Another Woman; Avalanche; Broadway Danny Rose; Crimes and Misdemeanors; Dandy in Aspic, A; Death on the Nile; Great Gatsby, The; Hannah and Her Sisters; Haunting of Julia, The; High Heels; Hurricane (1979); Husbands and Wives; Miami Rhapsody; Midsummer Night's Sex Comedy, A; Miracle at Midnight; New York Stories; Purple Rose of Cairo, The; Radio Days; Reckless; Rosemary's Baby; Secret Ceremony; See No Evil; September; Shadows and Fog; Supergirl; Widow's Peak; Zelig
Farrow, Tisa: And Hope to Die; Fingers; Search and Destroy; Some Call It Loving; Strange Shadows in an Empty Room; Zombie
Farugia, Lena: Gods Must Be Crazy II, The
Fassbinder, Rainer Werner: Ali: Fear Eats the Soul; American Soldier, The; Fox and His Friends; Germany In Autumn; Kamikaze 89; Querelle
Fastinetti, Nikki: Alien P.I.
Fat Boys, The: Disorderlies; Knights of the City; Krush Groove
Fat Joe: Urban Menace
Fataar, Ricky: Rutles, The (All You Need Is Cash)
Fatone, Joey: On the Line (2001)
Faulkner, Ben: Silent Fall

Faulkner, Graham: Brother Sun, Sister Moon
Faulkner, James: Albino; Maid, The
Faulkner, Sally: Alien Prey
Faulkner, Stephanie: Bus Is Coming, The
Fauna, Flora: Shatter Dead
Faunt, Jason: Totem
Faustina: Original Sins
Faustino, David: Killer Bud; Perfect Harmony
Faustino, Michael: Blank Check; Judgment
Faversham, William: Arizona Days
Favreau, Jon: Just Your Luck; Love & Sex; Made; Persons Unknown; Replacements, The; Rocky Marciano; Swingers; Very Bad Things
Fawcett, Allen: Blindside
Fawcett, Farrah: Apostle, The; Baby (2000); Between Two Women; Burning Bed, The; Cannonball Run; Children of the Dust; Double Exposure; Dr. T and the Women; Extremities; Man of the House; Murder in Texas; Murder on Flight 502; Myra Breckenridge; Poor Little Rich Girl: The Barbara Hutton Story; Red Light Sting, The; Saturn 3; See You in the Morning; Small Sacrifices; Substitute Wife, The; Sunburn
Fawcett, George: Son of the Sheik; Tempest; True Heart Susie; Wedding March, The
Fawkes, Michael: Child's Christmas in Wales, A (1986)
Fay, Ann: Somewhere in Sonora
Fay, Frank: Love Nest
Fay, Hugh: Little Annie Rooney
Faye, Alice: Alexander's Ragtime Band; Four Jills in a Jeep; Gang's All Here, The; Hello, Frisco, Hello; Hollywood Cavalcade; In Old Chicago; Magic of Lassie, The; On the Avenue; Poor Little Rich Girl (1936); Rose of Washington Square; State Fair; Stowaway; 365 Nights in Hollywood; Tin Pan Alley; Weekend in Havana
Faye, Frances: Pretty Baby
Faye, Herbie: Sgt. Bilko (TV Series)
Faylen, Frank: Copper Canyon; Flustered Comedy of Leon Errol, The; Gunfight at the O.K. Corral; Kid Galahad; Lost Weekend, The; McConnell Story, The; Monkey's Uncle, The; Perils of Pauline, The; Red Garters; Riot in Cell Block Eleven; Road to Rio
Fazenda, Louise: Keystone Comedies: Vol. 1–5; Noah's Ark
Fazio, Ron: Toxic Avenger Part II, The; Toxic Avenger Part III, The: The Last Temptation of Toxie
Feast, Michael: Caribbean Mystery, A
Featherstone, Angela: Dark Angel: The Ascent; Family of Cops; Guilty, The; Wedding Singer, The; Zero Effect
Feder, Frederique: Red
Federico, Luciano: Malena
Fedevich, John: Almost Famous
Feeney, Caroleen: Cadillac Ranch; Denise Calls Up
Fehmiu, Bekim: Deserter, The; Permission to Kill
Fehr, Brendan: Forsaken, The
Fehr, Oded: Deuce Bigalow: Male Gigolo; Mummy Returns, The
Feig, Peter: Zoo Radio
Feinstein, Alan: Two Worlds of Jennie Logan, The
Feizi, Salime: Color of Paradise, The
Fejto, Raphael: Au Revoir, Les Enfants
Feld, Fritz: Affairs of Annabel, The; Everything Happens at Night; Four Jacks and a Jill; Iceland; It's a Date; I've Always Loved You; Mexican Hayride; Noose Hangs High, The; Promises, Promises; World's Greatest Lover, The
Felder, Clarence: Hidden, The; Killing Floor, The
Feldman, Andrea: Heat
Feldman, Corey: Blown Away; Born Bad; 'Burbs, The; Dangerous Place, A; Dream a Little Dream; Dream a Little Dream 2; Edge of Honor; Evil Obsession; Friday the 13th—The Final Chapter; Goonies, The; License to Drive; Lipstick Camera; Lost Boys, The; Meatballs 4; National Lampoon's Last Resort; Red Line; Rock 'n' Roll High School Forever; Round Trip to Heaven; South Beach Academy; Stand by Me; Stepmonster; Tales from the Crypt Presents Bordello of Blood; Voodoo; Willa
Feldman, Marty: Adventure of Sherlock Holmes' Smarter Brother, The; Last Remake of Beau Geste, The; Sex with a Smile; Silent Movie; Slapstick of Another Kind; To See Such Fun; Yellowbeard; Young Frankenstein
Feldon, Barbara: Fitzwilly; Get Smart Again; No Deposit, No Return; Playmates; Smile; Sooner or Later
Feldshuh, Tovah: Amazing Howard Hughes, The; Blue Iguana; Brewster's Millions; Cheaper to Keep Her; Day in October, A; Happy Accidents; Holocaust; Idolmaker, The; Terror Out of the Sky; Walk on the Moon, A
Feliciano, Jose: Fargo
Feliciano, Nancy: Jacker 2: Descent to Hell
Fell, Norman: Boatniks, The; Boneyard, The; Bullitt; C.H.U.D. II (Bud the C.H.U.D.); Cleopatra Jones and the Casino of Gold; Fitzwilly; For the Boys; For the Love of It; Hexed; If It's Tuesday, This Must Be Belgium; On the Right Track; Paternity; Stone Killer, The
Feller, Bob: Life and Times of Hank Greenberg, The
Fellini, Federico: Alex in Wonderland; Ciao Federico!; Fellini's Roma
Fellowes, Rockcliffe: Regeneration
Felmy, Hansjor: Brainwashed
Felt, Asbestos: Killing Spree
Felton, Tom: Anna and the King; Borrowers, The; Harry Potter and the Sorcerer's Stone
Felton, Verna: Oklahoman, The
Fenech, Edwige: Phantom of Death; Sex with a Smile
Feng, Ku: Mighty Peking Man
Fengyi, Zhang: Emperor and the Assassin, The; Farewell My Concubine; Temptation of a Monk
Fenn, Sherilyn: Assassination File, The; Backstreet Dreams; Boxing Helena; Crime Zone; Desire and Hell at Sunset Motel; Diary of a Hitman; Dillinger; Don's Analyst, The; Fatal Instinct; Just Write; Lovelife; Meridian (Kiss of the Beast); Of Mice and Men; Outside Ozona; Ruby; Slave of Dreams; Three of Hearts; Two Moon Junction
Fennell, Tod: Stalked
Fenneman, George: You Bet Your Life (TV Series)
Fenton, Frank: Clay Pigeon, The
Fenton, Leslie: Strange Love of Molly Louvain, The; What Price Glory? (1926)
Fenton, Sarah Jane: Good Man in Africa, A
Fenton, Simon: Matinee
Feore, Colm: Beautiful Dreamers; Blades of Courage; Caveman's Valentine, The; Dr. Bethune; Escape, The; Hostile Waters; Lesser Evil, The; Night Falls on Manhattan; Pearl Harbor; Red Violin, The; Spider and the Fly, The; Storm of the Century; Striking Poses; Thirty-Two Short Films About Glenn Gould; Titus; Truman; Virginian, The
Feraco, Scott: Nasty Hero
Ferch, Heino: Winter Sleepers
Ferency, Adam: Interrogation
Ferguson, Al: Roamin' Wild; Tarzan the Mighty; Tarzan the Tiger
Ferguson, Andrew: Miracle Down Under
Ferguson, Chloe: Quiet Room, The
Ferguson, Colin: Prayer in the Dark, A
Ferguson, Craig: Big Tease, The; Life Without Dick; Saving Grace
Ferguson, Frank: Caught; They Won't Believe Me
Ferguson, Helen: Miss Lulu Bett
Ferguson, Matthew: Lilies
Ferguson, Phoebe: Quiet Room, The
Ferguson, Scott: Messenger, The; Small Time
Ferguson, Tom: Biohazard: The Alien Force
Fergusson, Karen: Angel at My Table, An
Fernán Gómez, Fernando: Belle Epoque; Butterfly; Half of Heaven; Spirit of the Beehive, The; Stilts, The (Los Zancos)
Fernandel: Angele; Fernandel the Dressmaker; Forbidden Fruit; Harvest (1937); Le Schpountz; Little World of Don Camillo, The; Nais; Pantaloons; Paris Holiday; Sheep Has Five Legs; Topaze; Well-Digger's Daughter, The
Fernandes, Miguel: Kurt Vonnegut's Monkey House; Lifeforce Experiment, The
Fernandez, Abel: Untouchables, The: Scarface Mob
Fernandez, Ana: Solas

Foley, David: Blast from the Past; High Stakes; It's Pat: The Movie; Kids in the Hall: Brain Candy; On the Line (2001); Sink or Swim
Foley, Jake: Octavia
Foley, Jennifer Crystal: 61*
Foley, Jeremy: Dante's Peak; Soccer Dog: The Movie
Foley, Scott: Forever Love
Folk, Abel: All Tied Up
Folland, Alison: All over Me; Boys Don't Cry
Follows, Megan: Anne of Avonlea; Anne of Green Gables; Back to Hannibal: The Return of Tom Sawyer and Huckleberry Finn; Cry in the Wind; Silver Bullet; Stacking; Termini Station
Folsom, Megan: Heartland
Fonda, Bridget: Aria; Balto; Bodies, Rest & Motion; Break Up; Camilla (1994); City Hall; Doc Hollywood; Finding Graceland; Frankenstein Unbound; Grace of My Heart; In the Gloaming; Iron Maze; It Could Happen to You; Jackie Brown; Jacob I Have Loved; Kiss of the Dragon; Lake Placid; Leather Jackets; Little Buddha; Monkeybone; Mr. Jealousy; Out of the Rain; Point of No Return; Road to Wellville, The; Rough Magic; Scandal; Shag, the Movie; Simple Plan, A; Single White Female; Singles; South of Heaven, West of Hell; Strapless; Touch; You Can't Hurry Love
Fonda, Henry: Advise and Consent; Ash Wednesday; Battle Force; Battle of the Bulge; Best Man, The; Big Hand for the Little Lady, A; Big Street, The; Boston Strangler, The; Cheyenne Social Club, The; Clarence Darrow; Drums Along the Mohawk; Fail-Safe; Firecreek; Fort Apache; Fugitive, The; Gideon's Trumpet; Grapes of Wrath, The; Great Smokey Roadblock, The; How the West Was Won; I Dream Too Much; Immortal Sergeant, The; In Harm's Way; Jesse James; Jezebel; Lady Eve, The; Longest Day, The; Mad Miss Manton, The; Madigan; Meteor; Midway; Mister Roberts; My Darling Clementine; My Name Is Nobody; Night Flight from Moscow; Oldest Living Graduate, The; On Golden Pond; Once Upon a Time in the West; Ox-Bow Incident, The; Return of Frank James, The; Rollercoaster; Roots: The Next Generation; Rounders, The; Sex and the Single Girl; Sometimes a Great Notion; Spencer's Mountain; Stage Struck; Swarm, The; Tales of Manhattan; Tentacles; That Certain Woman; There Was a Crooked Man; Tin Star, The; Too Late the Hero; Trail of the Lonesome Pine, The; 12 Angry Men; War and Peace; Warlock; Wrong Man, The; You Only Live Once; Young Mr. Lincoln; Yours, Mine and Ours
Fonda, Jane: Agnes of God; Any Wednesday; Barbarella; Barefoot in the Park; California Suite; Cat Ballou; Chase, The; China Syndrome, The; Circle of Love; Comes a Horseman; Coming Home; Dollmaker, The; Doll's House, A; Electric Horseman, The; Fun with Dick and Jane; Game Is Over, The; Joy House; Julia; Klute; Morning After, The; Nine to Five; Old Gringo, The; On Golden Pond; Period of Adjustment; Rollover; Stanley and Iris; Steelyard Blues; Tall Story; They Shoot Horses, Don't They?; Walk on the Wild Side
Fonda, Peter: Certain Fury; Deadfall; Dirty Mary, Crazy Larry; Don't Look Back; Easy Rider; Fatal Mission; Fighting Mad; Futureworld; High-Ballin'; Hired Hand, The; Hostage Tower, The; John Carpenter's Escape from L.A.; Jungle Heat; Killer Force; Last Movie, The (Chinchero); Lilith; Limey, The; Mercenary Fighters; Molly & Gina; Montana; Nadja; 92 in the Shade; Outlaw Blues; Passion of Ayn Rand, The; Race with the Devil; Rose Garden, The; Second Skin; South Beach; South of Heaven, West of Hell; Spasms; Split Image; Tammy and the Doctor; Thomas and the Magic Railroad; Trip, The; Ulee's Gold; Wanda Nevada; Wild Angels, The
Fondacaro, Phil: Blood Dolls; Creeps, The; Dollman vs. Demonic Toys
Fong, Benson: Charlie Chan in the Secret Service; Chinese Cat, The; Chinese Web, The; First Yank into Tokyo; Flower Drum Song; Girls! Girls! Girls!; Jinxed; Kung Fu—The Movie (1986); Scarlet Clue, The; Shanghai Cobra, The
Fong, Leo: Blind Rage; Low Blow
Fontaine, Frank: Stella
Fontaine, Jean: Sinister Urge, The
Fontaine, Joan: Beyond a Reasonable Doubt (1956); Bigamist, The; Born to Be Bad; Casanova's Big Night; Damsel in Distress, A; Decameron Nights; Emperor Waltz, The; Gunga Din; Ivanhoe; Jane Eyre; Letter from an Unknown Woman; Maid's Night Out, The; Quality Street; Rebecca; September Affair; Serenade; Suspicion; Until They Sail; Users, The; Voyage to the Bottom of the Sea; Witches, The; Women, The
Fontanel, Genevieve: Grain of Sand, The
Fontanne, Lynn: Guardsman, The
Fontes, Guilherme: Subway to the Stars
Foody, Ralph: Code of Silence
Foote, Hallie: Courtship; Habitation of Dragons, The; On Valentine's Day; 1918
Foran, Dick: Atomic Submarine, The; Black Legion; Boy Meets Girl; Brighty of the Grand Canyon; Dangerous (1935); Earthworm Tractors; Empty Holsters; Fighting 69th, The; Guest Wife; Horror Island; House of the Seven Gables, The; Mummy's Hand, The; My Little Chickadee; Petrified Forest, The; Private Buckaroo; Ride 'em Cowboy; Riders of Death Valley; Sisters, The (1938); Studs Lonigan; Winners of the West
Forbes, Brenda: Man Upstairs, The
Forbes, Bryan: Colditz Story, The; League of Gentlemen, The; Satellite in the Sky
Forbes, Francine: Splatter University
Forbes, Gary: Wiz Kid, The
Forbes, Mary: You Can't Cheat an Honest Man
Forbes, Michelle: Black Day Blue Night; John Carpenter's Escape from L.A.; Kalifornia; Swimming with Sharks
Forbes, Ralph: Lilies of the Field; Phantom Broadcast, The; Riptide; Three Musketeers, The
Forbes, Scott: Operation Pacific
Force, Full: House Party
Force, John: Visitors, The
Ford, Anitra: Big Bird Cage, The; Invasion of the Bee Girls
Ford, Bette: Landlady, The
Ford, Carol Ann: Dr. Who (TV series)
Ford, Constance: Last Hunt, The; Rome Adventure; Summer Place, A
Ford, Faith: Murder So Sweet; Weekend in the Country, A; You Talkin' to Me
Ford, Francis: Bad Lands (1939); Man from Monterey, The
Ford, Glenn: Affair in Trinidad; Americano, The; Appointment in Honduras; Big Heat, The; Blackboard Jungle, The; Border Shootout; Cimarron; Courtship of Eddie's Father, The; Day of the Assassin; Dear Heart; Don't Go Near the Water; Experiment in Terror; Fastest Gun Alive, The; Final Verdict; Four Horsemen of the Apocalypse; Gazebo, The; Gilda; Happy Birthday to Me; Human Desire; Interrupted Melody; Is Paris Burning?; It Started With a Kiss; Jubal; Lady in Question; Loves of Carmen, The; Lust for Gold; Man from Colorado, The; Man from the Alamo, The; Pocketful of Miracles; Raw Nerve; Return of October, The; Rounders, The; Sacketts, The; Santee; Smith!; So Ends Our Night; Stolen Life, A; Superman; Teahouse of the August Moon, The; Texas; 3:10 to Yuma; Torpedo Run; Violent Men, The; Virus; Visitor, The; White Tower, The
Ford, Harrison: Air Force One; American Graffiti; Apocalypse Now; Blade Runner; Clear and Present Danger; Conversation, The; Devil's Own, The; Empire Strikes Back, The; Force Ten from Navarone; Frantic; Frisco Kid, The; Fugitive, The; Hanover Street; Heroes; Indiana Jones and the Last Crusade; Indiana Jones and the Temple of Doom; More American Graffiti; Mosquito Coast, The; Patriot Games; Possessed, The (1977); Presumed Innocent; Raiders of the Lost Ark; Random Hearts; Regarding Henry; Return of the Jedi; Sabrina; Shadows; Six Days, Seven Nights; Star Wars; What Lies Beneath; Witness; Working Girl
Ford, Julia: Fatal Inversion, A
Ford, Maria: Alien Terminator; Angel of Destruction; Black Rose of Harlem; Bram Stoker's Burial of the Rats; Dance of the Damned; Dark Planet; Deathstalker IV: Match of the Titans; Final Judgment; Future Fear; Naked Obsession; Night Hunter; Showgirl Murders; Wasp Woman, The (1995)
Ford, Mick: Scum
Ford, Paul: Advise and Consent; Big Hand for the Little Lady, A; Comedians, The; Matchmaker, The; Music Man, The; Naked City, The; Russians Are Coming, the Russians Are Coming, The;

Fowley, Douglas: Along the Navajo Trail; Denver Kid; Desperate; Good Guys and the Bad Guys, The; Gun Smugglers; High and the Mighty, The; Homebodies; Hucksters, The; Kansas Pacific; Naked Jungle, The; One Body Too Many; Poor White Trash; Red River Shore; Rider from Tucson; Scared to Death; Secrets of the Wasteland; Wyatt Earp: Return to Tombstone
Fox, Bernard: Private Eyes, The; Strange Bedfellows; Titanic
Fox, C.: Track 16
Fox, David: Ordinary Magic
Fox, Earle: Scarlet Dawn
Fox, Edward: Anastasia: The Mystery of Anna; Battle of Britain; Big Sleep, The; Bounty, The; Cat and the Canary, The; Crucifer of Blood; Day of the Jackal, The; Dresser, The; Duellists, The; Edward and Mrs. Simpson; Force Ten from Navarone; Gandhi; Go-Between, The; Lost in Space (1998); Mirror Crack'd, The; Month by the Lake, A; Never Say Never Again; Prince Valiant; Robin Hood; Shaka Zulu; Shooting Party, The; Squeeze, The; Wild Geese II
Fox, Huckleberry: Blue Yonder, The; Misunderstood; Pharaoh's Army
Fox, James: Absolute Beginners; Afraid of the Dark; Chase, The; Circle of Passion; Doomsday Gun; Fall from Grace; Farewell to the King; Golden Bowl, The; Greystoke: The Legend of Tarzan, Lord of the Apes; Gulliver's Travels (1996) (Television); Heart of Darkness; High Season; Hostage; Isadora; King Rat; Leo Tolstoy's Anna Karenina (1997); Loneliness of the Long Distance Runner,The; Lover's Prayer; Mickey Blue Eyes; Mighty Quinn, The; Old Curiosity Shop, The; Patriot Games; Performance; Remains of the Day; Russia House, The; Servant, The; Sexy Beast; Thoroughly Modern Millie; Up at the Villa; Whistle Blower, The
Fox, Kerry: Affair, The; Angel at My Table, An; Country Life; Friends; Hanging Garden, The; Last Days of Chez Nous, The; Rainbow Warrior; Shallow Grave; Welcome to Sarajevo
Fox, Linda: Big Bust Out, The
Fox, Michael J.: American President, The; Back to the Future; Back to the Future II; Back to the Future III; Blue in the Face; Bright Lights, Big City; Casualties of War; Cold-Blooded; Doc Hollywood; For Love or Money; Frighteners, The; Greedy; Hard Way, The; High School, USA; Life with Mikey; Light of Day; Poison Ivy; Secret of My Success, The; Teen Wolf; Where the Rivers Flow North
Fox, Morgan: Flesh Gordon 2: Flesh Gordon meets the Cosmic Cheerleaders
Fox, Peter: Minor Miracle, A
Fox, Samantha: Night to Dismember, A
Fox, Sidney: Midnight; Murders in the Rue Morgue
Fox, Virginia: Buster Keaton Festival Vol. 1–3
Fox, Vivica A.: Booty Call; Double Take; Kingdom Come; Set It Off; Soul Food; Two Can Play That Game; Why Do Fools Fall in Love
Foxworth, Bo: Summer Dreams
Foxworth, Robert: Ants!; Beyond the Stars; Black Marble, The; Deathmoon; Double Standard; Frankenstein; Invisible Strangler; Prophecy (1979)
Foxx, Elizabeth: School Spirit
Foxx, Jamie: Ali; Any Given Sunday; Bait; Booty Call; Great White Hype, The; Held Up; Players Club, The; Truth About Cats and Dogs, The
Foxx, Redd: Cotton Comes to Harlem; Harlem Nights; Norman ... Is That You?
Foy, Charley: Wagons Roll at Night, The
Foy Jr., Eddie: Bells Are Ringing; Farmer Takes a Wife, The; Four Jacks and a Jill; Gidget Goes Hawaiian; Lucky Me; Pajama Game, The; 30 Is a Dangerous Age, Cynthia
Foyt, Victoria: Babyfever; Déjà Vu; Last Summer in the Hamptons
Frain, James: Hilary and Jackie; Loch Ness; Nothing Personal; Rasputin; Reindeer Games; Titus; Where the Heart Is
Frakes, Jonathan: Journey's End: The Saga of Star Trek:The Next Generation; Star Trek: First Contact; Star Trek: Generations; Star Trek: Insurrection; Star Trek: The Next Generation (TV Series)
Frampton, Peter: Sgt. Pepper's Lonely Hearts Club Band
France, C. V.: Skin Game, The (1931)
France, Ronald: Dirty Games
Francen, Victor: J'Accuse; Madame Curie; San Antonio; Tuttles of Tahiti, The
Franchi, Franco: Dr. Goldfoot and the Girl Bombs
Francine, Anne: Savages
Franciosa, Anthony: Across 110th Street; Assault on a Queen; Backstreet Dreams; Career; City Hall; Cricket, The; Curse of the Black Widow; Death House; Death Wish II; Double Threat; Drowning Pool, The; Face in the Crowd, A; Firepower; Ghost in the Noonday Sun; Long Hot Summer, The; Naked Maja, The; Period of Adjustment; Rio Conchos; Side Show; Stagecoach; Summer Heat; This Could Be the Night; Unsane; World Is Full of Married Men, The
Francis, Anna Belle: That's the Way I Like It
Francis, Anne: Bad Day at Black Rock; Battle Cry; Blackboard Jungle, The; Born Again; Don't Go Near the Water; Double-O Kid, The; Forbidden Planet; Haunts of the Very Rich; Laguna Heat; Lion Is in the Streets, A; Little Vegas; Love God?, The; Pancho Villa; Return (1984); Summer Holiday; Susan Slept Here
Francis, Arlene: All My Sons; Murders in the Rue Morgue; One, Two, Three; Thrill of It All, The
Francis, Bev: Pumping Iron II: The Women
Francis, Carol Ann: Shades of Love: Champagne for Two
Francis, Connie: Where the Boys Are (1960)
Francis, David Paul: Second Jungle Book, The: Mowgli and Baloo
Francis, Jan: Champions; Dracula
Francis, Kay: Cocoanuts; Four Jills in a Jeep; In Name Only; It's a Date; Little Men; Wonder Bar
Francis, Noel: Stone of Silver Creek
Francis, Robert: Caine Mutiny, The; Long Gray Line, The
Francis, Ryan: River Pirates, The
Franciscus, James: Amazing Dobermans; Beneath the Planet of the Apes; Cat O'Nine Tails; Good Guys Wear Black; Greek Tycoon, The; Killer Fish; Man Inside, The; Marooned; Miracle of the White Stallions; Nightkill; Secret Weapons; Valley of Gwangi; When Time Ran Out!
Francks, Don: Christmas Wife, The; Drying Up the Streets; Finian's Rainbow; Fish Hawk; Heck's Way Home; Terminal Choice
Francks, Rainbow Sun: Junior's Groove
Franco, James: James Dean (2001); Spider-Man; Whatever It Takes
Franco, Jess: Demoniac; Ilsa, the Wicked Warden
Franco, Margarita: Three Ninjas Kick Back
Franco, Ramon: Kiss Me a Killer; Shattered Image
François, Jacques: North Star (1996); Too Shy to Try
Franey, Billy: Somewhere in Sonora
Frank, Charles: Guide for the Married Woman, A; LBJ: The Early Years; Russkies; Tarantulas—The Deadly Cargo
Frank, Diana: Eyes of the Serpent; In the Time of Barbarians II
Frank, Evelyn: World of Strangers, A
Frank, Gary: Enemy Territory; Enola Gay: The Men, the Mission, the Atomic Bomb
Frank, Horst: Head, The (1959)
Frank, Jason David: Mighty Morphin Power Rangers: The Movie; Turbo: A Power Rangers Adventure
Frank, Joanna: Always
Frankel, Mark: For Roseanna; Leon the Pig Farmer; Season of Giants, A; Solitaire for 2; Young Catherine
Franken, Al: One More Saturday Night; Stuart Saves His Family
Franken, Steve: Can't Buy Me Love; Hardly Working; Sky Heist; Terror Out of the Sky; Time Travelers, The; Transylvania Twist
Frankeur, Paul: Jour de Fête; Le Gentleman D'Espom (Duke of the Derby); Milky Way, The; Un Singe en Hiver (A Monkey in Winter)
Frankham, David: Return of the Fly, The
Frankie Lymon and the Teenagers: Rock, Rock, Rock
Franklin, Diane: Better Off Dead; Terror Vision
Franklin, Don: Fast Forward
Franklin, George: Maximum Security
Franklin, Gloria: Drums of Fu Manchu

Franklin, John: Children of the Corn; Children of the Corn 666: Isaac's Return
Franklin, Pamela: And Soon the Darkness; Flipper's New Adventure; Food of the Gods; Horse Without a Head, The; Innocents, The (1961); Legend of Hell House, The; Night of the Following Day, The; Prime of Miss Jean Brodie, The; Satan's School for Girls; Tiger Walks, A; Witching, The (Necromancy)
Franklyn, Sabina: Worst Witch, The
Franklyn, William: Enemy from Space
Franks, Billy: Track 16
Franks, Chloe: Littlest Horse Thieves, The; Who Slew Auntie Roo?
Frann, Mary: Fatal Charm
Franquinha, Joey: Just Looking
Franz, Arthur: Abbott and Costello Meet the Invisible Man; Amazing Howard Hughes, The; Atomic Submarine, The; Flight to Mars; Hellcats of the Navy; Invaders from Mars; Jungle Patrol; Member of the Wedding, The; Monster on the Campus; Sands of Iwo Jima; Young Lions, The
Franz, Dennis: American Buffalo; Blow Out; Children of Fury; City of Angels; Die Hard 2: Die Harder; Kiss Shot; Package, The; Psycho II
Franz, Eduard: Burning Hills, The; Four Skulls of Jonathan Drake, The; Jazz Singer, The; Latin Lovers; Magnificent Yankee, The; Scar, The
Franzese, Daniel: Bully
Fraser, Bill: Captain's Paradise, The; Corn Is Green, The
Fraser, Brendan: Airheads; Bedazzled; Blast from the Past; Dudley Do-Right; Encino Man; George of the Jungle; Gods and Monsters; Monkeybone; Mrs. Winterbourne; Mummy, The; Mummy Returns, The; Passion of Darkly Noon, The; School Ties; Scout, The; Twenty Bucks; Twilight of the Golds, The; With Honors; Younger and Younger
Fraser, Brent: Little Death, The
Fraser, Duncan: Call of the Wild; Captains Courageous
Fraser, Elisabeth: Sammy, the Way-Out Seal; Sgt. Bilko (TV Series); Two for the Seesaw
Fraser, Hugh: Poirot (Series); Sharpe (TV Series)
Fraser, John: Repulsion; Study in Terror, A; Tunes of Glory
Fraser, Laura: Left Luggage; Titus; Virtual Sexuality
Fraser, Liz: Adventures of a Private Eye; Carry on Cruising; Chicago Joe and the Showgirl; Seaside Swingers
Fraser, Phyllis: Winds of the Wasteland
Fraser, Richard: Bedlam; White Pongo (Blond Gorilla)
Fraser, Ronald: Flight of the Phoenix, The; Moll Flanders
Fraser, Sally: Dangerous Charter; It's a Dog's Life; War of the Colossal Beast
Fraser, Shane: Angel 4: Undercover
Fraser, Tomiko: Head Over Heels
Frasser, Laura: Match, The
Frates, Robin: Arrival, The
Fratkin, Stuart: Remote
Frawley, William: Abbott and Costello Meet the Invisible Man; Adventures of Huckleberry Finn, The; Babe Ruth Story, The; Blondie in Society; Fighting Seabees, The; Flame of the Barbary Coast; Footsteps in the Dark; Harmony Lane; I Love Lucy (TV Series); Lady on a Train; Lemon Drop Kid, The; Mad About Music; Monsieur Verdoux; Mother Wore Tights; Princess Comes Across, The; Rancho Notorious; Rhythm on the River; Rose of Washington Square; Something to Sing About; Virginian, The; Whistling in Brooklyn
Frazee, Jane: Buck Privates; Hellzapoppin; Springtime in the Sierras; Under California Stars
Frazer, Robert: From a Far Country; Gangs of Sonora; White Zombie
Frazer, Rupert: Back Home; Girl in a Swing, The
Frazier, Ron: Dead Ahead: The Exxon Valdez Disaster; Head Office
Frazier, Sheila: Firehouse; Lazarus Syndrome, The; Superfly; Superfly T.N.T.; Three the Hard Way
Frechette, Mark: Zabriskie Point
Frechette, Peter: Empire City
Freddie and the Dreamers: Seaside Swingers
Frederick, Lynne: Amazing Mr. Blunden, The; Phase IV; Prisoner of Zenda, The; Schizo
Frederick, Pauline: Thank You, Mr. Moto
Frederick, Tara: Lotus Eaters, The
Frederick, Vicki: All the Marbles; Body Rock; Chopper Chicks in Zombietown
Fredro: Strapped
Freed, Alan: Go, Johnny, Go!; Rock, Rock, Rock
Freed, Bert: Billy Jack; Gazebo, The; Wild in the Streets
Freed, Sam: Call Me
Freeman, Colenton: Vampyr, The (1992)
Freeman, Eric: Silent Night, Deadly Night Part 2
Freeman, J. E.: Alien Resurrection; Copycat; Hard Traveling; Memphis
Freeman, Joan: Fastest Guitar Alive, The; Friday the 13th—The Final Chapter; Mooncussers; Panic in the Year Zero; Reluctant Astronaut, The; Tower of London
Freeman, Kathleen: Adventures of Topper, The; Blues Brothers 2000; Disorderly Orderly, The; Dragnet; House by the River; In the Mood; Ladies' Man, The (1961); Love Is Better Than Ever; Nutty Professor, The; Reckless Kelly; Rounders, The; Willies, The; Wrong Guys, The
Freeman, Mona: Black Beauty; Branded; Copper Canyon; Dear Wife; Heiress, The; Jumping Jacks; Mother Wore Tights; That Brennan Girl
Freeman, Morgan: Along Came a Spider; Amistad; Bonfire of the Vanities; Chain Reaction; Clean and Sober; Clinton and Nadine; Death of a Prophet; Deep Impact; Driving Miss Daisy; Glory; Hard Rain; High Crimes; Johnny Handsome; Kiss the Girls; Lean on Me; Moll Flanders; Nurse Betty; Outbreak; Power of One, The; Robin Hood: Prince of Thieves; Roll of Thunder, Hear My Cry; Seven; Shawshank Redemption, The; Street Smart; Sum of All Fears, The; That Was Then ... This Is Now; Under Suspicion (2000); Unforgiven (1992)
Freeman, Paul: Aces: Iron Eagle III; Devil's Arithmetic, The; Eminent Domain; Hit Woman: The Double Edge; Just Like a Woman; May Wine; Mighty Morphin Power Rangers: The Movie; Only Love; Raiders of the Lost Ark; Sakharov; Samson and Delilah; Sender, The; Shanghai Surprise; Whose Child Am I?; Without a Clue
Freeman Jr., Al: Detective, The; Down in the Delta; Malcolm X; My Sweet Charlie; Once Upon a Time ... When We Were Colored; Seven Hours to Judgment
Frehley, Ace: Kiss Meets the Phantom of the Park
Freiss, Stephane: Does This Mean We're Married?; King's Whore, The
French, Bill: Killing Edge, The
French, Bruce: Pipe Dreams
French, Ed: Breeders
French, George: Tarzan of the Apes
French, Leigh: Hollywood Knights, The; White Line Fever
French, Valerie: Four Skulls of Jonathan Drake, The; Jubal; 27th Day, The
French, Victor: Charro!; Little House on the Prairie (TV Series)
Fresh, Dave: Ganjasaurus Rex
Fresnay, Pierre: César; Fanny; Grand Illusion; Le Corbeau (The Raven (1943)); Marius; Monsieur Vincent
Fresson, Bernard: French Connection II, The; Hiroshima, Mon Amour; Place Vendome; Voyage of Terror: The Achille Lauro Affair
Frewer, Matt: Day My Parents Ran Away, The; Far from Home; Generation X; Honey, I Shrunk the Kids; Jailbait (2000); Kissinger and Nixon; Lawnmower Man 2: Jobe's War (Lawnmower Man: Beyond Cyberspace); Max Headroom; National Lampoon's Senior Trip; Positively True Adventures of the Alleged Texas Cheerleader-Murdering Mom, The; Quicksilver Highway; Short Time; Stand, The; Taking of Beverly Hills, The
Frey, Glenn: Let's Get Harry
Frey, Leonard: Boys in the Band, The; Fiddler on the Roof; Where the Buffalo Roam
Frey, Sami: Band of Outsiders; Black Widow; César and Rosalie; My Life and Times with Antonin Artaud; Nea (A Young Emmanuelle); Revenge of the Musketeers; Sand and Blood; Seven Deadly Sins, The; Sweet Movie

Freyd, Bernard: Alexina
Friberg, Ulf: Jerusalem
Fricke, Grayson: Past the Bleachers
Fricker, Brenda: Angels in the Outfield; Brides of Christ; Deadly Advice; Durango; Field, The; Home Alone 2: Lost in New York; Journey; Man of No Importance, A; Masterminds; My Left Foot; Resurrection Man; So I Married an Axe Murderer; Sound and the Silence,The; Time to Kill, A (1996); Utz; Woman of Independent Means, A
Frid, Jonathan: Best of Dark Shadows, The; Dark Shadows (TV Series); House of Dark Shadows; Seizure
Fridbjornsson, Bjorn Jorundur: Remote Control
Fridell, Squire: Pink Motel
Friedle, Will: My Date with the President's Daughter; Trojan War
Friedman, Budd: Gross Jokes
Friedman, Dave: Sore Losers
Friedman, Michael: Forest Warrior
Friedman, Peter: Blink; Heidi Chronicles, The; Safe; Single White Female
Friedrich, John: Final Terror, The; Small Circle of Friends, A; Thornbirds, The; Wanderers, The
Friel, Anna: Everlasting Piece, An; Land Girls, The; Rogue Trader; William Shakespeare's A Midsummer Night's Dream
Friell, Vincent: Restless Natives
Friels, Colin: Angel Baby; Back of Beyond; Class Action; Cosi; Darkman; Dingo; Good Man in Africa, A; Grievous Bodily Harm; Ground Zero; High Tide; Kangaroo; Malcolm; Monkey Grip; Mr. Reliable; Warm Nights on a Slow Moving Train
Friend, Philip: Pimpernel Smith
Frijda, Nelly: Question of Silence, A
Frisco, Joe: Riding High
Frith, Rebecca: Love Serenade
Fritsch, Thomas: Full Hearts and Empty Pockets
Fritsch, Willy: Spies; Woman in the Moon (Girl in the Moon; By Rocket to the Moon)
Fritz, Nikki: Where Evil Lies
Frizell, Lou: Stalking Moon, The; Summer of '42
Fröbe, Gert: $ (Dollars); Goldfinger; Is Paris Burning?; Serpent's Egg, The; Ten Little Indians; Those Daring Young Men in Their Jaunty Jalopies; Those Magnificent Men in Their Flying Machines; Thousand Eyes of Dr. Mabuse, The; Tonio Kroger
Froler, Samuel: Best Intentions, The
Frome, Milton: Ride 'em Cowgirl
Fromholz, Steve: Positive I.D.
Fromin, Troy: Adventures of the Kung Fu Rascals, The
Fronsoe, Susan: Biohazard: The Alien Force
Frost, Adam: Pact, The
Frost, Lindsay: Dead Heat; Monolith
Frost, Sadie: Bram Stoker's Dracula; Cisco Kid, The; Crimetime; Flypaper; Love, Honor & Obey; Magic Hunter; Pyromaniac's Love Story, A; Shopping; Splitting Heirs
Frost, Terry: Atom Man vs. Superman; Ghost Town Renegades; Man Who Cheated Himself, The; Waterfront
Frot, Catherine: Dinner Game, The
Frotscher, Donna: They Bite
Froud, Toby: Labyrinth
Fry, Stephen: Gosford Park; I.Q.; Jeeves and Wooster (TV Series); Peter's Friends; Relative Values; Wilde
Frydman, Basia: Slingshot, The
Frye, Brittain: Hide and Go Shriek
Frye, Dwight: Black Camel, The; Bride of Frankenstein; Crime of Dr. Crespi, The; Dead Men Walk; Dracula; Drums of Fu Manchu; Invisible Man, The; Vampire Bat, The
Frye, Soleil Moon: I've Been Waiting for You; Piranha; Pumpkinhead II: Bloodwings; Twisted Love
Frye, Virgil: Running Hot; Up from the Depths
Fryer, Eric: Terry Fox Story, The
Fuchs, Jason: Flipper
Fuchsberger, Joachim: Curse of the Yellow Snake, The
Fudge, Alan: Children of An Lac, The; My Demon Lover; Witness to the Execution
Fuente, Cristiàn de la: Driven
Fuentes, Daisy: Curdled
Fuerstein, Mark: Muse, The
Fugard, Athol: Meetings with Remarkable Men; Road to Mecca, The
Fugit, Patrick: Almost Famous
Fuizat, Allen: For the Love of Benji
Fuji, Tatsuya: In the Realm of Passion; In the Realm of the Senses
Fujioka, Hiroshi: Ghost Warrior; K2
Fujita, Susumu: Sanshiro Sugata
Fujiwara, Kei: Tetsuo: The Iron Man
Fulci, Lucio: Cat in the Brain, A
Fulford, Wendi: Warriors (1994)
Fuller, Barbara: Red Menace, The
Fuller, Brook: When Wolves Cry
Fuller, Dolores: Glen or Glenda; Jail Bait (1954)
Fuller, Jonathan: Bloodfist VI: Ground Zero; Castle Freak; Last Man Standing; Pit and the Pendulum, The; Suspect Device
Fuller, Kurt: Moonbase
Fuller, Lance: Apache Woman; Bride and the Beast, The; Kentucky Rifle
Fuller, Penny: Cat on a Hot Tin Roof; Elephant Man, The; George Washington: The Forging of a Nation; Lois Gibbs and the Love Canal; Miss Rose White; Piano for Mrs. Cimino, A
Fuller, Robert: Brain from Planet Arous, The; Donner Pass: The Road to Survival; Maverick; Return of the Seven; Whatever Happened to Aunt Alice?
Fuller, Samuel: Last Movie, The (Chinchero); Pierrot Le Fou; Return to Salem's Lot, A; State of Things, The; Tigrero: A Film That Was Never Made
Fullerton, Fiona: Alice's Adventures in Wonderland; Ghost in Monte Carlo, A; Shaka Zulu
Fulton, Christina: Girl with the Hungry Eyes, The; Hard Drive
Fulton, Rikki: Girl in the Picture, The
Fulton, Todd: Escapes
Fultz, Ronda: I Drink Your Blood
Funakoshi, Eiji: Fires on the Plain
Fung, Stephen: Gen-X Cops
Funicello, Annette: Babes in Toyland; Back to the Beach; Beach Blanket Bingo; Beach Party; Bikini Beach; Elfego Baca: Six Gun Law; Escapade in Florence; Horsemasters; How to Stuff a Wild Bikini; Lots of Luck; Misadventures of Merlin Jones, The; Monkey's Uncle, The; Muscle Beach Party; Shaggy Dog, The
Furey, John: Friday the 13th, Part II; Mutant on the Bounty; Wolves, The
Furlan, Mira: Babylon 5 (TV Series)
Furlong, Anthony: Planet Patrol
Furlong, Edward: American Heart; American History X; Animal Factory; Before and After; Brainscan; Detroit Rock City; Grass Harp, The; Home of Our Own, A; Little Odessa; Pecker; Pet Sematary Two; Terminator 2: Judgment Day
Furman, Roger: Georgia, Georgia
Fürmann, Benno: Anatomy; Princess and the Warrior, The
Furneaux, Yvonne: Master of Ballantrae, The; Mummy, The; Repulsion; Warriors, The
Furness, Betty: Aggie Appleby, Maker of Men; Swing Time
Furness, Deborra-Lee: Angel Baby; Shame; Waiting
Furst, Stephen: Dream Team, The; Magic Kid; Magic Kid 2; Midnight Madness; National Lampoon's Class Reunion; Silent Rage; Take Down; Unseen, The; Up the Creek
Furuya, Fumio: Sgt. Kabukiman N.Y.P.D.
Fury, Billy: That'll Be the Day
Fury, Ed: Wild Women of Wongo
Futterman, Dan: Birdcage, The; Breathing Room; Class of '61; Shooting Fish; Thicker Than Blood; Urbania; When Trumpets Fade
Fyfe, Mak: Excalibur Kid, The
Fyodora, Victoria: Target
Gabai, Richard: Hot Under the Collar
Gabay, Sasson: Escape: Human Cargo; Impossible Spy, The
Gabel, Martin: First Deadly Sin, The; Lady in Cement; Lord Love a Duck; Marnie; Smile, Jenny, You're Dead; Thief, The
Gabel, Michael: On the Block
Gabel, Scilla: Mill of the Stone Women
Gabela, Glen: Warriors from Hell

Gabin, Jean: Cat, The (1971) (Le Chat); Four Bags Full; French Can Can; Golgotha; Grand Illusion; Grisbi; La Bête Humaine; Le Cas du Dr. Laurent; Le Gentleman D'Espom (Duke of the Derby); Le Jour Se Leve (Daybreak (1939)); Le Plaisir; Les Misérables; Lower Depths (1936); Melodie en Sous-Sol (The Big Grab) (AnyNumber Can Win); Pepe Le Moko; Stormy Waters; Un Singe en Hiver (A Monkey in Winter); Zou Zou
Gable, Christopher: Boy Friend, The; Music Lovers, The; Rainbow, The
Gable, Clark: Across the Wide Missouri; Adventure; Any Number Can Play; Band of Angels; Betrayed; Boom Town; But Not for Me; Chained; China Seas; Command Decision; Comrade X; Dance, Fools, Dance; Dancing Lady; Forsaking All Others; Free Soul, A; Gone with the Wind; Hold Your Man; Homecoming; Honky Tonk; Hucksters, The; Idiot's Delight; It Happened One Night; It Started in Naples; Key to the City; King and Four Queens, The; Laughing Sinners; Lone Star; Love on the Run; Manhattan Melodrama; Misfits, The; Mogambo; Mutiny on the Bounty; Never Let Me Go; Night Nurse; No Man of Her Own; Painted Desert, The; Possessed; Red Dust; Run Silent, Run Deep; San Francisco; Saratoga; Soldier of Fortune; Somewhere I'll Find You; Strange Cargo; Strange Interlude; Susan Lenox: Her Fall and Rise; Tall Men, The; Teacher's Pet; Test Pilot; They Met in Bombay; To Please a Lady; Too Hot to Handle; Wife vs. Secretary
Gable, John Clark: Bad Jim
Gabor, Eva: Artists and Models; Don't Go Near the Water; Gigi; It Started With a Kiss; Last Time I Saw Paris, The; My Man Godfrey; New Kind of Love, A; Princess Academy, The; Truth About Women, The
Gabor, Miklos: Father
Gabor, Zsa Zsa: Beverly Hillbillies, The (1993); Boys' Night Out; Death of a Scoundrel; For the First Time; Lili; Lovely to Look At; Moulin Rouge; Picture Mommy Dead; Queen of Outer Space; Touch of Evil; We're Not Married
Gabriel, John: Sex and the College Girl
Gabrielle, Monique: Deathstalker II: Duel of the Titans
Gabrio, Gabriel: Harvest (1937)
Gades, Antonio: Blood Wedding; El Amor Brujo
Gadsden, Jacqueline: It
Gael, Anna: Therese and Isabelle
Gage, Kevin: Double Tap; Gunshy; Point Blank
Gage, Michael: Dee Snider's Strangeland
Gage, Patricia: Little Kidnappers; Rabid
Gagnon, Jacques: Mon Oncle Antoine
Gago, Jenny: My Family
Gahagan, Helen: She
Gail, Jane: Traffic in Souls
Gail, Max: Cardiac Arrest; Dangerous Touch; D.C. Cab; Deadly Target; Forest Warrior; Game of Love, The; Good Luck; Heartbreakers; Judgment in Berlin; Sodbusters; Street Crimes; Where Are the Children?
Gaines, Barry: Burglar From Hell; Jacker 2: Descent to Hell; Tales Till the End
Gaines, Boyd: Call Me; Sure Thing, The
Gainey, M. C.: Breakdown; Citizen Ruth; El Diablo; Leap of Faith; Ulterior Motives
Gains, Courtney: Can't Buy Me Love; King Cobra; Memphis Belle
Gainsbourg, Charlotte: Cement Garden, The; Jane Eyre; Le Petit Amour; Little Thief, The; Merci La Vie
Gainsbourg, Serge: Je Vous Aime (I Love You All)
Galabru, Michel: Choice of Arms, A; Holes, The; Judge and the Assassin, The; Uranus
Galan, Mapi: Killer Tongue
Galati, Tony: Dark Side, The; Darkside, The
Galbo, Cristina: Twice a Judas
Gale, David: Brain, The; Bride of Re-Animator; Guyver, The; Re-Animator; Syngenor
Gale, Ed: Chopper Chicks in Zombietown; Howard the Duck; Lifepod
Gale, Vincent: Escape, The
Galecki, Johnny: Bounce
Galeota, Jimmy: Clubhouse Detectives
Galiana, Maria: Solas
Galianos, Melissa: Laserhawk
Galiena, Anna: Being Human; Excellent Cadavers; Hairdresser's Husband, The; Jamon, Jamon; Leading Man, The; Rorret
Galina, Stacy: Children of the Corn V: Fields of Terror
Galipeau, Annie: Grey Owl
Gallagher, Bronagh: Commitments, The
Gallagher, David: Phenomenon
Gallagher, Helen: Strangers When We Meet
Gallagher, Megan: Crosscut; In a Stranger's Hands; Millennium; Trade Off
Gallagher, Michael: Ten Benny
Gallagher, Peter: American Beauty; Cafe Society; Caine Mutiny Court Martial, The; Center Stage; Cupid and Cate; Dreamchild; Fallen Angels; House on Haunted Hill; Idolmaker, The; Inconvenient Woman, An; Last Dance; Last Debate, The; Late for Dinner; Long Day's Journey into Night; Malice; Man Who Knew Too Little, The; Mother's Boys; Murder of Mary Phagan, The; Path to Paradise; Player, The; sex, lies and videotape; Short Cuts; Skag; Summer Lovers; Titanic; To Gillian on Her 37th Birthday; Underneath, The; Watch It; While You Were Sleeping; White Mile
Gallagher, Skeets: Bird of Paradise; Riptide
Gallagher, Stephen: Mrs. Parker and the Vicious Circle
Gallagher, Susan: Looking for Trouble
Galland, Philippe: Overseas
Gallander, James: Prisoner of Love
Gallardo, Camille: Of Love and Shadows
Gallardo, Carlos: El Mariachi
Gallardo, Jose: I Am Cuba
Galle, Matthew: Simple Justice
Galle, Raymond: Mauvaise Graine (Bad Seed)
Gallego, Gina: My Demon Lover
Galligan, Zach: All Tied Up; Caroline at Midnight; Cupid; Cyborg 3: The Recycler; Gremlins; Gremlins 2: The New Batch; Ice; Lawrenceville Stories, The; Mortal Passions; Psychic (1992); Rebel Storm; Round Trip to Heaven; Waxwork; Waxwork II: Lost in Time
Gallo, Carla: Spanking the Monkey
Gallo, George: Hide and Seek
Gallo, Mario: Revenge of the Ninja
Gallo, Vincent: Buffalo '66; Freeway 2: Confessions of a Trickbaby; Funeral, The; Palookaville; Truth or Consequences, N.M.
Gallo, William: Night of the Demons
Gallotte, Jean-François: Evil Within, The
Galloway, Don: Riding with Death; Rough Night in Jericho
Gam, Rita: Distortions; King of Kings (1961); Mohawk; Thief, The
Gamble, Mason: Dennis the Menace; Rushmore
Gamblin, Jacques: Dr. Akagi
Gamboa, Joonee: Chain, The
Gambon, Michael: Browning Version, The; Bullet to Beijing; Charlotte Gray; Clean Slate (1994); Cook, the Thief, His Wife & Her Lover, The; Dancing at Lughnasa; Gosford Park; Last September, The; Man of No Importance, A; Mary Reilly; Missing Link; Nothing Personal; Samson and Delilah; Sleepy Hollow; Squanto: A Warrior's Tale; Toys; Turtle Diary; Two Deaths; Wings of the Dove, The
Gammell, Robin: Circle of Two; His Bodyguard; Project X; Rituals
Gammon, James: Adventures of Huck Finn, The (1993); Ballad of Gregorio Cortez, The; Cabin Boy; Cell, The; Crisscross (1992); Deadly Encounter; Hi-Lo Country, The; I Love You to Death; Laguna Heat; Leaving Normal; Major League; Major League II; Milagro Beanfield War, The; Point Blank; Roe vs. Wade; Running Cool; Silver Bullet; Streets of Laredo; Traveller; Truman; Wild Bill; Wyatt Earp
Gampu, Ken: Act of Piracy; African Rage; American Ninja IV: The Annihilation; Dingaka; King Solomon's Mines; Naked Prey, The; Scavengers
Gance, Marguerite: La Chute de la Maison Usher
Gandolfini, James: Angie; Crimson Tide; Fallen; Get Shorty; Juror, The; Last Castle, The; Man Who Wasn't There, The

(2001); Mexican, The; 8MM; Night Falls on Manhattan; She's So Lovely; Sopranos, The (TV series); Terminal Velocity
Gang, Wu: Red Firecracker, Green Firecracker
Gange, Ray: Rude Boy
Ganios, Tony: Porky's Revenge; Wanderers, The
Gannon, Jamie: Shrieker
Ganoung, Richard: Billy's Hollywood Screen Kiss; Parting Glances
Gant, Mtume: Hurricane Streets
Gant, Richard: CB4; Nutty Professor II: The Klumps
Gantt, Leland: Affair, The
Gantzler, Peter: Italian for Beginners
Ganus, Paul: Crash and Burn; Silencer, The
Ganz, Bruno: American Friend, The; Bread and Tulips; Children of Nature; Circle of Deceit; Faraway, So Close; In the White City; Knife in the Head; Last Days of Chez Nous, The; Lumiere; Saint-Ex; Strapless; Wings of Desire
Gao, Jie: Xiu Xiu: The Sent Down Girl
Gaon, Yehoram: Operation Thunderbolt
Gaowa, Sigin: Women from the Lake of the Scented Souls
Garas, Kaz: Last Safari
Garay, Soo: Shot Through the Heart
Garbani, Ivo: Morgan the Pirate
Garber, Matthew: Gnome-Mobile, The; Mary Poppins
Garber, Victor: Kleptomania; Laughter on the 23rd Floor; Light Sleeper; Rodgers & Hammerstein's Cinderella; Sleepless in Seattle; Titanic
Garbiras, Nina: Bruiser
Garbo, Greta: Anna Christie; Anna Karenina; As You Desire Me; Camille; Conquest; Flesh and the Devil; Grand Hotel; Inspiration; Joyless Street; Kiss, The; Mata Hari; Mysterious Lady, The; Ninotchka; Painted Veil, The; Queen Christina; Romance; Single Standard, The; Susan Lenox: Her Fall and Rise; Two-Faced Woman; Wild Orchids; Woman of Affairs, A
Garcés, Iñigo: Devil's Backbone, The
Garcés, Paula: Clockstoppers
Garcia, Adam: Bootmen; Coyote Ugly; Riding in Cars with Boys
Garcia, Allan: Circus, The/A Day's Pleasure
Garcia, Andres: Dance of Death; Day of the Assassin
Garcia, Andy: American Roulette; Black Rain; Clinton and Nadine; Dead Again; Desperate Measures; Disappearance of Garcia Lorca, The; 8 Million Ways to Die; Godfather, Part III, The; Hero (1992); Hoodlum; Internal Affairs; Jennifer 8; Just the Ticket; Night Falls on Manhattan; Ocean's Eleven (2001); Show of Force, A; Stand and Deliver; Steal Big, Steal Little; Things to Do in Denver When You're Dead; Untouchables, The; When a Man Loves a Woman
Garcia, Darnell: Blind Rage
Garcia, Eddie: Beast of the Yellow Night; Debut, The
Garcia, Jerry: Grateful Dawg
Garcia, Lea: Black Orpheus
Garcia, Nicole: Beau Pere; Bolero; Corrupt; Mon Oncle d'Amerique; Overseas; Peril
Garcia, Raul: I Am Cuba
Garcia, Stênio: Me You Them
García, Cipriano: La Ciudad
Garcin, Ginette: Blue Country
Garcin, Henri: Eighth Day, The; Someone Behind the Door; Woman Next Door, The
Garde, Betty: Call Northside 777
Gardenia, Vincent: Age-Old Friends; Bang the Drum Slowly; Cold Turkey; Death Wish; Death Wish II; Firepower; Front Page, The; Heaven Can Wait; Home Movies; Kennedy (TV Miniseries); Last Flight of Noah's Ark; Little Murders; Little Shop of Horrors (1986); Lucky Luciano; Marciano; Moonstruck; Movers and Shakers; Skin Deep; Super, The; Tragedy of Flight 103, The: The Inside Story; Where's Poppa?
Gardère, Vincent: Night of the Hunted
Gardiner, Philip: Trees
Gardiner, Reginald: Androcles and the Lion; Born to Dance; Christmas in Connecticut; Damsel in Distress, A; Doctor Takes a Wife, The; Dolly Sisters, The; Everybody Sing; Halls of Montezuma; Horn Blows at Midnight, The; Immortal Sergeant, The; Man Who Came to Dinner, The; Marie Antoinette; Sundown; Wabash Avenue; Yank in the RAF, A
Gardner, Arthur: Assassin of Youth (Marijuana)
Gardner, Ava: Barefoot Contessa, The; Bhowani Junction; Bible, The; Cassandra Crossing, The; Earthquake; East Side, West Side; 55 Days at Peking; Ghosts on the Loose; Hucksters, The; Kidnapping of the President, The; Knights of the Round Table; Life and Times of Judge Roy Bean, The; Lone Star; Long Hot Summer, The; Mogambo; My Forbidden Past; Naked Maja, The; Night of the Iguana, The; On the Beach; One Touch of Venus; Pandora and the Flying Dutchman; Permission to Kill; Priest of Love; Regina; Sentinel, The; Seven Days in May; Show Boat; Singapore; Snows of Kilimanjaro, The; Whistle Stop
Gardner, Daniel: How U Like Me Now
Gardner, David: Bethune
Gardner, Devin: Kid Called Danger, A
Gardner, Hy: Girl Hunters, The
Gardner, Joan: Catherine the Great; Dark Journey; Man Who Could Work Miracles, The; Private Life of Don Juan, The
Gardner, Richard Harding: Deadly Daphne's Revenge
Gareth, Curt: Very Natural Thing, A
Garfield, Allen: Beverly Hills Cop II; Black Stallion Returns, The; Brinks Job, The; Candidate, The; Club Fed; Continental Divide; Conversation, The; Crime of the Century; Cry Uncle!; Cyborg 2; Desert Bloom; Diabolique; Family Prayers; Front Page, The; Get Crazy; Greetings; Hi Mom; Let It Ride; Majestic, The; Night Visitor (1989); One from the Heart; Putney Swope; Sketches of a Strangler; State of Things, The; Stunt Man, The
Garfield, Frank: Night of the Zombies
Garfield, John: Air Force; Body and Soul; Destination Tokyo; Fallen Sparrow, The; Force of Evil; Four Daughters; Gentlemen's Agreement; Hollywood Canteen; Humoresque; Juarez; Postman Always Rings Twice, The; Sea Wolf, The; Thank Your Lucky Stars; They Made Me a Criminal; Tortilla Flat
Garfield, John David: Savage Intruder, The
Garfield, Michael: Slugs, the Movie
Garfield Jr., John: Golden Voyage of Sinbad, The; That Cold Day in the Park
Garfunkel, Art: Boxing Helena; Carnal Knowledge; Catch-22; Short Fuse
Gargan, William: Aggie Appleby, Maker of Men; Animal Kingdom, The; Black Fury; Broadway Serenade; Canterville Ghost, The; Cheers for Miss Bishop; I Wake Up Screaming; Miss Annie Rooney; Rain; They Knew What They Wanted; Who Done It?; You Only Live Once
Gario, Gabriel: Pepe Le Moko
Garity, Troy: Bandits (2001)
Garko, Gianni: Night of the Devils
Garko, John: Have a Nice Funeral
Garland, Beverly: Alligator People, The; Blood Song (Haunted Symphony); Gamble on Love; Gundown at Sandoval; Gunslinger; It Conquered the World; It's My Turn; Pretty Poison; Say Goodbye, Maggie Cole; Swamp Women; Twice-Told Tales; Where the Red Fern Grows
Garland, Judy: Andy Hardy Meets a Debutante; Babes in Arms; Babes on Broadway; Broadway Melody of 1938; Child Is Waiting, A; Clock, The; Easter Parade; Everybody Sing; For Me and My Gal; Gay Purr-ee; Girl Crazy; Harvey Girls, The; I Could Go On Singing; In the Good Old Summertime; Judgment at Nuremberg; Life Begins for Andy Hardy; Listen, Darling; Little Nellie Kelly; Love Finds Andy Hardy; Meet Me in St. Louis; Pirate, The; Presenting Lily Mars; Star Is Born, A; Strike Up the Band; Summer Stock; That's Entertainment; Thoroughbreds Don't Cry; Thousands Cheer; Till the Clouds Roll By; Wizard of Oz, The; Words and Music; Ziegfeld Follies; Ziegfeld Girl
Garland, Richard: Attack of the Crab Monsters; Mutiny in Outer Space; Panic in the Year Zero; Undead, The
Garlick, Sean: Fortress
Garlicki, Piotr: Camouflage
Garlington, Lee: Babysitter, The
Garlington, Mary: Polyester
Garmon, Huw: Hedd Wyn
Garms, Justin: Gordy
Garneau, Constance: Strangers in Good Company

Garner, Alice: Love and Other Catastrophes
Garner, James: Americanization of Emily, The; Barbarians at the Gate; Boys' Night Out; Breathing Lessons; Cash McCall; Castaway Cowboy, The; Children's Hour, The; Dead Silence; Decoration Day; Distinguished Gentleman, The; Duel at Diablo; Fan, The; Fire in the Sky; Glitter Dome, The; Grand Prix; Great Escape, The; Hour of the Gun, The; Last Debate, The; Legalese; Marlowe; Maverick; Maverick (TV Series); Murphy's Romance; My Fellow Americans; My Name Is Bill W; Rockford Files, The (TV Series); Sayonara; Skin Game (1971); Space Cowboys; Streets of Laredo; Sunset; Support Your Local Gunfighter; Support Your Local Sheriff!; Tank; They Only Kill Their Masters; 36 Hours; Thrill of It All, The; Twilight; Up Periscope; Victor/Victoria; Wheeler Dealers, The
Garner, Jennifer: Dude, Where's My Car?; Rose Hill
Garner, Kelli: Bully
Garner, Peggy Ann: Betrayal; Cat, The (1966); In Name Only; Jane Eyre; Tree Grows in Brooklyn, A
Garnett, Gale: Mad Monster Party
Garofalo, Janeane: Adventures of Rocky and Bullwinkle, The; Big Trouble (2002); Bumblebee Flies Anyway, The; Bye Bye, Love; Clay Pigeons; Cold-Blooded; Copland; Dog Park; I Shot a Man in Vegas; Independent, The; Larger than Life; Matchmaker, The; Minus Man, The; Mystery Men; Reality Bites; Romy and Michele's High School Reunion; Steal This Movie; Sweethearts; Truth About Cats and Dogs, The; 200 Cigarettes; Wet Hot American Summer
Garofolo, Ettore: Mamma Roma
Garr, Teri: After Hours; Black Stallion, The; Black Stallion Returns, The; Changing Habits; Close Encounters of the Third Kind; Dumb and Dumber; Escape Artist, The; Firstborn; Full Moon in Blue Water; Head (1968); Honky Tonk Freeway; Let It Ride; Life Without Dick; Michael; Miracles; Mom and Dad Save the World; Mr. Mom; Oh, God!; One from the Heart; Out Cold; Perfect Alibi; Perfect Little Murder, A; Prime Suspect (1982) (Feature); Ready to Wear; Ronnie & Julie; Short Time; Simple Wish, A; Sting II, The; To Catch a King; Tootsie; Waiting for the Light; Witches' Brew; Young Frankenstein
Garralaga, Martin: Big Sombrero, The
Garrani, Ivo: Black Sunday; Hercules
Garrel, Maurice: Un Coeur en Hiver
Garrett, Betty: My Sister Eileen; Neptune's Daughter; On the Town; Take Me Out to the Ball Game; Words and Music
Garrett, Brad: Facade
Garrett, Hank: Blood Frenzy; Boys Next Door, The; Rosebud Beach Hotel, The (Nostell Hotel,The)
Garrett, Leif: Longshot (1981); Medicine Hat Stallion, The; Outsiders, The; Party Line; Shaker Run; Spirit of '76, The
Garrett, Lesley: Mikado, The
Garrett, Patsy: Benji; Dennis the Menace: Dinosaur Hunter; For the Love of Benji
Garrett, Teresa: It's in the Water
Garrick, Barbara: Ellen Foster; Sleepless in Seattle
Garrick, John: Just Imagine
Garrison, David: Homeboys
Garrone, Riccardo: Bang Bang Kid, The
Garson, Greer: Adventure; Goodbye, Mr. Chips; Happiest Millionaire, The; Julia Misbehaves; Julius Caesar; Madame Curie; Miniver Story, The; Mrs. Miniver; Mrs. Parkington; Pride and Prejudice; Random Harvest; Singing Nun, The; Sunrise at Campobello; That Forsyte Woman; When Ladies Meet
Garson, Willie: Out Cold (2001)
Garth, Daniel: Behind Locked Doors
Garth, Jennie: Beverly Hills 90210
Gartin, Christopher: Matters of the Heart; No Big Deal; Story Lady, The; Tremors 2: Aftershocks
Garvey, Steve: Bloodfist VI: Ground Zero; Original Kings Of Comedy, The
Garvie, Elizabeth: Pride and Prejudice
Garvin, Anita: Chump at Oxford, A; Laurel and Hardy Classics: Vol. 1–9
Garwood, John: Hell's Angels on Wheels
Gary, Lorraine: Jaws; Jaws: The Revenge; Jaws 2; Just You and Me, Kid; Pray for the Wildcats
Gascon, Jean: Man Called Horse, A
Gassman, Alessandro: Month by the Lake, A; Sacrilege; Steam: The Turkish Bath; Turkish Bath, The
Gassman, Vittorio: Abraham; Big Deal on Madonna Street; Bitter Rice; Catch as Catch Can; Family, The; Immortal Bachelor, The; Mambo; Miracle, The; Nude Bomb, The (Return of Maxwell Smart,The); Palermo Connection, The; Rhapsody; Sharky's Machine; Sleazy Uncle, The; Sleepers; Tempest; Tiger and The Pussycat, The; We All Loved Each Other So Much; Wedding, A (1978); Woman Times Seven
Gates, Anthony: L.A. Crackdown II
Gates, B. J.: Midnight Kiss
Gates, Larry: Hoodlum Priest, The; Hour of the Gun, The; Toys in the Attic; Young Savages, The
Gates, Nancy: Cheyenne Takes Over; Death of a Scoundrel; Suddenly; World Without End
Gates, William: Hoop Dreams
Gateson, Marjorie: Goin' to Town
Gatins, John: Leprechaun 3
Gatti, Jennifer: Blood Money (1999); Double Exposure
Gauger, Stephane: Six-String Samurai
Gaup, Mikkel: Pathfinder
Gauthier, Dan: Excessive Force II: Force on Force; Illegal in Blue
Gautier, Dick: Marathon; When Things Were Rotten (TV Series)
Gautier, Jean-Yves: Chef in Love, A
Gautreaux, David: Hearse, The
Gauzy, Dyna: Red Dwarf, The
Gavin, Erica: Caged Heat
Gavin, John: Back Street; Breath of Scandal, A; Imitation of Life; Jennifer; Madwoman of Chaillot, The; Midnight Lace; Psycho; Sophia Loren: Her Own Story; Thoroughly Modern Millie; Time to Love and a Time to Die, A
Gawthorne, Peter: Amazing Adventure
Gaxton, William: Best Foot Forward; Heat's On, The
Gay, Gregory: King of the Carnival
Gaye, Lisa: Class of Nuke 'em High 2: Subhumanoid Meltdown; Class of Nuke 'em High III; Sign of Zorro, The; Toxic Avenger Part II, The; Toxic Avenger Part III, The: The Last Temptation of Toxie
Gaye, Marvin: That Was Rock
Gayheart, Rebecca: Jawbreaker; Robin Cook's Invasion; Somebody Is Waiting; Too Smooth; Urban Legend
Gayle, Jackie: Bert Rigby, You're a Fool; Young at Heart Comedians, The
Gayle, Monica: Switchblade Sisters
Gaylord, Mitch: American Anthem; American Tiger; Animal Instincts
Gaynes, George: Dead Men Don't Wear Plaid; It Came Upon a Midnight Clear; Micki & Maude; Police Academy; Police Academy II: Their First Assignment; Police Academy III: Back in Training; Police Academy 6: City Under Siege; Police Academy: Mission to Moscow; Stepmonster; Tootsie; Vanya on 42nd Street
Gaynor, Janet: Star Is Born, A; Sunrise; Young in Heart, The
Gaynor, Mitzi: Birds and the Bees, The; Les Girls; South Pacific; Surprise Package; There's No Business Like Show Business; We're Not Married
Gayson, Eunice: Revenge of Frankenstein
Gazelle, Wendy: Hot Pursuit; Understudy, The: Graveyard Shift II
Gazzara, Ben: Anatomy of a Murder; Believe; Blindsided; Bloodline; Blue Moon; Bridge at Remagen, The; Buffalo '66; Convict Cowboy; Dogfighters, The; Early Frost, An; Farmer and Chase; Happiness; High Velocity; Illuminata; Killing of a Chinese Bookie; Ladykiller; Laugh for Joy (Passionate Thief) (1954); Lies Before Kisses; Neptune Factor, The; Opening Night; Parallel Lives; Passionate Thief, The (1961); Protector (1998); QB VII; Question of Honor, A; Quicker Than the Eye; Road House; Saint Jack; Secret Obsessions; Shadow Conspiracy; Spanish Prisoner, The; Stag; Tales of Ordinary Madness; They All Laughed; Thomas Crown Affair, The; Vicious Circles

Gazzo, Michael: Alligator; Blood Ties; Cookie; Fingers; Godfather, Part II, The; Kill Castro (Cuba Crossing, Mercenaries, Sweet Violent Tony)
Geary, Anthony: Antony and Cleopatra; Crack House; Dangerous Love; Disorderlies; High Desert Kill; Imposter, The; Johnny Got His Gun; Night Life; Night of the Warrior; Penitentiary III; Scorchers; UHF; You Can't Hurry Love
Geary, Cynthia: 8 Seconds; Northern Exposure (TV Series); When Time Expires
Gebrsellasie, Haile: Endurance
Gecks, Nicholas: Forever Young
Gedrick, Jason: Crossing the Bridge; Force, The; Heavenly Kid, The; Iron Eagle; Last Don, The; Massive Retaliation; Promised Land; Rooftops; Stacking; Summer Catch; Zoo Gang, The
Gee, Prunella: Witching Time
Geelbooi, Maria: Running Free
Geer, Ellen: Hard Traveling; Harold and Maude; On the Nickel
Geer, Will: Bandolero!; Billion Dollar Hobo, The; Black Like Me; Broken Arrow; Brother John; Bunco; Comanche Territory; Dear Dead Delilah; Executive Action; Intruder in the Dust; Jeremiah Johnson; Lust for Gold; Moving Violation; My Sister, My Love (The Mafu Cage); Napoleon and Samantha; President's Analyst, The; Reivers, The; Salt of the Earth; Seconds; Thanksgiving Story, The; To Please a Lady; Winchester '73; Woman Called Moses, A
Geeson, Judy: Berserk; Brannigan; Dominique Is Dead; Doomwatch; Executioner, The; Fear in the Night (Dynasty of Fear); 10 Rillington Place; To Sir with Love; Twinsanity
Geeson, Sally: Oblong Box, The
Gefner, Deborah: Exterminator 2, The
Gegauff, Danielle: Une Partie de Plaisir (Piece of Pleasure)
Gehman, Martha: Unveiled
Gehrig, Lou: Rawhide
Gehring, Ted: Gypsy Warriors, The
Gehringer, Charlie: Life and Times of Hank Greenberg, The
Geigel, Jennifer: Violent New Breed
Geldof, Bob: Pink Floyd: The Wall
Gelfant, Alan: Next Stop Wonderland
Gelin, Manuel: One Deadly Summer
Gélin, Daniel: Iran Days of Crisis; Is Paris Burning?; Killing Cars; La Ronde; Mademoiselle Striptease; Murmur of the Heart
Gellar, Sarah Michelle: Cruel Intentions; I Know What You Did Last Summer; Scream 2
Gelt, Grant: Mutant Species
Gemma, Giuliano: Corleone; Days of Wrath; Tex and the Lord of the Deep; Unsane; Warning, The; When Women Had Tails
Gemser, Laura: Quest for the Mighty Sword; Trap Them and Kill Them
Gendron, François-Eric: Blood of the Hunter; Boyfriends and Girlfriends; Cloud Waltzing; Not a Penny More, Not a Penny Less
Gene Vincent and His Blue Caps: Girl Can't Help It, The
Genesse, Bryan: Agent of Death; Armed and Deadly; Live Wire: Human Timebomb; Nightsiege-Project: Shadowchaser 2; Terminal Impact; Terminal Virus
Genest, Emile: Big Red; Incredible Journey, The; Nikki, Wild Dog of the North
Genn, Leo: Henry V; Immortal Battalion, The (The Way Ahead); Lady Chatterley's Lover; Miniver Story, The; Moby Dick; Quo Vadis (1951); Snake Pit, The; Strange Case of Dr. Jekyll and Mr. Hyde, The (1968); Ten Little Indians; Velvet Touch, The; Wooden Horse, The
Genovese, Mike: Code of Silence; Dark Angel: The Ascent; Invisible Kid, The; Triplecross
Gentile, Denise: Netherworld
Gentile, Robert: Fatally Yours; Strangers in the City
Gentle, Lili: Will Success Spoil Rock Hunter?
Gentry, Don: Breaker! Breaker!
Gentry, Mike Lloyd: Deadly Alliance
Gentry, Minnie: Georgia, Georgia
Gentry, Roger: Wizard of Mars, The
Genzel, Carrie: Virtual Seduction
Geoffrey, Paul: Excalibur
Geoffreys, Stephen: Chair, The; Fraternity Vacation; Fright Night; Heaven Help Us; Moon 44; 976-EVIL
George, Anthony: Untouchables, The: Scarface Mob
George, Betsy Lyn: Petticoat Planet
George, Chief Dan: Americathon; Cancel My Reservation; Dan Candy's Law (Alien Thunder); Harry and Tonto; Little Big Man; Outlaw Josey Wales, The; Smith!
George, Christopher: Angkor: Cambodia Express; Chisum; Cruise into Terror; Day of the Animals; Dixie Dynamite; El Dorado; Exterminator, The; Gates of Hell; Graduation Day; Grizzly; Man on a String; Pieces
George, Gladys: Flamingo Road; Hard Way, The; House Across the Bay, The; Lullaby of Broadway; Madame X; Marie Antoinette; Roaring Twenties, The
George, Gotz: Advertising Rules
George, Grace: Johnny Come Lately
George, Lynda Day: Ants!; Beyond Evil; Casino; Cruise into Terror; Day of the Animals; Junkman, The; Pieces; Young Warriors, The
George, Melissa: Limey, The
George, Rita: Hollywood Boulevard
George, Susan: Die Screaming, Marianne; Dirty Mary, Crazy Larry; Dr. Jekyll and Mr. Hyde; Enter the Ninja; House That Mary Bought, The; House Where Evil Dwells, The; Jack the Ripper; Jigsaw Man, The; Lightning, the White Stallion; Mandingo; Out of Season; Small Town in Texas, A; Sonny and Jed; Straw Dogs; Summer Heat; That Summer of White Roses; Tintorera; Tomorrow Never Comes; Venom
Georgeson, Tom: Fish Called Wanda, A; No Surrender
Georges-Picot, Olga: Children of Rage
Geralds, Jim: Le Voyage Imaginaire
Gerard, Charles: Bandits; Happy New Year (1973) (La Bonne Année)
Gerard, Danny: Robot in the Family
Gerard, George: Metamorphosis: The Alien Factor
Gerard, Gil: Buck Rogers in the 25th Century; Final Notice; Soldier's Fortune; Stepdaughter, The
Gerardi, Joan: Bikini Bistro
Geray, Steven: French Line, The; Gilda; Seventh Cross, The
Gerber, Jay: Cartier Affair, The
Gere, Richard: American Gigolo; And the Band Played On; Autumn in New York; Beyond the Limit; Bloodbrothers; Breathless; Cotton Club, The; Days of Heaven; Dr. T and the Women; Final Analysis; First Knight; Internal Affairs; Intersection; Jackal, The; King David; Looking for Mr. Goodbar; Miles from Home; Mothman Prophecies, The; Mr. Jones; No Mercy; Officer and a Gentleman, An; Power (1986); Pretty Woman; Primal Fear; Red Corner; Report to the Commissioner; Rhapsody in August; Runaway Bride; Sommersby; Strike Force; Unfaithful; Yanks
Geret, Georges: Diary of a Chambermaid; Very Curious Girl, A
Gerini, Claudia: Iris Blond
German, Gretchen: Man Called Sarge, A
Germann, Greg: Down to Earth; Joe Somebody; Sweet November (2001)
Gerrish, Frank: Partners in Crime
Gerroll, Daniel: Big Business; Eyes of a Witness
Gerron, Kurt: Blue Angel, The
Gerry, Alex: Bellboy, The
Gerry and the Pacemakers: That Was Rock
Gersak, Savina: Iron Warrior; Lone Runner; Midnight Ride
Gershon, Gina: Black & White (1998); Bound; Driven; Face/Off; Flinch; Guinevere; Insider, The; Joey Breaker; Legalese; Lies & Whispers; Love Matters; Lulu on the Bridge; One Tough Cop; Palmetto; Red Heat; Showgirls; This World, Then the Fireworks; Voodoo Dawn
Gerson, Betty Lou: Red Menace, The
Gerstein, Lisa: My Life's in Turnaround
Gerstle, Frank: Gang Busters
Gert, Valeska: Diary of a Lost Girl
Gertz, Jami: Crossroads; Don't Tell Her It's Me; Jersey Girl; Less Than Zero; Listen to Me; Lost Boys, The; Quicksilver; Renegades; Seven Girlfriends; Sibling Rivalry; Silence Like Glass; Solarbabies; Twister
Gesner, Zen: Wish Me Luck

Gilliam, Seth: Assault at West Point; Courage Under Fire; Jefferson in Paris; Tar
Gilliam, Terry: And Now for Something Completely Different; Life of Brian; Monty Python and the Holy Grail; Monty Python Live at the Hollywood Bowl; Monty Python's Flying Circus (TV Series); Monty Python's the Meaning of Life
Gillian, Tony: Ten Benny
Gilliard Jr., Lawrence: Lotto Land; Straight out of Brooklyn; Survive the Night
Gillies, Fiona: Frankenstein
Gilliland, Richard: Bug; Challenge of a Lifetime; Happy Hour; Killing in a Small Town; Star Kid
Gillin, Hugh: Psycho II; Psycho III
Gillin, Linda: Terror at the Red Wolf Inn (Terror House)
Gilling, Rebecca: Blue Lighting, The; Dangerous Life, A; Heaven Tonight; Naked Country, The; Return to Eden
Gillis, Ann: Adventures of Tom Sawyer, The; Little Men; Peck's Bad Boy with the Circus
Gillis, Jamie: Night of the Zombies
Gillmer, Caroline: Sorrento Beach
Gilman, Kenneth: Bedroom Eyes; Nights in White Satin; Scavengers
Gilmore, Craig: Living End, The
Gilmore, Danny: Lilies
Gilmore, Helen: Tom Sawyer
Gilmore, Margalo: Peter Pan; Woman's World
Gilmore, Virginia: Western Union
Gilmour, Ian: Dangerous Summer, A
Gilpin, Peri: Laughter on the 23rd Floor; Spring Forward
Gilyard, Clarence: Left Behind
Gilyard Jr., Clarence: One Riot, One Ranger; Walker: Texas Ranger
Giminez-Cacho, Daniel: Deep Crimson
Gimpel, Erica: Fence, The
Ging, Jack: Dear Detective; High Plains Drifter; Where the Red Fern Grows
Gingold, Hermione: Adventures of Sadie; Garbo Talks; Gay Purr-ee; Gigi; Music Man, The; Naked Edge, The
Ginsberg, Allen: Kerouac
Ginty, Robert: Act, The; Bounty Hunter; Coming Home; Exterminator, The; Exterminator 2, The; Harley Davidson and the Marlboro Man; Loverboy; Madhouse; Out on Bail; Programmed to Kill; Vietnam, Texas; Warrior of the Lost World
Giocante, Vahina: Marie Baie Des Anges
Giordana, Daniela: Badlands Drifter (Challenge of McKenna); Have a Nice Funeral
Giordano, Elizabeth: Warhead
Giorgi, Eleonora: Beyond Obsession; Inferno; Nudo di Donna (Portrait of a Woman, Nude); To Forget Venice
Giorgiade, Nick: Untouchables, The: Scarface Mob
Girachi, Mary: Miss Lulu Bett
Giradot, Annie: Organizer, The
Girard, Joe: Mystery of the Hooded Horsemen
Girard, Remy: Boys, The (1997)
Girard, Simone Elise: After the Storm
Girardot, Annie: Jupiter's Thigh; La Vie Continue; Le Cavaleur; Les Misérables; Love and the Frenchwoman; Mussolini and I; Rocco & His Brothers
Girardot, Hippolyte: Barjo; Jump Tomorrow
Giraud, Claude: Phedre
Giraud, Roland: Three Men and a Cradle
Giraudeau, Bernard: Bilitis; L'Année des Meduses; Passion of Love
Girolami, Enio: Final Defeat, The
Giron, Ali: Dead Man Out
Girotti, Massimo: Ossessione; Passion of Love; Red Tent, The; Stateline Motel; Teorema; Torture Chamber of Baron Blood, The; Wanton Contessa, The
Gish, Annabeth: Beautiful Girls; Desert Bloom; Don't Look Back; Hiding Out; Last Supper, The; Mystic Pizza; Scarlett; Shag, the Movie; SLC Punk; Steel; True Women; When He's Not a Stranger; Wyatt Earp
Gish, Dorothy: Hearts of the World; Home, Sweet Home (1914); Judith of Bethulia; Orphans of the Storm
Gish, Lillian: Birth of a Nation, The; Broken Blossoms; Comedians, The; Commandos Strike at Dawn; D. W. Griffith Triple Feature; Duel in the Sun; Follow Me, Boys!; Great Chase, The; Hambone and Hillie; Hearts of the World; His Double Life; Hobson's Choice; Home, Sweet Home (1914); Intolerance; Judith of Bethulia; Night of the Hunter; Orphans of the Storm; Portrait of Jennie; Scarlet Letter, The; Sweet Liberty; True Heart Susie; Unforgiven, The (1960); Way Down East; Wedding, A (1978); Whales of August, The; White Sister, The; Wind, The
Gisick, Michael: Darkness
Givens, Robin: Beverly Hills Madam; Blankman; Boomerang; Foreign Student; Penthouse, The; Rage in Harlem, A; Women of Brewster Place, The
Gladstone, Dana: Body Language; Presidio, The
Glanzelius, Anton: My Life as a Dog
Glas, Uschi: Tower of Screaming Virgins, The
Glaser, Étienne: MozartBrothers, The
Glaser, Paul Michael: Phobia; Princess Daisy
Glass, Ned: Dick Tracy Returns; Experiment in Terror; Kid Galahad; Requiem for a Heavyweight (1956) (Television); Street Music
Glassbourg, Adah: Rubberface
Glasser, Isabel: Circumstances Unknown; Forever Young; Pure Country; Surgeon, The; Tactical Assault
Glasser, Phillip: American Tail, An
Glaudini, Robert: Parasite
Glave, Matthew: Huntress, The
Glazer, Eugene: Substitute, The
Glazer, Steven: Aileen Wuornos: Selling of a Serial Killer
Gleason, Jackie: All Through the Night; Don't Drink the Water; Honeymooners, The: Lost Episodes (TV Series); Honeymooners, The (TV Series); Hustler, The; Izzy & Moe; Mr. Billion; Mr. Halpern and Mr. Johnson; Nothing in Common; Papa's Delicate Condition; Requiem for a Heavyweight (1962); Return of October, The; Smokey and the Bandit; Smokey and the Bandit II; Smokey and the Bandit III; Soldier in the Rain; Springtime in the Rockies; Sting II, The; Toy, The
Gleason, James: Arsenic and Old Lace; Bishop's Wife, The; Clock, The; Ex-Mrs. Bradford, The; Falcon Takes Over, The; Flying Fool, The; Footlight Serenade; Free Soul, A; Guy Named Joe, A; Helldorado; Here Comes Mr. Jordan; I'll See You in My Dreams; Jackpot, The; Key to the City; Last Hurrah, The; Manhattan Merry-Go-Round; Miss Grant Takes Richmond; Night of the Hunter; Return of October, The; Suddenly; Tree Grows in Brooklyn, A; Tycoon; What Price Glory; Yellow Cab Man, The
Gleason, Joanna: Edie & Pen; For Richer, for Poorer; F/X 2: The Deadly Art of Illusion; If These Walls Could Talk; Road Ends
Gleason, Lucille: Rhythm on the Range
Gleason, Paul: Breakfast Club, The; Brutal Truth, The; Challenge of a Lifetime; Day at the Beach; Die Hard; Doc Savage . . . , The Man of Bronze; Ewoks: The Battle for Endor; Forever Lulu; Fourth Story; Ghost Chase; Johnny Be Good; Komodo; Morgan Stewart's Coming Home; Night Game; No Code of Conduct; Pursuit of D. B. Cooper; Rich Girl; Running Cool; Supercarrier
Gleason, Russell: Flying Fool, The
Gledhill, Nicholas: Careful He Might Hear You
Gleeson, Brendan: Braveheart; General, The; Harrison's Flowers; I Went Down; Lake Placid; Mission: Impossible 2; Turbulence
Glen, Iain: Fools of Fortune; Lara Croft: Tomb Raider; Mountains of the Moon
Glenn, Cody: Border Shootout
Glenn, Evan: Too Smooth
Glenn, Roy: Carmen Jones
Glenn, Scott: Absolute Power; Angels Hard as They Come; As Summers Die; Baby Maker, The; Backdraft; Carla's Song; Challenge, The; Courage Under Fire; Edie & Pen; Extreme Justice; Fighting Mad; Firestorm; Hunt for Red October, The; Intrigue; Keep, The; Man on Fire; Miss Firecracker; More American Graffiti; My Heroes Have Always Been Cowboys; Night of the Running Man; Off Limits; Past Tense; Personal Best; Reckless; Right Stuff, The; River, The; Seventh Stream, The; Shadow Hunter; Shrieking, The; Silence of the Lambs; Silverado; Slaughter of the Innocents; Spy Within, The; Tall Tale: The Unbelievable Ad-

ventures of Pecos Bill; Training Day; Urban Cowboy; Verne Miller; Vertical Limit; Wild Geese II; Women & Men 2
Gless, Sharon: Hardhat and Legs; Hobson's Choice; Revenge of the Stepford Wives; Star Chamber, The; Tales of the Unexpected
Glib, Lesley: Lemora—Lady Dracula
Glick, Stacey: Brighton Beach Memoirs
Glogovac, Nebojsa: Cabaret Balkan; Vukovar
Glover, Brian: Alien 3; Kafka; Leon the Pig Farmer; McGuffin, The; Snow White: A Tale of Terror
Glover, Bruce: Big Bad Mama II; Ghost Town; Hider in the House; Night of the Scarecrow
Glover, Crispin: Back to the Future; Charlie's Angels; Chasers; Even Cowgirls Get the Blues; Fast Sofa; Hotel Room; Little Noises; Nurse Betty; River's Edge; Rubin & Ed; Twister; What's Eating Gilbert Grape?; Wild at Heart
Glover, Danny: America's Dream; Angels in the Outfield; Bat 21; Beloved; Bopha!; Buffalo Soldiers; Color Purple, The; Dead Man Out; Flight of the Intruder, The; Freedom Song; Gone Fishin'; Grand Canyon; Lethal Weapon; Lethal Weapon 2; Lethal Weapon 3; Lethal Weapon 4; Lonesome Dove; Mandela; Maverick; Memorial Day; Operation Dumbo Drop; Our Friend, Martin; Out; Places in the Heart; Predator 2; Pure Luck; Rage in Harlem, A; Raisin in the Sun, A; Royal Tenenbaums, The; Saint of Fort Washington, The; Silverado; Switchback; 3 A.M.; To Sleep with Anger; Witness
Glover, John: Apology; Assault at West Point; Automatic; Breaking Point; Chocolate War, The; Dead on the Money; Early Frost, An; Ed & His Dead Mother; El Diablo; 52 Pick-Up; Flash of Green, A; Gremlins 2: The New Batch; Killing Affair, A; Last Embrace, The; Love! Valour! Compassion!; Masquerade; Meet the Hollowheads; Night of the Running Man; Rocket Gibraltar; Scrooged; Season of Giants, A; Something Special; Traveling Man; What Ever Happened To … ?
Glover, Julian: Five Million Years to Earth; Hearts of Fire; Heat and Dust; Infiltrator, The; Mandela; Story of Jacob and Joseph, The; Theatre of Death; Treasure Island; Tusks
Glover, Kara: Caribe
Glover, Mark: Violent New Breed
Glover, Savion: Bamboozled; Bojangles; Wall, The (1998) (U.S.)
Glyn-Jones, David: Air Bud: World Pup
Glynn, Carlin: Continental Divide; Night Game; Trip to Bountiful, The
Go, Hiromi: Gonza the Spearman; Samurai Cowboy
Gobel, George: Alice Through the Looking Glass; Better Late than Never; Birds and the Bees, The; I Married a Woman; Young at Heart Comedians, The
Gobold, Cathy: Alex
Gocke, Justin: Witching of Ben Wagner, The
Godard, Jean-Luc: Contempt; First Name: Carmen
Godard, Tracy: Shadow Creature
Goddard, John: Naked Youth
Goddard, Mark: Blue Sunshine; Lost in Space (1998); Lost in Space (TV Series)
Goddard, Paulette: Cat and the Canary, The; Diary of a Chambermaid; Ghost Breakers; Great Dictator, The; Modern Times; Northwest Mounted Police; Pot O' Gold; Reap the Wild Wind; Second Chorus; So Proudly We Hail; Unconquered; Women, The; Young in Heart, The
Goddard, Trevor: Dead Tides; Fast Money; Illegal in Blue
Godfrey, Arthur: Flatbed Annie and Sweetie Pie: Lady Truckers; Glass Bottom Boat, The; Great Bank Hoax, The
Godfrey, Renee: Terror by Night
Godfrey, Terrie: Majorettes, The
Godin, Jacques: Being at Home with Claude; Man Inside, The
Godreche, Judith: Entropy; Man in the Iron Mask, The
Godunov, Alexander: Die Hard; Dogfighters, The; Money Pit, The; Runestone; Waxwork II: Lost in Time; Witness
Goethals, Angela: V. I. Warshawski
Goetz, Carl: Tom Sawyer
Goetz, Peter Michael: Beer; Father of the Bride Part II; Jumpin' Jack Flash; King Kong Lives; Tagget
Goetz, Scot: Living End, The
Goetzke, Bernhard: Destiny; Kriemhilde's Revenge; Siegfried
Goff, Norris: Dreaming Out Loud; So This Is Washington
Going, Joanna: Children of the Dust; Eden; Heaven; Inventing the Abbotts; Keys to Tulsa; Little City; Phantoms
Goiz, Silvia: La Ciudad
Golan, Gila: Catch as Catch Can; Our Man Flint; Valley of Gwangi
Gold, Jimmy: Frozen Limits, The
Gold, Tracey: Dance 'Til Dawn; Dirty Little Secret; Lots of Luck; Perfect Daughter, The; Shoot the Moon
Goldberg, Adam: All Over the Guy; Beautiful Mind, A; Dazed and Confused; Fast Sofa; Prophecy, The (1995); Saving Private Ryan
Goldberg, Jakub: Two Men and a Wardrobe
Goldberg, Whoopi: Adventures of Rocky and Bullwinkle, The; Alan Smithee Film, An—Burn Hollywood Burn; Alice in Wonderland; Associate, The; Bogus; Boys on the Side; Burglar (U.S.); Call Me Claus; Clara's Heart; Color Purple, The; Corrina, Corrina; Deep End of the Ocean, The; Eddie; Fatal Beauty; Ghost (1990); Ghosts of Mississippi; Homer and Eddie; How Stella Got Her Groove Back; In the Gloaming; Jumpin' Jack Flash; Kingdom Come; Kiss Shot; Little Rascals, The; Long Walk Home, The; Made in America; Monkeybone; Moonlight and Valentino; Naked in New York; National Lampoon's Loaded Weapon 1; Our Friend, Martin; Pagemaster, The; Player, The; Rat Race; Rodgers & Hammerstein's Cinderella; Sarafina!; Sister Act; Sister Act 2: Back in the Habit; Soapdish; Star Trek: Generations; Telephone, The; Theodore Rex
Goldblum, Jeff: Adventures of Buckaroo Banzai, The; Between the Lines; Beyond Suspicion; Beyond Therapy; Big Chill, The; Cats & Dogs; Death Wish; Deep Cover; Earth Girls Are Easy; Fathers & Sons; Favor, the Watch and the Very Big Fish,The; Fly, The; Framed; Great White Hype, The; Hideaway; Holy Man; Independence Day; Into the Night; Invasion of the Body Snatchers; Jurassic Park; Lost World, The: Jurassic Park; Lush Life; Mr. Frost; Next Stop, Greenwich Village; Nine Months; Powder; Rehearsal for Murder; Right Stuff, The; Shooting Elizabeth; Silverado; Strange Tales: Ray Bradbury Theater; Tall Guy, The; Thank God It's Friday; Threshold; Transylvania 6-5000; Trigger Happy (Mad Dog Time); Twisted Obsession; Vibes
Golden, Annie: American Astronaut, The; Forever Lulu; Hair; National Lampoon's Class of '86
Golden, Rachel: I Married a Vampire
Golden II, Norman D.: Cop and a Half
Goldin, Ricky Paul: Going Overboard; Hyper Sapian: People from Another Star
Golding, Meta: Quiet Days in Hollywood
Goldman, Philippe: Small Change
Goldoni, Lelia: Hysteria; Theatre of Death
Goldsby, Matthew: Student Bodies
Goldsmith, Clio: Cricket, The; Gift, The; Heat of Desire; Miss Right
Goldsmith, Jonathan: Phantom of the Mall—Eric's Revenge
Goldstein, Jenette: Aliens; Dead to Rights; Near Dark
Goldthwait, Bob: Burglar (U.S.); Freaked; Hot to Trot; One Crazy Summer; Police Academy 4: Citizens on Patrol; Police Academy III: Back in Training; Scrooged; Shakes the Clown; Sweethearts
Goldwyn, Tony: American Rhapsody, An; Bounce; Boys Next Door, The; Doomsday Gun; Ghost (1990); Iran Days of Crisis; Kiss the Girls; Kuffs; Last Word, The; Lesser Evil, The; Love Matters; Pelican Brief, The; Reckless; 6th Day, The; Substance of Fire, The; Taking the Heat; Traces of Red; Trouble on the Corner; Truman; Woman of Independent Means, A
Goleen, Frank Rozelaar: Goodnight, God Bless
Golino, Valeria: Big Top Pee-Wee; Clean Slate (1994); Detective School Dropouts; Four Rooms; Hot Shots; Hot Shots Part Deux; Immortal Beloved; Indian Runner, The; John Carpenter's Escape from L.A.; King's Whore, The; Occasional Hell, An; Rain Man; Somebody Is Waiting; Spanish Judges; Torrents of Spring; Year of the Gun
Golisano, Francesco: Miracle in Milan
Golonka, Arlene: Foxtrap; Hang 'em High; Last Married Couple in America, The; Survival Game
Golovine, Marina: Olivier, Olivier

Golubkina, Maria: Adam's Rib
Gombell, Minna: Block-Heads; Doomed Caravan; Pagan Love Song
Gomez, Carlos: Fools Rush In; Hostile Intentions
Gomez, Consuelo: El Mariachi
Gomez, Jamie: Silencer, The
Gomez, Jose Luis: Roads to the South
Gomez, Paloma: Valentina
Gomez, Panchito: Mi Vida Loca; Run for the Roses (Thoroughbred)
Gomez, Thomas: But Not for Me; Casbah; Force of Evil; Kim; Macao; Pittsburgh; Pony Soldier; Sherlock Holmes and the Voice of Terror; Singapore; Sorrowful Jones; That Midnight Kiss; Trapeze; Who Done It?
Gonzales, Barbara: Lotto Land
Gonzales, Dan Rivera: Men with Guns
Gonzales, Jerry: Calle 54
Gonzales, Peter: Fellini's Roma
Gonzalez, Clifton: 187
González, Rubén: Buena Vista Social Club, The
González González, Clifton: Wonderful Ice Cream Suit, The
Good, Maurice: Five Million Years to Earth
Goodall, Caroline: Casualties; Disclosure; Ring of Scorpio; Schindler's List; Silver Stallion, The; Sorrento Beach; Webber's World (At Home with the Webbers); White Squall
Goodall, Louise: My Name is Joe
Goodfellow, Joan: Buster and Billie; Flash of Green, A
Gooding, Omar: Baby Boy
Gooding Jr., Cuba: As Good as It Gets; Boyz N the Hood; Chill Factor; Daybreak (1993); Few Good Men, A; Gladiator; Instinct; Jerry Maguire; Judgment Night; Lightning Jack; Losing Isaiah; Men of Honor; Murder of Crows, A; Outbreak; Pearl Harbor; Rat Race; Snow Dogs; Tuskegee Airmen, The; What Dreams May Come
Goodliffe, Michael: One That Got Away, The
Goodman, Benny: Gang's All Here, The; Song Is Born, A
Goodman, Dody: Cool As Ice; Private Resort; Splash
Goodman, Greer: Tao of Steve, The
Goodman, John: Adventures of Rocky and Bullwinkle, The; Always; Arachnophobia; Babe, The (1992); Barton Fink; Big Easy, The; Big Lebowski, The; Blues Brothers 2000; Born Yesterday; Borrowers, The; Bringing Out the Dead; Coyote Ugly; Everybody's All-American; Fallen; Flintstones, The; Jack Bull, The; King Ralph; Kingfish: A Story of Huey P. Long; Matinee; Mother Night; My First Mister; One Night at McCool's; Pie in the Sky; Punchline; Raising Arizona; Revenge of the Nerds; Sea of Love; Stella; Storytelling; Streetcar Named Desire, A; True Stories; What Planet Are You From?; Wrong Guys, The
Goodman, Scott: MVP2: Most Vertical Primate
Goodrich, Deborah: Remote Control; Survival Game
Goodrow, Garry: Almos' a Man; Cardiac Arrest; Connection, The (1961); Glen and Randa; Steelyard Blues
Goodwin, Bill: Bathing Beauty; House of Horrors; It's a Great Feeling; Jolson Sings Again; Jolson Story, The; So Proudly We Hail; Spellbound
Goodwin, Harold: Abbott and Costello Meet the Keystone Kops; Tarzan and the Golden Lion
Goodwin, Kia Joy: Strapped
Goodwin, Laurel: Girls! Girls! Girls!; Papa's Delicate Condition
Goodwin, Michael: Sizzle
Goorjian, Michael A.: SLC Punk; Something More
Gora, Claudio: Catch as Catch Can
Goranson, Alicia: Boys Don't Cry
Gorbe, Janos: Round-Up, The
Gorcey, Bernard: Bowery Boys, The (Series)
Gorcey, David: Bowery Boys, The (Series); Pride of the Bowery
Gorcey, Elizabeth: Trouble with Dick, The
Gorcey, Leo: Bowery Boys, The (Series); Boys of the City; Pride of the Bowery; Road to Zanzibar
Gordon, Barry: Body Slam; Girl Can't Help It, The; Hands of a Stranger; Thousand Clowns, A
Gordon, Bobby: Big Business Girl
Gordon, Bruce: Curse of the Undead; Elephant Boy; Untouchables, The: Scarface Mob
Gordon, C. Henry: Charlie Chan at the Wax Museum; Gabriel over the White House; Tarzan's Revenge
Gordon, Carl: Piano Lesson, The
Gordon, Claire: Konga
Gordon, Colin: One That Got Away, The
Gordon, Dexter: Round Midnight
Gordon, Don: Beast Within, The; Borrower, The; Bullitt; Education of Sonny Carson, The; Final Conflict, The; Mack, The; Papillon; Skin Deep; Slaughter; Warbus; Z.P.G. (Zero Population Growth)
Gordon, Eve: Honey, We Shrunk Ourselves; I'll Be Home for Christmas; Paradise; Secret Passion of Robert Clayton, The; Switched at Birth
Gordon, Gale: All in a Night's Work; Our Miss Brooks (TV Series); Speedway; 30-Foot Bride of Candy Rock, The
Gordon, Gavin: Bat, The; Bitter Tea of General Yen, The; Matchmaker, The; Romance; Scarlet Empress, The
Gordon, Gerald: Force Five; Judas Project, The
Gordon, Hannah: Oh, Alfie
Gordon, Hannah Taylor: Jakob the Liar
Gordon, Jade: Sugar Town
Gordon, Jim: To Catch a Yeti
Gordon, Joyce: Killing 'Em Softly
Gordon, Julius: D.P.
Gordon, Keith: Back to School; Christine; Dressed to Kill; Home Movies; Kent State; Legend of Billie Jean, The; Silent Rebellion; Static
Gordon, Leo: Haunted Palace, The; Hondo; Hostile Guns; Intruder, The (1961); Maverick; Maverick (TV Series); McLintock!; My Name Is Nobody; Rage; Riot in Cell Block Eleven; Ten Wanted Men
Gordon, Mary: Double Wedding; Hound of the Baskervilles, The; Pearl of Death, The; Pot O' Gold; Sherlock Holmes and the Secret Weapon; Sherlock Holmes and the Voice of Terror; Texas Cyclone
Gordon, Philip: Bridge to Nowhere; Came a Hot Friday
Gordon, Robert: Loveless, The; Tom Sawyer
Gordon, Ruth: Abe Lincoln in Illinois; Action in the North Atlantic; Any Which Way You Can; Big Bus, The; Don't Go to Sleep; Every Which Way But Loose; Harold and Maude; Inside Daisy Clover; Lord Love a Duck; Maxie; Mugsy's Girls; My Bodyguard; North Star, The (1943); Prince of Central Park, The; Rosemary's Baby; Scavenger Hunt; Trouble with Spies, The; Two-Faced Woman; Whatever Happened to Aunt Alice?; Where's Poppa?
Gordon, Serena: Tale of Two Cities, A
Gordon, Stuart: Age of Innocence, The
Gordon, Susan: Picture Mommy Dead
Gordon-Levitt, Joseph: Along for the Ride; Angels in the Outfield; Great Elephant Escape, The; Holy Matrimony; Juror, The
Gore, Sandy: Brides of Christ
Gorg, Gwyn: Living the Blues
Gorham, Mel: Blue in the Face; Curdled
Goring, Marius: Barefoot Contessa, The; Circle of Danger; Ill Met by Moonlight; Night Ambush; Paris Express, The; Red Shoes, The; Spy in Black, The; Zeppelin
Gorkum, Harry Van: Escape Under Pressure
Gorman, Annette: Texas John Slaughter: Stampede at Bitter Creek
Gorman, Cliff: Angel; Boys in the Band, The; Cops and Robbers; Down Came a Blackbird; Hoffa; Justine; Night and the City; Night of the Juggler; Strike Force
Gorme, Eydie: Alice Through the Looking Glass
Gormley, Felim: Commitments, The
Gorney, Karen Lynn: Saturday Night Fever
Gorny, Frederic: Wild Reeds
Gorshin, Frank: Batman; Beverly Hills Bodysnatchers; Bloodmoon; Goliath Awaits; Hail Caesar; Hollywood Vice Squad; Hot Resort; Invasion of the Saucer Men; Meteor Man; Midnight; Sky Heist; Studs Lonigan; Sweet Justice; That Darn Cat; Underground Aces
Gorski, Tamara: Lost World, The; Picture Windows; Return to the Lost World; Striking Poses
Gortner, Marjoe: American Ninja III; Bobbie Jo and the Outlaw; Food of the Gods; Hellhole; Jungle Warriors; Marjoe; Pray

for the Wildcats; Sidewinder 1; Star Crash; Survivalist, The; Viva Knievel; Wild Bill
Gorton, Brad: Get Real
Gosch, Christopher: Get Real
Gosden, Freeman: Check and Double Check
Gosfield, Maurice: Sgt. Bilko (TV Series)
Gosling, Ryan: Murder by Numbers (2002)
Goss, David: Hollywood Cop
Gosselaar, Mark Paul: Dead Man on Campus; Kounterfeit; Necessary Parties; Specimen; Twisted Love; White Wolves: A Cry in the Wild II
Gossett Jr., Louis: Aces: Iron Eagle III; Bram Stoker's The Mummy; Carolina Skeletons; Choirboys, The; Cover-Up; Curse of the Starving Class; Dangerous Relations; Deep, The; Diggstown; Don't Look Back: The Story of Leroy "Satchel" Paige; El Diablo; Enemy Mine; Firewalker; Flashfire; Good Man in Africa, A; Goodbye, Miss 4th of July; Guardian, The; Highwayman, The; In His Father's Shoes; Inside; Inspectors, The; Iron Eagle; Iron Eagle II; Iron Eagle IV; It Rained All Night the Day I Left; It's Good to Be Alive; Jaws 3; J.D.'s Revenge; Josephine Baker Story, The; Keeper of the City; Laughing Policeman, The; Lazarus Syndrome, The; Little Ladies of the Night; Managua; Monolith; Murder on the Bayou; Officer and a Gentleman, An; Principal, The; Punisher, The; Raisin in the Sun, A; Return to Lonesome Dove; Roots; Roots—The Gift; Run for the Dream; Sadat; Skin Game (1971); Strange Justice; Sudie & Simpson; Terminal Countdown; Toy Soldiers; Travels with My Aunt; White Dawn, The; Zooman
Gostukhin, Vladimir: Close to Eden
Gotestam, Staffan: Brothers Lionheart, The
Gothard, Michael: King Arthur, The Young Warlord; Lifeforce; Scream and Scream Again; Valley, The
Gottfried, Gilbert: Aladdin & the King of Thieves; Problem Child; Silk Degrees
Gottli, Michael: Tales from the Gimli Hospital
Gottlieb, Carl: Cannonball
Gottschalk, Thomas: Driving Me Crazy; Ring of the Musketeer
Goudal, Jetta: White Gold
Goude, Ingrid: Killer Shrews, The
Gough, Lloyd: All My Sons; Green Hornet, The (TV Series); It's Good to Be Alive; Rancho Notorious
Gough, Michael: Advocate, The; Age of Innocence, The; Anna Karenina; Batman; Batman & Robin; Batman Returns; Berserk; Caravaggio; Crucible of Horror; Curse of the Crimson Altar; Horror Hospital; Horror of Dracula; Horrors of the Black Museum; Horse's Mouth, The; Konga; Out of Africa; Phantom of the Opera; Rob Roy, the Highland Rogue; Savage Messiah; Sleepy Hollow; Sword and the Rose, The (1953); They Came from Beyond Space; To the Lighthouse
Gould, Ben: Frankenstein Reborn!
Gould, Dana: Love Bug, The
Gould, Elliott: American History X; Beyond Justice; Big Hit, The; Bob & Carol & Ted & Alice; Boy Called Hate, A; Bugsy; Capricorn One; Conspiracy: The Trial of the Chicago 8; Cover Me; Dangerous, The (1984); Dangerous Love; Dead Men Don't Die; Devil and Max Devlin, The; Dirty Tricks; Escape to Athena; Falling in Love Again; Getting Straight; Glass Shield, The; Harry and Walter Go to New York; Hitz; I Love My Wife; I Will, I Will … for Now; Inside Out; Johns; Kill Shot; Lady Vanishes, The; Last Flight of Noah's Ark; Lemon Sisters, The; Lethal Obsession; Little Murders; Long Goodbye, The; M*A*S*H; Matilda; Mean Johnny Barrows; Muppet Movie, The; Muppets Take Manhattan, The; Naked Face, The; Night They Raided Minsky's, The; Night Visitor (1989); November Conspiracy, The; Ocean's Eleven (2001); Over the Brooklyn Bridge; Quick, Let's Get Married; S*P*Y*S; Silent Partner, The; Telephone, The; Vanishing Act; Wet and Wild Summer; Whiffs
Gould, Harold: Better Late than Never; Big Bus, The; Brown's Requiem; Fourth Wise Man, The; Front Page, The; Gambler, The; Gambler, Part II—The Adventure Continues, The; How to Break Up a Happy Divorce; Love and Death; Man in the Santa Claus Suit, The; My Giant; One and Only, The; Playing for Keeps; Red Light Sting, The; Romero; Seems Like Old Times; Sting, The
Gould, Jason: Prince of Tides, The
Goulet, Arthur: Silver Blaze
Goulet, Robert: Based on an Untrue Story; Gay Purr-ee; Naked Gun 2 1/2, The
Gourmet, Olivier: La Promesse
Goutine, Andrei: Luna Park
Gow, David: Hiroshima
Gowa, Siqin: Day the Sun Turned Cold, The
Gower, Andre: Monster Squad, The
Gowland, Gibson: Blind Husbands; Greed; Hell Harbor
Goya, Chantal: Masculine Feminine
Gozzi, Patricia: Sundays and Cybèle
Graas, John Christian: Philadelphia Experiment 2, The
Grable, Betty: Beautiful Blonde from Bashful Bend, The; College Swing; Dolly Sisters, The; Down Argentine Way; Farmer Takes a Wife, The; Follow the Fleet; Footlight Serenade; Four Jills in a Jeep; Gay Divorcée, The; Give Me a Sailor; Hold 'em Jail; How to Marry a Millionaire; I Wake Up Screaming; Moon over Miami; Mother Wore Tights; Pin-Up Girl; Song of the Islands; Springtime in the Rockies; Three Broadway Girls; Tin Pan Alley; Wabash Avenue; Yank in the RAF, A
Grabol, Sofie: Mifune
Grace, Anna: Girls Town
Grace, Carol: Gangster Story
Grace, Nickolas: Max Headroom; Robin Hood and the Sorcerer; Robin Hood: Herne's Son; Robin Hood: The Swords of Wayland; Salome's Last Dance; Solomon and Sheba; Tom & Viv
Gracen, Elizabeth: Final Mission; Lower Level
Grady, Ed L.: Last Game, The
Graf, David: Police Academy 5: Assignment: Miami Beach; Police Academy 4: Citizens on Patrol; Police Academy II: Their First Assignment; Police Academy III: Back in Training; Police Academy 6: City Under Siege; Police Academy: Mission to Moscow; Roseanne: An Unauthorized Biography; Suture
Graf, David Alan: Pups
Graff, Ilene: Ladybugs; South Pacific (2001)
Graff, Todd: Dominick and Eugene; Fly by Night; Framed; Opportunity Knocks
Graham, Bill: Bugsy
Graham, Cameron: Dream House
Graham, Currie: Survive the Night
Graham, Gary: Alien Nation, Dark Horizon; Arrogant, The; Dirty Dozen, The: The Deadly Mission; Last Warrior, The; Presence, The; Robot Jox; Steel
Graham, Gerrit: Annihilators, The; Bobbie Jo and the Outlaw; Break, The; Cannonball; Child's Play 2; C.H.U.D. II (Bud the C.H.U.D.); Demon Seed; Game of Love, The; Greetings; Home Movies; It's Alive III: Island of the Alive; Love Matters; National Lampoon's Class Reunion; National Lampoon's Favorite Deadly Sins; Philadelphia Experiment 2, The; Ratboy; Ratings Game, The; Son of Blob (Beware! The Blob); Spaceship (Naked Space); Terror Vision; Used Cars
Graham, Heather: Austin Powers: The Spy Who Shagged Me; Boogie Nights; Bowfinger; Diggstown; Don't Do It; Drugstore Cowboy; Entertaining Angels; From Hell; Guilty as Charged; License to Drive; Lost in Space (1998); Nowhere; O Pioneers!; Say It Isn't So; Shout (1991); Sidewalks of New York (2001); Six Degrees of Separation; Swingers; Terrified
Graham, Kirsty: Loch Ness
Graham, Lauren: One True Thing
Graham, Marcus: Dangerous Game (1990)
Graham, Ronny: New Faces; Ratings Game, The; World's Greatest Lover, The
Graham, Samaria: Children of the Corn IV: The Gathering
Graham, Sasha: Alien Agenda, The (TV Series); Bloodletting; Polymorph; Vicious Sweet, The
Graham, Sheilah: Girls Town
Graham, William: Just William's Luck
Grahame, Gloria: Bad and the Beautiful, The; Big Heat, The; Chilly Scenes of Winter; Crossfire; Greatest Show on Earth, The; Human Desire; In a Lonely Place; It Happened in Brooklyn; Macao; Man Who Never Was, The; Mansion of the Doomed; Merry Wives of Windsor, The; Merton of the Movies; Nesting, The; Not as a Stranger; Oklahoma!; Ride Beyond Vengeance;

Song of the Thin Man; Sudden Fear; Todd Killings, The; Woman's Secret, A
Grahame, Margot: Three Musketeers, The
Grammer, Kelsey: Anastasia; Dance 'Til Dawn; Down Periscope; 15 Minutes; Galaxies Are Colliding; Pentagon Wars, The; Real Howard Spritz, The
Gran, Albert: Hula
Grana, Sam: 90 Days
Granados, Daisy: Portrait of Teresa; Very Old Man with Enormous Wings, A
Granados, Rosario: Woman without Love, A
Grandin, Ethel: Traffic in Souls
Grandmaison, Maurice: Traffic in Souls
Grandy, Fred: Death Race 2000
Grange, Harold "Red": Galloping Ghost, The
Granger, Dorothy: Blue Montana Skies; Dangers of the Canadian Mounted
Granger, Farley: Arnold; Behave Yourself!; Deathmask; Enchantment; Hans Christian Andersen; Imagemaker, The; Man Called Noon, The; Night Flight from Moscow; Prowler, The; Purple Heart, The; Rope; Slasher; Small Town Girl; Strangers on a Train; They Call Me Trinity; They Live By Night; Wanton Contessa, The
Granger, Stewart: Adam and Evalyn; All the Brothers Were Valiant; Beau Brummell; Bhowani Junction; Caesar and Cleopatra; King Solomon's Mines; Last Hunt, The; Last Safari; Magic Bow, The; Man in Grey, The; North to Alaska; Prisoner of Zenda, The; Salome; Scaramouche; Sodom and Gomorrah; Wild Geese, The; Young Bess
Granstedt, Greta: Devil Horse, The
Grant, Barra: Daughters of Satan
Grant, Beth: Dance with Me; Dark Half, The; Rookie, The (2002)
Grant, Cary: Affair to Remember, An; Amazing Adventure; Arsenic and Old Lace; Awful Truth, The; Bachelor and the Bobby-Soxer, The; Bishop's Wife, The; Blonde Venus; Bringing Up Baby; Charade; Destination Tokyo; Every Girl Should Be Married; Father Goose; Grass Is Greener, The; Gunga Din; His Girl Friday; Holiday; Houseboat; Howards of Virginia, The; I Was a Male War Bride; I'm No Angel; In Name Only; Indiscreet; Monkey Business; Mr. Blandings Builds His Dream House; Mr. Lucky; My Favorite Wife; Night and Day; None But the Lonely Heart; North by Northwest; Notorious; Once Upon a Honeymoon; Only Angels Have Wings; Operation Petticoat; Penny Serenade; People Will Talk; Philadelphia Story, The; Pride and the Passion, The; She Done Him Wrong; Suspicion; Suzy; Sylvia Scarlett; Talk of the Town, The; That Touch of Mink; To Catch a Thief; Toast of New York, The; Topper; Walk, Don't Run
Grant, Charles: Playback
Grant, David Marshall: American Flyers; Bat 21; Breaking Point; Chamber, The; Forever Young; French Postcards; Happy Birthday, Gemini; Strictly Business
Grant, Donald: Monster in the Closet
Grant, Eldon: Big Fella
Grant, Faye: Omen IV: The Awakening; V; Vibrations
Grant, Frances: Man of the Frontier (Red River Valley); Oh! Susanna!; Traitor, The
Grant, Hugh: Awfully Big Adventure, An; Big Man; Bitter Moon; Bridget Jones's Diary; Englishman Who Went up a Hill But Came down a Mountain, The; Extreme Measures; Four Weddings and a Funeral; Impromptu; Jenny's War; Lair of the White Worm; Maurice; Mickey Blue Eyes; Night Train to Venice; Nine Months; Notting Hill; Our Sons; Remains of the Day; Rowing with the Wind; Sense and Sensibility; Sirens; Small Time Crooks
Grant, Jennifer: Savage
Grant, Kathryn: Anatomy of a Murder; Guns of Fort Petticoat; 7th Voyage of Sinbad, The
Grant, Kirby: Comin' Round the Mountain; In Society; Red River Range
Grant, Lee: Airport '77; Amati Girls, The; Balcony, The; Big Town, The; Billion for Boris, A; Buona Sera, Mrs. Campbell; Charlie Chan and the Curse of the Dragon Queen; Citizen Cohn; Damien: Omen II; Defending Your Life; Dr. T and the Women; For Ladies Only; In the Heat of the Night; Internecine Project, The; It's My Party; Little Miss Marker; Marooned; Middle of the Night; My Sister, My Love (The Mafu Cage); Plaza Suite; Portnoy's Complaint; Shampoo; Valley of the Dolls; Visiting Hours; Voyage of the Damned
Grant, Leon W.: Playing for Keeps
Grant, Micah: High Desert Kill
Grant, Ollie "Power": Black and White (2000)
Grant, Peter: Song Remains the Same, The
Grant, Rainer: Not Like Us
Grant, Richard E.: Age of Innocence, The; Bram Stoker's Dracula; Christmas Carol, A; Codename: Kyril; Cold Light of Day, The; Henry & June; How to Get Ahead in Advertising; Hudson Hawk; Jack and Sarah; L.A. Story; Little Vampire, The; Match, The; Merry War, A; Player, The; Posse; Ready to Wear; Serpent's Kiss, The; Spice World; Twelfth Night; Warlock; Withnail and I
Grant, Rodney A.: Dances with Wolves; Geronimo: An American Legend; Last Ride, The; Son of the Morning Star
Grant, Stacy: Fear, The: Halloween Night
Grant, Vince: French Exit
Grantham, Lucy: Last House on the Left
Granval, Charles: Boudu Saved from Drowning
Granville, Bonita: Ah, Wilderness; Breakfast in Hollywood; Cavalcade; Hitler's Children; Lone Ranger, The; Love Laughs at Andy Hardy; Mortal Storm, The; These Three
Grapewin, Charley: Alice Adams; Anne of Green Gables; Girl of the Golden West, The; Grapes of Wrath, The; Hell's House; Johnny Apollo; Listen, Darling; Of Human Hearts; One Frightened Night; Rhythm on the River; Three Comrades; Wizard of Oz, The
Grassle, Karen: Battered; Best Christmas Pageant Ever, The; Cocaine: One Man's Seduction; Harry's War; Little House on the Prairie (TV Series)
Grauman, Walter: Pleasure Palace
Gravel, Jacques Robert: Blind Trust (Pouvoir Intime)
Graver, Chris: Trick or Treat
Graves, Leslie: Piranha Part Two: The Spawning
Graves, Peter: Addams Family Values; Airplane!; Airplane II: The Sequel; Beginning of the End; Clonus Horror, The; Court-martial of Billy Mitchell, The; Encore; House on Haunted Hill; It Conquered the World; Killers from Space; Number One with a Bullet; Poor White Trash; President's Plane Is Missing, The; Red Planet Mars; Savannah Smiles; Sergeant Ryker; Stalag 17; Texas Across the River
Graves, Ralph: Batman and Robin (Adventures of Batmanand Robin); Dream Street; Extra Girl, The; Ladies of Leisure; That Certain Thing; Three Texas Steers
Graves, Rupert: Damage; Different for Girls; Dreaming of Joseph Lees; Fortunes of War; Handful of Dust, A; Intimate Relations; Madness of King George, The; Maurice; Mrs. Dalloway; Room with a View, A; Sweet Revenge; Where Angels Fear to Tread
Graves, Taylor: Miss Lulu Bett
Graves, Teresa: Get Christie Love!
Gravet, Fernand: Great Waltz, The
Gravina, Carla: Alfredo Alfredo; Tempter, The
Gravine, Cesare: Man Who Laughs, The
Gravy, Claudia: Yellow Hair and the Fortress of Gold
Gray, Billy: By the Light of the Silvery Moon; Day the Earth Stood Still, The; On Moonlight Bay; Seven Little Foys, The; Werewolves on Wheels
Gray, Carole: Curse of the Fly; Island of Terror
Gray, Charles: Beast Must Die, The; Devil Rides Out, The; Diamonds Are Forever; Dreams Lost, Dreams Found; Englishman Abroad, An; Jigsaw Man, The; Rocky Horror Picture Show, The; Unknown Terror, The
Gray, Coleen: Death of a Scoundrel; Kansas City Confidential; Killing, The; Kiss of Death; Leech Woman, The; Red River; Riding High; Tennessee's Partner
Gray, David Barry: Cops and Robbersons; Mr. Wonderful; Soldier Boyz
Gray, Dolores: Designing Woman; It's Always Fair Weather; Kismet; Opposite Sex, The (1956)
Gray, Donald: Flight from Vienna; Island of Desire
Gray, Dulcie: Mine Own Executioner

The; Onionhead; PT 109; Secret War of Harry Frigg, The; Sons of Katie Elder, The; Two Weeks in Another Town
Gregory, Lola: Coming Up Roses
Gregory, Mark: 1990: The Bronx Warriors; Thunder Warrior; Thunder Warrior II
Gregory, Natalie: Alice in Wonderland; Alice Through the Looking Glass
Gregory, Nick: Last Summer in the Hamptons
Gregory, Paul: Whoopee
Gregory, Tricia: Easier Said
Gregson, Joan: Sea People
Gregson, John: Captain's Table; Genevieve; Hans Brinker; Pursuit of the Graf Spee; Three Cases of Murder
Greif, Stephen: Great Riviera Bank Robbery, The
Greist, Kim: Duplicates; Homeward Bound: The Incredible Journey; Homeward Bound II: Lost in San Francisco; Houseguest; Last Exit to Earth; Manhunter; Payoff; Roswell; Throw Momma from the Train; Why Me?
Grellier, Michel: Holiday Hotel
Grenfell, Joyce: Americanization of Emily, The; Belles of St. Trinian's, The; Blue Murder at St. Trinian's; Old Dark House, The; Pickwick Papers, The
Grenier, Adrian: Adventures of Sebastian Cole, The; cecil b. Demented; Drive Me Crazy
Grenier, Zach: Swordfish
Grennan, Emmett: Killer Flick
Grenon, Macha: Dead Awake; Legends of the North; Sworn Enemies; Windsor Protocol, The
Gretsch, Joel: Legend of Bagger Vance, The
Grevill, Laurent: Camille Claudel
Grey, Anne: Number 17
Grey, Denise: Devil in the Flesh; Sputnik
Grey, Jennifer: Bloodhounds of Broadway; Case for Murder, A; Criminal Justice; Dirty Dancing; Eyes of a Witness; Ferris Bueller's Day Off; Lover's Knot; Since You've Been Gone; Stroke of Midnight; Wind (1992)
Grey, Joel: Buffalo Bill and the Indians; Cabaret; Christmas Carol, A; Come September; Dancer in the Dark; Dangerous, The (1984); Fantasticks, The; Kafka; Man on a String; Music of Chance, The; Queenie; Remo Williams: The Adventure Begins; Seven-Per-cent Solution, The; Venus Rising
Grey, Nan: House of the Seven Gables, The; Invisible Man Returns; Tower of London
Grey, Reatha: Soul Vengeance (Welcome Home Brother Charles)
Grey, Samantha: Night of the Zombies
Grey, Shirley: Hurricane Express; Mystery of the Marie Celeste, The (The Phantom Ship); Riding Tornado, The; Terror Aboard; Texas Cyclone; Uptown New York
Grey, Virginia: Another Thin Man; Big Store, The; Broadway Serenade; House of Horrors; Idiot's Delight; Jungle Jim; Love Has Many Faces; Mexican Hayride; Naked Kiss, The; Rose Tattoo, The; Slaughter Trail; Tarzan's New York Adventure; Threat, The; Whistling in the Dark
Grey, Zena: Max Keeble's Big Move
Greyeyes, Michael: Crazy Horse; Dance Me Outside; Magnificent Seven, The (TV Series)
Greyn, Clinton: Raid on Rommel
Gribbon, Harry: Ride Him Cowboy
Grieco, Richard: Apostate, The; Blackheart; Born to Run; Demolitionist, The; Heaven or Vegas; If Looks Could Kill; Inhumanoid; Mobsters; Mutual Needs; Suspicious Agenda; Tomcat: Dangerous Desires; Ultimate Deception; Vow to Kill, A; When Time Expires
Griem, Helmut: Cabaret; Children of Rage; Damned, The; Les Rendez-Vous D'Anna; Malou
Grier, David Alan: Beer; Blankman; Boomerang; In the Army Now; Jumanji; McHale's Navy; Return to Me; Tales from the Hood; 3 Strikes
Grier, Pam: Above the Law; Big Bird Cage, The; Bill and Ted's Bogus Journey; Bones; Bucktown; Class of 1999; Coffy; Drum; Fortress 2: Re-entry; Foxy Brown; Friday Foster; Ghosts of Mars; Greased Lightning; Holy Smoke; In Too Deep; Jackie Brown; John Carpenter's Escape from L.A.; Miami Vice: "The Prodigal Son"; On the Edge; Original Gangstas; Package, The; Posse; Scream, Blacula, Scream; Serial Killer; Sheba Baby; Something Wicked This Way Comes; 3 A.M.; Tough Enough; Twilight People; Vindicator, The
Grier, Rosey: Reggie's Prayer; Sophisticated Gents, The
Gries, Jonathan: Casualties; Four Eyes and Six Guns; Fright Night II; Get Shorty; Jackpot; Kill Me Again; Pucker Up and Bark Like a Dog; Running Scared
Griesemer, John: Where the Rivers Flow North
Grieve, Russ: Hills Have Eyes, The
Grifasi, Joe: Bad Medicine; Benny & Joon; Feud, The; Gentleman Bandit, The; Heavy; Hide in Plain Sight; Money Train; Naked Man, The; On the Yard; Still of the Night; Switching Goals
Griffeth, Simone: Patriot (1986)0
Griffies, Ethel: Billy Liar; Billy the Kid; Birds, The
Griffin, Eddie: Deuce Bigalow: Male Gigolo; Double Take; Foolish; John Q; Meteor Man; Walking Dead, The
Griffin, Joseph: First Degree; Road Rage; Striking Poses
Griffin, Kathy: It's Pat: The Movie
Griffin, Lynne: Strange Brew
Griffin, Merv: Alice Through the Looking Glass; Lonely Guy, The; Two-Minute Warning
Griffin, Rhonda: Creeps, The; Hideous
Griffin, Tod: She Demons
Griffith, Andy: Andy Griffith Show, The (TV Series); Face in the Crowd, A; Fatal Vision; Hearts of the West; Murder in Coweta County; Murder in Texas; No Time for Sergeants; No Time for Sergeants (Television); Onionhead; Pray for the Wildcats; Return to Mayberry; Rustler's Rhapsody; Savages; Spy Hard
Griffith, Corinne: Lilies of the Field
Griffith, Geraldine: Experience Preferred ... But Not Essential
Griffith, Hugh: Abominable Dr. Phibes, The; Canterbury Tales, The; Counterfeit Traitor, The; Cry of the Banshee; Diary of Forbidden Dreams; Dr. Phibes Rises Again; Hound of the Baskervilles, The; How to Steal a Million; Joseph Andrews; Last Days of Man on Earth, The; Legend of the Werewolf; Lucky Jim; Luther; Mutiny on the Bounty; Oliver; Run for Your Money, A; Start the Revolution Without Me; Tom Jones; Who Slew Auntie Roo?; Wuthering Heights
Griffith, James: Amazing Transparent Man, The; Blonde Ice; Bullwhip; Double Deal; Dynamo; Guns of Fort Petticoat
Griffith, Katharine: Pollyanna
Griffith, Kenneth: Englishman Who Went up a Hill But Came down a Mountain, The; Koroshi
Griffith, Kristin: Europeans, The; Rose Hill
Griffith, Melanie: Along for the Ride; Another Day in Paradise; Body Double; Bonfire of the Vanities; Born Yesterday; Buffalo Girls; cecil b. Demented; Cherry 2000; Crazy in Alabama; Drowning Pool, The; Fear City; In the Spirit; Joyride; Lolita; Milagro Beanfield War, The; Milk Money; Mulholland Falls; Night Moves; Nobody's Fool; Now and Then; Pacific Heights; Paradise; RKO 281; She's in the Army Now; Shining Through; Smile; Something Wild; Stormy Monday; Stranger Among Us, A; Tart; Two Much; Underground Aces; Women & Men: Stories of Seduction; Working Girl
Griffith, Raymond: White Tiger
Griffith, Rhiana: Pitch Black
Griffith, Thomas Ian: Blood of the Innocent; Crackerjack; Excessive Force; Hollow Point; John Carpenter's Vampires; Ulterior Motives
Griffith, Tom: Alien Factor, The
Griffith, Tracy: All Tied Up; Finest Hour, The; First Power, The; Skeeter
Griffiths, Linda: Lianna; Reno and the Doc; Sword of Gideon
Griffiths, Rachel: Blow; Blow Dry; Children of the Revolution; Cosi; Hilary and Jackie; Me Myself I; Muriel's Wedding; My Son the Fanatic; Rookie, The (2002); Welcome to Woop Woop
Griffiths, Richard: Blame It on the Bellboy; Funnybones; Guarding Tess; Harry Potter and the Sorcerer's Stone; King Ralph; Private Function, A; Shanghai Surprise; Sleepy Hollow; Whoops Apocalypse; Withnail and I
Griggs, Camilla: Bar Girls; Forced Vengeance
Griggs, Jeff: Forbidden Games
Grika, Johanna: Visitants, The

Grimaldi, Dan: Don't Go in the House
Grimes, Camryn: Swordfish
Grimes, Frank: Crystalstone; Dive, The
Grimes, Gary: Cahill—US Marshal; Class of '44; Culpepper Cattle Co., The; Gus; Summer of '42
Grimes, Scott: Critters; Critters 2: The Main Course; It Came Upon a Midnight Clear; Mystery, Alaska; Night Life
Grimes, Steven: Fatal Past
Grimes, Tammy: America; Can't Stop the Music; Modern Affair, A; No Big Deal; Trouble on the Corner
Grinberg, Anouk: Merci La Vie; My Man (Mon Homme)
Grint, Rupert: Harry Potter and the Sorcerer's Stone
Grisham, Jerry: Escapes
Grisman, David: Grateful Dawg
Grives, Steven: Dangerous Game (1990)
Grizzard, George: Attica; Bachelor Party; Caroline?; Comes a Horseman; Deliberate Stranger, The; From the Terrace; Iran Days of Crisis; Oldest Living Graduate, The; Stranger Within, The; Wrong Is Right
Groce, Larry: Heroes of the Heart
Grodenchik, Max: Rumpelstiltskin
Grodin, Charles: Beethoven; Beethoven's 2nd; Clifford; Couch Trip, The; Dave; 11 Harrowhouse; Grass Is Always Greener over the Septic Tank, The; Great Muppet Caper, The; Grown-Ups; Heart and Souls; Heartbreak Kid, The; Heaven Can Wait; Incredible Shrinking Woman, The; Ishtar; It's My Turn; King Kong; Last Resort; Lonely Guy, The; Midnight Run; Movers and Shakers; My Summer Story; Real Life; Seems Like Old Times; Sex and the College Girl; So I Married an Axe Murderer; Sunburn; Taking Care of Business; Woman in Red, The
Grody, Kathryn: Lemon Sisters, The
Grogan, C. P.: Comfort and Joy
Grogan, Clare: Gregory's Girl
Groh, David: Acts of Betrayal; Broken Vows; King Lear; Last Exit to Earth; Return of Superfly, The; Stoned Age, The
Gronemeyer, Herbert: Das Boot (The Boat); Spring Symphony
Groom, Sam: Baby Maker, The; Deadly Eyes; Deadly Games; Run for the Roses (Thoroughbred)
Gross, Arye: Arthur's Quest; Couch Trip, The; Coupe De Ville; Experts, The; For the Boys; Hexed; House II: The Second Story; In the Company of Spies; Matter of Degrees, A; Midnight Clear, A; Opposite Sex (And How to Live with Them), The (1993); Shaking the Tree; Soul Man
Gross, Edan: And You Thought Your Parents Were Weird; Halloween Tree, The
Gross, Loretta: Kill-Off, The
Gross, Mary: Casual Sex?; Couch Trip, The; Feds; Hot to Trot; Jailbait (2000); Santa Clause, The; Troop Beverly Hills
Gross, Michael: Alan and Naomi; Big Business; Cool As Ice; FBI Murders, The; Ground Control; Kounterfeit; Little Gloria, Happy at Last; Midnight Murders; Sometimes They Come Back Again; Tremors; Tremors 3: Back to Perfection; Tremors 2: Aftershocks; True Heart
Gross, Molly: Slaves to the Underground
Gross, Paul: Aspen Extreme; Buffalo Jump; Northern Extremes
Grossman, DePrise: Zarkorr! The Invader
Grossmith, George: Wedding Rehearsal
Grosso, Sonny: French Connection, The
Groth, Sylvester: Stalingrad
Grove, Richard: Army of Darkness; Scanner Cop
Grovenor, Linda: Die Laughing; Wheels of Fire
Grover, Edward: Strike Force
Groves, Robin: Nesting, The; Silver Bullet
Groves, Stewart: Raising Heroes
Grubb, Robert: Gallipoli
Grubbs, Gary: Ernest Green Story, The; Fatal Vision; JFK
Gruffudd, Ioan: 102 Dalmatians; Solomon and Gaenor
Grunberg, Klaus: More
Grundgens, Gustav: M
Gruner, Olivier: Angel Town; Automatic; Mercenary; Mercenary 2: Thick and Thin; Nemesis; Savage; Savate; Velocity Trap
Gryglaszewska, Halina: Double Life of Veronique, The
Gschnitzer, Julia: Inheritors, The
Guadagni, Nicky: Cube
Guard, Christopher: Return to Treasure Island
Guard, Dominic: Absolution; Picnic at Hanging Rock
Guard, Pippa: Daisies in December
Guardino, Harry: Adventures of Bullwhip Griffin, The; Dirty Harry; Enforcer, The; Five Pennies, The; Get Christie Love!; Hell Is for Heroes; Houseboat; Lovers and Other Strangers; Madigan; Matilda; Neon Empire, The; Pork Chop Hill; St. Ives; They Only Kill Their Masters; Whiffs
Guarnica, Lupe: Gloria
Gudmundsdottir, Bjork: Juniper Tree, The
Guedj, Vanessa: Le Grand Chemin (The Grand Highway)
Guerin, Michael: Curse of the Puppet Master
Guerra, Blanca: Danzon
Guerra, Ruy: Aguirre: Wrath of God
Guerra, Saverio: Summer of Sam
Guerrero, Evelyn: Cheech and Chong's Next Movie; Nice Dreams
Guerrero, Franco: Deathfight
Guerro, Álvaro: Amores Perros
Guesmi, Samir: Halfmoon
Guessan, Albertine: Faces of Women
Guest, Christopher: Best in Show; Beyond Therapy; Few Good Men, A; Girlfriends; Last Word, The; Little Shop of Horrors (1986); Long Riders, The; Piano for Mrs. Cimino, A; Return of Spinal Tap, The; Sticky Fingers; This Is Spinal Tap; Waiting for Guffman
Guest, Lance: Halloween II; Jaws: The Revenge; Last Starfighter, The; Mach 2; Plan B
Guest, Nicholas: Adrenalin: Fear the Rush; Brain Smasher ... A Love Story; Chrome Soldiers; Dollman; Long Riders, The; My Daughter's Keeper; Night Hunter; Puppet Master 5: The Final Chapter; Strange Case of Dr. Jekyll and Mr. Hyde,The (1989)
Guetary, Francois: Running Delilah
Guevara, Nacha: Miss Mary
Guffey, Cary: Mutant
Gugino, Carla: Buccaneers, The; Center of the World, The; Judas Kiss; Miami Rhapsody; Murder Without Motive; One, The; Red Hot; Snake Eyes; Son-in-Law; Spy Kids
Guidera, Anthony: Undercover
Guier, Adam: Pistol, The: The Birth of a Legend
Guilbert, Ann: Grumpier Old Men
Guilbert, Ann Morgan: Dick Van Dyke Show, The (TV Series)
Guild, Nancy: Abbott and Costello Meet the Invisible Man; Black Magic; Somewhere in the Night
Guilfoyle, James: Two Lost Worlds
Guilfoyle, Paul: Air Force One; Amelia Earhart: The Final Flight; Brother Orchid; Celtic Pride; Couch in New York, A; Crime of Dr. Crespi, The; Curiosity Kills; Final Analysis; Hoffa; In Dreams; L.A. Confidential; One Tough Cop; Random Hearts; Ransom; Virginian, The; Winterset
Guillaume, Robert: Cosmic Slop; Death Warrant; First Kid; His Bodyguard; Kid with the Broken Halo, The; Kid with the 200 I.Q., The; Lean on Me; Meteor Man; North and South; Penthouse, The; Run for the Dream; Seems Like Old Times; Superfly T.N.T.; Wanted: Dead or Alive; You Must Remember This
Guillemette, Peter: Bloody Murder
Guillemin, Sophie: With a Friend Like Harry
Guillen, Fernando: Women on the Verge of a Nervous Breakdown
Guillory, Sienna: Time Machine, The (2002)
Guinan, Francis: Mortal Sins (1992)
Guinee, Tim: Chain of Desire; John Carpenter's Vampires; Lily Dale; Pompatus of Love, The; Tai-Pan; Three Lives of Karen, The; Vietnam War Story—Part Two
Guinness, Alec: Bridge on the River Kwai, The; Brother Sun, Sister Moon; Captain's Paradise, The; Comedians, The; Cromwell; Damn the Defiant!; Detective, The; Dr. Zhivago; Fall of the Roman Empire, The; Foreign Field, A; Great Expectations; Handful of Dust, A; Hitler, the Last Ten Days; Horse's Mouth, The; Hotel Paradiso; Kafka; Kind Hearts and Coronets; Ladykillers, The; Last Holiday; Lavender Hill Mob, The; Lawrence of Arabia; Little Dorrit; Little Lord Fauntleroy; Lovesick; Majority of One, A; Malta Story, The; Man in the White

Suit, The; Monsignor Quixote; Murder by Death; Mute Witness; Oliver Twist; Passage to India, A; Prisoner, The (1955); Promoter, The; Quiller Memorandum, The; Raise the Titanic; Run for Your Money, A; Scrooge; Star Wars; Swan, The; To Paris with Love; To See Such Fun; Tunes of Glory
Guiomar, Julien: Leolo; Swashbuckler, The (1984)
Guirardeau, Bernard: Ridicule
Guiry, Tom: Lassie; Sandlot, The; Strike! (1998)
Guitierrez, Lorena: Crier, The
Guitry, Sacha: Pearls of the Crown, The
Gulager, Clu: Gambler, The; Glass House, The; Gunfighter (1997); Hidden, The; Hit Lady; Hunter's Blood; I'm Gonna Git You Sucka!; Lies; Living Proof: The Hank Williams Jr., Story; McQ; My Heroes Have Always Been Cowboys; Nightmare on Elm Street 2, A: Freddy's Revenge; Offspring, The; Other Side of Midnight, The; Prime Risk; Return of the Living Dead, The; Smile, Jenny, You're Dead; Summer Heat; Teen Vamp; Touched by Love; Uninvited, The; Willa
Gullette, Sean: Pi
Gulliver, Dorothy: Galloping Ghost, The; Shadow of the Eagle
Gulpilil, David: "Crocodile" Dundee; Mad Dog Morgan; Walkabout
Guma, Antonio: Lola's Game
Guma, Tony: Suburbans, The
Gummersal, Devon: Trading Favors
Gummersall, Devon: Lured Innocence
Gunn, David: Vampire Journals
Gunn, Janet: Carnosaur 3: Primal Species; Dark Prince: The Intimate Tales of Marquis de Sade; Night of the Running Man; Nurse, The
Gunn, Moses: Aaron Loves Angela; Amityville II: The Possession; Certain Fury; Cornbread, Earl and Me; Dixie Lanes; Haunts of the Very Rich; Heartbreak Ridge; Hot Rock, The; Killing Floor, The; Leonard Part 6; Memphis; Ninth Configuration, The; Perfect Harmony; Shaft; Shaft's Big Score!; Wild Rovers, The
Gunn, Peter: Blue Juice
Gunton, Bob: Ace Ventura: When Nature Calls; Broken Arrow; Buffalo Soldiers; Elvis Meets Nixon; Father Hood; Glimmer Man, The; In Pursuit of Honor; Ladykiller; Lois Gibbs and the Love Canal; Patch Adams; Perfect Storm, The; Rollover; Shawshank Redemption, The; Static
Guoli, Zhang: Story of Xinghua, The
Gupia, Kamlesh: Crystalstone
Gupta, Neena: Cotton Mary
Gupta, Pinaki Sen: Aparajito
Gurchenko, Lyudmilla: Siberiade
Gurie, Sigrid: Adventures of Marco Polo, The; Three Faces West
Gurney, Rachel: Upstairs, Downstairs
Gurry, Eric: Bad Boys; Something Special; Zoo Gang, The
Gurwitch, Annabelle: Changing Habits; Intimate Betrayal; Pizza Man
Guthrie, Arlo: Alice's Restaurant; Roadside Prophets; Woody Guthrie—Hard Travelin'
Guthrie, Tyrone: Beachcomber, The; Sidewalks of London
Gutierrez, Miguel: Bitter Sugar
Gutierrez, Zaide Silvia: El Norte
Gutowski, Rita: Sandman, The (1996)
Guttenberg, Steve: Amazon Women on the Moon; Bad Medicine; Bedroom Window, The; Big Green, The; Can't Stop the Music; Casper: A Spirited Beginning; Chicken Chronicles, The; Cocoon; Cocoon: The Return; Day After, The; Diner; Don't Tell Her It's Me; High Spirits; Home for the Holidays (1995); It Takes Two; Man Who Wasn't There, The; Miracle on Ice; Police Academy; Police Academy 4: Citizens on Patrol; Police Academy II: Their First Assignment; Police Academy III: Back in Training; Short Circuit; Surrender; Three Men and a Baby; Three Men and a Little Lady; Zeus and Roxanne
Gutteridge, Lucy: Little Gloria, Happy at Last; Top Secret; Trouble with Spies, The; Tusks
Guve, Bertil: Fanny and Alexander
Guy, DeJuan: One Man's Justice
Guy, Frank: One Man's Justice
Guy, Jasmine: America's Dream; Diamond Men; Perfect Crime
Guzaldo, Joe: Evil Has a Face; Smooth Talker
Guzman, Luis: Bone Collector, The; Carlito's Way; Count of Monte Cristo, The (2002); Jumpin' at the Boneyard; Limey, The; Luckytown Blues; Mr. Wonderful; Traffic
Gwenn, Edmund: Anthony Adverse; Bigamist, The; Challenge to Lassie; Cheers for Miss Bishop; Doctor Takes a Wife, The; Foreign Correspondent; Green Dolphin Street; Hills of Home; If I Were Rich; It's a Dog's Life; Lassie Come Home; Life with Father; Meanest Man in the World, The; Miracle on 34th Street; Skin Game, The (1931); Student Prince, The; Sylvia Scarlett; Them!; Trouble with Harry, The; Undercurrent; Waltzes from Vienna; Woman of Distinction, A
Gwyndaf, Gweirydd: Christmas Reunion, A
Gwynn, Michael: Revenge of Frankenstein
Gwynn, Peter: Nostradamus Kid, The
Gwynne, Anne: Arson Inc.; Black Friday; Dick Tracy Meets Gruesome; House of Frankenstein; King of the Bullwhip; Meteor Monster (Teenage Monster); Ride 'em Cowboy; Strange Case of Dr. Rx, The; Weird Woman
Gwynne, Fred: Any Friend of Nicholas Nickleby Is a Friend of Mine; Boy Who Could Fly, The; Car 54 Where Are You? (TV Series); Disorganized Crime; Ironweed; Littlest Angel, The; Man That Corrupted Hadleyburg, The; Munsters' Revenge, The; My Cousin Vinny; Mysterious Stranger, The; Pet Sematary; Secret of My Success, The; Shadows and Fog; Simon; So Fine; Vanishing Act; Water
Gwynne, Michael C.: Cherry 2000; Deadly Encounter; Guyana Tragedy, The: The Story of Jim Jones; Harry Tracy; Last of the Finest, The; Payday; Streets of L.A., The; Village of the Damned
Gyllenhaal, Jake: Bubble Boy; Donnie Darko; Highway; October Sky
Gyllenhaal, Maggie: cecil b. Demented
Gyngell, Kim: Boulevard of Broken Dreams; Heaven Tonight; Wacky World of Wills and Burke, The
Gynt, Greta: Human Monster, The (Dark Eyes of London); Sexton Blake and the Hooded Terror
Haade, William: Days of Old Cheyenne; Kid Galahad; Stage to Chino
Haag, Christina: Lost in the Bermuda Triangle
Haas, Hugo: Casbah; Holiday in Mexico; King Solomon's Mines; Merton of the Movies; Northwest Outpost; Private Affairs of Bel Ami, The
Haas, Lukas: Alan and Naomi; Boys (1996); Everyone Says I Love You; Johns; Lady in White; Leap of Faith; Mars Attacks!; Music Box, The; Rambling Rose; See You in the Morning; Shattered Spirits; Solarbabies; Testament; Warrior Spirit; Witness; Wizard of Loneliness, The
Haase, Cathy: Kill-Off, The
Habbema, Cox: Question of Silence, A
Habeck, Michael: Gigashadow
Habermann, Eva: Eating Pattern; Gigashadow; I Worship His Shadow; Tales from a Parallel Universe
Habich, Matthias: Coup De Grace; Straight for the Heart
Hack, Shelley: Finishing Touch, The; If Ever I See You Again; Me, Myself & I; Stepfather, The; Troll
Hacker, George: Manhattan Baby
Hackett, Buddy: Babe; Bud and Lou; God's Little Acre; It's a Mad Mad Mad Mad World; Loose Shoes; Love Bug, The; Muscle Beach Party; Music Man, The; Paulie; Wonderful World of the Brothers Grimm, The
Hackett, Claire: Gallowglass; Liam
Hackett, Joan: Escape Artist, The; Group, The; One Trick Pony; Only When I Laugh; Possessed, The (1977); Reflections of Murder; Support Your Local Sheriff!; Terminal Man, The; Will Penny
Hackett, John: Dead of Night
Hackett, Karl: Border Phantom; Desert Phantom; His Brother's Ghost; Prairie Rustlers; Sing, Cowboy, Sing; Take Me Back to Oklahoma; Traitor, The
Hackett, Sandy: Hamburger—The Motion Picture
Hackford, Taylor: First Works, Volumes 1 & 2
Hackl, Karl Heinz: Assisi Underground, The
Hackman, Gene: Absolute Power; All Night Long; Another Woman; Bat 21; Behind Enemy Lines; Birdcage, The; Bite the

Bullet; Bonnie and Clyde; Chamber, The; Cisco Pike; Class Action; Company Business; Conversation, The; Crimson Tide; Doctors' Wives; Domino Principle, The; Downhill Racer; Enemy of the State; Eureka; Extreme Measures; Firm, The; French Connection, The; French Connection II, The; Full Moon in Blue Water; Geronimo: An American Legend; Get Shorty; Hawaii; Heartbreakers; Heist (2001); Hoosiers; I Never Sang for My Father; Lilith; Loose Cannons; March or Die; Marooned; Mexican, The; Mississippi Burning; Misunderstood; Narrow Margin (1990); Night Moves; No Way Out; Package, The; Poseidon Adventure, The; Postcards from the Edge; Power (1986); Prime Cut; Quick and the Dead, The; Reds; Replacements, The; Riot; Royal Tenenbaums, The; Scarecrow; Split Decisions; Superman; Superman II; Superman IV: The Quest for Peace; Target; Twice in a Lifetime; Twilight; Uncommon Valor; Under Fire; Under Suspicion (2000); Unforgiven (1992); Wyatt Earp; Young Frankenstein; Zandy's Bride

Hada, Michiko: Mystery of Rampo, The

Hadary, Jonathan: As Is

Haddon, Dayle: Bedroom Eyes; Cyborg; French Woman, The; North Dallas Forty; Sex with a Smile

Hádek, Krystof: Dark Blue World

Haden, Sara: Anne of Green Gables; Life Begins for Andy Hardy; Life of Her Own, A; Love Laughs at Andy Hardy; Mad Love; Mr. Ace; Our Vines Have Tender Grapes; Poor Little Rich Girl (1936); Spitfire

Hadji-Lazaro, François: Dellamorte, Dellamore

Hadley, Reed: Baron of Arizona, The; Half-Breed, The; Kansas Pacific; Little Big Horn; Rimfire; Shock (1946); Whistling in the Dark; Zorro's Fighting Legion

Hafner, Ingrid: Philby, Burgess and Maclean: Spy Scandalof the Century

Haft, Linal: Soft Fruit

Hagalin, Sigridur: Children of Nature

Hagan, Jennifer: Gallagher's Travels

Hagan, Marianne: Halloween: The Curse of Michael Myers; I Think I Do

Hagan, Molly: French Exit; Miracle in Lane 2; Ringmaster

Hagar, Ivan: Behind Locked Doors

Hagen, Jean: Asphalt Jungle, The; Danny Thomas Show, The (TV Series); Dead Ringer; Latin Lovers; Life of Her Own, A; Panic in the Year Zero; Shaggy Dog, The; Singin' in the Rain

Hagen, Ross: Armed Response; Attack of the 60-Ft. Centerfold; B.O.R.N.; Commando Squad; Cyberzone; Kid with X-Ray Eyes, The; Night Creature; Phantom Empire, The (1986); Star Slammer; Warlords

Hagen, Uta: Other, The; Reversal of Fortune

Hager, Kristi: Sure Fire

Hagerty, Julie: Airplane!; Airplane II: The Sequel; Bad Medicine; Beyond Therapy; Bloodhounds of Broadway; Boys Will Be Boys; Freddy Got Fingered; Goodbye New York; Lost in America; Midsummer Night's Sex Comedy, A; Necessary Parties; Noises Off; Rude Awakening; Story of Us, The; Storytelling; What About Bob?; Wife, The

Hagerty, Michael G.: Rio Diablo

Haggard, Merle: Hillbillys in a Haunted House; Huckleberry Finn

Haggerty, Dan: Abducted; Abducted II; Angels Die Hard; California Gold Rush; Capture of Grizzly Adams, The; Cheyenne Warrior; Chilling, The; Desperate Women; Elves; Grizzly Mountain; Life and Times of Grizzly Adams, The; Little Patriot, The; Pink Angels; Soldier's Fortune; Spirit of the Eagle; Terror Out of the Sky

Haggerty, Dyland: Grizzly Mountain

Haggerty, H. B.: Four Deuces, The

Haggerty, Megan: Grizzly Mountain

Haggiag, Brahim: Battle of Algiers

Hagler, Marvin: Indio; Indio 2: The Revolt

Hagman, Larry: Big Bus, The; Deadly Encounter; Ensign Pulver; Fail-Safe; Group, The; Harry and Tonto; Intimate Strangers; Mother, Jugs, and Speed; Primary Colors; S.O.B.; Son of Blob (Beware! The Blob); Three in the Cellar

Hagney, Frank: Ride Him Cowboy

Hahn, Archie: Glory Years; Pray TV

Hahn, Jess: Mamma Dracula; Night of the Following Day, The

Hai, Ngo Quang: Vertical Ray of the Sun, The

Haid, Charles: Altered States; Capone; Chinatown Murders, The: Man Against the Mob; Cop; Cop for the Killing, A; Deathmoon; Execution of Private Slovik, The; Freeze Frame; Great Escape II, The; Hill Street Blues (TV Series); Night Breed; Rescue, The; Weekend War

Haiduk, Stacy: Beneficiary, The; Darwin Conspiracy, The; Yesterday's Target

Haig, Sid: Beyond Atlantis; Big Bird Cage, The; C.C. & Company; Coffy; Commando Squad; Warlords

Haig, Terry: Shades of Love: Champagne for Two

Haigh, Kenneth: Bitch, The; Robin and Marian

Haile, Tedesse: Endurance

Hailey, Leisha: All over Me

Haim, Corey: Blown Away; Double-O Kid, The; Dream a Little Dream; Dream a Little Dream 2; Dream Machine; Fast Getaway; Fast Getaway II; Fever Lake; Just One of the Girls; License to Drive; Life 101; Lost Boys, The; Lucas; Murphy's Romance; National Lampoon's Last Resort; Oh, What a Night; Prayer of the Rollerboys; Silver Bullet; Snowboard Academy; Watchers

Haines, Donald: Boys of the City; Pride of the Bowery

Haines, Patricia: Night Caller from Outer Space

Haines, Richard: Survivor

Haines, William: Show People; Tell It to the Marines

Haiyan, Zhang: Ermo

Haje, Khrystyne: Cyborg 3: The Recycler; Scanners 4: The Showdown

Haldane, Don: Nikki, Wild Dog of the North

Hale, Barbara: Boy with Green Hair, The; Buckskin; Clay Pigeon, The; First Yank into Tokyo; Jackpot, The; Jolson Sings Again; Last of the Comanches; Lion Is in the Streets, A; Oklahoman, The; 7th Cavalry; Seventh Victim, The; Window, The

Hale, Binnie: Love from a Stranger

Hale, Birdie M.: Blind Faith

Hale, Creighton: Cat and the Canary, The; Idol Dancer, The; Orphans of the Storm; Seven Footprints to Satan

Hale, Diana: My Friend Flicka

Hale, Georgia: Gold Rush, The

Hale, Georgina: Mahler

Hale, Jean: In Like Flint; St. Valentine's Day Massacre, The

Hale, Jonathan: Blondie; Blondie Has Servant Trouble; Blondie in Society; Blondie Knows Best; Charlie Chan's Secret; Saint in New York, The; Saint Strikes Back, The

Hale, Louise Closser: Shanghai Express; Today We Live

Hale, Michael: Devil Bat's Daughter

Hale, Monte: Missourians, The; Out California Way; Trail of Robin Hood

Hale, Nancy: Wyatt Earp: Return to Tombstone

Hale Jr., Alan: At Sword's Point; Battle Hymn; Big Trees, The; Fifth Musketeer, The; It Happens Every Spring; Rim of the Canyon; Short Grass; To the Shores of Tripoli; West Point Story, The

Hale Sr., Alan: Action in the North Atlantic; Adventures of Don Juan, The; Adventures of Marco Polo, The; Adventures of Mark Twain, The; Adventures of Robin Hood, The; Broadway Bill; Captains of the Clouds; Covered Wagon, The; Desperate Journey; Destination Tokyo; Dodge City; Fighting 69th, The; Footsteps in the Dark; Gentleman Jim; Last Days of Pompeii, The (1935); Lost Patrol, The; Man I Love, The; Man in the Iron Mask, The; My Girl Tisa; Night and Day; Of Human Bondage; Our Relations; Prince and the Pauper, The; Private Lives of Elizabeth and Essex, The; Pursued; Robin Hood; Santa Fe Trail; Sea Hawk, The; Sisters, The (1938); Smiling Ghost, The; Spirit of West Point, The; Stars in My Crown; Stella Dallas; Strawberry Blonde, The; Susan Lenox: Her Fall and Rise; Thin Ice; This Is the Army; Up Periscope; Virginia City

Haley, Brian: Baby's Day Out; Little Giants

Haley, Jack: Alexander's Ragtime Band; George White's Scandals; Higher and Higher; Moon over Miami; Movie Struck (Pick a Star); One Body Too Many; People Are Funny; Poor Little Rich Girl (1936); Rebecca of Sunnybrook Farm; Take It Big; Wizard of Oz, The

Haley, Jackie Earle: Bad News Bears, The; Bad News Bears Go to Japan, The; Bad News Bears in Breaking Training, The; Breaking Away; Damnation Alley (Survival Run); Dollman; Losin' It; Maniac Cop 3: Badge of Silence
Halicki, H. B.: Gone in 60 Seconds
Hall, Albert: Major Payne; Malcolm X; Rookie of the Year
Hall, Anthony: Sunset Park
Hall, Anthony Michael: Adventures of a Gnome Named Gnorm, The; Breakfast Club, The; Death Artist; Edward Scissorhands; Exit in Red; Freddy Got Fingered; Grave, The; Hail Caesar; Into the Sun; Johnny Be Good; National Lampoon's Vacation; Out of Bounds; Pirates of Silicon Valley; Six Degrees of Separation; Sixteen Candles; Texas; Trojan War; Weird Science
Hall, Arsenio: Amazon Women on the Moon; Coming to America; Harlem Nights
Hall, Brad: Limit Up; Troll
Hall, Bug: Honey, We Shrunk Ourselves; Little Rascals, The; Skipped Parts; Stupids, The
Hall, Carol E.: Love Your Mama
Hall, Charlie: Laurel and Hardy Classics: Vol. 1–9
Hall, Cleve: Twisted Nightmare
Hall, Delores: Leap of Faith
Hall, Ellen: Voodoo Man
Hall, Grayson: Adam at 6 A.M.; House of Dark Shadows; Night of Dark Shadows
Hall, Hanna: Homecoming; Virgin Suicides, The
Hall, Harriet: Witching of Ben Wagner, The
Hall, Huntz: Auntie Lee's Meat Pies; Bowery Boys, The (Series); Cyclone; Ratings Game, The; Valentino
Hall, Irma P.: Buddy; Family Thing, A; Midnight in the Garden of Good and Evil; Soul Food
Hall, James: Saturday Night Kid, The
Hall, Jerry: Savage Hearts
Hall, Jon: Ali Baba and the Forty Thieves; Arabian Nights; Charlie Chan in Shanghai; Cobra Woman; Gypsy Wildcat; Heartstopper; Hell Ship Mutiny; Hurricane, The; Invisible Agent; Invisible Man's Revenge, The; Kit Carson; Last of the Redmen; South of Pago Pago; Sudan; Tuttles of Tahiti, The
Hall, Juanita: Flower Drum Song
Hall, Kevin Peter: Misfits of Science; Predator
Hall, Landon: Maximum Security; Stolen Hearts
Hall, Lois: Pirates of the High Seas
Hall, Mark Edward: Across the Great Divide
Hall, Nathaniel: Livin' Large
Hall, Peter: Pedestrian, The
Hall, Philip Baker: Contender, The; Hard Eight; Implicated; Lost Souls; Magnolia; Rules of Engagement; Rush Hour; Secret Honor; Three O'Clock High
Hall, Porter: Arizona; Beautiful Blonde from Bashful Bend, The; Bulldog Drummond Escapes; Case of the Lucky Legs, The; Double Indemnity; General Died at Dawn, The; Great Moment, The; Intruder in the Dust; Miracle of Morgan's Creek, The; Princess Comes Across, The; Satan Met a Lady; Singapore; Story of Louis Pasteur, The; Sullivan's Travels; They Shall Have Music; Thin Man, The
Hall, Regina: Scary Movie 2
Hall, Rich: Million Dollar Mystery
Hall, Ron: Raw Target; Triple Impact
Hall, Ruth: Man from Monterey, The; Monkey Business; Ride Him Cowboy; Three Musketeers, The
Hall, Shana: Boogeyman 2, The
Hall, Shashawnee: Pet Shop
Hall, Thurston: Adventures of Topper, The; Affairs of Annabel, The; Amazing Dr. Clitterhouse, The; Black Room, The; Great Man's Lady, The; Great Moment, The; I Dood It; Rim of the Canyon; Secret Life of Walter Mitty, The; Song of Nevada; Theodora Goes Wild; Trapped by Television; Without Reservations; You Can't Cheat an Honest Man
Hall, Vondie Curtis: Turn It Up
Hall, Zooey: Fortune and Men's Eyes; I Dismember Mama
Hall Jr., Arch: Eegah!; Nasty Rabbit; Sadist, The; Wild Guitar
Hall Sr., Arch: Eegah!; Nasty Rabbit; Sadist, The; Wild Guitar
Hallahan, Charles: Dante's Peak; Going in Style; Pest, The; Tales of the Unexpected
Hallam, John: Murphy's War
Hall-Davies, Lillian: Farmer's Wife, The; Ring, The
Halldorsson, Gisli: Children of Nature
Hallgren, Frida: Slingshot, The
Halliday, Bryant: Devil Doll (1936)
Halliday, John: Bird of Paradise; Consolation Marriage; Finishing School; Terror Aboard
Hallier, Lori: Blindside; My Bloody Valentine; Running Wild
Hallinan, Olivia: Snoopers
Hallo, Dean: Blue Tiger
Halloren, Jane: Lianna
Hallum, John: It's in the Water
Hallyday, Johnny: Iron Triangle, The; Tales of Paris
Halop, Billy: Tom Brown's School Days (1940)
Halow, Bash: Lie Down with Dogs
Halpin, Luke: Flipper; Flipper's New Adventure; Flipper's Odyssey; Island of the Lost
Halprin, Daria: Zabriskie Point
Halsey, Brett: Atomic Submarine, The; Cat in the Brain, A; Ma and Pa Kettle at Home; Return of the Fly, The; Return to Peyton Place; Twice-Told Tales
Halsey, John: Rutles, The (All You Need Is Cash)
Halsted, Christopher: Haunting of Morella, The
Halston, Roger: Alien Terminator; Unknown Origin
Halton, Charles: Dr. Cyclops
Ham, Robert Mason: Magic Stone, The
Hama, Mie: You Only Live Twice
Hamamura, Jun: Zatoichi: The Blind Swordsman's Vengeance
Hamblin, John: Who Killed Baby Azaria?
Hamel, Veronica: Cannonball; Hill Street Blues (TV Series); New Life, A; Sessions
Hamer, Gerald: Scarlet Claw, The
Hamer, Rusty: Danny Thomas Show, The (TV Series)
Hamill, John: Beast in the Cellar, The
Hamill, Mark: Big Red One, The; Black Magic Woman; Corvette Summer; Empire Strikes Back, The; Eric; Guyver, The; John Carpenter Presents: Body Bags; Laserhawk; Midnight Ride; Night the Lights Went Out in Georgia, The; Raffle, The; Return of the Jedi; Silk Degrees; Slipstream; Star Wars; Time Runner; Village of the Damned; When Time Expires
Hamilton, Alexa: Death Spa
Hamilton, Antony: Howling IV; Mirrors; Samson and Delilah
Hamilton, Bernie: Bucktown; Losers, The
Hamilton, Carrie: Checkered Flag; Tokyo Pop
Hamilton, Dan: Romeo and Juliet
Hamilton, Dean: Rush Week
Hamilton, Derek: Extreme Days
Hamilton, Gay: Barry Lyndon
Hamilton, George: Amore! (1993); By Love Possessed; Dead Don't Die, The; Doc Hollywood; 8 Heads in a Duffel Bag; Evel Knievel; Express to Terror; From Hell to Victory; Godfather, Part III, The; Happy Hooker Goes to Washington, The; Hollywood Ending; Home from the Hill; Love at First Bite; Man Who Loved Cat Dancing, The; Monte Carlo; Once Is Not Enough; Once Upon a Crime; Playback; Poker Alice; Seekers, The; Sextette; Two Weeks in Another Town; Viva Maria!; Where the Boys Are (1960); Zorro, the Gay Blade
Hamilton, Jane: Beauty School; Slammer Girls; Wimps
Hamilton, John: TV's Best Adventures of Superman
Hamilton, Josh: Alive; Blowin' Smoke; Don't Look Back; House of Yes, The; Kicking and Screaming; Urbania; With Honors
Hamilton, Julie: Holy Smoke
Hamilton, Kipp: War of the Gargantuas
Hamilton, Linda: Beauty and the Beast (TV Series); Black Moon Rising; Children of the Corn; Club Med; Color of Courage, The; Dante's Peak; King Kong Lives; Mother's Prayer, A; Mr. Destiny; Rape and Marriage: The Rideout Case; Secret Weapons; Separate Lives; Shadow Conspiracy; Silent Fall; Skeletons in the Closet; Tag—The Assassination Game; Terminator, The; Terminator 2: Judgment Day
Hamilton, Lisa Gay: Drunks; House Divided, A; Jackie Brown; Palookaville; True Crime
Hamilton, Lois: Armed Response

Hamilton, Margaret: Anderson Tapes, The; Babes in Arms; Beautiful Blonde from Bashful Bend, The; Breaking the Ice; Broadway Bill; City Without Men; Daydreamer, The (1966); Invisible Woman, The; Night Strangler, The; People Will Talk; Red Pony, The; Sin of Harold Diddlebock (Mad Wednesday); Sun Comes Up, The; 13 Ghosts; Villain Still Pursued Her, The; Wabash Avenue; When's Your Birthday?; Wizard of Oz, The; You Only Live Once
Hamilton, Mark: Zarkorr! The Invader
Hamilton, Murray: Anatomy of a Murder; Boston Strangler, The; Brotherhood, The; Brubaker; Casey's Shadow; Drowning Pool, The; FBI Story, The; Hustler, The; Hysterical; If It's Tuesday, This Must Be Belgium; Jaws; Jaws 2; Last Days of Patton, The; No Time for Sergeants; No Way to Treat a Lady; 1941; Papa's Delicate Condition; Seconds; Sergeant Ryker; Spirit of St. Louis, The; Tall Story
Hamilton, Neil: Animal Kingdom, The; Laughing Sinners; Mysterious Dr. Fu Manchu; Return of Dr. Fu Manchu; Saint Strikes Back, The; Sin of Madelon Claudet, The; Tarzan and His Mate; Tarzan the Ape Man; Terror Aboard; They Meet Again; What Price Hollywood?; World Gone Mad, The
Hamilton, Paula: Four Days in July
Hamilton, Rich: Beware! Children at Play
Hamilton, Richard: In Country; On Deadly Ground
Hamilton, Ross: Island Fury
Hamilton, Suzanna: Brimstone and Treacle; 1984; Out of Africa; Tale of a Vampire
Hamilton, Ted: Pirate Movie, The
Hamilton, Tony: Fatal Instinct
Hamilton, Victoria: Victoria and Albert
Hamlin, Harry: Blue Skies Again; Clash of the Titans; Dinner at Eight; Disappearance; Ebbtide; Frogs for Snakes; Hitchhiker, The (Series); Hunted (1997); King of the Mountain; L.A. Law; Laguna Heat; Making Love; Movie Movie; Murder So Sweet; Save Me; Silent Predators; Target: Favorite Son; Under Investigation
Hamlin, Marilyn: Savage Weekend
Hammarsten, Gustav: Together
Hammel, Fritz: Scorpion Woman, The
Hammer: One Man's Justice
Hammer, Don: Danger
Hammon, Brandon: Soul Food
Hammond, John: Blue and the Gray, The
Hammond, Josh: Alien Arsenal
Hammond, Kay: Abraham Lincoln; Blithe Spirit; Five Golden Hours
Hammond, Nicholas: Amazing Spiderman, The; Chinese Web, The; King Richard II; Martian Chronicles, Parts I-III, The; Tempest, The (1983); Trouble in Paradise
Hammond, Patricia Lee: Dracula's Last Rites (1980)
Hammond, Peter: X—The Unknown
Hammond, Roger: Victoria and Albert
Hamnett, Olivia: Deadly Possession; Earthling, The; Last Wave, The
Hampden, Walter: Adventures of Mark Twain, The; Five Fingers
Hampshire, Susan: Cry Terror; Fighting Prince of Donegal, The; Living Free; Those Daring Young Men in Their Jaunty Jalopies; Three Lives of Thomasina, The
Hampton, James: Bunco; Condorman; Hangar 18; Hawmps!; Pump Up the Volume; Teen Wolf; Teen Wolf, Too
Hampton, Lionel: Song Is Born, A
Hampton, Paul: Hit! (1973); Never Forget; They Came from Within
Han, Kwon Taek: Lies (1999)
Han, Mary: Dynamo
Han, Ong Soo: Bloodsport II
Hana, Miya: What's Up, Tiger Lily?
Hanayagi, Shotaro: Story of the Late Chrysanthemums, The
Hancock, Barbara: Finian's Rainbow
Hancock, Herbie: Round Midnight; Stand by Me
Hancock, John: Catch the Heat; Collision Course; Traxx
Hancock, Sheila: Business Affair, A; Buster; Love and Death on Long Island
Hancock, Tony: Wrong Box, The
Handl, Irene: Adventures of a Private Eye; Morgan; Private Life of Sherlock Holmes, The; Wonderwall
Handler, Evan: Ransom
Handy, James: Dangerous Life, A; False Arrest; O. J. Simpson Story, The; Rave Review
Haney, Anne: Changing Habits; Liar, Liar; Mrs. Doubtfire
Haney, Carol: Pajama Game, The
Haney, Daryl: Concealed Weapon; Daddy's Boys
Hanin, Roger: Day of Atonement; My Other Husband
Hankerson, Barry L.: Pipe Dreams
Hankin, Larry: Out on a Limb; Prehysteria 2; TBone N Weasel
Hanks, Colin: Orange County
Hanks, Jim: Buford's Beach Bunnies; Xtro: Watch the Skies (Xtro 3)
Hanks, Steve: Island Claws
Hanks, Tom: Apollo 13; Bachelor Party; Big; Bonfire of the Vanities; Bosom Buddies (TV Series); 'Burbs, The; Cast Away; Dragnet; Every Time We Say Goodbye; Fallen Angels; Forrest Gump; Green Mile, The; He Knows You're Alone; Joe Versus the Volcano; League of Their Own, A; Man with One Red Shoe, The; Mazes and Monsters; Money Pit, The; Nothing in Common; Philadelphia; Punchline; Radio Flyer; Saving Private Ryan; Sleepless in Seattle; Splash; That Thing You Do!; Turner and Hooch; Volunteers; You've Got Mail
Hannah, Daryl: Addams Family Reunion; At Play in the Fields of the Lord; Attack of the 50-Foot Woman; Blade Runner; Clan of the Cave Bear; Crazy People; Diplomatic Siege; Final Terror, The; First Target; Gingerbread Man, The; Grumpier Old Men; Grumpy Old Men; Hard Country; Hi Life; Hide and Seek; High Spirits; Jackpot; Last Days of Frankie the Fly, The; Last Don, The; Legal Eagles; Little Rascals, The; Memoirs of an Invisible Man; My Favorite Martian; Pope of Greenwich Village, The; Real Blonde, The; Rear Window; Reckless; Roxanne; Splash; Steel Magnolias; Summer Lovers; Tie That Binds, The; Two Much; Walk to Remember, A; Wall Street
Hannah, John: Circus; Final Cut, The; Four Weddings and a Funeral; Hurricane, The; Love Bug, The; Mummy, The; Mummy Returns, The; Sliding Doors
Hannah, Page: My Man Adam; Shag, the Movie
Hannah, Will: Buckeye and Blue
Hann-Byrd, Adam: Digger; Halloween: H20; Ice Storm, The; Little Man Tate
Hannigan, Alyson: American Pie; American Pie 2; My Stepmother Is an Alien
Hannon, Lisa: That Darn Punk
Hano, Aki: Re-birth of Mothra II
Hanover, Donna: Series 7: The Contenders
Hans, Rhys: Twin Town
Hansard, Glen: Commitments, The
Hansen, Gale: Double Vision; Finest Hour, The; Shaking the Tree
Hansen, Gunnar: Freakshow; Hollywood Chainsaw Hookers; Mosquito; Texas Chainsaw Massacre, The
Hansen, Juliana: Perfect Family
Hansen, Martin: Hard Rock Nightmare
Hansen, Nicole: American Cyborg: Steel Warrior
Hansen, Patti: Hard to Hold
Hanson, Lars: Scarlet Letter, The; Walpurgis Night; Wind, The
Hanson, Peter: Branded; When Worlds Collide
Hanson, Tom: Hi-line, The
Hao, Zheng: Road Home, The (1999)
Hara, Setsuko: Early Summer; Idiot, The; Late Spring; No Regrets for Our Youth
Harada, Yoshio: Hunted, The (1995)
Haralde, Ralf: Framed
Harari, Clement: Train of Life
Hardaway, Anfernee: Blue Chips
Harden, Ernest: White Mama
Harden, Marcia Gay: Convict Cowboy; Crush (1994); Curtain Call; Desperate Measures; Fever; First Wives Club, The; Flubber; Late for Dinner; Meet Joe Black; Miller's Crossing; Path to Paradise; Pollock; Safe Passage; Space Cowboys; Spitfire Grill, The; Spy Hard; Used People

Harder, Christopher D.: 5 Dark Souls
Hardester, Crofton: 5 Dark Souls
Hardie, Kate: Croupier; Heart (1999)
Hardie, Raymond: Look Back in Anger
Hardie, Russell: Operator 13
Hardin, Jerry: Hot Spot; X-Files, The (TV Series)
Hardin, Melora: Chameleon; Erasable You; Lambada; Reckless Kelly
Hardin, Ty: Bad Jim; Berserk; Born Killer; Bronco (TV Series); Fire!; One Step to Hell; Palm Springs Weekend; PT 109; You're Jinxed Friend, You Just Met Sacramento
Harding, Ann: Animal Kingdom, The; Devotion; Love from a Stranger; Magnificent Yankee, The; Those Endearing Young Charms; Two Weeks with Love
Harding, June: Trouble with Angels, The
Harding, Lyn: Silver Blaze; Speckled Band, The; Triumph of Sherlock Holmes, The
Harding, Peter: Killing Time (1996)
Harding, Tonya: Breakaway
Hardison, Kadeem: Blind Faith; Def by Temptation; Dream Date; Gunmen; Panther; Renaissance Man; Sixth Man, The; Vampire in Brooklyn
Hardwick, Derek: Among the Cinders
Hardwicke, Cedric: Becky Sharp; Commandos Strike at Dawn; Desert Fox, The; Diane; Five Weeks in a Balloon; Ghost of Frankenstein; Ghoul, The; Helen of Troy; Howards of Virginia, The; Hunchback of Notre Dame, The; Invisible Agent; Invisible Man Returns; King Solomon's Mines; Les Misérables; Nicholas Nickleby; Nine Days a Queen; On Borrowed Time; Outer Limits, The (TV Series); Rope; Salome; Stanley and Livingstone; Sundown; Suspicion; Ten Commandments, The; Things to Come; Tom Brown's School Days (1940); Tycoon; Valley of the Sun; White Tower, The; Wilson; Wing and a Prayer, A; Winslow Boy, The
Hardwicke, Edward: Photographing Fairies; Shadowlands
Hardwicke, Stryker: Breathing Room
Hardy, Oliver: Air Raid Wardens; Atoll K (Utopia); Block-Heads; Bohemian Girl, The; Bonnie Scotland; Bullfighters, The; Chump at Oxford, A; Days of Thrills and Laughter; Devil's Brother, The; Fighting Kentuckian, The; Flying Deuces; Golden Age of Comedy, The; Great Guns; Hollywood Party; Laurel and Hardy Classics: Vol. 1–9; March of the Wooden Soldiers (Babes in Toyland (1934)); MGM's The Big Parade of Comedy; Movie Struck (Pick a Star); Nothing But Trouble; Our Relations; Pack Up Your Troubles; Pardon Us; Riding High; Saps at Sea; Sons of the Desert; Swiss Miss; Three Ages, The; Way Out West; When Comedy Was King; Zenobia
Hardy, Robert: All Creatures Great and Small; Dark Places; Gathering Storm; Jenny's War; Middlemarch; Sense and Sensibility; Shooting Party, The
Hardy, Trishalee: Little Ghost
Hare, Lumsden: She
Harelik, Mark: Barbarians at the Gate
Harewood, Dorian: Ambush Murders, The; American Christmas Carol, An; Full Metal Jacket; God Bless the Child; Jesse Owens Story, The; Kiss Shot; Pacific Heights; Roots: The Next Generation; Shattered Image; Sparkle; Triangle, The; 12 Angry Men; Walter and Henry
Harfouch, Corinna: Promise, The
Hargitay, Mariska: Finish Line; Jocks; Welcome to 18
Hargitay, Mickey: Bloody Pit of Horror; Lady Frankenstein; Promises, Promises; Will Success Spoil Rock Hunter?
Hargrave, T. J.: Prince of Central Park, The
Hargreaves, Amy: Brainscan
Hargreaves, Christine: Pink Floyd: The Wall
Hargreaves, John: Beyond Reasonable Doubt (1983); Careful He Might Hear You; Country Life; Don's Party; Killing of Angel Street, The; Long Weekend; Malcolm; My First Wife; Odd Angry Shot, The
Harker, Gordon: Champagne; Farmer's Wife, The
Harker, Susannah: Crucifer of Blood; Pride and Prejudice
Harkins, John: Birdy; Crime of the Century; One Shoe Makes It Murder; Rampage; Right of Way; This Gun for Hire
Harkishin, Jimmi: Bhaji on the Beach
Harlan, Dan: Blood, Guts, Bullets & Octane
Harlan, Kenneth: Shadow of the Eagle; Virginian, The
Harlan, Otis: Ride Him Cowboy; Telegraph Trail, The
Harlow, James: Safe House
Harlow, Jean: Bombshell; China Seas; Dinner at Eight; Girl from Missouri, The; Hold Your Man; Laurel and Hardy Classics: Vol. 1–9; Libeled Lady; Personal Property; Platinum Blonde; Public Enemy; Reckless; Red Dust; Red-Headed Woman; RiffRaff; Saratoga; Saturday Night Kid, The; Suzy; Wife vs. Secretary
Harlow, Shalom: Head Over Heels
Harmon, Deborah: Used Cars
Harmon, Mark: After the Promise; Casualties; Cold Heaven; Deliberate Stranger, The; Dillinger; Fear and Loathing in Las Vegas; Fourth Story; Goliath Awaits; Let's Get Harry; Long Road Home, The; Louis L'Amour's Crossfire Trail; Magic in the Water, The; Presidio, The; Prince of Bel Air; St. Elsewhere (TV Series); Stealing Home; Summer School; Sweet Bird of Youth; Till There Was You; Worth Winning; Wyatt Earp
Harmon, Tom: Spirit of West Point, The
Harmony, Christian: Doorway, The
Harmstorf, Raimund: Wolves, The
Harnett, Josh: Faculty, The; Halloween: H20
Harnick, Aaron: Judy Berlin
Harnois, Elisabeth: My Date with the President's Daughter
Harnos, Christine: Bloodhounds
Harnos, Kristina: Rescue, The
Harolde, Ralf: I'm No Angel
Harper, Frank: Twentyfourseven
Harper, Hill: He Got Game; Loving Jezebel; Skulls, The; Visit, The; Zooman
Harper, James: Mortal Sins (1990) (Dangerous Obsession)
Harper, Jessica: Blue Iguana; Imagemaker, The; Inserts; Mr. Wonderful; Pennies from Heaven; Phantom of the Paradise; Safe; Shock Treatment; Stardust Memories; Suspiria
Harper, Kamie: Friendship in Vienna, A
Harper, Marjory: Life and Times of Grizzly Adams, The
Harper, Robert: My Name Is Bill W; Nick Knight; Not Quite Human; Payoff
Harper, Samantha: Oh! Calcutta!
Harper, Tess: Amityville III: The Demon; Chiefs; Children of Fury; Crimes of the Heart; Criminal Law; Daddy's Dyin' and Who's Got the Will; Dark River: A Father's Revenge; Far North; Flashpoint; Her Alibi; Incident at Dark River; Ishtar; Man in the Moon, The; My Heroes Have Always Been Cowboys; My New Gun; Road to Galveston, The; Starflight One; Tender Mercies
Harper, Valerie: Blame It on Rio; Chapter Two; Don't Go to Sleep; Execution, The; Freebie and the Bean; Last Married Couple in America, The; Night Terror; Shadow Box, The; Thursday's Game
Harrelson, Brett: Dee Snider's Strangeland; From Dusk Till Dawn 2: Texas Blood Money; People vs. Larry Flynt, The
Harrelson, Woody: Cool Blue; Cowboy Way, The; Doc Hollywood; EDtv; Eye of the Demon; Hi-Lo Country, The; Indecent Proposal; Kingpin; Money Train; Natural Born Killers; Palmetto; People vs. Larry Flynt, The; Play It to the Bone; Sunchaser; Ted & Venus; Wag the Dog; Welcome to Sarajevo; White Men Can't Jump; Wildcats
Harring, Laura: Mulholland Drive; Rio Diablo
Harrington, Al: White Fang 2: Myth of the White Wolf
Harrington, Jay: Octopus (2000)
Harrington, Kate: Rachel, Rachel
Harrington, Kevin: Dish, The
Harrington, Laura: Dead Air; Linda; Maximum Overdrive; Midnight Cabaret; Perfect Witness
Harrington, Linda: Secret, The
Harrington, Pat: Affair, The; President's Analyst, The
Harrington, Peter: Time Chasers
Harris, Adeline: Texas John Slaughter: Stampede at Bitter Creek
Harris, Anita: Follow That Camel; Martians Go Home
Harris, Barbara: Dirty Rotten Scoundrels; Family Plot; Freaky Friday; Movie Movie; Nice Girls Don't Explode; North Avenue Irregulars, The; Oh Dad, Poor Dad—Mama's Hung You inthe

Closet and I'm Feeling So Sad; Peggy Sue Got Married; Plaza Suite; Seduction of Joe Tynan, The; Thousand Clowns, A
Harris, Barbara Eve: In His Father's Shoes
Harris, Brad: Fury of Hercules, The; Hercules; Rattler Kid; Samson; Seven Magnificent Gladiators, The
Harris, Bruklin: Dangerous Minds; Girls Town
Harris, Bud: Moon over Harlem
Harris, Christi: Night of the Demons 2
Harris, Cynthia: Edward and Mrs. Simpson; Izzy & Moe; Pancho Barnes; Reuben, Reuben
Harris, Danielle: Halloween IV: The Return of Michael Myers; Halloween V: The Revenge of Michael Myers; Killer Bud; Nightmare; Urban Legend
Harris, David: Badge of the Assassin; Dangerous Relations; Undercover
Harris, Dina: Ravage
Harris, Ed: Absolute Power; Abyss, The; Alamo Bay; Apollo 13; Beautiful Mind, A; Borderline; China Moon; Code Name: Emerald; Enemy at the Gates; Eye for an Eye; Firm, The; Flash of Green, A; Glengarry Glen Ross; Jackknife; Just Cause; Knightriders; Last Innocent Man, The; Milk Money; Needful Things; Nixon; Paris Trout; Places in the Heart; Pollock; Prime Gig, The; Riders of the Purple Sage; Right Stuff, The; Rock, The; Running Mates; Seekers, The; State of Grace; Stepmom; Sweet Dreams; Swing Shift; Third Miracle, The; To Kill a Priest; Truman Show, The; Under Fire; Walker
Harris, Emmylou: Down from the Mountain
Harris, Estelle: Addams Family Reunion; Chairman of the Board; Downhill Willie
Harris, Fred: Exterminators of the Year 3000
Harris, Gail: Forbidden Games
Harris, George: Prime Suspect 2
Harris, James: Sunset Park
Harris, Jamie: Savage Hearts
Harris, Jared: B. Monkey; Blue in the Face; Eternal, The; Happiness; I Shot Andy Warhol; Lush; Public Eye, The; Shadow Magic; Tall Tale: The Unbelievable Adventures of Pecos Bill
Harris, Jim: Squeeze Play
Harris, Jo Ann: Beguiled, The; Deadly Games
Harris, Jonathan: Lost in Space (TV Series)
Harris, Julie: Bell Jar, The; Carried Away; Christmas Wife, The; Dark Half, The; East of Eden; Ellen Foster; Gorillas in the Mist; Harper; Haunting, The; Hiding Place, The; Home for the Holidays (1972) (Television); Housesitter; I Am a Camera; Last of Mrs. Lincoln, The; Member of the Wedding, The; Reflections in a Golden Eye; Requiem for a Heavyweight (1962); Truth About Women, The; Voyage of the Damned; You're a Big Boy Now
Harris, Julius W.: Black Caesar; Friday Foster; Harley Davidson and the Marlboro Man; Hell Up in Harlem; Islands in the Stream; Shrunken Heads; Superfly; To Sleep with Anger
Harris, Kathryn: Broken Trust
Harris, Lara: All Tied Up; Dogfighters, The; Habitat; Inhumanoid; No Man's Land; Suicide Kings
Harris, Laura: Calling, The; Faculty, The; Highwayman, The
Harris, Lynn: Pleasure Unlimited
Harris, M. K.: Horseplayer; Slumber Party Massacre 3
Harris, Mel: Cameron's Closet; Desperate Motive; Firetrap; K-9; My Brother's Wife; Secretary, The; Sharon's Secret; Spider and the Fly, The; Suture; Wanted: Dead or Alive
Harris, Michael: Bar Girls; Dead Air; I Love You, Don't Touch Me!; Shattered Image; Soft Kill, The; Suture
Harris, Moira: Hellcab; One More Saturday Night
Harris, Neil Patrick: Clara's Heart; Cold Sassy Tree; Joan of Arc (1999); Man in the Attic, The; My Antonia; Purple People Eater; Starship Troopers
Harris, Phil: Buck Benny Rides Again; Dreaming Out Loud; Goodbye, My Lady; High and the Mighty, The; Melody Cruise; Wabash Avenue; Wheeler Dealers, The
Harris, Priscilla: Nights in White Satin
Harris, Richard: Abraham; Bible, The; Camelot; Cassandra Crossing, The; Count of Monte Cristo, The (2002); Cromwell; Cry, the Beloved Country; Deadly Trackers, The; Field, The; Game for Vultures; Gladiator; Grizzly Falls; Gulliver's Travels; Harry Potter and the Sorcerer's Stone; Hawaii; Hero, The (1971); Highpoint; Hunchback, The (1997); Juggernaut; King of the Wind; Last Word, The; Mack the Knife; Major Dundee; Man Called Horse, A; Man in the Wilderness; Martin's Day; Molly Maguires, The; Mutiny on the Bounty; 99 and 44/100 Percent Dead; Orca; Patriot Games; Red Desert; Return of a Man Called Horse, The; Robin and Marian; Savage Hearts; Shake Hands with the Devil; Silent Tongue; Smilla's Sense of Snow; Tarzan the Ape Man; This Is the Sea; This Sporting Life; Triumphs of a Man Called Horse; Unforgiven (1992); Wild Geese, The; Wreck of the Mary Deare, The; Wrestling Ernest Hemingway
Harris, Robert: Terrorists, The
Harris, Robert H.: How to Make a Monster
Harris, Robin: House Party; Mo' Better Blues; Sorority House Massacre 2
Harris, Robyn: Hard to Die
Harris, Rolf: Toby and the Koala Bear
Harris, Rosalind: Fiddler on the Roof
Harris, Rosemary: Beau Brummell; Chisholms, The; Heartbreak House; Little Riders, The; Ploughman's Lunch, The; Spider-Man; To the Lighthouse; Tom & Viv
Harris, Ross: Dog Trouble; Nightmare House; Testament
Harris, Stacy: Wyatt Earp: Return to Tombstone
Harris, Steve: Street Hunter
Harris, Wood: Remember the Titans
Harris, Zelda: Clover; Crooklyn
Harris Jr., Wendell B.: Chameleon Street
Harrison, Andrew: Littlest Horse Thieves, The
Harrison, Catherine: Blue Fire Lady; Empire State
Harrison, Emily: Curse of the Puppet Master
Harrison, Gavin: Public Enemy #1
Harrison, George: Imagine: John Lennon; Rutles, The (All You Need Is Cash)
Harrison, Gregory: Air Bud: Golden Receiver; Bare Essentials; Caught in the Act; Dangerous Pursuit; Duplicates; Enola Gay: The Men, the Mission, the Atomic Bomb; First Daughter; First Target; For Ladies Only; Hard Evidence; Hasty Heart; It's My Party; North Shore; Oceans of Fire; Razorback; Running Wild; Seduced
Harrison, Jenilee: Curse III: Blood Sacrifice; Fist of Iron; Illicit Behavior; Prime Target
Harrison, Kathleen: Christmas Carol, A; Ghoul, The; Night Must Fall
Harrison, Linda: Beneath the Planet of the Apes
Harrison, Noel: Déjà Vu
Harrison, Rex: Agony and the Ecstasy, The; Anastasia: The Mystery of Anna; Anna and the King of Siam; Ashanti; Blithe Spirit; Citadel, The; Cleopatra; Doctor Dolittle; Fifth Musketeer, The; Ghost and Mrs. Muir, The; Heartbreak House; Honey Pot, The; King Richard and the Crusaders; Major Barbara; Midnight Lace; My Fair Lady; Night Train to Munich (Night Train); Prince and the Pauper, The; Reluctant Debutante, The; Sidewalks of London; Staircase; Storm in a Teacup; Time to Die, A; Unfaithfully Yours
Harrison, Richard: Between God, the Devil and a Winchester; Empire of the Dark; His Name Was King; Place Called Trinity, A; Rescue Force
Harrison, Sandra: Blood of Dracula
Harrison, Susan: Sweet Smell of Success
Harrod, David: Blood on the Badge
Harrold, Kathryn: Best Legs in the 8th Grade, The; Bogie; Companion, The; Dead Solid Perfect; Deadly Desire; Heartbreakers; Hunter, The (1980); Into the Night; Modern Romance; Nightwing; Pursuit of D. B. Cooper; Rainbow Drive; Raw Deal; Sender, The; Yes, Giorgio
Harron, Dan: Really Weird Tales
Harron, Robert: Avenging Conscience, The; Hearts of the World; Home, Sweet Home (1914); Intolerance; Judith of Bethulia; Mother and the Law, The
Harrow, Lisa: Final Conflict, The; From a Far Country; Last Days of Chez Nous, The; Shaker Run; Sunday
Harry, Deborah: Forever Lulu; Hairspray; Heavy; Intimate Stranger; John Carpenter Presents: Body Bags; Satisfaction; Six Ways to Sunday; Tales from the Darkside, The Movie; Union City; Videodrome

Hart, Christopher: Addams Family Values
Hart, Christopher J.: Lady Terminator
Hart, David: Liam
Hart, Dolores: King Creole; Lonelyhearts; Loving You; Where the Boys Are (1960)
Hart, Dorothy: Naked City, The
Hart, Ian: BackBeat; Closer You Get, The; End of the Affair, The; Frogs for Snakes; Harry Potter and the Sorcerer's Stone; Hollow Reed; Hours and Times; Land and Freedom; Liam; Michael Collins; Monument Ave.; Nothing Personal; Wonderland (1999)
Hart, John: Blackenstein; Longhorn
Hart, Kevin: Lone Wolf
Hart, Linda: Get Shorty; Tin Cup
Hart, Melissa Joan: Drive Me Crazy; Sabrina, the Teenage Witch
Hart, Nadine: Robot Holocaust
Hart, Pam: Pi
Hart, Richard: Green Dolphin Street
Hart, Roxanne: Last Innocent Man, The; Meteorites!; Oh, God, You Devil!; Our Mother's Murder; Pulse; Samaritan: The Mitch Snyder Story; Special Bulletin; Tagget
Hart, Stacy: Get Real
Hart, Susan: Dr. Goldfoot and the Bikini Machine; Slime People, The
Hart, Teddy: Ma and Pa Kettle on Vacation
Hart, Veronica: RSVP
Hart, William S.: Hell's Hinges; Narrow Trail, The; Three-Word Brand, The; Tumbleweeds
Harte, Christine: Wish Me Luck
Harte, Jennifer: Prehysteria 2
Hartford, Glen: Hell Squad
Hartford, John: Down from the Mountain
Hartley, Daniel: Mystery Monsters
Hartley, Hal: Flirt
Hartley, Mariette: Encino Man; Improper Channels; M.A.D.D.: Mothers Against Drunk Driving; O'Hara's Wife; 1969; Ride the High Country; Silence of the Heart
Hartman, David: Island at the Top of the World, The
Hartman, Elizabeth: Beguiled, The; Group, The; Patch of Blue, A; Walking Tall; You're a Big Boy Now
Hartman, Jesse: Habit
Hartman, Lawrence: Zentropa
Hartman, Lisa: Bare Essentials; Bodily Harm; Full Exposure; Return of Eliot Ness, The; Take, The; Where the Boys Are '84
Hartman, Phil: Blind Date; CB4; Coneheads; Greedy; Houseguest; Jingle All the Way; Pagemaster, The; Pee-Wee Herman Show, The; Second Civil War, The; Sgt. Bilko; Small Soldiers; So I Married an Axe Murderer
Hartmann, Paul: Haunted Castle
Hartnell, William: Battle Hell; Dr. Who (TV series)
Hartner, Rona: Gadjo Dilo
Hartnett, Josh: Black Hawk Down; Blow Dry; 40 Days and 40 Nights; Here on Earth; O; Pearl Harbor; Virgin Suicides, The
Haruna, Kazuo: Silk Road, The
Harvest, Rainbow: Mirror Mirror; Old Enough
Harvey, Don: American Heart; Atom Man vs. Superman; Batman and Robin (Adventures of Batmanand Robin); Better Off Dead; Casualties of War; Con, The; Gang Busters; Prey of the Chameleon; Sawbones; Tank Girl
Harvey, Forrester: Chump at Oxford, A; Mystery Ranch
Harvey, Georgette: Chloe: Love is Calling You
Harvey, Joan: Hands of a Stranger
Harvey, John: Pin-Up Girl
Harvey, Laurence: Alamo, The; Butterfield 8; Dandy in Aspic, A; Darling; Escape to the Sun; I Am a Camera; King Richard and the Crusaders; Manchurian Candidate, The; Night Watch; Of Human Bondage; Romeo and Juliet; Room at the Top; Silent Enemy, The; Spy with a Cold Nose, The; Summer and Smoke; Three Men in a Boat; Truth About Women, The; Walk on the Wild Side; Wonderful World of the Brothers Grimm, The
Harvey, Paul: Call Northside 777; Helldorado; Meet Dr. Christian; Tournament Tempo
Harvey, Rodney: Guncrazy (1950); Mixed Blood
Harvey, Terence: Guncrazy (1950); Mixed Blood
Harvey, Tom: And Then You Die
Harwood, Bruce: X-Files, The (TV Series)
Hasegawa, Kazuo: Actor's Revenge, An; Chikamatsu Monogatari
Hasgawa, Machiko: Zatoichi: Masseur Ichi and a Chest ofGold
Hashemian, Mir Farrokh: Children of Heaven
Haskell, Colleen: Animal, The
Haskell, Peter: Christina; Cracker Factory; Riding the Edge
Hass, Dolly: Spy of Napoleon
Hasse, O. E.: Betrayed; Big Lift, The; State of Siege
Hasselhoff, David: Bail Out; Baywatch: The Movie; Cartier Affair, The; Final Alliance; Ring of the Musketeer; Star Crash; Terror at London Bridge; Witchery
Hassett, Marilyn: Bell Jar, The; Gypsy Angels; Massive Retaliation; Messenger of Death; Other Side of the Mountain, The; Other Side of the Mountain, Part II, The; Two-Minute Warning
Hasso, Signe: Heaven Can Wait; House on 92nd Street, The; Johnny Angel; Picture Mommy Dead; Reflection of Fear; Seventh Cross, The; Story of Dr. Wassell, The
Hasson, Ann: Romeo and Juliet
Hatch, Richard: Battlestar Galactica; Charlie Chan and the Curse of the Dragon Queen; Deadman's Curve; Delta Force, Commando Two; Ghetto Blaster; Hatfields and the McCoys, The; Heated Vengeance; Party Line; Prisoners of the Lost Universe
Hatcher, Teri: All Tied Up; Brain Smasher ... A Love Story; Cool Surface, The; Dead in the Water; Heaven's Prisoners; Running Mates; Since You've Been Gone; Soapdish; Spy Kids; Straight Talk; Tomorrow Never Dies; Two Days in the Valley
Hatfield, Hurd: Boston Strangler, The; Crimes of the Heart; Dragon Seed; El Cid; Her Alibi; King of Kings (1961); Left Handed Gun, The; Lies of the Twins; Picture of Dorian Gray, The
Hathaway, Amy: Last Exit to Earth
Hathaway, Anne: Princess Diaries, The
Hathaway, Noah: NeverEnding Story, The; Troll
Hatosy, Shawn: Anywhere But Here; Down to You; Faculty, The; John Q; Outside Providence; Witness Protection
Hattab, Yoram: Kadosh
Hattie, Hilo: Ma and Pa Kettle at Waikiki
Hatton, Raymond: Ace of Hearts; Arizona Bound; Below the Border; Covered Wagon Days; Dawn on the Great Divide; Down Texas Way; Forbidden Trails; Frontier Horizon; Frontier Pony Express; Ghost Town Law; Gunman from Bodie; Kansas Terrors; Lady Killer; Law and Order; Peck's Bad Boy; Rocky Mountain Rangers; Rough Riders' Roundup; Texas; Three Musketeers, The; Vigilantes Are Coming!; Virginian, The; Wagon Wheels; Wall Street Cowboy; West of the Law; Wyoming Outlaw
Hatton, Rondo: Brute Man, The; House of Horrors; In Old Chicago; Pearl of Death, The
Haudepin, Didier: Assassins de L'Ordre, Les (Law Breakers); This Special Friendship
Hauer, Rutger: Amelia Earhart: The Final Flight; Arctic Blue; Beyond Justice; Blade Runner; Blast; Bleeders; Blind Fury; Blind Side; Blood of Heroes; Blood of the Innocent; Bloodhounds of Broadway; Bone Daddy; Breed Apart, A; Buffy, the Vampire Slayer; Call of the Wild: The Dog of the Yukon; Chanel Solitaire; Crossworlds; Dandelions; Deadlock; Eating Pattern; Escape from Sobibor; Eureka; Fatherland; Flesh and Blood (Sword and the Rose, the (1985)); Forbidden Choices; Hitcher, The; Hostile Waters; Inside the Third Reich; Katie's Passion; Ladyhawke; Merlin (1998); Mr. Stitch; Mysteries; New World Disorder; Nighthawks; Nostradamus; Omega Doom; Osterman Weekend, The; Partners in Crime; Past Midnight; Precious Find; Redline; Soldier of Orange; Split Second; Surviving the Game; Tactical Assault; 10th Kingdom, The; Turbulence 3: Heavy Metal; Turkish Delight; Voyage; Wanted: Dead or Alive
Hauff, Thomas: Climb, The
Hauman, Constance: Madame Butterfly
Haun, Lindsey: Color of Friendship, The
Hauser, Cole: All Over Me; Good Will Hunting; Hart's War; Hi-Lo Country, The; Pitch Black
Hauser, Fay: Christmas Lilies of the Field; Jimmy the Kid; Jo Jo Dancer, Your Life Is Calling; Marvin and Tige
Hauser, Wings: Art of Dying, The; Beastmaster 2: Through the Portal of Time; Bedroom Eyes II; Carpenter, The; Coldfire; Dead

Man Walking; Deadly Force; Exiled in America; Frame Up; Homework; Hostage; Jo Jo Dancer, Your Life Is Calling; L.A. Bounty; Living to Die; Long Hot Summer, The; Mutant; Nightmare at Noon; No Safe Haven; Original Gangstas; Out of Sight Out of Mind; Pale Blood; Reason to Die; Siege of Firebase Gloria, The; Street Asylum; Tales from the Hood; 3:15—The Moment of Truth; Tough Guys Don't Dance; Vice Squad; Wilding, The Children of Violence; Wind, The

Haustein, Thomas: Christiane F.

Hautesserre, Francois: A La Mode

Havens, Richie: Greased Lightning

Haver, June: Dolly Sisters, The; Look for the Silver Lining; Love Nest

Haver, Phyllis: Buster Keaton Festival Vol. 1–3; Fig Leaves; What Price Glory? (1926)

Havers, Nigel: Burke and Wills; Burning Season, The; Chariots of Fire; Empire of the Sun; Farewell to the King; Little Princess, A; Whistle Blower, The

Haverstock, Thom: Skullduggery

Haverty, Liz: 5 Dead on the Crimson Canvas

Havoc, June: Brewster's Millions; Can't Stop the Music; Four Jacks and a Jill; Gentlemen's Agreement; Hello, Frisco, Hello

Haw, Alex: Following

Hawdon, Robin: When Dinosaurs Ruled the Earth

Hawes, Keeley: Last September, The; Retribution

Hawke, Ethan: Alive; Before Sunrise; Dad; Dead Poets Society; Explorers; Floundering; Gattaca; Great Expectations; Hamlet; Midnight Clear, A; Mystery Date; Newton Boys, The; Reality Bites; Rich in Love; Search and Destroy; Snow Falling on Cedars; Training Day; Waterland; White Fang; White Fang 2: Myth of the White Wolf

Hawkes, Chesney: Buddy's Song

Hawkes, John: Hardball; Roadracers

Hawkes, Terri: Killing Man, The

Hawkins, Corwin: Low Down Dirty Shame, A

Hawkins, Georgia: Doomed Caravan

Hawkins, Jack: Ben-Hur; Bonnie Prince Charlie; Bridge on the River Kwai, The; Cruel Sea, The; Elusive Pimpernel, The; Escape to the Sun; Fallen Idol, The; Land of the Pharaohs; League of Gentlemen, The; Malta Story, The; No Highway in the Sky; Prisoner, The (1955); Shalako; Tales that Witness Madness; Waterloo; Young Winston; Zulu

Hawkins, Jimmy: Annie Oakley (TV Series)

Hawkins, Screamin' Jay: Mystery Train

Hawkshaw, Jean: Wild Women of Wongo

Hawley, Richard: Captives

Hawn, Goldie: Best Friends; Bird on a Wire; Butterflies Are Free; Cactus Flower; Crisscross (1992); Death Becomes Her; Deceived; $ (Dollars); Duchess and the Dirtwater Fox, The; Everyone Says I Love You; First Wives Club, The; Foul Play; Girl from Petrovka, The; Housesitter; Lovers and Liars; One and Only, Genuine, Original Family Band, The; Out-of-Towners, The (1999); Overboard; Private Benjamin; Protocol; Seems Like Old Times; Shampoo; Sugarland Express, The; Swing Shift; There's a Girl in My Soup; Town & Country; Wildcats

Haworth, Jill: Exodus; Home for the Holidays (1972) (Television); In Harm's Way

Haworth, Vinton: Riding on Air

Hawthorne, Elizabeth: Alex

Hawthorne, Nigel: Amistad; Big Brass Ring, The; Call Me Claus; Demolition Man; Inside; Madeline; Madness of King George, The; Mapp & Lucia; Murder in Mind; Object of My Affection, The; Pope John Paul II; Tartuffe; Twelfth Night; Victoria and Albert; Winslow Boy, The; Yes, Prime Minister

Hawtrey, Charles: Carry on at Your Convenience; Carry on Cleo; Carry on Doctor; Carry on Nurse; Follow That Camel; Terrornauts, The

Hay, Christian: You're Jinxed Friend, You Just Met Sacramento

Hay, Colin: Wacky World of Wills and Burke, The

Hayakawa, Sessue: Bridge on the River Kwai, The; Cheat, The; Daughter of the Dragon; Green Mansions; Hell to Eternity; Swiss Family Robinson, The; Three Came Home; Tokyo Joe

Hayashi, Chizu: Zatoichi: The Blind Swordsman and theChess Expert

Hayashi, Marc: Chan Is Missing; Laser Man, The

Hayden, Dennis: One Man Army

Hayden, Julie: It's Pat: The Movie

Hayden, Linda: Madhouse; Shattered; Taste the Blood of Dracula

Hayden, Nora: Angry Red Planet, The

Hayden, Russell: Badmen of the Hills; Border Vigilantes; Doomed Caravan; Heart of Arizona; Heritage of the Desert; Hidden Gold; Hills of Old Wyoming; Hopalong Rides Again; In Old Colorado; In Old Mexico; Law of the Pampas; North of the Rio Grande; Pirates on Horseback; Range War; Renegade Trail; Santa Fe Marshal; Silver on the Sage; Stagecoach War; Texas Trail; Three Men from Texas; Wide-Open Town

Hayden, Sterling: Asphalt Jungle, The; Blue and the Gray, The; Crime of Passion; Denver and Rio Grande, The; Dr. Strangelove or How I Learned to Stop Worrying and Love the Bomb; Fighter Attack; Flat Top; Gas; Godfather, The; Johnny Guitar; Kansas Pacific; Killing, The; King of the Gypsies; Last Command, The; Last Days of Man on Earth, The; Long Goodbye, The; Prince Valiant; Shotgun; Spaghetti Western; Star, The (1952); Suddenly; Venom; Winter Kills

Haydn, Richard: Adventures of Bullwhip Griffin, The; And Then There Were None; Ball of Fire; Clarence, the Cross-Eyed Lion; Emperor Waltz, The; Five Weeks in a Balloon; Forever Amber; Jupiter's Darling; Mr. Music; Mutiny on the Bounty; Never Let Me Go; Please Don't Eat the Daisies; Singapore; Young Frankenstein

Haydon, Julie: Scoundrel, The

Hayek, Salma: Breaking Up; Desperado; Dogma; Faculty, The; 54; Fled; Fools Rush In; Hunchback, The (1997); Roadracers; Timecode; Velocity of Gary, The; Wild Wild West (1999)

Hayenga, Jeff: Unborn, The

Hayes, Allan: Neon Maniacs

Hayes, Allison: Attack of the 50-Foot Woman; Disembodied, The; Gunslinger; Hypnotic Eye, The; Mohawk; Undead, The; Unearthly, The; Zombies of Mora Tav

Hayes, Billie: Li'l Abner

Hayes, Carey: RSVP

Hayes, George "Gabby": Along the Navajo Trail; Arizona Kid; Bad Man of Deadwood; Badman's Territory; Bar-20 Rides Again; Bells of Rosarita; Blue Steel; Borderland; Broadway to Cheyenne; Call of the Prairie; Calling Wild Bill Elliott; Cariboo Trail; Carson City Kid; Dark Command; Death Valley Manhunt; Don't Fence Me In; Eagle's Brood; Heart of Arizona; Heart of the Golden West; Helldorado; Hidden Valley Outlaws; Hills of Old Wyoming; Hopalong Cassidy Returns; Hopalong Rides Again; In Old Caliente; In Old Mexico; In Old Santa Fe; Jesse James at Bay; Lawless Frontier; Lawless Nineties, The; Lights of Old Santa Fe; Lost City, The; Lucky Texan; Man from Utah, The; Melody Ranch; Mojave Firebrand; My Pal Trigger; 'Neath Arizona Skies; North of the Rio Grande; Phantom Broadcast, The; Plainsman, The; Rainbow Valley; Randy Rides Alone; Ranger and the Lady, The; Renegade Trail; Return of the Bad Men; Riders of Destiny; Robin Hood of the Pecos; Roll on Texas Moon; Romance on the Range; Saga of Death Valley; Silver on the Sage; Sons of the Pioneers; Star Packer, The; Sunset Serenade; Tall in the Saddle; Texas Rangers (1936); Texas Terror; Texas Trail; Three on the Trail; Trail Dust; Trail Street; Trailin' North; Utah; Wall Street Cowboy; War of the Wildcats; West of the Divide; Young Bill Hickok

Hayes, Helen: Airport; Anastasia; Arrowsmith; Candleshoe; Family Upside Down, A; Farewell to Arms, A; Herbie Rides Again; Murder with Mirrors; One of Our Dinosaurs Is Missing; Sin of Madelon Claudet, The; Skin Game, The (1931); Stage Door Canteen; Victory at Entebbe

Hayes, Isaac: Acting on Impulse; Counterforce; Final Judgment; Flipper; Good Idea; Guilty as Charged; Illtown; I'm Gonna Git You Sucka!; It Could Happen to You; Oblivion; Oblivion 2: Backlash; Posse; Prime Target; Robin Hood: Men in Tights; Six Ways to Sunday; Truck Turner; Uncle Sam

Hayes, Jerri: Black Sister's Revenge

Hayes, Linda: Romance on the Range

Hayes, Lucky: White Wolves II: Legend of the Wild

Hayes, Maggie: Girls Town

Hayes, Margaret: In Old Colorado
Hayes, Patricia: Corn Is Green, The; Fish Called Wanda, A; Willow
Hayes, Peter Lind: Five Thousand Fingers of Dr. T, The; Senator Was Indiscreet, The; Yin and Yang of Mr. Go, The
Hayes, Sean P.: Billy's Hollywood Screen Kiss
Hayes, Susan Seaforth: Dream Machine
Haygarth, Tony: Infiltrator, The
Hayman, Cyd: Godsend, The
Hayman, David: Behind the Lines; Gospel According to Vic, The; Hope and Glory; My Name is Joe; Sense of Freedom, A; Sid and Nancy
Hayman, Leslie: Virgin Suicides, The
Haymer, John: Four Deuces, The
Haymes, Dick: Four Jills in a Jeep; St. Benny the Dip; State Fair
Hayner, Daniel: Hallelujah!
Haynes, Linda: Drowning Pool, The; Latitude Zero; Rolling Thunder
Haynes, Lloyd: Good Guys Wear Black
Haynes, Roberta: Hell Ship Mutiny; Return to Paradise
Haynie, Jim: Bridges of Madison County, The; From Hollywood to Deadwood; Grand Tour: Disaster in Time; On the Edge; Out; Peacemaker, The (1997); Staying Together; Stephen King's Sleepwalkers; Too Much Sun
Hays, Kathryn: Ride Beyond Vengeance; Yuma
Hays, Lauren: Rebecca's Secret
Hays, Robert: Airplane!; Airplane II: The Sequel; California Gold Rush; Cat's Eye; Cyber Bandits; Dr. T and the Women; Fall of the House of Usher, The; Fifty/Fifty; Homeward Bound: The Incredible Journey; Homeward Bound II: Lost in San Francisco; Honeymoon Academy; Hot Chocolate; No Dessert Dad Until You Mow the Lawn; Raw Justice; Running Against Time; Scandalous; Take This Job and Shove It; Touched; Trenchcoat; Utilities
Hays, Steve: Trick
Haysbert, Dennis: Love and Basketball; Love Field; Major League: Back to the Minors; Minus Man, The; Mr. Baseball; Random Hearts; Return to Lonesome Dove; Standoff; Suture; Thirteenth Floor, The; Waiting to Exhale; What's Cooking?; Widow's Kiss
Hayshi, Henry: Pushed to the Limit
Hayter, David: Guyver 2: Dark Hero
Hayter, James: Big Fella; Pickwick Papers, The; Story of Robin Hood, The; Tom Brown's Schooldays (1950)
Hayward, Chad: Killing Game, The
Hayward, David: Accidental Meeting; Delusion; Fallen Angel; Red Alert
Hayward, Leland: Fear, The (1994)
Hayward, Louis: And Then There Were None; Anthony Adverse; Black Arrow, The (1948); Christmas Kid, The; Chuka; Dance, Girl, Dance; House by the River; Man in the Iron Mask, The; Rage of Paris, The; Saint in New York, The; Search for Bridey Murphy, The; Son of Monte Cristo, The; Strange Woman, The; Terror in the Wax Museum
Hayward, Susan: Adam Had Four Sons; Among the Living; Back Street; Beau Geste; Conqueror, The; David and Bathsheba; Deadline at Dawn; Demetrius and the Gladiators; Fighting Seabees, The; Hairy Ape, The; Honey Pot, The; House of Strangers; I Want to Live!; I'll Cry Tomorrow; Jack London; Lost Moment, The; Lusty Men, The; My Foolish Heart; Rawhide; Reap the Wild Wind; Say Goodbye, Maggie Cole; Smash-Up: The Story of a Woman; Snows of Kilimanjaro, The; Soldier of Fortune; Stolen Hours; They Won't Believe Me; Tulsa; Valley of the Dolls; Where Love Has Gone; Young and Willing
Haywood, Chris: Alex; Attack Force Z; Dogs in Space; Heatwave (1983); Kiss or Kill; Malcolm; Man of Flowers; Navigator: A Medieval Odyssey, The; Sweet Talker; Tale of Ruby Rose, The
Hayworth, Rita: Affair in Trinidad; Angels over Broadway; Blood and Sand; Charlie Chan in Egypt; Circus World; Cover Girl; Gilda; Hit the Saddle; Lady from Shanghai; Lady in Question; Loves of Carmen, The; Miss Sadie Thompson; Only Angels Have Wings; Pal Joey; Poppy Is Also a Flower, The; Renegade Ranger; Salome; Strawberry Blonde, The; Susan and God; Tales of Manhattan; They Came to Cordura; Tonight and Every Night; Trouble in Texas; You Were Never Lovelier; You'll Never Get Rich
Haze, Jonathan: Little Shop of Horrors, The (1960); Poor White Trash
Hazeldine, James: Business As Usual
Hazlehurst, Noni: Monkey Grip
He, Saifei: Temptress Moon
Head, Leon: Vampire Vixens from Venus
Head, Murray: French Woman, The; Sunday, Bloody Sunday
Headey, Lena: Gossip; Mrs. Dalloway; Onegin; Rudyard Kipling's The Jungle Book (1994); Summer House, The; Twice Upon A Yesterday; Waterland
Headly, Glenne: Bastard Out of Carolina; Breakfast of Champions; Dick Tracy; Dirty Rotten Scoundrels; Getting Even with Dad; Grand Isle; Hotel Room; Lonesome Dove; Making Mr. Right; Mortal Thoughts; Mr. Holland's Opus; My Own Country; Nadine; Ordinary Magic; Paperhouse; Pronto; Seize the Day; Sgt. Bilko; Two Days in the Valley; What's the Worst That Could Happen?; Winchell
Heald, Anthony: Deep Rising; 8MM; Proof of Life
Healey, Myron: Gang Busters; Incredible Melting Man, The; Kansas Pacific; Longhorn; Monsoon; Rage at Dawn; Unearthly, The; Varan, the Unbelievable
Healy, David: Sign of Four, The
Healy, Dorian: Young Soul Rebels
Healy, Katherine: Six Weeks
Healy, Mary: Five Thousand Fingers of Dr. T, The; Second Fiddle
Healy, Patricia: Sweet Poison; Ultraviolet
Healy, Ted: Dancing Lady; Hollywood Hotel; Lost Stooges, The; Mad Love; Operator 13
Healy-Louie, Miriam: No Telling
Heames, Darin: Fear, The (1994)
Heard, John: After Hours; Animal Factory; Awakenings; Beaches; Best Revenge; Betrayed; Between the Lines; Big; Cat People; Chilly Scenes of Winter; C.H.U.D.; Cutter's Way; Dead Ahead: The Exxon Valdez Disaster; Deceived; End of Innocence, The; Executive Power; First Love; Gladiator; Heart Beat; Heaven Help Us; Home Alone; Home Alone 2: Lost in New York; Men; Milagro Beanfield War, The; Mindwalk; Monday Night Mayhem; My Fellow Americans; O; On the Yard; 187; Out on a Limb; Package, The; Pact, The; Pelican Brief, The; Radio Flyer; Rambling Rose; Seventh Sign, The; Snake Eyes; Telephone, The; Trip to Bountiful, The; Violated; Waterland
Hearn, Ann: Dollmaker, The
Hearn, George: Annie, a Royal Adventure!; Barney's Great Adventure; Durango; Piano for Mrs. Cimino, A; Sanctuary of Fear; Sneakers; Sweeney Todd
Hearst, Patty: Bio-Dome; Cry-Baby
Hearst, Rick: Crossing the Line (1990)
Heath, Charlie: Leprechaun 2
Heath, Darrell: Don't Be a Menace to South Central while Drinking Your Juice in the 'Hood
Heath, Robin Lynn: Stranger, The
Heather, Jean: Last Round-Up
Heatherton, Joey: Bluebeard; Cry-Baby; Happy Hooker Goes to Washington, The; Where Love Has Gone
Heavener, David: L.A. Goddess; Outlaw Force; Prime Target
Heavy D: Big Trouble (2002)
Heche, Anne: Adventures of Huck Finn, The (1993); Beyond Suspicion; Donnie Brasco; Girls in Prison; I Know What You Did Last Summer; If These Walls Could Talk; John Q; Juror, The; Kingfish: A Story of Huey P. Long; O Pioneers!; One Kill; Pie in the Sky; Psycho; Return to Paradise; Six Days, Seven Nights; Third Miracle, The; Volcano; Wag the Dog; Walking and Talking; Wild Side
Hecht, Donatella: Flesh Eating Mothers
Hecht, Gina: One Night Stand
Hecht, Jessica: Intimate Betrayal
Heck, Angela: Tales from the Gimli Hospital
Heckart, Eileen: Bad Seed, The; Burnt Offerings; Butterflies Are Free; First Wives Club, The; Heller in Pink Tights; Hiding Place, The; Hot Spell; No Way to Treat a Lady; Somebody Up

Right Stuff, The; Shy People; Soldier's Daughter Never Cries, A; Splitting Heirs; Stunt Man, The; Swing Kids; Take This Job and Shove It; Tin Men; Tune in Tomorrow; With Six You Get Eggroll; World Apart, A

Hersholt, Jean: Cat and the Fiddle, The; Courageous Dr. Christian, The; Dr. Christian Meets the Women; Emma; Greed; Happy Landing; Heidi; Hell Harbor; Mask of Fu Manchu, The; Meet Dr. Christian; Melody for Three; Mr. Moto in Danger Island; One in a Million; Painted Veil, The; Remedy for Riches; Sin of Madelon Claudet, The; Skyscraper Souls; Student Prince in Old Heidelberg, The; Susan Lenox: Her Fall and Rise; They Meet Again

Herter, Gerard: Caltiki, the Immortal Monster; Go Kill and Come Back; Machine Gun Killers

Hervey, Irene: Charlie Chan in Shanghai; Count of Monte Cristo, The; Dude Ranger; Mr. Peabody and the Mermaid; Night Monster; Play Misty for Me

Herzog, Werner: Burden of Dreams; Man of Flowers; Tokyo-Ga

Heskin, Kam: Blackjack

Heslov, Grant: Dante's Peak

Hess, David: Last House on the Left; Let It Rock; Swamp Thing

Hess, Michelle: Taxi Dancers

Hess, Sandra: Beastmaster III: The Eye of Braxus; Mortal Kombat: Annihilation

Hess, Susan: Dress Gray

Hesseman, Howard: Amazon Women on the Moon; Big Bus, The; Diamond Trap, The; Doctor Detroit; Flight of the Navigator; Gridlock'd; Heat; Hot Chocolate; Inside Out; Little Miss Millions; Loose Shoes; Murder in New Hampshire; My Chauffeur; One Shoe Makes It Murder; Out of Sync; Police Academy II: Their First Assignment; Princess Who Had Never Laughed, The; Rubin & Ed; Silence of the Heart; Sunshine Boys, The; Tarantulas—The Deadly Cargo; Tunnelvision (1976)

Heston, Charlton: Agony and the Ecstasy, The; Airport 1975; Alaska; Antony and Cleopatra; Arrowhead; Avenging Angel, The (1995); Awakening, The; Ben-Hur; Beneath the Planet of the Apes; Big Country, The; Buccaneer, The; Call of the Wild; Chiefs; Crucifer of Blood; Diamond Head; Earthquake; El Cid; 55 Days at Peking; Four Musketeers, The; Gray Lady Down; Greatest Show on Earth, The; Greatest Story Ever Told, The; Hamlet; In the Mouth of Madness; Julius Caesar; Khartoum; Little Kidnappers; Major Dundee; Midway; Mother Lode; Mountain Men, The; Nairobi Affair; Naked Jungle, The; Omega Man, The; Order, The; Planet of the Apes; Pony Express; Prince and the Pauper, The; Proud Men; Ruby Gentry; Solar Crisis; Soylent Green; Ten Commandments, The; Thousand Heroes, A; Three Musketeers, The; Three Violent People; Tombstone; Touch of Evil; Town & Country; Treasure Island; True Lies; Two-Minute Warning; War Lord, The; Will Penny; Wreck of the Mary Deare, The

Heuring, Lori: In Crowd, The; True Blue

Hewett, Christopher: Producers, The; Ratboy

Hewett, Lauren: Echo of Thunder, The

Hewitt, Alan: Misadventures of Merlin Jones, The

Hewitt, Barbara: Equinox (The Beast) (1971)

Hewitt, Jennifer Love: Can't Hardly Wait; Heartbreakers; I Know What You Did Last Summer; I Still Know What You Did Last Summer; Telling You; Trojan War

Hewitt, Martin: Alien Predators; Crime Lords; Endless Love; Night Fire; Out of Control; Private War; White Ghost

Hewlett, David: Boys of St. Vincent; Cube; Desire and Hell at Sunset Motel; Penthouse, The; Pin; Scanners 2: The New Order

Hext, Tamera: Gates of Hell Part II: Dead Awakening

Hey, Virginia: Farscape (TV series); Obsession: A Taste for Fear

Heyden, Yvette: Tides of War

Heydt, Louis Jean: Great McGinty, The; Great Moment, The; Test Pilot; They Were Expendable

Heyerdahl, Christopher: Killing Yard, The; Silent Trigger

Heyl, John: Separate Peace, A

Heyman, Barton: Billy Galvin; Let's Scare Jessica to Death; Trial of the Cantonsville Nine, The; Valdez Is Coming

Heywood, Anne: Brain, The; I Want What I Want; Ninety Degrees in the Shade; Sadat; Scenes from a Murder; Shaming, The; Very Edge, The; What Waits Below

Heywood, Colin: Bloody New Year

Heywood, Pat: Rude Awakening; Wish You Were Here

Hezelhurst, Noni: Waiting

Hickey, Barry: Las Vegas Weekend

Hickey, Brendan: I Married a Vampire

Hickey, John Benjamin: Love! Valour! Compassion!; Only You

Hickey, Marguerite: Mirrors

Hickey, Tom: Last September, The; Raining Stones

Hickey, William: Any Man's Death; Bright Lights, Big City; Da; Forget Paris; Maddening, The; Major Payne; Mob Boss; Name of the Rose, The; Pink Cadillac; Prizzi's Honor; Puppet Master, The; Runestone; Tales from the Darkside, The Movie; Walls of Glass

Hickland, Catherine: Ghost Town; Witchery

Hickman, Darryl: Any Number Can Play; Fighting Father Dunne; Human Comedy, The; Island in the Sky; Johnny Shiloh; Keeper of the Flame; King Lear; Leave Her to Heaven; Men of Boys Town; Strange Love of Martha Ivers, The; Tea and Sympathy; Tingler, The

Hickman, Dwayne: Dr. Goldfoot and the Bikini Machine; High School, USA; How to Stuff a Wild Bikini

Hickman, Howard: Civilization; Kansas Terrors

Hicks, Catharine: Child's Play; Death Valley; Eight Days a Week; Fever Pitch; Laguna Heat; Like Father, Like Son; Peggy Sue Got Married; Razor's Edge, The; Redwood Curtain; Running Against Time; She's Out of Control; Souvenir; Spy; Star Trek IV: The Voyage Home

Hicks, Danny: Intruder (1988)

Hicks, Greg: Deadline

Hicks, Hilly: Amazing Spiderman, The; Cartier Affair, The

Hicks, Kevin: Blood Relations; Dance Me Outside; Final Notice

Hicks, Leonard: Santa Claus Conquers the Martians

Hicks, Michele: Twin Falls Idaho

Hicks, Redmond: She's Gotta Have It

Hicks, Russell: Captain America; Devil Dogs of the Air

Hicks, Seymour: Scrooge

Hicks, Taral: Belly; Bronx Tale, A

Hicks, William T.: Day of Judgment, A; Order of the Black Eagle

Hickson, Joan: At Bertram's Hotel; Body in the Library, The; Caribbean Mystery, A; Clockwise; 4:50 From Paddington; Great Expectations; Mirror Crack'd from Side to Side, The; Moving Finger, The; Murder at the Vicarage; Murder Is Announced, A; Murder She Said; Nemesis; Pocketful of Rye, A; Sleeping Murder; They Do It with Mirrors; Why Didn't They Ask Evans?

Hidalgo-Gato, Raymundo: El Super

Hidari, Sachiko: Insect Woman

Hiep, Nguyen Ngoc: Three Seasons

Higashiyama, Chiyeko: Tokyo Story

Higby, Mary Jane: Honeymoon Killers, The

Higby, Wilbur: True Heart Susie

Higgins, Anthony: Alive & Kicking; Bride, The; Cold Room, The; Draughtman's Contract, The; For Love or Money; Max Mon Amour; Quartet; Sweet Killing; Taste the Blood of Dracula; Young Sherlock Holmes

Higgins, Clare: Hellraiser; Hellraiser II: Hellbound

Higgins, Joel: First Affair; Killing at Hell's Gate

Higgins, John Michael: Best in Show; G.I. Jane; Late Shift, The; National Lampoon's Class of '86

Higgins, Michael: Courtship; On Valentine's Day; 1918; Paul's Case

Higgins, Paul: Retribution

Higginson, Jane: Silent Night, Deadly Night 5: The Toy Maker

Higginson, Tori: Jungleground

Hilario, Jonathan: Pig's Tale, A

Hilboldt, Lise: George Washington: The Forging of a Nation; Married Man, A; Noon Wine; Pudd'nhead Wilson; Sweet Liberty

Hildebrandt, Charles George: Return of the Alien's Deadly Spawn, The

Hildreth, Mark: Past Perfect

Hill, Arthur: Andromeda Strain, The; Dirty Tricks; Futureworld; Guardian, The; Harper; Killer Elite, The; Love Leads the Way; Murder in Space; One Magic Christmas; Ordeal of Dr. Mudd, The; Petulia; Prototype; Pursuit of Happiness, The; Return of

cust, The; Fever Lake; Fifth Floor, The; Final Alliance; From Dusk Till Dawn 2: Texas Blood Money; Inside Monkey Zetterland; Kansas City Massacre, The; Killer Elite, The; Last Ride of the Dalton Gang, The; Macho Callahan; Mark of the Beast, The; More American Graffiti; Mutant; Nightmare at Noon; November Conspiracy, The; Painted Hero; Posse; Rodeo Girl; Small Town in Texas, A; Smoky Mountain Christmas; Sweet Sixteen; Tentacles; Texas Payback; Time Served; Trapper County War; Uncle Sam; What Comes Around; White Lightning; Wyatt Earp: Return to Tombstone
Hopkins, Harold: Club, The; Sara Dane; Winds of Jarrah, The
Hopkins, Jermaine "Huggy": Juice; Phat Beach
Hopkins, Miriam: Barbary Coast, The; Becky Sharp; Carrie; Chase, The; Children's Hour, The; Dr. Jekyll and Mr. Hyde; Heiress, The; Old Maid, The; Savage Intruder, The; These Three; Virginia City
Hopkins, Telma: Bosom Buddies (TV Series); Kid with the Broken Halo, The; Trancers
Hoppe, Marianne: Ten Little Indians
Hoppe, Rolf: Palmetto
Hopper, Dennis: American Friend, The; Apocalypse Now; Apostate, The; Backtrack; Basquiat; Black Widow; Blood Red; Blue Velvet; Boiling Point; Carried Away; Chasers; Chattahoochee; Cheyenne (TV Series); Doublecrossed; Easy Rider; EDtv; Eye of the Storm; Flashback; Giant; Glory Stompers, The; Heart of Justice; Hoosiers; Inside Man, The; Jason and the Argonauts; Jesus' Son; King of the Mountain; Last Days of Frankie the Fly, The; Last Movie, The (Chinchero); Let It Rock; Luck of the Draw; Lured Innocence; Mad Dog Morgan; Meet the Deedles; My Science Project; Nails; Night Tide; O.C. & Stiggs; Osterman Weekend, The; Paris Trout; Pick-Up Artist, The; Planet of Blood (Queen of Blood); Rebel Without a Cause; Red Rock West; Riders of the Storm; River's Edge; Road Ends; Rumble Fish; Samson and Delilah; Search and Destroy; Source, The; Space Truckers; Speed; Stark; Straight to Hell; Sunset Heat; Super MarioBrothers, The; Texas Chainsaw Massacre 2, The; Ticker; Tracks; Trip, The; True Romance; Tycus; Waterworld; Wild Times; Witch Hunt
Hopper, Hal: Mudhoney
Hopper, Hedda: Alice Adams; As You Desire Me; Common Law, The; Maid's Night Out, The; Midnight; One Frightened Night; Racketeer; Skyscraper Souls; Speak Easily; Sunset Boulevard; Tarzan's Revenge
Hopper, William: Bad Seed, The; Deadly Mantis, The; Goodbye, My Lady; 20 Million Miles to Earth
Hopton, Russell: Lady Killer
Horan, Barbara: Malibu Bikini Shop, The; Triplecross
Horan, Gerard: Look Back In Anger
Hordern, Michael: Christmas Carol, A; Danny, The Champion of the World; Dark Obsession; Green Man, The; How I Won the War; Joseph Andrews; Lady Jane; Man Who Never Was, The; Middlemarch; Missionary, The; Old Curiosity Shop, The; Oliver Twist; Secret Garden, The; Sink the Bismarck; Story of Robin Hood, The; Suspicion; Trouble with Spies, The; Warriors, The; Where Eagles Dare; Windom's Way
Hori, Sami: Kadosh
Horino, Tad: Kung Pow!: Enter the Fist; Pacific Inferno
Horler, Sacha: Soft Fruit
Horn, Camilla: Faust; Tempest
Horn, Patrick Van: Swingers
Horne, Lena: Broadway Rhythm; Cabin in the Sky; Death of a Gunfighter; Duchess of Idaho; I Dood It; Ladies Sing the Blues, The; Panama Hattie; Stormy Weather; That's Entertainment! III; Thousands Cheer; Wiz, The; Ziegfeld Follies
Horneff, Wil: Born to Be Wild; Cash Crop
Horner, Penelope: Half a Sixpence
Horney, Brigitte: Baron Münchhausen (1943)
Horoks, Zbigniew: Dr. Petiot
Horovitch, David: 4:50 From Paddington; Mirror Crack'd from Side to Side, The; Murder at the Vicarage; They Do It with Mirrors
Horovitz, Adam: Lost Angels; Roadside Prophets
Horrocks, Jane: Absolutely Fabulous; Deadly Advice; Dressmaker, The; Getting It Right; Life Is Sweet; Little Voice; Second Best
Horse, Michael: Avenging, The; House of Cards; Legend of the Lone Ranger, The; Passenger 57
Horsford, Anna Maria: Murder Without Motive
Horsley, Lee: French Silk; Sword and the Sorcerer, The; 13 at Dinner
Horton, Clara: Tom Sawyer
Horton, Dan: Chippendales Murder, The
Horton, Edward Everett: Bluebeard's Eighth Wife; Cold Turkey; Front Page, The; Gang's All Here, The; Gay Divorcée, The; Here Comes Mr. Jordan; Holiday; I Married an Angel; Lady on a Train; Lost Horizon; Merry Widow, The; Pocketful of Miracles; Reaching for the Moon; Sex and the Single Girl; Shall We Dance?; Springtime in the Rockies; Top Hat; Ziegfeld Girl
Horton, Peter: Children of the Corn; Death Benefit; Side Out; Two Days in the Valley; Where the River Runs Black
Horton, Robert: Green Slime, The; Men of the Fighting Lady; Pony Soldier; Silver Blaze; Wagon Train (TV Series)
Hosea, Bobby: O. J. Simpson Story, The
Hoshi, Yuriko: Ghidrah, the Three-Headed Monster; Godzilla vs. Mothra; Kojiro
Hoskins, Bob: American Virgin; Balto; Beyond the Limit; Blue Ice; Brazil; Cousin Bette; Cry Terror; Don Quixote; Dunera Boys, The; Enemy at the Gates; Favor, the Watch and the Very Big Fish,The; Felicia's Journey; Heart Condition; Hook; Inner Circle, The; Inserts; Lassiter; Last Orders; Lonely Passion of Judith Hearne, The; Long Good Friday, The; Mermaids; Michael; Mona Lisa; Mussolini and I; Nixon; Passed Away; Pink Floyd: The Wall; Prayer for the Dying, A; Raggedy Rawney, The; Secret Agent, The; Shattered; Super MarioBrothers, The; Sweet Liberty; Twentyfourseven; White River; Who Framed Roger Rabbit
Hossack, Allison: Escape from Mars
Hossein, Robert: Battle of El Alamein, The; Bolero; Double Agents; Le Repos du Guerrier (Warrior's Rest)
Hotaru, Yukijiro: Zeram
Hotchkis, Joan: Last Game, The; Ode to Billy Joe
Hotton, Donald: Hearse, The
Hou, Chi Sui: Twin Warriors
Houdini, Harry: Man from Beyond, The
Houghton, Katharine: Ethan Frome; Guess Who's Coming to Dinner; Night We Never Met, The
Hounsou, Djimon: Amistad; Gladiator
House, Billy: People Will Talk
House, Ron: Bullshot (Bullshot Crummond)
Houseman, John: Another Woman; Babysitter, The; Bright Lights, Big City; Cheap Detective, The; Christmas without Snow, A; Displaced Person, The; Fog, The; Ghost Story; Gideon's Trumpet; Merry Wives of Windsor, The; Murder by Phone; Old Boyfriends; Our Town; Paper Chase, The; Rollerball; St. Ives; Three Days of the Condor; Wholly Moses!; Winds of War, The
Houser, Jerry: Bad Company; Class of '44; Summer of '42
Houser, Patrick: Hot Dog ... The Movie
Houston, Alan: Black and White (2000)
Houston, Cissy: Taking My Turn
Houston, Donald: Battle Hell; Doctor in the House; Maniac; Run for Your Money, A; 633 Squadron; Study in Terror, A; Where Eagles Dare
Houston, Renee: Horse's Mouth, The; Time Without Pity
Houston, Robert: Hills Have Eyes, The
Houston, Whitney: Bodyguard, The; Preacher's Wife, The; Rodgers & Hammerstein's Cinderella; Waiting to Exhale
Hove, Anders: Bloodlust: Subspecies III; Bloodstone: Subspecies II; Subspecies 4: Bloodstorm
Hoven, Adrian: Castle of the Creeping Flesh; Cave of the Living Dead
Hovey, Helen: Sadist, The
Hovis, Larry: Hogan's Heroes (TV Series)
Howard, Adam Coleman: Quiet Cool
Howard, Alan: Cook, the Thief, His Wife & Her Lover, The; Lord of the Rings, The: Fellowship of the Ring; Return of the Musketeers; Secret Rapture, The

Howard, Andrea: Nude Bomb, The (Return of Maxwell Smart,The)
Howard, Arliss: Beyond the Call; Crisscross (1992); Door to Door; For the Boys; Full Metal Jacket; Infiltrator, The; Iran Days of Crisis; Johns; Lesser Evil, The; Lost World, The: Jurassic Park; Man Who Captured Eichmann, The; Map of the World, A; Men Don't Leave; Old Man; Plain Clothes; Ruby; Sandlot, The; Somebody Has to Shoot the Picture; Tales of Erotica; Till Death Do Us Part; To Wong Foo, Thanks for Everything, Julie Newmar; Wilder Napalm; You Know My Name
Howard, Barbara: Running Mates
Howard, Brie: Android; Running Kind, The
Howard, Clint: Apollo 13; Arthur's Quest; Bigfoot: The Unforgettable Encounter; Body Armor; Carnosaur; Dentist 2, The: Brace Yourself; Disturbed; Evilspeak; Gentle Giant; Gung Ho (1985); Humanoids from the Deep; Ice Cream Man; Infested (Ticks); Leprechaun 2; Paper, The; Rock 'n' Roll High School; Santa with Muscles; Silent Night, Deadly Night 4—Initiation; Space Rangers (TV Series); Talion; Wraith, The
Howard, Curly: Lost Stooges, The; Stoogemania; Three Stooges, The (Volumes 1–10)
Howard, Frances: Swan, The
Howard, John: Arrest Bulldog Drummond; Bulldog Drummond Comes Back; Bulldog Drummond in Africa; Bulldog Drummond's Bride; Bulldog Drummond's Peril; Bulldog Drummond's Revenge; Bulldog Drummond's Secret Police; Club, The; High and the Mighty, The; Highest Honor, The; Invisible Woman, The; Lost Horizon; Love from a Stranger; Philadelphia Story, The; Undying Monster, The; Unknown Terror, The
Howard, Joyce: Night Has Eyes, The
Howard, Kathleen: It's a Gift
Howard, Ken: Country Girl, The; Murder in New Hampshire; 1776; Pudd'nhead Wilson; Real American Hero, The; Strange Interlude; Ulterior Motives
Howard, Kyle: Address Unknown; Paper Brigade, The
Howard, Leslie: Animal Kingdom, The; Devotion; 49th Parallel, The; Free Soul, A; Gone with the Wind; Intermezzo; Of Human Bondage; Petrified Forest, The; Pimpernel Smith; Pygmalion; Romeo and Juliet; Scarlet Pimpernel, The; Smilin' Through; Stand-In
Howard, Lewis: Hellzapoppin
Howard, Lisa: Bounty Hunters; Man Who Cheated Himself, The; Rolling Vengeance
Howard, Marion: Road Games
Howard, Marvin: Cremators, The
Howard, Mary: Abe Lincoln in Illinois; All over Town; Billy the Kid; Nurse Edith Cavell
Howard, Mel: Hester Street
Howard, Moe: Lost Stooges, The; Stoogemania; Three Stooges, The (Volumes 1–10)
Howard, Rance: Bigfoot: The Unforgettable Encounter
Howard, Ron: American Graffiti; Andy Griffith Show, The (TV Series); Bitter Harvest; Courtship of Eddie's Father, The; Eat My Dust; First Works, Volumes 1 & 2; Fugitive, The (TV Series); Grand Theft Auto; Huckleberry Finn; I'm a Fool; Independent, The; Migrants, The; More American Graffiti; Music Man, The; Return to Mayberry; Run Stranger Run; Shootist, The; Smoke; Village of the Giants
Howard, Ronald: Adventures of Sherlock Holmes, The (TV Series); Browning Version, The; Curse of the Mummy's Tomb, The; Koroshi
Howard, Shemp: Africa Screams; Arabian Nights; Bank Dick, The; Blondie Knows Best; Hellzapoppin; Pittsburgh; Stoogemania; Strange Case of Dr. Rx, The
Howard, Susan: Moonshine County Express; Night Games; Sidewinder 1
Howard, Terrence: Angel Eyes; Big Momma's House; Boycott; Glitter; Hart's War
Howard, Terrence DaShon: Sunset Park
Howard, Trevor: Albino; Battle of Britain; Bawdy Adventures of Tom Jones, The; Brief Encounter; Catch Me a Spy; Catholics; Charge of the Light Brigade, The; Clouded Yellow, The; Conduct Unbecoming; Dawning, The; Doll's House, A; Dust; Foreign Body; Gandhi; George Washington; Glory at Sea; Green for Danger; Hennessy; Hurricane (1979); I See a Dark Stranger; Immortal Battalion, The (The Way Ahead); Inside the Third Reich; Key, The; Last Remake of Beau Geste, The; Missionary, The; Morituri; Mutiny on the Bounty; Night Visitor, The (1970); Offence, The; Operation Crossbow; Persecution; Poppy Is Also a Flower, The; Run for the Sun; Ryan's Daughter; Sea Wolves, The; Shaka Zulu; Slavers; Stevie; Sword of the Valiant; Third Man, The; Unholy, The; Von Ryan's Express; Windwalker
Howard, Willie: Broadway Melody of 1938
Howarth, Kevin: Razor Blade Smile
Howat, Clark: Billy Jack
Howell, C. Thomas: Acting on Impulse; Baby Face Nelson; Big Fall, The; Breaking the Rules; Crimson Code; Curiosity Kills; Dangerous Indiscretion; Enemy Action; Far Out Man; Gettysburg; Grandview, U.S.A.; Hitcher, The; Hourglass; Into the Homeland; Jailbait (1992); Kid (1990); Nickel & Dime; Outsiders, The; Payback; Pure Danger; Red Dawn; Return of the Musketeers; Secret Admirer; Shameless; Shepherd; Side Out; Soul Man; Suspect Device; Sweeper, The; Tank; Tattle Tale; Teresa's Tattoo; That Night; Tiger's Tale, A; To Protect and Serve; Treacherous
Howell, Hoke: B.O.R.N.
Howell, Jeff: Cemetery Club, The
Howell, Jessica: Zeus and Roxanne
Howell, Kenneth: Pride of the Bowery
Howells, Ursula: Murder Is Announced, A
Howerd, Frankie: Carry on Doctor; Great St. Trinian's Train Robbery, The
Howes, Hans R.: Terminal Velocity
Howes, Reed: Chloe: Love is Calling You; Dawn Rider; Zorro Rides Again
Howes, Sally Ann: Admirable Crichton, The; Anna Karenina; Chitty Chitty Bang Bang; Dead of Night; Deathship; Nicholas Nickleby
Howland, Chris: Mad Executioners, The
Howland, Rick: To Catch a Yeti
Howlin, Olin: Blob, The; Santa Fe Saddlemates
Hoyo, George Del: Crying Child, The
Hoyos, Cristina: Blood Wedding; El Amor Brujo
Hoyos, Rodolfo: Brave One, The
Hoyt, Arthur: Great McGinty, The; His Private Secretary; Shriek in the Night, A; They Meet Again
Hoyt, John: Androcles and the Lion; Attack of the Puppet People; Black Castle, The; Brute Force; Casanova's Big Night; Curse of the Undead; Death of a Scoundrel; Desirée; Duel at Diablo; Flesh Gordon; In Search of Historic Jesus; Lost Continent, The; My Favorite Brunette; Operation C.I.A.; Star Trek: The Cage; Time Travelers, The; When Worlds Collide; Winter Meeting; X (The Man with the X-Ray Eyes)
Hrusínsky, Rudolf: Ninety Degrees in the Shade
Hsia, Lin Ching: Peking Opera Blues
Hsieh, Wang: Infra-Man
Hsio, Miao Ker: Chinese Connection, The
Hsueh, Nancy: Targets
Hu, Kelly: Scorpion King, The
Hu, Li: Day the Sun Turned Cold, The
Huang, Hae-Jin: Why Has Bhodi Dharma Left for the East?
Huang, Ying: Madame Butterfly
Huard, Patrick: Boys, The (1997)
Hubbard, Dana S.: Don't Let Your Meat Loaf
Hubbard, Ed: Vampires & Other Stereotypes
Hubbard, John: Mexican Hayride; Mummy's Tomb, The; You'll Never Get Rich
Hubbard, Tom: Two Lost Worlds
Huber, Harold: Charlie Chan in Rio; Klondike Annie
Hubert, Antoine: Le Grand Chemin (The Grand Highway)
Hubley, Season: Child in the Night; Elvis—The Movie; Hardcore; Key to Rebecca, The; Pretty Kill; Stepfather III: Father's Day; Total Exposure; Unspeakable Acts; Vice Squad
Hubley, Whip: Black Scorpion II: Aftershock; Desire and Hell at Sunset Motel; Russkies; Top Gun; Unveiled
Hubschmid, Paul: Funeral in Berlin
Huckabee, Cooper: Funhouse, The
Hudd, Walter: Elephant Boy

Huddleston, David: Bad Company; Big Lebowski, The; Double Exposure; Frantic; Gorp; M.A.D.D.: Mothers Against Drunk Driving; Santa Claus—The Movie; Tracker, The
Huddleston, Michael: Woman in Red, The; World's Greatest Lover, The
Hudson, Brett: Hysterical
Hudson, Elain: Who Killed Baby Azaria?
Hudson, Ernie: Basketball Diaries, The; Cherokee Kid, The; Clover; Collision Course; Congo; Cowboy Way, The; Crow, The; Dirty Dozen, The: The Fatal Mission; Ghostbusters; Ghostbusters II; Hand That Rocks the Cradle, The; Just Your Luck; Leviathan; Mr. Magoo; Never 2 Big; No Escape; Operation Delta Force; Penitentiary II; Red Letters; Shark Attack; Spacehunter: Adventures in the ForbiddenZone; Speechless; Stealth Fighter; Stranger in the Kingdom, A; Substitute, The; Sugar Hill; Tornado!; Trapper County War; Watcher, The; Weeds; Wrong Guys, The
Hudson, Gary: Force, The; Lights, Camera, Action, Love; Martial Outlaw; Mindtwister; Serial Killer; Sexual Intent; Texas Payback; Wild Cactus
Hudson, John: Screaming Skull, The; When Gangland Strikes
Hudson, Kate: About Adam; Almost Famous; Dr. T and the Women; Gossip
Hudson, Mark: Hysterical
Hudson, Oliver: Smokers, The
Hudson, Rochelle: Curly Top; Mr. Moto Takes a Chance; Mr. Skitch; She Done Him Wrong; Show Them No Mercy
Hudson, Rock: All That Heaven Allows; Ambassador, The; Avalanche; Battle Hymn; Bend of the River; Come September; Darling Lili; Devlin Connection III, The; Embryo; Giant; Gun Fury; Hornet's Nest; Ice Station Zebra; Lover Come Back; Magnificent Obsession; Man's Favorite Sport?; Martian Chronicles, Parts I-III, The; Mirror Crack'd, The; Pillow Talk; Seconds; Send Me No Flowers; Showdown; Something of Value; Strange Bedfellows; Tarnished Angels, The; Tobruk; Undefeated, The; Winchester '73; World War III; Written on the Wind
Hudson, Ruben Santiago: Rear Window; Solomon and Sheba
Hudson, Stephanie: Beach Babes 2: Cave Girl Island
Hudson, Toni: Just One of the Guys; Prime Risk; Uninvited, The
Hudson, William: Amazing Colossal Man, The; Attack of the 50-Foot Woman; Hysterical
Hudson Jr., Ernie: Wrecking Crew, The
Hues, Matthias: Alone in the Woods; Blackbelt; Bounty Tracker; Cyberzone; Digital Man; Fist of Iron; Mission of Justice; Suicide Ride; TC 2000
Huff, Brent: Armed Response; Final Justice; Stormquest
Huff, Shawn: Final Justice
Huffman, Cady: Space Marines
Huffman, David: Firefox; F.I.S.T.; St. Helens; Winds of Kitty Hawk, The; Witchcraft V: Dance with the Devil
Huffman, Felicity: Slight Case of Murder, A; Stephen King's Golden Years (TV Series)
Huffman, Kimberly: Sleeping with Strangers
Hufsey, Billy: Magic Kid; Off the Wall
Hugeny, Sharon: Majority of One, A
Hughes, Barnard: Cold Turkey; Da; Fantasticks, The; First Monday in October; Hospital, The; Incident, The; Lost Boys, The; Maxie; Midnight Cowboy; Odd Couple II, The; Past the Bleachers; Primal Secrets; Pursuit of Happiness, The; Rage; Sanctuary of Fear; Sister Act 2: Back in the Habit; Sisters (1973); Tron; Under the Biltmore Clock; Where Are the Children?; Where's Poppa?
Hughes, Brendan: Howling VI: The Freaks; Stranded; To Die For
Hughes, Carol: Flash Gordon Conquers the Universe; Man from Music Mountain; Stage Struck; Three Men on a Horse; Under Western Stars
Hughes, Finola: Above Suspicion; Aspen Extreme; Crying Child, The; Dark Side of Genius; Generation X; Staying Alive; Tycus
Hughes, Helen: Locked in Silence; Peanut Butter Solution, The
Hughes, John: That Sinking Feeling
Hughes, Kathleen: Cult of the Cobra
Hughes, Kay: Dick Tracy; Ride, Ranger, Ride; Vigilantes Are Coming!
Hughes, Kenneth: Adventures of Young Brave, The
Hughes, Kristen: Jane and the Lost City
Hughes, Lloyd: Drums of Jeopardy; Ella Cinders; Sweethearts on Parade; Where East Is East
Hughes, Mary Beth: Charlie Chan in Rio; Dressed to Kill; Great Flamarion, The; Ox-Bow Incident, The; Rimfire
Hughes, Miko: Cops and Robbersons; Fly Boy; Jack the Bear; Mercury Rising; Wes Craven's New Nightmare; Zeus and Roxanne
Hughes, Rhetta: Sweet Sweetback's Baadasssss Song
Hughes, Robin: Sometimes Aunt Martha Does Dreadful Things
Hughes, Stuart: Blades of Courage
Hughes, Wendy: Careful He Might Hear You; Dangerous Summer, A; Happy New Year (1987); Heist, The; Indecent Obsession, An; Kostas; Lonely Hearts; My Brilliant Career; My First Wife; Newsfront; Princess Caraboo; Return to Eden; Warm Nights on a Slow Moving Train; Wild Orchid 2: Two Shades of Blue; Woman Named Jackie, A
Hugh-Kelly, Daniel: Cujo; Nowhere to Hide
Hughley, D. L.: Brothers, The; Original Kings Of Comedy, The
Hui, Michael: Chinese Box
Hui, Ricky: Mr. Vampire (Vol. 1–4)
Huike, Zhang: Not One Less
Huison, Steve: Full Monty, The
Hulce, Tom: Amadeus; Animal House; Black Rainbow; Dominick and Eugene; Echo Park; Fearless; Heidi Chronicles, The; Inner Circle, The; Mary Shelley's Frankenstein; Parenthood; Slam Dance; 30-Sep-55; Those Lips, Those Eyes
Hulette, Gladys: Tol'able David
Hull, Dianne: Aloha, Bobby and Rose; Fifth Floor, The; New Adventures of Pippi Longstocking, The; Onion Field, The
Hull, Henry: Babes in Arms; Boys' Town; Fool Killer, The; High Sierra; Jesse James; Lifeboat; Master of the World; Midnight; Objective, Burma!; Portrait of Jennie; Proud Rebel, The; Return of Frank James, The; Return of Jesse James, The; Rimfire; Werewolf of London; Woman of the Town
Hull, Josephine: Arsenic and Old Lace; Harvey
Hulswit, Mart: Island of the Lost
Humbert, George: I Cover the Waterfront
Hume, Benita: It Happened in New Orleans; Last of Mrs. Cheney, The; Peck's Bad Boy with the Circus; Private Life of Don Juan, The; Suzy; Tarzan Escapes
Humphrey, Mark: Iron Eagle II
Humphrey, Renee: Cadillac Ranch; Fun; Jailbait (1992); Sex Monster, The
Humphreys, Judith: Hedd Wyn
Humphreys, Michael Connor: Forrest Gump
Humphries, Barry: Barry McKenzie Holds His Own; Leading Man, The; Les Patterson Saves the World
Hundar, Robert: Barry McKenzie Holds His Own; Leading Man, The; Les Patterson Saves the World
Hung, Chu Ngoc: Vertical Ray of the Sun, The
Hung, Sammo: Eastern Condors; Heart of Dragon; Millionaire's Express (Shanghai Express); Painted Faces; Paper Marriage; Project A (Part I); Zu: Warriors from the Magic Mountain
Hunnicutt, Arthur: Big Sky, The; Bounty Man, The; Broken Arrow; Devil's Canyon; Distant Drums; El Dorado; French Line, The; Harry and Tonto; Last Command, The; Lusty Men, The; Pinky; Red Badge of Courage, The; She Couldn't Say No
Hunnicutt, Gayle: Dream Lover; Legend of Hell House, The; Marlowe; Martian Chronicles, Parts I-III, The; Once in Paris; Return of the Man from U.N.C.L.E., The; Sell-Out, The; Silence Like Glass; Spiral Staircase, The; Target; Wild Angels, The
Hunt, Bonnie: Beethoven; Beethoven's 2nd; Getting Away with Murder; Green Mile, The; Jumanji; Kissing a Fool; Only You; Random Hearts; Return to Me
Hunt, Brad: Blindsided; Clubland; Dream with the Fishes; Fire Down Below
Hunt, Eleanor: Blue Steel; Whoopee
Hunt, Gareth: Bloodbath at the House of Death
Hunt, Helen: As Good as It Gets; Bill: On His Own; Cast Away; Curse of the Jade Scorpion, The; Dark River: A Father's Re-

venge; Dr. T and the Women; Incident at Dark River; Into the Badlands; Kiss of Death; Mr. Saturday Night; Murder in New Hampshire; Next of Kin; Only You; Pay It Forward; Pioneer Woman; Project X; Quarterback Princess; Trancers; Trancers II (The Return of Jack Deth); Trancers III: Deth Lives; Twister; Waterdance, The; What Women Want
Hunt, Jimmy: Invaders from Mars
Hunt, Linda: Bostonians, The; Dragonfly; Eleni; If Looks Could Kill; Kindergarten Cop; Rain Without Thunder; Ready to Wear; She-Devil; Silverado; Space Rangers (TV Series); Twenty Bucks; Waiting for the Moon; Year of Living Dangerously, The; Younger and Younger
Hunt, Marsha: Actors and Sin; Hell Town; Human Comedy, The; Johnny Got His Gun; Panama Hattie; Pride and Prejudice; Smash-Up: The Story of a Woman; Thunder Trail
Hunt, Martita: Admirable Crichton, The; Becket; Brides of Dracula; Great Expectations; Man in Grey, The; Song Without End; Three Men in a Boat; Wicked Lady, The
Hunter, Bill: Adventures of Priscilla, Queen of the Desert, The; Custodian, The; Death of a Soldier; Heatwave (1983); Hit, The (1984); Last Days of Chez Nous, The; Muriel's Wedding; Newsfront; Race the Sun; Rebel; Strictly Ballroom
Hunter, Ciara: Dangerous Prey
Hunter, Holly: Always; Animal Behavior; Broadcast News; Copycat; Crash (1996); Crazy in Love; End of the Line; Firm, The; Harlan County War; Home for the Holidays (1995); Jesus' Son; Life Less Ordinary, A; Living Out Loud; Miss Firecracker; Murder on the Bayou; Once Around; Piano, The; Positively True Adventures of the Alleged Texas Cheerleader-Murdering Mom, The; Raising Arizona; Roe vs. Wade; Svengali; Things You Can Tell Just by Looking at Her; Timecode; Urge to Kill
Hunter, Ian: Adventures of Robin Hood, The; Andy Hardy's Private Secretary; Billy the Kid; Bitter Sweet (1940); Broadway Melody of 1940; Broadway Serenade; Easy Virtue; Flame over India; Little Princess, The (1939); Order of the Black Eagle; Pursuit of the Graf Spee; Ring, The; Smilin' Through; Strange Cargo; Tarzan Finds a Son; That Certain Woman; Tower of London
Hunter, Jeffrey: Christmas Kid, The; Great Locomotive Chase, The; Guide for the Married Man, A; Hell to Eternity; King of Kings (1961); Last Hurrah, The; Private Navy of Sgt. O'Farrell, The; Searchers, The; Sergeant Rutledge; Seven Cities of Gold; Star Trek: The Cage; Star Trek: The Menagerie
Hunter, Kaki: Just the Way You Are; Porky's II: The Next Day; Porky's Revenge; Whose Life Is It, Anyway?
Hunter, Kim: Bad Ronald; Beneath the Planet of the Apes; Born Innocent; Comedian, The; Deadline USA; Escape from the Planet of the Apes; Kindred, The; Lilith; Out of the Cold; Planet of the Apes; Requiem for a Heavyweight (1956) (Television); Seventh Victim, The; Skokie; Streetcar Named Desire, A; Swimmer, The; Three Sovereigns for Sarah
Hunter, Matthew: Tearaway
Hunter, Morgan: Cyborg Soldier
Hunter, Ronald: Lazarus Syndrome, The; Three Sovereigns for Sarah
Hunter, Tab: Arousers, The; Battle Cry; Burning Hills, The; Cameron's Closet; Damn Yankees; Dark Horse; Grotesque; Hostile Guns; Island of Desire; Kid from Left Field, The; Loved One, The; Lust in the Dust; Pandemonium; Polyester; Ride the Wild Surf; Sea Chase, The; They Came to Cordura
Hunter, Thomas: Battle of the Commandos; Escape from the KGB; Vampire Happening
Hunter, Tony: Naked in the Sun
Huntington, Sam: Detroit Rock City; Jungle 2 Jungle
Huntley, Fred: Thundering Hoofs
Huntley, Raymond: I See a Dark Stranger; Immortal Battalion, The (The Way Ahead); Upstairs, Downstairs
Huppert, Isabelle: Amateur (1995); Bedroom Window, The; Cactus; Clean Slate (Coup de Torchon) (1981); Entre Nous (Between Us); Going Places; Heaven's Gate; Judge and the Assassin, The; La Cérémonie; La Separation; La Truite (The Trout); Lacemaker, The; Loulou; Madame Bovary; My Best Friend's Girl; School of Flesh; Sincerely Charlotte; Story of Women, The; Swindle, The; Violette
Hurdle, James: Climb, The
Hurkos, Peter: Boxoffice
Hurley, Elizabeth: Austin Powers: International Man of Mystery; Bedazzled; Dangerous Ground; EDtv; Kill Cruise; My Favorite Martian; Nightscare; Permanent Midnight; Rowing with the Wind; Samson and Delilah; Shameless
Hursey, Sherry: Avenging, The
Hurst, Brandon: Man Who Laughs, The
Hurst, Margaret: Meet the Navy
Hurst, Marguerite: Forgotten Silver
Hurst, Michael: Death Warmed Up; Desperate Remedies; Hercules and the Amazon Women; Hercules in the Underworld
Hurst, Paul: Big Stampede, The; Gun Smugglers; Missourians, The; Racketeer
Hurst, Ryan: Remember the Titans
Hurt, John: After Darkness; Alien; Aria; Captain Corelli's Mandolin; Champions; Contact; Dead Man; Deadline; Disappearance, The; East of Elephant Rock; Elephant Man, The; Even Cowgirls Get the Blues; Field, The; Frankenstein Unbound; From the Hip; Ghoul, The; Harry Potter and the Sorcerer's Stone; Heaven's Gate; Hit, The (1984); I, Claudius; Jake Speed; King Lear; King Ralph; Little Sweetheart; Lost Souls; Love and Death on Long Island; Midnight Express; Monolith; Naked Civil Servant, The; New Blood; Night Crossing; 1984; Osterman Weekend, The; Partners; Rob Roy; Scandal; Second Best; Shout, The (1979); Success Is the Best Revenge; 10 Rillington Place; White Mischief; Wild Bill
Hurt, Mary Beth: Affliction; Age of Innocence, The; Baby Girl Scott; Chilly Scenes of Winter; Compromising Positions; D.A.R.Y.L.; Defenseless; From the Journals of Jean Seberg; Light Sleeper; My Boyfriend's Back; Parents; Six Degrees of Separation; Slaves of New York; World According to Garp, The
Hurt, Wesley Ivan: Popeye
Hurt, William: Accidental Tourist, The; AI: Artificial Intelligence; Alice; Altered States; Big Brass Ring, The; Big Chill, The; Body Heat; Broadcast News; Changing Lanes; Children of a Lesser God; Couch in New York, A; Dark City; Doctor, The; Dune; Eyewitness; Flamingo Rising, The; 4th Floor, The; Gorky Park; I Love You to Death; Jane Eyre; Kiss of the Spider Woman; Lost in Space (1998); Michael; Mr. Wonderful; One True Thing; Plague, The; Second Best; Silent Witness; Smoke; Time of Destiny, A; Trial by Jury; Until the End of the World; Varian's War
Husky, Ferlin: Hillbillys in a Haunted House; Las Vegas Hillbillys
Huss, Jennifer: Polymorph; Vamps: Deadly Dream Girls
Hussey, Olivia: Bastard, The; Black Christmas; Cat and the Canary, The; Distortions; Escape 2000; Ivanhoe; Jesus of Nazareth; Man with Bogart's Face, The; Psycho 4: The Beginning; Quest of the Delta Knights; Romeo and Juliet; Save Me; Summertime Killer, The; Virus
Hussey, Ruth: Another Thin Man; Facts of Life; Honolulu; Madame X; Marine Raiders; Mr. Music; Northwest Passage; Philadelphia Story, The; Stars and Stripes Forever; Susan and God; Tender Comrade; Uninvited, The
Husted, Patrick: Claire Dolan
Huster, Francis: Another Man, Another Chance; Dinner Game, The; Edith and Marcel
Huston, Anjelica: Addams Family, The; Addams Family Values; Agnes Browne; And the Band Played On; Buffalo Girls; Buffalo '66; Cowboy and the Ballerina, The; Crimes and Misdemeanors; Crossing Guard, The; Dead, The; Enemies—A Love Story; Ever After; Gardens of Stone; Golden Bowl, The; Grifters, The; Handful of Dust, A; Ice Pirates; Lonesome Dove; Manhattan Murder Mystery; Mists of Avalon, The; Mr. North; Perez Family, The; Phoenix; Postman Always Rings Twice, The; Prizzi's Honor; Royal Tenenbaums, The; Swashbuckler (1976); Witches, The
Huston, Cissy: Road to Freedom: The Vernon Johns Story
Huston, Danny: Leo Tolstoy's Anna Karenina (1997)
Huston, John: Angela; Battle for the Planet of the Apes; Battle Force; Bible, The; Breakout; Cardinal, The; Casino Royale; Chinatown; Deserter, The; Fatal Attraction; Lovesick; Man in the Wilderness; Minor Miracle, A; Mr. Corbett's Ghost; Myra Breckenridge; Tentacles; Visitor, The; Wind and the Lion, The; Winter Kills; Word, The

Huston, Virginia: Flight to Mars; Nocturne
Huston, Walter: Abraham Lincoln; And Then There Were None; Ann Vickers; Criminal Code, The; December 7th: The Movie; Devil and Daniel Webster, The; Dodsworth; Dragon Seed; Duel in the Sun; Edge of Darkness; Gabriel over the White House; Law and Order; North Star, The (1943); Of Human Hearts; Outlaw, The; Rain; Rhodes of Africa (Rhodes); Shanghai Gesture, The; Summer Holiday; Transatlantic Tunnel; Treasure of the Sierra Madre; Virginian, The; Yankee Doodle Dandy
Hutchence, Michael: Dogs in Space
Hutchins, Will: Clambake; Maverick; Shooting, The
Hutchinson, Jeff: Rollerblade
Hutchinson, Josephine: Love Is Better Than Ever; Somewhere in the Night; Son of Frankenstein; Story of Louis Pasteur, The; Tender Years, The; Tom Brown's School Days (1940)
Hutchison, Doug: Bait; Green Mile, The
Hutchison, Fiona: Biggles—Adventures in Time; Rage
Hutson, Tracy: Rated X
Hutton, Betty: Annie Get Your Gun; Greatest Show on Earth, The; Here Come the Waves; Let's Dance; Miracle of Morgan's Creek, The; Perils of Pauline, The; Star Spangled Rhythm
Hutton, Brian: Carnival Rock
Hutton, Jim: Bachelor in Paradise; Don't Be Afraid of the Dark; Green Berets, The; Hallelujah Trail, The; Hellfighters; Honeymoon Machine, The; Horizontal Lieutenant, The; Major Dundee; Period of Adjustment; Psychic Killer; Time to Love and a Time to Die, A; Walk, Don't Run; Where the Boys Are (1960); Who's Minding the Mint?
Hutton, Lauren: American Gigolo; Caracara; Cradle Will Fall, The; Fear; Forbidden Sun; Gambler, The; Gator; Guilty as Charged; Lassiter; Malone; Millions; Missing Pieces; Monte Carlo; Once Bitten; Paper Lion; Paternity; Scandalous; Snow Queen; Starflight One; Time Stalkers; Trade Secrets; Viva Knievel; We the Jury; Wedding, A (1978); Welcome to L.A.; Zorro, the Gay Blade
Hutton, Marion: In Society
Hutton, Robert: Big Bluff, The; Casanova's Big Night; Hollywood Canteen; Invisible Invaders; Man in the Eiffel Tower, The; Naked Youth; Racket, The; Showdown at Boot Hill; Slime People, The; Steel Helmet, The; They Came from Beyond Space; Torture Garden
Hutton, Timothy: Aldrich Ames: Traitor Within; And Baby Makes Six; Beautiful Girls; City of Industry; Daniel; Dark Half, The; Deterrence; Everybody's All-American; Falcon and the Snowman, The; French Kiss; Friendly Fire; General's Daughter, The; Iceman; Last Word, The; Made in Heaven; Mr. and Mrs. Loving; Money Kings; Oldest Living Graduate, The; Ordinary People; Playing God; Q & A; Strangers; Substance of Fire, The; Taps; Temp, The; Time of Destiny, A; Torrents of Spring; Turk 182; Young Love, First Love; Zelda
Huy-Quan, Ke: Goonies, The
Hvenegaard, Pelle: Pelle the Conqueror
Hwang, Sin-Hye: 301/302
Hyams, Leila: Big House, The; Freaks; Girl in Every Port, A; Island of Lost Souls; Red-Headed Woman; Ruggles of Red Gap
Hyde, Jonathan: Anaconda; Jumanji; Plot to Kill Hitler, The; Richie Rich; Titanic
Hyde, Tracy: Melody
Hyde-White, Alex: Alien Within, The; Biggles—Adventures in Time; Ironclads; Phantom of the Opera; Romeo and Juliet; Silent Victim; Time Trackers; Unknown Origin; Wyatt Earp: Return to Tombstone
Hyde-White, Wilfrid: Adam and Evalyn; Betrayed; Browning Version, The; Chamber of Horrors; Conspirator; Flame over India; Ghosts of Berkeley Square; In Search of the Castaways; Last Holiday; Let's Make Love; Ten Little Indians; Trio; Truth About Women, The; Two-Way Stretch; Up the Creek; Winslow Boy, The
Hyer, Martha: Abbott and Costello Go to Mars; Battle Hymn; Best of Everything, The; Catch as Catch Can; Chase, The; Clay Pigeon, The; Delicate Delinquent, The; First Men in the Moon; Francis in the Navy; Gun Smugglers; House of 1,000 Dolls; Houseboat; Ice Palace; Lucky Me; My Man Godfrey; Night of the Grizzly, The; Paris Holiday; Picture Mommy Dead; Rustlers, The; Scarlet Spear, The; Some Came Running; Sons of Katie Elder, The
Hyland, Catherine: Vamping
Hyland, Diana: Boy in the Plastic Bubble, The; One Man's Way
Hylands, Scott: Coming Out Alive; Daddy's Gone A-Hunting; Fools; Halfback of Notre Dame, The
Hylton, Jane: Manster, The
Hyman, Flo: Order of the Black Eagle
Hymer, Warren: Case of the Curious Bride, The; Hitler—Dead or Alive; Kid Millions
Hynson, Mike: Endless Summer, The
Hyser, Joyce: Greedy; Just One of the Guys
Hytten, Olaf: Drums of Fu Manchu
Hyun, Lee Sang: Lies (1999)
Hywel, Dafydd: Coming Up Roses
Ibarra, Mirta: Guantanamera!; Strawberry and Chocolate; Up to a Certain Point
Ice Cube: Anaconda; Boyz N the Hood; Dangerous Ground; Friday; Glass Shield, The; Higher Learning; Players Club, The; Trespass
Ice T: Agent of Death; Air Rage; Body Count (1997) (direct to video); Final Voyage; Johnny Mnemonic; Judgment Day; Leprechaun in the Hood; Luck of the Draw; Mean Guns; New Jack City; Ricochet; Stealth Fighter; Surviving the Game; Tank Girl; Ticker; Trespass; Urban Menace; Wrecking Crew, The
Ichikawa, Raizo: Enjo; Shin Heinke Monogatari
Ida, Hiroki: Cyber Ninja
Ida, Kunihiko: Zeram
Ide, Rakkyo: Kikujiro
Idle, Eric: Adventures of Baron Münchausen, The; Alan Smithee Film, An—Burn Hollywood Burn; And Now for Something Completely Different; Around the World in 80 Days; Casper; Dudley Do-Right; Life of Brian; Mikado, The; Missing Pieces; Mom and Dad Save the World; Monty Python Live at the Hollywood Bowl; Monty Python's Flying Circus (TV Series); Monty Python's the Meaning of Life; National Lampoon's European Vacation; Nuns on the Run; Rutles, The (All You Need Is Cash); Splitting Heirs; To See Such Fun; Too Much Sun; Yellowbeard
Idol, Billy: Doors, The
Ieracitano, Guiseppe: Il Ladro Di Bambini (Stolen Children)
Ifans, Rhys: Heart (1999); Human Nature; Little Nicky; Love, Honor & Obey; Notting Hill; Replacements, The
Igawa, Hisashi: Rhapsody in August
Igughi, Takahito: Boiling Point
Igus, Darrow: Horrible Doctor Bones, The
Ihara, Tsuyoshi: Gamera: Guardian of the Universe
Ihnat, Steve: Hour of the Gun, The; Hunter (1971); Madigan
Ikebe, Ryo: Snow Country
Ikeda, Shoko: Operation Condor (Jackie Chan)
Iler, Robert: Sopranos, The (TV series)
Illery, Pola: Under the Roofs of Paris
Illusion, Justin: Terminal Impact
Iman: Exit to Eden; Heart of Darkness; Human Factor, The; Lies of the Twins; No Way Out; Star Trek VI: The Undiscovered Country
Imasheva, Albina: Beshkempir, The Adopted Son
Imes-Jackson, Mo'Nique: Two Can Play That Game
Imhoff, Gary: Angel in Training; Seniors, The
Imperioli, Michael: Flirt; Sopranos, The (TV series); Sweet Nothing
Imrie, Celia: Dark Adapted Eye, A; Hilary and Jackie; Oranges Are Not the Only Fruit
Ince, Elizabeth: Stitches (2001)
Incontrera, Annabella: Badlands Drifter (Challenge of McKenna); Bullet for Sandoval, A
Inescort, Frieda: Beauty for the Asking; Casanova's Big Night; Judge Steps Out, The; Return of the Vampire, The; Tarzan Finds a Son; Underworld Story; You'll Never Get Rich
Ingalls, Joyce: Deadly Force
Ingels, Marty: Horizontal Lieutenant, The; If It's Tuesday, This Must Be Belgium
Ingersoll, Amy: Knightriders

Ingham, Barrie: Antony and Cleopatra; Dr. Who and the Daleks; Josh Kirby, Time Warrior (Series)
Ingle, John: Suture
Ingraham, Bill: Butch Camp
Ingram, Jack: Atom Man vs. Superman; Ghost Town Renegades; Sea Hound, The; Sundown Riders
Ingram, Rex: Adventures of Huckleberry Finn, The; Cabin in the Sky; Dark Waters; Green Pastures; Talk of the Town, The; Thief of Bagdad, The
Inkizhinov, Valeri: Storm over Asia
Innes, Neil: Rutles, The (All You Need Is Cash)
Innocent, Harold: Canterville Ghost, The
Inoh, Shizuka: 8 1/2 Women
Inosanto, Danny: Game of Death
Interlenghi, Franco: I Vitelloni; Little World of Don Camillo, The; Shoeshine
Intrakanchit, Pisek: Bangkok Dangerous
Inwood, Steve: Human Shield, The; Staying Alive
Iorio, Jeffrey R.: Deadly Obsession
Ip, Grace: Gen-X Cops
Ipale, Aharon: Invisible: The Chronicles of Benjamin Knight
Irazoque, Enrique: Gospel According to Saint Matthew, The
Ireland, Jill: Assassination; Breakheart Pass; Breakout; Chato's Land; Chino; Cold Sweat; Death Wish II; Family, The; Hard Times; Love and Bullets; Mechanic, The; Rider on the Rain; Someone Behind the Door; Three Men in a Boat; Villa Rides
Ireland, John: All the King's Men; Arizona Bushwhackers; Badlands Drifter (Challenge of McKenna); Bushwhackers; Dead for a Dollar; Delta Fox; Doolins of Oklahoma; Escape to the Sun; Fall of the Roman Empire, The; Farewell My Lovely; 55 Days at Peking; Gangster, The; Gunfight at the O.K. Corral; Gunslinger; House of Seven Corpses, The; Kavik the Wolf Dog; Little Big Horn; Machine Gun Killers; Martin's Day; Messenger of Death; Miami Horror; Northeast of Seoul; Party Girl; Railroaded; Ransom; Red River; Return of Jesse James, The; Satan's Cheerleaders; Southern Yankee, A; Sundown; Swiss Conspiracy, The; Thunder Run; Tomorrow Never Comes; Treasure of the Amazon; Vengeance Valley; Walk in the Sun, A; We Are No Angels; Wild in the Country
Ireland, Kathy: Alien from L.A.; Amore! (1993); Backfire; Journey to the Center of the Earth; Miami Hustle; National Lampoon's Loaded Weapon 1; Necessary Roughness; Presence, The
Irissari, Tina: Devil, Probably, The
Irizarry, Vincent: Jackie Collins' Lucky Chances
Irlen, Steve: On the Make
Irons, Jeremy: Betrayal; Brideshead Revisited; Chinese Box; Chorus of Disapproval, A; Damage; Danny, The Champion of the World; Dead Ringers; Die Hard with a Vengeance; Dungeons & Dragons; French Lieutenant's Woman, The; House of the Spirits, The; Kafka; Lolita; M. Butterfly; Man in the Iron Mask, The; Mission, The; Moonlighting (1983); Nijinsky; Reversal of Fortune; Stealing Beauty; Swann in Love; Time Machine, The (2002); Waterland; Wild Duck, The
Irons, Samuel: Danny, The Champion of the World
Irons, Shaun: Jugular Wine
Ironside, Michael: Beyond Redemption; Black Ice; Children of the Corn: Revelation; Coming Out Alive; Common Bonds; Crime & Punishment in Suburbia; Cross Country; Dead Awake; Deadly Surveillance; Deadman's Revenge; Destiny to Order; Drop Dead Gorgeous; Extreme Prejudice; Father Hood; Ford: The Man & the Machine; Fortunes of War; Free Willy; Glass Shield, The; Guncrazy (1950); Hellcab; Hello, Mary Lou: Prom Night II; Highlander 2: The Quickening; Hostile Take Over; Jo Jo Dancer, Your Life Is Calling; Johnny 2.0; Killer Image; Killing Man, The; Major Payne; Mardi Gras for the Devil; McBain; Mind Field; Murder in Space; Neon City; Next Karate Kid, The; Nowhere to Hide; Payback; Point of Impact; Probable Cause; Red Scorpion 2; Red Sun Rising; Save Me; Scanners; Sins of Dorian Gray, The; Spacehunter: Adventures in the ForbiddenZone; Starship Troopers; Sweet Killing; Too Fast Too Young; Top Gun; Total Recall; Vagrant, The; Visiting Hours; Watchers
Irving, Amy: Anastasia: The Mystery of Anna; Benefit of the Doubt; Bossa Nova; Carrie; Carried Away; Competition, The; Confession, The; Crossing Delancey; Deconstructing Harry; Far Pavilions, The; Fury, The (1978); Heartbreak House; Honeysuckle Rose; I'm a Fool; I'm Not Rappaport; James Dean—A Legend in His Own Time; Kleptomania; Micki & Maude; Rage, The: Carrie 2; Show of Force, A; Turn of the Screw, The (1989); Voices; Yentl
Irving, Christopher: Dedicated Man, A
Irving, Clifford: F for Fake
Irving, George S.: Deadly Hero
Irwin, Bill: How the Grinch Stole Christmas; My Blue Heaven; Popeye; Scenes from a Mall; Stepping Out; Subway Stories
Irwin, Tom: Holiday Affair; Ladykiller
Isaacs, Jason: End of the Affair, The; Patriot, The; Solitaire for 2; Sweet November (2001)
Isaak, Chris: Grace of My Heart; Little Buddha; That Thing You Do!; Twin Peaks: Fire Walk with Me
Isabelle, Katherine: Ginger Snaps
Isakovic, Boris: Vukovar
Isfeld, Justin: Ice Cream Man
Ishibashi, Ryo: Blue Tiger
Ishida, Yuriko: Boiling Point
Ishikawa, Hiroshi: Godzilla vs. Gigan
Isobel, Katharine: Salt Water Moose
Isomura, Kenji: Heaven's Burning
Isunza, Agustin: Illusion Travels by Streetcar
Itami, Juzo: Family Game, The
Ito, Robert: John Woo's Once a Thief
Itonia: Blood Harvest
Iturbi, José: Holiday in Mexico; That Midnight Kiss; Three Daring Daughters; Two Girls and a Sailor
Itzin, Gregory: Fly Boy
Iures, Marcel: Hart's War; Unforgettable Summer, An
Iures, Michael: Peacemaker, The (1997)
Ivan, Daniel: Slaughter in San Francisco
Ivan, Rosalind: Pursuit to Algiers; Scarlet Street
Ivanek, Zeljko: Julian Po; Mass Appeal; Our Sons; Rat Pack, The; School Ties; Sender, The
Ivanov, Ivan: Bloodsport IV: The Dark Kumite
Ivashov, Vladimir: Ballad of a Soldier
Ivens, Terri: Trancers 5: Sudden Deth
Ivernel, Daniel: Diary of a Chambermaid
Ives, Burl: Baker's Hawk; Big Country, The; Cat on a Hot Tin Roof; Daydreamer, The (1966); Desire under the Elms; East of Eden; Ensign Pulver; Just You and Me, Kid; Roots; So Dear to My Heart; Station West; Summer Magic; Two Moon Junction; White Dog
Ivey, Dana: Addams Family Values; Adventures of Huck Finn, The (1993); Impostors, The; Kid, The (2000); Mumford; Simon Birch; Sleepless in Seattle
Ivey, Judith: Brighton Beach Memoirs; Compromising Positions; Decoration Day; Devil's Advocate; Everybody Wins; Hello Again; In Country; Long Hot Summer, The; Love Hurts; Mystery, Alaska; Sister, Sister; There Goes the Neighborhood; Washington Square; We Are the Children; What the Deaf Man Heard; Woman in Red, The
Ivgi, Moshe: Cup Final
Ivy, Bob: Phantasm IV: Oblivion
Iwai, Sharon: Great Wall, A
Iwasaski, Kaneko: Zatoichi: The Blind Swordsman and theChess Expert
Iwashita, Shima: Autumn Afternoon, An; Double Suicide; Red Lion
Izewska, Teresa: Kanal
Izumiya, Shigeru: Eijanaika (Why Not?)
Izzard, Eddie: Cat's Meow, The; Circus; Mystery Men; Shadow of the Vampire; Velvet Goldmine
Jablonska, Linda: Last Butterfly, The
Jackée: Ladybugs; Women of Brewster Place, The
Jackman, Hugh: Kate and Leopold; Someone Like You; Swordfish; X-Men
Jacks, Robert: Texas Chainsaw Massacre: The Next Generation
Jackson, Andrew: Twists of Terror

Jackson, Anne: Bell Jar, The; Folks; Funny About Love; Leave 'em Laughing; Lovers and Other Strangers; Out on a Limb; Rescuers, Stories of Courage, "TwoWomen"; Sam's Son; Secret Life of an American Wife, The; Tall Story
Jackson, Barry: Mr. Love
Jackson, Ernestine: Aaron Loves Angela
Jackson, Freda: Brides of Dracula
Jackson, Glenda: And Nothing But the Truth; Baby-Sitters Club, The; Beyond Therapy; Boy Friend, The; Business As Usual; Class of Miss MacMichael, The; Elizabeth R; Hedda; Hopscotch; House Calls; Incredible Sarah, The; King of the Wind; Lost and Found (1979); Marat/Sade; Music Lovers, The; Nasty Habits; Negatives; Rainbow, The; Return of the Soldier, The; Romantic Englishwoman, The; Sakharov; Salome's Last Dance; Stevie; Strange Interlude; Sunday, Bloody Sunday; Touch of Class, A; Turtle Diary; Women in Love
Jackson, Gordon: Fighting Prince of Donegal, The; Hamlet; Ipcress File, The; Madame Sin; Medusa Touch, The; Mutiny on the Bounty; Prime of Miss Jean Brodie, The; Russian Roulette; Shaka Zulu; Shooting Party, The; Tight Little Island; Town Like Alice, A; Tunes of Glory; Upstairs, Downstairs; Whistle Blower, The
Jackson, Ivan: World of Strangers, A
Jackson, Janet: Nutty Professor II: The Klumps; Poetic Justice
Jackson, John: Glimmer Man, The; Sudie & Simpson
Jackson, John M.: Deadman's Revenge; Ginger Ale Afternoon
Jackson, Jonathan: Camp Nowhere; Deep End of the Ocean, The; Prisoner of Zenda, Inc.
Jackson, Joshua: Cruel Intentions; Digger; Magic in the Water, The; Robin of Locksley; Ronnie & Julie; Skeletons in the Closet; Skulls, The; Urban Legend
Jackson, Kate: Adrift; Best of Dark Shadows, The; Death at Love House; Dirty Tricks; Listen to Your Heart; Loverboy; Making Love; Night of Dark Shadows; Satan's School for Girls; Thunder and Lightning
Jackson, Lamont: Class Act
Jackson, Lauren: Alex
Jackson, Lindsay: Secrets in the Attic
Jackson, Mallie: Hollywood Harry
Jackson, Marlon: Student Confidential
Jackson, Mary: Skinned Alive; Terror at the Red Wolf Inn (Terror House)
Jackson, Mel: Uninvited Guest
Jackson, Michael: Michael Jackson Moonwalker; Wiz, The
Jackson, Peter: Forgotten Silver
Jackson, Philip: Bad Behaviour; Little Voice; Poirot (Series)
Jackson, Richard Lee: Prisoner of Zenda, Inc.
Jackson, Sammy: Fastest Guitar Alive, The
Jackson, Samuel L.: Against the Wall; Amos & Andrew; Assault at West Point; Caveman's Valentine, The; Changing Lanes; Dead Man Out; Deep Blue Sea; Die Hard with a Vengeance; Eve's Bayou; Fluke; Fresh; Great White Hype, The; Hail Caesar; Hard Eight; Jackie Brown; Jumpin' at the Boneyard; Jurassic Park; Kiss of Death; Long Kiss Goodnight, The; Losing Isaiah; Menace II Society; Mob Justice; National Lampoon's Loaded Weapon 1; Negotiator, The; 187; Our Friend, Martin; Pulp Fiction; Red Violin, The; Rules of Engagement; Search for One-Eye Jimmy, The; Shaft; Sphere; Star Wars: Attack of the Clones; Star Wars: Episode I The Phantom Menace; Time to Kill, A (1996); True Romance; Unbreakable; White Sands
Jackson, Shar: Good Burger
Jackson, Sherry: Bare Knuckles; Danny Thomas Show, The (TV Series); Miracle of Our Lady of Fatima, The; Stingray; Trouble Along the Way
Jackson, Stoney: Black Scorpion II: Aftershock; Knights of the City; Up Against the Wall
Jackson, Thomas: Valley of the Zombies
Jackson, Tom: Grizzly Falls; Medicine River
Jackson, Victoria: Based on an Untrue Story; Casual Sex?; I Love You to Death; UHF
Jacob, Catherine: Tatie Danielle
Jacob, Irène: Big Brass Ring, The; Double Life of Veronique, The; Incognito; My Life So Far; Othello; Red; Spy Games; U.S. Marshals
Jacobi, Derek: Basil; Dead Again; Enigma; Gladiator; Gosford Park; Hamlet; Henry V; Human Factor, The; Hunchback (1982); I, Claudius; Inside the Third Reich; Little Dorrit; Love is the Devil; Odessa File, The; Othello; Philby, Burgess and Maclean: Spy Scandalof the Century; Secret Garden, The; Tenth Man, The
Jacobi, Doreen: Eating Pattern
Jacobi, Lou: Avalon; Better Late than Never; Everything You Always Wanted to Know About Sex but Were Afraid to Ask; I Don't Buy Kisses Anymore; I.Q.; Irma La Douce; Little Murders; Magician of Lublin, The; Next Stop, Greenwich Village; Roseland
Jacobs, André: Curse of the Crystal Eye; Prey for the Hunter
Jacobs, Emma: Murder on Line One
Jacobs, Michael Dean: Orgazmo
Jacobs, Steve: Alice to Nowhere; Father
Jacobson, Peter: Hit and Runway
Jacobsson, Ulla: Smiles of a Summer Night
Jacoby, Billy: Just One of the Guys
Jacoby, Bobby: Day My Parents Ran Away, The; Meet the Applegates; Night of the Demons 2; Wizard of the Lost Kingdom II
Jacoby, Scott: Bad Ronald; Baxter; To Die For; To Die For 2: Son of Darkness
Jacott, Carlos: Kicking and Screaming
Jacques, Hattie: Adventures of Sadie; Carry on Doctor
Jacquet, Roger: Occurrence at Owl Creek Bridge, An
Jade, Claude: Love on the Run; Stolen Kisses
Jaeckel, Richard: Attack!; Black Moon Rising; Cold River; Come Back, Little Sheba; Dark, The; Day of the Animals; Delta Force 2; Delta Fox; Devil's Brigade, The; Dirty Dozen, The: The Next Mission; Drowning Pool, The; Firehouse; Four for Texas; Gallant Hours, The; Ghetto Blaster; Green Slime, The; Grizzly; Guadalcanal Diary; Hoodlum Empire; Jaws of Death, The; Jungle Patrol; Kill, The; Latitude Zero; Martial Outlaw; Pacific Inferno; Sands of Iwo Jima; Sometimes a Great Notion; Starman; Supercarrier; 3:10 to Yuma; Ulzana's Raid; Violent Men, The; Walking Tall Part II; Wing and a Prayer, A
Jaenicke, Hannes: Restraining Order; Tigress, The
Jaffe, Chapelle: Confidential
Jaffe, Sam: Asphalt Jungle, The; Barbarian and the Geisha, The; Ben-Hur; Day the Earth Stood Still, The; Dunwich Horror, The; Gentlemen's Agreement; Guide for the Married Man, A; Gunga Din; Lost Horizon; On the Line; Scarlet Empress, The; 13 Rue Madeleine
Jaffrey, Madhur: Autobiography of a Princess; Shakespeare Wallah
Jaffrey, Saeed: Courtesans of Bombay; Deceivers, The; Diamond's Edge; Gandhi; Hullabaloo over George and Bonnie's Pictures; Masala; My Beautiful Laundrette
Jagger, Bianca: C.H.U.D. II (Bud the C.H.U.D.)
Jagger, Dean: Alligator; Cash McCall; Denver and Rio Grande, The; Elmer Gantry; End of the World; Evil Town; Executive Suite; Firecreek; Game of Death; Glass House, The; Honeymoon Machine, The; I Heard the Owl Call My Name; It's a Dog's Life; Jumbo; King Creole; Lindbergh Kidnapping Case, The; Nun's Story, The; Parrish; Private Hell 36; Proud Rebel, The; Pursued; Rawhide; Revolt of the Zombies; Robe, The; Sister Kenny; Smith!; Twelve O'Clock High; Valley of the Sun; Vanishing Point; Western Union; X—The Unknown
Jagger, Mick: Bent; Burden of Dreams; Freejack; Performance; Rutles, The (All You Need Is Cash)
Jaglom, Henry: Always; New Year's Day; Someone to Love; Venice/Venice
Jakobson, Maggie: New Year's Day
Jakoubek, Vaclav: Elementary School, The
Jakub, Lisa: Beautician and the Beast, The; Dream House; Lifeline; Matinee; Mrs. Doubtfire; Pig's Tale, A; Story Lady, The
Jamal-Warner, Malcolm: Drop Zone
James, Billy T.: Came a Hot Friday
James, Brian: Another 48 Hrs.; Armed and Dangerous; Arthur's Quest; Back in Business; Black Magic; Bombshell; Brain Smasher ... A Love Story; Brown's Requiem; Cabin Boy; Cherry 2000; Companion, The; Crimewave; Dark, The; Dead Man Walking; Enemy Mine; Evil Obsession; Fifth Element, The; Future Shock; Hong Kong '97; Horror Show, The; Hunter's Moon;

sus Cueball; Dillinger; Hidden Valley Outlaws; Mojave Firebrand; Return of the Bad Men; RiffRaff; Those Endearing Young Charms; Trail Street; Zombies on Broadway
Jeffreys, Chuck: Bloodmoon; Deathfight
Jeffries, Lang: Junkman, The
Jeffries, Lionel: Bhowani Junction; Blue Murder at St. Trinian's; Call Me Bwana; Camelot; Chitty Chitty Bang Bang; Colditz Story, The; Danny, The Champion of the World; Fanny; First Men in the Moon; Jekyll & Hyde; Letting the Birds Go Free; Murder Ahoy; Oh Dad, Poor Dad—Mama's Hung You inthe Closet and I'm Feeling So Sad; Prisoner of Zenda, The; Revenge of Frankenstein; Spy with a Cold Nose, The; Two-Way Stretch; Up the Creek; Who Slew Auntie Roo?; Wrong Arm of the Law, The
Jeffries, Todd: Colony, The (1995)
Jeffry, Doug: Don't Sleep Alone
Jeffs, Deanne: Midnight Dancer
Jei, Li Lin: Shaolin Temple
Jemison, Anna: Heatwave (1983); Smash Palace
Jemma, Dorothee: Hot Head
Jendly, Roger: Jonah Who Will Be 25 in the Year 2000
Jeni, Richard: Alan Smithee Film, An—Burn Hollywood Burn; Mask, The
Jenkin, Devon: Slammer Girls
Jenkins, "Butch": Human Comedy, The; Our Vines Have Tender Grapes; Summer Holiday
Jenkins, Allen: Amazing Dr. Clitterhouse, The; Ball of Fire; Big Wheel, The; Brother Orchid; Bureau of Missing Persons; Case of the Curious Bride, The; Case of the Howling Dog, The; Case of the Lucky Legs, The; Employees' Entrance; Five Came Back; Footsteps in the Dark; Hatbox Mystery, The; Marked Woman; Oklahoma Annie; Three Men on a Horse; Tin Pan Alley; Tomorrow at Seven; Wonder Man
Jenkins, Anthony: Blood Spell
Jenkins, Carol Mayo: Hollywood Heartbreak
Jenkins, Daniel H.: Florida Straits; O.C. & Stiggs; Tanner '88
Jenkins, Jane: Welcome to Hollywood
Jenkins, John: Patti Rocks
Jenkins, Ken: Edge of Honor
Jenkins, Megs: Innocents, The (1961)
Jenkins, Rebecca: Till Death Do Us Part
Jenkins, Richard: Couch in New York, A; Doublecrossed; Getting Out; Indian in the Cupboard, The; Little Nikita; Me, Myself & Irene; Random Hearts; Say It Isn't So; Witches of Eastwick, The; Wolf
Jenkins, Sam: Crew, The; Ed & His Dead Mother
Jenks, Frank: Corregidor; One Hundred Men and a Girl
Jenner, Bruce: Can't Stop the Music
Jenney, Lucinda: American Heart; Crazy/Beautiful; Next Door; Thinner; Verne Miller; Whoopee Boys, The
Jennings, Alex: Hunley, The
Jennings, Brent: Children of the Corn IV: The Gathering; Fixer, The; Live Wire; Nervous Ticks
Jennings, Bryon: Simple Twist of Fate, A
Jennings, Claudia: Deathsport; Great Texas Dynamite Chase, The; Truckstop Women
Jennings, DeWitt: Arrowsmith; Flesh and Blood (1922); Seven Footprints to Satan
Jennings, Joseph: Rock House
Jennings, Juanita: Laurel Avenue
Jennings, Maxine: Mr. Wong, Detective
Jennings, Tom: Stones of Death
Jennings, Waylon: Maverick; Sesame Street Presents Follow That Bird; Stagecoach
Jenrette, Rita: Zombie Island Massacre
Jens, Salome: Fool Killer, The; Harry's War; I'm Losing You; Jolly Corner, The; Savages; Seconds; Terror from the Year 5,000; Tomorrow's Child
Jensen, David: Schizopolis
Jensen, Erik: Horse for Danny, A
Jensen, Maren: Deadly Blessing
Jensen, Roy: Bandits
Jensen, Sara Indrio: Italian for Beginners
Jensen, Todd: Alien Chaser; Breeders; Cyborg Cop; Prey for the Hunter
Jenson, Sasha: Dazed and Confused; Dillinger & Capone; Twisted Love
Jeon, Hye Jin: Lies (1999)
Jeremiah, David: Midas Touch, The
Jeremy, Ron: They Bite
Jergens, Adele: Abbott and Costello Meet the Invisible Man; Dark Past, The; Fuller Brush Man, The; Ladies of the Chorus
Jergens, Diane: FBI Story, The
Jesse, Dan: Angel of H.E.A.T.
Jeter, Michael: Air Bud; Bank Robber; Boys Next Door, The; Drop Zone; Fisher King, The; Green Mile, The; Jurassic Park III; Mrs. Santa Claus; Naked Man, The; Sister Act 2: Back in the Habit; True Crime; Waterworld
Jett, Joan: Boogie Boy; Light of Day
Jett, Roger: Smithereens
Jewel: Ride with the Devil
Jewel, Jimmy: Arthur's Hallowed Ground
Jewell, Isabel: Ceiling Zero; Ciao! Manhattan; Evelyn Prentice; Go West, Young Man; Leopard Man, The; Little Men; Lost Horizon; Manhattan Melodrama; Marked Woman; Seventh Victim, The; Swing It, Sailor
Jézéquel, Julie: My Life and Times with Antonin Artaud
Ji, Liu: Red Sorghum
Jigme: Little Buddha
Jillette, Penn: Miami Vice: "The Prodigal Son"; Penn & Teller Get Killed
Jillian, Ann: Alice Through the Looking Glass; Ellis Island; Little White Lies; Mae West; Mr. Mom; Sammy, the Way-Out Seal
Jimenez, Luisa Maria: I Am Cuba
Jin, Elaine: Yi Yi
Jing, Ning: Red Firecracker, Green Firecracker
Jiraskova, Jirina: Ninety Degrees in the Shade
Jittlov, Mike: Wizard of Speed and Time, The
Jobert, Marlene: Catch Me a Spy; Le Secret; Masculine Feminine; Rider on the Rain; Swashbuckler, The (1984); Ten Days Wonder
Jodat, Shaghayegh: Gabbeh
Jodorowsky, Axel: Santa Sangre
Joel, Robert: Very Natural Thing, A
Joh, Kenzaburo: Zatoichi: Masseur Ichi and a Chest ofGold
Johann, Zita: Mummy, The
Johansen, David: Candy Mountain; Car 54, Where Are You? (1991); Desire and Hell at Sunset Motel; Freejack; Let It Ride; Mr. Nanny; Tales from the Darkside, The Movie
Johansson, Paul: Midnight Witness; Wishmaster 2: Evil Never Dies
Johansson, Scarlett: American Rhapsody, An; Ghost World; Horse Whisperer, The; Just Cause; Man Who Wasn't There, The (2001); Manny & Lo
Johar, I. S.: Flame over India; Maya
John, Elton: Stand by Me; Tommy
John, Gottfried: Chinese Boxes; Of Pure Blood
John, Lucien: Walkabout
Johnes, Alexandra: Zelly and Me
John-Jules, Danny: Blade II; Red Dwarf (TV Series)
Johnny Burnette Trio, The: Rock, Rock, Rock
Johns, Glynis: Adventures of Tartu; All Mine to Give; Another Time, Another Place; Court Jester, The; Dear Brigitte; Encore; 49th Parallel, The; Little Gloria, Happy at Last; Mary Poppins; No Highway in the Sky; Papa's Delicate Condition; Promoter, The; Ref, The; Rob Roy, the Highland Rogue; Shake Hands with the Devil; Sundowners, The; Superstar: Dare to Dream; Sword and the Rose, The (1953); That's Singing: The Best of Broadway; Under Milk Wood; Vault of Horror; While You Were Sleeping; Zelly and Me
Johns, Margo: Konga
Johns, Mervyn: Day of the Triffids, The; Dead of Night; Jamaica Inn; Never Let Go; Old Dark House, The; Quartet
Johns, Stratford: Great Expectations; Salome's Last Dance; Splitting Heirs; Wild Geese II
Johns, Tracy Camilla: She's Gotta Have It
Johnson, A. J.: I Got the Hook Up
Johnson, Adrienne-Joi: Baby Boy

Johnson, Amy Jo: Killing Mr. Griffin; Mighty Morphin Power Rangers: The Movie; Sweetwater
Johnson, Anne-Marie: Dream Date; Hollywood Shuffle; Robot Jox; Strictly Business; True Identity
Johnson, Anthony Rolfe: Gloriana
Johnson, Arch: Deathmask; Napoleon and Samantha
Johnson, Ariyan: Just Another Girl on the I.R.T.
Johnson, Arte: Alice in Wonderland; Alice Through the Looking Glass; Bud and Lou; Bunco; Evil Spirits; Evil Toons; Love at First Bite; Munchie; What Comes Around
Johnson, Ashley: Annie, a Royal Adventure!; Lionheart
Johnson, Ben: Back to Back; Bite the Bullet; Breakheart Pass; Champions; Cherry 2000; Chisum; Dillinger; Evening Star, The; Getaway, The; Grayeagle; Hang 'em High; Hunter, The (1980); Hustle; Junior Bonner; Last Picture Show, The; Major Dundee; Mighty Joe Young; My Heroes Have Always Been Cowboys; One-Eyed Jacks; Radio Flyer; Rare Breed, The (1966); Red Dawn; Rio Grande; Ruby Jean and Joe; Ruckus; Sacketts, The; Savage Bees, The; Shadow Riders, The; Shane; She Wore a Yellow Ribbon; Stranger on My Land; Sugarland Express, The; Terror Train; Tex; Three Godfathers, The; Tomboy and the Champ; Town That Dreaded Sundown, The; Train Robbers, The; Trespasses; Undefeated, The; Wagonmaster; Wild Bunch, The; Wild Times; Will Penny
Johnson, Beverly: Ashanti; Cover Girl Murders, The
Johnson, Bobby: Demon Wind
Johnson, Brad: Always; American Story, An; Annie Oakley (TV Series); Birds II, The: Land's End; Flight of the Intruder, The; Left Behind; Lone Justice 2; Philadelphia Experiment 2, The; Rough Riders; Siringo
Johnson, C. David: Aldrich Ames: Traitor Within; Legend of Gator Face, The
Johnson, Celia: Brief Encounter; Captain's Paradise, The; Kid for Two Farthings, A; Prime of Miss Jean Brodie, The; This Happy Breed; Unicorn, The
Johnson, Chic: All over Town; Country Gentlemen; Ghost Catchers, The; Hellzapoppin
Johnson, Christopher: Magic Stone, The
Johnson, Chubby: Fastest Gun Alive, The
Johnson, Clark: Blood Brothers; Junior's Groove; Model by Day; Silent Witness: What a Child Saw
Johnson, Don: Beulah Land; Born Yesterday; Boy and His Dog, A; Cease Fire; Dead-Bang; Goodbye Lover; Guilty as Sin; Harley Davidson and the Marlboro Man; Harrad Experiment, The; Hot Spot; In Pursuit of Honor; Long Hot Summer, The; Melanie; Miami Vice; Miami Vice: "The Prodigal Son"; Paradise; Rebels, The; Return to Macon County; Revenge of the Stepford Wives; Sweethearts' Dance; Tales of the Unexpected; Tin Cup; Zachariah
Johnson, Georgann: Front, The; Twilight Man
Johnson, Gil: Ruby Bridges
Johnson, Jack: Lost in Space (1998)
Johnson, Jim: Birthday Boy, The
Johnson, Johnnie: Chuck Berry Hail! Hail! Rock 'n' Roll
Johnson, Joseph Alan: Berserker
Johnson, Julanne: Thief of Bagdad, The
Johnson, Karen: Sensuous Wife, The
Johnson, Kathryn: Taming of the Shrew (1982)
Johnson, Kay: Madame Satan
Johnson, Kelly: Utu
Johnson, Kurt: Last Way Out, The; Sole Survivor
Johnson, Kyle: Learning Tree, The
Johnson, Laura: Chiller; Fatal Instinct; Judge and Jury; Lights, Camera, Action, Love; Murderous Vision; Nick Knight
Johnson, Lillian: Body and Soul
Johnson, Linda: Bandits of Dark Canyon
Johnson, Lynn-Holly: Alien Predators; For Your Eyes Only; Ice Castles; Out of Sight Out of Mind; Sisterhood, The; Watcher in the Woods, The; Where the Boys Are '84
Johnson, Margaret: Burn, Witch, Burn
Johnson, Mary: Treasure of Arne
Johnson, Michael: Lust for a Vampire
Johnson, Michelle: Beaks: the Movie; Blame It on Rio; Blood Ties; Body Shot; Donor, The; Driving Me Crazy; Far and Away; Genuine Risk; Glimmer Man, The; Incident at Deception Ridge; Jigsaw Murders, The; Slipping into Darkness; Till Murder Do Us Part; Waxwork; When the Bullet Hits the Bone; Wishful Thinking
Johnson, Noble: East of Borneo; Hawk of the Wilderness; King Kong; Mad Doctor of Market Street, The; Murders in the Rue Morgue; Mysterious Dr. Fu Manchu; Mystery Ranch; Ranger and the Lady, The; She; Ten Commandments, The
Johnson, Penny: Color of Friendship, The; Death Benefit; Imposter, The
Johnson, Raymond: Escape from Survival Zone
Johnson, Rebekah: Liberty Heights; Ruby Jean and Joe
Johnson, Rich: Foreign Student
Johnson, Richard: Amorous Adventures of Moll Flanders, The; Beyond the Door; Crucifer of Blood; Duel of Hearts; Haunting, The; Hennessy; Khartoum; Lara Croft: Tomb Raider; Never So Few; Operation Crossbow; Restless; Screamers; Spymaker: The Secret Life of Ian Fleming; Treasure Island; Turtle Diary; What Waits Below; Zombie
Johnson, Rita: Broadway Serenade; Edison, The Man; Here Comes Mr. Jordan; Honolulu; Letter of Introduction; My Friend Flicka; Naughty Nineties, The; Perfect Marriage; Smashing the Rackets; They Won't Believe Me
Johnson, Robin: Times Square
Johnson, Russell: Attack of the Crab Monsters; This Island Earth
Johnson, Ryan Thomas: Captain Nuke and the Bomber Boys; Carnosaur 2
Johnson, Scott: Whispering, The
Johnson, Stephen: Angel of H.E.A.T.
Johnson, Sunny: Dr. Heckyl and Mr. Hype
Johnson, Terry: Pleasure Unlimited
Johnson, Tony T.: Shadow Zone: The Undead Express
Johnson, Tor: Bride of the Monster; Meanest Man in the World, The
Johnson, Van: Battleground; Big Hangover, The; Brigadoon; Caine Mutiny, The; Command Decision; Delta Force, Commando Two; Divorce American Style; Doomsday Flight, The; Duchess of Idaho; Easy to Love; Go for Broke!; Guy Named Joe, A; Human Comedy, The; In the Good Old Summertime; It's a Big Country; Kidnapping of the President, The; Last Time I Saw Paris, The; Madame Curie; Men of the Fighting Lady; State of the Union; Thirty Seconds Over Tokyo; Three Days to a Kill; Thrill of a Romance; Two Girls and a Sailor; Weekend at the Waldorf; White Cliffs of Dover, The; Yours, Mine and Ours
Johnson), The Rock (Dwayne: Scorpion King, The
Johnson Jr., Mel: Hideous
Johnston, Bobby: Body Strokes (Siren's Call)
Johnston, Grace: God Bless the Child
Johnston, J. J.: Fixer, The
Johnston, John Dennis: In Pursuit of Honor; Miracle in the Wilderness; Pink Cadillac
Johnston, Johnnie: This Time For Keeps
Johnston, Katie: Clockmaker (1998)
Johnston, Kristen: Flintstones in Viva Rock Vegas, The
Johnston, Ollie: Frank and Ollie
Johnston, Shaun: Ms. Bear
Johnstone, Jane Anne: Dixie Dynamite
Jokovic, Mirjana: Eversmile New Jersey; Underground
Jolie, Angelina: Bone Collector, The; Cyborg 2; Foxfire; George Wallace; Girl, Interrupted; Gone in 60 Seconds; Hackers; Lara Croft: Tomb Raider; Life or Something Like It; Mojave Moon; Original Sin; Playing God; Pushing Tin; True Women
Jolivet, Pierre: Final Combat, The
Jolley, I. Stanford: Dangers of the Canadian Mounted; Death Rides the Plains; Scarlet Clue, The; Trail of the Silver Spurs; Violent Years, The
Jolly, Mike: Bad Guys
Jolson, Al: Go into Your Dance; Hallelujah, I'm A Bum; Hollywood Cavalcade; Jazz Singer, The; Rose of Washington Square; Wonder Bar
Jones, Allan: Day at the Races, A; Everybody Sing; Firefly, The; My Love for Yours (Honeymoon in Bali); Night at the Opera, A; One Night in the Tropics; Show Boat

Jones, Allison: Nightjohn
Jones, Angela: Curdled; Debt, The
Jones, Angus T.: Rookie, The (2002); See Spot Run
Jones, Ashley: Devil's Prey
Jones, Barbara: Desire
Jones, Barry: Brigadoon; Clouded Yellow, The; Glass Slipper, The; Number 17; Return to Paradise; Thirty-Nine Steps, The
Jones, Bruce: Raining Stones
Jones, Buck: Arizona Bound; Below the Border; Dawn on the Great Divide; Down Texas Way; Fighting Code; Fighting Ranger, The; Forbidden Trail; Forbidden Trails; Ghost Town Law; Gunman from Bodie; Ivory-Handled Gun, The; Law for Tombstone; Range Feud; Riders of Death Valley; Stone of Silver Creek; Sundown Rider, The; West of the Law; When a Man Sees Red
Jones, Carolyn: Addams Family, The (TV Series); Big Heat, The; Career; Color Me Dead; Eaten Alive; Hole in the Head, A; House of Wax; How the West Was Won; Ice Palace; Invasion of the Body Snatchers; King Creole; Last Train from Gun Hill; Little Ladies of the Night; Man Who Knew Too Much, The; Marjorie Morningstar; Seven Year Itch, The; Shaming, The; Tender Trap, The
Jones, Catherine Zeta: Phantom, The; Return of the Native, The; Splitting Heirs
Jones, Cherry: Cradle Will Rock; Erin Brockovich
Jones, Christopher: Looking Glass War, The; Ryan's Daughter; Three in the Attic; Wild in the Streets
Jones, Claude Earl: Bride of Re-Animator; Evilspeak
Jones, Cody: Goosebumps: The Haunted Mask; Running Wild
Jones, Damon: Pariah
Jones, David: Head (1968)
Jones, Dean: Any Wednesday; Beethoven; Blackbeard's Ghost; Born Again; Clear and Present Danger; Herbie Goes to Monte Carlo; Horse in the Gray Flannel Suit, The; Jailhouse Rock; Love Bug, The; Love Bug, The; Million Dollar Duck, The; Monkeys Go Home; Mr. Superinvisible; Never So Few; Other People's Money; Shaggy D.A., The; Snowball Express; Tea and Sympathy; That Darn Cat; That Darn Cat; Torpedo Run; Two on a Guillotine; Ugly Dachshund, The; Until They Sail
Jones, Desmond: Romance with a Double Bass
Jones, Dick: Last of the Pony Riders
Jones, Dickie: Westward Ho
Jones, Duane: Night of the Living Dead; To Die For
Jones, Eddie: Apprentice to Murder; Body Language
Jones, Freddie: And the Ship Sails On; Consuming Passions; Elephant Man, The; Firefox; Krull; Last Butterfly, The; Neverending Story III, The: Escape toFantasia; Romance with a Double Bass; Satanic Rites of Dracula, The; Son of Dracula; Twinsanity; Young Sherlock Holmes
Jones, Gemma: Bridget Jones's Diary; Cotton Mary; Devils, The; Sense and Sensibility; Theory of Flight, The; Wilde; Winslow Boy, The
Jones, Geraldine: Tall Guy, The
Jones, Gordon: Among the Living; Arizona Cowboy; Flying Tigers, The; Trail of Robin Hood; Trigger Jr.; Wistful Widow of Wagon Gap, The
Jones, Grace: Boomerang; Conan the Destroyer; Cyber Bandits; McCinsey's Island; Siesta; Vamp; View to a Kill, A
Jones, Griff Rhys: Misadventures of Mr. Wilt, The; Morons from Outer Space
Jones, Hatty: Madeline
Jones, Helen: Bliss
Jones, Henry: Bad Seed, The; Bramble Bush, The; California Gold Rush; Cash McCall; Deathtrap; Girl Can't Help It, The; Grifters, The; Napoleon and Samantha; Nowhere to Run; Rabbit Run; Support Your Local Sheriff!; 3:10 to Yuma; Will Success Spoil Rock Hunter?
Jones, James Earl: Allan Quartermain and the Lost City of Gold; Ambulance, The; Best of the Best; Bingo Long Traveling All-Stars and Motor Kings, The; Bloodtide; Bushido Blade; By Dawn's Early Light; City Limits; Clean Slate (1994); Clear and Present Danger; Comedians, The; Coming to America; Conan the Barbarian; Cry, the Beloved Country; Deadly Hero; Dr. Strangelove or How I Learned to Stop Worrying and Love the Bomb; End of the Road; Excessive Force; Exorcist II: The Heretic; Family Thing, A; Field of Dreams; Gang Related; Gardens of Stone; Great White Hope, The; Greatest, The; Grim Prairie Tales; Guyana Tragedy, The: The Story of Jim Jones; Heat Wave; Hunt for Red October, The; Ivory Hunters; Jefferson in Paris; Matewan; Merlin (1998); Meteor Man; My Little Girl; Our Friend, Martin; Patriot Games; Percy & Thunder; Piece of the Action, A; Rebound; Return of the Jedi; Road to Freedom: The Vernon Johns Story; Roots: The Next Generation; Sandlot, The; Scorchers; Second Civil War, The; Sommersby; Soul Man; Summer's End; Swashbuckler (1976); Three Fugitives; Undercover Angel; What the Deaf Man Heard
Jones, Janet: American Anthem; Flamingo Kid, The; Police Academy 5: Assignment: Miami Beach
Jones, Jeffrey: Avenging Angel, The (1995); Beetlejuice; Devil's Advocate; Dr. Dolittle 2; Ed Wood; Ferris Bueller's Day Off; Gambler, Part III—The Legend Continues, The; George Washington: The Forging of a Nation; Hanoi Hilton, The; Houseguest; Howard the Duck; Hunt for Red October, The; Mom and Dad Save the World; Out on a Limb; Over Her Dead Body; Pest, The; Ravenous; Sleepy Hollow; Stay Tuned; Transylvania 6-5000; Valmont; Who's Harry Crumb?; Without a Clue
Jones, Jennifer: Beat the Devil; Carrie; Dick Tracy's G-Men; Duel in the Sun; Frontier Horizon; Indiscretion of an American Wife; Love Is a Many-Splendored Thing; Madame Bovary; Man in the Gray Flannel Suit, The; Portrait of Jennie; Ruby Gentry; Since You Went Away; Song of Bernadette, The
Jones, Jerry: Dolemite
Jones, Jocelyn: Great Texas Dynamite Chase, The
Jones, Josephine Jacqueline: Black Venus; Warrior Queen
Jones, Ken: Melody
Jones, L. Q.: Ballad of Cable Hogue, The; Brotherhood of Satan; Bulletproof; Edge, The; Jack Bull, The; Lightning Jack; Lone Wolf McQuade; Patriot, The; Ride the High Country; River of Death; Standing Tall; Timerider; Tornado!; White Line Fever; Wild Bunch, The
Jones, Lisa: Life and Times of Grizzly Adams, The
Jones, Lucinda: Wild Duck, The
Jones, Marcia Mae: Mad About Music; Meet Dr. Christian; Misadventures of Buster Keaton, The; Old Swimmin' Hole, The; These Three
Jones, Marilyn: On the Block
Jones, Neal: Day at the Beach; Silent Prey
Jones, Nicholas: Not a Penny More, Not a Penny Less
Jones, Norman: Inspector Morse (TV Series)
Jones, Orlando: Bedazzled; Double Take; Evolution; Replacements, The; Say It Isn't So; Time Machine, The (2002)
Jones, Paul: Demons of the Mind
Jones, Peter: Hitchhiker's Guide to the Galaxy, The; Whoops Apocalypse
Jones, Richard: Good Old Boys, The
Jones, Richard T.: Black Rose of Harlem; Event Horizon; Kiss the Girls; Renaissance Man; Trigger Effect, The; Wood, The
Jones, Robert: Slaughter in San Francisco
Jones, Robert Earl: Displaced Person, The
Jones, Ronalda: Alligator Shoes
Jones, Rosie: Alice to Nowhere; Ganjasaurus Rex
Jones, Sam: American Strays; Ballistic; Davinci's War; Fist of Iron; Flash Gordon; In Gold We Trust; Jane and the Lost City; Lady Dragon 2; Maximum Force; My Chauffeur; Other Woman, The; Silent Assassins; Texas Payback; Thunder in Paradise; Under the Gun
Jones, Samantha: Get to Know Your Rabbit
Jones, Sharon Lee: Leapin' Leprechauns
Jones, Shirley: Bedtime Story; Carousel; Cheyenne Social Club, The; Children of An Lac, The; Courtship of Eddie's Father, The; Elmer Gantry; Girls of Huntington House; Music Man, The; Never Steal Anything Small; Oklahoma!; Shriek If You Know What I Did Last Friday the 13th; Silent Night, Lonely Night; Tank; Two Rode Together
Jones, Simon: Brideshead Revisited; For Love or Money; Hitchhiker's Guide to the Galaxy, The; Miracle on 34th Street; Operation Delta Force 2; Privates on Parade
Jones, Steve: Filth and the Fury, The; Great Rock and Roll Swindle, The

The; Havana; Kiss of the Spider Woman; Mack the Knife; Moon over Parador; Morning After, The; Onassis: The Richest Man in the World; One from the Heart; Organization, The; Panic in Needle Park; Penitent, The; Plague, The; Presumed Innocent; Romero; Rookie, The (1990); Street Fighter; Tango Bar; Tequila Sunrise; Trading Hearts
Julian, Janet: Choke Canyon; Ghost Warrior; Humongous; King of New York
Julien, Max: Getting Straight; Mack, The
Jump, Gordon: Bitter Vengeance
Jurado, Katy: Badlanders, The; Barabbas; Broken Lance; Bullfighter and the Lady, The; El Bruto (The Brute); High Noon; One-Eyed Jacks; Pat Garrett and Billy the Kid; Racers, The; Trapeze
Jurasik, Peter: Late Shift, The
Jurgens, Curt: And God Created Woman; Battle of Britain; Battle of the Commandos; Brainwashed; Breakthrough; Enemy Below, The; Goldengirl; Inn of the Sixth Happiness, The; Just a Gigolo; Mephisto Waltz, The; Miracle of the White Stallions; Mozart Story, The; Spy Who Loved Me, The; This Happy Feeling; Vault of Horror
Jurgens, Deana: Tin Man
Jurisic, Melita: Tale of Ruby Rose, The
Juross, Albert: Les Carabiniers
Justice, James Robertson: Captain Horatio Hornblower; Doctor at Large; Doctor at Sea; Doctor in Distress; Doctor in the House; Land of the Pharaohs; Le Repos du Guerrier (Warrior's Rest); Murder She Said; Rob Roy, the Highland Rogue; Story of Robin Hood, The; Sword and the Rose, The (1953); Tight Little Island
Justice, Katherine: Five Card Stud; Frasier the Lovable Lion (Frasier the Sensuous Lion)
Justin, John: Savage Messiah; Thief of Bagdad, The
Justin, Larry: Hollywood Meatcleaver Massacre
Justine, William: Bride and the Beast, The
Jutra, Claude: Mon Oncle Antoine
Kaake, Jeff: Border Shootout; Space Rangers (TV Series)
Kaalund, Lars: Italian for Beginners
Kaaren, Suzanne: Devil Bat, The
Kabo, Olga: Ice Runner
Kabongo, Dieudonné: Lumumba
Kaczmarek, Jane: All's Fair; D.O.A.; Door to Door; Heavenly Kid, The; Vice Versa
Kadler, Karen: Devil's Messenger, The
Kadochnikova, Larisa: Shadows of Forgotten Ancestors
Kagan, Diane: Barn Burning
Kagan, Elaine: Babyfever
Kagawa, Kyoko: Chikamatsu Monogatari
Kahan, Saul: Schlock
Kahler, Wolf: Dirty Dozen, The: The Deadly Mission; Raiders of the Lost Ark
Kahmhadze, Teimour: Chef in Love, A
Kahn, Madeline: Adventure of Sherlock Holmes' Smarter Brother, The; American Tail, An; Betsy's Wedding; Blazing Saddles; Cheap Detective, The; City Heat; Clue; First Family; For Richer, for Poorer; Happy Birthday, Gemini; Hideaways, The; High Anxiety; History of the World, Part One, The; Judy Berlin; Mixed Nuts; Muppet Movie, The; Paper Moon; Simon; Slapstick of Another Kind; Wholly Moses!; Yellowbeard; Young Frankenstein
Kaidanovsky, Alexander: Magic Hunter; Stalker
Kain, Amber: Mercy
Kain, Khalil: Bones; Juice; Love Jones; Zooman
Kaiser, Erwin: Dressed to Kill
Kaiser, Suki: Bloodhounds II; Virtual Assassin
Kaitan, Elizabeth: Assault of the Killer Bimbos; Petticoat Planet; South Beach Academy; Virtual Encounters
Kalem, Toni: Billy Galvin
Kalember, Patricia: Danielle Steel's Kaleidoscope
Kalevaars, Ingrid: Specimen
Kalfon, Jean-Pierre: Confidentially Yours; Valley, The
Kalifi, Mohsen: White Balloon, The
Kalinina, Daria: Welcome to the Dollhouse
Kalipha, Stefan: Born of Fire
Kallo, John: My Samurai
Kalmic, Lazar: Someone Else's America
Kaloper, Jagoda: WR: Mysteries of the Organism
Kalyagin, Alexander: Slave of Love, A; Unfinished Piece for the Player Piano, An (Unfinished Piece for a Mechanical Piano, An)
Kamamoto, Gayo: Zatoichi: The Blind Swordsman and theChess Expert
Kaman, Bob: Bloodfist
Kam-bo: Painted Faces
Kamekona, Danny: Robot Wars
Kamel, Stanley: Dancing with Danger
Kamerling, Antonie: Suite 16
Kaminska, Ida: Shop on Main Street, The
Kamm, Kris: Heroes of Desert Storm; When the Party's Over
Kamp-Groenveld, Alexandra: 2001: A Space Travesty
Kanakaredes, Melina: 15 Minutes
Kanakis, Anna: Warriors of the Wasteland
Kanaly, Steve: Balboa; Dillinger; Double Trouble; Fleshburn; Pumpkinhead II: Bloodwings; Scorpio One; Wind and the Lion, The
Kanan, Sean: Rich Girl
Kanaoka, Nodu: Tetsuo II: Body Hammer
Kanaventi, Munyaradzi: Running Wild
Kane, Alden: Prom Night IV—Deliver Us from Evil
Kane, Big Daddy: Posse
Kane, Bridget: Who's Who
Kane, Carol: Addams Family Values; American Strays; Annie Hall; Baby on Board; Big Bully; Crazysitter, The; Dog Day Afternoon; Even Cowgirls Get the Blues; Flashback; Games of Countess Dolingen of Gratz, The; Greatest Man in the World, The; Hester Street; In the Soup; Ishtar; Jumpin' Jack Flash; Lemon Sisters, The; License to Drive; Muppet Movie, The; My Blue Heaven; My First Mister; My Sister, My Love (The Mafu Cage); Norman Loves Rose; Office Killer; Over the Brooklyn Bridge; Pallbearer, The; Pandemonium; Princess Bride, The; Racing with the Moon; Scrooged; Secret Diary of Sigmund Freud, The; Sticky Fingers; Sunset Park; Ted & Venus; Transylvania 6-5000; Valentino; Wedding in White; When a Stranger Calls; When a Stranger Calls Back; World's Greatest Lover, The
Kane, Christian: Life or Something Like It
Kane, Irene: Killer's Kiss
Kane, Jimmy: Challenge to Be Free
Kane, Taylor: Dish, The
Ka'ne, Dayton: Hurricane (1979)
Kaner, Iris: Soldier of the Night
Kaneshiro, Takeshi: Chungking Express
Kang, Law: Crime Story
Kang, Patrick Lung: Black Mask
Kani, John: African Dream, An; Ghost and the Darkness, The; Killing Heat; Master Harold and the Boys; Options; Saturday Night at the Palace
Kanner, Alexis: Kings and Desperate Men: A Hostage Incident; Twinsanity
Kanter, Jennifer: Occultist, The
Kanter, Marin: Loveless, The
Kantner, China: Stoned Age, The
Kants, Ivar: Gallagher's Travels; Plumber, The
Kapelos, John: Deep End of the Ocean, The; Deep Red; Nick Knight
Kaplan, Gabe: Fast Break; Gabe Kaplan as Groucho; Nobody's Perfekt; Tulips
Kaplan, Marvin: New Kind of Love, A; Severed Arm, The
Kapoor, Shashi: Bombay Talkie; Deceivers, The; Heat and Dust; Householder, The; In Custody; Sammy and Rosie Get Laid; Shakespeare Wallah
Kaprisky, Valerie: Aphrodite; Breathless; Iran Days of Crisis; L'Année des Meduses
Kapture, Mitzi: His Bodyguard; Perfect Crime
Karabatsos, Ron: Hollywood Heartbreak; Rich Girl
Karasun, May: Lake Consequence
Karen, James: Fly Boy; Frankenstein Meets the Space Monster; Invaders from Mars; Piranha; Return of the Living Dead,

Kazan, Elia: City for Conquest
Kazan, Lainie: Associate, The; Big Hit, The; Cemetery Club, The; Crew, The; Cry for Love, A; Dayton's Devils; Delta Force, The; Harry and the Hendersons; I Don't Buy Kisses Anymore; Journey of Natty Gann, The; Lady in Cement; Love Is All There Is; Lust in the Dust; My Favorite Year; Obsessive Love; Pinocchio; Sunset Limousine; 29th Street; What's Cooking?
Kazann, Zitto: Slaughter of the Innocents
Kaznelson, Ayelet: Tao of Steve, The
Kazurinsky, Tim: Billion for Boris, A; Dinner at Eight; Neighbors; Police Academy 4: Citizens on Patrol; Police Academy III: Back in Training
Keach, James: Blue Hotel; Evil Town; Experts, The; FM; Long Riders, The; Love Letters; Man Who Broke 1000 Chains, The; Moving Violations; Razor's Edge, The; Wildcats
Keach, Stacy: All the Kind Strangers; Amanda and the Alien; American History X; Battle Force; Blue and the Gray, The; Butterfly; Children of the Corn 666: Isaac's Return; Class of 1999; Conduct Unbecoming; End of the Road; False Identity; Fat City; Forgotten, The; Future Fear; Gray Lady Down; Heart Is a Lonely Hunter, The; John Carpenter Presents: Body Bags; John Carpenter's Escape from L.A.; Killer Inside Me, The; Legend of the Lost Tomb; Life and Times of Judge Roy Bean, The; Long Riders, The; Luther; Mission of the Shark; Mistral's Daughter; New Centurions, The; New Crime City: Los Angeles 2020; Nice Dreams; Ninth Configuration, The; Pathfinder, The; Princess Daisy; Rio Diablo; Road Games; Rumor of War, A; Slave of the Cannibal God; Squeeze, The; Street People; Sunset Grill; Texas; That Championship Season; Up in Smoke; Watched!
Kean, Greg: Summer Dreams
Kean, Marie: Danny Boy; Dead, The; Lonely Passion of Judith Hearne, The
Keanan, Staci: Downhill Willie; Lisa
Keane, Dillie: Heaven's a Drag
Keane, Edward: Frontier Pony Express
Keane, James: Life on the Mississippi
Keane, Kerrie: Kung Fu—The Movie (1986); Malarek; Mistress; Nightstick; Obsessed; Perfect Daughter, The; Spasms
Kearney, Carolyn: Thing that Couldn't Die, The
Kearney, Gerard: War of the Buttons
Kearny, Stephen: Rikki and Pete
Keating, Larry: Above and Beyond; Francis Goes to the Races; George Burns and Gracie Allen Show, The (TV Series); Gypsy Colt; Incredible Mr. Limpet, The; Monkey Business; When Worlds Collide
Keaton, Buster: Adventures of Huckleberry Finn, The; Art of Buster Keaton, The; Beach Blanket Bingo; Boom in the Moon; Buster and Fatty; Buster Keaton Festival Vol. 1–3; Cameraman, The; College; Days of Thrills and Laughter; Doughboys; Forever and a Day; Free and Easy; Fuller Brush Man, The; Funny Thing Happened on the Way to the Forum, A; General, The; Great Chase, The; Hollywood Cavalcade; How to Stuff a Wild Bikini; In the Good Old Summertime; It's a Mad Mad Mad Mad World; Keaton Rides Again/Railroader; Li'l Abner; Limelight; Misadventures of Buster Keaton, The; Navigator, The (1924); Old Spanish Custom, An; Our Hospitality; Parlor, Bedroom and Bath; Seven Chances; Sherlock Jr.; Sidewalks of New York; Speak Easily; Spite Marriage; Steamboat Bill Jr.; Sunset Boulevard; Three Ages, The; Villain Still Pursued Her, The; What! No Beer?; When Comedy Was King
Keaton, Camille: I Spit on Your Grave
Keaton, Diane: Amelia Earhart: The Final Flight; Annie Hall; Baby Boom; Crimes of the Heart; Father of the Bride; Father of the Bride Part II; First Wives Club, The; Godfather, The; Godfather Epic, The; Godfather, Part II, The; Godfather, Part III, The; Good Mother, The; Hanging Up; Harry and Walter Go to New York; I Will, I Will … for Now; Interiors; Lemon Sisters, The; Little Drummer Girl, The; Looking for Mr. Goodbar; Love and Death; Lovers and Other Strangers; Manhattan; Manhattan Murder Mystery; Marvin's Room; Mrs. Soffel; Only Thrill, The; Play It Again, Sam; Reds; Running Mates; Shoot the Moon; Sister Mary Explains It All; Sleeper; Town & Country
Keaton, Joseph: Buster Keaton Festival Vol. 1–3; General, The
Keaton, Louise: Buster Keaton Festival Vol. 1–3
Keaton, Michael: Batman; Batman Returns; Beetlejuice; Clean and Sober; Desperate Measures; Dream Team, The; Gung Ho (1985); Jack Frost; Jackie Brown; Johnny Dangerously; Mr. Mom; Much Ado About Nothing; Multiplicity; My Life; Night Shift; One Good Cop; Our Hospitality; Pacific Heights; Paper, The; Speechless; Squeeze, The; Touch and Go; Working Stiffs
Keaton, Myra: Buster Keaton Festival Vol. 1–3
Keaton Jr., Buster: Our Hospitality
Keats, Ele: Lipstick Camera; Mother; White Dwarf
Keats, Steven: Friends of Eddie Coyle, The; Hester Street; In Dangerous Company
Keays-Byrne, Hugh: Blue Fin; Kangaroo; Mad Max
Kedrova, Lila: Bloodtide; Some Girls; Tell Me a Riddle; Testament; Torn Curtain; Zorba the Greek
Keefe, Dennis: Shadow Creature
Keegan, Andrew: Broken Hearts Club, The; Skateboard Kid 2, The; 10 Things I Hate About You
Keegan, Kari: Jason Goes to Hell: The Final Friday
Keehne, Virginya: Infested (Ticks)
Keel, Howard: Annie Get Your Gun; Arizona Bushwhackers; Armored Command; Calamity Jane; Day of the Triffids, The; Jupiter's Darling; Kismet; Kiss Me Kate; Lovely to Look At; Pagan Love Song; Rose Marie; Seven Brides for Seven Brothers; Show Boat; Texas Carnival; That's Entertainment! III; War Wagon, The
Keeler, Ruby: Dames; Flirtation Walk; Footlight Parade; 42nd Street; Go into Your Dance; Gold Diggers of 1933
Keeling, Rebecca: Snoopers
Keen, Geoffrey: Born Free; Cry, the Beloved Country; Dr. Syn, Alias the Scarecrow; Horrors of the Black Museum; Living Free; Number One of the Secret Service; Sink the Bismarck; Taste the Blood of Dracula
Keen, Malcolm: Lodger, The; Manxman, The
Keena, Monica: Crime & Punishment in Suburbia; Ripe; Snow White: A Tale of Terror
Keenan, Caroline: Killer Bud
Keene, Tom: Driftin' Kid; Dynamite Canyon; Lights of Old Santa Fe; Our Daily Bread; Plan 9 from Outer Space; Scarlet River; Trail of Robin Hood; Where Trails End
Keener, Catherine: Being John Malkovich; Box of Moonlight; Death to Smoochy; Johnny Suede; Living in Oblivion; 8MM; Real Blonde, The; Simpatico; Walking and Talking; Your Friends & Neighbors
Keeslar, Matt: Dune; Durango; Last Days of Disco, The; Psycho Beach Party; Splendor; Stupids, The; Texas Rangers (2001); Urbania
Kehkaial, Vladimir: Jugular Wine
Kehler, Jack: Blindsided
Kehoe, Jack: On the Nickel; Paper, The; Serpico; Servants of Twilight; Star Chamber, The
Keim, Claire: Girl, The (1999)
Keir, Andrew: Absolution; Catholics; Daleks—Invasion Earth 2150 A.D.; Dracula—Prince of Darkness; Dragonworld; Five Million Years to Earth; Rob Roy
Keitel, Harvey: Alice Doesn't Live Here Anymore; Bad Lieutenant; Blindside; Blue Collar; Blue in the Face; Border, The; Buffalo Bill and the Indians; Bugsy; Camorra; City of Industry; Clockers; Copland; Corrupt; Dangerous Game, A (1993); Death Watch; Duellists, The; Eagle's Wing; Exposed; Fairy Tale: A True Story; Falling in Love; Finding Graceland; Fingers; From Dusk Till Dawn; Holy Smoke; Imaginary Crimes; Inquiry, The; January Man, The; La Nuit de Varennes; Last Temptation of Christ, The; Little Nicky; Lulu on the Bridge; Mean Streets; Men's Club, The; Monkey Trouble; Mortal Thoughts; Mother, Jugs, and Speed; Off Beat; Piano, The; Pick-Up Artist, The; Point of No Return; Pulp Fiction; Reservoir Dogs; Rising Sun; Saturn 3; Shadrach; Sister Act; Smoke; Somebody to Love; Star Knight; Taxi Driver; Thelma & Louise; Three Seasons; Two Evil Eyes; Two Jakes, The; U-571; Ulysses' Gaze; Welcome to L.A.; Who's That Knocking at My Door?; Wise Guys; Young Americans, The
Keith, Brian: Alamo, The: Thirteen Days to Glory; Arrowhead; Deadly Companions, The; Death Before Dishonor; Dino; Entertaining Angels; Gambler Returns, The: Luck of the Draw; Hallelujah Trail, The; Hooper; Johnny Shiloh; Meteor; Moon Pilot;

Kelly, Tommy: Adventures of Tom Sawyer, The; Peck's Bad Boy with the Circus
Kelman, Paul: My Bloody Valentine
Kelsang, Hampa: Windhorse
Kelso, Bobby: Jack Knife Man, The
Kemmer, Ed: Earth vs. the Spider
Kemmerling, Warren: Eat My Dust
Kemp, Dan: Cry Blood, Apache
Kemp, Elizabeth: He Knows You're Alone; Killing Hour, The
Kemp, Gary: Bodyguard, The; Krays, The; Magic Hunter; Paper Marriage
Kemp, Jeremy: Angels and Insects; Belstone Fox, The; Blockhouse, The; Blue Max, The; Caravans; Darling Lili; East of Elephant Rock; George Washington; Leopard in the Snow; Operation Crossbow; Prisoner of Honor; Return of the Soldier, The; Sadat; When the Whales Came
Kemp, Lindsay: Savage Messiah
Kemp, Martin: Boca; Cyber Bandits; Embrace of the Vampire; Fleshtone; Krays, The; Sugar Town
Kemp, Sally: Last Hit, The
Kemp, Tina: Waltz Through the Hills
Kempe, Will: Hit the Dutchman; Pledge Night
Kemper, Charles: Intruder in the Dust
Kemper, Michael: Zombie Cop
Kempson, Rachel: Captive Heart; Déjà Vu
Kendal, Felicity: Shakespeare Wallah; Valentino
Kendal, Jennifer: Bombay Talkie
Kendall, Cavan: Sexy Beast
Kendall, Cy: King of the Pecos; Lonely Trail, The
Kendall, Geoffrey: Shakespeare Wallah
Kendall, Henry: Amazing Adventure; Rich and Strange
Kendall, Kay: Doctor in the House; Genevieve; Les Girls; Reluctant Debutante, The
Kendall, Suzy: Adventures of a Private Eye; Bird with the Crystal Plumage, The; Circus of Fear; Tales that Witness Madness; 30 Is a Dangerous Age, Cynthia; To Sir with Love; Torso
Kendall, Tony: When the Screaming Stops
Kenin, Alexa: Piano for Mrs. Cimino, A
Kennard, Malcolm: One Crazy Night
Kennedy, Angela: Wicked, The
Kennedy, Anne-Marie: My Name is Joe
Kennedy, Arthur: Air Force; Anzio; Bend of the River; Champion; City for Conquest; Crashout; Desperate Hours, The (1955); Desperate Journey; Elmer Gantry; Fantastic Voyage; Hail, Hero!; High Sierra; Lawrence of Arabia; Lusty Men, The; Man from Laramie, The; Minute to Pray, A Second to Die, A; Murder She Said; My Old Man's Place; Nevada Smith; Peyton Place; President's Plane Is Missing, The; Rancho Notorious; Sentinel, The; Shark! (Maneaters!); Signs of Life; Some Came Running; Summer Place, A; Tempter, The; They Died with Their Boots On; Window, The
Kennedy, Betty: Cheech and Chong's Next Movie
Kennedy, Bill: Two Lost Worlds
Kennedy, Deborah: Sum of Us, The
Kennedy, Douglas: Adventures of Don Juan, The; Amazing Transparent Man, The; Cariboo Trail; Fort Osage; Lone Ranger and the Lost City of Gold, The; South of St. Louis; Texas Rangers, The (1951)
Kennedy, Edgar: Air Raid Wardens; Cowboy Millionaire; Diplomaniacs; Dr. Christian Meets the Women; Double Wedding; Duck Soup; Hold 'em Jail; Hollywood Hotel; In Old California; In Person; Keystone Comedies: Vol. 1–5; Laurel and Hardy Classics: Vol. 1–9; Li'l Abner; Little Orphan Annie; Mad Wednesday (see also Sin of HaroldDiddlebock); My Dream Is Yours; Peck's Bad Boy with the Circus; Private Snuffy Smith; Remedy for Riches; Scarlet River; Sin of Harold Diddlebock (Mad Wednesday); Three Men on a Horse; Twentieth Century; When's Your Birthday?
Kennedy, George: Airport; Airport 1975; Airport '77; Airport '79: The Concorde; Bandolero!; Blue Knight, The; Bolero; Boston Strangler, The; Brain Dead; Brass Target; Cahill—US Marshal; Charade; Chattanooga Choo Choo; Cool Hand Luke; Counterforce; Creepshow 2; Death on the Nile; Deathship; Delta Force, The; Distant Justice; Double McGuffin, The; Driving Me Crazy; Earthquake; Eiger Sanction, The; Flight of the Phoenix, The; Gambler, Part III—The Legend Continues, The; Good Guys and the Bad Guys, The; Guns of the Magnificent Seven; Hired to Kill; Island of the Blue Dolphins; Jesse Owens Story, The; Just Before Dawn; Ministry of Vengeance; Mirage; Naked Gun, The; Naked Gun 33 1/3, The—The Final Insult; Naked Gun 2 1/2, The; Nightmare at Noon; Radioactive Dreams; Savage Dawn; Search and Destroy; Shenandoah; Sons of Katie Elder, The; Steel; Strait-Jacket; Terror Within, The; Thunderbolt and Lightfoot; Tick … Tick … Tick …; Uninvited, The; Virus; Wacko
Kennedy, Gerald: Newsfront
Kennedy, Graham: Club, The; Don's Party; Odd Angry Shot, The
Kennedy, Jamie: Bongwater; Bowfinger; Scream 2; Specials, The; Three Kings
Kennedy, Jayne: Body and Soul
Kennedy, Jo: Starstruck
Kennedy, Leon Isaac: Body and Soul; Hollywood Vice Squad; Knights of the City; Penitentiary; Penitentiary II; Penitentiary III
Kennedy, Maria Doyle: General, The; Miss Julie
Kennedy, Marklen: Witchcraft V: Dance with the Devil
Kennedy, Merle: Nemesis
Kennedy, Merna: Circus, The/A Day's Pleasure
Kennedy, Patricia: Country Life; Getting of Wisdom, The
Kennedy, Sarah: Jack Be Nimble
Kenner, Eliot: Running Wild
Kenney, James: Battle Hell
Kenney, June: Attack of the Puppet People; Earth vs. the Spider; Sorority Girl
Kenney, Sean: Corpse Grinders, The
Kensit, Patsy: Absolute Beginners; Angels and Insects; Bitter Harvest; Blame It on the Bellboy; Blue Tornado; Chicago Joe and the Showgirl; Does This Mean We're Married?; Dream Man; Fall from Grace; Full Eclipse; Grace of My Heart; Kill Cruise; Kleptomania; Lethal Weapon 2; Silas Marner; Time Bomb; Tunnel Vision (1994); Turn of the Screw (1992); Twenty-One
Kent, April: Incredible Shrinking Man, The
Kent, Arnold: Hula
Kent, Barbara: Oliver Twist; Vanity Fair
Kent, Chantellese: Home for Christmas; To Catch a Yeti
Kent, Elizabeth: Mindwarp
Kent, Gary: Satan's Sadists
Kent, Jean: Browning Version, The; Magic Bow, The; Woman in Question
Kent, Marjorie: Blondie Hits the Jackpot; Blondie Knows Best
Kent, Robert: Mr. Moto Takes a Chance
Kente, Dambisa: Friends
Kenyon, Gwen: Charlie Chan in the Secret Service
Kenyon, Sandy: Loch Ness Horror, The
Keogh, Alexia: Angel at My Table, An
Keogh, Danny: Shark Attack 2
Kepler, Shell: Homework
Keraga, Kelvin: Deadmate
Kercheval, Ken: Beretta's Island; Calamity Jane; Corporate Affairs; Devil Dog: The Hound of Hell
Kérien, Jean-Pierre: Muriel
Kerin, Jackie: Muriel
Kerman, Robert: Cannibal Holocaust; Emerald Jungle
Kerns, Joanna: American Summer, An; Bunny's Tale, A; Cross My Heart; Great Los Angeles Earthquake, The; Mistress; Nightman, The; No Dessert Dad Until You Mow the Lawn; Preppie Murder, The; Street Justice
Kerouac, Jack: Kerouac
Kerr, Bill: Coca Cola Kid, The; Dusty; Lighthorsemen, The; Miracle Down Under; Pirate Movie, The; Sweet Talker; Vigil; Year of Living Dangerously, The
Kerr, Bruce: Man from Snowy River, The
Kerr, Deborah: Affair to Remember, An; Arrangement, The; Black Narcissus; Bonjour Tristesse; Casino Royale; Chalk Garden, The; Courageous Mr. Penn; From Here to Eternity; Grass Is Greener, The; Hold the Dream; Hucksters, The; I See a Dark Stranger; Innocents, The (1961); Julius Caesar; King and I, The;

King Solomon's Mines; Life and Death of Colonel Blimp, The; Love on the Dole; Major Barbara; Naked Edge, The; Night of the Iguana, The; Prisoner of Zenda, The; Quo Vadis (1951); Sundowners, The; Tea and Sympathy; Witness for the Prosecution; Woman of Substance, A; Young Bess
Kerr, E. Katherine: Reuben, Reuben
Kerr, Edward: Above Suspicion; Legalese
Kerr, Elizabeth: Mork & Mindy (TV Series)
Kerr, John: Pit and the Pendulum, The; South Pacific; Tea and Sympathy
Kerr, Larry: Lost Missile, The
Kerr, Michael: Living the Blues
Kerr Jr., J. Herbert: Place Called Today, A
Kerr-Bell, Mamaengaroa: Once Were Warriors
Kerridge, Linda: Alien from L.A.; Down Twisted; Fade to Black; Mixed Blood; Surf 2
Kerrigan, J. M.: Black Beauty; Fastest Gun Alive, The; Lost Patrol, The
Kerrigan, J. Warren: Covered Wagon, The
Kerry, Norman: Bachelor Apartment; Merry-Go-Round, The; Phantom of the Opera; Unknown, The
Kersey, Paul: Missing Pieces
Kershaw, Doug: Zachariah
Kerwin, Brian: Antony and Cleopatra; Chisholms, The; Code Name: Chaos; Critical Choices; Flash (1998); Getting Away with Murder; Gold Diggers: The Secret of Bear Mountain; Hard Promises; Jack; King Kong Lives; Love Field; Murphy's Romance; Myth of Fingerprints, The; Power, Passion, and Murder; Real American Hero, The; Switched at Birth; Torch Song Trilogy; Unlikely Angel; Volcano: Fire on the Mountain; Wet Gold
Kerwin, Lance: Enemy Mine; Fourth Wise Man, The; Mysterious Stranger, The; Salem's Lot; Side Show; Snow Queen
Kerwin, William: Living Venus
Kessel, Sam: Together
Kessir, John: Cyber Tracker 2
Kesslar, Matt: Deli, The; Run of the Country, The
Kessler, Quin: She
Kessler, Robert: Lonely in America
Kessler, Wulf: White Rose, The
Kester, Ernest: Howling, The: New Moon Rising
Kestleman, Sara: Lady Jane; Lisztomania
Kestner, Boyd: Lethal Lolita—Amy Fisher: My Story
Kestner, Bryan: In Dark Places
Ketchum, Orville: Hard to Die
Kettle, Ross: Lethal Ninja
Key, Elizabeth: Blondes Have More Guns
Keyes, Evelyn: Before I Hang; Enchantment; Face Behind the Mask, The; Here Comes Mr. Jordan; Jolson Story, The; Lady in Question; Return to Salem's Lot, A; Slightly Honorable
Keyes, Irwin: Asylum; Godson, The
Keyloun, Mark: Mike's Murder; Separate Vacations
Keys-Hall, Michael: Blackout
Keystone Kops, The: Days of Thrills and Laughter; Dough and Dynamite/Knockout, The; Hollywood Cavalcade
Khajuria, Sarita: Bhaji on the Beach
Khamatova, Chulpan: Advertising Rules
Khambatta, Persis: Megaforce; Phoenix the Warrior; Warrior of the Lost World
Khan, Aamir: Earth
Khan, Cynthia: Fist of Steel
Khan, Michelle: Supercop; Wing Chun
Khan, Shaheen: Bhaji on the Beach
Khanh, Le: Vertical Ray of the Sun, The
Khanjian, Arsinée: Adjuster, The; Exotica; Fat Girl; Felicia's Journey; Speaking Parts
Khanna, Rahul: Earth
Kheradmad, Farhad: Life and Nothing More . . .
Khokhlova, Alexandra: By the Law
Khouadra, Nozha: Bye-Bye
Khouth, Gabe: Just One of the Girls
Khumalo, Leleti: Sarafina!
Kibbee, Guy: Babes in Arms; Blonde Crazy; Captain Blood; Captain January; Dames; Dixie Jamboree; Earthworm Tractors; Footlight Parade; Girl Crazy; Hold Your Man; Horn Blows at Midnight, The; It Started with Eve; Lady for a Day; Laughing Sinners; Let Freedom Ring; Little Lord Fauntleroy; Miss Annie Rooney; Of Human Hearts; Rain; Riding on Air; Strange Love of Molly Louvain, The; Three Comrades; Three Men on a Horse; Whistling in Dixie; Wonder Bar
Kiberlain, Sandrine: Beaumarchais the Scoundrel
Kid Rock: Joe Dirt
Kidd, Chris: Cry from the Mountain; Regenerated Man, The
Kidd, Delena: Victoria and Albert
Kidd, Michael: It's Always Fair Weather; Smile
Kidder, Margot: Amityville Horror, The; Beanstalk; Black Christmas; Bloodknot; Bounty Man, The; Clown at Midnight, The; Common Ground; Glitter Dome, The; Heartaches; Hi-line, The; Hitchhiker, The (Series); Junior's Groove; Keeping Track; Little Treasure; Louisiana; Maverick; Miss Right; Mob Story; 92 in the Shade; Quackser Fortune Has a Cousin in the Bronx; Quiet Day in Belfast, A; Reincarnation of Peter Proud, The; Sisters (1973); Some Kind of Hero; Superman; Superman II; Superman IV: The Quest for Peace; To Catch a Killer; Trenchcoat; Tribulation; Vanishing Act; Willie and Phil; Windrunner
Kidman, Nicole: Batman Forever; Billy Bathgate; Birthday Girl; BMX Bandits; Days of Thunder; Dead Calm; Eyes Wide Shut; Far and Away; Flirting; Malice; Moulin Rouge; Moulin Rouge (2001); My Life; Others, The; Peacemaker, The (1997); Portrait of a Lady, The; Practical Magic; To Die For; Wacky World of Wills and Burke, The
Kid'n'Play: House Party
Kieffer, Ray: Dance or Die
Kiel, Richard: Eegah!; Force Ten from Navarone; Human Duplicators, The; Hysterical; Las Vegas Hillbillys; Nasty Rabbit; Pale Rider; Silver Streak; So Fine; Spy Who Loved Me, The; They Went That-A-Way and That-A-Way; Think Big
Kiel, Sue: Red Heat; Survivor
Kier, Udo: Adventures of Pinocchio, The; Andy Warhol's Dracula; Andy Warhol's Frankenstein; Blade; Breaking the Waves; Dancer in the Dark; End of Days; Even Cowgirls Get the Blues; For Love or Money; Kingdom, The; Mark of the Devil; Salzburg Connection, The; Shadow of the Vampire; Spy Games; Story of O, The; Suspiria; Zentropa
Kiger, Susan: H.O.T.S.
Kihlstedt, Rya: Arctic Blue; Buccaneers, The; Home Alone 3
Kiil, Jorgen: Webmaster
Kikumai, Aya: Sonatine
Kilbride, Percy: Adventures of Mark Twain, The; Egg and I, The; George Washington Slept Here; Keeper of the Flame; Knickerbocker Holiday; Ma and Pa Kettle at Home; Ma and Pa Kettle (The Further Adventures of Ma and Pa Kettle); Ma and Pa Kettle at the Fair; Ma and Pa Kettle at Waikiki; Ma and Pa Kettle Back on the Farm; Ma and Pa Kettle Go to Town; Ma and Pa Kettle on Vacation; Riding High; RiffRaff; State Fair; Sun Comes Up, The; Welcome, Stranger
Kilburn, Terry: Black Beauty; Christmas Carol, A; Fiend without a Face
Kiley, Richard: Angel on My Shoulder; Final Days, The; George Washington; Little Prince, The; Looking for Mr. Goodbar; Night Gallery; Pendulum; Pray TV; Separate But Equal; Thornbirds, The
Kilian, Victor: Dangerous Passage; Dr. Cyclops; Mary Hartman, Mary Hartman (TV Series); Unknown World
Killion, Cynthia: Killing Game, The
Kilmer, Val: At First Sight; Batman Forever; Doors, The; Ghost and the Darkness, The; Gore Vidal's Billy the Kid; Heat; Island of Dr. Moreau, The; Kill Me Again; Man Who Broke 1000 Chains, The; Real Genius; Real McCoy, The; Red Planet; Saint, The (1997); Thunderheart; Tombstone; Top Gun; Top Secret; True Romance; Willow
Kilner, Kevin: Home Alone 3
Kilpatrick, Joy: Safe House
Kilpatrick, Lincoln: Hollywood Cop; Prison
Kilpatrick, Patrick: Cellar, The; Free Willy 3: The Rescue; Last Stand at Saber River; Scanners 4: The Showdown; Substitute, The: Failure Is Not an Option
Kim, Chu-Ryun: 301/302
Kim, Daniel Dae: American Shaolin: King of the Kickboxers II

Kim, Eva: Magic Stone, The
Kim, Evan: Dead Pool, The; Kentucky Fried Movie
Kim, Hang Yip: Undefeatable
Kim, Jacqueline: Brokedown Palace; Operator, The; Volcano
Kim, Miki: Primary Target
Kim, Sung-nyu: Chunhyang
Kimball, Anne: Monster from the Ocean Floor, The
Kimball, Bruce: Pink Angels
Kimberley, Maggie: Mummy's Shroud, The
Kimberly, Marla: Traffic
Kimbrough, Charles: Seduction of Joe Tynan, The; Sunday in the Park with George
Kimmel, Bruce: First Nudie Musical, The; Spaceship (Naked Space)
Kimmel, Dana: Friday the 13th, Part III
Kimura, Kazuya: Gonin
Kinchev, Konstantin: Burglar (Russian)
Kind, David: Quest of the Delta Knights
Kind, Richard: All-American Murder
Kindlon, Kevin: Heartstopper; Majorettes, The
Kinebrew, Carolyn: Messenger, The; Small Time
King, Adrienne: Friday the 13th; Friday the 13th, Part II
King, Alan: Author! Author!; Cat's Eye; Enemies—A Love Story; I, the Jury; Infiltrator, The; Just Tell Me What You Want; Memories of Me; Night and the City; Rush Hour 2
King, Andrea: Beast with Five Fingers, The; Lemon Drop Kid, The; Man I Love, The; Red Planet Mars
King, Atlas: Incredibly Strange Creatures Who Stopped Living and Became Mixed-Up Zombies, The; Thrill Killers, The
King, B. B.: Amazon Women on the Moon
King, Bernard: Fast Break
King, Billy: Hopalong Rides Again
King, Brad: Outlaws of the Desert; Riders of the Timberline; Secrets of the Wasteland; Stick to Your Guns; Twilight on the Trail
King, Brenda: Outlaws of the Desert; Riders of the Timberline; Secrets of the Wasteland; Stick to Your Guns; Twilight on the Trail
King, Caroline Junko: Three Ninjas Kick Back
King, Charles: Arizona Stagecoach; Below the Border; Broadway Melody, The; Caravan Trail; Desert Phantom; Enemy of the Law; Forbidden Trails; Ghost Town Law; His Brother's Ghost; In Early Arizona; Kid Ranger; Lawless Nineties, The; Lightnin' Crandall; Mystery of the Hooded Horsemen; Riders of the Rio Grande; Riders of the Rockies; Sing, Cowboy, Sing; Superman—The Serial; Unnamable, The; Where Trails End; Zorro's Fighting Legion
King, Claude: Behind the Mask; Three on the Trail
King, Dennis: Devil's Brother, The; Miracle, The
King, Dexter: Our Friend, Martin
King, Erik: Desperate Measures; Joey Breaker
King, James: Pearl Harbor; Slackers (2002)
King, John: Ace Drummond; Arizona Stagecoach; Boothill Bandits; Fugitive Valley; Renegade Girl; Saddle Mountain Roundup; Trail of the Silver Spurs
King, Lawrence: Abducted II
King, Loretta: Bride of the Monster
King, Mabel: Dead Men Don't Die; Wiz, The
King, Meegan: Sweater Girls
King, Perry: Andy Warhol's Bad; Choirboys, The; City in Fear; Class of 1984; Cracker Factory; Cry in the Night, A; Danielle Steel's Kaleidoscope; Different Story, A; Disaster at Silo 7; Hasty Heart; Jericho Fever; Killing Hour, The; Lipstick; Lords of Flatbush, The; Love's Savage Fury; Mandingo; Prize Pulitzer, The: The Roxanne Pulitzer Story; Search and Destroy; Switch; Wild Party, The
King, Regina: Down to Earth; Enemy of the State; Friday; How Stella Got Her Groove Back; Poetic Justice; Thin Line Between Love and Hate, A
King, Scott: Double Exposure
King, Stephen: Creepshow
King, Tony: Bucktown; Gordon's War; Report to the Commissioner
King, Walter Woolf: Go West; Swiss Miss
King, Wright: Wanted: Dead or Alive (TV Series)
King, Yolanda: Death of a Prophet; Our Friend, Martin; Selma Lord Selma
King, Zalman: Blue Sunshine; Smile, Jenny, You're Dead; Some Call It Loving; Tell Me a Riddle
King Sisters, The: Second Fiddle
Kingsford, Walter: Fingers at the Window
Kingsley, Ben: Alice in Wonderland; Assignment, The; Betrayal; Bugsy; Confession, The; Crime and Punishment; Dave; Death and the Maiden; Fifth Monkey, The; Gandhi; Harem; Joseph; Moses; Murderers Among Us: The Simon Wiesenthal Story; Pascali's Island; Photographing Fairies; Rules of Engagement; Schindler's List; Searching for Bobby Fischer; Sexy Beast; Silas Marner; Slipstream; Sneakers; Species; Survivors of the Holocaust; Turtle Diary; Twelfth Night; Weapons of Mass Distraction; What Planet Are You From?; Without a Clue
Kingsley, Danitza: Amazons
Kingsley, Susan: Dollmaker, The
Kingston, Alex: Croupier; Essex Boys; Moll Flanders
Kingston, Mark: Intimate Contact
Kingston, Natalie: His Private Secretary; Tarzan the Mighty; Tarzan the Tiger
Kinkade, Amelia: Night of the Demons 3; Night of the Demons 2
Kinmont, Kathleen: Art of Dying, The; CIA Codename Alexa; CIA II: Target: Alexa; Corporate Ladder; Final Impact; Final Round; Night of the Warrior; Renegade; Stranger in the House; Sweet Justice; Texas Payback
Kinnaman, Melanie: Friday the 13th, Part V—A New Beginning
Kinnear, Greg: As Good as It Gets; Dear God; Dinner with Friends; Gift, The; Loser; Mystery Men; Nurse Betty; Sabrina; Smile Like Yours, A; Someone Like You; We Were Soldiers; What Planet Are You From?; You've Got Mail
Kinnear, Roy: Diamond's Edge; Herbie Goes to Monte Carlo; Hound of the Baskervilles, The; Juggernaut; Madame Sin; Melody; Pirates; Return of the Musketeers; Taste the Blood of Dracula; Willy Wonka and the Chocolate Factory
Kinney, Kathy: Parting Glances
Kinney, Terry: Body Snatchers, The (1993); Devil in a Blue Dress; Fly Away Home; George Wallace; Good Old Boys, The; House of Mirth, The; JFK: Reckless Youth; No Mercy; Oxygen; Save the Last Dance; Talent for the Game; That Championship Season
Kinosita, Keisuke: Twenty-four Eyes
Kinsella, Neil: Octavia
Kinsey, Lance: Club Fed
Kinskey, Leonid: Can't Help Singing; Everything Happens at Night; Weekend in Havana
Kinski, Klaus: Aguirre: Wrath of God; Android; Buddy, Buddy; Bullet for the General, A; Burden of Dreams; Circus of Fear; Code Name: Wild Geese; Count Dracula; Counterfeit Traitor, The; Crawlspace; Dead Eyes of London; Deadly Sanctuary; Fitzcarraldo; For a Few Dollars More; French Woman, The; His Name Was King; Jack the Ripper; Little Drummer Girl, The; Operation Thunderbolt; Rough Justice; Ruthless Four, The; Schizoid; Secret Diary of Sigmund Freud, The; Shanghai Joe; Soldier, The; Star Knight; Time Stalkers; Time to Love and a Time to Die, A; Twice a Judas; Venom; Venus in Furs; Woyzeck
Kinski, Nastassja: American Rhapsody, An; Bella Mafia; Boarding School; Cat People; Claim, The; Crackerjack; Dying to Get Rich; Exposed; Faraway, So Close; Father's Day; For Your Love Only; Harem; Hotel New Hampshire, The; Magdalene; Maria's Lovers; Moon in the Gutter, The; One from the Heart; One Night Stand; Paris, Texas; Red Letters; Revolution; Savior; Somebody Is Waiting; Spring Symphony; Stay as You Are; Terminal Velocity; Tess; To the Devil, a Daughter; Torrents of Spring; Town & Country; Unfaithfully Yours; Wrong Move, The; Your Friends & Neighbors
Kirby, Bruce: Blood Money (1999); Mr. Wonderful
Kirby, Bruno: Basketball Diaries, The; Between the Lines; Birdy; Borderline; City Slickers; Donnie Brasco; Fallen Angels; Freshman, The; Golden Gate; Good Morning, Vietnam; Harrad Experiment, The; Modern Romance; Nitti: The Enforcer; Spy

Games; We're No Angels; When Harry Met Sally; Where the Buffalo Roam
Kirby, Jay: Sheriff of Las Vegas; Sundown Riders
Kirby, Leonard: Return of the Sand Fairy, The
Kirby, Michael: Swoon
Kirk, Jack: Pals of the Saddle
Kirk, James: National Lampoon's Golf Punks
Kirk, Justin: Love! Valour! Compassion!
Kirk, Laura: Lisa Picard is Famous
Kirk, Phyllis: Back from Eternity; House of Wax; Life of Her Own, A; Sad Sack, The
Kirk, Tommy: Absent-Minded Professor, The; Babes in Toyland; Bon Voyage!; Escapade in Florence; Horsemasters; Mars Needs Women; Misadventures of Merlin Jones, The; Monkey's Uncle, The; Old Yeller; Savage Sam; Shaggy Dog, The; Son of Flubber; Swiss Family Robinson, The; Unkissed Bride; Village of the Giants
Kirkham, Kathleen: Sky Pilot, The
Kirkland, Sally: Amnesia; Anna; Best of the Best; Blue; Bullseye; Cheatin' Hearts; Cold Feet; Double Jeopardy; Double Threat; EDtv; Fatal Games; Forever; Futz; Gunmen; High Stakes; Hit the Dutchman; In the Heat of Passion; JFK; Little Ghost; Paint It Black; Paranoia; Picture Windows; Primary Motive; Prime Time Murder; Revenge (1990); Talking Walls; Westing Game, The; Young Nurses, The
Kirkwood, Bryan: Devil's Prey
Kirkwood, Craig: Remember the Titans
Kirkwood, Gene: Night and the City
Kirov Ballet: Don Quixote
Kirsch, Stan: Highlander: The Gathering
Kirshner, Mia: Crow: City of Angels, The; Exotica; Johnny's Girl; Leo Tolstoy's Anna Karenina (1997); Love and Human Remains; Mad City; Not Another Teen Movie; Out of the Cold
Kirsten, Dorothy: Great Caruso, The
Kirtadze, Nino: Chef in Love, A
Kiser, Terry: Forest Warrior; Friday the 13th, Part VII: The New Blood; Hourglass; Into the Sun; Mannequin Two: On the Move; Offspring, The; Pet Shop; Rich Kids; Starflight One; Steel; Tammy & the T-Rex; Weekend at Bernie's; Weekend at Bernie's II
Kishi, Keiko: Kwaidan
Kishimoto, Kayoko: Fireworks; Kikujiro
Kissai, Csonger: Divided We Fall
Kissinger, Charles: Asylum of Satan
Kissner, Jeremy James: Dog of Flanders, A
Kistler, Darci: George Balanchine's The Nutcracker
Kitaen, Tawny: Bachelor Party; Dead Tides; Glory Years; Happy Hour; Hercules and the Circle of Fire; Hercules in the Underworld; Instant Justice; Playback; White Hot; Witchboard
Kitano, Takeshi: Boiling Point; Fireworks; Gonin; Johnny Mnemonic; Kikujiro; Sonatine; Violent Cop
Kitaoji, Kinya: Himatsuri
Kitchen, Michael: Doomsday Gun; Enchanted April; Fatherland; Fools of Fortune; Mrs. Dalloway; Out of Africa; Russia House, The
Kitt, Eartha: Boomerang; Erik the Viking; Ernest Scared Stupid; Fatal Instinct; Friday Foster; Harriet the Spy; Mark of the Hawk, The; New Faces; Unzipped
Kittles, Tory: Invincible
Kitzmiller, John: Cave of the Living Dead
Kizzier, Heath: Sons of Trinity, The
Klar, Norman: Hitchhikers
Klarwein, Eleonore: Peppermint Soda
Klausmeyer, Charles: Can It Be Love
Klein, Chris: American Pie; American Pie 2; Election; Here on Earth; Rollerball (2002); Say It Isn't So; We Were Soldiers
Klein, Gerald: Undefeatable
Klein, Larry: Sugar Town
Klein, Nic: Wheels: An Inline Story
Klein, Nita: Muriel
Klein, Robert: Bell Jar, The; Dangerous Curves; Labor Pains; Mixed Nuts; Next Stop Wonderland; Nobody's Perfekt; Owl and the Pussycat, The; Poison Ivy; Pursuit of Happiness, The
Kleiner, Towje: Train Killer, The
Klein-Rogge, Rudolf: Destiny; Dr. Mabuse, the Gambler (Parts I and II); Kriemhilde's Revenge; Spies; Testament of Dr. Mabuse
Klemp, Anna: Blue Sky
Klemperer, Werner: Hogan's Heroes (TV Series); Istanbul
Klenck, Margaret: Hard Choices
Kline, Kevin: Anniversary Party, The; Big Chill, The; Chaplin; Consenting Adults; Cry Freedom; Dave; Fierce Creatures; Fish Called Wanda, A; French Kiss; Grand Canyon; I Love You to Death; Ice Storm, The; In & Out; January Man, The; Life as a House; Pirates of Penzance, The; Princess Caraboo; Silverado; Soapdish; Sophie's Choice; Violets Are Blue; Wild Wild West (1999); William Shakespeare's A Midsummer Night's Dream
Kline, Val: Beach Girls, The
Kling, Heidi: D3: The Mighty Ducks; Mighty Ducks, The; Out on a Limb
Klintoe, Hanne: Loss of Sexual Innocence, The
Klisser, Evan J.: Hellgate
Klopfer, Eugen: Street, The
Klos, Elmar: Shop on Main Street, The
Kluga, Henlyk: Two Men and a Wardrobe
Klugman, Jack: Days of Wine and Roses (1962); Detective, The; Goodbye Columbus; I Could Go On Singing; Parallel Lives; 12 Angry Men; Twilight Zone, The (TV Series); Two-Minute Warning
Klusak, Jan: Report on the Party and the Guests, A
Knapp, Evalyn: His Private Secretary; In Old Santa Fe; Perils of Pauline, The; Rawhide
Knaup, Herbert: Run Lola Run
Knell, David: Life on the Mississippi
Knepper, Rob: Kidnapped in Paradise; Wild Thing; Zelda
Knievel, Evel: Viva Knievel
Knight, Christopher: Studs Lonigan
Knight, David: Demons 2; Nightmare; Who Shot Pat?
Knight, Esmond: Element of Crime, The; Waltzes from Vienna
Knight, Fuzzy: Adventures of Gallant Bess; Egg and I, The; Horror Island; Lone Star Trail; Operator 13; Rimfire; Trail of the Lonesome Pine, The
Knight, Gladys: Pipe Dreams
Knight, Jack: Class of 1999 II: The Substitute
Knight, Lily: Amati Girls, The
Knight, Michael E.: Date with an Angel; Hexed
Knight, Nic: Prince Brat and the Whipping Boy
Knight, Sandra: Frankenstein's Daughter; Terror, The
Knight, Shirley: Angel Eyes; As Good as It Gets; Endless Love; Group, The; If These Walls Could Talk; Indictment: The McMartin Trial; Juggernaut; Outer Limits, The (TV Series); Petulia; Playing for Time; Rain People, The; Secrets; Sender, The; Somebody Is Waiting; Stuart Saves His Family; Sweet Bird of Youth; Yarn Princess, The
Knight, Ted: Caddyshack
Knight, Trent: Charlie's Ghost; Forest Warrior; Invisible Mom; Skateboard Kid 2, The; Tin Soldier, The
Knight, Wayne: Chameleon; For Richer or Poorer; Jurassic Park; Rat Race; Space Jam
Knight, Wyatt: Porky's; Porky's II: The Next Day; Porky's Revenge
Knipper, Robert: Getting Out
Knittle, Kristen: Body Strokes (Siren's Call)
Knopf, Sascha: Black Male
Knott, Andrew: Black Beauty; Secret Garden, The
Knotts, Don: Andy Griffith Show, The (TV Series); Apple Dumpling Gang, The; Apple Dumpling Gang Rides Again, The; Big Bully; Ghost and Mr. Chicken, The; Gus; Herbie Goes to Monte Carlo; Hot Lead and Cold Feet; How to Frame a Figg; Incredible Mr. Limpet, The; Love God?, The; No Deposit, No Return; No Time for Sergeants; Private Eyes, The; Prizefighter, The; Reluctant Astronaut, The; Return to Mayberry; Shakiest Gun in the West, The
Knowles, Patric: Beauty for the Asking; Big Steal, The; Charge of the Light Brigade, The; Chisum; Elfego Baca: Six Gun Law; Five Came Back; Frankenstein Meets the Wolf Man; Hit the Ice; Monsieur Beaucaire; Strange Case of Dr. Rx, The; Terror in the Wax Museum; Three Came Home; Who Done It?; Wolf Man, The

Knox, Alexander: Commandos Strike at Dawn; Cry of the Innocent; Gorky Park; Judge Steps Out, The; Khartoum; Man in the Saddle; Operation Amsterdam; Puppet on a Chain; Sea Wolf, The; Sister Kenny; Sleeping Tiger, The; Tokyo Joe; Two of a Kind; Villa Rides; Wilson; Wreck of the Mary Deare, The
Knox, Elyse: Hit the Ice; Mummy's Tomb, The
Knox, Jacqueline: Little Patriot, The
Knox, Mickey: Dellamorte, Dellamore
Knox, Teddy: Frozen Limits, The
Knox, Terence: Children of the Corn II: The Final Sacrifice; Distortions; Humanoid Defender; Lies; Murder So Sweet; Rebel Love; Snow Kill; Spy Within, The; St. Elsewhere (TV Series); Tour of Duty; Tripwire
Knoxville, Johnny: Big Trouble (2002); Life Without Dick
Knudsen, Peggy: Copper Canyon; Istanbul; Never Say Goodbye
Knyphausen, Felix: Garden of Redemption, The
Knyvette, Sally: Blake's 7 (TV Series)
Ko, Su-Myong: Why Has Bhodi Dharma Left for the East?
Ko, U Aung: Beyond Rangoon
Kobayashi, Keiji: Godzilla 1985
Kobayashi, Megumi: Re-birth of Mothra II
Kobayashi, Tsuruko: Varan, the Unbelievable
Kober, Jeff: Automatic; Big Fall, The; First Power, The; Gold Coast; Hit List, The (1992); Keep the Change; Lone Justice; Lucky Stiff; One Man's Justice; Out of Bounds; Tank Girl; Viper
Koch, Sabrina: Alley Cats, The
Kodar, Oja: F for Fake
Kodetova, Barbora: Dune
Koenig, Tommy: National Lampoon's Class of '86
Koenig, Walter: Antony and Cleopatra; Moon Trap; Star Trek II: The Wrath of Khan; Star Trek III: The Search for Spock; Star Trek IV: The Voyage Home; Star Trek—The Motion Picture; Star Trek (TV Series); Star Trek V: The Final Frontier; Star Trek VI: The Undiscovered Country; Star Trek: Generations
Kogure, Gohei: Silk Road, The
Kogure, Michiyo: Geisha, A
Kohl, Lacey: Dead Simple
Kohler, Juliane: Aimee & Jaguar
Kohler Jr., Fred: Lawless Valley
Kohler Sr., Fred: Billy the Kid Returns; Deluge (1993); Fiddlin' Buckaroo; Lawless Valley; Old Ironsides; Texas Rangers (1936); Vigilantes Are Coming!
Kohner, Susan: By Love Possessed; Dino; Gene Krupa Story, The; Imitation of Life; To Hell and Back
Kohnert, Mary: Beyond the Door 3
Kohoutova, Kristyna: Alice
Koizumi, Hiroshi: Ghidrah, the Three-Headed Monster; Godzilla vs. Mothra; Mothra
Kolb, Clarence: Beware of Spooks; Honolulu; Sky's the Limit, The; Toast of New York, The
Kolker, Henry: Ghost Walks, The
Kollek, Amos: Double Edge; Goodbye New York; Whore 2
Koman, Jacek: Paperback Romance
Komarov, Sergei: By the Law
Komorowska, Liliana: Scanners 3: The Takeover
Komorowska, Maja: Contract; Year of the Quiet Sun
Kondazian, Karen: Mortal Sins (1992)
Konstam, Phyllis: Skin Game, The (1931)
Koo, Josephine: Police Story III—Super Cop
Koock, Guich: American Ninja; Square Dance
Kopecky, Milos: Baron Munchausen (1961)
Kopell, Bernie: When Things Were Rotten (TV Series)
Kopelow, Michael: Stoned Age, The
Kopins, Karen: Jake Speed; Once Bitten; Tracker, The
Korf, Mia: Blood Brothers; Silent Witness: What a Child Saw
Korikova, Yelena: Friend of the Deceased, A
Korjus, Miliza: Great Waltz, The
Korkes, Jon: Between the Lines
Korman, Harvey: Alice Through the Looking Glass; Americathon; Based on an Untrue Story; Betrayal of the Dove; Blazing Saddles; Bud and Lou; Curse of the Pink Panther, The; Dracula: Dead and Loving It; First Family; Gone Are the Days; Herbie Goes Bananas; High Anxiety; History of the World, Part One, The; Huckleberry Finn; Living Venus; Longshot, The (1985); Lord Love a Duck; Munchies
Kornbluth, Josh: Haiku Tunnel
Koromzay, Alix: Children of the Corn 666: Isaac's Return; Mimic 2
Korsmo, Charlie: Can't Hardly Wait; Doctor, The; Hook; What About Bob?
Kortman, Bob: Ivory-Handled Gun, The; Lonely Trail, The; Phantom Thunderbolt; Trail Drive; Vigilantes Are Coming!; Warning Shadows; Zorro Rides Again
Kortner, Fritz: Hands of Orlac; Pandora's Box; Warning Shadows
Korvin, Charles: Berlin Express; Ship of Fools
Korzun, Dina: Last Resort
Koscina, Sylva: Deadly Sanctuary; Hercules; Hercules Unchained; Hornet's Nest; Juliet of the Spirits; Manhunt (1973) (The Italian Connection); Secret War of Harry Frigg, The
Kosinski, Jerzy: Reds
Kosleck, Martin: All Through the Night; Flesh Eaters, The; Frozen Ghost, The; House of Horrors; Mummy's Curse, The; Nurse Edith Cavell; Pursuit to Algiers
Koslo, Paul: Conagher; Downdraft; Drive Like Lightning; Loose Cannons; Mr. Majestyk; Ransom; Robot Jox; Tomorrow Never Comes; Xtro II
Kossoff, David: Kid for Two Farthings, A; Unicorn, The
Kosti, Maria: Night of the Death Cult
Kosugi, Kane: Pray for Death
Kosugi, Sho: Black Eagle; Enter the Ninja; Journey of Honor; Pray for Death; Revenge of the Ninja
Kosyshin, Constantin: Friend of the Deceased, A
Koteas, Elias: Adjuster, The; Almost an Angel; Backstreet Dreams; Camilla (1994); Chain of Desire; Collateral Damage; Crash (1996); Cyborg 2; Desperate Hours (1990); Exotica; Fallen; Harrison's Flowers; Living Out Loud; Look Who's Talking Too; Lost Souls; Malarek; Novocaine; Power of Attorney; Prophecy, The (1995); Shot in the Heart; Sugartime; Teenage Mutant Ninja Turtles; Teenage Mutant Ninja Turtles III
Kotero, Apollonia: Back to Back; Ministry of Vengeance; Purple Rain
Kotto, Maka: Lumumba
Kotto, Yaphet: Across 110th Street; After the Shock; Alien; American Clock, The; Badge of the Assassin; Blue Collar; Brubaker; Chrome Soldiers; Dead Badge; Drum; Extreme Justice; Eye of the Tiger; Fighting Back; Five Card Stud; Freddy's Dead: The Final Nightmare; Friday Foster; Housewife; In Self Defense; Jigsaw Murders, The; Live and Let Die; Man and Boy; Midnight Run; Ministry of Vengeance; Nothing But a Man; Out of Sync; Park Is Mine, The; Pretty Kill; Puppet Masters, The; Rage; Raid on Entebbe; Report to the Commissioner; Running Man, The; Shark's Treasure; Star Chamber, The; Terminal Entry; Tripwire; Truck Turner; Two If By Sea; Warning Sign
Kotz, Adam: Shot Through the Heart
Kounde, Hubert: Café au Lait; Hate
Kovack, Nancy: Diary of a Madman; Enter Laughing; Frankie and Johnny
Kovacs, Ernie: Bell, Book and Candle; Ernie Kovacs: Television's Original Genius; Five Golden Hours; Kovacs; North to Alaska; Strangers When We Meet
Kovacs, Geza: Baby on Board
Kove, Martin: Baby Face Nelson; Final Equinox; Firehawk; Four Deuces, The; Future Shock; Grizzly Mountain; Judge and Jury; Karate Kid Part II, The; Karate Kid Part III, The; Mercenary; Nowhere Land; Outfit, The; Rambo: First Blood II; Renegade; Shootfighter; Steele Justice; White Light; Without Mercy; Wyatt Earp: Return to Tombstone
Koyama, Akiko: Violence at Noon
Kozak, Andreas: Red and the White, The
Kozak, Harley Jane: All I Want for Christmas; Amy Fisher Story, The; Android Affair, The; Arachnophobia; Dark Planet; Favor, The; Magic in the Water, The; Necessary Roughness; Taking of Beverly Hills, The
Kozelek, Mark: Almost Famous
Kozlowski, Linda: Almost an Angel; Backstreet Justice; "Crocodile" Dundee; "Crocodile" Dundee II; Crocodile Dundee in Los

Angeles; Neighbor, The; Pass the Ammo; Target: Favorite Son; Village of the Damned
Krabbé, Jeroen: Business for Pleasure; Code Name: Dancer; Crossing Delancey; Disappearance of Garcia Lorca, The; Farinelli Il Castrato; Flight of Rainbirds, A; For a Lost Soldier; Fourth Man, The; Fugitive, The; Immortal Beloved; Jumpin' Jack Flash; Kafka; King of the Hill; Living Daylights, The; No Mercy; Only Love; Prince of Tides, The; Punisher, The; Robin Hood; Secret Weapon; Soldier of Orange; Stalin; Till There Was You; Turtle Diary; World War III
Kraft, Evelyne: Mighty Peking Man
Krakowski, Jane: Dance with Me; Flintstones in Viva Rock Vegas, The; Go; Stepping Out
Kramer, Clare: Bring It On
Kramer, Eric Allen: Incredible Hulk Returns, The; Quest for the Mighty Sword
Kramer, Jeffrey: Halloween II; Hero and the Terror; Hollywood Boulevard; Jaws 2
Kramer, Joey: Flight of the Navigator
Kramer, Michael: Over the Edge
Kramer, Stepfanie: Terror at London Bridge
Kramer, Sylvia: Watch Me When I Kill
Krantz, Robert: Paradise Motel; Winners Take All
Kratka, Paul: Friday the 13th, Part III
Kratzig, Sadie: Confessions of a Sorority Girl
Kraus, Peter: Waltz King, The
Krause, Brian: December; Liars' Club, The; Naked Souls; Return to the Blue Lagoon; Stephen King's Sleepwalkers; Within the Rock
Krause, Gottfried: Deerslayer (1920)
Krause, Tina: Bloodletting
Krauss, Alison: Down from the Mountain
Krauss, Werner: Cabinet of Doctor Caligari, The; Jud Suss; Othello; Secrets of a Soul; Student of Prague; Waxworks
Kravchenko, Alexei: Come and See
Krebitz, Nicolette: Bandits
Kreischmann, Thomas: Stalingrad
Kresadlova, Vera: Larks on a String
Kresel, Lee: Mothra
Kretschmann, Thomas: Stendhal Syndrome, The
Kreuger, Kurt: Dark Corner, The; Enemy Below, The; Fear; Mademoiselle Fifi; Unfaithfully Yours
Kreuzer, Lisa: Alice in the City; American Friend, The; Birgit Haas Must Be Killed; Kings of the Road; L'Homme Blessé (The Wounded Man)
Kriegman, Michael: My Neighborhood
Kriel, Anneline: Kill and Kill Again
Kriener, Ulrike: Men ... (1985)
Krifia, Kamel: Kickboxer 4: Aggressor, The
Krige, Alice: Attila; Barfly; Calling, The; Chariots of Fire; Code Name: Chaos; Donor Unknown; Ghost Story; Habitat; Haunted Summer; Hidden in America; In the Company of Spies; Iran Days of Crisis; King David; Ladykiller; Little Vampire, The; Max and Helen; See You in the Morning; Star Trek: First Contact; Stephen King's Sleepwalkers; Tale of Two Cities, A
Krishna, Srinivas: Masala
Kristel, Sylvia: Arrogant, The; Beauty School; Casanova; Dracula's Widow; Emmanuelle; Fifth Musketeer, The; Game of Seduction; Goodbye Emmanuelle; Lady Chatterley's Lover; Mata Hari; Mysteries; Nude Bomb, The (Return of Maxwell Smart,The); Private School; Red Heat
Kristen, Ilene: Luscious (1997)
Kristen, Marta: Beach Blanket Bingo; Lost in Space (1998); Lost in Space (TV Series); Savage Sam; Terminal Island
Kristoff, Rom: Warbus
Kristofferson, Kris: Act of Passion; Alice Doesn't Live Here Anymore; Another Pair of Aces; Big Top Pee-Wee; Blade; Blade II; Blume in Love; Bring Me the Head of Alfredo Garcia; Cheatin' Hearts; Christmas in Connecticut; Cisco Pike; Convoy; Dance with Me; Fire Down Below; Flashpoint; Heaven's Gate; Knights; Last Days of Frank and Jesse James; Last Movie, The (Chinchero); Limbo; Lone Star; Millennium; Miracle in the Wilderness; Night of the Cyclone; No Place to Hide; Original Intent; Pair of Aces; Pat Garrett and Billy the Kid; Pharaoh's Army; Planet of the Apes (2001); Road Home, The (1995); Rollover; Sailor Who Fell from Grace with the Sea,The; Semi-Tough; Sodbusters; Soldier's Daughter Never Cries, A; Songwriter; Stagecoach; Star Is Born, A; Tracker, The; Trouble in Mind; Welcome Home
Krix, Cristof: Blue Hour, The
Kroeger, Gary: Man Called Sarge, A
Król, Joachim: Maybe, Maybe Not; Princess and the Warrior, The
Kroner, Josef: Shop on Main Street, The
Krook, Margaretha: Adventures of Picasso, The
Krowchuk, Chad: Heck's Way Home
Kruger, Alma: Craig's Wife
Kruger, Hardy: Barry Lyndon; Blue Fin; Flight of the Phoenix, The; Hatari!; Inside Man, The; One That Got Away, The; Paper Tiger; Red Tent, The; Sundays and Cybèle; Wild Geese, The; Wrong Is Right
Kruger, Otto: Another Thin Man; Chained; Colossus of New York, The; Corregidor; Dracula's Daughter; High Noon; Hitler's Children; I Am the Law; Jungle Captive; Magnificent Obsession; Saboteur; Young Philadelphians, The
Krull, Kendra: Unstrung Heroes
Krumholtz, David: Addams Family Values; Santa Clause, The; Sidewalks of New York (2001); Slums of Beverly Hills; 10 Things I Hate About You
Krupa, Gene: Benny Goodman Story, The; Glenn Miller Story, The
Krupa, Olek: Home Alone 3; Mac
Kruschen, Jack: Abbott and Costello Go to Mars; Angry Red Planet, The; Apartment, The; Cape Fear; Follow That Dream; Incredible Rocky Mountain Race, The; Julie; Lover Come Back; McLintock!; Satan's Cheerleaders; Unsinkable Molly Brown, The
Kruse, Line: Emma's Shadow
Krvitska, Tatiana: Friend of the Deceased, A
Kryll, Eve: Making Contact
Ksouri, Khaled: Halfmoon
Kudoh, Youki: Heaven's Burning; Picture Bride; Snow Falling on Cedars
Kudrow, Lisa: All Over the Guy; Analyze This; Clockwatchers; Hanging Up; Lucky Numbers; Opposite of Sex, The; Romy and Michele's High School Reunion
Kuhlman, Ron: Omega Syndrome; Shadow Play
Kuhn, Robert: Trespasses
Kulich, Vladmir: 13th Warrior, The
Kulky, Henry: Five Thousand Fingers of Dr. T, The; Wabash Avenue
Kulle, Jarl: Babette's Feast; Devil's Eye, The; Secrets of Women (Waiting Women); Smiles of a Summer Night
Kulp, Nancy: Beverly Hillbillies, The (TV Series); Strange Bedfellows
Kunen, James: Strawberry Statement, The
Kunsang: Little Buddha
Kunz, Simon: Parent Trap, The
Kuranda, Richard: J. Lyle
Kurata, Yasuaki: Fist of Legend
Kurnitzov, Alexander: Ice Runner
Kurosawa, Toshio: Evil of Dracula
Kurtha, Akbar: My Son the Fanatic
Kurtiz, Tuncel: Wall, The (1983) (Foreign)
Kurts, Alwyn: Earthling, The; Tim
Kurtz, Swoosie: Baja Oklahoma; Bright Lights, Big City; Bubble Boy; Citizen Ruth; Dangerous Liaisons; Image, The; Liar, Liar; Mating Season, The; My Own Country; Outside Ozona; Positively True Adventures of the Alleged Texas Cheerleader-Murdering Mom, The; Shock to the System, A; Stanley and Iris; Storybook; True Stories; Vice Versa; Wildcats; World According to Garp, The
Kurtzman, Katy: Child of Glass; Diary of a Teenage Hitchhiker
Kurz, Eva: Virus Knows No Morals, A
Kusakari, Tamiyo: Shall We Dance?
Kusatsu, Clyde: Dr. Strange; Dream Lover
Kuskabe, Yo: Madame Butterfly
Kusturica, Emir: Widow of St. Pierre, The

Lord of the Apes; Gunmen; Highlander; Highlander: Endgame; Highlander 2: The Quickening; Highlander: The Final Dimension; Highlander: The Gathering; Hunted, The (1995); Knight Moves; Love Songs (Paroles et Musique); Mean Guns; Mortal Kombat; North Star (1996); Priceless Beauty; Resurrection; Road Killers, The; Sicilian, The; Subway; To Kill a Priest; Why Me?
Lambert, Jack: Dick Tracy's Dilemma
Lambert, Martine: Love and the Frenchwoman
Lambert, Thomas: Merlin of the Crystal Cave
Lambton, Anne: Love is the Devil
Lamer, Susan: Hills Have Eyes, The
Lamont, Adele: Brain That Wouldn't Die, The
Lamont, Duncan: Evil of Frankenstein, The
Lamont, Marten: Federal Operator 99
Lamont, Molly: Awful Truth, The; Devil Bat's Daughter
Lamorisse, Pascal: Red Balloon, The; Voyage en Ballon (Stowaway to the Stars)
Lamos, Mark: Longtime Companion
LaMothe, Michelle: Strike a Pose
Lamour, Dorothy: Big Broadcast of 1938, The; Caught in the Draft; Creepshow 2; Death at Love House; Donovan's Reef; Greatest Show on Earth, The; Hurricane, The; Johnny Apollo; My Favorite Brunette; Road to Bali; Road to Hong Kong, The; Road to Morocco; Road to Rio; Road to Singapore; Road to Utopia; Road to Zanzibar; Swing High, Swing Low; They Got Me Covered
Lampe, Jutta: Marianne & Juliane
Lampert, Zohra: Alan and Naomi; Alphabet City; Connection (1973); Izzy & Moe; Lady of the House; Let's Scare Jessica to Death; Opening Night; Pay or Die
Lamprecht, Gunter: Berlin Alexanderplatz; Red Kiss (Rouge Baiser)
Lan, Wang: Wooden Man's Bride, The
Lancaster, Burt: Airport; All My Sons; Apache; Atlantic City; Barnum; Bird Man of Alcatraz; Brute Force; Buffalo Bill and the Indians; Cassandra Crossing, The; Child Is Waiting, A; Come Back, Little Sheba; Conversation Piece; Crimson Pirate, The; Criss Cross (1948); Devil's Disciple, The; Elmer Gantry; Executive Action; Field of Dreams; Flame and the Arrow, The; From Here to Eternity; Go Tell the Spartans; Gunfight at the O.K. Corral; Hallelujah Trail, The; His Majesty O'Keefe; Island of Dr. Moreau, The; Jim Thorpe—All American; Judgment at Nuremberg; Kentuckian, The; Lawman; Leopard, The; Little Treasure; Local Hero; Moses; On Wings of Eagles; 1900; Osterman Weekend, The; Professionals, The; Rainmaker, The; Rocket Gibraltar; Rose Tattoo, The; Run Silent, Run Deep; Scalphunters, The; Separate But Equal; Seven Days in May; Sorry, Wrong Number; Sweet Smell of Success; Swimmer, The; Tough Guys; Train, The; Trapeze; Twilight's Last Gleaming; Ulzana's Raid; Unforgiven, The (1960); Valdez Is Coming; Vengeance Valley; Vera Cruz; Victory at Entebbe; Voyage of Terror: The Achille Lauro Affair; Young Savages, The; Zulu Dawn
Lancaster, William: Moses
Lanchester, Elsa: Androcles and the Lion; Arnold; Beachcomber, The; Blackbeard's Ghost; Bride of Frankenstein; Easy Come, Easy Go; Forever and a Day; Glass Slipper, The; Inspector General, The; Lassie Come Home; Naughty Marietta; Northwest Outpost; Private Life of Henry the Eighth, The; Razor's Edge, The; Rembrandt; Secret Garden, The; Spiral Staircase, The; Terror in the Wax Museum; That Darn Cat; Witness for the Prosecution
Lanctot, Micheline: Apprenticeship of Duddy Kravitz, The
Land, Kena: Caged Heat 3000
Landa, Alfredo: Holy Innocents
Landau, David: Horse Feathers; Purchase Price, The; Street Scene
Landau, Juliet: Ravager; Theodore Rex
Landau, Martin: Access Code; Adventures of Pinocchio, The; Alone in the Dark; B.A.P.S; Being, The; By Dawn's Early Light; City Hall; Crimes and Misdemeanors; Cyclone; Ed Wood; EDtv; Empire State; Fall of the House of Usher, The; Gazebo, The; Hallelujah Trail, The; Intersection; Joseph; Last Word, The; Legacy of Lies; Legend of the Spirit Dog; Majestic, The; Max and Helen; Mistress; Neon Empire, The; Nevada Smith; No Place to Hide; North by Northwest; Outer Limits, The (TV Series); Paint It Black; Ready to Rumble; Return, The (1980); Rounders; Run If You Can; Sleepy Hollow; Sliver; Space 1999 (TV Series); Strange Shadows in an Empty Room; Sweet Revenge; They Call Me Mister Tibbs; Tucker: A Man and His Dream; 12:01; Without Warning; X-Files, The (1998)
Landen, Dindsdale: Morons from Outer Space
Lander, David L.: Funland; Masters of Menace; Steel and Lace; Wholly Moses!
Landers, Audrey: California Casanova; Chorus Line, A; Deadly Twins; Ghost Writer; Tennessee Stallion; Underground Aces
Landers, Judy: Club Fed; Deadly Twins; Doin' Time; Ghost Writer; Hellhole; Tennessee Stallion; Vega$
Landes, Michael: American Summer, An; Getting Personal
Landesberg, Steve: Blade; Final Notice; Leader of the Band; Little Miss Millions; Sodbusters
Landgard, Janet: Swimmer, The
Landgrebe, Gudrun: Berlin Affair, The; Woman in Flames, A
Landgren, Karl: Urban Warriors
Landham, Sonny: Fleshburn; Predator; Three Days to a Kill
Landi, Elissa: After the Thin Man; Corregidor; Count of Monte Cristo, The
Landi, Marla: Hound of the Baskervilles, The
Landi, Sal: Savage Streets; Xtro: Watch the Skies (Xtro 3)
Landis, Carole: Brass Monkey, The; Dance Hall; Four Jills in a Jeep; Having a Wonderful Crime; I Wake Up Screaming; Moon over Miami; One Million B.C.; Orchestra Wives; Out of the Blue; Three Texas Steers; Topper Returns; Wintertime
Landis, Jessie Royce: Boys' Night Out; Gidget Goes to Rome; Goodbye Again; I Married a Woman; It Happens Every Spring; My Man Godfrey; Swan, The; To Catch a Thief
Landis, John: Schlock
Landis, Nina: Komodo; Rikki and Pete
Landiss, Brent: Visitors, The
Lando, Joe: Any Place But Home; Doctor Quinn Medicine Woman
Landon, Laurene: All the Marbles; Armed Response; Yellow Hair and the Fortress of Gold
Landon, Michael: Bonanza (TV Series); Cheyenne (TV Series); I Was a Teenage Werewolf; Little House on the Prairie (TV Series)
Landon Jr., Michael: Bonanza (TV Series); Cheyenne (TV Series); I Was a Teenage Werewolf; Little House on the Prairie (TV Series)
Landry, Aude: Blood Relatives
Landry, Karen: Patti Rocks; Personals, The
Landry, Tamara: Beach Babes from Beyond
Landsberg, David: Detective School Dropouts
Lane, Abbe: Americano, The
Lane, Allan "Rocky": Bandits of Dark Canyon; Bells of Rosarita; Bronco (TV Series); Charlie Chan at the Olympics; Denver Kid; Law West of Tombstone; Maid's Night Out, The; Marshal of Cedar Rock; Marshal of Cripple Creek; Panama Lady; Santa Fe Uprising; Stagecoach to Denver; Stowaway; Tournament Tempo; Trail of Robin Hood; Vigilantes of Boomtown; Wild Frontier
Lane, Charles: But Not for Me; Dr. Jekyll and Mr. Hyde; Papa's Delicate Condition; Posse; 30-Foot Bride of Candy Rock, The; True Identity; White Sister, The
Lane, Colin: Broken Harvest
Lane, Diane: Big Town, The; Chaplin; Child Bride of Short Creek; Cotton Club, The; Descending Angel; Fallen Angels; Glass House, The (2001); Grace and Glorie; Gunshy; Hardball; Indian Summer; Jack; Judge Dredd; Knight Moves; Lady Beware; Little Romance, A; Lonesome Dove; Murder at 1600; My Dog Skip; My New Gun; Oldest Confederate Widow Tells All; Only Thrill, The; Outsiders, The; Perfect Storm, The; Priceless Beauty; Rumble Fish; Six Pack; Streetcar Named Desire, A; Streets of Fire; Touched by Love; Trigger Happy (Mad Dog Time); Unfaithful; Virginian, The; Vital Signs; Walk on the Moon, A; Westing Game, The; Wild Bill
Lane, Jocelyn: Tickle Me
Lane, Lenita: Bat, The

Lane, Lola: Buckskin Frontier; Deadline at Dawn; Four Daughters; Hollywood Hotel; Marked Woman
Lane, Michael: Gypsy Warriors, The
Lane, Mike: Curse of the Crystal Eye; Demon Keeper; Harder They Fall, The
Lane, Nathan: Addams Family Values; At First Sight; Birdcage, The; Boys Next Door, The; Frankie and Johnny; He Said, She Said; Isn't She Great; Jeffrey; Laughter on the 23rd Floor; Life with Mikey; Love's Labour's Lost; Mouse Hunt; Trixie
Lane, Priscilla: Arsenic and Old Lace; Four Daughters; Meanest Man in the World, The; Roaring Twenties, The; Saboteur; Silver Queen
Lane, Ray: Season of the Witch
Lane, Richard: Arabian Nights; Bullfighters, The; Hellzapoppin; Mr. Moto in Danger Island; Mr. Winkle Goes to War
Lane, Rosemary: Four Daughters; Hollywood Hotel; Oklahoma Kid, The; Return of Dr. X
Lane, Tim: Iron Warrior
Lane, Vicky: Jungle Captive
Lang, Charley: First Affair; Kent State
Lang, Fritz: Contempt
Lang, June (Vlasek): Bonnie Scotland
lang, k. d.: Eye of the Beholder
Lang, Katherine Kelly: Till the End of the Night
Lang, Melvin: Doomed to Die
Lang, Perry: Alligator; Body and Soul; Jennifer 8; Jocks; Little Vegas; Men of War; Mortuary Academy
Lang, Robert: Night Watch
Lang, Stephen: After the Storm; Amazing Panda Adventure, The; Another You; Band of the Hand; Death of a Salesman; Escape: Human Cargo; Fire Down Below; Gang in Blue; Gettysburg; Guilty as Sin; Hard Way, The; Last Exit to Brooklyn; Niagara Niagara; Occasional Hell, An; Project X; Shadow Conspiracy; Tall Tale: The Unbelievable Adventures of Pecos Bill; Tombstone
Langan, Glenn: Amazing Colossal Man, The; Forever Amber; Hangover Square; Mutiny in Outer Space; Snake Pit, The; Wing and a Prayer, A
Langdon, Harry: Golden Age of Comedy, The; Hallelujah, I'm A Bum; Strong Man, The; Zenobia
Langdon, Libby: Federal Hill
Langdon, Sue Ane: Cheyenne Social Club, The; Frankie and Johnny; Guide for the Married Man, A; Rounders, The; Roustabout; Without Warning
Lange, Artie: Bachelor, The; Dirty Work; Lost & Found (1999)
Lange, Claudie: Machine Gun Killers
Lange, Hope: Best of Everything, The; Beulah Land; Clear and Present Danger; Cooperstown; Death Wish; Fer-de-Lance; Ford: The Man & the Machine; I Am the Cheese; Just Cause; Nightmare on Elm Street 2, A: Freddy's Revenge; Peyton Place; Pleasure Palace; Pocketful of Miracles; Wild in the Country; Young Lions, The
Lange, Jessica: All That Jazz; Blue Sky; Cape Fear; Cat on a Hot Tin Roof; Country; Cousin Bette; Crimes of the Heart; Everybody's All-American; Far North; Frances; How to Beat the High Co$t of Living; Hush; King Kong; Losing Isaiah; Men Don't Leave; Music Box, The; Night and the City; O Pioneers!; Postman Always Rings Twice, The; Rob Roy; Streetcar Named Desire, A; Sweet Dreams; Thousand Acres, A; Titus; Tootsie
Lange, Romilly: Chamber of Horrors
Lange, Ted: Blade
Langedijk, Jack: Code Name Jaguar
Langella, Frank: And God Created Woman; Bad Company; Brainscan; Cutthroat Island; Dave; Diary of a Mad Housewife; Doomsday Gun; Dracula; Eddie; I'm Losing You; Junior; Lolita; Masters of the Universe; Men's Club, The; Moses; Ninth Gate, The; 1492: The Conquest of Paradise; Sphinx (1981); Those Lips, Those Eyes; True Identity; Twelve Chairs, The
Langenfeld, Sarah: Act, The
Langenkamp, Heather: Nightmare on Elm Street, A; Nightmare on Elm Street 3, A: The DreamWarriors; Wes Craven's New Nightmare
Langer, A. J.: John Carpenter's Escape from L.A.; Meet the Deedles
Langford, Frances: Born to Dance; Dixie Jamboree; Dreaming Out Loud; Girl Rush; Glenn Miller Story, The; Hollywood Hotel; People Are Funny; This Is the Army
Langham, Chris: Big Tease, The
Langham, Wallace: Sister Mary Explains It All
Langlet, Amanda: Pauline at the Beach
Langley, Michael: Heaven
Langlois, Lisa: Blood Relatives; Joy of Sex, The; Man Who Wasn't There, The; Mind Field; Nest, The; Transformations; Truth or Die
Langmann, Thomas: Night and Day
Langrick, Margaret: American Boyfriends; Cold Comfort; My American Cousin
Langrishe, Barry: Kiss or Kill
Langrishe, Caroline: Eagle's Wing
Langston, Murray: Night Patrol; Up Your Alley; Wishful Thinking
Langton, Brooke: Listen; Replacements, The
Langton, Jeff: Final Impact
Langton, Paul: Incredible Shrinking Man, The; Snow Creature, The
Langton-Lloyd, Robert: Mahabharata, The
Lanier, Jane: Mercy
Lanko, Vivian: Rejuvenator, The
Lannes, Georges: Circonstances Attenuantes
Lanoux, Victor: Cousin, Cousine; Dog Day; French Detective, The; Investigation; Lifeline; Louisiana; Make Room for Tomorrow; National Lampoon's European Vacation; One Wild Moment; Pardon Mon Affaire; Pardon Mon Affaire, Too!; Scene of the Crime; Shameless Old Lady, The; Woman at Her Window, A
Lansbury, Angela: All Fall Down; Amorous Adventures of Moll Flanders, The; Anastasia; Bedknobs and Broomsticks; Blue Hawaii; Breath of Scandal, A; Company of Wolves, The; Court Jester, The; Dear Heart; Death on the Nile; Gaslight; Greatest Story Ever Told, The; Harlow; Harvey Girls, The; Lady Vanishes, The; Lawless Street, A; Little Gloria, Happy at Last; Long Hot Summer, The; Manchurian Candidate, The; Mirror Crack'd, The; Mrs. Santa Claus; National Velvet; Picture of Dorian Gray, The; Pirates of Penzance, The; Private Affairs of Bel Ami, The; Reluctant Debutante, The; Samson and Delilah; Something for Everyone; State of the Union; Sweeney Todd; Three Musketeers, The; World of Henry Orient, The
Lansbury, David: Stranger in the Kingdom, A
Lansing, Joi: Atomic Submarine, The; Big Foot; Brave One, The; Hillbillys in a Haunted House; Hole in the Head, A
Lansing, Robert: Bittersweet Love; Blade Rider; Empire of the Ants; Equalizer, The: "Memories of Manon"; 4D Man; Grissom Gang, The; Island Claws; Life on the Mississippi; Namu, the Killer Whale; Nest, The; Scalpel; S.H.E.; Talion
Lantz, Walter: Bittersweet Love; Blade Rider; Empire of the Ants; Equalizer, The: "Memories of Manon"; 4D Man; Grissom Gang, The; Island Claws; Life on the Mississippi; Namu, the Killer Whale; Nest, The; Scalpel; S.H.E.; Talion
Lanvin, Gerard: Choice of Arms, A; My Man (Mon Homme); Taste of Others, The
Lanyer, Charles: Stepfather, The
Lanza, Mario: Because You're Mine; For the First Time; Great Caruso, The; Serenade; Seven Hills of Rome, The; That Midnight Kiss; Toast of New Orleans
LaPaglia, Anthony: Autumn in New York; Betsy's Wedding; Black Magic; Brilliant Lies; Bulletproof Heart; Chameleon; Client, The; Commandments; Criminal Justice; Custodian, The; Empire Records; Garden of Redemption, The; He Said, She Said; House of Mirth, The; Innocent Blood; Keeper of the City; Lansky; Lantana; Mortal Sins (1990) (Dangerous Obsession); Nitti: The Enforcer; One Good Cop; Paperback Romance; Past Tense; Phoenix; So I Married an Axe Murderer; Sweet and Lowdown; Trees Lounge; 29th Street; Whispers in the Dark
LaPaglia, Jonathan: Inferno
Lapensee, Francine: Demon Wind
LaPlante, Laura: Cat and the Canary, The; Last Warning, The
Lapotaire, Jane: Dark Angel, The; Eureka; Lady Jane; Spirit of the Dead; Surviving Picasso

Lara, Joe: American Cyborg: Steel Warrior; Final Equinox; Live Wire: Human Timebomb; Steel Frontier; Warhead
Larch, John: Miracle of the White Stallions; Play Misty for Me; Santee
Larcher, Taylor: Avenging, The
Lardnerward, Donald: My Life's in Turnaround
Largo, Diana: Battle of the Commandos
Lario, Veronica: Sotto Sotto
Larive, Leon: Children of Paradise, The
Larkin, Christopher: Flamingo Rising, The
Larkin, Mary: Psychomania
Laroque, Michele: Ma Vie En Rose
Larquey, Pierre: Le Corbeau (The Raven (1943))
Larroquette, John: Blind Date; Convicted; Defenders, The; Madhouse; Richie Rich; Second Sight; Stripes; 10th Kingdom, The; Walter and Henry
Larsen, Ham: Adventures of the Wilderness Family; Mountain Family Robinson; Wilderness Family, Part 2, The
Larsen, Keith: Flat Top; Whitewater Sam; Women of the Prehistoric Planet
Larsen, Thomas Bo: Celebration, The
Larson, Bobby: Leather Burners, The
Larson, Christine: Well, The
Larson, Darrell: City Limits; Danielle Steel's Fine Things; Mike's Murder; Miracle of the Heart; Uforia
Larson, Eric: Demon Wind; '68
Larson, Jack: TV's Best Adventures of Superman
Larson, Ryan: St. Francisville Experiment, The
Larson, Wolf: Expect No Mercy; Tracks of a Killer
Larsson, Anna-Lotta: Polar Bear King, The
Larsson, Dana: Music School, The
Larter, Ali: American Outlaws; Drive Me Crazy; Final Destination
LaRue, Jack: Christopher Strong; Dangerous Passage; Farewell to Arms, A; Gangs, Inc. (Paper Bullets); Go West, Young Man; In Old Caliente; Kennel Murder Case, The; Ride the Man Down; Road to Utopia; Santa Fe Uprising; Terror Aboard; To the Last Man
LaRue, Lash: Caravan Trail; Cheyenne Takes Over; Ghost Town Renegades; King of the Bullwhip; Stage to Mesa City; Stagecoach; Wild West
LaSalle, Martin: Pickpocket
LaSardo, Robert: Tiger Heart
Lascault, Catherine: Girl on the Bridge
Lascher, David: Call to Remember, A; White Squall
Laser, Dieter: Man Inside, The
Laskey, Kathleen: Lethal Lolita—Amy Fisher: My Story
Laskin, Michael: Personals, The
Lassander, Dagmar: Dandelions
Lasser, Louise: Bananas; Blood Rage; Crimewave; Everything You Always Wanted to Know About Sex but Were Afraid to Ask; For Ladies Only; Happiness; Mary Hartman, Mary Hartman (TV Series); Mystery Men; Night We Never Met, The; Requiem for a Dream; Rude Awakening; Sing; Slither
Lassez, Sarah: Clown at Midnight, The; Malicious; Roosters
Lassick, Sidney: Cool As Ice; Deep Cover; Further Adventures of Tennessee Buck, The; Out on Bail; Silent Madness; Sonny Boy; Unseen, The
Lassie: Magic of Lassie, The
Latell, Lyle: Dick Tracy versus Cueball; Dick Tracy's Dilemma
Latendresse, Sylvain: Stephanie, Nathalie, Caroline and Vincent
Latham, Louise: Crazy from the Heart; Love Field; Mass Appeal; Paradise; Pray TV; White Lightning
Lathan, Sanaa: Love and Basketball
Latifah, Queen: Living Out Loud; Set It Off
Latimore, Frank: Black Magic; Dolly Sisters, The; Shock (1946); 13 Rue Madeleine
Latt, Rachel: Nudist Colony of the Dead
Lattanzi, Matt: Blueberry Hill; Catch Me if You Can; Diving In; My Tutor; Rich and Famous
Lau, Damian: Legend of the Red Dragon
Lau, Jeff: Combination Platter
Lauck, Charles: So This Is Washington
Lauck, Chester: Dreaming Out Loud
Lauer, Andrew: Never on Tuesday; Screamers
Lauer, Justin: Creeps, The
Laufer, Jack: Man Who Captured Eichmann, The
Laufer, Joseph: Dangerous Prey
Laughlin, John: Crimes of Passion; Hills Have Eyes, The: Part Two; Midnight Crossing; Night Fire; Sexual Malice; Space Rage; Tons of Trouble
Laughlin, Tom: Billy Jack; Born Losers; Tall Story
Laughton, Charles: Abbott and Costello Meet Captain Kidd; Advise and Consent; Arch of Triumph; Barretts of Wimpole Street, The; Beachcomber, The; Canterville Ghost, The; Captain Kidd; Forever and a Day; Hobson's Choice; Hunchback of Notre Dame, The; If I Had a Million; Island of Lost Souls; It Started with Eve; Jamaica Inn; Les Misérables; Man in the Eiffel Tower, The; Mutiny on the Bounty; Old Dark House, The; Paradine Case, The; Private Life of Henry the Eighth, The; Rembrandt; Ruggles of Red Gap; Salome; Sidewalks of London; Spartacus; Strange Door, The; Tales of Manhattan; They Knew What They Wanted; This Land Is Mine; Tuttles of Tahiti, The; Witness for the Prosecution; Young Bess
Lauper, Cyndi: Life with Mikey; Off and Running; Opportunists, The; Vibes
Laurance, Mitchell: Stepfather II
Laure, Carole: Get Out Your Handkerchiefs; Sweet Country; Sweet Movie
Laure, Odette: Daddy Nostalgia
Laurel, Stan: Air Raid Wardens; Atoll K (Utopia); Block-Heads; Bohemian Girl, The; Bonnie Scotland; Bullfighters, The; Chump at Oxford, A; Days of Thrills and Laughter; Devil's Brother, The; Flying Deuces; Golden Age of Comedy, The; Great Guns; Hollywood Party; Laurel and Hardy Classics: Vol. 1–9; March of the Wooden Soldiers (Babes in Toyland (1934)); MGM's The Big Parade of Comedy; Movie Struck (Pick a Star); Nothing But Trouble; Our Relations; Pack Up Your Troubles; Pardon Us; Saps at Sea; Sons of the Desert; Swiss Miss; Way Out West; When Comedy Was King
Lauren, Ashley: Lurking Fear
Lauren, Dixie: 10 Violent Women
Lauren, Rod: Crawling Hand, The
Lauren, Tammy: Wes Craven's Wishmaster
Lauren, Veronica: Homeward Bound: The Incredible Journey; Homeward Bound II: Lost in San Francisco
Laurence, Ashley: Cupid; Felony; Hellraiser; Hellraiser II: Hellbound; Hellraiser 3: Hell on Earth; One Last Run; Savate; Triplecross; Warlock III: The End of Innocence
Laurence, Michael: Operator, The
Lauren-Herz, Andrea: Xtro: Watch the Skies (Xtro 3)
Laurenson, James: Cold Light of Day, The; House in the Hills, A; Rude Awakening
Laurent, Jacqueline: Le Jour Se Leve (Daybreak (1939))
Lauria, Dan: Great Los Angeles Earthquake, The; In the Line of Duty: Ambush in Waco; Mob Justice; Stakeout
Laurie, Hugh: Black Adder III (TV Series); Borrowers, The; Cousin Bette; Jeeves and Wooster (TV Series); Peter's Friends; Stuart Little
Laurie, Piper: Appointment with Death; Boss' Son, The; Bunker, The; Carrie; Children of a Lesser God; Crossing Guard, The; Dangerous Mission; Days of Wine and Roses, The (1958); Distortions; Dream a Little Dream; Faculty, The; Francis Goes to the Races; Grass Harp, The; Hustler, The; Inherit the Wind; Macbeth; Mae West; Other People's Money; Return to Oz; Rich in Love; Rising Son; Road to Galveston, The; Ruby; Skag; Son of Ali Baba; Storyville; Tiger Warsaw; Tim; Trauma; Twin Peaks (Movie); Twin Peaks (TV Series); Until They Sail; Wrestling Ernest Hemingway
Laurin, Marie: Talking Walls
Lauter, Ed: Big Score, The; Black Water; Breach of Trust; Breakheart Pass; Chicken Chronicles, The; Death Hunt; Death Wish III; Digital Man; Eureka; Extreme Justice; Family Plot; Gleaming the Cube; Jericho Mile, The; Last American Hero, The; Last Days of Patton, The; Longest Yard, The; Magic; Mercenary; Mulholland Falls; Murder So Sweet; Not Another Teen Movie; Rattled; Raven Hawk; Raw Deal; Real Genius; Revenge of the Nerds

II: Nerds in Paradise; Rocketeer, The; Stephen King's Golden Years (TV Series); Sweeper, The; 3:15—The Moment of Truth; Timerider; Trial by Jury; Under Investigation; Yuri Nosenko, KGB
Lauter, Harry: Hellcats of the Navy; Jungle Patrol; King of the Carnival
Lauterbach, Heiner: Men … (1985); Wiz Kid, The
Lavan, Rene: Bitter Sugar
Lavanant, Dominique: Monster, The
Lavant, Denis: Lovers on the Bridge
Lavelle, Sandie: Ladybird, Ladybird
Lavender, Ian: Adventures of a Private Eye
Laverick, June: Mania
Lavi, Daliah: Candide; Catlow; Spy with a Cold Nose, The; Ten Little Indians; Two Weeks in Another Town
Lavia, Gabriele: Deep Red; Inferno
Lavin, Linda: See You in the Morning
LaVorgna, Adam: I'll Be Home for Christmas
Law, Barbara: Bedroom Eyes
Law, John Phillip: African Rage; Alienator; Attack Force Z; Barbarella; Danger: Diabolik; Death Rides a Horse; Golden Voyage of Sinbad, The; Last Movie, The (Chinchero); Love Machine, The; My Magic Dog; Night Train to Terror; Tarzan the Ape Man; Tin Man
Law, Jude: AI: Artificial Intelligence; Enemy at the Gates; eXistenZ; Gattaca; Love, Honor & Obey; Midnight in the Garden of Good and Evil; Music from Another Room; Shopping; Talented Mr. Ripley, The; Wilde
Law, Phyllida: Much Ado About Nothing; Peter's Friends; Time Machine, The (2002); Winter Guest, The
Law, Tom: Shallow Grave
Lawford, Christopher: Blankman; Run
Lawford, Peter: Advise and Consent; April Fools, The; Buona Sera, Mrs. Campbell; Dead Ringer; Easter Parade; Exodus; Fantasy Island; Good News; Harlow; It Happened in Brooklyn; It Should Happen to You; Julia Misbehaves; Little Women; Man Called Adam, A; Mrs. Parkington; Never So Few; Ocean's Eleven; On an Island with You; Picture of Dorian Gray, The; Royal Wedding; Sky's the Limit, The; Son of Lassie; They Only Kill Their Masters; Two Sisters from Boston
Lawless, Lucy: Hercules and the Amazon Women; Women from Down Under
Lawley, Yvonne: Death in Brunswick
Lawrence, Adam: Drive-In Massacre
Lawrence, Barbara: Kronos; Letter to Three Wives, A; Star, The (1952); Street with No Name; Unfaithfully Yours
Lawrence, Bruno: Bridge to Nowhere; Efficiency Expert, The (Spotswood); Grievous Bodily Harm; Heart of the Stag; Jack Be Nimble; Quiet Earth, The; Rainbow Warrior; Rikki and Pete; Smash Palace; Treasure of the Yankee Zephyr; Utu
Lawrence, Carol: New Faces; Shattered Image; Summer of Fear
Lawrence, Cary: Canvas
Lawrence, Gail: Maniac
Lawrence, Gertrude: Rembrandt
Lawrence, Jim: High Country, The
Lawrence, Joey: Chains of Gold; Pulse; Tequila Body Shots; Urban Legends: Final Cut
Lawrence, Josie: Enchanted April
Lawrence, Marc: Asphalt Jungle, The; Charlie Chan at the Wax Museum; Cloak and Dagger; Dillinger; Don't Fence Me In; I Am the Law; Lady Scarface; Night Train to Terror; Pigs (Daddy's Deadly Darling); Revenge of the Pink Panther, The; Ruby; Sundown; Super Fuzz; Virginian, The
Lawrence, Mark Christopher: Fear of a Black Hat
Lawrence, Martin: Bad Boys; Big Momma's House; Black Knight; Blue Streak; Boomerang; House Party 2; Life; Nothing to Lose; Talkin' Dirty After Dark; Thin Line Between Love and Hate, A; What's the Worst That Could Happen?; You So Crazy
Lawrence, Matthew: Mrs. Doubtfire; Pulse
Lawrence, Michael: Came a Hot Friday; Price of Milk, The
Lawrence, Ronald William: Blackbelt 2: Fatal Force
Lawrence, Rosina: Charlie Chan's Secret; General Spanky
Lawrence, Scott: Laurel Avenue; Perfect Crime; Sometimes Aunt Martha Does Dreadful Things
Lawrence, Shirley: Satellite in the Sky
Lawrence, Steve: Alice Through the Looking Glass; Blues Brothers 2000; Express to Terror
Laws, Barry: Shadow Play
Lawson, Adam: Apex
Lawson, Bianca: Bones
Lawson, Charles: Four Days in July
Lawson, Cheryl: Dead Pit, The
Lawson, Leigh: Love Among the Ruins
Lawson, Linda: Night Tide
Lawson, Maggie: Model Behavior
Lawson, Priscilla: Flash Gordon: Rocketship (Spaceship to the Unknown; Perils from Planet Mongo)
Lawson, Shannon: Heck's Way Home
Lawson, Wilfrid: Danny Boy; Night Has Eyes, The; Pygmalion; Wrong Box, The
Lawton, Frank: Cavalcade; David Copperfield; Devil Doll, The (1936); Invisible Ray, The; Night to Remember, A; Winslow Boy, The
Laxdal, Jon: Polar Bear King, The
Laydu, Claude: Diary of a Country Priest
Layng, Lissa: Say Yes
Layton, Marcia: Cthulhu Mansion
Lazar, John: Night of the Scarecrow
Lazar, Paul: Buffalo Girls; Mickey Blue Eyes
Lazard, Justin: Brutal Truth, The; Dead Center; Species II
Lazarev, Alexander: Friend of the Deceased, A
Lazarev, Eugene: Ice Runner
Lazenby, George: Eyes of the Beholder; Fatally Yours; Gettysburg; On Her Majesty's Secret Service; Return of the Man from U.N.C.L.E., The; Saint Jack; Twin Sitters
Lazure, Gabrielle: Joshua Then and Now
Le, Hiep Thi: Heaven and Earth
Le Bihan, Samuel: Brotherhood of the Wolf
Le Calm, Renee: When the Cat's Away
Le Clainche, Charles: Man Escaped, A
Le Coq, Bernard: Van Gogh
Le Fleur, Art: Trancers
Le Mesurier, John: Brideshead Revisited; Brothers In Law; Five Golden Hours; Married Man, A
Le Roy, Eddie: No Time for Sergeants (Television)
le Vigan, Robert: Golgotha
Lea, Nicholas: John Woo's Once a Thief; Raffle, The; X-Files, The (TV Series)
Lea, Ron: Neighbor, The
Leach, Rosemary: D.P.; Hawk, The; Room with a View, A; That'll Be the Day; Turtle Diary
Leachman, Cloris: Amati Girls, The; Beverly Hillbillies, The (1993); Charley and the Angel; Crazy Mama; Daisy Miller; Danielle Steel's Fine Things; Dillinger; Dixie Changing Habits; Fade to Black; Foolin' Around; Hanging Up; Haunts of the Very Rich; Herbie Goes Bananas; High Anxiety; History of the World, Part One, The; Kiss Me Deadly; Last Picture Show, The; Love Hurts; Lovers and Other Strangers; Migrants, The; Muppet Movie, The; Music of the Heart; My Boyfriend's Back; Nobody's Girls; North Avenue Irregulars, The; Oldest Living Graduate, The; Prancer; Run Stranger Run; Scavenger Hunt; Shadow Play; Someone I Touched; S.O.S. Titanic; Steagle, The; Texasville; Thursday's Game; Walk Like a Man; Willa; Young Frankenstein
Leake, Damien: Killing Floor, The
Learned, Michael: All My Sons; Dragon: The Bruce Lee Story; Roots—The Gift; Thanksgiving Story, The; Touched by Love
Leary, Denis: Gunmen; Jesus' Son; Judgment Night; Matchmaker, The; Monument Ave.; National Lampoon's Favorite Deadly Sins; Neon Bible, The; Operation Dumbo Drop; Ref, The; Sand; Sandlot, The; Second Civil War, The; Silent Witness; Small Soldiers; Subway Stories; Suicide Kings; Thomas Crown Affair, The; True Crime; Two If By Sea; Underworld; Wag the Dog; Who's the Man?; Wide Awake
Leary, Timothy: Conceiving Ada; Hold Me, Thrill Me, Kiss Me; Roadside Prophets

Lease, Rex: Cyclone in the Saddle; Helldorado; Monster Walks, The
Léaud, Jean-Pierre: Day for Night; Diary of a Seducer; 400 Blows, The; Irma Vep; Last Tango in Paris; Le Départ; Le Gai Savoir (The Joy of Knowledge); Love on the Run; Masculine Feminine; Mother and the Whore, The; Oldest Profession, The; Pierrot Le Fou; Pigsty; Stolen Kisses; Two English Girls; Weekend
Leavins, Chris: Hanging Garden, The
Lebbos, Carmen: West Beirut
Lebedeff, Ivan: Goin' to Town
LeBlanc, Diana: Madonna: Innocence Lost
LeBlanc, Matt: Ed; Lost in Space (1998)
Lebowitz, Fran: Infamous Dorothy Parker, The
LeBrock, Kelly: Betrayal of the Dove; Hard Bounty; Hard to Kill; Tracks of a Killer; Weird Science; Woman in Red, The; Wrongfully Accused
Lebrun, Francoise: Mother and the Whore, The
Leclerc, Ginette: Baker's Wife, The; Man from Nowhere, The
Leclerc, Jean: Blown Away; Whispers
Lecomte, Cyril: Girl, The (1999)
Lecouer, Vincent: Deep in the Woods
Led Zeppelin: Song Remains the Same, The
Lederer, Francis: Bridge of San Luis Rey, The; Lisbon; Midnight; One Rainy Afternoon; Return of Dracula; Romance in Manhattan; Woman of Distinction, A
Ledford, Brandy: Zebra Lounge
Ledger, Heath: Knight's Tale, A; Monster's Ball; Patriot, The; 10 Things I Hate About You
Ledingham, David: Final Judgment
Ledoux, Fernand: La Bête Humaine; Stormy Waters
LeDoux, Jake: Summer's End
Ledoyen, Virginie: Beach, The; La Cérémonie; Single Girl
Leduc, Richard: Nous N'Irons Plus Au Bois
Leduke, Harrison: Laser Moon
Lee, Alan David: Sahara
Lee, Anna: Bedlam; Commandos Strike at Dawn; Ghost and Mrs. Muir, The; Hangmen Also Die; King Solomon's Mines; Man Who Lived Again, The; Prize, The; Seven Sinners
Lee, Bernard: Brain, The; Detective, The; Dr. No; Fallen Idol, The; Frankenstein and the Monster from Hell; Key, The; Last Holiday; Long Ago Tomorrow; Man with the Golden Gun, The; Pursuit of the Graf Spee; Rhodes of Africa (Rhodes); Spy Who Came in from the Cold, The; Spy Who Loved Me, The; Whistle Down the Wind; You Only Live Twice
Lee, Brandon: Bruce Lee: Curse of the Dragon; Crow, The; Kung Fu—The Movie (1986); Laser Mission; Rapid Fire; Showdown in Little Tokyo
Lee, Bruce: Bruce Lee: Curse of the Dragon; Chinese Connection, The; Enter the Dragon; Fists of Fury; Game of Death; Green Hornet, The (TV Series); Marlowe; Return of the Dragon
Lee, Canada: Cry, the Beloved Country; Lifeboat
Lee, Carl: Gordon's War; Superfly
Lee, Chen: Shanghai Joe
Lee, Christian: Invasion Earth: The Aliens Are Here
Lee, Christopher: Against All Odds (1968) (Kiss and Kill, Blood of Fu Manchu); Airport '77; Albino; Bear Island; Beat Girl; Captain America II: Death Too Soon; Caravans; Castle of Fu Manchu; Castle of the Living Dead; Circle of Iron; Circus of Fear; Corridor of Mirrors; Corridors of Blood; Count Dracula; Creeping Flesh, The; Crimson Pirate, The; Curse III: Blood Sacrifice; Curse of Frankenstein, The; Curse of the Crimson Altar; Dark Places; Death Train; Desperate Moves; Devil Rides Out, The; Devil's Undead, The; Dr. Terror's House of Horrors; Double Vision; Dracula A.D. 1972; Dracula and Son; Dracula Has Risen from the Grave; Dracula—Prince of Darkness; End of the World; Eye for an Eye; Far Pavilions, The; Five Golden Dragons; Four Musketeers, The; Funnyman; Girl, The; Goliath Awaits; Gorgon, The; Gremlins 2: The New Batch; Hannie Caulder; Hercules in the Haunted World; Hollywood Meatcleaver Massacre; Horror Express; Horror Hotel; Horror of Dracula; Hound of the Baskervilles, The; House of the Long Shadows; House That Dripped Blood, The; Howling II ... Your Sister Is a Werewolf; Jocks; Journey of Honor; Julius Caesar; Keeper, The; Killer Force; Land of Faraway, The; Lord of the Rings, The: Fellowship of the Ring; Magic Christian, The; Man with the Golden Gun, The; Moses; Moulin Rouge; Mummy, The; Murder Story; Oblong Box, The; 1941; Private Life of Sherlock Holmes, The; Pursuit of the Graf Spee; Rainbow Thief, The; Rasputin: The Mad Monk; Raw Meat; Return from Witch Mountain; Return of Captain Invincible, The; Return of the Musketeers; Rosebud Beach Hotel, The (Nostell Hotel,The); Russell Mulcahy's Tale of the Mummy; Salamander, The; Satanic Rites of Dracula, The; Scars of Dracula; Scott of the Antarctic; Scream and Scream Again; Scream of Fear; Serial; Shaka Zulu; Sherlock Holmes and the Deadly Necklace; Sherlock Holmes and the Incident at Victoria Falls; Sherlock Holmes and the Leading Lady; Skull, The; Sleepy Hollow; Star Wars: Attack of the Clones; Starship Invasions; Tale of Two Cities, A; Taste the Blood of Dracula; Terror of the Tongs, The; Theatre of Death; To the Devil, a Daughter; Torture Chamber of Dr. Sadism, The; Treasure Island; Virgin of Nuremberg (Horror Castle); Wicker Man, The
Lee, Conan: New York Cop
Lee, Cosette: Deranged
Lee, Danny: City War; Killer, The; Mighty Peking Man; Untold Story, The
Lee, Dexter: Sleepwalker
Lee, Dorothy: Hips, Hips, Hooray; Hook, Line and Sinker
Lee, Elizabeth: Something Weird
Lee, Gypsy Rose: My Lucky Star; Screaming Mimi; Stripper, The
Lee, Haan: Pushing Hands
Lee, Hey Young: Field of Honor
Lee, Hyo-jeong: Chunhyang
Lee, Janis: Blink of an Eye
Lee, Jason: Almost Famous; Big Trouble (2002); Chasing Amy; Dogma; Heartbreakers; Kissing a Fool; Mall Rats; Mumford; Vanilla Sky
Lee, Jason Scott: Dragon: The Bruce Lee Story; Map of the Human Heart; Murder in Mind; Rapa Nui; Rudyard Kipling's The Jungle Book (1994); Russell Mulcahy's Tale of the Mummy; Soldier
Lee, Jennifer: Sprung
Lee, Jesse: From the Mixed-Up Files of Mrs. Basile. Frankweiler
Lee, Joanna: Brain Eaters, The
Lee, Joie: Fathers & Sons; Mo' Better Blues
Lee, Jonah Ming: Magic Stone, The
Lee, Jonna: Making the Grade
Lee, Julian: My Samurai
Lee, Kaaren: Roadhouse 66
Lee, Kaiulani: Zelly and Me
Lee, Kang-sheng: Vive L'Amour
Lee, Kelly: Yi Yi
Lee, Lila: Blood and Sand; Country Gentlemen; Ex-Mrs. Bradford, The; Male and Female; Unholy Three
Lee, Linda Emery: Bruce Lee: Curse of the Dragon
Lee, Margaret: Five Golden Dragons
Lee, Mark: Blackwater Trail; Everlasting Secret Family, The; Gallipoli; Sahara
Lee, Mary: Song of Nevada
Lee, Michael: Temptation of a Monk
Lee, Michele: Bud and Lou; Fatal Image, The; How to Succeed in Business without Really Trying; Love Bug, The; Only with Married Men; Scandalous Me: The Jacqueline Susann Story
Lee, Miki: Mr. Nice Guy
Lee, Moon: Zu: Warriors from the Magic Mountain
Lee, Pamela Anderson: Barb Wire; Naked Souls
Lee, Peggy: Jazz Singer, The; Ladies Sing the Blues, The; Mr. Music; Pete Kelly's Blues
Lee, Pinky: In Old Amarillo; Lady of Burlesque
Lee, Rob: Virtual Encounters
Lee, Robbie: Switchblade Sisters
Lee, Robinne: Hav Plenty
Lee, Ruta: First and Ten; Funny Face
Lee, Sam: Gen-X Cops
Lee, Shannon: Cage II: Arena of Death, The; High Voltage

Lee, Sheryl: Angel's Dance; BackBeat; Bliss; Don't Do It; Fall Time; Homage; John Carpenter's Vampires; Kiss the Sky; Love, Lies and Murder; Mother Night; This World, Then the Fireworks; Twin Peaks: Fire Walk with Me
Lee, Sondra: Peter Pan
Lee, Sophie: Bootmen; Holy Smoke
Lee, Spike: Do the Right Thing; Drop Squad, The; First Works, Volumes 1 & 2; Girl 6; Jungle Fever; Malcolm X; Mo' Better Blues; School Daze; She's Gotta Have It
Lee, Stan: Jugular Wine
Lee, Stephen: Black Scorpion; Black Scorpion II: Aftershock; Dolls
Lee, Waise: Bullet in the Head; Wing Chun
Leeder, Stephen: Fatal Bond
Leeds, Andrea: Goldwyn Follies, The; Letter of Introduction; Real Glory, The; They Shall Have Music
Leeds, Andrew Harrison: Pig's Tale, A
Leeds, Elissa: Lights, Camera, Action, Love
Leeds, Lila: Show-Off, The
Leeds, Marcie: Wheels of Terror
Leeds, Peter: Ma and Pa Kettle Back on the Farm
Leegant, Dan: Signal 7
Leeman, Jacolyn: Lady Avenger
Leerhsen, Erica: Book of Shadows: Blair Witch 2
Leet, Scott: Out in Fifty
Leeves, Jane: Miracle on 34th Street
LeFevre, Adam: Mr. Wonderful; Ref, The; Return of the Secaucus 7
Lefévre, René: Crime of Monsieur Lange, The; Le Million; Sois Belle Et Tais-Toi (Just Another Pretty Face)
Leffler, Christian: Killer Flick
Lefkowitz, John: Hurry Up or I'll Be 30
LeGallienne, Eva: Devil's Disciple, The; Resurrection
LeGault, Lance: Pioneer Woman
Legge, Michael: Angela's Ashes
Legitimus, Darling: Sugarcane Alley
Legrand, Michel: Cleo from 5 to 7
Legrix, Laetitia: Come Undone
LeGros, James: Bad Girls; Boys (1996); Common Ground; Destiny Turns on the Radio; Don't Do It; Drugstore Cowboy; Floundering; Guncrazy (1950); Living in Oblivion; Marshal Law; My New Gun; Myth of Fingerprints, The; Nervous Ticks; Phantasm II; Point Break; Pronto; Safe; Scotland, PA; Serial Bomber; Wishful Thinking
Leguizamo, John: Body Count; Carlito's Way; Collateral Damage; Dr. Dolittle (1998); Executive Decision; Fan, The; Frogs for Snakes; Hangin' with the Homeboys; Moulin Rouge; Moulin Rouge (2001); Night Owl; Pest, The; Pyromaniac's Love Story, A; Spawn; Summer of Sam; Super MarioBrothers, The; To Wong Foo, Thanks for Everything, Julie Newmar; What's the Worst That Could Happen?; Whispers in the Dark; William Shakespeare's Romeo and Juliet
Lehman, Kristine: Bleeders
Lehman, Lillian: Mardi Gras for the Devil
Lehman, Manfred: Operation 'Nam
Lehmann, Beatrix: Candles at Nine; Staircase
Lehne, Fredric: Coward of the County; Dream Lover; Romeo and Juliet; This Gun for Hire
Lehne, John: American Hot Wax; Bound for Glory
Lehoczky, Bela: Hold Me, Thrill Me, Kiss Me
Lehr, Wendy: Marvelous Land of Oz, The
Lei, Huang: Life on a String
Leibman, Ron: Door to Door; Hot Rock, The; Just the Ticket; Night Falls on Manhattan; Norma Rae; Phar Lap; Rhinestone; Romantic Comedy; Seven Hours to Judgment; Up the Academy; Where's Poppa?; Zorro, the Gay Blade
Leifert, Don: Alien Factor, The
Leigh, Barbara: Boss; Student Nurses, The
Leigh, Cassandra: Alien Terminator; Caged Heat 3000
Leigh, Chyler: Not Another Teen Movie
Leigh, Janet: Angels in the Outfield; Bye Bye Birdie; Fog, The; Harper; Hills of Home; Holiday Affair; Houdini; It's a Big Country; Little Women; Manchurian Candidate, The; My Sister Eileen; Naked Spur, The; Perfect Furlough; Pete Kelly's Blues; Prince Valiant; Psycho; Scaramouche; That Forsyte Woman; Touch of Evil; Two Tickets to Broadway; Vikings, The; Words and Music
Leigh, Jennifer Jason: Angel City; Anniversary Party, The; Backdraft; Bastard Out of Carolina; Best Little Girl in the World, The; Big Picture, The; Buried Alive; Crooked Hearts; Dolores Claiborne; eXistenZ; Eyes of a Stranger; Fast Times at Ridgemont High; Flesh and Blood (Sword and the Rose, the (1985)); Georgia; Grandview, U.S.A.; Heart of Midnight; Hitcher, The; Hudsucker Proxy, The; Infamous Dorothy Parker, The; Kansas City; Killing of Randy Webster, The; Last Exit to Brooklyn; Love Letter, The; Men's Club, The; Miami Blues; Mrs. Parker and the Vicious Circle; Rush; Short Cuts; Single White Female; Sister, Sister; Skipped Parts; Thousand Acres, A; Undercover; Washington Square
Leigh, Nelson: World Without End
Leigh, Spencer: Caravaggio; Last of England, The
Leigh, Steven Vincent: China White; Deadly Bet; Sword of Honor
Leigh, Suzanna: Lost Continent, The; Lust for a Vampire; Paradise Hawaiian Style
Leigh, Tara: On the Make
Leigh, Taylor: Under Lock and Key
Leigh, Vivien: Anna Karenina; Caesar and Cleopatra; Dark Journey; Fire over England; Gone with the Wind; Roman Spring of Mrs. Stone, The; Ship of Fools; Sidewalks of London; Storm in a Teacup; Streetcar Named Desire, A; That Hamilton Woman; Waterloo Bridge
Leigh-Hunt, Barbara: Frenzy; Paper Mask
Leigh-Hunt, Ronald: Le Mans
Leighton, Laura: Seven Girlfriends
Leighton, Lillian: Peck's Bad Boy; Tumbleweeds
Leighton, Margaret: Best Man, The; Bonnie Prince Charlie; Carrington, V. C.; Elusive Pimpernel, The; From Beyond the Grave; Go-Between, The; Lady Caroline Lamb; Madwoman of Chaillot, The; Waltz of the Toreadors; Winslow Boy, The; X, Y and Zee
Leipnitz, Harold: Hell Hounds of Alaska
Leipzig, Dina: Blue Hour, The
Leis, Dan: Blood, Guts, Bullets & Octane
Leisure, David: Hollywood Safari; You Can't Hurry Love
Leitch, David: Death Warmed Up
Leitch, Donovan: And God Created Woman; Blob, The; Cutting Class; Dark Horse
Leith, Shayne: Warriors from Hell
Leith, Virginia: Brain That Wouldn't Die, The
Lelouch, Marie-Sophie: Bandits
Lemaire, Philippe: Blood Rose; Cartouche
LeMarco, Promise: Kolobos
LeMat, Paul: Aloha, Bobby and Rose; American Graffiti; Burning Bed, The; Caroline at Midnight; Children of Fury; Citizen's Band; Death Valley; Easy Wheels; Firehouse; Grave Secrets; Hanoi Hilton, The; Into the Homeland; Jimmy the Kid; Melvin and Howard; More American Graffiti; Night They Saved Christmas, The; On Wings of Eagles; P.K. & the Kid; Private Investigations; Puppet Master, The; Sensation; Strange Invaders; Woman with a Past
Lemay, Jeannine: Don't Mess with My Sister
LeMay, John D.: Jason Goes to Hell: The Final Friday
Lembeck, Harvey: Beach Blanket Bingo; Beach Party; Sgt. Bilko (TV Series)
Lembeck, Michael: Gorp; In-Laws, The; On the Right Track
Lemche, Kris: Ginger Snaps
Lemme, Steve: Super Troopers
Lemmon, Chris: Corporate Affairs; Going Undercover; Happy Hooker Goes Hollywood, The; Just Before Dawn; Just the Ticket; Lena's Holiday; That's Life; Thunder in Paradise; Thunder in Paradise II; Weekend Warriors
Lemmon, Jack: Airport '77; Apartment, The; April Fools, The; Avanti!; Bell, Book and Candle; Buddy, Buddy; China Syndrome, The; Dad; Days of Wine and Roses (1962); Ernie Kovacs: Television's Original Genius; For Richer, for Poorer; Fortune Cookie, The; Front Page, The; Getting Away with Murder; Glengarry Glen Ross; Good Neighbor Sam; Grass Harp, The; Great Race,

Levine, Ted: Betrayed; Bullet; Death Train; Ellen Foster; Evolution; Flubber; Fulfillment; Georgia; Harlan County War; Last Outlaw, The; Love at Large; Mad City; Mangler, The; Mob Justice; Moby Dick; Nowhere to Run; Silence of the Lambs; Switchback; Wild Wild West (1999)
Levinson, Barry: Quiz Show
Levis, Carroll: Brass Monkey, The
Levis, Patrick: Miracle in Lane 2
Levisetti, Emile: Alien Terminator; Where Evil Lies
Levitch, Ashlee: Star Kid
Levitt, Joseph Gordon: Halloween: H20; 10 Things I Hate About You
Levitt, Steve: Hunk
Levy, Eugene: Almost Heroes; American Pie; American Pie 2; Armed and Dangerous; Best in Show; Club Paradise; Down to Earth; Father of the Bride Part II; Going Berserk; Harrison Bergeron; I Love Trouble; Ladies Man, The (2000); Last Polka, The; Multiplicity; Speed Zone; Splash; Stay Tuned; Waiting for Guffman
Levy, Jeremy: Rich Kids
Lew, James: Balance of Power
Lewis, Al: Car 54, Where Are You? (1991); Car 54 Where Are You? (TV Series); Munsters' Revenge, The; My Grandpa Is a Vampire; Night Strangler, The; South Beach Academy
Lewis, Alun: Experience Preferred ... But Not Essential
Lewis, Charlotte: Bare Essentials; Decoy; Dial: Help; Embrace of the Vampire; Excessive Force; Glass Cage, The; Golden Child, The; Lipstick Camera; Men of War; Mutual Needs; Navajo Blues; Pirates; Storyville
Lewis, Clea: Rich Man's Wife, The
Lewis, Dawnn: Under Pressure
Lewis, Diana: Go West; Stephanie, Nathalie, Caroline and Vincent; Venus de Milo
Lewis, Elliott: Ma and Pa Kettle Go to Town
Lewis, Fiona: Dr. Phibes Rises Again; Dracula; Fury, The (1978); Innerspace; Lisztomania; Strange Behavior; Tintorera; Wanda Nevada
Lewis, Forrest: Monster of Piedras Blancas, The
Lewis, Gary: Billy Elliot
Lewis, Geoffrey: Any Which Way You Can; Bad Company; Bronco Billy; Catch Me if You Can; Culpepper Cattle Co., The; Dillinger; Disturbed; Double Impact; Every Which Way But Loose; High Plains Drifter; Lawnmower Man, The; Lust in the Dust; Macon County Line; Man without a Face, The; Matters of the Heart; My Name Is Nobody; National Lampoon's Last Resort; Night of the Comet; Only the Strong; Pancho Barnes; Pink Cadillac; Point of No Return; Return of a Man Called Horse, The; Return of the Man from U.N.C.L.E., The; Shadow Riders, The; Smile; Stitches; Tango and Cash; Thunderbolt and Lightfoot; Tilt; Trilogy of Terror II; Way of the Gun, The; When the Dark Man Calls; White Fang 2: Myth of the White Wolf; Wind and the Lion, The
Lewis, George J.: Big Sombrero, The; Federal Operator 99; G-Men vs. The Black Dragon; Sign of Zorro, The
Lewis, Gilbert: Gordon's War; Kid Who Loved Christmas, The; Touched
Lewis, Huey: Duets; Short Cuts
Lewis, Jarma: It's a Dog's Life
Lewis, Jenifer: Corrina, Corrina; Preacher's Wife, The
Lewis, Jenny: Foxfire; Friendship in Vienna, A; Runaway Father; Trading Hearts; Wizard, The
Lewis, Jerry: Arizona Dreams; Artists and Models; At War with the Army; Bellboy, The; Big Mouth, The; Boeing, Boeing; Caddy, The; Cinderfella; Cookie; Cracking Up; Delicate Delinquent, The; Disorderly Orderly, The; Don't Raise the Bridge, Lower the River; Errand Boy, The; Family Jewels, The; Funnybones; Hardly Working; Hollywood or Bust; Jumping Jacks; King of Comedy, The; Ladies' Man, The (1961); My Friend Irma; Nutty Professor, The; Patsy, The; Sad Sack, The; Slapstick of Another Kind; Which Way to the Front?
Lewis, Jerry Lee: American Hot Wax
Lewis, Joe E.: Private Buckaroo
Lewis, Juliette: Cape Fear; Crooked Hearts; Evening Star, The; 4th Floor, The; From Dusk Till Dawn; Husbands and Wives; Kalifornia; Mixed Nuts; National Lampoon's Christmas Vacation; Natural Born Killers; Romeo Is Bleeding; Strange Days; That Night; Too Young to Die; Way of the Gun, The; What's Eating Gilbert Grape?
Lewis, Justin: Blood & Donuts
Lewis, Leigh: To Catch a Yeti
Lewis, Linda: Alien Dead
Lewis, Matt: Edgar Allan Poe's Madhouse
Lewis, Matthew: Harry Potter and the Sorcerer's Stone
Lewis, Mitchell: Docks of New York, The
Lewis, Monica: Boxoffice; D.I., The
Lewis, Ralph: Avenging Conscience, The; Flesh and Blood (1922); Flying Serpent, The; Outside the Law; Somewhere in Sonora
Lewis, Rawle D.: Cool Runnings
Lewis, Richard: Drunks; Hugo Pool; Once Upon a Crime; Robin Hood: Men in Tights; That's Adequate; Wagons East; Weekend in the Country, A; Wrong Guys, The
Lewis, Robert Q.: Affair to Remember, An
Lewis, Ronald: Scream of Fear
Lewis, Sharon M.: Rude
Lewis, Sheldon: Monster Walks, The; Orphans of the Storm; Phantom, The; Seven Footprints to Satan
Lewis, Ted: Manhattan Merry-Go-Round
Lewis, Vicki: Huntress, The
Lewman, Lance: Breeders
Ley, John: BMX Bandits
Leyden, Michael Van: Singapore
Leyrado, Juan: Times to Come
Leysen, Johan: Egg
Leyton, Drue: Charlie Chan in London
Leyton, John: Schizo; Seaside Swingers
Lhermitte, Thierry: American Werewolf in Paris, An; Closet, The; Dinner Game, The; Little Indian, Big City; My Best Friend's Girl; My New Partner; Next Year If All Goes Well; Until September
Lhondup, Thilen: Himalaya
Li, Bruce: Dynamo
Li, Gong: Chinese Box; Emperor and the Assassin, The; Farewell My Concubine; Ju Dou; Raise the Red Lantern; Red Sorghum; Shanghai Triad; Story of Qiu Ju, The; Temptress Moon; To Live
Li, Jet: Black Mask; Fist of Legend; Jet Li's the Enforcer; Kiss of the Dragon; Legend, The; Legend of the Red Dragon; Lethal Weapon 4; Once Upon a Time in China; Once Upon a Time in China II; Once Upon a Time in China III; One, The; Romeo Must Die; Twin Warriors
Liang, Ning: Madame Butterfly
Liang-Yi, Guo: China, My Sorrow
Liapis, Peter: Ghoulies; Ghoulies IV
Liberace: Loved One, The; Sincerely Yours
Libert, Anne: Virgin Among the Living Dead, A
Libertini, Richard: All of Me; Big Trouble (1985); Don't Drink the Water; Fletch; Fletch Lives; Fourth Wise Man, The; Going Berserk; Nell; Popeye; Telling You; Vendetta
Liberty, Richard: Crazies, The; Day of the Dead
Libolt, Alain: Autumn Tale
Licata, Robert: Vicious Sweet, The
Licht, Jeremy: Comeback Kid, The; Next One, The
Lichtenstein, Mitchell: Streamers; Wedding Banquet, The
Liddell, Laura: Shakespeare Wallah
Liddy, G. Gordon: Adventures in Spying; Street Asylum; Super Force
Liebeneiner, Wolfgang: Liebelei
Lieber, Paul: Entertaining Angels
Lieberman, Wendy: Infamous Dorothy Parker, The
Lieh, Lo: Stranger and the Gunfighter, The
Lien, Jennifer: American History X; SLC Punk
Lieven, Albert: Brainwashed; Convoy; Seventh Veil, The
Lifford, Tina: Ernest Green Story, The; Mandela and De Klerk; Run for the Dream
Light, John: I'm a Fool
Lightfoot, Gordon: Harry Tracy
Lightstone, Marilyn: Lies My Father Told Me; Spasms

Ligon, Tom: Joyride
Lillard, Matthew: Dead Man's Curve; Dish Dogs; Love's Labour's Lost; Scream; Senseless; Serial Mom; She's All That; SLC Punk; Spanish Judges; Summer Catch; Tarantella; Thir13en Ghosts; Wing Commander
Lillie, Beatrice: On Approval; Thoroughly Modern Millie
Lilly, Robin: Beware! Children at Play
Lim, Gina: Bad Attitude
Lim, Steven: That's the Way I Like It
Lime, Yvonne: I Was a Teenage Werewolf
Limon, Dina: Boy Takes Girl
Lin, Brigitte: Bride with White Hair, The; Chungking Express; Jackie Chan's Police Force; Zu: Warriors from the Magic Mountain
Lin, Kevin: Temptress Moon
Lin, Traci: Class of 1999
Lincoln, Abbey: For Love of Ivy; Nothing But a Man
Lincoln, Andrew: Boston Kickout
Lincoln, Elmo: Adventures of Tarzan, The; Intolerance; Tarzan of the Apes; Wyoming Outlaw
Lincoln, Lar Park: Friday the 13th, Part VII: The New Blood; Princess Academy, The
Lincoln, Richard: Manny's Orphans (Come the Tigers)
Lincoln, Scott: Last Assassins
Lincoln, Warren: Power, The (1980)
Lind, Della: Swiss Miss
Lind, Greta: Rudy
Lind, Heather: Betrayal of the Dove
Lind, Traci: End of Violence, The; Model by Day; My Boyfriend's Back
Linda, Boguslaw: Masquerade
Lindberg, Chad: Fast and the Furious, The; October Sky
Lindblom, Gunnel: Hunger (1966); Silence, The; Virgin Spring, The; Winter Light
Linden, Doris: Private Snuffy Smith
Linden, Eric: Ah, Wilderness
Linden, Hal: Colony, The (1995); How to Break Up a Happy Divorce; I Do! I Do!; Killers in the House; Mr. Inside/Mr. Outside; My Wicked, Wicked Ways; New Life, A; Out to Sea; Ray Bradbury's Chronicles: The Martian Episodes; Starflight One
Linden, Jennie: Dr. Who and the Daleks; Women in Love
Linder, Cec: Quatermass and the Pit; Strange Tales: Ray Bradbury Theater
Linder, Crista: Days of Wrath
Linder, Max: Seven Years' Bad Luck
Linderman, Maggie: Vanishing, The
Lindfors, Viveca: Adventures of Don Juan, The; Cauldron of Blood; Exiled in America; Four in a Jeep; Girlfriends; King of Kings (1961); Last Summer in the Hamptons; Misplaced; Natural Enemies; Playing for Time; Rachel River; Silent Madness; Stargate; Story of Ruth, The; Voices; Way We Were, The; Zandalee
Lindgren, Lisa: Together
Lindinger, Natacha: Double Team
Lindley, Audra: Cannery Row; Desert Hearts; Heartbreak Kid, The; Revenge of the Stepford Wives; Spellbinder
Lindner, Carl Michael: Krippendorf's Tribe
Lindo, Delroy: Broken Arrow; Cider House Rules, The; Clockers; Crooklyn; Feeling Minnesota; First Time Felon; Get Shorty; Gone in 60 Seconds; Heist (2001); Last Castle, The; Life Less Ordinary, A; Malcolm X; One, The; Ransom; Romeo Must Die; Soul of the Game; Strange Justice; Winner, The
Lindon, Vincent: School of Flesh
Lindquist, Arthur: Regenerated Man, The
Lindsay, Margaret: Baby Face; Case of the Curious Bride, The; Cavalcade; Dangerous (1935); Devil Dogs of the Air; House of the Seven Gables, The; Lady Killer; Please Don't Eat the Daisies; Scarlet Street; Tammy and the Doctor
Lindsay, Robert: Bert Rigby, You're a Fool; Genghis Cohn; King Lear; Strike It Rich
Lindsey, George: Andy Griffith Show, The (TV Series); Return to Mayberry
Lindsey, Joseph: Amongst Friends; Public Enemy #1
Line, Helga: Nightmare Castle; When the Screaming Stops
Lineback, Richard: Baby Dance, The; Varsity Blues; Woman with a Past
Ling, Bai: Nobody's Girls; Red Corner; Somewhere in the City
Ling, Suzanne: Nobody's Girls; Red Corner; Somewhere in the City
Linh, Dan Pham: Indochine
Linke, Paul: Motel Hell; Time Flies When You're Alive
Linkletter, Art: Champagne for Caesar; People Are Funny
Linn, Rex: Breakdown; Last Stand at Saber River; Tin Cup
Linn, Teri Ann: Pure Danger
Linn-Baker, Mark: Bare Essentials; Laughter on the 23rd Floor; Me and Him; My Favorite Year; Noises Off
Linney, Laura: Absolute Power; Blind Spot; Congo; House of Mirth, The; Lush; Maze; Mothman Prophecies, The; Primal Fear; Running Mates; Simple Twist of Fate, A; Truman Show, The; Wild Iris; You Can Count on Me
Linnros, Henrik: Sunday's Children
Lino, Ivan: Just Imagine
Linstedt, Carl-Gustav: Man on the Roof
Linville, Larry: M*A*S*H (TV Series); No Dessert Dad Until You Mow the Lawn; Rock 'n' Roll High School Forever; School Spirit
Linz, Alex D.: Home Alone 3; Max Keeble's Big Move; One Fine Day
Lion, Leon M.: Amazing Adventure; Number 17
Liotard, Thérèse: My Father's Glory; My Mother's Castle; One Sings, the Other Doesn't
Liotta, Ray: Article 99; Blow; Copland; Corrina, Corrina; Dominick and Eugene; Field of Dreams; Goodfellas; Hannibal; Heartbreakers; John Q; Muppets From Space; No Escape; Operation Dumbo Drop; Phoenix; Rat Pack, The; Something Wild; Turbulence; Unforgettable; Unlawful Entry; Women & Men 2
Lipinski, Eugene: Aldrich Ames: Traitor Within; Moonlighting (1983); Riders of the Storm
Lipman, Maureen: Little Princess, A
Lipnicki, Jonathan: Jerry Maguire; Little Vampire, The; Stuart Little
Lipscomb, Dennis: Amazing Grace and Chuck; Blue Yonder, The; Crossroads; Eyes of Fire; First Power, The; Retribution; Sister, Sister; Slow Burn; Union City
Lipton, Peggy: Fatal Charm; Kinjite (Forbidden Subjects); Mod Squad, The (TV Series); Purple People Eater; Spider and the Fly, The; True Identity; Twin Peaks (Movie); Twin Peaks (TV Series); Twin Peaks: Fire Walk with Me
Lipton, Robert: Death Spa; Lethal Woman; Silent Night, Lonely Night; Woman, Her Men and Her Futon, A
Lira, Soia: Central Station
Lisi, Virna: Assault on a Queen; Challenge to White Fang; Christopher Columbus (1985); How to Murder Your Wife; Miss Right; Night Flight from Moscow; Queen Margot; Statue, The; When Wolves Cry
Lissauer, Trevor: Skateboard Kid, The
Lissek, Loon: Bloodmoon
Lister, Moira: Run for Your Money, A
Lister Jr., Tom "Tiny": I Got the Hook Up; Immortal Combat; Jackie Brown; Judgment Day; Little Nicky; Men of War; Next Friday; Phat Beach; Posse; Soulkeeper; Supreme Sanction
Litefoot: Indian in the Cupboard, The; Kull the Conqueror
Litel, John: Enchanted Forest, The; Flight to Mars; Northwest Trail; Pitfall; Return of Dr. X; Sister Kenny; Texas Lady; Virginia City
Lithgow, John: Adventures of Buckaroo Banzai, The; At Play in the Fields of the Lord; Baby Girl Scott; Blow Out; Civil Action, A; Cliffhanger; Day After, The; Distant Thunder; Don Quixote; Footloose; Glitter Dome, The; Good Man in Africa, A; Harry and the Hendersons; Hollow Point; Homegrown; Ivory Hunters; Love, Cheat & Steal; Manhattan Project, The; Memphis Belle; Mesmerized (Shocked); Obsession; Orange County; Out Cold; Pelican Brief, The; Princess Caraboo; Raising Cain; Redwood Curtain; Rich Kids; Ricochet; Santa Claus—The Movie; Shrek; Silent Fall; Traveling Man; Tuskegee Airmen, The; Twilight Zone—The Movie; 2010; World According to Garp, The; Wrong Man, The

Little, Cleavon: Blazing Saddles; Cotton Comes to Harlem; Don't Look Back: The Story of Leroy "Satchel" Paige; Double Exposure; Fletch Lives; FM; Gig, The; Greased Lightning; High Risk; Jimmy the Kid; Murder by Numbers (1989); Once Bitten; Salamander, The; Scavenger Hunt; Separate But Equal; Sky Is Gray, The; Surf 2; Toy Soldiers; Vanishing Point
Little, Kim: Sorority House Party
Little, Michelle: Appointment with Fear; My Demon Lover; Radioactive Dreams
Little, Natasha: Greenfingers
Little, Rich: Dirty Tricks; Happy Hour; Late Shift, The; Rich Little—One's a Crowd; Rich Little's Little Scams on Golf
Little Billy: Terror of Tiny Town, The
Little Nell: Jubilee; Rocky Horror Picture Show, The
Little Richard: Chuck Berry Hail! Hail! Rock 'n' Roll; Down and Out in Beverly Hills; Girl Can't Help It, The; Jimi Hendrix; Sunset Heat
Littlefield, Lucien: Bitter Tea of General Yen, The; Hell Town; Sheik, The; Tumbleweeds
Littman, Julian: MAD About Mambo
Liu, Emily: Pushing Hands
Liu, Eric: From Dusk Till Dawn
Liu, Lucy: Charlie's Angels; Flypaper; Shanghai Noon
Liu, Peiqi: Shadow Magic
Lively, Ernie: Accidental Meeting
Lively, Jason: Ghost Chase; Maximum Force; National Lampoon's European Vacation; Night of the Creeps
Lively, Robyn: Buckeye and Blue; Dream a Little Dream 2; Not Quite Human; Not Quite Human 2; Teen Witch
Livesey, Roger: Drums; Entertainer, The; League of Gentlemen, The; Life and Death of Colonel Blimp, The; Master of Ballantrae, The; Of Human Bondage
Livingston, Barry: Easy Wheels; Invisible Mom; Steel Sharks
Livingston, Margaret: Last Warning, The; Sunrise
Livingston, Richard B.: Reptilian
Livingston, Robert: Bells of Rosarita; Black Raven, The; Bold Caballero, The; Covered Wagon Days; Death Rides the Plains; Don't Fence Me In; Gangs of Sonora; Heart of the Rockies; Hit the Saddle; Kansas Terrors; Lone Star Raiders; Mule Train; Mysterious Desperado; Outlaws of Sonora; Range Defenders; Riders of the Black Hills; Riders of the Whistling Skull; Rocky Mountain Rangers; Trail Blazers; Under Texas Skies; Valley of the Zombies; Vigilantes Are Coming!; Winning of the West
Livingston, Ron: Body Shots; Office Space; Swingers
Livingstone, Mary: Jack Benny Program, The (TV Series)
Lizer, Kari: Hit Woman: The Double Edge
LL Cool J: Deep Blue Sea; Halloween: H20; In Too Deep; Kingdom Come; Out of Sync; Right to Remain Silent, The; Rollerball (2002); Woo
Llewellyn, Desmond: Living Daylights, The; Spy Who Loved Me, The; World Is Not Enough, The; You Only Live Twice
Llewellyn, Robert: Red Dwarf (TV Series)
Lloyd, Christopher: Addams Family, The; Addams Family Values; Alice in Wonderland; Amazing Stories (TV Series); Anastasia; Angels in the Outfield; Baby Geniuses; Back to the Future; Back to the Future II; Back to the Future III; Cadillac Ranch; Camp Nowhere; Changing Habits; Clue; Cowboy and the Ballerina, The; Dead Ahead: The Exxon Valdez Disaster; Dennis the Menace; Dream Team, The; Eight Men Out; It Came from the Sky; Miracles; My Favorite Martian; One Flew over the Cuckoo's Nest; Pagemaster, The; Premonition (1998); Quicksilver Highway; Radioland Murders; Rent-A-Kid; Right to Remain Silent, The; Schizoid; September Gun; Star Trek III: The Search for Spock; Streethawk; Suburban Commando; TBone N Weasel; Things to Do in Denver When You're Dead; Track 29; Twenty Bucks; Walk Like a Man; When Good Ghouls Go Bad; Who Framed Roger Rabbit; Why Me?; Wit
Lloyd, Emily: Boogie Boy; Chicago Joe and the Showgirl; Cookie; In Country; Real Thing, The; River Runs Through It, A; Scorchers; Under the Hula Moon; Wish You Were Here
Lloyd, Eric: Chameleon; Dunston Checks In; Santa Clause, The
Lloyd, George: Singapore
Lloyd, Harold: Days of Thrills and Laughter; Freshman, The; Grandma's Boy; Harold Lloyd's Comedy Classics; Mad Wednesday (see also Sin of HaroldDiddlebock); Milky Way, The; Safety Last; Sin of Harold Diddlebock (Mad Wednesday)
Lloyd, Jake: Star Wars: Episode I The Phantom Menace; Unhook the Stars
Lloyd, Jeremy: Bawdy Adventures of Tom Jones, The
Lloyd, Jimmy: Riders of the Whistling Pines; Sea Hound, The
Lloyd, John Bedford: Sweet Lorraine; Waiting for the Light
Lloyd, Kathleen: Car, The; Fly Boy; It Lives Again; Jayne Mansfield Story, The; Missouri Breaks, The; Take Down
Lloyd, Norman: Age of Innocence, The; Amityville 4: The Evil Escapes; Dead Poets Society; FM; Journey of Honor; Nude Bomb, The (Return of Maxwell Smart,The); Saboteur; St. Elsewhere (TV Series)
Lloyd, Sabrina: Father Hood
Lloyd, Sam: Death Artist
Lloyd, Sue: Ipcress File, The; Number One of the Secret Service
Lloyd, Susan: Breathing Room
Lloyd Jr., Harold: Frankenstein's Daughter; Married Too Young; Mutiny in Outer Space
Lo, Candy: Time and Tide
Lo, Ken: Crime Story
Lo Bianco, Tony: Ascent, The; Blood Ties; Bloodbrothers; Boiling Point; City Heat; City of Hope; Demon (God Told Me To); F.I.S.T.; Honeymoon Killers, The; Jane Austen's Mafia; Marciano; Mr. Inside/Mr. Outside; Rocky Marciano; Seven-Ups, The; Story of Jacob and Joseph, The; 10 Million Dollar Getaway, The; Tyson
Lo Verso, Enrico: Farinelli Il Castrato; Il Ladro Di Bambini (Stolen Children); La Scorta; L'America; Moses
Lobel, Bruni: Almost Angels
Loc, Goldie: Tha Eastsidaz
Loc, Le Van: Cyclo
Loc, Tone: Ace Ventura: Pet Detective; Blank Check; Freedom Strike; Posse; Surf Ninjas
Loc, Truong Thi: Scent of Green Papaya, The
Locane, Amy: Blue Sky; Bongwater; Bram Stoker's The Mummy; Carried Away; Criminal Hearts; Cry-Baby; Ebenezer; End of Summer; Going All the Way; Implicated; Lost Angels; Prefontaine; Route 9; School Ties
Lochary, David: Female Trouble; Mondo Trasho; Multiple Maniacs; Pink Flamingos
Locke, Bruce: Lone Tiger
Locke, Nancy: Hostage
Locke, Robert: '68
Locke, Sondra: Any Which Way You Can; Bronco Billy; Every Which Way But Loose; Gauntlet, The; Heart Is a Lonely Hunter, The; Outlaw Josey Wales, The; Ratboy; Reflection of Fear; Rosie; Sudden Impact; Tales of the Unexpected; Willard
Locke, Terrence: Goodbye, Norma Jean
Lockhart, Anne: Dark Tower; Joyride; Troll; Young Warriors, The
Lockhart, Calvin: Beast Must Die, The; Cotton Comes to Harlem; Dark of the Sun (Mercenaries) (1968); Let's Do It Again
Lockhart, Gene: Abe Lincoln in Illinois; Action in Arabia; Androcles and the Lion; Big Hangover, The; Billy the Kid; Blondie; Carousel; Christmas Carol, A; Devil and Daniel Webster, The; Earthworm Tractors; Edison, The Man; Girl in Every Port, A; Going My Way; Hangmen Also Die; His Girl Friday; Hoodlum Empire; House on 92nd Street, The; Listen, Darling; Man in the Gray Flannel Suit, The; Of Human Hearts; Sea Wolf, The; Sinners in Paradise; Something to Sing About; South of Pago Pago; Star of Midnight; Strange Woman, The; They Died with Their Boots On
Lockhart, June: All This and Heaven Too; Capture of Grizzly Adams, The; C.H.U.D. II (Bud the C.H.U.D.); Colony, The (1995); Deadly Games; Gift of Love, The; It's a Joke, Son!; Lost in Space (1998); Lost in Space (TV Series); Night They Saved Christmas, The; Out There; Rented Lips; Sergeant York; Sleep with Me; Son of Lassie; Strange Invaders; T-Men; Troll; Whisper Kills, A; Who Is the Black Dahlia?
Lockhart, Kathleen: Blondie; Christmas Carol, A; Mother Wore Tights

the Fighting Lady; Retreat Hell; Shack-Out on 101; Strategic Air Command; Three Secrets; Try and Get Me; Winning Team, The
Lovelace, Tim: Legion of the Night; Mosquito
Lovell, Jacqueline: Killer Eye, The
Lovelock, Raymond: Autopsy; One Russian Summer
Lover, Ed: Who's the Man?
Lovett, Dorothy: Courageous Dr. Christian, The; Dr. Christian Meets the Women; Meet Dr. Christian; Remedy for Riches; They Meet Again
Lovett, Lyle: Bastard Out of Carolina; Cookie's Fortune; Opposite of Sex, The; Player, The; Ready to Wear; Short Cuts
Lovgren, David: Something More
Lovitt, Gordon: Lies & Whispers
Lovitz, Jon: City Slickers II; Coneheads; Great White Hype, The; High School High; Last Resort; League of Their Own, A; Mom and Dad Save the World; Mr. Destiny; My Stepmother Is an Alien; National Lampoon's Loaded Weapon 1; North; Rat Race; Sand; Small Time Crooks; Three Amigos; Trapped in Paradise
Lovsky, Celia: I, Mobster
Low, Victor: Character (Karakter)
Lowe, Alex: Peter's Friends
Lowe, Arthur: Bawdy Adventures of Tom Jones, The; Lady Vanishes, The; Ruling Class, The
Lowe, Chad: Acceptable Risk; Apartment Complex, The; Apprentice to Murder; Highway to Hell; In the Presence of Mine Enemies; Nobody's Perfect; Quiet Days in Hollywood; Silence of the Heart; Siringo; Trueblood
Lowe, Edmund: Call Out the Marines; Chandu the Magician; Dillinger; Enchanted Forest, The; Every Day's a Holiday; Good Sam; Heller in Pink Tights; I Love You Again; In Old Arizona; What Price Glory? (1926); Wings of Eagles, The
Lowe, Rob: About Last Night ...; Austin Powers: The Spy Who Shagged Me; Bad Influence; Class; Escape Under Pressure; Finest Hour, The; First Degree; For Hire; Frank & Jesse; Hostile Intent; Hotel New Hampshire, The; Illegally Yours; Living in Peril; Masquerade; Midnight Man; Mulholland Falls; On Dangerous Ground; Oxford Blues; Proximity; St. Elmo's Fire; Specials, The; Square Dance; Stand, The; Stroke of Midnight; Tommy Boy; Wayne's World
Lowe, Susan: Desperate Living
Lowe Jr., Lloyd: Warden of Red Rock
Lowell, Carey: Dangerously Close; Down Twisted; Fierce Creatures; License to Kill; Me and Him; Road to Ruin (1991); Sleepless in Seattle
Lowens, Curt: Mandroid
Lowensohn, Elina: Amateur (1995); In the Presence of Mine Enemies; Nadja; Simple Men
Lowery, Andrew: Conspiracy of Fear, The; JFK: Reckless Youth; My Boyfriend's Back; School Ties
Lowery, Carolyn: Octopus (2000); Vicious Circles
Lowery, Robert: Arson Inc.; Batman and Robin (Adventures of Batmanand Robin); Dangerous Passage; Drums Along the Mohawk; House of Horrors; Johnny Reno; Mark of Zorro, The; McLintock!; Mummy's Ghost, The; Murder over New York; Revenge of the Zombies
Lowery, William: Nut, The
Lowitsch, Klaus: Despair; Gotcha!; Marriage of Maria Braun, The
Lowry, Judith: Effect of Gamma Rays on Man-in-the-Moon Marigolds, The
Lowry, Lynn: Crazies, The; Fighting Mad; Sugar Cookies; They Came from Within
Lowther, T. J.: Perfect World, A
Loy, Myrna: After the Thin Man; Ambassador's Daughter, The; Animal Kingdom, The; Another Thin Man; Ants!; April Fools, The; Arrowsmith; Bachelor and the Bobby-Soxer, The; Best Years of Our Lives, The; Broadway Bill; Connecticut Yankee, A; Consolation Marriage; Don Juan; Double Wedding; Emma; End, The; Evelyn Prentice; From the Terrace; Great Ziegfeld, The; I Love You Again; Jazz Singer, The; Just Tell Me What You Want; Libeled Lady; Lonelyhearts; Love Crazy; Love Me Tonight; Manhattan Melodrama; Mask of Fu Manchu, The; Midnight Lace; Mr. Blandings Builds His Dream House; Noah's Ark; Rains Came, The; Red Pony, The; Shadow of the Thin Man; Song of the Thin Man; Test Pilot; Thin Man, The; Thin Man Goes Home, The; Too Hot to Handle; Topaze; Vanity Fair; Wife vs. Secretary
Lozano, Manuel: Butterfly
Lozano, Margarita: Half of Heaven; Kaos; Night of the Shooting Stars; Viridiana
Lu, Kenneth: Combination Platter
Lu, Lisa: Have Gun, Will Travel (TV Series); Joy Luck Club, The; Temptation of a Monk
Lucan, Arthur: Vampire over London
Lucas, Charlie: Tea with Mussolini
Lucas, Joshua: Class of '61; Deep End, The; Session 9
Lucas, Laurent: With a Friend Like Harry
Lucas, Lisa: Migrants, The
Lucas, Wilfred: Chump at Oxford, A; I Cover the Waterfront; Pardon Us; Phantom, The
Lucas, Will: Pharaoh's Army
Lucas, William: Vampire Cop; X—The Unknown
Lucci, Susan: Anastasia: The Mystery of Anna; French Silk; Hit Woman: The Double Edge; Invitation to Hell; Lady Mobster; Mafia Princess
Lucero, Enrique: Return of a Man Called Horse, The; Shark! (Maneaters!)
Luchini, Fabrice: Beaumarchais the Scoundrel; Full Moon in Paris
Lucia, Chip: Hospital Massacre
Luckinbill, Laurence: Cocktail; Mating Season, The; Messenger of Death; Not for Publication; Star Trek V: The Final Frontier; To Heal a Nation
Lucking, Bill: Coast to Coast; Duplicates; Kung Fu—The Movie (1986); Return of a Man Called Horse, The
Ludlam, Charles: Big Easy, The; Forever Lulu
Ludwig, Ken: Moon Over Broadway
Ludwig, Pamela: Dead Man Walking; Over the Edge; Pale Blood; Rush Week
Luez, Laurette: Ballad of a Gunfighter
Luft, Lorna: Grease 2; Where the Boys Are '84
Lugosi, Bela: Abbott and Costello Meet Frankenstein; Ape Man, The; Black Camel, The; Black Cat, The; Black Dragons; Black Friday; Body Snatcher, The (1945); Bowery at Midnight; Boys from Brooklyn, The; Bride of the Monster; Chandu the Magician; Corpse Vanishes, The; Death Kiss, The; Deerslayer (1920); Devil Bat, The; Dracula; Frankenstein Meets the Wolf Man; Ghost of Frankenstein; Ghosts on the Loose; Glen or Glenda; Gorilla, The; Human Monster, The (Dark Eyes of London); International House; Invisible Ghost; Invisible Ray, The; Island of Lost Souls; Mark of the Vampire; Murder by Television; Murders in the Rue Morgue; Mysterious Mr. Wong, The; Mystery of the Marie Celeste, The (The Phantom Ship); Night Monster; Night of Terror; Ninotchka; One Body Too Many; Phantom Creeps, The; Plan 9 from Outer Space; Postal Inspector; Raven, The; Return of Chandu (Magician, The); Return of the Ape Man; Return of the Vampire, The; Scared to Death; Son of Frankenstein; SOS Coast Guard; Spooks Run Wild; Vampire over London; Voodoo Man; Warning Shadows; White Zombie; Wolf Man, The; You'll Find Out; Zombies on Broadway
Luhr, Bill: Slayground
Lui, Elaine: Bride with White Hair, The
Luisi, James: Red Light Sting, The
Lukas, Paul: Berlin Express; Deadline at Dawn; Dinner at the Ritz; Dodsworth; Four Horsemen of the Apocalypse; Fun in Acapulco; Ghost Breakers; Kim; Monster and the Girl, The; Secret of the Blue Room, The; Strange Cargo; Three Musketeers, The; 20,000 Leagues Under the Sea; Uncertain Glory; Watch on the Rhine
Lukather, Paul: Dinosaurus!; Hands of a Stranger
Luke, Edwin: Jade Mask, The
Luke, Jorge: Foxtrot; Pure Luck; Return of a Man Called Horse, The; Shark Hunter, The; Ulzana's Raid
Luke, Keye: Across the Pacific; Alice; Amsterdam Kill, The; Battle Hell; Charlie Chan at Monte Carlo; Charlie Chan at the Olympics; Charlie Chan at the Opera; Charlie Chan at the Racetrack; Charlie Chan in Paris; Charlie Chan in Shanghai; Charlie Chan on Broadway; Dead Heat; Feathered Serpent, The; First Yank into Tokyo; Good Earth, The; Gremlins; Kung Fu (1971);

Cromwell; Dementia 13; King Lear; King Lear; Lady Ice; Last Days of Man on Earth, The; Luther; Marat/Sade; Masque of the Red Death, The (1964); Rough Cut; Seance on a Wet Afternoon; Skull, The; Telefon; Very Edge, The; Young Winston
Mager, Jad: Blue Flame
Maggart, Brandon: Christmas Evil
Maggio, Pupella: Amarcord
Maggiorani, Lamberto: Bicycle Thief, The
Magimel, Benoit: Single Girl; Thieves (Les Voleurs)
Maglietta, Licia: Bread and Tulips
Magnani, Anna: Amore (1948); Bellissima; Fugitive Kind, The; Golden Coach, The; Laugh for Joy (Passionate Thief) (1954); Mamma Roma; Open City; Passionate Thief, The (1961); Rose Tattoo, The
Magnier, Pierre: Cyrano de Bergerac
Magnuson, Ann: Before and After; Caveman's Valentine, The; Checking Out; Love & Sex; Love at Large; Making Mr. Right; Night in the Life of Jimmy Reardon, A; Sleepwalker; Small Soldiers
Magon, Leslie: Unapproachable, The
Magri, Mike: Winterbeast
Maguire, Mary: Mysterious Mr. Moto
Maguire, Tobey: Cider House Rules, The; Fear and Loathing in Las Vegas; Ice Storm, The; Joyride; Pleasantville; Revenge of the Red Baron; Ride with the Devil; Spider-Man; Wonder Boys
Mahaffey, Valerie: National Lampoon's Senior Trip; They (They Watch); Women of Valor
Mahal, Taj: Outside Ozona; Rock and Roll Circus, The; Songcatcher; Sounder
Mahan, Larry: Good Old Boys, The
Maharis, George: Desperados, The; Land Raiders; Murder on Flight 502; Return to Fantasy Island; Sword and the Sorcerer, The
Maher, Bill: Cannibal Women in the Avocado Jungle of Death; Club Med; House II: The Second Story; Pizza Man
Maher, Joseph: Evil That Men Do, The; Frankenweenie; Funny Farm; Going Ape!; I.Q.; Under the Rainbow
Maheu, Gilles: Night Zoo
Mahjoub, Hossein: Color of Paradise, The
Mahler, Bruce: Funland; Police Academy II: Their First Assignment
Mahmud-Bey, Shiek: Night Falls on Manhattan
Mahoney, Jock: Away All Boats; Battle Hymn; Cow Town; Glory Stompers, The; Land Unknown, The; Nevadan, The; Rim of the Canyon; Their Only Chance; Time to Love and a Time to Die, A
Mahoney, John: Article 99; Barton Fink; Broken Hearts Club, The; Dinner at Eight; Frantic; Hudsucker Proxy, The; Image, The; In the Line of Fire; Love Hurts; Moonstruck; Primal Fear; Russia House, The; Say Anything; Secret Passion of Robert Clayton, The; She's the One; Striking Distance; Suspect; Target: Favorite Son; 10 Million Dollar Getaway, The; Unnatural Pursuits; Water Engine, The
Maiden, Sharon: Clockwise
Maiden, Tony: Spaced Out
Maier, Tim: Raw Courage
Mailer, Stephen: Getting In
Mailes, Charles: Thundering Hoofs
Main, Marjorie: Belle of New York, The; Egg and I, The; Friendly Persuasion; Harvey Girls, The; Heaven Can Wait; Honky Tonk; It's a Big Country; Johnny Come Lately; Long, Long Trailer, The; Ma and Pa Kettle at Home; Ma and Pa Kettle (The Further Adventures of Ma and Pa Kettle); Ma and Pa Kettle at the Fair; Ma and Pa Kettle at Waikiki; Ma and Pa Kettle Back on the Farm; Ma and Pa Kettle Go to Town; Ma and Pa Kettle on Vacation; Mr. Imperium; Rose Marie; Shepherd of the Hills, The; Show-Off, The; Stella Dallas; Summer Stock; Susan and God; Test Pilot; They Shall Have Music; Too Hot to Handle; Undercurrent; Wistful Widow of Wagon Gap, The; Woman's Face, A
Maina, Charles Gitonga: Air Up There, The
Mairesse, Valerie: Investigation; One Sings, the Other Doesn't; Sacrifice, The
Maitland, Marne: Fellini's Roma; Terror of the Tongs, The; Windom's Way
Majorino, Tina: Alice in Wonderland; Andre; Corrina, Corrina; Waterworld; When a Man Loves a Woman
Majors, Lee: Agency; Big Valley, The (TV Series); Bionic Woman, The; Cover Girl Murders, The; Cowboy and the Ballerina, The; Cyborg: The Six Million Dollar Man; Francis Gary Powers: The True Story of the U-2 Spy Incident; High Noon, Part Two; Keaton's Cop; Killer Fish; Last Chase, The; Liberation of L. B. Jones, The; Norseman, The; Out Cold (2001); Smoky Mountain Christmas; Starflight One; Steel; Trojan War; Will Penny
Makeba, Miriam: Sarafina!
Makepeace, Chris: Aloha Summer; Captive Hearts; Last Chase, The; Mazes and Monsters; Meatballs; My Bodyguard; Mysterious Stranger, The; Synapse; Terry Fox Story, The; Undergrads, The; Vamp
Maker, Mike: Sore Losers
Makharadze, Avtandil: Repentance
Maki, Claude: Brother
Makkena, Wendy: Air Bud; Camp Nowhere; Death Benefit; Sister Act; Sister Act 2: Back in the Habit
Mako: Armed Response; Balance of Power; Big Brawl, The; Bushido Blade; Conan the Barbarian; Dangerous Place, A; Eye for an Eye; Fatal Mission; Highlander: The Final Dimension; Hiroshima: Out of the Ashes; Island at the Top of the World, The; Killer Elite, The; Kung Fu—The Movie (1986); My Samurai; Pearl Harbor; Perfect Weapon; P.O.W.: The Escape; Red Sun Rising; Riot (1996) (TV Movie); Rising Sun; RoboCop 3; Sand Pebbles, The; Seven Years in Tibet; Sidekicks; Silent Assassins; Tucker: A Man and His Dream; Unremarkable Life, An; Wash, The
Maksimovic, Dragan: Meetings with Remarkable Men
Makuvachurna, Dominic: Jit
Mala: Hawk of the Wilderness; Tuttles of Tahiti, The
Malahide, Patrick: Beautician and the Beast, The; Heaven; Long Kiss Goodnight, The; Middlemarch; Two Deaths; Victoria and Albert
Malanowicz, Zygmunt: Knife in the Water
Malavoy, Christophe: Madame Bovary; Peril
Malberg, Henrik: Ordet
Malcolm, Christopher: Great Riviera Bank Robbery, The
Malden, Karl: Adventures of Bullwhip Griffin, The; Alice Through the Looking Glass; All Fall Down; Baby Doll; Billy Galvin; Bird Man of Alcatraz; Blue; Boomerang; Cat O'Nine Tails; Cheyenne Autumn; Cincinnati Kid, The; Dead Ringer; Fatal Vision; Fear Strikes Out; Gunfighter, The (1950); Gypsy; Halls of Montezuma; Hanging Tree, The; Hot Millions; Hotel; How the West Was Won; I Confess; Kiss of Death; Meteor; Miracle on Ice; Murderers' Row; Nevada Smith; Nuts; On the Waterfront; One-Eyed Jacks; Parrish; Patton; Pollyanna; Ruby Gentry; Skag; Sting II, The; Streetcar Named Desire, A; Summertime Killer, The; 13 Rue Madeleine; Urge to Kill; Wild Rovers, The
Malet, Arthur: Toys
Malet, Laurent: Invitation au Voyage; Roads to the South; Sword of Gideon
Malet, Pierre: Basileus Quartet
Malgras, Frederic: Marie Baie Des Anges
Malhotra, Pavan: Brothers in Trouble
Malick, Wendie: Madonna: Innocence Lost; North Shore Fish
Malidor, Lissette: La Truite (The Trout)
Malik, Art: City of Joy; Jewel in the Crown, The; Kid in King Arthur's Court, A; Living Daylights, The; Path to Paradise; True Lies; Turtle Beach (Killing Beach); Year of the Comet
Malina, Judith: Addams Family, The; Deli, The; Household Saints
Malinger, Ross: Little Bigfoot; Sleepless in Seattle; Sudden Death
Malkiewicz, Lisa: Jugular Wine
Malkin, Sam: Johnny & Clyde
Malkovich, John: Being John Malkovich; Con Air; Convent, The; Dangerous Liaisons; Death of a Salesman; Eleni; Empire of the Sun; Glass Menagerie, The; Heart of Darkness; In the Line of Fire; Jennifer 8; Killing Fields, The; Making Mr. Right; Man in the Iron Mask, The; Mary Reilly; Messenger: The Story of Joan of Arc, The; Mulholland Falls; Object of Beauty, The; Of Mice and Men; Places in the Heart; Portrait of a Lady, The; Queens Logic;

RKO 281; Rounders; Shadow of the Vampire; Shadows and Fog; Sheltering Sky, The; Time Regained; True West
Mallais-Borris, Rose: Alligator Shoes
Malleson, Miles: Brides of Dracula; Dead of Night; Horror of Dracula; Hound of the Baskervilles, The; Knight Without Armour; Nine Days a Queen
Malloy, Matt: Dr. T and the Women; In the Company of Men; Surviving Desire
Malloy, Tom: Gravesend
Malmsten, Birger: Night Is My Future; Secrets of Women (Waiting Women); Silence, The; Three Strange Loves
Malo, Gina: Chamber of Horrors
Malone, Bonz: Slam
Malone, Dorothy: Abduction; At Gunpoint; Battle Cry; Beach Party; Being, The; Big Sleep, The; Bushwhackers; Day Time Ended, The; Last Voyage, The; Little Ladies of the Night; Man of a Thousand Faces; Nevadan, The; Private Hell 36; Rest in Pieces; Shaming, The; Sincerely Yours; South of St. Louis; Tarnished Angels, The; Torpedo Alley; Warlock; Winter Kills; Written on the Wind; Young at Heart
Malone, Jena: Bastard Out of Carolina; Cheaters; Donnie Darko; Ellen Foster; For Love of the Game; Hidden in America; Hope; Life as a House; Stepmom
Malone, Karl: Rockwell: A Legend of the Wild West
Malone, Mike: Schizopolis
Maloney, Michael: Midwinter's Tale, A; Othello; Truly, Madly, Deeply
Maloney, Peter: Robot in the Family
Maltby, Katrina: Demon Keeper
Maltby, Lauren: I'll Be Home for Christmas
Maltin, Leonard: Forgotten Silver
Mamas and the Papas, The: Monterey Pop
Mamelok, Emil: Deerslayer (1920)
Mammone, Robert: Crossing, The
Mamo, Marc: Majority of One, A
Mamonov, Piotr: Taxi Blues
Man, Method: Black and White (2000); How High
Manasseri, Michael: When Danger Follows You Home
Mancini, Al: My Summer Story; Ticket, The
Mancini, Ray "Boom Boom": Dirty Dozen, The: The Fatal Mission; Mutants in Paradise; Oceans of Fire; Opposite Corners; Search for One-Eye Jimmy, The; Wishful Thinking
Mancini, Ric: Below the Belt; Penitentiary III; Triplecross
Mancuso, Nick: Blame It on the Night; Dark Prince: The Intimate Tales of Marquis de Sade; Deathship; Ex, The; Family Matter, A; Fatal Exposure; Flinch; Heartbreakers; Invader, The (1996); Last Train Home; Legend of Walks Far Woman, The; Lena's Holiday; Lies Before Kisses; Love Songs (Paroles et Musique); Mother Lode; Nightwing; Pact, The; Past Perfect; Provocateur; Rapid Fire; Suspicious Agenda; Takeover, The; Ticket to Heaven; Tribulation; Twists of Terror; Under Siege; Under Siege 2: Dark Territory
Mandalis, Elena: Only the Brave
Mandan, Robert: National Lampoon's Last Resort; Zapped!
Mandel, Howie: Fine Mess, A; Gas; Harrison Bergeron; Little Monsters; Princess Who Had Never Laughed, The; Shake, Rattle & Rock; St. Elsewhere (TV Series); Tribulation; Walk Like a Man
Mandell, Jonathan: Zipperface
Mander, Miles: Brighton Strangler, The; Captain Caution; Fingers at the Window; Pearl of Death, The; Phantom of the Opera; Return of the Vampire, The; Road to Singapore; Scarlet Claw, The; Tower of London
Mandylor, Costas: Crosscut; Delta of Venus; Double Take; Fatal Past; Fist of the North Star; Fury Within, The; Just Write; Last Exit to Earth; Stand-Ins; Stealth Fighter; Venus Rising
Mandylor, Louis: Life 101; Price of Glory; Set-Up, The
Manesse, Gaspard: Au Revoir, Les Enfants
Manetti, Larry: Exit; Take, The; Time Served
Manfredi, Nino: Alberto Express; Bread and Chocolate; Cafe Express; Down and Dirty; In Nome del Papa Re (In the Name of the Pope-King); Nudo di Donna (Portrait of a Woman, Nude); Spaghetti House; We All Loved Each Other So Much
Mang, William: Final Executioner, The
Mangano, Athony: Exchange, The
Mangano, Silvana: Bitter Rice; Conversation Piece; Dark Eyes; Death in Venice; Gold of Naples, The; Mambo; Oedipus Rex; Teorema; Ulysses
Mangold, Ernie: I Only Want You to Love Me
Manh, Tran: Three Seasons
Manheim, Camryn: Happiness; 10th Kingdom, The
Maniaci, Jim: Cyber Tracker; Cyber Tracker 2
Mann, Alakina: Others, The
Mann, Byron: Deadly Target; Invincible; Red Corner
Mann, Gabriel: American Virgin; Cherry Falls; Outside Providence; Things Behind the Sun
Mann, Hank: Abbott and Costello Meet the Keystone Kops; Call of the Prairie; City Lights
Mann, Leonard: Cut and Run; Night School; Wifemistress
Mann, Leslie: Cable Guy, The; George of the Jungle
Mann, Paul: Fiddler on the Roof
Mann, Sam: Hard Rock Zombies
Mann, Terrence: Chorus Line, A; Critters; Critters 2: The Main Course; 10 Million Dollar Getaway, The
Mann, Tracy: Fast Talking
Mannari, Guido: Cop in Blue Jeans, The
Manne, Shelley: Five Pennies, The
Manners, David: Bill of Divorcement, A; Death Kiss, The; Dracula; Mummy, The; Mystery of Edwin Drood, The; They Call It Sin; Three Broadway Girls
Manners, Sheila: Desert Phantom; Westward Ho
Mannheim, Lucie: High Command, The; Hotel Reserve; Thirty-Nine Steps, The
Manni, Ettore: Battle of El Alamein, The; City of Women; Hercules, Prisoner of Evil; Mademoiselle
Manning, Elizabeth: Deadmate
Manning, Hope: Old Corral
Manning, Irene: Yankee Doodle Dandy
Manning, Marilyn: Eegah!; Sadist, The
Manning, Ned: Dead-End Drive-In
Manning, Patricia: Hideous Sun Demon, The
Manning, Taryn: Crazy/Beautiful; Crossroads (2002)
Manoff, Dinah: Amati Girls, The; For Ladies Only; I Ought to Be in Pictures; Ordinary People; Staying Together; Welcome Home, Roxy Carmichael
Manojlovic, Miki: Artemisia; Cabaret Balkan; Every Other Weekend; Someone Else's America; Underground; When Father Was Away on Business
Manojlovic, Zorka: Someone Else's America
Mansfield, Jayne: Dog Eat Dog; Female Jungle; Girl Can't Help It, The; Guide for the Married Man, A; Las Vegas Hillbillys; Panic Button; Pete Kelly's Blues; Promises, Promises; Single Room Furnished; Underwater!; Will Success Spoil Rock Hunter?
Mansfield, Martha: Dr. Jekyll and Mr. Hyde
Manson, Jean: Young Nurses, The
Manson, Ted: Gordy
Mantee, Paul: Illusions
Mantegna, Joe: Above Suspicion; Airheads; Albino Alligator; Alice; Baby's Day Out; Body of Evidence; Bugsy; Call to Remember, A; Captain Nuke and the Bomber Boys; Comrades of Summer, The; Critical Condition; Eye for an Eye; Face Down; Fallen Angels; Family Prayers; For Better or Worse; For Hire; Forget Paris; Godfather, Part III, The; Homicide; Hoods; House of Games; Jerry and Tom; Last Don, The; Liberty Heights; Money Pit, The; National Lampoon's Favorite Deadly Sins; Persons Unknown; Queens Logic; Rat Pack, The; Searching for Bobby Fischer; State of Emergency; Suspect; Things Change; Thinner; Three Amigos; Turbulence 3: Heavy Metal; Underworld; Up Close and Personal; Wait Until Spring, Bandini; Water Engine, The; Weeds; Wonderful Ice Cream Suit, The
Mantel, Henriette: Brady Bunch Movie, The
Mantell, Joe: Marty (1953) (Television); Onionhead
Mantle, Clive: Robin Hood and the Sorcerer
Mantooth, Randolph: Agent Red; Enemy Action; Seekers, The; Terror at London Bridge
Manuel, Robert: Rififi
Manville, Lesley: Topsy-Turvy (1999)
Manz, Linda: Days of Heaven; Gummo; Longshot (1981); Orphan Train; Snow Queen

Mao, Angela: Enter the Dragon
Mara, Adele: I've Always Loved You; Nighttime in Nevada; Robin Hood of Texas; You Were Never Lovelier
Mara, Mary: Empire City
Marachuk, Steve: Piranha Part Two: The Spawning
Marais, Jean: Beauty and the Beast; Donkey Skin (Peau D'Âne); Elena and Her Men; Eternal Return, The; Les Parents Terribles; Orpheus; Stealing Beauty; Testament of Orpheus, The; White Nights
Maranne, Cindy: Slash Dance
Marcano, Joss: Delivery Boys
Marceau, Marcel: Silent Movie
Marceau, Sophie: Braveheart; Firelight; Fort Saganne; La Boum; Leo Tolstoy's Anna Karenina (1997); Lost & Found (1999); Police; Revenge of the Musketeers; William Shakespeare's A Midsummer Night's Dream; World Is Not Enough, The
Marcels, The: Twist Around the Clock
March, Eve: Song of Texas
March, Fredric: Adventures of Mark Twain, The; Alexander the Great; Anna Karenina; Anthony Adverse; Barretts of Wimpole Street, The; Best Years of Our Lives, The; Bridges at Toko-Ri, The; Death Takes a Holiday; Desperate Hours, The (1955); Dr. Jekyll and Mr. Hyde; Executive Suite; Hombre; I Married a Witch; Inherit the Wind; It's a Big Country; Les Misérables; Man in the Gray Flannel Suit, The; Mary of Scotland; Middle of the Night; Nothing Sacred; Seven Days in May; Smilin' Through; So Ends Our Night; Star Is Born, A; Susan and God; Tick … Tick … Tick …; Wild Party, The
March, Hal: Atomic Kid, The; George Burns and Gracie Allen Show, The (TV Series); My Sister Eileen; Send Me No Flowers
March, Jane: Circle of Passion; Color of Night; Dracula: The Dark Prince; Lover, The; Provocateur; Tarzan and the Lost City
March, Matthew: Spy Game
March, Tony: Shallow Grave
Marchal, Arlette: Hula; Wings
Marchal, Georges: Death in the Garden
Marchall, Steve: Night of the Creeps
Marchand, Corinne: Cleo from 5 to 7
Marchand, Guy: Cousin, Cousine; Entre Nous (Between Us); Heat of Desire; Holiday Hotel; Loulou; May Wine
Marchand, Henri: A Nous la Liberte
Marchand, Nancy: Bostonians, The; Brain Donors; Marty (1953) (Television); Naked Gun, The; Regarding Henry; Sabrina; Soldier's Home; Sopranos, The (TV series); Willa
Marchande, Teal: Planet Patrol
Marchini, Ron: Karate Cop; Omega Cop
Marcoux, Ted: Andersonville
Marcovicci, Andrea: Canterville Ghost, The; Front, The; Hand, The; Kings and Desperate Men: A Hostage Incident; Packin' It In; Smile, Jenny, You're Dead; Someone to Love; Spacehunter: Adventures in the ForbiddenZone; Stuff, The
Marcus, Jeff: Alien Nation, Dark Horizon
Marcus, Kipp: Jason Goes to Hell: The Final Friday
Marcus, Richard: Enemy Mine; Jesse
Marder, Jordan: Walking on Air
Mardirosian, Tom: Dark Half, The
Mare, Carolyn: Driller Killer, The
Mareze, Janie: La Chienne
Margo: Behind the Rising Sun; Lost Horizon; Who's Got the Action?; Winterset
Margolin, Janet: David and Lisa; Enter Laughing; Game of Love, The; Last Embrace, The; Morituri; Planet Earth; Pray for the Wildcats; Take the Money and Run
Margolin, Stuart: Class; Fine Mess, A; Futureworld; Guilty by Suspicion; Hi-line, The; Iron Eagle II; Running Hot; Women of the Prehistoric Planet
Margolis, Mark: Boss of Bosses; End of Days; Pi; Where the Rivers Flow North
Margolyes, Miriam: Age of Innocence, The; Different for Girls; Ed & His Dead Mother; End of Days; James and the Giant Peach; William Shakespeare's Romeo and Juliet
Margulies, David: Last Breath; Out on a Limb
Margulies, Julianna: Mists of Avalon, The; Newton Boys, The; Paradise Road; Price Above Rubies, A; Traveller; What's Cooking?
Marian, Ferdinand: Jud Suss
Maric, Milan: Wounds, The
Marie, Baby Rose: International House
Marie, Constance: My Family; Selena
Marie, Jeanne: International House; Young Nurses in Love
Marie, Lisa: Frogs for Snakes
Marie, Rose: Dick Van Dyke Show, The (TV Series); Lunch Wagon; Witchboard
Marielle, Jean-Pierre: One Wild Moment; Tous les Matins du Monde; Uranus
Marienthal, Eli: Slums of Beverly Hills; Unlikely Angel
Marin, Christian: Story of a Three Day Pass, The
Marin, Jacque: Herbie Goes to Monte Carlo
Marin, Richard "Cheech": After Hours; Born in East L.A.; Charlie's Ghost; Cisco Kid, The; Courtyard, The; Desperado; Echo Park; Far Out Man; From Dusk Till Dawn; Great White Hype, The; Million to Juan, A; Paulie; Picking up the Pieces; Ring of the Musketeer; Rude Awakening; Shrimp on the Barbie; Spy Kids; Tin Cup
Marin, Rikki: Things Are Tough All Over
Marinaro, Ed: Dancing with Danger; Diamond Trap, The; Game of Love, The; Gift of Love: The Daniel Huffman Story; Lethal Lolita—Amy Fisher: My Story
Marino, Dan: Ace Ventura: Pet Detective
Marion, Beth: Between Men
Marion, George F.: Anna Christie
Marioni, Saverio: Padre Padrone
Maris, Mona: Camila (1984); Falcon in Mexico, The
Marius, Robert: Triple Impact
Markel, Daniel: Dark Angel: The Ascent
Marken, Jane: Crazy for Love
Markes, Tony: In the Aftermath: Angels Never Sleep; Welcome to Hollywood
Markey, Enid: Civilization; Tarzan of the Apes
Markham, David: Richard's Things
Markham, Kika: Wonderland (1999)
Markham, Kiki: Two English Girls
Markham, Monte: Ginger in the Morning; Guns of the Magnificent Seven; Hot Pursuit; Hour of the Gun, The; Hustling; Jake Speed; Off the Wall; Piranha
Markov, Margaret: Hot Box, The
Marks, Alfred: Valentino
Marks, Shae: Return to Savage Beach
Markus, Winnie: Mozart Story, The
Marlaud, Philippe: Aviator's Wife, The
Marley, Ben: Pride of Jesse Hallman, The
Marley, Cedella: Joey Breaker
Marley, John: Amateur, The (1982); Blade; Car, The; Deathdream; Framed; Glitter Dome, The; Godfather, The; Greatest, The; It Lives Again; Joe Louis Story, The; Jory; Love Story; Mother Lode; On the Edge; Robbers of the Sacred Mountain; Threshold; Tribute; Utilities
Marlier, Carla: Melodie en Sous-Sol (The Big Grab) (Any Number Can Win)
Marlowe, Alan: Deadly Vengeance
Marlowe, Hugh: Bugles in the Afternoon; Casanova's Big Night; Castle of Evil; Day the Earth Stood Still, The; Earth vs. the Flying Saucers; Monkey Business; Mrs. Parkington; Night and the City; Rawhide; Twelve O'Clock High; World Without End
Marlowe, Linda: Green Man, The
Marlowe, Scott: Journey into Fear
Marly, Florence: Dr. Death: Seeker of Souls; Planet of Blood (Queen of Blood)
Marmont, Percy: Lisbon; Rich and Strange; Secret Agent, The; Young and Innocent
Marnhout, Heidi: Phantasm IV: Oblivion
Maroney, Kelli: Chopping Mall; Face Down; Night of the Comet
Maronna, Michael C.: Slackers (2002)
Maross, Joe: Salzburg Connection, The
Marotte, Carl: Breaking All the Rules; Twists of Terror

Marquand, Christian: And God Created Woman; Flight of the Phoenix, The
Marquand, Tina: Game Is Over, The; Texas Across the River
Marquardt, Peter: El Mariachi
Marques, Maria Elena: Pearl, The
Marquette, Chris: Noah; Tic Code, The
Marquette, Ron: Deadly Past; Public Access
Marquez, Esteban: Ascent to Heaven (Mexican Bus Ride)
Marquez, Evaristo: Burn!
Marriott, David: Operation War Zone
Marriott, Moore: Frozen Limits, The
Marrow, Jeff: Story of Ruth, The
Mars, Kenneth: Apple Dumpling Gang Rides Again, The; Beer; For Keeps; Illegally Yours; Police Academy 6: City Under Siege; Producers, The; Shadows and Fog; What's Up, Doc?; Yellowbeard; Young Frankenstein
Marsac, Maurice: Tarzan and the Trappers
Marsan, Eddie: Crime and Punishment
Marsden, James: Disturbing Behavior; Gossip; Public Enemy #1; Sugar and Spice
Marsden, Jimmy: No Dessert Dad Until You Mow the Lawn
Marsh, Garry: Just William's Luck
Marsh, Jamie: Beethoven's 3rd
Marsh, Jean: Changeling, The; Danny, The Champion of the World; Dark Places; Fatherland; Goliath Awaits; Return to Oz; Upstairs, Downstairs; Willow
Marsh, Joan: Charlie Chan on Broadway; Road to Zanzibar
Marsh, Mae: Avenging Conscience, The; Birth of a Nation, The; D. W. Griffith Triple Feature; Home, Sweet Home (1914); Intolerance; Judith of Bethulia; Mother and the Law, The; Tall Men, The; Three Godfathers, The; While the City Sleeps; White Rose, The
Marsh, Marian: Black Room, The; Crime and Punishment; Svengali; When's Your Birthday?
Marsh, Michele: Evil Town
Marsh, William: Proteus
Marshal, Alan: Conquest; House on Haunted Hill; Howards of Virginia, The; Lydia; Night Must Fall; Tom, Dick and Harry; White Cliffs of Dover, The
Marshal, Dodie: Easy Come, Easy Go
Marshall, Brenda: Background to Danger; Captains of the Clouds; Footsteps in the Dark; Smiling Ghost, The
Marshall, Bryan: Persuasion; Return to Snowy River, Part II
Marshall, Clark: Sidewalks of New York
Marshall, Connie: Mother Wore Tights
Marshall, Don: Terminal Island
Marshall, E. G.: Absolute Power; Bridge at Remagen, The; Cash McCall; Chase, The; Compulsion; Consenting Adults; Defenders, The; Eleanor: First Lady of the World; Interiors; Ironclads; Kennedy (TV Miniseries); Lazarus Syndrome, The; Littlest Angel, The; Miss Evers' Boys; Mountain, The; My Chauffeur; National Lampoon's Christmas Vacation; Nixon; Poppy Is Also a Flower, The; Power (1986); Pursuit of Happiness, The; Silver Chalice, The; 13 Rue Madeleine; Tommyknockers, The; 12 Angry Men; Two Evil Eyes
Marshall, Everett: Dixiana
Marshall, Garry: Forever Together; League of Their Own, A; Lost in America; Never Been Kissed; Soapdish; Twilight of the Golds, The
Marshall, Georges: French Way, The
Marshall, Herbert: Black Jack; Blonde Venus; Crack-Up; Enchanted Cottage, The; Five Weeks in a Balloon; Fly, The; Foreign Correspondent; Letter, The; List of Adrian Messenger, The; Little Foxes, The; Mad About Music; Midnight Lace; Moon and Sixpence, The; Murder; Painted Veil, The; Razor's Edge, The; Riptide; Secret Garden, The; Stage Struck; Underworld Story; Virgin Queen, The; When Ladies Meet; Woman Rebels, A
Marshall, James: Don't Do It; Few Good Men, A; Gladiator; Luck of the Draw; Soccer Dog: The Movie; Ticket, The; Vibrations
Marshall, Ken: Feds; Krull; Tilt
Marshall, Marion: I Was a Male War Bride
Marshall, Mike: La Grande Vadrouille
Marshall, Nancy: Frankenstein Meets the Space Monster
Marshall, Patricia: Good News
Marshall, Paula: Hellraiser 3: Hell on Earth; That Old Feeling
Marshall, Penny: Challenge of a Lifetime; Hard Way, The; Movers and Shakers
Marshall, Peter: Guide for the Married Woman, A
Marshall, Ruth: Love and Human Remains
Marshall, Sarah: Lord Love a Duck
Marshall, Sean: Pete's Dragon
Marshall, Trudy: Married Too Young
Marshall, Tully: Ball of Fire; Cat and the Canary, The; Covered Wagon, The; Hurricane Express; Intolerance; Night of Terror; Red Dust; Two-Fisted Law
Marshall, William: Blacula; Dinosaur Valley Girls; Othello; Scream, Blacula, Scream; Something of Value; That Brennan Girl
Marshall, Zena: Terrornauts, The
Marsillach, Cristina: Every Time We Say Goodbye; Terror at the Opera
Marston, John: Son of Kong, The
Marta, Darcy: Living End, The
Martel, Chris: Gruesome Twosome
Martel, June: Forlorn River
Martel, Wendy: Sorority House Massacre
Martell, Donna: Hills of Utah, The; Project Moon Base
Martell, Peter: Cobra, The (1967)
Martellis, Cynthia: Zooman
Marthouret, François: Sitcom
Marti, Luisito: Nueba Yol
Martin, Andra: Thing that Couldn't Die, The
Martin, Andrea: Believe; Boris and Natasha; Harrison Bergeron; Hedwig and the Angry Inch; Rude Awakening; Stepping Out; Ted & Venus; Too Much Sun; Wag the Dog; Worth Winning
Martin, Anne-Marie: Boogens, The; Hammered: The Best of Sledge
Martin, Barney: Arthur 2: On the Rocks; Pucker Up and Bark Like a Dog
Martin, Bill: Television Parts Home Companion
Martin, Caitlin: Crocodile
Martin, Christopher: Class Act; House Party 2; House Party 3
Martin, Crispin: Ali Baba and the Forty Thieves; Weekend in Havana
Martin, Damon: Amityville 1992: It's About Time; Ghoulies II
Martin, Dan: Laurel Avenue
Martin, Dean: Airport; All in a Night's Work; Ambushers, The; Artists and Models; At War with the Army; Bandolero!; Bells Are Ringing; Caddy, The; Cannonball Run; Cannonball Run II; Career; Five Card Stud; Four for Texas; Hollywood or Bust; Jumping Jacks; Kiss Me, Stupid; Murderers' Row; My Friend Irma; Ocean's Eleven; Rio Bravo; Robin & the Seven Hoods; Rough Night in Jericho; Showdown; Some Came Running; Sons of Katie Elder, The; Texas Across the River; Toys in the Attic; Who's Got the Action?; Young Lions, The
Martin, Dean Paul: Backfire; Heart Like a Wheel; Misfits of Science; Players
Martin, Deena: Swingers
Martin, Dewey: Big Sky, The; Flight to Fury; Land of the Pharaohs; Men of the Fighting Lady; Savage Sam
Martin, Dick: Carbon Copy
Martin, Duane: Above the Rim; Woo
Martin, D'Urville: Black Caesar; Blind Rage; Boss; Dolemite; Final Comedown, The; Hell Up in Harlem; Sheba Baby
Martin, George: Drunks
Martin, Jared: Quiet Cool; Twin Sitters
Martin, Jean: Battle of Algiers
Martin, Jill: Hawk of the Wilderness
Martin, John: Black Roses
Martin, Keil: Hill Street Blues (TV Series)
Martin, Kellie: Matinee
Martin, Lori: Cape Fear
Martin, Maribel: Blood Spattered Bride, The
Martin, Marion: Sinners in Paradise; They Got Me Covered
Martin, Marji: Hollywood Harry
Martin, Mary: Birth of the Blues; Night and Day; Peter Pan; Rhythm on the River

Martin, Millicent: Alfie; Stop the World I Want to Get Off
Martin, Nan: Doctor Detroit; For Love of Ivy; Golden Honeymoon, The; King Richard II; Other Side of the Mountain, Part II, The; Toys in the Attic
Martin, Pamela Sue: Buster and Billie; Cry in the Wild, A; Eye of the Demon; Girls of Huntington House; Lady in Red
Martin, Richard: Arizona Ranger; Brothers in the Saddle; Dynamite Pass; Gun Smugglers; Guns of Hate; Hot Lead; Marine Raiders; Mysterious Desperado; Rider from Tucson; Road Agent; Rustlers, The
Martin, Ross: Colossus of New York, The; Dead Heat on a Merry-Go-Round; Experiment in Terror; More Wild Wild West; Wild Wild West Revisited, The; Wild Wild West, The (TV series)
Martin, Rudolf: Dracula: The Dark Prince; Fall; Swordfish
Martin, Sallie: Say Amen, Somebody
Martin, Sandy: Scalpel; Vendetta
Martin, Steve: All of Me; And the Band Played On; Bowfinger; Dead Men Don't Wear Plaid; Dirty Rotten Scoundrels; Father of the Bride; Father of the Bride Part II; Grand Canyon; Housesitter; Jerk, The; Joe Gould's Secret; Kids Are Alright, The; L.A. Story; Leap of Faith; Little Shop of Horrors (1986); Lonely Guy, The; Man with Two Brains, The; Mixed Nuts; Movers and Shakers; Muppet Movie, The; My Blue Heaven; Novocaine; Out-of-Towners, The (1999); Parenthood; Pennies from Heaven; Planes, Trains and Automobiles; Roxanne; Sgt. Bilko; Simple Twist of Fate, A; Spanish Prisoner, The; Three Amigos
Martin, Strother: Attack!; Ballad of Cable Hogue, The; Better Late than Never; Brotherhood of Satan; Cool Hand Luke; Great Scout and Cathouse Thursday, The; Hannie Caulder; Hard Times; Love and Bullets; Magnetic Monster, The; Man Who Shot Liberty Valance, The; McLintock!; Nightwing; Pocket Money; Rooster Cogburn; Shenandoah; Slap Shot; Talion; Up in Smoke; Wild Bunch, The
Martin, Todd: Finger on the Trigger
Martin, Tony: Big Store, The; Casbah; Easy to Love; Here Come the Girls; Hit the Deck; Two Tickets to Broadway
Martindale, Margo: Critical Care; What Girls Learn
Martine, Daniel: Cause of Death
Martinelli, Elsa: Blood and Roses; Hatari!; Madigan's Millions; Maroc 7; Oldest Profession, The; Tenth Victim, The; Trial, The
Martines, Alessandra: Les Misérables
Martinez, A: Cherokee Kid, The; Double Tap; Hunt for the Night Stalker; Last Rites; One Night Stand; Powwow Highway; Where's the Money, Noreen?
Martinez, Fele: Lovers of the Arctic Circle; Open Your Eyes; Thesis
Martinez, Jorge: Catch the Heat
Martinez, Mario Ivan: Like Water for Chocolate
Martinez, Melissa: Our Song
Martinez, Olivier: Before Night Falls; Chambermaid on the Titanic, The; Horseman on the Roof, The; IP5: The Island of Pachyderms; My Man (Mon Homme); Unfaithful
Martinez, Patrice: Three Amigos
Martinez, Reinol: El Mariachi
Martinez, Vanessa: Limbo
Martinez, Vincent: School of Flesh
Martini, Derick: Smiling Fish & Goat on Fire
Martino, John: Truckstop Women
Martins, Camilla: Zero Kelvin
Martyn, Greg: Ellis Island
Marut, Marc: Paperboy, The
Marvin, Lee: Attack!; Bad Day at Black Rock; Big Heat, The; Big Red One, The; Cat Ballou; Comancheros, The; Death Hunt; Delta Force, The; Dirty Dozen, The; Dirty Dozen, The: The Next Mission; Dog Day; Donovan's Reef; Gorilla at Large; Gorky Park; Great Scout and Cathouse Thursday, The; Gun Fury; Hangman's Knot; Hell in the Pacific; I Died a Thousand Times; Killers, The; Klansman, The; Man Who Shot Liberty Valance, The; Monte Walsh; Not as a Stranger; Paint Your Wagon; Pete Kelly's Blues; Pocket Money; Point Blank; Prime Cut; Professionals, The; Raintree County; Sergeant Ryker; Shack-Out on 101; Ship of Fools; Shout at the Devil; Stranger Wore a Gun, The; Twilight Zone, The (TV Series); Wild One, The
Marwa, Emil: East Is East
Marx, Groucho: Copacabana; Double Dynamite; Girl in Every Port, A; Mr. Music; You Bet Your Life (TV Series)
Marx, Harpo: Stage Door Canteen
MarxBrothers, The: Animal Crackers; At the Circus; Big Store, The; Cocoanuts; Day at the Races, A; Duck Soup; Go West; Horse Feathers; Love Happy; Monkey Business; Night at the Opera, A; Night in Casablanca, A; Room Service
Marzio, Dulio: Two to Tango
Masak, Ron: Harper Valley P.T.A.
Mascarino, Pierrino: Clockmaker (1998)
Mascolo, Joseph: Shaft's Big Score!
Masé, Marino: Commandos; Les Carabiniers
Mashkov, Vladimir: Thief, The
Masina, Giulietta: Ginger and Fred; Il Bidone; Juliet of the Spirits; La Strada; Madwoman of Chaillot, The; Nights of Cabiria; Variety Lights; White Sheik, The
Maskell, Virginia: Only Two Can Play
Mason, Connie: Blood Feast
Mason, Hilary: Dolls; Meridian (Kiss of the Beast); Robot Jox
Mason, Jackie: Caddyshack II; Jerk, The
Mason, James: Assisi Underground, The; Autobiography of a Princess; Bad Man's River; Bloodline; Blue Max, The; Botany Bay; Boys from Brazil, The; Caught; Cold Sweat; Cross of Iron; Dangerous Summer, A; Desert Fox, The; Desert Rats, The; Destructors, The; East Side, West Side; 11 Harrowhouse; Evil Under the Sun; Fall of the Roman Empire, The; ffolkes; Five Fingers; Forever Darling; George Washington; Georgy Girl; Heaven Can Wait; High Command, The; Hotel Reserve; Inside Out; Ivanhoe; Jesus of Nazareth; Journey to the Center of the Earth; Julius Caesar; Kidnap Syndicate, The; Last of Sheila, The; Lolita; Lord Jim; Mackintosh Man, The; Madame Bovary; Man in Grey, The; Mandingo; Mill on the Floss, The; Murder by Decree; Night Has Eyes, The; North by Northwest; Odd Man Out; Pandora and the Flying Dutchman; Prince Valiant; Prisoner of Zenda, The; Salem's Lot; Seventh Veil, The; Shooting Party, The; Star Is Born, A; 20,000 Leagues Under the Sea; Verdict, The; Voyage of the Damned; Water Babies, The; Wicked Lady, The; Yin and Yang of Mr. Go, The
Mason, LeRoy: Apache Rose; Federal Operator 99; Helldorado; Hidden Valley Outlaws; Mojave Firebrand; Painted Stallion, The; Rainbow Valley; Rocky Mountain Rangers; Santa Fe Stampede; Song of Nevada; Texas Terror; When a Man Sees Red; Wyoming Outlaw
Mason, Madison: Dangerously Close
Mason, Marlyn: Christina
Mason, Marsha: Audrey Rose; Blume in Love; Broken Trust; Chapter Two; Cheap Detective, The; Cinderella Liberty; Dinner at Eight; Drop Dead Fred; Goodbye Girl, The; Heartbreak Ridge; I Love Trouble; Image, The; Lois Gibbs and the Love Canal; Max Dugan Returns; Nick of Time; Only When I Laugh; Promises in the Dark; Stella; Two Days in the Valley
Mason, Pamela: Navy vs. the Night Monsters, The
Mason, Tom: F/X 2: The Deadly Art of Illusion; Men Don't Leave; Return of the Man from U.N.C.L.E., The
Mason, Vivian: Lost Planet, The
Massari, Lea: Allonsonfan; And Hope to Die; Christ Stopped at Eboli; L'Aventura; Les Choses de la Vie (Things in Life, The); Les Rendez-Vous D'Anna; Murmur of the Heart; Story of a Love Story; Vengeance
Massen, Osa: Background to Danger; Iceland; Jack London; Master Race, The; My Love for Yours (Honeymoon in Bali); Rocketship X-M; Woman's Face, A; You'll Never Get Rich
Massey, Anna: Angels and Insects; Corn Is Green, The; Déjà Vu; Five Days One Summer; Frenzy; Haunted; Peeping Tom; Sakharov; Sweet William; Vault of Horror
Massey, Athena: Shadow of a Scream; Undercover; Unspeakable, The; Virtual Combat
Massey, Daniel: Incredible Sarah, The; Intimate Contact; Love with a Perfect Stranger; Star! (1968); Vault of Horror
Massey, Dick: Commitments, The
Massey, Edith: Desperate Living; Female Trouble; Multiple Maniacs; Mutants in Paradise; Pink Flamingos; Polyester
Massey, Gina: Thrillkill

Massey, Ilona: Balalaika; Frankenstein Meets the Wolf Man; Holiday in Mexico; Invisible Agent; Melody Master (The Great Awakening) (NewWine); Northwest Outpost; Rosalie
Massey, Raymond: Abe Lincoln in Illinois; Action in the North Atlantic; Arsenic and Old Lace; Chain Lightning; David and Bathsheba; Desert Song, The; Desperate Journey; Drums; East of Eden; Fountainhead, The; 49th Parallel, The; Hurricane, The; Naked and the Dead, The; Old Dark House, The; Omar Khayyam; Possessed; President's Plane Is Missing, The; Prisoner of Zenda, The; Reap the Wild Wind; Santa Fe Trail; Scarlet Pimpernel, The; Speckled Band, The; Things to Come; Woman in the Window
Massi, Mark: Silverlake Life: The View from Here
Massie, Paul: Sapphire
Massine, Leonide: Tales of Hoffman
Masson, Damien: 2001: A Space Travesty
Master P: Foolish; I Got the Hook Up
Masters, Ben: Celebrity; Deliberate Stranger, The; Dream Lover; Key Exchange; Making Mr. Right; Running Mates
Masterson, Chase: Married People, Single Sex
Masterson, Christopher: Scary Movie 2
Masterson, Fay: Apartment Complex, The; Avenging Angel, The (1995); Cops and Robbersons; Man without a Face, The; Power of One, The
Masterson, Mary Stuart: Amazing Stories (TV Series); Bad Girls; Bed of Roses; Benny & Joon; Chances Are; Digging to China; Florentine, The; Fried Green Tomatoes; Funny About Love; Gardens of Stone; Heaven's Prisoners; Immediate Family; Lily Dale; Mad at the Moon; Married to It; My Little Girl; Radioland Murders; Some Kind of Wonderful
Masterson, Peter: Stepford Wives, The
Masterson, Rod: Delta Heat
Masterson, Valerie: Voyage en Douce
Mastrantonio, Mary Elizabeth: Abyss, The; Class Action; Color of Money, The; Consenting Adults; Fools of Fortune; January Man, The; Limbo; Perfect Storm, The; Robin Hood: Prince of Thieves; Slam Dance; Three Wishes; Two Bits; White Sands; Witness Protection
Mastrogiacomo, Gina: Tall, Dark and Deadly
Mastroianni, Chiara: Diary of a Seducer; Ma Saison Preferée; Nowhere; Three Lives and Only One Death; Time Regained
Mastroianni, Marcello: Allonsonfan; Beyond Obsession; Big Deal on Madonna Street; Blood Feud; City of Women; Dark Eyes; Diary of Forbidden Dreams; Divine Nymph, The; Divorce—Italian Style; 8 1/2; Everybody's Fine; Fine Romance, A; Gabriela; Ginger and Fred; Henry IV; I Don't Want to Talk About It; La Dolce Vita; La Nuit de Varennes; Lunatics & Lovers; Macaroni; Marriage Italian Style; Massacre in Rome; Organizer, The; Poppy Is Also a Flower, The; Ready to Wear; Salut L'Artiste; Shoot Loud, Louder ... I Don't Understand; Slightly Pregnant Man, A; Special Day, A; Stay as You Are; Tenth Victim, The; Three Lives and Only One Death; Used People; Very Private Affair, A; White Nights; Wifemistress; Yesterday, Today and Tomorrow
Masur, Richard: Adam; Believers, The; Betrayal; Burning Bed, The; Cast the First Stone; Encino Man; Fallen Angel; Far from Home; Fire Down Below; Flashback; Forget Paris; George McKenna Story, The; Head Office; Heartburn; Hiroshima; It; License to Drive; Man without a Face, The; Mean Season, The; Mr. Horn; Multiplicity; My Girl; My Girl 2; My Science Project; Rent-a-Cop; Risky Business; Shoot to Kill; Six Degrees of Separation; 61*; Third Degree Burn; Walker; Who'll Stop the Rain
Matahi: Tabu
Matarazzo, Heather: Deli, The; Princess Diaries, The; Sorority Boys; Welcome to the Dollhouse
Mateos, Julian: Four Rode Out; Hellbenders, The
Materhofer, Ferdinand: Orphan Boy of Vienna, An
Mathé, Edouard: Vampires, The (1915) (Les Vampires)
Mather, Aubrey: House of Fear; Undying Monster, The
Matheron, Marie: Come Undone
Mathers, Jerry: Trouble with Harry, The
Matheson, Hans: Les Misérables
Matheson, Michelle: Howling VI: The Freaks
Matheson, Tim: Animal House; Best Legs in the 8th Grade, The; Black Sheep; Buried Alive; Buried Alive II; Dreamer; Drop Dead Fred; Eye of the Demon; Fletch; Forever Love; Impulse; Listen to Your Heart; Little Sex, A; Little White Lies; Longest Drive, The; Magnum Force; Midnight Heat; 1941; Quicksand: No Escape; Solar Crisis; Sometimes They Come Back; Speed Zone; Story of Us, The; Tails You Live, Heads You're Dead; Target of Suspicion; To Be or Not to Be; Trial & Error (1992); Twilight Man; Up the Creek; Very Brady Sequel, A
Mathew, Sue: Dangerous Indiscretion
Mathews, Carmen: Last Best Year, The; Sounder
Mathews, Frank: On the Bowery
Mathews, Kerwin: Battle Beneath the Earth; Devil at 4 O'-Clock, The; Jack the Giant Killer; Maniac; Nightmare in Blood; Octaman; 7th Voyage of Sinbad, The; Three Worlds of Gulliver, The; Waltz King, The
Mathews, Thom: Bloodmatch; Down Twisted; Friday the 13th, Part VI: Jason Lives; Heatseeker; Return of the Living Dead, The; Return of the Living Dead Part II
Mathie, Marion: Rumpole of the Bailey (TV Series)
Mathieson, Mark: Plan B
Mathieu, Ginett: Blue Country
Mathieu, Mireille: Slightly Pregnant Man, A
Mathis, Samantha: American President, The; American Psycho; Anything for Love; Broken Arrow; Freak City; How to Make an American Quilt; Jack and Sarah; Music of Chance, The; Pump Up the Volume; Super MarioBrothers, The; Thing Called Love, The; This Is My Life
Mathot, Oliver: Demoniac
Mathouret, Francois: Hot Chocolate
Matiko, Marie: Art of War, The
Matlin, Marlee: Bridge to Silence; Children of a Lesser God; Dead Silence; Freak City; Hear No Evil; It's My Party; Linguini Incident, The; Walker
Matlock, Glen: Filth and the Fury, The
Matmore, Daniel: Mangler, The
Matsuda, Eiko: In the Realm of the Senses
Matsuda, Seiko: Sweet Evil
Matsuda, Yusaku: Family Game, The
Mattausch, Dietrich: Wannsee Conference, The
Matte, Jean-Pierre: Warrior Spirit
Mattes, Eva: Celeste; In a Year of 13 Moons; Stroszek; Woyzeck
Matthau, Walter: Bad News Bears, The; Buddy, Buddy; Cactus Flower; Casey's Shadow; Charade; Charley Varrick; Couch Trip, The; Dennis the Menace; Earthquake; Ensign Pulver; Face in the Crowd, A; Fail-Safe; First Monday in October; Fortune Cookie, The; Front Page, The; Gangster Story; Grass Harp, The; Grumpier Old Men; Grumpy Old Men; Guide for the Married Man, A; Hanging Up; Hello, Dolly!; Hopscotch; House Calls; I Ought to Be in Pictures; I'm Not Rappaport; Incident, The; I.Q.; JFK; Kentuckian, The; King Creole; Kotch; Laughing Policeman, The; Life and Times of Hank Greenberg, The; Little Miss Marker; Lonely Are the Brave; Mirage; Movers and Shakers; New Leaf, A; Odd Couple, The; Odd Couple II, The; Onionhead; Out to Sea; Pete 'n' Tillie; Pirates; Plaza Suite; Secret Life of an American Wife, The; Strangers When We Meet; Sunshine Boys, The; Survivors, The; Taking of Pelham One Two Three, The; Who's Got the Action?
Matthes, Ulrich: Winter Sleepers
Matthew, James: Animal Instincts: The Seductress
Matthews, A. E.: Iron Duke, The; Made in Heaven
Matthews, Brian: Burning, The; Red Nights
Matthews, Carole: Swamp Women
Matthews, Christopher: Scars of Dracula; Scream and Scream Again
Matthews, Dakin: Revolver
Matthews, Delane: Invaders, The
Matthews, Devon: Wirey Spindell
Matthews, Francis: Corridors of Blood; McGuffin, The; Revenge of Frankenstein
Matthews, Jessie: Candles at Nine; Evergreen; Tom Thumb; Waltzes from Vienna
Matthews, Larry: Dick Van Dyke Show, The (TV Series)
Matthews, Lester: Raven, The; Werewolf of London

Matthews, Liesel: Air Force One; Little Princess, A
Matthews, Mandy: Ratcatcher
Matthews, Terumi: Madonna: Innocence Lost
Mattox, Martha: Haunted Gold
Mattson, Robin: Are You in the House Alone?; Bonnie's Kids; Island of the Lost; Namu, the Killer Whale; Return to Macon County
Mature, Victor: After the Fox; Androcles and the Lion; Betrayed; Captain Caution; Dangerous Mission; Demetrius and the Gladiators; Easy Living; Egyptian, The; Footlight Serenade; I Wake Up Screaming; Kiss of Death; Las Vegas Story, The; Long Haul; Million Dollar Mermaid; My Darling Clementine; No, No Nanette; One Million B.C.; Robe, The; Samson and Delilah; Samson and Delilah; Seven Day's Leave; Shanghai Gesture, The; Song of the Islands; Stella; Wabash Avenue
Maturin, Jack: Blood Dolls
Matuszak, John: Caveman; Dirty Dozen, The: The Fatal Mission; Down the Drain; Ice Pirates; One-Man Force
Mau, Les J. N.: Exchange, The
Mauch, Billy: Prince and the Pauper, The
Mauduech, Julie: Café au Lait
Mauldin, Bill: Red Badge of Courage, The
Maunder, Wayne: Seven Minutes, The
Maura, Carmen: Alice & Martin; Ay, Carmela!; Baton Rouge; Dark Habits; How to Be a Woman and Not Die in the Attempt; Law of Desire; Matador; Pepi, Luci, Bom and Other Girls; What Have I Done to Deserve This?; Women on the Verge of a Nervous Breakdown
Maurer, Joshua: Tour of Duty
Maurer, Peggy: I Bury the Living
Maurey, Nicole: Day of the Triffids, The; Diary of a Country Priest; Jayhawkers, The; Little Boy Lost
Mauri, Glauco: China Is Near
Maurier, Claire: 400 Blows, The
Mauro, Ralph: They Call Me Bruce?
Maurstad, Torval: Song of Norway
Maurus, Gerda: Spies; Woman in the Moon (Girl in the Moon; By Rocket to the Moon)
Maury, Derrel: Massacre at Central High
Max, Jean: J'Accuse
Maxey, Dawn: Ringmaster
Maxwell, Chenoa: Hav Plenty
Maxwell, James: One Day in the Life of Ivan Denisovich; Terrorists, The
Maxwell, Larry: Poison; Public Access
Maxwell, Lois: Corridor of Mirrors; Haunting, The; Man with the Golden Gun, The; Saint, The (TV Series); Satellite in the Sky; Spy Who Loved Me, The; Time Without Pity; You Only Live Twice
Maxwell, Marilyn: Arizona Bushwhackers; Critic's Choice; Forever Darling; Key to the City; Lemon Drop Kid, The; Lost in a Harem; Off Limits; Presenting Lily Mars; Show-Off, The; Summer Holiday
Maxwell, Paul: Madame Sin
May, Ann: Thundering Hoofs
May, April: Thundering Hoofs
May, Deborah: Caged Fear
May, Doris: Peck's Bad Boy
May, Elaine: Enter Laughing; In the Spirit; Luv; New Leaf, A; Small Time Crooks
May, Jodhi: Eminent Domain; House of Mirth, The; Last of the Mohicans, The; Sister, My Sister; World Apart, A
May, Julie: Hot Millions
May, Lola: Civilization
May, Mathilda: Becoming Colette; Jackal, The; Letters to an Unknown Lover; Lifeforce; Naked Tango; Only Love
May, Melinda: Hot Millions
May, Tracie: Hideous
Maya, Marlo: Flamenco
Mayall, Rik: Drop Dead Fred; Little Noises; Young Ones, The
Mayehoff, Eddie: Artists and Models; How to Murder Your Wife
Mayer, Chris: Survivor
Mayer, Debra: Blood Dolls; Stitches (2001)
Mayer, Ray: Swing It, Sailor
Mayes, Judith: Deadmate
Mayes, Kevin: Lie Down with Dogs
Mayfair, Mitzi: Four Jills in a Jeep
Mayfield, Curtis: Sparkle
Mayhew, Peter: Return of the Jedi
Maynard, Bill: Oddball Hall
Maynard, John: Dark Universe, The
Maynard, Ken: Come on Tarzan; Drum Taps; Fiddlin' Buckaroo; In Old Santa Fe; Phantom Thunderbolt; Trail Drive
Maynard, Kermit: Drum Taps; Night Riders, The; Stick to Your Guns; Trail of Robin Hood
Mayne, Ferdinand: Blue Murder at St. Trinian's; Fearless Vampire Killers, or, Pardon Me, But Your Teeth Are in My Neck, The; River of Diamonds; Secret Diary of Sigmund Freud, The; Vampire Happening
Mayniel, Juliette: Eyes Without a Face; Les Cousins
Maynor, Virginia: Man Beast
Mayo, Christine: Shock, The (1923)
Mayo, Virginia: Along the Great Divide; Best Years of Our Lives, The; Captain Horatio Hornblower; Castle of Evil; Devil's Canyon; Flame and the Arrow, The; French Quarter; Jack London; Kid from Brooklyn, The; King Richard and the Crusaders; Midnight Witness; Out of the Blue; Pearl of the South Pacific; Princess and the Pirate, The; Secret Life of Walter Mitty, The; Silver Chalice, The; Song Is Born, A; West Point Story, The; White Heat; Wonder Man
Mayron, Melanie: Boss' Wife, The; Checking Out; Girlfriends; Missing; My Blue Heaven; Ordeal in the Arctic; Sticky Fingers
Mays, Terra: Zoo Radio
Maza, Bob: Fringe Dwellers, The
Mazar, Debi: Bad Love; Beethoven's 2nd; Empire Records; Frogs for Snakes; Girl 6; Hush; Inside Monkey Zetterland; Meet Wally Sparks; Money for Nothing; Nowhere; She's So Lovely; So I Married an Axe Murderer; Space Truckers; Trouble on the Corner
Mazur, Monet: Raging Angels
Mazurki, Mike: Blood Alley; Challenge to Be Free; Four for Texas; Hell Ship Mutiny; Incredible Rocky Mountain Race, The; Magic of Lassie, The; Man with Bogart's Face, The; Mob Boss; Neptune's Daughter; Night and the City; Noose Hangs High, The; Shanghai Gesture, The; Some Like It Hot; Unconquered
Mazursky, Paul: Alex in Wonderland; Enemies—A Love Story; Faithful; First Works, Volumes 1 & 2; Into the Night; Man, a Woman and a Bank, A; Man Trouble; Miami Rhapsody; Scenes from the Class Struggle in Beverly Hills; Two Days in the Valley; Why Do Fools Fall in Love
Mazzarelli, Carmelo Di: L'America
Mazzello, Joseph: Cure, The; Jurassic Park; Radio Flyer; River Wild, The; Simon Birch; Star Kid; Three Wishes
MC Lyte: Fly by Night
McAbee, Cory: American Astronaut, The
McAfee, Anndi: Ice Cream Man
McAleer, Desmond: Four Days in July
McAlister, Jennifer: Serial
McAllister, Shawn: Looking for Trouble
McAllister, Ward: Looking for Trouble
McAnally, Ray: Danny Boy; Death of Adolf Hitler, The; Empire State; Great Expectations; Jack the Ripper; Mission, The; My Left Foot; No Surrender; Taffin; Very British Coup, A; We're No Angels
McAndrew, Marianne: Bat People; Hello, Dolly!; Seven Minutes, The
McArdle, John: Gallowglass
McArthur, Alex: Devil in the Flesh; Kiss the Girls; Ladykiller; Perfect Alibi; Race for Glory; Rampage; Sharon's Secret; Urge to Kill
McAteer, Desmond: Butterfly Kiss
McAuley, Annie: Recruits
McAvoy, May: Ben-Hur; Jazz Singer, The; Lady Windermere's Fan
McBain, Diane: Donner Pass: The Road to Survival; Parrish; Spinout
McBain, Robert: Deadline
McBeath, Tom: Quarantine

McBee, Deron Michael: In the Time of Barbarians; Killing Zone, The
McBride, Alex: Rats
McBride, Chi: Cosmic Slop; Kid, The (2000); Mercury Rising
McBroom, Marcia: Beyond the Valley of the Dolls
McCabe, Ruth: Snapper, The
McCabe, Tony: Something Weird
McCaffrey, James: Truth About Cats and Dogs, The
McCain, Frances Lee: Gremlins; Lookalike, The; Question of Faith; Real Life; Scandal in a Small Town
McCall, Mitzi: Opposite Sex (And How to Live with Them), The (1993)
McCalla, Irish: Hands of a Stranger; She Demons
McCallany, Holt: Out of Line; Search for One-Eye Jimmy, The
McCallister, Lon: Big Cat, The; Red House, The; Story of Seabiscuit, The
McCallum, David: Around the World Under the Sea; Deathgame; Haunting of Morella, The; King Solomon's Treasure; Man from U.N.C.L.E., The (TV Series); Night to Remember, A; Outer Limits, The (TV Series); Return of the Man from U.N.C.L.E., The; She Waits; Terminal Choice; Watcher in the Woods, The
McCambridge, Mercedes: All the King's Men; Cimarron; Deadly Sanctuary; Girls of Huntington House; Johnny Guitar; 99 Women; President's Plane Is Missing, The; Who Is the Black Dahlia?
McCamey, Shane: Legacy for Leonette
McCamus, Tom: First Degree; Man in Uniform, A; Passion of Ayn Rand, The; Sweet Hereafter, The
McCann, Chuck: Cameron's Closet; C.H.O.M.P.S.; Dracula: Dead and Loving It; Hamburger—The Motion Picture; Heart Is a Lonely Hunter, The; Projectionist, The; Rosebud Beach Hotel, The (Nostell Hotel,The); Storyville; They Went That-A-Way and That-A-Way; Thrashin'
McCann, Donal: Cal; Danny Boy; Dead, The; December Bride; Hard Way, The; Miracle, The; Stealing Beauty
McCann, Sean: Mind Field; Tracked; Trial & Error (1992)
McCann, Tara: Dracula Rising
McCardle, Brian: Ghost and the Darkness, The
McCarren, Fred: Boogens, The; Red Flag: The Ultimate Game
McCarthy, Andrew: Beniker Gang, The; Beyond Redemption; Class; Club Extinction; Courtyard, The; Dead Funny; Dream Man; Escape Clause; Fresh Horses; Getting In; Heaven Help Us; I'm Losing You; Kansas; Less Than Zero; Mannequin; Mrs. Parker and the Vicious Circle; Mulholland Falls; New World Disorder; Night of the Running Man; Only You; Pretty in Pink; St. Elmo's Fire; Stag; Waiting for the Moon; Weekend at Bernie's; Weekend at Bernie's II; Year of the Gun
McCarthy, Holis: Civil War Diary
McCarthy, Jenny: Baseketball; Python
McCarthy, Kevin: Ace High; Addams Family Reunion; Annapolis Story, An; Buffalo Bill and the Indians; Dan Candy's Law (Alien Thunder); Dark Tower; Dead on the Money; Distinguished Gentleman, The; Duplicates; Final Approach; Ghoulies III; Greedy; Hero at Large; Hostage; Hotel; Innerspace; Invasion of the Body Snatchers; Invitation to Hell; Judicial Consent; Just Cause; LBJ: The Early Years; Love or Money?; Midnight Hour; Mirage; My Tutor; Piranha; Poor Little Rich Girl: The Barbara Hutton Story; Prize, The; Ratings Game, The; Rose and the Jackal, The; Rosie; Sleeping Car, The; Steal Big, Steal Little; Those Lips, Those Eyes; UHF
McCarthy, Lin: D.I., The
McCarthy, Nobu: Karate Kid Part II, The; Pacific Heights; Wash, The
McCarthy, Sheila: Beautiful Dreamers; Friends, Lovers & Lunatics; George's Island; I've Heard the Mermaids Singing; Lotus Eaters, The; Paradise; Private Matter, A; Really Weird Tales; Stepping Out
McCarthy, Steven: Locked in Silence
McCarthy, Thomas: Saint Maybe
McCartney, Linda: Give My Regards to Broad Street
McCartney, Paul: Give My Regards to Broad Street
McCarty, John: Vampyre (1990)
McCarty, Mary: French Line, The
McCary, Rod: Through Naked Eyes
McCashin, Constance: Nightmare at Bittercreek; Obsessive Love
McCauley, Kevin: Trees
McClain, Cady: Simple Justice
McClanahan, Rue: Baby of the Bride; Modern Love; Pursuit of Happiness, The; This World, Then the Fireworks
McClanathan, Michael: Alice's Restaurant
McClarin, Curtis: Murder Without Motive
McCleery, Gary: Hard Choices
McCleery, Mick: Twisted Tales
McCleister, Tom: Haunting of Sea Cliff Inn, The
McClements, Catherine: Desperate Prey
McClinton, Delbert: Kleptomania
McClory, Sean: Dead, The; Fools of Fortune; Island in the Sky; My Chauffeur
McCloskey, Leigh: Accidental Meeting; Cameron's Closet; Dirty Laundry; Double Revenge; Fraternity Vacation; Hamburger—The Motion Picture; Inferno
McClung, Susan: Birch Interval, The
McClure, Doug: At the Earth's Core; Deadman's Revenge; Enemy Below, The; Firebird 2015 AD; Gambler Returns, The: Luck of the Draw; Gidget; Hell Hounds of Alaska; House Where Evil Dwells, The; Land That Time Forgot, The; Maverick; Omega Syndrome; People That Time Forgot, The; Playmates; Rebels, The; Shenandoah; Tapeheads; Unforgiven, The (1960)
McClure, Marc: After Midnight; Grim Prairie Tales; I Wanna Hold Your Hand; Perfect Match, The; Strange Behavior; Superman; Superman III; Superman IV: The Quest for Peace
McClure, Shaler: Sgt. Kabukiman N.Y.P.D.
McClure, Tane: Scorned 2
McClurg, Edie: Cinderella; Dance 'Til Dawn; Flubber; River Runs Through It, A; Stepmonster
McCluskey, Kenneth: Commitments, The
McCollum, Warren: Reefer Madness
McColm, Matt: Acts of Betrayal; Body Armor; Red Scorpion 2
McComas, Lorissa: Vamps: Deadly Dream Girls
McComb, Heather: New York Stories; Stay Tuned
McConaughey, Matthew: Amistad; Boys on the Side; Contact; EDtv; Frailty; Larger than Life; Lone Star; Newton Boys, The; Scorpion Spring; Texas Chainsaw Massacre: The Next Generation; Time to Kill, A (1996); U-571; Wedding Planner, The
McCord, Hugh: Blood, Guts, Bullets & Octane
McCord, Kent: Accidental Meeting; Illicit Behavior; Predator 2; Return of the Living Dead 3
McCormack, Catherine: Dancing at Lughnasa; Dangerous Beauty; Land Girls, The; Loaded; North Star (1996); Shadow of the Vampire; Spy Game; Tailor of Panama, The
McCormack, Eric: Free Enterprise; Lost World, The; Return to the Lost World
McCormack, Leigh: Long Day Closes, The
McCormack, Mary: Alarmist, The; Backfire; Big Tease, The; Cash Crop; K-Pax; Mystery, Alaska; Private Parts
McCormack, Patty: Adventures of Huckleberry Finn, The; All Mine to Give; Bad Seed, The; Mommy; Mommy 2: Mommy's Day; Silent Predators
McCormack, Will: American Outlaws
McCormick, Carolyn: You Know My Name
McCormick, Gilmer: Silent Night, Deadly Night
McCormick, Maureen: Idolmaker, The; Pony Express Rider; Take Down
McCormick, Myron: Hustler, The; Jolson Sings Again; No Time for Sergeants
McCormick, Pat: Doin' Time; Mr. Horn; Rented Lips; Smokey and the Bandit; Smokey and the Bandit II; Smokey and the Bandit III
McCourt, Emer: Boston Kickout; London Kills Me; Riff-Raff (1990)
McCowen, Alec: Age of Innocence, The; Dedicated Man, A; Forever Young; Frenzy; Hanover Street; Henry V; Loneliness of the Long Distance Runner,The; Never Say Never Again; Night to Remember, A; Personal Services; Stevie; Time Without Pity; Travels with My Aunt; Witches, The
McCoy, H.: Regeneration

McCoy, Matt: Bigfoot: The Unforgettable Encounter; Cool Surface, The; Dead On; Deepstar Six; Eyes of the Beholder; Fast Money; Hand That Rocks the Cradle, The; Hard Bounty; Hard Drive; Little Bigfoot; Rangers; Rent-A-Kid; Samurai Cowboy; Synapse; White Wolves: A Cry in the Wild II
McCoy, Steve: I Was a Teenage Zombie
McCoy, Sylvester: Dr. Who (TV series); Leapin' Leprechauns; Spellbreaker: Secret of the Leprechauns
McCoy, Tim: Aces and Eights; Arizona Bound; Below the Border; Bulldog Courage; Down Texas Way; End of the Trail; Fighting Shadows; Forbidden Trails; Ghost Patrol; Ghost Town Law; Gun Code; Gunman from Bodie; Riding Tornado, The; Roaring Guns; Run of the Arrow; Texas Cyclone; Traitor, The; Two-Fisted Law; West of the Law
McCoy, Tony: Bride of the Monster
McCracken, Jeff: Kent State; Running Brave; Summer of Fear
McCracken, Joan: Good News
McCrae, Scooter: Original Sins
McCrane, Paul: Fame; Portrait, The; Strapped
McCrary, Darius: Big Shots
McCrea, Jody: Beach Blanket Bingo; Beach Party; Cry Blood, Apache; Glory Stompers, The; Muscle Beach Party
McCrea, Joel: Barbary Coast, The; Bird of Paradise; Buffalo Bill; Come and Get It; Common Law, The; Cry Blood, Apache; Dead End; Foreign Correspondent; Four Faces West; Great Man's Lady, The; Great Moment, The; Interns Can't Take Money; Lost Squadron; More the Merrier, The; Most Dangerous Game, The; Oklahoman, The; Our Little Girl; Palm Beach Story, The; Primrose Path; Ramrod; Ride the High Country; South of St. Louis; Stars in My Crown; Sullivan's Travels; These Three; They Shall Have Music; Union Pacific; Virginian, The
McCrena, Brittany: Taxi Dancers
McCulloch, Bruce: Dog Park; Kids in the Hall: Brain Candy
McCulloch, Ian: Dr. Butcher, M.D. (Medical Deviate); Witching Time; Zombie
McCulloch, Kyle: Careful; Tales from the Gimli Hospital
McCullough, Julie: Big Bad Mama II; Round Trip to Heaven
McCullough, Lisa: Bloodsport II
McCullough, Suli: Don't Be a Menace to South Central while Drinking Your Juice in the 'Hood
McCurley, Matthew: North
McCurry, Natalie: Dead-End Drive-In
McCusker, Frank: Railway Station Man, The
McCutcheon, Bill: Tune in Tomorrow
McDade, Ross: This Is the Sea
McDaniel, Hattie: Alice Adams; Bride Walks Out, The; George Washington Slept Here; Gone with the Wind; Great Lie, The; In This Our Life; Johnny Come Lately; Judge Priest; Murder by Television; Never Say Goodbye; Operator 13; Saratoga; Shining Hour, The; Shopworn Angel, The; Show Boat; Since You Went Away; Zenobia
McDaniel, James: Road to Galveston, The
McDaniel, Tim: Ghost Chase
McDermott, Colleen: Night That Never Happened, The
McDermott, Dylan: Blue Iguana; Cowboy Way, The; Destiny Turns on the Radio; Fear Inside, The; Hamburger Hill; Hardware; Home for the Holidays (1995); In the Line of Fire; Into the Badlands; Jersey Girl; Miracle on 34th Street; Neon Empire, The; Texas Rangers (2001); Three to Tango; 'Til There Was You; Twister; Where Sleeping Dogs Lie
McDermott, Hugh: Devil Girl from Mars; Pimpernel Smith; Seventh Veil, The
McDermott, Shane: Airborne
McDevitt, Ruth: Homebodies
McDiarmid, Ian: Chernobyl: The Final Warning; Sleepy Hollow; Star Wars: Attack of the Clones; Star Wars: Episode I The Phantom Menace
McDonagh, Sean: Closer You Get, The
McDonald, Audra: Last Debate, The; Wit
McDonald, Christopher: Benefit of the Doubt; Boys Next Door, The; Chances Are; Conflict of Interest; Dirty Work; Eighteenth Angel, The; Fair Game; Fatal Exposure; Fatal Instinct; Happy Gilmore; House Arrest; Lawn Dogs; Leave It to Beaver; Monkey Trouble; My Teacher's Wife; Paramedics; Playroom; Quiz Show; Requiem for a Dream; Rich Man's Wife, The; Skulls, The; SLC Punk; Terminal Velocity; Thelma & Louise; Tuskegee Airmen, The; Unforgettable
McDonald, Francis: Bad Lands (1939); Girl in Every Port, A; Nomads of the North
McDonald, Garry: Wacky World of Wills and Burke, The
McDonald, Grace: Gung Ho! (1943)
McDonald, Ian: Ramrod
McDonald, Jack: Don Q, Son of Zorro
McDonald, Jennifer: Clean Shaven
McDonald, Joe: Mind Killer
McDonald, Kenneth: Coast Patrol, The
McDonald, Kevin: Godson, The; Kids in the Hall: Brain Candy
McDonald, Marie: Living in a Big Way; Promises, Promises; Tell It to the Judge
McDonald, Mary Ann: Love at First Sight
McDonald, Michael James: Unborn II, The
McDonald, Peter: Felicia's Journey; I Went Down; Opportunists, The; When Brendan Met Trudy
McDonald, Scott: Jack Frost (1997)
McDonnell, Mary: American Clock, The; Blue Chips; Dances with Wolves; Donnie Darko; Evidence of Blood; Grand Canyon; Independence Day; Matewan; Mumford; Passion Fish; Sneakers; Woman Undone
McDonough, Mary: Mom
McDonough, Neal: Blue River; Grace and Glorie; White Dwarf
McDonough, Robert: Magic Stone, The
McDormand, Frances: Almost Famous; Beyond Rangoon; Blood Simple; Butcher's Wife, The; Chattahoochee; Crazy in Love; Darkman; Fargo; Good Old Boys, The; Hidden Agenda; Hidden in America; Madeline; Man Who Wasn't There, The (2001); Mississippi Burning; Palookaville; Paradise Road; Passed Away; Primal Fear; Short Cuts; Talk of Angels; Wonder Boys
McDowall, Roddy: Adventures of Bullwhip Griffin, The; Alice in Wonderland; Alice Through the Looking Glass; Alien Within, The; Angel 4: Undercover; Arnold; Battle for the Planet of the Apes; Bedknobs and Broomsticks; Carmilla; Cat from Outer Space, The; Circle of Iron; Class of 1984; Cleopatra; Conquest of the Planet of the Apes; Cutting Class; Dead of Winter; Deadly Game; Dirty Mary, Crazy Larry; Double Trouble; Escape from the Planet of the Apes; Evil Under the Sun; Fatally Yours; Five Card Stud; Flood!; Fright Night; Fright Night II; Grass Harp, The; Heads; Holiday in Mexico; How Green Was My Valley; Inside Daisy Clover; It's My Party; Keys to the Kingdom, The; Laserblast; Lassie Come Home; Legend of Hell House, The; Lord Love a Duck; Macbeth; Mae West; Martian Chronicles, Parts I-III, The; Mean Johnny Barrows; Midnight Lace; Mirror, Mirror 2: Raven Dance; My Friend Flicka; Night Gallery; Planet of the Apes; Poseidon Adventure, The; Rabbit Test; Scavenger Hunt; Second Jungle Book, The: Mowgli and Baloo; Shakma; Son of Fury; Star Hunter; That Darn Cat; Thief of Baghdad (1978); Unknown Origin; Unlikely Angel; White Cliffs of Dover, The; Zany Adventures of Robin Hood, The
McDowell, Claire: Show-Off, The
McDowell, Malcolm: Asylum; Blue Thunder; Bopha!; Britannia Hospital; Buy and Cell; Caligula; Caller, The; Cat People; Chain of Desire; Class of 1999; Clockwork Orange, A; Collection, The; Compleat Beatles, The; Cyborg 3: The Recycler; Dangerous Indiscretion; Disturbed; Eye of the Snake; First 9 1/2 Weeks, The; Fist of the North Star; Get Crazy; Gigashadow; Gulag; Hugo Pool; If ...; Jezebel's Kiss; Just Visiting; Light in the Jungle, The; Little Riders, The; Long Ago Tomorrow; Look Back in Anger; Merlin & the Sword; Milk Money; Monte Carlo; Moon 44; My Life So Far; Night Train to Venice; O Lucky Man!; Star Trek: Generations; Sunset; Surgeon, The; Tank Girl; Terminal Countdown; Time After Time; Voyage of the Damned; Yesterday's Target
McDowell, Trevyn: Middlemarch
McEachin, James: Christina; Double Exposure; Honeyboy
McElduff, Ellen: Maximum Overdrive; Working Girls
McElhone, Natascha: Love's Labour's Lost; Mrs. Dalloway; Ronin; Surviving Picasso

McEnery, John: Bartleby; Land That Time Forgot, The; One Russian Summer; Pope John Paul II; Romeo and Juliet
McEnery, Peter: Entertaining Mr. Sloane; Fighting Prince of Donegal, The; Game Is Over, The; Moonspinners, The; Negatives
McEnroe, Annie: Hand, The; Howling II ... Your Sister Is a Werewolf; True Stories; Warlords of the 21st Century
McEntire, Reba: Buffalo Girls; Forever Love; Gambler Returns, The: Luck of the Draw; Little Rascals, The; Man from Left Field, The; Tremors
McEvoy, Barry: Everlasting Piece, An
McEwan, Geraldine: Henry V; Mapp & Lucia; Moses; Oranges Are Not the Only Fruit
McFadden, Gates: Star Trek: First Contact; Star Trek: Generations; Star Trek: The Next Generation (TV Series)
McFadden, Joseph: Small Faces
McFadden, Stephanie: Love Field
McFarland, Bob: Showgirl Murders
McFarland, Connie: Troll II
McFarland, Spanky: General Spanky; Kentucky Kernels; Peck's Bad Boy with the Circus; Trail of the Lonesome Pine, The
McFarlane, Andrew: Boulevard of Broken Dreams
McFerran, Douglas: Antitrust
McGaharin, Michael: Blondes Have More Guns
McGann, Mark: Business As Usual; John & Yoko: A Love Story
McGann, Paul: Afraid of the Dark; Alien 3; Dealers; Fairy Tale: A True Story; Paper Mask; Rainbow, The; Three Musketeers, The; Withnail and I
McGavin, Darren: American Clock, The; Billy Madison; Blood and Concrete, A Love Story; By Dawn's Early Light; Captain America; Child in the Night; Christmas Story, A; Court-martial of Billy Mitchell, The; Cyborg: The Six Million Dollar Man; Dead Heat; Delicate Delinquent, The; Diamond Trap, The; Firebird 2015 AD; From the Hip; Hangar 18; Hitchhiker, The (Series); Hot Lead and Cold Feet; Ike: The War Years; Man with the Golden Arm, The; Martian Chronicles, Parts I-III, The; Mission Mars; My Wicked, Wicked Ways; Night Stalker, The; Night Stalker, The: Two Tales of Terror (TV Series); Night Strangler, The; No Deposit, No Return; Perfect Harmony; Raw Deal; Say Goodbye, Maggie Cole; Summertime; Tribes; Turk 182
McGaw, Patrick: Amongst Friends; Basketball Diaries, The; Forbidden Choices; Malicious; Scorpion Spring
McGee, Jack: Space Rangers (TV Series)
McGee, Michi: In Gold We Trust
McGee, Vic: Wizard of Mars, The
McGee, Vonetta: Big Bust Out, The; Blacula; Detroit 9000 (Detroit Heat); Eiger Sanction, The; Repo Man; Scruples; To Sleep with Anger; You Must Remember This
McGee, William: Don't Look in the Basement
McGill, Bruce: As Summers Die; Citizen's Band; End of the Line; Good Old Boys, The; Hand, The; Last Boy Scout, The; Last Innocent Man, The; Legend of Bagger Vance, The; Little Vegas; Murder She Purred; My Cousin Vinny; No Mercy; Rosewood; 61*; Timecop; Waiting for the Moon; Whale for the Killing, A
McGill, Everett: Field of Honor; Heartbreak Ridge; Jezebel's Kiss; My Fellow Americans; People Under the Stairs, The; Quest for Fire; Silver Bullet; Straight Story, The; Under Siege 2: Dark Territory
McGill, Moyna: Strange Affair of Uncle Harry, The
McGillin, Howard: Where the Boys Are '84
McGillis, Kelly: Accused, The; At First Sight; Babe, The (1992); Cat Chaser; Grand Isle; Ground Control; House on Carroll Street, The; Made in Heaven; Reuben, Reuben; Top Gun; Unsettled Land; We the Jury; Winter People; Witness
McGinley, John C.: Animal, The; Article 99; Born to Be Wild; Car 54, Where Are You? (1991); Flypaper; Get Carter; Highlander 2: The Quickening; Highway; Jack Bull, The; Johns; Last Outlaw, The; Midnight Clear, A; Nothing to Lose; On Deadly Ground; Pentagon Wars, The; Platoon; Point Break; Prisoners of Inertia; Surviving the Game; Talk Radio; Three to Tango; Wagons East; Watch It
McGinley, Sean: Closer You Get, The; General, The; Informant, The
McGinley, Ted: Blue Tornado; Covert Assassin; Daybreak (2000); Every Mother's Worst Fear; Hostage Hotel; Linda; Major League: Back to the Minors; Revenge of the Nerds; Revenge of the Nerds III: The Next Generation; Revenge of the Nerds IV: Nerds in Love; Tails You Live, Heads You're Dead
McGinnis, Scott: Sky Bandits; You Can't Hurry Love
McGiver, John: Arnold; Fitzwilly; Gazebo, The; I Married a Woman; Love in the Afternoon; Man's Favorite Sport?; Period of Adjustment; Tom Sawyer
McGlone, Mike: Brothers McMullen, The; Hardball; One Tough Cop; She's the One
McGlynn, Mary Elizabeth: Invisible Dad
McGlynn Jr., Frank: Westward Ho
McGoohan, Patrick: Baby—Secret of the Lost Legend; Braveheart; Danger Man (TV Series); Dr. Syn, Alias the Scarecrow; Escape from Alcatraz; Hard Way, The; I Am a Camera; Ice Station Zebra; Kings and Desperate Men: A Hostage Incident; Koroshi; Man in the Iron Mask, The; Of Pure Blood; Phantom, The; Prisoner, The (1968) (TV Series); Scanners; Secret Agent (TV Series); Silver Streak; Three Lives of Thomasina, The; Three Sovereigns for Sarah; Time to Kill, A (1996)
McGovern, Elizabeth: Bedroom Window, The; Broken Trust; Clover; Favor, The; Flamingo Rising, The; Handmaid's Tale, The; House of Mirth, The; Johnny Handsome; King of the Hill; Lovesick; Me & Veronica; Native Son; Once Upon a Time in America (Long Version); Ordinary People; Racing with the Moon; Ragtime; She's Having a Baby; Shock to the System, A; Snow White and the Seven Dwarfs; Summer of Ben Tyler, The; Twice Upon A Yesterday; Wings of the Dove, The; Women & Men: Stories of Seduction
McGovern, Michael: Dirty Games
McGowan, Daniel: In His Life: The John Lennon Story
McGowan, Rose: Devil in the Flesh; Doom Generation, The; Going All the Way; Jawbreaker; Killing Yard, The; Last Stop; Monkeybone; Phantoms; Ready to Rumble; Scream; Southie
McGowan, Tom: Heavyweights
McGrady, Michael: Malevolence; Operation Delta Force 2
McGrath, Derek: Bloodsport IV: The Dark Kumite; Chameleon
McGrath, Douglas: Company Man
McGrath, Frank: Wagon Train (TV Series)
McGraw, Charles: Away All Boats; Bridges at Toko-Ri, The; Cimarron; Defiant Ones, The; Gangster, The; His Kind of Woman; Horizontal Lieutenant, The; Killer Inside Me, The; Ma and Pa Kettle Go to Town; Mad Ghoul, The; Narrow Margin, The (1952); One Minute to Zero; Pendulum; T-Men; Threat, The
McGraw, Melinda: Wrongfully Accused
McGreevey, Michael: Sammy, the Way-Out Seal
McGregor, Angela Punch: Island, The; Test of Love, A; We of the Never Never
McGregor, Ewan: Black Hawk Down; Blue Juice; Brassed Off; Eye of the Beholder; Life Less Ordinary, A; Little Voice; Moulin Rouge; Moulin Rouge (2001); Nightwatch; Pillow Book, The; Rogue Trader; Serpent's Kiss, The; Shallow Grave; Star Wars: Attack of the Clones; Star Wars: Episode I The Phantom Menace; Trainspotting; Velvet Goldmine
McGregor, Kenneth: Primal Scream
McGuire, Barry: Werewolves on Wheels
McGuire, Biff: Child of Glass; Last Word, The; Serpico; Werewolf of Washington
McGuire, Don: Fuller Brush Man, The; Threat, The
McGuire, Dorothy: Enchanted Cottage, The; Friendly Persuasion; Gentlemen's Agreement; Greatest Story Ever Told, The; Incredible Journey of Dr. Meg Laurel,The; Last Best Year, The; Make Haste to Live; Old Yeller; She Waits; Spiral Staircase, The; Summer Magic; Summer Place, A; Swiss Family Robinson, The; Till the End of Time; Tree Grows in Brooklyn, A
McGuire, James: Tuck Everlasting
McGuire, Jason: Pet Sematary Two
McGuire, John: Bells of San Angelo; Invisible Ghost; Stranger on the Third Floor
McGuire, Justin: Six-String Samurai
McGuire, Kathryn: Art of Buster Keaton, The; Navigator, The (1924); Sherlock Jr.
McGuire, Michael: Blade; Great Wallendas, The; Sanctuary of Fear

McHattie, Stephen: Belizaire the Cajun; Beverly Hills Cop 3; Call Me; Caribe; Convict Cowboy; Dark, The; Death Valley; James Dean—A Legend in His Own Time; Moving Violation; Salvation; Search for the Gods; Sticky Fingers; Tomorrow Never Comes; Ultimate Warrior, The
McHugh, Darren: Broken Harvest
McHugh, Frank: All Through the Night; Boy Meets Girl; Bullets or Ballots; City for Conquest; Devil Dogs of the Air; Ex-Lady; Fighting 69th, The; Footlight Parade; Going My Way; I Love You Again; Last Hurrah, The; Marine Raiders; Mighty Joe Young; Miss Grant Takes Richmond; Mystery of the Wax Museum; Roaring Twenties, The; Stage Struck; State Fair; Strange Love of Molly Louvain, The; Telegraph Trail, The; There's No Business Like Show Business; Three Men on a Horse; Tiger Walks, A; Tomorrow at Seven; Velvet Touch, The; Virginia City
McIlwaine, Robert: Soldier's Home
McIlwraith, David: Too Outrageous
McInnerny, Lizzy: Rowing with the Wind
McInnerny, Tim: 102 Dalmatians; Very British Coup, A
McIntire, Charles: War Arrow
McIntire, James: Gone in 60 Seconds
McIntire, John: As Summers Die; Away All Boats; Call Northside 777; Cloak and Dagger; Command Decision; Far Country, The; Flaming Star; Fugitive, The (TV Series); Heroes of the Heart; Honkytonk Man; Mark of the Hawk, The; Psycho; Rooster Cogburn; Rough Night in Jericho; Street with No Name; Summer and Smoke; Tin Star, The; Two Rode Together; Walk Softly, Stranger; Westward the Women; Winchester '73
McIntire, Tim: Aloha, Bobby and Rose; American Hot Wax; Fast-Walking; Gumball Rally, The; Sacred Ground; Sterile Cuckoo, The
McIntosh, Judy: Ebbtide
McIntyre, Joseph: Fantasticks, The
McKamy, Kim: Dreamaniac
McKay, David: Girl in the Picture, The; My Name is Joe
McKay, Doreen: Night Riders, The; Pals of the Saddle
McKay, John: Assault of the Rebel Girls (Cuban Rebel Girls); Niagara Niagara; Rocket Attack USA
McKay, Scott: Thirty Seconds Over Tokyo
McKay, Wanda: Black Raven, The; Bowery at Midnight; Corregidor; Monster Maker, The; Twilight on the Trail; Voodoo Man
McKean, Michael: Across the Moon; Best in Show; Big Picture, The; Book of Love; Brady Bunch Movie, The; Casper: A Spirited Beginning; Clue; Coneheads; D.A.R.Y.L.; Earth Girls Are Easy; Edie & Pen; Flashback; Hider in the House; Light of Day; Man Trouble; Memoirs of an Invisible Man; My First Mister; Nothing to Lose; Planes, Trains and Automobiles; Pompatus of Love, The; Return of Spinal Tap, The; Short Circuit 2; Teaching Mrs. Tingle; That Darn Cat; This Is Spinal Tap; True Crime; True Identity; Young Doctors in Love
McKee, Gina: Croupier; Wonderland (1999)
McKee, Lafe: Big Stampede, The; Man from Monterey, The; Mystery of the Hooded Horsemen; Rawhide; Ride Him Cowboy; Spirit of the West; Telegraph Trail, The; Warning Shadows
McKee, Lonette: Blind Faith; Brewster's Millions; Cotton Club, The; Cuba; Dangerous Passion; Gardens of Stone; Jungle Fever; Malcolm X; Round Midnight; Sparkle; Which Way Is Up?
McKee, Robin: DNA
McKeehan, Luke: Concrete Angels
McKellar, Don: eXistenZ; Exotica; HIghway 61; In the Presence of Mine Enemies; Last Night; Red Violin, The; When Night is Falling
McKellen, Ian: And the Band Played On; Apt Pupil; Ballad of Little Jo, The; Bent; Cold Comfort Farm; Gods and Monsters; Jack and Sarah; Keep, The; Lord of the Rings, The: Fellowship of the Ring; Plenty; Priest of Love; Rasputin; Richard III; Scandal; Scarlet Pimpernel, The; Shadow, The; Six Degrees of Separation; Swept from the Sea; Windmills of the Gods; X-Men
McKelvey, Mark: On the Make
McKenna, Alex: Joey; Stupids, The
McKenna, Seana: Hanging Garden, The
McKenna, Siobhan: Hungry Hill; King of Kings (1961); Of Human Bondage; Playboy of the Western World
McKenna, T. P.: Beast in the Cellar, The; Bleak House; Caribbean Mystery, A; Portrait of the Artist as a Young Man, A; Straw Dogs; To the Lighthouse
McKenna, Virginia: Born Free; Christian the Lion; Cruel Sea, The; Gathering Storm; Ring of Bright Water; Simba; Waterloo; Wreck of the Mary Deare, The
McKenzie, Jack: Silent Mouse
McKenzie, Jacqueline: Angel Baby; Deep Blue Sea; Mr. Reliable; On the Beach; Romper Stomper
McKenzie, Julia: Shirley Valentine; Those Glory Glory Days
McKenzie, Tim: Dead Easy; Gallipoli; Thirteenth Floor, The
McKeon, Doug: Breaking Home Ties; Comeback Kid, The; Heart of a Champion: The Ray Mancini Story; Mischief; On Golden Pond
McKeon, Nancy: Lightning Incident, The; Poison Ivy; Teresa's Tattoo; Where the Day Takes You
McKeon, Philip: Red Surf
McKern, Leo: Blue Lagoon, The; Candleshoe; Day the Earth Caught Fire, The; Foreign Field, A; French Lieutenant's Woman, The; Help!; Horse Without a Head, The; House on Garibaldi Street; King Lear; Ladyhawke; Massacre in Rome; Monsignor Quixote; Mouse That Roared, The; Murder with Mirrors; Nativity, The; Prisoner, The (1968) (TV Series); Reilly: The Ace of Spies; Rumpole of the Bailey (TV Series); Ryan's Daughter; Shoes of the Fisherman; Time Without Pity; Travelling North; X—The Unknown
McKidd, Kevin: Bedrooms and Hallways; Trainspotting
McKim, Robert: Hell's Hinges; Mark of Zorro, The; Strong Man, The
McKim, Sammy: Painted Stallion, The; Rocky Mountain Rangers
McKinney, Bill: Bronco Billy; City Slickers II; Final Justice; Heart Like a Wheel; Outlaw Josey Wales, The; Pink Cadillac
McKinney, Gregory: Brilliant Disguise, A
McKinney, Kurt: No Retreat, No Surrender
McKinney, Mark: Kids in the Hall: Brain Candy
McKinney, Nina Mae: Hallelujah!; Sanders of the River
McKinnon, Mona: Hellborn; Plan 9 from Outer Space
McKinnon, Ray: Goodbye Lover
McKnight, David: Terror in Paradise
McKrell, Jim: Love at the Top
McKuen, Rod: Rock, Pretty Baby
McLaglen, Victor: Call Out the Marines; Dishonored; Forever and a Day; Girl in Every Port, A; Gunga Din; Informer, The; Klondike Annie; Lady Godiva; Let Freedom Ring; Lost Patrol, The; Murder at the Vanities; Prince Valiant; Princess and the Pirate, The; Quiet Man, The; Rio Grande; Sea Devils; She Wore a Yellow Ribbon; South of Pago Pago; This Is My Affair; Trouble in the Glen; Wee Willie Winkie; What Price Glory? (1926); Whistle Stop
McLaren, Hollis: Outrageous; Too Outrageous; Vengeance Is Mine
McLaren, Malcolm: Great Rock and Roll Swindle, The
McLaren, Mary: New Frontier
McLarty, Ron: Feud, The; Mean Streak
McLaughlin, Bill: Border, The; Duchess and the Dirtwater Fox, The
McLaughlin, Duane: Runaway, The (2000)
McLaughlin, Ellen: Everything Relative
McLaughlin, Gibb: Farmer's Wife, The
McLaughlin, Laura: Twisted Tales
McLaughlin, Mark: Crocodile
McLaughlin, Maya: Children of the Night; Morrison Murders, The
McLean, Aloka: Lotus Eaters, The
McLean, Antoine: Hurricane Streets
McLean, David: Strangler, The
McLean, Lenny: Lock, Stock and Two Smoking Barrels
McLellan, Zoe: Dungeons & Dragons; Stonebrook
McLeod, Alex: Easier Said
McLeod, Catherine: Fabulous Texan, The; I've Always Loved You
McLeod, Gordon: Saint's Vacation, The
McLeod, Ken: Deadly Target; Trained to Fight

McLerie, Allyn Ann: Calamity Jane; Living Proof: The Hank Williams Jr., Story; Shining Season, A; Words and Music
McLiam, John: Showdown; Sleeper; Split Decisions
McLinden, Dursley: Diamond's Edge
McLish, Rachel: Aces: Iron Eagle III; Pumping Iron II: The Women; Raven Hawk
McLynn, Pauline: When Brendan Met Trudy
McLynont, Karen: Mr. Nice Guy
McMahon, Ed: Fun with Dick and Jane; Johnny Carson: His Favorite Moments; Kid from Left Field, The; Slaughter's Big Rip-Off
McMahon, Horace: Abbott and Costello Go to Mars; Delicate Delinquent, The; Never Steal Anything Small
McMahon, Julian: Wet and Wild Summer
McMahon, Shannon: Blood Sisters; Pledge Night
McManus, Don: Saved by the Light
McManus, James: La Cucaracha
McManus, Michael: Eating Pattern; Gigashadow; I Worship His Shadow; Speaking Parts; Tales from a Parallel Universe
McMartin, John: Dream Lover; Greatest Man in the World, The; Murrow; Native Son; Separate But Equal; Shock to the System, A; Who's That Girl
McMaster, Niles: Bloodsucking Freaks (The Incredible Torture Show)
McMillan, Andrew Ian: Kavik the Wolf Dog
McMillan, Dawn: Zeus and Roxanne
McMillan, Gloria: Our Miss Brooks (TV Series)
McMillan, Kenneth: Acceptable Risks; Armed and Dangerous; Blue Skies Again; Cat's Eye; Chilly Scenes of Winter; Dixie Changing Habits; Dune; Killing Hour, The; Malone; Reckless; Runaway Train; Three Fugitives; Whose Life Is It, Anyway?
McMillan, W. G.: Crazies, The
McMillan, Weston: Mortal Sins (1992)
McMillin, Michael: Midnight Kiss
McMullan, Jim: She's Dressed to Kill
McMurray, Sam: Addams Family Values; National Lampoon's Attack of the 5' 2" Women; Savage; Slappy and the Stinkers; Stone Cold
McMyler, Pamela: Dogpound Shuffle; Stick-Up, The
McNab, Mercedes: Escape from Atlantis; Savage Land
McNair, Barbara: Change of Habit; Organization, The; Stiletto; They Call Me Mister Tibbs; Venus in Furs
McNally, Kevin: Berlin Affair, The
McNally, Stephen: Air Raid Wardens; Black Castle, The; Criss Cross (1948); Devil's Canyon; For Me and My Gal; Make Haste to Live; Split Second; Thirty Seconds Over Tokyo; Tribute to a Bad Man; Winchester '73
McNamara, Brendan: War of the Buttons
McNamara, Brian: Black Water; Detective Sadie and Son; Mystery Date; When the Party's Over
McNamara, Ed: Strange Tales: Ray Bradbury Theater; Tramp at the Door
McNamara, Maggie: Moon Is Blue, The
McNamara, Pat: Daytrippers, The
McNamara, Ted: What Price Glory? (1926)
McNamara, William: Brylcreem Boys, The; Chasers; Copycat; Girl in the Cadillac; Implicated; Knockout; Natural Enemy; Radio Inside; Ringmaster; Stag; Storybook; Surviving the Game; Wild Flower (1991)
McNeal, Julia: Unbelievable Truth, The
McNear, Howard: Andy Griffith Show, The (TV Series)
McNeice, Ian: Ace Ventura: When Nature Calls; Beautician and the Beast, The; Dune; Life Less Ordinary, A
McNeil, Claudia: Raisin in the Sun, A; Roll of Thunder, Hear My Cry
McNeil, Kate: Escape Clause; Monkey Shines: An Experiment in Fear; One Kill
McNeil, Scott: Sleeping with Strangers
McNichol, Jimmy: Night Warning; Smokey Bites the Dust
McNichol, Kristy: Baby of the Bride; Dream Lover; End, The; Forgotten One, The; Just the Way You Are; Little Darlings; My Old Man; Night the Lights Went Out in Georgia, The; Only When I Laugh; Pirate Movie, The; Summer of My German Soldier; Two Moon Junction; White Dog; Women of Valor; You Can't Hurry Love
McOmie, Maggie: THX 1138
McPeak, Sandy: Born to Ride
McQuade, Kris: Two Friends
McQuarrie, Murdock: New Frontier
McQueen, Butterfly: I Dood It
McQueen, Chad: Firepower; Martial Law; Money to Burn; New York Cop; Nightforce; Number One Fan; Possessed by the Night; Red Line; Sexual Malice; Surface to Air
McQueen, Steve: Baby the Rain Must Fall; Blob, The; Bullitt; Cincinnati Kid, The; Getaway, The; Great Escape, The; Great St. Louis Bank Robbery, The; Hell Is for Heroes; Honeymoon Machine, The; Hunter, The (1980); Junior Bonner; Le Mans; Love with the Proper Stranger; Magnificent Seven, The; Nevada Smith; Never Love a Stranger; Never So Few; Papillon; Reivers, The; Sand Pebbles, The; Soldier in the Rain; Somebody Up There Likes Me; Thomas Crown Affair, The; Tom Horn; Towering Inferno, The; Wanted: Dead or Alive (TV Series); War Lover, The
McQuillan, Philip: In His Life: The John Lennon Story
McRae, Alan: Three Ninjas Kick Back
McRae, Carmen: Jo Jo Dancer, Your Life Is Calling
McRae, Frank: Batteries Not Included; Cannery Row; Dillinger; Farewell to the King; 48 Hrs.; Last Action Hero, The; Lightning Jack; Sketch Artist; Used Cars
McRae, Hilton: French Lieutenant's Woman, The
McRaney, Gerald: American Justice; Blind Vengeance; Dynamite and Gold; Grey Matter; Haunting Passion, The; Murder by Moonlight
McShane, Ian: Cheaper to Keep Her; Exposed; Grand Larceny; Great Riviera Bank Robbery, The; If It's Tuesday, This Must Be Belgium; Journey into Fear; Murders in the Rue Morgue; Ordeal by Innocence; Sexy Beast; Terrorists, The; Yesterday's Hero
McShane, Jenny: Shark Attack; Watcher, The
McSkimming, Jason: Excalibur Kid, The
McSorley, Gerard: Boxer, The; Felicia's Journey
McSweeney, Kathleen: Moonchild; Zombie Bloodbath 2
McTeer, Janet: Emily Bronte's Wuthering Heights; Saint-Ex; Songcatcher; Tumbleweeds
McVay, Stephanie: Edge of Seventeen
McVicar, Daniel: Alone in the Woods; Guardian Angel
McWhirter, Jillian: Beyond the Call of Duty; Dentist 2, The: Brace Yourself; Dune Warriors; Last Man Standing; Progeny; Stranglehold
McWilliams, Caroline: Rage
Meacham, Anne: Lilith
Mead, Courtland: Dragonworld; Stephen King's The Shining
Meade, Julia: Zotz!
Meade, Mary: T-Men
Meadows, Audrey: Honeymooners, The: Lost Episodes (TV Series); Honeymooners, The (TV Series); That Touch of Mink
Meadows, Jayne: Alice in Wonderland; Alice Through the Looking Glass; Enchantment; James Dean—A Legend in His Own Time; Lady in the Lake; Murder by Numbers (1989); Norman … Is That You?; Story of Us, The; Undercurrent
Meadows, Joyce: Brain from Planet Arous, The; Zebra in the Kitchen
Meadows, Kristen: Zero Tolerance
Meadows, Stephen: Sunstroke; Ultraviolet
Meadows, Tim: Ladies Man, The (2000)
Meager, Jill: 4:50 From Paddington
Meagher, Karen: Experience Preferred … But Not Essential; Threads
Meaney, Colm: Claire Dolan; Con Air; Doctor Quinn Medicine Woman; Englishman Who Went up a Hill But Came down a Mountain, The; Far and Away; 4 Days; Into the West; Money Kings; Monument Ave.; Mystery, Alaska; Road to Wellville, The; Scarlett; Snapper, The; Summer Fling; Under Siege; Van, The
Means, Angela: House Party 3
Means, Russell: Buffalo Girls; Last of the Mohicans, The; Pathfinder, The; Windrunner
Meara, Anne: Daytrippers, The; Heavyweights; Longshot, The (1985); Lovers and Other Strangers; My Little Girl; Out-of-Town-

ers, The (1970); Search for One-Eye Jimmy, The; That's Adequate
Meat Loaf: Black Dog; Everything That Rises; Fight Club; Leap of Faith; Mighty, The; Motorama; Outside Ozona; Rocky Horror Picture Show, The; Spice World; Squeeze, The; Stand by Me; To Catch a Yeti; Wayne's World
Medak, Karen: Galaxies Are Colliding; Treacherous Crossing
Medeiros, Michale: Infested (Ticks)
Mederov, Talai: Beshkempir, The Adopted Son
Medford, Kay: Ensign Pulver; Face in the Crowd, A; Funny Girl
Medina, Ofelia: Frida
Medina, Patricia: Abbott and Costello in the Foreign Legion; Botany Bay; Francis, the Talking Mule; Hotel Reserve; Jackpot, The; Latitude Zero; Mr. Arkadin (Confidential Report); Snow White and the Three Stooges; Thriller (TV Series)
Medway, Heather: Serpent's Lair
Medwetz, Anthony: Clockmaker (1998)
Medwin, Michael: Rattle of a Simple Man; Scrooge
Meed, Geoff: Kickboxer 5: Redemption
Meehan, Danny: Don't Drink the Water
Meek, Donald: Air Raid Wardens; Bathing Beauty; Blondie Takes a Vacation; Colonel Effingham's Raid; Du Barry Was a Lady; Hollywood Cavalcade; Jesse James; Keeper of the Flame; Little Miss Broadway; Love on the Run; Make a Wish; Mrs. Wiggs of the Cabbage Patch; Murder at the Vanities; Return of Frank James, The; Return of Peter Grimm, The; Romance in Manhattan; Stagecoach; State Fair; They Got Me Covered; Thin Man Goes Home, The; Toast of New York, The; Young Mr. Lincoln
Meek, Jeff: Night of the Cyclone
Meeker, George: Apache Rose; Hips, Hips, Hooray; Murder by Television; Night of Terror; Seven Doors to Death; Song of Nevada; Superman—The Serial; Tarzan's Revenge
Meeker, Ralph: Alpha Incident, The; Anderson Tapes, The; Battle Shock; Birds of Prey; Brannigan; Dead Don't Die, The; Detective, The; Food of the Gods; Four in a Jeep; Gentle Giant; Kiss Me Deadly; Mind Snatchers, The; My Boys Are Good Boys; Naked Spur, The; Night Games; Paths of Glory; Run of the Arrow; St. Valentine's Day Massacre, The; Winter Kills
Meeks, Edith: Poison
Meeks, Edward: Blood of the Hunter
Meffre, Armand: Blue Country; Here Comes Santa Claus
Megna, John: Ratings Game, The; To Kill a Mockingbird
Megowan, Don: Creation of the Humanoids; Lawless Street, A
Mehaffey, Blanche: Battling Orioles, The
Mehler, Tobias: Inspectors, The
Mehri, Jalal: Fearless Tiger
Meier, Shane: Andre
Meighan, Thomas: Male and Female
Meillon, John: Cars That Eat People (The Cars That Ate Paris); "Crocodile" Dundee; "Crocodile" Dundee II; Everlasting Secret Family, The; Fourth Wish, The; Frenchman's Farm; Ride a Wild Pony; Walkabout; Wild Duck, The
Meineke, Eva Marie: César and Rosalie
Meininger, Frederique: Lover, The
Meira, Tarcisio: Boca
Meisner, Gunter: In a Glass Cage
Mejia, Alfonso: Los Olvidados
Mekhralieva, Susanna: Prisoner of the Mountains
Melamed, Fred: Suspect
Melato, Mariangela: By the Blood of Others; Love and Anarchy; Seduction of Mimi, The; Summer Night; Swept Away; To Forget Venice
Melchior, Lauritz: Luxury Liner; This Time For Keeps; Thrill of a Romance; Two Sisters from Boston
Meldrum, Wendel: Hush Little Baby; Sodbusters
Melendez, Asdrubal: Very Old Man with Enormous Wings, A
Melendez, Ron: Children of the Corn III: Urban Harvest
Melford, Kim: Corvette Summer
Melia, Joe: Hitchhiker's Guide to the Galaxy, The; Privates on Parade; Sakharov
Melito, Joseph: 12 Monkeys
Mell, Marisa: Danger: Diabolik
Mellaney, Victor: Cyborg Soldier
Mellencamp, John: Falling from Grace
Melles, Sunnyi: 38 Vienna Before the Fall
Mellinger, Leonie: Lion and the Hawk, The
Mello, Breno: Black Orpheus
Mello, Tamara: Tortilla Soup
Melonas, Mac: Kid Called Danger, A
Meloni, Christopher: Bound; Souler Opposite, The; Wet Hot American Summer
Melson, Sara: Low Life, The
Melton, Sid: Lost Continent, The
Melville, Sam: Roughnecks
Melvin, Allan: Sgt. Bilko (TV Series)
Melvin, Murray: Taste of Honey, A
Memel, Steve: Savage Justice
Memphis, Ricky: La Scorta
Menchikov, Oleg: Burnt by the Sun; East-West
Mendaille, David: Kameradschaft
Mendel, Stephen: Midnight Heat; Provocateur
Mendelsohn, Ben: Cosi; Efficiency Expert, The (Spotswood)
Mendelson, Braddon: Nudist Colony of the Dead
Mendenhall, David: Going Bananas; Over the Top; Space Raiders; Streets; They Still Call Me Bruce
Mendes, Eva: All About the Benjamins
Mendez, Eva: Children of the Corn V: Fields of Terror
Mendez, Ray: Fast, Cheap and Out of Control
Mendonca, Mauro: Dona Flor and Her Two Husbands
Menese, Jose: Flamenco
Ménez, Bernard: Dracula and Son
Mengatti, John: Knights of the City; Meatballs Part II
Menglet, Alex: Georgia
Menina, Asha: House of Cards
Menjou, Adolphe: Across the Wide Missouri; Ambassador's Daughter, The; Are Parents People?; Bundle of Joy; Farewell to Arms, A; Front Page, The; Gold Diggers of 1935; Golden Boy; Goldwyn Follies, The; Hucksters, The; I Married a Woman; Letter of Introduction; Little Miss Marker; Marriage Circle, The; Milky Way, The; Morning Glory; Morocco; My Dream Is Yours; One Hundred Men and a Girl; One in a Million; Paths of Glory; Pollyanna; Roxie Hart; Sheik, The; Sorrows of Satan, The; Star Is Born, A; State of the Union; Step Lively; Swan, The; Three Musketeers, The; To Please a Lady; Woman of Paris, A; You Were Never Lovelier
Menshikov, Oleg: Prisoner of the Mountains
Menuhin, Yehudi: Magic Bow, The
Menzies, Heather: Captain America; Piranha
Menzies, Robert: Cactus
Meoli, Christian: Low Life, The
Mer, Juliano: Under the Domim Tree
Merasty, Bill: Legends of the North
Mercado, Patrick: Dreamlife of Angels, The
Merce, Jose: Flamenco
Mercer, Beryl: Cavalcade; Public Enemy; Supernatural
Mercer, Frances: Annabel Takes a Tour; Mad Miss Manton, The; Smashing the Rackets; Vivacious Lady
Mercer, Marian: Out on a Limb
Merchant, Veronica: Deep Crimson
Merchant, Vivien: Homecoming, The (1973); Offence, The; Under Milk Wood
Mercier, Michele: Call of the Wild; Global Affair, A; Shoot the Piano Player
Merckens, Marijke: Flight of Rainbirds, A
Mercouri, Melina: Dream of Passion, A; Nasty Habits; Never on Sunday; Once Is Not Enough; Stella; Topkapi
Mercure, Jean: Baxter
Mercure, Monique: Tramp at the Door
Mercurio, Micole: Turn of the Screw, The (1989); While You Were Sleeping
Mercurio, Paul: Anything for Love; Back of Beyond; Dark Planet; Exit to Eden; First 9 1/2 Weeks, The; Joseph; Strictly Ballroom; Welcome to Woop Woop
Mereader, Maria: Pardon My Trunk (Hello Elephant!)
Meredith, Burgess: Advise and Consent; Batman; Big Hand for the Little Lady, A; Burnt Offerings; Clash of the Titans; Day of the Locust, The; Diary of a Chambermaid; Foul Play; Full Moon in Blue Water; Great Bank Hoax, The; Grumpier Old Men;

the Unknown; Perils from Planet Mongo); Mrs. Wiggs of the Cabbage Patch; Mystery Ranch; Oklahoma Kid, The; Stick to Your Guns; Strangler of the Swamp; Tomorrow at Seven; Virginia City; Wyoming Outlaw; Yodelin' Kid from Pine Ridge
Middleton, Noelle: Carrington, V. C.
Middleton, Ray: Jubilee Trail; Lady for a Night; Lady from Louisiana
Middleton, Robert: Big Hand for the Little Lady, A; Court Jester, The; Friendly Persuasion; Law and Jake Wade, The; Lonely Man, The; Which Way to the Front?
Midkiff, Dale: Air Bud: World Pup; Any Place But Home; Blackmail; Elvis and Me; Love Potion #9; Magnificent Seven, The (TV Series); Pet Sematary; Visitors of the Night
Midler, Bette: Beaches; Bette Midler—Art or Bust; Big Business; Divine Madness; Down and Out in Beverly Hills; Drowning Mona; First Wives Club, The; For the Boys; Get Shorty; Gypsy; Hocus Pocus; Isn't She Great; Jinxed; Outrageous Fortune; Rose, The; Ruthless People; Scenes from a Mall; Stella; That Old Feeling
Midnite, Ethelbah: Escape to White Mountain
Mifune, Toshiro: Bad Sleep Well, The; Bushido Blade; Challenge, The; Drunken Angel; Grand Prix; Hell in the Pacific; Hidden Fortress, The; High and Low; Idiot, The; Journey of Honor; Life of Oharu; Lower Depths, The (1957); 1941; Paper Tiger; Picture Bride; Rashomon; Red Beard; Red Lion; Red Sun; Rikisha-Man; Samurai Saga; Samurai Trilogy, The; Sanjuro; Seven Samurai, The; Shadow of the Wolf; Shogun (Full-Length Version); Stray Dog; Sword of Doom; Throne of Blood; Winter Kills; Yojimbo; Zatoichi vs. Yojimbo
Migenes-Johnson, Julia: Bizet's Carmen; Mack the Knife
Mighty Clouds of Joy: Gospel
Miguel, Joelle: Four Adventures of Reinette and Mirabelle
Mihashi, Tatsuya: High and Low; What's Up, Tiger Lily?
Mihok, Dash: Thin Red Line, The; Whiteboyz
Mikani, Piro: L'America
Mikhailov, Viktor: Window to Paris
Mikhalkov, Andrej: Andrei Rublev
Mikhalkov, Nadia: Burnt by the Sun
Mikhalkov, Nikita: Burnt by the Sun; Siberiade
Miko, Izabella: Forsaken, The
Mikolaichuk, Ivan: Shadows of Forgotten Ancestors
Mikuni, Rentaro: Burmese Harp, The; Rikyu
Milan, Frank: Pals of the Saddle
Milan, George: Merlin's Shop of Mystical Wonders
Milan, Lita: I, Mobster; Left Handed Gun, The; Naked in the Sun; Never Love a Stranger; Poor White Trash
Milano, Alyssa: Body Count (1997) (direct to video); Canterville Ghost, The; Casualties of Love: The Long Island Lolita Story; Commando; Confessions of a Sorority Girl; Conflict of Interest; Dance 'Til Dawn; Embrace of the Vampire; Fear; Hugo Pool; Little Sister; Poison Ivy 2: Lily; Where the Day Takes You
Milano, Robert: Midnight Kiss
Miles, Adrianna: Werewolf
Miles, Bernard: Great Expectations; Never Let Me Go; Sapphire; Tom Thumb
Miles, Betty: Driftin' Kid
Miles, Chris Cleary: Second Best
Miles, Elaine: Northern Exposure (TV Series)
Miles, Joanna: American Clock, The; As Is; Blackout; Born Innocent; Bug; Friday the 13th: The Orphan; Heart of Justice; Judge Dredd; Ultimate Warrior, The; Water Engine, The
Miles, Kevin: Boulevard of Broken Dreams; Cars That Eat People (The Cars That Ate Paris)
Miles, Lillian: Reefer Madness
Miles, Peter: Red Pony, The
Miles, Sarah: Big Sleep, The; Blow-Up; Ghost in Monte Carlo, A; Hope and Glory; Lady Caroline Lamb; Man Who Loved Cat Dancing, The; Ordeal by Innocence; Queenie; Ryan's Daughter; Sailor Who Fell from Grace with the Sea,The; Servant, The; Silent Touch, The; Steaming; Those Magnificent Men in Their Flying Machines; Venom; White Mischief
Miles, Sherry: Velvet Vampire, The
Miles, Sylvia: Crossing Delancey; Denise Calls Up; Farewell My Lovely; Funhouse, The; Heat; Last Movie, The (Chinchero); Midnight Cowboy; 92 in the Shade; No Big Deal; Sentinel, The; She-Devil; Spike of Bensonhurst; Who Killed Mary What's 'Er Name?
Miles, Vera: And I Alone Survived; Autumn Leaves; Back Street; Brainwaves; Castaway Cowboy, The; FBI Story, The; Fire!; Follow Me, Boys!; Gentle Giant; Hellfighters; Man Who Shot Liberty Valance, The; Our Family Business; Outer Limits, The (TV Series); Psycho; Psycho II; Roughnecks; Run for the Roses (Thoroughbred); Searchers, The; Separate Lives; Sergeant Ryker; Those Calloways; Tiger Walks, A; Wrong Man, The
Milford, John: Chinese Web, The
Milford, Kim: Laserblast
Milford, Penelope: Blood Link; Cold Justice; Coming Home; Golden Seal, The; Last Word, The; Oldest Living Graduate, The; Rosie
Milian, Tomas: Blood and Guns (Tepepa); Boccaccio 70; Cat Chaser; Cop in Blue Jeans, The; Havana; Nails; Salome; Sonny and Jed; Winter Kills
Milicevic, Ivana: Head Over Heels
Milius, John: First Works, Volumes 1 & 2
Miljan, John: Belle of the Nineties; Charlie Chan in Paris; Emma; Ghost Walks, The; Lone Ranger and the Lost City of Gold, The; Mississippi; What! No Beer?
Millais, Hugh: Dogs of War, The
Millan, Tomas: Marilyn & Bobby: Her Final Affair
Millan, Victor: Boulevard Nights
Milland, Ray: Ambassador Bill; Attic, The; Beau Geste; Blackout; Blonde Crazy; Bugles in the Afternoon; Bulldog Drummond Escapes; Charlie Chan in London; Circle of Danger; Copper Canyon; Cruise into Terror; Dead Don't Die, The; Dial M for Murder; Doctor Takes a Wife, The; Escape to Witch Mountain; Everything Happens at Night; Forever and a Day; Frogs; Game for Vultures; Golden Earrings; It Happens Every Spring; Last Tycoon, The; Life of Her Own, A; Lisbon; Lost Weekend, The; Love Story; Man Alone, A; Masks of Death; Oliver's Story; Our Family Business; Panic in the Year Zero; Premature Burial, The; Quick, Let's Get Married; Reap the Wild Wind; Slavers; Starflight One; Swiss Conspiracy, The; Terror in the Wax Museum; Thief, The; Three Smart Girls; Uncanny, The; Uninvited, The; We're Not Dressing; Woman of Distinction, A; X (The Man with the X-Ray Eyes)
Millar, Marjie: When Gangland Strikes
Millardet, Patricia: Covert Assassin
Millbrook, Leo: My Magic Dog
Miller, Adelaide: Lonely in America
Miller, Allan: Warlock
Miller, Andrew: Cube; Last of the Dogmen
Miller, Ann: Easter Parade; Hit the Deck; Kiss Me Kate; Kissing Bandit, The; Lovely to Look At; Melody Ranch; Mulholland Drive; On the Town; Opposite Sex, The (1956); Room Service; Small Town Girl; Stage Door; Texas Carnival; That's Entertainment! III; Too Many Girls; Two Tickets to Broadway; Watch the Birdie; You Can't Take It with You
Miller, Barry: Fame; Peggy Sue Got Married; Sicilian, The
Miller, Bean: Rangers
Miller, Charles: Being Human; Little Kidnappers; Road to Ruin, The (1928)
Miller, Cheryl: Clarence, the Cross-Eyed Lion; Dr. Death: Seeker of Souls
Miller, Christa: Operator, The; Smiling Fish & Goat on Fire
Miller, David: Attack of the Killer Tomatoes; Ernest in the Army
Miller, Dean: Because You're Mine; Small Town Girl
Miller, Denise: Sooner or Later
Miller, Dennis: Disclosure; Joe Dirt; Madhouse; Murder at 1600; Net, The; Never Talk to Strangers; Tales from the Crypt Presents Bordello of Blood
Miller, Denny: Party, The
Miller, Dick: Apache Woman; Bucket of Blood, A; Carnival Rock; Dr. Heckyl and Mr. Hype; Evil Toons; Explorers; Far from Home; Ghost Writer; Gremlins; Gremlins 2: The New Batch; Gunslinger; Happy Hooker Goes Hollywood, The; Heart Like a Wheel; Hollywood Boulevard; Little Shop of Horrors, The

(1960); Matinee; Moving Violation; Mr. Billion; Night of the Creeps; Quake; Sorority Girl; Summer School Teachers; Trip, The; War of the Satellites; White Dog; Young Nurses, The
Miller, Elise: Lola's Game
Miller, Eve: Big Trees, The; Kansas Pacific; Winning Team, The
Miller, Frank: Jugular Wine
Miller, Garry: Amazing Mr. Blunden, The
Miller, Gary: Darkness
Miller, Glenn: Orchestra Wives
Miller, Helen: Being Human
Miller, Henry: Henry Miller Odyssey
Miller, Jason: Best Little Girl in the World, The; Dain Curse, The; Eternal, The; Exorcist, The; Light of Day; Mommy; Monsignor; Murdered Innocence; Ninth Configuration, The; Rudy; Toy Soldiers; Vengeance
Miller, Jean: Speak of the Devil
Miller, Jennifer: Terminal Impact
Miller, Jeremy: Emanon; Willies, The
Miller, John: Undefeatable
Miller, Jonny Lee: Afterglow; Behind the Lines; Dead Man's Walk; Dracula 2000; Hackers; Love, Honor & Obey; Mansfield Park; Plunkett & Macleane; Retribution; Trainspotting
Miller, Joshua: And You Thought Your Parents Were Weird
Miller, Kathleen: Fighting Mad; Strange New World
Miller, Kristine: Jungle Patrol
Miller, Larissa: Escape Under Pressure
Miller, Larry: Big Tease, The; Chairman of the Board; Corrina, Corrina; Dream Lover; Favor, The; For Richer or Poorer; Max Keeble's Big Move; Necessary Roughness; Nutty Professor, The; Nutty Professor II: The Klumps; Suburban Commando; 10 Things I Hate About You; Undercover Blues
Miller, Linda G.: Night of the Juggler
Miller, Lydia: Backlash
Miller, Mark: Ginger in the Morning; Mr. Sycamore; Savannah Smiles
Miller, Mark Thomas: Blue de Ville; Misfits of Science; Mom; Ski School
Miller, Marvin: Dead Reckoning; Hell Squad; Off Limits; Red Planet Mars
Miller, Mary: After Pilkington
Miller, Michael: Doc Savage ... , The Man of Bronze
Miller, Mike: Blastfighter
Miller, Patsy Ruth: Hunchback of Notre Dame, The
Miller, Penelope Ann: Adventures in Babysitting; Along Came a Spider; Along for the Ride; Awakenings; Break Up; Carlito's Way; Chaplin; Dead-Bang; Dead in a Heartbeat; Downtown; Freshman, The; Full Disclosure; Gun in Betty Lou's Handbag, The; Kindergarten Cop; Last Don, The; Little City; Other People's Money; Outside Ozona; Relic, The; Rocky Marciano; Ruby Bridges; Shadow, The; Witch Hunt; Year of the Comet
Miller, Rebecca: Consenting Adults; Murder of Mary Phagan, The; Wind (1992)
Miller, Roger: Lucky Luke
Miller, Sherry: Rent-A-Kid; Sabrina, the Teenage Witch; Scandalous Me: The Jacqueline Susann Story
Miller, Stephen E.: Home Is Where the Hart Is
Miller, Ty: Trancers 5: Sudden Deth; Trancers 4: Jack of Swords
Miller, Valarie Rae: All About the Benjamins
Miller, Walter: Dick Tracy's G-Men; Ghost Patrol; Ivory-Handled Gun, The; Lawless Valley; Lone Defender, The; Shadow of the Eagle; Street Scene
Millet, Christiane: Taste of Others, The
Millian, Andra: Stacy's Knights
Millican, James: Beyond the Purple Hills; Rimfire; Winning Team, The
Milligan, Spike: Alice's Adventures in Wonderland; Down Among the "Z" Men; Ghost in the Noonday Sun; To See Such Fun
Milliken, Angie: Dead Heart
Mills, Alley: Going Berserk; Tainted Blood
Mills, Donna: Alice Through the Looking Glass; Bunco; Curse of the Black Widow; False Arrest; Fire!; Haunts of the Very Rich; Incident, The; Murph the Surf; Play Misty for Me; Runaway Father; Stepford Husbands, The; Who Is the Black Dahlia?
Mills, Eddie: Dancer, Texas: Pop. 81
Mills, Hayley: Appointment with Death; Back Home; Chalk Garden, The; Daydreamer, The (1966); Endless Night; In Search of the Castaways; Moonspinners, The; Parent Trap, The; Pollyanna; Summer Magic; That Darn Cat; Tiger Bay; Trouble with Angels, The; Whistle Down the Wind
Mills, Hayword: Mississippi Blues
Mills, John: Africa—Texas Style!; Bean; Black Veil for Lisa, A; Cats; Chalk Garden, The; Chuka; Colditz Story, The; Dr. Strange; Frankenstein; Gandhi; Goodbye, Mr. Chips; Grave Indiscretion; Great Expectations; Hobson's Choice; In Which We Serve; King Rat; Lady Caroline Lamb; Martin Chuzzlewit; Masks of Death; Murder with Mirrors; Night of the Fox; Nine Days a Queen; Operation Crossbow; Quatermass Conclusion, The; Rocking Horse Winner, The; Ryan's Daughter; Sahara; Scott of the Antarctic; Swiss Family Robinson, The; Thirty-Nine Steps, The; This Happy Breed; Tiger Bay; Tunes of Glory; War and Peace; We Dive at Dawn; Who's That Girl; Woman of Substance, A; Wrong Box, The; Young Winston; Zulu Dawn
Mills, Johnny: Garden, The
Mills, Juliet: Avanti!; Barnaby and Me; Beyond the Door; Rare Breed, The (1966)
Mills, Kiri: Desperate Remedies
Mills, Samantha: Prehysteria
Mills, Tom: Luther, The Geek
Mills, Walter: High Country, The
Milne, Leslie: Vampire at Midnight
Milner, Martin: Columbo: Murder by the Book; Compulsion; Flood!; Francis in the Navy; Life with Father; Marjorie Morningstar; Operation Pacific; Pete Kelly's Blues; Seekers, The; Sweet Smell of Success; 13 Ghosts; Valley of the Dolls; Zebra in the Kitchen
Milo, Sandra: Bang Bang Kid, The; Dead for a Dollar; 8 1/2; General Della Rovere; Juliet of the Spirits; Vanina Vanini
Milos, Sofia: Order, The
Milot, Charles: French Connection II, The
Miltsakakis, Stefanos: Bloodsport IV: The Dark Kumite
Milushev, Boyan: Bird of Prey
Miluwi, John Omirah: Gorillas in the Mist
Mimieux, Yvette: Black Hole, The; Caper of the Golden Bulls, The; Dark of the Sun (Mercenaries) (1968); Devil Dog: The Hound of Hell; Diamond Head; Hit Lady; Jackson County Jail; Journey into Fear; Legend of Valentino; Monkeys Go Home; Neptune Factor, The; Obsessive Love; Platinum High School; Snowbeast; Three in the Attic; Time Machine, The; Toys in the Attic; Where the Boys Are (1960)
Minardos, Nico: Assault on Agathon; Daring Game
Minciotti, Esther: Marty (1953) (Television)
Mineau, Charlotte: Charlie Chaplin—The Early Years Vol. 1–4
Mineo, Sal: Cheyenne Autumn; Dino; Exodus; Gene Krupa Story, The; Rebel Without a Cause; Rock, Pretty Baby; Somebody Up There Likes Me; Tonka
Miner, Jan: Lenny; Willie and Phil
Miner, Rachel: Bully
Minevich, Borrah: One in a Million
Ming, Lau Siu: Eat a Bowl of Tea
Mingand, Pierre: Mauvaise Graine (Bad Seed)
Minjarez, Mike: Escape to White Mountain
Mink, Claudette: Children of the Corn: Revelation; Deadly Heroes
Minnelli, Liza: Arthur; Arthur 2: On the Rocks; Cabaret; Matter of Time, A; Muppets Take Manhattan, The; New York, New York; Parallel Lives; Rent-a-Cop; Silent Movie; Stepping Out; Sterile Cuckoo, The
Minns, Byron Keith: South Central
Minogue, Dannii: One Crazy Night
Minor, Shane: Shadow Creature
Minter, Kelly Jo: People Under the Stairs, The; Popcorn
Minter, Kristin: Cool As Ice; Flashfire; Savage; There Goes My Baby; Tick Tock
Minzhi, Wei: Not One Less
Miou-Miou: Dog Day; Dry Cleaning; Eighth Day, The; Entre Nous (Between Us); Going Places; Jonah Who Will Be 25 in the Year 2000; Josepha; La Lectrice (The Reader); Little Indian,

Big City; May Fools; Ménage; My Other Husband; Roads to the South; This Sweet Sickness
Mira, Brigitte: Ali: Fear Eats the Soul; Chinese Roulette; Every Man for Himself and God Against All; Kamikaze 89; Mother Kusters Goes to Heaven
Miracle, Irene: In the Shadow of Kilimanjaro; Last of Philip Banter, The; Puppet Master, The; Watchers II
Miranda, Carmen: Copacabana; Date with Judy, A; Doll Face; Down Argentine Way; Four Jills in a Jeep; Gang's All Here, The; Nancy Goes to Rio; Springtime in the Rockies; Weekend in Havana
Miranda, Isa: Dog Eat Dog; La Signora di Tutti; Man from Nowhere, The; Night Porter, The; Summertime
Miranda, John: Bloodthirsty Butchers
Miranda, Robert: Chips, the War Dog; Monkey Trouble
Mironova, Olga: Come and See
Mirren, Helen: Cal; Caligula; Collection, The; Comfort of Strangers, The; Cook, the Thief, His Wife & Her Lover, The; Critical Care; Dr. Bethune; Excalibur; Fiendish Plot of Dr. Fu Manchu, The; Gosford Park; Gospel According to Vic, The; Greenfingers; Hawk, The; Hussy; Last Orders; Long Good Friday, The; Losing Chase; Madness of King George, The; Mosquito Coast, The; Pascali's Island; Passion of Ayn Rand, The; Pledge, The; Prime Suspect 1; Prime Suspect 3; Prime Suspect 2; Prime Suspect: Scent of Darkness; Red King, White Knight; Royal Deceit; Savage Messiah; Some Mother's Son; Teaching Mrs. Tingle; 2010; When the Whales Came; Where Angels Fear to Tread
Mishima, Yukio: Black Lizard
Miss X: Vegas in Space
Mistral, Jorge: Wuthering Heights
Mistysyn, Stacy: Princes in Exile
Mitchell, Belle: Crazed
Mitchell, Cameron: Adventures of Gallant Bess; All Mine to Give; Andersonville Trial, The; Blood and Black Lace; Blood Link; Buck and the Preacher; Carousel; Crossing the Line (1990); Deadly Prey; Desirée; Dog Eat Dog; Escapade in Japan; Flight to Mars; Flood!; Frankenstein Island; Gambler, Part II—The Adventure Continues, The; Gorilla at Large; Hollywood Cop; Hombre; Homecoming; How to Marry a Millionaire; Klansman, The; Last Gun, The; Love Me or Leave Me; Low Blow; Man in the Saddle; Night Train to Terror; Nightforce; Nightmare in Wax (Crimes in the Wax Museum); No Justice; Pony Soldier; Rebel Rousers; Return to Fantasy Island; Ride in the Whirlwind; Slavers; Tall Men, The; Tomb, The; Without Warning
Mitchell, Colin: Combination Platter
Mitchell, Daryl: Black Knight; Galaxy Quest; Quiet Days in Hollywood; Sgt. Bilko
Mitchell, Duke: Boys from Brooklyn, The
Mitchell, Eddy: My Other Husband
Mitchell, Elizabeth: Frequency; Nurse Betty
Mitchell, Ella: Big Momma's House
Mitchell, Frank: 365 Nights in Hollywood
Mitchell, Gene: Takeover, The
Mitchell, Gordon: Fellini Satyricon; Giant of Metropolis, The; Shanghai Joe; She
Mitchell, Grant: Conflict; Dancing Lady; Ex-Mrs. Bradford, The; Footsteps in the Dark; Great Lie, The; Guest Wife; In Person; Man Who Came to Dinner, The; Peck's Bad Boy with the Circus; 365 Nights in Hollywood; Tomorrow at Seven
Mitchell, Guy: Red Garters
Mitchell, Heather: Everlasting Secret Family, The
Mitchell, Herb: Debt, The
Mitchell, James: Prodigal, The
Mitchell, John: Sea Shall Not Have Them, The
Mitchell, John Cameron: Band of the Hand; Hedwig and the Angry Inch; Misplaced
Mitchell, Joni: Last Waltz, The
Mitchell, Kel: Good Burger; Mystery Men
Mitchell, Kirsty: Attila
Mitchell, Laurie: Attack of the Puppet People
Mitchell, Millard: Gunfighter, The (1950); Here Come the Girls; Naked Spur, The
Mitchell, Mitch: Jimi Hendrix
Mitchell, Radha: High Art; Love and Other Catastrophes; Pitch Black
Mitchell, Red: 8 Seconds
Mitchell, Sasha: Class of 1999 II: The Substitute; Kickboxer 2: The Road Back; Kickboxer 3: Art of War; Kickboxer 4: Aggressor, The; Spike of Bensonhurst
Mitchell, Scoey: Jo Jo Dancer, Your Life Is Calling
Mitchell, Silas Weir: Patriot, The
Mitchell, Thomas: Adventure; Angels over Broadway; Bataan; Big Wheel, The; Black Swan, The; Buffalo Bill; By Love Possessed; Craig's Wife; Dark Mirror, The; Dark Waters; Fighting Sullivans, The (Sullivans, The); Gone with the Wind; High Noon; Hunchback of Notre Dame, The; Immortal Sergeant, The; It's a Wonderful Life; Joan of Paris; Keys to the Kingdom, The; Long Voyage Home, The; Lost Horizon; Only Angels Have Wings; Our Town; Outlaw, The; Pocketful of Miracles; Silver River; Song of the Islands; Stagecoach; Theodora Goes Wild; Toast of New Orleans; Trilogy of Terror II; While the City Sleeps; Wilson
Mitchell, Warren: Dunera Boys, The; Foreign Body; Knights and Emeralds; Meetings with Remarkable Men; Norman Loves Rose
Mitchell, Yvonne: Crucible of Horror; Demons of the Mind; Incredible Sarah, The; Sapphire; Tiger Bay
Mitchell-Leon, Carol: Getting Out
Mitchell-Smith, Ilan: Chocolate War, The; Identity Crisis; Journey to the Center of the Earth; Weird Science; Wild Life, The
Mitchum, Bentley: Demonic Toys; Ruby in Paradise; Shark Attack; Teenage Bonnie and Klepto Clyde
Mitchum, Chris: Big Foot; Big Jake; Biohazard: The Alien Force; Day Time Ended, The; Diamondbacks; Rio Lobo; Stingray; Striking Point; Summertime Killer, The
Mitchum, Jim: Blackout; Fatal Mission; Girls Town; Hollywood Cop; Jake Spanner Private Eye; Mercenary Fighters; Ransom; Thunder Road; Tramplers, The
Mitchum, John: Big Foot; Breakheart Pass; Dirty Harry; Enforcer, The; Escapes; High Plains Drifter; Hitler; Jake Spanner Private Eye; Outlaw Josey Wales, The; Paint Your Wagon; Telefon; Way West, The
Mitchum, Robert: Agency; Ambassador, The; Amsterdam Kill, The; Anzio; Backfire; Big Sleep, The; Big Steal, The; Blood on the Moon; Border Patrol; Breakthrough; Brotherhood of the Rose; Cape Fear; Cape Fear; Crossfire; Dead Man; El Dorado; Enemy Below, The; False Colors; Farewell My Lovely; Five Card Stud; Friends of Eddie Coyle, The; Girl Rush; Good Guys and the Bad Guys, The; Grass Is Greener, The; Gung Ho! (1943); Hearst and Davies Affair, The; His Kind of Woman; Holiday Affair; Home from the Hill; Hoppy Serves a Writ; Jake Spanner Private Eye; Last Tycoon, The; Leather Burners, The; Lone Star Trail; Longest Day, The; Lusty Men, The; Macao; Maria's Lovers; Matilda; Midnight Ride; Midway; Mr. North; My Forbidden Past; Night of the Hunter; Nightkill; Not as a Stranger; One Minute to Zero; One Shoe Makes It Murder; Out of the Past; Pursued; Rachel and the Stranger; Racket, The; Red Pony, The; River of No Return; Ryan's Daughter; Scrooged; Second Chance; Secret Ceremony; She Couldn't Say No; Story of G. I. Joe, The; Sundowners, The; That Championship Season; Thirty Seconds Over Tokyo; Thompson's Last Run; Thunder Road; Till the End of Time; Two for the Seesaw; Undercurrent; Villa Rides; War and Remembrance; Way West, The; Winds of War, The; Woman of Desire; Yakuza, The
Mitevska, Labina: Before the Rain; I Want You
Mitler, Matt: Occultist, The
Mitra, Rhona: Beowulf; Get Carter
Mitterer, Felix: Requiem for Dominic
Miu, Tse: Jet Li's the Enforcer
Mix, Tom: Dick Turpin; My Pal, the King
Miyagian, Eri: Summer Vacation: 1999
Miyamoto, Nobuko: Funeral, The; Minbo, or The Gentle Art of Japanese Extortion; Tampopo; Taxing Woman, A; Taxing Woman's Return, A
Miyeni, Eric: Dangerous Ground
Miyori, Kim: Antony and Cleopatra; John & Yoko: A Love Story; Punisher, The
Mizrahi, Isaac: For Love or Money; Unzipped

Mizrahi, Sarah: Unzipped
Mizuno, Kumi: War of the Gargantuas
Mo, Teresa: Hard Boiled
Moat, Bobby: Cool, Dry Place, A
Mobley, Mary Ann: Girl Happy; Harum Scarum
Mobley, Roger: Emil and the Detectives
Mobley, Stacey Leigh: Emil and the Detectives
Mocky, Jean-Pierre: Head Against the Wall
Modean, Jayne: Streethawk
Modesto, Sam: Buried Alive
Modine, Matthew: And the Band Played On; Birdy; Browning Version, The; Bye Bye, Love; Cutthroat Island; Equinox (1993); Fluke; Full Metal Jacket; Gamble, The; Gross Anatomy; Married to the Mob; Memphis Belle; Mrs. Soffel; Orphans; Pacific Heights; Private School; Real Blonde, The; Short Cuts; Streamers; Vision Quest; What the Deaf Man Heard; Wind (1992)
Modot, Gaston: Age of Gold; L'Age D'Or
Moeller, Ralph: Best of the Best 2; Viking Sagas, The
Moffat, Donald: Alamo Bay; Best of Times, The; Bourne Identity, The; Clear and Present Danger; Cookie's Fortune; Evening Star, The; Far North; Great Northfield Minnesota Raid, The; Housesitter; Love, Cheat & Steal; Necessary Parties; On the Nickel; Promises in the Dark; Regarding Henry; Right Stuff, The; Showdown; Teamster Boss: The Jackie Presser Story; Trapped in Paradise
Moffatt, Graham: Dr. Syn
Moffett, D. W.: Danielle Steel's Fine Things; In the Deep Woods; Kill Me Later; Lisa; Little Death, The; Misfit Brigade, The; Molly; Rough Magic; Stealing Beauty
Moffett, Gregory: Robot Monster
Moffett, Michelle: Deathstalker IV: Match of the Titans; Wild Cactus
Mog, Aribert: Ecstasy
Mogila, Linda: Cyrano de Bergerac
Mohammadi, Azize: Apple, The
Mohammadkhani, Aida: White Balloon, The
Mohner, Carl: Last Gun, The; Rififi; Sink the Bismarck
Mohr, Gerald: Angry Red Planet, The; Hunt the Man Down; Invasion USA (1952); King of the Cowboys; Son of Ali Baba; Terror in the Haunted House
Mohr, Jay: Cherry Falls; For Better or Worse; Go; Jane Austen's Mafia; Pay It Forward; Picture Perfect; Small Soldiers; Suicide Kings
Mohyeddin, Zia: Bombay Talkie; They Came from Beyond Space; We Are the Children
Moir, Alison: Johnny Suede
Moir, Richard: Heatwave (1983); Indecent Obsession, An
Mok, Karen: Black Mask
Mokae, Zakes: Dry White Season, A; Dust Devil; Master Harold and the Boys; Percy & Thunder; Rage in Harlem, A; Serpent and the Rainbow, The; Slaughter of the Innocents; World of Strangers, A
Mol, Gretchen: Just Looking; Music from Another Room; New Rose Hotel; Rounders; Thirteenth Floor, The
Molander, Karin: Thomas Graal's Best Child; Thomas Graal's Best Film
Moldovan, Florin: Gadjo Dilo
Molière Players, The: Alfred Hitchcock's Bon Voyage and Aventure Malgache
Molina, Alfred: American Friends; Before and After; Chocolat; Dead Man; Dudley Do-Right; Enchanted April; Hideaway; Impostors, The; Leo Tolstoy's Anna Karenina (1997); Letter to Brezhnev; Man Who Knew Too Little, The; Manifesto; Maverick; Meantime; Not Without My Daughter; Perez Family, The; Prick Up Your Ears; Scorpion Spring; Species; Texas Rangers (2001); Trial, The; White Fang 2: Myth of the White Wolf
Molina, Angela: Camorra; Demons in the Garden; Half of Heaven; Live Flesh; 1492: The Conquest of Paradise; Streets of Gold; That Obscure Object of Desire
Molina, Miguel: Law of Desire
Moll, Georgia: Misunderstood
Moll, Richard: Beanstalk; Dream Date; Dungeonmaster, The; Galaxis; Glass Cage, The; Highlander: The Gathering; House; Night Train to Terror; No Dessert Dad Until You Mow the Lawn; Secret Agent Club; Sidekicks; Storybook; Survivor; Sword and the Sorcerer, The; Think Big; Wicked Stepmother, The
Molnar, Tibor: Red and the White, The; Round-Up, The
Molone, Steve: Big Sweat, The
Moloney, Janel: Souler Opposite, The
Moltke, Alexandra: Dark Shadows (TV Series)
Momo, Alessandro: Malicious
Momoi, Kaori: Eijanaika (Why Not?)
Momsen, Taylor: How the Grinch Stole Christmas
Monaghan, Dominic: Lord of the Rings, The: Fellowship of the Ring
Monaghan, Marjorie: Nemesis; Space Rangers (TV Series)
Monahan, Dan: Porky's; Porky's II: The Next Day; Porky's Revenge; Up the Creek
Monahan, Tonia: Dominion; Edgar Allan Poe's Madhouse; Goblin; Prehistoric Bimbos in Armageddon City; Zombie Bloodbath
Moncrief, J. Michael: Legend of Bagger Vance, The
Moncrieff, Karen: Deathfight; Midnight Witness; Xtro: Watch the Skies (Xtro 3)
Mondy, Pierre: Gift, The; Sleeping Car Murders, The
Mones, Paul: Tuff Turf
Monet, Chaz: Ruby Bridges
Monfort, Sylvia: Le Cas du Dr. Laurent
Mong, William V.: Seven Footprints to Satan; What Price Glory? (1926)
Mongkolpisit, Pawalit: Bangkok Dangerous
Monk, Debra: Center Stage; Ellen Foster; Redwood Curtain
Monlaur, Yvonne: Brides of Dracula; Terror of the Tongs, The
Monnier, Antoine: Devil, Probably, The
Monnier, Valentine: Devilfish
Monoson, Lawrence: Black Rose of Harlem; Dangerous Love; Gaby, a True Story
Monot, Roland: Man Escaped, A
Monro, Truan: Prince Brat and the Whipping Boy
Monroe, Lochlan: Downhill Willie
Monroe, Marilyn: All About Eve; As Young as You Feel; Asphalt Jungle, The; Bus Stop; Clash by Night; Don't Bother to Knock; Gentlemen Prefer Blondes; How to Marry a Millionaire; Ladies of the Chorus; Let's Make It Legal; Let's Make Love; Love Happy; Love Nest; Misfits, The; Monkey Business; Niagara; Prince and the Showgirl, The; River of No Return; Seven Year Itch, The; Some Like It Hot; There's No Business Like Show Business; We're Not Married
Monroe, Sam: Tales from the Hood
Monroe, Steve: Kill-Off, The
Montagut, François: Strangers
Montalban, Carlos: Bananas
Montalban, Paolo: Rodgers & Hammerstein's Cinderella
Montalban, Ricardo: Across the Wide Missouri; Alice Through the Looking Glass; Battleground; Blue; Cheyenne Autumn; Conquest of the Planet of the Apes; Deserter, The; Escape from the Planet of the Apes; Fantasy Island; Fiesta; Kissing Bandit, The; Latin Lovers; Madame X; Mission to Glory; Naked Gun, The; Neptune's Daughter; On an Island with You; Return to Fantasy Island; Sayonara; Singing Nun, The; Star Trek II: The Wrath of Khan; Sweet Charity; Train Robbers, The; Two Weeks with Love
Montana, Bull: Son of the Sheik; Victory
Montana, Karla: Sweet 15
Montana, Monte: Down Dakota Way
Montand, Yves: César and Rosalie; Choice of Arms, A; Delusions of Grandeur; Goodbye Again; Grand Prix; IP5: The Island of Pachyderms; Is Paris Burning?; Jean De Florette; Let's Make Love; Manon of the Spring; My Geisha; Napoleon; On a Clear Day, You Can See Forever; Roads to the South; Sleeping Car Murders, The; State of Siege; Vincent, François, Paul and the Others; Wages of Fear, The; Z
Monte, Brenda: Unmade Beds
Monte, Marlo: Soul Vengeance (Welcome Home Brother Charles)
Monte, Mike: No Dead Heroes
Monteith, Kelly: Hollywood Boulevard II
Montell, Lisa: Nine Lives of Elfego Baca, The; World Without End
Montenegro, Fernanda: Central Station

Monteros, Rosenda: Battle Shock
Montesano, Enrico: Sotto Sotto
Montesi, Jorge: Death Target
Montesinos, Gino: Magic Stone, The
Montez, Maria: Ali Baba and the Forty Thieves; Arabian Nights; Cobra Woman; Follow the Boys; Gypsy Wildcat; Sudan; Valdez Is Coming
Montgomery, Belinda: Blackout; Man from Atlantis, The; Marciano; Miami Vice; Other Side of the Mountain, Part II, The; Silent Madness; Stone Cold Dead; Stone Fox, The; Todd Killings, The
Montgomery, Douglass: Cat and the Canary, The; Harmony Lane; Mystery of Edwin Drood, The
Montgomery, Elizabeth: Court-martial of Billy Mitchell, The; Thriller (TV Series)
Montgomery, Flora: When Brendan Met Trudy
Montgomery, George: From Hell to Borneo; Hostile Guns; Indian Uprising; Lone Ranger, The; Orchestra Wives; Roxie Hart; Texas Rangers, The (1951)
Montgomery, Julie: Revenge of the Nerds; Savage Justice
Montgomery, Lee: Baker's Hawk; Ben; Burnt Offerings; Girls Just Want to Have Fun; Into the Fire; Midnight Hour; Mutant; Prime Risk; Savage Is Loose, The
Montgomery, Robert: Big House, The; Divorcee, The; Forsaking All Others; Free and Easy; Here Comes Mr. Jordan; Inspiration; June Bride; Lady in the Lake; Last of Mrs. Cheney, The; Mr. and Mrs. Smith; Night Must Fall; Private Lives; Riptide; They Were Expendable
Monti, Ivana: Contraband
Monti, Maria: Fistful of Dynamite, A
Montiel, Sarita: Run of the Arrow; Serenade
Montorsi, Stefania: Mille Bolle Blu
Moody, David: Blue Knight, The
Moody, Elizabeth: Dead Alive
Moody, Jim: Bad Boys; Who's the Man?
Moody, Lynne: Las Vegas Lady; Last Light; White Dog
Moody, Ron: Dial M for Murder; Dogpound Shuffle; Ghost in Monte Carlo, A; Kid in King Arthur's Court, A; Legend of the Werewolf; Murder Most Foul; Oliver; Othello; Seaside Swingers; Twelve Chairs, The; Unidentified Flying Oddball; Wrong Is Right
Moog, Robert: Theremin: An Electronic Odyssey
Moon, Keith: That'll Be the Day; 200 Motels
Mooney, Maureen: Hell High
Mooney, William: Flash of Green, A
Moore, Alvy: Horror Show, The; Scream; Wild One, The
Moore, Archie: Adventures of Huckleberry Finn, The; Carpetbaggers, The
Moore, Ashleigh Aston: Now and Then
Moore, Candy: Tomboy and the Champ
Moore, Chase: Running Free
Moore, Christine: Lurkers; Prime Evil
Moore, Clayton: Black Dragons; Far Frontier; Helldorado; Kansas Pacific; Lone Ranger, The; Lone Ranger, The (TV Series); Lone Ranger and the Lost City of Gold, The; Riders of the Whistling Pines; Son of Monte Cristo, The
Moore, Cleo: Dynamite Pass; Hunt the Man Down; On Dangerous Ground
Moore, Colleen: Ella Cinders; Scarlet Letter, The; Sky Pilot, The; These Girls Won't Talk
Moore, Constance: Buck Rogers: Destination Saturn (Planet Outlaws); Show Business; Wives Under Suspicion; You Can't Cheat an Honest Man
Moore, Deborah: Midnight Man; On Dangerous Ground; Warriors of the Apocalypse
Moore, Demi: About Last Night ...; Butcher's Wife, The; Disclosure; Few Good Men, A; Ghost (1990); G.I. Jane; If These Walls Could Talk; Indecent Proposal; Juror, The; Mortal Thoughts; No Small Affair; Nothing But Trouble; Now and Then; One Crazy Summer; Parasite; Passion of Mind; St. Elmo's Fire; Scarlet Letter, The; Seventh Sign, The; Striptease; We're No Angels; Wisdom
Moore, Dennis: Arizona Bound; Black Market Rustlers; Colorado Serenade; Fast Talking; King of the Bullwhip; Lonely Trail, The; Purple Monster Strikes, The; Spooks Run Wild
Moore, Dickie: Bride Wore Red, The; Gabriel over the White House; Jive Junction; Little Men; Miss Annie Rooney; Oliver Twist; Out of the Past
Moore, Dudley: Adventures of Milo and Otis, The; Alice's Adventures in Wonderland; Arthur; Arthur 2: On the Rocks; Bedazzled; Best Defense; Blame It on the Bellboy; Crazy People; Foul Play; Hound of the Baskervilles, The; Like Father, Like Son; Lovesick; Micki & Maude; Parallel Lives; Romantic Comedy; Santa Claus—The Movie; Six Weeks; 10; 30 Is a Dangerous Age, Cynthia; Those Daring Young Men in Their Jaunty Jalopies; Unfaithfully Yours; Weekend in the Country, A; Wholly Moses!; Wrong Box, The
Moore, Duke: Plan 9 from Outer Space
Moore, Gar: Abbott and Costello Meet the Killer, Boris Karloff; Paisan; Underworld Story
Moore, Grace: One Night of Love
Moore, Irene: New Year's Day
Moore, James: Sinister Urge, The
Moore, Jenie: Vampire at Midnight
Moore, Joanna: Follow That Dream; Monster on the Campus
Moore, Juanita: Imitation of Life; Papa's Delicate Condition
Moore, Julianne: Assassins; Benny & Joon; Big Lebowski, The; Boogie Nights; Cast a Deadly Spell; Cookie's Fortune; End of the Affair, The; Evolution; Hannibal; Hellcab; Ideal Husband, An; Ladies Man, The (2000); Lost World, The: Jurassic Park; Magnolia; Map of the World, A; Myth of Fingerprints, The; Nine Months; Psycho; Roommates; Safe; Shipping News, The; Short Cuts; Surviving Picasso; Vanya on 42nd Street
Moore, Kieron: Anna Karenina; Arabesque; David and Bathsheba; Day of the Triffids, The; League of Gentlemen, The; Mine Own Executioner; Naked Heart, The; Satellite in the Sky
Moore, Mandy: Walk to Remember, A
Moore, Margy: Sherlock: Undercover Dog
Moore, Mary Tyler: Change of Habit; Dick Van Dyke Show, The (TV Series); Finnegan Begin Again; Flirting with Disaster; Gore Vidal's Lincoln; Just Between Friends; Keys to Tulsa; Labor Pains; Last Best Year, The; Ordinary People; Six Weeks; Thoroughly Modern Millie
Moore, Matt: Coquette; Deluge (1993); Pride of the Clan, The; Traffic in Souls; White Tiger
Moore, Mavor: Mortal Sins (1992)
Moore, Melba: Def by Temptation; Ellis Island
Moore, Melissa: Angel Fist; Hard to Die; One Man Army; Scream Dream; Sorority House Massacre 2; Vampire Cop
Moore, Michael J.: Deadly Stranger
Moore, Norma: Fear Strikes Out
Moore, Owen: As You Desire Me; Blackbird, The; High Voltage; Home, Sweet Home (1914); Keystone Comedies: Vol. 1–5
Moore, Paige: Wizard of Speed and Time, The
Moore, Patience: Cheap Shots
Moore, Pauline: Carson City Kid; Charlie Chan at Treasure Island; Trail Blazers
Moore, Rob: National Lampoon's Senior Trip
Moore, Roger: Bed and Breakfast; Bullseye; Cannonball Run; Diane; Escape to Athena; ffolkes; Fire, Ice & Dynamite; For Your Eyes Only; Interrupted Melody; Live and Let Die; Man Who Haunted Himself, The; Man with the Golden Gun, The; Maverick (TV Series); Miracle, The; Moonraker; Naked Face, The; Octopussy; Persuaders, The (TV Series); Quest, The; Rape of the Sabines; Saint, The (TV Series); Sea Wolves, The; Shout at the Devil; Spice World; Spy Who Loved Me, The; Street People; That Lucky Touch; View to a Kill, A; Wild Geese, The
Moore, Rudy Ray: Dolemite; Violent New Breed
Moore, Sheila: Ray Bradbury's Chronicles: The Martian Episodes
Moore, Shemar: Brothers, The
Moore, Shermar: Never 2 Big
Moore, Stephen: Clockwise
Moore, Terry: Beneath the 12-Mile Reef; Between Heaven and Hell; Beverly Hills Brats; Come Back, Little Sheba; Daddy Long Legs; Mighty Joe Young; Peyton Place; Platinum High School; Return of October, The; Shack-Out on 101; Two of a Kind
Moore, Thomas: Warriors of the Wasteland
Moore, Tim: Amos and Andy (TV Series)

Moore, Tom: Manhandled; Moon Over Broadway
Moore, Tyria: Aileen Wuornos: Selling of a Serial Killer
Moore, Victor: Heat's On, The; It's in the Bag; Louisiana Purchase; Star Spangled Rhythm; Swing Time; We're Not Married; Ziegfeld Follies
Moorehead, Agnes: Alice Through the Looking Glass; All That Heaven Allows; Bachelor in Paradise; Bat, The; Big Street, The; Black Jack; Citizen Kane; Conqueror, The; Dark Passage; Dear Dead Delilah; Hush ... Hush, Sweet Charlotte; Jane Eyre; Johnny Belinda; Journey into Fear; Left Hand of God, The; Lost Moment, The; Magnificent Ambersons, The; Magnificent Obsession; Main Street to Broadway; Meet Me in Las Vegas; Mrs. Parkington; Opposite Sex, The (1956); Our Vines Have Tender Grapes; Pollyanna; Raintree County; Seventh Cross, The; Show Boat; Since You Went Away; Singing Nun, The; Station West; Stratton Story, The; Summer Holiday; Swan, The; Twilight Zone, The (TV Series); What's the Matter with Helen?
Moorehead, Jean: Violent Years, The
Moorhead, Natalie: Dance, Fools, Dance; Heart of Arizona; Hook, Line and Sinker; Parlor, Bedroom and Bath
Moosbrugger, Christoph: Bloody Moon
Mooy, Genevieve: Dish, The
Moradi, Safar Ali: Taste of Cherry
Moraes, Drica: Bossa Nova
Morajele, Sechaba: Dangerous Ground
Morales, Esai: Bad Boys; Bloodhounds of Broadway; Burning Season, The; Deadlock 2; Disappearance of Garcia Lorca, The; Don't Do It; In the Army Now; La Bamba; My Family; Naked Tango; On Wings of Eagles; Principal, The; Rapa Nui; Scorpion Spring; Ultraviolet; Wonderful Ice Cream Suit, The
Moran, Dan: Mighty Aphrodite
Moran, Dolores: Horn Blows at Midnight, The; Man I Love, The
Moran, Erin: Galaxy of Terror
Moran, H. A.: Beggars of Life
Moran, Jackie: Adventures of Tom Sawyer, The; Buck Rogers: Destination Saturn (PlanetOutlaws); Meet Dr. Christian; Old Swimmin' Hole, The
Moran, Nick: Lock, Stock and Two Smoking Barrels; Musketeer, The; New Blood
Moran, Patrick: Biohazard: The Alien Force
Moran, Pauline: Poirot (Series)
Moran, Peggy: Horror Island; King of the Cowboys; Mummy's Hand, The
Moran, Polly: Red River Range; Show People; Tom Brown's School Days (1940)
Morane, Jacqueline: Picnic on the Grass
Moranis, Rick: Big Bully; Club Paradise; Flintstones, The; Ghostbusters; Ghostbusters II; Head Office; Honey, I Blew Up the Kid; Honey, I Shrunk the Kids; Honey, We Shrunk Ourselves; Last Polka, The; Little Giants; Little Shop of Horrors (1986); My Blue Heaven; Parenthood; Spaceballs; Splitting Heirs; Strange Brew; Streets of Fire; Wild Life, The
Morant, Richard: John & Yoko: A Love Story; Mahler
Morante, Laura: Tragedy of a Ridiculous Man
Moray, Yvonne: Terror of Tiny Town, The
Mordyukova, Nonna: Commissar, The
More, Camilla: In Search of the Serpent of Death
More, Kenneth: Admirable Crichton, The; Adventures of Sadie; Battle of Britain; Dark of the Sun (Mercenaries) (1968); Doctor in the House; Flame over India; Genevieve; Leopard in the Snow; Never Let Me Go; Night to Remember, A; Scott of the Antarctic; Scrooge; Sink the Bismarck; Slipper & the Rose, The; Tale of Two Cities, A; Thirty-Nine Steps, The; Unidentified Flying Oddball
Moreau, Jeanne: Alberto Express; Alex in Wonderland; Bride Wore Black, The; Chimes at Midnight (Falstaff); Diary of a Chambermaid; Elevator to the Gallows; Ever After; Fire Within, The; Foreign Field, A; Going Places; Heat of Desire; Immortal Story; Jules and Jim; Last Tycoon, The; Les Liaisons Dangereuses; Little Theatre of Jean Renoir, The; Lovers, The (1958); Lumiere; Mademoiselle; Map of the Human Heart; Monte Walsh; Mr. Klein; Old Lady Who Walked in the Sea, The; Proprietor, The; Querelle; Summer House, The; Train, The; Trial, The; Until the End of the World; Viva Maria!; Woman Is a Woman, A
Moreau, Marguerite: Queen of the Damned
Moreau, Nathaniel: Kissing Place, The; Tidy Endings
Moreau, Yolande: Amélie
Morehead, Elizabeth: Interceptor
Morel, Gael: Wild Reeds
Moreland, Mantan: Charlie Chan in the Secret Service; Chinese Cat, The; Dressed to Kill; Jade Mask, The; King of the Zombies; Meeting at Midnight; Next Time I Marry; Revenge of the Zombies; Scarlet Clue, The; Shanghai Cobra, The; Strange Case of Dr. Rx, The; Two-Gun Man from Harlem; Young Nurses, The
Moreland, Sherry: Fury of the Congo
Morell, Andre: Dark of the Sun (Mercenaries) (1968); Giant Behemoth, The; Hound of the Baskervilles, The; Mummy's Shroud, The; Plague of the Zombies; Quatermass and the Pit; Stolen Face; 10 Rillington Place; Vengeance of She, The
Morell, Joshua: Making Contact
Morelli, Laura: Last Orders
Morelli, Lino: Lunatics & Lovers
Moreno, Antonio: Bohemian Girl, The; Creature from the Black Lagoon; It
Moreno, Lisa: From Hell to Borneo
Moreno, Rita: Age Isn't Everything; Blue Moon; Boss' Son, The; Cry of Battle; Four Seasons, The; Happy Birthday, Gemini; I Like It Like That; King and I, The; Latin Lovers; Ma and Pa Kettle on Vacation; Marlowe; Night of the Following Day, The; Pagan Love Song; Pinero; Popi; Portrait of a Showgirl; Ritz, The; Seven Cities of Gold; Singin' in the Rain; Summer and Smoke; Toast of New Orleans; West Side Story
Morente, Enrique: Flamenco
Moretti, Linda: Postman, The (Il Postino)
Moretti, Nanni: Caro Diario; Palombella Rossa
Morevski, Abraham: Dybbuk, The
Morey, Bill: Real Men
Morgan, Alexandra: Deadly Games
Morgan, Audrey: Love Your Mama
Morgan, Carrie: Brigham City
Morgan, Chad: Whatever
Morgan, Chesty: Whatever
Morgan, Cindy: Tron
Morgan, David E.: Tron
Morgan, Debbi: Eve's Bayou; Jesse Owens Story, The; Love and Basketball
Morgan, Dennis: Captains of the Clouds; Christmas in Connecticut; Fighting 69th, The; Great Ziegfeld, The; Hard Way, The; In This Our Life; It's a Great Feeling; Kitty Foyle; Pearl of the South Pacific; Return of Dr. X; Thank Your Lucky Stars
Morgan, Emily: French Lieutenant's Woman, The
Morgan, Frank: Any Number Can Play; Balalaika; Bombshell; Boom Town; Broadway Melody of 1940; Broadway Serenade; Casanova Brown; Cat and the Fiddle, The; Courage of Lassie; Dimples; Great Ziegfeld, The; Green Dolphin Street; Hallelujah, I'm A Bum; Honky Tonk; Human Comedy, The; I Live My Life; Key to the City; Last of Mrs. Cheney, The; Mortal Storm, The; Naughty Marietta; Rosalie; Saratoga; Shop Around the Corner, The; Stratton Story, The; Summer Holiday; Sweethearts; Thousands Cheer; Tortilla Flat; White Cargo; White Cliffs of Dover, The; Wizard of Oz, The; Yolanda and the Thief
Morgan, Georgia: 10 Violent Women
Morgan, Harry: All My Sons; Apple Dumpling Gang, The; Apple Dumpling Gang Rides Again, The; Better Late than Never; Boots Malone; Cat from Outer Space, The; Charley and the Angel; Cimarron; Dragnet; Far Country, The; Flim-Flam Man, The; Frankie and Johnny; Gangster, The; Glenn Miller Story, The; Incident, The; It Started With a Kiss; More Wild Wild West; Not as a Stranger; Ox-Bow Incident, The; Roughnecks; Scandalous John; Shootist, The; Showdown, The (1950); Snowball Express; State Fair; Support Your Local Gunfighter; Support Your Local Sheriff!; Torch Song; Well, The; Wild Wild West Revisited, The; Wing and a Prayer, A
Morgan, Helen: Applause; Frankie and Johnny; Glorifying the American Girl; Go into Your Dance; Show Boat
Morgan, Jane: Our Miss Brooks (TV Series)

Morgan, Jaye P.: Night Patrol
Morgan, Michèle: Bluebeard; Cat and Mouse; Chase, The; Everybody's Fine; Fallen Idol, The; Higher and Higher; Joan of Paris; Lost Command; Naked Heart, The; Proud Ones, The; Stormy Waters
Morgan, Nancy: Americathon; Grand Theft Auto; Lucky Luke; Nest, The; Pray TV
Morgan, Priscilla: Pride and Prejudice
Morgan, Ralph: Dick Tracy vs. Crime Inc.; General Spanky; Kennel Murder Case, The; Last Round-Up; Little Men; Mannequin; Monster Maker, The; Night Monster; Rasputin and the Empress; Star of Midnight; Strange Interlude; Weird Woman; Wives Under Suspicion
Morgan, Read: Hollywood Harry
Morgan, Rhian: August
Morgan, Richard: Wicked, The
Morgan, Scott Wesley: Serial Mom
Morgan, Sidney: Juno and the Paycock
Morgan, Terence: Curse of the Mummy's Tomb, The; Hamlet
Morgan, Tim R.: Winterbeast
Morgan, Trevor: Barney's Great Adventure; Glass House, The (2001); Jurassic Park III; Rookie, The (2002); Sixth Sense, The
Morganti, Claudio: Palombella Rossa
Morgenstern, Madeleine: Francois Truffaut: Stolen Moments
Morgenstern, Maia: Ulysses' Gaze
Morghen, John: Make Them Die Slowly
Morguia, Ana Ofelia: Mary My Dearest
Mori, Claudia: Lunatics & Lovers
Mori, Kakuro: Story of the Late Chrysanthemums, The
Mori, Masayuki: Bad Sleep Well, The; Idiot, The; Princess Yang Kwei Fei; Rashomon; Ugetsu
Mori, Toshia: Bitter Tea of General Yen, The
Moriarty, Cathy: Another Stakeout; Burndown; But I'm a Cheerleader; Casper; Crazy in Alabama; Crimson Code; Digging to China; Dream with the Fishes; Gloria; Gun in Betty Lou's Handbag, The; Hugo Pool; Kindergarten Cop; Mambo Kings, The; Matinee; Me and the Kid; Neighbors; Opposite Corners; Pontiac Moon; P.U.N.K.S.; Raging Bull; Soapdish; White of the Eye
Moriarty, James: Chippendales Murder, The
Moriarty, Michael: Along Came a Spider; Bang the Drum Slowly; Blood Link; Calm at Sunset; Children of the Dust; Courage Under Fire; Crime of the Century; Dark Tower; Full Fathom Five; Hanoi Hilton, The; Holocaust; It's Alive III: Island of the Alive; James Dean (2001); Last Detail, The; Managua; My Old Man's Place; Nitti: The Enforcer; Out of Line; Pale Rider; Q; Report to the Commissioner; Return to Salem's Lot, A; Shiloh; Shiloh 2: Shiloh Season; Stuff, The; Tailspin; Troll; Who'll Stop the Rain; Winds of Kitty Hawk, The
Moriarty, P. H.: Dune; Lock, Stock and Two Smoking Barrels
Morice, Tara: Sorrento Beach; Strictly Ballroom
Morier-Genoud, Philippe: Au Revoir, Les Enfants
Moriggi, Francesca: Tree of the Wooden Clogs, The
Morin, Mayo: Clowns, The
Morina, Johnny: Boys of St. Vincent; Salt Water Moose
Morishita, Eri: Cyber Ninja
Morison, Patricia: Calling Dr. Death; Dressed to Kill; Fallen Sparrow, The; Lady on a Train; Song of the Thin Man; Song Without End; Without Love
Morita, Noriyuki "Pat": Alice Through the Looking Glass; Auntie Lee's Meat Pies; Babes in Toyland; Bloodsport II; Bloodsport III; Captive Hearts; Collision Course; Desert Heat; Even Cowgirls Get the Blues; For the Love of It; Hiroshima: Out of the Ashes; Honeymoon in Vegas; Karate Kid, The; Karate Kid Part II, The; Karate Kid Part III, The; King Cobra; Miracle Beach; Next Karate Kid, The; Reggie's Prayer; Thoroughly Modern Millie; Timemaster
Moritz, Louisa: Death Race 2000
Moritzen, Henning: Celebration, The; Memories of a Marriage
Moriyama, Yuko: Zeram
Morley, Karen: Beloved Enemy; Black Fury; Gabriel over the White House; Littlest Rebel, The; Mask of Fu Manchu, The; Mata Hari; Our Daily Bread; Sin of Madelon Claudet, The
Morley, Natasha: Kissed
Morley, Rita: Flesh Eaters, The
Morley, Robert: African Queen, The; Alice in Wonderland; Alice Through the Looking Glass; Alphabet Murders, The; Battle of the Sexes, The; Beat the Devil; Beau Brummell; Cromwell; Ghosts of Berkeley Square; Great Muppet Caper, The; High Road to China; Hot Millions; Hotel Paradiso; Human Factor, The; Istanbul: Keep Your Eyes Open; Loved One, The; Major Barbara; Marie Antoinette; Murder at the Gallop; Of Human Bondage; Oh, Heavenly Dog!; Old Dark House, The; Road to Hong Kong, The; Scavenger Hunt; Song of Norway; Study in Terror, A; Theatre of Blood; Trouble with Spies, The; Who Is Killing the Great Chefs of Europe?; Wind, The; Woman Times Seven
Mornell, Sara: Plan B
Moro, Alicia: Exterminators of the Year 3000
Morra, Gigio: Ciao Professore
Morrell, Leo: Crime Killer, The
Morrill, Priscilla: Last of Mrs. Lincoln, The; Right of Way
Morris, Adrian: Fighting Marines, The
Morris, Anita: Absolute Beginners; Aria; Bloodhounds of Broadway; Blue City; 18 Again; Little Miss Millions; Me and the Kid; Ruthless People; Sinful Life, A
Morris, Ann: Honolulu
Morris, Barboura: Atlas; Bucket of Blood, A; Sorority Girl; Wasp Woman (1960)
Morris, Chester: Bat Whispers, The; Big House, The; Divorcee, The; Five Came Back; Frankie and Johnny; Red-Headed Woman; She Creature, The; Smashing the Rackets; Tomorrow at Seven
Morris, Garrett: Black Rose of Harlem; Black Scorpion II: Aftershock; Cooley High; Critical Condition; Jackpot; Motorama; Santa with Muscles; Severed Ties; Stuff, The; Things We Did Last Summer; Twin Falls Idaho; Where's Poppa?
Morris, Glenn: Tarzan's Revenge
Morris, Greg: Vega$
Morris, Haviland: Home Alone 3; Love or Money?; Who's That Girl
Morris, Howard: Andy Griffith Show, The (TV Series); Boys' Night Out; End of the Line; Forty Pounds of Trouble; Life Stinks; Portrait of a Showgirl; 10 from Your Show of Shows; Transylvania Twist
Morris, Jane: Frankie and Johnny; Pet Shop
Morris, Jessica: Bloody Murder
Morris, Jonathon: Fantasticks, The; Subspecies 4: Bloodstorm; Vampire Journals
Morris, Judy: Between Wars; Plumber, The
Morris, Kathryn: Inherit the Wind
Morris, Kirk: Maciste in Hell
Morris, Marianne: Vampyres
Morris, Mary: Pimpernel Smith
Morris, Paul: Vamps: Deadly Dream Girls
Morris, Phil: Legal Deceit
Morris, Phyllis: Adventures of Tartu
Morris, Richard: Sea Lion, The
Morris, Stepen: North of the Rio Grande
Morris, Stephen: Hopalong Cassidy Returns
Morris, Wayne: Bushwhackers; Kid Galahad; Plunder Road; Return of Dr. X; Smiling Ghost, The; Stage to Tucson; Task Force; Time of Your Life, The
Morrisey, Betty: Circus, The/A Day's Pleasure
Morrison, Bill: Maximum Impact; Ozone; Zombie Cop
Morrison, Jennifer: Urban Legends: Final Cut
Morrison, Kenny: NeverEnding Story II, The; Quick and the Dead, The
Morrison, Temuera: Barb Wire; Once Were Warriors; Star Wars: Attack of the Clones; Vertical Limit
Morrison, Van: Last Waltz, The
Morrissette, Billy: Severed Ties
Morrissey, David: Captain Corelli's Mandolin; Hilary and Jackie; Waterland
Morrissey, Eamon: Eat the Peach; Seventh Stream, The
Morrow, Doretta: Because You're Mine
Morrow, Jeff: Creature Walks Among Us, The; Giant Claw, The; Kronos; Octaman; This Island Earth

Morrow, Jo: Dr. Death: Seeker of Souls; 13 Ghosts; Three Worlds of Gulliver, The
Morrow, Joshua: My Stepson, My Lover
Morrow, Mari: Uninvited Guest
Morrow, Rob: Labor Pains; Last Dance; Maze; Mother; Northern Exposure (TV Series); Only Love; Private Resort; Quiz Show
Morrow, Vic: Bad News Bears, The; Blackboard Jungle, The; Cimarron; Dirty Mary, Crazy Larry; Glass House, The; Men in War; 1990: The Bronx Warriors; Tom Sawyer; Tribute to a Bad Man; Twilight Zone—The Movie
Morse, Barry: Asylum; Changeling, The; Fugitive, The (TV Series); Fugitive, The: The Last Episode (TV Series); Love at First Sight; Sadat; Space 1999 (TV Series); Story of David, The; Tale of Two Cities, A; Whoops Apocalypse; Woman of Substance, A
Morse, David: Bait; Brotherhood of the Rose; Contact; Crazy in Alabama; Crossing Guard, The; Cry in the Wind; Dancer in the Dark; Desperate Hours (1990); Extreme Measures; Getaway, The; Green Mile, The; Hearts in Atlantis; Indian Runner, The; Inside Moves; Langoliers, The; Long Kiss Goodnight, The; Proof of Life; Prototype; Rock, The; Shattered Vows; St. Elsewhere (TV Series)
Morse, Helen: Caddie; Picnic at Hanging Rock; Town Like Alice, A
Morse, Laila: Nil by Mouth
Morse, Robert: Boatniks, The; Guide for the Married Man, A; How to Succeed in Business without Really Trying; Hunk; Loved One, The; Matchmaker, The; Oh Dad, Poor Dad—Mama's Hung You inthe Closet and I'm Feeling So Sad; That's Singing: The Best of Broadway; Where Were You When the Lights Went Out?
Morse, Stan: Striking Point
Morshower, Glen: Drive-In
Mortensen, Viggo: Albino Alligator; American Yakuza; Boiling Point; Carlito's Way; Crew, The; Crimson Tide; Daylight; Deception; G.I. Jane; Indian Runner, The; Leatherface—the Texas Chainsaw Massacre III; Lord of the Rings, The: Fellowship of the Ring; Passion of Darkly Noon, The; Perfect Murder, A; Prophecy, The (1995); Psycho; Reflecting Skin, The; 28 Days; Walk on the Moon, A; Young Americans, The
Mortimer, Caroline: Death of Adolf Hitler, The
Mortimer, Emily: Kid, The (2000)
Morton, Amy: Rookie of the Year
Morton, Dee Dee: Dakota
Morton, Gary: Postcards from the Edge
Morton, Greg: Postcards from the Edge
Morton, Joe: Alone in the Neon Jungle; Astronaut's Wife, The; Between the Lines; Blues Brothers 2000; Brother from Another Planet, The; City of Hope; Crossroads; Dragonfly; Executive Decision; Forever Young; Inkwell, The; Legacy of Lies; Lone Star; Miss Evers' Boys; Speed; Stranded; Tap; Terminator 2: Judgment Day; Trouble in Mind; Trouble on the Corner; Walking Dead, The; What Lies Beneath
Morton, Samantha: Dreaming of Joseph Lees; Emma; Jesus' Son; Sweet and Lowdown; This Is the Sea; Under the Skin
Mosby, John: Backfire
Moschin, Gastone: Joke of Destiny; Mr. Superinvisible; Oldest Profession, The
Moscovich, Maurice: Everything Happens at Night
Moscow, David: Big; Newsies; White Wolves: A Cry in the Wild II
Moseley, Bill: Silent Night, Deadly Night III: Better Watch Out!
Moser, Jeff: To Catch a Yeti
Moses, David: Daring Dobermans, The
Moses, Harry: Sweater Girls
Moses, Mark: Dead Men Don't Die; Hollywood Heartbreak; Tracker, The; Treehouse Hostage
Moses, Norman: Unearthing, The
Moses, William R.: Alien from L.A.; Circumstances Unknown; Double Exposure; Evil Has a Face; Fiancé, The; Fun; Haunting of Sea Cliff Inn, The; Mystic Pizza; Nurse, The
Moshesh, Nthati: Long Run, The
Moskow, Kenny: Overkill
Mosley, Roger E.: Greatest, The; Heart Condition; I Know Why the Caged Bird Sings; Jericho Mile, The; Mack, The; Pentathlon; Pray TV; Steel; Unlawful Entry
Moss, Arnold: Caper of the Golden Bulls, The; Loves of Carmen, The
Moss, Carrie-Anne: Crew, The; Matrix, The; Memento; New Blood; Red Planet; Sabotage
Moss, Darcy De: Forbidden Zone: Alien Abduction
Moss, Elisabeth: Earthly Possessions; Girl, Interrupted; Midnight's Child; Mumford
Moss, George: Riff-Raff (1990)
Moss, Jesse: Noah
Moss, Ronn: Hard Ticket to Hawaii; Hearts and Armour
Moss, Stewart: Bat People
Moss, Tegan: Sea People
Most, Donny: Huckleberry Finn
Mostel, Josh: Animal Behavior; Beverly Hills 90210; Billy Madison; City Slickers; City Slickers II; Compromising Positions; Great Expectations; Little Man Tate; Maddening, The; Matewan; Money Pit, The; Naked Tango; Radio Days; Stoogemania; Windy City
Mostel, Zero: Du Barry Was a Lady; Enforcer, The; Front, The; Funny Thing Happened on the Way to the Forum, A; Hot Rock, The; Journey into Fear; Mastermind; Panic in the Streets; Producers, The; Sirocco
Motoki, Masahiro: Gonin; Mystery of Rampo, The
Motulsky, Judy: Slithis
Mouchet, Catherine: Therese
Moulder-Brown, John: Deep End; King, Queen and Knave; Sleeping Murder
Moulin, Charles: Baker's Wife, The
Mount, Anson: Crossroads (2002); Urban Legends: Final Cut
Mouser, Dru: Tequila Body Shots
Mouton, Benjamin: Whore
Movin, Lisbeth: Day of Wrath
Movita: Wolf Call
Mowbray, Alan: Androcles and the Lion; Charlie Chan in London; Doughgirls, The; Every Girl Should Be Married; Girl from Missouri, The; Hollywood Hotel; In Person; It Happened in New Orleans; Ma and Pa Kettle at Home; Majority of One, A; Merton of the Movies; My Dear Secretary; On the Avenue; Roman Scandals; Rose Marie; So This Is Washington; Stand-In; Study in Scarlet, A; Terror by Night; That Uncertain Feeling; Topper Takes a Trip; Villain Still Pursued Her, The
Mower, Patrick: Black Beauty
Moy, Wood: Chan Is Missing
Moya, Angela: Luminarias
Moya, Pay: In the Soup
Moyer, Stephen: Prince Valiant
Moyer, Tawny: House of the Rising Sun
Moynahan, Bridget: Serendipity; Sum of All Fears, The
Moynihan, Bill: Creeps, The
Moyo, Alois: Power of One, The
Mr. T: D.C. Cab; Freaked; Penitentiary II; Rocky III; Straight Line
Mucari, Carlo: Tex and the Lord of the Deep
Mudugno, Enrica Maria: Kaos
Muel, Jean-Paul: House That Mary Bought, The
Mueller, Cookie: Female Trouble; Multiple Maniacs
Mueller, Dick: Omaha (The Movie)
Mueller, Maureen: In a Shallow Grave; Over Her Dead Body
Mueller-Stahl, Armin: Angry Harvest; Avalon; Colonel Redl; Forget Mozart; Game, The; Holy Matrimony; House of the Spirits, The; In the Presence of Mine Enemies; Jakob the Liar; Kafka; Last Good Time, The; Lola; Long Run, The; Music Box, The; Night on Earth; Peacemaker, The (1997); Power of One, The; Red Hot; Shine; Theodore Rex; Third Miracle, The; Thirteenth Floor, The; 12 Angry Men; Utz; X-Files, The (1998)
Mui, Anita: Better Tomorrow 3, A: Love and Death in Saigon; Jet Li's the Enforcer; Rumble in the Bronx
Muir, Gavin: Night Tide
Mukherji, Swapan: World of Apu, The
Mulcahy, Jack: Brothers McMullen, The
Muldaur, Diana: Beyond Reason; McQ; Other, The; Planet Earth; Return of Frank Cannon, The
Muldoon, Patrick: Arrival II, The; Black Cat Run; Chain of Command; Crimson Code; Rage and Honor II: Hostile Takeover

Mule, Francesco: When Women Lost Their Tails
Mulford, Nancy: Act of Piracy
Mulgrew, Kate: Danielle Steel's Daddy; Love Spell; Manions of America, The; Remo Williams: The Adventure Begins; Roots—The Gift; Round Numbers; Stranger Is Watching, A; Throw Momma from the Train
Mulhall, Jack: Buck Rogers: Destination Saturn (PlanetOutlaws); Flesh and Blood (1922); Invisible Ghost; Mysterious Dr. Satan; Mystery Squadron; Outlaws of Sonora; Saddle Mountain Roundup; Skull and Crown; Three Musketeers, The
Mulhare, Edward: Our Man Flint; Out to Sea; Outer Limits, The (TV Series); Von Ryan's Express
Mulhern, Matt: Biloxi Blues
Mulkey, Chris: Bound and Gagged: A Love Story; Dead Cold; Deadbolt; Ghost in the Machine; Heartbreak Hotel; Hometown Boy Makes Good; In Dangerous Company; Jack's Back; Patti Rocks; Psychopath (1997); Roe vs. Wade; Runaway Father; Silencer, The; Weapons of Mass Distraction; Write to Kill
Mull, Martin: Attention Shoppers; Bad Manners; Boss' Wife, The; Clue; Cutting Class; Dánce with Death; Day My Parents Ran Away, The; Edie & Pen; Far Out Man; FM; Home Is Where the Hart Is; How the West Was Fun; Lots of Luck; Mary Hartman, Mary Hartman (TV Series); Mr. Mom; Mr. Write; Mrs. Doubtfire; My Bodyguard; O.C. & Stiggs; Private School; Rented Lips; Serial; Sister Mary Explains It All; Ski Patrol; Take This Job and Shove It; Ted & Venus; Think Big
Mullally, Megan: Last Resort
Mullan, Carrie: Hideous Kinky
Mullan, Peter: Claim, The; Miss Julie; My Name is Joe; Session 9
Mullaney, Jack: Honeymoon Machine, The; Tickle Me
Mullany, Mitch: Breaks, The
Mullavey, Greg: C.C. & Company; I Dismember Mama; Mary Hartman, Mary Hartman (TV Series); Vultures
Mullen, Barbara: Corridor of Mirrors
Mullen, Leanne: Ratcatcher
Mullen, Marie: When Brendan Met Trudy
Mullen, Patty: Doom Asylum
Muller, Harrison: Final Executioner, The; She; 2020 Texas Gladiators; Violent Breed, The
Muller, Paul: Devil's Commandment, The; Nightmare Castle
Mulligan, Richard: Babes in Toyland; Big Bus, The; Doin' Time; Fine Mess, A; Gore Vidal's Lincoln; Group, The; Heavenly Kid, The; Hideaways, The; Little Big Man; Meatballs Part II; Poker Alice; Scavenger Hunt; S.O.B.; Teachers
Mulligan, Terry David: Hard Core Logo
Mullinar, Rod: Thirst
Mullins, Robin: Nell
Mulloney, Joe: Restless Natives
Mullowney, Deborah: Cellar Dweller
Mulroney, Dermot: Bad Girls; Bastard Out of Carolina; Bright Angel; Career Opportunities; Copycat; Goodbye Lover; Heart of Justice; How to Make an American Quilt; Kansas City; Last Outlaw, The; Living in Oblivion; Longtime Companion; My Best Friend's Wedding; Point of No Return; Samantha; Silent Tongue; Staying Together; Survival Quest; There Goes My Baby; Thing Called Love, The; Trigger Effect, The; Trixie; Where the Day Takes You; Where the Money Is; Young Guns
Mulroney, Kieran: Career Opportunities
Mulrooney, Lee: Resurrection Man
Mumba, Omero: Time Machine, The (2002)
Mummert, Danny: It's a Great Life
Mumy, Billy: Bless the Beasts and Children; Dear Brigitte; Lost in Space (TV Series); Sammy, the Way-Out Seal
Mumy, Seth: Three Wishes
Munch, Richard: Of Pure Blood
Munchkin, R. W.: L.A. Vice
Mundra, Michael Aniel: Across the Moon
Mundy, Kevin: Better Than Chocolate; Jailbait (2000)
Mune, Ian: Sleeping Dogs
Muni, Paul: Angel on My Shoulder; Black Fury; Commandos Strike at Dawn; Good Earth, The; I Am a Fugitive from a Chain Gang; Juarez; Last Angry Man, The; Life of Emile Zola, The; Scarface; Song to Remember, A; Story of Louis Pasteur, The
Muniz, Frankie: Big Fat Liar; Miracle in Lane 2; My Dog Skip
Muniz, Tommy: Crazy from the Heart
Munro, Caroline: At the Earth's Core; Captain Kronos: Vampire Hunter; Devil Within Her, The; Don't Open Till Christmas; Golden Voyage of Sinbad, The; Last Horror Film, The; Maniac; Night Owl; Slaughter High; Spy Who Loved Me, The; Star Crash
Munro, Janet: Crawling Eye, The; Darby O'Gill and the Little People; Day the Earth Caught Fire, The; Horsemasters; Third Man on the Mountain
Munro, Lochlyn: Camouflage; Dead Man on Campus
Munro, Neil: Confidential; Dancing in the Dark
Munroe, Fred: Longest Hunt, The
Munroe, Steve: Comic, The
Munshin, Jules: Easter Parade; Mastermind; On the Town; Take Me Out to the Ball Game
Munson, Ona: Lady from Louisiana; Red House, The; Shanghai Gesture, The
Munzuk, Maxim: Dersu Uzala
Muppets: Great Muppet Caper, The; Muppet Movie, The; Muppets Take Manhattan, The
Murase, Sachiko: Rhapsody in August
Murat, Jean: Carnival in Flanders; Eternal Return, The
Murata, Takehiro: Godzilla 2000; Minbo, or The Gentle Art of Japanese Extortion
Muravyova, Irina: Moscow Does Not Believe in Tears
Murdocco, Vince: Deathgame; Flesh Gordon 2: Flesh Gordon meets the Cosmic Cheerleaders
Murdock, George: Breaker! Breaker!; Certain Fury; Scorpio One; Strange Case of Dr. Jekyll and Mr. Hyde,The (1989)
Muresan, Gheorghe: My Giant
Murney, Christopher: Grace Quigley; Last Dragon, The; Secret of My Success, The
Murphy, Annette: Star Maps
Murphy, Audie: Arizona Raiders; Guns of Fort Petticoat; Red Badge of Courage, The; To Hell and Back; Unforgiven, The (1960)
Murphy, Ben: Chisholms, The; Cradle Will Fall, The; Riding with Death; Time Walker
Murphy, Brittany: Bongwater; Cherry Falls; Clueless; Common Ground; Devil's Arithmetic, The; Don't Say a Word; Girl, Interrupted; Prophecy II, The; Riding in Cars with Boys; Sidewalks of New York (2001); Summer Catch
Murphy, Carolyn: Liberty Heights
Murphy, Charlie: CB4
Murphy, Donald: Frankenstein's Daughter; Lord Love a Duck
Murphy, Donna: Center Stage; Last Debate, The; Star Trek: Insurrection
Murphy, Eddie: Another 48 Hrs.; Best Defense; Beverly Hills Cop; Beverly Hills Cop II; Beverly Hills Cop 3; Boomerang; Bowfinger; Coming to America; Distinguished Gentleman, The; Dr. Dolittle (1998); Dr. Dolittle 2; 48 Hrs.; Golden Child, The; Harlem Nights; Holy Man; Life; Metro; Nutty Professor, The; Nutty Professor II: The Klumps; Shrek; Trading Places; Vampire in Brooklyn
Murphy, Edna: Tarzan and the Golden Lion
Murphy, George: Bataan; Battleground; Broadway Melody of 1940; Broadway Melody of 1938; Broadway Rhythm; For Me and My Gal; Girl, a Guy and a Gob, A; Having a Wonderful Crime; It's a Big Country; Kid Millions; Letter of Introduction; Little Miss Broadway; Little Nellie Kelly; Show Business; Step Lively; This Is the Army; Tom, Dick and Harry
Murphy, Gerard: Waterworld
Murphy, Jack: Peter Pan
Murphy, Johnny: Commitments, The; Into the West
Murphy, Mary: Main Street to Broadway; Man Alone, A; Maverick Queen, The; Wild One, The
Murphy, Michael: Autobiography of Miss Jane Pittman, The; Breaking the Surface: The Greg Louganis Story; Caine Mutiny Court Martial, The; Class of Miss MacMichael, The; Clean Slate (1994); Cloak and Dagger; Count Yorga, Vampire; Dead Ahead: The Exxon Valdez Disaster; Folks; Great Bank Hoax, The; Kansas City; Manhattan; Mesmerized (Shocked); Phase IV; Salvador; Shocker; Strange Behavior; Tailspin; Tanner '88; That

Cold Day in the Park; Unmarried Woman, An; Year of Living Dangerously, The
Murphy, Reilly: Body Snatchers, The (1993)
Murphy, Rosemary: Any Wednesday; Ben; For the Boys; George Washington; Walking Tall
Murphy, Shannon: Firehouse
Murphy, Steve: No Justice
Murphy, Timothy Patrick: Sam's Son
Murray, Bill: Caddyshack; Charlie's Angels; Cradle Will Rock; Ed Wood; Ghostbusters; Ghostbusters II; Groundhog Day; Hamlet; Kingpin; Larger than Life; Little Shop of Horrors (1986); Loose Shoes; Mad Dog and Glory; Man Who Knew Too Little, The; Meatballs; Osmosis Jones; Quick Change; Razor's Edge, The; Rushmore; Scrooged; Space Jam; Stripes; Things We Did Last Summer; Tootsie; What About Bob?; Where the Buffalo Roam
Murray, Chic: Gregory's Girl
Murray, Christopher: Just Cause
Murray, Don: Advise and Consent; Baby the Rain Must Fall; Bus Stop; Conquest of the Planet of the Apes; Deadly Hero; Endless Love; Ghosts Can't Do It; Hearts Adrift; Hoodlum Priest, The; I Am the Cheese; Justin Morgan Had a Horse; Mistress; One Man's Way; Peggy Sue Got Married; Quarterback Princess; Radioactive Dreams; Scorpion; Shake Hands with the Devil; Sweet Love, Bitter
Murray, Guillermo: World of the Vampires
Murray, James: Crowd, The
Murray, Jan: Night Stalker, The: Two Tales of Terror (TV Series); Which Way to the Front?
Murray, John: Moving Violations
Murray, Mae: Bachelor Apartment; Merry Widow, The
Murray, Mick: Midnight Witness
Murtaugh, James: Rosary Murders, The
Murton, Lionel: Meet the Navy
Murton, Tom: Main Street to Broadway
Musante, Tony: Bird with the Crystal Plumage, The; Breaking Up Is Hard to Do; Collector's Item; Grissom Gang, The; Incident, The
Muscat, Angelo: Prisoner, The (1968) (TV Series)
Muse, Clarence: Black Stallion, The; Murder over New York
Musgrave, Robert: Bottle Rocket
Musidora: Vampires, The (1915) (Les Vampires)
Mustain, Minor: Snake Eater III: His Law
Musy, Allan: Warrior Spirit
Mutchie, Marjorie Ann: It's a Great Life
Muti, Ornella: Casanova; Once Upon a Crime; Oscar (1991); Somewhere in the City; Swann in Love; Tales of Ordinary Madness; Wait Until Spring, Bandini
Muza, Melvin: Street Hitz (Street Story)
Myers, Bruce: Governess, The
Myers, Carmel: Beau Brummell; Ben-Hur; Svengali
Myers, Cynthia: Beyond the Valley of the Dolls
Myers, Harry: City Lights
Myers, Kathleen: Dick Turpin
Myers, Kim: Illegally Yours; Nightmare on Elm Street 2, A: Freddy's Revenge
Myers, Mike: Austin Powers: International Man of Mystery; Austin Powers: The Spy Who Shagged Me; 54; Shrek; So I Married an Axe Murderer; Wayne's World; Wayne's World 2
Myerson, Alan: Steelyard Blues
Myles, Harry: Robo Vampire
Mynster, Karen-Lise: Sofie
N!Xau: Gods Must Be Crazy II, The
Nabors, Jim: Andy Griffith Show, The (TV Series); Return to Mayberry; Stroker Ace
Nachtergaele, Matheus: Four Days in September
Nader, George: Away All Boats; Carnival Story; House of 1,000 Dolls; Human Duplicators, The; Lady Godiva; Monsoon; Robot Monster
Nader, Michael: Finishing Touch, The; Flash, The (1990); Fled; Jackie Collins' Lucky Chances; Lady Mobster; Nick Knight
Naderi, Massoumeh: Apple, The
Nagase, Masatoshi: Cold Fever; Mystery Train
Nagel, Anne: Black Friday; Case of the Stuttering Bishop, The; Hoosier Schoolboy; Mad Doctor of Market Street, The; Mad Monster; Man Made Monster (The Atomic Monster); Spirit of West Point, The; Winners of the West
Nagel, Conrad: All That Heaven Allows; Ann Vickers; Divorcee, The; Kiss, The; Mysterious Lady, The
Nagy, Bill: Countess from Hong Kong, A
Naidu, Ajay: Touch and Go; Where the River Runs Black
Naiduk, Stacy: Steel and Lace
Nail, Jimmy: Diamond's Edge; Evita; Still Crazy
Nail, Joanne: Switchblade Sisters
Naish, J. Carrol: Across the Wide Missouri; Ann Vickers; Annie Get Your Gun; Beast with Five Fingers, The; Beau Geste; Behind the Rising Sun; Black Hand, The; Bulldog Drummond Comes Back; Bulldog Drummond in Africa; Calling Dr. Death; Clash by Night; CorsicanBrothers, The; Denver and Rio Grande, The; Down Argentine Way; Dracula vs. Frankenstein; Fighter Attack; Fugitive, The; Gung Ho! (1943); House of Frankenstein; Humoresque; Joan of Arc; Jungle Woman; Kissing Bandit, The; Last Command, The; Monster Maker, The; New Adventures of Charlie Chan, The (TVSeries); Rage at Dawn; Rio Grande; Sahara; Southerner, The; Strange Confession; That Midnight Kiss; Think Fast, Mr. Moto; This Could Be the Night; Thunder Trail; Toast of New Orleans; Waterfront; World Gone Mad, The
Naismith, Laurence: Amazing Mr. Blunden, The; Carrington, V. C.; Concrete Jungle, (1962) The (Criminal, The); Greyfriars Bobby; Man Who Never Was, The; Night to Remember, A; Persuaders, The (TV Series); Scrooge; Sink the Bismarck; World of Suzie Wong, The; Young Winston
Naito, Takashi: After Life
Najee-ullah, Mansoor: Death of a Prophet
Naji, Amir: Children of Heaven
Najimy, Kathy: Attention Shoppers; Hocus Pocus; Jeffrey; Nevada; Rat Race; Sister Act; Sister Act 2: Back in the Habit
Nakadai, Tatsuya: Face of Another, The; High and Low; Human Condition, The, Part One: No Greater Love; Human Condition, The, Part Two: The Roadto Eternity; Human Condition, The, Part Three: A Soldier's Prayer; Hunter in the Dark; Kagemusha; Kojiro; Kwaidan; Odd Obsession; Ran; Sanjuro; Sword of Doom; Wicked City, The (1992); Wolves, The
Nakagawa, Anna: Silk Road, The
Nakagawa, Ken: Living on Tokyo Time
Nakagawa, Roger: Escapade in Japan
Nakahara, Takeo: Godzilla 2000
Nakamura, Atsuo: Highest Honor, The
Nakamura, Ganjiro: Drifting Weeds
Nakamura, Kichiemon: Double Suicide
Nakamura, Knemon: Forty Seven Ronin
Nakamura, Toru: Blue Tiger; Gen-X Cops; New York Cop
Nakhapetov, Rodion: Slave of Love, A
Nalbach, Daniel: Gig, The
Nalder, Reggie: Day and the Hour; Mark of the Devil; Mark of the Devil, Part 2; Salem's Lot; Zoltan—Hound of Dracula
Naldi, Nita: Blood and Sand; Dr. Jekyll and Mr. Hyde; Ten Commandments, The
Namath, Joe: C.C. & Company; Chattanooga Choo Choo
Nance, Jack: Eraserhead; Little Witches; Meatballs 4; Twin Peaks (Movie); Twin Peaks (TV Series); Voodoo
Nance, John: Ghoulies
Nann, Erika: Mindtwister
Nanty, Isabelle: Tatie Danielle
Napaul, Neriah: Bikini Carwash Company 2
Naper, Marshall: Georgia
Napier, Alan: Across the Wide Missouri; Challenge to Lassie; Hangover Square; Hills of Home; House of the Seven Gables, The; Invisible Man Returns; Mademoiselle Fifi; Mole People, The; 36 Hours; Uninvited, The
Napier, Charles: Big Tease, The; Center of the Web; Citizen's Band; Ernest Goes to Jail; Eyes of the Beholder; Future Zone; Grifters, The; Hard Justice; Homicidal Impulse; Hunter's Moon; Incredible Hulk Returns, The; Indio 2: The Revolt; Instant Justice; Jury Duty; Last Embrace, The; Macon County Jail; Max Is Missing; Miami Blues; Night Stalker, The; One-Man Force; Philadelphia; Rambo: First Blood II; Renegade; Return to Frog-

Nelson, Barry: Bataan; Casino Royale; Island Claws; Johnny Eager; Pete 'n' Tillie; Rio Rita; Shadow of the Thin Man
Nelson, Bob: Brain Donors
Nelson, Bobby: Cyclone in the Saddle
Nelson, Craig T.: Action Jackson; All the Right Moves; ... And Justice for All; Call to Glory; Devil's Advocate; Diary of a Teenage Hitchhiker; Dirty Pictures; Fire Next Time, The; Ghosts of Mississippi; Huntress, The; I'm Not Rappaport; Josephine Baker Story, The; Killing Fields, The; Me and Him; Murderers Among Us: The Simon WiesenthalStory; Poltergeist; Poltergeist II: The Other Side; Probable Cause; Rachel River; Rage; Silkwood; Skulls, The; Troop Beverly Hills; Wag the Dog
Nelson, Danny: Blood Salvage
Nelson, David: Adventures of Ozzie and Harriet, The (TV Series); Cry-Baby; Peyton Place
Nelson, Dick: Great Guns
Nelson, Ed: Attack of the Crab Monsters; Boneyard, The; Brain Eaters, The; Bucket of Blood, A; Cries of Silence; For the Love of Benji; Return of Frank Cannon, The
Nelson, Gene: Lullaby of Broadway; Tea for Two; West Point Story, The
Nelson, Guy: Invasion of the Space Preachers
Nelson, Harriet: Adventures of Ozzie and Harriet, The (TV Series); Follow the Fleet; Kid with the 200 I.Q., The; Take It Big
Nelson, John Allen: Criminal Passion; Deathstalker III—The Warriors from Hell; Hunk; Killer Klowns from Outer Space; Saigon Commandos
Nelson, Judd: Billionaire Boys Club; Blackwater Trail; Blindfold: Acts of Obsession; Blue City; Breakfast Club, The; Cabin by the Lake; Caroline at Midnight; Circumstances Unknown; Conflict of Interest; Dark Asylum; Dark Backward, The; Entangled; Every Breath; Fandango; Far Out Man; Flinch; From the Hip; Hail Caesar; Hiroshima: Out of the Ashes; Light It Up; Making the Grade; New Jack City; Primary Motive; Relentless; St. Elmo's Fire; Steel
Nelson, June: Adventures of Ozzie and Harriet, The (TV Series)
Nelson, Kenneth: Boys in the Band, The
Nelson, Kris: Adventures of Ozzie and Harriet, The (TV Series)
Nelson, Lori: All I Desire; Day the World Ended, The; I Died a Thousand Times; Ma and Pa Kettle at the Fair; Ma and Pa Kettle at Waikiki; Mohawk; Revenge of the Creature; Underwater!
Nelson, Mari: Whore 2
Nelson, Michael J.: Mystery Science Theatre 3000: The Movie
Nelson, Ozzie: Adventures of Ozzie and Harriet, The (TV Series); Impossible Years, The; People Are Funny; Take It Big
Nelson, Peter: Crime Zone
Nelson, Rebecca: Surviving Desire
Nelson, Ricky: Adventures of Ozzie and Harriet, The (TV Series); Rio Bravo; Wackiest Ship in the Army, The
Nelson, Ruth: Awakenings; Haunting Passion, The; Wilson
Nelson, Sandra: Halfback of Notre Dame, The
Nelson, Sean: American Buffalo; Fresh; Stranger in the Kingdom, A; Wood, The
Nelson, Steven: Little Ninjas
Nelson, Tracy: Down and Out in Beverly Hills; Game of Love, The
Nelson, Willie: Amazons; Another Pair of Aces; Barbarosa; Coming Out of the Ice; Dynamite and Gold; Electric Horseman, The; Honeysuckle Rose; Last Days of Frank and Jesse James; Pair of Aces; Red-Headed Stranger, The; Songwriter; Stagecoach; Texas Guns; Thief (1981); Wag the Dog
Nemec, Corin: Drop Zone; Killer Bud; Lifeforce Experiment, The; Operation Dumbo Drop; Solar Crisis; Stand, The; War at Home, The; White Wolves II: Legend of the Wild
Nene, Sibongile: Jit
Neri, Francesca: Collateral Damage; Flight of the Innocent; Hannibal; Live Flesh; Outrage (1994)
Nero, Franco: Camelot; Challenge to White Fang; Confessions of a Police Captain; Die Hard 2: Die Harder; Django; Enter the Ninja; Force Ten from Navarone; Girl, The; High Crime; Kamikaze 89; Legend of Valentino; Long Live Your Death; Magdalene; Man with Bogart's Face, The; Querelle; Redneck; Salamander, The; Sardine: Kidnapped; Shark Hunter, The; Spaghetti Western; Sweet Country; Talk of Angels; Touch and Die; Tramplers, The; Tristana; Virgin and the Gypsy, The; Windmills of the Gods; Young Catherine
Nero, Toni: No Dead Heroes; Silent Night, Deadly Night
Nervo, Jimmy: Frozen Limits, The
Nesbitt, Cathleen: Affair to Remember, An; Desirée; Family Plot; Nicholas Nickleby; Staircase
Nesbitt, James: Go Now; Waking Ned Devine
Nesmith, Mike: Head (1968); Television Parts Home Companion
Nettleton, Lois: Bamboo Saucer (Collision Course); Brass; Butterfly; Deadly Blessing; Good Guys and the Bad Guys, The; Man in the Glass Booth; Manhunt for Claude Dallas; Period of Adjustment
Neubert, Keith: Sons of Trinity, The
Neufeld, Martin: Relative Fear
Neufield, Marc: Highlander: The Final Dimension
Neuman, Dorothy: Undead, The
Neuman, Jenny: Hell Night
Neuwirth, Bebe: Adventures of Pinocchio, The; Associate, The; Bugsy; Faculty, The; Green Card; Jumanji; Liberty Heights; Malice; Paint Job, The
Neville, Aaron: Zandalee
Neville, John: Adventures of Baron Münchausen, The; Baby's Day Out; Behind the Lines; Johnny 2.0; Sabotage; Song Spinner; Study in Terror, A; X-Files, The (1998); X-Files, The (TV Series)
Nevin, Brooke: Running Wild
Nevin, Robyn: Careful He Might Hear You; Fourth Wish, The; Irishman, The
Nevin, Rosa: Still Not Quite Human
Nevins, Claudette: Mask, The; Possessed, The (1977)
Nevinson, Gennie: Muriel's Wedding
New, Nancy: Bostonians, The
Newark, Derek: Bellman and True; Offence, The
Newbern, George: Doppelganger: The Evil Within; Evening Star, The; Father of the Bride; Father of the Bride Part II; It Takes Two; Little Sister; Paramedics; Witness to the Execution
Newbigin, Flora: Borrowers, The
Newburger, Marc: Curse of the Puppet Master
Newcomb, Jamie: Lone Wolf
Newell, William: Mysterious Dr. Satan
Newhart, Bob: Cold Turkey; First Family; Hell Is for Heroes; Hot Millions; In & Out; Little Miss Marker; Marathon; On a Clear Day, You Can See Forever; Thursday's Game
Newland, Michael: Big Bang Theory, The
Newley, Anthony: Alice in Wonderland; Alice Through the Looking Glass; Boris and Natasha; Doctor Dolittle; Garbage Pail Kids Movie, The; Good Idea; Old Curiosity Shop, The; Outrage!; Stagecoach; X—The Unknown
Newman, Alec: Dune
Newman, Barry: Amy; Bowfinger; Brown's Requiem; Having It All; Limey, The; Mirror Crack'd from Side to Side, The; Night Games; Salzburg Connection, The; True Blue; Vanishing Point
Newman, Emily: Woman Chaser, The
Newman, James L.: Silent Night, Deadly Night Part 2
Newman, Laraine: Alone in the Woods; American Hot Wax; Coneheads; Invaders from Mars; Perfect; Problem Child 2; Revenge of the Red Baron; Things We Did Last Summer; Tunnelvision (1976); Wholly Moses!; Witchboard 2
Newman, Nanette: Endless Game, The; Long Ago Tomorrow; Madwoman of Chaillot, The; Of Human Bondage; Seance on a Wet Afternoon; Wrong Arm of the Law, The; Wrong Box, The
Newman, Paul: Absence of Malice; Blaze; Buffalo Bill and the Indians; Butch Cassidy and the Sundance Kid; Cat on a Hot Tin Roof; Color of Money, The; Cool Hand Luke; Drowning Pool, The; Exodus; Fat Man and Little Boy; Fort Apache—The Bronx; From the Terrace; Harper; Harry and Son; Helen Morgan Story, The; Hombre; Hud; Hudsucker Proxy, The; Hustler, The; Lady L; Left Handed Gun, The; Life and Times of Judge Roy Bean, The; Long Hot Summer, The; Mackintosh Man, The; Message in a Bottle; Mr. and Mrs. Bridge; New Kind of Love, A; Nobody's Fool; Paris Blues; Pocket Money; Prize, The; Quintet; Secret War of Harry Frigg, The; Silent Movie; Silver Chalice, The; Slap Shot; Somebody Up There Likes Me; Sometimes a Great Notion; Sting,

Nirvana, Yana: Club Life
Nishida, Naomi: Godzilla 2000
Nishida, Toshiyuki: Silk Road, The
Nishio, John: Silk Road, The
Nissen, Heige: Leaves from Satan's Book
Nitschke, Ronald: Innocent, The; Sons of Trinity, The
Niven, Barbara: I Married a Monster; Under Lock and Key
Niven, David: Around the World in 80 Days; Ask Any Girl; Bachelor Mother; Bedtime Story; Beloved Enemy; Birds and the Bees, The; Bishop's Wife, The; Bluebeard's Eighth Wife; Bonjour Tristesse; Bonnie Prince Charlie; Candleshoe; Carrington, V. C.; Casino Royale; Charge of the Light Brigade, The; Curse of the Pink Panther, The; Dawn Patrol, The; Death on the Nile; Dinner at the Ritz; Dodsworth; Elusive Pimpernel, The; Enchantment; Escape to Athena; Eternally Yours; 55 Days at Peking; Guns of Navarone, The; Happy Go Lovely; Immortal Battalion, The (The Way Ahead); Impossible Years, The; King, Queen and Knave; Lady L; Moon Is Blue, The; Murder by Death; My Man Godfrey; No Deposit, No Return; Paper Tiger; Perfect Marriage; Pink Panther, The; Please Don't Eat the Daisies; Prisoner of Zenda, The; Real Glory, The; Rough Cut; Sea Wolves, The; Statue, The; Toast of New Orleans; Trail of the Pink Panther, The; Wuthering Heights
Niven, Kip: New Year's Evil
Nivola, Alessandro: Face/Off; I Want You; Jurassic Park III; Love's Labour's Lost; Mansfield Park; Reach the Rock
Nixon, Cynthia: Baby's Day Out; I Am the Cheese; Manhattan Project, The; Tanner '88
Nixon, John P.: Legend of Boggy Creek
Nixon, Marni: Taking My Turn
Niznik, Stephanie: Inferno
Nkake, Sandra: Girl, The (1999)
Noah, Jeffrey: Baby Monitor: Sound of Fear
Noakes, Tony: Breakaway
Noble, Chelsea: Instant Karma; Left Behind
Noble, Christian: Human Desires
Noble, Erin: Uninvited, The
Noble, James: Paramedics; You Talkin' to Me
Noble, Nancy Lee: Just for the Hell of It
Noble, Trisha: Private Eyes, The
Nocito, Renee: Track 16
Noel, Bernard: Married Woman, A
Noel, Chris: Cease Fire; Glory Stompers, The
Noel, Magali: Amarcord; Les Rendez-Vous D'Anna; Rififi
Noel-Noel: Sputnik
Noethen, Aldrich: Harmonists, The
Nogulich, Natalija: Dirty Dozen, The: The Fatal Mission; Hoffa; Homicide
Noiman, Rivka: Jesus
Noimura, Christopheren: Madame Butterfly
Noiret, Philippe: Birgit Haas Must Be Killed; Cinema Paradiso; Clean Slate (Coup de Torchon) (1981); Clockmaker, The (1973); Dead Tired (Grosse Fatigue); Fort Saganne; Holes, The; Judge and the Assassin, The; Jupiter's Thigh; Justine; Le Secret; Life and Nothing But; Murphy's War; My New Partner; Next Summer; Night Flight from Moscow; Postman, The (Il Postino); Purple Taxi, The; Return of the Musketeers; Revenge of the Musketeers; Three Brothers; Uranus; Woman at Her Window, A; Zazie dans le Metro
Nolan, Doris: Holiday
Nolan, Jeanette: Avalanche; Big Heat, The; Chamber of Horrors; Macbeth
Nolan, Kathleen: Amy; Lights, Camera, Action, Love; Night Stalker, The: Two Tales of Terror (TV Series)
Nolan, Lloyd: Bataan; Circus World; Dressed to Kill; Every Day's a Holiday; Fire!; Girl Hunters, The; Guadalcanal Diary; Hannah and Her Sisters; House Across the Bay, The; House on 92nd Street, The; Ice Station Zebra; Interns Can't Take Money; Island in the Sky; Johnny Apollo; Lady in the Lake; Last Hunt, The; Lemon Drop Kid, The; My Boys Are Good Boys; Peyton Place; Private Files of J. Edgar Hoover, The; Sergeant Ryker; Somewhere in the Night; Street with No Name; Sun Comes Up, The; Texas Rangers (1936); Tree Grows in Brooklyn, A
Nolan, Paul: Shapeshifter
Nolan, Tom: School Spirit; Up the Creek
Nolan and the Sons of the Pioneers, Bob: Apache Rose; Bells of Rosarita; Don't Fence Me In; Eyes of Texas; Helldorado; Nighttime in Nevada; Old Corral; Roll on Texas Moon; San Fernando Valley; Song of Nevada; Song of Texas
Nolot, Jacques: Under the Sand
Nolte, Brawley: Ransom
Nolte, Nick: Affliction; Afterglow; Another 48 Hrs.; Blue Chips; Breakfast of Champions; Cannery Row; Cape Fear; Deep, The; Down and Out in Beverly Hills; Everybody Wins; Extreme Prejudice; Farewell to the King; 48 Hrs.; Golden Bowl, The; Grace Quigley; Heart Beat; I Love Trouble; I'll Do Anything; Jefferson in Paris; Lorenzo's Oil; Mother Night; Mulholland Falls; New York Stories; Nightwatch; North Dallas Forty; Prince of Tides, The; Q & A; Return to Macon County; Simpatico; Teachers; Thin Red Line, The; Three Fugitives; Trixie; U-Turn; Under Fire; Weeds; Who'll Stop the Rain
None Credited: Godzilla vs. the Sea Monster; Gorath
Noni, Geula: Sallah
Nonyela, Valentine: Young Soul Rebels
Noonan, Tom: Collision Course; Last Action Hero, The; Opportunists, The; Pledge, The
Noonan, Tommy: Ambassador's Daughter, The; Bundle of Joy; Gentlemen Prefer Blondes; Girl Most Likely, The; Jungle Patrol; Monster Squad, The; Promises, Promises; Star Is Born, A; Three Nuts in Search of a Bolt; What Happened Was ...; Wife, The; Wolfen
Noone, Kathleen: Hearts Adrift
Norby, Ghita: Kingdom, The; Memories of a Marriage; Sofie
Norcia, Jo: Maximum Impact
Norden, Tommy: Flipper's Odyssey
Nordling, Jeffrey: Dangerous Heart; D3: The Mighty Ducks
Nordquist, Monica: Polar Bear King, The
Norgaard, Cartsen: D2: The Mighty Ducks
Noriega, Eduardo: Devil's Backbone, The; Open Your Eyes; Thesis
Noris, Saran: Invisible Dad
Norman, Robert: My Life So Far
Norman, Steve: Jet Benny Show, The
Norman, Susan: Poison
Norman, Zack: America; Babyfever; Cadillac Man; Romancing the Stone; Sitting Ducks
Normand, Mabel: Charlie Chaplin ... Our Hero; Extra Girl, The; Keystone Comedies: Vol. 1–5; When Comedy Was King
Norona, David: Mrs. Santa Claus
Norris, Aaron: Overkill
Norris, Bruce: Reach the Rock; Sixth Sense, The
Norris, Christopher: Eat My Dust; Summer of '42
Norris, Chuck: Braddock: Missing in Action III; Breaker! Breaker!; Bruce Lee: Curse of the Dragon; Code of Silence; Delta Force, The; Delta Force 2; Eye for an Eye; Firewalker; Force of One; Forced Vengeance; Forest Warrior; Game of Death; Good Guys Wear Black; Hellbound; Hero and the Terror; Hitman, The; Invasion U.S.A. (1985); Lone Wolf McQuade; Missing in Action; Missing in Action 2: The Beginning; Octagon, The; One Riot, One Ranger; Return of the Dragon; Sidekicks; Silent Rage; Slaughter in San Francisco; Top Dog; Walker: Texas Ranger
Norris, Edward: Mysterious Desperado; Show Them No Mercy
Norris, Fred: Private Parts
Norris, Joycelyn: Super Soul Brother
Norris, Lee: Hope
Norris, Mike: Born American; Delta Force 3; Ripper Man; Survival Game; Young Warriors, The
Norris, Terry: Innocence
North, Alan: Billy Galvin; Police Squad!
North, J. J.: Attack of the 60-Ft. Centerfold
North, Jay: Maya; Zebra in the Kitchen
North, Neil: Winslow Boy, The
North, Noelle: Slumber Party 57; Sweater Girls
North, Sheree: Breakout; Lawman; Madigan; Maniac Cop; Organization, The; Portrait of a Stripper; Real American Hero, The; Snatched; Trouble with Girls, The
North, Ted: Devil Thumbs a Ride, The

Northam, Jeremy: Emma; Fatal Inversion, A; Gloria; Golden Bowl, The; Happy, Texas; Ideal Husband, An; Mimic; Net, The; Voices From a Locked Room; Winslow Boy, The
Northcott, Ryan: Mystery, Alaska; Ripper: Letter from Hell
Nortier, Nadine: Mouchette
Norton, Adam: Who's Who
Norton, Alex: Comfort and Joy; Gregory's Girl; Sense of Freedom, A; Squanto: A Warrior's Tale
Norton, Barry: What Price Glory? (1926)
Norton, Charles: Check and Double Check
Norton, Edward: American History X; Death to Smoochy; Everyone Says I Love You; Fight Club; Keeping the Faith; People vs. Larry Flynt, The; Primal Fear; Rounders; Score, The
Norton, Jim: Cry of the Innocent; Sakharov
Norton, Ken: Drum; Oceans of Fire
Norton, Richard: China O'Brien 2; Cyber Tracker; Deathfight; Direct Hit; Gymkata; Lady Dragon; Mr. Nice Guy; Rage and Honor; Rage and Honor II: Hostile Takeover; Raiders of the Sun; Strategic Command; Tough and Deadly
Norvo, Red: Screaming Mimi
Norwood, Brandy: Rodgers & Hammerstein's Cinderella
Norwood Jr., Willie: Once Upon a Time ... When We Were Colored
Noseworthy, Jack: Barb Wire; Breakdown; Event Horizon; Place for Annie, A
Notarianni, Pietro: Malena
Notaro, Frank: Lethal Ninja
Noth, Christopher: Apology; Cast Away; Cold Around the Heart
Nottingham, Wendy: Topsy-Turvy (1999)
Nouri, Michael: American Yakuza; Between Two Women; Black Ice; Davinci's War; Finding Forrester; Flashdance; Fortunes of War; Gangster Wars; Hidden, The; Hidden II, The; Imagemaker, The; Inner Sanctum 2; Little Vegas; No Escape, No Return; Overkill; Project: Alien; Psychic (1992); Shattered Dreams; Thieves of Fortune; To the Limit; Total Exposure
Noury, Alain: Wanderer, The
Novack, Shelly: Most Wanted
Novak, Blaine: Strangers Kiss
Novak, Jane: Three-Word Brand, The
Novak, John: Call of the Wild: The Dog of the Yukon; Downdraft
Novak, Kim: Amorous Adventures of Moll Flanders, The; Bell, Book and Candle; Boys' Night Out; Eddy Duchin Story, The; Just a Gigolo; Kiss Me, Stupid; Liebestraum; Man with the Golden Arm, The; Middle of the Night; Mirror Crack'd, The; Of Human Bondage; Pal Joey; Picnic; Strangers When We Meet; Tales that Witness Madness; Vertigo; White Buffalo
Novak, Mel: Capital Punishment
Novarro, Ramon: Ben-Hur; Big Steal, The; Cat and the Fiddle, The; Heller in Pink Tights; Mata Hari; Student Prince in Old Heidelberg, The
Novello, Don: Gilda Live; Godfather, Part III, The; Just the Ticket; New York Stories; Pinocchio; Spirit of '76, The; Teenage Bonnie and Klepto Clyde
Novello, Ivor: Lodger, The; White Rose, The
Novello, Jay: Robin Hood of the Pecos
Nover, Matt: Blue Chips
Novo, Nacho: Red Squirrel, The
Novotna, Jarmila: Search, The
Nozick, Bruce: Hit the Dutchman; Killer Instinct
Nquyen, Ho: Alamo Bay
Ntshona, Winston: I Dreamed of Africa
Nubiola, Esther: Nico and Dani
Nucci, Danny: Big Squeeze, The; Code Name Jaguar; Friends and Lovers; Roosters; That Old Feeling
Nudi, Thinley: Cup, The
Nugent, Elliott: Romance; Unholy Three
Nunez Jr., Miguel A.: Slam Dunk Ernest
Nunn, Bill: Affair, The; Always Outnumbered; Blood Brothers; Canadian Bacon; Dangerous Heart; Do the Right Thing; Extreme Measures; Kiss the Girls; Last Seduction, The; Legend of 1900, The; Mr. and Mrs. Loving; Mo' Better Blues; Passing Glory; Regarding Henry; Silent Witness: What a Child Saw; Sister Act; Substitute, The: Failure Is Not an Option; Things to Do in Denver When You're Dead; Tic Code, The; True Crime; White Lie
Nunn, Larry: Men of Boys Town
Nureyev, Rudolf: Exposed; Valentino
Nusevic, Emira: Welcome to Sarajevo
Nussbaum, Danny: Beautiful People; Twentyfourseven
Nussbaum, Mike: Con, The
Nuti, Francesco: Pool Hustlers, The
Nutter, Bryan: Witchcraft VI: The Devil's Mistress
Nutter, Mayf: Hunter's Blood
Nuyen, France: China Cry; Deathmoon; Diamond Head; Joy Luck Club, The; Return to Fantasy Island
Nxomalo, Gideon: World of Strangers, A
Nye, Carrie: Divorce His: Divorce Hers
Nye, Louis: Alice Through the Looking Glass; Facts of Life; Stripper, The; 10 from Your Show of Shows; Wheeler Dealers, The
Nye, Raymond: Hard Hombre
Nyman, Lena: Autumn Sonata; I Am Curious Blue; I Am Curious Yellow
Nyqvist, Michael: Together
O., Billie: Secret Kingdom, The
O'Connell, Charlie: Devil's Prey
O'Connor, Frances: About Adam
O'Farill, Chico: Calle 54
O'Hare, Denis: Anniversary Party, The
Oakie, Jack: Affairs of Annabel, The; Annabel Takes a Tour; Great Dictator, The; Hello, Frisco, Hello; Iceland; If I Had a Million; Little Men; Lover Come Back; Murder at the Vanities; Song of the Islands; Texas Rangers (1936); Tin Pan Alley; Toast of New York, The; Uptown New York; Wild Party, The; Wintertime
Oakland, Simon: Chato's Land; I Want to Live!; Night Stalker, The: Two Tales of Terror (TV Series); Night Strangler, The; Psycho; Sand Pebbles, The; Scandalous John; Tony Rome
Oakman, Wheeler: End of the Trail; Ghost Patrol; Outside the Law; Peck's Bad Boy; Roaring Guns; Sundown Rider, The; Texas Cyclone; Two-Fisted Law
Oates, Simon: Terrornauts, The
Oates, Warren: And Baby Makes Six; Badlands (1973); Blue and the Gray, The; Blue Thunder; Border, The; Bring Me the Head of Alfredo Garcia; Brinks Job, The; Cockfighter; Crooks and Coronets (Sophie's Place); Dillinger; Dixie Dynamite; Drum; East of Eden; Gunfire; Hired Hand, The; In the Heat of the Night; Major Dundee; My Old Man; 92 in the Shade; Race with the Devil; Return of the Seven; Ride the High Country; Rise and Fall of Legs Diamond, The; Shooting, The; Sleeping Dogs; Smith!; Stripes; There Was a Crooked Man; Thief Who Came to Dinner, The; Tom Sawyer; Tough Enough; Two-Lane Blacktop; White Dawn, The; Wild Bunch, The
O'Banion, John: Judas Project, The
O'Bannon, Dan: Dark Star
Ober, Philip: Chloe: Love is Calling You; Ghost and Mr. Chicken, The; Magnificent Yankee, The; Mating Game, The
Oberon, Merle: Beloved Enemy; Berlin Express; Cowboy and the Lady, The; Dark Waters; Deep in My Heart; Desirée; Divorce of Lady X, The; Forever and a Day; Hotel; Interval; Lydia; Private Life of Don Juan, The; Private Life of Henry the Eighth, The; Scarlet Pimpernel, The; Song to Remember, A; That Uncertain Feeling; These Three; Wedding Rehearsal; Wuthering Heights
Oblilvian, Jack: Sore Losers
Obradors, Jacqueline: Six Days, Seven Nights; Tortilla Soup
Obregon, Ana: Bolero
Obregon, Rod: Tides of War
O'Brian, Hugh: Africa—Texas Style!; Beyond the Purple Hills; Broken Lance; Cruise into Terror; Fantasy Island; Gambler Returns, The: Luck of the Draw; Game of Death; Killer Force; Little Big Horn; Love Has Many Faces; Man from the Alamo, The; Murder on Flight 502; Probe; Return of Jesse James, The; Rocketship X-M; Seekers, The; Shootist, The; Son of Ali Baba; Ten Little Indians; There's No Business Like Show Business; Wyatt Earp: Return to Tombstone
O'Brian, Michael: Playboy of the Western World
O'Brian, Peter: Angel of Fury
O'Brian, Seamus: Bloodsucking Freaks (The Incredible Torture Show)
O'Brien, Ann: Vermont Is for Lovers

O'Brien, Austin: Last Action Hero, The; Lawnmower Man 2: Jobe's War (Lawnmower Man: Beyond Cyberspace); My Girl 2; Prehysteria
O'Brien, Colleen: Combination Platter
O'Brien, Dave: Boys of the City; Devil Bat, The; Enemy of the Law; Forbidden Trails; Gun Code; Gunman from Bodie; Lightnin' Crandall; Reefer Madness; Spooks Run Wild
O'Brien, Donald: Place Called Trinity, A; Quest for the Mighty Sword
O'Brien, Edmond: Admiral Was a Lady, The; Barefoot Contessa, The; Bigamist, The; Comedian, The; D-Day the Sixth of June; Denver and Rio Grande, The; D.O.A.; Doomsday Flight, The; Double Life, A; Fantastic Voyage; Girl, a Guy and a Gob, A; Girl Can't Help It, The; Great Impostor, The; Hunchback of Notre Dame, The; Julius Caesar; Last Voyage, The; Love God?, The; Lucky Luciano; Man Who Shot Liberty Valance, The; Moon Pilot; 99 and 44/100 Percent Dead; 1984; Pete Kelly's Blues; Rio Conchos; Seven Days in May; Stopover Tokyo; They Only Kill Their Masters; Two of a Kind; Up Periscope; White Heat; Wild Bunch, The
O'Brien, Edna: Hard Way, The
O'Brien, Erin: Onionhead
O'Brien, Eugene: Rebecca of Sunnybrook Farm
O'Brien, George: Arizona Legion; Cowboy Millionaire; Daniel Boone; Dude Ranger; Fig Leaves; Fort Apache; Lawless Valley; Marshal of Mesa City; Mystery Ranch; Noah's Ark; Renegade Ranger; She Wore a Yellow Ribbon; Stage to Chino; Sunrise; Triple Justice; Windjammer
O'Brien, Jeanne: Dirty Laundry
O'Brien, Joan: It Happened at the World's Fair
O'Brien, Kieran: Virtual Sexuality
O'Brien, Kim: Huckleberry Finn
O'Brien, Margaret: Amy; Canterville Ghost, The; Heller in Pink Tights; Jane Eyre; Journey for Margaret; Little Women; Madame Curie; Meet Me in St. Louis; Our Vines Have Tender Grapes; Secret Garden, The
O'Brien, Maria: Promised a Miracle; Smile
O'Brien, Myles: Forbidden Sins; Scorned 2
O'Brien, Niall: Broken Harvest; Class of '61
O'Brien, Pat: Angels with Dirty Faces; Bombardier; Bombshell; Boy Meets Girl; Boy with Green Hair, The; Bureau of Missing Persons; Ceiling Zero; Consolation Marriage; Crack-Up; Devil Dogs of the Air; End, The; Fighting Father Dunne; Fighting 69th, The; Flirtation Walk; Front Page, The; Having a Wonderful Crime; Hell's House; His Butler's Sister; Iron Major, The; Jubilee Trail; Knute Rockne—All American; Last Hurrah, The; Marine Raiders; Ragtime; RiffRaff; Slightly Honorable; Some Like It Hot; World Gone Mad, The
O'Brien, Patrick: Airborne
O'Brien, Richard: Dark City; Dungeons & Dragons; Jubilee; Rocky Horror Picture Show, The; Shock Treatment
O'Brien, Shauna: Fugitive Rage
O'Brien, Tom: Big Easy, The; Phantom, The
O'Brien, Trever: Homecoming; Midas Touch, The
O'Brien, Virginia: Du Barry Was a Lady; Harvey Girls, The; Lady Be Good; Merton of the Movies; Panama Hattie; Ship Ahoy; Thousands Cheer; Ziegfeld Follies
O'Brien-Moore, Erin: Black Legion; Little Men
O'Bryan, Patrick: 976-EVIL II: The Astral Factor
O'Bryan, Sean: Twilight of the Golds, The
O'Bryne, Colm: Snapper, The
O'Byrne, Brian F.: Bandits (2001); Everlasting Piece, An
O'Byrne, Kehli: Terminal Virus
Ocana, Susana: Skyline
O'Carroll, Brendan: Van, The
Occhipinti, Andrea: Blade in the Dark, A; Bolero; Running Away
Ochoa, Eliades: Buena Vista Social Club, The
Ochsenknecht, Uwe: Enlightenment Guaranteed; Men ... (1985)
O'Connell, Arthur: Anatomy of a Murder; Ben; Blondie's Blessed Event; Bus Stop; Cimarron; Fantastic Voyage; Follow That Dream; Gidget; Great Impostor, The; Great Race, The; Hiding Place, The; Huckleberry Finn; Kissin' Cousins; Man of the West; Misty; Monkey's Uncle, The; Operation Petticoat; Picnic; Reluctant Astronaut, The; Ride Beyond Vengeance; 7 Faces of Dr. Lao; Suppose They Gave a War and Nobody Came?; There Was a Crooked Man; They Only Kill Their Masters
O'Connell, Deirdre: Fearless; Lifeform; Pastime
O'Connell, Eddie: Absolute Beginners
O'Connell, Helen: I Dood It
O'Connell, Jerry: Blue River; Body Shots; Calendar Girl; Jerry Maguire; Joe's Apartment; Mission to Mars; Ollie Hopnoodle's Haven of Bliss; Scream 2; Stand by Me; Tomcats; What the Deaf Man Heard
O'Connell, Patrick: Endless Summer II
O'Connor, Brian: National Lampoon's Class of '86
O'Connor, Carroll: Brass; By Love Possessed; Convicted; Death of a Gunfighter; Devil's Brigade, The; Doctors' Wives; For Love of Ivy; Hawaii; Kelly's Heroes; Marlowe; Point Blank; Return to Me; 36 Hours to Die; Waterhole #3
O'Connor, Darren: Parker Adderson, Philosopher
O'Connor, Derrick: Dealers; End of Days; Hope and Glory
O'Connor, Donald: Alice in Wonderland; Beau Geste; Francis Goes to the Races; Francis in the Navy; Francis Joins the Wacs; Francis, the Talking Mule; I Love Melvin; Out to Sea; Private Buckaroo; Ragtime; Singin' in the Rain; There's No Business Like Show Business; Toys
O'Connor, Frances: AI: Artificial Intelligence; Bedazzled; Kiss or Kill; Love and Other Catastrophes; Mansfield Park
O'Connor, Glynnis: Boy in the Plastic Bubble, The; California Dreaming; Deliberate Stranger, The; Ellen Foster; Melanie; Ode to Billy Joe; Our Town; Past the Bleachers; Someone I Touched; Those Lips, Those Eyes; To Heal a Nation
O'Connor, Hazel: Breaking Glass
O'Connor, Hugh: My Left Foot; Red Hot; Three Musketeers, The; Young Poisoner's Handbook, The
O'Connor, Kevin: Bogie; Special Effects
O'Connor, Kevin J.: Candy Mountain; Deep Rising; F/X 2: The Deadly Art of Illusion; Hellcab; Lord of Illusions; Love Bug, The; Moderns, The; Mummy, The; No Escape; Peggy Sue Got Married; Tanner '88
O'Connor, Matt: Burglar From Hell
O'Connor, Renee: Darkman II: The Return of Durant; Hercules and the Lost Kingdom
O'Connor, Sinead: Butcher Boy, The
O'Connor, Terry: Breaker! Breaker!
O'Connor, Tim: Buck Rogers in the 25th Century
O'Connor, Una: Adventures of Don Juan, The; Cavalcade; Chained; Christmas in Connecticut; Invisible Man, The; Personal Property; Strawberry Blonde, The; Suzy; Witness for the Prosecution
O'Conor, Joseph: Black Windmill, The
Oda, Erika: After Life
O'Daniels, Barrie: Devil Horse, The
O'Day, Mollie: Chloe: Love is Calling You
O'Day, Nell: Arizona Stagecoach
O'Dea, Dennis: Captain Horatio Hornblower
O'Dea, Jimmy: Darby O'Gill and the Little People
O'Dea, Judith: Night of the Living Dead
Odell, Miranda: Witchcraft XI: Sisters in Blood
O'Dell, Bryan: Street Wars
O'Dell, Tony: Chopping Mall; Evils of the Night
Odetta: Autobiography of Miss Jane Pittman, The
Odette, Mary: She
Odom, George T.: Straight out of Brooklyn
O'Donnell, Cathy: Amazing Mr. X; Best Years of Our Lives, The; Man from Laramie, The; Miniver Story, The; Terror in the Haunted House; They Live By Night
O'Donnell, Chris: Bachelor, The; Batman & Robin; Batman Forever; Blue Sky; Chamber, The; Circle of Friends; Cookie's Fortune; Fried Green Tomatoes; In Love and War; Mad Love; Scent of a Woman; School Ties; Three Musketeers, The; Vertical Limit
O'Donnell, Rosie: Another Stakeout; Beautiful Girls; Car 54, Where Are You? (1991); Exit to Eden; Flintstones, The; Harriet the Spy; League of Their Own, A; Now and Then; Sleepless in Seattle; Wide Awake

O'Donnell, Spec: Little Annie Rooney
O'Donoghue, Michael: Suicide Club, The
O'Donovan, Ross: Starstruck
O'Driscoll, Martha: Fallen Sparrow, The; Ghost Catchers, The; Here Come the Co-Eds; House of Dracula
O'Dwyer, Marion: Agnes Browne
Oedekerk, Steve: High Strung; Kung Pow!: Enter the Fist
Ogata, Issey: Yi Yi
Ogata, Ken: Ballad of Narayama, The; Eijanaika (Why Not?); Mishima: A Life in Four Chapters; Vengeance Is Mine
Ogawa, Mayumi: Zatoichi: The Blind Swordsman's Vengeance
Ogier, Bulle: Candy Mountain; Celine and Julie Go Boating; Discreet Charm of the Bourgeoisie, The; Irma Vep; Les Tricheurs; Maitresse; Somewhere in the City; Valley, The; Venus Beauty Institute
Ogier, Pascale: Full Moon in Paris
Ogilvy, Ian: And Now the Screaming Starts; Anna Karenina; Conqueror Worm, The; Death Becomes Her; Invasion of Privacy; She Beast, The; Upstairs, Downstairs
O'Gorman, Dean: Young Hercules
O'Grady, Gail: Blackout; Celtic Pride; Nobody's Perfect; Spellcaster; That Old Feeling; Three Lives of Karen, The
O'Grady, Timothy E.: James Joyce's Women
Ogumbanjo, Femi: Loss of Sexual Innocence, The
Oh, Sandra: Double Happiness; Last Night
Oh, Soon-Tek: Death Wish IV: The Crackdown; Home of Our Own, A; Missing in Action 2: The Beginning; Red Sun Rising; Steele Justice; Yellow
O'Halloran, Brian: Clerks
O'Halloran, Jack: Dragnet; Hero and the Terror; Mob Boss
Ohana, Claudia: Erendira; Erotique; Luzia; Opera do Malandro
O'Hanlon Jr., George: Erendira; Erotique; Luzia; Opera do Malandro
O'Hara, Brett: Incredibly Strange Creatures Who Stopped Living and Became Mixed-Up Zombies, The
O'Hara, Catherine: After Hours; Beetlejuice; Best in Show; Betsy's Wedding; Heartburn; Home Alone; Home Alone 2: Lost in New York; Home Fries; Hope; Last Polka, The; Late Last Night; Little Vegas; Orange County; Paper, The; Really Weird Tales; Simple Twist of Fate, A; Summer Fling; Tall Tale: The Unbelievable Adventures of Pecos Bill; There Goes the Neighborhood; Waiting for Guffman; Wyatt Earp
O'Hara, David: Braveheart; Matchmaker, The; Oliver Twist
O'Hara, Jenny: Angie
O'Hara, Kareen: Go Kill and Come Back
O'Hara, Maureen: Against All Flags; At Sword's Point; Big Jake; Black Swan, The; Buffalo Bill; Comanche Territory; Dance, Girl, Dance; Deadly Companions, The; Fallen Sparrow, The; How Green Was My Valley; Hunchback of Notre Dame, The; Immortal Sergeant, The; Jamaica Inn; Lady Godiva; Lisbon; Long Gray Line, The; McLintock!; Miracle on 34th Street; Mr. Hobbs Takes a Vacation; Only the Lonely; Parent Trap, The; Quiet Man, The; Rare Breed, The (1966); Redhead from Wyoming, The; Rio Grande; Sinbad the Sailor; Spencer's Mountain; This Land Is Mine; To the Shores of Tripoli; War Arrow; Wings of Eagles, The; Woman's Secret, A
O'Hara, Quinn: Swingin' Summer, A
O'Hare, Michael: Babylon 5 (TV Series)
O'Hare, Sarah: Head Over Heels
Ohashi, Minako: Living on Tokyo Time
O'Heaney, Caitlin: He Knows You're Alone
O'Herlihy, Dan: Actors and Sin; At Sword's Point; Dead, The; Halloween III: Season of the Witch; Imitation of Life; Invasion USA (1952); Last Starfighter, The; Longest Drive, The; MacArthur; Macbeth; Odd Man Out; 100 Rifles; People, The; Rat Pack, The; RoboCop; RoboCop 2; Waltz Through the Hills; Waterloo
O'Herlihy, Gavan: Conagher
O'Herne, Pete: Bad Taste
Ohmart, Carol: House on Haunted Hill; Naked Youth; Spider Baby
Ohtomo, Osamu: 8Man
O'Hurley, John: Power Within, The
Oida, Yoshi: Pillow Book, The
Oja, Kimberly: Air Rage
Okada, Eiji: Hiroshima, Mon Amour; Traffic Jam; Ugly American, The; Woman in the Dunes
Okamura, Gerald: Power Within, The
O'Keefe, Alexis: Angel in Training
O'Keefe, Anne-Marie: City of the Vampires
O'Keefe, Dennis: Brewster's Millions; Broadway Bill; Dishonored Lady; Doll Face; Fighting Seabees, The; Great Dan Patch, The; Hangmen Also Die; I'm No Angel; Lady Scarface; Leopard Man, The; Sensations of 1945; Story of Dr. Wassell, The; T-Men; Topper Returns; You'll Find Out
O'Keefe, Doug: Specimen; When the Bullet Hits the Bone
O'Keefe, Jodi: She's All That
O'Keefe, Jodi Lyn: Halloween: H20; Whatever It Takes
O'Keefe, John: Conceiving Ada
O'Keefe, John E.: Out of the Rain
O'Keefe, Michael: Bridge to Silence; Caddyshack; Dark Secret of Harvest Home, The; Disaster at Silo 7; Edie & Pen; Fear; Great Santini, The; Hitchhiker, The (Series); Incident at Deception Ridge; Ironweed; Me & Veronica; Nate and Hayes; Nina Takes a Lover; Out of the Rain; Rumor of War, A; Slugger's Wife, The; Split Image; Too Young to Die; Whoopee Boys, The
O'Keefe, Paul: Daydreamer, The (1966)
O'Keeffe, Miles: Ator: The Fighting Eagle; Blade Master, The; Campus Man; Dead Tides; Diamondbacks; Drifter, The; Iron Warrior; Liberty and Bash; Lone Runner; Marked Man; Relentless II: Dead On; Shoot; Silent Hunter; Sword of the Valiant; Tarzan the Ape Man; Waxwork; Zero Tolerance
O'Kelly, Donal: Van, The
O'Kelly, Tim: Targets
Okking, Jens: Kingdom, The
Okumoto, Yuji: Hard Justice; Nemesis; Robot Wars
Olaf, Pierre: Little Theatre of Jean Renoir, The
Oland, Warner: Black Camel, The; Charlie Chan at Monte Carlo; Charlie Chan at the Olympics; Charlie Chan at the Opera; Charlie Chan at the Racetrack; Charlie Chan in Egypt; Charlie Chan in London; Charlie Chan in Paris; Charlie Chan in Shanghai; Charlie Chan on Broadway; Charlie Chan's Secret; Daughter of the Dragon; Dishonored; Drums of Jeopardy; Jazz Singer, The; Mysterious Dr. Fu Manchu; Painted Veil, The; Return of Dr. Fu Manchu; Shanghai Express; Tell It to the Marines; Werewolf of London
Olandt, Ken: Digital Man; Leprechaun; Super Force; Supercarrier
Olbrychski, Daniel: Birch Wood; Bolero; Deluge, The (Potop) (1973); Tin Drum, The; Wedding, The (1972)
Oldfield, Eric: Island Trader; Stones of Death
Oldham, Will: Matewan
Oldman, Gary: Air Force One; Basquiat; Bram Stoker's Dracula; Chattahoochee; Contender, The; Criminal Law; Fallen Angels; Fifth Element, The; Hannibal; Immortal Beloved; JFK; Lost in Space (1998); Meantime; Murder in the First; Prick Up Your Ears; Professional, The; Romeo Is Bleeding; Rosencrantz and Guildenstern Are Dead; Scarlet Letter, The; Sid and Nancy; State of Grace; Track 29; True Romance; We Think the World of You
Olds, Gabriel: Calendar Girl
O'Leary, Ann: Kiss the Girls Goodbye
O'Leary, Celine: Quiet Room, The
O'Leary, Matthew: Domestic Disturbance; Frailty
O'Leary, William: Flight of Black Angel; Hot Shots; In the Line of Duty: Ambush in Waco; Nice Girls Don't Explode
Olejnik, Craig: Teen Sorcery
Olen, Fred: Tomb, The
Oleynik, Larisa: 10 Things I Hate About You
Oliensis, Adam: Pompatus of Love, The
Olin, Ken: Evolution's Child; Game of Love, The; Queens Logic
Olin, Lena: Chocolat; Enemies—A Love Story; Havana; Mr. Jones; Mystery Men; Night and the Moment, The; Night Falls on Manhattan; Ninth Gate, The; Polish Wedding; Queen of the Damned; Romeo Is Bleeding; Unbearable Lightness of Being, The
Olita, Joseph: Amin: The Rise and Fall

Oliver, Barret: Cocoon; Cocoon: The Return; D.A.R.Y.L.; Frankenweenie; NeverEnding Story, The; Secret Garden, The
Oliver, Edna May: Ann Vickers; David Copperfield; Drums Along the Mohawk; Little Miss Broadway; Lydia; Nurse Edith Cavell; Romeo and Juliet; Rosalie; Saturday Night Kid, The; Second Fiddle; Story of Vernon and Irene Castle, The; Tale of Two Cities, A
Oliver, Gordon: Blondie
Oliver, Michael: Problem Child; Problem Child 2
Oliver, Robert Lee: Flesh Eating Mothers
Oliver, Rochelle: Courtship; On Valentine's Day; 1918
Oliver, Steven: Werewolves on Wheels
Oliver, Susan: Disorderly Orderly, The; Fugitive, The (TV Series); Gene Krupa Story, The; Ginger in the Morning; Guns of Diablo; Hardly Working; Star Trek: The Cage; Star Trek: The Menagerie; Tomorrow's Child
Oliver, Theresa: Twisted Tales
Oliveri, Robert: Honey, I Blew Up the Kid
Olivery, Jody: Delivery Boys
Olivier, Laurence: As You Like It; Battle of Britain; Betsy, The; Bounty, The; Boys from Brazil, The; Brideshead Revisited; Bridge Too Far, A; Carrie; Clash of the Titans; Clouds over Europe; Collection, The; Devil's Disciple, The; Divorce of Lady X, The; Dracula; Ebony Tower, The; Entertainer, The; Fire over England; 49th Parallel, The; Hamlet; Henry V; I Stand Condemned; Jazz Singer, The; Jigsaw Man, The; Khartoum; King Lear; Lady Caroline Lamb; Little Romance, A; Love Among the Ruins; Marathon Man; Mr. Halpern and Mr. Johnson; Nicholas and Alexandra; Othello; Pride and Prejudice; Prince and the Showgirl, The; Rebecca; Richard III; Seven-Per-cent Solution, The; Shoes of the Fisherman; Sleuth; Spartacus; That Hamilton Woman; Voyage 'Round My Father, A; Wagner; War Requiem; Wild Geese II; Wuthering Heights
Oliviero, Silvio: Graveyard Shift; Understudy, The: Graveyard Shift II
Olkewicz, Walter: Pronto; You Know My Name
Olmos, Edward James: American Me; Ballad of Gregorio Cortez, The; Blade Runner; Burning Season, The; Caught; Dead Man's Walk; Disappearance of Garcia Lorca, The; Gossip; Hollywood Confidential; Limbic Region, The; Miami Vice: "The Prodigal Son"; Million to Juan, A; Mirage; My Family; Roosters; Saving Grace; Selena; Slave of Dreams; Stand and Deliver; Talent for the Game; Triumph of the Spirit; Wall, The (1998) (U.S.); Wolfen; Wonderful Ice Cream Suit, The; Zoot Suit
Olmstead, Gertrude: Monster, The
O'Loughlin, Gerald S.: Pleasure Palace; Riot
Olsen, Ashley: Billboard Dad; How the West Was Fun; It Takes Two; Switching Goals
Olsen, Eric Christian: Arthur's Quest
Olsen, John: Visitors, The
Olsen, Mary-Kate: Billboard Dad; How the West Was Fun; It Takes Two; Switching Goals
Olsen, Moroni: Cobra Woman; Three Musketeers, The
Olsen, Ole: All over Town; Country Gentlemen; Ghost Catchers, The; Hellzapoppin
Olson, James: Amityville II: The Possession; Andromeda Strain, The; Commando; My Sister, My Love (The Mafu Cage); Rachel, Rachel; Rachel River; Someone I Touched; Strange New World
Olson, Nancy: Absent-Minded Professor, The; Big Jim McLain; Force of Arms; Mr. Music; Pollyanna; Smith!; Snowball Express; Son of Flubber; Union Station
Olund, Niclas: Slingshot, The
Olyphant, Timothy: Beyond Suspicion; Broken Hearts Club, The; Go; Gone in 60 Seconds; Rock Star; When Trumpets Fade
Omaggio, Maria Rosaria: Cop in Blue Jeans, The
O'Malley, Jason: Backstreet Dreams
O'Malley, Pat: Fighting Marines, The; Virginian, The
O'Mara, Kate: Horror of Frankenstein; Nativity, The; Vampire Lovers, The; Whose Child Am I?
Omori, Yoshiyuki: MacArthur's Children
Ondra, Anny: Blackmail; Manxman, The
O'Neal, Frederick: Free, White, and 21; Something of Value
O'Neal, Griffin: April Fool's Day; Assault of the Killer Bimbos; Escape Artist, The; Evil Lives; Hadley's Rebellion; Wraith, The
O'Neal, Patrick: Alvarez Kelly; Chamber of Horrors; El Condor; For the Boys; From the Terrace; In Harm's Way; Like Father, Like Son; Make Me an Offer; New York Stories; Q & A; Secret Life of an American Wife, The; Silent Night, Bloody Night; Stepford Wives, The; Stiletto; Under Siege; Way We Were, The; Where Were You When the Lights Went Out?
O'Neal, Ron: As Summers Die; Guyana Tragedy, The: The Story of Jim Jones; Mercenary Fighters; Original Gangstas; Red Dawn; Sophisticated Gents, The; St. Helens; Superfly; Superfly T.N.T.; Up Against the Wall; When a Stranger Calls
O'Neal, Ryan: Alan Smithee Film, An—Burn Hollywood Burn; Barry Lyndon; Chances Are; Driver, The; Faithful; Fever Pitch; Green Ice; Irreconcilable Differences; Love Story; Main Event, The; Man Upstairs, The; Oliver's Story; Paper Moon; Partners; Small Sacrifices; So Fine; Thief Who Came to Dinner, The; Tough Guys Don't Dance; What's Up, Doc?; Wild Rovers, The; Zero Effect
O'Neal, Shaquille: Blue Chips; Kazaam; Steel
O'Neal, Tatum: Bad News Bears, The; Certain Fury; Circle of Two; International Velvet; Little Darlings; Little Noises; Paper Moon
O'Neil, Barbara: All This and Heaven Too; I Am the Law; Tower of London
O'Neil, Colette: Dreams Lost, Dreams Found
O'Neil, Sally: 16 Fathoms Deep
O'Neil, Tricia: Are You in the House Alone?; Piranha Part Two: The Spawning
O'Neill, Amy: White Wolves: A Cry in the Wild II
O'Neill, Angela: River of Diamonds; Sorority House Massacre
O'Neill, Chris: BackBeat; James Joyce's Women
O'Neill, Dick: Buddy Holly Story, The; St. Ives; Wolfen
O'Neill, Ed: Adventures of Ford Fairlane, The; Bone Collector, The; Disorganized Crime; Dutch; Little Giants; Lucky Numbers; Prefontaine; Sibling Rivalry; 10th Kingdom, The; Wayne's World; When Your Lover Leaves
O'Neill, Fiona: Vampyr, The (1992)
O'Neill, Henry: Anthony Adverse; Case of the Lucky Legs, The; Girl Crazy; Honky Tonk; It Happened in New Orleans; Lady Killer; Return of October, The; Virginian, The; Whistling in Brooklyn; Whistling in the Dark; White Cargo
O'Neill, James: Count of Monte Cristo, The
O'Neill, Jennifer: Bad Love; Caravans; Cloud Dancer; Committed; Corporate Ladder; Cover Girl Murders, The; Force of One; Full Exposure; I Love N.Y.; Innocent, The; Invasion of Privacy; Lady Ice; Love's Savage Fury; Perfect Family; Psychic, The (1977); Reincarnation of Peter Proud, The; Rio Lobo; Scanners; Silver Strand; Steel; Summer of '42; Whiffs
O'Neill, Maggie: Under Suspicion
O'Neill, Ryan J.: Hollywood Safari
O'Neill, Shannon: Creeping Terror, The
O'Neill, Willa: One Crazy Night; Price of Milk, The
Ong, Alannah: Double Happiness
Ono, Masahiko: Boiling Point
Ono, Yoko: Imagine: John Lennon; Rock and Roll Circus, The; Satan's Bed
Onodera, Akira: Gamera: Guardian of the Universe
Onoe, Kikunosuke: Kojiro
Onorati, Peter: Dead Ahead; Donor Unknown; Firehouse; Just Looking; Not Like Us; Tycus
Ontiveros, Lupe: Candyman 3: Day of the Dead; Chuck & Buck
Ontkean, Michael: Blood of Others, The; Clara's Heart; Cold Front; Just the Way You Are; Legacy of Lies; Maid to Order; Making Love; Stepford Husbands, The; Street Justice; Summer of the Monkeys; Twin Peaks (Movie); Twin Peaks (TV Series); Voices; Willie and Phil; Witching, The (Necromancy)
Ooms, Amanda: Women on the Roof, The
Opatoshu, David: Forced Vengeance; Torn Curtain; Who'll Stop the Rain
Ophuls, Marcel: Francois Truffaut: Stolen Moments
Opiana, Marian: Man of Iron
Opinato, Mario: Muse, The

Oppenheimer, Alan: Invisible: The Chronicles of Benjamin Knight; Macbeth; Riding with Death; Trancers 4: Jack of Swords
Opper, Don: Android; Critters; Critters 2: The Main Course; Critters 3; Critters 4; Slam Dance
O'Quinn, Terry: Amityville: A New Generation; Black Widow; Blind Fury; Company Business; Cutting Edge, The; Don't Talk to Strangers; Forgotten One, The; Good Fight, The; Lipstick Camera; Millennium; My Samurai; My Stepson, My Lover; Pin; Prisoners of the Sun; Rocketeer, The; Shadow Warriors; Son of the Morning Star; Stepfather, The; Stepfather II; Tombstone; When the Time Comes; Wild Card
O'Rawe, Geraldine: Circle of Friends
Orbach, Jerry: Adventures of a Gnome Named Gnorm, The; Aladdin & the King of Thieves; California Casanova; Crimes and Misdemeanors; Delirious; Delusion; Dirty Dancing; F/X; Imagemaker, The; Last Exit to Brooklyn; Mr. Saturday Night; Out for Justice; Out on a Limb; Prince of the City; Straight Talk; That's Singing: The Best of Broadway; Toy Soldiers; Universal Soldier
Orbach, Ron: Love Crimes
Orbison, Roy: Fastest Guitar Alive, The
Ordung, Wyott: Monster from the Ocean Floor, The
O'Reilly, Cyril: Air Rage; Cool Surface, The; Dance of the Damned; Eruption; Shadow of a Scream; Unspeakable, The
O'Reilly, Harry: Hamburger Hill
O'Reilly, Robert: Moonbase
Orfani, Fereshteh Sadr: White Balloon, The
Oriel, Ray: Infested (Ticks)
Orla, Ressel: Spiders, The (1919)
Orlando, Tony: Rosie
Orlov, Dmitri: Alexander Nevsky
Ormeny, Tom: Agent on Ice
Ormond, Julia: Captives; First Knight; Legends of the Fall; Prime Gig, The; Sabrina; Smilla's Sense of Snow; Stalin; Varian's War; Young Catherine
Ormsby, Alan: Children Shouldn't Play with Dead Things
Ormsby, Anya: Children Shouldn't Play with Dead Things; Deathdream
Ornaghi, Luigi: Tree of the Wooden Clogs, The
O'Ross, Ed: Another 48 Hrs.; Full Metal Jacket; Hidden, The; Play Nice; Power Within, The; Red Heat; Terminal Countdown; Universal Soldier
O'Rourke, Heather: Poltergeist II: The Other Side; Poltergeist III
O'Rourke, Rachel: Eternal, The
Orozco, Marieta: Nico and Dani
Orozco, Regina: Deep Crimson
Orr, Christopher: Calm at Sunset; Robin Cook's Invasion
Orr, Veronica: Prehistoric Bimbos in Armageddon City; Witching, The (1994)
Orser, Leland: Resurrection; Very Bad Things
Orsi, Leigh Ann: Pet Shop
Orsini, Marini: Eddie and the Cruisers II: Eddie Lives!
Orsini, Umberto: César and Rosalie; Goodbye Emmanuelle; Mademoiselle; Woman at Her Window, A
Ortelli, Dyana: Luminarias
Orth, Debra: Billy the Kid Meets the Vampires
Orth, Zak: Down to You; Loser; Rose Hill; When Trumpets Fade
Ortnow, Richard: Trial by Jury
Orwig, Bob: No Justice
Osborne, John: Get Carter
Osborne, Vivienne: Captain Caution; Supernatural; Tomorrow at Seven
Osbourne, Ozzy: Trick or Treat
Oscarsson, Per: Doll; House of Angels; Hunger (1966); Night Visitor, The (1970); Secrets
O'Shea, Daniel: Hamburger Hill
O'Shea, Michael: Big Wheel, The; It Should Happen to You; Jack London; Lady of Burlesque; Last of the Redmen; Threat, The; Underworld Story
O'Shea, Milo: Barbarella; Broken Vows; Butcher Boy, The; Loot; Matchmaker, The; Medicine Hat Stallion, The; Once a Hero; Only the Lonely; Opportunity Knocks; Paddy; Pilot, The; Playboys, The; Romeo and Juliet; Sacco and Vanzetti
O'Shea, Niall: Agnes Browne
O'Shea, Paul: Among the Cinders
Oshima, Yukari: Millionaire's Express (Shanghai Express)
Osment, Haley Joel: AI: Artificial Intelligence; Bogus; Pay It Forward; Sixth Sense, The
Osmond, Cliff: Fortune Cookie, The; Invasion of the Bee Girls; Kiss Me, Stupid; Shark's Treasure
Osmond, Marie: Gift of Love, The; Side by Side: The True Story of the Osmond Family
Osorio, Yelba: Riot (1996) (TV Movie)
Osterhage, Jeff: Big Bad John; Buckeye and Blue; Masque of the Red Death (1989); Sex Crimes; Shadow Riders, The; Sky Bandits; South of Reno
Ostrander, William: Red Heat
Ostrum, Peter: Willy Wonka and the Chocolate Factory
Osugi, Ren: Fireworks
O'Sullivan, Billy: Robin of Locksley
O'Sullivan, Maureen: All I Desire; Anna Karenina; Barretts of Wimpole Street, The; Connecticut Yankee, A; Day at the Races, A; Devil Doll, The (1936); Hannah and Her Sisters; Just Imagine; Peggy Sue Got Married; Pride and Prejudice; River Pirates, The; Skyscraper Souls; Stranded; Strange Interlude; Tall T, The; Tarzan and His Mate; Tarzan Escapes; Tarzan Finds a Son; Tarzan the Ape Man; Tarzan's New York Adventure; Tarzan's Secret Treasure; Thin Man, The
Oteri, Cheri: Inspector Gadget; Love & Sex; Lured Innocence; Scary Movie
Otis, Carré: Exit in Red; Wild Orchid
O'Toole, Annette: Best Legs in the 8th Grade, The; Broken Vows; Cat People; Cross My Heart; Foolin' Around; 48 Hrs.; Here on Earth; Huntress, The; It; King of the Gypsies; Love at Large; Love Matters; One on One; Smile; Superman III; White Lie
O'Toole, Peter: Becket; Caligula; Club Paradise; Creator; Dark Angel, The; Fairy Tale: A True Story; Foxtrot; Goodbye, Mr. Chips; Gulliver's Travels (1996) (Television); High Spirits; How to Steal a Million; Joan of Arc (1999); King Ralph; Last Emperor, The; Lawrence of Arabia; Lion in Winter, The; Lord Jim; Man of La Mancha; Masada; Murphy's War; My Favorite Year; Night of the Generals; Phantoms; Rainbow Thief, The; Ruling Class, The; Seventh Coin, The; Strange Tales: Ray Bradbury Theater; Stunt Man, The; Supergirl; Svengali; Under Milk Wood; What's New, Pussycat?; Wings of Fame; Zulu Dawn
Otowa, Nobuko: Island, The; Onibaba
Ott, Angelica: Hell Hounds of Alaska
Ottaviano, Fred: Shoot
Otto, Barry: Bliss; Cosi; Custodian, The; Howling III; Kiss or Kill; Strictly Ballroom
Otto, Gotz: Tomorrow Never Dies
Otto, Miranda: Human Nature; Jack Bull, The; Last Days of Chez Nous, The; Love Serenade; Nostradamus Kid, The; What Lies Beneath
Ottoson, Carl: Reptilicus
Ouedraogo, Assita: La Promesse
Ouimet, Daniele: Daughters of Darkness
Ousdal, Sverre Anker: Insomnia
Ouspenskaya, Maria: Beyond Tomorrow; Dodsworth; Frankenstein Meets the Wolf Man; I've Always Loved You; Love Affair; Mortal Storm, The; Rains Came, The; Shanghai Gesture, The; Wolf Man, The
Outerbridge, Peter: Better Than Chocolate; Drop Dead Gorgeous; Escape from Mars; Kissed; Time Shifters, The
Outlaw, Geoff: Alice's Restaurant
Overall, Park: Gambler Returns, The: Luck of the Draw; House of Cards; Vanishing, The
Overman, Lynne: Broadway Bill; Caught in the Draft; Edison, The Man; Little Miss Marker; Midnight; Northwest Mounted Police; Silver Queen
Overton, Frank: Desire under the Elms; Fail-Safe; Lonelyhearts
Overton, Rick: Galaxies Are Colliding; Sinful Life, A
Owen, Chris: Angus; October Sky
Owen, Clive: Bent; Century; Class of '61; Close My Eyes; Croupier; Gosford Park; Greenfingers; Lorna Doone; Nobody's Children; Return of the Native, The; Rich Man's Wife, The
Owen, Garry: Blondie in Society

Owen, Granville: Li'l Abner
Owen, Megan: Clean Shaven
Owen, Michael: Dick Tracy vs. Crime Inc.
Owen, Reginald: Above Suspicion; Anna Karenina; Bride Wore Red, The; Cairo; Canterville Ghost, The; Captain Kidd; Challenge to Lassie; Christmas Carol, A; Conquest; Five Weeks in a Balloon; Great Ziegfeld, The; Hills of Home; I Married an Angel; Love on the Run; Madame Curie; Madame X; Miniver Story, The; Monsieur Beaucaire; Mrs. Miniver; National Velvet; Personal Property; Pirate, The; Queen Christina; Random Harvest; Real Glory, The; Red Garters; Reunion in France; Somewhere I'll Find You; Study in Scarlet, A; Tammy and the Doctor; Tarzan's Secret Treasure; They Met in Bombay; Thrill of It All, The; White Cargo; Woman of the Year; Woman's Face, A
Owen, Rena: Once Were Warriors
Owen, Seena: Victory
Owen, Timothy: Terminal Bliss
Owen, Tony: Norman Loves Rose
Owens, Ciaran: Agnes Browne; Angela's Ashes
Owens, Eamonn: Butcher Boy, The
Owens, Mark: Friday the 13th: The Orphan
Owens, Michelle: Midnight Kiss
Owens, Patricia: Fly, The; Hell to Eternity; Law and Jake Wade, The
Owens, Susie: They Bite
Owensby, Earl: Dogs of Hell; Rutherford County Line; Wolfman
Owsley, Monroe: Call Her Savage; Goin' to Town
Oxenberg, Catherine: Arthur's Quest; Lair of the White Worm; Overexposed; Ring of Scorpio; Swimsuit; Time Served
Oxenbould, Ben: Arthur's Quest; Lair of the White Worm; Overexposed; Ring of Scorpio; Swimsuit; Time Served
Oxley, David: Ill Met by Moonlight; Night Ambush
Oz, Frank: Blues Brothers 2000; Star Wars: Attack of the Clones; Star Wars: Episode I The Phantom Menace
Ozanne, Robert: Circonstances Attenuantes
Ozawa, Shoichi: Pornographers, The
Paar, Jack: Love Nest; Walk Softly, Stranger
Pace, Judy: Brian's Song; Cotton Comes to Harlem; Three in the Attic; Three in the Cellar
Pace, Roger: War of the Colossal Beast
Pace, Tom: Blood Orgy of the She Devils
Pacifici, Federico: Flight of the Innocent
Pacino, Al: ... And Justice for All; Any Given Sunday; Author! Author!; Bobby Deerfield; Carlito's Way; City Hall; Cruising; Devil's Advocate; Dick Tracy; Dog Day Afternoon; Donnie Brasco; Frankie and Johnny; Glengarry Glen Ross; Godfather, The; Godfather Epic, The; Godfather, Part II, The; Godfather, Part III, The; Heat; Insider, The; Looking for Richard; Panic in Needle Park; Revolution; Scarecrow; Scarface; Scent of a Woman; Sea of Love; Serpico; Two Bits
Pack, Roger Lloyd: Young Poisoner's Handbook, The
Pack, Stephanie: Hours and Times
Packard, Kelly: Little Bigfoot
Packer, David: Courtyard, The; Heartless; Running Kind, The; Silent Motive
Pacome, Maria: Daydreamer, The (1970) (Le Distrait)
Pacula, Joanna: Black Ice; Body Puzzle; Breaking Point; Business for Pleasure; Captain Nuke and the Bomber Boys; Death Before Dishonor; Deep Red; Escape from Sobibor; Every Breath; Eyes of the Beholder; Gorky Park; Haunted Sea, The; Heaven Before I Die; Husbands and Lovers; Kiss, The; Last Gasp; Marked for Death; My Giant; Not Like Us; Not Quite Paradise; Options; Sweet Lies; Timemaster; Tombstone; Under Investigation; Virus; Warlock: The Armageddon
Padden, Sarah: Lone Star Raiders
Padilla, Pilar: Bread and Roses
Padrao, Ana: My Daughter's Keeper
Pagan, Michael J.: How Stella Got Her Groove Back
Pagano, Bartolomeo: Cabiria
Page, Amy: Buford's Beach Bunnies
Page, Anita: Broadway Melody, The; Free and Easy; Our Modern Maidens; Sidewalks of New York; Skyscraper Souls
Page, Anthony: Rebel
Page, Corey: Dead Man on Campus
Page, Diamond Dallas: Ready to Rumble
Page, Dorothy: Ride 'em Cowgirl
Page, Gale: Amazing Dr. Clitterhouse, The; Four Daughters; Time of Your Life, The
Page, Genevieve: Belle de Jour; Day and the Hour; Private Life of Sherlock Holmes, The; Song Without End
Page, Geraldine: Beguiled, The; Blue and the Gray, The; Bride, The; Dear Heart; Dollmaker, The; Happiest Millionaire, The; Harry's War; Hitchhiker, The (Series); Hondo; Honky Tonk Freeway; I'm Dancing As Fast As I Can; Interiors; My Little Girl; Native Son; Pete 'n' Tillie; Pope of Greenwich Village, The; Summer and Smoke; Sweet Bird of Youth; Toys in the Attic; Trip to Bountiful, The; Walls of Glass; Whatever Happened to Aunt Alice?; White Nights; You're a Big Boy Now
Page, Grant: Road Games
Page, Harrison: Hammered: The Best of Sledge; Lionheart
Page, Joy: Bullfighter and the Lady, The; Fighter Attack; Kismet
Page, Ken: Cats
Page, Patti: Boys' Night Out
Page, Rebecca: Danny
Pagel, Justin: Thugs
Pages, Jean-François: Deep Trouble
Paget, Debra: Broken Arrow; Demetrius and the Gladiators; From the Earth to the Moon; Haunted Palace, The; Last Hunt, The; Love Me Tender; Omar Khayyam; Prince Valiant; Stars and Stripes Forever; Tales of Terror; Ten Commandments, The
Pagett, Nicola: Oliver's Story; Privates on Parade
Pagliero, Marcel: Dedee D'Anvers
Pagnol, Jacqueline: Nais; Topaze
Paige, Elaine: Cats
Paige, Janis: Angel on My Shoulder; Bachelor in Paradise; Hollywood Canteen; Love at the Top; Please Don't Eat the Daisies; Romance on the High Seas; Silk Stockings; Winter Meeting
Paige, Jo: Child's Christmas in Wales, A (1986)
Paige, Robert: Abbott and Costello Go to Mars; Blonde Ice; Can't Help Singing; Green Promise, The; Hellzapoppin; Monster and the Girl, The; Pardon My Sarong; Son of Dracula
Pailhas, Geraldine: Don Juan DeMarco; IP5: The Island of Pachyderms; Suite 16
Pain, Didier: My Father's Glory; My Mother's Castle
Paine, Heidi: Wizards of the Demon Sword
Paiva, Nestor: Ballad of a Gunfighter; Creature from the Black Lagoon; Falcon in Mexico, The; Nine Lives of Elfego Baca, The; Purple Heart, The; They Saved Hitler's Brain
Pajala, Turo: Ariel
Palagonia, Al: Summer of Sam
Palance, Holly: Best of Times, The; Tuxedo Warrior
Palance, Jack: Alice Through the Looking Glass; Alone in the Dark; Arrowhead; Attack!; Bagdad Café; Barabbas; Batman; Battle of the Commandos; Buffalo Girls; Chato's Land; City Slickers; City Slickers II; Cocaine Cowboys; Contempt; Cop in Blue Jeans, The; Cops and Robbersons; Cyborg 2; Deadly Sanctuary; Desperados, The; Dracula; Ebenezer; Four Deuces, The; Gor; Great Adventure, The; Halls of Montezuma; Hatfields and the McCoys, The; Hawk the Slayer; Hell's Brigade; Horsemen, The; I Died a Thousand Times; Keep the Change; Last Contract, The; Last Ride of the Dalton Gang, The; Lonely Man, The; Marco Polo; Monte Walsh; Outlaw of Gor; Panic in the Streets; Requiem for a Heavyweight (1956) (Television); Saddle Tramps; Second Chance; Sensuous Nurse, The; Shane; Silver Chalice, The; Solar Crisis; Strange Case of Dr. Jekyll and Mr. Hyde, The (1968); Sudden Fear; Tango and Cash; Torture Garden; Winter's End; Without Warning; Young Guns
Palazzolo, Michael: Curse of the Queerwolf
Palermo, Anthony: Serpent's Lair
Palfy, David: Storm
Palillo, Ron: Committed; Hellgate
Palin, Michael: American Friends; And Now for Something Completely Different; Brazil; Fierce Creatures; Fish Called Wanda, A; How to Irritate People; Jabberwocky; Life of Brian; Missionary, The; Monty Python and the Holy Grail; Monty Python Live at the Hollywood Bowl; Monty Python's Flying Cir-

cus (TV Series); Private Function, A; Ripping Yarns; Time Bandits
Palladino, Aleksa: Huntress, The; Manny & Lo
Palladino, Erik: U-571
Pallenberg, Anita: Barbarella; Performance
Pallette, Eugene: Adventures of Robin Hood, The; Bride Came C.O.D., The; Fighting Caravans; First Love; Gang's All Here, The; Heaven Can Wait; Intolerance; It's a Date; Kansan, The; Kennel Murder Case, The; Mark of Zorro, The; Mr. Skitch; My Man Godfrey; One Hundred Men and a Girl; Pin-Up Girl; Sensations of 1945; Shanghai Express; Silver Queen; Stowaway; Three Musketeers, The; Virginian, The; Young Tom Edison
Pallodino, Aleksa: Adventures of Sebastian Cole, The
Palme, Ulf: Dreams; Miss Julie
Palmer, Betsy: Fear, The: Halloween Night; Friday the 13th; Friday the 13th, Part II; Last Angry Man, The; Long Gray Line, The; Marty (1953) (Television); Still Not Quite Human; Tin Star, The
Palmer, Byron: Ma and Pa Kettle at Waikiki
Palmer, Geoffrey: Mrs. Brown
Palmer, Gregg: From Hell It Came; Scream; To Hell and Back; Zombies of Mora Tav
Palmer, Gretchen: I Got the Hook Up
Palmer, Lilli: Adorable Julia; Body and Soul; Boys from Brazil, The; But Not for Me; Chamber of Horrors; Cloak and Dagger; Counterfeit Traitor, The; Holcroft Covenant, The; Miracle of the White Stallions; Murders in the Rue Morgue; My Girl Tisa; Operation Crossbow; Secret Agent, The
Palmer, Maria: Days of Glory
Palmer, Paul: St. Francisville Experiment, The
Palmer, Peter: Li'l Abner
Palmer, Shirley: Somewhere in Sonora
Palminteri, Chazz: Analyze This; Boss of Bosses; Bronx Tale, A; Bullets over Broadway; Diabolique; Down to Earth; Excellent Cadavers; Faithful; Hurlyburly; Jade; Last Word, The; Mulholland Falls; Oscar (1991); Perez Family, The; Usual Suspects, The
Palomino, Carlos: Geronimo: An American Legend
Paltrow, Gwyneth: Anniversary Party, The; Bounce; Duets; Emma; Flesh and Bone; Great Expectations; Hard Eight; Hush; Jefferson in Paris; Moonlight and Valentino; Mrs. Parker and the Vicious Circle; Pallbearer, The; Perfect Murder, A; Royal Tenenbaums, The; Seven; Shakespeare in Love; Shallow Hal; Sliding Doors; Talented Mr. Ripley, The
Paluzzi, Luciana: Black Veil for Lisa, A; Carlton-Browne of the F.O.; Chuka; Green Slime, The; Manhunt (1973) (The Italian Connection); Muscle Beach Party; 99 Women; Powderkeg; Return to Peyton Place; Sensuous Nurse, The
Pan Chacon, Thales: Luzia
Pan-Andreas, George: Crime Killer, The
Panaro, Alessandra: Son of Captain Blood
Pandey, Nirmal: Bandit Queen
Panebianco, Richard: China Girl; Dogfight
Paneque, Miguel: Letters from the Park
Panes, Michael: Anniversary Party, The
Panettiere, Hayden: Joe Somebody; Remember the Titans
Pang, Adrian: That's the Way I Like It
Pang, Andrew: Corruptor, The
Pangborn, Franklin: All over Town; Call Out the Marines; Christmas in July; Great Moment, The; Hail the Conquering Hero; Horn Blows at Midnight, The; International House; My Dream Is Yours; Palm Beach Story, The; Romance on the High Seas; Sullivan's Travels; Swing High, Swing Low; Topper Takes a Trip; Vivacious Lady
Panjabi, Archie: East Is East
Pankin, Stuart: Beanstalk; Betrayal of the Dove; Dirt Bike Kid, The; Father & Scout; Hollywood Knights, The; Honey, We Shrunk Ourselves; Life Stinks; Love at Stake; Mannequin Two: On the Move; Second Sight; Squanto: A Warrior's Tale; Striptease
Pankow, John: Monkey Shines: An Experiment in Fear; Mortal Thoughts; Object of My Affection, The; Secret of My Success, The; Stranger Among Us, A; Talk Radio; To Live and Die in L.A.; Year of the Gun
Pankratov-Tchiorny, Alexandre: Jazzman
Pannach, Gerulf: Singing the Blues in Red
Pannelli, Nicola: In Love and War (2001)
Pantoliano, Joe: Baby's Day Out; Bad Boys; Better Way to Die, A; Bound; Downtown; El Diablo; Fugitive, The; Hoods; Immortals, The; Last of the Finest, The; Last Word, The; Matrix, The; Me and the Kid; Memento; Natural Enemy; New Blood; Ready to Rumble; Risky Business; Robot in the Family; Running Scared; Scenes from the Goldmine; Short Time; Spy Within, The; Steal Big, Steal Little; Tales from the Crypt (TV Series); Three of Hearts; U.S. Marshals; Used People; Zandalee
Pan-Yong, Yi: Why Has Bhodi Dharma Left for the East?
Paoleilei, James: Sudden Thunder
Paoli, Cecile: Near Misses
Paoming, Ku: Wooden Man's Bride, The
Papa, Anny: Blade in the Dark, A
Papas, Helen: Graveyard Shift
Papas, Irene: Assisi Underground, The; Brotherhood, The; Captain Corelli's Mandolin; Christ Stopped at Eboli; Dream of Kings, A; Erendira; Guns of Navarone, The; High Season; Into the Night; Iphigenia; Message, The (Mohammad, Messenger of God); Moonspinners, The; Moses; Sweet Country; Tribute to a Bad Man; Trojan Women, The; Z; Zorba the Greek
Papas, Laslo: Crazed
Paquin, Anna: Almost Famous; Amistad; Finding Forrester; Fly Away Home; Hurlyburly; Jane Eyre; Member of the Wedding, The; Piano, The; Walk on the Moon, A; X-Men
Paradis, Vanessa: Girl on the Bridge
Paragon, John: Echo Park
Paramore, Kiri: Last Days of Chez Nous, The
Paras, Dean: Too Smooth
Parducci, Michael: Gravesend; Hit and Runway
Pardue, Kip: Driven; Remember the Titans
Paré, Jessica: Lost and Delirious
Paré, Michael: Bad Moon; Blink of an Eye; Closer, The; Dangerous, The (1984); Deadly Heroes; Debt, The; Eddie and the Cruisers; Eddie and the Cruisers II: Eddie Lives!; Empire City; Hope Floats; Instant Justice; Into the Sun; Killing Streets; Last Hour, The; Moon 44; Philadelphia Experiment, The; Point of Impact; Raging Angels; Solar Force; Space Rage; Streets of Fire; Sunset Heat; Sworn Enemies; Triplecross; Village of the Damned; Warriors (1994); Women's Club, The; World Gone Wild
Paredes, Marisa: All About My Mother; Deep Crimson; Devil's Backbone, The; Flower of My Secret, The; High Heels
Parely, Mila: Rules of the Game, The
Parent, Monique: Blood Thirsty; Buford's Beach Bunnies; Dark Secrets
Parfitt, Judy: Dolores Claiborne; Hamlet; Jewel in the Crown, The; Office Romances
Parillaud, Anne: Frankie Starlight; Innocent Blood; La Femme Nikita; Man in the Iron Mask, The; Map of the Human Heart; Shattered Image
Paris, Cheryl: Sweet Bird of Youth
Paris, Jerry: Dick Van Dyke Show, The (TV Series); Wild One, The
Parisy, Andrea: La Grande Vadrouille
Park, Melissa: Where Evil Lies
Park, Ray: Star Wars: Episode I The Phantom Menace
Park, Reg: Hercules and the Captive Women; Hercules in the Haunted World; Hercules, Prisoner of Evil
Parker, Cecil: Admirable Crichton, The; Citadel, The; Heavens Above; Indiscreet; Ladykillers, The; Magic Bow, The; Man in the White Suit, The; Quartet; Saint's Vacation, The; Ships with Wings; Sons of the Sea; Stars Look Down, The; Storm in a Teacup; Study in Terror, A; Wreck of the Mary Deare, The
Parker, Cecilia: Ah, Wilderness; Andy Hardy Gets Spring Fever; Andy Hardy Meets a Debutante; Andy Hardy's Double Life; Love Finds Andy Hardy; Mystery Ranch; Painted Veil, The; Riders of Destiny; Trail Drive
Parker, Charlie: Celebrating Bird: The Triumph of Charlie Parker
Parker, Christopher: Red Nights
Parker, Cindy: Lovers' Lovers

Parker, Corey: Big Man on Campus; How I Got into College; Lost Language of Cranes, The; Mr. and Mrs. Loving
Parker, David M.: Xtro: Watch the Skies (Xtro 3)
Parker, Eddie: Tarantula
Parker, Eleanor: Above and Beyond; Chain Lightning; Dead on the Money; Escape from Fort Bravo; Escape Me Never; Hans Brinker; Hole in the Head, A; Home for the Holidays (1972) (Television); Home from the Hill; Interrupted Melody; King and Four Queens, The; Man with the Golden Arm, The; Naked Jungle, The; Never Say Goodbye; Oscar, The (1966); Panic Button; Return to Peyton Place; Scaramouche; She's Dressed to Kill; Sound of Music, The; Three Secrets; Tiger and The Pussycat, The
Parker, Ellen: Lost Missile, The
Parker, F. William: Jack Frost (1997)
Parker, Fess: Davy Crockett and the River Pirates; Davy Crockett, King of the Wild Frontier; Great Locomotive Chase, The; Hell Is for Heroes; Jayhawkers, The; Light in the Forest, The; Old Yeller; Them!; Westward Ho, the Wagons
Parker, Jameson: American Justice; Callie and Son; Curse of the Crystal Eye; Gathering, Part II, The; Prince of Darkness; Small Circle of Friends, A; Spy; White Dog
Parker, Jean: Beyond Tomorrow; Bluebeard; Dead Man's Eyes; Flying Blind; Flying Deuces; Gabriel over the White House; Ghost Goes West, The; Gunfighter, The (1950); Lawless Street, A; Little Women; One Body Too Many; Operator 13; Texas Rangers (1936); Zenobia
Parker, Kim: Fiend without a Face
Parker, Lara: Best of Dark Shadows, The; Foxfire Light; Night of Dark Shadows; Race with the Devil
Parker, Mary-Louise: Boys on the Side; Bullets over Broadway; Client, The; Cupid and Cate; Five Senses, The; Fried Green Tomatoes; Goodbye Lover; Grand Canyon; Legalese; Longtime Companion; Mr. Wonderful; Murder in Mind; Naked in New York; Place for Annie, A; Reckless; Saint Maybe; Sugartime
Parker, Molly: Center of the World, The; In the Shadows; Kissed; Wonderland (1999)
Parker, Monica: Coming Out Alive; Improper Channels
Parker, Nathaniel: Beverly Hills Ninja; Lover's Prayer; Othello; Squanto: A Warrior's Tale; War Requiem; Wide Sargasso Sea
Parker, Nicole: Incredibly True Adventure of Two Girls in Love, The
Parker, Nicole Ari: Dancing in September; Loving Jezebel; Remember the Titans
Parker, Noelle: Lethal Lolita—Amy Fisher: My Story; Twisted
Parker, Norman: Killing Hour, The
Parker, Paula Jai: Breaks, The; Cosmic Slop; Sprung
Parker, Sarah Jessica: Dudley Do-Right; Ed Wood; Extreme Measures; First Wives Club, The; Flight of the Navigator; Footloose; Girls Just Want to Have Fun; Hocus Pocus; Honeymoon in Vegas; If Lucy Fell; L.A. Story; Life Without Dick; Mars Attacks!; Miami Rhapsody; Somewhere, Tomorrow; State & Main; Striking Distance; Substance of Fire, The; 'Til There Was You
Parker, Suzy: Chamber of Horrors; Interns, The
Parker, Trey: Baseketball; Orgazmo
Parker, Wes: Cry from the Mountain
Parker, Willard: Hunt the Man Down
Parker Jr., Ray: Enemy Territory
Parkes, Shaun: Human Traffic
Parkins, Barbara: Asylum; Christina; Puppet on a Chain; Shout at the Devil; Snatched; To Catch a King; Valley of the Dolls
Parks, Larry: Jolson Sings Again; Jolson Story, The; Love Is Better Than Ever
Parks, Michael: Arizona Heat; Bible, The; China Lake Murders, The; Club Life; Death Wish V: The Face of Death; Deceiver; Dial M for Murder; ffolkes; Hard Country; Hitman, The; Julian Po; Niagara Niagara; Private Files of J. Edgar Hoover, The; Return of Josey Wales; Savage Bees, The; Savannah Smiles; Sidewinder 1; Storyville; Stranger by Night; Welcome to Spring Break
Parks, Tammy: Attack of the 60-Ft. Centerfold
Parks, Tom: Ladybugs
Parks, Tricia: L.A. Crackdown
Parlavecchio, Steve: Amongst Friends
Parlo, Dita: Amongst Friends
Parnell, Emory: Ma and Pa Kettle at the Fair; Ma and Pa Kettle Back on the Farm; Trail of Robin Hood
Parrilla, Lana: Spiders (2000)
Parrish, Helen: First Love; In Old California; Sunset Serenade; Three Smart Girls Grow Up; You'll Find Out
Parrish, Julie: Doberman Gang, The
Parrish, Leslie: Candyman, The; Li'l Abner; Manchurian Candidate, The
Parrish, Max: Hold Me, Thrill Me, Kiss Me
Parrish, Steve: Scanners 3: The Takeover
Parry, Natasha: Windom's Way
Parsekian, Tom: Hot Resort; Shattered Vows
Parsons, Estelle: American Clock, The; Bonnie and Clyde; Come Along with Me; Don't Drink the Water; For Pete's Sake; Freak City; Gentleman Bandit, The; I Never Sang for My Father; Looking for Richard; Love Letter, The; Private Matter, A; Rachel, Rachel; Watermelon Man
Parsons, Karyn: Ladies Man, The (2000); Major Payne
Parsons, Louella: Hollywood Hotel; Without Reservations
Parsons, Nancy: Motel Hell; Porky's II: The Next Day
Parsons, Shannon Michelle: Freakshow
Parsum, Mads: Webmaster
Parton, Dolly: Best Little Whorehouse in Texas, The; Beverly Hillbillies, The (1993); Nine to Five; Rhinestone; Smoky Mountain Christmas; Steel Magnolias; Straight Talk; Unlikely Angel
Partridge, Laurie Tait: Deadly Daphne's Revenge
Partridge, Ross: Amityville: A New Generation
Pas, Michael: Daens
Pascal, Christine: Clockmaker, The (1973); Round Midnight; Sincerely Charlotte
Pascal, Olivia: Bloody Moon
Pascaud, Nathale: Mr. Hulot's Holiday
Pasco, Isabelle: Deep Trouble; Prospero's Books
Pasco, Richard: Gorgon, The; Mrs. Brown
Pasdar, Adrian: Carlito's Way; Cookie; Ghost Brigade; Just Like a Woman; Last Good Time, The; Lost Capone, The; Made in USA; Near Dark; Pompatus of Love, The; Slave of Dreams; Streets of Gold; Torn Apart; Vital Signs; Wounded
Pashin, Yevgeni: Friend of the Deceased, A
Pasolini, Pier Paolo: Canterbury Tales, The
Pass, Cyndi: Bounty Tracker
Passalia, Antonio: Le Boucher (The Butcher)
Passanante, Jean: Return of the Secaucus 7
Passi, Christopher: Marvelous Land of Oz, The
Pastko, Earl: HIghway 61
Pastore, Louis: Agent on Ice
Pastore, Vincent: Mickey Blue Eyes; Sopranos, The (TV series)
Pastorelli, Robert: Bait; Eraser; Michael; Paint Job, The; Simple Wish, A; Sister Act 2: Back in the Habit; South Pacific (2001); Striking Distance; Yarn Princess, The
Pataki, Michael: Amazing Spiderman, The; Bat People; Graduation Day; Grave of the Vampire; Last Word, The; Pink Angels; Rocky IV; Zoltan—Hound of Dracula
Pate, Michael: Black Castle, The; Curse of the Undead; Hondo; Lawless Street, A; Mad Dog Morgan; McLintock!; Something of Value; Strange Door, The; Tower of London; Wild Duck, The
Paterson, Bill: Comfort and Joy; Coming Up Roses; Crush; Defense of the Realm; Diamond's Edge; Heart (1999); Odd Job, The; Return of the Musketeers; Truly, Madly, Deeply
Paterson, Pat: Charlie Chan in Egypt
Patey, Christian: L'Argent
Patil, Smita: Spices
Patinkin, Mandy: Adventures of Elmo in Grouchland, The; Alien Nation; Daniel; Dick Tracy; Doctor, The; House on Carroll Street, The; Hunchback, The (1997); Impromptu; Lulu on the Bridge; Maxie; Music of Chance, The; Night of the Juggler; Pinero; Princess Bride, The; Squanto: A Warrior's Tale; Strange Justice; Sunday in the Park with George; True Colors; Yentl
Paton, Angela: Con, The
Paton, Charles: Blackmail
Patric, Jason: After Dark, My Sweet; Denial; Frankenstein Unbound; Geronimo: An American Legend; Incognito; Journey of

August King, The; Lost Boys, The; Rush; Sleepers; Solarbabies; Speed 2: Cruise Control; Your Friends & Neighbors
Patrick, Barbara: Within the Rock
Patrick, Butch: Adventures of Milo in the Phantom Tollbooth, The
Patrick, Dennis: Dear Dead Delilah; Heated Vengeance; Joe
Patrick, Dorothy: Follow Me Quietly; Road Agent; Thunder Pass; Under Mexicali Stars
Patrick, Gail: Brewster's Millions; Death Takes a Holiday; Doctor Takes a Wife, The; Love Crazy; Mad About Music; Mississippi; Murder at the Vanities; Murders in the Zoo; My Man Godfrey; Phantom Broadcast, The; Wagon Wheels; Wives Under Suspicion
Patrick, Gregory: Bad Blood; Woman Obsessed, A
Patrick, Lee: Adventures of Topper, The; Black Bird, The; City for Conquest; Footsteps in the Dark; Fuller Brush Girl, The; In This Our Life; Mildred Pierce; Mrs. Parkington; Smiling Ghost, The; Somewhere I'll Find You
Patrick, Nigel: Battle of Britain; Browning Version, The; Encore; Executioner, The; League of Gentlemen, The; Mackintosh Man, The; Pandora and the Flying Dutchman; Pickwick Papers, The; Raintree County; Sapphire; Trio; Virgin Soldiers, The
Patrick, Robert: Asylum; Body Language; Body Shot; Cool Surface, The; Copland; Decoy; Double Dragon; Faculty, The; Fire in the Sky; Forgotten City; From Dusk Till Dawn 2: Texas Blood Money; Future Hunters; Hong Kong '97; Last Gasp; Only Thrill, The; Sink or Swim; Spy Kids; Striptease; Tactical Assault; Terminator 2: Judgment Day; Texas Rangers (2001); Zero Tolerance
Patry, Cherie: Kingdom of the Vampire
Patte, Jean-Marie: Rise of Louis XIV, The
Patten, Luana: Fun and Fancy Free; Home from the Hill; Johnny Tremain; Rock, Pretty Baby; So Dear to My Heart
Patterson, David: Secret Garden, The
Patterson, Elizabeth: Bill of Divorcement, A; Bluebeard's Eighth Wife; Colonel Effingham's Raid; Hold Your Man; Intruder in the Dust; I've Always Loved You; Love Me Tonight; Sky's the Limit, The; Tall Story; Welcome, Stranger
Patterson, Hank: El Paso Kid
Patterson, Jay: Double Exposure; Double Jeopardy; Excessive Force II: Force on Force
Patterson, Lee: Jack the Ripper
Patterson, Lorna: Imposter, The
Patterson, Neva: David and Lisa; Desk Set
Patterson, Sarah: Company of Wolves, The
Patterson, Scott: Alien Nation, Dark Horizon
Patton, Mark: Anna to the Infinite Power; Nightmare on Elm Street 2, A: Freddy's Revenge
Patton, Will: Armageddon; Belizaire the Cajun; Chinese Boxes; Client, The; Cold Heaven; Copycat; Deadly Desire; Dillinger; Entrapment; Everybody Wins; Fled; Gone in 60 Seconds; In the Deep Woods; In the Soup; Inventing the Abbotts; Jesus' Son; Judicial Consent; Midnight Edition; Mothman Prophecies, The; Murder on the Bayou; Natural Causes; No Way Out; Paint Job, The; Postman, The; Puppet Masters, The; Remember the Titans; Romeo Is Bleeding; Shock to the System, A; Spitfire Grill, The; Stars and Bars; Taking the Heat; Tollbooth; Wildfire
Patton-Hall, Michael: Escapes
Paukstelis, Tina Ona: 5 Dark Souls; Unearthing, The
Paul, Adrian: Cover Girl Murders, The; Dead Men Can't Dance; Dying to Get Rich; Highlander: Endgame; Highlander: The Gathering; Premonition (1998)
Paul, Alexandra: American Flyers; Baywatch: The Movie; Christine; Cyber Bandits; Death Train; Detonator II: Night Watch; Dragnet; 8 Million Ways to Die; Getting Physical; Millions; Paperboy, The; Piranha; Prey of the Chameleon; Spectre; Sunset Grill
Paul, Brian: Urban Jungle
Paul, David: Barbarians, The; Double Trouble; Think Big; Twin Sitters
Paul, Don Michael: Aloha Summer; Heart of Dixie, The; Rich Girl; Robot Wars; Rolling Vengeance; Winners Take All
Paul, Eugenia: Disembodied, The
Paul, Megan: Forest Warrior
Paul, Peter: Barbarians, The; Double Trouble; Think Big; Twin Sitters
Paul, Richard: Bloodfist III: Forced to Fight
Paul, Richard Joseph: Oblivion; Oblivion 2: Backlash; Stepsister, The; Under the Boardwalk; Vampirella
Paul, Rosemary: Dead Easy
Paul, Stuart: Emanon; Falling in Love Again
Paul, Zoe: L.I.P. Service (1999)
Pauley, Rebecca: Near Misses
Paulin, Scott: Captain America; Cat People; Deceit; From Hollywood to Deadwood; Grim Prairie Tales; Last of Philip Banter, The; Pump Up the Volume; Teen Wolf; To Heal a Nation; Tricks of the Trade; White Hot: The Mysterious Murder of Thelma Todd
Paull, Morgan: Fade to Black
Paull, Nicki: Boulevard of Broken Dreams
Paulsen, Albert: Gypsy Warriors, The; Laughing Policeman, The; Search for the Gods
Paulsen, Pat: Blood Suckers from Outer Space; Night Patrol; Where Were You When the Lights Went Out?
Paulsen, Rob: Perfect Match, The
Pavan, Marisa: Diane; Drum Beat; John Paul Jones; Man in the Gray Flannel Suit, The; Rose Tattoo, The; What Price Glory
Pavarotti, Luciano: Yes, Giorgio
Pavlovsky, Tato: Miss Mary
Pavlow, Muriel: Doctor in the House; Malta Story, The; Murder She Said
Pawley, Edward: Hoosier Schoolboy
Paxinou, Katina: For Whom the Bell Tolls; Miracle, The
Paxton, Bill: Apollo 13; Back to Back; Boxing Helena; Brain Dead; Bright Shining Lie, A; Dark Backward, The; Evening Star, The; Frailty; Frank & Jesse; Future Shock; Indian Summer; Last of the Finest, The; Mighty Joe Young; Monolith; Near Dark; Next of Kin; One False Move; Pass the Ammo; Predator 2; Simple Plan, A; Slipstream; Titanic; Tombstone; Traveller; Trespass; True Lies; Twister; U-571; Vagrant, The; Vertical Limit; Weird Science
Payan, Ilka Tanya: Florida Straits
Payant, Gilles: Big Red
Paymer, David: American President, The; Amistad; Bait; Carpool; Chill Factor; City Hall; Crime of the Century; Gang Related; Get Shorty; Heart and Souls; Lesser Evil, The; Mighty Joe Young; Mr. Saturday Night; Mumford; Nixon; Outside Ozona; Partners (2000); Payback; Quiz Show; Searching for Bobby Fischer; Sixth Man, The; Unforgettable
Payne, Allen: CB4; Jason's Lyric; Price Above Rubies, A; Tuskegee Airmen, The; Vampire in Brooklyn; Walking Dead, The
Payne, Bruce: Cisco Kid, The; Face the Evil; Full Eclipse; H. P. Lovecraft's Necronomicon: Book of the Dead; Highlander: Endgame; Kounterfeit; Nemesis; One Man's Justice; Operation Intercept; Passenger 57; Ravager; Ripper: Letter from Hell; Silence Like Glass; Sweepers; Switch; Warlock III: The End of Innocence
Payne, Eric: Gridlock'd
Payne, John: College Swing; Dodsworth; Dolly Sisters, The; Footlight Serenade; Hello, Frisco, Hello; Iceland; Kansas City Confidential; Razor's Edge, The; Slightly Scarlet; Springtime in the Rockies; Sun Valley Serenade; Tennessee's Partner; Tin Pan Alley; To the Shores of Tripoli; Weekend in Havana
Payne, Julie: Private School
Payne, Laurence: Tell-Tale Heart, The
Payne, Sally: Bad Man of Deadwood; Jesse James at Bay; Man from Music Mountain; Romance on the Range; Young Bill Hickok
Payne, Sandra: Moving Finger, The
Payne III, Carl Anthony: Breaks, The
Pays, Amanda: Cold Room, The; Dead on the Money; Exposure; Flash, The (1990); Kindred, The; Leviathan; Max Headroom; Off Limits; Oxford Blues; Solitaire for 2; 13 at Dinner
Payton, Barbara: Bride of the Gorilla; Drums in the Deep South; Kiss Tomorrow Goodbye; Only the Valiant
Payton-Wright, Pamela: Going in Style; Resurrection
Payvar, Puya: Life and Nothing More ...
Pazira, Niloufar: Kandahar
Pazos, Felipe: Old Man and the Sea, The

Pazzafini, Nello: Adios, Hombre
Peach, Mary: No Love for Johnnie
Peacock, Trevor: Merlin of the Crystal Cave
Peaker, E. J.: Four Deuces, The; Graduation Day; Hello, Dolly!
Pearce, Adrian: Warriors from Hell
Pearce, Alice: Kiss Me, Stupid; Thrill of It All, The
Pearce, Craig: Seventh Floor, The; Vicious
Pearce, Guy: Adventures of Priscilla, Queen of the Desert, The; Count of Monte Cristo, The (2002); Heaven Tonight; Hunting; L.A. Confidential; Memento; Ravenous; Rules of Engagement; Time Machine, The (2002)
Pearce, Jack: Great Northfield Minnesota Raid, The
Pearce, Jacqueline: Don't Raise the Bridge, Lower the River; Plague of the Zombies; Reptile, The
Pearce, Mary Vivian: Mondo Trasho; Multiple Maniacs; Pink Flamingos
Pearcy, Patricia: Delusion; Squirm
Pearl, Lady B.: Over the Line
Pearlman, Ron: Alien Resurrection
Pearlman, Stephen: Pi
Pearson, Neil: Secret Rapture, The
Pearson, Richard: Moving Finger, The
Pearson, Ted: Dick Tracy's G-Men
Peary, Harold: Look Who's Laughing; Seven Day's Leave
Pecic, Bogdan: Dead Next Door, The; Robot Ninja; Zombie Cop
Peck, Bob: After Pilkington; Edge of Darkness; Jurassic Park; Kitchen Toto, The; Slipstream
Peck, Cecilia: Ambition; Blue Flame; Portrait, The; Torn Apart
Peck, Craig: There's Nothing Out There
Peck, David: Gal Young 'Un
Peck, George: Curse of the Puppet Master
Peck, Gregory: Amazing Grace and Chuck; Arabesque; Behold a Pale Horse; Big Country, The; Blue and the Gray, The; Boys from Brazil, The; Bravados, The; Cape Fear; Cape Fear; Captain Horatio Hornblower; Captain Newman, M.D.; David and Bathsheba; Days of Glory; Designing Woman; Duel in the Sun; Gentlemen's Agreement; Gunfighter, The (1950); Guns of Navarone, The; How the West Was Won; Keys to the Kingdom, The; MacArthur; Mackenna's Gold; Man in the Gray Flannel Suit, The; Marooned; Mirage; Moby Dick; Moby Dick; Old Gringo, The; Omen, The; On the Beach; Only the Valiant; Other People's Money; Paradine Case, The; Pork Chop Hill; Portrait, The; Roman Holiday; Scarlet and the Black, The; Sea Wolves, The; Snows of Kilimanjaro, The; Spellbound; Stalking Moon, The; To Kill a Mockingbird; Twelve O'Clock High; Yearling, The
Peck, J. Eddie: Curse II—The Bite; Lambada
Peck, Josh: Max Keeble's Big Move
Peck, Tony: Brenda Starr
Peckinpah, Sam: Gunfire
Pecoraro, Susu: Camila (1984)
Pedersen, Maren: Witchcraft Through the Ages (HAXAN)
Pederson, Chris: Suburbia
Peel, David: Brides of Dracula
Peeples, Nia: Bloodhounds II; Blues Brothers 2000; Deadlock 2; Deepstar Six; I Don't Buy Kisses Anymore; Mr. Stitch; North Shore; Return to Lonesome Dove; Swimsuit
Peers, Joan: Applause; Parlor, Bedroom and Bath
Peet, Amanda: Body Shots; Changing Lanes; High Crimes; Saving Silverman; Whipped; Whole Nine Yards, The
Peil, Ed: Blue Steel
Pei-pei, Chang: Painted Faces
Pekic, Dusan: Wounds, The
Peldon, Ashley: Westing Game, The
Pelé: Hot Shot; Minor Miracle, A; Victory
Pelikan, Lisa: Ghoulies; Into the Badlands; Jennifer; Lionheart; Return to the Blue Lagoon
Pelka, Valentine: Rowing with the Wind
Pellay, Lanah: Eat the Rich
Pellegrino, Frank: Tarantella
Pellegrino, Mark: Cherokee Kid, The; Midnight Witness
Pelletier, Andrée: Bach and Broccoli
Pelletier, Michele-Barbara: Lotus Eaters, The
Pellicer, Pina: Macario
Pelligrino, Frank: Mickey Blue Eyes; Silent Prey
Pelloupaa, Matti: Ariel
Peluso, Jennifer: Freakshow
Pembroke, Percy: Adventures of Tarzan, The
Peña, Candela: All About My Mother
Peña, Elizabeth: Across the Moon; Aldrich Ames: Traitor Within; Batteries Not Included; Blue Steel; Contagious; Crossover Dreams; Dead Funny; Dee Snider's Strangeland; Down and Out in Beverly Hills; El Super; Invaders, The; Jacob's Ladder; La Bamba; Lone Star; Rush Hour; Second Civil War, The; Seven Girlfriends; Tortilla Soup; Waterdance, The
Penalver, Diana: Dead Alive
Pendelton, Gaylord: Interns Can't Take Money
Pendergrass, Teddy: Soup for One
Pendleton, Aidan: Andre
Pendleton, Austin: Associate, The; Four Eyes and Six Guns; 4th Floor, The; Great Smokey Roadblock, The; Guarding Tess; Hello Again; Mr. and Mrs. Bridge; Mr. Nanny; My Cousin Vinny; Proprietor, The; Rain Without Thunder; Short Circuit; Simon; Trial and Error (1997); Two Days in the Valley; Two Much; What's Up, Doc?
Pendleton, Nat: Another Thin Man; Buck Privates Come Home; Dr. Kildare's Strange Case; Girl from Missouri, The; Mad Doctor of Market Street, The; Manhattan Melodrama; Northwest Passage; Scared to Death; Shopworn Angel, The; Trapped by Television
Penghlis, Thaao: Lookalike, The
Penhaligon, Susan: Confessional, The; Land That Time Forgot, The; Leopard in the Snow; Nasty Habits; Patrick; Uncanny, The
Penhall, Bruce: Savage Beach
Penn, Christopher: All the Right Moves; At Close Range; Beethoven's 2nd; Best of the Best; Best of the Best 2; Boys Club, The; Corky Romano; Deceiver; Fist of the North Star; Florentine, The; Footloose; Funeral, The; Futurekick; Imaginary Crimes; Josh and S.A.M.; Made in USA; Mulholland Falls; Murder by Numbers (2002); One Tough Cop; Pale Rider; Pickle, The; Reservoir Dogs; Rumble Fish; Sacred Cargo; Short Cuts; To Wong Foo, Thanks for Everything, Julie Newmar; True Romance; Under the Hula Moon; Wild Life, The
Penn, Leo: Not Wanted
Penn, Matthew: Delta Force 3; Playing for Keeps
Penn, Sean: At Close Range; Bad Boys; Before Night Falls; Being John Malkovich; Carlito's Way; Casualties of War; Colors; Crackers; Dead Man Walking; Falcon and the Snowman, The; Fast Times at Ridgemont High; Game, The; Hugo Pool; Hurlyburly; I Am Sam; Judgment in Berlin; Killing of Randy Webster, The; Racing with the Moon; Shanghai Surprise; She's So Lovely; State of Grace; Sweet and Lowdown; Thin Red Line, The; U-Turn; Up at the Villa; We're No Angels
Pennell, Larry: FBI Story, The
Penner, Jonathan: Fool and His Money, A; Last Supper, The
Pennick, Jack: Operation Pacific
Penning, Wesley: Circle of Fear
Pennington, Ann: Madame Behave
Pennock, Chris: Great Texas Dynamite Chase, The
Penny, Joe: Bittersweet (1999); Blood Vows: The Story of a Mafia Wife; Bloody Birthday; Bodily Harm; Danger of Love; Gangster Wars; Whisper Kills, A
Penny, Ralph: Devil Commands, The
Penny, Sydney: Bernadette; Child of Darkness, Child of Light; Eye of the Snake; Hearts Adrift; Hyper Sapian: People from Another Star; Running Away
Penry-Jones, Rupert: Charlotte Gray; Virtual Sexuality
Pentony, Alan: Frankie Starlight
Penty, Doug: Chameleon III: Dark Angel
Peppard, George: Battle Beyond the Stars; Blue Max, The; Breakfast at Tiffany's; Carpetbaggers, The; Chinatown Murders, The: Man Against the Mob; Damnation Alley (Survival Run); Executioner, The; From Hell to Victory; Groundstar Conspiracy, The; Home from the Hill; How the West Was Won; Newman's Law; Night of the Fox; Operation Crossbow; Pendulum; Pork Chop Hill; Rough Night in Jericho; Silence Like Glass; Target Eagle; Tigress, The; Tobruk; Torn Between Two Lovers; Treasure of the Yankee Zephyr

Pepper, Barry: Battlefield Earth; Enemy of the State; Green Mile, The; Saving Private Ryan; 61*; We Were Soldiers
Pepper, John: Specters
Pera, Marilia: Central Station; Mixed Blood; Pixote
Pera, Radames: Kung Fu (1971)
Perabo, Piper: Adventures of Rocky and Bullwinkle, The; Coyote Ugly; Lost and Delirious
Perce, Joe: Don't Mess with My Sister
Percival, Lance: Darling Lili
Percy, Eileen: Down to Earth; Man from Painted Post, The; Reaching for the Moon; Wild and Woolly
Percy, Esme: Song of Freedom
Perec, Georges: Games of Countess Dolingen of Gratz, The
Peredes, Marisa: Vengeance
Pereio, Paulo Cesar: I Love You (Eu Te Amo)
Perella, Marco: Man with the Perfect Swing, The
Perera, Fia: Raising the Heights
Perez, George: Manhattan Merengue; Toy Soldiers
Perez, Jose: Off and Running; One Shoe Makes It Murder; Short Eyes
Perez, Rosie: Criminal Justice; Fearless; Human Nature; It Could Happen to You; Night on Earth; Somebody to Love; Subway Stories; 24-Hour Woman; Untamed Heart; White Men Can't Jump
Perez, Vincent: Bride of the Wind; Crow: City of Angels, The; Cyrano De Bergerac; I Dreamed of Africa; Indochine; Queen Margot; Queen of the Damned; Shot Through the Heart; Swept from the Sea; Talk of Angels; Time Regained
Pérez, Marco: Amores Perros
Perier, François: Gervaise; Le Samourai; Nights of Cabiria; Sylvia and the Phantom
Perkins, Anthony: Black Hole, The; Catch-22; Crimes of Passion; Daughter of Darkness; Deadly Companion; Demon in My View, A; Desire under the Elms; Edge of Sanity; Fear Strikes Out; ffolkes; Fool Killer, The; Friendly Persuasion; Glory Boys, The; Goodbye Again; Green Mansions; I'm Dangerous Tonight; In the Deep Woods; Les Misérables; Lonely Man, The; Mahogany; Matchmaker, The; Napoleon and Josephine: A Love Story; On the Beach; Pretty Poison; Psycho; Psycho 4: The Beginning; Psycho II; Psycho III; Ravishing Idiot, The; Sins of Dorian Gray, The; Someone Behind the Door; Tall Story; Ten Days Wonder; Tin Star, The; Trial, The; Winter Kills
Perkins, Elizabeth: About Last Night ...; Avalon; Big; Cats & Dogs; Doctor, The; Flintstones, The; From the Hip; He Said, She Said; I'm Losing You; Indian Summer; Love at Large; Miracle on 34th Street; Moonlight and Valentino; Over Her Dead Body; Rescuers, Stories of Courage, "TwoWomen"; Sweethearts' Dance; 28 Days; What Girls Learn
Perkins, Emily: Ginger Snaps
Perkins, Millie: Cockfighter; Diary of Anne Frank, The; Ensign Pulver; Gun in the House, A; Haunting Passion, The; Love in the Present Tense; Macbeth; Pistol, The: The Birth of a Legend; Ride in the Whirlwind; Shooting, The; Table for Five; Wild in the Country; Wild in the Streets
Perkins, Osgood: Scarface
Perles, Alfred: Henry Miller Odyssey
Perlich, Max: Born Yesterday; Georgia; Gummo; House on Haunted Hill; Independent, The; Lansky; Maverick; Real Thing, The; Rush; Terrified
Perlman, Rhea: Amazing Stories (TV Series); Canadian Bacon; Carpool; Houdini; Matilda; Over Her Dead Body; Ratings Game, The; Secret Cutting; Sunset Park; Ted & Venus; There Goes the Neighborhood
Perlman, Ron: Adventures of Huck Finn, The (1993); Beauty and the Beast (TV Series); Blade II; Blindman's Bluff; Body Armor; Cisco Kid, The; City of Lost Children, The; Cronos; Double Exposure; Frogs for Snakes; Island of Dr. Moreau, The; Last Supper, The; Magnificent Seven, The (TV Series); Name of the Rose, The; Price of Glory; Prince Valiant; Quest for Fire; Romeo Is Bleeding; Second Civil War, The; Sensation; Stephen King's Sleepwalkers; When the Bough Breaks
Pernel, Florence: Blue
Perra, J. W.: Planet Patrol
Perreau, Gigi: Girls Town; Journey to the Center of Time (Time Warp); Mr. Skeffington; My Foolish Heart; Yolanda and the Thief
Perri, Paul: Hit and Run
Perrier, Mireille: Toto the Hero
Perrin, Francis: Billy Ze Kick
Perrin, Jack: Painted Stallion, The
Perrin, Jacques: Cinema Paradiso; Donkey Skin (Peau D'Àne); Flight of the Innocent; Girl with a Suitcase; Love Songs (Paroles et Musique); 317th Platoon, The
Perrine, Valerie: Agency; Boiling Point; Border, The; Break, The; Bright Angel; Brown's Requiem; Can't Stop the Music; Electric Horseman, The; Last American Hero, The; Lenny; Magician of Lublin, The; Maid to Order; Mr. Billion; Slaughterhouse Five; Sweet Bird of Youth; Water; When Your Lover Leaves
Perrineau Jr., Harold: Edge, The; Smoke; William Shakespeare's Romeo and Juliet; Woman on Top
Perrino, Joseph: Bumblebee Flies Anyway, The
Perrins, Leslie: Nine Days a Queen; Triumph of Sherlock Holmes, The
Perry, DJ: Knight Chills
Perry, Felton: Dumb and Dumber; RoboCop 2; Talent for the Game
Perry, Gil: Sourdough
Perry, Jeff: Hard Promises; Kingfish: A Story of Huey P. Long; Playmaker
Perry, John Bennett: Fools Rush In; Last Fling, The
Perry, Luke: American Strays; Attention Shoppers; Buffy, the Vampire Slayer; 8 Seconds; Fifth Element, The; Florentine, The; Last Breath; Normal Life; Riot (1996) (TV Movie); Robin Cook's Invasion; Storm Tracker; Terminal Bliss; Triangle, The
Perry, Margaret: Go West, Young Man
Perry, Matthew: Almost Heroes; Fools Rush In; Three to Tango; Whole Nine Yards, The
Perry, Natasha: Midnight Lace
Perry, Rod: Black Godfather, The
Perry, Roger: Cat, The (1966); Count Yorga, Vampire; Revenge (1971) (Shelley Winters)
Perry, Susan: Knock on Any Door
Perryman, Clara: Escape to Love
Perschy, Maria: Castle of Fu Manchu; Man's Favorite Sport?; Vultures
Persky, Lisa Jane: Big Easy, The; Coneheads; Peggy Sue Got Married; Sure Thing, The
Persoff, Nehemiah: Al Capone; American Tail, An; Badlanders, The; Comancheros, The; Deadly Harvest; Eric; Francis Gary Powers: The True Story of the U-2 Spy Incident; Green Mansions; In Search of Historic Jesus; Marty (1953) (Television); Never Steal Anything Small; Psychic Killer; Sadat; Some Like It Hot; Wrong Man, The; Yentl
Persson, Essy: Mission Stardust
Pertwee, Jon: Adventures of a Private Eye; Carry on Cleo; Dr. Who (TV series); House That Dripped Blood, The; Number One of the Secret Service
Pertwee, Sean: Blue Juice; Deadly Voyage; Love, Honor & Obey; Shopping; Stiff Upper Lips
Peru, Dana: Gal Young 'Un
Perugorria, Jorge: Guantanamera!; Strawberry and Chocolate
Pesce, Franco: Have a Nice Funeral
Pesci, Joe: Betsy's Wedding; Bronx Tale, A; Casino; Easy Money; 8 Heads in a Duffel Bag; Eureka; Gone Fishin'; Goodfellas; Home Alone; Home Alone 2: Lost in New York; JFK; Jimmy Hollywood; Lethal Weapon 2; Lethal Weapon 3; Lethal Weapon 4; Man on Fire; My Cousin Vinny; Public Eye, The; Raging Bull; Super, The; With Honors
Pescow, Donna: Glory Years; Jake Speed; Saturday Night Fever
Peters, Bernadette: Alice; Annie; Heartbeeps; Impromptu; Jerk, The; Last Best Year, The; Longest Yard, The; Martian Chronicles, Parts I-III, The; Odyssey, The; Pennies from Heaven; Pink Cadillac; Rodgers & Hammerstein's Cinderella; Silent Movie; Slaves of New York; Sleeping Beauty; Sunday in the Park with George; Tulips
Peters, Brock: Ace High; Adventures of Huckleberry Finn, The; Broken Angel; Carmen Jones; Framed; Incredible Journey of Dr. Meg Laurel,The; Pawnbroker, The; Secret, The; Slaughter's

Big Rip-Off; Star Trek VI: The Undiscovered Country; Two-Minute Warning
Peters, Clark: Mona Lisa; Silver Dream Racer
Peters, Erika: Heroes Die Young
Peters, Fred: Tarzan and the Golden Lion
Peters, House: Human Hearts
Peters, Jean: Apache; As Young as You Feel; Broken Lance; It Happens Every Spring; Man Called Peter, A; Niagara; Pickup on South Street; Viva Zapata!
Peters, Kelly Jean: Pocket Money
Peters, Lauri: For Love of Ivy
Peters, Noel: Invisible Maniac
Peters, Rick: Elvis Meets Nixon
Peters, Scott: Girl Hunters, The
Peters, Werner: Corrupt Ones, The; 36 Hours
Petersen, Amy: Foolish
Petersen, Paul: Mommy 2: Mommy's Day
Petersen, William L.: Amazing Grace and Chuck; Anything for Love; Beast, The; Contender, The; Cousins; Deadly Currents; Fear; Gunshy; Hard Promises; Keep the Change; Kiss the Sky; Long Gone; Manhunter; Mulholland Falls; Passed Away; Rat Pack, The; Return to Lonesome Dove; Skulls, The; To Live and Die in L.A.; Young Guns II
Peterson, Amanda: Can't Buy Me Love; Fatal Charm; I Posed for Playboy; Windrunner
Peterson, Cassandra: Allan Quartermain and the Lost City of Gold; Echo Park
Peterson, Kimberlee: Homecoming; Legend of the Lost Tomb; Secret Cutting
Peterson, Margie: Strike a Pose
Peterson, Robert: Crude Oasis, The
Peterson, Stewart: Against a Crooked Sky; Pony Express Rider; Where the Red Fern Grows
Peterson, Vidal: Wizard of the Lost Kingdom
Petersons, Alexannder: Desperate Prey
Petherbridge, Edward: Lovers of Their Time; Strange Interlude
Petit, Philippe: Mondo
Petit, Victor: Night of the Death Cult; Return of the Evil Dead
Petrella, Ian: Christmas Story, A
Petrenko, Alexei: Rasputin
Petrie, Doris: Wedding in White
Petrillo, Sammy: Boys from Brooklyn, The
Petroff, Gloria: Two Lost Worlds
Petronijevic, Dan: My Horrible Year
Petrusic, Luka: I Want You
Pettersson, Birgitta: Virgin Spring, The
Pettet, Joanna: Blue; Casino Royale; Cry of the Innocent; Double Exposure; Evil, The; Group, The; Night of the Generals; Pioneer Woman; Robbery; Sweet Country; Terror in Paradise
Pettiet, Christopher: Goodbye Bird, The
Pettifer, Brian: Gospel According to Vic, The
Petty, Lori: Clubland; Firetrap; Free Willy; Glass Shield, The; In the Army Now; League of Their Own, A; Point Break; Relax ... It's Just Sex; Route 666; Serial Bomber; Tank Girl
Petty, Rose: Housekeeper, The
Petty, Tom: Postman, The
Pettyjohn, Angelique: Biohazard
Pevney, Joseph: Nocturne
Peyser, Penny: Frisco Kid, The; In-Laws, The; Wild Times
Pfeiffer, Dedee: Allnighter, The; Deadly Past; Double Exposure; Meat Loaf: To Hell and Back; Red Surf; Running Cool; Sandman (1992); Shoot; Up Close and Personal; Vamp
Pfeiffer, Michelle: Age of Innocence, The; Batman Returns; Callie and Son; Dangerous Liaisons; Dangerous Minds; Deep End of the Ocean, The; Fabulous Baker Boys, The; Falling in Love Again; Frankie and Johnny; Grease 2; Hollywood Knights, The; I Am Sam; Into the Night; Ladyhawke; Love Field; Married to the Mob; One Fine Day; Power, Passion, and Murder; Russia House, The; Story of Us, The; Sweet Liberty; Tequila Sunrise; Thousand Acres, A; To Gillian on Her 37th Birthday; Up Close and Personal; What Lies Beneath; William Shakespeare's A Midsummer Night's Dream; Witches of Eastwick, The; Wolf
Pflug, Jo Ann: Catlow; M*A*S*H; Night Strangler, The
Pfluger, Frederic: Girl on the Bridge
Phelan, Joe: South of Reno
Phelan, Mark: Spiders (2000)
Phelps, Buster: Little Orphan Annie
Phelps, Peter: Blackwater Trail; Lighthorsemen, The; Merlin; Starlight Hotel
Phelps, Robert: Lights, Camera, Action, Love
Phenice, Michael: 9 1/2 Ninjas
Phifer, Mekhi: Clockers; High School High; I Still Know What You Did Last Summer; Impostor; O; Soul Food; Uninvited Guest
Philbin, John: Crew, The; Martians Go Home; North Shore; Shy People
Philbin, Mary: Human Hearts; Man Who Laughs, The; Merry-Go-Round, The; Phantom of the Opera
Philbrook, James: Finger on the Trigger
Philipchuk, Misha: Thief, The
Philipe, Gérard: Beauties of the Night; Devil in the Flesh; Fanfan the Tulip; Le Rouge et le Noir; Les Liaisons Dangereuses; Proud Ones, The
Philippe, Ryan: Cruel Intentions; I Know What You Did Last Summer; Lifeform; White Squall
Philipps, Busy: Smokers, The
Philips, Emo: Journey to the Center of the Earth
Philips, Lee: Peyton Place
Philips, Mary: Farewell to Arms, A; Leave Her to Heaven
Philipson, Donna: Reptilian
Phillip, Lawrence King: Abducted
Phillippe, Ryan: Antitrust; 54; Gosford Park; Playing by Heart; Way of the Gun, The
Phillips, Angelina: Series 7: The Contenders
Phillips, Angie: Manny & Lo
Phillips, Bijou: Black and White (2000); Bully; Fast Sofa; Tart
Phillips, Bill: Flat Top
Phillips, Bobbie: Back in Action; Chameleon; Chameleon III: Dark Angel; Cover Girl Murders, The; Ring of Fire 3: Lion Strike; TC 2000
Phillips, Chynna: Goodbye, Miss 4th of July; Prize Pulitzer, The: The Roxanne Pulitzer Story
Phillips, Courtney: Return to the Blue Lagoon
Phillips, Gary: Whodunit?
Phillips, Gina: Breaking Free; Jeepers Creepers
Phillips, Grace: All the Vermeers in New York; Truth or Consequences, N.M.
Phillips, Howard: Last Mile, The
Phillips, James: In Gold We Trust
Phillips, Jean: Among the Living; Outlaws of the Desert
Phillips, John: Mummy's Shroud, The
Phillips, Joseph C.: Strictly Business
Phillips, Julianne: Big Bully; Fletch Lives; Seven Hours to Judgment; Skin Deep; Sweet Lies; Tidal Wave: No Escape; Vow to Kill, A; Where's the Money, Noreen?
Phillips, Kristie: Spitfire
Phillips, Leslie: August; Gamma People, The
Phillips, Lou Diamond: Ambition; Bats; Better Way to Die, A; Big Hit, The; Boulevard; Courage Under Fire; Dakota; Dangerous Touch; Dark Wind; Disorganized Crime; Extreme Justice; First Power, The; Harley; La Bamba; Renegades; Route 666; Shadow of the Wolf; Show of Force, A; Sioux City; Stand and Deliver; Supernova; Teresa's Tattoo; Undertow; Wharf Rat, The; Young Guns; Young Guns II
Phillips, Mackenzie: American Graffiti; Love Child; More American Graffiti; Rafferty and the Gold Dust Twins
Phillips, Michelle: American Anthem; Assault & Matrimony; Death Squad, The; Dillinger; Man with Bogart's Face, The; Scissors; Secrets of a Married Man; Sweetwater; Valentino
Phillips, Patricia: Shades of Love: Sincerely, Violet
Phillips, Peg: Northern Exposure (TV Series)
Phillips, Samantha: Deceit; Sexual Malice
Phillips, Sian: Age of Innocence, The; Attila; Borrowers, The; Carpathian Eagle; Doctor and the Devils, The; Goodbye, Mr. Chips; I, Claudius; Murphy's War; Under Milk Wood; Valmont
Phillips, Sydney Coale: Cause of Death
Phillips, Wendy: Bugsy
Phipps, Bill: Red River Shore

Phipps, Max: Dark Age; Nate and Hayes
Phipps, William: Wyatt Earp: Return to Tombstone
Phoenix, Gemma: Raining Stones
Phoenix, Joaquin: Clay Pigeons; Gladiator; Inventing the Abbotts; 8MM; Quills; Return to Paradise; To Die For; U-Turn; Yards, The
Phoenix, Leaf: Russkies; SpaceCamp
Phoenix, Rain: Even Cowgirls Get the Blues
Phoenix, River: Dogfight; Explorers; I Love You to Death; Indiana Jones and the Last Crusade; Little Nikita; Mosquito Coast, The; My Own Private Idaho; Night in the Life of Jimmy Reardon, A; Running on Empty; Silent Tongue; Sneakers; Stand by Me; Thing Called Love, The
Phuntsok, Sonam: Kundun
Pialat, Maurice: A Nos Amours; Under the Sun of Satan
Piantadosi, Joseph: Schlock
Piat, Jean: Tower of Screaming Virgins, The
Piazza, Ben: Children of An Lac, The; Consenting Adults; Guilty by Suspicion; Hanging Tree, The; Scene of the Crime
Pica, Tina: Yesterday, Today and Tomorrow
Picardo, Robert: Explorers; Gremlins 2: The New Batch; Jack's Back; 976-EVIL; Star Trek: First Contact; Wagons East
Picatto, Alexandra: Colony, The (1995)
Piccoli, Michel: Beaumarchais the Scoundrel; Belle de Jour; Beyond Obsession; Contempt; Danger: Diabolik; Dangerous Moves; Day and the Hour; Death in the Garden; Diary of a Chambermaid; Discreet Charm of the Bourgeoisie, The; Game Is Over, The; Genealogies of a Crime; Infernal Trio, The; La Belle Noiseuse; La Passante; La Puritaine; Lady L; Le Doulos; Les Choses de la Vie (Things in Life, The); L'Etat Sauvage (The Savage State); Mado; May Fools; Milky Way, The; Passion in the Desert; Peril; Phantom of Liberty, The; Sleeping Car Murders, The; Success Is the Best Revenge; Ten Days Wonder; Vincent, François, Paul and the Others; Wedding in Blood
Piccolo, Ottavia: Mado; Zorro
Picerni, Paul: Operation Pacific; Tanks Are Coming, The; To Hell and Back
Pichel, Irving: Dick Tracy's G-Men; Dracula's Daughter; General Spanky; Oliver Twist; Silver Streak
Pichler, Joe: When Good Ghouls Go Bad
Pickens, Slim: Apple Dumpling Gang, The; Blazing Saddles; Cowboys, The; Deserter, The; Dr. Strangelove or How I Learned to Stop Worrying and Love the Bomb; Ginger in the Morning; Hawmps!; Honeysuckle Rose; Howling, The; Mr. Billion; One-Eyed Jacks; 1941; Pat Garrett and Billy the Kid; Pink Motel; Pony Express Rider; Rancho Deluxe; Red River Shore; Rough Night in Jericho; Sacketts, The; Talion; Tom Horn; White Buffalo; White Line Fever; Will Penny
Pickens Jr., James: Gridlock'd
Picker, Josh: Alex
Pickering, Sarah: Little Dorrit
Pickett, Blake: Dark Universe, The
Pickett, Bobby: Frankenstein Sings
Pickett, Cindy: Atomic Dog; Call to Glory; Crooked Hearts; Deepstar Six; Echoes in the Darkness; Evolver; Ferris Bueller's Day Off; Goodbye Bird, The; Hot to Trot; Hysterical; Into the Homeland; Men's Club, The; Painted Hero; Stepdaughter, The; Stephen King's Sleepwalkers; Wild Card
Pickford, Jack: Goose Woman, The; Tom Sawyer
Pickford, Mary: Coquette; D. W. Griffith Triple Feature; Little Annie Rooney; Pollyanna; Poor Little Rich Girl, The (1917); Pride of the Clan, The; Rebecca of Sunnybrook Farm; Sparrows; Stella Maris; Taming of the Shrew, The
Pickles, Carolyn: Letting the Birds Go Free
Pickles, Christina: St. Elsewhere (TV Series)
Pickles, Vivian: Candleshoe; Elizabeth R; Harold and Maude; Suspicion
Pickup, Ronald: Danny, The Champion of the World; Fortunes of War; Pope John Paul II; Rector's Wife, The; Wagner
Picon, Molly: Come Blow Your Horn; Fiddler on the Roof; For Pete's Sake; Murder on Flight 502
Picot, Genevieve: Proof
Piddock, Jim: Best in Show
Pidgeon, Rebecca: Dawning, The; Heist (2001); Spanish Prisoner, The; State & Main; Winslow Boy, The
Pidgeon, Walter: Advise and Consent; Bad and the Beautiful, The; Big Red; Cinderella; Command Decision; Dark Command; Deep in My Heart; Executive Suite; Forbidden Planet; Funny Girl; Girl of the Golden West, The; Hit the Deck; Holiday in Mexico; House Across the Bay, The; How Green Was My Valley; It's a Date; Julia Misbehaves; Last Time I Saw Paris, The; Lindbergh Kidnapping Case, The; Listen, Darling; Madame Curie; Man Hunt (1941); Men of the Fighting Lady; Million Dollar Mermaid; Miniver Story, The; Mrs. Miniver; Mrs. Parkington; Murder on Flight 502; Neptune Factor, The; Saratoga; Shopworn Angel, The; That Forsyte Woman; Too Hot to Handle; Two-Minute Warning; Voyage to the Bottom of the Sea; Weekend at the Waldorf; White Cargo
Pieplu, Claude: Wedding in Blood
Pierce, Bradley: Borrowers, The; Jumanji
Pierce, Brock: First Kid; Legend of the Lost Tomb
Pierce, Chuck: Boggy Creek II
Pierce, David: Little Man Tate
Pierce, David Hyde: Isn't She Great; Mating Habits of the Earthbound Human,The; Nixon; Wet Hot American Summer
Pierce, James: Tarzan and the Golden Lion
Pierce, Jill: Cyborg Soldier
Pierce, Justin: Black Male; First Time Felon; Kids
Pierce, Maggie: Fastest Guitar Alive, The
Pierce, Stack: Enemy Unseen; Low Blow; Patriot (1986)0
Pierce, Wendell: It Could Happen to You
Pierce Jr., Charles B.: Norseman, The
Pierini, David: Last Way Out, The
Pierpoint, Eric: Alien Nation, Dark Horizon; Sex, Love, and Cold Hard Cash; Steel; Stranger, The
Pierre: 2001: A Space Travesty
Pierre, Roger: Mon Oncle d'Amerique
Pigaut, Roger: Simple Story, A
Pigg, Alexandra: Chicago Joe and the Showgirl; Letter to Brezhnev
Piggins, Chris: Lady of the Lake
Pigott-Smith, Tim: Hunchback (1982); Jewel in the Crown, The; Remains of the Day; Sweet William
Pilato, Joseph: Day of the Dead; Married People, Single Sex
Pilbeam, Nova: Man Who Knew Too Much, The; Nine Days a Queen; Young and Innocent
Pileggi, Mitch: Shocker; X-Files, The (TV Series)
Pilisi, Mark: Tearaway
Pilkington, Lorraine: Human Traffic; Miracle, The
Pill, Alison: Baby (2000); What Girls Learn
Pillars, Jeffrey: Ernest Rides Again
Pilleggi, Mitch: X-Files, The (1998)
Pillot, Mary: Trespasses
Pilmark, Soren: Kingdom, The
Pilon, Daniel: Obsessed
Pilon, Donald: Left for Dead; Pyx, The
Pinal, Silvia: Exterminating Angel, The; Shark! (Maneaters!); Simon of the Desert; Viridiana
Pinchette, Jean-François: Being at Home with Claude
Pinchot, Bronson: Beverly Hills Cop 3; Blame It on the Bellboy; Courage Under Fire; First Wives Club, The; Great American Sex Scandal, The; Hot Resort; It's My Party; Langoliers, The; Out of the Cold; Risky Business; Second Sight; Slappy and the Stinkers; True Romance
Pinchot, Rosamond: Three Musketeers, The
Pine, Larry: Sunday; Vanya on 42nd Street
Pine, Philip: Lost Missile, The
Pine, Robert: Apple Dumpling Gang Rides Again, The; Are You Lonesome Tonight; Empire of the Ants
Pinero, Miguel: Miami Vice; Streets of L.A., The
Pinkett, Jada: Bamboozled; If These Walls Could Talk; Inkwell, The; Jason's Lyric; Low Down Dirty Shame, A; Menace II Society; Nutty Professor, The; Scream 2; Set It Off; Tales from the Crypt: Demon Knight; Woo
Pinon, Dominique: Alien Resurrection; City of Lost Children, The; Delicatessen

Pinsent, Gordon: Case of Libel, A; John and the Missus; Silence of the North; Vow to Kill, A
Pinsent, Leah: Virus
Pintauro, Danny: Beniker Gang, The; Cujo
Pinter, Harold: Mansfield Park; Tailor of Panama, The
Pinto, Dan: Captured Alive
Pinto, Johnny: Off and Running
Pinza, Ezio: Mr. Imperium
Piper, Kelly: Maniac; Rawhead Rex
Piper, Roddy: Back in Action; Body Slam; Dead Tides; Hell Comes to Frogtown; Immortal Combat; Jungleground; Marked Man; No Contest; Sci-Fighters; Shepherd; They Live; Tough and Deadly
Piranha, P. Floyd: Redneck Zombies
Pires, David: Zoo Radio
Piro, Grant: Mr. Accident
Pirro, Mark: Polish Vampire in Burbank, A
Piscopo, Joe: Captain Nuke and the Bomber Boys; Dead Heat; Huck and the King of Hearts; Johnny Dangerously; Sidekicks; Two Bits & Pepper; Wise Guys
Pisier, Marie-France: Celine and Julie Go Boating; Chanel Solitaire; Cousin, Cousine; Francois Truffaut: Stolen Moments; French Postcards; Love on the Run; Miss Right; Nous N'Irons Plus Au Bois; Other Side of Midnight, The; Time Regained
Pistone, Kimberly: Blue de Ville
Pithey, Winsley: Saint, The (TV Series)
Pitillo, Maria: Dear God; Frank & Jesse; Godzilla (1998)
Pitoc, John Paul: Trick
Pitoeff, Sacha: Last Year at Marienbad
Pjtoniak, Anne: Agnes of God; Opportunists, The; Sister, Sister; Wizard of Loneliness, The
Pitt, Brad: Across the Tracks; Cool World; Cutting Class; Devil's Own, The; Favor, The; Fight Club; Interview with the Vampire; Johnny Suede; Kalifornia; Legends of the Fall; Meet Joe Black; Mexican, The; Ocean's Eleven (2001); River Runs Through It, A; Seven; Seven Years in Tibet; Sleepers; Snatch; Spy Game; Thelma & Louise; Too Young to Die; True Romance; 12 Monkeys
Pitt, Ingrid: House That Dripped Blood, The; Transmutations; Vampire Lovers, The; Where Eagles Dare; Wicker Man, The
Pitt, Michael: Bully; Hedwig and the Angry Inch; Murder by Numbers (2002)
Pitt, Norman: Saint, The (TV Series)
Pitts, Greg: Beethoven's 3rd
Pitts, ZaSu: Aggie Appleby, Maker of Men; Dames; Denver and Rio Grande, The; Eternally Yours; Francis Joins the Wacs; Francis, the Talking Mule; Greed; Guardsman, The; Life with Father; Mr. Skitch; Mrs. Wiggs of the Cabbage Patch; No, No Nanette; Nurse Edith Cavell; Perfect Marriage; Ruggles of Red Gap; This Could Be the Night; Thrill of It All, The; Wedding March, The
Piven, Jeremy: Crew, The; Don King: Only in America; Family Man, The; Grosse Pointe Blank; Highway; Judgment Night; Just Write; Kiss the Girls; Music from Another Room; PCU; Phoenix; Real Thing, The; Red Letters; Serendipity; 12:01; Twogether; Very Bad Things; Wavelength
Place, Mary Kay: Being John Malkovich; Big Chill, The; Bright Angel; Captain Ron; Citizen Ruth; Crazy from the Heart; Girl Who Spelled Freedom, The; Human Nature; Manny & Lo; Mary Hartman, Mary Hartman (TV Series); Modern Problems; More American Graffiti; My First Mister; New Life, A; New York, New York; Pecker; Rainmaker, The (1997); Samantha; Smooth Talk
Placido, Michele: Big Business; Forever Mary; L'America; Summer Night; Three Brothers
Plana, Tony: Backlash; Break of Dawn; Disorderlies; Havana; Hillside Stranglers, The; Knockout; Latino; Listen to Your Heart; Live Wire; One Good Cop; Romero; Rookie, The (1990); Salvador; Silver Strand; Streets of L.A., The; Sweet 15
Planchon, Roger: Return of Martin Guerre, The
Planer, Nigel: Young Ones, The
Plank, Scott: Dying to Remember; Marshal Law; Moonbase; Pastime; Saints & Sinners
Platt, Edward: Rebel Without a Cause; Rock, Pretty Baby
Platt, Louise: Captain Caution
Platt, Marc: Seven Brides for Seven Brothers; Tonight and Every Night
Platt, Oliver: Benny & Joon; Bicentennial Man; Bulworth; Dangerous Beauty; Diggstown; Dr. Dolittle (1998); Don't Say a Word; Executive Decision; Flatliners; Funnybones; Gun Shy; Impostors, The; Indecent Proposal; Infiltrator, The; Lake Placid; Ready to Rumble; Simon Birch; Tall Tale: The Unbelievable Adventures of Pecos Bill; Temp, The; Three Musketeers, The; Three to Tango; Time to Kill, A (1996)
Platters, The: Girl Can't Help It, The
Playten, Alice: Who Killed Mary What's 'Er Name?
Pleasence, Angela: Christmas Carol, A; Favor, the Watch and the Very Big Fish,The; Godsend, The
Pleasence, Donald: Advocate, The; All Quiet on the Western Front; Alone in the Dark; Ambassador, The; American Tiger; Barry McKenzie Holds His Own; Better Late than Never; Black Arrow (1984); Black Windmill, The; Blood Relatives; Breed Apart, A; Caribbean Mystery, A; Circus of Horrors; Count of Monte Cristo, The; Creepers; Cul-de-Sac; Deep Cover; Devil Within Her, The; Devonsville Terror, The; Dr. Jekyll and Mr. Hyde; Dracula; Escape from New York; Fantastic Voyage; Freakmaker; From Beyond the Grave; Great Escape II, The; Ground Zero; Hallelujah Trail, The; Halloween; Halloween II; Halloween IV: The Return of Michael Myers; Halloween: The Curse of Michael Myers; Halloween V: The Revenge of Michael Myers; Hanna's War; Horsemasters; House of Usher, The; Journey into Fear; Land of the Minotaur; Last Tycoon, The; Madwoman of Chaillot, The; Mania; Millions; Monster Club, The; Night Creature; Night of the Generals; No Love for Johnnie; Nothing Underneath; 1984; Operation 'Nam; Outer Limits, The (TV Series); Phantom of Death; Prince of Darkness; Raw Meat; River of Death; Sgt. Pepper's Lonely Hearts Club Band; Shadows and Fog; Shaming, The; Soldier Blue; Specters; Tale of Two Cities, A; Tales that Witness Madness; Telefon; Ten Little Indians; THX 1138; Tomorrow Never Comes; Treasure of the Amazon; Treasure of the Yankee Zephyr; Uncanny, The; Warrior of the Lost World; Warrior Queen; Wedding in White; Will Penny; You Only Live Twice
Pleshette, John: Kid with the Broken Halo, The; Paramedics
Pleshette, Suzanne: Adventures of Bullwhip Griffin, The; Alone in the Neon Jungle; Belarus File, The; Birds, The; Blackbeard's Ghost; Dixie Changing Habits; Forty Pounds of Trouble; Fugitive, The (TV Series); Hot Stuff; If It's Tuesday, This Must Be Belgium; Legend of Valentino; Nevada Smith; Oh, God! Book II; One Cooks, the Other Doesn't; Rome Adventure; Shaggy D.A., The; Support Your Local Gunfighter; Suppose They Gave a War and Nobody Came?; Ugly Dachshund, The
Plimpton, George: Easy Wheels; Fool and His Money, A; If Ever I See You Again; Just Cause
Plimpton, Martha: Beautiful Girls; Chantilly Lace; Daybreak (1993); Defenders, The; Defenders, The: Taking the First; Forbidden Choices; Goonies, The; I Shot Andy Warhol; I'm Not Rappaport; Inside Monkey Zetterland; Josh and S.A.M.; Last Summer in the Hamptons; Mosquito Coast, The; Music from Another Room; Parenthood; Pecker; River Rat, The; Running on Empty; Samantha; Shy People; Silence Like Glass; Stanley and Iris; Stars and Bars; Woman at War, A
Plimpton, Shelley: Glen and Randa
Plotnick, Jack: Chairman of the Board
Plowman, Melinda: Billy the Kid vs. Dracula
Plowright, Joan: Aldrich Ames: Traitor Within; Avalon; Brimstone and Treacle; Britannia Hospital; Dance with Me; Dedicated Man, A; Dennis the Menace; Dressmaker, The; Drowning by Numbers; Enchanted April; Entertainer, The; Equus; I Love You to Death; Jane Eyre; Last Action Hero, The; Mr. Wrong; 101 Dalmatians (1996); Place for Annie, A; Pyromaniac's Love Story, A; Return of the Native, The; Scarlet Letter, The; Sorrento Beach; Stalin; Summer House, The; Tea with Mussolini; Time Without Pity; Widow's Peak
Pluhar, Erika: Goalie's Anxiety at the Penalty Kick
Plumb, Eve: ... And God Spoke
Plummer, Amanda: Apartment Complex, The; Butterfly Kiss; Courtship; Daniel; Dollmaker, The; Don't Look Back; Drunks; Final Cut, The; Fisher King, The; Freeway; Hotel New Hampshire, The; Last Light; Million Dollar Hotel; Miss Rose White; Needful Things; Nostradamus; Prisoners of Inertia; Prophecy,

The (1995); Pulp Fiction; Right to Remain Silent, The; Simple Wish, A; So I Married an Axe Murderer; Static; World According to Garp, The
Plummer, Christopher: Amateur, The (1982); Battle of Britain; Beautiful Mind, A; Blackheart; Boss' Wife, The; Boy in Blue, The; Clown at Midnight, The; Conduct Unbecoming; Conspiracy of Fear, The; Crackerjack; Day that Shook the World, The; Dial M for Murder; Disappearance, The; Dolores Claiborne; Dracula 2000; Dragnet; Dreamscape; Eyewitness; Fall of the Roman Empire, The; Full Disclosure; Ghost in Monte Carlo, A; Hanover Street; Harrison Bergeron; Hidden Agenda (1998); Highpoint; I Love N.Y.; Inside Daisy Clover; Insider, The; International Velvet; Lily in Love; Man Who Would Be King, The; Mind Field; Money; Murder by Decree; Night of the Generals; Nuremberg; Ordeal by Innocence; Prototype; Pyx, The; Red-Blooded American Girl; Return of the Pink Panther, The; Royal Hunt of the Sun; Scarlet and the Black, The; Shadow Box, The; Shadow Dancing; Silent Partner, The; Skeletons; Somewhere in Time; Sound of Music, The; Souvenir; Spiral Staircase, The; Stage Struck; Star Crash; Star Trek VI: The Undiscovered Country; Thornbirds, The; 12 Monkeys; Waterloo; We the Jury; Where the Heart Is; Winchell; Wolf; Young Catherine
Plummer, Glenn: Menace II Society; Pastime; Pronto; Rangers; Showgirls; South Central; Substitute, The; Up Close and Personal
Plummer (voices), Christopher: American Tail, An
Png, Pierre: That's the Way I Like It
Podemski, Jennifer: Dance Me Outside
Podesta, Alejandra: I Don't Want to Talk About It
Podesta, Rossana: Helen of Troy; Hercules; Sensual Man, The; Sodom and Gomorrah; Ulysses; Virgin of Nuremberg (Horror Castle)
Podobed: Extraordinary Adventures of Mr. West in the Land of the Bolsheviks, The
Poe, Carey: Extraordinary Adventures of Mr. West in the Land of the Bolsheviks, The
Poelvoorde, Benoit: Man Bites Dog
Pogson, Kathryn: Overindulgence
Pogue, Ken: Blindman's Bluff; Climb, The; Contagious; Dead of Winter; Grey Fox, The; Keeping Track; One Magic Christmas; Run
Pohlmann, Eric: Horsemen, The; Surprise Package
Pohnel, Ron: No Retreat, No Surrender
Poindexter, Larry: American Ninja II; Sorceress
Pointer, Priscilla: Disturbed; Runaway Father
Poiret, Jean: Elegant Criminal, The; Last Metro, The; Tales of Paris
Poitier, Sidney: Band of Angels; Bedford Incident, The; Blackboard Jungle, The; Brother John; Buck and the Preacher; Children of the Dust; Cry, the Beloved Country; Defiant Ones, The; Duel at Diablo; For Love of Ivy; Free of Eden; Goodbye, My Lady; Greatest Story Ever Told, The; Guess Who's Coming to Dinner; In the Heat of the Night; Jackal, The; Let's Do It Again; Lilies of the Field; Little Nikita; Mandela and De Klerk; Mark of the Hawk, The; Organization, The; Paris Blues; Patch of Blue, A; Piece of the Action, A; Pressure Point; Raisin in the Sun, A; Separate But Equal; Shoot to Kill; Slender Thread, The; Sneakers; Something of Value; They Call Me Mister Tibbs; To Sir with Love; Uptown Saturday Night; Wilby Conspiracy, The
Poitier, Sydney Tamiia: Free of Eden
Polanski, Roman: Andy Warhol's Dracula; Back in the U.S.S.R.; Ciao Federico!; Dead Tired (Grosse Fatigue); Fearless Vampire Killers, or, Pardon Me, But Your Teeth Are in My Neck, The; Generation, A (1954); Pure Formality, A; Tenant, The
Pole, Edward Tudor: Kull the Conqueror
Poletti, Victor: And the Ship Sails On
Polic, II, Henry: When Things Were Rotten (TV Series)
Polis, Joel: Twilight Man
Polish, Mark: Twin Falls Idaho
Polito, Jon: Angel's Dance; Barton Fink; Bushwhacked; Crow, The; Equalizer, The: "Memories of Manon"; Fire with Fire; Just Your Luck; Miller's Crossing; Nowhere Land
Politoff, Haydee: Dracula's Great Love
Polivka, Boleslav: Divided We Fall
Polk, Brigid: Watched!
Pollack, Sydney: Changing Lanes; Eyes Wide Shut; Husbands and Wives; Player, The; Tootsie
Pollak, Cheryl: Crossing the Bridge; My Best Friend Is a Vampire; Night Life
Pollak, Kevin: Canadian Bacon; Casino; Chameleon; Clean Slate (1994); Deterrence; Dr. Dolittle 2; Don's Analyst, The; End of Days; Few Good Men, A; Grumpier Old Men; Grumpy Old Men; Hoods; House Arrest; Indian Summer; Miami Rhapsody; Opposite Sex (And How to Live with Them), The (1993); Outside Ozona; Ricochet; Ruby Bridges; Sex Monster, The; Steal This Movie; That Thing You Do!; 3,000 Miles to Graceland; Truth or Consequences, N.M.; Usual Suspects, The; Whole Nine Yards, The
Pollan, Tracy: Danielle Steel's Fine Things; Great Love Experiment, The; Stranger Among Us, A
Pollard, Michael J.: America; American Gothic; Arrival, The; Art of Dying, The; Between the Lines; Bonnie and Clyde; Enter Laughing; Heated Vengeance; Legend of Frenchie King, The; Motorama; Night Visitor (1989); Patriot (1986)0; Riders of the Storm; Roxanne; Season of Fear; Skeeter; Sleepaway Camp III; Split Second; Tango and Cash; Vengeance Is Mine; Wild Angels, The
Pollard, Snub: Arizona Days; Golden Age of Comedy, The; Harold Lloyd's Comedy Classics; Man of a Thousand Faces; Riders of the Rockies; Sing, Cowboy, Sing; White Legion
Pollard, Thommy: Penitentiary
Polley, Sarah: Adventures of Baron Münchausen, The; Claim, The; eXistenZ; Go; Guinevere; Jerry and Tom; Lantern Hill; Last Night; Sweet Hereafter, The
Pollock, Alexander: Cats & Dogs
Pollock, Channing: Judex
Pollock, Daniel: Romper Stomper
Pollock, Eileen: Far and Away
Polo, Teri: Arrival, The; Aspen Extreme; Born to Ride; Domestic Disturbance; Meet the Parents; Mystery Date; Prayer in the Dark, A; Quick
Polson, John: Back of Beyond; Mission: Impossible 2; Sum of Us, The
Pomeranc, Max: Fluke; Journey; Searching for Bobby Fischer
Pompei, Elena: Mines of Kilimanjaro
Poncela, Eusebio: Law of Desire
Pons, Lily: I Dream Too Much
Pons, Martina: Mummy and the Curse of the Jackals, The
Pontremoli, David: To Forget Venice
Pop, Iggy: Crow: City of Angels, The; Cry-Baby; Hardware
Pope, Carly: Cooler Climate, A
Popov, N.: October (Ten Days That Shook the World)
Poppel, Marc: Relentless II: Dead On
Porel, Marc: Psychic, The (1977)
Porizkova, Paulina: Anna; Arizona Dreams; Dark Asylum; Her Alibi; Partners in Crime; Wedding Bell Blues
Portal, Alexia: Autumn Tale
Portal, Louise: Decline of the American Empire, The
Portal, Robert: Stiff Upper Lips
Porter, Alisan: Curly Sue
Porter, Ashley: Young Nurses, The
Porter, Don: Bachelor in Paradise; Candidate, The; Christmas Coal Mine Miracle, The; Live a Little, Love a Little; Night Monster; White Line Fever
Porter, Eric: Antony and Cleopatra; Belstone Fox, The; Hands of the Ripper; Hennessy; Little Lord Fauntleroy; Lost Continent, The; Thirty-Nine Steps, The; Why Didn't They Ask Evans?
Porter, Jean: Bathing Beauty; San Fernando Valley; Till the End of Time
Porter, Maria: Henry Fool
Porter, Susie: Welcome to Woop Woop
Portman, Eric: Bedford Incident, The; Colditz Story, The; Corridor of Mirrors; Crimes of Stephen Hawke, The; 49th Parallel, The; Great Day; Naked Edge, The; One of Our Aircraft Is Missing; We Dive at Dawn
Portman, Natalie: Anywhere But Here; Beautiful Girls; Everyone Says I Love You; Heat; Mars Attacks!; Professional, The; Star

Wars: Attack of the Clones; Star Wars: Episode I The Phantom Menace; Where the Heart Is
Portnow, Richard: Donor Unknown; In Dangerous Company; Meet the Hollowheads
Portuondo, Omara: Buena Vista Social Club, The
Posey, Nicole: Beach Babes from Beyond
Posey, Parker: Anniversary Party, The; Best in Show; Clockwatchers; Daytrippers, The; Doom Generation, The; Drunks; Henry Fool; House of Yes, The; Josie and the Pussycats; Kicking and Screaming; Party Girl; Scream 3; SubUrbia; Sweetest Thing, The; Waiting for Guffman; You've Got Mail
Post, Markie: Glitz; I've Been Waiting for You; Scene of the Crime; Tricks of the Trade; Triplecross; Visitors of the Night
Post, Saskia: Dogs in Space
Posta, Adrienne: Adventures of a Private Eye
Postlethwaite, Pete: Alice in Wonderland; Amistad; Animal Farm; Brassed Off; Crimetime; Distant Voices/Still Lives; Dragonheart; In the Name of the Father; James and the Giant Peach; Lost World, The: Jurassic Park; Martin Chuzzlewit; Serpent's Kiss, The; Split Second; Suite 16; William Shakespeare's Romeo and Juliet
Postmaster P: Leprechaun in the Hood
Poston, Tom: Cold Turkey; Happy Hooker, The; Mork & Mindy (TV Series); Old Dark House, The; Soldier in the Rain; Story of Us, The; Thriller (TV Series); Up the Academy; Zotz!
Potapov, Alexander: Captive in the Land, A
Potente, Franka: Anatomy; Princess and the Warrior, The; Run Lola Run
Potter, Chris: Arachnid
Potter, Dennis: Dennis Potter: The Last Interview
Potter, Madeleine: Bostonians, The; Slaves of New York; Spellbreaker: Secret of the Leprechauns; Suicide Club, The
Potter, Martin: Ciao Federico!; Fellini Satyricon; Twinsanity
Potter, Michael: Female Trouble
Potter, Monica: Along Came a Spider; Cool, Dry Place, A; Head Over Heels; Heaven or Vegas; Patch Adams
Potter, Sally: Tango Lesson, The
Potts, Annie: Breaking the Rules; Corvette Summer; Flatbed Annie and Sweetie Pie: Lady Truckers; Ghostbusters; Ghostbusters II; Heartaches; Jumpin' Jack Flash; Pass the Ammo; Pretty in Pink; Texasville; Who's Harry Crumb?
Potts, Cliff: Last Ride of the Dalton Gang, The; M.A.D.D.: Mothers Against Drunk Driving; Silent Running
Potts, Nell: Effect of Gamma Rays on Man-in-the-Moon Marigolds, The
Pouget, Ely: Death Machine; Lawnmower Man 2: Jobe's War (Lawnmower Man: Beyond Cyberspace); Silent Victim
Poujouly, Georges: Elevator to the Gallows; Forbidden Games
Pounder, C.C.H.: Bagdad Café; Benny & Joon; Boycott; Disappearance of Christina, The; End of Days; Ernest Green Story, The; If These Walls Could Talk; Lifepod; Postcards from the Edge; Psycho 4: The Beginning; Race; Return to Lonesome Dove; RoboCop 3; Sliver; Third Degree Burn; When a Man Loves a Woman; White Dwarf; Zooman
Pounds, Louise: Farmer's Wife, The
Poupaud, Melvin: Diary of a Seducer; Genealogies of a Crime
Powell, Brittney: Airborne; Dragonworld
Powell, Charles: Call of the Wild: The Dog of the Yukon; Screamers
Powell, Clifton: Bones; Breaks, The; Pentagon Wars, The; Selma Lord Selma
Powell, Dick: Bad and the Beautiful, The; Blessed Event; Christmas in July; Cornered; Cry Danger; Dames; Flirtation Walk; Footlight Parade; 42nd Street; Gold Diggers of 1935; Gold Diggers of 1933; Hollywood Hotel; Midsummer Night's Dream, A; Murder My Sweet; On the Avenue; Pitfall; Stage Struck; Station West; Susan Slept Here
Powell, Eleanor: Born to Dance; Broadway Melody of 1940; Broadway Melody of 1938; Broadway Melody of 1936; Duchess of Idaho; Honolulu; I Dood It; Lady Be Good; Rosalie; Sensations of 1945; Ship Ahoy; Thousands Cheer
Powell, Jane: Athena; Date with Judy, A; Enchanted Island; Girl Most Likely, The; Hit the Deck; Holiday in Mexico; Luxury Liner; Nancy Goes to Rio; Rich, Young and Pretty; Royal Wedding; Seven Brides for Seven Brothers; Small Town Girl; Three Daring Daughters; Two Weeks with Love
Powell, Lee: Flash Gordon Conquers the Universe; Hi-Yo Silver; Lone Ranger, The
Powell, Lovelady: Happy Hooker, The
Powell, Randy: Talking About Sex
Powell, Robert: Dark Forces; Four Feathers, The; Frankenstein; Hunchback (1982); Jane Austen in Manhattan; Jesus of Nazareth; Jigsaw Man, The; Mahler; Merlin of the Crystal Cave; Secrets; Shaka Zulu; Spirit of the Dead; Thirty-Nine Steps, The; What Waits Below
Powell, William: After the Thin Man; Another Thin Man; Double Wedding; Evelyn Prentice; Ex-Mrs. Bradford, The; Feel My Pulse; Girl Who Had Everything, The; Great Ziegfeld, The; How to Marry a Millionaire; I Love You Again; It's a Big Country; Kennel Murder Case, The; Last Command, The; Last of Mrs. Cheney, The; Libeled Lady; Life with Father; Love Crazy; Manhattan Melodrama; Mister Roberts; Mr. Peabody and the Mermaid; My Man Godfrey; Reckless; Senator Was Indiscreet, The; Shadow of the Thin Man; Song of the Thin Man; Star of Midnight; Thin Man, The; Thin Man Goes Home, The; Ziegfeld Follies
Power, Chad: Three Ninjas; Three Ninjas Knuckle Up
Power, Taryn: Count of Monte Cristo, The; Sinbad and the Eye of the Tiger; Tracks
Power, Tyrone: Alexander's Ragtime Band; Black Swan, The; Blood and Sand; California Casanova; Eddy Duchin Story, The; Evil Lives; In Old Chicago; Jesse James; Johnny Apollo; Lloyd's of London; Long Gray Line, The; Marie Antoinette; Mark of Zorro, The; Pony Soldier; Rains Came, The; Rawhide; Razor's Edge, The; Rose of Washington Square; Second Fiddle; Shag, the Movie; Son of Fury; Thin Ice; Witness for the Prosecution; Yank in the RAF, A
Power Sr., Tyrone: Big Trail, The; Dream Street; Red Kimono, The
Powers, Alexandra: Dangerous Pursuit; Last Man Standing; Seventh Coin, The
Powers, Caroline Capers: Oracle, The
Powers, Leslie Ann: Hairspray
Powers, Mala: City That Never Sleeps; Colossus of New York, The; Cyrano De Bergerac; Daddy's Gone A-Hunting; Rage at Dawn; Tammy and the Bachelor; Unknown Terror, The
Powers, Stefanie: Die! Die! My Darling!; Escape to Athena; Experiment in Terror; Gone with the West; Good Idea; Herbie Rides Again; Invisible Strangler; Little Moon & Jud McGraw; Love Has Many Faces; Man Inside, The; McLintock!; Mistral's Daughter; Night Games; Palm Springs Weekend; Sky Heist; Survive the Night
Powers, Stephanie: Boatniks, The
Powers, Tom: Destination Moon; Station West; They Won't Believe Me
Powlas, Tracy: Crinoline Head
Powley, Bryan: Love from a Stranger
Pownall, Leon: Love and Hate
Powney, Clare: Girl, The
Prada, Anthony: Ma Saison Preferée
Pradier, Perrette: Burning Court, The
Prado, Lilia: Ascent to Heaven (Mexican Bus Ride); Illusion Travels by Streetcar
Praed, Michael: Nightflyers; Robin Hood and the Sorcerer; Robin Hood: The Swords of Wayland; To Die For 2: Son of Darkness
Prager, Sally: Hideaways, The
Prakash, Bhanu: Terrorist, The
Pralle, Arlene: Aileen Wuornos: Selling of a Serial Killer
Pras: Turn It Up
Prat, Eric: Tatie Danielle
Prather, Joan: Big Bad Mama; Deerslayer, The (1978); Rabbit Test; Smile
Pratt, Alan: Track 16
Pratt, Judson: Monster on the Campus
Pratt, Keri Lynn: Cruel Intentions 2; Smokers, The
Pratt, Kyla: Barney's Great Adventure; Dr. Dolittle 2
Pratt, Mike: Twinsanity
Pratt, Purnell: Mystery Squadron; Shriek in the Night, A

Pratt, Susan May: Center Stage; 10 Things I Hate About You
Preiss, Wolfgang: Battle of the Commandos; Cave of the Living Dead; Mad Executioners, The; Mill of the Stone Women; Raid on Rommel; Salzburg Connection, The; Thousand Eyes of Dr. Mabuse, The
Preisser, June: Babes in Arms; Strike Up the Band
Préjean, Albert: Crazy Ray, The; Italian Straw Hat, The; Le Voyage Imaginaire; Princess Tam Tam; Under the Roofs of Paris
Preminger, Otto: Stalag 17; They Got Me Covered
Prendes, Luis: Christmas Kid, The
Prentiss, Ann: Any Wednesday
Prentiss, Paula: Bachelor in Paradise; Black Marble, The; Born to Win; Buddy, Buddy; Honeymoon Machine, The; Horizontal Lieutenant, The; In Harm's Way; Last of the Red Hot Lovers; M.A.D.D.: Mothers Against Drunk Driving; Man's Favorite Sport?; Packin' It In; Parallax View, The; Saturday the 14th; Stepford Wives, The; What's New, Pussycat?; World of Henry Orient, The
Prentiss, Robert: Total Exposure
Presby, Shannon: New Kids, The
Prescott, Judy: Hit and Runway
Prescott, Nicole: Tar
Prescott, Robert: Bachelor Party
Presle, Micheline: Blood of Others, The; Chef in Love, A; Devil in the Flesh; French Way, The; Nea (A Young Emmanuelle); Prize, The; Time Out For Love
Presley, Elvis: Blue Hawaii; Change of Habit; Charro!; Clambake; Double Trouble; Easy Come, Easy Go; Elvis: The Lost Performances; Flaming Star; Follow That Dream; Frankie and Johnny; Fun in Acapulco; G.I. Blues; Girl Happy; Girls! Girls! Girls!; Harum Scarum; It Happened at the World's Fair; Jailhouse Rock; Kid Galahad; King Creole; Kissin' Cousins; Live a Little, Love a Little; Love Me Tender; Loving You; Paradise Hawaiian Style; Roustabout; Speedway; Spinout; Stay Away Joe; This Is Elvis; Tickle Me; Trouble with Girls, The; Viva Las Vegas; Wild in the Country
Presley, Priscilla: Adventures of Ford Fairlane, The; Naked Gun, The; Naked Gun 33 1/3, The—The Final Insult; Naked Gun 2 1/2, The
Presnell, Harve: Everything That Rises; Fargo; Julian Po; Paint Your Wagon; Tidal Wave: No Escape; Unsinkable Molly Brown, The; Whole Wide World, The
Pressly, Jaime: Not Another Teen Movie; 100 Girls; Poison Ivy: The New Seduction; Ringmaster; TICKER
Pressman, Lawrence: Gathering, The; Hanoi Hilton, The; Hellstrom Chronicle, The; Man from Atlantis, The; Man in the Glass Booth; Rehearsal for Murder; Streethawk
Presson, Essy: Therese and Isabelle
Presson, Jason: Explorers
Prestia, Jo: Dreamlife of Angels, The
Preston, Cyndy: Brain, The; Dark Side, The; Darkside, The; Premonition (1998); Prom Night III—Last Kiss
Preston, J. A.: Harvest of Fire; High Noon, Part Two; Real Life; Remo Williams: The Adventure Begins
Preston, Kelly: Addicted to Love; American Clock, The; Cheyenne Warrior; Citizen Ruth; Double Cross; Experts, The; 52 Pick-Up; For Love of the Game; Holy Man; Jack Frost; Jerry Maguire; Love Is a Gun; Metalstorm: The Destruction of Jared-Syn; Mischief; Mrs. Munck; Nothing to Lose; Only You; Perfect Bride, The; Run; Secret Admirer; SpaceCamp; Spellbinder; Tiger's Tale, A; Twins
Preston, Matt: Showgirl Murders
Preston, Mike: Metalstorm: The Destruction of Jared-Syn; Road Warrior, The
Preston, Robert: Beau Geste; Best of the Badmen; Blood on the Moon; Chisholms, The; Finnegan Begin Again; How the West Was Won; Junior Bonner; Last Starfighter, The; Mame; Man That Corrupted Hadleyburg, The; Music Man, The; Northwest Mounted Police; Outrage!; Reap the Wild Wind; Rehearsal for Murder; Semi-Tough; September Gun; S.O.B.; Sundowners, The; This Gun for Hire; Tulsa; Union Pacific; Victor/Victoria; Wake Island
Prete, Gian Carlo: Loves and Times of Scaramouche, The
Prevert, Pierre: Age of Gold
Previn, Soon-Yi: Wild Man Blues
Prevost, Daniel: Dinner Game, The
Prevost, Marie: Flying Fool, The; Hands Across the Table; Ladies of Leisure; Marriage Circle, The; Sin of Madelon Claudet, The; Sweethearts on Parade
Price, Alan: Don't Look Back; O Lucky Man!; Oh, Alfie
Price, Brenda: Robin Hood Gang, The
Price, Dennis: Five Golden Hours; Horror Hospital; Horror of Frankenstein; Hungry Hill; Kind Hearts and Coronets; Magic Bow, The; Murder Most Foul; Naked Truth (Your Past Is Showing); No Love for Johnnie; School for Scoundrels; Ten Little Indians; Tunes of Glory; Twins of Evil; Venus in Furs; Victim
Price, Hal: Desert Phantom
Price, Jamieson K.: Secret Kingdom, The
Price, Marc: Killer Tomatoes Eat France; Rescue, The; Trick or Treat
Price, Molly: Jersey Girl
Price, Rosalinda: Roaring Guns
Price, Stanley: Driftin' Kid
Price, Sue: Nemesis 4; Nemesis 3: Time Lapse; Nemesis 2
Price, Vincent: Abominable Dr. Phibes, The; Backtrack; Baron of Arizona, The; Bat, The; Bloodbath at the House of Death; Champagne for Caesar; Comedy of Terrors; Conqueror Worm, The; Cry of the Banshee; Dangerous Mission; Dead Heat; Diary of a Madman; Dr. Goldfoot and the Bikini Machine; Dr. Goldfoot and the Girl Bombs; Dr. Phibes Rises Again; Edward Scissorhands; Escapes; Fall of the House of Usher, The; Fly, The; Haunted Palace, The; Heart of Justice; His Kind of Woman; House of 1,000 Dolls; House of the Long Shadows; House of the Seven Gables, The; House of Wax; House on Haunted Hill; Invisible Man Returns; Journey into Fear; Keys to the Kingdom, The; Las Vegas Story, The; Last Man on Earth, The; Laura; Leave Her to Heaven; Madhouse; Masque of the Red Death, The (1964); Master of the World; Monster Club, The; Oblong Box, The; Offspring, The; Pit and the Pendulum, The; Private Lives of Elizabeth and Essex, The; Raven, The; Return of the Fly, The; Scavenger Hunt; Scream and Scream Again; Serenade; Shock (1946); Snow White and the Seven Dwarfs; Song of Bernadette, The; Tales of Terror; Theatre of Blood; Three Musketeers, The; Tingler, The; Tomb of Ligeia; Tower of London; Tower of London; Trouble with Girls, The; Twice-Told Tales; Whales of August, The; While the City Sleeps; Wilson
Prichard, Robert: Alien Space Avenger
Priest, Martin: Plot Against Harry, The
Priest, Pat: Easy Come, Easy Go; Incredible Two-Headed Transplant, The
Priestley, Jason: Beverly Hills 90210; Calendar Girl; Cold-Blooded; Common Ground; Eye of the Beholder; Highwayman, The; Love and Death on Long Island; Nowhere to Run; Quantum Leap (TV Series); Tombstone
Prieto, Paco Christian: Only the Strong; Street Law
Prim, Suzy: Mayerling
Prima, Barry: Ferocious Female Freedom Fighters
Prima, Louis: Manhattan Merry-Go-Round
Prime, Cheryl: Lovers of Their Time
Primus, Barry: Autopsy; Big Business; Black & White (1998); Boxcar Bertha; Brotherly Love; Cannibal Women in the Avocado Jungle of Death; Crime of the Century; Denial; Flipping; Gold Coast; Jake Speed; Macbeth; Night and the City; Portrait of a Showgirl; Talking Walls; Trade Off
Prince: Graffiti Bridge; Purple Rain; Under the Cherry Moon
Prince, Clayton: Hairspray
Prince, Faith: My Father, the Hero
Prince, John T.: Battling Orioles, The
Prince, William: Blade; City in Fear; Cyrano De Bergerac; Gauntlet, The; Greatest Man in the World, The; Objective, Burma!; Soldier, The; Spies Like Us; Sybil; Taking of Beverly Hills, The; Vice Versa
Principal, Victoria: I Will, I Will ... for Now; Life and Times of Judge Roy Bean, The; Mistress; Nightmare; Pleasure Palace
Prine, Andrew: Bandolero!; Callie and Son; Centerfold Girls; Christmas Coal Mine Miracle, The; Crypt of the Living Dead; Donner Pass: The Road to Survival; Eliminators, The; Evil, The; Generation (1969); Gettysburg; Grizzly; Last of the Mohicans;

Riders, The; Night the Lights Went Out in Georgia, The; Parent Trap, The; Postcards from the Edge; Right Stuff, Rookie, The (2002); Savior; Seniors, The; Something to Talk About; Suspect; Switchback; 30-Sep-55; Tough Enough; Traffic; Undercover Blues; Wilder Napalm; Wyatt Earp
Quaid, Randy: Adventures of Rocky and Bullwinkle, The; Apprenticeship of Duddy Kravitz, The; Bloodhounds of Broadway; Bound for Glory; Breakout; Bug Buster; Bye Bye, Love; Caddyshack II; Choirboys, The; Curse of the Starving Class; Days of Thunder; Dead Solid Perfect; Fool for Love; Foxes; Frankenstein; Freaked; Guyana Tragedy, The: The Story of Jim Jones; Hard Rain; Heartbeeps; Independence Day; Kingpin; Last Dance; Last Detail, The; Last Picture Show, The; Last Rites; LBJ: The Early Years; Legends of the North; Long Riders, The; Martians Go Home; Midnight Express; Moonshine Highway; Moving; National Lampoon's Christmas Vacation; Next Door; No Man's Land; Not Another Teen Movie; Of Mice and Men; Out Cold; Paper, The; Parents; Protector (1998); P.U.N.K.S.; Purgatory; Quick Change; Slugger's Wife, The; Streetcar Named Desire, A; Streets of Laredo; Sweet Country; Texasville; Vegas Vacation; Wild Life, The; Woman Undone; Wraith, The
Qualen, John: Adventure; Angels over Broadway; Arabian Nights; At Gunpoint; Big Hand for the Little Lady, A; Dark Waters; Doubting Thomas; Firecreek; Fugitive, The; Grapes of Wrath, The; Hans Christian Andersen; High and the Mighty, The; I'll Take Sweden; Jungle Book (1942); Melody Master (The Great Awakening) (NewWine); My Love for Yours (Honeymoon in Bali); Our Daily Bread; Passion; Prize, The; Scar, The; Shepherd of the Hills, The; 365 Nights in Hollywood; Three Musketeers, The
Qualls, DJ: Road Trip
Quan, Jonathan Ke: Breathing Fire
Quarry, Robert: Commando Squad; Count Yorga, Vampire; Cyberzone; Cyclone; Dr. Phibes Rises Again; Evil Spirits; Madhouse; Spirits; Teenage Exorcist; Warlords
Quarshie, Hugh: Church, The; Star Wars: Episode I The Phantom Menace
Quarter, James: Intimate Obsession
Quartermaine, Leon: As You Like It
Quast, Philip: Around the World in 80 Ways
Quayle, Anna: Chitty Chitty Bang Bang; Hard Day's Night, A
Quayle, Anthony: Anne of the Thousand Days; Bourne Identity, The; Damn the Defiant!; Dial M for Murder; Endless Game, The; Everything You Always Wanted to Know About Sex but Were Afraid to Ask; Guns of Navarone, The; Holocaust 2000; Key to Rebecca, The; Misunderstood; Moses; Murder by Decree; Poppy Is Also a Flower, The; Pursuit of the Graf Spee; QB VII; Story of David, The; Study in Terror, A; Tamarind Seed, The; Wrong Man, The
Queen Latifah: Bone Collector, The
Quennessen, Valerie: French Postcards; Summer Lovers
Quentin, John: Stendhal Syndrome, The; Terrorists, The
Quest, Ginger: Vegas in Space
Questel, Mae: Majority of One, A
Quester, Hugues: Tale of Springtime, A
Qui, Robert Do: Case for Murder, A
Quick, Diana: Brideshead Revisited; Misadventures of Mr. Wilt, The; Odd Job, The; Ordeal by Innocence
Quigley, Charles: Charlie Chan's Secret; Superman—The Serial; Woman's Face, A
Quigley, Linnea: Beach Babes from Beyond; Bimbo Movie Bash; Creepozoids; Hollywood Chainsaw Hookers; Jack-O; Kolobos; Pumpkinhead II: Bloodwings; Robot Ninja; Sorority Babes in the Slimeball Bowl-O-Rama; Virgin High; Witchtrap; Young Warriors, The
Quijada, Alfonso: Deathgame
Quill, Tim: Hamburger Hill; Staying Together; Suicide Ride; Thou Shalt Not Kill … Except
Quillan, Eddie: Dixie Jamboree; Mutiny on the Bounty; Young Mr. Lincoln
Quilley, Denis: King David; Lion and the Hawk, The; Privates on Parade
Quilligan, Veronica: Halfmoon
Quimette, Stephen: Destiny to Order
Quine, Richard: Babes on Broadway; Clay Pigeon, The; Little Men
Quinlan, Kathleen: American Story, An; Apollo 13; Blackout; Bodily Harm; Breakdown; Civil Action, A; Clara's Heart; Doors, The; Dreams Lost, Dreams Found; Event Horizon; Hanky Panky; I Never Promised You a Rose Garden; Independence Day; Last Light; Last Winter, The; Lawn Dogs; Lifeguard; My Giant; Perfect Alibi; Promise, The; Runner Stumbles, The; She's in the Army Now; Strays; Sunset; Trapped; Trial by Jury; Twilight Zone—The Movie; Warning Sign; Wild Thing; Zeus and Roxanne
Quinn, Aidan: All My Sons; Assignment, The; At Play in the Fields of the Lord; Avalon; Benny & Joon; Blink; Commandments; Crusoe; Desperately Seeking Susan; Early Frost, An; Handmaid's Tale, The; Haunted; In Dreams; Legends of the Fall; Lemon Sisters, The; Lies of the Twins; Looking for Richard; Mary Shelley's Frankenstein; Michael Collins; Mission, The; Music of the Heart; Perfect Witness; Playboys, The; Practical Magic; Private Matter, A; Reckless; Songcatcher; Stakeout; Stars Fell on Henrietta, The; This Is My Father
Quinn, Aileen: Annie
Quinn, Anthony: Across 110th Street; African Rage; Against All Flags; Back to Bataan; Barabbas; Behold a Pale Horse; Black Orchid, The; Black Swan, The; Blood and Sand; Blowing Wild; Buffalo Bill; Bulldog Drummond in Africa; Caravans; Children of Sanchez, The; China Sky; City for Conquest; Con Artists, The; Destructors, The; Don Is Dead, The; Dream of Kings, A; Ghost Breakers; Ghosts Can't Do It; Gotti; Greek Tycoon, The; Guadalcanal Diary; Guns of Navarone, The; Heller in Pink Tights; Hercules and the Amazon Women; Hercules and the Circle of Fire; Hercules and the Lost Kingdom; Hercules in the Underworld; High Risk; Hot Spell; Jungle Fever; La Strada; Last Action Hero, The; Last Train from Gun Hill; Lawrence of Arabia; Lion of the Desert; Lost Command; Lust for Life; Man of Passion, A; Message, The (Mohammad, Messenger of God); Mobsters; Old Man and the Sea, The; Onassis: The Richest Man in the World; Only the Lonely; Ox-Bow Incident, The; Regina; Requiem for a Heavyweight (1962); Revenge (1990); Road to Morocco; Road to Singapore; R.P.M. (Revolutions per Minute); Salamander, The; Seven Cities of Gold; Shoes of the Fisherman; Sinbad the Sailor; Somebody to Love; Swing High, Swing Low; They Died with Their Boots On; Tycoon; Ulysses; Union Pacific; Viva Zapata!; Waikiki Wedding; Walk in the Clouds, A; Walk in the Spring Rain, A; Warlock; Zorba the Greek
Quinn, Colin: Who's the Man?
Quinn, Daniel: Avenging Angel, The (1995); Band of the Hand; Reason to Believe, A; Scanner Cop; Scanners 4: The Showdown
Quinn, Elizabeth: Sound and the Silence,The
Quinn, Francesco: Dead Certain; Indio; Nowhere Land; Platoon; Priceless Beauty; Quo Vadis? (1985)
Quinn, Frank: Body Puzzle
Quinn, Glenn: Dr. Giggles
Quinn, J. C.: Babe, The (1992); Barfly; Crisscross (1992); Maximum Overdrive; Megaville; Prayer of the Rollerboys; Priceless Beauty; Violated
Quinn, James W.: Witchtrap
Quinn, Marian: Broken Harvest
Quinn, Martha: Bad Channels; Chopper Chicks in Zombietown; Motorama
Quinn, Pat: Alice's Restaurant; Unmarried Woman, An; Zachariah
Quinn, Patricia: Rocky Horror Picture Show, The; Witching Time
Quinones, Adolfo: Breakin'; Breakin' 2 Electric Boogaloo
Quintana, Rosita: Susanna
Quintano, Gene: Treasure of the Four Crowns
Quinteros, Lorenzo: Man Facing Southeast
Quivers, Robin: Private Parts
Quo, Beulah: Children of An Lac, The
Qurrassi, Sarfuddin: Salaam Bombay!
Quynh, Nguyen Nhu: Cyclo; Vertical Ray of the Sun, The
Ra, Sun: Mystery, Mr. Ra
Raab, Ellie: Eyes of an Angel
Raab, Kurt: Boarding School; Les Tricheurs; Mussolini and I; Satan's Brew; Why Does Herr R. Run Amok?

Raab, Robyn Lynne: Orgazmo
Raaz, Vijay: Monsoon Wedding
Rabal, Enrique: Man and the Monster, The
Rabal, Francisco: Camorra; Corleone; Eclipse, The; Goya in Bordeaux; Holy Innocents; Nazarin; Nun, The (La Religieuse); Saddle Tramps; Sorcerer; Stay as You Are; Stilts, The (Los Zancos); Viridiana
Rabal, Liberto: Live Flesh
Rabelo, José: La Ciudad
Racette, Francine: Au Revoir, Les Enfants; Dan Candy's Law (Alien Thunder); Disappearance, The; Lumiere
Rachins, Alan: Always; L.A. Law; Meet Wally Sparks; Showgirls; Star Quest; Stepsister, The
Racimo, Victoria: Ernest Goes to Camp; High Velocity; Mountain Men, The; Prophecy (1979); Search for the Gods
Rack, Tom: Xchange
Radcliffe, Daniel: Harry Potter and the Sorcerer's Stone
Radd, Ronald: King Lear; Saint, The (TV Series)
Rademakers, Fons: Daughters of Darkness
Radenburgh, Dawn: Facade
Radford, Basil: Captive Heart; Dead of Night; Night Train to Munich (Night Train); Passport to Pimlico; Tight Little Island; Winslow Boy, The; Young and Innocent
Radford, Natalie: Agent Red; Chippendales Murder, The; Tomcat: Dangerous Desires
Radner, Gilda: First Family; Gilda Live; Hanky Panky; Haunted Honeymoon; Movers and Shakers; Rutles, The (All You Need Is Cash); Things We Did Last Summer; Woman in Red, The
Radziwilowicz, Jerzy: Man of Iron; Man of Marble; Suspended
Rae, Bettina: Witching of Ben Wagner, The
Rae, Cassidy: Evolver; Extreme Days; National Lampoon's Favorite Deadly Sins
Rae, Charlotte: Car 54 Where Are You? (TV Series); Hair; Hot Rock, The; Thunder in Paradise; Worst Witch, The
Rafferty, Chips: Desert Rats, The; Sundowners, The; Wackiest Ship in the Army, The; Walk into Hell
Rafferty, Frances: Abbott and Costello in Hollywood; Mrs. Parkington
Raffetto, Michael: Seven Doors to Death
Raffin, Deborah: Claudia; Death Wish III; Demon (God Told Me To); For the Love of It; Forty Carats; Hanging on a Star; Jungle Heat; Killing at Hell's Gate; Morning Glory; Night of the Fox; Once Is Not Enough; Ransom; Scanners 2: The New Order; Sentinel, The; Touched by Love; Willa
Raft, George: Background to Danger; Casino Royale; Each Dawn I Die; Five Golden Dragons; Follow the Boys; Hammersmith Is Out; House Across the Bay, The; If I Had a Million; Johnny Angel; Man with Bogart's Face, The; Mr. Ace; Night after Night; Nocturne; Outpost in Morocco; Scarface; Sextette; Some Like It Hot; They Drive by Night; Whistle Stop
Raftery, James: Night Owl
Raftery, Matt: Witchouse
Ragland, Rags: Girl Crazy; Whistling in Brooklyn; Whistling in the Dark
Ragno, Joe: Day at the Beach
Ragsdale, William: Fright Night; Fright Night II; Mannequin Two: On the Move; National Lampoon's Favorite Deadly Sins
Railsback, Steve: Alligator II; Angela; Barb Wire; Blue Monkey; Deadly Games; Deadly Intent; Distortions; Ed Gein; Escape 2000; Final Mission; Forgotten, The; From Here to Eternity; Golden Seal, The; Helter Skelter; Lifeforce; Private Wars; Quake; Save Me; Scenes from the Goldmine; Scissors; Stranger in the House; Stunt Man, The; Sunstroke; Survivalist, The; Trick or Treat
Raimi, Sam: Indian Summer; Thou Shalt Not Kill ... Except
Raimi, Sonia: Tuck Everlasting
Raimi, Theodore: Lunatics: A Love Story; Skinner
Raimu: Baker's Wife, The; César; Fanny; Marius; Pearls of the Crown, The; Well-Digger's Daughter, The
Rain, Douglas: Oedipus Rex
Rainer, Luise: Good Earth, The; Great Waltz, The; Great Ziegfeld, The
Raines, Cristina: Duellists, The; Nightmares; Quo Vadis? (1985); Russian Roulette; Sentinel, The; Silver Dream Racer; Touched by Love
Raines, Ella: Hail the Conquering Hero; Impact; Ride the Man Down; Senator Was Indiscreet, The; Strange Affair of Uncle Harry, The; Tall in the Saddle
Raines, Frances: Breeders
Rainey, Ford: Bed and Breakfast; Cellar, The; My Sweet Charlie; Strangers: The Story of a Mother and a Daughter
Rains, Claude: Adventures of Robin Hood, The; Angel on My Shoulder; Anthony Adverse; Caesar and Cleopatra; Casablanca; Deception; Evil Mind, The (The Clairvoyant); Forever and a Day; Four Daughters; Here Comes Mr. Jordan; Invisible Man, The; Juarez; King's Row; Lisbon; Mr. Skeffington; Mr. Smith Goes to Washington; Mystery of Edwin Drood, The; Notorious; Now, Voyager; Paris Express, The; Passage to Marseilles; Phantom of the Opera; Prince and the Pauper, The; Sea Hawk, The; They Made Me a Criminal; White Tower, The; Wolf Man, The
Raisch, Bill: Fugitive, The (TV Series); Fugitive, The: The Last Episode (TV Series)
Raitt, John: Pajama Game, The
Rall, Tommy: Kiss Me Kate; My Sister Eileen
Ralli, Giovanna: Caper of the Golden Bulls, The; General Della Rovere
Ralph, Jessie: Camille; Double Wedding; Drums Along the Mohawk; Evelyn Prentice; Good Earth, The; Last of Mrs. Cheney, The; Little Lord Fauntleroy; Murder at the Vanities; They Met in Bombay
Ralph, Michael: Drop Squad, The; Woo
Ralph, Sheryl Lee: Deterrence; Distinguished Gentleman, The; Mighty Quinn, The; Mistress; To Sleep with Anger; Witch Hunt
Ralston, Esther: Old Ironsides; Oliver Twist; Peter Pan; Sadie McKee; To the Last Man
Ralston, Howard: Pollyanna
Ralston, Jobyna: Freshman, The; Wings
Ralston, Vera Hruba: Dakota; Fighting Kentuckian, The; Hoodlum Empire; Jubilee Trail
Ramallo, Fernando: Nico and Dani
Rambal, Enrique: Exterminating Angel, The
Rambeau, Marjorie: Any Number Can Play; Inspiration; Laughing Sinners; Man Called Peter, A; Man of a Thousand Faces; Min and Bill; Palooka; Primrose Path; Rains Came, The; Salome, Where She Danced; Torch Song
Ramberg, Sterling: Revenge of the Teenage Vixens from OuterSpace
Rambo, Dack: Hit Lady; River of Diamonds; Shades of Love: Lilac Dream
Ramer, Henry: Between Friends; Big Slice, The; Reno and the Doc
Ramey, Alan: Vampires from Outer Space
Ramezani, Mohsen: Color of Paradise, The
Ramirez, Frank: Miracle in Rome
Ramirez, Lydia: Street Hitz (Street Story)
Ramis, Harold: Baby Boom; Ghostbusters; Ghostbusters II; Stealing Home; Stripes
Ramokgopa, Tommy: Magic Garden, The
Ramones, The: Rock 'n' Roll High School
Ramos, David: Takeover, The
Ramos, Nick: Legend of Walks Far Woman, The
Ramos, Rudy: Blindsided; Open House; Quicksilver
Rampling, Charlotte: Angel Heart; Caravan to Vaccares; D.O.A.; Farewell My Lovely; Foxtrot; Georgy Girl; Invasion of Privacy; Knack ... and How to Get It, The; Mascara; Max Mon Amour; Night Porter, The; Orca; Purple Taxi, The; Sardine: Kidnapped; Stardust Memories; Under the Sand; Verdict, The; Wings of the Dove, The; Zardoz
Ramsay, Bruce: Alive; Dead Beat; Hellraiser: Bloodline
Ramsay Jr., Lynne: Ratcatcher
Ramsden, Frances: Mad Wednesday (see also Sin of Harold Diddlebock)
Ramsden, John: Howling, The: New Moon Rising

Ramsey, Anne: Final Cut, The; Homer and Eddie; Meet the Hollowheads; River Pirates, The; Say Yes; Throw Momma from the Train

Ramsey, Logan: Head (1968); Hoodlum Priest, The; Joy Sticks; King Richard II; Say Yes; Some Call It Loving

Ramsey, Marion: Police Academy 5: Assignment: Miami Beach; Police Academy II: Their First Assignment; Police Academy III: Back in Training

Ramsey, Natalie: Children of the Corn 666: Isaac's Return

Ramsey, Stephen: No Telling

Ramsey, Ward: Dinosaurus!

Ramson, Bert: Maverick

Ramus, Nick: Windwalker

Rand, John: Charlie Chaplin Cavalcade

Rand, Sally: Road to Yesterday, The

Randall, Ethan: Dutch; Evolver; Far Off Place, A

Randall, Lexi: Sarah, Plain and Tall; Skylark; War, The

Randall, Meg: Ma and Pa Kettle (The Further Adventures of Ma and Pa Kettle); Ma and Pa Kettle Back on the Farm; Ma and Pa Kettle Go to Town

Randall, Richard: Cross Mission

Randall, Stacie: Dream a Little Dream 2; Excessive Force II: Force on Force; Ghoulies IV; Trancers 5: Sudden Deth; Trancers 4: Jack of Swords

Randall, Tony: Adventures of Huckleberry Finn, The; Alphabet Murders, The; Boys' Night Out; Everything You Always Wanted to Know About Sex but Were Afraid to Ask; Fatal Instinct; Foolin' Around; Let's Make Love; Littlest Angel, The; Lover Come Back; Mating Game, The; Pillow Talk; Scavenger Hunt; Send Me No Flowers; 7 Faces of Dr. Lao; That's Adequate; Will Success Spoil Rock Hunter?

Randazzo, Peter: Trees

Randazzo, Teddy: Rock, Rock, Rock

Randell, Ron: I Am a Camera; Loves of Carmen, The

Randig, Ric: Splatter University

Randle, Theresa: Bad Boys; Beverly Hills Cop 3; CB4; Girl 6; Space Jam; Spawn; Sugar Hill

Randolph, Amanda: Amos and Andy (TV Series)

Randolph, Anders: Black Pirate, The

Randolph, Jane: Curse of the Cat People, The; Falcon's Brother, The; Railroaded; T-Men

Randolph, John: Adventures of Nellie Bly, The; American Clock, The; As Summers Die; Foreign Field, A; Killing at Hell's Gate; National Lampoon's Christmas Vacation; Prizzi's Honor; Seconds; Serpico; Sibling Rivalry; Wizard of Loneliness, The

Randolph, Joyce: Honeymooners, The: Lost Episodes (TV Series); Honeymooners, The (TV Series)

Randolph, Windsor Taylor: Amazons

Random, Robert: Vampire at Midnight

Rangel, Maria: Full Fathom Five

Ranger, Dan: Last Ride, The

Rankin, Claire: Face to Kill For, A

Rankin, Sean: Underground

Ranney, Juanita: Danger Zone, The (1986)

Ransen, Holger Juul: Kingdom, The

Ransom, Kenny: Prison for Children

Ransom, Tim: Dressmaker, The

Ransome, Prunella: Man in the Wilderness

Ransone, James: American Astronaut, The

Rapaport, Michael: Bamboozled; Beautiful Girls; Copland; Deep Blue Sea; Higher Learning; Illtown; Kicked in the Head; Kiss of Death; Kiss Toledo Goodbye; Men of Honor; Metro; Mighty Aphrodite; Naked Man, The; Pallbearer, The; Palmetto; 6th Day, The; Small Time Crooks; Subway Stories; True Romance; Zebrahead

Rapp, Anthony: Adventures in Babysitting; Dazed and Confused

Rappagna, Anna: Order of the Black Eagle

Rappaport, David: Bride, The; Mysteries

Rappaport, Sheeri: Little Witches

Rappaport, Stephen: ... And God Spoke

Rascel, Renato: Seven Hills of Rome, The

Rasche, David: Act of Passion; Big Tease, The; Bingo; Dead Weekend; Delirious; Fighting Back; Hammered: The Best of Sledge; Hostage Hotel; Innocent Man, An; Masters of Menace; Native Son; Out There; Silhouette; Special Bulletin; That Old Feeling

Rascoe, Stephanie: Positive I.D.

Rashad, Phylicia: Free of Eden; Loving Jezebel; Once Upon a Time ... When We Were Colored; Visit, The

Rasp, Fritz: Diary of a Lost Girl; Spies; Woman in the Moon (Girl in the Moon; By Rocket to the Moon)

Raspberry, James: I Was a Zombie for the FBI

Rassam, Julien: Accompanist, The

Rasulala, Thalmus: Adios Amigo; Autobiography of Miss Jane Pittman, The; Blacula; Born American; Bucktown; Bulletproof; Friday Foster; Mom and Dad Save the World; Sophisticated Gents, The

Rasumny, Mikhail: For Whom the Bell Tolls

Ratanasopha, Premsinee: Bangkok Dangerous

Ratchford, Jeremy: Moonshine Highway

Ratcliff, Sandy: Family Life

Rathbone, Basil: Above Suspicion; Adventures of Marco Polo, The; Adventures of Robin Hood, The; Adventures of Sherlock Holmes, The; Anna Karenina; Bathing Beauty; Captain Blood; Casanova's Big Night; Comedy of Terrors; Court Jester, The; David Copperfield; Dawn Patrol, The; Dressed to Kill; Fingers at the Window; Garden of Allah, The; Hillbillys in a Haunted House; Hound of the Baskervilles, The; House of Fear; If I Were King; Last Days of Pompeii, The (1935); Last Hurrah, The; Love from a Stranger; Magic Sword, The; Make a Wish; Mark of Zorro, The; Pearl of Death, The; Planet of Blood (Queen of Blood); Pursuit to Algiers; Rhythm on the River; Romeo and Juliet; Scarlet Claw, The; Sherlock Holmes and the Secret Weapon; Sherlock Holmes and the Spider Woman; Sherlock Holmes and the Voice of Terror; Sherlock Holmes Faces Death; Sherlock Holmes in Washington; Son of Frankenstein; Tale of Two Cities, A; Tales of Terror; Terror by Night; Tovaritch; Tower of London; Voyage to the Prehistoric Planet; We're No Angels; Woman in Green, The

Ratliff, Garette Patrick: Return to the Blue Lagoon

Ratner, Benjamin: Bounty Hunters

Ratner-Stauber, Tzvi: Family Prayers

Ratoff, Gregory: Here Comes Trouble; I'm No Angel; Skyscraper Souls; What Price Hollywood?

Rattray, Heather: Across the Great Divide; Adventures of the Wilderness Family; Basket Case 2; Mountain Family Robinson; Sea Gypsies, The; Wilderness Family, Part 2, The

Ratzenberger, John: House II: The Second Story; Tick Tock; Time Stalkers; Under Pressure

Rauch, Siegfried: Le Mans; Nous N'Irons Plus Au Bois

Rauscher, Aurore: Rendezvous in Paris

Rauum, Spencer: Wheels: An Inline Story

Raven, Mike: Wheels: An Inline Story

Raven, Stark: Shatter Dead

Raven-Symone: Dr. Dolittle 2

Ravera, Gina: Soul of the Game

Ravovit, Andrew: Magnificent Seven, The (TV Series)

Rawlinson, Herbert: Jail Bait (1954); Superman—The Serial

Rawls, Lou: Malevolence

Ray, Aldo: And Hope to Die; Biohazard; Bog; Boxoffice; Centerfold Girls; Dead Heat on a Merry-Go-Round; Evils of the Night; God's Little Acre; Gone with the West; Green Berets, The; Hollywood Cop; Inside Out; Little Moon & Jud McGraw; Men in War; Miss Sadie Thompson; Naked and the Dead, The; Pat and Mike; Psychic Killer; Shock'em Dead; Star Slammer; Terror on Alcatraz; We're No Angels

Ray, Allene: Phantom, The

Ray, Frankie: Invasion of the Star Creatures; Kiss the Girls Goodbye

Ray, Gene Anthony: Fame

Ray, James: Mass Appeal; She's Having a Baby

Ray, Johnnie: There's No Business Like Show Business

Ray, Leah: One in a Million; Thin Ice

Ray, Man: Avant Garde Program #2

Ray, Michel: Brave One, The; Tin Star, The

Ray, Nica: Cutting Moments

Ray, Nicholas: Lightning over Water

Ray, Sonny: Perils of Pauline, The

Raye, Lisa: Players Club, The
Raye, Martha: Alice in Wonderland; Big Broadcast of 1938, The; College Swing; Four Jills in a Jeep; Give Me a Sailor; Hellzapoppin; Jumbo; Monsieur Verdoux; Pin-Up Girl; Rhythm on the Range; Waikiki Wedding
Raymond, Bill: Where the Rivers Flow North
Raymond, Cyril: Brief Encounter
Raymond, Gary: Jason and the Argonauts; Playboy of the Western World
Raymond, Gene: Bride Walks Out, The; Ex-Lady; Hit the Deck; If I Had a Million; Mr. and Mrs. Smith; Plunder Road; Red Dust; Sadie McKee; Smilin' Through; Transatlantic Merry-Go-Round
Raymond, Lee: She Freak, The
Raymond, Lina: Gypsy Warriors, The
Raymond, Martin: Living the Blues
Raymond, Paula: Beast from 20,000 Fathoms, The; Blood of Dracula's Castle; Duchess of Idaho; Gun Riders, The
Raymond, Richard: Rats
Raymond, Ruth: Bad Blood; Woman Obsessed, A
Raymond, Usher: Light It Up; Texas Rangers (2001)
Raynor, Lavita: Belly
Raynor, Michael: Federal Hill
Rea, Peggy: In Country; Love Field; Made in America
Rea, Stephen: Angie; Bad Behaviour; Butcher Boy, The; Citizen X; Crime of the Century; Crying Game, The; Danny Boy; Doctor and the Devils, The; Double Tap; End of the Affair, The; Guinevere; In Dreams; Interview with the Vampire; Loose Connections; Michael Collins; Musketeer, The; Princess Caraboo; Ready to Wear; Sink or Swim; Snow in August; Still Crazy; Summer Fling; This Is My Father
Read, Barbara: Three Smart Girls
Read, Dolly: Beyond the Valley of the Dolls
Read, James: Harvest of Fire; Love Crimes; North and South; Poor Little Rich Girl: The Barbara Hutton Story; Remington Steele (TV series); Web of Deceit; When the Dark Man Calls
Reagan, Nancy: Rockin' Ronnie
Reagan, Ron: Rockin' Ronnie
Reagan, Ronald: Bedtime for Bonzo; Boy Meets Girl; Cattle Queen of Montana; Dark Victory; Desperate Journey; Hellcats of the Navy; Killers, The; King's Row; Knute Rockne—All American; Rockin' Ronnie; Santa Fe Trail; Tennessee's Partner; This Is the Army; Winning Team, The
Reason, Rex: Creature Walks Among Us, The; This Island Earth
Reason, Rhodes: Bronco (TV Series); Voodoo Island
Rebar, Alex: Incredible Melting Man, The
Rebbot, Saddy: My Life to Live
Rebhorn, James: Blank Check; Bright Shining Lie, A; Carlito's Way; Game, The; Guarding Tess; I Love Trouble; Mistrial; My Fellow Americans; Scent of a Woman; Scotland, PA; Snow Falling on Cedars; Talented Mr. Ripley, The; Will, G. Gordon Liddy
Reboux, Anaïs: Fat Girl
Rector, Jeff: Street Soldiers
Rector, Jerry: Rule #3
Redbone, Leon: Candy Mountain
Redd, Joyce: Ballad of a Gunfighter
Redding, Juli: Mission in Morocco
Redding, Otis: Monterey Pop
Redding, Wilma: Pacific Inferno
Reddy, Helen: Airport 1975; Pete's Dragon
Rede, Nina Pens: Gertrude
Redeker, Quinn: Coast to Coast; Spider Baby
Redfern, Linda: I Will Fight No More Forever
Redfield, Dennis: Dead and Buried; Pulse
Redfield, William: Connection, The (1961); Fantastic Voyage; Hot Rock, The; I Married a Woman; Morituri; Mr. Billion; New Leaf, A
Redford, Robert: All the President's Men; Barefoot in the Park; Bridge Too Far, A; Brubaker; Butch Cassidy and the Sundance Kid; Candidate, The; Chase, The; Downhill Racer; Electric Horseman, The; Great Gatsby, The; Great Waldo Pepper, The; Havana; Horse Whisperer, The; Hot Rock, The; Indecent Proposal; Inside Daisy Clover; Jeremiah Johnson; Last Castle, The; Legal Eagles; Natural, The; Out of Africa; Sneakers; Spy Game; Sting, The; Tell Them Willie Boy Is Here; This Property Is Condemned; Three Days of the Condor; Twilight Zone, The (TV Series); Up Close and Personal; Way We Were, The
Redgrave, Corin: Between Wars; Excalibur; Four Weddings and a Funeral; Persuasion
Redgrave, Lynn: Antony and Cleopatra; Big Bus, The; Everything You Always Wanted to Know About Sex but Were Afraid to Ask; Georgy Girl; Getting It Right; Gods and Monsters; Great American Sex Scandal, The; Happy Hooker, The; Long Live Your Death; Midnight; Morgan Stewart's Coming Home; Next Best Thing, The; Rehearsal for Murder; Shine; Silent Mouse; Sooner or Later; Strike! (1998); Varian's War; Virgin Soldiers, The; Walking on Air; What Ever Happened To ... ?
Redgrave, Michael: Browning Version, The; Captive Heart; Dam Busters, The; Dead of Night; Dr. Jekyll and Mr. Hyde; Go-Between, The; Goodbye, Mr. Chips; Hill, The; Importance of Being Earnest, The; Innocents, The (1961); Lady Vanishes, The; Loneliness of the Long Distance Runner,The; Mr. Arkadin (Confidential Report); Nicholas and Alexandra; 1984; Sea Shall Not Have Them, The; Secret Beyond the Door; Shake Hands with the Devil; Stars Look Down, The; Time Without Pity; Twinsanity; Wreck of the Mary Deare, The
Redgrave, Vanessa: Agatha; Ballad of the Sad Cafe, The; Bear Island; Bella Mafia; Blow-Up; Bostonians, The; Camelot; Charge of the Light Brigade, The; Consuming Passions; Cradle Will Rock; Deep Impact; Déjà Vu; Devils, The; Down Came a Blackbird; House of the Spirits, The; Howards End; Isadora; Julia; Little Odessa; Lulu on the Bridge; Mission: Impossible; Month by the Lake, A; Morgan; Mother's Boys; Mrs. Dalloway; Murder on the Orient Express; Orpheus Descending; Out of Season; Playing for Time; Pledge, The; Prick Up Your Ears; Seven-Per-cent Solution, The; Smilla's Sense of Snow; Snow White and the Seven Dwarfs; Steaming; They (They Watch); Three Sovereigns for Sarah; Trojan Women, The; Wagner; Wetherby; What Ever Happened To ... ?; Wilde; Yanks; Young Catherine
Redman: How High
Redman, Amanda: For Queen and Country; Richard's Things; Sexy Beast
Redmond, Liam: Ghost and Mr. Chicken, The; I See a Dark Stranger
Redmond, Moira: Nightmare
Redmond, Siobhan: Look Back In Anger
Rednikova, Yehaterina: Thief, The
Redondo, Emiliano: Black Venus
Redwine, Ted: Mystery Monsters; P.U.N.K.S.
Reed, Alan: Actors and Sin; Days of Glory; Seniors, The
Reed, Alyson: Chorus Line, A; Manhattan Merengue; Skin Deep
Reed, Dolores: Invasion of the Star Creatures
Reed, Donald: Man from Monterey, The
Reed, Donna: Babes on Broadway; Benny Goodman Story, The; Caddy, The; From Here to Eternity; Green Dolphin Street; Gun Fury; Hangman's Knot; Human Comedy, The; It's a Wonderful Life; Last Time I Saw Paris, The; Picture of Dorian Gray, The; Shadow of the Thin Man; They Were Expendable; Trouble Along the Way
Reed, Hal: Doberman Gang, The
Reed, Jennifer A.: Apart from Hugh
Reed, Jerry: Bat 21; Gator; High-Ballin'; Hot Stuff; Smokey and the Bandit; Smokey and the Bandit II; Smokey and the Bandit III; Survivors, The; What Comes Around
Reed, Kevin: Last Way Out, The
Reed, Laura: Prime Time Murder
Reed, Lou: Blue in the Face; Faraway, So Close; Get Crazy; One Trick Pony
Reed, Marshall: Sundown Riders; They Saved Hitler's Brain
Reed, Oliver: Adventures of Baron Münchausen, The; Beat Girl; Big Sleep, The; Black Arrow (1984); Blood in the Streets; Brood, The; Burnt Offerings; Captive; Captive Rage; Castaway; Christopher Columbus (1985); Class of Miss MacMichael, The; Condorman; Curse of the Werewolf, The; Dante's Inferno; Devils, The; Dr. Heckyl and Mr. Hype; Four Musketeers, The; Funnybones; Ghost in Monte Carlo, A; Gladiator; Gor; Great Scout and Cathouse Thursday, The; Hired to Kill; House of Usher, The; Lion

of the Desert; Marco Polo; Misfit Brigade, The; Oliver; One Russian Summer; Paranoiac; Prince and the Pauper, The; Prisoner of Honor; Ransom; Return of the Musketeers; Return to Lonesome Dove; Sell-Out, The; Severed Ties; Shuttered Room, The; Spasms; Sting II, The; Ten Little Indians; Three Musketeers, The; Tommy; Tomorrow Never Comes; Treasure Island; Venom; Women in Love; Z.P.G. (Zero Population Growth)
Reed, Pamela: Bean; Best of Times, The; Cadillac Man; Caroline?; Chattahoochee; Clan of the Cave Bear; Critical Choices; Goodbye People, The; Junior; Kindergarten Cop; Melvin and Howard; Passed Away; Proof of Life; Rachel River; Right Stuff, The; Tanner '88; Woman with a Past; Young Doctors in Love
Reed, Paul: Car 54 Where Are You? (TV Series)
Reed, Penelope: Amazons
Reed, Phillip: Klondike Annie; Last of the Mohicans, The; Madame X
Reed, Ralph: Reform School Girl; Wyatt Earp: Return to Tombstone
Reed, Rex: Myra Breckenridge
Reed, Robert: Boy in the Plastic Bubble, The; Brady Bunch, The (TV series); Bud and Lou; Casino; Death of a Centerfold; Haunts of the Very Rich; Pray for the Wildcats; Prime Target; Snatched; Star! (1968); Very Brady Christmas, A
Reed, Shanna: Don't Talk to Strangers; Mirrors; Rattled; Sister-In-Law, The; Welcome to Planet Earth
Reed, Susanne: Up from the Depths
Reed, Tracy: All the Marbles; Running Scared
Reed, Walter: Superman and the Mole Men
Reedus, Norman: Blade II; Dark Harbor; Gossip; Reach the Rock; Six Ways to Sunday
Rees, Angharad: Hands of the Ripper
Rees, Donough: Crush (1994)
Rees, Roger: Black Male; Bumblebee Flies Anyway, The; If Looks Could Kill; Mountains of the Moon; Robin Hood: Men in Tights; Stop! Or My Mom Will Shoot; Trouble on the Corner
Reese, Della: Harlem Nights; Kid Who Loved Christmas, The; Psychic Killer; Thin Line Between Love and Hate, A
Reese, Michelle: Night Stalker, The
Reeve, Christopher: Above Suspicion; Anna Karenina; Aviator, The; Black Fox; Blood Horse; Bostonians, The; Death Dreams; Deathtrap; Good Men and Bad; Great Escape II, The; Monsignor; Morning Glory; Mortal Sins (1992); Noises Off; Rear Window; Remains of the Day; Rose and the Jackal, The; Sea Wolf, The; Sleeping Beauty; Somewhere in Time; Speechless; Street Smart; Superman; Superman II; Superman III; Superman IV: The Quest for Peace; Switching Channels; Village of the Damned
Reeves, Eve: Behind Locked Doors
Reeves, George: Blue Gardenia, The; Bugles in the Afternoon; Great Lover, The; Hoppy Serves a Writ; Jungle Jim; Rancho Notorious; So Proudly We Hail; Strawberry Blonde, The; Superman and the Mole Men; TV's Best Adventures of Superman; Westward Ho, the Wagons
Reeves, Keanu: Babes in Toyland; Bill and Ted's Bogus Journey; Bill and Ted's Excellent Adventure; Bram Stoker's Dracula; Brotherhood of Justice; Chain Reaction; Devil's Advocate; Dream to Believe; Even Cowgirls Get the Blues; Feeling Minnesota; Gift, The; Hardball; I Love You to Death; Johnny Mnemonic; Last Time I Committed Suicide, The; Little Buddha; Matrix, The; Much Ado About Nothing; My Own Private Idaho; Night Before, The; Parenthood; Permanent Record; Point Break; Prince of Pennsylvania; Replacements, The; River's Edge; Speed; Sweet November (2001); Tune in Tomorrow; Walk in the Clouds, A; Watcher, The
Reeves, Lisa: Chicken Chronicles, The
Reeves, Mathonway: Child's Christmas in Wales, A (1986)
Reeves, Saskia: Antonia & Jane; Butterfly Kiss; Close My Eyes; December Bride; Different for Girls; Dune; Heart (1999)
Reeves, Scott: Edge of Honor; Friday the 13th, Part VIII: Jason Takes Manhattan; Hearts Adrift
Reeves, Steve: Athena; Goliath and the Barbarians; Hercules; Hercules Unchained; Jail Bait (1954); Last Days of Pompeii (1960); Morgan the Pirate
Reevis, Steve: Geronimo: An American Legend; Last of the Dogmen; Wild Bill
Regalbuto, Joe: Deadly Weapon; Raw Deal; Six Weeks; Streethawk
Regan, Mary: Heart of the Stag; Midnight Dancer; Sylvia
Regan, Phil: Go into Your Dance; Manhattan Merry-Go-Round; Sweet Adeline
Regan, Vincent: Black Knight
Regehr, Duncan: Monster Squad, The; My Wicked, Wicked Ways; Primo Baby
Regent, Benoit: Blue
Reggiani, Serge: Cat and Mouse; La Ronde; Le Doulos; Paris Blues; Vincent, François, Paul and the Others
Regina, Paul: Bounty Tracker; It's My Party
Regine: My New Partner; Robert et Robert
Regnier, Natacha: Dreamlife of Angels, The
Reicher, Frank: Captain America; Jade Mask, The; King Kong; Son of Kong, The
Reichmann, Wolfgang: Beethoven's Nephew
Reid, Alex: Arachnid
Reid, Beryl: Beast in the Cellar, The; Carry on Emmanuelle; Doctor and the Devils, The; Dr. Phibes Rises Again; Entertaining Mr. Sloane; Joseph Andrews; Killing of Sister George, The; Psychomania
Reid, Carl Benton: Athena; Indian Uprising; Pressure Point; Stage to Tucson
Reid, Christopher: Class Act; House Party 2; House Party 3
Reid, Elliott: Gentlemen Prefer Blondes; Thrill of It All, The; Woman's World
Reid, Kate: Andromeda Strain, The; Atlantic City; Circle of Two; Death of a Salesman; Deathship; Deceived; Fire with Fire; Heaven Help Us; Highpoint; Last Best Year, The; Signs of Life; This Property Is Condemned
Reid, Lehua: Point of Impact
Reid, Sheila: Winter Guest, The
Reid, Tara: American Pie 2; Big Lebowski, The; Body Shots; Dr. T and the Women; Josie and the Pussycats; Just Visiting; Urban Legend
Reid, Tim: Dead-Bang; Fourth War, The; It; You Must Remember This
Reid, Wallace: Roaring Road, The
Reif, Taryn: Blood Surf
Reifsnyder, Timothy: Wide Awake
Reilly, John C.: Anniversary Party, The; Boogie Nights; Boys (1996); Casualties of War; Dolores Claiborne; For Love of the Game; Georgia; Hard Eight; Hoffa; Incredible Journey of Dr. Meg Laurel,The; Magnolia; Never Been Kissed; Out on a Limb; Perfect Storm, The; River Wild, The; State of Grace; What's Eating Gilbert Grape?
Reilly, Robert: Frankenstein Meets the Space Monster
Reineke, Gary: Why Shoot the Teacher?
Reiner, Carl: Adventures of Rocky and Bullwinkle, The; Dead Men Don't Wear Plaid; Dick Van Dyke Show, The (TV Series); Fatal Instinct; Gazebo, The; Generation (1969); Gidget Goes Hawaiian; Guide for the Married Man, A; Ocean's Eleven (2001); Pinocchio; Right to Remain Silent, The; Russians Are Coming, the Russians Are Coming, The; Skokie; Spirit of '76, The; Summer School; 10 from Your Show of Shows
Reiner, Rob: Bullets over Broadway; Bye Bye, Love; EDtv; Enter Laughing; Mixed Nuts; Muse, The; Postcards from the Edge; Sleepless in Seattle; Spirit of '76, The; Story of Us, The; This Is Spinal Tap; Thursday's Game; Where's Poppa?
Reiner, Tracy: League of Their Own, A
Reinhold, Judge: As Good as Dead; Baby on Board; Bank Robber; Beethoven's 3rd; Beverly Hills Cop; Beverly Hills Cop II; Beverly Hills Cop 3; Black Magic; Coming Unglued; Daddy's Dyin' and Who's Got the Will; Dead in a Heartbeat; Fast Times at Ridgemont High; Floating Away; Four Eyes and Six Guns; Head Office; Homegrown; Hostage Train; Near Misses; Newsbreak; Off Beat; Over Her Dead Body; Promised a Miracle; Right to Remain Silent, The; Roadhouse 66; Running Scared; Ruthless People; Santa Clause, The; Soldier's Tale, A; Vice Versa; Wharf Rat, The; Zandalee
Reiniger, Scott: Dawn of the Dead

Reinking, Ann: All That Jazz; Micki & Maude; Movie Movie
Reis, Michelle: Legend, The; Wicked City, The (1992)
Reiser, Paul: Aliens; Bye Bye, Love; Crazy People; Cross My Heart; Family Prayers; Marrying Man, The; Mr. Write; Story of Us, The; Sunset Limousine
Rekert, Winston: Agnes of God; Cooler Climate, A; Eternal Evil; Glory! Glory!; Heartaches; High Stakes; Toby McTeague
Rekin, Dwayne: Cat, The (1966)
Remar, James: Across the Moon; Band of the Hand; Blink; Blowback; Born Bad; Boys on the Side; Cotton Club, The; Deadlock; Drugstore Cowboy; Fatal Charm; Fatal Instinct; 48 Hrs.; Hellraiser: Inferno; Indecency; Inferno; Miracle on 34th Street; One Good Turn; Phantom, The; Quest, The; Quiet Cool; Renaissance Man; Rent-a-Cop; Rites of Passage; Silence Like Glass; Strangers; Surgeon, The; Tigress, The; Warriors, The; What Lies Beneath; White Fang; Wild Bill; Windwalker
Remarque, Erich Maria: Time to Love and a Time to Die, A
Remay, Albert: Children of Paradise, The
Remberg, Erika: Cave of the Living Dead; Circus of Horrors
Remick, Lee: Anatomy of a Murder; Baby the Rain Must Fall; Blue Knight, The; Bridge to Silence; Competition, The; Days of Wine and Roses (1962); Detective, The; Europeans, The; Experiment in Terror; Face in the Crowd, A; Hallelujah Trail, The; Hennessy; Hustling; I Do! I Do!; Ike: The War Years; Jesse; Long Hot Summer, The; Loot; Medusa Touch, The; Mistral's Daughter; No Way to Treat a Lady; Of Pure Blood; Omen, The; QB VII; Snow Queen; Sometimes a Great Notion; Telefon; Torn Between Two Lovers; Tribute; Wheeler Dealers, The
Remsen, Bert: Borderline; Carny; Code of Silence; Daddy's Dyin' and Who's Got the Will; Dead Ringer; Hobson's Choice; Hugo Pool; Jack the Bear; Jezebel's Kiss; Ladykiller; Lies; Lookin' to Get Out; M.A.D.D.: Mothers Against Drunk Driving; Only the Lonely; Payback; Road Ends; Sting II, The; Thieves Like Us
Remsen, Kerry: Appointment with Fear
Remy, Albert: 400 Blows, The
Renaldo, Duncan: Border Patrol; Cisco Kid (TV Series); Covered Wagon Days; Fighting Seabees, The; Kansas Terrors; Outlaws of the Desert; Painted Stallion, The; Rocky Mountain Rangers; San Antonio Kid; South of the Border; Zorro Rides Again
Renan, Sergio: Debajo del Mundo (Under Earth)
Renant, Simone: Les Liaisons Dangereuses; That Man from Rio
Renaud, Madeleine: Stormy Waters
Renavent, Georges: East of Borneo
Renay, Liz: Desperate Living; Thrill Killers, The
Renderer, Scott: Poison
Rendorf, Sherry: Slaughterhouse
Renfro, Brad: Apt Pupil; Bully; Client, The; Cure, The; Ghost World; Skipped Parts; Sleepers; Tart; Telling Lies in America; Tom and Huck
Renhua, Na: Girl from Hunan
Renier, Jeremie: La Promesse
Renko, Serge: Rendezvous in Paris
Renna, Patrick: Address Unknown; Beanstalk; Blue River; Johnny Mysto; P.U.N.K.S.
Rennard, Deborah: Lionheart
Renner, Jeremy: National Lampoon's Senior Trip
Rennie, Callum Keith: Hard Core Logo; Last Night
Rennie, James: Illicit
Rennie, Michael: Battle of El Alamein, The; Day the Earth Stood Still, The; Demetrius and the Gladiators; Desirée; Devil's Brigade, The; Five Fingers; Hondo and the Apaches; Hotel; Mambo; Omar Khayyam; Phone Call from a Stranger; Ride Beyond Vengeance; Robe, The; Seven Cities of Gold; Ships with Wings; Soldier of Fortune; Third Man on the Mountain; Trio; Wicked Lady, The
Renniks, Lei: Sinyster
Reno, Ginetta: Leolo
Reno, Jean: Big Blue, The; Crimson Rivers, The; Final Combat, The; For Roseanna; French Kiss; Godzilla (1998); Just Visiting; Mission: Impossible; Professional, The; Rollerball (2002); Ronin
Reno, Kelly: Black Stallion, The; Black Stallion Returns, The; Brady's Escape
Renoir, Jean: La Bête Humaine
Renoir, Pierre: La Marseillaise; Madame Bovary
Renoir, Sophie: Boyfriends and Girlfriends
Renucci, Robin: King's Whore, The
Renvall, Johan: Dance
Renying, Zhou: King of Masks, The
Renzi, Eva: Bird with the Crystal Plumage, The; Funeral in Berlin
Renzi, Maggie: City of Hope; Passion Fish; Return of the Secaucus 7
Repo-Martell, Liisa: Critical Choices
Resines, Antonio: How to Be a Woman and Not Die in the Attempt; Skyline
Resnick, Amy: Haiku Tunnel
Resnick, Judith: Carnival of Blood
Ressel, Frank: Have a Nice Funeral
Restrepo, Juan David: Our Lady of the Assassins
Rettig, Tommy: At Gunpoint; Five Thousand Fingers of Dr. T, The; Jackpot, The; River of No Return
Reuben, Gloria: Dead Air; Nick of Time; Timecop
Reubens, Paul: Blow; Buddy; Dunston Checks In; Mystery Men; Pandemonium; South of Heaven, West of Hell
Revach, Zeev: Escape: Human Cargo
Revere, Anne: Birch Interval, The; Body and Soul; Devil Commands, The; Forever Amber; Gentlemen's Agreement; Howards of Virginia, The; Meanest Man in the World, The; National Velvet; Place in the Sun, A; Song of Bernadette, The; Star Spangled Rhythm; Thin Man Goes Home, The
Revill, Clive: Avanti!; George Washington; Ghost in the Noonday Sun; Legend of Hell House, The; Matilda; One of Our Dinosaurs Is Missing; Private Life of Sherlock Holmes, The
Revueltas, Rosoura: Salt of the Earth
Rex, Simon: Shriek If You Know What I Did Last Friday the 13th
Rey, Alejandro: Fun in Acapulco; High Velocity; Ninth Configuration, The; Pacific Connection, The; Rita Hayworth: The Love Goddess
Rey, Antonia: Tarantella
Rey, Fernando: Antony and Cleopatra; Black Arrow (1984); Discreet Charm of the Bourgeoisie, The; French Connection, The; French Connection II, The; High Crime; Hit, The (1984); Immortal Story; La Grande Bourgeoise; Last Days of Pompeii (1960); Light at the End of the World, The; Monsignor; Moon over Parador; Naked Tango; 1492: The Conquest of Paradise; Pantaloons; Quintet; Rustler's Rhapsody; Saving Grace; Seven Beauties; Star Knight; That Obscure Object of Desire; Tristana; Tunnel, The; Villa Rides; Viridiana
Rey, Mony: Mademoiselle
Reyes, Pia: Forbidden Zone: Alien Abduction
Reyes Jr., Ernie: Red Sonja; Surf Ninjas; Teenage Mutant Ninja Turtles II: The Secret of the Ooze
Reymond, Dominique: Come Undone
Reynal, Madeleine: Dr. Caligari
Reynaud, Janine: Castle of the Creeping Flesh
Reyne, James: Return to Eden
Reynolds, Adeline de Walt: Iceland
Reynolds, Burt: Armored Command; Best Friends; Best Little Whorehouse in Texas, The; Blade Rider; Boogie Nights; Breaking In; Cannonball Run; Cannonball Run II; Cherokee Kid, The; Citizen Ruth; City Heat; Cop and a Half; Crew, The; Deliverance; Driven; End, The; Everything You Always Wanted to Know About Sex but Were Afraid to Ask; Frankenstein and Me; Fuzz; Gator; Gunsmoke (TV Series); Hard Time; Heat; Hooper; Hostage Hotel; Hunter's Moon; Hustle; Longest Yard, The; Maddening, The; Malone; Man from Left Field, The; Man Who Loved Cat Dancing, The; Man Who Loved Women, The; Meet Wally Sparks; Modern Love; Mystery, Alaska; 100 Rifles; Operation C.I.A.; Paternity; Physical Evidence; Pups; Raven (1997); Rent-a-Cop; Rough Cut; Semi-Tough; Shamus; Shark! (Maneaters!); Sharky's Machine; Silent Movie; Smokey and the Bandit; Smokey and the Bandit II; Starting Over; Stick; Striptease; Stroker Ace; Switching Channels; Trigger Happy (Mad Dog Time); White Lightning

Reynolds, Debbie: Affairs of Dobie Gillis, The; Athena; Bundle of Joy; Catered Affair, The; Detective Sadie and Son; Divorce American Style; Gazebo, The; Gift of Love: The Daniel Huffman Story; Give a Girl a Break; Heaven and Earth; Hit the Deck; How the West Was Won; I Love Melvin; In & Out; It Started With a Kiss; Mating Game, The; Mother; Mr. Imperium; Singin' in the Rain; Singing Nun, The; Susan Slept Here; Tammy and the Bachelor; Tender Trap, The; That's Entertainment! III; That's Singing: The Best of Broadway; This Happy Feeling; Three Little Words; Two Weeks with Love; Unsinkable Molly Brown, The; What's the Matter with Helen?
Reynolds, Gene: Andy Hardy's Private Secretary; Bridges at Toko-Ri, The; Diane; Jungle Patrol; Mortal Storm, The; Of Human Hearts; Tuttles of Tahiti, The
Reynolds, Hayley: Lifeforce Experiment, The
Reynolds, Helene: Wintertime
Reynolds, Jacob: Gummo
Reynolds, Jay: Reincarnate, The
Reynolds, Joyce: Adventures of Mark Twain, The
Reynolds, Marjorie: Doomed to Die; Fatal Hour, The; His Kind of Woman; Holiday Inn; Monsieur Beaucaire; Mr. Wong in Chinatown; Robin Hood of the Pecos; That Midnight Kiss; Time of Their Lives, The
Reynolds, Michael J.: Lifeforce Experiment, The; Trial & Error (1992)
Reynolds, Nicola: Human Traffic
Reynolds, Patrick: Eliminators, The
Reynolds, Paul: Angelic Conversation; Let Him Have It
Reynolds, Quentin: Golden Earrings
Reynolds, Robert: Daughter of Darkness; Tunnel Vision (1994)
Reynolds, Ryan: Alarmist, The; Ordinary Magic
Reynolds, Simon: Gate II
Reynolds, Vera: Monster Walks, The; Road to Yesterday, The
Reynolds, William: Away All Boats; Land Unknown, The; Son of Ali Baba; Thing that Couldn't Die, The
Rhames, Ving: Baby Boy; Body Count; Bringing Out the Dead; Con Air; Dangerous Ground; Dave; Don King: Only in America; Drop Squad, The; Entrapment; Homicide; Kiss of Death; Long Walk Home, The; Mission: Impossible; Mission: Impossible 2; Out of Sight; Patty Hearst; People Under the Stairs, The; Pulp Fiction; Rising Son; Rosewood; Saint of Fort Washington, The; Striptease
Rhee, Phillip: Best of the Best; Best of the Best 2; Silent Assassins
Rhoades, Barbara: Shakiest Gun in the West, The
Rhodes, Cynthia: Curse of the Crystal Eye; Dirty Dancing; Runaway; Staying Alive
Rhodes, Donnelly: After the Promise; Dirty Work; Kurt Vonnegut's Monkey House; Showdown at Williams Creek
Rhodes, Earl: Sailor Who Fell from Grace with the Sea,The
Rhodes, Erik: Charlie Chan in Paris; Gay Divorcée, The; One Rainy Afternoon
Rhodes, Frank: Sandman (1992)
Rhodes, Hari: Detroit 9000 (Detroit Heat); Dream for Christmas, A; Woman Called Moses, A
Rhodes, Marjorie: Decameron Nights
Rhodin, Olof: Evil Ed
Rhue, Geoffrey: Squeeze
Rhue, Madlyn: Majority of One, A
Rhymes, Busta: Finding Forrester; Shaft
Rhys, Paul: Becoming Colette; Chaplin; Gallowglass; Nina Takes a Lover; Vincent and Theo
Rhys, Phillip: Fear, The: Halloween Night
Rhys-Davies, John: Best Revenge; Blood of the Innocent; Bloodsport III; Body Armor; Canvas; Cyborg Cop; Dark Prince: The Intimate Tales of Marquis de Sade; Double-O Kid, The; Firewalker; Great Expectations; In the Shadow of Kilimanjaro; Indiana Jones and the Last Crusade; Journey of Honor; King Solomon's Mines; Living Daylights, The; Lord of the Rings, The: Fellowship of the Ring; Lost World, The; Nativity, The; Raiders of the Lost Ark; Rebel Storm; Return to the Lost World; Ring of the Musketeer; Robot in the Family; Sadat; Sahara; Seventh Coin, The; Sunset Grill; Tusks; Unnamable II, The
Rhys-Davies (voices), John: Aladdin & the King of Thieves
Rhys-Meyers, Jonathan: Loss of Sexual Innocence, The; Velvet Goldmine
Rialson, Candice: Hollywood Boulevard; Summer School Teachers
Ribeiro, Alfonso: Infested (Ticks)
Ribisi, Giovanni: Boiler Room; Gift, The; Gone in 60 Seconds; Mod Squad, The; Saving Private Ryan; Shot in the Heart; SubUrbia
Ribisi, Marissa: 100 Girls
Ribon, Diego: Evil Clutch
Ribovska, Malka: Shameless Old Lady, The
Ricci, Christina: Addams Family, The; Addams Family Values; All Over the Guy; Bastard Out of Carolina; Bless the Child; Buffalo '66; Casper; Cemetery Club, The; Gold Diggers: The Secret of Bear Mountain; Ice Storm, The; Man Who Cried, The; Mermaids; Now and Then; Opposite of Sex, The; Pecker; Sleepy Hollow; Summer Fling; That Darn Cat; 200 Cigarettes
Ricci, Rona De: Pit and the Pendulum, The
Ricciarelli, Katia: Otello
Rice, Bill: Otello
Rice, Diana: Barney's Great Adventure
Rice, Florence: Double Wedding; Navy Blue and Gold; Riding on Air
Rice, Frank: Fiddlin' Buckaroo; Fighting Ranger, The; Ivory-Handled Gun, The; Somewhere in Sonora
Rice, Jeffrey D.: Warlords of Hell
Rice, Joan: His Majesty O'Keefe; Story of Robin Hood, The
Rice, Joel S.: Final Exam
Rice-Davies, Mandy: Absolute Beginners; Seven Magnificent Gladiators, The
Rice-Oxley, Mark: In His Life: The John Lennon Story
Rich, Adam: Devil and Max Devlin, The
Rich, Allan: Miami Hustle
Rich, Buddy: Ship Ahoy
Rich, Christopher: Prisoners of Inertia
Rich, Claude: Bride Wore Black, The; Elusive Corporal, The; Revenge of the Musketeers
Rich, Irene: Angel and the Badman; Beau Brummell; Champ, The; Lady in Question; Lady Windermere's Fan; Mortal Storm, The
Rich, Matty: Straight out of Brooklyn
Rich, Ron: Fortune Cookie, The
Rich, Victor: Sensuous Wife, The
Richard, Eric: Home Sweet Home (1982)
Richard, Fir-mine: Mama, There's a Man in Your Bed
Richard, Jean: Candide
Richard, Nathalie: Irma Vep; Up/Down/Fragile
Richard, Pierre: Chef in Love, A; Daydreamer, The (1970) (Le Distrait); Le Chêvre (The Goat); Les Comperes; Return of the Tall Blond Man with One Black Shoe, The; Tall Blond Man with One Black Shoe, The; Too Shy to Try
Ri'chard, Robert: In His Father's Shoes; Light It Up; Our Friend, Martin
Richards, A. J.: Sandman, The (1996)
Richards, Addison: Bad Lands (1939); Our Daily Bread; Rustlers, The
Richards, Ann: Badman's Territory; Sorry, Wrong Number
Richards, Ariana: Angus; Grand Tour: Disaster in Time; Jurassic Park; Switched at Birth
Richards, Beah: As Summers Die; Beloved; Dream for Christmas, A; Guess Who's Coming to Dinner; Purlie Victorious
Richards, David: Legend of the Spirit Dog
Richards, Denise: Drop Dead Gorgeous; Kill Shot; Starship Troopers; Tail Lights Fade; Tammy & the T-Rex; Valentine; Wild Things; World Is Not Enough, The
Richards, Evan: Down and Out in Beverly Hills; Dream Machine; Mute Witness; Society
Richards, Gordon: White Pongo (Blond Gorilla)
Richards, Grant: Four Skulls of Jonathan Drake, The
Richards, Hoyt: Hit and Runway
Richards, Jeff: Above and Beyond; Goldy, The Last of the Golden Bears; It's a Dog's Life; Opposite Sex, The (1956)
Richards, Keith: Chuck Berry Hail! Hail! Rock 'n' Roll; King of the Carnival

Richards, Kim: Escape to Witch Mountain; Meatballs Part II; Return from Witch Mountain; Tuff Turf
Richards, Lauren Ian: Witchcraft XI: Sisters in Blood
Richards, Lisa: Eating; Prince of Central Park, The; Rolling Thunder
Richards, Michael: Coneheads; David Copperfield; Problem Child; Ratings Game, The; So I Married an Axe Murderer; Transylvania 6-5000; Trial and Error (1997); UHF; Unstrung Heroes; Young Doctors in Love
Richards, Michele Lamar: Top Dog
Richards, Paul: Kiss Daddy Good Night; Unknown Terror, The
Richards, Simon: Home for Christmas
Richardson, Ian: B.A.P.S; Brazil; Cry Freedom; Foreign Affairs; Hound of the Baskervilles, The; Incognito; King and I, The; M. Butterfly; Marat/Sade; Midsummer Night's Dream, A; Monsignor Quixote; Plot to Kill Hitler, The; Sign of Four, The; Year of the Comet
Richardson, Jay: Fugitive Rage; Original Intent; Teenage Exorcist; Wizards of the Demon Sword
Richardson, Joely: Drowning by Numbers; Event Horizon; Hollow Reed; I'll Do Anything; In the Shadows; Loch Ness; 101 Dalmatians (1996); Patriot, The; Return to Me; Shining Through; Sister, My Sister; Wetherby
Richardson, John: Black Sunday; Torso; Vengeance of She, The
Richardson, Latanya: Nightman, The
Richardson, Lee: Amazing Grace and Chuck; Believers, The; Fly II, The; I Am the Cheese; Stranger Among Us, A; Sweet Lorraine; Tiger Warsaw
Richardson, Marie: Eyes Wide Shut
Richardson, Miranda: After Pilkington; Alice in Wonderland; Apostle, The; Bachelor, The; Big Brass Ring, The; Century; Crying Game, The; Damage; Dance with a Stranger; Designated Mourner, The; Empire of the Sun; Enchanted April; Evening Star, The; Fatherland; Get Carter; Kansas City; King and I, The; Merlin (1998); Night and the Moment, The; Saint-Ex; Sleepy Hollow; Tom & Viv; Transmutations; Twisted Obsession
Richardson, Natasha: Blow Dry; Comfort of Strangers, The; Fat Man and Little Boy; Favor, the Watch and the Very Big Fish,The; Gothic; Handmaid's Tale, The; Hostages; Month in the Country, A; Nell; Parent Trap, The; Past Midnight; Patty Hearst; Widow's Peak; Zelda
Richardson, Patricia: Dead Simple; Ulee's Gold
Richardson, Paul: On the Line
Richardson, Peter: Pope Must Diet, The; Supergrass, The
Richardson, Ralph: Alice's Adventures in Wonderland; Anna Karenina; Battle of Britain; Citadel, The; Clouds over Europe; Divorce of Lady X, The; Doll's House, A; Dragonslayer; Exodus; Fallen Idol, The; Four Feathers, The; Ghoul, The; Greystoke: The Legend of Tarzan, Lord of the Apes; Heiress, The; Invitation to the Wedding; Khartoum; Lady Caroline Lamb; Long Day's Journey into Night; Looking Glass War, The; Man in the Iron Mask, The; Man Who Could Work Miracles, The; O Lucky Man!; Richard III; Rollerball; Tales from the Crypt; Things to Come; Thunder in the City; Time Bandits; Wagner; Who Slew Auntie Roo?; Witness for the Prosecution; Wrong Box, The
Richardson, Russell: Ragdoll
Richardson, Salli: How U Like Me Now; Low Down Dirty Shame, A; Posse; Sioux City; Soul of the Game
Richardson, Sy: Cinderella; Nocturna; Repo Man; Straight to Hell; Street Asylum; Walker
Richert, Carole: Tous les Matins du Monde
Richert, William: My Own Private Idaho
Richings, Julian: Cube
Richman, Peter Mark: Black Orchid, The; Dempsey; Friday the 13th, Part VIII: Jason Takes Manhattan; Yuma
Richmond, Adrianne: Deadly Spygames
Richmond, Branscombe: Jericho Fever; Renegade; To the Limit
Richmond, Dean: Trippin'
Richmond, Kane: Adventures of Rex and Rinty; Lost City, The; Murder over New York; Spy Smasher
Richmond, Warner: New Frontier; Tol'able David
Richter, Andy: Cabin Boy; Dr. T and the Women
Richter, Deborah: Cyborg
Richter, Jason James: Cops and Robbersons; Free Willy; Free Willy 2: The Adventure Home; Free Willy 3: The Rescue; Laserhawk; Neverending Story III, The: Escape toFantasia
Richter, Paul: Kriemhilde's Revenge; Siegfried
Richwine, Maria: Sex Crimes
Richwood, Patrick: Dark Side of Genius
Rickles, Don: Beach Blanket Bingo; Bikini Beach; Enter Laughing; For the Love of It; Innocent Blood; Keaton's Cop; Kelly's Heroes; Muscle Beach Party; Run Silent, Run Deep; X (The Man with the X-Ray Eyes)
Rickman, Alan: Awfully Big Adventure, An; Blow Dry; Bob Roberts; Close My Eyes; Closet Land; Dark Harbor; Die Hard; Dogma; Fallen Angels; Galaxy Quest; Harry Potter and the Sorcerer's Stone; January Man, The; Judas Kiss; Michael Collins; Quigley Down Under; Rasputin; Robin Hood: Prince of Thieves; Sense and Sensibility; Truly, Madly, Deeply
Ricossa, Maria: Bojangles; Dead Man Out
Rideau, Stéphane: Come Undone; Wild Reeds
Riders of the Purple Sage: Far Frontier
Ridgely, John: Air Force; Man I Love, The
Ridgely, Robert: Philadelphia; Who Am I This Time?
Ridges, Stanley: Black Friday; Interns Can't Take Money; Lady Is Willing, The; Mad Miss Manton, The; Master Race, The; Mr. Ace; Possessed; Scoundrel, The; Sea Wolf, The; Silver on the Sage; Story of Dr. Wassell, The; Tarzan Triumphs; Winterset
Riebauer, Harry: Mad Executioners, The
Rieck, Billy: Warden of Red Rock
Riefenstahl, Leni: Blue Light, The; Tiefland
Riegert, Peter: Americathon; Animal House; Baby Dance, The; Barbarians at the Gate; Bojangles; Chilly Scenes of Winter; Cold-Blooded; Crossing Delancey; Ellis Island; Face Down; Gypsy; Hi Life; Infiltrator, The; Infinity; Jerry and Tom; Local Hero; Man in Love, A; Mask, The; News at Eleven; North Shore Fish; Oscar (1991); Passed Away; Passion of Mind; Pie in the Sky; Runestone; Scandalous Me: The Jacqueline Susann Story; Shock to the System, A; Stranger, The; Utz
Riehle, Richard: Dangerous Woman, A; Free Willy; Lightning Jack; Too Fast Too Young
Riemann, Katja: Bandits; Maybe, Maybe Not
Riffon, Marc: White Wolves: A Cry in the Wild II
Rifkin, Adam: Welcome to Hollywood
Rifkin, Ron: Boiler Room; Dragonfly; Keeping the Faith; Manhattan Murder Mystery; Negotiator, The; Norma Jean and Marilyn; Silent Running; Substance of Fire, The; Sunshine Boys, The; Warden, The; Wolf
Riga, Michelle: Birthday Boy, The
Rigaud, George: Quatorze Juliet
Rigby, Cathy: Challenge of a Lifetime; Great Wallendas, The
Rigby, Edward: Stars Look Down, The; Young and Innocent
Rigby, Terrence: Homecoming, The (1973); Sign of Four, The
Rigg, Diana: Avengers, The (TV Series); Bleak House; Evil Under the Sun; Genghis Cohn; Good Man in Africa, A; Great Muppet Caper, The; Hospital, The; Julius Caesar; King Lear; Little Night Music, A; Midsummer Night's Dream, A; Moll Flanders; On Her Majesty's Secret Service; Running Delilah; Samson and Delilah; Theatre of Blood; Victoria and Albert; Witness for the Prosecution; Worst Witch, The
Rigg, Rebecca: Efficiency Expert, The (Spotswood); Fortress; Hunting; Tunnel Vision (1994)
Rigzin, Tseshang: Horse Thief, The
Rijn, Brad: Perfect Strangers
Riker, Robin: Alligator; Stepmonster
Riley, Bridget "Baby Doll": Triple Impact
Riley, Elaine: Hills of Utah, The; Rider from Tucson
Riley, Jack: Attack of the Killer Tomatoes; Night Patrol
Riley, Jeannine: Electra Glide in Blue
Riley, Larry: Dead Solid Perfect
Riley, Lisa Jane: Butterfly Kiss
Riley, Michael: ... And God Spoke; Heck's Way Home; Perfectly Normal; To Catch a Killer
Rilla, Walter: Adventures of Tartu; Days of Wrath; Gamma People, The
Rin Tin Tin: Lone Defender, The
Rin Tin Tin Jr.: Adventures of Rex and Rinty; Skull and Crown

Rinaldi, Gerard: For Better and for Worse
Ringwald, Molly: Baja; Betsy's Wedding; Breakfast Club, The; Brutal Truth, The; Face the Music; For Keeps; Fresh Horses; Malicious; Office Killer; Packin' It In; Pick-Up Artist, The; P.K. & the Kid; Pretty in Pink; Sixteen Candles; Spacehunter: Adventures in the Forbidden Zone; Stand, The; Strike It Rich; Tempest; Women & Men: Stories of Seduction
Rinn, Brad: Smithereens
Rintoul, David: Pride and Prejudice
Rio, Nicole: Visitants, The
Riordan, Marjorie: Pursuit to Algiers
Rios, Orlando: Calle 54
Ripley, Fay: Mute Witness
Ripper, Michael: Curse of the Mummy's Tomb, The; Quatermass and the Pit
Ripploh, Frank: Taxi Zum Klo (Taxi to the Toilet)
Rippy, Leon: Eye of the Storm; Stargate
Risdon, Elisabeth: Crime and Punishment; Roll on Texas Moon
Riselle, Miriam: Tevye
Rispoli, Michael: Summer of Sam; Volcano; While You Were Sleeping
Ristanovski, Nikola: Cabaret Balkan
Ristovski, Lazar: Cabaret Balkan; Tito and Me
Ritchard, Cyril: Blackmail; Half a Sixpence; Hans Brinker; Peter Pan
Ritchie, Clint: Against a Crooked Sky
Ritchie, June: Kind of Loving, A
Ritchie, Lionel: Preacher's Wife, The
Ritt, Martin: Slugger's Wife, The
Ritter, Brent: Curse of the Blue Lights
Ritter, Jason: Mumford
Ritter, John: Americathon; Colony, The (1995); Comeback Kid, The; Dead Husbands; Hero at Large; In Love with an Older Woman; It; It Came from the Sky; Last Fling, The; Mercenary; Montana; My Brother's Wife; Noises Off; Nowhere; Other, The; Panic; Pray TV; Prison for Children; Problem Child; Problem Child 2; Real Men; Sink or Swim; Skin Deep; Sling Blade; Smoky Mountain Christmas; Stay Tuned; Sunset Limousine; Terror Tract; They All Laughed; Tricks of the Trade; Unnatural Causes; Wholly Moses!
Ritter, Kristin: Student Bodies
Ritter, Tex: Arizona Days; Deep in the Heart of Texas; Enemy of the Law; Lone Star Trail; Mystery of the Hooded Horsemen; Riders of the Rockies; Sing, Cowboy, Sing; Take Me Back to Oklahoma; Trouble in Texas
Ritter, Thelma: As Young as You Feel; Bird Man of Alcatraz; Boeing, Boeing; Daddy Long Legs; Farmer Takes a Wife, The; Hole in the Head, A; Incident, The; Misfits, The; New Kind of Love, A; Pickup on South Street; Pillow Talk; Rear Window; Titanic
Ritz, Harry: Silent Movie
RitzBrothers, The: Goldwyn Follies, The; Gorilla, The; On the Avenue; One in a Million; Three Musketeers, The
Riva, Emmanuelle: Hiroshima, Mon Amour
Rivas, Carlos: They Saved Hitler's Brain
Rivas, Geoffrey: Above Suspicion
Rivas, Monica: Bread and Roses
Rivera, Chita: Mayflower Madam; Sweet Charity
Rivera, Kirk: Body Moves
Rivera, Rene: Rangers
Rivero, Enrique: Blood of a Poet
Rivero, Jorge: Counterforce; Day of the Assassin; Fist Fighter; Priest of Love; Rio Lobo; Target Eagle; Werewolf
Rivers, Joan: Muppets Take Manhattan, The; Swimmer, The
Rivers, Victor: Chain, The; Fled
Riviere, George: Castle of Blood (Castle of Terror); Virgin of Nuremberg (Horror Castle)
Riviere, Julien: Ma Vie En Rose; Thieves (Les Voleurs)
Riviere, Marie: Autumn Tale; Aviator's Wife, The; Summer
Riza, Bella: Hideous Kinky
Rizzo, Gianni: Mission Stardust
Rjin, Brad: Special Effects
Roach, Bert: Last Warning, The
Roach, Rickey: Black Devil Doll from Hell
Roache, Linus: Hart's War; Priest; Shot Through the Heart; Wings of the Dove, The
Roanne, André: Diary of a Lost Girl
Roarke, Adam: Dirty Mary, Crazy Larry; Four Deuces, The; Hell's Angels on Wheels; Losers, The; Psych-Out; Sioux City; Stunt Man, The; Trespasses; Women of the Prehistoric Planet
Roarke, John: Mutant on the Bounty
Robards, Sam: AI: Artificial Intelligence; Donor Unknown; Fandango; Life as a House; Man Who Captured Eichmann, The; Not Quite Paradise; Pancho Barnes; Warden, The
Robards Jr., Jason: Adventures of Huck Finn, The (1993); All the President's Men; Any Wednesday; Ballad of Cable Hogue, The; Big Hand for the Little Lady, A; Black Rainbow; Boy and His Dog, A; Breaking Home Ties; Bright Lights, Big City; Burden of Dreams; By Love Possessed; Cabo Blanco; Chernobyl: The Final Warning; Christmas to Remember, A; Christmas Wife, The; Comes a Horseman; Day After, The; Divorce American Style; Dream a Little Dream; Enemy Within, The; Fools; Good Mother, The; Hour of the Gun, The; Hurricane (1979); Inconvenient Woman, An; Isadora; Johnny Got His Gun; Journey; Julia; Julius Caesar; Laguna Heat; Legend of the Lone Ranger, The; Long Day's Journey into Night; Long Hot Summer, The; Magnolia; Max Dugan Returns; Melvin and Howard; Mr. Sycamore; Murders in the Rue Morgue; My Antonia; Night They Raided Minsky's, The; Once Upon a Time in the West; Paper, The; Parenthood; Pat Garrett and Billy the Kid; Philadelphia; Quick Change; Raise the Titanic; Reunion; Sakharov; Something Wicked This Way Comes; Square Dance; St. Valentine's Day Massacre, The; Storyville; Thousand Acres, A; Thousand Clowns, A; Tora! Tora! Tora!; Trial, The; You Can't Take It with You
Robards Sr., Jason: Abraham Lincoln; Bedlam; Broadway Bill; Fighting Marines, The; Isle of the Dead; Mademoiselle Fifi; Rimfire
Robay, Terrance: Let It Rock
Robb, David: Dreams Lost, Dreams Found
Robb, R. D.: Eight Days a Week
Robbins, Brian: C.H.U.D. II (Bud the C.H.U.D.)
Robbins, Marty: Ballad of a Gunfighter
Robbins, Skeeter Bill: Hard Hombre
Robbins, Tim: Antitrust; Arlington Road; Bob Roberts; Bull Durham; Cadillac Man; Erik the Viking; Five Corners; High Fidelity; Howard the Duck; Hudsucker Proxy, The; Human Nature; I.Q.; Jacob's Ladder; Jungle Fever; Miss Firecracker; Mission to Mars; Nothing to Lose; Player, The; Ready to Wear; Shawshank Redemption, The; Short Cuts; Tapeheads
Robe, Whitney Yellow: Patriot, The
Rober, Richard: Port of New York
Roberson, David: O. J. Simpson Story, The
Roberson, Ken: Yellow Hair and the Fortress of Gold
Robert Mitchell Boys Choir: Blondie in Society
Roberts, Aled: Snoopers
Roberts, Allene: Knock on Any Door; Red House, The; Union Station
Roberts, Arthur: Deadly Vengeance; Femme Fontaine: Killer Babe for the CIA; Not of This Earth; Revenge of the Ninja
Roberts, Christian: Desperados, The; To Sir with Love
Roberts, Conrad: Mosquito Coast, The
Roberts, Darryl: How U Like Me Now
Roberts, David: Me Myself I
Roberts, Doris: All Over the Guy; Love in the Present Tense; My Giant; Number One with a Bullet; Once in Paris; Ordinary Heroes; Simple Justice
Roberts, Eliza: Dead End; Love Is a Gun
Roberts, Eric: Agent of Death; Ambulance, The; American Strays; Babyfever; Best of the Best; Best of the Best 2; Bittersweet (1999); Blood Red; By the Sword; Coca Cola Kid, The; Dead End; Descending Angel; Facade; Family Matter, A; Final Analysis; Freefall; Glass Cage, The; Grave, The; Hard Truth; Heaven's Prisoners; Immortals, The; It's My Party; King of the Gypsies; La Cucaracha; Lansky; Lonely Hearts; Lost Capone, The; Love, Cheat & Steal; Love Is a Gun; Luck of the Draw; Nature of the Beast; No Alibi; Nobody's Fool; Odyssey, The; Past Perfect; Paul's Case; Pope of Greenwich Village, The; Prophecy II, The; Public Enemy #1; Purgatory; Race Against Time;

Raggedy Man; Restraining Order; Rude Awakening; Runaway Train; Saved by the Light; Sensation; Slow Burn; Specialist, The; Star 80; To Heal a Nation; Voyage
Roberts, Glenn: Crater Lake Monster, The
Roberts, Ian: Power of One, The; Terminal Impact
Roberts, Jeremy: Running Time
Roberts, Jessica: Angel Fist
Roberts, Joe: Buster Keaton Festival Vol. 1–3
Roberts, Jordan: Butch Camp
Roberts, Julia: America's Sweethearts; Conspiracy Theory; Dying Young; Erin Brockovich; Everyone Says I Love You; Flatliners; Hook; I Love Trouble; Mary Reilly; Mexican, The; Michael Collins; My Best Friend's Wedding; Mystic Pizza; Notting Hill; Ocean's Eleven (2001); Pelican Brief, The; Pretty Woman; Ready to Wear; Runaway Bride; Satisfaction; Sleeping with the Enemy; Something to Talk About; Steel Magnolias; Stepmom
Roberts, Leonard: Love Jones
Roberts, Lynne: Billy the Kid Returns; Dick Tracy Returns; Dynamite Pass; Eyes of Texas; Frontier Pony Express; Heart of the Rockies; Hi-Yo Silver; Hunt the Man Down; In Old Caliente; Lone Ranger, The; Robin Hood of Texas; Rough Riders' Roundup
Roberts, Mariwin: Sun Bunnies
Roberts, Mark: Night of the Devils; Posse
Roberts, Michael D.: Night of the Devils; Posse
Roberts, Nia: Solomon and Gaenor
Roberts, Pernell: Bonanza (TV Series); Checkered Flag; Desire under the Elms; Four Rode Out; High Noon, Part Two; Magic of Lassie, The; Night Train to Katmandu; Ride Lonesome
Roberts, Rachel: Belstone Fox, The; Hostage Tower, The; O Lucky Man!; Picnic at Hanging Rock; This Sporting Life; When a Stranger Calls
Roberts, Rick: Love and Human Remains
Roberts, Roy: Enforcer, The; Force of Evil; He Walked by Night; King and Four Queens, The; Second Chance
Roberts, Shawn: Sea People
Roberts, Tanya: Almost Pregnant; Beastmaster, The; Body Slam; California Dreaming; Hearts and Armour; Inner Sanctum; Sheena; View to a Kill, A
Roberts, Teal: Fatal Games
Roberts, Ted Jan: Dangerous Place, A; Magic Kid; Magic Kid 2; Power Within, The; Tiger Heart
Roberts, Theodore: Miss Lulu Bett; Ten Commandments, The
Roberts, Tony: American Clock, The; Amityville III: The Demon; Annie Hall; 18 Again; Just Tell Me What You Want; Key Exchange; Midsummer Night's Sex Comedy, A; Million Dollar Duck, The; Our Sons; Packin' It In; Play It Again, Sam; Popcorn; Question of Honor, A; Seize the Day; Serpico; Switch; Taking of Pelham One Two Three, The
Roberts Jr., Jay: White Phantom
Robertson, Andrew: Cement Garden, The
Robertson, Barbara: Straight Story, The
Robertson, Cliff: All in a Night's Work; Autumn Leaves; Best Man, The; Charly; Days of Wine and Roses, The (1958); Dead Reckoning; Devil's Brigade, The; Dominique Is Dead; Ford: The Man & the Machine; Gidget; Girl Most Likely, The; Great Northfield Minnesota Raid, The; Honey Pot, The; Interns, The; John Carpenter's Escape from L.A.; Key to Rebecca, The; Love Has Many Faces; Mach 2; Malone; Midway; Naked and the Dead, The; Obsession; Out of Season; Outer Limits, The (TV Series); Picnic; Pilot, The; PT 109; Race; Renaissance Man; Shaker Run; Shoot; 633 Squadron; Spider-Man; Star 80; Three Days of the Condor; Too Late the Hero; Two of a Kind; Underworld U.S.A.; Wild Hearts Can't Be Broken; Wind (1992)
Robertson, Dale: Cariboo Trail; Dakota Incident; Devil's Canyon; Farmer Takes a Wife, The; Kansas City Massacre, The; Last Ride of the Dalton Gang, The; Melvin Purvis: G-Man
Robertson, Françoise: Minion, The
Robertson, Iain: Small Faces
Robertson, Jenny: Danger of Love; Jacob I Have Loved; Nightman, The
Robertson, Kathleen: Dog Park; Scary Movie 2; Splendor; Survive the Night
Robertson, Patricia: Attack of the Swamp Creature
Robertson, Robbie: Carny
Robeson, Paul: Big Fella; Body and Soul; Emperor Jones, The; Jericho; King Solomon's Mines; Sanders of the River; Show Boat; Song of Freedom; Tales of Manhattan
Robie, Wendy: People Under the Stairs, The
Robin, Dany: Tales of Paris; Topaz; Waltz of the Toreadors
Robin, Michel: Investigation; Le Chêvre (The Goat)
Robin, Teddie: Twin Dragons
Robins, Barry: Bless the Beasts and Children
Robins, Laila: Female Perversions; Innocent Man, An; Live Nude Girls; Planes, Trains and Automobiles; Welcome Home, Roxy Carmichael
Robins, Oliver: Poltergeist II: The Other Side
Robinson, Alexia: Candyman 3: Day of the Dead
Robinson, Amy: Mean Streets
Robinson, Andrew: Charley Varrick; Cobra (1986); Dirty Harry; Fatal Charm; Hellraiser; Into the Badlands; Not My Kid; Prime Target; Pumpkinhead II: Bloodwings; Shoot to Kill; Someone I Touched; Trancers III: Deth Lives; Verne Miller
Robinson, Ann: Dragnet; Midnight Movie Massacre; War of the Worlds, The
Robinson, Bill: Just Around the Corner; Little Colonel, The; Littlest Rebel, The; Rebecca of Sunnybrook Farm; Stormy Weather
Robinson, Bruce: Story of Adele H, The
Robinson, Charles Knox: Daring Dobermans, The; Psycho Sisters
Robinson, Chris: Amy; Savannah Smiles; Stanley; Viper
Robinson, Claudia: Wide Sargasso Sea
Robinson, David: Buford's Beach Bunnies
Robinson, Edward G.: Actors and Sin; All My Sons; Amazing Dr. Clitterhouse, The; Barbary Coast, The; Brother Orchid; Bullets or Ballots; Cheyenne Autumn; Cincinnati Kid, The; Double Indemnity; Good Neighbor Sam; Hell on Frisco Bay; Hole in the Head, A; House of Strangers; I Am the Law; Key Largo; Kid Galahad; Little Caesar; Mr. Winkle Goes to War; My Geisha; Never a Dull Moment; Our Vines Have Tender Grapes; Prize, The; Red House, The; Robin & the Seven Hoods; Scarlet Street; Sea Wolf, The; Seven Thieves; Song of Norway; Soylent Green; Stranger, The; Tales of Manhattan; Ten Commandments, The; Thunder in the City; Two Weeks in Another Town; Violent Men, The; Woman in the Window
Robinson, Frances: Red Barry
Robinson, Holly: Jacksons, The: An American Dream; Killers in the House
Robinson, Jackie: Jackie Robinson Story, The
Robinson, Jackson: Bikini Island
Robinson, Jay: Born Again; Demetrius and the Gladiators; Dying to Remember; King Richard II; Macbeth; Malibu Bikini Shop, The; My Man Godfrey; Othello; Robe, The; Three the Hard Way; Transylvania Twist
Robinson, Karen: Stalked
Robinson, Larry: Sgt. Kabukiman N.Y.P.D.
Robinson, Leon: Band of the Hand; Streetwalkin'
Robinson, Lucy: Emma
Robinson, Madeleine: Le Gentleman D'Espom (Duke of the Derby)
Robinson, Michael: Beware! Children at Play
Robinson, Paul Michael: Active Stealth; Capitol Conspiracy, The; Maximum Security
Robinson, Roger: Newman's Law
Robinson, Tony: Neverending Story III, The: Escape toFantasia
Robinson, Wendy Raquel: Ringmaster; Two Can Play That Game
Robison, Ian: Replicant
Robles, Frank: Crossover Dreams
Robles, German: Vampire, The
Robson, Flora: Beast in the Cellar, The; Black Narcissus; Caesar and Cleopatra; Catherine the Great; Dominique Is Dead; Fire over England; Great Day; Les Misérables; Murder at the Gallop; Restless; Romeo and Juliet; Sea Hawk, The; Tale of Two Cities, A; Wuthering Heights
Robson, Greer: Smash Palace

Robson, May: Adventures of Tom Sawyer, The; Anna Karenina; Bringing Up Baby; Dancing Lady; It Happened in New Orleans; Joan of Paris; Lady by Choice; Lady for a Day; Little Orphan Annie; Nurse Edith Cavell; Reckless; Red-Headed Woman; Star Is Born, A; Strange Interlude; Wife vs. Secretary
Robson, Wayne: And Then You Die; Cube; Harlan County War
Roc, Patricia: Black Jack; Circle of Danger; Wicked Lady, The
Rocard, Pascale: Rascals, The
Rocca, Daniela: Divorce—Italian Style; Empty Canvas, The
Rocca, Stefania: Love's Labour's Lost
Rocco, Alex: Badge of the Assassin; Blue Knight, The; Boris and Natasha; Detroit 9000 (Detroit Heat); Dudley Do-Right; Friends of Eddie Coyle, The; Gotcha!; Grass Is Always Greener over the Septic Tank, The; Hustling; Just Write; Lady in White; Nobody's Perfekt; P.K. & the Kid; Pope Must Diet, The; Rafferty and the Gold Dust Twins; Spy Within, The; Stanley; Stunt Man, The; That Thing You Do!; Wired
Rochambeau, Angelique de: Original Sins
Roche, Eugene: Case for Murder, A; Newman's Law; Oh, God, You Devil!; Possessed, The (1977); Rape and Marriage: The Rideout Case; Slaughterhouse Five; W; Woman Chaser, The
Roche, Sebastian: Hunley, The
Rochefort, Jean: Birgit Haas Must Be Killed; Clockmaker, The (1973); French Postcards; Hairdresser's Husband, The; I Sent a Letter to My Love; Le Cavaleur; Le Complot (The Conspiracy); My Mother's Castle; Pardon Mon Affaire; Pardon Mon Affaire, Too!; Ready to Wear; Return of the Tall Blond Man with One Black Shoe, The; Ridicule; Salut L'Artiste
Rochelle, Amy: Rebecca's Secret
Rochelle, Robin: Sorority Babes in the Slimeball Bowl-O-Rama
Rochette, Genevieve: Northern Passage
Rochon, Debbie: Alien Agenda, The (TV Series); Santa Claws
Rochon, Lela: Big Hit, The; Gang Related; Knock Off; Labor Pains; Legal Deceit; Mr. and Mrs. Loving; Ruby Bridges; Waiting to Exhale; Why Do Fools Fall in Love
Rock, Chris: Beverly Hills Ninja; CB4; Dr. Dolittle (1998); Dogma; Down to Earth; Lethal Weapon 4; New Jack City; Nurse Betty; Pootie Tang
Rock, Crissy: Ladybird, Ladybird
Rocket, Charles: Brain Smasher … A Love Story; Charlie's Ghost; Delirious; Down Twisted; Dumb and Dumber; Earth Girls Are Easy; It's Pat: The Movie; Tom and Huck
Rockmore, Clara: Theremin: An Electronic Odyssey
Rockwell, Jack: Silver on the Sage; Twilight on the Trail
Rockwell, Robert: Our Miss Brooks (TV Series); Red Menace, The
Rockwell, Sam: Box of Moonlight; Charlie's Angels; Galaxy Quest; Green Mile, The; Heist (2001); Jerry and Tom; Lawn Dogs; Mercy; Safe Men
Rodann, Ziva: Three Nuts in Search of a Bolt
Rodd, Marcia: Citizen's Band; Last Embrace, The; Little Murders
Rode, Ebbe: Topsy Turvy (1984)
Roderick, Sue: Hedd Wyn
Rodgers, Anton: Lillie
Rodgers, Maria Antoinette: Journey to Spirit Island
Rodgers, Marshall: Body and Soul
Rodgers, Michael: Thomas and the Magic Railroad
Rodgers, Tristan: Evil Lives
Rodman, Dennis: Cutaway; Double Team
Rodnunsky, Serge: Lovers' Lovers
Rodrick, Michael: Desolation Angels
Rodrigue, Madeline: Crazy Ray, The
Rodrigues, Percy: Brainwaves
Rodriguez, Celia: I Am Cuba
Rodriguez, Estelita: Along the Navajo Trail; Golden Stallion, The; In Old Amarillo
Rodriguez, Frank: Miami Hot Talk
Rodriguez, Freddy: Dead Presidents; Pest, The
Rodriguez, Michelle: Fast and the Furious, The; Girlfight; Resident Evil; 3 A.M.
Rodriguez, Paul: Born in East L.A.; Made in America; Mambo Café; Million to Juan, A; Miracles; Quicksilver; Race; Rough Magic; Tortilla Soup; Whoopee Boys, The
Rodriguez, Valente: Roosters
Rodway, Norman: Reilly: The Ace of Spies; Story of David, The
Roebuck, Daniel: Cave Girl; Disorganized Crime; Dudes; Final Destination; Fugitive, The; Glimpse of Hell, A; Killing Mind, The; Late Shift, The; River's Edge
Roerick, William: Love Machine, The
Roescher, Michael: Gordy
Roese, Amanda: Secrets in the Attic
Roeves, Maurice: Last of the Mohicans, The; Moses
Rogen, Mike: Punch the Clock
Rogers, Bill: Taste of Blood, A
Rogers, Charles "Buddy": Wings
Rogers, Dinah Anne: Legacy for Leonette
Rogers, Dora: Keystone Comedies: Vol. 1–5
Rogers, Ginger: Bachelor Mother; Barkleys of Broadway, The; Carefree; Cinderella; Fifth Avenue Girl; Finishing School; Flying Down to Rio; Follow the Fleet; 42nd Street; Gay Divorcée, The; Gold Diggers of 1933; Having a Wonderful Time; In Person; Kitty Foyle; Lucky Partners; Monkey Business; Once Upon a Honeymoon; Primrose Path; Quick, Let's Get Married; Roberta; Romance in Manhattan; Roxie Hart; Shall We Dance?; Shriek in the Night, A; Stage Door; Star of Midnight; Story of Vernon and Irene Castle, The; Swing Time; Tales of Manhattan; Tender Comrade; Thirteenth Guest, The; Tom, Dick and Harry; Top Hat; Vivacious Lady; Weekend at the Waldorf; We're Not Married
Rogers, Ina: Buford's Beach Bunnies
Rogers, Ingrid: Carlito's Way
Rogers, Ivan: Striking Point
Rogers, Jean: Ace Drummond; Charlie Chan in Panama; Flash Gordon: Rocketship (Spaceship to the Unknown; Perils from Planet Mongo); Tournament Tempo; Whistling in Brooklyn
Rogers, Jimmy: False Colors; Forty Thieves; Mystery Man; Texas Masquerade
Rogers, Kenny: Coward of the County; Gambler, The; Gambler, Part II—The Adventure Continues, The; Gambler, Part III—The Legend Continues, The; Gambler Returns, The: Luck of the Draw; Rio Diablo; Six Pack
Rogers, Michael: Dangerous Prey
Rogers, Mimi: Austin Powers: International Man of Mystery; Blue Skies Again; Bulletproof Heart; Dark Horse; Deadlock; Desperate Hours (1990); Devil's Arithmetic, The; Far From Home: The Adventures of YellowDog; Fourth Story; Full Body Massage; Ginger Snaps; Gung Ho (1985); Hider in the House; Ladykiller; Lost in Space (1998); Mighty Quinn, The; Mirror Has Two Faces, The; Monkey Trouble; Palermo Connection, The; Rapture, The; Reflections in the Dark; Rousters, The; Seven Girlfriends; Shooting Elizabeth; Someone to Watch Over Me; Street Smart; Tricks; Weapons of Mass Distraction; White Sands
Rogers, Paul: Homecoming, The (1973)
Rogers, Reg: Attila
Rogers, Roy: Along the Navajo Trail; Apache Rose; Arizona Kid; Bad Man of Deadwood; Bells of Coronado; Bells of Rosarita; Bells of San Angelo; Billy the Kid Returns; Carson City Kid; Dark Command; Don't Fence Me In; Down Dakota Way; Eyes of Texas; Far Frontier; Frontier Pony Express; Golden Stallion, The; Heart of the Golden West; Helldorado; Hollywood Canteen; In Old Amarillo; In Old Caliente; Jesse James at Bay; King of the Cowboys; Lights of Old Santa Fe; My Pal Trigger; Nighttime in Nevada; Old Corral; Ranger and the Lady, The; Robin Hood of the Pecos; Roll on Texas Moon; Romance on the Range; Rough Riders' Roundup; Roy Rogers Show, The (TV Series); Saga of Death Valley; San Fernando Valley; Silver Spurs; Son of Paleface; Song of Nevada; Song of Texas; Sons of the Pioneers; Springtime in the Sierras; Sunset Serenade; Trail of Robin Hood; Trigger Jr.; Under California Stars; Under Western Stars; Utah; Wall Street Cowboy; Young Bill Hickok
Rogers, Ruth: Hidden Gold; Night Riders, The
Rogers, Wayne: Chiefs; Gig, The; Girl Who Spelled Freedom, The; Goodbye Bird, The; Killing Time, The (1987); Lady from Yesterday, The; M*A*S*H (TV Series); Once in Paris; Pocket Money

Rogers, Will: Ambassador Bill; Connecticut Yankee, A; Doubting Thomas; Golden Age of Comedy, The; Headless Horseman, The; Judge Priest; Mr. Skitch
Rogers Jr., Roy: Arizona Bushwhackers
Rogers Jr., Will: Look for the Silver Lining
Rohde, Armin: Run Lola Run
Rohm, Maria: Call of the Wild
Rohmer, Eric: Francois Truffaut: Stolen Moments
Rohner, Clayton: Caroline at Midnight; I, Madman; Just One of the Guys; Modern Girls; Naked Souls; Nightwish; Private Investigations
Rohren, Amy: Ceremony
Rois, Sophie: Inheritors, The
Rojas, Eduardo Lopez: My Family
Rojas, Victor: It Could Happen to You; Max Is Missing
Rojo, Gustavo: Christmas Kid, The
Rojo, Helena: Aguirre: Wrath of God; Foxtrot; Mary, Mary, Bloody Mary
Rojo, Maria: Break of Dawn; Danzon; Mary My Dearest
Rojo, Ruben: Great Madcap, The
Roland, Eugenie Cisse: Faces of Women
Roland, Gilbert: Bad and the Beautiful, The; Barbarosa; Beneath the 12-Mile Reef; Between God, the Devil and a Winchester; Bullfighter and the Lady, The; Call Her Savage; Captain Kidd; French Line, The; Go Kill and Come Back; Miracle of Our Lady of Fatima, The; Pacific Connection, The; Poppy Is Also a Flower, The; Racers, The; Ruthless Four, The; Sacketts, The; Sea Hawk, The; She Done Him Wrong; Three Violent People; Thunder Bay; Thunder Trail; Treasure of Pancho Villa, The; Underwater!
Roland, Jeanne: Curse of the Mummy's Tomb, The
Roland Petit Dance Company: Black Tights
Rolfe, Guy: Alphabet Murders, The; Dolls; Puppet Master 5: The Final Chapter; Puppet Master Four; Puppet Master III: Toulon's Revenge; Retro Puppetmaster; Snow White and the Three Stooges; Thriller (TV Series)
Rolffes, Kirsten: Kingdom, The
Rolin, Judy: Alice Through the Looking Glass
Rollan, Henri: Crazy Ray, The
Rolle, Esther: Age-Old Friends; Down in the Delta; Driving Miss Daisy; House of Cards; I Know Why the Caged Bird Sings; My Fellow Americans; Nobody's Girls; P.K. & the Kid; Raisin in the Sun, A; Romeo and Juliet; Rosewood; Summer of My German Soldier; To Dance with the White Dog
Rolling Stones, The: Gimme Shelter; Let's Spend the Night Together; Rock and Roll Circus, The; That Was Rock
Rollins, Henry: Chase, The; Johnny Mnemonic; Jugular Wine
Rollins Jr., Howard: Children of Times Square, The; Drunks; For Us the Living: The Medgar Evers Story; King; On the Block; Soldier's Story, A
Rolston, Mark: Comrades of Summer, The; Shawshank Redemption, The
Romain, Yvonne: Circus of Horrors; Curse of the Werewolf, The; Devil Doll (1936)
Romaine, Katherine: Metamorphosis: The Alien Factor
Roman, Cathrine: Bloody New Year
Roman, Ruth: Baby, The; Beyond the Forest; Blowing Wild; Champion; Day of the Animals; Far Country, The; Impulse; Love Has Many Faces; Sacketts, The; Strangers on a Train; Three Secrets; Window, The
Romance, Viviane: Melodie en Sous-Sol (The Big Grab) (Any Number Can Win); Panique
Romand, Beatrice: Autumn Tale; Chloe in the Afternoon; Claire's Knee; Le Beau Mariage; Summer
Romanelli, Carla: Shanghai Joe
Romano, Andy: Chameleon; Heaven or Vegas; Two Bits
Romano, Rino: Club, The
Romans, Pierre: Dr. Petiot
Romanus, Richard: Couch Trip, The; Night Terror; Point of No Return; Protocol; Russian Roulette; Sitting Ducks; To Protect and Serve
Romanus, Robert: Bad Medicine; Dangerous Curves
Romay, Lina: Adventure; Demoniac; Erotikill; Heat's On, The; Ilsa, the Wicked Warden
Rome, Sydne: Diary of Forbidden Dreams; Just a Gigolo; Sex with a Smile; That Lucky Touch
Romer, Fred: Great Adventure, The
Romero, Cesar: Americano, The; Batman; Beautiful Blonde from Bashful Bend, The; Charlie Chan at Treasure Island; Computer Wore Tennis Shoes, The; Crooks and Coronets (Sophie's Place); Dance Hall; Happy Go Lovely; Happy Landing; Hot Millions; Julia Misbehaves; Latitude Zero; Little Princess, The (1939); Lost Continent, The; Lust in the Dust; Madigan's Millions; Mission to Glory; My Lucky Star; Now You See Him, Now You Don't; Ocean's Eleven; Orchestra Wives; Racers, The; Show Them No Mercy; Simple Justice; Springtime in the Rockies; Tales of Manhattan; Two on a Guillotine; Wee Willie Winkie; Weekend in Havana; Wintertime
Romero, Ned: Children of the Corn II: The Final Sacrifice; Deerslayer, The (1978); I Will Fight No More Forever; Last of the Mohicans; Lost Child, The; Magnificent Seven, The (TV Series); Medicine Hat Stallion, The
Romic, Monika: Vukovar
Romijn-Stamos, Rebecca: Rollerball (2002)
Rommel, Dave: Colony (1996)
Romney, Edana: Corridor of Mirrors
Romo, Daniela: One Man's Hero
Rondinella, Clelia: Star Maker, The
Ronet, Maurice: Beau Pere; Circle of Love; Elevator to the Gallows; Fire Within, The; La Balance; Purple Noon; Sphinx (1981); Swimming Pool, The
Ronettes, The: That Was Rock
Rongguang, Yu: Iron Monkey
Ronstadt, Linda: Chuck Berry Hail! Hail! Rock 'n' Roll; Pirates of Penzance, The
Rooker, Michael: Afterburn; Bastard Out of Carolina; Bone Collector, The; Bram Stoker's Shadowbuilder; Brown's Requiem; Cliffhanger; Dark Half, The; Days of Thunder; Deceiver; Hard Truth; Henry: Portrait of a Serial Killer; Here on Earth; JFK; Johnny & Clyde; Keys to Tulsa; Mall Rats; Newsbreak; Replicant; Rosewood; Tombstone
Rooney, Mickey: Adventures of Huckleberry Finn, The; Ah, Wilderness; Andy Hardy Gets Spring Fever; Andy Hardy Meets a Debutante; Andy Hardy's Double Life; Andy Hardy's Private Secretary; Atomic Kid, The; Babe: Pig in the City; Babes in Arms; Babes on Broadway; Big Wheel, The; Bill; Bill: On His Own; Black Stallion, The; Boys' Town; Boys Will Be Boys; Breakfast at Tiffany's; Bridges at Toko-Ri, The; Captains Courageous; Care Bears Movie, The; Chained; Comedian, The; Domino Principle, The; Erik the Viking; Evil Roy Slade; Find the Lady; Francis in the Haunted House; Fugitive, The (TV Series); Gambler Returns, The: Luck of the Draw; Girl Crazy; Home for Christmas; Hoosier Schoolboy; How to Stuff a Wild Bikini; Human Comedy, The; It Came Upon a Midnight Clear; It's a Mad Mad Mad Mad World; King of the Roaring Twenties; Leave 'em Laughing; Life Begins for Andy Hardy; Lightning, the White Stallion; Little Lord Fauntleroy; Love Finds Andy Hardy; Love Laughs at Andy Hardy; Magic of Lassie, The; Manhattan Melodrama; Manipulator, The; Maximum Force; Men of Boys Town; Midsummer Night's Dream, A; My Heroes Have Always Been Cowboys; My Pal, the King; National Velvet; Off Limits; Pete's Dragon; Platinum High School; Pulp; Reckless; Requiem for a Heavyweight (1962); Revenge of the Red Baron; Road Home, The (1995); Silent Night, Deadly Night 5: The Toy Maker; Strike Up the Band; Summer Holiday; Sweet Justice; That's Entertainment! III; Thoroughbreds Don't Cry; Thousands Cheer; Words and Music; Young Tom Edison
Roos, Camilla Overbye: Facade
Roose, Thorkild: Day of Wrath
Root, Amanda: Persuasion
Root, Stephen: Night of the Scarecrow; Office Space
Rooymans, Huib: Flight of Rainbirds, A
Roquevert, Noel: Fanfan the Tulip; Un Singe en Hiver (A Monkey in Winter); Voulez Vous Danser avec Moi? (Will You Dance with Me?)
Rosanoff, Frayne: Python
Rosario, Alex Del: Midnight Dancer

Rosato, Tony: Busted Up; City of Shadows; Diamond Fleece, The; Separate Vacations
Rosay, Françoise: Bizarre, Bizarre; Carnival in Flanders; Full Hearts and Empty Pockets; Naked Heart, The; Quartet; September Affair
Roscoe, Albert: Last of the Mohicans, The
Rose, Gabrielle: Adjuster, The; Speaking Parts; Sweet Hereafter, The
Rose, George: Devil's Disciple, The; Hideaways, The; Jack the Ripper; Night to Remember, A; Pirates of Penzance, The; You Can't Take It with You
Rose, James: Chain, The
Rose, Jamie: Chopper Chicks in Zombietown; In Love with an Older Woman; Rebel Love; To Die Standing
Rose, Lenny: Beach Babes 2: Cave Girl Island
Rose, Robin Pearson: Last Resort
Rose, Roger: Ski Patrol
Rose, Sherrie: Black Scorpion II: Aftershock; Devil in the Flesh; Double Threat; In Gold We Trust; Maximum Force; New Crime City: Los Angeles 2020
Roseanne: Backfield in Motion; Blue in the Face; Even Cowgirls Get the Blues; She-Devil
Rosenbaum, Michael: Sorority Boys
Rosenberg, Sarah: Foxfire
Rosenberg, Saturday: Encounter at Raven's Gate
Rosenberg, Stephen: Jacob Two-Two Meets the Hooded Fang
Rosenbloom, Maxie: Abbott and Costello Meet the Keystone Kops; Each Dawn I Die; I Married a Monster from Outer Space; Louisiana Purchase; Mr. Moto's Gamble; To the Shores of Tripoli
Rosenthal, Sheila: Not Without My Daughter
Ross, Alma: Tuttles of Tahiti, The
Ross, Andrew: Party Camp
Ross, Annie: Basket Case 3: The Progeny; Short Cuts
Ross, Anthony: Country Girl, The
Ross, Betsy King: Phantom Empire (1935); Radio Ranch (Men with Steel Faces, Phantom Empire)
Ross, Beverly: Crazed
Ross, Bud: Crazed
Ross, Charlotte: Foreign Student; Kidnapped in Paradise; Savage Land
Ross, Chelcie: Amos & Andrew; Chain Reaction; Legacy of Lies; Rudy
Ross, Diana: Lady Sings the Blues; Mahogany; Wiz, The
Ross, Frank: Saturday Night Kid, The
Ross, Gene: Encounter with the Unknown; Poor White Trash II
Ross, Joe E.: Car 54 Where Are You? (TV Series); Sgt. Bilko (TV Series); Slumber Party 57
Ross, Katharine: Betsy, The; Butch Cassidy and the Sundance Kid; Climate for Killing, A; Conagher; Donnie Darko; Final Countdown, The; Fools; Get to Know Your Rabbit; Graduate, The; Hellfighters; Legacy, The; Murder in Texas; Red-Headed Stranger, The; Rodeo Girl; Shadow Riders, The; Shenandoah; Singing Nun, The; Stepford Wives, The; Swarm, The; Tell Them Willie Boy Is Here; They Only Kill Their Masters; Wrong Is Right
Ross, Lee: Dreaming of Joseph Lees; Metroland
Ross, Marion: Evening Star, The; Teacher's Pet
Ross, Matt: Ed's Next Move
Ross, Matthew: Just Visiting
Ross, Merrie Lynn: Bobbie Jo and the Outlaw; Class of 1984
Ross, Natanya: Shadow Zone: The Undead Express
Ross, Ricco: Proteus
Ross, Shirley: Big Broadcast of 1938, The; Waikiki Wedding
Ross, Ted: Bingo Long Traveling All-Stars and Motor Kings, The; Fighting Back; Wiz, The
Rossellini, Isabella: Big Night; Blue Velvet; Cousins; Crime of the Century; Death Becomes Her; Don Quixote; Fallen Angels; Fearless; Funeral, The; Immortal Beloved; Impostors, The; Innocent, The; Ivory Hunters; Left Luggage; Lies of the Twins; Matter of Time, A; Merlin (1998); Odyssey, The; Siesta; Tough Guys Don't Dance; White Nights; Wild at Heart; Wyatt Earp; Zelly and Me
Rossetter, Kathryn: Whatever
Rossi, Frank: Criminal Mind, The
Rossi, Leo: Accused, The; Casualties of Love: The Long Island Lolita Story; Fast Getaway; Fast Getaway II; Felony; Heart Like a Wheel; Hit List (1988); Maniac Cop 2; Mutant Species; Rave Review; Relentless; Relentless II: Dead On; Relentless 3; River's Edge; Too Much Sun; We're Talking Serious Money; Where the Day Takes You
Rossi, Vittorio: Snake Eater 2, the Drug Buster
Rossi-Stuart, Giacomo: Curse of the Living Dead (Kill, Baby, Kill); Last Man on Earth, The; Shanghai Joe
Rossiter, Leonard: Britannia Hospital; Luther
Rossman, Charley: Buford's Beach Bunnies
Rossovich, Rick: Black Scorpion; Cover Me; Fatally Yours; Gambler Returns, The: Luck of the Draw; Legend of the Lost Tomb; Lords of Discipline, The; Miracle in Lane 2; Navy Seals; New Crime City: Los Angeles 2020; Paint It Black; Roxanne; Spellbinder; Telling You; Top Gun; Tropical Heat; Warning Sign
Rossum, Emmy: Songcatcher
Rotaeta, Felix: Pepi, Luci, Bom and Other Girls
Roth, Andrea: Club, The; Crossworlds; Divided by Hate; Executive Power; Hidden Agenda (1998); Stepdaughter, The
Roth, Celia: All About My Mother; Labyrinth of Passion
Roth, Gene: Big Sombrero, The; Earth vs. the Spider; Marshal of Cripple Creek; Pirates of the High Seas; She Demons
Roth, Joan: Luther, The Geek
Roth, Johnny: Bride and the Beast, The
Roth, Lillian: Alice, Sweet Alice (Communion, Holy Terror); Animal Crackers; Ladies They Talk About; Madame Satan
Roth, Matt: Blink
Roth, Tim: Bodies, Rest & Motion; Captives; Deceiver; Everyone Says I Love You; Four Rooms; Gridlock'd; Heart of Darkness; Hit, The (1984); Hoodlum; Jumpin' at the Boneyard; Legend of 1900, The; Little Odessa; Lucky Numbers; Meantime; Million Dollar Hotel; Musketeer, The; No Way Home; Planet of the Apes (2001); Pulp Fiction; Reservoir Dogs; Rob Roy; Rosencrantz and Guildenstern Are Dead; Vincent and Theo
Rothammer, Mathias: Snoopers
Rothe, Bendt: Gertrude
Rothman, John: Copycat
Rothrock, Cynthia: Angel of Fury; China O'Brien; China O'Brien 2; Fast Getaway; Fast Getaway II; Guardian Angel; Lady Dragon; Lady Dragon 2; Martial Law; Martial Law Two—Undercover; Millionaire's Express (Shanghai Express); Rage and Honor; Rage and Honor II: Hostile Takeover; Undefeatable
Rothwell, Carolyn: Van, The
Rotten, Johnny: Filth and the Fury, The
Rottlander, Yella: Alice in the City; Scarlet Letter (1973)
Rotundo, Paolo: Ugly, The
Rouan, Brigitte: Overseas; Post Coitum
Rouffe, Alida: Marius
Rounds, David: So Fine
Roundtree, Richard: Amityville: A New Generation; Any Place But Home; Bad Jim; Ballistic; Big Score, The; Bloodfist III: Forced to Fight; Body of Influence; Christmas in Connecticut; City Heat; Corky Romano; Crack House; Day of the Assassin; Deadly Rivals; Diamonds; Escape to Athena; Eye for an Eye; Firehouse; Game for Vultures; Gypsy Angels; Jocks; Last Contract, The; Maniac Cop; Miami Cops; Mindtwister; Night Visitor (1989); Once Upon a Time ... When We Were Colored; One Down, Two to Go; Opposing Force; Original Gangstas; Party Line; Q; Seven; Shaft; Shaft; Shaft's Big Score!; Steel; Theodore Rex; Time to Die, A; Young Warriors, The
Rounseville, Robert: Carousel; Tales of Hoffman
Rourke, Mickey: Angel Heart; Animal Factory; Another 9 1/2 Weeks; Barfly; Body Heat; Bullet; Desperate Hours (1990); Diner; Double Team; Eureka; Exit in Red; Fall Time; Francesco; Get Carter; Harley Davidson and the Marlboro Man; Homeboy; Johnny Handsome; Last Outlaw, The; Last Ride, The; 9 1/2 Weeks; Out in Fifty; Point Blank; Pope of Greenwich Village, The; Prayer for the Dying, A; Rainmaker, The (1997); Rape and Marriage: The Rideout Case; Rumble Fish; Thicker Than Blood; White Sands; Wild Orchid; Year of the Dragon
Rouse, Eddie: George Washington
Rouse, Mitch: Sweethearts
Roussel, Anne: Music Teacher, The

Runyon, Jennifer: Blue de Ville; Carnosaur; 18 Again; Killing Streets; Man Called Sarge, A; Quantum Leap (TV Series); To All a Good Night
Ruocheng, Ying: Last Emperor, The; Little Buddha
RuPaul: But I'm a Cheerleader; Mother's Prayer, A; Wigstock: The Movie
Rupe, Katja: Germany In Autumn
Ruscio, Elizabeth: Cast the First Stone; Death Benefit; Hider in the House
Rush, Barbara: Between Friends; Bramble Bush, The; Can't Stop the Music; Come Blow Your Horn; Hombre; It Came from Outer Space; Moon of the Wolf; Robin & the Seven Hoods; Seekers, The; Strangers When We Meet; Summer Lovers; Superdad; Web of Deceit; When Worlds Collide; Widow's Kiss; Young Lions, The; Young Philadelphians, The
Rush, Deborah: Big Business; In & Out; My Blue Heaven
Rush, Geoffrey: Children of the Revolution; Elizabeth; House on Haunted Hill; Lantana; Les Misérables; Mystery Men; Quills; Shakespeare in Love; Shine; Tailor of Panama, The
Rushbrook, Claire: Secrets and Lies; Spice World; Under the Skin
Rushton, Jared: Big; Cry in the Wild, A; Honey, I Shrunk the Kids; Pet Sematary Two; Yarn Princess, The
Rusic, Rita: Third Solution, The
Ruskin, Joseph: Firepower; Gypsy Warriors, The
Ruskin, Sheila: Caribbean Mystery, A
Rusler, Robert: Assassination Game, The; Final Embrace; Game of Love, The; Sometimes They Come Back; Thrashin'; Vamp
Russ, Tim: Heroes of Desert Storm
Russ, William: Aspen Extreme; Beer; Crazy from the Heart; Crisis at Central High; Dead of Winter; Disorganized Crime; Drive Like Lightning; Pastime; Raw Courage; Traces of Red; Unholy, The; Wanted: Dead or Alive; When Danger Follows You Home
Russel, Reb: Aspen Extreme; Beer; Crazy from the Heart; Crisis at Central High; Dead of Winter; Disorganized Crime; Drive Like Lightning; Pastime; Raw Courage; Traces of Red; Unholy, The; Wanted: Dead or Alive; When Danger Follows You Home
Russell, Andy: Copacabana
Russell, Betsy: Avenging Angel (1985); Delta Heat; Out of Control; Trapper County War
Russell, Bryan: Adventures of Bullwhip Griffin, The; Charlie, the Lonesome Cougar; Emil and the Detectives
Russell, Clive: Margaret's Museum; Oscar & Lucinda
Russell, Craig: Outrageous; Too Outrageous
Russell, Elizabeth: Corpse Vanishes, The; Curse of the Cat People, The
Russell, Gail: Angel and the Badman; Great Dan Patch, The; Moonrise; Uninvited, The; Wake of the Red Witch
Russell, Harold: Best Years of Our Lives, The
Russell, Jane: Double Dynamite; French Line, The; Gentlemen Prefer Blondes; His Kind of Woman; Johnny Reno; Las Vegas Story, The; Macao; Montana Belle; Outlaw, The; Paleface, The; Son of Paleface; Tall Men, The; Underwater!
Russell, John: Buckskin; Forever Amber; Hoodlum Empire; Hostile Guns; Jubilee Trail; Man in the Saddle; Oklahoma Annie; Outlaw Josey Wales, The; Pale Rider; Rio Bravo; Sun Shines Bright, The; Under the Gun
Russell, Karen: Dead Certain
Russell, Ken: Russia House, The
Russell, Keri: Dead Man's Curve; Eight Days a Week; MAD About Mambo; We Were Soldiers
Russell, Kimberly: Ghost Dad; O. J. Simpson Story, The
Russell, Kurt: Backdraft; Best of Times, The; Big Trouble in Little China; Breakdown; Captain Ron; Charley and the Angel; Christmas Coal Mine Miracle, The; Computer Wore Tennis Shoes, The; Elvis—The Movie; Escape from New York; Executive Decision; Follow Me, Boys!; Fugitive, The (TV Series); Guns of Diablo; Horse in the Gray Flannel Suit, The; John Carpenter's Escape from L.A.; Longest Drive, The; Mean Season, The; Now You See Him, Now You Don't; Overboard; Search for the Gods; Silkwood; Soldier; Stargate; Superdad; Swing Shift; Tango and Cash; Tequila Sunrise; Thing, The (1982); 3,000 Miles to Graceland; Tombstone; Unlawful Entry; Used Cars; Vanilla Sky; Winter People
Russell, Leon: Mad Dogs and Englishmen
Russell, Lisa Ann: Apex
Russell, Lucy: Following
Russell, Mary: Riders of the Whistling Skull
Russell, Nipsey: Car 54, Where Are You? (1991); Wildcats; Wiz, The
Russell, Rosalind: Auntie Mame; Citadel, The; Craig's Wife; Evelyn Prentice; Forsaking All Others; Gypsy; His Girl Friday; Majority of One, A; Never Wave at a WAC (Private Wore Skirts, The); Night Must Fall; Oh Dad, Poor Dad—Mama's Hung You in the Closet and I'm Feeling So Sad; Picnic; Reckless; Sister Kenny; Tell It to the Judge; They Met in Bombay; Trouble with Angels, The; Velvet Touch, The; Woman of Distinction, A; Women, The
Russell, Stefene: Plan 10 from Outer Space
Russell, T. E.: Linda
Russell, Theresa: Aria; Black Widow; Cold Heaven; Eureka; Grave Indiscretion; Impulse; Insignificance; Kafka; Last Tycoon, The; Physical Evidence; Proposition, The; Public Enemy #1; Razor's Edge, The; Spy Within, The; Straight Time; Thicker Than Water; Track 29; Trade Off; Whore; Wild Things
Russell, Tony: Soul Hustler
Russell, William: Dr. Who (TV series)
Russinova, Isabel: Tex and the Lord of the Deep
Russo, Gianni: Four Deuces, The
Russo, James: Bad Girls; Bittersweet (1999); Blue Iguana; China Girl; Cold Heaven; Condition Red; Dangerous Game, A (1993); Davinci's War; Deep Core; Detour; Donnie Brasco; Extremities; Freeway; Illicit Behavior; Intimate Stranger; Kiss Before Dying, A; Love to Kill; No Way Home; Postman, The; Real Thing, The; Secretary, The; Set-Up, The; Trauma; Under Oath; We're No Angels
Russo, Michael: Nitti: The Enforcer; Pure Danger; Unmade Beds
Russo, René: Adventures of Rocky and Bullwinkle, The; Big Trouble (2002); Buddy; Freejack; Get Shorty; In the Line of Fire; Lethal Weapon 3; Lethal Weapon 4; One Good Cop; Outbreak; Ransom; Thomas Crown Affair, The; Tin Cup
Russom, Leon: Long Road Home, The; Wing and a Prayer, A
Rust, Richard: Double Revenge
Ruth, Babe: Headin' Home; Pride of the Yankees, The
Rutherford, Ann: Adventures of Don Juan, The; Andy Hardy Gets Spring Fever; Andy Hardy's Double Life; Andy Hardy's Private Secretary; Fighting Marines, The; Lawless Nineties, The; Life Begins for Andy Hardy; Lonely Trail, The; Love Finds Andy Hardy; Melody Trail; Of Human Hearts; Orchestra Wives; Public Cowboy #1; Secret Life of Walter Mitty, The; They Only Kill Their Masters; Whistling in Brooklyn; Whistling in Dixie; Whistling in the Dark
Rutherford, Camilla: Gosford Park
Rutherford, Erik: Lady of the Lake
Rutherford, Kelly: Acceptable Risk; I Love Trouble
Rutherford, Margaret: Alphabet Murders, The; Blithe Spirit; Chimes at Midnight (Falstaff); Countess from Hong Kong, A; Importance of Being Earnest, The; Murder Ahoy; Murder at the Gallop; Murder Most Foul; Murder She Said; Passport to Pimlico; Smallest Show on Earth, The; To See Such Fun; V.I.P.s, The
Rutherford, Teri-Lynn: Raffle, The
Ruttan, Susan: Eye of the Demon; Funny About Love; L.A. Law
Ruymen, Ann: Private Parts
Ruysdael, Basil: Broken Arrow; Carrie
Ryabova, Svetlana: Adam's Rib
Ryan, Amy: In the Deep Woods
Ryan, Anne: Three O'Clock High
Ryan, Bridgit: Palookaville
Ryan, Edmon: Human Monster, The (Dark Eyes of London); Two for the Seesaw
Ryan, Eileen: Anywhere But Here
Ryan, Fran: Rebel Love; Suture
Ryan, Ger: Van, The
Ryan, Hilary: Getting of Wisdom, The

Sakaguchi, Seiji: Forced Vengeance
Sakai, Franky: Mothra
Sakall, S. Z.: Ball of Fire; Christmas in Connecticut; Devil and Miss Jones, The; Dolly Sisters, The; In the Good Old Summertime; It's a Big Country; It's a Date; Look for the Silver Lining; Lullaby of Broadway; My Dream Is Yours; Never Say Goodbye; Romance on the High Seas; San Antonio; Small Town Girl; Spring Parade; Tea for Two; Wintertime; Wonder Man
Sakamoto, Ryuichi: Merry Christmas, Mr. Lawrence
Sakata, Harold: Goldfinger; Impulse; Jaws of Death, The
Sakelaris, Anastasia: Aliens Among Us; Welcome to Planet Earth
Saks, Gene: Goodbye People, The; I.Q.; Nobody's Fool; One and Only, The; Prisoner of Second Avenue, The; Thousand Clowns, A
Salas, Fabian: Tango Lesson, The
Salazar, Abel: Brainiac, The; Curse of the Crying Woman, The; Man and the Monster, The; Vampire, The
Salcedo, Leopoldo: Cry of Battle
Saldana, Theresa: Angel Town; Defiance; Double Revenge; Evil That Men Do, The; I Wanna Hold Your Hand; Night Before, The; Raging Bull; Time Shifters, The
Saldana, Zoe: Center Stage; Crossroads (2002)
Sale, Chic: Fighting Westerner, The
Sale, Virginia: Hatbox Mystery, The
Salem, Kario: Jericho Fever; Savage; Underground Aces
Salen, Jesper: Slingshot, The
Salenger, Meredith: Bug Buster; Dream a Little Dream; Edge of Honor; Journey of Natty Gann, The; Kiss, The; Lake Placid; Night in the Life of Jimmy Reardon, A; Venus Rising; Village of the Damned
Salerno, Enrico Maria: Bird with the Crystal Plumage, The
Salerno, Mary Jo: Modern Affair, A
Sales, Leander: Don't Let Your Meat Loaf
Sales, Soupy: … And God Spoke
Salgueiro, Teresa: Lisbon Story
Salinas, Carmen: Danzon
Salinas, Raul: Drive By
Salinger, Diane: Morning After, The; One Night Stand; Pee-Wee's Big Adventure
Salinger, Matt: Babyfever; Captain America; Firehawk; Fortunes of War; Manhunt for Claude Dallas; Options
Sally Fraser: Giant from the Unknown
Salmi, Albert: Ambushers, The; Born American; Breaking In; Brothers Karamazov, The; Empire of the Ants; Hard to Hold; Hour of the Gun, The; Jesse; Kill Castro (Cuba Crossing, Mercenaries , Sweet Violent Tony); Lawman; Menace on the Mountain; Night Games; St. Helens; Steel; Unforgiven, The (1960)
Salmon, Colin: Prime Suspect 2
Salmon, Philip: Vampyr, The (1992)
Salonga, Lea: Redwood Curtain
Salt, Jennifer: Gargoyles (1972); Hi Mom; Sisters (1973); Wedding Party, The
Salt, Karen: Prince Brat and the Whipping Boy
Saltarrelli, Elizabeth: Bound and Gagged: A Love Story
Salvador, Phillip: Fight for Us
Salvatori, Renato: Big Deal on Madonna Street; Burn!; Organizer, The; Rocco & His Brothers; State of Siege
Salzberg, Brian: Begotten
Salzman, Mark: Iron & Silk
Sambrell, Aldo: Tex and the Lord of the Deep; Yellow Hair and the Fortress of Gold
Samms, Emma: Goliath Awaits; Humanoids from the Deep; Illusions; More Wild Wild West; Shrimp on the Barbie; Star Quest
Samoilov, Vladimir: Siberiade
Samoilova, Tatyana: Cranes Are Flying, The
Samples, Sheridan: Smile Like Yours, A
Sampson, Robert: Arrival, The; Dark Side of the Moon, The; Gates of Hell; Re-Animator; Robot Jox
Sampson, Tim: War Party
Sampson, Will: Buffalo Bill and the Indians; Fish Hawk; Insignificance; One Flew over the Cuckoo's Nest; Orca; Poltergeist II: The Other Side; Standing Tall; Vega$; White Buffalo
Sams, Jeffrey: Fly by Night; Hope; Just Write; Rose Hill; Run for the Dream
Samten, Lobsang: Kundun
Samuel, Joanne: Alison's Birthday; Gallagher's Travels; Mad Max
Samuels, Haydon: I Live With Me Dad
Samuelsson, Emma: Together
San, Lu Man: Scent of Green Papaya, The
San Giacomo, Laura: Apocalypse, The; Nina Takes a Lover; Once Around; Pretty Woman; Quigley Down Under; Right to Remain Silent, The; sex, lies and videotape; Sister Mary Explains It All; Stand, The; Stuart Saves His Family; Under Suspicion; Where the Day Takes You
San Juan, Antonia: All About My Mother
San Juan, Olga: Beautiful Blonde from Bashful Bend, The; Blue Skies
Sanchez, Jaime: Florida Straits
Sanchez, Marco: Last Debate, The
Sanchez, Pedro: Final Defeat, The; Go Kill and Come Back; White Fang and the Hunter
Sanchez, Roselyn: Rush Hour 2
Sanchez, Victoria: Code Name Jaguar
Sanchez-Gijon, Aitana: Chambermaid on the Titanic, The; Walk in the Clouds, A
Sancho, Fernando: Boldest Job in the West, The; Django Shoots First
Sancho, José: Arachnid
Sand, Paul: Can't Stop the Music; Great Bank Hoax, The; Hot Rock, The; Last Fling, The; Main Event, The; Wholly Moses!
Sanda, Dominique: Cabo Blanco; Conformist, The; Damnation Alley (Survival Run); Garden of the Finzi-Continis, The; Mackintosh Man, The; Nobody's Children; 1900; Steppenwolf; Story of a Love Story; Voyage en Douce
Sander, Casey: Crosscut; Summer Dreams
Sander, Otto: Wings of Desire
Sanders, George: Action in Arabia; All About Eve; Allegheny Uprising; Amorous Adventures of Moll Flanders, The; Bitter Sweet (1940); Black Jack; Black Swan, The; Candyman, The; Death of a Scoundrel; Doomwatch; Endless Night; Falcon Takes Over, The; Falcon's Brother, The; Five Golden Hours; Foreign Correspondent; Forever Amber; From the Earth to the Moon; Ghost and Mrs. Muir, The; Hangover Square; House of the Seven Gables, The; In Search of the Castaways; Ivanhoe; Jupiter's Darling; King Richard and the Crusaders; Last Voyage, The; Lloyd's of London; Man Hunt (1941); Moon and Sixpence, The; Mr. Moto's Last Warning; Nurse Edith Cavell; One Step to Hell; Picture of Dorian Gray, The; Private Affairs of Bel Ami, The; Psychomania; Quiller Memorandum, The; Rebecca; Saint in London, The; Saint Strikes Back, The; Samson and Delilah; Shot in the Dark, A; Solomon and Sheba; Son of Fury; Son of Monte Cristo, The; Strange Affair of Uncle Harry, The; Strange Woman, The; Sundown; Tales of Manhattan; This Land Is Mine; Village of the Damned; Voyage in Italy; While the City Sleeps
Sanders, Henry G.: Boss' Son, The; Rebel
Sanders, Hugh: Pride of St. Louis, The
Sanders, Jay O.: Angels in the Outfield; Big Green, The; Confession, The; Daylight; Down Came a Blackbird; Earthly Possessions; For Richer or Poorer; Hostages; JFK; Kiss the Girls; Matchmaker, The; Misfit Brigade, The; Nobody's Children; Silver Strand; Tumbleweeds; V. I. Warshawski
Sanders, Otto: Faraway, So Close
Sanders, Paul Austin: Dark Universe, The
Sanders, Peggie: Lady Avenger
Sanders, Richard: Neon City
Sanderson, William: Client, The; Deadly Weapon; Forest Warrior; George Wallace; Last Man Standing; Last Man Standing; Lonesome Dove; Mirror Mirror; Mirror, Mirror 2: Raven Dance; Raggedy Man; Return to Lonesome Dove; Savage Weekend; Wagons East
Sandifer, Elizabeth: Animal Instincts 2
Sandler, Adam: Airheads; Big Daddy; Billy Madison; Bulletproof; Going Overboard; Happy Gilmore; Little Nicky; Mixed Nuts; Waterboy, The; Wedding Singer, The
Sandler, William: Witness Protection
Sandlund, Debra: Victimless Crimes
Sandor, Steve: Bonnie's Kids; Dynamo; Stryker

Sandoval, Miguel: Breach of Trust; Crew, The; Dancing with Danger; Fixer, The; Get Shorty; Mrs. Winterbourne; Route 9; Wild Iris
Sandre, Didier: Autumn Tale
Sandrelli, Stefania: Alfredo Alfredo; Conformist, The; Divorce—Italian Style; Family, The; Jamon, Jamon; Of Love and Shadows; Partner; Seduced and Abandoned; Stealing Beauty; We All Loved Each Other So Much
Sandrini, Luis: El Professor Hippie
Sands, Billy: Sgt. Bilko (TV Series)
Sands, Diana: Georgia, Georgia; Raisin in the Sun, A
Sands, Johnny: Admiral Was a Lady, The
Sands, Julian: After Darkness; Black Water; Boxing Helena; Browning Version, The; Circle of Passion; Crazy in Love; Doctor and the Devils, The; End of Summer; Gothic; Grand Isle; Great Elephant Escape, The; Husbands and Lovers; Impromptu; Killing Fields, The; Leaving Las Vegas; Loss of Sexual Innocence, The; Mercy; Murder by Moonlight; Naked Lunch; Phantom of the Opera; Room with a View, A; Siesta; Tale of a Vampire; Turn of the Screw (1992); Vibes; Warlock; Warlock: The Armageddon; Witch Hunt
Sands, Sonny: Bellboy, The
Sands, Tommy: Babes in Toyland; Ensign Pulver; None But the Brave
Sands, Walter: Blonde Ice
Sandweiss, Ellen: Evil Dead, The
Sandy, Gary: Mommy 2: Mommy's Day; Unlikely Angel
Sanford, Erskine: Lady from Shanghai; Letter from an Unknown Woman
Sanford, Garwin: Maternal Instincts; Quarantine
Sanford, Isabel: Desperate Moves; Pucker Up and Bark Like a Dog
Sanford, Stanley: Laurel and Hardy Classics: Vol. 1–9
Sano, Shiro: Violent Cop
Sanoussi-Bliss, Pierre: Nobody Loves Me
Sansone, Patricia: Merlin's Shop of Mystical Wonders
Santagata, Alfonso: Palombella Rossa
Santamaria, Claudio: Besieged
Santana, Ernie: Sudden Thunder
Santiago, Ray: Girlfight
Santiago, Saundra: Miami Vice
Santini, Pierre: Dirty Dishes
Santoni, Reni: Anzio; Bad Boys; Cobra (1986); Dead Men Don't Wear Plaid; Dirty Harry; Dr. Dolittle (1998); Enter Laughing; Late Shift, The; They Went That-A-Way and That-A-Way
Santos, Joe: Blade; Blue Knight, The; Deadly Desire; Friends of Eddie Coyle, The; Mo' Money; Rockford Files, The (TV Series); Trial by Jury; Zandy's Bride
Sanville, Michael: Dreams Come True; First Turn-on, The
Sanz, Jorge: Belle Epoque; Lovers (1992); Valentina
Sapara, Ade: Crusoe
Sapienza, Johnny: Crusoe
Sara, Mia: Any Man's Death; Apprentice to Murder; Black Day Blue Night; Blindsided; Bullet to Beijing; By the Sword; Call of the Wild; Caroline at Midnight; Climate for Killing, A; Daughter of Darkness; Ferris Bueller's Day Off; Hard Time; Legend; Maddening, The; Pompatus of Love, The; Queenie; Set-Up, The; Shadows in the Storm; Stranger Among Us, A; Timecop; 20,000 Leagues Under the Sea; Undertow
Sarafian, Richard: Bound; Bugsy; Don Juan DeMarco; Gotti; Gunmen; Miami Hustle; Ruby; Terminal Velocity
Sarandon, Chris: Child's Play; Collision Course; Cuba; Dark Tide; Dog Day Afternoon; Forced March; Fright Night; Goodbye, Miss 4th of July; Just Cause; Lipstick; Little Men; Mayflower Madam; Osterman Weekend, The; Princess Bride, The; Protocol; Resurrected, The; Road Ends; Sentinel, The; Slaves of New York; Tailspin; Tale of Two Cities, A; Tales from the Crypt Presents Bordello of Blood; Temptress; Terminal Justice; Terminal Justice, Cybertech P.D.; When the Dark Man Calls; Whispers
Sarandon, Susan: Anywhere But Here; Atlantic City; Buddy System, The; Bull Durham; Client, The; Compromising Positions; Cradle Will Rock; Dead Man Walking; Dry White Season, A; Earthly Possessions; Front Page, The; Great Smokey Roadblock, The; Great Waldo Pepper, The; Hunger, The (1983); Illuminata; January Man, The; Joe; Joe Gould's Secret; King of the Gypsies; Light Sleeper; Little Women; Lorenzo's Oil; Loving Couples; Mussolini and I; Other Side of Midnight, The; Our Friend, Martin; Pretty Baby; Rocky Horror Picture Show, The; Safe Passage; Something Short of Paradise; Stepmom; Sweethearts' Dance; Tempest; Thelma & Louise; Twilight; White Palace; Who Am I This Time?; Witches of Eastwick, The; Women of Valor
Sarasohn, Lane: Groove Tube, The
Sarchet, Kate: Sweater Girls
Sardà, Rosa Maria: All About My Mother
Sardou, Fernand: Little Theatre of Jean Renoir, The
Sarelle, Leilani: Breach of Trust; Harvest, The (1992); Neon Maniacs
Sargent, Dick: Billie; Clonus Horror, The; Ghost and Mr. Chicken, The; Hardcore; Live a Little, Love a Little; Melvin Purvis: G-Man; Murder by Numbers (1989); Operation Petticoat; Teen Witch
Sargent, Richard: Tanya's Island
Sarky, Daniel: Emmanuelle
Sarne, Michael: Seaside Swingers
Sarrazin, Michael: Beulah Land; Bullet to Beijing; Captive Hearts; Caravans; Deadly Companion; Doomsday Flight, The; Fighting Back; Flim-Flam Man, The; For Pete's Sake; Groundstar Conspiracy, The; Gumball Rally, The; Joshua Then and Now; Keeping Track; Lena's Holiday; Loves and Times of Scaramouche, The; Malarek; Mascara; Pursuit of Happiness, The; Reincarnation of Peter Proud, The; Sometimes a Great Notion; They Shoot Horses, Don't They?; Thunder Point; Train Killer, The
Sarsgaard, Peter: Boys Don't Cry; Center of the World, The; Freak City
Sartain, Gailard: Ernest Goes to Jail; Fried Green Tomatoes; Getting Even with Dad; Grifters, The; Guilty by Suspicion; Leader of the Band; Murder in Mind; One Riot, One Ranger; Open Season; Patriot, The; Real McCoy, The; Stop! Or My Mom Will Shoot
Sasaki, Katsuhiko: Terror of Mechagodzilla
Sassaman, Nicole: Witchcraft V: Dance with the Devil
Sassard, Jacqueline: Accident; Bad Girls; Les Biches
Sassoon, Cat: Angel Fist; Bloodfist IV—Die Trying; Bloodfist VI: Ground Zero
Sastre, Ines: Best Man, The
Sastri, Lina: Excellent Cadavers
Satie, Erik: Avant Garde Program #2
Sato, Kei: Violence at Noon; Zatoichi: The Blind Swordsman's Vengeance
Sato, Koichi: Gonin; Silk Road, The
Saucedo, Rick "Elvis": Gonin; Silk Road, The
Saucier, Jason: Crawlers
Sauer, Gary: Unbelievable Truth, The
Saunders, Jennifer: Absolutely Fabulous; Midwinter's Tale, A; Muppet Treasure Island; Supergrass, The
Saunders, Justine: Fringe Dwellers, The
Saunders, Mary Jane: Sorrowful Jones
Saunders, Michael K.: Billy the Kid Meets the Vampires
Saunders, Pamela: Alien Warrior
Savage, Ann: Detour; Renegade Girl
Savage, Ben: Little Monsters
Savage, Brad: Islands in the Stream
Savage, Fred: Boy Who Could Fly, The; Little Monsters; Princess Bride, The; Vice Versa; Wizard, The
Savage, John: All the Kind Strangers; Amateur, The (1982); American Strays; Amnesia; Any Man's Death; Bad Company; Brady's Escape; Caribe; Carnosaur 2; CIA II: Target: Alexa; Club Vampire; Coming Out of the Ice; Dangerous, The (1984); Daybreak (1993); Deer Hunter, The; Do the Right Thing; Eric; Godfather, Part III, The; Hair; Hostile Intent; Hotel Colonial; Hunting; Inside Moves; Jack Bull, The; Managua; Maria's Lovers; Message in a Bottle; Nairobi Affair; One Good Turn; Onion Field, The; Primary Motive; Red Scorpion 2; Salvador; Shattered Image; Sister-in-Law, The; Takeover, The; They Nest; Virginian, The; White Squall
Savage, Vic: Creeping Terror, The

Schell, Maria: Brothers Karamazov, The; Christmas Lilies of the Field; Cimarron; Gervaise; Hanging Tree, The; Just a Gigolo; La Passante; Napoleon; 99 Women; Odessa File, The; Samson and Delilah; White Nights
Schell, Maximilian: Abraham; Assisi Underground, The; Black Hole, The; Castle, The; Chosen, The; Cross of Iron; Day that Shook the World, The; Deep Impact; Eighteenth Angel, The; Far Off Place, A; Freshman, The; Joan of Arc (1999); John Carpenter's Vampires; Judgment at Nuremberg; Julia; Left Luggage; Little Odessa; Man in the Glass Booth; Marlene; Miss Rose White; Odessa File, The; Pedestrian, The; Players; Rose Garden, The; St. Ives; Stalin; Telling Lies in America; Topkapi; Young Catherine; Young Lions, The
Schell, Ronnie: Fatal Instinct; Revenge of the Red Baron
Schellengberg, August: Black Robe; Confidential; Free Willy; Free Willy 2: The Adventure Home; Free Willy 3: The Rescue; Iron Will; Lakota Woman: Siege at Wounded Knee; Mark of Cain; Striker's Mountain; Tramp at the Door; True Heart
Schellhardt, Mary Kate: Free Willy 2: The Adventure Home
Schenck, Wolfgang: Effi Briest
Schenna and the villagers of Tehouda, Leila: Ramparts of Clay
Scherrer, Paul: Children of the Corn II: The Final Sacrifice
Scheydt, Karl: American Soldier, The
Schiaffino, Rosanna: Man Called Noon, The; Two Weeks in Another Town
Schiavelli, Vincent: Courtyard, The; Lord of Illusions; Lurking Fear; Milo; Playroom; Prince Brat and the Whipping Boy; Waiting for the Light
Schicha, Ralph: Savage Attraction
Schiff, Richard: Heaven
Schiffer, Claudia: Black and White (2000); Friends and Lovers; In Pursuit
Schildkraut, Joseph: Crusades, The; Diary of Anne Frank, The; Flame of the Barbary Coast; Garden of Allah, The; Idiot's Delight; King of Kings, The (1927); Life of Emile Zola, The; Man in the Iron Mask, The; Marie Antoinette; Monsieur Beaucaire; Mr. Moto Takes a Vacation; Northwest Outpost; Orphans of the Storm; Rains Came, The; Road to Yesterday, The; Shop Around the Corner, The; Viva Villa!
Schilling, Vivian: Future Shock; Savage Land
Schiltz, Delphine: Ponette
Schlachet, Daniel: Swoon
Schlatter, Charlie: All-American Murder; 18 Again; Heartbreak Hotel; Police Academy: Mission to Moscow; Sunset Heat
Schlesinger, John: Lost Language of Cranes, The
Schloss, Zander: That Darn Punk
Schmid, Helmut: Salzburg Connection, The
Schmidinger, Walter: Hanussen
Schmidt, Marlene: Scorchy
Schmied, Hellena: Barcelona
Schmitz, Sybille: Vampyr (1931)
Schnabel, Stefan: Anna; Dracula's Widow; Firefox; Mr. Inside/Mr. Outside
Schnarre, Monika: Fearless Tiger
Schneider, Betty: Paris Belongs to Us
Schneider, Carol: Everything Relative
Schneider, Charles: Zarkorr! The Invader
Schneider, Dan: Good Burger
Schneider, Dawn: Free Ride
Schneider, Edith: Of Pure Blood
Schneider, John: Cocaine Wars; Curse, The; Eddie Macon's Run; Ministry of Vengeance; Stagecoach; Texas
Schneider, Magda: Liebelei
Schneider, Maria: Jane Eyre; Last Tango in Paris; Mamma Dracula; Passenger, The
Schneider, Paul: George Washington
Schneider, Rob: Adventures of Pinocchio, The; Animal, The; Beverly Hillbillies, The (1993); Big Daddy; Deuce Bigalow: Male Gigolo; Down Periscope; Dying to Get Rich; Judge Dredd; Knock Off; Muppets From Space; Surf Ninjas
Schneider, Romy: Assassination of Trotsky, The; Boccaccio 70; Cardinal, The; César and Rosalie; Death Watch; Good Neighbor Sam; Hero, The (1971); Infernal Trio, The; La Passante; Les Choses de la Vie (Things in Life, The); Mado; Simple Story, A; Swimming Pool, The; Trial, The; What's New, Pussycat?; Woman at Her Window, A
Schock, Barbara: From Hollywood to Deadwood
Schoeffling, Michael: Belizaire the Cajun; Let's Get Harry; Mermaids; Sylvester; Vision Quest; Wild Hearts Can't Be Broken
Schoelen, Jill: Adventures in Spying; Babes in Toyland; Chiller; Curse II—The Bite; Cutting Class; Phantom of the Opera; Popcorn; Rich Girl; Stepfather, The; There Goes My Baby; When a Stranger Calls Back
Schoene, Reiner: Nobody's Children
Schoener, Ingeborg: Mr. Superinvisible
Schofield, Annabel: Body Armor; Exit in Red; Solar Crisis
Schofield, Drew: Sid and Nancy
Schofield, Katharine: Lion of Africa, The
Schofield, Nell: Puberty Blues
Schombing, Jason: Timecop
Schon, Margarete: Kriemhilde's Revenge; Siegfried
Schoppert, Bill: Personals, The
Schrader, Maria: Aimee & Jaguar; Nobody Loves Me
Schrage, Lisa: China White; Hello, Mary Lou: Prom Night II
Schreck, Max: Nosferatu
Schreiber, Avery: Dracula: Dead and Loving It; Galaxina; Hunk; Loose Shoes; Silent Scream; Swashbuckler (1976)
Schreiber, Liev: Daytrippers, The; Denise Calls Up; Hamlet; Hurricane, The; Jakob the Liar; Kate and Leopold; Phantoms; Ransom; RKO 281; Scream 2; Spring Forward; Sum of All Fears, The; Walk on the Moon, A; Walking and Talking
Schreier, Tom: Ripper, The
Schroder, Rick: Across the Tracks; Call of the Wild; Champ, The; Crimson Tide; Earthling, The; Ebenezer; Last Flight of Noah's Ark; Little Lord Fauntleroy; Lonesome Dove; Return to Lonesome Dove; Texas; There Goes My Baby
Schroeder, Barbet: Celine and Julie Go Boating; Six in Paris (Paris Vue par …)
Schub, Steven: Caught
Schubert, Heinz: Emil and the Detectives
Schubert, Karin: Bluebeard
Schuck, John: Blade; Butch and Sundance: The Early Days; Four Eyes and Six Guns; Hammersmith Is Out; Holy Matrimony; Outrageous Fortune; Second Sight; Thieves Like Us
Schue, Matt: Blade; Butch and Sundance: The Early Days; Four Eyes and Six Guns; Hammersmith Is Out; Holy Matrimony; Outrageous Fortune; Second Sight; Thieves Like Us
Schull, Amanda: Center Stage
Schulter, Ariane: 1-900
Schultz, Albert: Ebenezer
Schultz, Dwight: Alone in the Dark; Fat Man and Little Boy; Long Walk Home, The; Star Trek: First Contact; Temp, The; When Your Lover Leaves; Woman with a Past
Schultz, Jeff: Buying Time
Schultz, Tom: Eyes of the Serpent; In the Time of Barbarians II
Schulz, Brian: Thou Shalt Not Kill … Except
Schulze, Paul: Grind; Hand Gun
Schumacher, Wendy: Animal Instincts: The Seductress; Capitol Conspiracy, The; Fugitive Rage; Scorned 2
Schumm, Hans: Spy Smasher
Schunzel, Reinhold: Fortune's Fool; Golden Earrings; Threepenny Opera, The
Schurer, Erna: Blood Castle; Specters
Schuurman, Betty: Character (Karakter)
Schwan, Ivyann: Problem Child 2
Schwartz, Aaron: Heavyweights
Schwartz, Albert: Time Stands Still
Schwartz, Maurice: Tevye
Schwartz, Scott: Toy, The
Schwartz, Simon: Inheritors, The
Schwartzman, Jason: Rushmore; Slackers (2002)
Schwarzenegger, Arnold: Batman & Robin; Beretta's Island; Collateral Damage; Commando; Conan the Barbarian; Conan the Destroyer; Dave; End of Days; Eraser; Hercules Goes Bananas; Jayne Mansfield Story, The; Jingle All the Way; Junior; Kindergarten Cop; Last Action Hero, The; Predator; Pumping Iron; Raw Deal; Red Heat; Red Sonja; Running Man, The; 6th

Scratch, Derf: Du-Beat-E-O
Scribner, Don: Wild Man
Scrimm, Angus: Mindwarp; Phantasm II; Phantasm III: Lord of the Dead; Phantasm IV: Oblivion; Subspecies; Transylvania Twist
Scruggs, Linda: Las Vegas Lady
Scuddamore, Simon: Slaughter High
Scully, Samantha: Silent Night, Deadly Night III: Better Watch Out!
Scully, Sean: Almost Angels
Seacat, Sandra: Baby Dance, The
Seagal, Kentaro: Seamless
Seagal, Steven: Above the Law; Executive Decision; Exit Wounds; Fire Down Below; Glimmer Man, The; Hard to Kill; Marked for Death; My Giant; On Deadly Ground; Out for Justice; Patriot, The; Ticker; Under Siege; Under Siege 2: Dark Territory
Seago, Howie: Beyond Silence
Seagrave, Jocelyn: Moonbase
Seagrove, Jenny: Appointment with Death; Chorus of Disapproval, A; Deadly Game; Guardian, The; Hold the Dream; Sherlock Holmes and the Incident at Victoria Falls; Woman of Substance, A
Seal, Elizabeth: Philby, Burgess and Maclean: Spy Scandal of the Century
Seale, Douglas: Ernest Saves Christmas
Seales, Franklyn: Onion Field, The; Taming of the Shrew (1982)
Seamens, Sueanne: Majorettes, The
Searcy, Nick: Cast Away; Nell; Perfect Crime
Sears, Dejanet: In His Father's Shoes; Stand Off
Sears, Heather: Phantom of the Opera; Room at the Top
Seay, James: Amazing Colossal Man, The; Killers from Space
Sebanek, Josef: Loves of a Blonde
Sebastian, Dorothy: Free and Easy; Spite Marriage
Sebastian, Lobo: 187
Seberg, Jean: Airport; Bonjour Tristesse; Breathless; Fine Madness, A; Lilith; Macho Callahan; Mouse That Roared, The; Paint Your Wagon; Pendulum; Saint Joan; Time Out For Love
Secombe, Harry: Down Among the "Z" Men
Secor, Kyle: Children of Fury; Delusion; Drop Zone; Late for Dinner; Silent Victim; Untamed Heart
Seda, Jon: Dear God; I Like It Like That; Price of Glory; Selena; Sunchaser; 12 Monkeys
Sedden, Margaret: Headin' Home
Seddiqi, Bahare: Children of Heaven
Sedgewick, Edna: Red Barry
Sedgwick, Edie: Ciao! Manhattan
Sedgwick, Kyra: Born on the Fourth of July; Critical Care; Heart and Souls; Kansas; Labor Pains; Losing Chase; Low Life, The; Man Who Broke 1000 Chains, The; Miss Rose White; Montana; Mr. and Mrs. Bridge; Phenomenon; Pyrates; Singles; Something to Talk About; What's Cooking?; Women & Men 2
Sedgwick, Robert: Nasty Hero
Seeger, Pete: Woody Guthrie—Hard Travelin'
Seel, Ceri: Tripods
Seeley, Blossom: Blood Money
Seeley, Eileen: Jack Frost 2; Ruby Jean and Joe
Seely, Sybil: Buster Keaton Festival Vol. 1–3
Seff, Brian: Pee-Wee Herman Show, The
Segal, George: All's Fair; Army of One; Babysitter, The; Black Bird, The; Blume in Love; Born to Win; Bridge at Remagen, The; Carbon Copy; Cold Room, The; Direct Hit; Duchess and the Dirtwater Fox, The; Endless Game, The; Flirting with Disaster; For the Boys; Fun with Dick and Jane; Hot Rock, The; Houdini; Invitation to a Gunfighter; It's My Party; Killing 'Em Softly; King Rat; Last Married Couple in America, The; Look Who's Talking; Lost and Found (1979); Lost Command; Me, Myself & I; Mirror Has Two Faces, The; No Way to Treat a Lady; Not My Kid; November Conspiracy, The; Owl and the Pussycat, The; Picture Windows; Quiller Memorandum, The; Rollercoaster; Russian Roulette; Ship of Fools; St. Valentine's Day Massacre, The; Stick; Taking the Heat; Terminal Man, The; Touch of Class, A; Where's Poppa?; Who Is Killing the Great Chefs of Europe?; Who's Afraid of Virginia Woolf?; Zany Adventures of Robin Hood, The
Segal, Howard: Last Game, The
Segal, Robbin Zohra: Harem
Segall, Pamela: After Midnight; Bed of Roses; Gate II; Something Special
Segda, Dorotha: My 20th Century
Segel, Jason: Slackers (2002)
Seghal, Zohra: Bhaji on the Beach; Masala
Seghers, Mil: Antonia's Line
Segundo, Compay: Buena Vista Social Club, The
Seidelman, Susan: First Works, Volumes 1 & 2
Seigner, Emmanuelle: Bitter Moon; Frantic; Ninth Gate, The; Place Vendome
Seigner, Louis: Le Bourgeois Gentilhomme
Seigner, Mathilde: Dry Cleaning; Venus Beauty Institute; With a Friend Like Harry
Seitz, John: Forced March; Hard Choices; Out of the Rain
Sekiguchi, Yusuke: Kikujiro
Sekka, Johnny: Message, The (Mohammad, Messenger of God)
Selander, Hjalmar: Treasure of Arne
Selby, David: Best of Dark Shadows, The; Dying Young; Girl in Blue, The; Grave Secrets: The Legacy of Hilltop Drive; Headless Body in Topless Bar; Intersection; Night of Dark Shadows; Raise the Titanic; Rich and Famous; Up the Sandbox
Selby, Nicholas: Elizabeth R; Macbeth
Selby, Sarah: Huckleberry Finn
Seldes, Marian: Town & Country
Self, Doug: Men in Love
Sell, Jack M.: Deadly Spygames
Sellars, Elizabeth: Chalk Garden, The; Mummy's Shroud, The; Never Let Go; Three Cases of Murder; Voyage 'Round My Father, A
Sellecca, Connie: Brotherhood of the Rose; Captain America II: Death Too Soon; Last Fling, The
Selleck, Tom: Broken Trust; Bunco; Christopher Columbus: The Discovery (1992); Daughters of Satan; Folks; Gypsy Warriors, The; Her Alibi; High Road to China; In & Out; Innocent Man, An; Lassiter; Last Stand at Saber River; Louis L'Amour's Crossfire Trail; Love Letter, The; Most Wanted; Mr. Baseball; Myra Breckenridge; Quigley Down Under; Ruby Jean and Joe; Runaway; Running Mates; Sacketts, The; Shadow Riders, The; Terminal Island; Three Men and a Baby; Three Men and a Little Lady; Washington Affair, The
Sellem, Marie-Lou: Winter Sleepers
Sellers, Mary: Crawlers
Sellers, Peter: After the Fox; Alice's Adventures in Wonderland; Battle of the Sexes, The; Being There; Blockhouse, The; Bobo, The; Carlton-Browne of the F.O.; Casino Royale; Dr. Strangelove or How I Learned to Stop Worrying and Love the Bomb; Down Among the "Z" Men; Fiendish Plot of Dr. Fu Manchu, The; Ghost in the Noonday Sun; Heavens Above; I Love You Alice B. Toklas!; I'm All Right Jack; Ladykillers, The; Lolita; Magic Christian, The; Mouse That Roared, The; Murder by Death; Naked Truth (Your Past Is Showing); Never Let Go; Only Two Can Play; Party, The; Pink Panther, The; Pink Panther Strikes Again, The; Prisoner of Zenda, The; Return of the Pink Panther, The; Revenge of the Pink Panther, The; Road to Hong Kong, The; Shot in the Dark, A; Smallest Show on Earth, The; There's a Girl in My Soup; To See Such Fun; Tom Thumb; Trail of the Pink Panther, The; Two-Way Stretch; Up the Creek; Waltz of the Toreadors; What's New, Pussycat?; Woman Times Seven; World of Henry Orient, The; Wrong Arm of the Law, The; Wrong Box, The
Sellier, Georges: Red Balloon, The
Sellner, Gustav Rudolph: Pedestrian, The
Selzer, Milton: Miss Rose White
Sema, Chie: Tokyo Decadence
Seneca, Joe: Blob, The; Crossroads; Mississippi Masala; Murder on the Bayou; Road to Freedom: The Vernon Johns Story; Saint of Fort Washington, The; Wilma
Sennett, Mack: Abbott and Costello Meet the Keystone Kops; Hollywood Cavalcade
Serato, Massimo: Catch as Catch Can; Tenth Victim, The

Serban, Isidor: Gadjo Dilo
Serbedzija, Rade: Before the Rain; Broken English; Eyes Wide Shut; Lies & Whispers; Mighty Joe Young; Polish Wedding; Saint, The (1997); Truce, The
Sergei, Ivan: John Woo's Once a Thief; Opposite of Sex, The
Serio, Terry: Fast Lane Fever; Shout: The Story of Johnny O'Keefe
Serious, Yahoo: Mr. Accident; Reckless Kelly; Young Einstein
Serling, Rod: Encounter with the Unknown
Serna, Assumpta: Hidden Assassin; Managua; Matador; Sharpe (TV Series)
Serna, Pepe: American Me; Break of Dawn; Conagher; Force of One; Killer Inside Me, The; Rookie, The (1990); Streets of L.A., The
Sernas, Jacques: Goliath and the Vampires; Helen of Troy
Serner, Halan: Man on the Roof
Serra, Raymond: Alphabet City; Nasty Hero
Serra, Tony: Watched!
Serrano, Diego: 24-Hour Woman
Serrano, Nestor: After the Storm; Bait
Serrault, Michel: Artemisia; Associate, The; Beaumarchais the Scoundrel; Dr. Petiot; Holes, The; La Cage aux Folles; La Cage aux Folles II; La Cage aux Folles III, The Wedding; Love and the Frenchwoman; Nelly and Monsieur Arnaud; Old Lady Who Walked in the Sea, The; Swindle, The
Serre, Henri: Jules and Jim
Serres, Jacques: Blue Country; French Detective, The
Servaes, Daguey: Fortune's Fool
Servais, Jean: Angele; Liars, The; Rififi
Sesau, Mo: Young Soul Rebels
Sessions, Almira: Oklahoma Annie
Sessions, John: Sweet Revenge
Seth, Roshan: Buddha of Suburbia, The; Gandhi; Little Dorrit; London Kills Me; Mississippi Masala; My Beautiful Laundrette; Not Without My Daughter; Solitaire for 2
Sethna, Maia: Earth
Seton, Bruce: Demon Barber of Fleet Street, The; Love from a Stranger
Settle, Matthew: In Crowd, The; Lansky; U-571
Séty, Gérard: Van Gogh
Severance, Joan: Almost Pregnant; Another Pair of Aces; Bird on a Wire; Black Scorpion; Black Scorpion II: Aftershock; Criminal Passion; Dangerous Indiscretion; Hard Evidence; Illicit Behavior; In Dark Places; Lake Consequence; No Holds Barred; Payback; Profile for Murder; Runestone; See No Evil, Hear No Evil; Write to Kill
Severn, Billy: Enchanted Forest, The
Sevier, Corey: Summer of the Monkeys
Sevigny, Chloe: American Psycho; Boys Don't Cry; Gummo; Kids; Last Days of Disco, The; Map of the World, A; Palmetto; Trees Lounge
Seville, Carmen: Boldest Job in the West, The; Pantaloons
Seward, Jim: Last Broadcast, The
Sewell, George: Invasion UFO; Vengeance of She, The
Sewell, Rufus: Bless the Child; Carrington; Cold Comfort Farm; Dangerous Beauty; Dark City; Hamlet; Illuminata; Knight's Tale, A; Man of No Importance, A; Middlemarch
Sexton III, Brendan: Boys Don't Cry; Hurricane Streets; Session 9
Sexton Jr., Brendan: Welcome to the Dollhouse
Seyler, Athene: Make Mine Mink
Seyler, Cathy: Vampyre (1990)
Seymour, Anne: Desire under the Elms; Misty; Trancers
Seymour, Caroline: Gumshoe
Seymour, Clarine: Idol Dancer, The
Seymour, Jane: Are You Lonesome Tonight; Battlestar Galactica; Doctor Quinn Medicine Woman; East of Eden; Four Feathers, The; Haunting Passion, The; Head Office; Jack the Ripper; Lassiter; Live and Let Die; Matters of the Heart; Oh, Heavenly Dog!; Onassis: The Richest Man in the World; Praying Mantis; Scarlet Pimpernel, The; Sinbad and the Eye of the Tiger; Somewhere in Time; Story of David, The; Sunstroke; Tunnel, The; War and Remembrance
Seymour, Ralph: Longshot (1981)
Seyrig, Delphine: Black Windmill, The; Daughters of Darkness; Discreet Charm of the Bourgeoisie, The; Donkey Skin (Peau D'Àne); Grain of Sand, The; I Sent a Letter to My Love; Last Year at Marienbad; Milky Way, The; Muriel; Stolen Kisses; Window Shopping
Sezer, Serif: Yol
Shackelford, Ted: Baby of the Bride; Dying to Remember; Spider and the Fly, The; Sweet Revenge
Shackley, John: Tripods
Shadix, Glenn: Dark Side of Genius; Dunston Checks In; My Summer Story
Shafer, Bobby Ray: Psycho Cop 2
Shafer, Dirk: Man of the Year
Shaffer, Paul: Gilda Live
Shaffer, Stacey: Blood Screams
Shah, Naseeruddin: Monsoon Wedding
Shai, Patrick: Rhodes
Shain, Harvey: Hot Ice
Shakur, Tupac: Above the Rim; Bullet; Gang Related; Gridlock'd; Juice; Poetic Justice
Shakurov, Sergei: Siberiade
Shalet, Victoria: Haunted
Shalhoub, Tony: Barton Fink; Big Night; Civil Action, A; Galaxy Quest; Impostor; Impostors, The; Life Less Ordinary, A; Life or Something Like It; Man Who Wasn't There, The (2001); Men in Black; Paulie; Siege, The; Spy Kids; That Championship Season; Thir13en Ghosts; Tic Code, The
Shamata, Chuck: Death Weekend; Death Wish V: The Face of Death; Left for Dead; Mafia Princess; Night Friend
Shanath, Tamara: Cronos
Shandling, Garry: Dr. Dolittle (1998); Hurlyburly; Love Affair; Mixed Nuts; Night We Never Met, The; Town & Country; What Planet Are You From?
Shane, Briant: Till There Was You
Shane, George: Resurrection Man
Shane, Jim: Chasing Dreams
Shane, Rachel: Bridge of Dragons; Futuresport
Shane, Sara: King and Four Queens, The
Shaner, Michael: Angel Fist; Expert, The
Shankar, Mamata: Stranger, The
Shankar, Ravi: Monterey Pop
Shankley, Amelia: Little Princess, A
Shanklin, Doug: Dark Rider
Shanks, Don: Life and Times of Grizzly Adams, The
Shanks, Michael: Escape from Mars; Stargate SG-1
Shannon, Frank: Flash Gordon Conquers the Universe; Flash Gordon: Rocketship (Spaceship to the Unknown; Perils from Planet Mongo)
Shannon, Harry: Cow Town; Hunt the Man Down; Once Upon a Honeymoon; Song of Texas
Shannon, Michael J.: Prime Suspect 3
Shannon, Molly: My 5 Wives; Never Been Kissed; Night at the Roxbury, A; Osmosis Jones; Serendipity; Superstar: Dare to Dream; Wet Hot American Summer
Shannon, Peggy: Deluge (1993)
Shannon, Vicellous Reon: Dancing in September; Freedom Song; Hurricane, The
Shanta, James Anthony: Allnighter, The
Shaoujun, Tian: Story of Xinghua, The
Shapiro, Ken: Groove Tube, The
Sharif, Omar: Anastasia: The Mystery of Anna; Ashanti; Baltimore Bullet, The; Behold a Pale Horse; Beyond Justice; Bloodline; Crime & Passion; Dr. Zhivago; Far Pavilions, The; Funny Girl; Funny Lady; Grand Larceny; Green Ice; Gulliver's Travels (1996) (Television); Horsemen, The; Juggernaut; Last Valley, The; Lawrence of Arabia; Mackenna's Gold; Night of the Generals; Oh, Heavenly Dog!; Pleasure Palace; Poppy Is Also a Flower, The; Rainbow Thief, The; S.H.E.; Tamarind Seed, The; 13th Warrior, The; Top Secret
Sharifi, Elham: Color of Paradise, The
Sharkey, Ray: Act of Piracy; Body Rock; Caged Fear; Capone; Chrome Soldiers; Cop and a Half; Du-Beat-E-O; Heart Beat; Hellhole; Idolmaker, The; Neon Empire, The; No Mercy; Private Investigations; Rain Killer, The; Regina; Relentless II: Dead On;

Round Trip to Heaven; Scenes from the Class Struggle in Beverly Hills; Take, The; Urban Crossfire; Who'll Stop the Rain; Willie and Phil; Wired; Wise Guys; Zebrahead
Sharon, Bo: Shrunken Heads
Sharp, Anthony: Confessional, The
Sharp, Lesley: Naked
Sharpe, Albert: Darby O'Gill and the Little People; Return of October, The
Sharpe, Cornelia: Reincarnation of Peter Proud, The; S.H.E.
Sharpe, David: Colorado Serenade; Dick Tracy Returns; Three Texas Steers; Wyoming Outlaw
Sharpe, Karen: High and the Mighty, The
Sharplin, Clint: Heaven
Sharrett, Michael: Deadly Friend; Magic of Lassie, The
Shatner, Melanie: Alien Within, The; Bloodlust: Subspecies III; Unknown Origin
Shatner, William: Airplane II: The Sequel; Andersonville Trial, The; Babysitter, The; Big Bad Mama; Broken Angel; Brothers Karamazov, The; Crash of Flight 401; Devil's Rain, The; Free Enterprise; Impulse; Intruder, The (1961); Kidnapping of the President, The; Kingdom of the Spiders; National Lampoon's Loaded Weapon 1; People, The; Pioneer Woman; Pray for the Wildcats; Prisoner of Zenda, Inc.; Secrets of a Married Man; Star Trek II: The Wrath of Khan; Star Trek III: The Search for Spock; Star Trek IV: The Voyage Home; Star Trek—The Motion Picture; Star Trek (TV Series); Star Trek V: The Final Frontier; Star Trek VI: The Undiscovered Country; Star Trek: Generations; Star Trek: The Menagerie; Tekwar: The Original Movie; Thriller (TV Series); Twilight Zone, The (TV Series); Visiting Hours; White Comanche
Shattuck, Shari: Dead On; Death Spa; Mad About You; Out for Blood
Shaud, Grant: Distinguished Gentleman, The
Shaughnessy, Mickey: Adventures of Huckleberry Finn, The; Boatniks, The; Designing Woman; Don't Go Near the Water; Jailhouse Rock
Shaver, Helen: Believers, The; Best Defense; Born to Be Wild; Color of Money, The; Coming Out Alive; Desert Hearts; Dr. Bethune; Gas; Harry Tracy; High-Ballin'; Innocent Victim; Lost!; Morning Glory; Murder So Sweet; Open Season; Outer Limits: Sandkings; Pair of Aces; Park Is Mine, The; Poltergeist: The Legacy; Starship Invasions; Survive the Night; Tremors 2: Aftershocks; Trial & Error (1992); War Boy, The
Shaw, Alonna: Cyborg Cop
Shaw, Bill: Ghostriders
Shaw, C. Montague: Buck Rogers: Destination Saturn (PlanetOutlaws); Mysterious Dr. Satan; Riders of the Whistling Skull; Zorro's Fighting Legion
Shaw, Crystal: Laser Moon
Shaw, Fiona: Butcher Boy, The; Harry Potter and the Sorcerer's Stone; Jane Eyre; Last September, The; Leo Tolstoy's Anna Karenina (1997); London Kills Me; Mountains of the Moon; My Left Foot; Persuasion; Seventh Stream, The; Super MarioBrothers, The; Undercover Blues
Shaw, Ian: Moondance
Shaw, Joe: Kull the Conqueror; Rhodes
Shaw, Martin: Hound of the Baskervilles, The; Macbeth; Rhodes
Shaw, Reta: Pajama Game, The
Shaw, Robert: Battle of Britain; Battle of the Bulge; Black Sunday; Deep, The; Diamonds; Force Ten from Navarone; From Russia with Love; Jaws; Man for All Seasons, A; Reflection of Fear; Robin and Marian; Royal Hunt of the Sun; Sting, The; Swashbuckler (1976); Taking of Pelham One Two Three, The; Town Called Hell, A; Young Winston
Shaw, Sebastian: High Season; Spy in Black, The
Shaw, Stan: Boys in Company C, The; Busted Up; Court-martial of Jackie Robinson, The; Cutthroat Island; D.P.; Fear; Freedom Song; Fried Green Tomatoes; Gladiator, The (1986) (Television); Harlem Nights; Lifepod; Monster Squad, The; Rising Sun; Snake Eyes; TNT Jackson; Tough Enough; Truck Turner
Shaw, Steve: Child of Glass
Shaw, Susan: Junkman, The; Quartet
Shaw, Susan D.: Adventures of the Wilderness Family; Mountain Family Robinson; Wilderness Family, Part 2, The
Shaw, Victoria: Alvarez Kelly; Eddy Duchin Story, The
Shaw, Vinessa: Corky Romano; 40 Days and 40 Nights; Hocus Pocus; Ladybugs
Shaw, Winifred: Case of the Velvet Claws, The; Gold Diggers of 1935; Satan Met a Lady; Sweet Adeline
Shawlee, Joan: Francis Joins the Wacs
Shawn, Dick: Angel; Beer; Check Is in the Mail, The; Evil Roy Slade; It's a Mad Mad Mad Mad World; Love at First Bite; Maid to Order; Producers, The; Rented Lips; Secret Diary of Sigmund Freud, The; Young Warriors, The
Shawn, Michael: Midnight Kiss
Shawn, Wallace: Bostonians, The; Cemetery Club, The; Crackers; Critical Care; Curse of the Jade Scorpion, The; Double-O Kid, The; First Time, The; Heaven Help Us; House Arrest; Just Write; Micki & Maude; Moderns, The; Mom and Dad Save the World; My Dinner with Andre; Nice Girls Don't Explode; Nickel & Dime; Noah; Prick Up Your Ears; Prime Gig, The; Princess Bride, The; Scenes from the Class Struggle in Beverly Hills; Shadows and Fog; She's Out of Control; Vanya on 42nd Street; Vegas Vacation; We're No Angels; Wife, The
Shay, Dorothy: Comin' Round the Mountain
Shaya, Carol: Silent Prey
Shaye, Lin: Attention Shoppers
Shayne, Linda: Screwballs
Shayne, Robert: Dynamite Pass; Face of Marble, The; I, Mobster; King of the Carnival; Loaded Pistols; Marshal of Cedar Rock; Neanderthal Man, The; Rider from Tucson; Threat, The; War of the Satellites
She, Elizabeth: Howling, The: New Moon Rising
Shea, Eric: Castaway Cowboy, The
Shea, John: Adventures of Sebastian Cole, The; Backstreet Justice; Case of Deadly Force, A; Getting Personal; Honey, I Blew Up the Kid; Honeymoon; Hussy; Impossible Spy, The; Kennedy (TV Miniseries); Ladykiller; Missing; Nativity, The; New Life, A; Small Sacrifices; Stealing Home; Unsettled Land; Weekend in the Country, A; Windy City
Shea, Katt: Barbarian Queen; Preppies
Shea, Tom: Somewhere, Tomorrow
Shearer, Harry: Blood and Concrete, A Love Story; Godzilla (1998); Oscar (1991); Plain Clothes; Pure Luck; Return of Spinal Tap, The; Right Stuff, The; This Is Spinal Tap
Shearer, Moira: Black Tights; Peeping Tom; Red Shoes, The; Tales of Hoffman
Shearer, Norma: Barretts of Wimpole Street, The; Divorcee, The; Free Soul, A; He Who Gets Slapped; Idiot's Delight; Marie Antoinette; Private Lives; Riptide; Romeo and Juliet; Smilin' Through; Strange Interlude; Student Prince in Old Heidelberg, The; Women, The
Shearman, Alan: Bullshot (Bullshot Crummond)
Sheedy, Ally: Amnesia; Bad Boys; Betsy's Wedding; Blue City; Breakfast Club, The; Buried Alive II; Chantilly Lace; Fear; Fury Within, The; Haunting of Sea Cliff Inn, The; Heart of Dixie, The; High Art; Invader (1993); Lost Capone, The; Macon County Jail; Maid to Order; Man's Best Friend (1993); One Night Stand; Only the Lonely; Parallel Lives; St. Elmo's Fire; Short Circuit; Sugar Town; Tattle Tale; Tin Soldier, The; Twice in a Lifetime; Warden, The; Wargames; We Are the Children
Sheehan, Doug: FBI Murders, The
Sheeler, Todd: McCinsey's Island
Sheen, Charlie: Arrival, The; Being John Malkovich; Beyond the Law; Boys Next Door, The; Cadence; Chase, The; Courage Mountain; Deadfall; Eight Men Out; Ferris Bueller's Day Off; Free Money; Hot Shots; Hot Shots Part Deux; Lucas; Major League; Major League II; Men at Work; Money Talks; National Lampoon's Loaded Weapon 1; Navy Seals; No Code of Conduct; No Man's Land; Platoon; Rated X; Red Dawn; Rookie, The (1990); Shadow Conspiracy; Silence of the Heart; Terminal Velocity; Three for the Road; Three Musketeers, The; Under Pressure; Wall Street; Wraith, The; Young Guns
Sheen, Lucy: Ping Pong
Sheen, Martin: American President, The; Andersonville Trial, The; Apocalypse Now; Badlands (1973); Believers, The; Beverly

Hills Brats; Beyond the Stars; Boca; Born Wild; Break, The; Cadence; Captain Nuke and the Bomber Boys; Cassandra Crossing, The; Catholics; Cold Front; Consenting Adults; Conspiracy: The Trial of the Chicago 8; Da; Dead Zone, The; Dillinger & Capone; Eagle's Wing; Enigma; Entertaining Angels; Execution of Private Slovik, The; Final Countdown, The; Firestarter; Fourth Wise Man, The; Gandhi; Gettysburg; Ghost Brigade; Guardian, The; Gunfighter (1997); Hear No Evil; Hostile Waters; Incident, The; Judgment in Berlin; Kennedy (TV Miniseries); Little Girl Who Lives Down the Lane, The; Loophole; Maid, The; Man, Woman and Child; Missiles of October, The; Monument Ave.; News at Eleven; Nightbreaker; No Code of Conduct; No Drums, No Bugles; O; Original Intent; Out of the Darkness; Outer Limits, The (TV Series); Rage; Roswell; Sacred Cargo; Samaritan: The Mitch Snyder Story; Shattered Spirits; Siesta; Spawn; Storm Tracker; Stranger in the Kingdom, A; Subject Was Roses, The; Sweet Hostage; That Championship Season; Touch and Die; Trigger Fast; Wall Street; War at Home, The; When the Bough Breaks

Sheen, Michael: Gallowglass; Wilde

Sheen, Ramon: Man of Passion, A

Sheen, Ruth: High Hopes; Young Poisoner's Handbook, The

Sheer, William: Headin' Home; Regeneration

Sheffer, Craig: Baby Cakes; Bliss; Bloodknot; Blue Desert; Deep Core; Desperate Trail; Double Take; Executive Power; Eye of the Storm; Fire in the Sky; Fire with Fire; Flypaper; Grave, The; Hellraiser: Inferno; In Pursuit of Honor; Instant Karma; Maze; Miss Evers' Boys; Night Breed; Program, The; River Runs Through It, A; Road Killers, The; Sleep with Me; Some Kind of Wonderful; Split Decisions; That Was Then ... This Is Now; Turbulence 3: Heavy Metal; Turbulence 2

Sheffield, Johnny: Tarzan and the Leopard Woman; Tarzan Finds a Son; Tarzan Triumphs; Tarzan's New York Adventure; Tarzan's Secret Treasure

Sheffield, Reginald: Second Chance

Shegog, Clifford: Street Wars

Sheila E.: Krush Groove

Sheilds, Frank: Hoosier Schoolboy

Sheiner, David: Stone Killer, The

Shelby, LaRita: South Central

Sheldon, Barbara: Lucky Texan

Sheldon, Gene: Sign of Zorro, The; Toby Tyler

Shellen, Stephen: Casual Sex?; Damned River; Drop Dead Gorgeous; Lifeline; Luscious (1997); Luscious (1997); Model by Day; Modern Girls; River Runs Through It, A; Stand Off; Stepfather, The; Talking Walls

Shelley, Barbara: Blood of the Vampire; Cat Girl; Dracula—Prince of Darkness; Five Million Years to Earth; Gorgon, The; Rasputin: The Mad Monk; Village of the Damned

Shelley, Joshua: Front, The

Shelly, Adrienne: Big Girls Don't Cry—They Get Even; Grind; Hexed; Hold Me, Thrill Me, Kiss Me; Sleeping with Strangers; Teresa's Tattoo; Trust; Unbelievable Truth, The

Shelton, Deborah: Blind Vision; Body Double; Circuitry Man II: Plughead Rewired; Hunk; Nemesis; Silk Degrees

Shelton, John: Time of Their Lives, The

Shelton, Marley: Bubble Boy; Hercules in the Underworld; Lured Innocence; Sugar and Spice; Trojan War; Valentine; Warriors of Virtue

Shelton, Reid: First and Ten

Shenar, Paul: Bedroom Window, The; Best Seller; Brass; Deadly Force; Dream Lover; King Richard II; Raw Deal; Scarface

Sheng, Lei Lao: Story of Qiu Ju, The; Women from the Lake of the Scented Souls

Shenkman, Ben: Pi

Shentall, Susan: Romeo and Juliet

Shepard, Angela: Billy the Kid Meets the Vampires; Penpal Murders; Vampires from Outer Space

Shepard, Jewel: Caged Heat 2: Stripped of Freedom

Shepard, Patty: Blood Moon (Werewolf Versus the Vampire Woman, The); Man Called Noon, The; Rest in Pieces; Slugs, the Movie; Stranger and the Gunfighter, The

Shepard, Sam: Baby Boom; Black Hawk Down; Bright Angel; Country; Crimes of the Heart; Curtain Call; Days of Heaven; Defenseless; Fool for Love; Frances; Good Old Boys, The; Lily Dale; One Kill; Only Thrill, The; Pelican Brief, The; Purgatory; Raggedy Man; Resurrection; Right Stuff, The; Safe Passage; Shot in the Heart; Snow Falling on Cedars; Steel Magnolias; Streets of Laredo; Swordfish; Thunderheart; Voyager

Shephard, Hilary: Last Exit to Earth

Shephard, O-Lan: Out

Shepherd, Amanda: Hocus Pocus

Shepherd, Cybill: Alice; Chances Are; Daisy Miller; Guide for the Married Woman, A; Heartbreak Kid, The; Lady Vanishes, The; Last Picture Show, The; Last Word, The; Long Hot Summer, The; Married to It; Memphis; Moonlighting (1985) (TV Pilot); Muse, The; Once Upon a Crime; Return, The (1980); Secrets of a Married Man; Seduced; Silver Bears; Taxi Driver; Texasville; Which Way Home

Shepherd, Elizabeth: Invitation to the Wedding; Tomb of Ligeia

Shepherd, Jack: Twenty-One; Wonderland (1999)

Shepherd, Jean: Ollie Hopnoodle's Haven of Bliss

Shepherd, John: Friday the 13th, Part V—A New Beginning; Thunder Run

Shepherd, Morgan: Elvira, Mistress of the Dark; Max Headroom

Shepherd, Simon: Tales of Erotica

Sheppard, Delia: Animal Instincts; Homeboys II: Crack City

Sheppard, Patty: Crypt of the Living Dead

Sheppard, Paula E.: Alice, Sweet Alice (Communion, Holy Terror); Liquid Sky

Sheppard, W. Morgan: Escape, The

Sheppard, William: Treasure of Pirate's Point

Sher, Antony: Alive & Kicking; Erik the Viking; Genghis Cohn; Mrs. Brown; Shadey; Tartuffe; Young Poisoner's Handbook, The

Sherbedgia, Rade: Mission: Impossible 2; Snatch; South Pacific (2001)

Sheridan, Ann: Angels with Dirty Faces; Appointment in Honduras; Black Legion; City for Conquest; Dodge City; Doughgirls, The; Edge of Darkness; Fighting Westerner, The; George Washington Slept Here; Good Sam; I Was a Male War Bride; King's Row; Letter of Introduction; Man Who Came to Dinner, The; Mississippi; Murder at the Vanities; Opposite Sex, The (1956); Silver River; Stella; Thank Your Lucky Stars; They Drive by Night; They Made Me a Criminal

Sheridan, Dave: Scary Movie

Sheridan, Dinah: Genevieve; Railway Children, The

Sheridan, Gail: Hills of Old Wyoming; Hopalong Cassidy Returns

Sheridan, Jamey: All I Want for Christmas; Echo of Thunder, The; Life as a House; Lost Child, The; Stand, The; Stanley and Iris; Stranger Among Us, A; Talent for the Game; Whispers in the Dark; Wild America

Sheridan, Margaret: Thing (From Another World), The (1951)

Sheridan, Nicollette: Beverly Hills Ninja; Dead Husbands; Jackie Collins' Lucky Chances; Noises Off; Silver Strand; Spy Hard

Sheridan, Richard: Secret of Roan Inish, The

Sherman, Bobby: Get Crazy

Sherman, Ellen: Dr. Tarr's Torture Dungeon

Sherman, Kerry: Satan's Cheerleaders

Sherman, Lowell: Bachelor Apartment; Ladies of Leisure; Way Down East; What Price Hollywood?

Sherwood, David: Curse of the Crystal Eye

Sherwood, Madeleine: Broken Vows; Sweet Bird of Youth

Sherwood, Roberta: Courtship of Eddie's Father, The

Shetty, Shefali: Monsoon Wedding

Shevtsov, George: Love Serenade

Sheybal, Vladek: Wind and the Lion, The

Shi, Zhang: Temptress Moon

Shields, Aaron: Crude Oasis, The

Shields, Arthur: Daughter of Dr. Jekyll; Enchanted Island; King and Four Queens, The; Little Nellie Kelly; Quiet Man, The; River, The

Shields, Brooke: Alice, Sweet Alice (Communion, Holy Terror); Bachelor, The; Backstreet Dreams; Black and White (2000); Blue Lagoon, The; Born Wild; Brenda Starr; Diamond Trap, The; Endless Love; Freaked; Freeway; Just You and Me, Kid; King of the Gypsies; Muppets Take Manhattan, The; Pretty Baby; Sahara; Seventh Floor, The; Speed Zone; Tilt; Wanda Nevada; Wet Gold
Shields, Nicholas: Princes in Exile
Shields, Robert: Wild Wild West Revisited, The
Shiganoya, Benkei: Sisters of the Gion
Shigeta, James: Cage II: Arena of Death, The; China Cry; Die Hard; Flower Drum Song; Space Marines; Tomorrow's Child
Shih, Chang: Wooden Man's Bride, The
Shiina, Kippei: Gonin
Shilling, Marion: Common Law, The
Shiloh, Shmuel: Double Edge; Goodbye New York
Shimada, Shogo: Zatoichi: Masseur Ichi and a Chest ofGold
Shimada, Yoko: Hunted, The (1995); Shogun (Full-Length Version)
Shimizu, Jenny: Foxfire
Shimizu, Misa: Eel, The
Shimkus, Joanna: Six in Paris (Paris Vue par …); Virgin and the Gypsy, The
Shimono, Sab: Come See the Paradise; Shadow, The; Suture; Teenage Mutant Ninja Turtles III; Three Ninjas Kick Back
Shimura, Takashi: Bad Sleep Well, The; Drunken Angel; Godzilla, King of the Monsters; High and Low; Ikiru; No Regrets for Our Youth; Sanjuro; Sanshiro Sugata; Seven Samurai, The; Stray Dog; Throne of Blood
Shinas, Sofia: Hostile Intent; Hourglass
Shindô, Eitarô: Sisters of the Gion
Shiner, Ronald: Carry on Admiral
Shintaro, Katsu: Razor, The: Sword of Justice
Shipman, Gwynne: Trail Dust
Shipp, John Wesley: Flash, The (1990); NeverEnding Story II, The; Soft Deceit
Shirakawa, Yumi: H-Man, The
Shire, Talia: Bed and Breakfast; Blood Vows: The Story of a Mafia Wife; Chantilly Lace; Cold Heaven; Deadfall; Dunwich Horror, The; For Richer, for Poorer; Godfather, The; Godfather Epic, The; Godfather, Part II, The; Godfather, Part III, The; Landlady, The; Lured Innocence; New York Stories; Old Boyfriends; Prophecy (1979); Rad; Rocky; Rocky II; Rocky III; Rocky IV; Rocky V; Visit, The
Shirley, Aliesa: Sweet Sixteen
Shirley, Anne: Anne of Green Gables; Bombardier; Devil and Daniel Webster, The; Four Jacks and a Jill; Murder My Sweet; Stella Dallas
Shirt, J. C. White: Broken Chain, The
Shishido, Joe: 8Man
Shoaib, Samia: Pi
Shoemaker, Ann: House by the River
Shoemaker, Craig: Safe House
Shor, Dan: Mesmerized (Shocked); Strange Behavior; Strangers Kiss; Wise Blood
Shor, Miriam: Bedazzled; Hedwig and the Angry Inch
Shore, Dinah: Fun and Fancy Free; Up in Arms
Shore, Pauly: Bio-Dome; Bogus Witch Project, The; Curse of Inferno, The; Dream Date; Encino Man; In the Army Now; Jury Duty; Son-in-Law
Short, Antrum: Tom Sawyer
Short, Bobby: Blue Ice
Short, Dorothy: Reefer Madness; Trail of the Silver Spurs
Short, Kathryn: Goosebumps: The Haunted Mask
Short, Martin: Alice in Wonderland; Big Picture, The; Captain Ron; Clifford; Cross My Heart; Father of the Bride; Father of the Bride Part II; Get Over It; Innerspace; Jungle 2 Jungle; Mars Attacks!; Merlin (1998); Mumford; Pure Luck; Really Weird Tales; Simple Wish, A; Sunset Limousine; Three Amigos; Three Fugitives
Shortt, Pat: Closer You Get, The
Shou, Robin: Mortal Kombat; Mortal Kombat: Annihilation
Show, Grant: Texas; Treacherous Crossing; Woman, Her Men and Her Futon, A
Showalter, Max: Lord Love a Duck
Showalter, Michael: Wet Hot American Summer
Shower, Kathy: Commando Squad; Further Adventures of Tennessee Buck, The; L.A. Goddess; Out on Bail; Robo C.H.I.C.; Wild Cactus
Shrapnel, John: Body, The
Shriner, Kin: Crying Child, The; Cyberzone; Obsessive Love; Vendetta
Shriner, Wil: Time Trackers
Shrody, Eric: Big Bang Theory, The
Shropshire, Anne: Something to Talk About
Shubert, Nancy: Sagebrush Trail
Shue, Elisabeth: Adventures in Babysitting; Back to the Future II; Back to the Future III; Blind Justice; Call to Glory; Cocktail; Cousin Bette; Deconstructing Harry; Heart and Souls; Hollow Man; Karate Kid, The; Leaving Las Vegas; Link; Marrying Man, The; Molly; Palmetto; Radio Inside; Saint, The (1997); Soapdish; Trigger Effect, The; Twenty Bucks; Underneath, The
Shuford, Stephanie: Dreams Come True
Shull, Richard B.: Big Bus, The; Cockfighter; Fortune, The; Pack, The; Splash
Shum, Frankie: Crippled Masters, The
Shumaker, Helen: Haiku Tunnel
Shute, Anja: Tendres Cousines
Shutta, Ethel: Whoopee
Siani, Sabrina: Ator: The Fighting Eagle
Siao, Josephine: Legend, The
Sibbett, Jane: Arrival II, The; It Takes Two; Noah; Resurrected, The
Sibony, Clément: Deep in the Woods
Sicari, Joseph R.: Night School
Sidahl, Viveka: House of Angels
Siddig, Alexander: Vertical Limit
Sidney, Sylvia: Blood on the Sun; Come Along with Me; Corrupt; Damien: Omen II; Dead End; Death at Love House; Demon (God Told Me To); Early Frost, An; Finnegan Begin Again; Fury (1936); Having It All; Love from a Stranger; Mr. Ace; Pals; Sabotage; Shadow Box, The; Small Killing, A; Snowbeast; Street Scene; Summer Wishes, Winter Dreams; Trail of the Lonesome Pine, The; Used People; Wagons Roll at Night, The; You Only Live Once
Sieber, Maria: Scarlet Empress, The
Siebert, Charles: Blue Sunshine; Cry for Love, A; Incredible Hulk, The; Miracle Worker, The
Siemaszko, Casey: Amazing Stories (TV Series); Big Slice, The; Biloxi Blues; Breaking In; Crew, The; Limbo; Miracle of the Heart; Near Misses; Of Mice and Men; Rose Hill; Teresa's Tattoo; Three O'Clock High; Young Guns
Siemaszko, Nina: Power of Attorney; Saint of Fort Washington, The; Sawbones; Wild Orchid 2: Two Shades of Blue
Sierra, Gregory: Clones, The; Code Name: Dancer; Deep Cover; Gambler, Part II—The Adventure Continues, The; Low Down Dirty Shame, A; Miami Vice; Unspeakable Acts; Wonderful Ice Cream Suit, The
Siewkumar, Asha: Tropical Heat
Siffredi, Rocco: Romance
Sigel, Beanie: State Property
Sigler, Jamie Lynn: Sopranos, The (TV series)
Signorelli, Tom: Alice, Sweet Alice (Communion, Holy Terror); Crossover Dreams
Signoret, Simone: Cat, The (1971) (Le Chat); Day and the Hour; Death in the Garden; Dedee D'Anvers; Diabolique; I Sent a Letter to My Love; Is Paris Burning?; La Ronde; Madame Rosa; Room at the Top; Ship of Fools; Sleeping Car Murders, The; Widow Couderc
Sihol, Caroline: Tous les Matins du Monde
Sikes, Brenda: Cleopatra Jones; Mandingo
Sikes, Cynthia: Arthur 2: On the Rocks; Love Hurts; Oceans of Fire; Possums; St. Elsewhere (TV Series)
Sikharulidze, Jemal: Prisoner of the Mountains
Sikking, James B.: Dead Badge; Final Approach; Hill Street Blues (TV Series); In Pursuit of Honor; Man on a String; Morons from Outer Space; Narrow Margin (1990); Ollie Hopnoodle's

Haven of Bliss; Ordinary People; Pelican Brief, The; Soul Man; Tyson; Up the Creek
Silbar, Adam: Hot Moves
Silberg, Joshua: Ebenezer
Sillas, Karen: Beast, The; Female Perversions; Flirt; Reach the Rock; Simple Men; What Happened Was ...
Sills, Milton: Miss Lulu Bett
Silva, Henry: Above the Law; Allan Quartermain and the Lost City of Gold; Alligator; Bravados, The; Buck Rogers in the 25th Century; Bulletproof; Code of Silence; Day of the Assassin; Ghost Dog: The Way of the Samurai; Green Mansions; Harvest, The (1992); Jayhawkers, The; Law and Jake Wade, The; Love and Bullets; Lust in the Dust; Man and Boy; Manhunt (1973) (The Italian Connection); Megaforce; Never a Dull Moment; Possessed by the Night; Shoot; Tall T, The; Thirst; Three Days to a Kill; Violent Breed, The; Virus; Wrong Is Right
Silva, Trinidad: Night Before, The
Silvain, Eugene: Passion of Joan of Arc, The
Silveira, Lenor: Convent, The
Silver, Joe: Gig, The; Rabid; Switching Channels; They Came from Within; You Light Up My Life
Silver, Ron: Ali; Arrival, The; Beneficiary, The; Best Friends; Betrayal; Billionaire Boys Club; Black & White (1998); Blind Side; Blue Steel; Cutaway; Danger Zone; Deadly Outbreak; Dear Detective; Eat and Run; Enemies—A Love Story; Entity, The; Father's Revenge, A; Fellow Traveler; Forgotten Prisoners; Garbo Talks; Goodbye People, The; In the Company of Spies; Kissinger and Nixon; Lifepod; Live Wire; Married to It; Mr. Saturday Night; Oh, God, You Devil!; Reversal of Fortune; Shadow Zone: The Undead Express; Silent Rage; Skeletons; Timecop; Woman of Independent Means, A
Silvera, Frank: Appaloosa, The; Killer's Kiss; Miracle of Our Lady of Fatima, The; St. Valentine's Day Massacre, The; Stalking Moon, The; Valdez Is Coming
Silverheels, Jay: Broken Arrow; Lone Ranger, The; Lone Ranger, The (TV Series); Lone Ranger and the Lost City of Gold, The; Santee; War Arrow
Silverman, Jonathan: Age Isn't Everything; At First Sight; Breaking the Rules; Brighton Beach Memoirs; Caddyshack II; Challenge of a Lifetime; Class Action; For Richer, for Poorer; Freak City; French Exit; Girls Just Want to Have Fun; Inspectors, The; Little Big League; Little Sister; Odd Couple II, The; Sketch Artist II: Hands That See; Something About Sex; Stealing Home; Teresa's Tattoo; Traveling Man; 12:01; Weekend at Bernie's; Weekend at Bernie's II
Silvers, Phil: All Through the Night; Boatniks, The; Buona Sera, Mrs. Campbell; Cheap Detective, The; Chicken Chronicles, The; Cover Girl; Follow That Camel; Footlight Serenade; Forty Pounds of Trouble; Four Jills in a Jeep; Funny Thing Happened on the Way to the Forum, A; Guide for the Married Man, A; Happy Hooker Goes Hollywood, The; Hey Abbott!; It's a Mad Mad Mad Mad World; Lady Be Good; Lady Takes a Chance, A; Lucky Me; Roxie Hart; Sgt. Bilko (TV Series); Summer Stock; Tom, Dick and Harry
Silverston, Ben: Browning Version, The
Silverstone, Alicia: Babysitter, The; Batman & Robin; Blast from the Past; Clueless; Crush, The (1993); Excess Baggage; Hideaway; Love's Labour's Lost; True Crime
Silverstone, Ben: Get Real
Silvestre, Armand: Rock 'n' Roll Wrestling Women vs. the Aztec Mummy
Sim, Alastair: Belles of St. Trinian's, The; Blue Murder at St. Trinian's; Christmas Carol, A; Green for Danger; Littlest Horse Thieves, The; Ruling Class, The; School for Scoundrels; Stage Fright
Sim, Gerald: Dr. Jekyll and Sister Hyde; Long Ago Tomorrow
Sim, Sheila: Great Day
Simcoe, Anthony: Castle, The; Farscape (TV series)
Simm, John: Boston Kickout; Human Traffic
Simmons, Anthony: Sherlock: Undercover Dog
Simmons, Beverly: Buck Privates Come Home
Simmons, Gene: Kiss Meets the Phantom of the Park; Red Surf; Runaway; Trick or Treat; Wanted: Dead or Alive
Simmons, J. K.: Mexican, The; Spider-Man
Simmons, Jaason: Frankenstein Reborn!
Simmons, Jean: Adam and Evalyn; Androcles and the Lion; Big Country, The; Black Narcissus; Clouded Yellow, The; Dain Curse, The; Daisies in December; Dawning, The; Desirée; Divorce American Style; Dominique Is Dead; Egyptian, The; Elmer Gantry; Going Undercover; Grass Is Greener, The; Great Expectations; Great Expectations; Guys and Dolls; Hamlet; How to Make an American Quilt; Hungry Hill; Mr. Sycamore; Robe, The; Rough Night in Jericho; She Couldn't Say No; Small Killing, A; Spartacus; They Do It with Mirrors; This Could Be the Night; Thornbirds, The; Trio; Until They Sail; Young Bess
Simmons, Shadia: Color of Friendship, The
Simmrin, Joey: Midas Touch, The; Star Kid
Simms, Ginny: Broadway Rhythm
Simms, Hilda: Joe Louis Story, The
Simms, Larry: Blondie; Blondie Has Servant Trouble; Blondie Hits the Jackpot; Blondie in Society; Blondie Knows Best
Simms, Michael: Scarecrows
Simms, Mike: Bus Is Coming, The
Simon, François: Basileus Quartet; Christ Stopped at Eboli; Lumiere
Simon, Luc: Lancelot of the Lake
Simon, Michel: Bizarre, Bizarre; Boudu Saved from Drowning; Candide; Circonstances Attenuantes; Head, The (1959); La Chienne; Panique; Train, The; Two of Us, The
Simon, Paul: Annie Hall; One Trick Pony; Rutles, The (All You Need Is Cash)
Simon, Robert F.: Benny Goodman Story, The; Chinese Web, The; Nine Lives of Elfego Baca, The
Simon, Simone: Cat People; Curse of the Cat People, The; Devil and Daniel Webster, The; La Bête Humaine; La Ronde; Le Plaisir; Mademoiselle Fifi
Simon, Tania: Women from Down Under
Simonnett, Michelle: Bernadette
Simons, Frank: Blue Yonder, The
Simonsen, Lars: Twist and Shout
Simonson, Renée: Nothing Underneath
Simpson, Anna: Our Song
Simpson, Jimmi: Loser
Simpson, Monica: Concealed Weapon
Simpson, O. J.: Capricorn One; CIA Codename Alexa; Firepower; Hambone and Hillie; Killer Force; Klansman, The; Naked Gun, The; Naked Gun 33 1/3, The—The Final Insult; Naked Gun 2 1/2, The; No Place to Hide
Simpson, Raeanin: Little Heroes
Simpson, Ronald: Song of Freedom
Simpson, Russell: Border Patrol; Cabin in the Cotton; Grapes of Wrath, The; Human Hearts; Ma and Pa Kettle at the Fair; Spoilers, The; Virginia City; Virginian, The
Simpson, Sandy: Glory Years
Simpson, Terry: Deadline
Simpson, Tina May: Final Equinox
Sims, Aaron: Adventures of the Kung Fu Rascals, The
Sims, George: High Country, The
Sims, Jackson: Kill-Off, The
Sims, Joan: Carry on at Your Convenience; Carry on Behind; Carry on Cleo; Carry on Cowboy; Carry on Doctor; Carry on Emmanuelle; Follow That Camel; Last of the Blonde Bombshells, The; Love Among the Ruins; Murder Is Announced, A
Sinatra, Frank: Anchors Aweigh; Assault on a Queen; Can-Can; Cannonball Run II; Come Blow Your Horn; Detective, The; Devil at 4 O'Clock, The; Double Dynamite; First Deadly Sin, The; Four for Texas; From Here to Eternity; Guys and Dolls; High Society; Higher and Higher; Hole in the Head, A; It Happened in Brooklyn; Kings Go Forth; Kissing Bandit, The; Lady in Cement; Man with the Golden Arm, The; Manchurian Candidate, The; Meet Danny Wilson; Miracle of the Bells, The; Never So Few; None But the Brave; Not as a Stranger; Ocean's Eleven; On the Town; Pal Joey; Pride and the Passion, The; Robin & the Seven Hoods; Ship Ahoy; Some Came Running; Step Lively; Suddenly; Take Me Out to the Ball Game; Tender Trap, The; That's Entertainment; Tony Rome; Von Ryan's Express; Young at Heart
Sinatra, Nancy: Speedway; Wild Angels, The
Sinatra Jr., Frank: Man Called Adam, A

Sinbad: Cherokee Kid, The; Coneheads; First Kid; George of the Jungle; Good Burger; Houseguest; Jingle All the Way; Meteor Man; Necessary Roughness
Sinclair, Gordon John: Girl in the Picture, The; Gregory's Girl; That Sinking Feeling
Sinclair, Hugh: Circle of Danger; Corridor of Mirrors; Saint's Vacation, The
Sinclair, Kristian: Countryman
Sinclair, Madge: Almos' a Man; Coming to America; Conrack; Convoy; Cornbread, Earl and Me
Sinden, Donald: Captain's Table; Cruel Sea, The; Doctor in the House; Island at the Top of the World, The
Singer, Linda: Zombie Nightmare
Singer, Lori: Falcon and the Snowman, The; Footloose; Last Ride, The; Made in USA; Man with One Red Shoe, The; Short Cuts; Storm and Sorrow; Summer Heat; Sunset Grill; Trouble in Mind; Warlock
Singer, Marc: Beastmaster, The; Beastmaster 2: Through the Portal of Time; Beastmaster III: The Eye of Braxus; Berlin Conspiracy, The; Cyberzone; Dead Space; Deadly Game; Go Tell the Spartans; High Desert Kill; If You Could See What I Hear; Man Called Sarge, A; Savate; Sea Wolf, The; Silk Degrees; Sweet Justice; Two Worlds of Jennie Logan, The; Ultimate Desires; V; Watchers II
Singer, Ritchie: Encounter at Raven's Gate
Singer, Susie: Landlady, The
Singh, Greishma Makar: Little Buddha
Singhammer, Eva Maria: Heidi
Singleton, Penny: Blondie; Blondie Has Servant Trouble; Blondie Hits the Jackpot; Blondie in Society; Blondie Knows Best; Blondie Takes a Vacation; Blondie's Blessed Event; Boy Meets Girl; It's a Great Life
Singleton, Sam: Death of a Prophet
Sinise, Gary: Albino Alligator; Apollo 13; Forrest Gump; George Wallace; Impostor; Jack the Bear; Midnight Clear, A; Mission to Mars; My Name Is Bill W; Of Mice and Men; Ransom; Reindeer Games; Snake Eyes; Stand, The; That Championship Season; True West; Truman
Sinniger, Christina: Evil Within, The
Sirico, Tony: New York Cop; Sopranos, The (TV series)
Sirola, Joseph: Love Is a Gun
Sirtis, Marina: Journey's End: The Saga of Star Trek:The Next Generation; Star Trek: First Contact; Star Trek: Generations; Star Trek: The Next Generation (TV Series)
Sisero, Greg: Retro Puppetmaster
Sisk, Kathleen: Girl Who Spelled Freedom, The
Siskova, Anna: Divided We Fall
Sisqo: Get Over It
Sistillio, Troy: Raising Heroes
Sisto, Jeremy: Crew, The; Hideaway; Suicide Kings; White Squall
Sisto, Rocco: American Astronaut, The
Sisupal, Sonu: Terrorist, The
Sivero, Frank: Cop and a Half
Sizemore, Tom: American Story, An; Bad Love; Big Trouble (2002); Black Hawk Down; Bringing Out the Dead; Devil in a Blue Dress; Florentine, The; Heart and Souls; Heat; Match, The; Matter of Degrees, A; Passenger 57; Play It to the Bone; Red Planet; Relic, The; Saving Private Ryan; Strange Days; Striking Distance; Ticker; True Romance; Watch It; Where Sleeping Dogs Lie; Witness Protection; Wyatt Earp
Sjoman, Vilgot: I Am Curious Blue
Sjöström, Victor: Outlaw and His Wife, The; Phantom Chariot; Thomas Graal's Best Child; Thomas Graal's Best Film; Walpurgis Night; Wild Strawberries
Skaggs, Jimmie F.: Lost Capone, The
Skala, Lilia: Charly; Deadly Hero; Flashdance; Heartland; House of Games; Lilies of the Field; Men of Respect; Probe; Roseland; Ship of Fools
Skarsgard, Stellan: Amistad; Breaking the Waves; Deep Blue Sea; Glass House, The (2001); Good Evening Mr. Wallenberg; Good Will Hunting; Harlan County War; Insomnia; My Son the Fanatic; Noon Wine; Passion of Mind; Ronin; Savior; Slingshot, The; Timecode; Wind (1992); Women on the Roof, The; Zero Kelvin
Skarvellis, Jackie: Rats are Coming! The Werewolves Are Here!, The
Skelton, Red: Bathing Beauty; Clown, The; Du Barry Was a Lady; Fuller Brush Man, The; Having a Wonderful Time; I Dood It; Lady Be Good; Lovely to Look At; Merton of the Movies; Neptune's Daughter; Panama Hattie; Ship Ahoy; Show-Off, The; Southern Yankee, A; Texas Carnival; Thousands Cheer; Three Little Words; Watch the Birdie; Whistling in Brooklyn; Whistling in Dixie; Whistling in the Dark; Yellow Cab Man, The; Ziegfeld Follies
Skerla, Lena: Fire Within, The
Skerritt, Tom: Alien; Big Bad Mama; Big Man on Campus; Big Town, The; Child in the Night; China Lake Murders, The; Contact; Dangerous Summer, A; Dead Zone, The; Devil's Rain, The; Divided by Hate; Fighting Back; Fuzz; Heist, The; High Noon; Hitchhiker, The (Series); Ice Castles; Knight Moves; Maid to Order; M*A*S*H; Miles to Go; Nightmare at Bittercreek; Opposing Force; Poison Ivy; Poker Alice; Poltergeist III; Red King, White Knight; River Runs Through It, A; Rookie, The (1990); Silence of the North; SpaceCamp; Steel Magnolias; Texas Rangers (2001); Thieves Like Us; Top Gun; Turning Point, The; Up in Smoke; What the Deaf Man Heard; Wild Orchid 2: Two Shades of Blue; Wild Rovers, The; Wisdom
Skinner, Anita: Girlfriends; Sole Survivor
Skinner, Cornelia Otis: Uninvited, The
Skinner, Keith: Mademoiselle
Skipper, Pat: Dancing with Danger
Skipworth, Alison: Becky Sharp; Dangerous (1935); Doubting Thomas; If I Had a Million; Night after Night; Princess Comes Across, The; Satan Met a Lady
Skjonberg, Espen: One Day in the Life of Ivan Denisovich
Skoliar, Igor: Jazzman
Skolimowski, Jerzy: Big Shots; Circle of Deceit; White Nights
Skomarovsky, Vladimir: Black Eagle
Skvorecky, Josef: Report on the Party and the Guests, A
Skye, Ione: Carmilla; Gas, Food, Lodging; Girls in Prison; Guncrazy (1950); Mindwalk; Night in the Life of Jimmy Reardon, A; Rachel Papers; River's Edge; Samantha; Say Anything; Stranded
Skyler, Tristene: Book of Shadows: Blair Witch 2
Slabolepszy, Paul: Saturday Night at the Palace
Slade, Max Elliott: Three Ninjas; Three Ninjas Kick Back; Three Ninjas Knuckle Up
Sladen, Elizabeth: Dr. Who: Revenge of the Cybermen; Gulliver in Lilliput
Slaska, Aleksandra: Passenger, The
Slate, Jeremy: Born Losers; Centerfold Girls; Dead Pit, The; Dream Machine; Girls! Girls! Girls!; Hell's Angels '69; Mr. Horn; Sons of Katie Elder, The; Summer of Fear
Slater, Christian: Basil; Bed of Roses; Beyond the Stars; Broken Arrow; Contender, The; Gleaming the Cube; Hard Rain; Heathers; Interview with the Vampire; Jimmy Hollywood; Julian Po; Kuffs; Legend of Billie Jean, The; Mobsters; Murder in the First; Name of the Rose, The; Pump Up the Volume; Robin Hood: Prince of Thieves; Tales from the Darkside, The Movie; 3,000 Miles to Graceland; True Romance; Tucker: A Man and His Dream; Twisted; Untamed Heart; Very Bad Things; Where the Day Takes You; Wizard, The; Young Guns II
Slater, Helen: Betrayal of the Dove; Chantilly Lace; City Slickers; Happy Together; House in the Hills, A; Lassie; Legend of Billie Jean, The; No Way Back; Parallel Lives; Ruthless People; Secret of My Success, The; Sticky Fingers; Supergirl; 12:01
Slater, Justine: Bar Girls
Slater, Ryan: Amazing Panda Adventure, The
Slater, Suzanne: Mindtwister
Slattery, John: Cash Crop; Lily Dale
Slattery, Tony: Heaven's a Drag; Peter's Friends
Slaughter, Sgt.: Bad Guys
Slaughter, Tod: Crimes at the Dark House; Crimes of Stephen Hawke, The; Demon Barber of Fleet Street, The; Face at the Window, The; Never Too Late; Sexton Blake and the Hooded Terror; Ticket of Leave Man, The

ello; Prime of Miss Jean Brodie, The; Private Function, A; Quartet; Richard III; Room with a View, A; Secret Garden, The; Sister Act; Sister Act 2: Back in the Habit; Tea with Mussolini; Travels with My Aunt; V.I.P.s, The; Washington Square
Smith, Mel: Brain Donors; Misadventures of Mr. Wilt, The; Morons from Outer Space; Twelfth Night
Smith, Melanie: Night Hunter; Trancers III: Deth Lives
Smith, Mittie: Blue Yonder, The
Smith, Pam: Misty
Smith, Patricia: Spirit of St. Louis, The
Smith, Paul: Death Chase; Desert Kickboxer; Gor; Haunted Honeymoon; Jungle Warriors; Madron; Outlaw Force; Popeye; Red Sonja; Sadat; Salamander, The; Sno-Line; Sonny Boy; Terminal Entry; We Are No Angels
Smith, Queenie: Mississippi; My Sister Eileen
Smith, Rainbeaux: Slumber Party 57
Smith, Ray: King Lear
Smith, Rex: Danielle Steel's Once in a Lifetime; Passion to Kill, A; Pirates of Penzance, The; Snow White and the Seven Dwarfs; Sooner or Later; Streethawk; Transformations; Trial of the Incredible Hulk
Smith, Robert: Call Out the Marines
Smith, Roger: Never Steal Anything Small
Smith, Roger Guenveur: Color of Courage, The; Facade
Smith, Sammy: How to Succeed in Business without Really Trying
Smith, Shawn: Land Unknown, The; World Without End
Smith, Shawnee: Blob, The; Desperate Hours (1990); Summer School
Smith, Sheila: Taking My Turn
Smith, Shelley: Scruples
Smith, Sinjin: Side Out
Smith, Stephanie: Kiss the Girls Goodbye
Smith, Stephanie Ann: Under Lock and Key
Smith, T. Ryder: Brainscan
Smith, Ted: Adventures of the Kung Fu Rascals, The
Smith, Terri Susan: Basket Case
Smith, Will: Ali; Bad Boys; Enemy of the State; Independence Day; Legend of Bagger Vance, The; Made in America; Men in Black; Six Degrees of Separation; Wild Wild West (1999)
Smith, William: Angels Die Hard; Any Which Way You Can; B.O.R.N.; Boss; C.C. & Company; Commando Squad; Deadly Trackers, The; Fever Pitch; Frisco Kid, The; Gentle Savage; Grave of the Vampire; Invasion of the Bee Girls; L.A. Vice; Last American Hero, The; Losers, The; Maniac Cop; Platoon Leader; Red Dawn; Red Nights; Rockford Files, The (TV Series); Scorchy; Spirit of the Eagle; Twilight's Last Gleaming; Ultimate Warrior, The
Smith, Willie E.: Legend of Boggy Creek
Smith, Willie Mae Ford: Say Amen, Somebody
Smith, Yeardley: Ginger Ale Afternoon; Just Write; Maximum Overdrive
Smith-Cameron, J.: Gal Young 'Un; Harriet the Spy; Rage, The: Carrie 2
Smithers, Jan: Where the Lilies Bloom
Smitrovich, Bill: Futuresport; Killing Affair, A; Miami Vice; Millennium
Smits, Jimmy: Believers, The; Bless the Child; Cisco Kid, The; Fires Within; Glitz; L.A. Law; Last Word, The; Marshal Law; Million Dollar Hotel; Murder in Mind; My Family; Old Gringo, The; Price of Glory; Running Scared; Solomon and Sheba; Star Wars: Attack of the Clones; Switch; Tommyknockers, The; Vital Signs
Smits, Sonja: Dead Husbands; Spenser: Pale Kings & Princes; That's My Baby; Videodrome
Smokey Robinson and the Miracles: That Was Rock
Smollett, Jurnee: Eve's Bayou; Selma Lord Selma
Smoove, J. B.: Pootie Tang
Smothers, Dick: Alice Through the Looking Glass; Tales of the Unexpected; Yo-Yo Man
Smothers, Tom: Alice Through the Looking Glass; Get to Know Your Rabbit; Kids Are Alright, The; Pandemonium; Serial; Silver Bears; Speed Zone; Yo-Yo Man
Smurfit, Victoria: Ivanhoe; Run of the Country, The
Snaider, Meredith: Habit
Snape, William: Full Monty, The
Sneider, Eric: Captains Courageous
Snider, Dee: Dee Snider's Strangeland
Snipes, Wesley: America's Dream; Art of War, The; Blade; Blade II; Boiling Point; Demolition Man; Down in the Delta; Drop Zone; Fan, The; Futuresport; Jungle Fever; King of New York; Mo' Better Blues; Money Train; Murder at 1600; New Jack City; One Night Stand; Passenger 57; Rising Sun; Streets of Gold; Sugar Hill; To Wong Foo, Thanks for Everything, Julie Newmar; U.S. Marshals; Waterdance, The; White Men Can't Jump
Snodgress, Carrie: Across the Tracks; Attic, The; Ballad of Little Jo, The; Blueberry Hill; Death Benefit; Diary of a Mad Housewife; Ed Gein; 8 Seconds; Forsaken, The; Mission of the Shark; Murphy's Law; Night in Heaven, A; Pale Rider; Rabbit Run; Rose and the Jackal, The; Silent Night, Lonely Night; Stranger in the Kingdom, A; Trick or Treat; Wild Things; Woman with a Past
Snoop Dog: Wrecking Crew, The
Snow, Victoria: Kissing Place, The
Snowden, Jane: French Lessons
Snowden, Leigh: Creature Walks Among Us, The
Snowflake: Lawless Nineties, The; Lonely Trail, The
Snyder, Arlen Dean: Dear Detective; No Man's Land; Scalpel; Summer Dreams; Wheels of Terror
Snyder, Deb: Pushing Hands
Snyder, Drew: Blindfold: Acts of Obsession; Dance with Death; Night School; Project: Eliminator
Snyder, Maria: Prophecy, The (1995)
Snyder, Nancy: Plants Are Watching, The
Snyder, Suzanne: Killer Klowns from Outer Space
Snyder, Valerie Sedle: Merry Wives of Windsor, The
Sobel, David: Wish Me Luck
Sobieski, Leelee: Eyes Wide Shut; Glass House, The (2001); Here on Earth; Horse for Danny, A; Joan of Arc (1999); Joy Ride; My First Mister; Never Been Kissed; Soldier's Daughter Never Cries, A
Socas, Maria: Warrior and the Sorceress, The
Soderbergh, Steven: Schizopolis
Soderdahl, Lars: Brothers Lionheart, The
Soeberg, Camilla: Erotique; Manifesto
Sofaer, Abraham: Captain Sinbad; Elephant Walk; His Majesty O'Keefe; Journey to the Center of Time (Time Warp); Naked Jungle, The; Quo Vadis (1951)
Sofer, Rena: Stepsister, The; Twin Sitters
Softley, Ellen: I, Zombie
Sohn, Sonja: Slam
Sojin: Thief of Bagdad, The
Sokol, Marilyn: Foul Play; Something Short of Paradise
Sokoloff, Marla: Dude, Where's My Car?; Sugar and Spice; Whatever It Takes
Sokoloff, Vladimir: Baron of Arizona, The
Sola, Miguel Angel: Tango
Solanitsin, Anatoly: Stalker
Solar, Silvia: Finger on the Trigger
Solari, Chris: Crocodile
Solari, Rudy: Boss' Son, The
Solari, Suzanne: Rollerblade
Soler, Andres: El Bruto (The Brute)
Soler, Fernando: Great Madcap, The; Susanna
Soles, P. J.: Alienator; B.O.R.N.; Halloween; Little Bigfoot; Power Within, The; Rock 'n' Roll High School; Saigon Commandos; Stripes; Uncle Sam
Solli, Sergio: Ciao Professore
Solntseva, Yulia: Aelita: Queen of Mars; Cigarette Girl from Mosselprom, The
Sologne, Madeleine: Eternal Return, The
Solomin, Vitaly: Siberiade
Solomin, Yuri: Dersu Uzala
Solomon, Charles: Witchcraft II: The Temptress; Witchcraft III, The Kiss of Death; Witchcraft IV
Solomon, James: Song of Freedom
Solondz, Todd: Fear, Anxiety and Depression

The; Good Morning, Babylon; Indian Summer; Maria's Lovers; Oscar (1991); Prophecy 3: The Ascent; Rumble Fish; Texas Rangers (2001); Tie That Binds, The
Sparks, Ned: Blessed Event; Bride Walks Out, The; Going Hollywood; Magic Town; One in a Million; Sweet Adeline
Sparks, Omillio: State Property
Sparrowhawk, Leo: Out on Bail
Sparv, Camilla: Dead Heat on a Merry-Go-Round; Downhill Racer; Greek Tycoon, The; Survival Zone
Spaulding, Tracy: Striking Point
Speakman, Jeff: Deadly Outbreak; Escape from Atlantis; Expert, The; Perfect Weapon; Scorpio One; Street Knight
Spears, Aries: Out of Sync
Spears, Britney: Crossroads (2002)
Speciale, Linda: Screwballs
Speck, David: Client, The
Speckhahn, Holger: Anatomy
Spector, Daniel: Running Wild
Speedman, Scott: Duets
Speer, Hugo: Full Monty, The; Mainline Run; Swing
Speir, Dona: Fit to Kill; Hard Ticket to Hawaii; Savage Beach
Spell, George: Dream for Christmas, A; Man and Boy
Spelling, Tori: House of Yes, The; Scary Movie 2; Trick
Spelvin, Georgina: I Spit on Your Corpse
Spence, Bruce: … Almost; Mad Max Beyond Thunderdome; Rikki and Pete; Road Warrior, The; Where the Green Ants Dream
Spence, Sebastian: Boys of St. Vincent
Spencer, Bud: Ace High; Aladdin; Beyond the Law; Boot Hill; Massacre at Fort Holman (Reason to Live … A Reason to Die, A); Miami Supercops; Saddle Tramps; They Call Me Trinity; Trinity Is Still My Name; Troublemakers
Spencer, Chris: Don't Be a Menace to South Central while Drinking Your Juice in the 'Hood
Spencer, Danielle: Crossing, The
Spencer, Jeremy: Prince and the Showgirl, The
Spencer, John: Albino Alligator; Cafe Society; Cold Around the Heart; Negotiator, The; Presumed Innocent; Rock, The
Spencer, Marv: Killing Edge, The
Spengler, Volker: In a Year of 13 Moons; Satan's Brew
Sperandeo, Tony: La Scorta
Sperber, Wendie Jo: Bosom Buddies (TV Series); First Time, The; I Wanna Hold Your Hand; Moving Violations; Mr. Write
Sperberg, Fritz: Lucky Luke
Sperry, Corwyn: Sudden Thunder
Spice Girls: Spice World
Spicer, Jerry: Witchcraft VI: The Devil's Mistress
Spiegel, Scott: Dead Next Door, The; Robot Ninja; Skinned Alive
Spielberg, David: Effect of Gamma Rays on Man-in-the-Moon Marigolds, The; Silent Predators
Spielberg, Steven: Survivors of the Holocaust
Spiers, Stephen: Musketeer, The
Spiesser, Jacques: Baxter; Black and White in Color; La Truite (The Trout)
Spill, Stormy: Baxter; Black and White in Color; La Truite (The Trout)
Spillane, Mickey: Girl Hunters, The
Spilsbury, Klinton: Legend of the Lone Ranger, The
Spindler, Will: Last Five Days, The
Spinell, Joe: Big Score, The; Hollywood Harry; Last Horror Film, The; Maniac; Ninth Configuration, The; Operation War Zone; Star Crash; Strike Force; Vigilante
Spinella, Stephen: Love! Valour! Compassion!; Virtuosity
Spiner, Brent: Independence Day; Introducing Dorothy Dandridge; Out to Sea; Phenomenon; Pie in the Sky; Star Trek: First Contact; Star Trek: Generations; Star Trek: Insurrection; Star Trek: The Next Generation (TV Series)
Spinetti, Victor: Hard Day's Night, A; Help!
Spitz, Mark: Challenge of a Lifetime
Spolt, William: Rattler Kid
Spoonauer, Lisa: Clerks
Spottiswood, Greg: Looking for Miracles
Spradlin, G. D.: And I Alone Survived; Ed Wood; Formula, The; Long Kiss Goodnight, The; Lords of Discipline, The; North Dallas Forty; One on One; Riders of the Purple Sage; Tank; War of the Roses, The; Wrong Is Right
Spradling, Charlie: Angel of Destruction; Puppet Master II; To Sleep With a Vampire
Spriggs, Elizabeth: Sense and Sensibility; Those Glory Glory Days
Spring, Helen: Hazel Christmas Show, The (TV Series)
Springer, Gary: Bernice Bobs Her Hair
Springer, Jerry: Ringmaster; Since You've Been Gone
Springfield, Rick: Dead Reckoning; Hard to Hold; Nick Knight; Silent Motive
Springsteen, Pamela: Sleepaway Camp II: Unhappy Campers; Sleepaway Camp III
Sprinkle, Annie: My Father Is Coming
Sprouse, Cole: Big Daddy
Sprouse, Dylan: Big Daddy
Spybey, Dina: Julian Po; SubUrbia
Squire, Ronald: Encore
Squire, Sean: Passing Glory
Sridevi: God Is My Witness
St. Alban, Nancy: Durango
St. Claire, Taylore: Virtual Encounters
St. Cyr, Lili: I, Mobster
St. Gerard, Michael: Replikator: Cloned to Kill
St. Jacques, Raymond: Cotton Comes to Harlem; Final Comedown, The; Green Berets, The; Kill Castro (Cuba Crossing, Mercenaries , Sweet Violent Tony); Search for the Gods; Sophisticated Gents, The; Voodoo Dawn; Wild Pair, The
St. John, Al: Buster and Fatty; Charlie Chaplin … Our Hero; Cheyenne Takes Over; Death Rides the Plains; Hell Harbor; His Brother's Ghost; His Private Secretary; Keystone Comedies: Vol. 1–5; King of the Bullwhip; Lawman Is Born, A; Li'l Abner; Prairie Rustlers; Riders of Destiny; Sing, Cowboy, Sing; Stage to Mesa City
St. John, Betta: All the Brothers Were Valiant; Corridors of Blood; Horror Hotel
St. John, Howard: Born Yesterday; Don't Drink the Water; Li'l Abner
St. John, Jill: Act, The; Come Blow Your Horn; Concrete Jungle, The (1982); Diamonds Are Forever; Out There; Roman Spring of Mrs. Stone, The; Tony Rome
St. John, Michelle: Where the Spirit Lives
St. Louis, Dean: Coroner, The
St. Onge, Guylaine: Fatal Combat
St. Paule, Irma: Desecration
Stabile, Nick: Bride of Chucky
Stack, Don: Santa with Muscles
Stack, Joanna Leigh: Paradise Motel
Stack, Robert: Airplane!; Big Trouble (1985); Bullfighter and the Lady, The; Caddyshack II; Corrupt Ones, The; Dangerous Curves; Date with Judy, A; First Love; George Washington; High and the Mighty, The; Is Paris Burning?; Joe Versus the Volcano; John Paul Jones; Killer Bud; Last Voyage, The; Mortal Storm, The; Most Wanted; Mr. Music; Murder on Flight 502; Plain Clothes; Return of Eliot Ness, The; Tarnished Angels, The; To Be or Not to Be; Uncommon Valor; Untouchables, The: Scarface Mob; Written on the Wind
Stack (voices), Robert: Beavis and Butt-head Do America
Stacy, James: Double Exposure; Matters of the Heart; Posse; Swingin' Summer, A
Stadlen, Lewis J.: Between the Lines; Savages; Windy City
Staff, Kathy: Mary Reilly
Stafford, Chris: Edge of Seventeen
Stafford, Frederick: Battle of El Alamein, The; Topaz
Stafford, Jo: Ship Ahoy
Stafford, Jon: Crossing the Line (1990)
Stahelski, Chad: Nemesis 2
Stahl, Lisa: Shallow Grave
Stahl, Nick: Blue River; Bully; Disturbing Behavior; Lover's Prayer; Man without a Face, The; Safe Passage; Tall Tale: The Unbelievable Adventures of Pecos Bill
Staiola, Enzo: Bicycle Thief, The

Staley, James: Robot Wars
Staley, Joan: Ghost and Mr. Chicken, The
Stallone, Frank: Barfly; Fear; Heart of Midnight; Lethal Games; Order of the Eagle; Outlaw Force; Public Enemy #1; Ten Little Indians
Stallone, Jacqueline: Beach Babes from Beyond
Stallone, Sage: Fatally Yours
Stallone, Sylvester: Alan Smithee Film, An—Burn Hollywood Burn; Assassins; Cannonball; Cliffhanger; Cobra (1986); Copland; Daylight; Death Race 2000; Demolition Man; Driven; First Blood; F.I.S.T.; Get Carter; Judge Dredd; Lock Up; Lords of Flatbush, The; Nighthawks; Oscar (1991); Over the Top; Paradise Alley; Rambo III; Rambo: First Blood II; Rebel; Rhinestone; Rocky; Rocky II; Rocky III; Rocky IV; Rocky V; Specialist, The; Stop! Or My Mom Will Shoot; Tango and Cash; Victory
Stallybrass, Anne: Six Wives of Henry VIII, The (TV Series)
Stalmaster, Hal: Johnny Tremain
Stamos, John: Alice Through the Looking Glass; Born to Ride; Disappearance of Christina, The
Stamp, Terence: Adventures of Priscilla, Queen of the Desert, The; Alien Nation; Billy Budd; Bliss; Blue; Bowfinger; Collector, The; Divine Nymph, The; Far from the Madding Crowd; Genuine Risk; Hit, The (1984); Kiss the Sky; Legal Eagles; Limey, The; Link; Meetings with Remarkable Men; Real McCoy, The; Red Planet; Sicilian, The; Star Wars: Episode I The Phantom Menace; Superman II; Teorema; Thief of Baghdad (1978); Wall Street
Stanczak, Wadeck: Rendez-Vous; Scene of the Crime
Stander, Lionel: Beyond the Law; Black Bird, The; Boot Hill; Cul-de-Sac; Dandy in Aspic, A; Last Good Time, The; Loved One, The; Mad Wednesday (see also Sin of HaroldDiddlebock); Matilda; Mr. Deeds Goes to Town; New York, New York; Once Upon a Time in the West; Pulp; Scoundrel, The; Sensual Man, The; Sin of Harold Diddlebock (Mad Wednesday); Specter of the Rose, The; St. Benny the Dip; Unfaithfully Yours
Standing, Guy: Bulldog Drummond Escapes; Death Takes a Holiday; Lives of a Bengal Lancer, The
Standing, John: 8 1/2 Women; Legacy, The; Man Who Knew Too Little, The; Mrs. Dalloway; Nightflyers; Privates on Parade; Walk, Don't Run; X, Y and Zee
Stanford, Alan: Animal Farm
Stanford, Nathania: Return to the Lost World
Stang, Arnold: Hercules Goes Bananas; Man with the Golden Arm, The
Stanley, Alvah: Romeo and Juliet
Stanley, Edwin: Mysterious Dr. Satan
Stanley, Florence: Fortune, The; Prisoner of Second Avenue, The; Trapped in Paradise
Stanley, Forrest: Outlaws of the Desert
Stanley, Kim: Cat on a Hot Tin Roof; Danger; Frances; Goddess, The; Right Stuff, The; Seance on a Wet Afternoon
Stanley, Louise: Riders of the Rockies; Sing, Cowboy, Sing
Stanley, Pat: Ladies' Man, The (1961)
Stanley, Paul: I Heard the Owl Call My Name; Kiss Meets the Phantom of the Park
Stanley, Ralph: Down from the Mountain
Stanley, Rebecca: Eyes of Fire
Stanley, Taylor: Secret Cutting
Stansbury, Hope: Rats are Coming! The Werewolves Are Here!, The
Stansfield, Claire: Mind Ripper; Sensation; Sweepers; Swordsman, The
Stansfield, Lisa: Swing
Stanski, Ben: Burglar From Hell; Jacker 2: Descent to Hell; Tales Till the End
Stanton, Harry Dean: Against the Wall; Alien; Black Marble, The; Blue Tiger; Christine; Cisco Pike; Cockfighter; Dead Man's Walk; Death Watch; Dillinger; Down Periscope; Farewell My Lovely; Fire Down Below; Flatbed Annie and Sweetie Pie: Lady Truckers; Fool for Love; Fourth War, The; Hostages; Hotel Room; Last Temptation of Christ, The; Man Trouble; Man Who Cried, The; Mighty, The; Missouri Breaks, The; Mr. North; Never Talk to Strangers; 92 in the Shade; Oldest Living Graduate, The; One from the Heart; One Magic Christmas; Paris, Texas; Pat Garrett and Billy the Kid; Payoff; Playback; Pretty in Pink; Rafferty and the Gold Dust Twins; Rancho Deluxe; Rebel Rousers; Red Dawn; Repo Man; Ride in the Whirlwind; Rose, The; Sand; She's So Lovely; Slam Dance; Stars and Bars; Straight Story, The; Straight Time; Twin Peaks: Fire Walk with Me; Twister; Two-Lane Blacktop; Uforia; Where the Lilies Bloom; Wild at Heart; Wise Blood; Young Doctors in Love; Zandy's Bride
Stanton, John: Dusty; Great Expectations—The Untold Story; Kitty and the Bagman; Naked Country, The; Run, Rebecca, Run; Tai-Pan
Stanton, Maria: Voodoo Dolls
Stanton, Robert: Abbott and Costello in Hollywood; Dennis the Menace
Stanwyck, Barbara: All I Desire; Baby Face; Ball of Fire; Big Valley, The (TV Series); Bitter Tea of General Yen, The; Blowing Wild; Bride Walks Out, The; Cattle Queen of Montana; Christmas in Connecticut; Clash by Night; Crime of Passion; Cry Wolf; Double Indemnity; East Side, West Side; Escape to Burma; Executive Suite; Golden Boy; Great Man's Lady, The; Hollywood Canteen; Illicit; Interns Can't Take Money; Ladies of Leisure; Ladies They Talk About; Lady Eve, The; Lady of Burlesque; Mad Miss Manton, The; Maverick Queen, The; Meet John Doe; Night Nurse; Night Walker, The; Purchase Price, The; Remember the Night; Roustabout; Sorry, Wrong Number; Stella Dallas; Strange Love of Martha Ivers, The; This Is My Affair; Thornbirds, The; Titanic; To Please a Lady; Two Mrs. Carrolls, The; Union Pacific; Violent Men, The; Walk on the Wild Side
Stapel, Huub: Amsterdamned; Attic: The Hiding of Anne Frank; Lift, The
Stapleton, Jean: Baby (2000); Cinderella; Eleanor: First Lady of the World; Grown-Ups; Habitation of Dragons, The; Lily Dale; Michael; Up the Down Staircase; You've Got Mail
Stapleton, Maureen: Addicted to Love; Cocoon; Cocoon: The Return; Fan, The; Gathering, The; Gathering, Part II, The; Heartburn; Johnny Dangerously; Last Good Time, The; Little Gloria, Happy at Last; Lonelyhearts; Lost and Found (1979); Made in Heaven; Money Pit, The; Nuts; On the Right Track; Passed Away; Plaza Suite; Queen of the Stardust Ballroom; Reds; Runner Stumbles, The; Sweet Lorraine; Trading Mom
Stapley, Richard: Strange Door, The
Star, Holly: Prehistoric Bimbos in Armageddon City
Stark, Jonathan: House II: The Second Story; Project X
Stark, Koo: Emily
Starke, Anthony: Magnificent Seven, The (TV Series); Return of the Killer Tomatoes
Starr, Beau: Check Is in the Mail, The; Dead Air; Empire City; Glory Years; Halloween V: The Revenge of Michael Myers; Prisoner of Love
Starr, Blaze: Blaze Starr: The Original
Starr, Emerald: Men in Love
Starr, Fredro: Ride; Sunset Park
Starr, Mike: Clockers; Deli, The; Dumb and Dumber; Ed Wood; Gloria; Just Your Luck; Mad Dog and Glory; Mardi Gras for the Devil
Starr, Ringo: Alice in Wonderland; Caveman; Give My Regards to Broad Street; Kids Are Alright, The; Lisztomania; Magic Christian, The; Princess Daisy; Sextette; Son of Dracula; That'll Be the Day; 200 Motels
Starret, Jennifer: Frightmare
Starrett, Charles: Badmen of the Hills; Mask of Fu Manchu, The; Silver Streak
Starrett, Jack: Brothers in Arms; Cry Blood, Apache; Death Chase; First Blood; Mr. Horn; Nightwish
Statham, Jason: Ghosts of Mars; Lock, Stock and Two Smoking Barrels; One, The; Snatch; Turn It Up
Staunton, Imelda: Antonia & Jane; Crush; Deadly Advice; Much Ado About Nothing; Peter's Friends
Stavin, Mary: Opponent, The
Steadman, Alison: Abigail's Party; Blame It on the Bellboy; Clockwise; Kipperbang; Life Is Sweet; Misadventures of Mr. Wilt, The; Pride and Prejudice; Tartuffe
Steadman, Lynda: Career Girls
Steafel, Sheila: Bloodbath at the House of Death
Steckler, Ray Dennis: Las Vegas Weekend

Tenenbaums, The; There's Something About Mary; Your Friends & Neighbors; Zero Effect; Zoolander
Stiller, Jerry: Hairspray; Heavyweights; Hot Pursuit; Independent, The; Little Vegas; McGuffin, The; My 5 Wives; Nadine; On the Line (2001); Ritz, The; Seize the Day; Subway Stories; That's Adequate; Those Lips, Those Eyes; Zoolander
Stilwell, Diane: Mating Season, The; Perfect Match, The
Stimac, Slavko: Do You Remember Dolly Bell?
Stimely, Brett: Bloodstone
Stimson, Sara: Little Miss Marker
Sting: Bride, The; Brimstone and Treacle; Dune; Grave Indiscretion; Julia and Julia; Plenty; Quadrophenia; Stormy Monday
Stinston, John: Scared to Death
Stirling, Linda: Cherokee Flash; Purple Monster Strikes, The; San Antonio Kid; Santa Fe Saddlemates; Wagon Wheels Westward
Stock, Barbara: Verne Miller
Stock, Nigel: Prisoner, The (1968) (TV Series); Russian Roulette
Stockdale, Carl: Ivory-Handled Gun, The; Law for Tombstone; Stage to Chino
Stocker, Walter: They Saved Hitler's Brain
Stockwell, Dean: Air Force One; Alsino and the Condor; Anchors Aweigh; Backtrack; Beverly Hills Cop II; Blue Iguana; Blue Velvet; Boy with Green Hair, The; Buying Time; Chasers; Compulsion; Dune; Dunwich Horror, The; Gardens of Stone; Gentlemen's Agreement; In Pursuit; Kim; Langoliers, The; Last Movie, The (Chinchero); Limit Up; Living in Peril; Long Day's Journey into Night; Madonna: Innocence Lost; Married to the Mob; McHale's Navy; Mr. Wrong; Naked Souls; Pacific Connection, The; Palais Royale; Paris, Texas; Player, The; Psych-Out; Quantum Leap (TV Series); Restraining Order; Rites of Passage; Secret Garden, The; Shame; Smokescreen; Son of the Morning Star; Song of the Thin Man; Stars in My Crown; They Nest; Time Guardian, The; To Live and Die in L.A.; Tracks; Tucker: A Man and His Dream; Twilight Man; Werewolf of Washington; Win, Place or Steal; Wrong Is Right
Stockwell, Guy: It's Alive!; Santa Sangre; Tobruk; War Lord, The
Stockwell, John: Born to Ride; Christine; City Limits; Dangerously Close; I Shot a Man in Vegas; Legal Deceit; Losin' It; My Science Project; Nurse, The; Operation Intercept; Quarterback Princess; Radioactive Dreams; Stag; Top Gun
Stoddard, Malcolm: Godsend, The
Stodden, Nick: Shivers, The; Vampire Holocaust; Violent New Breed
Stojkovic, Andjela: Someone Else's America
Stoker, Austin: Assault on Precinct 13; Sheba Baby
Stokes, Barry: Alien Prey; Spaced Out
Stokey, Susan: Power, The (1980)
Stoklos, Randy: Side Out
Stokowski, Leopold: One Hundred Men and a Girl
Stole, Mink: But I'm a Cheerleader; Desperate Living; Female Trouble; Hairspray; Leather Jacket Love Story; Mondo Trasho; Multiple Maniacs; Pink Flamingos
Stoler, Shirley: Below the Belt; Displaced Person, The; Honeymoon Killers, The; Seven Beauties; Sticky Fingers
Stolhanske, Erik: Super Troopers
Stoll, Brad: Lost in Yonkers
Stoller, Fred: Downhill Willie
Stollery, David: Ten Who Dared; Westward Ho, the Wagons
Stoltz, Eric: Anaconda; Bodies, Rest & Motion; Code Name: Emerald; Common Ground; Discovery Program; Don't Look Back; Fast Times at Ridgemont High; Fluke; Fly II, The; Foreign Affairs; Grace of My Heart; Haunted Summer; Heart of Justice; Hi Life; House of Mirth, The; Inside; Keys to Tulsa; Kicking and Screaming; Killing Zoe; Lionheart; Little Women; Manifesto; Mask (1985); Memphis Belle; Money; Mr. Jealousy; Murder of Crows, A; My Horrible Year; Naked in New York; One Kill; Passion of Ayn Rand, The; Prophecy, The (1995); Pulp Fiction; Rob Roy; Running Hot; Sister, Sister; Sleep with Me; Some Kind of Wonderful; Surf 2; Things Behind the Sun; Two Days in the Valley; Waterdance, The; Woman at War, A
Stolze, Lena: Last Five Days, The; Nasty Girl, The; White Rose, The
Stone, Christopher: Annihilators, The; Cujo; Dying to Remember; Howling, The; Invisible Mom; Junkman, The
Stone, Dorothy: Revolt of the Zombies
Stone, Doug: Gordy
Stone, Fred: Alice Adams; Trail of the Lonesome Pine, The; Westerner, The
Stone, George E.: Last Mile, The; Viva Villa!
Stone, Harold J.: Big Mouth, The; Hardly Working; Legend of Valentino; Wrong Man, The; X (The Man with the X-Ray Eyes)
Stone, Lewis: All the Brothers Were Valiant; Andy Hardy Gets Spring Fever; Andy Hardy Meets a Debutante; Andy Hardy's Double Life; Andy Hardy's Private Secretary; Angels in the Outfield; Any Number Can Play; Big House, The; Bureau of Missing Persons; China Seas; Girl from Missouri, The; Grand Hotel; Inspiration; It's a Big Country; Key to the City; Life Begins for Andy Hardy; Lost World, The; Love Finds Andy Hardy; Love Laughs at Andy Hardy; Mask of Fu Manchu, The; Mata Hari; Nomads of the North; Prisoner of Zenda, The; Queen Christina; Red-Headed Woman; Romance; Sin of Madelon Claudet, The; Sun Comes Up, The; Suzy; Treasure Island; Wild Orchids; Woman of Affairs, A
Stone, Madison: Evil Toons
Stone, Martin: Letting the Birds Go Free
Stone, Matt: Baseketball
Stone, Michael: Bloody Murder; Malevolence
Stone, Milburn: Branded; Captive Wild Woman; Frozen Ghost, The; Gunsmoke (TV Series); Jungle Woman; Sinners in Paradise; Strange Confession; Sun Shines Bright, The; Young Mr. Lincoln
Stone, Oliver: Dave; First Works, Volumes 1 & 2
Stone, Philip: Moses
Stone, Sam: Dead Man Out
Stone, Sharon: Above the Law; Action Jackson; Allan Quartermain and the Lost City of Gold; Basic Instinct; Beyond the Stars; Casino; Cold Steel; Deadly Blessing; Diabolique; Diary of a Hitman; Gloria; He Said, She Said; Intersection; King Solomon's Mines; Last Dance; Mighty, The; Muse, The; Police Academy 4: Citizens on Patrol; Quick and the Dead, The; Scissors; Simpatico; Sliver; Specialist, The; Sphere; Total Recall; Where Sleeping Dogs Lie; Year of the Gun
Stone, Stuart: Boys Club, The
Stone, Yael: Me Myself I
Stones, Tammy: Neurotic Cabaret
Stonham, Kay: Home Sweet Home (1982)
Stoppa, Paolo: Miracle in Milan
Storch, Larry: Adventures Beyond Belief; Adventures of Huckleberry Finn, The; Better Late than Never; Captain Newman, M.D.; Fakeout; Forty Pounds of Trouble; Great Race, The; Incredible Rocky Mountain Race, The; Sex and the Single Girl; Without Warning
Storey, June: Blue Montana Skies; Colorado Sunset; Dance Hall; South of the Border; Strange Woman, The
Storey, Ruth: Blue Gardenia, The
Storhoi, Dennis: 13th Warrior, The
Storke, Adam: Lifepod; Mystic Pizza; National Lampoon's Attack of the 5' 2" Women; Stand, The
Storm, Gale: Revenge of the Zombies; Stampede; Texas Rangers, The (1951); Tom Brown's School Days (1940); Underworld Story
Stormare, Peter: Armageddon; Bruiser; Circus; Dancer in the Dark; Fargo; Million Dollar Hotel; 8MM; Purgatory; Somewhere in the City
Storti, Raymond: Wish Me Luck
Stossel, Ludwig: Bluebeard; Escape Me Never; House of Dracula; Pittsburgh; Pride of the Yankees, The; This Time For Keeps; Yolanda and the Thief
Stothard, Lisa: Bloodsport IV: The Dark Kumite
Stott, Ken: Boxer, The; Star Hunter
Stott, Ted: Plunkett & Macleane
Stovelbæk, Anette: Italian for Beginners
Stowe, Madeleine: Another Stakeout; Bad Girls; Blink; China Moon; Closet Land; General's Daughter, The; Impostor; Last of

Styles, Edwin: Adam and Evalyn
Suarez, Emma: Red Squirrel, The
Subkoff, Tara: All over Me; Black Circle Boys
Suchanek, Michal: Dirty Little Secret; Noah
Sucharetza, Marla: Whore 2
Suchet, David: Deadly Voyage; Don't Hang Up; Executive Decision; Harry and the Hendersons; Hunchback (1982); Iron Eagle; Last Innocent Man, The; Moses; Murrow; Poirot (Series); Sunday; 13 at Dinner; To Kill a Priest; Victoria and Albert; When the Whales Came; Wing Commander
Suddoth, Kohl: Bowfinger
Sudina, Marina: Mute Witness
Sugawara, Bunta: Distant Justice
Sugimura, Haruko: Late Chrysanthemums
Suh, Angie: Yellow
Sukapatana, Chintara: Good Morning, Vietnam
Sukowa, Barbara: Berlin Alexanderplatz; Lola; M. Butterfly; Marianne & Juliane; Sicilian, The; Third Miracle, The; Urbania; Voyager; Zentropa
Sulfaro, Giuseppe: Malena
Sullavan, Margaret: Mortal Storm, The; Shining Hour, The; Shop Around the Corner, The; Shopworn Angel, The; So Ends Our Night; Three Comrades
Sullivan, Barry: Another Time, Another Place; Any Number Can Play; Bad and the Beautiful, The; Buckskin; Caravans; Casino; Gangster, The; Julie; Kung Fu (1971); Life of Her Own, A; Maverick Queen, The; Mr. Imperium; Nancy Goes to Rio; Pat Garrett and Billy the Kid; Planet of the Vampires; Shark! (Maneaters!); Skirts Ahoy!; Strategic Air Command; Take a Hard Ride; Texas Lady; Washington Affair, The; Woman of the Town; Yuma
Sullivan, Brad: Bushwhacked; Fantasticks, The; Funny Farm; Orpheus Descending; Prince of Tides, The; Sister Act 2: Back in the Habit
Sullivan, Charlotte: Legend of Gator Face, The
Sullivan, Didi: Caltiki, the Immortal Monster
Sullivan, Don: Giant Gila Monster, The
Sullivan, Ed: Singing Nun, The
Sullivan, Erik Per: Unfaithful
Sullivan, Francis L.: Caesar and Cleopatra; Citadel, The; Joan of Arc
Sullivan, George: Rockwell: A Legend of the Wild West
Sullivan, Jean: Uncertain Glory
Sullivan, Liam: Magic Sword, The
Sullivan, Matthew: Max Is Missing
Sullivan, Sean Gregory: Howling VI: The Freaks
Sullivan, Susan: City in Fear; Deadman's Curve; Incredible Hulk, The; Ordeal of Dr. Mudd, The
Sullivan, Tom: Cocaine Cowboys
Sullivan, Trent: Me Myself I
Sumac, Yma: Omar Khayyam
Summer, Crystal: Double Blast
Summer, Donna: Thank God It's Friday
Summerour, Lisa: Philadelphia
Summers, Andy: Stand by Me
Summers, Bunny: Merlin's Shop of Mystical Wonders
Summers, Sylvia: Dreamaniac
Summerville, Slim: Charlie Chan in Reno; Jesse James; Rebecca of Sunnybrook Farm; Western Union
Sumpter, Donald: Black Panther, The
Sumpter, Jeremy: Frailty
Sun, Elizabeth: Groove
Sundberg, Clinton: Key to the City; Living in a Big Way
Sundland, Debra: Tough Guys Don't Dance
Sundquist, Bjorn: Dive, The; Shipwrecked
Sundquist, Gerry: Boarding School; Don't Open Till Christmas; Great Expectations; Meetings with Remarkable Men
Suplee, Ethan: Evolution; Remember the Titans
Supremes, The: That Was Rock
Surovy, Nicolas: Breaking Free; Man Who Captured Eichmann, The; Stark; 12:01; When Danger Follows You Home
Susa, Amber: American Summer, An
Susman, Tod: Only the Strong
Sust, David: In a Glass Cage
Sutherland, Catherine: Turbo: A Power Rangers Adventure
Sutherland, Dick: Grandma's Boy
Sutherland, Donald: Alex in Wonderland; Apprentice to Murder; Art of War, The; Assignment, The; Backdraft; Bear Island; Benefit of the Doubt; Bethune; Blood Relatives; Buffy, the Vampire Slayer; Casanova; Castle of the Living Dead; Citizen X; Crackers; Dan Candy's Law (Alien Thunder); Day of the Locust, The; Die! Die! My Darling!; Dirty Dozen, The; Disappearance, The; Disclosure; Dr. Bethune; Dr. Terror's House of Horrors; Don't Look Now; Dry White Season, A; Eagle Has Landed, The; Eminent Domain; Eye of the Needle; Fallen; Free Money; Gas; Great Train Robbery, The; Heaven Help Us; Hollow Point; Hunley, The; Instinct; Invasion of the Body Snatchers; JFK; Johnny Got His Gun; Kelly's Heroes; Kentucky Fried Movie; Klute; Lady Ice; Lifeforce Experiment, The; Little Murders; Lock Up; Lost Angels; Man, a Woman and a Bank, A; M*A*S*H; Max Dugan Returns; Murder by Decree; Natural Enemy; Nothing Personal; Oldest Confederate Widow Tells All; Ordeal by Innocence; Ordinary People; Outbreak; Panic; Puppet Masters, The; Quicksand: No Escape; Railway Station Man, The; Red Hot; Revolution; Rosary Murders, The; S*P*Y*S; Shadow Conspiracy; Shadow of the Wolf; Six Degrees of Separation; Space Cowboys; Start the Revolution Without Me; Steelyard Blues; Threshold; Time to Kill, A (1996); Trouble with Spies, The; Virus; Wolf at the Door; Younger and Younger
Sutherland, Kiefer: Amazing Stories (TV Series); Article 99; Bay Boy, The; Break Up; Bright Lights, Big City; Brotherhood of Justice; Chicago Joe and the Showgirl; Cowboy Way, The; Crazy Moon; Dark City; Eye for an Eye; Few Good Men, A; Flashback; Flatliners; Freeway; Ground Control; Hourglass; Killing Time, The (1987); Last Days of Frankie the Fly, The; Last Light; Lost Boys, The; 1969; Picking up the Pieces; Promised Land; Renegades; Right Temptation, The; Soldier's Sweetheart, A; Stand by Me; Three Musketeers, The; Time to Kill, A (1996); Truth or Consequences, N.M.; Twin Peaks: Fire Walk with Me; Vanishing, The; Young Guns; Young Guns II
Sutorius, James: Windy City
Sutton, Dudley: Devils, The; Leather Boys, The; Number One of the Secret Service; Orlando
Sutton, Emma: Goodnight, God Bless
Sutton, Grady: Great Moment, The; Lady Takes a Chance, A; Show-Off, The; Vivacious Lady; Waikiki Wedding
Sutton, John: Arrest Bulldog Drummond; Bat, The; Invisible Man Returns; Jane Eyre; Murder over New York; Second Woman, The; Yank in the RAF, A
Sutton, Kay: Lawless Valley; Li'l Abner; Saint in New York, The
Sutton, Lisa: Raw Courage
Sutton, Lori: Polish Vampire in Burbank, A
Sutton, Nick: Gummo
Sutton, Raymond: Dogpound Shuffle
Suvari, Mena: American Beauty; American Pie; American Pie 2; American Virgin; Loser; Musketeer, The; Sugar and Spice
Suzman, Janet: Black Windmill, The; Day in the Death of Joe Egg, A; Draughtman's Contract, The; Dry White Season, A; House on Garibaldi Street; Leon the Pig Farmer; Nicholas and Alexandra; Nuns on the Run; Priest of Love; Zany Adventures of Robin Hood, The
Suzuki, Mayu: Godzilla 2000
Suzuki, Seijun: Cold Fever
Svashenko, Semyon: Arsenal; Earth
Svenson, Bo: Choke Canyon; Curse II—The Bite; Deadly Impact; Delta Force, The; Final Chapter—Walking Tall; Frankenstein; Great Waldo Pepper, The; Heartbreak Ridge; Heartless; Last Contract, The; Night Warning; North Dallas Forty; Private Obsession; Snowbeast; Steel Frontier; Steele's Law; Three Days to a Kill; Thunder Warrior; Thunder Warrior II; Tides of War; Walking Tall Part II; White Phantom; Wizard of the Lost Kingdom
Sverak, Zdenek: Elementary School, The; Kolya
Swada, Ken: Mishima: A Life in Four Chapters
Swain, Chelse: Mangler 2, The
Swain, Dominique: Face/Off; Lolita; Smokers, The; Tart
Swain, Howard: Jon Jost's Frameup; Night of the Scarecrow

Swain, Mack: Gold Rush, The; Last Warning, The; Mockery; Three Charlies and a Phoney!
Swank, Hilary: Boys Don't Cry; Gift, The; Kounterfeit; Next Karate Kid, The; Quiet Days in Hollywood; Sometimes They Come Back Again
Swanson, Gary: Triplecross; Vice Squad
Swanson, Gloria: Indiscreet; Male and Female; Manhandled; Queen Kelly; Sadie Thompson; Sunset Boulevard; Three for Bedroom C; When Comedy Was King
Swanson, Jackie: Oblivion; Oblivion 2: Backlash
Swanson, Kristy: Buffy, the Vampire Slayer; Chase, The; Deadly Friend; Diving In; Dude, Where's My Car?; 8 Heads in a Duffel Bag; Flowers in the Attic; Getting In; Ground Control; Higher Learning; Highway to Hell; Mannequin Two: On the Move; Marshal Law; Phantom, The; Program, The; Supreme Sanction; Zebra Lounge
Swanson, Rochelle: Cyberzone; Deadly Outbreak; Hard Bounty; Mutual Needs
Swart, Rufus: Dust Devil
Swarts, Nick: Spiders (2000)
Swayze, Don: Beach Babes from Beyond; Body of Influence; Broken Trust; Edge of Honor; Money to Burn; Payback
Swayze, Marcia: Rule #3
Swayze, Patrick: Along for the Ride; Black Dog; City of Joy; Dirty Dancing; Donnie Darko; Father Hood; Ghost (1990); Grandview, U.S.A.; Next of Kin; North and South; Outsiders, The; Point Break; Red Dawn; Road House; Steel Dawn; Tall Tale: The Unbelievable Adventures of Pecos Bill; Three Wishes; Tiger Warsaw; To Wong Foo, Thanks for Everything, Julie Newmar
Sweaney, Debra: Savage Instinct
Swedberg, Heidi: Evolution's Child; Father & Scout; Ticket, The
Sweeney, Ann: Incredible Melting Man, The
Sweeney, Bob: George Burns and Gracie Allen Show, The (TV Series); Toby Tyler
Sweeney, D. B.: Blue Desert; Cutting Edge, The; Day in October, A; Eight Men Out; Fire in the Sky; Gardens of Stone; Hardball; Hear No Evil; Heaven Is a Playground; Introducing Dorothy Dandridge; Leather Jackets; Lonesome Dove; Memphis Belle; Miss Rose White; No Man's Land; Roommates
Sweeney, Joseph: 12 Angry Men
Sweeney, Julia: Beethoven's 3rd; God Said, Ha!; It's Pat: The Movie; Whatever It Takes
Sweet, Blanche: Anna Christie; Avenging Conscience, The; D. W. Griffith Triple Feature; Home, Sweet Home (1914); Judith of Bethulia
Sweet, Dolph: Below the Belt; King; Which Way Is Up?
Sweet, Gary: Indecent Obsession, An
Sweet, Vonte: Marshal Law; You Must Remember This
Sweeten, Madylin: Dog of Flanders, A
Swenson, Forrest: To All a Good Night
Swenson, Karl: Brighty of the Grand Canyon; Hanging Tree, The; Hour of the Gun, The
Swift, Clive: Raw Meat
Swift, David: Arthur's Hallowed Ground; Black Panther, The; Jack and Sarah
Swift, Francie: Fall; Last Breath
Swift, Paul: Multiple Maniacs
Swift, Susan: Harper Valley P.T.A.
Swinburne, Nora: Betrayed; River, The
Swinton, Tilda: Beach, The; Caravaggio; Conceiving Ada; Deep End, The; Edward II; Female Perversions; Garden, The; Last of England, The; Love is the Devil; Orlando; War Requiem; War Zone, The
Swit, Loretta: Beer; Best Christmas Pageant Ever, The; First Affair; Forest Warrior; Freebie and the Bean; M*A*S*H (TV Series); Race with the Devil; S.O.B.
Switzer, Bill: Locked in Silence; Mr. Rice's Secret
Switzer, Carl "Alfalfa": General Spanky; High and the Mighty, The; I Love You Again; Island in the Sky; Motorcycle Gang
Swofford, Ken: Black Roses; Bless the Beasts and Children; Gambler, Part II—The Adventure Continues, The; Hunter's Blood; Sky Heist
Swope, Topo: Tracks
Swope, Tracy Brooks: Inner Sanctum 2
Sydney, Basil: Dam Busters, The; Hamlet; Rhodes of Africa (Rhodes); Simba; Treasure Island
Sydney, Sylvia: Witching of Ben Wagner, The
Syed, Shafiq: Salaam Bombay!
Sykes, Eric: Heavens Above; Others, The; Spy with a Cold Nose, The
Sylvester, Harold: Cop for the Killing, A; Corrina, Corrina; Fast Break; Officer and a Gentleman, An; Trippin'; Uncommon Valor; Vision Quest
Sylvester, William: Devil Doll (1936); Gorgo; Riding with Death; 2001: A Space Odyssey
Sylvie: Forbidden Fruit; Little World of Don Camillo, The; Shameless Old Lady, The; Ulysses
Sylwan, Kari: Cries and Whispers
Syms, Sylvia: Asylum; Desperados, The; Intimate Contact; Murder Is Announced, A; Operation Crossbow; Shirley Valentine; Victim; World of Suzie Wong, The
Syron, Brian: Backlash
Szarabajka, Keith: Andre; Billy Galvin; Equalizer, The: "Memories of Manon"; Marie; Nightlife; Perfect World, A; Staying Together; Stephen King's Golden Years (TV Series)
Sze-Man, Tsang: Iron Monkey
Szeps, Henri: Run, Rebecca, Run
Szonert, Eliza: Dish, The
Szubanski, Magda: Babe; Babe: Pig in the City
Tabakov, Oleg: Oblomov; Unfinished Piece for the Player Piano, An (Unfinished Piece for a Mechanical Piano, An)
Tabatabai, Jasmin: Bandits
Tabori, Kristoffer: Marilyn & Bobby: Her Final Affair; Rappaccini's Daughter
Tadokoro, Yutaka: Tokyo Pop
Taeger, Ralph: Hondo and the Apaches
Tagawa, Cary-Hiroyuki: Art of War, The; Bridge of Dragons; Danger Zone; Dangerous, The (1984); Mortal Kombat; Natural Causes; Nemesis; Pearl Harbor; Phantom, The; Picture Bride; Provocateur; Rising Sun; Soldier Boyz; Space Rangers (TV Series)
Taggart, Ben: Man Made Monster (The Atomic Monster)
Taggart, Rita: Horror Show, The; Webber's World (At Home with the Webbers)
Taghmaoui, Said: Hate; Hideous Kinky
Tagore, Sharmila: Days and Nights in the Forest; World of Apu, The
Taguchi, Hiromasa: Shall We Dance?
Taguchi, Tomoroh: Tetsuo II: Body Hammer; Tetsuo: The Iron Man
Taimak: Last Dragon, The
Tainsh, Tracy: Frenchman's Farm
Tait, Marissa: Totem
Tait, Tristan: Rose Hill
Taka, Miiko: Walk, Don't Run
Takahashi, Etsushi: 8Man
Takaki, Mio: Berlin Affair, The
Takakura, Ken: Antarctica; Black Rain; Mr. Baseball; Yakuza, The
Takamine, Hideko: Mistress, The (1953); When a Woman Ascends the Stairs
Takarada, Akira: Godzilla vs. Monster Zero; Godzilla vs. Mothra; Latitude Zero; Minbo, or The Gentle Art of Japanese Extortion
Takarada, Junko: Traffic Jam
Takashima, Tadao: King Kong vs. Godzilla; Son of Godzilla
Takayama, Akira: Picture Bride
Takei, George: Bug Buster; Green Berets, The; Kissinger and Nixon; Live by the Fist; Oblivion; Oblivion 2: Backlash; Prisoners of the Sun; Red Line 7000; Star Trek II: The Wrath of Khan; Star Trek III: The Search for Spock; Star Trek IV: The Voyage Home; Star Trek—The Motion Picture; Star Trek (TV Series); Star Trek V: The Final Frontier; Star Trek VI: The Undiscovered Country; Star Trek: The Menagerie; Walk, Don't Run
Takenaka, Naoto: Gonin; Mystery of Rampo, The; Shall We Dance?
Takeshi, Beat: Brother

Talbert, Charlie: Angus
Talbot, Emilie: Ceremony
Talbot, Helen: Federal Operator 99
Talbot, Lyle: Adventures of Ozzie and Harriet, The (TV Series); Atom Man vs. Superman; Batman and Robin (Adventures of Batmanand Robin); Case of the Lucky Legs, The; Dixie Jamboree; Fury of the Congo; Glen or Glenda; Go West, Young Man; Jail Bait (1954); Ladies They Talk About; One Body Too Many; One Night of Love; Our Little Girl; Purchase Price, The; Second Fiddle; Shriek in the Night, A; Thirteenth Guest, The; Trapped by Television
Talbot, Nita: Amityville 1992: It's About Time; Chained Heat; Concrete Jungle, The (1982); Frightmare; I Married a Woman; Island Claws; Puppet Master II; Rockford Files, The (TV Series); Who's Got the Action?
Talbott, Gloria: Arizona Raiders; Cyclops, The; Daughter of Dr. Jekyll; Girls Town; I Married a Monster from Outer Space; Leech Woman, The; Talion
Talbott, Michael: Miami Vice
Taliaferro, Hal: Federal Operator 99; Hi-Yo Silver; Lone Ranger, The; Painted Stallion, The; Song of Texas
Taliferro, Michael: Replacements, The
Talking Heads: Stop Making Sense
Tallichet, Margaret: Stranger on the Third Floor
Talmadge, Constance: Intolerance
Talmadge, Natalie: Art of Buster Keaton, The; Our Hospitality
Talman, William: City That Never Sleeps; Crashout; One Minute to Zero; Racket, The
Talor, Venesa: Shandra, The Jungle Girl
Tam, Alan: Armour of God
Tamada, Paige: Santa Clause, The
Tamara: No, No Nanette
Tamba, Tetsuro: You Only Live Twice
Tambakis, Peter Anthony: Snow in August
Tamblyn, Amber: Johnny Mysto
Tamblyn, Russ: Attack of the 60-Ft. Centerfold; Blood Screams; Cimarron; Don't Go Near the Water; Fastest Gun Alive, The; Haunting, The; High School Confidential!; Hit the Deck; Invisible Mom; Johnny Mysto; Last Hunt, The; My Magic Dog; Necromancer; Peyton Place; Phantom Empire, The (1986); Retreat Hell; Running Mates; Satan's Sadists; Seven Brides for Seven Brothers; Tom Thumb; Twin Peaks (Movie); Twin Peaks (TV Series); War of the Gargantuas; West Side Story; Win, Place or Steal; Winning Team, The; Wizards of the Demon Sword; Wonderful World of the Brothers Grimm, The
Tambor, Jeffrey: Big Bully; Cocaine: One Man's Seduction; Girl, Interrupted; Gun in the House, A; House in the Hills, A; How the Grinch Stole Christmas; Life Stinks; Man Who Captured Eichmann, The; Man Who Wasn't There, The; Meet Joe Black; Muppets From Space; My Teacher's Wife; Pastime; Pollock; Sadat; Saturday the 14th; There's Something About Mary; Three O'Clock High; Weapons of Mass Distraction; Webber's World (At Home with the Webbers)
Tamerlis, Zoe: Ms. .45; Special Effects
Tamiroff, Akim: Alphaville; Anastasia; Battle Hell; Black Magic; Bridge of San Luis Rey, The; Can't Help Singing; Chained; CorsicanBrothers, The; Deadly Sanctuary; For Whom the Bell Tolls; Gangster, The; General Died at Dawn, The; Great McGinty, The; His Butler's Sister; Hotel Paradiso; Lt. Robin Crusoe, U.S.N.; Miracle of Morgan's Creek, The; Mr. Arkadin (Confidential Report); My Girl Tisa; My Love for Yours (Honeymoon in Bali); Naughty Marietta; Northwest Mounted Police; Outpost in Morocco; Panic Button; Sadie McKee; Story of Louis Pasteur, The; Tortilla Flat; Trial, The; Union Pacific
Tan, Madeline: That's the Way I Like It
Tan, Philip: Bloodsport II; Kung Pow!: Enter the Fist
Tanaka, Kinuyo: Life of Oharu; Mother; Sandakan No. 8; Sansho the Bailiff
Tanaka, Kunie: Evil of Dracula
Tanaka, Sara: Rushmore
Tanaka, Shinji: Island, The
Tanaka, Yoshiko: Black Rain
Tandy, Jessica: Batteries Not Included; Best Friends; Birds, The; Bostonians, The; Camilla (1994); Cocoon; Cocoon: The Return; Desert Fox, The; Driving Miss Daisy; Forever Amber; Fox-Fire; Fried Green Tomatoes; Gin Game, The; House on Carroll Street, The; Nobody's Fool; September Affair; Seventh Cross, The; Still of the Night; Story Lady, The; To Dance with the White Dog; Used People; World According to Garp, The
Tandy, Mark: Railway Station Man, The
Tanner, Mary: Something Special
Tanner, Tony: Stop the World I Want to Get Off
Tantai, Hassan: Kandahar
Tapping, Amanda: Stargate SG-1
Tara, Suzanne: Danger Zone, The (1986)
Tarantino, Brian: Summer of Sam
Tarantino, Quentin: Desperado; Destiny Turns on the Radio; Four Rooms; From Dusk Till Dawn; Reservoir Dogs; Sleep with Me; Somebody to Love
Taratorkin, Georgi: Crime and Punishment
Tardif, Rene: National Lampoon's Golf Punks
Tarding, Emil: Mifune
Tari, Le: Brotherhood of Death
Tarkenton, Fran: First and Ten
Tarkovsky, Andrei: Andrei Rublev
Tarrant, John: Starship
Tarrin: Monster from a Prehistoric Planet
Tashman, Lilyan: Bulldog Drummond; Frankie and Johnny; Riptide; Scarlet Dawn
Tassoni, Caralina C.: Evil Clutch
Tataryn, Sean: Leather Jacket Love Story
Tate, Larenz: Dead Presidents; Inkwell, The; Love Come Down; Love Jones; Menace II Society; Postman, The; Why Do Fools Fall in Love
Tate, Laura: Dead Space; Subspecies
Tate, Sharon: Ciao Federico!; Fearless Vampire Killers, or, Pardon Me, But Your Teeth Are in My Neck, The; Valley of the Dolls
Tati, Jacques: Jour de Fête; Mr. Hulot's Holiday; My Uncle (Mon Oncle); Parade; Playtime; Traffic
Tattoli, Elda: China Is Near
Tatum, Bradford: Stoned Age, The; Within the Rock
Taube, Sven-Bertil: Jerusalem; Puppet on a Chain
Tauber, Richard: Heart's Desire
Tautou, Audrey: Amélie; Venus Beauty Institute
Tavernier, Bertrand: Francois Truffaut: Stolen Moments
Tavernier, Nils: Beatrice; Post Coitum
Tavi, Tuvia: Paradise
Taxier, Arthur: Cover Girl Murders, The
Tayback, Tom: Undercover
Tayback, Vic: Alice Doesn't Live Here Anymore; Beverly Hills Bodysnatchers; Cheap Detective, The; Horseplayer; Lepke; Portrait of a Stripper; Rage; Weekend Warriors
Taye-Loren, Carolyn: Witchcraft V: Dance with the Devil
Taylor, Benedict: Black Arrow (1984); Duel of Hearts; Every Time We Say Goodbye; Far Pavilions, The
Taylor, Buck: Gunsmoke (TV Series); Gunsmoke: Return to Dodge; Pony Express Rider; Standing Tall
Taylor, Christine: Brady Bunch Movie, The; Breaking Free; Kiss Toledo Goodbye; Overnight Delivery; Something About Sex; Very Brady Sequel, A; Wedding Singer, The; Zoolander
Taylor, Clayton: Kid Called Danger, A; Robin Hood Gang, The
Taylor, Courtney: Cover Me; Tracks of a Killer
Taylor, Delores: Billy Jack
Taylor, Don: Father of the Bride; Father's Little Dividend; I'll Cry Tomorrow; Men of Sherwood Forest; Naked City, The
Taylor, Dub: Across the Rio Grande; Best of Times, The; Conagher; Creature from Black Lake; Falling from Grace; Gambler Returns, The: Luck of the Draw; Gator; Great Smokey Roadblock, The; Man and Boy; Man Called Horse, A; Moonshine County Express; My Heroes Have Always Been Cowboys; Parrish; Pat Garrett and Billy the Kid; Pony Express Rider; They Went That-A-Way and That-A-Way
Taylor, Elizabeth: Ash Wednesday; Beau Brummell; Between Friends; Big Hangover, The; Butterfield 8; Cat on a Hot Tin Roof; Cleopatra; Comedians, The; Conspirator; Courage of Lassie; Date with Judy, A; Divorce His: Divorce Hers; Dr. Faustus; Driver's Seat, The; Elephant Walk; Father of the Bride; Father's Little Dividend; Flintstones, The; Giant; Girl Who Had Everything,

The; Hammersmith Is Out; Ivanhoe; Jane Eyre; Julia Misbehaves; Lassie Come Home; Last Time I Saw Paris, The; Life with Father; Little Night Music, A; Little Women; Love Is Better Than Ever; Mirror Crack'd, The; National Velvet; Night Watch; Place in the Sun, A; Poker Alice; Raintree County; Reflections in a Golden Eye; Rhapsody; Rumor Mill, The; Sandpiper, The; Secret Ceremony; Suddenly, Last Summer; Sweet Bird of Youth; Taming of the Shrew, The; Under Milk Wood; Victory at Entebbe; V.I.P.s, The; Who's Afraid of Virginia Woolf?; Winter Kills; X, Y and Zee

Taylor, Estelle: Cimarron; Don Juan; Street Scene; Ten Commandments, The

Taylor, Forrest: Arizona Days; Colorado Serenade; Mystery of the Hooded Horsemen; Riders of Destiny; Song of Nevada; Sons of the Pioneers

Taylor, Grant: Long John Silver

Taylor, Holland: Bosom Buddies (TV Series); Cop and a Half; George of the Jungle; Happy Accidents; Keeping the Faith; Last Summer in the Hamptons; Next Stop Wonderland; She's Having a Baby; Steal Big, Steal Little

Taylor, Jack: Christmas Kid, The; Erotikill

Taylor, James: Two-Lane Blacktop

Taylor, Jana: Hell's Angels on Wheels

Taylor, Jennifer: Crude Oasis, The

Taylor, Joan: Apache Woman; Earth vs. the Flying Saucers; Rifleman, The (TV Series); Rose Marie; 20 Million Miles to Earth

Taylor, Jodie: Satan's Sadists

Taylor, John: Sugar Town

Taylor, Joshua: American Astronaut, The

Taylor, Joyce: Twice-Told Tales

Taylor, Kelli: Club, The

Taylor, Kent: Brain of Blood; Brides of the Beast; Crawling Hand, The; Death Takes a Holiday; I'm No Angel; Mrs. Wiggs of the Cabbage Patch; Satan's Sadists; Slightly Scarlet

Taylor, Kimberly: Beauty School

Taylor, Kit: Long John Silver

Taylor, Lawrence: Any Given Sunday

Taylor, Lili: Addiction, The; Arizona Dreams; Bright Angel; Cold Fever; Dogfight; Girls Town; Haunting, The; High Fidelity; Household Saints; I Shot Andy Warhol; Illtown; Impostors, The; Kicked in the Head; Mrs. Parker and the Vicious Circle; Mystic Pizza; Pecker; Ransom; Ready to Wear; Rudy; Short Cuts; Watch It

Taylor, Lindsay: Hard to Die

Taylor, Marjorie: Crimes of Stephen Hawke, The; Face at the Window, The; Ticket of Leave Man, The

Taylor, Mark L.: Eight Days a Week; Ratings Game, The

Taylor, Martha: Manhattan Baby

Taylor, Meshach: Mannequin; Mannequin Two: On the Move; Ultrawarrior; Virtual Seduction

Taylor, Monica: Big Bust Out, The

Taylor, Noah: Almost Famous; Flirting; Lara Croft: Tomb Raider; Nostradamus Kid, The; One Crazy Night; Shine; Year My Voice Broke, The

Taylor, Norma: Adventures of Rex and Rinty

Taylor, Regina: Children of the Dust; Hostile Waters; Spirit Lost; Strange Justice

Taylor, Renee: Love Is All There Is; White Palace

Taylor, Rip: Private Obsession; Things Are Tough All Over

Taylor, Robert: Above and Beyond; All the Brothers Were Valiant; Bataan; Billy the Kid; Broadway Melody of 1938; Broadway Melody of 1936; Camille; Conspirator; D-Day the Sixth of June; Gorgeous Hussy, The; Hondo and the Apaches; Ivanhoe; Johnny Eager; Johnny Tiger; Knights of the Round Table; Last Hunt, The; Law and Jake Wade, The; Miracle of the White Stallions; Night Walker, The; Party Girl; Personal Property; Quo Vadis (1951); This Is My Affair; Three Comrades; Undercurrent; Waterloo Bridge; Westward the Women; When Ladies Meet

Taylor, Rod: Ask Any Girl; Birds, The; Catered Affair, The; Chuka; Cry of the Innocent; Dark of the Sun (Mercenaries) (1968); Deadly Trackers, The; Glass Bottom Boat, The; Hotel; Man Who Had Power over Women, The; Open Season; Powderkeg; Raintree County; 36 Hours; Time Machine, The; Time to Die, A; Train Robbers, The; V.I.P.s, The; Welcome to Woop Woop; World Without End; Zabriskie Point

Taylor, Ruth: Headin' Home

Taylor, Sam: Living the Blues

Taylor, Sharon: Attack of the Killer Tomatoes

Taylor, Vaughn: It Should Happen to You

Taylor, Wally: Hidden Fears

Taylor, William: Downdraft

Taylor-Young, Leigh: Can't Stop the Music; Devlin Connection III, The; Honeymoon Academy; Horsemen, The; I Love You Alice B. Toklas!; Jagged Edge; Looker; Marathon; Secret Admirer

Tchkhikvadze, Ramaz: Chef in Love, A

Teague, Anthony: How to Succeed in Business without Really Trying

Teague, Marshall: Colony, The (1995); Dangerous Place, A; Fist of Iron; Guardian Angel

Teal, Ray: Burning Hills, The; Distant Drums; Jumping Jacks

Teale, Owen: Hawk, The; War Requiem

Tearle, Conway: Hurricane Express; Stella Maris; Vanity Fair

Tearle, Godfrey: Decameron Nights; One of Our Aircraft Is Missing

Teasdale, Verree: Fifth Avenue Girl; Terror Aboard

Tebbs, Susan: Littlest Horse Thieves, The

Tecsi, Sandor: '68

Ted Jan Roberts: Hollywood Safari

Tedd, Steven: Rough Justice

Tedeschi, Valeria Bruni: My Man (Mon Homme)

Tedford, Travis: Little Rascals, The

Tedrow, Irene: Two Worlds of Jennie Logan, The

Teefy, Maureen: Fame

Tell, Olive: Scarlet Empress, The

Teller: Fantasticks, The; Penn & Teller Get Killed

Temchen, Sybil: Body Shots; Passion of Ayn Rand, The; Ten Benny

Temple, Shirley: Baby Take a Bow; Bachelor and the Bobby-Soxer, The; Blue Bird, The; Bright Eyes; Captain January; Curly Top; Dimples; Fort Apache; Heidi; Just Around the Corner; Little Colonel, The; Little Miss Broadway; Little Miss Marker; Little Princess, The (1939); Littlest Rebel, The; Miss Annie Rooney; Our Little Girl; Poor Little Rich Girl (1936); Rebecca of Sunnybrook Farm; Since You Went Away; Stand Up and Cheer; Story of Seabiscuit, The; Stowaway; Susannah of the Mounties; Wee Willie Winkie

Templeton, Christopher: Hostage for a Day

Tempo, Nino: Girl Can't Help It, The

Tench, John: Operative, The

Tendeter, Kaye: Fall of the House of Usher, The

Tendeter, Stacey: Two English Girls

Tendler, Jesse R.: Secret, The

Tenessy, Hedi: Revolt of Job, The

Tennant, Victoria: All of Me; Best Seller; Chiefs; Dempsey; Flowers in the Attic; Handmaid's Tale, The; Holcroft Covenant, The; L.A. Story; Strangers Kiss; War and Remembrance; Whispers

Tenney, Anne: Castle, The

Tenney, Jon: Fools Rush In; Lassie; Lovelife; Music from Another Room; Twilight of the Golds, The; Watch It

Tenuta, Judy: Butch Camp

Tepper, William: Miss Right

ter Steege, Johanna: Immortal Beloved; Vanishing, The; Vincent and Theo

Terajima, Susumu: After Life; Fireworks

Terao, Akira: Akira Kurosawa's Dreams; Ran

Terekhova, Margarita: Mirror, The

Teresina: On the Make

Tergensen, Lee: Shot in the Heart; Wild Iris

Terhune, Max: Arizona Stagecoach; Black Market Rustlers; Boothill Bandits; Fugitive Valley; Heart of the Rockies; Hit the Saddle; Manhattan Merry-Go-Round; Night Riders, The; Outlaws of Sonora; Overland Stage Raiders; Pals of the Saddle; Range Defenders; Red River Range; Ride, Ranger, Ride; Riders of the Black Hills; Riders of the Whistling Skull; Saddle Mountain Roundup; Santa Fe Stampede; Three Texas Steers; Trail of the Silver Spurs

Terkel, Studs: Eight Men Out
Terlesky, John: Allnighter, The; Chopping Mall; Damned River; Deathstalker II: Duel of the Titans; When He's Not a Stranger
Termo, Leonard: Year of the Dragon
Terra, Scott: Shadrach
Terral, Boris: Post Coitum
Terrell, Cedrick: Whispering, The
Terrell, John: Five Heartbeats, The; She's Gotta Have It
Terrell, Steve: Invasion of the Saucer Men; Motorcycle Gang
Terrence, John: Merlin's Shop of Mystical Wonders
Terry, Carl: Firing Line, The
Terry, DeSean: God's Army
Terry, Edward: Luther, The Geek
Terry, John: Big Green, The; Dangerous Woman, A; Hawk the Slayer; Killing in a Small Town; Resurrected, The; Silhouette
Terry, Kim: Slugs, the Movie
Terry, Nigel: Caravaggio; Déjà Vu; Edward II; Excalibur; Lion in Winter, The; Sylvia
Terry, Paul: James and the Giant Peach
Terry, Philip: Balalaika; Born to Kill; George White's Scandals; Lost Weekend, The
Terry, Ruth: Heart of the Golden West
Terry, Sheila: Haunted Gold; Lawless Frontier; 'Neath Arizona Skies; Sphinx, The (1933)
Terry, William: Stage Door Canteen
Terry the Tramp: Hell's Angels '69
Terry-Thomas: Abominable Dr. Phibes, The; Blue Murder at St. Trinian's; Brothers In Law; Carlton-Browne of the F.O.; Danger: Diabolik; Daydreamer, The (1966); Dr. Phibes Rises Again; Don't Raise the Bridge, Lower the River; Hound of the Baskervilles, The; How to Murder Your Wife; I'm All Right Jack; It's a Mad Mad Mad Mad World; Lucky Jim; Make Mine Mink; Naked Truth (Your Past Is Showing); School for Scoundrels; Strange Bedfellows; Those Daring Young Men in Their Jaunty Jalopies; Those Magnificent Men in Their Flying Machines; Tom Thumb; Vault of Horror; Where Were You When the Lights Went Out?; Wonderful World of the Brothers Grimm, The
Terzieff, Laurent: A Coeur Joie (Head over Heels); Milky Way, The; Vanina Vanini
Tesreau, Krista: Breaking the Rules
Tessier, Genevieve: Real Howard Spritz, The
Tessier, Robert: Born Losers; Deep, The; Double Exposure; Last of the Mohicans; Lost Empire, The; Nightwish; No Safe Haven
Tessier, Valentine: Club des Femmes; Madame Bovary
Testi, Fabio: Ambassador, The; Blood in the Streets; Contraband; Garden of the Finzi-Continis, The; Gunfire; Mussolini and I; Stateline Motel
Testud, Sylvie: Beyond Silence
Teterson, Pete: Cold River
Tethong, Gyurme: Kundun
Tevini, Thierry: Tendres Cousines
Tewes, Lauren: China Lake Murders, The; Eyes of a Stranger
Texada, Tia: Nurse Betty
Texiere, Jacob: Leaves from Satan's Book
Teymouri, Sadou: Kandahar
Teyssedre, Anne: Tale of Springtime, A
Tha Dogg Pound: Show, The
Thal, Eric: Gun in Betty Lou's Handbag, The; Prisoner of Love; Puppet Masters, The; Samson and Delilah; Six Degrees of Separation; Stranger Among Us, A
Thalbach, Katharina: Good Evening Mr. Wallenberg
Thalia: Mambo Café
Thall, Benj: Homeward Bound: The Incredible Journey; Homeward Bound II: Lost in San Francisco
Thalman, Jim: No One Sleeps
Thames, Byron: Blame It on the Night; Seven Minutes in Heaven
Thatcher, Heather: Undying Monster, The
Thatcher, Torin: Affair in Trinidad; Crimson Pirate, The; Diane; From Hell to Borneo; Houdini; Istanbul; Jack the Giant Killer; 7th Voyage of Sinbad, The; Snows of Kilimanjaro, The; Strange Case of Dr. Jekyll and Mr. Hyde, The (1968)
Thate, Hilmar: Veronika Voss
Thaw, John: Business As Usual; Chaplin; Inspector Morse (TV Series); Killing Heat; Year in Provence, A
Thaxter, Phyllis: Jim Thorpe—All American; Living in a Big Way; Springfield Rifle; Thirty Seconds Over Tokyo; World of Henry Orient, The
Thayer, Brynn: Game of Love, The; Hero and the Terror
Thayer, Max: No Dead Heroes; No Retreat, No Surrender II
Thayer, Meg: Omega Cop
Thayer, Tina: Jive Junction
Theirse, Darryl: I Love You, Don't Touch Me!
Thelen, Jodi: Four Friends; One Night Stand
Theobald, Jeremy: Following
Theremin, Leon: Theremin: An Electronic Odyssey
Theriault, Serge: Boys, The (1997)
Theron, Charlize: Astronaut's Wife, The; Celebrity; Cider House Rules, The; Curse of the Jade Scorpion, The; Devil's Advocate; Hollywood Confidential; Legend of Bagger Vance, The; Men of Honor; Mighty Joe Young; Reindeer Games; Sweet November (2001); Trial and Error (1997); Two Days in the Valley; Yards, The
Theroux, Justin: Body Count (1997) (direct to video); Mulholland Drive; Sirens
Thesiger, Ernest: Brass Monkey, The; Bride of Frankenstein; Ghosts of Berkeley Square; Ghoul, The; Old Dark House, The
Thewlis, David: Besieged; Black Beauty; Dragonheart; Island of Dr. Moreau, The; Naked; Prime Suspect 3; Restoration; Seven Years in Tibet; Total Eclipse
Thibeau, Jack: Escape from Alcatraz
Thibeault, Debi: Cemetery High; Galactic Gigolo; Psychos in Love
Thicke, Alan: And You Thought Your Parents Were Weird; Any Place But Home; Betrayal of the Dove; Dance 'Til Dawn; Great American Sex Scandal, The; Not Quite Human; Not Quite Human 2; Obsessed; Scene of the Crime; Stepmonster; Still Not Quite Human; Thunder Point; Windsor Protocol, The
Thierry, Melanie: Legend of 1900, The
Thiess, Ursula: Monsoon
Thiessen, Tiffani-Amber: Hollywood Ending; Ladies Man, The (2000); Love Stinks; Shriek If You Know What I Did Last Friday the 13th
Thigpen, Kevin: Just Another Girl on the I.R.T.; Tar
Thinnes, Roy: Hindenburg, The; Invaders, The; Journey to the Far Side of the Sun; Rush Week; Satan's School for Girls; Scruples; Sizzle
Thirloway, Gregory: Inspectors, The; National Lampoon's Golf Punks
Thivisol, Victoire: Ponette
Thom, James: Virtual Assassin
Thomas, B. J.: Jory
Thomas, Betty: Hill Street Blues (TV Series); Homework; Prison for Children; Troop Beverly Hills; Tunnelvision (1976); When Your Lover Leaves
Thomas, Buckwheat: General Spanky
Thomas, Damien: Shogun (Full-Length Version); Sinbad and the Eye of the Tiger
Thomas, Danny: Danny Thomas Show, The (TV Series); I'll See You in My Dreams; Jazz Singer, The
Thomas, Dave: Boris and Natasha; Cold Sweat; Coneheads; Love at Stake; Moving; My Man Adam; Rat Race; Sesame Street Presents Follow That Bird; Strange Brew
Thomas, Eddie Kaye: American Pie 2
Thomas, Frank: Frank and Ollie
Thomas, Gareth: Blake's 7 (TV Series)
Thomas, George: Hide and Go Shriek
Thomas, Heather: Cyclone; Dirty Dozen, The: The Fatal Mission; Ford: The Man & the Machine; Hidden Obsession; Red-Blooded American Girl; Zapped!
Thomas, Heidi: Debt, The
Thomas, Henry: All the Pretty Horses; Bombshell; Cloak and Dagger; Curse of the Starving Class; E.T.—The Extra-Terrestrial; Fire in the Sky; Hijacking Hollywood; Indictment: The McMartin Trial; Legends of the Fall; Misunderstood; Moby Dick; Niagara Niagara; Psycho 4: The Beginning; Quest, The; Raggedy

Man; Riders of the Purple Sage; Suicide Kings; Taste for Killing, A; Valmont
Thomas, Isa: Flash of Green, A
Thomas, Jake: AI: Artificial Intelligence
Thomas, Jameson: Farmer's Wife, The; Scarlet Empress, The
Thomas, Jay: Killing Mr. Griffin; Mork & Mindy (TV Series); Mr. Holland's Opus; My Date with the President's Daughter; Smile Like Yours, A
Thomas, Jennifer: Desolation Angels
Thomas, Jonathan Taylor: Adventures of Pinocchio, The; Common Ground; I'll Be Home for Christmas; Man of the House; Tom and Huck; Wild America
Thomas, Kurt: Gymkata
Thomas, Marcus: Drowning Mona
Thomas, Marlo: Act of Passion; Consenting Adults; In the Spirit; Real Blonde, The
Thomas, Philip Michael: Death Drug; Miami Vice; Miami Vice: "The Prodigal Son"; Stigma; Streetfight (Coonskin); Wizard of Speed and Time, The
Thomas, Richard: All Quiet on the Western Front; Battle Beyond the Stars; Berlin Tunnel 21; Down, Out & Dangerous; Flood: A River's Rampage; Glory! Glory!; Hobson's Choice; Invaders, The; It; Last Summer; Linda; Living Proof: The Hank Williams Jr., Story; Mission of the Shark; Roots: The Next Generation; Thanksgiving Story, The; 30-Sep-55; Thousand Heroes, A; Todd Killings, The; Winning
Thomas, Robin: Amityville Dollhouse; Chameleon; Clockstoppers; Contender, The; From the Dead of Night; Memories of Murder
Thomas, Sean Patrick: Save the Last Dance
Thomas, Sian: Wedding Gift, The
Thomas, Tressa: Five Heartbeats, The
Thomas, William: Solomon and Gaenor
Thomason, Marsha: Black Knight
Thomassin, Florence: Mina Tannenbaum
Thomerson, Tim: Brain Smasher ... A Love Story; Cherry 2000; Crimson Code; Detour; Dollman; Dollman vs. Demonic Toys; Escape from Atlantis; Fade to Black; Flash, The (1990); Fleshtone; Gale Force; Glory Years; Harvest, The (1992); Hong Kong '97; Incredible Hulk Returns, The; Intimate Stranger; Iron Eagle; Metalstorm: The Destruction of Jared-Syn; Natural Causes; Near Dark; Nemesis; Nemesis 3: Time Lapse; Prime Time Murder; Spitfire; Tiger's Tale, A; Trancers; Trancers 5: Sudden Deth; Trancers 4: Jack of Swords; Trancers II (The Return of Jack Deth); Trancers III: Deth Lives; Vietnam, Texas; Volunteers; When Time Expires; Who's Harry Crumb?; Wrong Guys, The; Zone Troopers
Thompson, Alina: Marked Man
Thompson, Andrea: Doin' Time on Planet Earth
Thompson, Brian: Catch the Heat; Commando Squad; Doctor Mordrid; Hired to Kill; Mortal Kombat: Annihilation; Nightwish; Rage and Honor
Thompson, Christopher: Luzhin Defence, The
Thompson, Cindy Ann: Cave Girl
Thompson, David L.: Cat in the Brain, A
Thompson, Derek: Belfast Assassin
Thompson, Emma: Carrington; Dead Again; Fortunes of War; Henry V; Howards End; Impromptu; In the Name of the Father; Judas Kiss; Junior; Look Back In Anger; Much Ado About Nothing; My Father, the Hero; Peter's Friends; Primary Colors; Remains of the Day; Sense and Sensibility; Tall Guy, The; Winter Guest, The; Wit
Thompson, Fred Dalton: Aces: Iron Eagle III; Baby's Day Out; Barbarians at the Gate; Born Yesterday; Cape Fear; Class Action; Curly Sue; Die Hard 2: Die Harder; In the Line of Fire; Keep the Change; Thunderheart
Thompson, Gordon: Donor, The
Thompson, Jack: Breaker Morant; Broken Arrow; Burke and Wills; Caddie; Club, The; Earthling, The; Excess Baggage; Far Off Place, A; Flesh and Blood (Sword and the Rose, the (1985)); Ground Zero; Last Dance; Mad Dog Morgan; Man from Snowy River, The; Midnight in the Garden of Good and Evil; Original Sin; South Pacific (2001); Star Wars: Attack of the Clones; Sum of Us, The; Sunday Too Far Away; Trouble in Paradise; Turtle Beach (Killing Beach); Wind (1992); Woman of Independent Means, A
Thompson, Jody: Deathgame
Thompson, Judy: Teach Me Tonight
Thompson, Kay: Funny Face
Thompson, Kenan: Good Burger; Heavyweights
Thompson, Kenneth: Just Imagine; Sweethearts on Parade; White Gold
Thompson, Lea: All the Right Moves; Article 99; Back to the Future; Back to the Future II; Back to the Future III; Beverly Hillbillies, The (1993); Casual Sex?; Dennis the Menace; Going Undercover; Howard the Duck; Montana; Nightbreaker; Red Dawn; Right to Remain Silent, The; Some Kind of Wonderful; SpaceCamp; Substitute Wife, The; Wild Life, The; Wizard of Loneliness, The
Thompson, Marshall: Around the World Under the Sea; Bog; Clarence, the Cross-Eyed Lion; Crashout; Cult of the Cobra; East of Kilimanjaro; Fiend without a Face; First Man into Space, The; Homecoming; It! The Terror from Beyond Space; Show-Off, The; They Were Expendable; To Hell and Back; White Dog
Thompson, Michelle: My Sweet Suicide
Thompson, Rex: Eddy Duchin Story, The
Thompson, Sada: Indictment: The McMartin Trial; Our Town; Princess Daisy; Pursuit of Happiness, The
Thompson, Sarah: Cruel Intentions 2
Thompson, Shawn: Bram Stoker's Shadowbuilder; Future Fear; Hairspray; Heads; Sleeping with Strangers
Thompson, Sophie: Dancing at Lughnasa; Emma
Thompson, Susann: Ghosts of Mississippi
Thompson, Suzanne: High Noon
Thompson, Teri: Breakaway; Married People, Single Sex
Thompson, Weyman: Hot Shot
Thomsen, Ulrich: Celebration, The
Thomsett, Sally: Railway Children, The
Thomson, Anna: Cafe Society; Outside the Law
Thomson, Fred: Thundering Hoofs
Thomson, Kim: Great Expectations; Murder 101; Sherlock Holmes: Hands of a Murderer; Stealing Heaven
Thomson, Pat: Strictly Ballroom
Thomson, R. H.: And Then You Die; Bone Daddy; Ford: The Man & the Machine; Heaven on Earth; If You Could See What I Hear; Lotus Eaters, The; Quarrel, The; Surfacing; Ticket to Heaven
Thor, Cameron: Face Down
Thor, Larry: Amazing Colossal Man, The
Thorburn, June: Three Worlds of Gulliver, The; Tom Thumb
Thordsen, Kelly: Ugly Dachshund, The
Thorley, Ken: Escapes; Ghost in the Machine
Thorliefsson, Eggert: Remote Control
Thornbury, Bill: Phantasm; Phantasm IV: Oblivion
Thorndike, Sybil: Major Barbara; Nine Days a Queen; Prince and the Showgirl, The; Shake Hands with the Devil
Thorne, Callie: Ed's Next Move; Next Stop Wonderland; Wirey Spindell
Thorne, Dyanne: Ilsa, the Wicked Warden
Thorne, Zachary: Meat Loaf: To Hell and Back
Thorne-Smith, Courtney: Breach of Conduct; Chairman of the Board; Lucas; Revenge of the Nerds II: Nerds in Paradise; Summer School; Welcome to 18
Thornhill, Lisa: Enemy Action
Thornton, Billy Bob: Apostle, The; Armageddon; Bandits (2001); Don't Look Back; Homegrown; Man Who Wasn't There, The (2001); Monster's Ball; Primary Colors; Pushing Tin; Simple Plan, A; Sling Blade; South of Heaven, West of Hell; U-Turn; Winner, The
Thornton, Brad: Kickboxer 4: Aggressor, The
Thornton, David: Breathing Room; Off and Running
Thornton, Noley: Danielle Steel's Fine Things; Little Riders, The
Thornton, Sigrid: Great Expectations—The Untold Story; Lighthorsemen, The; Over the Hill; Return to Snowy River, Part II; Slate, Wyn, and Me; Trapped in Space
Thorogood, Maurice: House That Mary Bought, The

Thorsen, Sven-Ole: Abraxas Guardian of the Universe; Fatal Combat; Viking Sagas, The
Thorson, Linda: Act of Passion; Avengers, The (TV Series); Curtains; Sweet Liberty
Three Stooges, The: Dancing Lady; Snow White and the Three Stooges
Threlfall, David: Summer House, The
Thring, Frank: Mad Max Beyond Thunderdome
Throne, Malachi: It Takes a Thief (TV Series)
Throw, Lisa: Shandra, The Jungle Girl
Thrush, George: Vermont Is for Lovers
Thual, Jean-Yves: Red Dwarf, The
Thuillier, Luc: Monsieur Hire; Old Lady Who Walked in the Sea, The
Thulin, Ingrid: Brink of Life; Cries and Whispers; Damned, The; Four Horsemen of the Apocalypse; Hour of the Wolf; Magician, The; Moses; Silence, The; Wild Strawberries; Winter Light
Thundercloud, Chief: Badman's Territory; Hi-Yo Silver; Lone Ranger, The; Riders of the Whistling Skull
Thurman, Bill: Badman's Territory; Hi-Yo Silver; Lone Ranger, The; Riders of the Whistling Skull
Thurman, Uma: Adventures of Baron Münchausen, The; Avengers, The; Batman & Robin; Beautiful Girls; Dangerous Liaisons; Even Cowgirls Get the Blues; Final Analysis; Gattaca; Golden Bowl, The; Henry & June; Jennifer 8; Johnny Be Good; Kiss Daddy Good Night; Les Misérables; Mad Dog and Glory; Month by the Lake, A; Pulp Fiction; Robin Hood; Sweet and Lowdown; Truth About Cats and Dogs, The; Where the Heart Is
Thurseon, Debbie: Prey, The
Thursfield, Sophie: Sister, My Sister
Thurston, Carol: Story of Dr. Wassell, The
Tichy, Gerard: Summertime Killer, The
Ticotin, Rachel: Con Air; Critical Condition; Don Juan DeMarco; Falling Down; First Time Felon; Forever Together; Fort Apache—The Bronx; Full Disclosure; F/X 2: The Deadly Art of Illusion; Keep the Change; One Good Cop; Prison Stories: Women on the Inside; Steal Big, Steal Little; Total Recall; Turbulence; Warden of Red Rock; Wharf Rat, The; Where the Day Takes You
Tidof, Max: Harmonists, The
Tien, James: Fists of Fury
Tiernan, Andrew: Edward II
Tierney, Gene: Advise and Consent; Egyptian, The; Ghost and Mrs. Muir, The; Heaven Can Wait; Laura; Leave Her to Heaven; Left Hand of God, The; Never Let Me Go; Night and the City; Razor's Edge, The; Return of Frank James, The; Shanghai Gesture, The; Son of Fury; Sundown; Toys in the Attic
Tierney, Jacob: Dead End; Josh and S.A.M.; Neon Bible, The; This Is My Father
Tierney, Lawrence: Abduction; Born to Kill; Bushwhackers; Devil Thumbs a Ride, The; Dillinger; Dillinger; Female Jungle; Midnight; Prowler, The; Reservoir Dogs; Runestone; Southie; Those Endearing Young Charms; Two Days in the Valley; Wizards of the Demon Sword
Tierney, Maura: Forces of Nature; Instinct; Liar, Liar; Mercy; Oxygen; Primary Colors; Scotland, PA
Tierney, Patrick: Next of Kin
Tiffe, Angelo: Sword of Honor
Tiffin, Pamela: One, Two, Three; State Fair; Viva Max!
Tifo, Marie: Blind Trust (Pouvoir Intime)
Tigar, Kenneth: Gypsy Warriors, The; Little Bigfoot; Rage
Tighe, Kevin: Another 48 Hrs.; Avenging Angel, The (1995); Better Off Dead; Caught in the Act; City of Hope; Darwin Conspiracy, The; Double Cross; Geronimo: An American Legend; Jade; K-9; Man in Uniform, A; Men of War; Mumford; Race the Sun; What's Eating Gilbert Grape?; Winchell
Tikaram, Ramon: Kama Sutra: A Tale of Love
Tilbury, Peter: Nemesis
Tiller, Nadja: Burning Court, The; Tonio Kroger
Tiller, Patrick: Too Fast Too Young
Tillis, Mel: Uphill All the Way
Tilly, Jennifer: American Strays; Bella Mafia; Bird of Prey; Bound; Bride of Chucky; Bullets over Broadway; Crew, The; Double Cross; Edie & Pen; Embrace of the Vampire; Fabulous Baker Boys, The; Far from Home; Fast Sofa; Getaway, The; Heads; Hide and Seek; High Spirits; Hoods; House Arrest; Inside Out; Inventing the Abbotts; Let It Ride; Liar, Liar; Made in America; Man with a Gun; Moving Violations; Muse, The; Music from Another Room; Pompatus of Love, The; Relax … It's Just Sex; Remote Control; Rented Lips; Scorchers; Shadow of the Wolf; Silent Witness; Sister Mary Explains It All; Webber's World (At Home with the Webbers)
Tilly, Meg: Agnes of God; Big Chill, The; Body Snatchers, The (1993); Carmilla; Cat's Meow, The; Girl in a Swing, The; Impulse; Journey; Leaving Normal; Masquerade; Off Beat; One Dark Night; Primal Secrets; Psycho II; Sleep with Me; Tex; Two Jakes, The; Valmont
Tilton, Charlene: Border Shootout; Center of the Web; Deadly Bet; Diary of a Teenage Hitchhiker; Fall of the House of Usher, The; Silence of the Hams; Sweater Girls
Timberlake, Justin: Model Behavior
Timbrook, Corbin: Forbidden Sins
Timko, Johnny: Hot Moves
Timkul, Patharawarin: Bangkok Dangerous
Timmins, Cali: Hard Evidence; Takeover, The
Timmons, James: Kissed
Timothy, Christopher: All Creatures Great and Small
Timsit, Patrick: Little Indian, Big City
Tinapp, Barton: Dennis the Menace: Dinosaur Hunter
Tindall, Hilary: Max Headroom
Tinelli, Jaime: Sudden Death
Tingwell, Charles: Breaker Morant; Castle, The; Cry in the Dark, A; Innocence; Miracle Down Under; Murder Ahoy; Murder at the Gallop; Murder Most Foul; Murder She Said
Tinti, Gabriele: Trap Them and Kill Them
Tiny Tim: Blood Harvest
Tiplady, Brittany: Millennium
Tippitt, Wayne: Pipe Dreams
Tipple, Gordon: Time Runner
Tippo, Patti: Omega Syndrome
Tirelli, Jaime: Girlfight
Tishman, Keren: Chain of Command
Tittle, Bently: Dark Universe, The
Tobeck, Joel: Women from Down Under
Tobey, Kenneth: Beast from 20,000 Fathoms, The; Bigamist, The; Davy Crockett and the River Pirates; Davy Crockett, King of the Wild Frontier; Elfego Baca: Six Gun Law; I Was a Male War Bride; It Came from Beneath the Sea; Kiss Tomorrow Goodbye; Strange Invaders; Thing (From Another World), The (1951); This Time For Keeps; Wings of Eagles, The
Tobgyal, Orgyen: Cup, The
Tobias, George: Air Force; Balalaika; Bride Came C.O.D., The; Captains of the Clouds; City for Conquest; Judge Steps Out, The; Mildred Pierce; New Kind of Love, A; Objective, Burma!; Rawhide; Sergeant York; Set-Up, The; Seven Little Foys, The; Strawberry Blonde, The; This Is the Army
Tobias, Oliver: Breeders; Grizzly Falls; King Arthur, The Young Warlord; Mata Hari; Operation 'Nam; Stud, The; Wicked Lady, The
Tobin, Genevieve: Case of the Lucky Legs, The
Tobolowsky, Stephen: Basic Instinct; Black Dog; Bossa Nova; Dr. Jekyll and Ms. Hyde; Funny About Love; Glimmer Man, The; Grifters, The; Groundhog Day; Josh and S.A.M.; Memoirs of an Invisible Man; Mr. Magoo; My Father, the Hero; Operator, The
Todd, Ann: All This and Heaven Too; Danny Boy; Human Factor, The; Paradine Case, The; Scream of Fear; Seventh Veil, The; Ships with Wings; Son of Captain Blood; Time Without Pity
Todd, Beverly: Brother John; Clara's Heart; Don't Look Back: The Story of Leroy "Satchel" Paige; Jericho Mile, The; Ladies Club; Lean on Me; Moving; Vice Squad
Todd, Hallie: Check Is in the Mail, The
Todd, Harry: Jack Knife Man, The
Todd, Michael: Robot Ninja
Todd, Richard: Asylum; Battle Hell; D-Day the Sixth of June; Dam Busters, The; Dorian Gray; Man Called Peter, A; Never Let Go; Number One of the Secret Service; Operation Crossbow; Rob Roy, the Highland Rogue; Saint Joan; Sherlock Holmes and the Incident at Victoria Falls; Stage Fright; Story of Robin Hood,

The; Sword and the Rose, The (1953); Very Edge, The; Virgin Queen, The
Todd, Russell: Chopping Mall; One Last Run; Sweet Murder; Where the Boys Are '84
Todd, Saira: Bad Behaviour; Fatal Inversion, A
Todd, Thelma: Bohemian Girl, The; Call Her Savage; Cockeyed Cavaliers; Devil's Brother, The; Hips, Hips, Hooray; Horse Feathers; Monkey Business; Palooka; Seven Footprints to Satan; Speak Easily
Todd, Tony: Beastmaster III: The Eye of Braxus; Black Fox; Blood Horse; Bram Stoker's Shadowbuilder; Candyman; Candyman: Farewell to the Flesh; Candyman 3: Day of the Dead; Good Men and Bad; Ivory Hunters; Night of the Living Dead; Pandora Project, The; Sabotage; Wes Craven's Wishmaster
Todd, Trisha: Claire of the Moon
Todd, Zen: Killer Flick
Todeschini, Bruno: Va Savoir
Todorovic, Bora: Time of the Gypsies
Toffalo, Lino: Lunatics & Lovers
Tognazzi, Ricky: Blood Ties
Tognazzi, Ugo: Joke of Destiny; La Cage aux Folles; La Cage aux Folles II; La Cage aux Folles III, The Wedding; Pigsty; Tragedy of a Ridiculous Man
Toibin, Niall: Eat the Peach; Rawhead Rex
Tokui, Yu: Shall We Dance?
Tol, Henriette: Flight of Rainbirds, A
Tolan, Michael: Hour of the Gun, The
Tolbe, Joe: Men in Love
Toledo, Goya: Amores Perros
Toler, Sidney: Castle in the Desert; Charlie Chan at the Wax Museum; Charlie Chan at Treasure Island; Charlie Chan in City in Darkness; Charlie Chan in Honolulu; Charlie Chan in Panama; Charlie Chan in Reno; Charlie Chan in Rio; Charlie Chan in the Secret Service; Charlie Chan's Murder Cruise; Chinese Cat, The; Dead Men Tell; Double Wedding; Heritage of the Desert; It's in the Bag; Jade Mask, The; Law of the Pampas; Meeting at Midnight; Murder over New York; Night to Remember, A; Our Relations; Romance in Manhattan; Scarlet Clue, The; Shanghai Cobra, The; Speak Easily; Spitfire
Toles-Bey, John: Leap of Faith; Rage in Harlem, A; Waterworld
Tolkan, James: Bloodfist IV—Die Trying; Boiling Point; Masters of the Universe; Ministry of Vengeance; Opportunity Knocks; Question of Faith; Second Sight; Sketch Artist II: Hands That See; Viper; Weekend War
Tolo, Marilu: Beyond Fear; Confessions of a Police Captain; Long Live Your Death; Marriage Italian Style
Tom, David: Stay Tuned
Tom, Lauren: Joy Luck Club, The
Tom, Nicholle: Beethoven's 2nd
Tomanovich, Dara: Amnesia; Back in Business
Tomasina, Jeana: Beach Girls, The
Tomei, Adam: My Own Country
Tomei, Marisa: Chaplin; Four Rooms; Happy Accidents; My Cousin Vinny; My Own Country; Only Love; Only You; Oscar (1991); Paper, The; Perez Family, The; Since You've Been Gone; Slums of Beverly Hills; Someone Like You; Unhook the Stars; Untamed Heart; Watcher, The; Welcome to Sarajevo; What Women Want
Tomelty, Frances: Bellman and True; Blue Money; Bullshot (Bullshot Crummond); Field, The
Tomita, Tamlyn: Come See the Paradise; Joy Luck Club, The; Killing Jar, The; Picture Bride
Tomlin, Lily: All of Me; And the Band Played On; Beverly Hillbillies, The (1993); Big Business; Blue in the Face; Flirting with Disaster; Getting Away with Murder; Incredible Shrinking Woman, The; Kid, The (2000); Krippendorf's Tribe; Late Show, The; Nashville; Nine to Five; Search for Signs of Intelligent Life in the Universe, The; Shadows and Fog; Short Cuts; Tea with Mussolini
Tomlins, Jason: Live! From Death Row
Tomlinson, David: Bedknobs and Broomsticks; Carry on Admiral; Fiendish Plot of Dr. Fu Manchu, The; Made in Heaven; Mary Poppins; Pimpernel Smith; Three Men in a Boat; Up the Creek; Water Babies, The; Wooden Horse, The
Tomlinson, Ricky: Raining Stones; Riff-Raff (1990)
Tompkins, Angel: Don Is Dead, The; I Love My Wife; Prime Cut
Tompkins, Joan: I Love My Wife
Tompkinson, Stephen: Brassed Off
Tonby, Kristian: Littlest Viking, The
Tone, Franchot: Advise and Consent; Bombshell; Bride Wore Red, The; Dancing Lady; Dangerous (1935); Dark Waters; Every Girl Should Be Married; Five Graves to Cairo; Gabriel over the White House; Girl from Missouri, The; Gorgeous Hussy, The; Here Comes the Groom; His Butler's Sister; In Harm's Way; Lives of a Bengal Lancer, The; Love on the Run; Man in the Eiffel Tower, The; Mutiny on the Bounty; Quality Street; Reckless; Sadie McKee; Suzy; Three Comrades; Today We Live
Tong, Jacqueline: How to Get Ahead in Advertising
Tong, Kam: Have Gun, Will Travel (TV Series)
Tonke, Laura Maori: Winter Sleepers
Tono, Eijiro: Yojimbo
Tonsberg, Adam: Twist and Shout
Toomey, Regis: Arizona; Betrayal from the East; Beyond the Forest; Dive Bomber; Doughgirls, The; Dynamite Pass; Framed; High and the Mighty, The; Island in the Sky; Phantom Creeps, The; Skull and Crown; Station West; Strange Illusion
Toone, Geoffrey: Captain Sinbad; Terror of the Tongs, The
Tootoosis, Gordon: Call of the Wild; Stone Fox, The
Topaz, David: Goodbye New York
Topol: Fiddler on the Roof; Flash Gordon; For Your Eyes Only; House on Garibaldi Street; Left Luggage; Queenie; Sallah
Topol-Barzilai, Anat: Witchcraft
Torday, Terry: Tower of Screaming Virgins, The
Toren, Marta: Casbah; Paris Express, The; Sirocco
Torey, Roberta: Hans Brinker
Torgan, Kendra: Killing Time (1996)
Torgov, Sarah: Drying Up the Streets; If You Could See What I Hear
Tork, Peter: Head (1968)
Torme, Mel: Comedian, The; Girls Town; Good News; Higher and Higher; Man Called Adam, A; Words and Music
Tormey, John: Ghost Dog: The Way of the Samurai
Torn, Rip: Another Pair of Aces; Baby Doll; Balloon Farm; Beastmaster, The; Beautiful Dreamers; Beer; Betrayal; Birch Interval, The; Blue and the Gray, The; By Dawn's Early Light; Canadian Bacon; Cat on a Hot Tin Roof; City Heat; Cold Feet; Coma; Critic's Choice; Cross Creek; Dead Ahead: The Exxon Valdez Disaster; Defending Your Life; Dolly Dearest; Down Periscope; Extreme Prejudice; First Family; Flashpoint; Freddy Got Fingered; Heartland; Hit List (1988); How to Make an American Quilt; Jinxed; King of Kings (1961); Laguna Heat; Letter to My Killer; Man Who Fell to Earth, The; Manhunt for Claude Dallas; Men in Black; Nadine; One Trick Pony; Pair of Aces; Passing Glory; Payday; Pork Chop Hill; President's Plane Is Missing, The; Private Files of J. Edgar Hoover, The; Rape and Marriage: The Rideout Case; RoboCop 3; Seduction of Joe Tynan, The; Senseless; Shining Season, A; Silence Like Glass; Slaughter; Songwriter; Sophia Loren: Her Own Story; Stranger Is Watching, A; Summer Rental; Sweet Bird of Youth; Trial and Error (1997); Tropic of Cancer; Where the Rivers Flow North; You're a Big Boy Now
Torne, Regina: Like Water for Chocolate
Torocsik, Mari: Love
Torrence, David: City Girl
Torrence, Ernest: Covered Wagon, The; Fighting Caravans; Hunchback of Notre Dame, The; I Cover the Waterfront; King of Kings, The (1927); Peter Pan; Steamboat Bill Jr.; Tol'able David; Twelve Miles Out
Torrent, Ana: ¡Cria!; Nest, The; Spirit of the Beehive, The; Thesis
Torres, Fernanda: One Man's War
Torres, Liz: America; Bloodfist IV—Die Trying; Just Cause; More Wild Wild West; Thieves of Fortune
Torres, Raquel: Duck Soup; White Shadows in the South Seas
Torry, Guy: Animal, The; Don't Say a Word
Torry, Joe: Back in Business; Poetic Justice; Sprung; Tales from the Hood

Toto: Big Deal on Madonna Street; Gold of Naples, The; Hawks and the Sparrows, The; Laugh for Joy (Passionate Thief) (1954); Passionate Thief, The (1961)
Totter, Audrey: Any Number Can Play; Carpetbaggers, The; Jet Attack; Lady in the Lake; Set-Up, The
Toub, Shaun: Steel Sharks
Touliatos, George: Crackerjack; Firebird 2015 AD; Firepower; Heartaches; Left for Dead; Mortal Sins (1992); Robbers of the Sacred Mountain; Tracks of a Killer
Toumanova, Tamara: Days of Glory
Tousey, Sheila: Medicine River; Silent Tongue; Slaughter of the Innocents
Toussaint, Beth: Armed and Deadly; Blackmail; Breach of Conduct; Nightsiege-Project: Shadowchaser 2
Toussaint, Lorraine: America's Dream; Nightjohn
Tovar, Lupita: Dracula (Spanish)
Tower, Wade: Ripper, The
Towers, Constance: Horse Soldiers, The; Naked Kiss, The; Next Karate Kid, The; On Wings of Eagles; Sergeant Rutledge; Shock Corridor; Sylvester
Towles, Tom: Mad Dog and Glory
Towne, Aline: Radar Men from the Moon; Zombies of the Stratosphere (Satan's Satellites) (Serial)
Towne, Katherine: What Lies Beneath
Townes, Harry: Fitzwilly; Santee; Screaming Mimi
Townsend, Anna: Grandma's Boy
Townsend, Jill: Awakening, The; Oh, Alfie
Townsend, Omar: Party Girl
Townsend, Patrice: Always; Sitting Ducks
Townsend, Robert: Five Heartbeats, The; Hollywood Shuffle; Mercenary 2: Thick and Thin; Meteor Man; Mighty Quinn, The; Ratboy
Townsend, Stuart: About Adam; Queen of the Damned; Resurrection Man; Shooting Fish; Under the Skin
Townshend, Pete: Jimi Hendrix
Toyokawa, Etsushi: No Way Back
Tozzi, Giorgio: Torn Between Two Lovers
Tracey, Ian: Bloodhounds II; Dirty Little Secret
Trachtenberg, Michelle: Forever Together; Harriet the Spy; Inspector Gadget
Tracy, Greg: Forever Together; Harriet the Spy; Inspector Gadget
Tracy, Lee: Best Man, The; Betrayal from the East; Blessed Event; Bombshell; Doctor X; Strange Love of Molly Louvain, The
Tracy, Spencer: Adam's Rib; Bad Day at Black Rock; Boom Town; Boys' Town; Broken Lance; Captains Courageous; Cass Timberlane; Desk Set; Devil at 4 O'Clock, The; Dr. Jekyll and Mr. Hyde; Edison, The Man; Father of the Bride; Father's Little Dividend; Fury (1936); Guess Who's Coming to Dinner; Guy Named Joe, A; Inherit the Wind; It's a Mad Mad Mad Mad World; Judgment at Nuremberg; Keeper of the Flame; Last Hurrah, The; Libeled Lady; Mannequin; Men of Boys Town; Mountain, The; Northwest Passage; Old Man and the Sea, The; Pat and Mike; RiffRaff; San Francisco; Sea of Grass, The; Seventh Cross, The; Stanley and Livingstone; State of the Union; Test Pilot; Thirty Seconds Over Tokyo; Tortilla Flat; Without Love; Woman of the Year
Tracy, Steve: Desperate Moves
Trainor, Mary Ellen: Greedy; Little Giants; Tales from the Crypt (TV Series)
Trainor, Saxon: Magic in the Mirror
Tran, Tung Thanh: Good Morning, Vietnam
Trantow, Cordula: Castle, The; Hitler
Trask, Stephen: Hedwig and the Angry Inch
Traubel, Helen: Deep in My Heart; Ladies' Man, The (1961)
Trauth, Andrew James: Mysterious Museum
Travalena, Fred: Buy and Cell
Travanti, Daniel J.: Adam; Case of Libel, A; Eyes of a Witness; Fellow Traveler; Hill Street Blues (TV Series); Just Cause; Megaville; Midnight Crossing; Millennium; Murrow; Tagget; Wasp Woman, The (1995); Weep No More My Lady
Travers, Bill: Belstone Fox, The; Bhowani Junction; Born Free; Browning Version, The; Christian the Lion; Duel at Diablo; Gorgo; Ring of Bright Water; Romeo and Juliet; Smallest Show on Earth, The
Travers, Henry: Ball of Fire; Death Takes a Holiday; Edison, The Man; Girl, a Guy and a Gob, A; Invisible Man, The; It's a Wonderful Life; Madame Curie; Mrs. Miniver; On Borrowed Time; Primrose Path; Rains Came, The; Random Harvest; Shadow of a Doubt
Travis, June: Case of the Black Cat, The; Ceiling Zero; Star, The (1952)
Travis, Nancy: Anything for Love; Beyond Suspicion; Body Language; Bogus; Chaplin; Destiny Turns on the Radio; Fluke; Internal Affairs; Loose Cannons; Passed Away; Running Mates; So I Married an Axe Murderer; Three Men and a Baby; Three Men and a Little Lady; Vanishing, The
Travis, Randy: Black Dog; Boys Will Be Boys; Deadman's Revenge; Fire Down Below; Frank & Jesse; Texas; Texas Rangers (2001); White River
Travis, Richard: Man Who Came to Dinner, The; Missile to the Moon
Travis, Stacey: Bandits (2001); Dracula Rising; Hardware; Only the Strong; Suspect Device
Travis, Tony: Flesh Gordon 2: Flesh Gordon meets the Cosmic Cheerleaders
Travolta, Ellen: Are You in the House Alone?; Basket, The; Elvis—The Movie
Travolta, Joey: Basket, The; Beach Babes from Beyond; Davinci's War; Ghost Writer; Hunter's Blood; They Still Call Me Bruce; To the Limit; Wilding, The Children of Violence
Travolta, John: Battlefield Earth; Blow Out; Boy in the Plastic Bubble, The; Broken Arrow; Carrie; Chains of Gold; Civil Action, A; Devil's Rain, The; Domestic Disturbance; Dumb Waiter, The; Experts, The; Eyes of an Angel; Face/Off; General's Daughter, The; Get Shorty; Grease; Look Who's Talking; Look Who's Talking Now; Look Who's Talking Too; Lucky Numbers; Mad City; Michael; Our Friend, Martin; Perfect; Phenomenon; Primary Colors; Pulp Fiction; Saturday Night Fever; She's So Lovely; Shout (1991); Staying Alive; Swordfish; Two of a Kind; Urban Cowboy; White Man's Burden
Traylor, Susan: Broken Vessels
Treacher, Arthur: Curly Top; Heidi; In Society; Little Princess, The (1939); Mad About Music; Mary Poppins; My Lucky Star; Riptide; Satan Met a Lady; Stowaway; That Midnight Kiss; Thin Ice; Viva Villa!
Treanor, Michael: Three Ninjas; Three Ninjas Knuckle Up
Treas, Terri: Alien Nation, Dark Horizon; Deathstalker III—The Warriors from Hell; House IV; Ladykiller; Rage and Honor
Treat, Daniel: Shadrach
Trebor, Robert: My Demon Lover
Tree, David: Drums; Knight Without Armour; Pygmalion
Tree, Lady: Wedding Rehearsal
Treil, Laurence: Entangled
Trejo, Danny: Animal Factory; Bubble Boy; Desert Heat; From Dusk Till Dawn 2: Texas Blood Money; Point Blank; Spy Kids
Tremayne, Les: Angry Red Planet, The; Man Called Peter, A; Monolith Monsters, The; Monster of Piedras Blancas, The; Slime People, The; War of the Worlds, The
Tremblay, Johanne-Marie: Straight for the Heart
Tremko, Anne: Member of the Wedding, The
Trench, Alex: Oliver Twist
Trenholme, Helen: Case of the Howling Dog, The
Treniers, The: Girl Can't Help It, The
Trentini, Peggy: Human Desires
Trepechinska, Joanna: Paper Marriage
Trese, Adam: 40 Days and 40 Nights; Illtown; Palookaville
Trevarthen, Noel: Dusty
Treves, Frederick: Flame to the Phoenix, A; Paper Mask; Sleeping Murder
Trevino, Marco Antonio: Donna Herlinda and Her Son
Trevino, Vic: Firehawk; Kill Zone
Trevor, Austin: To Paris with Love
Trevor, Claire: Allegheny Uprising; Amazing Dr. Clitterhouse, The; Babe Ruth Story, The; Baby Take a Bow; Best of the Badmen; Born to Kill; Breaking Home Ties; Crack-Up; Dark Command; Dead End; High and the Mighty, The; Honky Tonk; Hood-

lum Empire; How to Murder Your Wife; Johnny Angel; Key Largo; Kiss Me Goodbye; Man without a Star; Marjorie Morningstar; Mountain, The; Murder My Sweet; Stagecoach; Stranger Wore a Gun, The; Stripper, The; Texas; Two Weeks in Another Town; Velvet Touch, The; Woman of the Town
Trevor, Norman: Dancing Mothers
Trickey, Paula: Base, The
Trieb, Tatjana: Beyond Silence
Trieste, Leopoldo: Henry IV; Shoot Loud, Louder ... I Don't Understand; Star Maker, The; White Sheik, The
Trifunovic, Sergej: Someone Else's America; 3 A.M.
Trigger: Billy the Kid Returns
Trigger, Sarah: Deadfall; El Diablo; Kid (1990); PCU
Trilling, Zoe: Night of the Demons 2; Tobe Hooper's Night Terrors
Trimble, Jerry: Breathing Fire; In the Name of Justice; Live by the Fist; One Man Army; Stranglehold
Trintignant, Jean-Louis: Act of Aggression; And God Created Woman; And Hope to Die; Bad Girls; Confidentially Yours; Conformist, The; Je Vous Aime (I Love You All); Le Secret; Les Biches; Les Liaisons Dangereuses; Les Violons du Bal; Man and a Woman, A; Man and a Woman, A: 20 Years Later; Merci La Vie; My Night at Maud's; Next Summer; Passion of Love; Red; Rendez-Vous; Seven Deadly Sins, The; Sleeping Car Murders, The; Under Fire; Z
Trintignant, Marie: Next Summer; Ponette; Wings of Fame
Tripp, Louis: Gate II
Tripplehorn, Jeanne: Basic Instinct; Firm, The; Mickey Blue Eyes; Night We Never Met, The; Office Killer; Old Man; Relative Values; Sliding Doors; Steal This Movie; 'Til There Was You; Timecode; Very Bad Things; Waterworld
Triska, Jan: Andersonville; Elementary School, The; My Antonia
Trissenaar, Elisabeth: Angry Harvest; Nobody Loves Me
Tristan, Dorothy: End of the Road; Griffin and Phoenix: A Love Story
Tritt, Travis: Rio Diablo
Troisi, Massimo: Hotel Colonial; Postman, The (Il Postino)
Trotter, Kate: Clarence
Trotter, Laura: Miami Horror
Troughton, David: Norman Conquests, The, Episode 1: Table Manners; Norman Conquests, The, Episode 3: Roundand Round the Garden; Norman Conquests, The, Episode 2: LivingTogether
Troughton, Patrick: Dr. Who (TV series); Frankenstein and the Monster from Hell; Sinbad and the Eye of the Tiger
Troup, Bobby: Five Pennies, The
Trowbridge, Charles: Captain America; Fatal Hour, The; Valley of the Zombies
Troxell, Richard: Madame Butterfly
Troy, Ellen: Dance
Troy, Phillip: Ice
Truax, Maude: Hula
Trudeau, Margaret: Kings and Desperate Men: A Hostage Incident
True, Jim: Affliction; Hudsucker Proxy, The; Normal Life; Singles
True, Rachel: Craft, The; Half Baked; Nowhere
Truex, Ernest: Adventures of Marco Polo, The; Bachelor Mother; Christmas in July; His Girl Friday
Truffaut, Ewa: Francois Truffaut: Stolen Moments
Truffaut, François: Close Encounters of the Third Kind; Day for Night; Green Room, The; Wild Child, The (L'Enfant Sauvage)
Truffaut, Laura: Francois Truffaut: Stolen Moments
Trujillo, Raul: Black Fox; Blood Horse; Clearcut; Good Men and Bad; Highlander: The Final Dimension; Medicine River
Truman, Jeff: Bliss
Truman, Ralph: Saint in London, The
Trumbo, Karen: Claire of the Moon
Trump, Marla Maples: Executive Decision
Truswell, Chris: Fast Talking
Tryon, Glenn: Battling Orioles, The
Tryon, Tom: Cardinal, The; Color Me Dead; Gundown at Sandoval; I Married a Monster from Outer Space; In Harm's Way; Moon Pilot; Story of Ruth, The; Texas John Slaughter: Stampede at BitterCreek; Three Violent People
Trzepiecinska, Joanna: Blood of the Innocent
Tsang, Eric: Gen-X Cops
Tsang, Ken: Police Story III—Super Cop
Tsarong, Tenzin Thuthob: Kundun
Tschechowa, Olga: Haunted Castle; Italian Straw Hat, The
Tse, Nicholas: Gen-X Cops; Time and Tide
Tse, Yang: Enter the Dragon
Tselikovskaya, Ludmila: Ivan the Terrible—Part I & Part II
Tsien, Wong Tsu: Chinese Ghost Story, A
Tsopei, Corinna: Man Called Horse, A
Tsubouchi, Mikiko: Zatoichi: Masseur Ichi and a Chest of Gold
Tsuchiya, Yoshio: Human Vapor, The
Tsui, Cathy: Time and Tide
Tsui, Elvis: Sex and Zen
Tsukamoto, Shinya: Tetsuo II: Body Hammer
Tsuneta, Fujio: Eel, The
Tsuruta, Koji: Samurai Trilogy, The
Tubb, Barry: Consenting Adults; Top Gun; Valentino Returns; Warm Summer Rain
Tubert, Marcelo: Tremors 2: Aftershocks
Tucci, Stanley: Alarmist, The; Beethoven; Big Night; Big Trouble (2002); Billy Bathgate; Daytrippers, The; Impostors, The; In the Soup; In Too Deep; It Could Happen to You; Joe Gould's Secret; Jury Duty; Kiss of Death; Life Less Ordinary, A; Men of Respect; Modern Affair, A; Montana; Pelican Brief, The; Public Eye, The; Sidewalks of New York (2001); Somebody to Love; Undercover Blues; William Shakespeare's A Midsummer Night's Dream; Winchell
Tucci, Tony: Gravesend
Tuck, Jennifer: Penpal Murders; Vampires from Outer Space
Tuck, Jessica: Lifepod; Mr. Write; O. J. Simpson Story, The; Wing and a Prayer, A
Tucker, Chris: Dead Presidents; Fifth Element, The; Friday; Jackie Brown; Money Talks; Rush Hour; Rush Hour 2
Tucker, Forrest: Abominable Snowman of the Himalayas, The; Adventures of Huckleberry Finn, The; Auntie Mame; Big Cat, The; Brimstone; Bugles in the Afternoon; Cancel My Reservation; Chisum; Coroner Creek; Cosmic Monsters, The; Crawling Eye, The; Final Chapter—Walking Tall; Finger Man; Hellfire; Hoodlum Empire; Incredible Rocky Mountain Race, The; Jubilee Trail; Keeper of the Flame; Melody Master (The Great Awakening) (NewWine); Montana Belle; Nevadan, The; Never Say Goodbye; Pony Express; Rage at Dawn; Real American Hero, The; Sands of Iwo Jima; Three Violent People; Thunder Run; Time Stalkers; Trouble in the Glen; Westerner, The
Tucker, Jerry: Dick Tracy Returns
Tucker, Jonathan: Deep End, The; 100 Girls; Virgin Suicides, The
Tucker, Michael: Assault & Matrimony; Checking Out; Day One; D2: The Mighty Ducks; For Love or Money; Goodbye People, The; L.A. Law; Radio Days; Spy; 'Til There Was You; Too Young to Die
Tucker, Sophie: Broadway Melody of 1938; Follow the Boys; Sensations of 1945; Thoroughbreds Don't Cry
Tucker, Tanya: Hard Country; Rebels, The
Tuckett, Jimmy: Clubland
Tudyk, Alan: Knight's Tale, A; 28 Days
Tufts, Sonny: Cat Women of the Moon; Easy Living; Glory at Sea; Here Come the Waves; So Proudly We Hail; Virginian, The
Tull, Jethro: Rock and Roll Circus, The
Tull, Patrick: Parting Glances
Tulleners, Tonny: Scorpion
Tullis Jr., Dan: Private Wars
Tully, Tom: Adventure; Branded; Coogan's Bluff; Jazz Singer, The; June Bride; Lady in the Lake; Love Is Better Than Ever; Love Me or Leave Me; Moon Is Blue, The; Northern Pursuit; Ruby Gentry; Soldier of Fortune; Trouble Along the Way; Virginian, The; Wackiest Ship in the Army, The
Tumbuan, Frans: Rage and Honor II: Hostile Takeover; Without Mercy
Tune, Tommy: Boy Friend, The
Tung, Bill: Police Story III—Super Cop

Tung, Jennifer: Kung Pow!: Enter the Fist
Tunney, Robin: Craft, The; Empire Records; End of Days; Julian Po; Montana; Niagara Niagara; Riders of the Purple Sage; Supernova; Vertical Limit
Turano, Robert: Federal Hill
Turco, Paige: Dead Funny; November Conspiracy, The; Teenage Mutant Ninja Turtles II: The Secret of the Ooze; Teenage Mutant Ninja Turtles III; Vibrations
Turkel, Ann: Fear, The (1994); Last Contract, The; 99 and 44/100 Percent Dead; Paper Lion
Turman, Glynn: Attica; Blue Knight, The; Buffalo Soldiers; Cooley High; Freedom Song; Gremlins; Hero Ain't Nothin' But a Sandwich, A; Inkwell, The; J.D.'s Revenge; Out of Bounds; Penitentiary II; Secrets of a Married Man
Turnbull, John: Silver Blaze
Turner, Barbara: Monster from Green Hell
Turner, Claramae: Carousel
Turner, Clive: Howling, The: New Moon Rising
Turner, Fred: Jack Knife Man, The
Turner, Guinevere: Go Fish
Turner, Hilary Shepard: Turbo: A Power Rangers Adventure
Turner, Isaac: Girl with the Hungry Eyes, The
Turner, Janine: Ambulance, The; Cliffhanger; Curse of Inferno, The; Leave It to Beaver; Northern Exposure (TV Series); Quantum Leap (TV Series)
Turner, Jim: My Samurai
Turner, Kathleen: Accidental Tourist, The; Baby Geniuses; Beautiful; Body Heat; Breed Apart, A; Crimes of Passion; House of Cards; Jewel of the Nile, The; Julia and Julia; Legalese; Man with Two Brains, The; Moonlight and Valentino; Naked in New York; Peggy Sue Got Married; Prizzi's Honor; Romancing the Stone; Serial Mom; Simple Wish, A; Switching Channels; Undercover Blues; V. I. Warshawski; Virgin Suicides, The; War of the Roses, The
Turner, Lana: Adventures of Marco Polo, The; Another Time, Another Place; Bachelor in Paradise; Bad and the Beautiful, The; Betrayed; Bittersweet Love; By Love Possessed; Cass Timberlane; Diane; Dr. Jekyll and Mr. Hyde; Green Dolphin Street; Homecoming; Honky Tonk; Imitation of Life; Johnny Eager; Latin Lovers; Life of Her Own, A; Love Finds Andy Hardy; Love Has Many Faces; Madame X; Mr. Imperium; Persecution; Peyton Place; Postman Always Rings Twice, The; Prodigal, The; Sea Chase, The; Somewhere I'll Find You; Three Musketeers, The; Weekend at the Waldorf; Who's Got the Action?; Witches' Brew; Ziegfeld Girl
Turner, Mae: Two-Gun Man from Harlem
Turner, Stephen Barker: Book of Shadows: Blair Witch 2
Turner, Tina: Mad Max Beyond Thunderdome; That Was Rock; Tommy
Turner, Tyrin: Menace II Society
Turpin, Ben: Golden Age of Comedy, The; Hollywood Cavalcade; Saps at Sea
Turturro, Aida: Angie; Deep Blue Sea; Jersey Girl; Junior; Sopranos, The (TV series); Tales of Erotica
Turturro, John: Backtrack; Barton Fink; Being Human; Box of Moonlight; Brain Donors; Clockers; Collateral Damage; Color of Money, The; Company Man; Cradle Will Rock; Do the Right Thing; Fearless; Five Corners; Grace of My Heart; Gung Ho (1985); Illuminata; Jungle Fever; Luzhin Defence, The; Mac; Man Who Cried, The; Men of Respect; Miller's Crossing; Mo' Better Blues; Monday Night Mayhem; Quiz Show; Rounders; Search and Destroy; Search for One-Eye Jimmy, The; Sicilian, The; Source, The; State of Grace; Sugartime; To Live and Die in L.A.; Truce, The; Unstrung Heroes
Turturro, Nicholas: Cosmic Slop; Excess Baggage; Federal Hill; Hellraiser: Inferno; Mercenary 2: Thick and Thin; Mob Justice; Search for One-Eye Jimmy, The
Tushingham, Rita: Awfully Big Adventure, An; Dream to Believe; Housekeeper, The; Knack … and How to Get It, The; Leather Boys, The; Mysteries; Paper Marriage; Spaghetti House; Swing; Taste of Honey, A; Under the Skin
Tutin, Dorothy: Alive & Kicking; Cromwell; Importance of Being Earnest, The; King Lear; Savage Messiah; Shooting Party, The; Six Wives of Henry VIII, The (TV Series); Tale of Two Cities, A
Tuttle, Lurene: Affairs of Dobie Gillis, The; Clonus Horror, The; Final Chapter—Walking Tall; Give a Girl a Break; Glass Slipper, The; Ma Barker's Killer Brood; Sincerely Yours; White Mama
Tuzman, Kaleil Isaza: Startup.com
Tweed, Shannon: Bimbo Movie Bash; Cannibal Women in the Avocado Jungle of Death; Cold Sweat; Face the Evil; Firing Line, The; Forbidden Sins; Hitchhiker, The (Series); Hot Dog … The Movie; Human Desires; Last Call; Last Hour, The; Lethal Woman; Meatballs III; Model by Day; Night Fire; Night Visitor (1989); No Contest; Possessed by the Night; Scorned
Twelvetrees, Helen: Painted Desert, The; State's Attorney
Twiggy: Boy Friend, The; Club Paradise; Doctor and the Devils, The; Istanbul: Keep Your Eyes Open; John Carpenter Presents: Body Bags; Madame Sousatzka; W
Twitty, Conway: Platinum High School
Twomey, Anne: Imagemaker, The; Rear Window; Scout, The
Tyler, Beverly: Voodoo Island
Tyler, Jeff: Tom Sawyer
Tyler, Judy: Jailhouse Rock
Tyler, Liv: Armageddon; Cookie's Fortune; Dr. T and the Women; Heavy; Inventing the Abbotts; Lord of the Rings, The: Fellowship of the Ring; One Night at McCool's; Onegin; Plunkett & Macleane; Silent Fall; Stealing Beauty; That Thing You Do!
Tyler, Sai: Under Lock and Key
Tyler, Tom: Adventures of Captain Marvel, The; Border Vigilantes; Brother Orchid; Brothers of the West; Forty-Niners; Last Outlaw, The; Mummy's Hand, The; Night Riders, The; Powdersmoke Range; Riders for Justice; Riders of the Rio Grande; Riders of the Timberline; Road Agent; Roamin' Wild; Talk of the Town, The; Westerner, The
Tyner, Charles: Hamburger—The Motion Picture; Harold and Maude; Incredible Journey of Dr. Meg Laurel,The; Jeremiah Johnson; Medicine Hat Stallion, The; Planes, Trains and Automobiles; Pulse
Tyrrell, Susan: Andy Warhol's Bad; Angel; Another Man, Another Chance; Avenging Angel (1985); Big Top Pee-Wee; Cry-Baby; Demolitionist, The; Far from Home; Fast-Walking; Fat City; Flesh and Blood (Sword and the Rose, the (1985)); Forbidden Zone; Killer Inside Me, The; Lady of the House; Liar's Moon; Loose Shoes; Night Warning; Poison Ivy: The New Seduction; Poker Alice; Powder; Rockula; Steagle, The; Tales of Ordinary Madness; Zandy's Bride
Tyson, Barbara: Baby Monitor: Sound of Fear; Resurrection
Tyson, Cathy: Business As Usual; Lost Language of Cranes, The; Mona Lisa; Priest; Serpent and the Rainbow, The
Tyson, Cicely: Acceptable Risks; Airport '79: The Concorde; Always Outnumbered; Autobiography of Miss Jane Pittman, The; Bustin' Loose; Comedians, The; Duplicates; Fried Green Tomatoes; Heart Is a Lonely Hunter, The; Heat Wave; Hero Ain't Nothin' But a Sandwich, A; Hoodlum; Kid Who Loved Christmas, The; King; Man Called Adam, A; Ms. Scrooge; Oldest Confederate Widow Tells All; Riot (1996) (TV Movie); Road to Galveston, The; Roots; Samaritan: The Mitch Snyder Story; Sounder; Wilma; Woman Called Moses, A; Women of Brewster Place, The
Tyson, Hayley: Ernest in the Army
Tyson, Mike: Black and White (2000)
Tyson, Richard: Battlefield Earth; Beneath the Bermuda Triangle; Dark Tide; Firetrap; Glass Cage, The; Kindergarten Cop; Pandora Project, The; Pharaoh's Army; Three O'Clock High; Two Moon Junction
Tyzack, Margaret: King's Whore, The; Mr. Love; Nemesis; Quatermass Conclusion, The
U2: U2: Rattle and Hum
Ubach, Alanna: Blue Moon; Clockwatchers; Denise Calls Up; Huntress, The; Just Your Luck
Ubarry, Hector: "Crocodile" Dundee II
Uchaneishvili, Levan: Legend of Suram Fortress, The
Udenio, Fabiana: Austin Powers: International Man of Mystery; Godson, The
Udvarnoky, Chris: Other, The
Udy, Claudia: Nightforce
Udy, Helene: Hollywood Detective, The; Sweet Murder

Uffindell-Phillips, Toby: Return of the Sand Fairy, The
Uggams, Leslie: Roots; Sizzle; Sugar Hill; Two Weeks in Another Town
Ulacia, Richard: Mixed Blood
Ullman, Tracey: Bullets over Broadway; Household Saints; I Love You to Death; I'll Do Anything; Panic; Plenty; Ready to Wear; Robin Hood: Men in Tights; Small Time Crooks
Ullmann, Liv: Autumn Sonata; Bay Boy, The; Cold Sweat; Cries and Whispers; Dangerous Moves; Emigrants, The; Forty Carats; Gaby, a True Story; Hour of the Wolf; Mindwalk; New Land, The; Night Visitor, The (1970); Passion of Anna, The; Persona; Richard's Things; Rose Garden, The; Scenes from a Marriage; Serpent's Egg, The; Wild Duck, The; Zandy's Bride
Ulric, Lenore: Camille; Northwest Outpost
Ulrich, Kim Johnston: Rumpelstiltskin
Ulrich, Skeet: Albino Alligator; As Good as It Gets; Boys (1996); Chill Factor; Craft, The; Newton Boys, The; Ride with the Devil; Scream; Soldier's Sweetheart, A; Touch
Umbers, Margaret: Bridge to Nowhere; Death Warmed Up
Umecka, Jolanta: Knife in the Water
Umeki, Miyoshi: Flower Drum Song; Horizontal Lieutenant, The; Sayonara
Umemura, Yôko: Sisters of the Gion
Unda, Emilia: Maedchen in Uniform
Underwood, Blair: Dangerous Relations; Heat Wave; Just Cause; Krush Groove; Mistrial; Posse; Rules of Engagement; Soul of the Game
Underwood, Jay: Boy Who Could Fly, The; Gumshoe Kid, The; Invisible Kid, The; Not Quite Human; Not Quite Human 2; Nurse, The; Possums; Raffle, The; Reason to Believe, A; Stalked; Still Not Quite Human; Wyatt Earp: Return to Tombstone
Unger, Deborah: Crash (1996); Game, The; Highlander: The Final Dimension; Hurricane, The; Keys to Tulsa; No Way Home; Payback; Till There Was You; Whispers in the Dark
Ungerer, Lilith: Why Does Herr R. Run Amok?
Union, Gabrielle: Bring It On;Brothers, The; 10 Things I Hate About You
Urban, Karl: Heaven; Price of Milk, The
Urbaniak, James: Henry Fool
Urbano, Maryann: Laser Man, The
Ure, Mary: Reflection of Fear; Where Eagles Dare; Windom's Way
Urecal, Minerva: Apache Rose; Ape Man, The; Corpse Vanishes, The; Oklahoma Annie; So This Is Washington
Urena, Fabio: Bronx War, The
Urich, Robert: Blindman's Bluff; Bunco; Captains Courageous; Endangered Species; Hit Woman: The Double Edge; Horse for Danny, A; Ice Pirates; In a Stranger's Hands; Invitation to Hell; Killing at Hell's Gate; Lonesome Dove; Magnum Force; Mistral's Daughter; Perfect Little Murder, A; Princess Daisy; Revolver; Spenser: Ceremony; Spenser: Pale Kings & Princes; Turk 182; Vega$
Urquhart, Robert: Battle Hell; Curse of Frankenstein, The; Knights of the Round Table
Urquidez, Benny: Bloodmatch
Urzi, Saro: Seduced and Abandoned
Usher, Guy: Devil Bat, The; Doomed to Die
Usher, Paul: Swing
Ustinov, Pavla: Thief of Baghdad (1978)
Ustinov, Peter: Alice in Wonderland; Appointment with Death; Around the World in 80 Days; Ashanti; Beau Brummell; Billy Budd; Blackbeard's Ghost; Charlie Chan and the Curse of the Dragon Queen; Comedians, The; Death on the Nile; Egyptian, The; Evil Under the Sun; Great Muppet Caper, The; Hammersmith Is Out; Hot Millions; Immortal Battalion, The (The Way Ahead); Lady L; Lion and the Hawk, The; Logan's Run; Lola Montes; Lorenzo's Oil; Old Curiosity Shop, The; One of Our Aircraft Is Missing; One of Our Dinosaurs Is Missing; Purple Taxi, The; Quo Vadis (1951); Spartacus; Stiff Upper Lips; Sundowners, The; Thief of Baghdad (1978); 13 at Dinner; Topkapi; Victoria and Albert; Viva Max!; We're No Angels
Utley, Darrell Thomas: Danielle Steel's Once in a Lifetime
Utsunomiya, Masayo: Irezumi (Spirit of Tattoo)
Vaananen, Kari: Amazon
Vaccaro, Brenda: Cookie; Dear Detective; Death Weekend; First Deadly Sin, The; For Keeps; Guyana Tragedy, The: The Story of Jim Jones; Heart of Midnight; Honor Thy Father; I Love My Wife; Lethal Games; Midnight Cowboy; Mirror Has Two Faces, The; Once Is Not Enough; Pride of Jesse Hallman, The; Supergirl; Ten Little Indians; Water; Zorro, the Gay Blade
Vadas, Kenny: Captains Courageous
Vadim, Annette: Blood and Roses; Les Liaisons Dangereuses
Vadim, Roger: Ciao! Manhattan
Vadis, Dan: Bronco Billy; Seven Magnificent Gladiators, The
Vahanian, Marc: Prince of Central Park, The
Vahle, Timothy: Forbidden Sins
Valandrey, Charlotte: House That Mary Bought, The; Orlando; Red Kiss (Rouge Baiser)
Valdes, Bebo: Calle 54
Valdez, Daniel: Zoot Suit
Vale, Virginia: Flustered Comedy of Leon Errol, The; Marshal of Mesa City; Stage to Chino; Triple Justice
Valen, Nancy: Final Embrace
Valens, Ritchie: Go, Johnny, Go!
Valenti, Chuck: Bronx Executioner, The
Valentine, Anthony: Carpathian Eagle; Dirty Dozen, The: The Fatal Mission; Father's Revenge, A; Robin Hood and the Sorcerer
Valentine, Karen: Hot Lead and Cold Feet; North Avenue Irregulars, The; Power Within, The; Return to Fantasy Island; Skeezer
Valentine, Kim: Grandma's House
Valentine, Scott: After the Shock; Carnosaur 3: Primal Species; Dangerous Pursuit; Deadtime Stories; Double Obsession; Homicidal Impulse; My Demon Lover; Object of Obsession; Out of Annie's Past; Paranoia; Secret Passion of Robert Clayton, The; Till the End of the Night; To Sleep With a Vampire; Unborn II, The; Write to Kill
Valentini, Mariella: Volere Volare
Valentino, Rudolph: Blood and Sand; Eagle, The; Moran of the Lady Letty; Sheik, The; Son of the Sheik
Valenza, Tasia: Rappin'
Valerie, Jeanne: Les Liaisons Dangereuses
Vallai, Peter: Magic Hunter
Vallance, Louise: Robbers of the Sacred Mountain
Vallee, Marcel: Topaze
Vallee, Rudy: Admiral Was a Lady, The; Bachelor and the Bobby-Soxer, The; Beautiful Blonde from Bashful Bend, The; How to Succeed in Business without Really Trying; It's in the Bag; Mad Wednesday (see also Sin of Harold Diddlebock); Palm Beach Story, The; People Are Funny; Second Fiddle; Sin of Harold Diddlebock (Mad Wednesday); Unfaithfully Yours; Vagabond Lover, The
Valleta, Amber: What Lies Beneath
Valletta, Al: Runaway Nightmare
Valli, Alida: Eyes Without a Face; Il Grido (Outcry, The); Miracle of the Bells, The; Month by the Lake, A; Oedipus Rex; Paradine Case, The; Spider's Stratagem, The; Suspiria; Third Man, The; Walk Softly, Stranger; Wanton Contessa, The; We the Living; White Tower, The
Valli, Frankie: Dirty Laundry; Opposite Corners
Valli, Romolo: Bobby Deerfield; Fistful of Dynamite, A
Vallin, Rick: Ghosts on the Loose; Jungle Jim; King of the Carnival; Last of the Redmen; Riders of the Rio Grande; Sea Hound, The
Vallod, Jean-Claude: Human Resources
Vallone, Raf: Almost Perfect Affair, An; Bitter Rice; Catholics; Christopher Columbus (1985); El Cid; Greek Tycoon, The; Gunfight, A; Harlow; Honor Thy Father; Nevada Smith; Other Side of Midnight, The; Season of Giants, A; Summertime Killer, The; Time to Die, A; Two Women
Valois, Valerie: Scanners 3: The Takeover
Van, Bobby: Affairs of Dobie Gillis, The; Bunco; Kiss Me Kate; Navy vs. the Night Monsters, The; Small Town Girl
van Allan, Richard: Vampyr, The (1992)
Van Ammelrooy, Willeke: Antonia's Line
Van Ark, Joan: Frogs; Red Flag: The Ultimate Game; Tainted Blood; When the Dark Man Calls

Van Atta, Lee: Dick Tracy; Undersea Kingdom
Van Bergen, Lewis: Pinocchio's Revenge; South of Reno
Van Buren, Mabel: Miss Lulu Bett
Van Cleef, Lee: Armed Response; Bad Man's River; Beast from 20,000 Fathoms, The; Beyond the Law; Blade Rider; Bravados, The; Captain Apache; China Gate; Code Name: Wild Geese; Commandos; Days of Wrath; Death Rides a Horse; El Condor; Escape from New York; For a Few Dollars More; Good the Bad and the Ugly, The; Gunfight at the O.K. Corral; Gypsy Colt; Hard Way, The; It Conquered the World; Jungle Raiders; Kansas City Confidential; Lonely Man, The; Man Alone, A; Man Who Shot Liberty Valance, The; Octagon, The; Ride Lonesome; Stranger and the Gunfighter, The; Take a Hard Ride; Ten Wanted Men; Thieves of Fortune; Tin Star, The; Tribute to a Bad Man
Van Dam, José: Music Teacher, The
van Damme, Gabrielle: Marquis
Van Damme, Jean-Claude: Black Eagle; Bloodsport; Cyborg; Death Warrant; Desert Heat; Double Impact; Double Team; Hard Target; Kickboxer; Knock Off; Legionnaire; Lionheart; Maximum Risk; No Retreat, No Surrender; Nowhere to Run; Order, The; Quest, The; Replicant; Street Fighter; Sudden Death; Timecop; Universal Soldier
van de Ven, Monique: Amsterdamned; Assault, The; Johnsons, The; Katie's Passion; Turkish Delight
Van Den Bergh, Gert: Naked Prey, The
van den Elsen, Sylvie: L'Argent
van der Beek, James: Angus; Cash Crop; Texas Rangers (2001); Varsity Blues
Van Der Velde, Nadine: Shadow Dancing
Van Der Vlis, Diana: X (The Man with the X-Ray Eyes)
Van Devere, Trish: Changeling, The; Day of the Dolphin, The; Deadly Currents; Hearse, The; Hollywood Vice Squad; Messenger of Death; Movie Movie; Savage Is Loose, The; Where's Poppa?
Van Dien, Casper: Beastmaster III: The Eye of Braxus; Cutaway; Kill Shot; Partners (2000); Python; Road Rage; Shark Attack; Sleepy Hollow; Starship Troopers; Tarzan and the Lost City; Time Shifters, The
Van Doren, Mamie: Francis Joins the Wacs; Free Ride; Girl in Black Stockings, The; Girls Town; High School Confidential!; Las Vegas Hillbillys; Navy vs. the Night Monsters, The; Running Wild; Teacher's Pet; Three Nuts in Search of a Bolt
van Dreelen, John: Great Wallendas, The
Van Dyke, Barry: Casino; Foxfire Light
Van Dyke, Conny: Framed; Hell's Angels '69
Van Dyke, Dick: Bye Bye Birdie; Chitty Chitty Bang Bang; Cold Turkey; Country Girl, The; Dick Tracy; Dick Van Dyke Show, The (TV Series); Divorce American Style; Fitzwilly; Lt. Robin Crusoe, U.S.N.; Mary Poppins; Never a Dull Moment; Runner Stumbles, The
Van Dyke, Jerry: Courtship of Eddie's Father, The; McLintock!; Run If You Can
Van Eyck, Peter: Brain, The; Bridge at Remagen, The; Run for the Sun; Spy Who Came in from the Cold, The; Thousand Eyes of Dr. Mabuse, The; Wages of Fear, The
Van Fleet, Jo: East of Eden; Gunfight at the O.K. Corral; I Love You Alice B. Toklas!; I'll Cry Tomorrow; King and Four Queens, The; Rose Tattoo, The
Van Hentenryck, Kevin: Basket Case; Basket Case 2; Basket Case 3: The Progeny
Van Herwijnen, Carol: Still Smokin'
Van Holt, Brian: Whipped
Van Horn, Patrick: Free Enterprise
Van Hoy, Cameron: Pups
van Huet, Fedja: Character (Karakter)
Van Kamp, Merete: Princess Daisy
Van Kempen, Ad: 1-900
Van Lent, Amber: Bloodsport III
Van Lidth, Erland: Alone in the Dark
Van Loon, Robert: Paisan
Van Ness, Jon: Bostonians, The; Hospital Massacre
Van Pallandt, Nina: American Gigolo; Assault on Agathon; Jungle Warriors; Long Goodbye, The
Van Patten, Dick: Charly; Dangerous Place, A; Diary of a Teenage Hitchhiker; Final Embrace; Gus; High Anxiety; Jake Spanner Private Eye; Love Is All There Is; Midnight Hour; Robin Hood: Men in Tights; Son of Blob (Beware! The Blob); Spaceballs; When Things Were Rotten (TV Series)
Van Patten, James: Nightforce; Tennessee Stallion; Young Warriors, The
Van Patten, Joyce: Billy Galvin; Breathing Lessons; Eleanor: First Lady of the World; Goddess, The; Housewife; Mikey and Nicky; Monkey Shines: An Experiment in Fear; St. Elmo's Fire; Stranger Within, The
Van Patten, Nels: One Last Run; Summer School
Van Patten, Timothy: Class of 1984; Curse IV: The Ultimate Sacrifice; Zone Troopers
Van Patten, Vincent: Break, The; Charley and the Angel; Chino; Hell Night; Rock 'n' Roll High School
Van Peebles, Mario: Ali; Blowback; Delivery Boys; Exterminator 2, The; Full Eclipse; Gang in Blue; Gunmen; Heartbreak Ridge; Highlander: The Final Dimension; Hot Shot; Identity Crisis; Jaws: The Revenge; Judgment Day; Killers in the House; Love Kills; New Jack City; Posse; Protector (1998); Rappin'; Riot (1996) (TV Movie); Solo; Stag; Terminal Velocity; 3:15—The Moment of Truth; Urban Crossfire
Van Peebles, Melvin: Calm at Sunset; Fist of the North Star; Gang in Blue; O.C. & Stiggs; Posse; Sophisticated Gents, The; Stephen King's The Shining; Sweet Sweetback's Baadasssss Song
Van Pellicom, Kristien: Innocence
Van Sickel, Dale: Dangers of the Canadian Mounted; King of the Rocketmen
Van Sloan, Edward: Before I Hang; Behind the Mask; Death Kiss, The; Deluge (1993); Dracula; Dracula's Daughter; Mummy, The; Riders of the Rio Grande
Van Tieghem, David: No Telling
Van Tongeren, Hans: Spetters
van Uchelen, Marc: Assault, The
Van Valkenburgh, Deborah: Brain Smasher ... A Love Story; Bunny's Tale, A; Phantom of the Ritz; Rampage; Warriors, The
Van Vooren, Monique: Andy Warhol's Frankenstein; Ash Wednesday; Sugar Cookies
Van Wormer, Steve: Groove; Meet the Deedles
Van Zandt, Steve: Sopranos, The (TV series)
Vance, Courtney B.: Adventures of Huck Finn, The (1993); Affair, The; Blind Faith; Boys Next Door, The; Cookie's Fortune; Dangerous Minds; Hamburger Hill; Last Supper, The; Panther; Percy & Thunder; Piano Lesson, The; Preacher's Wife, The; Space Cowboys; Tuskegee Airmen, The; 12 Angry Men; Urban Crossfire
Vance, Danitra: Jumpin' at the Boneyard; Limit Up; Sticky Fingers
Vance, Pruitt Taylor: Mumford
Vance, Vivian: Great Race, The; I Love Lucy (TV Series)
Vander, Musetta: Project Shadowchaser 3000
Vandergaw, Terra: '68
Vandernoot, Alexandra: Blood of the Hunter; Dinner Game, The; Highlander: The Gathering
Vandis, Titos: Young Doctors in Love
Vanel, Charles: Death in the Garden; Diabolique; Wages of Fear, The
Vanilla Ice: Cool As Ice; Hip-Hop Witch Movie, Da
Vanity: Action Jackson; Davinci's War; 52 Pick-Up; Highlander: The Gathering; Last Dragon, The; Memories of Murder; Neon City; South Beach; Tanya's Island
VanKamp, Merete: Lethal Woman
Vannicola, Joanne: Iron Eagle IV; Love and Human Remains
Varconi, Victor: Everything Happens at Night
Varden, Evelyn: Athena
Varden, Norma: Mademoiselle Fifi
Vardhan, Vishnu: Terrorist, The
Varela, Amanda: Falcon's Brother, The
Varela, Leonor: Blade II; Tailor of Panama, The
Vargas, Jacob: Mi Vida Loca; Selena
Vargas, John: In Dark Places

Vargas, Valentina: Dirty Games; Hellraiser: Bloodline; Tigress, The
Varma, Indira: Kama Sutra: A Tale of Love
Varney, Jim: Beverly Hillbillies, The (1993); Dr. Otto and the Riddle of the Gloom Beam; Ernest Goes to Africa; Ernest Goes to Camp; Ernest Goes to Jail; Ernest in the Army; Ernest Rides Again; Ernest Saves Christmas; Ernest Scared Stupid; Expert, The; Fast Food; Rousters, The; Slam Dunk Ernest; Snowboard Academy; Treehouse Hostage; Wilder Napalm
Varney, Reg: Great St. Trinian's Train Robbery, The
Varsi, Diane: Compulsion; I Never Promised You a Rose Garden; Johnny Got His Gun; People, The; Peyton Place; Sweet Love, Bitter; Wild in the Streets
Vartan, Michael: Dead Man's Curve; Mists of Avalon, The; Myth of Fingerprints, The; Never Been Kissed; Sand; Wild Flower (1993) (Fiorile)
Varty, John: Born Wild
Vasconcelos, Tito: Danzon
Vasquez, José Luis Lopez: Garden of Delights, The
Vasquez, Roberta: Fit to Kill
Vasut, Marek: Delta of Venus
Vattier, Robert: Le Schpountz
Vaughan, Alberta: Randy Rides Alone
Vaughan, Greg: Children of the Corn V: Fields of Terror; Poison Ivy: The New Seduction
Vaughan, Peter: Bleak House; Blockhouse, The; Die! Die! My Darling!; Fatherland; Forbidden; Haunted Honeymoon; Ideal Husband, An; Les Misérables; Remains of the Day; Straw Dogs
Vaughan, Sarah: Ladies Sing the Blues, The
Vaughan, Vanessa: Crazy Moon; Sound and the Silence,The
Vaughn, Martin: Phar Lap
Vaughn, Ned: Chips, the War Dog
Vaughn, Robert: Baseketball; Battle Beyond the Stars; Black Moon Rising; Blind Vision; Blue and the Gray, The; Brass Target; Bridge at Remagen, The; Bullitt; Captive Rage; C.H.U.D. II (Bud the C.H.U.D.); City in Fear; Delta Force, The; Going Under; Hangar 18; Hitchhiker, The (Series); Hour of the Assassin; Inside the Third Reich; Joe's Apartment; Julius Caesar; Kill Castro (Cuba Crossing, Mercenaries , Sweet Violent Tony); Magnificent Seven, The; Man from U.N.C.L.E., The (TV Series); McCinsey's Island; Nightstick; Nobody's Perfect; Pootie Tang; Prince of Bel Air; Question of Honor, A; Return of the Man from U.N.C.L.E., The; River of Death; Shaming, The; S.O.B.; Starship Invasions; Statue, The; Superman III; Transylvania Twist; Young Philadelphians, The
Vaughn, Vince: Cell, The; Clay Pigeons; Cool, Dry Place, A; Domestic Disturbance; Just Your Luck; Locusts, The; Lost World, The: Jurassic Park; Made; Prime Gig, The; Psycho; Return to Paradise; South of Heaven, West of Hell; Swingers
Vaughter, Marcus: Visitants, The
Vaugier, Emmanuelle: Halfback of Notre Dame, The
Vavrova, Dana: Brother of Sleep
Vawter, Ron: Philadelphia; Swoon
Ve Sota, Bruno: Attack of the Giant Leeches; Daughter of Horror; War of the Satellites
Vega, Alexa: Spy Kids
Vega, Isela: Barbarosa; Bring Me the Head of Alfredo Garcia; Deadly Trackers, The; Streets of L.A., The
Vega, Makenzie: Family Man, The
Vega, Vladimir: Ladybird, Ladybird
Veidt, Conrad: Above Suspicion; All Through the Night; Beloved Rogue; Cabinet of Doctor Caligari, The; Dark Journey; Hands of Orlac; Man Who Laughs, The; Spy in Black, The; Student of Prague; Thief of Bagdad, The; Waxworks; Whistling in the Dark; Woman's Face, A
Vel Johnson, Reginald: Die Hard; Die Hard 2: Die Harder; Great American Sex Scandal, The; Posse; Seven Hours to Judgment
Velasquez, Andres: Littlest Outlaw, The
Velasquez, Andy: Heaven Before I Die
Velazquez, Lorena: Rock 'n' Roll Wrestling Women vs. the Aztec Mummy
Velazquez, Patricia: Beowulf; Eruption
Veld, Hansman In't: Still Smokin'
Velez, Eddie: Bitter Vengeance; Doin' Time; Romero; Rooftops; Women's Club, The
Velez, Lauren: I Like It Like That; I Think I Do
Velez, Lupe: Hell Harbor; Hollywood Party; Mexican Spitfire; Palooka; Where East Is East
Velez, Martha: Star Maps
Venable, Evelyn: Alice Adams; Death Takes a Holiday; Harmony Lane; Heritage of the Desert; Little Colonel, The; Mrs. Wiggs of the Cabbage Patch
Venantini, Luca: Aladdin; Exterminators of the Year 3000
Venantini, Venantino: Final Justice
Vendeuil, Magali: Beauties of the Night
Veninger, Ingrid: Hush Little Baby
Vennera, Chick: Alone in the Woods; Beneath the Bermuda Triangle; Double Threat; High Risk; Milagro Beanfield War, The; Terror Within 2, The; Tycus
Venora, Diane: Bird; F/X; Hamlet; Heat; Insider, The; Jackal, The; Substitute, The; Surviving Picasso; Terminal Choice; 13th Warrior, The; True Crime; Wolfen
Ventantonio, John: Private Parts
Venton, Harley: Blood Ties
Ventura, Jesse: Abraxas Guardian of the Universe; Predator
Ventura, Lino: French Detective, The; Grisbi; Happy New Year (1973) (La Bonne Année); Les Grandes Gueules (Jailbirds' Vacation); Medusa Touch, The; Pain in the A—, A; Sword of Gideon
Ventura, Viviane: Battle Beneath the Earth
Venture, Richard: Scent of a Woman; Series 7: The Contenders
Vera, Billy: Baja Oklahoma; Finish Line
Vera, Victoria: Monster Dog
Vera-Ellen: Belle of New York, The; Happy Go Lovely; Kid from Brooklyn, The; On the Town; Three Little Words; White Christmas; Wonder Man; Words and Music
Verbeke, Natalia: Jump Tomorrow
Verdon, Gwen: Cocoon; Cocoon: The Return; Damn Yankees; Marvin's Room; Nadine
Verdone, Carlo: Iris Blond
Verdu, Maribel: Goya in Bordeaux; Lovers (1992)
Verdugo, Elena: Big Sombrero, The; Frozen Ghost, The; House of Frankenstein; Moon and Sixpence, The
Verea, Lisette: Night in Casablanca, A
Vereen, Ben: Buy and Cell; Ellis Island; Funny Lady; Gas-s-s-s; Roots; Zoo Gang, The
Vergara, Sofia: Big Trouble (2002)
Verhoeven, Simon: Bride of the Wind
Verica, Tom: 800 Leagues Down the Amazon; Lost in the Bermuda Triangle
Verley, Bernard: Chloe in the Afternoon; Milky Way, The
Verley, Françoise: Chloe in the Afternoon
Verlin, Melanie: Midnight
Verlo, Lisa: Midnight
Vermes, David: Hungarian Fairy Tale, A
Verne, Kaaren: All Through the Night; Sherlock Holmes and the Secret Weapon
Vernon, Anne: Therese and Isabelle
Vernon, Howard: Angel of Death; Awful Dr. Orloff, The; Blood Rose; Bob le Flambeur; Castle of the Creeping Flesh; Virgin Among the Living Dead, A; Women in Cell Block 9; Zombie Lake
Vernon, Jackie: Young at Heart Comedians, The
Vernon, John: Angela; Animal House; Bail Out; Black Windmill, The; Blue Monkey; Border Heat; Brannigan; Chained Heat; Charley Varrick; Curtains; Deadly Stranger; Dirty Harry; Dixie Lanes; Doin' Time; Double Exposure; Ernest Goes to Camp; Family of Cops; Hammered: The Best of Sledge; Herbie Goes Bananas; Hostage for a Day; Hunter (1971); I'm Gonna Git You Sucka!; Jungle Warriors; Justine; Killer Klowns from Outer Space; Malicious; Mob Story; Nightstick; Outlaw Josey Wales, The; Point Blank; Ray Bradbury's Chronicles: The MartianEpisodes; Savage Streets; Sodbusters; Topaz; Uncanny, The; W
Vernon, Kate: Alphabet City; Blackjack; Bloodknot; Dangerous Touch; Downdraft; Flood: A River's Rampage; Hostile Take Over; Last of Philip Banter, The; Malcolm X; Mob Story; Probable Cause; Roadhouse 66; Sister-In-Law, The; Soft Deceit

Vernon, Sherri: 10 Violent Women
Vernon, Ted: Scarecrows
Vernon, Wally: Happy Landing
Veron, Pablo: Tango Lesson, The
Veronis, Nick: Day at the Beach
Verrell, Cec: Mad at the Moon
Versini, Marie: Escape from the KGB
Versois, Odile: Cartouche; To Paris with Love
Verveen, Arie: Caught; Running Free; Thin Red Line, The
Vessel, Edy: Passionate Thief, The (1961)
Vessey, Trissa: Ghost Dog: The Way of the Samurai
Vetchy, Ondrej: Dark Blue World
Vetchy, Ondrez: Kolya
Vetri, Victoria: Invasion of the Bee Girls; When Dinosaurs Ruled the Earth
Veugelers, Marijke: Egg
Viallargeon, Paule: I've Heard the Mermaids Singing
Viard, Karen: Delicatessen
Vibert, Ronan: Shadow of the Vampire
Vicious, Sid: Filth and the Fury, The; Great Rock and Roll Swindle, The
Vickers, Martha: Big Bluff, The; Big Sleep, The; Captive Wild Woman; Man I Love, The
Vickers, Yvette: Attack of the 50-Foot Woman; Attack of the Giant Leeches; I, Mobster
Victor, Gloria: Invasion of the Star Creatures
Victor, Katherine: Wild World of Batwoman, The (She Was aHappy Vampire)
Victory, Francis: Headin' Home
Vida, Piero: Dead for a Dollar
Vidal, Christina: Life with Mikey
Vidal, Gore: Bob Roberts; Gattaca; With Honors
Vidal, Henri: Sois Belle Et Tais-Toi (Just Another Pretty Face); Voulez Vous Danser avec Moi? (Will You Dance with Me?)
Vidal, Lisa: Fall; I Like It Like That
Vidan, Richard: Scarecrows
Vidarte, Walter: Outrage (1994)
Videnovic, Gala: Hey, Babu Riba
Vidler, Steven: Encounter at Raven's Gate; Good Wife, The; Three's Trouble; Wrangler
Vidnovic, Martin: King and I, The
Vidor, Florence: Are Parents People?; Jack Knife Man, The; Marriage Circle, The; Virginian, The
Viellard, Eric: Boyfriends and Girlfriends
Vieluf, Vince: American Werewolf in Paris, An; Rat Race
Vigoda, Abe: Cheap Detective, The; Good Burger; Joe Versus the Volcano; Jury Duty; Just the Ticket; Keaton's Cop; Love Is All There Is; Newman's Law; Plain Clothes; Prancer; Sugar Hill; Underworld; Vasectomy
Viharo, Robert: Bare Knuckles; Happy Birthday, Gemini; Hide in Plain Sight
Vilan, Mayte: Bitter Sugar
Vilar, Antonio: Have a Nice Funeral
Vilches, Jordi: Nico and Dani
Villafana, Martin: Junior's Groove
Village People, The: Can't Stop the Music
Villaggio, Paolo: Ciao Professore
Villagra, Nelson: Last Supper, The
Villalonga, Marthe: Ma Saison Preferée
Villalpando, David: El Norte
Villard, Tom: Force Five; Heartbreak Ridge; One Crazy Summer; Parasite; Popcorn; Swimsuit; Trouble with Dick, The; Weekend Warriors
Villarias, Carlos: Dracula (Spanish)
Villarreal, Julio: Woman without Love, A
Villechaize, Herve: Forbidden Zone; Greaser's Palace; Man with the Golden Gun, The; One and Only, The; Return to Fantasy Island; Seizure
Villella, Michael: Slumber Party Massacre
Villemaire, James: Dead Silence; Gate II
Villeret, Jacques: Dinner Game, The; Edith and Marcel; Robert et Robert
Villiers, James: Alphabet Murders, The; Half a Sixpence; Saint Jack; Scarlet Pimpernel, The
Vince, Pruitt Taylor: Cell, The; China Moon; Heavy; Legend of 1900, The; Nobody's Fool; Nurse Betty
Vincent, Alex: Child's Play 2
Vincent, Brian: Black Dog; Blue Moon
Vincent, Cerina: Not Another Teen Movie
Vincent, Craig: French Exit
Vincent, Frank: Deli, The; Gotti; Grind; Mortal Thoughts; Raging Bull; Ten Benny
Vincent, Hélène: Ma Vie En Rose
Vincent, Jan-Michael: Abducted II; Alienator; Bandits; Beyond the Call of Duty; Big Wednesday; Bite the Bullet; Born in East L.A.; Buster and Billie; Crossfire; Damnation Alley (Survival Run); Deadly Embrace; Deadly Heroes; Defiance; Demonstone; Dirty Games; Enemy Territory; Hard Country; Hidden Obsession; Hit List (1988); Hooper; In Gold We Trust; Last Plane Out; Mechanic, The; Midnight Witness; Raw Nerve; Red Line; Return, The (1980); Tribes; Undefeated, The; White Line Fever; Winds of War, The; World's Greatest Athlete, The; Xtro II
Vincent, June: Can't Help Singing; Climax, The
Vincent, Romo: Naked Jungle, The
Vincent, Troy: Petticoat Planet
Vincent, Virginia: Hills Have Eyes, The; I Want to Live!
Vincz, Melanie: Lost Empire, The
Ving, Lee: Black Moon Rising; Dudes; Grave Secrets; Oceans of Fire; Scenes from the Goldmine; Taking of Beverly Hills, The
Vinshwa: Terrorist, The
Vinson, Gary: High School Caesar; Majority of One, A
Vinson, Helen: Beyond Tomorrow; Broadway Bill; I Am a Fugitive from a Chain Gang; In Name Only; They Call It Sin; Thin Man Goes Home, The; Transatlantic Tunnel
Vint, Alan: Badlands (1973); Ballad of Gregorio Cortez, The; Macon County Line; Panic in Needle Park
Vint, Jesse: Bobbie Jo and the Outlaw; Dempsey; Forbidden World; On the Line; Pigs (Daddy's Deadly Darling)
Vintas, Gustav: Vampire at Midnight
Vinton, Bobby: Big Jake
Virgili, Elisabetta: Great Adventure, The
Virieux, Denise: Northern Extremes
Visnjic, Goran: Deep End, The
Visser, Angela: Hot Under the Collar; Killer Tomatoes Eat France
Vita, Helen: Satan's Brew
Vita, Perlo: Rififi
Vitale, Mario: Stromboli
Vitale, Milly: Seven Little Foys, The
Vitali, Keith: No Retreat, No Surrender 3: Blood Brothers; Revenge of the Ninja
Viterelli, Joe: Analyze This; Black Rose of Harlem; Bullets over Broadway; Facade; Mickey Blue Eyes; Shallow Hal
Vithana, Kim: Bhaji on the Beach
Vitold, Michel: Judex
Vitte, Ray: Thank God It's Friday
Vittet, Judith: City of Lost Children, The
Vitti, Monica: Almost Perfect Affair, An; Eclipse, The; Immortal Bachelor, The; L'Aventura; Phantom of Liberty, The; Red Desert
Viva: Ciao! Manhattan; Cisco Pike; Forbidden Zone; State of Things, The
Vlady, Marina: Double Agents; Le Complot (The Conspiracy); Two or Three Things I Know About Her
Vlastas, Michael: Blackbelt 2: Fatal Force
Voe, Sandra: Winter Guest, The
Vogel, Darlene: Angel 4: Undercover; Decoy; Ring of Steel
Vogel, Jack: Lock and Load
Vogel, Mitch: Menace on the Mountain; Reivers, The
Vogler, Rudiger: Alice in the City; Kings of the Road; Lisbon Story; Marianne & Juliane; Wrong Move, The
Voight, Jon: Ali; Anaconda; Boys Will Be Boys; Champ, The; Chernobyl: The Final Warning; Coming Home; Conrack; Convict Cowboy; Deliverance; Desert Bloom; Dog of Flanders, A; Enemy of the State; Eternity; Fixer, The; General, The; Heat; Hour of the Gun, The; Lara Croft: Tomb Raider; Last of His Tribe, The; Lookin' to Get Out; Midnight Cowboy; Mission: Impossible; Odessa File, The; Rainbow Warrior; Rainmaker, The (1997); Re-

turn to Lonesome Dove; Rosewood; Runaway Train; Table for Five; Tin Soldier, The; U-Turn; Varsity Blues
Vojnov, Dimitrie: Tito and Me
Volante, Vicki: Horror of the Blood Monsters
Vold, Ingrid: To Sleep With a Vampire
Volger, Rudiger: Faraway, So Close
Volk, Daniel: Yo-Yo Man
Vollrath, Robert: Prehistoric Bimbos in Armageddon City
Volonté, Gian Maria: Bullet for the General, A; Christ Stopped at Eboli; Fistful of Dollars, A; For a Few Dollars More; Girl with a Suitcase; Lucky Luciano; Open Doors; Sacco and Vanzetti
Volter, Philippe: Music Teacher, The
Von Au, Michael: Nobody Loves Me
Von Bargen, Daniel: G.I. Jane; Inferno; Last Hit, The; Trouble on the Corner
von Blanc, Christina: Virgin Among the Living Dead, A
von Detten, Erik: Leave It to Beaver
von Dohlen, Lenny: Billy Galvin; Bird of Prey; Blind Vision; Dracula's Widow; Electric Dreams; Entertaining Angels; Eyes of the Beholder; Home Alone 3; Jennifer 8; Leaving Normal; Love Kills; One Good Turn; Tollbooth; Under the Biltmore Clock
von Flotow, Michelle: Phantom Love
von Franckenstein, Clement: Underground
Von Koszian, Johanna: For the First Time
von Omsteiner, Joel: Robot Holocaust; Slash Dance
Von Palleske, Heidi: Dead Ringers; Shepherd
von Praunheim, Rosa: Virus Knows No Morals, A
von Scherler, Sasha: Party Girl
von Seyffertitz, Gustav: Ambassador Bill; Dishonored; Down to Earth; Mysterious Lady, The; Shanghai Express; She; Sparrows; Student Prince in Old Heidelberg, The
Von Stroheim, Erich: As You Desire Me; Blind Husbands; Crime of Dr. Crespi, The; Five Graves to Cairo; Foolish Wives; Fugitive Road; Grand Illusion; Great Flamarion, The; Great Gabbo, The; Intolerance; Lost Squadron; Napoleon; So Ends Our Night; Sunset Boulevard; Unnatural; Wedding March, The
von Sydow, Max: Awakenings; Bachelor, The; Belarus File, The; Best Intentions, The; Brass Target; Brink of Life; Christopher Columbus (1985); Citizen X; Code Name: Emerald; Death Watch; Dreamscape; Duet for One; Dune; Emigrants, The; Exorcist, The; Exorcist II: The Heretic; Father; Flash Gordon; Flight of the Eagle; Foxtrot; Greatest Story Ever Told, The; Hannah and Her Sisters; Hawaii; Hiroshima: Out of the Ashes; Hostile Waters; Hour of the Wolf; Hurricane (1979); Jerusalem; Judge Dredd; Kiss Before Dying, A; Magician, The; March or Die; Miss Julie; Needful Things; Never Say Never Again; New Land, The; Night Visitor, The (1970); Passion of Anna, The; Pelle the Conqueror; Quiller Memorandum, The; Red King, White Knight; Samson and Delilah; Seventh Seal, The; Silent Touch, The; Snow Falling on Cedars; Steppenwolf; Strange Brew; Target Eagle; Three Days of the Condor; Through a Glass Darkly; Ultimate Warrior, The; Until the End of the World; Victory; Virgin Spring, The; Voyage of the Damned; What Dreams May Come; Winter Light
von Trotta, Margarethe: American Soldier, The; Beware of a Holy Whore; Coup De Grace; Gods of the Plague
von Waggenheim, Gustav: Nosferatu; Woman in the Moon (Girl in the Moon; By Rocket to the Moon)
Von Zell, Harry: George Burns and Gracie Allen Show, The (TV Series); Son of Paleface; Strange Affair of Uncle Harry, The
von Zerneck, Danielle: Dangerous Curves; La Bamba; My Science Project; Under the Boardwalk
Voskovec, George: Barbarosa; Skag; Spy Who Came in from the Cold, The; 12 Angry Men; 27th Day, The
Vosloo, Arnold: Darkman II: The Return of Durant; Darkman III: Die, Darkman, Die; Diary of a Serial Killer; Finishing Touch, The; Hard Target; Mummy, The; Mummy Returns, The; Progeny; Zeus and Roxanne
Vostricil, Jan: Fireman's Ball, The
Votrian, Peter J.: Fear Strikes Out
Voutsinas, Andreas: Dream of Passion, A
Voyagis, Yorgo: Bourne Identity, The; Little Drummer Girl, The; Running Delilah
Vrana, Vlasta: Hawk's Vengeance; Lifeforce Experiment, The
Vreeken, Ron: Deathfight
Vrhovec, Janez: Man Is Not A Bird
Vrooman, Spencer: Pet Shop
Vujcic, Aleksandra: Broken English
Vullemin, Philippe: Mystery of Alexina, The
Vultaggio, Lisa: Mortal Sins (1992)
Vye, Murvyn: Escape to Burma; Golden Earrings; Pearl of the South Pacific; Road to Bali; Voodoo Island
Vyskocil, Ivan: Report on the Party and the Guests, A
Wachs, Caitlin: Air Bud: World Pup
Waddell, Justine: Dracula 2000
Waddington, Steven: Carrington; Edward II; Ivanhoe; Last of the Mohicans, The
Wade, Ernestine: Amos and Andy (TV Series)
Wade, Russell: Renegade Girl; Sundown Riders
Wade, Stuart: Meteor Monster (Teenage Monster); Monster from the Ocean Floor, The
Wade, Tyrone: Alien Force
Waggoner, Lyle: Gypsy Angels; Journey to the Center of Time (Time Warp); Surf 2; Wizards of the Demon Sword; Women of the Prehistoric Planet
Wagner, Agnieszka: Truce, The
Wagner, Chuck: Sisterhood, The
Wagner, Cristie: She-Devils on Wheels
Wagner, David: Pet Shop
Wagner, Jack: Dirty Little Secret; Swimsuit; Trapped in Space
Wagner, Kristina Malandro: Double Dragon
Wagner, Lindsay: Bionic Woman, The; Callie and Son; Contagious; Convicted; Danielle Steel's Once in a Lifetime; From the Dead of Night; High Risk; Incredible Journey of Dr. Meg Laurel,The; Martin's Day; Nighthawks; Nightmare at Bittercreek; Paper Chase, The; Princess Daisy; Ricochet; Rockford Files, The (TV Series); Shattered Dreams; Treacherous Crossing; Two Worlds of Jennie Logan, The
Wagner, Natasha Gregson: Another Day in Paradise; Dead Beat; Dragstrip Girl; Mind Ripper; Molly & Gina; Quiet Days in Hollywood; Stranger Than Fiction; Substitute, The; Tainted Blood; Urban Legend
Wagner, Robert: Affair, The; Airport '79: The Concorde; Austin Powers: International Man of Mystery; Austin Powers: The Spy Who Shagged Me; Beneath the 12-Mile Reef; Between Heaven and Hell; Broken Lance; Curse of the Pink Panther, The; Death at Love House; Deep Trouble; Dragon: The Bruce Lee Story; False Arrest; Halls of Montezuma; Harper; I Am the Cheese; It Takes a Thief (TV Series); Let's Make It Legal; Longest Day, The; Madame Sin; Mountain, The; Parallel Lives; Pink Panther, The; Prince Valiant; Stars and Stripes Forever; Stopover Tokyo; This Gun for Hire; Titanic; To Catch a King; Trail of the Pink Panther, The; War Lover, The; What Price Glory; Wild Things; Windmills of the Gods; Winning
Wagner, Thomas: Dead On; Marilyn & Bobby: Her Final Affair; Pinocchio's Revenge
Wagner, Wende: Green Hornet, The (TV Series)
Wagstaff, Elsie: Whistle Down the Wind
Wah, Yuen: Police Story III—Super Cop; Supercop
Wahl, Adam: Deadmate
Wahl, Ken: Dirty Dozen, The: The Next Mission; Favor, The; Fort Apache—The Bronx; Gladiator, The (1986) (Television); Jinxed; Omega Syndrome; Purple Hearts; Running Scared; Soldier, The; Taking of Beverly Hills, The; Treasure of the Yankee Zephyr; Wanderers, The
Wahlberg, Donnie: Black Circle Boys; Body Count; Diamond Men; Never 2 Big; Purgatory; Sixth Sense, The; Southie
Wahlberg, Mark: Big Hit, The; Boogie Nights; Corruptor, The; Fear; Perfect Storm, The; Planet of the Apes (2001); Renaissance Man; Rock Star; Substitute, The; Three Kings; Traveller; Yards, The
Wahlberg, Robert: Exchange, The
Wainwright, James: Private Files of J. Edgar Hoover, The; Survivors, The; Warlords of the 21st Century; Woman Called Moses, A
Waitaire, Gnarnay Yarrahe: Dead Heart
Waite, Liam: Second Skin

Waite, Ralph: Bodyguard, The; Crash and Burn; Five Easy Pieces; Gentleman Bandit, The; Last Summer; Lawman; On the Nickel; Red Alert; Sioux City; Stone Killer, The; Thanksgiving Story, The
Waites, Thomas: Clan of the Cave Bear; On the Yard; Verne Miller; Warriors, The
Waits, Tom: At Play in the Fields of the Lord; Bram Stoker's Dracula; Candy Mountain; Cold Feet; Down by Law; Ironweed; Mystery Men; Rumble Fish; Short Cuts
Wajnberg, Marc-Henri: Mamma Dracula
Wakabayashi, Akiko: You Only Live Twice
Wakao, Ayako: Geisha, A
Wakayama, Tomisaburo: Bad News Bears Go to Japan, The; Irezumi (Spirit of Tattoo); Lone Wolf and Cub: Sword of Vengeance; Shogun Assassin
Wakeham, Deborah: House of the Rising Sun
Wakely, Jimmy: Across the Rio Grande
Walbrook, Anton: Dangerous Moonlight (Suicide Squadron); 49th Parallel, The; Gaslight; La Ronde; Life and Death of Colonel Blimp, The; Lola Montes; Red Shoes, The; Saint Joan
Walburn, Raymond: Christmas in July; Count of Monte Cristo, The; Hail the Conquering Hero; Key to the City; Let Freedom Ring; Louisiana Purchase; Mad Wednesday (see also Sin of HaroldDiddlebock); Sin of Harold Diddlebock (Mad Wednesday); Thin Ice
Walcott, Gregory: Jet Attack; Plan 9 from Outer Space; Prime Cut
Walcott, Jersey Joe: Harder They Fall, The
Walcott, William: Down to the Sea in Ships
Walcutt, John: Return (1984)
Walczewski, Marek: Passenger, The
Walden, Lynette: Almost Blue; Saved by the Light; Silencer, The
Walden, Robert: Bloody Mama; Blue Sunshine; Kansas City Massacre, The; Memorial Day
Waldhorn, Gary: After Pilkington
Waldron, Shawna: Little Giants
Walerstein, Marcela: Disappearance of Garcia Lorca, The
Wales, Ethel: Border Vigilantes; Saturday Night Kid, The
Wales, Wally: Traitor, The
Walken, Christopher: Addiction, The; All-American Murder; America's Sweethearts; At Close Range; Batman Returns; Biloxi Blues; Blast from the Past; Brainstorm; Business Affair, A; Comfort of Strangers, The; Communion; Day of Atonement; Dead Zone, The; Deadline; Deer Hunter, The; Dogs of War, The; Eternal, The; Excess Baggage; Funeral, The; Heaven's Gate; Homeboy; Illuminata; King of New York; Kiss Toledo Goodbye; Last Embrace, The; Last Man Standing; McBain; Milagro Beanfield War, The; Mind Snatchers, The; Mistress; Mouse Hunt; New Rose Hotel; Next Stop, Greenwich Village; Nick of Time; Opportunists, The; Prophecy, The (1995); Prophecy II, The; Prophecy 3: The Ascent; Pulp Fiction; Roseland; Sarah, Plain and Tall; Scam; Scotland, PA; Search and Destroy; Skylark; Sleepy Hollow; Suicide Kings; Things to Do in Denver When You're Dead; Touch; True Romance; Vendetta; View to a Kill, A; Wayne's World 2; Who Am I This Time?; Wild Side; Winter's End
Walker, Albertina: Leap of Faith
Walker, Ally: Happy, Texas; Kazaam; Seventh Coin, The; Someone to Die For; Universal Soldier; When the Bough Breaks
Walker, Arnetia: Love Crimes
Walker, Christopher: Echo Park
Walker, Clint: Baker's Hawk; Bounty Man, The; Cheyenne (TV Series); Deadly Harvest; Dirty Dozen, The; Gambler Returns, The: Luck of the Draw; Hysterical; Maya; Night of the Grizzly, The; None But the Brave; Pancho Villa; Send Me No Flowers; Snowbeast; White Buffalo; Yuma
Walker, Corban: Frankie Starlight
Walker, Dominic: Power of One, The
Walker, Eamonn: Once in the Life
Walker, Eric: Ewok Adventure, The
Walker, Fiona: Norman Conquests, The, Episode 1: Table Manners; Norman Conquests, The, Episode 3: Roundand Round the Garden; Norman Conquests, The, Episode 2: LivingTogether
Walker, Helen: Brewster's Millions; Call Northside 777; Impact; My Dear Secretary; People Are Funny
Walker, Jimmie: Doin' Time; Frankenstein Sings; Going Bananas; Let's Do It Again
Walker, Joyce: Education of Sonny Carson, The
Walker, Justin: Born Bad; Humanoids from the Deep
Walker, Kathryn: Blade; Dangerous Game (1990); Murder of Mary Phagan, The; Neighbors; Rich Kids; Special Bulletin; Whale for the Killing, A; Winds of Kitty Hawk, The
Walker, Kim: Deadly Weapon; Heathers; Reason to Believe, A
Walker, Liza: Wavelength
Walker, Lou: Nightman, The
Walker, Marcy: Hot Resort; Midnight's Child
Walker, Matthew: Intimate Relations
Walker, Nancy: Best Foot Forward; Forty Carats; Girl Crazy; Lucky Me; Thursday's Game
Walker, Nella: They Call It Sin
Walker, Nicholas: Amnesia
Walker, Paul: Fast and the Furious, The; Joy Ride; Meet the Deedles; Skulls, The; Tammy & the T-Rex; Varsity Blues
Walker, Polly: Curtain Call; Dark Harbor; Enchanted April; For Roseanna; Lorna Doone; Sliver; Talk of Angels; Trial, The
Walker, Robert: Bataan; Clock, The; Madame Curie; One Touch of Venus; Sea of Grass, The; Since You Went Away; Song of Love; Strangers on a Train; Thirty Seconds Over Tokyo; Till the Clouds Roll By; Vengeance Valley
Walker, Sarah: Gloriana; Housekeeping
Walker, Sydney: Mrs. Doubtfire; Prelude to a Kiss
Walker, Terry: Take Me Back to Oklahoma
Walker, Zena: Dresser, The
Walker Jr., Robert: Angkor: Cambodia Express; Ensign Pulver; Evil Town; Gone with the West; Hambone and Hillie; Heated Vengeance; Little Moon & Jud McGraw; Son of Blob (Beware! The Blob)
Walkers, Cheryl: Stage Door Canteen
Walkinshaw, Hughston: Omaha (The Movie)
Wall, Max: Jabberwocky; We Think the World of You
Wallace, Anzac: Utu
Wallace, Basil: Marked for Death
Wallace, Bill: Avenging Force
Wallace, Chris: New Year's Evil
Wallace, Coley: Joe Louis Story, The
Wallace, David: Babysitter, The; Humongous; Mazes and Monsters
Wallace, Dee: Alligator II; Child Bride of Short Creek; Club Life; Critters; Cujo; E.T.—The Extra-Terrestrial; Frighteners, The; Hills Have Eyes, The; Howling, The; Huck and the King of Hearts; I'm Dangerous Tonight; Invisible Mom; Jimmy the Kid; Miracle Down Under; Nevada; Popcorn; Road Home, The (1995); Secret Admirer; Shadow Play; Skateboard Kid 2, The; Skeezer; Skeletons; Stranger on My Land; Whale for the Killing, A; Witness to the Execution
Wallace, George: Gross Jokes; Radar Men from the Moon; 3 Strikes; Wash, The (2001)
Wallace, Jack: Bear, The
Wallace, Jean: Big Combo, The; Man in the Eiffel Tower, The; Native Son; Sword of Lancelot
Wallace, Julie T.: Lunatic, The
Wallace, Linda: Charlie, the Lonesome Cougar
Wallace, Marcia: Pray TV
Wallace, Morgan: Billy the Kid Returns; Dream Street; Orphans of the Storm
Wallace, Rowena: Blackwater Trail
Wallace, Sue: Experience Preferred ... But Not Essential
Wallach, Eli: Ace High; Article 99; Associate, The; Baby Doll; Christopher Columbus (1985); Cinderella Liberty; Circle of Iron; Danger; Deep, The; Domino Principle, The; Executioner's Song, The; Family Matter, A; Firepower; Girlfriends; Godfather, Part III, The; Good the Bad and the Ugly, The; How to Steal a Million; Hunter, The (1980); Impossible Spy, The; Keeping the Faith; Legacy of Lies; Long Live Your Death; Lord Jim; Magnificent Seven, The; Misfits, The; Mistress; Moonspinners, The; Movie Movie; Night and the City; Nuts; Poppy Is Also a Flower, The; Pride of Jesse Hallman, The; Salamander, The; Sam's Son;

Sentinel, The; Seven Thieves; Skokie; Stateline Motel; Teamster Boss: The Jackie Presser Story; Tough Guys; Two Jakes, The; Two Much; Winter Kills
Wallach, Roberta: Effect of Gamma Rays on Man-in-the-Moon Marigolds, The
Waller, David: 4:50 From Paddington
Waller, Eddy: Bandits of Dark Canyon; Denver Kid; Marshal of Cedar Rock; Wild Frontier
Waller, Fats: Stormy Weather
Walley, Deborah: Beach Blanket Bingo; Benji; Bon Voyage!; Gidget Goes Hawaiian; Severed Arm, The; Spinout; Summer Magic
Wallis, Shani: Arnold; Oliver; Terror in the Wax Museum
Walls, Kevin Patrick: Soulkeeper
Walsh, Angela: Distant Voices/Still Lives
Walsh, Brigid Conley: Day My Parents Ran Away, The; Quest of the Delta Knights
Walsh, Dale: New Adventures of Tarzan
Walsh, Dermot: Ghost Ship; Tell-Tale Heart, The
Walsh, Dylan: Arctic Blue; Changing Habits; Congo; Divided by Hate; Eden; Final Voyage; Men; Nobody's Fool; Radio Inside
Walsh, Gabriel: Returning, The
Walsh, Gwynyth: Blue Monkey; Challengers, The; Limbic Region, The; Soft Deceit
Walsh, J. T.: Babysitter, The; Black Day Blue Night; Blue Chips; Breakdown; Client, The; Crazy People; Crime of the Century; Defenseless; Few Good Men, A; Gang in Blue; Good Morning, Vietnam; Grifters, The; Hidden Agenda (1998); Hoffa; Hope; Iron Maze; Last Seduction, The; Little Death, The; Miracle on 34th Street; Morning Glory; Needful Things; Negotiator, The; Nixon; Persons Unknown; Pleasantville; Red Rock West; Russia House, The; Sacred Cargo; Silent Fall; Sniper; True Identity; Wired
Walsh, Johnny: Wild Women of Wongo
Walsh, Kathleen: Killer Flick
Walsh, Kay: Dr. Syn, Alias the Scarecrow; Encore; Greyfriars Bobby; Horse's Mouth, The; Last Holiday; Scrooge; Sons of the Sea; Stage Fright; This Happy Breed; Tunes of Glory; Witches, The
Walsh, Kenneth: Climb, The; Habitat; Lost!; Reno and the Doc
Walsh, M. Emmet: Albino Alligator; Back to School; Best of Times, The; Bitter Harvest; Blade Runner; Blood Simple; Camp Nowhere; Cannery Row; Catch Me if You Can; Chairman of the Board; Chattahoochee; Clean and Sober; Cops and Robbersons; Criminal Hearts; Critters; Dead Badge; Dear Detective; Deliberate Stranger, The; Erasable You; Fletch; Four Eyes and Six Guns; Fourth Story; Get to Know Your Rabbit; High Noon, Part Two; Hitchhiker, The (Series); Killer Image; Killing Jar, The; Missing in Action; Music of Chance, The; Narrow Margin (1990); Panther; Probable Cause; Raw Courage; Red Alert; Red Scorpion; Relative Fear; Scandalous; Snow Dogs; Straight Time; Sunset; War Party; White Sands; Wild Card; Wildcats; Wilder Napalm
Walsh, Matthew Jason: City of the Vampires; Kingdom of the Vampire; Midnight 2; Zombie Bloodbath 2
Walsh, Raoul: Sadie Thompson
Walsh, Sally: Old Curiosity Shop, The
Walsh, Sydney: Homewrecker; To Die For
Walston, Ray: Apartment, The; Blood Relations; Blood Salvage; Damn Yankees; Fall of the House of Usher, The; Fast Times at Ridgemont High; From the Hip; Galaxy of Terror; Happy Hooker Goes to Washington, The; House Arrest; Kid with the Broken Halo, The; Kiss Me, Stupid; Man of Passion, A; My Favorite Martian; O.C. & Stiggs; Of Mice and Men; Popcorn; Popeye; Private School; Rad; Silver Streak; Ski Patrol; South Pacific; Stand, The; Sting, The; Tall Story; Tricks; Westing Game, The
Walter, Harriet: Good Father, The; Governess, The; May Fools; Merry War, A; Sense and Sensibility; Turtle Diary
Walter, Jerry: Nightmare in Blood
Walter, Jessica: Dr. Strange; Execution, The; Flamingo Kid, The; Going Ape!; Goldengirl; Grand Prix; Group, The; Home for the Holidays (1972) (Television); Lilith; Miracle on Ice; PCU; Play Misty for Me; Scruples; She's Dressed to Kill; Spring Fever; Victory at Entebbe
Walter, Lisa Ann: Eddie; Parent Trap, The
Walter, Rita: Cry from the Mountain
Walter, Tracey: Buffalo Girls; City Slickers; Conan the Destroyer; Delusion; Entertaining Angels; Mortuary Academy; Raggedy Man; Repo Man; Silence of the Lambs; Something Wild
Walter Hawkins and the Hawkins Family: Gospel
Walters, James: Shout (1991)
Walters, Julie: Billy Elliot; Buster; Educating Rita; Intimate Relations; Just Like a Woman; Lover's Prayer; Mack the Knife; Personal Services; Prick Up Your Ears; Sister, My Sister; Stepping Out; Summer House, The; Wedding Gift, The
Walters, Laurie: Harrad Experiment, The
Walters, Luana: Aces and Eights; Arizona Bound; Assassin of Youth (Marijuana); Badmen of the Hills; Corpse Vanishes, The; Down Texas Way; Drums of Fu Manchu; End of the Trail; Mexicali Rose; Tulsa Kid
Walters, Melora: Cabin Boy; Magnolia
Walters, Susan: Cop for the Killing, A; Elvis and Me; Galaxies Are Colliding; I Married a Monster
Walters, Thorley: Murder She Said; People That Time Forgot, The; Phantom of the Opera; Sherlock Holmes and the Deadly Necklace; Sign of Four, The
Walthall, Henry B.: Abraham Lincoln; Avenging Conscience, The; Birth of a Nation, The; Chandu the Magician; Devil Doll, The (1936); Helldorado; Home, Sweet Home (1914); Judge Priest; Judith of Bethulia; Last Outlaw, The; Ride Him Cowboy; Scarlet Letter, The; Scarlet Letter, The; Somewhere in Sonora; Strange Interlude; Viva Villa!; Warning Shadows
Walton, Douglas: Charlie Chan in London
Walton, Helen: Wolfheart's Revenge
Walton, John: Kangaroo; Lighthorsemen, The
Waltz, Lisa: Brighton Beach Memoirs
Walz, Marin: Boat Is Full, The
Wanamaker, Sam: Aviator, The; Baby Boom; Competition, The; Concrete Jungle, (1962) The (Criminal, The); Covert Assassin; Detective Sadie and Son; From Hell to Victory; Guilty by Suspicion; Judgment in Berlin; My Girl Tisa; Our Family Business; Private Benjamin; Pure Luck; Raw Deal; Running Against Time; Sell-Out, The; Spiral Staircase, The; Spy Who Came in from the Cold, The; Superman IV: The Quest for Peace
Wanamaker, Zoe: Prime Suspect 1; Tales of the Unexpected
Wanberg, Alexander: Mamma Dracula
Wang, Bo Z.: Pushing Hands
Wang, Faye: Chungking Express
Wang, Fei: Amazing Panda Adventure, The
Wang, George: Have a Nice Funeral
Wang, Jean: Iron Monkey
Wang, Joey: Reincarnation of Golden Lotus, The
Wang, Lai: Pushing Hands
Wang, Peter: Great Wall, A; Laser Man, The
Wang, Steve: Adventures of the Kung Fu Rascals, The
Wang, Wengqiang: Xiu Xiu: The Sent Down Girl
Wang, Yu-Wen: Eat Drink Man Woman
Wangchuk, Jamyang Jamtsho: Seven Years in Tibet
Wangiel, Karma: Himalaya
Warbeck, David: Black Cat, The; Miami Horror; Seven Doors of Death
Warburton, Patrick: Big Trouble (2002); Camouflage; Dish, The; Woman Chaser, The
Ward, Amelita: Jungle Captive
Ward, B. J.: Opposite Sex (And How to Live with Them), The (1993)
Ward, Burt: Alien Force; Batman; Beach Babes from Beyond; Robo C.H.I.C.; Robot Ninja; Smooth Talker; Virgin High
Ward, Clark: Eagle, The
Ward, Dave Oren: Pariah
Ward, Debra: Black Cobra 3
Ward, Donal Lardner: Suburbans, The
Ward, Douglas Turner: Man and Boy
Ward, Fannie: Cheat, The
Ward, Felix: Spookies
Ward, Fred: Backtrack; Big Business; Cast a Deadly Spell; Chain Reaction; Circus; Corky Romano; Crimson Code; Dangerous Beauty; Dark Wind; Equinox (1993); ... First Do No Harm;

Florida Straits; Forgotten City; Four Eyes and Six Guns; Full Disclosure; Henry & June; Miami Blues; Naked Gun 33 1/3, The—The Final Insult; Noon Wine; Off Limits; Player, The; Prince of Pennsylvania; Remo Williams: The Adventure Begins; Right Stuff, The; Secret Admirer; Short Cuts; Silkwood; Southern Comfort; Summer Catch; Swing Shift; Thunderheart; Timerider; Tremors; Tremors 2: Aftershocks; Two Small Bodies; Uforia; Uncommon Valor; Wild Iris
Ward, James: Red Line 7000
Ward, Jonathan: Mac and Me; White Water Summer
Ward, Lyman: Ferris Bueller's Day Off; Mikey; Taking of Beverly Hills, The
Ward, Mackenzie: Sons of the Sea
Ward, Mary: Surviving Desire
Ward, Megan: Amityville 1992: It's About Time; Arcade; Crash and Burn; Encino Man; Freaked; Joe's Apartment; PCU; Rated X; Tick Tock; Trancers III: Deth Lives
Ward, Merideth: Wheels: An Inline Story
Ward, Nelson E.: Mainline Run
Ward, Rachel: After Dark, My Sweet; Against All Odds (1984); Ascent, The; Black Magic; Christopher Columbus: The Discovery (1992); Dead Men Don't Wear Plaid; Double Jeopardy; Final Terror, The; Fortress; Good Wife, The; Hotel Colonial; How to Get Ahead in Advertising; My Stepson, My Lover; Night School; On the Beach; Sharky's Machine; Thornbirds, The; Wide Sargasso Sea
Ward, Richard: Across 110th Street; Mandingo
Ward, Robin: Thrillkill
Ward, Roger: Escape 2000; Mad Max
Ward, Roy: Ugly, The
Ward, Sela: Child of Darkness, Child of Light; Double Jeopardy; Fugitive, The; Haunting of Sarah Hardy, The; Hello Again; My Fellow Americans; Nothing in Common; Rainbow Drive; Rescuers, Stories of Courage, "Two Women"; Steele Justice
Ward, Simon: Children of Rage; Dracula; Four Feathers, The; Hitler, the Last Ten Days; Holocaust 2000; Monster Club, The; Supergirl; Young Winston; Zulu Dawn
Ward, Sophie: Big Fall, The; Casanova; Class of '61; Dark Adapted Eye, A; Emily Bronte's Wuthering Heights; Summer Story, A; Young Sherlock Holmes
Ward, Susan: In Crowd, The
Ward, Wally: Chocolate War, The; Invisible Kid, The
Ward, Zack: Star Hunter
Warde, Anthony: Buck Rogers: Destination Saturn (PlanetOutlaws); Dangers of the Canadian Mounted
Warden, Jack: Alice Through the Looking Glass; All the President's Men; … And Justice for All; Apprenticeship of Duddy Kravitz, The; Aviator, The; Being There; Beyond the Poseidon Adventure; Brian's Song; Bullets over Broadway; Bulworth; Carbon Copy; Chairman of the Board; Champ, The; Chu Chu and the Philly Flash; Crackers; Dead Solid Perfect; Death on the Nile; Dirty Work; Dog of Flanders, A; Donovan's Reef; Dreamer; Ed; Everybody Wins; Great Muppet Caper, The; Guilty as Sin; Heaven Can Wait; Hobson's Choice; Judgment; Man on a String; Man Who Loved Cat Dancing, The; Mighty Aphrodite; Night and the City; Passed Away; Presidio, The; Problem Child; Problem Child 2; Raid on Entebbe; Run Silent, Run Deep; September; Shampoo; So Fine; Sporting Club, The; Toys; 12 Angry Men; Used Cars; Verdict, The; While You Were Sleeping; White Buffalo
Warden, Jonathan: Greetings
Ward-Lealand, Jennifer: Desperate Remedies; Ugly, The
Ware, Herta: Crazy in Love; Lonely Hearts
Ware, Irene: Chandu the Magician; Raven, The
Warfield, Chris: Dangerous Charter
Warfield, Emily: Man in the Moon, The
Warhol, Andy: Cocaine Cowboys; Driver's Seat, The
Waring, Todd: Love and Murder
Warlock, Billy: Honor Thy Father & Mother: The Menendez Killings; Hot Shot; Opposite Corners; Society; Steel Sharks; Swimsuit
Warnat, Kimberly: Ms. Bear
Warnecke, Gordon: Fatal Inversion, A; My Beautiful Laundrette
Warner, David: Ballad of Cable Hogue, The; Beastmaster III: The Eye of Braxus; Blue Hotel; Cast a Deadly Spell; Christmas Carol, A; Code Name: Chaos; Company of Wolves, The; Cross of Iron; Doll's House, A; Felony; Final Equinox; Frankenstein; From Beyond the Grave; Grave Secrets; H. P. Lovecraft's Necronomicon: Book of the Dead; Holocaust; Hostile Take Over; Houdini; Island, The; John Carpenter Presents: Body Bags; Leading Man, The; Lost World, The; Magdalene; Man with Two Brains, The; Midsummer Night's Dream, A; Money Talks; Morgan; Naked Souls; Nightwing; Old Curiosity Shop, The; Omen, The; Providence; Quest of the Delta Knights; Rasputin; Return to the Lost World; Silver Bears; S.O.S. Titanic; Spymaker: The Secret Life of Ian Fleming; Star Trek V: The Final Frontier; Star Trek VI: The Undiscovered Country; Straw Dogs; Teenage Mutant Ninja Turtles II: The Secret of the Ooze; Thirty-Nine Steps, The; Time After Time; Time Bandits; Titanic; Tripwire; Tron; Tryst; Unnamable II, The; Waxwork; Wing Commander
Warner, Gary: Lurkers
Warner, H. B.: Adventures of Marco Polo, The; Arrest Bulldog Drummond; Bulldog Drummond in Africa; Bulldog Drummond's Bride; Bulldog Drummond's Peril; Bulldog Drummond's Secret Police; CorsicanBrothers, The; Girl of the Golden West, The; King of Kings, The (1927); Let Freedom Ring; Lost Horizon; Nurse Edith Cavell; Rains Came, The; Supernatural; Topper Returns
Warner, Jack: Captive Heart; Christmas Carol, A; Quatermass Experiment, The
Warner, Julie: Doc Hollywood; Indian Summer; Mr. Murder; Mr. Saturday Night; Puppet Masters, The; Tommy Boy; Wedding Bell Blues
Warner, Malcolm-Jamal: Restaurant; Tuskegee Airmen, The; Tyson
Warner, Steven: Little Prince, The
Warnock, Grant: Waterland
Warren, E. Alyn: Tarzan the Fearless
Warren, Estella: Driven; Planet of the Apes (2001)
Warren, Gary: Railway Children, The
Warren, James: Three for Bedroom C
Warren, Janet: Jade Mask, The; Twonky, The
Warren, Jennifer: Angel City; Another Man, Another Chance; Choice, The; Fatal Beauty; Intruder Within, The; Mutant; Slap Shot; Swap, The (Sam's Song)
Warren, Kiersten: Bicentennial Man; Grave Secrets: The Legacy of Hilltop Drive; Painted Hero
Warren, Kimberly: Blast; Mean Guns
Warren, Lesley Ann: Apology; Baja Oklahoma; Betrayal; Beulah Land; Bird of Prey; Burglar (U.S.); Choose Me; Cinderella; Clue; Color of Night; Cop; Joseph; Legend of Valentino; Life Stinks; Limey, The; Love Kills; Natural Enemy; Night in Heaven, A; One and Only, Genuine, Original Family Band, The; Portrait of a Showgirl; Portrait of a Stripper; Pure Country; Songwriter; Treasure of the Yankee Zephyr; Trixie; Twin Falls Idaho; Victor/Victoria; Worth Winning
Warren, Marc: Boston Kickout
Warren, Michael: Hill Street Blues (TV Series); Norman … Is That You?
Warren, Mike: Butterflies Are Free; Fast Break; Heaven Is a Playground; Kid Who Loved Christmas, The
Warren, Nancy: Where's the Money, Noreen?
Warren, Todd: Sleeping with Strangers
Warren G: Show, The
Warrender, Harry: Pandora and the Flying Dutchman
Warrick, Ruth: China Sky; Citizen Kane; CorsicanBrothers, The; Great Dan Patch, The; Guest in the House; Iron Major, The; Journey into Fear; Let's Dance; Mr. Winkle Goes to War; Ride Beyond Vengeance
Warrington, Don: Bloodbath at the House of Death; Lion of Africa, The
Warry-Smith, Dan: Legend of Gator Face, The
Warwick, James: Partners in Crime (Secret Adversary) (TV Series); Seven Dials Mystery, The; Why Didn't They Ask Evans?
Warwick, John: Face at the Window, The; Ticket of Leave Man, The
Warwick, Richard: If…; Lost Language of Cranes, The

Warwick, Robert: Adventures of Don Juan, The; Bold Caballero, The; Gangster's Boy; In a Lonely Place; Kismet; Private Lives of Elizabeth and Essex, The; Sudan; Sullivan's Travels; Woman's Face, A
Washbourne, Mona: Billy Liar; Brides of Dracula; Brideshead Revisited; Collector, The; Driver's Seat, The; Stevie
Washburn, Beverly: Wagon Train (TV Series)
Washburn, Bryant: Falcon in Mexico, The; Night of Terror; Return of Chandu (Magician, The)
Washburne, Rick: Comrades in Arms; Little Patriot, The
Washington, Blue: Haunted Gold
Washington, Denzel: Bone Collector, The; Carbon Copy; Courage Under Fire; Crimson Tide; Cry Freedom; Devil in a Blue Dress; Fallen; For Queen and Country; George McKenna Story, The; Glory; He Got Game; Heart Condition; Hurricane, The; John Q; Malcolm X; Mighty Quinn, The; Mississippi Masala; Mo' Better Blues; Much Ado About Nothing; Pelican Brief, The; Philadelphia; Power (1986); Preacher's Wife, The; Remember the Titans; Ricochet; Siege, The; St. Elsewhere (TV Series); Training Day; Virtuosity
Washington, Dinah: Ladies Sing the Blues, The
Washington, Isaiah: Always Outnumbered; Dancing in September; Exit Wounds; Girl 6; Joe Torre: Curveballs Along the Way; Love Jones; Mr. and Mrs. Loving; Romeo Must Die; True Crime
Washington, Kenneth: Hogan's Heroes (TV Series)
Washington, Kerry: Our Song
Washio, Isako: Fist of the North Star
Wass, Ted: Canterville Ghost, The; Curse of the Pink Panther, The; Longshot, The (1985); Oh, God, You Devil!; Pancho Barnes; Sheena; Triplecross
Wasserman, Jerry: Cooler Climate, A; Operative, The; Quarantine
Wasson, Craig: Body Double; Escape Under Pressure; Four Friends; Ghost Story; Go Tell the Spartans; Men's Club, The; Nightmare on Elm Street 3, A: The DreamWarriors; Schizoid; Sister-In-Law, The; Skag; Strapped; Trapped in Space
Watanabe, Eriko: Shall We Dance?
Watanabe, Fumio: Lone Wolf and Cub: Sword of Vengeance
Watanabe, Gedde: Gung Ho (1985); Vamp; Volunteers
Watanabe, Tetsu: Fireworks; Sonatine
Watase, Tsunehiko: Antarctica
Waterman, Dennis: Cold Justice; Scars of Dracula
Waterman, Felicity: Freedom Strike; Lena's Holiday; Miracle Beach; Thunder in Paradise
Waters, Crystal: Wigstock: The Movie
Waters, Ethel: Cabin in the Sky; Cairo; Member of the Wedding, The; Pinky; Tales of Manhattan
Waters, John: Alice to Nowhere; Attack Force Z; Boulevard of Broken Dreams; Breaker Morant; Ebbtide; Grievous Bodily Harm; Heaven Tonight; Miracle Down Under; Three's Trouble; Which Way Home
Waters, Muddy: Last Waltz, The
Waterston, Sam: Assault at West Point; Capricorn One; Captive in the Land, A; Crimes and Misdemeanors; Dempsey; Eagle's Wing; Enemy Within, The; Finnegan Begin Again; Friendly Fire; Generation (1969); Gore Vidal's Lincoln; Great Gatsby, The; Hannah and Her Sisters; Heaven's Gate; House Divided, A; Interiors; Journey into Fear; Journey of August King, The; Just Between Friends; Killing Fields, The; Lantern Hill; Man in the Moon, The; Mindwalk; Miracle at Midnight; Nightmare Years, The; Proprietor, The; Rancho Deluxe; Reflections of Murder; September; Serial Mom; Shadow Conspiracy; Sweet William; Trade Secrets; Warning Sign; Welcome Home; Who Killed Mary What's 'Er Name?
Watford, Gwen: Body in the Library, The; Fall of the House of Usher, The; Ghoul, The; Taste the Blood of Dracula
Watkin, Ian: Body in the Library, The; Fall of the House of Usher, The; Ghoul, The; Taste the Blood of Dracula
Watkin, Pierre: Atom Man vs. Superman; Shock (1946); Story of Seabiscuit, The; Superman—The Serial; Two Lost Worlds
Watkins, Gary: Wheels of Fire
Watkins, Linda: From Hell It Came
Watkins, Tionne T-Boz: Belly
Watkins, Tuc: I Think I Do
Watson, Alberta: Best Revenge; Destiny to Order; Hitman, The; Keep, The; Spanking the Monkey; Women of Valor
Watson, Anthony: Long Day Closes, The
Watson, Barry: Sorority Boys; Teaching Mrs. Tingle
Watson, Bill: Stingray
Watson, Bobs: Men of Boys Town; On Borrowed Time
Watson, Douglas: Parker Adderson, Philosopher; Trial of the Cantonsville Nine, The
Watson, Emily: Angela's Ashes; Boxer, The; Breaking the Waves; Cradle Will Rock; Gosford Park; Hilary and Jackie; Luzhin Defence, The; Metroland; Trixie
Watson, Emma: Harry Potter and the Sorcerer's Stone
Watson, Jack: King Arthur, The Young Warlord; Schizo; Sleeping Murder; Wild Geese, The
Watson, Jennia: Ragdoll
Watson, Lucile: Emperor Waltz, The; Footsteps in the Dark; Great Lie, The; Julia Misbehaves; Made for Each Other; My Forbidden Past; Thin Man Goes Home, The; Three Smart Girls; Tomorrow Is Forever; Uncertain Glory; Waterloo Bridge
Watson, Michael: Subspecies
Watson, Mills: Heated Vengeance; Kansas City Massacre, The
Watson, Minor: Adventures of Huckleberry Finn, The; Beyond the Forest; Jackie Robinson Story, The; Navy Blue and Gold; Star, The (1952); Virginian, The
Watson, Moray: Body in the Library, The; Pride and Prejudice
Watson, Muse: Acts of Betrayal; From Dusk Till Dawn 2: Texas Blood Money; I Still Know What You Did Last Summer; Something to Talk About
Watson, Vernee: Death Drug
Watt, Marty: Almost You
Watt, Nathan: Unstrung Heroes
Watt, Richard C.: Deathshot
Watters, William: Eegah!; Wild Guitar
Wattis, Richard: Colditz Story, The; Importance of Being Earnest, The
Watts, Naomi: Brides of Christ; Children of the Corn IV: The Gathering; Mulholland Drive; Persons Unknown; Tank Girl
Wauthion, Claire: Flight of Rainbirds, A
Waxman, Al: Collision Course; Hitman, The; Iron Eagle IV; Live Wire; Malarek; Meatballs III; Mob Story; Rescuers, Stories of Courage, "Two Women"; Spasms; Summer's End; Tulips; Wild Horse Hank
Way, Eileen: Queen of Hearts
Wayans, Damon: Bamboozled; Blankman; Bulletproof; Celtic Pride; Earth Girls Are Easy; Great White Hype, The; Last Boy Scout, The; Major Payne; Mo' Money
Wayans, Keenen Ivory: Glimmer Man, The; I'm Gonna Git You Sucka!; Low Down Dirty Shame, A
Wayans, Kim: Floundering; Talking About Sex
Wayans, Marlon: Above the Rim; Don't Be a Menace to South Central while Drinking Your Juice in the 'Hood; Dungeons & Dragons; Mo' Money; Requiem for a Dream; Scary Movie; Scary Movie 2; Senseless; Sixth Man, The
Wayans, Shawn: Don't Be a Menace to South Central while Drinking Your Juice in the 'Hood; New Blood; Scary Movie; Scary Movie 2
Wayborn, Kristine: Little Ghost
Wayne, David: Adam's Rib; American Christmas Carol, An; Andromeda Strain, The; Apple Dumpling Gang, The; As Young as You Feel; Front Page, The; How to Marry a Millionaire; Huckleberry Finn; Last Angry Man, The; Poker Alice; Portrait of Jennie; Prizefighter, The; Sad Sack, The; Stella; Survivalist, The; Tender Trap, The; Three Faces of Eve, The; We're Not Married
Wayne, Ethan: Operation 'Nam
Wayne, John: Alamo, The; Allegheny Uprising; Angel and the Badman; Baby Face; Back to Bataan; Barbarian and the Geisha, The; Big Jake; Big Jim McLain; Big Stampede, The; Big Trail, The; Blood Alley; Blue Steel; Brannigan; Cahill—US Marshal; Chisum; Circus World; Comancheros, The; Conqueror, The; Cowboys, The; Dakota; Dark Command; Dawn Rider; Donovan's Reef; El Dorado; Fighting Kentuckian, The; Fighting Seabees, The; Flame of the Barbary Coast; Flying Leathernecks; Flying Tigers, The; Fort Apache; Frontier Horizon; Greatest Story Ever

Weiss, Shaun: Heavyweights
Weisser, Morgan: Long Road Home, The; Mother
Weisser, Norbert: Adrenalin: Fear the Rush; Android; Arcade; Deceit; Heatseeker; My Antonia; Nemesis 4; Nemesis 3: Time Lapse; Omega Doom; Radioactive Dreams; Riders of the Purple Sage
Weissmuller, Johnny: Fury of the Congo; Jungle Jim; Tarzan and His Mate; Tarzan and the Leopard Woman; Tarzan Escapes; Tarzan Finds a Son; Tarzan the Ape Man; Tarzan Triumphs; Tarzan's New York Adventure; Tarzan's Secret Treasure
Weist, Lucinda: Haunting of Sea Cliff Inn, The
Weisz, Rachel: Chain Reaction; Enemy at the Gates; Going All the Way; I Want You; Land Girls, The; Mummy, The; Mummy Returns, The; Stealing Beauty; Swept from the Sea
Weitz, Bruce: Breaking the Surface: The Greg Louganis Story; Death of a Centerfold; Hill Street Blues (TV Series); Landlady, The; Liars' Club, The; Mach 2; Molly & Gina; No Place to Hide; O. J. Simpson Story, The; Rainbow Drive; Velocity Trap; Windrunner
Weitz, Chris: Chuck & Buck
Weitz, Paul: Chuck & Buck
Welch, Elisabeth: Big Fella; Song of Freedom
Welch, Gillian: Down from the Mountain
Welch, Joseph: Anatomy of a Murder
Welch, Niles: Phantom, The
Welch, Raquel: Bandolero!; Bedazzled; Bluebeard; Chairman of the Board; Fantastic Voyage; Four Musketeers, The; Fuzz; Hannie Caulder; Lady in Cement; Last of Sheila, The; Legend of Walks Far Woman, The; Magic Christian, The; Mother, Jugs, and Speed; Myra Breckenridge; Oldest Profession, The; 100 Rifles; Restless; Scandal in a Small Town; Shoot Loud, Louder ... I Don't Understand; Swingin' Summer, A; Tainted Blood; Three Musketeers, The; Tortilla Soup; Trouble in Paradise; Wild Party, The
Welch, Tahnee: Cocoon; Cocoon: The Return; Criminal Mind, The; Johnny 2.0; Lethal Obsession; Night Train to Venice
Weld, Tuesday: Author! Author!; Cincinnati Kid, The; Falling Down; Feeling Minnesota; Five Pennies, The; Heartbreak Hotel; I'll Take Sweden; Looking for Mr. Goodbar; Lord Love a Duck; Once Upon a Time in America (Long Version); Pretty Poison; Reflections of Murder; Return to Peyton Place; Rock, Rock, Rock; Serial; Soldier in the Rain; Thief (1981); Who'll Stop the Rain; Wild in the Country
Welden, Ben: Kid Galahad
Welker, Frank: Pagemaster, The
Welland, Colin: Spymaker: The Secret Life of Ian Fleming
Weller, Frederick: Business of Strangers, The; Stonewall
Weller, Mary Louise: Evil, The; Forced Vengeance
Weller, Peter: Adventures of Buckaroo Banzai, The; Apology; Cat Chaser; Decoy; Diplomatic Siege; Dracula: The Dark Prince; End of Summer; Fifty/Fifty; Firstborn; Just Tell Me What You Want; Killing Affair, A; Leviathan; Naked Lunch; New Age, The; Of Unknown Origin; Rainbow Drive; Road to Ruin (1991); RoboCop; RoboCop 2; Screamers; Substitute Wife, The; Sunset Grill; Tunnel, The; Women & Men: Stories of Seduction
Welles, Gwen: Between the Lines; Desert Hearts; Eating; Hit! (1973); New Year's Day; Sticky Fingers
Welles, Mel: Attack of the Crab Monsters; Commando Squad; Dr. Heckyl and Mr. Hype; Little Shop of Horrors, The (1960); She Beast, The
Welles, Orson: Battle of Austerlitz, The; Black Magic; Blood and Guns (Tepepa); Butterfly; Casino Royale; Chimes at Midnight (Falstaff); Citizen Kane; Compulsion; F for Fake; Follow the Boys; Get to Know Your Rabbit; Immortal Story; Is Paris Burning?; It's All True; Jane Eyre; Journey into Fear; Lady from Shanghai; Long Hot Summer, The; Macbeth; Man for All Seasons, A; Mr. Arkadin (Confidential Report); Moby Dick; Muppet Movie, The; Napoleon; Othello; Scene of the Crime; Someone to Love; Stranger, The; Ten Days Wonder; Third Man, The; Three Cases of Murder; Tomorrow Is Forever; Touch of Evil; Trial, The; Trouble in the Glen; V.I.P.s, The; Voyage of the Damned; Waterloo; Witching, The (Necromancy)
Welles, Steve: Puppet Master II
Welles, Virginia: Francis in the Haunted House
Welling, Miki: Alex's Apartment
Wellington, James: Too Fast Too Young
Welliver, Titus: Once in the Life; Zero Tolerance
Wellman Jr., William: Black Caesar; Born Losers; Swingin' Summer, A
Wells, Dawn: Return to Boggy Creek; Town That Dreaded Sundown, The
Wells, Doris: Oriane
Wells, Jacqueline: Black Cat, The; Kansas Terrors; Ranger and the Lady, The; Tarzan the Fearless
Wells, Mel: Wizard of the Lost Kingdom II
Wells, Tico: Five Heartbeats, The; Mississippi Masala
Wells, Tracy: Mirror, Mirror 2: Raven Dance
Wells, Vernon: Circle of Fear; Circuitry Man; Circuitry Man II: Plughead Rewired; Enemy Unseen; Last Man Standing; Road Warrior, The; Stranglehold
Welsh, John: Nightmare
Welsh, Kenneth: Adrift; And Then You Die; Big Slice, The; Dead Silence; Death Wish V: The Face of Death; Escape Clause; Good Fight, The; Joe Torre: Curveballs Along the Way; Last Best Year, The; Love and Hate; Loyalties; Margaret's Museum; Screwball Academy; Straight Line; War Boy, The
Welti, Lisa: Don't Sleep Alone
Wen, Jiang: Emperor's Shadow, The
Wen, Ming-Na: Hong Kong '97; Joy Luck Club, The; One Night Stand; Star Quest; Street Fighter
Wences, Señor: Mother Wore Tights
Wenders, Wim: Lightning over Water
Wendt, George: Alice in Wonderland; Aliens Among Us; Guilty by Suspicion; Gung Ho (1985); Hostage for a Day; House; Man of the House; Outside Providence; Plain Clothes; Spice World; Welcome to Planet Earth
Weng, Jian: Red Sorghum
Wenli, Jiang: Story of Xinghua, The
Wenner, Jann: Perfect
Went, Johanna: Living End, The
Wentworth, Alexandra: Love Bug, The
Wepper, Fritz: Bridge, The; Final Combat, The
Werle, Barbara: Gone with the West; Little Moon & Jud McGraw
Werner, Oskar: Fahrenheit 451; Jules and Jim; Lola Montes; Ship of Fools; Shoes of the Fisherman; Spy Who Came in from the Cold, The; Voyage of the Damned
Wernicke, Otto: Testament of Dr. Mabuse
Wert, Doug: Assassination Game, The; Baby Face Nelson; Dracula Rising; Wasp Woman, The (1995)
Wesley, Charles: Murdercycle
Wessel, Dick: Dick Tracy versus Cueball; Gazebo, The; Pitfall
Wesson, Dick: Destination Moon; Jim Thorpe—All American
Wesson, Eileen: Zarkorr! The Invader
Wesson, Jessica: Flipper
West, Adam: Batman; Doin' Time on Planet Earth; For the Love of It; Happy Hooker Goes Hollywood, The; Joyride; Mad About You; New Age, The; Omega Cop; One Dark Night; Tammy and the Doctor; Young Philadelphians, The; Zombie Nightmare
West, Chandra: Puppet Master 5: The Final Chapter; Puppet Master Four; Something More; Universal Soldier II: Brothers in Arms
West, Charles: D. W. Griffith Triple Feature
West, Dean: Blood Harvest
West, Dominic: Rock Star; 28 Days; William Shakespeare's A Midsummer Night's Dream
West, Dottie: Aurora Encounter
West, Jeremy: Curse IV: The Ultimate Sacrifice
West, Joel: Blood Surf
West, Julian: Vampyr (1931)
West, Kevin: Santa with Muscles
West, Mae: Belle of the Nineties; Every Day's a Holiday; Go West, Young Man; Goin' to Town; Heat's On, The; I'm No Angel; Klondike Annie; My Little Chickadee; Myra Breckenridge; Night after Night; Sextette; She Done Him Wrong
West, Martin: Swingin' Summer, A
West, Samuel: Carrington; Howards End; Stiff Upper Lips

Whitfield, Lynn: Color of Courage, The; Eve's Bayou; George McKenna Story, The; Josephine Baker Story, The; Junior's Groove; State of Emergency; Taking the Heat; Thin Line Between Love and Hate, A
Whitfield, Mitchell: Best Men; Dogfight; I Love You, Don't Touch Me!; My Cousin Vinny
Whitfield, Raymond: How U Like Me Now
Whitford, Bradley: Billy Madison; Masterminds; Muse, The; My Fellow Americans; Red Corner
Whiting, Barbara: Beware, My Lovely
Whiting, Jack: Give Me a Sailor
Whiting, Leonard: Romeo and Juliet; Royal Hunt of the Sun
Whiting, Margaret: Sinbad and the Eye of the Tiger; Taking My Turn
Whitley, Ray: Land of the Open Range; Renegade Ranger
Whitlow, Jill: Adventures Beyond Belief; Ghost Chase; Night of the Creeps; Thunder Run; Twice Dead
Whitman, Ernest: Among the Living
Whitman, Mae: Gingerbread Man, The; Hope Floats; One Fine Day; When a Man Loves a Woman
Whitman, Stuart: Captain Apache; Comancheros, The; Crazy Mama; Crime of Passion; Day and the Hour; Delta Fox; Demonoid; Eaten Alive; Girl in Black Stockings, The; Kill Castro (Cuba Crossing, Mercenaries, Sweet Violent Tony); Las Vegas Lady; Mean Johnny Barrows; Mob Boss; Monster Club, The; Omega Cop; Private Wars; Ransom; Revenge (1971) (Shelley Winters); Rio Conchos; Ruby; Run for the Roses (Thoroughbred); Sandman (1992); Seekers, The; Shatter; Smooth Talker; Story of Ruth, The; Strange Shadows in an Empty Room; Texas Guns; Those Magnificent Men in Their Flying Machines; Treasure of the Amazon; Trial by Jury; Vultures; Walker: Texas Ranger; White Buffalo; Wounded Heart
Whitmore, James: Above and Beyond; All My Sons; All the Brothers Were Valiant; Asphalt Jungle, The; Battleground; Because You're Mine; Black Like Me; Chato's Land; Chuka; Eddy Duchin Story, The; First Deadly Sin, The; Force of One; Girl Who Had Everything, The; Give 'em Hell, Harry!; Glory! Glory!; Golden Honeymoon, The; Guns of the Magnificent Seven; Harrad Experiment, The; High Crime; I Will Fight No More Forever; It's a Big Country; Kiss Me Kate; Madigan; Majestic, The; McConnell Story, The; Next Voice You Hear, The; Nuts; Old Explorers; Rage; Relic, The; Serpent's Egg, The; Shawshank Redemption, The; Them!; Tora! Tora! Tora!; Waterhole #3; Where the Red Fern Grows; Word, The
Whitmore Jr., James: Boys in Company C, The; Gypsy Warriors, The
Whitney, Grace Lee: Star Trek (TV Series)
Whitrow, Benjamin: Belfast Assassin; Pride and Prejudice
Whitt, Garland: Blind Faith
Whittaker, Forest: Ready to Wear
Whitten, Frank: Vigil
Whitten, Margaret: Two-Gun Man from Harlem
Whitthorne, Paul: Critters 4
Whittington, Shawn: Barn Burning
Whittle, Brenton: Sara Dane
Whitton, Margaret: Best of Times, The; Big Girls Don't Cry—They Get Even; Little Monsters; Major League; Man without a Face, The; 9 1/2 Weeks; Secret of My Success, The; Trial by Jury
Whitty, May: Conquest; Lady Vanishes, The; Lassie Come Home; Madame Curie; Mrs. Miniver; Night Must Fall; Return of October, The; Suspicion; This Time For Keeps; White Cliffs of Dover, The
Whitworth, James: Planet of the Dinosaurs
Whitworth, Johnny: Empire Records; Somebody Is Waiting
Who, The: Kids Are Alright, The; Monterey Pop; Rock and Roll Circus, The
Wholihan, Kit: Islander, The
Whorf, Richard: Chain Lightning; Keeper of the Flame; Midnight; Yankee Doodle Dandy
Whylie, James: Place of Weeping
Wickes, Mary: Blondie's Blessed Event; By the Light of the Silvery Moon; Don't Go Near the Water; How to Murder Your Wife; I'll See You in My Dreams; June Bride; Ma and Pa Kettle at Home; Man Who Came to Dinner, The; On Moonlight Bay; Postcards from the Edge; Sister Act; Sister Act 2: Back in the Habit; Touched by Love
Wickham, Jeffrey: Terrorists, The
Wickham, Saskia: Leo Tolstoy's Anna Karenina (1997)
Wicki, Bernhard: Crime & Passion; Killing Cars; Love in Germany, A; Mysterious Stranger, The; Spring Symphony
Wicks, Rebecca: Jack-O
Widdoes, Kathleen: Mafia Princess; Without a Trace
Widmark, Richard: Alamo, The; All God's Children; Alvarez Kelly; Bear Island; Bedford Incident, The; Blackout; Broken Lance; Cheyenne Autumn; Cold Sassy Tree; Coma; Death of a Gunfighter; Domino Principle, The; Don't Bother to Knock; Final Option, The; Halls of Montezuma; Hanky Panky; How the West Was Won; Judgment at Nuremberg; Kiss of Death; Law and Jake Wade, The; Madigan; Mr. Horn; Murder on the Bayou; Night and the City; Panic in the Streets; Pickup on South Street; Road House; Rollercoaster; Run for the Sun; Saint Joan; Sell-Out, The; Street with No Name; Swarm, The; Texas Guns; To the Devil, a Daughter; Trap, The; True Colors; Tunnel of Love, The; Twilight's Last Gleaming; Two Rode Together; Warlock; Way West, The; Whale for the Killing, A; When the Legends Die
Wieck, Dorothea: Maedchen in Uniform
Wiemann, Mathias: Fear
Wiesendanger, Alex: Little Buddha
Wiesinger, Kai: BackBeat
Wiesmeiser, Lynda: Wheels of Fire
Wiest, Dianne: Associate, The; Birdcage, The; Bright Lights, Big City; Bullets over Broadway; Cookie; Cops and Robbersons; Drunks; Edward Scissorhands; Footloose; Hannah and Her Sisters; Horse Whisperer, The; I Am Sam; Independence Day; Little Man Tate; Lost Boys, The; Parenthood; Practical Magic; Radio Days; Scout, The; September; 10th Kingdom, The
Wiggins, Al: My Stepson, My Lover
Wiggins, Chris: American Christmas Carol, An; Fish Hawk; High-Ballin'; Kavik the Wolf Dog; King of the Grizzlies; Why Shoot the Teacher?
Wignacci, Darlene: Psycho Girls
Wilborn, Carlton: Dance
Wilby, James: Behind the Lines; Cotton Mary; Handful of Dust, A; Howards End; Maurice; Summer Story, A; Tale of Two Cities, A
Wilcox, Claire: Forty Pounds of Trouble
Wilcox, Frank: Clay Pigeon, The
Wilcox, Larry: Dirty Dozen, The: The Next Mission; Last Ride of the Dalton Gang, The; Sky Heist
Wilcox, Lisa: Nightmare on Elm Street 5, A: The Dream Child; Nightmare on Elm Street 4, A: The DreamMaster
Wilcox, Mary: Beast of the Yellow Night
Wilcox, Robert: Dreaming Out Loud; Man They Could Not Hang, The; Mysterious Dr. Satan
Wilcox, Shannon: Hollywood Harry; Triplecross
Wilcox-Horne, Colin: Baby Maker, The
Wilcoxon, Henry: Against a Crooked Sky; Cleopatra; Corsican-Brothers, The; Crusades, The; Dragnet; If I Were King; Jericho; Last of the Mohicans, The; Man in the Wilderness; Miniver Story, The; Mrs. Miniver; Mysterious Mr. Moto; Pony Express Rider; Tarzan Finds a Son; Two Worlds of Jennie Logan, The; War Lord, The
Wild, Christopher: Knights and Emeralds
Wild, Jack: Melody; Oliver
Wild, Susanne: Invisible Adversaries
Wilde, Cornel: At Sword's Point; Big Combo, The; Fifth Musketeer, The; Forever Amber; Gargoyles (1972); Greatest Show on Earth, The; Leave Her to Heaven; Naked Prey, The; Norseman, The; Omar Khayyam; Passion; Road House; Shark's Treasure; Song to Remember, A; Sword of Lancelot; Wintertime; Woman's World
Wilde, Lois: Brothers of the West; Hopalong Rides Again; Undersea Kingdom
Wilde, Steven: Shaking the Tree
Wilder, Gene: Adventure of Sherlock Holmes' Smarter Brother, The; Alice in Wonderland; Another You; Blazing Saddles; Bonnie and Clyde; Everything You Always Wanted to Know About Sex but Were Afraid to Ask; Frisco Kid, The; Funny About Love; Hanky Panky; Haunted Honeymoon; Little Prince, The;

Producers, The; Quackser Fortune Has a Cousin in the Bronx; See No Evil, Hear No Evil; Silver Streak; Start the Revolution Without Me; Stir Crazy; Thursday's Game; Willy Wonka and the Chocolate Factory; Woman in Red, The; World's Greatest Lover, The; Young Frankenstein
Wilder, Giselle: Unexpected Encounters
Wilder, James: Nevada; Our Mother's Murder; Prey of the Chameleon; Scorchers; Zombie High
Wilding, Michael: Convoy; Courtney Affair, The; Egyptian, The; Glass Slipper, The; In Which We Serve; Naked Edge, The; Ships with Wings; Stage Fright; Torch Song; Under Capricorn; Waterloo; World of Suzie Wong, The
Wildman, John: American Boyfriends; My American Cousin
Wildman, Steve: Super Soul Brother
Wildman, Valerie: Inner Sanctum
Wildsmith, Dawn: Surf Nazis Must Die; Wizards of the Demon Sword
Wiles, Jason: Kicking and Screaming; Roadracers; Windrunner
Wiley, Jan: Dick Tracy vs. Crime Inc.
Wilferson, Guy: Enemy of the Law
Wilhoite, Kathleen: Campus Man; Everybody Wins; Fire in the Sky; Live! From Death Row; Lorenzo's Oil; Murphy's Law; Nurse Betty; Pay It Forward; Tales of Erotica; Undercover; Witchboard
Wilker, José: Bye Bye Brazil; Dona Flor and Her Two Husbands; Medicine Man
Wilkerson, Guy: Hanging Tree, The
Wilkes, Donna: Angel
Wilkinson, Elizabeth: Suburban Roulette
Wilkinson, June: Bellboy and the Playgirls, The; Sno-Line
Wilkinson, Tom: Black Knight; Essex Boys; Full Monty, The; Ghost and the Darkness, The; Governess, The; Letting the Birds Go Free; Oscar & Lucinda; Paper Mask; Pocketful of Rye, A; Priest; Rush Hour; Sylvia; Wetherby; Wilde
Willard, Fred: Americathon; Best in Show; High Strung; How to Beat the High Co$t of Living; Lots of Luck; Moving Violations; Prehysteria! 3; Roxanne; Sodbusters; Waiting for Guffman
Willenborg, Amber: Basket, The
Willes, Jean: King and Four Queens, The
Willett, Chad: Annie O; Joan of Arc (1999)
Willette, Jo Ann: Welcome to 18
William, Warren: Arizona; Case of the Curious Bride, The; Case of the Howling Dog, The; Case of the Lucky Legs, The; Case of the Velvet Claws, The; Cleopatra; Employees' Entrance; Firefly, The; Go West, Young Man; Lady for a Day; Madame X; Man in the Iron Mask, The; Private Affairs of Bel Ami, The; Satan Met a Lady; Skyscraper Souls; Stage Struck; Wives Under Suspicion; Wolf Man, The
Williams, Adam: Fear Strikes Out
Williams, Amir: Silent Witness: What a Child Saw
Williams, Anson: I Married a Centerfold
Williams, Barbara: Bone Daddy; City of Hope; Digger; Family of Cops; Indecency; Jo Jo Dancer, Your Life Is Calling; Joe Torre: Curveballs Along the Way; Oh, What a Night; Spenser: Ceremony; Spenser: Pale Kings & Princes; Thief of Hearts; Tiger Warsaw; Watchers
Williams, Bill: Buckskin; Cariboo Trail; Clay Pigeon, The; Deadline at Dawn; Son of Paleface; Stratton Story, The; Those Endearing Young Charms; Torpedo Alley; Woman's Secret, A
Williams, Billy Dee: Alien Intruder; Batman; Bingo Long Traveling All-Stars and Motor Kings, The; Brian's Song; Chiefs; Christmas Lilies of the Field; Dangerous Passion; Driving Me Crazy; Empire Strikes Back, The; Fear City; Final Comedown, The; Glass House, The; Hard Time; Hit! (1973); Hostage Tower, The; Imposter, The; Jacksons, The: An American Dream; Ladies Man, The (2000); Lady Sings the Blues; Mahogany; Marvin and Tige; Mask of Death; Moving Target; Nighthawks; Number One with a Bullet; Oceans of Fire; Out of Towners, The (1970); Percy & Thunder; Return of the Jedi; Steel Sharks; Triplecross; Visit, The
Williams, Brook: Plague of the Zombies
Williams, Burt: Public Access
Williams, Cara: Doctors' Wives; Never Steal Anything Small
Williams, Carlton: Crooklyn
Williams, Caroline: Stepfather II; Texas Chainsaw Massacre 2, The
Williams, Cindy: American Graffiti; Big Man on Campus; Bingo; Conversation, The; First Nudie Musical, The; Gas-s-s-s; Meet Wally Sparks; Migrants, The; More American Graffiti; Rude Awakening; Son of Blob (Beware! The Blob); Spaceship (Naked Space); Stepford Husbands, The; Travels with My Aunt; Tricks of the Trade; Uforia
Williams, Clara: Hell's Hinges
Williams, Cress: Doom Generation, The
Williams, Cynda: Black Rose of Harlem; Condition Red; Gang in Blue; Ghost Brigade; Introducing Dorothy Dandridge; Mo' Better Blues; One False Move; Relax ... It's Just Sex; Spirit Lost; Sweeper, The; Tales of Erotica
Williams, Darnell: How U Like Me Now
Williams, Dean: Distant Voices/Still Lives
Williams, Diahn: Deadly Hero
Williams, Dick Anthony: Gardens of Stone; Gun in the House, A; Mo' Better Blues; Sophisticated Gents, The; Tap
Williams, Edy: Bad Girls from Mars; Hellhole; Mankillers; Secret Life of an American Wife, The; Seven Minutes, The
Williams, Emlyn: Citadel, The; Iron Duke, The; Jamaica Inn; Major Barbara; Stars Look Down, The; Wreck of the Mary Deare, The
Williams, Esther: Andy Hardy's Double Life; Bathing Beauty; Dangerous When Wet; Duchess of Idaho; Easy to Love; Fiesta; Jupiter's Darling; Million Dollar Mermaid; Neptune's Daughter; On an Island with You; Pagan Love Song; Skirts Ahoy!; Take Me Out to the Ball Game; Texas Carnival; That's Entertainment; That's Entertainment! III; This Time For Keeps; Thrill of a Romance; Ziegfeld Follies
Williams, Gareth: Palookaville
Williams, Grant: Brain of Blood; Incredible Shrinking Man, The; Leech Woman, The; Monolith Monsters, The; PT 109
Williams, Guinn: American Empire; Bad Lands (1939); Billy the Kid; Flirtation Walk; Littlest Rebel, The; Man of the Forest; Mystery Squadron; Noah's Ark; Phantom, The; Phantom Broadcast, The; Powdersmoke Range; Riders of Death Valley; Silver Queen; Station West; Vigilantes Are Coming!; Virginia City; Wolfheart's Revenge; You Only Live Once; You'll Never Get Rich
Williams, Guy: Captain Sinbad; Lost in Space (TV Series); Sign of Zorro, The
Williams, Hal: Don't Look Back: The Story of Leroy "Satchel" Paige; On the Nickel
Williams, Harland: Dog Park; Down Periscope; Half Baked; Rocketman; Sorority Boys
Williams, Heathcote: Orlando; Tango Lesson, The
Williams, Hugh: Human Monster, The (Dark Eyes of London); One of Our Aircraft Is Missing; Ships with Wings
Williams, Ian: Heaven's a Drag
Williams, Ian Patrick: Bad Channels
Williams, Jamie: Forever Together; Second Jungle Book, The: Mowgli and Baloo
Williams, Jane: Small Time
Williams, Jason: Danger Zone, The (1986); Flesh Gordon; Vampire at Midnight
Williams, JoBeth: Adam; American Dreamer; Backlash; Big Chill, The; Chantilly Lace; Child in the Night; Day After, The; Desert Bloom; Dutch; Endangered Species; Final Appeal; It Came from the Sky; Jungle 2 Jungle; Just Write; Kramer vs. Kramer; Little City; Me, Myself & I; Memories of Me; My Name Is Bill W; Parallel Lives; Poltergeist; Poltergeist II: The Other Side; Ruby Jean and Joe; Sex, Love, and Cold Hard Cash; Stir Crazy; Stop! Or My Mom Will Shoot; Switch; Teachers; Victim of Love; Welcome Home; When Danger Follows You Home; Wyatt Earp
Williams, John: Alfred Hitchcock Presents (TV Series); Dial M for Murder; Paradine Case, The; Sabrina; To Catch a Thief; Will Success Spoil Rock Hunter?; Witness for the Prosecution; Young Philadelphians, The
Williams, Kate: Melody
Williams, Kelli: Lifepod; Sweetwater; There Goes My Baby; Till Murder Do Us Part; Wavelength; Zapped Again

Williams, Kenneth: Carry on at Your Convenience; Carry on Behind; Carry on Cleo; Carry on Cowboy; Carry on Cruising; Carry on Doctor; Carry on Emmanuelle; Carry on Nurse; Follow That Camel
Williams, Kent: Sister-In-Law, The
Williams, Kimberly: Cold-Blooded; Father of the Bride; Father of the Bride Part II; Follow the Stars Home; Indian Summer; Safe House; 10th Kingdom, The; War at Home, The
Williams, Lia: Shot Through the Heart
Williams, Lynn Red: Mortal Kombat: Annihilation
Williams, Malinda: Dancing in September; High School High; Uninvited Guest
Williams, Mark: Borrowers, The; Trained to Fight
Williams, Megan: Anzacs
Williams, Michael: Educating Rita
Williams, Michael C.: Blair Witch Project, The
Williams, Michelle: Dick; Halloween: H20; Killing Mr. Griffin; Lassie; Timemaster
Williams, Olivia: Body, The; Emma; Mood Swingers; Postman, The; Rushmore; Sixth Sense, The
Williams, Paul: Battle for the Planet of the Apes; Cheap Detective, The; Headless Body in Topless Bar; Muppet Movie, The; Night They Saved Christmas, The; November Men, The; Phantom of the Paradise; Smokey and the Bandit; Smokey and the Bandit II; Smokey and the Bandit III; Stone Cold Dead; Wild Wild West Revisited, The
Williams, Peter: Jungleground; Robin Hood and the Sorcerer
Williams, Rhys: Corn Is Green, The; Fastest Gun Alive, The; Hills of Home; Raintree County; Showdown, The (1950); Strange Woman, The
Williams, Robert: Platinum Blonde
Williams, Robin: Adventures of Baron Münchausen, The; Aladdin & the King of Thieves; Awakenings; Being Human; Best of Times, The; Bicentennial Man; Birdcage, The; Cadillac Man; Club Paradise; Dead Again; Dead Poets Society; Death to Smoochy; Deconstructing Harry; Father's Day; Fisher King, The; Flubber; Good Morning, Vietnam; Good Will Hunting; Hamlet; Hook; Jack; Jakob the Liar; Jumanji; Mork & Mindy (TV Series); Moscow on the Hudson; Mrs. Doubtfire; Nine Months; Patch Adams; Popeye; Secret Agent, The; Seize the Day; Survivors, The; Toys; What Dreams May Come; World According to Garp, The
Williams, Saul: Slam
Williams, Scot: BackBeat
Williams, Simon: Odd Job, The
Williams, Spencer: Two-Gun Man from Harlem
Williams, Steven: Corrina, Corrina; Deep Red; Jason Goes to Hell: The Final Friday; Missing in Action 2: The Beginning; Revolver; Route 666; X-Files, The (TV Series)
Williams, Treat: Dead Heat; Deadly Hero; Deep End of the Ocean, The; Deep Rising; Dempsey; Devil's Own, The; Echoes in the Darkness; Escape: Human Cargo; Final Verdict; Flashpoint; Gale Force; Hair; Hand Gun; Heart of Dixie, The; Hollywood Ending; Johnny's Girl; Late Shift, The; Max and Helen; Men's Club, The; Mulholland Falls; Night of the Sharks; Once Upon a Time in America (Long Version); 1941; Parallel Lives; Phantom, The; Prince of the City; Pursuit of D. B. Cooper; Ritz, The; Skeletons in the Closet; Smooth Talk; Streetcar Named Desire, A; Substitute, The: Failure Is Not an Option; Sweet Lies; Things to Do in Denver When You're Dead; Third Degree Burn; Third Solution, The; 36 Hours to Die; Till Death Do Us Part; Venomous; Water Engine, The
Williams, Van: Green Hornet, The (TV Series)
Williams, Vanessa L.: Adventures of Elmo in Grouchland, The; Another You; Candyman; Dance with Me; Don Quixote; Drop Squad, The; Eraser; Full Exposure; Futuresport; Harley Davidson and the Marlboro Man; Hoodlum; Jacksons, The: An American Dream; Odyssey, The; Shaft; Soul Food; Under the Gun
Williams, Wade Andrew: Route 9
Williams, Wendy O.: Pucker Up and Bark Like a Dog; Reform School Girls
Williams II, Ernest: Black Sister's Revenge
Williams III, Clarence: Against the Wall; Dangerous Relations; Deep Cover; 52 Pick-Up; Frogs for Snakes; General's Daughter, The; George Wallace; Half Baked; Hoodlum; Immortals, The; Legend of 1900, The; Maniac Cop 2; Mod Squad, The (TV Series); My Heroes Have Always Been Cowboys; Rebound; Reindeer Games; Shepherd; Sprung; Sugar Hill
Williams Jr., Hank: Willa
Williams Jr., Spencer: Amos and Andy (TV Series); Bronze Buckaroo
Williamson, David: Resurrection Man
Williamson, Fred: Adios Amigo; Big Score, The; Black Caesar; Black Cobra 3; Blackjack; Blind Rage; Boss; Bucktown; Children of the Corn V: Fields of Terror; Deadly Impact; Deadly Intent; Delta Force, Commando Two; Express to Terror; Foxtrap; From Dusk Till Dawn; Hell Up in Harlem; Mean Johnny Barrows; One Down, Two to Go; Original Gangstas; Silent Hunter; South Beach; Steele's Law; Submerged; Take a Hard Ride; Three Days to a Kill; Three the Hard Way; Vigilante; Warrior of the Lost World; Warriors of the Wasteland
Williamson, Mykelti: Ali; Buffalo Soldiers; Con Air; First Power, The; Forrest Gump; Heat; Miami Vice; Soul of the Game; Species II; Three Kings; Truth or Consequences, N.M.; Waiting to Exhale; You Talkin' to Me
Williamson, Nicol: Advocate, The; Black Widow; Cheap Detective, The; Christopher Columbus (1985); Excalibur; Hamlet; Human Factor, The; I'm Dancing As Fast As I Can; Passion Flower; Return to Oz; Robin and Marian; Seven-Per-cent Solution, The; Venom; Wilby Conspiracy, The
Williamson, Phillip: Angelic Conversation
Willingham, Noble: Career Opportunities; City Slickers II; Fire in the Sky; Last Boy Scout, The; Pastime; Sweet Poison; Up Close and Personal
Willis, Bruce: Armageddon; Bandits (2001); Billy Bathgate; Blind Date; Bonfire of the Vanities; Breakfast of Champions; Color of Night; Death Becomes Her; Die Hard; Die Hard 2: Die Harder; Die Hard with a Vengeance; Fifth Element, The; Hart's War; Hudson Hawk; In Country; Jackal, The; Kid, The (2000); Last Boy Scout, The; Last Man Standing; Mercury Rising; Moonlighting (1985) (TV Pilot); Mortal Thoughts; National Lampoon's Loaded Weapon 1; Nobody's Fool; North; Pulp Fiction; Siege, The; Sixth Sense, The; Story of Us, The; Striking Distance; Sunset; That's Adequate; 12 Monkeys; Unbreakable; Whole Nine Yards, The
Willis, Hope Alexander: Pack, The
Willis, Matt: Return of the Vampire, The; So Dear to My Heart
Willman, Noel: Kiss of the Vampire; Reptile, The
Wills, Chill: Alamo, The; Allegheny Uprising; Arizona Legion; Billy the Kid; Boom Town; Deadly Companions, The; Francis Joins the Wacs; Harvey Girls, The; Honky Tonk; Kentucky Rifle; Lawless Valley; Loaded Pistols; Man from the Alamo, The; McLintock!; Mr. Billion; Pat Garrett and Billy the Kid; Ride the Man Down; Rio Grande; Rounders, The; Steagle, The; Tarzan's New York Adventure; Tulsa; Western Union; Westerner, The; Wheeler Dealers, The; Yearling, The
Wills, James "Kimo": Tao of Steve, The
Wilson, Barbara: Invasion of the Animal People
Wilson, Breck: Escape from Atlantis
Wilson, Brian: Theremin: An Electronic Odyssey
Wilson, Bridgette: Billy Madison; House on Haunted Hill; Love Stinks; Mortal Kombat; Nevada; Stepsister, The; Suburbans, The; Sweet Evil
Wilson, Chrystale: Players Club, The
Wilson, Daniel: Wait Until Spring, Bandini
Wilson, David Lee: Pariah
Wilson, Dennis: Two-Lane Blacktop
Wilson, Don: Jack Benny Program, The (TV Series)
Wilson, Don "The Dragon": Blackbelt; Bloodfist; Bloodfist 2; Bloodfist III: Forced to Fight; Bloodfist IV—Die Trying; Bloodfist V: Human Target; Bloodfist VI: Ground Zero; Capitol Conspiracy, The; Cyber Tracker; Cyber Tracker 2; Hollywood Safari; Magic Kid; Night Hunter; Operation Condor (Don "The Dragon" Wilson); Out for Blood; Power Within, The; Red Sun Rising; Ring of Fire 3: Lion Strike; Virtual Combat
Wilson, Dooley: Cairo

Wilson, Elizabeth: Addams Family, The; Believers, The; Grace Quigley; Happy Hooker, The; Incredible Shrinking Woman, The; Little Murders; Prisoner of Second Avenue, The; Quiz Show; Regarding Henry; Where Are the Children?; You Can't Take It with You
Wilson, Flip: Fish That Saved Pittsburgh, The; Uptown Saturday Night
Wilson, Frank: Emperor Jones, The
Wilson, Georges: Attack of the Killer Tomatoes; Empty Canvas, The; Make Room for Tomorrow
Wilson, Jackie: Go, Johnny, Go!
Wilson, Jim: Charlie, the Lonesome Cougar
Wilson, Julie: This Could Be the Night
Wilson, Kristen: Bulletproof; Dr. Dolittle 2; Dungeons & Dragons
Wilson, Kym: Brides of Christ
Wilson, Lambert: Belly of an Architect, The; Blood of Others, The; Five Days One Summer; Frankenstein; Jefferson in Paris; Leading Man, The; Red Kiss (Rouge Baiser); Rendez-Vous; Sahara; Strangers
Wilson, Lois: Covered Wagon, The; Deluge (1993); Miss Lulu Bett; Show-Off, The; Vanishing American, The
Wilson, Luke: Best Men; Blue Streak; Bongwater; Bottle Rocket; Dog Park; Home Fries; Legally Blonde; My Dog Skip; Royal Tenenbaums, The; Soul Survivors
Wilson, Mara: Balloon Farm; Matilda; Miracle on 34th Street; Mrs. Doubtfire; Simple Wish, A; Thomas and the Magic Railroad
Wilson, Marie: Boy Meets Girl; Girl in Every Port, A; Mr. Hobbs Takes a Vacation; My Friend Irma; Never Wave at a WAC (Private Wore Skirts, The); Private Affairs of Bel Ami, The; Satan Met a Lady
Wilson, Mary Louise: Cheap Shots
Wilson, Nancy: Big Score, The; Meteor Man
Wilson, Owen: Anaconda; Behind Enemy Lines; Bottle Rocket; Haunting, The; Minus Man, The; Permanent Midnight; Shanghai Noon; Zoolander
Wilson, Paul: Brainwaves; Devonsville Terror, The
Wilson, Perry: Fear Strikes Out
Wilson, Peta: Mercy
Wilson, Rachel: Mystery, Alaska
Wilson, Rita: Jingle All the Way; Mixed Nuts; Now and Then; Runaway Bride; Sleepless in Seattle; Story of Us, The; That Thing You Do!; Volunteers
Wilson, Robert Brian: Silent Night, Deadly Night
Wilson, Roger: Porky's; Porky's II: The Next Day; Power of Attorney
Wilson, Scott: Aviator, The; Blue City; Clay Pigeons; Femme Fatale; Flesh and Bone; Geronimo: An American Legend; Grissom Gang, The; In Cold Blood; Jesse; Malone; Mother; Ninth Configuration, The; On the Line; Pure Luck; Right Stuff, The; Shiloh; Shiloh 2: Shiloh Season; Tracker, The; Year of the Quiet Sun
Wilson, Sheree: Fraternity Vacation; Hellbound; News at Eleven; One Riot, One Ranger; Walker: Texas Ranger
Wilson, Stuart: Crossworlds; Death and the Maiden; Edie & Pen; Here on Earth; Highest Honor, The; Lethal Weapon 3; Luzhin Defence, The; Mask of Zorro, The; No Escape; Romance on the Orient Express; Teenage Mutant Ninja Turtles III; Vertical Limit; Wetherby
Wilson, Teddy: Benny Goodman Story, The
Wilson, Terry: Wagon Train (TV Series)
Wilson, Thomas F.: Action Jackson; Back to the Future; Back to the Future II; Back to the Future III; High Strung
Wilson, Tom: Chaplin Revue, The; Madame Behave
Wilson, Trey: Bull Durham; Drive-In; Great Balls of Fire; Raising Arizona
Wilson-Sampras, Bridgette: Just Visiting; Wedding Planner, The
Wilton, Penelope: Blame It on the Bellboy; Borrowers, The; Carrington; Clockwise; Cry Freedom; Norman Conquests, The, Episode 1: Table Manners; Norman Conquests, The, Episode 3: Roundand Round the Garden; Norman Conquests, The, Episode 2: LivingTogether; Secret Rapture, The; Singleton's Pluck; Victoria and Albert
Wiltsie, Jennifer: Wirey Spindell
Wimmer, Brian: Bittersweet (1999); Blue Flame; Dangerous Pursuit; Dead Badge; Late for Dinner; Lipstick Camera; Maddening, The
Winchell, Paul: Which Way to the Front?
Winchester, Anna-Maria: Chain Reaction; Deadly Possession
Wincott, Jeff: Deadly Bet; Donor, The; Fatal Combat; Future Fear; Gunshy; Killing Man, The; Last Man Standing; Martial Law Two—Undercover; Martial Outlaw; Mission of Justice; Profile for Murder; Street Law; Undertaker's Wedding, The; Universal Soldier II: Brothers in Arms; When the Bullet Hits the Bone
Wincott, Michael: Alien Resurrection; Along Came a Spider; Basquiat; Before Night Falls; Crow, The; Dead Man; Hidden Agenda (1998); Metro; 1492: The Conquest of Paradise; Strange Days; Wild Horse Hank
Windom, William: Attack of the 50-Foot Woman; Back to Hannibal: The Return of Tom Sawyer and Huckleberry Finn; Children of the Corn IV: The Gathering; Dennis the Menace: Dinosaur Hunter; Detective, The; Escape from the Planet of the Apes; Funland; Grandview, U.S.A.; Hour of the Gun, The; Leave 'em Laughing; Miracle on 34th Street; Now You See Him, Now You Don't; One Man's Way; She's Having a Baby; Sommersby; Space Rage
Windsor, Barbara: Study in Terror, A
Windsor, Marie: Abbott and Costello Meet the Mummy; Cat Women of the Moon; Critic's Choice; Double Deal; Force of Evil; Girl in Black Stockings, The; Good Guys and the Bad Guys, The; Hellfire; Humanoid Defender; Killing, The; Little Big Horn; Narrow Margin, The (1952); Outpost in Morocco; Showdown, The (1950); Swamp Women; Trouble Along the Way
Windsor, Romy: Big Bad John; House of Usher, The; Howling IV
Windust, Penelope: Iron Will
Winfield, Paul: Assassination File, The; Back to Hannibal: The Return of Tom Sawyer and Huckleberry Finn; Big Shots; Blue and the Gray, The; Blue City; Breathing Lessons; Brother John; Conrack; Damnation Alley (Survival Run); Death Before Dishonor; Gordon's War; Hero Ain't Nothin' But a Sandwich, A; High Velocity; Huckleberry Finn; It's Good to Be Alive; King; Knockout; Legend of Gator Face, The; Presumed Innocent; Serpent and the Rainbow, The; Sophisticated Gents, The; Sounder; Strategic Command; Twilight's Last Gleaming; Tyson; White Dog; White Dwarf
Winfrey, Oprah: Beloved; Color Purple, The; Native Son; Our Friend, Martin; Women of Brewster Place, The
Wing, Leslie: Cowboy and the Ballerina, The; Retribution
Wing, Tang Tak: Trained to Fight
Winger, Debra: Betrayed; Black Widow; Cannery Row; Dangerous Woman, A; Everybody Wins; Forget Paris; French Postcards; Leap of Faith; Legal Eagles; Made in Heaven; Mike's Murder; Officer and a Gentleman, An; Shadowlands; Sheltering Sky, The; Slumber Party 57; Terms of Endearment; Thank God It's Friday; Urban Cowboy; Wilder Napalm
Wingett, Mark: Quadrophenia
Winkler, Angela: Knife in the Head; Lost Honor of Katharina Blum, The; Sheer Madness; Tin Drum, The
Winkler, Henry: American Christmas Carol, An; Ground Control; Heroes; Katherine; Lords of Flatbush, The; Night Shift; One and Only, The; P.U.N.K.S.; Waterboy, The
Winkler, Matthew: 5 Dark Souls
Winn, Kitty: Man on a String; Panic in Needle Park
Winninger, Charles: Babes in Arms; Beyond Tomorrow; Broadway Rhythm; Every Day's a Holiday; Fighting Caravans; Lady Takes a Chance, A; Little Nellie Kelly; Living in a Big Way; Night Nurse; Nothing Sacred; Pot O' Gold; Show Boat; State Fair; Sun Shines Bright, The; Three Smart Girls; Three Smart Girls Grow Up; Torpedo Alley
Winningham, Mare: Better Off Dead; Boys Next Door, The; Everything That Rises; Eye on the Sparrow; Fatal Exposure; George Wallace; Georgia; God Bless the Child; Hard Promises; Intruders; Letter to My Killer; Made in Heaven; Miracle Mile; Nobody's Fool; St. Elmo's Fire; Shy People; Turner and Hooch; Under Pressure; War, The; Wyatt Earp

Winslet, Kate: Hamlet; Heavenly Creatures; Hideous Kinky; Holy Smoke; Jude; Kid in King Arthur's Court, A; Quills; Sense and Sensibility; Titanic
Winslow, George: Gentlemen Prefer Blondes
Winslow, Michael: Alphabet City; Buy and Cell; Going Under; Police Academy; Police Academy 5: Assignment: Miami Beach; Police Academy 4: Citizens on Patrol; Police Academy II: Their First Assignment; Police Academy III: Back in Training; Police Academy 6: City Under Siege; Police Academy: Mission to Moscow; Spaceballs; Tag—The Assassination Game; Think Big
Winston, Matt: Wes Craven's New Nightmare
Winston, McKinley: Urban Jungle
Winstone, Ray: Agnes Browne; Ladybird, Ladybird; Last Orders; Love, Honor & Obey; Nil by Mouth; Scum; Sexy Beast; War Zone, The
Wint, Maurice Dean: Cube
Winter, Alex: Bill and Ted's Bogus Journey; Bill and Ted's Excellent Adventure; Freaked; Haunted Summer
Winter, Edward: Act of Passion; Porky's II: The Next Day
Winter, George: Merlin of the Crystal Cave
Winter, Ophelie: 2001: A Space Travesty
Winter, Vincent: Gorgo; Horse Without a Head, The; Three Lives of Thomasina, The
Winters, D.D.: Tanya's Island
Winters, Dean: Undercover Angel
Winters, Deborah: Blue Sunshine; Class of '44; Kotch; Tarantulas—The Deadly Cargo
Winters, Grant: College
Winters, Jonathan: Adventures of Rocky and Bullwinkle, The; Alice Through the Looking Glass; Fish That Saved Pittsburgh, The; It's a Mad Mad Mad Mad World; Longshot, The (1985); Loved One, The; Moon over Parador; More Wild Wild West; Oh Dad, Poor Dad—Mama's Hung You inthe Closet and I'm Feeling So Sad; Russians Are Coming, the Russians Are Coming, The; Say Yes; Shadow, The; Viva Max!
Winters, Laska: Seven Footprints to Satan
Winters, Loren: Freeway Maniac
Winters, Nathan Forrest: Clownhouse
Winters, Roland: Feathered Serpent, The; To Please a Lady; West Point Story, The
Winters, Shelley: Alfie; Alice in Wonderland; Backfire; Balcony, The; Behave Yourself!; Bloody Mama; Blume in Love; Buona Sera, Mrs. Campbell; Cleopatra Jones; Déjà Vu; Delta Force, The; Diamonds; Diary of Anne Frank, The; Double Life, A; Elvis—The Movie; Enter Laughing; Executive Suite; Greatest Story Ever Told, The; Harper; Heavy; I Am a Camera; I Died a Thousand Times; Initiation of Sarah, The; Journey into Fear; King of the Gypsies; Knickerbocker Holiday; Lolita; Magician of Lublin, The; Mambo; Meet Danny Wilson; Mrs. Munck; Next Stop, Greenwich Village; Night of the Hunter; Over the Brooklyn Bridge; Patch of Blue, A; Phone Call from a Stranger; Pickle, The; Place in the Sun, A; Portrait of a Lady, The; Poseidon Adventure, The; Purple People Eater; Raging Angels; Revenge (1971) (Shelley Winters); Scalphunters, The; Shattered; S.O.B.; Stepping Out; Tenant, The; Tentacles; That Lucky Touch; Treasure of Pancho Villa, The; Unremarkable Life, An; Visitor, The; Weep No More My Lady; What's the Matter with Helen?; Who Slew Auntie Roo?; Wild in the Streets; Winchester '73; Young Savages, The
Winton, Sandy: Me Myself I
Winwood, Estelle: Dead Ringer; Glass Slipper, The; Magic Sword, The; Misfits, The; Swan, The; This Happy Feeling
Wirth, Billy: Boys on the Side; Children of the Dust; Fence, The; Final Mission; Judicial Consent; Space Marines; Venus Rising; War Party
Wisden, Robert: Captains Courageous; Every Mother's Worst Fear
Wisdom, Norman: To See Such Fun
Wisdom, Robert: Lifeform; Secret Cutting; Storytelling
Wise, Cela: Deadly Rivals
Wise, Greg: Feast of July
Wise, Ray: Body Shot; Chase, The; Endless Descent; Ghost Brigade; Journey of Natty Gann, The; Rising Sun; Season of Fear; Sunstroke; Swamp Thing; Twin Peaks: Fire Walk with Me
Wiseman, Debra: Mrs. Santa Claus
Wiseman, Don: Red Alert
Wiseman, Joseph: Dr. No; Journey into Fear; Prodigal, The; Seize the Day; Silver Chalice, The; Unforgiven, The (1960); Viva Zapata!
Wiseman, Michael: Judgment Night
Wisoff, Jill: Fear, Anxiety and Depression
Wite, Michael Jai: Ringmaster
Withers, Googie: Country Life; Dead of Night; Night and the City; On Approval; One of Our Aircraft Is Missing
Withers, Grant: Bells of Coronado; Doomed to Die; Fatal Hour, The; Fighting Marines, The; Final Extra, The; Goin' to Town; Hellfire; Hoodlum Empire; Lady Takes a Chance, A; Mr. Wong, Detective; Mr. Wong in Chinatown; Nighttime in Nevada; Oklahoma Annie; Road to Ruin, The (1928); Trigger Jr.; Utah
Withers, Jane: Bright Eyes; Captain Newman, M.D.
Witherspoon, Cora: Bank Dick, The; I've Always Loved You; Madame X; On the Avenue; Personal Property
Witherspoon, John: Friday; I Got the Hook Up; Next Friday; Ride; Sprung; Talkin' Dirty After Dark; Vampire in Brooklyn
Witherspoon, Reese: American Psycho; Cruel Intentions; Election; Far Off Place, A; Fear; Freeway; Jack the Bear; Legally Blonde; Man in the Moon, The; Overnight Delivery; Pleasantville; Return to Lonesome Dove; S.F.W.; Trumpet of the Swan, The; Twilight
Withrow, Glenn: Pass the Ammo
Witney, Michael: W
Witt, Alicia: Bongwater; cecil b. Demented; Fun; Mr. Holland's Opus; Urban Legend
Witt, Kathryn: Cocaine Wars
Witter, Karen: Perfect Match, The
Wixted, Kevin: Magic in the Mirror
Wlaschiha, Tom: No One Sleeps
Wodoslavsky, Stefas: 90 Days
Wöhler, Gustav Peter: Enlightenment Guaranteed
Wokalek, Johana: Aimee & Jaguar
Wolcott, Abigail: Hellgate
Wolders, Robert: Interval
Wolf, Bryan: Beyond the Doors
Wolf, Hilary: Big Girls Don't Cry—They Get Even
Wolf, Kelly: Day in October, A; Stephen King's Graveyard Shift (1990)
Wolf, Scott: Double Dragon; Go; Teenage Bonnie and Klepto Clyde; Welcome to Hollywood; White Squall
Wolfe, Ian: Bedlam; Brighton Strangler, The; Copper Canyon; Diane; Diary of a Madman; Homebodies; Houdini; Julia Misbehaves; Magnificent Yankee, The; One Man's Way; Pearl of Death, The; Scarlet Claw, The; Son of Monte Cristo, The
Wolfe, Jim: Chillers; Invasion of the Space Preachers
Wolfe, Nancy: Helter Skelter
Wolfe, Nancy Allison: Bar Girls
Wolff, Frank: Atlas; Last Gun, The; When Women Had Tails; When Women Lost Their Tails
Wolff, Rikard: House of Angels
Wolfit, Donald: Blood of the Vampire; Satellite in the Sky
Wolfman Jack: Deadman's Curve; Hanging on a Star; Midnight
Wolford, Josh: Forest Warrior
Wolheim, Louis: All Quiet on the Western Front; Danger Lights; Dr. Jekyll and Mr. Hyde; Tempest
Wollter, Sven: House of Angels; Man on the Roof
Woloshyn, Illya: Hush Little Baby
Wong, Anna May: Daughter of the Dragon; Impact; Peter Pan; Shanghai Express; Study in Scarlet, A; Thief of Bagdad, The
Wong, Anthony: Untold Story, The
Wong, B. D.: Executive Decision; Father of the Bride; Father of the Bride Part II; Jurassic Park; Men of War; Mystery Date; Seven Years in Tibet; Slappy and the Stinkers
Wong, Jadine: I Drink Your Blood
Wong, Janet: Bustin' Loose
Wong, Michael: John Woo's Once a Thief
Wong, Ronald: People's Hero
Wong, Russell: China Cry; China Girl; China White; Eat a Bowl of Tea; Prophecy II, The; Romeo Must Die

Wong, Victor: Big Trouble in Little China; Dim Sum: A Little Bit of Heart; Eat a Bowl of Tea; Golden Child, The; Ice Runner; Last Emperor, The; Prince of Darkness; Shanghai Surprise; Son of Kong, The; Three Ninjas; Three Ninjas Kick Back; Three Ninjas Knuckle Up; Tremors
Won-Sop, Sin: Why Has Bhodi Dharma Left for the East?
Wontner, Arthur: Genevieve; Silver Blaze; Triumph of Sherlock Holmes, The
Wood, Andy: Annihilators, The; Ghost Warrior
Wood, Annabella: Bloodthirsty Butchers
Wood, Britt: Hidden Gold; Range War
Wood, Cindi: Hoodlum Priest, The
Wood, Clive: Crucifer of Blood; Treasure Island
Wood, David: If…
Wood, Elijah: Adventures of Huck Finn, The (1993); Avalon; Black and White (2000); Bumblebee Flies Anyway, The; Child in the Night; Deep Impact; Faculty, The; Flipper; Forever Young; Good Son, The; Ice Storm, The; Lord of the Rings, The: Fellowship of the Ring; North; Oliver Twist; Paradise; Radio Flyer; War, The
Wood, Evan Rachel: Digging to China
Wood, Frank: Thirteen Days
Wood, Freeman: Buster Keaton Festival Vol. 1–3
Wood, Gordon: Forty-Niners
Wood, Harley: Border Phantom
Wood, Helen: Charlie Chan at the Racetrack; Give a Girl a Break
Wood, John: Body, The; Citizen X; Ideal Husband, An; Jane Eyre; Jumpin' Jack Flash; Lady Jane; Ladyhawke; Orlando; Purple Rose of Cairo, The; Rasputin; Sabrina; Shadowlands; Summer House, The; Victoria and Albert; Wargames; Which Way to the Front?; Young Americans, The
Wood, Lana: Grayeagle; Justin Morgan Had a Horse; Place Called Today, A; Searchers, The
Wood, Natalie: Affair, The; Bob & Carol & Ted & Alice; Brainstorm; Burning Hills, The; Cash McCall; Cracker Factory; From Here to Eternity; Ghost and Mrs. Muir, The; Great Race, The; Green Promise, The; Gypsy; Inside Daisy Clover; Jackpot, The; Kings Go Forth; Last Married Couple in America, The; Love with the Proper Stranger; Marjorie Morningstar; Meteor; Miracle on 34th Street; Rebel Without a Cause; Searchers, The; Sex and the Single Girl; Silver Chalice, The; Splendor in the Grass; Star, The (1952); This Property Is Condemned; Tomorrow Is Forever; West Side Story
Wood, Peggy: Story of Ruth, The
Wood, Robert: White Fang and the Hunter
Wood, Salvador: Death of a Bureaucrat
Wood, Thomas: Blood Feast; 2,000 Maniacs
Wood, Wilson: Zombies of the Stratosphere (Satan's Satellites) (Serial)
Wood Jr., Edward D.: Fugitive Girls; Hellborn; Love Feast, The; Sensuous Wife, The
Woodard, Alfre: Blue Chips; Bopha!; Crooklyn; Down in the Delta; Extremities; Grand Canyon; Gun in Betty Lou's Handbag, The; Heart and Souls; How to Make an American Quilt; K-Pax; Killing Floor, The; Love and Basketball; Mandela; Member of the Wedding, The; Miss Evers' Boys; Miss Firecracker; Mumford; Passion Fish; Piano Lesson, The; Primal Fear; Rich in Love; Scrooged; Star Trek: First Contact; Unnatural Causes; What's Cooking?
Woodard, Charlayne: Buffalo Girls; Run for the Dream
Woodbine, Bokeem: Big Hit, The; Black Male; Dead Presidents; Jason's Lyric; Panther; Sacrifice (2000); Strapped; Wishmaster 2: Evil Never Dies
Woodbury, Heather: Habit
Woodbury, Joan: Bulldog Courage; Chinese Cat, The; Eagle's Brood; Gangs, Inc. (Paper Bullets); King of the Zombies; Northwest Trail; Sunset Serenade; Time Travelers, The
Woode, Margo: Bullfighters, The
Woodland, Lauren: Doorway, The
Woodlawn, Holly: Billy's Hollywood Screen Kiss; Trash
Woodruff, Largo: Bill; Bill: On His Own; Coward of the County; Funhouse, The
Woods, Barbara Alyn: Dance with Death; Eden (TV Series); Ghoulies IV
Woods, Bill: Maniac
Woods, Donald: Anthony Adverse; Beast from 20,000 Fathoms, The; Beauty for the Asking; Bridge of San Luis Rey, The; Case of the Stuttering Bishop, The; Corregidor; Heritage of the Desert; Mexican Spitfire; Never Say Goodbye; Sea Devils; Story of Louis Pasteur, The; Sweet Adeline; 13 Ghosts; Wonder Man
Woods, Edward: Public Enemy; Tarzan the Fearless
Woods, Eric: Mutual Needs
Woods, Harry: Adventures of Rex and Rinty; Blue Montana Skies; Down Texas Way; Haunted Gold; In Early Arizona; Lawless Nineties, The; Range Defenders; Range Feud; Ranger and the Lady, The; West of the Law; Winners of the West
Woods, James: Against All Odds (1984); Another Day in Paradise; Badge of the Assassin; Best Seller; Boost, The; Casino; Cat's Eye; Chaplin; Choirboys, The; Citizen Cohn; Contact; Cop; Curse of the Starving Class; Diggstown; Dirty Pictures; Disappearance of Aimee, The; Eyewitness; Fallen Angels; Fast-Walking; For Better or Worse; General's Daughter, The; Getaway, The; Ghosts of Mississippi; Gift of Love, The; Hard Way, The; Immediate Family; In Love and War; Incredible Journey of Dr. Meg Laurel,The; Indictment: The McMartin Trial; John Carpenter's Vampires; John Q; Joshua Then and Now; Kicked in the Head; Killer: A Journal of Murder; Love and War; Mighty Aphrodite; My Name Is Bill W; Next Door; Nixon; Once Upon a Time in America (Long Version); Onion Field, The; Riding in Cars with Boys; Salvador; Specialist, The; Split Image; Straight Talk; Summer of Ben Tyler, The; True Believer; True Crime; Videodrome; Virgin Suicides, The; Women & Men: Stories of Seduction
Woods, Kevin Jamal: Little Rascals, The
Woods, Michael: Blindfold: Acts of Obsession; Haunting of Sarah Hardy, The; Hit Woman: The Double Edge; Lady Beware; Omen IV: The Awakening
Woods, Nan: China Beach (TV Series)
Woods, Robert: Badlands Drifter (Challenge of McKenna); Machine Gun Killers; Savage Guns
Woods, Sara: Sweeney Todd
Woodson, Jack: Edge of Darkness
Woodthorpe, Peter: Evil of Frankenstein, The; Inspector Morse (TV Series)
Woodville, Katherine: Posse
Woodvine, John: Assault on Agathon; Edge of Darkness
Woodward, Edward: Appointment, The; Breaker Morant; Champions; Christmas Carol, A; Christmas Reunion, A; Codename: Kyril; Equalizer, The: "Memories of Manon"; Final Option, The; Gulliver's Travels (1996) (Television); King David; Merlin & the Sword; Mister Johnson; Sherlock Holmes: Hands of a Murderer; Wicker Man, The
Woodward, Joanne: Big Hand for the Little Lady, A; Blind Spot; Breathing Lessons; Christmas to Remember, A; Crisis at Central High; Drowning Pool, The; Effect of Gamma Rays on Man-in-the-Moon Marigolds, The; End, The; Fine Madness, A; Foreign Affairs; From the Terrace; Fugitive Kind, The; Glass Menagerie, The; Harry and Son; Long Hot Summer, The; Mr. and Mrs. Bridge; New Kind of Love, A; Paris Blues; Rachel, Rachel; Shadow Box, The; Streets of L.A., The; Stripper, The; Summer Wishes, Winter Dreams; Sybil; They Might Be Giants; Three Faces of Eve, The; Winning
Woodward, Jonathon M.: Wit
Woodward, Morgan: Final Chapter—Walking Tall; Firecreek; Girls Just Want to Have Fun; Small Town in Texas, A; Which Way Is Up?; Wyatt Earp: Return to Tombstone; Yuma
Woodward, Tim: Dark Angel, The; Europeans, The; Prime Suspect: Scent of Darkness; Salome
Woof, Emily: Photographing Fairies
Wooldridge, Susan: Frankenstein; Hope and Glory; How to Get Ahead in Advertising; Jewel in the Crown, The; Loyalties
Wooley, Sheb: Hoosiers; Rawhide (TV Series)
Woollcott, Alexander: Scoundrel, The
Woolley, Monty: As Young as You Feel; Everybody Sing; Girl of the Golden West, The; Kismet; Man Who Came to Dinner, The; Midnight; Night and Day; Since You Went Away; Three Comrades

Fighting Lady; Mirrors; Mission to Glory; Mr. Imperium; My Dear Secretary; Neptune's Daughter; Orca; Patsy, The; Perfect Furlough; Phone Call from a Stranger; Piano for Mrs. Cimino, A; Piranha; Point Blank; Prime Risk; Promise Her Anything; Requiem for a Heavyweight (1956) (Television); Return of the Man from U.N.C.L.E., The; Royal Wedding; Running Wild; Shack-Out on 101; Smith!; Snowball Express; Somewhere I'll Find You; Son of Flubber; Song of the Thin Man; Texas Carnival; That Midnight Kiss; Three Little Words; Three Musketeers, The; Time to Love and a Time to Die, A; Untouchables, The: Scarface Mob; Viva Max!; War Wagon, The; Wavelength; Weekend at the Waldorf; Without Love
Wynter, Dana: Connection (1973); D-Day the Sixth of June; Invasion of the Body Snatchers; List of Adrian Messenger, The; Santee; Shake Hands with the Devil; Sink the Bismarck; Something of Value
Wynter, Sarah: Bride of the Wind; Lost Souls; Race Against Time; 6th Day, The
Wynters, Charlotte: Ivory-Handled Gun, The
Wynyard, Diana: Cavalcade; Gaslight
Wyss, Amanda: Better Off Dead; Black Magic Woman; Bloodfist IV—Die Trying; Checkered Flag; My Mother's Secret Life; Powwow Highway; Shakma; To Die For; To Die For 2: Son of Darkness
Xia, Yu: Shadow Magic
Xiao, Wang: Shanghai Triad
Xiaotuang, Deng: Girl from Hunan
Xin, Cun: Shower
Xing, Yufei: Shadow Magic
Xu, Zhu: King of Masks, The
Xuejian, Li: Emperor and the Assassin, The
Xueqi, Wang: Yellow Earth
Xuereb, Salvator: Ravager
Yaconelli, Frank: Driftin' Kid
Yadin, Yossi: Lies My Father Told Me
Yagher, Jeff: Lower Level; Madonna: Innocence Lost; Wing and a Prayer, A
Yakusho, Koji: Eel, The; Shall We Dance?
Yam, Simon: Bullet in the Head; Tongs
Yama, Akihiro Maru: Black Lizard
Yamada, Isuzu: Osaka Elegy; Sisters of the Gion
Yamaguchi, Isamu: Flunky, Work Hard!
Yamaguchi, Sayaka: Re-birth of Mothra II
Yamamoto, Mirai: Who Am I?
Yamanaka, Joe: Ulterior Motives
Yamashita, Tadashi: Capital Punishment
Yamauchi, Akira: Godzilla vs. the Smog Monster
Yamauchi, Takaya: MacArthur's Children
Yamazaki, Tsutomu: Funeral, The; High and Low; Rikyu; Taxing Woman, A
Yancy, Emily: Cotton Comes to Harlem
Yanez, Eduardo: Held Up; Miami Hustle
Yang, Gao: Red Firecracker, Green Firecracker
Yang, Kuei-Mei: Eat Drink Man Woman; Vive L'Amour
Yani, Rossana: White Comanche
Yankovic, "Weird Al": UHF
Yankovsky, Oleg: Nostalghia
Yanne, Jean: Bandits; Hanna K.; Indochine; Le Boucher (The Butcher); This Man Must Die; Weekend
Yanni, Rosanna: Sonny and Jed
Yao, Hsiao: Mighty Peking Man
Yares, Coco: Annie O
Yarlett, Claire: Blackout
Yarmush, Michael: Losing Chase
Yarnall, Celeste: Velvet Vampire, The
Yarnell, Lorene: Spaceballs; Wild Wild West Revisited, The
Yasbeck, Amy: Bloodhounds II; Dead Husbands; Dracula: Dead and Loving It; Mask, The; Problem Child; Problem Child 2; Robin Hood: Men in Tights; Something About Sex
Yasui, Shoji: Burmese Harp, The
Yates, Cassie: Evil, The; FM; Listen to Your Heart; Of Mice and Men; St. Helens
Yates, Kim: Teach Me Tonight
Yates, Marjorie: Black Panther, The; Long Day Closes, The; Very British Coup, A; Wetherby
Yearwood, Richard: Silent Witness: What a Child Saw
Yedidia, Mario: Warriors of Virtue
Yee, Kelvin Han: Great Wall, A
Yeh, Sally: Killer, The; Laser Man, The; Peking Opera Blues
Yelchin, Anton: Hearts in Atlantis
Yelykomov, Oleg: Burglar (Russian)
Yen, Donnie: Highlander: Endgame; Iron Monkey; Once Upon a Time in China II; Wing Chun
Yen, Zhang Zhi: American Shaolin: King of the Kickboxers II
Yen-Khe, Tran Nu: Cyclo; Scent of Green Papaya, The; Vertical Ray of the Sun, The
Yeoh, Michelle: Crouching Tiger, Hidden Dragon; Police Story III—Super Cop; Tomorrow Never Dies; Twin Warriors
Yeon, Kim Tae: Lies (1999)
Yesno, John: King of the Grizzlies
Yeung, Bolo: Bloodsport; Fearless Tiger; Shootfighter; Shootfighter 2: Kill or Be Killed; TC 2000
Yi, Ding: Amazing Panda Adventure, The
Yi, Maria: Fists of Fury
Yi, Tian: Blue Kite, The
Ying, Lam Ching: Mr. Vampire (Vol. 1–4)
Yip, Amy: Sex and Zen
Yip, David: Ping Pong
Yip, Francoise: Black Mask; Rumble in the Bronx
Yniguez, Richard: Boulevard Nights; Dirty Dozen, The: The Fatal Mission; Jake Spanner Private Eye
Yoakam, Dwight: Don't Look Back; Little Death, The; Minus Man, The; Newton Boys, The; Painted Hero; Panic Room; Roswell; Sling Blade; South of Heaven, West of Hell; When Trumpets Fade
Yoba, Malik: Cool Runnings; Ride
Yohn, Erica: Corrina, Corrina; Jack the Bear
Yokoshimaru, Hiroku: Legend of the Eight Samurai
Yokoyama, Makoto: Cyber Ninja
Yokoyama, Megumi: Gonin
Yonamine, Ace: Replacements, The
Yonne, Jean: A La Mode
York, Amanda: Scrubbers
York, Dick: Inherit the Wind; My Sister Eileen; Thriller (TV Series)
York, Jeff: Davy Crockett and the River Pirates; Great Locomotive Chase, The; Savage Sam; Westward Ho, the Wagons
York, John J.: House of the Rising Sun; Steel and Lace
York, Kathleen: Cries of Silence; Dead Men Can't Dance; Thompson's Last Run; Winners Take All
York, Michael: Accident; Austin Powers: International Man of Mystery; Austin Powers: The Spy Who Shagged Me; Cabaret; Conduct Unbecoming; Dark Planet; Duel of Hearts; Fall from Grace; Four Musketeers, The; Island of Dr. Moreau, The; Justine; Last Remake of Beau Geste, The; Lethal Obsession; Logan's Run; Murder on the Orient Express; Night of the Fox; Not of This Earth; Phantom of Death; Return of the Musketeers; Riddle of the Sands; Ripper, The; Romeo and Juliet; Something for Everyone; Success Is the Best Revenge; Sword of Gideon; Taming of the Shrew, The; Three Musketeers, The; True Women; Wide Sargasso Sea; Zeppelin
York, Rachel: Dead Center; Killer Instinct; Terror Tract
York, Susannah: Alice; Awakening, The; Battle of Britain; Christmas Carol, A; Conduct Unbecoming; Diamond's Edge; Falling in Love Again; Illusions; Killing of Sister George, The; Land of Faraway, The; Loophole; Man for All Seasons, A; Shout, The (1979); Silent Partner, The; Summer Story, A; That Lucky Touch; Tom Jones; Tunes of Glory; X, Y and Zee
Yorkin, Bud: For the Boys
Yoshiyuki, Kazuko: In the Realm of Passion
Yost, David: Mighty Morphin Power Rangers: The Movie
You, Frances: Double Happiness
You, Ge: Emperor's Shadow, The; To Live
Youb, Sammy Den: Madame Rosa
Younessi, Rojin: Time for Drunken Horses, A
Young, Aden: Black Robe; Cosi; Cousin Bette; Hotel de Love; In the Shadows; Over the Hill

Young, Alan: Androcles and the Lion; Baker's Hawk; Beverly Hills Cop 3; Time Machine, The; Tom Thumb
Young, Artie: Bronze Buckaroo
Young, Audrey: Wistful Widow of Wagon Gap, The
Young, Benny: Funnyman
Young, Bruce A.: Blink; What Ever Happened To . . . ?
Young, Burt: All the Marbles; Amityville II: The Possession; Back to School; Backstreet Dreams; Betsy's Wedding; Beverly Hills Brats; Blood Red; Bright Angel; Carnival of Blood; Chinatown; Choirboys, The; Club Fed; Convoy; Deli, The; Diving In; Excessive Force; Family Matter, A; Florentine, The; Going Overboard; Kicked in the Head; Killer Elite, The; Lookin' to Get Out; Mickey Blue Eyes; North Star (1996); Once Upon a Time in America (Long Version); Over the Brooklyn Bridge; Rocky; Rocky II; Rocky IV; Rocky V; Summer to Remember, A; Twilight's Last Gleaming; Undertaker's Wedding, The; Wait Until Spring, Bandini
Young, Calvin: Challenge, The
Young, Carleton: Double Deal; Pride of the Bowery; Reefer Madness; Smash-Up: The Story of a Woman; Smokey Trails; Zorro's Fighting Legion
Young, Chris: Book of Love; December; PCU; Runestone
Young, Clara Kimball: Return of Chandu (Magician, The)
Young, Clifton: Trail of Robin Hood
Young, Damian: Amateur (1995)
Young, David: Mary, Mary, Bloody Mary
Young, Desmond: Desert Fox, The
Young, Dey: Back in the U.S.S.R.; Conflict of Interest; Doin' Time; Murder 101; No Place to Hide; Not Quite Human 2; Rock 'n' Roll High School; True Heart
Young, Emily Mae: Undercover Angel
Young, Faron: Daniel Boone, Trail Blazer
Young, Gig: Air Force; Ask Any Girl; Bring Me the Head of Alfredo Garcia; City That Never Sleeps; Desperate Hours, The (1955); Escape Me Never; Game of Death; Girl Who Had Everything, The; Hunt the Man Down; Kid Galahad; Killer Elite, The; Lovers and Other Strangers; Lust for Gold; Only the Valiant; Pitfall; Shuttered Room, The; Slaughter Trail; Strange Bedfellows; Teacher's Pet; Tell It to the Judge; That Touch of Mink; They Shoot Horses, Don't They?; Three Musketeers, The; Torch Song; Tunnel of Love, The; Wake of the Red Witch; Young at Heart
Young, Harrison: Reptilian
Young, Karen: Almost You; Birdy; Criminal Law; Daylight; Heat; Hoffa; Jaws: The Revenge; Little Sweetheart; Mercy; Night Game; 9 1/2 Weeks; 10 Million Dollar Getaway, The; Wife, The
Young, Kristy: Gordy
Young, Loretta: Along Came Jones; Big Business Girl; Bishop's Wife, The; Crusades, The; Doctor Takes a Wife, The; Employees' Entrance; Eternally Yours; Farmer's Daughter, The; Heroes for Sale; Key to the City; Night to Remember, A; Perfect Marriage; Platinum Blonde; Rachel and the Stranger; Stranger, The; They Call It Sin
Young, Nat: Palm Beach
Young, Nedrick: Captain Scarlett; Dead Men Walk
Young, Neil: Last Waltz, The; Love at Large; '68
Young, Noah: Battling Orioles, The; Safety Last
Young, Otis: Blood Beach; Last Detail, The
Young, Paul: Another Time, Another Place; Girl in the Picture, The
Young, Polly Ann: Invisible Ghost; Man from Utah, The
Young, Ric: Corruptor, The; Dragon Chow
Young, Richard: Assassin; Friday the 13th, Part V—A New Beginning; Love at the Top; Saigon Commandos
Young, Robert: Bride Walks Out, The; Bride Wore Red, The; Cairo; Canterville Ghost, The; Crossfire; Enchanted Cottage, The; Half-Breed, The; Honolulu; Journey for Margaret; Lady Be Good; Mortal Storm, The; Navy Blue and Gold; Northwest Passage; Second Woman, The; Secret Agent, The; Shining Hour, The; Sin of Madelon Claudet, The; Spitfire; Stowaway; Strange Interlude; That Forsyte Woman; They Won't Believe Me; Those Endearing Young Charms; Three Comrades; Today We Live; Western Union
Young, Roland: And Then There Were None; Great Lover, The; Guardsman, The; His Double Life; King Solomon's Mines; Let's Dance; Madame Satan; Man Who Could Work Miracles, The; No, No Nanette; One Rainy Afternoon; Ruggles of Red Gap; St. Benny the Dip; Topper; Topper Returns; Topper Takes a Trip; Two-Faced Woman; Wedding Rehearsal; Young in Heart, The
Young, Rozwill: Who's the Man?
Young, Sean: Ace Ventura: Pet Detective; Amati Girls, The; Baby—Secret of the Lost Legend; Blade Runner; Blue Ice; Boost, The; Cousins; Dr. Jekyll and Ms. Hyde; Dune; Even Cowgirls Get the Blues; Evil Has a Face; Fatal Instinct; Fire Birds; Forever; Hold Me, Thrill Me, Kiss Me; Invader, The (1996); Jane Austen in Manhattan; Kiss Before Dying, A; Love Crimes; Men; Mirage; Model by Day; No Way Out; Once Upon a Crime; Proprietor, The; Secret Cutting; Sketch Artist; Stripes; Under the Biltmore Clock; Wall Street; Witness to the Execution; Young Doctors in Love
Young, Soo: Secrets of the Wasteland
Young, Stephen: Between Friends; Lifeguard; Patton; Spring Fever
Young, William Allen: Wisdom
Young Il, Oh: Yongary—Monster from the Deep
Youngblood, Rob: Kill Zone
Youngfellow, Barrie: It Came Upon a Midnight Clear; Nightmare in Blood
Youngman, Henny: Amazon Women on the Moon; Young at Heart Comedians, The
Youngs, Gail: Belizaire the Cajun
Youngs, Jim: Hot Shot; Nobody's Fool; Out of Control; Skeeter; You Talkin' to Me
Yowlachie, Chief: Painted Hills, The
Yu, Lu: Windhorse
Yu, Wang: Windhorse
Yuan, Liu Zhong: Life on a String
Yuelin, Zhao: Road Home, The (1999)
Yujuan, Wu: Women from the Lake of the Scented Souls
Yukiji, Asaoka: Razor, The: Sword of Justice
Yulin, Harris: Bad Dreams; Believers, The; Candy Mountain; Clear and Present Danger; Cutthroat Island; End of the Road; Fatal Beauty; Heart of Justice; Hostile Waters; Kansas City Massacre, The; Last Hit, The; Looking for Richard; Melvin Purvis: G-Man; Multiplicity; Parker Adderson, Philosopher; Rush Hour 2; Short Fuse; Steel; Stuart Saves His Family; Tailspin; Truman; Watched!
Yumei, Wang: Wooden Man's Bride, The
Yune, Johnny: They Call Me Bruce?; They Still Call Me Bruce
Yune, Rick: Fast and the Furious, The; Snow Falling on Cedars
Yun-Fat, Chow: Anna and the King; Better Tomorrow, A; Better Tomorrow 2, A; Better Tomorrow 3, A: Love and Death in Saigon; City on Fire; City War; Corruptor, The; Crouching Tiger, Hidden Dragon; Hard Boiled; Killer, The; Once a Thief; Prison on Fire; Replacement Killers, The
Yung, Victor Sen: Across the Pacific; Bonanza (TV Series); Charlie Chan at Treasure Island; Charlie Chan in Honolulu; Charlie Chan in Panama; Charlie Chan in Reno; Charlie Chan's Murder Cruise; Dead Men Tell; Feathered Serpent, The; She Demons
Yurka, Blanche: At Sword's Point; Bridge of San Luis Rey, The; City for Conquest; One Body Too Many
Yuying, Feng: Not One Less
Yuzawa, Shingo: Traffic Jam
Zabka, William: Back to School; High Voltage; Karate Kid Part II, The; Power Within, The; Shootfighter; Shootfighter 2: Kill or Be Killed; Tiger's Tale, A
Zabor, Jacques: Voyage en Douce
Zaborin, Lila: Blood Orgy of the She Devils
Zabriskie, Grace: Ambition; Burning Bed, The; Chain of Desire; Child's Play 2; Even Cowgirls Get the Blues; Hometown Boy Makes Good; Intimate Stranger; M.A.D.D.: Mothers Against Drunk Driving; Megaville; Passion of Darkly Noon, The; Servants of Twilight
Zacharias, Ann: Nea (A Young Emmanuelle)
Zacharias, John: Montenegro
Zacherley: Horrible Horror

DIRECTOR INDEX

Aarnikoski, Douglas: Highlander: Endgame
Aaron, Paul: Deadly Force; Different Story, A; Force of One; In Love and War; Love and War; Maxie; Miracle Worker, The
Abashidze, Dodo: Legend of Suram Fortress, The
Abbott, Abdul Malik: State Property
Abbott, George: Damn Yankees; Pajama Game, The; Too Many Girls
Abbott, Norman: Working Stiffs
Abdykalykov, Aktan: Beshkempir, The Adopted Son
Abel, Robert: Beshkempir, The Adopted Son
Abernathy, Lewis: House IV
Abrahams, Derwin: Border Vigilantes; Northwest Trail; Secrets of the Wasteland
Abrahams, Jim: Airplane!; Big Business; ... First Do No Harm; Hot Shots; Hot Shots Part Deux; Jane Austen's Mafia; Police Squad!; Ruthless People; Top Secret; Welcome Home, Roxy Carmichael
Abramson, Neil: Ringmaster
Abugov, Jeff: Mating Habits of the Earthbound Human,The
Abuladze, Tenghiz: Repentance
Acevski, Jon: Freddie as F.R.O.7
Acin, Javan: Hey, Babu Riba
Ackerman, Robert Allen: Baby (2000); Safe Passage
Acomba, David: Night Life
Adams, Catlin: Sticky Fingers
Adams, Daniel: Fool and His Money, A; Primary Motive
Adams, Doug: Blackout
Adamson, Al: Blood of Dracula's Castle; Brain of Blood; Dracula vs. Frankenstein; Five Bloody Graves; Gun Riders, The; Horror of the Blood Monsters; I Spit on Your Corpse; Satan's Sadists
Adamson, Andrew: Shrek
Adetuyi, Robert: Turn It Up
Adidge, Pierre: Mad Dogs and Englishmen
Adler, Carine: Under the Skin
Adler, Gilbert: Tales from the Crypt Presents Bordello of Blood
Adler, Jerry: National Lampoon's Class of '86
Adler, Joseph: Nightmare House; Sex and the College Girl
Adler, Lou: Up in Smoke
Adlon, Percy: Bagdad Café; Celeste; Last Five Days, The; Rosalie Goes Shopping; Sugarbaby; Younger and Younger
Adreon, Franklin: King of the Carnival
Aguirre, Javier: Dracula's Great Love
Ahern, Mats: Istanbul: Keep Your Eyes Open
Aizawa, Masahiro: Digimon: The Movie
Akerman, Chantal: Couch in New York, A; Les Rendez-Vous D'Anna; News from Home; Night and Day; Toute Une Nuit; Window Shopping
Akiyama, Katsuhito: Gall Force; Gall Force 2
Akkad, Moustapha: Lion of the Desert; Message, The (Mohammad, Messenger of God)
Alan, Jordan: Terminal Bliss
Alan, Pat: Shootfighter
Alber, Kevin: Where Evil Lies
Alberti, Irene von: Halfmoon
Albicocco, Jean Gabriel: Wanderer, The
Albright, Carlton J.: Luther, The Geek
Alcala, Felix Enriquez: Fire Down Below
Alda, Alan: Betsy's Wedding; Four Seasons, The; New Life, A; Sweet Liberty
Aldis, Will: Stealing Home
Aldrich, Adell: Kid from Left Field, The
Aldrich, Robert: All the Marbles; Apache; Attack!; Autumn Leaves; Choirboys, The; Dirty Dozen, The; Flight of the Phoenix, The; Four for Texas; Frisco Kid, The; Grissom Gang, The; Hush ... Hush, Sweet Charlotte; Hustle; Killing of Sister George, The; Kiss Me Deadly; Longest Yard, The; Sodom and Gomorrah; Too Late the Hero; Twilight's Last Gleaming; Ulzana's Raid; Vera Cruz; What Ever Happened to Baby Jane?
Alea, Tomas Gutierrez: Death of a Bureaucrat; Guantanamera!; Last Supper, The; Letters from the Park; Memories of Underdevelopment; Strawberry and Chocolate; Up to a Certain Point
Alessandrini, Goffredo: We the Living
Alexander, Bill: Tartuffe
Alexander, Jason: For Better or Worse; Just Looking
Alexander, Scott: Screwed
Alexson, Tracey: Labor Pains
Algar, James: Fantasia 2000; Legend of Sleepy Hollow, The (1949); Vanishing Prairie, The
Algrant, Dan: Naked in New York
Alk, Howard: Janis
Allan, Don: Jungleground
Allcroft, Britt: Thomas and the Magic Railroad
Allegret, Marc: Fanny; Lady Chatterley's Lover; Loves of Three Queens; Mademoiselle Striptease; Naked Heart, The; Sois Belle Et Tais-Toi (Just Another Pretty Face); Tales of Paris; Zou Zou
Allegret, Yves: Dedee D'Anvers; Proud Ones, The
Allen, A. K.: Ladies Club
Allen, Charles: Major Rock
Allen, Corey: Avalanche; Brass; Last Fling, The; Man in the Santa Claus Suit, The; Return of Frank Cannon, The; Thunder and Lightning
Allen, David: Dungeonmaster, The; Puppet Master II
Allen, Debbie: Out of Sync
Allen, Fred: Ride Him Cowboy
Allen, Irving: Slaughter Trail
Allen, Irwin: Beyond the Poseidon Adventure; Five Weeks in a Balloon; Swarm, The; Towering Inferno, The; Voyage to the Bottom of the Sea
Allen, James: Burndown
Allen, Kevin: Big Tease, The; Twin Town
Allen, Lewis: Another Time, Another Place; At Sword's Point; Perfect Marriage; Suddenly; Those Endearing Young Charms; Uninvited, The
Allen, Woody: Alice; Annie Hall; Another Woman; Bananas; Broadway Danny Rose; Bullets over Broadway; Celebrity; Crimes and Misdemeanors; Curse of the Jade Scorpion, The; Deconstructing Harry; Everyone Says I Love You; Everything You Always Wanted to Know About Sex but Were Afraid to Ask; Hannah and Her Sisters; Hollywood Ending; Husbands and Wives; Interiors; Love and Death; Manhattan; Manhattan Murder Mystery; Midsummer Night's Sex Comedy, A; Mighty Aphrodite; New York Stories; Purple Rose of Cairo, The; Radio Days; September; Shadows and Fog; Sleeper; Small Time Crooks; Stardust Memories; Sweet and Lowdown; Take the Money and Run; What's Up, Tiger Lily?; Zelig
Allers, Roger: Lion King, The
Allio, Rene: Shameless Old Lady, The
Allison, John: Taming of the Shrew (1982)
Almereyda, Michael: Eternal, The; Hamlet; Nadja; Twister
Almo, John: RSVP
Almodóvar, Pedro: All About My Mother; Dark Habits; Flower of My Secret, The; High Heels; Kika; Labyrinth of Passion; Law of Desire; Live Flesh; Matador; Pepi, Luci, Bom and Other Girls; Tie Me Up! Tie Me Down!; What Have I Done to Deserve This?; Women on the Verge of a Nervous Breakdown
Almond, Paul: Captive Hearts; Prep School
Alonzo, John A.: FM; Portrait of a Stripper
Alston, Emmett: Little Ninjas; New Year's Evil
Altman, Robert: Aria; Beyond Therapy; Brewster McCloud; Buffalo Bill and the Indians; Caine Mutiny Court Martial, The; Come Back to the Five and Dime, Jimmy Dean, Jimmy Dean; Cookie's Fortune; Countdown; Dr. T and the Women; Dumb Waiter, The; Fool for Love; Gingerbread Man, The; Gosford Park; James Dean Story, The; Kansas City; Long Goodbye, The;

M*A*S*H; McCabe and Mrs. Miller; Nashville; O.C. & Stiggs; Player, The; Popeye; Quintet; Ready to Wear; Secret Honor; Short Cuts; Streamers; Tanner '88; That Cold Day in the Park; Thieves Like Us; Vincent and Theo; Wedding, A (1978)
Alton, Robert: Merton of the Movies; Pagan Love Song
Alves, Joe: Jaws 3
Amamiya, Keita: Cyber Ninja; Zeram
Amar, Denis: Caged Heart, The (L'Addition)
Amateau, Rod: Bushwhackers; Drive-In; Garbage Pail Kids Movie, The; High School, USA; Monsoon; Seniors, The; Statue, The
Amelio, Gianni: Il Ladro Di Bambini (Stolen Children); L'America; Open Doors
Amenabar, Alejandro: Open Your Eyes; Others, The; Thesis
Amenta, Pino: Boulevard of Broken Dreams; Heaven Tonight
Amiel, Jon: Copycat; Entrapment; Man Who Knew Too Little, The; Queen of Hearts; Sommersby; Tune in Tomorrow
Amir, Gideon: P.O.W.: The Escape
Amoruso, Marina: Legends of the American West (Series)
Amurri, Franco: Flashback; Monkey Trouble
Amyes, Julian: Great Expectations; Jane Eyre; Murder at the Vicarage
Anand, Mukul S.: God Is My Witness
Anciano, Dominic: Love, Honor & Obey
Anders, Allison: Border Radio; Four Rooms; Gas, Food, Lodging; Grace of My Heart; Mi Vida Loca; Sugar Town; Things Behind the Sun
Anderson, Andy: Positive I.D.
Anderson, Brad: Happy Accidents; Next Stop Wonderland; Session 9
Anderson, Clyde: Monster Dog
Anderson, Gerry: Invasion UFO
Anderson, J. Todd: Naked Man, The
Anderson, Jane: Baby Dance, The
Anderson, John Murray: King of Jazz, The
Anderson, Kurt: Bounty Tracker; Dead Cold; Martial Law Two—Undercover; Martial Outlaw
Anderson, Lindsay: Britannia Hospital; Glory! Glory!; If …; Look Back in Anger; O Lucky Man!; This Sporting Life; Whales of August, The
Anderson, Michael: Around the World in 80 Days; Battle Hell; Captains Courageous; Conduct Unbecoming; Dam Busters, The; Doc Savage … , The Man of Bronze; Dominique Is Dead; Logan's Run; Martian Chronicles, Parts I-III, The; Millennium; Murder by Phone; Naked Edge, The; 1984; Operation Crossbow; Orca; Quiller Memorandum, The; Sea Wolf, The; Separate Vacations; Shake Hands with the Devil; Shoes of the Fisherman; Summer of the Monkeys; Sword of Gideon; Wreck of the Mary Deare, The; Young Catherine
Anderson, P. T.: Magnolia
Anderson, Paul: Event Horizon; Mortal Kombat; Resident Evil; Shopping; Soldier
Anderson, Paul Thomas: Boogie Nights; Hard Eight
Anderson, Robert: Young Graduates
Anderson, Stephen: Dead Men Can't Dance; Discovery Program; South Central
Anderson, Wes: Bottle Rocket; Royal Tenenbaums, The; Rushmore
Andreacchio, Mario: Napoleon
Andreef, Christina: Soft Fruit; Women from Down Under
Andrei, Yannick: Beyond Fear
Andrew, Tim: Don't Sleep Alone; Lola's Game
Andrieu, Michel: Weep No More My Lady
Angel, Chris: Beyond Redemption; Fear, The: Halloween Night
Angelo, Robert: Forbidden Sins; Mutual Needs
Angelopoulos, Theo: Ulysses' Gaze
Angelou, Maya: Down in the Delta
Anjou, Erik: Cool Surface, The
Annakin, Ken: Battle of the Bulge; Call of the Wild; Cheaper to Keep Her; Fifth Musketeer, The; Longest Day, The; New Adventures of Pippi Longstocking, The; Paper Tiger; Pirate Movie, The; Quartet; Story of Robin Hood, The; Swiss Family Robinson, The; Sword and the Rose, The (1953); Third Man on the Mountain; Those Daring Young Men in Their Jaunty Jalopies; Those Magnificent Men in Their Flying Machines; Three Men in a Boat; Trio
Annaud, Jean-Jacques: Bear, The; Black and White in Color; Enemy at the Gates; Hot Head; Lover, The; Name of the Rose, The; Quest for Fire; Seven Years in Tibet
Annett, Paul: Adventures of Sherlock Holmes, The (Series); Beast Must Die, The; Partners in Crime (Secret Adversary) (TV Series); Tales of the Unexpected; Witching of Ben Wagner, The
Anno, Hideaki: Gunbuster—Vols. 1–3
Anselmo, Reverge:
Anspaugh, David: Fresh Horses; Hoosiers; Moonlight and Valentino; Rudy
Anthony, Joseph: All in a Night's Work; Career; Matchmaker, The; Rainmaker, The; Tomorrow
Anthony, Robert: Without Mercy
Antier, Paul: Dead in a Heartbeat
Antonelli, John: Kerouac
Antonijevic, Peter: Savior
Antonio, Lou: Between Friends; Breaking Up Is Hard to Do; Gypsy Warriors, The; Last Prostitute, The; Lies Before Kisses; Mayflower Madam; Pals; Real American Hero, The; Silent Victory: The Kitty O'Neil Story; Someone I Touched; Taste for Killing, A; 13 at Dinner; This Gun for Hire
Antonioni, Michelangelo: Blow-Up; Classic Foreign Shorts: Volume 2; Eclipse, The; Il Grido (Outcry, The); L'Aventura; Passenger, The; Red Desert; Zabriskie Point
Anwarv, Ackyl: Angel of Fury
Aoki, Tetsuro: Devil Hunter Yohko
Apostolof, Stephen C.: Hot Ice
Apostolou, Scott: Mutants in Paradise
Appleby, Daniel: Bound and Gagged: A Love Story
Apstein, Norman: Ice Cream Man
Apted, Michael: Agatha; Always Outnumbered; Blink; Class Action; Coal Miner's Daughter; Collection, The; Continental Divide; Critical Condition; Extreme Measures; Firstborn; Gorillas in the Mist; Gorky Park; Incident at Oglala; Kipperbang; Long Way Home, The; Moving the Mountain; Nell; Squeeze, The; 35 Up; Thunderheart; 28 Up; World Is Not Enough, The
Aragón, Manuel Gutiérrez: Demons in the Garden; Half of Heaven
Araki, Gregg: Doom Generation, The; Living End, The; Nowhere; Splendor
Aranda, Vicente: Blood Spattered Bride, The; Lovers (1992)
Arau, Alfonso: Like Water for Chocolate; Picking up the Pieces; Walk in the Clouds, A
Arbuckle, Roscoe: Art of Buster Keaton, The; Buster and Fatty; Keystone Comedies: Vol. 1–5
Arcady, Alexandre: Day of Atonement
Arcand, Denys: Decline of the American Empire, The; Jesus of Montreal; Love and Human Remains
Archainbaud, George: Dangerous Venture; False Colors; Framed; Hoppy Serves a Writ; Hunt the Man Down; Kansan, The; Last of the Pony Riders; Lost Squadron; Mystery Man; Silent Conflict; State's Attorney; Texas Masquerade; Winning of the West; Woman of the Town
Ardolino, Emile: Chances Are; Dirty Dancing; George Balanchine's The Nutcracker; Gypsy; Sister Act; Three Men and a Little Lady
Argento, Dario: Bird with the Crystal Plumage, The; Cat O'-Nine Tails; Creepers; Deep Red; Inferno; Phantom of the Opera; Stendhal Syndrome, The; Suspiria; Terror at the Opera; Trauma; Two Evil Eyes; Unsane
Aristarian, Adolfo: Stranger, The
Arkin, Alan: Little Murders
Arkoff, Samuel Z.: Alakazam the Great
Arkush, Allan: Caddyshack II; Deathsport; Elvis Meets Nixon; Get Crazy; Heartbeeps; Hollywood Boulevard; Rock 'n' Roll High School; Shake, Rattle & Rock
Arliss, Leslie: Man in Grey, The; Night Has Eyes, The; Wicked Lady, The

Armitage, George: Grosse Pointe Blank; Miami Blues
Armstrong, Andy: Moonshine Highway
Armstrong, Gillian: Charlotte Gray; Fires Within; High Tide; Last Days of Chez Nous, The; Little Women; Mrs. Soffel; My Brilliant Career; Oscar & Lucinda; Starstruck
Armstrong, Michael: Mark of the Devil
Armstrong, Moira: Letting the Birds Go Free
Armstrong, Robin B.: Pastime
Armstrong, Ronald K.: Bugged!
Armstrong, Vic: Army of One
Arnaz, Lucie: Lucy and Desi: A Home Movie
Arner, Gwen: Matter of Principle, A; Necessary Parties
Arno, Eddie: Murder Story
Arnold, Frank: Josh Kirby, Time Warrior (Series); Waltz Through the Hills
Arnold, Jack: Bachelor in Paradise; Boss; Brady Bunch, The (TV series); Creature from the Black Lagoon; Global Affair, A; High School Confidential!; Incredible Shrinking Man, The; It Came from Outer Space; Monster on the Campus; Mouse That Roared, The; Revenge of the Creature; Swiss Conspiracy, The; Tarantula
Arnold, Newt: Bloodsport; Hands of a Stranger
Aronofsky, Darren: Pi; Requiem for a Dream
Aronson, Josh: Sound and Fury
Arranovitch, Semeon: I Was Stalin's Bodyguard
Arsenault, Jeffrey: Night Owl
Artenstein, Isaac: Break of Dawn
Arteta, Miguel: Chuck & Buck; Star Maps
Arthur, Karen: Bridge to Silence; Bunny's Tale, A; Disappearance of Christina, The; Jacksons, The: An American Dream; Lady Beware; Lost Child, The; My Sister, My Love (The Mafu Cage); Return to Eden; Secret, The; True Women
Arzner, Dorothy: Bride Wore Red, The; Christopher Strong; Craig's Wife; Dance, Girl, Dance; Wild Party, The
Asbury, Kelly: Spirit: Stallion of the Cimarron
Ascot, Anthony: Have a Nice Funeral
Ash: Big Bang Theory, The; Pups
Ashby, Hal: Being There; Bound for Glory; Coming Home; 8 Million Ways to Die; Harold and Maude; Last Detail, The; Let's Spend the Night Together; Lookin' to Get Out; Shampoo; Slugger's Wife, The
Ashe, Richard: Track of the Moon Beast
Asher, John Mallory: Kounterfeit
Asher, Robert: Make Mine Mink
Asher, William: Beach Blanket Bingo; Beach Party; Bikini Beach; How to Stuff a Wild Bikini; I Love Lucy (TV Series); Movers and Shakers; Muscle Beach Party; Night Warning; 27th Day, The
Ashida, Toyoo: Fist of the North Star
Ashley, Christopher: Jeffrey
Askin, Peter: Company Man
Askoldov, Aleksandr: Commissar, The
Aslanian, Samson: Torment
Asquith, Anthony: Browning Version, The; Carrington, V. C.; I Stand Condemned; Importance of Being Earnest, The; Pygmalion; V.I.P.s, The; We Dive at Dawn; Winslow Boy, The; Woman in Question
Assayas, Olivier: Irma Vep
Assonitis (Oliver Hellman), Ovidio: Beyond the Door; Madhouse; Tentacles
Athens, J. D.: Cannibal Women in the Avocado Jungle of Death; Pizza Man
Atkins, David: Novocaine
Atkins, Thomas: Silver Streak
Attenborough, Richard: Bridge Too Far, A; Chaplin; Chorus Line, A; Cry Freedom; Gandhi; Grey Owl; In Love and War; Magic; Shadowlands; Young Winston
Attias, Daniel: Silver Bullet; Sopranos, The (TV series)
Attwood, David: Moll Flanders; Shot Through the Heart; Wild West
Aubrey, Jay: Looking for Trouble
Aucion, Guillaume Martin: Oh! Calcutta!
Audley, Michael: Mark of the Hawk, The
Auer, Gabriel: Eyes of the Birds
Auer, John H.: City That Never Sleeps; Crime of Dr. Crespi, The; Wheel of Fortune
Auerbach, Gary: Just Your Luck
August, Bille: Best Intentions, The; House of the Spirits, The; Jerusalem; Les Misérables; Pelle the Conqueror; Smilla's Sense of Snow; Twist and Shout
Aured, Carlos: Horror Rises from the Tomb; House of Psychotic Women
Auster, Paul: Lulu on the Bridge
Auster, Sam: Screen Test
Austin, Michael: Princess Caraboo
Austin, Phil: Eat or Be Eaten
Austin, Ray: Highlander: The Gathering; Return of the Man from U.N.C.L.E., The; Space 1999 (TV Series); Zany Adventures of Robin Hood, The
Autant-Lara, Claude: Devil in the Flesh; Four Bags Full; Le Rouge et le Noir; Oldest Profession, The; Sylvia and the Phantom
Auzins, Igor: We of the Never Never
Avakian, Aram: Cops and Robbers; 11 Harrowhouse; End of the Road
Avallone, Marcello: Specters
Avalon, Phil: Fatal Bond
Avalos, Stefan: Last Broadcast, The
Avary, Roger: Killing Zoe; Mr. Stitch
Avati, Pupi: Best Man, The; Story of Boys and Girls
Avedis, Howard: Fifth Floor, The; Scorchy
Avellana, José Mari: Blackbelt 2: Fatal Force
Averback, Hy: Chamber of Horrors; Guide for the Married Woman, A; I Love You Alice B. Toklas!; M*A*S*H (TV Series); She's in the Army Now; Suppose They Gave a War and Nobody Came?; Where the Boys Are '84; Where Were You When the Lights Went Out?
Avery, Belle: Malevolence
Avery, Rick: Deadly Outbreak; Expert, The
Avila, Carlos: Price of Glory
Avildsen, John G.: Cry Uncle!; Desert Heat; 8 Seconds; For Keeps; Formula, The; Happy New Year (1987); Joe; Karate Kid, The; Karate Kid Part II, The; Karate Kid Part III, The; Lean on Me; Neighbors; Night in Heaven, A; Power of One, The; Rocky; Rocky V; Save the Tiger
Avildsen, Tom: Things Are Tough All Over
Avis, Meiert: Far from Home
Avitabile, Tom: Silent Prey
Avnet, Jon: Between Two Women; Fried Green Tomatoes; Red Corner; Up Close and Personal; War, The
Axel, Gabriel: Babette's Feast; Royal Deceit
Axelrod, George: Lord Love a Duck; Secret Life of an American Wife, The
Axmith, George: Angel 4: Undercover
Ayala, Fernando: El Professor Hippie
Aykroyd, Dan: Nothing But Trouble
Azzopardi, Mario: Bone Daddy; Nowhere to Hide; On Hostile Ground; Stargate SG-1; Time Shifters, The
B., Beth: Salvation; Two Small Bodies
Babbit, Jamie: But I'm a Cheerleader
Babenco, Hector: At Play in the Fields of the Lord; Ironweed; Kiss of the Spider Woman; Pixote
Babin, Charles: Mask of Fu Manchu, The
Bach, Jean: Great Day in Harlem, A
Bachmann, Gideon: Ciao Federico!
Bacon, Kevin: Losing Chase
Bacon, Lloyd: Action in the North Atlantic; Boy Meets Girl; Brother Orchid; Devil Dogs of the Air; Fighting Sullivans, The (Sullivans, The); Footlight Parade; Footsteps in the Dark; 42nd Street; French Line, The; Fuller Brush Girl, The; It Happens Every Spring; Knute Rockne—All American; Marked Woman; Miss Grant Takes Richmond; Oklahoma Kid, The; She Couldn't Say No; Silver Queen; Wonder Bar
Badat, Randall: Surf 2
Bader, Kwyn: Loving Jezebel
Badger, Clarence: It

Badger, Phillip: Forgotten One, The
Badham, John: American Flyers; Another Stakeout; Assassins; Bingo Long Traveling All-Stars and Motor Kings, The; Bird on a Wire; Blue Thunder; Dracula; Drop Zone; Floating Away; Hard Way, The; Incognito; Jack Bull, The; Last Debate, The; Nick of Time; Point of No Return; Reflections of Murder; Saturday Night Fever; Short Circuit; Stakeout; Wargames; Whose Life Is It, Anyway?
Badiyi, Reza S.: Of Mice and Men; Police Squad!
Bae, Yong-Kyun: Why Has Bhodi Dharma Left for the East?
Baer, Max: Ode to Billy Joe
Bagby Jr., Milton: Rebel Love
Baggott, King: Human Hearts; Tumbleweeds
Bagle, James: Stones of Death
Bahr, Fax: Hearts of Darkness
Baigelman, Steven: Feeling Minnesota
Bail, Chuck: Choke Canyon; Cleopatra Jones and the Casino of Gold; Gumball Rally, The
Bailey, Derek: Gloriana
Bailey, Fenton: Eyes of Tammy Faye, The
Bailey, John: China Moon; Search for Signs of Intelligent Life in the Universe, The
Bailey, Norma: Secret Cutting
Bailey, Patrick: Door to Door
Bailey, Richard: Win, Place or Steal
Baird, Stuart: Executive Decision; U.S. Marshals
Baker, Graham: Alien Nation; Beowulf; Born to Ride; Final Conflict, The; Impulse
Baker, Howard: Persuasion
Baker, Mark H.: Lifeform
Baker, Robert S.: Hellfire Club, The; Jack the Ripper
Baker, Roy Ward: And Now the Screaming Starts; Asylum; Dr. Jekyll and Sister Hyde; Don't Bother to Knock; Five Million Years to Earth; Masks of Death; Monster Club, The; Night to Remember, A; One That Got Away, The; Saint, The (TV Series); Scars of Dracula; Seven Brothers Meet Dracula, The; Vampire Lovers, The; Vault of Horror
Baker, Sharon R.: Cartoons Go to War
Bakshi, Ralph: Cool World; Fire and Ice; Fritz the Cat; Heavy Traffic; Hey Good Lookin'; Lord of the Rings, The; Streetfight (Coonskin); Wizards
Balaban, Bob: Last Good Time, The; My Boyfriend's Back; Parents
Balaban, Burt: Stranger from Venus
Balasko, Josiane: French Twist
Balch, Anthony: Horror Hospital
Baldanello, Gianfranco: This Man Can't Die
Balden, Jim: Gamble on Love; Lights, Camera, Action, Love
Baldi, Ferdinando: Duel of Champions; Treasure of the Four Crowns
Baldwin, Peter: Brady Bunch, The (TV series); Lots of Luck; Meet Wally Sparks; Very Brady Christmas, A
Baldwin, Thomas: Order of the Eagle
Bale, Paul Trevor: Littlest Viking, The
Baledon, Rafael: Curse of the Crying Woman, The; Man and the Monster, The
Ballard, Carroll: Black Stallion, The; Fly Away Home; Never Cry Wolf; Wind (1992)
Ballard, John: Friday the 13th: The Orphan
Baluzy, George: Black Male
Bamer, Rolf: Kill, The
Bamford, Roger: Rumpole of the Bailey (TV Series)
Bancroft, Anne: Fatso
Bancroft, Tony: Mulan
Band, Albert: Doctor Mordrid; Ghoulies II; I Bury the Living; Prehysteria; Prehysteria 2; Robot Wars; Tramplers, The; Zoltan—Hound of Dracula
Band, Charles: Blood Dolls; Crash! (1977); Crash and Burn; Creeps, The; Doctor Mordrid; Dollman vs. Demonic Toys; Dungeonmaster, The; Hideous; Meridian (Kiss of the Beast); Metalstorm: The Destruction of Jared-Syn; Parasite; Prehysteria; Trancers; Trancers II (The Return of Jack Deth)
Banderas, Antonio: Crazy in Alabama
Bank, Mirra: Nobody's Girls
Banks, Monty: Great Guns
Bannerman, Bill: Air Bud: World Pup
Banno, Yoshimitu: Godzilla vs. the Smog Monster
Baran, Jack: Destiny Turns on the Radio
Barba, Norberto: Blue Tiger; Lost in the Bermuda Triangle; Solo
Barbash, Uri: Beyond the Walls; Unsettled Land
Barbato, Randy: Eyes of Tammy Faye, The
Barbera, Joseph: Hey There, It's Yogi Bear; Jetsons: The Movie; Man Called Flintstone, A
Barclay, Paris: America's Dream; Cherokee Kid, The; Don't Be a Menace to South Central while Drinking Your Juice in the 'Hood
Barden, James H.: Judas Project, The
Barish, Leora: Venus Rising
Barker, Clive: Clive Barker's Salome and The Forbidden; Hellraiser; Lord of Illusions; Night Breed
Barker, Nicholas: Unmade Beds
Barkett, Steve: Empire of the Dark
Barma, Claude: Tales of Paris
Barmettler, Joseph L.: In the Time of Barbarians
Barnet, Boris: Girl with the Hatbox, The
Barnett, Ivan: Fall of the House of Usher, The
Barnett, Ken: Dark Tower
Barnett, Steve: Hollywood Boulevard II; Mindwarp; Mission of Justice; Scanners 4: The Showdown
Barnette, Neema: Run for the Dream; Spirit Lost
Baron, Allen: Foxfire Light; Night Stalker, The: Two Tales of Terror (TV Series)
Barr, Douglas: Conundrum; Dead Badge; Frame by Frame
Barreto, Bruno: Bossa Nova; Carried Away; Dona Flor and Her Two Husbands; Four Days in September; Gabriela; Happily Ever After; Heart of Justice; One Tough Cop; Show of Force, A; Story of Fausta, The
Barreto, Fabio: Luzia
Barrett, Lezli-An: Business As Usual
Barrett, Shirley: Love Serenade
Barron, Arthur: Jolly Corner, The; Parker Adderson, Philosopher
Barron, Steve: Adventures of Pinocchio, The; Coneheads; Electric Dreams; Merlin (1998); Teenage Mutant Ninja Turtles
Barron, Zelda: Forbidden Sun; Shag, the Movie
Barry, Christopher: Tripods
Barry, Ian: Blackwater Trail; Chain Reaction; Crimebroker; Diamond of Jeru, The; Inferno; Joey; Ring of Scorpio; Wrangler
Barry, Wesley E.: Creation of the Humanoids
Barski, Roger J.: Chains
Barsky, Bud: Coast Patrol, The
Bartel, Paul: Cannonball; Death Race 2000; Eating Raoul; Longshot, The (1985); Lust in the Dust; Not for Publication; Private Parts; Scenes from the Class Struggle in Beverly Hills
Bartkowiak, Andrzej: Exit Wounds; Romeo Must Die
Bartlett, Hall: Children of Sanchez, The; Jonathan Livingston Seagull
Bartlett, Richard: Ollie Hopnoodle's Haven of Bliss; Rock, Pretty Baby
Bartman, William: O'Hara's Wife
Barton, Charles: Abbott and Costello Meet Frankenstein; Abbott and Costello Meet the Killer, Boris Karloff; Africa Screams; Amos and Andy (TV Series); Buck Privates Come Home; Fighting Westerner, The; Forlorn River; Hell Town; Ma and Pa Kettle at the Fair; Mexican Hayride; Noose Hangs High, The; Shaggy Dog, The; Thunder Trail; Time of Their Lives, The; Toby Tyler; Wagon Wheels; Wistful Widow of Wagon Gap, The
Barton, Peter: Kill Castro (Cuba Crossing, Mercenaries , Sweet Violent Tony)
Barwood, Hal: Warning Sign
Barwood, Nick: Nasty Hero
Barzman, Paolo: For Better and for Worse
Baskin, Richard: Sing
Bass, Jules: Around the World in 80 Days; Daydreamer, The (1966); Flight of Dragons, The; Hobbit, The; Last Unicorn, The;

Mad, Mad Monsters, The; Mad Monster Party; Twenty Thousand Leagues Under the Sea (1972)
Bass, Kim: Ballistic
Bass, Saul: Phase IV
Bassoff, Lawrence: Hunk
Bassol, Vincent: Phantom 2040 (TV Series)
Bat-Adam, Michal: Boy Takes Girl
Batalov, Alexi: Overcoat, The
Batchelor, Joy: Animal Farm
Battersby, Bradley: Blue Desert; Red Letters
Battersby, Roy: Cracker (TV Series); Mr. Love
Battiato, Giacomo: Blood Ties; Hearts and Armour
Battle, Murray: Stand Off
Bauer, Evgenii: Early Russian Cinema: Before the Revolutions (Vol. 1–10)
Baumander, Lewis: Future Fear
Baumbach, Noah: Kicking and Screaming; Mr. Jealousy
Bava, Lamberto: Blade in the Dark, A; Demons; Demons 2; Frozen Terror
Bava, Mario: Beyond the Door 2; Black Sabbath; Black Sunday; Blood and Black Lace; Curse of the Living Dead (Kill, Baby, Kill); Danger: Diabolik; Devil in the House of Exorcism, The; Dr. Goldfoot and the Girl Bombs; Hercules in the Haunted World; House of Exorcism, The; Planet of the Vampires; Torture Chamber of Baron Blood, The; Twitch of the Death Nerve
Baxley, Craig R.: Action Jackson; Deep Red; I Come in Peace; Stone Cold; Storm of the Century; Twilight Man; Under Pressure
Baxter, John: Love on the Dole
Bay, Michael: Armageddon; Bad Boys; Pearl Harbor; Rock, The
Bayer, Rolf: Pacific Inferno
Bayly, Stephen: Coming Up Roses; Diamond's Edge
Beaird, David: It Takes Two; My Chauffeur; Octavia; Pass the Ammo; Scorchers
Beairsto, Rick: Close to Home
Beard, Glynn: Crier, The
Bearde, Chris: Hysterical
Beattie, Alan: Delusion
Beatty, Warren: Bulworth; Dick Tracy; Heaven Can Wait; Reds
Beaudin, Jean: Being at Home with Claude
Beaudine, William: Ape Man, The; Billy the Kid vs. Dracula; Bowery Boys, The (Series); Boys from Brooklyn, The; Face of Marble, The; Feathered Serpent, The; Ghosts on the Loose; Jesse James Meets Frankenstein's Daughter; Little Annie Rooney; Mom and Dad; Sparrows; Ten Who Dared; Voodoo Man; Westward Ho, the Wagons
Beaumont, Gabrielle: Beastmaster III: The Eye of Braxus; Carmilla; Death of a Centerfold; Godsend, The; Gone Are the Days
Beaumont, Harry: Beau Brummell; Broadway Melody, The; Dance, Fools, Dance; Laughing Sinners; Our Dancing Daughters; Show-Off, The; When's Your Birthday?
Bechard, Gorman: Cemetery High; Galactic Gigolo; Psychos in Love
Beck, Donald R.: Journey's End: The Saga of Star Trek:The Next Generation
Beck, George: Behave Yourself!
Beck, Martin: Last Game, The
Beck, Steve: Thir13en Ghosts
Becker, Harold: Black Marble, The; Boost, The; City Hall; Domestic Disturbance; Malice; Mercury Rising; Onion Field, The; Sea of Love; Taps; Vision Quest
Becker, Jacques: Grisbi
Becker, Jean: One Deadly Summer
Becker, Josh: Lunatics: A Love Story; Running Time; Thou Shalt Not Kill . . . Except
Becker, Terry: Thirsty Dead, The; Ulterior Motives
Becket, James: Natural Causes
Beckett, Jack: Please Don't Eat My Mother!
Bedford, Terry: Slayground
Beebe, Ford: Ace Drummond; Adventures of Rex and Rinty; Buck Rogers: Destination Saturn (PlanetOutlaws); Challenge to Be Free; Flash Gordon Conquers the Universe; Invisible Man's Revenge, The; Night Monster; Phantom Creeps, The; Red Barry; Riders of Death Valley; Shadow of the Eagle; Winners of the West
Beeman, Greg: Bushwhacked; License to Drive; Miracle in Lane 2; Mom and Dad Save the World
Beesley, Matt Earl: Point Blank
Behar, Andrew: Intimate Betrayal; Tie-Died: Rock 'n' Roll's Most Dedicated Fans
Behrens, Gloria: Wiz Kid, The
Beineix, Jean-Jacques: Betty Blue; Diva; IP5: The Island of Pachyderms; Moon in the Gutter, The
Beinstock, Marc: Beneficiary, The
Belateche, Irving: Implicated
Belen, Ana: How to Be a Woman and Not Die in the Attempt
Belgard, Arnold: East of Kilimanjaro
Bell, A. Dean: Backfire
Bell, Alan: Hitchhiker's Guide to the Galaxy, The; Ripping Yarns
Bell, Jeffrey: Radio Inside
Bell, Martin: American Heart; Hidden in America; Streetwise
Bellamy, Earl: Against a Crooked Sky; Desperate Women; Fire!; Flood!; Sidewinder 1; Trackers, The; Walking Tall Part II
Bellisario, Donald P.: Last Rites; Quantum Leap (TV Series)
Bellocchio, Marco: China Is Near; Henry IV
Bellon, Yannick: Rape of Love (L'Amour Violé)
Belmont, Vera: Red Kiss (Rouge Baiser)
Belson, Jerry: Jekyll & Hyde—Together Again; Surrender
Belvaux, Rémy: Man Bites Dog
Bemberg, Maria Luisa: Camila (1984); I Don't Want to Talk About It; Miss Mary
Benabib, Roberto: Little City
Bender, Jack: Call to Remember, A; Child's Play 3; In Love with an Older Woman; It Came from the Sky; Killing Mr. Griffin; Lone Justice 2; Midnight Hour; My Brother's Wife; Shattered Vows; Tricks of the Trade
Bender, Joel: Midnight Kiss; Returning, The; Rich Girl
Benedek, Laslo: Assault on Agathon; Daring Game; Kissing Bandit, The; Namu, the Killer Whale; Night Visitor, The (1970); Outer Limits, The (TV Series); Port of New York; Wild One, The
Benedict, Terry: Painted Hero
Benigni, Roberto: Johnny Stecchino; Life Is Beautiful; Monster, The
Benjamin, Martin: Last Party, The
Benjamin, Richard: City Heat; Downtown; Laughter on the 23rd Floor; Little Nikita; Made in America; Mermaids; Milk Money; Money Pit, The; Mrs. Winterbourne; My Favorite Year; My Stepmother Is an Alien; Pentagon Wars, The; Racing with the Moon
Benner, Richard: Happy Birthday, Gemini; Outrageous; Too Outrageous
Bennet, Spencer Gordon: Arizona Bound; Atom Man vs. Superman; Atomic Submarine, The; Batman and Robin (Adventures of Batmanand Robin); Calling Wild Bill Elliott; Federal Operator 99; Gunman from Bodie; Lost Planet, The; Masked Marvel, The; Mojave Firebrand; Pirates of the High Seas; Purple Monster Strikes, The; Superman—The Serial
Bennett, Bill: Backlash; Kiss or Kill; Two If By Sea
Bennett, Compton: Glory at Sea; King Solomon's Mines; Seventh Veil, The; That Forsyte Woman
Bennett, Edward: Poirot (Series); Woman at War, A
Bennett, Gary: Rain Without Thunder
Bennett, Richard: Harper Valley P.T.A.
Bennett, Rick: Balance of Power
Bennett, Rodney: Monsignor Quixote; Rumpole of the Bailey (TV Series)
Benson, Leon: Flipper's New Adventure
Benson, Robby: Modern Love; White Hot
Bentley, Thomas: Silver Blaze
Benton, Robert: Bad Company; Billy Bathgate; Kramer vs. Kramer; Late Show, The; Nadine; Nobody's Fool; Places in the Heart; Still of the Night; Twilight
Benveniste, Michael: Flesh Gordon

Beraud, Luc: Heat of Desire
Bercovici, Luca: Bittersweet (1999); Chain, The; Dark Tide; Ghoulies; Granny, The; Luck of the Draw; Rockula
Beresford, Bruce: Aria; Barry McKenzie Holds His Own; Black Robe; Breaker Morant; Bride of the Wind; Club, The; Crimes of the Heart; Don's Party; Double Jeopardy; Driving Miss Daisy; Fringe Dwellers, The; Getting of Wisdom, The; Good Man in Africa, A; Her Alibi; King David; Last Dance; Mister Johnson; Paradise Road; Puberty Blues; Rich in Love; Silent Fall; Tender Mercies
Berg, Peter: Very Bad Things
Berg, Rudolf Van Den: Cold Light of Day, The
Berger, Howard: Original Sins
Berger, Ludwig: Thief of Bagdad, The
Berger, Pamela: Magic Stone, The
Bergeron, Eric "Bibo": Road to El Dorado, The
Bergman, Andrew: Freshman, The; Honeymoon in Vegas; Isn't She Great; It Could Happen to You; So Fine; Striptease
Bergman, Daniel: Sunday's Children
Bergman, David: Horrible Horror
Bergman, Ingmar: After the Rehearsal; All These Women; Autumn Sonata; Brink of Life; Cries and Whispers; Devil's Eye, The; Dreams; Fanny and Alexander; From the Lives of the Marionettes; Hour of the Wolf; Lesson in Love, A; Magic Flute, The; Magician, The; Monika; Night Is My Future; Passion of Anna, The; Persona; Port of Call; Sawdust and Tinsel; Scenes from a Marriage; Secrets of Women (Waiting Women); Serpent's Egg, The; Seventh Seal, The; Silence, The; Smiles of a Summer Night; Summer Interlude; Three Strange Loves; Through a Glass Darkly; Virgin Spring, The; Wild Strawberries; Winter Light
Bergman, Martin: Weekend in the Country, A
Bergone, Serge: Last Gun, The
Bergqvist, Stig: Rugrats in Paris
Berke, Lester: Lost Missile, The
Berke, William: Arson Inc.; Badmen of the Hills; Betrayal from the East; Falcon in Mexico, The; Fury of the Congo; Jungle Jim; Renegade Girl
Berkeley, Busby: Babes in Arms; Babes on Broadway; For Me and My Gal; Gang's All Here, The; Girl Crazy; Gold Diggers of 1935; Hollywood Hotel; Small Town Girl; Stage Struck; Strike Up the Band; Take Me Out to the Ball Game; They Made Me a Criminal
Berkowitz, Myles: 20 Dates
Berlanti, Greg: Broken Hearts Club, The
Berlin, Abby: Blondie Knows Best; Double Deal
Berliner, Alain: Ma Vie En Rose; Passion of Mind
Berlinger, Joe: Book of Shadows: Blair Witch 2; Brother's Keeper; Paradise Lost: The Child Murders at Robin Hood Hills
Berman, Harvey: Wild Ride, The
Berman, Monty: Hellfire Club, The; Jack the Ripper
Berman, Ted: Black Cauldron, The; Fox and the Hound
Berna, Thomas: Colony (1996)
Bernard, Chris: Letter to Brezhnev
Bernard, Michael: Nights in White Satin
Bernds, Edward L.: Blondie Hits the Jackpot; Bowery Boys, The (Series); Queen of Outer Space; Reform School Girl; Return of the Fly, The; World Without End
Bernette, M. Neema: Better Off Dead
Bernhard, Jack: Blonde Ice
Bernhardt, Curtis: Beau Brummell; Conflict; Interrupted Melody; Kisses for My President; Miss Sadie Thompson; Possessed; Sirocco; Stolen Life, A
Bernstein, Adam: It's Pat: The Movie; Six Ways to Sunday
Bernstein, Armyan: Cross My Heart; Windy City
Bernstein, Walter: Little Miss Marker; Women & Men 2
Berri, Claude: Je Vous Aime (I Love You All); Jean De Florette; Le Sex Shop; Manon of the Spring; One Wild Moment; Tchao Pantin; Two of Us, The; Uranus
Berry, Bill: Brotherhood of Death; Off the Mark
Berry, Ian: Seventh Floor, The
Berry, John: Angel on My Shoulder; Bad News Bears Go to Japan, The; Captive in the Land, A; Casbah; Honeyboy; Maya; Pantaloons
Berry, Tom: Amityville Curse, The
Bertolucci, Bernardo: Before the Revolution; Besieged; Conformist, The; Grim Reaper, The; Last Emperor, The; Last Tango in Paris; Little Buddha; 1900; Partner; Sheltering Sky, The; Spider's Stratagem, The; Stealing Beauty; Tragedy of a Ridiculous Man
Bertucelli, Jean-Louis: Ramparts of Clay
Berwick, Irvin: Monster of Piedras Blancas, The
Beshears, James: Homework
Bessada, Milad: Quiet Day in Belfast, A
Bessie, Dan: Hard Traveling
Besson, Luc: Big Blue, The; Fifth Element, The; Final Combat, The; La Femme Nikita; Messenger: The Story of Joan of Arc, The; Professional, The; Subway
Betancor, Antonio J.: Valentina
Betuel, Jonathan: My Science Project; Theodore Rex
Betwick, Wayne: My Science Project; Theodore Rex
Bharadwaj, Radha: Basil; Closet Land
Bianchi, Edward: Fan, The; Off and Running
Bianchini, Paolo: Machine Gun Killers
Biberman, Abner: Running Wild
Biberman, Herbert J.: Master Race, The; Salt of the Earth
Bido, Anthony: Watch Me When I Kill
Bierman, Robert: Apology; Merry War, A; Vampire's Kiss
Bigelow, Kathryn: Blue Steel; Loveless, The; Near Dark; Point Break; Strange Days; Wild Palms
Bill, Tony: Beyond the Call; Crazy People; Five Corners; Harlan County War; Home of Our Own, A; My Bodyguard; Next Door; Oliver Twist; Six Weeks; Untamed Heart
Billington, Kevin: Light at the End of the World, The
Bilson, Bruce: Chattanooga Choo Choo; North Avenue Irregulars, The
Bilson, Danny: Wrong Guys, The; Zone Troopers
Binder, John: Uforia
Binder, Mike: Blankman; Crossing the Bridge; Indian Summer; Sex Monster, The
Binder, Steve: Give 'em Hell, Harry!; That Was Rock
Bindley, William: Eighteenth Angel, The; Freeze Frame; Johnny & Clyde; Judicial Consent
Binet, Catherine: Games of Countess Dolingen of Gratz, The
Bing, Steve: Every Breath
Binyon, Claude: Here Come the Girls; Stella
Birch, Patricia: Grease 2
Bird, Antonia: Mad Love; Priest; Ravenous
Bird, Brad: Amazing Stories (TV Series); Iron Giant, The
Birkin, Andrew: Burning Secret; Cement Garden, The; Desire
Birkin, John: Mr. Bean
Birkinshaw, Alan: House of Usher, The; Ten Little Indians
Birri, Fernando: Very Old Man with Enormous Wings, A
Bischoff, Sam: Last Mile, The
Bishop, Larry: Trigger Happy (Mad Dog Time)
Bivens, Loren: Trespasses
Bixby, Bill: Another Pair of Aces; Baby of the Bride; Death of the Incredible Hulk, The; Trial of the Incredible Hulk
Bjorknan, Stig: Georgia, Georgia
Black, Darby: Sweepers
Black, Eric: Witching, The (1994)
Black, Noel: Golden Honeymoon, The; I'm a Fool; Man, a Woman and a Bank, A; Pretty Poison; Prime Suspect (1982) (Feature); Private School; Quarterback Princess
Black, Trevor: Goldy, The Last of the Golden Bears
Blackburn, Richard: Lemora—Lady Dracula
Blaine, Cullen: R.O.T.O.R.
Blaine, Rick: Teach Me Tonight
Blair, David: Wax
Blair, George: Hypnotic Eye, The; Missourians, The; Tournament Tempo; Under Mexicali Stars
Blair, Jon: Anne Frank Remembered; Schindler
Blair, Les: Bad Behaviour
Blair, Mark: Confessions of a Serial Killer

Blake, Andrew: Miami Hot Talk
Blake, T. C.: Nightflyers
Blakemore, Michael: Country Life; Privates on Parade
Blakeney, Eric: Gun Shy
Blanc, Michel: Dead Tired (Grosse Fatigue)
Blanchard, John: Last Polka, The; Really Weird Tales; Shriek If You Know What I Did Last Friday the 13th
Blank, Les: Burden of Dreams; Mance Lipscomb: A Well-Spent Life
Blanks, Jamie: Urban Legend; Valentine
Blatty, William Peter: Exorcist III: Legion; Ninth Configuration, The
Blaustein, Berry: Beyond the Mat
Bleckner, Jeff: Beast, The; Brotherly Love; Rear Window; Target: Favorite Son; When Your Lover Leaves; White Water Summer
Blier, Bertrand: Beau Pere; Buffet Froid (Cold Cuts); Get Out Your Handkerchiefs; Going Places; Ménage; Merci La Vie; My Best Friend's Girl; My Man (Mon Homme); Too Beautiful for You
Block, Bruce: Princess Academy, The
Bloom, Jason: Bio-Dome; Dead Simple; Overnight Delivery
Bloom, Jeffrey: Blood Beach; Dogpound Shuffle; Flowers in the Attic; Stick-Up, The
Bloom III, George Jay: Brothers in Arms
Bloomfield, George: Deadly Companion; Nothing Personal; To Kill a Clown
Blot, Phillippe: Arrogant, The; Running Wild
Blumenthal, Andy: Bloodfist 2
Bluth, Don: All Dogs Go to Heaven; American Tail, An; Anastasia; Hans Christian Andersen's Thumbelina; Land Before Time, The; Rock-a-Doodle; Secret of NIMH, The; Titan A.E.; Troll in Central Park, A
Blystone, John G.: Block-Heads; Dick Turpin; Great Guy; Our Hospitality; Swiss Miss
Blyth, David: Death Warmed Up; My Grandpa Is a Vampire; Red-Blooded American Girl
Blyth, Jeff: Cheetah
Bnarbic, Paul: Cold Front
Bochner, Hart: High School High; PCU
Bodon, Jean: Hidden Fears
Bodrov, Sergei: Prisoner of the Mountains; Running Free
Boetticher, Budd: Bullfighter and the Lady, The; Decision at Sundown; Man from the Alamo, The; Ride Lonesome; Rise and Fall of Legs Diamond, The; Tall T, The
Bogart, Paul: Cancel My Reservation; Canterville Ghost, The; Class of '44; Heidi Chronicles, The; Marlowe; Oh, God, You Devil!; Power, Passion, and Murder; Skin Game (1971); Torch Song Trilogy
Bogayevicz, Yurek: Anna; Exit in Red; Three of Hearts
Bogdanovich, Josef: Boxoffice
Bogdanovich, Peter: Cat's Meow, The; Daisy Miller; Illegally Yours; Last Picture Show, The; Mask (1985); Noises Off; Paper Moon; Picture Windows; Rescuers, Stories of Courage, "Two Women"; Saint Jack; Targets; Texasville; They All Laughed; Thing Called Love, The; What's Up, Doc?
Bogner, Willy: Fire, Ice & Dynamite
Bohus, Ted A.: Regenerated Man, The; Vampire Vixens from Venus
Bohusz, Michael: Uninvited, The
Boisrone, Michel: Catherine & Co.; Love and the Frenchwoman; Tales of Paris; Voulez Vous Danser avec Moi? (Will You Dance with Me?)
Boisset, Yves: Dog Day; Purple Taxi, The
Boivan, Jerome: Barjo; Baxter
Bokanowski, Patrick: L'Ange (The Angel)
Boleslawski, Richard: Garden of Allah, The; Last of Mrs. Cheney, The; Les Misérables; Operator 13; Painted Veil, The; Rasputin and the Empress; Theodora Goes Wild
Boll, Heinrich: Germany In Autumn
Bologna, Joseph: Love Is All There Is
Bolognini, Mauro: Husbands and Lovers; La Grande Bourgeoise; Oldest Profession, The
Bolotin, Craig: Light It Up; That Night
Bolson, William T.: Sleeping with Strangers
Bolt, Ben: Big Town, The; Space Rangers (TV Series)
Bolt, Robert: Lady Caroline Lamb
Bond, Timothy: Deadly Harvest; Goosebumps: The Haunted Mask; Lost World, The; Return to the Lost World; Running Wild
Bond III, James: Def by Temptation
Bondarchuk, Sergei: War and Peace; Waterloo
Bonerz, Peter: Nobody's Perfekt; Police Academy 6: City Under Siege; When Things Were Rotten (TV Series)
Bonifer, Mike: Lipstick Camera
Bonk, Ron: City of the Vampires; Vicious Sweet, The
Bonnard, Mario: Last Days of Pompeii (1960)
Bonniere, René: Dream Man; Halfback of Notre Dame, The
Bonns, Miguel Iglesias: Night of the Howling Beast
Bookwalter, J. R.: Dead Next Door, The; Kingdom of the Vampire; Ozone; Polymorph; Robot Ninja; Sandman, The (1996)
Boorman, John: Beyond Rangoon; Deliverance; Emerald Forest, The; Excalibur; Exorcist II: The Heretic; General, The; Hell in the Pacific; Hope and Glory; Point Blank; Tailor of Panama, The; Where the Heart Is; Zardoz
Boos, H. Gordon: Forgotten City; Red Surf
Booth, Connie: Fawlty Towers (TV Series)
Borau, José Luis: On the Line
Borchers, Donald P.: Grave Secrets
Borden, John: Native Americans, The
Borden, Lizzie: Erotique; Love Crimes; Working Girls
Boris, Robert: Buy and Cell; Frank & Jesse; Oxford Blues; Steele Justice
Borman, Arthur: ... And God Spoke
Bornedal, Ole: Nightwatch
Borris, Clay: Alligator Shoes; Prom Night IV—Deliver Us from Evil; Quiet Cool; Someone to Die For; Suspicious Agenda
Borsos, Phillip: Dr. Bethune; Far From Home: The Adventures of YellowDog; Grey Fox, The; Mean Season, The; One Magic Christmas
Bortman, Michael: Crooked Hearts
Borzage, Frank: Farewell to Arms, A; Flirtation Walk; His Butler's Sister; History Is Made at Night; I've Always Loved You; Mannequin; Moonrise; Mortal Storm, The; Shining Hour, The; Smilin' Through; Stage Door Canteen; Strange Cargo; Three Comrades
Boskovich, John: Without You I'm Nothing
Boulting, John: Heavens Above; I'm All Right Jack; Lucky Jim
Boulting, Roy: Brothers In Law; Heavens Above; Last Word, The; Moving Finger, The; Run for the Sun; There's a Girl in My Soup
Bourguignon, Serge: A Coeur Joie (Head over Heels); Sundays and Cybèle
Bourla, David: When Time Expires
Bouvier, Robert: City in Panic
Bovon, Jean: Messin' with the Blues
Bowab, John: Gabe Kaplan as Groucho; Love at the Top
Bowen, David R.: Secret Life of Jeffrey Dahmer, The
Bowen, Jenny: Street Music; Wizard of Loneliness, The
Bowen, John: Dark Secrets; Lethal Games
Bowers, George: Body and Soul; Hearse, The; My Tutor; Private Resort
Bowes, Tom: Two Moon July
Bowey, John R.: Mutator
Bowman, Richard: Tick, The (TV Series)
Bowman, Rob: Airborne; X-Files, The (1998)
Bowser, Kenneth: In a Shallow Grave
Box, Muriel: Rattle of a Simple Man; Truth About Women, The
Boxell, Tim: Aberration
Boyd, Daniel: Chillers; Heroes of the Heart; Invasion of the Space Preachers
Boyd, Don: East of Elephant Rock; Kleptomania; Twenty-One
Boyd, Julianne: Eubie!
Boyer, Jean: Circonstances Attenuantes; Crazy for Love; Fernandel the Dressmaker
Boyle, Danny: Beach, The; Life Less Ordinary, A; Shallow Grave; Trainspotting

Boyum, Steve: Meet the Deedles
Bozzetto, Bruno: Allegro Non Troppo
Bradbury, Robert N.: Between Men; Blue Steel; Dawn Rider; Forbidden Trails; Kid Ranger; Lawless Frontier; Lucky Texan; Man from Utah, The; Rainbow Valley; Riders of Destiny; Riders of the Rockies; Sing, Cowboy, Sing; Star Packer, The; Texas Terror; Trail Beyond, The; Trouble in Texas; West of the Divide; Westward Ho
Braddock, Reb: Curdled
Bradford, Samuel: Teen Vamp
Bradley, Al: Cross Mission; Iron Warrior; Miami Cops
Bradley, David: They Saved Hitler's Brain
Bradshaw, John: Big Slice, The; Breakout; Full Disclosure; Lethal Tender; Specimen; That's My Baby; Undertaker's Wedding, The
Bradshaw, Randy: Blades of Courage; Last Train Home; Song Spinner
Brahm, John: Guest in the House; Hangover Square; Man from U.N.C.L.E., The (TV Series); Miracle of Our Lady of Fatima, The; Singapore; Thriller (TV Series); Undying Monster, The; Wintertime
Brakhage, Stan: Dog Star Man
Bralver, Bob: Midnight Ride; Rush Week
Brambilla, Marco: Demolition Man; Excess Baggage
Branagh, Kenneth: Dead Again; Hamlet; Henry V; Love's Labour's Lost; Mary Shelley's Frankenstein; Midwinter's Tale, A; Much Ado About Nothing; Peter's Friends
Brand, Joshua: Pyromaniac's Love Story, A
Brand, Larry: Drifter, The; Masque of the Red Death (1989); Overexposed; Paranoia; Till the End of the Night
Brander, Richard: Sizzle Beach, U.S.A.
Brando, Marlon: One-Eyed Jacks
Brandon, Clark: Skeeter
Brandstrom, Charlotte: Business Affair, A; Road to Ruin (1991); Sweet Revenge
Brannon, Fred: Dangers of the Canadian Mounted; King of the Rocketmen; Purple Monster Strikes, The; Radar Men from the Moon; Zombies of the Stratosphere (Satan's Satellites) (Serial)
Braoude, Patrick: Great, My Parents Are Divorcing
Brascia, Dominick: Evil Laugh; Hard Rock Nightmare
Brass, Tinto: Caligula
Brault, Michel: Paper Wedding
Brauman, Jack: Zombie Nightmare
Brauner, Franklin: Wild Side
Braunsteen, Joseph: Rest in Pieces
Braverman, Charles: Brotherhood of Justice; Hit and Run; Prince of Bel Air
Bray, Kevin: All About the Benjamins
Brayne, William: Flame to the Phoenix, A
Breakston, George: Manster, The; Scarlet Spear, The
Brealey, Gil: Test of Love, A
Breathnach, Paddy: Blow Dry; I Went Down
Breen, Julian: Alien Arsenal; Frankenstein Reborn!; Prehysteria! 3
Breen, Richard L.: Stopover Tokyo
Breillat, Catherine: Fat Girl; Romance
Breiman, Valerie: Love & Sex
Brel, Jacques: Franz
Brelis, Tia: Trading Mom
Brellat, Catherine: 36 Fillette
Breman, Valerie: Going Overboard
Bren, Milton H.: Three for Bedroom C
Brenon, Herbert: Dancing Mothers; Peter Pan
Brescia, Alfonso: White Fang and the Hunter
Bresciani, Andrea: Through the Looking Glass
Bresson, Robert: Devil, Probably, The; Diary of a Country Priest; Lancelot of the Lake; L'Argent; Man Escaped, A; Mouchette; Pickpocket
Brest, Martin: Beverly Hills Cop; Going in Style; Meet Joe Black; Midnight Run; Scent of a Woman
Bretherton, Howard: Bar-20 Rides Again; Below the Border; Call of the Prairie; Carson City Cyclone; Dawn on the Great Divide; Down Texas Way; Eagle's Brood; Ghost Town Law; Hidden Valley Outlaws; In Old Colorado; Ladies They Talk About; Outlaws of the Desert; Pirates of the Prairie; Riders of the Rio Grande; San Antonio Kid; Three on the Trail; Twilight on the Trail; West of the Law
Brewer, Otto: Phantom Empire (1935); Postal Inspector; Radio Ranch (Men with Steel Faces, Phantom Empire)
Breziner, Salome: Fast Sofa; Occasional Hell, An; Tollbooth
Briant, Michael E.: Dr. Who: Revenge of the Cybermen
Brice, Monte: Dr. Who: Revenge of the Cybermen
Brickman, Marshall: Lovesick; Manhattan Project, The; Simon; Sister Mary Explains It All
Brickman, Paul: Men Don't Leave; Risky Business
Bridges, Alan: Brief Encounter; D.P.; Out of Season; Pudd'nhead Wilson; Return of the Soldier, The; Shooting Party, The
Bridges, Beau: Seven Hours to Judgment; Wild Pair, The
Bridges, James: Baby Maker, The; Bright Lights, Big City; China Syndrome, The; Mike's Murder; Paper Chase, The; Perfect; 30-Sep-55; Urban Cowboy
Bright, Matthew: Freeway; Freeway 2: Confessions of a Trickbaby
Brill, Steven: Heavyweights; Late Last Night; Little Nicky
Brinckerhoff, Burt: Can You Hear the Laughter? The Story of Freddie Prinze; Cracker Factory; Remington Steele (TV series)
Britten, Lawrence: Whose Child Am I?
Brizzi, Gaetan: Fantasia 2000
Brock, Deborah: Rock 'n' Roll High School Forever; Slumber Party Massacre II
Brocka, Lino: Fight for Us
Broderick, John: Swap, The (Sam's Song); Warrior and the Sorceress, The
Broderick, Matthew: Infinity
Brodie, Kevin: Dog of Flanders, A; Mugsy's Girls; Treacherous
Bromell, Henry: Panic
Bromfield, Rex: Cafe Romeo; Home Is Where thé Hart Is; Love at First Sight; Melanie
Bromley-Davenport, Harry: Erasable You
Bromski, Jacek: Alice
Brook, Clive: On Approval
Brook, Peter: King Lear; Lord of the Flies; Mahabharata, The; Marat/Sade; Meetings with Remarkable Men
Brookner, Howard: Bloodhounds of Broadway
Brooks, Adam: Almost You
Brooks, Albert: Defending Your Life; Lost in America; Modern Romance; Mother; Muse, The; Real Life
Brooks, Bob: Tattoo
Brooks, James L.: As Good as It Gets; Broadcast News; I'll Do Anything; Terms of Endearment
Brooks, Joseph: If Ever I See You Again; Invitation to the Wedding; You Light Up My Life
Brooks, Mel: Blazing Saddles; Dracula: Dead and Loving It; High Anxiety; History of the World, Part One, The; Life Stinks; Producers, The; Robin Hood: Men in Tights; Silent Movie; Spaceballs; Twelve Chairs, The; Young Frankenstein
Brooks, Richard: Battle Circus; Bite the Bullet; Blackboard Jungle, The; Brothers Karamazov, The; Cat on a Hot Tin Roof; Catered Affair, The; Deadline USA; $ (Dollars); Elmer Gantry; Fever Pitch; In Cold Blood; Last Hunt, The; Last Time I Saw Paris, The; Looking for Mr. Goodbar; Lord Jim; Professionals, The; Something of Value; Sweet Bird of Youth; Wrong Is Right
Brooks, Robert: Who Shot Pat?
Broomfield, Nick: Aileen Wuornos: Selling of a Serial Killer; Chicken Ranch; Dark Obsession; Heidi Fleiss, Hollywood Madame; Monster in a Box
Bross, Eric: Chippendales Murder, The; On the Line (2001); Restaurant; Stranger Than Fiction; Ten Benny
Brower, Otto: Devil Horse, The; Fighting Caravans; Hard Hombre; Law of the Sea; Scarlet River; Spirit of the West
Brown, Barry: Cloud Dancer
Brown, Barry Alexander: Lonely in America
Brown, Bruce: Endless Summer, The; Endless Summer II

Brown, Clarence: Ah, Wilderness; Angels in the Outfield; Anna Christie; Anna Karenina; Chained; Conquest; Eagle, The; Edison, The Man; Emma; Flesh and the Devil; Free Soul, A; Goose Woman, The; Gorgeous Hussy, The; Human Comedy, The; Idiot's Delight; Inspiration; Intruder in the Dust; It's a Big Country; Last of the Mohicans, The; National Velvet; Of Human Hearts; Possessed; Rains Came, The; Romance; Sadie McKee; Song of Love; They Met in Bombay; To Please a Lady; White Cliffs of Dover, The; Wife vs. Secretary; Woman of Affairs, A; Yearling, The
Brown, Drew: Ah, Wilderness; Angels in the Outfield; Anna Christie; Anna Karenina; Chained; Conquest; Eagle, The; Edison, The Man; Emma; Flesh and the Devil; Free Soul, A; Goose Woman, The; Gorgeous Hussy, The; Human Comedy, The; Idiot's Delight; Inspiration; Intruder in the Dust; It's a Big Country; Last of the Mohicans, The; National Velvet; Of Human Hearts; Possessed; Rains Came, The; Romance; Sadie McKee; Song of Love; They Met in Bombay; To Please a Lady; White Cliffs of Dover, The; Wife vs. Secretary; Woman of Affairs, A; Yearling, The
Brown, Edwin Scott: Prey, The
Brown, Evert: This Is America, Charlie Brown
Brown, Georg Stanford: Alone in the Neon Jungle; Dangerous Relations; Miracle of the Heart; Roots: The Next Generation; Vietnam War Story
Brown, Gregory: Dead Man Walking; Stranger by Night; Street Asylum
Brown, Harry: Knickerbocker Holiday
Brown, Jim: Woody Guthrie—Hard Travelin'
Brown, Karl: White Legion
Brown, Larry: Pink Angels
Brown, Mark: Two Can Play That Game
Brown, Melville: Check and Double Check
Brown, Mitch: Deathshot
Brown, Richard: True Story of Frankenstein, The
Brown, Rowland: Blood Money
Brown, William H.: Casino Royale
Browning, Kirk: You Can't Take It with You
Browning, Philip: Shapeshifter
Browning, Ricou: Daring Game
Browning, Tod: Blackbird, The; Devil Doll, The (1936); Dracula; Freaks; Mark of the Vampire; Outside the Law; Unknown, The; West of Zanzibar; Where East Is East; White Tiger
Brownlow, Kevin: Buster Keaton: A Hard Act to Follow; Unknown Chaplin
Brownrigg, S. F.: Don't Look in the Basement; Poor White Trash II; Thinkin' Big
Bruce, James: Headless Body in Topless Bar; Love to Kill; Suicide Club, The
Bruce, John: Adventures of Sherlock Holmes, The (Series)
Bruestle, Martin: Sopranos, The (TV series)
Brunel, Adrian: Old Spanish Custom, An
Bruno, John: Virus
Brusati, Franco: Bread and Chocolate; Sleazy Uncle, The; To Forget Venice
Brustellin, Alf: Germany In Autumn
Bryant, Charles: Salome
Bryden, Bill: Aria
Buchanan, Larry: Beyond the Doors; Free, White, and 21; Goodbye, Norma Jean; Loch Ness Horror, The; Mars Needs Women
Buchowetzki, Dimitri: Othello; Swan, The
Buchs, Julio: Bullet for Sandoval, A
Buck, Chris: Tarzan (1999)
Buck, Douglas: Cutting Moments
Buckalew, Bethel: My Boys Are Good Boys
Buckhantz, Allan A.: Last Contract, The
Bucksey, Colin: Blue Money; Curiosity Kills; Dealers; McGuffin, The; Midnight's Child
Bucquet, Harold S.: Adventures of Tartu; Dr. Kildare's Strange Case; Dragon Seed; On Borrowed Time; Without Love
Budd, Colin: Hurricane Smith
Budd, Robin: Return to Never Land
Buechler, John Carl: Cellar Dweller; Dungeonmaster, The; Friday the 13th, Part VII: The New Blood; Ghoulies III; Troll
Bugajski, Richard: Clearcut; Interrogation
Bui, Tony: Three Seasons
Buitenhuis, Penelope: Boulevard
Bulajic, Veljko: Day that Shook the World, The
Bunce, Alan: Babar: The Movie
Bunche, Peter Gathings: Never 2 Big
Buntzman, Mark: Exterminator 2, The
Buñuel, Joyce: Dirty Dishes
Buñuel, Luis: Age of Gold; Ascent to Heaven (Mexican Bus Ride); Belle de Jour; Criminal Life of Archibaldo de la Cruz,The; Death in the Garden; Diary of a Chambermaid; Discreet Charm of the Bourgeoisie, The; El (This Strange Passion); El Bruto (The Brute); Exterminating Angel, The; Great Madcap, The; Illusion Travels by Streetcar; L'Age D'Or; Land Without Bread; Los Olvidados; Milky Way, The; Nazarin; Phantom of Liberty, The; Simon of the Desert; Susanna; That Obscure Object of Desire; Tristana; Un Chien Andalou; Viridiana; Woman without Love, A; Wuthering Heights
Buravsky, Aleksandr: Out of the Cold
Buravsky, Alexander: Sacred Cargo
Burchett, Mark: Vamps: Deadly Dream Girls
Burdeau, George: Native Americans, The
Burdis, Ray: Love, Honor & Obey
Burge, Robert: Keaton's Cop; Vasectomy
Burge, Stuart: Julius Caesar; Othello
Burke, James: In Dark Places
Burke, Martyn: Last Chase, The; Pirates of Silicon Valley
Burke, William: Dangerous Passage
Burkin, Stuart: Cash Crop
Burman, Tom: Meet the Hollowheads
Burnama, Jopi: Ferocious Female Freedom Fighters
Burnett, Charles: Glass Shield, The; Nightjohn; Selma Lord Selma; To Sleep with Anger
Burnett, J. Max: Possums
Burnett, Robert Meyer: Free Enterprise
Burns, Allan: Just Between Friends
Burns, Edward: Brothers McMullen, The; No Looking Back; She's the One; Sidewalks of New York (2001)
Burns, Keith: Ernie Kovacs: Television's Original Genius
Burns, Ken: Baseball: A Film by Ken Burns; Civil War, The; Thomas Jefferson
Burns, Ric: Way West, The
Burr, Jeff: Johnny Mysto; Leatherface—the Texas Chainsaw Massacre III; Night of the Scarecrow; Offspring, The; Pumpkinhead II: Bloodwings; Puppet Master 5: The Final Chapter; Puppet Master Four; Stepfather II; Werewolf Reborn!
Burrowes, Geoff: Return to Snowy River, Part II; Run
Burrows, James: Partners
Burrus, Ron: Getting Personal
Burstall, Tim: Attack Force Z; Great Expectations—The Untold Story; Kangaroo; Naked Country, The; Nightmare at Bittercreek
Burton, David: Fighting Caravans; Lady by Choice
Burton, Geoff: Sum of Us, The
Burton, Kenneth J.: Merlin's Shop of Mystical Wonders
Burton, Richard: Dr. Faustus
Burton, Sean: Curse III: Blood Sacrifice
Burton, Tim: Batman; Batman Returns; Beetlejuice; Ed Wood; Edward Scissorhands; Frankenweenie; Mars Attacks!; Pee-Wee's Big Adventure; Planet of the Apes (2001); Sleepy Hollow
Buscemi, Steve: Animal Factory; Trees Lounge
Buschmann, Christel: Comeback
Bushell, Anthony: Terror of the Tongs, The
Bushnell Jr., William H.: Four Deuces, The
Butler, David: April in Paris; Bright Eyes; By the Light of the Silvery Moon; Calamity Jane; Captain January; Caught in the Draft; Connecticut Yankee, A; Doubting Thomas; It's a Great Feeling; Just Imagine; King Richard and the Crusaders; Little Colonel, The; Littlest Rebel, The; Look for the Silver Lining; Lullaby of Broadway; Princess and the Pirate, The; Road to Mo-

rocco; San Antonio; Story of Seabiscuit, The; Tea for Two; Thank Your Lucky Stars; They Got Me Covered; You'll Find Out

Butler, George: Pumping Iron; Pumping Iron II: The Women

Butler, Robert: Blue Knight, The; Computer Wore Tennis Shoes, The; Hot Lead and Cold Feet; James Dean—A Legend in His Own Time; Moonlighting (1985) (TV Pilot); Night of the Juggler; Now You See Him, Now You Don't; Out on a Limb; Scandalous John; Star Trek: The Cage; Strange New World; Turbulence; Underground Aces; Up the Creek; White Mile

Butoy, Hendel: Fantasia 2000; Rescuers Down Under

Butterworth, Jez: Birthday Girl

Buzby, Zane: Last Resort

Buzzell, Edward: At the Circus; Best Foot Forward; Go West; Honolulu; Neptune's Daughter; Ship Ahoy; Song of the Thin Man; Woman of Distinction, A

Bye, Ed: Red Dwarf (TV Series)

Byrne, David: True Stories

Byrum, John: Heart Beat; Inserts; Razor's Edge, The; Whoopee Boys, The

Byrum, Rob: Scandalous

Bythewood, Reggie Rock: Dancing in September

C.K., Louis: Pootie Tang

Caan, James: Hide in Plain Sight

Cabanne, Christy: Dixie Jamboree; Jane Eyre; Last Outlaw, The; Mummy's Hand, The; One Frightened Night; Scared to Death; World Gone Mad, The

Cabot, Ellen: Beach Babes from Beyond; Beach Babes 2: Cave Girl Island; Blonde Heaven; Deadly Embrace

Cacoyannis, Michael: Iphigenia; Stella; Story of Jacob and Joseph, The; Sweet Country; Trojan Women, The; Zorba the Greek

Cadiff, Andy: Leave It to Beaver

Caesar, Richard: Calling, The

Cahn, Edward L.: Four Skulls of Jonathan Drake, The; Invasion of the Saucer Men; Invisible Invaders; It! The Terror from Beyond Space; Jet Attack; Law and Order; Motorcycle Gang; She Creature, The; Suicide Battalion; Voodoo Woman; Zombies of Mora Tav

Caiano, Mario: Adios, Hombre; Nightmare Castle; Shanghai Joe

Cain, Christopher: Amazing Panda Adventure, The; Gone Fishin'; Next Karate Kid, The; Principal, The; Pure Country; Rose Hill; Stone Boy, The; That Was Then ... This Is Now; Wheels of Terror; Where the River Runs Black; Young Guns

Cajayon, Gene: Debut, The

Calenda, Antonio: One Russian Summer

Callas, John: Lone Wolf

Callaway, Thomas L.: Murdercycle

Callner, Marty: Pee-Wee Herman Show, The

Callow, Simon: Ballad of the Sad Cafe, The

Camacho, Art: Little Bigfoot; Power Within, The

Camerini, Mario: Ulysses

Cameron, James: Abyss, The; Aliens; Piranha Part Two: The Spawning; Terminator, The; Terminator 2: Judgment Day; Titanic; True Lies

Cameron, Ken: Brides of Christ; Fast Talking; Good Wife, The; Miracle at Midnight; Monkey Grip; Oldest Confederate Widow Tells All

Cameron, Ray: Bloodbath at the House of Death

Camfield, Douglas: Ivanhoe

Cammell, Donald: Demon Seed; Performance; White of the Eye

Camp, Joe: Benji; Benji the Hunted; Double McGuffin, The; For the Love of Benji; Hawmps!; Oh, Heavenly Dog!

Campanile, Pasquale Festa: When Women Had Tails; When Women Lost Their Tails

Campbell, Doug: Cupid; Perfect Tenant, The; Season of Fear; Zapped Again

Campbell, Graeme: Blood Relations; Deadlock 2; Dream House; Into the Fire; Man in the Attic, The; Volcano: Fire on the Mountain

Campbell, Martin: Cast a Deadly Spell; Criminal Law; Defenseless; Edge of Darkness; Goldeneye; Mask of Zorro, The; No Escape; Vertical Limit

Campion, Anna: Loaded

Campion, Jane: Angel at My Table, An; Holy Smoke; Piano, The; Portrait of a Lady, The; Sweetie; Two Friends

Campisi, Gabriel: Alien Agenda, The (TV Series)

Campogalliani, Carlo: Goliath and the Barbarians

Campus, Michael: Education of Sonny Carson, The; Mack, The; Z.P.G. (Zero Population Growth)

Camus, Marcel: Black Orpheus

Camus, Mario: Holy Innocents

Candy, John: Hostage for a Day

Cannistraro, Richard: Violated

Cannon, Danny: I Still Know What You Did Last Summer; Judge Dredd; Phoenix; Young Americans, The

Cannon, Dyan: End of Innocence, The

Cantet, Laurent: Human Resources

Canutt, Yakima: Dangers of the Canadian Mounted; Federal Operator 99

Capitani, Giorgio: Lobster for Breakfast; Ruthless Four, The

Capon, Naomi: Six Wives of Henry VIII, The (TV Series)

Cappello, Frank: American Yakuza; No Way Back

Capra, Berndt: Mindwalk

Capra, Frank: Arsenic and Old Lace; Bitter Tea of General Yen, The; Broadway Bill; Here Comes the Groom; Hole in the Head, A; It Happened One Night; It's a Wonderful Life; Ladies of Leisure; Lady for a Day; Lost Horizon; Meet John Doe; Mr. Deeds Goes to Town; Mr. Smith Goes to Washington; Platinum Blonde; Pocketful of Miracles; Riding High; State of the Union; Strange Case of the Cosmic Rays, The; Strong Man, The; That Certain Thing; You Can't Take It with You

Carax, Léos: Lovers on the Bridge

Carayiannis, Costa: Land of the Minotaur

Carbol, Larry: Ghost Warrior

Carbonnaux, Norbert: Candide

Card, Lamar: Clones, The

Cardenas, Hernan: Island Claws

Cardiff, Jack: Dark of the Sun (Mercenaries) (1968); Freakmaker; My Geisha

Cardinal, Roger: Malarek

Cardona Jr., René: Beaks: the Movie; Tintorera; Treasure of the Amazon

Cardona Sr., René: Rock 'n' Roll Wrestling Women vs. the Aztec Ape; Rock 'n' Roll Wrestling Women vs. the Aztec Mummy

Cardone, J. S.: Black Day Blue Night; Climate for Killing, A; Forsaken, The; Outside Ozona; Shadow Hunter; Shadowzone; True Blue

Cardos, John "Bud": Act of Piracy; Dark, The; Day Time Ended, The; Kingdom of the Spiders; Mutant; Outlaw of Gor

Care, Peter: Act of Piracy; Dark, The; Day Time Ended, The; Kingdom of the Spiders; Mutant; Outlaw of Gor

Carew, Topper: Talkin' Dirty After Dark

Carle, Gilles: Blood of the Hunter

Carlei, Carlo: Flight of the Innocent; Fluke

Carley, Kurt Mac: Sexual Intent

Carlino, Lewis John: Class; Great Santini, The; Sailor Who Fell from Grace with the Sea, The

Carlsen, Henning: Hunger (1966); Wolf at the Door; World of Strangers, A

Carnage, Art: Horrible Doctor Bones, The; L.I.P. Service (1999)

Carnahan, Joe: Blood, Guts, Bullets & Octane

Carnahan, Matthew: Black Circle Boys

Carné, Marcel: Assassins de L'Ordre, Les (Law Breakers); Bizarre, Bizarre; Children of Paradise, The; Le Jour Se Leve (Daybreak (1939)); Les Visiteurs Du Soir

Carner, Charles Robert: Fixer, The

Caro, Marc: City of Lost Children, The; Delicatessen

Caron, Glenn Gordon: Clean and Sober; Love Affair; Picture Perfect; Wilder Napalm

Chechik, Jeremiah S.: Avengers, The; Benny & Joon; Diabolique; National Lampoon's Christmas Vacation; Tall Tale: The Unbelievable Adventures of Pecos Bill
Cheek, Douglas: C.H.U.D.
Chekmayan, Ara: Forever James Dean
Chelsom, Peter: Funnybones; Hear My Song; Mighty, The; Serendipity; Town & Country
Chen, Joan: Autumn in New York; Xiu Xiu: The Sent Down Girl
Chenal, Pierre: Crime and Punishment; Man from Nowhere, The; Native Son
Cher: If These Walls Could Talk
Chereau, Patrice: L'Homme Blessé (The Wounded Man); Queen Margot
Cherot, Christopher Scott: Hav Plenty
Cherry, John: Hav Plenty
Cherry III, John R.: Dr. Otto and the Riddle of the Gloom Beam; Ernest Goes to Africa; Ernest Goes to Camp; Ernest Goes to Jail; Ernest in the Army; Ernest Rides Again; Ernest Saves Christmas; Ernest Scared Stupid; Slam Dunk Ernest
Chetwynd, Lionel: Color of Justice; Hanoi Hilton, The; Varian's War
Cheveldave, Randolph: Deathgame
Chiaramonte, Andrew: Twogether
Chiodo, Stephen: Killer Klowns from Outer Space
Chionglo, Mel: Midnight Dancer
Chivers, Collin: Michael Jackson Moonwalker
Cholodenko, Lisa: High Art
Chomsky, Marvin J.: Anastasia: The Mystery of Anna; Attica; Billionaire Boys Club; Brotherhood of the Rose; Deliberate Stranger, The; Evel Knievel; Holocaust; Inside the Third Reich; Little Ladies of the Night; Murph the Surf; Nairobi Affair; Roots; Shaming, The; Tank; Victory at Entebbe
Chong, Thomas: Cheech and Chong's Next Movie; Corsican Brothers, The; Far Out Man; Nice Dreams; Still Smokin'
Chopra, Joyce: Danger of Love; Lemon Sisters, The; Murder in New Hampshire; Smooth Talk
Chouraqui, Elie: Harrison's Flowers; Love Songs (Paroles et Musique); Man on Fire
Christensen, Benjamin: Mockery; Seven Footprints to Satan; Witchcraft Through the Ages (HAXAN)
Christian, Nathaniel: California Casanova; Club Fed
Christian, Roger: Battlefield Earth; Final Cut, The; Masterminds; Nostradamus; Sender, The; Starship; Underworld
Christian-Jaque: Legend of Frenchie King, The; Love and the Frenchwoman; Nana; Pearls of the Crown, The
Christopher, Bojesse: Out in Fifty
Christopher, Mark: 54
Chubbuck, Lyndon: Kiss Toledo Goodbye; Naked Souls; Right Temptation, The
Chudnow, Byron: Amazing Dobermans; Daring Dobermans, The; Doberman Gang, The
Chudnow, David: Amazing Dobermans
Chukhrai, Grigori: Ballad of a Soldier
Chukhrai, Pavel: Thief, The
Chun, Oxide Pang: Bangkok Dangerous
Chung, Sun: City War
Ciccoritti, Gerard: Graveyard Shift; Paris France; Prayer in the Dark, A; Psycho Girls; Understudy, The: Graveyard Shift II
Cicero, Nando: Twice a Judas
Cimber, Matt: Butterfly; Fakeout; Single Room Furnished; Time to Die, A; Yellow Hair and the Fortress of Gold
Cimino, Michael: Deer Hunter, The; Desperate Hours (1990); Heaven's Gate; Sicilian, The; Sunchaser; Thunderbolt and Lightfoot; Year of the Dragon
Civirani, Osvaldo: Dead for a Dollar
Clabaugh, Richard: Python
Clair, René: A Nous la Liberte; And Then There Were None; Avant Garde Program #2; Beauties of the Night; Crazy Ray, The; Forever and a Day; Ghost Goes West, The; I Married a Witch; Italian Straw Hat, The; Le Million; Le Voyage Imaginaire; Love and the Frenchwoman; Quatorze Juliet; Under the Roofs of Paris
Clark, B. D.: Galaxy of Terror; Protector (1998)
Clark, Bob: American Clock, The; Baby Geniuses; Black Christmas; Children Shouldn't Play with Dead Things; Christmas Story, A; Deathdream; From the Hip; Loose Cannons; Murder by Decree; My Summer Story; Porky's; Porky's II: The Next Day; Rhinestone; Tribute; Turk 182
Clark, Brandon: Alligator II
Clark, Colbert: Mystery Squadron; Three Musketeers, The; Warning Shadows
Clark, Duane: Bitter Harvest; Shaking the Tree
Clark, Greydon: Danse Macabre; Final Justice; Forbidden Dance, The; Joy Sticks; Killer Instinct; Out of Sight Out of Mind; Return, The (1980); Satan's Cheerleaders; Skinheads; Uninvited, The; Wacko; Without Warning
Clark, James B.: Dog of Flanders, A; Flipper; Island of the Blue Dolphins; Misty; My Side of the Mountain
Clark, Jim: Madhouse
Clark, John: Fast Lane Fever
Clark, Larry: Another Day in Paradise; Bully; Kids
Clark, Lawrence Gordon: Belfast Assassin; Midnight Man; On Dangerous Ground; Romance on the Orient Express
Clark, Matt: Da
Clark, William: Goodbye Bird, The; Windrunner
Clarke, Alan: Scum
Clarke, James Keneim: Going Undercover
Clarke, Malcolm: Voices From a Locked Room
Clarke, Robert: Hideous Sun Demon, The
Clarke, Shirley: Connection, The (1961)
Clarke-Williams, Zoe: Men
Clavell, James: Last Valley, The; To Sir with Love
Claxton, William F.: Bonanza (TV Series)
Clayton, Jack: Great Gatsby, The; Innocents, The (1961); Lonely Passion of Judith Hearne, The; Room at the Top; Something Wicked This Way Comes
Cleese, John: Fawlty Towers (TV Series)
Clegg, Tom: Any Man's Death; Children of the Full Moon; House That Bled to Death, The; Inside Man, The; McVicar; Sharpe (TV Series); Stroke of Midnight
Clemens, Brian: Captain Kronos: Vampire Hunter
Clemens, William: Case of the Stuttering Bishop, The; Case of the Velvet Claws, The
Clement, Dick: Bullshot (Bullshot Crummond); Catch Me a Spy; Water
Clement, René: And Hope to Die; Day and the Hour; Forbidden Games; Gervaise; Is Paris Burning?; Joy House; Purple Noon; Rider on the Rain
Clements, Ron: Aladdin; Great Mouse Detective, The; Hercules (Animated) (1997); Little Mermaid, The
Clifford, Graeme: Burke and Wills; Caracara; Deception; Frances; Gleaming the Cube; Last Don, The; Past Tense; Turn of the Screw, The (1989)
Clift, Dension: Mystery of the Marie Celeste, The (The Phantom Ship)
Clifton, Elmer: Assassin of Youth (Marijuana); Captain America; Cyclone in the Saddle; Days of Old Cheyenne; Deep in the Heart of Texas; Down to the Sea in Ships; Not Wanted; Seven Doors to Death; Skull and Crown
Clifton, Peter: Song Remains the Same, The
Cline, Eddie: Art of Buster Keaton, The; Bank Dick, The; Breaking the Ice; Buster Keaton Festival Vol. 1–3; Cowboy Millionaire; Dude Ranger; Ghost Catchers, The; Hook, Line and Sinker; My Little Chickadee; Never Give a Sucker an Even Break; Peck's Bad Boy with the Circus; Private Buckaroo; Private Snuffy Smith; Three Ages, The; Villain Still Pursued Her, The
Cloche, Maurice: Monsieur Vincent
Clokey, Art: Gumby The Movie
Cloos, Hans Peter: Germany In Autumn
Clouse, Robert: Amsterdam Kill, The; Big Brawl, The; Black Belt Jones; China O'Brien; China O'Brien 2; Deadly Eyes; Enter the Dragon; Force Five; Game of Death; Gymkata; Pack, The; Ultimate Warrior, The

Clouzot, Henri-Georges: Diabolique; Jenny Lamour; Le Corbeau (The Raven (1943)); Manon; Mystery of Picasso, The; Wages of Fear, The
Clucher, E. B.: Sons of Trinity, The; They Call Me Trinity; Trinity Is Still My Name
Clurman, Harold: Deadline at Dawn
Clyde, Craig: Little Heroes
Coates, Lewis: Adventures of Hercules, The; Hercules; Star Crash
Coburn, Glenn: Blood Suckers from Outer Space
Cochran, Stacy: Boys (1996); My New Gun
Cocteau, Jean: Beauty and the Beast; Blood of a Poet; Les Parents Terribles; Orpheus; Testament of Orpheus, The
Coe, Fred: Thousand Clowns, A
Coe, Wayne: Grim Prairie Tales
Coen, Joel: Barton Fink; Big Lebowski, The; Blood Simple; Fargo; Hudsucker Proxy, The; Man Who Wasn't There, The (2001); Miller's Crossing; Raising Arizona
Cohen, Daniel: Diamond Men
Cohen, Eli: Quarrel, The; Soft Kill, The; Under the Domim Tree
Cohen, Howard R.: Deathstalker IV: Match of the Titans; Saturday the 14th; Space Raiders; Time Trackers
Cohen, Jem: Benjamin Smoke
Cohen, Joel: Frankenstein Sings
Cohen, Larry: Ambulance, The; As Good as Dead; Black Caesar; Demon (God Told Me To); Hell Up in Harlem; Housewife; It Lives Again; It's Alive!; It's Alive III: Island of the Alive; Original Gangstas; Perfect Strangers; Private Files of J. Edgar Hoover, The; Q; Return to Salem's Lot, A; Special Effects; Stuff, The; Wicked Stepmother, The
Cohen, Martin B.: Rebel Rousers
Cohen, Peter M.: Whipped
Cohen, Rob: Daylight; Dragon: The Bruce Lee Story; Dragonheart; Fast and the Furious, The; Rat Pack, The; Skulls, The; Small Circle of Friends, A
Cohen, S. E.: Martial Law
Cohen, Steve: Devil in the Flesh; Tough and Deadly
Cohen, Thomas A.: Massive Retaliation
Cohn, Alan: Dead Man on Campus
Cohn, Michael: Interceptor; Snow White: A Tale of Terror; When the Bough Breaks
Cohn, Peter: Drunks
Coke, Cyril: Pride and Prejudice
Cokliss, Harley: Black Moon Rising; Hercules and the Lost Kingdom; Malone; Warlords of the 21st Century
Cole, Henry: Shameless
Cole, Marcus: From the Mixed-Up Files of Mrs. Basile. Frankweiler
Cole, Nigel: Saving Grace
Cole, Tristan DeVere: Dive, The
Cole, William: Unveiled
Coleman, Lionel: I'm the One That I Want
Coles, John David: Good Fight, The; Rising Son; Signs of Life
Colizzi, Giuseppe: Ace High; Boot Hill
Colla, Richard A.: Battlestar Galactica; Don't Look Back: The Story of Leroy "Satchel" Paige; Fuzz; Prize Pulitzer, The: The Roxanne Pulitzer Story; Storm and Sorrow; Ultimate Deception
Collachia, Jeanne: Bread and Salt
Collard, Cyril: Savage Nights
Collector, Robert: Red Heat
Collier, James F.: China Cry; Cry from the Mountain; Hiding Place, The
Collins, Bob: Bronx Executioner, The
Collins, Boon: Abducted; Abducted II; Spirit of the Eagle
Collins, Edward: Evil Town
Collins, Lewis D.: Longhorn
Collins, Max Allan: Mommy; Mommy 2: Mommy's Day
Collins, Robert: Gideon's Trumpet; Life and Assassination of the Kingfish,The; Mafia Princess; Our Family Business
Collinson, Peter: African Rage; Earthling, The; House on Garibaldi Street; Italian Job, The; Man Called Noon, The; Sell-Out, The; Spiral Staircase, The; Ten Little Indians; Tomorrow Never Comes
Collum, Jason Paul: 5 Dark Souls
Colombo, Fernando: Skyline; Star Knight
Colpaert, Carl: Crew, The; Delusion; Facade; In the Aftermath: Angels Never Sleep
Columbus, Chris: Adventures in Babysitting; Bicentennial Man; Harry Potter and the Sorcerer's Stone; Heartbreak Hotel; Home Alone; Home Alone 2: Lost in New York; Mrs. Doubtfire; Nine Months; Only the Lonely; Stepmom
Comencini, Luigi: Misunderstood; Till Marriage Do Us Part
Comfort, Lance: Courageous Mr. Penn; Great Day
Compton, J. C.: Buckeye and Blue
Compton, Richard: Angels Die Hard; Deadman's Curve; Macon County Line; Ransom; Return to Macon County; Super Force; Wild Times
Condon, Bill: Candyman: Farewell to the Flesh; Dead in the Water; Gods and Monsters; Murder 101; Sister, Sister; White Lie
Coninx, Syijn: Daens
Conn, Nicole: Claire of the Moon
Connell, Myles: Opportunists, The
Connelly, Marc: Green Pastures
Connelly, Theresa: Polish Wedding
Connon, Raymond: Swing It, Sailor
Connor, Kevin: At the Earth's Core; From Beyond the Grave; Goliath Awaits; Hollywood Detective, The; Iran Days of Crisis; Land That Time Forgot, The; Lion of Africa, The; Little Riders, The; Motel Hell; Old Curiosity Shop, The; People That Time Forgot, The; Sunset Grill
Conrad, Claude: Birthday Boy, The
Conrad, Patrick: Mascara
Conrad, Robert: Bandits; Crossfire
Conrad, William: Side Show; Two on a Guillotine
Conte, Therese: Chasing Dreams
Contner, James A.: Cover Girl Murders, The; Hitler's Daughter; Return of Eliot Ness, The; 10 Million Dollar Getaway, The
Convy, Bert: Weekend Warriors
Conway, Gary: Sara Dane
Conway, Jack: Boom Town; Dragon Seed; Girl from Missouri, The; Honky Tonk; Hucksters, The; Julia Misbehaves; Let Freedom Ring; Libeled Lady; Love Crazy; Our Modern Maidens; Red-Headed Woman; Saratoga; Tale of Two Cities, A; Too Hot to Handle; Twelve Miles Out; Unholy Three; Viva Villa!
Conway, James L.: Boogens, The; Donner Pass: The Road to Survival; Hangar 18; Incredible Rocky Mountain Race, The; Last of the Mohicans
Coogan, Rif: Invisible Maniac; Psycho Cop 2
Cook, Barry: Mulan
Cook, Bruce R.: Nightwish
Cook, Donovan: Return to Never Land
Cook, Fielder: Big Hand for the Little Lady, A; Hideaways, The; I Know Why the Caged Bird Sings; Member of the Wedding, The; Patterns; Seize the Day
Cook, Lorna: Spirit: Stallion of the Cimarron
Cook, Philip: Beyond the Rising Moon (Star Quest); Invader (1993)
Cook, Troy: Takeover, The
Cooke, Alan: King Lear
Cooke, William: Freakshow
Coolidge, Martha: Angie; Bare Essentials; Crazy in Love; Flamingo Rising, The; Hammered: The Best of Sledge; Introducing Dorothy Dandridge; Joy of Sex, The; Lost in Yonkers; Out to Sea; Plain Clothes; Rambling Rose; Real Genius; Three Wishes; Valley Girl
Cooney, Michael: Jack Frost (1997); Jack Frost 2
Cooper, Hal: Brady Bunch, The (TV series)
Cooper, Jackie: Hammered: The Best of Sledge; Izzy & Moe; Leave 'em Laughing; Marathon; M*A*S*H (TV Series); Night They Saved Christmas, The; Rodeo Girl; Rosie; White Mama
Cooper, Merian C.: Chang; King Kong
Cooper, Peter H.: Ordinary Heroes

Cooper, Stuart: Bitter Vengeance; Bloodhounds II; Chameleon; Dancing with Danger; Dead Ahead; Disappearance, The; Hunted (1997); Long Hot Summer, The; Out of Annie's Past; Payoff; Ticket, The
Coppola, Christopher: Deadfall; Dracula's Widow; Gunfighter (1997)
Coppola, Francis Ford: Apocalypse Now; Bellboy and the Playgirls, The; Bram Stoker's Dracula; Conversation, The; Cotton Club, The; Dementia 13;. Finian's Rainbow; Gardens of Stone; Godfather, The; Godfather Epic, The; Godfather, Part II, The; Godfather, Part III, The; Jack; New York Stories; One from the Heart; Outsiders, The; Peggy Sue Got Married; Rain People, The; Rainmaker, The (1997); Rumble Fish; Tucker: A Man and His Dream; You're a Big Boy Now
Coppola, Sofia: Virgin Suicides, The,
Coraci, Frank: Murdered Innocence; Waterboy, The; Wedding Singer, The
Corbiau, Gerard: Farinelli Il Castrato; Music Teacher, The
Corbucci, Bruno: Aladdin; Cop in Blue Jeans, The; Miami Supercops
Corbucci, Sergio: Con Artists, The; Django; Hellbenders, The; Sonny and Jed; Super Fuzz
Corcoran, Bill: Sherlock Holmes and the Incident at Victoria Falls; Survive the Night
Corea, Nicholas: Incredible Hulk Returns, The
Corley, David L.: Angel's Dance
Corley, David R.: Executive Power
Corlish, Frank B.: Longest Hunt, The
Corman, Roger: Apache Woman; Atlas; Attack of the Crab Monsters; Bloody Mama; Bucket of Blood, A; Carnival Rock; Creature from the Haunted Sea, The; Day the World Ended, The; Fall of the House of Usher, The; Frankenstein Unbound; Gas-s-s-s; Gunslinger; Haunted Palace, The; I, Mobster; Intruder, The (1961); It Conquered the World; Little Shop of Horrors, The (1960); Machine-Gun Kelly; Masque of the Red Death, The (1964); Pit and the Pendulum, The; Premature Burial, The; Raven, The; Saga of the Viking Women and Their Voyage to the Waters of the Great Sea Serpent, The (Viking Women and the Sea Serpent, The); Sorority Girl; St. Valentine's Day Massacre, The; Swamp Women; Tales of Terror; Terror, The; Tomb of Ligeia; Tower of London; Trip, The; Undead, The; War of the Satellites; Wasp Woman (1960); Wild Angels, The; X (The Man with the X-Ray Eyes)
Corneau, Alain: Choice of Arms, A; Fort Saganne; Tous les Matins du Monde
Cornelius, Henry: Genevieve; I Am a Camera; Passport to Pimlico
Cornell, John: Almost an Angel; "Crocodile" Dundee II
Cornfield, Hubert: Night of the Following Day, The; Plunder Road; Pressure Point
Cornwell, Stephen: Killing Streets; Marshal Law; Philadelphia Experiment 2, The
Corona, Alfonso: Deathstalker III—The Warriors from Hell; World of the Vampires
Corr, Eugene: Desert Bloom
Correll, Charles: Cry in the Wind; Deadly Desire; Fortune Dane; In the Deep Woods; Stepsister, The
Correll, Richard: Ski Patrol
Corrente, Michael: American Buffalo; Federal Hill; Outside Providence
Corrigan, Lloyd: Daughter of the Dragon
Corson, Ian: Malicious
Cort, Bud: Ted & Venus
Corti, Axel: King's Whore, The
Cosby Jr., William H.: King's Whore, The
Coscarelli, Don: Beastmaster, The; Phantasm; Phantasm II; Phantasm III: Lord of the Dead; Phantasm IV: Oblivion; Survival Quest
Cosmatos, George Pan: Cassandra Crossing, The; Cobra (1986); Escape to Athena; Leviathan; Massacre in Rome; Of Unknown Origin; Rambo: First Blood II; Restless; Shadow Conspiracy; Tombstone
Costa, Mario: Rough Justice
Costa-Gavras, Constantin: Betrayed; Hanna K.; Mad City; Missing; Music Box, The; Sleeping Car Murders, The; State of Siege; Z
Costner, Kevin: Dances with Wolves; Postman, The
Coto, Manny: Cover-Up; Dr. Giggles; Playroom; Star Kid
Cottafari, Vittorio: Goliath and the Dragon; Hercules and the Captive Women
Cotter, John: Mountain Family Robinson
Couffer, Jack: Living Free; Nikki, Wild Dog of the North; Ring of Bright Water
Coughlan, Ian: Alison's Birthday
Coulter, Allen: Stephen King's Golden Years (TV Series)
Courtland, Jerome: Diamonds on Wheels
Couturie, Bill: Dear America: Letters Home from Vietnam; Ed
Covert, Michael: American Strays
Covington, Hil: Adventures in Spying
Cowan, Rich: Basket, The
Cowan, Will: Thing that Couldn't Die, The
Coward, Noel: In Which We Serve
Cowen, William: Oliver Twist
Cox, Alex: Repo Man; Sid and Nancy; Straight to Hell; Walker; Winner, The
Cox, Brian: Scorpion Spring
Cox, James: Highway
Cox, Mitchell: Rule #3
Cox, Paul: Cactus; Innocence; Kostas; Lonely Hearts; Man of Flowers; My First Wife; Woman's Tale, A
Crabtree, Arthur: Fiend without a Face; Horrors of the Black Museum; Quartet
Crain, William: Blacula; Dr. Black and Mr. Hyde
Crane, Kenneth: Manster, The; Monster from Green Hell
Craven, Jay: Stranger in the Kingdom, A; Where the Rivers Flow North
Craven, Wes: Chiller; Deadly Blessing; Deadly Friend; Hills Have Eyes, The; Hills Have Eyes, The: Part Two; Invitation to Hell; Last House on the Left; Music of the Heart; Nightmare on Elm Street, A; People Under the Stairs, The; Scream; Scream 3; Scream 2; Serpent and the Rainbow, The; Shocker; Summer of Fear; Swamp Thing; Vampire in Brooklyn; Wes Craven's New Nightmare
Crawford, Wayne: Crime Lords
credited!, Not: Charlie, the Lonesome Cougar; Down Under; Johnny Carson: His Favorite Moments; Revenge of Dr. X, The; Spaghetti Western
Creme, Lol: Lunatic, The
Cremin, Kevin G.: Siringo
Crenna, Richard: Better Late than Never
Cribben, Mik: Beware! Children at Play
Crichton, Charles: Battle of the Sexes, The; Dead of Night; Fish Called Wanda, A; Lavender Hill Mob, The
Crichton, Michael: Coma; Great Train Robbery, The; Looker; Physical Evidence; Runaway; Westworld
Crichton, Robin: Silent Mouse
Crisp, Donald: Don Q, Son of Zorro; Navigator, The (1924)
Crispino, Armando: Autopsy; Commandos
Cristallini, Giorgio: You're Jinxed Friend, You Just Met Sacramento
Cristofer, Michael: Body Shots; Original Sin
Croghan, Emma-Kate: Love and Other Catastrophes
Crombie, Donald: Caddie; Irishman, The; Killing of Angel Street, The; Kitty and the Bagman
Cromwell, John: Abe Lincoln in Illinois; Ann Vickers; Anna and the King of Siam; Dead Reckoning; Enchanted Cottage, The; Goddess, The; I Dream Too Much; In Name Only; Little Lord Fauntleroy; Made for Each Other; Of Human Bondage; Prisoner of Zenda, The; Racket, The; Since You Went Away; So Ends Our Night; Son of Fury; Spitfire; Tom Sawyer
Cronenberg, David: Brood, The; Crash (1996); Dead Ringers; Dead Zone, The; eXistenZ; Fly, The; M. Butterfly; Naked Lunch; Rabid; Scanners; They Came from Within; Videodrome
Crooke, Evan: Killing Jar, The
Crosland, Alan: Beloved Rogue; Case of the Howling Dog, The; Don Juan; Jazz Singer, The

Crouch, William Forest: Reet, Petite and Gone
Crounse, Avery: Cries of Silence; Eyes of Fire; Invisible Kid, The
Crowe, Cameron: Almost Famous; Jerry Maguire; Say Anything; Singles; Vanilla Sky
Crowe, Christopher: Off Limits; Whispers in the Dark
Cruise, Tom: Fallen Angels
Crump, Owen: Gateway to the Mind
Cruze, James: Covered Wagon, The; Great Gabbo, The; Helldorado; I Cover the Waterfront; Mr. Skitch; Old Ironsides; Roaring Road, The
Crystal, Billy: Forget Paris; Mr. Saturday Night; 61*
Cuaron, Alfonso: Fallen Angels; Great Expectations; Little Princess, A
Cuerda, Jose Luis: Butterfly
Cuesta, Michael: L.I.E.
Cukor, George: Adam's Rib; Bhowani Junction; Bill of Divorcement, A; Born Yesterday; Camille; Corn Is Green, The; David Copperfield; Dinner at Eight; Double Life, A; Gaslight; Heller in Pink Tights; Holiday; It Should Happen to You; Justine; Keeper of the Flame; Les Girls; Let's Make Love; Life of Her Own, A; Little Women; Love Among the Ruins; My Fair Lady; Pat and Mike; Philadelphia Story, The; Rich and Famous; Romeo and Juliet; Song Without End; Star Is Born, A; Susan and God; Sylvia Scarlett; Travels with My Aunt; Two-Faced Woman; What Price Hollywood?; Woman's Face, A; Women, The
Cullingham, Mark: Cinderella; Dead on the Money; Princess Who Had Never Laughed, The
Cumming, Alan: Anniversary Party, The
Cummings, Bill: Bad Attitude
Cummings, Howard: Courtship
Cummings, Irving: Curly Top; Dolly Sisters, The; Double Dynamite; Down Argentine Way; Everything Happens at Night; Flesh and Blood (1922); Hollywood Cavalcade; In Old Arizona; Just Around the Corner; Little Miss Broadway; Louisiana Purchase; Poor Little Rich Girl (1936); Springtime in the Rockies
Cummins, James: Boneyard, The
Cundey, Dean: Honey, We Shrunk Ourselves
Cundieff, Rusty: Fear of a Black Hat; Sprung; Tales from the Hood
Cunha, Richard: Frankenstein's Daughter; Giant from the Unknown; Missile to the Moon; She Demons
Cunningham, Sean S.: Deepstar Six; Friday the 13th; Manny's Orphans (Come the Tigers); New Kids, The; Stranger Is Watching, A
Curran, William: Love, Cheat & Steal
Currier, Lavinia: Passion in the Desert
Curtis, Dan: Burnt Offerings; Curse of the Black Widow; Dead of Night; Dracula; Express to Terror; House of Dark Shadows; Intruders; Kansas City Massacre, The; Last Ride of the Dalton Gang, The; Love Letter, The; Me and the Kid; Melvin Purvis: G-Man; Night of Dark Shadows; Night Strangler, The; Trilogy of Terror; Trilogy of Terror II; War and Remembrance; Winds of War, The
Curtis, Douglas: Sleeping Car, The
Curtis, Jack: Flesh Eaters, The
Curtis-Hall, Vondie: Glitter; Gridlock'd
Curtiz, Michael: Adventures of Huckleberry Finn, The; Adventures of Robin Hood, The; Angels with Dirty Faces; Black Fury; Breath of Scandal, A; Cabin in the Cotton; Captain Blood; Captains of the Clouds; Casablanca; Case of the Curious Bride, The; Charge of the Light Brigade, The; Comancheros, The; Dive Bomber; Doctor X; Dodge City; Egyptian, The; Female; Flamingo Road; Force of Arms; Four Daughters; Helen Morgan Story, The; I'll See You in My Dreams; Jazz Singer, The; Jim Thorpe—All American; Kennel Murder Case, The; Kid Galahad; King Creole; Life with Father; Mildred Pierce; My Dream Is Yours; Mystery of the Wax Museum; Night and Day; Noah's Ark; Passage to Marseilles; Private Lives of Elizabeth and Essex, The; Proud Rebel, The; Romance on the High Seas; Santa Fe Trail; Sea Hawk, The; Sea Wolf, The; Strange Love of Molly Louvain, The; This Is the Army; Trouble Along the Way; Virginia City; We're No Angels; White Christmas; Yankee Doodle Dandy; Young Man with a Horn
Cybulski, Mary: Hellcab
Cypher, Julie: Teresa's Tattoo
Cyran, Catherine: Hostile Intentions; In the Heat of Passion II: Unfaithful; Sawbones; True Heart; White Wolves: A Cry in the Wild II
Czinner, Paul: As You Like It; Catherine the Great
Da Costa, Morton: Auntie Mame; Music Man, The
Daalder, Renee: Habitat; Massacre at Central High
Daboul, Samer: Suicide Ride
Dahl, John: Joy Ride; Kill Me Again; Last Seduction, The; Red Rock West; Rounders; Unforgettable
Dahlin, Bob: Monster in the Closet
Dahms, Heinrich: My Daughter's Keeper
Daldry, Stephen: Billy Elliot
Dale, Holly: Blood & Donuts
Dalen, Zale: Expect No Mercy
Dali, Salvador: Un Chien Andalou
Dallamano, Massimo: Black Veil for Lisa, A; Dorian Gray
D'Almeida, Neville: Lady on the Bus
Dalrymple, Ian: Storm in a Teacup
Dalva, Robert: Black Stallion Returns, The
D'Amato (Aristide Massaccesi), Joe: Buried Alive; Trap Them and Kill Them
Damiani, Damiano: Amityville II: The Possession; Bullet for the General, A; Confessions of a Police Captain; Empty Canvas, The; Inquiry, The; Warning, The
Damski, Mel: Badge of the Assassin; For Ladies Only; Happy Together; Legend of Walks Far Woman, The; Mischief; Wild Card; Yellowbeard
D'Andrea, Anthony: Thrillkill
Daniel, Rod: Beethoven's 2nd; K-9; Like Father, Like Son; Super, The; Teen Wolf
Daniels, Harold: Poor White Trash; Terror in the Haunted House
Daniels, Marc: I Married Joan (TV Series); Planet Earth; Star Trek (TV Series); Star Trek: The Menagerie
Danielsson, Tage: Adventures of Picasso, The
D'Anna, Claude: Salome
Danniel, Danniel: Egg
Danska, Herbert: Sweet Love, Bitter
Dante, Joe: Amazon Women on the Moon; 'Burbs, The; Explorers; Gremlins; Gremlins 2: The New Batch; Hollywood Boulevard; Howling, The; Innerspace; Matinee; Piranha; Police Squad!; Second Civil War, The; Small Soldiers; Twilight Zone—The Movie
Danton, Ray: Crypt of the Living Dead; Psychic Killer; Tales of the Unexpected; Vietnam War Story
D'Antoni, Philip: Seven-Ups, The
Danus, Richard: No Place to Hide
Darabont, Frank: Buried Alive; Green Mile, The; Majestic, The; Shawshank Redemption, The
Darby, Jonathan: Enemy Within, The; Hush
Dardenne, Luc: La Promesse
Darling, Joan: Check Is in the Mail, The; First Love; Mary Hartman, Mary Hartman (TV Series); Willa
Darlow, Michael: Merlin of the Crystal Cave
Darnell, Eric: Antz
D'Arrast, Harry: Topaze
Dash, Julie: Daughters of the Dust
Dash, Sean: Breakaway
Dassin, Jules: Brute Force; Canterville Ghost, The; Circle of Two; Dream of Passion, A; Naked City, The; Never on Sunday; Night and the City; Reunion in France; Rififi; Topkapi
Daugherty, Herschel: Light in the Forest, The; Wagon Train (TV Series)
Davenport, Harry: Xtro; Xtro II; Xtro: Watch the Skies (Xtro 3)
Davenport, Harry Bromley: Adventures of Young Brave, The
Daves, Delmer: Badlanders, The; Broken Arrow; Dark Passage; Demetrius and the Gladiators; Destination Tokyo; Drum Beat; Hanging Tree, The; Hollywood Canteen; Jubal; Kings Go Forth; Never Let Me Go; Parrish; Red House, The; Rome Ad-

venture; Spencer's Mountain; Summer Place, A; Task Force; 3:10 to Yuma
David, Charles: Lady on a Train
David, Lorena: Eastside
David, Pierre: Scanner Cop; Serial Killer
Davidson, Boaz: American Cyborg: Steel Warrior; Going Bananas; Hospital Massacre; Outside the Law; Solar Force
Davidson, Gordon: Trial of the Cantonsville Nine, The
Davidson, John-Paul: Grave Indiscretion
Davidson, Martin: Eddie and the Cruisers; Hard Promises; Heart of Dixie, The; Hero at Large; Long Gone; Lords of Flatbush, The
Davies, Howard: Secret Rapture, The
Davies, John: Married Man, A; Sleeping Murder; Why Didn't They Ask Evans?
Davies, John Howard: Mr. Bean
Davies, Robert: Saturday Night at the Palace
Davies, Terence: Distant Voices/Still Lives; House of Mirth, The; Long Day Closes, The; Neon Bible, The
Davies, Valentine: Benny Goodman Story, The
Davis, Andrew: Above the Law; Chain Reaction; Code of Silence; Collateral Damage; Final Terror, The; Fugitive, The; Package, The; Perfect Murder, A; Steal Big, Steal Little; Under Siege
Davis, B. J.: White Ghost
Davis, Barry: Don't Hang Up
Davis, Beau: Laser Mission
Davis, Desmond: Clash of the Titans; Love with a Perfect Stranger; Nice Girl Like Me, A; Ordeal by Innocence; Sign of Four, The
Davis, Eddie: Cisco Kid (TV Series); Color Me Dead
Davis, Gary: Conflict of Interest
Davis, John A.: Jimmy Neutron, Boy Genius
Davis, Julie: All Over the Guy; I Love You, Don't Touch Me!; Witchcraft VI: The Devil's Mistress
Davis, Lee: 3 A.M.
Davis, Michael: Eight Days a Week; 100 Girls
Davis, Michael Paul: Beanstalk
Davis, Mick: Match, The
Davis, Ossie: Cotton Comes to Harlem; Gordon's War
Davis, Peter: Hearts and Minds
Davis, Tamra: Best Men; Billy Madison; CB4; Crossroads (2002); Guncrazy (1950); Half Baked; Skipped Parts
Dawn, Norman: Two Lost Worlds
Dawn, Vincent: Rats; Strike Commando
Dawson, Anthony M.: Castle of Blood (Castle of Terror); Code Name: Wild Geese; Hercules, Prisoner of Evil; Indio; Indio 2: The Revolt; Invasion of the Flesh Hunters; Jungle Raiders; Killer Fish; Mr. Superinvisible; Stranger and the Gunfighter, The; Take a Hard Ride; Virgin of Nuremberg (Horror Castle)
Day, Ernest: Green Ice
Day, Robert: Avengers, The (TV Series); Corridors of Blood; First Man into Space, The; Grass Is Always Greener over the Septic Tank, The; Haunted Strangler, The; Initiation of Sarah, The; Lady from Yesterday, The; Man with Bogart's Face, The; Quick and the Dead, The; Scruples; Two-Way Stretch
Dayan, Josee: Hot Chocolate
Dayton, Lyman: Avenging, The; Baker's Hawk; Dream Machine
De Arminan, Jaime: Nest, The
De Baroncelli, Jacques: French Way, The
De Bont, Jan: Haunting, The; Speed; Speed 2: Cruise Control; Twister
De Bosio, Gianfranco: Moses
de Broca, Philippe: Cartouche; Jupiter's Thigh; King of Hearts; Le Cavaleur; Le Magnifique; Louisiana; Oldest Profession, The; Seven Deadly Sins, The; That Man from Rio
de Cordova, Frederick: Bedtime for Bonzo; Frankie and Johnny; I'll Take Sweden; Jack Benny Program, The (TV Series)
De Filippo, Eduardo: Shoot Loud, Louder ... I Don't Understand
de Gaetano, Alessandro: Project: Metalbeast
De Heer, Rolf: Alien Visitor; Encounter at Raven's Gate; Quiet Room, The
De Jong, Ate: Drop Dead Fred; Flight of Rainbirds, A; Highway to Hell
de la Bouillerie, Hubert: Apocalypse, The; Right to Remain Silent, The
de Leon, Gerardo: Brides of the Beast
De Leon, Marcus: Big Squeeze, The; Kiss Me a Killer
de Lussanet, Paul: Mysteries
De Martino, Alberto: Blood Link; Django Shoots First; Holocaust 2000; Scenes from a Murder; Tempter, The
de Mille, William C.: His Double Life; Miss Lulu Bett
De Niro, Robert: Bronx Tale, A
de Ossorio, Amando: Night of the Death Cult; Return of the Evil Dead; Tombs of the Blind Dead; When the Screaming Stops
De Palma, Brian: Blow Out; Body Double; Bonfire of the Vanities; Carlito's Way; Carrie; Casualties of War; Dressed to Kill; Fury, The (1978); Get to Know Your Rabbit; Greetings; Hi Mom; Home Movies; Mission: Impossible; Mission to Mars; Obsession; Phantom of the Paradise; Raising Cain; Scarface; Sisters (1973); Snake Eyes; Untouchables, The; Wedding Party, The; Wise Guys
De Santis, Giuseppe: Bitter Rice
de Segonzac, Jean: Mimic 2
De Sica, Vittorio: After the Fox; Bicycle Thief, The; Boccaccio 70; Garden of the Finzi-Continis, The; Gold of Naples, The; Indiscretion of an American Wife; Marriage Italian Style; Miracle in Milan; Shoeshine; Two Women; Umberto D; Woman Times Seven; Yesterday, Today and Tomorrow
De Sota, Bruno: Invasion of the Star Creatures
de Souza, Stephen: Street Fighter
de Toth, André: Dark Waters; House of Wax; Last of the Comanches; Man in the Saddle; Morgan the Pirate; Pitfall; Ramrod; Springfield Rifle; Stranger Wore a Gun, The
De Witt, Elmo: Enemy Unseen
Dear, William: Angels in the Outfield; Balloon Farm; Harry and the Hendersons; If Looks Could Kill; Television Parts Home Companion; Timerider; Wild America
Dearden, Basil: Captive Heart; Dead of Night; Khartoum; League of Gentlemen, The; Man Who Haunted Himself, The; Persuaders, The (TV Series); Sapphire; Smallest Show on Earth, The; Victim
Dearden, James: Cold Room, The; Kiss Before Dying, A; Pascali's Island; Rogue Trader
DeBello, John: Attack of the Killer Tomatoes; Happy Hour; Killer Tomatoes Eat France; Killer Tomatoes Strike Back; Return of the Killer Tomatoes
DeCaprio, Al: Sgt. Bilko (TV Series)
DeCerchio, Tom: Celtic Pride
Deck, James D.: Ravager
Decker, Craig: Spike & Mike's Festival of Animation
Decoin, Henri: Love and the Frenchwoman
DeConcini, Ennio: Hitler, the Last Ten Days
DeCoteau, David: Creepozoids; Curse of the Puppet Master; Dreamaniac; Lady Avenger; Leather Jacket Love Story; Petticoat Planet; Puppet Master III: Toulon's Revenge; Skeletons; Sorority Babes in the Slimeball Bowl-O-Rama; Witchouse
Deem, Miles: Savage Guns
DeFelitta, Frank: Dark Night of the Scarecrow; Scissors; Two Worlds of Jennie Logan, The
DeFelitta, Raymond: Cafe Society
DeFranco, Robert: Telling You
DeGuere, Philip: Dr. Strange
Dehlaui, Jamil: Born of Fire
Deimel, Mark: Perfect Match, The
Dein, Edward: Curse of the Undead; Leech Woman, The; Shack-Out on 101
Deitch, Donna: Common Ground; Criminal Passion; Desert Hearts; Devil's Arithmetic, The; Prison Stories: Women on the Inside; Women of Brewster Place, The
DeJarnett, Steve: Cherry 2000; Miracle Mile

Dekker, Fred: Monster Squad, The; Night of the Creeps; RoboCop 3
Del Monte, Peter: Invitation au Voyage; Julia and Julia
Del Prete, Deborah: Simple Justice
Del Ruth, Roy: Alligator People, The; Babe Ruth Story, The; Blessed Event; Blonde Crazy; Born to Dance; Broadway Melody of 1938; Broadway Melody of 1936; Broadway Rhythm; Bureau of Missing Persons; Chocolate Soldier, The; Du Barry Was a Lady; Employees' Entrance; Happy Landing; Kid Millions; Lady Killer; My Lucky Star; On Moonlight Bay; On the Avenue; Topper Returns; West Point Story, The
del Toro, Guillermo: Blade II; Cronos; Devil's Backbone, The; Mimic
Delannoy, Jean: Bernadette; Eternal Return, The; Love and the Frenchwoman; This Special Friendship
Delfiner, Suzanne: Bernadette; Eternal Return, The; Love and the Frenchwoman; This Special Friendship
Delia, Francis: Freeway
D'Elia, Bill: Feud, The
Dell, Jeffrey: Carlton-Browne of the F.O.
Delman, Jeffrey S.: Deadtime Stories
Delon, Nathalie: Sweet Lies
Delpeut, Peter: Forbidden Quest
Delplanque, Lionel: Deep in the Woods
DeLuca, Rudy: Transylvania 6-5000
DeLuise, Dom: Boys Will Be Boys; Hot Stuff
DeLuise, Michael: Almost Pregnant
Dembo, Richard: Dangerous Moves
Demetrakas, Johanna: Out of Line
Demeyer, Paul: Rugrats in Paris
DeMichel, Helen: Tarantella
Demichell, Tulio: Son of Captain Blood
DeMille, Cecil B.: Cheat, The; Cleopatra; Crusades, The; Greatest Show on Earth, The; King of Kings, The (1927); Madame Satan; Male and Female; Northwest Mounted Police; Plainsman, The; Reap the Wild Wind; Road to Yesterday, The; Samson and Delilah; Story of Dr. Wassell, The; Ten Commandments, The; Ten Commandments, The; Unconquered; Union Pacific
Demme, Jonathan: Beloved; Caged Heat; Citizen's Band; Cousin Bobby; Crazy Mama; Fighting Mad; Last Embrace, The; Married to the Mob; Melvin and Howard; Philadelphia; Silence of the Lambs; Something Wild; Stop Making Sense; Subway Stories; Swimming to Cambodia; Swing Shift; Who Am I This Time?
Demme, Ted: Beautiful Girls; Blow; Life; Monument Ave.; Ref, The; Who's the Man?
DeMoro, Pierre: Hellhole; Savannah Smiles
Dempsey, Patrick: Ava's Magical Adventure
Demy, Jacques: Donkey Skin (Peau D'Àne); Lola; Seven Deadly Sins, The; Slightly Pregnant Man, A; Umbrellas of Cherbourg, The
Denis, Jean-Pierre: Field of Honor
Dennis, Charles: Reno and the Doc
Dennis, Claire: Chocolat
Densham, Pen: Houdini; Kiss, The; Moll Flanders; Zoo Gang, The
Deodato, Ruggero: Barbarians, The; Cannibal Holocaust; Cut and Run; Dial: Help; Lone Runner; Phantom of Death
DePalma, Frank: Private War
DePew, Joseph: Beverly Hillbillies Go Hollywood, The
Deray, Jacques: Borsalino; Swimming Pool, The
Derek, John: Bolero; Fantasies; Ghosts Can't Do It; Tarzan the Ape Man
Derrickson, Scott: Hellraiser: Inferno
Deruddere, Dominique: Suite 16; Wait Until Spring, Bandini
des Rozier, Hughes: Blue Jeans
DeSalvo, Anne: Amati Girls, The
Deschanel, Caleb: Crusoe; Escape Artist, The
Desfontanes, Henri: Queen Elizabeth
DeSimone, Tom: Concrete Jungle, The (1982); Hell Night; Reform School Girls
Desmarais, James: Road Lawyers and Other Briefs
Desmond, Brian: River of Unrest
D'Esposito, Louis: Opposite Corners
Deutch, Howard: Article 99; Getting Even with Dad; Great Outdoors, The; Grumpier Old Men; Odd Couple II, The; Pretty in Pink; Replacements, The; Some Kind of Wonderful
Deval, Jacques: Club des Femmes
Devenish, Ross: Bleak House; Overindulgence; Touch of Frost, A (TV Series)
Devereaux, Maurice: Lady of the Lake
Deville, Michel: La Lectrice (The Reader); Peril; Voyage en Douce
DeVito, Danny: Amazing Stories (TV Series); Death to Smoochy; Hoffa; Matilda; Ratings Game, The; Throw Momma from the Train; War of the Roses, The
Devor, Robinson: Woman Chaser, The
Dewey, Richard Lloyd: Rockwell: A Legend of the Wild West
DeWolf, Patrick: Innocent Lies
Dexter, John: I Want What I Want; Virgin Soldiers, The
Dey, Tom: Shanghai Noon
Deyries, Bernard: Shanghai Noon
Dhomme, Sylvain: Seven Deadly Sins, The
Di Leo, Fernando: Kidnap Syndicate, The; Manhunt (1973) (The Italian Connection); Violent Breed, The
Di Leo, Mario: Final Alliance
Diamonde, Lucian S.: Forbidden Zone: Alien Abduction
DiBergi, Jim: Return of Spinal Tap, The
Dichter, Jon: Operator, The
DiCillo, Tom: Box of Moonlight; Johnny Suede; Living in Oblivion; Real Blonde, The
Dick, Kirby: Sick: The Life and Death of Bob Flanagan, Supermasochist
Dick, Nigel: Dead Connection; Deadly Intent; Private Investigations
Dickerson, Ernest R.: Blind Faith; Bones; Bulletproof; Futuresport; Juice; Monday Night Mayhem; Strange Justice; Surviving the Game; Tales from the Crypt: Demon Knight
Dickinson, Thorold: Gaslight; High Command, The
Dickson, Lance: Hollywood Heartbreak
Dickson, Paul: Satellite in the Sky
Didden, Marc: Istanbul
Diege, Samuel: Ride 'em Cowgirl
Diegues, Carlos: Bye Bye Brazil; Subway to the Stars
Dienstag, Alan: Moneytree, The
Dieterle, William: Boots Malone; Devil and Daniel Webster, The; Elephant Walk; Hunchback of Notre Dame, The; Juarez; Kismet; Life of Emile Zola, The; Omar Khayyam; Portrait of Jennie; Quick, Let's Get Married; Salome; Satan Met a Lady; Scarlet Dawn; September Affair; Story of Louis Pasteur, The
Dignam, Erin: Denial
Dilello, Richard: Riot (1996) (TV Movie)
Diling, Bert: Dead Easy
Dillon, John Francis: Behind the Mask; Call Her Savage
DiMarco, Steve: Back in Action; Prisoner of Love
Dimsey, Ross: Blue Fire Lady
Dimster-Denk, Dennis: Mikey
Dindal, Mark: Cats Don't Dance; Emperor's New Groove, The
Dingo, Pece: Midnight Cabaret
Dingwall, John: Custodian, The
Dinner, Michael: Crew, The; Heaven Help Us; Hot to Trot; Off Beat
Dippe, Mark A. Z.: Spawn
Dirlam, John: Fatal Instinct
DiSalle, Mark: Kickboxer; Perfect Weapon
Disney, Walt: Fantasia; Fun and Fancy Free; Officer and a Duck, An (Limited Gold Edition 2); Peter and the Wolf; Pinocchio; Three Caballeros, The
Ditchburn, Robbie: Deadline
Dixon, Ivan: Percy & Thunder
Dixon, Jamie: Bram Stoker's Shadowbuilder
Dixon, Ken: Slave Girls from Beyond Infinity
Dizdar, Jasmin: Beautiful People
Dmytryk, Edward: Alvarez Kelly; Anzio; Back to Bataan; Behind the Rising Sun; Bluebeard; Broken Lance; Caine Mutiny,

The; Captive Wild Woman; Carpetbaggers, The; Cornered; Crossfire; Devil Commands, The; Hitler's Children; Left Hand of God, The; Mirage; Mountain, The; Murder My Sweet; Raintree County; Shalako; Soldier of Fortune; Tender Comrade; Till the End of Time; Walk on the Wild Side; Warlock; Where Love Has Gone; Young Lions, The
Dobb, Tony: Blue Tornado
Dobbs, Frank Q.: Uphill All the Way
Dobkin, David: Clay Pigeons
Dobson, Kevin James: Gold Diggers: The Secret of Bear Mountain; Miracle in the Wilderness; Squizzy Taylor
Docter, Peter: Monsters, Inc.
Dodson, James: Deadly Rivals; Quest of the Delta Knights
Dohler, Don: Alien Factor, The
Doillon, Jacques: La Puritaine; Ponette
Dolman, Martin: American Tiger; Hands of Steel
Dominik, Andrew: Chopper
Donahue, Patrick G.: Savage Instinct
Donaldson, Roger: Bounty, The; Cadillac Man; Cocktail; Dante's Peak; Getaway, The; Marie; No Way Out; Sleeping Dogs; Smash Palace; Species; Thirteen Days; White Sands
Donavan, Tom: Love Spell
Done, Harris: Firetrap; Storm Tracker
Donehue, Vincent J.: Lonelyhearts; Peter Pan; Sunrise at Campobello
Donen, Stanley: Arabesque; Bedazzled; Blame It on Rio; Charade; Damn Yankees; Deep in My Heart; Funny Face; Give a Girl a Break; Grass Is Greener, The; Indiscreet; It's Always Fair Weather; Little Prince, The; Love Is Better Than Ever; Movie Movie; On the Town; Pajama Game, The; Royal Wedding; Saturn 3; Seven Brides for Seven Brothers; Singin' in the Rain; Staircase; Surprise Package; Two for the Road
Dong, Arthur: Coming Out Under Fire
Doniger, Walter: Mad Bull
Donnelly, Thomas Michael: Garden of Redemption, The; Soldier's Sweetheart, A
Donnelly, Tom: Blindsided; Quicksilver
Donner, Clive: Babes in Toyland; Charlie Chan and the Curse of the Dragon Queen; Christmas Carol, A; Luv; Merlin & the Sword; Not a Penny More, Not a Penny Less; Nude Bomb, The (Return of Maxwell Smart,The); Oliver Twist; Scarlet Pimpernel, The; Stealing Heaven; Terror Stalks the Class Reunion; Thief of Baghdad (1978); To Catch a King; What's New, Pussycat?
Donner, Richard: Conspiracy Theory; Fugitive, The (TV Series); Goonies, The; Inside Moves; Ladyhawke; Lethal Weapon; Lethal Weapon 2; Lethal Weapon 3; Lethal Weapon 4; Maverick; Omen, The; Radio Flyer; Scrooged; Superman; Tales from the Crypt (TV Series); Toy, The; Twilight Zone, The (TV Series); Wanted: Dead or Alive (TV Series)
Donoghue, Mary Agnes: Paradise
Donohue, Jack: Assault on a Queen; Babes in Toyland; Lucky Me; Watch the Birdie; Yellow Cab Man, The
Donohue, John Clark: Marvelous Land of Oz, The
Donovan, Jim: Provocateur
Donovan, King: Promises, Promises
Donovan, Martin: Apartment Zero; Death Dreams; Mad at the Moon; Somebody Is Waiting; Substitute, The
Donovan, Paul: Def-Con 4; George's Island; I Worship His Shadow; Northern Extremes; Tomcat: Dangerous Desires
Doob, Nick: Down from the Mountain
Doran, Thomas: Spookies
Dorfmann, Jacques: Shadow of the Wolf
Dornhelm, Robert: Cold Feet; Echo Park; Requiem for Dominic
Dörrie, Doris: Enlightenment Guaranteed; Me and Him; Men … (1985); Nobody Loves Me
Dotan, Shimon: Finest Hour, The; Sworn Enemies; Warriors (1994)
Douchet, Jean: Six in Paris (Paris Vue par …)
Doueiri, Ziad: West Beirut
Douglas, Gordon: Black Arrow, The (1948); Call Me Bwana; Chuka; Detective, The; Dick Tracy versus Cueball; Doolins of Oklahoma; First Yank into Tokyo; Follow That Dream; General Spanky; Girl Rush; Great Missouri Raid, The; Harlow; If You Knew Susie; In Like Flint; Kiss Tomorrow Goodbye; Lady in Cement; McConnell Story, The; Nevadan, The; Only the Valiant; Rio Conchos; Robin & the Seven Hoods; Saps at Sea; Sincerely Yours; Slaughter's Big Rip-Off; Them!; They Call Me Mister Tibbs; Tony Rome; Up Periscope; Viva Knievel; Young at Heart; Zenobia; Zombies on Broadway
Douglas, Kirk: Posse
Douglas, Peter: Tiger's Tale, A
Doumani, Lorenzo: Amore! (1993); Bug Buster; Knockout; Mad About You; Storybook
Douy, Max: Seven Deadly Sins, The
Dovzhenko, Alexander: Arsenal; Earth; Zvenigora
Dowling, Kevin: Last Rites; Mojave Moon; Sum of Us, The
Downey, Robert: America; Greaser's Palace; Hugo Pool; Putney Swope; Rented Lips; Too Much Sun; Up the Academy
Doyle, Tim: Road Lawyers and Other Briefs
Drach, Michel: Les Violons du Bal
Dragin, Bert L.: Summer Camp Nightmare; Twice Dead
Dragojevic, Srdjan: Wounds, The
Dragoti, Stan: Love at First Bite; Man with One Red Shoe, The; Mr. Mom; Necessary Roughness; She's Out of Control
Drake, Jim: Based on an Untrue Story; Legacy for Leonette; Mary Hartman, Mary Hartman (TV Series); Police Academy 4: Citizens on Patrol; Speed Zone
Drake, Oliver: Across the Rio Grande; Mummy and the Curse of the Jackals, The
Drake, T. Y.: Keeper, The
Draskovic, Boro: Vukovar
Draven, Danny: Horrorvision
Drazan, Anthony: Hurlyburly; Imaginary Crimes; Zebrahead
Dreesen, Lance W.: Terror Tract
Dresch, Fred: My Samurai
Dreville, Jean: Sputnik
Drew, Di: Right Hand Man, The; Trouble in Paradise
Dreyer, Carl: Day of Wrath; Gertrude; Leaves from Satan's Book; Master of the House (Du Skal Aere Din Hustru); Ordet; Passion of Joan of Arc, The; Vampyr (1931)
Dreyfuss, Richard: Anything for Love
Dridi, Karim: Bye-Bye
Driscoll, Richard: Comic, The
Driver, Charla: Deadly Target
Driver, John: Marvelous Land of Oz, The
Driver, Sara: Sleepwalker
Drove, Antonio: Tunnel, The
Drury, David: Defense of the Realm; Forever Young; Hostile Waters; Intrigue; Prime Suspect 3; Rhodes; Split Decisions
Druxman, Michael B.: Doorway, The
Dryfoos, Susan W.: Line King, The
Dryhurst, Michael: Hard Way, The
Drysdale, Lee: Leather Jackets
Du Chau, Frederik: Quest for Camelot
Dubin, Charles S.: Cinderella; Gathering, Part II, The; Moving Violation; Roots: The Next Generation; Silent Rebellion
Dubov, Adam: Dead Beat
Dubroux, Daniele: Diary of a Seducer
Duchemin, Remy: A La Mode
Dudley, Terence: All Creatures Great and Small
Duffell, Peter: Experience Preferred … But Not Essential; Far Pavilions, The; House That Dripped Blood, The; Inside Out; King of the Wind; Letters to an Unknown Lover
Duffy, Martin: Bumblebee Flies Anyway, The
Dugan, Dennis: Beverly Hills Ninja; Big Daddy; Brain Donors; Happy Gilmore; Problem Child; Saving Silverman
Dugdale, George: Slaughter High
Dugowson, Martine: Mina Tannenbaum
Duguay, Christian: Adrift; Art of War, The; Assignment, The; Joan of Arc (1999); Live Wire; Model by Day; Scanners 3: The Takeover; Scanners 2: The New Order; Screamers
Duigan, John: Flirting; Journey of August King, The; Lawn Dogs; Leading Man, The; Molly; Romero; Sirens; Wide Sargasso Sea; Winter of Our Dreams; Year My Voice Broke, The

Duke, Bill: America's Dream; Cemetery Club, The; Deep Cover; Hoodlum; Killing Floor, The; Rage in Harlem, A; Raisin in the Sun, A; Sister Act 2: Back in the Habit
Duke, Daryl: Griffin and Phoenix: A Love Story; I Heard the Owl Call My Name; Payday; President's Plane Is Missing, The; Silent Partner, The; Tai-Pan; Thornbirds, The
Dumoulin, Georges: Nous N'Irons Plus Au Bois
Duncan, Patrick: 84 Charlie Mopic; Live! From Death Row
Duncan, Peter: Children of the Revolution
Dunham, Duwayne: Homeward Bound: The Incredible Journey; Little Giants
Dunne, Griffin: Addicted to Love; Lisa Picard is Famous; Practical Magic
Dunne, Philip: Wild in the Country
Dunning, George: Yellow Submarine
Dunsky, Evan: Alarmist, The
Dupeyron, Francois: La Machine
Dupont, E. A.: Neanderthal Man, The; Variety
Duran, Ciro: Tropical Snow
Durand, Rudy: Tilt
Durgay, Attila: Matt the Gooseboy
Durlow, David: Tailspin
Durston, David E.: I Drink Your Blood; Stigma
Dutcher, Richard: Brigham City; God's Army
Dutton, Charles S.: First Time Felon
Duvall, Robert: Angelo, My Love; Apostle, The
Duvivier, Julien: Anna Karenina; Black Jack; Burning Court, The; Diabolically Yours; Golgotha; Great Waltz, The; Little World of Don Camillo, The; Lydia; Panique; Pepe Le Moko; Tales of Manhattan
Dwan, Allan: Around the World; Brewster's Millions; Cattle Queen of Montana; Enchanted Island; Escape to Burma; Gorilla, The; Heidi; Hollywood Party; Iron Mask, The; Look Who's Laughing; Manhandled; Montana Belle; Northwest Outpost; Passion; Pearl of the South Pacific; Rebecca of Sunnybrook Farm; Restless Breed, The; Robin Hood; Sands of Iwo Jima; Slightly Scarlet; Tennessee's Partner; Three Musketeers, The
Dwan, Robert: You Bet Your Life (TV Series)
Dyal, H. Kaye: Project: Eliminator
Dyke, Robert: Moon Trap
Dylan, Jesse: How High
Dzhordzhadze, Nan: Chef in Love, A
Dziki, Waldemar: Young Magician, The
Eady, David: Three Cases of Murder
Earnshaw, Ellen: Human Desires
Eason, B. Reeves "Breezy": Adventures of Rex and Rinty; Blue Montana Skies; Empty Holsters; Fighting Marines, The; Galloping Ghost, The; Law for Tombstone; Man of the Frontier (Red River Valley); Phantom Empire (1935); Radio Ranch (Men with Steel Faces, Phantom Empire); Rimfire; Undersea Kingdom
Eason, Walter B.: Sea Hound, The
Eastman, Allan: Crazy Moon; Danger Zone; Ford: The Man & the Machine; War Boy, The
Eastwood, Clint: Absolute Power; Bird; Bridges of Madison County, The; Bronco Billy; Eiger Sanction, The; Firefox; Gauntlet, The; Heartbreak Ridge; High Plains Drifter; Honkytonk Man; Midnight in the Garden of Good and Evil; Outlaw Josey Wales, The; Pale Rider; Perfect World, A; Play Misty for Me; Rookie, The (1990); Space Cowboys; Sudden Impact; True Crime; Unforgiven (1992); White Hunter Black Heart
Ebata, Hiroyuki: Dog Soldier: Shadows of the Past
Eberhardt, Thom: Captain Ron; Face Down; Gross Anatomy; Night Before, The; Night of the Comet; Sole Survivor; Without a Clue
Ebishima, Toyo: Serendipity, the Pink Dragon
Ecare, Desire: Faces of Women
Echevarria, Nicolas: Cabeza de Vaca
Edel, Uli: Body of Evidence; Christiane F.; Confessions of a Sorority Girl; Last Exit to Brooklyn; Little Vampire, The; Mists of Avalon, The; Purgatory; Rasputin; Tyson
Edgren, Gustaf: Walpurgis Night
Edmunds, Don: Bare Knuckles
Edwards, Anthony: Charlie's Ghost
Edwards, Blake: Blind Date; Breakfast at Tiffany's; Curse of the Pink Panther, The; Darling Lili; Days of Wine and Roses (1962); Experiment in Terror; Fine Mess, A; Great Race, The; Man Who Loved Women, The; Micki & Maude; Operation Petticoat; Party, The; Perfect Furlough; Peter Gunn (TV Series); Pink Panther, The; Pink Panther Strikes Again, The; Return of the Pink Panther, The; Revenge of the Pink Panther, The; Shot in the Dark, A; Skin Deep; S.O.B.; Son of the Pink Panther; Sunset; Switch; Tamarind Seed, The; 10; That's Life; This Happy Feeling; Trail of the Pink Panther, The; Victor/Victoria; Wild Rovers, The
Edwards, Dan: Black Cobra 3
Edwards, Dave: Secret Garden, The
Edwards, George: Attic, The
Edwards, Henry: Juggernaut; Scrooge
Edwards, Vince: Mission Galactica: The Cylon Attack
Edzard, Christine: Little Dorrit
Egerton, Mark: Winds of Jarrah, The
Eggeling: Avant Garde Program #2
Eggleston, Colin: Long Weekend; Wicked, The
Egleson, Jan: Last Hit, The; Shock to the System, A
Egoyan, Atom: Adjuster, The; Exotica; Family Viewing; Felicia's Journey; Next of Kin; Speaking Parts; Sweet Hereafter, The
Eichorn, Franz: Violent Years, The
Eisenman, Rafael: Business for Pleasure; Lake Consequence
Eisenstein, Sergei: Alexander Nevsky; Battleship Potemkin, The; Ivan the Terrible—Part I & Part II; October (Ten Days That Shook the World); Strike (1924)
Elanjian Jr., George: Syngenor
Elfman, Richard: Forbidden Zone; Shrunken Heads
Elfont, Harry: Can't Hardly Wait; Josie and the Pussycats
Elias, Michael: Lush Life; No Laughing Matter
Eliasberg, Jan: Past Midnight
Elikann, Larry: Blue River; Disaster at Silo 7; Fever; God Bless the Child; Great Los Angeles Earthquake, The; Great Wallendas, The; Inconvenient Woman, An; Mother's Prayer, A; One Against the Wind; Poison Ivy; Story Lady, The; Stranger on My Land; Unexpected Family, An
Elkayem, Ellory: They Nest
Ellenshaw, Harrison: Dead Silence
Ellin, Doug: Kissing a Fool; Phat Beach
Elliot, Michael: Fatal Games; King Lear
Elliott, Lang: Cage; Cage II: Arena of Death, The; Private Eyes, The
Elliott, Scott: Map of the World, A
Elliott, Stephan: Adventures of Priscilla, Queen of the Desert, The; Eye of the Beholder; Frauds; Welcome to Woop Woop
Elliotts, Paul: Great Adventure, The
Ellis, Bob: Nostradamus Kid, The; Warm Nights on a Slow Moving Train
Ellis, David R.: Homeward Bound II: Lost in San Francisco
Ellison, James: Don't Go in the House
Elman, Luis: Matt the Gooseboy
Elvey, Maurice: Evil Mind, The (The Clairvoyant); School for Scandal; Sons of the Sea; Spy of Napoleon; Transatlantic Tunnel
Elwes, Cassian: Blue Flame
Emerson, John: Down to Earth; His Picture in the Papers; Reaching for the Moon; Wild and Woolly
Emes, Ian: Knights and Emeralds
Emmerich, Roland: Ghost Chase; Godzilla (1998); Independence Day; Making Contact; Moon 44; Patriot, The; Stargate; Universal Soldier
Enders, Robert: Stevie
Endfield, Cy: Mysterious Island; Try and Get Me; Underworld Story; Zulu
Engel, Thomas E.: Rich Little—One's a Crowd
English, John: Adventures of Captain Marvel, The; Adventures of Red Ryder; Arizona Days; Beyond the Purple Hills; Captain America; Cow Town; Dead Man's Gulch; Death Valley Manhunt; Dick Tracy Returns; Dick Tracy vs. Crime Inc.; Dick

Tracy's G-Men; Don't Fence Me In; Drums of Fu Manchu; Gangs of Sonora; Hawk of the Wilderness; Hi-Yo Silver; Hills of Utah, The; Last Round-Up; Loaded Pistols; Lone Ranger, The; Mule Train; Mysterious Dr. Satan; Riders for Justice; Riders of the Whistling Pines; Rim of the Canyon; San Fernando Valley; Utah; Zorro Rides Again; Zorro's Fighting Legion
Englund, George: Christmas to Remember, A; Dixie Changing Habits; Ugly American, The; Zachariah
Englund, Robert: 976-EVIL
Enrico, Robert: Le Secret; Les Grandes Gueules (Jailbirds' Vacation); Occurrence at Owl Creek Bridge, An
Enright, Ray: China Sky; Coroner Creek; Dames; Earthworm Tractors; Gung Ho! (1943); Iron Major, The; Return of the Bad Men; South of St. Louis; Spoilers, The; Tomorrow at Seven; Trail Street; Wagons Roll at Night, The
Enyedi, Ildiko: Magic Hunter; My 20th Century
Ephron, Nora: Lucky Numbers; Michael; Mixed Nuts; Sleepless in Seattle; This Is My Life; You've Got Mail
Epstein, Jean: La Chute de la Maison Usher
Epstein, Marcelo: Body Rock
Epstein, Robert: Celluloid Closet, The; Common Threads: Stories from the Quilt
Eram, Rene: Sweet Evil; Voodoo
Erdman, Dave: Soundstage: Blues Summit in Chicago
Ereira, Alan: Crusades, The
Erice, Victor: Spirit of the Beehive, The
Erman, John: Attic: The Hiding of Anne Frank; Boys Next Door, The; Breathing Lessons; Carolina Skeletons; Child of Glass; Early Frost, An; Eleanor: First Lady of the World; Ellen Foster; Last Best Year, The; My Old Man; Only Love; Our Sons; Outer Limits, The (TV Series); Roots: The Next Generation; Scarlett; Stella; Streetcar Named Desire, A; Victoria and Albert; When the Time Comes
Erschbamer, George: Bounty Hunters; Final Round; Flinch; Marco Polo; Snake Eater; Snake Eater III: His Law; Snake Eater 2, the Drug Buster
Ersgard, Jack: Backlash; Invisible: The Chronicles of Benjamin Knight; Living in Peril; Mandroid
Ersgard, Joakim: Acts of Betrayal; Visitors, The
Erskine, Chester: Androcles and the Lion; Egg and I, The; Frankie and Johnny; Girl in Every Port, A; Midnight
Esper, Dwain: Maniac; Sex Madness
Esposito, Joe: South Beach Academy
Essex, Harry: Cremators, The; Octaman
Estevez, Emilio: Men at Work; Rated X; War at Home, The; Wisdom
Esway, Alexander: Mauvaise Graine (Bad Seed)
Eubanks, Corey Michael: Bigfoot: The Unforgettable Encounter; Two Bits & Pepper
Eustache, Jean: Mother and the Whore, The
Evans, Bruce A.: Kuffs
Evans, David Mickey: Beethoven's 3rd; First Kid; Sandlot, The
Evans, John: Black Godfather, The
Evans, Marc: Resurrection Man; Thicker Than Water
Evans, Roger D.: Jet Benny Show, The
Everitt, Tim: Fatally Yours; Too Fast Too Young
Export, Valie: Invisible Adversaries
Eyre, Chris: Smoke Signals
Eyre, Richard: Loose Connections; Ploughman's Lunch, The; Singleton's Pluck
Eyres, John: Armed and Deadly; Conspiracy of Fear, The; Goodnight, God Bless; Judge and Jury; Monolith; Nightsiege-Project: Shadowchaser 2; Octopus (2000); Project Shadowchaser 3000; Ripper: Letter from Hell
Ezra, Mark: Savage Hearts
Faber, Christian: Bail Jumper
Faenza, Roberto: Bachelor, The; Corrupt
Faiman, Peter: "Crocodile" Dundee; Dutch
Fairchild, William: Horsemasters; Silent Enemy, The
Faircloth, Tommy: Crinoline Head
Fairfax, Ferdinand: Nate and Hayes; Rescue, The; Spymaker: The Secret Life of Ian Fleming
Fakasaku, Kinji: Tora! Tora! Tora!
Falk, Harry: Beulah Land; Death Squad, The; High Desert Kill; Night the City Screamed, The; Scene of the Crime; Sophisticated Gents, The
Falkenstein, Jun: Tigger Movie, The
Fall, Jim: Trick
Famuyiwa, Rick: Wood, The
Fanaka, Jamaa: Black Sister's Revenge; Penitentiary; Penitentiary II; Penitentiary III; Soul Vengeance (Welcome Home Brother Charles); Street Wars
Fancher, Hampton: Minus Man, The
Fansten, Jacques: Cross My Heart
Färberböck, Max: Aimee & Jaguar
Fargo, James: Caravans; Enforcer, The; Every Which Way But Loose; Forced Vengeance; Game for Vultures; Riding the Edge
Farino, Ernest: Josh Kirby, Time Warrior (Series); Steel and Lace
Farmanara, Bahman: Smell of Camphor, Fragrance of Jasmine
Farmer, Donald: Scream Dream; Vampire Cop
Farrelly, Bobby: Kingpin; Me, Myself & Irene; Osmosis Jones; Shallow Hal; There's Something About Mary
Farrelly, Peter: Dumb and Dumber; Kingpin; Me, Myself & Irene; Osmosis Jones; Shallow Hal; There's Something About Mary
Farris, John: Dear Dead Delilah
Farrow, John: Back from Eternity; Botany Bay; Commandos Strike at Dawn; Copper Canyon; Five Came Back; His Kind of Woman; Hondo; John Paul Jones; Saint Strikes Back, The; Sea Chase, The; Wake Island
Farwagi, André: Boarding School
Fasano, John: Black Roses
Fassbinder, Rainer Werner: Ali: Fear Eats the Soul; American Soldier, The; Berlin Alexanderplatz; Beware of a Holy Whore; Bitter Tears of Petra Von Kant, The; Chinese Roulette; Despair; Effi Briest; Fox and His Friends; Germany In Autumn; Gods of the Plague; I Only Want You to Love Me; In a Year of 13 Moons; Lili Marleen; Lola; Marriage of Maria Braun, The; Merchant of Four Seasons, The; Mother Kusters Goes to Heaven; Querelle; Satan's Brew; Veronika Voss; Why Does Herr R. Run Amok?
Faulkner, Brenden: Spookies
Faure, William C.: Shaka Zulu
Favreau, Jon: Made
Fawcett, John: Boys Club, The; Ginger Snaps
Fearnley, Neill L.: Black Ice; Escape from Mars; Johnny 2.0
Feferman, Linda: Seven Minutes in Heaven
Fei, Xie: Girl from Hunan; Women from the Lake of the Scented Souls
Feijoo, Beda Docampo: Debajo del Mundo (Under Earth)
Feist, Felix: Big Trees, The; Deluge (1993); Devil Thumbs a Ride, The; Donovan's Brain; George White's Scandals; Man Who Cheated Himself, The; Threat, The
Feldman, Dennis: Real Men
Feldman, Gene: Danny
Feldman, John: Dead Funny
Feldman, Jon Harmon: Lovelife
Feldman, Marty: Last Remake of Beau Geste, The; When Things Were Rotten (TV Series)
Fellini, Federico: Amarcord; And the Ship Sails On; Boccaccio 70; Casanova; City of Women; Clowns, The; 8 1/2; Fellini Satyricon; Fellini's Roma; Ginger and Fred; I Vitelloni; Il Bidone; Juliet of the Spirits; La Dolce Vita; La Strada; Nights of Cabiria; Orchestra Rehearsal; Variety Lights; White Sheik, The
Fenady, Georg: Arnold; Terror in the Wax Museum
Fengler, Michael: Why Does Herr R. Run Amok?
Fenton, Leslie: Saint's Vacation, The
Fenton, Thomas: Striking Point
Feraldo, Claude: Trade Secrets
Feret, René: Alexina; Mystery of Alexina, The
Ferguson, Larry: Beyond the Law; Gunfighter's Moon
Ferguson, Michael: Glory Boys, The

Ford, Eugene: Charlie Chan at Monte Carlo; Charlie Chan on Broadway
Ford, Greg: Daffy Duck's Quackbusters
Ford, Howard: Mainline Run
Ford, John: Arrowsmith; Cheyenne Autumn; December 7th: The Movie; Donovan's Reef; Drums Along the Mohawk; Fort Apache; Fugitive, The; Grapes of Wrath, The; Horse Soldiers, The; How Green Was My Valley; How the West Was Won; Hurricane, The; Informer, The; Judge Priest; Last Hurrah, The; Long Gray Line, The; Long Voyage Home, The; Lost Patrol, The; Man Who Shot Liberty Valance, The; Mary of Scotland; Mister Roberts; Mogambo; My Darling Clementine; Quiet Man, The; Rio Grande; Searchers, The; Sergeant Rutledge; She Wore a Yellow Ribbon; Stagecoach; Straight Shooting; Sun Shines Bright, The; They Were Expendable; Three Godfathers, The; Two Rode Together; Wagonmaster; Wee Willie Winkie; What Price Glory; Wings of Eagles, The; Young Mr. Lincoln
Ford, Philip: Bandits of Dark Canyon; Denver Kid; Rodeo King and the Senorita; Valley of the Zombies; Vegas in Space; Wild Frontier
Ford, Ron: Alien Agenda, The (TV Series); Alien Force; Witchcraft XI: Sisters in Blood
Ford, Steve: Dungeonmaster, The
Forde, Eugene: Charlie Chan in London; Charlie Chan's Murder Cruise; Dressed to Kill
Fordyce, Ian: How to Irritate People
Forman, Milos: Amadeus; Fireman's Ball, The; Hair; Loves of a Blonde; Man on the Moon; One Flew over the Cuckoo's Nest; People vs. Larry Flynt, The; Ragtime; Valmont
Forman, Tom: Shadows; Virginian, The
Forster, Marc: Monster's Ball
Forster, Robert: Hollywood Harry
Forsyth, Bill: Being Human; Breaking In; Comfort and Joy; Gregory's Girl; Housekeeping; Local Hero; That Sinking Feeling
Forte, John: MAD About Mambo
Fortenberry, John: Jury Duty; Night at the Roxbury, A
Fosse, Bob: All That Jazz; Cabaret; Lenny; Star 80; Sweet Charity
Foster, Giles: Consuming Passions; Innocent Victim; Rector's Wife, The; Silas Marner
Foster, Jodie: Home for the Holidays (1995); Little Man Tate
Foster, Lewis R.: Crashout; Dakota Incident; Laurel and Hardy Classics: Vol. 1–9; Sign of Zorro, The; Tonka
Foster, Norman: Brighty of the Grand Canyon; Charlie Chan at Treasure Island; Charlie Chan in Panama; Charlie Chan in Reno; Davy Crockett and the River Pirates; Davy Crockett, King of the Wild Frontier; Journey into Fear; Mr. Moto Takes a Chance; Mr. Moto Takes a Vacation; Mr. Moto's Last Warning; Mysterious Mr. Moto; Nine Lives of Elfego Baca, The; Rachel and the Stranger; Sign of Zorro, The; Tell It to the Judge; Thank You, Mr. Moto; Think Fast, Mr. Moto
Fournier, Claude: Dan Candy's Law (Alien Thunder)
Fowler, Robert: Below the Belt
Fowler Jr., Gene: I Married a Monster from Outer Space; I Was a Teenage Werewolf; Showdown at Boot Hill
Fox, Marilyn: Return of the Sand Fairy, The
Fox, Michael D.: Vamps: Deadly Dream Girls
Fox, Wallace: Bowery at Midnight; Corpse Vanishes, The; Pillow of Death; Powdersmoke Range
Frakas, Michael: Prime Risk
Fraker, William: Legend of the Lone Ranger, The; Monte Walsh; Reflection of Fear
Frakes, Jonathan: Clockstoppers; Star Trek: First Contact; Star Trek: Insurrection
Franchot, Pascal: Milo
Franciolini, Gianni: Pardon My Trunk (Hello Elephant!)
Francis, Freddie: Brain, The; Creeping Flesh, The; Doctor and the Devils, The; Dr. Terror's House of Horrors; Dracula Has Risen from the Grave; Evil of Frankenstein, The; Ghoul, The; Hysteria; Jigsaw Man, The; Legend of the Werewolf; Nightmare; Paranoiac; Skull, The; Son of Dracula; Tales from the Crypt; Tales that Witness Madness; They Came from Beyond Space; Torture Garden; Vampire Happening
Francis, Karl: And Nothing But the Truth
Francisci, Pietro: Hercules; Hercules Unchained
Franck, Joe: Mortal Kombat: The Animated Movie
Franco, Jess (Jesus): Against All Odds (1968) (Kiss and Kill, Blood of Fu Manchu); Angel of Death; Awful Dr. Orloff, The; Bloody Moon; Castle of Fu Manchu; Count Dracula; Deadly Sanctuary; Demoniac; Erotikill; Ilsa, the Wicked Warden; Jack the Ripper; 99 Women; Venus in Furs; Virgin Among the Living Dead, A; Women in Cell Block 9
Franju, Georges: Eyes Without a Face; Head Against the Wall; Judex
Frank, Carol: Sorority House Massacre
Frank, Christopher: Josepha; L'Année des Meduses
Frank, Melvin: Above and Beyond; Buona Sera, Mrs. Campbell; Court Jester, The; Duchess and the Dirtwater Fox, The; Facts of Life; Jayhawkers, The; Li'l Abner; Lost and Found (1979); Prisoner of Second Avenue, The; Strange Bedfellows; Touch of Class, A; Walk Like a Man
Frank, Robert: Candy Mountain
Frank, T. C.: Born Losers
Frankel, Cyril: Permission to Kill; Very Edge, The; Witches, The
Frankel, David: Miami Rhapsody
Frankenheimer, John: Against the Wall; All Fall Down; Andersonville; Bird Man of Alcatraz; Black Sunday; Burning Season, The; Challenge, The; Comedian, The; Days of Wine and Roses, The (1958); Dead-Bang; 52 Pick-Up; Fourth War, The; French Connection II, The; George Wallace; Grand Prix; Holcroft Covenant, The; Horsemen, The; Island of Dr. Moreau, The; Manchurian Candidate, The; 99 and 44/100 Percent Dead; Prophecy (1979); Reindeer Games; Ronin; Seconds; Seven Days in May; Story of a Love Story; Train, The; Year of the Gun; Young Savages, The
Franklin, Carl: Devil in a Blue Dress; Full Fathom Five; High Crimes; Laurel Avenue; Nowhere to Run; One False Move; One True Thing
Franklin, Chester M.: Vanity Fair
Franklin, Howard: Larger than Life; Public Eye, The; Quick Change
Franklin, Jeff: Love Stinks
Franklin, Jim: Ripping Yarns
Franklin, Richard: Beauty and the Beast (TV Series); Brilliant Lies; Cloak and Dagger; F/X 2: The Deadly Art of Illusion; Link; Patrick; Psycho II; Road Games; Running Delilah; Sorrento Beach
Franklin, Sidney: Barretts of Wimpole Street, The; Good Earth, The; Guardsman, The; Private Lives; Smilin' Through; Wild Orchids
Franklin, Wendell J.: Bus Is Coming, The
Fraser, Christopher: Summer City
Fraser, Harry: Broadway to Cheyenne; Chained for Life; Enemy of the Law
Frausto, Juan: Drive By
Frawley, James: Assault & Matrimony; Big Bus, The; Fraternity Vacation; Muppet Movie, The; Sins of the Mind; Spies, Lies, and Naked Thighs
Frazer, Henry: 'Neath Arizona Skies; Randy Rides Alone
Frears, Stephen: Dangerous Liaisons; Grifters, The; Gumshoe; Hero (1992); Hi-Lo Country, The; High Fidelity; Hit, The (1984); Liam; Mary Reilly; My Beautiful Laundrette; Prick Up Your Ears; Sammy and Rosie Get Laid; Snapper, The; Van, The
Freda, Riccardo: Devil's Commandment, The; Maciste in Hell
Freed, Herb: Beyond Evil; Graduation Day; Survival Game
Freed, Mark: Shock'em Dead
Freedman, Jerrold: Best Kept Secrets; Borderline; Native Son; Seduced; Streets of L.A., The; Thompson's Last Run
Freeland, Jason: Brown's Requiem
Freeland, Thornton: Be Yourself; Brass Monkey, The; Flying Down to Rio; Jericho; They Call It Sin; Whoopee
Freeman, Hal: Blood Frenzy

Freeman, Joan: Satisfaction; Streetwalkin'
Freeman, Morgan: Bopha!
Freeman, Morgan J.: Hurricane Streets
Fregonese, Hugo: Blowing Wild; Decameron Nights
Freiser, Eric: Warlock III: The End of Innocence
Freleng, Friz: Daffy Duck's Movie: Fantastic Island; Looney, Looney, Looney Bugs Bunny Movie; 1001 Rabbit Tales
French, Harold: Adam and Evalyn; Encore; Paris Express, The; Quartet; Rob Roy, the Highland Rogue; Trio
French, Lloyd: Laurel and Hardy Classics: Vol. 1–9
Frend, Charles: Cruel Sea, The; Run for Your Money, A; Scott of the Antarctic
Fresco, Rob: Dirty Little Secret; Evil Has a Face
Freund, Karl: Mad Love; Mummy, The
Freundlich, Bart: Myth of Fingerprints, The
Frey, Jeff: Blood Thirsty
Fridriksson, Fridrik Thor: Children of Nature; Cold Fever
Fried, Randall: Heaven Is a Playground
Friedberg, Rick: Off the Wall; Pray TV; Spy Hard
Friedenberg, Dick: Snow in August
Friedenberg, Richard: Deerslayer, The (1978); Education of Little Tree, The; Life and Times of Grizzly Adams, The; Mr. and Mrs. Loving
Friedgen, Bud: That's Entertainment! III
Friedkin, William: Blue Chips; Boys in the Band, The; Brinks Job, The; Cruising; Deal of the Century; Exorcist, The; French Connection, The; Guardian, The; Jade; Night They Raided Minsky's, The; Rampage; Rules of Engagement; Sorcerer; To Live and Die in L.A.; 12 Angry Men
Friedlander, Louis: Raven, The
Friedman, Adam: To Sleep With a Vampire
Friedman, Anthony: Bartleby
Friedman, Ed: Secret of the Sword, The
Friedman, Jeffrey: Celluloid Closet, The; Common Threads: Stories from the Quilt
Friedman, Ken: Made in USA
Friedman, Peter: Silverlake Life: The View from Here
Friedman, Richard: Deathmask; Doom Asylum; Forever Together; Phantom of the Mall—Eric's Revenge; Scared Stiff
Friend, Martyn: 4:50 From Paddington; Rumpole of the Bailey (TV Series)
Frost, David: Ring of Steel
Frost, Harvey: Midnight Heat; National Lampoon's Golf Punks; Tracks of a Killer
Frost, Lee: Dixie Dynamite; Private Obsession
Frost, Mark: Storyville
Fruet, William: Bedroom Eyes; Blue Monkey; Death Weekend; Search and Destroy; Spasms; Wedding in White
Fry, Benjamin: Wavelength
Frye, E. Max: Amos & Andrew
Fuest, Robert: Abominable Dr. Phibes, The; And Soon the Darkness; Aphrodite; Devil's Rain, The; Dr. Phibes Rises Again; Last Days of Man on Earth, The; Revenge of the Stepford Wives; Wuthering Heights
Fugard, Athol: Road to Mecca, The
Fukasaku, Kinji: Black Lizard; Green Slime, The; Samurai Reincarnation; Virus
Fukuda, Jun: Dragon Knight; Godzilla vs. Gigan; Godzilla vs. Mechagodzilla; Godzilla vs. the Sea Monster; Son of Godzilla
Fukutomi, Hiroshi: Battle Angel
Fulci, Lucio: Black Cat, The; Cat in the Brain, A; Challenge to White Fang; Contraband; Dangerous Obsession; Gates of Hell; House by the Cemetery; Lizard In A Woman's Skin, A; Manhattan Baby; New York Ripper, The; Psychic, The (1977); Seven Doors of Death; Zombie
Fuller, Fleming B.: Prey of the Chameleon
Fuller, Samuel: Baron of Arizona, The; Big Red One, The; China Gate; Naked Kiss, The; Pickup on South Street; Run of the Arrow; Shark! (Maneaters!); Shock Corridor; Steel Helmet, The; Underworld U.S.A.; White Dog
Fuller, Tex: Stranded
Fumihiko, Takayama: Bubblegum Crisis, Vols. 1–8
Fuqua, Antoine: Bait; Replacement Killers, The; Training Day
Furey, Lewis: Shades of Love: Champagne for Two; Shadow Dancing
Furie, Sidney J.: Appaloosa, The; Boys in Company C, The; Entity, The; Hide and Seek; Hit! (1973); Hollow Point; Ipcress File, The; Iron Eagle; Iron Eagle II; Iron Eagle IV; Lady Sings the Blues; Ladybugs; Leather Boys, The; My 5 Wives; Purple Hearts; Road Rage; Superman IV: The Quest for Peace; Taking of Beverly Hills, The
Furst, Stephen: Magic Kid 2
Fywell, Tim: Dark Adapted Eye, A; Fatal Inversion, A; Gallowglass; Norma Jean and Marilyn
Gabai, Richard: Hot Under the Collar; Virgin High
Gable, Martin: Lost Moment, The
Gabor, Pal: Brady's Escape
Gabourie, Mitchell: Buying Time
Gabriel, Mike: Pocahontas; Rescuers Down Under
Gaetano, Alessandro de: Butch Camp
Gaffney, Robert: Frankenstein Meets the Space Monster
Gage, George: Fleshburn
Gage, John: Velvet Touch, The
Gaines, Barry: Jacker 2: Descent to Hell; Tales Till the End
Gainville, René: Associate, The; Le Complot (The Conspiracy)
Gale, Charles: Captain Nuke and the Bomber Boys
Gale, John: Firing Line, The
Gale, Ricardo Jacques: Alien Intruder; Eyes of the Serpent; In the Time of Barbarians II
Galeen, Henrik: Student of Prague
Gallagher, John: Blue Moon; Deli, The; Street Hunter
Gallen, Joel: Not Another Teen Movie
Gallerani, Andrew: Just Write
Gallo, Fred: Black Rose of Harlem; Dead Space; Dracula Rising; Finishing Touch, The
Gallo, George: Double Take; Trapped in Paradise; 29th Street
Gallo, Vincent: Buffalo '66
Gallop, Frank: Great Chase, The
Gallu, Samuel: Theatre of Death
Gance, Abel: Abel Gance's Beethoven; Battle of Austerlitz, The; J'Accuse; Napoleon
Gannaway, Albert C.: Daniel Boone, Trail Blazer
Gans, Christophe: Brotherhood of the Wolf; H. P. Lovecraft's Necronomicon: Book of the Dead
Garabidian, Armand: Silk Degrees
Garcia, David: Sex Crimes
Garcia, Nicole: Every Other Weekend; Place Vendome
Garcia, Risa Bramon: 200 Cigarettes
Garcia, Rodrigo: Things You Can Tell Just by Looking at Her
Gardner, Herb: Goodbye People, The; I'm Not Rappaport
Gardner, Richard Harding: Deadly Daphne's Revenge; Sherlock: Undercover Dog
Gárdos, Éva: American Rhapsody, An
Garen, Leo: Shrieking, The
Garland, Patrick: Doll's House, A
Garmes, Lee: Actors and Sin; Angels over Broadway
Garnett, Tay: Bataan; Challenge to Be Free; Cheers for Miss Bishop; China Seas; Eternally Yours; Flying Fool, The; Joy of Living; Main Street to Broadway; Mrs. Parkington; One Minute to Zero; Postman Always Rings Twice, The; Seven Sinners; Slightly Honorable; Stand-In
Garrett, Roy: Eyes Behind the Stars
Garris, Mick: Critters 2: The Main Course; Psycho 4: The Beginning; Quicksilver Highway; Stand, The; Stephen King's Sleepwalkers; Stephen King's The Shining
Gasnier, Louis J.: Reefer Madness
Gast, Leon: Hell's Angels Forever; When We Were Kings
Gates, Jim: Hey Abbott!
Gates, Martin: Adventures of Mole, The
Gatlif, Tony: Gadjo Dilo; Latcho Drom; Mondo
Gaubert, Jean-Marie: Just Visiting
Gaudioz, Tony: Border Heat
Gaup, Nils: North Star (1996); Pathfinder; Shipwrecked
Gavaldon, Roberto: Littlest Outlaw, The; Macario
Gawer, Eleanor: Slipping into Darkness

Gogh, Theo van: 1-900
Golan, Menahem: Deadly Heroes; Delta Force, The; Diamonds; Enter the Ninja; Escape to the Sun; Hanna's War; Hit the Dutchman; Lepke; Lupo; Mack the Knife; Magician of Lublin, The; Operation Thunderbolt; Over the Brooklyn Bridge; Over the Top; Silent Victim
Gold, Greg: House of the Rising Sun
Gold, Jack: Catholics; Escape from Sobibor; Little Lord Fauntleroy; Medusa Touch, The; Murrow; Naked Civil Servant, The; Return of the Native, The; Rose and the Jackal, The; Sakharov; Tenth Man, The
Goldbacher, Sandra: Governess, The
Goldbeck, Willis: Love Laughs at Andy Hardy
Goldberg, Dan: Feds
Goldberg, Eric: Fantasia 2000; Pocahontas
Goldberg, Gary David: Dad
Goldberg, Howard: Eden
Goldblatt, Mark: Dead Heat; Punisher, The
Golden, Dan: Bram Stoker's Burial of the Rats; Naked Obsession; Terminal Virus
Goldenberg, Michael: Bed of Roses
Golding, Paul: Pulse
Goldman, Gary: Anastasia; Hans Christian Andersen's Thumbelina; Titan A.E.; Troll in Central Park, A
Goldman, Jill: Bad Love
Goldman, Martin: Legend of the Spirit Dog
Goldsmid, Peter: Road to Mecca, The
Goldstein, Allan A.: Blackout; Common Bonds; Death Wish V: The Face of Death; Lawrenceville Stories, The; Outside Chance of Maximilian Glick, The; Synapse; 2001: A Space Travesty; Virus
Goldstein, Amy: Silencer, The
Goldstein, Scott: Ambition; Walls of Glass
Goldstone, James: Brother John; Calamity Jane; Eric; Kent State; Outer Limits, The (TV Series); Rita Hayworth: The Love Goddess; Rollercoaster; Star Trek (TV Series); Swashbuckler (1976); They Only Kill Their Masters; When Time Ran Out!; Winning
Goldthwait, Bob: Shakes the Clown
Goldwyn, Tony: Someone Like You; Walk on the Moon, A
Gomer, Steve: Barney's Great Adventure; Fly by Night; Sunset Park; Sweet Lorraine
Gomez, Nick: Drowning Mona; Illtown; New Jersey Drive
Gondry, Michel: Human Nature
Gonzalez, Reuben: Mambo Café
Gonzalez, Servando: Fool Killer, The
Goodhew, Philip: Intimate Relations
Goodkind, Saul: Buck Rogers: Destination Saturn (PlanetOutlaws); Phantom Creeps, The
Goodman, Barak: Daley: The Last Boss
Goodman, Jenniphr: Tao of Steve, The
Goodson, Tony: And You Thought Your Parents Were Weird
Goodwin, Fred: Curse II—The Bite
Goodwins, Leslie: Bronco (TV Series); Dragnet; Mexican Spitfire; Mummy's Curse, The
Gordon, Bert I.: Amazing Colossal Man, The; Attack of the Puppet People; Beginning of the End; Cyclops, The; Earth vs. the Spider; Empire of the Ants; Food of the Gods; Mad Bomber, The; Magic Sword, The; Picture Mommy Dead; Satan's Princess; Village of the Giants; War of the Colossal Beast; Witching, The (Necromancy)
Gordon, Bryan: Career Opportunities; Discovery Program; Pie in the Sky
Gordon, Dennie: Joe Dirt
Gordon, James: Fabulous Villains, The
Gordon, Keith: Chocolate War, The; Midnight Clear, A; Mother Night; Wild Palms
Gordon, Michael: Boys' Night Out; Cyrano De Bergerac; Impossible Years, The; Pillow Talk; Texas Across the River
Gordon, Robert: Bonanza (TV Series); It Came from Beneath the Sea; Joe Louis Story, The; Revenge of the Red Baron
Gordon, Steve: Arthur
Gordon, Stuart: Castle Freak; Daughter of Darkness; Dolls; Fortress; From Beyond; Outer Limits: Sandkings; Pit and the Pendulum, The; Re-Animator; Robot Jox; Space Truckers; Wonderful Ice Cream Suit, The
Gordy, Berry: Mahogany
Goren, Serif: Yol
Goretta, Claude: Lacemaker, The
Gorg, Alan: Living the Blues
Gormley, Charles: Gospel According to Vic, The
Gornick, Michael: Creepshow 2; Stephen King's Golden Years (TV Series); Tales from the Darkside, Vol. I
Gorris, Marleen: Antonia's Line; Luzhin Defence, The; Mrs. Dalloway; Question of Silence, A
Gorsky, Alexander: Don Quixote
Goscinny, René: Lucky Luke: The Ballad of the Daltons
Gosha, Hideo: Hunter in the Dark; Wolves, The
Goslar, Jurgen: Albino; Slavers
Gosnell, Raja: Big Momma's House; Home Alone 3; Never Been Kissed
Gosse, Bob: Niagara Niagara
Gothar, Peter: Time Stands Still
Gottlieb, Carl: Amazon Women on the Moon; Caveman
Gottlieb, Franz: Curse of the Yellow Snake, The
Gottlieb, Lisa: Across the Moon; Cadillac Ranch; Just One of the Guys
Gottlieb, Max: Raising the Heights
Gottlieb, Michael: Kid in King Arthur's Court, A; Mannequin; Mr. Nanny
Gottschalk, Robert: Dangerous Charter
Gould, Heywood: Mistrial; One Good Cop; Trial by Jury
Goulding, Alf: Chump at Oxford, A
Goulding, Edmund: Dark Victory; Dawn Patrol, The; Forever and a Day; Grand Hotel; Great Lie, The; Old Maid, The; Razor's Edge, The; Reaching for the Moon; Riptide; That Certain Woman; We're Not Married
Goursand, Anne: Another 9 1/2 Weeks; Embrace of the Vampire; Poison Ivy 2: Lily
Gove, William: Apostate, The
Governor, Richard: Ghost Town
Graef-Marino, Gustavo: Diplomatic Siege
Graham, David C.: Undertaker and His Pals, The
Graham, William A.: Acceptable Risk; Amazing Howard Hughes, The; And I Alone Survived; Birds of Prey; Change of Habit; Deadly Encounter; Doomsday Flight, The; Fugitive, The (TV Series); George Washington: The Forging of a Nation; Get Christie Love!; Gore Vidal's Billy the Kid; Guyana Tragedy, The: The Story of Jim Jones; Harry Tracy; Last Days of Frank and Jesse James; M.A.D.D.: Mothers Against Drunk Driving; Man Who Captured Eichmann, The; Montana; Mr. Inside/Mr. Outside; Orphan Train; Proud Men; Rage; Return to the Blue Lagoon; Secrets of a Married Man; Supercarrier; Waterhole #3; Where the Lilies Bloom
Grammatikor, Vladimir: Land of Faraway, The
Granier-Deferre, Pierre: Cat, The (1971) (Le Chat); French Detective, The; Widow Couderc; Woman at Her Window, A
Grant, Brian: Immortals, The; Love Kills; Sensation; Sweet Poison
Grant, James Edward: Angel and the Badman
Grant, Julian: Angel and the Badman
Grant, Lee: Down and Out in America; Staying Together; Tell Me a Riddle
Grant, Michael: Fatal Attraction
Grasshoff, Alex: Billion for Boris, A
Grau, Jorge: Blood Castle
Grauman, Walter: Are You in the House Alone?; Disembodied, The; Lady in a Cage; Most Wanted; Nightmare on the 13th Floor; Outrage!; Pleasure Palace; Scene of the Crime; 633 Squadron
Graver, Gary: Angel in Training; Crossing the Line (1990); Evil Spirits; Party Camp; Trick or Treat
Graves, Alex: Casualties; Crude Oasis, The
Gray, Edward: Mafia: The History of the Mob in America
Gray, F. Gary: Friday; Negotiator, The; Set It Off

Gray, James: Little Odessa; Yards, The
Gray, Jerome: Traxx
Gray, John: American Story, An; Billy Galvin; Born to Be Wild; Glimmer Man, The; Hunley, The; Lost Capone, The; Place for Annie, A; Seventh Stream, The; When He's Not a Stranger
Gray, Mike: Wavelength
Grede, Kjell: Good Evening Mr. Wallenberg
Greek, Janet: Spellbinder
Green, Alfred E.: Baby Face; Copacabana; Dangerous (1935); Disraeli; Ella Cinders; Fabulous Dorseys, The; Four Faces West; Invasion USA (1952); Jackie Robinson Story, The; Jolson Story, The; Mr. Winkle Goes to War; South of Pago Pago; Thoroughbreds Don't Cry
Green, Bruce Seth: Hunt for the Night Stalker; In Self Defense; Rags to Riches; Running Against Time
Green, David: Children of the Dust
Green, David Gordon: George Washington
Green, Guy: Diamond Head; Incredible Journey of Dr. Meg Laurel,The; Luther; Once Is Not Enough; Patch of Blue, A; Walk in the Spring Rain, A
Green, Jack: Traveller
Green, Joseph: Brain That Wouldn't Die, The
Green, Terry: Cold Justice
Green, Tom: Freddy Got Fingered
Green, Walon: Hellstrom Chronicle, The
Greenaway, Peter: Belly of an Architect, The; Cook, the Thief, His Wife & Her Lover, The; Draughtman's Contract, The; Drowning by Numbers; 8 1/2 Women; Pillow Book, The; Prospero's Books; Zed and Two Noughts, A
Greenburg, Richard Alan: Little Monsters
Greene, Danford B.: Secret Diary of Sigmund Freud, The
Greene, David: After the Promise; Bella Mafia; Buster; Choice, The; Count of Monte Cristo, The; Fatal Vision; Fire Birds; Friendly Fire; Gray Lady Down; Guardian, The; Hard Country; In a Stranger's Hands; Madame Sin; Miles to Go; Penthouse, The; Prototype; Rehearsal for Murder; Shuttered Room, The; Small Sacrifices; Triplecross; Vanishing Act; What Ever Happened To … ?; World War III
Greene, Herbert: Cosmic Man, The
Greengrass, Paul: Theory of Flight, The
Greenspan, Bud: Wilma
Greenstands, Arthur: Wilma
Greenwald, Maggie: Ballad of Little Jo, The; Home Remedy; Kill-Off, The; Songcatcher
Greenwald, Robert: Breaking Up; Burning Bed, The; Flatbed Annie and Sweetie Pie: Lady Truckers; Forgotten Prisoners; Hear No Evil; Shattered Spirits; Steal This Movie; Sweethearts' Dance; Woman of Independent Means, A; Xanadu
Greenwalt, David: Secret Admirer
Grefe, William: Impulse; Jaws of Death, The; Stanley
Gregg, Colin: To the Lighthouse; We Think the World of You
Greggio, Ezio: Silence of the Hams
Greif, Leslie: Keys to Tulsa
Gremillon, Jean: Pattes Blanches (White Paws); Stormy Waters
Gremm, Wolf: Kamikaze 89
Grenfield, Luke: Animal, The
Grenier, Marc S.: Dead Awake
Grenville, Edmond T.: Beat Girl
Gréville, Edmond: Liars, The; Princess Tam Tam
Greyson, John: Lilies; Urinal
Gribbins, James: Shadow Creature
Gribble, Mike: Spike & Mike's Festival of Animation
Gries, Tom: Breakheart Pass; Breakout; Connection (1973); Fools; Glass House, The; Greatest, The; Helter Skelter; Lady Ice; Migrants, The; 100 Rifles; QB VII; Will Penny
Grieve, Andrew: Lorna Doone; Suspicion
Grieve, Ken: Adventures of Sherlock Holmes, The (Series)
Griffi, Giuseppe Patroni: Collector's Item; Divine Nymph, The; Driver's Seat, The
Griffith, Charles B.: Dr. Heckyl and Mr. Hype; Eat My Dust; Smokey Bites the Dust; Up from the Depths; Wizard of the Lost Kingdom II
Griffith, D. W.: Abraham Lincoln; Avenging Conscience, The; Birth of a Nation, The; Broken Blossoms; D. W. Griffith Triple Feature; Dream Street; Hearts of the World; Home, Sweet Home (1914); Idol Dancer, The; Intolerance; Judith of Bethulia; Mother and the Law, The; Orphans of the Storm; Sally of the Sawdust; Sorrows of Satan, The; True Heart Susie; Way Down East; White Rose, The
Griffith, Edward H.: Animal Kingdom, The; My Love for Yours (Honeymoon in Bali); Sky's the Limit, The; Young and Willing
Griffiths, Mark: Cheyenne Warrior; Cry in the Wild, A; Heroes Stand Alone; Max Is Missing; Running Hot; Tactical Assault; Ultraviolet
Grillo, Gary: American Justice
Grimaldi, Hugo: Human Duplicators, The; Mutiny in Outer Space
Grimm, Douglas K.: Laser Moon
Grindé, Nick: Before I Hang; Hitler—Dead or Alive; Man They Could Not Hang, The; Stone of Silver Creek
Grint, Alan: Adventures of Sherlock Holmes, The (Series); Secret Garden, The
Grinter, Brad F.: Flesh Feast
Grisman, Gillian: Grateful Dawg
Grissell, Wallace: Federal Operator 99
Grissmer, John: Blood Rage; Scalpel
Grlic, Rajko: That Summer of White Roses
Grosbard, Ulu: Deep End of the Ocean, The; Falling in Love; Georgia; Straight Time; Subject Was Roses, The; True Confessions
Gross, Larry: 3:15—The Moment of Truth
Gross, Yoram: Dot and the Bunny; Toby and the Koala Bear
Grossman, Adam: Sometimes They Come Back Again
Grossman, David: Yo-Yo Man
Grossman, Douglas: Hell High
Grossman, Goetz: Tar
Grossman, Sam: Van, The
Grosvenor, Charles: Once Upon a Forest
Grune, Karl: Street, The
Gruza, Jerzy: Alice
Guenette, Robert: Man Who Saw Tomorrow, The
Guercio, James William: Electra Glide in Blue
Guerra, Ruy: Erendira; Opera do Malandro
Guerrieri, Romolo: Final Executioner, The
Guerrini, Mino: Mines of Kilimanjaro
Guest, Christopher: Almost Heroes; Attack of the 50-Foot Woman; Best in Show; Big Picture, The; Waiting for Guffman
Guest, Cliff: Disturbance, The
Guest, Val: Abominable Snowman of the Himalayas, The; Carry on Admiral; Casino Royale; Day the Earth Caught Fire, The; Enemy from Space; Just William's Luck; Killer Force; Men of Sherwood Forest; Persuaders, The (TV Series); Quatermass Experiment, The; Up the Creek; When Dinosaurs Ruled the Earth
Guggenheim, Charles: Great St. Louis Bank Robbery, The
Guggenheim, Davis: Gossip
Guillermin, John: Blue Max, The; Bridge at Remagen, The; Death on the Nile; El Condor; King Kong; King Kong Lives; Never Let Go; Sheena; Towering Inferno, The; Tracker, The; Waltz of the Toreadors
Guiol, Fred L.: Battling Orioles, The
Guitry, Sacha: Napoleon; Pearls of the Crown, The
Guney, Yilmaz: Wall, The (1983) (Foreign)
Gunn, Gilbert: Cosmic Monsters, The
Gunnarsson, Sturla: Joe Torre: Curveballs Along the Way; We the Jury
Guralnick, Robert: Joe Torre: Curveballs Along the Way; We the Jury
Gurney Jr., Robert: Terror from the Year 5,000
Guterman, Lawrence: Cats & Dogs
Guthrie, Tyrone: Oedipus Rex
Gutierrez, Sebastian: Judas Kiss
Gutman, Nathaniel: Deadline; Linda; When the Dark Man Calls
Guttfreund, Andre: Femme Fatale

Guzman, Claudio: Hostage Tower, The; Willa
Gyllenhaal, Stephen: Certain Fury; Dangerous Woman, A; Homegrown; Killing in a Small Town; Losing Isaiah; Paris Trout; Promised a Miracle; Question of Faith; Warden, The; Warden of Red Rock; Waterland
Gyongyossy, Imre: Revolt of Job, The
Gyorgy, Appel: Pebble and the Penguin, The
Haak, Diane: Secrets in the Attic
Haas, Charles: Girls Town; New Adventures of Charlie Chan, The (TVSeries); Outer Limits, The (TV Series); Platinum High School
Haas, George: Friends and Lovers
Haas, Philip: Angels and Insects; Music of Chance, The; Up at the Villa
Haber, Mark: Daisies in December
Hachuel, Herve: Last of Philip Banter, The
Hackford, Taylor: Against All Odds (1984); Bound by Honor; Chuck Berry Hail! Hail! Rock 'n' Roll; Devil's Advocate; Dolores Claiborne; Everybody's All-American; Idolmaker, The; Officer and a Gentleman, An; Proof of Life; White Nights
Haedrick, Rolf: Among the Cinders
Haft, Jeremy: Crimson Code; Grizzly Mountain
Hafter, Petra: Demon in My View, A
Hagen, Ross: B.O.R.N.
Haggard, Mark: First Nudie Musical, The
Haggard, Piers: Back Home; Fiendish Plot of Dr. Fu Manchu, The; Fulfillment; Lifeforce Experiment, The; Quatermass Conclusion, The; Return to Treasure Island; Summer Story, A; Venom
Haggis, Paul: Red Hot
Hagman, Larry: Son of Blob (Beware! The Blob)
Hagmann, Stuart: Strawberry Statement, The; Tarantulas—The Deadly Cargo
Haid, Charles: Buffalo Soldiers; Children of Fury; Cooperstown; Iron Will; Nightman, The; Riders of the Purple Sage
Haig, Roul: Okefenokee
Haigney, Michael: Pokémon the Movie 2000; Pokémon 3
Haines, Fred: Steppenwolf
Haines, Randa: Children of a Lesser God; Dance with Me; Doctor, The; Wrestling Ernest Hemingway
Haines, Richard W.: Alien Space Avenger; Class of Nuke 'em High; Splatter University
Halas, John: Animal Farm
Haldane, Don: Reincarnate, The
Hale, William: Murder in Texas; Murder of Mary Phagan, The; One Shoe Makes It Murder; Red Alert; S.O.S. Titanic
Haley Jr., Jack: Love Machine, The; That's Entertainment
Halicki, H. B.: Gone in 60 Seconds; Junkman, The
Hall, Alexander: Because You're Mine; Doctor Takes a Wife, The; Forever Darling; Goin' to Town; Great Lover, The; Here Comes Mr. Jordan; I Am the Law; Little Miss Marker
Hall, Anthony Michael: Hail Caesar
Hall, Gary Skeen: Prime Time Murder
Hall, Godfrey: Undefeatable
Hall, Ivan: Kill and Kill Again; Kill or Be Killed
Hall, Kenneth J.: Evil Spawn; Ghost Writer
Hall, Mark: Wind in the Willows, The
Hall, Peter: Homecoming, The (1973); Midsummer Night's Dream, A; Never Talk to Strangers; Orpheus Descending
Hallenbeck, Bruce G.: Vampyre (1990)
Haller, Daniel: Buck Rogers in the 25th Century; Die, Monster, Die!; Dunwich Horror, The; Paddy
Hallowell, Todd: Love or Money?
Hallstrom, Lasse: Children of Noisy Village, The; Chocolat; Cider House Rules, The; My Life as a Dog; Once Around; Shipping News, The; Something to Talk About; What's Eating Gilbert Grape?
Halperin, Victor: Revolt of the Zombies; Supernatural; White Zombie
Halvorson, Gary: Adventures of Elmo in Grouchland, The; Country Girl, The
Hamann, Craig: Boogie Boy
Hamatsu, Mamoru: Heroic Legend of Arislan; Heroic Legend of Arislan: The Age of Heroes
Hamburg, John: Safe Men
Hamer, Robert: Dead of Night; Detective, The; Kind Hearts and Coronets; School for Scoundrels; To Paris with Love
Hamilton, David: Bilitis; Tendres Cousines
Hamilton, Dean: Road Home, The (1995); Savage Land; Strike a Pose
Hamilton, Guy: Battle of Britain; Colditz Story, The; Devil's Disciple, The; Diamonds Are Forever; Evil Under the Sun; Force Ten from Navarone; Funeral in Berlin; Goldfinger; Live and Let Die; Man with the Golden Gun, The; Mirror Crack'd, The; Remo Williams: The Adventure Begins
Hamilton, John: Code Name Jaguar
Hamilton, Strathford: Betrayal of the Dove; Blueberry Hill; Diving In; Escape from Atlantis; Proposition, The; Set-Up, The; Temptation
Hamilton-Wright, Michael: Mangler 2, The
Hamm, Nick: Talk of Angels
Hammer, Robert: Don't Answer the Phone
Hammond, Peter: Dark Angel, The; Inspector Morse (TV Series)
Hampton, Christopher: Carrington; Secret Agent, The
Hampton (Riccardo Freda), Robert: Caltiki, the Immortal Monster; Ghost, The (1963); Horrible Dr. Hichcock, The (Terror of Dr. Hichcock, The)
Hanbury, Victor: Hotel Reserve
Hancock, John: Bang the Drum Slowly; California Dreaming; Let's Scare Jessica to Death; Prancer; Steal the Sky; Weeds
Hancock, John Lee: Rookie, The (2002)
Hand, David: Bambi; Snow White and the Seven Dwarfs
Handler, Ken: Delivery Boys
Handley, Alan: Alice Through the Looking Glass
Hanks, Tom: Fallen Angels; That Thing You Do!
Hanna, William: Hey There, It's Yogi Bear; Jetsons: The Movie; Man Called Flintstone, A
Hannah, Eric: Extreme Days
Hannam, Ken: Sunday Too Far Away
Hannant, Brian: Time Guardian, The
Hanooka, Izhak: Red Nights
Hansel, Marion: Dust
Hansen, Ed: Bikini Carwash Company, The; Robo C.H.I.C.
Hanson, Curtis: Arousers, The; Bad Influence; Bedroom Window, The; Children of Times Square, The; Hand That Rocks the Cradle, The; L.A. Confidential; Losin' It; River Wild, The; Wonder Boys
Hanson, John: Northern Lights; Wild Rose
Hardwick, Gary: Brothers, The
Hardwicke, Cedric: Forever and a Day
Hardy, Joseph: Love's Savage Fury; Users, The
Hardy, Robin: Fantasist, The; Wicker Man, The
Hardy, Rod: Buffalo Girls; High Noon; Rio Diablo; Sara Dane; Thirst; 20,000 Leagues Under the Sea
Hare, David: Designated Mourner, The; Strapless; Wetherby
Hargrove, Dean: Dear Detective
Hark, Tsui: Better Tomorrow 3, A: Love and Death in Saigon; Double Team; Knock Off; Once Upon a Time in China; Once Upon a Time in China II; Once Upon a Time in China III; Peking Opera Blues; Time and Tide; Twin Dragons; We're Going to Eat You!; Zu: Warriors from the Magic Mountain
Harlan, Veidt: Jud Suss
Harlin, Renny: Adventures of Ford Fairlane, The; Born American; Cliffhanger; Cutthroat Island; Deep Blue Sea; Die Hard 2: Die Harder; Driven; Long Kiss Goodnight, The; Nightmare on Elm Street 4, A: The DreamMaster; Prison
Harling, Robert: Evening Star, The
Harlow, John: Candles at Nine
Harmon, Robert: Eyes of an Angel; Gotti; Hitcher, The; Nowhere to Run
Harrington, Curtis: Dead Don't Die, The; Devil Dog: The Hound of Hell; Mata Hari; Night Tide; Planet of Blood (Queen of Blood); Ruby; What's the Matter with Helen?; Who Slew Auntie Roo?

Hemmings, David: Christmas Reunion, A; Dark Horse; Just a Gigolo; Key to Rebecca, The; Quantum Leap (TV Series); Treasure of the Yankee Zephyr
Henabery, Joseph E.: Leather Burners, The; Man from Painted Post, The
Hendershot, Eric: Kid Called Danger, A; Robin Hood Gang, The
Henderson, Clark: Circle of Fear; Primary Target; Saigon Commandos; Warlords of Hell
Henderson, John: Borrowers, The; Loch Ness
Henenlotter, Frank: Basket Case; Basket Case 2; Basket Case 3: The Progeny; Brain Damage
Henkel, Kim: Texas Chainsaw Massacre: The Next Generation
Henoershot, Eric: Clubhouse Detectives
Henreid, Paul: Battle Shock; Dead Ringer
Henry, Buck: First Family; Heaven Can Wait
Henson, Brian: Muppet Christmas Carol, The; Muppet Treasure Island
Henson, Jim: Dark Crystal, The; Great Muppet Caper, The; Labyrinth
Henson, Robby: Pharaoh's Army
Henzell, Perry: Harder They Come, The
Herbert, Henry: Emily
Herbert, Martin: Miami Horror; Strange Shadows in an Empty Room
Herd, Kelli: It's in the Water
Herek, Stephen: Bill and Ted's Excellent Adventure; Critters; Don't Tell Mom the Babysitter's Dead; Holy Man; Life or Something Like It; Mighty Ducks, The; Mr. Holland's Opus; 101 Dalmatians (1996); Rock Star; Three Musketeers, The
Herman, Albert: Delinquent Daughters; Take Me Back to Oklahoma; Warning Shadows
Herman, Chip: Burglar From Hell
Herman, Jean: Honor Among Thieves
Herman, Mark: Blame It on the Bellboy; Brassed Off; Little Voice
Herman, Philip: Tales Till the End
Hermosillo, Jaime Humberto: Donna Herlinda and Her Son; Mary My Dearest
Heroux, Denis: Uncanny, The
Herrier, Mark: Popcorn
Herrington, Rowdy: Gladiator; Jack's Back; Murder of Crows, A; Road House
Herron, W. Blake: Skin Art
Hershman, Joel: Greenfingers; Hold Me, Thrill Me, Kiss Me
Herskovitz, Marshall: Dangerous Beauty; Jack the Bear
Hertel, Gene: Showgirl Murders
Herwitz, Samuel: On the Make
Herz, Michael: First Turn-on, The; Sgt. Kabukiman N.Y.P.D.; Sugar Cookies; Toxic Avenger, The; Toxic Avenger Part II, The; Toxic Avenger Part III, The: The Last Temptation of Toxie; Troma's War
Herzfeld, John: Casualties of Love: The Long Island Lolita Story; Don King: Only in America; Father's Revenge, A; 15 Minutes; Preppie Murder, The; Two Days in the Valley; Two of a Kind
Herzog, Werner: Aguirre: Wrath of God; Every Man for Himself and God Against All; Fitzcarraldo; Heart of Glass; Stroszek; Where the Green Ants Dream; Woyzeck
Hess, David: To All a Good Night
Hess, Eugene: Don't Do It
Hess, Jon: Excessive Force; Watchers
Hessler, Gordon: Cry of the Banshee; Girl in a Swing, The; Golden Voyage of Sinbad, The; Journey of Honor; Kiss Meets the Phantom of the Park; Misfit Brigade, The; Murders in the Rue Morgue; Oblong Box, The; Out on Bail; Pray for Death; Scream and Scream Again; Tales of the Unexpected
Heston, Charlton: Antony and Cleopatra; Mother Lode
Heston, Fraser: Alaska; Crucifer of Blood; Needful Things; Treasure Island
Hewitt, David L.: Bloodsuckers, The; Journey to the Center of Time (Time Warp); Wizard of Mars, The
Hewitt, Jean: Blood of Dracula's Castle
Hewitt, Paul: Wild Palms
Hewitt, Peter: Bill and Ted's Bogus Journey; Borrowers, The; Tom and Huck
Hewitt, Rod: Dangerous, The (1984); Debt, The; Verne Miller
Heyes, Douglas: Powderkeg; Thriller (TV Series); Twilight Zone, The (TV Series)
Heynemann, Laurent: Birgit Haas Must Be Killed; Old Lady Who Walked in the Sea, The
Hibbs, Jesse: To Hell and Back
Hick, Jochen: No One Sleeps
Hickenlooper, George: Big Brass Ring, The; Ghost Brigade; Hearts of Darkness; Low Life, The; Persons Unknown
Hickner, Steve: Prince of Egypt
Hickox, Anthony: Full Eclipse; Hellraiser 3: Hell on Earth; Invasion of Privacy; Jill the Ripper; Payback; Prince Valiant; Sundown; Warlock: The Armageddon; Waxwork; Waxwork II: Lost in Time
Hickox, Douglas: Blackout; Brannigan; Entertaining Mr. Sloane; Hound of the Baskervilles, The; Mistral's Daughter; Theatre of Blood; Zulu Dawn
Hickox, James D. R.: Blood Surf; Children of the Corn III: Urban Harvest
Hicks, Katherine: Knight Chills
Hicks, Scott: Hearts in Atlantis; Shine; Snow Falling on Cedars
Higgin, Howard: Hell's House; High Voltage; Painted Desert, The; Racketeer
Higgins, Colin: Best Little Whorehouse in Texas, The; Foul Play; Nine to Five
Hiken, Nat: Car 54 Where Are You? (TV Series); Love God?, The
Hill, Bob: Car 54 Where Are You? (TV Series); Love God?, The
Hill, George: Big House, The; Min and Bill; Tell It to the Marines
Hill, George Roy: Butch Cassidy and the Sundance Kid; Funny Farm; Great Waldo Pepper, The; Hawaii; Little Drummer Girl, The; Little Romance, A; Period of Adjustment; Slap Shot; Slaughterhouse Five; Sting, The; Thoroughly Modern Millie; Toys in the Attic; World According to Garp, The; World of Henry Orient, The
Hill, Jack: Big Bird Cage, The; Chamber of Fear; Coffy; Foxy Brown; Macabre Serenade; Sinister Invasion; Snake People; Spider Baby; Switchblade Sisters
Hill, James: Belstone Fox, The; Black Beauty; Born Free; Christian the Lion; Corrupt Ones, The; Seaside Swingers; Study in Terror, A
Hill, Robert: Adventures of Tarzan, The; Tarzan the Fearless
Hill, Terence: Lucky Luke; Troublemakers
Hill, Tim: Max Keeble's Big Move; Muppets From Space
Hill, Walter: Another 48 Hrs.; Brewster's Millions; Crossroads; Driver, The; Extreme Prejudice; 48 Hrs.; Geronimo: An American Legend; Hard Times; Johnny Handsome; Last Man Standing; Long Riders, The; Red Heat; Southern Comfort; Streets of Fire; Tales from the Crypt (TV Series); Trespass; Warriors, The; Wild Bill
Hillenbrand, David: King Cobra
Hillenbrand, Scott: King Cobra
Hiller, Arthur: Addams Family, The (TV Series); Americanization of Emily, The; Author! Author!; Babe, The (1992); Carpool; Hospital, The; In-Laws, The; Lonely Guy, The; Love Story; Making Love; Man in the Glass Booth; Man of La Mancha; Married to It; Miracle of the White Stallions; Nightwing; Out of Towners, The (1970); Outrageous Fortune; Plaza Suite; Popi; Promise Her Anything; Romantic Comedy; See No Evil, Hear No Evil; Silver Streak; Taking Care of Business; Teachers; Tobruk; Wheeler Dealers, The
Hillman, David Michael: Strangeness, The
Hillman, Wiliam Byron: Double Exposure
Hills, David: Ator: The Fighting Eagle; Blade Master, The; Quest for the Mighty Sword
Hills, Paul: Boston Kickout
Hillyer, Lambert: Dracula's Daughter; Fighting Code; Forbidden Trail; Hatbox Mystery, The; Invisible Ray, The; Narrow

Trail, The; Shock, The (1923); Sundown Rider, The; Sundown Riders; Three-Word Brand, The
Hilton, Arthur: Cat Women of the Moon; Misadventures of Buster Keaton, The; Return of Jesse James, The
Hilton-Jacobs, Lawrence: Quiet Fire
Hiltzik, Robert: Sleepaway Camp
Himelstein, Howard: Power of Attorney
Hinzman, Bill: Majorettes, The
Hippolyte, Alexander Gregory: Animal Instincts; Animal Instincts 2; Animal Instincts: The Seductress; Body of Influence; Object of Obsession; Undercover
Hirano, Toshihiro: Dangaio; Vampire Princess Miyu
Hiroaki, Gooda: Bubblegum Crisis, Vols. 1–8
Hiroya, Oohira: Riding Bean
Hiroyuki, Fukushima: Bubblegum Crash, Vols. 1–3; Ten Little Gall Force/Scramble Wars
Hiroyuki, Ochi: Armitage III: Electro Blood
Hirsch, Bettina: Munchies
Hirsch, Karl T.: Killer Bud
Hirtz, Dagmar: Moondance
Hiscott, Leslie S.: Triumph of Sherlock Holmes, The
Hitchcock, Alfred: Alfred Hitchcock Presents (TV Series); Alfred Hitchcock's Bon Voyage and Aventure Malgache; Birds, The; Blackmail; Champagne; Dial M for Murder; Easy Virtue; Family Plot; Farmer's Wife, The; Foreign Correspondent; Frenzy; I Confess; Jamaica Inn; Juno and the Paycock; Lady Vanishes, The; Lifeboat; Lodger, The; Man Who Knew Too Much, The; Manxman, The; Marnie; Mr. and Mrs. Smith; Murder; North by Northwest; Notorious; Number 17; Paradine Case, The; Psycho; Rear Window; Rebecca; Rich and Strange; Ring, The; Rope; Sabotage; Saboteur; Secret Agent, The; Shadow of a Doubt; Skin Game, The (1931); Spellbound; Stage Fright; Strangers on a Train; Suspicion; Thirty-Nine Steps, The; To Catch a Thief; Topaz; Torn Curtain; Trouble with Harry, The; Under Capricorn; Vertigo; Waltzes from Vienna; Wrong Man, The; Young and Innocent
Hittleman, Carl K.: Kentucky Rifle
Hitzig, Rupert: Backstreet Dreams; Night Visitor (1989); Nowhere Land
Hively, Jack B.: Adventures of Huckleberry Finn, The; California Gold Rush; Four Jacks and a Jill; Panama Lady
Ho, Yim: Day the Sun Turned Cold, The
Hobbs, Fredric: Day the Sun Turned Cold, The
Hobbs, Lyndall: Back to the Beach
Hobin, Bill: Judy Garland and Friends
Hoblit, Gregory: Class of '61; Fallen; Frequency; Hart's War; L.A. Law; Primal Fear; Roe vs. Wade
Hoch, Klaus: Flypaper
Hochberg, Victoria: Jacob I Have Loved; Sweet 15
Hodges, Mike: Black Rainbow; Croupier; Flash Gordon; Florida Straits; Get Carter; Hitchhiker, The (Series); Morons from Outer Space; Prayer for the Dying, A; Pulp; Terminal Man, The
Hodi, Jeno: Deadly Obsession; Triplecross
Hodson, Christopher: Partners in Crime (Secret Adversary) (TV Series)
Hoey, Michael: Navy vs. the Night Monsters, The
Hoffman, Antony: Red Planet
Hoffman, Herman: Invisible Boy, The; It's a Dog's Life
Hoffman, Jerzy: Deluge, The (Potop) (1973)
Hoffman, John: Strange Confession
Hoffman, Michael: One Fine Day; Promised Land; Restless Natives; Restoration; Soapdish; Some Girls; William Shakespeare's A Midsummer Night's Dream
Hoffman, Peter: Valentino Returns
Hoffs, Tamar Simon: Allnighter, The
Hofmeyr, Gary: Dirty Games; Light in the Jungle, The
Hofsiss, Jack: Cat on a Hot Tin Roof; Elephant Man, The; I'm Dancing As Fast As I Can; Oldest Living Graduate, The
Hogan, David: Barb Wire
Hogan, James: Arrest Bulldog Drummond; Bulldog Drummond Escapes; Bulldog Drummond's Bride; Bulldog Drummond's Peril; Bulldog Drummond's Secret Police; Final Extra, The; Mad Ghoul, The
Hogan, P. J.: Muriel's Wedding; My Best Friend's Wedding
Hoge, Bob: Godson, The
Holcomb, Rod: Captain America; Cartier Affair, The; Chains of Gold; China Beach (TV Series); Convict Cowboy; Dead to Rights; ER: The Series Premiere; Red Light Sting, The; Royce; Stark
Holden, Lansing C.: She
Holender, Adam: Twisted
Holland, Agnieszka: Angry Harvest; Europa, Europa; Olivier, Olivier; Secret Garden, The; Shot in the Heart; Third Miracle, The; To Kill a Priest; Total Eclipse; Washington Square
Holland, Savage Steve: Better Off Dead; How I Got into College; One Crazy Summer
Holland, Todd: Krippendorf's Tribe; Wizard, The
Holland, Tom: Child's Play; Fatal Beauty; Fright Night; Langoliers, The; Temp, The; Thinner
Hollander, Eli: Out
Holleb, Alan: School Spirit
Holmes, Ben: Maid's Night Out, The; Saint in New York, The
Holmes, Fred: Dakota; Harley
Holofcener, Nicole: Walking and Talking
Holt, Seth: Nanny, The; Scream of Fear
Holzberg, Roger: Midnight Crossing
Holzman, Allan: Forbidden World; Intimate Stranger; Out of Control; Programmed to Kill; Survivors of the Holocaust
Holzman, Edward: Body Strokes (Siren's Call); Forbidden Games
Honda, Inoshiro: Dagora, the Space Monster; Ghidrah, the Three-Headed Monster; Godzilla, King of the Monsters; Godzilla vs. Monster Zero; Godzilla vs. Mothra; Godzilla's Revenge; Gorath; H-Man, The; Half Human; Human Vapor, The; King Kong vs. Godzilla; Latitude Zero; Mothra; Mysterians, The; Rodan; Terror of Mechagodzilla; Varan, the Unbelievable; War of the Gargantuas
Hong, Elliot: They Call Me Bruce?
Hong, Hwa I.: Dynamo
Hook, Harry: Kitchen Toto, The; Last of His Tribe, The; Lord of the Flies
Hooks, Kevin: Black Dog; Color of Friendship, The; Fled; Heat Wave; Murder Without Motive; Passenger 57; Roots—The Gift; Strictly Business; Vietnam War Story
Hool, Lance: Missing in Action 2: The Beginning; One Man's Hero; Steel Dawn
Hooper, Tobe: Apartment Complex, The; Crocodile; Eaten Alive; Funhouse, The; I'm Dangerous Tonight; Invaders from Mars; Lifeforce; Mangler, The; Poltergeist; Salem's Lot; Spontaneous Combustion; Texas Chainsaw Massacre, The; Texas Chainsaw Massacre 2, The; Tobe Hooper's Night Terrors
Hoover, Claudia: Double Exposure
Hope, Margot: Femme Fontaine: Killer Babe for the CIA
Hopkins, Anthony: August
Hopkins, Arthur: His Double Life
Hopkins, Joel: Jump Tomorrow
Hopkins, John: Torment
Hopkins, Stephen: Blown Away; Dangerous Game (1990); Ghost and the Darkness, The; Judgment Night; Lost in Space (1998); Nightmare on Elm Street 5, A: The Dream Child; Predator 2; Under Suspicion (2000)
Hopper, Dennis: Backtrack; Chasers; Colors; Easy Rider; Hot Spot; Last Movie, The (Chinchero)
Hopper, Jerry: Addams Family, The (TV Series); Fugitive, The (TV Series); Madron; Pony Express
Horian, Richard: Student Confidential
Horiuchi, Yasuhiro: 8Man
Horn, Leonard: Hunter (1971); Outer Limits, The (TV Series)
Hornady, Jeffrey: Shout (1991)
Horne, James W.: All over Town; Bohemian Girl, The; Bonnie Scotland; College; Green Archer; Laurel and Hardy Classics: Vol. 1–9; Way Out West
Horner, Harry: Beware, My Lovely; New Faces; Red Planet Mars

Horton, Peter: Amazon Women on the Moon; Cure, The
Horvat, Aleks: Sweethearts
Hoskins, Bob: Raggedy Rawney, The
Hoskins, Dan: Chopper Chicks in Zombietown
Hossein, Robert: Double Agents
Hostettler, Joe: Young at Heart Comedians, The
Houck Jr., Joy N.: Creature from Black Lake; Grey Matter
Hough, John: American Gothic; Biggles—Adventures in Time; Black Arrow (1984); Brass Target; Dirty Mary, Crazy Larry; Duel of Hearts; Escape to Witch Mountain; Ghost in Monte Carlo, A; Howling IV; Legend of Hell House, The; Return from Witch Mountain; Triumphs of a Man Called Horse; Twins of Evil; Watcher in the Woods, The
Hous, Robert: Shogun Assassin
Houston, Bobby: Bad Manners; Caged Fear; Trust Me
Hoven, Adrian: Dandelions; Mark of the Devil, Part 2
Hovis, Michael: Man with the Perfect Swing, The
Howard, Adam Coleman: Dark Harbor
Howard, Cy: Lovers and Other Strangers
Howard, David: Arizona Legion; Daniel Boone; In Old Santa Fe; Marshal of Mesa City; Mystery Ranch; Mystery Squadron; Renegade Ranger; Triple Justice
Howard, Frank: Helter-Skelter Murders, The
Howard, Karin: Tigress, The
Howard, Leslie: Pimpernel Smith; Pygmalion
Howard, Richard: Ground Control
Howard, Ron: Apollo 13; Backdraft; Beautiful Mind, A; Cocoon; EDtv; Far and Away; Grand Theft Auto; Gung Ho (1985); How the Grinch Stole Christmas; Night Shift; Paper, The; Parenthood; Ransom; Splash; Willow
Howard, Sandy: One Step to Hell
Howard, William K.: Backdoor to Heaven; Cat and the Fiddle, The; Evelyn Prentice; Johnny Come Lately; Princess Comes Across, The; White Gold
Howe, Matthew: Original Sins
Howell, C. Thomas: Big Fall, The; Hourglass; Pure Danger
Howitt, Peter: Antitrust; Sliding Doors
Howson, Frank: Hunting
Hoyt, Harry: Lost World, The
Hrebejk, Jan: Divided We Fall
Hsu, Dachin: Pale Blood
Hsu, Talun: Witchcraft V: Dance with the Devil
Hu, Ann: Shadow Magic
Huang, George: Swimming with Sharks; Trojan War
Hua-Shan: Infra-Man
Hubert, Jean-Loup: Le Grand Chemin (The Grand Highway); Next Year If All Goes Well
Hudlin, Reginald: Boomerang; Cosmic Slop; Great White Hype, The; House Party; Ladies Man, The (2000)
Hudlin, Warrington: Cosmic Slop
Hudson, Gary: Thunder Run
Hudson, Hugh: Chariots of Fire; Greystoke: The Legend of Tarzan, Lord of the Apes; I Dreamed of Africa; Lost Angels; My Life So Far; Revolution
Huemer, Peter Ily: Kiss Daddy Good Night
Huestis, Marc: Men in Love
Huey, David: Capital Punishment
Huff, Brent: Final Justice
Huggins, Roy: Hangman's Knot
Hugh, R. John: Deadly Encounter; Naked in the Sun
Hughes, Albert: Dead Presidents; From Hell; Menace II Society
Hughes, Bronwen: Forces of Nature; Harriet the Spy
Hughes, Carol: Missing Link
Hughes, David: Missing Link
Hughes, Howard: Outlaw, The
Hughes, John: Breakfast Club, The; Curly Sue; Ferris Bueller's Day Off; Planes, Trains and Automobiles; She's Having a Baby; Sixteen Candles; Uncle Buck; Weird Science
Hughes, Ken: Casino Royale; Chitty Chitty Bang Bang; Cromwell; Internecine Project, The; Long Haul; Night School; Of Human Bondage; Oh, Alfie; Sextette
Hughes, Robert C.: Down the Drain; Hunter's Blood
Hughes, Terry: Barnum; Butcher's Wife, The; Monty Python Live at the Hollywood Bowl; Mrs. Santa Claus; Ripping Yarns; Sunset Limousine
Hui, Ann: Song of the Exile
Hulette, Don: Breaker! Breaker!; Tennessee Stallion
Hulme, Ron: Fearless Tiger
Humberstone, H. Bruce: Charlie Chan at the Olympics; Charlie Chan at the Opera; Charlie Chan at the Racetrack; Charlie Chan in Honolulu; Desert Song, The; Happy Go Lovely; Hello, Frisco, Hello; I Wake Up Screaming; Iceland; Pin-Up Girl; Sun Valley Serenade; Tarzan and the Trappers; Ten Wanted Men; To the Shores of Tripoli; Wonder Man
Hung, Sammo: Dragons Forever; Eastern Condors; Heart of Dragon; Millionaire's Express (Shanghai Express); Mr. Nice Guy; Paper Marriage
Hung, Tran Anh: Cyclo; Scent of Green Papaya, The; Vertical Ray of the Sun, The
Hung, Wong Kee: Mr. Vampire (Vol. 1–4)
Hunsicker, Jackson: Oddball Hall
Hunt, Bonnie: Return to Me
Hunt, Christopher: Eat and Run
Hunt, David: Sudden Thunder; Triple Impact
Hunt, Edward: Alien Warrior; Bloody Birthday; Brain, The; Starship Invasions
Hunt, Maurice: Pagemaster, The
Hunt, Paul: Clones, The; Merlin; Twisted Nightmare
Hunt, Peter H.: It Came Upon a Midnight Clear; Life on the Mississippi; Mysterious Stranger, The; 1776; Skeezer
Hunt, Peter R.: Assassination; Death Hunt; Eyes of a Witness; Gulliver's Travels; Hyper Sapian: People from Another Star; On Her Majesty's Secret Service; Shout at the Devil; Wild Geese II
Hunt, Pixote: Fantasia 2000
Hunter, T. Hayes: Ghoul, The
Hunter, Tim: Beverly Hills 90210; Lies of the Twins; Mean Streak; Mean Streak; Paint It Black; River's Edge; Saint of Fort Washington, The; Sylvester; Tex
Hunter (Massimo Pupillo), Max: Bloody Pit of Horror
Huppert, Caroline: Sincerely Charlotte
Hurley, Graham: Titanic: The Nightmare and the Dream
Hurran, Nick: Virtual Sexuality
Hurst, Brian Desmond: Christmas Carol, A; Dangerous Moonlight (Suicide Squadron); Hungry Hill; Malta Story, The; Playboy of the Western World; Simba
Hurst, Michael: New Blood
Hurtz, William: Little Nemo: Adventures in Slumberland
Hurwitz, Harry: Fleshtone; Projectionist, The; Rosebud Beach Hotel, The (Nostell Hotel, The); That's Adequate
Hussein, Waris: And Baby Makes Six; Callie and Son; Coming Out of the Ice; Divorce His: Divorce Hers; Edward and Mrs. Simpson; Fall from Grace; Intimate Contact; Little Gloria, Happy at Last; Melody; Onassis: The Richest Man in the World; Princess Daisy; Quackser Fortune Has a Cousin in the Bronx; Summer House, The; Switched at Birth
Huston, Anjelica: Agnes Browne; Bastard Out of Carolina
Huston, Danny: Becoming Colette; Maddening, The; Mr. Corbett's Ghost; Mr. North
Huston, Jimmy: Final Exam; My Best Friend Is a Vampire; Wharf Rat, The
Huston, John: Across the Pacific; African Queen, The; Annie; Asphalt Jungle, The; Barbarian and the Geisha, The; Beat the Devil; Bible, The; Casino Royale; Dead, The; Fat City; In This Our Life; Key Largo; Life and Times of Judge Roy Bean, The; List of Adrian Messenger, The; Mackintosh Man, The; Maltese Falcon, The; Man Who Would Be King, The; Misfits, The; Moby Dick; Moulin Rouge; Night of the Iguana, The; Phobia; Prizzi's Honor; Red Badge of Courage, The; Reflections in a Golden Eye; Treasure of the Sierra Madre; Under the Volcano; Unforgiven, The (1960); Victory; Wise Blood
Hutchison, Clint: Terror Tract
Hutton, Brian G.: First Deadly Sin, The; High Road to China; Kelly's Heroes; Night Watch; Where Eagles Dare; X, Y and Zee
Hutton, Robert: Slime People, The
Hutton, Timothy: Digging to China

Huyck, Willard: Best Defense; French Postcards; Howard the Duck
Hyams, Nessa: Leader of the Band
Hyams, Peter: Capricorn One; Death Target; End of Days; Hanover Street; Musketeer, The; Narrow Margin (1990); Outland; Presidio, The; Relic, The; Running Scared; Star Chamber, The; Stay Tuned; Sudden Death; Timecop; 2010
Hytner, Nicholas: Center Stage; Crucible, The; Madness of King George, The; Object of My Affection, The
Ibanez, Juan: Chamber of Fear; Dance of Death; Macabre Serenade; Sinister Invasion; Snake People
Ice Cube: Players Club, The
Ichaso, Leon: Bitter Sugar; Crossover Dreams; El Super; Fear Inside, The; Free of Eden; Pinero; Sugar Hill; Take, The; Zooman
Ichikawa, Kon: Actor's Revenge, An; Burmese Harp, The; Enjo; Fires on the Plain; Odd Obsession
Ide, Yasunori: Burn Up!
Idle, Eric: Rutles, The (All You Need Is Cash)
Iida, Tstutomu: Devilman Vol. 1–2
Ikehiro, Kazuo: Zatoichi: Masseur Ichi and a Chest ofGold
Illsley, Mark: Happy, Texas
Im, Kwon-taek: Chunhyang
Imagawa, Yasuhiro: Giant Robo
Imamura, Shohei: Ballad of Narayama, The; Black Rain; Eel, The; Eijanaika (Why Not?); Insect Woman; Pornographers, The; Vengeance Is Mine
Imhoof, Markus: Boat Is Full, The
Inagaki, Hiroshi: Kojiro; Rikisha-Man; Samurai Saga; Samurai Trilogy, The
Inamura, Shobei: Dr. Akagi
Iñárritu, Alejandro Gonzalez: Amores Perros
Ince, Thomas: Civilization
Indovina, Franco: Catch as Catch Can; Oldest Profession, The
Ingraham, Lloyd: American Aristocracy, An
Ingram, Malcolm: Tail Lights Fade
Ingster, Boris: Guns of Diablo; Judge Steps Out, The; Stranger on the Third Floor
Ingvordsen, J. Christian: Comrades in Arms; Firehouse; Little Patriot, The; Mob War; Outfit, The; Search and Destroy
Innocenti, Markus: Murder Story
Ionesco, Eugene: Seven Deadly Sins, The
Ireland, Dan: Velocity of Gary, The; Whole Wide World, The
Ireland, O'Dale: High School Caesar
Irmas, Matthew: Edie & Pen; When the Party's Over
Irvin, John: Champions; City of Industry; Crazy Horse; Dogs of War, The; Eminent Domain; Freefall; Ghost Story; Hamburger Hill; Month by the Lake, A; Next of Kin; Raw Deal; Robin Hood; Turtle Diary; When Trumpets Fade; Widow's Peak
Irvin, Sam: Acting on Impulse; Guilty as Charged; Oblivion; Oblivion 2: Backlash; Out There
Irving, David: C.H.U.D. II (Bud the C.H.U.D.); Night of the Cyclone
Irving, Richard: Cyborg: The Six Million Dollar Man; Jesse Owens Story, The
Isaac, James: Horror Show, The
Isaacs, Ronnie: Warriors from Hell
Isacsson, Kris: Down to You
Isasi, Antonio: Summertime Killer, The; Vengeance
Iscove, Robert: Boys and Girls; Flash, The (1990); Lawrenceville Stories, The; Mission of the Shark; Rodgers & Hammerstein's Cinderella; Shattered Dreams; She's All That; That's Singing: The Best of Broadway
Ishiguro, Noboru: Orguss, Vols. 1–4
Ishii, Takashi: Gonin
Israel, Neal: Americathon; Bachelor Party; Breaking the Rules; Moving Violations; Surf Ninjas; Tunnelvision (1976)
Israelson, Peter: Side Out
Itami, Juzo: Funeral, The; Minbo, or The Gentle Art of Japanese Extortion; Tampopo; Taxing Woman, A; Taxing Woman's Return, A
Ivory, James: Autobiography of a Princess; Bombay Talkie; Bostonians, The; Courtesans of Bombay; Europeans, The; Golden Bowl, The; Heat and Dust; Householder, The; Howards End; Hullabaloo over George and Bonnie's Pictures; Jane Austen in Manhattan; Jefferson in Paris; Maurice; Mr. and Mrs. Bridge; Quartet; Remains of the Day; Room with a View, A; Roseland; Savages; Shakespeare Wallah; Slaves of New York; Soldier's Daughter Never Cries, A; Surviving Picasso; Wild Party, The
Ivy, Bob: Dark Rider
Jablin, David: Don's Analyst, The; National Lampoon's Favorite Deadly Sins
Jabor, Arnaldo: I Love You (Eu Te Amo)
Jackson, David S.: Death Train; Detonator II: Night Watch
Jackson, Donald G.: Hell Comes to Frogtown; Return to Frogtown; Rollerblade
Jackson, Douglas: Dead End; Deadbolt; Natural Enemy; Paperboy, The; Stalked; Strange Tales: Ray Bradbury Theater; Twists of Terror; Whispers
Jackson, G. Philip: Replikator: Cloned to Kill
Jackson, George: House Party 2
Jackson, Jalil: Lady Terminator
Jackson, Larry: Bugs Bunny, Superstar
Jackson, Lewis: Christmas Evil
Jackson, Mick: Bodyguard, The; Chattahoochee; Clean Slate (1994); Indictment: The McMartin Trial; L.A. Story; Threads; Very British Coup, A; Volcano; Yuri Nosenko, KGB
Jackson, Pat: Encore; King Arthur, The Young Warlord; Prisoner, The (1968) (TV Series)
Jackson, Peter: Bad Taste; Dead Alive; Forgotten Silver; Frighteners, The; Heavenly Creatures; Lord of the Rings, The: Fellowship of the Ring; Meet the Feebles
Jackson, Richard: Big Bust Out, The
Jackson, Wilfred: Alice in Wonderland; Cinderella; Lady and the Tramp; Peter Pan
Jacobs, Alan: Nina Takes a Lover
Jacobs, Jerry P.: Dangerous Place, A; Freedom Strike
Jacobs, Jon: Girl with the Hungry Eyes, The
Jacobs, Werner: Heidi
Jacobson, Rick: Bloodfist VI: Ground Zero; Night Hunter; Reasons of the Heart; Ring of Fire 3: Lion Strike; Shadow Warriors; Star Quest; Strategic Command; Suspect Device; Unborn II, The
Jacobsson, Anders: Evil Ed
Jacoby, Joseph: Great Bank Hoax, The; Hurry Up or I'll Be 30
Jacopetti, Gualtiero: Mondo Cane II
Jacquot, Benoit: School of Flesh; Single Girl
Jaeckin, Just: Emmanuelle; French Woman, The; Lady Chatterley's Lover; Story of O, The
Jaffe, Stanley: Without a Trace
Jaglom, Henry: Always; Babyfever; Can She Bake a Cherry Pie?; Déjà Vu; Eating; Last Summer in the Hamptons; New Year's Day; Sitting Ducks; Someone to Love; Tracks; Venice/Venice
Jaimes, Sam: Snoopy: The Musical; Snoopy's Reunion; This Is America, Charlie Brown; Why, Charlie Brown, Why?
Jaissle, Matt: Legion of the Night
Jamain, Patrick: Honeymoon
James, Alan: Come on Tarzan; Dick Tracy; Phantom Thunderbolt; Red Barry; SOS Coast Guard; Trail Drive; When a Man Sees Red
James, Pedr: Martin Chuzzlewit
James, Steve: Hoop Dreams; Passing Glory; Prefontaine
Jameson, Jerry: Airport '77; Bat People; Cowboy and the Ballerina, The; High Noon, Part Two; Killing at Hell's Gate; Raise the Titanic; Starflight One; Terror on the 40th Floor
Jancso, Miklos: Red and the White, The; Round-Up, The
Janger, Lane: Just One Time
Janis, Conrad: November Conspiracy, The
Jankel, Annabel: D.O.A.; Max Headroom; Super Mario Brothers, The
Janot, Charles: Lucy and Desi: Before the Laughter
Jaoui, Agnès: Taste of Others, The
Jaque, Christian: Fanfan the Tulip

Jarman, Derek: Angelic Conversation; Aria; Caravaggio; Edward II; Garden, The; In the Shadow of the Sun; Jubilee; Last of England, The; War Requiem
Jarmusch, Jim: Dead Man; Down by Law; Ghost Dog: The Way of the Samurai; Mystery Train; Night on Earth; Stranger Than Paradise
Jarrott, Charles: Amateur, The (1982); Anne of the Thousand Days; Boy in Blue, The; Condorman; Last Flight of Noah's Ark; Littlest Horse Thieves, The; Night of the Fox; Other Side of Midnight, The; Poor Little Rich Girl: The Barbara Hutton Story; Strange Case of Dr. Jekyll and Mr. Hyde, The (1968)
Jarvi-Laturi, Ilkka: Spy Games
Jason, Leigh: Bride Walks Out, The; Lady for a Night; Mad Miss Manton, The; Out of the Blue
Jean, Mark: Homecoming
Jean, Vadim: Leon the Pig Farmer; Nightscare; Real Howard Spritz, The
Jeffrey, Tom: Odd Angry Shot, The
Jeffries, Lionel: Amazing Mr. Blunden, The; Baxter; Railway Children, The; Water Babies, The
Jeffries, Richard: Bloodtide
Jenkins, Michael: Rebel; Sweet Talker
Jenkins, Tamara: Slums of Beverly Hills
Jensen, Jeff: Watcher, The
Jenson, Vicky: Shrek
Jenz, Tom: Ladies Sing the Blues, The
Jessner, Leopold: Backstairs
Jeunet, Jean-Pierre: Alien Resurrection; Amélie; City of Lost Children, The; Delicatessen
Jewison, Norman: Agnes of God; ... And Justice for All; Best Friends; Bogus; Cincinnati Kid, The; Dinner with Friends; Fiddler on the Roof; F.I.S.T.; Forty Pounds of Trouble; Hurricane, The; In Country; In the Heat of the Night; Jesus Christ, Superstar; Moonstruck; Only You; Other People's Money; Picture Windows; Rollerball; Russians Are Coming, the Russians Are Coming, The; Send Me No Flowers; Soldier's Story, A; Thomas Crown Affair, The; Thrill of It All, The
Jhabvala, Ruth Prawer: Courtesans of Bombay
Jianxin, Huang: Wooden Man's Bride, The
Jimenez, Neal: Waterdance, The
Jing, Wong: Legend of the Red Dragon
Jiras, Robert: I Am the Cheese
Ji-Shun, Duan: Go-Masters, The
Jittlov, Mike: Wizard of Speed and Time, The
Joannon, Léo: Atoll K (Utopia)
Joanou, Phil: Entropy; Fallen Angels; Final Analysis; Heaven's Prisoners; State of Grace; Three O'Clock High; U2: Rattle and Hum; Wild Palms
Jobson, Dickie: Countryman
Jodorowsky, Alejandro: Rainbow Thief, The; Santa Sangre
Jodrell, Steve: Shame
Joens, Michael: My Little Pony: The Movie
Joffe, Arthur: Alberto Express; Harem
Joffe, Mark: Cosi; Efficiency Expert, The (Spotswood); Grievous Bodily Harm; Matchmaker, The
Joffe, Roland: City of Joy; Fat Man and Little Boy; Goodbye Lover; Killing Fields, The; Mission, The; Scarlet Letter, The
Johnson, Alan: Solarbabies; To Be or Not to Be
Johnson, Clark: Boycott
Johnson, David C.: Drop Squad, The; Riot (1996) (TV Movie)
Johnson, Hugh: Chill Factor
Johnson, Irvin: Fist of Steel
Johnson, Jed: Andy Warhol's Bad
Johnson, John H.: Curse of the Blue Lights
Johnson, Kenneth: Alien Nation, Dark Horizon; Incredible Hulk, The; Short Circuit 2; Steel; V
Johnson, Lamont: Broken Chain, The; Crisis at Central High; Dangerous Company; Execution of Private Slovik, The; Gore Vidal's Lincoln; Groundstar Conspiracy, The; Gunfight, A; Last American Hero, The; Lipstick; My Sweet Charlie; One on One; Paul's Case; Spacehunter: Adventures in the ForbiddenZone; Thousand Heroes, A; Twilight Zone, The (TV Series); Unnatural Causes
Johnson, Mark Steven: Simon Birch
Johnson, Nunnally: Man in the Gray Flannel Suit, The; Three Faces of Eve, The
Johnson, Patrick Read: Angus; Baby's Day Out; Spaced Invaders; When Good Ghouls Go Bad
Johnson, Tim: Antz
Johnston, Aaron Kim: For the Moment
Johnston, Jim: Blue de Ville
Johnston, Joe: Honey, I Shrunk the Kids; Jumanji; Jurassic Park III; October Sky; Pagemaster, The; Rocketeer, The
Johnstone, Tucker: Blood Salvage
Jonasson, Oskar: Remote Control
Jones, Amy: Love Letters; Maid to Order; Slumber Party Massacre
Jones, Amy Holden: Rich Man's Wife, The
Jones, Brian Thomas: Rejuvenator, The
Jones, Buck: Law for Tombstone
Jones, Chris: Escape from Survival Zone
Jones, Chuck: Adventures of Milo in the Phantom Tollbooth, The; Bugs Bunny/Road Runner Movie, The; 1001 Rabbit Tales
Jones, David: Betrayal; Christmas Carol, A; Christmas Wife, The; 84 Charing Cross Road; Jackknife; Look Back In Anger; Trial, The; Unexpected Life, An
Jones, David Hugh: Confession, The
Jones, Dick: Extra Girl, The
Jones, Don: Sweater Girls
Jones, F. Richard: Bulldog Drummond
Jones, Gary: Mosquito; Spiders (2000)
Jones, Harmon: As Young as You Feel; Bullwhip; Gorilla at Large; Pride of St. Louis, The
Jones, James Cellan: Fortunes of War
Jones, Kirk: Waking Ned Devine
Jones, L. Q.: Boy and His Dog, A
Jones, Mark: Leprechaun; Rumpelstiltskin
Jones, Philip J.: Cause of Death; Wish Me Luck
Jones, Terry: Erik the Viking; Life of Brian; Monty Python's the Meaning of Life; Personal Services
Jones, Tommy Lee: Good Old Boys, The
Jonker, Leif: Darkness
Jonze, Spike: Being John Malkovich
Jordan, Glenn: Barbarians at the Gate; Buddy System, The; Displaced Person, The; Dress Gray; Echoes in the Darkness; Frankenstein; Jesse; Legalese; Les Misérables; Lois Gibbs and the Love Canal; Mass Appeal; Night Ride Home; O Pioneers!; Only When I Laugh; Sarah, Plain and Tall; Streetcar Named Desire, A; Winter's End
Jordan, Kevin: Smiling Fish & Goat on Fire
Jordan, Neil: Butcher Boy, The; Company of Wolves, The; Crying Game, The; Danny Boy; End of the Affair, The; High Spirits; In Dreams; Interview with the Vampire; Michael Collins; Miracle, The; Mona Lisa; We're No Angels
Jordon, Glenn: To Dance with the White Dog
Jorfald, Knut W.: Littlest Viking, The
Joseph, Eugine: Spookies
Joslin, Tom: Silverlake Life: The View from Here
Jost, Jon: All the Vermeers in New York; Jon Jost's Frameup; Sure Fire
Jourdan, Pierre: Phedre
Joyce, Maurice: Doug's 1st Movie
Joyner, C. Courtney: Lurking Fear; Trancers III: Deth Lives
Jubenvill, Ken: Ebenezer
Judge, Mike: Beavis and Butt-head Do America; Beavis and Butt-head (TV Series); Office Space
Judkins, Ron: Hi-line, The
Julian, Rupert: Merry-Go-Round, The; Phantom of the Opera
Julien, Isaac: Young Soul Rebels
Junde, Cui: Story of Xinghua, The
Junger, Gil: Black Knight; 10 Things I Hate About You
Juran, Nathan: Attack of the 50-Foot Woman; Black Castle, The; Brain from Planet Arous, The; Deadly Mantis, The; First Men in the Moon; Hellcats of the Navy; Jack the Giant Killer; Land Raiders; 7th Voyage of Sinbad, The; 20 Million Miles to Earth

Juranville, Jacques: Le Gentleman D'Espom (Duke of the Derby)
Jutra, Claude: By Design; Mon Oncle Antoine; Surfacing
Kachivas, Lou: Secret of the Sword, The
Kachyna, Karel: Last Butterfly, The
Kaczender, George: Agency; Chanel Solitaire; Girl in Blue, The; In Praise of Older Women; Maternal Instincts; Pretty Kill
Kadár, Ján: Blue Hotel; Lies My Father Told Me; Shop on Main Street, The
Kadison, Ellis: Cat, The (1966)
Kadokawa, Haruki: Heaven and Earth; Legend of the Eight Samurai
Kagan, Bertrand Tager: Phantom 2040 (TV Series)
Kagan, Jeremy Paul: Big Fix, The; Big Man on Campus; By the Sword; Chosen, The; Conspiracy: The Trial of the Chicago 8; Descending Angel; Doctor Quinn Medicine Woman; Heroes; Journey of Natty Gann, The; Katherine; Roswell; Sleeping Beauty; Sting II, The
Kahn, Richard: Harlem Rides the Range
Kahn, Richard C.: Bronze Buckaroo; Two-Gun Man from Harlem
Kaige, Chen: Emperor and the Assassin, The; Farewell My Concubine; Life on a String; Temptress Moon; Yellow Earth
Kaiserman, Connie: My Little Girl
Kalatozov, Mikhail K.: Cranes Are Flying, The; I Am Cuba; Red Tent, The
Kalin, Tom: Swoon
Kalmanowicz, Max: Dreams Come True
Kalvert, Scott: Basketball Diaries, The
Kamelson, Bill: Souler Opposite, The
Kamen, Jay: Transformations
Kaminski, Janusz: Lost Souls
Kamiya, Jun: Girl from Phantasia
Kamler, Piotr: Chronopolis
Kampmann, Steven: Stealing Home
Kane, Dennis: French Quarter
Kane, Joseph: Arizona Kid; Bad Man of Deadwood; Billy the Kid Returns; Brimstone; Carson City Kid; Dakota; Fighting Marines, The; Flame of the Barbary Coast; Frontier Pony Express; Git Along, Little Dogies; Heart of the Golden West; Heart of the Rockies; Hoodlum Empire; In Old Caliente; Jesse James at Bay; Jubilee Trail; King of the Cowboys; King of the Pecos; Lawless Nineties, The; Lonely Trail, The; Man from Music Mountain; Maverick Queen, The; Melody Trail; Oh! Susanna!; Old Corral; Public Cowboy #1; Ranger and the Lady, The; Ride, Ranger, Ride; Ride the Man Down; Robin Hood of the Pecos; Romance on the Range; Rough Riders' Roundup; Saga of Death Valley; Silver Spurs; Song of Nevada; Song of Texas; Sons of the Pioneers; Springtime in the Rockies; Sunset Serenade; Under Western Stars; Undersea Kingdom; Wall Street Cowboy; Yodelin' Kid from Pine Ridge; Young Bill Hickok
Kanefsky, Rolf: There's Nothing Out There
Kaneko, Shusuke: Gamera: Guardian of the Universe; H. P. Lovecraft's Necronomicon: Book of the Dead; Summer Vacation: 1999
Kanevski, Vitaly: Freeze—Die—Come to Life
Kanew, Jeff: Eddie Macon's Run; Gotcha!; Natural Enemies; Revenge of the Nerds; Tough Guys; Troop Beverly Hills; V. I. Warshawski
Kanganis, Charles: No Escape, No Return; Race the Sun; Time to Die, A
Kanievska, Marek: Another Country; Less Than Zero; Where the Money Is
Kanin, Garson: Bachelor Mother; Great Man Votes, The; My Favorite Wife; Next Time I Marry; They Knew What They Wanted; Tom, Dick and Harry
Kanner, Alexis: Kings and Desperate Men: A Hostage Incident
Kanter, Hal: For the Love of It; I Married a Woman; Loving You
Kaplan, Betty: Of Love and Shadows
Kaplan, Deborah: Can't Hardly Wait; Josie and the Pussycats
Kaplan, Ed: Chips, the War Dog; Primal Secrets; Walking on Air
Kaplan, Jonathan: Accused, The; Bad Girls; Brokedown Palace; Fallen Angels; Gentleman Bandit, The; Heart Like a Wheel; Immediate Family; Love Field; Mr. Billion; Over the Edge; Picture Windows; Project X; Truck Turner; Unlawful Entry; White Line Fever
Kaplan, Nelly: Nea (A Young Emmanuelle); Very Curious Girl, A
Kaplan, Richard: Eleanor Roosevelt Story, The
Kaplan, Ted: Warbus
Kapland, Henry: Best of Dark Shadows, The
Kapur, Shekhar: Bandit Queen; Elizabeth
Karaim, Lee: Kiss the Girls Goodbye
Karan, Bill: Gang Busters
Karaszewski, Larry: Screwed
Karbelnikoff, Michael: Last Ride, The; Mobsters
Kardos, Leslie: Small Town Girl
Karlson, Phil: Ben; Big Cat, The; Framed; Hell to Eternity; Hornet's Nest; Kansas City Confidential; Kid Galahad; Ladies of the Chorus; Shanghai Cobra, The; Texas Rangers, The (1951); Untouchables, The: Scarface Mob; Walking Tall
Karman, Janice: Chipmunk Adventure, The
Karmel, Pip: Me Myself I
Karn, Bill: Ma Barker's Killer Brood
Karson, Eric: Angel Town; Black Eagle; Octagon, The; Opposing Force
Kar-Wai, Wong: Chungking Express
Kasdan, Jake: Orange County; Zero Effect
Kasdan, Lawrence: Accidental Tourist, The; Big Chill, The; Body Heat; French Kiss; Grand Canyon; I Love You to Death; Mumford; Silverado; Wyatt Earp
Kass, Sam Henry: Search for One-Eye Jimmy, The
Kassovitz, Mathieu: Café au Lait; Crimson Rivers, The; Hate
Kassovitz, Peter: Jakob the Liar; Make Room for Tomorrow
Kastle, Leonard: Honeymoon Killers, The
Kastner, Daphina: French Exit
Katansky, Ivan: S.S. Hell Camp
Katayama, Kazuyashi: Appleseed; Rumik World: The Supergal
Katkin, Brian: Enemy Action
Katleman, Michael: Bloodhounds; Spider and the Fly, The
Katselas, Milton: Butterflies Are Free; Forty Carats; Report to the Commissioner; Strangers: The Story of a Mother and a Daughter
Katsuhito, Akiyama: Bubblegum Crisis, Vols. 1–8; Sol Bianca
Katsumata, Tomoharu: Arcadia of My Youth
Katz, Douglas: Age Isn't Everything
Katzin, Lee H.: Bastard, The; Break, The; Dirty Dozen, The: The Deadly Mission; Dirty Dozen, The: The Fatal Mission; Hondo and the Apaches; Jake Spanner Private Eye; Le Mans; Man from Atlantis, The; Restraining Order; Salzburg Connection, The; Savages; Sky Heist; Space 1999 (TV Series); Terror Out of the Sky; Whatever Happened to Aunt Alice?; World Gone Wild
Katzman, Sam: Brothers of the West
Kaufer, Jonathan: Soup for One
Kaufman, George S.: Senator Was Indiscreet, The
Kaufman, James: Backstab; Night of the Demons 3; Whiskers
Kaufman, Lloyd: Sgt. Kabukiman N.Y.P.D.; Stuff Stephanie in the Incinerator; Toxic Avenger Part II, The; Toxic Avenger Part III, The: The Last Temptation of Toxie
Kaufman, Phil: Great Northfield Minnesota Raid, The; Henry & June; Invasion of the Body Snatchers; Right Stuff, The; Rising Sun; Unbearable Lightness of Being, The; Wanderers, The; White Dawn, The
Kaufman, Philip: Quills
Kaurismaki, Aki: Ariel
Kaurismaki, Mika: Amazon; Condition Red; Tigrero: A Film That Was Never Made
Kavanagh, Denis: Flight from Vienna
Kawadri, Anwar: Claudia; In Search of the Serpent of Death
Kawajiri, Yoshiaki: Cyber City Oedo 808; Demon City Shinjuku; Neo-Tokyo; Wicked City (1995)
Kawamori, Shoji: Macross Plus

Kawamura, Takamitsu: Gargoyles: The Movie (1994)
Kawasaki, Hiroshi: Record of Lodoss War
Kawasaki, Kikuo: Lured Innocence
Kaweski, Mike: Phantom 2040 (TV Series)
Kay, Gilbert: White Comanche
Kay, Stephen: Last Time I Committed Suicide, The
Kay, Stephen T.: Get Carter
Kaye, John: Along for the Ride
Kaye, Tony: American History X
Kaylor, Robert: Carny; Nobody's Perfect
Kazan, Elia: Arrangement, The; Baby Doll; Boomerang; East of Eden; Face in the Crowd, A; Gentlemen's Agreement; Last Tycoon, The; On the Waterfront; Panic in the Streets; Pinky; Sea of Grass, The; Splendor in the Grass; Streetcar Named Desire, A; Tree Grows in Brooklyn, A; Viva Zapata!
Kazan, Nicholas: Dream Lover
Keach, James: Camouflage; False Identity; Forgotten, The; Praying Mantis; Stars Fell on Henrietta, The; Sunstroke
Keating, David: Summer Fling
Keating, Kevin: Hell's Angels Forever
Keaton, Buster: Art of Buster Keaton, The; Buster Keaton Festival Vol. 1–3; General, The; Navigator, The (1924); Our Hospitality; Seven Chances; Sherlock Jr.; Three Ages, The
Keaton, Diane: Hanging Up; Heaven; Unstrung Heroes; Wild Flower (1991)
Keen, Bob: Proteus; Sir Arthur Conan Doyle's The Lost World; To Catch a Yeti
Keene, Nietzchka: Juniper Tree, The
Keeslar, Don: Bog; Capture of Grizzly Adams, The
Keeter, Worth: Dogs of Hell; Illicit Behavior; Order of the Black Eagle; Scorpio One; Snapdragon; Trapper County War; Wolfman
Keeve, Douglas: Unzipped
Keglevic, Peter: Kill Cruise
Kehoe, Casey: Cutting Moments
Keighley, William: Adventures of Robin Hood, The; Bride Came C.O.D., The; Bullets or Ballots; Each Dawn I Die; Fighting 69th, The; George Washington Slept Here; Green Pastures; Ladies They Talk About; Man Who Came to Dinner, The; Master of Ballantrae, The; Prince and the Pauper, The; Street with No Name
Keith, David: Curse, The; Further Adventures of Tennessee Buck, The
Keith, Harvey: Jezebel's Kiss; Stand-Ins
Keller, Frederick King: Eyes of the Amaryllis; Tuck Everlasting; Vamping
Keller, Harry: Gundown at Sandoval; Marshal of Cedar Rock; Red River Shore; Tammy and the Doctor; Texas John Slaughter: Stampede at BitterCreek
Keller, Worth: L.A. Bounty
Kelley, John Patrick: Locusts, The
Kellis, Nick: Locusts, The
Kelljan, Bob: Count Yorga, Vampire; Scream, Blacula, Scream
Kellman, Barnet: Key Exchange; Slappy and the Stinkers; Straight Talk
Kellogg, David: Cool As Ice; Inspector Gadget
Kellogg, Ray: Giant Gila Monster, The; Green Berets, The; Killer Shrews, The
Kelly, Gene: Cheyenne Social Club, The; Guide for the Married Man, A; Hello, Dolly!; Invitation to the Dance; It's Always Fair Weather; On the Town; Singin' in the Rain; That's Entertainment Part II; Tunnel of Love, The
Kelly, James: Beast in the Cellar, The
Kelly, Nancy: Thousand Pieces of Gold
Kelly, Patrick: Beer
Kelly, Richard: Donnie Darko
Kelly, Ron: King of the Grizzlies
Kelly, Rory: Sleep with Me
Kempner, Aviva: Life and Times of Hank Greenberg, The
Kemp-Welch, Joan: Romeo and Juliet
Kendall, Nicholas: Mr. Rice's Secret
Kenichi, Yatagai: Ten Little Gall Force/Scramble Wars
Kenji, Misumi: Razor, The: Sword of Justice
Kennedy, Burt: Alamo, The: Thirteen Days to Glory; All the Kind Strangers; Big Bad John; Deserter, The; Dynamite and Gold; Good Guys and the Bad Guys, The; Hannie Caulder; Killer Inside Me, The; More Wild Wild West; Return of the Seven; Rounders, The; Suburban Commando; Support Your Local Gunfighter; Support Your Local Sheriff!; Texas Guns; Train Robbers, The; Trouble with Spies, The; War Wagon, The; Wild Wild West Revisited, The
Kennedy, Ken: Mission to Glory
Kennedy, Lou: Breathing Fire
Kennedy, Michael: Caribe; Hard Evidence; Red Scorpion 2; Robin of Locksley; Swordsman, The; Talons of the Eagle
Kennedy, Tom: Time Walker
Kent, Larry: High Stakes
Kentis, Chris: Grind
Kenton, Erle C.: Ghost of Frankenstein; House of Dracula; House of Frankenstein; Island of Lost Souls; Melody for Three; Pardon My Sarong; Remedy for Riches; They Meet Again; Who Done It?
Kerbosch, Roeland: For a Lost Soldier
Kern, James V.: Doughgirls, The; Never Say Goodbye; Second Woman, The; Two Tickets to Broadway
Kernochan, Sarah: Marjoe; Strike! (1998)
Kerr, Frank: Trueblood
Kerrigan, Justin: Human Traffic
Kerrigan, Lodge H.: Claire Dolan; Clean Shaven
Kershner, Irvin: Empire Strikes Back, The; Eyes of Laura Mars, The; Fine Madness, A; Flim-Flam Man, The; Hoodlum Priest, The; Never Say Never Again; Raid on Entebbe; Return of a Man Called Horse, The; RoboCop 2; S*P*Y*S; Traveling Man; Up the Sandbox
Kervyn, Emmanuel: Rabid Grannies
Keshishian, Alek: Truth or Dare; With Honors
Kessler, Bruce: Cruise into Terror; Deathmoon; Simon, King of the Witches
Kessler, Stephen: Independent, The; Vegas Vacation
Keusch, Michael: Double Cross; Huck and the King of Hearts; Just One of the Girls; Lena's Holiday; Samurai Cowboy
Khleifi, Michel: Wedding in Galilee, A
Khun, Tom: Bruce Lee: Curse of the Dragon
Kiarostami, Abbas: Life and Nothing More ...; Taste of Cherry; Wind Will Carry Us, The
Kidron, Beeban: Antonia & Jane; Oranges Are Not the Only Fruit; Swept from the Sea; To Wong Foo, Thanks for Everything, Julie Newmar; Used People
Ki-duk, Kim: Yongary—Monster from the Deep
Kiersch, Fritz: Children of the Corn; Gor; Into the Sun; Shattered Image; Stranger, The; Tuff Turf; Under the Boardwalk; Winners Take All
Kieslowski, Krzysztof: Blue; Double Life of Veronique, The; Red; White
Kijowski, Janusz: Masquerade
Kikoine, Gerard: Edge of Sanity
Kikuchi, Michitaka: Silent Mobius
Killough, Jon: Skinned Alive
Killy, Edward: Land of the Open Range; Stage to Chino
Kimbrough, Clinton: Young Nurses, The
Kimmel, Bruce: Spaceship (Naked Space)
Kimmins, Anthony: Bonnie Prince Charlie; Captain's Paradise, The; Mine Own Executioner
Kincade, John: Back to Back; Terminal Entry
Kincaid, Tim: Breeders; Occultist, The; Robot Holocaust; She's Back
King, Alex: Angkor: Cambodia Express
King, Allan Winton: By Way of the Stars; Kurt Vonnegut's Monkey House; Silence of the North; Termini Station
King, Burton: Man from Beyond, The
King, George: Crimes at the Dark House; Crimes of Stephen Hawke, The; Demon Barber of Fleet Street, The; Face at the Window, The; Sexton Blake and the Hooded Terror; Ticket of Leave Man, The
King, Henry: Alexander's Ragtime Band; Black Swan, The; Bravados, The; Carousel; David and Bathsheba; Gunfighter,

The (1950); Hell Harbor; In Old Chicago; Jesse James; Lloyd's of London; Love Is a Many-Splendored Thing; She Goes to War; Snows of Kilimanjaro, The; Song of Bernadette, The; Stanley and Livingstone; Twelve O'Clock High; White Sister, The; Wilson; Yank in the RAF, A
King, Louis: Bulldog Drummond Comes Back; Bulldog Drummond in Africa; Bulldog Drummond's Revenge; Charlie Chan in Egypt; Dangerous Mission
King, Rick: Forced March; Hard Choices; Hot Shot; Kickboxer 3: Art of War; Killing Time, The (1987); Passion to Kill, A; Prayer of the Rollerboys; Quick; Road Ends; Terminal Justice; Terminal Justice, Cybertech P.D.
King, Rob: Something More
King, Robert Lee: Psycho Beach Party
King, Stephen: Maximum Overdrive
King, Zalman: Boca; Delta of Venus; Two Moon Junction; Wild Orchid; Wild Orchid 2: Two Shades of Blue; Wildfire
King Jr., Woodie: Death of a Prophet
Kinney, Jack: Legend of Sleepy Hollow, The (1949)
Kinosita, Keisuke: Twenty-four Eyes
Kinugasa, Teinosuke: Gate of Hell
Kirby, John Mason: Savage Weekend
Kirkpatrick, Harry: Welcome to Spring Break
Kirman, Leonard: Carnival of Blood
Kirsh, John: Jesus
Kishon, Ephraim: Sallah
Kitano, Takeshi: Boiling Point; Brother; Fireworks; Kikujiro; Sonatine; Violent Cop
Kitrosser, Martin: Daddy's Girl; Fiancé, The; Silent Night, Deadly Night 5: The Toy Maker
Kizer, R. J.: Godzilla 1985; Hell Comes to Frogtown
Kjellin, Alf: Girls of Huntington House; Man from U.N.C.L.E., The (TV Series)
Klane, Robert: Thank God It's Friday; Weekend at Bernie's II
Klapisch, Cedric: When the Cat's Away
Klaus, Damian: Futurekick
Klausner, Josh: 4th Floor, The
Klein, Dennis: One More Saturday Night
Kleiser, Randal: Big Top Pee-Wee; Blue Lagoon, The; Boy in the Plastic Bubble, The; Flight of the Navigator; Gathering, The; Getting It Right; Grandview, U.S.A.; Grease; Honey, I Blew Up the Kid; It's My Party; Summer Lovers; White Fang
Klenhard, Walter: Baby Monitor: Sound of Fear; Disappearance; Haunting of Sea Cliff Inn, The
Kletter, Richard: Android Affair, The; Dangerous Indiscretion
Kleven, Max: Bail Out; Deadly Stranger; Night Stalker, The; Ruckus
Klick, Roland: Let It Rock
Klimov, Elem: Come and See; Rasputin
Klimovsky, Leon: Badlands Drifter (Challenge of McKenna); Blood Moon (Werewolf Versus the Vampire Woman, The); Rattler Kid
Kline, Robert: First Works, Volumes 1 & 2
Kloves, Steve: Fabulous Baker Boys, The; Flesh and Bone
Kluge, Alexander: Germany In Autumn
Klus, Rita: Twisted Tales
Kneitel, Seymour: Superman Cartoons
Knights, Robert: Dawning, The; Dedicated Man, A; Double Vision; Ebony Tower, The; Lovers of Their Time
Knowles, Bernard: Magic Bow, The
Kobayashi, Masaki: Human Condition, The, Part One: No Greater Love; Human Condition, The, Part Two: The Roadto Eternity; Human Condition, The, Part Three: A Soldier's Prayer; Kwaidan
Kobayashi, Toshiaki: Magical Twilight
Koch, Chris: Snow Day
Koch, Howard W.: Badge 373; Frankenstein 1970; Girl in Black Stockings, The
Koch, Phillip: Pink Nights
Koch, Ulrike: Saltmen of Tibet, The
Koepp, David: Stir of Echoes; Trigger Effect, The
Kohner, Pancho: Mr. Sycamore
Kokkinos, Ana: Only the Brave
Kolbe, Winrich: Darwin Conspiracy, The
Kollek, Amos: Double Edge; Forever Lulu; Goodbye New York; High Stakes; Whore 2
Koller, Xavier: Journey of Hope; Squanto: A Warrior's Tale
Komack, James: Porky's Revenge
Kon, Satoshi: Perfect Blue
Konchalovsky, Andrei: Duet for One; Homer and Eddie; Inner Circle, The; Maria's Lovers; Odyssey, The; Runaway Train; Shy People; Siberiade; Tango and Cash
Kong, Jackie: Being, The; Blood Diner; Night Patrol
Konparu, Tomoko: Rumik World: The Supergal
Kopple, Barbara: American Dream; Harlan County, U.S.A.; Wild Man Blues
Korda, Alexander: Fire over England; Lilies of the Field; Marius; Private Life of Don Juan, The; Private Life of Henry the Eighth, The; Rembrandt; That Hamilton Woman; Wedding Rehearsal
Korda, Zoltán: Cry, the Beloved Country; Drums; Elephant Boy; Four Feathers, The; If I Were Rich; Jungle Book (1942); Sahara; Sanders of the River
Kore-eda, Hirokazu: After Life
Korine, Harmony: Gummo
Kornbluth, Jacob: Haiku Tunnel
Korty, John: Autobiography of Miss Jane Pittman, The; Baby Girl Scott; Cast the First Stone; Christmas without Snow, A; Ewok Adventure, The; Eye on the Sparrow; Getting Out; Gift of Love: The Daniel Huffman Story; Haunting Passion, The; Long Road Home, The; Ms. Scrooge; Music School, The; Oliver's Story; People, The; Redwood Curtain; They (They Watch); Twice Upon a Time; Who Are the Debolts and Where Did They Get 19 Kids?
Korzenioswsky, Waldemar: Chair, The
Kosminsky, Peter: Emily Bronte's Wuthering Heights
Koster, Henry: Bishop's Wife, The; D-Day the Sixth of June; Dear Brigitte; Desirée; First Love; Flower Drum Song; Harvey; Inspector General, The; It Started with Eve; Man Called Peter, A; Mr. Hobbs Takes a Vacation; My Man Godfrey; Naked Maja, The; No Highway in the Sky; One Hundred Men and a Girl; Rage of Paris, The; Robe, The; Singing Nun, The; Spring Parade; Stars and Stripes Forever; Story of Ruth, The; Three Smart Girls; Three Smart Girls Grow Up; Two Sisters from Boston; Virgin Queen, The; Wabash Avenue
Kotani, Tom: Bushido Blade
Kotcheff, Ted: Apprenticeship of Duddy Kravitz, The; Family of Cops; First Blood; Folks; Fun with Dick and Jane; Hidden Assassin; Joshua Then and Now; North Dallas Forty; Split Image; Switching Channels; Uncommon Valor; Weekend at Bernie's; Who Is Killing the Great Chefs of Europe?; Winter People
Kouf, Jim: Disorganized Crime; Gang Related; Miracles
Kovacs, Ernie: Kovacs
Kovacs, Steven: '68
Kovalyov, Igor: Rugrats Movie, The
Kowalski, Bernard: Attack of the Giant Leeches; Macho Callahan; Marciano; Nativity, The; Stiletto
Krabbe, Jeroen: Left Luggage
Kragh-Jacobsen, Soeren: Emma's Shadow; Mifune
Kramer, Frank: We Are No Angels
Kramer, Jerry: Michael Jackson Moonwalker; Modern Girls
Kramer, Remi: High Velocity
Kramer, Stanley: Bless the Beasts and Children; Defiant Ones, The; Domino Principle, The; Guess Who's Coming to Dinner; Inherit the Wind; It's a Mad Mad Mad Mad World; Judgment at Nuremberg; Not as a Stranger; On the Beach; Pride and the Passion, The; R.P.M. (Revolutions per Minute); Runner Stumbles, The; Ship of Fools
Kramreither, Anthony: Thrillkill
Krasna, Norman: Ambassador's Daughter, The; Big Hangover, The
Krasny, Paul: Back to Hannibal: The Return of Tom Sawyer and Huckleberry Finn; Christina
Kraume, Lars: Advertising Rules
Kress, Harold F.: Painted Hills, The
Kret, Randolph: Pariah

Kriegman, Michael: My Neighborhood
Krish, John: Man Who Had Power over Women, The
Krishna, Srinivas: Masala
Krishnamma, Suri: Man of No Importance, A
Krishtofovich, Vyacheslav: Adam's Rib; Friend of the Deceased, A
Kroeker, Allan: Age-Old Friends; Heaven on Earth; Showdown at Williams Creek; Tramp at the Door
Krogstad, Karl: Last Ride, The
Krohn, Bill: It's All True
Kroll, Jon: Amanda and the Alien
Kronsberg, Jeremy Joe: Going Ape!
Kroon, Piet: Osmosis Jones
Kroopnick, Steve: Treasures of the Titanic
Kroyer, Bill: Ferngully—The Last Rainforest
Krueger, Lisa: Manny & Lo
Krueger, Michael: Mind Killer
Kubilos, Robert: Dish Dogs
Kubrick, Stanley: Barry Lyndon; Clockwork Orange, A; Dr. Strangelove or How I Learned to Stop Worrying and Love the Bomb; Eyes Wide Shut; Full Metal Jacket; Killer's Kiss; Killing, The; Lolita; Paths of Glory; Seafarers, The; Shining, The; Spartacus; 2001: A Space Odyssey
Kuleshov, Lev: By the Law; Extraordinary Adventures of Mr. West in the Land of the Bolsheviks, The
Kulijanov, Lev: Crime and Punishment
Kulik, Buzz: Around the World in 80 Days; Bad Ronald; Brian's Song; Code Name: Dancer; From Here to Eternity; George Washington; Hunter, The (1980); Jackie Collins' Lucky Chances; Lindbergh Kidnapping Case, The; Pioneer Woman; Riot; Sergeant Ryker; Shamus; Twilight Zone, The (TV Series); Villa Rides; Women of Valor
Kull, Edward: New Adventures of Tarzan; Tarzan and the Green Goddess
Kulle, Victor: Illusions
Kumai, Kei: Sandakan No. 8
Kumble, Roger: Cruel Intentions; Cruel Intentions 2; Sweetest Thing, The
Kumel, Harry: Daughters of Darkness
Kurahara, Koreyoshi: Antarctica; Hiroshima
Kureishi, Hanif: London Kills Me
Kurosawa, Akira: Akira Kurosawa's Dreams; Bad Sleep Well, The; Dersu Uzala; Dodes 'Ka-Den; Drunken Angel; Hidden Fortress, The; High and Low; Idiot, The; Ikiru; Kagemusha; Lower Depths, The (1957); No Regrets for Our Youth; Ran; Rashomon; Red Beard; Rhapsody in August; Sanjuro; Sanshiro Sugata; Seven Samurai, The; Stray Dog; Throne of Blood; Yojimbo
Kurotsuchi, Mitsuo: Traffic Jam
Kurtzman, Robert: Demolitionist, The; Wes Craven's Wishmaster
Kurys, Diane: Entre Nous (Between Us); Man in Love, A; Peppermint Soda
Kusama, Karyn: Girlfight
Kushner, Donald: First and Ten
Kusturica, Emir: Arizona Dreams; Do You Remember Dolly Bell?; Time of the Gypsies; Underground; When Father Was Away on Business
Kuzui, Fran Rubel: Buffy, the Vampire Slayer; Tokyo Pop
Kwapis, Ken: Beautician and the Beast, The; Beniker Gang, The; Dunston Checks In; He Said, She Said; Noah; Sesame Street Presents Follow That Bird; Vibes
Kwietniowski, Richard: Love and Death on Long Island
Kwitny, Jeff: Beyond the Door 3
Kyriazi, Paul: Omega Cop
Kyzystek, Waldemar: Suspended
La Cava, Gregory: Big News; Feel My Pulse; Fifth Avenue Girl; Gabriel over the White House; Living in a Big Way; My Man Godfrey; Primrose Path; Running Wild; Stage Door
La Rocque, Stephen: Samantha
La Salle, Eriq: Rebound
LaBrie, Richard: Good Luck
Labrune, Jeanne: Sand and Blood
LaBute, Neil: In the Company of Men; Nurse Betty; Your Friends & Neighbors
Lachman, Harry: Baby Take a Bow; Castle in the Desert; Charlie Chan in Rio; Dead Men Tell; Murder over New York; Our Relations
Ladd, Diane: Mrs. Munck
LaDuca, Rob: Lion King II: Simba's Pride
Lafia, John: Blue Iguana; Chameleon III: Dark Angel; Child's Play 2; Man's Best Friend (1993)
Lagomarsino, Ron: Dinner at Eight; Running Mates
LaGravanese, Richard: Living Out Loud
Lahiff, Craig: Deadly Possession; Ebbtide; Heaven's Burning
Lahti, Christine: Anything for Love; My First Mister
Laing, John: Beyond Reasonable Doubt (1983)
LaLoggia, Frank: Fear No Evil; Lady in White; Mother
Laloux, René: Fantastic Planet
Lam, Ringo: City on Fire; Maximum Risk; Prison on Fire; Replicant; Twin Dragons
Lamas, Lorenzo: CIA II: Target: Alexa
Lambert, Mary: Clubland; Dragstrip Girl; Grand Isle; In Crowd, The; My Stepson, My Lover; Pet Sematary; Pet Sematary Two; Siesta
Lamberti, Mark: Lost Stooges, The
Lamont, Charles: Abbott and Costello Go to Mars; Abbott and Costello in the Foreign Legion; Abbott and Costello Meet Captain Kidd; Abbott and Costello Meet Dr. Jekyll and Mr. Hyde; Abbott and Costello Meet the Invisible Man; Abbott and Costello Meet the Keystone Kops; Abbott and Costello Meet the Mummy; Comin' Round the Mountain; Francis in the Haunted House; Hit the Ice; Ma and Pa Kettle at Home; Ma and Pa Kettle (The Further Adventures of Ma and Pa Kettle); Ma and Pa Kettle Go to Town; Ma and Pa Kettle on Vacation; Salome, Where She Danced
Lamore, Marsh: Secret of the Sword, The
Lamorisse, Albert: Red Balloon, The; Voyage en Ballon (Stowaway to the Stars)
Lan, U: Girl from Hunan
Lancaster, Burt: Kentuckian, The
Landers, Lew: Adventures of Gallant Bess; Annabel Takes a Tour; Bad Lands (1939); Dynamite Pass; Enchanted Forest, The; Return of the Vampire, The; Smashing the Rackets; Torpedo Alley
Landis, James: Nasty Rabbit; Sadist, The
Landis, John: Amazon Women on the Moon; American Werewolf in London, An; Animal House; Beverly Hills Cop 3; Blues Brothers, The; Blues Brothers 2000; Coming to America; Dying to Get Rich; Innocent Blood; Into the Night; Kentucky Fried Movie; Oscar (1991); Schlock; Spies Like Us; Stupids, The; Three Amigos; Trading Places; Twilight Zone—The Movie
Landon, Michael: It's Good to Be Alive; Little House on the Prairie (TV Series); Sam's Son
Landres, Paul: Flipper's Odyssey; Go, Johnny, Go!; Return of Dracula; Wyatt Earp: Return to Tombstone
Lane, Andrew: Desperate Motive; Jake Speed; Lonely Hearts; Mortal Passions; Secretary, The; Trade Off
Lane, Charles: True Identity
Lane, David: Invasion UFO
Lane, Rocky: All's Fair
Laneuville, Eric: Ernest Green Story, The; George McKenna Story, The
Lanfield, Sidney: Addams Family, The (TV Series); Hound of the Baskervilles, The; Lemon Drop Kid, The; Meanest Man in the World, The; My Favorite Blonde; One in a Million; Second Fiddle; Skirts Ahoy!; Sorrowful Jones; Station West; Thin Ice; You'll Never Get Rich
Lang, Fritz: Beyond a Reasonable Doubt (1956); Big Heat, The; Blue Gardenia, The; Clash by Night; Cloak and Dagger; Destiny; Dr. Mabuse, the Gambler (Parts I and II); Fury (1936); Hangmen Also Die; House by the River; Human Desire; Kriemhilde's Revenge; M; Man Hunt (1941); Metropolis (1926); Metropolis (1984 Musical Version); Rancho Notorious; Return of Frank James, The; Scarlet Street; Secret Beyond the Door; Siegfried; Spiders, The (1919); Spies; Testament of Dr.

Mabuse; Thousand Eyes of Dr. Mabuse, The; Western Union; While the City Sleeps; Wolfheart's Revenge; Woman in the Moon (Girl in the Moon; By Rocket to the Moon); Woman in the Window; You Only Live Once
Lang, Krzysztof: Paper Marriage
Lang, Michel: Gift, The; Holiday Hotel
Lang, Perry: Little Vegas; Men of War
Lang, Richard: Change of Seasons, A; Don't Go to Sleep; Fantasy Island; Kung Fu—The Movie (1986); Mountain Men, The; Texas; Vega$; Word, The
Lang, Rocky: Nervous Ticks; Race for Glory
Lang, Walter: Blue Bird, The; But Not for Me; Can-Can; Desk Set; Jackpot, The; King and I, The; Little Princess, The (1939); Moon over Miami; Mother Wore Tights; Red Kimono, The; Snow White and the Three Stooges; Song of the Islands; State Fair; There's No Business Like Show Business; Tin Pan Alley; Weekend in Havana
Langley, Noel: Adventures of Sadie; Pickwick Papers, The; Search for Bridey Murphy, The
Langston, Murray: Wishful Thinking
Langton, Simon: Act of Passion; Anna Karenina; Casanova; Laguna Heat; Pride and Prejudice; Upstairs, Downstairs; Whistle Blower, The
Langway, Douglas: Raising Heroes
Lanoff, Lawrence: Miami Hustle; Temptress
Lantieri, Michael: Komodo
Lantz, Walter: World of Andy Panda, The
Lanza, Anthony M.: Glory Stompers, The; Incredible Two-Headed Transplant, The
Lapine, James: Earthly Possessions; Impromptu; Life with Mikey; Sunday in the Park with George
Lardnerward, Donald: My Life's in Turnaround
Large, Brian: Elektra
Larkin, Christopher: Very Natural Thing, A
Larraz, Joseph: House That Vanished, The; Vampyres
Larry, Sheldon: Terminal Choice
Larsen, Keith: Whitewater Sam
Lasseter, John: Bug's Life, A; Toy Story; Toy Story 2
Lathan, Stan: Almos' a Man; Beat Street; Sky Is Gray, The
Latshaw, Steve: Biohazard: The Alien Force; Dark Universe, The; Jack-O
Latt, David Michael: Sorority House Party
Lattuada, Alberto: Christopher Columbus (1985); Cricket, The; Stay as You Are; Variety Lights
Laughlin, Michael: Mesmerized (Shocked); Strange Behavior; Strange Invaders
Laughlin, Tom: Billy Jack
Laughton, Charles: Night of the Hunter
Launder, Frank: Belles of St. Trinian's, The; Blue Murder at St. Trinian's; Great St. Trinian's Train Robbery, The; I See a Dark Stranger
Launer, Dale: Love Potion #9
Lautner, Georges: Icy Breasts; La Cage aux Folles III, The Wedding; My Other Husband
Lauzon, Jean-Claude: Leolo; Night Zoo
Laven, Arnold: Monster That Challenged the World, The; Rough Night in Jericho
Lavin, Julianna: Live Nude Girls
Lavut, Martin: Palais Royale; Smokescreen
Law, Alex: Painted Faces
Law, Clara: Erotique; Reincarnation of Golden Lotus, The; Temptation of a Monk
Law, Joe: Crippled Masters, The
Lawick, Hugo van: Leopard Son, The
Lawrence, Denny: Archer's Adventure
Lawrence, Diarmuid: Emma
Lawrence, Marc: Pigs (Daddy's Deadly Darling)
Lawrence, Martin: Thin Line Between Love and Hate, A
Lawrence, Quentin: Crawling Eye, The
Lawrence, Ray: Bliss; Lantana
Lawton, J. F.: Hunted, The (1995)
Layton, Joe: Littlest Angel, The
Lazarus, Paul: Seven Girlfriends
Le Chanois, Jean-Paul: Le Cas du Dr. Laurent; L'Ecole Buissonniere; Les Misérables; Passion for Life
Le Moine, Yvonne: Red Dwarf, The
Leach, Wilford: Pirates of Penzance, The; Wedding Party, The
Leacock, Philip: Angel City; Curse of King Tut's Tomb, The; Thanksgiving Story, The; Three Sovereigns for Sarah; War Lover, The
Leader, Tony: Children of the Damned; Lost in Space (TV Series)
Lean, David: Blithe Spirit; Bridge on the River Kwai, The; Brief Encounter; Dr. Zhivago; Great Expectations; Hobson's Choice; In Which We Serve; Lawrence of Arabia; Oliver Twist; Passage to India, A; Ryan's Daughter; Summertime; This Happy Breed
Lear, Norman: Cold Turkey
Leary, Denis: National Lampoon's Favorite Deadly Sins
Lease, Maria: Dolly Dearest
Leaver, Don: Avengers, The (TV Series); Touch of Frost, A (TV Series); Witching Time
LeBorg, Reginald: Calling Dr. Death; Dead Man's Eyes; Diary of a Madman; Jungle Woman; Mummy's Ghost, The; Psycho Sisters; Voodoo Island; Weird Woman
Leboursier, Raymond: Nais
Lecallier, Adeline: Nais
Leconte, Patrice: Girl on the Bridge; Hairdresser's Husband, The; Monsieur Hire; Ridicule; Widow of St. Pierre, The
Leddy, Bruce: My Teacher's Wife
Leder, Herbert J.: Candyman, The
Leder, Mimi: Deep Impact; Pay It Forward; Peacemaker, The (1997); Woman with a Past
Leder, Paul: Exiled in America; Frame Up; I Dismember Mama; Molly & Gina; Murder by Numbers (1989); Sketches of a Strangler; Vultures
Lederer, Charles: Fingers at the Window; Never Steal Anything Small
Lederman, D. Ross: End of the Trail; Range Feud; Riding Tornado, The; Tarzan's Revenge; Texas Cyclone; Two-Fisted Law
Leduc, Paul: Frida
Lee, Ang: Crouching Tiger, Hidden Dragon; Eat Drink Man Woman; Ice Storm, The; Pushing Hands; Ride with the Devil; Sense and Sensibility; Wedding Banquet, The
Lee, Bruce: Return of the Dragon
Lee, Chris Chan: Yellow
Lee, Damian: Agent Red
Lee, Damien: Abraxas Guardian of the Universe; Donor, The; Fatal Combat; Food of the Gods Part II; Last Man Standing; Moving Target; Ski School; Street Law; When the Bullet Hits the Bone
Lee, Daniel: Black Mask
Lee, Evan: Hollywood Meatcleaver Massacre
Lee, Iara: Synthetic Pleasures
Lee, Jack: Captain's Table; Wooden Horse, The
Lee, Malcolm: Best Man, The
Lee, Norman: Chamber of Horrors
Lee, Robert: Operative, The; Virtual Assassin
Lee, Rowland V.: Bridge of San Luis Rey, The; Captain Kidd; Count of Monte Cristo, The; Love from a Stranger; Mysterious Dr. Fu Manchu; One Rainy Afternoon; Return of Dr. Fu Manchu; Sea Lion, The; Son of Frankenstein; Son of Monte Cristo, The; Three Musketeers, The; Toast of New York, The; Tower of London
Lee, Spike: Bamboozled; Clockers; Crooklyn; Do the Right Thing; Get on the Bus; Girl 6; He Got Game; Jungle Fever; Malcolm X; Mo' Better Blues; Original Kings Of Comedy, The; School Daze; She's Gotta Have It; Summer of Sam
Lee, Thomas: Supernova
Leeds, Herbert: Charlie Chan in City in Darkness; Mr. Moto in Danger Island
Leeson, Lynn Hershman: Conceiving Ada
Leet, Scott: Out in Fifty
Lefler, Doug: Hercules and the Circle of Fire
Legend, Johnny: Sleazemania Strikes Back
Legge, Michael: Alien Agenda, The (TV Series)

Legrand, François: Tower of Screaming Virgins, The
Lehman, Ernest: Portnoy's Complaint
Lehmann, Michael: Airheads; 40 Days and 40 Nights; Heathers; Hudson Hawk; Meet the Applegates; My Giant; Truth About Cats and Dogs, The
Lehner, Peter: Megaville
Leiberman, Robert: Will, G. Gordon Liddy
Leibovit, Arnold: Puppetoon Movie, The
Leifer, Neil: Trading Hearts; Yesterday's Hero
Leigh, Jennifer Jason: Anniversary Party, The
Leigh, Mike: Abigail's Party; Career Girls; Four Days in July; High Hopes; Home Sweet Home (1982); Life Is Sweet; Meantime; Naked; Secrets and Lies; Topsy-Turvy (1999); Who's Who
Leighton, Eric: Dinosaur
Leiner, Danny: Dude, Where's My Car?
Leisen, Mitchell: Big Broadcast of 1938, The; Death Takes a Holiday; Girl Most Likely, The; Golden Earrings; Hands Across the Table; Lady Is Willing, The; Midnight; Murder at the Vanities; Remember the Night; Swing High, Swing Low
Leitch, Christopher: Courage Mountain; I've Been Waiting for You; Teen Wolf, Too
Leitzes, Jennifer: Montana
Leker, Larry: All Dogs Go to Heaven 2
Leland, David: Big Man; Checking Out; Land Girls, The; Wish You Were Here
Lelouch, Claude: And Now, My Love; Another Man, Another Chance; Bandits; Bolero; Cat and Mouse; Edith and Marcel; Happy New Year (1973) (La Bonne Année); Les Misérables; Man and a Woman, A; Man and a Woman, A: 20 Years Later; Robert et Robert
LeMattre, Debra: Seamless
Lemmo, James: Dream a Little Dream 2; Heart; Relentless 3; Tripwire; We're Talking Serious Money
Lemmon, Jack: Kotch
Lemmons, Kasi: Caveman's Valentine, The; Eve's Bayou
Lemont, John: Konga
Lemorande, Rusty: Journey to the Center of the Earth; Turn of the Screw (1992)
Leni, Paul: Cat and the Canary, The; Last Warning, The; Man Who Laughs, The; Waxworks
Lenica, Jan: Ubu and the Great Gidouille
Lennon, Terry: Daffy Duck's Quackbusters
Lent, Dean: Border Radio
Lente, Miklos: Oddballs
Lenzi, Umberto: Battle of the Commandos; Bridge to Hell; Emerald Jungle; Make Them Die Slowly; Paranoia
Leo, Malcolm: This Is Elvis
Leonard, Brett: Dead Pit, The; Hideaway; Lawnmower Man, The; Virtuosity
Leonard, Robert Z.: Broadway Serenade; Clown, The; Dancing Lady; Divorcee, The; Duchess of Idaho; Firefly, The; Girl of the Golden West, The; Great Ziegfeld, The; In the Good Old Summertime; Maytime; Nancy Goes to Rio; New Moon; Pride and Prejudice; Strange Interlude; Susan Lenox: Her Fall and Rise; Weekend at the Waldorf; When Ladies Meet; Ziegfeld Girl
Leonard, Sheldon: Danny Thomas Show, The (TV Series)
Leonard, Terry: Death Before Dishonor
Leondopoulos, Jordon: Swap, The (Sam's Song)
Leone, John: Great Smokey Roadblock, The
Leone, Sergio: Fistful of Dollars, A; Fistful of Dynamite, A; For a Few Dollars More; Good the Bad and the Ugly, The; Once Upon a Time in America (Long Version); Once Upon a Time in the West
Leonetti, John R.: Mortal Kombat: Annihilation
Leong, Po-Chih: Banana Cop; Cabin by the Lake; Ping Pong
Lerner, Carl: Black Like Me
Lerner, Dan: Shame
Lerner, Irving: Cry of Battle; Royal Hunt of the Sun; Studs Lonigan
LeRoy, Mervyn: Anthony Adverse; Any Number Can Play; Bad Seed, The; Devil at 4 O'Clock, The; East Side, West Side; FBI Story, The; Gold Diggers of 1933; Gypsy; Homecoming; I Am a Fugitive from a Chain Gang; Johnny Eager; Latin Lovers; Little Caesar; Little Women; Lovely to Look At; Madame Curie; Majority of One, A; Million Dollar Mermaid; Mister Roberts; No Time for Sergeants; Quo Vadis (1951); Random Harvest; Rose Marie; Sweet Adeline; Thirty Seconds Over Tokyo; Three Men on a Horse; Three on a Match; Waterloo Bridge; Without Reservations
Lessac, Michael: House of Cards
Lester, Mark L.: Armed and Dangerous; Base, The; Blowback; Bobbie Jo and the Outlaw; Class of 1984; Class of 1999; Commando; Double Take; Ex, The; Extreme Justice; Firestarter; Night of the Running Man; Public Enemy #1; Sacrifice (2000); Showdown in Little Tokyo; Truckstop Women
Lester, Richard: Butch and Sundance: The Early Days; Cuba; Four Musketeers, The; Funny Thing Happened on the Way to the Forum, A; Hard Day's Night, A; Help!; How I Won the War; Juggernaut; Knack ... and How to Get It, The; Petulia; Return of the Musketeers; Ritz, The; Robin and Marian; Superman II; Superman III; Three Musketeers, The
Letterier, François: Goodbye Emmanuelle
Lettich, Sheldon: Double Impact; Last Warrior, The (2000); Lionheart; Only the Strong; Order, The
Letts, Barry: Gulliver in Lilliput
Leung, Tony: Bloodmoon
Leva, Gary: Plan B
Levant, Brian: Beethoven; Flintstones, The; Flintstones in Viva Rock Vegas, The; Jingle All the Way; Problem Child 2; Snow Dogs
Leven, Jeremy: Don Juan DeMarco
Levering, Joseph: In Early Arizona
Levesque, Michel: Werewolves on Wheels
Levey, Jay: UHF
Levey, William A.: Blackenstein; Committed; Happy Hooker Goes to Washington, The; Hellgate; Lightning, the White Stallion; Slumber Party 57
Levi, Alan J.: Deadman's Revenge; Quantum Leap (TV Series); Riding with Death
Levi, Jefery: Invincible
Levick, David: Gospel
Levin, Henry: Ambushers, The; Desperados, The; Farmer Takes a Wife, The; Jolson Sings Again; Journey to the Center of the Earth; Lonely Man, The; Man from Colorado, The; Murderers' Row; Run for the Roses (Thoroughbred); Two of a Kind; Warriors, The; Where the Boys Are (1960); Wonderful World of the Brothers Grimm, The
Levin, Marc: Last Party, The; Slam; Whiteboyz
Levin, Peter: Comeback Kid, The; Gone to Texas; Rape and Marriage: The Rideout Case
Levin, Thunder: Evil Lives
Levine, Michael: Checkered Flag
Levine, Paul: Operation Intercept
Levinson, Barry: Avalon; Bandits (2001); Bugsy; Diner; Disclosure; Everlasting Piece, An; Good Morning, Vietnam; Jimmy Hollywood; Liberty Heights; Natural, The; Rain Man; Sleepers; Sphere; Tin Men; Toys; Wag the Dog; Young Sherlock Holmes
Levitow, Abe: Adventures of Milo in the Phantom Tollbooth, The; Gay Purr-ee; Mr. Magoo's Christmas Carol
Levy, Eugene: Once Upon a Crime; Sodbusters
Levy, Jefery: Inside Monkey Zetterland; S.F.W.
Levy, Ralph: Bedtime Story; Beverly Hillbillies, The (TV Series); George Burns and Gracie Allen Show, The (TV Series)
Levy, Scott: Alien Within, The; Baby Face Nelson; Beneath the Bermuda Triangle; Piranha; Spectre; Unknown Origin
Levy, Shawn: Address Unknown; Big Fat Liar
Levy, Shuki: Blind Vision; Turbo: A Power Rangers Adventure
Lewin, Albert: Moon and Sixpence, The; Pandora and the Flying Dutchman; Picture of Dorian Gray, The; Private Affairs of Bel Ami, The
Lewin, Ben: Favor, the Watch and the Very Big Fish,The; Georgia; Paperback Romance
Lewis, Al: Our Miss Brooks (TV Series)
Lewis, Christopher: Ripper, The
Lewis, David: Dangerous Curves
Lewis, Diana: Venus de Milo

Lewis, Herschell Gordon: Blood Feast; Color Me Blood Red; Gruesome Twosome; Just for the Hell of It; Living Venus; She-Devils on Wheels; Something Weird; Suburban Roulette; Taste of Blood, A; 2,000 Maniacs; Wizard of Gore, The
Lewis, Jerry: Bellboy, The; Big Mouth, The; Cracking Up; Errand Boy, The; Family Jewels, The; Hardly Working; Ladies' Man, The (1961); Nutty Professor, The; Patsy, The; Which Way to the Front?
Lewis, Joseph H.: Big Combo, The; Boys of the City; Gun Crazy; Invisible Ghost; Lawless Street, A; Mad Doctor of Market Street, The; Pride of the Bowery; Retreat Hell; Return of October, The; 7th Cavalry
Lewis, Mark: Gordy
Lewis, Robert: Circumstances Unknown; Crying Child, The; Dead Reckoning; Don't Talk to Strangers; Lady Killers; Memories of Murder; Perfect Crime; S.H.E.; Summer to Remember, A
Lewis, Robert Michael: Child Bride of Short Creek; Fallen Angel; Pray for the Wildcats
Lewnes, Pericles: Redneck Zombies
Liapis, Peter: Stepdaughter, The
Liatowitsch, Daniel: Kolobos
Libman, Leslie: Path to Paradise
Libov, Howard: Midnight Edition
Lichtenstein, Demian: 3,000 Miles to Graceland
Liconti, Carlo: Concrete Angels
Lieberman, Jeff: Blue Sunshine; Just Before Dawn; Remote Control; Squirm
Lieberman, Robert: All I Want for Christmas; D3: The Mighty Ducks; Fire in the Sky; Table for Five; Titanic
Liebman, Max: 10 from Your Show of Shows
Lifshitz, Sébastien: Come Undone
Lifton, Jimmy: Mirror, Mirror 2: Raven Dance
Light, Warren: Night We Never Met, The
Lima, Kevin: Goofy Movie, A; 102 Dalmatians; Tarzan (1999)
Liman, Doug: Getting In; Go; Swingers
Lincoln, F. J.: Wild Man
Lindberg, Per: June Night
Lindenmuth, Kevin J.: Alien Agenda, The (TV Series); Twisted Tales; Vampires & Other Stereotypes
Linder, Max: Seven Years' Bad Luck
Lindsay, Lance: Star Crystal
Lindsay-Hogg, Michael: As Is; Brideshead Revisited; Frankie Starlight; Habitation of Dragons, The; Let It Be; Master Harold and the Boys; Murder by Moonlight; Nasty Habits; Object of Beauty, The; Rock and Roll Circus, The; Running Mates; Strange Case of Dr. Jekyll and Mr. Hyde,The (1989); Thumbelina
Lindtberg, Leopold: Four in a Jeep
Link, Caroline: Beyond Silence
Link, Ron: Zombie High
Linklater, Richard: Before Sunrise; Dazed and Confused; Newton Boys, The; Slacker; SubUrbia; Waking Life
Linson, Art: Where the Buffalo Roam; Wild Life, The
Lion, Mickey: House of Exorcism, The
Lipman, David: Road Lawyers and Other Briefs
Lipstadt, Aaron: Android; Blood Money (1999); City Limits; Pair of Aces
Lisberger, Steven: Animalympics; Hot Pursuit; Slipstream; Tron
Lishman, Eda Lever: Primo Baby
Lister, David: Rutanga Tapes, The; Trigger Fast
Lit, Law: Mr. Vampire (Vol. 1–4)
Litten, Peter Mackenzie: Heaven's a Drag
Littin, Miguel: Alsino and the Condor
Little, Dwight H.: Bloodstone; Boss of Bosses; Free Willy 2: The Adventure Home; Halloween IV: The Return of Michael Myers; Marked for Death; Murder at 1600; Phantom of the Opera; Rapid Fire
Littman, Lynne: Freak City; Testament
Litvak, Anatole: All This and Heaven Too; Amazing Dr. Clitterhouse, The; Anastasia; City for Conquest; Goodbye Again; Mayerling; Night of the Generals; Sisters, The (1938); Snake Pit, The; Sorry, Wrong Number; Tovaritch
Lively, Gerry: Body Moves
Livingston, Christopher: Hit and Runway
Livingston, Jennie: Paris Is Burning
Livingston, Robert H.: Taking My Turn
Livingston, William: Great Indian Railway, The
Livingstone, Joe: Robo Vampire
Llosa, Luis: Anaconda; Crime Zone; 800 Leagues Down the Amazon; Hour of the Assassin; Sniper; Specialist, The
Lloyd, Frank: Blood on the Sun; Cavalcade; Howards of Virginia, The; If I Were King; Last Command, The; Mutiny on the Bounty; Oliver Twist
Lloyd, Harold: Harold Lloyd's Comedy Classics
Lloyd, Norman: Tales of the Unexpected
Lo, Lucas: No Retreat, No Surrender 3: Blood Brothers
Loach, Kenneth: Bread and Roses; Carla's Song; Family Life; Hidden Agenda; Ladybird, Ladybird; Land and Freedom; My Name is Joe; Raining Stones; Riff-Raff (1990); Singing the Blues in Red
Loader, Jayne: Atomic Cafe, The
Lobl, Victor: Beauty and the Beast (TV Series); Eden (TV Series)
Locke, Sondra: Impulse; Ratboy; Trading Favors
Loftis, Norman: Messenger, The; Small Time
Logan, Bob: Meatballs 4; Repossessed; Up Your Alley
Logan, Bruce: Vendetta
Logan, Joshua: Bus Stop; Camelot; Ensign Pulver; Fanny; Paint Your Wagon; Picnic; Sayonara; South Pacific; Tall Story
Logan, Stanley: Falcon's Brother, The
Logan, Tom: Shakma
Logothetis, Dimitri: Body Shot; Closer, The
Loma, J. Anthony: Counterforce; Man of Passion, A; Target Eagle
Loman (Jose Antonio De La Loma), Joseph: Boldest Job in the West, The
Lomas, Raoul: Minor Miracle, A
Lombardo, Lou: P.K. & the Kid; Russian Roulette
Lommel, Ulli: Big Sweat, The; Boogeyman, The; Brainwaves; Cocaine Cowboys; Devonsville Terror, The; Warbirds
Loncraine, Richard: Bellman and True; Brimstone and Treacle; Deep Cover; Haunting of Julia, The; Missionary, The; Richard III; Wedding Gift, The
London, James: Place Called Trinity, A
London, Jerry: Chiefs; Ellis Island; Haunting of Sarah Hardy, The; Kiss Shot; Manhunt for Claude Dallas; Rent-a-Cop; Scarlet and the Black, The; Season of Giants, A; Shogun (Full-Length Version); Victim of Love
London, Roy: Diary of a Hitman
Lonergan, Kenneth: You Can Count on Me
Long, Stanley: Adventures of a Private Eye
Longo, Robert: Johnny Mnemonic
Longon, Humphrey: Battle Force
Longstreet, Harry S.: Perfect Daughter, The; Sex, Love, and Cold Hard Cash; Vow to Kill, A
Lopez, Temistocles: Bird of Prey; Chain of Desire
Lord, Del: Trapped by Television
Lord, Jean-Claude: Eddie and the Cruisers II: Eddie Lives!; Landslide; Mind Field; Toby McTeague; Vindicator, The; Visiting Hours
Lord, Peter: Chicken Run
Lord, Stephen: Fall of the House of Usher, The
Lorentz, Pare: Plow That Broke the Plains, The
Loring, Ken: Combat Killers
Losey, Joseph: Accident; Assassination of Trotsky, The; Boy with Green Hair, The; Concrete Jungle, (1962) The (Criminal, The); Doll's House, A; Go-Between, The; La Truite (The Trout); Mr. Klein; Roads to the South; Romantic Englishwoman, The; Secret Ceremony; Servant, The; Sleeping Tiger, The; Steaming; Time Without Pity
Lotterby, Sydney: Yes, Prime Minister
Lottimer, Eb: Love Matters; Twisted Love
Louis, Larry: Body Puzzle
Lounguine, Pavel: Luna Park; Taxi Blues
Lounsbery, John: Rescuers, The

Lourie, Eugene: Beast from 20,000 Fathoms, The; Colossus of New York, The; Giant Behemoth, The; Gorgo
Louzil, Eric: Class of Nuke 'em High 2: Subhumanoid Meltdown; Class of Nuke 'em High III; Wilding, The Children of Violence
Loventhal, Charlie: First Time, The; Mr. Write; My Demon Lover
Lovy, Robert: Circuitry Man II: Plughead Rewired
Lovy, Steven: Circuitry Man; Circuitry Man II: Plughead Rewired
Low, Stephen: Titanica
Lowe, Lucas: American Shaolin: King of the Kickboxers II
Lowe, William: Slaughter in San Francisco
Lowenstein, Richard: Dogs in Space
Lowry, Dick: Attila; Cop for the Killing, A; Coward of the County; Diamond of Jeru, The; FBI Murders, The; Follow the Stars Home; Gambler, The; Gambler, Part II—The Adventure Continues, The; Gambler, Part III—The Legend Continues, The; Gambler Returns, The: Luck of the Draw; Horse for Danny, A; In the Line of Duty: Ambush in Waco; Jayne Mansfield Story, The; Last Stand at Saber River; Living Proof: The Hank Williams Jr., Story; Midnight Murders; Mr. Murder; Murder with Mirrors; Smokey and the Bandit III; Till Murder Do Us Part; Urban Crossfire; Wet Gold
Loy, Nanni: Cafe Express; Where's Piccone?
Lubin, Arthur: Ali Baba and the Forty Thieves; Black Friday; Buck Privates; Escapade in Japan; Francis Goes to the Races; Francis in the Navy; Francis Joins the Wacs; Francis, the Talking Mule; Hold That Ghost; Impact; Incredible Mr. Limpet, The; Lady Godiva; Maverick (TV Series); Phantom of the Opera; Ride 'em Cowboy
Lubitsch, Ernst: Bluebeard's Eighth Wife; Gypsy Blood; Heaven Can Wait; Lady Windermere's Fan; Marriage Circle, The; Merry Widow, The; Ninotchka; One Arabian Night; Passion; Shop Around the Corner, The; Student Prince in Old Heidelberg, The; That Uncertain Feeling; To Be or Not to Be
Luby, S. Roy: Arizona Stagecoach; Black Market Rustlers; Boothill Bandits; Border Phantom; Desert Phantom; Fugitive Valley; Saddle Mountain Roundup; Trail of the Silver Spurs
Lucas, George: American Graffiti; Star Wars; Star Wars: Attack of the Clones; Star Wars: Episode I The Phantom Menace; THX 1138
Lucas, Phil: Native Americans, The
Lucente, Francesco: Virgin Queen of St. Francis High, The
Lucidi, Maurizio: Saddle Tramps; Stateline Motel; Street People
Ludman, Larry: Deadly Impact; Operation 'Nam; Thunder Warrior; Thunder Warrior II
Ludwig, Edward: Big Jim McLain; Big Wheel, The; Bonanza (TV Series); Fabulous Texan, The; Fighting Seabees, The; Wake of the Red Witch
Luhrmann, Baz: Moulin Rouge (2001); Strictly Ballroom; William Shakespeare's Romeo and Juliet
Luke, Eric: Not Quite Human 2; Still Not Quite Human
Luketic, Robert: Legally Blonde
Lumet, Sidney: Anderson Tapes, The; Critical Care; Danger; Daniel; Deathtrap; Dog Day Afternoon; Equus; Fail-Safe; Family Business; Fugitive Kind, The; Garbo Talks; Gloria; Group, The; Guilty as Sin; Hill, The; Just Tell Me What You Want; Long Day's Journey into Night; Morning After, The; Murder on the Orient Express; Network; Night Falls on Manhattan; Offence, The; Pawnbroker, The; Power (1986); Prince of the City; Q & A; Running on Empty; Serpico; Stage Struck; Stranger Among Us, A; 12 Angry Men; Verdict, The; Wiz, The
Luna, Bigas: Anguish; Chambermaid on the Titanic, The; Jamon, Jamon
Lupino, Ida: Bigamist, The; Not Wanted; Trouble with Angels, The
Lurie, Rod: Contender, The; Deterrence; Last Castle, The
Lusk, Don: Pirates of Dark Waters, The: The Saga Begins
Luske, Hamilton: Alice in Wonderland; Cinderella; Lady and the Tramp; One Hundred and One Dalmatians; Peter Pan; Reluctant Dragon, The
Lussier, Patrick: Dracula 2000; Prophecy 3: The Ascent
Lustig, Dana: Kill Me Later; Wedding Bell Blues
Lustig, William: Hit List (1988); Maniac; Maniac Cop; Maniac Cop 2; Maniac Cop 3: Badge of Silence; Relentless; Uncle Sam; Vigilante
Luther, Salvo: Forget Mozart
Lyman, Michel: Phantom 2040 (TV Series)
Lynch, David: Blue Velvet; Dune; Elephant Man, The; Eraserhead; Hotel Room; Industrial Symphony No. 1 The Dream of the Broken Hearted; Lost Highway; Mulholland Drive; Straight Story, The; Twin Peaks (Movie); Twin Peaks: Fire Walk with Me; Wild at Heart
Lynch, Jennifer Chambers: Boxing Helena
Lynch, Paul: Blindside; Bullies; Cross Country; Dream to Believe; Drop Dead Gorgeous; Face the Evil; Humongous; No Contest; Prom Night; Really Weird Tales; Star Trek: The Next Generation (TV Series)
Lyne, Adrian: Fatal Attraction; Flashdance; Foxes; Indecent Proposal; Jacob's Ladder; Lolita; 9 1/2 Weeks; Unfaithful
Lynn, Jonathan: Clue; Distinguished Gentleman, The; Greedy; My Cousin Vinny; Nuns on the Run; Sgt. Bilko; Trial and Error (1997); Whole Nine Yards, The
Lyon, Francis D.: Castle of Evil; Cult of the Cobra; Great Locomotive Chase, The; Oklahoman, The; Tomboy and the Champ
Ma, Jingle: Tokyo Raiders
Maak, Karoly: Cat's Play
Maas, Dick: Amsterdamned; Lift, The; Silent Witness
Mabe, Byron: She Freak, The
MacArthur, Charles: Scoundrel, The
Macartney, Syd: Prince Brat and the Whipping Boy
MacCorkindale, Simon: House That Mary Bought, The
MacDonald, David: Devil Girl from Mars; Never Too Late
MacDonald, Heather: Ballot Measure 9
Macdonald, Hettie: Beautiful Thing
MacDonald, Peter: Legionnaire; Mo' Money; Neverending Story III, The: Escape toFantasia; Rambo III
MacFadden, Hamilton: Black Camel, The; Stand Up and Cheer
MacFarland, Mike: Hanging on a Star; Pink Motel
MacGregor, Sean: Gentle Savage
Machaty, Gustav: Ecstasy
Mack, Brice: Jennifer
Mackay, David: Breaking Free; Lesser Evil, The; Route 9; Turbulence 2
Mackendrick, Alexander: Ladykillers, The; Man in the White Suit, The; Sweet Smell of Success; Tight Little Island
Mackenzie, John: Act of Vengeance; Aldrich Ames: Traitor Within; Beyond the Limit; Deadly Voyage; Fourth Protocol, The; Infiltrator, The; Last of the Finest, The; Long Good Friday, The; Ruby; Sense of Freedom, A; Voyage
MacKenzie, Philip Charles: Attention Shoppers
Mackenzie, Will: Perfect Harmony; Worth Winning
MacKinnon, Gillies: Behind the Lines; Hideous Kinky; Last of the Blonde Bombshells, The; Playboys, The; Simple Twist of Fate, A; Small Faces
MacLachlan, Duncan: Second Jungle Book, The: Mowgli and Baloo
Maclean, Alison: Crush (1994); Jesus' Son
MacLean, Stephen: Around the World in 80 Ways
Macy, W. H.: Lip Service (1988)
Madden, David: Separate Lives
Madden, John: Captain Corelli's Mandolin; Ethan Frome; Golden Gate; Grown-Ups; Mrs. Brown; Shakespeare in Love
Madden, Lee: Hell's Angels '69; Night Creature
Maddin, Guy: Careful; Tales from the Gimli Hospital
Maddock, Brent: Tremors 3: Back to Perfection
Madison, Alan: Trouble on the Corner
Madjidi, Majid: Children of Heaven
Madsen, Kenneth: Day in October, A
Magalhaes, Ana Maria: Erotique
Magar, Guy: Children of the Corn: Revelation; Retribution; Stepfather III: Father's Day

Maggenti, Maria: Incredibly True Adventure of Two Girls in Love, The
Magnatta, Constantino: Dark Side, The; Darkside, The
Magni, Luigi: In Nome del Papa Re (In the Name of the Pope-King)
Magnoli, Albert: American Anthem; Born to Run; Dark Planet; Purple Rain; Street Knight
Magnuson, John: Lenny Bruce Performance Film, The
Maguire, Sharon: Bridget Jones's Diary
Magyar, Dezso: Rappaccini's Daughter
Mahaffey, Redge: Life 101
Maharaj, Anthony: Deathfight
Mahon, Barry: Assault of the Rebel Girls (Cuban Rebel Girls); Rocket Attack USA
Mailer, Norman: Tough Guys Don't Dance
Main, Stewart: Desperate Remedies
Mainka, Maximiliane: Germany In Autumn
Maitland, George: Invasion Earth: The Aliens Are Here
Majidi, Majid: Color of Paradise, The
Mak, Michael: Sex and Zen
Makavejev, Dusan: Coca Cola Kid, The; Innocence Unprotected; Man Is Not A Bird; Manifesto; Montenegro; Sweet Movie; WR: Mysteries of the Organism
Makhmalbaf, Mohsen: Gabbeh; Kandahar
Makhmalbaf, Samirah: Apple, The
Makin, Kelly: Kids in the Hall: Brain Candy; Mickey Blue Eyes; National Lampoon's Senior Trip
Makino, Shigeto: Record of Lodoss War
Makk, Karoly: Lily in Love; Love
Malenfant, Robert: Landlady, The; Nurse, The
Malick, Terence: Badlands (1973); Days of Heaven; Thin Red Line, The
Malle, Louis: Alamo Bay; Atlantic City; Au Revoir, Les Enfants; Crackers; Damage; Elevator to the Gallows; Fire Within, The; Lovers, The (1958); May Fools; Murmur of the Heart; My Dinner with Andre; Pretty Baby; Vanya on 42nd Street; Very Private Affair, A; Viva Maria!; Zazie dans le Metro
Mallet, David: Cats
Mallon, James: Mystery Science Theatre 3000: The Movie
Malloy, Brendan: Out Cold (2001)
Malloy, Emmett: Out Cold (2001)
Malmuth, Bruce: Hard to Kill; Man Who Wasn't There, The; Nighthawks; Pentathlon; Where Are the Children?
Malone, Mark: Bulletproof Heart; Hoods; Last Stop
Malone, Nancy: I Married a Monster
Malone, William: House on Haunted Hill; Scared to Death
Mamet, David: Heist (2001); Homicide; House of Games; Oleanna; Spanish Prisoner, The; State & Main; Things Change; Winslow Boy, The
Mamin, Yuri: Window to Paris
Mamoru, Oshii: Ghost in the Shell
Mamoulian, Rouben: Applause; Becky Sharp; Blood and Sand; Dr. Jekyll and Mr. Hyde; Golden Boy; Love Me Tonight; Mark of Zorro, The; Queen Christina; Silk Stockings; Summer Holiday
Manchevski, Milcho: Before the Rain
Mancuso (Joe d'Amato), Kevin: 2020 Texas Gladiators
Mandel, Jeff: Elves; Robo C.H.I.C.
Mandel, Robert: Big Shots; F/X; Independence Day; Perfect Witness; School Ties; Substitute, The; Touch and Go
Mandelberg, Artie: His Bodyguard; Where's the Money, Noreen?
Mandoki, Luis: Angel Eyes; Born Yesterday; Gaby, a True Story; Message in a Bottle; When a Man Loves a Woman; White Palace
Mandt, Neil: Arthur's Quest; Hijacking Hollywood
Manduke, Joseph: Cornbread, Earl and Me; Gumshoe Kid, The; Omega Syndrome
Manfredi, Nino: Nudo di Donna (Portrait of a Woman, Nude)
Mangine, Joseph: Neon Maniacs
Mangold, James: Copland; Girl, Interrupted; Heavy; Kate and Leopold
Mankiewicz, Francis: And Then You Die; Love and Hate
Mankiewicz, Joseph L.: All About Eve; Barefoot Contessa, The; Cleopatra; Five Fingers; Ghost and Mrs. Muir, The; Guys and Dolls; Honey Pot, The; House of Strangers; Julius Caesar; Letter to Three Wives, A; People Will Talk; Sleuth; Somewhere in the Night; Suddenly, Last Summer; There Was a Crooked Man
Mankiewicz, Tom: Delirious; Dragnet; Taking the Heat
Mankiewirk, Henry: Hell's Brigade
Mann, Abby: King
Mann, Anthony: Bend of the River; Cimarron; Dandy in Aspic, A; Desperate; El Cid; Fall of the Roman Empire, The; Far Country, The; Glenn Miller Story, The; God's Little Acre; Great Flamarion, The; He Walked by Night; Man from Laramie, The; Man of the West; Men in War; Naked Spur, The; Railroaded; Serenade; Strategic Air Command; T-Men; Thunder Bay; Tin Star, The; Winchester '73
Mann, Daniel: Butterfield 8; Come Back, Little Sheba; Dream of Kings, A; For Love of Ivy; Hot Spell; I'll Cry Tomorrow; Interval; Journey into Fear; Last Angry Man, The; Man Who Broke 1000 Chains, The; Matilda; Our Man Flint; Playing for Time; Rose Tattoo, The; Teahouse of the August Moon, The; Who's Got the Action?; Willard
Mann, Delbert: All Quiet on the Western Front; Birch Interval, The; Dear Heart; Desire under the Elms; Fitzwilly; Francis Gary Powers: The True Story of the U-2 Spy Incident; Ironclads; Last Days of Patton, The; Love Leads the Way; Lover Come Back; Marty (1953) (Television); Marty (1955); Middle of the Night; Night Crossing; She Waits; That Touch of Mink; Torn Between Two Lovers
Mann, Farhad: Lawnmower Man 2: Jobe's War (Lawnmower Man: Beyond Cyberspace); Nick Knight; Return to Two-Moon Junction
Mann, Michael: Ali; Heat; Insider, The; Jericho Mile, The; Keep, The; Last of the Mohicans, The; Manhunter; Thief (1981)
Mann (Santos Alocer), Edward: Cauldron of Blood
Manning, Jack: Merry Wives of Windsor, The
Manning, Michelle: Blue City
Manoogian, Peter: Arena; Demonic Toys; Dungeonmaster, The; Eliminators, The; Enemy Territory; Midas Touch, The; Seedpeople
Manos, Guy: Cutaway
Manos, Mark S.: Huntress: Spirit of the Night
Mansfield, Mike: Stand by Me
Mansfield, Scott: Deadly Games
Mantello, Joe: Love! Valour! Compassion!
Manuli, Guido: Volere Volare
Manzarek, Ray: Doors, the Soft Parade
Manzor, Rene: Legends of the North; Warrior Spirit
Marcarelli, Robert: Original Intent
Marcel, Terry: Hawk the Slayer; Jane and the Lost City; Prisoners of the Lost Universe
March, Alex: Firehouse; Mastermind; Paper Lion
Marchent, Joaquin Romero: Firehouse; Mastermind; Paper Lion
Marconi, David: Harvest, The (1992)
Marcum, G. D.: Gates of Hell Part II: Dead Awakening
Marcus, Adam: Jason Goes to Hell: The Final Friday
Marcus, Mitch: Boy Called Hate, A; Knocking on Death's Door
Marcus, Paul: Break Up; Prime Suspect: Scent of Darkness
Marcus, Philip: Terror on Alcatraz
Marendino, James: SLC Punk
Marfori, Andreas: Evil Clutch
Margolin, Stuart: Family Matter, A; Glitter Dome, The; How the West Was Fun; Medicine River; Paramedics; Salt Water Moose; Shining Season, A
Margolis, Jeff: Family Matter, A; Glitter Dome, The; How the West Was Fun; Medicine River; Paramedics; Salt Water Moose; Shining Season, A
Marin, Edwin L.: Abilene Town; Cariboo Trail; Christmas Carol, A; Death Kiss, The; Everybody Sing; Invisible Agent; Johnny Angel; Listen, Darling; Miss Annie Rooney; Mr. Ace;

Nocturne; Show Business; Study in Scarlet, A; Tall in the Saddle
Marin, Richard "Cheech": Born in East L.A.
Marinos, Lex: Indecent Obsession, An
Maris, Peter: Can It Be Love; Diplomatic Immunity; Ministry of Vengeance; Terror Squad; Viper
Mark, Mary Ellen: Streetwise
Marker, Russ: Yesterday Machine, The
Markes, Anthony: Bikini Island
Markes, Tony: Welcome to Hollywood
Markham, Monte: Neon City
Markiw, Gabriel: Mob Story
Markiw, Jancarlo: Mob Story
Markle, Fletcher: Incredible Journey, The
Markle, Peter: Avenging Angel, The (1995); Bat 21; Breaking Point; El Diablo; Four Eyes and Six Guns; Hot Dog … The Movie; Last Days of Frankie the Fly, The; Mob Justice; Nightbreaker; Personals, The; Wagons East; White Dwarf
Markovic, Goran: Tito and Me
Markowitz, Murray: Left for Dead
Markowitz, Robert: Afterburn; Belarus File, The; Dangerous Life, A; Decoration Day; Love, Lies and Murder; My Mother's Secret Life; Pray TV; Too Young to Die; Tuskegee Airmen, The; Voices
Marks, Arthur: Bonnie's Kids; Bucktown; Detroit 9000 (Detroit Heat); Friday Foster; J.D.'s Revenge
Marks, Ross: Twilight of the Golds, The
Marks, Ross Kagan: Homage
Marlowe, Brad: Webber's World (At Home with the Webbers)
Marlowe, Derek: Adventures of Sherlock Holmes, The (Series)
Marmorstein, Malcolm: Dead Men Don't Die
Marnham, Christian: Lethal Woman
Marois, Jean-Pierre: American Virgin
Marquand, Richard: Eye of the Needle; Hearts of Fire; Jagged Edge; Legacy, The; Return of the Jedi; Until September
Marquette, Jacques: Meteor Monster (Teenage Monster)
Marr, Leon: Dancing in the Dark
Marsh, William: Mood Swingers
Marshall, Frank: Alive; Arachnophobia; Congo
Marshall, Garry: Beaches; Dear God; Exit to Eden; Flamingo Kid, The; Frankie and Johnny; Nothing in Common; Overboard; Pretty Woman; Princess Diaries, The; Runaway Bride; Young Doctors in Love
Marshall, George: Blue Dahlia, The; Boy, Did I Get a Wrong Number!; Destry Rides Again; Fancy Pants; Gazebo, The; Ghost Breakers; Goldwyn Follies, The; Guns of Fort Petticoat; Houdini; How the West Was Won; It Started With a Kiss; Laurel and Hardy Classics: Vol. 11; Mating Game, The; Monsieur Beaucaire; My Friend Irma; Off Limits; Pack Up Your Troubles; Papa's Delicate Condition; Perils of Pauline, The; Pot O' Gold; Red Garters; Sad Sack, The; Show Them No Mercy; Star Spangled Rhythm; Texas; 365 Nights in Hollywood; Valley of the Sun; You Can't Cheat an Honest Man
Marshall, Mannie: Unexpected Encounters
Marshall, Penny: Awakenings; Big; Jumpin' Jack Flash; League of Their Own, A; Preacher's Wife, The; Renaissance Man; Riding in Cars with Boys; Working Stiffs
Marshall, Tonie: Venus Beauty Institute
Martin, Charles: Death of a Scoundrel; My Dear Secretary
Martin, Darnell: I Like It Like That
Martin, D'Urville: Dolemite
Martin, Eugenio: Horror Express; Pancho Villa
Martin, Frank: John Huston—The Man, the Movies, the Maverick
Martin, Gene: Bad Man's River
Martin, James Aviles: Flesh Eating Mothers
Martin, Michael: I Got the Hook Up; Tha Eastsidaz
Martin, Richard: Air Bud: Golden Receiver; Elizabeth R; Wounded
Martin, Richard Wayne: No Justice
Martin, Steve: Bowfinger
Martin, Steven M.: Theremin: An Electronic Odyssey
Martin, Wrye: Unearthing, The
Martinez, Chuck: Nice Girls Don't Explode
Martinez, Rene: Super Soul Brother
Martini, Richard: Limit Up; You Can't Hurry Love
Martino, Francesco: Dr. Butcher, M.D. (Medical Deviate)
Martino, Raymond: Davinci's War; Skyscraper; To the Limit
Martino, Sergio: Opponent, The; Screamers; Sex with a Smile; Slave of the Cannibal God; Torso
Martins, Marina: Tons of Trouble
Martins, W. Mel: Alex's Apartment
Martinson, Leslie: Atomic Kid, The; Batman; Cheyenne (TV Series); Kid with the Broken Halo, The; Kid with the 200 I.Q., The; Maverick (TV Series); PT 109
Marton, Andrew: Africa—Texas Style!; Around the World Under the Sea; Clarence, the Cross-Eyed Lion; Gypsy Colt; King Solomon's Mines; Longest Day, The; Men of the Fighting Lady
Marvin, Mike: Hamburger—The Motion Picture; Wraith, The
Marvin, R.: Renegade
Mas, Juan A.: Coroner, The
Masahiro, Tanaka: Riding Bean
Masaki, Shin-Ichi: Humanoid, The
Masami, Oobari: Bubblegum Crisis, Vols. 1–8
Masano, Anton Giulio: Atom Age Vampire
Mascarelli, Robert: I Don't Buy Kisses Anymore
Maseba, Yutaka: Ambassador Magma
Massetti, Ivana: Domino
Massi, Stelvio: Fearless
Massot, Joe: Song Remains the Same, The; Wonderwall
Master P: I Got the Hook Up
Masters, Quentin: Dangerous Summer, A; Stud, The
Masterson, Peter: Arctic Blue; Blood Red; Full Moon in Blue Water; Lily Dale; Night Game; Only Thrill, The; Trip to Bountiful, The
Mastorakis, Nico: Blind Date; Double Exposure; Hired to Kill; In the Cold of the Night; Next One, The; Nightmare at Noon; Wind, The
Mastrocinque, Camillo: Full Hearts and Empty Pockets
Mastroianni, Armand: Cameron's Closet; Deep Trouble; Distortions; Double Revenge; First Daughter; First Target; He Knows You're Alone; Killing Hour, The; Robin Cook's Invasion; Supernaturals, The
Masuda, Toshio: Tora! Tora! Tora!
Matalon, Eddy: Blackout; Sweet Killing
Maté, Rudolph: Branded; Dark Past, The; Deep Six, The; D.O.A.; For the First Time; Second Chance; Three Violent People; Union Station; Violent Men, The; When Worlds Collide
Matheson, Tim: Breach of Conduct; Buried Alive II; In the Company of Spies; Tails You Live, Heads You're Dead
Mathias, Sean: Bent
Matmor, Daniel: Homeboys II: Crack City; Urban Jungle
Matsumiya, Masuzumi: Wannabes
Matsutani, Rainer: Eating Pattern
Matsuura, Johei: Crying Freeman, Vols. 1–3
Matsuzono, Tohru: Rumik World: Laughing Target
Mattei, Bruno: Night of the Zombies; Seven Magnificent Gladiators, The
Mattei, Marius: Moving Target
Matthau, Charles: Doin' Time on Planet Earth; Grass Harp, The
Matthau, Walter: Gangster Story
Matthews, Paul: Breeders
Mattison, Bunny: Great Mouse Detective, The
Mattison, Sally: Slumber Party Massacre 3
Mattson, Arne: Doll; Girl, The
Mauri, Roberto: Animal Called Man, An; Slaughter of the Vampires
Maxwell, Garth: Jack Be Nimble
Maxwell, Peter: Highest Honor, The; Run, Rebecca, Run; Secret Agent (TV Series)
Maxwell, Ronald F.: Gettysburg; Little Darlings; Night the Lights Went Out in Georgia, The
May, Bradford: Darkman II: The Return of Durant; Darkman III: Die, Darkman, Die; Devil's Prey; Drive Like Lightning;

Legacy of Lies; Lethal Lolita—Amy Fisher: My Story; Madonna: Innocence Lost; Marilyn & Bobby: Her Final Affair; Mortal Sins (1992)
May, Elaine: Heartbreak Kid, The; Ishtar; Mikey and Nicky; New Leaf, A
May, Joe: House of the Seven Gables, The; Invisible Man Returns
Mayberry, Russ: Brady Bunch, The (TV series); Challenge of a Lifetime; Fer-de-Lance; Probe; Rebels, The; Side by Side: The True Story of the Osmond Family; Unidentified Flying Oddball
Maybury, John: Love is the Devil
Mayer, Gerald: Man Inside, The
Mayers, Janet: Letter to My Killer
Mayersberg, Paul: Captive; Nightfall
Mayfield, Les: American Outlaws; Blue Streak; Encino Man; Flubber; Miracle on 34th Street
Maylam, Tony: Burning, The; Riddle of the Sands; Sins of Dorian Gray, The; Split Second
Maynard, Ken: Fiddlin' Buckaroo
Mayo, Archie: Adventures of Marco Polo, The; Angel on My Shoulder; Black Legion; Case of the Lucky Legs, The; Go into Your Dance; House Across the Bay, The; Illicit; Night after Night; Night in Casablanca, A; Orchestra Wives; Petrified Forest, The; Svengali; They Shall Have Music
Mayron, Melanie: Baby-Sitters Club, The
Maysles, Albert: Gimme Shelter
Maysles, David: Gimme Shelter
Mazin, Craig: Specials, The
Mazo, Michael: Crackerjack; Downdraft; Time Runner
Mazursky, Paul: Alex in Wonderland; Blume in Love; Bob & Carol & Ted & Alice; Down and Out in Beverly Hills; Enemies—A Love Story; Faithful; Harry and Tonto; Moon over Parador; Moscow on the Hudson; Next Stop, Greenwich Village; Pickle, The; Scenes from a Mall; Tempest; Unmarried Woman, An; Willie and Phil; Winchell
Mazzolla, Russ: Planet Patrol
Mazzucato, Paolo: Moonbase
McAbee, Cory: American Astronaut, The
McAnuff, Des: Adventures of Rocky and Bullwinkle, The; Cousin Bette
McBrearty, Don: Child's Christmas in Wales, A (1986); Coming Out Alive; Really Weird Tales; Strange Tales: Ray Bradbury Theater
McBrearty, John: Sorority Girls and the Creature from Hell
McBride, Jim: Big Easy, The; Blood Ties; Breathless; David Holzman's Diary; Glen and Randa; Great Balls of Fire; Informant, The; Meat Loaf: To Hell and Back; Pronto; Wrong Man, The
McCain, Howard: No Dessert Dad Until You Mow the Lawn; Shadow of a Scream; Unspeakable, The
McCall, Cheryl: Streetwise
McCall, Rod: Cheatin' Hearts
McCanlies, Tim: Dancer, Texas: Pop. 81
McCann, Tim: Desolation Angels
McCarey, Leo: Affair to Remember, An; Awful Truth, The; Belle of the Nineties; Bells of St. Mary's, The; Duck Soup; Going My Way; Good Sam; Indiscreet; Love Affair; Milky Way, The; Once Upon a Honeymoon; Ruggles of Red Gap
McCarey, Ray: So This Is Washington; You Can't Fool Your Wife
McCarthy, John P.: Forty-Niners; Trailin' North
McCarthy, Michael: Operation Amsterdam; Thieves of Fortune
McCarthy, Peter: Floundering
McCathy, John Michael: Sore Losers
McClary, J. Michael: Annie O; Curse of the Starving Class
McClatchy, Greggor: Vampire at Midnight
McCleery, Mick: Alien Agenda, The (TV Series); Track 16; Twisted Tales
McCord, Jonas: Body, The
McCormick, Bret: Blood on the Badge
McCormick, Nelson: Kill Shot
McCowan, George: Frogs; Murder on Flight 502; Return to Fantasy Island
McCrae, Scooter: Shatter Dead
McCubbin, Peter: Home for Christmas
McCulloch, Bruce: Dog Park; Superstar: Dare to Dream
McCullough, Jim: Aurora Encounter
McDonald, Bruce: Dance Me Outside; Hard Core Logo; HIghway 61; Scandalous Me: The Jacqueline Susann Story
McDonald, Frank: Along the Navajo Trail; Bells of Rosarita; Big Sombrero, The; Flying Blind; Gun Smugglers; Lights of Old Santa Fe; My Pal Trigger; One Body Too Many; Take It Big; Thunder Pass; Wyatt Earp: Return to Tombstone
McDonald, J. Farrell: Patchwork Girl of Oz, The
McDonald, Michael James: Crazysitter, The; Death Artist
McDonald, Rodney: Deep Core; Scorned 2; Steel Sharks; Surface to Air
McDougall, Charles: Heart (1999)
McDougall, Don: Bonanza (TV Series); Chinese Web, The; Riding with Death
McDougall, Francine: Sugar and Spice
McElwee, Ross: Sherman's March
McEveety, Bernard: Brotherhood of Satan; Longest Drive, The; Napoleon and Samantha; Ride Beyond Vengeance; Roughnecks
McEveety, Vincent: Amy; Apple Dumpling Gang Rides Again, The; Castaway Cowboy, The; Charley and the Angel; Firecreek; Gunsmoke: Return to Dodge; Gus; Herbie Goes Bananas; Herbie Goes to Monte Carlo; Menace on the Mountain; Million Dollar Duck, The; Smoke; Star Trek (TV Series); Superdad
McGann, William: American Empire; Case of the Black Cat, The; Dr. Christian Meets the Women; In Old California
McGaugh, W. F.: New Adventures of Tarzan
McGavin, Darren: Run Stranger Run
McGehee, Scott: Deep End, The; Suture
McGinnis, Scott: Caroline at Midnight; Last Gasp
McGoohan, Patrick: Prisoner, The (1968) (TV Series)
McGowan, Darrell: Showdown, The (1950)
McGowan, J. P.: Drum Taps; Hurricane Express; Tarzan and the Golden Lion
McGowan, Robert: Old Swimmin' Hole, The
McGowan, Stuart E.: Billion Dollar Hobo, The; Showdown, The (1950); They Went That-A-Way and That-A-Way
McGrath, Douglas: Company Man; Emma
McGrath, Joseph: Bliss of Mrs. Blossom, The; Casino Royale; Magic Christian, The; 30 Is a Dangerous Age, Cynthia
McGrath, Martin: Wet and Wild Summer
McGuane, Thomas: 92 in the Shade
McGuckian, Mary: This Is the Sea
McGuire, Don: Delicate Delinquent, The
McHenry, Doug: House Party 2; Jason's Lyric; Kingdom Come
McIntyre, C. J.: Border Shootout
McIntyre, Chris: Backstreet Justice; Captured Alive
McIntyre, Thom: Rutherford County Line
McKay, Cole: Game, The; Star Hunter
McKay, Jim: Girls Town; Our Song
McKay, John: Crush
McKellar, Don: Last Night
McKellips, Paul: Reggie's Prayer
McKeown, Douglas: Return of the Alien's Deadly Spawn, The
McKimmie, Jackie: Waiting
McLachlan, Duncan: Born Wild; Double-O Kid, The; Scavengers
McLaglen, Andrew V.: Bandolero!; Blue and the Gray, The; Breakthrough; Cahill—US Marshal; Chisum; Devil's Brigade, The; Dirty Dozen, The: The Next Mission; ffolkes; Have Gun, Will Travel (TV Series); Hellfighters; McLintock!; Monkeys Go Home; On Wings of Eagles; Rare Breed, The (1966); Sahara; Sea Wolves, The; Shadow Riders, The; Shenandoah; Undefeated, The; Way West, The; Wild Geese, The
McLennan, Don: Slate, Wyn, and Me
McLeod, Norman Z.: Casanova's Big Night; Horse Feathers; It's a Gift; Kid from Brooklyn, The; Lady Be Good; Let's Dance; Little Men; Monkey Business; Never Wave at a WAC (Private

Wore Skirts, The); Paleface, The; Panama Hattie; Road to Rio; Secret Life of Walter Mitty, The; Topper; Topper Takes a Trip
McLoughlin, Tom: Date with an Angel; Fire Next Time, The; Friday the 13th, Part VI: Jason Lives; Journey; One Dark Night; Sometimes They Come Back; Yarn Princess, The
McMurray, Mary: At Bertram's Hotel; Office Romances
McNally, David: Coyote Ugly
McNamara, Sean: Casper: A Spirited Beginning; P.U.N.K.S.; Treehouse Hostage
McNaughton, Ian: And Now for Something Completely Different; Monty Python's Flying Circus (TV Series)
McNaughton, John: Borrower, The; Girls in Prison; Henry: Portrait of a Serial Killer; Lansky; Mad Dog and Glory; Normal Life; Sex, Drugs, Rock & Roll; Wild Things
McPherson, John: Dirty Work; Fade to Black; Incident at Deception Ridge; Strays
McQ: Charlie's Angels
McQuarrie, Christopher: Way of the Gun, The
McRae, Henry: Tarzan the Tiger
McTiernan, John: Die Hard; Die Hard with a Vengeance; Hunt for Red October, The; Last Action Hero, The; Medicine Man; Nomads; Predator; Rollerball (2002); 13th Warrior, The; Thomas Crown Affair, The
McWhinnie, Donald: Elizabeth R; Mapp & Lucia
Mead, Nick: Bank Robber; Swing
Meadows, Shane: Twentyfourseven
Meckler, Nancy: Alive & Kicking; Sister, My Sister
Medak, Peter: Babysitter, The; Changeling, The; David Copperfield; Day in the Death of Joe Egg, A; Ghost in the Noonday Sun; Hunchback, The (1997); Krays, The; Let Him Have It; Men's Club, The; Negatives; Odd Job, The; Pinocchio; Pontiac Moon; Romeo Is Bleeding; Ruling Class, The; Snow Queen; Snow White and the Seven Dwarfs; Species II; Zorro, the Gay Blade
Medem, Julio: Lovers of the Arctic Circle; Red Squirrel, The
Medford, Don: Fugitive, The: The Last Episode (TV Series); Organization, The; Sizzle
Medoway, Cary: Heavenly Kid, The; Paradise Motel
Meerapfel, Jeanine: Malou
Meffre, Pomme: Grain of Sand, The
Megahey, Leslie: Advocate, The
Megahy, Francis: Carpathian Eagle; Great Riviera Bank Robbery, The; Red Sun Rising; Taffin
Mehrez, Alan: Bloodsport II; Bloodsport III
Mehta, Deepa: Camilla (1994); Earth
Mehta, Ketan: Spices
Meins, Gus: Gentleman from California; March of the Wooden Soldiers (Babes in Toyland (1934))
Meisel, Myron: It's All True
Mekas, Adolfas: Brig, The
Mekas, Jonas: Brig, The
Melançon, André: Bach and Broccoli
Melchior, Ib: Angry Red Planet, The; Time Travelers, The
Mele, Arthur N.: Soldier's Fortune
Melendez, Bill: Bon Voyage, Charlie Brown; Boy Named Charlie Brown, A; Lion, the Witch and the Wardrobe, The; Play It Again, Charlie Brown; Race for Your Life, Charlie Brown; Snoopy, Come Home; This Is America, Charlie Brown; You're Not Elected, Charlie Brown
Melford, George: Dracula (Spanish); East of Borneo; Moran of the Lady Letty; Sheik, The
Melkonian, James: Stoned Age, The
Mellencamp, John: Falling from Grace
Melton, Frank: Othello
Melville, Jean-Pierre: Bob le Flambeur; Le Doulos; Le Samourai; Les Enfants Terribles
Menaul, Chris: Fatherland; Feast of July; Passion of Ayn Rand, The; Prime Suspect 1
Menaul, Christopher: One Kill
Mendelsohn, Eric: Judy Berlin
Mendeluk, George: Doin' Time; Kidnapping of the President, The; Meatballs III; Stone Cold Dead
Mendes, Lothar: Man Who Could Work Miracles, The
Mendes, Sam: American Beauty
Mendez, Fernando: Vampire, The
Mendez, Mike: Bimbo Movie Bash
Menendez, Ramon: Money for Nothing; Stand and Deliver
Menges, Chris: Crisscross (1992); Second Best; World Apart, A
Meng-Hua, Ho: Mighty Peking Man
Menshov, Vladimir: Moscow Does Not Believe in Tears
Menzel, Jiri: Closely Watched Trains; Larks on a String
Menzies, William Cameron: Chandu the Magician; Drums in the Deep South; Invaders from Mars; Things to Come
Merchant, Ismail: Cotton Mary; Courtesans of Bombay; In Custody; Proprietor, The
Meredino, James: Hard Drive
Meredith, Burgess: Man in the Eiffel Tower, The; Yin and Yang of Mr. Go, The
Merendino, James: Real Thing, The; Terrified
Merhi, Jalal: Operation Golden Phoenix
Merhi, Joseph: CIA Codename Alexa; Direct Hit; Executive Target; Final Impact; Killing Game, The; L.A. Crackdown; L.A. Crackdown II; L.A. Vice; Last Man Standing; Magic Kid; Maximum Force; Rage; Riot; Sweeper, The; Zero Tolerance
Merhige, E. Elias: Shadow of the Vampire
Merhige, Edmund Elias: Begotten
Merino, J. L.: Blood Castle
Merlet, Agnes: Artemisia
Merrick, Ian: Black Panther, The
Merrill, Kieth: Harry's War; Take Down; Windwalker
Merriweather, George: Blondes Have More Guns
Merriwether (Arch Hall Sr.), Nicholas: Eegah!
Merwin, David: Eegah!
Mesa, Roland: Revenge of the Nerds III: The Next Generation
Mesa, William: DNA; Galaxis
Meshekoff, Matthew: Opposite Sex (And How to Live with Them), The (1993)
Messina, Philip F.: Spy
Metcalfe, Tim: Killer: A Journal of Murder
Metter, Alan: Back to School; Billboard Dad; Girls Just Want to Have Fun; Moving; Police Academy: Mission to Moscow
Metzger, Alan: China Lake Murders, The; Fatal Exposure; New Eden
Metzger, Radley: Alley Cats, The; Cat and the Canary, The; Daniella by Night; Therese and Isabelle
Meyer, Andrew: Night of the Cobra Woman
Meyer, David: Mafia: The History of the Mob in America
Meyer, Jean: Le Bourgeois Gentilhomme
Meyer, Kevin: Civil War Diary; Invasion of Privacy; Perfect Alibi; Under Investigation
Meyer, Nicholas: Company Business; Day After, The; Deceivers, The; Star Trek II: The Wrath of Khan; Star Trek VI: The Undiscovered Country; Time After Time; Vendetta; Volunteers
Meyer, Russ: Beyond the Valley of the Dolls; Mudhoney; Seven Minutes, The
Meyer, Turi: Candyman 3: Day of the Dead
Meyers, Dave: Foolish
Meyers, Janet: Ripper, The
Meyers, Nancy: Parent Trap, The; What Women Want
Meza, Eric: Breaks, The; House Party 3
Michaels, Bret: No Code of Conduct
Michaels, Ellyn: Rebecca's Secret
Michaels, Nolan T.: American Flatulators
Michaels, Richard: Backfield in Motion; Berlin Tunnel 21; Blue Skies Again; Father & Scout; Heart of a Champion: The Ray Mancini Story; Lethal Charm; One Cooks, the Other Doesn't; Sadat; Silence of the Heart
Michalakis, John Elias: I Was a Teenage Zombie
Micheaux, Oscar: Body and Soul
Michell, Roger: Buddha of Suburbia, The; Changing Lanes; Notting Hill; Persuasion
Michener, Dave: Great Mouse Detective, The; Once Upon a Forest
Mihaileanu, Radu: Train of Life

Mihalka, George: Bullet to Beijing; Eternal Evil; Hostile Take Over; My Bloody Valentine; Psychic (1992); Relative Fear; Straight Line; Thunder Point; Windsor Protocol, The
Mikamoto, Yasuyoshi: Orguss, Vols. 1–4
Mikels, Ted V.: Astro-Zombies; Black Klansman, The; Blood Orgy of the She Devils; Corpse Grinders, The; 10 Violent Women
Mikesch, Elfi: Astro-Zombies; Black Klansman, The; Blood Orgy of the She Devils; Corpse Grinders, The; 10 Violent Women
Mikhalkov, Nikita: Burnt by the Sun; Close to Eden; Dark Eyes; Oblomov; Slave of Love, A; Unfinished Piece for the Player Piano, An (Unfinished Piece for a Mechanical Piano, An)
Mileham, Michael: Pushed to the Limit
Miles, Christopher: Priest of Love; That Lucky Touch; Virgin and the Gypsy, The
Milestone, Hank: From Hell to Victory
Milestone, Lewis: All Quiet on the Western Front; Arch of Triumph; Edge of Darkness; Front Page, The; General Died at Dawn, The; Hallelujah, I'm A Bum; Halls of Montezuma; Lucky Partners; Mutiny on the Bounty; North Star, The (1943); Ocean's Eleven; Pork Chop Hill; Purple Heart, The; Rain; Red Pony, The; Strange Love of Martha Ivers, The; Walk in the Sun, A
Milius, John: Big Wednesday; Conan the Barbarian; Dillinger; Farewell to the King; Flight of the Intruder, The; Red Dawn; Rough Riders; Wind and the Lion, The
Milland, Ray: Lisbon; Man Alone, A; Panic in the Year Zero
Millar, Gavin: Danny, The Champion of the World; Dreamchild; Retribution; Tidy Endings
Millar, Stuart: Rooster Cogburn; When the Legends Die
Miller, Bennett: Cruise, The
Miller, Claude: Accompanist, The; Little Thief, The; This Sweet Sickness
Miller, Dan T.: Screamers
Miller, David: Back Street; Billy the Kid; Bittersweet Love; Captain Newman, M.D.; Diane; Executive Action; Flying Tigers, The; Hail, Hero!; Lonely Are the Brave; Love Happy; Midnight Lace; Opposite Sex, The (1956); Sudden Fear
Miller, George: Andre; Anzacs; Aviator, The; Babe: Pig in the City; Chain Reaction; Frozen Assets; Goodbye, Miss 4th of July; Great Elephant Escape, The; Les Patterson Saves the World; Lorenzo's Oil; Mad Max; Mad Max Beyond Thunderdome; Man from Snowy River, The; Miracle Down Under; NeverEnding Story II, The; Over the Hill; Road Warrior, The; Silver Strand; Tidal Wave: No Escape; Twilight Zone—The Movie; Witches of Eastwick, The; Zeus and Roxanne
Miller, Harvey: Bad Medicine; Getting Away with Murder
Miller, Ira: Loose Shoes
Miller, J. C.: No Dead Heroes
Miller, Jason: That Championship Season
Miller, Jonathan: Long Day's Journey into Night
Miller, Michael: Case of Deadly Force, A; Dangerous Passion; Danielle Steel's Daddy; Danielle Steel's Once in a Lifetime; Jackson County Jail; National Lampoon's Class Reunion; Silent Rage
Miller, Neal: Under the Biltmore Clock
Miller, Paul: Pest, The
Miller, Randall: Class Act; Houseguest; Sixth Man, The
Miller, Robert Ellis: Any Wednesday; Baltimore Bullet, The; Bed and Breakfast; Brenda Starr; Girl from Petrovka, The; Hawks; Heart Is a Lonely Hunter, The; Reuben, Reuben
Miller, Sidney: 30-Foot Bride of Candy Rock, The
Miller, Troy: Jack Frost
Milligan, Andy: Bloodthirsty Butchers; Legacy of Horror; Rats are Coming! The Werewolves Are Here!, The
Milloy, Travis: Thugs
Mills, Alec: Bloodmoon; Dead Sleep
Milner, Dan: From Hell It Came
Milo, Tom E.: Smooth Talker
Milton, Robert: Devotion
Minahan, Daniel: Series 7: The Contenders
Miner, Michael: Deadly Weapon
Miner, Steve: Big Bully; Forever Young; Friday the 13th, Part II; Friday the 13th, Part III; Halloween: H20; House; Lake Placid; My Father, the Hero; Soul Man; Texas Rangers (2001); Warlock; Wild Hearts Can't Be Broken
Mingay, David: Rude Boy
Minghella, Anthony: English Patient, The; Mr. Wonderful; Talented Mr. Ripley, The; Truly, Madly, Deeply
Mingozzi, Gianfranco: Sardine: Kidnapped
Minion, Joe: Daddy's Boys
Minkoff, Rob: Lion King, The; Stuart Little
Minnelli, Vincente: American in Paris, An; Bad and the Beautiful, The; Band Wagon, The; Bells Are Ringing; Brigadoon; Cabin in the Sky; Clock, The; Courtship of Eddie's Father, The; Designing Woman; Father of the Bride; Father's Little Dividend; Four Horsemen of the Apocalypse; Gigi; Home from the Hill; I Dood It; Kismet; Long, Long Trailer, The; Lust for Life; Madame Bovary; Matter of Time, A; Meet Me in St. Louis; On a Clear Day, You Can See Forever; Pirate, The; Reluctant Debutante, The; Sandpiper, The; Some Came Running; Tea and Sympathy; Two Weeks in Another Town; Undercurrent; Yolanda and the Thief; Ziegfeld Follies
Mintz, Murphy: Cardiac Arrest
Mirkin, David: Heartbreakers; Romy and Michele's High School Reunion
Mirvish, Dan: Omaha (The Movie)
Misiorowski, Bob: Blink of an Eye; Blood of the Innocent; Point of Impact; Shark Attack
Misumi, Kenji: Lone Wolf and Cub: Sword of Vengeance; Shogun Assassin; Zatoichi: The Blind Swordsman and theChess Expert
Mitchell, David: City of Shadows; Downhill Willie; Killing Man, The; Mask of Death
Mitchell, Gene: Flipping
Mitchell, John Cameron: Hedwig and the Angry Inch
Mitchell, Mike: Deuce Bigalow: Male Gigolo
Mitchell, Oswald: Danny Boy
Mitchell, Sollace: Call Me
Miterrand, Frederic: Madame Butterfly
Miyazaki, Hayao: Castle of Cagliostro, The; Lupin III: Tales of the Wolf (TV Series); My Neighbor Totoro; Princess Mononoke
Miyoshi, Kunio: Re-birth of Mothra II
Mizoguchi, Kenji: Chikamatsu Monogatari; Forty Seven Ronin; Geisha, A; Life of Oharu; Osaka Elegy; Princess Yang Kwei Fei; Sansho the Bailiff; Shin Heinke Monogatari; Sisters of the Gion; Story of the Late Chrysanthemums, The; Street of Shame; Ugetsu
Mizrahi, Moshe: Every Time We Say Goodbye; I Sent a Letter to My Love; La Vie Continue; Madame Rosa
Mizuno, Kazunori: Record of Lodoss War
Moctezuma, Juan Lopez: Dr. Tarr's Torture Dungeon; Mary, Mary, Bloody Mary
Moder, Richard: Bionic Woman, The
Moeller, Phillip: Break of Hearts
Moffitt, John: Love at Stake
Mogherini, Flavio: Lunatics & Lovers
Moguy, Leonide: Action in Arabia; Whistle Stop
Möhr, Hanro: Hostage
Moland, Hans Petter: Zero Kelvin
Molander, Gustav: Dollar; Intermezzo; Only One Night
Moleon, Rafael: Baton Rouge
Molina, Jack: Craving, The
Molina, William H.: Last Assassins
Molinaro, Edouard: Beaumarchais the Scoundrel; Dracula and Son; Just the Way You Are; La Cage aux Folles; La Cage aux Folles II; Pain in the A—, A; Ravishing Idiot, The; Seven Deadly Sins, The
Moll, Dominik: With a Friend Like Harry
Moll, James: Last Days, The
Moloney, Paul: I Live With Me Dad
Monahan, Dave: Adventures of Milo in the Phantom Tollbooth, The
Mondshein, Andrew: Evidence of Blood

Mones, Paul: Fathers & Sons; Saints & Sinners
Monger, Christopher: Englishman Who Went up a Hill But Came down a Mountain, The; Just Like a Woman; Waiting for the Light
Monicelli, Mario: Big Deal on Madonna Street; Laugh for Joy (Passionate Thief) (1954); Lovers and Liars; Organizer, The; Passionate Thief, The (1961)
Monnier, Philippe: Tale of Two Cities, A
Monroe, Madison: Phantom Love
Monroe, Phil: Bugs Bunny/Road Runner Movie, The
Montagne, Edward: Reluctant Astronaut, The; They Went That-A-Way and That-A-Way
Montaldo, Giuliano: Sacco and Vanzetti; Time to Kill (1990)
Montero, Roberto: Monster of the Island, The; Slasher
Montes, Eduardo: Double Obsession
Montesi, Jorge: Bloodknot; Hush Little Baby; Omen IV: The Awakening; Soft Deceit; Turbulence 3: Heavy Metal; Visitors of the Night
Montgomery, George: From Hell to Borneo
Montgomery, Monty: Loveless, The
Montgomery, Patrick: Compleat Beatles, The
Montgomery, Robert: Gallant Hours, The; Lady in the Lake
Moody, Ralph: Stage to Tucson
Moodysson, Lukas: Together
Moore, Charles Philip: Angel of Destruction; Blackbelt; Dance with Death; Demon Wind
Moore, John: Behind Enemy Lines
Moore, Michael: Big One, The; Buckskin; Canadian Bacon; Fastest Guitar Alive, The; Paradise Hawaiian Style; Roger & Me; Talion
Moore, Richard: Circle of Iron
Moore, Robert: Chapter Two; Cheap Detective, The; Murder by Death; Thursday's Game
Moore, Simon: Under Suspicion
Moore, Tara: Tusks
Moore, Tom: Danielle Steel's Fine Things; 'Night, Mother; Return to Boggy Creek
Moorhouse, Jocelyn: How to Make an American Quilt; Proof; Thousand Acres, A
Mora, Philippe: Back in Business; Beast Within, The; Breed Apart, A; Communion; Death of a Soldier; Howling II … Your Sister Is a Werewolf; Howling III; Mad Dog Morgan; Mercenary 2: Thick and Thin; Precious Find; Return of Captain Invincible, The
Morahan, Andy: Highlander: The Final Dimension; Murder in Mind
Morahan, Christopher: After Pilkington; Clockwise; Jewel in the Crown, The; Paper Mask; Unnatural Pursuits
Moranis, Rick: Strange Brew
Mordente, Tony: Love in the Present Tense
Mordillat, Gérard: Billy Ze Kick; My Life and Times with Antonin Artaud
Moreau, Jeanne: Lumiere
Moreton, David: Edge of Seventeen
Moretti, Nanni: Caro Diario; Palombella Rossa
Morgan, W. T.: Matter of Degrees, A
Morita, Yoshimitsu: Family Game, The
Moriyama, Yuuji: Urusei Yatsura (TV Series) Vols. 1–45
Morneau, Louis: Bats; Carnosaur 2; Final Judgment; Quake; To Die Standing
Moroder, Giorgio: Metropolis (1984 Musical Version)
Morris, David: Patti Rocks; Vietnam War Story—Part Two
Morris, David Burton: Hometown Boy Makes Good; Jersey Girl; Three Lives of Karen, The
Morris, Ernest: Tell-Tale Heart, The
Morris, Errol: Dark Wind; Fast, Cheap and Out of Control; Mr. Death: The Rise and Fall of Fred A. Leuchter Jr.; Thin Blue Line, The; Vernon, Florida
Morris, Howard: Don't Drink the Water; Who's Minding the Mint?; With Six You Get Eggroll
Morrison, Bruce: Shaker Run; Tearaway
Morrissette, Billy: Scotland, PA
Morrissey, Kevin: Witchcraft IV
Morrissey, Paul: Andy Warhol's Dracula; Andy Warhol's Frankenstein; Beethoven's Nephew; Flesh; Heat; Hound of the Baskervilles, The; Mixed Blood; Spike of Bensonhurst; Trash
Morrisson, Paul: Solomon and Gaenor
Morrow, Rob: Maze
Morse, Hollingsworth: Daughters of Satan; Justin Morgan Had a Horse
Morse, Terrel O.: Unknown World
Morse, Terry: Fog Island; Godzilla, King of the Monsters
Morton, Rocky: D.O.A.; Max Headroom; Super Mario Brothers, The
Morton, Vincent: Windrider
Moses, Ben: Nickel & Dime
Moses, Gilbert: Fish That Saved Pittsburgh, The
Moses, Harry: Assault at West Point
Mosher, Gregory: Life in the Theater, A; Prime Gig, The
Moshinsky, Elijah: Genghis Cohn; Green Man, The
Moskov, George: Married Too Young
Moskowitz, Steward: Adventures of an American Rabbit, The
Mosquera, Gustavo: Times to Come
Mostow, Jonathan: Beverly Hills Bodysnatchers; Breakdown; Flight of Black Angel; U-571
Mottola, Greg: Daytrippers, The
Mourneau, Louis: Soldier Boyz
Mowbray, Malcolm: Don't Tell Her It's Me; Out Cold; Private Function, A; Sweet Revenge
Moxey, John Llewellyn: Bounty Man, The; Children of An Lac, The; Circus of Fear; Cradle Will Fall, The; Detective Sadie and Son; Home for the Holidays (1972) (Television); Horror Hotel; Intimate Strangers; Lady Mobster; Mating Season, The; Night Stalker, The; Sanctuary of Fear; Through Naked Eyes
Moyle, Alan: Empire Records; Gun in Betty Lou's Handbag, The; Jailbait (2000); Pump Up the Volume; Times Square; Xchange
Mulcahy, Russell: Blue Ice; Highlander; Highlander 2: The Quickening; On the Beach; Razorback; Real McCoy, The; Resurrection; Ricochet; Russell Mulcahy's Tale of the Mummy; Shadow, The; Silent Trigger
Mullen, Mark: Cool Blue
Müller, Ray: Wonderful Horrible Life of Leni Riefenstahl
Mulligan, Robert: Baby the Rain Must Fall; Bloodbrothers; Clara's Heart; Come September; Fear Strikes Out; Great Impostor, The; Inside Daisy Clover; Kiss Me Goodbye; Love with the Proper Stranger; Man in the Moon, The; Other, The; Pursuit of Happiness, The; Same Time Next Year; Stalking Moon, The; Summer of '42; To Kill a Mockingbird; Up the Down Staircase
Mulot, Claude: Black Venus; Blood Rose
Munch, Christopher: Hours and Times
Munchkin, Richard W.: Dance or Die; Deadly Bet; Evil Obsession; Fist of Iron; Guardian Angel; Out for Blood; Texas Payback
Mundhra, Jag: Jigsaw Murders, The; L.A. Goddess; Last Call; Open House; Other Woman, The; Sexual Malice; Tropical Heat; Wild Cactus
Mune, Ian: Bridge to Nowhere; Came a Hot Friday
Mungia, Lance: Six-String Samurai
Muniz, Angel: Nueba Yol
Munk, Andrej: Passenger, The
Muñoz, Alex: Riot (1996) (TV Movie)
Munroe, Cynthia: Wedding Party, The
Murakami, Jimmy T.: Battle Beyond the Stars; When the Wind Blows
Murakami, Ryu: Tokyo Decadence
Murakawa, Toru: Distant Justice; New York Cop
Murch, Walter: Return to Oz
Murlowski, John: Amityville: A New Generation; Automatic; Return of the Family Man; Santa with Muscles; Secret Agent Club
Murnau, F. W.: City Girl; Faust; Haunted Castle; Last Laugh, The; Nosferatu; Sunrise; Tabu
Muro, Jim: Street Trash
Murphy, Blair: Jugular Wine

Murphy, Dudley: Emperor Jones, The
Murphy, Eddie: Harlem Nights
Murphy, Edward: Heated Vengeance
Murphy, Geoff: Blind Side; Don't Look Back; Fortress 2: Reentry; Freejack; Last Outlaw, The; Magnificent Seven, The (TV Series); Quiet Earth, The; Race Against Time; Red King, White Knight; Under Siege 2: Dark Territory; Utu; Young Guns II
Murphy, Maurice: Wet and Wild Summer
Murphy, Patrick Michael: Elvis: The Lost Performances
Murphy, Ralph: Spirit of West Point, The
Murphy, Richard: Wackiest Ship in the Army, The
Murphy, Tab: Last of the Dogmen
Murray, Bill: Quick Change
Murray, Katrina: Secret Garden, The
Murray, Robin: Dance
Murray, William: Primal Scream
Musallam, Izidore K.: Heaven Before I Die
Musca, Tom: Race
Musker, John: Aladdin; Great Mouse Detective, The; Hercules (Animated) (1997); Little Mermaid, The
Muspratt, Victoria: Inhumanoid; Macon County Jail; Teen Sorcery
Mutrux, Floyd: Aloha, Bobby and Rose; American Hot Wax; Hollywood Knights, The; There Goes My Baby
Myers, Zion: Sidewalks of New York
Myerson, Alan: Holiday Affair; Police Academy 5: Assignment: Miami Beach; Steelyard Blues; Television Parts Home Companion
Myles, Bruce: Ground Zero
Myrick, Daniel: Blair Witch Project, The
Nadel, Arthur H.: Clambake
Nagahama, Tadao: Starbirds
Nagaoka, Akinori: Record of Lodoss War
Nagaoka, Yasuchika: New Cutey Honey, The
Nagy, Ivan: Captain America II: Death Too Soon; Deadly Hero; Gun in the House, A; Skinner
Nahon, Chris: Kiss of the Dragon
Nair, Mira: Kama Sutra: A Tale of Love; Mississippi Masala; Monsoon Wedding; My Own Country; Perez Family, The; Salaam Bombay!
Nakano, Desmond: White Man's Burden
Nakayama, Hisashi: Digimon: The Movie
Nalluri, Bharat: Killing Time (1996)
Nankin, Michael: Midnight Madness
Napolitano, Joe: Contagious
Naranjo, Lisandro Duque: Miracle in Rome
Narizzano, Silvio: Blue; Body in the Library, The; Class of Miss MacMichael, The; Die! Die! My Darling!; Georgy Girl; Loot; Redneck; Why Shoot the Teacher?
Naruse, Mikio: Flunky, Work Hard!; Late Chrysanthemums; Mother; When a Woman Ascends the Stairs; Wife! Be Like a Rose!
Natali, Vincenzo: Cube
Naud, Bill: Whodunit?
Nava, Gregory: El Norte; My Family; Selena; Time of Destiny, A; Why Do Fools Fall in Love
Nazarro, Ray: Dog Eat Dog; Indian Uprising; Kansas Pacific
Neame, Ronald: Chalk Garden, The; First Monday in October; Foreign Body; Gambit; Hopscotch; Horse's Mouth, The; I Could Go On Singing; Man Who Never Was, The; Meteor; Odessa File, The; Poseidon Adventure, The; Prime of Miss Jean Brodie, The; Promoter, The; Scrooge; Tunes of Glory; Windom's Way
Needham, Hal: Body Slam; Cannonball Run; Cannonball Run II; Hooper; Hostage Hotel; Megaforce; Rad; Smokey and the Bandit; Smokey and the Bandit II; Stroker Ace; Villain, The
Needham, John: Chuck Amuck: The Movie
Neff, Thomas L.: Running Mates
Negrin, Alberto: Mussolini and I; Voyage of Terror: The Achille Lauro Affair
Negroponte, Michel: Jupiter's Wife
Negulesco, Jean: Best of Everything, The; Daddy Long Legs; How to Marry a Millionaire; Humoresque; Johnny Belinda; Phone Call from a Stranger; Road House; Three Came Home; Titanic; Woman's World
Neilan, Marshall: Chloe: Love is Calling You; Rebecca of Sunnybrook Farm; Stella Maris; Sweethearts on Parade; Vagabond Lover, The
Neill, Roy William: Black Room, The; Dr. Syn; Dressed to Kill; Frankenstein Meets the Wolf Man; Gypsy Wildcat; House of Fear; Pearl of Death, The; Pursuit to Algiers; Scarlet Claw, The; Sherlock Holmes and the Secret Weapon; Sherlock Holmes and the Spider Woman; Sherlock Holmes Faces Death; Sherlock Holmes in Washington; Terror by Night; Woman in Green, The
Neilson, James: Adventures of Bullwhip Griffin, The; Bon Voyage!; Dr. Syn, Alias the Scarecrow; Gentle Giant; Johnny Shiloh; Moon Pilot; Mooncussers; Moonspinners, The; Summer Magic
Neira, Daniel: Immortal Combat
Neitz, Alvin J.: Phantom, The
Nel, Frans: American Kickboxer
Nelson, Art J.: Creeping Terror, The
Nelson, David: Last Plane Out
Nelson, Dusty: Necromancer; White Phantom
Nelson, Gary: Allan Quartermain and the Lost City of Gold; Black Hole, The; Freaky Friday; Get Smart Again; Jimmy the Kid; Lookalike, The; Murder in Coweta County; Pride of Jesse Hallman, The; Revolver; Santee
Nelson, Gene: Harum Scarum; Kissin' Cousins
Nelson, Jack: Tarzan the Mighty
Nelson, Jessie: Corrina, Corrina; I Am Sam
Nelson, Ozzie: Adventures of Ozzie and Harriet, The (TV Series)
Nelson, Ralph: Charly; Christmas Lilies of the Field; Duel at Diablo; Embryo; Father Goose; Hero Ain't Nothin' But a Sandwich, A; Lady of the House; Lilies of the Field; Requiem for a Heavyweight (1956) (Television); Requiem for a Heavyweight (1962); Soldier Blue; Soldier in the Rain; Tick ... Tick ... Tick ...; Wilby Conspiracy, The
Nelson, Tim Blake: O
Nemec, Jan: Report on the Party and the Guests, A
Nepomuceno, Luis: Pacific Connection, The
Nesher, Avi: Doppelganger: The Evil Within; Mercenary; Savage; She; Time Bomb
Neufeld, Max: Orphan Boy of Vienna, An
Neumann, Kurt: Carnival Story; Fly, The; It Happened in New Orleans; Kronos; Make a Wish; Mohawk; My Pal, the King; Return of the Vampire, The; Rocketship X-M; Secret of the Blue Room, The; Son of Ali Baba; Tarzan and the Leopard Woman
Newbrook, Peter: Spirit of the Dead
Newell, Mike: Amazing Grace and Chuck; Awakening, The; Awfully Big Adventure, An; Dance with a Stranger; Donnie Brasco; Enchanted April; Four Weddings and a Funeral; Good Father, The; Into the West; Man in the Iron Mask, The; Pushing Tin
Newfield, Sam: Aces and Eights; Arizona Gunfighter; Black Raven, The; Bulldog Courage; Dead Men Walk; Death Rides the Plains; Flying Serpent, The; Ghost Patrol; His Brother's Ghost; Lawman Is Born, A; Lightnin' Crandall; Lost Continent, The; Mad Monster; Monster Maker, The; Prairie Rustlers; Roaring Guns; Star Hunter; Terror of Tiny Town, The; Traitor, The; White Pongo (Blond Gorilla)
Newland, John: Don't Be Afraid of the Dark; Legend of Hillbilly John, The
Newlin, Martin: Crawlers; Witchery
Newman, Joseph M.: Great Dan Patch, The; Jungle Patrol; King of the Roaring Twenties; Love Nest; Pony Soldier; This Island Earth
Newman, Paul: Effect of Gamma Rays on Man-in-the-Moon Marigolds, The; Glass Menagerie, The; Harry and Son; Rachel, Rachel; Shadow Box, The; Sometimes a Great Notion
Newmeyer, Fred: Freshman, The; General Spanky; Grandma's Boy; Safety Last
Niami, Ramin: Somewhere in the City

Odell, David: Martians Go Home
Odets, Clifford: None But the Lonely Heart
O'Donoghue, Michael: None But the Lonely Heart
Odorisio, Luciano: Sacrilege
Oedekerk, Steve: Ace Ventura: When Nature Calls; Kung Pow!: Enter the Fist; Nothing to Lose
O'Fallon, Peter: Suicide Kings
O'Ferrall, George More: Three Cases of Murder
Ofteringer, Suzanne: Nico Icon
Ogilvie, George: Crossing, The; Mad Max Beyond Thunderdome
Ogorodnikov, Valery: Burglar (Russian)
Ogrodnik, Mo: Ripe
O'Hara, Gerry: Bitch, The; Leopard in the Snow; Maroc 7
O'Hara, Terrence: Perfect Bride, The
O'Haver, Tommy: Billy's Hollywood Screen Kiss; Get Over It
O'Herlihy, Michael: Cry of the Innocent; Fighting Prince of Donegal, The; Medicine Hat Stallion, The; One and Only, Genuine, Original Family Band, The; Smith!
Ohlmeyer, Don: Heroes of Desert Storm
O'Horgan, Tom: Futz
Okamoto, Kihachi: Red Lion; Sword of Doom; Zatoichi vs. Yojimbo
Okawara, Takao: Godzilla 2000
Okazaki, Steven: Living on Tokyo Time
Okuda, Seiji: Crystal Triangle
Okuwaki, Masahara: Dirty Pair: Affair on Nolandia
Okuyama, Kazuyoshi: Mystery of Rampo, The
Old Jr., John: Blastfighter; Devilfish
Oldman, Gary: Nil by Mouth
Oldoini, Enrico: Bye Bye, Baby
Olen Ray, Fred: Air Rage
Oliansky, Joel: Competition, The
Olin, Ken: In Pursuit of Honor; White Fang 2: Myth of the White Wolf
Oliver, David: Cave Girl
Oliver, Robert H.: Dr. Frankenstein's Castle of Freaks
Oliver, Ron: Prom Night III—Last Kiss; Tales from a Parallel Universe
Oliver, Ruby L.: Love Your Mama
Olivera, Hector: Barbarian Queen; Cocaine Wars; Funny Dirty Little War (No Habra Mas Penas ni Olvido); Two to Tango; Wizard of the Lost Kingdom
Oliveria, Manoel de: Convent, The
Olivier, Laurence: Hamlet; Henry V; Prince and the Showgirl, The; Richard III
Ollstein, Marty: Dangerous Love
Olmi, Ermanno: Tree of the Wooden Clogs, The
Olmos, Edward James: American Me
O'Malley, David: Easy Wheels
Omori, Kazuki: Godzilla Versus Biollante
Onchi, Hideo: Toward the Terra
O'Neal, Ron: Superfly T.N.T.; Up Against the Wall
O'Neans, Douglas F.: Sno-Line
O'Neil, Robert Vincent: Angel; Avenging Angel (1985)
Ophuls, Marcel: Hotel Terminus: The Life and Times of Klaus Barbie; Sorrow and the Pity, The
Ophüls, Max: Caught; Earrings of Madame De ..., The; La Ronde; La Signora di Tutti; Le Plaisir; Letter from an Unknown Woman; Liebelei; Lola Montes
Oppenheimer, Peer J.: Terror in Paradise
Ordung, Wyott: Monster from the Ocean Floor, The
Orlando, Dominic: Knights of the City
Orme, Stuart: Heist, The; Ivanhoe; Puppet Masters, The; Sherlock Holmes: Hands of a Murderer
Ormerod, James: Frankenstein
Ormond, Ron: King of the Bullwhip
Ormrod, Peter: Eat the Peach
Ormsby, Alan: Deranged
Orona, Gary: Bikini Carwash Company 2
Orr, James: Breaking All the Rules; Man of the House; Mr. Destiny; They Still Call Me Bruce
Ortega, Kenny: Hocus Pocus; Newsies
Osamu, Kamijoo: Riding Bean
Osborne, Aaron: Caged Heat 3000; Zarkorr! The Invader
Oshii, Mamoru: Patlabor: The Mobile Police
Oshii, Mamoru: Urusei Yatsura: Only You; Urusei Yatsura: Beautiful Dreamer
Oshima, Nagisa: Cruel Story of Youth; In the Realm of Passion; In the Realm of the Senses; Max Mon Amour; Merry Christmas, Mr. Lawrence; Violence at Noon
Osmond, Cliff: Penitent, The
O'Steen, Sam: Best Little Girl in the World, The; Queen of the Stardust Ballroom; Sparkle
Osten, Suzanne: Mozart Brothers, The
O'Sullivan, Thaddeus: December Bride; Nothing Personal
Oswald, Gerd: Brainwashed; Crime of Passion; Outer Limits, The (TV Series); Paris Holiday; Screaming Mimi; Star Trek (TV Series)
Othenin-Girard, Dominique: After Darkness; Halloween V: The Revenge of Michael Myers; Night Angel; Omen IV: The Awakening
Otomo, Katsuhiro: Akira; Neo-Tokyo
Ottman, John: Urban Legends: Final Cut
Otto, Linda: Unspeakable Acts
Ottoni, Filippo: Detective School Dropouts
Ouellette, Jean Paul: Unnamable, The; Unnamable II, The
Oury, Gerard: Delusions of Grandeur; La Grande Vadrouille
Owen, Cliff: Bawdy Adventures of Tom Jones, The; Vengeance of She, The; Wrong Arm of the Law, The
Oz, Frank: Dark Crystal, The; Dirty Rotten Scoundrels; Housesitter; In & Out; Indian in the Cupboard, The; Little Shop of Horrors (1986); Muppets Take Manhattan, The; Score, The; What About Bob?
Ozawa, S.: Street Fighter
Ozgenturk, Ali: Horse, The
Ozon, François: Under the Sand
Ozpetek, Ferzan: Steam: The Turkish Bath; Turkish Bath, The
Ozu, Yasujiro: Autumn Afternoon, An; Drifting Weeds; Early Summer; Equinox Flower; Late Spring; Tokyo Story
Ozun, François: Sitcom
Pabst, G. W.: Diary of a Lost Girl; Don Quixote; Joyless Street; Kameradschaft; Love of Jeanne Ney; Pandora's Box; Secrets of a Soul; Threepenny Opera, The; Westfront 1918
Pacino, Al: Looking for Richard
Padget, Calvin Jackson: Battle of El Alamein, The
Page, Anthony: Absolution; Bill; Bill: On His Own; Chernobyl: The Final Warning; Forbidden; Heartbreak House; I Never Promised You a Rose Garden; Lady Vanishes, The; Middlemarch; Missiles of October, The; Monte Carlo; Nightmare Years, The; Scandal in a Small Town
Pagnol, Marcel: Angele; Baker's Wife, The; César; Harvest (1937); Le Schpountz; Topaze; Well-Digger's Daughter, The
Paizs, John: Invasion
Pakula, Alan J.: All the President's Men; Comes a Horseman; Consenting Adults; Devil's Own, The; Dream Lover; Klute; Orphans; Parallax View, The; Pelican Brief, The; Presumed Innocent; Rollover; See You in the Morning; Sophie's Choice; Starting Over; Sterile Cuckoo, The
Pal, George: 7 Faces of Dr. Lao; Time Machine, The; Tom Thumb; Wonderful World of the Brothers Grimm, The
Pal, Laszlo: Journey to Spirit Island
Palcy, Euzhan: Dry White Season, A; Killing Yard, The; Ruby Bridges; Sugarcane Alley
Pallenberg, Raspo: Cutting Class
Palm, Anders: Dead Certain; Murder on Line One
Palmer, John: Ciao! Manhattan
Palmer, Tony: 200 Motels; Wagner
Palmer Jr., Thomas: Forever
Palmieri, Matt: Sand
Palmisano, Conrad E.: Busted Up; Space Rage
Paltrow, Bruce: Duets; Little Sex, A
Palud, Herve: Little Indian, Big City
Panahi, Jafar: White Balloon, The
Panama, Norman: Barnaby and Me; Court Jester, The; I Will, I Will ... for Now; Road to Hong Kong, The; Trap, The

Pan-Andreas, George: Crime Killer, The
Panaro, Gino: Cutting Moments
Pang, Danny: Bangkok Dangerous
Papamichael, Phedon: Dark Side of Genius; Sketch Artist
Papatakis, Nico: Les Abysses
Paradise, Michael J.: Visitor, The
Paradisi, Giulio: Spaghetti House
Paragon, John: Double Trouble; Ring of the Musketeer; Twin Sitters
Parajanov, Sergi: Color of Pomegranates, The; Legend of Suram Fortress, The; Shadows of Forgotten Ancestors
Paras, Dean: Too Smooth
Parco, Paul Salvatore: Deadly Alliance; Pucker Up and Bark Like a Dog
Parda, Joseph A.: 5 Dead on the Crimson Canvas
Parello, Chuck: Ed Gein
Paris, Domonic: Dracula's Last Rites (1980)
Paris, Jerry: Don't Raise the Bridge, Lower the River; Evil Roy Slade; Grasshopper, The; How to Break Up a Happy Divorce; Make Me an Offer; Never a Dull Moment; Only with Married Men; Police Academy II: Their First Assignment; Police Academy III: Back in Training; Viva Max!
Parish, Richard C.: Don't Raise the Bridge, Lower the River; Evil Roy Slade; Grasshopper, The; How to Break Up a Happy Divorce; Make Me an Offer; Never a Dull Moment; Only with Married Men; Police Academy II: Their First Assignment; Police Academy III: Back in Training; Viva Max!
Parisot, Dean: Framed; Galaxy Quest; Home Fries
Park, Adam: Wishful Thinking
Park, Chui-Soo: 301/302
Park, Nick: Chicken Run; Wallace & Gromit: A Close Shave; Wallace & Gromit: A Grand Day Out; Wallace & Gromit: The Wrong Trousers
Parker, Alan: Angel Heart; Angela's Ashes; Birdy; Bugsy Malone; Come See the Paradise; Commitments, The; Evita; Fame; Midnight Express; Mississippi Burning; Pink Floyd: The Wall; Road to Wellville, The; Shoot the Moon
Parker, Albert: Black Pirate, The
Parker, Brian: Inspector Morse (TV Series)
Parker, Cary: Girl in the Picture, The
Parker, Christine: Women from Down Under
Parker, David: Bimbo Movie Bash; Dead Hate the Living, The
Parker, John: Daughter of Horror
Parker, Norton S.: Road to Ruin, The (1928)
Parker, Oliver: Ideal Husband, An; Othello
Parker, Percy G.: Castle of the Creeping Flesh
Parker, Trey: Orgazmo; South Park: Bigger, Longer & Uncut
Parkinson, Andrew: I, Zombie
Parkinson, Eric: Future Shock
Parks, Hugh: Shakma; Shoot
Parks, Michael: Return of Josey Wales
Parks Jr., Gordon: Aaron Loves Angela; Learning Tree, The; Shaft; Shaft's Big Score!; Superfly; Three the Hard Way
Parolini, Gianfranco: Fury of Hercules, The; Samson
Parr, John H.: Prey for the Hunter; Pursuit
Parr, Larry: Soldier's Tale, A
Parriott, James D.: Heart Condition; Misfits of Science
Parrish, Robert: Bobo, The; Casino Royale; Cry Danger; Destructors, The; Journey to the Far Side of the Sun; Mississippi Blues; Town Called Hell, A
Parrott, James: Laurel and Hardy Classics: Vol. 1–9; Pardon Us
Parry, Gordon: Tom Brown's Schooldays (1950)
Parsons, John: Watched!
Parsons, Nicholas: Dead Heart
Part, Michael: Starbirds
Pascal, Gabriel: Caesar and Cleopatra; Major Barbara
Pascal, Michel: Francois Truffaut: Stolen Moments
Paseornek, Michael: Vibrations
Paskaljevic, Goran: Cabaret Balkan; Someone Else's America
Pasolini, Pier Paolo: Accattone; Arabian Nights; Canterbury Tales, The; Decameron, The; Gospel According to Saint Matthew, The; Hawks and the Sparrows, The; Love Meetings; Mamma Roma; Medea; Oedipus Rex; Pigsty; Salo: 120 Days of Sodom; Teorema
Pasquin, John: Joe Somebody; Jungle 2 Jungle; Nightmare; Santa Clause, The
Passer, Ivan: Born to Win; Creator; Crime & Passion; Cutter's Way; Fourth Story; Haunted Summer; Silver Bears; Stalin
Pastrone, Giovanni: Cabiria
Pataki, Michael: Cinderella; Mansion of the Doomed
Patchett, Tom: Best Legs in the 8th Grade, The
Pate, Jonas: Deceiver; Grave, The
Pate, Josh: Deceiver
Pate, Michael: Tim
Patel, Raju: In the Shadow of Kilimanjaro
Paterson, Daniel M.: Girlfriend from Hell
Paterson, Iain: Hidden Agenda (1998)
Paton, Stuart: 20,000 Leagues Under the Sea
Patrick, Daniel: Haunted Sea, The
Patrick, Matthew: Hider in the House; Tainted Blood
Patrick, Michael: Drop Dead Gorgeous
Patterson, John: Grave Secrets: The Legacy of Hilltop Drive; Taken Away
Patterson, Willi: Dreams Lost, Dreams Found
Pattinson, Michael: ... Almost; Ground Zero; Limbic Region, The; One Crazy Night
Patton-Spruill, Robert: Body Count; Squeeze
Patzack, Peter: Lethal Obsession
Paul, Byron: Lt. Robin Crusoe, U.S.N.
Paul, Don: Road to El Dorado, The
Paul, Stefan: Jimmy Cliff—Bongo Man
Paul, Steven: Eternity; Falling in Love Again; Slapstick of Another Kind
Paul, Stuart: Emanon
Paulikovski, Paul: Last Resort
Paulsen, David: Schizoid
Pavia, Mark: Night Flier, The
Pavlou, George: Rawhead Rex; Transmutations
Pavone, Michael: Chameleon
Paxton, Bill: Frailty
Payne, Alexander: Citizen Ruth; Election
Payne, Dave: Under Oath
Payne, David: Addams Family Reunion; Alien Terminator; Aliens Among Us; Concealed Weapon; Criminal Hearts; Not Like Us
Payson, John: Joe's Apartment
Pearce, Michael: James Joyce's Women
Pearce, Richard: Country; Dead Man Out; Family Thing, A; Final Days, The; Heartland; Leap of Faith; Long Walk Home, The; No Mercy; Sessions; South Pacific (2001); Thicker Than Blood; Threshold; Witness Protection
Pearl, Steven: At First Sight
Pearlman, Jordan Walker: Visit, The
Pecas, Max: Daniella by Night
Peck, Brian: Willies, The
Peck, Raoul: Lumumba
Peck, Ron: Empire State
Peckinpah, David: When Danger Follows You Home
Peckinpah, Sam: Ballad of Cable Hogue, The; Bring Me the Head of Alfredo Garcia; Convoy; Cross of Iron; Deadly Companions, The; Getaway, The; Junior Bonner; Killer Elite, The; Major Dundee; Osterman Weekend, The; Pat Garrett and Billy the Kid; Ride the High Country; Straw Dogs; Wild Bunch, The
Peeples, Quinton: Joyride
Peerce, Larry: Ash Wednesday; Bell Jar, The; Court-martial of Jackie Robinson, The; Elvis and Me; Goodbye Columbus; Hard to Hold; Incident, The; Love Child; Murder So Sweet; Neon Empire, The; Other Side of the Mountain, The; Other Side of the Mountain, Part II, The; Prison for Children; Queenie; Separate Peace, A; Sporting Club, The; That Was Rock; Two-Minute Warning; Wired; Woman Named Jackie, A
Peeters, Barbara: Summer School Teachers
Pelaez, Antonio: Crystalstone
Pelissier, Anthony: Encore; Rocking Horse Winner, The

Pellerin, Jack: Laserhawk
Pellerin, Jean: Clown at Midnight, The; Daybreak (2000); Escape Under Pressure; For Hire
Pelletier, Andre: Voodoo Dolls
Pellington, Mark: Arlington Road; Going All the Way; Mothman Prophecies, The
Pellizzari, Monica: Women from Down Under
Peltier, Melissa: Titanic
Penczner, Marius: I Was a Zombie for the FBI
Penn, Arthur: Alice's Restaurant; Bonnie and Clyde; Chase, The; Dead of Winter; Four Friends; Inside; Left Handed Gun, The; Little Big Man; Miracle Worker, The; Missouri Breaks, The; Night Moves; Penn & Teller Get Killed; Portrait, The; Target
Penn, Leo: Dark Secret of Harvest Home, The; Judgment in Berlin; Lost in Space (TV Series); Man Called Adam, A
Penn, Sean: Crossing Guard, The; Indian Runner, The; Pledge, The
Pennebaker, D. A.: Don't Look Back; Down from the Mountain; Monterey Pop; Moon Over Broadway; War Room, The
Pennell, Eagle: Last Night at the Alamo
Peoples, David: Blood of Heroes
Pepin, Richard: Cyber Tracker; Cyber Tracker 2; Dark Breed; Epicenter; Firepower; T-Force; Terminal Countdown
Peploe, Clare: High Season; Rough Magic
Peploe, Mark: Afraid of the Dark
Perello, Hope: Howling VI: The Freaks; Pet Shop
Perennou, Marie: Microcosmos
Perez, Jack: America's Deadliest Home Video; La Cucaracha
Perier, Etienne: Investigation; Zeppelin
Perisic, Zoran: Sky Bandits
Perkins, Anthony: Lucky Stiff; Psycho III
Perry, Dein: Bootmen
Perry, Frank: Compromising Positions; David and Lisa; Diary of a Mad Housewife; Hello Again; Last Summer; Mommie Dearest; Monsignor; Rancho Deluxe; Skag; Swimmer, The
Persky, Bill: Serial
Pesce, P. J.: Desperate Trail
Peters, Brooke L.: Unearthly, The
Peters, Charlie: Music from Another Room; Passed Away
Peters, Christina: Smokers, The
Petersen, Wolfgang: Air Force One; Das Boot (The Boat); Enemy Mine; For Your Love Only; In the Line of Fire; NeverEnding Story, The; Outbreak; Perfect Storm, The; Shattered
Peterson, Kristine: Critters 3; Deadly Dreams; Hard Truth; Kickboxer 5: Redemption; Lower Level; Slaves to the Underground
Petipa, Marius: Don Quixote
Petit, Christopher: Caribbean Mystery, A; Chinese Boxes
Petri, Elio: Tenth Victim, The
Petrie, Ann: Mother Teresa
Petrie, Daniel: Bay Boy, The; Betsy, The; Bramble Bush, The; Buster and Billie; Calm at Sunset; Cocoon: The Return; Dollmaker, The; Fort Apache—The Bronx; Inherit the Wind; Kissinger and Nixon; Lassie; Lifeguard; Moon of the Wolf; My Name Is Bill W; Neptune Factor, The; Raisin in the Sun, A; Resurrection; Rocket Gibraltar; Silent Night, Lonely Night; Six Pack; Spy with a Cold Nose, The; Square Dance; Stolen Hours; Sybil; Walter and Henry; Wild Iris
Petrie, Donald: Associate, The; Favor, The; Grumpy Old Men; Miss Congeniality; My Favorite Martian; Mystic Pizza; Opportunity Knocks; Richie Rich
Petrie, Jeanette: Mother Teresa
Petrie Jr., Daniel: Dead Silence; In the Army Now; Toy Soldiers
Petroni, Giulio: Blood and Guns (Tepepa); Death Rides a Horse
Pevney, Joseph: Away All Boats; Cash McCall; Contract for Life: The S.A.D.D. Story; Istanbul; Man of a Thousand Faces; Meet Danny Wilson; Night of the Grizzly, The; Star Trek (TV Series); Strange Door, The; Tammy and the Bachelor; Torpedo Run; Who Is the Black Dahlia?
Peyser, John: Centerfold Girls; Four Rode Out
Pfleghar, Michel: Oldest Profession, The
Phelps, William: North Shore
Philibert, Nicolas: In the Land of the Deaf
Philips, Lee: Barnum; Blind Vengeance; Blue Lighting, The; Hardhat and Legs; Mae West; On the Right Track; Samson and Delilah; Silent Motive; Stranger Within, The; Sweet Hostage; Windmills of the Gods
Phillipe, Harald: Escape from the KGB
Phillips, Bill: There Goes the Neighborhood
Phillips, John Michael: Mikado, The
Phillips, Lou Diamond: Dangerous Touch; Sioux City
Phillips, Maurice: Another You; Over Her Dead Body; Riders of the Storm
Phillips, Nick: Criminally Insane
Phillips, Todd: Road Trip
Pialat, Maurice: A Nos Amours; Loulou; Police; Under the Sun of Satan; Van Gogh
Piché, Jean-Marc: Minion, The
Pichel, Irving: Colonel Effingham's Raid; Dance Hall; Destination Moon; Martin Luther; Miracle of the Bells, The; Most Dangerous Game, The; Mr. Peabody and the Mermaid; She; They Won't Believe Me; Tomorrow Is Forever
Pichul, Vasily: Little Vera
Pickett, Rex: From Hollywood to Deadwood
Pierce, Arthur C.: Las Vegas Hillbillys; Women of the Prehistoric Planet
Pierce, Charles B.: Boggy Creek II; Grayeagle; Legend of Boggy Creek; Norseman, The; Sacred Ground; Town That Dreaded Sundown, The
Pierce, Kimberly: Boys Don't Cry
Pierson, Carl: New Frontier
Pierson, Frank: Citizen Cohn; Dirty Pictures; King of the Gypsies; Lakota Woman: Siege at Wounded Knee; Looking Glass War, The; Somebody Has to Shoot the Picture; Star Is Born, A; Truman
Pilichino, Margarita: Anna Karenina
Pillsbury, Sam: Free Willy 3: The Rescue; Into the Badlands; Starlight Hotel; Zandalee
Piluso, Mario: Halloween Tree, The
Ping, He: Red Firecracker, Green Firecracker
Ping, Yuen Wo: Wing Chun
Pinion, Efren C.: Blind Rage
Pink, Sidney: Christmas Kid, The; Finger on the Trigger; Reptilicus
Pinoteau, Claude: La Boum
Pinsent, Gordon: John and the Missus
Pinsker, Seth: Hidden II, The
Pintilie, Lucian: Unforgettable Summer, An
Pintoff, Ernest: Blade; Lunch Wagon; St. Helens; Who Killed Mary What's 'Er Name?
Pipelow, John: Dee Snider's Strangeland
Piper, Brett: Dinosaur Babes; Nymphoid Barbarian in Dinosaur Hell, A; They Bite
Pires, Gilbert: Act of Aggression
Pirosh, Robert: Go for Broke!
Pirro, Mark: Buford's Beach Bunnies; Curse of the Queerwolf; Nudist Colony of the Dead; Polish Vampire in Burbank, A
Pistor, Peter: Fence, The; In Pursuit
Pitkethly, Lawrence: American Cinema
Pitre, Glen: Belizaire the Cajun; Time Served
Pittman, Bruce: Blood Brothers; Confidential; Flood: A River's Rampage; Harrison Bergeron; Hello, Mary Lou: Prom Night II; Locked in Silence; Mark of Cain; No Alibi; Silent Witness: What a Child Saw; Strange Tales: Ray Bradbury Theater; Where the Spirit Lives
Piznarski, Mark: Death Benefit; Here on Earth
Platt, Lucas: Girl in the Cadillac
Pleckaitis, Michael: Trees
Plone, Allen: Phantom of the Ritz; Sweet Justice
Plympton, Bill: I Married a Strange Person; J. Lyle; Tune, The
Poague, John R.: In the Name of Justice
Podeswa, Jeremy: Five Senses, The
Poe, Amos: Alphabet City; Dead Weekend; Frogs for Snakes

Down Twisted; Heatseeker; Hong Kong '97; Kickboxer 2: The Road Back; Kickboxer 4: Aggressor, The; Knights; Mean Guns; Nemesis; Nemesis 4; Nemesis 3: Time Lapse; Nemesis 2; Omega Doom; Radioactive Dreams; Raven Hawk; Spitfire; Sword and the Sorcerer, The; Ticker; Urban Menace; Wrecking Crew, The
Qamar, A. C.: Deadly Vengeance
Quaid, Dennis: Everything That Rises
Quested, John: Loophole
Quine, Richard: Bell, Book and Candle; Hotel; How to Murder Your Wife; My Sister Eileen; Oh Dad, Poor Dad—Mama's Hung You inthe Closet and I'm Feeling So Sad; Paris When It Sizzles; Prisoner of Zenda, The; Sex and the Single Girl; Strangers When We Meet; W; World of Suzie Wong, The
Quinn, Anthony: Buccaneer, The
Quinn, James: Blindman's Bluff
Quinn, John: Total Exposure
Quinn, Paul: This Is My Father
Quintano, Gene: Honeymoon Academy; National Lampoon's Loaded Weapon 1; Why Me?
Quinterio, Carlo U.: Night Train to Venice
Quintero, Jose: Roman Spring of Mrs. Stone, The
Quisenberry, Byron: Scream
Rabenalt, Arthur Maria: Unnatural
Rademakers, Fons: Assault, The; Rose Garden, The
Rademakers, Lili: Diary of a Mad Old Man
Rader, Peter: Grandma's House; Hired to Kill
Radford, Michael: Another Time, Another Place; B. Monkey; 1984; Postman, The (Il Postino); White Mischief
Radler, Robert: Best of the Best; Best of the Best 2; Substitute, The: Failure Is Not an Option
Radomski, Eric: Batman: Mask of the Phantasm
Raeburn, Michael: Jit; Killing Heat
Rafelson, Bob: Black Widow; Blood and Wine; Five Easy Pieces; Head (1968); King of Marvin Gardens, The; Man Trouble; Mountains of the Moon; Poodle Springs; Postman Always Rings Twice, The; Stay Hungry; Tales of Erotica
Raffanini, Piccio: Obsession: A Taste for Fear
Rafferty, Kevin: Atomic Cafe, The
Rafferty, Pierce: Atomic Cafe, The
Raffill, Stewart: Across the Great Divide; Adventures of the Wilderness Family; Grizzly Falls; High Risk; Ice Pirates; Mac and Me; Mannequin Two: On the Move; Philadelphia Experiment, The; Sea Gypsies, The; Tammy & the T-Rex
Rafkin, Alan: Ghost and Mr. Chicken, The; How to Frame a Figg; Shakiest Gun in the West, The
Raglin, Tim: Thumbelina
Railsback, Steve: Spy Within, The
Raimi, Sam: Army of Darkness; Crimewave; Darkman; Evil Dead, The; Evil Dead 2; For Love of the Game; Gift, The; Quick and the Dead, The; Simple Plan, A; Spider-Man
Raimondi, Paul: Crosscut
Rainone, Frank: Brooklyn State of Mind, A; Me and the Mob
Rakoff, Alvin: Deathship; Dirty Tricks; King Solomon's Treasure; Mr. Halpern and Mr. Johnson; Voyage 'Round My Father, A
Ramati, Alexander: Assisi Underground, The
Rambaldi, Vittorio: Decoy
Ramirez, Robert: Brave Little Toaster Goes to Mars, The
Ramis, Harold: Analyze This; Bedazzled; Caddyshack; Club Paradise; Groundhog Day; Multiplicity; National Lampoon's Vacation; Stuart Saves His Family
Ramsay, Lynne: Ratcatcher
Rand, Patrick: Mom
Randall, Addison: Killing Zone, The
Randas, Lance: Maximum Impact; Zombie Cop
Randel, Tony: Amityville 1992: It's About Time; Children of the Night; Fist of the North Star; Hellraiser II: Hellbound; Infested (Ticks); One Good Turn; Rattled
Rankin Jr., Arthur: Around the World in 80 Days; Flight of Dragons, The; Hobbit, The; Last Unicorn, The; Mad, Mad Monsters, The; Twenty Thousand Leagues Under the Sea (1972); Willie McBean and His Magic Machine
Ransen, Mort: Margaret's Museum; Shades of Love: Sincerely, Violet
Ransick, Whitney: Hand Gun
Rao, Krishna: Crossworlds
Raphael, Frederic: Women & Men: Stories of Seduction
Rapp, Philip: Adventures of Topper, The; I Married Joan (TV Series)
Rappaport, Mark: From the Journals of Jean Seberg
Rappeneau, Jean-Paul: Cyrano De Bergerac; Horseman on the Roof, The; Swashbuckler, The (1984)
Rapper, Irving: Adventures of Mark Twain, The; Born Again; Brave One, The; Corn Is Green, The; Deception; Marjorie Morningstar; Miracle, The; Now, Voyager; Rhapsody in Blue; Sextette
Rash, Steve: Buddy Holly Story, The; Can't Buy Me Love; Eddie; Held Up; Queens Logic; Son-in-Law; Under the Rainbow
Raskin, Jay: I Married a Vampire
Raskov, Daniel: Masters of Menace
Rasmussen, Lars: Littlest Viking, The
Rathborne, Tina: Zelly and Me
Ratner, Brett: Family Man, The; Money Talks; Rush Hour; Rush Hour 2
Ratoff, Gregory: Adam Had Four Sons; Black Magic; Corsican Brothers, The; Footlight Serenade; Heat's On, The; Intermezzo; Rose of Washington Square
Rautenbach, Jans: No One Cries Forever
Ravenscroft, Alan: Titanic: A Question of Murder
Ravich, Rand: Astronaut's Wife, The
Rawi, Ousama: Housekeeper, The
Rawlins, John: Arabian Nights; Arizona Ranger; Dick Tracy Meets Gruesome; Dick Tracy's Dilemma; Sherlock Holmes and the Voice of Terror; Sudan
Ray, Albert: Shriek in the Night, A; Thirteenth Guest, The
Ray, Bernard B.: Roamin' Wild; Smokey Trails
Ray, Fred Olen: Active Stealth; Alien Dead; Alienator; Armed Response; Attack of the 60-Ft. Centerfold; Bad Girls from Mars; Beverly Hills Vamp; Biohazard; Capitol Conspiracy, The; Commando Squad; Cyberzone; Cyclone; Evil Toons; Fugitive Rage; Hollywood Chainsaw Hookers; Inner Sanctum; Inner Sanctum 2; Invisible Dad; Invisible Mom; Mach 2; Maximum Security; Mindtwister; Mob Boss; Operation Condor (Don "The Dragon" Wilson); Phantom Empire, The (1986); Possessed by the Night; Scalps; Spirits; Star Slammer; Tomb, The; Venomous; Warlords; Wizards of the Demon Sword
Ray, Man: Avant Garde Program #2; Man Ray Classic Shorts
Ray, Nicholas: Born to Be Bad; 55 Days at Peking; Flying Leathernecks; In a Lonely Place; Johnny Guitar; King of Kings (1961); Knock on Any Door; Lusty Men, The; On Dangerous Ground; Party Girl; Rebel Without a Cause; They Live By Night; Woman's Secret, A
Ray, Satyajit: Adversary, The; Aparajito; Days and Nights in the Forest; Devi (The Goddess); Distant Thunder; Home and the World; Pather Panchali; Stranger, The; Two Daughters; World of Apu, The
Raye, Michael: Laserblast
Raymond, Alan: Elvis '56; Sweet Home Chicago
Raymond, Ed: Submerged
Raymond, Jack: Speckled Band, The
Raymond, Susan: Elvis '56; Sweet Home Chicago
Raynr, David: Trippin'; Whatever It Takes
Razatos, Spiro: Class of 1999 II: The Substitute; Fast Getaway
Reardon, John: Whoops Apocalypse
Rebane, Bill: Alpha Incident, The; Blood Harvest
Red, Eric: Bad Moon; Body Parts; Cohen and Tate; Undertow
Redford, Robert: Horse Whisperer, The; Legend of Bagger Vance, The; Milagro Beanfield War, The; Ordinary People; Quiz Show; River Runs Through It, A
Redmond, Lee: Final Mission
Reed, Bill: Secret of the Sword, The
Reed, Carol: Agony and the Ecstasy, The; Fallen Idol, The; Immortal Battalion, The (The Way Ahead); Key, The; Kid for Two Farthings, A; Night Train to Munich (Night Train); Odd Man

Out; Oliver; Stars Look Down, The; Third Man, The; Trapeze; Unicorn, The
Reed, Jerry: What Comes Around
Reed, Joel M.: Bloodsucking Freaks (The Incredible Torture Show); Night of the Zombies
Reed, Luther: Dixiana
Reed, Peyton: Bring It On; Love Bug, The
Reed, Ted: Nut, The
Rees, Clive: Blockhouse, The; When the Whales Came
Rees, Jerry: Brave Little Toaster, The; Marrying Man, The
Reeve, Christopher: In the Gloaming
Reeve, Geoffrey: Caravan to Vaccares; Puppet on a Chain; Souvenir
Reeves, George: TV's Best Adventures of Superman
Reeves, Matt: Pallbearer, The
Reeves, Michael: Conqueror Worm, The; She Beast, The
Regan, Patrick: Kiss Daddy Goodbye
Reggio, Godfrey: Koyaanisqatsi; Powaqqatsi
Reichert, Mark: Union City
Reichmann, Thomas: Mingus
Reid, Alastair: Inspector Morse (TV Series); Shattered; Teamster Boss: The Jackie Presser Story
Reid, Max: Eye of the Snake; Wild Thing
Reid, Tim: Little Mermaid, The; Once Upon a Time … When We Were Colored
Reilly, William: Men of Respect
Reiner, Carl: All of Me; Bert Rigby, You're a Fool; Dead Men Don't Wear Plaid; Dick Van Dyke Show, The (TV Series); Enter Laughing; Fatal Instinct; Jerk, The; Man with Two Brains, The; Oh, God!; One and Only, The; Sibling Rivalry; Summer Rental; Summer School; That Old Feeling; Where's Poppa?
Reiner, Jeffrey: Blood and Concrete, A Love Story; Evolution's Child; Huntress, The; Serpent's Lair; Trouble Bound
Reiner, Lucas: Spirit of '76, The
Reiner, Rob: American President, The; Few Good Men, A; Ghosts of Mississippi; Misery; North; Princess Bride, The; Stand by Me; Story of Us, The; Sure Thing, The; This Is Spinal Tap; When Harry Met Sally
Reinhardt, Gottfried: Betrayed
Reinhardt, Max: Midsummer Night's Dream, A
Reinisch, Deborah: Caught in the Act
Reinl, Harald: Chariots of the Gods; Hell Hounds of Alaska; Torture Chamber of Dr. Sadism, The
Reis, Irving: All My Sons; Bachelor and the Bobby-Soxer, The; Big Street, The; Crack-Up; Enchantment; Falcon Takes Over, The; Hitler's Children
Reisner, Allen: All Mine to Give
Reisner, Charles F.: Art of Buster Keaton, The; Steamboat Bill Jr.
Reisz, Karel: Everybody Wins; French Lieutenant's Woman, The; Gambler, The; Isadora; Morgan; Sweet Dreams; Who'll Stop the Rain
Reitherman, Wolfgang: Aristocats, The; Jungle Book, The (1967); One Hundred and One Dalmatians; Rescuers, The; Robin Hood; Sword in the Stone, The; Wind in the Willows, The
Reitman, Ivan: Dave; Evolution; Father's Day; Ghostbusters; Ghostbusters II; Junior; Kindergarten Cop; Legal Eagles; Meatballs; Six Days, Seven Nights; Stripes; Twins
Reitz, Edgar: Germany In Autumn
Rémy, Christopher: Clockmaker (1998)
René, Norman: Longtime Companion; Prelude to a Kiss; Reckless
Renoir, Jean: Boudu Saved from Drowning; Crime of Monsieur Lange, The; Day in the Country, A; Diary of a Chambermaid; Elena and Her Men; Elusive Corporal, The; French Can Can; Golden Coach, The; Grand Illusion; La Bête Humaine; La Chienne; La Marseillaise; Little Theatre of Jean Renoir, The; Lower Depths (1936); Madame Bovary; Picnic on the Grass; River, The; Rules of the Game, The; Southerner, The; Testament of Dr. Cordelier, The; This Land Is Mine; Toni
Resnais, Alain: Hiroshima, Mon Amour; Last Year at Marienbad; Melo; Mon Oncle d'Amerique; Muriel; Providence; Stavisky
Resnick, Adam: Cabin Boy
Resnikoff, Robert: First Power, The
Restaino, Elvis: Bloodsport IV: The Dark Kumite
Resteghini, Dale Anthony: Hip-Hop Witch Movie, Da
Revier, Harry: Lost City, The
Revon, Bernard: Rascals, The
Reynolds, Burt: End, The; Gator; Hard Time; Man from Left Field, The; Sharky's Machine; Stick
Reynolds, C.D.H.: Day of Judgment, A
Reynolds, Don: His Name Was King
Reynolds, Gene: M*A*S*H (TV Series); Truth or Die
Reynolds, Kevin: Beast, The; Count of Monte Cristo, The (2002); Fandango; 187; Rapa Nui; Robin Hood: Prince of Thieves; Waterworld
Reynolds, Scott: Heaven; Ugly, The
Reynolds, Sheldon: Adventures of Sherlock Holmes, The (TV Series)
Reynolds, Ursi: Ganjasaurus Rex
Rezyka, Mark: South of Reno
Rhine, Robert: Road Lawyers and Other Briefs
Rhodes, Michael Ray: Entertaining Angels; Fourth Wise Man, The; Killing Mind, The; Matters of the Heart
Rice, David: Quiet Thunder
Rich, David Lowell: Airport '79: The Concorde; Chu Chu and the Philly Flash; Convicted; Enola Gay: The Men, the Mission, the Atomic Bomb; Family Upside Down, A; Hearst and Davies Affair, The; Madame X; Northeast of Seoul; Satan's School for Girls; Story of David, The
Rich, John: Boeing, Boeing; Brady Bunch, The (TV series); Clarence Darrow; Easy Come, Easy Go; Roustabout
Rich, Matty: Inkwell, The; Straight out of Brooklyn
Rich, Richard: Black Cauldron, The; Fox and the Hound; King and I, The; Swan Princess, The; Trumpet of the Swan, The
Richard, Jeff: Berserker
Richard, Pierre: Daydreamer, The (1970) (Le Distrait); Too Shy to Try
Richards, Cybil: Shandra, The Jungle Girl; Virtual Encounters
Richards, Dick: Culpepper Cattle Co., The; Death Valley; Farewell My Lovely; Heat; Man, Woman and Child; March or Die; Rafferty and the Gold Dust Twins
Richards, Lloyd: Piano Lesson, The; Roots: The Next Generation
Richardson, Jeff: That Darn Punk
Richardson, John: Dusty
Richardson, Mark: Robot in the Family
Richardson, Peter: Eat the Rich; Pope Must Diet, The; Supergrass, The
Richardson, Tony: Blue Sky; Border, The; Charge of the Light Brigade, The; Entertainer, The; Hamlet; Hotel New Hampshire, The; Joseph Andrews; Loneliness of the Long Distance Runner,The; Look Back in Anger; Loved One, The; Mademoiselle; Taste of Honey, A; Tom Jones; Women & Men: Stories of Seduction
Richert, William: Night in the Life of Jimmy Reardon, A; Winter Kills
Richman, Meg: In the Shadows
Richmond, Anthony: Déjà Vu; Night of the Sharks
Richter, Ota: Skullduggery
Richter, W. D.: Adventures of Buckaroo Banzai, The; Late for Dinner
Rickman, Alan: Winter Guest, The
Rickman, Tom: River Rat, The
Ridley, John: Cold Around the Heart
Ridley, Philip: Passion of Darkly Noon, The; Reflecting Skin, The
Riead, William: Scorpion
Riefenstahl, Leni: Blue Light, The; Tiefland; Triumph of the Will
Riesner, Charles F.: Big Store, The; Lost in a Harem; Manhattan Merry-Go-Round
Riffel, J.: House on Tombstone Hill, The

Rifkin, Adam: Chase, The; Dark Backward, The; Detroit Rock City; Never on Tuesday; Something About Sex; Welcome to Hollywood
Riker, David: La Ciudad
Riklis, Eran: Cup Final
Riley, H. Anne: Animal Behavior
Rilla, Wolf: Village of the Damned
Rin, Taro: X
Ripley, Arthur: Chase, The; Thunder Road
Ripoll, Maria: Tortilla Soup; Twice Upon A Yesterday
Ripploh, Frank: Taxi Zum Klo (Taxi to the Toilet)
Ripstein, Arturo: Deep Crimson; Foxtrot
Risi, Dino: How Funny Can Sex Be?; Running Away; Tiger and The Pussycat, The
Risi, Marco: Forever Mary
Ritchie, Aileen: Closer You Get, The
Ritchie, Guy: Lock, Stock and Two Smoking Barrels; Snatch
Ritchie, Michael: Almost Perfect Affair, An; Bad News Bears, The; Candidate, The; Cops and Robbersons; Couch Trip, The; Diggstown; Divine Madness; Downhill Racer; Fantasticks, The; Fletch; Fletch Lives; Golden Child, The; Island, The; Positively True Adventures of the Alleged Texas Cheerleader-Murdering Mom, The; Prime Cut; Scout, The; Semi-Tough; Simple Wish, A; Smile; Survivors, The; Wildcats
Ritelis, Viktors: Crucible of Horror
Ritt, Martin: Back Roads; Black Orchid, The; Brotherhood, The; Casey's Shadow; Conrack; Cross Creek; Front, The; Great White Hope, The; Hombre; Hud; Long Hot Summer, The; Molly Maguires, The; Murphy's Romance; Norma Rae; Nuts; Paris Blues; Pete 'n' Tillie; Sounder; Spy Who Came in from the Cold, The; Stanley and Iris
Ritter, Tim: Alien Agenda, The (TV Series); Killing Spree; Screaming for Sanity: Truth or Dare 3; Wicked Games
Rivers, Joan: Rabbit Test
Rivette, Jacques: Celine and Julie Go Boating; La Belle Noiseuse; Nun, The (La Religieuse); Paris Belongs to Us; Up/Down/Fragile; Va Savoir
Rizenberg, Frederick A.: Gospel
Roach, Chris: Thirteenth Floor, The
Roach, Hal: One Million B.C.
Roach, Jay: Austin Powers: International Man of Mystery; Austin Powers: The Spy Who Shagged Me; Meet the Parents; Mystery, Alaska
Roach, M. Ray: Zoo Radio
Roach Jr., Hal: One Million B.C.
Roarke, Adam: Trespasses
Robak, Alain: Evil Within, The
Robbie, Seymour: C.C. & Company
Robbins, Brian: Good Burger; Hardball; Ready to Rumble; Show, The; Varsity Blues
Robbins, Jerome: West Side Story
Robbins, Matthew: Batteries Not Included; Bingo; Corvette Summer; Dragonslayer; Legend of Billie Jean, The
Robbins, Tim: Bob Roberts; Cradle Will Rock; Dead Man Walking
Robe, Mike: Child in the Night; News at Eleven; Return to Lonesome Dove; Son of the Morning Star; Urge to Kill
Robert, Genevieve: Casual Sex?
Robert, Vincent: Fear, The (1994)
Robert, Yves: My Father's Glory; My Mother's Castle; Pardon Mon Affaire; Pardon Mon Affaire, Too!; Return of the Tall Blond Man with One Black Shoe, The; Salut L'Artiste; Tall Blond Man with One Black Shoe, The
Robert Lee: Hostage Train
Roberts, Alan: Happy Hooker Goes Hollywood, The; Karate Cop; Round Trip to Heaven; Save Me
Roberts, Chris: Wing Commander
Roberts, Darryl: How U Like Me Now
Roberts, Deborah: Frankenstein General Hospital
Roberts, John: Paulie; War of the Buttons
Roberts, Stephen: Ex-Mrs. Bradford, The; Romance in Manhattan; Star of Midnight
Robertson, Cliff: Pilot, The
Robertson, David: Firebird 2015 AD
Robertson, John S.: Dr. Jekyll and Mr. Hyde; Little Orphan Annie; Our Little Girl; Single Standard, The
Robertson, Joseph F.: Auntie Lee's Meat Pies; Love Feast, The; Sensuous Wife, The
Robertson, Michael: Back of Beyond
Robertson, Tom G.: River Pirates, The
Robins, Herb: Worm Eaters, The
Robins, John: Hot Resort
Robinson, Bruce: How to Get Ahead in Advertising; Jennifer 8; Withnail and I
Robinson, John Mark: All Tied Up; Kid (1990); Roadhouse 66
Robinson, Les: Walk into Hell
Robinson, Paul D.: Last Flight to Hell
Robinson, Phil: Ferngully 2: The Magical Rescue
Robinson, Phil Alden: Field of Dreams; Freedom Song; In the Mood; Sneakers; Sum of All Fears, The
Robinson, Ted: Shout: The Story of Johnny O'Keefe
Robison, Arthur: Warning Shadows
Robson, Mark: Bedlam; Bridges at Toko-Ri, The; Champion; Daddy's Gone A-Hunting; Earthquake; From the Terrace; Harder They Fall, The; Home of the Brave; Inn of the Sixth Happiness, The; Isle of the Dead; Lost Command; My Foolish Heart; Peyton Place; Prize, The; Return to Paradise; Seventh Victim, The; Valley of the Dolls; Von Ryan's Express
Rocco, Marc: Dream a Little Dream; Murder in the First; Scenes from the Goldmine; Where the Day Takes You
Rocha, Glauber: Black God (White Devil)
Rochat, Eric: Fifth Monkey, The
Roche, Sean: Chasing Dreams
Rockwell, Alexandre: Four Rooms; In the Soup; Somebody to Love
Roddam, Franc: Aria; Bride, The; K2; Lords of Discipline, The; Moby Dick; Quadrophenia; War Party
Rodnunsky, Serge: Dead Tides; Final Equinox; Lovers' Lovers; Newsbreak
Rodriguez, Paul: Million to Juan, A
Rodriguez, Robert: Desperado; El Mariachi; Faculty, The; Four Rooms; From Dusk Till Dawn; Roadracers; Spy Kids
Roe, Chris: Pop & Me
Roeg, Nicolas: Aria; Castaway; Cold Heaven; Don't Look Now; Eureka; Full Body Massage; Heart of Darkness; Insignificance; Man Who Fell to Earth, The; Performance; Samson and Delilah; Sweet Bird of Youth; Track 29; Two Deaths; Walkabout; Witches, The
Roemer, Michael: Nothing But a Man; Plot Against Harry, The
Roessler, Rick: Slaughterhouse
Roffman, Julian: Mask, The
Rogell, Albert S.: Admiral Was a Lady, The; Li'l Abner; Thundering Hoofs; War of the Wildcats
Rogers, Charles R.: Bohemian Girl, The; Devil's Brother, The; Laurel and Hardy Classics: Vol. 1–9
Rogers, Doug: Dennis the Menace: Dinosaur Hunter
Rogers, James B.: American Pie 2; Say It Isn't So
Rogers, Maclean: Down Among the "Z" Men
Rogosin, Lionel: Come Back Africa; On the Bowery
Rohmer, Eric: Autumn Tale; Aviator's Wife, The; Boyfriends and Girlfriends; Chloe in the Afternoon; Claire's Knee; Four Adventures of Reinette and Mirabelle; Full Moon in Paris; Le Beau Mariage; My Night at Maud's; Pauline at the Beach; Rendezvous in Paris; Six in Paris (Paris Vue par ...); Summer; Tale of Springtime, A
Roley, Sutton: Snatched
Rollin, Jean: Living Dead Girl; Night of the Hunted; Zombie Lake
Rollins, Bernie: Getting Over
Roman, Phil: Tom & Jerry: the Movie
Romanek, Mark: Static
Romero, Eddie: Beast of the Yellow Night; Beyond Atlantis; Brides of the Beast; Twilight People
Romero, George A.: Bruiser; Crazies, The; Creepshow; Dark Half, The; Dawn of the Dead; Day of the Dead; Knightriders;

Martin; Monkey Shines: An Experiment in Fear; Night of the Living Dead; Season of the Witch; Two Evil Eyes
Romero, Joey: Savage Justice
Romine, Charles: Behind Locked Doors
Rondell, Ronnie: No Safe Haven
Roodt, Darrell: Cry, the Beloved Country; Dangerous Ground; Father Hood; Place of Weeping; Sarafina!; Second Skin
Room, Abram: Bed and Sofa
Rooney, Darrell: Lady and the Tramp II: Scamp's Adventure; Lion King II: Simba's Pride
Roos, Don: Bounce; Opposite of Sex, The
Root, Wells: Bold Caballero, The
Ropelewski, Tom: Look Who's Talking Now; Madhouse
Roper, Mark: Alien Chaser; Live Wire: Human Timebomb; Warhead
Rose, Bernard: Candyman; Chicago Joe and the Showgirl; Immortal Beloved; Leo Tolstoy's Anna Karenina (1997); Paperhouse
Rose, Lee: Color of Courage, The; What Girls Learn
Rose, Les: Gas
Rose, Mickey: Student Bodies
Rose, Reuben: Screwball Academy
Rosen, Dan: Dead Man's Curve
Rosen, Gary: Sink or Swim
Rosen, Martin: Plague Dogs, The; Stacking; Watership Down
Rosen, Phil: Charlie Chan in the Secret Service; Chinese Cat, The; Gangs, Inc. (Paper Bullets); Jade Mask, The; Little Men; Meeting at Midnight; Phantom Broadcast, The; Return of the Ape Man; Scarlet Clue, The; Sphinx, The (1933); Spooks Run Wild
Rosen, Robert L.: Raw Courage
Rosenberg, Anita: Assault of the Killer Bimbos
Rosenberg, Craig: Hotel de Love
Rosenberg, Stuart: Amityville Horror, The; April Fools, The; Brubaker; Cool Hand Luke; Drowning Pool, The; Laughing Policeman, The; Love and Bullets; My Heroes Have Always Been Cowboys; Pocket Money; Pope of Greenwich Village, The; Voyage of the Damned
Rosenberg, Tanya: Blood Games
Rosenbloom, Dale: Shiloh
Rosenblum, Ralph: Any Friend of Nicholas Nickleby Is a Friend of Mine; Greatest Man in the World, The; Man That Corrupted Hadleyburg, The
Rosenfeld, Keva: Twenty Bucks
Rosenfelt, Scott: Family Prayers
Rosenthal, Rick: American Dreamer; Bad Boys; Birds II, The: Land's End; Devlin; Distant Thunder; Halloween II; Russkies
Rosenthal, Robert J.: Zapped!
Rosi, Francesco: Big Rip-off, The; Bizet's Carmen; Christ Stopped at Eboli; Lucky Luciano; Palermo Connection, The; Three Brothers; Truce, The
Rosman, Mark: Blue Yonder, The; Evolver; Force, The; Invader, The (1996); Model Behavior
Rosner, Mark: Empire City
Ross, Benjamin: RKO 281; Young Poisoner's Handbook, The
Ross, Gary: Pleasantville
Ross, Herbert: Boys on the Side; California Suite; Dancers; Footloose; Funny Lady; Goodbye Girl, The; Goodbye, Mr. Chips; I Ought to Be in Pictures; Last of Sheila, The; Max Dugan Returns; My Blue Heaven; Nijinsky; Owl and the Pussycat, The; Pennies from Heaven; Play It Again, Sam; Protocol; Secret of My Success, The; Seven-Per-Cent Solution, The; Steel Magnolias; Sunshine Boys, The; True Colors; Turning Point, The; Undercover Blues
Rossati, Nello: Sensuous Nurse, The; Tides of War
Rossellini, Roberto: Amore (1948); Fear; General Della Rovere; Open City; Paisan; Rise of Louis XIV, The; Stromboli; Vanina Vanini; Voyage in Italy
Rossen, Robert: Alexander the Great; All the King's Men; Body and Soul; Hustler, The; Lilith; Mambo; They Came to Cordura
Rossi, Franco: Quo Vadis? (1985)
Rosson, Arthur: Long Long Trail
Rostrup, Kaspar: Memories of a Marriage
Roth, Bobby: Baja Oklahoma; Boss' Son, The; Dead Solid Perfect; Game of Love, The; Heartbreakers; Keeper of the City; Man Inside, The; Rainbow Drive
Roth, Joe: America's Sweethearts; Coupe De Ville; Revenge of the Nerds II: Nerds in Paradise; Streets of Gold
Roth, Lynn: Changing Habits
Roth, Phillip: Apex; Digital Man; Prototype X29A; Velocity Trap
Roth, Tim: War Zone, The
Rothman, Stephanie: Student Nurses, The; Terminal Island; Velvet Vampire, The
Rothstein, Richard: Hitchhiker, The (Series)
Rotundo, Nick: Gladiator Cop II: The Swordsman
Rouan, Brigitte: Overseas; Post Coitum
Rouch, Jean: Six in Paris (Paris Vue par ...)
Rouffio, Jaques: La Passante
Rouse, Russell: Caper of the Golden Bulls, The; Fastest Gun Alive, The; Oscar, The (1966); Thief, The; Well, The
Roussel, Jeannine: Lady and the Tramp II: Scamp's Adventure
Rousselot, Philippe: Serpent's Kiss, The
Rowe, George: Fatal Mission
Rowe, Peter: Lost!
Rowland, E. G.: Final Defeat, The
Rowland, Roy: Bugles in the Afternoon; Five Thousand Fingers of Dr. T, The; Girl Hunters, The; Hit the Deck; Hollywood Party; Meet Me in Las Vegas; Our Vines Have Tender Grapes; Seven Hills of Rome, The; Two Weeks with Love
Royle, David: Mafia: The History of the Mob in America
Rozema, Patricia: I've Heard the Mermaids Singing; Mansfield Park; When Night is Falling
Ruane, John: Death in Brunswick
Rubbo, Michael: Peanut Butter Solution, The
Ruben, Andy: Club Vampire
Ruben, J. Walter: Ace of Aces; RiffRaff
Ruben, Joseph: Dreamscape; Good Son, The; Gorp; Joyride; Money Train; Return to Paradise; Sister-in-Law, The; Sleeping with the Enemy; Stepfather, The; True Believer
Ruben, Katt Shea: Dance of the Damned; Last Exit to Earth; Poison Ivy; Streets
Rubens, Percival: Survival Zone; Sweet Murder
Rubie, Howard: Island Trader
Rubin, Bruce Joel: My Life
Rubinek, Saul: Jerry and Tom
Rubini, Sergio: Station, The
Rubino, John: Lotto Land
Rudolph, Alan: Afterglow; Breakfast of Champions; Choose Me; Endangered Species; Equinox (1993); Love at Large; Made in Heaven; Moderns, The; Mortal Thoughts; Mrs. Parker and the Vicious Circle; Nightmare Circus (Barn of the Living Dead) (Terror Circus); Songwriter; Trixie; Trouble in Mind; Welcome to L.A.
Rudolph, Louis: Double Standard
Rudolph, Oscar: Brady Bunch, The (TV series); Twist Around the Clock
Ruggles, Wesley: Arizona; Cimarron; I'm No Angel; No Man of Her Own; Somewhere I'll Find You
Ruiz, Raúl: Genealogies of a Crime; Three Lives and Only One Death
Ruiz, Raúl: Instant Justice; Shattered Image; Time Regained
Rumar, Craig T.: Instant Justice
Rupe, Katja: Germany In Autumn
Rush, Richard: Color of Night; Freebie and the Bean; Getting Straight; Hell's Angels on Wheels; Psych-Out; Stunt Man, The
Ruskin, Coby: When Things Were Rotten (TV Series)
Rusnak, Josef: Quiet Days in Hollywood; Thirteenth Floor, The
Russell, Charles: Blob, The; Eraser; Mask, The; Nightmare on Elm Street 3, A: The DreamWarriors
Russell, Chuck: Bless the Child; Scorpion King, The
Russell, David O.: Flirting with Disaster; Spanking the Monkey; Three Kings

Russell, Jay: End of the Line; My Dog Skip
Russell, Ken: Altered States; Boy Friend, The; Crimes of Passion; Dante's Inferno; Devils, The; Gothic; Lair of the White Worm; Lisztomania; Mahler; Music Lovers, The; Prisoner of Honor; Rainbow, The; Salome's Last Dance; Savage Messiah; Tales of Erotica; Tommy; Tracked; Valentino; Whore; Women & Men: Stories of Seduction; Women in Love
Russell, William D.: Best of the Badmen; Green Promise, The; Hazel Christmas Show, The (TV Series)
Russo, Aaron: Rude Awakening
Russo, John: Heartstopper; Midnight; Midnight 2; Santa Claws
Rust, John: Smurfs and the Magic Flute, The
Rustam, Mardi: Evils of the Night
Ruzowitzky, Stefan: Anatomy; Inheritors, The
Ryan, Frank: Call Out the Marines; Can't Help Singing
Ryan, Terence: Brylcreem Boys, The
Ryan, William: Reach the Rock
Ryazanov, Eldar: Forgotten Tune for the Flute, A
Rydell, Mark: Cinderella Liberty; Cowboys, The; Crime of the Century; For the Boys; Harry and Walter Go to New York; Intersection; James Dean (2001); On Golden Pond; Reivers, The; River, The; Rose, The
Rye, Renny: Poirot (Series)
Ryman, John: Galaxies Are Colliding
Rymer, Judy: Who Killed Baby Azaria?
Rymer, Michael: Angel Baby; In Too Deep; Queen of the Damned
Ryu, Taiji: Record of Lodoss War
Ryutaro, Nakamura: Legend of Crystania
Sabal, Rob: Escape to White Mountain
Sabella, Paul: All Dogs Go to Heaven 2
Sachs, William: Galaxina; Hitz; Incredible Melting Man, The; Last Hour, The
Sackheim, Daniel: Glass House, The (2001)
Sacks, Alan: Du-Beat-E-O
Saeta, Eddie: Dr. Death: Seeker of Souls
Safran, Henri: Norman Loves Rose; Wild Duck, The
Sagal, Boris: Angela; Dial M for Murder; Girl Happy; Ike: The War Years; Masada; Night Gallery; Omega Man, The; Peter Gunn (TV Series)
Sagan, Leontine: Maedchen in Uniform
Saget, Bob: Dirty Work
Saia, Louis: Boys, The (1997)
Sakaguchi, Hironobu: Final Fantasy: The Spirits Within
Sakai, Akio: Record of Lodoss War
Sakakibara, Motonori: Final Fantasy: The Spirits Within
Saks, Gene: Barefoot in the Park; Brighton Beach Memoirs; Cactus Flower; Fine Romance, A; Last of the Red Hot Lovers; Mame; Odd Couple, The
Saldanha, Carlos: Ice Age
Sale, Richard: Let's Make It Legal
Sales, Leander: Don't Let Your Meat Loaf
Salkow, Sidney: City Without Men; Last Man on Earth, The; Twice-Told Tales
Salle, David: Search and Destroy
Salles Jr., Walter: Central Station; Exposure
Salomon, Mikael: Far Off Place, A; Glimpse of Hell, A; Hard Rain
Saltzman, Mark: Three Ninjas Kick Back
Salva, Victor: Clownhouse; Jeepers Creepers; Nature of the Beast; Powder; Rites of Passage
Salvador, Jaime: Boom in the Moon
Salvatores, Gabriele: Mediterraneo
Salwen, Hal: Denise Calls Up
Salzman, Barnard: Diamondbacks
Salzman, Glen: Rubberface
Samperi, Salvatore: Malicious
Samples, Keith: Smile Like Yours, A
Samson, Barry: Ice Runner; Yesterday's Target
Samuels, Stuart: Rockin' Ronnie
Samuelson, G. B.: She
San Fernando, Manuel: Rock 'n' Roll Wrestling Women vs. the Aztec Mummy
Sanchez, Eduardo: Blair Witch Project, The
Sanders, Denis: Elvis—That's the Way It Is; Invasion of the Bee Girls; One Man's Way
Sandgren, Ake: Slingshot, The
Sandrich, Jay: For Richer, for Poorer; Seems Like Old Times
Sandrich, Mark: Aggie Appleby, Maker of Men; Buck Benny Rides Again; Carefree; Cockeyed Cavaliers; Follow the Fleet; Gay Divorcée, The; Here Come the Waves; Hips, Hips, Hooray; Holiday Inn; Melody Cruise; Shall We Dance?; So Proudly We Hail; Top Hat; Woman Rebels, A
Sands, Sompote: Crocodile
Sands, Trever: Suicide Ride
Sanford, Arlene: I'll Be Home for Christmas; Very Brady Sequel, A
Sanforth, Clifford: Murder by Television
Sanger, Jonathan: Code Name: Emerald; Down Came a Blackbird
Sangster, Jimmy: Fear in the Night (Dynasty of Fear); Horror of Frankenstein; Lust for a Vampire
Santell, Alfred: Hairy Ape, The; Having a Wonderful Time; Interns Can't Take Money; Jack London; Winterset
Santiago, Cirio H.: Angel Fist; Beyond the Call of Duty; Caged Heat 2: Stripped of Freedom; Dune Warriors; Field of Fire; Firehawk; Future Hunters; Kill Zone; Live by the Fist; One Man Army; Raiders of the Sun; Sisterhood, The; Stranglehold; Stryker; TNT Jackson; Vampire Hookers (Sensuous Vampires); Wheels of Fire
Santley, Joseph: Cocoanuts; Harmony Lane; Melody Ranch
Santostefano, Damon: Severed Ties; Three to Tango
Saperstein, David: Beyond the Stars; Killing Affair, A
Sarafian, Deran: Alien Predators; Back in the U.S.S.R.; Death Warrant; Gunmen; Interzone; Road Killers, The; Terminal Velocity; To Die For
Sarafian, Richard C.: Eye of the Tiger; Gangster Wars; I Spy (TV Series); Man in the Wilderness; Man Who Loved Cat Dancing, The; Street Justice; Sunburn; Vanishing Point
Sargent, Joseph: Abraham; Bojangles; Caroline?; Coast to Coast; Colossus: The Forbin Project; Crime and Punishment; Day One; Goldengirl; Hustling; Incident, The; Ivory Hunters; Jaws: The Revenge; MacArthur; Man from U.N.C.L.E., The (TV Series); Man on a String; Mandela and De Klerk; Manions of America, The; Memorial Day; Miss Evers' Boys; Miss Rose White; My Antonia; Never Forget; Nightmares; Of Pure Blood; Passion Flower; Skylark; Streets of Laredo; Taking of Pelham One Two Three, The; Tomorrow's Child; Tribes; Wall, The (1998) (U.S.); White Lightning
Sargenti, Marina: Child of Darkness, Child of Light; Mirror Mirror
Sarin, Vic: Cold Comfort; Hearts Adrift; In His Father's Shoes; Left Behind; Legend of Gator Face, The; Sea People; Spenser: Pale Kings & Princes; Wounded Heart
Sarne, Michael: Myra Breckenridge
Sarno, Jonathan: Plants Are Watching, The
Sasdy, Peter: Devil Within Her, The; Devil's Undead, The; Doomwatch; Hands of the Ripper; King Arthur, The Young Warlord; Lonely Lady, The; Rude Awakening; Sherlock Holmes and the Leading Lady; Taste the Blood of Dracula
Sassone, Oley: Bloodfist III: Forced to Fight; Fast Getaway II; Final Embrace; Playback
Satenstein, Frank: Honeymooners, The: Lost Episodes (TV Series); Honeymooners, The (TV Series)
Satlof, Ron: Humanoid Defender
Sato, Junya: Go-Masters, The; Silk Road, The
Sato, Shimako: Tale of a Vampire
Sauer, Ernest G.: Beauty School; Bikini Bistro
Saura, Carlos: Ay, Carmela!; Blood Wedding; ¡Cría!; El Amor Brujo; Flamenco; Garden of Delights, The; Goya in Bordeaux; Hunt, The; Mama Turns 100; Outrage (1994); Stilts, The (Los Zancos); Tango
Sautet, Claude: César and Rosalie; Les Choses de la Vie (Things in Life, The); Mado; Nelly and Monsieur Arnaud; Sim-

ple Story, A; Un Coeur en Hiver; Vincent, François, Paul and the Others
Savalas, Telly: Beyond Reason
Saville, Philip: Buccaneers, The; Fellow Traveler; Mandela; Max and Helen; Metroland; Secrets; Shadey; Those Glory Glory Days; Wonderland
Saville, Victor: Conspirator; Dark Journey; Evergreen; Forever and a Day; Green Dolphin Street; Iron Duke, The; Kim; Silver Chalice, The; Stop the World I Want to Get Off; Storm in a Teacup; Tonight and Every Night
Savini, Tom: Night of the Living Dead
Savoca, Nancy: Dogfight; Household Saints; If These Walls Could Talk; True Love; 24-Hour Woman
Sax, Geoffrey: Broken Trust; Ruby Jean and Joe
Saxon, John: Death House
Sayadian, Stephen: Dr. Caligari
Sayles, John: Baby, It's You; Brother from Another Planet, The; City of Hope; Eight Men Out; Lianna; Limbo; Lone Star; Matewan; Men with Guns; Passion Fish; Return of the Secaucus 7; Secret of Roan Inish, The
Sbardellati, James: Under the Gun
Scaini, Stefan: Prisoner of Zenda, Inc.
Scanlan, Joseph L.: Nightstick; Spring Fever
Scardino, Don: Me & Veronica
Scarpaci, Philip: Doll in the Dark, A
Scarpelli, Umberto: Giant of Metropolis, The
Schaack, Michael: Pippi Longstocking
Schachter, Steven: Above Suspicion; Con, The; Slight Case of Murder, A; Water Engine, The
Schaefer, Armand: Hurricane Express; Sagebrush Trail; 16 Fathoms Deep; Three Musketeers, The
Schaefer, George: Best Christmas Pageant Ever, The; Bunker, The; Doctors' Wives; Generation (1969); Last of Mrs. Lincoln, The; Macbeth; Man Upstairs, The; Pendulum; People vs. Jean Harris; Piano for Mrs. Cimino, A; Right of Way
Schaeffer, Eric: Fall; If Lucy Fell; My Life's in Turnaround; Wirey Spindell
Schaeffer, Franky: Baby on Board; Rebel Storm; Wired to Kill
Schaffner, Franklin J.: Best Man, The; Boys from Brazil, The; Islands in the Stream; Lionheart; Nicholas and Alexandra; Our Town; Papillon; Patton; Planet of the Apes; Sphinx (1981); Stripper, The; War Lord, The; Welcome Home; Yes, Giorgio
Schain, Don: Ginger; Girls Are for Loving; Place Called Today, A
Schamoni, Peter: Spring Symphony
Schatzberg, Jerry: Clinton and Nadine; Honeysuckle Rose; Misunderstood; No Small Affair; Panic in Needle Park; Reunion; Scarecrow; Seduction of Joe Tynan, The; Street Smart
Scheepmaker, Hans: Field of Honor
Scheerer, Robert: Adam at 6 A.M.; Hans Brinker; How to Beat the High Co$t of Living; World's Greatest Athlete, The
Scheinman, Andrew: Little Big League
Schell, Maximilian: Marlene; Pedestrian, The
Schellerup, Henning: Adventures of Nellie Bly, The; In Search of Historic Jesus
Schenkel, Carl: Eye of the Demon; Hitchhiker, The (Series); Knight Moves; Mighty Quinn, The; Missing Pieces; Silence Like Glass; Silhouette; Surgeon, The; Tarzan and the Lost City
Schenkman, Richard: Pompatus of Love, The
Schepisi, Fred: Barbarosa; Cry in the Dark, A; Fierce Creatures; Iceman; I.Q.; Last Orders; Mr. Baseball; Plenty; Roxanne; Russia House, The; Six Degrees of Separation
Scher, J. Noyes: Prisoners of Inertia
Scherfig, Lone: Italian for Beginners
Schertzinger, Victor: Birth of the Blues; Mikado, The; One Night of Love; Rhythm on the River; Road to Singapore; Road to Zanzibar; Something to Sing About; Uptown New York
Schibli, Paul: Nutcracker Prince, The
Schiffman, Suzanne: Sorceress, The (1988)
Schiller, Greta: Paris Was a Woman
Schiller, Lawrence: Double Exposure; Double Jeopardy; Executioner's Song, The; Hey, I'm Alive!; Plot to Kill Hitler, The
Schilling, Tom: Cinderella
Schirk, Keinz: Wannsee Conference, The
Schlagman, Eric L.: Punch the Clock
Schlaich, Frieder: Halfmoon
Schlamme, Thomas: Bette Midler—Art or Bust; Crazy from the Heart; Kingfish: A Story of Huey P. Long; Miss Firecracker; So I Married an Axe Murderer; Spalding Gray: Terrors of Pleasure; You So Crazy
Schlatter, George: Norman … Is That You?
Schlesinger, John: Believers, The; Billy Liar; Cold Comfort Farm; Darling; Day of the Locust, The; Englishman Abroad, An; Eye for an Eye; Falcon and the Snowman, The; Far from the Madding Crowd; Honky Tonk Freeway; Innocent, The; Kind of Loving, A; Madame Sousatzka; Marathon Man; Midnight Cowboy; Next Best Thing, The; Pacific Heights; Separate Tables; Sunday, Bloody Sunday; Yanks
Schlöndorff, Volker: Circle of Deceit; Coup De Grace; Death of a Salesman; Germany In Autumn; Handmaid's Tale, The; Lost Honor of Katharina Blum, The; Murder on the Bayou; Palmetto; Swann in Love; Tin Drum, The; Voyager
Schlossberg-Cohen, Jay: Night Train to Terror
Schmidt, Rob: Crime & Punishment in Suburbia
Schmoeller, David: Arrival, The; Crawlspace; Curse IV: The Ultimate Sacrifice; Mysterious Museum; Netherworld; Puppet Master, The; Secret Kingdom, The
Schnabel, Julian: Basquiat; Before Night Falls
Schneider, Jane: Women from Down Under
Schneider, Paul: Baby Cakes; Dance 'Til Dawn; Honor Thy Father & Mother: The Menendez Killings; Roseanne: An Unauthorized Biography; Something Special
Schnitzer, Robert: Kandyland; Premonition, The (1975); Rebel
Schoedsack, Ernest B.: Chang; Dr. Cyclops; King Kong; Last Days of Pompeii, The (1935); Mighty Joe Young; Most Dangerous Game, The; Son of Kong, The
Schoemann, Michael: Magic Voyage, The
Schoendoerffer, Pierre: 317th Platoon, The
Scholes, Roger: Tale of Ruby Rose, The
Schoolnik, Skip: Hide and Go Shriek
Schrader, Leonard: Naked Tango
Schrader, Paul: Affliction; American Gigolo; Blue Collar; Cat People; Comfort of Strangers, The; Hardcore; Light of Day; Light Sleeper; Mishima: A Life in Four Chapters; Patty Hearst; Touch; Witch Hunt
Schreibman, Myrl A.: Angel of H.E.A.T.; Liberty and Bash
Schreiner, William: Sinful Life, A
Schreyer, John: Naked Youth
Schroeder, Barbet: Barfly; Before and After; Desperate Measures; General Idi Amin Dada; Kiss of Death; Koko: A Talking Gorilla; Les Tricheurs; Maitresse; More; Murder by Numbers (2002); Our Lady of the Assassins; Reversal of Fortune; Single White Female; Valley, The
Schroeder, Frank C.: Pistol, The: The Birth of a Legend
Schroeder, Michael: Cover Me; Cyborg 2; Cyborg 3: The Recycler; Damned River; Glass Cage, The; Mortuary Academy; Out of the Dark; Relentless II: Dead On
Schubert, Peter: Germany In Autumn
Schulman, Tom: 8 Heads in a Duffel Bag
Schultz, Carl: Blue Fin; Careful He Might Hear You; Deadly Currents; Seventh Sign, The; Travelling North; Which Way Home
Schultz, John: Drive Me Crazy
Schultz, Michael: Car Wash; Carbon Copy; Cooley High; Disorderlies; For Us the Living: The Medgar Evers Story; Greased Lightning; Great American Sex Scandal, The; Killers in the House; Krush Groove; Last Dragon, The; Livin' Large; Scavenger Hunt; Sgt. Pepper's Lonely Hearts Club Band; Time Stalkers; Which Way Is Up?
Schulz, Bob: Robbers of the Sacred Mountain
Schulze, Douglas: Hellmaster
Schumacher, Joel: Batman & Robin; Batman Forever; Client, The; Cousins; D.C. Cab; Dying Young; Falling Down; Flatliners; Flawless; Incredible Shrinking Woman, The; Lost Boys, The; 8MM; St. Elmo's Fire; Time to Kill, A (1996)

Schunzel, Reinhold: Balalaika; Fortune's Fool; Melody Master (The Great Awakening) (NewWine)
Schuster, Harold: Breakfast in Hollywood; Dinner at the Ritz; Finger Man; Marine Raiders; My Friend Flicka; So Dear to My Heart; Tender Years, The
Schuttes, Jan: Dragon Chow
Schwartz, Douglas: Baywatch: The Movie; Thunder in Paradise; Thunder in Paradise II
Schwartz, Maurice: Tevye
Schwartz, Stefan: Shooting Fish
Schwarzenegger, Arnold: Christmas in Connecticut
Schwimmer, David: Since You've Been Gone
Sciamma, Alberto: Killer Tongue
Scoffield, Jon: To See Such Fun
Scola, Ettore: Down and Dirty; Family, The; La Nuit de Varennes; Le Bal; Macaroni; Passion of Love; Special Day, A; We All Loved Each Other So Much
Scorsese, Martin: After Hours; Age of Innocence, The; Alice Doesn't Live Here Anymore; Boxcar Bertha; Bringing Out the Dead; Cape Fear; Casino; Color of Money, The; Goodfellas; King of Comedy, The; Kundun; Last Temptation of Christ, The; Last Waltz, The; Mean Streets; New York, New York; New York Stories; Raging Bull; Taxi Driver; Two by Scorsese; Who's That Knocking at My Door?
Scott, Campbell: Big Night
Scott, Cynthia: Strangers in Good Company
Scott, Darin: Love & a .45
Scott, Ewing: Windjammer
Scott, Gene: Mystery Island
Scott, George C.: Andersonville Trial, The; Rage; Savage Is Loose, The
Scott, Jake: Plunkett & Macleane
Scott, James: Strike It Rich
Scott, Michael: Dangerous Heart; Heck's Way Home; Ladykiller; Sharon's Secret
Scott, Oz: Bustin' Loose; Spanish Judges
Scott, Ridley: Alien; Black Hawk Down; Black Rain; Blade Runner; Duellists, The; G.I. Jane; Gladiator; Hannibal; Legend; 1492: The Conquest of Paradise; Someone to Watch Over Me; Thelma & Louise; White Squall
Scott, Sherman: Kid with X-Ray Eyes, The
Scott, T.J.: TC 2000; Young Hercules
Scott, Tony: Beverly Hills Cop II; Crimson Tide; Days of Thunder; Enemy of the State; Fan, The; Hunger, The (1983); Last Boy Scout, The; Revenge (1990); Spy Game; Top Gun; True Romance
Scribner, George: Oliver & Company
Seacat, Sandra: In the Spirit
Seagal, Steven: On Deadly Ground
Seale, James: Asylum
Seale, John: Till There Was You
Sears, Cynthia L.: Till There Was You
Sears, Fred F.: Earth vs. the Flying Saucers; Giant Claw, The
Sears, Phil: Ripper Man
Sears, Richard: Bongwater
Seaton, George: Airport; Big Lift, The; Counterfeit Traitor, The; Country Girl, The; Little Boy Lost; Miracle on 34th Street; Showdown; Teacher's Pet; 36 Hours
Sebastian, Beverly: Delta Fox; Gator Bait II—Cajun Justice; Rocktober Blood; Running Cool
Sebastian, Jonathan: Voyage to the Prehistoric Planet
Sedan, Mike: Married People, Single Sex; Night Fire
Sedgwick, Edward: Air Raid Wardens; Beware of Spooks; Cameraman, The; Doughboys; Free and Easy; Ma and Pa Kettle Back on the Farm; Movie Struck (Pick a Star); Parlor, Bedroom and Bath; Riding on Air; Southern Yankee, A; Speak Easily; Spite Marriage; What! No Beer?
Sedwick, John: Best of Dark Shadows, The; Dark Shadows (TV Series)
Seed, Paul: Affair, The; Dead Ahead: The Exxon Valdez Disaster
Seely, Bob: Rover Dangerfield
Segal, Alex: No Time for Sergeants (Television); Story of David, The
Segal, Peter: My Fellow Americans; Naked Gun 33 1/3, The—The Final Insult; Nutty Professor II: The Klumps; Tommy Boy
Segall, Stuart: Drive-In Massacre; Illegal in Blue
Seidelman, Arthur Allan: Body Language; Caller, The; Children of Rage; Dying to Remember; Friendship in Vienna, A; Glory Years; Grace and Glorie; Harvest of Fire; Hercules Goes Bananas; Kid Who Loved Christmas, The; Macbeth; Poker Alice; Rescue Me; Runaway, The (2000); Summer of Ben Tyler, The; Trapped in Space
Seidelman, Susan: Cookie; Cooler Climate, A; Desperately Seeking Susan; Making Mr. Right; She-Devil; Smithereens; Tales of Erotica
Seiler, Lewis: Charlie Chan in Paris; Doll Face; Guadalcanal Diary; Here Comes Trouble; Pittsburgh; Smiling Ghost, The; Tanks Are Coming, The; Winning Team, The
Seiter, William A.: Allegheny Uprising; Big Business Girl; Dimples; Diplomaniacs; Four Jills in a Jeep; In Person; It's a Date; Lady Takes a Chance, A; Little Giant; Make Haste to Live; One Touch of Venus; Roberta; Room Service; Sons of the Desert; Stowaway; Susannah of the Mounties; This Is My Affair; Way Back Home; You Were Never Lovelier
Seitz, George B.: Andy Hardy Meets a Debutante; Andy Hardy's Double Life; Andy Hardy's Private Secretary; Danger Lights; Drums of Jeopardy; Fighting Ranger, The; Kit Carson; Last of the Mohicans, The; Life Begins for Andy Hardy; Love Finds Andy Hardy; Vanishing American, The
Seitzman, Michael: Farmer and Chase
Sekely, Steve: Day of the Triffids, The; Revenge of the Zombies; Scar, The; Waterfront
Selander, Lesley: Arizona Bushwhackers; Border Patrol; Brothers in the Saddle; Buckskin Frontier; Doomed Caravan; Fighter Attack; Flat Top; Flight to Mars; Fort Osage; Forty Thieves; Guns of Hate; Heart of Arizona; Heritage of the Desert; Hidden Gold; Hopalong Rides Again; Lone Ranger and the Lost City of Gold, The; Mysterious Desperado; Out California Way; Phantom of the Plains; Pirates on Horseback; Range War; Renegade Trail; Rider from Tucson; Riders of the Timberline; Road Agent; Robin Hood of Texas; Rustlers, The; Santa Fe Marshal; Sheriff of Las Vegas; Short Grass; Shotgun; Silver on the Sage; Stagecoach War; Stampede; Stick to Your Guns; Three Men from Texas; Wide-Open Town
Selick, Henry: James and the Giant Peach; Monkeybone; Nightmare Before Christmas, The
Selignac, Arnaud: Eye of the Wolf; Northern Passage
Sell, Jack M.: Deadly Spygames
Sellier Jr., Charles E.: Annihilators, The; Silent Night, Deadly Night
Selman, David: Fighting Shadows; Texas Trail
Seltzer, David: Lucas; Punchline; Shining Through
Selwyn, Edgar: Sin of Madelon Claudet, The; Skyscraper Souls
Selznick, Aran: Care Bears Movie, The
Semler, Dean: Firestorm; Patriot, The
Sena, Dominic: Gone in 60 Seconds; Kalifornia; Swordfish
Senelka, Peter: Teen Alien
Senensky, Ralph: Dream for Christmas, A
Sennett, Mack: Charlie Chaplin … Our Hero; Dough and Dynamite/Knockout, The; These Girls Won't Talk
Sequi, Mario: Cobra, The (1967)
Sereny, Eva: Foreign Student
Seresin, Michael: Homeboy
Serious, Yahoo: Mr. Accident; Reckless Kelly; Young Einstein
Serreau, Coline: Mama, There's a Man in Your Bed; Three Men and a Cradle
Sessa, Alex: Amazons; Stormquest
Setbon, Philip: Mr. Frost
Sewell, Vernon: Blood Beast Terror, The; Curse of the Crimson Altar; Ghost Ship; Ghosts of Berkeley Square
Seymour, Jeff: Rave Review
Sgarro, Nicholas: Fortune Dane; Happy Hooker, The
Shackleton, Michael: Survivor

Sidney, George: Anchors Aweigh; Annie Get Your Gun; Bathing Beauty; Bye Bye Birdie; Cass Timberlane; Eddy Duchin Story, The; Half a Sixpence; Harvey Girls, The; Holiday in Mexico; Jupiter's Darling; Key to the City; Kiss Me Kate; Pal Joey; Scaramouche; Show Boat; Thousands Cheer; Three Musketeers, The; Viva Las Vegas; Young Bess
Sidney, Scott: Madame Behave; Tarzan of the Apes
Siegel, David: Deep End, The; Suture
Siegel, Don: Annapolis Story, An; Beguiled, The; Big Steal, The; Black Windmill, The; Charley Varrick; Coogan's Bluff; Dirty Harry; Escape from Alcatraz; Flaming Star; Hell Is for Heroes; Invasion of the Body Snatchers; Jinxed; Killers, The; Madigan; Private Hell 36; Riot in Cell Block Eleven; Rough Cut; Shootist, The; Telefon; Two Mules for Sister Sara
Sigl, Robert: Gigashadow
Signorelli, James: Easy Money; Elvira, Mistress of the Dark; Hotel Room
Sijie, Dai: China, My Sorrow
Silberg, Joel: Bad Guys; Breakin'; Catch the Heat; Lambada; Rappin'
Silberling, Brad: Casper; City of Angels
Sillen, Peter: Benjamin Smoke
Silver, Andrew: Return (1984)
Silver, Joan Micklin: Bernice Bobs Her Hair; Between the Lines; Big Girls Don't Cry—They Get Even; Chilly Scenes of Winter; Crossing Delancey; Finnegan Begin Again; Hester Street; In the Presence of Mine Enemies; Loverboy; Prison Stories: Women on the Inside; Private Matter, A
Silver, Marisa: He Said, She Said; Indecency; Old Enough; Permanent Record; Vital Signs
Silver, Raphael D.: On the Yard
Silver, Ron: Lifepod
Silver, Scott: Johns; Mod Squad, The
Silverman, David: Monsters, Inc.
Silverstein, Elliot: Car, The; Cat Ballou; Flashfire; Man Called Horse, A
Silvester, Dario: Between God, the Devil and a Winchester
Simandl, Lloyd A.: Dangerous Prey; Ultimate Desires
Simenon, Marc: By the Blood of Others
Simeone, Lawrence L.: Blindfold: Acts of Obsession; Cop-Out; Eyes of the Beholder
Simmonds, Allen: Striker's Mountain
Simmons, Anthony: Little Sweetheart
Simmons, Kendrick: Celebrating Bird: The Triumph of Charlie Parker
Simo, Sandor: Train Killer, The
Simon, Adam: Brain Dead; Carnosaur
Simon, Francis: Chicken Chronicles, The
Simon, Juan Piquer: Cthulhu Mansion; Endless Descent; Pieces; Slugs, the Movie
Simon, Roger L.: Lies & Whispers; My Man Adam
Simon, S. Sylvan: Abbott and Costello in Hollywood; Fuller Brush Man, The; Lust for Gold; Rio Rita; Son of Lassie; Whistling in Brooklyn; Whistling in Dixie; Whistling in the Dark
Simoneau, Yves: Amelia Earhart: The Final Flight; Blind Trust (Pouvoir Intime); Dead Man's Walk; Free Money; Memphis; Mother's Boys; Nuremberg; Perfectly Normal; 36 Hours to Die; Till Death Do Us Part
Simpson, Jane: Little Witches; Number One Fan
Simpson, Megan: Alex
Simpson, Michael A.: Fast Food; Funland; Impure Thoughts; Sleepaway Camp II: Unhappy Campers; Sleepaway Camp III
Simpson, Peter: Prom Night III—Last Kiss
Sinatra, Frank: None But the Brave
Sinclair, Andrew: Tuxedo Warrior; Under Milk Wood
Sinclair, Harry: Price of Milk, The
Sindell, Gerald: H.O.T.S.
Singer, Alexander: Bunco; Captain Apache; Lost in Space (TV Series); Love Has Many Faces
Singer, Bryan: Apt Pupil; Public Access; Usual Suspects, The; X-Men
Singh, Tarsem: Cell, The
Singleton, John: Baby Boy; Boyz N the Hood; Higher Learning; Poetic Justice; Rosewood; Shaft
Singleton, Ralph S.: Stephen King's Graveyard Shift (1990)
Sinise, Gary: Miles from Home; Of Mice and Men; True West
Sinkel, Bernhard: Germany In Autumn
Sinofsky, Bruce: Brother's Keeper; Paradise Lost: The Child Murders at Robin Hood Hills
Sinyor, Gary: Bachelor, The; Leon the Pig Farmer; Solitaire for 2; Stiff Upper Lips
Siodmak, Curt: Bride of the Gorilla; Magnetic Monster, The
Siodmak, Robert: Cobra Woman; Crimson Pirate, The; Criss Cross (1948); Dark Mirror, The; Son of Dracula; Spiral Staircase, The; Strange Affair of Uncle Harry, The
Sipes, Andrew: Fair Game
Sirk, Douglas: All I Desire; All That Heaven Allows; Battle Hymn; Imitation of Life; Magnificent Obsession; Tarnished Angels, The; Time to Love and a Time to Die, A; Written on the Wind
Sissel, Sandi: Chicken Ranch
Sitch, Rob: Castle, The; Dish, The
Sivan, Santosh: Terrorist, The
Sivo, Yuri: Mortal Sins (1990) (Dangerous Obsession)
Sjoberg, Alf: Miss Julie
Sjoman, Vilgot: I Am Curious Blue; I Am Curious Yellow
Sjorgen, John: Money to Burn; Red Line
Sjöström, Victor: He Who Gets Slapped; Outlaw and His Wife, The; Phantom Chariot; Scarlet Letter, The; Wind, The
Skahill, Bix: Life Without Dick
Skerritt, Tom: Divided by Hate
Skjoldbjærg, Erik: Insomnia
Skogland, Kari: Children of the Corn 666: Isaac's Return; Zebra Lounge
Skolimowski, Jerzy: Deep End; King, Queen and Knave; Le Départ; Lightship, The; Moonlighting (1983); Shout, The (1979); Success Is the Best Revenge; Torrents of Spring
Skoog, Susan: Whatever
Slapczynski, Richard: Through the Looking Glass
Slater, Christian: Anything for Love
Slater, Guy: Pocketful of Rye, A
Slatzer, Robert F.: Big Foot
Slee, Mike: Big Foot
Sloan, Brian: I Think I Do
Sloan, Holly Goldberg: Big Green, The
Sloan, Victoria: Shrieker
Sloane, Paul: Consolation Marriage; Terror Aboard
Sloane, Rick: Visitants, The
Slocum, James: American Summer, An
Slovin, Karl: Sex and the Other Man
Sluizer, George: Crimetime; Utz; Vanishing, The; Vanishing, The
Smallcombe, John: African Dream, An
Smart, Ralph: Quartet
Smawley, Robert J.: American Eagle; River of Diamonds
Smight, Jack: Airport 1975; Damnation Alley (Survival Run); Fast Break; Harper; Illustrated Man, The; Intimate Power; Loving Couples; Midway; No Way to Treat a Lady; Number One with a Bullet; Rabbit Run; Roll of Thunder, Hear My Cry; Secret War of Harry Frigg, The
Smiley, Rob: Our Friend, Martin
Smith, Bernie: You Bet Your Life (TV Series)
Smith, Brian J.: Body of Influence 2
Smith, Bruce: Bebe's Kids
Smith, Bud: Johnny Be Good
Smith, Charles Martin: Air Bud; Boris and Natasha; Fifty/Fifty; Trick or Treat
Smith, Chris: American Movie
Smith, Cliff: Ace Drummond
Smith, Clive: Pippi Longstocking; Rock and Rule
Smith, Howard: Marjoe
Smith, John N.: Boys of St. Vincent; Cool, Dry Place, A; Dangerous Minds; Sugartime
Smith, Kevin: Chasing Amy; Clerks; Dogma; Jay and Silent Bob Strike Back; Mall Rats

Smith, Marshall: Satan's Bed
Smith, Mel: Bean; Radioland Murders; Tall Guy, The
Smith, Peter: No Surrender
Smith, Richard Dana: Dentist 2, The: Brace Yourself
Smith, Roy Allen: Land Before Time II, The; Land Before Time III, The
Smith, Yvonne: Ray Charles: The Genius of Soul
Smithee, Alan: Appointment with Fear; Bloodsucking Pharaohs in Pittsburgh; Call of the Wild; Death of a Gunfighter; Fatal Charm; Ghost Fever; Gypsy Angels; Hellraiser: Bloodline; I Love N.Y.; Let's Get Harry; Morgan Stewart's Coming Home; O. J. Simpson Story, The; Raging Angels; Shrimp on the Barbie; Solar Crisis; Stitches; Sub Down
Smoke, Stephen: Final Impact; Street Crimes
Smolan, Sandy: Rachel River
Snedon, Greg: Dunera Boys, The
Snider, Skott: Miracle Beach
Snyder, Robert: Henry Miller Odyssey
Soavi, Michele: Church, The; Dellamorte, Dellamore; Sect, The
Sobel, Mark: Access Code; Ordeal in the Arctic; Sweet Revenge; Trial & Error (1992)
Soderbergh, Steven: Erin Brockovich; Fallen Angels; Kafka; King of the Hill; Limey, The; Ocean's Eleven (2001); Out of Sight; Schizopolis; sex, lies and videotape; Traffic; Underneath, The
Softley, Iain: BackBeat; East Is East; Hackers; K-Pax; Wings of the Dove, The
Sokolow, Alec: Frankenstein Sings
Solberg, Helena: Carmen Miranda: Bananas Is My Business
Solberg, Russell: Payback; Raven (1997)
Soldini, Silvio: Bread and Tulips
Sole, Alfred: Alice, Sweet Alice (Communion, Holy Terror); Pandemonium; Tanya's Island
Solinas, Piernico: Touch and Die
Sollima, Sergio: Blood in the Streets; Family, The
Solomon, Courtney: Dungeons & Dragons
Solondz, Todd: Fear, Anxiety and Depression; Happiness; Storytelling; Welcome to the Dollhouse
Solt, Andrew: Imagine: John Lennon; This Is Elvis
Solum, Ola: Polar Bear King, The
Solvay, Paul: Devil's Wedding Night, The
Sommers, Stephen: Adventures of Huck Finn, The (1993); Catch Me if You Can; Deep Rising; Mummy, The; Mummy Returns, The; Rudyard Kipling's The Jungle Book (1994)
Song, Kamoon: Pocahontas
Sonnenfeld, Barry: Addams Family, The; Addams Family Values; Big Trouble (2002); For Love or Money; Get Shorty; Men in Black; Wild Wild West (1999)
Soref, Dror: Seventh Coin, The
Sorin, Carlos: Eversmile New Jersey
Sortor, Ronnie: Ravage; Sinyster
Sorvino, Paul: That Championship Season
Sotirakis, Dimitri: Beverly Hills Brats
Sotos, Jim: Hot Moves; Sweet Sixteen
Spacey, Kevin: Albino Alligator
Sparber, Isadore: Superman Cartoons
Sparr, Robert: Swingin' Summer, A
Speer, Martin: Hasty Heart
Speiser, Aaron: Talking About Sex
Spence, Greg: Children of the Corn IV: The Gathering; Prophecy II, The
Spence, Michael: Edge of Honor; Legend of the Spirit Dog
Spence, Richard: Blind Justice; Different for Girls; New World Disorder
Spencer, Alan: Hexed
Spencer, Brenton: Blown Away; Club, The
Spencer, Jane: Little Noises
Spera, Robert: Leprechaun in the Hood; Witchcraft
Spheeris, Penelope: Beverly Hillbillies, The (1993); Black Sheep; Boys Next Door, The; Decline of Western Civilization, The; Dudes; Hollywood Vice Squad; Little Rascals, The; Prison Stories: Women on the Inside; Senseless; Suburbia; Wayne's World
Spicer, Bryan: For Richer or Poorer; McHale's Navy; Mighty Morphin Power Rangers: The Movie
Spiegel, Scott: From Dusk Till Dawn 2: Texas Blood Money; Intruder (1988)
Spielberg, Steven: AI: Artificial Intelligence; Always; Amazing Stories (TV Series); Amistad; Close Encounters of the Third Kind; Color Purple, The; Columbo: Murder by the Book; Duel; Empire of the Sun; E.T.—The Extra-Terrestrial; Hook; Indiana Jones and the Last Crusade; Indiana Jones and the Temple of Doom; Jaws; Jurassic Park; Lost World, The: Jurassic Park; Night Gallery; 1941; Raiders of the Lost Ark; Saving Private Ryan; Schindler's List; Sugarland Express, The; Tiny Toons Adventures: How I Spent MyVacation; Twilight Zone—The Movie
Spiers, Bob: Absolutely Fabulous; Spice World; That Darn Cat
Spinelli, Martin J.: Sourdough
Spink, Philip: Ronnie & Julie
Spiridakis, Tony: Last Word, The
Spiro, Lev J.: Welcome to Planet Earth
Sporn, Michael: Marzipan Pig, The
Sporup, Murray Douglas: Rock, Baby, Rock It
Spottiswoode, Roger: Air America; And the Band Played On; Best of Times, The; Hiroshima; Last Innocent Man, The; Pursuit of D. B. Cooper; Shoot to Kill; 6th Day, The; Stop! Or My Mom Will Shoot; Terror Train; Third Degree Burn; Time Flies When You're Alive; Tomorrow Never Dies; Turner and Hooch; Under Fire
Spotton, John: Keaton Rides Again/Railroader
Sprackling, Simon: Funnyman
Sprecher, Jill: Clockwatchers
Spring, Tim: Double Blast; Raw Target; Reason to Die
Springsteen, R. G.: Arizona Cowboy; Hellfire; Hostile Guns; Johnny Reno; Marshal of Cripple Creek; Oklahoma Annie; Red Menace, The; Santa Fe Uprising; Stagecoach to Denver; Vigilantes of Boomtown; Wagon Wheels Westward; When Gangland Strikes
Spry, Robin: Cry in the Night, A; Drying Up the Streets; Keeping Track; Obsessed
Squire, Anthony: Mission in Morocco
Squiteri, Pasquale: Corleone; Third Solution, The
St. Clair, Malcolm: Are Parents People?; Bullfighters, The; Buster Keaton Festival Vol. 1–3; Show-Off, The
Stabile, Salvatore: Gravesend
Stafford, Stephen: Hit Woman: The Double Edge; I Posed for Playboy
Stagliano, Nick: Florentine, The
Stagnaro, Juan Bautista: Debajo del Mundo (Under Earth)
Stahl, Eric Steven: Final Approach; Safe House
Stahl, John M.: Immortal Sergeant, The; Keys to the Kingdom, The; Leave Her to Heaven; Letter of Introduction
Stahl, Ray: Scarlet Spear, The
Stallone, Sylvester: Paradise Alley; Rocky II; Rocky III; Rocky IV; Staying Alive
Stanford, Jeremy: Stepmonster
Stanley, John: Nightmare in Blood
Stanley, Richard: Dust Devil; Fly Boy; Hardware; Treasure of Pirate's Point
Stanojevic, Stanislav: Notorious Nobodies
Stanski, Ben: Tales Till the End
Stanzler, Jeff: Jumpin' at the Boneyard
Stapleford, Betty: Zombie Army
Star, Bruce: Boogeyman 2, The
Starewicz, Ladislaw: Early Russian Cinema: Before the Revolutions (Vol. 1–10)
Starr, Steven: Joey Breaker
Starrett, Jack: Cleopatra Jones; Cry Blood, Apache; Final Chapter—Walking Tall; Losers, The; Mr. Horn; Race with the Devil; Slaughter; Small Town in Texas, A; Summer Heat
Staub, Ralph: Country Gentlemen
Steckler, Len: Mad Bull

Steckler, Ray Dennis: Incredibly Strange Creatures Who Stopped Living and Became Mixed-Up Zombies, The; Rat Pfink a Boo Boo; Thrill Killers, The; Wild Guitar
Steensland, David: Escapes
Steensland, Mark: Last Way Out, The
Stegani, Giorgio: Beyond the Law
Stein, Darren: Jawbreaker
Stein, Herb: Escape to Love
Stein, Jeff: Kids Are Alright, The
Stein, Ken: Killer Instinct; Rain Killer, The
Stein, Paul: Common Law, The; Heart's Desire
Steinberg, David: Going Berserk; Paternity; Switching Goals
Steinberg, Michael: Bodies, Rest & Motion; Waterdance, The
Steinberg, Ziggy: Boss' Wife, The
Steinmann, Danny: Friday the 13th, Part V—A New Beginning; Savage Streets
Stelling, Jos: Pointsman, The; Rembrandt—1669
Stellman, Martin: For Queen and Country
Stembridge, Gerard: About Adam
Stephani, Frederick: Flash Gordon: Rocketship (Spaceship to the Unknown; Perils from Planet Mongo)
Stephen, A. C.: Fugitive Girls; Orgy of the Dead; Pleasure Unlimited; Sun Bunnies
Stephenson, John: Animal Farm
Sterling, William: Alice's Adventures in Wonderland
Stern, Daniel: Rookie of the Year
Stern, Leonard: Just You and Me, Kid; Missing Pieces
Stern, Noah: Pyrates
Stern, Sandor: Amityville 4: The Evil Escapes; Assassin; Dangerous Pursuit; Duplicates; Glitz; Jericho Fever; John & Yoko: A Love Story; Pin; Web of Deceit
Stern, Steven H.: Ambush Murders, The; Black Fox; Blood Horse; Breaking the Surface: The Greg Louganis Story; Devil and Max Devlin, The; Draw; Final Notice; Getting Physical; Good Men and Bad; Love and Murder; Mazes and Monsters; Miracle on Ice; Money; Morning Glory; Murder in Space; Not Quite Human; Obsessive Love; Park Is Mine, The; Portrait of a Showgirl; Rolling Vengeance; Small Killing, A; Undergrads, The; Weekend War; Young Love, First Love
Stern, Tom: Freaked
Stettner, Patrick: Business of Strangers, The
Stevens, Andrew: Crash Dive; Scorned; Skateboard Kid 2, The; Terror Within 2, The; Virtual Combat
Stevens, Arnold: Attack of the Swamp Creature
Stevens, Art: Fox and the Hound; Rescuers, The
Stevens, David: Kansas; Town Like Alice, A
Stevens, George: Alice Adams; Damsel in Distress, A; Diary of Anne Frank, The; Giant; Greatest Story Ever Told, The; Gunga Din; I Remember Mama; Kentucky Kernels; More the Merrier, The; Penny Serenade; Place in the Sun, A; Quality Street; Shane; Swing Time; Talk of the Town, The; Vivacious Lady; Woman of the Year
Stevens, Neal: Stitches (2001)
Stevens, Robert: Never Love a Stranger
Stevens, Warren A.: Lone Tiger
Stevens Jr., George: Separate But Equal
Stevenson, Andy: Knights and Armor
Stevenson, Rick: Magic in the Water, The
Stevenson, Robert: Absent-Minded Professor, The; Bedknobs and Broomsticks; Blackbeard's Ghost; Darby O'Gill and the Little People; Dishonored Lady; Forever and a Day; Gnome-Mobile, The; Herbie Rides Again; In Search of the Castaways; Island at the Top of the World, The; Jane Eyre; Joan of Paris; Johnny Tremain; Kidnapped; King Solomon's Mines; Las Vegas Story, The; Love Bug, The; Man Who Lived Again, The; Mary Poppins; Misadventures of Merlin Jones, The; Monkey's Uncle, The; My Forbidden Past; Nine Days a Queen; Old Yeller; One of Our Dinosaurs Is Missing; Shaggy D.A., The; Son of Flubber; That Darn Cat; Tom Brown's School Days (1940); Walk Softly, Stranger
Stewart, Alan A.: Ghetto Blaster
Stewart, Alan L.: Ghostriders
Stewart, Douglas Day: Listen to Me; Thief of Hearts
Stewart, Jean: Long Run, The
Stewart, John: Hidden Obsession
Stewart, Peter: Gun Code
Stewart Jr., Douglas M.: Gun Code
Stiller, Ben: Cable Guy, The; Reality Bites; Zoolander
Stiller, Mauritz: Thomas Graal's Best Child; Thomas Graal's Best Film; Treasure of Arne
Stillman, Whit: Barcelona; Last Days of Disco, The; Metropolitan
Stix, John: Great St. Louis Bank Robbery, The
Stock, Mark: Midnight Movie Massacre
Stockwell, John: Cheaters; Crazy/Beautiful; Undercover
Stoeffhaas, Jerry: Cheap Shots
Stoller, Bryan Michael: Undercover Angel
Stoloff, Ben: Affairs of Annabel, The; It's a Joke, Son!; Night of Terror; Palooka; Sea Devils; Transatlantic Merry-Go-Round
Stoloff, Victor: Washington Affair, The
Stoltz, Eric: My Horrible Year
Stone, Andrew L.: Julie; Last Voyage, The; Sensations of 1945; Song of Norway; Stormy Weather
Stone, Norman: Mirror Crack'd from Side to Side, The; They Do It with Mirrors
Stone, Oliver: Any Given Sunday; Born on the Fourth of July; Doors, The; Hand, The; Heaven and Earth; JFK; Natural Born Killers; Nixon; Platoon; Salvador; Seizure; Talk Radio; U-Turn; Wall Street
Stone, Virginia Lively: Run If You Can
Stones, Tad: Aladdin & the King of Thieves; Return of Jafar, The
Stopkewich, Lynne: Kissed
Stoppard, Tom: Rosencrantz and Guildenstern Are Dead
Storm, Howard: Mork & Mindy (TV Series); Once Bitten
Strayer, Frank: Blondie; Blondie Has Servant Trouble; Blondie in Society; Blondie Takes a Vacation; Blondie's Blessed Event; Daring Young Man, The; Fugitive Road; Ghost Walks, The; It's a Great Life; Monster Walks, The; Vampire Bat, The
Streisand, Barbra: Mirror Has Two Faces, The; Prince of Tides, The; Yentl
Streitfeld, Susan: Female Perversions
Strick, Joseph: Balcony, The; Portrait of the Artist as a Young Man, A; Tropic of Cancer
Strick, Wesley: Tie That Binds, The
Strickland, John: Prime Suspect 2
Strock, Herbert L.: Blood of Dracula; Crawling Hand, The; Devil's Messenger, The; How to Make a Monster; I Was a Teenage Frankenstein; Witches' Brew
Strock, Robert L.: Bronco (TV Series)
Stromberg, William R.: Crater Lake Monster, The
Stroud, Richard: Deadline
Stryker, Jonathan: Curtains
Stuart, Jeb: Switchback
Stuart, Mel: Chisholms, The; I Love My Wife; If It's Tuesday, This Must Be Belgium; Sophia Loren: Her Own Story; Willy Wonka and the Chocolate Factory
Stuckey, Dave: Lugosi, The Forgotten King
Sturges, John: Bad Day at Black Rock; By Love Possessed; Chino; Eagle Has Landed, The; Escape from Fort Bravo; Great Escape, The; Gunfight at the O.K. Corral; Hallelujah Trail, The; Hour of the Gun, The; Ice Station Zebra; It's a Big Country; Joe Kidd; Last Train from Gun Hill; Law and Jake Wade, The; Magnificent Seven, The; Magnificent Yankee, The; Marooned; McQ; Never So Few; Old Man and the Sea, The; Underwater!
Sturges, Preston: Beautiful Blonde from Bashful Bend, The; Christmas in July; Great McGinty, The; Great Moment, The; Hail the Conquering Hero; Lady Eve, The; Mad Wednesday (see also Sin of HaroldDiddlebock); Miracle of Morgan's Creek, The; Palm Beach Story, The; Sin of Harold Diddlebock (Mad Wednesday); Sullivan's Travels; Unfaithfully Yours
Sturridge, Charles: Brideshead Revisited; Fairy Tale: A True Story; Foreign Field, A; Gulliver's Travels (1996) (Television); Handful of Dust, A; Where Angels Fear to Tread
Styles, Eric: Dreaming of Joseph Lees; Relative Values

Styles, Richard: Shallow Grave
Styron, Susanna: Shadrach
Suarez, Bobby A.: Warriors of the Apocalypse
Suarez, Gonzalo: Rowing with the Wind
Subiela, Eliseo: Man Facing Southeast
Sugai, Hisashi: Roots Search
Suissa, Daniele J.: Shades of Love: The Rose Cafe
Sullivan, Daniel: Substance of Fire, The
Sullivan, Fred G.: Cold River
Sullivan, Kevin: Anne of Avonlea; Anne of Green Gables; Cosmic Slop; How Stella Got Her Groove Back; Lantern Hill; Looking for Miracles
Sullivan, Kevin Rodney: America's Dream; Soul of the Game
Sullivan, Tim: Jack and Sarah
Summers, Jeremy: Five Golden Dragons; House of 1,000 Dolls
Summers, Walter: Human Monster, The (Dark Eyes of London); River of Unrest
Sun, Shirley: Iron & Silk
Sundstrom, Cedric: American Ninja III; American Ninja IV: The Annihilation; Captive Rage
Sundstrom, Neal: Howling V—The Rebirth
Sunseri, Jack A.: Chilling, The
Suo, Masayuki: Shall We Dance?
Surjik, Stephen: Wayne's World 2; Weapons of Mass Distraction
Suso, Henry: Deathsport
Sutherland, A. Edward: Beyond Tomorrow; Every Day's a Holiday; Flying Deuces; Follow the Boys; Having a Wonderful Crime; International House; Invisible Woman, The; Mississippi; Mr. Robinson Crusoe; Murders in the Zoo; One Night in the Tropics
Sutherland, Edward: Saturday Night Kid, The
Sutherland, Hal: Journey Back to Oz; Pinocchio and the Emperor of the Night
Sutherland, Kiefer: Last Light; Truth or Consequences, N.M.
Svankmajer, Jan: Alice
Svatek, Peter: Bleeders; Call of the Wild: The Dog of the Yukon; Sci-Fighters
Sverák, Jan: Dark Blue World; Elementary School, The; Kolya
Swackhamer, E. W.: Amazing Spiderman, The; Are You Lonesome Tonight; Dain Curse, The; Death at Love House; Longshot (1981); Man and Boy; Night Terror; Perfect Family; Rousters, The; Secret Passion of Robert Clayton, The; Terror at London Bridge; Winds of Kitty Hawk, The
Swaim, Bob: Half-Moon Street; La Balance; Masquerade; Target of Suspicion
Swanbeck, John: Big Kahuna, The
Swanson, Donald: Magic Garden, The
Sweeney, Bob: Return to Mayberry
Sweeney, Julia: God Said, Ha!
Swenson, Charles: Mouse and His Child, The; Twice Upon a Time
Swerdlove, Larry: Skateboard Kid, The
Swickard, Charles: Hell's Hinges
Swift, David: Good Neighbor Sam; How to Succeed in Business without Really Trying; Interns, The; Parent Trap, The; Pollyanna
Swift, Lela: Best of Dark Shadows, The; Dark Shadows (TV Series)
Swimmer, Saul: Mrs. Brown You've Got a Lovely Daughter
Swirnoff, Brad: Tunnelvision (1976)
Switzer, Michael: Forever Love; Lightning Incident, The; Nitti: The Enforcer; Past the Bleachers; Summer Dreams; Unlikely Angel
Sykes, Peter: Demons of the Mind; Jesus; To the Devil, a Daughter
Sylbert, Paul: Steagle, The
Szabó, István: Colonel Redl; Father; Hanussen; Meeting Venus; Mephisto; 25, Firemen's Street
Szulzinger, Boris: Mamma Dracula
Szwarc, Jeannot: Bug; Enigma; Grand Larceny; Jaws 2; Murders in the Rue Morgue; Santa Claus—The Movie; Somewhere in Time; Supergirl
Taav, Michael: Paint Job, The
Tabak, Matthew: Beyond Suspicion
Tabet, Sylvio: Beastmaster 2: Through the Portal of Time
Tabio, Juan Carlos: Guantanamera!; Strawberry and Chocolate
Tacchella, Jean-Charles: Blue Country; Cousin, Cousine
Tadashi, Okuda: Riding Bean
Taft, Gene: Blame It on the Night
Tahimik, Kidlat: Perfumed Nightmare
Taicher, Robert: Inside Out
Tai-Kit, Mak: Wicked City, The (1992)
Takabayashi, Yoichi: Irezumi (Spirit of Tattoo)
Takacs, Tibor: Bad Blood; Deadly Past; Gate, The; Gate II; I, Madman; Redline; Sabotage; Sabrina, the Teenage Witch
Takahata, Isao: Grave of the Fireflies
Takakjian, Glen: Metamorphosis: The Alien Factor
Takamasa, Ikegami: A.D. Police Files, Vols. 1–3
Takamoto, Iwao: Charlotte's Web
Takamoto, Yoshihiro: Record of Lodoss War: Chronicles of the Heroic Knight
Takayama, Hideki: Urotsukidoji II: Legend of the Demon Womb; Urotsukidoji: Legend of the Overfiend
Takeshi, Mori: Otaku No Video
Talalay, Rachel: Freddy's Dead: The Final Nightmare; Ghost in the Machine; Tank Girl
Talbot, Paul: Freakshow
Talbot, Robert: Mystery Monsters
Talmadge, Richard: Devil Horse, The; Project Moon Base
Tamahori, Lee: Along Came a Spider; Edge, The; Mulholland Falls; Once Were Warriors
Tamayo, Augusto: Ultrawarrior
Tampa, Harry: Nocturna
Tanaka, Shigeo: Gamera Versus Barugon
Tanaka, Tokuzo: Zatoichi: The Blind Swordsman's Vengeance
Tannen, Terrell: Shadows in the Storm
Tannen, William: Flashpoint; Hero and the Terror
Tanner, Alain: In the White City; Jonah Who Will Be 25 in the Year 2000
Tanovic, Danis: No Man's Land (2001)
Tansey, Robert Emmett: Caravan Trail; Colorado Serenade; Driftin' Kid; Dynamite Canyon; Where Trails End; Wild West; Wildfire
Taplitz, Daniel: Black Magic; Commandments; Nightlife
Tarantino, Quentin: Four Rooms; Jackie Brown; Pulp Fiction; Reservoir Dogs
Tarkovsky, Andrei: Andrei Rublev; Mirror, The; My Name Is Ivan; Nostalghia; Sacrifice, The; Solaris; Stalker
Taro, Rin: Dagger of Kamui, The; Doomed Megalopolis, Parts 1–4; Neo-Tokyo
Tash, Max: Running Kind, The
Tashlin, Frank: Alphabet Murders, The; Artists and Models; Cinderfella; Disorderly Orderly, The; Girl Can't Help It, The; Glass Bottom Boat, The; Hollywood or Bust; Private Navy of Sgt. O'Farrell, The; Son of Paleface; Susan Slept Here; Will Success Spoil Rock Hunter?
Tass, Nadia: Mr. Reliable; Pure Luck; Rikki and Pete
Tassie, Paul: Pig's Tale, A
Tate, Martin: Totem
Tati, Jacques: Jour de Fête; Mr. Hulot's Holiday; My Uncle (Mon Oncle); Parade; Playtime; Traffic
Tato, Anna Maria: Night and the Moment, The
Tatoulis, John: Silver Stallion, The
Taurog, Norman: Adventures of Tom Sawyer, The; Birds and the Bees, The; Blue Hawaii; Boys' Town; Broadway Melody of 1940; Bundle of Joy; Caddy, The; Dr. Goldfoot and the Bikini Machine; Double Trouble; G.I. Blues; Girl Crazy; Girls! Girls! Girls!; Hold 'em Jail; It Happened at the World's Fair; Jumping Jacks; Little Nellie Kelly; Live a Little, Love a Little; Mad About Music; Men of Boys Town; Mrs. Wiggs of the Cabbage Patch; Onionhead; Palm Springs Weekend; Presenting Lily

Mars; Rhythm on the Range; Rich, Young and Pretty; Speedway; Spinout; That Midnight Kiss; Tickle Me; Toast of New Orleans; We're Not Dressing; Words and Music; Young Tom Edison
Tausik, David: Blood Song (Haunted Symphony); Homicidal Impulse
Taverna, Michele: Managua
Tavernier, Bertrand: Beatrice; Clean Slate (Coup de Torchon) (1981); Clockmaker, The (1973); Daddy Nostalgia; Death Watch; Judge and the Assassin, The; Life and Nothing But; Mississippi Blues; Revenge of the Musketeers; Round Midnight; Sunday in the Country, A
Taviani, Paolo: Allonsonfan; Good Morning, Babylon; Kaos; Night of the Shooting Stars; Padre Padrone; Wild Flower (1993) (Fiorile)
Taviani, Vittorio: Allonsonfan; Good Morning, Babylon; Kaos; Night of the Shooting Stars; Padre Padrone; Wild Flower (1993) (Fiorile)
Taylor, Alan: Palookaville
Taylor, Baz: Near Misses; Shooting Elizabeth; Tattle Tale
Taylor, Don: Damien: Omen II; Diamond Trap, The; Escape from the Planet of the Apes; Final Countdown, The; Great Scout and Cathouse Thursday, The; Listen to Your Heart; My Wicked, Wicked Ways; Night Games; Red Flag: The Ultimate Game; Ride the Wild Surf; Secret Weapons; September Gun; Tom Sawyer
Taylor, Finn: Dream with the Fishes
Taylor, Jud: Broken Vows; Christmas Coal Mine Miracle, The; City in Fear; Clover; Danielle Steel's Kaleidoscope; FoxFire; Great Escape II, The; Old Man and the Sea, The; Out of the Darkness; Packin' It In; Question of Honor, A; Revenge (1971) (Shelley Winters); Say Goodbye, Maggie Cole; Search for the Gods
Taylor, Ray: Cheyenne Takes Over; Dick Tracy; Flash Gordon Conquers the Universe; Ghost Town Renegades; Ivory-Handled Gun, The; Lone Star Trail; Mystery of the Hooded Horsemen; Painted Stallion, The; Perils of Pauline, The; Rawhide; Return of Chandu (Magician, The); Riders of Death Valley; Stage to Mesa City; Vigilantes Are Coming!; Winners of the West
Taylor, Renee: Love Is All There Is
Taylor, Richard: Stingray
Taylor, Robert: Heidi's Song; Nine Lives of Fritz the Cat
Taylor, Roderick: Instant Karma
Taylor, Sam: Ambassador Bill; Coquette; Freshman, The; Nothing But Trouble; Safety Last; Taming of the Shrew, The; Tempest
Taylor, William Desmond: Tom Sawyer
Taymor, Julie: Titus
Tchernia, Pierre: Holes, The
Teague, Lewis: Alligator; Cat's Eye; Collision Course; Cujo; Deadlock; Fighting Back; Jewel of the Nile, The; Lady in Red; Navy Seals; Saved by the Light; TBone N Weasel; Triangle, The
Teche, Gary: Nevada
Téchiné, André: Alice & Martin; Ma Saison Preferée; Rendez-Vous; Scene of the Crime; Thieves (Les Voleurs); Wild Reeds
Telford, Frank: Bamboo Saucer (Collision Course)
Temple, Julien: Absolute Beginners; Bullet; Earth Girls Are Easy; Filth and the Fury, The; Great Rock and Roll Swindle, The
Templeton, George: Sundowners, The
Tennant, Andy: Amy Fisher Story, The; Anna and the King; Ever After; Fools Rush In; It Takes Two; Keep the Change
Tennent, Joseph: Retro Puppetmaster
Tenney, Del: Horror of Party Beach, The
Tenney, Kevin S.: Arrival II, The; Cellar, The; Night of the Demons; Peacemaker (1990); Pinocchio's Revenge; Tick Tock; Witchboard; Witchboard 2; Witchtrap
Tennyson, Pen: Convoy
Tent, Kevin: Ultrawarrior
Terada, Kazuo: Gargoyles: The Movie (1994)
Terasawa, Buichi: Raven Tengu Kabuto
Terlesky, John: Chain of Command; Judgment Day; Pandora Project, The; Supreme Sanction
Teshigahara, Hiroshi: Face of Another, The; Rikyu; Woman in the Dunes
Tess, Nadia: Malcolm
Tessari, Duccio: Beyond Justice; Long Live Your Death; Tex and the Lord of the Deep; Zorro
Tetsu, Dezuki: Urusei Yatsura: Inaba the Dreammaker
Tetzlaff, Ted: Fighting Father Dunne; RiffRaff; White Tower, The; Window, The
Teuber, Monica: Magdalene
Tewkesbury, Joan: Cold Sassy Tree; Old Boyfriends; Strangers; Sudie & Simpson; Tenth Month, The
Tewksbury, Peter: Emil and the Detectives; Stay Away Joe; Trouble with Girls, The
Tezuka, Osamu: Legend of the Forest
Thau, Leon: Save the Lady
The Beatles: Magical Mystery Tour
The Klein Brothers: Wheels: An Inline Story
Theakston, Graham: Money Kings; Tripods
Thiele, Rolf: Tonio Kroger
Thiele, William: Tarzan Triumphs
Thies, Christopher: Winterbeast
Thomas, Albie: Palm Beach
Thomas, Antony: Code Name: Chaos
Thomas, Betty: Brady Bunch Movie, The; Dr. Dolittle (1998); Late Shift, The; Only You; Private Parts; 28 Days
Thomas, Dave: Experts, The; Strange Brew
Thomas, Gerald: Carry on at Your Convenience; Carry on Behind; Carry on Cleo; Carry on Cowboy; Carry on Cruising; Carry on Doctor; Carry on Emmanuelle; Carry on Nurse; Follow That Camel
Thomas, John G.: Arizona Heat; Tin Man
Thomas, Ralph: Clouded Yellow, The; Doctor at Large; Doctor at Sea; Doctor in Distress; Doctor in the House; No Love for Johnnie; Tale of Two Cities, A; Thirty-Nine Steps, The
Thomas, Ralph L.: Apprentice to Murder; Terry Fox Story, The; Ticket to Heaven
Thomas, Scott: Silent Assassins
Thomas, Theodore: Frank and Ollie
Thomason, Harry: Encounter with the Unknown
Thompson, Brett: Adventures in Dinosaur City
Thompson, Byron W.: Stonebrook
Thompson, Caroline: Black Beauty; Buddy
Thompson, Chris: Bosom Buddies (TV Series)
Thompson, Ernest: 1969
Thompson, J. Lee: Ambassador, The; Battle for the Planet of the Apes; Blue Knight, The; Cabo Blanco; Cape Fear; Conquest of the Planet of the Apes; Death Wish IV: The Crackdown; Evil That Men Do, The; Firewalker; Flame over India; Greek Tycoon, The; Guns of Navarone, The; Happy Birthday to Me; Huckleberry Finn; King Solomon's Mines; Kinjite (Forbidden Subjects); Mackenna's Gold; Messenger of Death; Murphy's Law; Reincarnation of Peter Proud, The; St. Ives; Taras Bulba; Ten to Midnight; Tiger Bay; White Buffalo
Thompson, Robert C.: Bud and Lou; Dog Trouble
Thomsen, Christian Braad: Ladies on the Rocks
Thomson, Chris: Meteorites!; Morrison Murders, The; Swimsuit; Three's Trouble; Trucks
Thor, Cameron: Brutal Truth, The
Thornhill, Michael: Between Wars; Everlasting Secret Family, The
Thornton, Billy Bob: All the Pretty Horses; Sling Blade
Thorpe, Jerry: All God's Children; Kung Fu (1971); Lazarus Syndrome, The; Possessed, The (1977); Smile, Jenny, You're Dead
Thorpe, Richard: Above Suspicion; Adventures of Huckleberry Finn, The; All the Brothers Were Valiant; Athena; Black Hand, The; Challenge to Lassie; Date with Judy, A; Double Wedding; Fiesta; Fun in Acapulco; Girl Who Had Everything, The; Great Caruso, The; Honeymoon Machine, The; Horizontal Lieutenant, The; It's a Big Country; Ivanhoe; Jailhouse Rock; Knights of the Round Table; Lone Defender, The; Night Must Fall; On an Island with You; Prisoner of Zenda, The; Prodigal, The; Student Prince, The; Sun Comes Up, The; Tarzan Escapes;

Tung-shing, Yee: People's Hero
Tunnicliffe, Gary J.: Within the Rock
Turko, Rosemarie: Dungeonmaster, The
Turner, Ann: Celia, Child of Terror
Turner, Brad: Inspectors, The; Roswell: The Aliens Attack
Turner, Chester T.: Black Devil Doll from Hell
Turner, Clive: Howling, The: New Moon Rising
Turner, Paul: Hedd Wyn
Turner, Robert: Digger
Turteltaub, Jon: Cool Runnings; Driving Me Crazy; Instinct; Phenomenon; Think Big; Three Ninjas; While You Were Sleeping
Turtletaub, Jon: Kid, The (2000)
Turturro, John: Illuminata; Mac
Tuttle, Frank: Hell on Frisco Bay; Roman Scandals; This Gun for Hire; Waikiki Wedding
Twohy, David N.: Arrival, The; Grand Tour: Disaster in Time; Pitch Black
Tych, Jean: Great Expectations
Tykwer, Tom: Princess and the Warrior, The; Run Lola Run; Winter Sleepers
Uchida, Yorihisa: Guy: Awakening of the Devil; Guy II: Second Target
Uemura, Osamu: Rumik World: Firetripper
Ullmann, Liv: Faithless; Sofie
Ulmer, Edgar G.: Amazing Transparent Man, The; Black Cat, The; Bluebeard; Daughter of Dr. Jekyll; Detour; Jive Junction; Man from Planet X, The; Moon over Harlem; Naked Venus; St. Benny the Dip; Strange Illusion; Strange Woman, The
Ulrich, Carl: Stephanie, Nathalie, Caroline and Vincent
Umgelter, Fritz: Bellboy and the Playgirls, The
Underwood, Ron: City Slickers; Heart and Souls; Mighty Joe Young; Speechless; Tremors
Ungar, George: Champagne Safari, The
Unger, Lawrence: Intimate Obsession
Unknown!: Street of Forgotten Women, The
Unkrich, Lee: Monsters, Inc.
Uno, Michael Toshiyuki: Blind Spot; Face to Kill For, A; Road to Galveston, The; Vietnam War Story—Part Two; Wash, The; Without Warning: The James Brady Story
Urayama, K.: Taro, the Dragon Boy
Urbishi, Rocco: George Carlin: Jammin' in New York
Ureles, Jeff: Cheap Shots
Urveta, Chano: Brainiac, The; Witch's Mirror, The
Usher, Kinka: Mystery Men
Ustinov, Peter: Billy Budd; Hammersmith Is Out; Lady L; Lion and the Hawk, The
Uys, Jamie: Dingaka; Gods Must Be Crazy, The; Gods Must Be Crazy II, The
Vacek, Jack: Rock House
Vadim, Roger: And God Created Woman; And God Created Woman; Barbarella; Blood and Roses; Circle of Love; Game Is Over, The; Game of Seduction; Hitchhiker, The (Series); Le Repos du Guerrier (Warrior's Rest); Les Liaisons Dangereuses; Seven Deadly Sins, The
Vajda, Marian D.: Snoopers
Valdez, Luis: Cisco Kid, The; La Bamba; Zoot Suit
Valenti, Frank: Delta Force, Commando Two
Valenzuela, Jose Luis: Luminarias
Valère, Jean: Time Out For Love
Valerii, Tonino: Days of Wrath; Massacre at Fort Holman (Reason to Live … A Reason to Die, A); My Name Is Nobody
Vallelonga, Nick: Brilliant Disguise, A; Corporate Ladder
Valli, Eric: Himalaya
Van Ackeren, Robert: Woman in Flames, A
Van Atta, Don: Bosom Buddies (TV Series)
Van Damme, Jean-Claude: Quest, The
Van Den Berg, Rudolf: Johnsons, The
van Diem, Mike: Character (Karakter)
Van Dormael, Jaco: Eighth Day, The; Toto the Hero
Van Dusen, Bruce: Cold Feet
Van Dyke, W. S.: After the Thin Man; Andy Hardy Gets Spring Fever; Another Thin Man; Bitter Sweet (1940); Cairo; Forsaking All Others; I Live My Life; I Love You Again; I Married an Angel; Journey for Margaret; Love on the Run; Manhattan Melodrama; Marie Antoinette; Naughty Marietta; Personal Property; Rosalie; Rose Marie; San Francisco; Shadow of the Thin Man; Sweethearts; Tarzan the Ape Man; Thin Man, The; White Shadows in the South Seas
Van Heerden, Andre: Tribulation
Van Horn, Buddy: Any Which Way You Can; Dead Pool, The; Pink Cadillac
Van Peebles, Mario: Love Kills; New Jack City; Panther; Posse
Van Peebles, Melvin: Gang in Blue; Identity Crisis; Story of a Three Day Pass, The; Sweet Sweetback's Baadasssss Song; Watermelon Man
Van Sant, Gus: Drugstore Cowboy; Even Cowgirls Get the Blues; Finding Forrester; Good Will Hunting; My Own Private Idaho; Psycho; Tales of Erotica; To Die For
Vane, Norman Thaddeus: Club Life; Frightmare; Midnight; Taxi Dancers
Vanwagenen, Sterling: Alan and Naomi
Vanzina, Carlo: Gamble, The; Millions; Nothing Underneath
Varda, Agnes: Cleo from 5 to 7; Le Bonheur; Le Petit Amour; One Sings, the Other Doesn't; Vagabond
Varnel, Marcel: Chandu the Magician; Frozen Limits, The
Vart, Henri: Secret Obsessions
Vasallo, Carlos: Day of the Assassin
Vasiliev, Georgi: Chapayev
Vasiliev, Sergei: Chapayev
Vasquez, Joseph B.: Bronx War, The; Hangin' with the Homeboys; Manhattan Merengue; Street Hitz (Street Story)
Veber, Francis: Closet, The; Le Chêvre (The Goat); Les Comperes; Out on a Limb; Three Fugitives
Vecchietti, Alberto: Monster of the Island, The
Vega, Pastor: Portrait of Teresa
Vejar, Mike: Quantum Leap (TV Series)
Veloz, David: Permanent Midnight
Vendramini, Danny: Desperate Prey
Vennera, Chick: Angel in Training
Ventura, Michael: I'm Almost Not Crazy: John Cassavetes—The Man and His Work
Venturini, Edward: Headless Horseman, The; In Old Mexico
Verber, Francis: Dinner Game, The
Verbinski, Gore: Mexican, The; Mouse Hunt
Verdone, Carlo: Iris Blond
Verducci, Pat: True Crime
Verheyen, Jan: Little Death, The
Verhoeven, Michael: Killing Cars; Nasty Girl, The; White Rose, The
Verhoeven, Paul: Basic Instinct; Flesh and Blood (Sword and the Rose, the (1985)); Fourth Man, The; Hitchhiker, The (Series); Hollow Man; Katie's Passion; RoboCop; Showgirls; Soldier of Orange; Spetters; Starship Troopers; Total Recall; Turkish Delight
Verklan, Laura: Lincoln Assassination, The
Verneuil, Henri: Forbidden Fruit; Love and the Frenchwoman; Melodie en Sous-Sol (The Big Grab) (Any Number Can Win); Night Flight from Moscow; Sheep Has Five Legs; Un Singe en Hiver (A Monkey in Winter)
Vernon, Henry: Danger Zone, The (1986)
Verona, Stephen F.: Lords of Flatbush, The; Pipe Dreams; Talking Walls
Veronis, Nick: Day at the Beach
VeSota, Bruno: Brain Eaters, The; Female Jungle
Vicario, Marco: Sensual Man, The; Wifemistress
Vickers, Lindsey C.: Appointment, The
Vidor, Charles: Cover Girl; Gilda; Hans Christian Andersen; It's a Big Country; Lady in Question; Love Me or Leave Me; Loves of Carmen, The; Rhapsody; Song to Remember, A; Song Without End; Swan, The; Tuttles of Tahiti, The
Vidor, King: Beyond the Forest; Big Parade, The; Bird of Paradise; Champ, The; Citadel, The; Comrade X; Crowd, The; Duel in the Sun; Fountainhead, The; Hallelujah!; Jack Knife Man, The; Man without a Star; Northwest Passage; Our Daily Bread; Ruby Gentry; Show People; Sky Pilot, The; Solomon and Sheba; Stella Dallas; Street Scene; Texas Rangers (1936); Tol'able David; War and Peace
Viertel, Berthold: Rhodes of Africa (Rhodes)

Vigne, Daniel: One Woman or Two; Return of Martin Guerre, The; Strangers
Vignola, Robert: Scarlet Letter, The
Vigo, Jean: Zero for Conduct
Viktor: Alien P.I.
Vila, Camilo: Options; Unholy, The
Vilencia, Jeff: Sleazemania Strikes Back
Villalobos, Reynaldo: Conagher; Hollywood Confidential
Villaronga, Agustin: In a Glass Cage
Vilsmaier, Joseph: Brother of Sleep; Harmonists, The; Stalingrad
Vince, Robert: MVP2: Most Vertical Primate
Vincent, Christian: La Separation
Vincent, Chuck: Bad Blood; Bedroom Eyes II; Preppies; Sensations; Sex Appeal; Slammer Girls; Summer Camp; Thrilled to Death; Warrior Queen; Wimps; Woman Obsessed, A; Young Nurses in Love
Vint, Jerry: Bad Blood; Bedroom Eyes II; Preppies; Sensations; Sex Appeal; Slammer Girls; Summer Camp; Thrilled to Death; Warrior Queen; Wimps; Woman Obsessed, A; Young Nurses in Love
Vinterberg, Thomas: Celebration, The
Vinton, Will: Adventures of Mark Twain, The
Viola, Joe: Angels Hard as They Come; Hot Box, The
Virgien, Norton: Rugrats Movie, The
Virgo, Clement: Junior's Groove; Love Come Down; Rude
Visconti, Luchino: Bellissima; Boccaccio 70; Conversation Piece; Damned, The; Death in Venice; Innocent, The; Leopard, The; Ossessione; Rocco & His Brothers; Wanton Contessa, The; White Nights
Vitale, Tony: Kiss Me Guido
Vittorie, Joseph: Criminal Mind, The
Vogel, Virgil: Beulah Land; Big Valley, The (TV Series); Invasion of the Animal People; Land Unknown, The; Mole People, The; One Riot, One Ranger; Streethawk
Vogelsang, Judith: Heartless
Vohrer, Alfred: Dead Eyes of London
Voight, Jon: Tin Soldier, The
Voizard, Marc: Hawk's Vengeance; Marked Man; Shades of Love: Lilac Dream
Volk, Paul G.: Steel Frontier; Sunset Strip
Vollman, Tom: Alien Agenda, The (TV Series)
von Baky, Josef: Baron Münchhausen (1943)
Von Fristch, Gunther: Curse of the Cat People, The
Von Furstenberg, Vieth: Curse of the Cat People, The
von Garnier, Katja: Bandits
von Mende, H. Todd: Easier Said
von Praunheim, Rosa: Virus Knows No Morals, A
von Ratony, Akos: Cave of the Living Dead
von Scherler Mayer, Daisy: Madeline; Party Girl; Woo
von Sternberg, Josef: Blonde Venus; Blue Angel, The; Crime and Punishment; Dishonored; Docks of New York, The; Last Command, The; Macao; Morocco; Scarlet Empress, The; Shanghai Express; Shanghai Gesture, The; Underworld
Von Stroheim, Erich: Merry Widow, The
Von Stroheim, Erich: Blind Husbands; Foolish Wives; Greed; Queen Kelly; Wedding March, The
von Theumer, Ernst R.: Jungle Warriors
von Trier, Lars: Breaking the Waves; Element of Crime, The; Kingdom, The; Zentropa
von Trier, Lars: Dancer in the Dark
von Trotta, Margarethe: Marianne & Juliane; Promise, The; Sheer Madness
Vorhaus, Bernard: Amazing Mr. X; Courageous Dr. Christian, The; Lady from Louisiana; Meet Dr. Christian; Three Faces West
Voss, Kurt: Amnesia; Baja; Body Count (1997) (direct to video); Border Radio; Genuine Risk; Horseplayer; Poison Ivy: The New Seduction; Sugar Town
Votocek, Otakar: Wings of Fame
Wachowski, Andy: Bound; Matrix, The
Wachowski, Larry: Bound; Matrix, The
Wacks, Jonathan: Ed & His Dead Mother; Mystery Date; Powwow Highway
Waddington, Andrucha: Me You Them
Wade, Alan: Julian Po
Wadleigh, Michael: Wolfen; Woodstock
Waggner, George: Climax, The; Fighting Kentuckian, The; Horror Island; Man Made Monster (The Atomic Monster); Operation Pacific; Wolf Call; Wolf Man, The
Wagner, Bruce: I'm Losing You
Wagner, Paul: Windhorse
Wain, David: Wet Hot American Summer
Wainwright, Rupert: Blank Check; Dillinger; Discovery Program; Stigmata
Waite, Ralph: On the Nickel
Wajda, Andrzej: Ashes and Diamonds; Birch Wood; Danton; Generation, A (1954); Kanal; Love in Germany, A; Man of Iron; Man of Marble; Wedding, The (1972)
Walas, Chris: Fly II, The; Vagrant, The
Waldman, Grant Austin: Teenage Exorcist
Walker, Dorian: Making the Grade; Teen Witch
Walker, Giles: 90 Days; Ordinary Magic; Princes in Exile
Walker, Hal: At War with the Army; Road to Bali; Road to Utopia
Walker, Nancy: Can't Stop the Music
Walker, Pete: Confessional, The; Die Screaming, Marianne; House of the Long Shadows; Schizo
Walker, Rob: Circus
Walker, Stuart: Mystery of Edwin Drood, The; Werewolf of London
Walkow, Gary: Hammered: The Best of Sledge; Trouble with Dick, The
Wallace, Craig: Cutting Moments
Wallace, David: Crusades, The; King Tut: The Face of Tutankhamun
Wallace, Joshua: Diary of a Serial Killer
Wallace, Randall: Man in the Iron Mask, The; We Were Soldiers
Wallace, Richard: Bombardier; Captain Caution; Fallen Sparrow, The; Girl, a Guy and a Gob, A; It's in the Bag; Little Minister, The; Night to Remember, A; Sinbad the Sailor; Tycoon; Young in Heart, The
Wallace, Rick: Acceptable Risks
Wallace, Stephen: For Love Alone; Prisoners of the Sun; Turtle Beach (Killing Beach)
Wallace, Tommy Lee: Aloha Summer; Comrades of Summer, The; Fright Night II; Halloween III: Season of the Witch; It; Presence, The; Witness to the Execution
Waller, Anthony: American Werewolf in Paris, An; Guilty, The; Mute Witness
Wallerstein, Herb: Snowbeast
Walsh, John: Ed's Next Move
Walsh, Kieron J.: When Brendan Met Trudy
Walsh, Matthew Jason: Bloodletting
Walsh, Raoul: Along the Great Divide; Background to Danger; Band of Angels; Battle Cry; Big Trail, The; Blackbeard the Pirate; Captain Horatio Hornblower; College Swing; Dark Command; Desperate Journey; Distant Drums; Gentleman Jim; Going Hollywood; Gun Fury; High Sierra; Horn Blows at Midnight, The; In Old Arizona; King and Four Queens, The; Klondike Annie; Lion Is in the Streets, A; Man I Love, The; Naked and the Dead, The; Northern Pursuit; Objective, Burma!; Pursued; Regeneration; Roaring Twenties, The; Sadie Thompson; Silver River; Strawberry Blonde, The; Tall Men, The; They Died with Their Boots On; They Drive by Night; Thief of Bagdad, The; Uncertain Glory; What Price Glory? (1926); White Heat
Walters, Charles: Ask Any Girl; Barkleys of Broadway, The; Belle of New York, The; Dangerous When Wet; Don't Go Near the Water; Easter Parade; Easy to Love; Glass Slipper, The; Good News; High Society; Jumbo; Lili; Please Don't Eat the Daisies; Summer Stock; Tender Trap, The; Texas Carnival; Torch Song; Unsinkable Molly Brown, The; Walk, Don't Run
Walton, Fred: April Fool's Day; Courtyard, The; Dead Air; Hadley's Rebellion; Homewrecker; Rosary Murders, The; Step-

Tokyo-Ga; Until the End of the World; Wings of Desire; Wrong Move, The
Wendkos, Paul: Betrayal; Blood Vows: The Story of a Mafia Wife; Celebrity; Cocaine: One Man's Seduction; Cry for Love, A; Execution, The; From the Dead of Night; Gidget; Gidget Goes Hawaiian; Gidget Goes to Rome; Great Escape II, The; Guns of the Magnificent Seven; Haunts of the Very Rich; Honor Thy Father; I Spy (TV Series); Johnny Tiger; Mephisto Waltz, The; Ordeal of Dr. Mudd, The; White Hot: The Mysterious Murder of Thelma Todd; Wing and a Prayer, A; Woman Called Moses, A
Wenk, Richard: Just the Ticket; National Lampoon's Attack of the 5' 2" Women; Vamp
Werker, Alfred: Adventures of Sherlock Holmes, The; At Gunpoint; Devil's Canyon; He Walked by Night; Shock (1946)
Werner, Jeff: Die Laughing
Werner, Peter: Barn Burning; Battered; Call Me Claus; Don't Cry, It's Only Thunder; Hiroshima: Out of the Ashes; I Married a Centerfold; Image, The; LBJ: The Early Years; Lone Justice; No Man's Land; Substitute Wife, The
Wertmuller, Lina: All Screwed Up; Blood Feud; Camorra; Ciao Professore; Joke of Destiny; Love and Anarchy; Night Full of Rain, A; Seduction of Mimi, The; Seven Beauties; Sotto Sotto; Summer Night; Swept Away
Wesley, William: Route 666; Scarecrows
West, Jake: Razor Blade Smile
West, Roland: Bat Whispers, The; Monster, The
West, Simon: Con Air; General's Daughter, The; Lara Croft: Tomb Raider
Weston, Armand: Nesting, The
Weston, Eric: Evilspeak; Iron Triangle, The; Marvin and Tige; To Protect and Serve
Wetzl, Fulvio: Rorret
Wetzler, Gwen: Secret of the Sword, The
Wexler, Haskell: Latino; Medium Cool
Whale, James: Bride of Frankenstein; Frankenstein; Invisible Man, The; Man in the Iron Mask, The; Old Dark House, The; Show Boat; Sinners in Paradise; Wives Under Suspicion
Wharmby, Tony: Covert Assassin; Equalizer, The: "Memories of Manon"; Kissing Place, The; Lillie; Partners in Crime (Secret Adversary) (TV Series); Seven Dials Mystery, The; Sorry, Wrong Number; Treacherous Crossing
Whatham, Claude: Buddy's Song; Elizabeth R; Murder Elite; Sweet William; That'll Be the Day
Wheat, Jim: After Midnight; Ewoks: The Battle for Endor; Lies
Wheat, Ken: After Midnight; Ewoks: The Battle for Endor; Lies
Wheatley, David: Hostages; Nobody's Children
Wheeler, Anne: Better Than Chocolate; Loyalties
Whelan, Tim: Badman's Territory; Clouds over Europe; Divorce of Lady X, The; Higher and Higher; Mill on the Floss, The; Rage at Dawn; Seven Day's Leave; Sidewalks of London; Step Lively; Texas Lady; Thief of Bagdad, The
Whitaker, Forest: Hope Floats; Strapped; Waiting to Exhale
White, Alan: Risk
White, Jules: Sidewalks of New York
White, Sam: People Are Funny
White, Steve: Amityville Dollhouse
White, Wally: Lie Down with Dogs
Whitelaw, Alexander: Vicious Circles
Whitesell, John: Calendar Girl; See Spot Run
Whitman, Philip H.: His Private Secretary
Whitmore II, Preston A.: Walking Dead, The
Whorf, Richard: Champagne for Caesar; It Happened in Brooklyn; Love from a Stranger; Luxury Liner; Till the Clouds Roll By
Whyte, Michael: Railway Station Man, The
Wiard, William: Tom Horn
Wickes, David: Frankenstein; Hitchhiker, The (Series); Jack the Ripper; Jekyll & Hyde; Silver Dream Racer
Wicki, Bernhard: Bridge, The; Longest Day, The; Morituri
Widen, Gregory: Prophecy, The (1995)
Widerberg, Bo: Elvira Madigan; Man on the Roof
Wiederhorn, Ken: Eyes of a Stranger; House in the Hills, A; Meatballs Part II; Return of the Living Dead Part II; Shock Waves (Death Corps)
Wiemer, Robert: Anna to the Infinite Power; Night Train to Katmandu; Somewhere, Tomorrow
Wiene, Robert: Cabinet of Doctor Caligari, The; Hands of Orlac
Wilbur, Crane: Bat, The
Wilcox, Fred M.: Courage of Lassie; Forbidden Planet; Hills of Home; Lassie Come Home; Secret Garden, The; Three Daring Daughters
Wilcox, Herbert: Courtney Affair, The; Forever and a Day; Lilacs in the Spring (Let's Make Up); London Melody; No, No Nanette; Nurse Edith Cavell; Trouble in the Glen
Wild, Andrew: Spenser: Ceremony
Wild, Nettie: Place Called Chiapas, A
Wilde, Cornel: Naked Prey, The; Shark's Treasure; Sword of Lancelot
Wilde, Ted: Battling Orioles, The
Wilder, Billy: Apartment, The; Avanti!; Buddy, Buddy; Double Indemnity; Emperor Waltz, The; Fedora; Five Graves to Cairo; Fortune Cookie, The; Front Page, The; Irma La Douce; Kiss Me, Stupid; Lost Weekend, The; Love in the Afternoon; Mauvaise Graine (Bad Seed); One, Two, Three; Private Life of Sherlock Holmes, The; Sabrina; Seven Year Itch, The; Some Like It Hot; Spirit of St. Louis, The; Stalag 17; Sunset Boulevard; Witness for the Prosecution
Wilder, Gene: Adventure of Sherlock Holmes' Smarter Brother, The; Haunted Honeymoon; Woman in Red, The; World's Greatest Lover, The
Wilder, John: Breaking Home Ties
Wilder, W. Lee: Big Bluff, The; Killers from Space; Manfish; Snow Creature, The
Wilding, Gavin: Listen; Premonition (1998); Raffle, The; Stag
Wiles, Gordon: Charlie Chan's Secret; Gangster, The; Ginger in the Morning
Wiley, Ethan: Children of the Corn V: Fields of Terror; House II: The Second Story
Wilkinson, Charles: Breach of Trust; Quarantine
Willeg, Edward: Mad Executioners, The
Williams, Anson: All-American Murder; Dream Date; Little White Lies; Perfect Little Murder, A
Williams, Bob: Gross Jokes
Williams, Elmo: Hell Ship Mutiny
Williams, Hype: Belly
Williams, Larry: Path to Paradise
Williams, Matt: Where the Heart Is
Williams, Oscar: Death Drug; Final Comedown, The
Williams, Paul: Mirage; Miss Right; November Men, The
Williams, Richard: Arabian Knight
Williams, Scott: Man with Two Heads
Williams, Stephen: Shadow Zone: The Undead Express
Williams, Tod: Adventures of Sebastian Cole, The
Williamson, Fred: Adios Amigo; Big Score, The; Foxtrap; Mean Johnny Barrows; One Down, Two to Go; Silent Hunter; South Beach; Steele's Law; Three Days to a Kill
Williamson, Kevin: Teaching Mrs. Tingle
Willing, Nick: Alice in Wonderland; Jason and the Argonauts; Photographing Fairies
Wills, J. Elder: Big Fella; Song of Freedom
Wilson, Andy: Playing God
Wilson, Hugh: Blast from the Past; Burglar (U.S.); Dudley Do-Right; First Wives Club, The; Guarding Tess; Police Academy; Rustler's Rhapsody
Wilson, Jim: Stacy's Knights
Wilson, Richard: Al Capone; Invitation to a Gunfighter; It's All True; Pay or Die; Three in the Attic
Wilson, S. S.: Tremors 2: Aftershocks
Wilson, Sandy: American Boyfriends; Harmony Cats; My American Cousin
Wilson, Yale: Truth or Dare? A Critical Madness
Wimmer, Kurt: One Man's Justice
Winant, Scott: 'Til There Was You

Wincer, Simon: Crocodile Dundee in Los Angeles; Dark Forces; D.A.R.Y.L.; Echo of Thunder, The; Escape: Human Cargo; Flash (1998); Free Willy; Girl Who Spelled Freedom, The; Harley Davidson and the Marlboro Man; Lighthorsemen, The; Lightning Jack; Lonesome Dove; LOUIS L'AMOUR'S CROSSFIRE TRAIL; Murder She Purred; Operation Dumbo Drop; Phantom, The; Phar Lap; Quigley Down Under
Windom, Lawrence: Headin' Home
Windust, Bretaigne: Enforcer, The; June Bride; Winter Meeting
Winer, Harry: House Arrest; JFK: Reckless Youth; Mirrors; SpaceCamp
Winfrey, Jonathan: Assassination Game, The; Black Scorpion; Black Scorpion II: Aftershock; Carnosaur 3: Primal Species; Excessive Force II: Force on Force; Legend of the Lost Tomb; New Crime City: Los Angeles 2020
Winick, Gary: Out of the Rain; Sweet Nothing; Tic Code, The
Winkler, Charles: Disturbed; Rocky Marciano; You Talkin' to Me
Winkler, David: Finding Graceland
Winkler, Henry: Cop and a Half; Memories of Me; Smoky Mountain Christmas
Winkler, Irwin: At First Sight; Guilty by Suspicion; Life as a House; Net, The; Night and the City
Winkless, Terence H.: Berlin Conspiracy, The; Bloodfist; Corporate Affairs; Ladykiller; Nest, The; Not of This Earth; Rage and Honor; Westing Game, The; White Wolves II: Legend of the Wild
Winner, James: Night That Never Happened, The
Winner, Michael: Appointment with Death; Big Sleep, The; Bullseye; Chato's Land; Chorus of Disapproval, A; Death Wish; Death Wish II; Death Wish III; Firepower; Lawman; Mechanic, The; Nightcomers, The; Scream for Help; Sentinel, The; Stone Killer, The; Wicked Lady, The
Winning, David: Killer Image; Profile for Murder; Storm; Turbo: A Power Rangers Adventure
Winograd, Peter: One Last Run
Winsor, Terry: Essex Boys
Winston, Stan: Adventures of a Gnome Named Gnorm, The; Pumpkinhead
Winter, Alex: Freaked
Winterbottom, Michael: Butterfly Kiss; Claim, The; Go Now; I Want You; Jude; Welcome to Sarajevo; Wonderland (1999)
Winters, David: Dr. Jekyll and Mr. Hyde; Last Horror Film, The; Thrashin'
Winters, Paul: Freeway Maniac
Winterstein, Frank: Sherlock Holmes and the Deadly Necklace
Wiper, Scott: Better Way to Die, A
Wisbar, Frank: Devil Bat's Daughter; Strangler of the Swamp
Wise, Herbert: Castle of the Living Dead; Elizabeth R; Gathering Storm; I, Claudius; Norman Conquests, The, Episode 1: Table Manners; Norman Conquests, The, Episode 3: Roundand Round the Garden; Norman Conquests, The, Episode 2: Living-Together; Pope John Paul II; Skokie; Strange Interlude; 10th Kingdom, The
Wise, Kirk: Atlantis: The Lost Empire; Beauty and the Beast; Hunchback of Notre Dame, The
Wise, Robert: Andromeda Strain, The; Audrey Rose; Blood on the Moon; Body Snatcher, The (1945); Born to Kill; Curse of the Cat People, The; Day the Earth Stood Still, The; Desert Rats, The; Executive Suite; Haunting, The; Helen of Troy; Hindenburg, The; I Want to Live!; Mademoiselle Fifi; Rooftops; Run Silent, Run Deep; Sand Pebbles, The; Set-Up, The; Somebody Up There Likes Me; Sound of Music, The; Star! (1968); Star Trek—The Motion Picture; This Could Be the Night; Three Secrets; Tribute to a Bad Man; Two for the Seesaw; Until They Sail; West Side Story
Wiseman, Carol: Does This Mean We're Married?; Face the Music; Little Princess, A; May Wine
Wishman, Doris: Bad Girls Go to Hell; Blaze Starr: The Original; Night to Dismember, A
Witcher, Theodore: Love Jones
Withrow, Stephen: Friends, Lovers & Lunatics
Witliff, William: Red-Headed Stranger, The
Witney, William: Adventures of Captain Marvel, The; Adventures of Red Ryder; Apache Rose; Arizona Raiders; Bells of Coronado; Bells of San Angelo; Dick Tracy Returns; Dick Tracy vs. Crime Inc.; Dick Tracy's G-Men; Down Dakota Way; Drums of Fu Manchu; Eyes of Texas; Far Frontier; G-Men vs. The Black Dragon; Golden Stallion, The; Hawk of the Wilderness; Helldorado; Hi-Yo Silver; In Old Amarillo; Island of Dr. Moreau, The; Lone Ranger, The; Master of the World; Mysterious Dr. Satan; Nighttime in Nevada; Outcast, The; Painted Stallion, The; Paratroop Command; Roll on Texas Moon; SOS Coast Guard; Springtime in the Sierras; Spy Smasher; Trail of Robin Hood; Trigger Jr.; Under California Stars; Zorro Rides Again; Zorro's Fighting Legion
Wolcott, James L.: Wild Women of Wongo
Wolf, Fred: Mouse and His Child, The; Point, The
Wolfe, Donald: Savage Intruder, The
Wolk, Andy: Criminal Justice; Defenders, The; Defenders, The: Taking the First; Traces of Red
Wolk, Peter: Defenders, The: Taking the First
Wolman, Dan: Soldier of the Night; Up Your Anchor
Wolodarsky, M. Wallace: Cold-Blooded; Sorority Boys
Wong, Che-Kirk: Big Hit, The; Crime Story
Wong, James: Final Destination; One, The
Wong, Kar-wai: In the Mood for Love
Woo, Jang Sun: Lies (1999)
Woo, John: Better Tomorrow, A; Better Tomorrow 2, A; Blackjack; Broken Arrow; Bullet in the Head; Face/Off; Hard Boiled; Hard Target; John Woo's Once a Thief; Killer, The; Mission: Impossible 2; Once a Thief
Wood, Sam: Casanova Brown; Command Decision; Day at the Races, A; Devil and Miss Jones, The; For Whom the Bell Tolls; Goodbye, Mr. Chips; Guest Wife; Hold Your Man; King's Row; Kitty Foyle; Madame X; Navy Blue and Gold; Night at the Opera, A; Our Town; Peck's Bad Boy; Pride of the Yankees, The; Stratton Story, The
Wood Jr., Edward D.: Bride of the Monster; Glen or Glenda; Hellborn; Jail Bait (1954); Night of the Ghouls; Plan 9 from Outer Space; Sinister Urge, The
Woodhead, Leslie: Endurance; Tragedy of Flight 103, The: The Inside Story
Woodman, William: King Richard II; Romeo and Juliet; Tempest, The (1983)
Woodruff, Frank: Lady Scarface
Woods, Jack: Equinox (The Beast) (1971)
Woods, Mark: Witchcraft II: The Temptress
Woodward, Joanne: Come Along with Me
Woodward, John: Neurotic Cabaret
Wool, Abbe: Roadside Prophets
Woolnough, Jeff: First Degree; Universal Soldier II: Brothers in Arms
Woo-Ping, Yuen: Twin Warriors
Workman, Chuck: Andy Warhol: Superstar; Source, The; Stoogemania
Worsley, Wallace: Ace of Hearts; Hunchback of Notre Dame, The
Worswick, Clark: Agent on Ice
Worth, Aaron: 9 1/2 Ninjas
Worth, David: Chain of Command; Kickboxer; Lady Dragon; Lady Dragon 2; Shark Attack 2; Warrior of the Lost World
Wortmann, Sonke: Maybe, Maybe Not
Woster, Eric: Sandman (1992)
Wragge, Martin: Last Warrior, The
Wray, John Griffith: Anna Christie
Wrede, Caspar: One Day in the Life of Ivan Denisovich; Terrorists, The
Wright, Alexander: Fast Money; First 9 1/2 Weeks, The
Wright, Allen: Slow Bullet
Wright, Geoffrey: Cherry Falls; Romper Stomper
Wright, Mack V.: Haunted Gold; Hit the Saddle; Man from Monterey, The; Range Defenders; Riders of the Whistling

Skull; Sea Hound, The; Somewhere in Sonora; Vigilantes Are Coming!; Winds of the Wasteland
Wright, Tenny: Big Stampede, The; Telegraph Trail, The
Wright, Thomas: Bodily Harm; Chrome Soldiers; Deadly Game; Fatal Image, The; Highlander: The Gathering; No Holds Barred; Snow Kill
Wrye, Donald: Born Innocent; Ice Castles; Not in This Town
Wuhl, Robert: Open Season
Wurlitzer, Rudy: Candy Mountain
Wyler, William: Ben-Hur; Best Years of Our Lives, The; Big Country, The; Carrie; Children's Hour, The; Collector, The; Come and Get It; Dead End; Desperate Hours, The (1955); Dodsworth; Friendly Persuasion; Funny Girl; Heiress, The; How to Steal a Million; Jezebel; Letter, The; Liberation of L. B. Jones, The; Little Foxes, The; Mrs. Miniver; Roman Holiday; These Three; Westerner, The; Wuthering Heights
Wyles, David: Man with a Gun
Wynn, Bob: Resurrection of Zachary Wheeler, The
Wynn, Tracy Keenan: Hit Lady
Wynne, Paul: Bombshell
Wynorski, Jim: Big Bad Mama II; Chopping Mall; Deathstalker II: Duel of the Titans; Final Voyage; Gale Force; Ghoulies IV; Hard Bounty; Hard to Die; Haunting of Morella, The; Little Miss Millions; Lost Empire, The; Munchie; Munchie Strikes Back; 976-EVIL II: The Astral Factor; Not of This Earth; Rangers; Return of the Swamp Thing; Sorceress; Sorority House Massacre 2; Stealth Fighter; Transylvania Twist; Vampirella; Wasp Woman, The (1995)
Wynorsky, Jim: Pandora Project, The
Xhonneux, Henri: Marquis
Xiaowen, Zhou: Emperor's Shadow, The; Ermo
Yablonsky, Yabo: Manipulator, The
Yabuki, Kimio: Twelve Months
Yaitanes, Greg: Double Tap; Hard Justice
Yakin, Boaz: Fresh; Price Above Rubies, A; Remember the Titans
Yamamoto, Michio: Evil of Dracula
Yamamoto, Yoshikio: Rei-Rei
Yamashita, Takaaki: Digimon: The Movie
Yamazaki, Kazuo: Urusei Yatsura (TV Series) Vols. 1–45; Urusei Yatsura: Remember Love
Yanagimachi, Mitsuo: Himatsuri; Shadow of China
Yang, Edward: Yi Yi
Yang, Zhang: Shower
Yansen, Louis: Misplaced
Yarbrough, Jean: Brute Man, The; Creeper, The; Devil Bat, The; Here Come the Co-Eds; Hillbillys in a Haunted House; House of Horrors; In Society; King of the Zombies; Lost in Alaska; Naughty Nineties, The
Yari, Bob: Mindgames
Yasuhiko, Yoshikazu: Venus Wars, The
Yasuyuki, Noda: Bubblegum Crash, Vols. 1–3
Yatagai, Kenichi: Bubblegum Crash, Vols. 1–3
Yates, Hal: Flustered Comedy of Leon Errol, The
Yates, Peter: Breaking Away; Bullitt; Curtain Call; Deep, The; Don Quixote; Dresser, The; Eleni; Eyewitness; For Pete's Sake; Friends of Eddie Coyle, The; Hot Rock, The; House on Carroll Street, The; Innocent Man, An; Koroshi; Krull; Mother, Jugs, and Speed; Murphy's War; Robbery; Roommates; Run of the Country, The; Suspect; Year of the Comet
Yates, Rebecca: Rubberface
Yau, Herman: Untold Story, The
Yeager, Steve: On the Block
Yeaton, Brook: Ice
Yeaworth Jr., Irvin S.: Blob, The; Dinosaurus!; 4D Man
Yellen, Linda: Chantilly Lace; End of Summer; Parallel Lives
Yen, Chang Hsin: Shaolin Temple
Yevtushenko, Yevgenii: Kindergarten
Yimou, Zhang: Not One Less; Road Home, The (1999)
Yoakam, Dwight: South of Heaven, West of Hell
Yolles, Edie: That's My Baby
Yonis, Jeff: Bloodfist V: Human Target; Born Bad; Humanoids from the Deep
Yorkin, Bud: Arthur 2: On the Rocks; Come Blow Your Horn; Divorce American Style; Love Hurts; Start the Revolution Without Me; Thief Who Came to Dinner, The; Twice in a Lifetime
Yoshida, Hiroaki: Iron Maze
Yoshiomi: Iron Maze
Young, Freddie: Arthur's Hallowed Ground
Young, Harold: Dreaming Out Loud; Frozen Ghost, The; Jungle Captive; Mummy's Tomb, The; Scarlet Pimpernel, The
Young, John Scaret: Sirens
Young, Lance: Bliss
Young, Lee Doo: Silent Assassins
Young, Robert: Doomsday Gun; Fierce Creatures; Getting Gotti; Hostage; Jeeves and Wooster (TV Series); Robin Hood: Herne's Son; Robin Hood: The Swords of Wayland; Romance with a Double Bass; Soldier's Home; Splitting Heirs; World Is Full of Married Men, The; Worst Witch, The
Young, Robert M.: Ballad of Gregorio Cortez, The; Caught; Dominick and Eugene; Extremities; One Trick Pony; Rich Kids; Roosters; Saving Grace; Short Eyes; Slave of Dreams; Solomon and Sheba; Talent for the Game; Triumph of the Spirit; We Are the Children
Young, Robert W.: Scandalous
Young, Roger: Bitter Harvest; Bourne Identity, The; Double-crossed; Gulag; Joseph; Kiss the Sky; Lassiter; Mercy Mission (The Rescue of Flight 711); Moses; Squeeze, The; Two of a Kind
Young, Terence: Amorous Adventures of Moll Flanders, The; Black Tights; Bloodline; Cold Sweat; Corridor of Mirrors; Dr. No; From Russia with Love; Klansman, The; Poppy Is Also a Flower, The; Red Sun; Thunderball; Wait Until Dark; When Wolves Cry
Younger, Ben: Boiler Room
Youngson, Robert: Days of Thrills and Laughter; Golden Age of Comedy, The; MGM's The Big Parade of Comedy; When Comedy Was King
Yu, Ronny: Bride of Chucky; Bride with White Hair, The; China White; Warriors of Virtue
Yuasa, Noriyaki: Gamera the Invincible; Gamera Versus Gaos; Gamera Versus Guiron; Gamera Versus Zigra
Yuen, Corey: Jet Li's the Enforcer; Legend, The; No Retreat, No Surrender; No Retreat, No Surrender II
Yuen, Galen: Riot (1996) (TV Movie)
Yuen, Woo-Ping: Fist of Legend; Iron Monkey
Yuhas, Robert: Infamous Dorothy Parker, The
Yukich, Jim: Double Dragon
Yune, Johnny: They Still Call Me Bruce
Yust, Larry: Homebodies; Say Yes
Yuyama, Kunihiko: Goshogun—The Time Stranger; Pokémon the First Movie: Mewtwo Strikes Back; Pokémon the Movie 2000; Pokémon 3
Yuzna, Brian: Bride of Re-Animator; Dentist, The; H. P. Lovecraft's Necronomicon: Book of the Dead; Progeny; Return of the Living Dead 3; Silent Night, Deadly Night 4—Initiation; Society
Zabalza, José Maria: Fury of the Wolf Man
Zacharias, Alfredo: Bandits; Bees, The; Crossfire; Demonoid
Zacharias, Steve: Revenge of the Nerds IV: Nerds in Love
Zahr, Raja: Revenge of the Nerds IV: Nerds in Love
Zaillian, Steven: Civil Action, A; Searching for Bobby Fischer
Zaks, Jerry: Marvin's Room
Zala, Nancy: Round Numbers
Zaloum, Alain: Canvas; Suspicious Minds
Zambrano, Benito: Solas
Zamm, Alex: Chairman of the Board; My Date with the President's Daughter
Zampi, Mario: Five Golden Hours; Naked Truth (Your Past Is Showing)
Zanke, Susanne: Scorpion Woman, The
Zanuck, Lili Fini: Rush
Zanussi, Krzysztof: Camouflage; Catamount Killing, The; Contract; From a Far Country; Silent Touch, The; Unapproachable, The; Year of the Quiet Sun
Zaorski, Janusz: Baritone

Zaphiratos, Fabrice A.: Bloodbeat
Zappa, Frank: 200 Motels
Zarchi, Meir: Don't Mess with My Sister; I Spit on Your Grave
Zarindast, Tony: Werewolf
Zaslove, Alan: Return of Jafar, The
Zea, Kristi: Women & Men 2
Zeffirelli, Franco: Brother Sun, Sister Moon; Champ, The; Endless Love; Hamlet; Jane Eyre; Jesus of Nazareth; La Traviata; Otello; Romeo and Juliet; Taming of the Shrew, The; Tea with Mussolini
Zeglio, Primo: Mission Stardust; Morgan the Pirate
Zeig, Sandra: Girl, The (1999)
Zeilinger, Jimmy: Little Sister
Zeisler, Alfred: Amazing Adventure
Zeltser, Yuri: Black & White (1998); Eye of the Storm; Playmaker
Zeman, Karel: Baron Munchausen (1961)
Zemeckis, Robert: Amazing Stories (TV Series); Back to the Future; Back to the Future II; Back to the Future III; Cast Away; Contact; Death Becomes Her; Forrest Gump; I Wanna Hold Your Hand; Romancing the Stone; Tales from the Crypt (TV Series); Used Cars; What Lies Beneath; Who Framed Roger Rabbit
Zetlin, Barry: Dogfighters, The
Zetterling, Mai: Hitchhiker, The (Series); Scrubbers
Zhang, Yimou: Ju Dou; Raise the Red Lantern; Red Sorghum; Shanghai Triad; Story of Qiu Ju, The; To Live
Zhelyabuzhsky, Yuri: Cigarette Girl from Mosselprom, The
Zhuangzhuang, Tian: Blue Kite, The; Horse Thief, The
Zidi, Claude: My New Partner
Zieff, Howard: Dream Team, The; Hearts of the West; House Calls; Main Event, The; My Girl; My Girl 2; Private Benjamin; Slither; Unfaithfully Yours
Ziehl, Scott: Broken Vessels; Proximity
Ziehm, Howard: Flesh Gordon; Flesh Gordon 2: Flesh Gordon meets the Cosmic Cheerleaders
Zielinski, Rafal: Babe; Fun; Ginger Ale Afternoon; Jailbait (1992); National Lampoon's Last Resort; Night of the Warrior; Recruits; Screwballs; Spellcaster
Ziller, Paul: Back in Action; Bloodfist IV—Die Trying; Breaking Point; Deadly Surveillance; Ms. Bear; Pledge Night; Probable Cause; Shootfighter 2: Kill or Be Killed; Virtual Seduction
Zimmerman, Vernon: Fade to Black
Zinberg, Michael: Accidental Meeting
Zinnemann, Fred: Behold a Pale Horse; Day of the Jackal, The; Five Days One Summer; From Here to Eternity; High Noon; Julia; Man for All Seasons, A; Member of the Wedding, The; Men, The (1950); Nun's Story, The; Oklahoma!; Search, The; Seventh Cross, The; Sundowners, The
Zinner, Peter: Salamander, The
Zito, Joseph: Abduction; Friday the 13th—The Final Chapter; Invasion U.S.A. (1985); Missing in Action; Prowler, The; Red Scorpion
Zivkovich, Milas: Concealed Weapon
Zlotoff, Lee David: Spitfire Grill, The
Zonca, Erick: Dreamlife of Angels, The
Zondag, Dick: We're Back! A Dinosaur's Story
Zondag, Ralph: Dinosaur; We're Back! A Dinosaur's Story
Zucker, David: Airplane!; Baseketball; Naked Gun, The; Naked Gun 2 1/2, The; Police Squad!; Ruthless People; Top Secret
Zucker, Jerry: Airplane!; First Knight; Ghost (1990); Police Squad!; Rat Race; Ruthless People; Top Secret
Zucker (Massimo Pupillo), Ralph: Terror Creatures from the Grave
Zuckerman, Steve: North Shore Fish
Zuniga, Frank: Fist Fighter; Golden Seal, The; Wilderness Family, Part 2, The
Zurinaga, Marcos: Disappearance of Garcia Lorca, The; Tango Bar
Zurlini, Valerio: Girl with a Suitcase
Zwart, Harald: One Night at McCool's
Zwerin, Charlotte: Gimme Shelter
Zwick, Edward: About Last Night …; Courage Under Fire; Glory; Having It All; Leaving Normal; Legends of the Fall; Siege, The; Special Bulletin
Zwick, Joel: Bosom Buddies (TV Series); Second Sight
Zwicky, Karl: Vicious
Zwigoff, Terry: Crumb; Ghost World

ACADEMY AWARD WINNERS

1927–28

Best Picture:	WINGS
Best Actor:	Emil Jannings, in THE LAST COMMAND and THE WAY OF ALL FLESH
Best Actress:	Janet Gaynor, in SEVENTH HEAVEN, STREET ANGEL, and SUNRISE
Best Director:	Frank Borzage, for SEVENTH HEAVEN

1928–29

Best Picture:	BROADWAY MELODY
Best Actor:	Warner Baxter, in IN OLD ARIZONA
Best Actress:	Mary Pickford, in COQUETTE
Best Director:	Frank Lloyd, for THE DIVINE LADY

1929–30

Best Picture:	ALL QUIET ON THE WESTERN FRONT
Best Actor:	George Arliss, in DISRAELI
Best Actress:	Norma Shearer, in THE DIVORCÉE
Best Director:	Lewis Milestone, for ALL QUIET ON THE WESTERN FRONT

1930–31

Best Picture:	CIMARRON
Best Actor:	Lionel Barrymore, in A FREE SOUL
Best Actress:	Marie Dressler, in MIN AND BILL
Best Director:	Norman Taurog, for SKIPPY

1931–32

Best Picture:	GRAND HOTEL
Best Actor:	Wallace Beery, in THE CHAMP Fredric March, in DR. JEKYLL AND MR. HYDE (tie)
Best Actress:	Helen Hayes, in THE SIN OF MADELON CLAUDET
Best Director:	Frank Borzage, for BAD GIRL

1932–33

Best Picture:	CAVALCADE
Best Actor:	Charles Laughton, in THE PRIVATE LIFE OF HENRY VIII
Best Actress:	Katharine Hepburn, in MORNING GLORY
Best Director:	Frank Lloyd, for CAVALCADE

1934

Best Picture:	IT HAPPENED ONE NIGHT
Best Actor:	Clark Gable, in IT HAPPENED ONE NIGHT
Best Actress:	Claudette Colbert, in IT HAPPENED ONE NIGHT
Best Director:	Frank Capra, for IT HAPPENED ONE NIGHT

1935

Best Picture:	MUTINY ON THE BOUNTY
Best Actor:	Victor McLaglen, in THE INFORMER
Best Actress:	Bette Davis, in DANGEROUS
Best Director:	John Ford, for THE INFORMER

1936

Best Picture: THE GREAT ZIEGFELD
Best Actor: Paul Muni, in THE STORY OF LOUIS PASTEUR
Best Actress: Luise Rainer, in THE GREAT ZIEGFELD
Best Director: Frank Capra, for MR. DEEDS GOES TO TOWN

1937

Best Picture: THE LIFE OF EMILE ZOLA
Best Actor: Spencer Tracy, in CAPTAINS COURAGEOUS
Best Actress: Luise Rainer, in THE GOOD EARTH
Best Director: Leo McCarey, for THE AWFUL TRUTH

1938

Best Picture: YOU CAN'T TAKE IT WITH YOU
Best Actor: Spencer Tracy, in BOYS TOWN
Best Actress: Bette Davis, in JEZEBEL
Best Director: Frank Capra, for YOU CAN'T TAKE IT WITH YOU

1939

Best Picture: GONE WITH THE WIND
Best Actor: Robert Donat, in GOODBYE, MR. CHIPS
Best Actress: Vivien Leigh, in GONE WITH THE WIND
Best Director: Victor Fleming, for GONE WITH THE WIND

1940

Best Picture: REBECCA
Best Actor: James Stewart, in THE PHILADELPHIA STORY
Best Actress: Ginger Rogers, in KITTY FOYLE
Best Director: John Ford, for THE GRAPES OF WRATH

1941

Best Picture: HOW GREEN WAS MY VALLEY
Best Actor: Gary Cooper, in SERGEANT YORK
Best Actress: Joan Fontaine, in SUSPICION
Best Director: John Ford, for HOW GREEN WAS MY VALLEY

1942

Best Picture: MRS. MINIVER
Best Actor: James Cagney, in YANKEE DOODLE DANDY
Best Actress: Greer Garson, in MRS. MINIVER
Best Director: William Wyler, for MRS. MINIVER

1943

Best Picture: CASABLANCA
Best Actor: Paul Lukas, in WATCH ON THE RHINE
Best Actress: Jennifer Jones, in THE SONG OF BERNADETTE
Best Director: Michael Curtiz, for CASABLANCA

1944

Best Picture: GOING MY WAY
Best Actor: Bing Crosby, in GOING MY WAY
Best Actress: Ingrid Bergman, in GASLIGHT
Best Director: Leo McCarey, for GOING MY WAY

1945

Best Picture: THE LOST WEEKEND
Best Actor: Ray Milland, in THE LOST WEEKEND
Best Actress: Joan Crawford, in MILDRED PIERCE
Best Director: Billy Wilder, for THE LOST WEEKEND

1946

Best Picture: THE BEST YEARS OF OUR LIVES
Best Actor: Fredric March, in THE BEST YEARS OF OUR LIVES
Best Actress: Olivia de Havilland, in TO EACH HIS OWN
Best Director: William Wyler, for THE BEST YEARS OF OUR LIVES

1947

Best Picture: GENTLEMAN'S AGREEMENT
Best Actor: Ronald Coleman, in A DOUBLE LIFE
Best Actress: Loretta Young, in THE FARMER'S DAUGHTER
Best Director: Elia Kazan, for GENTLEMAN'S AGREEMENT

1948
Best Picture: HAMLET
Best Actor: Laurence Olivier, in HAMLET
Best Actress: Jane Wyman, in JOHNNY BELINDA
Best Director: John Huston, for TREASURE OF THE SIERRA MADRE

1949
Best Picture: ALL THE KING'S MEN
Best Actor: Broderick Crawford, in ALL THE KING'S MEN
Best Actress: Olivia de Havilland, in THE HEIRESS
Best Director: Joseph L. Mankiewicz, for A LETTER TO THREE WIVES

1950
Best Picture: ALL ABOUT EVE
Best Actor: José Ferrer, in CYRANO DE BERGERAC
Best Actress: Judy Holliday, in BORN YESTERDAY
Best Director: Joseph L. Mankiewicz, for ALL ABOUT EVE

1951
Best Picture: AN AMERICAN IN PARIS
Best Actor: Humphrey Bogart, in THE AFRICAN QUEEN
Best Actress: Vivien Leigh, in A STREETCAR NAMED DESIRE
Best Director: George Stevens, for A PLACE IN THE SUN

1952
Best Picture: THE GREATEST SHOW ON EARTH
Best Actor: Gary Cooper, in HIGH NOON
Best Actress: Shirley Booth, in COME BACK, LITTLE SHEBA
Best Director: John Ford, for THE QUIET MAN

1953
Best Picture: FROM HERE TO ETERNITY
Best Actor: William Holden, in STALAG 17
Best Actress: Audrey Hepburn, in ROMAN HOLIDAY
Best Director: Fred Zinnemann, for FROM HERE TO ETERNITY

1954
Best Picture: ON THE WATERFRONT
Best Actor: Marlon Brando, in ON THE WATERFRONT
Best Actress: Grace Kelly, in THE COUNTRY GIRL
Best Director: Elia Kazan, for ON THE WATERFRONT

1955
Best Picture: MARTY
Best Actor: Ernest Borgnine, in MARTY
Best Actress: Anna Magnani, in THE ROSE TATTOO
Best Director: Delbert Mann, for MARTY

1956
Best Picture: AROUND THE WORLD IN 80 DAYS
Best Actor: Yul Brynner, in THE KING AND I
Best Actress: Ingrid Bergman, in ANASTASIA
Best Director: George Stevens, for GIANT

1957
Best Picture: THE BRIDGE ON THE RIVER KWAI
Best Actor: Alec Guinness, in THE BRIDGE ON THE RIVER KWAI
Best Actress: Joanne Woodward, in THE THREE FACES OF EVE
Best Director: David Lean, for THE BRIDGE ON THE RIVER KWAI

1958
Best Picture: GIGI
Best Actor: David Niven, in SEPARATE TABLES
Best Actress: Susan Hayward, in I WANT TO LIVE!
Best Director: Vincente Minnelli, for GIGI

1959
Best Picture: BEN-HUR
Best Actor: Charlton Heston, in BEN-HUR
Best Actress: Simone Signoret, in ROOM AT THE TOP
Best Director: William Wyler, for BEN-HUR

1960

Best Picture:	THE APARTMENT
Best Actor:	Burt Lancaster, in ELMER GANTRY
Best Actress:	Elizabeth Taylor, in BUTTERFIELD 8
Best Director:	Billy Wilder, for THE APARTMENT

1961

Best Picture:	WEST SIDE STORY
Best Actor:	Maximilian Schell, in JUDGMENT AT NUREMBERG
Best Actress:	Sophia Loren, in TWO WOMEN
Best Director:	Robert Wise and Jerome Robbins, for WEST SIDE STORY

1962

Best Picture:	LAWRENCE OF ARABIA
Best Actor:	Gregory Peck, in TO KILL A MOCKINGBIRD
Best Actress:	Anne Bancroft, in THE MIRACLE WORKER
Best Director:	David Lean, for LAWRENCE OF ARABIA

1963

Best Picture:	TOM JONES
Best Actor:	Sidney Poitier, in LILIES OF THE FIELD
Best Actress:	Patricia Neal, in HUD
Best Director:	Tony Richardson, for TOM JONES

1964

Best Picture:	MY FAIR LADY
Best Actor:	Rex Harrison, in MY FAIR LADY
Best Actress:	Julie Andrews, in MARY POPPINS
Best Director:	George Cukor, for MY FAIR LADY

1965

Best Picture:	THE SOUND OF MUSIC
Best Actor:	Lee Marvin, in CAT BALLOU
Best Actress:	Julie Christie, in DARLING
Best Director:	Robert Wise, for THE SOUND OF MUSIC

1966

Best Picture:	A MAN FOR ALL SEASONS
Best Actor:	Paul Scofield, in A MAN FOR ALL SEASONS
Best Actress:	Elizabeth Taylor, in WHO'S AFRAID OF VIRGINIA WOOLF?
Best Director:	Fred Zinnemann, for A MAN FOR ALL SEASONS

1967

Best Picture:	IN THE HEAT OF THE NIGHT
Best Actor:	Rod Steiger, in IN THE HEAT OF THE NIGHT
Best Actress:	Katharine Hepburn, in GUESS WHO'S COMING TO DINNER
Best Director:	Mike Nichols, for THE GRADUATE

1968

Best Picture:	OLIVER!
Best Actor:	Cliff Robertson, in CHARLY
Best Actress:	Katharine Hepburn, in THE LION IN WINTER Barbra Streisand, in FUNNY GIRL (tie)
Best Director:	Carol Reed, for OLIVER!

1969

Best Picture:	MIDNIGHT COWBOY
Best Actor:	John Wayne, in TRUE GRIT
Best Actress:	Maggie Smith, in THE PRIME OF MISS JEAN BRODIE
Best Director:	John Schlesinger, for MIDNIGHT COWBOY

1970

Best Picture:	PATTON
Best Actor:	George C. Scott, in PATTON
Best Actress:	Glenda Jackson, in WOMEN IN LOVE
Best Director:	Franklin J. Schaffner, for PATTON

1971

Best Picture:	THE FRENCH CONNECTION
Best Actor:	Gene Hackman, in THE FRENCH CONNECTION
Best Actress:	Jane Fonda, in KLUTE
Best Director:	William Friedkin, for THE FRENCH CONNECTION

1972

Best Picture: THE GODFATHER
Best Actor: Marlon Brando, in THE GODFATHER
Best Actress: Liza Minnelli, in CABARET
Best Director: Bob Fosse, for CABARET

1973

Best Picture: THE STING
Best Actor: Jack Lemmon, in SAVE THE TIGER
Best Actress: Glenda Jackson, in A TOUCH OF CLASS
Best Director: George Roy Hill, for THE STING

1974

Best Picture: THE GODFATHER, PART II
Best Actor: Art Carney, in HARRY AND TONTO
Best Actress: Ellen Burstyn, in ALICE DOESN'T LIVE HERE ANYMORE
Best Director: Francis Ford Coppola, for THE GODFATHER, PART II

1975

Best Picture: ONE FLEW OVER THE CUCKOO'S NEST
Best Actor: Jack Nicholson, in ONE FLEW OVER THE CUCKOO'S NEST
Best Actress: Louise Fletcher, in ONE FLEW OVER THE CUCKOO'S NEST
Best Director: Milos Forman, for ONE FLEW OVER THE CUCKOO'S NEST

1976

Best Picture: ROCKY
Best Actor: Peter Finch, in NETWORK
Best Actress: Faye Dunaway, in NETWORK
Best Director: John G. Avildsen, for ROCKY

1977

Best Picture: ANNIE HALL
Best Actor: Richard Dreyfuss, in THE GOODBYE GIRL
Best Actress: Diane Keaton, in ANNIE HALL
Best Director: Woody Allen, for ANNIE HALL

1978

Best Picture: THE DEER HUNTER
Best Actor: Jon Voight, in COMING HOME
Best Actress: Jane Fonda, in COMING HOME
Best Director: Michael Cimino, for THE DEER HUNTER

1979

Best Picture: KRAMER VS. KRAMER
Best Actor: Dustin Hoffman, in KRAMER VS. KRAMER
Best Actress: Sally Field, in NORMA RAE
Best Director: Robert Benton, for KRAMER VS. KRAMER

1980

Best Picture: ORDINARY PEOPLE
Best Actor: Robert De Niro, in RAGING BULL
Best Actress: Sissy Spacek, in COAL MINER'S DAUGHTER
Best Director: Robert Redford, for ORDINARY PEOPLE

1981

Best Picture: CHARIOTS OF FIRE
Best Actor: Henry Fonda, in ON GOLDEN POND
Best Actress: Katharine Hepburn, in ON GOLDEN POND
Best Director: Warren Beatty, for REDS

1982

Best Picture: GANDHI
Best Actor: Ben Kingsley, in GANDHI
Best Actress: Meryl Streep, in SOPHIE'S CHOICE
Best Director: Richard Attenborough, for GANDHI

1983

Best Picture: TERMS OF ENDEARMENT
Best Actor: Robert Duvall, in TENDER MERCIES
Best Actress: Shirley MacLaine, in TERMS OF ENDEARMENT
Best Director: James L. Brooks, for TERMS OF ENDEARMENT

1984

Best Picture: AMADEUS
Best Actor: F. Murray Abraham, in AMADEUS
Best Actress: Sally Field, in PLACES IN THE HEART
Best Director: Milos Forman, for AMADEUS

1985

Best Picture: OUT OF AFRICA
Best Actor: William Hurt, in KISS OF THE SPIDER WOMAN
Best Actress: Geraldine Page, in THE TRIP TO BOUNTIFUL
Best Director: Sydney Pollack, for OUT OF AFRICA

1986

Best Picture: PLATOON
Best Actor: Paul Newman, in THE COLOR OF MONEY
Best Actress: Marlee Matlin, in CHILDREN OF A LESSER GOD
Best Director: Oliver Stone, for PLATOON

1987

Best Picture: THE LAST EMPEROR
Best Actor: Michael Douglas, in WALL STREEET
Best Actress: Cher, in MOONSTRUCK
Best Director: Bernardo Bertolucci, for THE LAST EMPEROR

1988

Best Picture: RAIN MAN
Best Actor: Dustin Hoffman, in RAIN MAN
Best Actress: Jodie Foster, in THE ACCUSED
Best Director: Barry Levinson, for RAIN MAN

1989

Best Picture: DRIVING MISS DAISY
Best Actor: Daniel Day-Lewis, in MY LEFT FOOT
Best Actress: Jessica Tandy, in DRIVING MISS DAISY
Best Director: Oliver Stone, for BORN ON THE FOURTH OF JULY

1990

Best Picture: DANCES WITH WOLVES
Best Actor: Jeremy Irons, in REVERSAL OF FORTUNE
Best Actress: Kathy Bates, in MISERY
Best Director: Kevin Costner, for DANCES WITH WOLVES

1991

Best Picture: THE SILENCE OF THE LAMBS
Best Actor: Anthony Hopkins, in THE SILENCE OF THE LAMBS
Best Actress: Jodie Foster, in THE SILENCE OF THE LAMBS
Best Director: Jonathan Demme, for THE SILENCE OF THE LAMBS

1992

Best Picture: UNFORGIVEN
Best Actor: Al Pacino, in SCENT OF A WOMAN
Best Actress: Emma Thompson, in HOWARD'S END
Best Director: Clint Eastwood, for UNFORGIVEN

1993

Best Picture: SCHINDLER'S LIST
Best Actor: Tom Hanks, in PHILADELPHIA
Best Actress: Holly Hunter, in THE PIANO
Best Director: Steven Spielberg, for SCHINDLER'S LIST

1994

Best Picture: FORREST GUMP
Best Actor: Tom Hanks, in FORREST GUMP
Best Actress: Jessica Lange, in BLUE SKY
Best Director: Robert Zemeckis, for FORREST GUMP

1995

Best Picture: BRAVEHEART
Best Actor: Nicolas Cage, in LEAVING LAS VEGAS
Best Actress: Susan Sarandon, in DEAD MAN WALKING
Best Director: Mel Gibson, for BRAVEHEART

1996

Best Picture: THE ENGLISH PATIENT
Best Actor: Geoffrey Rush, in SHINE
Best Actress: Frances McDormand, in FARGO
Best Director: Anthony Minghella, for THE ENGLISH PATIENT

1997

Best Picture: TITANIC
Best Actor: Jack Nicholson, in AS GOOD AS IT GETS
Best Actress: Helen Hunt, in AS GOOD AS IT GETS
Best Director: James Cameron, for TITANIC

1998

Best Picture: SHAKESPEARE IN LOVE
Best Actor: Roberto Benigni, in LIFE IS BEAUTIFUL
Best Actress: Gwyneth Paltrow, in SHAKESPEARE IN LOVE
Best Director: Steven Spielberg, for SAVING PRIVATE RYAN

1999

Best Picture: AMERICAN BEAUTY
Best Actor: Kevin Spacey, in AMERICAN BEAUTY
Best Actress: Hilary Swank, in BOYS DON'T CRY
Best Director: Sam Mendes, for AMERICAN BEAUTY

2000

Best Picture: GLADIATOR
Best Actor: Russell Crowe, in GLADIATOR
Best Actress: Julia Roberts, in ERIN BROCKOVICH
Best Director: Steven Soderbergh, for TRAFFIC

2001

Best Picture: A BEAUTIFUL MIND
Best Actor: Denzel Washington, in TRAINING DAY
Best Actress: Halle Berry, in MONSTER'S BALL
Best Director: Ron Howard, for A BEAUTIFUL MIND

COMPLETE ALTERNATE TITLES LIST

Addict, see *Born to Win*
Adventures of Batman and Robin, see *Batman and Robin*
Akaza, God of Vengeance, see *Crash (1977)*
Alien Terror, see *Sinister Invasion*
Alien Thunder, see *Dan Candy's Law*
Alistair Maclean's Nightwatch, see *Detonator II*
All Forgotten, see *Lover's Prayer*
All the Mornings of the World, see *Tous les Matins du Monde*
All You Need Is Cash, see *Rutles, The*
American Woman, see *Closer You Get, The*
Asphyx, The, see *Spirit of the Dead*
Assault Force, see *ffolkes*
Babes in Toyland (1934), see *March of the Wooden Soldiers*
Bad, see *Andy Warhol's Bad*
Bandera Bandits, see *Sonny and Jed*
Barn of the Naked Dead, see *Nightmare Circus*
Baron Blood, see *Torture Chamber of Baron Blood, The*
Battle of the River Plate, The, see *Pursuit of the Graf Spee*
Battling Hoofer, see *Something to Sing About*
Bay Coven, see *Eye of the Demon*
Bay of Blood, see *Twitch of the Death Nerve*
Beethoven (1937), see *Abel Gance's Beethoven*
Bela Lugosi Meets a Brooklyn Gorilla, see *Boys from Brooklyn, The*
Bells, see *Murder by Phone*
Below Utopia, see *Body Count* (1997, direct to video)
Beware! The Blob, see *Son of Blob*
Beyond, The, see *Seven Doors of Death*
Beyond Forgiveness, see *Blood of the Innocent*
Beyond the Darkness, see *Buried Alive (1979)*
Big Grab, The, see *Melodie en Sous-sol*
Black Magic Mansion, see *Cthulhu Mansion, The*
Blond Gorilla, see *White Pongo*
Blood In, Blood Out, see *Bound by Honor*
Blood Island, see *The Shuttered Room*
Blood Money, see *Clinton and Nadine*
Blood of Fu Manchu, see *Against All Odds (1968)*
Body Bags, see *John Carpenter's Body Bags*
Born to the West, see *Hell Town*
Brain Dead, see *Dead Alive*
Brain Machine, The, see *Grey Matter*
Brides of Blood, see *Brides of the Beast*
Bronco Busters, see *Gone with the West*
Brute, The, see *El Bruto*
Bud the C.H.U.D., see *C.H.U.D. II*
Bullshot Crummond, see *Bullshot*
By Rocket to the Moon, see *Woman in the Moon*
Call Him Mr. Shatter, see *Shatter*
Call It Murder, see *Midnight (1934)*
Carmen, see *Bizet's Carmen*
Carnage, see *Twitch of the Death Nerve*
Cars That Ate Paris, see *Cars That Eat People*
Casebook of Sherlock Holmes, see *Adventures of Sherlock Holmes, The (Series)*
Castle of Terror, see *Castle of Blood*
Castle of the Walking Dead, see *Torture Chamber of Dr. Sadism*
Cemetery Man, see *Dellamorte, Dellamore*
Challenge of McKenna, see *Badlands Drifter*
Chasing Beauties, see *Loving Jezebel*
China 9, Liberty 7, see *Gunfire*
Chincero, see *Last Movie, The*
Christmas Tree, The, see *When Wolves Cry*
Christmas Vacation, see *National Lampoon's Christmas Vacation*
City in Fear (1972), see *A Place Called Today*
City of the Living Dead, see *Gates of Hell*
Clairvoyant, The, see *Evil Mind, The*
Class of '86, see *National Lampoon's Class of '86*
Class Reunion, see *National Lampoon's Class Reunion*
Cold Cuts, see *Buffet Froid*
Collision Course, see *Bamboo Saucer*
Colony Mutation, see *Colony (1996)*
Communion, see *Alice, Sweet Alice*
Confidential Report, see *Mr. Arkadin*
Conspiracy, The, see *Le Complot*
Coup de Torchon, see *Clean Slate*
Creature Wasn't Nice, The, see *Spaceship*
Creature's Revenge, The, see *Brain of Blood*
Creeping Unknown, The, see *Quatermass Experiment, The*
Cries in the Night, see *Funeral Home*
Crimes in the Wax Museum, see *Nightmare in Wax*
Criminal, The, see *Concrete Jungle*
Crimson Cult, The, see *Curse of the Crimson Altar*
Crisis in the Kremlin: The Last Days of the Soviet Union, see *Assassination Game, The*
Crossroads of Destiny, see *Macon County Jail*
Cuba Crossing, see *Kill Castro*
Cuban Rebel Girls, see *Assault of the Rebel Girls*
Daddy's Deadly Darling, see *Pigs*
Dark Eyes of London, see *Human Monster, The*
Day of Anger, see *Days of Wrath*
Daybreak (1939), see *Le Jour Se Leve*
Dead Babies, see *Mood Swingers*
Dead Kids, see *Strange Behavior*
Death Corps, see *Shock Waves*
Death Ride, see *Crash (1977)*
Deathline, see *Raw Meat*
Der Golem, Wie er in Die Welt Kam, see *Golem, The (How He Came into the World)*
Der Todesking, see *The Death King*
Destination Saturn, see *Buck Rogers: Destination Saturn*
Detonator, see *Death Train*
Detroit Heat, see *Detroit 9000*
Devil's Daughter, see *The Sect*
Devil's Envoy, The, see *Les Visiteurs du Soir*
Dirty Outlaws, The, see *Big Rip-Off, The*
Dr. Terror's Gallery of Terrors, see *Bloodsuckers, The*
Don't Open the Door, see *Friday the 13th: The Orphan*
Don't Turn the Other Cheek, see *Long Live Your Death*
Dracula's Dog, see *Zolton—Hound of Dracula*
Du Skal Here Din Hustro, see *Master of the House*
Dynasty of Fear, see *Fear in the Night*
Eaten Alive by Cannibals, see *Emerald Jungle*
Emanuelle and the Last Cannibals, see *Trap Them and Kill Them*
Eu Te Amo, see *I Love You*
European Vacation, see *National Lampoon's European Vacation*
Even More Ripping Yarns, see *Ripping Yarns*
Exorcism and Black Masses, see *Demoniac*
Eyes of Dr. Chaney, The, see *Mansion of the Doomed*
Eyes of Evil, see *Thousand Eyes of Dr. Mabuse, The*
Falstaff, see *Chimes at Midnight*
Fear, The, see *Gates of Hell*
Fear in the City of the Living Dead, see *Gates of Hell*
Fighter, The, see *Savate*

Final Programme, The, see *Last Days of Man on Earth, The*
Floating Weeds, see *Drifting Weeds*
Folks at the Red Wolf Inn, The, see *Terror at the Red Wolf Inn*
Forbidden Subjects, see *Kinjite*
Forever Lulu, see *Along for the Ride*
Fra Diavalo, see *Devil's Brother, The*
Frankenstein '88, see *Vindicator, The*
Frantic (1957), see *Elevator to the Gallows*
Frasier the Sensitive Lion, see *Frasier the Lovable Lion*
Friday Night Date, A, see *Road Rage*
Fruit Machine, The, see *Wonderland*
Gallery of Horrors, see *Bloodsuckers, The*
Gamera, see *Gamera the Invincible*
Gamma 693, see *Night of the Zombies*
Gird City, see *And Nothing But the Truth*
Girl in the Moon, see *Woman in the Moon*
Go Figure, see *Va Savoir*
God Told Me To, see *Demon*
Good Day to Die, A, see *Children of the Dust*
Graduation, The, see *The Prowler*
Greta the Mad Butcher, Ilsa—Absolute Power, see *Ilsa the Wicked Warden*
Hangover, The, see *Female Jungle*
Hannah, Queen of Vampires, see *Crypt of the Living Dead*
Harvest, see *Cash Crop*
Haunted Symphony, see *Blood Song*
Head over Heels, see *A Coeur Joie*
Heads I Kill You . . . Tails You're Dead!, see *Guns for Dollars*
Hellfire, see *Blood Song*
Here Come the Tigers, see *Manny's Orphans*
Hollow Triumph, see *The Scar*
Holy Terror, see *Alice, Sweet Alice*
Horror Castle, see *Virgin of Nuremburg*
House of Evil, see *Macabre Serenade*
House of the Damned, see *Spectre*
House of the Dark Stairway, see *A Blade in the Dark*
Hungry Pets, see *Please Don't Eat My Mother*
Hungry Wives, see *Season of the Witch*
I Hate Your Guts, see *The Intruder*
I Love You All, see *Je Vous Aime*
Il Postino, see *Postman, The (1994)*
In the Bleak Midwinter, see *Midwinter's Tale, A*
In the Light of the Moon, see *Ecl Gein*
Incredible Invasion, see *Sinister Invasion*
Incredible Torture Show, The, see *Bloodsucking Freaks*
Invasion Force, see *Hangar 18*
It Can Be Done, Amigo, see *Saddle Tramps*
It Lives by Night, see *Bat People*
It Runs in the Family, see *My Summer Story*
Jailbird's Vacation, see *Les Grandes Gueules*
Joe Palooka, see *Palooka*
Joy of Knowledge, see *Le Gai Savoir*
Just Another Pretty Face, see *Sois Belle Et Tais-Toi*
Kill, Baby, Kill, see *Curse of the Living Dead*
Killing Beach, see *Turtle Beach*
King of the City, see *Club Life*
King of the Witches, see *Simon, King of the Witches*
Kirlian Witness, The, see *Plants Are Watching, The*
Kiss and Kill, see *Against All Odds (1968)*
Kiss of the Beast, see *Meridian*
Knockout, The, see *Dough & Dynamite*
Krocodylus, see *Blood Surf*
L'Addition, see *Caged Heart*
L'Amour Violé, see *Rape of Love*
La Bonne Année, see *Happy New Year*
La Decade Prodigieuse, see *Ten Days Wonder*
Last Elephant, The, see *Ivory Hunters*
Last Patrol, The, see *Last Warrior, The*
Last Survivor, The, see *Cannibal*
Law Breakers, see *Assassins de L'Ordre, Les*
Le Chat, see *Cat, The*
Le Dernier Combat, see *Final Combat, The*
Le Distrait, see *Daydreamer, The*
Legend of Blood Castle, The, see *Blood Castle*
Legend of the Seven Golden Vampires, The, see *Seven Brothers Meet Dracula, The*
Legendary Curse of Lemora, see *Lemora: Lady Dracula*
Lemora: A Child's Tale of the Supernatural, see *Lemora: Lady Dracula*
Leon, see *Professional, The*
Les Vampires, see *Vampires, The*
Line of Fire, see *Swap, The (Sam's Song)*
Los Zancos, see *Stilts, The*
Loves of Irina, see *Erotikill*
Macabro, see *Frozen Terror*
Mad Mission, see *Aces Go Places*
Maddest Story Ever Told, The, see *Spider Baby*
Mafu Cage, see *My Sister, My Love*
Malice in Wonderland, see *Rumor Mill, The*
Maneaters!, see *Shark!*
Margaret Bourke White, see *Double Exposure*
Marijuana, see *Assassin of Youth*
Marquis De Sade, see *Dark Prince: The Intimate Tales of Marquis De Sade*
Matt Riker, see *Mutant Hunt*
Medical Deviate, see *Dr. Butcher, MD*
Memed My Hawk, see *Lion and the Hawk, The*
Men with Steel Faces & Phantom Empire, see *Radio Ranch*
Mercenaries (1978), see *Kill Castro*
Mercenaries, The (1968), see *Dark of the Sun*
Mexican Bus Ride, see *Ascent to Heaven*
Michael Angel, see *Apostate, The*
Mind Warp, see *Grey Matter*
Missing in Action III, see *Braddock: Missing in Action III*
Mohammed, Messenger of God, see *Message, The*
Monkey in Winter, see *Un Singe en Hiver*
Monster Mash, see *Frankenstein Sings*
More Ripping Yarns, see *Ripping Yarns*
Murder at the Baskervilles, see *Silver Blaze*
Murder by the Book, see *Columbo: Murder by the Book*
Mutations, see *Freakmaker*
My Favorite Season, see *Ma Saison Préferée*
My Son, the Vampire, see *Vampire over London*
Naked Space, see *Spaceship*
National Lampoon's Animal House, see *Animal House*
Necromancy, see *Witching, The*
Night Train, see *Night Train to Munich*
No Habrá Más Penas Ni Olvido, see *Funny, Dirty Little War*
North Sea Hijack, see *ffolkes*
Northwest Frontier, see *Flame Over India*
No-Tell Hotel, The, see *Rosebud Beach Hotel, The*
Old Mother Riley Meets the Vampire, see *Vampire over London*
One by One, see *The Majorettes*
Orphan, The, see *Friday the 13th: The Orphan*
Outcry, The, see *Il Grido*
Paroles et Musique, see *Love Songs*
Party, Inc., see *Party Girls*
Passion of Beatrice, The, see *Beatrice*
Passionate Thief, see *Laugh for Joy*
Payment in Blood, see *Final Defeat, The*
P. C. H., see *Kill Shot*
Perils from Planet Mongo, see *Flash Gordon: Rocketship*
Phantom Tollbooth, The, see *Adventures of Milo in the Phantom Tollbooth, The*

Pick a Star, see *Movie Struck*
Piece of Pleasure, see *Une Partie de Plaisir*
Place Called Today, see *City in Fear*
Planet Outlaws, see *Buck Rogers: Destination Saturn*
Portrait of a Woman, Nude, see *Nudo di Donna*
Potop, see *Deluge, The*
Prague Duet, see *Lies & Whispers*
Pranks, see *Dorm That Dripped Blood, The*
Private Wore Skirts, The, see *Never Wave at a WAC*
Proud Ones, The, see *Horse of Pride, The*
Psycho Circus, see *Circus of Fear*
Quatermass II: Enemy from Space, see *Enemy from Space*
Queen of Blood, see *Planet of Blood*
Raven, The (1943), see *Le Corbeau*
Reader, The, see *La Lectrice*
Reason to Live . . . Reason to Die, A, see *Massacre at Fort Holman*
Red River Valley, see *Man of the Frontier*
Return from the Past, see *Bloodsuckers, The*
Return of Maxwell Smart, The, see *Nude Bomb, The*
Revenge of the Zombie, see *Kiss Daddy Goodbye*
Revolutions Per Minute, see *R.P.M.*
Rhodes, see *Rhodes of Africa*
Ripper, see *Fear City*
Ripper of Notre Dame, see *Demoniac*
Rise of Catherine the Great, The, see *Catherine the Great*
Rocket to the Moon, see *Cat Women of the Moon*
Rocky Mountain Mystery, see *Fighting Westerner, The*
Rouge Baiser, see *Red Kiss*
St. Martin's Lane, see *Sidewalks of London*
Sandstorm, see *Sand*
Scandal Man, see *L'Odeur des Fauves*
Scarface Mob, The, see *Untouchables: Scarface Mob*
Scream and Die, see *House That Vanished, The*
Scream of the Demon Lover, see *Blood Castle*
Secret Adversary, see *Partners in Crime*
Secret Life of Ian Fleming, The, see *Spymaker: The Secret Life of Ian Fleming*
Secret of Dorian Gray, The, see *Dorian Gray*
Sensuous Vampires, see *Vampire Hookers*
Seven Notes in Black, see *The Psychic*
Shame (1961), see *Intruder, The*
She Was a Hippy Vampire, see *Wild World of Batwoman, The*
Shocked, see *Mesmerized*
Smuggler, The, see *Contraband*
Sophie's Place, see *Crooks and Coronets*
Space Zombies, see *Astro Zombies*
Spaceship to the Unknown, see *Flash Gordon: Rocketship*
Spider Woman, see *Sherlock Holmes and the Spider Woman*
Spirit of Tattoo, see *Irezumi*
Spotswood, see *Efficiency Expert, The*
Star Quest, see *Beyond the Rising Moon*
Stowaway to the Stars, see *Voyage en Ballon*
Suicide Squadron, see *Dangerous Moonlight*
Sullivans, The, see *Fighting Sullivans, The*
Survival Run (1977), see *Damnation Alley*
Survival Run (1979), see *Soldier of Orange*
Sweet, Violent Tony, see *Kill Castro*
Sword and the Rose, The, see *Flesh and Blood*
Taste for Flesh and Blood, A, see *Invasion for Flesh and Blood*
Taxi to the Toilet, see *Taxi Zum Klo*
Teenage Monster, see *Meteor Monster*
Ten Days That Shook the World, see *October*
Tenebrae, see *Unsane*
Tepepa, see *Blood and Guns*
Terror Circus, see *Nightmare Circus*
Terror House, see *Terror at the Red Wolf Inn*
Terror of Dr. Hichcock, The, see *Horrible Dr. Hichcock, The*
They Call Me Hallelujah, see *Guns for Dollars*
They Watch, see *They*
Thief and the Cobbler, The, see *Arabian Knight*
Things in Life, The, see *Les Choses de la Vie*
This Strange Passion, see *El*
Thrill Seeker, see *Time Shifters*
Ticks, see *Infested*
Time Warp, see *Journey to the Center of Time*
Top of the Food Chain, see *Invasion*
Trout, The, see *La Truite*
Twilight of the Dead, see *Gates of Hell*
Under Earth, see *Debajo del Mundo*
Underworld, see *Transmutations*
Unfinished Piece for a Mechanical Piano, An, see *Unfinished Piece for the Player Piano*
Utopia, see *Atoll K*
Vacation, see *National Lampoon's Vacation*
Valley Obscured by Clouds, see *Valley, The*
Vampire Men of the Lost Planet, see *Horror of the Blood Monsters*
Vampires, The, see *Goliath and the Vampires*
Vengeful Dead, The, see *Kiss Daddy Goodbye*
Vig, see *Money Kings*
Viking Women and the Sea Serpent, The, see *Saga of the Viking Women and Their Voyage to the Waters of the Great Sea Serpent, The*
Viktor Vogel, see *Advertising Rules*
Vivid, see *Luscious*
Waiting Woman, see *Secrets of Women*
Walking Tall: The Final Chapter, see *Final Chapter—Walking Tall*
Warriors Rest, see *Le Repos du Guerrier*
Way Ahead, The, see *Immortal Battalion, The*
Welcome to Oblivion, see *Ultrawarrior*
Werewolf Versus the Vampire Woman, The, see *Blood Moon*
Whiskey Galore, see *Tight Little Island*
Whispering Shadow, The, see *Warning Shadows*
White Paws, see *Pattes Blanches*
Who Knows?, see *Va Savoir*
Will You Dance with Me?, see *Voulez Vous Danser avec Moi?*
Wishmaster, see *Wes Craven's Wishmaster*
Witchfinder General, see *Conquerer Worm, The*
Wounded Man, The, see *L'Homme Blessé*
Y2K, see *Terminal Countdown*
Young Emmanuelle, A, see *Nea*
Your Past Is Showing, see *Naked Truth*
Zombie Holocaust, see *Dr. Butcher, MD*

BARRON'S

PSAT/NMSQT*

16TH EDITION

Sharon Weiner Green, M.A.
Former Instructor in English
Merritt College
Oakland, California

Ira K. Wolf, Ph.D.
President, PowerPrep, Inc.
Former High School Teacher, College Professor,
and University Director of Teacher Preparation

BARRON'S

ABOUT THE AUTHORS

Sharon Green started helping prepare students for the PSAT and SAT as a 13-year-old assistant at her father's college entrance tutoring course; she has never stopped since. A National Merit Scholar, she holds degrees from Harvard College, New York University School of Education, and the University of California at Berkeley. Her test preparation books, all published by Barron's, run the gamut from the California High School Proficiency Examination to the GRE. Whenever she can dig her way out from under multiple dictionaries, Sharon enjoys folk dancing, reading Jane Austen and science fiction, and watching Little League baseball.

Dr. Ira Wolf, who earned his bachelor's, master's, and doctoral degrees at Tufts, Yale, and Rutgers, respectively, has had a long career in math education. In addition to teaching math at the high school level for several years, he was a professor of mathematics at Brooklyn College and the Director of the Mathematics Teacher Preparation program at SUNY Stony Brook.

Dr. Wolf has been helping students prepare for the PSAT, SAT, ACT, and SAT Subject Tests in Math for more than 35 years. He is the founder and president of PowerPrep, Inc., a test preparation company on Long Island that currently works with more than 1,000 high school students each year.

All inquiries should be addressed to:
Barron's Educational Series, Inc.
250 Wireless Boulevard
Hauppauge, NY 11788
www.barronseduc.com

International Standard Serial No.: 1941-7055 (print with CD-ROM)

ISBN: 978-0-7641-4795-1 (book)
ISBN: 978-1-4380-7167-1 (book/CD-ROM package)

PRINTED IN THE UNITED STATES OF AMERICA
9 8 7 6 5 4 3 2 1

Contents

Preface

Welcome to the sixteenth edition of *Barron's PSAT/NMSQT*. If you are preparing for the PSAT, this is the book you need.

This sixteenth edition updates America's leading book focused on the PSAT. Along with the best of the time-tested features of earlier editions, today's sixteenth edition provides much, much more.

- It clears up misconceptions you may have about the test—although there's a Writing Skills section, you *don't* have to write an essay!—and gives you a brief rundown of the entire test.
- It features four full-length sample tests modeled on the PSAT in length and difficulty, four crucial "dress rehearsals" for the day you walk into the examination room. If you purchased this book with a CD-ROM, you have two additional tests for practice.
- It prepares you for the Writing Skills section, teaching you how to spot errors and polish rough drafts so that you can shine on the PSAT and eventually on the SAT.
- It briefs you on vocabulary-in-context and reading comprehension questions, giving you key tips on how to tackle these important verbal question types.
- It takes you step by step through the double reading passages, showing you how to work your way through a pair of reading passages without wasting effort or time.
- It introduces you to the non-multiple-choice questions in the Mathematics section, teaching you shortcuts to solving problems and entering your own answers on a sample grid.
- It offers you advice on how (and when) to use a calculator in dealing with both multiple-choice and "grid-in" questions.
- It contains a separate chapter that reviews every math topic you need to know.
- It gives you the 300-word PSAT High-Frequency Word List, 300 vital words that have been shown by computer analysis to occur and reoccur on actual published PSATs, plus Barron's PSAT Basic Word List, more than 1,300 words that you'll want to master as you work to build a college-level vocabulary. (For quick review, you can consult the list of Basic Word Parts.)

Most important, it teaches you the special tactics and strategies essential for scoring high on the PSAT.

No other book tells you as much about the test. No other book offers you as many questions modeled on the PSAT.

The PSAT is your chance to get yourself set for the all-important SAT. It's also your chance to qualify for some of the nation's most prestigious college scholarships. Go for your personal best; take the time to learn how to prepare for the PSAT.

This sixteenth edition of *Barron's PSAT/NMSQT* is evidence of Barron's ongoing commitment to make this publication America's outstanding PSAT study guide.

PSAT/NMSQT Test Format

Section 1 Critical Reading 8 sentence completions 4 short-paragraph reading comprehension 12 long-passage reading comprehension	25 minutes	24 questions
1-MINUTE BREAK		
Section 2 Math 20 multiple-choice	25 minutes	20 questions
1-MINUTE BREAK		
Section 3 Critical Reading 5 sentence completions 4 short-paragraph reading comprehension 15 long-passage reading comprehension	25 minutes	24 questions
5-MINUTE BREAK		
Section 4 Mathematics 8 multiple-choice 10 student-produced response (grid-in)	25 minutes	18 questions
1-MINUTE BREAK		
Section 5 Writing Skills 20 improving sentences 14 identifying sentence errors 5 improving paragraphs	30 minutes	39 questions

Acknowledgments

The authors gratefully acknowledge all those sources who granted permission to use materials from their publications:

Pages 14–15, 126–127: From *Summer of '49* by David Halberstam, © 1989 by David Halberstam. Reprinted by permission of HarperCollins Publishers Inc.

Pages 15, 127: From *Take Time for Paradise,* © 1989 by the Estate of A. Bartlett Giamatti.

Page 35: From *Life Nature Library: The Forest* by Peter Farb and the editors of Time-Life Books, © Time-Life Books Inc., pp. 75–76.

Pages 36–37: From "Introduction" from *Bury My Heart at Wounded Knee: An Indian History of the American West* by Dee Brown, Copyright © 1970 by Dee Brown. Reprinted by arrangement with Henry Holt & Co., LLC.

Page 44: From *Modern Dancer's Primer for Action,* by Martha Graham, © 1941 by PUP. Reprinted by permission of Princeton University Press.

Pages 44–45: From *Chez Panisse Menu Cookbook* by Alice Waters, copyright © 1982 by Alice L. Waters. Used by permission of Random House, Inc.

Pages 104, 106, 108, 112, 114, 116, 118: From "The Odds Are You're Innumerate" by John Allen Paulos in *The New York Times Book Review,* © by the New York Times Co., January 1, 1989, pp. 16–17. Reprinted by permission.

Page 383: From *King Solomon's Ring* by Konrad Z. Lorenz, © 1952, Harper & Row, pp. 128–129.

Page 384: Excerpts from *Renaissance to Modern Tapestries in The Metropolitan Museum of Art* (pp. 4–6) by Edith Appleton Standen. © 1987, the Metropolitan Museum of Art. Reprinted courtesy of the Metropolitan Museum of Art.

Page 391: Excerpt from "Yonder Peasant, Who Is He?" in *Memories of a Catholic Girlhood,* copyright 1948 and renewed 1975 by Mary McCarthy, p. 57. Reprinted with permission by Houghton Mifflin Harcourt Publishing Company.

Page 392: From *Reinventing Womanhood* by Caroline G. Heilbrun. Copyright © 1979 by Caroline G. Heilbrun. Used by permission of W. W. Norton & Company, Inc., pp. 56–57.

Pages 422–423: From "Huge Conservation Effort Aims to Save Vanishing Architect of the Savannah" by William K. Stevens, © 2001 by the New York Times Co. Reprinted by permission.

Page 430: From "Let's Say You Wrote Badly This Morning" by David Huddle in *The Writing Habit,* University Press of New England, Lebanon, NH. Reprinted with permission.

Pages 430–431: From "My Two One-Eyed Coaches" by George Garrett. © Copyright George Garrett. Originally published in the *Virginia Quarterly Review*, vol. 63, no. 2.

Page 459: From "The Tornado" by John T. Snow in *Scientific American Inc.,* April 1984, pp. 41–42. Reprinted with permission. Copyright © 1984 Scientific American, a division of Nature America, Inc. All rights reserved.

Pages 460–461: From *An American Childhood* by Annie Dillard, © 1987 by Annie Dillard. Reprinted by permission of Harper Collins Publishers Inc.

Page 468: Excerpt from "Women and Fiction" in *Granite & Rainbows* by Virginia Woolf, copyright 1958 by Leonard Woolf and renewed 1986 by M.T. Parsons, Executor of Leonard Sidney Woolf, reprinted with permission by Houghton Mifflin Harcourt Publishing Company, pp. 43–44.

Pages 468–469: From Showalter, Elaine, *A Literature of Their Own.* © 1977 Princeton University Press, 2005 renewed PUP, 1999 exp. Paperback edition, pp. 10–12. Reprinted by permission of Princeton University Press.

Page 499: From *Black Americans in the Roosevelt Era* by John B. Kirby, University of Tennessee Press, © 1980.

Page 507: From "The Feeling of Flying" by Samuel Hynes. First published in *The Sewanee Review,* vol. 95, no. 1, Winter, 1987, © 1987 by Samuel Hynes. Reprinted with permission of the editor.

Pages 507–508: From "The Stunt Pilot" by Annie Dillard, © 1989, in *The Best American Essays,* Ticknor & Fields.

ON THE CD

Test One, Section 1, Questions 10–15: Excerpts from *Composing a Life,* copyright © 1989 by Mary Catherine Bateson, pp. 1–2 and 4–7. Used by permission of Grove/Atlantic, Inc.

Test One, Section 1, Questions 16–24: From "Chapter 3. Overview: Fighting Back" by Darlene Clark Hine, from *The Eyes on the Prize Civil Rights Reader* by Clayborne Carson et al., copyright © 1987, 1991 by Blackside Inc. Used by permission of Viking Penguin, a division of Penguin Group (USA) Inc.

Test One, Section 3, Passage 2: From *The Greenpeace Book of Dolphins* edited by John May, © 1990. Reprinted by permission of Greenpeace.

Test Two, Section 1, Questions 16–24: From "W. E. B. Du Bois: Protagonist of the Afro-American Protest" in *Black Leaders of the Twentieth Century* edited by John Hope Franklin and August Meier. Copyright 1982 by the Board of Trustees of the University of Illinois. Used with permission of University of the Illinois Press.

Test Two, Section 3, Passage 1: From *The Soul of the Night* by Chet Raymo, © 1985, pp. 68–70. With permission of the author.

PART ONE

INTRODUCTION

Note the following icons, used throughout this book:

Time saver

Educated guess

Did you notice?

Look it up; math reference fact

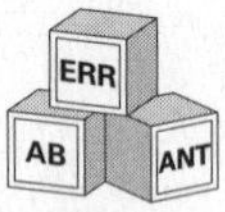

Prefixes, roots, and suffixes

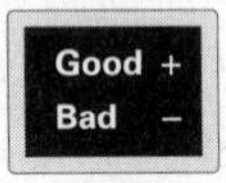

Positive or negative?

Helpful Hint

Caution!

Calculator use is recommended

The PSAT/National Merit Scholarship Qualifying Test

Your plan to take the PSAT/NMSQT is perhaps your first concrete step toward planning a college career. The PSAT/NMSQT and the SAT—what do they mean to you? When do you take them? What sort of hurdles do you face? How do these tests differ from the tests you ordinarily face in school? In this section we answer these basic questions so that you will be able to move on to the following chapters and concentrate on preparing yourself for this test.

Some Basic Questions Answered

What Is the PSAT/NMSQT?

The PSAT/NMSQT is the first step in getting ready for the SAT. It is given only in mid-October. Most schools administer the exam on a Saturday; some, however, give it three days earlier on Wednesday. You will take the PSAT on the day it is offered in your school.

The test consists of five sections: two test critical reading skills, two test mathematical reasoning skills, and one tests writing skills. The time allowed for each of the reading and math sections is twenty-five minutes; the time allowed for the writing skills section is thirty minutes.

Why Is the Test Called the PSAT/NMSQT?

The "P" in PSAT stands for "preliminary." So first and foremost the PSAT is the Preliminary SAT. As such, its job is to familiarize students with the types of questions that are on the SAT and to help students assess their strengths and weaknesses.

The PSAT also serves as the National Merit Scholarship Qualifying Test (NMSQT). Approximately 50,000 students nationally gain recognition in the NMSQT competition by earning high scores on the PSAT.

Who Takes the PSAT/NMSQT?

Essentially, all high school students who plan to take the SAT take the PSAT in October of their junior year. In addition, about 50 percent of sophomores take the PSAT for practice. **Note:** You will take the PSAT either in tenth *and* eleventh grade or just in eleventh grade; no one takes the PSAT only in tenth grade. Also, you can only qualify for recognition in the National Merit Scholarship competition as a junior. Even if you had perfect scores on the PSAT as a sophomore, you would have to take it again as a junior to receive a National Merit letter of commendation or to qualify as a semifinalist.

What Are Merit Scholarships?

Merit Scholarships are prestigious national awards that carry with them a chance for solid financial aid. Conducted by NMSC, an independent, nonprofit organization with offices at 1560 Sherman Avenue, Suite 200, Evanston, Illinois 60201-4897, the Merit Program today is supported by grants from more than 500 corporations, private foundations, colleges and universities, and other organizations. The top-scoring PSAT/NMSQT participants in every state are named Semifinalists. Those who advance to Finalist standing compete for one-time National Merit $2500 Scholarships and renewable, four-year Merit Scholarships, which may be worth as much as $10,000 a year for four years.

Check out Merit Scholarships at *www.nationalmerit.org.*

What Is the National Achievement Scholarship Program for Outstanding Black Students?

This program is aimed at honoring and assisting promising African-American high school students throughout the country. It is also administered by NMSC. Students who enter the Merit Program by taking the PSAT/NMSQT and who are also eligible to participate in the Achievement program mark a space on their test answer sheets asking to enter this competition as well. Top-scoring African-American students in each of the regions established for the competition compete for nonrenewable National Achievement $2500 Scholarships and for four-year Achievement Scholarships supported by many colleges and corporate organizations.

Note: To be considered for this program, you *must* mark the appropriate space on your answer sheet.

Check out the National Achievement Scholarship Program at *www.nationalmerit.org.*

How Can the PSAT/NMSQT Help Me?

If you are a high school junior, it will help you gauge your potential scores on the SAT that you will take in the spring. It will give you some idea of which colleges you should apply to in your senior year. It will give you access to scholarship competitions. It will definitely give you practice in answering multiple-choice questions, where timing is an important factor.

In addition, you may choose to take advantage of the College Board's Student Search Service. This service is free for students who fill out the biographical section of the PSAT/NMSQT. If you fill out this section, you will receive mail from colleges and search programs.

How Do I Apply for This Test?

You apply through your school. Fees, when required, are collected by your school. Fee waivers are available for students whose families cannot afford the test fee; if this applies to you, talk to your counselor.

The test is given in October. In December the results are sent to your school and to the scholarship program that you indicated on your answer sheet in the examination room. Your school will send you your score report.

What if I Am a Home-Schooled Student?

If you are a home-schooler, you must make arrangements with the principal or counselor of a nearby high school (public or independent) to take the test. Do not wait until the school year starts to make your arrangements. If you want to take the test in October, start the process the previous June.

Because you are a home-schooler, your score report is supposed to be sent to your home address. When you fill out your answer sheet, you must enter the state's home school code in the school code section of the answer sheet. This will ensure that you will receive your score report. You should be able to get this number from the exam proctor or supervisor.

What Makes the PSAT Different from Other Tests?

The PSAT is trying to measure your ability to reason using facts that are part of your general knowledge or facts that are included in your test booklet. You are not required to recall any history or literature or science. You are not even required to recall most math formulas—they are printed right in the test booklet.

Your score depends upon how many questions you answer correctly. You can't go too slowly, but, accuracy is more important than speed. You have to pace yourself so that you don't sacrifice speed to gain accuracy (or sacrifice accuracy to gain speed).

The biggest mistake most students make is trying to answer too many questions. It is better to answer fewer questions correctly, even if you have to leave some out at the end of a section. See page 11 for a full discussion of how to pace yourself.

How Is the PSAT Different from the SAT?

The PSAT is a mini-version of the SAT. For most students, it serves as a practice test. The PSAT takes two hours and ten minutes; the SAT takes almost twice as long. You have to answer fewer reading, math, and writing skills questions on the PSAT than you do on the SAT; however, the questions are similar in level of difficulty.

Unlike the SAT, the PSAT has *no* essay-writing section. *You do <u>not</u> have to write an essay*. Your school may recommend that you participate in the College Board's practice essay-writing program, *Score Write*. However, your participation in *Score Write* will *not* affect your PSAT score.

How Is the PSAT Scored?

The PSAT has three parts: critical reading, math, and writing skills. On each part you will receive a score between 20 and 80, and a combined Selection Index, which is the sum of your three scores. For example, if your score report listed scores of 53 in critical reading, 61 in math, and 48 in writing skills, your Selection Index would be 53 + 61 + 48 = 162.

Score Report

Critical Reading	Math	Writing Skills	Selection Index
53	61	48	162

For each individual score, as well as the Selection Index, you will receive a percentile ranking that shows how your scores compare with those of the other students who took the PSAT the same day you did.

Because SAT scores range from 200 to 800, many students multiply their PSAT scores by 10 to make them look like SAT scores. So, if you earned the scores given in the previous paragraph, you might say that your PSAT score was a 1620.

How Are the Results of Your PSAT/NMSQT Reported?

About six to eight weeks after the test, you will receive, through your school, the following:

1. an official score report that includes:
   a) the answer you gave for each question
   b) the correct answer for each question
   c) the difficulty level of each question
   d) a Selection Index, which is used to determine eligibility for NMSC programs
2. a copy of the original test booklet that you used in the examination room

Can I Do Anything if I Miss the Test but Still Want to Participate in Scholarship Competitions?

If you fail to take the PSAT/NMSQT because you were ill or involved in an emergency, you still may be able to qualify for a National Merit or National Achievement Scholarship. You need to contact the NMSC to find out about alternative testing arrangements that would enable you to take part in the National Merit competitions.

If you are of Hispanic descent, you need to contact the National Hispanic Scholar Recognition Program run by the College Board. You can arrange to be considered for this program by communicating with The College Board, Suite 600, 1233 20th Street NW, Washington, DC 20036.

How to Approach the PSAT/NMSQT

TEST-TAKING TACTICS

What Tactics Can Help Me When I Take the PSAT?

1. **Memorize the directions given in this book for each type of question.** These are only slightly different from the exact words you'll find on the PSAT you'll take. During the test, you won't have to waste even a few seconds reading any directions or sample questions.

2. **Know the format of the test.** The number and kinds of questions will break down roughly as follows:

   48 Critical Reading Questions (2 sections, 25 minutes each)

   38 Math Questions (2 sections, 25 minutes each)

   39 Writing Skills Questions (1 section, 30 minutes)

   See the chart on page vi for the breakdown within each section.

3. **Expect easy questions at the beginning of many sets of the same question type.** Within these sets (except for the reading comprehension and improving paragraph questions), the questions progress from easy to difficult. In other words, the first sentence completion question in a set will be easier than the last sentence completion in that set. Similarly, the first grid-in question will be much easier than the last grid-in question.

4. **Take advantage of the easy questions to boost your score.** Each question is worth the same number of points. Whether it is easy or difficult, whether it takes you ten seconds or two minutes to answer, you get the same number of points for each question you answer correctly. Your job is to answer as many questions as you possibly can without rushing ahead so fast that you make careless errors and lose points for failing to give some questions enough thought. So take enough time to get those easy questions right!

5. ***First* answer all the easy questions; *then* tackle the hard ones if you have time.** The questions in each segment of the test get harder as you go along (except for the reading comprehension and improving paragraph questions). But there's no rule that says you have to answer the questions in order. You're allowed to skip. So skip the hard sentence completion questions and move on to the short reading passages right away. If you finish all the reading and still have time, you can go back to the hard sentence completion questions you skipped. Test-wise students know when it's time to move on. Test-wise students also know how to keep track of what they have skipped. Be sure to mark skipped questions in your test booklet. Be sure to skip that number on your answer sheet. Always be aware of where you are on the answer sheet.

6. **Eliminate as many wrong answers as you can and then make an educated guess.** Deciding between two choices is easier than deciding among five. Whenever you guess, every answer choice you eliminate improves your chances of guessing correctly.

7. **Change answers *only* if you have a reason for doing so.** Don't give in to last-minute panic. It's usually better for you not to change your answers on a sudden hunch or whim.

8. **Calculators are permitted in the test room, so bring along a calculator that you are comfortable using.** No question on the test will *require* the use of a calculator, but a calculator will be helpful for some questions. **Note:** Make sure that whatever calculator you bring is on the College Board's approved list. They do not permit pocket organizers, calculators with keypads, laptops, and so on. For a complete list of authorized and unauthorized calculators, go to *http://www.collegeboard.org/student/testing/psat/about/calculator.html.*

9. **Remember that you are allowed to write anything you want in your test booklet. Make good use of it.** Circle questions you skip, and put big question marks next to questions you answer but are unsure about. In sentence completion questions, circle or underline key words such as *although*, *therefore*, *not*, and so on. In reading passages, circle key words and underline or put a mark in the margin next to any major point. On math questions, mark up diagrams, adding lines when necessary. And, of course, use all the space provided to solve the problem. In short, write anything that will help you, using whatever symbols you like. But remember, the only thing that counts is what you enter on your answer sheet. No one will ever see anything that you write in your test booklet.

10. **Be careful not to make any stray marks on your answer sheet.** This test is graded by a machine, and a machine cannot tell the difference between an accidental mark and a filled-in answer. When the machine sees two marks instead of one, the answer is marked wrong.

11. **Check frequently to make sure you are answering the questions in the right spots.** No machine is going to notice that you made a mistake early in the test, that you answered question 4 in the space for question 5, and that all your following answers are in the wrong place. One way to avoid this problem is to mark your answers in your test booklet and transfer them to your answer sheet by blocks.

12. **Line up your test book with your answer sheet to avoid making careless errors.** Whether you choose to fill in the answers question by question or in blocks, you will do so most efficiently if you keep your test booklet and your answer sheet aligned.

13. **Be particularly careful in marking the student-produced responses on the math grid.** Before you fill in the appropriate blanks in the grid, write your answer at the top of the columns. Then go down each column and make sure you fill in the right spaces.

14. **Don't get bogged down on any one question.** By the time you get to the actual PSAT, you should have a fair idea of how much time to spend on each question. If a question is taking too long, leave it and go on to the next question. This is no time to try to show the world that you can stick to a job no matter how long it takes. All the machine that grades the test will notice is that after a certain point you didn't have any correct answers.

REDUCING ANXIETY

How Can I Prevent PSAT Anxiety from Setting In?

1. The best way to prepare for any test you ever take is to get a good night's sleep before the test so that you are well rested and alert.

2. Eat breakfast for once in your life. You have a full morning ahead of you; you should have a full stomach as well.

3. Allow plenty of time for getting to the test site. Taking a test is pressure enough. You don't need the extra tension that comes from worrying about whether you will get there on time.

4. Be aware of the amount of time the test is going to take. There are five sections. They will take two hours and ten minutes total. Add to that a five-minute break after the third section, one-minute breaks between the others, plus thirty minutes for paper pushing. If the test starts at 8:00 A.M., don't make a dentist appointment for 11:00 A.M. You can't possibly get there on time, and you'll just spend the last half hour of the test worrying about it.

5. The College Board tells you to bring two sharpened No. 2 pencils to the test. Bring four. They don't weigh much, and this might be the one day in the decade when two pencil points decide to break. Bring full-size pencils, not little stubs. They are easier to write with, and you might as well be comfortable.

6. Speaking of being comfortable, wear comfortable clothes. This is a test, not a fashion show. Aim for the layered look. Wear something light, but bring a sweater. The test room may be hot, or it may be cold. You can't change the room, but you can put on the sweater.

7. Bring a watch or small travel clock, which you may keep on your desk. You need one. The room in which you take the test may not have a clock, and some proctors are not very good about posting the time on the blackboard. Don't depend on them. Each time you begin a test section, write down in your booklet the time according to your watch. That way you will always know how much time you have left. **Note:** Make sure that whatever watch or small clock you bring is a *silent* timepiece. The College Board does not permit you to bring any timer or watch with an audible alarm into the testing room. No beeps!

8. Smuggle in some quick energy in your pocket—trail mix, raisins, a candy bar. Even if the proctors don't let you eat in the test room, you can still grab a bite en route to the restrooms during the five-minute break. Taking the test can leave you feeling drained and in need of a quick pickup—bring along your favorite comfort food.

9. There will be a break after the third section. Use this period to clear your thoughts. Take a few deep breaths. Stretch. Close your eyes and imagine yourself floating or sunbathing. In addition to being under mental pressure, you're under physical pressure from sitting so long in an uncomfortable seat with a No. 2 pencil clutched in your hand. Anything you can do to loosen up and get the kinks out will ease your body and help the oxygen get to your brain.

10. Most important of all, remember: very little, if anything, is riding on the result of this test. If you do poorly, no one will know; your PSAT scores are not reported to the colleges to which you plan to apply. So relax!

GUESSING

If you try answering a question on the PSAT, but are unsure of the correct answer, should you guess?

The answer to the above question is very simple: in general, *it pays to guess*. To understand why this is so and why so many people are confused about it, you must understand how the PSAT is scored.

Two types of scores are associated with the PSAT: raw scores and scaled scores. First, three raw scores are calculated—one for each part of the test. Each raw score is then converted to a scaled score between 20 and 80. If you multiply a PSAT scaled score by 10, it becomes equivalent to an SAT scaled score. So, for example, a PSAT score of 56 is equivalent to an SAT score of 560.

On the PSAT, every question is worth exactly the same amount: 1 raw score point. A correct answer to a critical reading question for which you may have to read a whole paragraph is worth no more than a correct response to a sentence completion question that you can answer in a few seconds. You get no more credit for a correct answer to the hardest math question than you do for the easiest. For each question that you answer correctly, you receive 1 raw score point. For each multiple-choice question that you answer incorrectly, you lose ¼ point. Questions that you leave out have no effect on your score. So on each of the PSAT's three parts—critical reading, math, and writing skills—the raw score is calculated as follows:

$$(\text{\# of correct answers}) - \left(\frac{\text{\# of incorrect multiple-choice answers}}{4}\right) = \text{Raw Score}$$

There are 48 critical reading questions on the PSAT, 24 in each section. Let's assume that on each of the two sections you leave out the last 5 questions because you run out of time, and of the first 19 questions, you answer 15 correctly and 4 incorrectly. What would your raw score be? For the 30 correct answers you would earn 30 points and for the 8 incorrect answers you would lose $\frac{8}{4} = 2$ points. So your raw score on the critical reading part would be $30 - 2 = 28$, which would be converted to a scaled score of about 56.

In this scenario, what would happen to your score if during your last few seconds, you quickly bubbled in an answer for each of the 10 questions that you didn't have time to answer? Since there are five choices for each question, on average you would answer one-fifth of them correctly and four-fifths of them incorrectly. That is, you would probably get about 2 right and 8 wrong. How would that affect your score? Well, for 2 right answers you would gain 2 raw score points, and for 8 wrong answers you would lose $\frac{8}{4} = 2$ raw score points. So your raw score, and hence your scaled score, would be the same. If you were lucky and answered 3 questions correctly or a bit unlucky and answered only 1 question correctly, your raw score, and hence your scaled score, would go up or down slightly, but most likely it would remain the same. This leaves us with the following important conclusion:

On average, on the PSAT, wild guessing does not affect your score.

Although, as we have just seen, on average wild guessing doesn't affect your score, *educated guessing* can have an enormous effect on your score—it can increase it dramatically! To see what we mean by educated guessing and how it can increase your score on the PSAT, let's look at two examples. The first is a sentence completion question.

1. In Victorian times, countless Egyptian mummies were ground up to produce dried mummy powder, hailed by quacks as a near-magical ----, able to cure a wide variety of ailments.

(A) toxin (B) diagnosis (C) symptom
(D) panacea (E) placebo

Clearly, what is needed is a word such as *medicine*—something capable of curing ailments. Let's assume that you know that *toxin* means poison; so you immediately eliminate A. You also know that although *diagnosis* and *symptom* are medical terms, neither means a medicine or a cure; so you eliminate B and C. You now know that the correct answer must be D or E, but unfortunately you have no idea what *panacea* or *placebo* means. You *could* guess, but you don't want to be wrong; after all, there's that ¼-point penalty for incorrect answers. So, should you leave it out? Absolutely not. *You must guess!* We'll explain why and how in a moment, but first let's look at the other example, this time a math one.

2. From 2000 to 2010 the number of students participating in a school's community service program increased by 25 percent. If the number of participants in 2010 was P, how many students participated in 2000?

(A) $0.75P$
(B) $0.80P$
(C) $1.20P$
(D) $1.25P$
(E) $1.50P$

Even if you are not very good at percent problems (especially when they involve letters!), you should realize that since participation in the program increased, the number of students who participated in 2000 must be *less than P.* So you know the answer must be A or B. What do you do? Do you guess and risk losing points for a wrong answer, or do you leave it out because you have no idea which answer is correct? *You must guess!*

Suppose that on the entire PSAT there are 16 questions on which you can eliminate three of the five answer choices, as we did on the two examples above, but you have no idea whatsoever about which of the two remaining choices is correct. What would be the result of guessing on those questions? You would probably get about 8 right answers and 8 wrong answers. Would that be good or bad? *It would be great!* For the 8 right answers you would earn 8 raw score points, but for the 8 wrong answers you would lose only $\frac{8}{4} = 2$ raw score points. Those 16 guesses gained you 6 raw score points, which would raise your scaled score by about 5 points (50 SAT points). You can't give up 50 points because you're afraid to guess.

When you take the PSAT, what if you find questions on which you can eliminate only one or two of the answer choices? You still have to guess. Remember—if you can't eliminate anything and you take wild guesses, you will break even. Whenever you can eliminate any choices at all, you must guess.

As you read this book, you will learn strategies that will enable you to narrow down the choices on every question you attempt. So the only questions you should leave out are the ones you didn't attempt, because you ran out of time.

If you read a question but are unsure of the answer, use one of the strategies in this book to narrow down the choices and guess!

PACING

The biggest mistake that most students make when they take the PSAT is that they try to answer too many questions. Therefore, an important strategy is to slow down and answer fewer questions. Let's see why this is true.

Section 2 of a PSAT is always a math section with 20 multiple-choice questions. The questions in this section are presented in order of difficulty. Although this varies slightly from test to test, typically questions 1–6 are considered easy, questions 7–14 are considered medium, and questions 15–20 are considered hard. Even within the groups, the questions increase in difficulty: questions 7 and 14, for example, may both be ranked medium, but question 14 will definitely be harder than question 7. Of course, this depends slightly on each student's math skills. Some students might find question 8 or 9 or even 10 to be easier than question 7, but everyone will find questions 11 and 12 to be harder than questions 1 and 2, and questions 19 and 20 to be harder than questions 13 and 14.

However, all questions have the same value. You earn 1 point for a correct answer to question 1, which might take you only fifteen seconds to solve, and 1 point for a correct answer to question 20, which might take two or three minutes to solve. Knowing that it will probably take at least ten minutes to answer the last 5 questions, many students try to race through the first 15 questions in fifteen minutes or less and, as a result, miss many questions that they could have answered correctly, had they slowed down.

Suppose Michael rushed through questions 1–15 and got 9 right answers and 6 wrong ones and then worked on the 5 hardest questions and got 2 right and 3 wrong. His raw score would be $8\frac{3}{4}$: 11 for the 11 correct answers minus $2\frac{1}{4}$ points for the 9 wrong answers. Had he gone slowly and carefully, and not made any careless errors on the easy and medium questions, he might have run out of time and not answered any of the 5 hard questions at the end. But if spending all twenty-five minutes on the first 15 questions meant that he answered 13 correctly, 2 incorrectly, and omitted 5, his raw score would have been $12\frac{1}{2}$. If Michael had a similar improvement on Section 4, the other math section, his scaled score would have been about 7 points (70 SAT points) higher.

The only questions on the PSAT that do not proceed from easy to difficult are the reading comprehension questions; but the sentence completion questions at the beginning of each reading section do. So when a section begins with 8 sentence completions, for example, a winning strategy is to answer the 5 easy and medium ones, intentionally skip the 3 hardest ones, and go directly to the reading questions. It would be a shame to have to leave out a few reading questions that might be easy or medium because you wasted too much time trying to answer some very hard sentence completions, which you might very well miss, anyway. It is not only OK to intentionally leave out questions on the PSAT, for almost all students, even very good ones, it is advisable to do so. So it is worth repeating:

The biggest mistake that most students make when they take the PSAT is that they try to answer too many questions.

Sample PSAT Questions

The purpose of this section is to familiarize you with the kinds of questions that appear on the PSAT by presenting questions like those on recent PSATs. Knowing what to expect when you take the examination is an important step in preparing for the test and succeeding in it.

If you wish, you can head straight for the diagnostic test that follows to learn about your strengths and weaknesses as a test taker and to get a sense of how well you might do on the PSAT. However, before you tackle the diagnostic test, we recommend that you take a few minutes to acquaint yourself with the kinds of questions you're going to encounter.

The directions that precede the various types of questions are similar to those on the PSAT. For all except the student-produced response questions, you are to choose the best answer and fill in the corresponding blank on the answer sheet.

CRITICAL READING

There are two types of questions on the Critical Reading portion of the PSAT:

- sentence completion questions
- reading comprehension questions

The critical reading questions on the PSAT are in Section 1 (questions 1–24) and Section 3 (questions 25–48). You are allowed twenty-five minutes to complete each section.

	Sentence Completion	Short Passages	Long Passages
Section 1	1–8	9–12 [2 passages]	13–24 [2 passages]
Section 3	25–29	30–33 [2 passages]	34–48 [2 passages]
	13 questions total	8 questions total	27 questions total

Sentence Completion

Sentence completion questions are straightforward fill-in-the-blank questions. Each group of sentence completion questions starts with easy questions and gets harder as it goes along.

Sentence Completion Directions

Each of the following sentences contains one or two blanks; these blanks indicate that a word or set of words has been left out. Below the sentence are five words or phrases, lettered A through E. Select the word or set of words that best completes the sentence.

EXAMPLE:

Fame is ----; today's rising star is all too soon tomorrow's washed-up has-been.

(A) rewarding (B) gradual (C) essential
(D) spontaneous (E) transitory

Ⓐ Ⓑ Ⓒ Ⓓ ●

1. Folk dancing is ---- senior citizens, and it is also economical; they need neither great physical agility nor special equipment to enjoy participating in the dance.

(A) bewildering to (B) thrilling for
(C) foreign to (D) appropriate for
(E) impracticable for

2. Holding her infant son, the new mother felt an ---- greater than any other joy she had known.

(A) affluence (B) incentive (C) assurance
(D) incredulity (E) elation

3. The author maintained that his insights were not ---- but had been made independently of others.

(A) derivative (B) esoteric (C) fallacious
(D) hypothetical (E) concise

4. Suspicious of the ---- actions of others, the critic Edmund Wilson was in many ways a ---- man, unused to trusting anyone.

(A) altruistic . . cynical
(B) questionable . . contrite
(C) generous . . candid
(D) hypocritical . . cordial
(E) benevolent . . dauntless

5. Although Roman original contributions to government, jurisprudence, and engineering are commonly acknowledged, the artistic legacy of the Roman world continues to be judged widely as ---- the magnificent Greek traditions that preceded it.

(A) an improvement on (B) an echo of
(C) a resolution of (D) a precursor of
(E) a consummation of

6. ---- though she appeared, her journals reveal that her outward maidenly reserve concealed a passionate nature unsuspected by her family and friends.

(A) Effusive (B) Suspicious (C) Tempestuous
(D) Domineering (E) Reticent

7. Crabeater seal, the common name of *Lobodon carcinophagus*, is ----, since the animal's staple diet is not crabs, but krill.

(A) a pseudonym (B) a misnomer
(C) an allusion (D) a digression
(E) a compromise

Answer Explanations

Sentence Completion Questions

1. **(D)** *Because* senior citizens don't need great physical agility to enjoy folk dancing, it is an *appropriate* activity for them. It is not by definition *thrilling* for them.

2. **(E)** If the missing word is an emotion greater than *any other joy*, then it too must be a form of joy. *Elation* is a feeling of great joy.

3. **(A)** If the author got his insights independently, then he did not get or derive them from the insights of other people. In other words, his insights were not *derivative*.

4. **(A)** Someone given to distrusting the motives and actions of others is by definition *cynical*. Such a person would question even the *altruistic*, unselfish deeds of others, suspecting there to be ulterior motives for these charitable acts.

5. **(B)** The view of Rome's contributions to government, law, and engineering is wholly positive: these original additions to human knowledge are generally acknowledged or recognized. *In contrast*, Rome's original contributions to art are *not* recognized; they are seen as just an *echo* or imitation of the art of ancient Greece.

   Note that *Although* sets up the contrast here.

6. **(E)** Her outward appearance was one of "maidenly reserve" (self-restraint; avoidance of intimacy). Thus, she seemed to be *reticent* (reserved; disinclined to speak or act freely), even though she actually felt things passionately.

7. **(B)** Because these seals eat far more krill than crabs, it *misnames* them to call them crabeater seals. The term is thus a *misnomer*, a name that's wrongly applied to someone or something.

   Beware of eye-catchers. Choice A is incorrect. A *pseudonym* isn't a mistaken name; it's a false name that an author adopts.

Critical Reading

Your ability to read and understand the kind of material found in college texts and the more serious magazines is tested in the critical reading section of the PSAT/NMSQT. There are two types of passages on the test, short passages and long passages. Short passages are approximately 100 words in length; long passages generally range from 400–850 words. Some passages are paired: you will be asked to answer two or three questions that compare the viewpoints of two passages on the same subject.

Critical Reading Directions

The passages below are followed by questions on their content; questions following a pair of related passages may also be based on the relationship between the paired passages. Answer the questions on the basis of what is stated or implied in the passages and in any introductory material that may be provided.

Questions 8 and 9 are based on the following passage.

"Ladybug, ladybug, fly away home. Your house is on fire; your children do roam." Few farmers would seek to chase away ladybugs, or ladybird beetles, with this familiar children's rhyme, for ladybugs are known as the farmer's friend. Clusters of ladybugs are often gathered and sold to farmers, who employ them to control the spread of insect pests. In 1888, for example, when California's orange orchards were threatened by an outbreak of cottony-cushion scale, farmers imported the Australian ladybird beetle to devour the scale. In less than two years, the ladybugs had saved the orchards.

8. The quotation in the opening lines of the passage primarily serves to

(A) alert the ladybugs to an actual danger
(B) introduce the passage's subject informally
(C) demonstrate a common misapprehension
(D) provide a critical literary allusion
(E) diminish the importance of ladybird beetles

9. As used in line 12, the word "scale" most likely refers to

(A) a form of cotton
(B) a variety of insect
(C) a type of orange
(D) a plant nutrient
(E) a measure of weight

Questions 10–16 are based on the following passages.

The following passages are excerpted from books on America's national pastime, baseball.

Passage 1

DiMaggio had size, power, and speed. McCarthy, his longtime manager, liked to say that DiMaggio might have stolen 60 bases a season if he had given him the green light. Stengel, his new manager, was equally impressed, and when DiMaggio was on base he would point to him as an example of the perfect base runner. "Look at him," Stengel would say as DiMaggio ran out a base hit, "he's always watching the ball. He isn't watching second base. He isn't watching third base. He knows they haven't been moved. He isn't watching the ground, because he knows they haven't built a canal or a swimming pool since he was last there. He's watching the ball and the outfielder, which is the one thing that is different on every play."

DiMaggio complemented his natural athletic ability with astonishing physical grace. He played the outfield, he ran the bases, and he batted not just effectively but with rare style. He would glide rather than run, it seemed, always smooth, always ending up where he wanted to be just when he wanted to be there. If he appeared to play effortlessly, his teammates knew otherwise. In his first season as a Yankee, Gene Woodling, who played left field, was struck by the sound of DiMaggio chasing a fly ball. He sounded like a giant truck horse on the loose, Woodling thought, his feet thudding down hard on the grass. The great, clear noises in the open space enabled Woodling to measure the distances between them without looking.

He was the perfect Hemingway hero, for Hemingway in his novels romanticized the man who exhibited grace under pressure, who withheld any emotion lest it soil the purer statement of his deeds. DiMaggio was that kind of hero; his grace and skill were always on display, his emotions always concealed. This stoic grace was not achieved without a terrible price: DiMaggio was a man wound tight. He suffered from insomnia and ulcers. When he sat and watched the game he chain-smoked and drank endless cups of coffee. He was ever conscious of his obligation to play well. Late in his career, when his legs were bothering him and the Yankees had a comfortable lead in a pennant race, columnist Jimmy Cannon asked him why he played so hard—the games, after all, no longer meant so much. "Because there might be somebody out there who's never seen me play before," he answered.

Passage 2

Athletes and actors—let actors stand for the set of performing artists—share much. They share the need to make gestures as fluid and economical as possible, to make out of a welter of choices the single, precisely right one. They share the need for thousands of hours of practice in order to train the body to become the perfect, instinctive instrument to express. Both athlete and actor, out of that abundance of emotion, choice, strategy, knowledge of the terrain, mood of spectators, condition of others in the ensemble, secret awareness of injury or weakness, and as nearly an absolute *concentration* as possible so that all externalities are integrated, all distraction absorbed to the self, must be able to change the self so successfully that it changes us.

When either athlete or actor can bring all these skills to bear and focus them, then he or she will achieve that state of complete intensity and complete relaxation—complete coherence or integrity between what the performer wants to do and what the performer has to do. Then, the performer is free; for then, all that has been learned, by thousands of hours of practice and discipline and by repetition of pattern, becomes natural. Then, intellect is upgraded to the level of an instinct. The body follows commands that precede thinking.

When athlete and artist achieve such self-knowledge that they transform the self so that we are re-created, it is finally an exercise in power. The individual's power to dominate, on stage or field, invests the whole arena around the locus of performance with his or her power. We draw from the performer's energy, just as we scrutinize the performer's vulnerabilities, and we criticize as if we were equals (we are not) what is displayed. This is why all performers dislike or resent the audience as much as they need and enjoy it. Power flows in a mysterious circuit from performer to spectator (I assume a "live" performance) and back, and while cheers or applause are the hoped-for outcome of performing, silence or gasps are the most desired, for then the moment has occurred—then domination is complete, and as the performer triumphs, a unity rare and inspiring results.

10. In Passage 1, Stengel is most impressed by DiMaggio's

(A) indifference to potential dangers
(B) tendency to overlook the bases in his haste
(C) ability to focus on the variables
(D) proficiency at fielding fly balls
(E) overall swiftness and stamina

11. It can be inferred from the content and tone of Stengel's comment (lines 7–15) that he would regard a base runner who kept his eye on second base with

(A) trepidation (B) approbation
(C) resignation (D) exasperation
(E) tolerance

12. The phrase "a man wound tight" (lines 39–40) means a man

(A) wrapped in confining bandages
(B) living in constricted quarters
(C) under intense emotional pressure
(D) who drank alcohol to excess
(E) who could throw with great force

13. Which best describes what the author is doing in the parenthetical comment "let actors stand for the set of performing artists" (lines 51–52)?

(A) indicating that actors should rise out of respect for the arts
(B) defining the way in which he is using a particular term
(C) encouraging actors to show tolerance for their fellow artists
(D) emphasizing that actors are superior to other performing artists
(E) correcting a misinterpretation of the role of actors

14. To the author of Passage 2, freedom for performers depends on

(A) their subjection of the audience
(B) their willingness to depart from tradition
(C) the internalization of all they have learned
(D) their ability to interpret material independently
(E) the absence of injuries or other weaknesses

15. The author's attitude toward the concept of the equality of spectators and performers (lines 83–87) is one of

(A) relative indifference
(B) mild skepticism
(C) explicit rejection
(D) strong embarrassment
(E) marked perplexity

16. The author of Passage 2 would most likely react to the characterization of DiMaggio presented in lines 43–50 by pointing out that DiMaggio probably

(A) felt some resentment of the spectator whose good opinion he supposedly sought
(B) never achieved the degree of self-knowledge that would have transformed him
(C) was unaware that his audience was surveying his weak points
(D) was a purely instinctive natural athlete
(E) was seldom criticized by his peers

Answer Explanations

Critical Reading Questions

8. **(B)** Rather than launch immediately into a formal discussion of the beneficial qualities of ladybugs or ladybird beetles, the author chooses to *introduce the subject informally* by quoting a familiar nursery rhyme.

9. **(B)** Cottony-cushion scale is just one of the insect pests combatted by ladybird beetles. The correct answer is Choice B, *a variety of insect*.

10. **(C)** Stengel's concluding sentence indicates that DiMaggio watches "the one thing that is different on every play." In other words, DiMaggio *focuses on the variables*, the factors that change from play to play.

11. **(D)** The sarcastic tone of Stengel's comment suggests that he would be *exasperated* or irritated by a base runner who had his eye on second base when he should have been watching the ball and the outfielder.

12. **(C)** Look at the sentences following this phrase. They indicate that DiMaggio was a man *under intense emotional pressure*, one who felt so much stress that he developed ulcers and had problems getting to sleep.

13. **(B)** The author is taking a moment away from his argument to make sure the reader knows exactly who the subjects of his comparison are. He is not simply comparing athletes and actors. He is comparing athletes and *all* performing artists, "the set of performing artists," to use his words. Thus, in his side comment, he is *defining* how he intends to use the word *actors* throughout the discussion.

14. **(C)** Performers are free when all they have learned becomes so natural, so internalized, that it seems instinctive. In other words, freedom depends on *the internalization* of what they have learned.

15. **(C)** The author bluntly states that we spectators are not the performers' equals. Thus, his attitude toward the concept is one of *explicit rejection*.

16. **(A)** Passage 1 indicates DiMaggio always played hard to live up to his reputation and to perform well for anyone in the stands who had never seem him play before. Clearly, he wanted the spectators to have a good opinion of him. Passage 2, however, presents a more complex picture of the relationship between the performer and his audience. On the one hand, the performer needs the audience, needs its good opinion and its applause. On the other hand, the performer also resents the audience, resents the way spectators freely point out his weaknesses and criticize his art. Thus, the author of Passage 2 might well point out that DiMaggio *felt some resentment* of the audience, whom he hoped to impress with his skill.

MATHEMATICS

There are two types of questions on the Mathematics portion of the PSAT:

1. multiple-choice questions
2. grid-in questions

The math questions are in Sections 2 and 4 of the PSAT. You have twenty-five minutes to work on each section.

- Section 2 has 20 multiple-choice questions (Questions 1–20)
- Section 4 has 8 multiple-choice questions (Questions 21–28) followed by 10 grid-in questions (Questions 29–38).

Within each group, the questions are presented approximately in order of increasing difficulty. In fact, on the score report, which you will receive about seven or eight weeks after taking the PSAT, each question will be rated E (Easy), M (Medium), or H (Hard), depending on how many students answered that question correctly. A typical ranking of the math questions would be as follows:

	Easy	Medium	Hard
Section 2: Multiple-choice	1–6	7–14	15–20
Section 4: Multiple-choice	21–22	23–25	26–28
Section 4: Grid-in	29–31	32–35	36–38

As a result, the amount of time you spend on any one question should vary greatly.

Multiple-Choice Questions

Twenty-eight of the 38 mathematics questions on the PSAT are multiple-choice questions. Although you have certainly taken multiple-choice tests before, the PSAT uses a few different types of questions in these sections, and you must become familiar with all of them. By far, the most common type of question is one in which you are asked to solve a problem. The straightforward way to answer such a question is to do the necessary work, get the solution, then look at the five choices and choose the one that corresponds to your answer. In Chapter 6 we will discuss other techniques for answering these questions, but for now let's look at a couple of examples.

EXAMPLE 1

What is the average (arithmetic mean) of –2, –1, 0, 1, 2, 3, and 4?

(A) 0

(B) $\frac{3}{7}$

(C) 1

(D) $\frac{7}{6}$

(E) $\frac{7}{2}$

To solve this problem requires only that you know how to find the average of a set of numbers. Ignore the fact that this is a multiple-choice question. *Don't even look at the choices.*

- Calculate the average by adding the 7 numbers and dividing by 7.
- $\frac{-2 + -1 + 0 + 1 + 2 + 3 + 4}{7} = \frac{7}{7} = 1.$
- Now look at the five choices. Find 1, listed as Choice C, and blacken in C on your answer sheet.

EXAMPLE 2

Emily was born on Wednesday, April 16, 2008. Her sister Erin was born exactly 1200 days later. On what day of the week was Erin born?

(A) Tuesday
(B) Thursday
(C) Friday
(D) Saturday
(E) Sunday

Again, you are not helped by the fact that this question is a multiple-choice question. You need to determine the day of the week on which Erin was born and then select the choice that matches your answer.

- The 7 days keep repeating in exactly the same order: 1 day after Emily was born was a Thursday, 2 days after Emily was born was a Friday, and so on. Make a table.

	Thurs.	**Fri.**	**Sat.**	**Sun.**	**Mon.**	**Tues.**	**Wed.**
Days after Emily	1	2	3	4	5	6	7
was born	8	9	10	11	12	13	14
	and so on.						

- Note that whenever the number of days is a multiple of 7 (7, 14, 21, . . . , 70, . . .) a whole number of weeks has gone by, and it is again a Wednesday.
- If 1200 were a multiple of 7, the 1200th day would be a Wednesday.
- Is it? To find out, use your calculator: $1200 \div 7 = 171.4285\ldots$
- 1200 days is <u>not</u> a whole number of weeks; it is a little more than 171 weeks.
- Since $171 \times 7 = 1197$, the 1197th day completes the 171st week and hence is a Wednesday.
- The 1198th day starts the next week. It is a Thursday; the 1199th day is a Friday; and the 1200th day is a Saturday.
- The answer is D.

Note: Did you notice that the solution didn't use the fact that Emily was born on April 16, 2008? This is unusual. Occasionally, but not often, a PSAT problem contains extraneous information.

In contrast to Examples 1 and 2, some questions *require* you to look at all five choices in order to find the answers. Consider Example 3.

EXAMPLE 3

For any numbers a and b: let the operation ☺ be defined by $a ☺ b = a^2 + b^2$. Which of the following is *not* equal to 6 ☺ 8?

(A) -10 ☺ 0
(B) -8 ☺ -6
(C) 9 ☺ $\sqrt{19}$
(D) (6 ☺ 9) − (4 ☺ 1)
(E) 2(3 ☺ 4)

The words *which of the following* alert you to the fact that you are going to have to examine each of the five choices and determine which of them satisfies the stated condition—in this case, that it is *not* equal to 6 ☺ 8.

Do not be concerned that you have never seen the symbol "☺" used this way before. No one has. On the PSAT there is almost always at least one question that uses a symbol that the test makers have made up. All you have to do is read the question very carefully and follow the directions exactly. In this case we have: 6 ☺ 8 = $6^2 + 8^2 = 36 + 64 = 100$.

Now check each of the five choices, and find the one that is *not* equal to 100.

(A) -10 ☺ 0 = $(-10)^2 + 0^2 = 100 + 0 = 100$
(B) -8 ☺ -6 = $(-8)^2 + (-6)^2 = 64 + 36 = 100$
(C) 9 ☺ $\sqrt{19}$ = $9^2 + (\sqrt{19})^2 = 81 + 19 = 100$
(D) (6 ☺ 9) − (4 ☺ 1) = $(6^2 + 9^2) - (4^2 + 1^2) = (36 + 81) - (16 + 1) = 117 - 17 = 100$
(E) 2(3 ☺ 4) = $2(3^2 + 4^2) = 2(9 + 16) = 2(25) = 50$, which is *not* equal to 100.

So, the correct answer is E.

Another kind of multiple-choice question that appears on the PSAT is the Roman numeral-type question. These questions consist of three statements labeled I, II, and III. The five answer choices give various possibilities for which of the statements are true. So, really, a Roman numeral question consists of three separate true–false questions. Here is a typical example.

EXAMPLE 4

In $\triangle ABC$, $AB = 3$ and $BC = 4$. Which of the following could be the perimeter of $\triangle ABC$?

I. 8
II. 12
III. 16

(A) I only
(B) II only
(C) I and II only
(D) II and III only
(E) I, II, and III

- Note that "I. 8" is simply an abbreviation of the statement, "The perimeter of $\triangle ABC$ could be 8." The same is true for "II. 12" and "III. 16." To solve this problem, examine each of the three statements independently.

I. Could the perimeter be 8? If it were, then the third side would be 1. But in any triangle, the smallest side must be greater than the difference of the other two sides. So, the third side must be *greater* than $4 - 3 = 1$. It cannot equal 1. I is false.

II. Could the perimeter be 12? That is, could the third side be 5? Yes. The three sides could be 3, 4, and 5. In fact, the most common right triangle to appear on the PSAT is a 3-4-5 right triangle. II is true.

III. Could the perimeter be 16? If it were, then the third side would be 9. But in any triangle, the largest side must be less than the sum of the other two sides. So, the third side must be less than $4 + 3 = 7$. It cannot equal 9. III is false.

- Only statement II is true. The answer is B.

Grid-In Questions

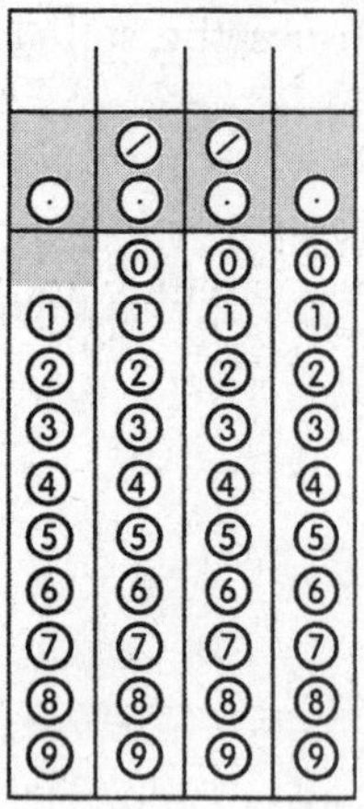

Ten of the 38 mathematics questions on the PSAT are what the College Board calls student-produced response questions. These are the only questions on the PSAT that are not multiple-choice. Since the answers to these questions are entered on a special grid, they are usually referred to as *grid-in* questions. Except for the method of entering your answer, this type of question is probably the one with which you are most familiar. In your math class, most homework problems and test questions require you to determine an answer and write it down, and this is what you will do on the grid-in problems. The only difference is that on the PSAT, you must record your answer on a special grid, such as the one shown, so that it can be read by a computer.

There is no deduction for wrong answers to grid-in questions, so if you can't solve a problem, you should always guess.

Here is a typical grid-in question.

EXAMPLE 5

John has a rectangular garden. He decides to enlarge it by increasing its length by 20% and its width by 30%. If the area of the new garden is a times the area of the original garden, what is the value of a?

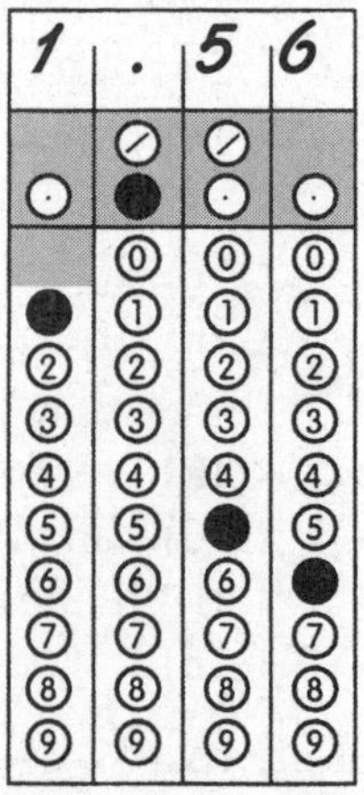

Solution. From the wording of the question, it is clear that the answer does not depend on the actual original dimensions. Therefore, pick an easy value. For example, assume that the original garden is a square whose sides are 10. Since 20% of 10 is 2 and 30% of 10 is 3, then the new garden is a 12 by 13 rectangle. Therefore, the area of the original garden is $10 \times 10 = 100$, and the area of the new garden is $12 \times 13 = 156$. So $156 = a(100)$, and $a = 1.56$.

To enter this answer, you write 1.56 in the four spaces at the top of the grid and blacken in the appropriate circle under each space. In the first column, under the 1, blacken the oval marked 1; in the second column, under the decimal point, blacken the oval with the decimal point; in the third column, under the 5, blacken the oval marked 5; and finally, in the fourth column, under the 6, blacken the oval marked 6.

Note that the only symbols that appear in the grid are the digits from 0 to 9, a decimal point, and a fraction bar (/). The grid does not have a minus sign, so *answers to grid-in problems can never be negative*. In Chapter 5, you will read suggestions for the best way to fill in grids. You will also learn the special rules concerning the proper way to grid-in fractions, mixed numbers, and decimals that won't fit in the grid's four columns. When you take the diagnostic test, just enter your answers exactly as was done in Example 5.

WRITING SKILLS

The Writing Skills section consists of 39 questions to be answered in thirty minutes. A typical test has 20 improving sentences questions, 14 identifying sentence errors questions, and 5 improving paragraphs questions.

Improving Sentences Questions

The improving sentences questions test your ability to select the wording that makes the strongest sentence—the clearest, the smoothest, the most compact.

Improving Sentences Directions

Some or all parts of the following sentences are underlined. The first answer choice, (A), simply repeats the underlined part of the sentence. The other four choices present four alternative ways to phrase the underlined part. Select the answer that produces the most effective sentence, one that is clear and exact, and blacken the appropriate space on your answer sheet. In selecting your choice, be sure that it is standard written English and that it expresses the meaning of the original sentence.

EXAMPLE:

The first biography of author Eudora Welty came out in 1998, <u>and she was eighty-nine years old at the time.</u>

(A) and she was eighty-nine years old at the time
(B) at the time when she was eighty-nine
(C) upon becoming an eighty-nine year old
(D) when she was eighty-nine
(E) at the age of eighty-nine years old

Ⓐ Ⓑ Ⓒ ● Ⓔ

1. <u>More than any animal</u>, the wolverine exemplifies the unbridled ferocity of "nature red in tooth and claw."

(A) More than any animal
(B) More than any other animal
(C) More than another animal
(D) Unlike any animal
(E) Compared to other animals

2. The reviewer knew that Barbara Cartland had written several Gothic <u>novels, she didn't remember any of their titles.</u>

(A) novels, she didn't remember any of their titles
(B) novels, however she didn't remember any of their titles
(C) novels, their titles, however, she didn't remember
(D) novels without remembering any of their titles
(E) novels, but she remembered none of their titles

3. I think the United States will veto the resolution imposing sanctions against Israel <u>regardless of the desires of the Arab nations</u> for strong action.

(A) regardless of the desires of the Arab nations
(B) irregardless of the Arab nations' desires
(C) regardless of the Arab nations desires
(D) irregardless of the Arab nation's desires
(E) mindful of the desires of the Arab nations

Answer Explanations

1. **(B)** Choice B includes the necessary word *other*, which makes the comparison correct. Choice D changes the meaning of the sentence by its implication that the wolverine is *not* an animal.
2. **(E)** Choices A, B, and C are run-on sentences. Choice D changes the meaning of the sentence by implying that it was Barbara Cartland who could not remember the titles.
3. **(A)** *Irregardless* in Choices B and D is incorrect. Also, in Choices C and D, the case of *nations* is incorrect. The correct form of the plural possessive case of *nation* is *nations'*. Choice E changes the meaning of the sentence; in fact, it reverses it.

Identifying Sentence Errors

The identifying sentence errors questions test your ability to spot faults in usage and sentence structure.

Identifying Sentence Errors Directions

The sentences in this section may contain errors in grammar, usage, choice of words, or idioms. There is either just one error per sentence, or the sentence is correct. Some words or phrases are underlined and lettered; everything else in the sentence is correct.

If an underlined word or phrase is incorrect, choose that letter; if the sentence is correct, select No error. Then blacken the appropriate space on your answer sheet.

EXAMPLE:

The region has a climate so severe that (A) plants growing there (B) rarely had been (C) more than twelve inches high (D). No error (E) Ⓐ Ⓑ ● Ⓓ Ⓔ

4. Despite the fact that (A) some states (B) have resisted, Congress have passed (C) legislation permitting (D) highway speed limits to 65 miles per hour on rural Interstates. No error (E)

5. J. M. Barrie's *Peter Pan,* which (A) originated as (B) a play for children, later was reworked (C) as a novel, a popular animated film, and it was turned into a hit musical comedy (D). No error (E)

6. Joe DiMaggio, whose (A) style was one of quiet excellence (B), was consistently the New York Yankees' outstanding player (C) during (D) his thirteen years on the team. No error (E)

7. When Ms. Rivera was (A) truly (B) happy, she does not constantly (C) complain that (D) she has no purpose in life. No error (E)

Answer Explanations

4. **(C)** Error in subject-verb agreement. The antecedent, *Congress*, is singular. Change *have passed* to *has passed.*
5. **(D)** Error in parallelism. All sentence parts listed in a series should have the same form. Change *it was turned into a hit musical comedy* to *a hit musical comedy.*
6. **(E)** Sentence is correct.
7. **(A)** Error in sequence of tenses. The sentence should read: *When Ms. Rivera is truly happy, she does not constantly complain.*

Improving Paragraphs Questions

The improving paragraphs questions test your ability to polish an essay by combining sentences or manipulating sentence parts. You may need to arrange sentences to improve the essay's logical organization or to pick evidence to strengthen the writer's argument.

Improving Paragraphs Directions

The passage below is the unedited draft of a student's essay. Some of the essay needs to be rewritten to make the meaning clearer and more precise. Read the essay carefully.

The essay is followed by questions about changes that might improve all or part of its organization, development, sentence structure, use of language, appropriateness to the audience, or use of standard written English. Choose the answer that most clearly and effectively expresses the student's intended meaning. Indicate your choice by filling in the corresponding space on the answer sheet.

[1] As people grow older, quite obviously, the earth does too. **[2]** And with the process of the earth aging, we must learn to recycle. **[3]** The idea of using things over and over again to conserve our supply of natural resources is a beautiful one. **[4]** Those who don't see how easy it is to recycle should be criticized greatly.

[5] As we become more aware of the earth's problems, we all say "Oh, I'd like to help." **[6]** However, so few really do get involved. **[7]** Recycling is a simple, yet effective place to start. **[8]** Taking aluminum cans to the supermarket to be recycled is an ingenious idea. **[9]** It attracts those who want the money (5 cents a can), and it is also a convenient place to go to. **[10]** In addition, in almost every town, there is a Recycling Center. **[11]** I know that there are separate bins for paper, bottles, cans, etc. **[12]** This is a convenient service to those who recycle. **[13]** It is so easy to drive a few blocks to a center to drop off what needs to be recycled. **[14]** This is just another simple example of how easy it really is to recycle and to get involved. **[15]** Those who don't see its simplicity should be criticized for not doing their part to help make the world a better place.

[16] When I go to other people's houses and see aluminum cans in the garbage, I can honestly say I get enraged. **[17]** Often I say, "Why don't you just recycle those cans instead of throwing them out?" **[18]** What makes me even more angry is when they say "We have no time to recycle them." **[19]** Those people, I feel, should be criticized for not recycling in the past and should be taught a lesson about our earth and how recycling can conserve it.

8. Which of the following most effectively expresses the underlined portion of sentence 2 below?

And <u>with the process of the earth aging</u>, we must learn to recycle.

(A) with the aging process of the earth
(B) the process of the earth's aging
(C) as the earth ages
(D) with the aging earth's process
(E) as the process of the earth's aging continues

9. Considering the essay as a whole, which of the following best explains the main purpose of the second paragraph?

(A) to explain the historical background of the topic
(B) to provide a smooth transition between the first and third paragraphs
(C) to define terms introduced in the first paragraph
(D) to give an example of an idea presented in the first paragraph
(E) to present a different point of view on the issue being discussed

10. Which of the sentences below most effectively combines sentences 10, 11, and 12?

(A) Recycling centers offer recyclers convenience by providing separate bins for paper, bottles, and cans and by being located in almost every town.
(B) Recycling centers, located in almost every town, serve recyclers by providing convenient bins to separate paper, bottles, and cans.
(C) Almost every town has a recycling center with separate bins for paper, bottles, and cans, and this is a convenient service for people who want to recycle.
(D) People who want to recycle will find recycling centers in almost every town, providing a convenient separation of paper, bottles, and cans into bins.
(E) For the convenience of recyclers, separate bins for paper, bottles, and cans are provided by almost every town's recycling center.

Answer Explanations

8. **(C)** This question asks you to find an alternative to a rather awkward group of words, composed of two phrases, *with the process* and *of the earth aging*. The second is graceless and ungrammatical. It should have read *of the earth's aging*, because in standard usage, nouns and pronouns modifying gerunds are usually written as possessives. Knowing what it should have been, however, is not much help in answering the question. You still must select from the five alternatives the one best way to express the essay writer's idea. In the context of the whole sentence, two of the choices, B and D, make no sense at all. A also borders on incomprehensibility. Left with C and E, the better choice is C because it is more concise and it expresses exactly what the writer intended.

9. **(D)** To answer this question, you need to have read the whole essay. You also need to know the way individual paragraphs function in an essay—any essay. Here, all five choices describe legitimate uses of a paragraph, but they don't all apply to this particular essay. Choices A, C, and E can be quickly discarded. Choice B is a possibility because in a unified essay every paragraph (except the first and last) in some sense serves as a bridge between paragraphs. Because the second paragraph is the longest in the essay, however, its main function is probably more than transitional. In fact, it develops by example an idea originating in the first paragraph—how easy it is to recycle. Therefore, D is the best choice.

10. **(B)** In a series of short sentences, every idea carries equal weight. By combining short sentences, writers may emphasize the important ideas and subordinate the others. To answer this question, then, you have to decide which idea expressed by the three sentences ought to be emphasized. Since two of the sentences (11 and 12) refer to the convenient arrangement of recycling centers, that's the point to stress. In the context of the whole essay, the other sentence (10), which pertains to the location of recycling centers, contains less vital information. Usually, the main point of a sentence is contained in the main, or independent, clause, and secondary ideas are found in subordinate, or dependent, clauses.

    With that principle in mind, read each of the choices. A and C give equal weight to the location and convenience of recycling centers. D stresses the location rather than the convenience. E subordinates properly but changes the meaning. Therefore, B is the correct answer. In B, information about the location of recycling centers is contained in a subordinate clause included parenthetically inside the main clause.

TACTICAL WRAP-UP

1. Memorize the directions given in this book for each type of question.
2. Know the format of the test.
3. Expect easy questions at the beginning of many sets of the same question type.
4. Take advantage of the easy questions to boost your score.
5. First answer all the easy questions; then tackle the hard ones if you have time.
6. Eliminate as many wrong answers as you can and then make an educated guess.
7. Change answers *only* if you have a reason for doing so.
8. Calculators are permitted on the math portion of the test, so bring along a calculator that you are comfortable using.
9. Remember that you are allowed to write anything you want in your test booklet. Make good use of it.
10. Be careful not to make any stray marks on your answer sheet.
11. Check frequently to make sure you are answering the questions in the right spots.
12. Line up your test book with your answer sheet to avoid making careless errors.
13. Be particularly careful in marking the student-produced responses on the math grids.
14. Don't get bogged down on any one question.

PART TWO

KNOW YOUR STRENGTHS

A Diagnostic Test

On the following pages you will find a sample PSAT test. Take this test, following the directions below; then score your answers and go over the results using the self-rating guides provided. This should give you a fairly good sense of what your score would be if you didn't do any special preparation for the test.

Once you've done this, you'll be in good shape to come with up with a review plan that meets your needs. You'll know which types of questions you have to practice, which topics in math you must review, which reading skills you have to concentrate on, and which writing skills you need to improve.

HERE'S WHAT YOU NEED TO KNOW:

- Each correct answer is worth 1 point (raw score).
- Except for 10 grid-in math questions in Section 4, every question on the PSAT is multiple-choice.
- The multiple-choice questions have a ¼-point penalty for wrong answers.
- There is *no* penalty for wrong answers on the 10 grid-in math questions.
- If you don't answer a question, your raw score is not affected.

SIMULATE TEST CONDITIONS (TAKE THIS DIAGNOSTIC PSAT AS IF IT'S THE REAL THING)

Total Time: 2 hours, 10 minutes*

- Find a quiet place to work.
- Keep an accurate record of your time.
- If you finish a section early, do not start the next section. Use the remaining minutes to check your work.
- Read the questions closely.
- Work carefully, even if it means you don't get to all the questions.
- Do not spend too much time on questions that seem hard for you.
- If time permits, go back to any questions you left out.
- Do not guess wildly, but whenever you can eliminate one or two answer choices, make an educated guess.

*This does not count the short breaks between the sections (see page vi).

Answer Sheet–Diagnostic Test

Each mark should completely fill the appropriate space, and should be as dark as all other marks. Make all erasures complete. Traces of an erasure may be read as an answer.

Section 1 – Critical Reading
25 minutes

1 Ⓐ Ⓑ Ⓒ Ⓓ Ⓔ
2 Ⓐ Ⓑ Ⓒ Ⓓ Ⓔ
3 Ⓐ Ⓑ Ⓒ Ⓓ Ⓔ
4 Ⓐ Ⓑ Ⓒ Ⓓ Ⓔ
5 Ⓐ Ⓑ Ⓒ Ⓓ Ⓔ
6 Ⓐ Ⓑ Ⓒ Ⓓ Ⓔ
7 Ⓐ Ⓑ Ⓒ Ⓓ Ⓔ
8 Ⓐ Ⓑ Ⓒ Ⓓ Ⓔ
9 Ⓐ Ⓑ Ⓒ Ⓓ Ⓔ
10 Ⓐ Ⓑ Ⓒ Ⓓ Ⓔ
11 Ⓐ Ⓑ Ⓒ Ⓓ Ⓔ
12 Ⓐ Ⓑ Ⓒ Ⓓ Ⓔ
13 Ⓐ Ⓑ Ⓒ Ⓓ Ⓔ
14 Ⓐ Ⓑ Ⓒ Ⓓ Ⓔ
15 Ⓐ Ⓑ Ⓒ Ⓓ Ⓔ
16 Ⓐ Ⓑ Ⓒ Ⓓ Ⓔ
17 Ⓐ Ⓑ Ⓒ Ⓓ Ⓔ
18 Ⓐ Ⓑ Ⓒ Ⓓ Ⓔ
19 Ⓐ Ⓑ Ⓒ Ⓓ Ⓔ
20 Ⓐ Ⓑ Ⓒ Ⓓ Ⓔ
21 Ⓐ Ⓑ Ⓒ Ⓓ Ⓔ
22 Ⓐ Ⓑ Ⓒ Ⓓ Ⓔ
23 Ⓐ Ⓑ Ⓒ Ⓓ Ⓔ
24 Ⓐ Ⓑ Ⓒ Ⓓ Ⓔ

Section 2 – Math
25 minutes

1 Ⓐ Ⓑ Ⓒ Ⓓ Ⓔ
2 Ⓐ Ⓑ Ⓒ Ⓓ Ⓔ
3 Ⓐ Ⓑ Ⓒ Ⓓ Ⓔ
4 Ⓐ Ⓑ Ⓒ Ⓓ Ⓔ
5 Ⓐ Ⓑ Ⓒ Ⓓ Ⓔ
6 Ⓐ Ⓑ Ⓒ Ⓓ Ⓔ
7 Ⓐ Ⓑ Ⓒ Ⓓ Ⓔ
8 Ⓐ Ⓑ Ⓒ Ⓓ Ⓔ
9 Ⓐ Ⓑ Ⓒ Ⓓ Ⓔ
10 Ⓐ Ⓑ Ⓒ Ⓓ Ⓔ
11 Ⓐ Ⓑ Ⓒ Ⓓ Ⓔ
12 Ⓐ Ⓑ Ⓒ Ⓓ Ⓔ
13 Ⓐ Ⓑ Ⓒ Ⓓ Ⓔ
14 Ⓐ Ⓑ Ⓒ Ⓓ Ⓔ
15 Ⓐ Ⓑ Ⓒ Ⓓ Ⓔ
16 Ⓐ Ⓑ Ⓒ Ⓓ Ⓔ
17 Ⓐ Ⓑ Ⓒ Ⓓ Ⓔ
18 Ⓐ Ⓑ Ⓒ Ⓓ Ⓔ
19 Ⓐ Ⓑ Ⓒ Ⓓ Ⓔ
20 Ⓐ Ⓑ Ⓒ Ⓓ Ⓔ

Section 3 – Critical Reading
25 minutes

25 Ⓐ Ⓑ Ⓒ Ⓓ Ⓔ
26 Ⓐ Ⓑ Ⓒ Ⓓ Ⓔ
27 Ⓐ Ⓑ Ⓒ Ⓓ Ⓔ
28 Ⓐ Ⓑ Ⓒ Ⓓ Ⓔ
29 Ⓐ Ⓑ Ⓒ Ⓓ Ⓔ
30 Ⓐ Ⓑ Ⓒ Ⓓ Ⓔ
31 Ⓐ Ⓑ Ⓒ Ⓓ Ⓔ
32 Ⓐ Ⓑ Ⓒ Ⓓ Ⓔ
33 Ⓐ Ⓑ Ⓒ Ⓓ Ⓔ
34 Ⓐ Ⓑ Ⓒ Ⓓ Ⓔ
35 Ⓐ Ⓑ Ⓒ Ⓓ Ⓔ
36 Ⓐ Ⓑ Ⓒ Ⓓ Ⓔ
37 Ⓐ Ⓑ Ⓒ Ⓓ Ⓔ
38 Ⓐ Ⓑ Ⓒ Ⓓ Ⓔ
39 Ⓐ Ⓑ Ⓒ Ⓓ Ⓔ
40 Ⓐ Ⓑ Ⓒ Ⓓ Ⓔ
41 Ⓐ Ⓑ Ⓒ Ⓓ Ⓔ
42 Ⓐ Ⓑ Ⓒ Ⓓ Ⓔ
43 Ⓐ Ⓑ Ⓒ Ⓓ Ⓔ
44 Ⓐ Ⓑ Ⓒ Ⓓ Ⓔ
45 Ⓐ Ⓑ Ⓒ Ⓓ Ⓔ
46 Ⓐ Ⓑ Ⓒ Ⓓ Ⓔ
47 Ⓐ Ⓑ Ⓒ Ⓓ Ⓔ
48 Ⓐ Ⓑ Ⓒ Ⓓ Ⓔ

Remove answer sheet by cutting on dotted line

Section 4 – Math

25 minutes

21 Ⓐ Ⓑ Ⓒ Ⓓ Ⓔ
22 Ⓐ Ⓑ Ⓒ Ⓓ Ⓔ
23 Ⓐ Ⓑ Ⓒ Ⓓ Ⓔ
24 Ⓐ Ⓑ Ⓒ Ⓓ Ⓔ
25 Ⓐ Ⓑ Ⓒ Ⓓ Ⓔ
26 Ⓐ Ⓑ Ⓒ Ⓓ Ⓔ
27 Ⓐ Ⓑ Ⓒ Ⓓ Ⓔ
28 Ⓐ Ⓑ Ⓒ Ⓓ Ⓔ

29

30

31

32

33

34

35

36

37

38

Section 5 – Writing Skills

30 minutes

1 Ⓐ Ⓑ Ⓒ Ⓓ Ⓔ
2 Ⓐ Ⓑ Ⓒ Ⓓ Ⓔ
3 Ⓐ Ⓑ Ⓒ Ⓓ Ⓔ
4 Ⓐ Ⓑ Ⓒ Ⓓ Ⓔ
5 Ⓐ Ⓑ Ⓒ Ⓓ Ⓔ
6 Ⓐ Ⓑ Ⓒ Ⓓ Ⓔ
7 Ⓐ Ⓑ Ⓒ Ⓓ Ⓔ
8 Ⓐ Ⓑ Ⓒ Ⓓ Ⓔ
9 Ⓐ Ⓑ Ⓒ Ⓓ Ⓔ
10 Ⓐ Ⓑ Ⓒ Ⓓ Ⓔ
11 Ⓐ Ⓑ Ⓒ Ⓓ Ⓔ
12 Ⓐ Ⓑ Ⓒ Ⓓ Ⓔ
13 Ⓐ Ⓑ Ⓒ Ⓓ Ⓔ
14 Ⓐ Ⓑ Ⓒ Ⓓ Ⓔ
15 Ⓐ Ⓑ Ⓒ Ⓓ Ⓔ
16 Ⓐ Ⓑ Ⓒ Ⓓ Ⓔ
17 Ⓐ Ⓑ Ⓒ Ⓓ Ⓔ
18 Ⓐ Ⓑ Ⓒ Ⓓ Ⓔ
19 Ⓐ Ⓑ Ⓒ Ⓓ Ⓔ
20 Ⓐ Ⓑ Ⓒ Ⓓ Ⓔ
21 Ⓐ Ⓑ Ⓒ Ⓓ Ⓔ
22 Ⓐ Ⓑ Ⓒ Ⓓ Ⓔ
23 Ⓐ Ⓑ Ⓒ Ⓓ Ⓔ
24 Ⓐ Ⓑ Ⓒ Ⓓ Ⓔ
25 Ⓐ Ⓑ Ⓒ Ⓓ Ⓔ
26 Ⓐ Ⓑ Ⓒ Ⓓ Ⓔ
27 Ⓐ Ⓑ Ⓒ Ⓓ Ⓔ
28 Ⓐ Ⓑ Ⓒ Ⓓ Ⓔ
29 Ⓐ Ⓑ Ⓒ Ⓓ Ⓔ
30 Ⓐ Ⓑ Ⓒ Ⓓ Ⓔ
31 Ⓐ Ⓑ Ⓒ Ⓓ Ⓔ
32 Ⓐ Ⓑ Ⓒ Ⓓ Ⓔ
33 Ⓐ Ⓑ Ⓒ Ⓓ Ⓔ
34 Ⓐ Ⓑ Ⓒ Ⓓ Ⓔ
35 Ⓐ Ⓑ Ⓒ Ⓓ Ⓔ
36 Ⓐ Ⓑ Ⓒ Ⓓ Ⓔ
37 Ⓐ Ⓑ Ⓒ Ⓓ Ⓔ
38 Ⓐ Ⓑ Ⓒ Ⓓ Ⓔ
39 Ⓐ Ⓑ Ⓒ Ⓓ Ⓔ

SECTION 1/CRITICAL READING

TIME: 25 MINUTES

24 QUESTIONS (1–24)

Directions: For each question in this section, select the best answer from among the choices given and fill in the corresponding circle on the answer sheet.

Each sentence below has one or two blanks, each blank indicating that something has been omitted. Beneath the sentence are five words or sets of words labeled A through E. Choose the word or set of words that, when inserted in the sentence, best fits the meaning of the sentence as a whole.

EXAMPLE:

Medieval kingdoms did not become constitutional republics overnight; on the contrary, the change was ----.

(A) unpopular (B) unexpected
(C) advantageous (D) sufficient (E) gradual

Ⓐ Ⓑ Ⓒ Ⓓ ●

1. For Miró, art became a ---- ritual: paper and pencils were holy objects to him, and he worked as though he were performing a religious rite.
(A) superficial (B) sacred (C) banal
(D) cryptic (E) futile

2. Many Wright scholars, striving for accurate reconstructions of the architect's life, have been ---- by the palpable ---- and smoke screens of Wright's autobiography.
(A) delighted..truths (B) amazed..facts
(C) vexed..errors (D) confused..precision
(E) entertained..omissions

3. A certain ---- in Singer's prose always keeps one at arm's length from his protagonist's emotions.
(A) detachment (B) lyricism (C) fluency
(D) brevity (E) rhythm

4. The books' topics are no less varied than their bindings, for their prolific author has ---- specialization as energetically as some of his colleagues have ---- it.
(A) resisted..pursued
(B) admired..supported
(C) endorsed..accepted
(D) defended..attacked
(E) repudiated..deliberated

5. The mayfly is an ---- creature: its adult life lasts little more than a day.
(A) elegant (B) ephemeral (C) idiosyncratic
(D) impulsive (E) omnivorous

GO ON TO NEXT PAGE ▶

Directions: The passages below are followed by questions on their content; questions following a pair of related passages may also be based on the relationship between the paired passages. Answer the questions on the basis of what is stated or implied in the passages and in any introductory material that may be provided.

Questions 6–9 are based on the following passage.

Passage 1

Knighthoods are not what they used to be. Members of the press have had a field day with the recent knighting of Mick Jagger, rock and roll's perennial bad boy. Though Sir Mick, as he is now to be called, is not the first rock and roller to be dubbed a knight—Sir Elton John was knighted in 1997, Sir Paul McCartney in 1996—he is the most notorious. One reporter even quipped that Jagger's trip to Buckingham Palace was not his first experience with royal hospitality: in 1967 he had spent a night in Her Majesty's Prison, Brixton, convicted of drug possession.

Passage 2

What factors led to the decline of the armored knight? Although some scholars have hypothesized that developing technology, in particular the invention of firearms, rendered knights in armor obsolete, this suggestion seems unlikely. On the contrary, throughout the Middle Ages and well into the fifteenth century, technological developments contributed to the effectiveness of the chivalry, enabling them to consolidate their positions both politically and economically. Rather than technological obsolescence spelling the doom of these mounted warriors, it seems more likely that changes in basic army structure—the development of the modern professional army, based on the Swiss model—and the high costs of outfitting themselves with steeds and armor led many knights to abandon their careers as professional fighting men.

6. The reaction of the press to the news of Jagger's knighting (lines 2–4) can best be characterized as one of

(A) indifference
(B) disappointment
(C) outrage
(D) envy
(E) glee

7. The phrase "royal hospitality" (line 10) is being used

(A) literally
(B) ironically
(C) colloquially
(D) descriptively
(E) objectively

8. Both passages make the point that the institution of knighthood

(A) glorifies professional fighting men
(B) has undergone changes over time
(C) reached its high point in the fifteenth century
(D) depends on technological progress
(E) requires a mounted order of chivalry

9. Which best expresses the relationship between Passage 2 and Passage 1?

(A) Passage 2 provides a technical explanation for the examples cited in Passage 1.
(B) Passage 2 advocates particular changes as a result of the situation described in Passage 1.
(C) Passage 2 expresses reservations about the value of a tradition whose vitality is acclaimed in Passage 1.
(D) Passage 2 offers historical perspective on an institution whose current guise is mocked in Passage 1.
(E) Passage 2 questions an assumption underlying the ideas expressed in Passage 1.

GO ON TO NEXT PAGE ►

Directions: Each passage below is followed by questions based on its content. Answer the questions following each passage on the basis of what is stated or implied in that passage and in any introductory material that may be provided.

Questions 10–15 are based on the following passage.

The world's tropical rain forests contain varieties of plant and animal life found nowhere else on earth. The following passage presents background information on the epiphytes and their relatives the strangler trees, fascinating specimens of rain forest plant life.

The great trees furnish support for much of the other plant life of the forest. Climbers are abundant, much more so than elsewhere. Greedy for light, they have various adaptations for hoisting themselves to the upper canopy—some are twiners, others are equipped with tendrils, hooks or suckers. An entire group of plants is unfitted to start low and climb high to reach the light. These are epiphytes, plants that grow on trees without parasitizing them or deriving any advantage except a platform near the sun. They are extraordinarily common. However, in order to grow close to the sunlight, they have had to pay a price—they have lost their root connection with the forest floor and its abundant moisture. For soil, they must often make do with the small amounts of debris that lodge in crannies in the trees, with dust from the atmosphere and organic matter and seeds deposited by ants that often nest in the roots of epiphytes—a small but vital source of humus and minerals. So well have these plants managed to create their own environment that the spoonfuls of soil in which they grow do not differ significantly from normal soil in microbiological processes.

Some of the epiphytes have developed remarkable adaptations for conserving water. Many are encased in a waxy layer that retards evaporation. The roots of some orchids have a spongy tissue that not only soaks up water but also carries on photosynthesis. The staghorn fern accumulates water-holding humus in a sort of bucket structure at the base of its leaves. The large group of tropical plants known as bromeliads are living cisterns—their long branching leaves spring from the same place around the stem, and overlap so tightly at their bases that they can hold water, as much as four-and-a-half quarts in a large plant. These bromeliad tanks become a center of life, holding breeding frogs, snails and aquatic insects, all of which add to the supply of nutrients in the water. Hairs at the base of the leaves line the tank and perform the job of absorbing water and nutrients, making the bromeliad independent of a root connection with the soil.

The problems of living in the dark rain forest, and the unusual efforts made to rise into the sun, are best symbolized by the strangler trees. They achieve their place in the sun by stealth. The strangler begins life as an epiphyte, its seed germinating high up in the fork of a large tree. The seedling puts out two kinds of roots: one seizes the branch and serves as a grapple to hold the plant in place, and the other dangles like a cable, growing steadily closer to the soil. Until it makes contact with the ground, the strangler grows like any other epiphyte, obtaining small quantities of water and nutrients from the debris in the tree crevice. But once the descending root reaches the soil its source of supply is increased enormously and the plant's growth quickens. It sprouts more leaves high in the canopy and grows upward toward a sunlit window between the leaves; a maze of additional feeding cables descends to the soil and eventually the supporting tree is encased in a network of them. It was once thought that the strangler kills the forest giant by the simple process of enwrapping it and preventing its trunk from expanding, but it is now known that it actually squeezes its host to death. As the hold tightens, the strangler's roots thicken to a marked degree, preparing for the time when it will need props to stand by itself in the sunlight it has captured. The host finally expires, thoroughly encased inside the "trunk" (actually the fused roots) of the strangler tree which now stands on its own pedestal as a member of the high forest canopy.

10. According to the passage, some epiphytes are particularly adapted to

(A) the floor of the tropical rain forest
(B) a sunless environment
(C) the dissipation of rainwater
(D) drawing sustenance from a host
(E) the retention of liquid

GO ON TO NEXT PAGE ▶

11. It can be inferred from the passage that one of the following is true of epiphytes.

(A) They lack root systems.
(B) They do not require large amounts of soil for growth.
(C) They are incapable of photosynthesis.
(D) They are hard to perceive in the dense rain forest canopy.
(E) They need different nutrients than other plants do.

12. The passage can best be described as

(A) enthusiastic exhortation
(B) sophisticated analysis
(C) straightforward description
(D) indirect exposition
(E) forceful argument

13. The author states all of the following about the strangler tree EXCEPT

(A) It eventually becomes self-supporting.
(B) Its feeding cables ascend toward the forest canopy.
(C) Its roots extend far from its point of germination.
(D) It undergoes a rapid growth spurt.
(E) Its roots become conspicuously larger.

14. In line 72, "marked" most nearly means

(A) noticeable
(B) branded
(C) graded
(D) doomed
(E) unique

15. Which of the following does the passage suggest about the strangler tree?

(A) It needs only a small supply of nutrients for full growth.
(B) All its roots seek the forest floor.
(C) It outgrows its need for its host.
(D) It is killed by the forest giant that supports it.
(E) It eventually sheds its feeder cables.

Questions 16–24 are based on the following passage.

The passage below is excerpted from the introduction to Bury My Heart at Wounded Knee, *written in 1970 by the Native American historian Dee Brown.*

Line

Since the exploratory journey of Lewis and Clark to the Pacific Coast early in the nineteenth century, the number of published accounts describing the "opening" of the American West has risen into the thousands. The greatest concentration of recorded experience and observation came out of the thirty-year span between 1860 and 1890—the period covered by this book. It was an incredible era of violence, greed, audacity, sentimentality, undirected exuberance, and an almost reverential attitude toward the ideal of personal freedom for those who already had it.

During that time the culture and civilization of the American Indian was destroyed, and out of that time came virtually all the great myths of the American West—tales of fur traders, mountain men, steamboat pilots, goldseekers, gamblers, gunmen, cavalrymen, cowboys, harlots, missionaries, schoolmarms, and homesteaders. Only occasionally was the voice of the Indian heard, and then more often than not it was recorded by the pen of a white man. The Indian was the dark menace of the myths, and even if he had known how to write in English, where would he have found a printer or a publisher?

Yet they are not all lost, those Indian voices of the past. A few authentic accounts of American western history were recorded by Indians either in pictographs or in translated English, and some managed to get published in obscure journals, pamphlets, or books of small circulation. In the late nineteenth century, when the white man's curiosity about Indian survivors of the wars reached a high point, enterprising newspaper reporters frequently interviewed warriors and chiefs and gave them an opportunity to express their opinions on what was happening in the West. The quality of these interviews varied greatly, depending upon the abilities of the interpreters, or upon the inclination of the Indians to speak freely. Some feared reprisals for telling the truth, while others delighted in hoaxing reporters with tall tales and shaggy-dog stories.

GO ON TO NEXT PAGE ▶

Contemporary newspaper statements by Indians must therefore be read with skepticism, although some of them are masterpieces of irony and others burn with outbursts of poetic fury.

Among the richest sources of first-person statements by Indians are the records of treaty councils and other formal meetings with civilian and military representatives of the United States government. Isaac Pitman's new stenographic system was coming into vogue in the second half of the nineteenth century, and when Indians spoke in council a recording clerk sat beside the official interpreter.

Even when the meetings were in remote parts of the West, someone usually was available to write down the speeches, and because of the slowness of the translation process, much of what was said could be recorded in longhand. Interpreters quite often were half-bloods who knew spoken languages but seldom could read or write. Like most oral peoples they and the Indians depended upon imagery to express their thoughts, so that the English translations were filled with graphic similes and metaphors of the natural world. If an eloquent Indian had a poor interpreter, his words might be transformed to flat prose, but a good interpreter could make a poor speaker sound poetic.

Most Indian leaders spoke freely and candidly in councils with white officials, and as they became more sophisticated in such matters during the 1870's and 1880's, they demanded the right to choose their own interpreters and recorders. In this latter period, all members of the tribes were free to speak, and some of the older men chose such opportunities to recount events they had witnessed in the past, or sum up the histories of their peoples. Although the Indians who lived through this doom period of their civilization have vanished from the earth, millions of their words are preserved in official records. Many of the more important council proceedings were published in government documents and reports.

Out of all these sources of almost forgotten oral history, I have tried to fashion a narrative of the conquest of the American West as the victims experienced it, using their own words whenever possible. Americans who have always looked westward when reading about this period should read this book facing eastward.

This is not a cheerful book, but history has a way of intruding upon the present, and perhaps those who read it will have a clearer understanding of what the American Indian is, by knowing what he was. They may learn something about their own relationship to the earth from a people who were true conservationists. The Indians knew that life was equated with the earth and its resources, that America was a paradise, and they could not comprehend why the intruders from the East were determined to destroy all that was Indian as well as America itself.

16. A main concern of the author in this passage is to
(A) denounce the white man for his untrustworthiness and savagery
(B) evaluate the effectiveness of the military treaty councils
(C) argue for the improved treatment of Indians today
(D) suggest that Indian narratives of the conquest of the West are similar to white accounts
(E) introduce the background of the original source materials for his text

17. In line 4, the quotation marks around the word "opening" serve to
(A) emphasize the author's belief that the conquest of the West took place much earlier
(B) demonstrate the uniqueness of the author's choice of words
(C) indicate the author's disagreement with a term in common use
(D) emphasize the need for the word to be stressed when it is spoken aloud
(E) criticize the rapid growth in number of these published accounts

18. In lines 5–6, "concentration" most nearly means
(A) memory
(B) attention
(C) diligence
(D) imprisonment
(E) cluster

GO ON TO NEXT PAGE ▶

19. According to the passage, nineteenth-century newspaper accounts of interviews with Indians are variable in quality for which of the following reasons?

I. Lack of skill on the part of the translators
II. The tendency of the reporters to overstate what they were told by the Indians
III. The Indians' misgivings about possible retaliations

(A) I only
(B) III only
(C) I and II only
(D) I and III only
(E) I, II, and III

20. The author's tone in describing the Indian survivors can best be described as

(A) skeptical (B) detached (C) elegiac
(D) obsequious (E) impatient

21. The author is most impressed by which aspect of the English translations of Indian speeches?

(A) Their vividness of imagery
(B) Their lack of frankness
(C) The inefficiency of the process
(D) Their absence of sophistication
(E) Their brevity of expression

22. In line 69, "flat" most nearly means

(A) smooth (B) level (C) pedestrian
(D) horizontal (E) unequivocal

23. The author most likely suggests that Americans should read this book facing eastward

(A) in an inappropriate attempt at levity
(B) out of respect for Western superstitions
(C) in order to read by natural light
(D) because the Indians came from the East
(E) to identify with the Indians' viewpoint

24. In line 101, "equated with" most nearly means

(A) reduced to an average with
(B) necessarily tied to
(C) numerically equal to
(D) fulfilled by
(E) differentiated by

IF YOU FINISH IN LESS THAN 25 MINUTES, YOU MAY CHECK YOUR WORK ON THIS SECTION ONLY. DO NOT TURN TO ANY OTHER SECTION IN THE TEST.

STOP

SECTION 2 /MATHEMATICS

TIME: 25 MINUTES

20 QUESTIONS (1–20)

Directions:

For each question in this section, determine which of the five choices is correct, and blacken that choice on your answer sheet. You may use any blank space on the page for your work.

NOTES:

- You may use a calculator whenever you believe it will be helpful.
- Use the diagrams provided to help you solve the problems. Unless you see the phrase <u>Note:</u> Figure not drawn to scale under a diagram, it has been drawn as accurately as possible. Unless it is stated that a figure is three dimensional, you may assume that it lies in a plane.

Reference

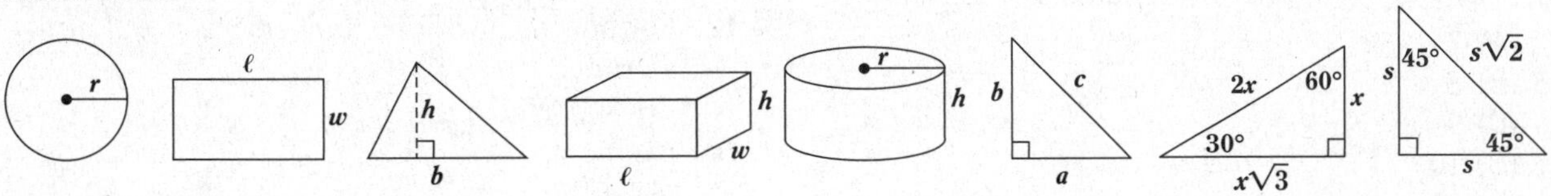

$A = \pi r^2$ $C = 2\pi r$ | $A = \ell w$ | $A = \frac{1}{2}bh$ | $V = \ell wh$ | $V = \pi r^2 h$ | $c^2 = a^2 + b^2$ | **Special Right Triangles**

Number of degrees in a circle: 360

Sum of the measures, in degrees, of the three angles of a triangle: 180

1. If $4x = 12$, then $12x =$

(A) 4
(B) 6
(C) 24
(D) 36
(E) 48

2. Which of the following numbers has the same digit in the hundreds and hundredths places?

(A) 3300.0033
(B) 3335.3553
(C) 3353.5353
(D) 3357.3573
(E) 3357.7533

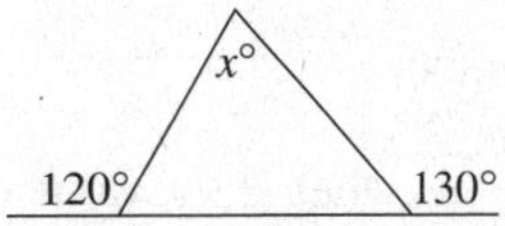

3. In the figure above, what is the value of x?

(A) 50
(B) 60
(C) 70
(D) 110
(E) It cannot be determined from the information given.

4. For how many integers n is it true that $n^2 - 10$ is negative?

(A) 5
(B) 6
(C) 7
(D) 10
(E) More than 10

GO ON TO NEXT PAGE ▶

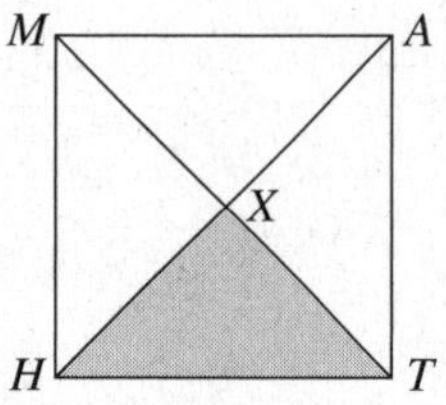

5. In the figure above, *MATH* is a square. If $MX = 3$, what is the area of the shaded triangle?

(A) $\frac{9}{4}$
(B) $\frac{9\sqrt{3}}{4}$
(C) 4.5
(D) 9
(E) 18

6. If $7x + 5 = 74$, what is the value of $\sqrt{7x - 5}$?

(A) 7
(B) 8
(C) 9
(D) 10
(E) 11

7. How many primes less than 100 are divisible by 3?

(A) none
(B) 1
(C) more than 1 but less than 33
(D) 33
(E) more than 33

8. If $f(x) = x^2 - 2^x$, what is the value of $f(3)$?

(A) -17
(B) -1
(C) 0
(D) 1
(E) 17

9. If Michael can paint $\frac{2}{5}$ of a room in an hour at this rate, how many rooms can he paint in *h* hours?

(A) $\frac{2h}{5}$
(B) $\frac{5h}{2}$
(C) $h - \frac{2}{5}$
(D) $\frac{2}{5h}$
(E) $\frac{5}{2h}$

10. If $x^2 + 1 = 50$, which of the following could be the value of $x + 1$?

(A) -8
(B) -6
(C) $\sqrt{50}$
(D) 6
(E) 7

11. Evelyn's average (arithmetic mean) on her six math tests this marking period is 80. Fortunately for Evelyn, her teacher drops each student's lowest grade; doing so raises Evelyn's average to 90. What was her lowest grade?

(A) 20
(B) 25
(C) 30
(D) 40
(E) 50

12. For how many prime numbers p is $p + 1$ also a prime?

(A) None
(B) 1
(C) 2
(D) 3
(E) More than 3

Questions 13 and 14 refer to the following definition.

$\boxed{W \quad X \quad Y \quad Z}$ is a *number bar* if $W + Z = X + Y$ and $2W = 3X$.

13. If $\boxed{3 \quad X \quad Y \quad 7}$ is a *number bar*, what is the value of Y?

(A) 0
(B) 2
(C) 4
(D) 6
(E) 8

14. If $\boxed{W \quad X \quad Y \quad W}$ is a *number bar*, $Y =$

(A) $\frac{3}{4}W$
(B) W
(C) $\frac{4}{3}W$
(D) $3W$
(E) $4W$

GO ON TO NEXT PAGE ▶

15. If m is an integer, which of the following could be true?

I. $\frac{16}{m}$ is an odd integer
II. $\frac{m}{16}$ is an odd integer
III. $16m$ is an odd integer

(A) I only
(B) II only
(C) III only
(D) I and II only
(E) I, II, and III

16. What is the volume, in cubic inches, of a cube whose surface area is 60 square inches?

(A) $10\sqrt{10}$
(B) $15\sqrt{15}$
(C) $60\sqrt{60}$
(D) 1000
(E) 3375

17. In rectangle $PQRS$, diagonal PR makes a 60° angle with side PS. If $PR = 10$, what is the area of the rectangle?

(A) $25\sqrt{2}$
(B) $25\sqrt{3}$
(C) 48
(D) 50
(E) 100

18. If $25 - 2\sqrt{x} = 7$, then $x =$

(A) -81
(B) 9
(C) 36
(D) 49
(E) 81

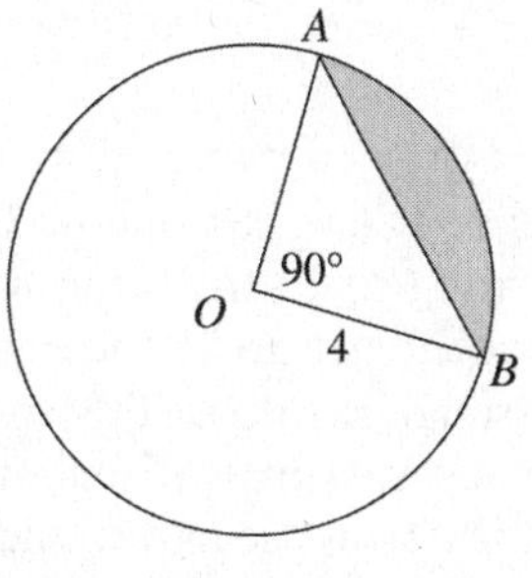

19. In the figure above, the radius of circle O is 4, and $m\angle AOB = 90°$. What is the perimeter of the shaded region?

(A) $4 + 2\pi$
(B) $4\sqrt{2} + \pi$
(C) $4\sqrt{2} + 2\pi$
(D) $4\sqrt{3} + \pi$
(E) $4\sqrt{3} + 2\pi$

20. Because her test turned out to be more difficult than she intended it to be, a teacher decided to adjust the grades by deducting only half the number of points a student missed. For example, if a student missed 20 points, she received a 90 instead of an 80. Before the grades were adjusted Mary's grade was G. What was her grade after the adjustment?

(A) $50 + \frac{G}{2}$
(B) $\frac{1}{2}(100 - G)$
(C) $100 - \frac{G}{2}$
(D) $\frac{100 - G}{2}$
(E) $G + 25$

IF YOU FINISH IN LESS THAN 25 MINUTES, YOU MAY CHECK YOUR WORK ON THIS SECTION ONLY. DO NOT TURN TO ANY OTHER SECTION IN THE TEST.

STOP

SECTION 3 /CRITICAL READING

TIME: 25 MINUTES

24 QUESTIONS (25–48)

Directions: For each question in this section, select the best answer from among the choices given and fill in the corresponding circle on the answer sheet.

Each sentence below has one or two blanks, each blank indicating that something has been omitted. Beneath the sentence are five words or sets of words labeled A through E. Choose the word or set of words that, when inserted in the sentence, best fits the meaning of the sentence as a whole.

EXAMPLE:

Medieval kingdoms did not become constitutional republics overnight; on the contrary, the change was ----.

(A) unpopular (B) unexpected
(C) advantageous (D) sufficient (E) gradual

Ⓐ Ⓑ Ⓒ Ⓓ ●

25. Feeling ---- about her latest victories, the tennis champion looked smugly at the row of trophies on her mantelpiece.

(A) downcast (B) agitated (C) indifferent
(D) complacent (E) philosophical

26. Normally an individual thunderstorm lasts about 45 minutes, but under certain conditions the storm may ----, becoming ever more severe, for as long as four hours.

(A) wane (B) moderate (C) persist
(D) vacillate (E) disperse

27. The newest fiber-optic cables that carry telephone calls cross-country are made of glass so ---- that a piece 100 miles thick is clearer than a standard windowpane.

(A) fragile (B) immaculate (C) tangible
(D) transparent (E) iridescent

28. Her employers could not complain about her work because she was ---- in the ---- of her duties.

(A) derelict..performance
(B) importunate..observance
(C) meticulous..postponement
(D) assiduous..execution
(E) hidebound..conception

29. Decorated in ---- style, his home contained bits and pieces of furnishings from widely divergent periods, strikingly juxtaposed to create a unique decor.

(A) an aesthetic (B) a lyrical (C) a traditional
(D) an eclectic (E) a perfunctory

30. Equipped with mechanisms that deliberately delay sprouting, woodland seeds often seem sadly ---- to germinate.

(A) prone (B) reluctant (C) qualified
(D) prolific (E) modified

31. Soap operas and situation comedies, though given to distortion, are so derivative of contemporary culture that they are inestimable ---- the attitudes and values of our society in any particular decade.

(A) contradictions of (B) antidotes to
(C) indices of (D) prerequisites for
(E) determinants of

32. Although eighteenth-century English society as a whole did not encourage learning for its own sake in women, nonetheless it illogically ---- women's sad lack of education.

(A) palliated (B) postulated
(C) decried (D) brooked
(E) vaunted

GO ON TO NEXT PAGE ▶

Directions: Each of the passages below precedes two questions based on its content. Answer the questions following each passage on the basis of what is stated or implied in that passage.

Questions 33 and 34 are based on the following passage.

One of the world's most celebrated crusaders for social justice and peace is South Africa's Archbishop Desmond Tutu. Despite his prominence, however, Archbishop Tutu has always made time for his people. On the day in 1984 that he was named winner of the Nobel Peace Prize, reporters and photographers mobbed the seminary where he was staying. A press conference was hastily set up. Just as it was to begin, the archbishop's student assistant entered the courtyard, returning from a family funeral. Leaving the microphones and cameras behind, the archbishop went to comfort her. The world press could wait; her grief could not.

33. The anecdote about Archbishop Tutu serves primarily to demonstrate his
(A) fame (B) anguish (C) distraction
(D) compassion (E) peacefulness

34. In lines 3–4, "prominence" most nearly means
(A) projection (B) high altitude
(C) land elevation (D) emphasis (E) renown

Questions 35 and 36 are based on the following passage.

Although most of the world's active volcanoes are located along the edges of the great shifting plates that make up Earth's surface, there are more than 100 isolated areas of volcanic activity far from the nearest plate boundary. Geologists call these volcanic areas hot spots. Lying deep in the interior of a plate, hot spots or intra-plate volcanoes are sources of magma, the red-hot, molten material within the earth's crust. These intra-plate volcanoes often form volcanic chains, trails of extinct volcanoes. Such volcanic chains serve as landmarks signaling the slow but relentless passage of the plates.

35. The term "hot spot" is being used in the passage
(A) rhetorically (B) colloquially
(C) technically (D) ambiguously
(E) ironically

36. Hot spots differ from other areas of volcanic activity in their
(A) temperature (B) location (C) composition
(D) volatility (E) relevance

Diagnostic Test

GO ON TO NEXT PAGE ▶

Directions: The passages below are followed by questions on their content; questions following a pair of related passages may also be based on the relationship between the paired passages. Answer the questions on the basis of what is stated or implied in the passages and in any introductory material that may be provided.

Questions 37–48 are based on the following passages.

In Passage 1, the author, the dancer-choreographer Martha Graham, draws on her experience as a dancer to generalize about her art. In Passage 2, the author, California chef Alice Waters, presents her approach to cooking, as practiced at her restaurant, Chez Panisse.

Passage 1

I am a dancer. My experience has been with dance as an art.

Each art has an instrument and a medium. The instrument of the dance is the human body; the medium is movement. The body has always been to me a thrilling wonder, a dynamo of energy, exciting, courageous, powerful; a delicately balanced logic and proportion. It has not been my aim to evolve or discover a new method of dance training, but rather to dance significantly. To dance significantly means "through the medium of discipline and by means of a sensitive, strong instrument, to bring into focus unhackneyed movement: a human being."

I did not want to be a tree, a flower, or a wave. In a dancer's body, we as audience must see *ourselves*, not the imitated behavior of everyday actions, not the phenomena of nature, not exotic creatures from another planet, but something of the miracle that is a human being, motivated, disciplined, concentrated.

Technique and training have never been a substitute for that condition of awareness which is talent, for that complete miracle of balance which is genius, but it can give plasticity and tension, freedom and discipline, balancing one against the other. It can awaken memory of the race through muscular memory of the body. Training and technique are means to strength, to freedom, to spontaneity.

Contrary to popular belief, spontaneity as one sees it in dance or in theater, is not wholly dependent on emotion at that instant. It is the condition of emotion objectified. It plays that part in theater that light plays in life. It illumines. It excites. Spontaneity is essentially dependent on energy, upon the strength necessary to perfect timing. It is the result of perfect timing to the Now. It is not essentially intellectual or emotional, but is nerve reaction.

To me, the acquirement of nervous, physical, and emotional concentration is the one element possessed to the highest degree by the truly great dancers of the world. Its acquirement is the result of discipline, of energy in the deep sense. That is why there are so few great dancers.

A great dancer is not made by technique alone any more than a great statesman is made by knowledge alone. Both possess true spontaneity. Spontaneity in behavior, in life, is due largely to complete health; on the stage to a technical use—often so ingrained by proper training as to seem instinctive—of nervous energy. Perhaps what we have always called intuition is merely a nervous system organized by training to perceive.

Passage 2

Flexibility is an essential component of good cooking. You should never feel locked in to a recipe or a menu unless it involves a basic principle regarding procedure or technique such as those involved in breadmaking and pastry. I don't ever want to write anything in this book that is so precise that the reader must invoke great powers of concentration on every last detail in order to ensure the success of a recipe or a dinner; ingredients are simply too variable. I want to *suggest* the expected taste; I want to *suggest* the appearance of the complete dish; I want to *suggest* the combination of ingredients; and I want to *suggest* the overall harmony and balance of the meal. Then it will be up to you to determine the correct balance and composition. Perhaps the garlic is sharp and strong and you will use it sparingly in a particular presentation, or you may find the garlic to be sweet and fresh and you will want to use twice as much!

GO ON TO NEXT PAGE ►

Learn to trust your own instincts. A good cook needs only to have positive feelings about food in general, and about the pleasures of eating and cooking. I have known some cooks who did not seem to discover pleasure and gratification in things culinary. At the restaurant, I look for employees who are interested in working in the kitchen for reasons above and beyond those of simply needing a job, any job. This applies equally to the home cook: a cook who dislikes food is a bad cook. Period. Even an ambivalent cook is a bad cook. Yet a person who responds to the cooking processes and the mound of fresh ingredients with a genuine glow of delight is likely to be, or become, a very good cook indeed. Technical skills can be acquired and perfected along the way, but dislike or ambivalence toward food cannot always be overcome.

In the early stages of my culinary pursuits, I cooked as I had seen cooking done in France. I copied some of the more traditional cooks, and I stayed within the bounds they had laid out so carefully because I didn't trust my own instincts yet. Having imitated their styles, I found that with time and experience, their fundamental principles had become a part of my nature and I began to understand why they had done certain things in a particular way. Then I could begin to develop a different and more personal style based on the ingredients available to me here in California.

37. Graham rejects movement in dance that is

(A) jerky (B) spontaneous (C) brief
(D) trite (E) natural

38. In saying that she "did not want to be a tree, a flower, or a wave" (lines 15–16), Graham

(A) emphasizes that dancers must express their humanity
(B) reveals an innate discomfort with natural phenomena
(C) suggests a budding desire to imitate other phenomena
(D) conveys a sense of unsatisfied longings
(E) indicates impatience with how long such transformations take

39. In line 25, "plasticity" most nearly means

(A) nervous energy
(B) strength and endurance
(C) mobility and pliancy
(D) organic coherence
(E) muscular memory

40. According to Graham, most people believe that spontaneous theatrical moments

(A) are the product of disciplined rehearsal and training
(B) happen only because the actor is gripped by a sudden emotion
(C) are dependent on the audience's willingness to suspend their disbelief
(D) depends upon the quickness of the actor's reaction time
(E) are more objective than subjective

41. Graham attempts to clarify the function of spontaneity in dance or theater (lines 34–36) by means of

(A) a digression
(B) an analogy
(C) a hypothesis
(D) an anecdote
(E) a quotation

42. In Passage 2, Waters is discussing cooking from the point of view of

(A) a chef on the verge of opening her own restaurant
(B) someone uninformed about traditional methods of French cuisine
(C) an accomplished practitioner of the culinary arts
(D) a gifted home cook and collector of recipes
(E) a professional determined to outstrip her competitors

43. Waters uses the example of the garlic (lines 71–75) to show

(A) the variability of ingredients
(B) the importance of every last detail
(C) her insistence on fresh ingredients
(D) the need to be a flexible shopper
(E) her preference for strong flavors

GO ON TO NEXT PAGE ▶

44. In writing her cookbook, Waters is trying to

(A) anticipate any pitfalls those using her recipes might run into
(B) provide precise measurements for her readers to follow
(C) limit herself to basic principles and procedures
(D) dictate the spices going into each meal
(E) allow scope for the reader's own culinary initiative

45. To Waters, to produce superior results, the cook must possess

(A) an excellent sense of smell
(B) first-rate technical skills
(C) the finest kitchen equipment
(D) detailed recipes to follow
(E) a love of her medium

46. In lines 81–84 Waters indicates she seeks restaurant employees who share her

(A) level of expertise
(B) classical French training
(C) enjoyment of culinary processes
(D) willingness to work long hours
(E) respect for tradition

47. In these passages, both Graham and Waters are

(A) examining their consciences
(B) presenting their artistic creeds
(C) criticizing their opponents
(D) analyzing their impact on their fields
(E) reassessing their chosen professions

48. Waters and Graham seem alike in that they both

(A) have an abundant supply of nervous energy
(B) benefited from extensive classical training
(C) occasionally distrust their own instincts
(D) are passionately involved with their art
(E) believe in maintaining a positive attitude

IF YOU FINISH IN LESS THAN 25 MINUTES, YOU MAY CHECK YOUR WORK ON THIS SECTION ONLY. DO NOT TURN TO ANY OTHER SECTION IN THE TEST.

STOP

SECTION 4/MATHEMATICS

TIME: 25 MINUTES

18 QUESTIONS (21–38)

Directions:

For questions 21–28, determine which of the five choices is correct, and blacken that choice on your answer sheet. You may use any blank space on the page for your work.

NOTES:

- You may use a calculator whenever you believe it will be helpful.
- Use the diagrams provided to help you solve the problems. Unless you see the phrase Note: Figure not drawn to scale under a diagram, it has been drawn as accurately as possible. Unless it is stated that a figure is three dimensional, you may assume that it lies in a plane.

Reference

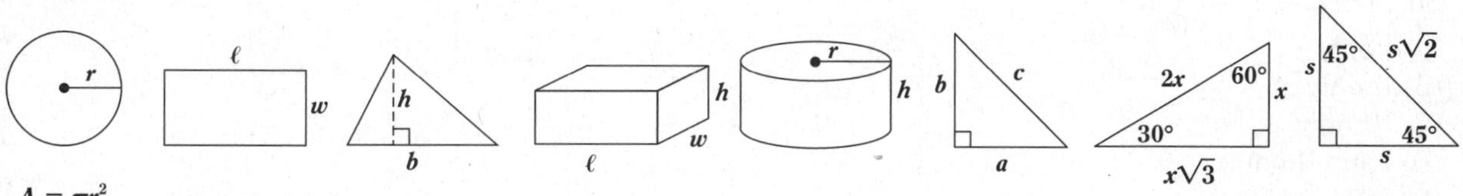

$A = \pi r^2$ $C = 2\pi r$ $A = \ell w$ $A = \frac{1}{2}bh$ $V = \ell wh$ $V = \pi r^2 h$ $c^2 = a^2 + b^2$ **Special Right Triangles**

Number of degrees in a circle: 360

Sum of the measures, in degrees, of the three angles of a triangle: 180

21. If $7d + 5 = 5d + 7$, what is the value of d?

(A) −1
(B) 0
(C) 1
(D) 5
(E) 7

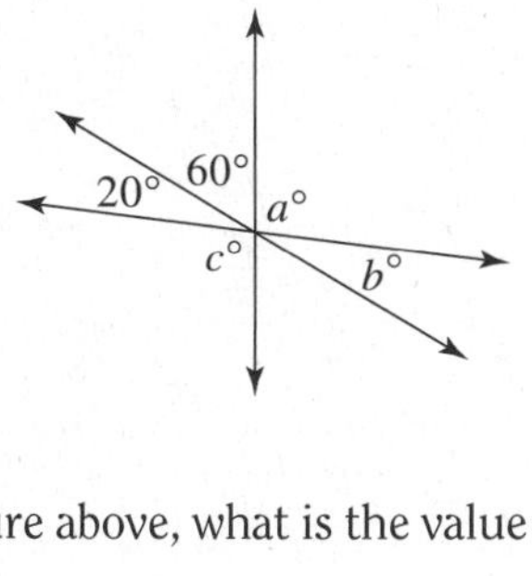

22. In the figure above, what is the value of $a + b + c$?

(A) 210
(B) 220
(C) 240
(D) 270
(E) 280

23. If $5\sqrt{x} + 1 = 46$, what is the value of x?

(A) 1
(B) 3
(C) 9
(D) 81
(E) 729

24. If $x^2 = y^2$, which of the following must be true?

(A) $x = y$
(B) $x = -y$
(C) $y = |x|$
(D) $x = |y|$
(E) $|x| = |y|$

GO ON TO NEXT PAGE ▶

<u>Questions 25 and 26</u> refer to the following definition.

For all integers a and b, *let the operation* ✣ *be defined by*:

$$a ✣ b = a, \text{ if } a + b \text{ is even;}$$
$$a ✣ b = b, \text{ if } a + b \text{ is odd.}$$

25. What is the value of -5 ✣ 5?

(A) 10
(B) 5
(C) 0
(D) -5
(E) -10

26. If $a \neq b$ and a ✣ $b = 10$, which of the following could be true?

I. $a + b$ is even
II. $a + b$ is odd
III. b ✣ $a = 10$

(A) I only
(B) II only
(C) III only
(D) I and II only
(E) I, II, and III

27. A bag contains 4 red, 5 white, and 6 blue marbles. Sarah begins removing marbles from the bag at random, one at a time. What is the least number of marbles she must remove to be sure that she has at least one of each color?

(A) 3
(B) 6
(C) 9
(D) 12
(E) 15

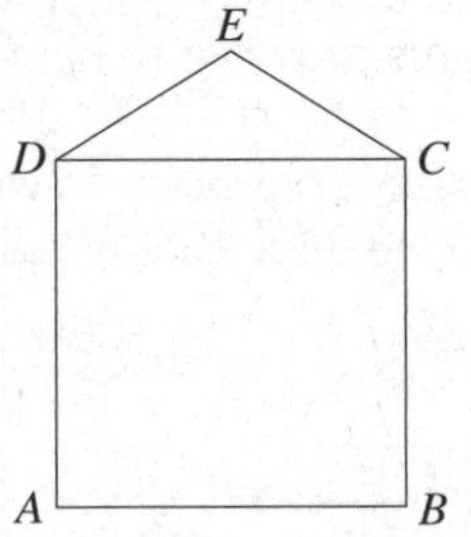

<u>Note</u>: Figure not drawn to scale

28. In the figure above, $ED = EC$, the area of square $ABCD$ is 100, and the area of $\triangle DEC$ is 10. Find the distance from A to E.

(A) 11
(B) 12
(C) $\sqrt{146}$
(D) 13
(E) $\sqrt{\ 44}$

GO ON TO NEXT PAGE ▶

Student-Produced Response Directions

In questions 29–38, first solve the problem, and then enter your answer on the grid provided on the answer sheet. The instructions for entering your answers follow.

- First, write your answer in the boxes at the top of the grid.
- Second, grid your answer in the columns below the boxes.
- Use the fraction bar in the first row or the decimal point in the second row to enter fractions and decimals.

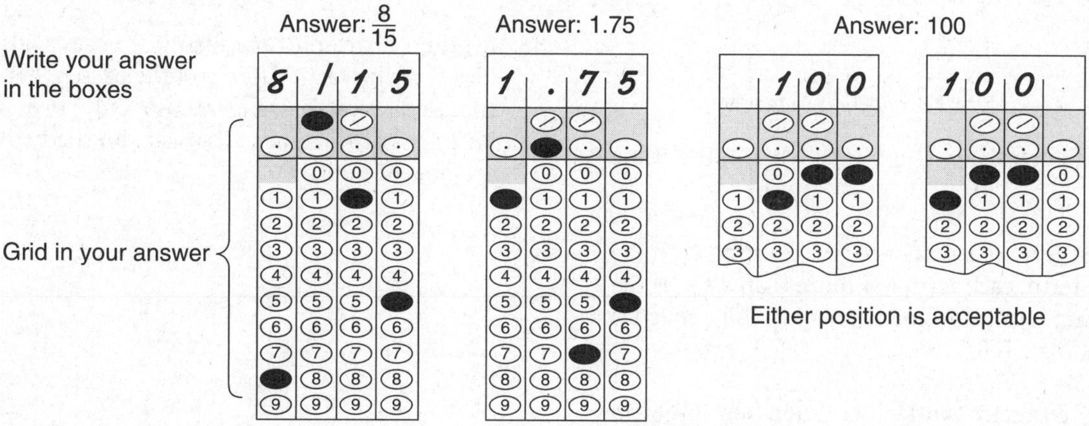

- Grid only one space in each column.
- Entering the answer in the boxes is recommended as an aid in gridding but is not required.
- The machine scoring your exam can read only what you grid, so you **must grid-in your answers correctly to get credit.**
- If a question has more than one correct answer, grid-in only one of them.
- The grid does not have a minus sign; so no answer can be negative.
- A mixed number *must* be converted to an improper fraction or a decimal before it is gridded. Enter $1\frac{1}{4}$ as $\frac{5}{4}$ or 1.25; the machine will interpret 11/4 as $\frac{11}{4}$ and mark it wrong.
- **All decimals must be entered as accurately as possible.** Here are three acceptable ways of gridding

$$\frac{3}{11} = 0.272727\ldots$$

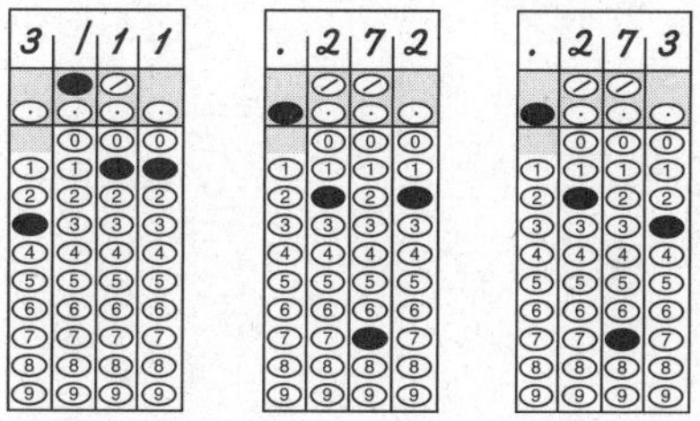

- Note that rounding to .273 is acceptable because you are using the full grid, but you would receive **no credit** for .3 or .27, because they are less accurate.

29. If $5 - w = 4.99$, then what is the value of w?

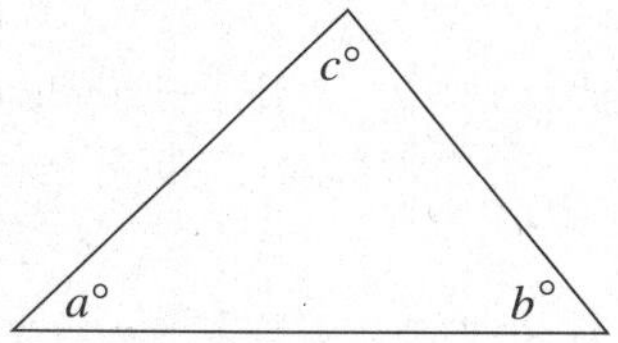

30. If, in the figure above, $a{:}b{:}c = 5{:}7{:}12$, what is the value of c?

31. If $xy = 30$ and $x = -6$, what is the value of $x^2 - y^2$?

32. If 25% of x equals 35% of x, what is 45% of x?

GO ON TO NEXT PAGE ▶

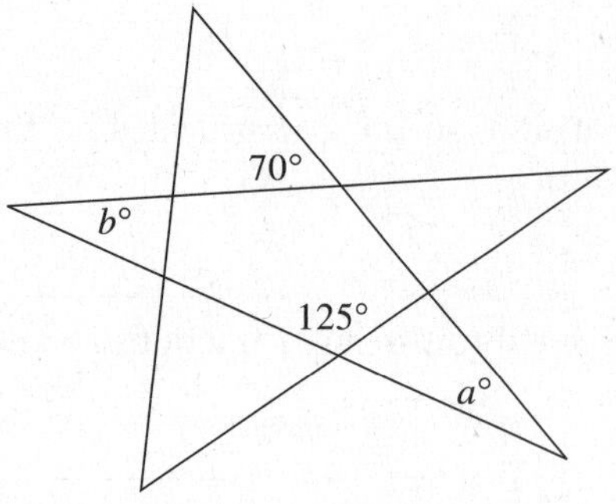

Note: Figure not drawn to scale

33. In the figure above, if $a = 30$, what is the value of b?

34. The first term of a sequence is 2. Starting with the second term, each term is 1 more than 2 times the preceding term. How many terms of this sequence are less than 100?

35. In the correctly worked out addition problem below, each letter represents a different digit. What is the number ABC?

$$\begin{array}{r} 2B \\ 4B \\ +\ 6B \\ \hline ABC \end{array}$$

36. If circle O has its center at (1, 1), and line l is tangent to circle O at P (4, −4), then what is the slope of l?

37. What is the height, in feet, of a rectangular box whose width and length are 5 feet and 7 feet, respectively, and whose total surface area is 298 square feet?

38. A group charters three identical buses and occupies $\frac{4}{5}$ of the seats. After $\frac{1}{4}$ of the passengers leave, the remaining passengers use only two of the buses. What fraction of the seats on the two buses are now occupied?

IF YOU FINISH IN LESS THAN 25 MINUTES, YOU MAY CHECK YOUR WORK ON THIS SECTION ONLY. DO NOT TURN TO ANY OTHER SECTION IN THE TEST.

STOP

SECTION 5/WRITING SKILLS

TIME: 30 MINUTES

39 QUESTIONS (1–39)

Directions: For each question in this section, select the best answer from among the choices given and fill in the corresponding circle on the answer sheet.

Some or all parts of the following sentences are underlined. The first answer choice, (A), simply repeats the underlined part of the sentence. The other four choices present four alternative ways to phrase the underlined part. Select the answer that produces the most effective sentence, one that is clear and exact, and blacken the appropriate space on your answer sheet. In selecting your choice, be sure that it is standard written English and that it expresses the meaning of the original sentence.

EXAMPLE:

The first biography of author Eudora Welty came out in 1998, <u>and she was eighty-nine years old at the time.</u>

(A) and she was eighty-nine years old at the time
(B) at the time when she was eighty-nine
(C) upon becoming an eighty-nine year old
(D) when she was eighty-nine
(E) at the age of eighty-nine years old

Ⓐ Ⓑ Ⓒ Ⓓ ●

1. <u>If he was to decide to go to college</u>, I, for one, would recommend that he plan to go to Yale.

(A) If he was to decide to go to college
(B) If he were to decide to go to college
(C) Had he decided to go to college
(D) In the event that he decides to go to college
(E) Supposing he was to decide to go to college

2. <u>Except for you and I, everyone brought</u> a present to the party.

(A) Except for you and I, everyone brought
(B) With the exception of you and I, everyone brought
(C) Except for you and I, everyone had brought
(D) Except for you and me, everyone brought
(E) Except for you and me, everyone had brought

3. <u>Had I realized how close</u> I was to failing, I would not have gone to the party.

(A) Had I realized how close
(B) If I would have realized how close
(C) Had I had realized how close
(D) When I realized how close
(E) If I realized how close

4. <u>Being a realist</u>, I could not accept his statement that supernatural beings had caused the disturbance.

(A) Being a realist
(B) Due to the fact that I am a realist
(C) Being that I am a realist
(D) Being as I am a realist
(E) Realist that I am

5. Having finished the marathon in record-breaking time, <u>the city awarded him its Citizen's Outstanding Performance Medal.</u>

(A) the city awarded him its Citizen's Outstanding Performance Medal
(B) the city awarded the Citizen's Outstanding Performance Medal to him
(C) he was awarded the Citizen's Outstanding Performance Medal by the city
(D) the Citizen's Outstanding Performance Medal was awarded to him
(E) he was awarded by the city the Citizen's Outstanding Performance Medal

GO ON TO NEXT PAGE ▶

6. The football team's winning its first game of the season excited the student body.

(A) The football team's winning its first game of the season
(B) The football team having won its first game of the season
(C) Having won its first game of the season, the football team
(D) Winning its first game of the season, the football team
(E) The football team winning its first game of the season

7. Anyone interested in the use of computers can learn much if you have access to a copy of *PC Magazine* or of *MacUser*.

(A) if you have access to
(B) if he or she has access to
(C) if access is available to
(D) by access to
(E) from access to

8. I have to make dinner, wash the dishes, do my homework, and then relaxing.

(A) to make dinner, wash the dishes, do my homework, and then relaxing
(B) to make dinner, washing the dishes, my homework, and then relaxing
(C) to make dinner, wash the dishes, doing my homework, and then relax
(D) to prepare dinner, wash the dishes, do my homework, and then relaxing
(E) to make dinner, wash the dishes, do my homework, and then relax

9. The climax occurs when he asks who's in the closet.

(A) occurs when he asks who's
(B) is when he asks who's
(C) occurs when he is asking who's
(D) is when he is asking who's
(E) occurs when he asked who's

10. Setting up correct bookkeeping procedures is important to any new business, it helps to obtain the services of a good accountant.

(A) is important to any new business, it helps
(B) are important to any new business, it
(C) is important to any new business, therefore, try
(D) is important to any new business; it helps
(E) are important to any new business, so try

11. The grocer hadn't hardly any of those kind of canned goods.

(A) hadn't hardly any of those kind
(B) hadn't hardly any of those kinds
(C) had hardly any of those kind
(D) had hardly any of those kinds
(E) had scarcely any of those kind

12. Having spent five years in the Appalachian Mountains collecting mountain ballads, an anthology entitled *English Folk Songs from the Southern Appalachians* was produced by Olive Dame Campbell

(A) an anthology entitled *English Folk Songs from the Southern Appalachians* was produced by Olive Dame Campbell
(B) Olive Dame Campbell produced an anthology entitled *English Folk Songs from the Southern Appalachians*
(C) Olive Dame Campbell's anthology entitled *English Folk Songs from the Southern Appalachians* was produced
(D) an anthology entitled *English Folk Songs from the Southern Appalachians* has been produced by Olive Dame Campbell
(E) there is an anthology entitled *English Folk Songs from the Southern Appalachians* produced by Olive Dame Campbell

13. Juan broke his hip, he has not and possibly never will be able to run the mile again.

(A) hip, he has not and possibly never will be able to run
(B) hip; he has not been able to run and possibly never will be able to run
(C) hip; he has not and possibly never will be able to run
(D) hip, he has not been and possibly never would be able to run
(E) hip; he has not and possibly will never be able to run

14. I came late to class today; the reason being that the bus broke down.

(A) today; the reason being that
(B) today, the reason being that
(C) today because
(D) today;
(E) today; since

GO ON TO NEXT PAGE ►

15. Young children's fevers are erratic, furthermore they can spike unpredictably, and, just as unpredictably, can subside.

(A) erratic, furthermore they can spike unpredictably, and, just as unpredictably, can subside
(B) erratic; nevertheless, they can spike unpredictably, and, just as unpredictably, they can subside
(C) erratic, and can spike unpredictably, and, just as unpredictable, they can subside
(D) erratic: they can spike unpredictably, and, just as unpredictably, can subside
(E) erratic, they can spike just as unpredictably as they can subside

16. Of all the characters in *A Christmas Carol*, sweet and saintly Tiny Tim is the more beloved.

(A) Of all the characters in *A Christmas Carol*, sweet and saintly Tiny Tim is the more beloved.
(B) Of all the characters in *A Christmas Carol*, sweet and saintly Tiny Tim was the more beloved.
(C) In *A Christmas Carol*, of all the characters, sweet and saintly Tiny Tim is the more beloved.
(D) Of all the characters in *A Christmas Carol*, sweet and saintly Tiny Tim is the most beloved.
(E) Sweet and saintly Tiny Tim is more beloved than all the characters in *A Christmas Carol*.

17. The history of the past quarter century illustrates how a president may increase his power to act aggressively in international affairs, and he does not consider the wishes of Congress.

(A) affairs, and he does not consider the wishes of Congress
(B) affairs, therefore he did not consider the wishes of Congress
(C) affairs without considering the wishes of Congress
(D) affairs, but he does not consider what Congress wishes
(E) affairs, and he may not have considered the wishes of Congress

18. With the exception of a few publications like *The New York Times*, American newspapers tend to ignore world news unless the event to be reported immediately affects American citizens.

(A) unless the event to be reported immediately affects American citizens
(B) unless the event being reported immediately effects American citizens
(C) except the event to be reported has immediately affected American citizens
(D) unless the event immediately to be reported affecting American citizens
(E) unless the immediate event they reported affects American citizens

19. When he was a war correspondent during the Spanish Civil War (1936–1939), the American novelist Ernest Hemingway has written movingly about the struggle of the Republican forces against General Francisco Franco's Nationalist troops.

(A) Hemingway has written movingly about the struggle
(B) Hemingway has written while moving about the struggle
(C) Hemingway has written movingly from the struggle
(D) Hemingway has been writing movingly about the struggle
(E) Hemingway wrote movingly about the struggle

20. Fearful that Rome's hungry, restless throngs might grow unruly, Roman emperors catered to the masses, providing the mob with bread and circuses.

(A) emperors catered to the masses, providing the mob with bread
(B) emperors catered to the masses, provided that the mob with bread
(C) emperors catered for the masses, providing the mob with bread
(D) emperors catered to the masses, they provided the mob with bread
(E) emperors catered for the masses by providing the mob with bread

GO ON TO NEXT PAGE ▶

The sentences in this section may contain errors in grammar, usage, choice of words, or idioms. There is either just one error per sentence, or the sentence is correct. Some words or phrases are underlined and lettered; everything else in the sentence is correct.

If an underlined word or phrase is incorrect, choose that letter; if the sentence is correct, select No error. Then blacken the appropriate space on your answer sheet.

EXAMPLE:

The region has a climate so severe that (A) plants growing there (B) rarely had been (C) more than twelve inches high. (D) No error (E)

Ⓐ Ⓑ ● Ⓓ Ⓔ

21. In order to (A) conserve valuable gasoline, motorists had ought to (B) check their speedometers while (C) driving along the highways since it is (D) very easy to exceed 55 miles per hour while driving on open roads. No error (E)

22. The book must (A) be old, for (B) its cover is torn (C) bad. (D) No error (E)

23. Not one (A) of the children has ever sang (B) in public (C) before. (D) No error (E)

24. Neither you nor I (A) can realize the affect (B) his behavior will have (C) on his chances for promotion. (D) No error (E)

25. The apparently (A) obvious solution to (B) the problem was overlooked (C) by many of (D) the contestants. No error (E)

26. After (A) he had drank (B) the warm milk, he began to feel sleepy (C) and finally decided (D) to go to bed. No error (E)

27. Without hardly (A) a moment's delay, the computer began to (B) print out (C) the answer to (D) the problem. No error (E)

28. Of (A) the two candidates for this newly formed (B) government position, Ms. Rivera is the most qualified (C) because (D) of her experience in the field. No error (E)

29. Diligence and honesty as well as (A) being intelligent (B) are (C) qualities that personnel directors look for when (D) they interview applicants. No error (E)

30. Neither the San Francisco earthquake or (A) the subsequent (B) fire was (C) able to destroy the spirit (D) of the city dwellers. No error (E)

GO ON TO NEXT PAGE ►

31. The impatient customer (A) had scarcely enough (B) money to pay (C) the clerk at (D) the checkout counter. No error (E)

32. The principal (A) of equal justice for all (B) is one (C) of the cornerstones of the democratic way of life. (D) No error (E)

33. Although alchemy anticipated science in its belief that (A) physical reality was determined by (B) an unvarying (C) set of natural laws, the alchemist's experimental method was not hardly (D) scientific. No error (E)

34. If (A) anyone calls (B) while the delegates are in conference, tell them (C) the chairman will return the call (D) after the meeting. No error (E)

GO ON TO NEXT PAGE ►

Improving Paragraphs Directions

The passage below is the unedited draft of a student's essay. Some of the essay needs to be rewritten to make the meaning clearer and more precise. Read the essay carefully.

The essay is followed by questions about changes that might improve all or part of its organization, development, sentence structure, use of language, appropriateness to the audience, or use of standard written English. Choose the answer that most clearly and effectively expresses the student's intended meaning. Indicate your choice by filling in the corresponding space on the answer sheet.

[1] There are many reasons making it cruel to keep animals penned up in zoos for the sole purpose of letting families gawk at caged creatures. **[2]** There has to be a better reason to imprison animals than merely to allow visitors to drop a quarter into a food dispenser so that one can feed the monkeys or the elephant. **[3]** One might argue that it is educational. **[4]** If someone is so dumb that they don't know what a zebra looks like, they should pull out an encyclopedia and look it up. **[5]** Humans have no right to pull animals from their natural environment and to seal their fate forever behind a set of cold metal bars. **[6]** Animals need to run free and live, but by putting them in zoos we are disrupting and disturbing nature.

[7] Then there is the issue of sanitary conditions for animals at the zoo. **[8]** When the animals have been at the zoo for a while they adopt a particular lifestyle. **[9]** They lounge around all day, and they're fed at a particular time. **[10]** They get used to that. **[11]** That means that they would never again be able to be placed back in their natural environment. **[12]** They would never survive. **[13]** And if they reproduce while in captivity, the offspring are born into an artificial lifestyle. **[14]** After a few generations the animals become totally different from their wild and free ancestors, and visitors to the zoo see animals hardly resembling the ones living in their natural habitat.

[15] The vicious cycle should be stopped before it is too late. **[16]** The whole idea of a zoo is cruel. **[17]** If zoos are not cruel and if, as some people say, they serve a useful purpose, then why not put homo sapiens on display, too?

35. Which is the most effective revision of the underlined segment of sentence 1 below?

<u>There are many reasons making it cruel to keep animals penned up in zoos</u> for the sole purpose of letting families gawk at caged creatures.

(A) Many reasons exist for the cruelty of keeping animals penned up in zoos
(B) It is a cruel practice to keep animals penned up in zoos
(C) The reasons are numerous to object to the cruelty experienced by animals locked in cages
(D) There are several reasons for it being cruel toward animals to lock them up in zoos
(E) Locking up animals in zoos a cruel practice especially

36. Taking sentence 3 into account, which of the following is the most effective revision of sentence 4?

(A) Reading about animals in the encyclopedia rather than studying them first hand.
(B) In the encyclopedia you can gain more information about zebras and other animals.
(C) Viewing the animal in a zoo is clearly more informative than looking at a picture in a book.
(D) Doesn't everyone know what a zebra looks like, even little children?
(E) But if someone is so dumb that they don't know what a zebra looks like, they should look it up in an encyclopedia.

GO ON TO NEXT PAGE ►

37. Which of the following reasons most accurately describes the author's intention in the selection of words used in the underlined segment of sentence 5 below?

Humans have no right to pull animals from their natural environment and to seal their fate forever behind a set of cold metal bars.

(A) to inform the reader that animals in the zoo live in cages
(B) to propose a solution to the plight of animals in the zoo
(C) to arouse in the reader an emotional response to the problem
(D) to appeal to the reader to weigh both sides of the issue
(E) to convince the reader that animals don't enjoy being in the zoo

38. Which of the following revisions of sentence 7 is the best topic sentence for paragraph 2?

(A) Life in captivity causes animals to change.
(B) No one favors zoos that deliberately try to change the lifestyle of animals in captivity.
(C) Living conditions for animals in the zoo are ordinarily harsh and cruel.
(D) Living in the zoo, conditions for animals affect them permanently.
(E) Life in the zoo for animals is not a bowl of cherries.

39. Which revision most effectively combines sentences 10, 11, and 12?

(A) Because they would never be able to survive again back in their natural environment, they grow used to being fed.
(B) Having grown used to regular feedings, the animals would be unable to survive back in their native environment.
(C) Growing accustomed to that, placing them back in their native habitat and being unable to survive on their own.
(D) They, having gotten used to being fed regularly, in their natural environment would never survive.
(E) Being unable to survive back in their natural environment, the animals have grown accustomed to regular feedings.

IF YOU FINISH IN LESS THAN 30 MINUTES, YOU MAY CHECK YOUR WORK ON THIS SECTION ONLY. DO NOT TURN TO ANY OTHER SECTION IN THE TEST.

STOP

Answer Key

Section 1 Critical Reading

1. **B**	6. **E**	11. **B**	16. **E**	21. **A**
2. **C**	7. **B**	12. **C**	17. **C**	22. **C**
3. **A**	8. **B**	13. **B**	18. **E**	23. **E**
4. **A**	9. **D**	14. **A**	19. **D**	24. **B**
5. **B**	10. **E**	15. **C**	20. **C**	

Section 2 Mathematics

1. **D**	5. **C**	9. **A**	13. **E**	17. **B**
2. **C**	6. **B**	10. **B**	14. **C**	18. **E**
3. **C**	7. **B**	11. **C**	15. **D**	19. **C**
4. **C**	8. **D**	12. **B**	16. **A**	20. **A**

Section 3 Critical Reading

25. **D**	30. **B**	35. **C**	40. **B**	45. **E**
26. **C**	31. **C**	36. **B**	41. **B**	46. **C**
27. **D**	32. **C**	37. **D**	42. **C**	47. **B**
28. **D**	33. **D**	38. **A**	43. **A**	48. **D**
29. **D**	34. **E**	39. **C**	44. **E**	

Section 4 Mathematics

21. **C**	23. **D**	25. **D**	27. **D**
22. **B**	24. **E**	26. **D**	28. **D**

29.
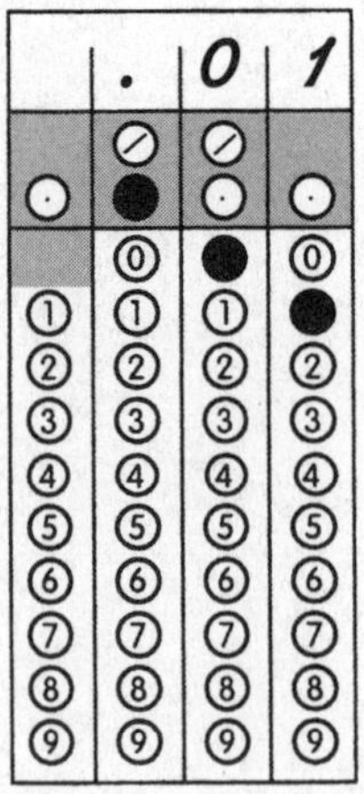

30.
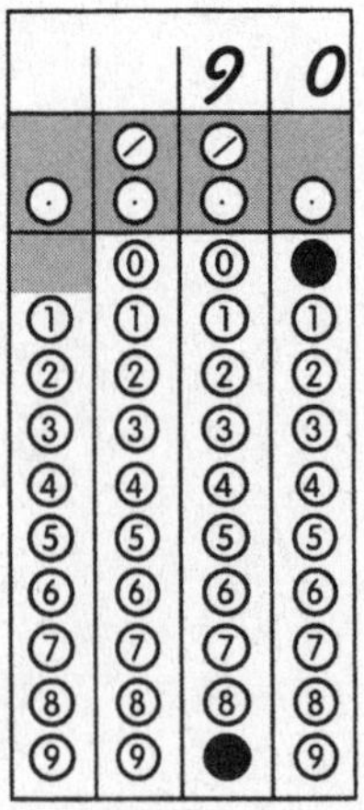

31.
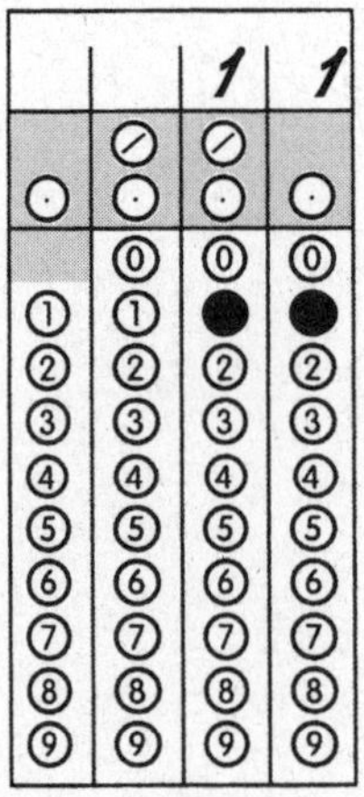

32.
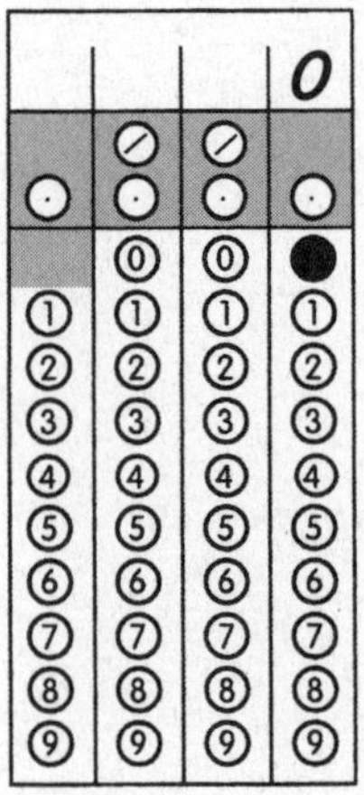

33.
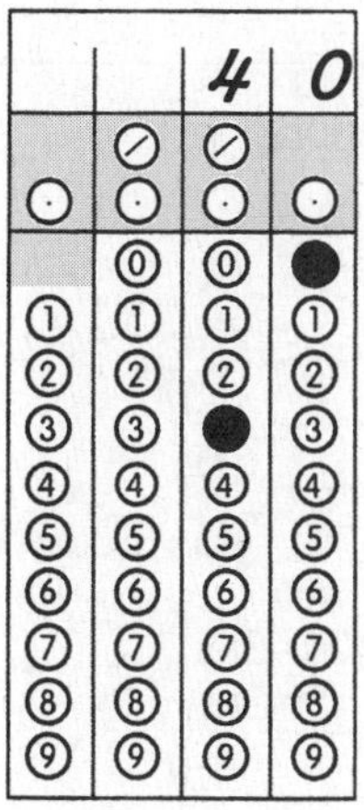

34.
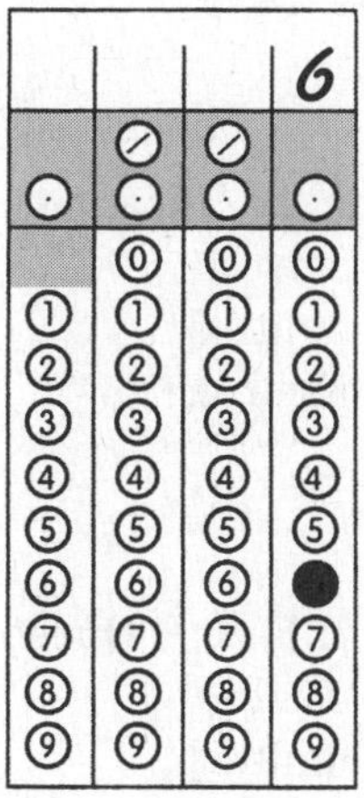

35.
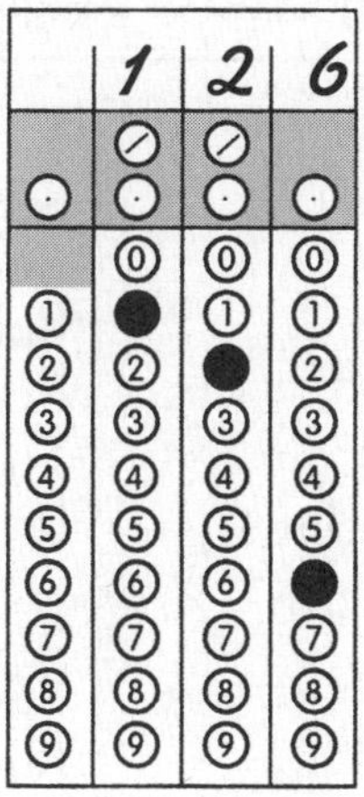

36.
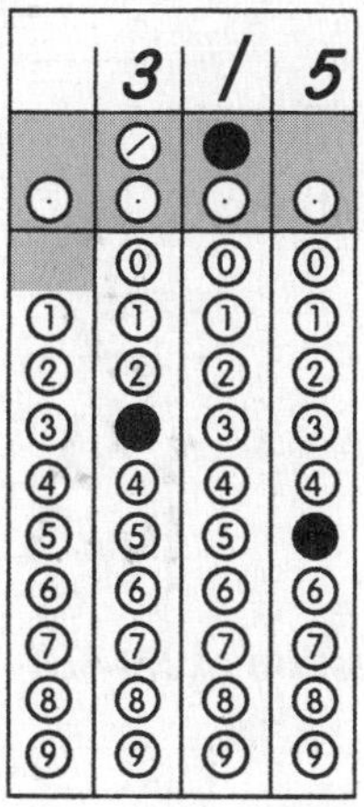

or .6

37.
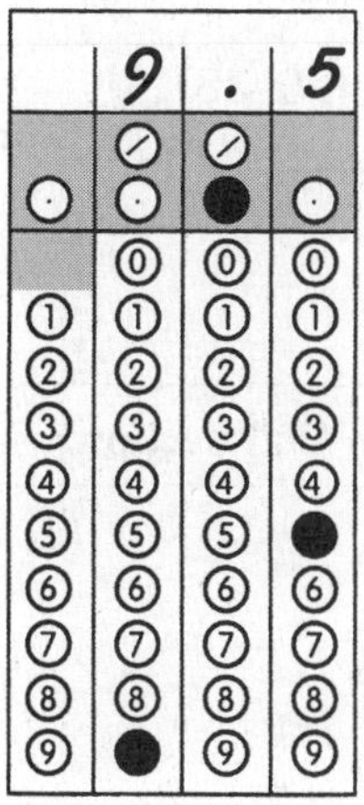

38.
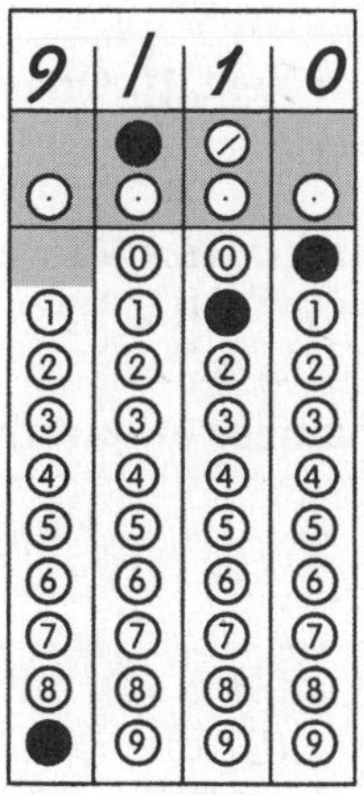

or .9

Section 5 Writing Skills

1. **B**
2. **D**
3. **A**
4. **A**
5. **C**
6. **A**
7. **B**
8. **E**
9. **A**
10. **D**
11. **D**
12. **B**
13. **B**
14. **C**
15. **D**
16. **D**
17. **C**
18. **A**
19. **E**
20. **A**
21. **B**
22. **D**
23. **B**
24. **B**
25. **E**
26. **B**
27. **A**
28. **C**
29. **B**
30. **A**
31. **E**
32. **A**
33. **D**
34. **C**
35. **B**
36. **C**
37. **C**
38. **A**
39. **B**

Scoring Chart—Diagnostic Test

Critical Reading Sections

Section 1: 24 Questions (1–24)

Number correct	13	(A)
Number omitted	1	(B)
Number incorrect	6	(C)
$\frac{1}{4}$ (C)	3/2	(D)
(A) − (D)	16.5	Raw Score I

Section 3: 24 Questions (25–48)

Number correct	_________	(A)
Number omitted	_________	(B)
Number incorrect	_________	(C)
$\frac{1}{4}$ (C)	_________	(D)
(A) − (D)	_________	Raw Score II

Total Critical Reading Raw Score

Raw Scores I + II _________

Mathematics Sections

Section 2: 20 Questions (1–20)

Number correct	_________	(A)
Number omitted	_________	(B)
Number incorrect	_________	(C)
$\frac{1}{4}$ (C)	_________	(D)
(A) − (D)	_________	Raw Score I

Section 4: First 8 Questions (21–28)

Number correct	_________	(A)
Number omitted	_________	(B)
Number incorrect	_________	(C)
$\frac{1}{4}$ (C)	_________	(D)
(A) − (D)	_________	Raw Score II

Section 4: Next 10 Questions (29–38)

Number correct	_________	Raw Score III

Total Mathematics Raw Score

Raw Scores I + II + III _________

NOTE: In each section (A) + (B) + (C) should equal the number of questions in that section.

Writing Skills Section

Section 5: 39 Questions (1–39)

Number correct	_________	(A)
Number omitted	_________	(B)
Number incorrect	_________	(C)
$\frac{1}{4}$ (C)	_________	(D)

Writing Skills Raw Score

(A) − (D) _________

Evaluation Chart

Study your score. Your raw score is an indication of your probable achievement on the PSAT/NMSQT. As a guide to the amount of work you need or want to do with this book, study the following.

Raw Score			Self-Rating
Critical Reading	*Mathematics*	*Writing Skills*	
42–48	35–38	33–39	Superior
37–41	30–34	28–32	Very good
32–36	25–29	23–27	Good
26–31	21–24	17–22	Above average
20–25	17–20	12–16	Average
12–19	10–16	7–11	Below average
less than 12	less than 10	less than 7	Inadequate

ANSWER EXPLANATIONS

Section 1 Critical Reading

1. **(B)** For Miró, art was holy or *sacred*. Note how the second clause clarifies what kind of ritual art became for Miró.

   Choice A is incorrect. *Superficial* means shallow or not profound. If Miró worked as though he were performing a religious rite, he would not think of creating art as superficial. Choice C is incorrect. *Banal* means commonplace or trite. If Miró looked on paper and pencil as holy objects, he would not regard his art as banal. Choice D is incorrect. *Cryptic* means mysterious or obscure. The word has no necessary connection with holiness. Choice E is incorrect. *Futile* means useless or pointless. The word makes no sense in this context.

2. **(C)** The key term here is "smoke screen," something designed to obscure or mislead. How would accuracy-loving scholars react to an autobiography filled with misleading remarks? They would be *vexed* (annoyed) by the smoke screens and other misleading *errors*.

   Choice A is incorrect. How would Wright scholars react to the misleading, deceptive smoke screens in Wright's autobiography? They definitely would not have been *delighted* or pleased by them. Choice B is incorrect. While Wright scholars might have been *amazed* or surprised by misleading smoke screens in Wright's autobiography, their reaction is likely to have been far more negative. Choice D is incorrect. While Wright scholars might have been *confused* or puzzled by misleading smoke screens in Wright's autobiography, their reaction is likely to have been far more negative. Choice E is incorrect. Wright scholars are unlikely to have been *entertained* or amused by *omissions* (lapses) and misleading smoke screens in Wright's autobiography.

3. **(A)** To be kept "at arm's length" from someone's emotions is to feel an emotional distance between you and that person. Singer's own quality of uninvolvement or *detachment* makes the reader feel distant from his main character.

   Choice B is incorrect. *Lyricism* refers to emotional, poetic expression. It would be more likely to put the reader in touch with the character's emotions than to distance the reader from what the character feels. Choice C is incorrect. *Fluency* means ease in speech or writing. That would be unlikely to distance the reader from what the character feels. Choice D is incorrect. *Brevity* means conciseness or terseness, the ability to express much in a few words. That would be unlikely to distance the reader from what the character feels. Choice E is incorrect. *Rhythm* is the recurrence of a pattern (in writing) or a beat (in music). Again, that would be unlikely to distance the reader from what the character feels.

4. **(A)** Break down the sentence. The prolific (highly productive) author has written many different books, bound in many different bindings. The fact that the books' topics vary as much as their bindings indicates the author has not specialized in any one topic. Instead, he has *resisted* or fought specialization as strongly as some other writers have *pursued* it.

   Choice B is incorrect. The author has not specialized in one topic; he has not *admired* or looked positively on specialization. Choice C is incorrect. The author has not specialized in one topic; he has not *endorsed* or formally approved specialization. Choice D is incorrect. The author has not specialized in one topic; he has not *defended* or supported specialization. Choice E is incorrect. The author has not gone so far as to *repudiate* or disown specialization. In addition, it makes little sense to say that his colleagues have energetically *deliberated* or thought about specialization.

5. **(B)** If the mayfly's adult life lasts for such a short time, it clearly is an *ephemeral* (short-lived, fleeting) creature. Note how the second clause clarifies what the author means by *ephemeral.*

   Choice A is incorrect. *Elegant* means tastefully refined or graceful. You are looking for a word that means short-lived. Choice C is incorrect. *Idiosyncratic* means quirky or peculiar to an individual. You are looking for a word that means short-lived. Choice D is incorrect. *Impulsive* means rash or impetuous. You are looking for a word that means short-lived. Choice E is incorrect. *Omnivorous* means eating both animal and plant food. You are looking for a word that means short-lived.

6. **(E)** Reporters "have had a field day" commenting on the controversial knighting. In other words, they have had an occasion for unrestrained ridicule and hilarity, to which their response has been one of pure *glee* (high-spirited delight, often prompted by a malicious joy in someone else's discomfiture).

7. **(B)** Consider that the original instance of royal hospitality to which the reporter refers is a night in a prison cell. Does that sound hospitable to you? Clearly, the reporter is using the phrase *ironically*, in an amusingly surprising way.

8. **(B)** The opening sentence of Passage 1 is "Knighthoods are not what they used to be." The opening sentence of Passage 2 is "What factors led to the decline of the armored knight?" Although the passages greatly differ in focus and tone, both make the point that the institution of knighthood has *undergone changes over time.*

9. **(D)** Passage 2 discusses the institution of knighthood from the Middle Ages through the fifteenth century: it *offers historical perspective* on the institution. Passage 1 discusses the current *guise* or form the institution takes today, with rock-and-roll knights whose not-so-shining reputations the author cheerfully *mocks* (makes fun of). The correct answer is Choice D: *Passage 2 offers historical perspective on an institution whose current guise is mocked in Passage 1.*

10. **(E)** The second paragraph discusses the various methods epiphytes adopt in order to retain or conserve moisture.

    Choice A is incorrect. Epiphytes have lost their root connection with the forest floor. Choice B is incorrect. Epiphytes seek the sun; they are not adapted to a sunless environment. Choice C is incorrect. Epiphytes have developed ways to conserve rainwater, not to dissipate or squander it. Choice D is incorrect. Epiphytes are not parasites; they do not derive nourishment ("sustenance") from the tree trunks to which they attach themselves.

11. **(B)** The first paragraph states that epiphytes grow in "spoonfuls" of soil. We can infer from this that they do not need particularly large amounts of soil for growth.

    Choice A is incorrect. Although epiphytes have lost their root connection with the forest floor, they do possess root systems. Choice C is incorrect. The passage states that the roots of some orchids carry on photosynthesis; epiphytes clearly are not incapable of photosynthesis. Choice D is incorrect. Nothing in the passage suggests epiphytes are hard to spot. Choice E is incorrect. Epiphytes have "managed to create their own environment" so well that the soil in which they grow does not differ significantly from normal soil in microbiological processes. This fact does not suggest that their need for nutrients differs from that of plants that grow in normal soil.

12. **(C)** Epiphytes are described in a straightforward, direct manner.

    Choice A is incorrect. The author is not exhorting or urging anyone to do anything. Choice B is incorrect. The author is not analyzing epiphytes, that is, thoroughly studying each of the individual features that comprise these plants in order to understand their structure. He is simply saying what they are like. Choice D is incorrect. The author is being direct rather than indirect in presenting what he knows about epiphytes. Choice E is incorrect. The author is not being particularly forceful in his presentation; neither is he presenting an argument.

13. **(B)** The strangler tree's feeding cables do not ascend toward the canopy; they descend to the forest floor. You can double-check your answer by using the process of elimination.

    The strangler tree eventually stands on its own pedestal or supports itself. You can eliminate Choice A. One set of the strangler tree's roots (the "feeding cable") extends all the way from high up in the fork of the host tree down to the forest floor. You can eliminate Choice C. When the feeder cable reaches the soil, the plant's growth quickens. You can eliminate Choice D. The strangler's roots "thicken to a marked degree," becoming *conspicuously larger*. You can eliminate Choice E. Only Choice B is left. It is the correct answer.

14. **(A)** The roots thicken to a marked or *noticeable* degree, eventually growing thick enough to support the strangler tree.

15. **(C)** The concluding sentence states that the host expires and the strangler tree stands on its own pedestal of thickened roots (its original feeding cables, now fused together). Thus, the strangler tree has *outgrown its need for its host*.

16. **(E)** Throughout the passage the author presents and comments on the nature of the original documents that form the basis for his historical narrative. Thus, it is clear that a major concern of his is to *introduce* these "sources of almost forgotten oral history" to his readers.

    Choice A is incorrect. The author clearly regrets the fate of the Indians. However, he does not take this occasion to denounce or condemn the white man. Choice B is incorrect. While the author discusses the various treaty councils, he does not evaluate or judge how effective they were. Choice C is incorrect. The author never touches on the current treatment of Indians. Choice D is incorrect. The author indicates no such thing.

17. **(C)** Because Brown looks on the conquest of the West from a Native American perspective, he views it as the tragic destruction of Indian civilization rather than as the heroic opening of new, uncivilized territory by European civilization. Thus, by putting quotation marks around the word "opening," Brown indicates his *disagreement with* the notion of "the opening of the West," *a term in common use* in typical narratives of the period.

18. **(E)** Of all the thousands of published descriptions of the opening of the West, the greatest concentration or *cluster* of accounts date from the period of 1860 to 1890.

19. **(D)** You can arrive at the correct choice by the process of elimination.

    Statement I is true. The passage states that the quality of the interviews depended on the interpreters' abilities. Inaccuracies could creep in because of the translators' lack of skill. Therefore, you can eliminate Choice B.

    Statement II is untrue. The passage indicates that the Indians sometimes exaggerated, telling the reporters tall tales. It does not indicate that the reporters in turn overstated what they had been told. Therefore, you can eliminate Choices C and E.

    Statement III is true. The passage indicates that the Indians sometimes were disinclined to speak the whole truth because they feared reprisals (retaliation) if they did. Therefore, you can eliminate Choice A.

    Only Choice D is left. It is the correct answer.

20. **(C)** Brown speaks of the Indians who lived through the "doom period of their civilization," the victims of the conquest of the American West. In doing so, his tone can best be described as *elegiac*, expressing sadness about their fate and lamenting their vanished civilization.

21. **(A)** In the fifth paragraph Brown comments upon the "graphic similes and metaphors of the natural world" found in the English translations of Indian speeches. Thus, he is impressed by their *vividness of imagery*.

22. **(C)** Commenting about inadequate interpreters who turned eloquent Indian speeches into "flat" prose, Brown is criticizing the translations for their *pedestrian*, unimaginative quality.

23. **(E)** Brown has tried to create a narrative of the winning of the West from the victims' perspective. In asking his readers to read the book facing eastward (the way the Indians would have been looking when they first saw the whites headed west), he is asking them metaphorically to look at things from the Indians' point of view.

24. **(B)** In the sentence immediate preceding the one in which this phrase appears, Brown calls the Indians "true conservationists." Such conservationists know that life is *necessarily tied to* the earth and to its resources and that by destroying these resources by imbalancing the equation, so to speak, you destroy life itself.

Section 2 Mathematics

For many problems, the explanation provides a reference to one or more **KEY FACTS** from Chapter 7. These are the mathematical facts that you need to solve that problem. If a solution refers to **KEY FACT J2**, for example, the solution depends on the second **KEY FACT** discussed in Section J of Chapter 7.

For some problems, an alternative solution, indicated by two asterisks (**), follows the first solution. When this occurs, usually one of the solutions is the direct mathematical one and the other is based on one of the tactics discussed in Chapters 6 and 7.

See page 234 for an explanation of the symbol $\Rightarrow$, which is used in several answer explanations.

1. **(D)** $4x = 12 \Rightarrow x = 3 \Rightarrow 12x = 36$.

2. **(C)** Just look at each number carefully. The hundreds place is the third from the left of the decimal point and the hundredths place is the second to the right of the decimal point: 3<u>3</u>53.5<u>3</u>53.

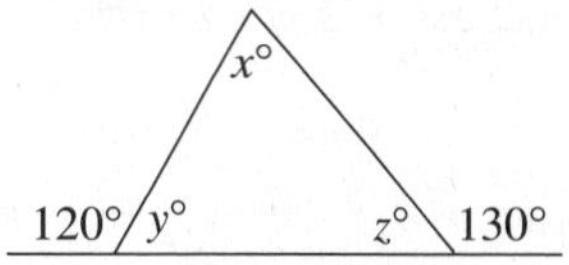

3. **(C)** In the figure above, by **KEY FACT J1**, $x + y + z = 180$, and by **KEY FACT I2**, $y = 60$ and $z = 50$. Therefore,

   $$x = 180 - (50 + 60) = 180 - 110 = 70.$$

4. **(C)** The expression $n^2 - 10$ is negative whenever $n^2 < 10$. This is true for all integers between -3 and 3 inclusive: $-3, -2, -1, 0, 1, 2, 3$—7 in all.

5. **(C)** The diagonals of a square bisect each other and bisect the right angles. So the measure of $\angle XHT$ and $\angle XTH$ are each 45°, and $\triangle HXT$ is a 45-45-90 right triangle. Therefore,

   $$MX = 3 \Rightarrow XT = 3 \Rightarrow XH = 3, \text{ and}$$
   $$\text{area of } \triangle HXT = \tfrac{1}{2}(3)(3) = 4.5.$$

   $MX = 3 \Rightarrow MT = 6$. By **KEY FACT K6, the area of a square equals $\frac{d^2}{2}$, where d is the length of a diagonal. So the area of square *MATH* is $\frac{1}{2}(6)^2 = 18$, and the area of the shaded triangle is $18 \div 4 = 4.5$.

6. **(B)** $7x + 5 = 74 \Rightarrow 7x = 69 \Rightarrow 7x - 5 = 64$. So $\sqrt{7x - 5} = \sqrt{64} = 8$. (Note that, since the given equation and what you want both involve $7x$, you should *not* solve for x.)

7. **(B)** 3 is the only prime divisible by 3.

8. **(D)** $f(3) = 3^2 - 2^3 = 9 - 8 = 1$.

9. **(A)** Just multiply: $\frac{2}{5}(h) = \frac{2h}{5}$.
Use **TACTIC 6-2 and pick an easy-to-use number for h: 2, for example. Michael can paint $\frac{2}{5}$ of a room in the first hour and another $\frac{2}{5}$ of a room in the second hour, for a total of $\frac{4}{5}$ of a room. Check the choices. Only $\frac{2h}{5}$ equals $\frac{4}{5}$ when $h = 2$.

10. **(B)** $x^2 + 1 = 50 \Rightarrow x^2 = 49 \Rightarrow x = 7$ or $x = -7$. Therefore, $x + 1 = 8$ or $x + 1 = -6$. Since 8 is not one of the choices, the answer is -6.

11. **(C)** On her 6 tests combined, Evelyn earned a total of $6 \times 80 = 480$ points (see **KEY FACT E1**). The total of her 5 best grades is $5 \times 90 = 450$ points. So, her lowest grade was $480 - 450 = 30$.

12. **(B)** Of the two consecutive integers p and $p + 1$, one is odd and one is even. Since 2 is the only even prime number, there is only one possibility:

$p = 2$ and $p + 1 = 3$. ($p = 1$ and $p + 1 = 2$ does *not* work, because 1 is *not* a prime number.)

13. **(E)** Since $W = 3$ and $Z = 7$, then

$$W + Z = 10 \Rightarrow X + Y = 10$$

Since $3X = 2W = 2(3) = 6$, $X = 2$ and $Y = 8$.

14. **(C)** Here $Z = W$. So by definition of a number bar, $W + Z = X + Y \Rightarrow 2W = X + Y$; but the definition also states that $2W = 3X$, so $X = \frac{2}{3}W$. Therefore,

$$2W = \frac{2}{3}W + Y \Rightarrow Y = \frac{4}{3}W.$$

15. **(D)** Check each statement.
- Could $\frac{16}{m}$ be odd? Yes, if $m = 16$, then $\frac{16}{m} = 1$, an odd integer. (I is true.)
- Could $\frac{m}{16}$ be an odd integer? Sure, it could be any odd integer; for example, if $m = 16$, $\frac{m}{16} = 1$, and if $m = 80$, $\frac{m}{16} = 5$. (II is true.)
- Could $16m$ be odd? No, the product of 16 and any integer is even. (III is false.)
- Only statements I and II are true.

16. **(A)** By **KEY FACT M2**, if e is the edge of the cube, the surface area, A, is $6e^2$ and the volume, V, is e^3. Then

$$A = 6e^2 = 60 \Rightarrow e^2 = 10 \Rightarrow e = \sqrt{10} \Rightarrow$$
$$V = \left(\sqrt{10}\right)^3 = \left(\sqrt{10}\right)\left(\sqrt{10}\right)\left(\sqrt{10}\right) = 10\sqrt{10}.$$

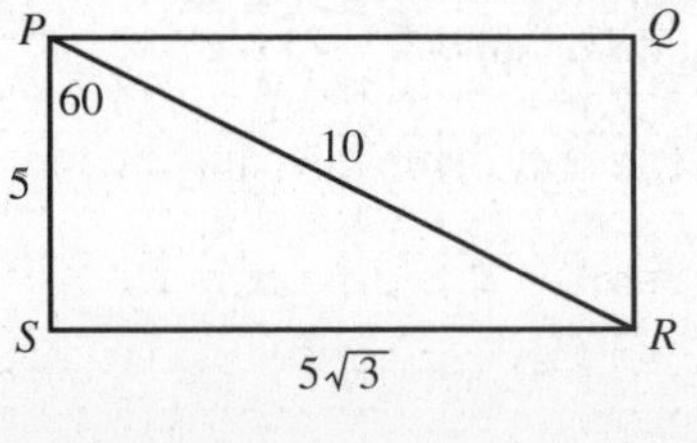

17. **(B)** PR is the hypotenuse of a 30-60-90 right triangle. By **KEY FACT J11**, PS, the leg opposite the 30° angle, is 5 (half the hypotenuse), and SR is $5\sqrt{3}$. So the area of the rectangle is $5 \times 5\sqrt{3} = 25\sqrt{3}$.

18. **(E)** $25 - 2\sqrt{x} = 7 \Rightarrow -2\sqrt{x} = -18 \Rightarrow \sqrt{x} = 9 \Rightarrow x = 9^2 = 81$.

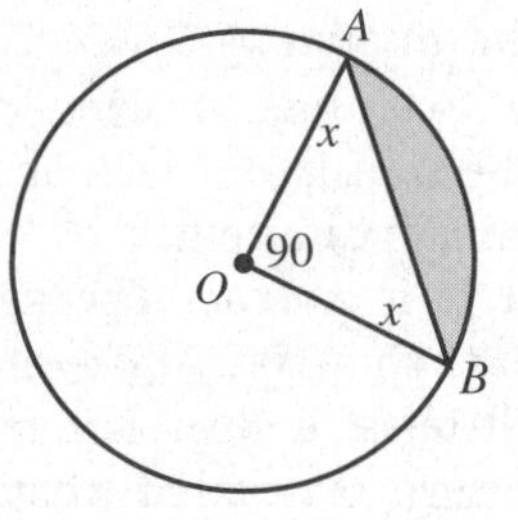

19. **(C)** Since each radius is 4, $OA = OB$ and $\triangle AOB$ is an isosceles right triangle. So by **KEY FACT J5**, $AB = 4\sqrt{2}$. The length of arc AB is $\frac{90}{360} = \frac{1}{4}$ of the circumference, which by **KEY FACT L4** is $2\pi(4) = 8\pi$; so the length of arc $AB = 2\pi$. The perimeter of the region, then, is $4\sqrt{2} + 2\pi$.

20. **(A)** If Mary earned a grade of G on the test, she missed $(100 - G)$ points. In adjusting the grades, the teacher decided to deduct only half that number: $\frac{100-G}{2}$. So Mary's new grade was

$$100 - \left(\frac{100-G}{2}\right) = 100 - 50 + \frac{G}{2} = 50 + \frac{G}{2}.$$

**Pick a number for G. For example, if G is 80, as explained in the question, Mary's adjusted grade would be 90. Only Choice A is equal to 90 when G is 80.

Section 3 Critical Reading

25. **(D)** The key word here is *smugly*. The tennis champion is smug or *complacent* about her victories.

Choice A is incorrect. *Downcast* means sad. A smug, self-satisfied tennis champion would be unlikely to feel downcast about winning victories. Choice B is incorrect. *Agitated* means anxious or disturbed. A smug, self-satisfied tennis champion would be unlikely to feel agitated about winning victories. Choice C is incorrect. *Indifferent* means uncaring or neutral. A smug, self-satisfied tennis champion would be unlikely to be indifferent to having won victories. Choice E is incorrect. *Philosophical* means calm and stoical, governed by reason rather than emotion. The tennis champion, however, is not entirely philosophical; she looks on her trophies smugly, viewing them with satisfaction.

26. **(C)** *But* signals a contrast. Normally thunderstorms last for a short time. However, sometimes they last or *persist* for a long time. Note the effect of the phrase "becoming ever more severe." If the storm keeps on getting worse, it is not *waning* (declining), *moderating* (becoming less severe), *vacillating* (wavering), or *dispersing* (being scattered).

27. **(D)** Why is this 100-mile-thick piece of glass clearer than a standard windowpane? *Because* the glass is exceptionally *transparent*. The "so . . . that" structure signals cause and effect.

Choice A is incorrect. *Fragile* means breakable. The sentence emphasizes the clearness of the glass, not its fragility. Choice B is incorrect. *Immaculate* means perfectly clean. The sentence emphasizes the clearness of the glass, not its cleanliness. Choice C is incorrect. *Tangible* means able to be touched. The sentence emphasizes the clearness of the glass, not its tangibility. Choice E is incorrect. *Iridescent* means lustrous and rainbowlike. The sentence emphasizes the clearness of the glass, not its iridescence.

28. **(D)** The *assiduous* or diligent *execution* (performance) of one's job would give one's employer no cause for complaint. Note the signal word *because* indicating the sentence's cause and effect structure.

Choice A is incorrect. *Derelict* means neglectful in the performance of one's duties. Her employers would have had every right to complain if she had been derelict in the performance of her duties. Choice B is incorrect. *Importunate* means annoyingly demanding and overeager. It is related to the word *persistent*, but has negative connotations. The first missing word should be entirely positive. Choice C is incorrect. *Meticulous* means painstaking and careful. However, employers would not necessarily be happy to have an employee who was meticulous about postponing or putting off doing her work. Choice E is incorrect. *Hidebound* means narrow-minded and unwilling to change. Employers might easily have complaints about an employee who was hidebound in her notion of what her duties were.

29. **(D)** Something *eclectic* is by definition composed of items drawn from many different sources. In this case, the style of interior decoration is eclectic.

Choice A is incorrect. *Aesthetic* means characterized by a love of beauty. The key phrase here is "bits and pieces . . . from widely divergent periods." The author is not emphasizing the beauty of the style of decoration; he is emphasizing its unusual variety. Choice B is incorrect. *Lyrical* means musical or songlike. The word is an unlikely choice to describe a style of decoration. Choice C is incorrect. *Traditional* means customary or established. A unique mix of furnishings from very different periods would be unlikely to be described as customary or traditional. Choice E is incorrect. *Perfunctory* means hasty and superficial; it also can mean uninterested. Neither meaning makes sense in the context.

30. **(B)** One expects seeds to germinate or sprout within a relatively short period of time. However, for woodland seeds, the process takes longer than normal; the seeds seem sadly *reluctant* to sprout.

Choice A is incorrect. *Germinate* means to put forth shoots or sprout. If the mechanisms delay sprouting, then the woodland seeds would not be unfortunately *prone* or inclined to germinate. Choice C is incorrect. *Qualified* means fitted or competent to do something. It makes no sense in the context. Choice D is incorrect. *Prolific* means highly productive or fruitful. If the mechanisms delay the seeds' sprouting, then the seeds would not be sadly *prolific* or productive. Choice E is incorrect. *Modified* means changed. It makes no sense in the context.

31. **(C)** Because these shows are highly derivative of (stem from) our culture, they reflect what our culture is like. Thus, they are good *indices* (indicators or signs) of our culture's attitudes and values. *Indices* is the plural form of *index*.

Choice A is incorrect. The soap operas are derivative of contemporary culture; they are based on or derived from it. They do not *contradict* or disagree with it. Choice B is incorrect. Because soap operas are derived from contemporary culture, they are unlikely to be *antidotes* or medicines that can serve to counteract its effects. Choice D is incorrect. Soap operas are derivative of contemporary culture; they are based on or derived from it. Thus, they cannot be *prerequisites* (preconditions or requirements that must be met *before* something can occur) for contemporary culture. Choice E is incorrect. According to the author, soap operas are derivative of contemporary culture; they are based on or derived from it. Thus, they are unlikely be *determinants* (determining agents) of the culture from which they derive.

32. **(C)** Given that English society didn't encourage women to get an education, you would expect it not to care that women were uneducated. However, English society was illogical: it *decried* or expressed its disapproval of women's lack of education.

Choice A is incorrect. *Palliated* means alleviated or relieved without curing. It makes no sense in the context. Choice B is incorrect. *Postulated* means assumed without proof, or claimed. It makes little sense here. Choice D is incorrect. *Brooked* means tolerated or endured. It makes little sense here. Choice E is incorrect. *Vaunted* means boasted or bragged about. It makes little sense here.

33. **(D)** The passage depicts Archbishop Tutu's *compassion,* his feeling for someone in need that leads him to ignore the importunate demands of the press. Choice B is incorrect: it is the distressed student assistant who feels grief or anguish, not the archbishop.

34. **(E)** The archbishop's prominence is his fame or *renown.*

35. **(C)** The author uses the term "hot spot" to indicate a geological phenomenon; she uses the term *technically,* as it is used by geologists.

    Choice B is incorrect. In its informal, or colloquial, sense, a hot spot is a nightclub.

36. **(B)** The opening sentence states that "most of the world's active volcanoes are located along the edges of the great shifting plates." However, there are "isolated areas of volcanic activity" that are located "far from the nearest plate boundary." These hot spots differ from other areas of volcanic activity in their *location*: they occur within the plates, not along the plates' edges.

37. **(D)** Graham's goal is "to bring into unhackneyed movement." Thus, she rejects movement in dance that is hackneyed or *trite*.

38. **(A)** Graham insists that, in the dancer's body, the audience must see themselves, "something of the miracle that is a human being." In rejecting the idea of their imitating natural phenomena (trees, flowers, waves), she emphasizes that dancers must embody or *express their humanity*.

39. **(C)** Graham is pairing opposite qualities that are held in balance by training and technique. Thus, technique and training give freedom and its opposite, discipline; tension and its opposite, plasticity (*mobility and pliancy*).

40. **(B)** What do most people believe? Most people believe that spontaneity in dance or in theater *is* wholly dependent on emotion at that moment. That is what Graham refers to as the "popular belief." It is the belief that spontaneous theatrical moments *happen only because the actor is gripped by a sudden emotion*.

41. **(B)** Graham draws an *analogy* or comparison between the function of spontaneity in dance or theater and that of light in life.

42. **(C)** Waters is an experienced cook and restaurateur, an *accomplished practitioner of the culinary arts*.

    You can determine the answer to this question by using the process of elimination. Waters is not a cook on the verge of opening a restaurant or simply a gifted home cook; she has run her own restaurant for years, long enough to have developed criteria for hiring employees (lines 81–84). Therefore, you can eliminate Choices A and D. She is not uninformed about traditional methods of French cooking; she served her culinary apprenticeship in France. You can eliminate Choice B. Though she is a professional, there is nothing in the passage to suggest that she is set on outstripping her competition. You can eliminate Choice E. Only Choice C is left; it is the correct answer.

43. **(A)** Sometimes sharp and strong, sometimes sweet and fresh, garlic varies in quality. Waters uses the example of the garlic to show the *variability of ingredients*.

44. **(E)** Waters stresses that she is only making suggestions and that it is up to the reader to "determine the correct balance and composition" of the meal. Thus, she is trying to *allow scope* (room) *for the reader's own culinary initiative*.

45. **(E)** Waters states firmly that "a person who responds to the cooking processes and the mound of fresh ingredients with a genuine glow of delight is likely to be, or become, a very good cook indeed." Thus, to be a good cook, one who will produce superior results, one must have *a love of one's medium* (material for artistic expression; in this case, food).

46. **(C)** Waters is looking for employees who will take great personal satisfaction in what they are doing, people who enjoy the *culinary processes*.

47. **(B)** Waters and Graham are expressing their belief as artists in spontaneity, in flexibility, in energy, in joy. They are *presenting their artistic creeds*.

48. **(D)** Graham and Waters resemble one another in their marked enthusiasm and love for their work. Both clearly *are passionately involved with their art*.

Section 4 Mathematics

MULTIPLE-CHOICE QUESTIONS

For many problems, the explanation provides a reference to one or more **KEY FACTS** from Chapter 7. These are the mathematical facts that you need to solve that problem. If a solution refers to **KEY FACT J2**, for example, the solution depends on the second **KEY FACT** discussed in Section J of Chapter 7.

For some problems, an alternative solution, indicated by two asterisks (**), follows the first solution. When this occurs, usually one of the solutions is the direct mathematical one and the other is based on one of the tactics discussed in Chapters 6 and 7.

See page 234 for an explanation of the symbol ⇒, which is used in several answer explanations.

21. **(C)** Solve the given equation using the six-step method discussed in Section 9-G.

$$7d + 5 = 5d + 7 \Rightarrow$$
$$2d + 5 = 7 \Rightarrow 2d = 2 \Rightarrow d = 1.$$

Use **TACTIC 6-1. Test the answer choices, starting with C, which happens to work.

22. **(B)** The unmarked angle opposite the 60° angle also measures 60° (**KEY FACT I4**), and the sum of the measures of all six angles in the diagram is 360° (**KEY FACT I3**). Then,

$$360 = a + b + c + 20 + 60 + 60 =$$
$$a + b + c + 140.$$

Subtracting 140 from each side, we get

$$a + b + c = 220.$$

23. **(D)** If $5\sqrt{x} + 1 = 46$, then $5\sqrt{x} = 45$, and so $\sqrt{x} = 9$ and $x = 81$.

24. **(E)** If $y = 1$, then x could be 1 or -1; so neither Choice A nor Choice B is correct. If $x = 1$ and $y = -1$, Choice C is wrong, and if $y = 1$ and $x = -1$, Choice D is wrong. Only Choice E is correct.

$$**x^2 = y^2 \Rightarrow x^2 - y^2 = 0 \Rightarrow (x - y)(x + y) = 0$$

Therefore,

$$x - y = 0 \text{ or } x + y = 0 \Rightarrow$$
$$x = y \text{ or } x = -y \Rightarrow |x| = |y|$$

25. **(D)** Since $-5 + 5 = 0$, and since 0 is an even integer, $-5 \oplus 5 = -5$.

26. **(D)**
- Could $a + b$ be even? Yes, if $a = 10$ and $b = 2$, then $a + b$ is even and $a \oplus b = 10$.
- Could $a + b$ be odd? Yes, if $a = 1$ and $b = 10$, then $a + b$ is odd and $a \oplus b = 10$.
- Could $b \oplus a = 10$? No. If $b \oplus a$ were 10, then $b \oplus a$ would be equal to $a \oplus b$, which would imply that $a = b$, contrary to the given information.
- Statements I and II only are true.

27. **(D)** If Sarah were really unlucky, what could go wrong in her attempt to get one marble of each color? Well, her first 11 picks *might* yield 6 blue marbles and 5 white ones. But then the twelfth marble would be red, and she would have at least one of each color. The answer is 12.

28. **(D)** Since the area of square $ABCD$ is 100, each side is 10. In the diagram, draw in line segment $\overline{AE}$ and line segment $\overline{EXY}$ perpendicular to $\overline{AB}$ and $\overline{CD}$, and then label the diagram.

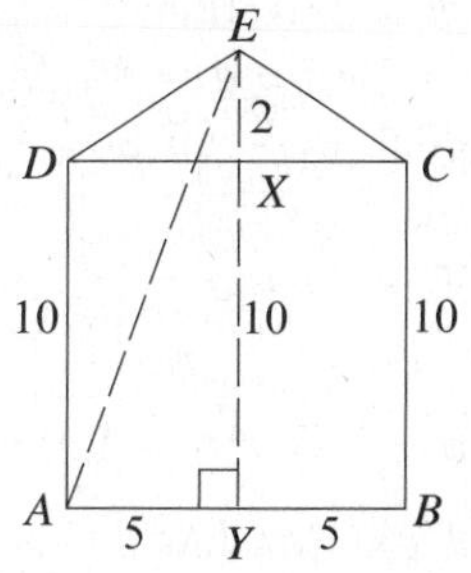

$XY = 10$ since it is the same length as a side of the square. $\overline{EX}$ is the height of $\triangle ECD$, whose base is 10 and whose area is 10. So $10 = \frac{1}{2}(10)(EX) \Rightarrow EX = 2$, and so $EY = 12$.
Since $\triangle ECD$ is isosceles, $DX = 5$; so $AY = 5$. Finally, recognize $\triangle AYE$ as a 5-12-13 right triangle, or use the Pythagorean theorem to find the hypotenuse, AE, of the triangle:

$$(AE)^2 = 5^2 + 12^2 = 25 + 144 = 169,$$
so $AE = 13$.

GRID-IN QUESTIONS

29. **(.01)** First, add w to each side of the given equation, and then subtract 4.99:

$$5 - w = 4.99 \Rightarrow 5 = 4.99 + w \Rightarrow w = .01.$$

30. **(90)** In a ratio problem write the letter x after each number (**TACTIC D-1**). Then $a = 5x$, $b = 7x$, and $c = 12x$; and since, by **KEY FACT J1**, the sum of the measures of the angles of a triangle is 180°:

$$5x + 7x + 12x = 180 \Rightarrow 24x = 180 \Rightarrow x = 7.5.$$
So $c = 12x = 12(7.5) = 90$.

31. **(11)** Since $xy = 30$ and $x = -6$, we have $y = -5$. So $x^2 - y^2 = (-6)^2 + (-5)^2 = 36 - 25 = 11$.

32. **(0)** For any numbers a and b, if $a \neq b$ and $ax = bx$, then x must be 0. Therefore,
25% of $x = 35\%$ of $x \Rightarrow x = 0 \Rightarrow 45\%$ of $x = 0$.

33. **(40)** Consider the diagram below in which several additional angles have been labeled and repeatedly use **KEY FACTS I2, I4,** and **J1.**

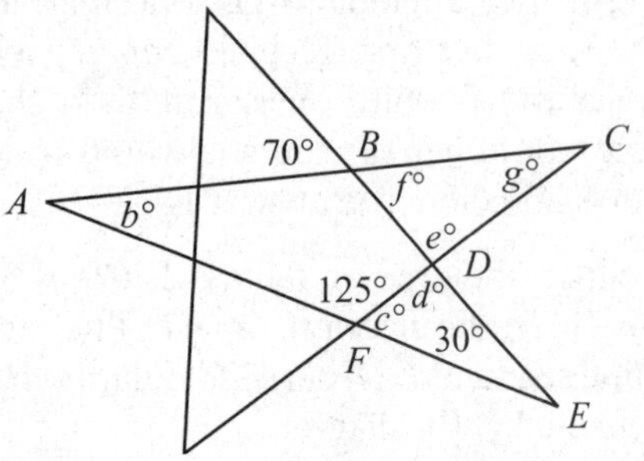

Since $125 + c = 180$, then $c = 55$; so in $\triangle DEF$, $55 + 30 + d = 180 \Rightarrow d = 95$. Also, since vertical angles are equal, $e = 95$ and $f = 70$. Then in $\triangle BCD$,

$$95 + 70 + g = 180 \Rightarrow g = 15.$$

Finally, in $\triangle CAF$,

$$15 + 125 + b = 180 \Rightarrow b = 40.$$

34. **(6)** Write out the first few terms being careful to follow the directions. The first term is 2. The second term is 1 more than 2 times the first term: $2(2) + 1 = 5$. The third term is 1 more than 2 times the second term: $2(5) + 1 = 11$. Continuing in this way, you find that the terms less than 100 are: 2, 5, 11, 23, 47, 95. There are 6 of them.

35. **(126)** In the tens column, $2 + 4 + 6 = 12$; so if nothing was carried from the units column, $A = 1$ and $B = 2$. In fact, this works, because if $B = 2$, the units column adds up to 6, and $ABC = 126$.

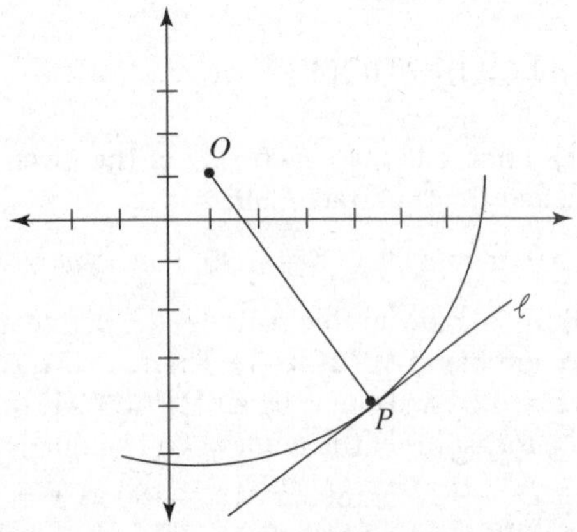

36. $\left(\frac{3}{5}\text{ or }.6\right)$ A quick sketch can eliminate a few choices and guard against carelessness. From the diagram, we see that the slope of l is positive (**KEY FACT N5**), and so we can eliminate choices A and B. By **KEY FACT N4**, the slope of $\overline{OP}$ is $\frac{-4-1}{4-1} = \frac{-5}{3}$. Since by **KEY FACT N6**, $\overline{OP} \perp l$, the slope of l is the negative reciprocal of $-\frac{5}{3}$, namely $\frac{3}{5}$.

37. **(9.5)** By **KEY FACT M2**, the surface area of a rectangular box is given by $A = 2(\ell w + wh + \ell h)$. Replacing w by 5, ℓ by 7, and A by 298, we get

$$298 = 2(35 + 5h + 7h) = 70 + 24h.$$

Therefore, $24h = 228$ and $h = 9.5$.

38. $\left(\frac{9}{10}\text{ or }.9\right)$ If there are x seats on each bus, then the group is using $\frac{4}{5}(3x) = \frac{12}{5}x$ seats. After $\frac{1}{4}$ of the passengers get off, $\frac{3}{4}$ of them, or $\frac{3}{4}\left(\frac{12}{5}x\right) = \frac{9}{5}x$ remain. The fraction of the $2x$ seats now being used on the two buses is

$$\frac{\frac{9}{5}x}{2x} = \frac{\frac{9}{5}}{2} = \frac{9}{10}.$$

**To avoid working with x, assume there are 20 seats on each bus. At the beginning, the group is using $\frac{4}{5}$ of the 60 seats on the three buses: $\frac{4}{5}(60) = 48$. When $\frac{1}{4}$ of the 48 people left, 12 left and the 36 remaining people used $\frac{36}{40} = \frac{9}{10}$ of the 40 seats on the two buses.

Section 5 Writing Skills

1. **(B)** Choice B corrects the misuse of the subjunctive.
2. **(D)** Choice D corrects the error in the case of the pronoun. Choice E corrects the error in case but introduces an error in tense.
3. **(A)** The clause is correct.
4. **(A)** Sentence is correct.
5. **(C)** Error in modification and word order. Choice C corrects the dangling participle.
6. **(A)** Sentence is correct.
7. **(B)** This corrects the unnecessary switch in the pronouns, *anyone–you*.
8. **(E)** Error in parallelism. *Relax* matches *make*, *wash*, and *do*.
9. **(A)** Sentence is correct.
10. **(D)** Comma splice. The run-on sentence is corrected by the use of a semicolon.

11. **(D)** Error in following conventions. Choice D corrects the double negative *hadn't hardly* and the misuse of *those* with *kind*.

12. **(B)** Error in modification and word order. Choice B corrects the dangling participle.

13. **(B)** Comma splice. In Choice B, the run-on sentence is corrected by the use of a semicolon, and the omission of the past participle *been* is also corrected.

14. **(C)** Errors in following conventions. Choice C expresses the author's meaning directly and concisely. All other choices are either indirect or ungrammatical.

15. **(D)** Incorrect conjunction. The conjunction *furthermore* fails to link the two clauses logically. Choice D corrects the error by eliminating the incorrect conjunction and substituting a colon to separate the two main clauses. (A colon may separate two main clauses when the second explains the first. In Choice D, the second clause ["they . . . subside"] explains in what way young children's fevers are erratic.)

16. **(D)** Error in degree of comparison. Because there are many characters in *A Christmas Carol,* you must describe Tiny Tim as the *most* beloved of them all.

17. **(C)** Wordiness. Choice C eliminates the unnecessary words.

18. **(A)** Sentence is correct.

19. **(E)** Error in sequence of tenses. Because Hemingway worked as a correspondent at a definite time in the past (during the Spanish Civil War), the verb should be in the past tense ("wrote"), not the present perfect tense ("has written").

20. **(A)** Sentence is correct.

21. **(B)** Error in diction. Change *had ought* to *ought*.

22. **(D)** Adjective and adverb confusion. Change *bad* to *badly*.

23. **(B)** Error in tense. Change *has sang* to *has sung*.

24. **(B)** Error in diction. Change *affect* to *effect*.

25. **(E)** Sentence is correct.

26. **(B)** Error in verb. Change *had drank* to *had drunk*.

27. **(A)** Error in diction. Since *without hardly* is a double negative, change *without hardly* to either *without* or *with hardly*.

28. **(C)** Error in comparison of modifiers. Incorrect use of the superlative. Change *most* to *more*.

29. **(B)** Error in parallelism. Change *being intelligent* to *intelligence*.

30. **(A)** Error in diction. Change *or* to *nor*.

31. **(E)** Sentence is correct.

32. **(A)** Error in diction. Change *principal* to *principle*.

33. **(D)** Double negative. Do not combine *hardly* with *not*. Either say the alchemist's method was not scientific, or say that it was hardly scientific.

34. **(C)** Error in agreement. Change *them* to *him* or *her*.

35. **(B)** Choice A is awkwardly constructed. The phrase *for the cruelty of keeping animals* is cumbersome. Moreover, the sentence suggests that cruelty to animals can be justified—the opposite of what the writer intended to say.
    Choice B states the idea clearly and economically. It is the best answer.
    Choice C is wordy and awkwardly expressed.
    Choice D is wordy and awkwardly expressed.
    Choice E, which lacks a main verb, is a sentence fragment.

36. **(C)** Choice A is a sentence fragment. It lacks a main verb.
    Choice B contradicts the idea that zoos can be educational.
    Choice C accurately develops the idea introduced in sentence 3 that zoos can be educational. It is the best answer.
    Choice D is irrelevant to the idea in sentence 3.
    Choice E is written with a hostile and inappropriate tone.

37. **(C)** Choice A is not the best answer because most readers probably know that zoos house animals in cages. Moreover, highly charged language is not ordinarily used merely to pass along information.
    Choice B is unrelated to the words in question.
    Choice C is the best answer. The choice of words is meant to shock and disturb the reader.
    Choice D suggests that the author is trying to be objective, but the words in question are hardly objective.
    Choice E describes the purpose of the entire essay but not the particular words in question.

38. **(A)** Choice A introduces the main idea of the paragraph. It is the best answer.
    Choice B raises an issue not mentioned in the remainder of the paragraph. Thereofre, it is not a good topic sentence of the paragraph.

Choice C contains an idea not discussed in the paragraph. The paragraph focuses on how animals behave in captivity, not on living conditions at the zoo.

Choice D contains a dangling modifier. The phrase *Living in the zoos* should modify *animals* instead of *conditions.*

Choice E contains a frivolous cliché that is not consistent with the tone of the essay.

39. **(B)** Choice A is grammatically correct, but it reverses the cause-effect relationship stated by the original sentences.

Choice B accurately and economically conveys the ideas of the original sentences. It is the best answer.

Choice C is a sentence fragment. It lacks a main verb. The *-ing* forms of verbs (e.g., *growing, placing, being*) may not be used as the main verb without a helping verb, as in was growing, is placing, and so on.

Choice D is grammatically correct but stylistically awkward mainly because the subject *They* is too far removed from the verb *would . . . survive.*

Choice E is virtually meaningless because the cause-effect relationship has been reversed.

PART THREE

CRITICAL READING

CHAPTER 1

The Sentence Completion Question

The sentence completion questions ask you to choose the best way to complete a sentence from which one or two words have been omitted. You must be able to recognize the logic, style, and tone of the sentence so that you can choose the answer that makes sense in this context. You must also be able to recognize the way words are normally used.

The sentences cover a wide variety of topics of the sort you have probably encountered in your general reading. However, this is not a test of your general knowledge. You may feel more comfortable if you are familiar with the topic the sentence is discussing, but you should be able to handle any of the sentences using your understanding of the English language.

TIPS FOR HANDLING SENTENCE COMPLETION QUESTIONS

Tip 1

Before you look at the answer choices, read the sentence, substituting the word "blank" for the missing word. Think of words you know that might make sense in the context. You may not come up with the exact word, but you may come up with a synonym. You will definitely have a feel for what word belongs in the frame.

EXAMPLE 1

See how the first tip works in dealing with the following sentence:

> The psychologist set up the experiment to test the rat's ________: he wished to see how well the rat adjusted to the changing conditions it had to face.

Even before you look at the answer choices, you can figure out what the answer *should* be.

Look at the sentence. The psychologist is trying to test the rat's "blank." In other words, the psychologist is trying to test some particular quality or characteristic of the rat. What quality? How do you get the answer?

Look at the second part of the sentence, the part following the colon (the second clause, in technical terms). This clause defines or clarifies what the psychologist is trying to test. He is trying to see how well the rat adjusts. What words does this suggest to you? *Flexibility*, possibly, or *adjustment* comes to mind. Either of these words could logically complete the sentence's thought.

Here are the five answer choices given:

(A) reflexes (B) communicability (C) stamina
(D) sociability (E) adaptability

Which one is the best synonym for *flexibility* or *adjustment*? Clearly, the closest synonym is *adaptability*, Choice E.

To make sure you are correct, reread the sentence, substituting the word *adaptability* in the blank.

> The psychologist set up the experiment to test the rat's adaptability: he wished to see how well the rat adjusted to the changing conditions it had to face.

The correct answer is Choice E.

Power Practice

Practice Tip 1 as you work through the following questions, step by step.

1. It is foolish to boast about your wealth or accomplishments; no one likes a ____________________.

   What word makes sense in the context?
   Write down your word: ____________________

Now look at the answer choices:

(A) miser (B) turncoat (C) braggart
(D) charlatan (E) mentor

Reread the sentence, substituting your answer choice in the blank.

2. Usually several skunks live together; however, adult male striped skunks are ____________________ during the summer.

   What word makes sense in the context?
   Write down your word: ____________________

Now look at the answer choices:

(A) nocturnal (B) solitary (C) predatory
(D) cooperative (E) dormant

Reread the sentence, substituting your answer choice in the blank.

3. Justice Brandeis was noted for his legal ______________ : his biographers often comment about the keenness of his insights into the workings of the law.

   What word makes sense in the context?
   Write down your word: ______________

Now look at the answer choices:

(A) ethics (B) malpractice (C) defense
(D) acumen (E) representation

Reread the sentence, substituting your answer choice in the blank.

Check Your Answers:

1. **(C)** A *braggart* is a boaster.
2. **(B)** *Solitary* means alone, without companions.
3. **(D)** *Acumen* means shrewdness, keenness of judgment.

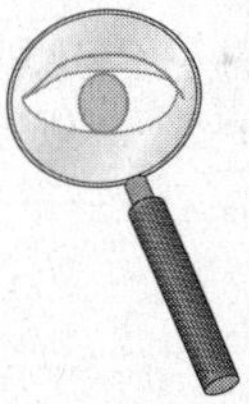

DID YOU NOTICE?

Each of the sentences in the preceding questions is actually two statements linked by a semicolon (;) or a colon (:). The punctuation mark is your clue that the two statements support each other.

A semicolon signals you that the second statement develops the idea expressed in the first statement.

Statement 1: It is foolish to boast about your wealth or accomplishments.

Why?

Statement 2: No one likes a braggart.

A colon signals you that the second statement serves to explain or clarify the first. It gives examples, or it defines terms.

Statement 1: Justice Brandeis was noted for his legal acumen.

What is legal acumen?

Statement 2: His biographers often comment about *the keenness of his insights into the workings of the law.*

Legal acumen is keenness of insight into the workings of the law.

Tip 2

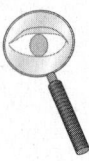

Look for words or phrases that indicate a contrast between one idea and another—words like *although, however, despite,* or *but.* In such cases, an antonym or near-antonym for another word in the sentence may be the correct answer.

EXAMPLE 2

See how the second tip works in dealing with the following sentence:

> We expected the winner of the race to be jubilant about his victory, but he was ________ instead.

How do you expect someone to feel who has won a victory? Even if you do not know the word *jubilant,* you can guess that it means overjoyed and triumphant.

But signals a contrast. The winner is *not* jubilant. Instead, he is the opposite of jubilant: he is sad.

Here are the five answer choices given:

(A) triumphant (B) mature (C) morose
(D) talkative (E) culpable

You are looking for an antonym of *jubilant. Triumphant* is a synonym of *jubilant,* not an antonym; its antonym is *sad* or *disappointed.* You can cross out Choice A. *Mature* means grown-up; its antonym is *immature.* You can cross out Choice B. The next choice, *morose,* may be an unfamiliar word to you. For the moment, skip Choice C. The antonym of *talkative* is *silent* or *uncommunicative.* You can cross out Choice D. *Culpable* means guilty; its antonym is *innocent.* You can cross out Choice E. Only Choice C is left. *Morose* means gloomy and ill-humored; it is the opposite of *jubilant.*

Power Practice

Practice Tip 2 as you work through the following questions, step by step.

1. Although it appeared quite ________ , the vase was actually very sturdy; even a fall from the top shelf left it undamaged.

Although signals a contrast. The vase is actually *sturdy* (tough). Even a fall does not shatter or damage it. However, the vase appears to be the opposite of sturdy. You are looking for the antonym of *sturdy.* What word makes sense in the context?

Write down your word: ______________________________

Now look at the answer choices:

(A) expensive (B) floral (C) capacious
(D) ornate (E) fragile

Reread the sentence, substituting your answer choice in the blank.

2. Despite his seemingly hopeless position, Bond felt ________ that he would escape from the trap.

Despite signals a contrast. Bond's position seems hopeless. He is caught in a trap. However, Bond feels the opposite of hopeless. You are looking for the antonym of *hopeless*. What word makes sense in the context?

Write down your word: ____________________________

Now look at the answers:

(A) problematic (B) dubious (C) optimistic
(D) unwarranted (E) tolerant

Reread the sentence, substituting your answer choice in the blank.

3. Most birds of prey hunt by day; owls, however, are ________ hunters.

However signals a contrast. Owls do the opposite of what most birds of prey do. You are looking for the antonym of *by day*. What word makes sense in the context?

Write down your word: ____________________________

Now look at the answer choices:

(A) migratory (B) nocturnal (C) persistent
(D) clandestine (E) fierce

HOW'S YOUR WORD POWER?
Did you know all the words in the answer choices? Look up any unfamiliar words in our Word List, in a dictionary, or online at sites like *www.onelook.com* or *www.dictionary.com*.

Check Your Answers:

1. **(E)** The opposite of sturdy or durable is *fragile*.
2. **(C)** The opposite of hopeless is *optimistic* or hopeful.
3. **(B)** Unlike most birds of prey, owls do not hunt by day. They hunt by night. They are *nocturnal* hunters.

Tip 3

Look for words or phrases that indicate support for a concept—words such as *likewise, similarly, in the same way, and, in addition, additionally,* and *also*. What follows logically develops the writer's idea. In such cases, a synonym or near-synonym for another word in the sentence may provide the correct answer.

EXAMPLE 3

See how the third tip works in dealing with the following sentence:

> The simplest animals are those whose bodies are least complex in structure, and that do the same things done by all animals, such as eating, breathing, moving, and feeling, in the most ________ way.

The transition word *and* signals you that the writer intends to develop the idea of simplicity introduced in the sentence. Which of the answer choices is closest in meaning to *simplest* and to *least complex*?

Here are the five answer choices given:

(A) haphazard (B) bizarre (C) advantageous
(D) primitive (E) unique

You are looking for a word that develops the idea of simplicity, possibly a synonym for the word *simplest*. In biology class, you most likely learned that primitive life forms were simple in structure, and that the more complex forms of life evolved later. Clearly, Choice D, *primitive*, is best. It is the only answer choice that develops the idea of simplicity.

Power Practice

Practice Tip 3 as you work through the following questions, step by step.

1. Studies have shown that women are faster than men at certain precision manual tasks; moreover, they also ________ men in arithmetic calculation and in recalling landmarks from a route.

Moreover signals support. You are looking for a word that supports and develops the idea of women being *faster than* men at certain tasks. What word makes sense in the context?

Write down your word: ____________________

Now look at the answer choices:

(A) outnumber (B) conspire against (C) acknowledge
(D) outperform (E) lag behind

Reread the sentence, substituting your answer choice in the blank.

2. After the El Salvadoran rebels ousted President Hernandez Martinez, the revolution spread to Guatemala, whose authoritarian president was similarly ________ .

Similarly signals support. You are looking for a word that supports and develops the idea of being *ousted* (forced out). What word makes sense in the context?

Write down your word: ____________________________

Now look at the answer choices:

(A) overthrown (B) nominated (C) elected
(D) derided (E) astounded

Reread the sentence, substituting your answer choice in the blank.

3. During World War II, Finland was conspicuous for its refusal to take sides with either warring power, while Sweden likewise refused to do anything that might damage its traditional________ .

Likewise signals support. Finland and Sweden both acted in a similar way. You are looking for a word or phrase that develops the idea of Finland's *refusal to take sides*. What word makes sense in the context?

Write down your word: ____________________________

Now look at the answer choices:

(A) monarchy (B) neutrality (C) economy
(D) belligerence (E) dignity

Reread the sentence, substituting your answer choice in the blank.

Check Your Answers:

1. **(D)** According to the studies, women *outperform* (do better than) men at certain tasks.
2. **(A)** The president was *overthrown* (removed from power; thrown out of office).
3. **(B)** Sweden did not want to damage its traditional *neutrality*. Like Finland, it refused to take sides.

Tip 4

Look for words or phrases that indicate that one thing causes another—words like *because*, *since*, *therefore*, or *thus*.

EXAMPLE 4

See how the fourth tip works in dealing with the following sentence:

Because her delivery was ________ , the effect of her speech on the voters was nonexistent.

Because signals a relationship of cause and effect. One thing causes another. Which of the answer choices expresses such a logical relationship?

Here are the five answer choices given:

(A) halting (B) plausible (C) moving
(D) respectable (E) audible

What sort of delivery would cause a speech to have no effect? Obviously you would not expect a *moving* (eloquent) delivery to have such a poor result. A *halting* or stumbling speech, however, might logically have little or no effect on its audience. Thus, Choice A is best.

Power Practice

Practice Tip 4 as you work through the following questions, step by step.

1. We ran out of food toward the middle of the day, so by the time we returned to camp that evening we were ________ .

So signals cause and effect. You are looking for a word that expresses the effect of running out of food on a group of campers. What word makes sense in the context?

Write down your word: ______________________

Now look at the answer choices:

(A) footsore (B) reckless (C) envious
(D) ravenous (E) tasteless

Reread the sentence, substituting your answer choice in the blank.

2. He valued his colleagues for the soundness of their opinions and therefore ________ with them often.

Therefore signals cause and effect. You are looking for a word that expresses the result of a person's valuing his colleagues' sound (sensible) opinions. What word makes sense in the context?

Write down your word: ____________________

Now look at the answer choices:

(A) differed (B) consulted (C) embarked
(D) celebrated (E) struggled

Reread the sentence, substituting your answer choice in the blank.

3. Since the polar bear uses Arctic sea ice as a platform from which to hunt and feed upon seals, to seek mates and breed, and to travel long distances, any threat to the existence of sea ice would have ________ effect on all stages of the animal's life cycle.

Since signals cause and effect. You are looking for a word that expresses the effect on the polar bear of a threat to its habitat. What word makes sense in the context?

Write down your word: ____________________

Now look at the answer choices:

(A) an innocuous (B) a characteristic (C) a detrimental
(D) a peripheral (E) a positive

Reread the sentence, substituting your answer choice in the blank.

Check Your Answers:

1. **(D)** A day of hiking on an empty stomach would result in people being *ravenous* (very hungry).
2. **(B)** *Because* he valued his colleagues' sensible opinions, he *consulted* or discussed matters with them.
3. **(C)** Something that threatened the polar bear's habitat by definition would have *a detrimental* (harmful) effect on its life cycle.

Tip 5

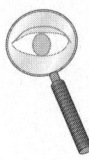

Look for signals that indicate a word is being defined—phrases such as *in other words, that is,* or *which means,* and special punctuation clues. Commas, hyphens, and parentheses all are used to set off definitions.

EXAMPLE 5

See how the fifth tip works in dealing with the following sentence:

> As a child, Menuhin was considered a _________ , gifted with extraordinary musical ability.

This sentence is a straightforward definition. The missing word is defined in the section set off by the comma. Ask yourself what word in the dictionary is defined as a person *gifted with extraordinary musical ability*?

Here are the five answer choices given:

(A) heretic (B) prodigy (C) mendicant
(D) renegade (E) precursor

Menuhin was a child *prodigy*. The correct answer is Choice B.

Power Practice

Practice Tip 5 as you work through the following questions, step by step.

1. In her old age, Miss Emily became ________; in other words, she grew to shun society, preferring to live alone in her decaying house.

The phrase *in other words* signals a definition. Whatever word you choose has something to do with avoiding society. What word makes sense in the context?

Write down your word: ____________________

Now look at the answer choices:

(A) forgetful (B) reclusive (C) obdurate
(D) ironic (E) avaricious

Reread the sentence, substituting your answer choice in the blank.

2. Gladiators were trained in the use of the net and the ________ (three-pronged spear).

The phrase in the parentheses defines the missing word. What word makes sense in the context?

Write down your word: ______________________

Now look at the answer choices:

(A) rapier (B) implement (C) crescent
(D) triage (E) trident

Reread the sentence, substituting your answer choice in the blank.

3. I am a habitual ________, that is, a person who puts off doing things until another day.

The phrase *that is* signals a definition. Whatever word you choose should mean someone who delays doing what he or she ought to do. What word makes sense in the context?

Write down your word: ______________________

Now look at the answer choices:

(A) miser (B) ingrate (C) proponent
(D) procrastinator (E) debunker

Reread the sentence, substituting your answer choice in the blank.

Check Your Answers:

1. **(B)** By definition, someone who shuns or avoids society is *reclusive.* Miss Emily acts like a recluse or hermit.
2. **(E)** A gladiator's three-pronged weapon is a *trident*.
3. **(D)** A person who habitually puts off doing things is a *procrastinator*.

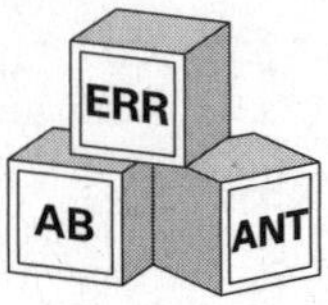

Tip 6

If you're having vocabulary trouble, look for familiar word parts—prefixes, suffixes, and roots—in unfamiliar words.

EXAMPLE 6

See how the sixth tip works in dealing with the following sentence:

After a tragedy, many people claim to have had a ________ of disaster.

Some of the following answer choices are unfamiliar words that you can figure out if you know the meaning of the prefixes, suffixes, and roots involved.

Here are the five answer choices given:

(A) deviation (B) proclamation (C) presentiment
(D) brink (E) verdict

Go through the answer choices, trying to figure out the meaning of any unfamiliar words by breaking them down into parts.

Deviation — The prefix *de-* means down or away.
The root *via* means way or road.
A *deviation* is a departure from the way, that is, a divergence or difference.

Does this word work in the context? If it does not, you can eliminate Choice A.

Proclamation — The prefix *pro-* means forward or in favor of.
The root *clam* means cry out.
A *proclamation* is a public statement or announcement, something cried out to the people.

Does this word work in the context? If it does not, you can eliminate Choice B.

Presentiment — The prefix *pre-* means before.
The root *sens* means feel. A *sentiment* is a feeling.
A *presentiment* is something you feel before it happens, a premonition or foreboding.

Presentiment works in the context. Your best answer is Choice C.

Power Practice

Practice Tip 6 as you work through the following questions, step by step.

1. Breaking with established artistic traditions, Dalí was a genius whose ________ works infuriated the traditionalists of his day.

The opening phrase is your key to the meaning of the missing word. What word makes sense in the context?

Write down your word: ____________________

Now look at the answer choices:

(A) derivative (B) magnanimous (C) insignificant
(D) uncontroversial (E) heterodox

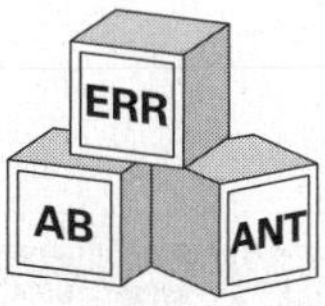

Break down any unfamiliar words into parts. Reread the sentence, substituting your answer choice in the blank.

2. The Declaration of Independence proclaimed the ________ of the American colonies and an end to English rule.

The phrase *an end to English rule* is a strong clue to the meaning of the missing word. What word makes sense in the context?

Write down your word: ____________________

Now look at the answer choices:

(A) manipulation (B) consecration (C) abasement
(D) autonomy (E) heresy

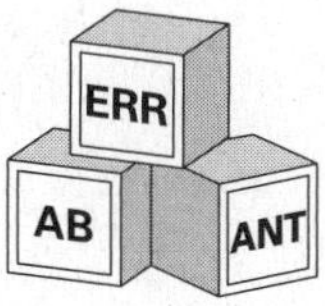

Break down any unfamiliar words into parts. Reread the sentence, substituting your answer choice in the blank.

3. After many years of working together as a comedy duo, Dean Martin and Jerry Lewis ended their ________ on a sour note.

The opening phrase is your key to the meaning of the missing word. What word makes sense in the context?

Write down your word: ____________________

Now look at the answer choices:

(A) resolution (B) tenacity (C) collaboration
(D) duplicity (E) commemoration

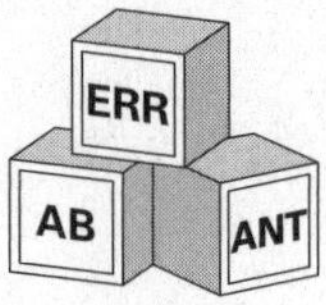

Break down any unfamiliar words into parts. Reread the sentence, substituting your answer choice in the blank.

Check Your Answers:

1. **(E)** The prefix *hetero-* means other. The root *dox-* means opinion. In breaking with established artistic traditions, Dalí created works that were *heterodox* (unorthodox; not in accordance with established opinions).
2. **(D)** The prefix *auto-* means self. The root *nom-* means law or custom. The Declaration proclaimed the colonies' *autonomy* or right of self-government.
3. **(C)** The prefix *col-* means with or together. The root *labor* of course means work. The comedians ended their *collaboration*.

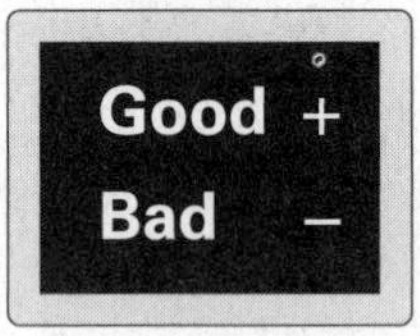

Tip 7

Work out whether the missing word is positive (+) or negative (–). Then test the answer choices for their positive or negative sense, eliminating those that don't work.

EXAMPLE 7

See how the seventh tip works in the following sentence.

> No matter how hard Ichabod tried to appear smooth and debonair, he still struck those who met him as a particularly ________ young man.

The sentence contrasts Ichabod's desired image—smooth and debonair (both positive terms)—with the actual negative impression he makes. You are looking for a negative term. Ask yourself what negative words would describe a young man who is *not* smooth and debonair (suave; sophisticated; elegant).

Here are the five answer choices given:

(A) heroic (B) promising (C) mendacious
(D) ungainly (E) precocious

TIME FOR AN EDUCATED GUESS
At this point, even if you do not know the meaning of the words *mendacious* and *ungainly*, you *must* guess.

Heroic (gallant; brave), *promising* (likely to turn out well), and *precocious* (unusually advanced, especially mentally) are all positive terms. Since you are looking for a negative term, you can eliminate Choices A, B, and E.

Both *mendacious* and *ungainly* are negative terms. *Mendacious* means untruthful. Ichabod isn't being untruthful; he's just unsuccessful at looking cool and suave. No matter how hard he tries, he still looks *ungainly*: ungraceful and clumsy, the opposite of smooth. The correct answer is Choice D.

Power Practice

Practice Tip 7 as you work through the following questions, step by step.

Good +
Bad −

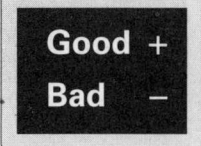

1. When the students were told that the popular class trip to Washington, D.C. had been cancelled for lack of funds, they predictably were greatly ________ .

Analyze the sentence to see whether the missing word is positive or negative. The opening clause is your key to the meaning of the missing word. What word makes sense in the context?

Write down your word: ______________________

Now look at the answer choices:

(A) relieved (B) accommodated (C) disgruntled
(D) emancipated (E) disseminated

Reread the sentence, substituting your answer choice in the blank.

2. Eugene Lang was a public ________ , creating scholarships that enabled hundreds of poor children to attend college.

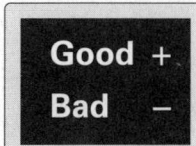

Good +
Bad −

Analyze the sentence to see whether the missing word is positive or negative. The long descriptive phrase is your key to the meaning of the missing word. What word makes sense in the context?

Write down your word: ______________________

Now look at the answer choices:

(A) partisan (B) benefactor (C) misanthrope
(D) official (E) nuisance

Reread the sentence, substituting your answer choice in the blank.

3. Although General Benedict Arnold originally distinguished himself by his brave service in the Continental Army, his later betrayal of the American cause so________ his name that few people today recognize his contribution to America's independence.

Good +
Bad −

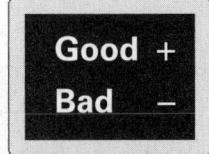

Analyze the sentence to see whether the missing word is positive or negative. The phrase "his later betrayal of the American cause" is your key to the meaning of the missing word. What word makes sense in the context?

Write down your word: ____________________

Now look at the answer choices:

(A) exalted (B) blackened (C) misconstrued
(D) proclaimed (E) cleared

Reread the sentence, substituting your answer choice in the blank.

Check Your Answers:

1. **(C)** The students' reaction to losing their trip clearly is negative. They are *disgruntled* (displeased and sulky).
2. **(B)** Someone who creates scholarships enabling poor children to attend college is a public *benefactor* (one who does good works).
3. **(B)** What effect would betraying a cause have on someone's good name? Clearly, it would have a negative effect. Arnold's betrayal *blackened* his name.

Tip 8

In a sentence completion question with two blanks, eliminate answer choices by testing one blank at a time. First read through the entire sentence and decide which blank you want to work on. Then insert the appropriate word of each answer pair in that blank. Ask yourself whether this particular word makes sense in this blank. If a word makes *no* sense in the sentence, you can eliminate that answer pair.

EXAMPLE 8

See how the eighth tip works in the following sentence.

The author portrays research psychologists not as disruptive ________ in the field of psychotherapy, but as effective ________ working ultimately toward the same ends as the psychotherapists.

Two additional tips can help you answer this question. **Tip 2:** Look for words that signal a contrast. The *not as...but as* structure signals a contrast; the missing words may be antonyms or near-antonyms. **Tip 7:** Test the answer choices for their positive or negative sense, eliminating those that don't work.

Good +
Bad −

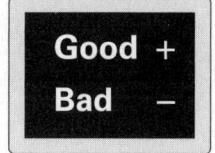

Here are the five answer choices given:

(A) proponents..opponents
(B) antagonists..pundits
(C) interlocutors..surrogates
(D) meddlers..usurpers
(E) intruders..collaborators

Turn to the second part of the sentence. The research psychologists are portrayed as effective "blanks" working ultimately toward the same ends as the psychotherapists. The key phrase here is "working ultimately toward the same ends." Thus, the research psychologists are in effect working together with the psychotherapists to achieve a common goal. This immediately suggests that the correct answer is *collaborators*, Choice E. Test the first word of that answer pair in the first blank. The adjective "disruptive" suggests that the first missing word is negative in tone. *Intruders* (people who rudely or inappropriately barge in) definitely have negative connotations. Choice E continues to look good.

Reread the sentence with both words in place, making sure both words make sense. "The author portrays research psychologists not as disruptive intruders in the field of psychotherapy, but as effective collaborators working ultimately toward the same ends as the psychotherapists." Both words make perfect sense. The correct answer is Choice E.

Power Practice

Practice Tip 8 as you work through the following questions, step by step.

1. Barbara's new classmates were neither _________ nor ________: they were not unfriendly, but they were not precisely welcoming either.

Quickly decide which blank you are going to test. The second clause (the part following the colon) is your key to the meaning of both missing words. What word makes sense in the blank you have chosen?

Write down your word: ______________________

Now look at the answer choices:

(A) curious..intelligent
(B) aloof..scholarly
(C) standoffish..cordial
(D) magnanimous..pragmatic
(E) diligent..affable

Eliminate any answer pair that did not work in the blank you tested. Then work on the other blank. Reread the sentence, substituting *both words* of your answer pair in the blanks.

2. Although his personal appearance is ________, the homework that he hands in is always neat, well-organized, and ________ executed.

Quickly decide which blank you are going to test. The contrast signal *Although* is your key to the meaning of both missing words. What word makes sense in the blank you have chosen?

Write down your word: ____________________

Now look at the answer choices:

(A) immaculate..flawlessly
(B) disheveled.. poorly
(C) stylish..indifferently
(D) curious..hastily
(E) unkempt..meticulously

Eliminate any answer pair that did not work in the blank you tested. Then work on the other blank. Reread the sentence, substituting *both words* of your answer pair in the blanks.

3. Scrooge's hatred of ________ grew so strong that he came to regard people who spent any money at all on Christmas presents and holiday entertainments as ________.

Quickly decide which blank you are going to test. The cause-and-effect signal "so..that" is your key to the meaning of both missing words. What word makes sense in the blank you have chosen?

Write down your word: ____________________

Now look at the answer choices:

(A) parsimony..ingrates
(B) philanthropy..misers
(C) extravagance..wastrels
(D) frugality..traitors
(E) seclusion..prodigals

Eliminate any answer pair that did not work in the blank you tested. Then work on the other blank. Reread the sentence, substituting *both words* of your answer pair in the blanks.

Check Your Answers:

1. **(C)** Barbara's classmates were not unfriendly and *standoffish* (cold and aloof). However, they were also not welcoming and *cordial* (warm and friendly).
2. **(E)** Although the student's appearance is *unkempt* (untidy; uncared for), his homework is *meticulously* (carefully and properly) executed.
3. **(C)** Scrooge hates *extravagance* (excessive or unnecessary spending). Because of this, he looks on people who spend money on things he regards unnecessary as *wastrels* (spendthrifts).

Practice Exercises

The following exercises are set up to give even National Merit Scholars a challenge. If you don't get every answer right, it's No Big Deal. Just do your best, and check the answer explanations for tips on how to do even better next time round.

EXERCISE A

1. Although the play was not praised by the critics, it did not ________ thanks to favorable word-of-mouth comments.

   (A) succeed (B) translate
   (C) function (D) close
   (E) continue

2. Because the hawk is ________ bird, farmers try to keep it away from their chickens.

   (A) a migratory (B) an ugly
   (C) a predatory (D) a reclusive
   (E) a huge

3. If you are trying to make a strong impression on your audience, you cannot do so by being understated, tentative, or ________.

   (A) hyperbolic (B) restrained
   (C) argumentative (D) authoritative
   (E) expressive

4. Despite the mixture's ________ nature, we found that by lowering its temperature in the laboratory we could dramatically reduce its tendency to vaporize.

   (A) resilient (B) homogeneous
   (C) insipid (D) volatile
   (E) acerbic

5. Milton's poem *Lycidas* is renowned as an example of ________ verse, for it laments the death of the young clergyman Edward King.

   (A) satiric (B) moribund
   (C) elegiac (D) free
   (E) didactic

6. Despite his ________ appearance, he was chosen by his employer for a job that required neatness and polish.

   (A) disheveled (B) impressive
   (C) prepossessing (D) aloof
   (E) tardy

7. The earthquake caused some damage, but the tidal wave that followed was more ________ because it ________ many villages.

   (A) culpable..bypassed
   (B) surreptitious..absorbed
   (C) deleterious..renovated
   (D) beneficial..congested
   (E) devastating..inundated

8. Several manufacturers now make biodegradable forms of plastic: some plastic six-pack rings, for example, gradually ________ when exposed to sunlight.

   (A) harden (B) stagnate
   (C) inflate (D) propagate
   (E) decompose

9. Although Barbara Tuchman never earned a graduate degree, she nevertheless ________ a scholarly career as a historian noted for her vivid style and ________ erudition.

(A) interrupted..flawed
(B) relinquished..immense
(C) abandoned..capricious
(D) pursued..prodigious
(E) followed..scanty

10. Since the chief executive officer had promised to give us a definite answer to our proposal, we were ________ by his ________ reply.

(A) pleased..equivocal
(B) vexed..negative
(C) annoyed..noncommittal
(D) delighted..perfunctory
(E) baffled..decisive

EXERCISE B

1. The insurance company rejected his application for accident insurance, because his ________ occupation made him a poor risk.

(A) desultory (B) haphazard
(C) esoteric (D) hazardous
(E) sedentary

2. No other artist rewards the viewer with more sheer pleasure than Miró: he is one of those blessed artists who combine profundity and ________.

(A) education (B) wisdom
(C) faith (D) depth
(E) fun

3. The tapeworm is an example of ________ organism, one that lives within or on another creature, deriving some or all of its nutriment from its host.

(A) a hospitable (B) an exemplary
(C) a parasitic (D) an autonomous
(E) a protozoan

4. The young woman was quickly promoted when her employers saw how ________ she was.

(A) indigent (B) indifferent
(C) assiduous (D) irresolute
(E) cursory

5. Though she was theoretically a friend of labor, her voting record in Congress ________ that impression.

(A) implied (B) created
(C) confirmed (D) belied
(E) maintained

6. The reasoning in this editorial is so ________ that I cannot see how anyone can be ________ by it.

(A) coherent..convinced
(B) astute..persuaded
(C) cogent..moved
(D) specious..deceived
(E) dispassionate..incriminated

7. To ________ the problem of contaminated chicken, the panel recommends shifting inspections from cursory visual checks to a more scientifically ________ random sampling for bacterial and chemical contamination.

(A) alleviate..rigorous
(B) eliminate..perfunctory
(C) analyze..symbolic
(D) document..unreliable
(E) obviate..dubious

8. Unable to hide his ________ for the police commissioner, the inspector imprudently made ________ remarks about his superior officer.

(A) disdain..detached
(B) respect..ambiguous
(C) liking..unfathomable
(D) contempt..interminable
(E) scorn..scathing

9. We were amazed that a woman who had been up to now the most ________ of public speakers could, in a single speech, electrify an audience and bring them cheering to their feet.

   (A) enthralling (B) accomplished
   (C) pedestrian (D) auspicious
   (E) masterful

10. Shy and hypochondriacal, Madison was ________ at public gatherings; his character made him a most ________ lawmaker and practicing politician.

    (A) ambivalent..conscientious
    (B) uncomfortable..unlikely
    (C) inaudible..fervent
    (D) aloof..gregarious
    (E) awkward..effective

EXERCISE C

1. In place of the more general debate about abstract principles of government that many delegates expected, the Constitutional Convention put ________ proposals on the table.

   (A) theoretical (B) vague
   (C) concrete (D) tentative
   (E) redundant

2. He was so ________ in meeting the payments on his car that the finance company threatened to seize the automobile.

   (A) dilatory (B) mercenary
   (C) solvent (D) diligent
   (E) compulsive

3. The child was so spoiled by her indulgent parents that she pouted and became ________ when she did not receive all of their attention.

   (A) discreet (B) suspicious
   (C) elated (D) sullen
   (E) tranquil

4. Modern architecture has abandoned the use of ________ trimming on buildings and has concentrated on an almost Greek simplicity of line.

   (A) flamboyant (B) austere
   (C) inconspicuous (D) hypothetical
   (E) derivative

5. We lost confidence in him because he never ________ the grandiose promises he had made.

   (A) forgot about
   (B) reneged on
   (C) tired of
   (D) delivered on
   (E) retreated from

6. Perhaps because something in us instinctively distrusts such displays of natural fluency, some readers approach John Updike's fiction with ________.

   (A) indifference (B) suspicion
   (C) veneration (D) enthusiasm
   (E) eloquence

7. Because she had a reputation for ________, we were surprised and pleased when she greeted us so ________.

   (A) insolence..informally
   (B) insouciance..cordially
   (C) graciousness..amiably
   (D) arrogance..disdainfully
   (E) aloofness..affably

8. Just as disloyalty is the mark of the traitor, ________ is the mark of the ________.

   (A) timorousness..hero
   (B) temerity..renegade
   (C) avarice..philanthropist
   (D) cowardice..craven
   (E) vanity..flatterer

9. We now know that what constitutes practically all of matter is empty space: relatively enormous ________ in which revolve infinitesimal particles so ________ that they have never been seen or photographed.

(A) crescendos..minute
(B) enigmas..static
(C) conglomerates..vague
(D) abstractions..colorful
(E) voids..small

10. Brilliant yet disturbing, James Baldwin's *The Fire Next Time* is both so eloquent in its passion and so ________ in its candor that it is bound to ________ any reader.

(A) bitter..soothe
(B) romantic..appall
(C) searing..unsettle
(D) indifferent..disappoint
(E) frank..bore

EXERCISE D

1. The scientist maintains that any hypothesis must explain what has already been discovered and must be constantly ________ by future findings.

(A) confirmed (B) invalidated
(C) disregarded (D) equaled
(E) reversed

2. Traffic speed limits are set at a level that achieves some balance between the danger of ________ speed and the desire of most people to travel as quickly as possible.

(A) minimal (B) normal
(C) prudent (D) inadvertent
(E) excessive

3. Written in an engaging style, the book provides a comprehensive overview of European wines that should prove inviting to everyone from the virtual ________ to the experienced connoisseur.

(A) prodigal (B) novice
(C) zealot (D) miser
(E) glutton

4. In view of the interrelationships among the African-American leaders treated in this anthology, a certain amount of ________ among some of the essays presented is inevitable.

(A) overlapping (B) inaccuracy
(C) pomposity (D) exaggeration
(E) objectivity

5. Most Antarctic animals ________ depend on the tiny shrimplike krill, either feeding on them directly, like the humpback whale, or consuming species that feed on them.

(A) seldom (B) ultimately
(C) needlessly (D) immediately
(E) marginally

6. Andy Warhol was an inspired ________ of his own art: he had a true gift for publicity.

(A) assessor (B) promoter
(C) curator (D) benefactor
(E) luminary

7. Japan's industrial success is ________ in part to its tradition of group effort and ________ , as opposed to the tradition of individual personal achievement common in many other industrial nations.

   (A) responsive..independence
   (B) related..misdirection
   (C) equivalent..solidarity
   (D) subordinate..individuality
   (E) attributable..cooperation

8. Aimed at ________ European attempts to seize territory in the Americas, the Monroe Doctrine was a strong warning to ________ foreign powers.

   (A) abetting..impertinent
   (B) eliminating..credulous
   (C) assisting..remote
   (D) preventing..overt
   (E) curbing..predatory

9. Because he was cynical, he was reluctant to ________ the ________ of any kind act until he had ruled out all possible hidden uncharitable motives.

   (A) question..benevolence
   (B) acknowledge..wisdom
   (C) credit..unselfishness
   (D) endure..loss
   (E) witness..outcome

10. The concept of individual freedom grew from political and moral convictions that ________ the closed and ________ world of feudalism into a more open and dynamic society.

   (A) galvanized..vibrant
   (B) converted..irreverent
   (C) transformed..hierarchical
   (D) recast..vital
   (E) merged..unregulated

EXERCISE E

1. Some students are ________ in choosing their classes; that is, they want to take only the courses for which they see immediate value.

   (A) theoretical (B) impartial
   (C) pragmatic (D) idealistic
   (E) opinionated

2. Chaotic in conception but not in ________, Kelly's canvases are as neat as the proverbial pin.

   (A) conceit (B) theory
   (C) execution (D) origin
   (E) intent

3. Although Josephine Tey was arguably as good a mystery writer as Agatha Christie, she was clearly far less ________ than Christie, having written only six books in comparison to Christie's sixty.

   (A) coherent (B) prolific
   (C) equivocal (D) pretentious
   (E) gripping

4. In the North American tribes, men were the representational artists, creating drawings of hunters and animals; women, on the other hand, traditionally ________ abstract, geometrical compositions.

   (A) devised (B) shunned
   (C) decried (D) impersonated
   (E) prefigured

5. The counselor viewed divorce not as a single circumscribed event but as ________ of changing family relationships—as a process that begins during the failing marriage and extends over many years.

(A) a continuum (B) an episode
(C) a parody (D) a denial
(E) an elimination

6. The systems analyst hesitated to talk to strangers about her highly specialized work, because she feared it was too ________ for people uninitiated in the field to understand.

(A) intriguing (B) derivative
(C) frivolous (D) esoteric
(E) rudimentary

7. Lavish in visual beauty, the film *Lawrence of Arabia* nevertheless boasts ________ of style: it knows how much can be shown in a single shot, how much can be said in a few words.

(A) nonchalance (B) economy
(C) autonomy (D) frivolity
(E) arrogance

8. The verbose and ________ style of the late Victorian novel is totally unlike the ________ of a minimalist like Hemingway.

(A) chatty..prolixity
(B) awkward..consistency
(C) redundant..terseness
(D) eloquent..logistics
(E) concise..floridity

9. Both the popular shows *China Beach* and *Tour of Duty* reflect the way dissent has become ________ in America; what were radical antiwar attitudes in the 1960s are now ________ TV attitudes.

(A) domesticated..mainstream
(B) obsolete..militant
(C) meaningful..unfashionable
(D) sensationalized..trite
(E) troublesome..conventional

10. He was a ________ employee, but the ________ and exhaustive research that he performed made it worthwhile for his employers to put up with his difficult moods.

(A) domineering..biased
(B) congenial..exemplary
(C) popular..pretentious
(D) fastidious..garbled
(E) cantankerous..meticulous

Answer Key

EXERCISE A

1. **D**	3. **B**	5. **C**	7. **E**	9. **D**
2. **C**	4. **D**	6. **A**	8. **E**	10. **C**

EXERCISE B

1. **D**	3. **C**	5. **D**	7. **A**	9. **C**
2. **E**	4. **C**	6. **D**	8. **E**	10. **B**

EXERCISE C

1. **C**	3. **D**	5. **D**	7. **E**	9. **E**
2. **A**	4. **A**	6. **B**	8. **D**	10. **C**

EXERCISE D

1. **A**	3. **B**	5. **B**	7. **E**	9. **C**
2. **E**	4. **A**	6. **B**	8. **E**	10. **C**

EXERCISE E

1. **C**	3. **B**	5. **A**	7. **B**	9. **A**
2. **C**	4. **A**	6. **D**	8. **C**	10. **E**

Answer Explanations

EXERCISE A

1. **(D)** Because the word-of-mouth comments were good, the play did not *close*. Watch out for the word *not*. It's a small but important word, one easy to overlook.
2. **(C)** The hawk is a *predatory* bird; it preys on chickens and other small creatures.
3. **(B)** You will not make a strong impression on your audience if you are *restrained* (reserved; reticent).
4. **(D)** By definition, a *volatile* (unstable) mixture tends to vaporize or evaporate.
5. **(C)** By definition, *elegiac* (like an elegy; sorrowful) verse is melancholy; often, such verse laments a death.
6. **(A)** *Despite* is a contrast clue. Despite his *disheveled* (untidy) appearance, he got a job that required him to be neat.
7. **(E)** The tidal wave was *devastating* (extremely destructive) because it *inundated* (flooded) many villages.
8. **(E)** By definition, biodegradable products *decompose* (disintegrate; break down).
9. **(D)** Barbara Tuchman *pursued* (followed) a scholarly career. She was famous for her vivid style and her *prodigious* (exceptional; extraordinary) erudition. Note that the second missing word must be positive. If you tested the second blank first, you could have eliminated Choices A, C, and E.
10. **(C)** A person who had been promised a definite answer would most likely be *annoyed* by a *noncommittal* (evasive; vague; indefinite) reply.

EXERCISE B

1. **(D)** A *hazardous* (dangerous) occupation would make someone a poor insurance risk.
2. **(E)** The artist combines profundity and *fun*. The sentence's first clause is your key to the meaning of the missing word.
3. **(C)** An organism that derives some or all of its nourishment from a host is by definition *parasitic*.
4. **(C)** Employers would most likely promote an *assiduous* (diligent; hard-working) worker.
5. **(D)** The Congresswoman voted against bills that would have benefited labor. Her voting record *belied* (contradicted) the impression that she was a friend of labor.
6. **(D)** *Specious* (faulty) reasoning would be unlikely to *deceive* (fool) anyone.
7. **(A)** The panel wishes to *alleviate* (ease; lessen) the problem by switching to a more *rigorous* (exact) method of the inspection.
8. **(E)** The inspector could not hide his *scorn* for his superior officer. Instead, he imprudently (unwisely) made *scathing* (scornful; cutting) remarks about his boss.
9. **(C)** People would most likely be surprised to have a dull, *pedestrian* speaker make an electrifying, dynamic speech.
10. **(B)** Because he was shy, Madison was *uncomfortable* at public gatherings. His shyness and his hypochondria (excessive worrying about his health) made him an *unlikely* person to be involved in politics.

EXERCISE C

1. **(C)** Instead of discussing abstract principles, the Convention dealt with *concrete* (specific; actual) proposals.
2. **(A)** He was *dilatory* (tardy; slow) in making his car payments.
3. **(D)** The child pouted (showed her displeasure) and became *sullen* (angry; sulky) when her parents ignored her. Note that you are looking for a negative word.
4. **(A)** The sentence contrasts the simple lines of modern architecture with the *flamboyant* (showy; flashy) trimming on older buildings.
5. **(D)** Someone who never *delivered on* (lived up to) the promises he made would soon cause people to distrust him.
6. **(B)** Some readers approach Updike's fluent prose with *suspicion* (doubt; mistrust). They distrust his fluency.
7. **(E)** Because she had a reputation for *aloofness* (coldness; standoffishness), they were pleasantly surprised when she greeted them *affably* (warmly; cordially). Note the cause and effect signal here.
8. **(D)** *Cowardice* is the mark of the *craven* (coward).

9. **(E)** Matter consists of *voids* (empty spaces) in which extremely *small* particles revolve. The opening clause contains your key to the first missing word.
10. **(C)** Baldwin's book is so *searing* (severely critical; scorching) in its frankness or candor that it is bound to *unsettle* (disturb) any reader. The opening phrase "Brilliant yet disturbing" is your key to the missing words.

EXERCISE D

1. **(A)** A hypothesis must be *confirmed* (corroborated; backed up) by future discoveries. Otherwise, it will be proven worthless.
2. **(E)** *Excessive* (extreme) speed is dangerous.
3. **(B)** The book should interest a wide range of readers: everyone from the *novice* (beginner) wine-taster to the experienced connoisseur.
4. **(A)** The African-American leaders discussed in the essays were involved with one another in various ways. (There were *interrelationships* among them.) Therefore, it makes sense for there to be some *overlapping* (elements in common) among the essays.
5. **(B)** Most of these animals *ultimately* (in the end) get their nourishment from krill, either directly, by eating krill themselves, or indirectly, by feeding on other species that eat krill.
6. **(B)** Someone who has a gift for publicity clearly would be a good *promoter* (publicity organizer; advocate) of his own art.
7. **(E)** Japan's success is *attributable* (can be ascribed or credited) to Japan's tradition of group effort and *cooperation* (working together). The contrast signal "as opposed to" provides a key to the meaning of the second missing word.
8. **(E)** The Monroe Doctrine was aimed at *curbing* (restraining) attempts to seize land by *predatory* (plundering; exploiting) foreign powers. Note that the second missing word must be negative.
9. **(C)** Someone cynical (disbelieving) would be reluctant to *credit* (believe) the *unselfishness* of any kind act without checking further.
10. **(C)** Altered political and moral convictions *transformed* (changed) the *hierarchical* (organized by rank; ruled by a closed elite) world of feudalism into a more dynamic society.

EXERCISE E

1. **(C)** *Pragmatic* (practical) students choose classes that have immediate value.
2. **(C)** The sentence contrasts the conception of Kelly's paintings with their *execution* (implementation; the way the idea is carried out).
3. **(B)** Tey was less *prolific* (productive) than Christie: she wrote fewer books.
4. **(A)** Women *devised* (created; planned) abstract designs.
5. **(A)** The counselor saw divorce as a *continuum* (a continuous whole that can be divided only arbitrarily) or ongoing process.
6. **(D)** Something highly specialized that is hard to discuss with people uninitiated in the field is by definition *esoteric* (obscure; arcane; only for initiates).
7. **(B)** By accomplishing a great deal with just a few words or a single shot, the film demonstrates *economy* (efficient use of resources) of style. The contrast clue *nevertheless* sets up the contrast between the film's lavishness or extravagance of visual beauty and its economy of style.
8. **(C)** The late Victorian novel tends to be wordy and *redundant* (repetitive). The novels of Hemingway tend to be *terse* (concise and to the point). Note the contrast signal *unlike*.
9. **(A)** Dissent has become *domesticated* (tame); radical attitudes are now *mainstream* (conventional).
10. **(E)** A *cantankerous* (bad-tempered) person by definition has difficult moods. Employers would not put up with such a difficult employee unless he did exceptionally good work, in this case, *meticulous* (extremely careful) and exhaustive research.

SENTENCE COMPLETION WRAP-UP

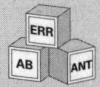

1. Before you look at the answer choices, read the sentence, substituting the word "blank" for the missing word.
2. Look for words or phrases that indicate a contrast between one idea and another—words like *although, however, despite,* or *but*.
3. Look for words or phrases that indicate support for a concept—words such as *likewise, similarly, in the same way, and, in addition, additionally,* and *also*.
4. Look for words or phrases that indicate that one thing causes another—words like *because, since, therefore*, or *thus*.
5. Look for signals that indicate a word is being defined—phrases such as *in other words, that is,* or *which means*, and special punctuation clues, such as commas, hyphens, and parentheses.
6. If you're having vocabulary trouble, look for familiar word parts—prefixes, suffixes, and roots—in unfamiliar words.
7. Work out whether the missing word is positive (+) or negative (–). Then test the answer choices for their positive or negative sense, eliminating those that don't work.
8. In a sentence completion question with two blanks, eliminate answer choices by testing one blank at a time.

Improving Critical Reading Comprehension

CHAPTER 2

Now more than ever, doing well on the critical reading questions can make the difference between success and failure on the PSAT. The most numerous questions in each verbal section, they are also the most time-consuming and the ones most likely to bog you down. However, you can handle them, and this chapter will show you how.

FREQUENTLY ASKED QUESTIONS

1. **How can I become a better reader?**
Read, Read, Read!
Just do it.
There is no substitute for extensive reading to prepare you for the PSAT and for college work. The only way to build up your proficiency in reading is by reading books of all kinds. As you read, you will develop speed, stamina, and the ability to comprehend the printed page. But if you want to turn yourself into the kind of reader the colleges are looking for, you must develop the habit of reading—closely and critically—every day.

2. **What sort of material should I read?**
Challenge yourself. Don't limit your reading to light fiction, graphic novels, and Xbox reviews. Branch out a bit. Try to develop an interest in as many fields as you can.
Check out some of these magazines:

- *The New Yorker*
- *Smithsonian*
- *The New York Review of Books*
- *National Geographic*
- *Natural History*
- *Harper's Magazine*

Explore popular encyclopedias on the Web. You'll find articles on literature, music, science, philosophy, history, the arts—the whole range of fields touched on by the PSAT. If you take time to sample these fields, you won't find the subject matter of the reading passages on the PSAT strange.

3. **On the PSAT, is it better to read the passage first or the questions first?** The answer is, it depends on the passage, and *it depends on you*. If you are a super fast reader faced with one of the 100-word short reading passages, you may want to head for the questions first. It all depends on how good your visual memory is and on how good at scanning you are. If you're not a speed demon at reading, your best move may be to skim the whole passage before you read the questions. Only you can decide which method suits you best.

> **KNOW YOURSELF**
>
> What Kind of Reader Are *You*?
>
> - A slow but steady reader, able to work your way through hard mateiral if you're given enough time?
> - A super fast reader, able to skim whole pages in barely no time at all?
> - A careful reader?
> - A careless reader?
>
> In figuring out what approach will work *best* for you on the critical reading sections of the test, you need to know what kind of reader you are.

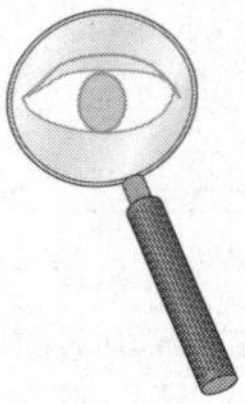

THE QUESTIONS-FIRST APPROACH

- As you read each question, be on the lookout for key words, either in the question itself or among the answer choices.
- Run your eye down the passage, looking for those key words or their synonyms. (That's called *scanning.*)
- When you spot a key word in a sentence, read that sentence and a couple of sentences around it.
- Decide whether you can confidently answer the question on the basis of just that part of the passage.
- Check to see whether your answer is correct.

GENERAL TIPS: WORKING YOUR WAY THROUGH THE READING SECTIONS

1. **Tackle the short passages before the long ones.** Use them as a warm-up for the longer passages that follow.

2. **Tackle passages with familiar subjects before passages with unfamiliar ones.** It's hard to concentrate when you read about something wholly unfamiliar to you. Give yourself a break. In each section, first tackle the reading passage that interests you or deals with the topic about which you have a clue. Then move on to the other passage. You'll do better that way.

3. **If you are stumped by a tough reading question, move on, but do *not* skip the other questions on that passage.** Remember, the critical reading questions following each passage are not arranged in order of difficulty. They tend to be arranged sequentially: questions on paragraph 1 come before questions on paragraph 2. So try *all* the questions on the passage. That tough question may be just one question away from one that's easy for you.

4. **Do not zip back and forth between passages.** Stick with one passage until you feel sure you've answered all the questions you can on that passage. (If you don't, you'll probably have to waste time rereading the passage when you come back to it.) Before moving on to the next passage, be sure to go back over any questions you marked to come back to. In answering other questions on the passage, you may have acquired some information that will help you answer the questions you skipped.

5. **Read as fast as you can with understanding, but don't force yourself to rush.** Do not worry about the time. If you worry about not finishing the test, you will start taking shortcuts and miss the correct answer in your rush.

6. **Try to anticipate what the passage will be about.** As you read the italicized introductory material and tackle the passage's opening sentences, ask yourself who or what the author is talking about.

7. **Read with a purpose.** Try to spot what kind of writing this is, what techniques are used, who its intended audience is, and how the author feels about the subject. Be on the lookout for names, dates, and places. In particular, try to remember where in the passage the author makes major points. Then, when you start looking for the phrase or sentence that will justify your answer choice, you may be able to save time by zipping back to that section of the passage without having to reread the whole thing.

8. **Read the footnotes.** Duh!

9. **When you tackle the questions, go back to the passage to check each answer choice.** Do not rely on your memory, and above all, do not ignore the passage and just answer questions based on other things you've read. Remember, the questions are asking you about what this author has to say about the subject, not about what some other author you once read said about it in another book.

10. **Use the line references in the questions to get quickly to the correct spot in the passage.** It takes less time to locate a line number than to spot a word or phrase. Use the line numbers to orient yourself in the text.

11. **When dealing with the double passages, tackle them one at a time.** The questions are organized sequentially: questions about Passage 1 come before questions about Passage 2. So, do things in order. First read Passage 1; then jump straight to the questions and answer all the questions on Passage 1. Next read Passage 2; then answer all the questions on Passage 2. Finally, tackle the two or three questions that refer to both passages. Go back to both passages as needed.

    Occasionally a couple of questions referring to both passages will come before the questions on Passage 1. Do not let this throw you. Use your common sense. You've just read the first passage. Skip the one or two questions on both passages, and head straight for the questions about Passage 1. Answer them. Then read Passage 2. Answer the questions on Passage 2. Finally, go back to the questions you skipped and answer them (plus any other questions at the end of the set that refer to both passages). This is not rocket science. One thing, though: whenever you skip from question to question or from passage to passage, *be sure you are filling in the right spaces on your answer sheet*.

12. **Watch out for words or phrases in the questions that can clue you in to the kind of question being asked.** If you can recognize just what a given question is asking for, you'll be better able to tell which particular reading tactic to apply.

Now that you have a general idea about how to work your way through the reading sections, it's time to think about how to handle the different reading question types.

- **Vocabulary**—quick questions (you have to figure out the meaning of an individual word)
- **Main Idea**—big picture questions (you have to figure out the central point the author is trying to make)
- **Specific Detail**—narrow focus questions (you have to zoom in on specific facts)
- **Inference**—logic questions (you have to figure out what the author is suggesting or stating indirectly)
- **Attitude/Tone**—emotion questions (you have to figure out how the author feels about something or someone)
- **Literary Technique**—technical questions (you have to know the meaning of literary terms)
- **Logic/Application**—advanced logic questions (you have to judge the strength or weakness of the author's argument and figure out how it might apply in other situations)

On the following pages you will get to work through several questions of each type, learning to handle them as you go. All these questions are based on a long reading passage from *The New York Times*. You may find the passage challenging, but you can take as much time as you need to figure it out.

The following passage is taken from an article on mathematical and scientific illiteracy published in The New York Times *in January 1989, as Ronald and Nancy Reagan left the White House.*

The abstractness of mathematics is a great obstacle for many intelligent people. Such people may readily understand narrative particulars, but strongly resist impersonal generalities. Since numbers, science, and such generalities are intimately related, this resistance can lead to an almost willful mathematical and scientific illiteracy. Numbers have appeal for many only if they're associated with them personally—hence part of the attraction of astrology, biorhythms, Tarot cards and the I Ching, all individually customized "sciences."

Mathematical illiteracy and the attitudes underlying it provide in fact a fertile soil for the growth of pseudoscience. In *Pseudoscience and Society in Nineteenth-Century America,* Arthur Wrobel remarks that belief in phrenology, homeopathy, and hydropathy was not confined to the poor and the ignorant, but pervaded much of nineteenth-century literature. Such credulity is not as extensive in contemporary literature, but astrology is one pseudoscience that does seem to engage a big segment of the reading public. Literary allusions to it abound, appearing in everything from Shakespeare to Dom DeLillo's *Libra*. A 1986 Gallup poll showed that 52 percent of American teenagers subscribe to it, as does at least 50 percent of the nation's departing First Couple.

Given these figures, it may not be entirely inappropriate to note here that no mechanism through which the alleged zodiacal influences exert themselves has ever been specified by astrologers. Gravity certainly cannot account for these natal influences, since even the gravitational pull of the attending obstetrician is orders of magnitude greater than that of the relevant planet or planets. Nor is there any empirical evidence; top astrologers (as determined by their peers) have failed repeatedly to associate personality profiles with astrological data at a rate higher than that of chance. Neither of these fatal objections to astrology, of course, is likely to carry much weight with literate but innumerate people who don't estimate magnitudes or probabilities, or who are over-impressed by vague coincidences yet unmoved by overwhelming statistical evidence.

VOCABULARY QUESTIONS

Vocabulary-in-context questions are easy to spot. They look like this:

In line 13, "frabbledrab" most nearly means

(A) snipsnop
(B) kangasplat
(C) replix
(D) oggitty
(E) thrumble

Tip 1

Tackle vocabulary-in-context questions the same way you do sentence completion questions. First, read the sentence, substituting "blank" for the word in quotes. Think of words you know that might make sense in the context. Then test each answer choice, substituting it in the sentence for the word in quotes. Ask yourself whether this particular answer choice makes sense in the specific context.

Vocabulary Power Practice

WORDS HAVE MULTIPLE MEANINGS

A *run* in baseball is ***not*** the same thing as a *run* in your stocking.

1. In line 11, "confined" most nearly means

(A) enclosed
(B) jailed
(C) isolated
(D) restricted
(E) preached

2. In line 14, "engage" most nearly means

(A) hire
(B) reserve
(C) attract
(D) confront
(E) interlock

Vocabulary-in-context questions take hardly any time to answer. If you're running out of time, answer them first.

3. In line 16, "subscribe to" most nearly means

(A) sign up for
(B) agree with
(C) write about
(D) suffer from
(E) pay for

Check Your Answers

1. **(D)** The original sentence states that "belief...was not ________ to the poor and the ignorant, but pervaded much of nineteenth-century literature." Non-scientific belief was widespread in the nineteenth century; it pervaded or filled the literature of the period. Therefore, it was not *restricted* or confined to poor, ignorant people, but had spread to the well-to-do, literate classes.

Note that *many* of the answer choices could be substitutes for "confined" *in other contexts*. For example, if the sentence were "The dogcatcher *confined* dozens of stray animals in the pound," Choice A, *enclosed*, would be the best word to substitute. Your job is to spot which meaning of the word works this time.

2. **(C)** Again, look at the sentence, substituting "blank" for the key word. "Astrology...does seem to *blank* a big segment of the reading public." What word would make sense in the context? Summarize what's going on. The author is reacting to the strong hold that astrology has on the reading public. Despite its being a pseudoscience, astrology has managed to *attract* or involve many members of the reading public. The correct answer is Choice C.
3. **(B)** "52 percent of American teenagers *blank* it, as does at least 50 percent of the nation's departing First Couple." The author has been talking about how many people have been attracted or drawn to astrology. Many of these people have been more or less won over by it: they accept it as a valid belief. Thus, the teenagers (and the Reagans) who *subscribe to* astrology *agree with* it, going along with its doctrines. Once again, you've found a word that makes sense in context.

The following passage is taken from an article on mathematical and scientific illiteracy published in The New York Times *in January 1989, as Ronald and Nancy Reagan left the White House.*

The abstractness of mathematics is a great obstacle for many intelligent people. Such people may readily understand narrative particulars, but strongly resist impersonal generalities. Since numbers, science, and such generalities are intimately related, this resistance can lead to an almost willful mathematical and scientific illiteracy. Numbers have appeal for many only if they're associated with them personally—hence part of the attraction of astrology, biorhythms, Tarot cards and the I Ching, all individually customized "sciences."

Mathematical illiteracy and the attitudes underlying it provide in fact a fertile soil for the growth of pseudoscience. In *Pseudoscience and Society in Nineteenth-Century America,* Arthur Wrobel remarks that belief in phrenology, homeopathy, and hydropathy was not confined to the poor and the ignorant, but pervaded much of nineteenth-century literature. Such credulity is not as extensive in contemporary literature, but astrology is one pseudoscience that does seem to engage a big segment of the reading public. Literary allusions to it abound, appearing in everything from Shakespeare to Dom DeLillo's *Libra*. A 1986 Gallup poll showed that 52 percent of American teenagers subscribe to it, as does at least 50 percent of the nation's departing First Couple.

Given these figures, it may not be entirely inappropriate to note here that no mechanism through which the alleged zodiacal influences exert themselves has ever been specified by astrologers. Gravity certainly cannot account for these natal influences, since even the gravitational pull of the attending obstetrician is orders of magnitude greater than that of the relevant planet or planets. Nor is there any empirical evidence; top astrologers (as determined by their peers) have failed repeatedly to associate personality profiles with astrological data at a rate higher than that of chance. Neither of these fatal objections to astrology, of course, is likely to carry much weight with literate but innumerate people who don't estimate magnitudes or probabilities, or who are over-impressed by vague coincidences yet unmoved by overwhelming statistical evidence.

MAIN IDEA QUESTIONS

Main idea questions look like this:

> Which of the following best states the central thought of the passage?
> The primary purpose of the passage is to…
> In the second paragraph of the passage, the author primarily stresses that…

Tip 2

When asked to find a passage's main idea, be sure to check the opening and summary sentences of each paragraph. Authors often orient readers with a sentence that expresses a paragraph's main idea concisely. Although such *topic sentences* may appear anywhere in the paragraph, you can usually find them in the opening or closing sentences.

In PSAT reading passages, topic sentences are sometimes implied rather than stated directly. If you cannot find a topic sentence, ask yourself these questions:

- Who or what is this passage about?
- What feature of this subject is the author talking about?
- What is the author trying to get across about this feature of the subject?

You'll be on your way to locating the passage's main idea.

Main Idea Power Practice

1. In the final paragraph of the passage, the author stresses that
   (A) astrologers are working to discover the mechanisms through which the zodiac affects human lives
   (B) the planets are able to influence people in mysterious, imperceptible ways
   (C) top astrologers strive to maintain accurate personality profiles of their clientele
   (D) astrologers have been unable to corroborate their theories scientifically
   (E) astrologers are more mechanically minded than mathematically literate

2. The author's primary purpose throughout the passage is to
   (A) contrast astrology and other contemporary pseudosciences with phrenology, homeopathy, and hydropathy
   (B) trace the development of the current belief in astrology to its nineteenth-century roots
   (C) apologize for the rise of mathematical and scientific illiteracy in the present day
   (D) disprove the difficulty of achieving universal mathematical and scientific literacy
   (E) relate mathematical illiteracy to the prevalence of invalid pseudoscientific beliefs today

Check Your Answers

1. **(D)** The author spends the final paragraph debunking (discrediting; exposing) the claims of astrologers. To their claim that the planets in the heavens at the time of one's birth influence one's destiny, he retorts that the attending physician exerts more gravitational pull on the infant than the distant planets do. To their claim that astrological data can be used to predict personality types, he retorts that no valid correlation exists between astrological predictions and the results of scientifically legit-

imate personality profiles. Throughout the paragraph, he stresses that *astrologers have been unable to corroborate* (confirm or back up) *their theories scientifically*.

2. **(E)** Go back to the passage and look at the opening sentences of the three paragraphs and the final sentence of the third paragraph. (The shaded bits.) What are these sentences talking about? Mathematical illiteracy. What aspect of mathematical illiteracy are they talking about? They're talking about how it *relates to the prevalence* (widespread acceptance) of astrology and other *invalid pseudoscientific beliefs today*.

   Choice A is incorrect. Although the author mentions phrenology and the other pseudosciences, he never contrasts them with astrology. Choice B is incorrect; although the author discusses astrology at length, his chief purpose is to use astrology as an example of a contemporary pseudoscientific belief, not to trace its nineteenth-century connections. Choice C is incorrect; the author is irritated by the state of mathematical and scientific illiteracy today, not apologetic about it. Choice D is incorrect; nothing in the passage supports it.

The following passage is taken from an article on mathematical and scientific illiteracy published in The New York Times *in January 1989, as Ronald and Nancy Reagan left the White House.*

The abstractness of mathematics is a great obstacle for many intelligent people. Such people may readily understand narrative particulars, but strongly resist impersonal generalities. Since numbers, science, and such generalities are intimately related, this resistance can lead to an almost willful mathematical and scientific illiteracy. Numbers have appeal for many only if they're associated with them personally—hence part of the attraction of astrology, biorhythms, Tarot cards and the I Ching, all individually customized "sciences."

Mathematical illiteracy and the attitudes underlying it provide in fact a fertile soil for the growth of pseudoscience. In *Pseudoscience and Society in Nineteenth-Century America,* Arthur Wrobel remarks that belief in phrenology, homeopathy, and hydropathy was not confined to the poor and the ignorant, but pervaded much of nineteenth-century literature. Such credulity is not as extensive in contemporary literature, but astrology is one pseudoscience that does seem to engage a big segment of the reading public. Literary allusions to it abound, appearing in everything from Shakespeare to Dom DeLillo's *Libra*. A 1986 Gallup poll showed that 52 percent of American teenagers subscribe to it, as does at least 50 percent of the nation's departing First Couple.

Given these figures, it may not be entirely inappropriate to note here that no mechanism through which the alleged zodiacal influences exert themselves has ever been specified by astrologers. Gravity certainly cannot account for these natal influences, since even the gravitational pull of the attending obstetrician is orders of magnitude greater than that of the relevant planet or planets. Nor is there any empirical evidence; top astrologers (as determined by their peers) have failed repeatedly to associate personality profiles with astrological data at a rate higher than that of chance. Neither of these fatal objections to astrology, of course, is likely to carry much weight with literate but innumerate people who don't estimate magnitudes or probabilities, or who are over-impressed by vague coincidences yet unmoved by overwhelming statistical evidence.

SPECIFIC DETAIL QUESTIONS

Specific detail questions often begin like this:

According to the author, what is the reason for...
The "fatal objections" to astrology referred to in line 25 are...
To the author, a belief in astrology is...

Tip 3

When you answer specific detail questions, point to the precise words in the passage that support your answer choice. You must be *sure* that the answer you select is in the passage. That means you must find a word or sentence or group of sentences that justifies your choice. Do *not* pick an answer just because it agrees with your personal opinions or with information on the subject that you've gotten from other sources.

FACT VS. OPINION

Fact: In 1986, a Gallup poll sampled American teenagers' views on astrology.
(You can verify this by checking old newspaper reports and Gallup poll publications.)

Opinion: Patsy believes that people born under the sign of Scorpio are passionate.
(Well, that's what *she* believes...)

Specific Detail Power Practice

1. Which of the following best summarizes the reason given in lines 1–5 for the extent of mathematical and scientific illiteracy today?

   (A) Many intelligent people dislike the intimacy of the connection between numbers and science.
   (B) Many otherwise intelligent people have difficulty dealing with impersonal, abstract concepts.
   (C) Intelligent people prefer speaking in generalities to narrating particular incidents.
   (D) Few people are able to appreciate the benefits of an individually customized science.
   (E) People today no longer cherish their personal associations with numbers.

2. According to the author, "phrenology, homeopathy, and hydropathy" (lines 10–11) are all

   (A) scholarly allusions
   (B) pseudosciences
   (C) branches of astrology
   (D) forms of society
   (E) mechanisms

3. The "figures" referred to in line 18 are the

   (A) pseudosciences
   (B) literary references
   (C) prominent political leaders
   (D) numbers involved in calculating horoscopes
   (E) statistics concerning believers in astrology

4. The term "innumerate" (line 26) is best interpreted to mean

   (A) various in kind
   (B) too numerous to count
   (C) scientifically sophisticated
   (D) unable to use mathematics
   (E) indifferent to astrology

Check Your Answers

1. **(B)** In the opening lines, the author states that the abstractness of mathematics is a problem for many intelligent people. People resist dealing with abstractions ("impersonal generalities"). However, to work in science or math, you must deal with abstractions: numbers, science, and abstractions are "intimately connected." *Because* many otherwise intelligent people have difficulty dealing with impersonal, abstract concepts, these people wind up mathematically and scientifically illiterate. That, according to the author, is the reason for much of the mathematical and scientific illiteracy we see today. The correct answer is Choice B.
2. **(B)** Phrenology, homeopathy, and hydropathy are three beliefs mentioned in the book titled *Pseudoscience and Society in Nineteenth-Century America.* Throughout the passage, the author is critical of various beliefs he categorizes as unscientific. He groups such beliefs together as *pseudosciences*, false sciences in which many otherwise intelligent individuals believe. Phrenology is the belief that the shape of your skull indicates your character traits and mental abilities. Homeopathy is the belief that you can cure disease by giving someone who is ill extremely small doses of a substance that would produce in someone healthy symptoms similar to those of the disease. Hydropathy is the belief that you can cure disease by giving someone ill huge amounts of water (both internally and externally). To the author, all three beliefs are *pseudosciences*.

   Note the phrase "to the author." The question is not asking you what *you* think about phrenology, homeopathy, and hydropathy. It is asking you what *the author* thinks of these beliefs.
3. **(E)** The paragraph immediately preceding line 18 gives the percentage of American teenagers who go along with astrology. It also refers to the well-known fact that Nancy Reagan (half of "the nation's departing First Couple") believed in astrology (she followed the advice of astrologers in setting up her husband's engagements during his presidency) and that her husband might possibly have believed in it as well. Thus, the figures referred to are *statistics concerning believers in astrology.*
4. **(D)** The author contrasts the word "innumerate" with the word "literate." Since *illiterate* means unable to read, *innumerate* must mean unable to use mathematics.

   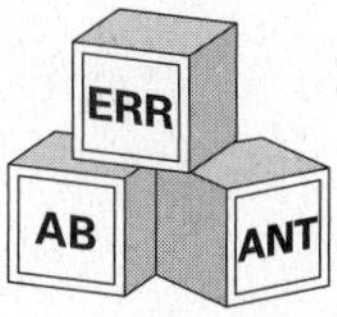

   You can use your knowledge of word parts to answer this question. *In-* means not; *numer-* means number. *Innumerate* means not having numbers, unable to use numbers. Watch out, however, for eye-catchers. *Innumerable* means uncountable, too many or too numerous for anyone to count.

The following passage is taken from an article on mathematical and scientific illiteracy published in The New York Times *in January 1989, as Ronald and Nancy Reagan left the White House.*

The abstractness of mathematics is a great obstacle for many intelligent people. Such people may readily understand narrative particulars, but strongly resist impersonal generalities. Since numbers, science, and such generalities are intimately related, this resistance can lead to an almost willful mathematical and scientific illiteracy. Numbers have appeal for many only if they're associated with them personally—hence part of the attraction of astrology, biorhythms, Tarot cards and the I Ching, all individually customized "sciences."

Mathematical illiteracy and the attitudes underlying it provide in fact a fertile soil for the growth of pseudoscience. In *Pseudoscience and Society in Nineteenth-Century America,* Arthur Wrobel remarks that belief in phrenology, homeopathy, and hydropathy was not confined to the poor and the ignorant, but pervaded much of nineteenth-century literature. Such credulity is not as extensive in contemporary literature, but astrology is one pseudoscience that does seem to engage a big segment of the reading public. Literary allusions to it abound, appearing in everything from Shakespeare to Dom DeLillo's *Libra*. A 1986 Gallup poll showed that 52 percent of American teenagers subscribe to it, as does at least 50 percent of the nation's departing First Couple.

Given these figures, it may not be entirely inappropriate to note here that no mechanism through which the alleged zodiacal influences exert themselves has ever been specified by astrologers. Gravity certainly cannot account for these natal influences, since even the gravitational pull of the attending obstetrician is orders of magnitude greater than that of the relevant planet or planets. Nor is there any empirical evidence; top astrologers (as determined by their peers) have failed repeatedly to associate personality profiles with astrological data at a rate higher than that of chance. Neither of these fatal objections to astrology, of course, is likely to carry much weight with literate but innumerate people who don't estimate magnitudes or probabilities, or who are over-impressed by vague coincidences yet unmoved by overwhelming statistical evidence.

INFERENCE QUESTIONS

Inference questions often begin like this:

The author implies that...
The passage suggests that...
It can be inferred from the passage that...
The author would most likely...
The author probably considers...

Tip 4

When you answer inference questions, look for what the passage logically suggests, but does *not* directly state. Inference questions require you to use your judgment. You are drawing a conclusion based on what you have read in the text. Think about what the passage suggests. You must not take anything directly stated in the passage as an inference. Instead, you must look for clues in the passage that you can use in coming up with your own conclusion. Then you should choose as your answer a statement that logically follows from the information the author has given you.

Inference Power Practice

1. Lines 5–7 ("Numbers . . . 'sciences'") suggest that the author thinks the individually customized sciences that he mentions are

   (A) impersonal
   (B) rewarding
   (C) personally appealing
   (D) fundamentally sound
   (E) unscientific

> **DID YOU NOTICE?**
> There are quotation marks around the word "sciences." Quotation marks often indicate that the word in quotes is being used in a special sense.

2. The author most likely regards the lack of empirical evidence for astrology as

   (A) an oversight on the part of the astrologers
   (B) a key argument against its validity
   (C) a flaw that will be corrected in time
   (D) the unfortunate result of too small a sampling
   (E) a major reason to keep searching for fresh data

Check Your Answers

1. **(E)** Note the quotation marks around the word *sciences.* They are your clue that the author does not regard astrology, biorhythms, Tarot cards, and the I Ching as real sciences. Instead, he considers them *unscientific.*
2. **(B)** The final sentence of the paragraph characterizes these absences of empirical evidence as "fatal objections to astrology." In general, the author sees astrology as invalid, a pseudoscience, not a real science. If he were handed empirical experimental data that supported astrological theory, he probably would have a harder time rejecting it so sharply. Thus, he most likely regards the lack of empirical, observable evidence for astrology as *a key argument against its validity*.

The following passage is taken from an article on mathematical and scientific illiteracy published in The New York Times *in January 1989, as Ronald and Nancy Reagan left the White House.*

The abstractness of mathematics is a great obstacle for many intelligent people. Such people may readily understand narrative particulars, but strongly resist impersonal generalities. Since numbers, science, and such generalities are intimately related, this resistance can lead to an almost willful mathematical and scientific illiteracy. Numbers have appeal for many only if they're associated with them personally—hence part of the attraction of astrology, biorhythms, Tarot cards and the I Ching, all individually customized "sciences."

Mathematical illiteracy and the attitudes underlying it provide in fact a fertile soil for the growth of pseudoscience. In *Pseudoscience and Society in Nineteenth-Century America,* Arthur Wrobel remarks that belief in phrenology, homeopathy, and hydropathy was not confined to the poor and the ignorant, but pervaded much of nineteenth-century literature. Such credulity is not as extensive in contemporary literature, but astrology is one pseudoscience that does seem to engage a big segment of the reading public. Literary allusions to it abound, appearing in everything from Shakespeare to Dom DeLillo's *Libra*. A 1986 Gallup poll showed that 52 percent of American teenagers subscribe to it, as does at least 50 percent of the nation's departing First Couple.

Given these figures, it may not be entirely inappropriate to note here that no mechanism through which the alleged zodiacal influences exert themselves has ever been specified by astrologers. Gravity certainly cannot account for these natal influences, since even the gravitational pull of the attending obstetrician is orders of magnitude greater than that of the relevant planet or planets. Nor is there any empirical evidence; top astrologers (as determined by their peers) have failed repeatedly to associate personality profiles with astrological data at a rate higher than that of chance. Neither of these fatal objections to astrology, of course, is likely to carry much weight with literate but innumerate people who don't estimate magnitudes or probabilities, or who are over-impressed by vague coincidences yet unmoved by overwhelming statistical evidence.

ATTITUDE/TONE QUESTIONS

Attitude/tone questions often look like this:

> The author's attitude toward...is...
> The author regards the idea that...with...
> The author's tone in the passage...

Tip 5

When asked to figure out an author's attitude or tone, look for words that convey emotion, express values, or paint pictures. These images and descriptive phrases get the author's feelings across.

Attitude/Tone Power Practice

1. The author's attitude toward believers in astrology can best be described as one of
   (A) grudging respect
   (B) amused tolerance
   (C) open disdain
   (D) disguised hostility
   (E) puzzled fascination

2. The author's tone in referring to the nation's departing First Couple can best be described as
   (A) respectful
   (B) nostalgic
   (C) negative
   (D) mocking
   (E) effusive

KNOW YOUR ATTITUDES
(If you don't know any of these words, look them up.)

SAD	*somber, melancholy, pessimistic, regretful*
HAPPY	*optimistic, sanguine, amused*
EVIL GRIN	*mocking, sardonic, sarcastic, ironic, cynical, disdainful*
ANGRY	*irate, outraged, incensed*
FOOLISH	*baffled, puzzled, bemused, bewildered*
SURPRISED	*astonished, astounded, awestruck*
EMBARRASSED	*discomfited, mortified*
WHATEVER	*indifferent, ambivalent, equivocal*

Check Your Answers

1. **(C)** The author states that people who believe in astrology are the sort who are "over-impressed by vague coincidences." Clearly, he feels that people should not be impressed by such vague coincidences. In his opinion, astrology as a science is fatally flawed. He looks down on the innumerate souls who continue to believe in it despite all the evidence against it. Thus, his attitude toward those who believe in astrology is one of *open disdain* or contempt.
2. **(D)** In saying that at least 50 percent of the Reagans subscribes to a belief in astrology, the author is making a little joke. He is referring to Nancy Reagan's dependence on astrologers and, at the same time, implying that 100 percent of the Reagans, that is, the first lady *and* the president, may believe in a subject he considers nonsensical. Even the term *First Couple*, all dressed up in capital letters, has a mocking ring. The correct answer is *mocking*, Choice D.

The following passage is taken from an article on mathematical and scientific illiteracy published in The New York Times *in January 1989, as Ronald and Nancy Reagan left the White House.*

The abstractness of mathematics is a great obstacle for many intelligent people. Such people may readily understand narrative particulars, but strongly resist impersonal generalities. Since numbers, science, and such generalities are intimately related, this resistance can lead to an almost willful mathematical and scientific illiteracy. Numbers have appeal for many only if they're associated with them personally—hence part of the attraction of astrology, biorhythms, Tarot cards and the I Ching, all individually customized "sciences."

Mathematical illiteracy and the attitudes underlying it provide in fact a fertile soil for the growth of pseudoscience. In *Pseudoscience and Society in Nineteenth-Century America,* Arthur Wrobel remarks that belief in phrenology, homeopathy, and hydropathy was not confined to the poor and the ignorant, but pervaded much of nineteenth-century literature. Such credulity is not as extensive in contemporary literature, but astrology is one pseudoscience that does seem to engage a big segment of the reading public. Literary allusions to it abound, appearing in everything from Shakespeare to Dom DeLillo's *Libra*. A 1986 Gallup poll showed that 52 percent of American teenagers subscribe to it, as does at least 50 percent of the nation's departing First Couple.

Given these figures, it may not be entirely inappropriate to note here that no mechanism through which the alleged zodiacal influences exert themselves has ever been specified by astrologers. Gravity certainly cannot account for these natal influences, since even the gravitational pull of the attending obstetrician is orders of magnitude greater than that of the relevant planet or planets. Nor is there any empirical evidence; top astrologers (as determined by their peers) have failed repeatedly to associate personality profiles with astrological data at a rate higher than that of chance. Neither of these fatal objections to astrology, of course, is likely to carry much weight with literate but innumerate people who don't estimate magnitudes or probabilities, or who are over-impressed by vague coincidences yet unmoved by overwhelming statistical evidence.

LITERARY TECHNIQUE QUESTIONS

Literary technique questions often look like this:

> Which of the following best describes the development of this passage?
> In presenting the argument, the author does all of the following EXCEPT...
> The statement in lines 8–9 is an example of...
> In the passage, the author makes the central point primarily by...

Tip 6

Familiarize yourself with the common terms used to describe an author's technique. Even if you don't learn them all, once you've mastered a few, you'll be in a good position to eliminate incorrect answer choices and make an educated guess among the rest.

COMMON LITERARY TERMS

allusion	reference to something
analogy	comparison; similarity of functions or properties; likeness
anecdote	short account of an incident (often autobiographical)
antithesis	direct opposite
argumentative	presenting a logical argument
assertion	positive statement; declaration
cite	to refer to; to quote as an authority
euphemism	mild or indirect expression substituted for one felt offensive or harsh (Example: "Downsizing employees" is a euphemism for firing them.)
expository	concerned with explaining ideas, facts, etc.
generalization	simplification; general idea or principle
metaphor	an expression used to suggest a similarity between two things that are not literally equivalent (Example: "He's a tiger!")
narrative (adj.)	relating to telling a story
paradox	statement that contradicts itself (Example: "I always lie.")
rhetorical	relating to the effective use of language
thesis	the central idea in a piece of writing; a point to be defended

Literary Technique Power Practice

1. The opening sentence of the second paragraph contains an example of

   (A) an apology
   (B) a metaphor
   (C) a paradox
   (D) a euphemism
   (E) an understatement

2. The author's point about the popularity of astrology is made through both

   (A) personal testimony and generalizations
   (B) assertions and case histories
   (C) comparisons and anecdotes
   (D) literary and statistics references
   (E) observation and analogy

Check Your Answers

1. **(B)** The phrase "a fertile soil for...growth" is an example of *a metaphor*. People's attitudes aren't really dirt.
2. **(D)** The author offers as evidence of astrology's popularity both *literary references* (allusions to Dom DeLillo's *Libra* and to Shakespeare) and *statistics* based on Gallup poll figures.

The following passage is taken from an article on mathematical and scientific illiteracy published in The New York Times *in January 1989, as Ronald and Nancy Reagan left the White House.*

The abstractness of mathematics is a great obstacle for many intelligent people. Such people may readily understand narrative particulars, but strongly resist impersonal generalities. Since numbers, science, and such generalities are intimately related, this resistance can lead to an almost willful mathematical and scientific illiteracy. Numbers have appeal for many only if they're associated with them personally—hence part of the attraction of astrology, biorhythms, Tarot cards and the I Ching, all individually customized "sciences."

Mathematical illiteracy and the attitudes underlying it provide in fact a fertile soil for the growth of pseudoscience. In *Pseudoscience and Society in Nineteenth-Century America,* Arthur Wrobel remarks that belief in phrenology, homeopathy, and hydropathy was not confined to the poor and the ignorant, but pervaded much of nineteenth-century literature. Such credulity is not as extensive in contemporary literature, but astrology is one pseudoscience that does seem to engage a big segment of the reading public. Literary allusions to it abound, appearing in everything from Shakespeare to Dom DeLillo's *Libra*. A 1986 Gallup poll showed that 52 percent of American teenagers subscribe to it, as does at least 50 percent of the nation's departing First Couple.

Given these figures, it may not be entirely inappropriate to note here that no mechanism through which the alleged zodiacal influences exert themselves has ever been specified by astrologers. Gravity certainly cannot account for these natal influences, since even the gravitational pull of the attending obstetrician is orders of magnitude greater than that of the relevant planet or planets. Nor is there any empirical evidence; top astrologers (as determined by their peers) have failed repeatedly to associate personality profiles with astrological data at a rate higher than that of chance. Neither of these fatal objections to astrology, of course, is likely to carry much weight with literate but innumerate people who don't estimate magnitudes or probabilities, or who are over-impressed by vague coincidences yet unmoved by overwhelming statistical evidence.

LOGIC/APPLICATION QUESTIONS

Logic/application questions look like this:

> With which of the following statements would the author be most in agreement?
>
> The author's argument would be most weakened by the discovery of which of the following?
>
> The author's contention would be most clearly strengthened if which of the following were found to be true?

Tip 7

Think about how the ideas in the passage are logically organized. Break down the author's argument. The author is making a point. Ask yourself which statements support that point. How could you attack that point? What other statements could you make to support it?

Logic/application questions take lots of time to think through. If you're running out of time, you may want to skip that logic question and try a detail or vocabulary one.

Why get bogged down answering one time-consuming question when in the same amount of time you can answer two less demanding ones?

Logic/Application Power Practice

1. Which of the following would most weaken the author's assumption that mathematical and scientific literacy would make people less likely to believe in a pseudoscience such as astrology?
   (A) Assertions by professional astrologers that astrology has a firm scientific basis in astronomy.
   (B) Anecdotal reports that an individual astrologer has been known to use a calculator in computing horoscopes.
   (C) Poll results showing that the percentage of American teenagers believing in astrology has radically decreased since 1989.
   (D) Evidence that the majority of practicing astrologers have also taught mathematics or a scientific discipline.
   (E) A statement by ex-president Reagan denying that he had ever believed in astrology.

BE ON THE LOOKOUT FOR QUALIFIERS

Little words like "somewhat," "often," and "almost" limit the meaning of other words. Little words, but they can have a big impact. Which would you rather have the Terminator say, "No problem," or "Almost no problem"?

2. With which of the following statements would the author be most likely to disagree?
   (A) Phrenology may be of some interest to sociologists and cultural historians, but it has no real value as a scientific discipline.
   (B) A rigorous training in mathematics would benefit young people by equipping them to estimate magnitudes and probabilities.
   (C) People were somewhat less apt to be taken in by pseudoscientific claims in the nineteenth century than they are today.
   (D) Despite the weight of the evidence against astrology, scientifically illiterate individuals will continue to believe in it.
   (E) Determining biorhythms and computing astrological horoscopes may require people to perform some mathematical calculations.

Check Your Answers

1. **(D)** If we assume that people who have professionally taught math or science are therefore not mathematically and scientifically illiterate, and if we also assume that practicing astrologers believe in astrology, then *evidence that the majority of practicing astrologers have also taught mathematics or a scientific discipline* would clearly weaken the author's assumption that mathematical and scientific literacy would make people less likely to believe in astrology.
2. **(C)** You can answer this question by using the process of elimination.

   The key word here is "disagree." Examine each statement in turn, asking yourself whether it does or does not reflect the author's point of view. Eliminate every answer choice with which the author would agree.

   First check Choice A. Phrenology is one of the pseudosciences mentioned in the second paragraph; clearly, the author would agree *it has no real value as a scientific discipline* or field of study. You can eliminate Choice A.

   Next check Choice B. In the concluding sentence of the passage, the author mentions the failure to estimate magnitudes and probabilities as a characteristic of innumerate, mathematically illiterate people. The author wishes people to be mathematically *literate*; therefore, he would agree that *a rigorous training in mathematics* that enabled them to estimate magnitudes and probabilities *would benefit young people*. You can eliminate Choice B.

   In the second paragraph, the author states that belief in various pseudosciences "pervaded much of nineteenth-century literature"; it was widespread in earlier days. He then asserts that "such credulity is not as extensive in contemporary literature." In other words, the author argues that *people are somewhat less apt to be taken in by pseudoscientific claims today than they were a century ago*. This directly contradicts what is stated in Choice C. Therefore, Choice C is most likely the correct answer.

   Double-check yourself. Test the other two answer choices.

   In lines 25–28, the author states directly that the "fatal objections to astrology" he has just pointed out are unlikely to convince the innumerate scientifically illiterate believers in astrology that the powers of the zodiac are nonexistent. Clearly, the author would agree that *scientifically illiterate individuals will continue to believe* in astrology despite the evidence. You can eliminate Choice D.

   The author asserts that the only numbers that appeal to some people are ones with which they have personal associations—numbers connected to individual biorhythms or astrological horoscopes, for example. Given this personal connection with numbers, even non-mathematically inclined individuals might wind up having *to perform mathematical computations*, though the author would most likely look down on such computations as unscientific. You can eliminate Choice E.

   Only Choice C is left. As you suspected, it is the correct answer.

Practice Exercises

SHORT PASSAGES

Passage 1

Too many parents force their children into group activities. They are concerned about the child who loves to do things alone, who prefers a solitary walk with a camera to a game of ball. They want their sons to be "team players" and their daughters "good mixers." In such foolish fears lie the beginnings of the blighting of individuality, the thwarting of personality, the stealing of the wealth of one's capital for living joyously and well in a confused world. What America needs is a new army of defense, manned by young men and women who, through guidance and confidence, encouragement and wisdom, have built up values for themselves and away from crowds and companies.

1. According to the passage, too many parents push their children to be

   (A) unnecessarily gregarious
   (B) foolishly timorous
   (C) pointlessly extravagant
   (D) acutely individualistic
   (E) financially dependent

2. The primary point the author wishes to make is that

   (A) young people need time to themselves
   (B) group activities are harmful to children
   (C) parents knowingly thwart their children's personalities
   (D) independent thinking is of questionable value
   (E) America needs universal military training

3. The author puts quotation marks around the words *team players* and *good mixers* to indicate that he

   (A) is using vocabulary that is unfamiliar to the reader
   (B) intends to define these terms later in the course of the passage
   (C) can readily distinguish these terms from one another
   (D) prefers not to differentiate roles by secondary factors such as gender
   (E) refuses to accept the assumption that these are entirely positive values

4. By "the wealth of one's capital for living joyously and well in a confused world" (lines 9–11), the author most likely means the

   (A) financial security that one attains from one's individual professional achievements
   (B) riches that parents thrust upon children who would far prefer to be left alone to follow their own inclinations
   (C) hours spent in solitary pursuits that enable one to develop into an independent, confident adult
   (D) happy memories of childhood days spent in the company of good friends
   (E) profitable financial and personal contacts young people make when they engage in group activities

Passage 2

"Sticks and stones can break my bones,
But names will never harm me."

No doubt you are familiar with this childhood rhyme; perhaps, when you were younger, you frequently invoked whatever protection it could offer against unpleasant epithets. But like many popular slogans and verses, this one will not bear too close scrutiny. For names will hurt you. Sometimes you may be the victim, and find yourself an object of scorn, humiliation, and hatred just because other people have called you certain names. At other times you may not be the victim, but clever speakers and writers may, through name-calling, blind your judgment so that you will follow them in a course of action wholly opposed to your own interests or principles. Name-calling can make you gullible to propaganda which you might otherwise readily see through and reject.

5. The author's primary purpose in quoting the rhyme in lines 1 and 2 is to
   (A) remind readers of their childhood vulnerabilities
   (B) emphasize the importance of maintaining one's good name
   (C) demonstrate his conviction that only physical attacks can harm us
   (D) affirm his faith in the rhyme's ability to shield one from unpleasant epithets
   (E) introduce the topic of speaking abusively about others

6. By "this one will not bear too close scrutiny" (lines 8–9), the author means that
   (A) the statement will no longer seem valid if you examine it closely
   (B) the literary quality of the verse does not improve on closer inspection
   (C) people who indulge in name-calling are embarrassed when they are in the spotlight
   (D) the author cannot stand having his comments looked at critically
   (E) a narrow line exists between analyzing a slogan and overanalyzing it

7. According to the passage, name-calling may make you more susceptible to
   (A) poetic language
   (B) biased arguments
   (C) physical abuse
   (D) risky confrontations
   (E) offensive epithets

8. The author evidently believes that slogans and verses frequently
   (A) appeal to our better nature
   (B) are disregarded by children
   (C) are scorned by unprincipled speakers
   (D) represent the popular mood
   (E) oversimplify the situation

Passage 3

The following passage was written by Phillips Brooks, a nineteenth-century Anglican bishop.

To keep clear of concealment, to keep clear of the need of concealment, to do nothing which you might not do out on the middle of Boston Common at noonday—I cannot say how more and more it seems to me the glory of a young person's life. It is an awful hour when the first necessity of hiding anything comes. The whole life is different thenceforth. When there are questions to be feared and eyes to be avoided and subjects which must not be touched, then the bloom of life is gone. Put off that day as long as possible. Put it off forever if you can.

9. The author regards the occasion when one first must conceal something as
   (A) anticlimactic
   (B) insignificant
   (C) fleeting
   (D) momentous
   (E) enviable

10. The author's tone throughout the passage can best be described as
    (A) hostile
    (B) condescending
    (C) playful
    (D) earnest
    (E) impersonal

11. The passage as a whole can best be described as
    (A) an apology
    (B) a rebuttal
    (C) an exhortation
    (D) an understatement
    (E) a paradox

Passage 4

The following passage was written by a twentieth-century naturalist.

We were about a quarter mile away when quiet swept over the colony. A thousand or more heads periscoped. Two thousand eyes glared. Save for our wading, the world's business had stopped. A thousand avian personalities were concentrated on us, and the psychological force of this was terrific. Contingents of home-coming feeders, suddenly aware of four strange specks moving across the lake, would bank violently and speed away. Then the chain reaction began. Every throat in that rookery let go with a concatenation of wild, raspy, terrorized trumpet bursts. With all wings now fully spread and churning, and quadrupling the color mass, the birds began to move as one, and the sky was filled with the sound of Judgment Day.

12. The author's primary purpose in this passage is to
    (A) explain a natural catastrophe
    (B) issue a challenge
    (C) criticize an expedition
    (D) evoke an experience
    (E) document an experiment

13. The "four strange specks" (line 9) are
    (A) wild birds
    (B) animal predators
    (C) intruding humans
    (D) unusual clouds
    (E) members of the colony

14. In line 10, "bank" most nearly means
    (A) cover
    (B) heap up
    (C) count on
    (D) tilt laterally
    (E) reserve carefully

15. The visitors' response to the episode described in this passage was most likely one of
    (A) impatience
    (B) trepidation
    (C) outrage
    (D) grief
    (E) awe

Passage 5

How is a newborn star formed? For the answer to this question, we must look to the familiar physical concept of gravitational instability. It is a simple concept, long-known to scientists, having been first recognized by Isaac Newton in the late 1600's.

Let us envision a cloud of interstellar atoms and molecules, slightly admixed with dust. This cloud of interstellar gas is static and uniform. Suddenly, something occurs to disturb the gas, causing one small area within it to condense. As this small area increases in density, becoming slightly denser than the gas around it, its gravitational field likewise increases somewhat in strength. More matter now is attracted to the area, and its gravity becomes even stronger; as a result, it starts to contract, in process increasing in density even more. This in turn further increases its gravity, so that it accumulates still more matter and contracts further still. And so the process continues, until finally the small area of gas gives birth to a gravitationally bound object, a newborn star.

16. The primary purpose of the passage is to
    (A) demonstrate the evolution of the meaning of a term
    (B) support a theory considered outmoded
    (C) depict the successive stages of a phenomenon
    (D) establish the pervasiveness of a process
    (E) describe a static condition

17. In line 11, "disturb" most nearly means
    (A) hinder
    (B) perplex
    (C) unsettle
    (D) pester
    (E) inconvenience

18. It can be inferred from the passage that the author views the information contained within it as
    (A) controversial but irrefutable
    (B) commonly accepted and factual
    (C) speculative and unprofitable
    (D) original but obscure
    (E) sadly lacking in elaboration

19. The author provides information that answers which of the following questions?
    I. How does the small region's increasing density affect its gravitational field?
    II. What causes the disturbance that changes the cloud from its original static state?
    III. What is the end result of the gradually increasing concentration of the small region of gas?
    (A) I only
    (B) II only
    (C) I and II only
    (D) I and III only
    (E) I, II, and III

20. Throughout the passage, the author's manner of presentation is
    (A) argumentative
    (B) convoluted
    (C) anecdotal
    (D) expository
    (E) hyperbolic

LONG PASSAGES

Passage 1

Although patience is the most important quality a treasure hunter can have, the trade demands a certain amount of courage, too. I have my share of guts, but make no boast about ignoring the hazards of diving. As all good divers know, the business of plunging into an alien world with an artificial air supply as your only link to the world above can be as dangerous as stepping into a den of lions. Most of the danger rests within the diver himself.

The devil-may-care diver who shows great bravado underwater is the worst risk of all. He may lose his bearings in the glimmering dim light that penetrates the sea and become separated from his diving companions. He may dive too deep, too long and suffer painful, sometimes fatal, bends.

He may surface too quickly and force his lungs to squeeze their supply of high pressure air into his bloodstream, causing an embolism—a bubble of air in the blood—which often kills. He may become trapped in a submarine rockslide, get lost in an underwater cave, or be chopped to bits by a marauding shark. These are not occasional dangers such as crossing a street in busy traffic. They are always with you underwater. At one time or another, I have faced all of them except bends and embolism, which can be avoided by common sense and understanding of human physical limits beneath the surface.

Once, while salvaging brass from the sunken hulk of an old steel ship, I brushed lightly against a huge engine cylinder, which looked as if it were as solid as it was on the day the ship was launched. Although the pressure of my touch was hardly enough to topple a toy soldier, the heavy mass of cast iron collapsed, causing a chain reaction in which the rest of the old engine crumbled. Tons of iron dropped all around me. Sheer luck saved me from being crushed. I have been wary of swimming around steel shipwrecks ever since.

1. The author's attitude toward divers who show "great bravado underwater" (lines 12–13) is primarily one of
   (A) admiration for their courage
   (B) resentment of their success
   (C) distaste for their methods
   (D) disapproval of their rashness
   (E) dismay over their laziness

2. The passage most probably appeared in
   (A) a short story
   (B) an autobiographical article
   (C) a diver's logbook
   (D) an article in an encyclopedia
   (E) a manual of skin diving instructions

3. Which of the following does the author not do?
   (A) define a term
   (B) give an example
   (C) make a comparison
   (D) pose a question
   (E) list a possibility

4. According to the passage, the solidity of the steel engine cylinder was
   (A) flawless
   (B) massive
   (C) flexible
   (D) illusory
   (E) fortunate

5. In line 42, "sheer" most nearly means
   (A) steep
   (B) pure
   (C) sharp
   (D) filmy
   (E) abrupt

Passage 2

The following passage is taken from a basic geology text.

Rocks which have solidified directly from molten materials are called igneous rocks. Igneous rocks are commonly referred to as primary rocks because they are the original source of material found in sedimentaries and metamorphics. Igneous rocks compose the greater part of the earth's crust, but they are generally covered at the surface by a relatively thin layer of sedimentary or metamorphic rocks. Igneous rocks are distinguished by the following characteristics: (1) they contain no fossils; (2) they have no regular arrangement of layers; and (3) they are nearly always made up of crystals.

Sedimentary rocks are composed largely of minute fragments derived from the disintegration of existing rocks and in some instances from the remains of animals. As sediments are transported, individual fragments are sorted according to size. Distinct layers of such sediments as gravel, sand, and clay build up, as they are deposited by water and occasionally wind. These sediments vary in size with the material and the power of the eroding agent. Sedimentary materials are laid down in layers called strata.

When sediments harden into sedimentary rocks, the names applied to them change to indicate the change in physical state. Thus, small stones and gravel cemented together are known as conglomerates; cemented sand becomes sandstone; and hardened clay becomes shale. In addition to these, other sedimentary rocks such as limestone frequently result from the deposition of dissolved material. The ingredient parts are normally precipitated by organic substances, such as the shells of clams or hard skeletons of other marine life.

Both igneous and sedimentary rocks may be changed by pressure, heat, solution, or cementing action. When individual grains from existing rocks tend to deform and interlock, they are called metamorphic rocks. For example, granite, an igneous rock, may be metamorphosed into a gneiss or a schist. Limestone, a sedimentary rock, when subjected to heat and pressure may become marble, a metamorphic rock. Shale under pressure becomes slate.

6. The primary purpose of the passage is to
   (A) explain the factors that may cause rocks to change in form
   (B) show how the scientific names of rocks reflect the rocks' composition
   (C) present a new hypothesis about the nature of rock formation
   (D) define and describe several diverse kinds of rocks
   (E) explain why rocks are basic parts of the earth's structure

7. In line 29, "state" most nearly means
   (A) mood
   (B) pomp
   (C) territory
   (D) predicament
   (E) condition

8. According to the passage, igneous rocks are characterized by
   (A) their inability to be changed by heat or pressure
   (B) the wealth of fossils they incorporate
   (C) their granular composition
   (D) their relative rarity
   (E) their lack of regular strata

9. The passage contains information that would answer which of the following questions?
   I. Which elements form igneous rocks?
   II. What produces sufficient pressure to alter a rock?
   III. Why is marble called a metamorphic rock?
   (A) I only
   (B) III only
   (C) I and II only
   (D) II and III only
   (E) I, II, and III

10. The author does all of the following EXCEPT
    (A) provide an example
    (B) define a term
    (C) describe a process
    (D) cite an authority
    (E) enumerate specific attributes

DOUBLE PASSAGES

The following set of paired passages is the same set that appeared at the beginning of the book. The questions following the paired passages, however, will be new to you. The passages are excerpted from books on America's national pastime, baseball.

Passage 1

DiMaggio had size, power, and speed. McCarthy, his longtime manager, liked to say that DiMaggio might have stolen 60 bases a season if he had given him the green light. Stengel, his new manager, was equally impressed, and when DiMaggio was on base he would point to him as an example of the perfect base runner. "Look at him," Stengel would say as DiMaggio ran out a base hit, "he's always watching the ball. He isn't watching second base. He isn't watching third base. He knows they haven't been moved. He isn't watching the ground, because he knows they haven't built a canal or a swimming pool since he was last there. He's watching the ball and the outfielder, which is the one thing that is different on every play."

DiMaggio complemented his natural athletic ability with astonishing physical grace. He played the outfield, he ran the bases, and he batted not just effectively but with rare style. He would glide rather than run, it seemed, always smooth, always ending up where he wanted to be just when he wanted to be there. If he appeared to play effortlessly, his teammates knew otherwise. In his first season as a Yankee, Gene Woodling, who played left field, was struck by the sound of DiMaggio chasing a fly ball. He sounded like a giant truck horse on the loose, Woodling thought, his feet thudding down hard on the grass. The great, clear noises in the open space enabled Woodling to measure the distances between them without looking.

He was the perfect Hemingway hero, for Hemingway in his novels romanticized the man who exhibited grace under pressure, who withheld any emotion lest it soil the purer statement of his deeds. DiMaggio was that kind of hero; his grace and skill were always on display, his emotions always concealed. This stoic grace was not achieved without a terrible price: DiMaggio was a man wound tight. He suffered from insomnia and ulcers. When he sat and watched the game he chain smoked and drank endless cups of coffee. He was ever conscious of his obligation to play well. Late in his career, when his legs were bothering him and the Yankees had a comfortable lead in a pennant race, columnist Jimmy Cannon asked him why he played so hard—the games, after all, no longer meant so much. "Because there might be somebody out there who's never seen me play before," he answered.

Passage 2

Athletes and actors—let actors stand for the set of performing artists—share much. They share the need to make gestures as fluid and economical as possible, to make out of a welter of choices the single, precisely right one. They share the need for thousands of hours of practice in order to train the body to become the perfect, instinctive instrument to express. Both athlete and actor, out of that abundance of emotion, choice, strategy, knowledge of the terrain, mood of spectators, condition of others in the ensemble, secret awareness of injury or weakness, and as merely an absolute concentration as possible so that all externalities are integrated, all distraction absorbed to the self, must be able to change the self so successfully that it changes us.

When either athlete or actor can bring all these skills to bear and focus them, then he or she will achieve that state of complete intensity and complete relaxation—complete coherence or integrity between what the performer wants to do and what the performer has to do. Then, the performer is free; for then, all that has been learned, by thousands of hours of practice and discipline and by repetition of pattern, becomes natural. Then, intellect is upgraded to the level of an instinct. The body follows commands that precede thinking.

When athlete and artist achieve such self-knowledge that they transform the self so that we are recreated, it is finally an exercise in power. The individual's power to dominate, on stage or field, invests the whole arena around the locus of performance with his or her power. We draw from the performer's energy, just as we scrutinize the performer's vulnerabilities, and we criticize as if we were equals (we are not) what is displayed. This is why all performers dislike or resent the audience as much as they need and enjoy it. Power flows in a mysterious circuit from performer to spectator (I assume a "live" performance) and back, and while cheers or applause are the hoped-for outcome of performing, silence or gasps are the most desired, for then the moment has occurred—then domination is complete, and as the performer triumphs, a unity rare and inspiring results.

11. Stengel's comments in lines 8–17 serve chiefly to
    - (A) point out the stupidity of the sort of error he condemns
    - (B) suggest the inevitability of mistakes in running bases
    - (C) show it is easier to spot problems than to come up with answers
    - (D) answer the criticisms of DiMaggio's baserunning
    - (E) modify his earlier position on DiMaggio's ability

12. In line 28, "struck" most nearly means
    - (A) halted
    - (B) slapped
    - (C) afflicted
    - (D) enamored
    - (E) impressed

13. By quoting Woodling's comment on DiMaggio's running (lines 29–32), the author most likely intends to emphasize
    (A) his teammates' envy of DiMaggio's natural gifts
    (B) how much exertion went into DiMaggio's moves
    (C) how important speed is to a baseball player
    (D) Woodling's awareness of his own slowness
    (E) how easily DiMaggio was able to cover territory

14. In the last paragraph of Passage 1, the author acknowledges which negative aspect of DiMaggio's heroic image?
    (A) His overemphasis on physical grace
    (B) His emotional romanticism
    (C) The uniformity of his performance
    (D) The obligation to answer the questions of reporters
    (E) The burden of living up to his reputation

15. The author makes his point about DiMaggio's prowess through all the following except
    (A) literary allusion
    (B) quotations
    (C) personal anecdotes
    (D) generalization
    (E) understatement

16. In line 56, "stand for" most nearly means
    (A) tolerate
    (B) represent
    (C) advocate
    (D) withstand
    (E) surpass

17. In lines 73–74, "bring all these skills to bear" most nearly means
    (A) come to endure
    (B) carry toward
    (C) apply directly
    (D) cause to behave
    (E) induce birth

18. Why, in line 99, does the author of Passage 2 assume a "live" performance?
    (A) His argument assumes a mutual involvement between performer and spectator that can occur only when both are physically present.
    (B) He believes that televised and filmed images give a false impression of the performer's ability to the spectators.
    (C) He fears the use of "instant replay" and other broadcasting techniques will cause performers to resent spectators even more strongly.
    (D) His argument dismisses the possibility of combining live performances with filmed segments.
    (E) He prefers audiences not to have time to reflect about the performance they have just seen.

19. Which of the following characteristics of the ideal athlete mentioned in Passage 2 is NOT illustrated by the anecdotes about DiMaggio in Passage 1?
    (A) Knowledge of the terrain
    (B) Secret awareness of injury or weakness
    (C) Consciousness of the condition of other teammates
    (D) Ability to make gestures fluid and economical
    (E) Absolute powers of concentration

20. Which of the following statements is best supported by a comparison of the two passages?
    (A) Both passages focus on the development of a specific professional athlete.
    (B) The purpose of both passages is to compare athletes with performing artists.
    (C) The development of ideas in both passages is similar.
    (D) Both passages examine the nature of superior athletic performance.
    (E) Both passages discuss athletic performance primarily in abstract terms.

Answer Key

SHORT PASSAGES

1. **A**	6. **A**	11. **C**	16. **C**
2. **A**	7. **B**	12. **D**	17. **C**
3. **E**	8. **E**	13. **C**	18. **B**
4. **C**	9. **D**	14. **D**	19. **D**
5. **E**	10. **D**	15. **E**	20. **D**

LONG PASSAGES

1. **D**	3. **D**	5. **B**	7. **E**	9. **B**
2. **B**	4. **D**	6. **D**	8. **E**	10. **D**

DOUBLE PASSAGES

11. **A**	13. **B**	15. **E**	17. **C**	19. **C**
12. **E**	14. **E**	16. **B**	18. **A**	20. **D**

Answer Explanations

SHORT PASSAGES

1. **(A)** The passage criticizes parents who force their children into group activities and push them to be *unnecessarily gregarious* (social; outgoing).
   Word Parts Clue: The root *greg-* means crowd. Gregarious people like crowds.
2. **(A)** The author is in favor of doing things on one's own and pursuing individual interests. Therefore, he feels that *young people need time to themselves.*
3. **(E)** Quotation marks often indicate that words are being used in a special sense.
   Here, the author puts quotes around *team players* and *good mixers* to show that he does not believe being a team player or a social mixer is an entirely good thing. In other words, he *refuses to accept the assumption that these are entirely positive values.*
4. **(C)** The author believes that by developing one's individual personality, one stores up the confidence and strong sense of self one needs to do well in adult life. Thus, "the wealth of one's capital" consists of the *hours spent in solitary pursuits that enable one to develop into an independent, confident adult.*
5. **(E)** Authors frequently use a quotation—a proverb, an epigram, a bit of verse—to introduce a topic. Here the author quotes the rhyme to *introduce the topic of speaking abusively about others,* that is, name-calling.
6. **(A)** The rhyme says names will never harm you; the author says the opposite: names *will* hurt you. The author's point is that, if you think closely about what the rhyme is saying, you'll realize it isn't true. In other words, *the statement will no longer seem valid if you examine it closely.*
7. **(B)** The passage's concluding sentence states that "Name-calling can make you gullible to propaganda which you might otherwise readily see through and reject."
   In other words, name-calling can make you susceptible (vulnerable) to the *biased arguments* and half-truths of the propagandists.
8. **(E)** Go back to the sentence where the author mentions slogans and verses. What does it say? "(L)ike many popular slogans and verses, this one will not bear too close scrutiny." The author evidently believes that such popular slogans and

bits of verse frequently do not hold up under close examination. They don't tell the whole story. Instead, they *oversimplify the situation.*

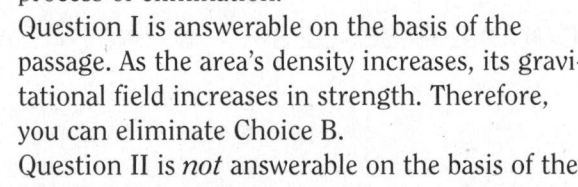

9. **(D)** The author calls the occasion on which one first must hide something "an awful hour" and says one's "whole life is different" afterwards. Clearly, he regards the occasion as *momentous* (crucial; highly significant).
10. **(D)** The author is dead serious about his subject; his tone throughout the passage is *earnest* (intensely serious and sincere).
11. **(C)** Throughout the passage Bishop Brooks is urging young people to live virtuously and honorably, so that they never have any dark secrets they feel they must hide. Thus, the passage can best be described as *an exhortation* (a speech or address communicating urgent advice or recommendations).
    Did you already know the word *exhortation*? If not, you still had a good chance of answering this question correctly. Remember the process of elimination? If you go through the answer choices crossing out the ones you know are wrong, you'll be in a great position to make an educated guess.
12. **(D)** The author is *evoking* (imaginatively creating; producing a vivid impression of) *an experience* that a group of naturalists had visiting a rookery (colony or breeding ground of wild birds).
13. **(C)** The "four strange specks" of whom the birds become aware are the naturalists, the *intruding humans* who have invaded the birds' territory.
14. **(D)** Think of how birds fly. They swoop, they wheel, they bank, that is, *tilt laterally*, tipping as they go into a turn.
15. **(E)** The author describes the scene in vivid terms: trumpet bursts, churning wings, a sky "filled with the sound of judgment day." Clearly, the most likely response on the part of the visiting naturalists would have been *awe* (mixed reverence, fear, and wonder).
    Note how the words that painted pictures helped you identify the emotion the visitors most likely felt.
16. **(C)** The entire second paragraph serves to describe or *depict the successive stages of* the formation of a gravitationally bound object. (*Successive stages* are steps that follow in order, one after another.) Key words that let you know that the passage is depicting the successive stages of a phenomenon are: *now, even more, further, further still,* and *finally.*
17. **(C)** The process of gravitational instability begins when something occurs to *unsettle* or disturb the static cloud of gas so that one small region becomes a little denser than the gas around it.
18. **(B)** To the author, the concept is both *commonly accepted* (it has been known since Newton's day) *and factual* (it is a simple, realistic concept, based on fact).
19. **(D)** You can answer this question by using the process of elimination.
    Question I is answerable on the basis of the passage. As the area's density increases, its gravitational field increases in strength. Therefore, you can eliminate Choice B.
    Question II is *not* answerable on the basis of the passage. The passage nowhere states what disturbs the gas. Therefore, you can eliminate Choices C and E.
    Question III is answerable on the basis of the passage. The end result of the process is the formation of a gravitationally bound object, a newborn star. Therefore, you can eliminate Choice A.
    Only Choice D is left. It is the correct answer.
20. **(D)** The author's manner of presentation is *expository*: he is explaining a physical concept.

LONG PASSAGES

1. **(D)** The author clearly criticizes divers who fail to treat the underwater perils they face with proper caution. Condemning their devil-may-care bravado (swaggering pretense of courage; bluster), he shows his *disapproval of their rashness*.
   Choice C is incorrect. To feel distaste for something is to have no particular liking for it. You might have a personal distaste for drinking coffee, for example, but have no problem with other people's drinking some. The author here is strongly critical of the devil-may-care divers whose lack of caution exposes them to mortal danger.
2. **(B)** The personal, chatty tone and the use of the first person pronoun ("I have my share of guts," "I have been wary") suggest that this passage most likely appeared in *an autobiographical article.*

3. **(D)** You can answer this question by using the process of elimination.
Does the author *define a term*? Yes. He defines the word *embolism.* You can eliminate Choice A.
Does the author *give an example*? Yes. He gives examples of different underwater perils. You can eliminate Choice B.
Does the author *make a comparison*? Yes. He compares the danger of deep-sea diving to the danger of "stepping into a den of lions." You can eliminate Choice C.
Does the author *pose a question*? Scan the passage looking for a question mark. If you don't see one, the author most likely did *not* ask any questions. Therefore, Choice D is probably the correct answer. To be sure you are right, check Choice E.
Does the author *list a possibility*? Yes. He lists all the possible dangers that a devil-may-care, careless diver may face. You can eliminate Choice E.
Only Choice D is left. It is the correct answer.
4. **(D)** The engine cylinder *looked* solid but fell apart at a touch. Its solidity was *illusory* (deceptive; like an illusion).
5. **(B)** The author was saved by *pure* luck.
6. **(D)** Throughout the passage, the author attempts to *define and describe several diverse kinds of rocks*.
When you look for a passage's *primary* purpose, you are trying to discover its chief intent *as a whole*. Do not be misled into selecting an answer that is true as far as it goes but does not hold true for the passage as a whole. For example, one purpose of the passage is to *explain the factors that may cause rocks to change in form.* However, this is not the passage's primary purpose.
7. **(E)** Sandstone's new name reflects the change in sand's physical state or *condition.*
8. **(E)** According to the passage, igneous rocks "have no regular arrangement of layers." Thus, they can be characterized by *their lack of regular strata* (layers).
9. **(B)** You can answer this question by using the process of elimination.
Question I is *not* answerable on the basis of the passage. The passage nowhere states which elements go into forming igneous rocks. Therefore, you can eliminate Choices A, C, and E.
Question II is *not* answerable on the basis of the passage. The passage nowhere states what force produces enough pressure to make a rock change from one physical state to another. Therefore, you can eliminate Choice D.
Only Choice B is left, and it is the correct answer. Question III is answerable on the basis of the passage. Marble is called a metaphoric rock because it comes into existence when limestone, a sedimentary rock, is subjected to heat and pressure and undergoes a metamorphosis or change.
10. **(D)** You can use the process of elimination to answer this question.
Does the author *provide an example*? Yes. He gives the example of limestone as a type of sedimentary rock. You can eliminate Choice A.
Does the author *define a term*? Yes. He defines *igneous rocks, sedimentary rocks, metamorphic rocks.* You can eliminate Choice B.
Does the author *describe a process*? Yes. In paragraph 2 he describes how sedimentary rocks are formed. You can eliminate Choice C.
Does the author *cite* or refer to *an authority* (expert)? Scan the passage looking for people's names and for titles of books (Clue: they'll begin with capital letters). If you don't see one, the author most likely did *not* cite an authority. Therefore, Choice D is probably the correct answer. To be sure you are right, check Choice E.
Does the author *enumerate* (list) *specific attributes* or characteristics? Yes. He lists three characteristics that distinguish igneous rocks. You can eliminate Choice E.
Only Choice D is left. It is the correct answer.

DOUBLE PASSAGES

11. **(A)** Manager Stengel's sarcastic comments about the mistakes DiMaggio *doesn't* make indicate just how dumb the manager thinks it is to look down at the ground when you should have your attention on the outfielder and the ball. Clearly, if one of his players made such an error, Stengel's response would be to say, "What's the matter, stupid? Are you afraid you're going to fall in a ditch down there?"
12. **(E)** Woodling was struck, or *impressed,* by the sound of DiMaggio's running; he found the impact of DiMaggio's feet hitting the ground

impressive.

13. **(B)** Note the context of the reference to Woodling. In the sentence immediately before it, the author says that, if DiMaggio "appeared to play effortlessly, his teammates knew otherwise." The author then introduces a comment by Woodling, one of DiMaggio's teammates. Woodling knew a great deal of effort went into DiMaggio's playing: he describes how DiMaggio's feet pounded as he ran. Clearly, the force of DiMaggio's running is mentioned to illustrate *how much exertion went into DiMaggio's moves*.
14. **(E)** In the final paragraph, the author describes DiMaggio pushing himself to play hard, despite his injuries. DiMaggio does this because he is trying to live up to the image his public has of him. He feels *the burden of living up to his reputation*.
15. **(E)** You can answer this technique question by using the process of elimination.
    Does the author make use of *literary allusions* (references to literature)? Yes. He makes an allusion to the novels of Ernest Hemingway. You can eliminate Choice A.
    Does the author make use of *quotations*? Yes. He quotes the comments of Casey Stengel and of DiMaggio himself. You can eliminate Choice B.
    Does the author make use of *personal anecdotes*? Yes. He tells an anecdote or story about Gene Woodling's first impression of DiMaggio. You can eliminate Choice C.
    Does the author make use of *generalizations* (general statements)? Yes. He makes several generalizations about DiMaggio ("He was the perfect Hemingway hero..."). You can eliminate Choice D.
    Does the author make use of *understatements*? (Understatements are a form of irony in which you purposely describe something as if it is weaker or less than it really is. To say "Joe DiMaggio was a pretty good hitter" is an understatement.) No. The author always expresses himself emphatically, using strong, extremely positive words to describe his subject. He never uses any understatements. Therefore, the correct answer is Choice E.
16. **(B)** At this point, the questions on Passage 2 begin. In this brief aside or side comment, the author is defining how he intends to use a word. He wishes to use the word *actors* to stand for, or *represent*, all other performers. This way every time he makes his comparison between athletes and performers he won't have to list all the various sorts of performing artists (actors, dancers, singers, acrobats, clowns) who resemble athletes in their need for physical grace, extensive rehearsal, and total concentration.
17. **(C)** The author has been describing the wide range of skills a performer uses in crafting an artistic or athletic performance. It is by taking these skills and *applying them directly* and with concentration to the task at hand that the performer achieves his or her goal.
18. **(A)** Although a spectator may feel powerfully involved with the filmed or televised image of a performer, the filmed image is unaffected by the spectator's feelings. Thus, for power to "flow in a mysterious circuit" from performer to spectator *and back*, the assumption is that *both performer and spectator must be physically present*.
19. **(C)** Although DiMaggio's teammates clearly were aware of his condition (as the Woodling anecdote illustrates), none of the anecdotes in Passage 1 indicate or even suggest that DiMaggio was specifically *conscious of his teammates' condition*.
    You can answer this question by using the process of elimination.
    Do the anecdotes about DiMaggio show that he had *knowledge of the terrain*? Yes. In running bases, DiMaggio never lets himself be distracted by looking at the bases or down at the ground; as Stengel says, he knows where they are. Clearly he knows the terrain. You can eliminate Choice A.
    Do the anecdotes about DiMaggio show that he had a *secret awareness of injury or weakness*? Yes. When DiMaggio's legs are failing him late in his career, he still pushes himself to perform well for the fan in the stands who hasn't seen him play before. In doing so, he takes into account his secret awareness of his legs' weakness. You can eliminate Choice B.
    Do the anecdotes about DiMaggio show that he had an *ability to make gestures fluid and economical*? Yes. Gliding rather than running, always smooth, never wasting a glance on inessentials, DiMaggio clearly shows that he can move fluidly and economically. You can eliminate Choice D.

Do the anecdotes about DiMaggio show that he had *absolute powers of concentration*? Yes. Running bases, DiMaggio *always* keeps his eye on the ball and the outfielder; he concentrates absolutely on them. You can eliminate Choice E. Only Choice C is left. It is the correct answer.

20. **(D)** Although one passage presents an abstract discussion of the nature of the ideal athlete and the other describes the achievements and character of a specific superior athlete, *both passages examine the nature of superior athletic performance*.

READING WRAP-UP

1. Tackle the short passages before the long ones.
2. Tackle passages with familiar subjects before passages with unfamiliar ones.
3. If you are stumped by a tough reading question, move on, but do *not* skip the other questions on that passage without giving them a shot.
4. Whenever you skip a question, *be sure you are filling in the right spaces on your answer sheet*.
5. Do not zip back and forth between passages.
6. Read as fast as you can with understanding, but don't force yourself to rush.
7. Try to anticipate what the passage will be about.
8. Read with a purpose.
9. Read the footnotes.
10. When you tackle the questions, go back to the passage to check each answer choice.
11. Use the line references in the questions to get quickly to the correct spot in the passage.
12. When dealing with the double passages, tackle them one at a time.
13. Be on the lookout for words or phrases in the questions that can clue you in to the kind of question being asked.
14. Tackle vocabulary-in-context questions the same way you do sentence completion questions, substituting "blank" for the word in quotes.
15. When asked to find a passage's main idea, be sure to check the opening and summary sentences of each paragraph.
16. When you answer specific detail questions, point to the precise words in the passage that support your answer choice.
17. When you answer inference questions, look for what the passage logically suggests, but does *not* directly state.
18. When asked to figure out an author's attitude or tone, look for words that convey emotion, express values, or paint pictures.
19. Familiarize yourself with the common terms used to describe an author's technique.
20. Think about how the ideas in the passage are logically organized.

Building Your Vocabulary

CHAPTER 3

Recognizing the meaning of words is essential to comprehending what you read. The more you stumble over unfamiliar words in a text, the more you have to take time out to look up words in your dictionary, the more likely you are to wind up losing track of what the author has to say.

To succeed in college, you must develop a college-level vocabulary. You must familiarize yourself with technical words in a wide variety of fields, mastering each field's special vocabulary. You must learn to use these words, and reuse them until they become second nature to you. The time you put in now learning vocabulary-building techniques for the PSAT will pay off later on and not just on the PSAT.

LONG-RANGE STRATEGY

There is only one effective long-range strategy for vocabulary building: READ.

Read—widely and well. Sample different fields—physics, art history, political science, geology—and different styles. Extensive reading is the one sure way to make your vocabulary grow.

As you read, however, take some time to acquaint yourself specifically with the kinds of words you must know to do well on the PSAT. No matter how little time you have before the test, you still can familiarize yourself with the sort of vocabulary you will be facing on the PSAT. First, look over the 300 words you will find on our PSAT high-frequency word list (pages 136–137): each of these 300 words, ranging from everyday words such as *ample* and *meek* to less commonly known ones such as *esoteric* and *pervasive* has appeared (as answer choices or as question words) at least four times in PSATs in the past two decades.

Next, proceed to master these high-frequency words. First check off the words you think you know. Then *look up all 300 words and their definitions in our abridged basic word list* (pages 138–187). Pay particular attention to the words you thought you knew. See whether any of them are defined in an unexpected way. If they are, make a special note of them. As you know from the preceding chapters, the PSAT often stumps students with questions based on unfamiliar meanings of familiar-looking words.

Not only will looking over the high-frequency word list reassure you that you *do* know some PSAT-type words; but also it may well help you on the actual day of the test. These words have turned up on recent tests; some of them may appear on the test you take.

A PLAN FOR USING THE WORD LIST

For those of you who wish to work your way through the word list and feel the need for a plan, we recommend that you follow the procedure described below in order to use the lists most profitably:

1. Set aside a definite time each day for the study of a list.
2. Devote at least one hour to each list.
3. First, go through the list looking at the short, simple-looking words (six letters at most). Mark those you don't know. In studying, pay particular attention to them.
4. Go through the list again looking at the longer words. Pay particular attention to words with more than one meaning and familiar-looking words that have unusual definitions that come as a surprise to you. Many tests make use of these secondary definitions.
5. List unusual words on index cards so that you can shuffle and review them from time to time. (Study no more than five cards at a time.)
6. Use the illustrative sentences in the list as models and make up new sentences of your own.

For each word, the following is provided:

- The word (printed in heavy type)
- Its part of speech (abbreviated)
- A brief definition
- A sentence illustrating the word's use

Whenever appropriate, related words are provided, together with their parts of speech. The forty-eight word lists are arranged in alphabetical order.

PSAT High-Frequency Word List

absolve
abstract
accessible
acclaim
accommodate
acknowledge
acrimony
adversary
adverse
aesthetic
affable
affinity
alleviate
altruistic
ambiguous
ambivalence
amenable
ample
antagonism
apathy
apprehension
apprenticeship
appropriate
aristocracy
aspire
assert
assumption
authentic
autonomous
aversion
banal
beneficial
benign
betray
brittle
buoyant
candor
captivate
caricature
censor
chronicle
circumspect
cite
cliché
coalesce
collaborate
compliance
component
composure
compromise
condone
confirm
conformity
confront
congenial
conscientious
consistency
consolidation
contentious
convention
convoluted
corrosion
curtail
dawdle
dearth
debilitate
decorous
decry
defamation
deference
defiance
degenerate
demean
denounce
depict

deplete
deplore
derision
derivative
detached
deterrent
didactic
diffident
digression
discernible
disclaimer
disclose
discord
discrepancy
disgruntled
disinterested
dismiss
disparage
disparate
dispatch
dispel
disperse
dissent
dissipate
distinction
divulge
docile
doctrine
dogmatic
eclectic
eclipse
elated
elicit
elusive
embellish
endorse
enhance
enigma
entice
enumerate
ephemeral
erode
erratic
erroneous
esoteric
espouse
esteem
excerpt
exemplary
exonerate
expedite
exploit
facilitate
fallacious
farce
fastidious
fawning
feasible
fervor
flippant
forthright
frail
frivolous
garrulous
generate
genre
gluttonous
gratify
gregarious
hackneyed
hamper
hindrance
hostility
hypocritical
hypothetical
iconoclastic
immutable
impede
imperceptible
implacable
implement
implication
impromptu
incarcerate
incongruity
inconsequential
inconsistency
incorporate
indict
indifferent
induce
industrious
inept
infallible
ingenious
ingenuous
ingrate
inherent
initiate
innate
innocuous
inscrutable
insightful
intangible
integrity
intricacy
introspective
irony
judicious
languid
larceny
lethargic
loathe
malice
meek
meticulous
misconception
misrepresent
mock
monarchy
monotony
mutability
naïveté
nocturnal
nonchalance
nostalgia
notorious
nurture
obnoxious
obscure
opaque
optimist
orator
ostentatious
outmoded
pacifist
pacify
paradox
patronize
pedantic
perjury
perpetual
pervasive
pessimism
petulant
phenomena
philanthropist
plagiarize
potency
pragmatic
precedent
predator
premise
premonition
presumptuous
prevail
prey
profound
proliferation
prolific
prologue
prominent
promote
prophetic
prosperity
provocative
prudent
ramble
random
recluse
refute
rejuvenate
relinquish
renown
reprehensible
repudiate
reserved
resignation
resolution
resolve
restraint
retain
reticent
reverent
ruthless
satirize
scrutinize
seclusion
serenity
sever
severity
singular
skeptical
steadfast
stoic
stratagem
subdued
subversive
superficial
superfluous
suppress
surpass
susceptible
suspend
sustain
symmetry
synthesis
taciturn
tedious
temper
temperament
termination
thwart
toxic
transcendent
transparent
trepidation
turbulence
urbane
utopia
vacillate
versatile
volatile
voracious
wary

Basic Word List

The abridged Basic Word List follows. *Do not let this list overwhelm you.* You do not need to memorize every word. An entry preceded by a bullet (•) is a High-Frequency Word.

Word List 1 abase–accommodate

abase V. lower; humiliate. Defeated, Queen Zenobia was forced to *abase* herself before the conquering Romans, who forced her to march before the emperor Aurelian in the procession celebrating his triumph.

abate V. subside; decrease; lessen. Rather than leaving immediately, they waited for the storm to *abate*. abatement, N.

abdicate V. renounce; give up. When Edward VIII *abdicated* the British throne to marry the woman he loved, he surprised the entire world. When the painter Gauguin *abdicated* his family responsibilities to run off to Samoa, he surprised no one at all.

aberration N. deviation from the expected or the normal; mental irregularity or disorder. Survivors of a major catastrophe are likely to exhibit *aberrations* of behavior because of the trauma they have experienced. aberrant, ADJ. and N.

abet V. encourage; aid. She was accused of aiding and *abetting* the drug dealer by engaging in a money-laundering scheme to help him disguise his illegal income. abettor, N.

abeyance N. suspended action. The deal was held in *abeyance* until her arrival.

abject ADJ. hopeless and crushed; servile and spiritless; wretched. On the streets of New York, the homeless live in *abject* poverty, lying huddled in doorways to find shelter from the wind.

abrade V. wear away by friction; scrape; erode. The sharp rocks *abraded* the skin on her legs; so she put iodine on her *abrasions*.

abscond V. depart secretly to avoid capture. The teller who *absconded* with the bonds was not captured until someone recognized him from his photograph on *America's Most Wanted*.

absolute ADJ. complete; totally unlimited; certain. Although the king of Siam was an *absolute* monarch, he did not want to behead his unfaithful wife without *absolute* evidence of her infidelity.

• **absolve** V. pardon (an offense); free from blame. The father confessor *absolved* him of his sins. absolution, N.

abstain V. refrain; hold oneself back voluntarily from an action or practice (especially one regarded as improper or unhealthy). After considering the effect of alcohol on his athletic performance, he decided to *abstain* from drinking while he trained for the race. abstinence, N.; abstinent or abstemious, ADJ.

• **abstract** ADJ. theoretical; not concrete; nonrepresentational. To him, hunger was an *abstract* concept; he had never missed a meal.

abstruse ADJ. obscure; profound; difficult to understand. She carries around *abstruse* works of philosophy, not because she understands them but because she wants her friends to think she does.

accelerate V. move faster. In our science class, we learn how falling bodies *accelerate*.

• **accessible** ADJ. easy to approach; obtainable. We asked our guide whether the ruins were *accessible* on foot.

accessory N. additional object; useful but not essential thing. The *accessories* she bought cost more than the dress. also ADJ.

• **acclaim** V. applaud; announce with great approval. The NBC sportscasters *acclaimed* every American victory in the Olympics and lamented every American defeat. acclamation, acclaim, N.

accolade N. award of merit. In the world of public relations, a Clio is the highest *accolade* an advertising campaign can receive.

• **accommodate** V. provide lodgings. Mary asked the room clerk whether the hotel would be able to *accommodate* the tour group on such short notice. accommodations, N.

• **accommodate** V. oblige or help someone; adjust or bring into harmony; adapt. Mitch always did everything possible to *accommodate* his elderly relatives, from driving them to medical appointments to helping them with paperwork. accommodating, ADJ. (secondary meaning)

Word List 2 accomplice–alacrity

accomplice N. partner in crime. Because he had provided the criminal with the lethal weapon, he was arrested as an *accomplice* in the murder.

• **acknowledge** V. recognize; admit. Although Ira *acknowledged* that the Beatles' tunes sounded pretty dated nowadays, he still preferred them to the punk rock songs his nephews played.

acquittal N. declaration of innocence; deliverance from a charge. His *acquittal* by the jury surprised those who had thought him guilty. acquit, V.

• **acrimony** N. bitterness of words or manner. The candidate attacked his opponent with great *acrimony.* acrimonious, ADJ.

acumen N. mental keenness. His business *acumen* helped him to succeed where others had failed.

adamant ADJ. hard; inflexible. Bronson played the part of a revenge-driven man, *adamant* in his determination to punish the criminals who had destroyed his family. adamancy, N.

adapt V. alter; modify. Some species of animals have become extinct because they could not *adapt* to a changing environment.

addiction N. compulsive, habitual need. His *addiction* to drugs caused his friends much grief.

adhere V. stick fast to. I will *adhere* to this opinion until someone comes up with solid proof that I am wrong. adhesive, ADJ.

adjacent ADJ. adjoining; neighboring; close by. Philip's best friend Jason lived only four houses away, close but not immediately *adjacent.*

adjudicate V. pass legal judgment on; sit in judgment. Do you trust Judge Judy to *adjudicate* disputes impartially?

admonish V. warn; scold. The preacher *admonished* his listeners to change their wicked ways. admonition, N.

adroit ADJ. skillful; nimble. The juggler's admirers particularly enjoyed his *adroit* handling of difficult balancing tricks.

adulation N. flattery; admiration. The rock star relished the *adulation* she received from her groupies and yes-men.

adulterate V. make impure by adding inferior or tainted substances. It is a crime to *adulterate* foods without informing the buyer; when consumers learned that the manufacturer had *adulterated* its apple juice by mixing it with water, they protested vigorously.

• **adversary** N. opponent. "Aha!" cried Holmes. "Watson, I suspect this delay is the work of my old *adversary* Professor Moriarty." adversarial, ADJ.

• **adverse** ADJ. unfavorable; hostile. The recession had a highly *adverse* effect on Father's investment portfolio: he lost so much money that he could no longer afford the butler and the upstairs maid. adversity, N.

adversity N. poverty; misfortune. We must learn to meet *adversity* gracefully.

advocate V. urge; plead for. Noted abolitionists such as Frederick Douglass and Sojourner Truth *advocated* the eradication of the Southern institution of slavery. also N.

• **aesthetic** ADJ. artistic; dealing with or capable of appreciation of the beautiful. The beauty of Tiffany's stained glass appealed to Alice's *aesthetic* sense. aesthete, N.

• **affable** ADJ. easily approachable; warmly friendly. Accustomed to cold, aloof supervisors, Nicholas was amazed by how *affable* his new employer was.

affected ADJ. artificial; pretended; assumed in order to impress. His *affected* mannerisms—his "Harvard" accent, his air of boredom, his flaunting of obscure foreign words—irritated many of us who had known him before he had gone away to school. affectation, N.

• **affinity** N. kinship; attraction to. She felt an *affinity* with all who suffered; their pains were her pains. Her brother, in contrast, had an *affinity* for political wheeling and dealing; he manipulated people shamelessly, not caring who got hurt.

affirmation N. positive assertion; confirmation; solemn pledge by one who refuses to take an oath. Despite Tom's *affirmations* of innocence, Aunt Polly still suspected he had eaten the pie. affirm, V.

affix V. add on; fasten; attach. First the registrar had to *affix* her signature to the license; then she had to *affix* her official seal.

affluence N. wealth; prosperity; abundance. Galvanized by his sudden, unexpected *affluence,* the lottery winner dashed out to buy himself a brand new Ferrari. affluent, ADJ.

affront V. insult; offend. Accustomed to being treated with respect, Miss Challoner was *affronted* by Vidal's offensive behavior.

aggregate V. gather; accumulate. Before the Wall Street scandals, dealers in so-called junk bonds managed to *aggregate* great wealth in short periods of time. aggregation, N.

agility N. nimbleness. The acrobat's *agility* amazed and thrilled the audience. agile, ADJ.

agitate V. stir up; disturb. Her fiery remarks further *agitated* the already angry mob.

alacrity N. cheerful promptness. Phil and Dave were raring to get off to the mountains; they packed up their ski gear and climbed into the van with *alacrity.*

Word List 3 alias–ancillary

alias N. an assumed name. John Smith's *alias* was Bob Jones. also ADV.

alienate V. make hostile; separate. Her attempts to *alienate* the two friends failed because they had complete faith in each other.

• **alleviate** V. relieve; lessen. This should *alleviate* the pain; if it does not, we will use stronger drugs.

alloy V. mix; make less pure; lessen or moderate. Our delight at the victory was *alloyed* by our concern for the pitcher, who injured his pitching arm in the game.

allude V. refer indirectly. Try not to mention divorce in John's presence because he will think you are *alluding* to his marital problems with Jill.

allure V. entice; attract. *Allured* by the song of the sirens, the helmsman steered the ship toward the reef. also N.

allusion N. indirect reference. When Amanda said to the ticket scalper, "One hundred bucks? What do you want, a pound of flesh?," she was making an *allusion* to Shakespeare's *Merchant of Venice*.

aloft ADV. upward. The sailor climbed *aloft* into the rigging. To get into a loft bed, you have to climb *aloft*.

aloof ADJ. apart; reserved; standoffish. People thought James was a snob because he remained *aloof* while all the rest of the group conversed.

altercation N. noisy quarrel; heated dispute. In that hot-tempered household, no meal ever came to a peaceful conclusion; the inevitable *altercation* occasionally even ended in blows.

• **altruistic** ADJ. unselfishly generous; concerned for others. The star received no fee for appearing at the benefit; it was a purely *altruistic* act. altruism, N.

amalgam N. mixture of different elements; alloy. In character, King Gustav was a strange *amalgam* of hard-headed practicality and religious zeal. amalgamate, V.

• **ambiguous** ADJ. unclear or doubtful in meaning. The proctor's *ambiguous* instructions thoroughly confused us; we didn't know which columns we should mark and which we should leave blank. ambiguity, N.

• **ambivalence** N. having contradictory or conflicting emotional attitudes. Torn between loving her parents one minute and hating them the next, she was confused by the *ambivalence* of her feelings. ambivalent, ADJ.

ambulatory ADJ. able to walk; not bedridden. Jonathan was a highly *ambulatory* patient; not only did he refuse to be confined to bed, but also he insisted on riding his skateboard up and down the halls.

ameliorate V. improve; make more satisfactory. Carl became a union organizer because he wanted to join the fight to *ameliorate* working conditions in the factory.

• **amenable** ADJ. readily managed; willing to give in; agreeable; submissive. A born snob, Wilbur was *amenable* to any suggestions from those he looked up to, but he resented advice from his supposed inferiors. Unfortunately, his incorrigible snobbery was not *amenable* to improvement.

amiable ADJ. agreeable; lovable; warmly friendly. In *Little Women*, Beth is the *amiable* daughter whose loving disposition endears her to all who have dealings with her.

amorous ADJ. moved by sexual love; loving. "Love them and leave them" was the motto of the *amorous* Don Juan.

amorphous ADJ. formless; lacking shape or definition. As soon as we have decided on our itinerary, we shall send you a copy; right now, our plans are still *amorphous*.

• **ample** ADJ. abundant. Bond had *ample* opportunity to escape. Why did he let us catch him?

amplify V. broaden or clarify by expanding; intensify; make stronger. Charlie Brown tried to *amplify* his remarks, but he was drowned out by jeers from the audience. Lucy, however, used a loudspeaker to *amplify* her voice and drowned out all the hecklers.

anachronism N. something regarded as outmoded; something or someone misplaced in time. In today's world of personal copiers and fax machines, the old-fashioned mimeograph machine is clearly an *anachronism*; even the electric typewriter seems *anachronistic* next to a laptop PC.

analogy N. similarity; parallelism. A well-known *analogy* compares the body's immune system with an army whose defending troops are the lymphocytes or white blood cells. *Analogies* are useful, but you can't take them too far: cells, after all, are not soldiers; there is no boot camp for lymphocytes.

anarchist N. person who seeks to overturn the established government; advocate of abolishing authority. Denying she was an *anarchist,* Katya maintained she wished only to make changes in our government, not to destroy it entirely.

anarchy N. absence of governing body; state of disorder. For weeks China was in a state of *anarchy*, with soldiers shooting down civilians in the streets and rumors claiming that Premier Deng was dead. Foreigners fleeing the country reported conditions were so *anarchic* that it was a miracle they escaped.

ancillary ADJ. serving as an aid or accessory; auxiliary. In an *ancillary* capacity Doctor Watson was helpful; however, Holmes could not trust the good doctor to solve a perplexing case on his own. also N.

Word List 4 animated–aristocracy

animated ADJ. lively; spirited. Jim Carrey's facial expressions are highly *animated:* when he played Ace Ventura, he looked practically rubber-faced.

animosity N. active enmity. Mr. Fang incurred the *animosity* of the party's rulers because he advocated limitations of their power.

anomaly N. irregularity; something out of place or abnormal. A bird that cannot fly is an *anomaly.* A classical harpist in the middle of a heavy metal band is *anomalous;* she is also inaudible.

• **antagonism** N. hostility; active resistance. Barry showed his *antagonism* toward his new stepmother by ignoring her whenever she tried talking to him. antagonistic, ADJ.

antecedents N. preceding events or circumstances that influence what comes later; ancestors or early background. Susi Bechhofer's ignorance of her Jewish background had its *antecedents* in the chaos of World War II. Smuggled out of Germany and adopted by a Christian family, she knew nothing of her birth and *antecedents* until she was reunited with her family in 1989.

anticlimax N. letdown in thought or emotion. After the fine performance in the first act, the rest of the play was an *anticlimax.* anticlimactic, ADJ.

antipathy N. aversion; dislike. Tom's extreme *antipathy* for disputes keeps him from getting into arguments with his temperamental wife. Noise in any form is *antipathetic* to him. Among his particular *antipathies* are honking cars, boom boxes, and heavy metal rock.

antiquated ADJ. obsolete; outdated. Accustomed to editing his papers on word processors, Philip thought typewriters were too *antiquated* for him to use.

antiseptic N. substance that prevents infection. It is advisable to apply an *antiseptic* to any wound, no matter how slight or insignificant. also ADJ.

antithesis N. contrast; direct opposite of or to. This tyranny was the *antithesis* of all that he had hoped for, and he fought it with all his strength.

• **apathy** N. lack of caring; indifference. A firm believer in democratic government, she could not understand the *apathy* of people who never bothered to vote. She wondered whether they had ever cared or whether they had always been *apathetic.*

aplomb N. poise; assurance. Gwen's *aplomb* in handling potentially embarrassing moments was legendary around the office; when one of her clients broke a piece of her best crystal, she coolly picked up her own goblet and hurled it into the fireplace.

apocryphal ADJ. untrue; made up. To impress his friends, Tom invented *apocryphal* tales of his adventures in the big city.

apostate N. one who abandons his religious faith or political beliefs. Because he switched from one party to another, his former friends shunned him as an *apostate.*

append V. attach. I shall *append* this chart to my report. When you *append* a bibliography to a text, you have just created an *appendix.*

• **apprehension** N. fear; discernment; capture. The tourist refused to drive his rental car through downtown Miami because he felt some *apprehension* that he might be carjacked.

• **apprenticeship** N. time spent as a novice learning a trade from a skilled worker. As a child, Pip had thought it would be wonderful to work as Joe's *apprentice;* now he hated his *apprenticeship* and scorned the blacksmith's trade.

• **appropriate** ADJ. fitting or suitable; pertinent. Madonna spent hours looking for a suit that would be *appropriate* to wear at a summer wedding.

• **appropriate** V. acquire; take possession of for one's own use; set aside for a special purpose. The ranchers *appropriated* lands that had originally been intended for Indian use. In response, Congress *appropriated* additional funds for the Bureau of Indian Affairs.

arable ADJ. fit for growing crops. The first settlers wrote home glowing reports of the New World, praising its vast acres of *arable* land ready for the plow.

arbiter N. a person with power to decide a dispute; judge. As an *arbiter* in labor disputes, she is skillful: she balances the demands of both sides and hands down rulings with which everyone agrees. As an *arbiter* of style, however, she is worthless: she wears such unflattering outfits that no woman in her right mind would imitate her.

arbitrary ADJ. unreasonable or capricious; randomly selected without any reason; based solely on one's unrestricted will or judgment. The coach claimed the team lost because the umpire made some *arbitrary* calls.

archipelago N. group of closely located islands. When Gauguin looked at the map and saw the *archipelagoes* in the South Seas, he longed to visit them.

arduous ADJ. hard; strenuous. Bob's *arduous* efforts had sapped his energy. Even using a chain saw, he found chopping down trees an *arduous,* time-consuming task.

aria N. operatic solo. At her Metropolitan Opera audition, Marian Anderson sang an *aria* from the opera *Norma.*

arid ADJ. dry; barren. The cactus has adapted to survive in an *arid* environment.

• **aristocracy** N. hereditary nobility; privileged class. Americans have mixed feelings about hereditary *aristocracy:* we say all men are created equal, but we describe people who bear themselves with grace and graciousness as natural *aristocrats.*

Word List 5 arrogance–authoritative

arrogance N. pride; haughtiness. Convinced that Emma thought she was better than anyone else in the class, Ed rebuked her for her *arrogance.*

articulate ADJ. effective; distinct. Her *articulate* presentation of the advertising campaign impressed her employers. also V.

ascendancy N. controlling influence. President Marcos failed to maintain his *ascendancy* over the Philippines. He was overthrown by the forces of Corazon Aquino when she *ascended* to power.

ascetic ADJ. practicing self-denial; austere. The wealthy, self-indulgent young man felt oddly drawn to the strict, *ascetic* life led by members of some monastic orders. also N.

• **aspire** V. seek to attain; long for. Because he *aspired* to a career in professional sports, Philip enrolled in a graduate program in sports management. aspiration, N.

assail V. assault. He was *assailed* with questions after his lecture.

• **assert** V. state strongly or positively; insist on or demand recognition of (rights, claims, etc). When Jill *asserted* that nobody else in the junior class had such an early curfew, her parents *asserted* themselves, telling her that if she didn't get home by nine o'clock, she would be grounded for the week. assertion, N.

assiduous ADJ. diligent. It took Rembrandt weeks of *assiduous* labor before he was satisfied with his self-portrait. assiduity, N.

assuage V. ease or lessen (pain); Jilted by Jane, Dick tried to *assuage* his heartache by indulging in ice cream.

• **assumption** N. something taken for granted; taking over or taking possession of. The young princess made the foolish *assumption* that the regent would not object to her *assumption* of power. assume, V.

assurance N. promise or pledge; certainty; self-confidence. When Guthrie gave Guinness his *assurance* rehearsals were going well, he spoke with such *assurance* that Guinness felt relieved. assure, V.; assured, ADJ.

astute ADJ. wise; shrewd; keen. As tutor, she made *astute* observations about how to take multiple-choice tests. She was an *astute* observer: she noticed every tiny detail and knew exactly how important each one was.

asylum N. place of refuge; safety. Fleeing persecution, the political refugee sought *asylum* in the United States.

atrophy V. waste away. After three months in a cast, Stan's biceps had *atrophied* somewhat; however, he was sure that if he pumped iron for a while he would soon build it up.

attain V. reach or accomplish; gain. It took Bolingbroke years to *attain* his goal of gaining the throne.

attentive ADJ. watching carefully; considerate; thoughtful. Spellbound, the *attentive* audience watched the final game of the match, never taking their eyes from the ball. Stan's *attentive* daughter slipped a sweater over his shoulders without distracting his attention from the game.

attire N. clothing (especially, splendid clothes). At the Academy Awards ceremony, the television host commented on the highly fashionable *attire* worn by the nominees. also N.

attribute N. essential quality. His outstanding *attribute* was his kindness.

attribute V. ascribe or credit (to a cause); regard as characteristic of a person or thing. I *attribute* Andrea's success in science to the encouragement she received from her parents.

attrition N. gradual decrease in numbers; reduction in the work force without firing employees; wearing away of opposition by means of harassment. In the 1960s urban churches suffered from *attrition* as members moved from the cities to the suburbs. Rather than fire staff members, church leaders followed a policy of *attrition,* allowing elderly workers to retire without replacing them.

audacity N. boldness. Luke could not believe his own *audacity* in addressing the princess. Where did he get the nerve?

augment V. increase. Armies *augment* their forces by calling up reinforcements; teachers *augment* their salaries by taking odd jobs. Lexy *augments* her salary by working in a record store. Her *augmentation* of wealth has not been great; however, she has *augmented* her record collection considerably.

aura N. distinctive atmosphere; luminous glow. Radiant with happiness, the bride seemed surrounded by an *aura* of brightness.

auspicious ADJ. favoring success; fortunate. With favorable weather conditions, it was an *auspicious* moment to set sail. Prospects for trade were good: under such promising *auspices* we were bound to thrive. Thomas, however, had doubts: a paranoid, he became suspicious whenever conditions seemed *auspicious.*

austere ADJ. forbiddingly stern; severely simple and unornamented. The headmaster's *austere* demeanor tended to scare off the more timid students, who never visited his study willingly. The room reflected the man, for it was *austere* and bare, like a monk's cell, with no touches of luxury to moderate its *austerity.*

• **authentic** ADJ. genuine. The art expert was able to distinguish the *authentic* van Gogh painting from the forged copy. authenticate, V.

authoritative ADJ. having the weight of authority; overbearing and dictatorial. Impressed by the young researcher's well-documented presentation, we accepted her analysis of the experiment as *authoritative.*

Word List 6 autonomous–blasphemy

• **autonomous** ADJ. self-governing. This island is a colony; however, in most matters, it is *autonomous* and receives no orders from the mother country. The islanders are an independent lot and would fight to preserve their *autonomy.*

autopsy N. examination of a dead body; postmortem. The medical examiner ordered an *autopsy* to determine the cause of death. also V.

avarice N. greediness for wealth. King Midas is a perfect example of *avarice,* for he was so greedy that he wished everything he touched would turn to gold.

averse ADJ. reluctant. The reporter was *averse* to revealing the sources of his information.

• **aversion** N. firm dislike. Bert had an *aversion* to yuppies; Alex had an *aversion* to punks. Their mutual *aversion* was so great that they refused to speak to one another.

avert V. prevent; turn aside. "Watch out!" she cried, hoping to *avert* an accident. She *averted* her eyes from the dead cat on the highway.

avid ADJ. greedy; eager for. Abner was *avid* for pleasure and partied with great *avidity.*

awe N. solemn wonder. The tourists gazed with *awe* at the tremendous expanse of the Grand Canyon.

babble V. chatter idly. The little girl *babbled* about her dolls and pets.

badger V. pester; annoy; harass. Madge was forced to change her telephone number because she was *badgered* by obscene phone calls.

baffle V. frustrate; perplex. The new code *baffled* the enemy agents.

balk V. foil or thwart; stop short; refuse to go on. When the warden learned that several inmates were planning to escape, he took steps to *balk* their attempt. However, he *balked* at punishing them by shackling them to the walls of their cells.

• **banal** ADJ. hackneyed; commonplace; trite; lacking originality. The hack writer's worn-out clichés made his comic sketch seem *banal.* He even resorted to the *banality* of having someone slip on a banana peel!

bane N. cause of ruin; curse. Lucy's little brother was the *bane* of her existence: his attempts to make her life miserable worked so well that she could have fed him some ratsbane for having such a *baneful* effect.

bastion N. stronghold; something seen as a source of protection. The villagers fortified the town hall, hoping this improvised *bastion* could protect them from the guerrilla raids.

begrudge V. resent. I *begrudge* every minute I have to spend attending meetings; they're a complete waste of time.

beguile V. mislead or delude; cheat; pass time. With flattery and big talk of easy money, the con men *beguiled* Kyle into betting his allowance on the shell game. Broke, Kyle *beguiled* himself during the long hours by playing solitaire.

belie V. contradict; give a false impression of. His coarse, hard-bitten exterior *belied* his underlying sensitivity.

benefactor N. gift giver; patron. In later years Scrooge became Tiny Tim's *benefactor* and gave him many gifts.

• **beneficial** ADJ. helpful; advantageous; useful. Tiny Tim's cheerful good nature had a *beneficial* influence on Scrooge's disposition.

beneficiary N. person entitled to benefits or proceeds of an insurance policy or will. In Scrooge's will, he made Tiny Tim his *beneficiary.* Everything he left would go to the benefit of young Tim.

benevolent ADJ. generous; charitable. Mr. Fezziwig was a *benevolent* employer, who wished to make Christmas merrier for young Scrooge and his other employees.

• **benign** ADJ. kindly; favorable; not malignant. Though her *benign* smile and gentle bearing made Miss Marple seem a sweet little old lady, in reality she was a tough-minded, shrewd observer of human nature. benignity, N.

bestial ADJ. beastlike; brutal. According to legend, the werewolf was able to abandon its human shape to take on a *bestial* form.

bestow V. confer. The president wished to *bestow* great honors upon the hero.

• **betray** V. be unfaithful; reveal (unconsciously or unwillingly). The spy *betrayed* his country by selling military secrets to the enemy. When he was taken in for questioning, the tightness of his lips *betrayed* his fear of being caught.

biased ADJ. slanted; prejudiced. Because the judge played golf regularly with the district attorney's father, we feared he might be *biased* in the prosecution's favor. bias, N.

bizarre ADJ. fantastic; violently contrasting. The plot of the novel was too *bizarre* to be believed.

bland ADJ. soothing; mild; dull. Unless you want your stomach lining to be eaten away, stick to a *bland* diet. blandness, N.

blandishment N. flattery. Despite the salesperson's *blandishments,* the customer did not buy the outfit.

blare N. loud, harsh roar; screech. I don't know which is worse: the steady *blare* of a teenager's boom box deafening your ears or a sudden blaze of flashbulbs dazzling your eyes.

blasphemy N. irreverence; sacrilege; cursing. In my father's house, the Dodgers were the holiest of holies; to cheer for another team was to utter words of *blasphemy.* blasphemous, ADJ.

Word List 7 blatant–cant

blatant ADJ. flagrant; conspicuously obvious; loudly offensive. To the unemployed youth from Dublin, the "No Irish Need Apply" placard in the shop window was a *blatant* mark of prejudice.

blithe ADJ. gay; joyous; carefree. Without a care in the world, Beth went her *blithe,* light-hearted way.

bloat V. expand or swell (with water or air); puff up with conceit. Constant flattery from his hangers-on *bloated* the heavyweight champion's already sizable ego.

boisterous ADJ. rough and noisy; rowdy; stormy. The unruly crowd of demonstrators became even more *boisterous* when the mayor tried to quiet them.

bolster V. support; reinforce. The debaters amassed file boxes full of evidence to *bolster* their arguments.

boon N. blessing; benefit. The recent rains that filled our empty reservoirs were a *boon* to the whole community.

boundless ADJ. unlimited; vast. Mike's energy was *boundless:* the greater the challenge, the more vigorously he tackled the job.

bountiful ADJ. abundant; graciously generous. Thanks to the good harvest, we had a *bountiful* supply of food, and we could be as *bountiful* as we liked in distributing food to the needy.

bourgeois ADJ. middle class; selfishly materialistic; dully conventional. Technically, anyone who belongs to the middle class is *bourgeois,* but, given the word's connotations, most people resent it if you call them that.

boycott V. refrain from buying or using. In an effort to stop grape growers from using pesticides that harmed the farm workers' health, Cesar Chavez called for consumers to *boycott* grapes.

brackish ADJ. somewhat salty. Following the stream, we noticed its fresh, springlike water grew increasingly *brackish* as we drew nearer to the bay.

brandish V. wave around; flourish. Alarmed, Doctor Watson wildly *brandished* his gun until Holmes told him to put the thing away before he shot himself.

breach N. breaking of contract or duty; fissure; gap. Jill sued Jack for *breach* of promise, claiming he had broken his promise to marry her. They found a *breach* in the enemy's fortifications and penetrated their lines. also V.

brevity N. conciseness. Since you are charged for every transmitted word, *brevity* is essential when you send a telegram or cablegram.

brine N. salt water; seawater (as opposed to fresh). If you pack a peck of peppers in *brine,* what do you get? A peck of pickled peppers! briny, ADJ.

• **brittle** ADJ. easily broken; difficult. My employer's self-control was as *brittle* as an eggshell. Her *brittle* personality made it difficult for me to get along with her.

brochure N. pamphlet. This free *brochure* on farming was issued by the Department of Agriculture.

brusque ADJ. blunt; abrupt. Jill was offended by Jack's *brusque* reply; he had no right to be so impatient with her.

bungle V. mismanage; blunder. Don't botch this assignment, Bumstead; if you *bungle* the job, you're fired!

• **buoyant** ADJ. able to float; cheerful and optimistic. When the boat capsized, her *buoyant* life jacket kept Jody afloat. Scrambling back on board, she was still in a *buoyant* mood, certain that despite the delay she'd win the race. buoyancy, N.

burgeon V. bloom; develop rapidly; flourish. From its start as a small Seattle coffeehouse, Starbucks seemed to *burgeon* almost overnight into a major national chain.

bustle V. move about energetically; teem. David and the children *bustled* about the house getting in each other's way as they tried to pack for the camping trip.

buttress V. support or prop up. The government is considering price supports to *buttress* the declining economy. The huge cathedral walls were supported by flying *buttresses.* also N.

cajole V. coax; wheedle. Jill tried to *cajole* Jack into buying her a fur coat, but no matter how much she coaxed him, he wouldn't give in to her *cajolery.*

calamity N. disaster; misery. As news of the *calamity* spread, offers of relief poured in to the stricken community. calamitous, ADJ.

calligraphy N. beautiful writing; excellent penmanship. In the Middle Ages, before a novice scribe was allowed to copy an important document, he had to spend years practicing *calligraphy.*

callous ADJ. hardened; unfeeling. Carl had worked in the hospital for so many years that he was *callous* to the suffering in the wards. It was as if he had a *callus* on his soul.

camaraderie N. good-fellowship. What Ginger loved best about her job was the sense of *camaraderie* she and her coworkers shared.

• **candor** N. frankness; open honesty. Jack can carry *candor* too far: when he told Jill his honest opinion of her, she nearly slapped his face. Instead of being so *candid,* try keeping your opinions to yourself.

canine ADJ. related to dogs; doglike. Some days the *canine* population of Berkeley seems almost to outnumber the human population.

cant N. insincere, hypocritical speech; "pious" talk; jargon of thieves. Shocked by news of the minister's extramarital love affairs, the worshippers dismissed his talk about the sacredness of marriage as mere *cant. Cant* is a form of hypocrisy: those who can, pray; those who can't, pretend.

Word List 8 capricious–choreography

capricious ADJ. unpredictable; fickle. The storm was *capricious:* it changed course constantly. Jill was *capricious,* too: she changed boyfriends almost as often as she changed clothes.

caption N. title; chapter heading; text under illustration. The capricious *captions* that accompany "The Far Side" cartoons are almost as funny as the pictures. also V.

• **captivate** V. charm; fascinate. Although he was predisposed to dislike Elizabeth, Darcy found himself *captivated* by her charm and wit.

cardiac ADJ. pertaining to the heart. Since no one in his family had ever had *cardiac* problems, Bill was unconcerned about the possibility of a heart attack.

• **caricature** N. exaggerated picture or description; distortion. The cartoonist's *caricature* of Senator Foghorn grossly exaggerated the size of the senator's nose and ears. also V.

carping ADJ. finding fault. A *carping* critic is a nit-picker, someone who loves to point out flaws. carp, V.

caste N. one of the hereditary classes in Hindu society; social stratification; prestige. She bore a mark on her forehead signifying she was a Brahmin, a member of the highest *caste*.

castigation V. punishment, severe criticism. Sensitive to even mild criticism, Virginia Woolf could not bear the *castigation* that she met in certain reviews. castigate, V.

casualty N. serious or fatal accident. The number of *casualties* on this holiday weekend was high.

catacomb N. subterranean cemetery; underground passageway. Londoners refer to their *catacomb*-like subway system as the Underground.

catastrophe N. calamity; disaster. The 1906 San Francisco earthquake was a *catastrophe* that destroyed most of the city.

caustic ADJ. burning; sarcastically biting. The critic's *caustic* review humiliated the actors, who resented his cutting remarks.

cede V. yield (title, territory) to; surrender formally. Eventually the descendants of England's Henry II were forced to *cede* their French territories to the King of France.

• **censor** N. inspector overseeing public morals; official who prevents publication of offensive material. Because certain passages in his novel *Ulysses* had been condemned by the *censor,* James Joyce was unable to publish the novel in England for many years.

censure V. blame; criticize. Though I don't blame Tony for leaving Tina, I do *censure* him for failing to pay child support.

cerebral ADJ. pertaining to the brain or intellect. The content of philosophical works is *cerebral* in nature and requires much thought.

cessation N. stopping. The airline workers threatened a *cessation* of all work if management failed to meet their demands. cease, V.

chafe V. warm by rubbing; make sore (by rubbing). Chilled, he *chafed* his hands before the fire. The collar of his school uniform *chafed* Tom's neck, but not as much the school's strict rules *chafed* his spirit. also N.

chaff N. husks and stems left over when grain has been threshed; worthless, leftover by-products. When you separate the wheat from the *chaff,* be sure you throw out the *chaff.*

chagrin N. vexation (caused by humiliation or injured pride); disappointment. Embarrassed by his parents' shabby, working-class appearance, Doug felt their visit to his school would bring him nothing but *chagrin.* Someone filled with *chagrin* doesn't grin: he's too mortified.

chameleon N. lizard that changes color in different situations. Like the *chameleon,* the candidate assumed the political thinking of every group he met.

chaotic ADJ. in utter disorder. He tried to bring order into the *chaotic* state of affairs. chaos, N.

charlatan N. quack; pretender to knowledge. When they realized that the Wizard didn't know how to get them back to Kansas, Dorothy and her friends were sure they'd been duped by a *charlatan.*

chary ADJ. cautious; sparing or restrained about giving. A prudent, thrifty, New Englander, DeWitt was as *chary* of investing money in junk bonds as he was *chary* of paying people unnecessary compliments.

chasm N. abyss. They could not see the bottom of the *chasm.*

chastise V. punish physically; scold verbally. "Spare the rod and spoil the child," Miss Watson said, grabbing her birch wand and proceeding to *chastise* poor Huck thoroughly.

chauvinist N. blindly devoted patriot. *Chauvinists* cannot recognize any faults in their country, no matter how flagrant they may be. Likewise, a male *chauvinist* cannot recognize how biased he is in favor of his own sex, no matter how flagrant that may be.

chicanery N. trickery; deception. Those sneaky lawyers misrepresented what occurred, made up all sorts of implausible alternative scenarios to confuse the jurors, and in general depended on *chicanery* to win the case.

choreography N. art of representing dances in written symbols; arrangement of dances. Merce Cunningham has begun to use a computer in designing *choreography:* a software program allows him to compose arrangements of possible moves and to view them immediately onscreen.

Word List 9 chronic–compute

chronic ADJ. long established (as a disease). The doctors were finally able to attribute his *chronic* headaches and nausea to traces of formaldehyde gas in his apartment.

• **chronicle** V. report; record (in chronological order). The gossip columnist was paid to *chronicle* the latest escapades of the socially prominent celebrities. also N.

circumscribe V. limit; confine. Although I do not wish to *circumscribe* your activities, I must insist that you complete this assignment before you start anything else.

• **circumspect** ADJ. prudent; cautious. Investigating before acting, she tried always to be *circumspect.*

• **cite** V. quote; refer to; commend. Because Virginia could *cite* hundreds of biblical passages from memory, her pastor *cited* her for her studiousness. citation, N.

clairvoyant ADJ., N. having foresight; fortune-teller. Cassandra's *clairvoyant* warning was not heeded by the Trojans. clairvoyance, N.

clandestine ADJ. secret. After avoiding their chaperone, the lovers had a *clandestine* meeting.

claustrophobia N. fear of being shut in. If Santa Claus got stuck in a chimney and couldn't get out, would he wind up suffering from *claustrophobia*?

clemency N. disposition to be lenient; mildness, as of the weather. The lawyer was pleased when the case was sent to Judge Smith's chambers because Smith was noted for her *clemency* toward first offenders. We decided to eat dinner in the garden to enjoy the unexpected *clemency* of the weather.

• **cliché** N. phrase dulled in meaning by repetition. High school compositions are often marred by such *clichés* as "strong as an ox."

climactic ADJ. relating to the highest point. When Jack reached the *climactic* portions of the book, he could not stop reading. climax, N.

clique N. small exclusive group. Fitzgerald wished that he belonged to the *clique* of popular athletes and big men on campus who seemed to run Princeton's social life.

• **coalesce** V. combine; fuse. The brooks *coalesced* into one large river. When minor political parties *coalesce,* their *coalescence* may create a major coalition.

coalition N. association; union. Jesse Jackson's Rainbow *Coalition* brought together people of many different races and creeds.

cogitate V. think over. *Cogitate* on this problem; the solution will come.

coincidence N. two or more things occurring at the same time by chance. Was it just a *coincidence* that John and she had chanced to meet at the market for three days running, or was he deliberately trying to seek her out? coincident, ADJ.

• **collaborate** V. work together. Two writers *collaborated* in preparing this book.

colossal ADJ. huge. Radio City Music Hall has a *colossal* stage.

collusion N. conspiring in a fraudulent scheme. The swindlers were found guilty of *collusion.* collude, V.

comely ADJ. attractive; agreeable. I would rather have a poor but *comely* wife than a rich and homely one.

commiserate V. feel or express pity or sympathy for. Her friends *commiserated* with the widow.

compact ADJ. tightly packed; firm; brief. His short, *compact* body was better suited to wrestling than to basketball.

compact N. agreement; contract. The signers of the Mayflower *Compact* were establishing a form of government.

comparable ADJ. similar. People whose jobs are *comparable* in difficulty should receive *comparable* pay.

compatible ADJ. harmonious; in harmony with. They were *compatible* neighbors, never quarreling over unimportant matters. compatibility, N.

compile V. assemble; gather; accumulate. We planned to *compile* a list of the words most frequently used on SAT examinations. compilation, N.

complacent ADJ. self-satisfied; smug. Feeling *complacent* about his latest victories, he looked smugly at the row of trophies on his mantelpiece. complacency, N.

complement V. complete; make perfect. The waiter recommended a glass of port to *complement* the cheese. also N.

• **compliance** N. readiness to yield; conformity in fulfilling requirements. Bill was so bullheaded that we never expected his easy *compliance* to our requests. As an architect, however, Bill recognized that his design for the new school had to be in *compliance* with the local building code.

• **component** N. element; ingredient. I wish all the *components* of my stereo system were working at the same time.

• **composure** N. mental calmness. Even the latest work crisis failed to shake her *composure*.

compress V. close; squeeze; contract. She *compressed* the package under her arm.

• **compromise** V. adjust or settle by making mutual concessions; endanger the interests or reputation of. Sometimes the presence of a neutral third party can help adversaries *compromise* their differences. Unfortunately, your presence at the scene of the dispute *compromises* our claim to neutrality in this matter. also N.

compute V. reckon; calculate. He failed to *compute* the interest; so his bank balance was not accurate.

Word List 10 concerted–contention

concerted ADJ. mutually agreed on; done together. All the Girl Scouts made a *concerted* effort to raise funds for their annual outing. When the movie star appeared, his fans let out a *concerted* sigh.

concise ADJ. brief but comprehensive. The instructions were *concise* and to the point: they included every necessary detail and not one word more. Precision indicates exactness; *concision* indicates compactness. To achieve *conciseness,* cut out unnecessary words.

concoct V. prepare by combining; make up in concert. How did the inventive chef ever *concoct* such a strange dish? concoction, N.

concurrent ADJ. happening at the same time. In America, the colonists were resisting the demands of the mother country; at the *concurrent* moment in France, the middle class was sowing the seeds of rebellion. The two revolutionary movements took place *concurrently.*

condescend V. act conscious of descending to a lower level; patronize. Though Jill was a star softball player in college, when she played a pickup game at the local park she never *condescended* to her teammates or acted as if she thought herself superior to them. condescension. N.

condole V. express sympathetic sorrow. Bill's friends gathered to *condole* with him over his loss. Those unable to attend the funeral sent letters of *condolence.*

• **condone** V. overlook voluntarily; forgive. Unlike the frail widow, who indulged her only son and *condoned* his mischievous behavior, the boy's stern uncle did nothing but scold.

confine V. shut in; restrict. The terrorists had *confined* their prisoner in a small room. However, they had not chained him to the wall or done anything else to *confine* his movements further. confinement, N.

• **confirm** V. corroborate; verify; support. I have several witnesses who will *confirm* my account of what happened.

conflagration N. great fire. In the *conflagration* that followed the 1906 earthquake, much of San Francisco burned to the ground.

• **conformity** N. agreement or compliance; actions in agreement with prevailing social customs. In *conformity* with the bylaws of the Country Dance and Song Society, I am submitting a petition nominating Susan Murrow as president of the society. Because Kate had always been a rebellious child, we were surprised by her *conformity* to the standards of behavior prevalent at her new school.

• **confront** V. face someone or something; encounter, often in a hostile way. Fearing his wife's hot temper, Stanley was reluctant to *confront* her about her skyrocketing credit card bills.

congeal V. freeze; coagulate. His blood *congealed* in his veins as he saw the dreaded monster rush toward him.

• **congenial** ADJ. pleasant; friendly. My father loved to go out for a meal with *congenial* companions.

connotation N. suggested or implied meaning of an expression. Foreigners frequently are unaware of the *connotations* of the words they use.

consensus N. general agreement. Every time the garden club members had nearly reached a *consensus* about what to plant, Mistress Mary, quite contrary, disagreed.

consequence N. self-importance; pomposity. Convinced of his own importance, the actor strutted about the dressing room with such an air of *consequence* that it was hard for his valet to keep a straight face. consequential, ADJ.

• **consistency** N. harmony of parts; dependability; uniformity; degree of thickness. Holmes judged puddings and explanations on their *consistency*: he liked his puddings without lumps and his explanations without contradictions or improbabilities. consistent, ADJ.

console V. lessen sadness or disappointment; give comfort. When her father died, Marius did his best to *console* Cosette.

• **consolidation** N. unification; process of becoming firmer or stronger. The recent *consolidation* of several small airlines into one major company has left observers of the industry wondering whether room still exists for the "little guy" in aviation. consolidate, V.

conspicuous ADJ. easily seen; noticeable; striking. Janet was *conspicuous* both for her red hair and for her height.

constituent N. resident of a district represented by an elected official. The congressman received hundreds of letters from angry *constituents* after the Equal Rights Amendment failed to pass.

constraint N. compulsion; repression of feelings. There was a feeling of *constraint* in the room because no one dared to criticize the speaker. constrain, V.

contagion N. infection. Fearing *contagion,* the health authorities took great steps to prevent the spread of the disease.

contempt N. scorn; disdain. The heavyweight boxer looked on ordinary people with *contempt,* scorning them as weaklings who couldn't hurt a fly. We thought it was *contemptible* of him to be *contemptuous* of people for being weak.

contention N. claim; thesis. It is our *contention* that, if you follow our tactics, you will boost your score on the PSAT. contend, V.

Word List 11 contentious–curtail

• **contentious** ADJ. quarrelsome. Disagreeing violently with the referees' ruling, the coach became so *contentious* that they threw him out of the game.

context N. writings preceding and following the passage quoted. Because these lines are taken out of *context,* they do not convey the message the author intended.

contingent ADJ. dependent on; conditional. Cher's father informed her that any increase in her allowance was *contingent* on the quality of her final grades. contingency, N.

contingent N. group that makes up part of a gathering. The New York *contingent* of delegates at the Democratic National Convention was a boisterous, sometimes rowdy lot.

contortion N. twisting; distortion. Watching the *contortions* of the gymnast as he twisted and heaved his body from one side to the other of the pommel horse, we were awed by his strength and flexibility.

contrite ADJ. penitent. Her *contrite* tears did not influence the judge when he imposed sentence.

• **convention** N. social or moral custom; established practice. Flying in the face of *convention,* George Sand shocked society by taking lovers and wearing men's clothes.

converge V. approach; tend to meet; come together. African-American men from all over the United States *converged* on Washington to take part in the historic Million Man march.

convert N. one who has adopted a different religion or opinion. On his trip to Japan, though the president spoke at length about the merits of American automobiles, he made few *converts* to his beliefs. also V.

conviction N. judgment that someone is guilty of a crime; strongly held belief. Even her *conviction* for murder did not shake Peter's *conviction* that Harriet was innocent of the crime.

• **convoluted** ADJ. complex and involved; intricate; winding; coiled. Talk about twisted! The new tax regulations are so *convoluted* that even my accountant can't unravel their mysteries.

cordial ADJ. gracious; heartfelt. Our hosts greeted us at the airport with a *cordial* welcome and a hearty hug.

corroborate V. confirm; support. Though Huck was quite willing to *corroborate* Tom's story, Aunt Polly knew better than to believe either of them.

• **corrosion** N. destruction by chemical action. The *corrosion* of the girders supporting the bridge took place so gradually that no one suspected any danger until the bridge suddenly collapsed. corrode, V.

cosmic ADJ. pertaining to the universe; vast. *Cosmic* rays derive their name from the fact that they bombard the earth's atmosphere from outer space. cosmos, N.

cosmopolitan ADJ. sophisticated. Her years in the capital had transformed her into a *cosmopolitan* young woman highly aware of international affairs.

countenance V. approve; tolerate. He refused to *countenance* such rude behavior on their part.

covert ADJ. secret; hidden; implied. Investigations of the Central Intelligence Agency and other secret service networks reveal that such *covert* operations can get out of control.

covetous ADJ. avaricious; eagerly desirous of. The child was *covetous* by nature and wanted to take the toys belonging to his classmates. covet, V.

cower V. shrink quivering, as from fear. The frightened child *cowered* in the corner of the room.

crass ADJ. very unrefined; grossly insensible. The film critic deplored the *crass* commercialism of moviemakers who abandon artistic standards in order to make a quick buck.

credibility N. believability. Because the candidate had made some pretty unbelievable promises, we began to question the *credibility* of everything she said.

credulity N. belief on slight evidence; gullibility; naïveté. Con artists take advantage of the *credulity* of inexperienced investors to swindle them out of their savings. credulous, ADJ.

criterion N. standard used in judging. What *criterion* did you use when you selected this essay as the prizewinner? criteria, Pl.

cryptic ADJ. mysterious; hidden; secret. Thoroughly baffled by Holmes's *cryptic* remarks, Watson wondered whether Holmes was intentionally concealing his thoughts about the crime.

culinary ADJ. relating to cooking. Many chefs attribute their *culinary* skill to the wise use of spices.

cull V. pick out; reject. Every month the farmer *culls* the nonlaying hens from his flock and sells them to the local butcher. also N.

culmination N. attainment of highest point. Her inauguration as president of the United States marked the *culmination* of her political career. culminate, V.

culpable ADJ. deserving blame. Corrupt politicians who condone the illegal activities of gamblers are equally *culpable.*

cumbersome ADJ. heavy; hard to manage. He was burdened down with *cumbersome* parcels.

curb V. restrain. The overly generous philanthropist had to *curb* his beneficent impulses before he gave away all his money and left himself with nothing.

cursory ADJ. casual; hastily done. Because a *cursory* examination of the ruins indicates the possibility of arson, we believe the insurance agency should undertake a more extensive investigation of the fire's cause.

• **curtail** V. shorten; reduce. When Elton asked Cher for a date, she said she was really sorry she couldn't go out with him, but her dad had ordered her to *curtail* her social life.

Word List 12 cynical–demolish

cynical ADJ. skeptical or distrustful of human motives. *Cynical* from birth, Sidney was suspicious whenever anyone give him a gift "with no strings attached." cynic, N.

dabble V. work at in a nonserious fashion; splash around. The amateur painter *dabbled* at art, but seldom produced a finished piece. The children *dabbled* their hands in the bird bath, splashing one another gleefully.

daunt V. intimidate; frighten. "Boast all you like of your prowess. Mere words cannot *daunt* me," the *dauntless* hero answered the villain.

• **dawdle** V. loiter; waste time. At the mall, Mother grew impatient with Jo and Amy because they tended to *dawdle* as they went from store to store.

• **dearth** N. scarcity. The *dearth* of skilled labor compelled the employers to open trade schools.

debase V. reduce in quality or value; lower in esteem; degrade. In *The King and I,* Anna refuses to kneel down and prostrate herself before the king, for she feels that to do so would *debase* her position, and she will not submit to such *debasement.*

• **debilitate** V. weaken; enfeeble. Michael's severe bout of the flu *debilitated* him so much that he was too tired to go to work for a week.

decadence N. decay or decline, especially moral; self-indulgence. We named our best-selling ice cream flavor "chocolate *decadence*" because only truly self-indulgent people would treat themselves to something so calorific and cholesterol laden.

decipher V. decode. I could not *decipher* the doctor's handwriting.

• **decorous** ADJ. proper. Prudence's *decorous* behavior was praised by her teachers, who wished they had a classroom full of such polite and proper little girls. decorum, N.

decoy N. lure or bait. The wild ducks were not fooled by the *decoy.* also V.

• **decry** V. express strong disapproval of; disparage. The founder of the Children's Defense Fund, Marian Wright Edelman, strongly *decries* the lack of financial and moral support for children in America today.

deducible ADJ. derived by reasoning. If we accept your premise, your conclusions are easily *deducible.*

deface V. mar; disfigure. If you *deface* a library book, you will have to pay a hefty fine.

• **defamation** N. harming a person's reputation. *Defamation* of character may result in a slander suit. If rival candidates persist in *defaming* one another, the voters may conclude that all politicians are crooks.

defeatist ADJ. attitude of one who is ready to accept defeat as a natural outcome. If you maintain your *defeatist* attitude, you will never succeed. also N.

• **deference** N. courteous regard for another's wish. In *deference* to the minister's request, please do not take photographs during the wedding service.

• **defiance** N. opposition; willingness to resist. In learning to read and write in *defiance* of his master's orders, Frederick Douglass showed exceptional courage. defy, V.

definitive ADJ. final; complete. Carl Sandburg's *Abraham Lincoln* may be regarded as the *definitive* work on the life of the Great Emancipator.

defrock V. strip a priest or minister of church authority. We knew the minister had violated church regulations, but we had not realized his offense was serious enough for people to seek to *defrock* him.

defunct ADJ. dead; no longer in use or existence. The lawyers sought to examine the books of the *defunct* corporation.

• **degenerate** V. become worse; deteriorate. As the fight dragged on, the champion's style *degenerated* until he could barely keep on his feet.

deign V. condescend; stoop. The celebrated fashion designer would not *deign* to speak to a mere seamstress; his overburdened assistant had to convey the master's wishes to the lowly workers assembling his great designs.

delete V. erase; strike out. Less is more: if you *delete* this paragraph, the composition will have more appeal.

deleterious ADJ. harmful. If you believe that smoking is *deleterious* to your health (and the surgeon general certainly does), then quit!

delineate V. portray; depict; sketch. Using only a few descriptive phrases, Jane Austen *delineates* the character of Mr. Collins so well that we can predict his every move. delineation, N.

delirium N. mental disorder marked by confusion. In his *delirium,* the drunkard saw pink panthers and talking pigs. Perhaps he wasn't *delirious;* he might just have wandered into a movie.

delusion N. false belief; hallucination. Don suffers from *delusions* of grandeur: he thinks he's a world-famous author when he's published just one paperback book.

• **demean** V. degrade; humiliate. Standing on his dignity, he refused to *demean* himself by replying to the offensive letter. If you truly believed in the dignity of labor, you would not think it would *demean* you to work as a janitor.

demeanor N. behavior; bearing. His sober *demeanor* quieted the noisy revelers.

demolish V. destroy; tear down. Before building a new hotel along the waterfront, the construction company had to *demolish* several rundown warehouses on that site. demolition, N.

Word List 13 demur–dichotomy

demur V. object (because of doubts, scruples); hesitate. When offered a post on the board of directors, David *demurred*: he had doubts about taking on the job because he was unsure he could handle it in addition to his other responsibilities.

demure ADJ. grave; serious; coy. She was *demure* and reserved, a nice modest girl whom any young man would be proud to take home to his mother.

• **denounce** V. condemn; criticize. The reform candidate *denounced* the corrupt city officials for having betrayed the public's trust. denunciation, N.

deny V. contradict; refuse. Do you *deny* his story, or do you support what he says? How could Pat *deny* the truth of the accusation that he'd been swiping the Oreos when he'd been caught with his hand in the cookie jar? denial, N.

• **depict** V. portray. In this sensational exposé, the author *depicts* John Lennon as a drug-crazed neurotic. Do you question the accuracy of this *depiction* of Lennon?

• **deplete** V. reduce; exhaust. We must wait until we *deplete* our present inventory before we order replacements.

• **deplore** V. regret strongly; express grief over. Although Ann Landers *deplored* the disintegration of the modern family, she recognized that not every marriage could be saved.

deprecate V. express disapproval of; protest against. A firm believer in old-fashioned courtesy, Miss Post *deprecated* the unfortunate modern tendency to address new acquaintances by their first names. deprecatory, ADJ.

depreciate V. lessen in value. If you neglect this property, it will *depreciate.*

deprivation N. loss. In prison she faced the sudden *deprivation* of rights she had taken for granted: the right to stay up late reading a book, the right to privacy, the right to make a phone call to a friend.

derelict ADJ. abandoned; negligent. The *derelict* craft was a menace to navigation. Whoever abandoned it in mid harbor was *derelict* in living up to his or her responsibilities as a boat owner. dereliction, N.

• **derision** N. ridicule; mockery. Greeting his pretentious dialogue with *derision,* the critics refused to consider his play seriously. deride, V.

• **derivative** ADJ. unoriginal; derived from another source. Although her early poetry was clearly *derivative* in nature, the critics felt she had promise and eventually would find her own voice.

desecrate V. profane; violate the sanctity of. The soldiers *desecrated* the temple, shattering the altar and trampling the holy objects underfoot.

designation N. identifying name; appointment to a position or office. For years the president's home had no proper *designation*; eventually it was called the White House. Given Gary's background in accounting, his *designation* as treasurer came as no surprise to his fellow board members.

despise V. look on with scorn; regard as worthless or distasteful. Mr. Bond, I *despise* spies; I look down on them as mean, *despicable,* honorless men, whom I would cheerfully wipe from the face of the earth.

despondent ADJ. depressed; gloomy. To the dismay of his parents, William became so seriously *despondent* after he broke up with Jan that they despaired of finding a cure for his gloom. despondency, N.

desultory ADJ. aimless; haphazard; digressing at random. In prison Malcolm X set himself the task of reading straight through the dictionary; to him, reading was purposeful, not *desultory.*

• **detached** ADJ. emotionally removed; calm and objective; indifferent. A psychoanalyst must maintain a *detached* point of view and stay uninvolved with her patients' personal lives. detachment, N. (secondary meaning)

determination N. resolve; measurement or calculation; decision. Nothing could shake his *determination* that his children would get the best education that money could buy. Thanks to my pocket calculator, my *determination* of the answer to the problem took only seconds of my time.

• **deterrent** N. something that discourages; hindrance. Does the threat of capital punishment serve as a *deterrent* to potential killers? deter, V.

detrimental ADJ. harmful; damaging. The candidate's acceptance of major financial contributions from a well-known racist ultimately proved *detrimental* to his campaign, for he lost the backing of many of his early grassroots supporters. detriment, N.

deviate V. turn away from (a principle, norm); depart; diverge. Richard never *deviated* from his daily routine: every day he set off for work at eight o'clock, had his sack lunch (peanut butter on whole wheat) at 12:15, and headed home at the stroke of five.

devious ADJ. roundabout; erratic; not straightforward. The Joker's plan was so *devious* that it was only with great difficulty we could follow its shifts and dodges.

dexterous ADJ. skillful. The magician was so *dexterous* that we could not follow him as he performed his tricks.

diagnosis N. art of identifying a disease; analysis of a condition. In medical school Margaret developed her skill at *diagnosis,* learning how to read volumes from a rapid pulse or a hacking cough. diagnose, V.; diagnostic, ADJ.

dichotomy N. split; branching into two parts (especially contradictory ones). Willie didn't know how to resolve the *dichotomy* between his ambition to go to college and his childhood longing to run away to join the circus. Then he heard about Ringling Brothers Circus College, and he knew he'd found the perfect school.

Word List 14 didactic–disparate

• **didactic** ADJ. teaching; instructional. Pope's lengthy poem *An Essay on Man* is too *didactic* for my taste: I dislike it when poets turn preachy and moralize.

diehard N. unyielding opponent (to a measure, position, etc.). Even the popular new president could not win support for his universal health care plan from the *diehards* in his party.

• **diffident** ADJ. shy; lacking confidence; reserved. Can a naturally *diffident* person become a fast-talking, successful used car salesman?

diffuse ADJ. wordy; rambling; spread out (like a gas). If you pay authors by the word, you tempt them to produce *diffuse* manuscripts rather then brief ones. diffusion, N.

• **digression** N. wandering away from the subject. Nobody minded when Professor Renoir's lectures wandered away from their official theme; his *digressions* were always more fascinating than the topic of the day. digress, V.

dilemma N. problem; choice of two unsatisfactory alternatives. In this *dilemma,* he knew no one to whom he could turn for advice.

dilettante N. aimless follower of the arts; amateur; dabbler. He was not serious in his painting; he was rather a *dilettante.*

diligence N. steadiness of effort; persistent hard work. Her employers were greatly impressed by her *diligence* and offered her a partnership in the firm. diligent, ADJ.

dilute V. make less concentrated; reduce in strength. She preferred her coffee *diluted* with milk.

diminutive ADJ. small in size. Looking at the tiny gymnast, we were amazed that anyone so *diminutive* could perform with such power.

din N. continued loud noise. The *din* of the jackhammers outside the classroom window drowned out the lecturer's voice. also V.

dirge N. lament with music. The funeral *dirge* stirred us to tears.

disavowal N. denial; disclaiming. His *disavowal* of his part in the conspiracy was not believed by the jury. disavow, V.

• **discernible** ADJ. distinguishable; perceivable. The ships in the harbor were not *discernible* in the fog.

discerning ADJ. mentally quick and observant; having insight. Though no genius, the star was sufficiently *discerning* to tell her true friends from the countless phonies who flattered her.

• **disclaimer** N. denial of a legal claim or right; disavowal. Though reporter Joe Klein issued a *disclaimer* stating that he was *not* Anonymous, the author of *Primary Colors,* eventually he admitted that he had written the controversial novel. disclaim, V.

• **disclose** V. reveal. Although competitors offered him bribes, he refused to *disclose* any information about his company's forthcoming product. disclosure, N.

disconcert V. confuse; upset; embarrass. The lawyer was *disconcerted* by the evidence produced by her adversary.

• **discord** N. lack of harmony; conflict; Watching Tweedledum battle Tweedledee, Alice wondered what had caused this pointless *discord.*

discount V. discredit; reduce in price. Be prepared to *discount* what he has to say about his ex-wife.

• **discrepancy** N. lack of consistency; contradiction; difference. "Observe, Watson, the significant *discrepancies* between Sir Percy's original description of the crime and his most recent testimony. What do these contradictions suggest?"

discriminating ADJ. able to see differences; prejudiced. A superb interpreter of Picasso, she was sufficiently *discriminating* to judge the most complex works of modern art. [secondary meaning] discrimination, N.

discursive ADJ. digressing; rambling. As the lecturer wandered from topic to topic, we wondered what if any point there was to his *discursive* remarks.

disdain V. view with scorn or contempt. In the film *Funny Face,* the bookish heroine *disdained* fashion models for their lack of intellectual interests. also N.

disembark V. go ashore; unload cargo from a ship. Before the passengers could *disembark,* they had to pick up their passports from the ship's purser.

• **disgruntled** ADJ. discontented; sulky and dissatisfied. The numerous delays left the passengers feeling *disgruntled.* disgruntle, V.

disheveled ADJ. untidy. Your *disheveled* appearance will hurt your chances in this interview.

• **disinterested** ADJ. unprejudiced. Given the judge's political ambitions and the lawyers' financial interest in the case, the only *disinterested* person in the courtroom may have been the court reporter.

dismay V. discourage; frighten. The huge amount of work she had left to do *dismayed* her. also N.

• **dismiss** V. put away from consideration; reject. Believing in John's love for her, she *dismissed* the notion that he might be unfaithful. [secondary meaning]

• **disparage** V. belittle. A doting mother, Emma was more likely to praise her son's crude attempts at art than to *disparage* them.

• **disparate** ADJ. basically different; unrelated. Unfortunately, Tony and Tina have *disparate* notions of marriage: Tony sees it as a carefree extended love affair, while Tina sees it as a solemn commitment to build a family and a home.

Word List 15 disparity–duplicity

disparity N. difference; condition of inequality. Their *disparity* in rank made no difference at all to the prince and Cinderella.

dispassionate ADJ. calm; impartial. Known in the company for his cool judgment, Bill could impartially examine the causes of a problem, giving a *dispassionate* analysis of what had gone wrong, and go on to suggest how to correct the mess.

• **dispatch** N. speediness; prompt execution; message sent with all due speed. Young Napoleon defeated the enemy with all possible *dispatch*; he then sent a *dispatch* to headquarters, informing his commander of the great victory. also V.

• **dispel** V. scatter; cause to vanish. The bright sunlight eventually *dispelled* the morning mist.

• **disperse** V. scatter. The police fired tear gas into the crowd to *disperse* the protesters.

disputatious ADJ. argumentative; fond of arguing. Convinced he knew more than his lawyers, Tom was a *disputatious* client, ready to argue about the best way to conduct the case.

dissemble V. disguise; pretend. Even though John tried to *dissemble* his motive for taking modern dance, we all knew he was there not to dance but to meet girls.

disseminate V. distribute; spread; scatter (like seeds). By their use of the Internet, propagandists have been able to *disseminate* their pet doctrines to new audiences around the globe.

• **dissent** V. disagree. In the recent Supreme Court decision, Justice Kennedy *dissented* from the majority opinion. also N.

dissertation N. formal essay. In order to earn a graduate degree from many of our universities, a candidate is frequently required to prepare a *dissertation* on some scholarly subject.

dissident ADJ. dissenting; rebellious. In the purge that followed the student demonstrations at Tiananmen Square, the government hunted down the *dissident* students and their supporters. also N.

• **dissipate** V. squander; waste; scatter. He is a fine artist, but we fear he may *dissipate* his gifts if he keeps wasting his time doodling on napkins.

dissuade V. persuade not to do; discourage. Since Tom could not *dissuade* Huck from running away from home, he decided to run away with him. dissuasion, N.

• **distinction** N. honor; contrast; discrimination. A holder of the Medal of Honor, George served with great *distinction* in World War II. He made a *distinction,* however, between World War II and Vietnam, which he considered an immoral conflict.

distort V. twist out of shape. It is difficult to believe the newspaper accounts of the riots because of the way some reports *distort* and exaggerate the actual events. distortion, N.

divergent ADJ. differing; deviating. Since graduating from medical school, the two doctors have taken *divergent* paths, the one going on to become a nationally prominent surgeon, the other dedicating himself to a small family practice in his hometown. divergence, N.

diverse ADJ. differing in some characteristics; various. The professor suggested *diverse* ways of approaching the assignment and recommended that we choose one of them. diversity, N.

diversion N. act of turning aside; pastime. After studying for several hours, he needed a *diversion* from work. divert, V.

• **divulge** V. reveal. No lover of gossip, Charlotte would never *divulge* anything that a friend told her in confidence.

• **docile** ADJ. obedient; easily managed. As *docile* as he seems today, that old lion was once a ferocious, snarling beast.

• **doctrine** N. teachings, in general; particular principle (religious, legal, etc.) taught. He was so committed to the *doctrines* of his faith that he was unable to evaluate them impartially.

document V. provide written evidence. She kept all the receipts from her business trip in order to *document* her expenses for the firm. also N.

• **dogmatic** ADJ. opinionated; arbitrary; doctrinal. We tried to discourage Doug from being so *dogmatic* but never could convince him that his opinions might be wrong.

dormant ADJ. sleeping; lethargic; latent. At fifty her long-*dormant* ambition to write flared up once more; within a year she had completed the first of her great historical novels.

doubtful ADJ. uncertain; undecided. From the outset, the outcome of the battle was *doubtful*: we had no certainty that we were going to win.

downcast ADJ. disheartened; sad. Cheerful and optimistic by nature, Beth was never *downcast* despite the difficulties she faced.

draconian ADJ. extremely severe. When the principal canceled the senior prom because some seniors had been late to school that week, we thought the *draconian* punishment was far too harsh for such a minor violation of the rules.

dregs N. sediment; worthless residue. David poured the wine carefully to avoid stirring up the *dregs.*

dross N. waste matter; worthless impurities. Many methods have been devised to separate the valuable metal from the *dross.*

ductile ADJ. malleable; flexible; pliable. Copper is an extremely *ductile* material: you can stretch it into the thinnest of wires, bend it, even wind it into loops.

duplicity N. double-dealing; hypocrisy. When Tanya learned that Mark had been two-timing her, she was furious at his *duplicity.*

Word List 16 duty–enhance

duty N. tax on imported or exported goods. Because he was too stingy to pay the *duty* on the watch he'd bought in Switzerland, Rex foolishly tried to smuggle it through Customs.

dwindle V. shrink; reduce. The food in the lifeboat gradually *dwindled* away to nothing.

ebb V. recede; lessen. Mrs. Dalloway sat on the beach and watched the tide *ebb.* also N.

ebullient ADJ. showing excitement; overflowing with enthusiasm. Her *ebullient* nature could not be repressed; she was always bubbling over with exuberance. ebullience, N.

eccentric ADJ. irregular; odd; whimsical; bizarre. The comet veered dangerously close to the earth in its *eccentric* orbit. eccentricity, N.

• **eclectic** ADJ. composed of elements drawn from disparate sources. His style of interior decoration was *eclectic:* bits and pieces of furnishings from widely divergent periods strikingly juxtaposed to create a unique decor. eclecticism, N.

• **eclipse** V. darken; extinguish; surpass. The new stock market high *eclipsed* the previous record set in 1995.

ecstasy N. rapture; joy; any overpowering emotion. When Allison received her long-hoped-for letter of acceptance from Harvard, she was in *ecstasy.* ecstatic, ADJ.

effervescence N. inner excitement or exuberance; bubbling from fermentation or carbonation. Nothing depressed Sue for long; her natural *effervescence* soon reasserted itself. Soda that loses its *effervescence* goes flat. effervescent, ADJ., effervesce, V.

effrontery N. insolent boldness. Lady Bracknell was shocked that Jack, a man of no rank or breeding, had possessed the *effrontery* to court the daughter of a noble family.

egotistical ADJ. excessively self-centered; self-important; conceited. Typical *egotistical* remark: "But enough of this chit-chat about you and your little problems. Let's talk about what's really important: *Me!*"

egregious ADJ. notorious; gross; shocking. She was an *egregious* liar; we all knew better than to believe a word she said.

• **elated** ADJ. overjoyed; in high spirits. Grinning from ear to ear, Carl Lewis was clearly *elated* by his ninth Olympic gold medal. elation, N.

• **elicit** V. draw out (by discussion); call forth. The camp counselor's humorous remarks finally *elicited* a smile from the shy new camper.

eloquence N. expressiveness; persuasive speech. The crowds were stirred by Martin Luther King's *eloquence.* eloquent, ADJ.

elucidate V. explain; enlighten. He was called upon to *elucidate* the disputed points in his article.

• **elusive** ADJ. evasive; baffling; hard to grasp. Trying to pin down exactly when the contractors would be done remodeling the house, Nancy was frustrated by their *elusive* replies. elude, V.

emanate V. issue forth. A strong odor of sulphur *emanated* from the spring.

emancipate V. set free. At first, the attempts of the abolitionists to *emancipate* the slaves were unpopular in New England as well as in the South.

• **embellish** V. adorn. We enjoyed my mother-in-law's stories about how she came here from Russia, in part because she *embellished* the bare facts of the journey with humorous anecdotes and vivid descriptive details.

embrace V. hug; adopt or espouse; accept readily; encircle; include. Clasping Maid Marian in his arms, Robin Hood *embraced* her lovingly. In joining the outlaws in Sherwood Forest, she had openly *embraced* their cause.

empathy N. ability to identify with another's feelings, ideas, etc. What made Ann such a fine counselor was her *empathy,* her ability to put herself in her client's place and feel his emotions as if they were her own. empathize, V.

empirical ADJ. based on experience. He distrusted hunches and intuitive flashes; he placed his reliance entirely on *empirical* data.

emulate V. imitate; rival. In a brief essay, describe a person you admire, someone whose virtues you would like to *emulate.*

encumber V. burden. Some people *encumber* themselves with too much luggage when they go for short trips.

• **endorse** V. approve; support. Everyone waited to see which one of the rival candidates for the city council the mayor would *endorse.* endorsement, N. (secondary meaning).

enduring ADJ. lasting; surviving. Keats believed in the *enduring* power of great art, which would outlast its creators' brief lives. endure, V.

energize V. invigorate; make forceful and active. Rather than exhausting Maggie, dancing *energized* her.

engage V. attract; hire; pledge oneself; confront. "Your case has *engaged* my interest, my lord," said Holmes. "You may *engage* my services."

engaging ADJ. charming; attractive. Everyone liked Nancy's pleasant manners and *engaging* personality.

engender V. cause; produce. To receive praise for real accomplishments *engenders* self-confidence in a child.

engross V. occupy fully. John was so *engrossed* in his studies that he did not hear his mother call.

• **enhance** V. increase; improve. You can *enhance* your chances of being admitted to the college of your choice by learning to write well; an excellent essay can *enhance* any application.

Word List 17 enigma–explicate

• **enigma** N. puzzle; mystery. "What *do* women want?" asked Dr. Sigmund Freud. Their behavior was an *enigma* to him.

enterprising ADJ. ready to undertake ambitious projects. An *enterprising* young man, Matt saw business opportunities on every side and was always eager to capitalize on them.

• **entice** V. lure; attract; tempt. She always tried to *entice* her baby brother into mischief.

• **enumerate** V. list; mention one by one. Huck hung his head in shame as Miss Watson *enumerated* his many flaws.

enunciate V. speak distinctly. Stop mumbling! How will people understand you if you do not *enunciate*?

• **ephemeral** ADJ. short-lived; fleeting. The mayfly is an *ephemeral* creature: its adult life lasts little more than a day.

epic N. long heroic poem, novel, or similar work of art. Kurosawa's film *Seven Samurai* is an *epic* portraying the struggle of seven warriors to destroy a band of robbers. also ADJ.

epilogue N. short speech at conclusion of dramatic work. The audience was so disappointed in the play that many did not remain to hear the *epilogue.*

equivocal ADJ. ambiguous; intentionally misleading. Rejecting the candidate's *equivocal* comments on tax reform, the reporters pressed him to state clearly where he stood on the issue. equivocate, V.

• **erode** V. eat away. The limestone was *eroded* by the dripping water until only a thin shell remained. erosion, N.

• **erratic** ADJ. odd; unpredictable. Investors become anxious when the stock market appears *erratic.*

• **erroneous** ADJ. mistaken; wrong. I thought my answer was correct, but it was *erroneous.*

eschew V. avoid. Hoping to present himself to his girlfriend as a totally reformed character, he tried to *eschew* all the vices, especially chewing tobacco and drinking bathtub gin.

• **esoteric** ADJ. hard to understand; known only to the chosen few. *New Yorker* short stories often included *esoteric* allusions to obscure people and events; the implication was, if you were in the in-crowd, you'd get the reference; if you came from Cleveland, you would not.

• **espouse** V. adopt; support. She was always ready to *espouse* a worthy cause.

• **esteem** V. respect; value; Jill *esteemed* Jack's taste in music, but she deplored his taste in clothes.

estranged ADJ. separated; alienated. The *estranged* wife sought a divorce. estrangement, N.

ethereal ADJ. light; heavenly; unusually refined. In Shakespeare's *The Tempest,* the spirit Ariel is an *ethereal* creature, too airy and unearthly for our mortal world.

euphemism N. mild expression used in place of an unpleasant one. Until recently, many American southerners avoided the word *bull* in polite speech, replacing it by a *euphemism,* such as *he-cow* or *male beast.*

euphonious ADJ. pleasing in sound. *Euphonious* even when spoken, the Italian language is particularly pleasing to the ear when sung. euphony, N.

evenhanded ADJ. impartial; fair. Do men and women receive *evenhanded* treatment from their teachers, or, as recent studies suggest, do teachers pay more attention to male students than to females?

eventuality N. possible occurrence. The government instituted new security procedures to prepare for the *eventuality* of a terrorist attack.

evocative ADJ. tending to call up (emotions, memories). Scent can be remarkably *evocative:* the aroma of pipe tobacco *evokes* the memory of my father; a whiff of talcum powder calls up images of my daughter as a child.

exacting ADJ. extremely demanding. Cleaning the ceiling of the Sistine Chapel was an *exacting* task, one that demanded extremely meticulous care on the part of the restorers. exaction, N.

• **excerpt** N. selected passage (written or musical). The cinematic equivalent of an *excerpt* from a novel is a clip from a film.

exculpate V. clear from blame. Though Sid came up with excuse after excuse to *exculpate* himself, Samantha still blamed him for his conduct.

execute V. put into effect; carry out; put to death. The prima ballerina *executed* the pirouette so badly that the infuriated choreographer was ready to tear out his hair. execution, N.

• **exemplary** ADJ. serving as a model; outstanding. At commencement the dean praised Ellen for her *exemplary* behavior as class president.

• **exonerate** V. acquit; exculpate. The defense team feverishly sought fresh evidence that might *exonerate* its client.

expansive ADJ. outgoing and sociable; broad and extensive; able to increase in size. Mr. Fezziwig was in an *expansive* humor, cheerfully urging his guests to join in the Christmas feast. Looking down on his *expansive* paunch, he sighed: if his belly *expanded* any further, his pants would need an *expansive* waistline.

expedient ADJ. suitable to achieve a particular end; practical; politic. A pragmatic politician, he was guided by what was *expedient* rather than by what was ethical. expediency, N.

• **expedite** V. hasten. Because we are on a tight schedule, we hope you will be able to *expedite* the delivery of our order. expeditious, ADJ.

explicate V. explain; interpret; clarify. Harry Levin *explicated* James Joyce's often bewildering novels with such clarity that even *Finnegan's Wake* seemed comprehensible to his students.

Word List 18 explicit–fleeting

explicit ADJ. totally clear; definite; outspoken. Don't just hint around that you're dissatisfied: be *explicit* about what's bugging you.

• **exploit** N. deed or action, particularly a brave deed. Raoul Wallenberg was noted for his *exploits* in rescuing Jews from Hitler's forces.

exploit V. make use of, sometimes unjustly. Cesar Chavez fought attempts to *exploit* migrant farmworkers in California. exploitation, N.

expunge V. wipe out; remove; destroy. If you hit the "Delete" key by mistake, you can accidentally *expunge* an entire block of text.

expurgate V. clean; remove offensive parts of a book. The editors felt that certain passages in the book had to be *expurgated* before it could be used in the classroom.

extraneous ADJ. not essential; superfluous. No wonder Ted can't think straight! His mind is so cluttered up with *extraneous* trivia, he can't concentrate on the essentials.

extrapolate V. infer; project from known data into the unknown; make a conjecture. On the basis of what they could *extrapolate* from the results of the primaries on Super Tuesday, the networks predicted that John McCain would be the Republican candidate for the presidency.

extricate V. free; disentangle. The fox could not *extricate* itself from the trap.

exuberant ADJ. joyfully enthusiastic; flamboyant; lavish; abundant. I was bowled over by Amy's *exuberant* welcome. What an enthusiastic greeting!

fabricate V. build; lie. If we *fabricate* the buildings in this project out of standardized sections, we can reduce construction cost considerably. Because of

Jack's tendency to *fabricate,* Jill had trouble believing a word he said.

facile ADJ. easily accomplished; ready or fluent; superficial. Words came easily to Jonathan: he was a *facile* speaker and prided himself on being ready to make a speech at a moment's notice.

• **facilitate** V. help bring about; make less difficult. Rest and proper nourishment should *facilitate* the patient's recovery.

• **fallacious** ADJ. false; misleading. Paradoxically, *fallacious* reasoning does not always yield erroneous results: even though your logic may be faulty, the answer you get may nevertheless be correct. fallacy, N.

fallible ADJ. liable to err. I know I am *fallible,* but I feel confident that I am right this time.

• **farce** N. broad comedy; mockery. Nothing went right; the entire interview degenerated into a *farce.* farcical, ADJ.

• **fastidious** ADJ. difficult to please; squeamish. Bobby was such a *fastidious* eater that he would eat a sandwich only if his mother first cut off every scrap of crust.

• **fawning** ADJ. seeking favor by cringing and flattering; obsequious. "Stop crawling around like a boot-licker, Uriah! I can't stand your flattery and *fawning* ways." fawn, V.

• **feasible** ADJ. practical. Was it *feasible* to build a new stadium for the Yankees on New York's West Side? Without additional funding, the project was clearly unrealistic.

feint N. trick; shift; sham blow. Fooled by his opponent's *feint,* the boxer unwisely dropped his guard. also V.

ferment N. agitation; commotion. With the breakup of the Soviet Union, much of Eastern Europe was in a state of *ferment.*

• **fervor** N. glowing ardor; intensity of feeling. At the protest rally, the students cheered the strikers and booed the dean with equal *fervor.* fervent, fervid, ADJ.

fester V. provoke keen irritation or resentment. Joe's insult *festered* in Anne's mind for days and made her too angry to speak to him.

fetid ADJ. having a foul, disgusting odor. Change the kitty litter in the cat box right now! No self-respecting cat would use a litter box with such a *fetid* smell.

fetter V. shackle. The prisoner was *fettered* to the wall.

fiasco N. total failure. Tanya's attempt to look sophisticated by smoking was a *fiasco:* she lit the wrong end of the cigarette, choked when she tried to inhale, and burned a hole in her boyfriend's couch.

fiery ADJ. easily provoked; passionate; burning. By reputation, redheads have *fiery* tempers; the least little thing can cause them to explode.

finesse N. delicate skill. The *finesse* and adroitness with which the surgeon wielded her scalpel impressed the observers in the operating theater.

finite ADJ. having an end; limited. Though Bill really wanted to win the pie-eating contest, the capacity of his stomach was *finite,* and he had to call it quits after eating only seven cherry pies.

firebrand N. hothead; troublemaker. The police tried to keep track of all the local *firebrands* when the president came to town.

fissure N. crevice. The mountain climbers secured footholds in tiny *fissures* in the rock.

fitful ADJ. spasmodic; intermittent. After several *fitful* attempts, he decided to postpone the start of the project until he felt more energetic.

fleeting ADJ. transitory; vanishing quickly. The glory of a New England autumn is *fleeting*: the first gust of wind strips the trees of their colorful leaves.

Word List 19 flippant–garble

• **flippant** ADJ. lacking proper seriousness. When Mark told Mona he loved her, she dismissed his earnest declaration with a *flippant* "Oh, you say that to all the girls!" flippancy, N.

flout V. reject; mock. The headstrong youth *flouted* all authority; he refused to be curbed.

fluctuate V. waver; shift. The water pressure in our shower *fluctuates* wildly; you start rinsing yourself off with a trickle, and, two minutes later, a blast of water nearly knocks you down.

fluency N. smoothness of speech. He spoke French with *fluency* and ease.

foible N. weakness; slight fault. We can overlook the *foibles* of our friends; no one is perfect.

foliage N. masses of leaves. Every autumn before the leaves fell, he promised himself he would drive through New England to admire the colorful fall *foliage.*

forbearance N. patience. We must use *forbearance* in dealing with him because he is still weak from his illness.

foreboding N. premonition of evil. Suspecting no conspiracies against him, Caesar gently ridiculed his wife's *forebodings* about the ides of March.

foreshadow V. give an indication beforehand; portend; prefigure. In retrospect, political analysts realized that Yeltsin's defiance of the attempted coup *foreshadowed* his emergence as the dominant figure of the new Russian republic.

foresight N. ability to foresee future happenings; careful provision for the future. A shrewd investor, she had the *foresight* to buy land just before the current real estate boom.

forestall V. prevent by taking action in advance. By setting up a prenuptial agreement, the prospective bride and groom hoped to *forestall* any potential arguments about money in the event of a divorce.

forfeit V. lose; surrender. Convicted murderers *forfeit* the right to inherit anything from their victims; the law does not allow them to benefit financially from their crimes.

forgo V. give up; do without. Determined to lose weight over the summer, Michelle decided to *forgo* dessert until she could fit into a size eight again.

formidable ADJ. inspiring fear or apprehension; difficult; awe inspiring. In the film *Meet the Parents,* the hero is understandably nervous about meeting his fiancée's father, a *formidable* CIA agent.

• **forthright** ADJ. outspoken; frank. Never afraid to call a spade a spade, she was perhaps too *forthright* to be a successful party politician.

fortuitous ADJ. accidental; by chance. Though he pretended their encounter was *fortuitous,* he'd actually been hanging around her usual haunts for the past two weeks, hoping she'd turn up.

foster V. rear; encourage. According to the legend, Romulus and Remus were *fostered* by a she-wolf who raised the abandoned infants as her own. also ADJ.

• **frail** ADJ. weak. The delicate child seemed too *frail* to lift the heavy carton.

franchise N. right granted by authority; right to vote; business licensed to sell a product in a particular territory. The city issued a *franchise* to the company to operate surface transit lines on the streets for 99 years. For most of American history, women lacked the right to vote: not until the early twentieth century was the *franchise* granted to women. Stan owns a Carvel's ice cream *franchise* in Chinatown.

frantic ADJ. wild. At the time of the collision, many people became *frantic* with fear.

fraudulent ADJ. cheating; deceitful. The government seeks to prevent *fraudulent* and misleading advertising.

• **frivolous** ADJ. lacking in seriousness; self-indulgently carefree; relatively unimportant. Though Nancy enjoyed Bill's *frivolous,* lighthearted companionship, she sometimes wondered whether he could ever be serious. frivolity, N.

fugitive ADJ. fleeting or transient; elusive; fleeing. How can a painter capture on canvas the *fugitive* beauty of clouds moving across the sky? also N.

fundamental V. basic; primary; essential. The committee discussed all sorts of side issues without ever getting down to addressing the *fundamental* problem.

furtive ADJ. stealthy; sneaky. Noticing the *furtive* glance the customer gave the diamond bracelet on the counter, the jeweler wondered whether he had a potential shoplifter on his hands.

fusion N. union; coalition. The opponents of the political party in power organized a *fusion* of disgruntled groups and became an important element in the election.

futile ADJ. useless; hopeless; ineffectual. It is *futile* for me to try to get any work done around here while the telephone is ringing every thirty seconds. futility, N.

gainful ADJ. profitable. After having been out of work for six months, Brenda was excited by the prospect of *gainful* employment.

gale N. windstorm; gust of wind; emotional outburst (laughter, tears). The Weather Channel warned viewers about a rising *gale,* with winds of up to 60 miles per hour.

galvanize V. stimulate by shock; stir up; revitalize. News that the prince was almost at their door *galvanized* the ugly stepsisters into a frenzy of combing and primping.

garble V. mix up; jumble; distort. A favorite party game involves passing a whispered message from one person to another, till, by the time it reaches the last player, everyone has totally *garbled* the message.

Word List 20 garish–hazardous

garish ADJ. overbright in color; gaudy. She wore a gaudy rhinestone necklace with an excessively *garish* gold lamé dress.

• **garrulous** ADJ. loquacious; wordy; talkative. My Uncle Henry can outtalk any three people I know. He is the most *garrulous* person in Cayuga County. garrulity, N.

gastric ADJ. pertaining to the stomach. Clutching his stomach and grimacing broadly, the acting student feigned *gastric* distress.

gavel N. hammerlike tool; mallet. "Sold!" cried the auctioneer, banging her *gavel* on the table to indicate she'd accepted the final bid.

genealogy N. record of descent; lineage. He was proud of his *genealogy* and constantly referred to the achievements of his ancestors.

• **generate** V. cause; produce; create. In his first days in office, President Obama managed to *generate* a new mood of optimism; we hoped he could *generate* a few new jobs.

generic ADJ. characteristic of an entire class or species. Sue knew so many computer programmers who spent their spare time playing fantasy games that she began to think that playing Dungeons & Dragons was a *generic* trait.

• **genre** N. particular variety of art or literature. Both a short story writer and a poet, Langston Hughes proved himself equally skilled in either *genre*.

genteel ADJ. well-bred; elegant. We are looking for a man with a *genteel* appearance who can inspire confidence by his cultivated manner.

germane ADJ. pertinent; bearing upon the case at hand. The lawyer objected that the witness's testimony was not *germane* to the case and should be ignored by the jury.

gibberish N. nonsense; babbling. "Did you hear that fool boy spouting *gibberish* about monsters from outer space? I never heard anything so nonsensical in all my . . ."

giddy ADJ. lighthearted; dizzy. The silly, *giddy* young girls rode ride after ride on the Tilt-a-Whirl until they were *giddy* and sick.

gingerly ADV. very carefully. To separate egg whites, first crack the egg *gingerly,* avoiding breaking the yolk.

glimmer V. shine erratically; twinkle. In the darkness of the cavern, the glowworms hanging from the cavern roof *glimmered* like distant stars.

gloss over V. explain away. No matter how hard he tried to talk around the issue, the president could not *gloss over* the fact that he had raised taxes after all.

glower V. scowl. The angry boy *glowered* at his father.

• **gluttonous** ADJ. greedy for food. The *gluttonous* boy ate all the cookies.

gorge N. small, steep-walled canyon. The white-water rafting guide warned us about the rapids farther downstream, where the river cut through a narrow *gorge*.

gorge V. stuff oneself. The gluttonous guest *gorged* himself, cramming food into his mouth as fast as he could.

grandeur N. impressiveness; stateliness; majesty. No matter how often he hiked through the mountains, David never failed to be struck by the *grandeur* of the Sierra Nevada range.

grandiose ADJ. pretentious; high-flown; ridiculously exaggerated; impressive. The aged matinee idol still had *grandiose* notions of his supposed importance in the theatrical world.

graphic ADJ. pertaining to the art of delineating; vividly described. I was particularly impressed by the *graphic* presentation of the storm.

• **gratify** V. please. Amy's success in her new job *gratified* her parents.

gratuitous ADJ. given freely; unwarranted; uncalled for. Quit making *gratuitous* comments about my driving; no one asked you for your opinion.

• **gregarious** ADJ. sociable. Typically, party-throwers are *gregarious;* hermits are not.

guile N. deceit; duplicity; wiliness; cunning. Iago uses considerate *guile* to trick Othello into believing that Desdemona has been unfaithful.

gullible ADJ. easily deceived. Overly *gullible* people have only themselves to blame if they fall for scams repeatedly. As the saying goes, "Fool me once, shame on you. Fool me twice, shame on me."

• **hackneyed** ADJ. commonplace; trite. When the reviewer criticized the movie for its *hackneyed* plot, we agreed; we had seen similar stories hundreds of times before.

• **halting** ADJ. hesitant; faltering. Novice extemporaneous speakers often talk in a *halting* fashion as they grope for the right words.

• **hamper** V. obstruct. The new mother didn't realize how much the effort of caring for an infant would *hamper* her ability to keep an immaculate house.

harangue N. noisy speech. In her lengthy *harangue,* the principal berated the offenders. also V.

harass V. to annoy by repeated attacks. When he could not pay his bills as quickly as he had promised, he was *harassed* by his creditors.

harbor V. provide a refuge for; hide. The church *harbored* illegal aliens who were political refugees.

haughtiness N. pride; arrogance. When she realized that Darcy believed himself too good to dance with his inferiors, Elizabeth took great offense at his *haughtiness.*

hazardous ADJ. dangerous. Your occupation is too *hazardous* for insurance companies to consider your application.

Word List 21 headstrong–imbue

headstrong ADJ. stubborn; willful; unyielding. Because she refused to marry the man her parents had chosen for her, everyone scolded Minna and called her a foolish *headstrong* girl.

heckle V. harass; taunt; jeer at. The home team's fans mercilessly *heckled* the visiting pitcher, taunting him whenever he let anyone get on base.

heed V. pay attention to; consider. We hope you *heed* our advice and get a good night's sleep before the test. also N.

herculean ADJ. very strong; extremely difficult to perform; like the mythological hero Hercules.

Muscles rippling, the action hero was a *herculean* figure, lifting enormous weights with ease.

heresy N. opinion contrary to popular belief; opinion contrary to accepted religion. Galileo's assertion that the earth moved around the sun directly contradicted the religious teachings of his day; as a result, he was tried for *heresy*. heretic, N.

hermetic ADJ. sealed by fusion so as to be airtight. After you sterilize the bandages, place them in a container and seal it with a *hermetic* seal to protect them from contamination by airborne bacteria.

hermit N. someone who chooses to live in solitude; recluse. Abandoning society, Thoreau chose to go off and live in the woods like a *hermit*.

hiatus N. gap; pause. Except for a brief two-year *hiatus,* during which she enrolled in the Peace Corps, Ms. Clements has devoted herself to her medical career.

hibernate V. sleep throughout the winter. Bears are one of the many species of animals that *hibernate*. hibernation, N.

hierarchy N. arrangement by rank or standing; authoritarian body divided into ranks. To be low man on the totem pole is to have an inferior place in the *hierarchy*.

• **hindrance** N. block; obstacle. Stalled cars along the highway are a *hindrance* to traffic that tow trucks should remove without delay. hinder, V.

homespun ADJ. domestic; made at home. *Homespun* wit like *homespun* cloth was often coarse and plain.

• **hostility** N. unfriendliness; hatred. Children who have been the sole objects of their parents' attention often feel *hostility* toward a new baby in the family, resenting the newcomer who has taken their place.

humane ADJ. marked by kindness or consideration. It is ironic that the *Humane* Society sometimes must show its compassion toward mistreated animals by killing them to put them out of their misery.

humble ADJ. modest; not proud. He spoke with great feeling of how much he loved his *humble* home, which he would not trade for a palace. humility, N.

husband V. use sparingly; conserve; save. Marathon runners must *husband* their energy so that they can keep going for the entire distance.

hyperbole N. exaggeration; overstatement. As far as I'm concerned, Apple's claims about the new computer are pure *hyperbole:* no machine is that good!

• **hypocritical** ADJ. pretending to be virtuous; deceiving. It was *hypocritical* of Martha to say such nice things about my poetry to me and then make fun of my verses behind my back. hypocrisy, N.

• **hypothetical** ADJ. based on assumptions or hypotheses; supposed. Suppose you are accepted by Harvard, Stanford, and Brown. Which one would you choose to attend? Remember, this is only a *hypothetical* situation. hypothesis, N.

• **iconoclastic** ADJ. attacking cherished traditions. Deeply *iconoclastic,* Jean Genet deliberately set out to shock conventional theatergoers with his radical plays.

ideology N. system of ideas of a group. For people who had grown up believing in the communist *ideology,* it was hard to adjust to capitalism.

idiom N. expression whose meaning as a whole differs from the meanings of its individual words; distinctive style. The phrase "to lose one's marbles" is an *idiom:* if I say that Joe's lost his marbles, I'm not asking you to find some for him. I'm telling you *idiomatically* that he's crazy.

idiosyncrasy N. individual trait, usually odd in nature; eccentricity. One of Richard Nixon's little *idiosyncrasies* was his liking for ketchup on cottage cheese. One of Hannibal Lecter's little *idiosyncrasies* was his liking for human flesh.

ignite V. kindle; light. When Desi crooned "Baby, light my fire," literal-minded Lucy looked around for some paper to *ignite*.

ignoble ADJ. unworthy; base in nature; not noble. Sir Galahad was so pure in heart that he could never stoop to perform an *ignoble* deed.

illuminate V. brighten; clear up or make understandable; enlighten. Just as a lamp can *illuminate* a dark room, a perceptive comment can *illuminate* a knotty problem.

illusory ADJ. deceptive; not real. Unfortunately, the costs of running the lemonade stand were so high that Tom's profits proved *illusory*.

imbalance N. lack of balance or symmetry; disproportion. To correct racial *imbalance* in the schools, school boards have bussed black children into white neighborhoods and white children into black ones.

imbibe V. drink in. The dry soil *imbibed* the rain quickly.

imbue V. permeate completely; dye thoroughly; fill. The sight of her grandparents' names inscribed on the wall of Ellis Island *imbued* Sarah with a sense of her special heritage as the descendant of immigrants.

Word List 22 immaterial–incarcerate

immaterial ADJ. unimportant; irrelevant; intangible. Though Kit said it was wholly *immaterial* whether she had a birthday party or not, we wanted to throw her a party.

imminent ADJ.; near at hand; impending. Rosa was such a last-minute worker that she could never start writing a paper till the deadline was *imminent*.

immobilize V. make unable to move. For a moment, Peter's fear of snakes *immobilized* him; then the use of his limbs returned to him and he bolted from the room.

immune ADJ. resistant to; free or exempt from. Fortunately, Florence had contracted chicken pox as a child and was *immune* to it when her baby broke out in spots.

• **immutable** ADJ. unchangeable. All things change over time; nothing is *immutable.*

impair V. injure; hurt. Drinking alcohol can *impair* your ability to drive safely; if you're going to drink, don't drive.

impart V. give or convey; communicate. A born dancer, she *imparted* her love of movement to her audience with every step she took.

impartial ADJ. not biased; fair. Knowing she could not be *impartial* about her own child, Jo refused to judge any match in which Billy was competing.

impassable ADJ. not able to be traveled or crossed. A giant redwood had fallen across the highway, blocking all four lanes: the road was *impassable.*

impasse N. predicament offering no escape; deadlock; dead end. The negotiators reported they had reached an *impasse* in their talks and had little hope of resolving the deadlock swiftly.

impecunious ADJ. without money. Though Scrooge claimed he was too *impecunious* to give alms, he easily could have afforded to be charitable.

• **impede** v. hinder; block; delay. A series of accidents *impeded* the launching of the space shuttle.

impel V. drive or force onward. A strong feeling of urgency *impelled* her; if she failed to finish the project right then, she knew that she would never get it done.

• **imperceptible** ADJ. unnoticeable; undetectable. Fortunately, the stain on the blouse was *imperceptible* after the blouse had gone through the wash.

impermeable ADJ. impervious; not permitting passage through its substance. Sue chose a raincoat made of Gore-Tex because the material was *impermeable* to liquids.

impertinent ADJ. insolent; rude. His neighbors' *impertinent* curiosity about his lack of dates angered Ted. It was downright rude of them to ask him such personal questions.

imperturbable ADJ. calm; placid; composed. In the midst of the battle, the Duke of Wellington remained *imperturbable* and in full command of the situation despite the hysteria and panic all around him. imperturbability, N.

impetuous ADJ. violent; hasty; rash. "Leap before you look" was the motto suggested by one particularly *impetuous* young man.

impiety N. irreverence; lack of respect for God. When members of the youth group draped the church in toilet paper one Halloween, the minister reprimanded them for their *impiety.* impious, ADJ.

• **implacable** ADJ. incapable of being pacified. Relentlessly seeking revenge, Madame Defarge was the *implacable* enemy of the Evremonde family.

• **implement** V. put into effect; supply with tools. The mayor was unwilling to *implement* the plan until she was sure it had the governor's backing. also N.

implicate V. incriminate; show to be involved. Here's the deal: If you agree to take the witness stand and *implicate* your partners in crime, the prosecution will recommend that the judge go easy in sentencing you.

• **implication** N. something hinted at or suggested. When Miss Watson said she hadn't seen her purse since the last time Jim was in the house, the *implication* was that she suspected Jim had taken it. imply, V.

implicit ADJ. understood but not stated. Jack never told Jill he adored her; he believed his love was *implicit* in his deeds.

importune V. beg persistently. Democratic and Republican phone solicitors *importuned* her for contributions so frequently that she decided to give nothing to either party.

impotent ADJ. weak; ineffective. Although he wished to break the nicotine habit, he found himself *impotent* to resist the craving for a cigarette.

• **impromptu** ADJ. without previous preparation; off the cuff; on the spur of the moment. The judges were amazed that she could make such a thorough, well-supported presentation in an *impromptu* speech.

inadvertently ADV. unintentionally; by oversight; carelessly. Judy's great fear was that she might *inadvertently* omit a question on the exam and mismark her whole answer sheet.

inane ADJ. silly; senseless. There's no point in what you're saying. Why are you bothering to make such *inane* remarks? inanity, N.

inanimate ADJ. lifeless. She was asked to identify the still and *inanimate* body.

inarticulate ADJ. speechless; producing indistinct speech. He became *inarticulate* with rage and uttered sounds without meaning.

incapacitate V. disable. During the winter, many people were *incapacitated* by respiratory ailments.

• **incarcerate** V. imprison. The civil rights workers were willing to be arrested and even *incarcerated* if by their imprisonment they could serve the cause.

Word List 23 incentive–infallible

incentive N. spur; motive. Mike's strong desire to outshine his big sister was all the *incentive* he needed to do well in school.

incessant ADJ. uninterrupted; unceasing. In a famous TV commercial, the frogs' *incessant* croaking goes on and on until eventually it turns into a single word: "Bud-weis-er."

incipient ADJ. beginning; in an early stage. I will go to sleep early for I want to break an *incipient* cold.

incite V. arouse to action; goad; motivate; induce to exist. In a fiery speech, Mario *incited* his fellow students to go out on strike to protest the university's anti-affirmative-action stand.

inclusive ADJ. tending to include all. The comedian turned down the invitation to join the Players' Club, saying any club that would let him in was too *inclusive.*

• **incongruity** N. lack of harmony; absurdity. The *incongruity* of his wearing sneakers with formal attire amused the observers. incongruous, ADJ.

incoherent ADJ. unintelligible; muddled; illogical. The excited fan blushed and stammered, her words becoming almost *incoherent* in the thrill of meeting her favorite rock star face to face. incoherence, N.

• **inconsequential** ADJ. insignificant; unimportant. Brushing off Ali's apologies for having broken the wine glass, Tamara said, "Don't worry about it; it's *inconsequential.*"

• **inconsistency** N. state of being self-contradictory; lack of uniformity or steadiness. How are lawyers different from agricultural inspectors? While lawyers check *inconsistencies* in witnesses' statements, agricultural inspectors check *inconsistencies* in Grade A eggs. inconsistent, ADJ.

• **incorporate** V. introduce something into a larger whole; combine; unite. Breaking with precedent, President Truman ordered the military to *incorporate* blacks into every branch of the armed services. also ADJ.

incorporeal ADJ. lacking a material body; insubstantial. Although Casper the friendly ghost is an *incorporeal* being, he and his fellow ghosts make a decided impact on the physical world.

incorrigible ADJ. uncorrectable. Though Widow Douglass hoped to reform Huck, Miss Watson pronounced him *incorrigible* and said he would come to no good end.

incredulous ADJ. unwilling or unable to believe; skeptical. When Marco claimed he hadn't eaten the jelly doughnut, Joyce took one *incredulous* look at his smeared face and laughed.

incrustation N. hard coating or crust. In dry dock, we scraped off the *incrustation* of dirt and barnacles that covered the hull of the ship.

incumbent N. officeholder. The newly elected public official received valuable advice from the previous *incumbent.* also ADJ.

indefatigable ADJ. tireless. Although the effort of taking out the garbage tired Wayne out for the entire morning, when it came to partying, he was *indefatigable.*

indelible ADJ. not able to be erased. The *indelible* ink left a permanent mark on my shirt. Young Bill Clinton's meeting with President Kennedy made an *indelible* impression on the youth.

• **indict** V. charge. The district attorney didn't want to *indict* the suspect until she was sure she had a strong enough case to convince a jury. indictment, N.

• **indifferent** ADJ. unmoved or unconcerned by; mediocre. Because Consuela felt no desire to marry, she was *indifferent* to Edward's constant proposals. Not only was she *indifferent* to him personally, but she felt that, given his general silliness, he would make an *indifferent* husband.

indigenous ADJ. native. Cigarettes are made of tobacco, a plant *indigenous* to the New World.

indisputable ADJ. too certain to be disputed. In the face of these *indisputable* statements, I withdraw my complaint.

indomitable ADJ. unconquerable; unyielding. Focusing on her final vault despite her twisted ankle, gymnastics star Kerri Strug proved she had an *indomitable* will to win.

indubitable ADJ. unable to be doubted; unquestionable. Auditioning for the chorus line, Molly was an *indubitable* hit: the director fired the leading lady and hired Molly in her place!

• **induce** V. persuade; bring about. After the quarrel, Tina said nothing could *induce* her to talk to Tony again. inducement, N.

indulgent ADJ. humoring; yielding; lenient. Jay's mom was excessively *indulgent:* she bought him every Nintendo cartridge and video game on the market. She *indulged* Jay so much, she spoiled him rotten.

• **industrious** ADJ. diligent; hard-working. Look busy when the boss walks past your desk; it never hurts to appear *industrious.* industry, N.

ineffable ADJ. unutterable; unable to be expressed in speech. Looking down at her newborn daughter, Ruth felt such *ineffable* joy that, for the first time in her adult life, she had no words to convey what was in her heart.

• **inept** ADJ. lacking skill; unsuited; incompetent. The *inept* glove maker was all thumbs. ineptitude, ineptness, N.

inevitable ADJ. unavoidable. Though death and taxes are both supposedly *inevitable,* some people avoid paying taxes for years.

• **infallible** ADJ. unerring; faultless. Jane refused to believe the pope was *infallible,* reasoning: "All human beings are capable of error. The pope is a human being. Therefore, the pope is capable of error."

Word List 24 infamous–insurgent

infamous ADJ. notoriously bad. Charles Manson and Jeffrey Dahmer are both *infamous* killers.

infer V. deduce; conclude. From the students' glazed looks, it was easy for me to *infer* that they were bored out of their minds. inference, N.

infernal ADJ. pertaining to hell; devilish. Batman was baffled: he could think of no way to hinder the Joker's *infernal* scheme to destroy the city.

infinitesimal ADJ. exceedingly small; so small as to be almost nonexistent. Making sure everyone was aware she was on an extremely strict diet, Melanie said she would have only an *infinitesimal* sliver of pie.

infraction N. violation (of a rule or regulation); breach. When Dennis Rodman butted heads with the referee, he committed a clear *infraction* of NBA rules.

• **ingenious** ADJ. clever; resourceful. Kit admired the *ingenious* way that her computer keyboard opened up to reveal the built-in CD-ROM below. ingenuity, N.

• **ingenuous** ADJ. naive and trusting; young; unsophisticated. The woodsman had not realized how *ingenuous* Little Red Riding Hood was until he heard that she had gone off for a walk in the woods with the Big Bad Wolf.

• **ingrate** N. ungrateful person. That *ingrate* Bob sneered at the tie I gave him.

ingratiate V. make an effort to become popular with others. In *All About Eve,* the heroine, an aspiring actress, wages a clever campaign to *ingratiate* herself with Margo Channing, an established star.

• **inherent** ADJ. firmly established by nature or habit. Katya's *inherent* love of justice caused her to champion anyone she considered treated unfairly by society.

inhibit V. restrain; retard or prevent. Only two things *inhibited* him from taking a punch at Mike Tyson: Tyson's left hook and Tyson's right jab. The protective undercoating on my car *inhibits* the formation of rust.

• **initiate** V. begin; originate; receive into a group. The college is about to *initiate* a program for reducing math anxiety among students.

inkling N. hint. This came as a complete surprise to me as I did not have the slightest *inkling* of your plans.

inlet N. small bay; narrow passage between islands; entrance. Seeking shelter from the gale, Drake sailed the *Golden Hind* into a protected *inlet,* where he hoped to wait out the storm.

• **innate** ADJ. inborn. Mozart's parents soon recognized young Wolfgang's *innate* talent for music.

• **innocuous** ADJ. harmless. An occasional glass of wine with dinner is relatively *innocuous* and should have no ill effect on you.

innovation N. change; introduction of something new. Although Richard liked to keep up with all the latest technological *innovations,* he didn't always abandon tried-and-true techniques in favor of something new. innovate, V.

inopportune ADJ. untimely; poorly chosen. A punk rock concert is an *inopportune* setting for a quiet conversation.

inordinate ADJ. unrestrained; excessive. She had an *inordinate* fondness for candy, eating two or three boxes in a single day.

inquisitor N. questioner (especially harsh); investigator. Fearing being grilled ruthlessly by the secret police, Masha faced her *inquisitors* with trepidation.

insatiable ADJ. not easily satisfied; greedy. Welty's thirst for knowledge was *insatiable;* she was in the library day and night.

• **inscrutable** ADJ. impenetrable; not readily understood; mysterious. Experienced poker players try to keep their expressions *inscrutable,* hiding their reactions to the cards behind a so-called poker face.

insidious ADJ. treacherous; stealthy; sly. The fifth column is *insidious* because it works secretly within our territory for our defeat.

• **insightful** ADJ. discerning; perceptive. Sol thought he was very *insightful* about human behavior, but he was actually clueless as to why people acted the way they did.

insinuate V. hint; imply; creep in. When you say I look robust, do you mean to *insinuate* that I'm getting fat?

insipid ADJ. lacking in flavor; dull. Flat prose and flat ginger ale are equally *insipid*: both lack sparkle.

insolence N. impudent disrespect; haughtiness. How dare you treat me so rudely! The manager will hear of your *insolence.* insolent, ADJ.

insolvent ADJ. bankrupt; lacking money to pay. When rumors that he was *insolvent* reached his creditors, they began to press him to pay the money he owed them. insolvency, N.

insomnia N. wakefulness; inability to sleep. He refused to join us in a midnight cup of coffee because he claimed it gave him *insomnia.*

instigate V. urge; start; provoke. Rumors of police corruption led the mayor to *instigate* an investigation into the department's activities.

insubordination N. disobedience; rebelliousness. At the slightest hint of *insubordination* from the sailors of the *Bounty,* Captain Bligh had them flogged; finally, they mutinied.

insubstantial ADJ. lacking substance; insignificant; frail. His hopes for a career in acting proved *insubstantial;* no one would cast him, even in an *insubstantial* role.

insurgent ADJ. rebellious. Because the *insurgent* forces had occupied the capital and had gained control of the railway lines, several of the war correspondents covering the uprising predicted a rebel victory.

Word List 25 insurrection–jeopardize

insurrection N. rebellion; uprising. In retrospect, given how badly the British treated the American colonists, the eventual *insurrection* seems inevitable.

• **intangible** ADJ. not able to be perceived by touch; vague. Though the financial benefits of his Oxford post were meager, Lewis was drawn to it by its *intangible* rewards: prestige, intellectual freedom, the fellowship of his peers.

• **integrity** N. uprightness; wholeness. Lincoln, whose personal *integrity* has inspired millions, fought a civil war to maintain the *integrity* of the Republic, that these United States might remain undivided for all time.

interminable ADJ. endless. Although his speech lasted for only twenty minutes, it seemed *interminable* to his bored audience.

intermittent ADJ. periodic; on and off. The outdoor wedding reception had to be moved indoors to avoid the *intermittent* showers that fell all afternoon.

interrogate V. question closely; cross-examine. Knowing that the Nazis would *interrogate* him about his background, the secret agent invented a cover story that would help him meet their questions.

intimidate V. frighten. I'll learn karate and then those big bullies won't be able to *intimidate* me any more.

intransigence N. refusal of any compromise; stubbornness. When I predicted that the strike would be over in a week, I didn't expect to encounter such *intransigence* from both sides. intransigent, ADJ.

• **intricacy** N. complexity; knottiness. Philip spent many hours designing mazes of such great *intricacy* that none of his classmates could solve them. intricate, ADJ.

intrigue V. fascinate; interest. Holmes's air of reserve *intrigued* Irene Adler; she wanted to know just what made the great detective tick.

intrinsic ADJ. essential; inherent; built-in. Although my grandmother's china has little *intrinsic* value, I shall always cherish it for the memories it evokes.

• **introspective** ADJ. looking within oneself. Though young Francis of Assisi led a wild and worldly life, even he had *introspective* moments during which he examined his soul.

intrude V. trespass; enter as an uninvited person. She hesitated to *intrude* on their conversation.

intuition N. immediate insight; power of knowing without reasoning. Even though Tony denied that anything was wrong, Tina trusted her *intuition* that something was bothering him. intuitive, ADJ.

inundate V. overwhelm; flood; submerge. This semester I am *inundated* with work: you should see the piles of paperwork flooding my desk. Until the great dam was build, the waters of the Nile used to *inundate* the river valley every year.

invalidate V. discredit; nullify. The relatives who received little or nothing sought to *invalidate* the will by claiming that the deceased had not been in his right mind when he signed the document.

invective N. abuse. He had expected criticism but not the *invective* that greeted his proposal.

inviolable ADJ. secure from corruption, attack, or violation; unassailable. Batman considered his oath to keep the people of Gotham City safe *inviolable:* nothing on earth could make him break this promise.

irascible ADJ. irritable; easily angered. Pop had what people call a hair-trigger temper; he was a hot-tempered, *irascible* guy.

irksome ADJ. annoying; tedious. The petty rules and regulations Bill had to follow at work irritated him: he found them uniformly *irksome.*

• **irony** N. hidden sarcasm or satire; use of words that seem to mean the opposite of what they actually mean. Gradually his listeners began to realize that the excessive praise he was lavishing on his opponent was actually *irony;* he was in fact ridiculing the poor fool.

irrational ADJ. illogical; lacking reason; insane. Many people have such an *irrational* fear of snakes that they panic at the sight of a harmless garter snake.

irrelevant ADJ. not applicable; unrelated. No matter how *irrelevant* the patient's mumblings may seem, they give us some indications of what he has on his mind.

isolate V. keep apart; pinpoint; quarantine. The medical researchers *isolated* themselves in a remote village. Until they could *isolate* the cause of the plague and develop an effective vaccine, they had to avoid potential carriers of the disease. Anyone infected they *isolated* immediately.

itinerant ADJ. wandering; traveling. He was an *itinerant* peddler and traveled through Pennsylvania and Virginia selling his wares. also N.

jabber V. chatter rapidly or unintelligibly. Why does the fellow insist on *jabbering* away in French when I can't understand a word he says?

jargon N. language used by a special group; technical terminology; gibberish. The computer salesmen at the store used a *jargon* of their own that we simply couldn't follow; we had no idea what they were jabbering about.

jaunty ADJ. lighthearted; animated; easy and carefree. In *Singing in the Rain,* Gene Kelly sang and danced his way through the lighthearted title number in a properly *jaunty* style.

jeopardize V. endanger; imperil; put at risk. You can't give me a D in chemistry; you'll *jeopardize* my chances of getting into M.I.T. jeopardy, N.

Word List 26 jocose–lurk

jocose ADJ. giving to joking. The salesman was so *jocose* that many of his customers suggested that he become a stand-up comic.

jocular ADJ. said or done in jest. Although Bill knew the boss hated jokes, he couldn't resist making one *jocular* remark. jocularity, N.

• **judicious** ADJ. sound in judgment; wise. At a key moment in his life, he made a *judicious* investment that was the foundation of his later wealth.

justification N. good or just reason; defense; excuse. The jury found him guilty of the more serious charge because they could see no possible *justification* for his actions.

juxtapose V. place side by side. You'll find it easier to compare the two paintings if you *juxtapose* them.

kindle V. start a fire; inspire. One of the first things Ben learned in the Boy Scouts was how to *kindle* a fire by rubbing two dry sticks together. Her teacher's praise for her poetry *kindled* a spark of hope inside Maya.

knit V. contract into wrinkles; grow together. Whenever David worries, his brow *knits* in a frown. When he broke his leg, he sat around the house all day waiting for the bones to *knit.*

laborious ADJ. demanding much work or care; tedious. In putting together his dictionary of the English language, Doctor Johnson undertook a *laborious* task.

laconic ADJ. brief and to the point. Many of the characters portrayed by Clint Eastwood are *laconic* types, rugged men of few words.

laggard ADJ. slow; sluggish. The sailor had been taught not to be *laggard* in carrying out orders. lag, N., V.

lair N. wild animal's living place; den; hideaway. Jack London called his remote dwelling place the *Lair* of the Wolf.

lament V. grieve; express sorrow. Even advocates of the war *lamented* the loss of so many lives in combat. lamentation, N.

lampoon V. ridicule. This hilarious article *lampoons* the pretensions of some movie moguls. also N.

• **languid** ADJ. weary; feeble; listless; apathetic. The chronic invalid's most recent siege of illness left her *languid* and drooping. languor, N. languish, V.

• **larceny** N. theft. Because of the prisoner's long record of thefts, the district attorney refused to reduce the charge from grand *larceny* to petty *larceny.*

latent ADJ. potential but undeveloped; dormant; hidden. Polaroid pictures are popular at parties, because you can see the *latent* photographic image gradually appear before your eyes.

laud V. praise. The NFL *lauded* Boomer Esiason's efforts to raise money to combat cystic fibrosis. laudable, laudatory, ADJ.

leaven V. cause to rise or grow lighter; mix in something that transforms, alleviates, or enlivens. As bread dough is *leavened,* it puffs up, expanding in volume. also N.

lenience N. mildness; permissiveness. Considering the gravity of the offense, we were surprised by the *lenience* of the sentence. also leniency; lenient, ADJ.

lethal ADJ. deadly. It is unwise to leave *lethal* weapons where children may find them.

• **lethargic** ADJ. drowsy; dull. The stuffy room made her *lethargic:* she felt as if she was about to nod off.

levity N. lack of seriousness; lightness. Stop giggling and wiggling around in your seats: such *levity* is improper in church.

libel N. defamatory statement; act of writing something that smears a person's character. If Batman wrote that the Joker was a dirty, rotten, mass-murdering criminal, could the Joker sue Batman for *libel*?

lilliputian ADJ. extremely small. Tiny and delicate, the model was built on a *lilliputian* scale. also N.

linger V. loiter or dawdle; continue or persist. Hoping to see Juliet pass by, Romeo *lingered* outside the Capulet house for hours. Though Mother made stuffed cabbage on Monday, the smell *lingered* around the house for days.

loath ADJ. reluctant; disinclined. Fearing for her son's safety, the overprotective mother was *loath* to let him go on the class trip.

• **loathe** V. detest. Booing and hissing, the audience showed how much they *loathed* the wicked villain.

lofty ADJ. very high. Though Barbara Jordan's fellow students used to tease her about her *lofty* ambitions, she rose to hold one of the highest positions in the land.

longevity N. long life. When he reached 90, the old man was proud of his *longevity.*

loquacious ADJ. talkative. She is very *loquacious* and can speak on the telephone for hours.

lucid ADJ. easily understood; clear; intelligible. Her explanation was *lucid* enough for a child to grasp.

lucrative ADJ. profitable. He turned his hobby into a *lucrative* profession.

lugubrious ADJ. mournful; funereal. Gloomy Gus walked around town with a *lugubrious* expression on his face.

luminous ADJ. shining; issuing light. The sun is a *luminous* body.

lure V. entice; attract. Baiting his hook with the latest fly he had put together, Grandpa Joe swore that this new fly was so attractive that it could *lure* the wariest trout out of hiding.

lurk V. stealthily lie in waiting; slink; exist unperceived. "Who knows what evils *lurk* in the hearts of men? The Shadow knows!"

Word List 27 luxuriant–meticulous

luxuriant ADJ. abundant; rich and splendid; fertile. Lady Godiva was completely covered by her *luxuriant* hair.

maelstrom N. whirlpool. The canoe was tossed about in the *maelstrom*.

magnanimous ADJ. generous. Philanthropists by definition are *magnanimous;* misers, by definition, are not. magnanimity, N.

• **malice** N. hatred; spite. Jealous of Cinderella's beauty, her wicked stepsisters expressed their *malice* by forcing her to do menial tasks.

malign V. speak evil of; bad-mouth; defame. Her hatred of her ex-husband ran so deep that she *maligned* anyone who even casually dated him.

malignant ADJ. having an evil influence; virulent. This is a *malignant* disease; we may have to use drastic measures to stop its spread.

malleable ADJ. capable of being shaped by pounding; impressionable. Gold is a *malleable* metal, easily shaped into bracelets and rings. Fagin hoped Oliver was a *malleable* lad, easily shaped into a thief.

manifest ADJ. evident; visible; obvious. Digby's embarrassment when he met Madonna was *manifest:* his ears turned bright pink, he kept scuffing one shoe in the dirt, and he couldn't look her in the eye.

marked ADJ. noticeable; targeted for vengeance. He walked with a *marked* limp, a souvenir of an old I.R.A. attack. As British ambassador, he knew he was a *marked* man.

marshal V. put in order. At a debate tournament, extemporaneous speakers have only a minute or two to *marshal* their thoughts before they address their audience.

martinet N. strict disciplinarian. Captain Bligh was a *martinet* who observed each regulation to the letter.

massive ADJ. solid or heavy; large in scope; severe. The bust of Beethoven emphasizes his high forehead and *massive* brow. The composer suffered a *massive* hearing loss that left him unable to hear the music the orchestra played.

materialism N. preoccupation with physical comforts and things. By its nature, *materialism* is opposed to idealism, for where the *materialist* emphasizes the needs of the body, the idealist emphasizes the needs of the soul. materialistic, ADJ.

maverick N. rebel; nonconformist. To the masculine literary establishment, George Sand, with her insistence on wearing trousers and smoking cigars, was clearly a *maverick* who fought her proper womanly role.

mawkish ADJ. mushy and gushy; sentimental; maudlin. Whenever Gigi and her boyfriend would sigh and get all lovey-dovey, her little brother would shout, "Yuck!," protesting their *mawkish* behavior.

maxim N. proverb; a truth pithily stated. Aesop's fables illustrate moral *maxims*.

meager ADJ. scanty; inadequate. Still hungry after his *meager* serving of porridge, Oliver Twist asked for a second helping.

mealymouthed ADJ. indirect in speech; hypocritical; evasive. Rather than tell Jill directly what he disliked, Jack made a few *mealymouthed* comments and tried to change the subject.

meander V. wind or turn in its course. Needing to stay close to a source of water, he followed every twist and turn of the stream as it *meandered* through the countryside.

mediate V. settle a dispute through the services of an outsider. King Solomon was asked to *mediate* a dispute between two women, each of whom claimed to be the mother of the same child.

mediocre ADJ. ordinary; commonplace. We were disappointed because he gave a rather *mediocre* performance in this role.

meditation N. reflection; thought. She reached her decision only after much *meditation*.

• **meek** ADJ. quiet and obedient; spiritless. Can Lois Lane see through Superman's disguise and spot the superhero masquerading as the *meek,* timorous Clark Kent?

melancholy ADJ. gloomy; morose; blue. To Eugene, stuck in his small town, a train whistle was a *melancholy* sound, for it made him think of all the places he would never get to see.

mellifluous ADJ. sweetly or smoothly flowing; melodious. What a *mellifluous* language Italian is! Even the street vendors' cries sound like little songs.

mentor N. counselor; teacher. During this very trying period, she could not have had a better *mentor,* for her adviser was sympathetic and understanding.

mercantile ADJ. concerning trade. Selling candy bars to his classmates whose parents had packed their lunch boxes with apples and carrot sticks, George clearly was destined to be a *mercantile* success.

mercenary ADJ. interested in money or gain. Andy's every act was prompted by *mercenary* motives: his first question was always, "What's in it for me?"

mercurial ADJ. capricious; changing; fickle. Quick as quicksilver to change, he was *mercurial* in nature and therefore unreliable.

mesmerize V. hypnotize; fascinate. On a long stretch of road between Fresno and Los Angeles, the open highway began to *mesmerize* Richard; he pulled over to the side of the road and rested to free himself from highway hypnosis.

• **meticulous** ADJ. excessively careful; painstaking; scrupulous. Martha Stewart, a *meticulous* housekeeper, fusses about each and every detail that goes into making up her perfect home.

Word List 28 migratory–nadir

migratory ADJ. wandering. The return of the *migratory* birds to the northern sections of this country is a harbinger of spring.

ministration N. act of giving care; attending to someone's needs. Red Cross founder Florence Nightingale was honored for her *ministrations* to wounded soldiers during the Crimean War.

minute ADJ. extremely small. The twins resembled one another closely; only *minute* differences set them apart.

misanthrope N. one who hates mankind. In *Gulliver's Travels,* Swift portrays human beings as vile, degraded beasts; for this reason, some critics consider him a *misanthrope.*

• **misconception** N. misunderstanding; misinterpretation. I'm afraid you are suffering from a *misconception,* Mr. Collins: I do not want to marry you at all.

misconstrue v. interpret incorrectly; misjudge. She took the passage seriously rather than humorously because she *misconstrued* the author's ironic tone.

miserly ADJ. stingy; mean. The *miserly* old man greedily counted the gold coins he had hoarded over the years.

misnomer N. wrong name; incorrect designation. His tyrannical conduct proved to us all that his nickname, King Eric the Just, was a *misnomer.*

• **misrepresent** V. give a false or incorrect impression, usually intentionally. The ad "Lovely Florida building site with water view" *misrepresented* the property, which was actually ten acres of bottomless swamp.

mitigate V. appease; moderate. Nothing Jason did could *mitigate* Medea's anger; she refused to forgive him for betraying her.

mobile ADJ. movable; not fixed. The *mobile* blood bank operated by the Red Cross visited our neighborhood today. mobility, N.

• **mock** V. ridicule; imitate, often in derision. It is unkind to *mock* anyone; it is stupid to *mock* anyone significantly bigger than you. mockery, N.

mode N. prevailing style; manner; way of doing something. The rock star had to have her hair done in the latest *mode:* frizzed, with occasional moussed spikes for variety. Henry plans to adopt a simpler *mode* of life: he is going to become a mushroom hunter and live off the land.

mollify V. soothe. The airline customer service representative tried to *mollify* the angry passenger by offering her a seat in first class.

momentous ADJ. very important. When Marie and Pierre Curie discovered radium, they had no idea of the *momentous* impact their discovery would have upon society.

• **monarchy** N. government under a single ruler. Though England today is a *monarchy,* there is some question whether it will be one in 20 years, given the present discontent at the prospect of Prince Charles as king.

monochromatic ADJ. having only one color. Most people who are color blind actually can distinguish several colors; some, however, have a truly *monochromatic* view of a world all in shades of gray.

• **monotony** N. sameness leading to boredom. What could be more deadly dull than the *monotony* of punching numbers into a computer hour after hour?

monumental ADJ. massive; immense. Writing a dictionary is a *monumental* task; so is reading one.

moratorium N. suspension of activity; authorized period of delay (of a payment, etc.). If we declare a *moratorium* and delay collecting all debts for six months, I am sure the farmers will be able to meet their bills.

morose ADJ. ill-humored; sullen; melancholy. Forced to take early retirement, Bill acted *morose* for months; then, all of a sudden, he shook off his sullen mood and was his usual cheerful self.

morsel N. small bit of food. "No, thank you, Aunt Polly," he said. "I'm so stuffed I can't eat another *morsel.*"

mortify V. humiliate; punish the flesh. She was so *mortified* by her blunder that she ran to her room in tears.

muddle V. confuse; mix up. His thoughts were *muddled* and chaotic. also N.

mural N. wall painting. The walls of the Chicano Community Center are covered with *murals* painted in the style of Diego Rivera, the great Mexican artist.

murky ADJ. dark and gloomy; thick with fog; vague. The *murky* depths of the swamp were so dark that you couldn't tell the vines and branches from the snakes.

muse V. ponder. For a moment he *mused* about the beauty of the scene, but his thoughts soon changed as he recalled his own personal problems. also N.

• **mutability** N. ability to change in form; fickleness. Going from rags to riches and then back to rags again, the bankrupt financier was a victim of the *mutability* of fortune.

muted ADJ. silent; muffled; toned down. Thanks to the thick, sound-absorbing walls of the cathedral, only *muted* traffic noise reached the worshippers within.

mutinous ADJ. unruly; rebellious. The captain had to use force to quiet his *mutinous* crew.

myriad N. very large number. *Myriads* of mosquitoes from the swamps invaded our village every evening at twilight. also ADJ.

nadir N. lowest point. Although few people realized it, the Dow-Jones averages had reached their *nadir* and would soon begin an upward surge.

Word List 29 naïveté–obnoxious

• **naïveté** N. quality of being unsophisticated; simplicity; artlessness; gullibility. Touched by the *naïveté* of sweet, convent-trained Cosette, Marius pledges himself to protect her innocence. naive, ADJ.

narrative ADJ. related to telling a story. A born teller of tales, Olsen used her impressive *narrative* skills to advantage in her story, "I Stand Here Ironing."

navigable ADJ. wide and deep enough to allow ships to pass through; able to be steered. So much sand had built up at the bottom of the canal that the waterway was barely *navigable*.

nebulous ADJ. vague; hazy; cloudy. After 20 years, she had only a *nebulous* memory of her grandmother's face.

negligence N. neglect; failure to take reasonable care. Tommy failed to put back the cover on the well after he fetched his pail of water; because of his *negligence,* Kitty fell in.

negligible ADJ. so small, trifling, or unimportant that it may be easily disregarded. Because the damage to his car had been *negligible,* Michael decided he wouldn't bother to report the matter to his insurance company.

neologism N. new or newly coined word or phrase. As we invent new devices and professions, we must also invent *neologisms* such as "microcomputer" and "astronaut" to describe them.

neophyte N. recent convert; beginner. This mountain slope contains slides that will challenge experts as well as *neophytes*.

• **nocturnal** ADJ. relating to, occurring, or active in the night. Mr. Jones obtained a watchdog to prevent the *nocturnal* raids on his chicken coops.

• **nonchalance** N. indifference; lack of concern; composure. Cool, calm, and collected under fire, James Bond shows remarkable *nonchalance* in the face of danger.

nondescript ADJ. undistinctive; ordinary. The private detective was a *nondescript* fellow with no outstanding features, the sort of person one would never notice in a crowd.

nonentity N. person or thing of no importance; nonexistence. Don't dismiss John as a *nonentity*; in his quiet way, he's very important to the firm.

• **nostalgia** N. homesickness; longing for the past. My grandfather seldom spoke of life in the old country; he had little patience with *nostalgia*. nostalgic, ADJ.

notable ADJ. conspicuous; important; distinguished. Normally *notable* for his calm in the kitchen, today the head cook was shaking, for the *notable* chef Julia Child was coming to dinner.

• **notorious** ADJ. disreputable; widely known; scandalous. To the starlet, any publicity was good publicity: if she couldn't have a good reputation, she'd settle for being *notorious*. notoriety, N.

novelty N. something new; newness. The computer is no longer a *novelty* around the office; every office has one. novel, ADJ.

novice N. beginner. Even a *novice* at working with computers can install *Barron's Computer Study Program for the SAT* by following the easy steps outlined in the user's manual.

nozzle N. projecting spout; tapering tube. Did you leave the garden hose on? I see a trail of water leaking from its *nozzle*.

nucleus N. central point or core; component of protoplasm; central part of atom. Kathryn, Lexy, and Steven formed the *nucleus* of the debate team, which eventually grew to include most of the senior class.

nullify V. to make invalid; make null or void. Once the contract was *nullified,* it no longer had any legal force.

• **nurture** V. nourish; educate; foster. The Head Start program attempts to *nurture* pre-kindergarten children so that they will do well when they enter public school. also N.

nutrient N. nourishing substance. As a budding nutritionist, Kim has learned to design diets that contain foods rich in important basic *nutrients*.

obdurate ADJ. stubborn. The manager was *obdurate* in refusing to discuss the workers' grievances.

obfuscate V. confuse; muddle; make unclear. Occasionally in talking with patients, doctors seem to use medical terms to *obfuscate* rather than to inform them about the state of their health.

objective ADJ. not influenced by emotions; fair. Even though he was her son, she tried to be *objective* about his behavior.

objective N. goal; aim. A degree in medicine was her ultimate *objective.*

obligatory ADJ. required; legally or morally binding. It is *obligatory* that books borrowed from the library be returned within two weeks.

oblique ADJ. indirect; slanting (deviating from the perpendicular or from a straight line). Casting a quick, *oblique* glance at the reviewing stand, the sergeant ordered the company to march "*Oblique* Right."

obliterate V. destroy completely. In the film *Independence Day* the explosion *obliterated* the White House, vaporizing it completely.

oblivion N. obscurity; forgetfulness. After a brief period of popularity, Hurston's works fell into *oblivion;* no one bothered to reprint them or even to read them any more.

oblivious ADJ. inattentive or unmindful; wholly absorbed. Deep in her book, Nancy was *oblivious* of the noisy squabbles of her brother and his friends.

• **obnoxious** ADJ. offensive; objectionable. A sneak and a tattletale, Sid was an *obnoxious* little brat.

Word List 30 obscure–painstaking

• **obscure** ADJ. dark; vague; unclear. Even after I read the poem a fourth time, its meaning was still *obscure.* obscurity, N.

• **obscure** V. darken; make unclear. At times he seemed purposely to *obscure* his meaning, preferring mystery to clarity.

obsequious ADJ. slavishly attentive; servile; fawning; sycophantic. Why are some waiters in fancy restaurants so *obsequious*? What makes them think diners want to have people fawning all over them?

obsessive ADJ. related to thinking about something constantly; preoccupying. Ballet, which had been a hobby, began to dominate her life; her love of dancing became *obsessive.*

obsolescent ADJ. going out of use. Given how quickly computer technology changes, I've had to reconcile myself to the fact that, no matter how up-to-date a system I buy, it's practically *obsolescent* as soon as I've gotten it out of its box.

obsolete ADJ. outmoded. "Hip" is an *obsolete* expression; it went out with love beads and tie-dye shirts.

obtrude V. push (oneself or one's ideas) forward or intrude; butt in; stick out or extrude. Because Fanny was reluctant to *obtrude* her opinions about child raising upon her daughter-in-law, she kept a close watch on her tongue. obtrusive, ADJ.

offensive ADJ. attacking; insulting; distasteful. Getting into street brawls is no minor matter for professional boxers, who are required by law to restrict their *offensive* impulses to the ring.

officious ADJ. meddlesome; excessively pushing in offering one's services. After her long flight, Jill just wanted to nap, but the *officious* bellboy was intent on showing her all the special features of the deluxe suite.

olfactory ADJ. concerning the sense of smell. A wine taster must have a discriminating palate and a keen *olfactory* sense, for a good wine appeals both to the taste buds and to the nose.

ominous ADJ. threatening. Those clouds are *ominous;* they suggest a severe storm is on the way.

omnivorous ADJ. eating both plant and animal food; devouring everything. Some animals, including man, are *omnivorous* and eat both meat and vegetables; others are either carnivorous or herbivorous.

• **opaque** ADJ. not transparent; impenetrable to light. The *opaque* window shade kept the sunlight out of the room. opacity, N.

opportunist N. individual who sacrifices principles for expediency by taking advantage of circumstances. Forget ethics! He's such an *opportunist* that he'll vote in favor of any deal that will give him a break.

opprobrium N. public disgrace or reproach; vilification. How did the Republicans manage to turn the once-honored name of "liberal" into a term of *opprobrium?*

opt V. decide in favor of; choose. Given the choice between the movie and the folk dance, Sharon *opted* to go to the dance.

• **optimist** N. person who looks on the good side. The pessimist says the glass is half empty; the *optimist* says it is half full.

opulence N. extreme wealth; luxuriousness; abundance. The glitter and *opulence* of the ballroom took Cinderella's breath away. opulent, ADJ.

• **orator** N. public speaker. The abolitionist Frederick Douglass was a brilliant *orator* whose speeches brought home to his audience the evils of slavery.

ordeal N. severe trial or affliction. June was so painfully shy that it was an *ordeal* for her to speak up when the teacher called on her in class.

ornate ADJ. excessively or elaborately decorated. The furnishings of homes that were shown on *Lifestyles of the Rich and Famous* tended to be highly *ornate.*

• **ostentatious** ADJ. showy; pretentious; trying to attract attention. Trump's latest casino in Atlantic City is the most *ostentatious* gambling palace in the East: it easily outglitters its competitors. ostentation, N.

outlandish ADJ. bizarre; peculiar; unconventional. The eccentric professor who engages in markedly *outlandish* behavior is a stock figure in novels with an academic setting.

• **outmoded** ADJ. no longer stylish; old-fashioned. Unconcerned about keeping in style, Lenore was perfectly happy to wear *outmoded* clothes as long as they were clean and unfrayed.

outwit V. outsmart; trick. By disguising himself as an old woman, Holmes was able to *outwit* his pursuers and escape capture.

overbearing ADJ. bossy; arrogant; decisively important. Certain of her own importance and of the unimportance of everyone else, Lady Bracknell was intolerably *overbearing* in her manner. "In choosing a husband," she said, "good birth is of *overbearing* importance; compared to that, neither wealth nor talent signifies."

overt ADJ. open to view. According to the United States Constitution, a person must commit an *overt* act before he or she may be tried for treason.

• **pacifist** N. one opposed to force; antimilitarist. Shooting his way through the jungle, Rambo was clearly not a *pacifist*.

• **pacify** V. soothe; make calm or quiet; subdue. Dentists criticize the practice of giving fussy children sweets to *pacify* them.

painstaking ADJ. expending or showing diligent care and great effort. The new high-frequency word list is the result of *painstaking* efforts on the part of our research staff.

Word List 31 palatable–perjury

palatable ADJ. agreeable; pleasing to the taste. Neither Jack's underbaked opinions nor his overcooked casseroles were *palatable* to me.

pallid ADJ. pale; wan. Because his occupation required that he work at night and sleep during the day, he had an exceptionally *pallid* complexion.

panacea N. cure-all; remedy for all diseases. Some people claim that vitamin C is a *panacea* that can cure everything from cancer to the common cold.

pandemonium N. wild tumult. When the ships collided in the harbor, *pandemonium* broke out among the passengers.

parable N. short tale illustrating a moral principle. In the *parable* of the good shepherd, Jesus encourages his followers to seek those who have strayed from the flock.

• **paradox** N. something apparently contradictory in nature; statement that looks false but is actually correct. Richard presents a bit of a *paradox,* for he is a card-carrying member of both the National Rifle Association and the relatively pacifist American Civil Liberties Union.

paragon N. model of perfection. The class disliked him because the teacher was always pointing him out as a *paragon* of virtue.

paramount ADJ. foremost in importance; supreme. Proper nutrition and hygiene are of *paramount* importance in adolescent development and growth.

parched ADJ. extremely dry; very thirsty. The *parched* desert landscape seemed hostile to life.

parody N. humorous imitation; spoof; takeoff; travesty. The show *Forbidden Broadway* presents *parodies* spoofing the year's new productions playing on Broadway.

partial ADJ. incomplete; having a liking for something. In this issue we have published only a *partial* list of contributors because we lack space to acknowledge everyone. I am extremely *partial* to chocolate eclairs.

partisan ADJ. one-sided; prejudiced; committed to a party. On certain issues of principle, she refused to take a *partisan* stand but let her conscience be her guide. also N.

partition V. divide into parts. Before their second daughter was born, Jason and Lizzie decided each child needed a room of her own, and so they *partitioned* a large bedroom into two small but separate rooms. also N.

passive ADJ. not active; acted upon. Mahatma Gandhi urged his followers to pursue a program of *passive* resistance rather than resort to violence and acts of terrorism.

passport N. legal document identifying the bearer as a citizen of a country and allowing him or her to travel abroad. In arranging your first trip abroad, be sure to allow yourself enough time to apply for and receive your *passport*: you won't be allowed to travel without one.

pastoral ADJ. rural; simple and peaceful; idyllic; relating to shepherds. Tired of city living, David dreamed of moving to the country and enjoying the tranquillity of *pastoral* life.

• **patronize** V. support; act superior toward; be a customer of. Penniless artists hope to find some wealthy art lover who will *patronize* them. If a wine steward *patronized* me because he saw I knew nothing about fine wine, I'd refuse to *patronize* his restaurant.

paucity N. scarcity; lack. They closed the restaurant because the *paucity* of customers made it a losing proposition to operate.

- **pedantic** ADJ. showing off learning; bookish. Leavening his decisions with humorous, down-to-earth anecdotes, Judge Walker was not at all the *pedantic* legal scholar. pedant, N.

pedestrian ADJ. ordinary; unimaginative. Unintentionally boring, he wrote page after page of *pedestrian* prose. (secondary meaning)

peerless ADJ. having to equal; incomparable. To his admirers, the reigning operatic tenor of his generation, Luciano Pavarotti, was *peerless*; no one could compare with him.

pendulum N. suspended body that swings freely. Watching the swinging *pendulum* of the grandfather clock, Johnny swayed from side to side, echoing its movement.

penitent ADJ. feeling regret or sorrow for one's offenses; repentant. When he realized the enormity of his crime, he became remorseful and *penitent.* also N.

perceptive ADJ. insightful; aware; wise. Although Maud was a generally *perceptive* critic, she had her blind spots: she could never see flaws in the work of her friends.

perdition N. damnation; complete ruin. Praying for salvation, young Steven feared he was damned to eternal *perdition.*

peremptory ADJ. demanding and leaving no choice. From Jack's *peremptory* knock on the door, Jill could tell he would not give up until she let him in.

perfidious ADJ. treacherous; disloyal. When Caesar realized that Brutus had betrayed him, he reproached his *perfidious* friend. perfidy, N.

perfunctory ADJ. superficial; not thorough; lacking interest, care, or enthusiasm. Giving the tabletop only a *perfunctory* swipe with her dust cloth, Betty promised herself she'd clean it more thoroughly tomorrow.

- **perjury** N. false testimony while under oath. Rather than lie under oath and perhaps be indicted for *perjury,* the witness chose to take the Fifth Amendment, refusing to answer any questions on the grounds that he might incriminate himself.

Word List 32 permutation–ponderous

permutation N. transformation; rearrangement of elements. I'm pretty sure Ted's phone number ends in 5236 or some *permutation* of those digits.

pernicious ADJ. very destructive. Crack cocaine has had a *pernicious* effect on urban society: it has destroyed families, turned children into drug dealers, and increased the spread of violent crimes.

perpetrate V. commit an offense. Only an insane person could *perpetrate* such a horrible crime.

- **perpetual** ADJ. everlasting. Ponce de León hoped to find the legendary fountain of *perpetual* youth. perpetuity, N.

perpetuate V. make something last; preserve from extinction. Some critics attack *The Adventures of Huckleberry Finn* because they believe Twain's book *perpetuates* a false image of blacks in this country.

peruse V. read with care. After the conflagration that burned down her house, Joan closely *perused* her home insurance policy to discover exactly what benefits her coverage provided her. perusal, N.

- **pervasive** ADJ. pervading; spread throughout every part. Despite airing them for several hours, she could not rid her clothes of the *pervasive* odor of mothballs that clung to them. pervade, V.

perverse ADJ. stubbornly wrongheaded; wicked and perverted. When Jack was in a *perverse* mood, he would do the opposite of whatever Jill asked him. When Hannibal Lecter was in a *perverse* mood, he ate the flesh of his victims.

- **pessimism** N. belief that life is basically bad or evil; gloominess. Considering how well you have done in the course so far, you have no real reason for such *pessimism* about your final grade.
- **petulant** ADJ. touchy; peevish. If you'd had hardly any sleep for three nights and people kept on phoning and waking you up, you'd sound pretty *petulant,* too.
- **phenomena** N. Pl. observable facts or events. We kept careful records of the *phenomena* we noted in the course of these experiments.
- **philanthropist** N. lover of mankind; doer of good. In his role as *philanthropist* and public benefactor, John D. Rockefeller Sr., donated millions to charity; as an individual, however, he was a tight-fisted old man.

phlegmatic ADJ. not easily excited to action or emotional displays; calm; sluggish. The nurse was a cheerful but *phlegmatic* person, untroubled by sudden emergencies.

pious ADJ. devout; religious. The challenge for church members today is how to be *pious* in the best sense, that is, to be devout without becoming hypocritical or sanctimonious. piety, N.

pique V. provoke or arouse; annoy. "I know something *you* don't know," said Lucy, trying to *pique* Ethel's interest.

pique N. irritation; resentment. She showed her *pique* at her loss by refusing to appear with the other contestants at the end of the competition.

pivotal ADJ. crucial; key; vital. The new "smart weapons" technology played a *pivotal* role in the quick resolution of the war with Iraq.

placate V. pacify; conciliate. The store manager, trying to *placate* the angry customer, offered to replace the damaged merchandise or to give back her money right away.

placid ADJ. calm; peaceful. Looking at the storm-tossed waters of the lake, Bob wondered why they ever called it Lake *Placid.*

• **plagiarize** V. steal another's ideas and pass them off as one's own. The teacher could tell that the student had *plagiarized* parts of his essay; she could recognize whole paragraphs straight from *Barron's Book Notes.*

platitude N. trite remark; commonplace statement. In giving advice to his son, old Polonius expressed himself only in *platitudes;* every word out of his mouth was commonplace.

plausible ADJ. having a show of truth but open to doubt; specious. Your mother made you stay home from school because she needed you to program the VCR? I'm sorry, you'll have to come up with a more *plausible* excuse than that.

plethora N. excess; overabundance. She offered a *plethora* of excuses for her shortcomings.

pliable ADJ. flexible; yielding; adaptable. In remodeling the bathroom, we have replaced all the old, rigid lead pipes with new, *pliable* copper tubing.

plight N. condition, state (especially a bad state or condition); predicament. Loggers, unmoved by the *plight* of the spotted owl, plan to keep on logging whether or not they ruin the owl's habitat.

pluck N. courage. Even the enemies of young Indiana Jones were impressed by the boy's *pluck* in trying to rescue the archaeological treasure they had stolen. plucky, ADJ.

plunder N. loot; takings from a raid. Rubbing his hands with glee, the robber gloated over his ill-gotten *plunder.* also V.

podium N. pedestal; raised platform. The audience applauded as the conductor made his way to the *podium.*

polemical ADJ. aggressive in verbal attack; disputatious. Lexy was a master of *polemical* rhetoric; she should have worn a T-shirt with the slogan "Born to Debate."

ponderous ADJ. weighty; unwieldy. His humor lacked the light touch; his jokes were always *ponderous.*

Word List 33 pore–preside

pore V. study deeply; stare. In doing research on the SAT, we *pored* over back issues of *Scientific American* to locate articles from which reading passages had been excerpted.

porous ADJ. full of pores; like a sieve. Dancers like to wear *porous* clothing because it allows the ready passage of air.

portend V. foretell; presage. The king did not know what these omens might *portend* and asked his soothsayers to interpret them.

portly ADJ. stout; corpulent. The salesclerk diplomatically referred to the overweight customer as not fat but *portly.*

posterity N. descendants; future generations. We hope to leave a better world to *posterity.*

• **potency** N. power; effectiveness; influence. Looking at the expiration date on the cough syrup bottle, we wondered whether the medication still retained its *potency.* potent, ADJ.

potentate N. monarch; sovereign. The *potentate* spent more time at Monte Carlo than he did at home on his throne.

practical ADJ. based on experience; useful. Sharon gained *practical* experience in hospital work by acting as an emergency room volunteer.

• **pragmatic** ADJ. practical (as opposed to idealistic); concerned with the practical worth or impact of something. This coming trip to France should provide me with a *pragmatic* test of the value of my conversational French class.

prairie N. vast, level, or slightly rolling tract of grassland. The *prairie* is "big sky" country: your views are unobstructed by buildings or trees.

prate V. speak foolishly; boast idly. Despite Elizabeth's obvious disinclination for the topic, Mr. Collins *prated* on and on about his wonderful prospects as a husband, thanks to his noble patron, Lady Catherine de Burgh.

prattle V. babble. Baby John *prattled* on and on about the cats and his ball and the Cookie Monster.

preamble N. introductory statement. In the *preamble* to the Constitution, the purpose of the document is set forth.

precarious ADJ. uncertain; risky. Saying the stock would be a *precarious* investment, the broker advised her client against purchasing it.

• **precedent** N. something preceding in time that may be used as an authority or guide for future action. If I buy you a car for your sixteenth birthday, your brothers will want me to buy them cars when they turn sixteen, too; I can't afford to set such an expensive *precedent.*

precipitate ADJ. rash; premature; abrupt; hasty; sudden. Though I was angry enough to resign on the spot, I had enough sense to keep myself from quitting a job in such a *precipitate* fashion.

precipitous ADJ. steep; overhasty. This hill is difficult to climb because it is so *precipitous;* one slip, and our descent will be *precipitous* as well.

preclude V. make impossible; eliminate. Because the band was already booked to play in Hollywood on New Year's Eve, that booking *precluded* their accepting the New Year's Eve gig in London they were offered.

precursor N. forerunner. Though Gray and Burns share many traits with the Romantic poets who followed them, most critics consider them *precursors* of the Romantic movement, not true Romantics.

• **predator** N. creature that seizes and devours another animal; person who robs or exploits others. Not just cats, but a wide variety of *predators*—owls, hawks, weasels, foxes—catch mice for dinner. A carnivore is by definition *predatory,* for it *preys* on weaker creatures.

predetermine V. predestine; settle or decide beforehand; influence markedly. Romeo and Juliet believed that Fate had *predetermined* their meeting. Bea gathered estimates from caterers, florists, and stationers so that she could *predetermine* the costs of holding a catered buffet. Philip's love of athletics *predetermined* his choice of a career in sports marketing.

predilection N. partiality; preference. Although my mother wrote all sorts of poetry over the years, she had a definite *predilection* for occasional verse.

preeminent ADJ. outstanding; superior. The king traveled to Boston because he wanted the *preeminent* surgeon in the field to perform the operation.

preempt V. head off; forestall by acting first; appropriate for oneself; supplant. Hoping to *preempt* any attempts by the opposition to make educational reform a hot political issue, the candidate set out her own plan to revitalize the public schools. preemptive, ADJ.

prelate N. church dignitary. The archbishop of Moscow and other high-ranking *prelates* visited the Russian Orthodox seminary.

• **premise** N. assumption; postulate. Acting on the *premise* that there's no fool like an old fool, P. T. Barnum hired a 90-year-old clown for his circus.

• **premonition** N. forewarning. In horror movies, the hero often has a *premonition* of danger, yet he foolishly ignores it.

preposterous ADJ. absurd; ridiculous. When he tried to downplay his youthful experiments with marijuana by saying he hadn't inhaled, we all thought, "What a *preposterous* excuse!"

prescience N. ability to foretell the future. Given the current wave of Japan bashing, it does not take *prescience* for me to foresee problems in our future trade relations with Japan.

preside V. act as president or chairman; exercise control. When the club president cannot attend a meeting, the vice president will *preside* over that session.

Word List 34 prestige–prophetic

prestige N. impression produced by achievements or reputation. Many students want to go to Harvard College not for the education offered but for the *prestige* of Harvard's name.

• **presumptuous** ADJ. taking liberties; overstepping bounds; nervy. I thought it was *presumptuous* of Mort to butt into Bishop Tutu's talk with Mrs. Clinton and ask them for their autographs; I wouldn't have had the nerve.

pretentious ADJ. ostentatious; pompous; making unjustified claims; overly ambitious. None of the other prizewinners are wearing their medals; isn't it a bit *pretentious* of you to wear yours?

• **prevail** V. triumph; predominate; prove superior in strength, power, or influence; be current. A radical committed to social change, Reed had no patience with the conservative views that *prevailed* in the America of his day. prevalent, ADJ.; prevailing, ADJ.

prevaricate V. lie. Some people believe that to *prevaricate* in a good cause is justifiable and regard their false statement as a "white lie."

• **prey** N. target of a hunt; victim. In *Stalking the Wild Asparagus,* Euell Gibbons has as his *prey* not wild beasts but wild plants. also V.

privation N. hardship; want. In his youth, he knew hunger and *privation.*

procrastinate V. postpone; delay or put off. Looking at four years of receipts and checks he still had to sort through, Bob was truly sorry he had *procrastinated* for so long and not finished filing his taxes long ago.

prodigal ADJ. wasteful; reckless with money. Don't be so *prodigal* spending my money; when you've earned some money, you can waste it as much as you want! also N.

prodigious ADJ. marvelous; enormous. Watching the champion weight lifter heave the weighty barbell to shoulder height and then boost it overhead, we marveled at his *prodigious* strength.

prodigy N. highly gifted child; extraordinary accomplishment or event. Menuhin was a *prodigy,* performing wonders on his violin when he was barely eight years old.

profane V. violate; desecrate; treat unworthily. The members of the mysterious Far Eastern cult sought to kill the British explorer because he had *profaned* the sanctity of their holy goblet by using it as an ashtray. also ADJ.

profligate N. dissipated; wasteful; wildly immoral. Although surrounded by wild and *profligate* companions, she nevertheless managed to retain some sense of decency.

• **profound** ADJ. deep; not superficial; complete. Freud's remarkable insights into human behavior caused his fellow scientists to honor him as a *profound* thinker. profundity, N.

profusion N. overabundance; lavish expenditure; excess. Freddy was so overwhelmed by the *profusion* of choices on the menu that he knocked over his wine glass and soaked his host. He made *profuse* apologies to his host, the waiter, the busboy, the people at the next table, and the man in the men's room giving out paper towels.

progenitor N. ancestor. The Roth family, whose *progenitors* emigrated from Germany early in the nineteenth century, settled in Peru, Illinois.

• **proliferation** N. rapid growth; spread; multiplication. Times of economic hardship inevitably encourage the *proliferation* of countless get-rich-quick schemes. proliferate, V.

• **prolific** ADJ. abundantly fruitful. My editors must assume I'm a *prolific* writer: they expect me to revise six books this year!

• **prologue** N. introduction (to a poem or play). In the *prologue* to *Romeo and Juliet*, Shakespeare introduces the audience to the feud between the Montagues and the Capulets.

prolong V. make longer; draw out; lengthen. In their determination to discover ways to *prolong* human life, doctors fail to take into account that longer lives are not always happier ones.

• **prominent** ADJ. conspicuous; notable; sticking out. Have you ever noticed that Prince Charles's *prominent* ears make him resemble the big-eared character in *Mad* comics?

promontory N. high point of land jutting out into a body of water; headland. They erected a lighthouse on the *promontory* to warn approaching ships of their nearness to the shore.

• **promote** V. help to flourish; advance in rank; publicize. Founder of the Children's Defense Fund, Marian Wright Edelman ceaselessly *promotes* the welfare of young people everywhere.

promulgate V. proclaim a doctrine or law; make known by official publication. When Moses came down from the mountaintop all set to *promulgate* God's commandments, he was shocked to discover his followers worshipping a golden calf.

prone ADJ. inclined to; prostrate. She was *prone* to sudden fits of anger during which she would lie *prone* on the floor, screaming and kicking her heels.

propagate V. multiply; spread. Since bacteria *propagate* more quickly in unsanitary environments, it is important to keep hospital rooms clean.

propensity N. natural inclination. Convinced of his own talent, Sol has an unfortunate *propensity* to belittle the talents of others.

property N. quality or aspect; belongings; land. In science class we learned that each element has certain physical and chemical *properties*.

• **prophetic** ADJ. foretelling the future. I have no magical *prophetic* powers; when I predict what will happen, I base my predictions on common sense. prophesy, V.

Word List 35 proponent–qualified

proponent N. supporter; backer. In the Senate, *proponents* of the universal health care measure lobbied to gain additional support for the controversial legislation.

propriety N. fitness; correct conduct. Miss Manners counsels her readers so that they may behave with due *propriety* in any social situation and not embarrass themselves.

prosaic ADJ. dull and unimaginative; matter-of-fact; factual. Though the ad writers had come up with a wildly imaginative campaign to publicize the company's newest product, the head office rejected it for a more *prosaic,* down-to-earth approach.

• **prosperity** N. good fortune; financial success; physical well-being. Promising to stay together "for richer, for poorer," the newlyweds vowed to be true to one another in *prosperity* and hardship alike.

protagonist N. principal character; leading actor. Emma, the *protagonist* of Jane Austen's novel, is an overindulged young woman convinced of her ability as a matchmaker.

prototype N. original work used as a model by others. The National Air and Space Museum displays the Wright brothers' first plane, the *prototype* of all the American aircraft that came after.

protract V. prolong. Seeking to delay the union members' vote, the management team tried to *protract* the negotiations endlessly, but the union representatives saw through their strategy.

protrude V. stick out. His fingers *protruded* from the holes in his gloves. protrusion, N.

protuberance N. protrusion; bulge. A ganglionic cyst is a fluid-filled tumor that develops near a joint membrane or tendon sheath and that bulges beneath the skin, forming a *protuberance.*

provident ADJ. displaying foresight; thrifty; preparing for emergencies. In his usual *provident* manner, he had insured himself against this type of loss.

provincial ADJ. pertaining to a province; limited in outlook; unsophisticated. As *provincial* governor, Sir Henry administered the queen's law in his remote corner of Canada. Caught up in local problems, out of touch with London news, he became sadly *provincial.*

provisional ADJ. tentative. Kim's acceptance as an American Express cardholder was *provisional:* before issuing her a card, American Express wanted to check her employment record and credit history.

• **provocative** ADJ. arousing anger or interest; annoying. In a typically *provocative* act, the bully kicked sand into the weaker man's face.

proximity N. nearness. Blind people sometimes develop a compensatory ability to sense the *proximity* of objects around them.

• **prudent** ADJ. cautious; careful. A miser hoards money not because he is *prudent* but because he is greedy. prudence, N.

prune V. cut away; trim. With the help of her editor, she was able to *prune* her manuscript into publishable form.

pseudonym N. pen name. Samuel Clemens's *pseudonym* was Mark Twain.

puerile ADJ. childish; immature. Throwing tantrums? You should have outgrown such *puerile* behavior years ago.

pugnacious ADJ. combative; disposed to fight. "Put up your dukes!" he cried, making a fist to show how *pugnacious* he was.

pulverize V. crush or grind into dust. Before sprinkling the dried herbs into the stew, Michael first *pulverized* them into a fine powder.

pummel V. beat or pound with fists. Swinging wildly, Pammy *pummeled* her brother around the head and shoulders.

punctilious ADJ. laying stress on niceties of conduct or form; minutely attentive to fine points (perhaps too much so). Percy is *punctilious* about observing the rules of etiquette whenever Miss Manners invites him to stay. punctiliousness, N.

pungent ADJ. stinging; sharp in taste or smell; caustic. The *pungent* odor of ripe Limburger cheese appealed to Simone but made Stanley gag.

puny ADJ. insignificant; tiny; weak. Our *puny* efforts to stop the flood were futile.

purge V. remove or get rid of something unwanted; free from blame or guilt; cleanse or purify. The Communist government *purged* the party to get rid of members suspected of capitalist sympathies. also N.

purveyor N. furnisher of foodstuffs; caterer. As *purveyor* of rare wines and viands, he traveled through France and Italy every year in search of new products to sell.

quack N. charlatan; impostor. Don't let that *quack* fool you with his wild claims; he can't cure what ails you. quackery, N.

quagmire N. soft wet boggy land; complex or dangerous situation from which it is difficult to free oneself. Up to her knees in mud, Myra wondered how on earth she was going to extricate herself from this *quagmire*.

qualified ADJ. limited; restricted. Unable to give the candidate full support, the mayor gave him only a *qualified* endorsement. (secondary meaning)

Word List 36 quandary–reconcile

quandary N. dilemma. When both Harvard and Stanford accepted Lori, she was in a *quandary* as to which school she should attend.

quarry N. victim; object of a hunt. The police closed in on their *quarry*.

quarry V. dig into. They *quarried* blocks of marble out of the hillside. also N.

quell V. extinguish; put down; quiet. Miss Minchin's demeanor was so stern and forbidding that she could *quell* any unrest among her students with one intimidating glance.

quench V. douse or extinguish; assuage or satisfy. What's the favorite song of the fire department? "Baby, *Quench* My Fire!"

querulous ADJ. fretful; whining. Even the most agreeable toddlers can begin to act *querulous* if they miss their nap.

quibble N. minor objection or complaint. Aside from a few hundred teensy-weensy *quibbles* about the set, the script, the actors, the director, the costumes, the lighting, and the props, the hypercritical critic loved the play. also V.

quip N. witty jest; wisecrack; taunt. Whenever the reporters asked him a tough question, he never gave them a straight answer but joked around, tossing off one-liners and humorous *quips*. also V.

quiver V. tremble; shake. The bird dog's nose twitched and his whiskers *quivered* as he strained eagerly against the leash. also N.

quiver N. case for arrows. Robin Hood reached back and plucked one last arrow from his *quiver*. (secondary meaning)

quixotic ADJ. idealistic but impractical. Simon's head is in the clouds; he constantly comes up with *quixotic*, unworkable schemes.

rabid ADJ. like a fanatic; furious. He was a *rabid* follower of the Dodgers and watched them play whenever he could go to the ball park.

raconteur N. storyteller. My father was a gifted *raconteur* with an unlimited supply of anecdotes.

rally V. call up or summon (forces, vital powers, etc.); revive or recuperate. Washington quickly *rallied* his troops to fight off the British attack. The patient had been sinking throughout the night, but at dawn she *rallied* and made a complete recovery.

• **ramble** V. wander aimlessly (physically or mentally). Listening to the teacher *ramble*, Shelby wondered whether he'd ever get to the point. also N.

rampant ADJ. growing in profusion; unrestrained. In the garden, the weeds were *rampant*: they killed all the flowers that had been planted in the spring. In the city, crime was *rampant*: the burglars and muggers were out of control.

ramshackle ADJ. rickety; falling apart. The boys propped up the *ramshackle* clubhouse with a couple of boards.

rancid ADJ. having the odor of stale fat. The *rancid* odor that filled the ship's galley nauseated the crew.

rancor N. bitterness; deep-seated hatred. Thirty years after the war, she could not let go of the past but still felt an implacable *rancor* against the foe.

• **random** ADJ. without definite purpose, plan, or aim; haphazard. Although the sponsor of the raffle claimed all winners were chosen at *random,* people had their suspicions when the grand prize went to the sponsor's brother-in-law.

rant V. rave; talk excitedly; scold; make a grandiloquent speech. When he heard that I'd totaled the family car, Dad began to *rant* at me like a complete madman.

rarefied ADJ. made less dense [of a gas]. The mountain climbers had difficulty breathing in the *rarefied* atmosphere. rarefy, V.

raucous ADJ. harsh and shrill; disorderly and boisterous. The *raucous* crowd of New Year's Eve revelers got progressively noisier as midnight drew near.

raze V. destroy completely. Spelling is important: to raise a building is to put it up; to *raze* a building is to tear it down.

reactionary ADJ. recoiling from progress; politically ultraconservative. Opposing the use of English in worship services, *reactionary* forces in the church fought to reinstate the mass in Latin.

rebuff V. snub; beat back. She *rebuffed* his invitation so smoothly that he did not realize he had been snubbed.

recalcitrant ADJ. obstinately stubborn. Which animal do you think is more *recalcitrant*, a pig-headed pig or a stubborn mule?

recant V. disclaim or disavow; retract a previous statement; openly confess error. Those who can, keep true to their faith; those who can't, *recant.*

recapitulate V. summarize. Let us *recapitulate* what has been said thus far before going ahead.

recession N. withdrawal; time of low economic activity. The slow *recession* of the floodwaters created problems for the crews working to restore power to the area.

reciprocate V. repay in kind. It was kind of Donna to have us over to dinner; I'd like us to *reciprocate* in some way, if we can.

• **recluse** N. hermit; loner. Disappointed in love, Miss Emily became a *recluse;* she shut herself away in her empty mansion and refused to see another living soul. reclusive, ADJ.

reconcile V. correct inconsistencies; become friendly after a quarrel. Every time we try to *reconcile* our checkbook with the bank statement, we quarrel. However, despite these monthly lovers' quarrels, we always manage to *reconcile.*

Word List 37 recount–renovate

recount V. narrate or tell; count over again. About to *recount* the latest adventure of Sherlock Holmes, Watson lost track of exactly how many cases Holmes had solved and refused to begin his tale until he'd *recounted* them one by one.

rectify V. set right; correct. You had better send a check to *rectify* your account before American Express cancels your credit card.

rectitude N. uprightness; moral virtue; correctness of judgment. The Eagle Scout was a model of *rectitude.*

recumbent ADJ. reclining; lying down completely or in part. The command "at ease" does not permit you to take a *recumbent* position.

recuperate V. recover. The doctors were worried because the patient did not *recuperate* as rapidly as they had expected.

recurrent ADJ. occurring again and again. Because Phil suffered from *recurrent* ear infections, the doctors were concerned that these periodic attacks might eventually affect his hearing.

redundant ADJ. superfluous; repetitious; excessively wordy. The bottle of wine I brought to Bob's was certainly *redundant:* how was I to know Bob owned a winery? In your essay, you repeat several points unnecessarily; try to be less *redundant* in the future. redundancy, N.

refine V. free from impurities; perfect. Just as you can *refine* sugar by removing bits of cane and other unwanted material, you can *refine* verse by removing awkward metaphors and polishing rough rhymes. refinement, N.

reflect V. consider or deliberate; show; mirror. Mr. Collins *reflected* on Elizabeth's rejection of his proposal. Did it *reflect* her true feelings, he wondered. Looking at his *reflection* in the mirror, he refused to believe that she could reject such a fine figure of a man.

refraction N. bending of a ray of light. Insert a stick in a glass of water and look at it carefully. It looks bent because of the *refraction* of the light by the water.

refrain V. abstain from; resist. Whenever he heard a song with a lively chorus, Sol could never *refrain* from joining in on the refrain.

refrain N. chorus. Whenever he heard a song with a lively chorus, Sol could never refrain from joining in on the *refrain.*

• **refute** V. disprove. At his trial, Socrates attempted to *refute* the claims of those who accused him of corrupting the youth of Athens through his teachings.

regress V. move backward to an earlier, generally more primitive state. Although Timmy outgrew his need for a pacifier well over a year ago, occasionally when he's tired or nervous, he *regresses* and starts sucking his thumb.

reiterate V. repeat. He *reiterated* the warning to make sure that everyone understood it.

rejoinder N. retort; comeback; reply. When someone has been rude to me, I find it particularly satisfying to come up with a quick *rejoinder.*

• **rejuvenate** V. make young again. The charlatan claimed that his elixir would *rejuvenate* the aged and weary.

relegate V. banish to an inferior position; delegate; assign. After Ralph dropped his second tray of drinks that week, the manager swiftly *relegated* him to a minor post cleaning up behind the bar.

relevant ADJ. pertinent; referring to the case in hand. How *relevant* Virginia Woolf's essays are to women writers today; it's as if Woolf in the 1930s foresaw our current literary struggles. relevancy, N.

relic N. surviving remnant; memento. Egypt's Department of Antiquities prohibits tourists from taking mummies and other ancient *relics* out of the country. Mike keeps his photos of his trip to Egypt in a box with other *relics* of his travels.

• **relinquish** V. give up something with reluctance; yield. Once you get used to fringe benefits like expense account meals and a company car, it's very hard to *relinquish* them.

relish V. savor; enjoy. Watching Peter enthusiastically chow down, I thought, "Now there's a man who *relishes* a good dinner!" also N.

reminiscence N. recollection. Her *reminiscences* of her experiences are so fascinating that she ought to write a book.

remiss ADJ. negligent. The prison guard was accused of being *remiss* in his duty when the prisoner escaped.

remnant N. remainder. I suggest that you wait until the store places the *remnants* of these goods on sale.

remonstrance N. protest; objection. The authorities were deaf to the pastor's *remonstrances* about the lack of police protection in the area. remonstrate, V.

remorse N. guilt; self-reproach. The murderer felt no *remorse* for his crime.

remunerative ADJ. lucrative; rewarding. Because work as an insurance agent was far more *remunerative* than work as a church organist, Ives eventually resigned from his church job. remuneration, N.

renegade N. deserter; traitor. Because he had abandoned his post and joined forces with the Indians, his fellow officers considered the hero of *Dances with Wolves* a *renegade.* also ADJ.

renounce V. abandon; disown; repudiate. Even though she knew she would be burned at the stake as a witch, Joan of Arc refused to *renounce* her belief that her voices came from God. renunciation, N.

renovate V. restore to good condition; renew. We *renovated* our kitchen, replacing the old cabinets and countertop and installing new appliances.

Word List 38 renown–reticent

• **renown** N. fame. For many years an unheralded researcher, Barbara McClintock gained international *renown* when she won the Nobel Prize in physiology and medicine.

rent N. rip; split. Kit did an excellent job of mending the *rent* in the lining in her coat. rend, V.

repatriate V. return to one's own country. Although the Western powers hoped to *repatriate* the refugees swiftly, they were unable to do so because of the still dangerous conditions in the refugees' homeland.

repeal V. revoke; annul. What would the effect on our society be if we decriminalized drug use by *repealing* the laws against the possession and sale of narcotics?

repel V. drive away; disgust. At first, the Beast's ferocious appearance *repelled* Beauty, but she came to love the tender heart hidden behind that beastly exterior.

repertoire N. list of works of music, drama, etc., a performer is prepared to present. The opera company decided to include *Madame Butterfly* in its *repertoire* for the following season.

replenish V. fill up again. Before she could take another backpacking trip, Carla had to *replenish* her stock of freeze-dried foods.

• **reprehensible** ADJ. deserving blame. Shocked by the viciousness of the bombing, politicians of every party uniformly condemned the terrorists' *reprehensible* deed.

repress V. restrain; hold back; crush; suppress. Anne's parents tried to curb her impetuosity without *repressing* her boundless high spirits.

reprieve N. temporary stay. During the twenty-four-hour *reprieve,* the lawyers sought to make the stay of execution permanent. also V.

reprimand V. reprove severely; rebuke. Every time Ermengarde made a mistake in class, she was afraid that Miss Minchin would *reprimand* her and tell her father how badly she was doing in school. also N.

reproachful ADJ. expressing disapproval. He never could do anything wrong without imagining the *reproachful* look in his mother's eye.

reprove V. censure; rebuke. Though Aunt Bea at times would *reprove* Opie for inattention in church, she believed he was at heart a God-fearing lad.

• **repudiate** V. disown; disavow. On separating from Tony, Tina announced that she would *repudiate* all debts incurred by her soon-to-be ex-husband.

repulsion N. distaste; act of driving back. Hating bloodshed, she viewed war with *repulsion*. Even defensive battles distressed her, for the *repulsion* of enemy forces is never accomplished bloodlessly.

reputable ADJ. respectable. If you want to buy antiques, look for a *reputable* dealer; far too many dealers today pass off fakes as genuine antiques.

rescind V. cancel. Because of the public outcry against the new taxes, the senator proposed a bill to *rescind* the unpopular financial measure.

• **reserved** ADJ. self-controlled; careful in expressing oneself. They made an odd couple: she was outspoken and uninhibited; he was cautious and *reserved.* (secondary meaning)

• **resignation** N. patient submissiveness; statement that one is quitting a job. If Bob Cratchit had not accepted Scrooge's bullying with such *resignation,* he might have gotten up the nerve to hand in his *resignation.* resigned, ADJ.

resilient ADJ. elastic; having the power of springing back. Highly *resilient,* steel makes excellent bedsprings. resilience, N.

• **resolution** N. determination. Nothing could shake his *resolution* that his children would get the best education that money could buy. resolute, ADJ.

• **resolve** V. decide; settle; solve. "I have *resolved,* Watson, to travel to Bohemia to *resolve* the dispute between Irene Adler and the King. In my absence, do your best to *resolve* any mysteries that arise."

resonant ADJ. echoing; resounding; deep and full in sound. The deep, *resonant* voice of the actor James Earl Jones makes him particularly effective when he appears on stage.

respiration N. breathing. The doctor found that the patient's years of smoking had adversely affected both his lung capacity and his rate of *respiration.* respire, V.

restive ADJ. restlessly impatient; obstinately resisting control. Waiting impatiently in line to see Santa Claus, even the best-behaved children grow *restive* and start to fidget.

• **restraint** N. moderation or self-control; controlling force; restriction. Control yourself, young lady! Show some *restraint!*

resumption N. taking up again; recommencement. During summer break, Don had not realized how much he missed university life; at the *resumption* of classes, however, he felt marked excitement and pleasure. resume, V.

resurge V. rise again; flow to and fro. It was startling to see the spirit of nationalism *resurge* as the Soviet Union disintegrated into a loose federation of ethnic and national groups. resurgence, N.

• **retain** V. keep; employ. Fighting to *retain* his seat in Congress, Senator Foghorn *retained* a new manager to head his reelection campaign.

retaliation N. repayment in kind (usually for bad treatment). Because everyone knew the Princeton Band had stolen Brown's mascot, the whole Princeton student body expected some sort of *retaliation* from Brown. retaliate, V.

• **reticent** ADJ. reserved; uncommunicative; inclined to be silent. Fearing his competitors might get advance word about his plans from talkative staff members, Hughes preferred *reticent* employees to loquacious ones.

Word List 39 retract–saturate

retract V. withdraw; take back. When I saw how Fred and his fraternity brothers had trashed the frat house, I decided to *retract* my offer to let them use our summer cottage for the weekend. retraction, N.

retrieve V. recover; find and bring in. The dog was intelligent and quickly learned to *retrieve* the game killed by the hunter.

retroactive ADJ. taking effect prior to its enactment (as a law) or imposition (as a tax). Because the new pension law was *retroactive* to the first of the year, even though Martha had retired in February, she was eligible for the pension.

revelry N. boisterous merrymaking. New Year's Eve is a night of *revelry.*

• **reverent** ADJ. respectful; worshipful. Though I bow my head in church and recite the prayers, sometimes I don't feel properly *reverent.* revere, V.

revoke V. cancel; retract. Repeat offenders who continue to drive under the influence of alcohol face having their driver's license permanently *revoked.*

revulsion N. sudden, violent change of feeling; distaste; repugnance. Normally Cecil had a good appetite, but when he felt seasick he viewed his shipboard supper with *revulsion.*

rift N. opening made by splitting; open space; break in friendly relations. After the recent earthquake, geologists observed several fresh *rifts* in the Hayward hills. Through a *rift* in the dense clouds the pilot glimpsed a beacon light far below. Unsure how he had offended Jo, Laurie tried to think of some way to mend the *rift* in their friendship.

rigid ADJ. stiff and unyielding; strict; hard and unbending. By living with a man to whom she was not married, George Eliot broke Victorian society's most *rigid* rule of respectable behavior.

rigor N. severity. Many settlers could not stand the *rigors* of the New England winters.

rile V. vex; irritate. Red had a hair-trigger temper: he was an easy man to *rile.*

rivulet N. small stream. As the rains continued, the small trickle of water running down the hillside grew into a *rivulet* that threatened to wash away a portion of the slope.

rousing ADJ. lively; stirring. "And now, let's have a *rousing* welcome for TV's own Roseanne Barr, who'll lead us in a *rousing* rendition of 'The Star Spangled Banner.'"

ruddy ADJ. reddish; healthy looking. Santa Claus's *ruddy* cheeks nicely complement Rudolph the Reindeer's bright red nose.

rue V. regret; lament; mourn. Tina *rued* the night she met Tony and wondered how she'd ever fallen for such a jerk. rueful, ADJ.

rummage V. ransack; thoroughly search. When we *rummaged* through the trunks in the attic, we found many souvenirs of our childhood days. also N.

rupture N. act of breaking; fracture; break in harmony or peaceful relations. The *rupture* of gas lines caused by the earthquake contributed greatly to the fire that ensued.

ruse N. trick; stratagem. Because they wanted to decorate the living room for their mother's surprise birthday party, the girls tried to think of some good *ruse* to lure her out of the house for a couple of hours.

• **ruthless** ADJ. pitiless; cruel. Captain Hook was a dangerous, *ruthless* villain who would stop at nothing to destroy Peter Pan.

saboteur N. one who commits sabotage; destroyer of property. Members of the Resistance acted as *saboteurs,* blowing up train lines to prevent supplies from reaching the Nazi army.

saccharine ADJ. cloyingly sweet. She tried to ingratiate herself, speaking sweetly and smiling a *saccharine* smile.

sagacious ADJ. keen; shrewd; having insight. Holmes is far too *sagacious* to be fooled by a simple trick like that. sagacity, N.

salutary ADJ. tending to improve; beneficial; wholesome. The punishment had a *salutary* effect on the boy, for he became a model student.

sanction V. approve; ratify. Nothing will convince me to *sanction* the engagement of my daughter to such a worthless young man.

sap V. diminish; undermine. The element kryptonite has an unhealthy effect on Superman: it *saps* his strength.

sarcasm N. scornful remarks; stinging rebuke. Though Ralph tried to ignore the mocking comments of his supposed friends, their *sarcasm* wounded him deeply.

sate V. satisfy to the full; cloy. Its hunger *sated,* the lion dozed.

satiate V. satisfy fully. Having stuffed themselves until they were *satiated,* the guests were so full they were ready for a nap.

• **satirize** V. mock. Cartoonist Gary Trudeau often *satirizes* contemporary politicians; through the comments of the *Doonesbury* characters, Trudeau ridicules political corruption and folly. satirical, ADJ.

saturate V. soak thoroughly. Thorough watering is the key to lawn care: you must *saturate* your new lawn well to encourage its growth.

Word List 40 saunter–shyster

saunter V. stroll slowly. Too tired for his usual brisk walk, Stan *sauntered* through the park, taking time to enjoy the spring flowers.

savant N. learned scholar. Despite all her academic honors, Dr. Diamond refused to be classed as a *savant:* considering herself a simple researcher, she refused to describe herself in such grandiose terms.

savory ADJ. tasty; pleasing, attractive, or agreeable. Julia Child's recipes enable amateur chefs to create *savory* delicacies for their guests.

scamper V. run about playfully. Looking forward to the game of hide-and-seek, the children *scampered* off to find good spots in which to hide.

scanty ADJ. meager; insufficient. Thinking his helping of food was *scanty,* Oliver Twist asked for more.

scapegoat N. someone who bears the blame for others. After the *Challenger* disaster, NASA searched for *scapegoats* on whom they could cast the blame.

scavenge V. hunt through discarded materials for usable items; search, especially for food. If you need parts for an old car that the dealers no longer have in stock, try *scavenging* for odd bits and pieces at the auto wreckers' yards. scavenger, N.

schism N. division; split. Let us not widen the *schism* by further bickering.

scintillate V. sparkle; flash. I enjoy her dinner parties because the food is excellent and the conversation *scintillates.*

scrupulous ADJ. conscientious; extremely thorough. Though Alfred is *scrupulous* in fulfilling his duties at work, he is less conscientious about his obligations to his family and friends.

• **scrutinize** V. examine closely and critically. Searching for flaws, the sergeant *scrutinized* every detail of the private's uniform.

scuffle V. struggle confusedly; move off in a confused hurry. The twins briefly *scuffled,* wrestling to see which of them would get the toy. When their big brother yelled, "Let go of my Gameboy!" they *scuffled* off down the hall.

seasoned ADJ. experienced. Though pleased with her new batch of rookies, the basketball coach wished she had a few more *seasoned* players on the team. (secondary meaning)

• **seclusion** N. isolation; solitude. One moment she loved crowds; the next, she sought *seclusion*.

sect N. separate religious body; faction. As university chaplain, she sought to address universal religious issues and not limit herself to concerns of any one *sect*.

secular ADJ. worldly; not pertaining to church matters. The church leaders decided not to interfere in *secular* matters.

sedate ADJ. calm and composed; grave. To calm the agitated pony, we teamed him with a *sedate* mare that easily accepted the harness.

sedition N. resistance to authority; insubordination; rebellion. Her words, though not treasonous in themselves, were calculated to arouse thoughts of *sedition*. seditious, ADJ.

seep V. leak through; trickle. After all the times we'd tried to repair the leaky roof, we were discouraged to see the water *seep* through the ceiling once again.

sensory ADJ. pertaining to the physical senses. Blasted by sound waves, dazzled by flashing lights, jostled by crowds, a newcomer to rock concerts can suffer from *sensory* overload.

sequester V. isolate; retire from public life; segregate; seclude. Banished from his kingdom, the wizard Prospero *sequestered* himself on a desert island.

serendipity N. gift for finding valuable or desirable things by accident; accidental good fortune or luck. Many scientific discoveries are a matter of *serendipity*: Newton was not sitting there thinking about gravity when the apple dropped on his head.

• **serenity** N. calmness; placidity. The *serenity* of the sleepy town was shattered by a tremendous explosion.

servile ADJ. slavishly submissive; fawning; cringing. Constantly fawning over his employer, Uriah Heep was a *servile* creature.

servitude N. slavery; compulsory labor. Born a slave, Douglass resented his life of *servitude* and plotted to escape to the North.

• **sever** V. cut; separate. Dr. Guillotin invented a machine that could neatly *sever* an aristocratic head from its equally aristocratic body.

• **severity** N. harshness; intensity; austerity; rigidity. The *severity* of Jane's migraine attack was so great that she took to her bed for a week.

shackle V. chain; fetter. In a chain gang, convicts are *shackled* together to prevent their escape. also N.

shambles N. wreck; mess; slaughterhouse. After the hurricane, the Carolina coast was a *shambles*. After the New Year's Eve party, the apartment was a *shambles*.

shimmer V. glimmer intermittently. The moonlight *shimmered* on the water as the moon broke through the clouds for a moment. also N.

shortcomings N. failures; deficiencies. Aware of his own *shortcomings* as a public speaker, the candidate worked closely with debate coaches to prepare for the coming campaign.

shrewd ADJ. clever; astute. A *shrewd* investor, he took clever advantage of the fluctuations of the stock market.

shun V. keep away from. Cherishing his solitude, the recluse *shunned* the company of other human beings.

shyster N. lawyer using questionable methods. The respectable attorney was horrified to learn that his newly discovered half brother was nothing but a cheap *shyster*.

Word List 41 simile–spoke

simile N. comparison of one thing with another, using the word *like* or *as*. "My love is like a red, red rose" is a *simile*.

simplistic ADJ. oversimplified. Though Jack's solution dealt adequately with one aspect of the problem, it was *simplistic* in failing to consider various complications that might arise.

simulate V. feign; pretend. The judge ruled that the accused racketeer had *simulated* insanity and was in fact sane enough to stand trial.

• **singular** ADJ. unique; extraordinary; odd. Though the young man tried to understand Father William's *singular* behavior, he still found it odd that the old man incessantly stood on his head. singularity, N.

sinister ADJ. evil; conveying a sense of ill omen. Aware of the Penguin's *sinister* purpose, Batman wondered how he could save Gotham City from the ravages of his evil enemy.

sinuous ADJ. winding; bending in and out; not morally honest. The snake moved in a *sinuous* manner.

• **skeptical** ADJ. doubting; suspending judgment until having examined the evidence supporting a point of view. I am *skeptical* about this project; I want some proof that it can work. skepticism, N.

skulk V. move furtively and secretly. He *skulked* through the less fashionable sections of the city in order to avoid meeting any of his former friends.

slacken V. slow up; loosen. As they passed the finish line, the runners *slackened* their pace.

slag N. residue from smelting metal; dross; waste matter. The blast furnace had a special opening at the bottom to allow the workers to remove the worthless *slag*.

slapdash ADJ. haphazard; careless; sloppy. From the number of typos and misspellings I found in it, it's clear that Mario proofread the report in a remarkably *slapdash* fashion.

slather V. spread abundantly. Johnny *slathered* jelly on his toast so generously that it oozed over the edge and dripped on the clean tablecloth below.

slothful ADJ. lazy. Lying idly on the sofa while others worked, Reggie denied he was *slothful:* "I just supervise better lying down."

sluggish ADJ. slow; lazy; lethargic. After two nights without sleep, she felt *sluggish* and incapable of exertion.

smelt V. melt or blend ores, changing their chemical composition. The furnaceman *smelts* tin with copper to create a special alloy used in making bells.

smolder V. burn without flame; be liable to break out at any moment. The rags *smoldered* for hours before they burst into flame.

smuggler N. one who illegally moves goods across national borders. Suspecting Randy might be a *smuggler,* the customs inspector made a thorough search of his luggage but found nothing illicit.

sneer V. smile or laugh contemptuously; make an insulting comment or face. "I could paint better than that with both hands tied behind my back," *sneered* Marvin.

sobriety N. moderation (especially regarding indulgence in alcohol); seriousness. Neither falling-down drunks nor stand-up comics are noted for *sobriety.* sober, ADJ.

sodden ADJ. soaked; dull, as if from drink. He set his *sodden* overcoat near the radiator to dry.

solemnity N. seriousness; gravity. The minister was concerned that nothing should disturb the *solemnity* of the marriage service.

soliloquy N. talking to oneself. Dramatists use the *soliloquy* as a device to reveal a character's innermost thoughts and emotions.

somber ADJ. gloomy; depressing; dark; drab. Dull brown and charcoal gray are pretty *somber* colors; can't you wear something bright?

somnolent ADJ. half asleep. The heavy meal and the overheated room made us all *somnolent* and indifferent to the speaker.

soporific ADJ. sleep-causing; marked by sleepiness. Professor Pringle's lectures were so *soporific* that even he fell asleep in class. also N.

sordid ADJ. vile; filthy; wretched; mean. Talk show hosts seem willing to discuss any topic, no matter how *sordid* and disgusting it may be.

spartan ADJ. avoiding luxury and comfort; sternly disciplined. Looking over the bare, unheated room with its hard cot, he wondered what he was doing in such *spartan* quarters. Only his *spartan* sense of duty kept him at his post.

spat N. squabble; minor dispute. What had started out as a mere *spat* escalated into a full-blown argument.

specious ADJ. seemingly reasonable but incorrect; misleading (often intentionally). To claim that, because houses and birds both have wings, both can fly, is extremely *specious* reasoning.

speculate V. theorize or ponder; assume a financial risk; gamble. Students of the stock market *speculate* that the seeds of the financier's downfall were planted when he *speculated* heavily in junk bonds.

spendthrift N. someone who wastes money. Easy access to credit encourages people to turn into *spendthrifts* who shop till they drop.

splendor N. magnificence; grandeur; brilliance. Awed by the glittering chandeliers and finely costumed courtiers, Cinderella was overwhelmed by the *splendor* of the ball.

spoke N. radiating bar supporting the rim of a wheel. The repair man at the bicycle shop took less than half an hour to fix the bent *spokes* on Bob's rear wheel.

Word List 42 spontaneity–subsequent

spontaneity N. lack of premeditation; naturalness; freedom from constraint. When Betty and Jennifer met, Jen impulsively hugged her roommate-to-be, but Betty drew back, unprepared for such *spontaneity.* spontaneous, ADJ.

sporadic ADJ. occurring irregularly. Although you can still hear *sporadic* outbursts of laughter and singing outside, the big Halloween parade has passed; the party's over till next year.

spurious ADJ. false; counterfeit; forged; illogical. The hero of Jonathan Gash's mystery novels is an antique dealer who gives the reader advice on how to tell *spurious* antiques from the real thing.

spurt V. gush forth; squirt. Water suddenly *spurted* from the fountain and splashed Bert right in the face.

squabble N. minor quarrel; bickering. Children invariably get involved in petty *squabbles;* wise parents know when to interfere and when to let the children work things out on their own.

squalor N. filth; degradation; dirty, neglected state. With rusted, broken-down cars in its yard, trash piled up on the porch, and tar paper peeling from the roof, the shack was the picture of *squalor.*

squander V. waste. If you *squander* your allowance on candy and comic books, you won't have any money left to buy the new box of crayons you want.

stagnant ADJ. motionless; stale; dull. Mosquitoes commonly breed in ponds of *stagnant* water. Mike's career was *stagnant;* it wasn't going anywhere, and neither was he! stagnate, V.

staid ADJ. sober; sedate. The wild parties at the fraternity house appealed to the jocks and slackers, but appalled the more *staid* and serious students on campus.

stalemate N. deadlock. Negotiations between the union and the employers have reached a *stalemate*: neither side is willing to budge from its previously stated position.

stalwart ADJ. strong and vigorous; unwaveringly dependable. We thought the congressman was a *stalwart* Democrat until he voted against the president's health care plan.

stamina N. strength; staying power. I doubt that she has the *stamina* to run the full distance of the marathon race.

stanza N. division of a poem. We all know the first *stanza* of the "The Star Spangled Banner." Does anyone know the last?

static ADJ. unchanging; lacking development. Why watch chess on TV? I like watching a game with action, not something *static* where nothing seems to be going on. stasis, N.

statute N. law enacted by the legislature. The *statute* of limitations sets the limits on how long you have to take legal action in specific cases.

• **steadfast** ADJ. loyal; unswerving. Penelope was *steadfast* in her affections, faithfully waiting for Ulysses to return from his wanderings.

stem V. check the flow. The paramedic used a tourniquet to *stem* the bleeding from the slashed artery.

stem from V. arise from. Morton's problems in school *stemmed from* his poor study habits.

stereotyped ADJ. oversimplified; lacking individuality; seen as a type. My chief objection to the book is that the characters are *stereotyped;* they don't come across as real people with individual quirks, fears, and dreams. stereotype, N., V.

stifle V. suppress; extinguish; inhibit. Halfway through the boring lecture, Laura gave up trying to *stifle* her yawns.

stodgy ADJ. stuffy; boringly conservative. For a young person, Winston seems remarkably *stodgy*: you'd expect someone his age to show a little more life.

• **stoic** ADJ. impassive; unmoved by joy or grief. I wasn't particularly *stoic* when I had my flu shot; I squealed like a stuck pig. also N.

stolid ADJ. unruffled; impassive; dull. Marianne wanted a romantic, passionate suitor like Willoughby, not a *stolid*, unimaginative one like Colonel Brandon.

• **stratagem** N. deceptive scheme. Though Wellington's forces seemed to be in full retreat, in reality their withdrawal was a *stratagem* intended to lure the enemy away from its sheltered position.

strident ADJ. loud and harsh; insistent. Whenever Sue became angry, she tried not to raise her voice; she had no desire to appear *strident*.

stringent ADJ. binding; rigid; strict. Protesting that the school dress code was too *stringent*, Katya campaigned to have the rules relaxed.

stupefy V. make numb; stun; amaze. Disapproving of drugs in general, Laura refused to take sleeping pills or any other medicine that might *stupefy* her. stupefaction, N.

stupor N. state of apathy; daze; lack of awareness. The paramedics shook the unconscious man but could not rouse him from his drunken *stupor*.

• **subdued** ADJ. less intense; quieter. Bob liked the *subdued* lighting at the restaurant because he thought it was romantic. I just thought it was dimly lit.

subjective ADJ. existing in the mind, rather than in the object itself; opposite of objective; personal. Your analysis is highly *subjective*; you have permitted your emotions and your opinions to color your thinking.

sublime ADJ. exalted; noble and uplifting; utter. Lucy was in awe of Desi's *sublime* musicianship, while he was in awe of her *sublime* naïveté.

subordinate ADJ. occupying a lower rank; inferior; submissive. Bishop Proudie's wife expected all the *subordinate* clergy to behave with great deference to the wife of their superior.

subsequent ADJ. following; later. In *subsequent* lessons, we shall take up more difficult problems.

Word List 43 subside–tarry

subside V. sink to a low(er) level; grow quiet, less active, or less violent. The doctor assured us that the fever would eventually *subside*.

subsidiary N. something secondary in importance or subordinate; auxiliary. The Turner Broadcasting System is a wholly owned *subsidiary* of AOL Time Warner. First deal with the critical issues, then with the *subsidiary* ones. also ADJ.

substantial ADJ. ample; solid; in essentials. The scholarship represented a *substantial* sum of money.

substantiate V. establish by evidence; verify; support. These endorsements from satisfied customers *substantiate* our claim that Barron's *PSAT/NMSQT* is the best PSAT-prep book on the market.

subtlety N. perceptiveness; ingenuity; delicacy. Never obvious, she expressed herself with such *subtlety* that her remarks went right over the heads of most of her audience. subtle, ADJ.

• **subversive** ADJ. tending to overthrow or destroy. At first glance, the notion that styrofoam cups may actually be more ecologically sound than paper cups strikes most environmentalists as *subversive.*

succinct ADJ. brief; terse; compact. Don't bore your audience with excess verbiage: be *succinct.*

succulent ADJ. juicy; full of richness. To some people, Florida citrus fruits are more *succulent* than those from California. also N.

suffragist N. advocate of voting rights (for women). In recognition of her efforts to win the vote for women, Congress authorized coining a silver dollar honoring the *suffragist* Susan B. Anthony.

• **superficial** ADJ. trivial; shallow. Since your report gave only a *superficial* analysis of the problem, I cannot give you more than a passing grade.

• **superfluous** ADJ. excessive; unnecessary. Please try not to include so many *superfluous* details in your report; just give me the bare facts. superfluity, N.

supplant V. replace; usurp. Did the other woman actually *supplant* Princess Diana in Prince Charles's affections, or did Charles never love Diana at all?

supple ADJ. flexible; pliant. Years of yoga exercises made Grace's body *supple.*

• **suppress** V. crush; subdue; inhibit. Too polite to laugh in anyone's face, Roy did his best to *suppress* his amusement at Ed's inane remark.

surfeit V. satiate; stuff; indulge to excess in anything. Every Thanksgiving we are *surfeited* with an overabundance of holiday treats. also N.

• **surpass** V. exceed. Her PSAT scores *surpassed* our expectations.

surreptitious ADJ. secret; furtive; sneaky. Hoping to discover where Mom had hidden the Christmas presents, Tommy took a *surreptitious* peek into the master bedroom closet.

• **susceptible** ADJ. impressionable; easily influenced; having little resistance, as to a disease; receptive to. Said the patent medicine man to the extremely *susceptible* customer, "Buy this new miracle drug, and you will no longer be *susceptible* to the common cold."

• **suspend** V. defer or postpone; expel or eject; halt or discontinue; hang from above. When the judge *suspended* his sentence, Bill breathed a sigh of relief. When the principal *suspended* her from school, Wanda tried to look as if she didn't care. When the trapeze artist broke her arm, she had to *suspend* her activities: she no longer could be *suspended* from her trapeze.

• **sustain** V. experience; support; nourish. Stuart *sustained* such a severe injury that the doctors feared he would be unable to work to *sustain* his growing family.

swill V. drink greedily. Singing "Yo, ho, ho, and a bottle of rum," Long John Silver and his fellow pirates *swilled* their grog.

swindler N. cheat. She was gullible and trusting, an easy victim for the first *swindler* who came along.

sycophant N. servile flatterer; bootlicker. Fed up with the toadies and flatterers who made up his entourage, the star cried, "Get out, all of you! I'm sick to death of *sycophants!*"

• **symmetry** N. arrangement of parts so that balance is obtained; congruity. Something lopsided by definition lacks *symmetry.*

• **synthesis** N. combining parts into a whole. Now that we have succeeded in isolating this drug, our next problem is to plan its *synthesis* in the laboratory. synthesize, V.

• **taciturn** ADJ. habitually silent; talking little. The stereotypical cowboy is a *taciturn* soul, answering lengthy questions with "Yep" or "Nope."

tactile ADJ. pertaining to the organs or sense of touch. His callused hands had lost their *tactile* sensitivity.

taint V. contaminate; cause to lose purity; modify with a trace of something bad. One speck of dirt on your utensils may contain enough germs to *taint* an entire batch of preserves.

tangential ADJ. peripheral; only slightly connected; digressing. Despite Clark's attempts to distract her with *tangential* remarks, Lois kept on coming back to her main question: why couldn't he come out to dinner with Superman and her?

tantalize V. tease; torture with disappointment. Tom *tantalized* his younger brother, holding the ball just too high for Jimmy to reach.

tarry V. delay; dawdle. We can't *tarry* if we want to get to the airport on time.

Word List 44 tedious–transcendent

• **tedious** ADJ. boring; tiring. The repetitious nature of work on the assembly line made Martin's job very *tedious.* tedium, N.

• **temper** V. moderate; tone down or restrain; toughen (steel). Not even her supervisor's grumpiness could *temper* Nancy's enthusiasm for her new job.

• **temperament** N. characteristic frame of mind; disposition; emotional excess. Although the twins look alike, they differ markedly in *temperament*: Todd is calm, but Rod is excitable. Racket-throwing tennis star John McEnroe was famed for his displays of *temperament.*

temperate ADJ. restrained; self-controlled; moderate in respect to temperature. Try to be *temperate* in your eating this holiday season; if you control your appetite, you won't gain too much weight.

tempestuous ADJ. stormy; impassioned; violent. Racket-throwing tennis star John McEnroe was famed for his displays of *tempestuous* temperament.

tenet N. doctrine; dogma. The agnostic did not accept the *tenets* of their faith.

tentative ADJ. hesitant; not fully worked out or developed; experimental; not definite or positive. Unsure of his welcome at the Christmas party, Scrooge took a *tentative* step into his nephew's drawing room.

tenuous ADJ. thin; weak; unsubstantial. Napoleon's alliance with Russia quickly proved *tenuous*: it disintegrated altogether in 1812.

• **termination** N. end. Though the time for *termination* of the project was near, we still had a lot of work to finish before we shut up shop.

terrestrial ADJ. earthly (as opposed to celestial); pertaining to the land. In many science fiction films, alien invaders from outer space plan to destroy all *terrestrial* life.

terse ADJ. concise; abrupt; pithy. There is a fine line between speech that is *terse* and to the point and speech that is too abrupt.

theocracy N. government run by religious leaders. Though some Pilgrims aboard the *Mayflower* favored the establishment of a *theocracy* in New England, many of their fellow voyagers preferred a nonreligious form of government.

theoretical ADJ. not practical or applied; hypothetical. Bob was better at applied engineering and computer programming than he was at *theoretical* physics and math. While I can still think of some *theoretical* objections to your plan, you've convinced me of its basic soundness.

therapeutic ADJ. curative. Now better known for its racetrack, Saratoga Springs first gained attention for the *therapeutic* qualities of its famous "healing waters."

thrifty ADJ. careful about money; economical. A *thrifty* shopper compares prices before making major purchases.

thrive V. prosper; flourish. Despite the impact of the recession on the restaurant trade, Philip's cafe *thrived.*

• **thwart** V. baffle; frustrate. Batman searched for a way to *thwart* the Joker's evil plan to destroy Gotham City.

tiff ADJ. minor quarrel; fit of annoyance. Whenever the Kramdens had a *tiff,* Ralph would bluster, "That's it, Alice!" and storm out of the apartment.

tiller N. handle used to move a boat's rudder (to steer). Fearing the wind might shift suddenly and capsize the skiff, Tom kept one hand on the *tiller* at all times.

timidity N. lack of self-confidence or courage. If you are to succeed as a salesman, you must first lose your *timidity* and fear of failure.

tirade N. extended scolding; denunciation; harangue. Every time the boss holds a meeting, he goes into a lengthy *tirade,* scolding us for everything from tardiness to padding our expenses.

titanic ADJ. gigantic. *Titanic* waves beat against the majestic S.S. *Titanic,* driving it against the concealed iceberg.

title N. right or claim to possession; mark of rank; name (of a book, film, etc.). Though the penniless Duke of Ragwort no longer had *title* to the family estate, he still retained his *title* as head of one of England's oldest families. The *title* of his autobiography was *From Riches to Rags*.

toady N. servile flatterer; yes man. Never tell the boss anything he doesn't wish to hear: he doesn't want an independent adviser, he just wants a *toady.* also V.

torpor N. lethargy; sluggishness; dormancy. Throughout the winter, nothing aroused the bear from his *torpor:* he would not emerge from hibernation until spring. torpid, ADJ.

torrent N. rushing stream; flood. Day after day of heavy rain saturated the hillside until the water ran downhill in *torrents.* torrential, ADJ.

totter V. move unsteadily; sway, as if about to fall. On unsteady feet, the drunk *tottered* down the hill to the nearest bar.

• **toxic** ADJ. poisonous. Caution: poison! Manufacturers put the skull and crossbones on bottles of iodine to warn purchasers that iodine is *toxic* if taken internally. toxicity, N.

tractable ADJ. docile; easily managed. Although Susan seemed a *tractable* young woman, she had a stubborn streak of independence that occasionally led her to defy the powers-that-be when she felt they were in the wrong.

traduce V. slander; malign. His opponents tried to *traduce* the candidate's reputation by spreading rumors about his past.

• **transcendent** ADJ. surpassing; exceeding ordinary limits; superior. Standing on the hillside watching the sunset through the Golden Gate was a *transcendent* experience for Lise: it was so beautiful it surpassed her wildest dreams.

Word List 45 transcribe–unfeasible

transcribe V. copy. It took hours for the secretary to *transcribe* his shorthand notes of the conference into a form others could read.

transgression N. violation of a law; sin. Forgive us our *transgressions;* we know not what we do. transgress, V.

transient ADJ. momentary; temporary; staying for a short time. Lexy's joy at finding the perfect Christmas gift for Phil was *transient;* she still had to find presents for Roger, Laura, Allison, and Uncle Bob. Located near the airport, this hotel caters to a largely *transient* trade.

transition N. going from one state of action to another. During the period of *transition* from oil heat to gas heat, the furnace will have to be shut off.

transitory ADJ. impermanent; fleeting. Fame is *transitory*: today's rising star is all too soon tomorrow's washed-up has-been. transitoriness, N.

translucent ADJ. partly transparent. We could not recognize the people in the next room because of the *translucent* curtains that separated us.

• **transparent** ADJ. easily detected; permitting light to pass through freely. Bobby managed to put an innocent look on his face; to his mother, however, his guilt was *transparent*.

travail N. painful physical or mental labor; drudgery; torment. Like every other high school student she knew, Sherry detested the yearlong *travail* of cramming for the SAT.

trek N. travel; journey. The tribe made their *trek* farther north that summer in search of game. also V.

trenchant ADJ. cutting; keen. With *trenchant* wit, Frank Rich made some highly cutting remarks as he panned another dreadful play.

• **trepidation** N. fear; nervous apprehension. As she entered the office of the dean of admissions, Sharon felt some *trepidation* about how she would do in her interview.

trifling ADJ. trivial; unimportant. Why bother going to see a doctor for such a *trifling,* everyday cold?

trigger V. set off. John is touchy today; say one word wrong and you'll *trigger* an explosion.

trite ADJ. hackneyed; commonplace. The *trite* and predictable situations on many television programs turn off viewers, who respond by turning off their sets.

trivial ADJ. trifling; unimportant. Too many magazines ignore newsworthy subjects and feature *trivial* gossip about celebrities.

trough N. container for feeding farm animals; lowest point (of a wave, business cycle, etc.). The hungry pigs struggled to get at the fresh swill in the *trough*. The surfer rode her board, coasting along in the *trough* between two waves.

troupe N. group of stage performers; touring company. Was Will Kemp a member of Shakespeare's *troupe* of players when they performed at the Globe?

truism N. self-evident truth. Many a *truism* is summed up in a proverb; for example, "Marry in haste, repent at leisure."

turbid ADJ. muddy; having the sediment disturbed. The water was *turbid* after the children had waded through it.

• **turbulence** N. state of violent agitation. Warned of approaching *turbulence* in the atmosphere, the pilot told the passengers to fasten their seat belts.

turgid ADJ. swollen; distended. The *turgid* river threatened to overflow the levees and flood the countryside.

turmoil N. great commotion and confusion. Lydia running off with a soldier! Mother fainting at the news! The Bennet household was in *turmoil.*

typhoon N. tropical hurricane or cyclone. If you liked *Twister,* you'll love *Typhoon!*

tyranny N. oppression; cruel government. Frederick Douglass fought against the *tyranny* of slavery throughout his entire life. tyrant, N.

ubiquitous ADJ. being everywhere; omnipresent. That Christmas "The Little Drummer Boy" seemed *ubiquitous*: Justin heard the tune everywhere he went.

ultimate ADJ. final; not susceptible to further analysis. Scientists are searching for the *ultimate* truths.

unanimity N. complete agreement. We were surprised by the *unanimity* with which members of both parties accepted our proposals. unanimous, ADJ.

unassuming ADJ. modest. He is so *unassuming* that some people fail to realize how great a man he really is.

unbecoming ADJ. unattractive; improper. What an *unbecoming* dress Mona is wearing! That girl has no color sense. At the court martial the captain was charged with conduct *unbecoming* an officer.

undermine V. weaken; sap. The recent corruption scandals have *undermined* many people's faith in the city government.

underscore V. emphasize. Addressing the jogging class, Kim *underscored* the importance to runners of good nutrition.

undulating ADJ. moving with a wavelike motion. The Hilo Hula Festival was an *undulating* sea of grass skirts.

unearth V. dig up. When they *unearthed* the city, the archaeologists found many relics of an ancient civilization.

unequivocal ADJ. plain; obvious. My answer to your proposal is an *unequivocal* and absolute "No."

unfazed ADJ. not bothered; unworried. Surrounded by armed opponents, Bond nevertheless appeared completely *unfazed* by his danger.

unfeasible ADJ. not practical or workable. Roy's plan to enlarge the living room by knocking down a couple of internal walls proved *unfeasible* when he discovered that those walls were holding up the roof.

Word List 46 unfounded–venerate

unfounded ADJ. baseless; not based on fact. Cher feared that her boyfriend was unfaithful; fortunately, her suspicions proved to be *unfounded*.

ungainly ADJ. awkward; clumsy; unwieldy. "If you want to know whether Nick's an *ungainly* dancer, check out my bruised feet," said Nora. Anyone who has ever tried to carry a bass fiddle knows it's an *ungainly* instrument.

uniformity N. sameness; monotony. At *Persons Magazine*, we strive for *uniformity* of style; as a result, all of our writers wind up sounding exactly alike.

unintimidating ADJ. unfrightening. Though Phil had expected to feel overawed when he met Joe Montana, he found the world-famous quarterback friendly and *unintimidating.*

unique ADJ. without an equal; single in kind. You have the *unique* distinction of being the only student whom I have had to fail in this course.

universal ADJ. characterizing or affecting all; present everywhere. At first, no one shared Christopher's opinions; his theory that the world was round was met with *universal* disbelief.

unnerve V. upset; weaken. His wartime experiences left Tom badly shaken; any sudden noise could *unnerve* him, reducing him to a quivering wreck.

unprecedented ADJ. novel; unparalleled. Margaret Mitchell's book *Gone with the Wind* was an *unprecedented* success.

unravel V. disentangle; solve. With equal ease Miss Marple *unraveled* tangled balls of yarn and baffling murder mysteries.

unrequited ADJ. not reciprocated. Suffering the pangs of *unrequited* love, Olivia rebukes Cesario for his hard-heartedness.

unscathed ADJ. unharmed. Juan's parents prayed that he would come home from the war *unscathed.*

unseemly ADJ. unbecoming; indecent; in poor taste. When he put whoopie cushions on all the seats in the funeral parlor, Seymour's conduct was most *unseemly.*

unsightly ADJ. unpleasant to look at; ugly. Although James was an experienced emergency room nurse, he occasionally became queasy when faced with a particularly *unsightly* injury.

unsullied ADJ. spotlessly clean; unstained. The reputation of our school is *unsullied,* young ladies; you must conduct yourself modestly and discreetly so that you never disgrace our good name.

unwarranted ADJ. unjustified; groundless; undeserved. We could not understand Martin's *unwarranted* rudeness to his mother's guests.

upbraid V. severely scold; reprimand. Not only did Miss Minchin *upbraid* Ermengarde for her disobedience, but she hung her up by her braids from a coat rack in the classroom.

uphold V. give support; keep from sinking; lift up. Bold Sir Robin was ready to fight to the death to *uphold* the honor of his lady.

upright ADJ. honest; ethical; erect; perpendicular. An *upright* person acts straight: he does not cheat. An *upright* post stands straight: it does not lean.

uproarious ADJ. marked by commotion; extremely funny; very noisy. The *uproarious* comedy hit *Ace Ventura: Pet Detective* starred Jim Carrey, whose comic mugging provoked gales of *uproarious* laughter from audiences coast to coast.

• **urbane** ADJ. suave; refined; elegant. Country-bred and naïve, Anna felt out of place among her *urbane* and sophisticated new classmates. urbanity, N.

usurp V. seize another's power or rank. The revolution ended when the victorious rebel general succeeded in *usurping* the throne.

• **utopia** N. ideal place, state, or society. Fed up with this imperfect universe, Don would have liked to run off to Shangri-la or some other fictitious *utopia.* utopian, ADJ.

• **vacillate** V. waver; fluctuate. Uncertain which suitor she ought to marry, the princess *vacillated,* saying now one, now the other. vacillation, N.

vacuous ADJ. empty; lacking in ideas; stupid. The politician's *vacuous* remarks annoyed the audience, who had hoped to hear more than empty platitudes.

vagabond N. wanderer; tramp. In summer, college students wander the roads of Europe like carefree *vagabonds.* also ADJ.

validate V. confirm; ratify. I will not publish my findings until I *validate* my results.

vanguard N. advance guard of a military force; forefront of a movement. When no enemy was in sight, the duke of Plaza Toro marched in the *vanguard* of his troops, but once the bullets flew above, he headed for the rear.

vantage N. position giving an advantage. They fired upon the enemy from behind the trees, walls, and any other point of *vantage* they could find.

vapid ADJ. dull and unimaginative; insipid and flavorless. "*Bor*-ing!" said Cheryl, as she suffered through yet another *vapid* lecture about Dead White Male Poets.

vehement ADJ. forceful; intensely emotional; with marked vigor. Alfred became so *vehement* in describing what was wrong with the Internal Revenue Service that he began jumping up and down and frothing at the mouth. vehemence, N.

veneer N. thin layer; cover. Deceived by Victor's *veneer* of sophistication, casual acquaintances failed to perceive his fundamental shallowness.

venerate V. revere. In Tibet today, the common people still *venerate* their traditional spiritual leader, the Dalai Lama.

Word List 47 venturesome–whiff

venturesome ADJ. bold. A group of *venturesome* women were the first to scale Mt. Annapurna.

veracity N. truthfulness. Asserting his *veracity,* young George Washington proclaimed, "Father, I cannot tell a lie!"

verbose ADJ. wordy. Someone mute can't talk; someone *verbose* can hardly stop talking.

verdant ADJ. green; lush in vegetation. Monet's paintings of the *verdant* fields were symphonies in green.

verisimilitude N. appearance of truth; likelihood. Critics praised her for the *verisimilitude* of her performance as Lady Macbeth. She was completely believable.

• **versatile** ADJ. having many talents; capable of working in many fields. She was a *versatile* athlete, earning varsity letters in basketball, hockey, and track.

vertigo N. severe dizziness. When you test potential airplane pilots for susceptibility to spells of *vertigo,* be sure to hand out airsick bags.

vicarious ADJ. acting as a substitute; done by a deputy. Though Maud was too meek to talk back to anyone, she got a *vicarious* kick out of Rita's sharp retorts.

vicissitude N. change of fortune. Humbled by life's *vicissitudes,* the last emperor of China worked as a lowly gardener in the palace over which he had once ruled.

vie V. contend; compete. Politicians *vie* with one another, competing for donations and votes.

vigor N. active strength. Although he was over 70 years old, Jack had the *vigor* of a man in his prime. vigorous, ADJ.

vindicate V. clear from blame; exonerate; justify or support. The lawyer's goal was to *vindicate* her client and prove him innocent on all charges. The critics' extremely favorable reviews *vindicate* my opinion that *The Madness of King George* is a brilliant movie.

vindictive ADJ. out for revenge; malicious. Divorce sometimes brings out a *vindictive* streak in people; when Tony told Tina he wanted a divorce, she poured green Jello into the aquarium and turned his tropical fish into dessert.

virtuoso N. highly skilled artist. The promising young cellist Yo-Yo Ma grew into a *virtuoso* whose *virtuosity* on the violin thrilled millions.

virulent ADJ. extremely poisonous; hostile; bitter. Laid up with a *virulent* case of measles, Vera blamed her doctors because her recovery took so long. In fact, she became quite *virulent* on the subject of the quality of modern medical care.

vise N. tool for holding work in place. Before filing its edges, the keysmith took the blank key and fixed it firmly between the jaws of a *vise.*

vivacious ADJ. animated; lively. The hostess on *The Morning News* was a bit too bubbly and *vivacious* for me to take before I'd had my first cup of coffee.

• **volatile** ADJ. changeable; explosive; evaporating rapidly. The political climate today is extremely *volatile*: no one can predict what the electorate will do next. Maria Callas's temper was extremely *volatile*: the only thing you could predict was that she was sure to blow up. Ethyl chloride is an extremely *volatile* liquid: it evaporates instantly.

voluble ADJ. fluent; glib; talkative. Excessively *voluble* speakers suffer from logorrhea: they run off at the mouth a lot!

voluminous ADJ. extensive; bulky; large. Despite her family burdens, she kept up a *voluminous* correspondence with her friends. A caftan is a *voluminous* garment; most people wearing one look as if they're draped in a small tent.

• **voracious** ADJ. ravenous. The wolf is a *voracious* animal, its hunger never satisfied.

vulnerable ADJ. susceptible to wounds. His opponents could not harm Achilles, who was *vulnerable* only in his heel.

waive V. give up a claim or right voluntarily; refrain from enforcing; postpone considering. Although technically prospective students had to live in Piedmont to attend high school there, occasionally the school *waived* the residence requirement in order to enroll promising athletes.

wallow V. roll in; indulge in; become helpless. The hippopotamus loves to *wallow* in pools of mud. The horror film addict loves to *wallow* in tales of blood.

wanderlust N. strong longing to go off traveling. The cowboy had a bad case of *wanderlust;* he could never settle down.

wane V. decrease in size or strength; draw gradually to an end. When lit, does a wax candle *wane?*

wanton ADJ. unrestrained; willfully malicious; unchaste. Pointing to the stack of bills, Sheldon criticized Sarah for her *wanton* expenditures. In response, Sarah accused Sheldon of making an unfounded, *wanton* attack.

warble V. sing; babble. Every morning the birds *warbled* outside her window. also N.

• **wary** ADJ. very cautious. The spies grew *wary* as they approached the sentry.

wayward ADJ. ungovernable; unpredictable; contrary. Miss Watson warned Huck that if he didn't mend his ways she would ship him off to a school for *wayward* youths.

wheedle V. cajole; coax; deceive by flattery. She knows she can *wheedle* almost anything she wants from her father.

whet V. sharpen; stimulate. The odors from the kitchen are *whetting* my appetite; I will be ravenous by the time the meal is served.

whiff N. puff or gust (of air, scent, etc.); hint. The slightest *whiff* of Old Spice cologne brought memories of George to her mind.

Word List 48 whimsical–zephyr

whimsical N. capricious; fanciful. In *Mrs. Doubtfire,* the hero is a playful, *whimsical* man who takes a notion to dress up as a woman so that he can look after his children, who are in the custody of his ex-wife. whimsy, N.

whittle V. pare; cut off bits. As a present for Aunt Polly, Tom *whittled* some clothespins out of a chunk of wood.

willful ADJ. intentional; headstrong. Donald had planned to kill his wife for months; clearly, her death was a case of deliberate, *willful* murder, not a crime of passion committed by a hasty, *willful* youth unable to foresee the consequences of his deeds.

wile N. trick intended to deceive; stratagem. At the end of the movie, the hero sees through the temptress's *wiles* and returns to his sweetheart back home.

wily ADJ. cunning; artful. If coyotes are supposed to be such sneaky, *wily* creatures, how does Road Runner always manage to outwit Wile E. Coyote?

winnow V. sift; separate good parts from bad. This test will *winnow* out the students who study from those who never open a book.

withdrawn ADJ. introverted; remote. Rebuffed by his colleagues, the initially outgoing young researcher became increasingly *withdrawn.*

wither V. shrivel; decay. Cut flowers are beautiful for a day, but all too soon they *wither.*

withhold V. hold back; desist from giving; keep possession of. The tenants decided to *withhold* a portion of the rent until the landlord kept his promise to renovate the building.

wretch N. miserable person; vile, despicable person. Tina felt sorry for the poor *wretches* who stood shivering in the rain. However, she was furious with that *wretch* Tony, who stood her up.

wry ADJ. twisted; with a humorous twist. We enjoy Dorothy Parker's verse for its *wry* wit.

zeal N. eager enthusiasm. Wang's *zeal* was contagious; soon all his fellow students were busily making posters, inspired by his ardent enthusiasm for the cause. zealous, ADJ.

zenith N. highest point; culmination. When the film star's career was at its *zenith,* she was in such great demand that producers told her to name her own price.

zephyr N. gentle breeze; west wind. When these *zephyrs* blow, it is good to be in an open boat under a full sail.

Basic Word Parts

In addition to reviewing the High-Frequency Word List, what other quick vocabulary-building tactics can you follow when you face a test deadline?

One good approach is to learn how to build up (and tear apart) words. You know that words are made up of other words: the *room* in which you *store* things is the *storeroom;* the person whose job is to *keep* the *books* is the *bookkeeper.*

Just as words are made up of other words, words are also made up of word parts: prefixes, suffixes, and roots. A knowledge of these word parts and their meanings can help you determine the meanings of unfamiliar words.

Most modern English words are derived from Anglo-Saxon (Old English), Latin, and Greek. Because few students nowadays study Latin and Greek (and even fewer study Anglo-Saxon!), the majority of high school juniors and seniors lack a vital tool for unlocking the meaning of unfamiliar words.

Build your vocabulary by mastering basic word parts. Learning thirty key word parts can help you unlock the meaning of over 10,000 words. Learning fifty key word parts can help you unlock the meaning of over 100,000!

COMMON PREFIXES

Prefixes are syllables that precede the root or stem and change or refine its meaning.

Prefix	Meaning	Illustration
ab, abs	from, away from	*abduct* lead away, kidnap *abjure* renounce *abject* degraded, cast down
ad, ac, af, ag, an, ap, as, as, at	to, forward	*adit* entrance *adjure* request earnestly *admit* allow entrance *accord* agreement, harmony *affliction* distress *aggregation* collection *annexation* add to *apparition* ghost *arraignment* indictment *assumption* arrogance, the taking for granted *attendance* presence, the persons present
ambi	both	*ambidextrous* skilled with both hands *ambiguous* of double meaning *ambivalent* having two conflicting emotions
an, a	without	*anarchy* lack of government *anemia* lack of blood *amoral* without moral sense
ante	before	*antecedent* preceding event or word *antediluvian* ancient (before the flood) *antenuptial* before the wedding

Prefix	Meaning	Illustration
anti	against, opposite	*antipathy* hatred *antiseptic* against infection *antithetical* exactly opposite
arch	chief, first	*archetype* original *archbishop* chief bishop *archaeology* study of first or ancient times
be	over, thoroughly	*bedaub* smear over *befuddle* confuse thoroughly *beguile* deceive, charm thoroughly
bi	two	*bicameral* composed of two houses (Congress) *biennial* every two years *bicycle* two-wheeled vehicle
cata	down	*catastrophe* disaster *cataract* waterfall *catapult* hurl (throw down)
circum	around	*circumnavigate* sail around (the globe) *circumspect* cautious (looking around) *circumscribe* limit (place a circle around)
com, co, col, con, cor	with, together	*combine* merge with *commerce* trade with *communicate* correspond with *coeditor* joint editor *collateral* subordinate, connected *conference* meeting *corroborate* confirm
contra, contro	against	*contravene* conflict with *controversy* dispute
de	down, away	*debase* lower in value *decadence* deterioration *decant* pour off
demi	partly, half	*demigod* partly divine being
di	two	*dichotomy* division into two parts *dilemma* choice between two bad alternatives
dia	across	*diagonal* across a figure *diameter* distance across a circle *diagram* outline drawing
dis, dif	not, apart	*discord* lack of harmony *differ* disagree (carry apart) *disparity* condition of inequality; difference
dys	faulty, bad	*dyslexia* faulty ability to read *dyspepsia* indigestion
ex, e	out	*expel* drive out *extirpate* root out *eject* throw out

Prefix	Meaning	Illustration
extra, extro	beyond, outside	*extracurricular* beyond the curriculum *extraterritorial* beyond a nation's bounds *extrovert* person interested chiefly in external objects and actions
hyper	above; excessively	*hyperbole* exaggeration *hyperventilate* breathe at an excessive rate
hypo	beneath; lower	*hypoglycemia* low blood sugar
in, il, im, ir	not	*inefficient* not efficient *inarticulate* not clear or distinct *illegible* not readable *impeccable* not capable of sinning; flawless *irrevocable* not able to be called back
in, il, im, ir	in, on, upon	*invite* call in *illustration* something that makes clear *impression* effect upon mind or feelings *irradiate* shine upon
inter	between, among	*intervene* come between *international* between nations *interjection* a statement thrown in
intra, intro	within	*intramural* within a school *introvert* person who turns within himself
macro	large, long	*macrobiotic* tending to prolong life *macrocosm* the great world (the entire universe)
mega	great, million	*megalomania* delusions of grandeur *megaton* explosive force of a million tons of TNT
meta	involving change	*metamorphosis* change of form
micro	small	*microcosm* miniature universe *microbe* minute organism *microscopic* extremely small
mis	bad, improper	*misdemeanor* minor crime; bad conduct *mischance* unfortunate accident *misnomer* wrong name
mis	hatred	*misanthrope* person who hates mankind *misogynist* woman-hater
mono	one	*monarchy* government by one ruler *monotheism* belief in one god
multi	many	*multifarious* having many parts *multitudinous* numerous
neo	new	*neologism* newly coined word *neophyte* beginner; novice
non	not	*noncommittal* undecided *nonentity* person of no importance

Prefix	Meaning	Illustration
ob, oc, of, op	against	*obloquy* infamy; disgrace *obtrude* push into prominence *occlude* close; block out *offend* insult *opponent* someone who struggles against; foe
olig	few	*oligarchy* government by a few
pan	all, every	*panacea* cure-all *panorama* unobstructed view in all directions
para	beyond, related	*parallel* similar *paraphrase* restate; translate
per	through, completely	*permeable* allowing passage through *pervade* spread throughout
peri	around, near	*perimeter* outer boundary *periphery* edge *periphrastic* stated in a roundabout way
poly	many	*polygamist* person with several spouses *polyglot* speaking several languages
post	after	*postpone* delay *posterity* generations that follow *posthumous* after death
pre	before	*preamble* introductory statement *prefix* word part placed before a root/stem *premonition* forewarning
prim	first	*primordial* existing at the dawn of time *primogeniture* state of being the first born
pro	forward, in favor of	*propulsive* driving forward *proponent* supporter
proto	first	*prototype* first of its kind
pseudo	false	*pseudonym* pen name
re	again, back	*reiterate* repeat *reimburse* pay back
retro	backward	*retrospect* looking back *retroactive* effective as of a past date
se	away, aside	*secede* withdraw *seclude* shut away *seduce* lead astray
semi	half, partly	*semiannual* every six months *semiconscious* partly conscious
sub, suc, suf, sug, sup, sus	under, less	*subway* underground road *subjugate* bring under control *succumb* yield; cease to resist *suffuse* spread through *suggest* hint *suppress* put down by force *suspend* delay

Prefix	Meaning	Illustration
super, sur	over, above	*supernatural* above natural things *supervise* oversee *surtax* additional tax
syn, sym, syl, sys	with, together	*synchronize* time together *synthesize* combine together *sympathize* pity; identify with *syllogism* explanation of how ideas relate *system* network
tele	far	*telemetry* measurement from a distance *telegraphic* communicated over a distance
trans	across	*transport* carry across *transpose* reverse, move across
ultra	beyond, excessive	*ultramodern* excessively modern *ultracritical* exceedingly critical
un	not	*unfeigned* not pretended; real *unkempt* not combed; disheveled *unwitting* not knowing; unintentional
under	below	*undergird* strengthen underneath *underling* someone inferior
uni	one	*unison* oneness of pitch; complete accord *unicycle* one-wheeled vehicle
vice	in place of	*vicarious* acting as a substitute *viceroy* governor acting in place of a king
with	away, against	*withhold* hold back; keep *withstand* stand up against; resist

COMMON ROOTS AND STEMS

Roots are basic words which have been carried over into English. *Stems* are variations of roots brought about by changes in declension or conjugation.

Root or Stem	Meaning	Illustration
ac, acr	sharp	*acrimonious* bitter; caustic *acerbity* bitterness of temper *acidulate* to make somewhat acid or sour
aev, ev	age, era	*primeval* of the first age *coeval* of the same age or era *medieval or mediaeval* of the middle ages
ag, act	do	*act* deed *agent* doer
agog	leader	*demagogue* false leader of people *pedagogue* teacher (leader of children)
agri, agrari	field	*agrarian* one who works in the field *agriculture* cultivation of fields *peregrination* wandering (through fields)
ali	another	*alias* assumed (another) name *alienate* estrange (turn away from another)
alt	high	*altitude* height *altimeter* instrument for measuring height
alter	other	*altruistic* unselfish, considering others *alter ego* a second self
am	love	*amorous* loving, especially sexually *amity* friendship *amicable* friendly
anim	mind, soul	*animadvert* cast criticism upon *unanimous* of one mind *magnanimity* greatness of mind or spirit
ann, enn	year	*annuity* yearly remittance *biennial* every two years *perennial* present all year; persisting for several years
anthrop	man	*anthropology* study of man *misanthrope* hater of mankind *philanthropy* love of mankind; charity
apt	fit	*aptitude* skill *adapt* make suitable or fit
aqua	water	*aqueduct* passageway for conducting water *aquatic* living in water *aqua fortis* nitric acid (strong water)

Root or Stem	Meaning	Illustration
arch	ruler, first	*archaeology* study of antiquities (study of first things) *monarch* sole ruler *anarchy* lack of government
aster	star	*astronomy* study of the stars *asterisk* starlike type character (*) *disaster* catastrophe (contrary star)
aud, audit	hear	*audible* able to be heard *auditorium* place where people may be heard *audience* hearers
auto	self	*autocracy* rule by one person (self) *automobile* vehicle that moves by itself *autobiography* story of one's own life
belli	war	*bellicose* inclined to fight *belligerent* inclined to wage war *rebellious* resisting authority
ben, bon	good	*benefactor* one who does good deeds *benevolence* charity (wishing good) *bonus* something extra above regular pay
biblio	book	*bibliography* list of books *bibliophile* lover of books *Bible* The Book
bio	life	*biography* writing about a person's life *biology* study of living things *biochemist* student of the chemistry of living things
breve	short	*brevity* briefness *abbreviate* shorten *breviloquent* marked by brevity of speech
cad, cas	to fall	*decadent* deteriorating *cadence* intonation, musical movement *cascade* waterfall
cap, capt, cept, cip	to take	*capture* seize *participate* take part *precept* wise saying (originally a command)
capit, capt	head	*decapitate* remove (cut off) someone's head *captain* chief
carn	flesh	*carnivorous* flesh-eating *carnage* destruction of life *carnal* fleshly
ced, cess	to yield, to go	*recede* go back, withdraw *antecedent* that which goes before *process* go forward
celer	swift	*celerity* swiftness *decelerate* reduce swiftness *accelerate* increase swiftness

Root or Stem	Meaning	Illustration
cent	one hundred	*century* one hundred years *centennial* hundredth anniversary *centipede* many-footed, wingless animal
chron	time	*chronology* timetable of events *anachronism* a thing out of time sequence *chronicle* register events in order of time
cid, cis	to cut, to kill	*incision* a cut (surgical) *homicide* killing of a man *fratricide* killing of a brother
cit, citat	to call, to start	*incite* stir up, start up *excite* stir up *recitation* a recalling (or repeating) aloud
civi	citizen	*civilization* society of citizens, culture *civilian* member of community *civil* courteous
clam, clamat	to cry out	*clamorous* loud *declamation* speech *acclamation* shouted approval
claud, claus, clos, clud	to close	*claustrophobia* fear of close places *enclose* close in *conclude* finish
cognosc, cognit	to learn	*agnostic* lacking knowledge, skeptical *incognito* traveling under assumed name *cognition* knowledge
compl	to fill	*complete* filled out *complement* that which completes something *comply* fulfill
cord	heart	*accord* agreement (from the heart) *cordial* friendly *discord* lack of harmony
corpor	body	*incorporate* organize into a body *corporeal* pertaining to the body, fleshly *corpse* dead body
cred, credit	to believe	*incredulous* not believing, skeptical *credulity* gullibility *credence* belief
cur	to care	*curator* person who has the care of something *sinecure* position without responsibility *secure* safe
curr, curs	to run	*excursion* journey *cursory* brief *precursor* forerunner
da, dat	to give	*data* facts, statistics *mandate* command *date* given time

Root or Stem	Meaning	Illustration
deb, debit	to owe	*debt* something owed *indebtedness* debt *debenture* bond
dem	people	*democracy* rule of the people *demagogue* (false) leader of the people *epidemic* widespread (among the people)
derm	skin	*epidermis* skin *pachyderm* thick-skinned quadruped *dermatology* study of skin and its disorders
di, diurn	day	*diary* a daily record of activities, feelings, etc. *diurnal* pertaining to daytime
dic, dict	to say	*abdicate* renounce *diction* speech *verdict* statement of jury
doc, doct	to teach	*docile* obedient; easily taught *document* something that provides evidence *doctor* learned person (originally, teacher)
domin	to rule	*dominate* have power over *domain* land under rule *dominant* prevailing
duc, duct	to lead	*viaduct* arched roadway *aqueduct* artificial waterway
dynam	power, strength	*dynamic* powerful *dynamite* powerful explosive *dynamo* engine making electrical power
ego	I	*egoist* person who is self-interested *egotist* selfish person *egocentric* revolving about self
erg, urg	work	*energy* power *ergatocracy* rule of the workers *metallurgy* science and technology of metals
err	to wander	*error* mistake *erratic* not reliable, wandering *knight-errant* wandering knight
eu	good, well, beautiful	*eupeptic* having good digestion *eulogize* praise *euphemism* substitution of pleasant way of saying something blunt
fac, fic, fec, fect	to make, to do	*factory* place where things are made *fiction* manufactured story *affect* cause to change
fall, fals	to deceive	*fallacious* misleading *infallible* not prone to error, perfect *falsify* lie
fer, lat	to bring, to bear	*transfer* bring from one place to another *translate* bring from one language to another *conifer* bearing cones, as pine trees

Root or Stem	Meaning	Illustration
fid	belief, faith	*infidel* nonbeliever, heathen *confidence* assurance, belief
fin	end, limit	*confine* keep within limits *finite* having definite limits
flect, flex	bend	*flexible* able to bend *deflect* bend away, turn aside
fort	luck, chance	*fortuitous* accidental, occurring by chance *fortunate* lucky
fort	strong	*fortitude* strength, firmness of mind *fortification* strengthening *fortress* stronghold
frag, fract	break	*fragile* easily broken *infraction* breaking of a rule *fractious* unruly, tending to break rules
fug	flee	*fugitive* someone who flees *refuge* shelter, home for someone fleeing
fus	pour	*effusive* gushing, pouring out *diffuse* widespread (poured in many directions)
gam	marriage	*monogamy* marriage to one person *bigamy* marriage to two people at the same time *polygamy* having many wives or husbands at the same time
gen, gener	class, race	*genus* group of animals with similar traits *generic* characteristic of a class *gender* class organized by sex
grad, gress	go, step	*digress* go astray (from the main point) *regress* go backwards *gradual* step by step, by degrees
graph, gram	writing	*epigram* pithy statement *telegram* instantaneous message over great distance *stenography* shorthand (writing narrowly)
greg	flock, herd	*gregarious* tending to group together, as in a herd *aggregate* group, total *egregious* conspicuously bad; shocking
helio	sun	*heliotrope* flower that faces the sun *heliograph* instrument that uses the sun's rays to send signals
it, itiner	journey, road	*exit* way out *itinerary* plan of journey
jac, jact, jec	to throw	*projectile* missile; something thrown forward *trajectory* path taken by thrown object *ejaculatory* casting or throwing out
jur, jurat	to swear	*perjure* testify falsely *jury* group of men and women sworn to seek the truth *adjuration* solemn urging

Root or Stem	Meaning	Illustration
labor, laborat	to work	*laboratory* place where work is done *collaborate* work together with others *laborious* difficult
leg, lect, lig	to choose, to read	*election* choice *legible* able to be read *eligible* able to be selected
leg	law	*legislature* law-making body *legitimate* lawful *legal* lawful
liber, libr	book	*library* collection of books *libretto* the "book" of a musical play *libel* slander (originally found in a little book)
liber	free	*liberation* the act of setting free *liberal* generous (giving freely); tolerant
log	word, study	*entomology* study of insects *etymology* study of word parts and derivations *monologue* speech by one person
loqu, locut	to talk	*soliloquy* speech by one individual *loquacious* talkative *elocution* speech
luc	light	*elucidate* enlighten *lucid* clear *translucent* allowing some light to pass through
magn	great	*magnify* enlarge *magnanimity* generosity, greatness of soul *magnitude* greatness, extent
mal	bad	*malevolent* wishing evil *malediction* curse *malefactor* evildoer
man	hand	*manufacture* create (make by hand) *manuscript* written by hand *emancipate* free (let go from the hand)
mar	sea	*maritime* connected with seafaring *submarine* undersea craft *mariner* seaman
mater, matr	mother	*maternal* pertaining to motherhood *matriarch* female ruler of a family, group, or state *matrilineal* descended on the mother's side
mit, miss	to send	*missile* projectile *dismiss* send away *transmit* send across
mob, mot, mov	move	*mobilize* cause to move *motility* ability to move *immovable* not able to be moved

Root or Stem	Meaning	Illustration
mon, monit	to warn	*admonish* warn *premonition* foreboding *monitor* watcher (warner)
mori, mort	to die	*mortuary* funeral parlor *moribund* dying *immortal* not dying
morph	shape, form	*amorphous* formless, lacking shape *metamorphosis* change of shape *anthropomorphic* in the shape of man
mut	change	*immutable* not able to be changed *mutate* undergo a great change *mutability* changeableness, inconstancy
nat	born	*innate* from birth *prenatal* before birth *nativity* birth
nav	ship	*navigate* sail a ship *circumnavigate* sail around the world *naval* pertaining to ships
neg	deny	*negation* denial *renege* deny, go back on one's word *renegade* turncoat, traitor
nomen	name	*nomenclature* act of naming, terminology *nominal* in name only (as opposed to actual) *cognomen* surname, distinguishing nickname
nov	new	*novice* beginner *renovate* make new again *novelty* newness
omni	all	*omniscient* all-knowing *omnipotent* all-powerful *omnivorous* eating everything
oper	to work	*operate* work *cooperation* working together
pac	peace	*pacify* make peaceful *pacific* peaceful *pacifist* person opposed to war
pass	feel	*dispassionate* free of emotion *impassioned* emotion-filled *impassive* showing no feeling
pater, patr	father	*patriotism* love of one's country (fatherland) *patriarch* male ruler of a family, group, or state *paternity* fatherhood
path	disease, feeling	*pathology* study of diseased tissue *apathetic* lacking feeling; indifferent *antipathy* hostile feeling

Root or Stem	Meaning	Illustration
ped, pod	foot	*impediment* stumbling block; hindrance *tripod* three-footed stand *quadruped* four-footed animal
ped	child	*pedagogue* teacher of children *pediatrician* children's doctor
pel, puls	to drive	*compulsion* a forcing to do *repel* drive back *expel* drive out, banish
pet, petit	to seek	*petition* request *appetite* craving, desire *compete* vie with others
phil	love	*philanthropist* benefactor, lover of humanity *Anglophile* lover of everything English *philanderer* one involved in brief love affairs
pon, posit	to place	*postpone* place after *positive* definite, unquestioned (definitely placed)
port, portat	to carry	*portable* able to be carried *transport* carry across *export* carry out (of country)
poten	able, powerful	*omnipotent* all-powerful *potentate* powerful person *impotent* powerless
psych	mind	*psychology* study of the mind *psychosis* mental disorder *psychopath* mentally ill person
put, putat	to trim, to calculate	*putative* supposed (calculated) *computation* calculation *amputate* cut off
quer, ques, quir, quis	to ask	*inquiry* investigation *inquisitive* questioning *query* question
reg, rect	rule	*regicide* murder of a ruler *regent* ruler *insurrection* rebellion; overthrow of a ruler
rid, ris	to laugh	*derision* scorn *risibility* inclination to laughter *ridiculous* deserving to be laughed at
rog, rogat	to ask	*interrogate* question *prerogative* privilege
rupt	to break	*interrupt* break into *bankrupt* insolvent *rupture* a break
sacr	holy	*sacred* holy *sacrilegious* impious, violating something holy *sacrament* religious act

Root or Stem	Meaning	Illustration
sci	to know	*science* knowledge *omniscient* knowing all *conscious* aware
scop	watch, see	*periscope* device for seeing around corners *microscope* device for seeing small objects
scrib, script	to write	*transcribe* make a written copy *script* written text *circumscribe* write around, limit
sect	cut	*dissect* cut apart *bisect* cut into two pieces
sed, sess	to sit	*sedentary* inactive (sitting) *session* meeting
sent, sens	to think, to feel	*consent* agree *resent* show indignation *sensitive* showing feeling
sequi, secut, seque	to follow	*consecutive* following in order *sequence* arrangement *sequel* that which follows *non sequitur* something that does not follow logically
solv, solut	to loosen	*absolve* free from blame *dissolute* morally lax *absolute* complete (not loosened)
somn	sleep	*insomnia* inability to sleep *somnolent* sleepy *somnambulist* sleepwalker
soph	wisdom	*philosopher* lover of wisdom *sophisticated* worldly wise
spec, spect	to look at	*spectator* observer *aspect* appearance *circumspect* cautious (looking around)
spir	breathe	*respiratory* pertaining to breathing *spirited* full of life (breath)
string, strict	bind	*stringent* strict *constrict* become tight *stricture* limit, something that restrains
stru, struct	build	*constructive* helping to build *construe* analyze (how something is built)
tang, tact, ting	to touch	*tangent* touching *contact* touching with, meeting *contingent* depending upon
tempor	time	*contemporary* at same time *extemporaneous* impromptu *temporize* delay

Root or Stem	Meaning	Illustration
ten, tent	to hold	*tenable* able to be held *tenure* holding of office *retentive* holding; having a good memory
term	end	*interminable* endless *terminate* end
terr	land	*terrestrial* pertaining to earth *subterranean* underground
therm	heat	*thermostat* instrument that regulates heat *diathermy* sending heat through body tissues
tors, tort	twist	*distort* twist out of true shape or meaning *torsion* act of twisting *tortuous* twisting
tract	drag, pull	*distract* pull (one's attention) away *intractable* stubborn, unable to be dragged *attraction* pull, drawing quality
trud, trus	push, shove	*intrude* push one's way in *protrusion* something sticking out
urb	city	*urban* pertaining to a city *urbane* polished, sophisticated (pertaining to a city dweller) *suburban* outside of a city
vac	empty	*vacuous* lacking content, empty-headed *evacuate* compel to empty an area
vad, vas	go	*invade* enter in a hostile fashion *evasive* not frank; eluding
veni, vent, ven	to come	*intervene* come between *prevent* stop *convention* meeting
ver	true	*veracious* truthful *verify* check the truth *verisimilitude* appearance of truth
verb	word	*verbose* wordy *verbiage* excessive use of words *verbatim* word for word
vers, vert	turn	*vertigo* turning dizzy *revert* turn back (to an earlier state) *diversion* something causing one to turn aside
via	way	*deviation* departure from the way *viaduct* roadway (arched) *trivial* trifling (small talk at crossroads)
vid, vis	to see	*vision* sight *evidence* things seen *vista* view

Root or Stem	Meaning	Illustration
vinc, vict, vanq	to conquer	*invincible* unconquerable *victory* winning *vanquish* defeat
viv, vit	alive	*vivisection* operating on living animals *vivacious* full of life *vitality* liveliness
voc, vocat	to call	*avocation* calling, minor occupation *provocation* calling or rousing the anger of *invocation* calling in prayer
vol	wish	*malevolent* wishing someone ill *voluntary* of one's own will
volv, volut	to roll	*revolve* roll around *evolve* roll out, develop *convolution* coiled state

COMMON SUFFIXES

Suffixes are syllables that are added to a word. Occasionally, they change the meaning of the word; more frequently, they serve to change the grammatical form of the word (noun to adjective, adjective to noun, noun to verb).

Suffix	Meaning	Illustration
able, ible	capable of (adjective suffix)	*portable* able to be carried *interminable* not able to be limited *legible* able to be read
ac, ic	like, pertaining to (adjective suffix)	*cardiac* pertaining to the heart *aquatic* pertaining to the water *dramatic* pertaining to the drama
acious, icious	full of (adjective suffix)	*audacious* full of daring *perspicacious* full of mental perception *avaricious* full of greed
al	pertaining to (adjective or noun suffix)	*maniacal* insane *final* pertaining to the end *logical* pertaining to logic
ant, ent	full of (adjective or noun suffix)	*eloquent* pertaining to fluid, effective speech *suppliant* pleader (person full of requests) *verdant* green
ary	like, connected with (adjective or noun suffix)	*dictionary* book connected with words *honorary* with honor *luminary* celestial body
ate	to make (verb suffix)	*consecrate* to make holy *enervate* to make weary *mitigate* to make less severe
ation	that which is (noun suffix)	*exasperation* irritation *irritation* annoyance
cy	state of being (noun suffix)	*democracy* government ruled by the people *obstinacy* stubbornness *accuracy* correctness
eer, er, or	person who (noun suffix)	*mutineer* person who rebels *lecher* person who lusts *censor* person who deletes improper remarks
escent	becoming (adjective suffix)	*evanescent* tending to vanish *pubescent* arriving at puberty
fic	making, doing (adjective suffix)	*terrific* arousing great fear *soporific* causing sleep
fy	to make (verb suffix)	*magnify* enlarge *petrify* turn to stone *beautify* make beautiful
iferous	producing, bearing (adjective suffix)	*pestiferous* carrying disease *vociferous* bearing a loud voice

Suffix	Meaning	Illustration
il, ile	pertaining to, capable of (adjective suffix)	*puerile* pertaining to a boy or child *ductile* capable of being hammered or drawn *civil* polite
ism	doctrine, belief (noun suffix)	*monotheism* belief in one god *fanaticism* excessive zeal; extreme belief
ist	dealer, doer (noun suffix)	*fascist* one who believes in a fascist state *realist* one who is realistic *artist* one who deals with art
ity	state of being (noun suffix)	*annuity* yearly grant *credulity* state of being unduly willing to believe *sagacity* wisdom
ive	like (adjective suffix)	*expensive* costly *quantitative* concerned with quantity *effusive* gushing
ize, ise	make (verb suffix)	*victimize* make a victim of *rationalize* make rational *harmonize* make harmonious *enfranchise* make free or set free
oid	resembling, like (adjective suffix)	*ovoid* like an egg *anthropoid* resembling man *spheroid* resembling a sphere
ose	full of (adjective suffix)	*verbose* full of words *lachrymose* full of tears
osis	condition (noun suffix)	*psychosis* diseased mental condition *neurosis* nervous condition *hypnosis* condition of induced sleep
ous	full of (adjective suffix)	*nauseous* full of nausea *ludicrous* foolish
tude	state of (noun suffix)	*fortitude* state of strength *beatitude* state of blessedness *certitude* state of sureness

PART FOUR

WRITING SKILLS

Chapter 4: Improving Written Expression

CHAPTER 4

Improving Written Expression

You definitely want to study hard when you prepare for the writing skills section of the PSAT: a good score on this section of the test may make all the difference between your becoming a National Merit finalist and your coming out a runner-up.

There are three different kinds of questions on the writing skills section of the PSAT: improving sentences, identifying sentence errors, and improving paragraphs. More than half of them, twenty questions out of thirty-nine, involve choosing the best of five different versions of a sentence.

The writing skills questions test your ability to recognize clear, correct standard written English, the kind of writing your college professors will expect on the papers you turn in to them. You'll be expected to know basic grammar, such as subject-verb agreement, pronoun-antecedent agreement, correct verb tense, correct sentence structure, and correct diction. You'll need to know how to recognize a dangling participle and how to spot when two parts of a sentence are not clearly connected. You'll also need to know when a paragraph is (or isn't) properly developed and organized.

Improving Sentences

The most numerous questions in the Writing Skills section involve spotting the form of a sentence that works best. In these improving sentences questions, you will be presented with five different versions of the same sentence; you must choose the *best* one. Here are the directions:

Improving Sentences Directions:
Some or all parts of the following sentences are underlined. The first answer choice, (A), simply repeats the underlined part of the sentence. The other four choices present four alternative ways to phrase the underlined part. Select the answer that produces the most effective sentence, one that is clear and exact, and blacken the appropriate space on your answer sheet. In selecting your choice, be sure that it is standard written English and that it expresses the meaning of the original sentence.

EXAMPLE:

The first biography of author Eudora Welty came out in 1998, and she was eighty-nine years old at the time.

(A) and she was eighty-nine years old at the time
(B) at the time when she was eighty-nine
(C) upon becoming an eighty-nine year old
(D) when she was eighty-nine
(E) at the age of eighty-nine years old

Ⓐ Ⓑ Ⓒ ● Ⓔ

TIPS FOR HANDLING IMPROVING SENTENCES QUESTIONS

Tip 1

If you spot an error in the underlined section, eliminate Choice A and any other answer that contains the same error. If something in the underlined section of a sentence correction question strikes you as an obvious error, you can immediately ignore Choice A, which is *always* a repetition of the original underlined section, and any other answer choices that repeat the error. Remember, you still don't have to be able to explain what is wrong. You just need to find a correct equivalent. If the error you found in the underlined section is absent from more than one of the answer choices, look over those choices again to see if they add any new errors.

EXAMPLE 1

See how the first tip works in dealing with the following sentence:

Being as I had studied for the test with a tutor, I was confident.

(A) Being as I had studied for the test
(B) Being as I studied for the test
(C) Since I studied for the test
(D) Since I had studied for the test
(E) Because I studied for the test

Being as is unacceptable as a conjunction in standard written English. Therefore, you can eliminate Choices A and B right away. *Since* and *Because* are both acceptable conjunctions, so you have to look more closely at Choices C, D, and E. The only other changes these choices make are in the tense of the verb. Since the studying occurred before the taking of the test, the past perfect tense, *had studied,* is correct, so the answer is Choice D.

Tip 2

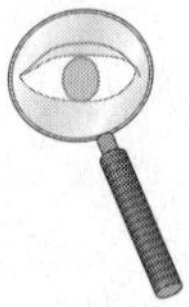

If you don't spot an error in the underlined section, look at the answer choices to see what is changed. Sometimes it's hard to spot what's wrong with the underlined section in a sentence correction question. When that happens, turn to the answer choices. Find the changes in the answers. The changes will tell you what kind of error is being tested. When you substitute the answer choices in the original sentence, ask yourself which of these choices makes the sentence seem clearest to you. That may well be the correct answer choice.

EXAMPLE 2

See how the second tip works in dealing with the following sentence:

> Even the play's most minor characters work together with extraordinary skill, their interplay creates a moving theatrical experience.
>
> (A) their interplay creates a moving theatrical experience
> (B) a moving theatrical experience is created by their interplay
> (C) and their interplay creates a moving theatrical experience
> (D) and a moving theatrical experience being the creation of their interplay
> (E) with their interplay they create a moving theatrical experience

Look at the underlined section of the sentence. Nothing seems wrong with it. It could stand on its own as an independent sentence: *Their interplay creates a moving theatrical experience*. Choices B and E are similar to it, for both could stand as independent sentences. Choices C and D, however, are not independent sentences; both begin with the linking word *and*. The error needing correction here is the common comma splice, in which two sentences are carelessly linked with only a comma. Choice C corrects this error in the simplest way possible, adding the word *and* to tie these sentences together.

Tip 3

Make sure that all parts of the sentence are logically connected. Not all parts of a sentence are created equal. Some parts should be subordinated to the rest, connected with subordinating conjunctions or relative pronouns, not just added on with *and*. Overuse of *and* frequently makes sentences sound babyish. Compare "We had dinner at the Hard Rock Cafe, and we went to a concert" with "After we had dinner at the Hard Rock Cafe, we went to a concert."

EXAMPLE 3

See how the third tip works in dealing with the following sentence:

> The rock star always had enthusiastic fans and they loved him.
>
> (A) and they loved him
> (B) and they loving him
> (C) what loved him
> (D) who loved him
> (E) which loved him

The original version of this sentence doesn't have any grammatical errors, but it is a poor sentence because it doesn't connect its two clauses logically. The second clause ("and they loved him") is merely adding information about the fans, so it should be turned into an adjective clause, introduced by a relative pronoun. Choices D and E both seem to work, but you know that *which* should never be used to refer to people, so Choice D is obviously the correct answer.

Tip 4

Make sure that all sentence parts listed as a series are similar in form. If they are not, the sentence suffers from a lack of parallel structure. The sentence "I'm taking classes in algebra, history, and how to speak French" lacks parallel structure. *Algebra* and *history* are nouns, names of subjects. The third subject should also be a noun: *conversational French.*

EXAMPLE 4

See how the fourth tip works in dealing with the following sentence:

In this chapter we'll analyze both types of questions, suggest useful techniques for tackling them, providing some sample items for you to try.

(A) suggest useful techniques for tackling them, providing some sample items for you to try
(B) suggest useful techniques for tackling them, providing some sample items which you can try
(C) suggest useful tactics for tackling them, and provide some sample items for you to try
(D) and suggest useful techniques for tackling them by providing some sample items for you to try
(E) having suggested useful techniques for tackling them and provided some sample items for you to try

To answer questions like this correctly, you must pay particular attention to what the sentence means. You must first decide whether *analyzing, suggesting,* and *providing* are logically equal in importance here. Since they are—all are activities that "we" will do—they should be given equal emphasis. Only Choice C provides the proper parallel structure.

Tip 5

Pay particular attention to the shorter answer choices. (This tactic also applies to certain paragraph correction questions.) Good prose is economical. Often the correct answer choice will be the shortest, most direct way of making a point. If you spot no grammatical errors or errors in logic in a concise answer choice, it may well be right.

EXAMPLE 5

See how the fifth tip works in dealing with the following sentence:

The turning point in the battle of Waterloo probably was Blucher, who was arriving in time to save the day.

(A) Blucher, who was arriving
(B) Blucher, in that he arrived
(C) Blucher's arrival
(D) when Blucher was arriving
(E) that Blucher had arrived

Which answer choice uses the fewest words? Choice C, *Blucher's arrival.* It also happens to be the right answer.

Choice C is both concise in style and correct in grammar. Look back at the original sentence. Strip it of its modifiers, and what is left? "The turning point . . . was Blucher." A turning point is not a person; it is a *thing.* The turning point in the battle was not Blucher, but Blucher's *action,* the thing he did. The correct answer is Choice C, *Blucher's arrival.* Pay particular attention to such concise answer choices. If a concise choice sounds natural when you substitute it for the original underlined phrase, it's a reasonable guess.

Identifying Sentence Errors

Almost one-third of the Writing Skills questions on the PSAT, fourteen of the thirty-nine, to be exact, are identifying sentence errors questions in which you have to find an error in the underlined section of a sentence. You do *not* have to correct the sentence or explain what is wrong. Here are the directions.

Identifying Sentence Errors Directions:
The sentences in this section may contain errors in grammar, usage, choice of words, or idioms. There is either just one error per sentence, or the sentence is correct. Some words or phrases are underlined and lettered; everything else in the sentence is correct.

If an underlined word or phrase is incorrect, choose that letter; if the sentence is correct, select No error. Then blacken the appropriate space on your answer sheet.

EXAMPLE:

These fields have soil so rich that (A) corn growing here (B) commonly had stood (C) more than six feet tall (D). No error (E).

Ⓐ Ⓑ ● Ⓓ Ⓔ

TIPS FOR HANDLING IDENTIFYING SENTENCE ERRORS QUESTIONS

Tip 6

Remember that the error, if there is one, must be in an underlined part of the sentence. You don't have to worry about improvements that could be made in the rest of the sentence. For example, if you have a sentence in which the subject is plural and the verb is singular, you could call either one the error. But if only the verb is underlined, the error for that sentence is the verb.

EXAMPLE 6

See how the sixth tip works in dealing with the following sentence:

> If one follows the discipline of Hatha Yoga, you know the critical
> A B
> importance of physical purification to render the body fit for the
> C D
> practice of higher meditation. No error
> E

What's wrong with the sentence above? Look at Choice B. The writer makes an abrupt, unnecessary shift in person, switching from the pronoun one ("one follows") to the pronoun you ("you know"). There are two ways to fix this sentence. You can rewrite it like this:

> If you follow the discipline of Hatha Yoga, you know the critical importance of physical purification to render the body fit for the practice of higher meditation.

You can also rewrite it like this:

> If one follows the discipline of Hatha Yoga, one knows the critical importance of physical purification to render the body fit for the practice of higher meditation.

However, your job is not to rewrite the sentence. Your job is simply to spot the error, and that error *must be in an underlined part*. In answering error identification questions, focus on the underlined portions of the sentence. Don't waste your time thinking of other ways to make the sentence work.

Tip 7

Use your ear for the language. Remember, you don't have to name the error, or be able to explain why it is wrong. All you have to do is recognize that something *is* wrong. On the early, easy questions in the set, if a word or phrase sounds wrong to you, it probably is, even if you don't know why.

EXAMPLE 7

See how the seventh tip works in dealing with the following sentence:

> In my history class I learned why the American colonies
> A B
> opposed the British, how they organized the militia, and
> C
> the accomplishments of the Continental Congress. No error
> D E

When you got to Choice D, the last section of the sentence, did "the accomplishments of the Continental Congress" sound funny to you—awkward, strange, wooden? Even though you didn't know exactly what was wrong, did something feel off there? If so, congratulations: you have a good ear.

If you followed your instincts and chose Choice D as the error, you were right. The error is a lack of parallel structure. The sentence is listing three things you learned, and they should all be in the same form. Your ear expects the pattern to be the same. Since the first two items listed are clauses, the third should be too: "In my history class I learned why the American colonies opposed the British, how they organized the militia, and what the Continental Congress accomplished."

Tip 8

Look first for the most common errors. Be systematic: check the underlined sections one by one. Most of the sentences will have errors. If you are having trouble finding mistakes, check for some of the more common ones: subject-verb agreement, pronoun-antecedent problems, misuse of adjectives and adverbs, dangling modifiers. But look for errors only in the underlined parts of the sentence.

EXAMPLE 8

See how the eighth tip works in dealing with the following sentence:

> Marilyn and <u>I</u> (A) ran as <u>fast</u> (B) as we could, but we missed our train, <u>which</u> (C) made <u>us</u> (D) late for work. <u>No error</u> (E)

Imagine that you have this sentence, and you can't see what is wrong with it. Start at the beginning and check each answer choice. *I* is part of the subject, so it is the right case: after all, you wouldn't say "Me ran fast." *Fast* can be an adverb, so it is being used correctly here. *Which* is a pronoun, and needs a noun for its antecedent. The only available noun is *train*, but that doesn't make sense (the train didn't make us late—*missing* the train made us late.) So there is your error, Choice C.

Tip 9

Remember that not every sentence contains an error. Ten to twenty percent of the time, the sentence is correct as it stands. Do not get so caught up in hunting for errors that you start seeing errors that aren't there. If no obvious errors strike your eye and the sentence sounds natural to your ear, go with Choice E: No error.

Improving Paragraphs

In the improving paragraphs questions, you will confront a flawed student essay followed by five questions. In some cases, you must select the answer choice that best rewrites and combines portions of two separate sentences. In others, you must decide where in the essay a sentence best fits. In still others, you must choose what sort of additional information would most strengthen the writer's argument. Here are the directions.

Improving Paragraphs Directions:
The passage below is the unedited draft of a student's essay. Some of the essay needs to be rewritten to make the meaning clearer and more precise. Read the essay carefully.

The essay is followed by five questions about changes that might improve all or part of its organization, development, sentence structure, use of language, appropriateness to the audience, or use of standard written English. Choose the answer that most clearly and effectively expresses the student's intended meaning. Indicate your choice by filling in the corresponding space on the answer sheet.

TIPS FOR HANDLING IMPROVING PARAGRAPHS QUESTIONS

Tip 10

First read the passage; then read the questions. Whether you choose to skim the student essay quickly or to read it closely, you need to have a reasonable idea of what the student author is trying to say before you set out to correct this rough first draft.

Tip 11

First tackle the questions that ask you to improve individual sentences; then tackle the ones that ask you to strengthen the passage as a whole. In the sentence correction questions, you've just been weeding out ineffective sentences and selecting effective ones. Here you're doing more of the same. It generally takes less time to spot an effective sentence than it does to figure out a way to strengthen an argument or link up two paragraphs.

Tip 12

Consider whether the addition of signal words or phrases—transitions—would strengthen the passage or particular sentences within it. If the essay is trying to contrast two ideas, it might benefit from the addition of a contrast signal.

Contrast Signals: *although, despite, however, in contrast, nevertheless, on the contrary, on the other hand.*

If one portion of the essay is trying to support or continue a thought developed elsewhere in the passage, it might benefit from the addition of a support signal.

Support Signals: *additionally, furthermore, in addition, likewise, moreover.*

If the essay is trying to indicate that one thing causes another, it might benefit from the addition of a cause-and-effect signal.

Cause-and-Effect Signals: *accordingly, as a result of, because, consequently, hence, therefore, thus.*

Pay particular attention to answer choices that contain such signal words.

Tip 13

When you tackle the questions, *go back to the passage* to verify each answer choice. See whether your revised version of a particular sentence sounds right in its context. Ask yourself whether your choice follows naturally from the sentence before.

Common Grammar and Usage Errors

Some errors are more common than others in this section. Here are a dozen that appear frequently on the examination. Watch out for them when you do the practice exercises and when you take the PSAT.

The Run-On Sentence

Mary's party was very exciting, it lasted until 2 A.M.
It is raining today, I need a raincoat.

You may also have heard this error called a comma splice. It can be corrected by making two sentences instead of one:

Mary's party was very exciting. It lasted until 2 A.M.

or by using a semicolon in place of the comma:

Mary's party was very exciting; it lasted until 2 A.M.

or by proper compounding:

Mary's party was very exciting and lasted until 2 A.M.

You can also correct this error with proper subordination. The second example above could be corrected:

Since it is raining today, I need a raincoat.
It is raining today, and so I need a raincoat.

The Sentence Fragment

Since John was talking during the entire class, making it impossible for anyone to concentrate.

This is the opposite of the first error. Instead of too much in one sentence, here you have too little. Do not be misled by the length of the fragment. It must have a main clause before it can be a complete sentence. All you have in this example is the cause. You still need a result. For example, the sentence could be corrected:

Since John's talking during the entire class made it impossible for anyone to concentrate, the teacher had him stay after school.

Error in the Case of a Noun or Pronoun

Between you and I, this test is not really very difficult.

Case problems usually involve personal pronouns, which are in the nominative case (*I, he, she, we, they, who*) when they are used as subjects or predicate nominatives and in the objective case (*me, him, her, us, them, whom*) when they are used as direct objects, indirect objects, and objects of prepositions. In this example, if you realize that *between* is a preposition, you know that *I* should be changed to the objective *me* because it is the object of a preposition.

Error in Subject-Verb Agreement

Harvard College, along with several other Ivy League schools, are sending students to the conference.

Phrases starting with *along with* or *as well as* or *in addition to* that are placed in between the subject and the verb do not affect the verb. The subject of this sentence is *Harvard College,* so the verb should be *is sending.*

There is three bears living in that house.

Sentences that begin with *there* have the subject after the verb. The subject of this sentence is *bears,* so the verb should be *are.*

Error in Pronoun-Number Agreement

Every one of the girls on the team is trying to do their best.

Every pronoun must have a specific noun or noun substitute for an antecedent, and it must agree with that antecedent in number (singular or plural). In this example, *their* refers to *one* and must be singular:

Every one of the girls on the team is trying to do her best.

Error in the Tense or Form of a Verb

After the sun set behind the mountain, a cool breeze sprang up and brought relief from the heat.

Make sure the verbs in a sentence appear in the proper sequence of tenses, so that it is clear what happened when. Since, according to the sentence, the breeze did not appear until after the sun had finished setting, the setting belongs in the past perfect tense:

After the sun had set behind the mountain, a cool breeze sprang up and brought relief from the heat.

Error in Logical Comparison

I can go to California or Florida. I wonder which is best.

When you are comparing only two things, you should use the comparative form of the adjective, not the superlative:

I wonder which is better.

Comparisons must also be complete and logical.

The rooms on the second floor are larger than the first floor.

It would be a strange building that had rooms larger than an entire floor. Logically, this sentence should be corrected to

The rooms on the second floor are larger than those on the first floor.

Adjective and Adverb Confusion

She did good on the test.

They felt badly about leaving their friends.

These are the two most common ways that adjectives and adverbs are misused. In the first example, when you are talking about how someone did, you want the adverb *well,* not the adjective *good:*

She did well on the test.

In the second example, after a linking verb like *feel,* you want a predicate adjective to describe the subject:

They felt bad about leaving their friends.

Error in Modification and Word Order

Reaching for the book, the ladder slipped out from under him.

A participial phrase at the beginning of the sentence should describe the subject of the sentence. Since it doesn't make sense to think of a ladder reaching for a book, this participle is left dangling with nothing to modify. The sentence needs some rewriting:

When he reached for the book, the ladder slipped out from under him.

Error in Parallelism

In his book on winter sports, the author discusses ice-skating, skiing, hockey, and how to fish in an ice-covered lake.

Logically, equal and similar ideas belong in similar form. This shows that they are equal. In this sentence, the author discusses four sports, and all four should be presented the same way:

In his book on winter sports, the author discusses ice skating, skiing, hockey, and fishing in an ice-covered lake.

Error in Diction or Idiom

The affects of the storm could be seen everywhere.

Your ear for the language will help you handle these errors, especially if you are accustomed to reading standard English. These questions test you on words that are frequently misused, on levels of usage (informal versus formal), and on standard English idioms. In this example, the verb *affect,* meaning "to influence," has been confused with the noun *effect,* meaning "result."

The effects of the storm could be seen everywhere.

The exercises that follow will give you practice in answering the three types of questions you'll find on the Identifying Sentence Errors questions, Improving Sentence questions, and Improving Paragraph questions. When you have completed each exercise, check your answers against the answer key. Then, read the answer explanations for any questions you either answered incorrectly or omitted.

Practice Exercises

The sentences in this section may contain errors in grammar, usage, choice of words, or idioms. There is either just one error per sentence, or the sentence is correct. Some words or phrases are underlined and lettered; everything else in the sentence is correct.

If an underlined word or phrase is incorrect, choose that letter; if the sentence is correct, select No error. Then blacken the appropriate space on your answer sheet.

EXAMPLE:

These fields have soil so rich that corn
A
growing here commonly had stood more
B C
than six feet tall. No error Ⓐ Ⓑ ● Ⓓ Ⓔ
D E

1. We were already to leave for the amusement park
A B
when John's car broke down; we were forced to
C D
postpone our outing. No error
E

2. By order of the Student Council, the wearing of
A B
slacks by we girls in school has been permitted.
C D
No error
E

3. Each one of the dogs in the show require a special
A B C
kind of diet. No error
D E

4. The major difficulty confronting the authorities
A
was the reluctance of the people to talk; they had
B C
been warned not to say nothing to the police.
D
No error
E

5. If I were you, I would never permit him
A B
to take part in such an exhausting and painful
C D
activity. No error
E

6. Stanford White, who is one of America's
A
most notable architects, have designed many
B C
famous buildings, among them the original
D
Madison Square Garden. No error
E

7. The notion of allowing the institution of slavery
A B
to continue to exist in a democratic society had no
C
appeal to either the violent followers of John
Brown nor the peaceful disciples of Sojourner
D
Truth. No error
E

8. Some students prefer watching filmstrips to
A
textbooks because they feel uncomfortable with
B C
the presentation of information in a non-oral form.
D
No error
E

9. There was so much conversation in back of me
A B
that I couldn't hear the actors on the stage.
C D
No error
E

10. This book is too elementary; it can help neither
A B
you nor I. No error
C D E

11. In a way _we_ (A) may say _that_ (B) we _have reached_ (C) the _end of_ (D) the Industrial Revolution. _No error_ (E)

12. _Although_ (A) the books are _altogether_ (B) on the shelf, _they_ (C) are not arranged in _any kind of_ (D) order. _No error_ (E)

13. The _reason for_ (A) my _prolonged absence_ (B) from class _was_ (C) _because_ (D) I was ill for three weeks. _No error_ (E)

14. _According to_ (A) researchers, the weapons and work implements _used by_ (B) Cro-Magnon hunters appear _being_ (C) _actually quite_ (D) "modern." _No error_ (E)

15. Since we were caught _completely unawares_ (A), the _affect_ (B) of Ms. Rivera's remarks _was startling;_ (C) some were shocked, _but_ (D) others were angry. _No error_ (E)

16. The committee _had intended_ (A) both _you and I_ (B) to speak at the assembly; _however,_ (C) _only_ (D) one of us will be able to talk. _No error_ (E)

17. The existence of rundown "welfare hotels," _in which_ (A) homeless families _reside_ (B) at enormous _cost to_ (C) the taxpayer, provides a shameful _commentary of_ (D) America's commitment to house the poor. _No error_ (E)

18. We have heard that the _principal_ (A) has decided _whom_ (B) the prizewinners _will be_ (C) _and_ (D) will announce the names in the assembly today. _No error_ (E)

19. _As soon as_ (A) the sun _had rose_ (B) _over_ (C) the mountains, the valley became _unbearably hot_ (D) and stifling. _No error_ (E)

20. _They_ (A) are both _excellent books_ (B), but this one _is_ (C) _best_ (D). _No error_ (E)

21. Although the news _had come_ (A) as a surprise _to all_ (B) in the room, both Jane and Oprah tried to do _her_ (C) work _as though_ (D) nothing had happened. _No error_ (E)

22. _Even_ (A) well-known fashion designers have difficulty staying on top _from one season to another_ (B) _because of_ (C) _changeable moods_ (D) and needs in the marketplace. _No error_ (E)

23. Arms control has been _under discussion_ (A) for decades with the former Soviet Union, _but_ (B) solutions _are still_ (C) _alluding_ (D) the major powers. _No error_ (E)

24. Perhaps sports enthusiasts are realizing _that_ (A) jogging is _not easy on_ (B) joints and tendons, for the _latest_ (C) fad _is being walking_ (D). _No error_ (E)

25. Technological advances can cause factual data to
A
become obsolete within a short time; yet, students
B C
should concentrate on reasoning skills, not facts.
D
No error
E

26. If anyone cares to join me in this campaign, either
A B C
now or in the near future, they will be welcomed
D
gratefully. No error
E

27. The poems with which he occasionally
A
desired to regale the fashionable world were
B
invariably bad—stereotyped, bombastic, and
C
even ludicrous. No error
D E

28. Ever since the quality of teacher education came
A B
under public scrutiny, suggestions for upgrading
C
the profession are abounding. No error
D E

29. Because the door was locked and bolted, the police
A
were forced to break into the apartment through
B C D
the bedroom window. No error
E

30. I will always remember you standing by me
A B C D
offering me encouragement. No error
E

31. With special training, capuchin monkeys
can enable quadriplegics as well as other
A B
handicapped individuals to become
C
increasingly independent. No error
D E

32. Contrary to what had previously been reported, the
A
conditions governing the truce between Libya and
B
Chad arranged by the United Nations has not yet
C D
been revealed. No error
E

33. Avid readers generally either admire or dislike
A
Ernest Hemingway's journalistic style of writing;
B
few have no opinion of him. No error
C D E

34. In 1986, the nuclear disaster at Chernobyl
has aroused intense speculation about the long-
A B
term effects of radiation that continued for
C
the better part of a year. No error
D E

35. Howard Hughes, who became the subject of
A B
bizarre rumors as a result of his extreme
C
reclusiveness, was well-known as an aviator,
industrialist, and in producing motion pictures.
D
No error
E

Some or all parts of the following sentences are underlined. The first answer choice, (A), simply repeats the underlined part of the sentence. The other four choices present four alternative ways to phrase the underlined part. Select the answer that produces the most effective sentence, one that is clear and exact, and blacken the appropriate space on your answer sheet. In selecting your choice, be sure that it is standard written English and that it expresses the meaning of the original sentence.

EXAMPLE:

The first biography of author Eudora Welty came out in 1998, and she was eighty-nine years old at the time.

(A) and she was eighty-nine years old at the time
(B) at the time when she was eighty-nine
(C) upon becoming an eighty-nine year old
(D) when she was eighty-nine
(E) at the age of eighty-nine years old

Ⓐ Ⓑ Ⓒ ● Ⓔ

36. The child is neither encouraged to be critical or to examine all the evidence before forming an opinion.

(A) neither encouraged to be critical or to examine
(B) neither encouraged to be critical nor to examine
(C) either encouraged to be critical or to examine
(D) encouraged either to be critical nor to examine
(E) not encouraged either to be critical or to examine

37. The process by which the community influence the actions of its members is known as social control.

(A) influence the actions of its members
(B) influences the actions of its members
(C) had influenced the actions of its members
(D) influences the actions of their members
(E) will influence the actions of its members

38. Play being recognized as an important factor improving mental and physical health and thereby reducing human misery and poverty.

(A) Play being recognized as
(B) By recognizing play as
(C) Their recognizing play as
(D) Recognition of it being
(E) Play is recognized as

39. To be sure, there would be scarcely any time left over for other things if school children would have been expected to have considered all sides of every matter on which they hold opinions.

(A) would have been expected to have considered
(B) should have been expected to have considered
(C) were expected to consider
(D) will be expected to have considered
(E) were expected to be considered

40. Using it wisely, leisure promotes health, efficiency and happiness.

(A) Using it wisely
(B) If it is used wisely
(C) Having used it wisely
(D) Because of its wise use
(E) Because of usefulness

41. In giving expression to the play instincts of the human race, new vigor and effectiveness are afforded by recreation to the body and to the mind.

(A) new vigor and effectiveness are afforded by recreation to the body and to the mind
(B) recreation affords new vigor and effectiveness to the body and to the mind
(C) there are afforded new vigor and effectiveness to the body and to the mind
(D) by recreation the body and the mind are afforded new vigor and effectiveness
(E) to the body and to the mind afford new vigor and effectiveness to themselves by recreation

42. Depending on skillful suggestion, argument is seldom used in advertising.

(A) Depending on skillful suggestion, argument is seldom used in advertising.
(B) Argument is seldom used in advertising, which depends instead on skillful suggestion.
(C) Skillful suggestion is depended on by advertisers instead of argument.
(D) Suggestion, which is more skillful, is used in place of argument by advertisers.
(E) Instead of suggestion, depending on argument is used by skillful advertisers.

43. When this war is over, no nation will either be isolated in war or peace.

(A) either be isolated in war or peace
(B) be either isolated in war or peace
(C) be isolated in neither war nor peace
(D) be isolated either in war or in peace
(E) be isolated neither in war or peace

44. Thanks to the prevailing westerly winds, dust blowing east from the drought-stricken plains travels halfway across the continent to fall on the cities of the East Coast.

(A) blowing east from the drought-stricken plains
(B) that, blowing east from the drought-stricken plains,
(C) from the drought-stricken plains and blows east
(D) that is from the drought-stricken plains blowing east
(E) blowing east that is from the plains that are drought-stricken

45. Americans are learning that their concept of a research worker toiling alone in a laboratory and who discovers miraculous cures has been highly idealized and glamorized.

(A) toiling alone in a laboratory and who discovers miraculous cures
(B) toiling alone in a laboratory and discovers miraculous cures
(C) toiling alone in a laboratory to discover miraculous cures
(D) who toil alone in the laboratory and discover miraculous cures
(E) has toiled alone hoping to discover miraculous cures

46. However many mistakes have been made in our past, the tradition of America, not only the champion of freedom but also fair play, still lives among millions who can see light and hope scarcely anywhere else.

(A) not only the champion of freedom but also fair play
(B) the champion of not only freedom but also of fair play
(C) the champion not only of freedom but also of fair play
(D) not only the champion but also freedom and fair play
(E) not the champion of freedom only, but also fair play

47. Examining the principal movements sweeping through the world, it can be seen that they are being accelerated by the war.

(A) Examining the principal movements sweeping through the world, it can be seen
(B) Having examined the principal movements sweeping through the world, it can be seen
(C) Examining the principal movements sweeping through the world can be seen
(D) Examining the principal movements sweeping through the world, we can see
(E) It can be seen examining the principal movements sweeping through the world

48. The FCC is broadening its view on what constitutes indecent programming, radio stations are taking a closer look at their broadcasters' materials.

(A) The FCC is broadening its view on what constitutes indecent programming
(B) The FCC, broadening its view on what constitutes indecent programming, has caused
(C) The FCC is broadening its view on what constitutes indecent programming, as a result
(D) Since the FCC is broadening its view on what constitutes indecent programming
(E) The FCC, having broadened its view on what constitutes indecent programming

49. As district attorney, Elizabeth Holtzman not only had the responsibility of supervising a staff of dedicated young lawyers but she had the task of maintaining good relations with the police also.

(A) but she had the task of maintaining good relations with the police also
(B) but she also had the task of maintaining good relations with the police
(C) but also had the task of maintaining good relations with the police
(D) but she had the task to maintain good relations with the police also
(E) but also she had the task to maintain good relations with the police

50. Many politicians are now trying to take uncontroversial positions on issues; the purpose being to allow them to appeal to as wide a segment of the voting population as possible.

(A) issues; the purpose being to allow them to appeal
(B) issues in order to appeal
(C) issues, the purpose is to allow them to appeal
(D) issues and the purpose is to allow them to appeal
(E) issues; that was allowing them to appeal

Directions: The passage below is the unedited draft of a student's essay. Some of the essay needs to be rewritten to make the meaning clearer and more precise. Read the essay carefully.

The essay is followed by six questions about changes that might improve all or part of its organization, development, sentence structure, use of language, appropriateness to the audience, or use of standard written English. Choose the answer that most clearly and effectively expresses the student's intended meaning. Indicate your choice by filling in the corresponding space on the answer sheet.

[1] Throughout history, people have speculated about the future. **[2]** Will it be a utopia? they wondered. **[3]** Will injustice and poverty be eliminated? **[4]** Will people accept ethnic diversity, learning to live in peace? **[5]** Will the world be clean and unpolluted? **[6]** Or will technology aid us in creating a trap for ourselves we cannot escape, for example such as the world in *1984*? **[7]** With the turn of the millennium just around the corner these questions are in the back of our minds.

[8] Science fiction often portrays the future as a technological Garden of Eden. **[9]** With interactive computers, TVs and robots at our command, we barely need to lift a finger to go to school, to work, to go shopping, and education is also easy and convenient. **[10]** Yet, the problems of the real twentieth century seem to point in another direction. **[11]** The environment, far from improving, keeps deteriorating. **[12]** Wars and other civil conflicts breakout regularly. **[13]** The world's population is growing out of control. **[14]** The majority of people on earth live in poverty. **[15]** Many of them are starving. **[16]** Illiteracy is a problem in most poor countries. **[17]** Diseases and malnourishment is very common. **[18]** Rich countries like the U.S.A. don't have the resources to help the "have-not" countries.

[19] Instead, think instead of all the silly inventions such as tablets you put in your toilet tank to make the water blue, or electric toothbrushes. **[20]** More money is spent on space and defense than on education and health care. **[21]** Advancements in agriculture can produce enough food to feed the whole country, yet people in the U.S. are starving.

[22] Although the USSR is gone, the nuclear threat continues from small countries like Iran. **[23]** Until the world puts its priorities straight, we can't look for a bright future in the twenty-first century, despite the rosy picture painted for us by the science fiction writers.

51. Considering the context of paragraph 1, which of the following is the best revision of sentence 6?

(A) Or will technology create a trap for ourselves from which we cannot escape, for example the world in *1984*?
(B) Or will technology aid people in creating a trap for themselves that they cannot escape; for example, the world in *1984*?
(C) Or will technology create a trap from which there is no escape, as it did in the world in *1984*?
(D) Or will technology trap us in an inescapable world, for example, it did so in the world of *1984*?
(E) Perhaps technology will aid people in creating a trap for themselves from which they cannot escape, just as they did it in the world of *1984*.

52. With regard to the essay as a whole, which of the following best describes the writer's intention in paragraph 1?

(A) to announce the purpose of the essay
(B) to compare two ideas discussed later in the essay
(C) to take a position on the essay's main issue
(D) to reveal the organization of the essay
(E) to raise questions that will be answered in the essay

53. Which of the following is the best revision of the underlined segment of sentence 9 below?

[9] With interactive computers, TVs and robots at our command, we barely need to lift a finger to go to school, to work, <u>to go shopping, and education is also easy and convenient</u>.

(A) and to go shopping, while education is also easy and convenient
(B) to go shopping, and getting an education is also easy and convenient
(C) to go shopping as well as educating ourselves are all easy and convenient
(D) to shop, and an easy and convenient education
(E) to shop, and to get an easy and convenient education

54. Which of the following is the most effective way to combine sentences 14, 15, 16, and 17?

(A) The majority of people on earth are living in poverty and are starving, with illiteracy, and disease and being malnourished are also a common problems.
(B) Common problems for the majority of people on earth are poverty, illiteracy, diseases, malnourishment, and many are illiterate.
(C) The majority of people on earth are poor, starving, sick, malnourished, and illiterate.
(D) Common among the poor majority on earth is poverty, starvation, disease, malnourishment, and illiteracy.
(E) The majority of the earth's people living in poverty with starvation, disease, malnourishment and illiteracy a constant threat.

55. Considering the sentences that precede and follow sentence 19, which of the following is the most effective revision of sentence 19?

(A) Instead they are devoting resources on silly inventions such as tablets to make toilet tank water blue or electric toothbrushes.
(B) Instead, they waste their resources on producing silly inventions like electric toothbrushes and tablets for bluing toilet tank water.
(C) Think of all the silly inventions: tablets you put in your toilet tank to make the water blue and electric toothbrushes.
(D) Instead, tablets you put in your toilet tank to make the water blue or electric toothbrushes are examples of useless products on the market today.
(E) Instead of spending on useful things, think of all the silly inventions such as tablets you put in your toilet tank to make the water blue or electric toothbrushes.

56. Which of the following revisions would most improve the overall coherence of the essay?

(A) moving sentence 7 to paragraph 2
(B) moving sentence 10 to paragraph 1
(C) moving sentence 22 to paragraph 2
(D) deleting sentence 8
(E) deleting sentence 23

Answer Key

1. **A**	11. **E**	21. **C**	31. **E**	41. **B**	51. **C**
2. **C**	12. **B**	22. **E**	32. **D**	42. **B**	52. **E**
3. **B**	13. **D**	23. **D**	33. **D**	43. **D**	53. **E**
4. **D**	14. **C**	24. **D**	34. **A**	44. **A**	54. **C**
5. **E**	15. **B**	25. **C**	35. **D**	45. **C**	55. **B**
6. **C**	16. **B**	26. **D**	36. **E**	46. **C**	56. **C**
7. **D**	17. **D**	27. **E**	37. **B**	47. **D**	
8. **B**	18. **B**	28. **D**	38. **E**	48. **D**	
9. **B**	19. **B**	29. **E**	39. **C**	49. **C**	
10. **D**	20. **D**	30. **C**	40. **B**	50. **B**	

Answer Explanations

1. **(A)** Error in diction. Should be *all ready. All ready* means the group is ready; *already* means prior to a given time, previously.
2. **(C)** Error in pronoun case. Should be *us.* The expression *us girls* is the object of the preposition *by.*
3. **(B)** Error in subject-verb agreement. Should be *requires.* Verb should agree with the subject (*each one*).
4. **(D)** Should be *to say anything. Not to say nothing* is a double negative.
5. **(E)** Sentence is correct.
6. **(C)** Error in subject-verb agreement. Since the subject is Stanford White (singular), change *have designed* to *has designed.*
7. **(D)** Error in use of correlatives. Change *nor* to *or.* The correct form of the correlative pairs *either* with *or.*
8. **(B)** Error in parallel structure. Change *textbooks* to *reading textbooks.* To have parallel structure, the linked sentence elements must share the same grammatical form.
9. **(B)** Error in diction. Change *in back of* to *behind.*
10. **(D)** Error in pronoun case. Should be *me.* Pronoun is the object of the verb *can help.*
11. **(E)** Sentence is correct.
12. **(B)** Error in diction. Should be *all together. All together* means in a group; *altogether* means entirely.
13. **(D)** Improper use of *because.* Change to *that* (*The reason . . . was that . . .*).
14. **(C)** Incorrect verbal. Change the participle *being* to the infinitive *to be.*
15. **(B)** Error in diction. Change *affect* (a verb meaning to influence or pretend) to *effect* (a noun meaning result).
16. **(B)** Error in pronoun case. Should be *me.* Subjects of infinitives are in the objective case.
17. **(D)** Error in idiom. Change *commentary of* to *commentary on.*
18. **(B)** Error in pronoun case. Should be *who.* The pronoun is the predicate complement of *will be* and is in the nominative case.
19. **(B)** Should be *had risen.* The past participle of the verb *to rise* is *risen.*
20. **(D)** Error in comparison of modifiers. Should be *better.* Do not use the superlative when comparing two things.
21. **(C)** Error in pronoun-number agreement. Should be *their* instead of *her.* The antecedent of the pronoun is *Jane and Oprah* (plural).
22. **(E)** Sentence is correct.
23. **(D)** Error in diction. Change *alluding* (meaning to refer indirectly) to *eluding* (meaning to evade).
24. **(D)** Confusion of verb and gerund (verbal noun). Change *is being walking* to *is walking.*
25. **(C)** Error in coordination and subordination. Change *yet* to *therefore* or another similar connector to clarify the connection between the clauses.

26. **(D)** Error in pronoun-number agreement. Should be *he* or *she*. The antecedent of the pronoun is *anyone* (singular).

27. **(E)** Sentence is correct.

28. **(D)** Error in sequence of tenses. Change *are abounding* to *have abounded.* The present perfect tense talks about an action that occurs at one time, but is seen in relation to another time.

29. **(E)** Sentence is correct.

30. **(C)** Error in pronoun case. Should be *your.* The pronoun modifying a gerund (verbal noun) should be in the possessive case.

31. **(E)** Sentence is correct.

32. **(D)** Error in subject-verb agreement. Since the subject is *conditions* (plural), change *has* to *have.*

33. **(D)** Error in pronoun. Since the sentence speaks about Hemingway's style rather than about Hemingway, the phrase should read *of it,* not *of him.*

34. **(A)** Error in sequence of tenses. Change *has aroused* to *aroused.* The present perfect tense (*has aroused*) is used for indefinite time. In this sentence, the time is defined as *the better part of a year*.

35. **(D)** Lack of parallel structure. Change *in producing motion pictures* to *motion picture producer.*

36. **(E)** This question involves two aspects of correct English. *Neither* should be followed by *nor; either* by *or.* Choices A and D are, therefore, incorrect. The words *neither . . . nor* and *either . . . or* should be placed before the two items being discussed—*to be critical* and *to examine*. Choice E meets both requirements.

37. **(B)** This question tests agreement. Errors in subject-verb agreement and pronoun-number agreement are both involved. *Community* (singular) needs a singular verb, *influences.* Also, the pronoun that refers to *community* should be singular *(its)*.

38. **(E)** Error in following conventions. This is an incomplete sentence or fragment. The sentence needs a verb to establish a principal clause. Choice E provides the verb (*is recognized*) and presents the only complete sentence in the group.

39. **(C)** *Would have been expected* is incorrect as a verb in a clause introduced by the conjunction *if. Had been expected* or *were expected* is preferable. *To have considered* does not follow correct sequence of tense and should be changed to *to consider.*

40. **(B)** Error in modification and word order. One way of correcting a dangling participle is to change the participial phrase to a clause. Choices B and D substitute clauses for the phrase. However, Choice D changes the meaning of the sentence. Choice B is correct.

41. **(B)** Error in modification and word order. As it stands, the sentence contains a dangling modifier. This is corrected by making *recreation* the subject of the sentence, in the process switching from the passive to the active voice. Choice E also provides a subject for the sentence; however, the meaning of the sentence is changed in Choice E.

42. **(B)** Error in modification and word order. As presented, the sentence contains a dangling parti-ciple, *depending.* Choice B corrects this error. The other choices change the emphasis presented by the author.

43. **(D)** Error in word order. *Either . . . or* should precede the two choices offered (*in war* and *in peace*).

44. **(A)** Sentence is correct.

45. **(C)** Error in parallelism. In the underlined phrase, you will find two modifiers of *worker-toiling* and *who discovers.* The first is a participial phrase, and the second a clause. This results in an error in parallel structure. Choice B also has an error in parallel structure. Choice C corrects this by eliminating one of the modifiers of *worker.* Choice D corrects the error in parallel structure but introduces an error in agreement between subject and verb—*who* (singular) and *toil* (plural). Choice E changes the tense and also the meaning of the original sentence.

46. **(C)** Error in parallelism. Parallel structure requires that *not only* and *but also* immediately precede the words they limit.

47. **(D)** Error in modification and word order. Choices A, B, and E are incorrect because of the dangling participle. Choice C is incoherent. Choice D correctly eliminates the dangling participle by introducing the subject *we.*

48. **(D)** Error in comma splice. The punctuation in Choices A and C creates a run-on sentence. Choices B and E are both ungrammatical. Choice D corrects the run-on sentence by changing the beginning clause into the adverb clause that starts with the subordinating conjunction *since.*

49. **(C)** Error in parallelism. Since the words *not only* immediately precede the verb in the first half of the sentence, the words *but also* should immediately precede the verb in the second half. This error in parallel structure is corrected in Choice C.

50. **(B)** Error in coordination and subordination. The punctuation in Choices A, C, D, and E creates an incomplete sentence or fragment. Choice B corrects the error by linking the elements with *in order to.*

51. **(C)** Choice A is awkward and shifts the pronoun usage in the paragraph from third to first person. Choice B is awkward and contains a semicolon error. A semicolon is used to separate two independent clauses. The material after the semicolon is a sentence fragment. Choice C is succinctly and accurately expressed. It is the best answer. Choice D contains a comma splice between *world* and *for.* A comma may not be used to join two independent clauses. Choice E is awkwardly expressed and contains the pronoun *it,* which lacks a clear referent.

52. **(E)** Choice A indirectly describes the purpose of paragraph 1 but does not identify the writer's main intention. Choices B, C, and D fail to describe the writer's main intention. Choice E accurately describes the writer's main intention. It is the best answer.

53. **(E)** Choice A is grammatically correct but cumbersome. Choice B contains an error in parallel construction. The clause that begins *and getting* is not grammatically parallel to the previous items on the list. Choice C contains a mixed construction. The first and last parts of the sentence are grammatically unrelated. Choice D contains faulty parallel structure. Choice E is correct and accurately expressed. It is the best answer.

54. **(C)** Choice A is wordy and awkwardly expressed. Choice B contains an error in parallel structure. The clause *and many are illiterate* is not grammatically parallel to the previous items on the list of problems. Choice C is concise and accurately expressed. It is the best answer. Choice D is concise, but it contains an error in subject-verb agreement. The subject is *poverty, starvation . . . etc.,* which requires a plural verb; the verb *is* is singular. Choice E is a sentence fragment; it has no main verb.

55. **(B)** Choice A contains an error in idiom. The standard phrase is *devoting to,* not *devoting on.* Choice B ties sentence 19 to the previous sentence and is accurately expressed. It is the best answer. Choice C fails to improve the coherence of the paragraph. Choice D is unrelated to the context of the paragraph. Choice E is insufficiently related to the context of the paragraph.

56. **(C)** Choice A should stay put because it provides a transition between the questions in paragraph 1 and the beginning of paragraph 2. Choice B is a pivotal sentence in paragraph 2 and should not be moved. Choice C fits the topics of paragraph 2; therefore, sentence 22 should be moved to paragraph 2. Choice C is the best answer. Choice D is needed as an introductory sentence in paragraph 2. It should not be deleted. Choice E provides the essay with a meaningful conclusion and should not be deleted.

WRITING SKILLS WRAP-UP

Improving Sentences Questions

1. If you spot an error in the underlined section, eliminate any answer that contains the same error.
2. If you don't spot an error in the underlined section, look at the answer choices to see what is changed.
3. Make sure that all parts of the sentence are logically connected.
4. Make sure that all sentence parts listed as a series are similar in form.
5. Pay particular attention to the shorter answer choices.

Identifying Sentence Errors Questions

6. Remember that the error, if there is one, must be in an underlined part of the sentence.
7. Use your ear for the language.
8. Look first for the most common errors. Be systematic: check the underlined sections one by one.
9. Remember that not every sentence contains an error. Ten to twenty percent of the time, go with Choice E: No error.

Improving Paragraphs Questions

10. First read the passage; then read the questions.
11. First tackle the questions that ask you to improve individual sentences; then tackle the ones that ask you to strengthen the passage as a whole.
12. Consider whether the addition of signal words or phrases—transitions—would strengthen the passage or particular sentences within it.
13. When you tackle the questions, *go back to the passage to verify each answer choice.*

PART FIVE

MATHEMATICS

CHAPTER 5

Introduction to the Mathematics Sections

Part Five consists of three chapters. This first brief chapter serves as an introduction to the mathematics part of the PSAT. Please do not skip it—take the few minutes necessary to carefully read everything in this chapter. It gives some valuable information about the organization of the math part of this book, as well as some important information about the test itself. It discusses the use of calculators on the test and explains the directions for both types of math questions.

Chapter 6 includes a discussion of all the essential tactics and strategies that good test takers need to know to do their best on the math part of the PSAT. The explanation of each tactic is followed by sample problems to solve using that particular tactic. The chapter ends with a set of exercises to test your understanding of the tactics discussed. If you master Chapter 6, you will be able to significantly improve your score on the math part of the PSAT.

Chapter 7 contains a review of the mathematics you need to know in order to do well on the PSAT, as well as hundreds of sample problems patterned on actual test questions. The chapter is conveniently divided into eighteen short sections (Section A through Section R), each on a different topic—percents, ratios, averages, triangles, circles, and so on.

WHEN TO STUDY CHAPTERS 6 AND 7

How much time you initially devote to Chapter 7 should depend on your math skills. If you are an excellent student who consistently earns A's in math class, you can skip the instructional parts of Chapter 7 for now. If, while doing the practice tests in Part Six, you find that you keep making mistakes on certain types of problems (averages, percents, geometry, for example) or they take you too long, you should study the appropriate sections of Chapter 7. Even if your math skills are excellent and you don't need the review, you should do the sample questions in those sections; they are an excellent source of additional PSAT questions. If you know that your math skills are not very good, it is advisable to review the material in Chapter 7 and work out the problems *before* tackling the practice tests in Part Six.

No matter how good you are in math, *you should carefully read Chapter 6*. In that chapter you will learn techniques for (1) getting the correct answer to problems that you don't know how to solve and (2) getting the correct answer more quickly on those that you do know how to do.

SUGGESTED STUDY PLAN

1. Review the rules given in Part One of this book on how to pace yourself and when to guess.
2. Study the rules for the math part of the test that are presented in this chapter, including the use of calculators and the way to handle grid-in questions.
3. Study the math test-taking strategies presented in Chapter 6.
4. Take the diagnostic test at the beginning of this book to help you identify your areas of weakness
5. Study those sections of Chapter 7 that cover the topics you are weak in.
6. Take the practice tests at the end of this book.

AN IMPORTANT SYMBOL

Throughout the book, the symbol $\Rightarrow$ is used to indicate that one step in the solution of a problem follows *immediately* from the preceding one and that no explanation is necessary. You should read

$2x = 12 \Rightarrow x = 6$ as
$2x = 12$, *which implies that* $x = 6$, or, *since* $2x = 12$, *then* $x = 6$.

Here is a sample solution to the following problem using $\Rightarrow$:

What is the value of $3x^2 - 7$ when $x = -5$?

$x = -5 \Rightarrow x^2 = (-5)^2 = 25 \Rightarrow 3x^2 = 3(25) = 75 \Rightarrow 3x^2 - 7 = 75 - 7 = 68.$

When the reason for a step is not obvious, $\Rightarrow$ is not used; rather, an explanation is given, often including a reference to a **KEY FACT** from Chapter 7. In many solutions, some steps are explained, while others are linked by the $\Rightarrow$ symbol, as in the following example:

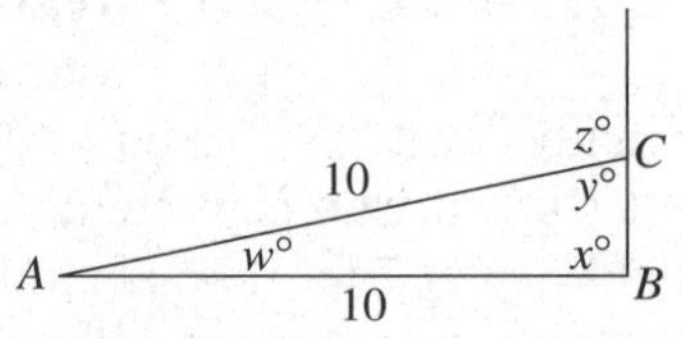

In the diagram above, if $w = 10$, what is the value of z?

- By **KEY FACT J1**, $w + x + y = 180$.
- Since $\triangle ABC$ is isosceles, $x = y$ [**KEY FACT J5**].
- Therefore, $w + 2y = 180 \Rightarrow 10 + 2y = 180 \Rightarrow 2y = 170 \Rightarrow y = 85$.
- Finally, since $y + z = 180$ [**KEY FACT I2**], $85 + z = 180 \Rightarrow z = 95$.

USE OF THE CALCULATOR

There isn't a single question on the PSAT for which a calculator is required. In fact, for most questions a calculator is completely useless. There are several questions, however, for which a calculator *could* be used, and since calculators are permitted, you should definitely bring one with you when you take the PSAT. As you go through the hundreds of practice math questions in this book, you should have available the calculator you intend to take to the test, and you should use it whenever you think it is appropriate. You will probably use it more at the beginning of your review because, as you go through this book, you will learn more and more strategies to help you solve problems easily without doing tedious calculations.

If you forget to bring a calculator to the actual test, you will not be able to use one, since none will be provided, and you will not be allowed to share one with a friend. For exactly the same reason, be sure that you have new batteries in your calculator or that you bring a spare, because if your calculator fails during the test, you will have to finish without one.

What Calculator Should You Use?

Almost any four-function, scientific, or graphing calculator is acceptable. Since you don't "need" a calculator at all, you don't "need" any particular type. There is absolutely no advantage to having a graphing calculator, but we do recommend a scientific calculator, since it is occasionally useful to have parentheses keys, ( ); a reciprocal key, $\frac{1}{x}$; and an exponent key, y^x or ^. All scientific calculators have these features. If you tend to make mistakes working with fractions, you might want to get a calculator that can do fractional arithmetic. With such a calculator, for example, you can add $\frac{1}{3}$ and $\frac{1}{5}$ by entering 1/3 + 1/5; the readout will be 8/15, not the decimal 0.5333333.

Do not buy a new calculator right before you take the PSAT. The best advice is to use a calculator you are completely familiar with—the one you always use in your math class. If you don't have one or want to get a different one, *buy it now* and become familiar with it. Do all the practice exams in this book with the same calculator you intend to bring to the test.

When Should Calculators Be Used?

If you have strong math skills and are a good test-taker, you will probably use your calculator infrequently, if at all, since, for one thing, strong math students can do a lot of basic arithmetic just as accurately, and faster, in their heads or on paper than with a calculator. A less obvious but more important point is that students who are good test-takers will realize that many problems can be solved without doing any calculations at all (mental, written, or with a calculator); they will solve those problems in less time than it takes to pick a calculator up. On the other hand, if you are less confident about your mathematical ability or your test-taking skills, you will probably find your calculator a useful tool.

NOTE: Throughout this book, this icon  will be placed next to a problem where the use of a calculator is recommended. As you will see, this judgment is very subjective. Sometimes a question can be answered in a few seconds with no calculations whatsoever, *if* you see the best approach. In that case, the use of a calculator would *not* be recommended. If you don't see the easy way, however, and have to do some arithmetic, you may prefer to use a calculator.

Let's look at two sample questions on which some students would use calculators frequently, others less frequently, and still others not at all.

EXAMPLE 1

If $16 \times 25 \times 36 = (4a)^2$, what is the value of a?

(A) 6 (B) 15 (C) 30 (D) 36 (E) 60

(i) Heavy calculator use: WITH A CALCULATOR multiply: $16 \times 25 \times 36 = 14400$. Observe that $(4a)^2 = 16a^2$, and so $16a^2 = 14{,}400$. WITH A CALCULATOR divide: $a^2 = 14{,}400 \div 16 = 900$. Finally, WITH A CALCULATOR take the square root: $a = \sqrt{900} = 30$. The answer is C.

(ii) Light calculator use: Immediately notice that you can "cancel" the 16 on the left-hand side with the 4^2 on the right-hand side. WITH A CALCULATOR: multiply $25 \times 36 = 900$, and WITH A CALCULATOR take the square root of 900.

(iii) No calculator use: Cancel the 16 and the 4^2. Notice that $25 = 5^2$ and $36 = 6^2$; so $a^2 = 5^2 \times 6^2 = 30^2$, and $a = 30$.

EXAMPLE 2 (GRID-IN)

If the length of a diagonal of a rectangle is 15, and if one of the sides is 9, what is the perimeter?

Whether or not you intend to use your calculator, the first thing to do is to draw a diagram.

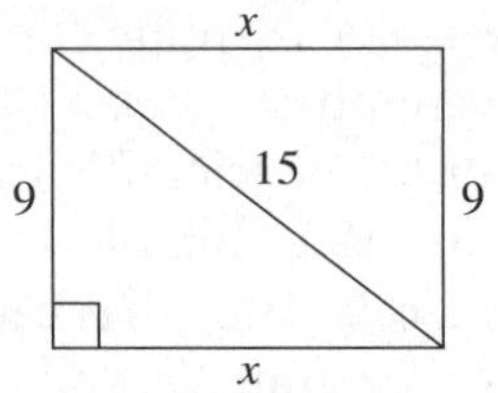

(i) Heavy calculator use: By the Pythagorean theorem, $x^2 + 9^2 = 15^2$. Observe that $9^2 = 81$, and WITH A CALCULATOR evaluate: $15^2 = 225$. Then WITH A CALCULATOR subtract: $225 - 81 = 144$. So, $x^2 = 144$. Hit the square root key on your calculator to get $x = 12$. Finally, WITH A CALCULATOR add to find the perimeter: $9 + 12 + 9 + 12 = 42$.

(ii) Light calculator use: Everything is the same as in (i) except *some* of the calculations can be done mentally: finding the square root of 144 and adding to find the perimeter.

(iii) No calculator use: *All of the calculations* are done mentally, or, better yet, *no calculations are done at all*, because you immediately see that each half of the rectangle is a 9-12-15 right triangle (a 3-4-5 right triangle in which each side was multiplied by 3), and you add up the sides in your head.

Here are three final comments on the use of calculators:

1. The reason that calculators are of limited value on the PSAT is that no calculator can *do* mathematics. *You* have to know the mathematics and the way to apply it. A calculator cannot tell you whether to multiply or divide or that on a particular question you should use the Pythagorean theorem.
2. No PSAT problem ever requires tedious calculations. However, if you don't see how to avoid calculating, just do it—*don't spend a lot of time looking for a shortcut that will save you a little time!*
3. Most students use calculators more than they should, but if you can solve a problem with a calculator that you might otherwise miss, use the calculator.

HELPFUL HINT

In general, you should do very little arithmetic using paper and pencil. If you can't do it mentally, use your calculator. In particular, avoid long division and multiplication in which the factors have two or more digits. If you know that $15^2 = 225$, terrific; if not, it is better to use your calculator than to multiply with paper and pencil.

DIRECTIONS FOR MATHEMATICS SECTIONS

On the first page of Section 2 (the first math section), you will see the following instructions for multiple-choice questions.

Multiple-Choice Directions

For each question in this section, determine which of the five choices is correct and blacken that choice on your answer sheet. You may use any blank space on the page for your work.

NOTES:

- You may use a calculator whenever you believe it will be helpful.
- Use the diagrams provided to help you solve the problems. Unless you see the phrase Note: Figure not drawn to scale under a diagram, it has been drawn as accurately as possible. Unless it is stated that a figure is three dimensional, you may assume that it lies in a plane.

On the first page of Section 4 (the second math section), you will see the same directions for questions 21–28.

In the middle of Section 4 of your PSAT, you will see the following directions for handling questions 29–38, the student-produced response questions, the only questions on the PSAT that are not multiple-choice. Because the answers to these questions are entered in special grids, they are usually referred to as grid-in questions.

Student-Produced Response Directions

In questions 29–38, first solve the problem, and then enter your answer on the grid provided on the answer sheet. The instructions for entering your answers follow.

- First, write your answer in the boxes at the top of the grid.
- Second, grid your answer in the columns below the boxes.
- Use the fraction bar in the first row or the decimal point in the second row to enter fractions and decimals.

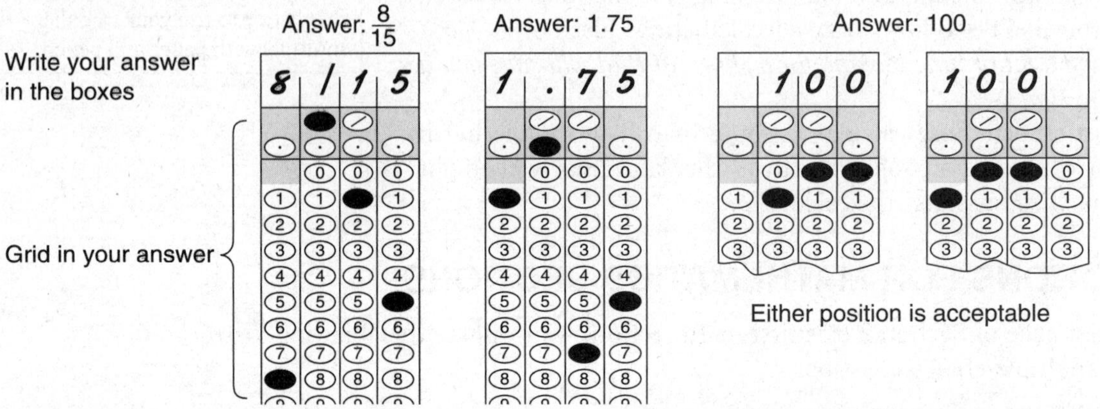

- Grid only one space in each column.
- Entering the answer in the boxes is recommended as an aid in gridding but is not required.
- The machine scoring your exam can read only what you grid, so you **must grid-in your answers correctly to get credit.**
- If a question has more than one correct answer, grid-in only one of them.
- The grid does not have a minus sign; so no answer can be negative.
- A mixed number *must* be converted to an improper fraction or a decimal before it is gridded. Enter $1\frac{1}{4}$ as $\frac{5}{4}$ or 1.25; the machine will interpret 11/4 as $\frac{11}{4}$ and mark it wrong.

- **All decimals must be entered as accurately as possible.** Here are three acceptable ways of gridding

$$\frac{3}{11} = 0.272727\ldots$$

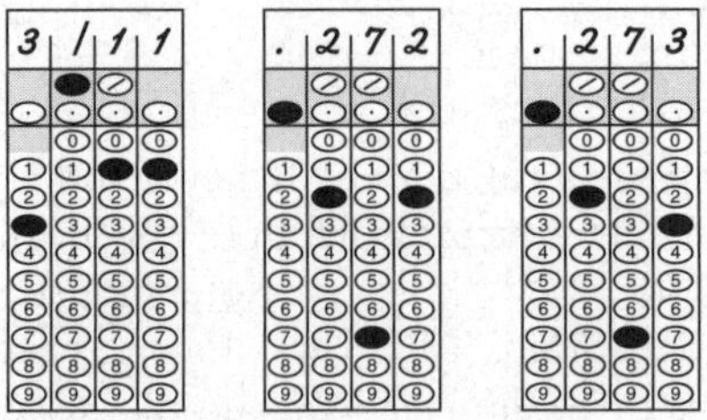

- Note that rounding to .273 is acceptable because you are using the full grid, but you would receive **no credit** for .3 or .27, because they are less accurate.

In addition to the directions for multiple-choice questions, the first page of each math section has a box labeled "Reference" that contains the following mathematical facts:

Reference

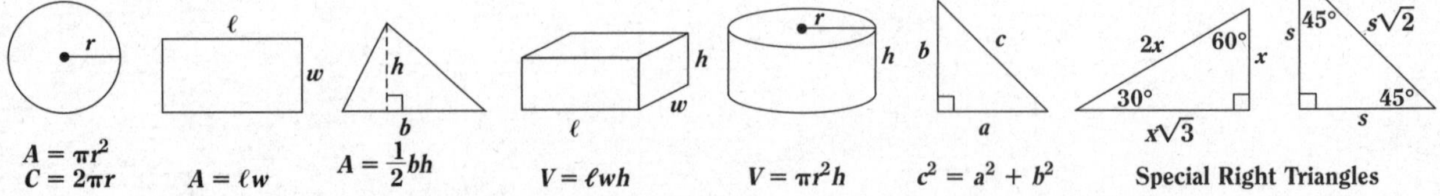

Number of degrees of arc in a circle: 360

Sum of the measures, in degrees, of the angles of a triangle: 180

Many books advise that since these formulas are printed in the exam booklet, students can always look them up as needed and, therefore, don't have to learn or review them. Even the College Board's official guide, *SAT Preparation Booklet*, states:

> *The test doesn't require you to memorize formulas. Commonly used formulas are provided in the test booklet at the beginning of each mathematical section.*

HELPFUL HINT

As you prepare for this test, learn the directions for each section. When you take the PSAT, do not waste even one second reading directions.

This is very poor advice. During the test, you don't want to spend any of your valuable time looking up facts that you can learn now. All of these "commonly used formulas" and other important facts are presented in Chapter 7, where each of them is highlighted and identified as a "Reference Fact." As you learn and review these facts, you should commit them to memory.

INSTRUCTIONS FOR GRID-IN QUESTIONS

On the math part of the PSAT, questions 29–38 are the student-produced response questions. This is the type of question that is most familiar—you solve a problem and then write the answer on your answer sheet. The only difference is that on the PSAT, *after* you write the answer on your answer sheet, you must then enter the answer on a special grid that can be read by a computer. For this reason, these questions are usually referred to as grid-ins.

To be sure you get credit for these questions, you need to know the guidelines for gridding-in your answers. Not all of this information is given in the directions printed in the exam booklet; so you should carefully read each of the ten rules below.

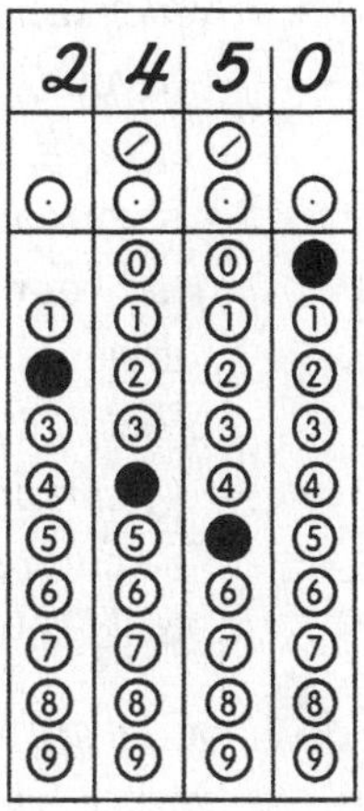

Your answer sheet will have ten grids, one for each question. Each one will look like the grid shown here. After solving a problem, the first step is to write the answer in the four boxes at the top of the grid. You then blacken the appropriate space under each box. For example, if your answer to a question is 2450, you write 2450 at the top of the grid, one digit in each box, and then in each column blacken the space that contains the number you wrote at the top of the column. This is not difficult, but there are some special rules concerning grid-in questions; so let's go over them before you practice gridding-in some numbers.

1. The only symbols that appear in the grid are the digits 0 to 9, a decimal point, and a slash (/), used to write fractions. Keep in mind that, since there is no negative sign, *the answer to every grid-in question must be a positive number or 0.*

2. You will receive credit for a correct answer no matter where you grid it. For example, the answer 17 could be gridded in any of three positions:

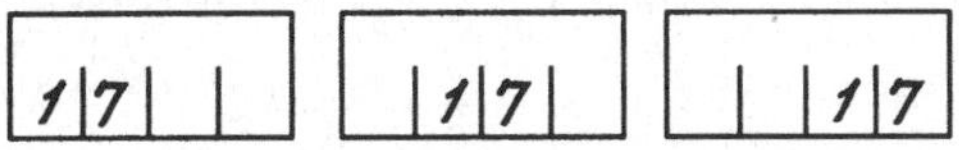

Nevertheless, we suggest that you consistently *write all your answers* the way numbers are usually displayed—*to the right, with blank spaces at the left.*

1/2	.4	.25	6
$\frac{1}{2}$	.4	.25	6

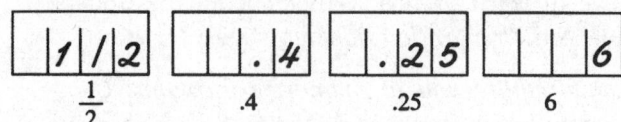

3. *Never round off your answers.* If a decimal answer will fit in the grid and you round it off, your answer will be marked wrong. For example, if the answer is .148 and you rounded it to the nearest hundredth and entered .15, you would receive *no credit.* If a decimal answer will not fit in the grid, enter a decimal point in the first column, followed by the first three digits. For example, if your answer is 0.373737 . . . , enter it as .373. You would receive credit if you rounded it to .374, but don't. You might occasionally make a mistake in rounding, whereas you'll *never* make a mistake if you just copy the first three digits. Note: If the correct answer has more than two decimal digits, *you must use all four columns of the grid.*

4. *Never write a 0 before the decimal point.* The first column of the grid doesn't even have a 0 in it. If the correct answer is 0.3333 . . . , you must grid it as .333. You can't grid 0.33, and 0.3 is not accurate enough.

5. *Never simplify fractions.*
   - If your answer is a fraction that will fit in the grid, such as $\frac{2}{3}$ or $\frac{4}{18}$ or $\frac{6}{34}$, *just enter it.* Don't waste time reducing it or converting it to a decimal.
   - If your answer is a fraction that won't fit in the grid, do not attempt to reduce it; use your calculator to *convert it to a decimal.* For example, $\frac{24}{65}$ won't fit in a grid; it would require five spaces: 2 4 / 6 5. Do not waste even a few seconds trying to reduce it; just divide on your calculator, and enter .369. Unlike $\frac{24}{65}$, the fraction $\frac{24}{64}$ *can be reduced*—to $\frac{12}{32}$, which doesn't help, or to $\frac{6}{16}$ or $\frac{3}{8}$, both of which could be entered. *Don't do it!* It takes time, and you might make a mistake. You won't make a mistake if you just use your calculator: 24 ÷ 64 = .375.

6. *Be aware that you can never enter a mixed number.* If your answer is $2\frac{1}{2}$, you *cannot* leave a space and enter it as 2 1/2. Also if you enter [21/2], the machine will read it as $\frac{21}{2}$ and mark it wrong. You must enter $2\frac{1}{2}$ as the improper fraction $\frac{5}{2}$ or as the decimal 2.5.

7. Sometimes grid-in questions have more than one correct answer. On these questions you are to *grid-in only one of the acceptable answers.* For example, if a question asked for a positive number less than 100 which was divisible by both 5 and 7, you could enter *either* 35 *or* 70, but not both.

8. There is no penalty for a wrong answer to a grid-in question. Therefore, you might as well guess.

9. Be sure to *grid every answer carefully.* The computer does not read what you have written in the boxes; it reads only the answer in the grid. If the correct answer to a question is 100 and you write 100 in the boxes but accidentally grid-in 200, you get *no* credit.

10. If you know that the answer to a question is 100, can you just grid it in and not bother writing it on top? Yes, you will get full credit, and so some books recommend that you don't waste time writing the answer. This is terrible advice. Instead, *write each answer in the boxes.* It takes less than two seconds per answer to do this, and it definitely cuts down on careless errors in gridding. More important, if you go back to check your work, it is much easier to read what's in the boxes than what's in the grid.

Now, check your understanding of these guidelines. Use the empty grids below to enter each of the following numbers.

1. 123 **2.** $\frac{7}{11}$ **3.** $2\frac{3}{4}$ **4.** $\frac{8}{30}$

5. 0 **6.** $\frac{48}{80}$ **7.** 1.1111 . . . **8.** $\frac{19}{15}$

1.
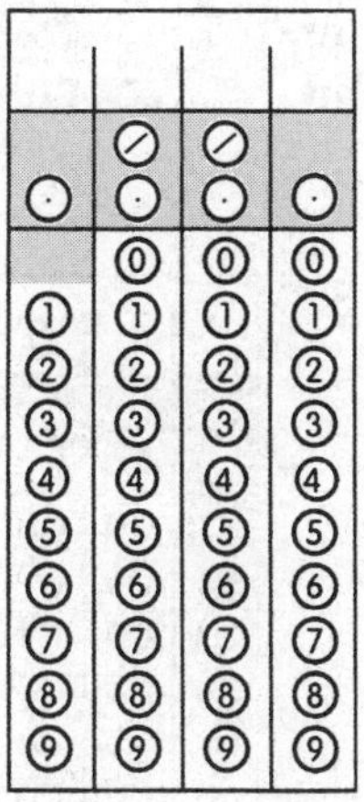

2.
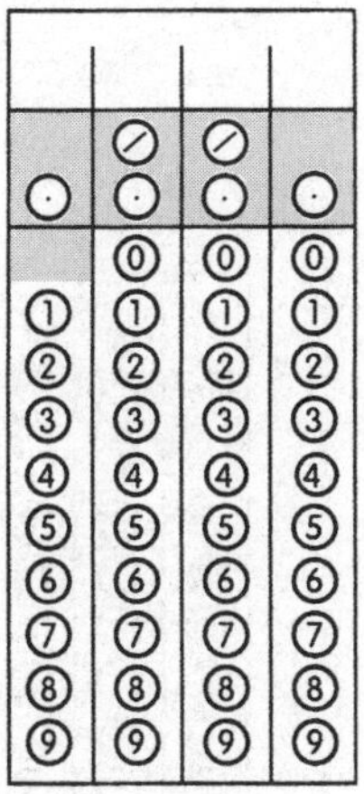

3.
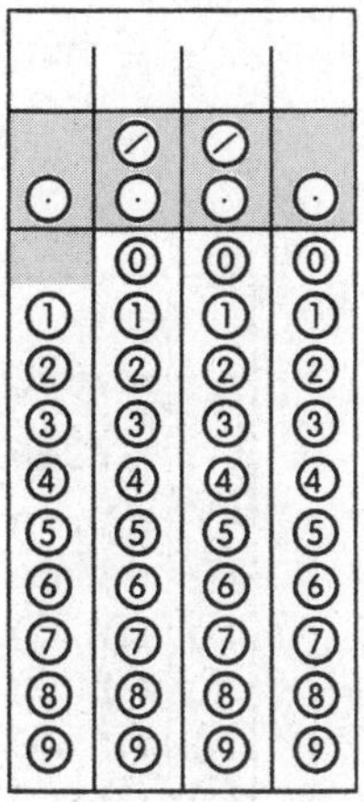

4.
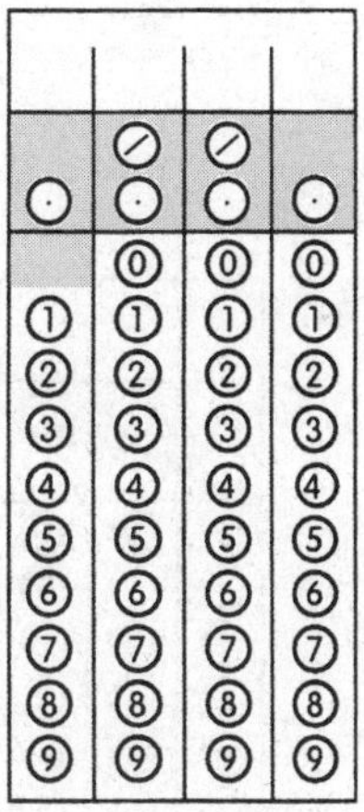

5.
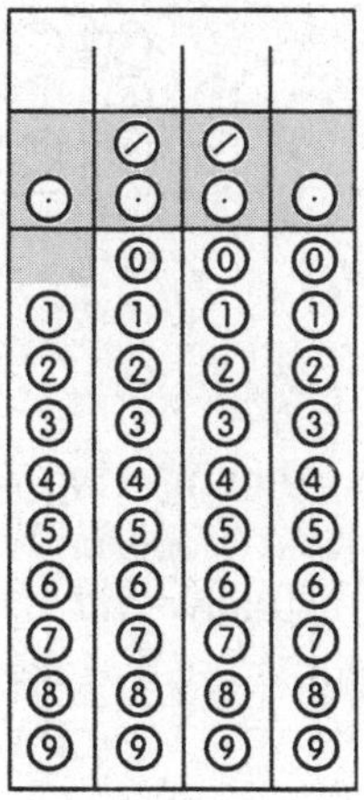

6.
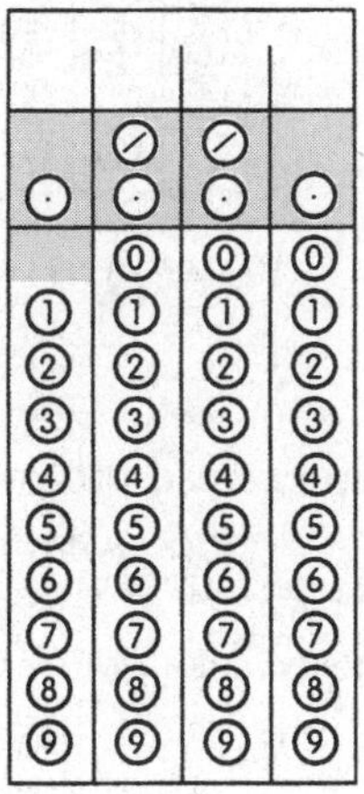

7.
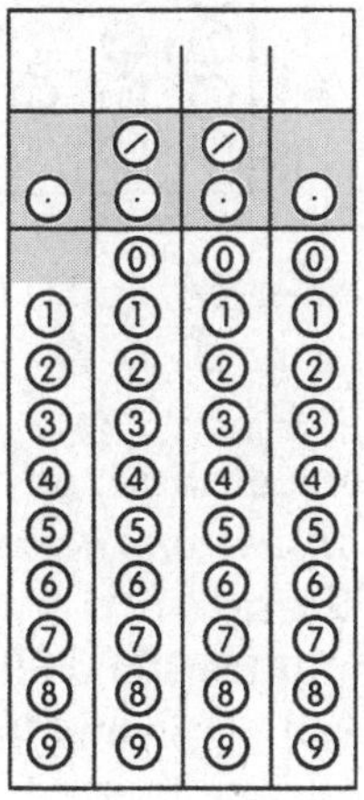

8.
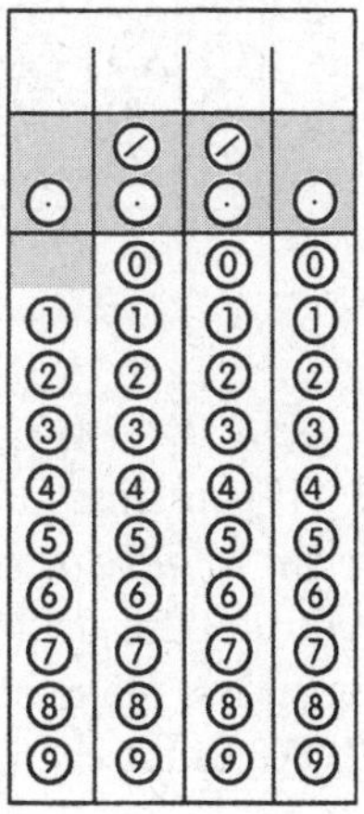

Solutions. Each grid contains the answer we recommend. Other acceptable answers, if any, are written below each grid.

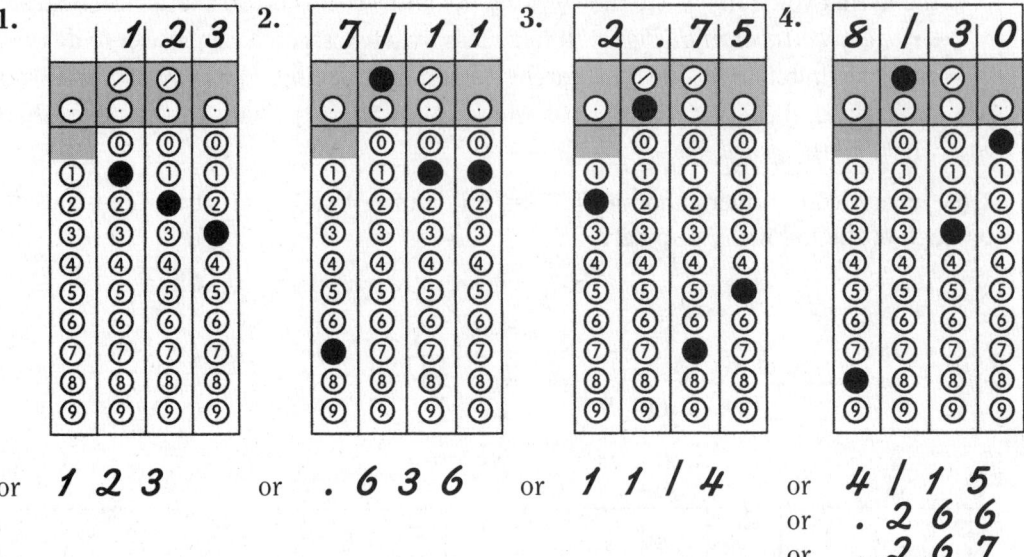

1.
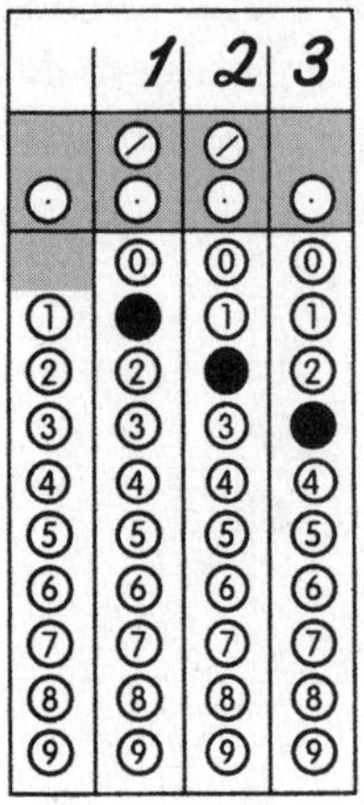

or 1 2 3

2.
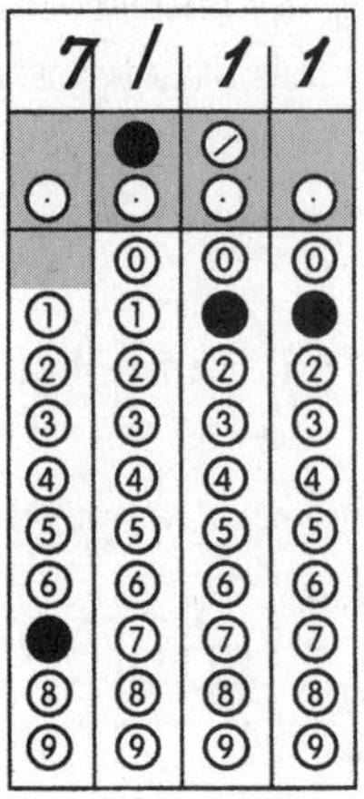

or . 6 3 6

3.
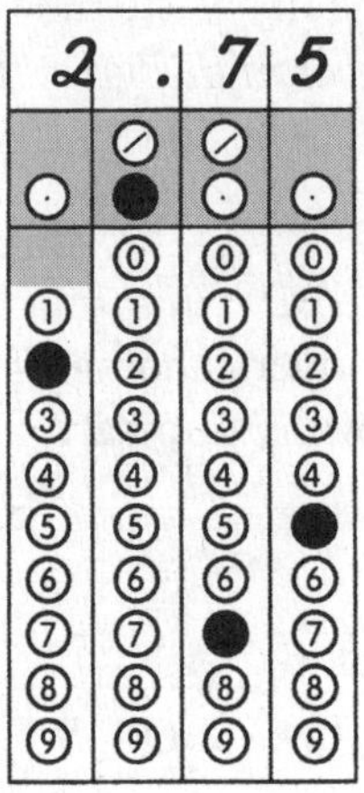

or 1 1 / 4

4.
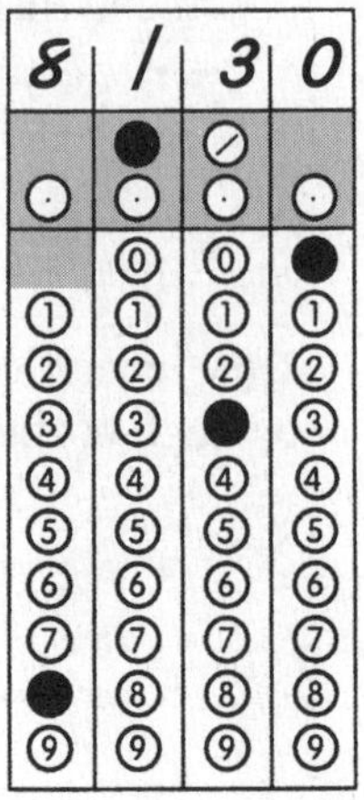

or 4 / 1 5
or . 2 6 6
or . 2 6 7

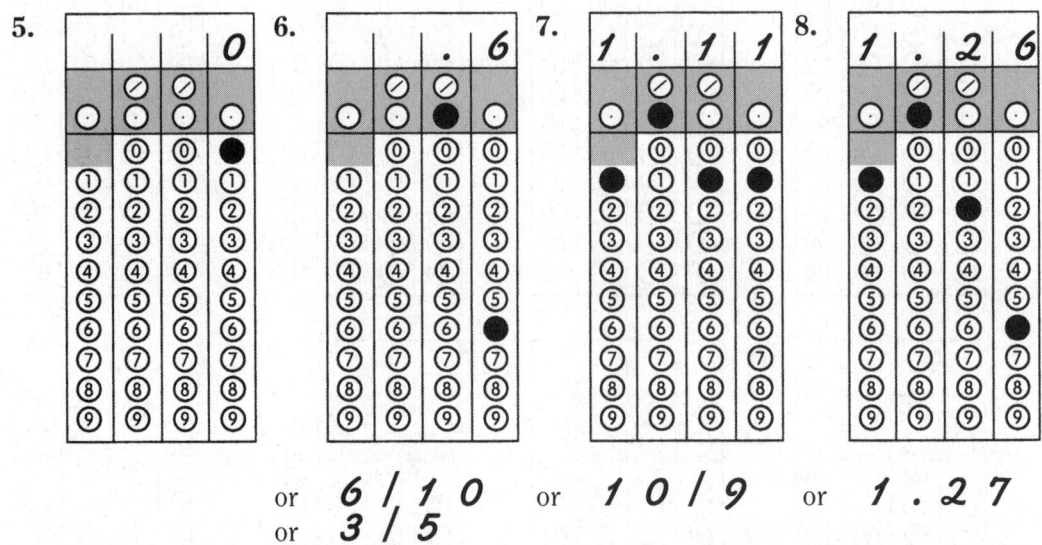

5.
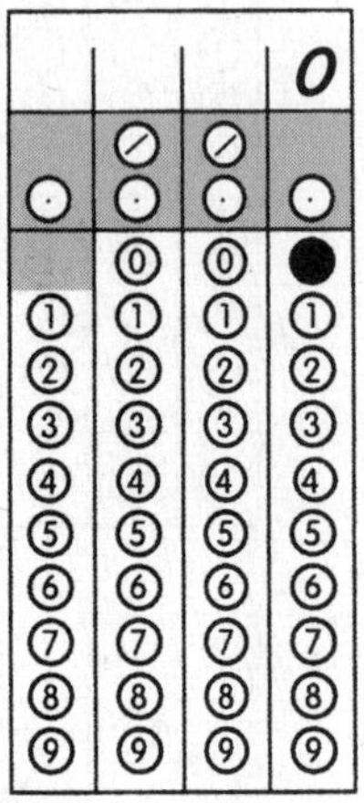

6.
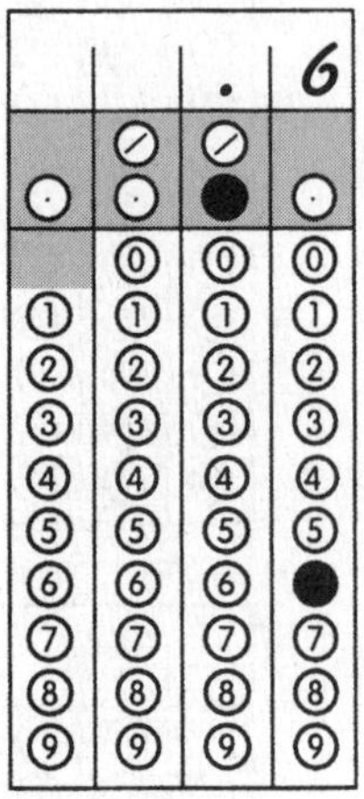

or 6 / 1 0
or 3 / 5

7.
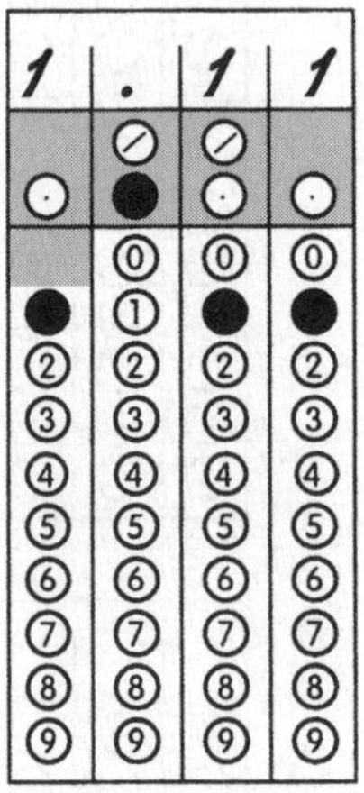

or 1 0 / 9

8.
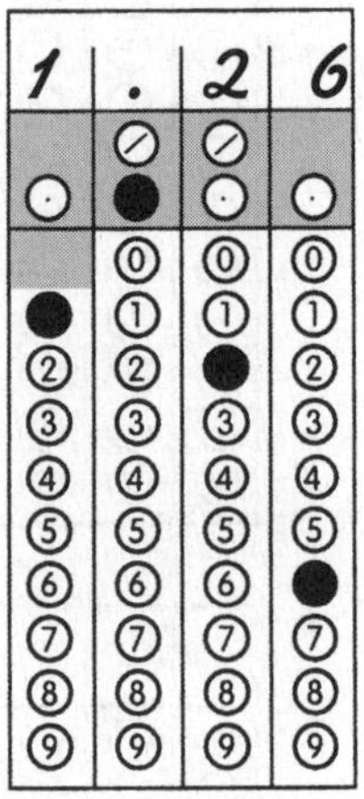

or 1 . 2 7

If you missed even one of these, go back and reread the rules on gridding. *You never want to have a correct answer and get no credit because you didn't grid it properly*. When you do the grid-in problems on the practice PSATs in this book, actually grid in the answers. Make sure you understand all of these rules *now*. When you actually take the PSAT, don't even look at the gridding instructions.

Tactics and Strategies

CHAPTER 6

In this chapter you will learn important strategies to help you answer both the multiple-choice and grid-in questions on the PSAT. However, as invaluable as these tactics are, use them only when you need them. If you know how to solve a problem and are confident that you can do so accurately and reasonably quickly, JUST DO IT!

TACTIC

6-1 Test the choices, starting with C

TACTIC 6-1, often called *backsolving,* is useful when you are asked to solve for an unknown and you understand what needs to be done to answer the question but you want to avoid doing the algebra. The idea is simple: Test the various choices to see which one is correct.

NOTE: On the PSAT the answers to virtually all numerical multiple-choice questions are listed in either increasing or decreasing order. Consequently, Choice C is the middle value, and in applying **TACTIC 6-1**, *you should always start with Choice C.* For example, assume that Choices A, B, C, D, and E are given in increasing order. Try Choice C. If it works, you've found the answer. If Choice C doesn't work, you should know whether you need to test a larger number or a smaller one, and that information permits you to eliminate two more choices. If Choice C is too small, you need a larger number, and so Choices A and B are out; if Choice C is too big, eliminate Choices D and E, which are even larger.

Examples 1 and 2 illustrate the proper use of **TACTIC 6-1**.

EXAMPLE 1

If the average (arithmetic mean) of 5, 6, 7, and x is 10, what is the value of x?

(A) 8
(B) 13
(C) 18
(D) 22
(E) 28

Solution. Use **TACTIC 6-1**. Test Choice C: $x = 18$.

- Is the average of 5, 6, 7, and 18 equal to 10?
- No: $\frac{5 + 6 + 7 + 18}{4} = \frac{36}{4} = 9$, which is *too small.*
- Eliminate Choice C, and, since for the average to be 10, x must be *greater* than 18, eliminate Choices A and B, as well.

- Try Choice D: $x = 22$. Is the average of 5, 6, 7, and 22, equal to 10?
- Yes: $\frac{5+6+7+22}{4} = \frac{40}{4} = 10$. The answer is Choice D.

Remember that every problem that can be solved using **TACTIC 6-1** can be solved directly, usually in less time. Therefore, we again stress: *If you are confident that you can solve a problem quickly and accurately, just do so.*

See Section 7-E on averages for a direct method for solving Example 1 that is *faster* than backsolving. If you know that method, you should use it, and save **TACTIC 6-1** for those problems that you can't easily solve directly.

EXAMPLE 2

Judy is now twice as old as Adam, but six years ago, she was five times as old as he was. How old is Judy now?

(A) 8
(B) 16
(C) 20
(D) 24
(E) 32

Solution. Use **TACTIC 6-1** and backsolve starting with Choice C. If Judy is now 20, Adam is 10, and six years ago, they would have been 14 and 4. Since Judy would have been less than five times as old as Adam, eliminate Choices C, D, and E, and try a smaller value. If Judy is now 16, Adam is 8; six years ago, they would have been 10 and 2. That's it; 10 *is* five times 2. The answer is Choice B. (See Example 4 in Section 7-H on word problems for the correct algebraic solution.)

Some tactics allow you to eliminate a few choices so that you can make an educated guess. On those problems where it can be used, **TACTIC 6-1** *always* gets you the right answer. The only reason not to use it on a particular problem is that you can *easily* solve the problem directly.

TACTIC

6-2 Replace variables with numbers

Mastery of **TACTIC 6-2** is critical for anyone developing good test-taking skills. This tactic can be used whenever the five choices involve the variables in the question. There are three steps:

1. Replace each letter with an easy-to-use number.
2. Solve the problem using those numbers.
3. Evaluate each of the five choices with the numbers you chose to see which choice is equal to the answer you obtained.

Examples 3 and 4 illustrate the proper use of **TACTIC 6-2**.

EXAMPLE 3

If a is equal to the sum of b and c, which of the following is equal to the difference of b and c?

(A) $a - b - c$
(B) $a - b + c$
(C) $a - c$
(D) $a - 2c$
(E) $a - b - 2c$

Solution.

- Choose three easy-to-use numbers that satisfy $a = b + c$: for example, $a = 5$, $b = 3$, $c = 2$.
- Then, solve the problem with these numbers: the difference of b and c is $3 - 2 = 1$.
- Finally, check each of the five choices to see which one is equal to 1:

(A) Does $a - b - c = 1$?	No.	$5 - 3 - 2 = 0$
(B) Does $a - b + c = 1$?	No.	$5 - 3 + 2 = 4$
(C) Does $a - c = 1$?	No.	$5 - 2 = 3$
(D) Does $a - 2c = 1$?	Yes!	$5 - 2(2) = 5 - 4 = 1$
(E) Does $a - b - 2c = 1$?	No.	$5 - 3 - 2(2) = 2 - 4 = -2$

- The answer is Choice D.

EXAMPLE 4

If the sum of five consecutive even integers is t, then, in terms of t, what is the greatest of these integers?

(A) $\frac{t-20}{5}$
(B) $\frac{t-10}{5}$
(C) $\frac{t}{5}$
(D) $\frac{t+10}{5}$
(E) $\frac{t+20}{5}$

Solution.

- Choose five easy-to-use consecutive even integers: 2, 4, 6, 8, 10. Then their sum, t, is 30.
- Solve the problem with these numbers: the greatest of these integers is 10.
- When $t = 30$, the five choices are $\frac{10}{5}, \frac{20}{5}, \frac{30}{5}, \frac{40}{5}, \frac{50}{5}$.
- Only $\frac{50}{5}$, Choice E, is equal to 10.

Of course, if your algebra skills are good, Examples 3 and 4 can be solved without using **TACTIC 6-2**. The important point is that if you are uncomfortable with the correct algebraic solution, you don't have to omit these questions. You can use **TACTIC 6-2** and *always* get the correct answer.

Example 5 is somewhat different. You are asked to reason through a word problem involving only variables. Most students find problems like

HELPFUL HINT

Replace the letters with numbers that are easy to use, not necessarily ones that make sense. It is perfectly OK to ignore reality. A school can have 2 students, apples can cost 10 dollars each, trains can go 5 miles per hour or 1000 miles per hour—it doesn't matter.

this one mind-boggling. Here, the use of **TACTIC 6-2** is essential. Without it, most students would find Example 5 very difficult, if not impossible.

EXAMPLE 5

A vendor sells h hot dogs and s sodas. If a hot dog costs twice as much as a soda, and if the vendor takes in a total of d dollars, how many *cents* does a soda cost?

(A) $\frac{100d}{s+2h}$

(B) $\frac{s+2h}{100d}$

(C) $\frac{100}{d(s+2h)}$

(D) $100d(s+2h)$

(E) $\frac{d}{100(s+2h)}$

Solution.

- Replace h, s, and d with three easy-to-use numbers. Suppose a soda costs 50¢ and a hot dog \$1.00. Then if he sold 2 sodas and 3 hot dogs, he took in \$4.00.
- Which of the choices equals 50 when $s = 2$, $h = 3$, and $d = 4$?
- Only Choice A: $\frac{100(4)}{2+2(3)} = \frac{400}{8} = 50$.

Of course, when you check the choices, you should use your calculator whenever necessary. However, you do not need to determine the value of each choice; you only need to know if it is the correct choice. In Example 5, Choices B and E are small fractions and could not possibly equal 50, and Choice D is clearly greater than 50; so don't waste your time evaluating them. Only Choices A and C are even possible.

TACTIC 6-3 Choose an appropriate number

TACTIC 6-3 is similar to **TACTIC 6-2**, in that we pick convenient numbers. However, no variable is given in the problem. **TACTIC 6-3** is especially useful in problems involving fractions, ratios, and percents.

EXAMPLE 6

On a certain college committee, $\frac{2}{3}$ of the members are female and $\frac{3}{8}$ of the females are varsity athletes. If $\frac{3}{5}$ of the committee members are not varsity athletes, what fraction of the members of the committee are male varsity athletes?

(A) $\frac{3}{20}$

(B) $\frac{11}{60}$

(C) $\frac{1}{4}$

(D) $\frac{2}{5}$

(E) $\frac{5}{12}$

In problems involving fractions, the best number to use is the least common denominator of all the fractions. In problems involving percents, the easiest number to use is 100.

Solution. Since the lowest common denominator (LCD) of the three fractions is 120, assume that the committee has 120 members. Then there are $\frac{2}{3} \times 120 = 80$ females. Of the 80 females, $\frac{3}{8} \times 80 = 30$ are varsity athletes. Since $\frac{3}{5} \times 120 = 72$ committee members are not varsity athletes, then $120 - 72 = 48$ are varsity athletes; of these, 30 are female and the other 18 are male. Finally, the fraction of the members of the committee who are male varsity athletes is $\frac{18}{120} = \frac{3}{20}$ (Choice A).

EXAMPLE 7

From 1995 to 2000 the sales of a book decreased by 80%. If the sales in 2005 were the same as in 1995, by what percent did they increase from 2000 to 2005?

(A) 80%
(B) 100%
(C) 120%
(D) 400%
(E) 500%

Solution. Since this problem involves percents, assume that 100 copies of the book were sold in 1995 (and 2005). Sales dropped by 80 (80% of 100) to 20 in 2000 and then increased by 80, from 20 back to 100, in 2005. By **KEY FACT C5**, the percent increase was

$$\frac{\text{the actual increase}}{\text{the original amount}} \times 100\% = \frac{80}{20} \times 100\% = 400\% \text{ (Choice D).}$$

TACTIC

6-4 Eliminate absurd choices and guess

When you have no idea how to solve a problem, eliminate all the absurd choices and guess from among the remaining ones.

During the course of a PSAT, you will probably find at least a few multiple-choice questions that you read but have no idea how to solve. *Do not automatically omit these questions!* Often two or three of the answers are absurd. Eliminate them and *guess*. Occasionally, four of the choices are absurd. When this occurs, your answer is no longer a guess.

What makes a choice absurd? Here are a few things to note. Even if you don't know how to solve a problem, you may realize that

- the answer must be positive, but some of the choices are negative.
- the answer must be even, but some of the choices are odd.
- a ratio must be less than 1, but some choices are greater than or equal to 1.

Let's look at five examples. In some of them the information given is intentionally insufficient to solve the problem, but you will still be able to determine that some of the answers are absurd. Even when there is enough information to solve the problem, don't. Rather, see if you can determine which choices are absurd and should therefore be eliminated.

EXAMPLE 8

A region inside a semicircle of radius r is shaded. What is its area?

(A) $\frac{1}{4}\pi r^2$
(B) $\frac{1}{3}\pi r^2$
(C) $\frac{1}{2}\pi r^2$
(D) $\frac{2}{3}\pi r^2$
(E) $\frac{3}{4}\pi r^2$

Solution. Even if you have no idea how to find the area of the shaded region, you should know that since the area of a circle is πr^2, the area of a semicircle is $\frac{1}{2}\pi r^2$. So the area of the shaded region must be *less than* $\frac{1}{2}\pi r^2$. Eliminate Choices C, D, and E. On an actual problem, if the diagram is drawn to scale, you may be able to make an educated guess between Choices A and B. If not, just choose one or the other.

EXAMPLE 9

The average of 5, 10, 15, and x is 20. What is x?

(A) 0
(B) 20
(C) 25
(D) 45
(E) 50

Solution. If the average of four numbers is 20, and three of them are less than 20, the other one must be greater than 20. Eliminate Choices A and B and guess. If you further realize that since 5 and 10 are *a lot* less than 20, x will be *a lot* more than 20, then eliminate Choice C, as well.

EXAMPLE 10

A prize of $27,000 is to be divided in some ratio among three people. What is the largest share?

(A) $18,900
(B) $13,500
(C) $8100
(D) $5400
(E) $2700

Solution. If the prize were divided equally, each share would be worth $9000. If it is divided unequally, the largest share must be *more than* $9000; so eliminate Choices C, D, and E. In an actual question, you would be told what the ratio is, and that information might enable you to eliminate Choice A or Choice B. If not, you would just guess.

EXAMPLE 11

A jar contains only red and blue marbles. The ratio of the number of red marbles to the number of blue marbles is 5:3. What percent of the marbles are blue?

(A) 37.5%
(B) 50%
(C) 60%
(D) 62.5%
(E) 80%

Solution. Since there are 5 red marbles for every 3 blue ones, there are fewer blue ones than red ones. Therefore, *fewer than half* (50%) of the marbles are blue. Eliminate Choices B, C, D, and E. The answer is Choice A.

EXAMPLE 12

Square *WXYZ* is divided into two unequal regions. If $WX = 4$, which of the following could be the area of the larger region?

(A) 8π
(B) $8\pi - 32$
(C) $16 - 8\pi$
(D) $32 - 8\pi$
(E) $8\pi - 16$

Solution. Since the area of the square is 16, the area of the larger region must be more than 8. Since π is slightly more than 3, 8π (which appears in each choice) is somewhat more than 24, approximately 25. Check the choices:

- (A) $8\pi \approx 25$, which is more than the area of the whole square.
- (B) $8\pi - 32$ is negative. Clearly impossible!
- (C) $16 - 8\pi$ is also negative.
- (D) $32 - 8\pi \approx 7$, which is too small.
- (E) $8\pi - 16 \approx 9$. The answer must be E.

TACTIC

6-5 Draw a diagram

On any geometry question for which a figure is not provided, draw one (as accurately as possible) in your test booklet. Often looking at the diagram will lead you to the correct method. Sometimes, as in Example 13 on the following page, a careful examination of the diagram is sufficient to actually determine the correct answer.

EXAMPLE 13

A rectangle is 7 times as long as it is wide. If the width is w, what is the length of a diagonal?

(A) $2w\sqrt{5}$

(B) $5w\sqrt{2}$

(C) $7w$

(D) $8w$

(E) $50w$

Solution. First draw a rectangle that is 7 times as large as it is wide. (By marking off 7 widths, you should be able to do this quite accurately.) Then draw in a diagonal.

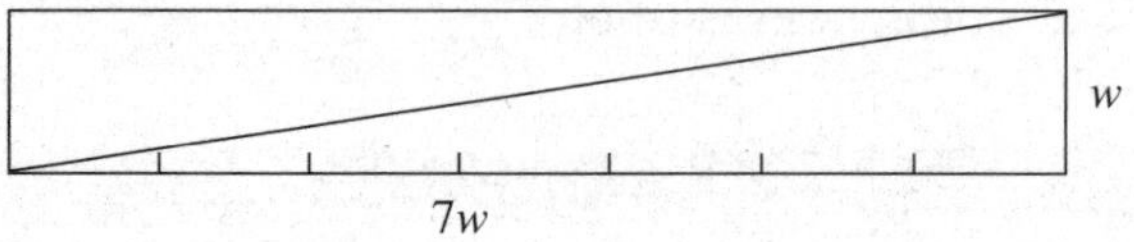

You probably realize that you can use the Pythagorean theorem to find the length of the diagonal, but by looking at the diagram, you should see that the diagonal is just slightly larger than the length, $7w$. Now check each answer choice using your calculator when necessary. Clearly, the answer is not $7w$, and $50w$ is way too big. Eliminate Choices C and E. Even Choice D, $8w$, is probably too big, but don't eliminate it until you use your calculator to test Choices A and B. $2\sqrt{5} \approx 4.5$, which is clearly too small; $5\sqrt{2} \approx 7.07$, which looks just right. Choose Choice B.

TACTIC

6-6 Use diagrams wisely. If a diagram is drawn to scale, trust it.

Remember that every diagram that appears on the PSAT has been drawn as accurately as possible, *unless* you see "Note: Figure not drawn to scale."

In figures that are drawn to scale, the following are true: line segments that appear to be the same length, *are* the same length; if an angle clearly looks obtuse, it *is* obtuse; and if one angle appears larger than another, you may assume that it *is* larger.

Examples 14, 15, and 16 below all contain diagrams that have been drawn to scale. Of course, each of these relatively easy examples has a correct mathematical solution, but for practice use **TACTIC 6-6** to eliminate as many choices as possible by simply looking at the given diagram.

HELPFUL HINT

On the PSAT, if you know how to solve a geometry problem, just do it. However, if you don't know how and if there is a diagram that has been drawn to scale, do not leave it out. Trusting the diagram to be accurate, you can always eliminate some of the choices and make an educated guess.

EXAMPLE 14

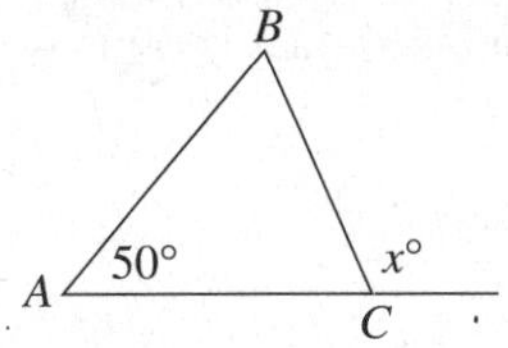

If in the figure above $AB = AC$, what is the value of x ?

(A) 135
(B) 125
(C) 115
(D) 65
(E) 50

Solution. Clearly, the angle is obtuse; so x is greater than 90, and so you can immediately eliminate Choices D and E. You can "measure" x more accurately by drawing a couple of lines in the diagram. Draw in $\overline{DC}$ perpendicular to AC. Then, $x = 90°$ plus the measure of □*DCB*. To estimate the measure of □*DCB*, draw in $\overline{EC}$, which bisects □*ACD*, a 90° angle. This creates angle *ECD*, a 45° angle, and it is clear that the measure of □*DCB* is about half of that, say 23°. So, x is about $90 + 23 = 113$. The answer must be Choice C, 115.

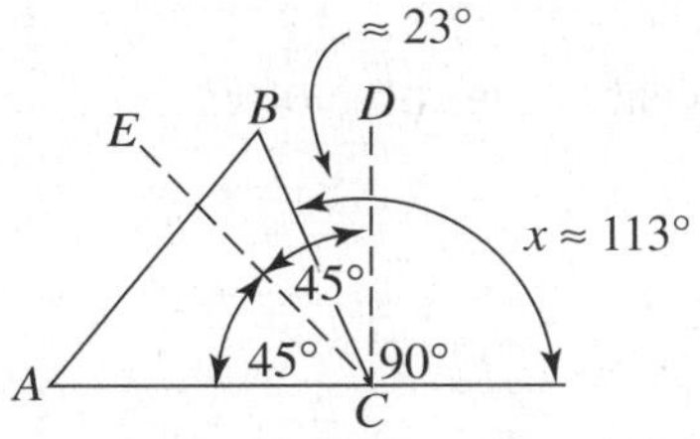

EXAMPLE 15

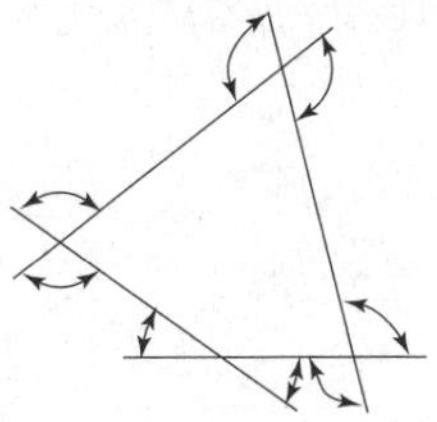

In the figure above, what is the sum of the measures of all the marked angles?

(A) 360°
(B) 540°
(C) 720°
(D) 900°
(E) 1080°

Solution. Make your best estimate of each angle and add them up. The five choices are so far apart that even if you're off by 15° or more on some of the angles, you'll get the right answer. The sum of the estimates shown is 690°; so the correct answer *must* be 720° (Choice C).

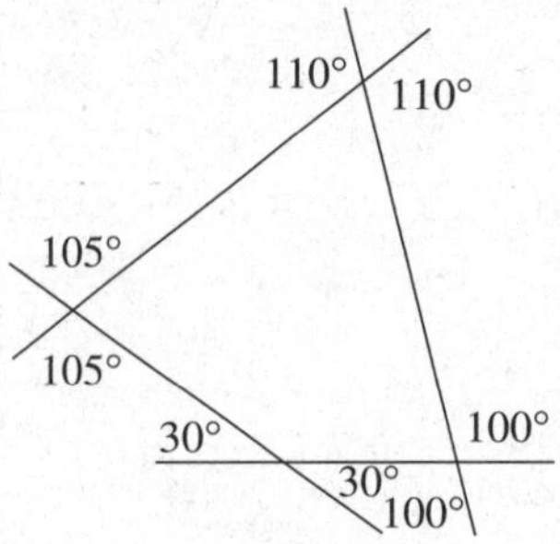

EXAMPLE 16

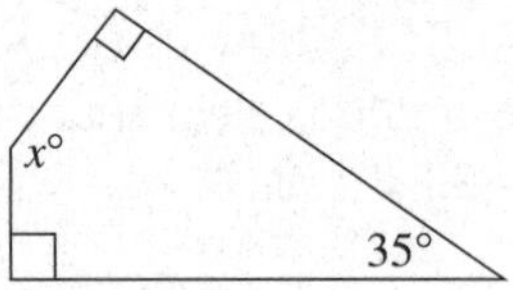

In the figure above, what is the value of x?

(A) 120
(B) 130
(C) 145
(D) 160
(E) 175

Solution. Since the diagram is drawn to scale, trust it. Look at x: it appears to be *about* $90 + 50 = 140$; it is *definitely* less than 160. Also, y is clearly less than 45; so x is greater than 135. The answer must be 145 (Choice C).

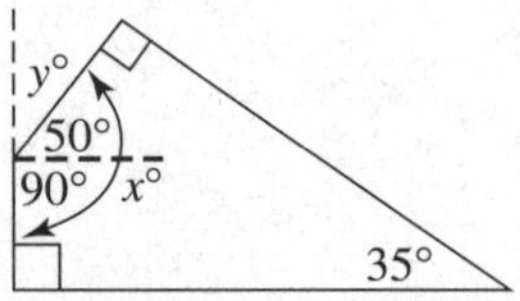

TACTIC

6-7 Use diagrams wisely. If a diagram is not drawn to scale, redraw it to scale.

In figures that are not drawn to scale, make *no* assumptions. Lines that look parallel might not be; an angle that appears to be obtuse, might, in fact, be acute; two line segments might have the same length even though one looks twice as long as the other.

In the examples illustrating **TACTIC 6-6**, all of the diagrams were drawn to scale, and we were able to use the diagrams to our advantage. When diagrams have not been drawn to scale, you must be more careful.

HELPFUL HINT

In order to redraw a diagram to scale, ask yourself, "What is wrong with the original diagram?" If an angle is marked 45°, but in the figure it looks like a 75° angle, redraw it. If two line segments appear to be parallel, but you have not been told that they are, redraw them so that they are clearly not parallel. If two segments appear to have the same length, but one is marked 5 and the other 10, redraw them so that the second segment is twice as long as the first.

EXAMPLE 17

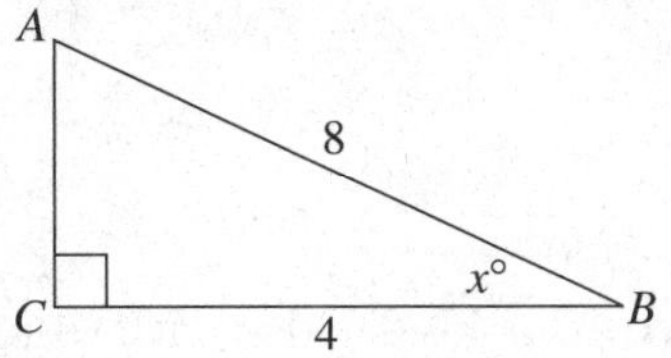

Note: Figure not drawn to scale

In $\triangle ABC$, what is the value of x?

(A) 15
(B) 30
(C) 45
(D) 60
(E) 75

Solution. In what way is this figure not drawn to scale? $AB = 8$ and $BC = 4$, but in the figure, AB is not nearly twice as long as BC. Although the figure is not drawn to scale, the square symbol at angle C indicates that angle C is a right angle. So draw a right triangle in which AB *is* twice as long as BC. Now you can see that x is about 60 (Choice D).

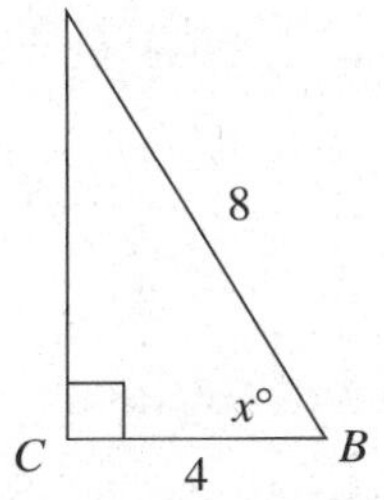

In fact, x is exactly 60. If the hypotenuse of a right triangle is twice the length of one of the legs, then the triangle is a 30-60-90 triangle, and the angle formed by the hypotenuse and that leg is 60° (See Section 7-J).

EXAMPLE 18

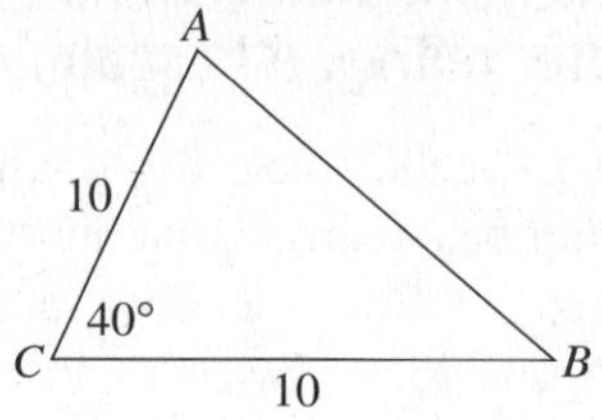

Note: Figure not drawn to scale

In the figure above, which of the following statements *could* be true?

I. $AB < AC$
II. $AB > AC$
III. Area of $\triangle ABC = 50$

(A) None
(B) I only
(C) II only
(D) I and III only
(E) II and III only

Solution. In the given diagram, *AB* is longer than *AC*, which is 10. But, we know that we *cannot trust the diagram*. Actually, there are two things wrong: angle *C* is labeled 40° but looks much more like 60° or 70°, and *AC* and *BC* are each labeled 10, but *BC* is much longer. Redraw the triangle with a smaller angle and two sides of the same length.

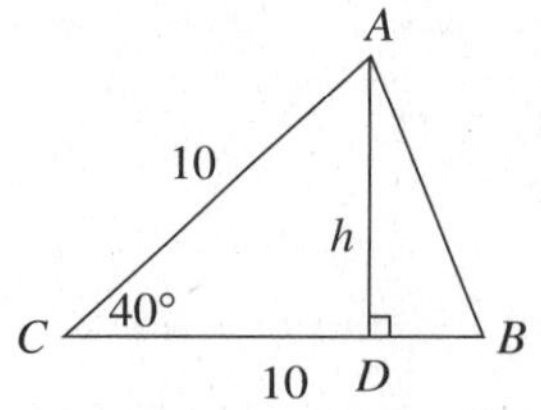

Now just look: $\overline{AB}$ is clearly shorter than $\overline{AC}$. So I is true and II is false. If you draw in altitude $\overline{AD}$, it is also clear that h is less than 10.

$$A = \frac{1}{2}bh = \frac{1}{2}(10)h = 5h < 5 \times 10 = 50$$

The area must be less than 50. III is false. Only I is true (Choice B).

TACTIC

6-8

Subtract to find shaded regions

Whenever part of a figure is shaded and part is unshaded, the straightforward way to find the area of the shaded portion is to find the area of the entire figure and subtract from it the area of the unshaded region. Occasionally, you may see an easy way to calculate the shaded area directly, but usually you should subtract.

EXAMPLE 19

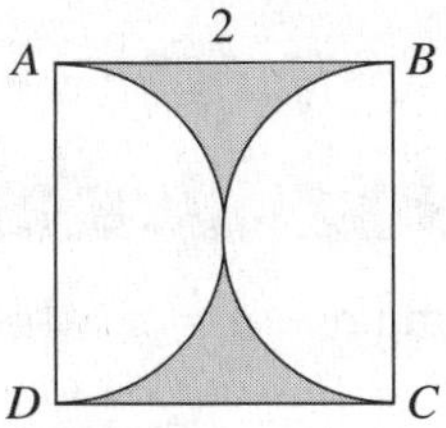

In the figure above, the shaded region is bounded by two semicircles and two sides of square $ABCD$. If $AB = 2$, what is the area of the shaded region?

(A) $4 - 2\pi$
(B) $4 - \pi$
(C) $4 + 2\pi$
(D) $16 - 4\pi$
(E) $4\pi - 16$

Solution. The entire region is a square whose area is 4. Since each semicircle has a diameter of 2 (hence a radius of 1), together they form a circle of radius 1. The area of such a circle is $\pi(1)^2 = \pi$. So, the area of the shaded region is $4 - \pi$ (Choice B).

TACTIC

6-9 Add equations

When a question involves two equations, almost always the best strategy is to either add them or subtract. If there are three or more equations, just add them.

EXAMPLE 20

If $4x + y = 23$ and $x - 2y = 8$, what is the average of x and y?

(A) 0
(B) 2.5
(C) 3
(D) 3.5
(E) 5

HELPFUL HINT: Usually, answering a question that involves two or more equations does not require you to solve them.

Solution. Add the two equations:

$$\begin{array}{rrcrcr} & 4x & + & y & = & 23 \\ + & x & - & 2y & = & 8 \\ \hline & 5x & - & y & = & 31 \end{array}$$

This does not appear to help, so try subtracting the two equations:

$$\begin{array}{rrcrcr} & 4x & + & y & = & 23 \\ - & x & - & 2y & = & 8 \\ \hline & 3x & + & 3y & = & 15 \end{array}$$

Divide each side by 3:

$$x + y = 5$$

The average of x and y is their sum divided by 2:

$$\frac{x+y}{2} = \frac{5}{2} = 2.5$$

The answer is Choice B.

NOTE: You *could have* actually solved for x and y $[x = 6, y = -1]$ and then taken their average. However, that method would have been more time-consuming and unnecessary.

EXAMPLE 21

If $a - b = 1$, $b - c = 2$, and $c - a = d$, what is the value of d?

(A) -3
(B) -1
(C) 1
(D) 3
(E) It cannot be determined from the information given.

Solution. Since there are more than two equations, add them:

$$\begin{array}{r} a - b = 1 \\ b - c = 2 \\ + \; c - a = d \\ \hline 0 = 3 + d \Rightarrow d = -3 \end{array}$$

The answer is Choice A.

TACTIC 6-10 Systematically make lists

When a question asks "how many," often the best strategy is to make a list. If you do this it is important that you make the list in a *systematic* fashion so that you don't inadvertently leave something out. Often, shortly after starting the list, you can see a pattern developing and can figure out how many more entries there will be without writing them all down.

Listing things systematically means writing them in numerical order (if the entries are numbers) or in alphabetical order (if the entries are letters). If the answer to "how many" is a small number (as in Example 22), just list all possibilities. If the answer is a large number (as in Example 23), start the list and write enough entries until you see a pattern.

EXAMPLE 22

The sum of three positive integers is 20. If one of them is 5, what is the greatest possible value of the product of the other two?

Solution. Since one of the integers is 5, the sum of the other two is 15. Systematically, list all possible pairs, (a, b), of positive integers whose sum is 15, and check their products. First let $a = 1$, then 2, and so on.

a	b	ab
1	14	14
2	13	26
3	12	36
4	11	44
5	10	50
6	9	54
7	8	56

The answer is 56.

EXAMPLE 23

A palindrome is a number, such as 74,947, that reads the same forward and backward. How many palindromes are there between 200 and 800?

> HELPFUL HINT
>
> Don't list *all* the possibilities. STOP as soon as you see the pattern.

Solution. First, write down the numbers in the 200s that end in 2: 202, 212, 222, 232, 242, 252, 262, 272, 282, 292

Now write the numbers beginning and ending in 3: 303, 313, 323, 333, 343, 353, 363, 373, 383, 393

By now you should see the pattern: there are ten numbers beginning with a 2, ten beginning with 3, and there will be ten beginning with 4, 5, 6, and 7 for a total of $6 \times 10 = 60$ palindromes.

TACTIC

6-11 Handle strange symbols properly

On almost all PSATs, there are a few questions that use symbols, such as: ⊕, □, ☺, ✠, or ✤, that you have never before seen in a mathematics problem. How can you answer such a question? Don't panic! It's easy—you are always told exactly what the symbol means! All you have to do is follow the directions carefully.

When there are two questions using the same symbol, the first question is usually easy and involves only numbers; the second is more difficult and usually contains variables.

Examples 24 and 25 refer to the following definition.

If a and b are unequal positive numbers, let the operation ☺ be defined by

$$a \,☺\, b = \frac{a+b}{a-b}$$

EXAMPLE 24

What is the value of 6 ☺ 2?

(A) 2
(B) 3
(C) 4
(D) 8
(E) 12

Solution. The definition of ☺ tells us that whenever two numbers surround a "happy face," we are to form a fraction in which the numerator is their sum and the denominator is their difference. So, 6 ☺ 2 is the fraction whose numerator is $6 + 2 = 8$ and whose denominator is $6 - 2 = 4$: $\frac{8}{4} = 2$ (Choice A).

EXAMPLE 25

If $c ☺ d = 3$, which of the following is true?

(A) $c = 3d$
(B) $c = 2d$
(C) $c = d$
(D) $d = 2c$
(E) $d = 3c$

Solution. $c ☺ d = 3 \Rightarrow \frac{c+d}{c-d} = 3 \Rightarrow c + d = 3c - 3d \Rightarrow 4d = 2c \Rightarrow c = 2d$ (Choice B).

Practice Exercises

None of these exercises *requires* the use of the tactics that you just learned. However, as you try each one, even if you know the correct mathematical solution, before solving it, think about which of the tactics could be used. An answer key follows the questions.

MULTIPLE-CHOICE QUESTIONS

1. If the average (arithmetic mean) of 10, 20, 30, 40, and a is 50, what is the value of a?

(A) 50
(B) 60
(C) 100
(D) 150
(E) 250

2. Larry has 250 marbles, all red, white, and blue, in the ratio of 1:3:6, respectively. How many blue marbles does he have?

(A) 25
(B) 75
(C) 100
(D) 125
(E) 150

3. If w whistles cost c cents, how many whistles can you get for d dollars?

(A) $\frac{100dw}{c}$
(B) $\frac{dw}{100c}$
(C) $100cdw$
(D) $\frac{dw}{c}$
(E) cdw

4. If x% of w is 10, what is w?

(A) $\frac{10}{x}$
(B) $\frac{100}{x}$
(C) $\frac{1000}{x}$
(D) $\frac{x}{100}$
(E) $\frac{x}{10}$

5. If 8% of c is equal to 12% of d, which of the following is equal to $c + d$?

(A) $1.5d$
(B) $2d$
(C) $2.5d$
(D) $3d$
(E) $5d$

6. On a certain legislative committee, $\frac{3}{8}$ of the committee members are Republicans. If $\frac{2}{3}$ of the members are men and $\frac{3}{5}$ of the men are Democrats, what fraction of the members are Democratic women?

(A) $\frac{3}{20}$
(B) $\frac{9}{40}$
(C) $\frac{1}{4}$
(D) $\frac{2}{5}$
(E) $\frac{5}{12}$

7. Kim receives a commission of \$25 for every \$2,000 worth of merchandise she sells. What percent is her commission?

(A) $1\frac{1}{4}$%
(B) $2\frac{1}{2}$%
(C) 5%
(D) 25%
(E) 125%

8. From 1990 to 1995, the value of one share of stock of *XYZ* corporation increased by 25%. If the value was D dollars in 1995, what was the value in 1990?

(A) $1.75D$
(B) $1.25D$
(C) $1.20D$
(D) $.80D$
(E) $.75D$

9. What is the value of p if p is positive and $p \times p \times p = p + p + p$?

(A) $\frac{1}{3}$
(B) $\sqrt{3}$
(C) 3
(D) $3\sqrt{3}$
(E) 9

10. What is 4% of 5%?

(A) .09%
(B) .20%
(C) 2.0%
(D) 9%
(E) 20%

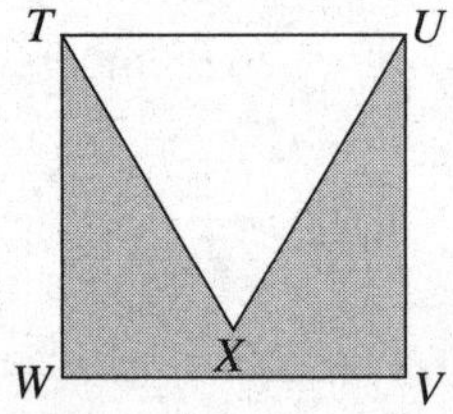

11. In the figure above, $TUVW$ is a square and TUX is an equilateral triangle. If $VW = 2$, what is the area of the shaded region?

(A) $\sqrt{3}$
(B) 2
(C) 3
(D) $4 - 2\sqrt{3}$
(E) $4 - \sqrt{3}$

12. If $12a + 3b = 1$ and $7b - 2a = 9$, what is the average (arithmetic mean) of a and b?

(A) 0.1
(B) 0.5
(C) 1
(D) 2.5
(E) 5

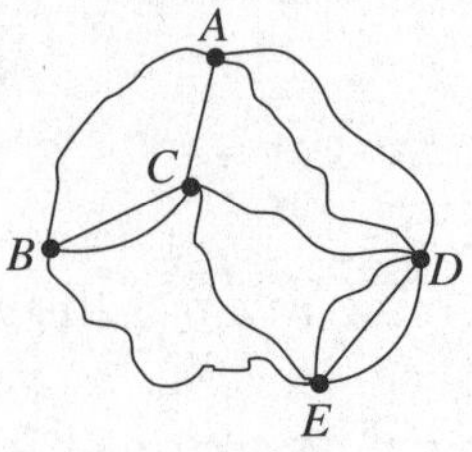

13. The map above shows all the roads connecting five towns. How many different ways are there to go from A to E if you may not return to a town after you leave it and you may not go through both C and D?

(A) 8
(B) 12
(C) 16
(D) 24
(E) 32

Questions 14–15 refer to the following definition.

For any numbers a, b, c a ✪ b ✪ $c = abc - (a + b + c)$.

14. What is the value of 3 ✪ 5 ✪ 2?

(A) 0
(B) 5
(C) 10
(D) 20
(E) 30

15. For what positive number x is it true that x ✪ $2x$ ✪ $3x = 0$?

(A) 0
(B) 1
(C) 2
(D) 3
(E) 6

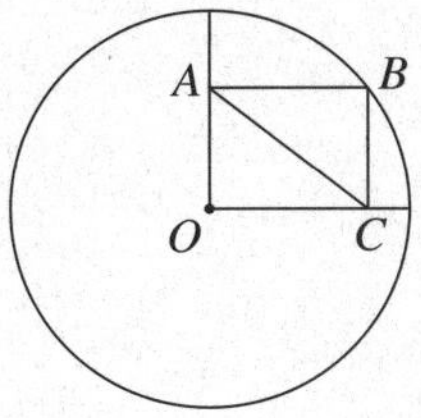

16. In the figure above, if the radius of circle O is 10, what is the length of diagonal AC of rectangle $OABC$?

(A) $\sqrt{2}$
(B) $\sqrt{10}$
(C) $5\sqrt{2}$
(D) 10
(E) $10\sqrt{2}$

GRID-IN QUESTIONS

17. What is the area of a rectangle whose length is twice its width and whose perimeter is equal to the perimeter of a square whose area is 1? __________

18. For how many integers between 1 and 1000 is at least one of the digits a 9? ____________________

Answer Key

Next to the answer for each question is the number of the tactic that would be most helpful in answering the question, in the event that you do not see the direct solution.

1. D (TACTIC 6-1)

2. E (TACTIC 6-1)

3. A (TACTIC 6-2)

4. C (TACTIC 6-2)

5. C (TACTIC 6-3)

6. B (TACTIC 6-3)

7. A (TACTIC 6-4)

8. D (TACTIC 6-4)

9. B (TACTIC 6-1)

10. B (TACTIC 6-4)

11. E (TACTIC 6-8)

12. B (TACTIC 6-9)

13. B (TACTIC 6-10)

14. D (TACTIC 6-11)

15. B (TACTIC 6-11)

16. D (TACTIC 6-6)

17. $\frac{8}{9}$ (TACTIC 6-5)

18. 271 (TACTIC 6-10)

CHAPTER 7

Review of PSAT Mathematics

Arithmetic

To do well on the PSAT, you need to feel comfortable with most topics of basic arithmetic. The first five sections of Chapter 7 provide you with a review of the basic arithmetic operations, signed numbers, fractions and decimals, ratios, percents, and averages. Because you will have a calculator with you at the test, you will not have to do long division, multiply three-digit numbers, or perform any other tedious calculations using paper and pencil. If you use a calculator with fraction capabilities, you can even avoid finding least common denominators and reducing fractions.

*The solutions to more than one-third of the math questions on the PSAT depend on your knowing the **KEY FACTS** in these sections. Be sure to review them all.*

7-A BASIC ARITHMETIC CONCEPTS

A ***set*** is a collection of "things" that have been grouped together in some way. Those "things" are called the ***elements*** or ***members***. For example:

If A is the set of states in the United States, then California is an element of A.
If B is the set of letters in the English alphabet, then z is a member of B.
If C is the set of even integers, then 46 is in C.

The ***union*** of two sets, A and B, is the set consisting of all the elements that are in A or B or both. Note that this includes those elements that are in A and B. The union is represented as $A \cup B$.

The ***intersection*** of two sets, A and B, is the set consisting only of those elements that are in both A and B. The intersection is represented as $A \cap B$.

In describing a set of numbers, we usually list the elements inside a pair of braces. For example, let A be the set of prime numbers less than 10, and let B be the set of even positive integers less than 10.

$$A = \{2, 3, 5, 7\} \qquad B = \{2, 4, 6, 8\}$$
$$A \cup B = \{2, 3, 4, 5, 6, 7, 8\}$$
$$A \cap B = \{2\}$$

The ***solution set*** of an equation is the set of all numbers that satisfy the equation.

EXAMPLE 1

If $C = \{-2, -1, 0, 1, 2\}$ and D is the set that consists of the squares of each of the elements of C, how many numbers are elements of D?

Solution. 0 is in D (since $0^2 = 0$); 1 is in D (since $1^2 = 1$); and 4 is in D (since $2^2 = 4$). These are the only elements of D; so D has 3 elements. Note that $(-1)^2 = 1$ and $(-2)^2 = 4$, but we have already listed 1 and 4. $D = \{0, 1, 4\}$.

Let's start our review of arithmetic by reviewing the most important sets of numbers and their properties. On the PSAT the word *number* always means *real number*, a number that can be represented by a point on the number line.

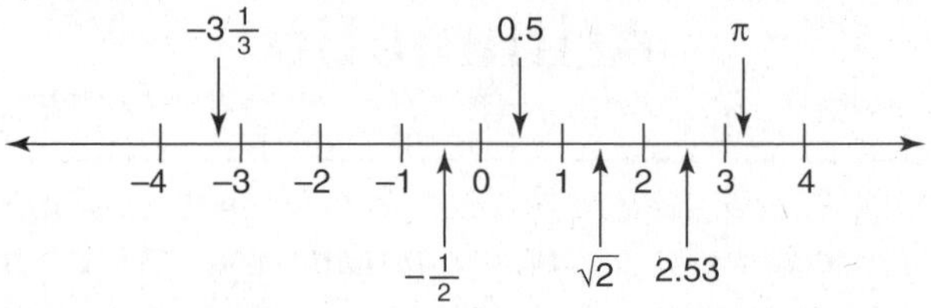

Signed Numbers

The numbers to the right of 0 on the number line are called ***positive*** and those to the left of 0 are called ***negative***. Note that 0 is neither positive nor negative. Negative numbers must be written with a *negative sign* (-3); positive numbers can be written with a *plus sign* ($+3$) but are usually written without a sign (3). All numbers can be called *signed numbers*.

The ***absolute value*** of a number a, denoted $|a|$, is the distance between a and 0 on the number line. Since 5 is 5 units to the right of 0 on the number line and -5 is 5 units to the left of 0, both have an absolute value of 5:

$$|5| = 5 \quad \text{and} \quad |-5| = 5$$

EXAMPLE 2

How many integers are solutions of the inequality $|x| < 5$?

(A) 0
(B) 4
(C) 8
(D) 9
(E) infinitely many

Solution. There are infinitely many *numbers* whose absolute value is less than 5, but only 9 of them are *integers*.

$$-4, -3, -2, -1, 0, 1, 2, 3, 4 \text{ (Choice D).}$$

In arithmetic we are basically concerned with the addition, subtraction, multiplication, and division of numbers. The table below gives the terms for the results of these operations.

Operation	Symbol	Result	Example	
Addition	$+$	***Sum***	16 is the sum of 12 and 4	$12 + 4 = 16$
Subtraction	$-$	***Difference***	8 is the difference of 12 and 4	$12 - 4 = 8$
Multiplication*	$\times$	***Product***	48 is the product of 12 and 4	$12 \times 4 = 48$
Division	$\div$	***Quotient***	3 is the quotient of 12 and 4	$12 \div 4 = 3$

*In certain situations, multiplication can also be indicated by a dot, parentheses, or the juxtaposition of symbols without any sign: $2^2 \cdot 2^4$, $3(4)$, $3(x + 2)$, $3a$, $4abc$.

Given any two numbers a and b, you can *always* find their sum, difference, product, and quotient (with a calculator, if necessary), but you can *never divide by zero.*

$0 \div 7 = 0$, but $7 \div 0$ is meaningless

EXAMPLE 3

What is the sum of the product and quotient of 8 and 8?

Solution. Product: $8 \times 8 = 64$. Quotient: $8 \div 8 = 1$. Sum: $64 + 1 = 65$.

Key Fact A1

For any number a: $a \times 0 = 0$. Conversely, if the product of two or more numbers is 0, *at least one* of them must be 0.

If $ab = 0$, then $a = 0$ or $b = 0$.
If $rst = 0$, then $r = 0$ or $s = 0$ or $t = 0$.

EXAMPLE 4

What is the product of all the integers from -5 to 5, inclusive?

Solution. Before reaching for your calculator, look and think. You are asked for the product of eleven numbers, one of which is 0. So, by **KEY FACT A1**, the product is 0.

Key Fact A2

The product and quotient of two positive numbers or two negative numbers is positive; the product and quotient of a positive number and a negative number is negative.

$12 \times 2 = 24$ $\quad$ $12 \times (-2) = -24$ $\quad$ $(-12) \times 2 = -24$ $\quad$ $(-12) \times (-2) = 24$
$12 \div 2 = 6$ $\quad$ $12 \div (-2) = -6$ $\quad$ $(-12) \div 2 = -6$ $\quad$ $(-12) \div (-2) = 6$

To determine whether a product of more than two numbers is positive or negative, count the number of negative factors.

Key Fact A3

- The product of an *even* number of negative factors is positive.
- The product of an *odd* number of negative factors is negative.

EXAMPLE 5

Which of the following are equal to $(-1)^{25}$?

I. $(-1)^{100}$
II. $-(1)^{100}$
III. $-(-1)^{100}$

(A) I only
(B) II only
(C) III only
(D) II and III only
(E) I, II, and III

Solution. Since 25 is odd and 100 is even, $(-1)^{25} = -1$, whereas $(-1)^{100} = 1$. (I is false.) Since $1^{100} = 1$, $-(1)^{100} = -1$. II is true. Since $(-1)^{100} = 1$, $-(-1)^{100} = -1$. III is true. Only II and III are true (Choice D).

Key Fact A4

- The sum of two positive numbers is positive.
- The sum of two negative numbers is negative.

$$6 + 2 = 8 \quad (-6) + (-2) = -8$$

- To find the sum of a positive and a negative number, find the difference of their absolute values and use the sign of the number with the larger absolute value.

To calculate $6 + (-2)$ or $(-6) + 2$, take the *difference*, $6 - 2 = 4$, and use the sign of the number whose absolute value is 6:

$$6 + (-2) = 4 \quad (-6) + 2 = -4$$

Key Fact A5

To subtract signed numbers, change the problem to an addition problem, by changing the sign of what is being subtracted, and use **KEY FACT A4**.

$$2 - 6 = 2 + (-6) = -4 \qquad 2 - (-6) = 2 + (6) = 8$$

$$(-2) - (-6) = (-2) + (6) = 4 \qquad (-2) - 6 = (-2) + (-6) = -8$$

In each case, the minus sign was changed to a plus sign, and either the 6 was changed to -6 or the -6 was changed to 6.

> All arithmetic involving signed numbers can be accomplished on *any* calculator, but not all calculators handle negative numbers the same way. Be sure you know how to enter negative numbers and how to use them on *your* calculator. It is a good idea to always put negative numbers in parentheses.

Integers

The ***integers*** are $\{\ldots, -4, -3, -2, -1, 0, 1, 2, 3, 4, \ldots\}$
The ***positive integers*** are $\{1, 2, 3, 4, 5, \ldots\}$
The ***negative integers*** are $\{\ldots, -5, -4, -3, -2, -1\}$

Consecutive integers are two or more integers written in sequence in which each integer is 1 more than the preceding one. For example:

$$22, 23 \qquad 6, 7, 8, 9$$

$$-2, -1, 0, 1 \qquad n, n+1, n+2, n+3, \ldots$$

> **CAUTION:** Never assume that *number* means *integer*: 3 is not the only number between 2 and 4—there are infinitely many,

EXAMPLE 6

If $0 < x < 3$ and $2 < y < 8$, what is the largest integer value of $x + y$?

Solution. If x and y are integers, the largest value of $x + y$ is $2 + 7 = 9$. However, even though $x + y$ is to be an integer, neither x nor y must be. If $x = 2.5$ and $y = 7.5$, then $x + y = 10$, which must be the largest integer value, since clearly $x + y < 11$.

The sum, difference, and product of two integers is *always* an integer; the quotient of two integers may be an integer, but not necessarily. The quotient $37 \div 10$ can be expressed as $\frac{37}{10}$ or $3\frac{7}{10}$ or 3.7. If the quotient is to be an integer, you can also say that the quotient is 3 and there is a *remainder* of 7. It depends upon your point of view. For example, if 37 pounds of rice is to be divided into 10 bags, each bag will hold 3.7 pounds; but if 37 books are to be divided among 10 people, each one will get 3 books and there will be 7 left over (the remainder).

To find the remainder when 100 is divided by 7, divide on your calculator: $100 \div 7 = 14.285714\ldots$ This tells you that the quotient is 14. Ignore everything to the right of the decimal point. To find the remainder, multiply: $14 \times 7 = 98$, and then subtract: $100 - 98 = 2$.

> The standard way to find quotients and remainders is to use long division. But on the PSAT, you should *never* do long division; you should use your calculators.

EXAMPLE 7

If the remainder when a is divided by 7 is 2 and the remainder when b is divided by 7 is 4, what is the remainder when ab is divided by 7?

(A) 0
(B) 1
(C) 3
(D) 6
(E) 8

Solution. a can be any number that is 2 more than a multiple of 7: 9, 16, 23, ... b can be any number that is 4 more than a multiple of 7: 11, 18, 25, ...

For simplicity, let $a = 9$ and $b = 11$. Then $ab = 99$, and when 99 is divided by 7, the quotient is 14 and the remainder is 1 (Choice B).

If a and b are integers, the following four terms are synonymous:

a is a ***divisor*** of b	a is a ***factor*** of b
b is ***divisible*** by a	b is a ***multiple*** of a

All these statements mean that, when b is divided by a, there is no remainder (or, more precisely, the remainder is 0). For example:

3 is a divisor of 12.	3 is a factor of 12.
12 is divisible by 3.	12 is a multiple of 3.

1 is *not* a prime number.

The only positive divisor of 1 is 1. All other positive integers have at least two positive divisors: 1 and itself, and possibly many more. For example, 6 is divisible by 1 and 6, as well as 2 and 3, whereas 7 is divisible only by 1 and 7. Positive integers, such as 7, which have *exactly two* positive divisors are called ***prime numbers*** or ***primes***. Here are the first few primes:

2, 3, 5, 7, 11, 13, 17, 19, 23.

Memorize this list—it will come in handy. Note that 1 is *not* a prime.

EXAMPLE 8

What is the sum of the largest prime factor of 26 and the largest prime factor of 28?

Solution.
The factors of 26 are 1, 2, 13, and 26. The largest *prime* factor is 13.
The factors of 28 are 1, 2, 4, 7, 14, and 28. The largest *prime* factor is 7.
The sum of 13 and 7 is 20.

NOTE

0 is an even integer.

The ***even numbers*** are all the integer multiples of 2: $\{\ldots, -4, -2, 0, 2, 4, 6, \ldots\}$
The ***odd numbers*** are the integers not divisible by 2: $\{\ldots, -5, -3, -1, 1, 3, 5, \ldots\}$

Key Fact A6

1. If two integers are both even or both odd, their sum and difference are even.
2. If one integer is even and the other odd, their sum and difference are both odd.
3. The product of two integers is even unless both of them are odd.

Exponents and Roots

Repeated addition of the same number is indicated by multiplication:

$$11 + 11 + 11 + 11 + 11 + 11 + 11 = 7 \times 11$$

Repeated multiplication of the same number is indicated by an exponent:

$$11 \times 11 \times 11 \times 11 \times 11 \times 11 \times 11 = 11^7$$

In the expression 11^7, 11 is called the ***base*** and 7 is the ***exponent***.

Although most of the exponents you will encounter on the PSAT are positive integers, you may occasionally see 0, negative integers, and rational numbers used as exponents. All of these are defined in the next **KEY FACT**.

Key Fact A7

For any number b and positive integer n:

- $b^0 = 1$
- $b^1 = b$
- $b^n = b \times b \times \ldots \times b$, where b is used as a factor n times
- $b^{-n} = \frac{1}{b^n}$
- $b^{\frac{1}{n}} = \sqrt[n]{b}$

For example,

$2^0 = 1$ $\quad 2^1 = 2$ $\quad 2^4 = 2 \times 2 \times 2 \times 2 = 16$

$2^{-4} = \frac{1}{2^4} = \frac{1}{16}$ $\quad 16^{\frac{1}{4}} = \sqrt[4]{16} = 2$

Now consider the following four calculations.

(i) $5^4 \times 5^3 = (5 \times 5 \times 5 \times 5) \times (5 \times 5 \times 5) = 5^7 = 5^{4+3}$

(ii) $\frac{5^6}{5^4} = \frac{\cancel{5} \times \cancel{5} \times \cancel{5} \times \cancel{5} \times 5 \times 5}{\cancel{5} \times \cancel{5} \times \cancel{5} \times \cancel{5}_1} = 5 \times 5 = 5^2 = 5^{6-4}$

(iii) $(5^2)^3 = (5 \times 5)^3 = (5 \times 5) \times (5 \times 5) \times (5 \times 5) = 5^6 = 5^{2 \times 3}$

(iv) $5^3 \times 6^3 = (5 \times 5 \times 5) \times (6 \times 6 \times 6) = (5 \times 6)(5 \times 6)(5 \times 6) = (5 \times 6)^3$

These four examples illustrate the following important laws of exponents.

Key Fact A8

For any numbers b, c, m, and n:

(i) $b^m b^n = b^{m+n}$ (ii) $\frac{b^m}{b^n} = b^{m-n}$ (iii) $(b^m)^n = b^{mn}$ (iv) $b^m c^m = (bc)^m$

EXAMPLE 9

If $5^a \times 5^b = 5^{50}$, what is the average (arithmetic mean) of a and b?

Solution. Since $5^a \times 5^b = 5^{a+b}$, we see that $a + b = 50 \Rightarrow \frac{a+b}{2} = 25$.

EXAMPLE 10

What is the value of $16^{\frac{3}{4}}$?

Solution. By **KEY FACT A8** (iii), $16^{\frac{3}{4}} = (16^{\frac{1}{4}})^3 = (\sqrt[4]{16})^3 = 2^3 = 8$.

Squares and Square Roots

The exponent that appears most often on the PSAT is 2. It is used to form the square of a number, as in πr^2 (the area of a circle), $a^2 + b^2 = c^2$ (Pythagorean theorem), or $x^2 - y^2$ (the difference of two squares). Therefore, it is helpful to recognize the ***perfect squares***, numbers that are the squares of integers. The squares of the integers from 0 to 15 are as follows:

x	0	1	2	3	4	5	6	7	8	9	10	11	12	13	14	15
x^2	0	1	4	9	16	25	36	49	64	81	100	121	144	169	196	225

There are two numbers that satisfy the equation $x^2 = 4$: $x = 2$ and $x = -2$. The positive number, 2, is called the ***principal square root*** of 4 and is denoted by the symbol $\sqrt{4}$. Clearly, each perfect square has a square root: $\sqrt{0} = 0$, $\sqrt{16} = 4$, $\sqrt{49} = 7$, and $\sqrt{121} = 11$. It is an important fact, however, that *every* positive number has a square root.

Key Fact A9

For any positive number a, there is a positive number b that satisfies the equation $b^2 = a$. That number is called the principal square root of a and is written $b = \sqrt{a}$. Therefore, for any positive number a: $\sqrt{a} \times \sqrt{a} = (\sqrt{a})^2 = a$.

The only difference between $\sqrt{4}$ and $\sqrt{5}$ is that $\sqrt{4}$ is an integer, whereas $\sqrt{5}$ is not. Since 5 is greater than 4, we know that $\sqrt{5}$ is greater than $\sqrt{4} = 2$. In fact, $(2.2)^2 = 4.84$, which is close to 5, and $(2.23)^2 = 4.9729$, which is very close to 5. So, $\sqrt{5} \approx 2.23$. Using the square root key on your calculator, you can find the value of any square root to several decimal places of accuracy, much more than you need for the PSAT.

EXAMPLE 11

What is the circumference of a circle whose area is 10π?

(A) 5π
(B) 10π
(C) $\pi\sqrt{10}$
(D) $2\pi\sqrt{10}$
(E) $\pi\sqrt{20}$

Solution. Since the area of a circle is given by the formula $A = \pi r^2$, we have

$$\pi r^2 = 10\pi \Rightarrow r^2 = 10 \Rightarrow r = \sqrt{10}.$$

The circumference is given by the formula $C = 2\pi r$, so $C = 2\pi\sqrt{10}$ (Choice D). (See Section 7-L on circles.)

PEMDAS

> HELPFUL HINT
>
> Every scientific and graphing calculator automatically follows PEMDAS, but to be sure of getting the right answer, you must enter the numbers carefully, always using parentheses around negative numbers, fractions, and even around numerators and denominators that are not single numbers.

When a calculation requires performing more than one operation, it is important to carry out the operations in the correct order. For decades students have memorized the sentence, "Please Excuse My Dear Aunt Sally," or just the first letters, PEMDAS, to remember the proper order of operations. The letters stand for:

- Parentheses: First do whatever appears in parentheses, following PEMDAS within the parentheses also, if necessary.
- Exponents: Next evaluate all terms with exponents.
- Multiplication and Division: Do all multiplications and divisions *in order from left to right*—do not multiply first and then divide.
- Addition and Subtraction: Finally, do all additions and subtractions *in order from left to right*—do not add first and then subtract.

Here are some worked-out examples.

1. $10 + 4 \times 2 = 10 + 8 = 18$ [Multiply before you add.]
   $(10 + 4) \times 2 = 14 \times 2 = 28$ [First add in the parentheses.]
2. $16 \div 2 \times 4 = 8 \times 4 = 32$ [Just go from left to right.]
   $16 \div (2 \times 4) = 16 \div 8 = 2$ [First multiply in the parentheses.]
3. $5 \times 2^3 = 5 \times 8 = 40$ [Do exponents first.]
   $(5 \times 2)^3 = 10^3 = 1000$ [First multiply in the parentheses.]
4. $10 + 15 \div (2 + 3) = 10 + 15 \div 5 = 10 + 3 = 13$ [Do parentheses first, then divide.]
5. $100 - 2^2(3 + 4 \times 5) = 100 - 2^2(23) = 100 - 4(23) = 100 - 92 = 8$
   [Do parentheses first (using PEMDAS), then the exponent, then multiplication.]

Key Fact A10

(The distributive law) For any real numbers a, b, and c:

$$a(b + c) = ab + ac \qquad a(b - c) = ab - ac$$

and if $a \neq 0$

$$\frac{b + c}{a} = \frac{b}{a} + \frac{c}{a} \qquad \frac{b - c}{a} = \frac{b}{a} - \frac{c}{a}$$

> HELPFUL HINT
>
> Be sure you use the distributive law with both multiplication and division whenever you can.

EXAMPLE 12

Which of the following is equivalent to $\frac{x^5 + x^4}{x^4}$ for all nonzero numbers x?

(A) $x + 1$
(B) x^5
(C) $x^5 + 1$
(D) $x + x^4$
(E) x^{16}

Solution. $\frac{x^5 + x^4}{x^4} = \frac{x^5}{x^4} + \frac{x^4}{x^4} = x + 1$ (Choice A).

Practice Exercises

MULTIPLE-CHOICE QUESTIONS

1. For how many integers n, is it true that $n^2 = n^3$?

(A) None
(B) 1
(C) 2
(D) 4
(E) More than 4

2. If $x \blacklozenge y$ represents the number of integers greater than x and less than y, what is the value of $-\pi \blacklozenge \pi$?

(A) 0
(B) 3
(C) 4
(D) 6
(E) 7

3. Which of the following is equal to $(5^8 \times 5^9)^{10}$?

(A) 5^{27}
(B) 5^{82}
(C) 5^{170}
(D) 5^{720}
(E) 25^{720}

4. If p and q are primes greater than 100, which of the following must be true?

I. $p + q$ is even
II. pq is odd
III. $p^2 - q^2$ is even

(A) I only
(B) II only
(C) I and II only
(D) I and III only
(E) I, II, and III

5. If $(5^a)(5^b) = \frac{5^c}{5^d}$, what is d in terms of a, b, and c?

(A) $\frac{c}{ab}$
(B) $c - a - b$
(C) $a + b - c$
(D) $c - ab$
(E) $\frac{c}{a + b}$

GRID-IN QUESTIONS

6. A number is "nifty" if it is a multiple of 2 or 3. How many nifty numbers are there between -11 and 11?

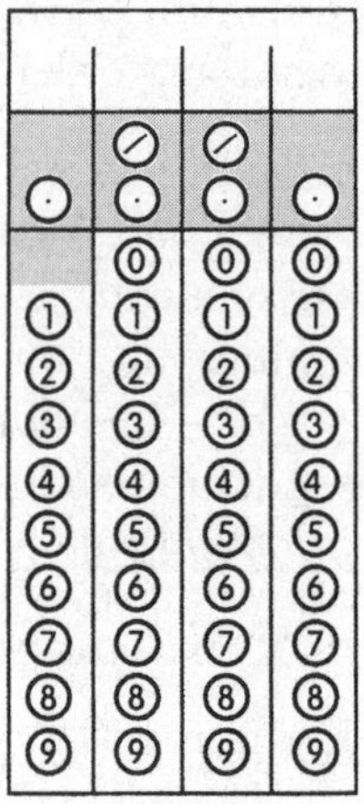

7. If for any positive integer n, $\tau(n)$ represents the number of positive divisors of n, what is the value of $\tau(\tau(\tau(12)))$?

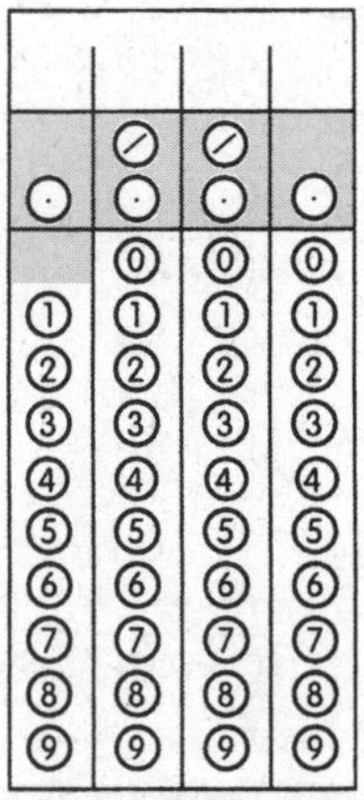

8. If the product of four consecutive integers is equal to one of the integers, what is the largest possible value of one of the integers?

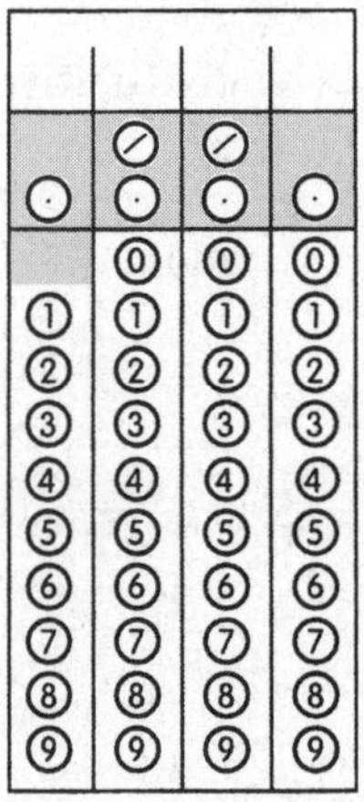

9. At Ben's Butcher Shop, 199 pounds of chopped meat is being divided into packages, each weighing 2.5 pounds. How many pounds of meat are left when there isn't enough to make another whole package?

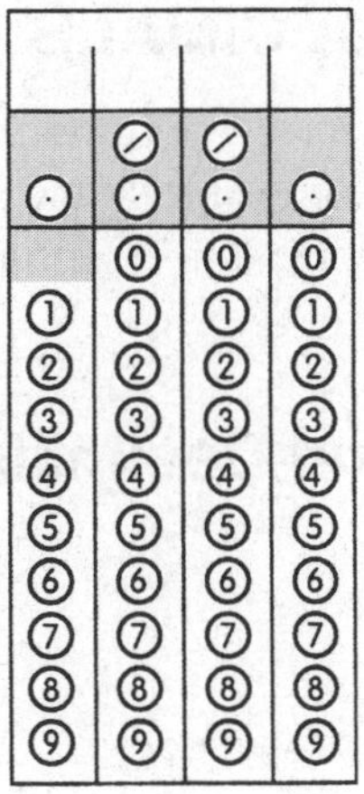

10. What is the largest number, x, that can be entered in the grid such that $\sqrt{x}$ is an integer?

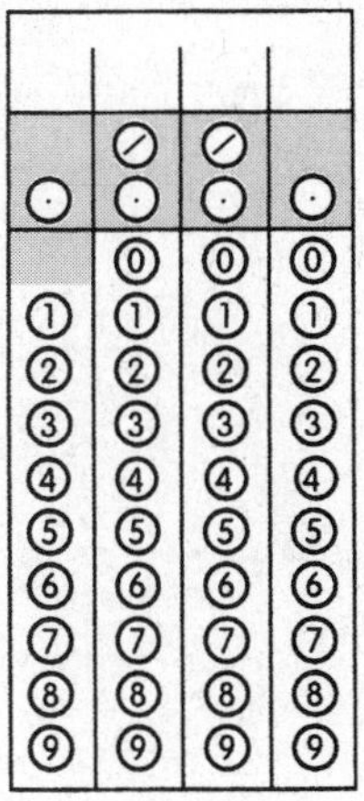

Answer Key

1. C **2.** E **3.** C **4.** E **5.** B

6.

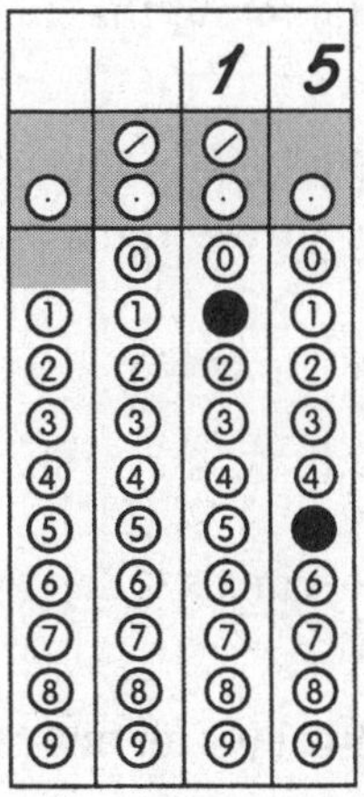

7.

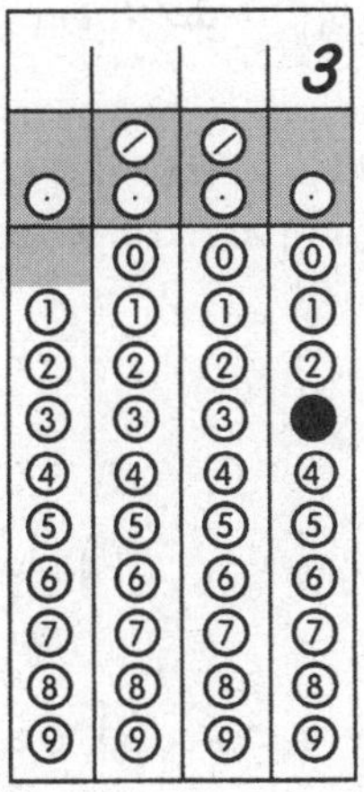

8.

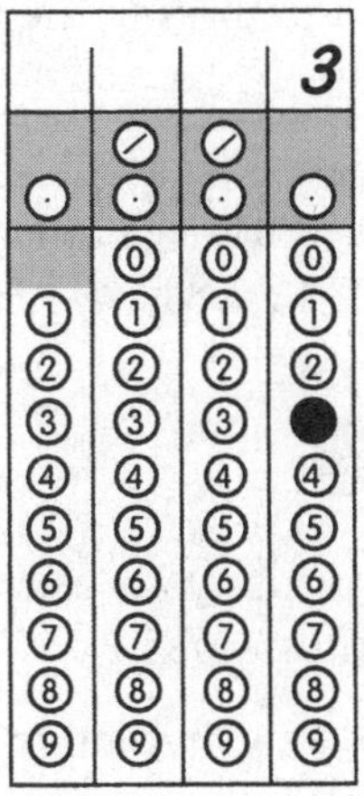

9.

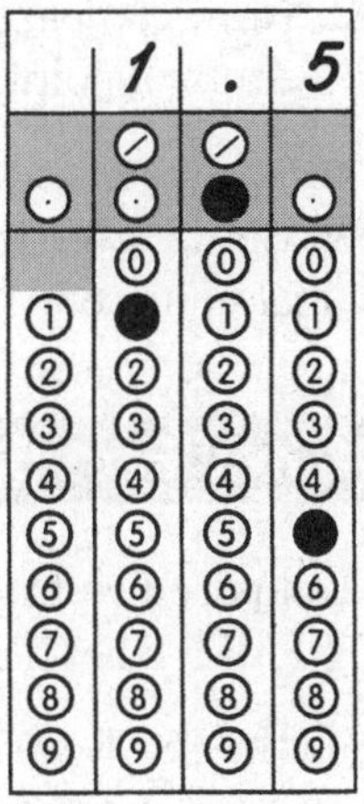

10.

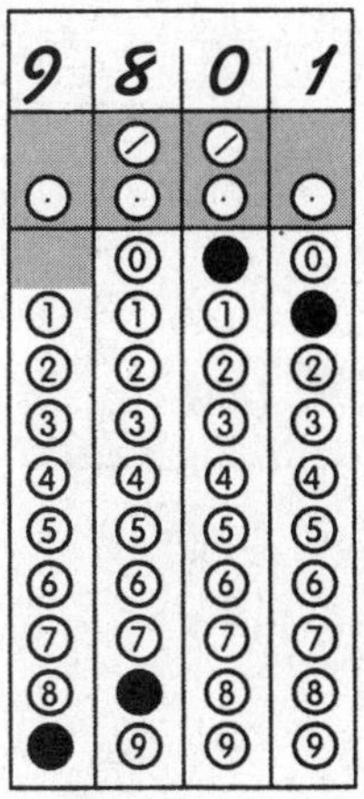

7-B FRACTIONS AND DECIMALS

Several questions on the PSAT involve fractions or decimals. In this section we will present all of the important facts you need to know for the PSAT. Even if you are using a calculator that has fraction capabilities, it is essential that you review all of this material thoroughly.

Comparing Fractions and Decimals

Key Fact B1

To compare two decimals, follow these rules:

- Whichever number has the greater number to the left of the decimal point is greater: since $10 > 9$, $10.001 > 9.896$ and since $1 > 0$, $1.234 > 0.8$.
- If the numbers to the left of the decimal point are equal (or if there are no numbers to the left of the decimal point), proceed as follows:

  1. If the numbers do not have the same number of digits to the right of the decimal point, add zeros to make the number of digits equal.
  2. Now, compare the numbers to the right of the decimal point (*ignoring* the decimal point itself).

For example, to compare 1.83 and 1.823, add a zero to the end of 1.83, forming 1.830. Now, thinking of them as whole numbers, compare the numbers to the right of the decimal point: $830 > 823 \Rightarrow 1.830 > 1.823$.

Key Fact B2

To compare two fractions, use your calculator to convert them to decimals. Then apply **KEY FACT B1**. This *always* works.

On the PSAT, *never* do long division to convert a fraction to a decimal (or for any other reason). Use your calculator.

To compare $\frac{1}{3}$ and $\frac{3}{8}$, use your calculator: $\frac{1}{3} = .333\ldots$ and $\frac{3}{8} = .375$. Since $.375 > .333$, $\frac{3}{8} > \frac{1}{3}$.

Key Fact B3

KEY FACTS B1 and **B2** apply to *positive* decimals and fractions. Clearly, any positive number is greater than any negative number. For negative decimals and fractions, note that if $a > b$, then $-a < -b$.

$$\frac{3}{8} > \frac{1}{3} \Rightarrow -\frac{1}{3} > -\frac{3}{8} \quad \text{and} \quad .83 > .829 \Rightarrow -.83 < -.829$$

Arithmetic Operations with Decimals and Fractions

Using a calculator saves time and avoids careless errors. If you know that $12 \times 12 = 144$ and that $1.2 \times 1.2 = 1.44$, fine, but if you're not sure, use your calculator rather than paper and pencil. You should even use your calculator to multiply $.2 \times .2$ if there's any chance that you would write 0.4 instead of 0.04 as the answer.

> HELPFUL HINT
>
> On the PSAT, *all* decimal arithmetic (including whole numbers) that you can't easily do mentally should be done on your calculator.

Key Fact B4

To multiply two fractions, multiply their numerators and multiply their denominators:

$$\frac{3}{5} \times \frac{4}{7} = \frac{3 \times 4}{5 \times 7} = \frac{12}{35}.$$

Key Fact B5

To multiply a fraction by any other number, write that number as a fraction whose denominator is 1:

$$\frac{3}{5} \times 7 = \frac{3}{5} \times \frac{7}{1} = \frac{21}{5} \qquad \frac{3}{4} \times \pi = \frac{3}{4} \times \frac{\pi}{1} = \frac{3\pi}{4}$$

TACTIC B1

Reduce fractions before multiplying (divide the numerator and the denominator by a common factor).

EXAMPLE 1

Express the product, $\frac{3}{4} \times \frac{8}{9} \times \frac{15}{16}$, in lowest terms.

Solution. If you just multiply the numerators and denominators (with a calculator, of course), you get $\frac{360}{576}$, which is a nuisance to reduce. Also, dividing on your calculator won't help, since your answer is supposed to be a fraction in lowest terms. It is better to use **TACTIC B1** and reduce first:

$$\frac{{}^{1}\cancel{3}}{4} \times \frac{{}^{1}\cancel{8}}{\cancel{9}_{\cancel{3}_{1}}} \times \frac{{}^{5}\cancel{15}}{\cancel{16}_{2}} = \frac{1 \times 1 \times 5}{4 \times 1 \times 2} = \frac{5}{8}.$$

TACTIC B2

When a problem requires you to find a fraction of a number, multiply.

EXAMPLE 2

If $\frac{5}{8}$ of the 320 seniors at Central High School are girls, and $\frac{4}{5}$ of the senior girls are taking a science course, how many senior girls are NOT taking a science course?

(A) 40
(B) 70
(C) 160
(D) 200
(E) It cannot be determined from the information given.

Solution. There are $\frac{5}{\cancel{8}} \times \cancel{320}^{40} = 200$ senior girls. Of these, $\frac{4}{\cancel{5}} \times \cancel{200}^{40} = 160$ are taking science. Then, $200 - 160 = 40$ are not taking science (Choice A).

CALCULATOR HINT

If you are going to use your calculator, enter the numbers without reducing. Given the choice of multiplying $\frac{48}{128} \times 80$ or $\frac{3}{8} \times 80$, *you* would prefer the second option, but with *your calculator,* the first one is just as easy.

The ***reciprocal*** of any nonzero number x, is the number $\frac{1}{x}$. The reciprocal of the fraction $\frac{a}{b}$ is the fraction $\frac{b}{a}$.

Key Fact B6

To divide any number by a fraction, multiply that number by the reciprocal of the fraction:

$$20 \div \frac{2}{3} = \frac{20}{1} \times \frac{3}{2} = 30 \qquad \frac{3}{5} \div \frac{2}{3} = \frac{3}{5} \times \frac{3}{2} = \frac{9}{10}$$

EXAMPLE 3

A certain real estate course takes 36 hours to complete. If the course is divided into 40-minute classes, how many times does the class meet?

Solution. First, note that 40 minutes $= \frac{40}{60}$ hour $= \frac{2}{3}$ hour. Then, $36 \div \frac{2}{3} = \frac{36}{1} \times \frac{3}{2} = 54$.

NOTE: In this problem, you could have avoided fractions by changing 36 hours to $36 \times 60 = 2{,}160$ minutes and then dividing: $2{,}160 \div 40 = 54$.

Key Fact B7

To add or subtract fractions with the same denominator, add or subtract the numerators and keep the denominator:

$$\frac{4}{9} + \frac{1}{9} = \frac{5}{9} \quad \text{and} \quad \frac{4}{9} - \frac{1}{9} = \frac{3}{9} = \frac{1}{3}$$

To add or subtract fractions with different denominators, first rewrite the fractions as equivalent fractions with the same denominators:

$$\frac{1}{6} + \frac{3}{4} = \frac{2}{12} + \frac{9}{12} = \frac{11}{12}$$

NOTE: The *easiest* denominator to get is the product of the denominators ($6 \times 4 = 24$, in this example), but the *best* denominator to use is the *least common denominator,* which is the *least common multiple* (LCM) of the denominators (12 in this case). Using the least common denominator minimizes the amount of reducing that is necessary to express the answer in lowest terms.

EXAMPLE 4

Michael had a baseball card collection. Sally took $\frac{1}{3}$ of his cards and Heidi took $\frac{1}{4}$ of them. What fraction of his cards did Michael have left?

EXAMPLE 5

Michael had a baseball card collection. Sally took $\frac{1}{3}$ of his cards and Heidi took $\frac{1}{4}$ of what was left. What fraction of his cards did Michael have left?

Solution 4. $\frac{1}{3} + \frac{1}{4} = \frac{4}{12} + \frac{3}{12} = \frac{7}{12}$ of the cards were taken; so Michael had $\frac{5}{12}$ of them left.

Solution 5. $\frac{1}{3} + \frac{1}{6} = \frac{2}{6} + \frac{1}{6} = \frac{3}{6} = \frac{1}{2}$ of the cards were taken; so Michael had $\frac{1}{2}$ of them left.

CAUTION: Be sure to read questions carefully. In Example 4, Heidi took $\frac{1}{4}$ of the cards. In Example 5, however, she took only $\frac{1}{4}$ of the $\frac{2}{3}$ that were left after Sally took her cards: she took $\frac{1}{4} \times \frac{2}{3} = \frac{1}{6}$ of the cards.

Arithmetic Operations with Mixed Numbers

A ***mixed number*** is a number such as $3\frac{1}{2}$, which consists of an integer followed by a fraction. It is an abbreviation for the *sum* of the number and the fraction; so, $3\frac{1}{2}$ is an abbreviation for $3 + \frac{1}{2}$. Every mixed number can be written as an improper fraction, and every improper fraction can be written as a mixed number:

$$3\frac{1}{2} = 3 + \frac{1}{2} = \frac{3}{1} + \frac{1}{2} = \frac{6}{2} + \frac{1}{2} = \frac{7}{2} \quad \text{and} \quad \frac{7}{2} = \frac{6}{2} + \frac{1}{2} = 3 + \frac{1}{2} = 3\frac{1}{2}$$

Key Fact B8

To write a mixed number as an improper fraction or an improper fraction as a mixed number, follow these rules:

1. To write a mixed number ($3\frac{1}{2}$) as an improper fraction, multiply the whole number (3) by the denominator (2), add the numerator (1), and write the sum over the denominator (2): $\frac{3 \times 2 + 1}{2} = \frac{7}{2}$.
2. To write an improper fraction ($\frac{7}{2}$) as a mixed number, divide the numerator by the denominator; the quotient (3) is the whole number. Place the remainder (1) over the denominator to form the fractional part $\left(\frac{1}{2}\right)$: $3\frac{1}{2}$.

CAUTION: You can *never* grid-in a mixed number. You must change it to an improper fraction or a decimal. (See Chapter 5.)

Key Fact B9

To add mixed numbers, add the integers and add the fractions:

- $5\frac{1}{4} + 3\frac{2}{3} = (5 + 3) + \left(\frac{1}{4} + \frac{2}{3}\right) = 8 + \left(\frac{3}{12} + \frac{8}{12}\right) = 8 + \frac{11}{12} = 8\frac{11}{12}$
- $5\frac{3}{4} + 3\frac{2}{3} = (5 + 3) + \left(\frac{3}{4} + \frac{2}{3}\right) = 8 + \left(\frac{9}{12} + \frac{8}{12}\right) = 8 + \frac{17}{12} = 8 + 1\frac{5}{12} =$

  $8 + 1 + \frac{5}{12} = 9\frac{5}{12}$

Key Fact B10

To subtract mixed numbers, subtract the integers and also subtract the fractions. If, however, the fraction in the second number is greater than the fraction in the first number, you first have to borrow 1 from the integer part. For example, since $\frac{2}{3} > \frac{1}{4}$, you can't subtract $5\frac{1}{4} - 3\frac{2}{3}$ until you borrow 1 from the 5:

$$5\frac{1}{4} = 5 + \frac{1}{4} = (4 + 1) + \frac{1}{4} = 4 + \left(1 + \frac{1}{4}\right) = 4 + \frac{5}{4}.$$

HELPFUL HINT

All arithmetic operations on mixed numbers can be done directly on your calculator. There is no need to change the mixed numbers to improper fractions or to borrow.

Now, you have

$$5\frac{1}{4} - 3\frac{2}{3} = 4\frac{5}{4} - 3\frac{2}{3} = (4 - 3) + \left(\frac{5}{4} - \frac{2}{3}\right) =$$

$$1 + \left(\frac{15}{12} - \frac{8}{12}\right) = 1\frac{7}{12}.$$

Key Fact B11

To multiply or divide mixed numbers, change them to improper fractions:

$$1\frac{2}{3} \times 3\frac{1}{4} = \frac{5}{3} \times \frac{13}{4} = \frac{65}{12} = 5\frac{5}{12}$$

HELPFUL HINT

Remember that on the PSAT, if you ever get stuck on a fraction problem, you can always convert the fractions to decimals and do all the work on your calculator.

Practice Exercises

MULTIPLE-CHOICE QUESTIONS

1. The school band has 24 boys and 16 girls. What fraction of the band members are girls?

(A) $\frac{2}{5}$

(B) $\frac{3}{5}$

(C) $\frac{2}{3}$

(D) $\frac{3}{4}$

(E) $\frac{3}{2}$

2. Adam had a baseball card collection. One day he gave Noah $\frac{1}{5}$ of cards; the following day he gave Pete $\frac{3}{8}$ of the cards he had left. What fraction of his original collection did Adam still have?

(A) $\frac{3}{10}$

(B) $\frac{17}{40}$

(C) $\frac{1}{2}$

(D) $\frac{23}{40}$

(E) $\frac{7}{10}$

3. For how many integers n between 20 and 30 is it true that $\frac{3}{n}$, $\frac{5}{n}$, and $\frac{7}{n}$ are all in lowest terms?

(A) 2
(B) 3
(C) 4
(D) 5
(E) 6

4. What fractional part of a week is 63 hours?

(A) $\frac{7}{24}$

(B) $\frac{3}{8}$

(C) $\frac{24}{63}$

(D) $\frac{4}{7}$

(E) $\frac{7}{9}$

5. If $\frac{3}{7}$ of a number is 35, what is $\frac{6}{7}$ of that number?

(A) 6
(B) 15
(C) 17.5
(D) 30
(E) 70

GRID-IN QUESTIONS

6. $\frac{5}{8}$ of 24 is equal to $\frac{15}{7}$ of what number?

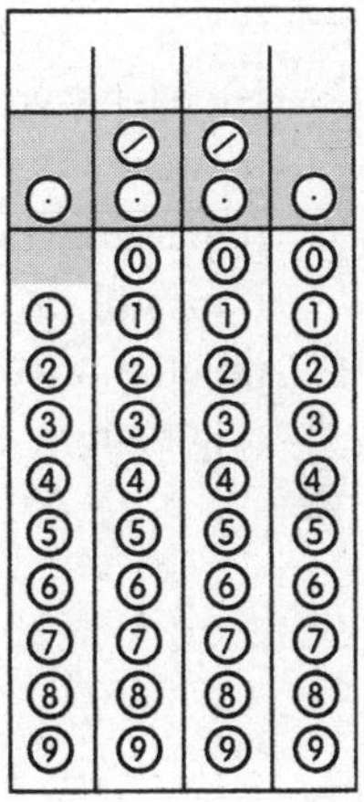

7. If $5a = 3$ and $3b = 5$, what is the value of $\frac{a}{b}$?

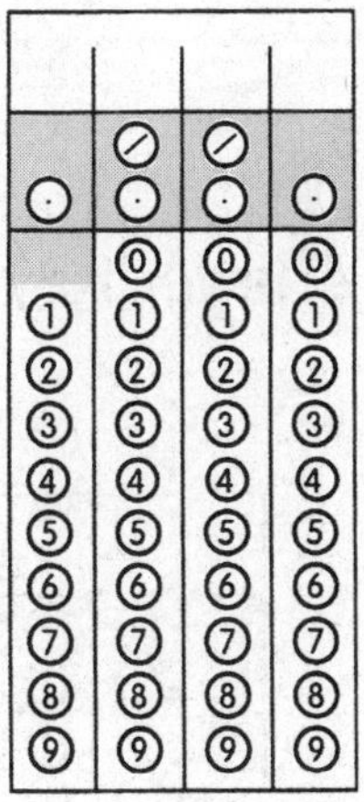

8. What is a possible value of x if $\frac{2}{3} < \frac{1}{x} < \frac{7}{9}$?

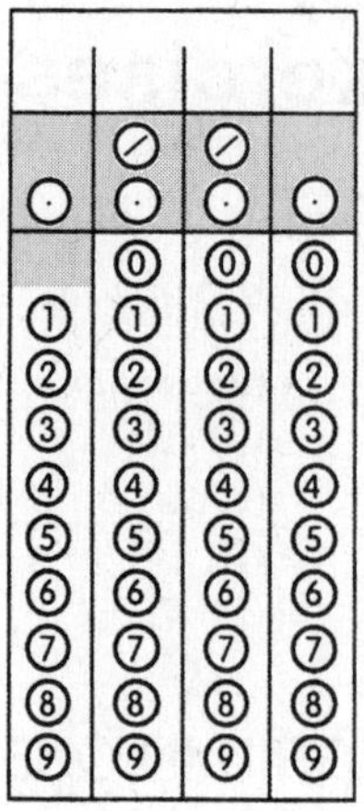

9. Michael gave $\frac{1}{12}$ of his money to Sally and $\frac{1}{5}$ of his remaining money to Heidi. If he still had \$704, how much money did he have originally?

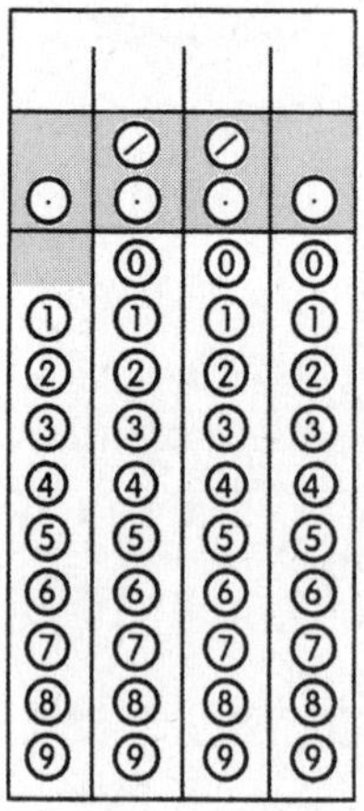

10. Let $A = \{1, 2, 3\}$ and $B = \{2, 3, 4\}$, and let C be the set consisting of the 9 fractions whose numerators are in A and whose denominators are in B. What is the product of all of the numbers in C?

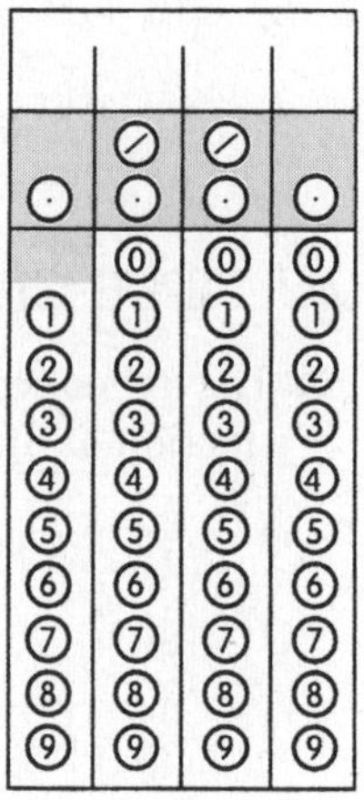

Answer Key

1. A

2. C

3. C

4. B

5. E

6.

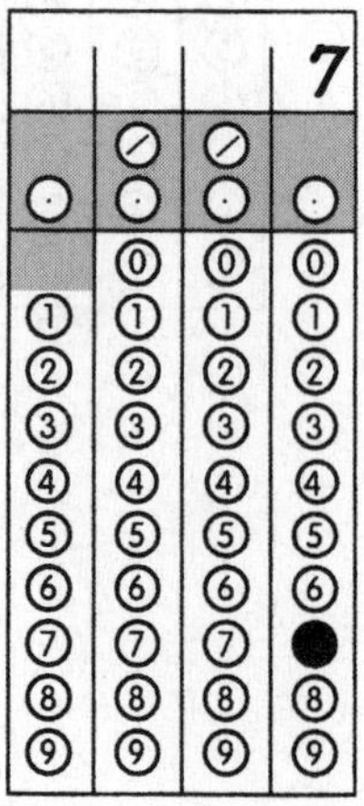

7.

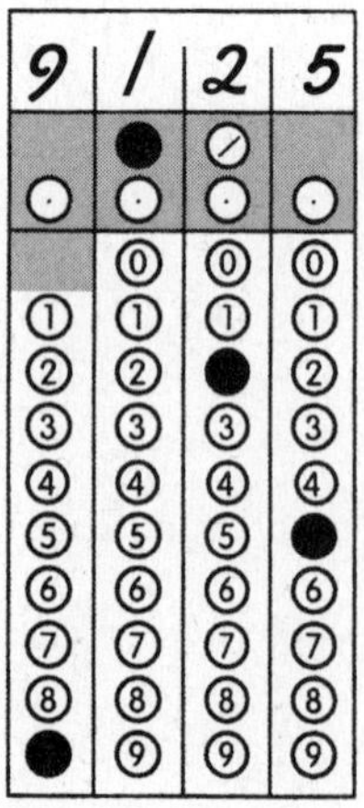

8.

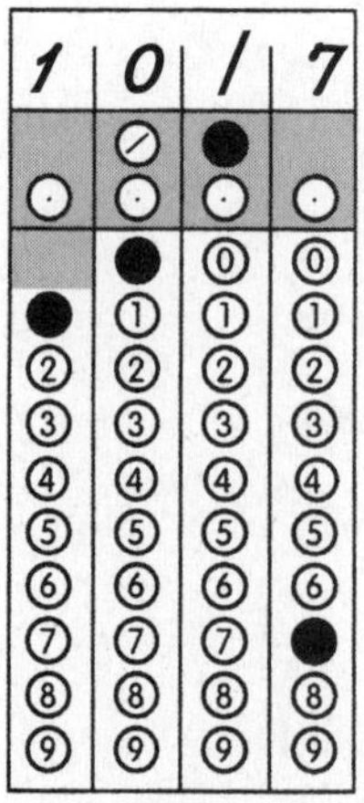

9.

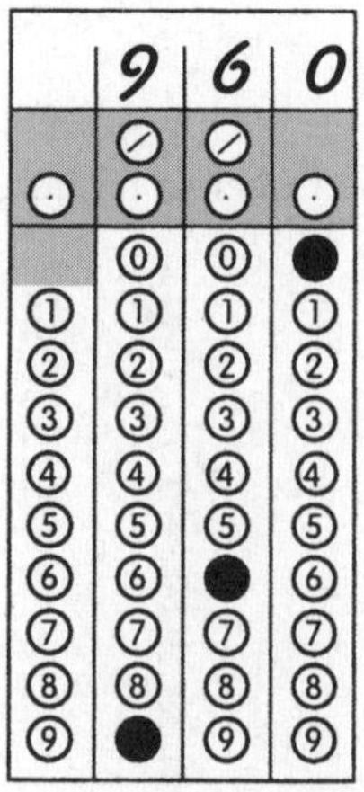

10.

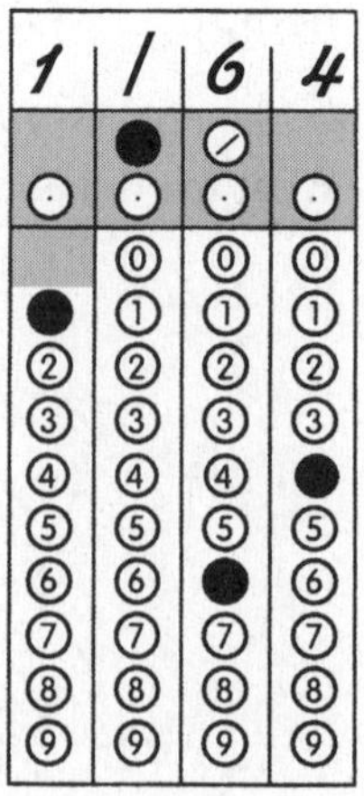

7-C PERCENTS

The word *percent* means hundredth. We use the symbol % to express the word "percent." For example, "15 percent" means "15 hundredths" and can be written with a % symbol, as a fraction, or as a decimal: $15\% = \frac{15}{100} = .15$.

Key Fact C1

To convert a percent to a decimal or a percent to a fraction, follow these rules:

1. To convert a percent to a decimal, drop the % symbol and move the decimal point two places to the left, adding zeros if necessary. (Remember that we assume that there is a decimal point to the right of any whole number.)
2. To convert a percent to a fraction, drop the % symbol, write the number over 100, and reduce.

$$25\% = .25 = \frac{25}{100} = \frac{1}{4} \qquad 100\% = 1.00 = \frac{100}{100}$$

$$12.5\% = .125 = \frac{12.5}{100} = \frac{125}{1000} = \frac{1}{8}$$

$$1\% = .01 = \frac{1}{100} \qquad \frac{1}{2}\% = .5\% = .005 = \frac{.5}{100} = \frac{1}{200}$$

$$250\% = 2.50 = \frac{250}{100} = \frac{5}{2}$$

Key Fact C2

To convert a decimal to a percent or a fraction to a percent, follow these rules:

1. To convert a decimal to a percent, move the decimal point two places to the right, adding zeros if necessary, and add the % symbol.
2. To convert a fraction to a percent, first convert the fraction to a decimal, and then complete step 1.

$$.375 = 37.5\% \qquad .3 = 30\% \qquad 1.25 = 125\% \qquad 10 = 1000\%$$

$$\frac{3}{4} = .75 = 75\% \qquad \frac{1}{3} = .33333... = 33.333...\% = 33\frac{1}{3}\%$$

You should be familiar with the following basic conversions.

$$\frac{1}{4} = 25\% \qquad \frac{1}{3} = 33\frac{1}{3}\% \qquad \frac{1}{2} = 50\% \qquad \frac{2}{3} = 66\frac{2}{3}\% \qquad \frac{3}{4} = 75\%$$

Any problem involving percents can be done on your calculator (even if your calculator doesn't have a % key): to find 25% of 32, write 25% as a decimal and multiply: $32 \times .25 = 8$. Consider these three questions:

(i) What is 35% of 200?
(ii) 70 is 35% of what number?
(iii) 70 is what percent of 200?

Each question can be answered easily by using your calculator, but you must first set up the question properly so that you know what to multiply or divide. In each case, there is one unknown; call it x. Now, just translate each sentence, replacing "is" with "=" and the unknown by x.

(i) $x = 35\%$ of $200 \Rightarrow x = .35 \times 200 = 70$.
(ii) $70 = 35\%$ of $x \Rightarrow 70 = .35x \Rightarrow x = 70 \div .35 = 200$.
(iii) $70 = x\%$ of $200 \Rightarrow 70 = \frac{x}{100}(200) \Rightarrow x = 35$.

Another way to handle questions such as these is to set up the proportion $\frac{is}{of} = \frac{\%}{100}$. To use this method, think of "is," "of," and "%" as variables.

In each percent problem you are given two of them and need to find the third, which you label x. Of course, you then solve such equations by cross-multiplying. For example, the three problems we just solved could be handled as follows:

(i) <u>What</u> <u>is</u> 35% of 200? (Let x = the "is" number.)

$$\frac{x}{200} = \frac{35}{100} \Rightarrow 100x = 35(200) = 7000 \Rightarrow x = 70$$

(ii) 70 is 35% <u>of</u> <u>what</u> <u>number</u>? (Let x = the "of" number.)

$$\frac{70}{x} = \frac{35}{100} \Rightarrow 7000 = 35x \Rightarrow x = 200$$

(iii) 70 is <u>what</u> <u>%</u> of 200? (Let x = the %.)

$$\frac{70}{200} = \frac{x}{100} \Rightarrow 200x = 7000 \Rightarrow x = 35$$

EXAMPLE 1

Justin gave 30% of his baseball cards to Judy and 25% to Lior. If he still had 540 cards, how many did he have originally?

Solution. Originally, Justin had 100% of the cards (all of them). Since he gave away 55% of them, he had 100% − 55% = 45% of them left. So, 540 is 45% of what number? $540 = .45x \Rightarrow x = 540 \div .45 = 1200$.

EXAMPLE 2

After Sharon gave 157 baseball cards to Zach and 95 to Samir, she still had 348 left. What percent of her cards did Sharon give away?

Solution. Sharon gave away a total of 252 cards and had 348 left. Therefore, she started with 252 + 348 = 600 cards. So, 252 is what percent of 600?

$$252 = \frac{x}{\cancel{100}}(\overset{6}{\cancel{600}}) \Rightarrow 6x = 252 \Rightarrow x = 252 \div 6 = 42.$$

Sharon gave away 42% of her cards.

Key Fact C3

For any positive number a: $a\%$ of 100 is a. For example: 17.2% of 100 is 17.2; 600% of 100 is 600; and $\frac{1}{5}\%$ of $100 = \frac{1}{5}$.

TACTIC

C1 **In any problem involving percents, try to use the number 100.**

EXAMPLE 3

In 1980 the populations of Madison and Monroe were the same. From 1980 to 1990, however, the population of Madison increased by 25% while the population of Monroe decreased by 25%. In 1990, the population of Monroe was what percent of the population of Madison?

(A) 25%
(B) 50%
(C) 60%
(D) $66\frac{2}{3}\%$
(E) $166\frac{2}{3}\%$

Solution. Assume that in 1980 the population of each town was 100. Then, since 25% of 100 is 25, in 1990, the populations were 100 + 25 = 125 (Madison) and 100 − 25 = 75 (Monroe). Then, in 1990, Monroe's population was $\frac{75}{125} = \frac{3}{5} = 60\%$ of Madison's.

Key Fact C4

For any positive numbers a and b: $a\%$ of $b = b\%$ of a.

Percent Increase and Percent Decrease

Key Fact C5

The ***percent increase*** of a quantity is

$$\frac{\text{the actual increase}}{\text{the original amount}} \times 100\%.$$

The ***percent decrease*** of a quantity is

$$\frac{\text{the actual decrease}}{\text{the original amount}} \times 100\%.$$

For example:

- If the price of a radio goes from \$60 to \$75, the actual increase is \$15, and the percent increase is $\frac{15}{60} \times 100\% = \frac{1}{4} \times 100\% = 25\%$.
- If a \$75 radio is on sale for \$60, the actual decrease in price is \$15, and the percent decrease is $\frac{\cancel{15}^{1}}{\cancel{75}_{5}} \times 100\% = \frac{1}{5} \times 100\% = 20\%$.

CAUTION: Percents over 100%, which come up most often on questions involving percent increases, are often confusing for many students. Be sure you understand that 100% of a particular number is that number, 200% of a number is 2 times the number, and 1000% of a number is 10 times the number.

Notice that the percent increase in going from 60 to 75 is *not* the same as the percent decrease in going from 75 to 60.

If the value of an investment rises from \$1000 to \$5000, the investment is now worth 5 times, or 500%, as much as it was originally, but there has been only a 400% increase in value:

$$\frac{\text{the actual increase}}{\text{the original amount}} \times 100\% =$$

$$\frac{4000}{1000} \times 100\% = 4 \times 100\% = 400\%.$$

EXAMPLE 4

The value of an investment doubled every 5 years from 1980 to 1995. What was the percent increase in the value during this time?

Solution. The value doubled 3 times from, say, \$100 in 1980 to \$200 in 1985, to \$400 in 1990, and to \$800 in 1995. So the value in 1995 was 8 times the value in 1980, but this was an increase of \$700 or 700%.

Practice Exercises

MULTIPLE-CHOICE QUESTIONS

1. Ron bought a \$60 sweater on sale at 10% off. How much did he pay, including 5% sales tax?

(A) \$51.00
(B) \$53.50
(C) \$55.00
(D) \$56.70
(E) \$57.00

2. What is 5% of 10% of 40%?

(A) 0.002%
(B) 0.2%
(C) 2%
(D) 20%
(E) 2,000%

3. What percent of 25 is b?

(A) $\frac{b}{25}$
(B) $\frac{b}{4}$
(C) $\frac{25}{b}$
(D) $\frac{4}{b}$
(E) $4b$

4. 10 is $\frac{1}{10}$% of what number?

(A) .01
(B) 1
(C) 100
(D) 1,000
(E) 10,000

5. On a test consisting of 80 questions, Susan answered 75% of the first 60 questions correctly. What percent of the other 20 questions does she need to answer correctly for her grade on the entire exam to be 80%?

(A) 85%
(B) 87.5%
(C) 90%
(D) 95%
(E) 100%

GRID-IN QUESTIONS

6. A supermarket reduced the price per pound of whole chickens by 20%. How many pounds of chicken can now be purchased for the amount of money that used to buy 20 pounds of chicken?

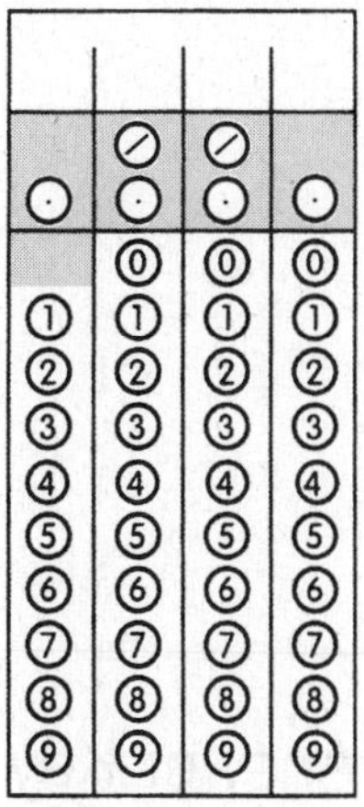

7. If c is a positive number, 300% of c is what percent of $300c$?

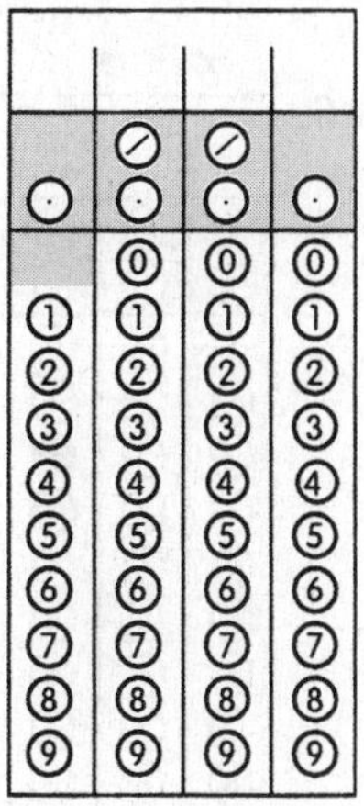

8. If 25 students took an exam and 7 of them failed, what percent of them passed?

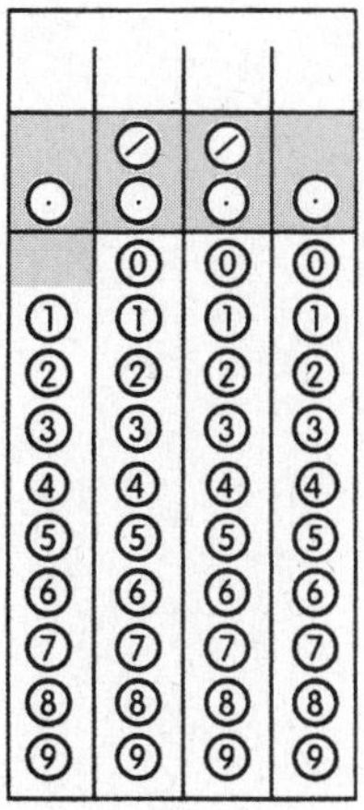

9. A college has 3000 students. If 23.5% of them are freshmen, 29.2% of them are sophomores, and 27% of them are juniors, how many are seniors?

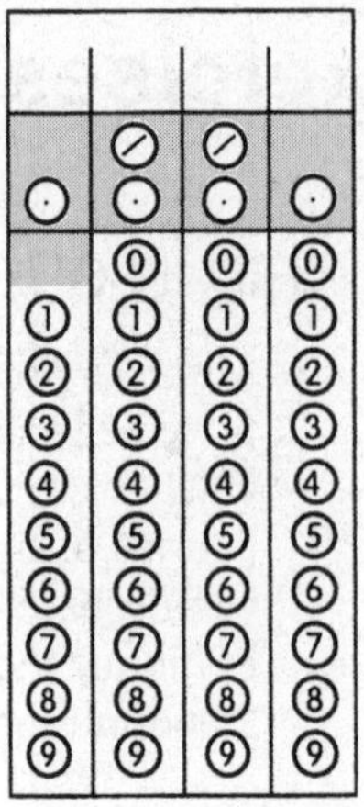

10. There are twice as many girls as boys in a science class. If 30% of the girls and 45% of the boys have already completed their lab reports, what percent of the students have not yet finished their reports?

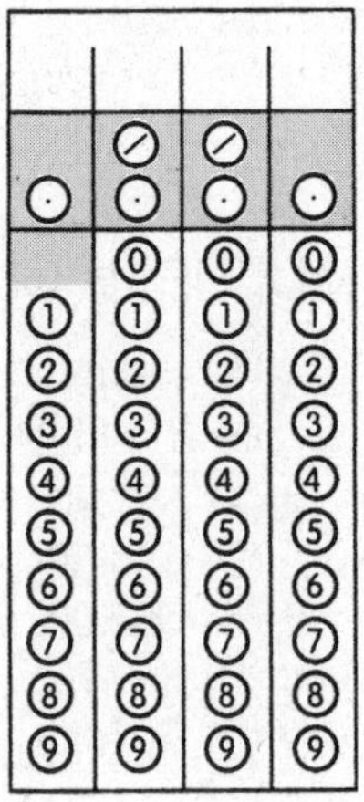

Answer Key

1. D **2.** B **3.** E **4.** E **5.** D

6.

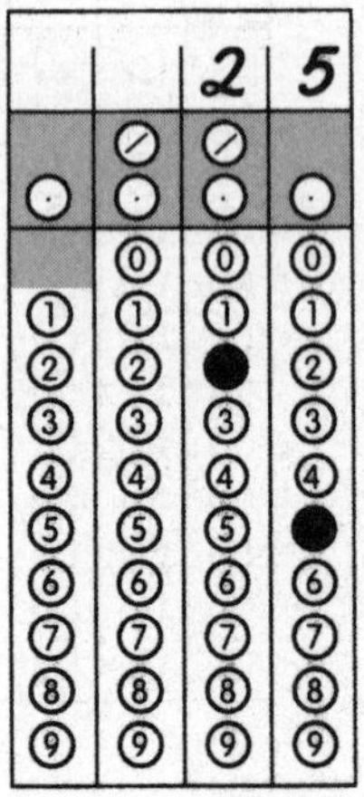

7.

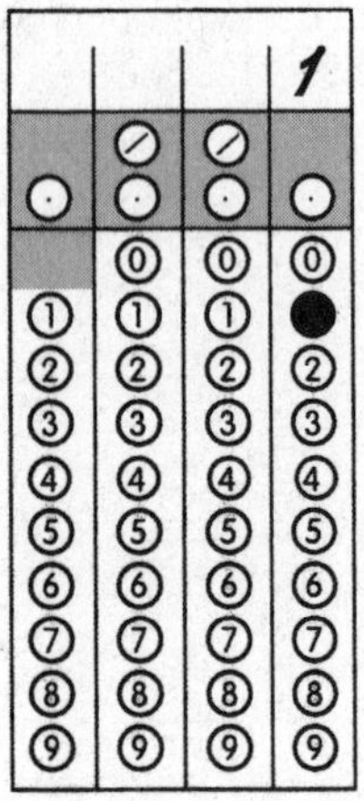

8.

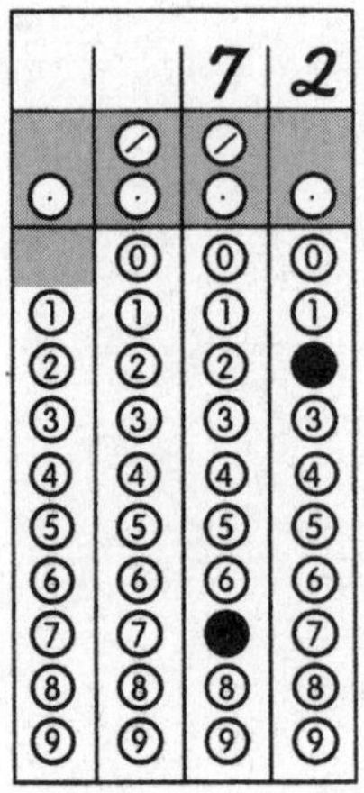

9.

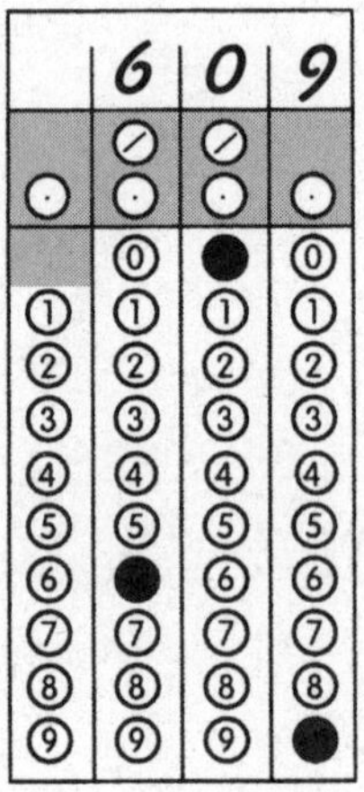

10.

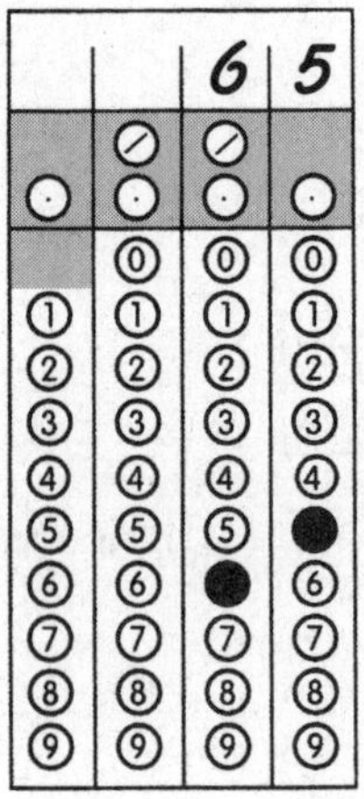

7-D RATIOS AND PROPORTIONS

A ***ratio*** is a fraction that compares two quantities that are measured in the *same* units. One quantity is the numerator of the fraction, and the other quantity is the denominator.

For example, if there are 6 boys and 16 girls in the chess club, we say that the ratio of the number of boys to the number of girls in the club is 6 to 16, or $\frac{6}{16}$, often written as 6:16. Since a ratio is just a fraction, it can be reduced or converted to a decimal or a percent. The following are all different ways to express the same ratio:

6 to 16   6:16 $\frac{6}{16}$ 3 to 8   3:8 $\frac{3}{8}$ .375   37.5%

Key Fact D1

If a set of objects is divided into two groups in the ratio of a:b, then the first group contains $\frac{a}{a+b}$ of the objects and the second group contains $\frac{b}{a+b}$ of the objects.

EXAMPLE 1

A jar contains only red and blue marbles. If the ratio of the number of blue marbles to the number of red marbles in the jar is 2:3, what percent of the marbles are red?

Solution. The red marbles constitute $\frac{3}{2+3} = \frac{3}{5} = 60\%$ of the total number.

EXAMPLE 2

If 35% of the students in the honor society are male, what is the ratio of male students to female students in the society?

Solution. Assume that there are 100 students in the society; then 35 of them are male, and $100 - 35 = 65$ of them are female. So, the ratio of males to females is $\frac{35}{65} = \frac{7}{13}$.

HELPFUL HINT: In problems involving percents, the best number to use is 100.

If we know a ratio, we *cannot* determine from that fact alone how many objects there are. In Example 1 above, since the ratio of blue marbles to red marbles is 2:3, there *might be* 2 blue marbles and 3 red ones, but *not necessarily*—there might be 200 blue marbles and 300 red ones, since the ratio 200:300 clearly reduces to 2:3. In the same way, all of the following are possibilities for the distribution of marbles.

Blue	4	6	8	20	400	8,000	**$2x$**
Red	6	9	12	30	600	12,000	**$3x$**

The important thing to observe is that the number of red marbles can be *any* multiple of 3, as long as the number of blue marbles is the *same* multiple of 2.

Key Fact D2

If two numbers are in the ratio of a:b, then for some number x, the first number is ax and the second number is bx.

TACTIC

D1

In any ratio problem, write the letter *x* after each number and use some given information to solve for *x*.

EXAMPLE 3

If the ratio of boys to girls at a pep rally is 4:5, which of the following CANNOT be the number of children at the pep rally?

(A) 27
(B) 45
(C) 108
(D) 120
(E) 360

Solution. If $4x$ and $5x$ are the number of boys and girls at the pep rally, respectively, then the number of children present is $4x + 5x = 9x$. Therefore, the number of children must be a multiple of 9. Only 120 (Choice D), is not divisible by 9.

Ratios can be extended to three or four or more terms. For example, we can say that the ratio of freshmen to sophomores to juniors to seniors in the school play is 2:3:5:3, which means that for every 2 freshmen in the play, there are 3 sophomores, 5 juniors, and 2 seniors.

EXAMPLE 4

If the measures of the three angles in a triangle are in the ratio of 5:6:7, what is the measure of the largest angle?

Solution. Let the measures of the three angles be $5x$, $6x$, and $7x$. Since in any triangle the sum of the measures of the three angles is 180° (**KEY FACT J1**):

$$5x + 6x + 7x = 180 \Rightarrow 18x = 180 \Rightarrow x = 10.$$

Therefore, the measure of the largest angle is $7 \times 10 = 70°$.

A ***proportion*** is an equation that states that two ratios are equivalent. Since ratios are just fractions, any equation such as $\frac{4}{6} = \frac{10}{15}$, in which each side is a single fraction, is a proportion. Usually, the proportions you encounter on the PSAT involve one or more variables.

TACTIC

D2

Solve proportions by cross-multiplying: if $\frac{a}{b} = \frac{c}{d}$, then $ad = bc$.

EXAMPLE 5

If $\frac{2}{7} = \frac{x}{91}$, what is the value of x?

Solution. Cross-multiply: $2(91) = 7x \Rightarrow 182 = 7x \Rightarrow x = 26$.

A ***rate*** is a fraction that compares two quantities measured in *different* units. The word *per* often appears in rate problems: miles per hour, dollars per week, cents per ounce, children per classroom, and so on.

TACTIC D3

Set up rate problems just like ratio problems.
Solve the proportions by cross-multiplying.

EXAMPLE 6

Susan completed 25 math exercises in 35 minutes. At this rate, how many exercises can she do in 42 minutes?

Solution. Handle this rate problem exactly like a ratio problem. Set up a proportion and cross-multiply:

$$\frac{\text{exercises}}{\text{minutes}} = \frac{25}{35} = \frac{x}{42} \Rightarrow 35x = 25 \times 42 = 1050 \Rightarrow x = 30.$$

On the PSAT, many rate problems involve only variables. These problems are handled in exactly the same way.

EXAMPLE 7

If a apples cost c cents, how many apples can be bought for d dollars?

(A) $100acd$

(B) $\frac{100d}{ac}$

(C) $\frac{ad}{100c}$

(D) $\frac{c}{100ad}$

(E) $\frac{100ad}{c}$

Solution. First change d dollars to $100d$ cents, and set up a proportion: $\frac{\text{apples}}{\text{cents}} = \frac{a}{c} = \frac{x}{100d}$. Now cross-multiply:

$$100ad = cx \Rightarrow x = \frac{100ad}{c} \text{ (Choice E).}$$

Rate problems are examples of ***direct variation***. We say that one variable ***varies directly*** with a second variable or that the two variables are ***directly proportional*** if their quotient is a constant. So if y is directly proportional to x, there is a constant k, such that $\frac{y}{x} = k$. The constant is the rate of increase or decrease. In Example 6, the number of math exercises Susan does varies directly with the number of minutes she spends on them. Susan's rate of solving is $\frac{5}{7}$ exercises per minute.

$$\text{The quotient } \frac{\text{exercises}}{\text{minutes}} \text{ is constant: } \frac{25}{35} = \frac{5}{7} \text{ and } \frac{30}{42} = \frac{5}{7}.$$

Notice that when two quantities vary directly, as the first quantity increases or decreases, so does the other. In Example 6 as the number of exercises increases, the number of minutes it takes Susan to do them also increases.

EXAMPLE 8

If x and y are directly proportional and $x = 12$ when $y = 3$, what is x when $y = 12$?

Solution. Since x and y are directly proportional, their quotient is a constant. So $\frac{12}{3} = 4 = \frac{x}{12} \Rightarrow x = 48$.

Occasionally on the PSAT you will encounter problems in which as one quantity increases, the other decreases. Problems such as these are usually examples of ***inverse variation***. We say that one variable ***varies inversely*** with a second variable or that the two variables are ***inversely proportional*** if their product is a constant. So if y is inversely proportional to x, there is a constant k such that $xy = k$.

EXAMPLE 9

If x and y are inversely proportional and $x = 12$ when $y = 3$, what is x when $y = 12$?

Solution. Since x and y are inversely proportional, their product is a constant. Since $xy = 12 \times 3 = 36$, if $y = 12$, then $x(12) = 36$, and so $x = 3$.

EXAMPLE 10

A landscaper has enough money on hand to hire six workers for ten days. Assuming each worker earns the same amount of money per day, for how many days could the landscaper meet his payroll if he hires fifteen workers?

(A) 4
(B) 6
(C) 12
(D) 15
(E) 25

Solution. As the number of workers increases, the number of days the money will last decreases. So this is an example of inverse variation. The product (workers) × (days) remains constant.

$$(6 \text{ workers}) \times (10 \text{ days}) = 60 \text{ worker-days} = (15 \text{ workers}) \times (d \text{ days}) \Rightarrow d = 4.$$

Practice Exercises

MULTIPLE-CHOICE QUESTIONS

1. If the ratio of boys to girls in the French Club is 2:3, what percent of the club members are girls?

   (A) $33\frac{1}{3}\%$
   (B) 40%
   (C) 60%
   (D) $66\frac{2}{3}\%$
   (E) It cannot be determined from the information given.

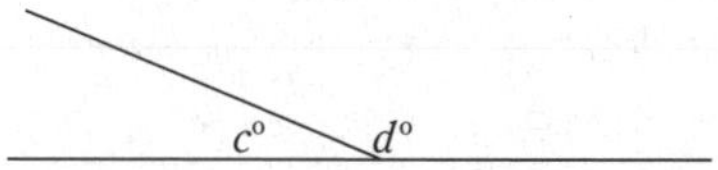

Note: Figure not drawn to scale.

2. In the diagram above, $c{:}d = 5{:}7$. What is $d - c$?

   (A) 15
   (B) 30
   (C) 75
   (D) 105
   (E) 165

3. The measures of the three angles in a triangle are in the ratio of 1:1:2. Which of the following must be true?

   I. The triangle is isosceles.
   II. The triangle is a right triangle.
   III. The triangle is equilateral.

   (A) None
   (B) I only
   (C) II only
   (D) I and II only
   (E) I and III only

4. Gilda can grade t tests in $\frac{1}{x}$ hours. At this rate, how many tests can she grade in x hours?

   (A) tx
   (B) tx^2
   (C) $\frac{1}{t}$
   (D) $\frac{x}{t}$
   (E) $\frac{1}{tx}$

5. Kerry can polish i inches of a railing in m minutes. At this rate, how many feet can he polish in h hours?

   (A) $\frac{5hi}{m}$
   (B) $\frac{60hi}{m}$
   (C) $\frac{hi}{12m}$
   (D) $\frac{5m}{hi}$
   (E) $5him$

GRID-IN QUESTIONS

6. If $\frac{a}{9} = \frac{9}{2a}$, what is the value of a^2?

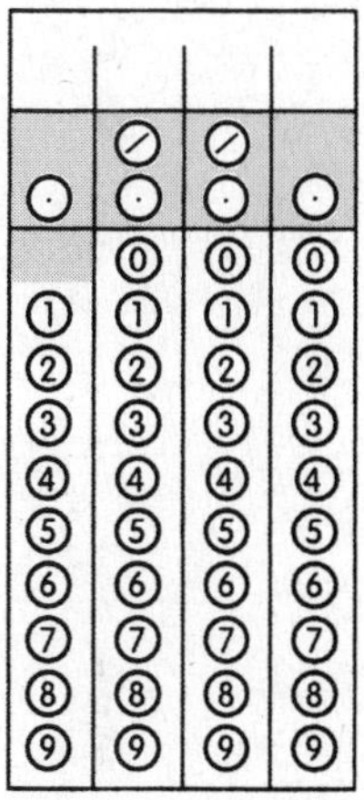

7. Roselle can read 36 pages per hour. At this rate, how many pages can she read in 36 minutes?

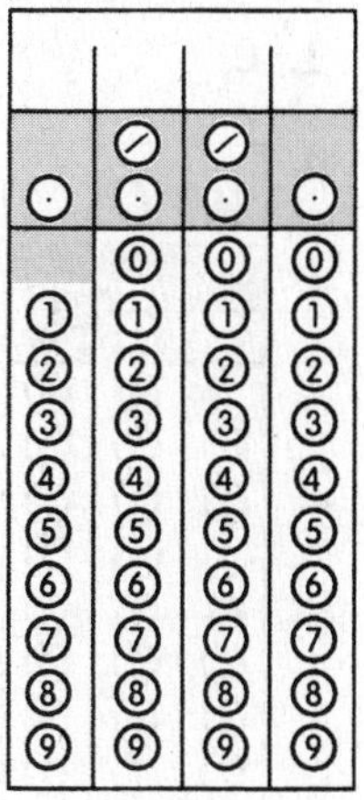

8. If $3a = 2b$ and $3b = 5c$, what is the ratio of a to c?

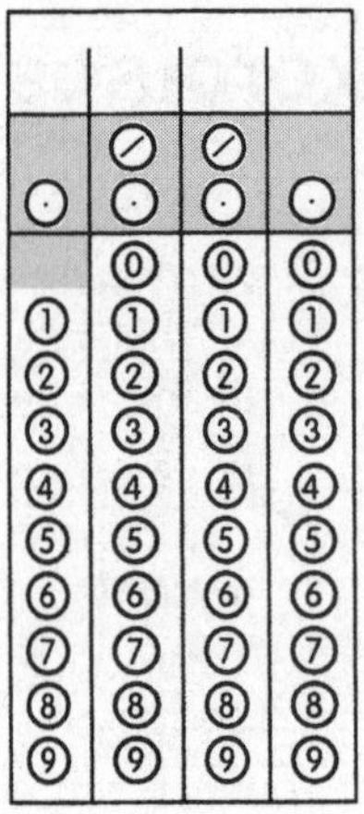

10. If a varies directly with b^2, and if $b = 4$ when $a = 3$, what is the value of a when $b = 8$?

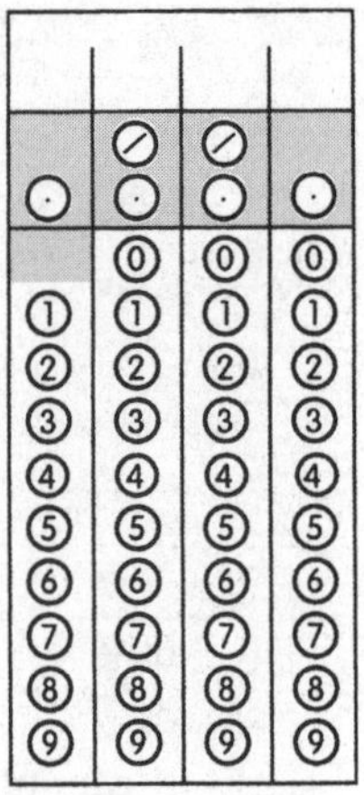

9. In a quadrilateral, the ratio of the measures of the four angles is 5:6:6:7. What is the degree measure of the largest angle?

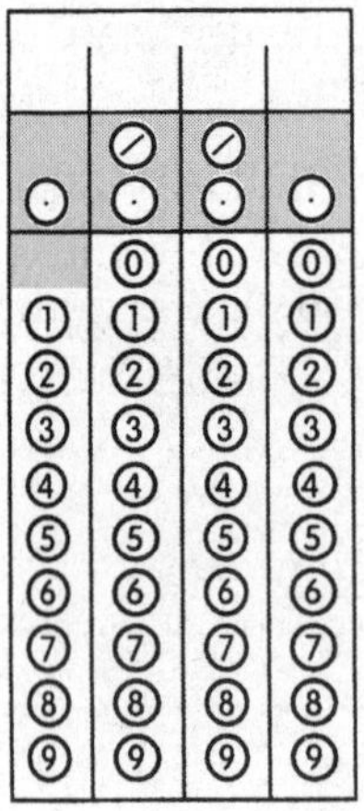

Answer Key

1. C **2.** B **3.** D **4.** B **5.** A

6.

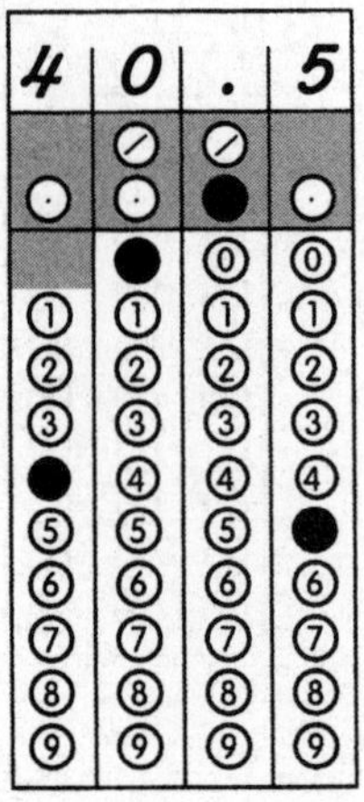

7.

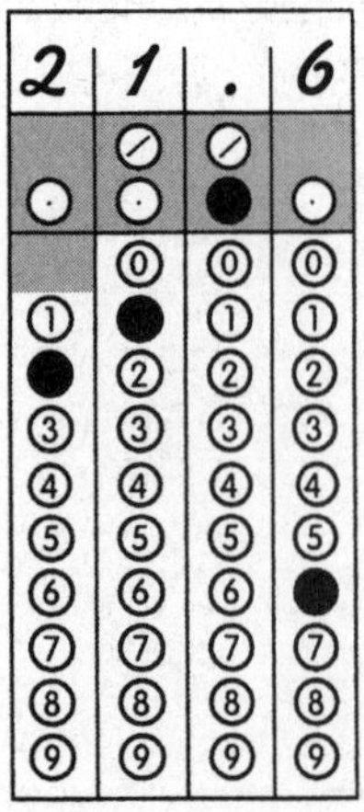

8.

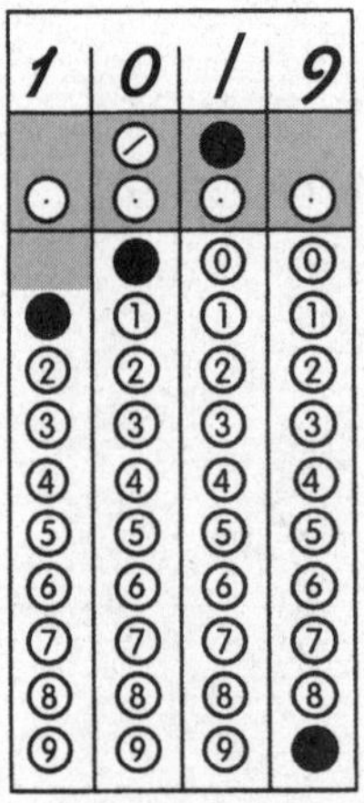

9.

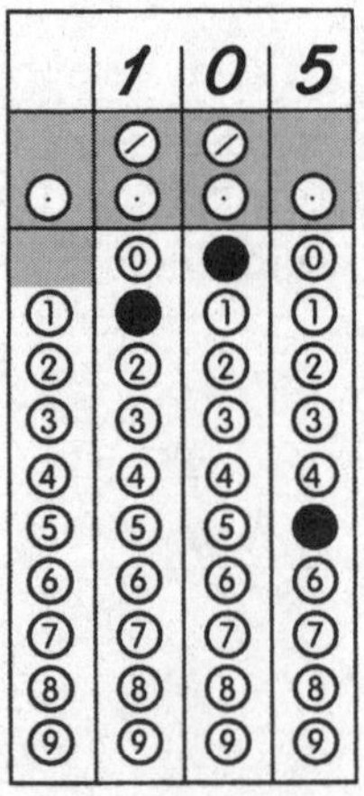

10.

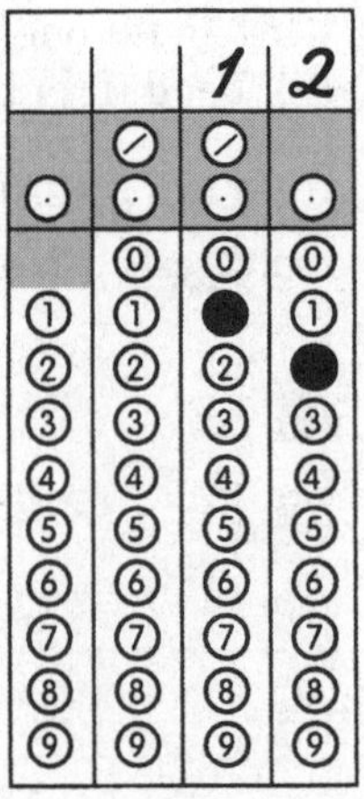

7-E AVERAGES

The ***average*** of a set of n numbers is the sum of those numbers divided by n.

$$\text{Average} = \frac{\text{the sum of the } n \text{ numbers}}{n} \quad \text{or simply} \quad A = \frac{\text{sum}}{n}.$$

If you took three math tests so far this year and your grades were 81, 93, and 78, to calculate your average, you would add the three grades and divide by 3:

$$\frac{81 + 93 + 78}{3} = \frac{252}{3} = 84.$$

The technical name for this is *arithmetic mean*, and on the PSAT those words always appear in parentheses—for example, "What is the average (arithmetic mean) of 81, 93, and 78?"

Very often on the PSAT, you are *not* asked to find an average; rather, you are given the average of a set of numbers and asked to provide some other information. The key to solving all of these problems is to first find the sum of the numbers. Since $A = \frac{\text{sum}}{n}$, multiplying both sides by n yields this equation: sum $= nA$.

Key Fact E1

If the average of a set of n numbers is A, the sum of those numbers is nA.

EXAMPLE 1

The average (arithmetic mean) of Carol's grades on the 6 French tests that she has taken this year is 86. If her average after the first 4 tests was 83, what was the average of her fifth and sixth tests?

(A) 84.5
(B) 87.5
(C) 89
(D) 90
(E) 92

Solution.

- Carol has earned a total of $6 \times 86 = 516$ points.
- On her first 4 tests she earned $4 \times 83 = 332$ points.
- On her last 2 tests Carol earned $516 - 332 = 184$ points.
- Carol's average on her last 2 tests is $\frac{184}{2} = 92$ (Choice E).

EXAMPLE 2

In Mr. Walsh's biology class, the average (arithmetic mean) of the grades earned by the 15 girls was 90, and the average grade earned by the 10 boys was 80. What was the class average?

The answer to this question is *not* 85. When we combine two or more averages to form a single average, we cannot take the average of the averages. We must assign each average its proper *weight*. In this case, more students earned 90 then 80, so the class average must be closer to 90 than to 80—surely greater than 85. Here is the solution.

- The 15 girls earned a total of $15 \times 90 = 1350$ points.
- The 10 boys earned a total of $10 \times 80 = 800$ points.
- Together the 25 students earned a total of $1350 + 800 = 2150$ points.
- The class average was $2150 \div 25 = 86$.

The solution to Example 2 can be expressed as a single fraction:

$$\frac{15(90) + 10(80)}{25} = \frac{1350 + 800}{25} = \frac{2150}{25} = 86.$$

Two other terms that are associated with averages are ***median*** and ***mode***. In a set of n numbers that are arranged in increasing order, the ***median*** is the middle number (if n is odd) or the average of the two middle numbers (if n is even). The ***mode*** is the number in the set that occurs most often.

EXAMPLE 3

In 1998, Judith sold 9 paintings. The selling prices were: \$500, \$1100, \$1200, \$500, \$1200, \$5000, \$700, \$500, \$4000. What is the average (arithmetic mean) of the median and mode of this set of data?

Solution. The first step is to write the data in increasing order:

500, 500, 500, 700, <u>1100</u>, 1200, 1200, 4000, 5000.

The median is 1100, the middle number. The mode is 500, the number that appears more times than any other. The average of the median and the mode is

$$\frac{1100 + 500}{2} = \frac{1600}{2} = 800.$$

Practice Exercises

MULTIPLE-CHOICE QUESTIONS

1. If the average (arithmetic mean) of 15, 16, 17, and w is 18, what is the value of w ?

(A) 16.5
(B) 18
(C) 24
(D) 48
(E) 72

2. Linda's average (arithmetic mean) on 4 tests is 80. What does she need on her fifth test to raise her average to 84?

(A) 82
(B) 84
(C) 92
(D) 96
(E) 100

3. If $x + y = 5$, $y + z = 8$, and $z + x = 9$, what is the average (arithmetic mean) of x, y, and z?

(A) $\frac{11}{3}$
(B) $\frac{11}{2}$
(C) $\frac{22}{3}$
(D) 11
(E) 22

4. If $a + b = 3(c + d)$, which of the following is the average (arithmetic mean) of a, b, c, and d ?

(A) $\frac{c+d}{4}$
(B) $\frac{3(c+d)}{8}$
(C) $\frac{c+d}{2}$
(D) $\frac{3(c+d)}{4}$
(E) $c + d$

5. Which of the following is the average (arithmetic mean) of $x^2 - 10$, $30 - x^2$, and $6x + 10$?

(A) $2x + 10$
(B) $2x + 30$
(C) $3x + 15$
(D) $2x^2 + 6x + 30$
(E) $6x + 10$

GRID-IN QUESTIONS

6. What is the average (arithmetic mean) of the positive integers from 1 to 50, inclusive?

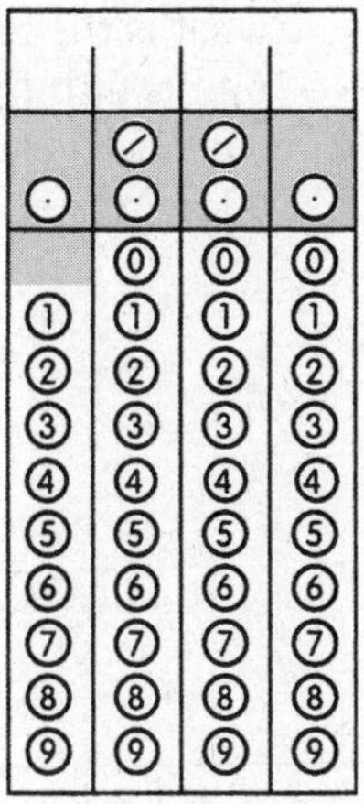

7. If $20a + 20b = 70$, what is the average (arithmetic mean) of a and b?

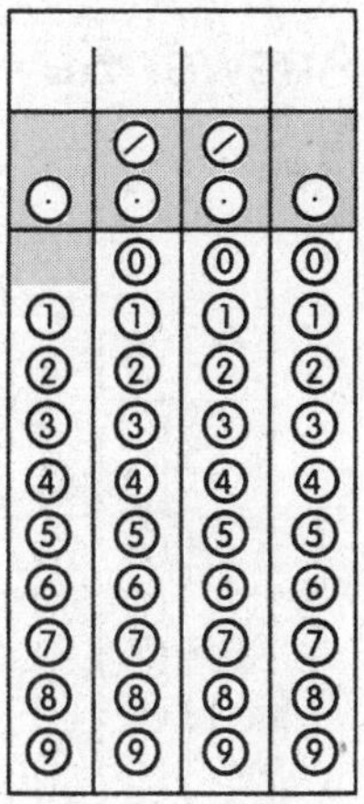

8. What is the average (arithmetic mean), in degrees, of the measures of the five angles in a pentagon?

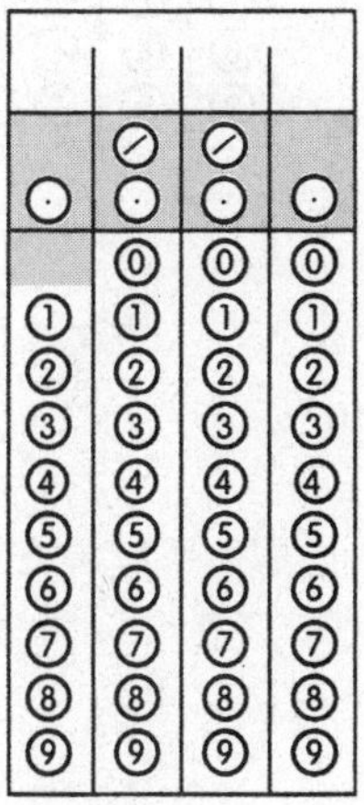

9. Jason's average (arithmetic mean) on 4 tests is 80. Assuming he can earn no more than 100 on any test, what is the least he can earn on his fifth test and still have a chance for an 85 average after 7 tests?

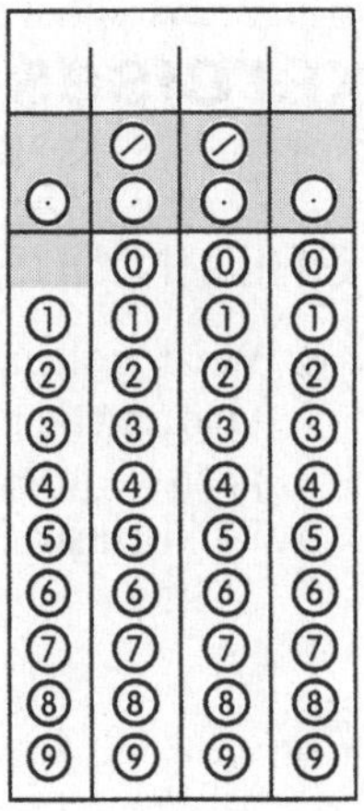

10. Let M be the median and m the mode of the following set of numbers: 20, 80, 30, 50, 80, 100. What is the average (arithmetic mean) of M and m?

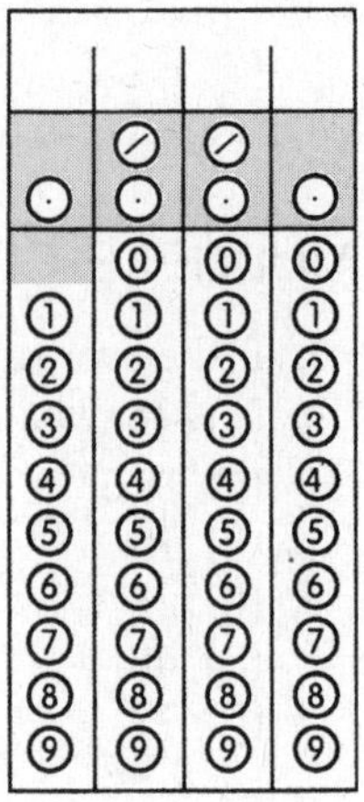

Answer Key

1. C **2.** E **3.** A **4.** E **5.** A

6.

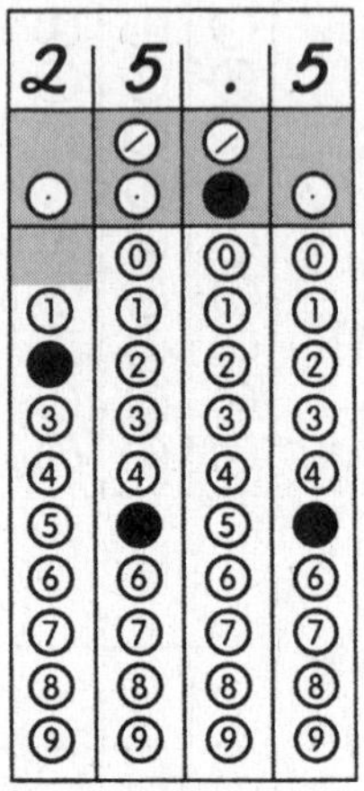

7.

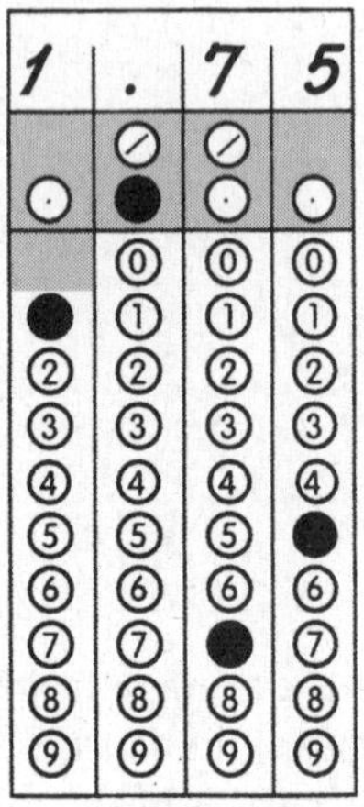

8.

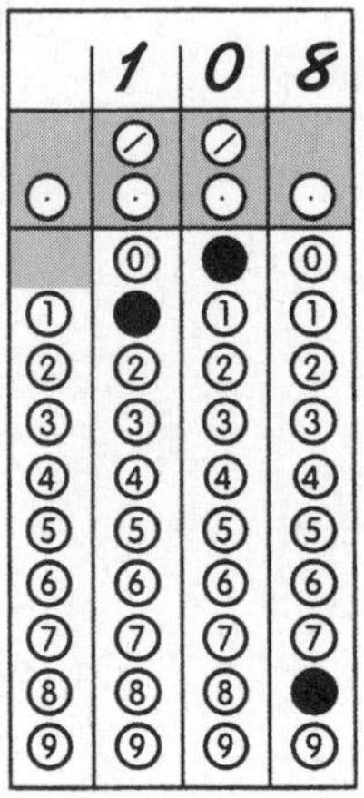

9.

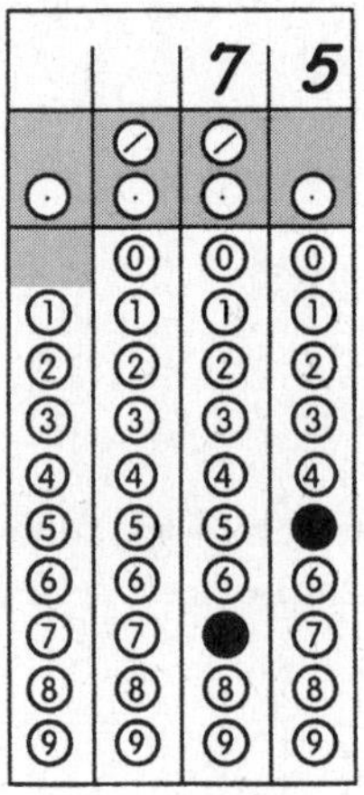

10.

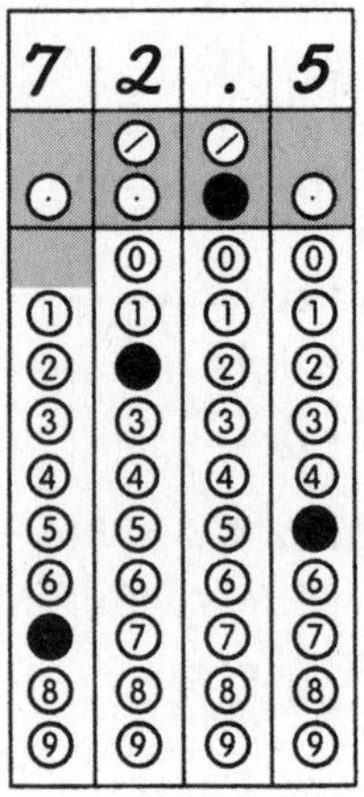

Algebra

For the PSAT you need to know only a small part of the algebra normally taught in a high school elementary algebra course and none of the material taught in an intermediate or advanced algebra course. In Sections 7-F, 7-G, and 7-H, we will review only those topics that you absolutely need for the PSAT.

7-F POLYNOMIALS

Even though the terms *monomial, binomial, trinomial,* and *polynomial* are not used on the PSAT, you need to be able to work with simple polynomials, and these terms will make it easy to discuss the important concepts.

- A ***monomial*** is any number or variable or product of numbers and variables. Each of the following are monomials:

$$3 \qquad -4 \qquad x \qquad y \qquad 3x \qquad -4xyz \qquad 5x^3 \qquad 1.5xy^2 \qquad a^3b^4$$

The number that appears in front of the variables in a monomial is called the ***coefficient***. The coefficient of $5x^3$ is 5. If there is no number, the coefficient is 1 or -1, because x means $1x$ and $-ab^2$ means $-1ab^2$.

- A ***polynomial*** is a monomial or the sum of two or more monomials. Each monomial that makes up the polynomial is called a ***term*** of the polynomial.

Polynomials that have two terms are called **binomials**, and polynomials that have three terms are called **trinomials**. The table below gives examples of each type.

Monomials	Binomials	Trinomials
x^2	$2x^2 + 3$	$x^2 + 5x - 1$
$3abc$	$3x^2 - 7$	$w^2 - 2w + 1$
$-a^2b^3$	$a^2b + b^2a$	$a^2 + 2ab + b^2$

Two terms are called *like terms* if they have exactly the same variables and exponents; they can differ only in their coefficients: $5a^2b$ and $-3a^2b$ are like terms, whereas a^2b and b^2a are not.

On the PSAT, you are often asked to evaluate a polynomial for specific values of the variables.

EXAMPLE 1

What is the value of $-2a^2b + ab$ when $a = -6$ and $b = 0.5$?

Solution. Rewrite the expression, replacing the letters a and b by the numbers -6 and 0.5, respectively. First, write each number in parentheses and then evaluate:

$$-2(-6)^2(0.5) + (-6)(0.5) =$$
$$-2(36)(0.5) + (-3) =$$
$$-36 - 3 = -39.$$

CAUTION: Be sure you follow PEMDAS: Handle exponents before the other operations. For example, in Example 1, you cannot multiply -2 by -6, get 12, and then square 12. You must first square -6, and then multiply by -2.

Key Fact F1

The only terms of a polynomial that can be combined are like terms.

Key Fact F2

To add two polynomials, put a plus sign between them, erase the parentheses, and combine like terms.

EXAMPLE 2

What is the sum of $5x^2 + 10x - 7$ and $3x^2 - 4x + 2$?

HELPFUL HINT: To add, subtract, multiply, and divide polynomials, use the usual laws of arithmetic. To avoid careless errors, write each polynomial in parentheses before performing any arithmetic operations.

Solution.
$(5x^2 + 10x - 7) + (3x^2 - 4x + 2) =$
$5x^2 + 10x - 7 + 3x^2 - 4x + 2 =$
$(5x^2 + 3x^2) + (10x - 4x) + (-7 + 2) =$
$8x^2 + 6x - 5.$

Key Fact F3

To subtract two polynomials, change the minus sign between them to a plus sign and change the sign of every term in the second parentheses. Then use **KEY FACT F2** to add them: erase the parentheses and combine like terms.

EXAMPLE 3

Subtract $3x^2 - 4x + 2$ from $5x^2 + 10x - 7$.

CAUTION: Make sure you get the order right in a subtraction problem.

Solution. Be careful. Start with the second polynomial and subtract the first:
$(5x^2 + 10x - 7) - (3x^2 - 4x + 2) =$
$(5x^2 + 10x - 7) + (-3x^2 + 4x - 2) =$
$2x^2 + 14x - 9$

Key Fact F4

To multiply monomials, first multiply their coefficients and then multiply their variables, by adding the exponents (see Section 7-A).

EXAMPLE 4

What is the product of $5xy^3z^5$ and $-2x^3y$?

Solution. $(5xy^3z^5)(-2x^2y) = 5(-2)(x)(x^3)(y^3)(y)(z^5) = -10x^4y^4z^5$.

All other polynomials are multiplied by using the distributive property.

Key Fact F5

To multiply a monomial by any polynomial, just multiply each term of the polynomial by the monomial.

EXAMPLE 5

What is the product of $2a$ and $3a^2 - 6ab + b^2$?

Solution. $2a(3a^2 - 6ab + b^2) = 6a^3 - 12a^2b + 2ab^2$.

On the PSAT, the only other polynomials that you could be asked to multiply are two binomials.

Key Fact F6

To multiply two binomials, use the so-called FOIL method, which is really nothing more than the distributive law. Multiply each term in the first parentheses by each term in the second parentheses and simplify by combining terms, if possible.

$$(2x - 7)(3x + 2) = \underbrace{(2x)(3x)}_{\text{First terms}} + \underbrace{(2x)(2)}_{\text{Outer terms}} + \underbrace{(-7)(3x)}_{\text{Inner terms}} + \underbrace{(-7)(2)}_{\text{Last terms}} = 6x^2+4x-21x-14 = 6x^2-17x-14$$

EXAMPLE 6

What is the value of $(x - 3)(x + 4) - (x - 5)(x + 6)$?

Solution. First, multiply both pairs of binomials:

$$(x - 3)(x + 4) = x^2 + 4x - 3x - 12 = x^2 + x - 12$$
$$(x - 5)(x + 6) = x^2 + 6x - 5x - 30 = x^2 + x - 30$$

Now, subtract: $(x^2 + x - 12) - (x^2 + x - 30) = x^2 + x - 12 - x^2 - x + 30 = 18$.

Key Fact F7

The three most important binomial products on the PSAT are

- $(x - y)(x + y) = x^2 - y^2$
- $(x - y)^2 = x^2 - 2xy + y^2$
- $(x + y)^2 = x^2 + 2xy + y^2$

HELPFUL HINT: If you memorize these products, you won't have to multiply the binomials out each time you need them.

EXAMPLE 7

If $a - b = 9.2$ and $a + b = 5$, what is the value of $a^2 - b^2$?

Solution. The moment you see $a^2 - b^2$, you should think $(a - b)(a + b)$. So, $a^2 - b^2 = (a - b)(a + b) = (9.2)(5) = 46$.

On the PSAT, the only division of polynomials you will have to do is to divide a polynomial by a monomial. You will *not* have to do long division of polynomials.

Key Fact F8

To divide a polynomial by a monomial, use the distributive property.

EXAMPLE 8

What is the quotient when $24a^2b + 9ab^3c$ is divided by $6ab$?

Solution. By the distributive property, $\frac{24a^2b + 9ab^3c}{6ab} = \frac{24a^2b}{6ab} + \frac{9ab^3c}{6ab}$.

Now simplify each fraction: $4a + \frac{3}{2}b^2c$.

Occasionally on the PSAT you will be asked to simplify an algebraic expression. To do so, you will probably have to do some simple factoring.

Key Fact F9

To factor a polynomial, the first step is *always* to use the distributive property to remove the greatest common factor of all the terms.

For example:

$$6xy + 8yz = 2y(3x + 4z)$$
$$x^3 + x^2 + x = x(x^2 + x + 1)$$

Key Fact F10

To factor a trinomial, use trial and error to find the binomials whose product is that trinomial.

For example:

$$x^2 - 4x + 4 = (x - 2)(x - 2)$$
$$x^2 - 2x - 15 = (x - 5)(x + 3)$$
$$2x^2 + 12x + 16 = 2(x^2 + 6x + 8) = 2(x + 4)(x + 2)$$

EXAMPLE 9

Which of the following is equivalent to $\frac{2x^2 - 8}{x^2 - 4x + 4}$?

(A) 2

(B) $\frac{2(x+2)}{x-2}$

(C) $\frac{2(x+4)}{x-4}$

(D) $\frac{2x+2}{x-2}$

(E) $\frac{6}{4x-4}$

Solution.

$$\frac{2x^2-8}{x^2-4x+4}=\frac{2\left(x^2-4\right)}{(x-2)(x-2)}=\frac{2\cancel{(x-2)}(x+2)}{\cancel{(x-2)}(x-2)}=\frac{2(x+2)}{x-2}\ \text{(Choice B).}$$

In Example 9, when $x = 3$, the value of $\dfrac{2x^2-8}{x^2-4x+4}$ is

$$\frac{2(3)^2-8}{3^2-4(3)+4}=\frac{18-8}{9-12+4}=\frac{10}{1}=10.$$

HELPFUL HINT

If you ever get stuck trying to simplify an algebraic expression, you can plug in a number and test the answers.

Only Choice B is 10 when $x = 3$: $\dfrac{2(3+2)}{3-2}=\dfrac{2(5)}{1}=10.$

Note that this does not depend on the choice of x. You can verify, for example, that if $x = 6$, the original expression and the correct answer choice are both equal to 4.

Practice Exercises

MULTIPLE-CHOICE QUESTIONS

1. If $x^2 + y^2 = 36$ and $(x + y)^2 = 64$, what is the value of xy?

(A) 7
(B) 14
(C) 28
(D) 100
(E) It cannot be determined from the information given.

2. What is the value of $(500{,}001)^2 - (499{,}999)^2$?

(A) 2
(B) 4
(C) 1,000,000
(D) 2,000,000
(E) 1,000,000,000,000

3. If $\frac{1}{x} + \frac{1}{y} = \frac{1}{z}$ and $xy = z$, what is the average of x and y?

(A) 0
(B) $\frac{1}{2}$
(C) 1
(D) $\frac{z}{2}$
(E) $\frac{x+y}{2z}$

4. What is the average (arithmetic mean) of $x^2 + 2x - 3$, $3x^2 - 2x - 3$, and $30 - 4x^2$?

(A) $\frac{8x^2 + 4x + 24}{3}$
(B) $\frac{8x^2 + 24}{3}$
(C) $\frac{24 - 4x}{3}$
(D) -12
(E) 8

5. What is the value of $x^2 - 10x + 25$ when $x = 95$?

(A) 90
(B) 100
(C) 950
(D) 8,100
(E) 10,000

GRID-IN QUESTIONS

6. If $a^2 + b^2 = 4$ and $(a - b)^2 = 2$, what is the value of ab?

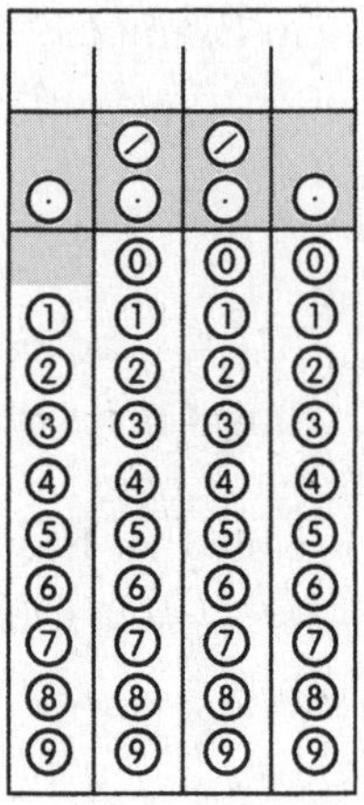

7. What is the value of $\frac{c^2 - d^2}{c - d}$ when $c = 23.4$ and $d = 34.5$?

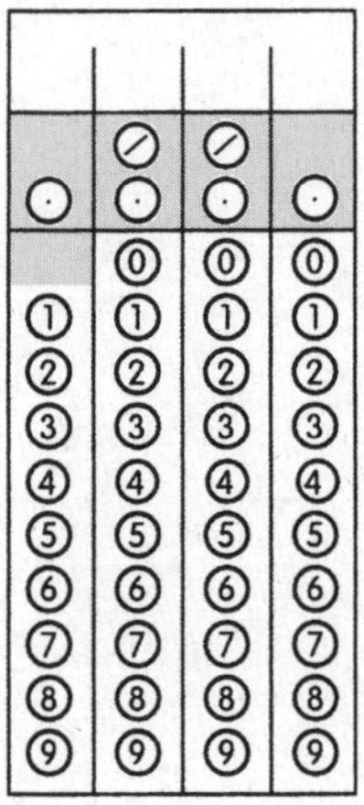

8. If $x^2 - y^2 = 80$ and $x - y = 16$, what is the average of x and y?

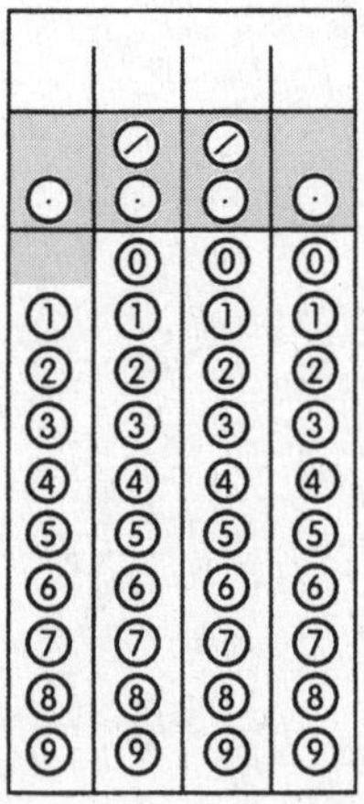

9. What is the value of $(2x + 3)(x + 6) - (2x - 5)(x + 10)$?

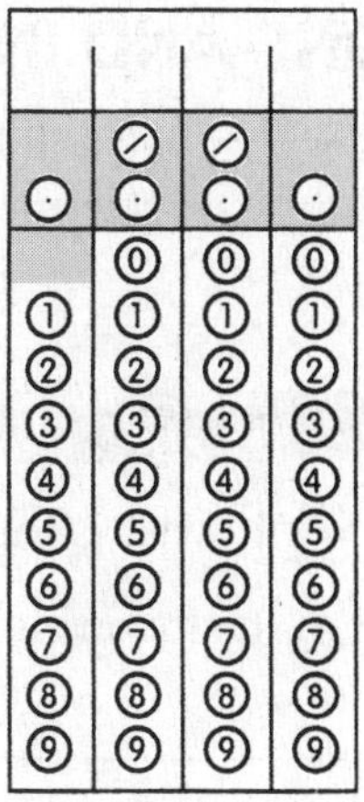

10. If $\left(\frac{1}{a} + a\right)^2 = 144$, what is the value of $\frac{1}{a^2} + a^2$?

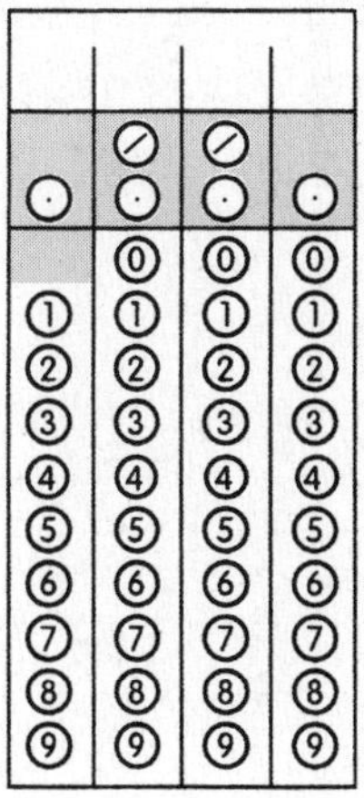

Answer Key

1. B **2.** D **3.** B **4.** E **5.** D

6.

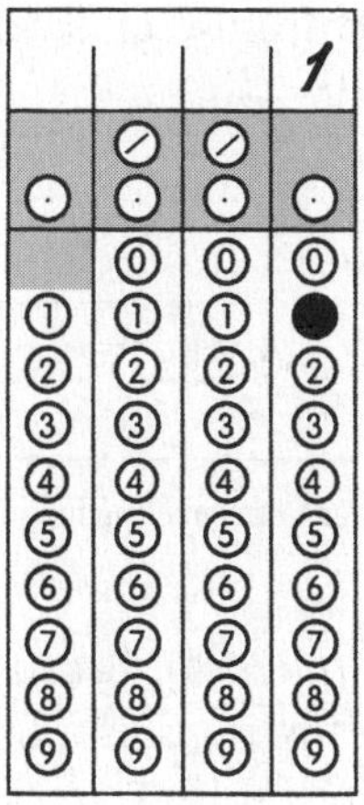

7.

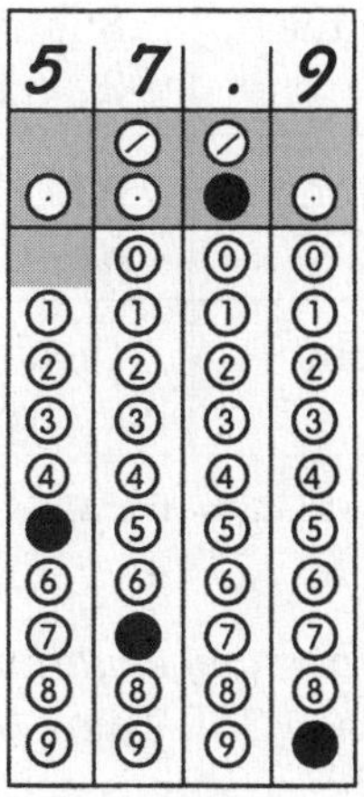

8.

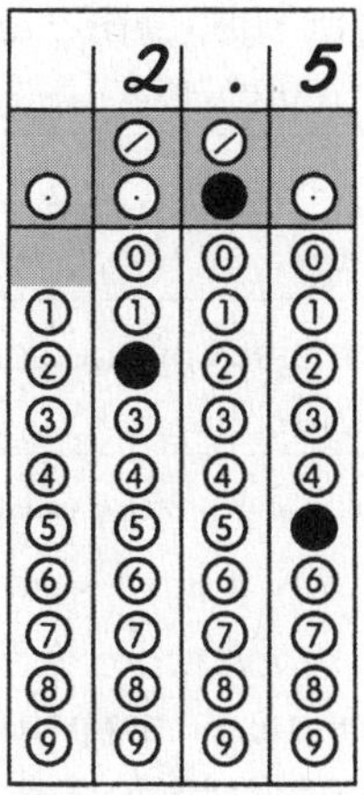

9.

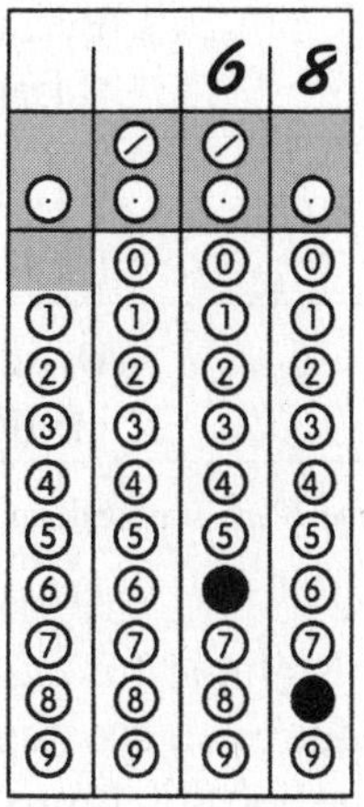

10.

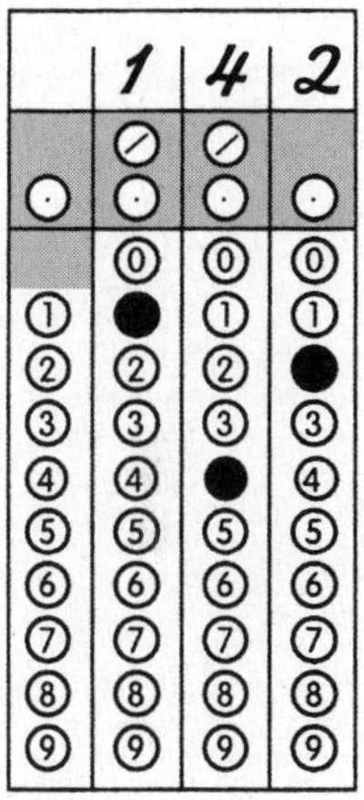

7-G SOLVING EQUATIONS AND INEQUALITIES

Most of the equations and inequalities that you will have to solve on the PSAT have only one variable and no exponents. A simple six-step method, illustrated below, can be used on all of them.

EXAMPLE 1

If $\frac{1}{2}x + 3(x - 2) = 2(x + 1) + 1$, what is the value of x ?

Solution. Follow the steps outlined in the following table.

Step	What to Do	Example
1	Remove fractions and decimals by multiplying both sides by the Lowest Common Denominator (LCD).	Multiply each term by 2: $x + 6(x - 2) = 4(x + 1) + 2$
2	Remove all parentheses by using the distributive property.	$x + 6x - 12 = 4x + 4 + 2$
3	Combine like terms on each side.	$7x - 12 = 4x + 6$
4	By adding or subtracting, get all the variables on one side.	Subtract $4x$ from each side: $3x - 12 = 6$
5	By adding or subtracting, get all the plain numbers on the other side.	Add 12 to each side: $3x = 18$
6	Divide both sides by the coefficient of the variable.	Divide both sides by 3: $x = 6$

Note: If you start with an inequality and in Step 6 you divide by a negative number, remember to reverse the inequality.

Example 1 *is actually much more difficult than any equation on the PSAT,* because it requires all six steps. This never happens on the PSAT. Think of the six steps as a list of questions that must be answered. Ask whether each step is necessary. If it isn't, move on to the next one; if it is, do it.

Let's look at Example 2, which does not require all six steps.

EXAMPLE 2

For what real number x is it true that $4(2x - 7) = x$?

(A) -4
(B) -1
(C) 0
(D) 1
(E) 4

Solution. Do whichever of the six steps are necessary.

Step	Question	Yes/No	What to Do
1	Are there any fractions or decimals?	No	
2	Are there any parentheses?	Yes	Get rid of them: $8x - 28 = x$.
3	Are there any like terms to combine?	No	
4	Are there variables on both sides?	Yes	Subtract x from each side: $7x - 28 = 0$
5	Is there a plain number on the same side as the variable?	Yes	Add 28 to each side: $7x = 28$
6	Does the variable have a coefficient?	Yes	Divide both sides by 7: $x = 4$

TACTIC G1

Memorize these six steps in order, and use this method whenever you have to solve this type of equation or inequality.

Sometimes on the PSAT, you are given an equation with several variables and asked to solve for one of them in terms of the others.

TACTIC G2

When you have to solve for one variable in terms of the others, treat all of the others as if they were numbers, and apply the six-step method.

EXAMPLE 3

If $r = 5s - 2t$, what is the value of s in terms of r and t?

Solution. To solve for s, treat r and t as numbers, and use the six-step method with s as the only variable.

Step	Question	Yes/No	What to Do
1	Are there any fractions or decimals?	No	
2	Are there any parentheses?	No	
3	Are there any like terms to combine?	No	
4	Are there variables on both sides?	No	Remember: The only variable is s.
5	Is there a plain number on the same side as the variable?	Yes	Remember: We're considering t as a number, and it is on the same side as s, the variable. Add $2t$ to both sides: $r + 2t = 5s$
6	Does the variable have a coefficient?	Yes	Divide both sides by 5: $s = \frac{r + 2t}{5}$

> **HELPFUL HINT**
> In applying the six-step method, you should not actually make a table, as we did in Examples 1–3, since it would be too time consuming. Instead, use the method as a guideline and mentally go through each step, doing only those that are required.

The six-step method can also be used if a variable is in a denominator. Just be sure to start with Step 1 and get rid of the fraction.

EXAMPLE 4

If $\frac{1}{2x} + \frac{2}{3} = \frac{4}{3x}$, then $x =$

Solution. Multiply each term by $6x$, the LCD,

$$6x\left(\frac{1}{2x}\right) + 6x\left(\frac{2}{3}\right) = 6x\left(\frac{4}{3x}\right) \Rightarrow 3 + 4x = 8 \Rightarrow 4x = 5 \Rightarrow x = \frac{5}{4} \text{ (or 1.25)}$$

Occasionally, on the PSAT you will have to solve an equation, such as $2\sqrt{x} - 7 = 5$, that involves a square root. Proceed normally, treating the square root as your variable, using whichever of the six steps are necessary until you have that square root equal to a number. Then square both sides.

EXAMPLE 5

If $2\sqrt{x} - 7 = 5$, then $x =$

Solution.

Add 7 to each side:	$2\sqrt{x} = 12$
Divide each side by 2:	$\sqrt{x} = 6$
Now square each side:	$(\sqrt{x})^2 = 6^2 \Rightarrow x = 36$

Systems of Linear Equations

The equations $x + y = 10$ and $x - y = 2$ each have infinitely many solutions. However, there is only one pair of numbers, $x = 6$ and $y = 4$, which satisfy both equations simultaneously: $6 + 4 = 10$ and $6 - 4 = 2$. These numbers are the only solution of the *system of equations*: $x + y = 10$ and $x - y = 2$.

A system of equations is a set of two or more equations involving two or more variables. To solve such a system, you must find values for each of the variables that will make each equation true. On the PSAT, the most useful method is to add or subtract the equations (usually add).

TACTIC

G3 **To solve a system of equations, add or subtract them. If there are more than two equations, add them.**

EXAMPLE 6

If $2x + y = 10$ and $x - y = 2$, then what is the value of xy?

Solution. Add the two equations:

$$\begin{array}{rl} & 2x + y = 10 \\ + & \underline{\;\; x - y = \;\;2} \\ & 3x \qquad = 12 \quad \text{so, } x = 4 \end{array}$$

Replacing x by 4 in $x - y = 2$ yields $y = 2$. So, $xy = (4)(2) = 8$.

EXAMPLE 7

If $3a + 5b = 10$ and $5a + 3b = 30$, what is the average (arithmetic mean) of a and b ?

(A) 2.5
(B) 4
(C) 5
(D) 20
(E) It cannot be determined from the information given.

HELPFUL HINT

On the PSAT, most problems involving systems of equations do not require you to solve the system. These problems usually ask for something other than the value of each variable. Read the questions very carefully, circle what you need, and do not do more than is required.

Solution. Add the two equations:

$$\begin{array}{rl} & 3a + 5b = 10 \\ + & \underline{5a + 3b = 30} \\ & 8a + 8b = 40 \end{array}$$

Divide both sides by 8: $a + b = 5$

The average of a and b is: $\dfrac{a+b}{2} = \dfrac{5}{2} = 2.5$ (Choice A)

NOTE: It is not only unnecessary to first solve for a and b ($a = 7.5$ and $b = -2.5$), but because it is so much more time consuming, it would be foolish to do so.

Practice Exercises

MULTIPLE-CHOICE QUESTIONS

1. If $5x + 12 = 5 - 2x$, what is the value of x ?

(A) $-\frac{17}{7}$
(B) -3
(C) -1
(D) 1
(E) $\frac{17}{7}$

2. If $\frac{1}{a - b} = 6$, then $a =$

(A) $b + 6$
(B) $b - 6$
(C) $b + \frac{1}{6}$
(D) $b - \frac{1}{6}$
(E) $\frac{1 - 6b}{6}$

3. If $\frac{1}{3}x + \frac{1}{6}x + \frac{1}{9}x = 33$, what is the value of x ?

(A) 3
(B) 18
(C) 27
(D) 54
(E) 72

4. If $ax - b = c - dx$, what is the value of x in terms of a, b, c, and d?

(A) $\frac{b + c}{a + d}$
(B) $\frac{c - b}{a - d}$
(C) $\frac{b + c - d}{a}$
(D) $\frac{c - b}{a + d}$
(E) $\frac{c}{b} - \frac{d}{a}$

5. If $\frac{a + 2b + 3c}{3} = \frac{a + 2b}{2}$, then $c =$

(A) $\frac{a + 2b}{6}$
(B) $\frac{a + 2b}{3}$
(C) $\frac{a + 2b}{2}$
(D) $a + 2b$
(E) $\frac{1}{2}$

GRID-IN QUESTIONS

6. If $9x + 10 = 32$, what is the value of $9x - 10$?

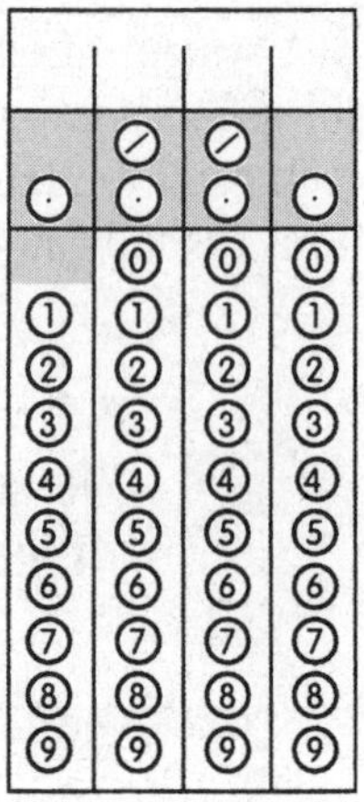

7. If $7x - 3 = 11$, what is the value of $(7x - 3)^2$?

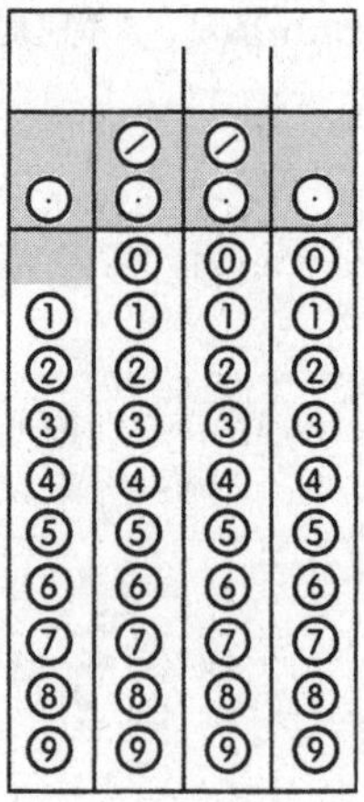

8. If $a = 2b$, $3b = 4c$, and $5c = 6a - 7$, what is the value of c?

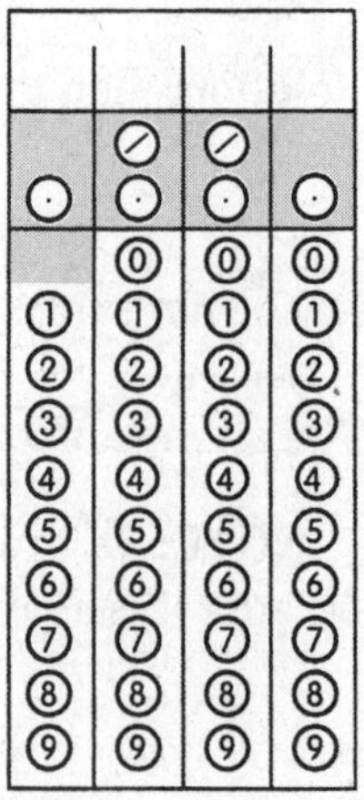

9. If $7y - 5x = 3$, what is the smallest integer value of x for which $y > 75$?

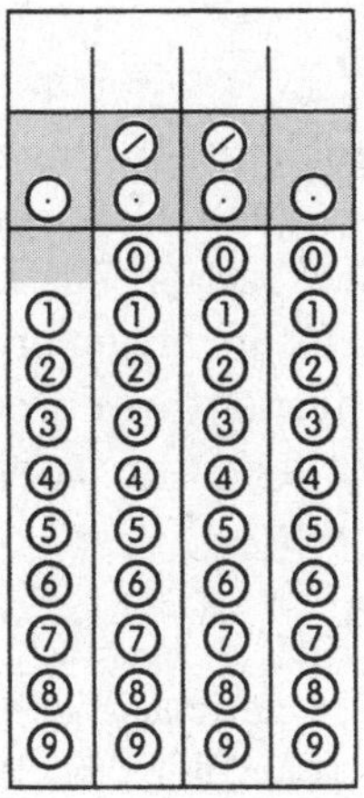

10. If $x^2 + 5 < 6$ and $2x^2 + 7 > 8$, what is one possible value of x?

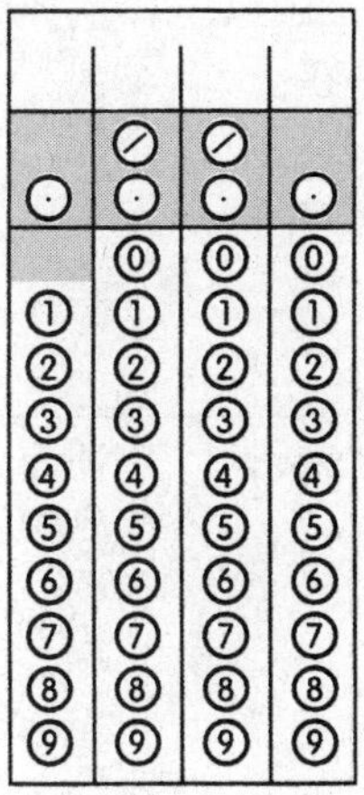

Answer Key

1. C **2.** C **3.** D **4.** A **5.** A

6.

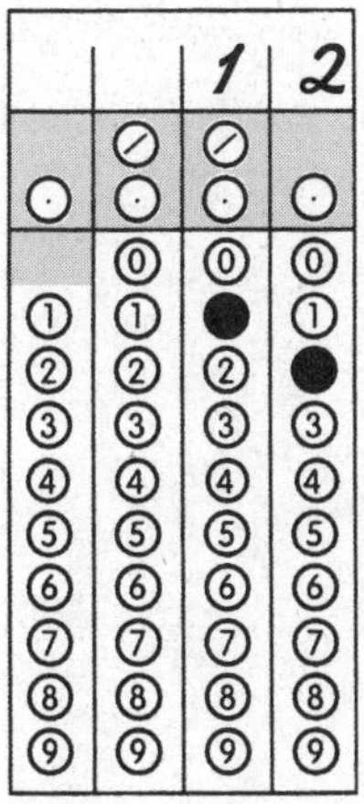

7.

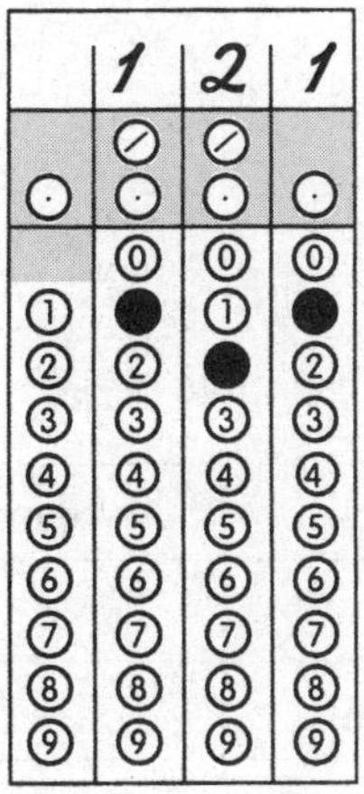

8.

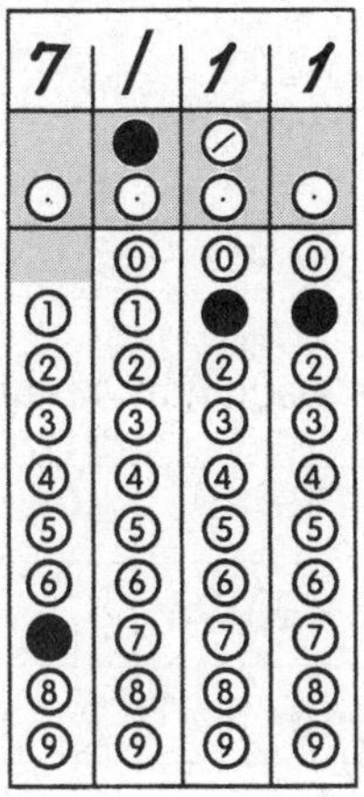

9.

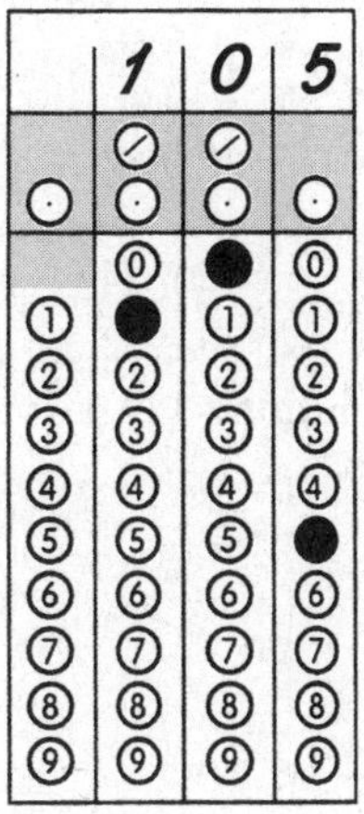

10.

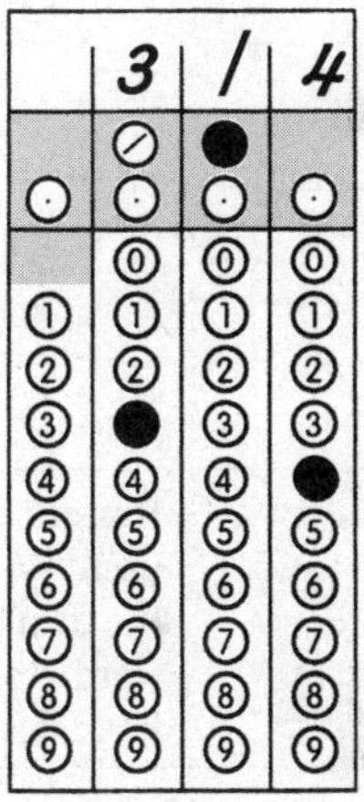

or any number satisfying $.71 < x < 1$

7-H WORD PROBLEMS

A typical PSAT has several word problems. In this chapter you have already seen word problems on consecutive integers in Section 7-A, fractions in Section 7-B, percents in Section 7-C, ratios and proportions in Section 7-D, and averages in Section 7-E. Later in this chapter you will see word problems involving probability, circles, triangles, and other geometric figures. A few of these problems can be solved with just arithmetic, but most of them require basic algebra.

HELPFUL HINT: In problems involving ages, remember that "years ago" means you need to subtract, and "years from now" means you need to add.

Age Problems

Example 1 below is the same as Example 2 in Chapter 6. In Chapter 6 you were shown how to solve it by backsolving; now we will show you the correct algebraic solution.

EXAMPLE 1

Judy is now twice as old as Adam, but six years ago, she was five times as old as he was. How old is Judy now?

(A) 8
(B) 16
(C) 20
(D) 24
(E) 32

Solution. Let x = Adam's age now, and fill in the table below.

HELPFUL HINT: It is often very useful to organize the data from a word problem in a table.

	Judy	Adam
Now	$2x$	x
6 years ago	$2x - 6$	$x - 6$

Now translate: Judy's age six years ago was five times Adam's age:

$$2x - 6 = 5(x - 6)$$
$$2x - 6 = 5x - 30 \Rightarrow 24 = 3x \Rightarrow x = 8.$$

Adam is now 8. However, 8 is *not* the answer. The question could have asked for Adam's age now or six years ago or at any time. It could have asked for Judy's age at any time or for their combined ages. What it did ask for is Judy's age now, which is 16, twice Adam's age (Choice B).

HELPFUL HINT: In all word problems on the PSAT, circle what you're looking for in your exam booklet. Don't answer the wrong question!

Distance Problems

All distance problems involve one of three variations of the same formula:

$$\text{distance} = \text{rate} \times \text{time} \quad \text{rate} = \frac{\text{distance}}{\text{time}}$$

$$\text{time} = \frac{\text{distance}}{\text{rate}}$$

These are usually abbreviated, $d = rt$, $r = \frac{d}{t}$, and $t = \frac{d}{r}$.

EXAMPLE 2

Justin drove 1 mile, from Exit 10 to Exit 11 on the thruway, at 50 miles per hour. Adam drove the same distance at 60 miles per hour. How many *seconds* longer did it take Justin than Adam to drive that mile?

Solution. The time to drive 1 mile at 50 miles per hour is given by

$$t = \frac{1 \text{ mile}}{50 \text{ miles per hour}} = \frac{1}{50} \text{ hour} = \frac{1}{50} \times 60 \text{ minutes} =$$

$$\frac{6}{5} \text{ minutes} = 1\frac{1}{5} \text{ minutes}$$

The time to drive 1 mile at 60 miles per hour is given by

$$t = \frac{1 \text{ mile}}{60 \text{ miles per hour}} = \frac{1}{60} \text{ hour} = 1 \text{ minute.}$$

The difference is $\frac{1}{5}$ minute $= \frac{1}{5}$ (60 seconds) $=$ 12 seconds.

Note that the solution to Example 2 used the time formula but required only arithmetic, not algebra. Example 3 requires an algebraic solution.

EXAMPLE 3

Eve drove from her home to college at an average speed of 60 miles per hour. Returning over the same route, due to construction delays, she was able to average only 45 miles per hour. If the return trip took 30 minutes longer, how many miles did she drive each way?

(A) 1.5
(B) 2
(C) 2.5
(D) 90
(E) 180

Solution. Let x = the number of hours it took to go. Then to return, it took $x + 0.5$ hours (*not* $x + 30$). Now make a table.

	Rate	Time	Distance
going	60	x	$60x$
returning	45	$x + 0.5$	$45(x + 0.5)$

Since she drove the same distance going and returning:

$$60x = 45(x + 0.5) \Rightarrow 60x = 45x + 22.5 \Rightarrow 15x = 22.5 \Rightarrow x = 1.5.$$

Now be sure to answer the correct question. Choices A, B, and C are the time, in hours, for going, returning, and the round-trip; Choices D and E are the distances each way and round-trip. You could have been asked for any of the five. If you circled what you're looking for, you won't make a careless mistake. Eve drove 60(1.5) = 90 miles each way, and so the correct answer is Choice D.

The d in $d = rt$ stands for "distance," but it could represent any type of work that is performed at a certain rate r for a certain amount of time t. Example 3 did not have to be about distance. Instead of driving 90 miles at 45 miles per hour for 2 hours, Eve could have read 90 pages at a rate of 45 pages per hour for 2 hours or planted 90 flowers at the rate of 45 flowers per hour for 2 hours or typed 90 words at a rate of 45 words per minute for 2 minutes.

HELPFUL HINT

Most algebraic word problems on the PSAT are not too difficult. If you get stuck on one, however, don't despair. Use one or more of the tactics that you learned in Chapter 6, especially backsolving, to eliminate choices and, if necessary, guess.

Practice Exercises

MULTIPLE-CHOICE QUESTIONS

1. In 7 years Danielle will be twice as old as she was 8 years ago. How old is Danielle now?

(A) 7
(B) 15
(C) 23
(D) 30
(E) 37

2. In the morning, Alan drove 100 miles at the rate of 60 miles per hour; in the afternoon, he drove another 100 miles at the rate of 40 miles per hour. What was his average rate of speed, in miles per hour, for the day?

(A) 45
(B) 48
(C) 50
(D) 52
(E) 55

3. In a family of three, the father weighed 5 times as much as the child, and the mother weighed $\frac{3}{4}$ as much as the father. If the three of them weighed a total of 390 pounds, how much did the mother weigh?

(A) 40
(B) 100
(C) 125
(D) 150
(E) 200

4. At 7:00 P.M., the hostess of the party remarked that only $\frac{1}{4}$ of her guests had arrived so far but that as soon as 10 more showed up, $\frac{1}{3}$ of the guests would be there. How many people were invited?

(A) 20
(B) 32
(C) 80
(D) 120
(E) 144

5. If the sum of 5 consecutive integers is S, what is the largest of those integers in terms of S?

(A) $\frac{S-10}{5}$

(B) $\frac{S+4}{4}$

(C) $\frac{S+5}{4}$

(D) $\frac{S-5}{2}$

(E) $\frac{S+10}{5}$

GRID-IN QUESTIONS

6. A box contains only red, yellow, and green jelly beans. The number of red jelly beans is $\frac{4}{5}$ the number of green ones, and the number of green ones is $\frac{3}{4}$ the number of yellow ones. If there are 470 jelly beans in all, how many of them are yellow?

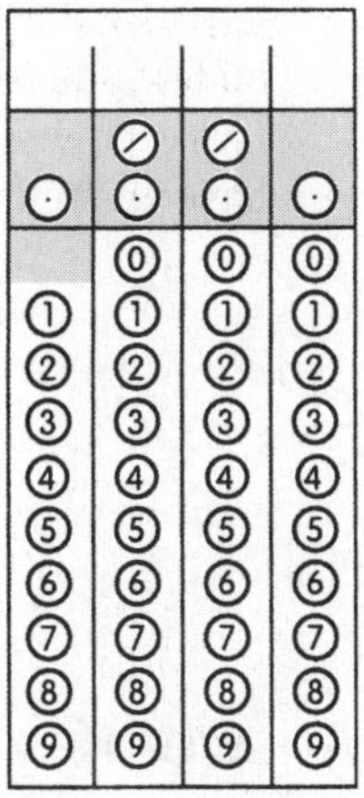

7. On a certain project the only grades awarded were 75 and 100. If 85 students completed the project and the average of their grades was 85, how many earned 100?

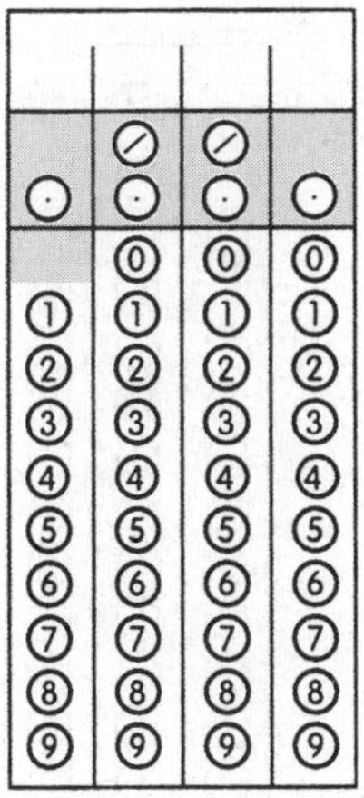

8. Since 1953, when Frank graduated from high school, he has gained two pounds every year. In 1983 he was 40% heavier than in 1953. What percent of his 1998 weight was his 1983 weight?

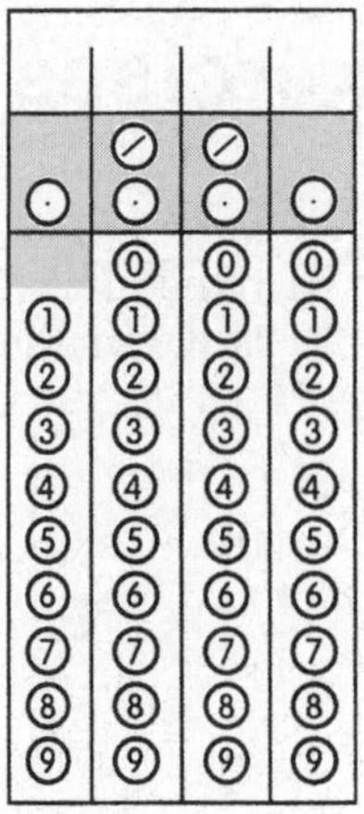

9. The number of baseball cards in Neil's collection is 80% of the number in Larry's collection. If Neil has 80 fewer baseball cards than Larry, how many do they have altogether?

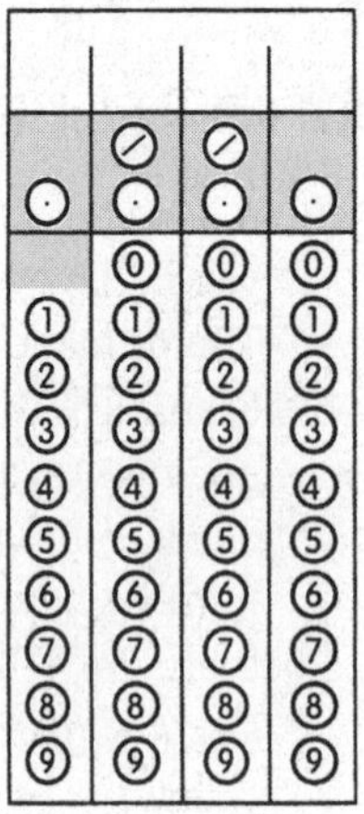

10. What is the greater of two numbers whose product is 700, if the sum of the two numbers exceeds their difference by 20?

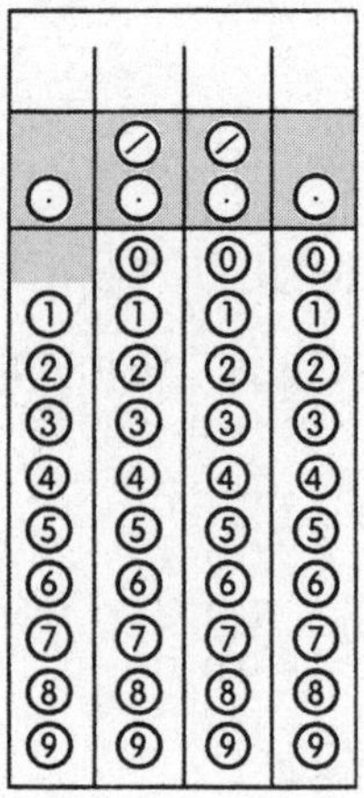

Answer Key

1. C **2.** B **3.** D **4.** D **5.** E

6.

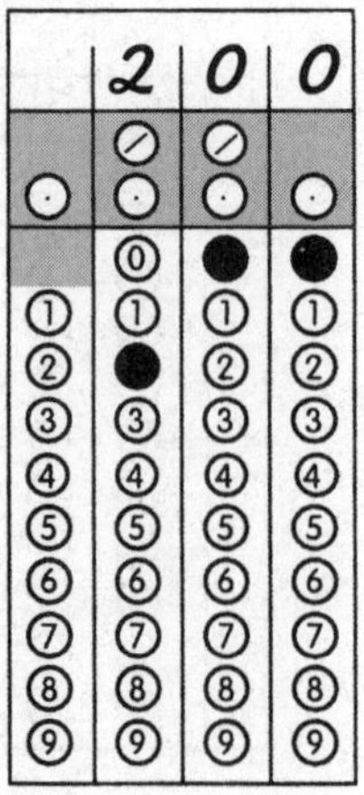

7.

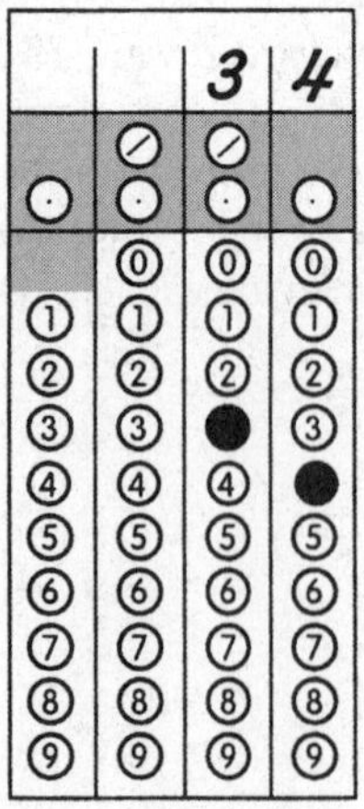

8.

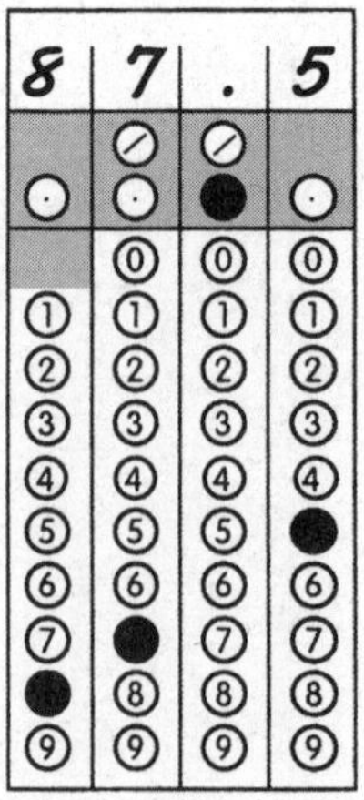

9.

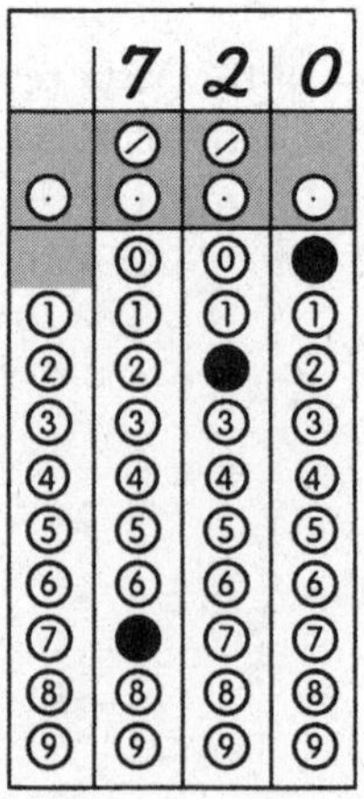

10.

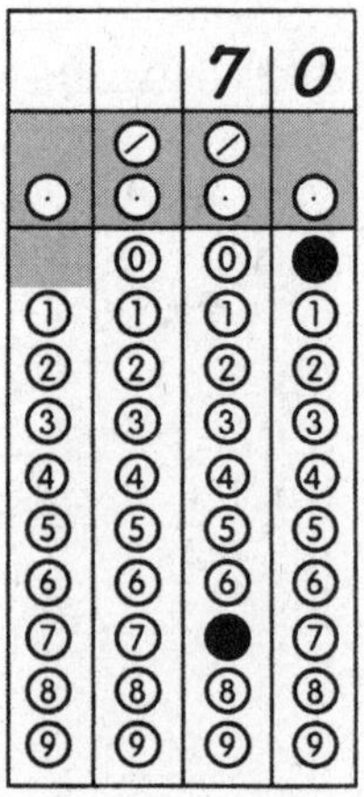

Geometry

Although about 30 percent of the math questions on the PSAT involve geometry, you need to know only a relatively small number of facts—far fewer than you would learn in a geometry course—and, of course, you don't need to provide proofs. In the next six sections we will review all of the geometry that you need to know to do well on the PSAT. Also, we will present the material exactly as it appears on the PSAT, using the same vocabulary and notation, which may be slightly different from the terminology you have used in your math classes.

7-I LINES AND ANGLES

An ***angle*** is formed by the intersection of two line segments, rays, or lines. The point of intersection is called the ***vertex***. On the PSAT, angles are always measured in degrees.

Key Fact I1

Angles are classified according to their degree measures.

- An ***acute*** angle measures less than 90° (Figure 1).
- A ***right*** angle measures 90° (Figure 2).
- An ***obtuse*** angle measures more than 90° but less than 180° (Figure 3).
- A ***straight*** angle measures 180° (Figure 4).

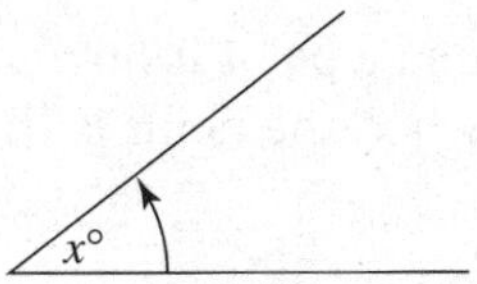

$x < 90$

Figure 1

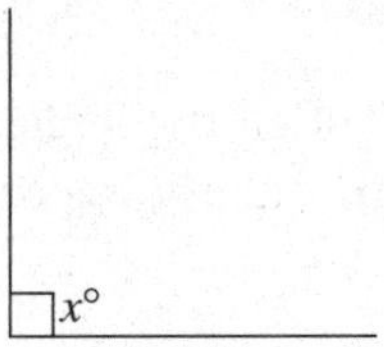

$x = 90$

Figure 2

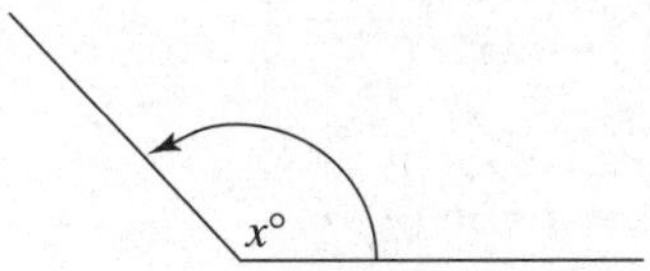

$90 < x < 180$

Figure 3

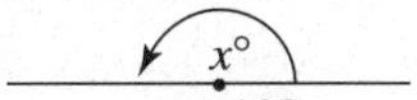

$x = 180$

Figure 4

NOTE

A small square like the one in Figure 2 at left *always* means that the angle is a right angle. On the PSAT, if an angle has a square in it, it must be a 90° angle, *even if the figure has not been drawn to scale.*

Key Fact I2

If two or more angles form a straight angle, the sum of their measures is 180°.

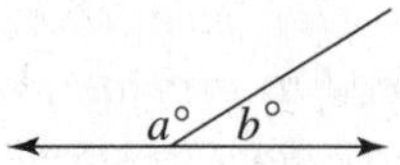

$a + b = 180$

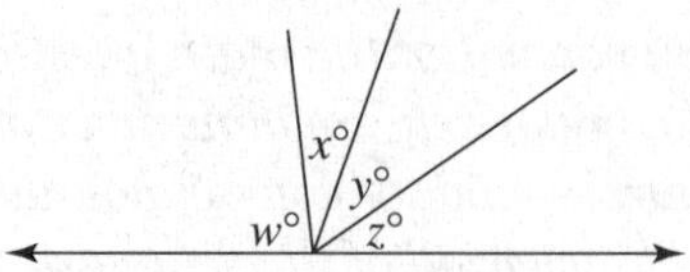

$w + x + y + z = 180$

EXAMPLE 1

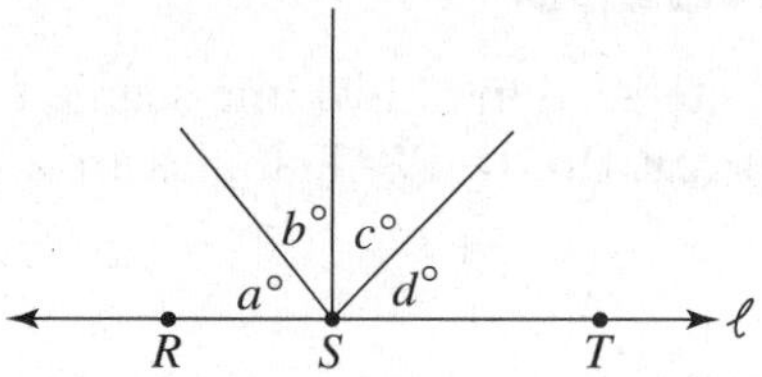

In the figure above, R, S, and T are all on line ℓ. What is the average of a, b, c, and d?

Solution. Since $\angle RST$ is a straight angle, by **KEY FACT I2**, $a + b + c + d = 180$, and so their average is $\frac{180}{4} = 45$.

Key Fact I3

The sum of the measures of all the angles around a point is 360°.

NOTE: This fact is particularly important when the point is the center of a circle, as we shall see in Section 7-L.

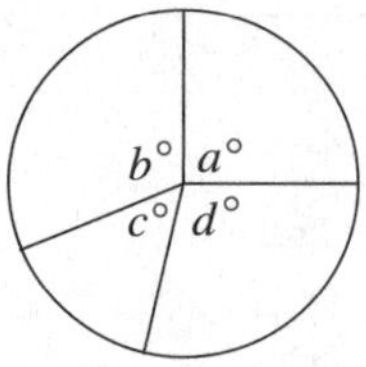

$a + b + c + d = 360$

When two lines intersect, four angles are formed. The two angles in each pair of opposite angles are called ***vertical angles***.

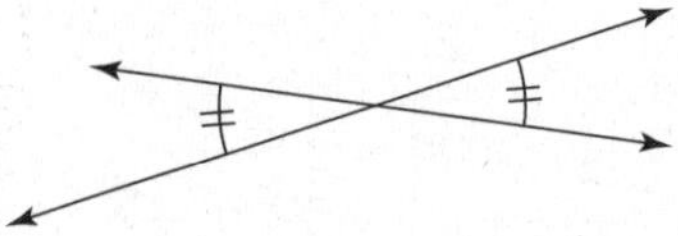

Key Fact I4

Vertical angles have equal measures.

EXAMPLE 2

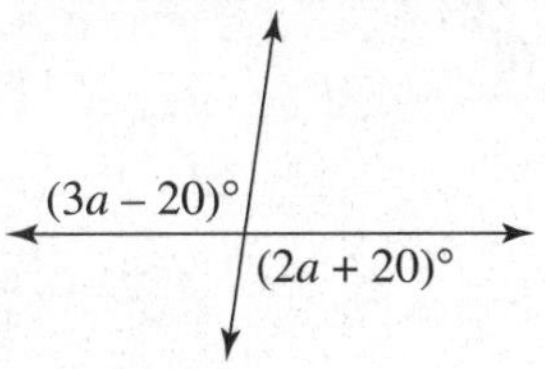

In the figure above, what is the value of a?

Solution. Because vertical angles are equal, $3a - 20 = 2a + 20 \Rightarrow a = 40$.

Two lines that intersect to form right angles are called ***perpendicular***.

Two lines that never intersect are said to be ***parallel***. So, parallel lines form no angles. However, if a third line, called a ***transversal***, intersects a pair of parallel lines, eight angles are formed; the relationships among these angles are very important.

Key Fact I5

If a pair of parallel lines is cut by a transversal that is not perpendicular to the parallel lines,

- Four of the angles are acute, and four are obtuse.
- All four acute angles are equal: $a = c = e = g$.
- All four obtuse angles are equal: $b = d = f = h$.
- The sum of any acute angle and any obtuse angle is 180°; for example, $d + e = 180$, $c + f = 180$, $b + g = 180$, . . .

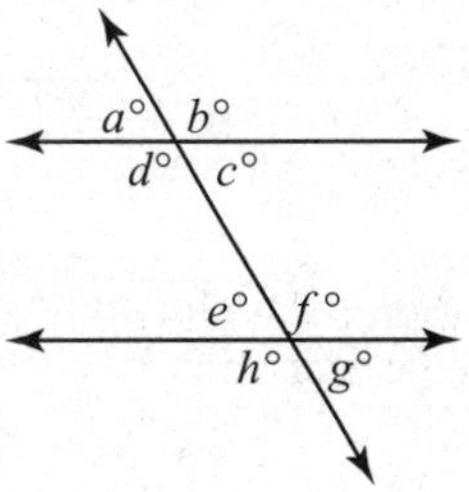

HELPFUL HINT

You must know **KEY FACT I5**—almost every PSAT has questions based on it. However, you do *not* need to know the special terms you learned in your geometry class for these pairs of angles; those terms are not used on the PSAT.

EXAMPLE 3

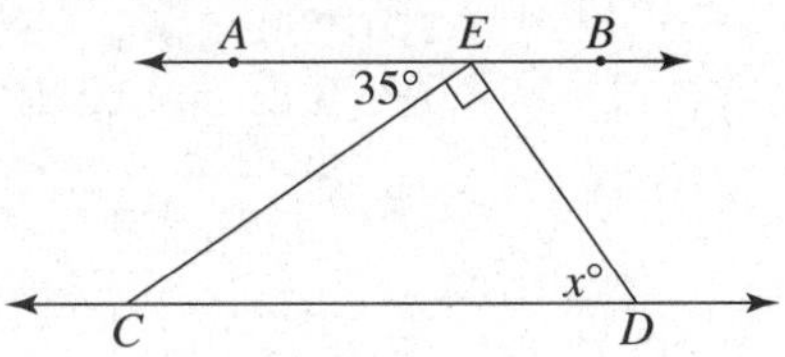

In the figure above, $\overleftrightarrow{AB}$ is parallel to $\overleftrightarrow{CD}$. What is the value of x?

Solution. Let y be the measure of $\angle BED$. Then, by **KEY FACT I2**,

$$35 + 90 + y = 180 \Rightarrow 125 + y = 180 \Rightarrow y = 55.$$

Since $\overleftrightarrow{AB}$ and $\overleftrightarrow{CD}$ are parallel, by **KEY FACT I5**, $x = y \Rightarrow x = 55$.

Practice Exercises

MULTIPLE-CHOICE QUESTIONS

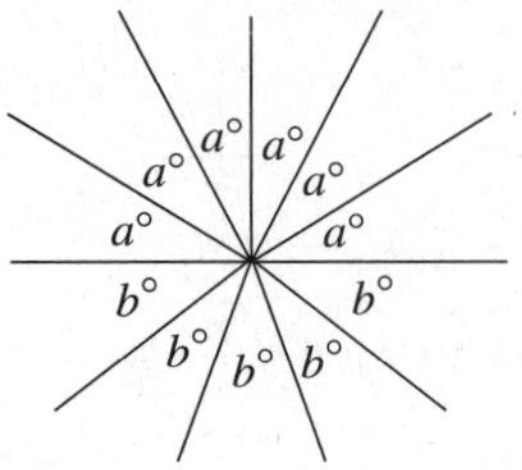

1. In the figure above, what is the value of $\frac{b+a}{b-a}$?
   (A) 6
   (B) 11
   (C) 30
   (D) 36
   (E) 66

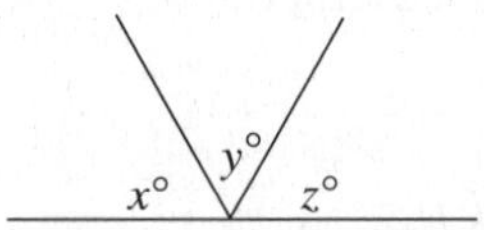

Note: Figure not drawn to scale

2. In the figure above, $x{:}y = 3{:}5$ and $z{:}y = 2{:}1$. What is the measure of the largest angle?
   (A) 60
   (B) 90
   (C) 100
   (D) 120
   (E) 150

3. What is the measure of the smaller angle formed by the minute and hour hands of a clock at 1:40?
   (A) 120°
   (B) 135°
   (C) 150°
   (D) 170°
   (E) 180°

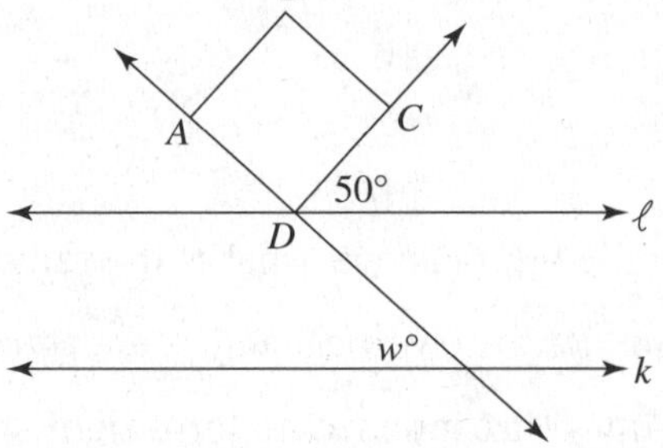

4. In the figure above, lines k and ℓ are parallel, and line ℓ passes through D, one of the vertices of square $ABCD$. What is the value of w?
   (A) 30
   (B) 40
   (C) 45
   (D) 50
   (E) 60

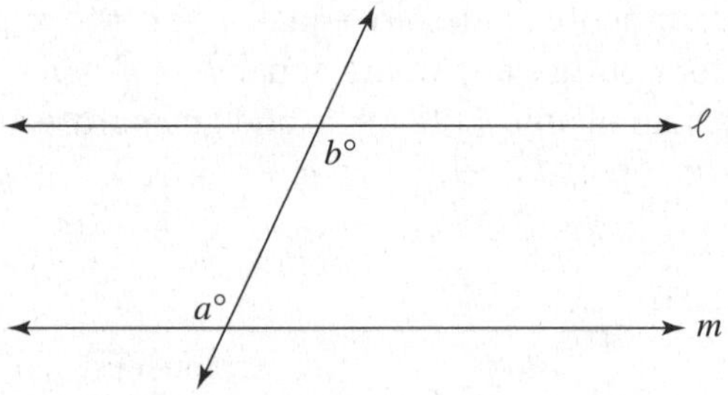

Note: Figure not drawn to scale

5. In the figure above, $\ell \parallel m$. Which of the following statements about $a + b$ is true?
   (A) $a + b < 180$
   (B) $a + b = 180$
   (C) $180 < a + b \leq 270$
   (D) $270 < a + b \leq 360$
   (E) It cannot be determined from the information given.

GRID-IN QUESTIONS

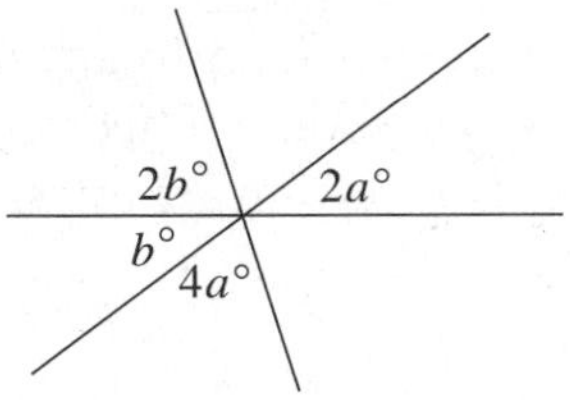

6. In the figure above, what is the value of b?

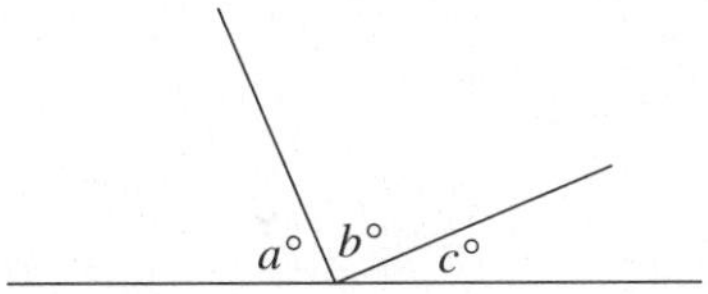

7. In the figure above, if a:b:c = 3:4:1, what is the value of a?

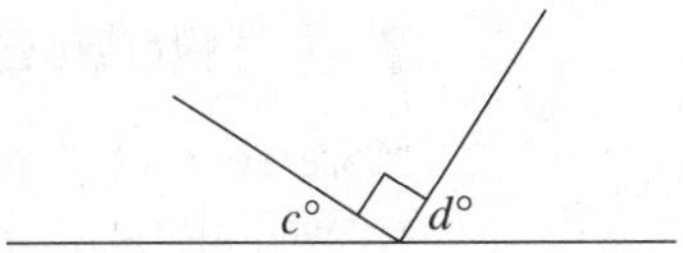

8. In the figure above, what is the value of c if d:c = 3:2?

9. A, B, and C are points on a line with B between A and C. Let M and N be the midpoints of $\overline{AB}$ and $\overline{BC}$, respectively. If $AB = 3BC$, what is $\frac{AB}{MN}$?

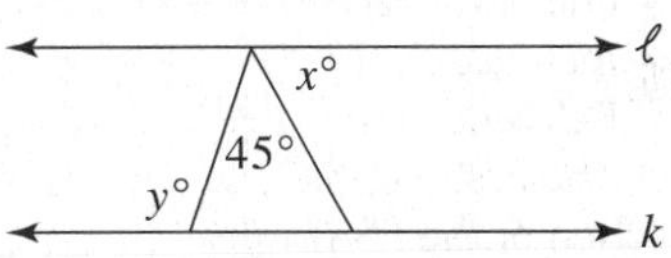

10. In the figure above, lines k and l are parallel. What is the value of $y - x$?

6.
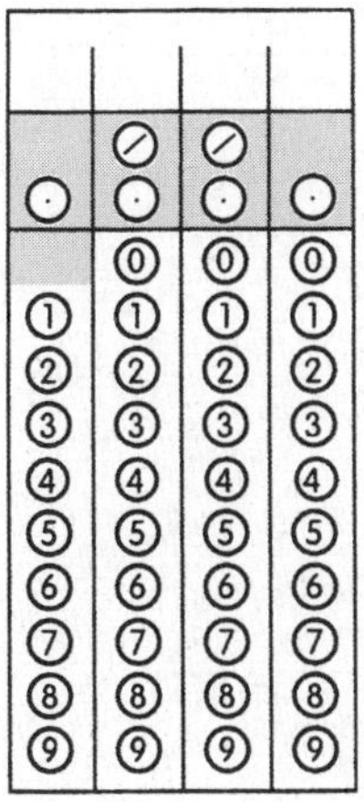

7.
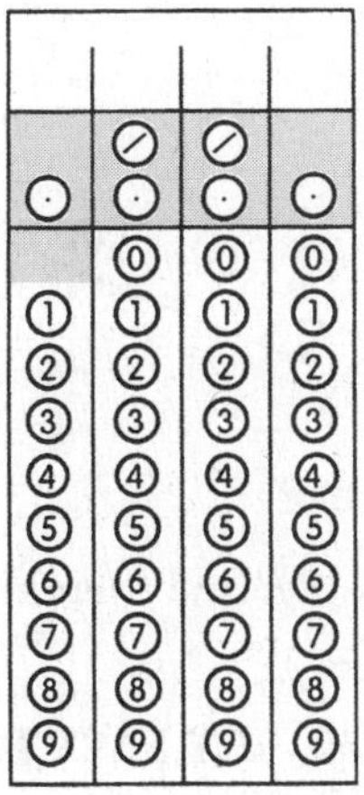

8.
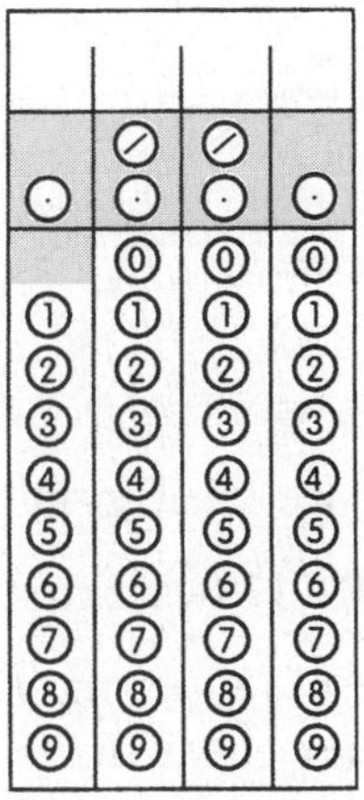

9.
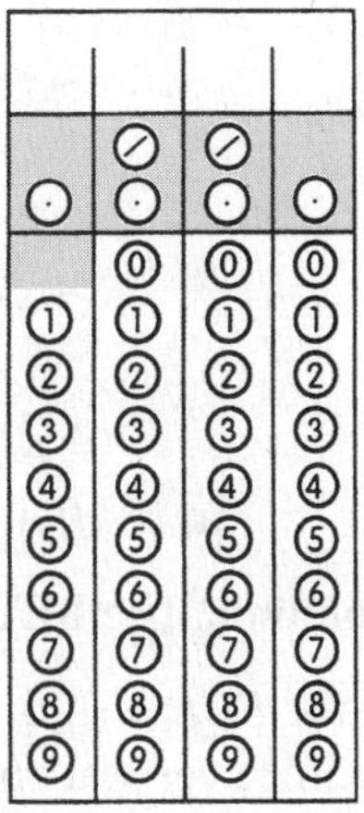

10.
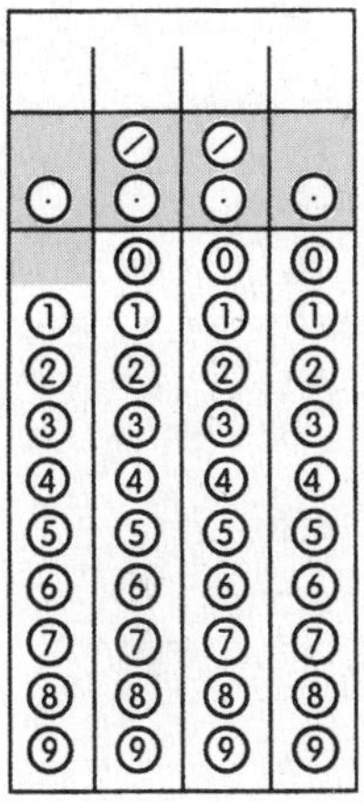

Answer Key

1. B **2.** C **3.** D **4.** B **5.** E

6.
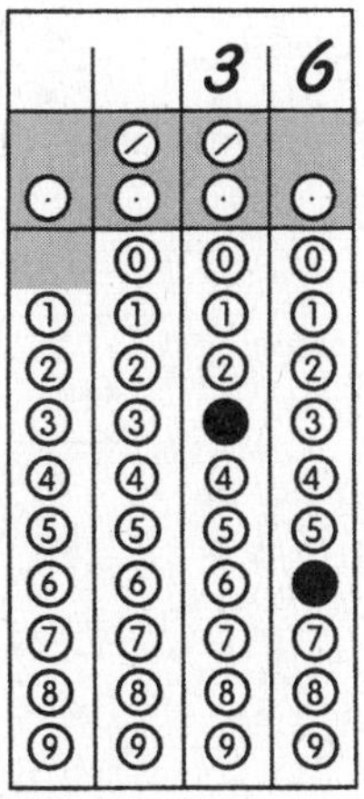

7.
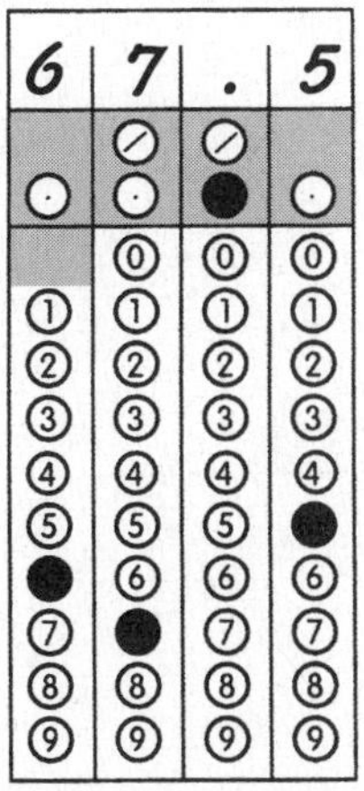

8.
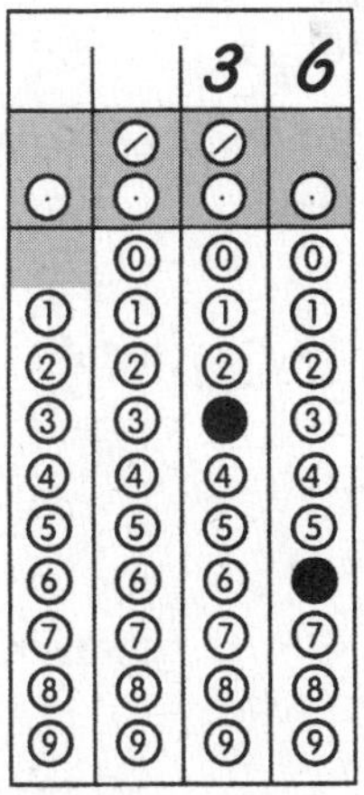

9.
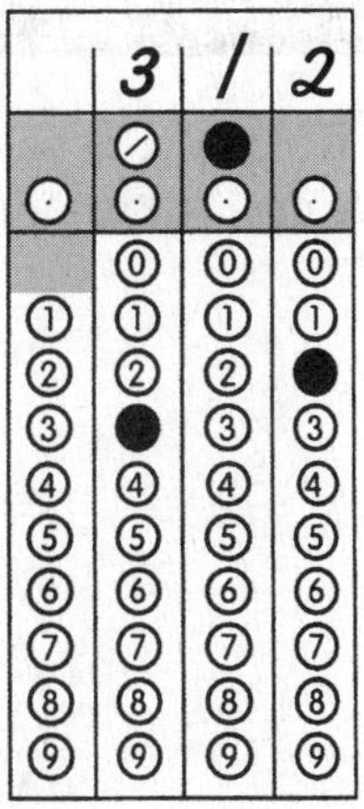

10.
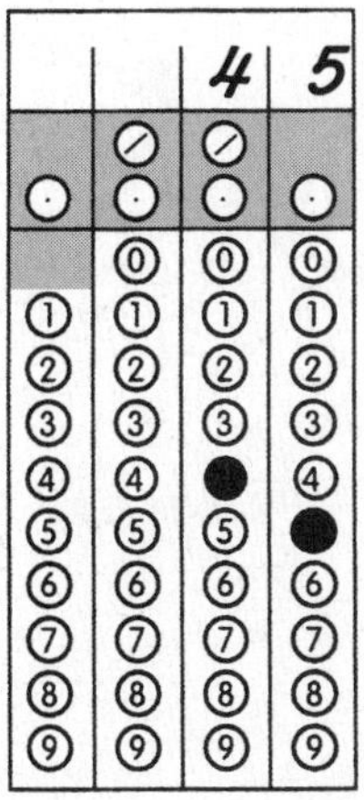

7-J TRIANGLES

More geometry questions on the PSAT pertain to triangles than to any other topic. To answer these questions correctly, you need to know several important facts about the angles and sides of triangles. The **KEY FACTS** in this section are extremely useful. *Be sure you learn them all.*

Key Fact J1

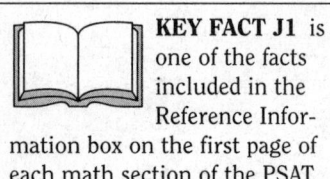

KEY FACT J1 is one of the facts included in the Reference Information box on the first page of each math section of the PSAT.

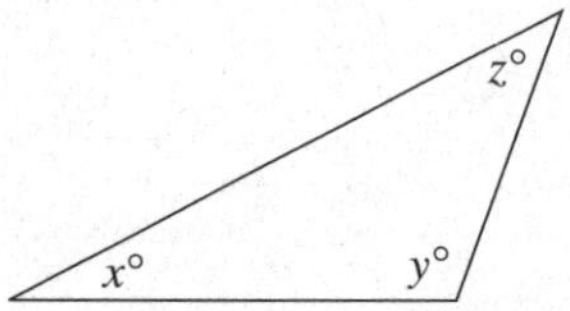

$x + y + z = 180.$

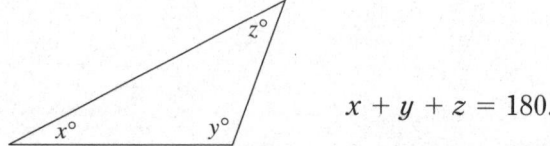

In any triangle, the sum of the measures of the three angles is 180°.

EXAMPLE 1

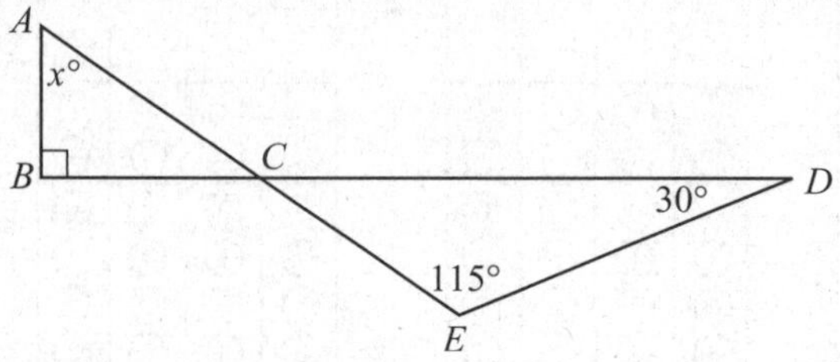

In the figure above, what is the value of x?

Solution. Use **KEY FACT J1** twice: first, in $\triangle CDE$ and then in $\triangle ABC$.

- $m\angle DCE + 115 + 30 = 180 \Rightarrow m\angle DCE + 145 = 180 \Rightarrow m\angle DCE = 35$
- Since vertical angles are equal, $m\angle ACB = 35$ [**KEY FACT I4**]
- $x + 90 + 35 = 180 \Rightarrow x + 125 = 180 \Rightarrow x = 55$

An ***exterior angle*** of a triangle is an angle formed by one side of the triangle and the extension of another side.

Key Fact J2

The measure of an exterior angle of a triangle is equal to the sum of the measures of the two opposite interior angles.

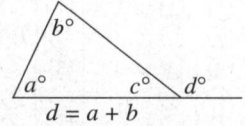

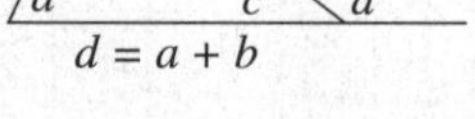

$d = a + b$

EXAMPLE 2

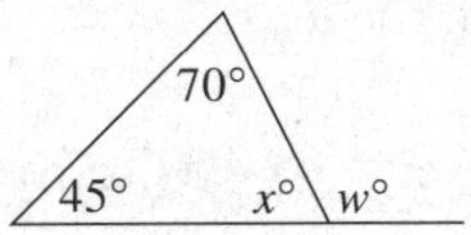

In the figure above, what is the value of w?

Solution. By **KEY FACT J2**: $w = 45 + 70 = 115$.

Key Fact J3

In any triangle

- the longest side is opposite the largest angle.
- the shortest side is opposite the smallest angle.
- sides with the same length are opposite angles with the same measure.

A triangle with two equal sides is called ***isosceles***; it has two equal angles. A triangle with three equal sides is called ***equilateral***; it has three equal angles, each of which measures 60°.

EXAMPLE 3

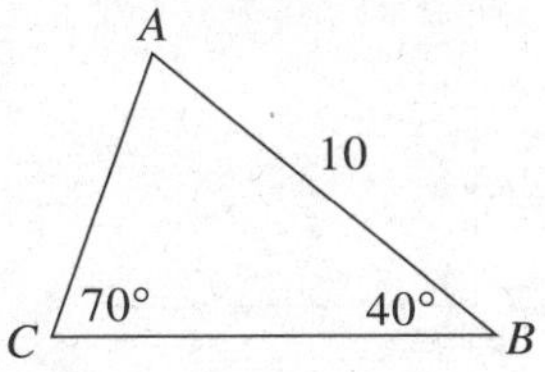

Note: Figure not drawn to scale

Which of the following statements about $\triangle ABC$ in the figure above must be true?

I. $m\angle A = 70°$
II. $BC = 10$
III. Perimeter of $\triangle ABC = 30$

(A) I only
(B) II only
(C) I and II only
(D) I and III only
(E) I, II, and III

Solution.

- By **KEY FACT J1**, $m\angle A + 70 + 40 = 180 \Rightarrow m\angle A = 70$. (I is true.)
- Therefore, $m\angle A = m\angle C$, and by **KEY FACT J3**, $BC = 10$. (II is true.)
- Since $\angle B$ is the smallest angle, AC is the smallest side. In particular, it is less than 10.
- Therefore, the perimeter is less than 30. (III is false.)
- Only I and II are true (Choice C).

Right triangles are triangles that have one right angle and two acute ones. The side opposite the 90° angle is called the **hypotenuse**, and by **KEY FACT J3**, it is the longest side. The other two sides are called the ***legs***.

EXAMPLE 4

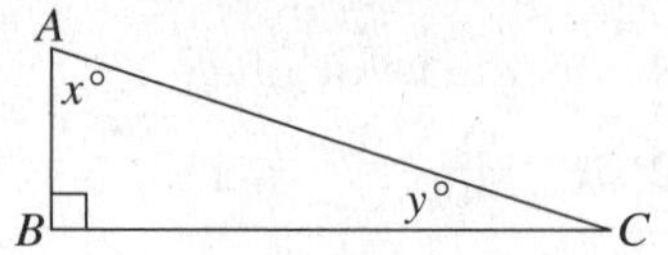

In the figure above, what is the average (arithmetic mean) of x and y?

Solution. Since the diagram indicates that $\triangle ABC$ is a right triangle, then, by **KEY FACT J1**, $90 + x + y = 180 \Rightarrow x + y = 90$. The average of x and y is $\frac{x+y}{2} = \frac{90}{2} = 45$.

The most important facts concerning right triangles are the **Pythagorean theorem** and its converse, which are given in **KEY FACT J4**.

Key Fact J4

If a, b, and c are the lengths of the sides of a triangle, with $a \leq b \leq c$, then the triangle is a right triangle if and only if $a^2 + b^2 = c^2$.

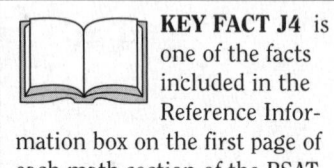

KEY FACT J4 is one of the facts included in the Reference Information box on the first page of each math section of the PSAT.

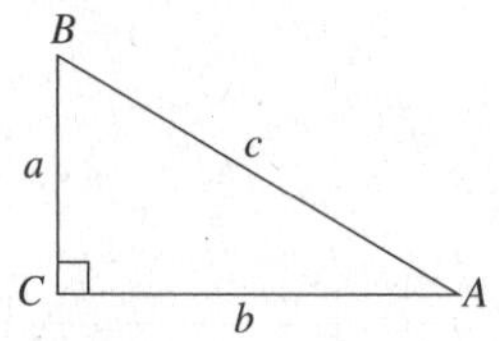

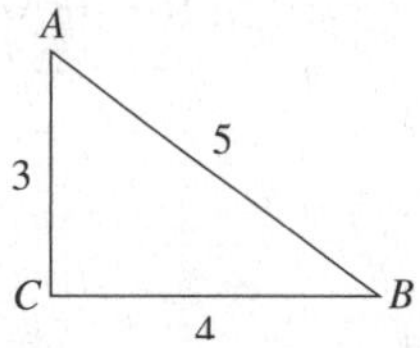

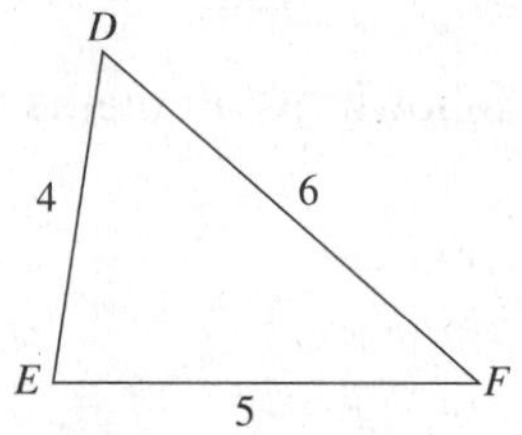

Since $3^2 + 4^2 = 5^2$, $\triangle ABC$ is a right triangle, whereas $\triangle DEF$ is not a right triangle, since $4^2 + 5^2 \neq 6^2$.

EXAMPLE 5

Which of the following are *not* the sides of a right triangle?

(A) 6, 8, 10
(B) 1, 1, $\sqrt{2}$
(C) 1, $\sqrt{3}$, 2
(D) $\sqrt{3}$, $\sqrt{4}$, $\sqrt{5}$
(E) 5, 12, 13

Solution. Just check each of the choices.

A: $6^2 + 8^2 = 36 + 64 = 100 = 10^2$ These *are* the sides of a right triangle.
B: $1^2 + 1^2 = 1 + 1 = 2 = (\sqrt{2})^2$ These *are* the sides of a right triangle.
C: $1^2 + (\sqrt{3})^2 = 1 + 3 = 4 = 2^2$ These *are* the sides of a right triangle.
D: $(\sqrt{3})^2 + (\sqrt{4})^2 = 3 + 4 = 7 \neq (\sqrt{5})^2$ These *are not* the sides of a right triangle.
E: $5^2 + 12^2 = 25 + 144 = 169 = 13^2$ These *are* the sides of a right triangle.

The answer is Choice D.

On the PSAT, the most common right triangles whose sides are *integers* are the 3-4-5 triangle and its multiples, such as 6-8-10 and 30-40-50.

Let x = length of each leg, and h = length of the hypotenuse, of an isosceles right triangle. By the Pythagorean theorem (**KEY FACT J4**), $x^2 + x^2 = h^2$. Then, $2x^2 = h^2$, and $h = \sqrt{2x^2} = x\sqrt{2}$.

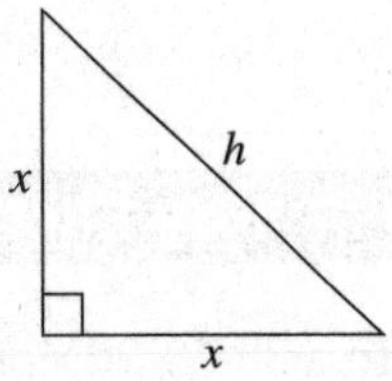

Key Fact J5

In a 45-45-90 right triangle, the sides are x, x, and $x\sqrt{2}$.

In a 45-45-90 right triangle:

- Multiply the length of a leg by $\sqrt{2}$ to find the length of the hypotenuse.
- Divide the hypotenuse by $\sqrt{2}$ to find the length of each leg.

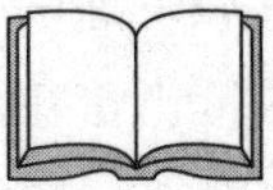

KEY FACT J5 is one of the facts included in the Reference Information box on the first page of each math section of the PSAT.

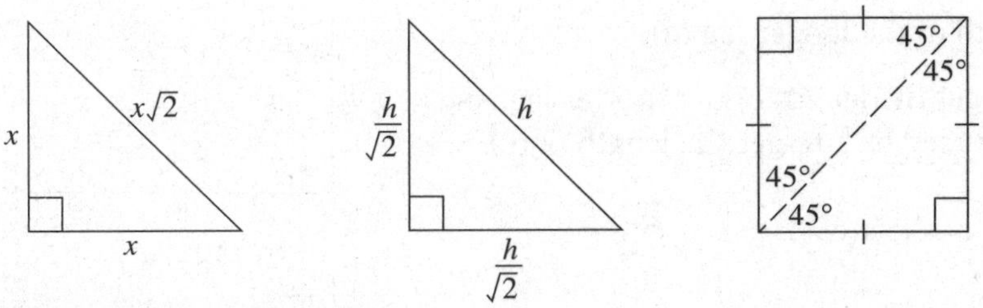

Key Fact J6

A diagonal of a square divides the square into two isosceles right triangles.

An ***altitude*** of a triangle is a line segment drawn from a vertex, perpendicular to the opposite side.

Key Fact J7

An altitude divides an equilateral triangle into two 30-60-90 right triangles.

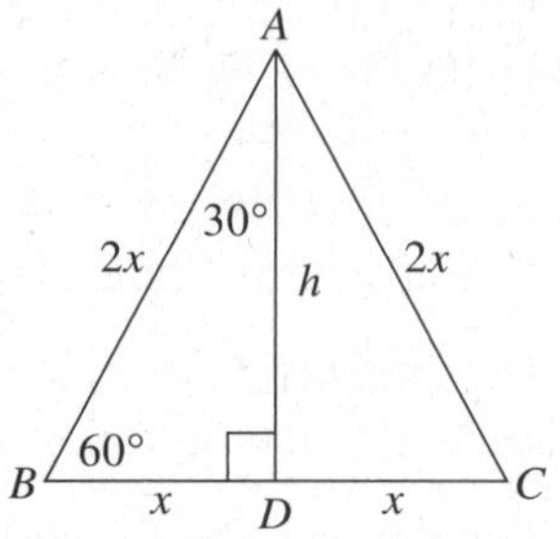

Let $2x$ be the length of each side of equilateral triangle ABC, in which altitude AD is drawn. Then $\triangle ABD$ is a 30-60-90 right triangle, and its sides are x, $2x$, and h. By the Pythagorean theorem,

$$x^2 + h^2 = (2x)^2 = 4x^2, \text{ so } h^2 = 3x^2,$$
$$\text{and } h = \sqrt{3x^2} = x\sqrt{3}.$$

Key Fact J8

In a 30-60-90 right triangle the sides are x, $x\sqrt{3}$, and $2x$.

KEY FACT J8 is one of the facts included in the Reference Information box on the first page of each math section of the PSAT.

In a 30-60-90 right triangle:

If you know the length of the shorter leg (x),

- multiply it by $\sqrt{3}$ to get the length of the longer leg, and
- multiply it by 2 to get the length of the hypotenuse.

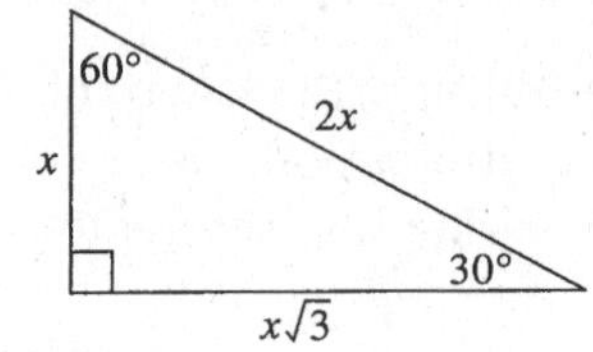

If you know the length of the longer leg (a),

- divide it by $\sqrt{3}$ to get the length of the shorter leg, and
- multiply the shorter leg by 2 to get the length of the hypotenuse.

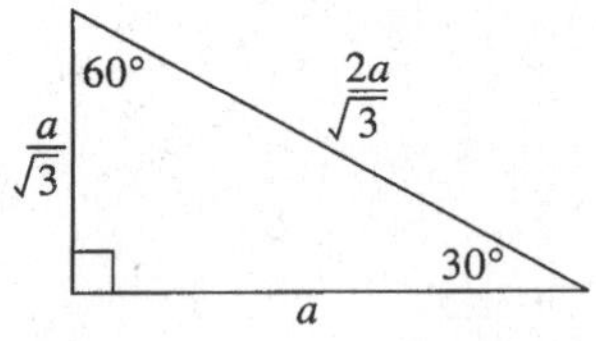

If you know the length of the hypotenuse (h),

- divide it by 2 to get the length of the shorter leg, and
- multiply the shorter leg by $\sqrt{3}$ to get the length of the longer leg.

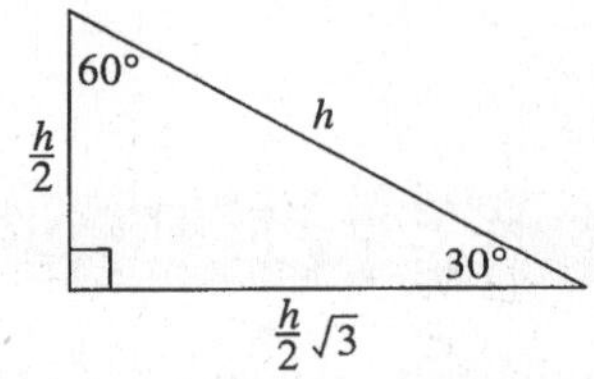

EXAMPLE 6

What is the area of a square whose diagonal is 4?

(A) 4
(B) 8
(C) 16
(D) $4\sqrt{3}$
(E) $16\sqrt{3}$

Solution. Draw a diagonal in a square of side s, creating a 45-45-90 right triangle. By **KEY FACT J6**,

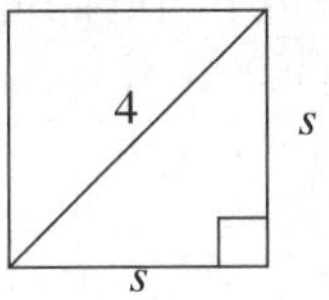

$$s = \frac{2}{\sqrt{2}} \text{ and } A = s^2 = \left(\frac{4}{\sqrt{2}}\right)^2 = \frac{16}{2} = 8.$$ The answer is Choice B.

EXAMPLE 7

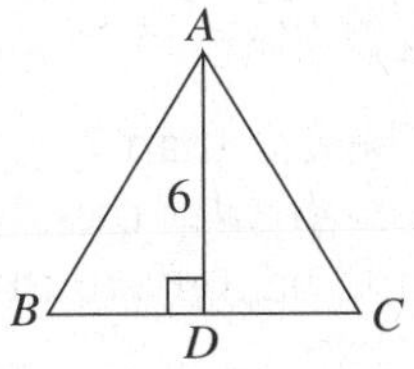

In equilateral triangle ABC, the length of altitude AD is 6. What is the perimeter of $\triangle ABC$?

(A) 18

(B) $6\sqrt{3}$

(C) $12\sqrt{3}$

(D) $18\sqrt{3}$

(E) 36

Solution. Use **KEY FACT J8.**

- Divide the longer leg, AD, of right triangle ADB by $\sqrt{3}$ to get the shorter leg, BD:

$$\frac{6}{\sqrt{3}} = \frac{6}{\sqrt{3}} \times \frac{\sqrt{3}}{\sqrt{3}} = \frac{6\sqrt{3}}{3} = 2\sqrt{3}.$$

- Multiply BD by 2 to get side BC. Then $BC = 2(2\sqrt{3}) = 4\sqrt{3}$.
- Finally, multiply BC by 3 to get the perimeter of $\triangle ABC$: $3(4\sqrt{3}) = 12\sqrt{3}$.
- The answer is Choice C.

Key Fact J9

(Triangle Inequality)

- The sum of the lengths of any two sides of a triangle is greater than the length of the third side.
- The difference of the lengths of any two sides of a triangle is less than the length of the third side.

EXAMPLE 8

If the lengths of two of the sides of a triangle are 7 and 8, which of the following could be the length of the third side?

I. 1
II. 2
III. 15

(A) None
(B) I only
(C) II only
(D) I and II only
(E) I, II, and III

Solution. Use **KEY FACT J9**.

- The length of the third side must be *less* than $7 + 8 = 15$. So III is false.
- The length of the third side must be *greater* than $8 - 7 = 1$. So I is false.
- *Any* number between 1 and 15 could be the length of the third side. So II is true.
- The answer is Choice C.

Key Fact J10

The area of a triangle is given by $A = \frac{1}{2}bh$, where b is the base and h is the height.

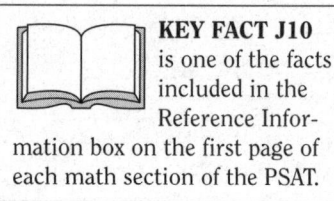

KEY FACT J10 is one of the facts included in the Reference Information box on the first page of each math section of the PSAT.

Note:
1. *Any* side of the triangle can be taken as the base.
2. The height is the altitude drawn to the base from the opposite vertex.
3. In a right triangle, either leg can be the base and the other the height.
4. The height may be outside the triangle. [See the figure below.]

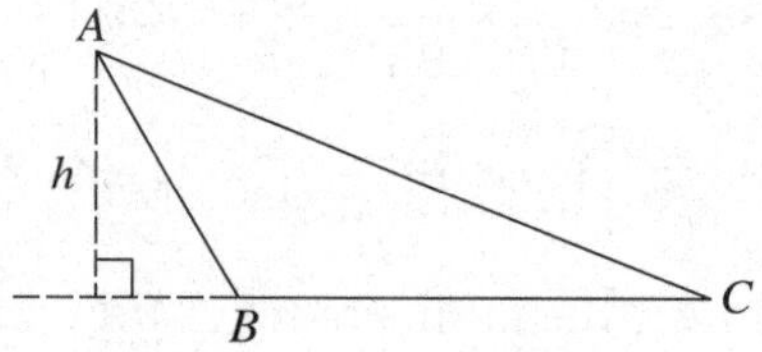

In the figure below:
If AC is the base, BD is the height. If AB is the base, CE is the height. If BC is the base, AF is the height.

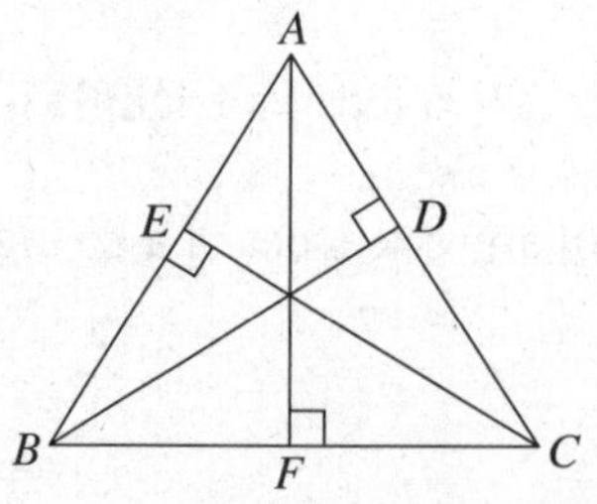

EXAMPLE 9

What is the area of an equilateral triangle whose sides are 10?

(A) 30
(B) $25\sqrt{3}$
(C) 50
(D) $50\sqrt{3}$
(E) 100

Solution. Draw an equilateral triangle and one of its altitudes.

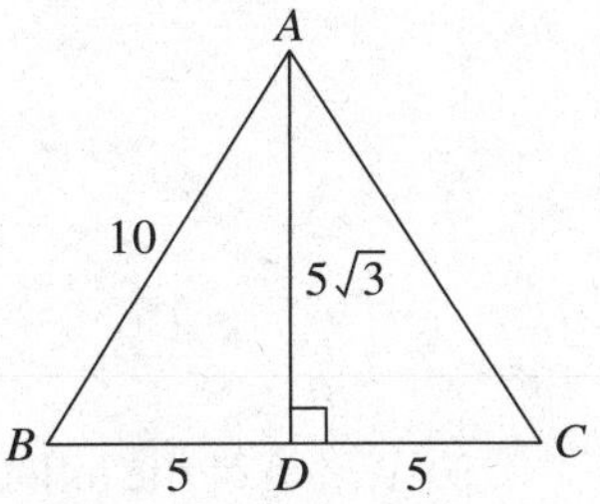

- By **KEY FACT J7**, $\triangle ABD$ is a 30-60-90 right triangle.
- By **KEY FACT J8**, $BD = 5$ and $AD = 5\sqrt{3}$.
- The area of $\triangle ABC = \frac{1}{2}(10)(5\sqrt{3}) = 25\sqrt{3}$ (Choice B).

Replacing 10 by s in Example 10 yields a very useful result.

Key Fact J11

If A represents the area of an equilateral triangle with side s, then $A = \frac{s^2\sqrt{3}}{4}$.

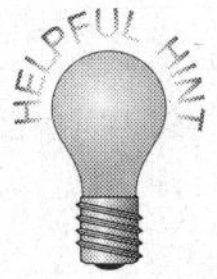

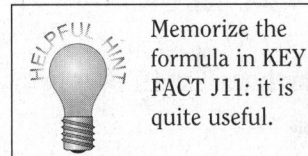

Memorize the formula in KEY FACT J11: it is quite useful.

Practice Exercises

MULTIPLE-CHOICE QUESTIONS

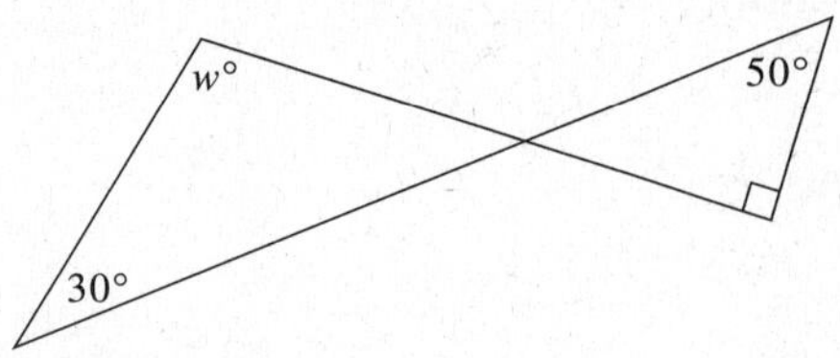

1. In the figure above, what is the value of w?

(A) 90
(B) 100
(C) 110
(D) 120
(E) 130

2. Two sides of a right triangle are 5 and 7. Which of the following could be the length of the third side?

I. $\sqrt{24}$
II. $\sqrt{54}$
III. $\sqrt{74}$

(A) I only
(B) II only
(C) I and II
(D) I and III
(E) I, II, and III

<u>Questions 3 and 4</u> refer to the following figure.

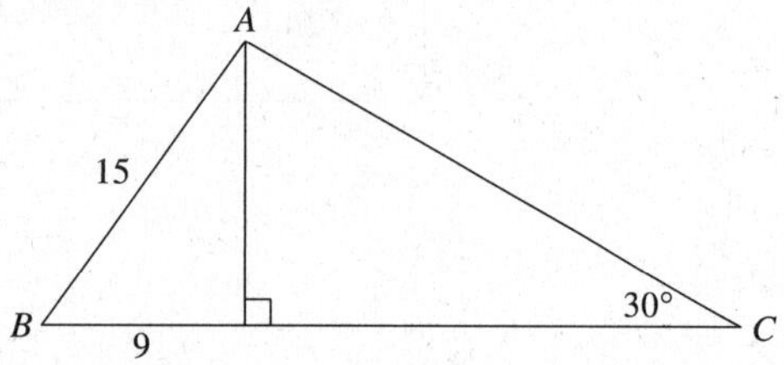

3. What is the perimeter of $\triangle ABC$?

(A) 48
(B) $48 + 12\sqrt{2}$
(C) $48 + 12\sqrt{3}$
(D) 72
(E) It cannot be determined from the information given.

4. What is the area of $\triangle ABC$?

(A) 108
(B) $54 + 72\sqrt{2}$
(C) $54 + 72\sqrt{3}$
(D) 198
(E) It cannot be determined from the information given.

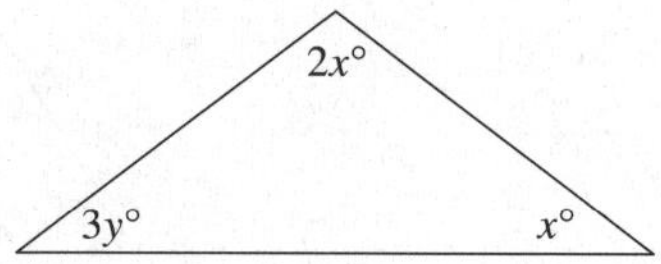

5. Which of the following expresses a true relationship between x and y in the figure above?

(A) $y = 60 - x$
(B) $y = x$
(C) $x + y = 90$
(D) $y = 180 - 3x$
(E) $x = 90 - 3y$

GRID-IN QUESTIONS

6. If the difference between the measures of the two smaller angles of a right triangle is 6°, what is the measure, in degrees, of the smallest angle?

7. What is the smallest integer x for which x, $x + 5$, and $2x - 15$ could be the lengths of the sides of a triangle?

8. If the measures of the angles of a triangle are in the ratio of 1:2:3 and if the length of the smallest side is 10, what is the length of the longest side?

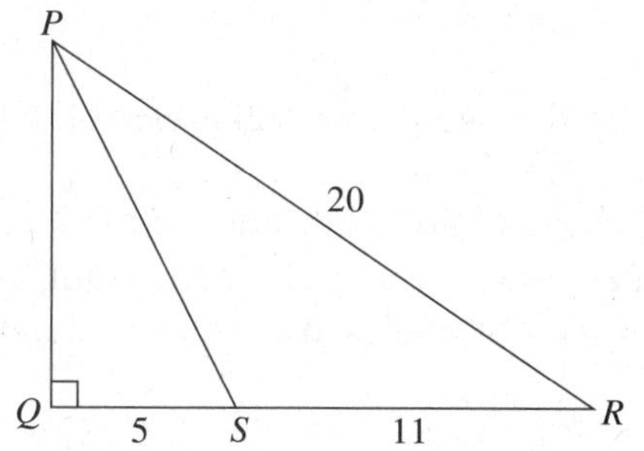

9. In the figure above, what is the value of *PS*?

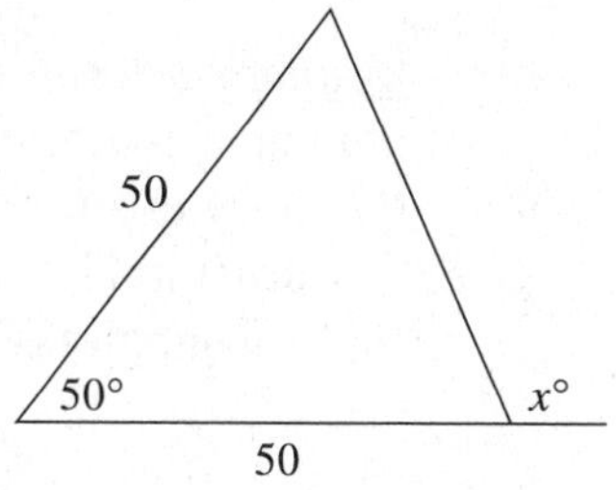

10. In the figure above, what is the value of x?

6.
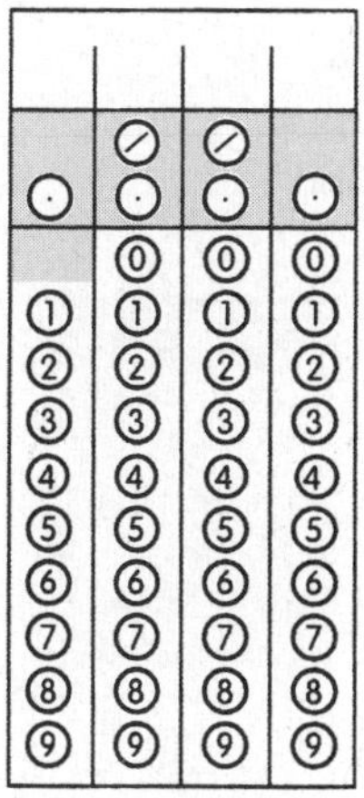

7.
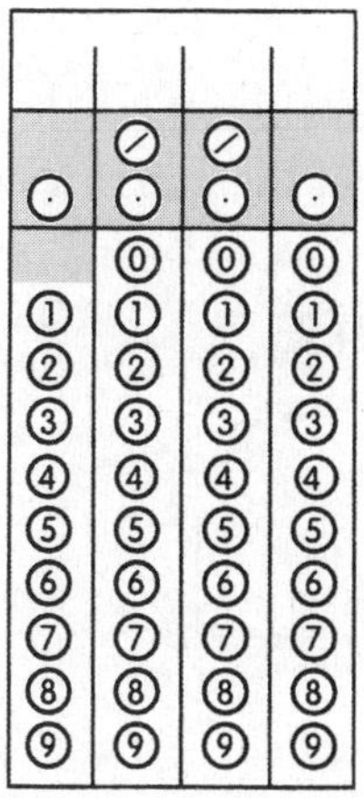

8.
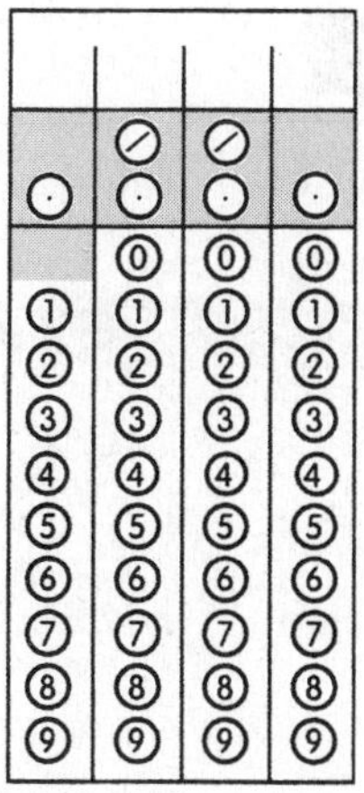

9.
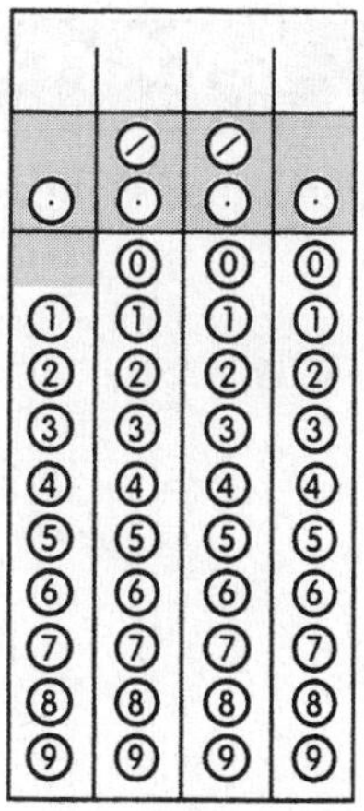

10.
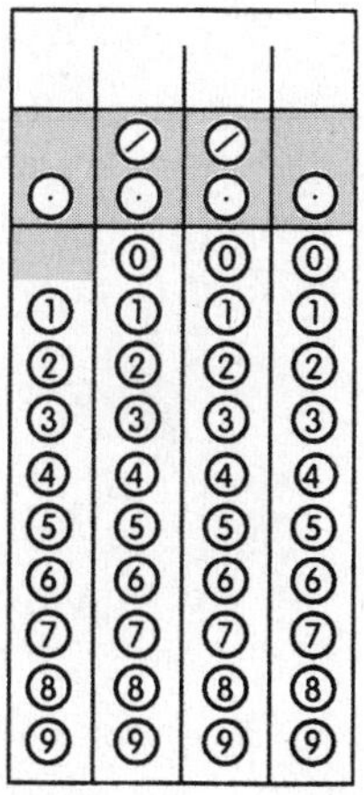

Answer Key

1. C **2.** D **3.** C **4.** C **5.** A

6.
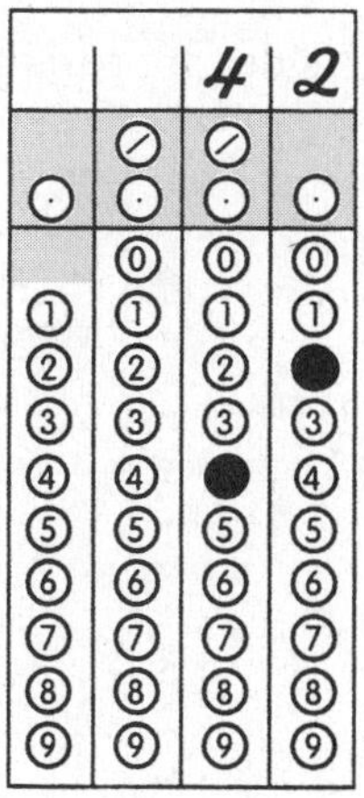

7.
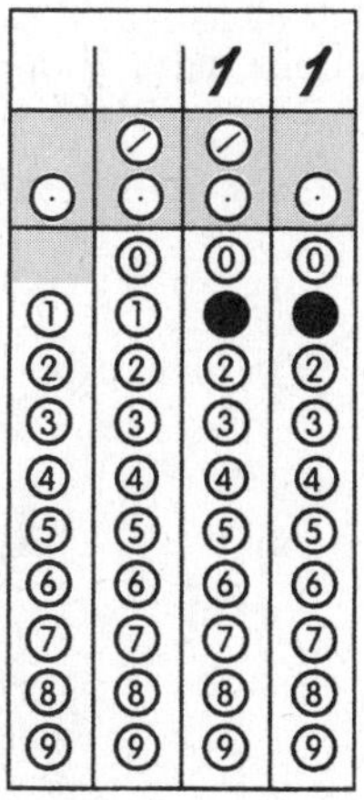

8.
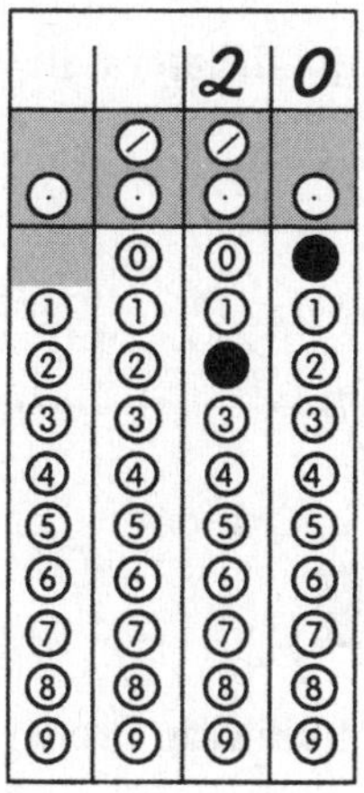

9.
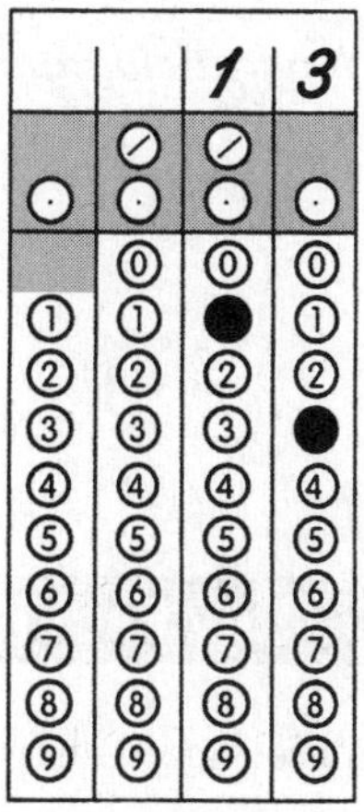

10.
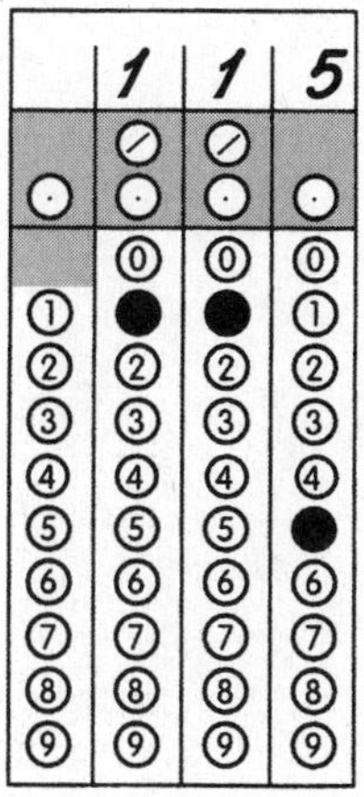

7-K QUADRILATERALS

A ***quadrilateral*** is a polygon with four sides. In this section we will present the key facts you need to know about three special quadrilaterals.

Every quadrilateral has two diagonals. If you draw in either one, you will divide the quadrilateral into two triangles. Since the sum of the measures of the three angles in each of the triangles is 180°, the sum of the measures of the angles in the quadrilateral is 360°.

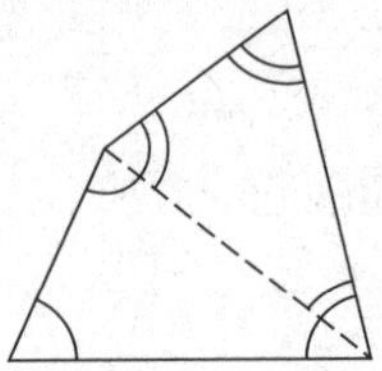

Key Fact K1

In any quadrilateral, the sum of the measures of the four angles is 360°.

EXAMPLE 1

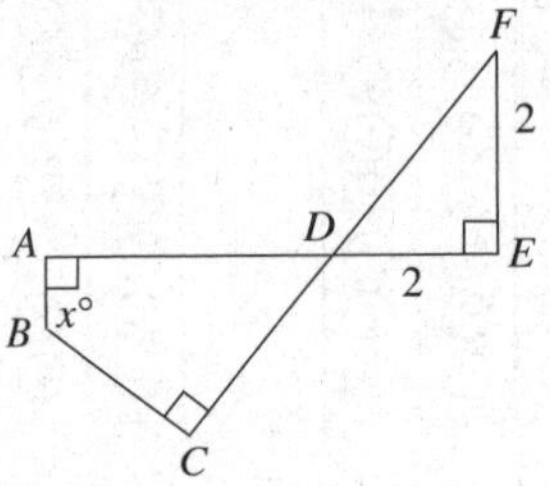

In the figure above, what is the value of x?

Solution. Since $\triangle DEF$ is an isosceles right triangle, $m\angle EDF = 45°$; also, since the two angles at vertex D are vertical angles, their measures are equal. Therefore, the measure of $\angle ADC$ is 45°. Finally, since the sum of the measures of all four angles of $ABCD$ is 360°:

$$45 + 90 + 90 + x = 360 \Rightarrow 225 + x = 360 \Rightarrow x = 135.$$

A ***parallelogram*** is a quadrilateral in which both pairs of opposite sides are parallel.

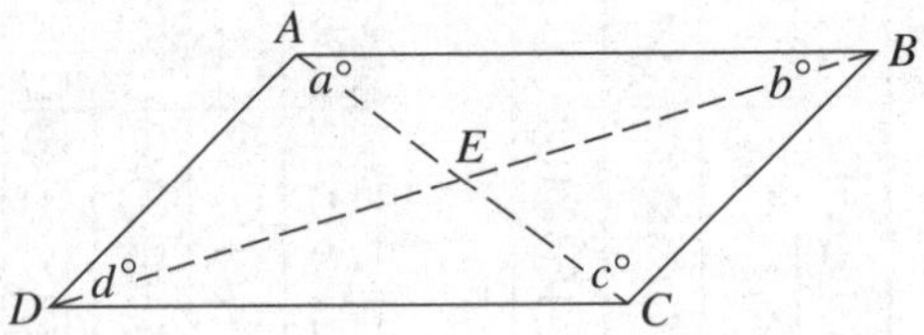

Key Fact K2

Parallelograms have the following properties:

- Opposite sides are equal: $AB = CD$ and $AD = BC$.
- Opposite angles are equal: $a = c$ and $b = d$.
- Adjacent angles add up to 180°: $a + b = b + c = c + d = a + d = 180$.
- The diagonals bisect each other: $AE = EC$ and $DE = EB$.

EXAMPLE 2

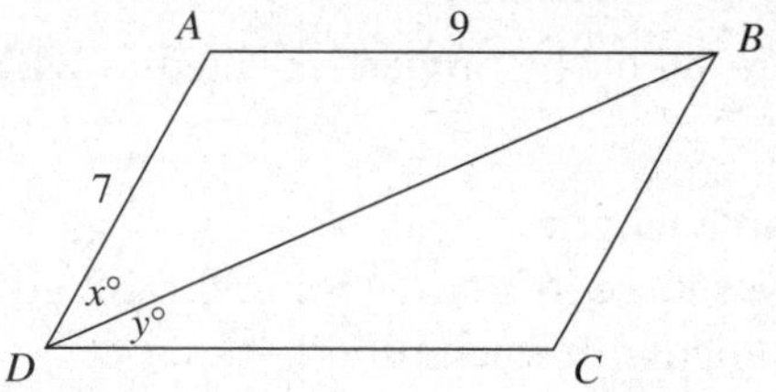

In the figure above, *ABCD* is a parallelogram. Which of the following statements must be true?

(A) $x < y$
(B) $x = y$
(C) $x > y$
(D) $x + y < 90$
(E) $x + y > 90$

Solution. Since $\overline{AB}$ and $\overline{CD}$ are parallel line segments cut by transversal $\overline{BD}$, $m\angle ABD = y°$. In $\triangle ABD$ $AB > AD$, so by **KEY FACT J3**, the measure of the angle opposite $\overline{AB}$ is greater than the measure of the angle opposite $\overline{AD}$. Therefore, $x > y$ (Choice C).

A ***rectangle*** is a parallelogram in which all four angles are right angles. Two adjacent sides of a rectangle are usually called the ***length*** (l) and the ***width*** (w).

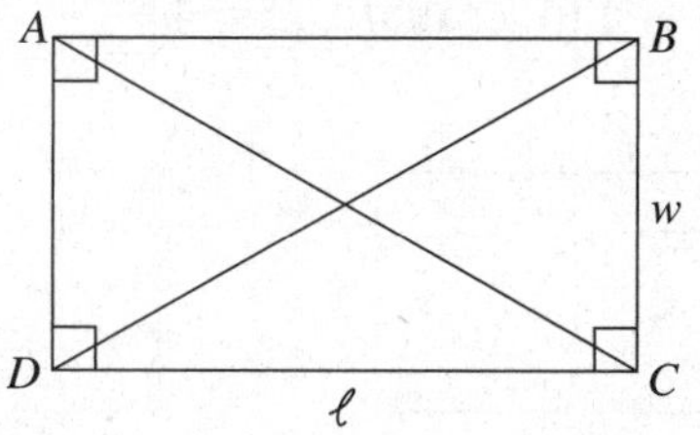

Key Fact K3

Since a rectangle is a parallelogram, all of the properties listed in **KEY FACT K2** hold for rectangles. In addition,

- The measure of each angle in a rectangle is 90°.
- The diagonals of a rectangle have the same length: $AC = BD$.

A ***square*** is a rectangle in which all four sides have the same length.

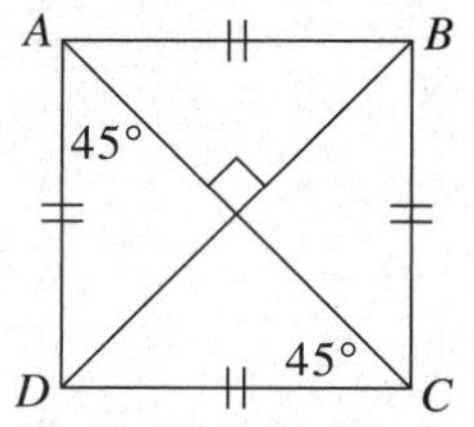

Key Fact K4

Since a square is a rectangle, all of the properties listed in **KEY FACTS K2** and **K3** hold for squares. In addition,

- All four sides have the same length.
- Each diagonal divides the square into two 45-45-90 right triangles.
- The diagonals are perpendicular to each other: $AC \perp BD$.

EXAMPLE 3

What is the length of each side of a square if its diagonals are 8?

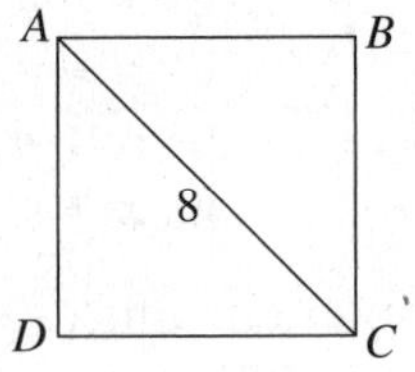

Solution. Draw a diagram. In square *ABCD*, diagonal *AC* is the hypotenuse of a 45-45-90 right triangle, and side *AB* is a leg of that triangle. By **KEY FACT J5**,

$$AB = \frac{AC}{\sqrt{2}} = \frac{8}{\sqrt{2}} \times \frac{\sqrt{2}}{\sqrt{2}} = \frac{8\sqrt{2}}{2} = 4\sqrt{2}.$$

The ***perimeter*** (*P*) of any polygon is the sum of the lengths of all its sides.

Key Fact K5

In a rectangle, $P = 2(\ell + w)$, and in a square, $P = 4s$.

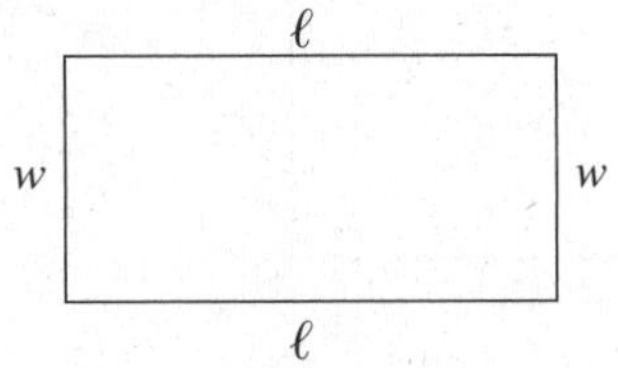

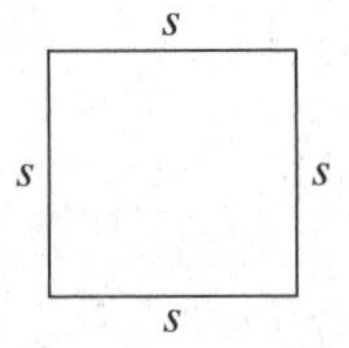

$P = \ell + w + \ell + w = 2(\ell + w)$ $\quad$ $P = s + s + s + s = 4s$

EXAMPLE 4

A rectangle is divided into two squares, each with a perimeter of 10. What is the perimeter of the rectangle?

(A) 10
(B) 12.5
(C) 15
(D) 17.5
(E) 20

Solution. Don't do anything until you have drawn a diagram.

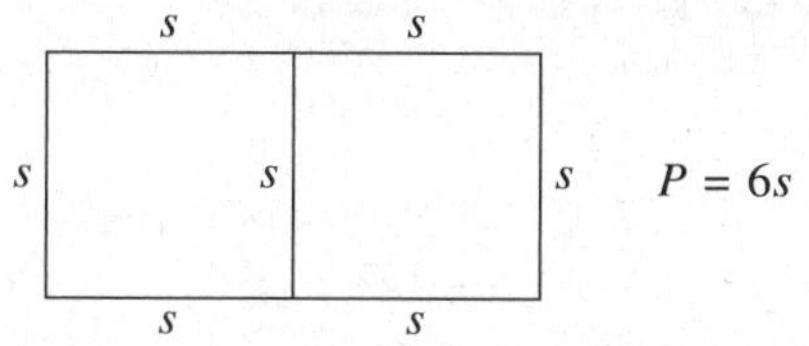

Since the perimeter of each square is 10, the length of each side is $10 \div 4 = 2.5$. Therefore, the perimeter of the rectangle is $6 \times 2.5 = 15$ (Choice C).

In Section 9-J we reviewed the formula for the ***area*** of a triangle. You also need to know the area formulas for a parallelogram, rectangle, and square.

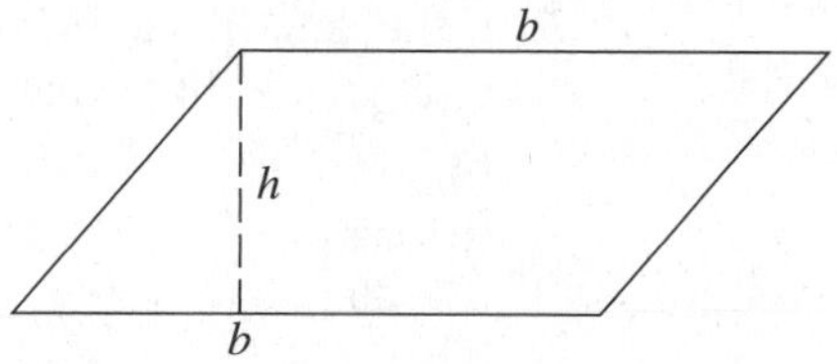

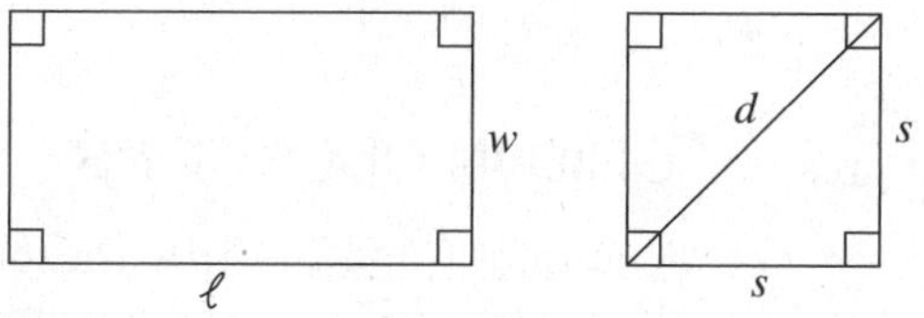

The formula for the area of a rectangle, given in **KEY FACT K6** is one of the facts included in the Reference Information box on the first page of each math section of the PSAT.

Key Fact K6

Here are the area formulas you need to know:

- For a parallelogram: $A = bh$
- For a rectangle: $A = \ell w$
- For a square: $A = s^2$ or $A = \frac{1}{2}d^2$

EXAMPLE 5

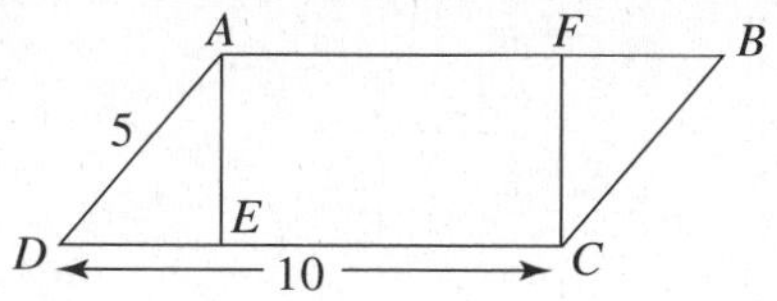

In the figure above, the area of parallelogram *ABCD* is 40. What is the area of rectangle *AFCE*?

(A) 20
(B) 24
(C) 28
(D) 32
(E) 36

Solution. Since the base *CD*, is 10 and the area of *ABCD* is 40, the height *AE* must be 4. Then $\triangle AED$ must be a 3-4-5 right triangle with $DE = 3$, which implies that $EC = 7$. The area of the rectangle is $7 \times 4 = 28$ (Choice C).

Practice Exercises

MULTIPLE-CHOICE QUESTIONS

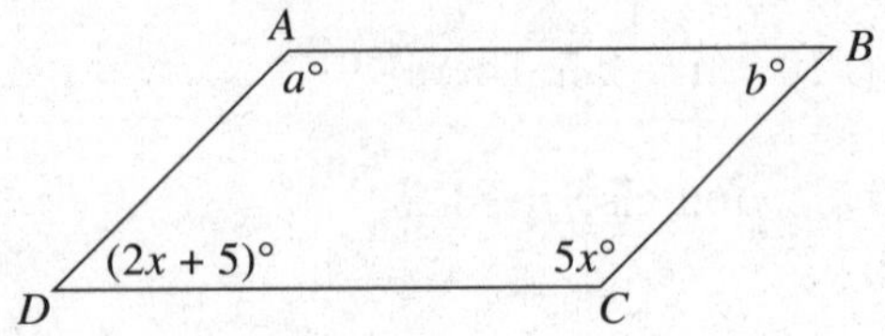

1. In the figure above, *ABCD* is a parallelogram. What is the value of $a - b$?

(A) 25
(B) 55
(C) 70
(D) 90
(E) 125

2. What is the perimeter of a rectangle whose area is 21?

(A) 10
(B) 20
(C) 21
(D) 44
(E) It cannot be determined from the information given.

3. The length of a rectangle is 10 more than the side of a square, and the width of the rectangle is 10 less than the side of the square. If the area of the square is 125, what is the area of the rectangle?

(A) 25
(B) 115
(C) 125
(D) 135
(E) 225

4. What is the area of a square whose diagonals are 12?

(A) $5\sqrt{2}$
(B) $50\sqrt{2}$
(C) 72
(D) 144
(E) $144\sqrt{2}$

5. If the length of a rectangle is 4 times its width, and if its area is 144, what is its perimeter?

(A) 6
(B) 24
(C) 30
(D) 60
(E) 96

GRID-IN QUESTIONS

Questions 6 and 7 refer to the following figure, in which *M, N, O,* and *P* are the midpoints of the sides of rectangle *ABCD*.

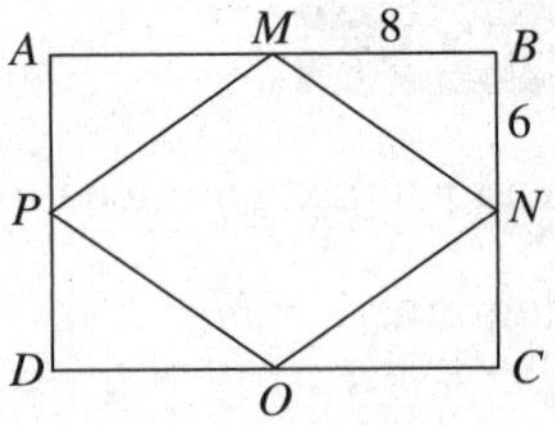

6. What is the perimeter of quadrilateral *MNOP*?

7. What is the area of quadrilateral *MNOP*?

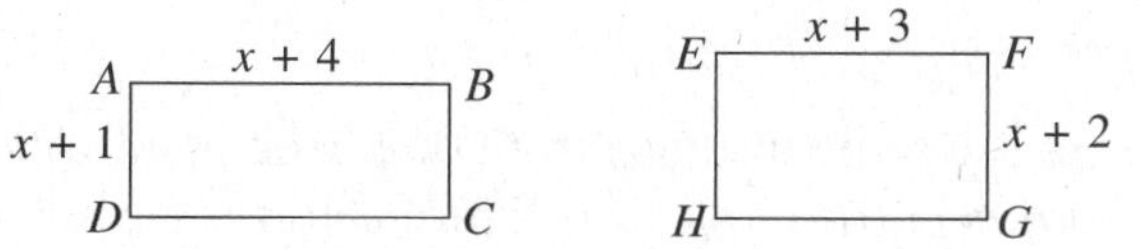

8. If in the figures above, the area of rectangle $ABCD$ is 100, what is the area of rectangle $EFGH$?

9. In quadrilateral $PQRS$, the measure of angle S is 20 more than the average of the measures of the other three. What is the measure of angle S?

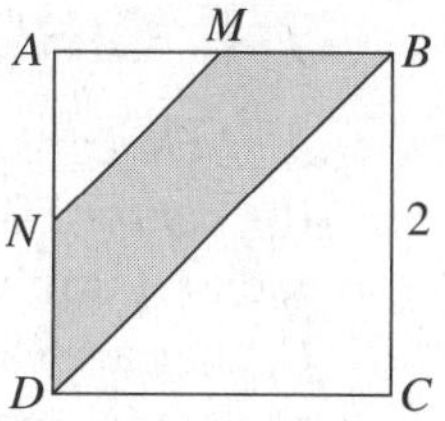

10. If in the figure above, M and N are the midpoints of two of the sides of square $ABCD$, what is the area of the shaded region?

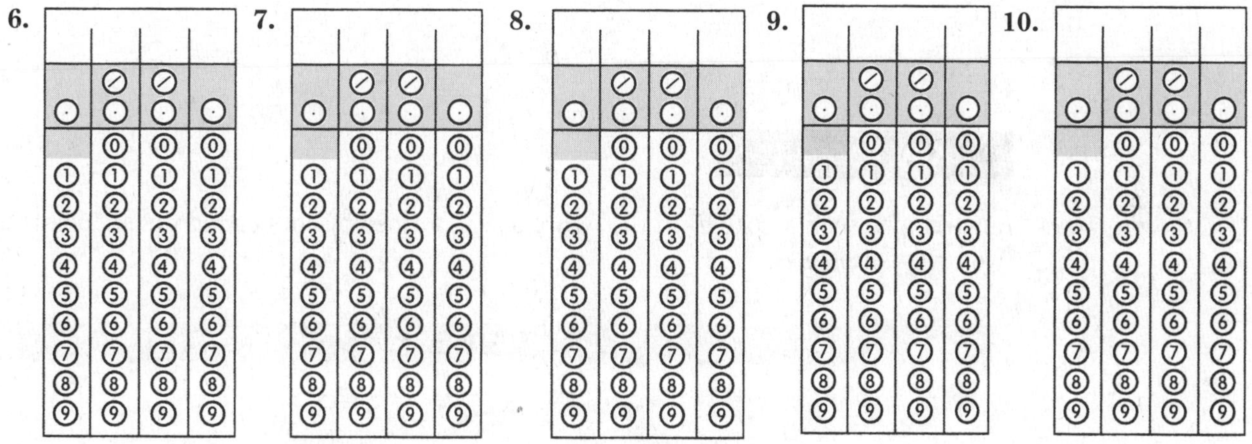

Answer Key

1. C **2.** E **3.** A **4.** C **5.** D

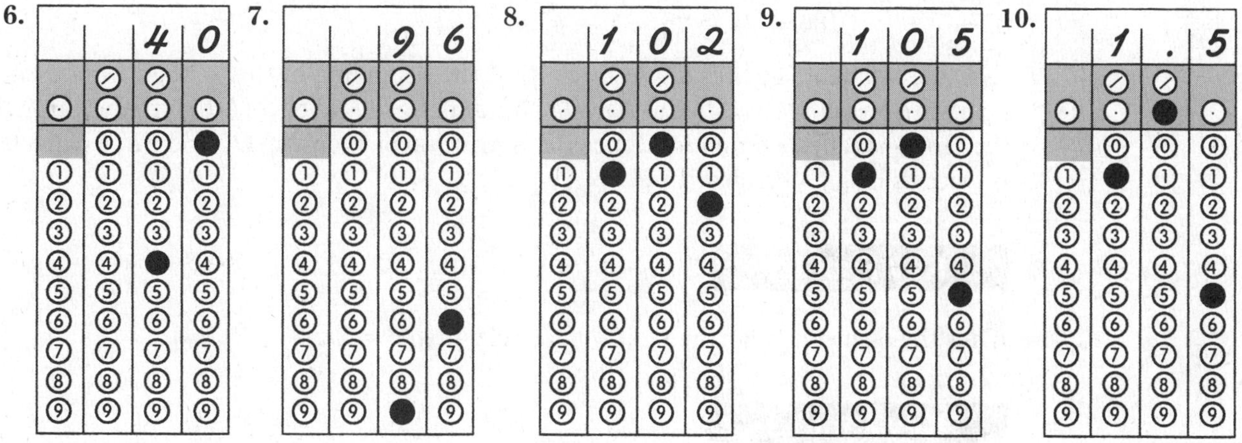

7-L CIRCLES

A ***circle*** consists of all the points that are the same distance from one fixed point called the ***center***. That distance is called the ***radius*** of the circle. The figure below is a circle of radius 1 unit whose center is at the point O. Since A, B, C, D, and E are all points on circle O, they are each 1 unit from O. The word ***radius*** is also used to represent any of the line segments joining the center and a point on the circle. The plural of *radius* is *radii*. In circle O, $\overline{OA}$, $\overline{OB}$, $\overline{OC}$, $\overline{OD}$, and $\overline{OE}$ are all radii. If a circle has radius r, each of the radii is r units long.

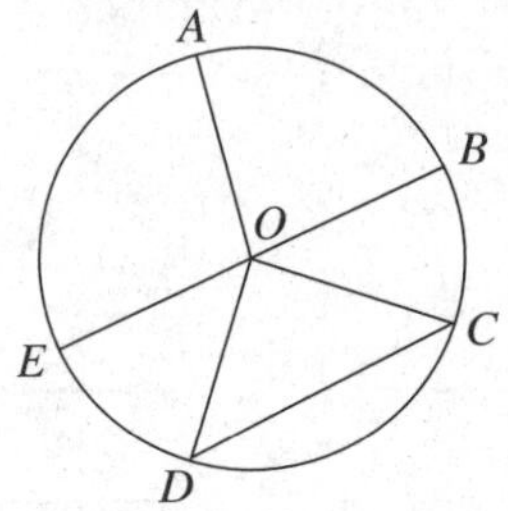

Key Fact L1

Any triangle, such as $\triangle COD$ in the figure above, formed by connecting the endpoints of two radii, is isosceles.

EXAMPLE 1

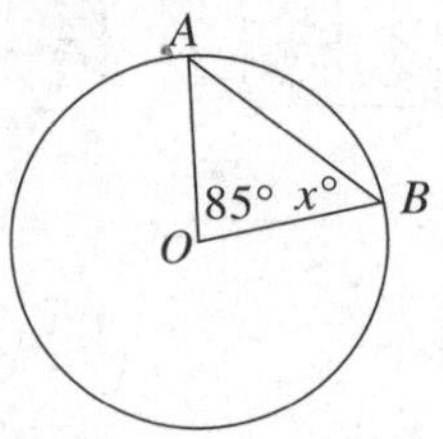

If A and B are points on circle O, what is the value of x?

Solution. Since $\triangle AOB$ is isosceles, angles A and B have the same measure. So $85 + x + x = 180 \Rightarrow 2x = 95 \Rightarrow x = 47.5$.

A line segment, such as $\overline{CD}$ in circle O at the beginning of this section, whose endpoints are on a circle, is called a ***chord***. A chord such as $\overline{BE}$ in circle O that passes through the center is called a ***diameter***. Since $\overline{BE}$ is made up of two radii, $\overline{OB}$ and $\overline{OE}$, a diameter is twice as long as a radius.

Key Fact L2

If d is the diameter and r the radius of a circle, then $d = 2r$.

Key Fact L3

A diameter is the longest chord that can be drawn in a circle.

EXAMPLE 2

A, *B*, and *C*, the three vertices of right triangle *ABC*, all lie on a circle whose radius is 4. Which of the following statements *could* be true?

I. The hypotenuse of $\triangle ABC$ is 10
II. The perimeter of $\triangle ABC$ is 25
III. The area of $\triangle ABC$ is 35

(A) None
(B) I only
(C) II only
(D) III only
(E) I, II, and III

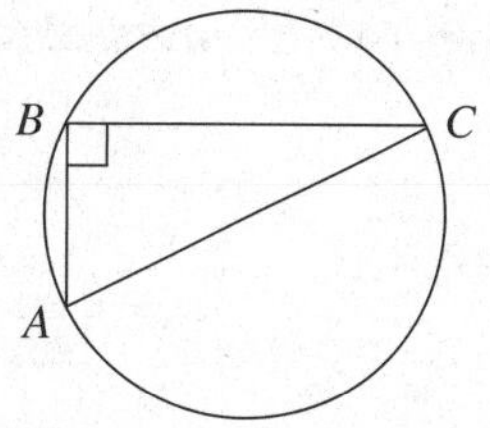

Solution. Since the radius is 4, the diameter is 8. Since each side of $\triangle ABC$ is a chord, none of the sides can be greater than 8; so *AC* cannot be 10 (I is false), and the perimeter can surely not exceed 24 (II is false). Since the area of a right triangle can be calculated using one of the legs as the base and the other as the height, the area cannot exceed $\frac{1}{2}(8)(8) = 32$ and so cannot equal 35 (III is false). None of the statements is true (Choice A).

The total length around a circle is called the ***circumference*** of the circle. In every circle the ratio of the circumference to the diameter is exactly the same and is denoted by the symbol π (the Greek letter pi).

Key Fact L4

For every circle,

$$\pi = \frac{\text{circumference}}{\text{diameter}} = \frac{C}{d} \quad \text{or} \quad C = \pi d \quad \text{or} \quad C = 2\pi r$$

$C = 2\pi r$ is one of the facts included in the Reference Information box on the first page of each math section of the PSAT.

Key Fact L5

The value of π is *approximately* 3.14.

HELPFUL HINT

On almost every question on the PSAT that involve circles, you are expected to leave your answer in terms of π; so don't multiply by 3.14 unless you need to. If you need an approximation—to test a choice, for example—then use the π-key on your calculator.

EXAMPLE 3

If the circumference of a circle is equal to the perimeter of a square whose sides are π, what is the radius of the circle?

Solution. If each side of the square is π, then its perimeter is 4π. Since the circumference of the circle is equal to the perimeter of the square, $C = 4\pi$. But $C = 2\pi r$, and so $2\pi r = 4\pi \Rightarrow r = 2$.

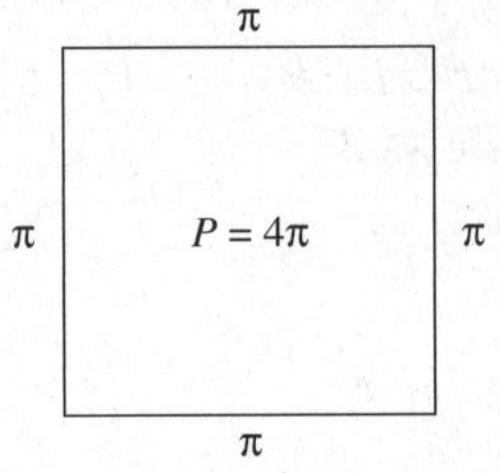

An ***arc*** consists of two points on a circle and all the points between them. If two points, such as P and Q in circle O, are the endpoints of a diameter, they divide the circle into two arcs called ***semicircles***. On the PSAT, *arc AB* always refers to the small arc joining A and B.

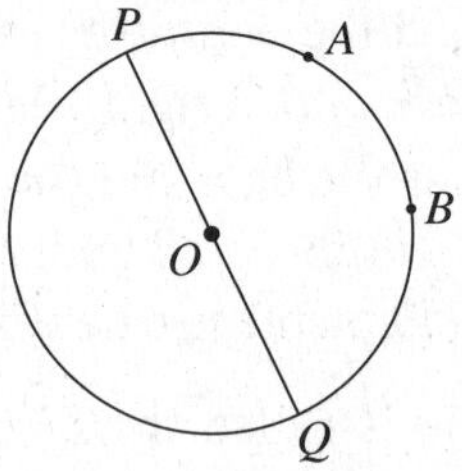

An angle whose vertex is at the center of a circle is called a ***central angle***.

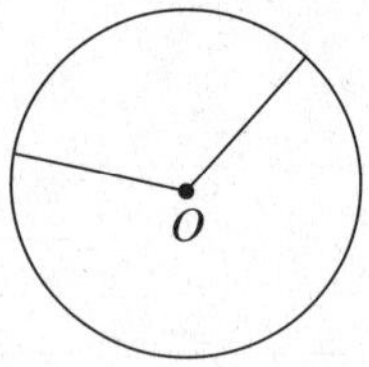

Key Fact L6

The degree measure of a complete circle is 360°.

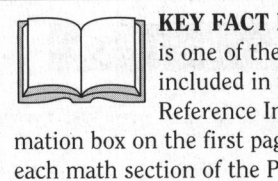

KEY FACT L6 is one of the facts included in the Reference Information box on the first page of each math section of the PSAT.

Key Fact L7

The degree measure of an arc equals the degree measure of the central angle that intercepts it.

CAUTION: Degree measure is *not* a measure of length. In these circles, arcs *AB* and *CD* each measure 72°, even though arc *CD* is much longer.

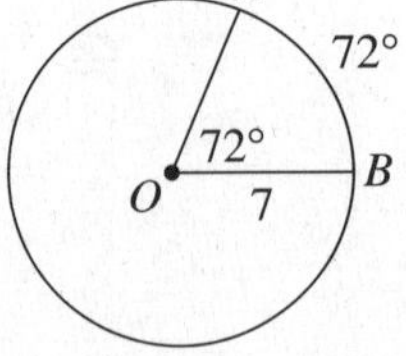

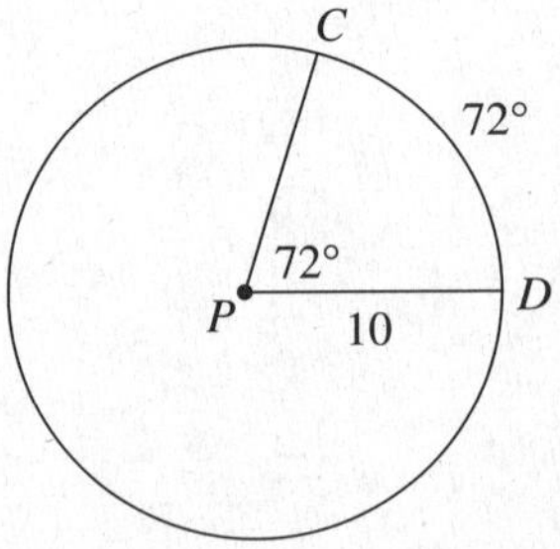

How long *is* arc *CD*? Since the radius of circle *P* is 10, its diameter is 20, and its circumference is 20π. Since there are 360° in a circle, arc *CD* is $\frac{72}{360}$, or $\frac{1}{5}$, of the circumference: $\frac{1}{5}(20\pi) = 4\pi$.

Key Fact L8

The formula for the area of a circle of radius r is $A = \pi r^2$.

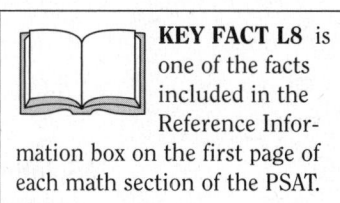

KEY FACT L8 is one of the facts included in the Reference Information box on the first page of each math section of the PSAT.

The area of circle *P*, above, is $\pi(10)^2 = 100\pi$ square units. The area of sector *CPD* is $\frac{1}{5}$ of the area of the circle: $\frac{1}{5}(100\pi) = 20\pi$.

Key Fact L9

If an arc measures $x°$, the length of the arc is $\frac{x}{360}(2\pi r)$, and the area of the sector formed by the arc and two radii is $\frac{x}{360}(\pi r^2)$.

Examples 4 and 5 refer to the figure below, in which the radius of the inner circle is 4 and the radius of the outer circle is 6.

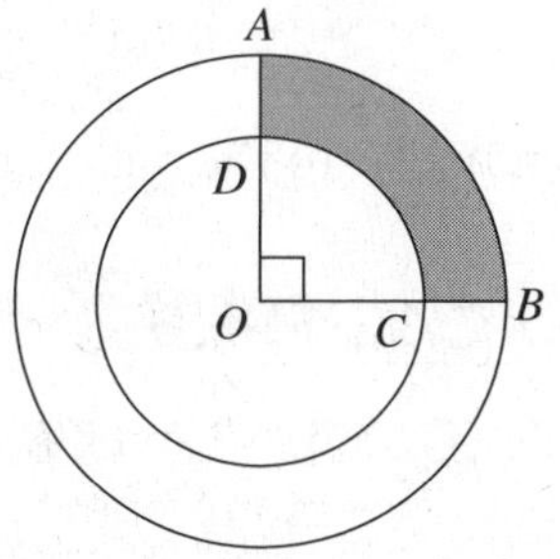

EXAMPLE 4

What is the area of the shaded region, *ABCD*?

(A) 4π
(B) 5π
(C) 9π
(D) 16π
(E) 20π

Solution. To find the area of *ABCD*, subtract the area of sector *DOC* from the area of sector *AOB*. Since $m\angle AOB$ is 90°, each sector is a quarter-circle.

The area of $AOB = \frac{1}{4}\pi(6)^2 = \frac{1}{4}(36\pi) = 9\pi$.

The area of $COD = \frac{1}{4}\pi(4)^2 = \frac{1}{4}(16\pi) = 4\pi$.

So the area of $ABCD = 9\pi - 4\pi = 5\pi$ (Choice B).

EXAMPLE 5

What is the perimeter of the shaded region, *ABCD*?

(A) 5π
(B) $2 + 5\pi$
(C) $4 + 5\pi$
(D) $4 + 20\pi$
(E) $4 + 24\pi$

Solution. Arcs *AB* and *CD* are each quarter-circles, and so their lengths are $\frac{1}{4}$ of the circumferences of circles whose diameters are 8 and 12.

$$AB = \frac{1}{4}(12\pi) = 3\pi \qquad CD = \frac{1}{4}(8\pi) = 2\pi$$

The lengths of line segments *AD* and *BC* are each $6 - 4 = 2$. So the perimeter is $2 + 2 + 3\pi + 2\pi = 4 + 5\pi$ (Choice C).

A line that touches a circle at exactly one point is called a ***tangent***. In the figure below, line *l* is ***tangent*** to circle *O* at point *P*.

Key Fact L10

A line tangent to a circle is perpendicular to the radius drawn to the point of contact.

EXAMPLE 6

If line *l* is tangent to circle *O* at point *P* and if *B* is a point on *l* such that $PB = 8$ and $OB = 10$, what is the radius of the circle?

Solution. Draw a diagram and label it. By **KEY FACT L10**, radius $\overline{OP}$ is perpendicular to *l*. Therefore, $\triangle OPB$ is a right triangle.

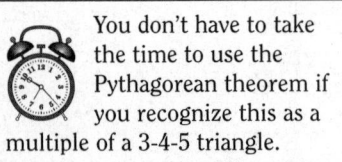

You don't have to take the time to use the Pythagorean theorem if you recognize this as a multiple of a 3-4-5 triangle.

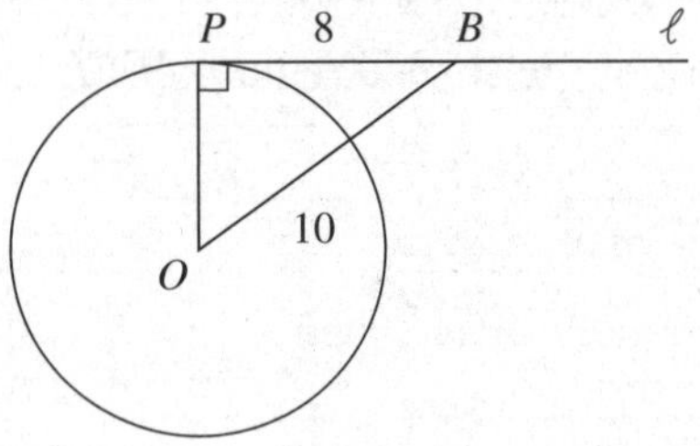

By the Pythagorean theorem,

$$OP^2 + 8^2 = 10^2 \Rightarrow OP^2 + 64 = 100 \Rightarrow OP^2 = 36 \Rightarrow OP = 6.$$

Practice Exercises

MULTIPLE-CHOICE QUESTIONS

Questions 1 and 2 refer to the following figure.

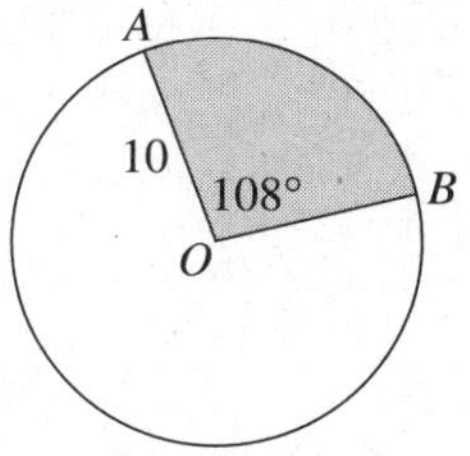

1. What is the length of arc AB?
   (A) 3π
   (B) 6π
   (C) 12π
   (D) 18π
   (E) 30π

2. What is the area of the shaded sector?
   (A) 3π
   (B) 6π
   (C) 12π
   (D) 18π
   (E) 30π

3. What is the circumference of a circle whose area is 100π?
   (A) 10
   (B) 20
   (C) 10π
   (D) 20π
   (E) 25π

4. What is the area of a circle whose circumference is π?
   (A) $\frac{\pi}{4}$
   (B) $\frac{\pi}{2}$
   (C) π
   (D) 2π
   (E) 4π

5. What is the area of a circle whose radius is the diagonal of a square whose area is 4?
   (A) 2π
   (B) $2\pi\sqrt{2}$
   (C) 4π
   (D) 8π
   (E) 16π

GRID-IN QUESTIONS

6. The circumferences of two circles are in the ratio of 3:5. What is the ratio of the area of the smaller circle to the area of the larger circle?

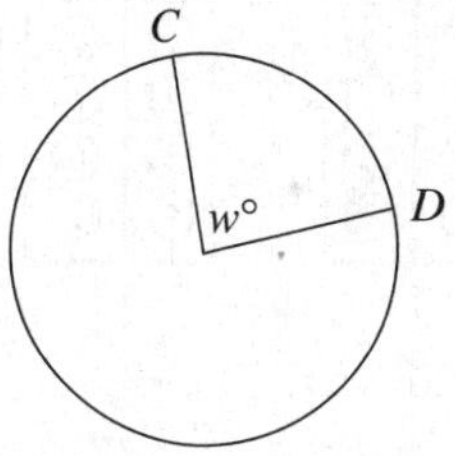

7. In the figure above, the ratio of the length of arc CD to the circumference of the circle is 2:9. What is the value of w?

8. The circumference of a circle is $a\pi$ units, and the area of the circle is $b\pi$ square units. If $a = b$, what is the radius of the circle?

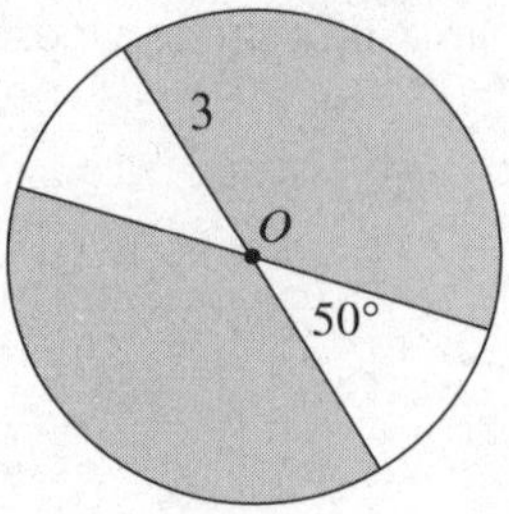

9. In the figure above, the radius of circle O is 3, and the area of the shaded region is $k\pi$. What is the value of k?

10. If the area of a circle whose diameter is π, is written as $a\pi^b$, what is the value of ab?

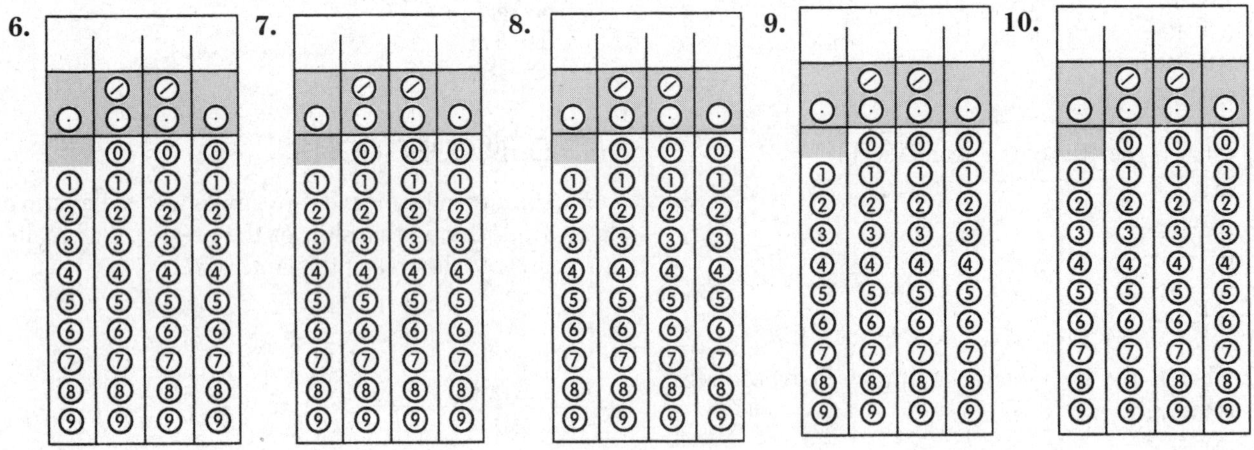

Answer Key

1. B **2.** E **3.** D **4.** A **5.** D

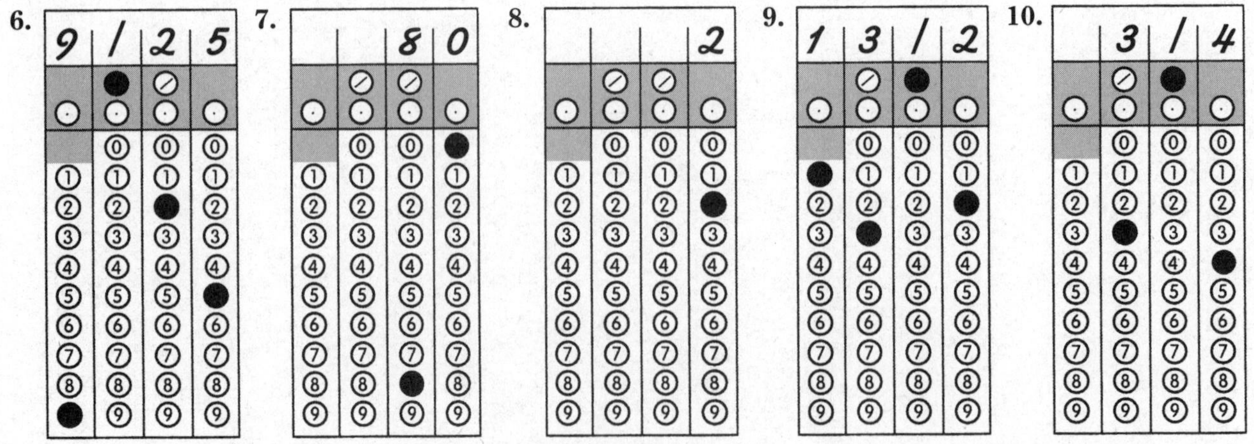

7-M SOLID GEOMETRY

There is very little solid geometry on the PSAT. Basically, all you need to know are the formulas for the volume and surface areas of rectangular solids (including cubes) and cylinders.

A ***rectangular solid*** or ***box*** is a solid formed by six rectangles, called ***faces***. The sides of the rectangles are called ***edges***. As shown in the diagram below, the edges are called the ***length***, ***width***, and ***height***. A ***cube*** is a rectangular solid in which the length, width, and height are equal, so all the edges are the same length.

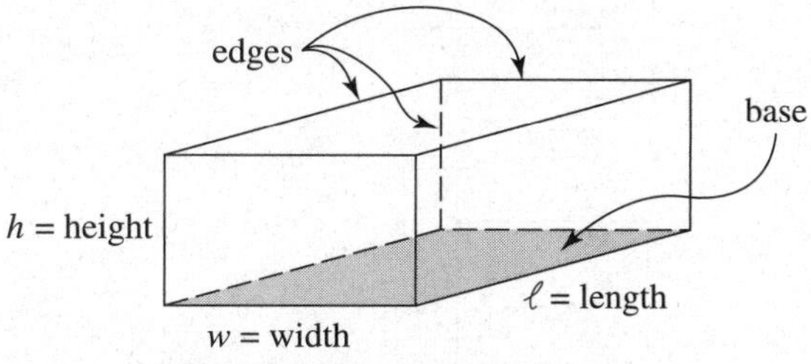

RECTANGULAR SOLID

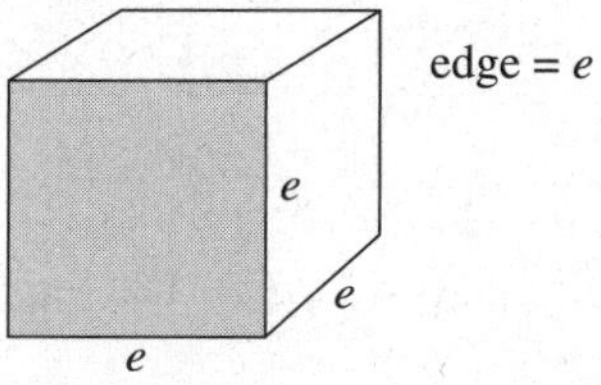

CUBE

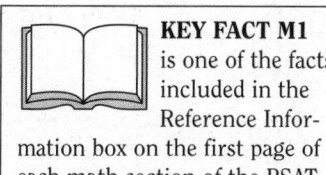

KEY FACT M1 is one of the facts included in the Reference Information box on the first page of each math section of the PSAT.

Key Fact M1

The formula for the volume of a rectangular solid is $V = \ell wh$.

In a cube, all the edges are equal. Therefore, if e is the edge, the formula for the volume is $V = e^3$.

EXAMPLE 1

The base of a rectangular tank is 3 feet wide and 4 feet long; the height of the tank is 10 inches. If water is pouring into the tank at the rate of 3 cubic feet per hour, how many *minutes* will be required to fill the tank?

Solution. Draw a picture. Change all units to feet. Then the volume of the tank is $3 \times 4 \times \frac{5}{6} = 10$ cubic feet. At 3 cubic feet per hour, the required time is $\frac{10}{3}$ hours $= \frac{10}{3}(60) = 200$ minutes.

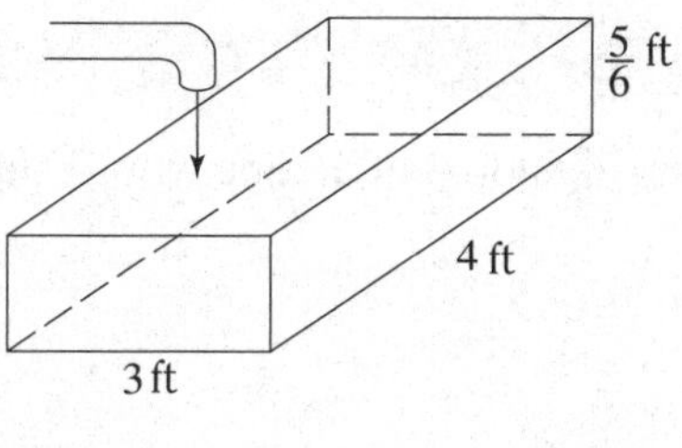

To find the ***surface area*** of a rectangular solid, add the area of the six rectangular faces. Since the top and bottom faces are equal, the front and back faces are equal, and the left and right faces are equal, we can calculate the area of one face from each pair and then double the sum. In a cube, each of the six faces has the same area.

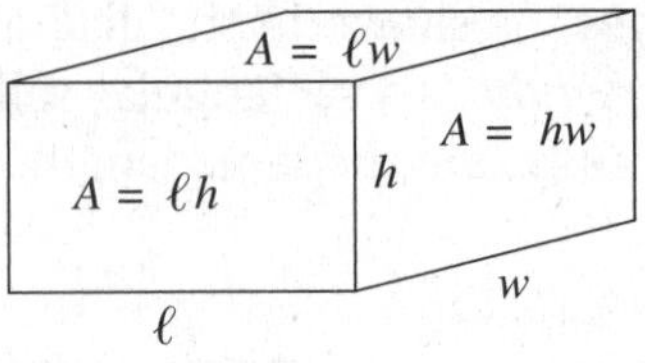

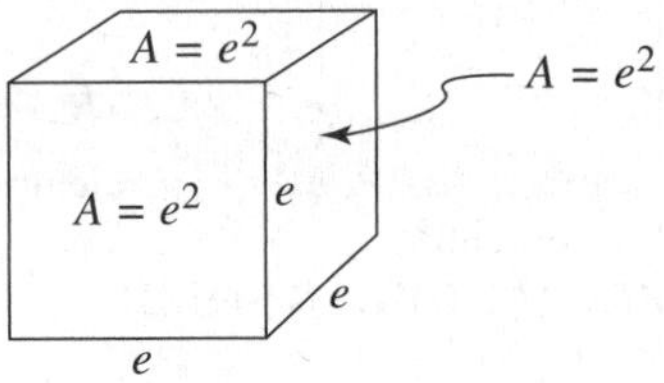

Key Fact M2

The surface area of a rectangular solid is $A = 2(lw + \ell h + wh)$. The surface area of a cube is $A = 6e^2$.

EXAMPLE 2

The volume of a cube is v cubic yards, and its surface area is a square feet. If $v = a$, what is the length in inches of each edge?

Solution. Draw a diagram. If e is the length of the edge in yards, then $3e$ is the length in feet, and $36e$ is the length in inches. Therefore, $v = e^3$ and $a = 6(3e)^2 = 6(9e^2) = 54e^2$.

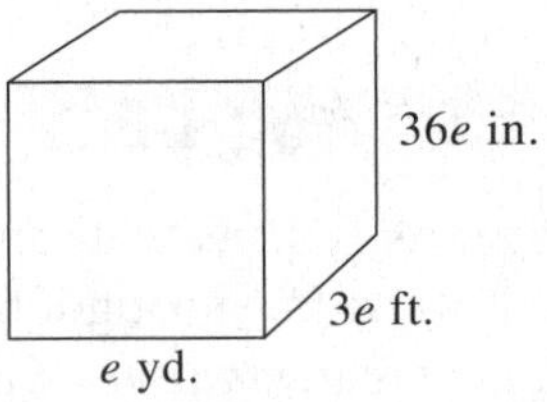

Since $v = a$, $e^3 = 54e^2 \Rightarrow e = 54$; the length of each edge is $36(54) = 1944$ inches.

A ***diagonal*** of a box is a line segment joining a vertex on the top of the box to the opposite vertex on the bottom.

EXAMPLE 3

What is the length of a diagonal of a cube whose sides are 1?

Solution. Draw a diagram and label it. Since the base is a 1×1 square, the length of diagonal $\overline{AC}$ is $\sqrt{2}$. Then $\overline{AD}$, a diagonal of the cube, is the hypotenuse of right triangle ACD whose legs are 1 and $\sqrt{2}$; so

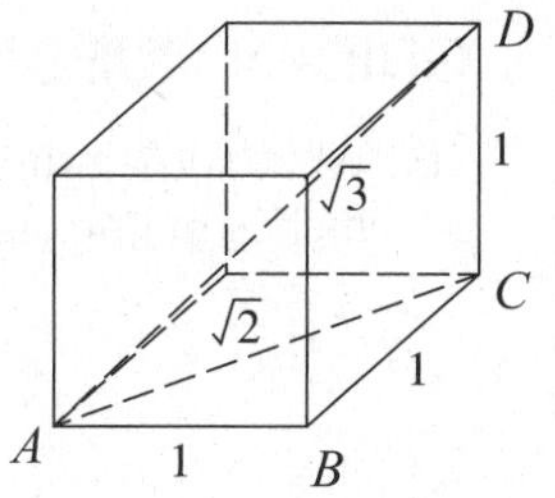

$$(AD)^2 = 1^2 + (\sqrt{2})^2 = 1 + 2 = 3, \text{ and } AD = \sqrt{3}.$$

A ***cylinder*** is similar to a rectangular solid except that the base is a circle instead of a rectangle. The volume of a cylinder is the area of its circular base (πr^2) times its height (h).

KEY FACT M3 is one of the facts included in the Reference Information box on the first page of each math section of the PSAT.

Key Fact M3

The formula for the volume, V, of a cylinder whose circular base has radius r and whose height is h is $V = \pi r^2 h$.

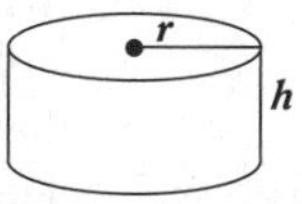

EXAMPLE 4

What is the height of a cylinder whose diameter is 10 and whose volume is 100π?

Solution. Since the diameter is 10, the radius is 5.

$$V = 100\pi = \pi r^2 h = \pi(5^2)h = 25\pi h \Rightarrow h = 4.$$

Practice Exercises

MULTIPLE-CHOICE QUESTIONS

1. What is the volume, in cubic feet, of a rectangular solid whose length, width, and height are 1 foot 3 inches, 1 foot 4 inches, and 1 foot 6 inches?

(A) 2.5
(B) 2.912
(C) 3.375
(D) 49
(E) 4320

2. The volume of a cube is a cubic feet and its surface area is b square feet. If $a = b$, what is the length, in feet, of each edge?

(A) 1
(B) 2
(C) 6
(D) 12
(E) 36

3. What is the volume of a cube whose surface area is 150?

(A) 25
(B) 100
(C) 125
(D) 1000
(E) 15,625

4. What is the surface area of a cube whose volume is 64?

(A) 16
(B) 64
(C) 96
(D) 128
(E) 384

5. The height and radius of a cylinder are each equal to the edge of a cube. What is the ratio of the volume of the cube to the volume of the cylinder?

(A) $\frac{1}{\pi}$
(B) π
(C) π^2
(D) π^3
(E) It cannot be determined from the information given.

GRID-IN QUESTIONS

6. What is the number of cubic inches in one cubic foot?

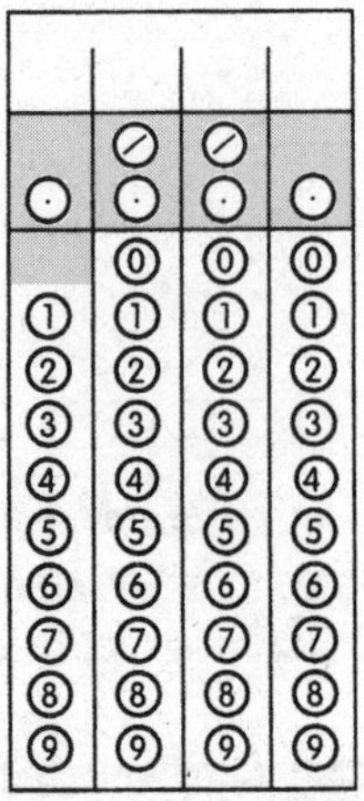

7. What is the volume, in cubic centimeters, of a cube in which the sum of the lengths of all the edges is 6 centimeters?

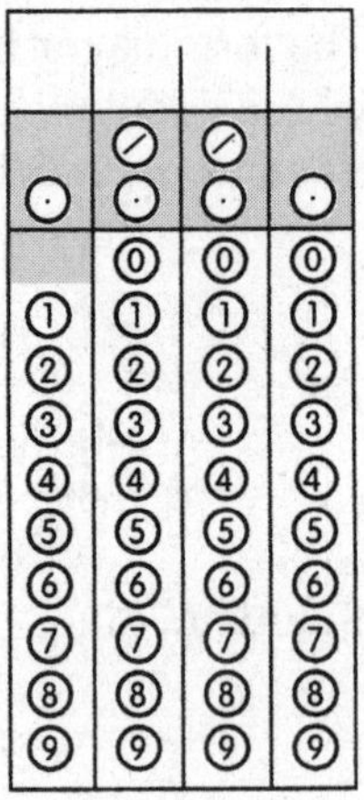

8. A solid metal cube with sides of 3 inches is placed in a rectangular tank whose length, width, and height are 3, 4, and 5 inches, respectively. What is the volume, in cubic inches, of water that the tank can now hold?

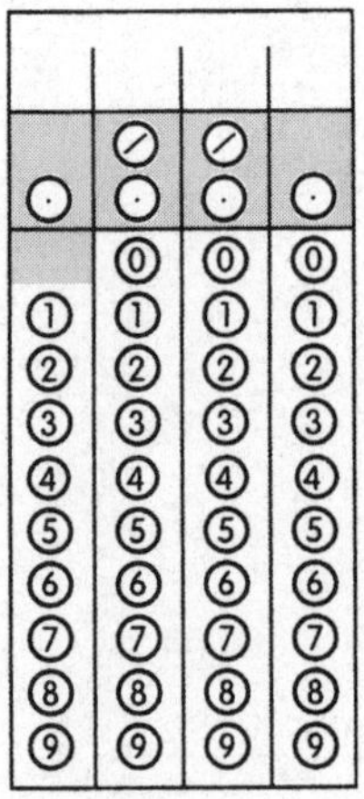

9. A rectangular tank has a base that is 16 inches by 5 inches and a height of 18 inches. If the tank is half full of water, by how many inches will the water level rise if 260 cubic inches of water are poured into it?

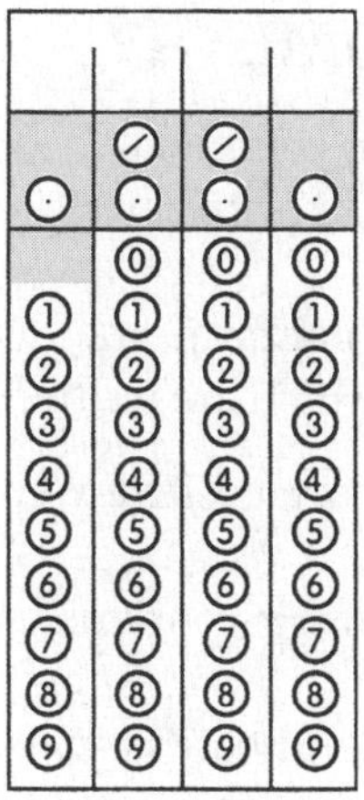

10. The base of a rectangular tank is 2 feet wide and 4 feet long; the height of the tank is 20 inches. If water is pouring into the tank at the rate of 2 cubic inches per second, how many *hours* will be required to fill the tank?

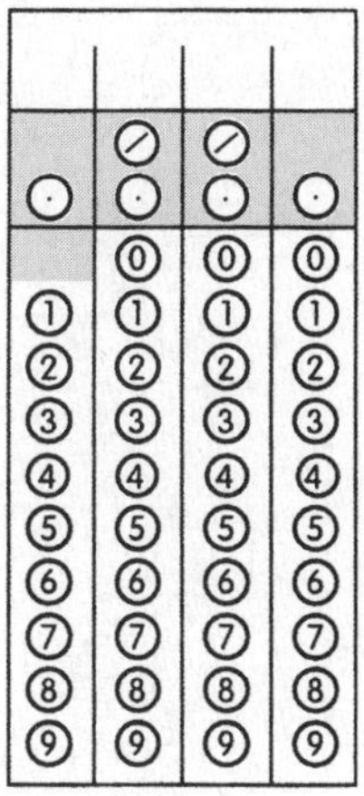

Answer Key

1. A

2. C

3. C

4. C

5. A

6.

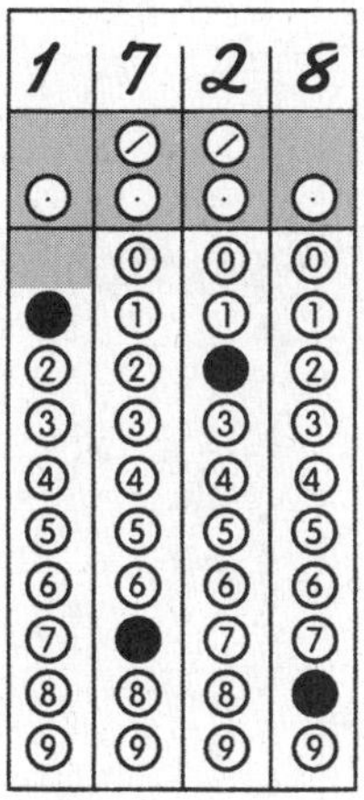

7.

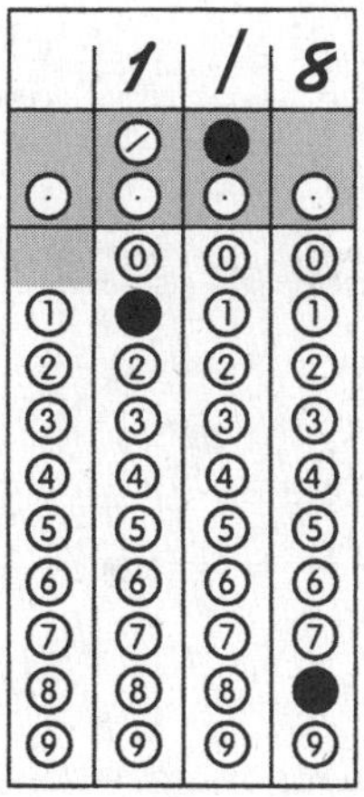

8.

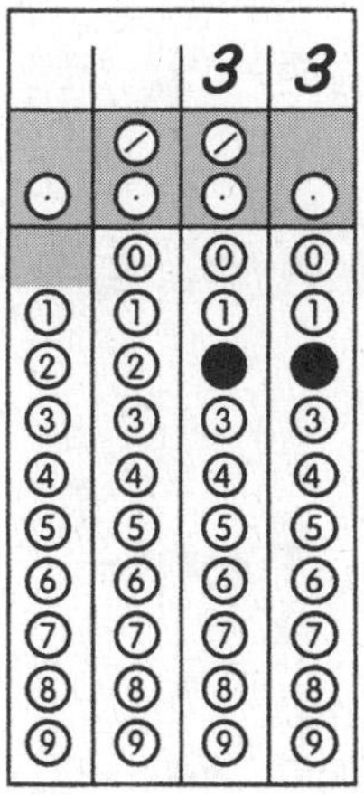

9.

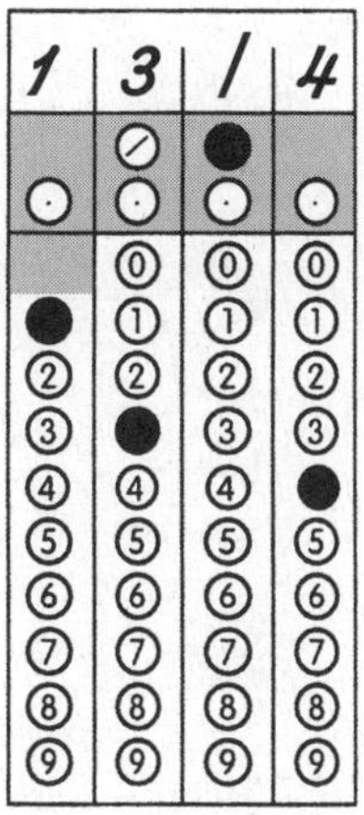

10.

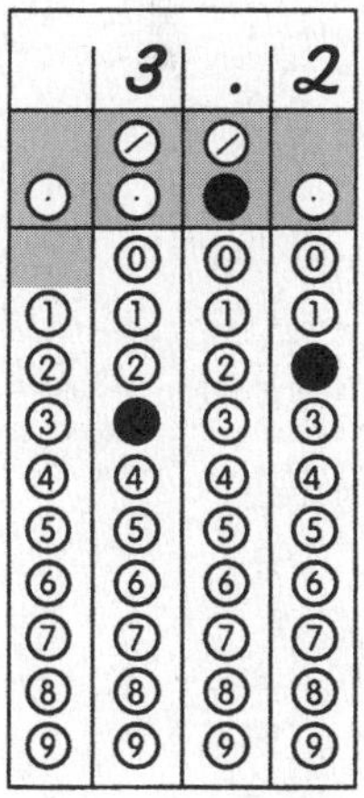

7-N COORDINATE GEOMETRY

The PSAT has very few questions on coordinate geometry. Most often they deal with the coordinates of points and occasionally with the slope of a line. You are *never* required to draw a graph.

In coordinate geometry, each point in the plane is assigned two numbers, an ***x*-coordinate** and a ***y*-coordinate**, which are written as an ordered pair, **(x, y)**.

- Points to the right of the y-axis have positive x-coordinates, and those to the left have negative x-coordinates.
- Points above the x-axis have positive y-coordinates, and those below it have negative y-coordinates.
- If a point is on the x-axis, its y-coordinate is 0.
- If a point is on the y-axis, its x-coordinate is 0.

For example, point A in the figure below is labeled (2, 3) since it is 2 units to the right of the y-axis and 3 units above the x-axis. Similarly, $B(-3, -5)$ is 3 units to the left of the y-axis and 5 units below the x-axis.

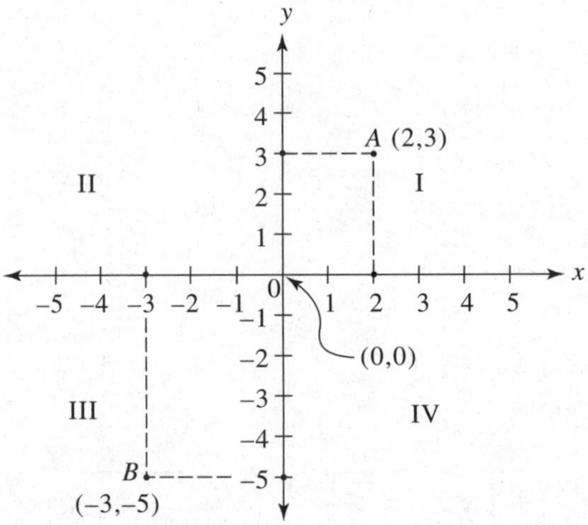

EXAMPLE 1

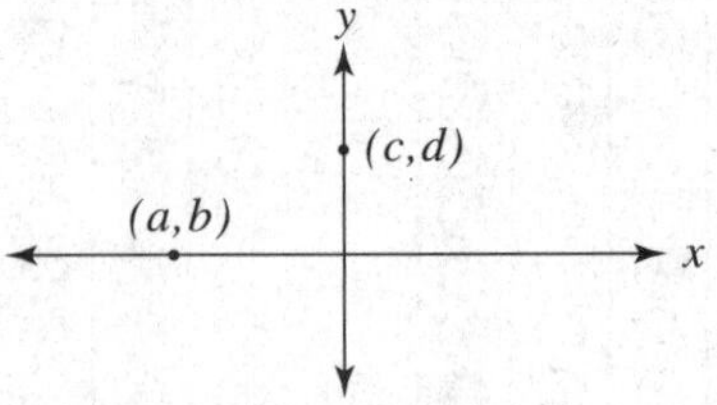

In the diagram above, which of the following must be true?

I. $a + b < ab$
II. $c + d < cd$
III. $a + b < c + d$

(A) I only
(B) II only
(C) III only
(D) I and III only
(E) I, II, and III

Solution. Since (a, b) is on the x-axis, $b = 0$. Therefore, $ab = 0$ and $a + b = a$, which is negative, since (a, b) is to the left of the y-axis. Since any negative number is less than 0, $a + b < ab$ (I is true). Since (c, d) is on the y-axis, $c = 0$. Therefore, $cd = 0$ and $c + d = d$, which is positive since (c, d) is above the x-axis. So $cd < c + d$ (II is false). Since $a + b$ is negative and $c + d$ is positive, $a + b < c + d$ (III is true). Only statements I and III are true (Choice D).

Often a question requires you to calculate the distance between two points. This is easiest when the points lie on the same horizontal or vertical line.

HELPFUL HINT: If two points have been plotted on a graph and if they have the same x-coordinates or y-coordinates, you can find the distance between them by counting boxes.

Key Fact N1

- All the points on a horizontal line have the same y-coordinate. To find the distance between any two of them, subtract the smaller x-coordinate from the larger x-coordinate.
- All the points on a vertical line have the same x-coordinate. To find the distance between any two of them, subtract the smaller y-coordinate from the larger y-coordinate.

CAUTION: To find the distance between two points that do *not* lie on the same horizontal or vertical line, you cannot count boxes and you cannot subtract; you *must* use the distance formula or the Pythagorean theorem.

Key Fact N2

The distance d, between two points, $A(x_1, y_1)$ and $B(x_2, y_2)$, can be calculated using the distance formula:

$$d = \sqrt{(x_2 - x_1)^2 + (y_2 - y_1)^2}.$$

EXAMPLE 2

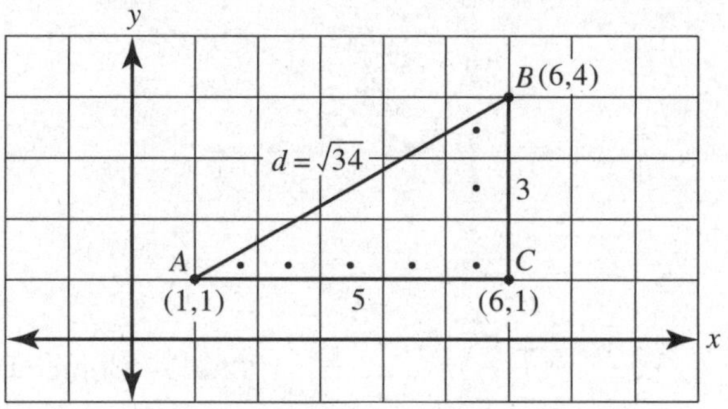

What is the perimeter of $\triangle ABC$, in the figure above?

(A) 13
(B) 16
(C) $8 + \sqrt{34}$
(D) $10 + \sqrt{34}$
(E) $8 + \sqrt{74}$

Solution. By counting boxes or subtracting, you find that the distance from A to C is $6 - 1 = 5$, and the distance from B to C is $4 - 1 = 3$. To find the distance from A to B, use the distance formula:

$$AB = \sqrt{(6-1)^2 + (4-1)^2} = \sqrt{(5)^2 + (3)^2} = \sqrt{25+9} = \sqrt{34}$$

So the perimeter is $5 + 3 + \sqrt{34} = 8 + \sqrt{34}$ (Choice C).

Key Fact N3

If $P(x_1, y_1)$ and $Q(x_2, y_2)$ are any two points, then the midpoint, M, of segment $\overline{PQ}$ is the point whose coordinates are $\left(\frac{x_1+x_2}{2}, \frac{y_1+y_2}{2}\right)$.

EXAMPLE 3

ABCD is a rectangle whose vertices are at A (2, 0), B (0, 3), C (6, 7), and D (8, 4). If the diagonals intersect at E, what are the coordinates of E?

(A) (2, 3.5)
(B) (3, 5)
(C) (4, 0.5)
(D) (4, 3.5)
(E) (8, 7)

Solution. Since, by **KEY FACT K2**, the diagonals of a parallelogram (and, hence, a rectangle) bisect each other, E is the midpoint of diagonal AC:

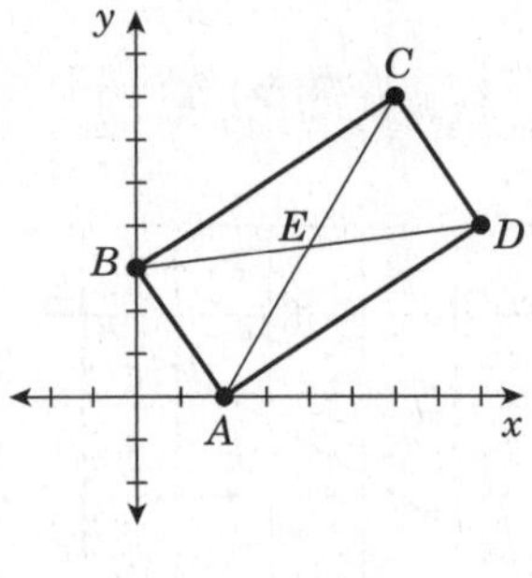

HELPFUL HINT

You should make a quick sketch. This often allows you to see the correct answer and always allows you to eliminate choices that are clearly wrong.

$$E = \left(\frac{2+6}{2}, \frac{7+0}{2}\right) = \left(\frac{8}{2}, \frac{7}{2}\right) = (4, 3.5) \text{ (Choice D).}$$

The ***slope*** of a line is a number that indicates how steep the line is.

Key Fact N4

- Vertical lines do not have slopes.
- To find the slope of any nonvertical line, proceed as follows:

1. Choose any 2 points $A(x_1, y_1)$ and $B(x_2, y_2)$ on the line.
2. Take the differences of the y-coordinates, $y_2 - y_1$, and the x-coordinates, $x_2 - x_1$.
3. Divide. Slope $= \frac{y_1 - y_2}{x_1 - x_2}$.

EXAMPLE 4

What is the slope of the line that passes through (0, 3) and (4, 0)?

Solution. Use the slope formula: $\frac{0-3}{4-0} = \frac{-3}{4} = -\frac{3}{4}$.

Key Fact N5

- The slope of any horizontal line is 0.
- The slope of any line that goes up as you move from left to right is positive.
- The slope of any line that goes down as you move from left to right is negative.

EXAMPLE 5

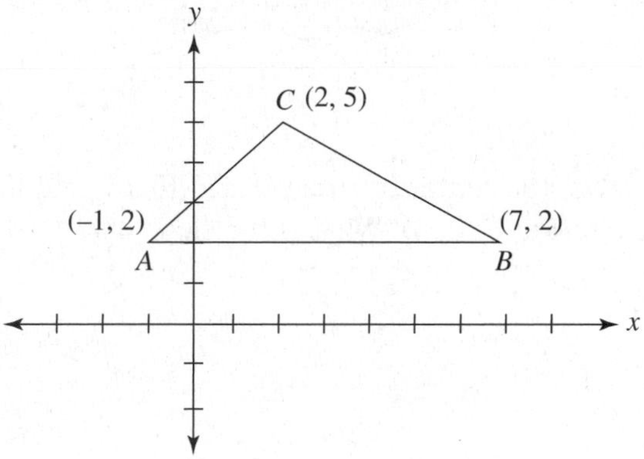

In the figure above, let r, s, and t represent the slopes of line segments $\overline{AB}$, $\overline{BC}$, and $\overline{AC}$, respectively. Which of the following is true?

(A) $r < s < t$
(B) $r < t < s$
(C) $s < r < t$
(D) $s < t < r$
(E) $t < r < s$

Solution. Since $\overline{AB}$ is horizontal, its slope is 0: $r = 0$; since $\overline{BC}$ goes down as you move from left to right, its slope is negative: $s < 0$; and since $\overline{AC}$ goes up as you move from left to right, its slope is positive: $t > 0$. Therefore,

$$s < r < t \text{ (Choice C)}.$$

Note that you *could have* calculated the slopes of $\overline{AC}$ and $\overline{BC}$, but it was unnecessary to do so.

Key Fact N6

- If two nonvertical lines are parallel, their slopes are equal.
- If two nonvertical lines are perpendicular, the product of their slopes is -1.

If the product of two numbers, a and b, is -1, then $ab = -1 \Rightarrow a = -\frac{1}{b}$. So another way to express the second part of **KEY FACT N6** is to say that *if two nonvertical lines are perpendicular, then the slope of one is the negative reciprocal of the slope of the other.*

EXAMPLE 6

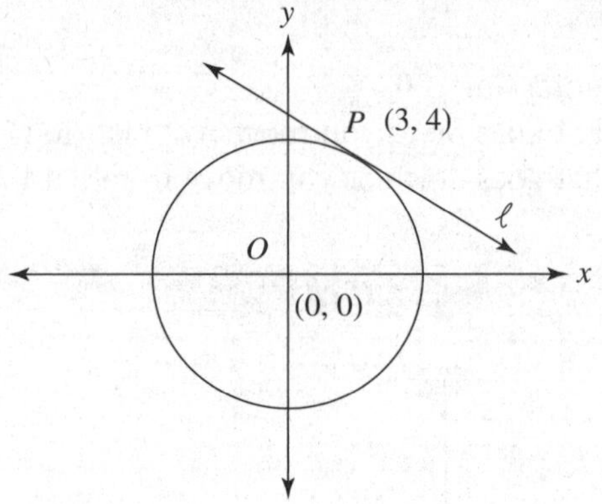

In the figure above, the center of circle O is at (0, 0), and line l is tangent to the circle at P (3, 4). What is the slope of l?

(A) $-\frac{4}{3}$

(B) $-\frac{3}{4}$

(C) 0

(D) $\frac{3}{4}$

(E) $\frac{4}{3}$

Solution. From the diagram, it is clear that the slope of l is negative; so the answer must be (A) or (B). In fact, the slope of radius $\overline{OP}$ is $\frac{4-0}{3-0} = \frac{3}{4}$. By **KEY FACT L10**, $\overline{OP} \perp l$, and so, by **KEY FACT N6**, the slope of l is the negative reciprocal of $\frac{4}{3}$. The slope of l is $-\frac{3}{4}$ (Choice B).

On the PSAT you won't have to graph a straight line (or anything else), but you should recognize the equations of straight lines.

Key Fact N7

For any real numbers a, b, m:

- The equation of a vertical line can be written as $x = a$.
- The equation of any nonvertical line can be written as $y = mx + b$.
- In the equation $y = mx + b$, m is the slope of the line, and b is the y-intercept.
- If $m = 0$, the line is horizontal, and its equation is $y = b$.

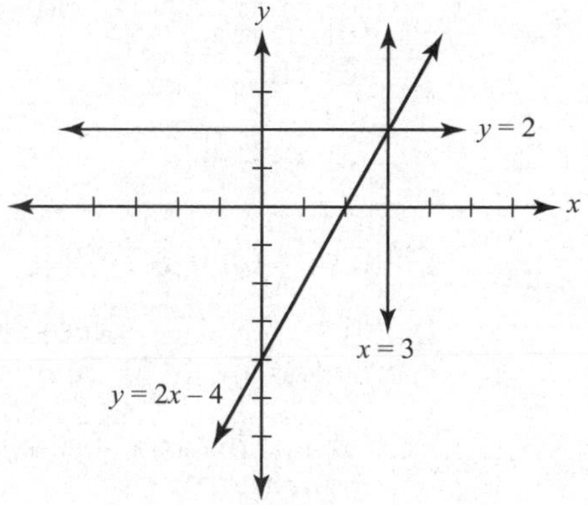

EXAMPLE 7

Which of the following is an equation of a line that is parallel to the line whose equation is $y = 2x - 3$?

(A) $y = 2x + 3$
(B) $y = -2x - 3$
(C) $y = \frac{1}{2}x + 3$
(D) $y = -\frac{1}{2}x + 3$
(E) $y = -\frac{1}{2}x - 3$

Solution. By **KEY FACT N7**, the slope of the line $y = 2x - 3$ is 2. By **KEY FACT N6**, parallel lines have equal slopes. Only Choice A, $y = 2x + 3$, is also the equation of a line whose slope is 2.

Practice Exercises

MULTIPLE-CHOICE QUESTIONS

1. What is the area of the rectangle, three of whose vertices are the points $A(2, 2)$, $B(6, 4)$, and $C(7, 2)$?

(A) 10
(B) 25
(C) 40
(D) 50
(E) 100

2. A circle whose center is at $(2, -3)$ passes through the point $(4, 4)$. What is the area of the circle?

(A) 5π
(B) 37π
(C) 53π
(D) 85π
(E) It cannot be determined from the information given.

3. $B(7, -7)$ is a point on a circle whose center is at $(3, 5)$. If AB is a diameter of the circle, what is the slope of AB?

(A) -3
(B) $-\frac{1}{3}$
(C) $\frac{1}{3}$
(D) 3
(E) It cannot be determined from the information given.

4. What is the slope of the line that passes through $(0, a)$ and $(b, 0)$, where $b \neq 0$?

(A) $\frac{a}{b}$
(B) $-\frac{a}{b}$
(C) $\frac{b}{a}$
(D) $-\frac{b}{a}$
(E) It cannot be determined from the information given.

5. A circle whose center is at $(6, 8)$ passes through the origin. Which of the following points is NOT on the circle?

(A) $(12, 0)$
(B) $(6, -2)$
(C) $(16, 8)$
(D) $(-2, 12)$
(E) $(-4, 8)$

GRID-IN QUESTIONS

Questions 6 and 7 concern parallelogram $ABCD$, whose coordinates are $A(-6, 2)$, $B(-3, 6)$, $C(4, 6)$, $D(1, 2)$.

6. What is the area of parallelogram $ABCD$?

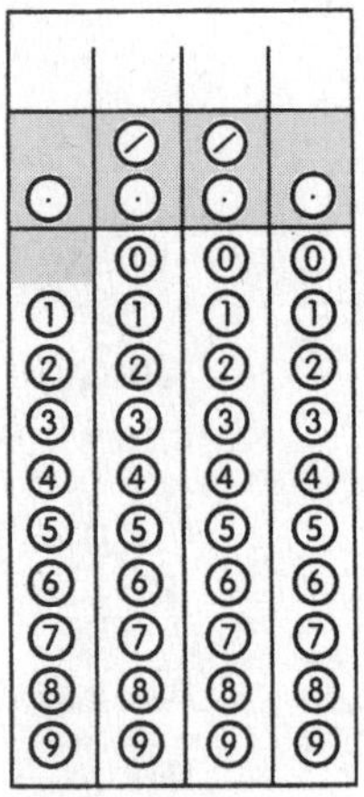

7. What is the perimeter of parallelogram $ABCD$?

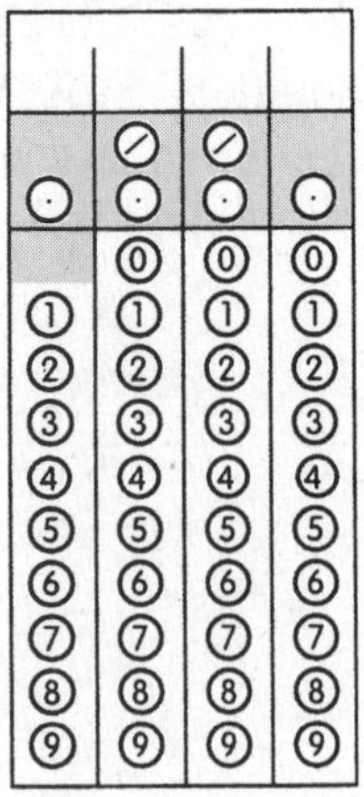

8. If the coordinates of $\triangle JKL$ are $J(0, 0)$, $K(8, 0)$, and $L(2, 6)$, what is the sum of the slopes of the three sides of the triangle?

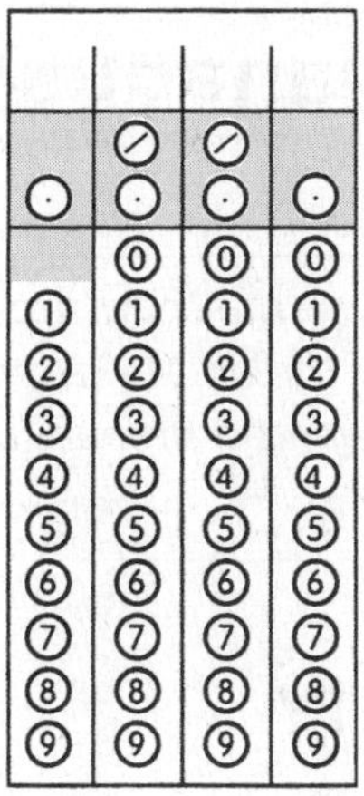

9. If $P(-3, 3)$ and $Q(1, -2)$ are the endpoints of one side of square $PQRS$, what is the area of the square?

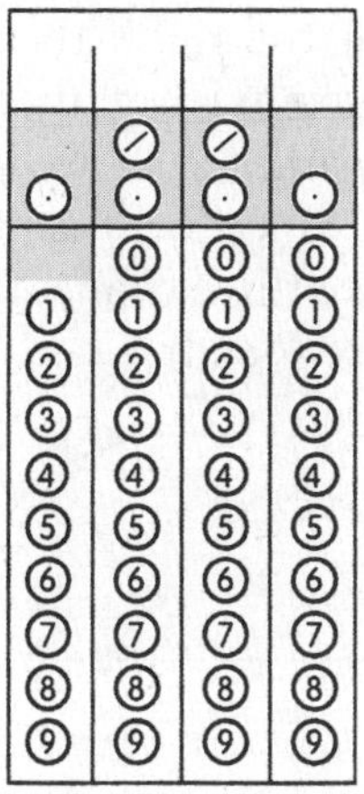

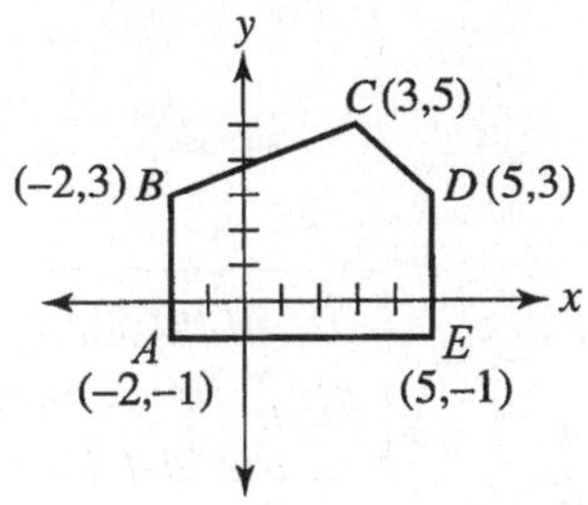

10. What is the area of pentagon *ABCDE*?

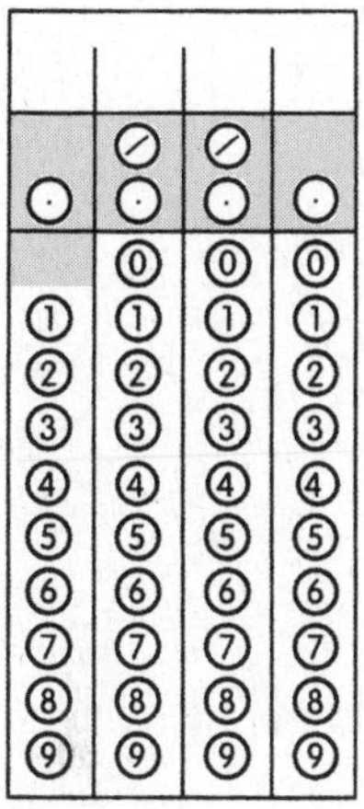

Answer Key

1. A **2.** C **3.** A **4.** B **5.** D

6.

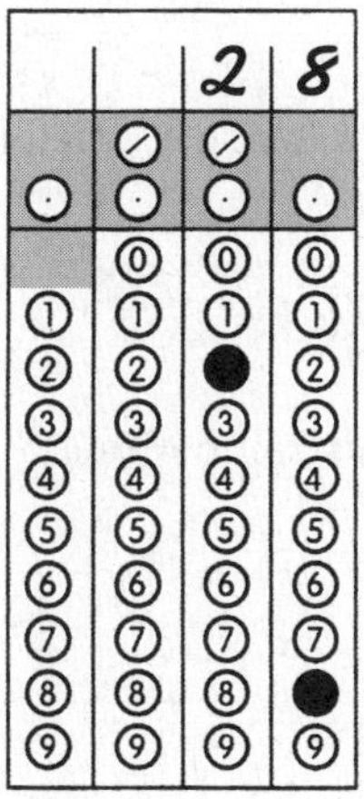

7.

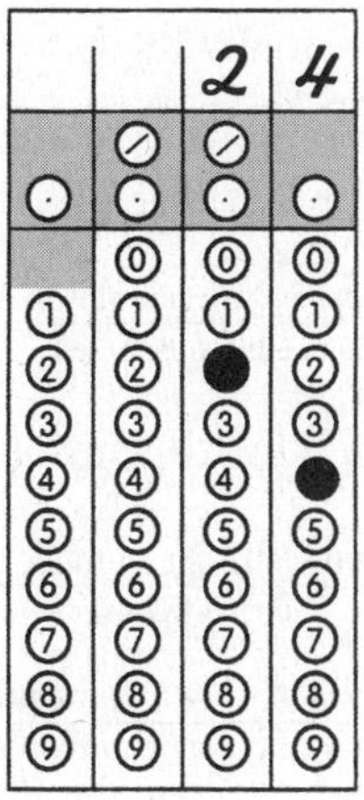

8.

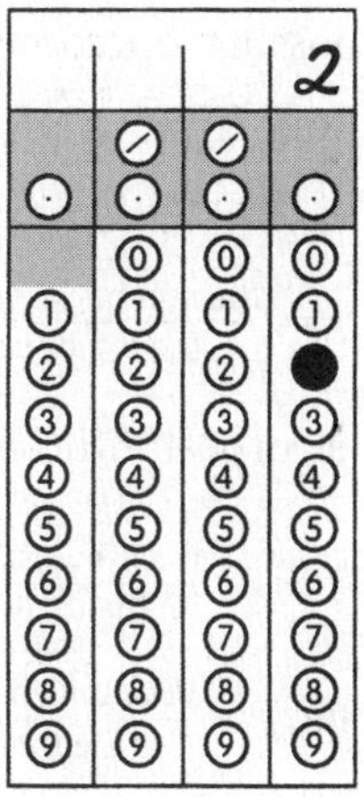

9.

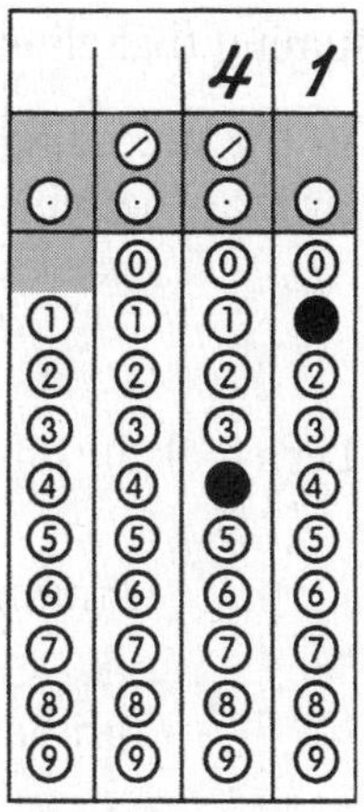

10.

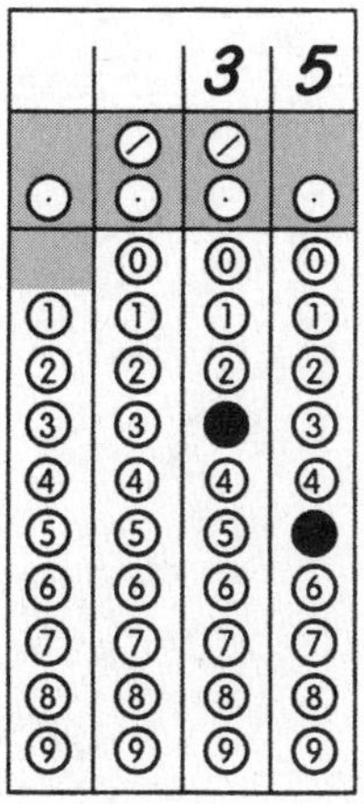

Miscellaneous Topics

About 90 percent of the questions on the PSAT are on arithmetic, algebra, and geometry. The remaining 10 percent of the questions are on miscellaneous topics covered in the last four sections of this chapter: probability, sequences, data interpretation, and functions.

7-O BASIC PROBABILITY

The ***probability*** that an ***event*** will occur is a number between 0 and 1, usually written as a fraction, which indicates how likely it is that the event will happen. For example, if you spin the spinner at the right, there are four possible outcomes: it is equally likely that the spinner will stop in any of the four regions. There is one chance in four that it will stop in the region marked 2. So we say that the probability of spinning a 2 is one-fourth and write $P(2) = \frac{1}{4}$. Since 2 is the only even number on the spinner we could also say $P(\text{even}) = \frac{1}{4}$. There are three chances in four that the spinner will land in a region with an odd number in it, so $P(\text{odd}) = \frac{3}{4}$.

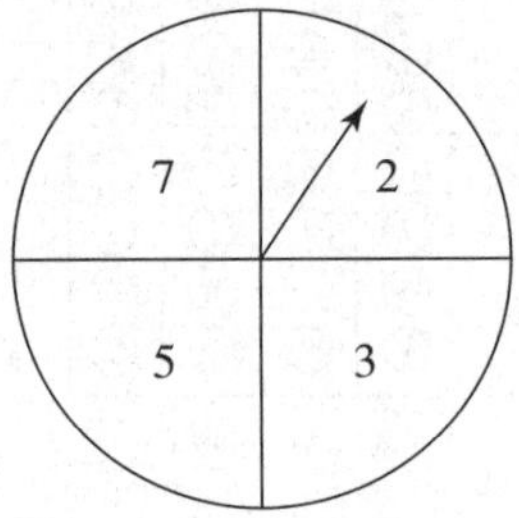

Key Fact O1

If E is any event, the probability that E will occur is given by

$$P(E) = \frac{\text{the number of favorable outcomes}}{\text{the total number of possible outcomes}}$$

assuming that all of the possible outcomes are equally likely.

In the preceding example, each of the four regions is the same size; so it is equally likely that the spinner will land on the 2, 3, 5, or 7. Therefore,

$$P(\text{odd}) = \frac{\text{the number of ways of getting an odd number}}{\text{the total number of possible outcomes}} = \frac{3}{4}.$$

Let's look at some other probabilities associated with spinning this spinner once:

$$P(\text{number} > 8) = \frac{\text{the number of ways of getting a number} > 8}{\text{the total number of possible outcomes}} = \frac{0}{4} = 0$$

$$P(\text{prime number}) = \frac{\text{the number of ways of getting a prime number}}{\text{the total number of possible outcomes}} = \frac{4}{4} = 1$$

$$P(\text{number} < 5) = \frac{\text{the number of ways of getting a number} < 5}{\text{the total number of possible outcomes}} = \frac{2}{4} = \frac{1}{2}$$

Key Fact O2

Let E be an event and $P(E)$ the probability it will occur.

Then with reference to the example above:

- If E is *impossible* (such as getting a number greater than 8), $P(E) = 0$.
- If it is *certain* that E will occur (such as getting a prime number), $P(E) = 1$.
- In all cases $0 \leq P(E) \leq 1$.
- The probability that event E will *not* occur is $1 - P(E)$.
- If 2 or more events constitute all the outcomes, the sum of their probabilities is 1.

  [For example, $P(\text{even}) + P(\text{odd}) = \frac{1}{4} + \frac{3}{4} = 1$].
- The more likely it is that an event will occur, the higher its probability (the closer to 1 it is); the less likely it is that an event will occur, the lower its probability (the closer to 0 it is).

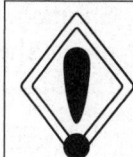

CAUTION: The answer to a probability question can *never* be negative and can *never* be greater than 1.

EXAMPLE 1

A two-digit number is chosen at random. What is the probability that the number chosen is a multiple of 9?

Solution. There are 90 two-digit numbers (all of the integers between 10 and 99, inclusive). Of these 90 numbers, 10 of them (18, 27, 36, . . . , 99) are multiples of 9. Therefore,

$$\text{probability} = \frac{\text{the number of favorable outcomes}}{\text{the total number of possible outcomes}} = \frac{10}{90} = \frac{1}{9}.$$

Key Fact O3

If an experiment is done two (or more) times, the probability that first one event will occur and then a second event will occur is the product of the probabilities.

EXAMPLE 2

The spinner at the beginning of this section is spun three times. What is the probability that it never lands on the 2?

(A) $\frac{1}{64}$

(B) $\frac{1}{4}$

(C) $\frac{27}{64}$

(D) $\frac{3}{4}$

(E) $\frac{9}{4}$

Solution. We want the probability that on each of the three spins the spinner lands on one of the three odd numbers. Since $P(\text{odd}) = \frac{3}{4}$, by **KEY FACT O3**, the probability of three consecutive odd numbers is

$$P(\text{odd 1st time}) \times P(\text{odd 2nd time}) \times P(\text{odd 3rd time}) = \frac{3}{4} \times \frac{3}{4} \times \frac{3}{4} = \frac{27}{64}.$$

Occasionally, on a PSAT there will be a question that relates to probability and geometry. The next **KEY FACT** will help you deal with that type of question.

Key Fact O4

If a point is chosen at random inside a geometrical figure, the probability that the chosen point lies in a particular region is

$$\frac{\text{the area of that region}}{\text{the area of the whole figure}}$$

EXAMPLE 3

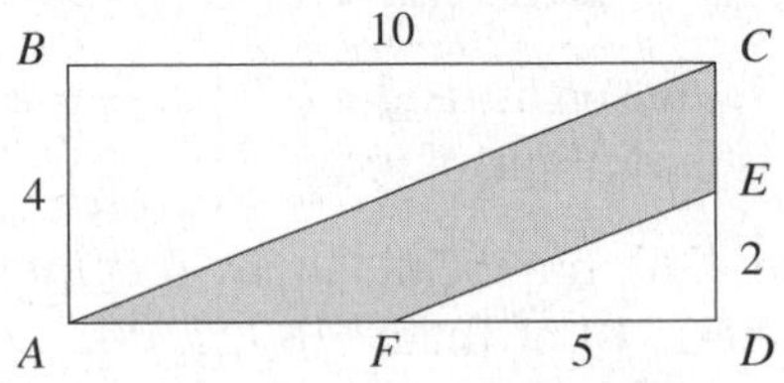

If a point is chosen at random inside rectangle *ABCD*, what is the probability that the point lies in the shaded region?

Solution. The area of rectangle *ABCD* is $4 \times 10 = 40$. The area of right triangle *ABC* is $\frac{1}{2}(4 \times 10) = 20$, and the area of right triangle *EDF* is $\frac{1}{2}(2 \times 5) = 5$. So the total area of the white region is $20 + 5 = 25$, and the area of the shaded region is $40 - 25 = 15$. The probability that the chosen point lies inside the shaded region is $\frac{15}{40} = \frac{3}{8}$.

Practice Exercises

MULTIPLE-CHOICE QUESTIONS

Questions 1–3 refer to a jar that contains 5 marbles, 1 of each of the colors red, white, blue, green, and yellow.

1. If four marbles are removed from the jar, what is the probability that the yellow one was removed?

(A) $\frac{1}{20}$

(B) $\frac{1}{5}$

(C) $\frac{1}{4}$

(D) $\frac{4}{5}$

(E) $\frac{5}{4}$

2. If one marble is removed from the jar, what is the probability that it is red, white, or blue?

(A) $\frac{1}{15}$

(B) $\frac{1}{5}$

(C) $\frac{2}{5}$

(D) $\frac{3}{5}$

(E) $\frac{5}{3}$

3. If two marbles are removed from the jar, what is the probability that each of them is red, white, or blue?

(A) $\frac{6}{25}$

(B) $\frac{3}{10}$

(C) $\frac{9}{25}$

(D) $\frac{2}{3}$

(E) $\frac{6}{5}$

4. The Smiths have two children. If their older child is a boy, what is the probability that their younger child is also a boy?

(A) $\frac{1}{4}$

(B) $\frac{1}{3}$

(C) $\frac{1}{2}$

(D) $\frac{2}{3}$

(E) $\frac{3}{4}$

5. The Kleins have two children. What is the probability that both of their children are boys?

(A) $\frac{1}{4}$

(B) $\frac{1}{3}$

(C) $\frac{1}{2}$

(D) $\frac{2}{3}$

(E) $\frac{3}{4}$

GRID-IN QUESTIONS

6. If three coins are flipped, what is the probability that there are more heads than tails?

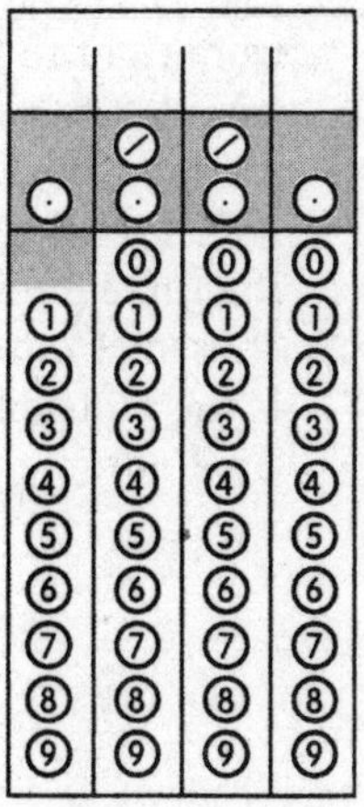

7. A box contains 10 slips of paper, each with a different number from 1 to 10 written on it. If one slip is removed at random, what is the probability that the number selected is a multiple of 2 or 3?

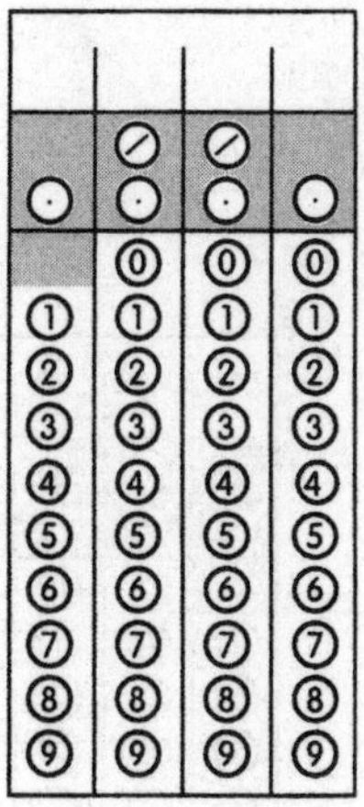

8. If two people are chosen at random, what is the probability that they were born on different days of the week?

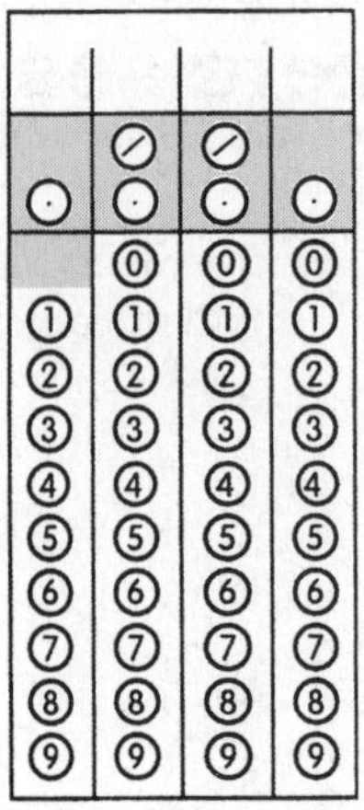

9. A number is a *palindrome* if it reads exactly the same from right to left as it does from left to right. For example, 66, 818, and 2552 are all palindromes. If a three-digit number is chosen at random, what is the probability that it is a palindrome?

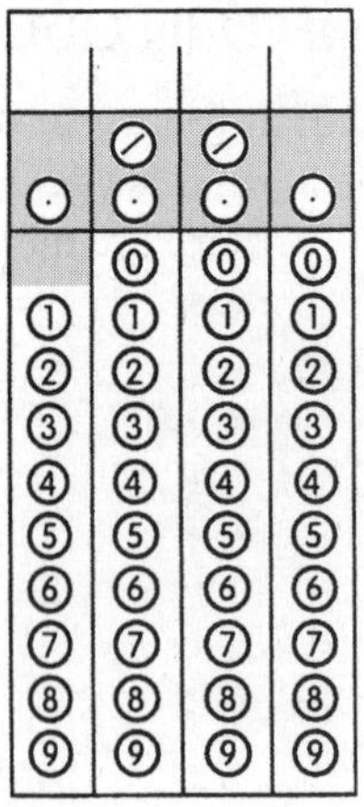

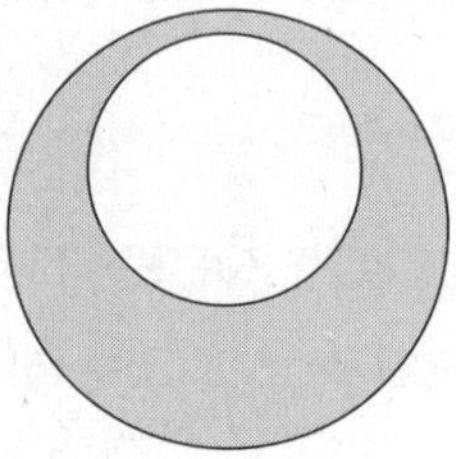

10. In the diagram above, the radius of the large circle is 5 and the radius of the small circle is 3. If a point is chosen at random inside the large circle, what is the probability that the point lies inside the small white circle?

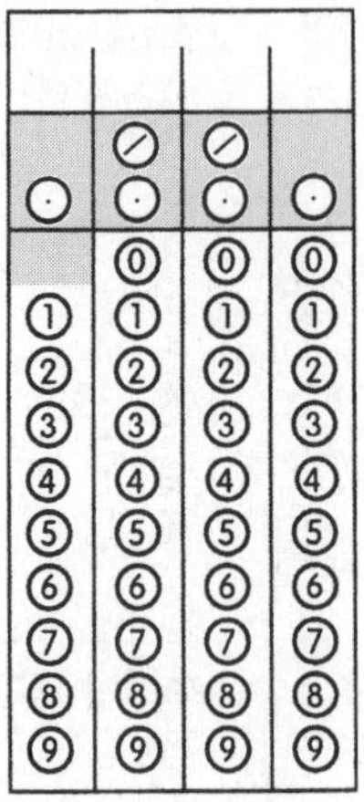

Answer Key

1. D

2. D

3. B

4. C

5. A

6.

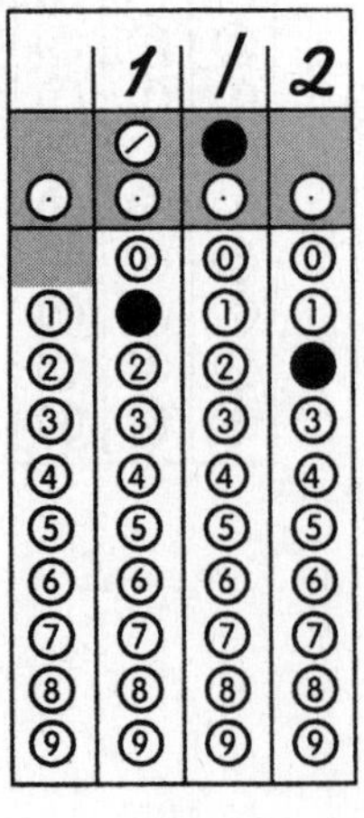

or .5

7.

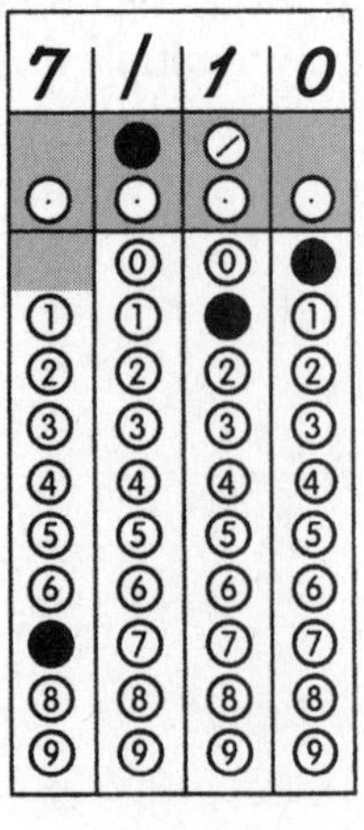

or . 7

8.

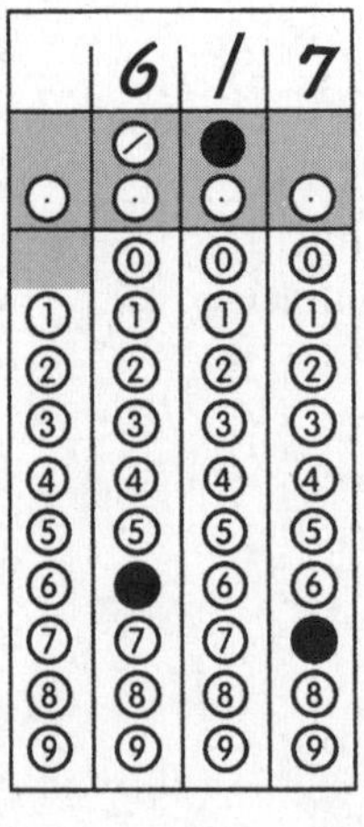

9.

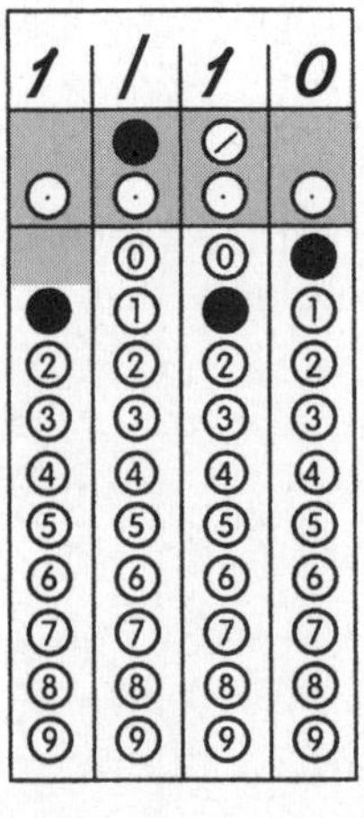

10.

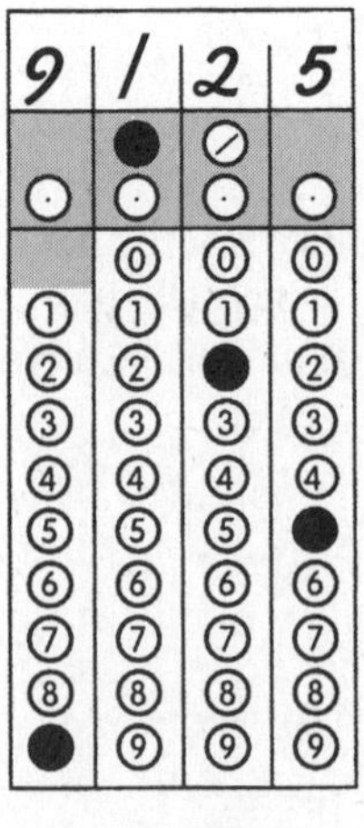

or .36

7-P SEQUENCES

There are three types of sequences that occasionally appear on the PSAT: *arithmetic sequences*, *geometric sequences*, and *repeating sequences*.

An ***arithmetic sequence*** is a sequence in which the *difference* between any two consecutive terms is the same. For example, the sequence 8, 11, 14, 17, 20, . . . is an arithmetic sequence in which the common difference is 3. An easy way to find the nth term of such a sequence is to start with the first term and add the common difference $n-1$ times. In this example, the fifth term is 20, which can be obtained by taking the first term, 8, and adding the common difference, 3, four times: $8 + 4(3) = 8 + 12 = 20$.

KEY FACT P1 gives the formula for finding the nth term of any arithmetic sequence.

Key Fact P1

If $a_1, a_2, a_3, \ldots$ is an arithmetic sequence whose common difference is d, then $a_n = a_1 + (n-1)\,d$.

EXAMPLE 1

What is the 100th term of the sequence 8, 11, 14, 17, 20, . . . ?

Solution. This is an arithmetic sequence whose first term is 8 and whose comman difference is 3. So by **KEY FACT P1**

$$a_{100} = a_1 + 99d = 8 + 99(3) = 8 + 297 = 305.$$

A ***geometric sequence*** is a sequence in which the *ratio* between any two consecutive terms is the same. For example, the sequence 2, 8, 32, 128, 512, . . . is a geometric sequence: the ratios $\frac{8}{2}, \frac{32}{8}, \frac{128}{32}$ are all equal to 4.

An easy way to find the nth term of a geometric sequence is to start with the first term and multiply it by the common ratio $n-1$ times. For example, in the sequence 2, 8, 32, 128, 512, . . . the fourth term is 128, which can be obtained by taking the first term, 2, and multiplying it by the common ratio, 4, three times: $2 \times 4 \times 4 \times 4 = 2 \times 4^3 = 2 \times 64 = 128$. The next **KEY FACT** gives the formula for finding the nth term of a geometric sequence.

Key Fact P2

If $a_1, a_2, a_3, \ldots$ is a geometric sequence whose common ratio is r, then $a_n = a_1\,(r)^{n-1}$.

EXAMPLE 2

What is the 100th term of the sequence 2, 8, 32, 128, 512, . . . ?

(A) 2^{99}
(B) 2^{100}
(C) 2×4^{99}
(D) 2×4^{100}
(E) 2×4^{101}

Solution. This is a geometric series whose first term is 2 and whose common ratio is 4. So by **KEY FACT P2**,

$$a_{100} = a_1(r)^{99} = 2 \times 4^{99} \text{ (Choice C).}$$

A ***repeating sequence*** is a sequence in which a certain number of terms repeat indefinitely. Each of the following is a repeating sequence

(i) $-1, 0, 1, -1, 0, 1, -1, 0, 1, \ldots$
(ii) $1, 4, 2, 8, 5, 7, 1, 4, 2, 8, 5, 7, \ldots$
(iii) red, white, blue, green, red, white, blue, green, . . .

On the PSAT, questions concerning repeating sequences usually ask you to find a particular term of the sequence, such as the 100th term or 1000th term. So you need to have a procedure for finding the term you want. For example, let's find the 500th term of the sequence 1, 4, 2, 8, 5, 7, 1, 4, 2, 8, 5, 7, . . . Think of this as a sequence in which the set {1, 4, 2, 8, 5, 7} of 6 numbers keeps repeating. Since the last number in the set is 7, if we write down 1 set or 2 sets or 3 sets or 10 sets, the last number will be 7. So the 6th, 12th, 18th, and 60th terms are all 7. In general, if n is a multiple of 6, the nth term is 7. So the 30th term, the 666th term, and the 6,000,000th terms are all 7. To answer the question, "What is the 500th term?" the first thing you should do is divide 500 by 6. If 500 is a multiple of 6, the answer will be 7. Using your calculator, you find that $500 \div 6 = 83.333$. So 500 is not a multiple of 6. When 500 is divided by 6, the *integer* quotient is 83 (ignore the decimal portion). This means that in the first 500 terms of the sequence, the set {1, 4, 2, 8, 5, 7} repeats 83 times. Since $83 \times 6 = 498$, the 498th term is 7. The 499th term starts the next set; it is 1 and the 500th term is 4.

TACTIC P1

To find the nth term of a repeating sequence, divide n by the number of terms that repeat. If r is the integer remainder, then the nth term is the same as the rth term.

In the worked-out example preceding **TACTIC P1**, we found the 500th term of the sequence 1, 4, 2, 8, 7, 1, 4, 2, 8, 7, . . . Using **TACTIC P1**, we would proceed as follows:

$500 \div 6 = 83.333 \Rightarrow$ the quotient is 83. Then $83 \times 6 = 498$ and $500 - 498 = 2$. The remainder is 2, and so the 500th term is the same as the 2nd term, namely 4.

Practice Exercises

MULTIPLE-CHOICE QUESTIONS

1. What is the 100th term of the sequence 4, 9, 14, 19, 24, . . . ?

(A) 494
(B) 499
(C) 504
(D) 509
(E) 514

2. Consider the sequence 2, 6, 18, 54, 162, . . . What is the 25th term?

(A) 3^{24}
(B) 3^{25}
(C) 2×3^{24}
(D) 2×3^{25}
(E) 6^{24}

3. If today is Saturday, what day will it be 500 days from today?

(A) Saturday
(B) Sunday
(C) Tuesday
(D) Wednesday
(E) Friday

4. If it is now September, what month will it be 555 months from now?

(A) April
(B) June
(C) September
(D) November
(E) December

5. The first term of sequence I is 2 and each subsequent term is 2 more than the preceding term. The first term of sequence II is 2 and each subsequent term is 2 times the preceding term. What is the ratio of the 32nd term of sequence II to the 32nd term of sequence I?

(A) 1
(B) 2
(C) 2^{26}
(D) 2^{27}
(E) 2^{32}

GRID-IN QUESTIONS

6. The first term of a sequence is 1 and every term after the first one is 1 more than the square of the preceding term. What is the fifth term?

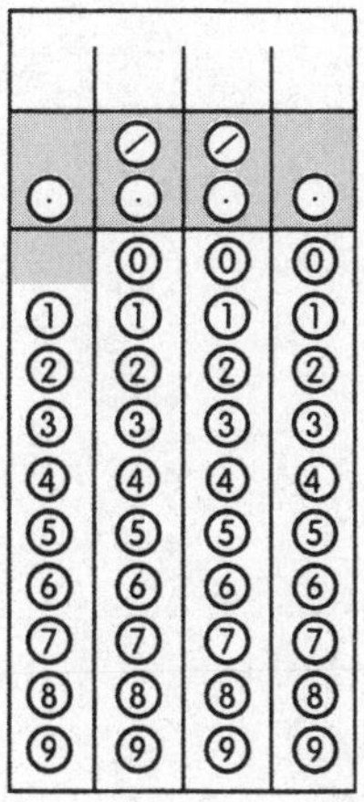

7. The first two terms of a sequence are 5 and 7. Each term after the second one is found by taking the average (arithmetic mean) of all the preceding terms. What is the 50th term of this sequence?

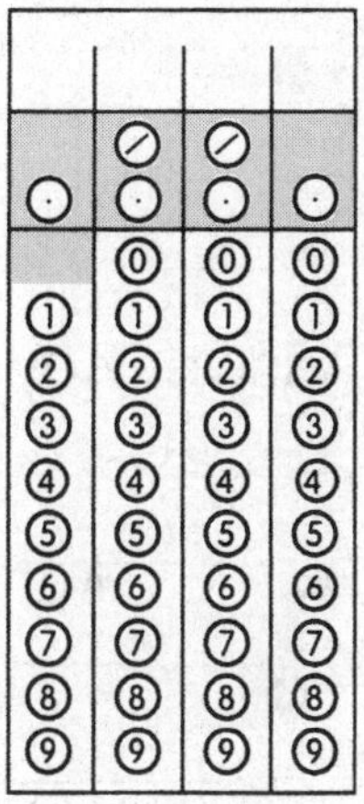

8. Consider the sequence 2, 6, 18, 54, 162, . . . If the 77th term is a and the 80th term is b, what is the value of $\frac{b}{a}$?

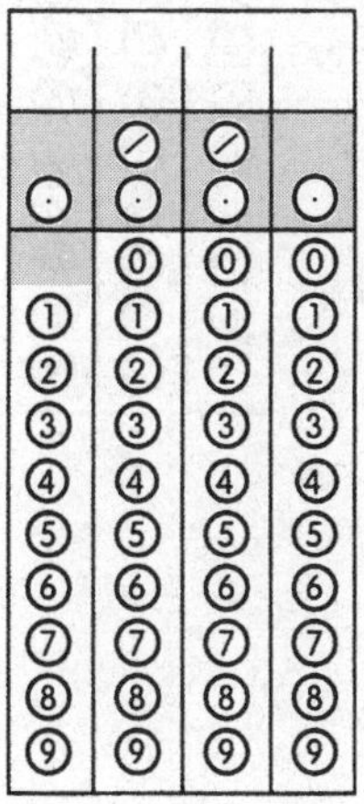

9. Consider the sequence 1, 2, 3, 1, 2, 3, 1, 2, 3, . . . What is the sum of the first 100 terms?

10. In a certain sequence the difference between any two consecutive terms is 4. If the 20th term is 100, what is the 2nd term?

Answer Key

1. B **2.** C **3.** C **4.** E **5.** C

6. 677

7. 6

8. 27

9. 199

10. 28

7-Q INTERPRETATION OF DATA

On the PSAT, charts and graphs are *always* drawn to scale.

On the PSAT it is likely that there will be one or two questions that will require you to interpret the data that appear in some type of table or graph. Occasionally you will be asked two questions based on the same set of data. In this case, the first question is usually quite easy, requiring only that you *read* the information in the table or graph. The second question is usually a little more challenging and may ask you to *interpret* the data or *manipulate* them or *make a prediction* based on them.

The data can be presented in the columns of a table or displayed graphically. The graphs that appear most often are circle graphs, bar graphs, line graphs, and scatter-plot graphs. In this section, we will illustrate each of these and give examples of the types of questions that may be asked.

Line Graphs

A ***line graph*** indicates how one or more quantities change over time. The horizontal axis is usually marked off in units of time; the units on the vertical axis can represent almost any type of numerical data: dollars, weights, exam grades, number of people, and so on.

Here is a typical line graph:

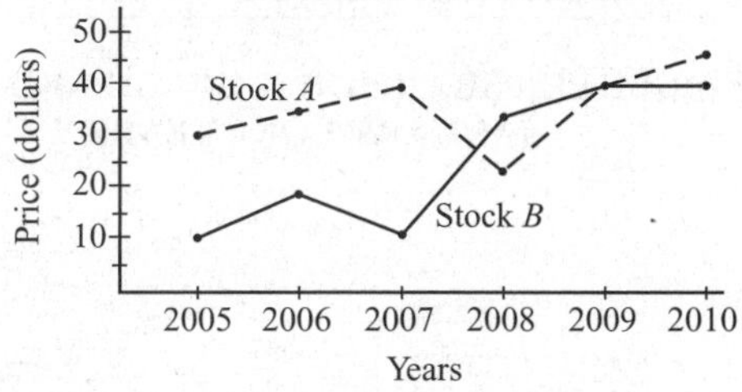

Before reading even one of the questions based on the above graph, you should have acquired *at least* the following information: (i) the graph gives the values of two different stocks; (ii) the graph covers the period from January 1, 2005, to January 1, 2010; (iii) during that time, both stocks rose in value. There are several questions that could be asked about the data in this graph. Here are two examples.

EXAMPLE 1

On January 1 of what year was the ratio of the value of a share of stock A to the value of a share of stock B the greatest?

(A) 2005
(B) 2006
(C) 2007
(D) 2008
(E) 2010

Solution. From 2008 to 2010, the values of the two stocks were fairly close; so those years are not candidates. In 2007 the ratio was 40 : 10 or 4 : 1 or 4. In 2006 the ratio was 35 : 15 or 7 : 3 or 2.33. In 2005 the ratio was 30 : 10 or 3 : 1 or 3. The ratio was greatest in 2007 (Choice C).

EXAMPLE 2

What was the average yearly increase in the value of a share of stock *A* from 2005 to 2010?

Solution. Over the five-year period from January 1, 2005, to January 1, 2010, the value of a share of stock *A* rose from \$30 to \$45, an increase of \$15. The average yearly increase was \$15 ÷ 5 years, or \$3 per year.

Tables and Bar Graphs

The same information that was given in the preceding line graph could have been presented in a ***table*** or in a ***bar graph***.

In a bar graph, the taller the bar, the greater the value of the quantity. Bar graphs can also be drawn horizontally; in this case the longer the bar, the greater the quantity.

PRICE PER SHARE OF STOCKS *A* AND *B* ON JANUARY 1 OF 6 YEARS

	Prices (dollars)					
Stock	2005	2006	2007	2008	2009	2010
Stock *A*	30	35	40	25	40	45
Stock *B*	10	20	15	35	40	40

PRICE PER SHARE OF STOCKS *A* AND *B* ON JANUARY 1 OF 6 YEARS

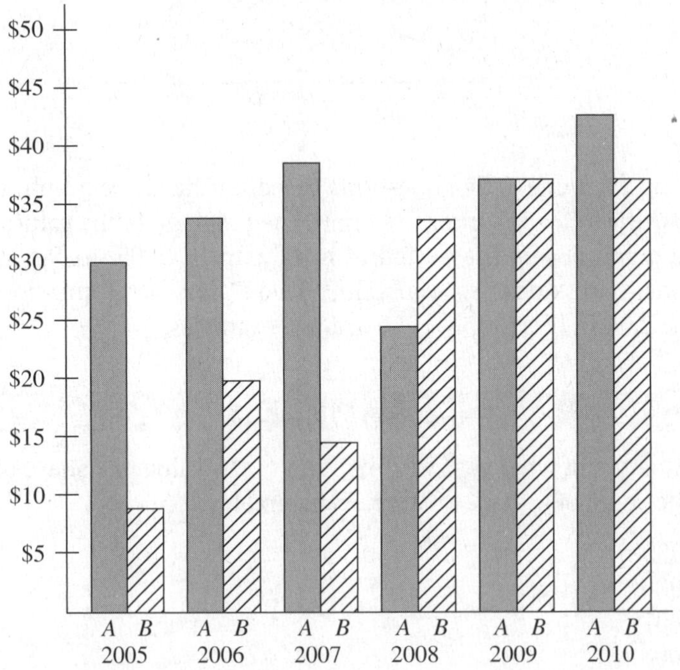

In a slight variation of the horizontal bar graph, the bars are replaced by a string of icons, or symbols. For example, the graph on the following page, in which each picture of a person represents 100 students, conveys information about the languages studied by the students at State College in 2010.

NUMBERS OF STUDENTS ENROLLED IN LANGUAGE COURSES AT STATE COLLEGE IN 2010

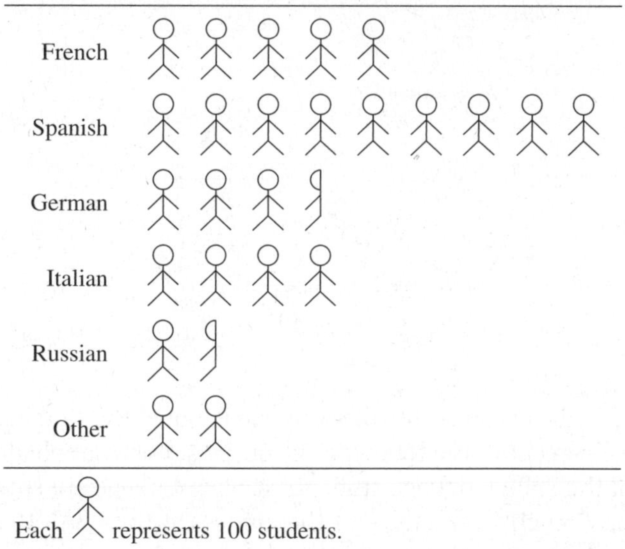

EXAMPLE 3

If the "Other" category includes five languages, what is the average (arithmetic mean) number of students studying each language offered at the college?

Solution. First determine the total number of students taking a language course. Either get the number for each language and add or just count the number of icons: there are 24 full icons and 2 half icons for a total of 25 icons, representing 2500 students. The 2500 students are divided among 10 languages (the 5 languages listed plus the 5 in the "Other" category): $2500 \div 10 = 250$.

EXAMPLE 4

If the number of students studying Italian next year is the same as the number taking Spanish this year, by what percent will the number of students taking Italian increase?

Solution. The number of students taking Italian would increase by 500 from 400 to 900. This represents a $\frac{500}{400} \times 100\% = 125\%$ increase.

Circle Graphs

A ***circle graph*** is another way to present data. In a circle graph, which is sometimes called a ***pie chart***, the circle is divided into sectors, with the size of each sector exactly proportional to the quantity it represents. For example, the information included in the previous graph is presented in the circle graph below.

NUMBERS OF STUDENTS ENROLLED IN LANGUAGE COURSES AT STATE COLLEGE IN 2010

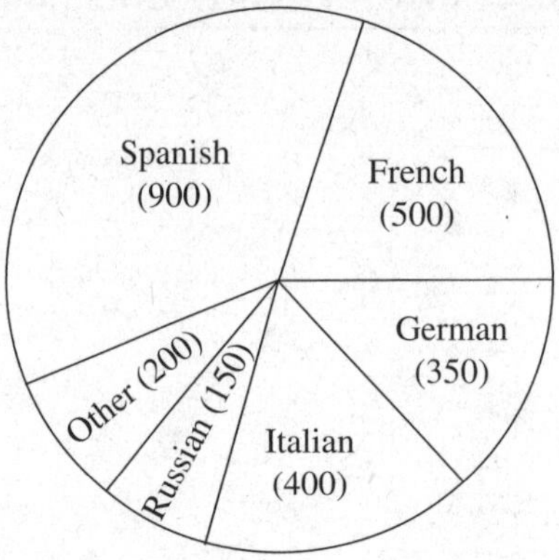

Usually on the PSAT, in each sector of the circle is noted the number of degrees of its central angle or the percent of the total data it contains. For example, in the circle graph above, since 500 of the 2500 language students at State College are studying French, the sector representing French is exactly $\frac{1}{5}$ of the circle. On the PSAT this sector could be marked either 72° ($\frac{1}{5}$ of 360°) or 20% ($\frac{1}{5}$ of 100%), as in the graphs below.

DISTRIBUTION OF THE 2500 STUDENTS ENROLLED IN LANGUAGE COURSES

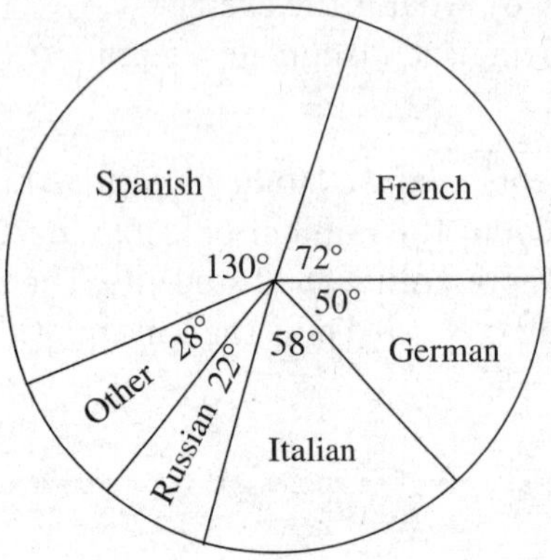

DISTRIBUTION OF THE 2500 STUDENTS ENROLLED IN LANGUAGE COURSES

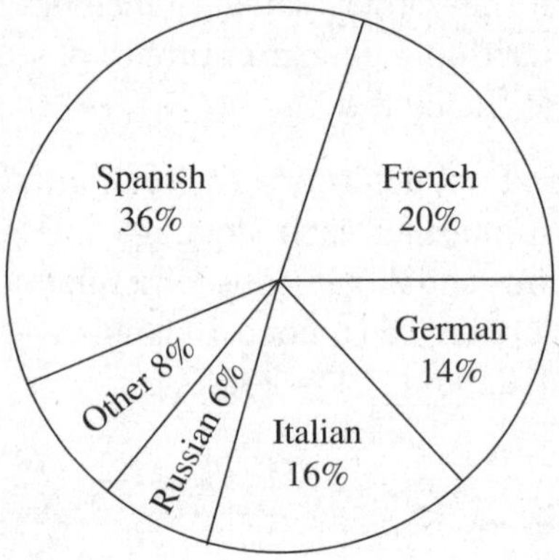

Practice Exercises

MULTIPLE-CHOICE QUESTIONS

Questions 1 and 2 refer to the following graph.

BAKER FAMILY HOUSEHOLD BUDGET IN 2010

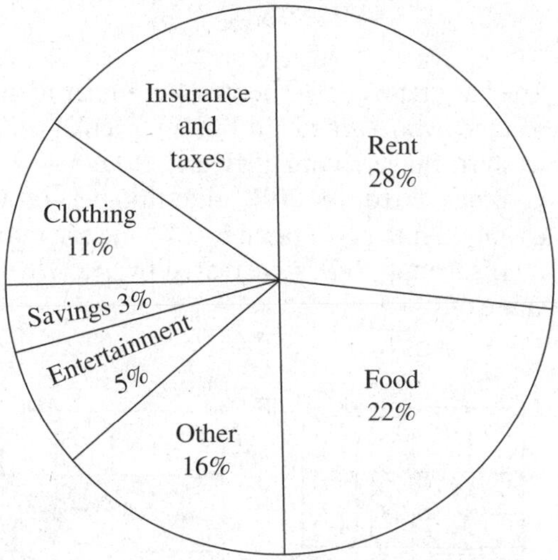

1. If the Baker's income in 2010 was $40,000, how much more did they spend on insurance and taxes than they did on clothing?
   (A) $1600
   (B) $2000
   (C) $3200
   (D) $4400
   (E) $6000

2. What is the degree measure of the central angle of the sector representing insurance and taxes?
   (A) 45
   (B) 54
   (C) 60
   (D) 72
   (E) 90

Questions 3 and 4 refer to the following graph.

MATH SAT SCORES OF JUNIORS AT WESTSIDE HIGH SCHOOL

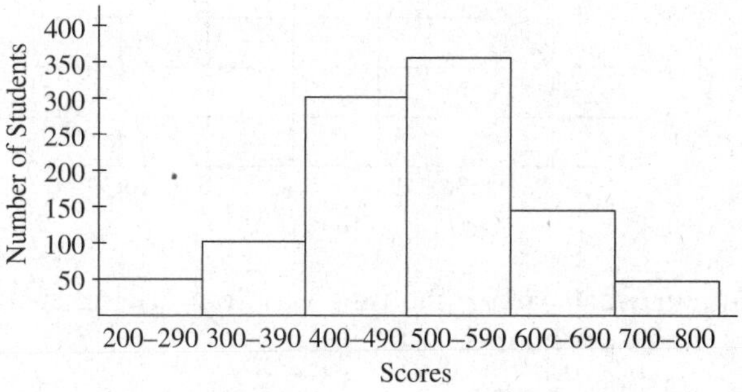

3. How many juniors at Westside High School took the SAT?
   (A) 1000
   (B) 1100
   (C) 1200
   (D) 1250
   (E) 1300

4. To the nearest 5%, what percent of the juniors had Math SAT scores of less than 600?
   (A) 70
   (B) 75
   (C) 80
   (D) 85
   (E) It cannot be determined from the information given.

Questions 5 and 6 refer to the following graph.

SPEEDS AT WHICH TOM DROVE BETWEEN
8:00 A.M. AND 10:30 A.M. ON SUNDAY MORNING

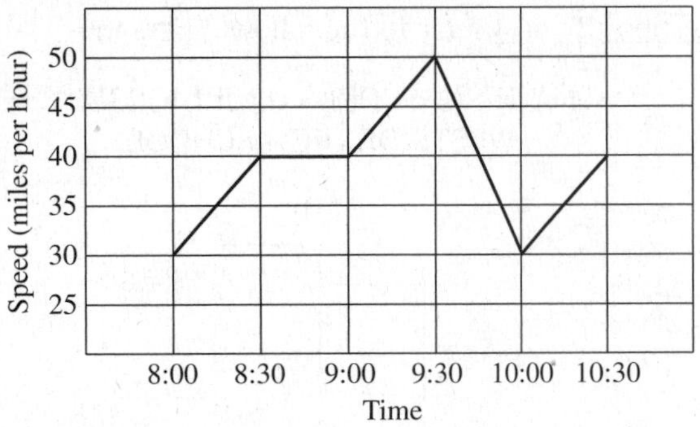

5. For what part of the time was Tom driving at 40 miles per hour or faster?

(A) 20%
(B) 25%
(C) $33\frac{1}{3}\%$
(D) 40%
(E) 50%

6. How far, in miles, did Tom drive between 8:30 and 9:00?

(A) 0
(B) 20
(C) 30
(D) 40
(E) It cannot be determined from the information given.

GRID-IN QUESTIONS

DISTRIBUTION OF GRADES ON
THE FINAL EXAM IN PHYSICS

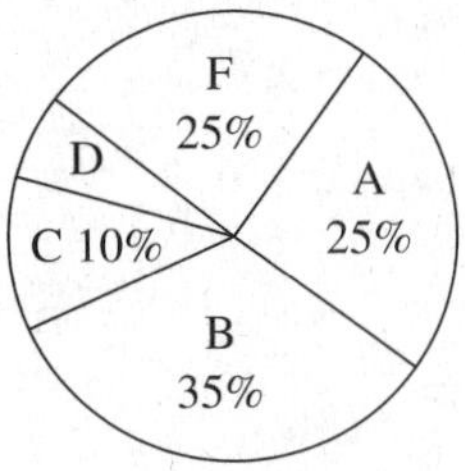

7. On the basis of the data in the graph above, if 300 students took the physics exam, how many earned a grade of D?

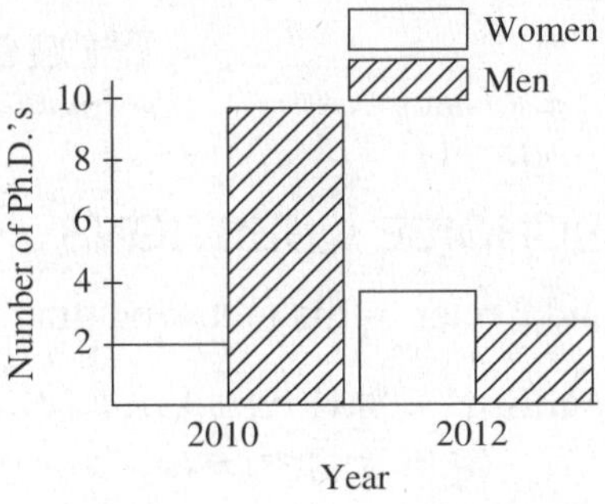

8. The bar graph above shows the number of men and women who earned Ph.D.'s in French at Southwestern University in 2010 and 2012.

From 2010 to 2012 the number of women earning Ph.D.'s increased by $x\%$, and the number of men earning Ph.D.'s decreased by $y\%$. What is the value of $x - y$?

7.

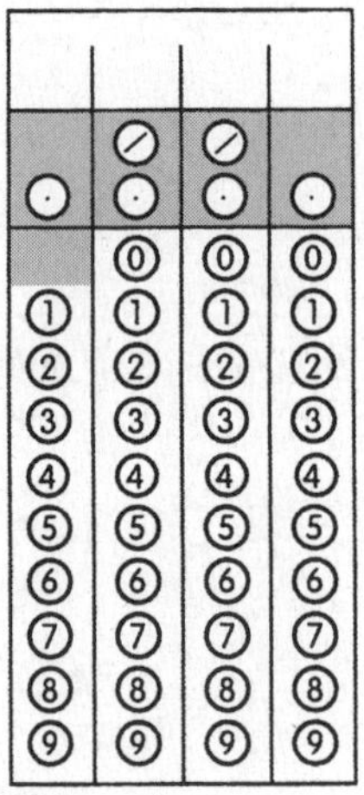

8.

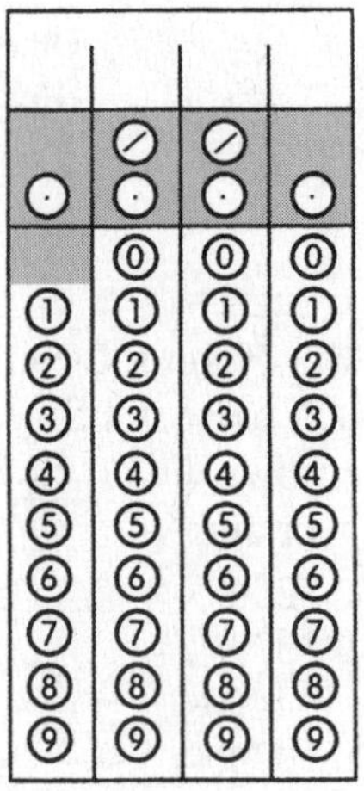

Answer Key

1. A
2. B
3. A
4. C
5. E
6. B

7.

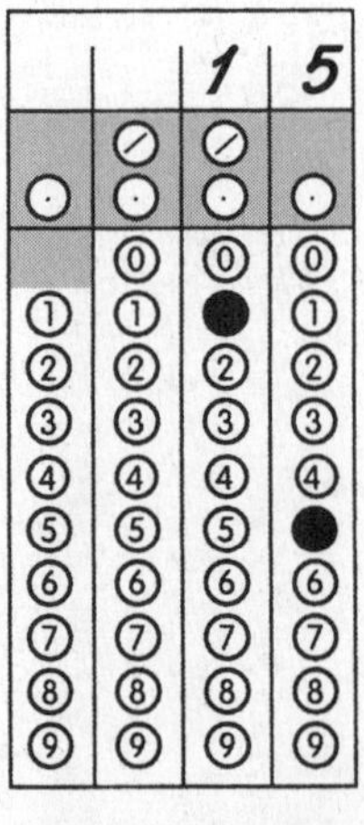

8.

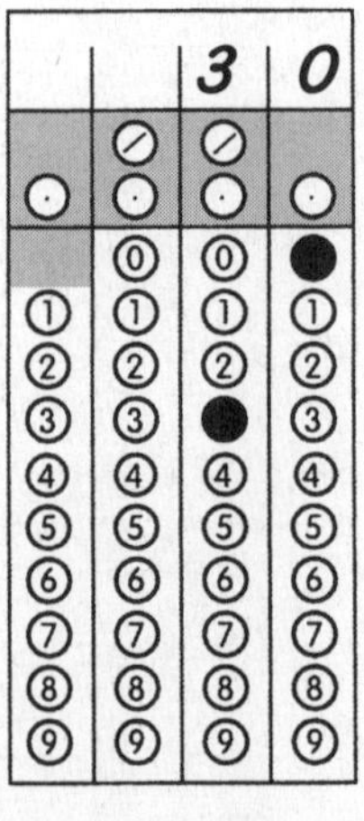

7-R FUNCTIONS

Very little of what is taught about functions in high school math classes is tested on the PSAT. In this section we will review only those basic facts about functions and their graphs that you need to know for the PSAT.

As used on the PSAT, a ***function*** is a rule that assigns to each number in one set a number in another set. The function is usually designated by the letter f, although other letters, such as g and h, are sometimes used. The numbers in the first set are labeled x, and the number in the second set to which x is assigned by the function is designated by the letter y or by $f(x)$.

For example, the function that assigns to each real number x, the number $2x + 3$, can be written $y = 2x + 3$ or $f(x) = 2x + 3$.

The number assigned to 5 is $2(5) + 3 = 10 + 3 = 13$, and the number assigned to -5 is $2(-5) + 3 = -10 + 3 = -7$.

To express these facts, we write

$f(5) = 13$ and $f(-5) = -7$.

The proper way to think of the function $f(x) = 2x + 3$ is that f takes *anything* and assigns to it 2 times *that thing* plus 3:

$$f(\textit{anything}) = 2(\textit{that thing}) + 3$$

- $f(100) = 2(100) + 3 = 203$
- $f(a) = 2a + 3$
- $f(x^2) = 2x^2 + 3$
- $f(0) = 2(0) + 3 = 0 + 3 = 3$
- $f(a + b) = 2(a + b) + 3$
- $f(2x^2 + 3) = 2(2x^2 + 3) + 3 = 4x^2 + 9$

EXAMPLE 1

If $f(x) = x^2 + 2x$, what is $f(3) + f(-3)$?

Solution. $f(3) = 3^2 + 2(3) = 9 + 6 = 15$
$f(-3) = (-3)^2 + 2(-3) = 9 - 6 = 3$

Therefore, $f(3) + f(-3) = 15 + 3 = 18$.

EXAMPLE 2

If $f(x) = x^2 + 2x$, what is $f(x + 2)$?

(A) $x^2 + 2x + 4$
(B) $x^2 + 2x + 8$
(C) $x^2 + 6x + 4$
(D) $x^2 + 6x + 8$
(E) $x^3 + 4x^2 + 4x$

Solution. $f(x + 2) = (x + 2)^2 + 2(x + 2) = (x^2 + 4x + 4) + (2x + 4) = x^2 + 6x + 8$ (Choice D).

EXAMPLE 3

Let $f(x) = x^2 + 2x$ and $g(x) = x^2 - 2x$. If $g(4) = a$ and $f(a) = b$, what is the value of b?

Solution. $g(4) = 4^2 - 2(4) = 16 - 8 = 8$; so $a = 8$. Then

$f(a) = f(8) = 8^2 + 2(8) = 64 + 16 = 80$. So $b = 80$.

The graph of a function, f, is a certain set of points in the coordinate plane. The point (x, y) is on the graph of f if and only if $y = f(x)$. So, for example, the graph of $f(x) = 2x + 3$ consists of all points (x, y) such that $y = 2x + 3$. Since $f(5) = 13$ and $f(-5) = -7$, then (5, 13) and (–5, –7) are both points on the graph of $f(x) = 2x + 3$. On the PSAT you may have to know whether a certain point is on the graph of a given function, but you won't have to actually graph the function.

EXAMPLE 4

Which of the following is NOT a point on the graph of $f(x) = x^2 + \frac{4}{x^2}$?

(A) (1, 5)
(B) (–1, 5)
(C) (2, 5)
(D) (–2, –5)
(E) (4, 16.25)

Solution.

$f(1) = 1^2 + \frac{4}{1^2} = 1 + 4 = 5 \Rightarrow$ (1, 5) *is* a point on the graph.

$f(-1) = (-1)^2 + \frac{4}{(-1)^2} = 1 + 4 = 5 \Rightarrow$ (–1, 5) *is* a point on the graph.

$f(2) = 2^2 + \frac{4}{2^2} = 4 + 1 = 5 \Rightarrow$ (2, 5) *is* a point on the graph.

$f(-2) = (-2)^2 + \frac{4}{(-2)^2} = 4 + 1 = 5 \neq -5 \Rightarrow$ (–2, –5) is *NOT* a point on the graph.

The answer is Choice D.

Practice Exercises

MULTIPLE-CHOICE QUESTIONS

1. If $f(x) = 2x - x^2$, what is the value of $f(-2)$?

(A) –8
(B) –4
(C) 0
(D) 4
(E) 8

2. If $f(x) = 3x + 5$ and $f(2) = a$, what is $f(a)$?

(A) 11
(B) 13
(C) 25
(D) 38
(E) 121

3. If $f(x) = 3x + 5$ and $g(x) = 5x + 3$, what is $g(6) - f(6)$?

(A) 0
(B) 6
(C) 10
(D) 26
(E) 56

4. Let $f(x) = 3x + 5$ and $g(x) = 5x + 3$. If $f(2) = a$ and $g(a) = b$, what is b?

(A) 11
(B) 24
(C) 44
(D) 58
(E) 143

5. If $f(x) = 3x - 5$ and $(2, b)$ is a point on the graph of $y = f(x)$, then $b =$

(A) –1
(B) 1
(C) 3
(D) 5
(E) 11

GRID-IN QUESTIONS

6. If $f(x) = 3x + 5$ and $(a, 20)$ is a point on the graph of $y = f(x)$, then what is the value of a?

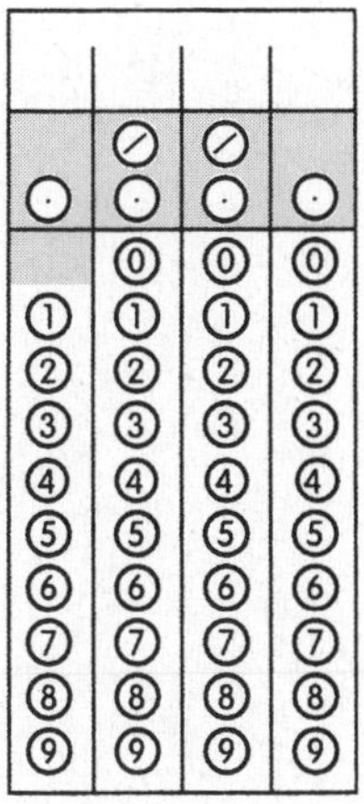

7. If $f(x) = 2^x + x^2$, what is $f(1)$?

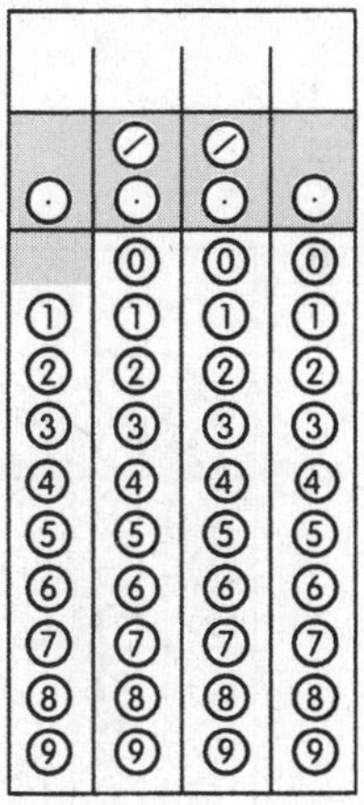

8. Let $f(x) = x^2 + 1$ and $g(x) = 1 - x^2$. If $g(3) = a$ and $f(a) = b$, what is b?

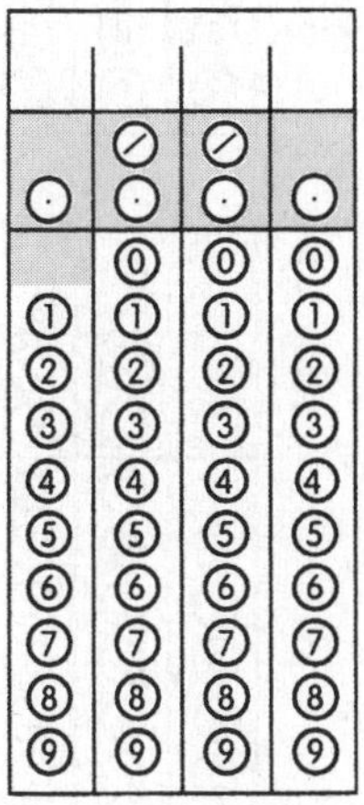

9. If $f(x) = x^2 + 1$ and $f(3) = a$, what is $f(a)$?

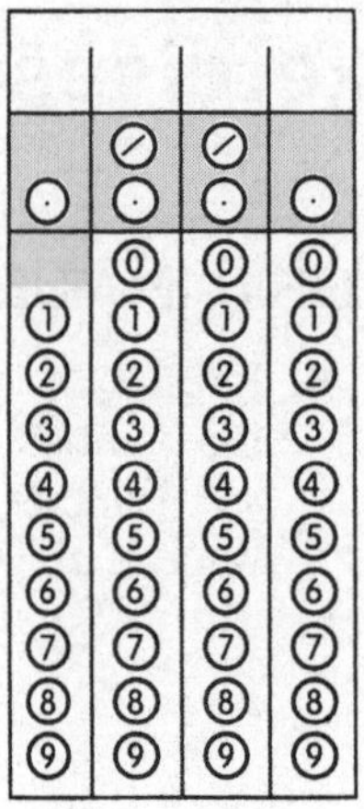

10. If $f(x) = 4 - x^2$ and (a, b) is a point on the graph of $y = f(x)$, what is the greatest possible value of b?

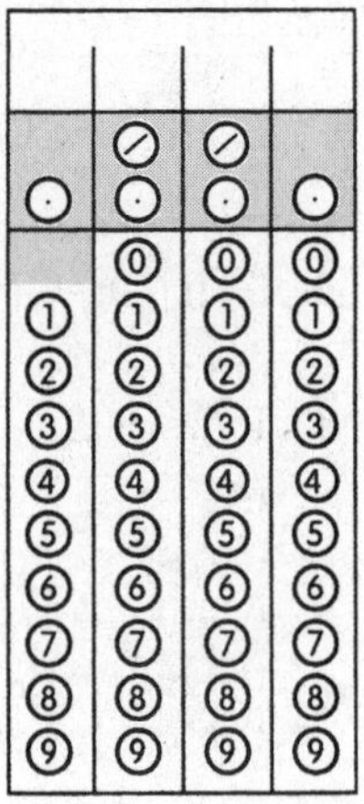

Answer Key

1. A **2.** D **3.** C **4.** D **5.** B

6.

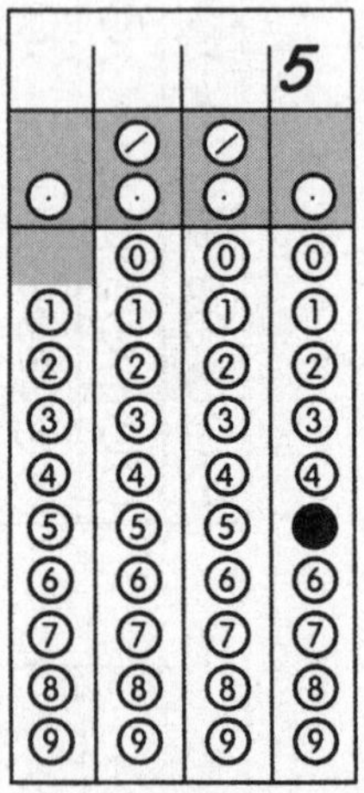

7.

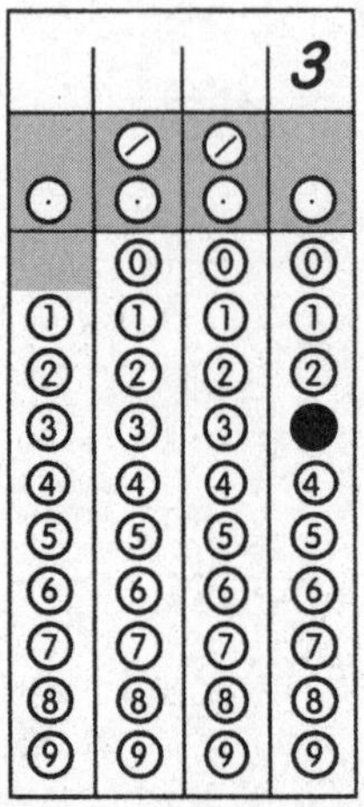

8.

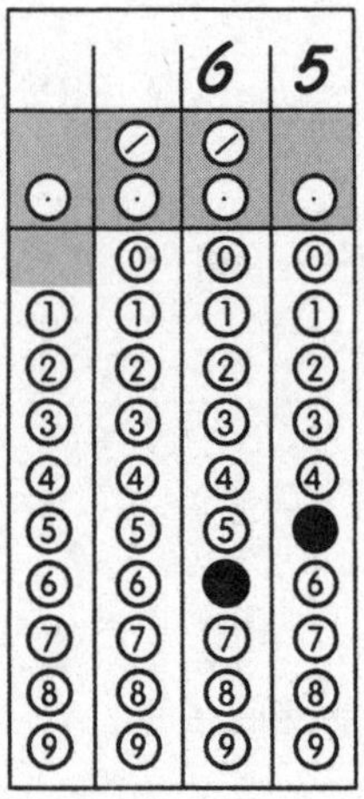

9.

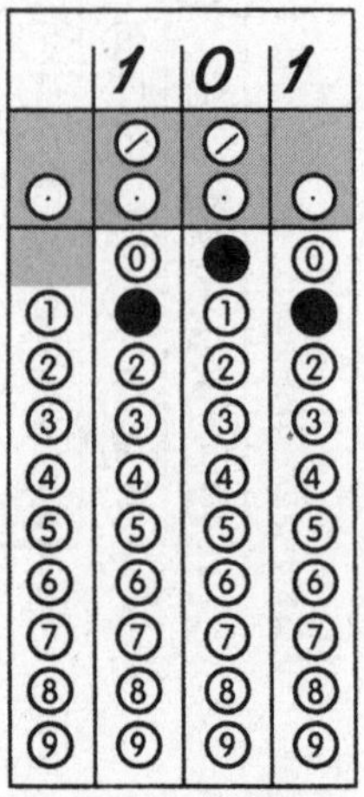

10.

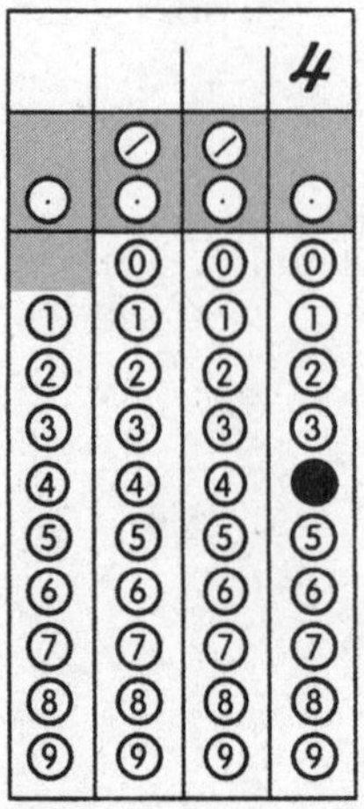

PART SIX

TEST YOURSELF

Four Practice Tests

Four Practice Tests

A two-hour and ten-minute test can be exhausting. Here are some tips that will help you cope on the day of the test:

- Build up your stamina. You have to get used to answering tough questions for more than two hours straight. Take these four practice tests under timed conditions. Try to stay focused the entire time. This practice will pay off when you take the actual test.
- Be well rested on the day of the test. Last-minute cramming will only tire you out. Try to organize your study plan so that you can quit prepping a few days before you take the test. Above all, get a good night's sleep the night before the test.
- Bring a timepiece, preferably the same one you have been using while you have been taking your practice exams. Remember, no beeps or rings! You are not allowed to use a watch or timer with an audible alarm.
- Wear layers. You don't want to be too hot or too cold.
- As you take the test, use the short breaks to stretch and get out the kinks. Breathe in deeply, and let go of the tension as you breathe out. You've done a good job preparing, so think positive, and relax.

Answer Sheet—Practice Test 1

Each mark should completely fill the appropriate space, and should be as dark as all other marks. Make all erasures complete. Traces of an erasure may be read as an answer.

Section 1 – Critical Reading

25 minutes

1 Ⓐ Ⓑ Ⓒ Ⓓ Ⓔ
2 Ⓐ Ⓑ Ⓒ Ⓓ Ⓔ
3 Ⓐ Ⓑ Ⓒ Ⓓ Ⓔ
4 Ⓐ Ⓑ Ⓒ Ⓓ Ⓔ
5 Ⓐ Ⓑ Ⓒ Ⓓ Ⓔ
6 Ⓐ Ⓑ Ⓒ Ⓓ Ⓔ
7 Ⓐ Ⓑ Ⓒ Ⓓ Ⓔ
8 Ⓐ Ⓑ Ⓒ Ⓓ Ⓔ
9 Ⓐ Ⓑ Ⓒ Ⓓ Ⓔ
10 Ⓐ Ⓑ Ⓒ Ⓓ Ⓔ
11 Ⓐ Ⓑ Ⓒ Ⓓ Ⓔ
12 Ⓐ Ⓑ Ⓒ Ⓓ Ⓔ
13 Ⓐ Ⓑ Ⓒ Ⓓ Ⓔ
14 Ⓐ Ⓑ Ⓒ Ⓓ Ⓔ
15 Ⓐ Ⓑ Ⓒ Ⓓ Ⓔ
16 Ⓐ Ⓑ Ⓒ Ⓓ Ⓔ
17 Ⓐ Ⓑ Ⓒ Ⓓ Ⓔ
18 Ⓐ Ⓑ Ⓒ Ⓓ Ⓔ
19 Ⓐ Ⓑ Ⓒ Ⓓ Ⓔ
20 Ⓐ Ⓑ Ⓒ Ⓓ Ⓔ
21 Ⓐ Ⓑ Ⓒ Ⓓ Ⓔ
22 Ⓐ Ⓑ Ⓒ Ⓓ Ⓔ
23 Ⓐ Ⓑ Ⓒ Ⓓ Ⓔ
24 Ⓐ Ⓑ Ⓒ Ⓓ Ⓔ

Section 2 – Math

25 minutes

1 Ⓐ Ⓑ Ⓒ Ⓓ Ⓔ
2 Ⓐ Ⓑ Ⓒ Ⓓ Ⓔ
3 Ⓐ Ⓑ Ⓒ Ⓓ Ⓔ
4 Ⓐ Ⓑ Ⓒ Ⓓ Ⓔ
5 Ⓐ Ⓑ Ⓒ Ⓓ Ⓔ
6 Ⓐ Ⓑ Ⓒ Ⓓ Ⓔ
7 Ⓐ Ⓑ Ⓒ Ⓓ Ⓔ
8 Ⓐ Ⓑ Ⓒ Ⓓ Ⓔ
9 Ⓐ Ⓑ Ⓒ Ⓓ Ⓔ
10 Ⓐ Ⓑ Ⓒ Ⓓ Ⓔ
11 Ⓐ Ⓑ Ⓒ Ⓓ Ⓔ
12 Ⓐ Ⓑ Ⓒ Ⓓ Ⓔ
13 Ⓐ Ⓑ Ⓒ Ⓓ Ⓔ
14 Ⓐ Ⓑ Ⓒ Ⓓ Ⓔ
15 Ⓐ Ⓑ Ⓒ Ⓓ Ⓔ
16 Ⓐ Ⓑ Ⓒ Ⓓ Ⓔ
17 Ⓐ Ⓑ Ⓒ Ⓓ Ⓔ
18 Ⓐ Ⓑ Ⓒ Ⓓ Ⓔ
19 Ⓐ Ⓑ Ⓒ Ⓓ Ⓔ
20 Ⓐ Ⓑ Ⓒ Ⓓ Ⓔ

Section 3 – Critical Reading

25 minutes

25 Ⓐ Ⓑ Ⓒ Ⓓ Ⓔ
26 Ⓐ Ⓑ Ⓒ Ⓓ Ⓔ
27 Ⓐ Ⓑ Ⓒ Ⓓ Ⓔ
28 Ⓐ Ⓑ Ⓒ Ⓓ Ⓔ
29 Ⓐ Ⓑ Ⓒ Ⓓ Ⓔ
30 Ⓐ Ⓑ Ⓒ Ⓓ Ⓔ
31 Ⓐ Ⓑ Ⓒ Ⓓ Ⓔ
32 Ⓐ Ⓑ Ⓒ Ⓓ Ⓔ
33 Ⓐ Ⓑ Ⓒ Ⓓ Ⓔ
34 Ⓐ Ⓑ Ⓒ Ⓓ Ⓔ
35 Ⓐ Ⓑ Ⓒ Ⓓ Ⓔ
36 Ⓐ Ⓑ Ⓒ Ⓓ Ⓔ
37 Ⓐ Ⓑ Ⓒ Ⓓ Ⓔ
38 Ⓐ Ⓑ Ⓒ Ⓓ Ⓔ
39 Ⓐ Ⓑ Ⓒ Ⓓ Ⓔ
40 Ⓐ Ⓑ Ⓒ Ⓓ Ⓔ
41 Ⓐ Ⓑ Ⓒ Ⓓ Ⓔ
42 Ⓐ Ⓑ Ⓒ Ⓓ Ⓔ
43 Ⓐ Ⓑ Ⓒ Ⓓ Ⓔ
44 Ⓐ Ⓑ Ⓒ Ⓓ Ⓔ
45 Ⓐ Ⓑ Ⓒ Ⓓ Ⓔ
46 Ⓐ Ⓑ Ⓒ Ⓓ Ⓔ
47 Ⓐ Ⓑ Ⓒ Ⓓ Ⓔ
48 Ⓐ Ⓑ Ⓒ Ⓓ Ⓔ

Remove answer sheet by cutting on dotted line

Section 4 – Math

25 minutes

21 Ⓐ Ⓑ Ⓒ Ⓓ Ⓔ
22 Ⓐ Ⓑ Ⓒ Ⓓ Ⓔ
23 Ⓐ Ⓑ Ⓒ Ⓓ Ⓔ
24 Ⓐ Ⓑ Ⓒ Ⓓ Ⓔ
25 Ⓐ Ⓑ Ⓒ Ⓓ Ⓔ
26 Ⓐ Ⓑ Ⓒ Ⓓ Ⓔ
27 Ⓐ Ⓑ Ⓒ Ⓓ Ⓔ
28 Ⓐ Ⓑ Ⓒ Ⓓ Ⓔ

29

30

31

32

33

34

35

36

37

38

Section 5 – Writing

30 minutes

1 Ⓐ Ⓑ Ⓒ Ⓓ Ⓔ
2 Ⓐ Ⓑ Ⓒ Ⓓ Ⓔ
3 Ⓐ Ⓑ Ⓒ Ⓓ Ⓔ
4 Ⓐ Ⓑ Ⓒ Ⓓ Ⓔ
5 Ⓐ Ⓑ Ⓒ Ⓓ Ⓔ
6 Ⓐ Ⓑ Ⓒ Ⓓ Ⓔ
7 Ⓐ Ⓑ Ⓒ Ⓓ Ⓔ
8 Ⓐ Ⓑ Ⓒ Ⓓ Ⓔ
9 Ⓐ Ⓑ Ⓒ Ⓓ Ⓔ
10 Ⓐ Ⓑ Ⓒ Ⓓ Ⓔ
11 Ⓐ Ⓑ Ⓒ Ⓓ Ⓔ
12 Ⓐ Ⓑ Ⓒ Ⓓ Ⓔ
13 Ⓐ Ⓑ Ⓒ Ⓓ Ⓔ
14 Ⓐ Ⓑ Ⓒ Ⓓ Ⓔ
15 Ⓐ Ⓑ Ⓒ Ⓓ Ⓔ
16 Ⓐ Ⓑ Ⓒ Ⓓ Ⓔ
17 Ⓐ Ⓑ Ⓒ Ⓓ Ⓔ
18 Ⓐ Ⓑ Ⓒ Ⓓ Ⓔ
19 Ⓐ Ⓑ Ⓒ Ⓓ Ⓔ
20 Ⓐ Ⓑ Ⓒ Ⓓ Ⓔ
21 Ⓐ Ⓑ Ⓒ Ⓓ Ⓔ
22 Ⓐ Ⓑ Ⓒ Ⓓ Ⓔ
23 Ⓐ Ⓑ Ⓒ Ⓓ Ⓔ
24 Ⓐ Ⓑ Ⓒ Ⓓ Ⓔ
25 Ⓐ Ⓑ Ⓒ Ⓓ Ⓔ
26 Ⓐ Ⓑ Ⓒ Ⓓ Ⓔ
27 Ⓐ Ⓑ Ⓒ Ⓓ Ⓔ
28 Ⓐ Ⓑ Ⓒ Ⓓ Ⓔ
29 Ⓐ Ⓑ Ⓒ Ⓓ Ⓔ
30 Ⓐ Ⓑ Ⓒ Ⓓ Ⓔ
31 Ⓐ Ⓑ Ⓒ Ⓓ Ⓔ
32 Ⓐ Ⓑ Ⓒ Ⓓ Ⓔ
33 Ⓐ Ⓑ Ⓒ Ⓓ Ⓔ
34 Ⓐ Ⓑ Ⓒ Ⓓ Ⓔ
35 Ⓐ Ⓑ Ⓒ Ⓓ Ⓔ
36 Ⓐ Ⓑ Ⓒ Ⓓ Ⓔ
37 Ⓐ Ⓑ Ⓒ Ⓓ Ⓔ
38 Ⓐ Ⓑ Ⓒ Ⓓ Ⓔ
39 Ⓐ Ⓑ Ⓒ Ⓓ Ⓔ

SECTION 1/CRITICAL READING

TIME: 25 MINUTES
24 QUESTIONS (1–24)

Directions: For each question in this section, select the best answer from among the choices given and fill in the corresponding circle on the answer sheet.

Each sentence below has one or two blanks, each blank indicating that something has been omitted. Beneath the sentence are five words or sets of words labeled A through E. Choose the word or set of words that, when inserted in the sentence, best fits the meaning of the sentence as a whole.

EXAMPLE:

Medieval kingdoms did not become constitutional republics overnight; on the contrary, the change was ----.

(A) unpopular (B) unexpected
(C) advantageous (D) sufficient (E) gradual

Ⓐ Ⓑ Ⓒ Ⓓ ●

1. Unhappily, the psychology experiment was ---- by the subjects' awareness of the presence of observers in their midst.

(A) muted (B) palliated (C) marred
(D) clarified (E) concluded

2. Until James learned to be more ---- about writing down his homework assignments, he seldom knew when any assignment was due.

(A) obdurate (B) contrary (C) opportunistic
(D) methodical (E) literate

3. Despite all the advertisements singing the ---- of the new product, she remained ---- its merits, wanting to see what *Consumer Reports* had to say about its claims.

(A) virtues..an optimist about
(B) praises..a skeptic about
(C) joys..a convert to
(D) defects..a cynic about
(E) advantages..a believer in

4. After working on the project night and day for two full months, Sandy felt that she had earned a ----.

(A) penalty (B) scolding (C) degree
(D) chore (E) respite

5. Even though the basic organization of the brain does not change after birth, details of its structure and function remain ---- for some time, particularly in the cerebral cortex.

(A) plastic (B) immutable (C) essential
(D) unknown (E) static

GO ON TO NEXT PAGE ▶

Directions: The passages below precede questions based on their content or the relationship between the passages. Answer the questions that follow on the basis of what is stated or implied in the passage.

Questions 6–9 are based on the following passages.

Passage 1

Spiders, and in particular hairy spiders, possess a highly developed sense of touch. Tarantulas, for example, perceive three distinct types of touch: a light whisper that flutters the sensitive leg hairs; a smooth rubbing of the body hair; a steady pressure against the body wall. Press a pencil against the tarantula's body wall and it will back away cautiously without reacting defensively. However, if the tarantula sees the pencil approaching from above, the motion will excite a defensive reaction: it will rear up, lifting its front legs and baring its fangs, maintaining this attack stance until the pencil stops moving.

Passage 2

"The eensy-weensy spider climbed up the waterspout..."

Tarantulas are the world's largest spiders. The very largest live in the jungles of South America, and, in the days when bananas were transported as large bunches on stalks, tarantulas often were accidentally imported with the fruit. Stout-bodied and hairy, tarantulas can create great panic among arachnophobes (people who fear spiders). Actually, these large spiders are gentle giants, whose temperaments do not match their intimidating appearance. Docile and non-aggressive, tarantulas do not bite unless they are severely provoked. Even if they do bite, their bites are not particularly dangerous; they are about as painful as bee stings, and should be treated similarly.

6. In Passage 1, the author's attitude toward tarantulas can best be described as

(A) apprehensive (B) sentimental
(C) approving (D) objective (E) defensive

7. In line 10, "excite" most nearly means

(A) irritate (B) delight (C) stimulate
(D) exhilarate (E) discompose

8. Which statement best expresses the relationship between the two passages?

(A) Passage 1 describes its subject by supplying details with which the author of Passage 2 would disagree.
(B) Passage 1 provides scientific observations of the subject, while Passage 2 offers a popular introduction to the subject.
(C) Passage 1 presents its subject in highly figurative terms, while Passage 2 is more technical in nature.
(D) Both Passage 1 and Passage 2 assume readers will have an automatically negative response to the subject under discussion.
(E) Passage 2 is objective in its presentation, while Passage 1 is more personal in tone.

9. Which generalization about tarantulas is supported by both passages?

(A) They have a marked degree of intelligence.
(B) Their gentleness belies their frightening looks.
(C) They have been unfairly maligned by arachnophobes.
(D) They are capable of acting to defend themselves.
(E) They are easily intimidated by others.

GO ON TO NEXT PAGE ▶

Directions: Each passage below is followed by questions based on its content. Answer the questions following each passage on the basis of what is stated or implied in that passage and in any introductory material that may be provided.

Questions 10–15 are based on the following passage.

The following passage is from a book written by the naturalist Konrad Lorenz and published in 1952.

In the chimney the autumn wind sings the song of the elements, and the old firs before my study window wave excitedly with their arms and sing so loudly in chorus that I can hear their sighing melody through the double panes. Suddenly, from above, a dozen black, streamlined projectiles shoot across the piece of clouded sky for which my window forms a frame. Heavily as stones they fall, fall to the tops of the firs where they suddenly sprout wings, become birds and then light feather rags that the storm seizes and whirls out of my line of vision, more rapidly than they were borne into it.

I walk to the window to watch this extraordinary game that the jackdaws are playing with the wind. A game? Yes, indeed, it is a game, in the most literal sense of the word: practiced movements, indulged in and enjoyed for their own sake and not for the achievement of a special object. And rest assured, these are not merely inborn, purely instinctive actions, but movements that have been carefully learned. All these feats that the birds are performing, their wonderful exploitation of the wind, their amazingly exact assessment of distances and, above all, their understanding of local wind conditions, their knowledge of all the up-currents, air pockets and eddies—all this proficiency is no inheritance, but, for each bird, an individually acquired accomplishment.

And look what they do with the wind! At first sight, you, poor human being, think that the storm is playing with the birds, like a cat with a mouse, but soon you see, with astonishment, that it is the fury of the elements that here plays the role of the mouse and that the jackdaws are treating the storm exactly as the cat its unfortunate victim. Nearly, but only nearly, do they give the storm its head, let it throw them high, high into the heavens, till they seem to fall upwards, then, with a casual flap of a wing, they turn themselves over, open their pinions for a fraction of a second from below against the wind, and dive—with an acceleration far greater than that of a falling stone—into the depths below. Another tiny jerk of the wing and they return to their normal position and, on close-reefed sails, shoot away with breathless speed into the teeth of the gale, hundreds of yards to the west: this all playfully and without effort, just to spite the stupid wind that tries to drive them towards the east. The sightless monster itself must perform the work of propelling the birds through the air at a rate of well over 80 miles an hour; the jackdaws do nothing to help beyond a few lazy adjustments of their black wings. Sovereign control over the power of the elements, intoxicating triumph of the living organism over the pitiless strength of the inorganic!

10. The "arms" mentioned in line 3 are

(A) wings (B) storm winds
(C) heraldic emblems (D) branches
(E) missiles

11. According to the passage, the bird's skill in adapting to wind conditions is

(A) genetically determined
(B) limited
(C) undependable
(D) dependent on the elements
(E) gained through practice

12. In line 20, "rest assured" most likely means

(A) sleep securely
(B) others are certain
(C) be confident
(D) remain poised
(E) in their sure leisure

13. The "sightless monster" mentioned in line 50 is

(A) an unobservant watcher
(B) a falling stone
(C) an airplane
(D) the powerful windstorm
(E) a blind predator

GO ON TO NEXT PAGE ►

14. Throughout the passage, the author is most impressed by
- (A) the direction-finding skills of the birds
- (B) the jackdaws' superhuman strength
- (C) his inability to join the jackdaws in their game
- (D) the fleeting nature of his encounter with the birds
- (E) the jackdaws' mastery of the forces of nature

15. The author does all of the following EXCEPT
- (A) use a metaphor
- (B) argue a cause
- (C) clarify a term
- (D) describe a behavior
- (E) dismiss a notion

Questions 16–24 are based on the following passage.

The passage below, taken from a museum bulletin, discusses tapestry making as an art form.

Tapestries are made on looms. Their distinctive weave is basically simple: the colored weft threads interface regularly with the monochrome warps, as in darning or plain cloth, but as they do so, they form a design by reversing their direction when a change of color is needed. The wefts are beaten down to cover the warps completely. The result is a design or picture that is the fabric itself, not one laid upon a ground like an embroidery, a print, or brocading. The back and front of a tapestry show the same design. The weaver always follows a preexisting model, generally a drawing or painting, known as the cartoon, which in most cases he reproduces as exactly as he can. Long training is needed to become a professional tapestry weaver. It can take as much as a year to produce a yard of very finely woven tapestry.

Tapestry-woven fabrics have been made from China to Peru and from very early times to the present day, but large wall hangings in this technique, mainly of wool, are typically Northern European. Few examples predating the late fourteenth century have survived, but from about 1400 tapestries were an essential part of aristocratic life. The prince or great nobleman sent his plate and his tapestries ahead of him to furnish his castles before his arrival as he traveled through his domains; both had the same function, to display his wealth and social position. It has frequently been suggested that tapestries helped to heat stone-walled rooms, but this is a modern idea; comfort was of minor importance in the Middle Ages. Tapestries were portable grandeur, instant splendor, taking the place, north of the Alps, of painted frescoes further south. They were hung without gaps between them, covering entire walls and often doors as well. Only very occasionally were they made as individual works of art such as altar frontals. They were usually commissioned or bought as sets, or "chambers," and constituted the most important furnishings of any grand room, except for the display of plate, throughout the Middle Ages and the sixteenth century. Later, woven silks, ornamental wood carving, stucco decoration, and painted leather gradually replaced tapestry as expensive wall coverings, until at last wallpaper was introduced in the late eighteenth century and eventually swept away almost everything else.

By the end of the eighteenth century, the "tapestry-room" [a room with every available wall surface covered with wall hangings] was no longer fashionable: paper had replaced wall coverings of wool and silk. Tapestries, of course, were still made, but in the nineteenth century they often seem to have been produced mainly as individual works of art that astonish by their resemblance to oil paintings, tours de force woven with a remarkably large number of wefts per inch. In England during the second half of the century, William Morris attempted to reverse this trend and to bring tapestry weaving back to its true principles, those he considered to have governed it in the Middle Ages. He imitated medieval tapestries in both style and technique, using few warps to the inch, but he did not make sets; the original function for which tapestry is so admirably suited—completely covering the walls of a room and providing sumptuous surroundings for a life of pomp and splendor—could not be revived. Morris's example has been followed, though with less imitation of medieval style, by many weavers of the present century, whose coarsely woven cloths hang like single pictures and can be admired as examples of contemporary art.

GO ON TO NEXT PAGE ▶

16. Tapestry weaving may be characterized as which of the following?

I. Time-consuming
II. Spontaneous in concept
III. Faithful to an original

(A) I only
(B) III only
(C) I and II only
(D) I and III only
(E) II and III only

17. In lines 1–2, "distinctive" most nearly means

(A) characteristic (B) stylish
(C) discriminatory (D) eminent
(E) articulate

18. Renaissance nobles carried tapestries with them to demonstrate their

(A) piety (B) consequence
(C) aesthetic judgment (D) need for privacy
(E) dislike for cold

19. In line 9, "ground" most nearly means

(A) terrain (B) dust (C) thread (D) base
(E) pigment

20. The statement in line 31 ("but this . . . idea") is best described as an example of

(A) a definition of a central concept
(B) an acknowledgment of a principle
(C) a dismissal of a common view
(D) an emotional refutation
(E) a moral proclamation

21. In line 40, the quotation marks around the word "chambers" serve to

(A) emphasize the inadequacy of the particular choice of words
(B) point out the triteness of the term
(C) indicate the use of a colloquialism
(D) illustrate the need for the word to be stressed when spoken aloud
(E) indicate the word is being used in a special sense

22. The author regards William Morris (lines 60–64) as

(A) a bold innovator
(B) an uninspired hack
(C) a medieval nobleman
(D) a cartoonist
(E) a traditionalist

23. In contrast to nineteenth-century tapestries, contemporary tapestries

(A) are displayed in sets of panels
(B) echo medieval themes
(C) faithfully copy oil paintings
(D) have a less fine weave
(E) indicate the owner's social position

24. The primary purpose of the passage is to

(A) explain the process of tapestry making
(B) contrast Eastern and Western schools of tapestry
(C) analyze the reasons for the decline in popularity of tapestries
(D) provide a historical perspective on tapestry making
(E) advocate a return to a more colorful way of life

IF YOU FINISH IN LESS THAN 25 MINUTES, YOU MAY CHECK YOUR WORK ON THIS SECTION ONLY. DO NOT TURN TO ANY OTHER SECTION IN THE TEST.

STOP

SECTION 2 /MATHEMATICS

TIME: 25 MINUTES

20 QUESTIONS (1–20)

Directions:

For each question in this section, determine which of the five choices is correct, and blacken that choice on your answer sheet. You may use any blank space on the page for your work.

NOTES:

- You may use a calculator whenever you believe it will be helpful.
- Use the diagrams provided to help you solve the problems. Unless you see the phrase Note: Figure not drawn to scale under a diagram, it has been drawn as accurately as possible. Unless it is stated that a figure is three dimensional, you may assume that it lies in a plane.

Reference

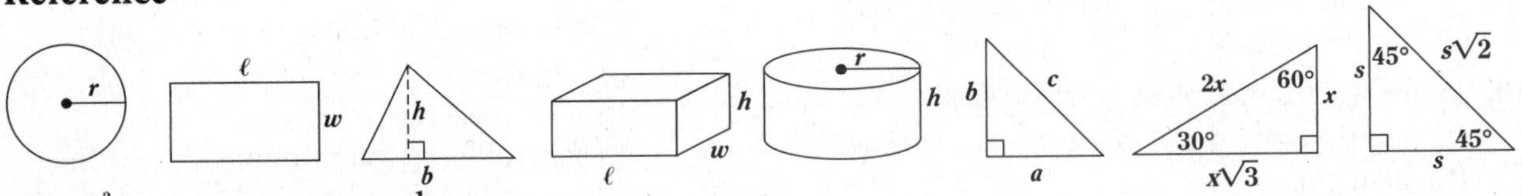

$A = \pi r^2$ $C = 2\pi r$ $A = \ell w$ $A = \frac{1}{2}bh$ $V = \ell wh$ $V = \pi r^2 h$ $c^2 = a^2 + b^2$ **Special Right Triangles**

Number of degrees in a circle: 360

Sum of the measures, in degrees, of the three angles of a triangle: 180

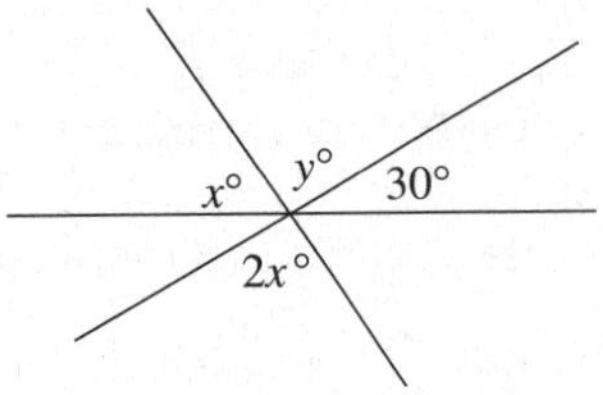

1. In the figure above, what is the value of y?

(A) 50
(B) 70
(C) 90
(D) 100
(E) 140

2. If $(a + 12) - 12 = 12$, then $a =$

(A) -12
(B) 0
(C) 12
(D) 24
(E) 36

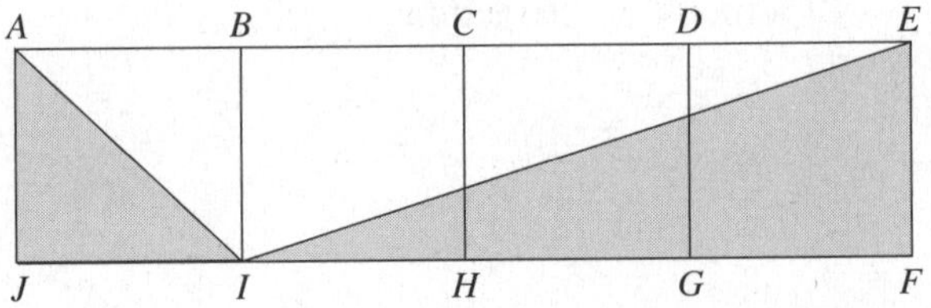

3. In the figure above, rectangle $AEFJ$ is divided into four equal squares. What is the ratio of the area of the shaded region to the area of the white region?

(A) 1:2
(B) 3:5
(C) 5:8
(D) 1:1
(E) 5:3

4. The Albertville Little League raised some money. They used 72% of the money to buy uniforms, 19% for equipment, and the remaining \$243 for a team party. How much money did the team raise?

(A) \$2400
(B) \$2450
(C) \$2500
(D) \$2600
(E) \$2700

5. If it is now 1:30, what time will it be when the hour hand has moved through an angle of 20°?

(A) 1:45
(B) 1:50
(C) 2:00
(D) 2:10
(E) 2:15

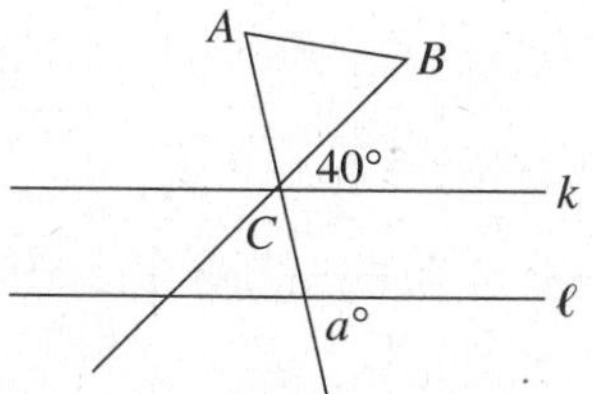

6. In the figure above, lines k and ℓ are parallel, and line k passes through C, one of the vertices of equilateral triangle ABC. What is the value of a?

(A) 40
(B) 50
(C) 60
(D) 80
(E) 90

7. If the difference of two numbers is less than the sum of the numbers, which of the following must be true?

(A) Neither number is positive.
(B) At least one of the numbers is positive.
(C) Exactly one of the numbers is positive.
(D) Both numbers are positive.
(E) None of these statements must be true.

8. 20 is what percent of C?

(A) $20C\%$
(B) $\frac{1}{20C}\%$
(C) $\frac{20}{C}\%$
(D) $\frac{200}{C}\%$
(E) $\frac{2000}{C}\%$

9. Two sides of a right triangle are 5 and 9. Which of the following could be the length of the third side?

I. $\sqrt{56}$
II. $\sqrt{76}$
III. $\sqrt{106}$

(A) I only
(B) III only
(C) I and II only
(D) I and III only
(E) I, II, and III

10. Which of the following is an equation of a line that is parallel to the line whose equation is $y = 2x - 3$?

(A) $y = 2x + 3$
(B) $y = -2x - 3$
(C) $y = \frac{1}{2}x - 3$
(D) $y = -\frac{1}{2}x + 3$
(E) $y = -\frac{1}{2}x - 3$

11. If n is an integer and n, $n + 1$, and $n + 2$ are the lengths of the sides of a triangle, which of the following could be the value of n?

I. 1
II. 3
III. 13

(A) I only
(B) II only
(C) III only
(D) II and III only
(E) I, II, and III

12. A bank raised the minimum payment on its charge accounts from \$10 to \$20 per month. What was the percent increase in the minimum monthly pament?

(A) 10%
(B) 20%
(C) 50%
(D) 100%
(E) 200%

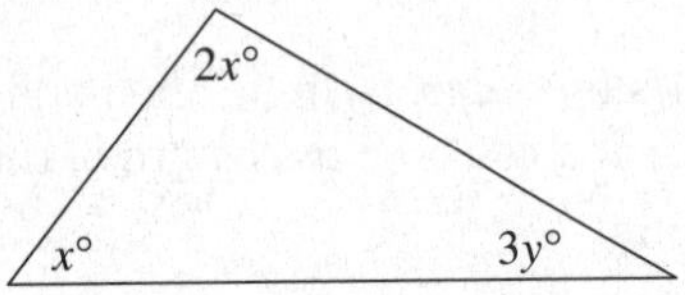

13. For the figure above, which of the following is an expression for y in terms of x?

(A) x
(B) $60 - x$
(C) $x - 60$
(D) $180 - 3x$
(E) $90 - x$

Questions 14 and 15 refer to the following definition.

For any number x, $\|x\| = \frac{2}{3}x^2$.

14. What is the value of $\|6^2\|$?

(A) 16
(B) 24
(C) 144
(D) 576
(E) 864

15. If $y = \frac{2}{3}x$, which of the following is an expression for $\|y\|$ in terms of x?

(A) $\frac{2}{3}x^3$
(B) $\frac{4}{9}x^2$
(C) $\frac{4}{9}x^3$
(D) $\frac{8}{27}x^2$
(E) $\frac{8}{27}x^3$

16. If $f(x) = 9x + 9^x$, what is the value of $f\left(\frac{1}{2}\right)$?

(A) 3
(B) 6
(C) 7.5
(D) 9
(E) 9.9

17. The road from Jack's house to Jill's is exactly 10 kilometers. At different times, Jack and Jill each left home and walked toward the other's house. They walked at the same rate, and they met at noon, 4 kilometers from Jill's house. If Jack left at 10:00, at what time did Jill leave?

(A) 9:40
(B) 10:00
(C) 10:40
(D) 11:00
(E) 11:20

18. The Northport High School French Club has twice as many female members as male members. One day, the percentage of female members attending a meeting of the club was twice the percentage of male members. What percent of those attending the meeting were males?

(A) 20%
(B) 25%
(C) $33\frac{1}{3}$%
(D) 50%
(E) It cannot be determined from the information given.

19. If a and b are the lengths of the legs of a right triangle whose hypotenuse is 10 and whose area is 20, what is the value of $(a + b)^2$?

(A) 100
(B) 120
(C) 140
(D) 180
(E) 200

20. A lottery prize worth d dollars was to be divided equally among 4 winners. It was subsequently discovered that there were 2 additional winners, and the prize would now be divided equally among all the winners. How much more money, in dollars, would each original winner have received if the additional winners were not discovered?

(A) $\frac{d}{12}$
(B) $\frac{d}{6}$
(C) $\frac{d}{4}$
(D) $\frac{12}{d}$
(E) $\frac{6}{d}$

IF YOU FINISH IN LESS THAN 25 MINUTES, YOU MAY CHECK YOUR WORK ON THIS SECTION ONLY. DO NOT TURN TO ANY OTHER SECTION IN THE TEST.

STOP

SECTION 3/CRITICAL READING

TIME: 25 MINUTES

24 QUESTIONS (25–48)

Directions: For each question in this section, select the best answer from among the choices given and fill in the corresponding circle on the answer sheet.

Each sentence below has one or two blanks, each blank indicating that something has been omitted. Beneath the sentence are five words or sets of words labeled A through E. Choose the word or set of words that, when inserted in the sentence, best fits the meaning of the sentence as a whole.

EXAMPLE:

Medieval kingdoms did not become constitutional republics overnight; on the contrary, the change was ----.

(A) unpopular (B) unexpected
(C) advantageous (D) sufficient (E) gradual

Ⓐ Ⓑ Ⓒ Ⓓ ●

25. Nothing anyone could say was able to alter North's ---- that his attempt to lie to Congress was justified.

(A) demand (B) conviction (C) maxim
(D) fear (E) ambivalence

26. Excessive use of coal and oil eventually may ---- the earth's supply of fossil fuels, leaving us in need of a new source of energy.

(A) replenish (B) magnify (C) merge
(D) deplete (E) redirect

27. Contemporary authorities have come to ---- the use of "healthy" in place of "healthful"; however, they still reject the use of "disinterested" in place of "uninterested."

(A) condone (B) evaluate (C) imitate
(D) disdain (E) repudiate

28. Michael's severe bout of the flu ---- him so much that he was too tired to go to work for a week.

(A) recuperated (B) diagnosed
(C) incarcerated (D) captivated
(E) debilitated

29. Though Alec Guinness was determined to make a name for himself on the stage, when he considered the uncertainties of an actor's life, his ---- wavered.

(A) resolution (B) reverence (C) affectation
(D) theatricality (E) skepticism

30. In *Gulliver's Travels,* Swift's intent is ----; he exposes the follies of English society by ridiculing the follies of the Lilliputians.

(A) elegiac (B) prophetic (C) satirical
(D) questionable (E) derivative

31. Even the threat of sudden death could not ---- the intrepid pilot and explorer Beryl Markham; a true ----, she risked her life countless times to set records for flying small planes.

(A) intimidate..patrician
(B) divert..renegade
(C) interest..dilettante
(D) daunt..daredevil
(E) survive..firebrand

32. As an indefatigable consumer advocate, Ralph Nader is constantly engaged in ---- the claims of unscrupulous merchandisers and cautioning the public to exercise a healthy ----.

(A) asserting..autonomy
(B) deflating..prodigality
(C) debunking..skepticism
(D) affirming..indifference
(E) exaggerating..optimism

GO ON TO NEXT PAGE ▶

Directions: Each of the passages below precedes two questions based on its content. Answer the questions following each passage on the basis of what is stated or implied in that passage.

Questions 33 and 34 are based on the following passage.

Can prison reform people, positively transforming their lives? Some who answer yes to this question point to the example of Malcolm Little, later known as Malcolm X. *The Autobiography of Malcolm X* describes how Malcolm, a high school dropout, in prison set himself the task of reading straight through the dictionary; to him, reading was purposeful, not aimless, and he plowed his way through its hundreds of pages, from A for *aardvark* to Z for *zymurgy*.

33. The author's attitude toward Malcolm's activities in prison can best be described as

(A) nostalgic (B) pessimistic
(C) condescending (D) approving
(E) apologetic

34. In line 8, "plowed" most nearly means

(A) harrowed (B) cultivated
(C) plunged recklessly (D) prepared hastily
(E) proceeded steadily

Questions 35 and 36 are based on the following passage.

Many primates live together in an organized troop or social group that includes members of all ages and both sexes. Such troops always move compactly together in a stable social unit. A typical primate troop characteristically exhibits a ranking hierarchy among the males in the troop. This ranking hierarchy serves to alleviate conflict within the troop. The highest-ranking male or males defend, control, and lead the troop; the strong social bond among members and their safety is maintained.

35. According to the passage, primate societies are

(A) generally unstable
(B) hierarchically flexible
(C) extremely competitive
(D) dominated by adult males
(E) frequently in conflict with each other

36. According to the passage, the hierarchic structure within a troop serves to

(A) protect the members of the troop
(B) facilitate food gathering
(C) establish friendships within the group
(D) keep members of other troops from joining
(E) teach the youngest members how to survive

GO ON TO NEXT PAGE ►

Directions: The passages below are followed by questions on their content; questions following a pair of related passages may also be based on the relationship between the paired passages. Answer the questions on the basis of what is stated or implied in the passages and in any introductory material that may be provided.

Questions 37–48 are based on the following passages.

The following passages present two portraits of grandmothers. In Passage 1, Mary McCarthy shares her memories of her Catholic grandmother, who raised McCarthy and her brother after their parents' death. In Passage 2, Caroline Heilbrun tells of her Jewish grandmother, who died when Heilbrun was ten.

Passage 1

Luckily, I am writing a memoir and not a work of fiction, and therefore I do not have to account for my grandmother's unpleasing character and look for the Oedipal fixation or the traumatic experience which would give her that clinical authenticity that is nowadays so desirable in portraiture. I do not know how my grandmother got the way she was; I assume, from family photographs and from the inflexibility of her habits, that she was always the same, and it seems as idle to inquire into her childhood as to ask what was ailing Iago or look for the error in toilet-training that was responsible for Lady Macbeth. My grandmother's sexual history, bristling with infant mortality in the usual style of her period, was robust and decisive: three tall, handsome sons grew up, and one attentive daughter. Her husband treated her kindly. She had money, many grandchildren, and religion to sustain her. White hair, glasses, soft skin, wrinkles, needlework—all the paraphernalia of motherliness were hers; yet it was a cold, grudging, disputatious old woman who sat all day in her sunroom making tapestries from a pattern, scanning religious periodicals, and setting her iron jaw against any infraction of her ways.

Combativeness was, I suppose, the dominant trait in my grandmother's nature. An aggressive churchgoer, she was quite without Christian feeling; the mercy of the Lord Jesus had never entered her heart. Her piety was an act of war against the Protestant ascendancy. The religious magazines on her table furnished her not with food for meditation but with fresh pretexts for anger; articles attacking birth control, divorce, mixed marriages, Darwin, and secular education were her favorite reading. The teachings of the Church did not interest her, except as they were a rebuke to others; "Honor thy father and thy mother," a commandment she was no longer called upon to practice, was the one most frequently on her lips. The extermination of Protestantism, rather than spiritual perfection, was the boon she prayed for. Her mind was preoccupied with conversion; the capture of a soul for God much diverted her fancy—it made one less Protestant in the world. Foreign missions, with their overtones of good will and social service, appealed to her less strongly; it was not a *harvest* of souls that my grandmother had in mind.

This pugnacity of my grandmother's did not confine itself to sectarian enthusiasm. There was the defense of her furniture and her house against the imagined encroachments of visitors. With her, this was not the gentle and tremulous protectiveness endemic in old ladies, who fear for the safety of their possessions with a truly touching anxiety, inferring the fragility of all things from the brittleness of their old bones and hearing the crash of mortality in the perilous tinkling of a tea-cup. My grandmother's sentiment was more autocratic: she hated having her chairs sat in or her lawns stepped on or the water turned on in her basins, for no reason at all except pure officiousness; she even grudged the mailman his daily promenade up her sidewalk. Her home was a center of power, and she would not allow it to be derogated by easy or democratic usage. Under her jealous eye, its social properties had atrophied, and it functioned in the family structure simply as a political headquarters. The family had no friends, and entertaining was held to be a foolish and unnecessary courtesy as between blood relations. Holiday dinners fell, as a duty, on the lesser members of the organization: the daughters and daughters-in-law (converts from the false religion) offered up Baked Alaska on a platter like the head of John the Baptist, while the old people sat enthroned at the table, and only their digestive processes acknowledged, with rumbling, enigmatic salvos, the festal day.

GO ON TO NEXT PAGE ▶

Passage 2

My grandmother, one of Howe's sustaining women, not only ruled the household with an arm of iron, but kept a store to support them all, her blond, blue-eyed husband enjoying life rather than struggling through it. My grandmother was one of those powerful women who know that they stand between their families and an outside world filled with temptations to failure and shame. I remember her as thoroughly loving. But there can be no question that she impaired her six daughters for autonomy as thoroughly as if she had crippled them—more so. The way to security was marriage; the dread that stood in the way of this was sexual dalliance, above all pregnancy. The horror of pregnancy in an unmarried girl is difficult, perhaps, to recapture now. For a Jewish girl not to be a virgin on marriage was failure. The male's rights were embodied in her lack of sexual experience, in the knowledge that he was the first, the owner.

All attempts at autonomy had to be frustrated. And of course, my grandmother's greatest weapon was her own vulnerability. She had worked hard, only her daughters knew how hard. She could not be comforted or repaid—as *my* mother would feel repaid—by a daughter's accomplishments, only by her marriage.

37. McCarthy's attitude toward her grandmother is best described as

(A) tolerant (B) appreciative (C) indifferent (D) nostalgic (E) sardonic

38. In line 10, "idle" most nearly means

(A) slothful (B) passive (C) fallow (D) useless (E) unoccupied

39. According to McCarthy, a portrait of a character in a work of modern fiction must have

(A) photographic realism
(B) psychological validity
(C) sympathetic attitudes
(D) religious qualities
(E) historical accuracy

40. McCarthy's primary point in describing her grandmother's physical appearance (lines 19–25) is best summarized by which of the following axioms?

(A) Familiarity breeds contempt.
(B) You can't judge a book by its cover.
(C) One picture is worth more than ten thousand words.
(D) There's no smoke without fire.
(E) Blood is thicker than water.

41. By describing the typical old woman's fear for the safety of her possessions (in lines 53–60), McCarthy emphasizes that

(A) her grandmother feared the approach of death
(B) old women have dangerously brittle bones
(C) her grandmother possessed considerable wealth
(D) her grandmother had different reasons for her actions
(E) visitors were unwelcome in her grandmother's home

42. In line 68, "properties" most nearly means

(A) belongings (B) aspects (C) holdings (D) titles (E) acreage

43. Heilbrun is critical of her grandmother primarily because

(A) she would not allow her husband to enjoy himself
(B) she could not accept her own vulnerability
(C) she fostered a sense of sexual inadequacy
(D) she discouraged her daughters' independence
(E) she physically injured her children

44. By describing the extent of the feeling against pregnancy in unmarried girls (lines 94–99), Heilbrun helps the reader understand

(A) her fear of being scorned as an unwed mother
(B) why her grandmother strove to limit her daughters' autonomy
(C) her disapproval of contemporary sexual practices
(D) her awareness of her mother's desire for happiness
(E) how unforgiving her grandmother was

GO ON TO NEXT PAGE ▶

45. In stating that her grandmother's greatest weapon was her own vulnerability (lines 101–102), Heilbrun implies that her grandmother got her way by exploiting her children's

(A) sense of guilt
(B) innocence of evil
(C) feeling of indifference
(D) abdication of responsibility
(E) lack of experience

46. Both passages mention which of the following as being important to the writer's grandmother?

(A) governing the actions of others
(B) contributing to religious organizations
(C) protecting her children's virtue
(D) marrying off her daughters
(E) being surrounded by a circle of friends

47. Which technique is used in Passage 1 but not in Passage 2?

(A) relating the author's own experience
(B) stating an opinion
(C) making an assertion
(D) drawing a contrast
(E) making literary references

48. McCarthy would most likely react to the characterization of her grandmother, like Heilbrun's grandmother, as one of the "sustaining women" (lines 81–82) by pointing out that

(A) this characterization is not in good taste
(B) the characterization fails to account for her grandmother's piety
(C) the details of the family's social life support this characterization
(D) her grandmother's actual conduct is not in keeping with this characterization
(E) this characterization slightly exaggerates her grandmother's chief virtue

IF YOU FINISH IN LESS THAN 25 MINUTES, YOU MAY CHECK YOUR WORK ON THIS SECTION ONLY. DO NOT TURN TO ANY OTHER SECTION IN THE TEST.

STOP

SECTION 4/MATHEMATICS

TIME: 25 MINUTES
18 QUESTIONS (21–38)

Directions:

For questions 21–28, determine which of the five choices is correct, and blacken that choice on your answer sheet. You may use any blank space on the page for your work.

NOTES:

- You may use a calculator whenever you believe it will be helpful.
- Use the diagrams provided to help you solve the problems. Unless you see the phrase
  Note: Figure not drawn to scale
  under a diagram, it has been drawn as accurately as possible. Unless it is stated that a figure is three dimensional, you may assume that it lies in a plane.

Reference

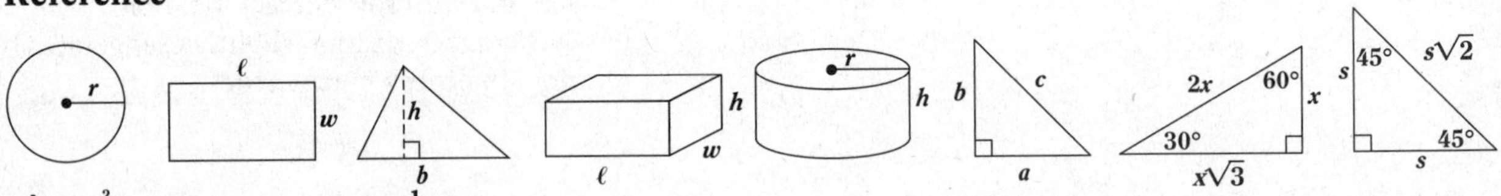

$A = \pi r^2$ $C = 2\pi r$ | $A = \ell w$ | $A = \frac{1}{2}bh$ | $V = \ell wh$ | $V = \pi r^2 h$ | $c^2 = a^2 + b^2$ | Special Right Triangles

Number of degrees in a circle: 360
Sum of the measures, in degrees, of the three angles of a triangle: 180

21. If the ratio of the number of boys to girls in a club is 2:3, what percent of the club members are girls?

(A) $33\frac{1}{3}\%$
(B) 40%
(C) 50%
(D) 60%
(E) $66\frac{2}{3}\%$

22. The Salem Soccer League is divided into d divisions. Each division has t teams, and each team has p players. How many players are there in the entire league?

(A) $\frac{pt}{d}$
(B) $\frac{dt}{p}$
(C) $\frac{d}{pt}$
(D) $d + t + p$
(E) dtp

23. Which of the following is *NOT* a solution of $3x^2 + 2y = 5$?

(A) $x = 1$ and $y = 1$
(B) $x = -1$ and $y = 1$
(C) $x = 1$ and $y = -1$
(D) $x = 3$ and $y = -11$
(E) $x = -3$ and $y = -11$

24. Sally wrote the number 1 on 1 slip of paper, the number 2 on 2 slips of paper, the number 3 on 3 slips of paper, the number 4 on 4 slips of paper, the number 5 on 5 slips of paper, and the number 6 on 6 slips of paper. All the slips of paper were placed in a bag, and Lana drew one slip at random. What is the probability that the number on the slip Lana drew was odd?

(A) $\frac{1}{9}$
(B) $\frac{1}{7}$
(C) $\frac{3}{7}$
(D) $\frac{1}{2}$
(E) $\frac{4}{7}$

GO ON TO NEXT PAGE ▶

25. If $|x| = |y|$, which of the following must be true?

I. $-x = -y$
II. $x^2 = y^2$
III. $x^3 = y^3$

(A) I only
(B) II only
(C) I and II only
(D) II and III only
(E) I, II, and III

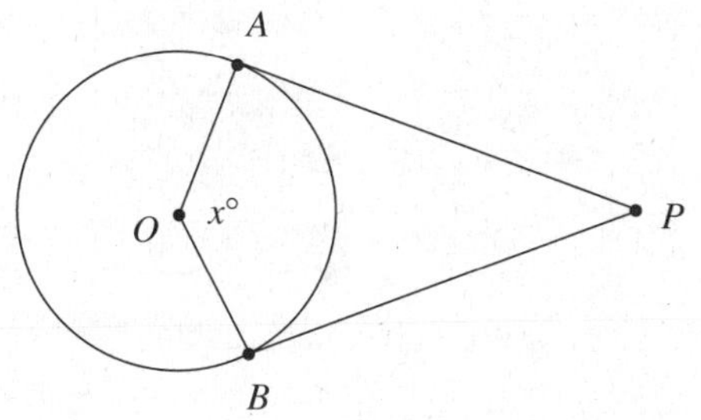

26. In the figure above, $\overline{PA}$ and $\overline{PB}$ are tangent to circle O. If $m\angle P = 50°$, what is the value of x?

(A) 50
(B) 90
(C) 120
(D) 130
(E) 150

27. Which of the following expressions is equal to $2^{3x} + 2^{3x} + 2^{3x} + 2^{3x}$?

(A) 2^{3x+2}
(B) 2^{3x+4}
(C) 2^{6x}
(D) 2^{12x}
(E) 2^{9x^2}

28. The circumference of circle II is 4 feet longer than the circumference of circle I. How many feet longer is the radius of circle II than the radius of circle I?

(A) $\frac{1}{4\pi}$
(B) $\frac{2}{\pi}$
(C) $\frac{1}{\pi}$
(D) 2
(E) It cannot be determined from the information given.

Student-Produced Response Directions

In questions 29–38, first solve the problem, and then enter your answer on the grid provided on the answer sheet. The instructions for entering your answers follow.

- First, write your answer in the boxes at the top of the grid.
- Second, grid your answer in the columns below the boxes.
- Use the fraction bar in the first row or the decimal point in the second row to enter fractions and decimals.

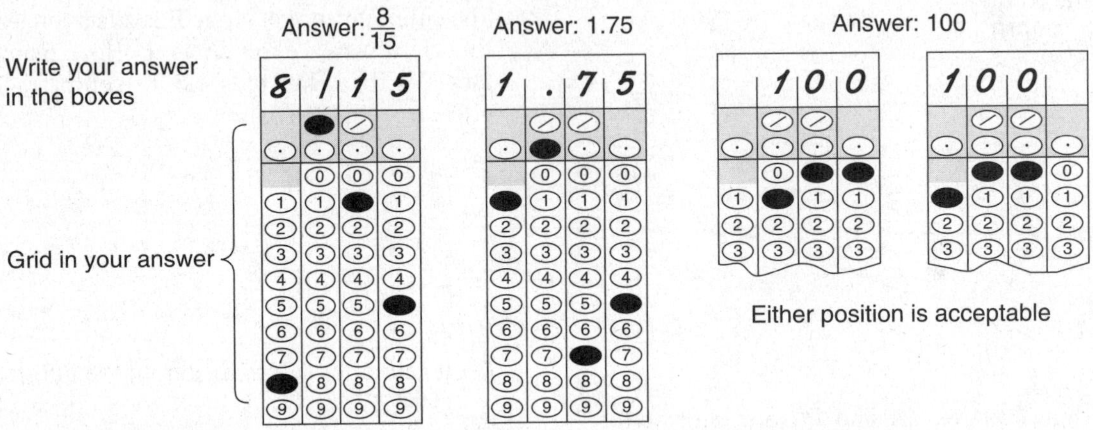

- Grid only one space in each column.
- Entering the answer in the boxes is recommended as an aid in gridding but is not required.
- The machine scoring your exam can read only what you grid, so you **must grid-in your answers correctly to get credit.**
- If a question has more than one correct answer, grid-in only one of them.
- The grid does not have a minus sign; so no answer can be negative.
- A mixed number *must* be converted to an improper fraction or a decimal before it is gridded. Enter $1\frac{1}{4}$ as $\frac{5}{4}$ or 1.25; the machine will interpret 11/4 as $\frac{11}{4}$ and mark it wrong.
- **All decimals must be entered as accurately as possible.** Here are three acceptable ways of gridding $\frac{3}{11} = 0.272727\ldots$

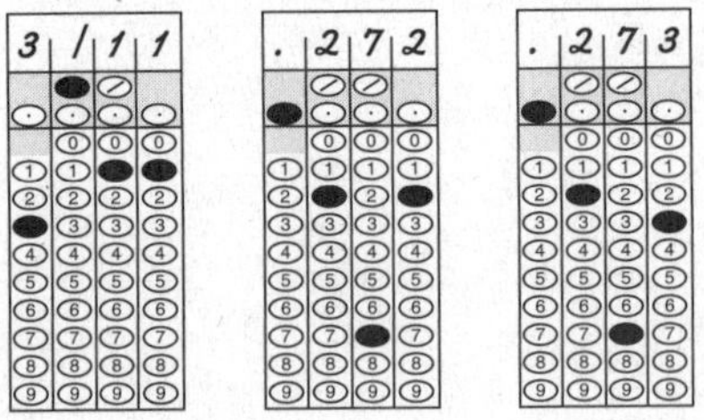

- Note that rounding to .273 is acceptable because you are using the full grid, but you would receive **no credit** for .3 or .27, because they are less accurate.

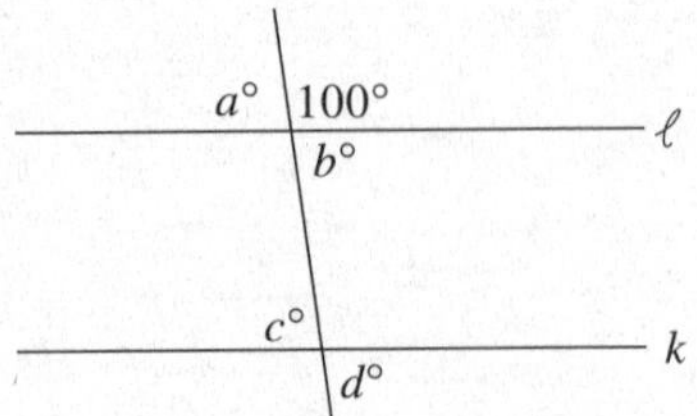

Lines ℓ and k are parallel.

29. In the figure above, what is the value of $a + b + c + d$?

30. If $a = 6$ and $b = -6$, what is the value of $2a - 3b$?

31. If A is the median of {1, 2, 3, 4, 5, 6} and B is the median of {1, 2, 3, 4, 5, 6, 7}, what is the average (arithmetic mean) of A and B?

GO ON TO NEXT PAGE ▶

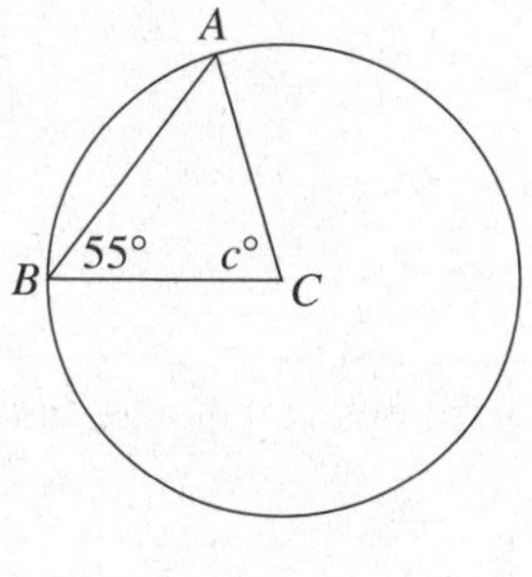

32. In the figure above, C is the center of the circle. What is the value of c?

33. If Elaine drove 190 kilometers between 12:00 noon and 3:20 P.M., what was her average speed, in kilometers per hour?

34. From 2000 until 2010 the value of an investment increased by 10% every year. The value of that investment on January 1, 2006, was how many times greater than the value on January 1, 2004?

35. How many two-digit numbers do not contain the digit 9?

36. If the average (arithmetic mean) of five numbers is 95 and the average of three of them is 100, what is the average of the other two?

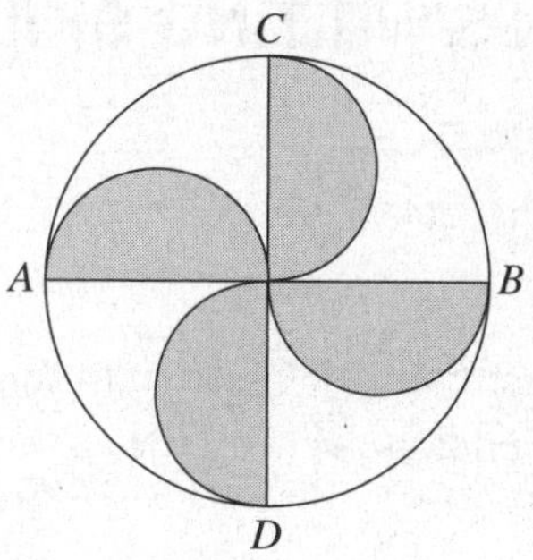

37. In the circle above, diameters AB and CD are perpendicular, and each of the four shaded regions is a semicircle. The shaded area is how many times the white area?

38. When a group of people were tested for a rare disease, 99.6% of them were found not to have the disease. If 10 people did have the disease, how many people were tested?

IF YOU FINISH IN LESS THAN 25 MINUTES, YOU MAY CHECK YOUR WORK ON THIS SECTION ONLY. DO NOT TURN TO ANY OTHER SECTION IN THE TEST.

STOP

SECTION 5/WRITING SKILLS

TIME: 30 MINUTES

39 QUESTIONS (1–39)

Directions: For each question in this section, select the best answer from among the choices given and fill in the corresponding circle on the answer sheet.

Some or all parts of the following sentences are underlined. The first answer choice, (A), simply repeats the underlined part of the sentence. The other four choices present four alternative ways to phrase the underlined part. Select the answer that produces the most effective sentence, one that is clear and exact, and blacken the appropriate space on your answer sheet. In selecting your choice, be sure that it is standard written English and that it expresses the meaning of the original sentence.

EXAMPLE:

The first biography of author Eudora Welty came out in 1998, and she was eighty-nine years old at the time.

(A) and she was eighty-nine years old at the time
(B) at the time when she was eighty-nine
(C) upon becoming an eighty-nine year old
(D) when she was eighty-nine
(E) at the age of eighty-nine years old

Ⓐ Ⓑ Ⓒ ● Ⓔ

1. Although serfs were lucky to drink their ale from cracked wooden bowls, nobles customarily drunk their wine from elaborately chased drinking horns.

(A) drunk their wine from
(B) have drinked their wine from
(C) drank their wine from
(D) had drunken their wine from
(E) drinking their wine from

2. Before the search party reached the scene of the accident, the rain began to fall, making rescue efforts more difficult.

(A) the rain began to fall
(B) the rain had began to fall
(C) it began to rain
(D) the rain had begun to fall
(E) it started to rain

3. For many students, keeping a journal during college seems satisfying their need for self-expression.

(A) keeping a journal during college seems satisfying their need
(B) keeping a journal during college seems to satisfy their need
(C) keeping a journal during college seeming satisfying their need
(D) to keep a journal during college seems satisfying their need
(E) the keeping of a journal during college seems to satisfy their need

4. Peter Martins began to develop his own choreographic style, but he was able to free himself from the influence of Balanchine.

(A) style, but he was able to
(B) style; but he was able to
(C) style only when he was able to
(D) style only when he is able to
(E) style: only when he was able to

5. Irregardless of the outcome of this dispute, our two nations will remain staunch allies.

(A) Irregardless of the outcome
(B) Regardless of how the outcome
(C) With regard to the outcome
(D) Regardless of the outcome
(E) Disregarding the outcome

GO ON TO NEXT PAGE ▶

6. With the onset of winter, the snows began to fall, we were soon forced to remain indoors most of the time.

(A) the snows began to fall, we were soon forced to remain indoors
(B) the snows began to fall; we were soon forced to remain indoors
(C) the snows began to fall; we are soon forced to remain indoors
(D) the snows began to fall, having forced us to remain indoors
(E) the snows begin to fall; we were soon forced to remain indoors

7. "Araby," along with several other stories from Joyce's *Dubliners*, are going to be read at Town Hall by the noted Irish actor Brendan Coyle.

(A) are going to be read
(B) were going to be read
(C) are gone to be read
(D) is going to be read
(E) is gone to be read

8. In 1980 the Democrats lost not only the executive branch, but also their majority in the United States Senate.

(A) lost not only the executive branch but also their majority
(B) lost not only the executive branch but also its majority
(C) not only lost the executive branch but also their majority
(D) lost the executive branch but also their majority
(E) lost not only the executive branch but their majority also

9. Before considering an applicant for this job, he must have a degree in electrical engineering as well as three years in the field.

(A) Before considering an applicant for this job, he must have
(B) Before considering an applicant for this job, he should have
(C) We will not consider an applicant for this job without
(D) To consider an applicant for this job, he must have
(E) We will not consider an applicant for this job if he does not have

10. To invest intelligently for the future, mutual funds provide an excellent opportunity for the average investor.

(A) To invest intelligently for the future, mutual funds
(B) As an intelligent investment for the future, mutual funds
(C) Investing intelligently for the future, mutual funds
(D) To invest with intelligence, mutual funds
(E) Having invested intelligently, you must determine that mutual funds

11. When you remodel your home, your renovations must be in compliance to the local building code.

(A) must be in compliance to the local building code
(B) must be in compliance with the local building code
(C) must comply to the local building code
(D) must have been in compliance to the local building code
(E) must have been in compliance with the local building code

12. Although bothered by constant heckling from their traditional rivals, the home team's response was to stick to the coach's game plan and defeat their opponents.

(A) the home team's response was to stick to the coach's game plan and defeat their opponents
(B) the home team's response was to stick to the coach's game plan and defeat its opponents
(C) the home team's response is about sticking to the coach's game plan and defeating their opponents
(D) the home team responded with sticking to the coach's game plan and they defeated their opponents
(E) the home team responded by sticking to the coach's game plan and defeating their opponents

13. Mary is as fast as, if not faster than, anyone in her class and should be on the team.

(A) as fast as, if not faster than, anyone
(B) as fast, if not faster than, anyone else
(C) as fast as, if not more fast than, anyone
(D) as fast as, if not faster than, anyone else
(E) as swift as, if not faster than, anyone

GO ON TO NEXT PAGE ▶

14. Senator Schumer is one of the legislators who are going to discuss the budget with the president.

(A) one of the legislators who are going
(B) one of the legislators who is going
(C) one of the legislators who has gone
(D) one of the legislators who is gone
(E) one of the legislators who were gone

15. New research studies show that alcohol and tobacco are as harmful to elderly women as elderly men.

(A) are as harmful to elderly women as elderly men
(B) are so harmful to elderly women as elderly men
(C) being as harmful to elderly women as elderly men
(D) are as harmful to elderly women as to elderly men
(E) are as harmful to elderly women as to men being elderly

16. Chronic fatigue syndrome is not a normal condition; rather, it is an abnormal response to stress factors such as anxiety or infection.

(A) condition; rather, it is an abnormal response to stress factors such as
(B) condition, it is a rather abnormal response to stress factors such as
(C) condition; but it is an abnormal response to stress factors such as
(D) condition rather, it is an abnormal response to stress factors like
(E) condition, rather it is a way of responding abnormally to such stress factors as

17. A cynic is when someone has a tendency to disbelieve that any actions can have wholly unselfish motivations.

(A) A cynic is when someone has a tendency to disbelieve that any actions can have wholly unselfish motivations.
(B) Someone who has a tendency to disbelieve that any actions can have wholly unselfish motivations, and he is a cynic.
(C) A cynic is when someone tends not to believe that any actions might have had wholly unselfish motivations.
(D) A cynic is someone which has a tendency to disbelieve that any actions can be wholly unselfishly motivated.
(E) A cynic is someone who tends to disbelieve that any actions can have wholly unselfish motivations.

18. When NASA has been informed of the dangerous weather conditions, the head of the space agency decided to postpone the shuttle launch.

(A) When NASA has been informed of the dangerous weather conditions
(B) Because NASA having been informed of the dangerous weather conditions
(C) Although NASA was informed with the dangerous weather conditions
(D) When NASA was informed of the dangerous weather conditions
(E) When NASA has been informed with the dangerous weather conditions

19. Henry James wrote the play *Guy Domville* primarily because he hoped revitalizing of his waning literary career.

(A) he hoped revitalizing of his waning literary career
(B) he hoped revitalizing of his literary career that was waning
(C) his hoping was the revitalizing of his waning literary career
(D) he hoped to revitalize his waning literary career
(E) he hoped revitalizing of his literary career that had waned

20. While strolling in Golden Gate Park one day, seeing the carousel with its elegantly carved horses delighted the young couple.

(A) seeing the carousel with its elegantly carved horses delighted the young couple
(B) the sight of the carousel with its elegantly carved horses delighted the young couple
(C) the young couple was delighted by the sight of the carousel with its elegantly carved horses
(D) the carousel delighted the young couple with its elegantly carved horses when they saw it
(E) to have seen the carousel's elegantly carved horses delighted the young couple

GO ON TO NEXT PAGE ▶

The sentences in this section may contain errors in grammar, usage, choice of words, or idioms. There is either just one error per sentence, or the sentence is correct. Some words or phrases are underlined and lettered; everything else in the sentence is correct.

If an underlined word or phrase is incorrect, choose that letter; if the sentence is correct, select No error. Then blacken the appropriate space on your answer sheet.

EXAMPLE:

The region has a climate so severe that (A) plants growing there (B) rarely had been (C) more than twelve inches high (D). No error (E)

Ⓐ Ⓑ ● Ⓓ Ⓔ

21. Being that (A) my car is getting its (B) annual tune-up, I will not be (C) able to pick you up (D) tomorrow morning. No error (E)

22. The average taxpayer can't hardly (A) believe that income tax fraud is so widespread as (B) to justify (C) the precautions that the authorities have taken (D). No error (E)

23. No one but (A) he (B) knew what (C) questions were going (D) to be asked on this test. No error (E)

24. You are being quite (A) cynical when you say that the reason (B) we have such a large (C) turnout is because (D) we are serving refreshments. No error (E)

25. Although (A) I am playing (B) golf for more than (C) three years, I cannot manage to break (D) 90. No error (E)

26. Studies have found (A) that a mild salt solution is more affective (B) than (C) the commercial preparations available in drug stores in the treatment of (D) this ailment. No error (E)

27. If (A) I have to make a choice between (B) John, Henry and her (C), I think I'll select Henry because of his self-control during (D) moments of stress. No error (E)

28. In order to (A) raise public consciousness concerning environmental problems, you (B) should distribute leaflets, write to your representative (C) in Congress, as well as signing (D) the necessary petitions. No error (E)

GO ON TO NEXT PAGE ►

29. Members of a scientific expedition discovered the
Titanic, which sank after it struck an iceberg,
A B
furthermore it was not possible for them to
C
raise it. No error
D E

30. Scientists show that change, whether good or bad,
A B
leads to stress and that the accumulation from
C D
stress-related changes can cause major illness.
No error
E

31. We have spent all together too much money on
A B
this project; we have exceeded our budget and
C
can expect no additional funds until the beginning
D
of the new year. No error
E

32. Between thirty and forty students seem willing to
A B
volunteer; the rest are not planning to participate
C D
in the program. No error
E

33. The horse that won the trophies differed with the
A B
other horses in overall appearance as well as
C D
ability. No error
E

34. The business executive, planning to attend the
A
conference in New Orleans, could not decide
B
whether to travel on or remaining at the hotel was
C
the better choice. No error
D E

GO ON TO NEXT PAGE ►

Improving Paragraphs Directions

The passage below is the unedited draft of a student's essay. Some of the essay needs to be rewritten to make the meaning clearer and more precise. Read the essay carefully.

The essay is followed by questions about changes that might improve all or part of its organization, development, sentence structure, use of language, appropriateness to the audience, or use of standard written English. Choose the answer that most clearly and effectively expresses the student's intended meaning. Indicate your choice by filling in the corresponding space on the answer sheet.

[1] In the twentieth century, women have held a major part in influencing social change and social status. **[2]** In such developing countries as Saudi Arabia, restrictions on women are gradually being lifted, and they have gained the right to be in public without your head covered.

[3] In the area of social status, women have fought for better treatment and more respect. **[4]** An example of this is the fight for women in the workplace. **[5]** Not long ago most women stayed at home and took care of their families, while their husbands worked at white collar and blue collar jobs. **[6]** But now many women work as doctors, lawyers, and other established positions. **[7]** Women are finally out in the work force competing with men for the same jobs.

[8] In the area of politics and government, many women have attained high positions. **[9]** Hillary Rodham Clinton became a role model for many young women in this country. **[10]** Two women are now members of the U.S. Supreme Court. **[11]** Several women also are governors, senators and representatives. **[12]** There will never again be an all-male cabinet. **[13]** Ever since women's suffrage, women have won the rights reserved for men. **[14]** The result was that women now have a voice in the actions of our country.

[15] In the areas of health, medicine, sciences, and the military, women have also come into their own. **[16]** Although the world still has a long way to go before women achieve total equality with men, the twentieth century may long be remembered as the time when the first steps were taken.

35. Considering the essay as a whole, which revision of sentence 1 would serve best as the essay's opening sentence?

(A) The social status of women has undergone a major change during the twentieth century.
(B) Twentieth century women will have a major influence in changing their social status.
(C) As a major influence in the twentieth century, women have had their social status changed.
(D) Under the influence of twentieth century women, their status has changed.
(E) Being influenced by social change in the twentieth century, the status of women has changed.

36. Which is the most effective revision of the underlined segment of sentence 2 below?

In such developing countries as Saudi Arabia, restrictions on women are gradually being lifted, and they have gained the right to be in public without your head covered.

(A) for example, women are gaining rights like the one to be in public bareheaded
(B) which means that they have gained the right to be in public with their heads uncovered
(C) and they have the right, for example, for you to go bareheaded in public
(D) and women now have gained the right to be bareheaded in public
(E) to the extent that women can exercise the right of going into public with their head uncovered

GO ON TO NEXT PAGE ►

37. Which revision of sentence 8 provides the best transition between the second and the third paragraphs?

(A) The competition has extended into politics and government, where many women have replaced men in high positions.
(B) Irregardless, in the field of politics and government many women have attained high positions.
(C) High positions in government and politics have been attained by women.
(D) Among the jobs that women have attained are in politics and government.
(E) The world of politics and government has changed because women have attained high positions.

38. Sentence 8 is the topic sentence of the third paragraph. Which of the following is the best revision of sentence 9?

(A) The wife of the president, Hillary Rodham Clinton, made herself a role model for many young American women.
(B) In the 1992 national election, Hillary Rodham Clinton helped her husband win the presidency of the United States.
(C) After seven years as prime minister of England, Margaret Thatcher was finally defeated by a male, John Major.
(D) While she was the leader of India, Indira Ghandi was assassinated.
(E) In recent years both Margaret Thatcher of England and Indira Ghandi of India, for example, served as leaders of their countries.

39. Which sentence in the third paragraph should be revised or deleted because it contributes least to the development of the main idea of the paragraph?

(A) Sentence 10 (B) Sentence 11
(C) Sentence 12 (D) Sentence 13
(E) Sentence 14

IF YOU FINISH IN LESS THAN 30 MINUTES, YOU MAY CHECK YOUR WORK ON THIS SECTION ONLY. DO NOT TURN TO ANY OTHER SECTION IN THE TEST.

STOP

Answer Key

Section 1 Critical Reading

1. **C**	6. **D**	11. **E**	16. **D**	21. **E**
2. **D**	7. **C**	12. **C**	17. **A**	22. **E**
3. **B**	8. **B**	13. **D**	18. **B**	23. **D**
4. **E**	9. **D**	14. **E**	19. **D**	24. **D**
5. **A**	10. **D**	15. **B**	20. **C**	

Section 2 Mathematics

1. **D**	5. **D**	9. **D**	13. **B**	17. **C**
2. **C**	6. **D**	10. **A**	14. **E**	18. **A**
3. **D**	7. **B**	11. **D**	15. **D**	19. **D**
4. **E**	8. **E**	12. **D**	16. **C**	20. **A**

Section 3 Critical Reading

25. **B**	30. **C**	35. **D**	40. **B**	45. **A**
26. **D**	31. **D**	36. **A**	41. **D**	46. **A**
27. **A**	32. **C**	37. **E**	42. **B**	47. **E**
28. **E**	33. **D**	38. **D**	43. **D**	48. **D**
29. **A**	34. **E**	39. **B**	44. **B**	

Section 4 Mathematics

21. **D**	23. **C**	25. **B**	27. **A**
22. **E**	24. **C**	26. **D**	28. **B**

29.
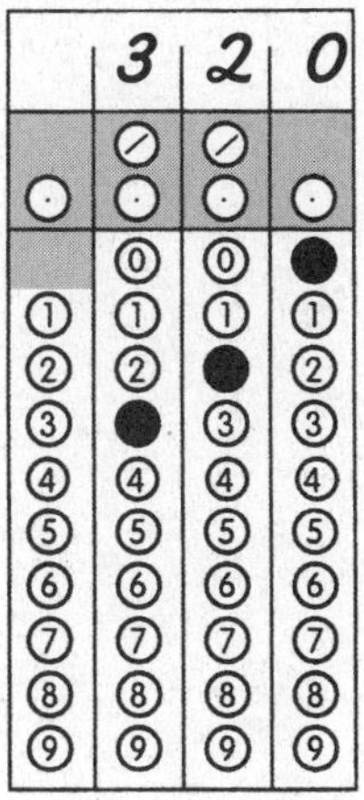

30.
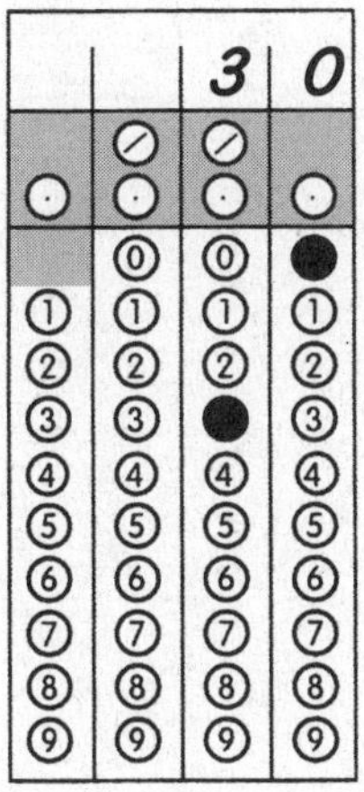

31.
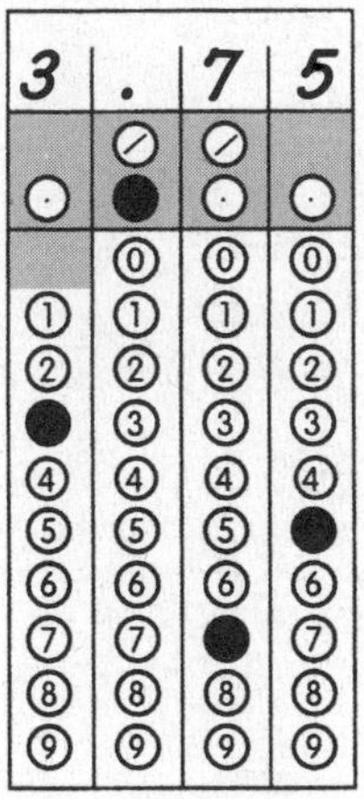

or 1 5 / 4

32.
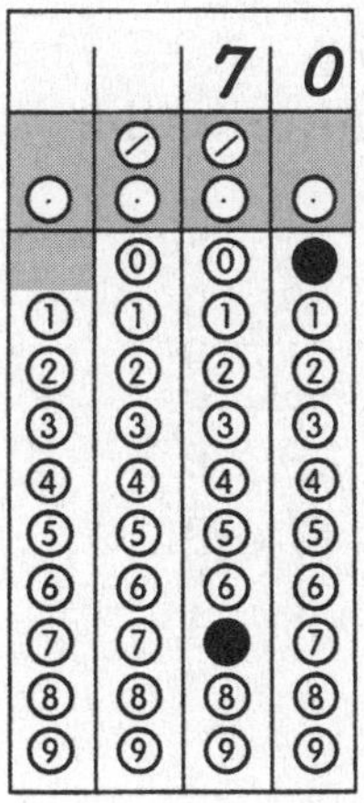

33.
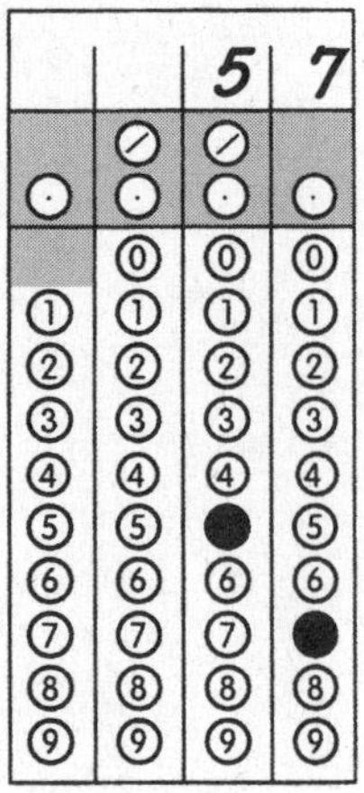

34.
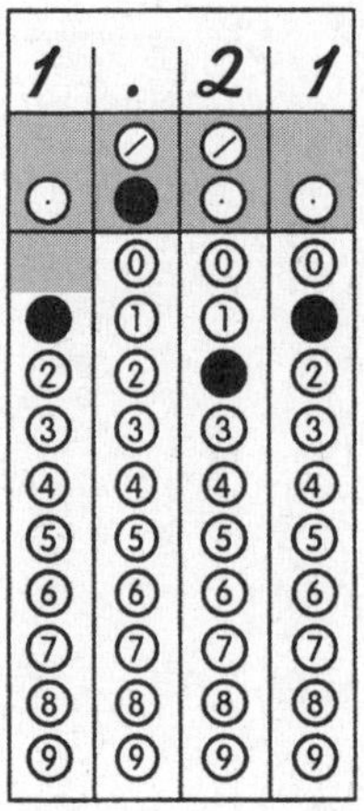

35.
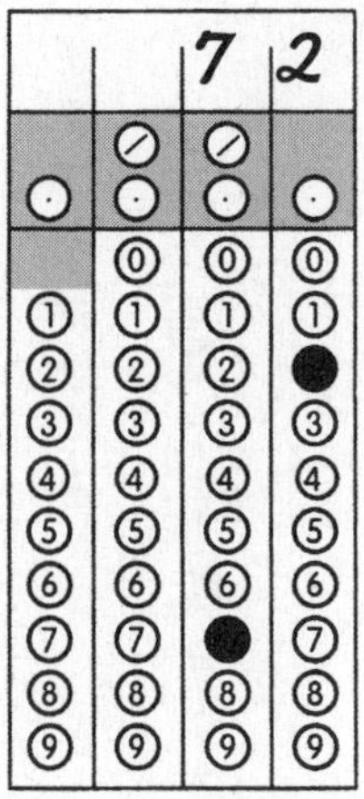

36.
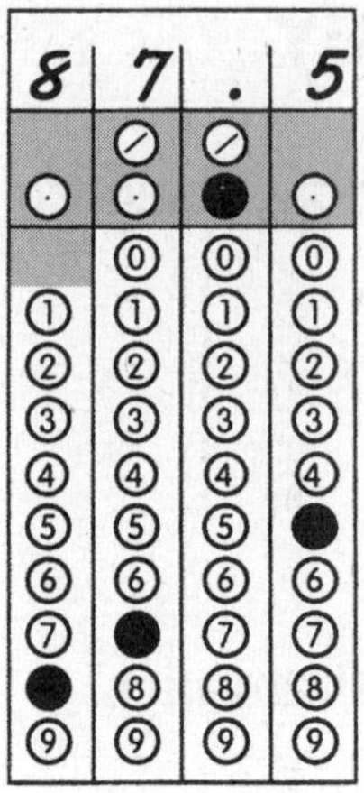

37.
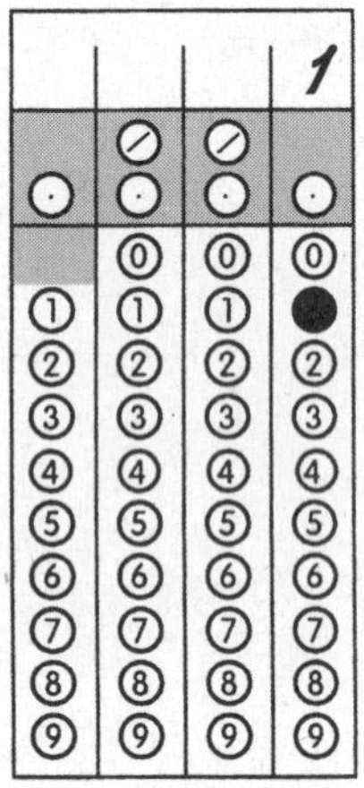

38.
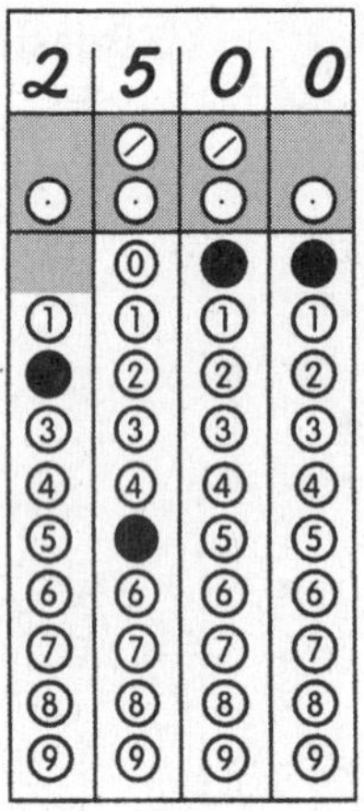

Section 5 Writing Skills

1. **C**
2. **D**
3. **B**
4. **C**
5. **D**
6. **B**
7. **D**
8. **A**
9. **E**
10. **B**
11. **B**
12. **E**
13. **D**
14. **A**
15. **D**
16. **A**
17. **E**
18. **D**
19. **D**
20. **C**
21. **A**
22. **A**
23. **B**
24. **D**
25. **B**
26. **B**
27. **B**
28. **D**
29. **C**
30. **D**
31. **A**
32. **E**
33. **B**
34. **C**
35. **A**
36. **D**
37. **A**
38. **E**
39. **E**

Scoring Chart—Practice Test 1

Critical Reading Sections

Section 1: 24 Questions (1–24)

Number correct ________ (A)
Number omitted ________ (B)
Number incorrect ________ (C)
$\frac{1}{4}$ (C) ________ (D)
(A) − (D) ________ Raw Score I

Section 3: 24 Questions (25–48)

Number correct ________ (A)
Number omitted ________ (B)
Number incorrect ________ (C)
$\frac{1}{4}$ (C) ________ (D)
(A) − (D) ________ Raw Score II

Total Critical Reading Raw Score

Raw Scores I + II ________

Mathematics Sections

Section 2: 20 Questions (1–20)

Number correct ________ (A)
Number omitted ________ (B)
Number incorrect ________ (C)
$\frac{1}{4}$ (C) ________ (D)
(A) − (D) ________ Raw Score I

Section 4: First 8 Questions (21–28)

Number correct ________ (A)
Number omitted ________ (B)
Number incorrect ________ (C)
$\frac{1}{4}$ (C) ________ (D)
(A) − (D) ________ Raw Score II

Section 4: Next 10 Questions (29–38)

Number correct ________ Raw Score III

Total Mathematics Raw Score

Raw Scores I + II + III ________

NOTE: In each section (A) + (B) + (C) should equal the number of questions in that section.

Writing Skills Section

Section 5: 39 Questions (1–39)

Number correct ________ (A)
Number omitted ________ (B)
Number incorrect ________ (C)
$\frac{1}{4}$ (C) ________ (D)

Writing Skills Raw Score

(A) − (D) ________

Evaluation Chart

Study your score. Your raw score is an indication of your probable achievement on the PSAT/NMSQT. As a guide to the amount of work you need or want to do with this book, study the following.

Raw Score			**Self-Rating**
Critical Reading	*Mathematics*	*Writing Skills*	
42–48	35–38	33–39	Superior
37–41	30–34	28–32	Very good
32–36	25–29	23–27	Good
26–31	21–24	17–22	Above average
20–25	17–20	12–16	Average
12–19	10–16	7–11	Below average
less than 12	less than 10	less than 7	Inadequate

ANSWER EXPLANATIONS

Section 1 Critical Reading

1. **(C)** The use of "unhappily" tells us that the experiment was somehow damaged or *marred* by the presence of observers. It makes no sense for the psychology experiment to have been *muted* (hushed), *palliated* (mitigated; alleviated), or *clarified* (made clear) by the subjects becoming aware of the presence of observers around them. Likewise, while the subjects' awareness of the presence of observers in their midst might have caused the experiment to be hastily *concluded* (ended), that is not the best possible answer choice.

2. **(D)** James didn't know when assignments were due because there was something wrong with the way he wrote them down. He was not orderly or *methodical* about it. Basically, James was careless about writing down his assignments. That is the reason he seldom knew when they were due. It would not have helped him to be more *obdurate* (stubborn and unyielding), more *contrary* (stubbornly willful or opposed), or more *literate* (well read). To be *opportunistic* is to base one's actions on effectiveness or expediency rather than on ethical principles. The word makes no sense in the context.

3. **(B)** The word "despite" signals a contrast. Despite the advertised *praises*, she had doubts—she remained *a skeptic* about the product. Note also that "singing the praises of" is a cliché, a customary phrase. Choice A is incorrect. It makes no sense to say that *despite* ads expressing admiration for a product's *virtues* (good qualities) the woman still was *optimistic* or hopeful about its merits. Choice C is incorrect. It makes no sense to say that *despite* ads expressing admiration for a product's *joys* the woman still was *converted to* a belief in its merits. Choice D is incorrect. *Defects* are flaws. Note that the first missing word must be positive in nature. No advertisers would sing (express admiration for) the bad points of a product they were trying to sell. Choice E is incorrect. It makes no sense to say that *despite* ads expressing admiration for a product's *advantages* (favorable qualities) the woman still was *a believer in* its merits.

4. **(E)** Again, think of your own answer before looking at the choices. What would you need after two full months of solid work? A rest, or *respite*. It makes no sense for Sandy to feel that she had earned a *penalty* (punishment), *scolding* (rebuke), *degree* (academic award), or *chore* (unpleasant task). She felt she had earned a rest.

5. **(A)** The phrase "even though" tells us that there will be a contrast. This requires a word that is opposite in meaning to "does not change." *Plastic* can mean adaptable or pliable when used as an adjective, as it is here. Choice B is incorrect. *Immutable* means unchangeable. For some time after birth, the details of the brain's structure and function *are* able to change or adapt. Choice C is incorrect. *Essential* (absolutely necessary) makes no sense in the context. Choice D is incorrect. *Unknown* (not discovered or identified; obscure) makes no sense in the context. Choice E is incorrect. *Static* means showing little or no change. For some time after birth, the details of the brain's structure and function *do* change or adapt.

6. **(D)** The author's presentation of factual information about tarantulas is scientifically *objective* (impartial).

7. **(C)** To excite a defensive response is to *stimulate* or arouse that reaction.

8. **(B)** Passage 1 describes what you would see if you subjected a tarantula to various forms of stimuli (pressing a pencil against its body-wall, holding a pencil above it, etc.). In other words, it *provides scientific observations of the subject* (the tarantula). Passage 2, in contrast, offers highly general, chatty information about tarantulas, providing *a popular introduction to the subject.*

9. **(D)** You can answer this question by using the process of elimination.
   Do both passages indicate that tarantulas have a marked degree of intelligence? Nothing in either passage suggests this. You can eliminate Choice A.

Note the following icons, used throughout this book:

Time saver	Look it up; math reference fact	Helpful Hint
Educated guess	Prefixes, roots, and suffixes	Caution!
Did you notice?	Positive or negative?	Calculator use is recommended

Do both passages indicate that the tarantulas' gentleness belies (contradicts) their frightening looks? No. Although Passage 2 states that tarantulas are gentler creatures than their appearance suggests, Passage 1 says nothing about their being gentle. You can eliminate Choice B.

Do both passages indicate that tarantulas have been maligned (slandered; bad-mouthed) by arachnophobes? No. Passage 1 says nothing at all about arachnophobes. You can eliminate Choice C.

Do both passages indicate that tarantulas are capable of acting to defend themselves? Yes. Passage 1 portrays a tarantula's defensive reaction to a perceived threat: the spider immediately goes into its attack stance. Passage 2 indicates that tarantulas will bite if they are severely provoked; thus, they *are capable of acting to defend themselves*. The correct answer is most likely Choice D.

Confirm your answer choice by checking Choice E. Do both passages indicate that tarantulas are easily intimidated (frightened) by others? No. Nothing in either passage indicates this. You can eliminate Choice E.

Only Choice D is left. It is the correct answer.

10. **(D)** Blown about by the storm, the *branches* of the fir trees move from side to side: "the old firs . . . wave excitedly with their arms."

11. **(E)** The author states that the jackdaw's proficiency is not inherited or innate, but "an individually acquired accomplishment." In other words, it has been *gained through practice*.

12. **(C)** The author is stressing that you can *be* sure or *confident* of the truth of what he says.

13. **(D)** The "sightless monster" is the "stupid wind" that tries to dive the jackdaws toward the east. Note how the author personifies the wind, writing as if the wind had some degree of human intelligence and responsiveness.

14. **(E)** The concluding sentence of the passage celebrates the birds' "Sovereign control over the power of the elements," in other words, their *mastery of the forces of nature*. Though Choice B may seem tempting, you can rule it out: Lorenz emphasizes the storm's strength ("the pitiless strength of the inorganic"), not the strength of the birds. Choices A, C, and D are unsupported by the passage.

15. **(B)** The author uses several metaphors ("close-reefed sails," "the teeth of the gale," etc.) and clarifies what he means by the term *game*. He describes the jackdaws' behavior in detail and dismisses the notion that their behavior is purely instinctive. However, he never *argues a cause*.

16. **(D)** Tapestry weaving is time-consuming, taking "as much as a year to produce a yard." In addition, it is faithful to the original ("The weaver always follows a preexisting model."). It is not, however, spontaneous in concept.

17. **(A)** The author mentions tapestry's distinctive or *characteristic* weave as something that distinguishes tapestry-woven materials from other fabrics (prints, brocades, etc.).

18. **(B)** By using tapestries "to display his wealth and social position," the nobleman is using them to demonstrate his *consequence* or importance.

19. **(D)** The "ground" upon which embroidery is laid is the cloth *base* upon which the embroiderer stitches a design.

20. **(C)** The author refers to the suggestion that tapestries served primarily as a source of warmth only to *dismiss* or reject the idea. To prove his point he asserts that comfort had little importance in medieval times.

21. **(E)** Here the word "chambers" *is being used in a special sense* to mean a set of wall hangings made to fit a specific room.

22. **(E)** In describing Morris as someone who attempted to bring back tapestry making to its true, medieval principles, the author depicts him as a *traditionalist*, someone who attempts to preserve or restore ancient cultural practices or beliefs.

23. **(D)** In comparison to the tightly-woven tapestries of the nineteenth-century, present-day wall hangings are described as "coarsely woven cloths." Thus, they *have a less fine weave* than their predecessors.

24. **(D)** Although the passage explains the process of tapestry making and mentions that large wall hangings are Western rather than Eastern in origin, Choices A and B do not reflect the passage's primary purpose. This purpose is to *provide a historical perspective on tapestry making*.

Section 2 Mathematics

For many problems, the explanation provides a reference to one or more **KEY FACTS** from Chapter 7. These are the mathematical facts that you need to solve that problem. If a solution refers to **KEY FACT J2**, for example, the solution depends on the second **KEY FACT** discussed in Section J of Chapter 7.

For some problems, an alternative solution, indicated by two asterisks (**), follows the first solution. When this occurs, usually one of the solutions is the direct mathematical one and the other is based on one of the tactics discussed in Chapters 6 and 7.

See page 234 for an explanation of the symbol $\Rightarrow$, which is used in several answer explanations.

1. **(D)** Since $x + y + 30 = 180$ and $y = 2x$, we get
$$x + 2x + 30 = 180 \Rightarrow 3x = 150 \Rightarrow$$
$$x = 50 \Rightarrow y = 2x = 100.$$

2. **(C)** The left-hand side of $(a + 12) - 12 = 12$ is just a. So, $a = 12$.
Of course, you can use **TACTIC 6-1: backsolve, starting (and ending) with C.

3. **(D)** Let each side of the small squares be 1. Then each square has area 1, and the area of rectangle *AEFJ* is 4. The shaded area consists of $\triangle AJI$ and $\triangle EFI$. The white region is $\triangle AEI$, whose area is $\frac{1}{2}(4)(1) = 2$. The area of the shaded region is $4 - 2 = 2$, and so the ratio of the areas is $2:2 = 1:1$.
**Just look at the diagram. Exactly half of square *ABIJ* and exactly half of rectangle *BEFI* are shaded. The areas of the shaded and white regions are equal.

4. **(E)** Since 72% + 19% = 91%, the \$243 spent on the party represents the other 9% of the money raised. Then $.09m = 243 \Rightarrow m = 243 \div .09 = 2700$.

5. **(D)** Every hour the hour hand moves through 30° ($\frac{1}{12}$ of 360°). So it will move through 20° in $\frac{2}{3}$ of an hour or 40 minutes; 40 minutes after 1:30 is 2:10.

6. **(D)** Since *ABC* is an equilateral triangle, $x = 60$. So, $60 + 40 + y = 180 \Rightarrow y = 80$. Then by **KEY FACT I6** (when parallel lines are cut by a transversal, the four acute angles have the same measure), $y = a$. So, $a = 80$.

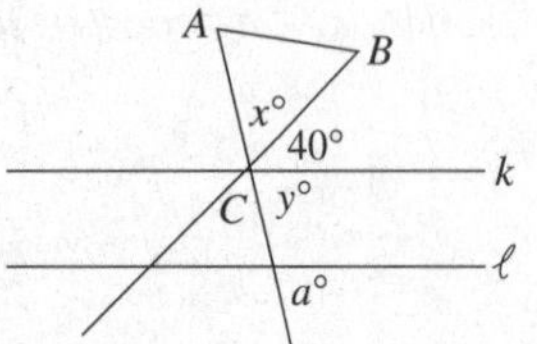

Use **TACTIC 6-6 (trust the diagram)—*a* appears to be slightly less than a 90° angle.

7. **(B)** Let x and y be the two numbers:
$x < y < x + y \Rightarrow -y < y \Rightarrow 0 < 2y \Rightarrow y$ is positive. Therefore, at least one of the numbersis positive. (Note that there are no restrictions on x.)

8. **(E)** Solve the equation $20 = \frac{x}{100}C$:
$$2000 = xC \Rightarrow x = \frac{2000}{C}\%.$$
Use **TACTIC 6-3: substitute an easy-to-use number: 20 is 100% of 20. Which of the choices is equal to 100% when $C = 20$? Only $\frac{2000}{C}\%$.

9. **(D)** Whenever we know two of the three sides of a right triangle, we can find the third side by using the Pythagorean theorem. First, assume that the two given sides are both legs, and let x represent the hypotenuse. Then
$$x^2 = 5^2 + 9^2 = 25 + 81 = 106 \Rightarrow x = \sqrt{106}$$
and III is true. Now assume that one side is a leg and that the longer side is the hypotenuse; let y represent the other leg. Then
$$5^2 + y^2 = 9^2 \Rightarrow 25 + y^2 = 81 \Rightarrow$$
$$y^2 = 56 \Rightarrow y = \sqrt{56}$$
and I is true. Therefore, I and III only are true.

10. **(A)** By **KEY FACT N7**, the slope of the line $y = 2x - 3$ is 2. By **KEY FACT N6**, parallel lines have equal slopes. Only Choice A, $y = 2x + 3$, also has a slope equal to 2.

11. **(D)** Just check each choice. Is there a triangle whose sides are 1, 2, 3? No, the sum of any two sides of a triangle must be *greater* than the third side (**KEY FACT J12**). (I is false.) Are there triangles whose sides are 3, 4, 5 and 13, 14, 15. Yes. (II and III are true.) Statements II and III only are true.

12. **(D)** By **KEY FACT C5**, the percent increase in the bank's charge is $\frac{\text{the actual increase}}{\text{the original amount}} \times 100\%$. The charge was originally \$10 and the actual increase was \$10. So, the percent increase is
$$\frac{10}{10} \times 100 = 100\%.$$

13. **(B)** Since the sum of the three measures is 180°:
$$180 = x + 2x + 3y = 3x + 3y = 3(x + y)$$
So, $x + y = 60$ and $y = 60 - x$.
Use **TACTIC 6-3: pick an easy-to-use value for x. Note that in the diagram x appears to be about 50, but you can pick any value: say 10. Then
$$10 + 20 + 3y = 180 \Rightarrow 3y = 150 \Rightarrow y = 50.$$
Which of the choices equals 10 when y is 50? Only $60 - x$.

14. **(E)** $\|6^2\| = \frac{2}{3}(6^2)^2 = \frac{2}{3}(36)^2 = \frac{2}{3}(1296) = 864$.

15. **(D)** $\|y\| = \|\frac{2}{3}x\| = \frac{2}{3}\left(\frac{2}{3}x\right)^2 = \frac{2}{3}\left(\frac{4}{9}x^2\right) = \frac{8}{27}x^2$.

    Use **TACTIC 6-2: replace the variables with numbers. Let $x = 3$. Then $y = \frac{2}{3}(3) = 2$, and $\|2\| = \frac{2}{3}(2)^2 = \frac{2}{3}(4) = \frac{8}{3}$. Which of the choices is equal to $\frac{8}{3}$ when $x = 3$? Only $\frac{8}{27}x^2$.

16. **(C)** $f\left(\frac{1}{2}\right) = 9\left(\frac{1}{2}\right) + 9^{\frac{1}{2}} = 4.5 + \sqrt{9} = 4.5 + 3 = 7.5$.

17. **(C)** Jill walked 4 kilometers and Jack walked 6 kilometers; so Jill walked $\frac{4}{6} = \frac{2}{3}$ the distance that Jack walked. Since their rates were the same, she did it in $\frac{2}{3}$ the time: $\frac{2}{3}$ of 2 hours is $\frac{4}{3}$ of an hour, or 1 hour and 20 minutes. She left at 10:40.
    **Jack walked 6 kilometers in exactly 2 hours; so, he was walking at a rate of 3 kilometers per hour. Jill walked 4 kilometers, also at 3 kilometers per hour; so her walking time was $4 \div 3$ or $1\frac{1}{3}$ hours ($t = d \div r$: See Section 7-H). Therefore, Jill left $1\frac{1}{3}$ hours, or 1 hour and 20 minutes, before noon—at 10:40.

18. **(A)** Even if you can do the algebra, this type of problem is easier by using **TACTIC 6-3**: choose easy-to-use numbers. Assume that there are 100 females and 50 males in the club and that 20% of the females and 10% of the males attended the meeting. Then, 20 females and 5 males were there, and 5 is 20% of 25, the total number attending.

19. **(D)** $(a + b)^2 = a^2 + 2ab + b^2 = (a^2 + b^2) + 2ab$. By the Pythagorean theorem, $a^2 + b^2 = 10^2 = 100$; and since the area is 20, $\frac{1}{2}ab = 20 \Rightarrow ab = 40$, and $2ab = 80$. Then

    $$(a^2 + b^2) + 2ab = 100 + 80 = 180.$$

20. **(A)** Originally the fund of d dollars was to be divided among 4 winners, in which case each of them would have received $\frac{d}{4}$ dollars. Instead, the fund was divided among 6 winners, and each received $\frac{d}{6}$ dollars. This represents a loss to each of the original winners of $\frac{d}{4} - \frac{d}{6} = \frac{3d}{12} - \frac{2d}{12} = \frac{d}{12}$ dollars.

    **Unless you are comfortable with the algebra, plug in a number for d; say $d = 24$. Then the 4 winners would have received $24 \div 4 = 6$ dollars each. Now the 6 winners will receive $24 \div 6 = 4$ dollars each, a difference of \$2. Which of the choices is equal to 2 when $d = 24$? Only $\frac{d}{12}$.

Section 3 Critical Reading

25. **(B)** Remember to think of your own answer before looking at the choices. North clearly had a strong belief; no one's words could convince him otherwise. This would guide you to choose *conviction*, one meaning of which is belief.

    Choice A is incorrect. *Demand* means requirement or forceful request. It is not the *best* word in the context of the sentence. Choice C is incorrect. A *maxim* is a proverbial saying or rule of conduct. It is not the *best* word in the context of the sentence. Choice D is incorrect. *Fear* makes no sense in the context of the sentence.

    Choice E is incorrect. *Ambivalence* means uncertainty or conflict of ideas. It makes no sense in the context of the sentence.

26. **(D)** If we are likely to be in need of a new source of energy, we must be about to run out of the old source of fuel. This would happen if we *deplete* or exhaust our supply. The phrase "excessive use" is also a clue that we may be running out, through using too much. Excessive use of fossil fuels clearly would not *replenish* (refill; restock) or *magnify* (enlarge) the supply of coal and oil. Likewise, it would not *merge* (combine) or *redirect* (reroute; send elsewhere) the supply of fossil fuels.

27. **(A)** The word "however" signals a contrast. The sentence says the authorities reject the use of "disinterested." Therefore, *in contrast*, they accept or *condone* the use of "healthy." You are looking for a word that is opposite in meaning to *reject*. None of the remaining choices—*evaluate* (assess), *imitate* (copy), *disdain* (look down on; scorn), *repudiate* (disown; deny)—have that meaning.

28. **(E)** The flu weakened or *debilitated* Michael, leaving him too tired to return to work. *Recuperated* (regained health), *diagnosed* (identified an illness), *incarcerated* (imprisoned; confined), and *captivated* (enchanted; enthralled) all make no sense in this context.

29. **(A)** The word "though" also signals a contrast. Although Alec Guinness had his mind set on becoming an actor, his determination or *resolution* wavered. Note that *resolution* is not just a statement of intent; it can mean firmness of intent as well. It was Guinness's determination to become an actor that momentarily wavered, not his *reverence* (awed respect; veneration), *affectation* (artificiality of manner), *theatricality* (staginess), or *skepticism* (unbelief; doubting attitude).

30. **(C)** The key word here is "ridiculing," meaning making fun of or mocking. In writing *Gulliver's Travels*, Swift means to mock or make fun of his society: his intent is *satirical* (sarcastic and cutting). It is not *elegiac* (expressing sorrow), *prophetic* (visionary; oracular), or *derivative* (imitative; unoriginal). It certainly is not *questionable* (dubious or disputable).

31. **(D)** Someone who risks his or her life frequently is a *daredevil*. Since the threat of death does not keep Markham from such activities, the first missing word must be *daunt*, meaning to frighten or lessen one's courage.

    Choice A is incorrect. Remember, *both* words of your answer choice must fit the meaning of the sentence as a whole. *Intimidate* means frighten or threaten. It is a good choice for the first blank. However, a *patrician* is an aristocrat, a person of high rank. Such persons are not by definition people who customarily risk their lives. Choice B is incorrect. Neither *divert* (redirect; distract) nor *renegade* (turncoat; traitor) complete the sentence properly. Choice C is incorrect. A *dilettante* is a dabbler or casual participant in an activity. In risking her life countless times to set records, clearly Markham was no dabbler at flying small planes. Choice E is incorrect. A *firebrand* is an agitator or troublemaker. Markham was a risk taker, not a troublemaker.

32. **(C)** "Unscrupulous merchandisers" make false claims. *Debunking* means exposing falseness in something. Nader, who is an advocate or protector of the consumer, teaches people to be suspicious and to exercise *skepticism*. Note that "exercising skepticism" is a cliché, a very commonly used phrase.

    Choice A is incorrect. A consumer advocate would not be engaged in *asserting* (insisting on; affirming) the claims of dishonest merchandisers. Choice B is incorrect. While a consumer advocate might become involved in *deflating* (belittling; puncturing) the claims of dishonest merchandisers, there's no way he or she would have warned the public to exercise a healthy *prodigality* (wastefulness). Choice D is incorrect. A consumer advocate would not be engaged in *affirming* (supporting; confirming) the claims of dishonest merchandisers. Choice E is incorrect. A consumer advocate would not be engaged in *exaggerating* (overstating) the claims of dishonest merchandisers, nor would he or she warn the public to exercise a healthy *optimism* (hopefulness).

33. **(D)** The author's attitude is clearly *approving*: she notes that some commentators cite Malcolm's change in prison as an example of positive transformation; she also uses words with positive connotations ("purposeful") to describe Malcolm's method of tackling his task.

34. **(E)** In plowing his way through the dictionary, Malcolm *proceeded steadily* and purposefully from the beginning to the end.

35. **(D)** Lines 8–9 of the passage say that in primate troops, males "defend, control and lead the troop." Therefore, the troops are *dominated by adult males*.

36. **(A)** The passage says that the ranking hierarchy lessens conflict within the troop. Therefore, it is meant to *protect the members of the troop* from internal strife.

37. **(E)** In candidly exposing her grandmother's flaws, the author exhibits a *sardonic* or scornful and sarcastic attitude.

38. **(D)** McCarthy sees as little point in speculating about her grandmother's childhood as she does in wondering about the toilet training of a fictional character like Lady Macbeth. Such speculations are, to McCarthy's mind, idle or *useless*.

39. **(B)** The author states (somewhat ironically) that modern fictional characters must have "clinical authenticity." In other words, they must appear to be genuine or *valid* in *psychological* terms.

40. **(B)** Although the grandmother's outward appearance was soft and motherly, her essential nature was hard as nails. Clearly, you cannot judge a book (person) by its cover (outward appearance).

41. **(D)** McCarthy is building up a portrait of her grandmother as a pugnacious, autocratic person. She describes the fear old ladies have for their belongings as a very human (and understandable) reaction: aware of their own increasing fragility (and eventual death), old ladies identify with their fragile possessions and are protective of them. McCarthy's grandmother was also protective of her belongings, but she was not the typical "gentle and tremulous" elderly woman. She was a petty tyrant and had decidedly *different reasons for her actions*.

42. **(B)** Because her grandmother was more interested in maintaining her power than in being hospitable, the social properties or *aspects* of the family home had withered and decayed till no real sociability existed.

43. **(D)** Heilbrun's central criticism is that her grandmother "impaired her six daughters for autonomy" or independence. In other words, *she discouraged her daughters' independence*.

44. **(B)** Heilbrun realizes that people nowadays may have difficulty understanding what motivated her grandmother to control her daughters' lives and restrict their autonomy so thoroughly. By describing how great the horror of pregnancy in an unmarried girl was, she helps the reader understand *why her grandmother* acted as she did.

45. **(A)** By dwelling on how hard she had worked to support her daughters and how much she would be hurt if they failed to pay her back by making good marriages, Heilbrun's grandmother exploited their *sense of guilt*.

46. **(A)** The common factor in both grandmothers' lives is their need to govern the *actions of others*. McCarthy's grandmother tyrannized everyone from the mailman to her daughters and daughters-in-law; Heilbrun's grandmother "ruled the household with an arm of iron," governing her daughters' lives.

47. **(E)** McCarthy refers casually to Iago and Lady Macbeth, key figures in Shakespeare's tragedies. Heilbrun makes no such *literary references*.

48. **(D)** While Heilbrun's grandmother was a "sustaining woman" who provided for her family, McCarthy's grandmother was a grudging woman, not a sustaining one. Thus, McCarthy would most likely point out that *her grandmother's actual conduct is not in keeping with this characterization*.

Section 4 Mathematics

For many problems, the explanation provides a reference to one or more **KEY FACTS** from Chapter 7. These are the mathematical facts that you need to solve that problem. If a solution refers to **KEY FACT J2**, for example, the solution depends on the second **KEY FACT** discussed in Section J of Chapter 7.

For some problems, an alternative solution, indicated by two asterisks (**), follows the first solution. When this occurs, usually one of the solutions is the direct mathematical one and the other is based on one of the tactics discussed in Chapters 6 and 7.

See page 234 for an explanation of the symbol $\Rightarrow$, which is used in several answer explanations.

21. **(D)** Since the ratio of the number of boys to girls is 2:3, the number of boys is $2x$, the number of girls is $3x$, and the total number of members is $2x + 3x = 5x$. So the girls make up $\frac{3x}{5x} = \frac{3}{5} = 60\%$ of the members.

22. **(E)** Since d divisions each have t teams, multiply to get dt teams, and since each team has p players, multiply the number of teams (dt) by p to get the total number of players: dtp.

Use **TACTIC 6-2. Choose easy-to-use numbers for t, d, and p. For example, assume that there are 2 divisions, each with 4 teams So, there are $2 \times 4 = 8$ teams. Then assume that each of the teams has 10 players, for a total of $8 \times 10 = 80$ players. Now check the five choices. Which one is equal to 80 when $d = 2$, $t = 4$, and $p = 10$? Only dtp.

23. **(C)** Test each set of values to see which one does not work. Only Choice C, $x = 1$ and $y = -1$ does not work: $3(1)^2 + 2(-1) = 3 - 2 = 1$, not 5. The other choices all work.

24. **(C)** There is a total of $1 + 2 + 3 + 4 + 5 + 6 = 21$ slips of paper. Since odd numbers are written on $1 + 3 + 5 = 9$ of them, the probability of drawing an odd number is $\frac{9}{21} = \frac{3}{7}$.

25. **(B)** If $|x| = |y|$, then $x = y$ or $x = -y$. So $x^2 = y^2$ or $x^2 = (-y)^2 = y^2$. (II is true.) If $x = 1$ and $y = -1$, then both I and III are false. Only statement II is true.

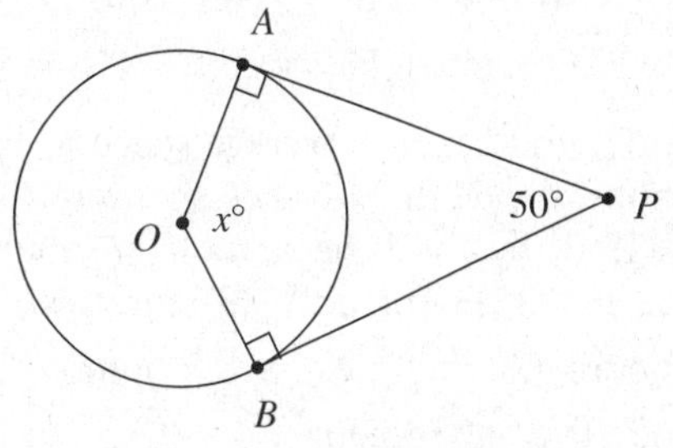

26. **(D)** Since $\overline{OA}$ and $\overline{OB}$ are radii drawn to the points of contact of two tangents, by **KEY FACT L10**, $\overline{OA} \perp \overline{PA}$ and $\overline{OB} \perp \overline{PB}$. So angles A and B are right angles. Finally, by **KEY FACT K1**, the sum of the measures of the four angles in any quadrilateral is 360; so, $90 + 90 + 50 + x = 360$. Therefore, $230 + x = 360$, and $x = 130$.

27. **(A)** $2^{3x} + 2^{3x} + 2^{3x} + 2^{3x} = 4(2^{3x}) = 2^2(2^{3x}) = 2^{3x+2}$.
**Let $x = 1$; then $2^{3x} = 2^3 = 8$, and

$$2^{3x} + 2^{3x} + 2^{3x} + 2^{3x} = 8 + 8 + 8 + 8 = 32.$$

Which of the choices equals 32 when $x = 1$? Only 2^{3x+2} ($2^5 = 32$).

28. **(B)** Let r and R be the radii of circle I and circle II, respectively.

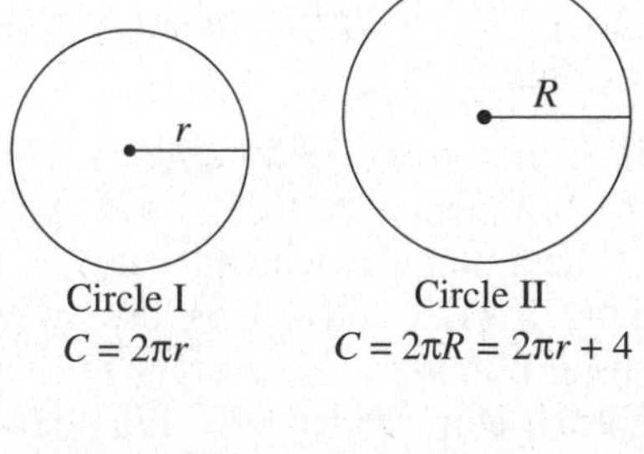

Since the circumference of circle I is $2\pi r$, the circumference of circle II is $2\pi r + 4 = 2(\pi r + 2)$. But, of course, the circumference of circle II is also $2\pi R$. Therefore, $2\pi R = 2(\pi r + 2)$. Dividing by 2, we get $\pi R = \pi r + 2$. Now, dividing by π, we get $R = r + \frac{2}{\pi}$.

29. **(320)** Since $a + 100 = 180$, $a = 80$. But since ℓ and k are parallel, the four acute angles are all equal: $80 = a = b = c = d$, so their sum is $4 \times 80 = 320$.

30. **(30)** Evaluate: $2(6) - 3(-6) = 12 + 18 = 30$.

31. **($\mathbf{3.75}$ or $\mathbf{\frac{15}{4}}$)** The median of the 7 numbers 1, 2, 3, 4, 5, 6, 7 is the middle one: 4. The median of the 6 numbers 1, 2, 3, 4, 5, 6 is the average of the two middle ones: $\frac{3+4}{2} = 3.5$. Finally, the average of 4 and 3.5 is 3.75 or $\frac{15}{4}$.

32. **(70)** Since all of the radii of a circle have the same length, $CA = CB$. Therefore,

$$m\angle A = m\angle B = 55°, \text{ and}$$

$$c = 180 - (55 + 55) = 180 - 110 = 70.$$

33. **(57)** To find Elaine's average speed in kilometers per hour, divide the distance she went, in kilometers (190), by the time it took, in hours. Elaine drove for 3 hours and 20 minutes, which is $3\frac{1}{3}$ hours (20 minutes $= \frac{20}{60}$ hour $= \frac{1}{3}$ hour). Elaine's average speed is

$$190 \div 3\frac{1}{3} = 190 \div \frac{10}{3} = \overset{19}{\cancel{190}} \times \frac{3}{\cancel{10}} = 57.$$

34. **(1.21)** Since this is a percent problem, assume the value of the investment on January 1, 2004 was \$100. Since 10% of 100 is 10, one year later the value of the investment had increased by \$10 to \$110. Now, 10% of 110 is 11, so in the next year the value increased by \$11 to \$121. Finally, 121 is 1.21×100.

35. **(72)** There are 90 two-digit numbers (the integers from 10 to 99 inclusive). To find out how many of them do not contain the digit 9, calculate how many of them *do* contain the digit 9, and subtract that number from 90. There are a total of 18 two-digit numbers that contain the digit 9—the 10 numbers from 90 to 99 plus the 8 other numbers that end in 9: 19, 29, . . . , 89. Finally, there are $90 - 18 = 72$ two-digit numbers that do not contain the digit 9.

36. **(87.5)** If the average of 5 numbers is 95, the sum of those numbers is $5 \times 95 = 475$. Similarly, the sum of the 3 numbers whose average is 100 is 300, leaving 175 $(475 - 300)$ as the sum of the 2 remaining numbers. The average of these 2 numbers is their sum divided by 2: $175 \div 2 = 87.5$.

**Assume that the five numbers are 100, 100, 100, x, and y. Then we have $\frac{100+100+100+x+y}{5} = 95$. So, $300 + x + y = 475$. So, $x + y = 175$, and $\frac{x+y}{2} = \frac{175}{2} = 87.5$.

37. **(1)** Assume that the radius of the large circle is 2. Then the area of the circle is 4π. The radius of each semicircle is 1, and since the area of a circle of radius 1 is π, the area of each semicircle is $\frac{1}{2}\pi$, and the total shaded area is $4\left(\frac{1}{2}\pi\right) = 2\pi$. Since the shaded area is exactly one-half of the circle, the white area is also one-half of the circle. The areas are equal, and so the shaded area is 1 times the white area.

38. **(2500)** If 99.6% of the people tested did not have the disease, then 0.4% of them did have the disease. If x = the number of people tested, then $10 = 0.004x \Rightarrow x = 10 \div .004 = 2500$.

Section 5 Writing Skills

1. **(C)** Choice C uses *drank*, the correct form of the irregular verb *drink*.

2. **(D)** Error in tense. Change *began* to *had begun*.

3. **(B)** Error in idiom. *Seems satisfying their need* is unidiomatic. *Seems to satisfy their need* is correct.

4. **(C)** Error in coordination and subordination. Choice C corrects the error in conjunction use.

5. **(D)** Error in following conventions. *Irregardless* is a nonstandard use of *regardless*.

6. **(B)** Comma splice. The run-on sentence is corrected in Choice B.

7. **(D)** Errors in subject-verb agreement. The phrase *along with several other stories* is not part of the subject of the sentence. The subject is *"Araby"* (singular); the verb should be *is going to be read* (singular).

8. **(A)** Sentence is correct. Choice B introduces an error in agreement. Choices C, D, and E misuse the *not only . . . but also* construction.

9. **(E)** Error in modification and word order. The dangling modifier is corrected in Choice E.

10. **(B)** Error in modification and word order. The dangling construction is corrected in Choices B and E. However, only Choice B retains the meaning of the original sentence.

11. **(B)** Error in idiom. Choice B properly replaces the incorrect preposition *to* with the correct preposition, *with*. Although Choice E also properly replaces the incorrect preposition, it introduces a new error involving the sequence of tenses.

12. **(E)** Dangling participle. A participial phrase modifies or describes a noun. Was the *response* bothered by the rival team's heckling? No. The *home team* was bothered by the heckling. Choice E corrects the dangling participle without introducing any fresh errors.

13. **(D)** Error in logical comparison. The faulty comparison is corrected in Choice D.

14. **(A)** The original sentence is correct. The subject of *are going* is *legislators* (plural). Therefore, Choices B, C, and D are incorrect. Choice E changes the meaning of the original sentence.

15. **(D)** Incomplete comparison. They are as harmful *to* women as they are *to* men.

16. **(A)** Sentence is correct.

17. **(E)** Error in usage. Do not use *when* or *where* after *is* in making a definition.

18. **(D)** Error in sequence of tenses. The present perfect tense ("has been informed") indicates some vague time before now, or a time that lasts up to the present. NASA, however, was told about the dangerous weather conditions at a definite time in the past. Therefore, you should use either the simple past tense ("was informed") or the past perfect tense ("had been informed") here.

19. **(D)** Error in idiom. Either James hoped *for* the revitalization of his career, or he hoped *to* revitalize it. In this case, the verbal *to revitalize* is correct.

20. **(C)** Dangling modifier. Ask yourself who are strolling in the park. Choice C rearranges the words in the sentence to make "While strolling in Golden Gate Park one day" clearly refer to "the young couple."

21. **(A)** Error in diction. Change *Being that* to *Since.*

22. **(A)** Error in following conventions. Double negative. Change *can't* to *can.*

23. **(B)** Error in pronoun case. *But,* as used in this sentence, is a preposition meaning *except*. Change *he* to *him.*

24. **(D)** Error in following conventions. Change *reason . . . is because* to *reason . . . is that.*

25. **(B)** Error in tense. Change *am playing* to *have been playing.*

26. **(B)** Error in diction. Change *affective* to *effective.*

27. **(B)** Error in diction. Use *among* rather than *between* when you are dealing with three or more items.

28. **(D)** Error in parallelism. Change *as well as signing* to *and sign* in order to match the other items in the list.

29. **(C)** Error in coordination and subordination. Incorrect sentence connector. Change *furthermore* to the coordinating conjunction *but* to clarify the relationship between the clauses.

30. **(D)** Error in idiom. Change *accumulation from* to *accumulation of.*

31. **(A)** Error in diction. *Altogether* is correct.

32. **(E)** Sentence is correct.

33. **(B)** Error in idiom. Change *differ with* (which indicates a difference of opinion) to *differ from* (which indicates a difference in appearance).

34. **(C)** Error in parallelism. Change *remaining at* to the infinitive *to remain at* in order to match *to travel on.*

35. **(A)** Choice A accurately describes the content of the essay. The original introductory sentence is misleading. The essay is about changes in the status of women, not about the role women played in causing the changes. It is the best answer.

    Choice B is a variation of the original introductory sentence but the use of the future verb tense fails to convey the actual content of the essay.

    Choice C is a confusing sentence consisting of two illogically unrelated clauses.

    Choice D fails to convey the contents of the essay. It also contains the pronoun *their,* which does not have a clear antecedent.

    Choice E is virtually meaningless. It also contains a dangling participle. The phrase that begins *Being influenced . . .* should modify *women,* not *status.*

36. **(D)** Choice A inserts a comma splice between *lifted* and *for example*. Two independent clauses should be separated by a period or semicolon.

    Choice B contains the pronoun *they,* which lacks a specific reference.

    Choice C improperly shifts pronouns from third person to second person.

    Choice D is effectively expressed. It is the best answer.

    Choice E is cumbersome and awkwardly worded. The phrase *the right of going into public* contains an idiom error. The correct phrase is *right to go into public.*

37. **(A)** Choice A provides a smooth transition by alluding to the discussion of competition in the second paragraph and introducing the main topic of the third. A is the best answer.

    Choice B uses a nonstandard transitional word *irregardless,* which in the context makes no sense.

    Choice C contains no specifically transitional material.

    Choice D would be a decent transition were it not for its mixed construction. The first half of the sentence doesn't fit grammatically with the second half.

    Choice E introduces a new idea that is unrelated to the content of the third paragraph.

38. **(E)** Choice A is illogical; becoming role model is not an example of attaining a high position in politics and government.

    Choice B is not a good example of attaining a high position in politics.

    Choice C is irrelevant. Margaret Thatcher's defeat is not an example of an achievement in politics and government.

    Choice D is slightly off the mark. The sentence emphasizes Indira Ghandi's assassination instead of her leadership.

    Choice E gives two examples of women who have attained a high position in politics and government. It is the best answer.

39. **(E)** All the sentences except sentence 14 support the idea stated in the topic sentence, that women have made gains in politics and government. Threfore, Choice E is the best answer.

Answer Sheet–Practice Test 2

Each mark should completely fill the appropriate space, and should be as dark as all other marks. Make all erasures complete. Traces of an erasure may be read as an answer.

Section 1 – Critical Reading

25 minutes

1 Ⓐ Ⓑ Ⓒ Ⓓ Ⓔ
2 Ⓐ Ⓑ Ⓒ Ⓓ Ⓔ
3 Ⓐ Ⓑ Ⓒ Ⓓ Ⓔ
4 Ⓐ Ⓑ Ⓒ Ⓓ Ⓔ
5 Ⓐ Ⓑ Ⓒ Ⓓ Ⓔ
6 Ⓐ Ⓑ Ⓒ Ⓓ Ⓔ
7 Ⓐ Ⓑ Ⓒ Ⓓ Ⓔ
8 Ⓐ Ⓑ Ⓒ Ⓓ Ⓔ
9 Ⓐ Ⓑ Ⓒ Ⓓ Ⓔ
10 Ⓐ Ⓑ Ⓒ Ⓓ Ⓔ
11 Ⓐ Ⓑ Ⓒ Ⓓ Ⓔ
12 Ⓐ Ⓑ Ⓒ Ⓓ Ⓔ
13 Ⓐ Ⓑ Ⓒ Ⓓ Ⓔ
14 Ⓐ Ⓑ Ⓒ Ⓓ Ⓔ
15 Ⓐ Ⓑ Ⓒ Ⓓ Ⓔ
16 Ⓐ Ⓑ Ⓒ Ⓓ Ⓔ
17 Ⓐ Ⓑ Ⓒ Ⓓ Ⓔ
18 Ⓐ Ⓑ Ⓒ Ⓓ Ⓔ
19 Ⓐ Ⓑ Ⓒ Ⓓ Ⓔ
20 Ⓐ Ⓑ Ⓒ Ⓓ Ⓔ
21 Ⓐ Ⓑ Ⓒ Ⓓ Ⓔ
22 Ⓐ Ⓑ Ⓒ Ⓓ Ⓔ
23 Ⓐ Ⓑ Ⓒ Ⓓ Ⓔ
24 Ⓐ Ⓑ Ⓒ Ⓓ Ⓔ

Section 2 – Math

25 minutes

1 Ⓐ Ⓑ Ⓒ Ⓓ Ⓔ
2 Ⓐ Ⓑ Ⓒ Ⓓ Ⓔ
3 Ⓐ Ⓑ Ⓒ Ⓓ Ⓔ
4 Ⓐ Ⓑ Ⓒ Ⓓ Ⓔ
5 Ⓐ Ⓑ Ⓒ Ⓓ Ⓔ
6 Ⓐ Ⓑ Ⓒ Ⓓ Ⓔ
7 Ⓐ Ⓑ Ⓒ Ⓓ Ⓔ
8 Ⓐ Ⓑ Ⓒ Ⓓ Ⓔ
9 Ⓐ Ⓑ Ⓒ Ⓓ Ⓔ
10 Ⓐ Ⓑ Ⓒ Ⓓ Ⓔ
11 Ⓐ Ⓑ Ⓒ Ⓓ Ⓔ
12 Ⓐ Ⓑ Ⓒ Ⓓ Ⓔ
13 Ⓐ Ⓑ Ⓒ Ⓓ Ⓔ
14 Ⓐ Ⓑ Ⓒ Ⓓ Ⓔ
15 Ⓐ Ⓑ Ⓒ Ⓓ Ⓔ
16 Ⓐ Ⓑ Ⓒ Ⓓ Ⓔ
17 Ⓐ Ⓑ Ⓒ Ⓓ Ⓔ
18 Ⓐ Ⓑ Ⓒ Ⓓ Ⓔ
19 Ⓐ Ⓑ Ⓒ Ⓓ Ⓔ
20 Ⓐ Ⓑ Ⓒ Ⓓ Ⓔ

Section 3 – Critical Reading

25 minutes

25 Ⓐ Ⓑ Ⓒ Ⓓ Ⓔ
26 Ⓐ Ⓑ Ⓒ Ⓓ Ⓔ
27 Ⓐ Ⓑ Ⓒ Ⓓ Ⓔ
28 Ⓐ Ⓑ Ⓒ Ⓓ Ⓔ
29 Ⓐ Ⓑ Ⓒ Ⓓ Ⓔ
30 Ⓐ Ⓑ Ⓒ Ⓓ Ⓔ
31 Ⓐ Ⓑ Ⓒ Ⓓ Ⓔ
32 Ⓐ Ⓑ Ⓒ Ⓓ Ⓔ
33 Ⓐ Ⓑ Ⓒ Ⓓ Ⓔ
34 Ⓐ Ⓑ Ⓒ Ⓓ Ⓔ
35 Ⓐ Ⓑ Ⓒ Ⓓ Ⓔ
36 Ⓐ Ⓑ Ⓒ Ⓓ Ⓔ
37 Ⓐ Ⓑ Ⓒ Ⓓ Ⓔ
38 Ⓐ Ⓑ Ⓒ Ⓓ Ⓔ
39 Ⓐ Ⓑ Ⓒ Ⓓ Ⓔ
40 Ⓐ Ⓑ Ⓒ Ⓓ Ⓔ
41 Ⓐ Ⓑ Ⓒ Ⓓ Ⓔ
42 Ⓐ Ⓑ Ⓒ Ⓓ Ⓔ
43 Ⓐ Ⓑ Ⓒ Ⓓ Ⓔ
44 Ⓐ Ⓑ Ⓒ Ⓓ Ⓔ
45 Ⓐ Ⓑ Ⓒ Ⓓ Ⓔ
46 Ⓐ Ⓑ Ⓒ Ⓓ Ⓔ
47 Ⓐ Ⓑ Ⓒ Ⓓ Ⓔ
48 Ⓐ Ⓑ Ⓒ Ⓓ Ⓔ

Remove answer sheet by cutting on dotted line

Section 4 – Math

25 minutes

21 Ⓐ Ⓑ Ⓒ Ⓓ Ⓔ
22 Ⓐ Ⓑ Ⓒ Ⓓ Ⓔ
23 Ⓐ Ⓑ Ⓒ Ⓓ Ⓔ
24 Ⓐ Ⓑ Ⓒ Ⓓ Ⓔ
25 Ⓐ Ⓑ Ⓒ Ⓓ Ⓔ
26 Ⓐ Ⓑ Ⓒ Ⓓ Ⓔ
27 Ⓐ Ⓑ Ⓒ Ⓓ Ⓔ
28 Ⓐ Ⓑ Ⓒ Ⓓ Ⓔ

29

	/	/	
.	.	.	.
	0	0	0
1	1	1	1
2	2	2	2
3	3	3	3
4	4	4	4
5	5	5	5
6	6	6	6
7	7	7	7
8	8	8	8
9	9	9	9

30

	/	/	
.	.	.	.
	0	0	0
1	1	1	1
2	2	2	2
3	3	3	3
4	4	4	4
5	5	5	5
6	6	6	6
7	7	7	7
8	8	8	8
9	9	9	9

31

	/	/	
.	.	.	.
	0	0	0
1	1	1	1
2	2	2	2
3	3	3	3
4	4	4	4
5	5	5	5
6	6	6	6
7	7	7	7
8	8	8	8
9	9	9	9

32

	/	/	
.	.	.	.
	0	0	0
1	1	1	1
2	2	2	2
3	3	3	3
4	4	4	4
5	5	5	5
6	6	6	6
7	7	7	7
8	8	8	8
9	9	9	9

33

	/	/	
.	.	.	.
	0	0	0
1	1	1	1
2	2	2	2
3	3	3	3
4	4	4	4
5	5	5	5
6	6	6	6
7	7	7	7
8	8	8	8
9	9	9	9

34

	/	/	
.	.	.	.
	0	0	0
1	1	1	1
2	2	2	2
3	3	3	3
4	4	4	4
5	5	5	5
6	6	6	6
7	7	7	7
8	8	8	8
9	9	9	9

35

	/	/	
.	.	.	.
	0	0	0
1	1	1	1
2	2	2	2
3	3	3	3
4	4	4	4
5	5	5	5
6	6	6	6
7	7	7	7
8	8	8	8
9	9	9	9

36

	/	/	
.	.	.	.
	0	0	0
1	1	1	1
2	2	2	2
3	3	3	3
4	4	4	4
5	5	5	5
6	6	6	6
7	7	7	7
8	8	8	8
9	9	9	9

37

	/	/	
.	.	.	.
	0	0	0
1	1	1	1
2	2	2	2
3	3	3	3
4	4	4	4
5	5	5	5
6	6	6	6
7	7	7	7
8	8	8	8
9	9	9	9

38

	/	/	
.	.	.	.
	0	0	0
1	1	1	1
2	2	2	2
3	3	3	3
4	4	4	4
5	5	5	5
6	6	6	6
7	7	7	7
8	8	8	8
9	9	9	9

Section 5 – Writing

30 minutes

1 Ⓐ Ⓑ Ⓒ Ⓓ Ⓔ
2 Ⓐ Ⓑ Ⓒ Ⓓ Ⓔ
3 Ⓐ Ⓑ Ⓒ Ⓓ Ⓔ
4 Ⓐ Ⓑ Ⓒ Ⓓ Ⓔ
5 Ⓐ Ⓑ Ⓒ Ⓓ Ⓔ
6 Ⓐ Ⓑ Ⓒ Ⓓ Ⓔ
7 Ⓐ Ⓑ Ⓒ Ⓓ Ⓔ
8 Ⓐ Ⓑ Ⓒ Ⓓ Ⓔ
9 Ⓐ Ⓑ Ⓒ Ⓓ Ⓔ
10 Ⓐ Ⓑ Ⓒ Ⓓ Ⓔ
11 Ⓐ Ⓑ Ⓒ Ⓓ Ⓔ
12 Ⓐ Ⓑ Ⓒ Ⓓ Ⓔ
13 Ⓐ Ⓑ Ⓒ Ⓓ Ⓔ
14 Ⓐ Ⓑ Ⓒ Ⓓ Ⓔ
15 Ⓐ Ⓑ Ⓒ Ⓓ Ⓔ
16 Ⓐ Ⓑ Ⓒ Ⓓ Ⓔ
17 Ⓐ Ⓑ Ⓒ Ⓓ Ⓔ
18 Ⓐ Ⓑ Ⓒ Ⓓ Ⓔ
19 Ⓐ Ⓑ Ⓒ Ⓓ Ⓔ
20 Ⓐ Ⓑ Ⓒ Ⓓ Ⓔ
21 Ⓐ Ⓑ Ⓒ Ⓓ Ⓔ
22 Ⓐ Ⓑ Ⓒ Ⓓ Ⓔ
23 Ⓐ Ⓑ Ⓒ Ⓓ Ⓔ
24 Ⓐ Ⓑ Ⓒ Ⓓ Ⓔ
25 Ⓐ Ⓑ Ⓒ Ⓓ Ⓔ
26 Ⓐ Ⓑ Ⓒ Ⓓ Ⓔ
27 Ⓐ Ⓑ Ⓒ Ⓓ Ⓔ
28 Ⓐ Ⓑ Ⓒ Ⓓ Ⓔ
29 Ⓐ Ⓑ Ⓒ Ⓓ Ⓔ
30 Ⓐ Ⓑ Ⓒ Ⓓ Ⓔ
31 Ⓐ Ⓑ Ⓒ Ⓓ Ⓔ
32 Ⓐ Ⓑ Ⓒ Ⓓ Ⓔ
33 Ⓐ Ⓑ Ⓒ Ⓓ Ⓔ
34 Ⓐ Ⓑ Ⓒ Ⓓ Ⓔ
35 Ⓐ Ⓑ Ⓒ Ⓓ Ⓔ
36 Ⓐ Ⓑ Ⓒ Ⓓ Ⓔ
37 Ⓐ Ⓑ Ⓒ Ⓓ Ⓔ
38 Ⓐ Ⓑ Ⓒ Ⓓ Ⓔ
39 Ⓐ Ⓑ Ⓒ Ⓓ Ⓔ

SECTION 1/CRITICAL READING

TIME: 25 MINUTES

24 QUESTIONS (1–24)

Directions: For each question in this section, select the best answer from among the choices given and fill in the corresponding circle on the answer sheet.

Each sentence below has one or two blanks, each blank indicating that something has been omitted. Beneath the sentence are five words or sets of words labeled A through E. Choose the word or set of words that, when inserted in the sentence, best fits the meaning of the sentence as a whole.

EXAMPLE:

Medieval kingdoms did not become constitutional republics overnight; on the contrary, the change was ----.

(A) unpopular (B) unexpected
(C) advantageous (D) sufficient (E) gradual

Ⓐ Ⓑ Ⓒ Ⓓ ●

1. Impressed by the extraordinary potential of the new superconductor, scientists predict that its use will ---- the computer industry, creating new products overnight.

(A) justify (B) alienate (C) nullify
(D) revolutionize (E) overestimate

2. No matter how ---- the revelations of the coming year may be, they will be hard put to match those of the past decade, which have ---- transformed our view of the emergence of Mayan civilization.

(A) minor..dramatically
(B) profound..negligibly
(C) striking..radically
(D) bizarre..nominally
(E) questionable..possibly

3. Few other plants can grow beneath the canopy of the sycamore tree, whose leaves and pods produce a natural herbicide that leaches into the soil, ---- other plants that might compete for water and nutrients.

(A) inhibiting (B) distinguishing
(C) nourishing (D) encouraging
(E) refreshing

4. Black women authors such as Zora Neale Hurston, originally ---- by both white and black literary establishments to obscurity as minor novelists, are being rediscovered by black feminist critics today.

(A) inclined (B) relegated (C) subjected
(D) diminished (E) characterized

5. Critics of the movie version of *The Color Purple* ---- its saccharine, overoptimistic mood as out of keeping with the novel's more ---- tone.

(A) applauded..somber
(B) condemned..hopeful
(C) acclaimed..positive
(D) denounced..sanguine
(E) decried..acerbic

Practice Test 2

GO ON TO NEXT PAGE ▶

Directions: The passages below precede questions based on their content or the relationship between the passages. Answer the questions that follow on the basis of what is stated or implied in the passage.

Questions 6–9 are based on the following passages.

Passage 1

There was a time when poetry mattered in America—a time when T. S. Eliot could fill a football stadium with poetry fans, when literature enjoyed a central place in our culture, and young men and women dreamed about becoming writers. That time is long gone. Today if young people dream of writing at all, they dream of writing rap songs or sitcom scripts, pop lit, not enduring works of art.

Passage 2

Recently a children's book about writing poetry came out. It was called *Poetry Matters*. In essence, that's the question poets face today. Does poetry matter? As Billy Collins wrote, "One of the ridiculous aspects of being a poet is the huge gulf between how seriously we take ourselves and how generally we are ignored by everybody else." We think that what we write matters, but for the most part, in America no one cares. It may be different elsewhere on the globe—Ossip Mandelstam once maintained that only in Russia was poetry respected because there it got people killed. Here, we don't get killed, but we're dying anyway.

6. In Passage 1, the reference to the football stadium (line 3) serves primarily to

(A) demonstrate the connection between sports and poetry
(B) show Eliot's deep appreciation of football
(C) emphasize the popularity of poetry in the period
(D) suggest a potential site for poetry readings today
(E) point out Eliot's enduring vision

7. In line 4, "enjoyed" most nearly means

(A) fancied
(B) relished
(C) possessed
(D) appreciated
(E) flourished

8. In Passage 2, the statement "we're dying anyway" (line 22) is an example of

(A) an apology
(B) a metaphor
(C) a euphemism
(D) a hypothesis
(E) an understatement

9. The authors of Passage 1 and Passage 2 agree that

(A) poetry plays a significant role in modern culture
(B) poets must take themselves seriously if poetry is to survive
(C) rap songs are a valid form of poetic expression
(D) poetry is more appealing to children than to adults
(E) the climate for poetry in America is inauspicious

Practice Test 2

GO ON TO NEXT PAGE ▶

Directions: Each passage below is followed by questions based on its content. Answer the questions following each passage on the basis of what is stated or implied in that passage and in any introductory material that may be provided.

Questions 10–15 are based upon the following passage.

In the following passage from Jane Austen's novel Pride and Prejudice, *the heroine Elizabeth Bennet faces an unexpected encounter with her father's cousin (and prospective heir), the clergyman Mr. Collins.*

It was absolutely necessary to interrupt him now.

"You are too hasty, Sir," she cried. "You forget that I have made no answer. Let me do it without further loss of time. Accept my thanks for the compliment you are paying me. I am very sensible of the honour of your proposals, but it is impossible for me to do otherwise than decline them."

"I am not now to learn," replied Mr. Collins with a formal wave of the hand, "that it is usual with young ladies to reject the addresses of the man whom they secretly mean to accept, when he first applies for their favour; and that sometimes the refusal is repeated a second or even a third time. I am therefore by no means discouraged by what you have just said, and shall hope to lead you to the altar ere long."

"Upon my word, Sir," cried Elizabeth, "your hope is rather an extraordinary one after my declaration. I do assure you that I am not one of those young ladies (if such young ladies there are) who are so daring as to risk their happiness on the chance of being asked a second time. I am perfectly serious in my refusal. You could not make *me* happy, and I am convinced that I am the last woman in the world who would make *you* so. Nay, were your friend Lady Catherine to know me, I am persuaded she would find me in every respect ill qualified for the situation."

"Were it certain that Lady Catherine would think so," said Mr. Collins very gravely—"but I cannot imagine that her ladyship would at all disapprove of you. And you may be certain that when I have the honour of seeing her again I shall speak in the highest terms of your modesty, economy, and other amiable qualifications."

"Indeed, Mr. Collins, all praise of me will be unnecessary. You must give me leave to judge for myself, and pay me the compliment of believing what I say. I wish you very happy and very rich, and by refusing your hand, do all in my power to prevent your being otherwise. In making me the offer, you must have satisfied the delicacy of your feelings with regard to my family, and may take possession of Longbourn estate whenever it falls, without any self-reproach. This matter may be considered, therefore, as finally settled." And rising as she thus spoke, she would have quitted the room, had not Mr. Collins thus addressed her.

"When I do myself the honour of speaking to you next on this subject I shall hope to receive a more favourable answer than you have now given me; though I am far from accusing you of cruelty at present, because I know it to be the established custom of your sex to reject a man on the first application, and perhaps you have even now said as much to encourage my suit as would be consistent with the true delicacy of the female character."

"Really, Mr. Collins," cried Elizabeth with some warmth, "you puzzle me exceedingly. If what I have hitherto said can appear to you in the form of encouragement, I know not how to express my refusal in such a way as may convince you of its being one."

10. It can be inferred that in the paragraphs immediately preceding this passage

(A) Elizabeth and Mr. Collins quarreled
(B) Elizabeth met Mr. Collins for the first time
(C) Mr. Collins asked Elizabeth to marry him
(D) Mr. Collins gravely insulted Elizabeth
(E) Elizabeth discovered that Mr. Collins was a fraud

11. In line 6, "sensible" most nearly means

(A) logical
(B) perceptible
(C) sound in judgment
(D) keenly aware
(E) appreciable

12. Instead of having the intended effect, Elizabeth's initial refusal of Mr. Collins (lines 3–8)

(A) causes her to rethink rejecting him
(B) makes him less inclined to wed
(C) gives her the opportunity to consider other options
(D) persuades him she dislikes him intensely
(E) fails to put an end to his suit

GO ON TO NEXT PAGE ▶

13. It can be inferred from lines 30–33 that Mr. Collins

(A) will take Elizabeth's words seriously
(B) admires Elizabeth's independence
(C) is very disappointed by her decision
(D) would accept Lady Catherine's opinion
(E) means his remarks as a joke

14. The reason Elizabeth insists all praise of her "will be unnecessary" (lines 37–38) is that she

(A) feels sure Lady Catherine will learn to admire her in time
(B) is too shy to accept compliments readily
(C) has no intention of marrying Mr. Collins
(D) believes a clergyman should be less effusive
(E) values her own worth excessively

15. On the basis of his behavior in this passage, Mr. Collins may best be described as

(A) malicious in intent
(B) both obtuse and obstinate
(C) unsure of his acceptance
(D) kindly and understanding
(E) sensitive to Elizabeth's wishes

Questions 16–24 are based on the following passage.

African elephants now are an endangered species. The following passage, taken from a newspaper article written in 1989, discusses the potential ecological disaster that might occur if the elephant were to become extinct.

The African elephant—mythic symbol of a continent, keystone of its ecology and the largest land animal remaining on earth—has become the object of one of the biggest, broadest international efforts yet mounted to turn a threatened species off the road to extinction. But it is not only the elephant's survival that is at stake, conservationists say. Unlike the endangered tiger, unlike even the great whales, the African elephant is in great measure the architect of its environment. As a voracious eater of vegetation, it largely shapes the forest-and-savanna surroundings in which it lives, thereby setting the terms of existence for millions of other storied animals—from zebras to gazelles to giraffes and wildebeests—that share its habitat. And as the elephant disappears, scientists and conservationists say, many other species will also disappear from vast stretches of forest and savanna, drastically altering and impoverishing whole ecosystems.

Just as the American buffalo was hunted almost to extinction a century ago, so the African elephant is now the victim of an onslaught of commercial killing, stimulated in this case by soaring global demand for ivory. Most of the killing is illegal, and conservationists say that although the pressure of human population and development contributes to the elephants' decline, poaching is by far the greatest threat. The elephant may or may not be on the way to becoming a mere zoological curiosity like the buffalo, but the trend is clear.

In an atmosphere of mounting alarm among conservationists, a new international coordinating group backed by 21 ivory-producing and ivory-consuming countries has met and adopted an ambitious plan of action. Against admittedly long odds, the multinational rescue effort is aimed both at stopping the slaughter of the elephants in the short term and at nurturing them as a vital "keystone species" in the long run.

It is the elephant's metabolism and appetite that make it a disturber of the environment and therefore an important creator of habitat. In a constant search for the 300 pounds of vegetation it must have every day, it kills small trees and underbrush and pulls branches off big trees as high as its trunk will reach. This creates innumerable open spaces in both deep tropical forests and in the woodlands that cover part of the African savannas. The resulting patchwork, a mosaic of vegetation in various stages of regeneration, in turn creates a greater variety of forage that attracts a greater variety of other vegetation-eaters than would otherwise be the case.

In studies over the last 20 years in southern Kenya near Mount Kilimanjaro, Dr. David Western has found that when elephants are allowed to roam the savannas naturally and normally, they spread out at "intermediate densities." Their foraging creates a mixture of savanna woodlands (what the Africans call bush) and grassland. The result is a highly diverse array of other plant-eating species: those like the zebra, wildebeest and gazelle, that graze; those like the giraffe, bushbuck and lesser kudu, that browse on tender shoots, buds, twigs and leaves; and plant-eating primates like the baboon and vervet monkey. These herbivores attract carnivores like the lion and cheetah.

GO ON TO NEXT PAGE ▶

When the elephant population thins out, Dr. Western said, the woodlands become denser and the grazers are squeezed out. When pressure from poachers forces elephants to crowd more densely onto reservations, the woodlands there are knocked out and the browsers and primates disappear.

Something similar appears to happen in dense tropical rain forests. In their natural state, because the overhead forest canopy shuts out sunlight and prevents growth on the forest floor, rain forests provide slim pickings for large, hoofed plant-eaters. By pulling down trees and eating new growth, elephants enlarge natural openings in the canopy, allowing plants to regenerate on the forest floor and bringing down vegetation from the canopy so that smaller species can get at it.

In such situations, the rain forest becomes hospitable to large plant-eating mammals such as bongos, bush pigs, duikers, forest hogs, swamp antelopes, forest buffaloes, okapis, sometimes gorillas and always a host of smaller animals that thrive on secondary growth. When elephants disappear and the forest reverts, the larger animals give way to smaller, nimbler animals like monkeys, squirrels and rodents.

16. The passage is primarily concerned with

(A) explaining why elephants are facing the threat of extinction
(B) explaining difficulties in providing sufficient forage for plant eaters
(C) explaining how the elephant's impact on its surroundings affects other species
(D) distinguishing between savannas and rain forests as habitats for elephants
(E) contrasting elephants with members of other endangered species

17. In line 5, "mounted" most nearly means

(A) ascended
(B) increased
(C) launched
(D) attached
(E) exhibited

18. In the opening paragraph, the author mentions tigers and whales in order to emphasize which point about the elephant?

(A) Like them, it faces the threat of extinction.
(B) It is herbivorous rather than carnivorous.
(C) It moves more ponderously than either the tiger or the whale.
(D) Unlike them, it physically alters its environment.
(E) It is the largest extant land mammal.

19. A necessary component of the elephant's ability to transform the landscape is its

(A) massive intelligence
(B) fear of predators
(C) ravenous hunger
(D) lack of grace
(E) ability to regenerate

20. It can be inferred from the passage that

(A) the lion and the cheetah commonly prey upon elephants
(B) the elephant is dependent upon the existence of smaller plant-eating mammals for its survival
(C) elephants have an indirect effect on the hunting patterns of certain carnivores
(D) the floor of the tropical rain forest is too overgrown to accommodate larger plant-eating species
(E) the natural tendency of elephants is to crowd together in packs

21. In lines 40 and 41, the quotation marks around the phrase "keystone species" serve to

(A) emphasize the triteness of the phrase
(B) contradict the literal meaning of the term
(C) indicate the author's desire to write colloquially
(D) imply the phrase has ironic connotations
(E) indicate the phrase is being used in a special or technical sense

GO ON TO NEXT PAGE ▶

22. The passage contains information that would answer which of the following questions?

I. How does the elephant's foraging affect its surroundings?
II. How do the feeding patterns of gazelles and giraffes differ?
III. What occurs in the rain forest when the elephant population dwindles?

(A) I only
(B) II only
(C) I and II only
(D) II and III only
(E) I, II, and III

23. In line 91, "host" most nearly means

(A) food source for parasites
(B) very large number
(C) provider of hospitality
(D) military force
(E) angelic company

24. Which of the following statements best expresses the author's attitude toward the damage to vegetation caused by foraging elephants?

(A) It is a regrettable by-product of the feeding process.
(B) It is a necessary but undesirable aspect of elephant population growth.
(C) It fortuitously results in creating environments suited to diverse species.
(D) It has the unexpected advantage that it allows scientists access to the rain forest.
(E) It reinforces the impression that elephants are a disruptive force.

IF YOU FINISH IN LESS THAN 25 MINUTES, YOU MAY CHECK YOUR WORK ON THIS SECTION ONLY. DO NOT TURN TO ANY OTHER SECTION IN THE TEST.

STOP

SECTION 2 /MATHEMATICS

TIME: 25 MINUTES

20 QUESTIONS (1–20)

Directions:

For each question in this section, determine which of the five choices is correct, and blacken that choice on your answer sheet. You may use any blank space on the page for your work.

NOTES:

- You may use a calculator whenever you believe it will be helpful.
- Use the diagrams provided to help you solve the problems. Unless you see the phrase <u>Note:</u> Figure not drawn to scale under a diagram, it has been drawn as accurately as possible. Unless it is stated that a figure is three dimensional, you may assume that it lies in a plane.

Reference

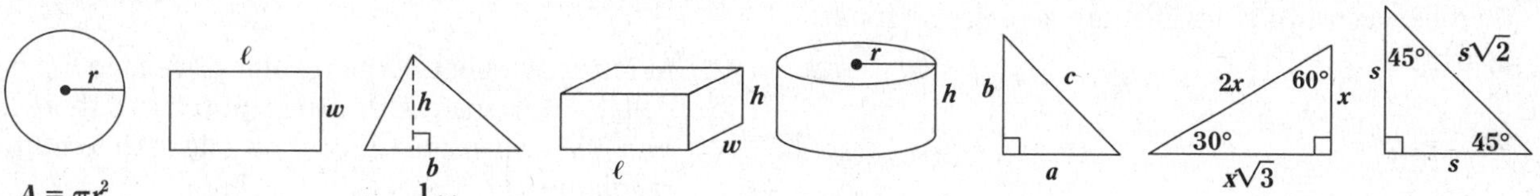

$A = \pi r^2$, $C = 2\pi r$ — $A = \ell w$ — $A = \frac{1}{2}bh$ — $V = \ell wh$ — $V = \pi r^2 h$ — $c^2 = a^2 + b^2$ — **Special Right Triangles**

Number of degrees in a circle: 360
Sum of the measures, in degrees, of the three angles of a triangle: 180

1. If $b - 8 = 0$, what is the value of $b + 8$?

(A) −16
(B) −8
(C) 0
(D) 8
(E) 16

2. Isaac has twice as many toys as Sidney. If Isaac has t toys, how many does Sidney have?

(A) $2t$
(B) t^2
(C) $\frac{t}{2}$
(D) $\frac{2}{t}$
(E) $t + 2$

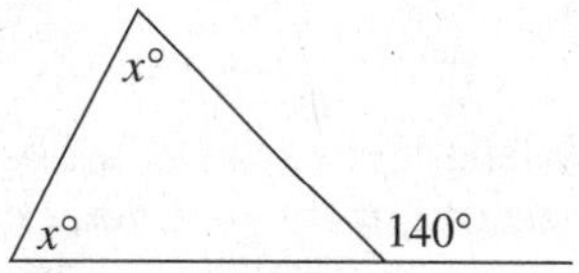

3. In the figure above, what is the value of x?

(A) 40
(B) 60
(C) 70
(D) 80
(E) 140

4. What is the value of n if $10^{2n+1} = 1{,}000{,}000$?

(A) 2
(B) 2.5
(C) 3
(D) 5
(E) 6

GO ON TO NEXT PAGE ►

5. What is the product of 1.5 and 1.7 rounded to the nearest tenth?

(A) 2.2
(B) 2.5
(C) 2.6
(D) 3.0
(E) 3.2

6. A square has the same area as a circle of diameter 4. What is the length of each side of the square?

(A) $2\sqrt{\pi}$
(B) $4\sqrt{\pi}$
(C) 2π
(D) 4π
(E) 8π

7. On a map, $\frac{1}{3}$ inch represents 14 miles. What is the length, in inches, of the line segment drawn on the map between two cities that are actually 30 miles apart?

(A) $\frac{7}{15}$
(B) $\frac{5}{7}$
(C) $\frac{3}{4}$
(D) $1\frac{2}{5}$
(E) 10

8. What is the length of each of the six equal sides of a regular hexagon, if the perimeter of the hexagon is equal to the perimeter of a square whose area is 36?

(A) 4
(B) 6
(C) 12
(D) 24
(E) 36

9. If for any number b, the operations ◇ and ◆ are defined by b◇ $= b + 1$ and ◆b $= b - 1$, which of the following is NOT equal to (3◇)(◆5)?

(A) (1◇)(◆9)
(B) 7◇ + ◆9
(C) (4◇)(◆4)
(D) (7◇)(◆3)
(E) 15◇ ÷ ◆2

10. If $\frac{n+2}{5}$ is an integer, what is the remainder when n is divided by 5?

(A) 1
(B) 2
(C) 3
(D) 4
(E) It cannot be determined from the information given.

11. The day of a quiz, only Michelle was absent. The average (arithmetic mean) grade of the other students was 85. When Michelle took a makeup quiz, her grade was 30, which lowered the class's average to 80. How many students are in the class?

(A) 8
(B) 9
(C) 10
(D) 11
(E) 12

12. At Music Warehouse the regular price for a CD is d dollars. How many CDs can be purchased there for m dollars when the CDs are on sale at 20% off the regular price?

(A) $\frac{4d}{5m}$
(B) $\frac{4m}{5d}$
(C) $\frac{5d}{4m}$
(D) $\frac{5m}{4d}$
(E) $\frac{md}{20}$

13. In a group of 40 people, 13 own dogs and 18 own cats. If 16 have neither a dog nor a cat, how many people have both?

(A) 0
(B) 3
(C) 6
(D) 7
(E) 11

14. How many integers are solutions of the inequality $3|x| + 1 < 16$?

(A) 0
(B) 4
(C) 8
(D) 9
(E) Infinitely many

GO ON TO NEXT PAGE ▶

15. Each of the 15 members of a club owns a certain number of teddy bears. The following chart shows the number of teddy bears owned.

Number of Teddy Bears	Number of Members
6	2
8	5
10	4
13	4

What is the average (arithmetic mean) of the median and the mode of this set of data?

(A) 4.5
(B) 8
(C) 8.5
(D) 9
(E) 9.5

16. What is the value of $3^{\frac{1}{2}} \times 3^{\frac{1}{3}} \times 3^{\frac{1}{6}}$?

(A) $3^{\frac{1}{36}}$
(B) $3^{\frac{1}{11}}$
(C) $27^{\frac{1}{36}}$
(D) $27^{\frac{1}{11}}$
(E) 3

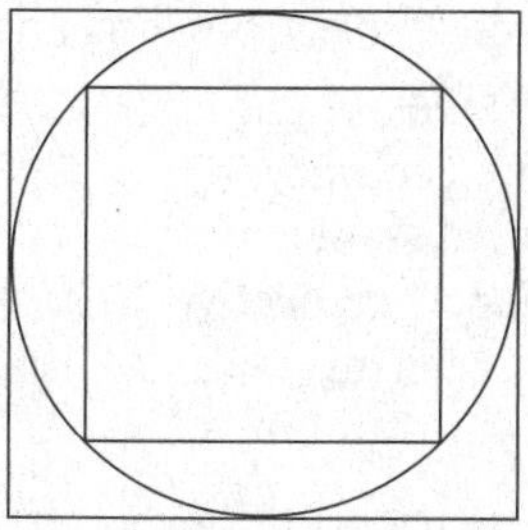

17. In the figure above, the small square is inscribed in the circle, which is inscribed in the large square. What is the ratio of the area of the large square to the area of the small square?

(A) $\sqrt{2}$:1
(B) $\sqrt{3}$:1
(C) 2:1
(D) $2\sqrt{2}$:1
(E) It cannot be determined from the information given.

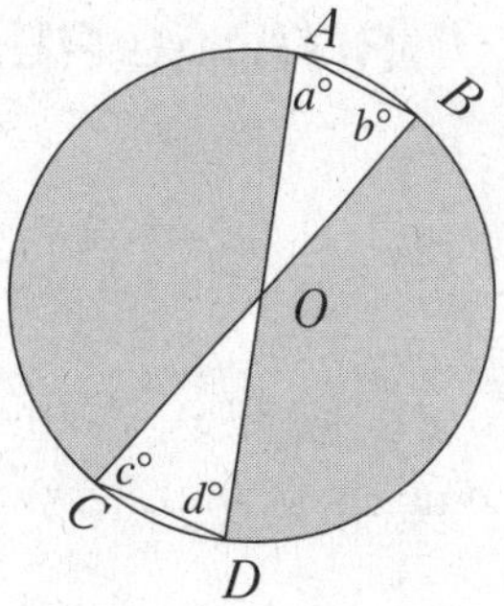

18. In the figure above, O is the center of the circle and $AD = 10$. If the area of the shaded region is 20π, what is the value of $a + b + c + d$?

(A) 144
(B) 216
(C) 240
(D) 270
(E) 288

19. If $r + 2s = a$ and $r - 2s = b$, which of the following is an expression for rs?

(A) ab
(B) $\frac{a + b}{2}$
(C) $\frac{a - b}{2}$
(D) $\frac{a^2 - b^2}{4}$
(E) $\frac{a^2 - b^2}{8}$

20. If a is increased by 25% and b is decreased by 25%, the resulting numbers will be equal. What is the ratio of a to b?

(A) $\frac{3}{5}$
(B) $\frac{3}{4}$
(C) $\frac{1}{1}$
(D) $\frac{4}{3}$
(E) $\frac{5}{3}$

IF YOU FINISH IN LESS THAN 25 MINUTES, YOU MAY CHECK YOUR WORK ON THIS SECTION ONLY. DO NOT TURN TO ANY OTHER SECTION IN THE TEST.

STOP

Practice Test 2

SECTION 3/CRITICAL READING

TIME: 25 MINUTES

24 QUESTIONS (25–48)

Directions: For each question in this section, select the best answer from among the choices given and fill in the corresponding circle on the answer sheet.

Each sentence below has one or two blanks, each blank indicating that something has been omitted. Beneath the sentence are five words or sets of words labeled A through E. Choose the word or set of words that, when inserted in the sentence, best fits the meaning of the sentence as a whole.

EXAMPLE:

Medieval kingdoms did not become constitutional republics overnight; on the contrary, the change was ----.

(A) unpopular (B) unexpected
(C) advantageous (D) sufficient (E) gradual

Ⓐ Ⓑ Ⓒ Ⓓ ●

25. In order that they may be able to discriminate wisely among the many conflicting arguments put before them, legislators must be trained to ---- the truth.

(A) confuse (B) condemn (C) ignore
(D) condone (E) discern

26. In their new collections of lighthearted, provocative dresses, French fashion designers are gambling that even ---- professional women are ready for a bit of ---- in style.

(A) strict..reticence
(B) serious..frivolity
(C) elegant..tradition
(D) modern..harmony
(E) unsentimental..propriety

27. The airline customer service representative tried to ---- the ---- passenger by offering her a seat in first class.

(A) pacify..placid
(B) thwart..irate
(C) divert..grateful
(D) authorize..listless
(E) mollify..angry

28. People who find themselves unusually ---- and ready to drowse off at unexpected moments may be suffering from a hormonal imbalance.

(A) lethargic (B) distracted (C) obdurate
(D) benign (E) perfunctory

29. The expression "he passed away" is ---- for "he died."

(A) a reminder (B) a commiseration
(C) a simile (D) a euphemism
(E) an exaggeration

30. Despite the enormous popularity and influence of his book, *Thunder Out of China*, White's career ----.

(A) soared (B) endured (C) accelerated
(D) revived (E) foundered

31. Written just after Martin Luther King's assassination, Lomax's book has all the virtues of historical ---- but lacks the greater virtue of historical ----, which comes from long and mature reflection upon events.

(A) precision..accuracy
(B) criticism..distance
(C) immediacy..perspective
(D) outlook..realism
(E) currency..testimony

32. Relishing his triumph, Kevin Costner especially ---- the chagrin of the critics who had predicted his ----.

(A) regretted..success
(B) acknowledged..comeback
(C) understated..bankruptcy
(D) distorted..mortification
(E) savored..failure

Directions: Each of the passages below precedes two questions based on its content. Answer the questions following each passage on the basis of what is stated or implied in that passage.

Questions 33 and 34 are based on the following passage.

Little vegetation grows in the vast South African tableland known as the Nama Karroo. The open plateau, home to springboks and other members of the antelope family, seems a rocky, inhospitable place. Yet the springboks find sustenance, searching among the rocks and pebbles, and coming up with mouthfuls of "stones" which they munch contentedly. These stones are in actuality plants, members of the genus Lithops, some of the strangest succulents in the world. Nature has camouflaged these stone plants so well that even trained botanists have trouble telling them apart from the rocks surrounding them.

33. The quotation marks around the word "stones" (line 7) primarily serve to emphasize that the plants

(A) are extraordinarily hard
(B) are inedible by humans
(C) are not literally stones
(D) can be recognized by antelopes
(E) survive in an arid environment

34. The context suggests that a succulent (line 10) is most likely

(A) a rock form
(B) an antelope
(C) a desert insect
(D) a type of camouflage
(E) a kind of plant

Questions 35 and 36 are based on the following passage.

Echoing leaders in the field such as Noam Chomsky, many linguists argue that the capacity for language is a uniquely human property. They contend that chimpanzees and related primates are incapable of using language because their brains lack the human brain structures that make language. Other researchers, however, disagree, citing experiments in which apes have been taught to use symbolic communication systems, such as American Sign Language. In one study, for example, Georgia State professor E. Sue Savage-Rambaugh has worked with a "keyboard" consisting of 400 symbols to communicate with bonobos (also known as pygmy chimpanzees).

35. In line 3, "property" most nearly means

(A) trait (B) wealth (C) ownership
(D) oddity (E) affliction

36. Savage-Rambaugh and Chomsky disagree in their evaluations of

(A) primates' value in experimental research
(B) primates' abilities in language acquisition
(C) primates' abilities to manipulate artifacts
(D) researchers' knowledge of American Sign Language
(E) researchers' impartiality in primate studies

Directions: The passages below are followed by questions on their content; questions following a pair of related passages may also be based on the relationship between the paired passages. Answer the questions on the basis of what is stated or implied in the passages and in any introductory material that may be provided.

Questions 37–48 are based on the following passages.

The following passages are excerpted from two recent essays that relate writing to sports. The author of Passage 1 deals with having had a novel rejected by his publisher. The author of Passage 2 explores how his involvement in sports affected his writing career.

Passage 1

In consigning this manuscript to a desk drawer, I am comforted by the behavior of baseball players. There are *no* pitchers who do not give up home runs, there are *no* batters who do not strike out. There are *no* major league pitchers or batters who have not somehow learned to survive giving up home runs and striking out. That much is obvious.

What seems to me less obvious is how these "failures" must be digested, or put to use, in the overall experience of the player. A jogger once explained to me that the nerves of the ankle are so sensitive and complex that each time a runner sets his foot down, hundreds of messages are conveyed to the runner's brain about the nature of the terrain and the requirements for weight distribution, balance, and muscle-strength. I'm certain that the ninth-inning home run that Dave Henderson hit off Donny Moore registered complexly and permanently in Moore's mind and body and that the next time Moore faced Henderson, his pitching was informed by his awful experience of October 1986. Moore's continuing baseball career depended to some extent on his converting that encounter with Henderson into something useful for his pitching. I can also imagine such an experience destroying an athlete, registering in his mind and body in such a negative way as to produce a debilitating fear.

Of the many ways in which athletes and artists are similar, one is that, unlike accountants or plumbers or insurance salesmen, to succeed at all they must perform at an extraordinary level of excellence. Another is that they must be willing to extend themselves irrationally in order to achieve that level of performance. A writer doesn't have to write all-out all the time, but he or she must be ready to write all-out any time the story requires it. Hold back and you produce what just about any literate citizen can produce, a "pretty good" piece of work. Like the cautious pitcher, the timid writer can spend a lifetime in the minor leagues.

And what more than failure—the strike out, the crucial home run given up, the manuscript criticized and rejected—is more likely to produce caution or timidity? An instinctive response to painful experience is to avoid the behavior that produced the pain. To function at the level of excellence required for survival, writers like athletes must go against instinct, must absorb their failures and become stronger, must endlessly repeat the behavior that produced the pain.

Passage 2

The athletic advantages of this concentration, particularly for an athlete who was making up for the absence of great natural skill, were considerable. Concentration gave you an edge over many of your opponents, even your betters, who could not isolate themselves to that degree. For example, in football if they were ahead (or behind) by several touchdowns, if the game itself seemed to have been settled, they tended to slack off, to ease off a little, certainly to relax their own concentration. It was then that your own unwavering concentration and your own indifference to the larger point of view paid off. At the very least you could deal out surprise and discomfort to your opponents.

But it was more than that. Do you see? The ritual of physical concentration, of acute engagement in a small space while disregarding all the clamor and demands of the larger world, was the best possible lesson in precisely the kind of selfish intensity needed to create and to finish a poem, a story, or a novel. This alone mattered while all the world going on, with and without you, did not.

I was learning first in muscle, blood, and bone, not from literature and not from teachers of literature or the arts or the natural sciences, but from coaches, in particular this one coach who paid me enough attention to influence me to teach some things to myself. I was learning about art and life through the abstraction of athletics in much the same way that a soldier is, to an extent, prepared for war by endless parade ground drill. His body must learn to be a soldier before heart, mind, and spirit can.

GO ON TO NEXT PAGE ▶

Ironically, I tend to dismiss most comparisons of athletics to art and to "the creative process." But only because, I think, so much that is claimed for both is untrue. But I have come to believe—indeed I have to believe it insofar as I believe in the validity and efficacy of art—that what comes to us first and foremost through the body, as a sensuous affective experience, is taken and transformed by mind and self into a thing of the spirit. Which is only to say that what the body learns and is taught is of enormous significance—at least until the last light of the body fails.

37. Why does the author of Passage 1 consign his manuscript to a desk drawer?

(A) to protect it from the inquisitive eyes of his family
(B) to prevent its getting lost or disordered
(C) because his publisher wishes to take another look at it
(D) because he chooses to watch a televised baseball game
(E) to set it aside as unmarketable in its current state

38. Why is the author of Passage 1 "comforted by the behavior of baseball players" (lines 1–8)?

(A) He treasures the timeless rituals of America's national pastime.
(B) He sees he is not alone in having to confront failure and move on.
(C) He enjoys watching the frustration of the batters who strike out.
(D) He looks at baseball from the viewpoint of a behavioral psychologist.
(E) He welcomes any distraction from the task of revising his novel.

39. What function in the passage is served by the discussion of the nerves in the ankle in lines 11–17?

(A) It provides a momentary digression from the overall narrative flow.
(B) It emphasizes how strong a mental impact Henderson's home run must have had on Moore.
(C) It provides scientific confirmation of the neuromuscular abilities of athletes.
(D) It illustrates that the author's interest in sports is not limited to baseball alone.
(E) It conveys a sense of how confusing it is for the mind to deal with so many simultaneous messages.

40. In line 19, "registered" most nearly means

(A) enrolled formally
(B) expressed without words
(C) corresponded exactly
(D) made an impression
(E) qualified officially

41. The attitude of the author of Passage 1 to accountants, plumbers, and insurance salesmen (lines 30–36) can best be described as

(A) respectful
(B) cautious
(C) superior
(D) cynical
(E) hypocritical

42. In the concluding paragraphs of Passage 1, the author appears to

(A) romanticize the writer as someone heroic in his or her accomplishments
(B) deprecate athletes for their inability to react to experience instinctively
(C) minimize the travail that artists and athletes endure to do their work
(D) advocate the importance of literacy to the common citizen
(E) suggest a cautious approach would reduce the likelihood of future failure

43. The author of Passage 2 prizes

(A) his innate athletic talent
(B) the respect of his peers
(C) his ability to focus
(D) the gift of relaxation
(E) winning at any cost

44. In line 61, "settled" most nearly means

(A) judged
(B) decided
(C) reconciled
(D) pacified
(E) inhabited

45. What does the author mean by "indifference to the larger point of view" (lines 64–65)?

(A) inability to see the greater implications of the activity in which you were involved
(B) hostility to opponents coming from larger, better trained teams
(C) reluctance to look beyond your own immediate concerns
(D) refusing to care how greatly you might be hurt by your opponents
(E) being more concerned with the task at hand than with whether you win or lose

GO ON TO NEXT PAGE ▶

46. What is the function of the phrase "to an extent" in line 82?

(A) It denies a situation.
(B) It conveys a paradox.
(C) It qualifies a statement.
(D) It represents a metaphor.
(E) It minimizes a liability.

47. The author finds it ironic that he tends to "dismiss most comparisons of athletics to art" (lines 86–87) because

(A) athletics is the basis for great art
(B) he finds comparisons generally unhelpful
(C) he is making such a comparison
(D) he typically is less cynical
(E) he rejects the so-called creative process

48. The authors of both passages would agree that

(A) the lot of the professional writer is more trying than that of the professional athlete
(B) athletics has little to do with the actual workings of the creative process
(C) both artists and athletes learn hard lessons in the course of mastering their art
(D) it is important to concentrate on the things that hurt us in life
(E) participating in sports provides a distraction from the isolation of a writer's life

Practice Test 2

IF YOU FINISH IN LESS THAN 25 MINUTES, YOU MAY CHECK YOUR WORK ON THIS SECTION ONLY. DO NOT TURN TO ANY OTHER SECTION IN THE TEST.

STOP

SECTION 4/MATHEMATICS

TIME: 25 MINUTES

18 QUESTIONS (21–38)

Directions:

For questions 21–28, determine which of the five choices is correct, and blacken that choice on your answer sheet. You may use any blank space on the page for your work.

NOTES:

- You may use a calculator whenever you believe it will be helpful.
- Use the diagrams provided to help you solve the problems. Unless you see the phrase
  Note: Figure not drawn to scale
  under a diagram, it has been drawn as accurately as possible. Unless it is stated that a figure is three dimensional, you may assume that it lies in a plane.

Reference

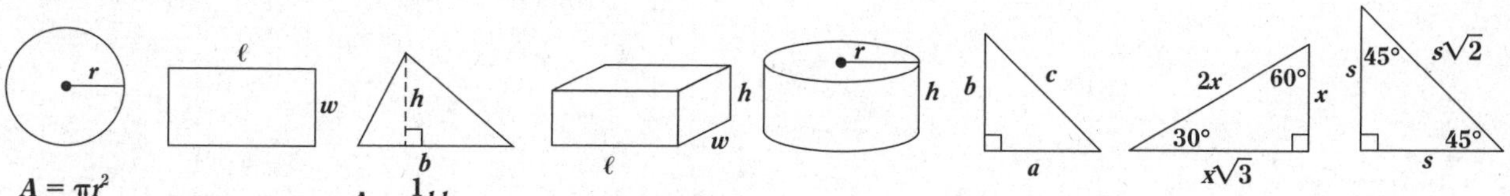

$A = \pi r^2$
$C = 2\pi r$ $\quad A = \ell w \quad A = \frac{1}{2}bh \quad V = \ell wh \quad V = \pi r^2 h \quad c^2 = a^2 + b^2$ **Special Right Triangles**

Number of degrees in a circle: 360
Sum of the measures, in degrees, of the three angles of a triangle: 180

21. If a basket of fruit contains 5 pounds of apples, 3 pounds of oranges, and 1 pound of pears, by weight, what fraction of the fruit is oranges?

(A) $\frac{1}{9}$
(B) $\frac{1}{5}$
(C) $\frac{1}{3}$
(D) $\frac{3}{8}$
(E) $\frac{1}{2}$

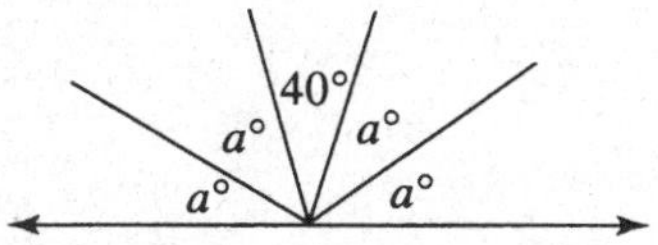

22. In the figure above, what is the value of a?

(A) 30
(B) 35
(C) 36
(D) 45
(E) 80

23. If $\frac{5}{8}$ of the members of a chess club are boys, what is the ratio of girls to boys in the club?

(A) $\frac{3}{13}$
(B) $\frac{5}{13}$
(C) $\frac{3}{5}$
(D) $\frac{5}{3}$
(E) $\frac{8}{5}$

24. A rectangle has a perimeter equal to the circumference of a circle of radius 3. If the width of the rectangle is 3, what is its length?

(A) $3\pi - 3$
(B) $4.5\pi - 3$
(C) $6\pi - 3$
(D) $9\pi - 3$
(E) $3\pi + 3$

GO ON TO NEXT PAGE ▶

25. If p, q, and r are prime numbers greater than 5, which of the following could be true?

I. $p - q$ is prime
II. $p + q$ is prime
III. $p + q + r$ is prime

(A) I only
(B) II only
(C) I and II only
(D) I and III only
(E) I, II, and III

26. If A (3, −2) and B (7, 2) are the endpoints of a diameter of a circle, what is the area of the circle?

(A) $2\sqrt{2}\pi$
(B) $4\sqrt{2}\pi$
(C) 8π
(D) 16π
(E) 32π

27. If $13 - 2\sqrt{x} = 7$, then what is the value of x?

(A) −9
(B) 6
(C) 9
(D) 16
(E) There is no value of x that satisfies the equation.

28. The estate of a wealthy man was distributed as follows: 10% to his wife, 5% divided equally among his 3 children, 5% divided equally among his 5 grandchildren, and the balance to a charitable trust. If the trust received $1,000,000, how much did each grandchild inherit?

(A) $10,000
(B) $12,500
(C) $20,000
(D) $62,500
(E) $100,000

Practice Test 2

GO ON TO NEXT PAGE ▶

Student-Produced Response Directions

In questions 29–38, first solve the problem, and then enter your answer on the grid provided on the answer sheet. The instructions for entering your answers follow.

- First, write your answer in the boxes at the top of the grid.
- Second, grid your answer in the columns below the boxes.
- Use the fraction bar in the first row or the decimal point in the second row to enter fractions and decimals.

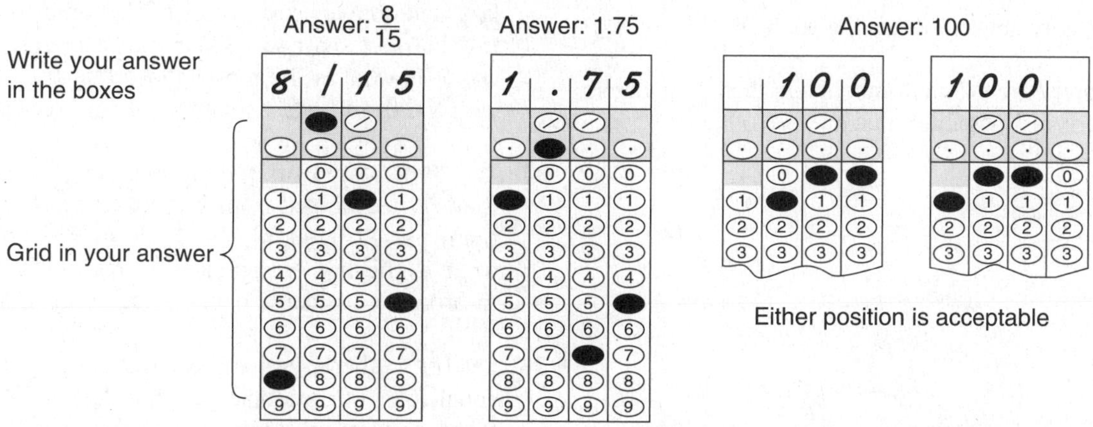

- Grid only one space in each column.
- Entering the answer in the boxes is recommended as an aid in gridding but is not required.
- The machine scoring your exam can read only what you grid, so you **must grid-in your answers correctly to get credit.**
- If a question has more than one correct answer, grid-in only one of them.
- The grid does not have a minus sign; so no answer can be negative.
- A mixed number *must* be converted to an improper fraction or a decimal before it is gridded. Enter $1\frac{1}{4}$ as $\frac{5}{4}$ or 1.25; the machine will interpret 11/4 as $\frac{11}{4}$ and mark it wrong.
- **All decimals must be entered as accurately as possible.** Here are three acceptable ways of gridding

$$\frac{3}{11} = 0.272727\ldots$$

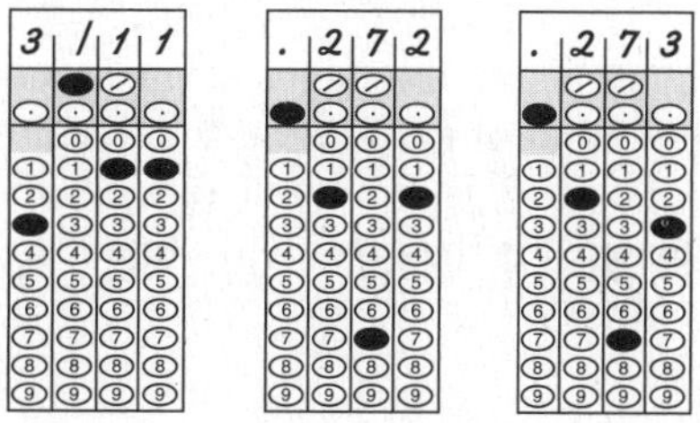

- Note that rounding to .273 is acceptable because you are using the full grid, but you would receive **no credit** for .3 or .27, because they are less accurate.

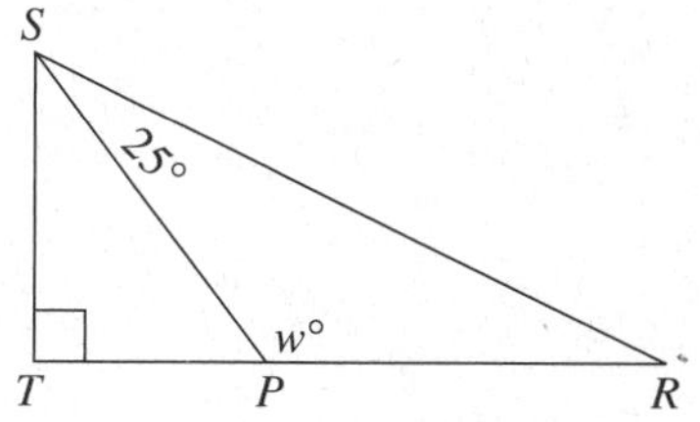

29. In the figure above, if *PS* bisects $\angle RST$, what is the value of w?

30. There are 150 people in line outside a ballpark. If Peter is the 10th person from the front and Wendy is the 110th person from the front, how many people are there between Peter and Wendy?

GO ON TO NEXT PAGE ▶

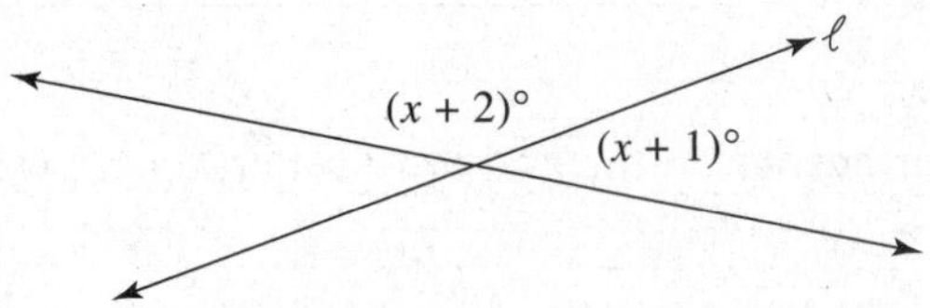

Note: Figure not drawn to scale

31. In the figure above, what is the value of x?

32. If r, s, and t are prime numbers less than 15, what is the greatest possible value of $\frac{r-s}{t}$?

33. If $\frac{2}{x} + \frac{3}{4} = \frac{4}{5}$, then $x =$

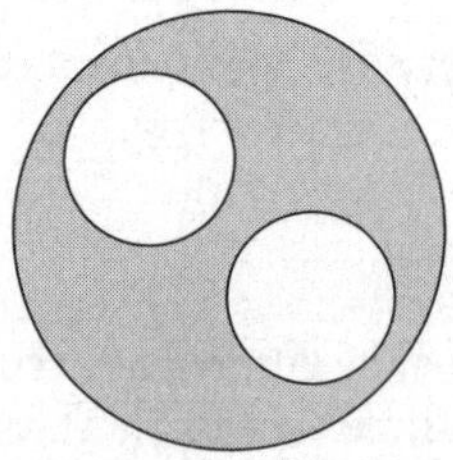

Note: Figure not drawn to scale

34. In the figure above, the radius of the large circle is 3 and the radius of each of the small white circles is 1. If a point, P, is chosen at random inside the big circle, what is the probability that P lies in the shaded region?

35. Two circles have diameters of 12 inches and 10 inches, respectively. The area of the larger circle is what percent *more* than the area of the smaller circle? (Grid-in your answer without a percent sign.)

36. One hundred dollars has been divided among five people. Each one received a whole number of dollars, and no two people received the same amount. If the largest share was \$35 and the smallest share was \$10, what is the most money that the person with the third largest share could have received?

37. Twenty-five students took a quiz, and the grades they earned ranged from 2 to 10. If exactly 22 of them passed by earning a grade of 7 or higher, what is the highest possible average (arithmetic mean) the class could have earned on the quiz?

38. Let $[x]$ = the largest integer that is less than or equal to x. For example, $[2.66] = 2$ and $[5] = 5$. What is the value of $[2\pi] - [-2\pi]$?

IF YOU FINISH IN LESS THAN 25 MINUTES, YOU MAY CHECK YOUR WORK ON THIS SECTION ONLY. DO NOT TURN TO ANY OTHER SECTION IN THE TEST.

STOP

Practice Test 2

SECTION 5/WRITING SKILLS

TIME: 30 MINUTES

39 QUESTIONS (1–39)

Directions: For each question in this section, select the best answer from among the choices given and fill in the corresponding circle on the answer sheet.

Some or all parts of the following sentences are underlined. The first answer choice, (A), simply repeats the underlined part of the sentence. The other four choices present four alternative ways to phrase the underlined part. Select the answer that produces the most effective sentence, one that is clear and exact, and blacken the appropriate space on your answer sheet. In selecting your choice, be sure that it is standard written English and that it expresses the meaning of the original sentence.

EXAMPLE:

The first biography of author Eudora Welty came out in 1998, and she was eighty-nine years old at the time.

(A) and she was eighty-nine years old at the time
(B) at the time when she was eighty-nine
(C) upon becoming an eighty-nine year old
(D) when she was eighty-nine
(E) at the age of eighty-nine years old

Ⓐ Ⓑ Ⓒ ● Ⓔ

1. Fifty-three thousand shouting enthusiasts filled the stadium, they had come to watch the first game of the season and to cheer the home team.

(A) enthusiasts filled the stadium, they had come
(B) enthusiasts filled the stadium to come
(C) enthusiasts, filling the stadium, had come
(D) enthusiasts filled the stadium; and had come
(E) enthusiasts filling the stadium, who had come

2. Cecil Sharp wrote the initial volume of *The Country Dance Book* because he wanted preserving of Britain's traditional dances before they were totally forgotten.

(A) he wanted preserving of
(B) he had wanted the preserving of
(C) he wanted to preserve
(D) his desire was the preservation of
(E) he has wanted to preserve

3. Finally reviewing the extensive evidence against the defendant, he was found guilty.

(A) Finally reviewing the extensive evidence against the defendant,
(B) Reviewing the extensive evidence against the defendant,
(C) The jury finally reviewed the extensive evidence against the defendant,
(D) When the jury finally reviewed the extensive evidence against the defendant,
(E) The jury finally reviewed the evidence against the defendant,

4. Paul Gauguin was married and had family responsibilities and he ran away to the South Seas to paint.

(A) Paul Gauguin was married and had family responsibilities and he
(B) Although being married and having family responsibilities, Paul Gauguin
(C) Although Paul Gauguin was married and had family responsibilities, he
(D) Being married, and therefore having family responsibilities, Paul Gauguin
(E) Despite the fact that Paul Gauguin was married and had family responsibilities, he

Practice Test 2

GO ON TO NEXT PAGE ▶

5. A key difference between mice and voles is tail length, a mouse's tail is twice as long as the tail of a vole.
   (A) length, a mouse's tail is
   (B) length; a mouse's tail is
   (C) length, the tail of a mouse is
   (D) length; a mouse's tail, it is
   (E) length, mice's tails are

6. As a retired executive, he is now busier than ever; he makes his living by speaking before business and philanthropic groups, writing books and articles, and he is a director of three major corporations.
   (A) by speaking before business and philanthropic groups, writing books and articles, and he is a director of
   (B) by speaking before business and philanthropic groups, and he writes books and articles as well as being a director of
   (C) by speaking before business and philanthropic groups, and he writes books and articles, and directs
   (D) by speaking before business and philanthropic groups, writing books and articles, and directing
   (E) by speaking before business and philanthropic groups, in addition to writing books and articles, and he is a director of

7. President Reagan established a special commission for the space program; the purpose being to investigate the causes of the *Challenger* disaster.
   (A) program; the purpose being to
   (B) program; whose purpose being to
   (C) program, the purpose was to
   (D) program to
   (E) program; in order to

8. When Harriet Tubman decided to help runaway slaves escape to the North, she knew that her mission would bring her into danger in both South and North.
   (A) When Harriet Tubman decided to help runaway slaves escape
   (B) When Harriet Tubman decides to help runaway slaves escape
   (C) When Harriet Tubman decided about helping runaway slaves escape
   (D) After the decision by Harriet Tubman to help runaway slaves escape
   (E) After Harriet Tubman's making of the decision to help runaway slaves escape

9. The growing impoverishment of women and children in American society distresses Senator Feinstein, and she is also infuriated.
   (A) distresses Senator Feinstein, and she is also infuriated
   (B) distresses Senator Feinstein, infuriating her
   (C) distresses and infuriates Senator Feinstein
   (D) is distressing Senator Feinstein, making her infuriated
   (E) is a cause of distress to Senator Feinstein, and of a fury

10. Being a successful reporter demands powers of observation, fluency, and persistence.
   (A) Being a successful reporter demands
   (B) Being a successful reporter who demands
   (C) To be a successful reporter who demands
   (D) Being a successful reporter demanding
   (E) To be a successful reporter demanding

11. Had I been at the scene of the accident, I could have administered first aid to the victims.
   (A) Had I been at the scene of the accident
   (B) If I were at the scene of the accident
   (C) If I was at the scene of the accident
   (D) I should have been at the scene of the accident
   (E) I should have been at the scene of the accident, and

12. The Northern Lights, or Aurora Borealis, is so named because it is a light display that takes place in the northern skies.
   (A) because it is a light display that takes place
   (B) as a light display taking place
   (C) because of taking place
   (D) due to the fact that it is a light display
   (E) contrary to the fact of taking place

13. It is not for you to assume responsibility; it is rather me who is the guilty person in this matter.
   (A) me who is
   (B) me who am
   (C) I who is
   (D) I who are
   (E) I who am

GO ON TO NEXT PAGE ►

14. Brightly colored birds soared to and fro, indifferent with the ships that traversed the blue Caribbean waters.

(A) Brightly colored birds soared to and fro, indifferent with the ships that traversed
(B) Brightly colored birds soared to and from, indifferent with the ships which traversed
(C) Brightly colored birds soared to and fro, indifferent to the ships that traversed
(D) Bright colored birds soared to and fro, indifferently with the ships, they traversed
(E) Brighly colored birds soaring to and fro, indifferent with the ships that traversed

15. The Metropolitan Museum of Art's collection of medieval sculptures, like so many other aspects of the museum, have benefited significantly from the generosity of J. Pierpont Morgan, the financier.

(A) sculptures, like so many other aspects of the museum, have benefited significantly from
(B) sculptures, like so many other aspects of the museum, have significant benefits from
(C) sculptures, like so many other aspects of the museum, has benefited significantly from
(D) sculptures, similar to many other aspects of the museum, have benefited significantly from
(E) sculptures, like so many other aspects of the museum, have benefited significantly through

16. Native Americans did not fare well in the mission system, perishing in vast numbers from measles and other diseases introduced by the Spanish.

(A) fare well in the mission system, perishing
(B) fare good in the mission system, perishing
(C) fare well in the mission system, they perished
(D) fare well from the mission system, perishing
(E) fare well in the mission system, despite perishing

17. Standoffish and reserved, Charles Lindbergh was uncomfortable with the applause he received from the crowds which have cheered his historic flight.

(A) received from the crowds which have cheered his historic flight
(B) receives from the crowds which cheer his historic flight
(C) received from the cheering crowds about his historic flight
(D) received from the crowds when they cheer his historic flight
(E) received from the crowds that cheered his historic flight

18. Study-abroad programs can enhance students' acquisition of a foreign language, improve their knowledge of the host culture, and even their world views can be transformed.

(A) culture, and even their world views can be transformed
(B) culture, and even can transform their world views
(C) culture, and their world views can even be transformed
(D) culture, and even transform their world views
(E) culture, and even transforming their world views

19. Once dried and pinned as specimens, dragonflies lose most of their color and become increasing fragile.

(A) Once dried and pinned as specimens, dragonflies lose most of their color and become increasing fragile.
(B) Once dried and pinned as a specimen, dragonflies lose most of their color and become increasing fragile.
(C) Once they have been dried and pinned as specimens, dragonflies lose most of their color, becoming increasing fragile.
(D) They were once dried and pinned as specimens, and then dragonflies lose most of their color and become increasingly fragile.
(E) Once dried and pinned as specimens, dragonflies lose most of their color and become increasingly fragile.

20. By the time Jews began to arrive in the United States in significant numbers in the early twentieth century, they already have established an affinity with political liberalism in Europe.

(A) they already have established an affinity with
(B) they all ready have established an affinity with
(C) they already have established an affinity for
(D) an affinity had already been established by them toward
(E) they already had established an affinity with

Practice Test 2

GO ON TO NEXT PAGE ►

The sentences in this section may contain errors in grammar, usage, choice of words, or idioms. There is either just one error per sentence, or the sentence is correct. Some words or phrases are underlined and lettered; everything else in the sentence is correct.

If an underlined word or phrase is incorrect, choose that letter; if the sentence is correct, select No error. Then blacken the appropriate space on your answer sheet.

EXAMPLE:

The region has a climate so severe that plants
A
growing there rarely had been more than twelve
B C
inches high. No error
D E

Ⓐ Ⓑ ● Ⓓ Ⓔ

21. After his heart attack, he was ordered to lay in bed
A B C
and rest for two weeks. No error
D E

22. While my aunt and I were traveling through our
A B C
national parks, my aunt was frightened by a bear.
D
No error
E

23. Only recently, the newly organized football
A B
association added two new teams to their league.
C D
No error
E

24. In view of the controversy with the school board,
A
neither the teachers nor the principal are being
B C
considered for salary increases at this time.
D
No error
E

25. While we have rummaged through the attic, we
A B
found not only an album of our trip to Europe
C
but also a multitude of old news clippings.
D
No error
E

26. Of all the members of the United States team,
A B
Greg Lemond was the first to win the prestigious
C D
Tour de France bike race. No error
E

27. Before we adopt this legislation, we ought to
A B
consider the affect the new law will have on our
C D
retired and disabled citizens. No error
E

28. The legendary Mark McGwire has established
A
an enviable record, and it probably will not
B C
be broken during the next fifty years. No error
D E

29. Toni Cade Bambara, who is a black American
A
writer, has been active in civil rights and women's
B
issues, nor is she attuned to Afro-American
C D
relationships. No error
E

30. The boom in sales of video cassette recorders can
A
be attributed to numerous things, including being
B C D
price reduction and the growth of rental stores.
No error
E

Practice Test 2

GO ON TO NEXT PAGE ▶

31. After a six-month study semester abroad, she was happy to get home to comfortable familiar surroundings and appetizing food. No error
(A: After; B: was; C: happy; D: comfortable familiar; E: No error)

32. The conductor's uncompromising manner at the podium sometimes created friction with orchestral players, who saw him as dictatorial. No error
(A: uncompromising; B: friction with; C: who; D: as; E: No error)

33. Because he has been warned only about the danger of walking on the railroad trestle, he dared several of his friends to walk on the tracks. No error
(A: has been warned; B: only; C: walking; D: several of; E: No error)

34. Where is it possible to find if it was James Russell Lowell or Henry Wadsworth Longfellow who wrote "Hiawatha"? No error
(A: if; B: was; C: or; D: who; E: No error)

Improving Paragraphs Directions

The passage below is the unedited draft of a student's essay. Some of the essay needs to be rewritten to make the meaning clearer and more precise. Read the essay carefully.

The essay is followed by questions about changes that might improve all or part of its organization, development, sentence structure, use of language, appropriateness to the audience, or use of standard written English. Choose the answer that most clearly and effectively expresses the student's intended meaning. Indicate your choice by filling in the corresponding space on the answer sheet.

[1] Although some people believe that certain celebrations have no point, celebrations are one of the few things that all people have in common. **[2]** They take place everywhere. **[3]** Listing all of them would be an impossible task. **[4]** People of all kinds look forward to celebrations for keeping traditions alive for generation after generation. **[5]** Those who criticize celebrations do not understand the human need to preserve tradition and culture.

[6] In the Muslim religion, the Ead is a celebration. **[7]** It begins as soon as Ramadan (the fasting month) is over. **[8]** During the Ead, families gather together. **[9]** New clothes are bought for children, and they receive money from both family and friends. **[10]** Also, each family, if they can afford it, slaughters a sheep or a cow. **[11]** They keep a small fraction of the meat, and the rest they must give to the poor. **[12]** They also donate money to a mosque.

[13] Many celebrations involve eating meals. **[14]** In the United States, people gather together on Thanksgiving to say thank you for their blessings by having a huge feast with turkey, sweet potatoes, and cranberry sauce. **[15]** Christmas and Easter holiday dinners are a custom in the Christian religion. **[16]** They have a roast at Christmas. **[17]** At Easter they serve ham. **[18]** The Jewish people celebrate Passover with a big meal called a seder. **[19]** They say prayers, drink wine, and sing songs to remember how Jews suffered centuries ago when they escaped from slavery in Egypt.

[20] A celebration is held each year to honor great people like Dr. Martin Luther King. **[21]** His birthday is celebrated because of this man's noble belief in equality of all races. **[22]** People wish to remember not only his famous speeches, including "I Have A Dream," but also about him being assassinated in Memphis in 1968. **[23]** He died while fighting for the equality of minorities. **[24]** Unlike religious celebrations, celebrations for great heroes like Martin Luther King are for all people everywhere in the world. **[25]** He is a world-class hero and he deserved the Nobel Prize for Peace that he won.

35. To improve the unity of the first paragraph, which of the following is the best sentence to delete?

(A) sentence 1
(B) sentence 2
(C) sentence 3
(D) sentence 4
(E) sentence 5

36. In the context of the third paragraph, which is the best way to combine sentences 15, 16, and 17?

(A) A roast at Christmas, ham at Easter—that's what Christians eat.
(B) Christians customarily serve a roast for Christmas dinner, at Easter ham is eaten.
(C) At customary holiday dinners, Christians eat a roast at Christmas and ham is for Easter dinner.
(D) Christians often celebrate the Christmas holiday with a roast for dinner and Easter with a traditional ham.
(E) Christmas and Easter dinners are the custom in the Christian religion, where they have a roast at Christmas and ham at Easter.

GO ON TO NEXT PAGE ►

37. In an effort to provide a more effective transition between paragraphs 3 and 4, which of the following would be the best revision of sentence 20 below?

A celebration is held each year to honor great people like Dr. Martin Luther King.

(A) There are also some celebrations to honor great people like Dr. Martin Luther King.
(B) Martin Luther King is also celebrated in the United States.
(C) In the United States, celebrating to honor great people like Dr. Martin Luther King has become a tradition.
(D) In addition to observing religious holidays, people hold celebrations to honor great leaders like Dr. Martin Luther King.
(E) Besides holding religion-type celebrations, celebrations to honor great people like Dr. Martin Luther King are also held.

38. Which is the best revision of the underlined segment of sentence 22 below?

People wish to remember not only his famous speeches, including "I Have A Dream," but <u>also about him being assassinated</u> in Memphis in 1968.

(A) that his assassination occurred
(B) about his being assassination
(C) the fact that he was assassinated
(D) about the assassination, too,
(E) his assassination

39. Considering the essay as a whole, which one of the following best explains the main function of the last paragraph?

(A) to summarize the main idea of the essay
(B) to refute a previous argument stated in the essay
(C) to give an example
(D) to provide a solution to a problem
(E) to evaluate the validity of the essay's main idea

Practice Test 2

IF YOU FINISH IN LESS THAN 30 MINUTES, YOU MAY CHECK YOUR WORK ON THIS SECTION ONLY. DO NOT TURN TO ANY OTHER SECTION IN THE TEST.

STOP

Answer Key

Section 1 Critical Reading

1. **D**	6. **C**	11. **D**	16. **C**	21. **E**
2. **C**	7. **C**	12. **E**	17. **C**	22. **E**
3. **A**	8. **B**	13. **D**	18. **D**	23. **B**
4. **B**	9. **E**	14. **C**	19. **C**	24. **C**
5. **E**	10. **C**	15. **B**	20. **C**	

Section 2 Mathematics

1. **E**	5. **C**	9. **C**	13. **D**	17. **C**
2. **C**	6. **A**	10. **C**	14. **D**	18. **E**
3. **C**	7. **B**	11. **D**	15. **D**	19. **E**
4. **B**	8. **A**	12. **D**	16. **E**	20. **A**

Section 3 Critical Reading

25. **E**	30. **E**	35. **A**	40. **D**	45. **E**
26. **B**	31. **C**	36. **B**	41. **C**	46. **C**
27. **E**	32. **E**	37. **E**	42. **A**	47. **C**
28. **A**	33. **C**	38. **B**	43. **C**	48. **C**
29. **D**	34. **E**	39. **B**	44. **B**	

Section 4 Mathematics

21. **C**	23. **C**	25. **D**	27. **C**
22. **B**	24. **A**	26. **C**	28. **B**

29.

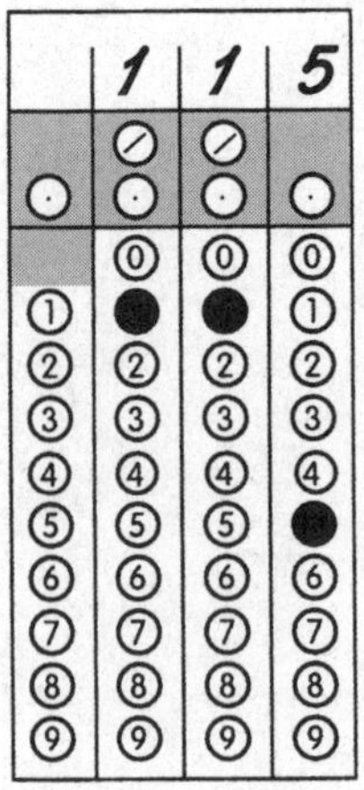

30.

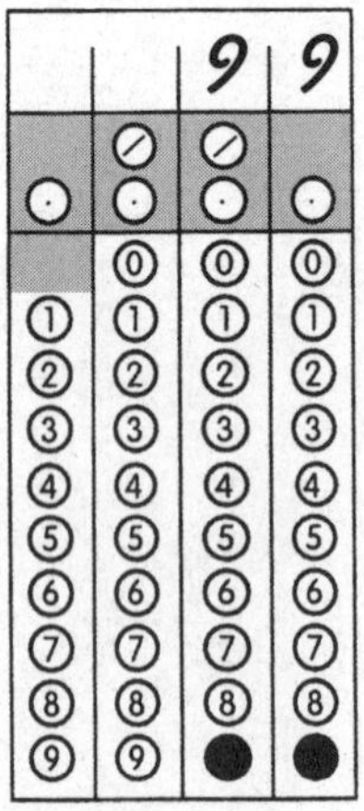

31.

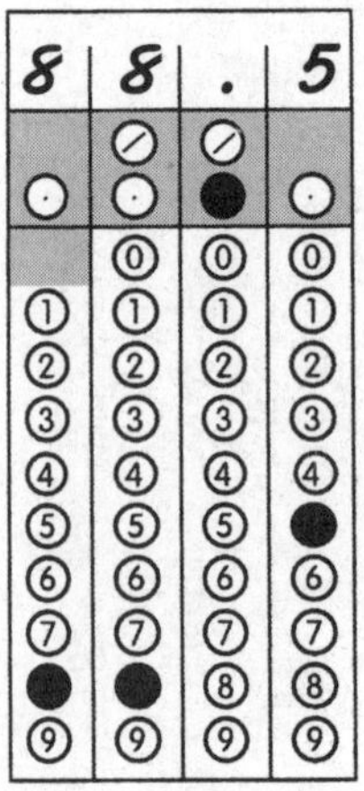

32.

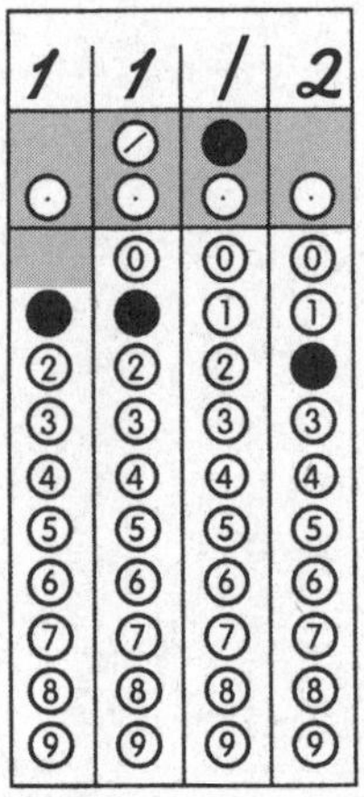

or ***5.5***

33.
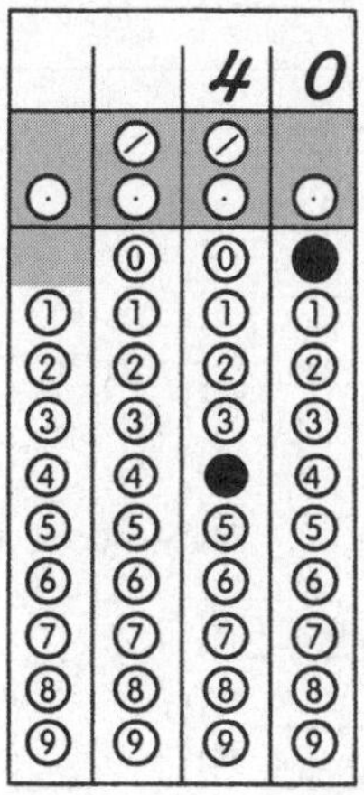

34.
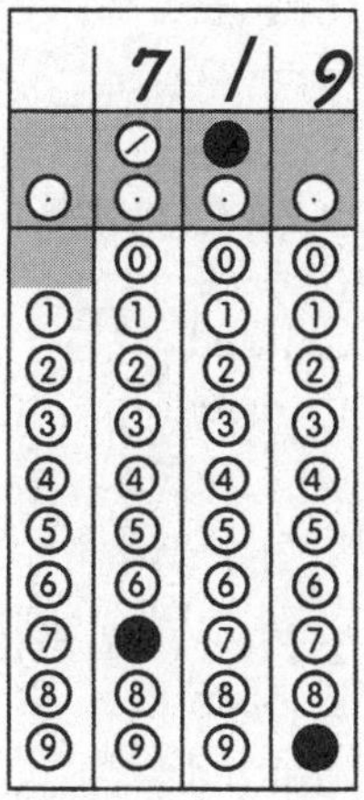

or *.777* or *.778*

35.
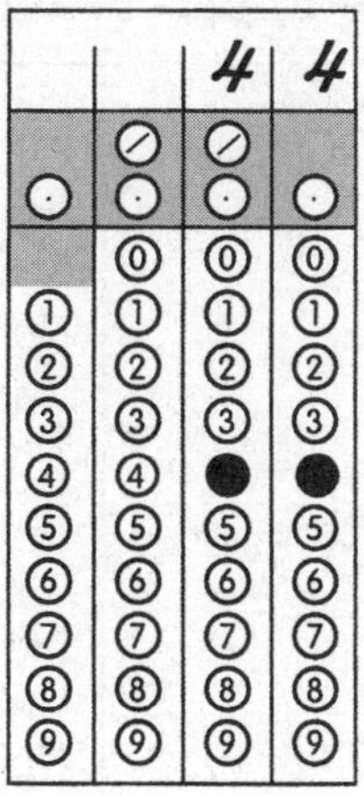

36.
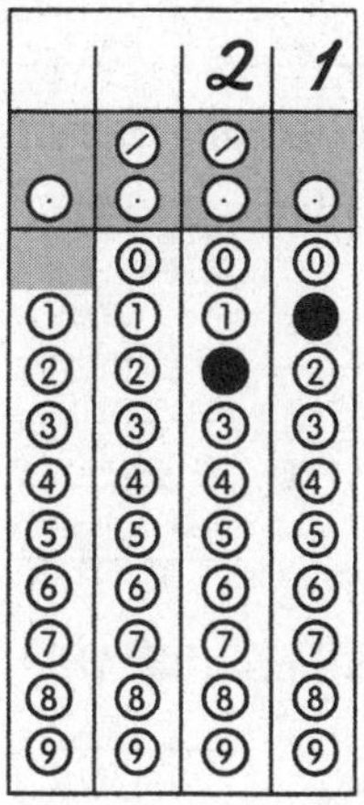

37.
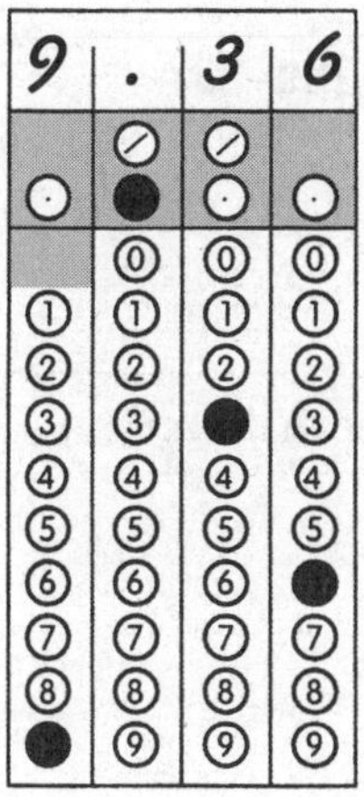

38.
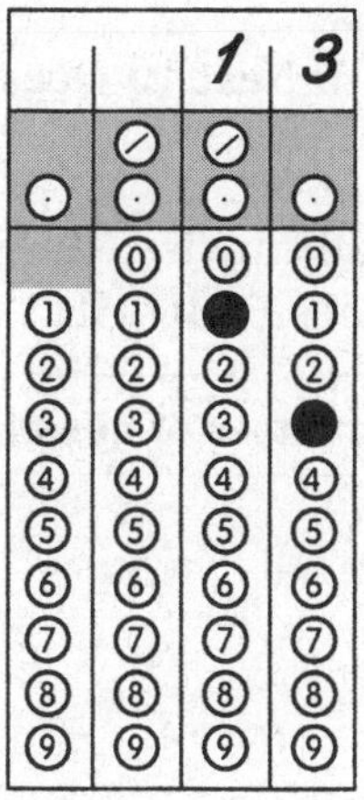

Section 5 Writing Skills

1.	**C**	9.	**C**	17.	**E**	25.	**A**	33.	**A**
2.	**C**	10.	**A**	18.	**D**	26.	**E**	34.	**A**
3.	**D**	11.	**A**	19.	**E**	27.	**C**	35.	**C**
4.	**C**	12.	**A**	20.	**E**	28.	**C**	36.	**D**
5.	**B**	13.	**E**	21.	**C**	29.	**C**	37.	**D**
6.	**D**	14.	**C**	22.	**E**	30.	**D**	38.	**E**
7.	**D**	15.	**C**	23.	**D**	31.	**D**	39.	**C**
8.	**A**	16.	**A**	24.	**C**	32.	**E**		

Scoring Chart—Practice Test 2

Critical Reading Sections

Section 1: 24 Questions (1–24)

Number correct ________ (A)
Number omitted ________ (B)
Number incorrect ________ (C)
$\frac{1}{4}$ (C) ________ (D)
(A) − (D) ________ Raw Score I

Section 3: 24 Questions (25–48)

Number correct ________ (A)
Number omitted ________ (B)
Number incorrect ________ (C)
$\frac{1}{4}$ (C) ________ (D)
(A) − (D) ________ Raw Score II

Total Critical Reading Raw Score

Raw Scores I + II ________

Mathematics Sections

Section 2: 20 Questions (1–20)

Number correct ________ (A)
Number omitted ________ (B)
Number incorrect ________ (C)
$\frac{1}{4}$ (C) ________ (D)
(A) − (D) ________ Raw Score I

Section 4: First 8 Questions (21–28)

Number correct ________ (A)
Number omitted ________ (B)
Number incorrect ________ (C)
$\frac{1}{4}$ (C) ________ (D)
(A) − (D) ________ Raw Score II

Section 4: Next 10 Questions (29–38)

Number correct ________ Raw Score III

Total Mathematics Raw Score

Raw Scores I + II + III ________

NOTE: In each section (A) + (B) + (C) should equal the number of questions in that section.

Writing Skills Section

Section 5: 39 Questions (1–39)

Number correct ________ (A)
Number omitted ________ (B)
Number incorrect ________ (C)
$\frac{1}{4}$ (C) ________ (D)

Writing Skills Raw Score

(A) − (D) ________

Evaluation Chart

Study your score. Your raw score is an indication of your probable achievement on the PSAT/NMSQT. As a guide to the amount of work you need or want to do with this book, study the following.

Raw Score			Self-Rating
Critical Reading	*Mathematics*	*Writing Skills*	
42–48	35–38	33–39	Superior
37–41	30–34	28–32	Very good
32–36	25–29	23–27	Good
26–31	21–24	17–22	Above average
20–25	17–20	12–16	Average
12–19	10–16	7–11	Below average
less than 12	less than 10	less than 7	Inadequate

ANSWER EXPLANATIONS

Section 1 Critical Reading

1. **(D)** Such an extraordinarily useful material would *revolutionize* or make radical changes in an industry. The key word here is "Impressed." This tells you that the missing word must be positive in nature. You can immediately eliminate *alienate* (estrange; make unfriendly) and *nullify* (invalidate; make futile). Likewise, *justify* (warrant; show to be just or right) and *overestimate* (overrate; give excessive importance to) make no sense in the context.

2. **(C)** A contrast is set up here by the expression "no matter how." It tells us that, although future "revelations" (surprising news) may be *striking*, they will not equal past ones. These past revelations *radically* transformed or thoroughly changed our view.

   Choice A is incorrect. *Minor* means unimportant. It makes no sense in the context. Choice B is incorrect. *Profound* (very deep; great) revelations would make great changes in our view of the emergence of Mayan civilization. It makes no sense to say such revelations would have transformed it *negligibly* (insignificantly; only in a minor way). Choice D is incorrect. It makes no sense to say that truly *bizarre* (strange; weird) revelations would have transformed our view of the emergence of Mayan civilization only *nominally* (minimally; in name only). Choice E is incorrect. *Questionable* means dubious or debatable. It makes no sense in the context.

3. **(A)** Since "few other plants can grow beneath the canopy of the sycamore," it must be *inhibiting* or restraining the other plants. What is an herbicide? It is something that kills plants. It definitely does not *nourish* (feed; nurture), *encourage*, or *refresh* them. It makes no sense to say that it *distinguishes* (recognizes differences between; perceives) them.

4. **(B)** Certain authors have been *relegated* or sent off to "obscurity," a state of being hidden or forgotten. There they must be "rediscovered."

   Choice A is incorrect. *Inclined* means mentally disposed or apt to do something. It makes no sense in this context. Choice C is incorrect. *Subjected* means made vulnerable to or exposed to. Although it is a possible answer choice, it is not the word that *best* fits the meaning of the sentence as a whole. Choice D is incorrect. *Diminished* means lessened or made smaller. It would be unidiomatic to describe someone or something as being "diminished to obscurity." Choice E is incorrect. *Characterized* means described. It makes no sense to describe someone or something as being "characterized to obscurity."

5. **(E)** Critics sometimes praise but more often *decry* or condemn things. Here the critics see the "saccharine" (too sweet) mood of the movie as inconsistent with the *acerbic* (sour, bitter) tone of the book. The key phrase here is "out of keeping." It signals a contrast. The movie's tone is overly optimistic. The book's tone, therefore, cannot be optimistic. *Hopeful* and *sanguine* are synonyms for *optimistic*. Therefore, you can eliminate Choices B and D. Similarly, critics of the movie dislike its being so sugary and overoptimistic. The critics condemn the change of tone; they do not *applaud* or *acclaim* (praise) it.

6. **(C)** If poetry fans can fill an entire football stadium, there must be a lot of them. Thus, the reference to the football stadium suggests the size of the audience for poetry and thus *emphasizes the popularity of poetry in the period.*

7. **(C)** To say that literature enjoyed a central place in the culture is to say that literature *possessed* or occupied such a place.

8. **(B)** The statement "we're dying anyway" is an example of a *metaphor* or implicit comparison. The author does not mean that he and his fellow poets are literally dying; they are dying metaphorically (figuratively), for their poetry does not matter to anyone, and to be ignored feels like death.

9. **(E)** The time when poetry mattered "is long gone." In America "no one cares." Clearly the authors of Passage 1 and Passage 2 agree that *the climate for poetry in America is inauspicious* (unfavorable).

Note the following icons, used throughout this book:

Time saver	Look it up; math reference fact	Helpful Hint
Educated guess	Prefixes, roots, and suffixes	Caution!
Did you notice?	Positive or negative?	Calculator use is recommended

10. **(C)** Among other clues, Mr. Collins states that he hopes to lead Elizabeth "to the altar ere long."

11. **(D)** Elizabeth is "sensible of the honour" Mr. Collins is paying her by proposing. She is all too *keenly aware* of his intentions and wants nothing to do with them.

12. **(E)** Elizabeth expects that by refusing Mr. Collins's proposal, she will *put an end to his suit*; that is the result she desires. However, her rejection *fails* to have this intended effect. Instead, Mr. Collins in his stubbornness and conceit continues to pursue her and even takes her refusal as an encouraging sign.

13. **(D)** Mr. Collins breaks off in the middle of a sentence that begins, "Were it certain that Lady Catherine would think so—." He then finishes it awkwardly by saying, "but I cannot imagine that her ladyship would at all disapprove of you." By implication, his unspoken thought was that, if Lady Catherine *didn't* approve of Elizabeth, then Mr. Collins wouldn't want to marry her after all.

14. **(C)** Mr. Collins plans to praise Elizabeth to Lady Catherine in order to ensure Lady Catherine's approval of his bride. Elizabeth insists all such praise will be unnecessary because she *has no intention of marrying Mr. Collins* and thus has no need of Lady Catherine's approval.

15. **(B)** *Obtuse* means thickheaded, and *obstinate* means stubborn. Both apply to Mr. Collins, who can't seem to understand that Elizabeth is telling him "no."

16. **(C)** The author's emphasis is on the elephant as an important "creator of habitat" for other creatures.

17. **(C)** To mount an effort to rescue an endangered species is to *launch* or initiate a campaign.

18. **(D)** The elephant is the architect of its environment in that it *physically alters its environment*, transforming the landscape around it.

19. **(C)** The author states that it is the elephant's metabolism and appetite—in other words, its voracity or *ravenous hunger*—that leads to its creating open spaces in the woodland and transforming the landscape.

20. **(C)** Since the foraging of elephants creates a varied landscape that attracts a diverse group of plant-eating animals and since the presence of these plant eaters in turn attracts carnivores, it follows that elephants *have an indirect effect on the hunting patterns of carnivores*.

21. **(E)** Here the phrase "keystone species" *is being used in a special or technical sense* to mean a species whose very presence contributes to a diversity of life and whose extinction would consequently lead to the extinction of other forms of life.

22. **(E)** You can arrive at the correct answer choice through the process of elimination.

Question I is answerable on the basis of the passage. The elephant's foraging opens up its surroundings by knocking down trees and stripping off branches. Therefore, you can eliminate Choices B and D.

Question II is answerable on the basis of the passage. Gazelles are grazers; giraffes are browsers. Therefore, you can eliminate Choice A.

Question III is answerable on the basis of the passage. The concluding sentence states that when elephants disappear, the forest reverts. Therefore, you can eliminate Choice C.

Only Choice E is left. It is the correct answer.

23. **(B)** The author is listing the many species that depend on the elephant as a creator of habitat. Thus, the host of smaller animals is the *very large number* of these creatures that thrive in the elephant's wake.

24. **(C)** The author is in favor of the effect of elephants on the environment; he feels an accidental or *fortuitous result* of their foraging is that it allows a greater variety of creatures to exist in mixed-growth environments.

Section 2 Mathematics

For many problems, the explanation provides a reference to one or more **KEY FACTS** from Chapter 7. These are the mathematical facts that you need to solve that problem. If a solution refers to **KEY FACT J2**, for example, the solution depends on the second **KEY FACT** discussed in Section J of Chapter 7.

For some problems, an alternative solution, indicated by two asterisks (**), follows the first solution. When this occurs, usually one of the solutions is the direct mathematical one and the other is based on one of the tactics discussed in Chapters 6 and 7.

See page 234 for an explanation of the symbol ⇒, which is used in several answer explanations.

1. **(E)** $b - 8 = 0 \Rightarrow b = 8 \Rightarrow b + 8 = 16$.

2. **(C)** If Isaac has twice as many toys as Sydney, then Sydney has half as many as Isaac: $\frac{t}{2}$. This is so easy that you shouldn't have to plug in a number, but you could: If Isaac has 10 toys, then Sydney has 5, and only Choice C equals 5 when t is 10.

3. **(C)** By **KEY FACT J2**, the measure of an exterior angle of a triangle is equal to the sum of the measures of the two opposite interior angles; so

$140 = x + x = 2x \Rightarrow x = 70.$

**Let the third angle in the triangle be y. Then $140 + y = 180 \Rightarrow y = 40$; and

$40 + x + x = 180 \Rightarrow x = 70.$

4. **(B)** Since $1{,}000{,}000 = 10^6$, then

$$2n + 1 = 6 \Rightarrow 2n = 5 \Rightarrow n = 2.5.$$

5. **(C)** Use your calculator: $1.5 \times 1.7 = 2.55$, which, to the nearest tenth, is 2.6.

6. **(A)** Since the circle's diameter is 4, its radius is 2, and by **KEY FACT L8** its area is $\pi(2)^2 = 4\pi$. Since the area of the square is also 4π, the length of each side is $\sqrt{4\pi} = 2\sqrt{\pi}$.

7. **(B)** Set up a proportion and cross-multiply:

$$\frac{\text{inches}}{\text{miles}} = \frac{\frac{1}{3}}{14} = \frac{x}{30}.$$

Then, $14x = 30\left(\frac{1}{3}\right) = 10$, and $x = \frac{10}{14} = \frac{5}{7}$.

8. **(A)** Since the area of the square is 36, its sides are 6, and its perimeter is 24. Since the perimeter of the hexagon is also 24, each of its six sides is 4.

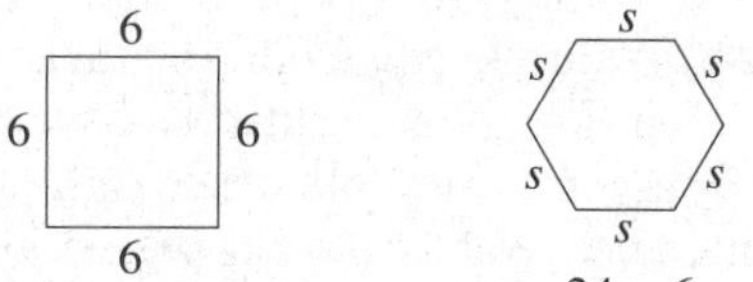

$P = 24$ $\qquad$ $24 = 6s$, $s = 4$

9. **(C)** The first step is to calculate (3◇)(◆5):

(3◇)(◆5) = $(3 + 1)(5 - 1) = 4 \times 4 = 16$.

Now check each answer until you find one that is NOT equal to 16.

A: (1◇)(◆9) = $(1 + 1)(9 - 1) = (2)(8) = 16$.
B: (7◇)(◆9) = $(7 + 1) + (9 - 1) = 8 + 8 = 16$.
C: (4◇)(◆4) = $(4 + 1)(4 - 1) = 5 \times 3 \neq 16$.

10. **(C)** Pick an integer for $\frac{n+2}{5}$, say 2. Then

$$\frac{n+2}{5} = 2 \Rightarrow n + 2 = 10 \Rightarrow n = 8,$$

and 5 goes into 8 once with a remainder of 3.

11. **(D)** Let n represent the number of students in the class other than Michelle. These n students earned a total of $85n$ points (**TACTIC E1**). When Michelle was included, there were $n + 1$ students who earned a total of $85n + 30$ points. Since the class average was then 80:

$$80 = \frac{85n + 30}{n + 1} \Rightarrow$$
$$85n + 30 = 80(n + 1) = 80n + 80 \Rightarrow$$

$5n = 50 \Rightarrow n = 10$, and so $n + 1 = 11$.

Use **TACTIC 6-1: backsolve, starting with Choice C. If there were 10 children in the class, the 9 students other than Michelle would have earned $9 \times 85 = 765$ points, and so including Michelle, the total number of points earned would have been $765 + 30 = 795$ points. The class average, then, would have been $\frac{795}{10} = 79.5$, which is just a little too low. Eliminate Choices A, B, and C, and try Choice D, which works.

12. **(D)** At the regular price, a CD costs d dollars; at 20% off, each one costs 80% of d dollars:

$$\frac{80}{100}(d) = \frac{80d}{100} = \frac{4d}{5} \text{ dollars.}$$

To find out how many you can buy, divide the amount of money, m, by the price per CD, $\frac{4d}{5}$:

$$m \div \frac{4d}{5} = m\left(\frac{5}{4d}\right) = \frac{5m}{4d}.$$

Use **TACTIC 6-3 and plug in easy-to-use numbers. If CDs regularly cost \$10, then on sale at 20% off, they cost \$8 each. How many can be purchased on sale for \$40? The answer is 5. Which of the choices equals 5 when $d = 10$ and $m = 40$? Only $\frac{5m}{4d}$.

13. **(D)** Since 16 of the 40 people have neither a dog nor a cat, 24 people have at least one, possibly both. Since 18 of those 24 have cats, 6 of them have dogs, but no cat. But since 13 have dogs, it must be that 7 dog owners also have cats.

**A Venn diagram may make this easier.

Let x = the number of people who have both a cat and a dog.

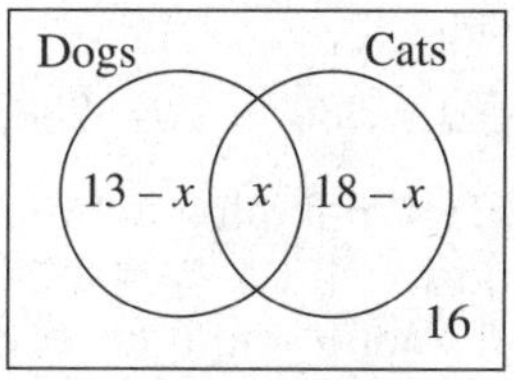

$$(13 - x) + x + (18 - x) = 24 \Rightarrow$$
$$31 - x = 24 \Rightarrow x = 7.$$

14. **(D)** $3|x| + 1 < 16 \Rightarrow 3|x| < 15 \Rightarrow |x| < 5$. There are 9 integers whose absolute value is less than 5: $-4, -3, -2, -1, 0, 1, 2, 3, 4$.

15. **(D)** The mode is 8, since more people have 8 teddy bears than any other number. Since there are 15 members, the median is the eighth piece of data when arranged in increasing order; so the median is 10. Finally, the average of 8 and 10 is 9.

16. **(E)** By **KEY FACT A21**,

$$3^{\frac{1}{2}} \times 3^{\frac{1}{3}} \times 3^{\frac{1}{6}} = 3^{\left(\frac{1}{2}+\frac{1}{3}+\frac{1}{6}\right)} = 3^1 = 3$$

**Just enter the given expression into your calculator.

17. **(C)** Label the diagram as shown below, letting *s* and *S* be the sides of squares *ABCD* and *EFGH*, respectively.

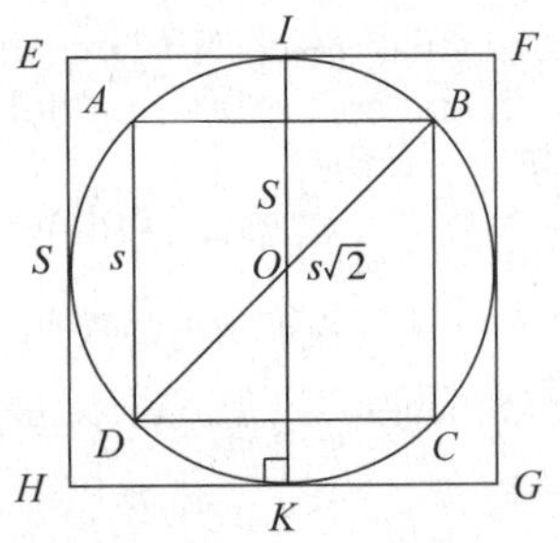

Since $\triangle DAB$ is a 45-45-90 right triangle, $BD = s\sqrt{2}$. Draw line segment $\overline{IK}$ through center *O* and perpendicular to $\overline{GH}$. Then $IK = HE = S$. Notice that *BD* and *IK* are each diameters of circle *O*, so $BD = IK$, which means that

$$S = s\sqrt{2} \Rightarrow \frac{S}{s} = \sqrt{2} \Rightarrow \frac{S^2}{s^2} = 2.$$

Since s^2 and S^2 are the areas of the squares, the desired ratio is 2 : 1.

18. **(E)** Since the diameter of the circle is 10, the radius is 5 and the area is 25π. Also, since the area of the shaded region is 20π, it is $\frac{20}{25} = \frac{4}{5}$ of the circle, and the white area is $\frac{1}{5}$ of the circle. Then the sum of the measures of the two white central angles is $\frac{1}{5}$ of 360°, or 72°. The sum of the measures of all six angles in the two triangles is $2 \times 180° = 360°$; so

$a + b + c + d = 360 - 72 = 288.$

19. **(E)** Use **TACTIC 6-3**: plug in numbers for *r* and *s*. Let $r = 2$ and $s = 1$. So $2s = 2$, $a = 4$ and $b = 0$. Now, plug in 4 for *a* and 0 for *b* and see which of the five choices is equal to 2. Only E works: $\frac{a^2 - b^2}{8} = \frac{4^2 - 0^2}{8} = \frac{16}{8} = 2.$

**Here is the correct algebraic solution.

Add the two equations:

$$\begin{array}{r} r + 2s = a \\ + \; r - 2s = b \\ \hline 2r = a + b \end{array}$$

Divide by 2: $r = \frac{a+b}{2}$

Now, multiply the second equation by -1 and add it to the first:

$$\begin{array}{r} r + 2s = a \\ + \; -r + 2s = -b \\ \hline 4s = a - b \end{array}$$

Divide by 4: $s = \frac{a-b}{4}$

So, $rs = \frac{a+b}{2} \cdot \frac{a-b}{4} = \frac{a^2 - b^2}{8}.$

This is the type of algebra you want to avoid.

20. **(A)** $a + 25\%(a) = 1.25a$, and $b - 25\%(b) = 0.75b$.

So, $1.25a = .75b$, and $\frac{a}{b} = \frac{.75}{1.25} = \frac{75}{125} = \frac{3}{5}$

**If after increasing *a* and decreasing *b*, the results are equal, *a* must be smaller than *b*. So, *the ratio of a to b must be less than 1*. Eliminate Choices C, D, and E. Now, either test Choices A and B, or just guess. To test Choice B, pick two numbers in the ratio of 3 to 4—30 and 40, for example. Then, 30 increased by 25% is 37.5, and 40 decreased by 25% is 30. The results are not equal; so eliminate Choice B. The answer is $\frac{3}{5}$. (Note that 50 decreased by 25% *is* 37.5.)

Section 3 Critical Reading

25. **(E)** To make the correct decisions, the lawmakers must be able to *discern* or recognize the truth. It would be counterproductive to have lawmakers *confuse* (bewilder), *condemn* (blame), or *ignore* (pay no attention to) the truth. To have them *condone* (excuse or overlook) the truth would not make them better able to make wise decisions.

26. **(B)** There is a chance that *serious* women may not be attracted by an inappropriate *frivolity* or lightheartedness in style—hence the gamble. Lighthearted, provocative dresses are unlikely examples of *reticence* (restraint; reserve), *tradition* (established custom), *harmony* (friendly agreement), or *propriety* (socially appropriate behavior).

27. **(E)** A customer service agent would try to *mollify* or soothe an *angry* passenger by giving her an upgrade to a better class of service.

Choice A is incorrect. *Placid* means calm. The customer service representative would have no need to *pacify* (calm) an already placid passenger. Choice B is incorrect. *Thwart* means frustrate. Offering the passenger a seat in first class would not thwart her. Choice C is incorrect. *Divert* means distract or entertain. The passenger is grateful; the customer service representative does not need to divert her. Choice D is incorrect. *Authorize* means approve or give permission. *Listless* means weary and uninterested. Neither word makes sense in the context.

28. **(A)** If falling asleep at times you wouldn't normally wish to, you clearly would strike yourself as unusually *lethargic* (drowsily slow to respond; sluggish; listless). The key phrase here is "ready to drowse off." *Distracted* means preoccupied. *Obdurate* means pig-headedly stubborn. *Benign* means kindly; it can also mean harmless. *Perfunctory* means done routinely and without enthusiasm. None of these words conveys a sense of drowsiness.

29. **(D)** A *euphemism* is by definition a mild expression used in place of a more unpleasant or distressing one. The blunt expression "he died" is unpleasantly direct for some people, who substitute the vague euphemism "he passed away."

    Choice A is incorrect. A *reminder* is a memory aid. Choice B is incorrect. A *commiseration* is an expression of sympathy. Choice C is incorrect. A *simile* is a figure of speech drawing a comparison between two things. "My love is like a red, red rose" is an example of a simile. Choice E is incorrect. An *exaggeration* is an overstatement. "I could eat a horse" is an example of an exaggeration.

30. **(E)** *Despite* signals a contrast. If someone writes an enormously popular book, you would expect his career to prosper. Instead, White's career *foundered* or came to grief. Contrary to expectations, White's career did not do well. The missing word clearly must be negative. *Soared* (flew high; ascended to new heights), *endured* (survived; lasted through hardships), *accelerated* (gathered speed; progressed faster), and *revived* (flourished again) all are positive terms.

31. **(C)** Because it was written immediately after the assassination, the book has *immediacy*, but it lacks *perspective*; the author had not had enough time to distance himself from his immediate reactions to the event and think about it. The key phrases here are "just after Martin Luther King's assassination" and "long and mature reflection upon events."

    Choice A is incorrect. *Precision* (exactness) and *accuracy* (correctness) are synonyms. The author is drawing a contrast between the virtues the book has and the virtues it lacks. The missing words must be antonyms or near-antonyms. Choice B is incorrect. *Criticism* or assessment makes no sense in the context. Choice D is incorrect. Neither *outlook* (viewpoint; attitude) nor *realism* (theory of representing real life accurately without idealizing it) makes sense in the context. Choice E is incorrect. *Currency* is the quality of being prevalent or current. *Testimony* is the solemn declaration made by a witness under oath. Neither word makes sense in the context.

32. **(E)** The key word here is "chagrin." Because Costner has triumphed, the critics who predicted his *failure* feel chagrin (great annoyance mixed with disappointment or humiliation). Costner, for his part, greatly enjoys his success and especially enjoys or *savors* their embarrassment and vexation. Costner enjoys his critics' mortification. He does not *regret* (feel sorry for) it, *understate* (minimize) it, or *distort* (misrepresent or twist) it. He does more than merely *acknowledge* it (grant that it exists).

33. **(C)** The next sentence says that these stones in actuality are plants. Thus, the quotation marks around the word "stones" serve to underscore that these stonelike objects *are not literally stones*.

34. **(E)** Examine the context: "These stones are in actuality *plants*, members of the genus Lithops, some of the strangest succulents in the world." A succulent is clearly *a kind of plant*.

35. **(A)** Chomsky and others contend that the capacity for language is a uniquely human property or *trait*.

36. **(B)** Where Chomsky and Savage-Rambaugh differ has to do with the primates' capacity to use language, in other words, their *abilities in language acquisition*.

37. **(E)** The italicized introduction states that the author has had his manuscript rejected by his publisher. He is consigning or committing it to a desk drawer *to set it aside as unmarketable*.

38. **(B)** The rejected author identifies with these baseball players, who constantly must face "failure." *He sees he is not alone in having to confront failure and move on.*

39. **(B)** The author uses the jogger's comment to make a point about the *mental impact Henderson's home run must have had on Moore*. He reasons that, if each step a runner takes sends so many complex messages to the brain, then Henderson's ninth-inning home run must have flooded Moore's brain with messages, impressing its image indelibly in Moore's mind.

40. **(D)** The author is talking of the impact of Henderson's home run on Moore's mind. Registering in Moore's mind, the home run *made an impression* on him.

41. **(C)** The author looks on himself as someone who "to succeed at all . . . must perform at an extraordinary level of excellence." This level of excellence, he maintains, is not demanded of accountants, plumbers, and insurance salesmen, and he seems to pride himself on belonging to such a demanding profession. Thus, his attitude to members of less demanding professions can best be described as *superior*.

42. **(A)** The description of the writer defying his pain and extending himself irrationally to create a "masterpiece" despite the rejections of critics and publishers is a highly romantic one that elevates *the writer as someone heroic in his or her accomplishments*.

43. **(C)** The author of Passage 2 discusses the advantages of his ability to concentrate. Clearly, he prizes *his ability to focus* on the task at hand.

44. **(B)** When one football team is ahead of another by several touchdowns and there seems to be no way for the second team to catch up, the outcome of the game appears *decided* or settled.

45. **(E)** The "larger point of view" focuses on what to most people is the big question: the outcome of the game. The author is indifferent to this larger point of view. Concentrating on his own performance, he is *more concerned with the task at hand than with* winning or losing the game.

46. **(C)** Parade ground drill clearly does not entirely prepare a soldier for the reality of war. It only does so "to an extent." By using this phrase, the author is *qualifying his statement*, making it less absolute.

47. **(C)** One would expect someone who dismisses or rejects most comparisons of athletics to art to avoid making such comparisons. The author, however, *is making such a comparison*. This reversal of what would have been expected is an instance of irony.

48. **(C)** To learn to overcome failure, to learn to give one's all in performance, to learn to focus on the work of the moment, to learn "the selfish intensity needed to create and to finish a poem, a story, or a novel"—these are hard lessons that *both athletes and artists learn*.

Practice Test 2

Section 4 Mathematics

For many problems, the explanation provides a reference to one or more **KEY FACTS** from Chapter 7. These are the mathematical facts that you need to solve that problem. If a solution refers to **KEY FACT J2**, for example, the solution depends on the second **KEY FACT** discussed in Section J of Chapter 7.

For some problems, an alternative solution, indicated by two asterisks (**), follows the first solution. When this occurs, usually one of the solutions is the direct mathematical one and the other is based on one of the tactics discussed in Chapters 6 and 7.

See page 234 for an explanation of the symbol ⇒, which is used in several answer explanations.

21. **(C)** The weight of the fruit is $5 + 3 + 1 = 9$ pounds, of which 3 pounds are oranges. Hence, the desired fraction is $\frac{3}{9} = \frac{1}{3}$.

22. **(B)** Since the sum of the five angles is 180°:

$$4a + 40 = 180 \Rightarrow 4a = 140 \Rightarrow a = 35.$$

23. **(C)** Use **TACTIC 6-3** and choose an easy-to-use number. Since $\frac{5}{8}$ of the members are boys, assume there are 8 members, 5 of whom are boys. Then the other 3 are girls, and the ratio of girls to boys is 3 to 5, or $\frac{3}{5}$.

24. **(A)** Refer to the figures below.

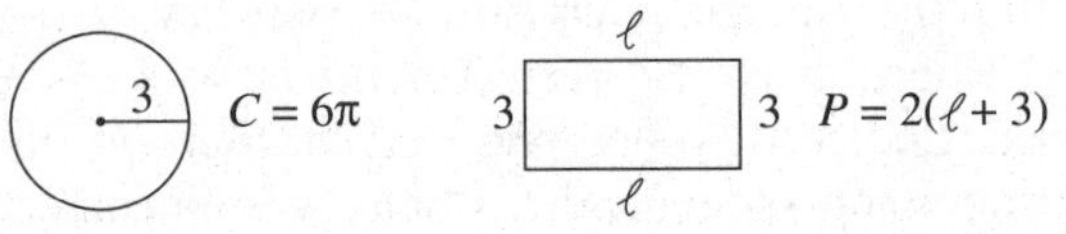

The circumference of a circle of radius 3 is 6π (**KEY FACT L4**). By **KEY FACT K5**, the perimeter of a rectangle is $2(\ell + w)$, so $6\pi = 2(\ell + 3)$. So, $\ell + 3 = 3\pi$ and $\ell = 3\pi - 3$.

25. **(D)** $13 - 11 = 2$, so I could be true. Since $5 + 7 + 11 = 23$, III could be true. Since all primes greater than 5 are odd, $p + q$ must be even and so cannot be a prime. (Statement II is false.) Statements I and III only are true.

26. **(C)** Use the distance formula, **KEY FACT N2**, to calculate the length of diameter $\overline{AB}$:

$$AB = \sqrt{(7-3)^2 + (2-(-2))^2} = \sqrt{4^2 + 4^2} = \sqrt{32}.$$

So the diameter is $\sqrt{32}$ and the radius is $\frac{\sqrt{32}}{2}$.

Then, by **KEY FACT L8**, the area is

$$A = \pi r^2 = \pi\left(\frac{\sqrt{32}}{2}\right)^2 = \pi\left(\frac{32}{4}\right) = 8\pi.$$

Note: You do not need to simplify $\sqrt{32}$. You also don't need to use your calculator to evaluate $\sqrt{32}$, but if you do, don't round off. Take whatever appears in your calculator's window, divide it by 2 and then square it—you will get exactly 8. Of course, *do not* multiply by 3.14.

27. **(C)** $13 - 2\sqrt{x} = 7 \Rightarrow -2\sqrt{x} = -6 \Rightarrow \sqrt{x} = 3$. So, $x = 9$.

You can use **TACTIC 6-1 and backsolve. Choice C, 9, works.

28. **(B)** The trust received 80% of the estate (10% went to the man's wife, 5% to his children, and 5% to his grandchildren). If E represents the value of the estate, then $0.80E = 1{,}000{,}000$. Therefore,

$$E = 1{,}000{,}000 \div .80 = 1{,}250{,}000.$$

Each grandchild received 1% (one fifth of 5%) of the estate: $.01 \times \$1{,}250{,}000 = \$12{,}500$.

29. **(115)** We can find any or all of the angles in the figure. One way to get w is to note that since $\overline{PS}$ is an angle bisector, the measure of $\angle PST = 25$ and so, by **KEY FACT J2**, $w = 25 + 90 = 115$.

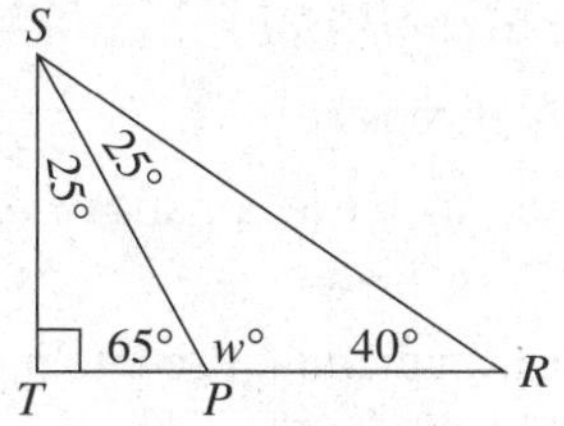

30. **(99)** From the 109 people in front of Wendy, remove Peter plus the 9 people in front of Peter: $109 - 10 = 99$.

31. **(88.5)** $(x + 1) + (x + 2) = 180 \Rightarrow 2x + 3 = 180$. So, $2x = 177 \Rightarrow x = 88.5$.

32. $\left(\frac{11}{2} \text{ or } 5.5\right)$ To make the fraction $\frac{r-s}{t}$ as large as possible, make the numerator, $r - s$, as large as you can, and the denominator t, as small as you can. So let t be 2, the smallest prime. In order for the difference $r - s$ to be as large as possible, let r be large, and subtract as little as possible. Therefore, let r be 13, the largest prime less than 15, and let s be 2, the smallest prime. (Note that the question did not say that s and t had to be different, only that they had to be primes.) Finally,

$$\frac{r-s}{t} = \frac{13-2}{2} = \frac{11}{2} \text{ or } 5.5.$$

33. **(40)** To solve the equation $\frac{2}{x} + \frac{3}{4} = \frac{4}{5}$, subtract $\frac{3}{4}$ from each side:

$$\frac{2}{x} + \frac{3}{4} = \frac{4}{5} \Rightarrow \frac{2}{x} = \frac{1}{20} \Rightarrow x = 40$$

Note: Do not waste time getting a common denominator; just use your calculator.

34. $\left(\frac{7}{9} \text{ or } .777 \text{ or } .778\right)$ Since the radius of the large circle is 3 by **KEY FACT L8**, its area is 9π. Each of the small circles has a radius of 1 and an area of π. So the total area of the white region is 2π, leaving 7π for the area of the shaded region. Therefore, the probability that P lies in the shaded region is $\frac{7\pi}{9\pi} = \frac{7}{9}$.

35. **(44)** Since the diameters of the circles are in the ratio of 12:10 or 6:5, the ratio of their areas is $6^2{:}5^2 = 36{:}25$. Convert the ratio to a percent:

$$36:25 = \frac{36}{25} = \frac{144}{100} = 144\%.$$

So, the area of the large circle is 144% of the area of the small one, or is 44% *more* than the area of the small one.

**With your calculator, actually calculate the areas. The radius of the large circle is 6, so its area is $\pi(6)^2 = 36\pi$. Similarly, the radius of the small circle is 5 and its area is $\pi(5)^2 = 25\pi$. The difference in the areas is $36\pi - 25\pi = 11\pi$, and 11π is 44% of 25π $\left(\frac{11\pi}{25\pi} = \frac{11}{25} = \frac{44}{100}\right)$.

36. **(21)** For the third place share to be as large as possible, the fourth place share must be as small as possible. However, it must be more than 10, so let it be 11. Then the amount, in dollars, left for second and third place is $100 - (35 + 11 + 10) = 100 - 56 = 44$. So, the second place share could be \$23 and the third place share \$21.

37. **(9.36)** For the average to be as high as possible, each student needs to have scored the maximum number of points. Therefore, assume that each of the 22 students who passed earned a grade of 10, that only one student earned a 2, and that the other two students who failed each earned a 6, the highest possible failing grade. Then the average is $\frac{10(22) + 2 + 2(6)}{25} = \frac{234}{25} = 9.36$.

38. **(13)** Since π is approximately 3.14, 2π is approximately 6.28, and $[2\pi] = 6$. Now, be careful: -2π is approximately -6.28, and the largest integer less than -6.28 is -7. Finally,

$$[2\pi] - [-2\pi] = 6 - (-7) = 6 + 7 = 13.$$

Section 5 Writing Skills

1. **(C)** Comma splice. Choices A, D, and E are run-on sentences. Choice B is constructed awkwardly.

2. **(C)** The verb *want* (meaning wish or desire) customarily is followed by the infinitive. Sharp wished *to preserve* or save the old folk dances.

3. **(D)** This choice corrects the dangling modifier.

4. **(C)** Error in coordination and subordination. The subordinating conjunction *Although* best connects the sentence's two clauses.

5. **(B)** Comma splice. Choices A, C, and E are run-on sentences; Choice D is unidiomatic.

6. **(D)** Error in parallelism. Parallel structure is maintained in Choice D.

7. **(D)** Choices A, B, and E contain sentence fragments; Choice C creates a comma splice.

8. **(A)** Sentence is correct. The past tense and the subordinating conjunction *when* are correctly used in Choice A.

9. **(C)** Choice C expresses the author's meaning directly and concisely. All other choices are either indirect or ungrammatical.

10. **(A)** Choices B, C, D, and E are sentence fragments.

11. **(A)** Sentence is correct.

12. **(A)** Sentence is correct.

13. **(E)** The errors in pronoun case and subject-verb agreement are corrected in Choice E. *I* should be used instead of *me* because it is the predicate nominative of the verb *is*. *Who*, having as its antecedent the pronoun *I*, is a first-person singular pronoun. The first-person singular verb *am* should be used.

14. **(C)** Error in idiomatic usage. The birds are indifferent *to* the ships.

15. **(C)** Error in subject-verb agreement. The subject of the sentence, *collection*, is singular; the verb should be singular as well.

16. **(A)** Sentence is correct.

17. **(E)** Error in sequence of tenses. *Was* and *received* are in the simple past tense. Both indicate a definite time in the past. *Have cheered* is in the present perfect tense. It indicates sometime before now but not a definite time. The sequence is illogical.

18. **(D)** Error in parallelism. Choice D corrects the lack of parallel structure.

19. **(E)** Adjective-adverb confusion. The dragonflies become *increasingly* fragile.

20. **(E)** Error in sequence of tenses. The *had* before *established* indicates a time prior to *began to arrive*.

21. **(C)** Error in diction. Use *lie* instead of *lay*.

22. **(E)** Sentence is correct.

23. **(D)** Error in pronoun number agreement. Since antecedent is *association*, change *their* to *its*.

24. **(C)** Error in subject-verb agreement. In a neither-nor construction the verb agrees with the noun or pronoun that comes immediately before the verb. *Principal is being considered* is correct.

25. **(A)** Error in tense. Change *have rummaged* to *were rummaging*.

26. **(E)** Sentence is correct.

27. **(C)** Error in diction. Use *effect* instead of *affect*.

28. **(C)** Error in coordination and subordination. Delete the comma and substitute *that* for *and it*. The second clause describes McGwire's record.

29. **(C)** Error in coordination and subordination. Change *nor is she* to *and she is* to clarify the relationship between the clauses.

30. **(D)** Error in diction. The word *being* is unnecessary. Change *including being* to *including*.

31. **(D)** Adjective and adverb confusion. Change *comfortable* to *comfortably*.

32. **(E)** Sentence is correct.

33. **(A)** Error in tense. Change *has been warned* to *had been warned*.

34. **(A)** Error in diction. Use *if* to indicate a condition. Substitute *whether*.

35. **(C)** All sentences except sentence 3 contribute to the paragraph's main point, that celebrations help to unite people and keep traditions alive. Therefore, Choice C is the best answer.

36. **(D)** Choice A is fresh, but its tone is not consistent with the rest of the essay.
    Choice B contains a comma splice between *dinner* and *at*.
    Choice C emphasizes the idea properly but contains an error in parallel construction.
    Choice D places the emphasis where it belongs and expresses the idea effectively. It is the best answer.
    Choice E is repetitious, and it contains an error in pronoun reference. The pronoun *they* has no specific referent.

37. **(D)** Choice A does not provide a significantly better transition.
    Choice B does nothing to improve the relationship between paragraphs 3 and 4.
    Choice C is awkwardly worded and does not include transitional material.
    Choice D provides an effective transition between paragraphs. It is the best answer.
    Choice E tries to provide a transition, but it is wordy and it contains a dangling participle.

38. **(E)** Choice A places emphasis on the location of the assassination instead of on the event itself, an emphasis that the writer did not intend.
    Choice B contains a nonstandard usage. The phrase *to remember about* is not standard.
    Choice C is grammatically correct but wordy.
    Choice D is the same as B.
    Choice E is a succinct and proper revision. It is the best answer.

39. **(C)** The main purpose of the last paragraph is to provide an example of a celebration that unites people and preserves tradition. Therefore, Choice C is the best answer.

Answer Sheet—Practice Test 3

Each mark should completely fill the appropriate space, and should be as dark as all other marks. Make all erasures complete. Traces of an erasure may be read as an answer.

Section 1 – Critical Reading 25 minutes	Section 2 – Math 25 minutes	Section 3 – Critical Reading 25 minutes
1 Ⓐ Ⓑ Ⓒ Ⓓ Ⓔ	1 Ⓐ Ⓑ Ⓒ Ⓓ Ⓔ	25 Ⓐ Ⓑ Ⓒ Ⓓ Ⓔ
2 Ⓐ Ⓑ Ⓒ Ⓓ Ⓔ	2 Ⓐ Ⓑ Ⓒ Ⓓ Ⓔ	26 Ⓐ Ⓑ Ⓒ Ⓓ Ⓔ
3 Ⓐ Ⓑ Ⓒ Ⓓ Ⓔ	3 Ⓐ Ⓑ Ⓒ Ⓓ Ⓔ	27 Ⓐ Ⓑ Ⓒ Ⓓ Ⓔ
4 Ⓐ Ⓑ Ⓒ Ⓓ Ⓔ	4 Ⓐ Ⓑ Ⓒ Ⓓ Ⓔ	28 Ⓐ Ⓑ Ⓒ Ⓓ Ⓔ
5 Ⓐ Ⓑ Ⓒ Ⓓ Ⓔ	5 Ⓐ Ⓑ Ⓒ Ⓓ Ⓔ	29 Ⓐ Ⓑ Ⓒ Ⓓ Ⓔ
6 Ⓐ Ⓑ Ⓒ Ⓓ Ⓔ	6 Ⓐ Ⓑ Ⓒ Ⓓ Ⓔ	30 Ⓐ Ⓑ Ⓒ Ⓓ Ⓔ
7 Ⓐ Ⓑ Ⓒ Ⓓ Ⓔ	7 Ⓐ Ⓑ Ⓒ Ⓓ Ⓔ	31 Ⓐ Ⓑ Ⓒ Ⓓ Ⓔ
8 Ⓐ Ⓑ Ⓒ Ⓓ Ⓔ	8 Ⓐ Ⓑ Ⓒ Ⓓ Ⓔ	32 Ⓐ Ⓑ Ⓒ Ⓓ Ⓔ
9 Ⓐ Ⓑ Ⓒ Ⓓ Ⓔ	9 Ⓐ Ⓑ Ⓒ Ⓓ Ⓔ	33 Ⓐ Ⓑ Ⓒ Ⓓ Ⓔ
10 Ⓐ Ⓑ Ⓒ Ⓓ Ⓔ	10 Ⓐ Ⓑ Ⓒ Ⓓ Ⓔ	34 Ⓐ Ⓑ Ⓒ Ⓓ Ⓔ
11 Ⓐ Ⓑ Ⓒ Ⓓ Ⓔ	11 Ⓐ Ⓑ Ⓒ Ⓓ Ⓔ	35 Ⓐ Ⓑ Ⓒ Ⓓ Ⓔ
12 Ⓐ Ⓑ Ⓒ Ⓓ Ⓔ	12 Ⓐ Ⓑ Ⓒ Ⓓ Ⓔ	36 Ⓐ Ⓑ Ⓒ Ⓓ Ⓔ
13 Ⓐ Ⓑ Ⓒ Ⓓ Ⓔ	13 Ⓐ Ⓑ Ⓒ Ⓓ Ⓔ	37 Ⓐ Ⓑ Ⓒ Ⓓ Ⓔ
14 Ⓐ Ⓑ Ⓒ Ⓓ Ⓔ	14 Ⓐ Ⓑ Ⓒ Ⓓ Ⓔ	38 Ⓐ Ⓑ Ⓒ Ⓓ Ⓔ
15 Ⓐ Ⓑ Ⓒ Ⓓ Ⓔ	15 Ⓐ Ⓑ Ⓒ Ⓓ Ⓔ	39 Ⓐ Ⓑ Ⓒ Ⓓ Ⓔ
16 Ⓐ Ⓑ Ⓒ Ⓓ Ⓔ	16 Ⓐ Ⓑ Ⓒ Ⓓ Ⓔ	40 Ⓐ Ⓑ Ⓒ Ⓓ Ⓔ
17 Ⓐ Ⓑ Ⓒ Ⓓ Ⓔ	17 Ⓐ Ⓑ Ⓒ Ⓓ Ⓔ	41 Ⓐ Ⓑ Ⓒ Ⓓ Ⓔ
18 Ⓐ Ⓑ Ⓒ Ⓓ Ⓔ	18 Ⓐ Ⓑ Ⓒ Ⓓ Ⓔ	42 Ⓐ Ⓑ Ⓒ Ⓓ Ⓔ
19 Ⓐ Ⓑ Ⓒ Ⓓ Ⓔ	19 Ⓐ Ⓑ Ⓒ Ⓓ Ⓔ	43 Ⓐ Ⓑ Ⓒ Ⓓ Ⓔ
20 Ⓐ Ⓑ Ⓒ Ⓓ Ⓔ	20 Ⓐ Ⓑ Ⓒ Ⓓ Ⓔ	44 Ⓐ Ⓑ Ⓒ Ⓓ Ⓔ
21 Ⓐ Ⓑ Ⓒ Ⓓ Ⓔ		45 Ⓐ Ⓑ Ⓒ Ⓓ Ⓔ
22 Ⓐ Ⓑ Ⓒ Ⓓ Ⓔ		46 Ⓐ Ⓑ Ⓒ Ⓓ Ⓔ
23 Ⓐ Ⓑ Ⓒ Ⓓ Ⓔ		47 Ⓐ Ⓑ Ⓒ Ⓓ Ⓔ
24 Ⓐ Ⓑ Ⓒ Ⓓ Ⓔ		48 Ⓐ Ⓑ Ⓒ Ⓓ Ⓔ

Remove answer sheet by cutting on dotted line

Section 4 – Math

25 minutes

21 Ⓐ Ⓑ Ⓒ Ⓓ Ⓔ
22 Ⓐ Ⓑ Ⓒ Ⓓ Ⓔ
23 Ⓐ Ⓑ Ⓒ Ⓓ Ⓔ
24 Ⓐ Ⓑ Ⓒ Ⓓ Ⓔ
25 Ⓐ Ⓑ Ⓒ Ⓓ Ⓔ
26 Ⓐ Ⓑ Ⓒ Ⓓ Ⓔ
27 Ⓐ Ⓑ Ⓒ Ⓓ Ⓔ
28 Ⓐ Ⓑ Ⓒ Ⓓ Ⓔ

29 | 30 | 31 | 32 | 33 | 34 | 35 | 36 | 37 | 38

(Each grid: / / ; . . . . ; 0 0 0 ; 1–9 in four columns)

Section 5 – Writing

30 minutes

1 Ⓐ Ⓑ Ⓒ Ⓓ Ⓔ
2 Ⓐ Ⓑ Ⓒ Ⓓ Ⓔ
3 Ⓐ Ⓑ Ⓒ Ⓓ Ⓔ
4 Ⓐ Ⓑ Ⓒ Ⓓ Ⓔ
5 Ⓐ Ⓑ Ⓒ Ⓓ Ⓔ
6 Ⓐ Ⓑ Ⓒ Ⓓ Ⓔ
7 Ⓐ Ⓑ Ⓒ Ⓓ Ⓔ
8 Ⓐ Ⓑ Ⓒ Ⓓ Ⓔ
9 Ⓐ Ⓑ Ⓒ Ⓓ Ⓔ
10 Ⓐ Ⓑ Ⓒ Ⓓ Ⓔ
11 Ⓐ Ⓑ Ⓒ Ⓓ Ⓔ
12 Ⓐ Ⓑ Ⓒ Ⓓ Ⓔ
13 Ⓐ Ⓑ Ⓒ Ⓓ Ⓔ
14 Ⓐ Ⓑ Ⓒ Ⓓ Ⓔ
15 Ⓐ Ⓑ Ⓒ Ⓓ Ⓔ
16 Ⓐ Ⓑ Ⓒ Ⓓ Ⓔ
17 Ⓐ Ⓑ Ⓒ Ⓓ Ⓔ
18 Ⓐ Ⓑ Ⓒ Ⓓ Ⓔ
19 Ⓐ Ⓑ Ⓒ Ⓓ Ⓔ
20 Ⓐ Ⓑ Ⓒ Ⓓ Ⓔ
21 Ⓐ Ⓑ Ⓒ Ⓓ Ⓔ
22 Ⓐ Ⓑ Ⓒ Ⓓ Ⓔ
23 Ⓐ Ⓑ Ⓒ Ⓓ Ⓔ
24 Ⓐ Ⓑ Ⓒ Ⓓ Ⓔ
25 Ⓐ Ⓑ Ⓒ Ⓓ Ⓔ
26 Ⓐ Ⓑ Ⓒ Ⓓ Ⓔ
27 Ⓐ Ⓑ Ⓒ Ⓓ Ⓔ
28 Ⓐ Ⓑ Ⓒ Ⓓ Ⓔ
29 Ⓐ Ⓑ Ⓒ Ⓓ Ⓔ
30 Ⓐ Ⓑ Ⓒ Ⓓ Ⓔ
31 Ⓐ Ⓑ Ⓒ Ⓓ Ⓔ
32 Ⓐ Ⓑ Ⓒ Ⓓ Ⓔ
33 Ⓐ Ⓑ Ⓒ Ⓓ Ⓔ
34 Ⓐ Ⓑ Ⓒ Ⓓ Ⓔ
35 Ⓐ Ⓑ Ⓒ Ⓓ Ⓔ
36 Ⓐ Ⓑ Ⓒ Ⓓ Ⓔ
37 Ⓐ Ⓑ Ⓒ Ⓓ Ⓔ
38 Ⓐ Ⓑ Ⓒ Ⓓ Ⓔ
39 Ⓐ Ⓑ Ⓒ Ⓓ Ⓔ

SECTION 1/CRITICAL READING

TIME: 25 MINUTES
24 QUESTIONS (1–24)

Directions: For each question in this section, select the best answer from among the choices given and fill in the corresponding circle on the answer sheet.

Each sentence below has one or two blanks, each blank indicating that something has been omitted. Beneath the sentence are five words or sets of words labeled A through E. Choose the word or set of words that, when inserted in the sentence, best fits the meaning of the sentence as a whole.

EXAMPLE:

Medieval kingdoms did not become constitutional republics overnight; on the contrary, the change was ----.

(A) unpopular (B) unexpected
(C) advantageous (D) sufficient (E) gradual

Ⓐ Ⓑ Ⓒ Ⓓ ●

1. Though he was reputedly a skilled craftsman, the judging committee found his work ---- and lacking in polish.
   (A) crude (B) accomplished
   (C) distinguished (D) adequate
   (E) conceptual

2. Taxonomy—the branch of biology that describes and classifies living creatures—has ---- for approximately 1.4 million creatures.
   (A) need (B) names (C) sanctions
   (D) relevance (E) scope

3. During the height of the mating season, disputes often erupt in the small rookery where space is ---- and male egrets must ---- a patch on which to build their nests.
   (A) inadequate..mull over
   (B) circumscribed..rule out
   (C) unavailable..pick through
   (D) unconditional..seek out
   (E) limited..vie for

4. Because he could not support the cures he obtained with scientific data, he was accused by some skeptics of being ----.
   (A) a zealot (B) an artist (C) a mendicant
   (D) a charlatan (E) a dilettante

5. Critics have been misled by Tennessee Williams's obvious ---- exaggerated theatrical gestures into ---- his plays as mere melodramas, "full of sound and fury, signifying nothing."
   (A) disinclination for..disparaging
   (B) repudiation of..misrepresenting
   (C) indulgence in..acclaiming
   (D) propensity for..denigrating
   (E) indifference to..lauding

GO ON TO NEXT PAGE ▶

Directions: The passages below are followed by questions based on their content; questions following a pair of related passages may also be based on the relationship between the paired passages. Answer the questions on the basis of what is stated or implied in the passages and in any introductory material that may be provided.

Questions 6–9 are based on the following passages.

Passage 1

True scientists are no strangers to hard work. To prove a hypothesis or confirm a discovery, they conduct test after test, examining their subject from every possible angle that might cast fresh light upon it. They never jump to conclusions, but inch by methodical inch creep up upon them, slowly, unerringly, surely. This is the essence of modern scientific method, the method championed by Boyle and Hooke and other seventeenth century experimental scientists.

Passage 2

According to the naturalist Donald Culross Peattie, many scientists reject the idea of scientific intuition. In Peattie's words, they "rely utterly on the celebrated inductive method of reasoning: the facts are to be exposed, and we have to conclude from them only what we must." Peattie acknowledges the soundness of this rule for ordinary researchers (minds "that can do no better"), but nevertheless derides this step-by-step, fact-by-fact method as plodding. He points to Einstein, who, working in a patent office, suddenly, out of the blue, had his famous insight $e = mc^2$. "First he dreamed it; then he knew it; then, rather for others' sake, he proved it." This is how the really great advances in science are made.

6. The author of Passage 1 characterizes true scientists as all of the following EXCEPT

(A) systematic (B) deliberate (C) accurate
(D) diligent (E) inspired

7. In lines 8–9, "championed" most nearly means

(A) challenged (B) triumphed (C) espoused
(D) overpowered (E) defeated

8. Unlike the author of Passage 1, the author of Passage 2 makes use of

(A) scientific data
(B) direct citation
(C) historical references
(D) first person narration
(E) positive assertions

9. The author of Passage 1 would most likely respond to the first three sentences of Passage 2 (lines 11–20) by arguing that Peattie

(A) refuses to acknowledge any contributions to scientific knowledge by ordinary researchers
(B) minimizes the value of intuition to the advancement of science
(C) fails to appreciate the virtues of the inductive method sufficiently
(D) misunderstands the way in which scientists apply the inductive method
(E) fails to distinguish between the inductive and deductive methods of reasoning

Practice Test 3

GO ON TO NEXT PAGE ▶

Directions: Each passage below is followed by questions based on its content. Answer the questions following each passage on the basis of what is stated or implied in that passage and in any introductory material that may be provided.

Questions 10–15 are based on the following passage.

Noted for their destructiveness, tornadoes have long fascinated both scientists and the public at large. The following passage is from a magazine article on tornadoes written in 1984.

A tornado is the product of a thunderstorm, specifically of the interaction of a strong thunderstorm with winds in the troposphere (the active layer of the atmosphere that extends nine to 17 kilometers up from the ground). The process by which a tornado is formed is one in which a small fraction of the tremendous energy of the thunderstorm, whose towering cumulonimbus cloud can be 10 to 20 kilometers across and more than 17 kilometers high, is concentrated in an area no more than several hundred meters in diameter. Before going into the process in detail let me first describe the phenomenon itself.

A tornado is a vortex; air rotates around the tornado's axis about as fast as it moves toward and along the axis. Drawn by greatly reduced atmospheric pressure in the central core, air streams into the base of the vortex from all directions through a shallow layer a few tens of meters deep near the ground. In the base the air turns abruptly to spiral upward around the core and finally merges, at the hidden upper end of the tornado, with the airflow in the parent cloud. The pressure within the core may be as much as 10 percent less than that of the surrounding atmosphere; about the same difference as that between sea level and an altitude of one kilometer. Winds in a tornado are almost always cyclonic, which in the Northern Hemisphere means counterclockwise.

The vortex frequently—not always—becomes visible as a funnel cloud hanging part or all of the way to the ground from the generating storm. A funnel cloud forms only if the pressure drop in the core exceeds a critical value that depends on the temperature and the humidity of the inflowing air. As air flows into the area of lower pressure, it expands and cools; if it cools enough, the water vapor in it condenses and forms droplets. The warmer and drier the inflowing air is, the greater the pressure drop must be for condensation to occur and a cloud to form. Sometimes no condensation funnel forms, in which case the tornado reveals itself only through the dust and debris it carries aloft.

A funnel can be anywhere from tens of meters to several kilometers long, and where it meets the parent cloud its diameter ranges from a few meters to hundreds of meters. Usually it is cone-shaped, but short, broad, cylindrical pillars are formed by very strong tornadoes, and long, rope-like tubes that trail off horizontally are also common. Over a tornado's brief lifetime (never more than a few hours) the size and shape of the funnel may change markedly, reflecting changes in the intensity of the winds or in the properties of the inflowing air. Its color varies from a dirty white to gray to dark blue gray when it consists mostly of water droplets, but if the core fills with dust, the funnel may take on a more exotic hue, such as the red of west Oklahoma clay. Tornadoes can also be noisy, often roaring like a freight train or a jet engine. This may result from the interaction of the concentrated high winds with the ground.

10. Tornadoes are characterized by which of the following?

I. Brevity of duration
II. Intense concentration of energy
III. Uniformity of shape

(A) I only
(B) II only
(C) I and II only
(D) II and III only
(E) I, II, and III

11. The sentence in lines 12–13 ("Before . . . itself") functions in the passage primarily as

(A) a transition
(B) a concession
(C) an apology
(D) a criticism
(E) a refutation

GO ON TO NEXT PAGE ▶

12. In line 16, "Drawn" most nearly means
(A) elongated (B) sketched (C) drained
(D) inferred (E) pulled

13. The passage suggests that which of the following is true of a tornado?
(A) Its winds are invariably counterclockwise.
(B) It can last for days at a time.
(C) Its funnel cloud will not form if the air is cool and dry.
(D) It exceeds its parent cloud in size.
(E) It responds to changes in temperature and humidity.

14. According to the author, a direct relation may exist between the color a tornado takes on and
(A) the composition of the terrain it passes over
(B) the intensity of the winds it concentrates
(C) the particular shape of funnel it forms
(D) the direction in which its winds rotate
(E) the degree of noise involved

15. In the final paragraph the author does all of the following EXCEPT
(A) suggest a hypothesis
(B) provide a concrete example
(C) indicate a time span
(D) argue a viewpoint
(E) use a simile

Questions 16–24 are based on the following passage.

The following passage is an excerpt from "An American Childhood," *the autobiography of the writer Annie Dillard published in 1987.*

Outside in the neighborhoods, learning our way around the streets, we played among the enormous stone monuments of the millionaires—both those tireless Pittsburgh founders of the heavy industries from which the nation's wealth derived (they told us at school) and the industrialists' couldn't-lose bankers and backers, all of whom began as canny boys, the stories of whose rises to riches adults still considered inspirational to children.

We were unthinkingly familiar with the moguls' immense rough works as so much weird scenery on long drives. We saw the long, low-slung stripes of steel factories by the rivers; we saw pyramidal heaps of yellow sand at glassworks by the shining railroad tracks; we saw rusty slag heaps on the outlying hilltops, and coal barges tied up at the docks. We recognized, on infrequent trips downtown, the industries' smooth corporate headquarters, each to its own soaring building—Gulf Oil, Alcoa, U.S. Steel, Koppers Company, Pittsburgh Plate Glass, Mellon Bank. Our classmates' fathers worked in these buildings, or at nearby corporate headquarters for Westinghouse Electric, Jones & Laughlin Steel, Allegheny Ludlum, Westinghouse Air Brake, and H. J. Heinz.

The nineteenth-century industrialists' institutions—galleries, universities, hospitals, churches, Carnegie libraries, the Carnegie Museum, Frick Park, Mellon Park—were, many of them, my stomping grounds. These absolute artifacts of philanthropy littered the neighborhoods with marble. Millionaires' encrusted mansions, now obsolete and turned into parks or art centers, weighed on every block. They lent their expansive, hushed moods to the Point Breeze neighborhoods where we children lived and where those fabulous men had lived also, or rather had visited at night in order to sleep. Everywhere I looked, it was the Valley of the Kings, their dynasty just ended, and their monuments intact but already out of fashion.

All these immensities wholly dominated the life of the city. So did their several peculiar social legacies: their powerful Calvinist mix of piety and acquisitiveness, which characterized the old and new Scotch-Irish families and the nation they

GO ON TO NEXT PAGE ►

helped found; the wall-up hush of what was, by my day, old money—amazing how fast it ages if you let it alone—and the clang and roar of making that money; the owners' Presbyterian churches, their anti-Catholicism, anti-Semitism, Republicanism, and love of continuous work; their dogmatic practicality; their easy friendliness; their Pittsburgh-centered innocence, and, paradoxically, their egalitarianism.

For all the insularity of the old guard, Pittsburgh was always an open and democratic town. "Best-natured people I ever went among," a Boston visitor noted two centuries earlier. In colonial days, everybody went to balls, regardless of rank. No one had any truck with aristocratic pretensions—hadn't they hated the British lords in Ulster? People who cared to rave about their bloodlines, Mother told us, had stayed in Europe, which deserved them. We were vaguely proud of living in a city so full of distinctive immigrant groups, among which we never thought to number ourselves. We had no occasion to visit the steep hillside neighborhoods—Polish, Hungarian, Rumanian, Italian, Slav—of the turn-of-the-century immigrants who poured the steel and stirred the glass and shoveled the coal.

We children played around the moguls' enormous pale stone houses, restful as tombs, set back just so on their shaded grounds. Henry Clay Frick's daughter, unthinkably old, lived alone in her proud, sinking mansion; she had lived alone all her life. No one saw her. Men mowed the wide lawns and seeded them, and pushed rollers over them, over the new grass seed and musket balls and arrowheads, over the big trees' roots, bones, shale, coal.

We knew bits of this story, and we knew none of it. We knew that before big industry there had been small industry here—H. J. Heinz setting up a roadside stand to sell horseradish roots from his garden. There were the makers of cannonballs for the Civil War. There were the braggart and rowdy flatboat men and keelboat men, and the honored steamboat builders and pilots. There were local men getting rich in iron and glass manufacturing and trade downriver. There was a whole continentful of people passing through, native-born and immigrant men and women who funneled down Pittsburgh, where two rivers converged to make a third river. It was the gateway to the West; they piled onto flatboats and launched out into the Ohio River singing, to head for new country. There had been a Revolutionary War, and before that the French and Indian War. And before that, and first of all, had been those first settlers come walking bright-eyed in, into nowhere from out of nowhere, the people who, as they said, "broke wilderness," the pioneers. This was the history.

16. The opening paragraph suggests the author regards the inspirational tales of the lives of the industrialists with a sense of

(A) optimism (B) reverence (C) discomfort
(D) irony (E) envy

17. The author and her fellow children regarded the enormous buildings as

(A) unnatural phenomena to observe
(B) a backdrop to their lives
(C) a challenge to the imagination
(D) signs of excessive consumption
(E) intimations of immortality

18. The author calls the moguls fabulous (line 37) because they were

(A) fictitious (B) celebrated (C) wonderful
(D) startling (E) affluent

19. The author's remark in lines 48 and 49 ("amazing how fast . . . alone") can best be described as

(A) an extended metaphor
(B) an ironic aside
(C) a faulty hypothesis
(D) a concrete example
(E) a personal reminiscence

20. By "People who cared to rave about their bloodlines . . . had stayed in Europe, which deserved them" (lines 63–65), the author's mother means

(A) only Europe was worthy enough to have citizens descended from noble blood
(B) aristocrats tended to be disinclined to travel
(C) Americans were ashamed of their lack of noble birth, and therefore avoided Europe
(D) it served Europe right if all those snobs who boasted about their lineage stayed right there
(E) it was madness for an American to try to trace his bloodlines; only a European could succeed

GO ON TO NEXT PAGE ▶

21. The author uses the description of the Frick lawns in lines 78–82 chiefly to help

(A) indicate the opulence of the moguls' lifestyle
(B) counteract the isolation of Henry Clay Frick's daughter
(C) convey a sense of Pittsburgh's buried past
(D) highlight the distinction between the moguls and their employees
(E) argue in favor of preserving open spaces in cities

22. The opening sentence of the last paragraph (lines 83–84) presents the reader with

(A) a euphemism (B) an epitaph (C) a simile
(D) a paradox (E) a reminiscence

23. In the phrase "broke wilderness" (line 103), "broke" most likely means

(A) shattered (B) bankrupted (C) unraveled
(D) interrupted (E) penetrated

24. The passage's closing paragraph is organized according to

(A) geographical principles
(B) reverse chronological order
(C) cause and effect
(D) personal recollections
(E) extensive quotations

IF YOU FINISH IN LESS THAN 25 MINUTES, YOU MAY CHECK YOUR WORK ON THIS SECTION ONLY. DO NOT TURN TO ANY OTHER SECTION IN THE TEST.

STOP

SECTION 2 /MATHEMATICS

TIME: 25 MINUTES

20 QUESTIONS (1–20)

Directions:

For each question in this section, determine which of the five choices is correct, and blacken that choice on your answer sheet. You may use any blank space on the page for your work.

NOTES:

- You may use a calculator whenever you believe it will be helpful.
- Use the diagrams provided to help you solve the problems. Unless you see the phrase

Note: Figure not drawn to scale

under a diagram, it has been drawn as accurately as possible. Unless it is stated that a figure is three dimensional, you may assume that it lies in a plane.

Reference

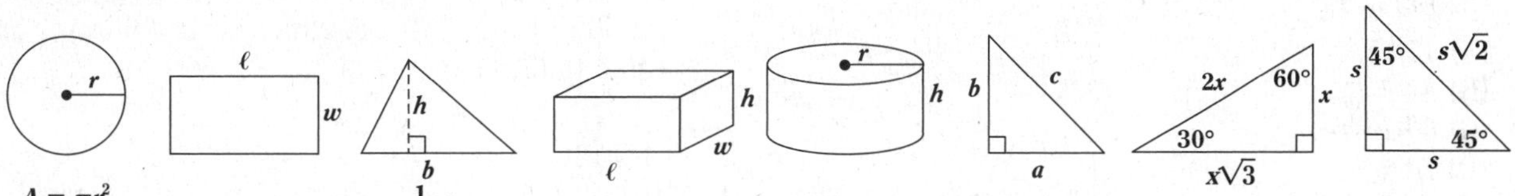

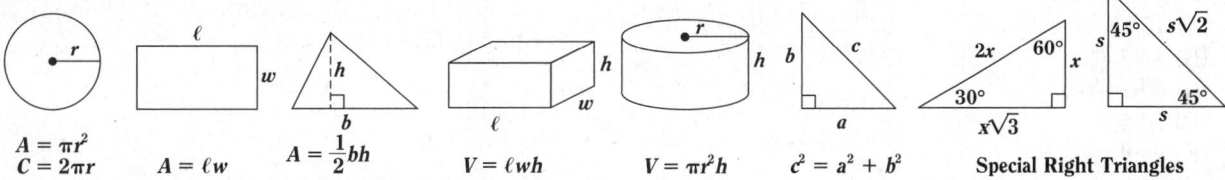

$A = \pi r^2$ $C = 2\pi r$ | $A = \ell w$ | $A = \frac{1}{2}bh$ | $V = \ell wh$ | $V = \pi r^2 h$ | $c^2 = a^2 + b^2$ | **Special Right Triangles**

Number of degrees in a circle: 360

Sum of the measures, in degrees, of the three angles of a triangle: 180

1. If Mr. Beck earns \$16 per hour, how many hours will he have to work in order to earn \$88?

(A) 5
(B) 5.5
(C) 6.5
(D) 23.5
(E) 1408

2. Sarah saves \$8 every day. If 11 days ago she had \$324, how many dollars will she have 11 days from now?

(A) 148
(B) 236
(C) 412
(D) 500
(E) 566

3. Which of the following is an expression for "the product of 7 and the average (arithmetic mean) of a and b?"

(A) $\frac{7a + b}{2}$

(B) $\frac{7a + 7b}{2}$

(C) $\frac{7 + a + b}{3}$

(D) $7 + \frac{a + b}{2}$

(E) $\frac{7 + 7a + 7b}{3}$

4. If $\frac{3}{4}$ of a number is 7 more than $\frac{1}{6}$ of the number, what is $\frac{5}{3}$ of the number?

(A) 12
(B) 15
(C) 18
(D) 20
(E) 24

GO ON TO NEXT PAGE ▶

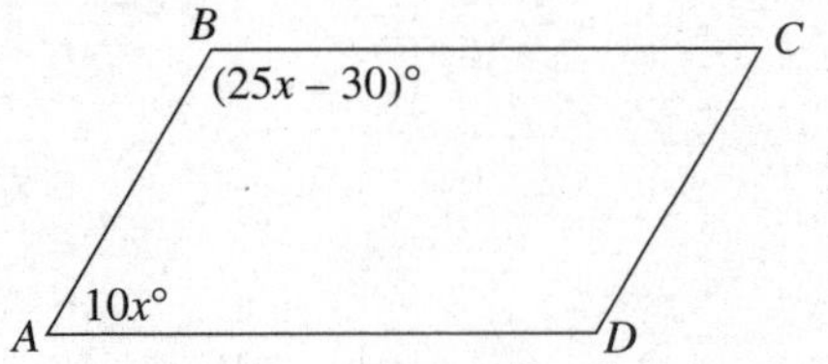

5. In parallelogram $ABCD$ above, what is the value of x?

(A) 2
(B) 4
(C) 6
(D) 20
(E) 60

6. An operation, ∗, is defined as follows: for any positive numbers a and b, $a*b = \sqrt{a+\sqrt{b}}$. Which of the following is an integer?

(A) 11∗5
(B) 4∗9
(C) 4∗16
(D) 7∗4
(E) 9∗9

7. A factory that is open exactly 25 days each month produces 64 engines each day it is open. How many years will it take to produce 96,000 engines?

(A) fewer than 5
(B) 5
(C) more than 5 but less than 10
(D) 10
(E) more than 10

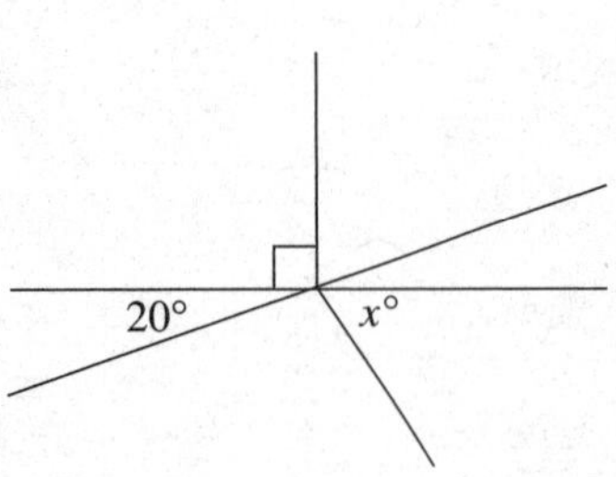

8. In the figure above, what is the value of x?

(A) 20
(B) 70
(C) 60
(D) 110
(E) It cannot be determined from the information given.

9. If $x - y = 5$, and $x^2 - y^2 = 75$, what is the value of y?

(A) −10
(B) −5
(C) 5
(D) 10
(E) $5\sqrt{2}$

10. Julie inherited 40% of her father's estate. After paying a tax equal to 30% of her inheritance, what percent of her father's estate did she own?

(A) 10%
(B) 12%
(C) 18%
(D) 28%
(E) 30%

11. For any positive integer $n > 1$: $n!$ represents the product of the first n positive integers. For example, $3! = 1 \times 2 \times 3 = 6$. Which of the following are equal to $(3!)(4!)$?

I. 7!
II. 12!
III. 4! + 5!

(A) None
(B) I only
(C) III only
(D) I and III
(E) I, II, and III

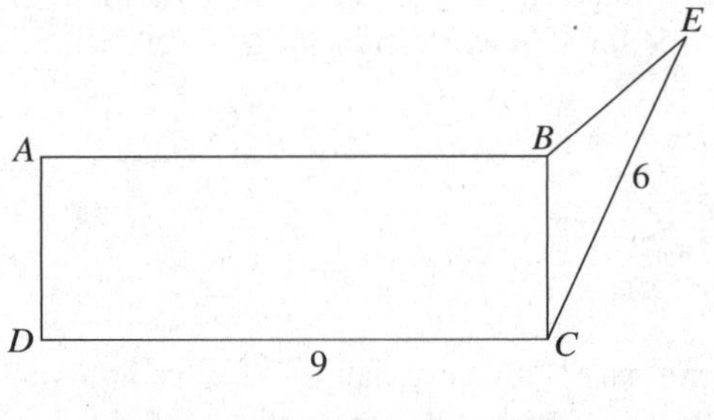

12. In the figure above, $BC = BE$. If R represents the perimeter of rectangle $ABCD$ and T represents the perimeter of triangle CBE, what is the value of $R - T$?

(A) 3
(B) 12
(C) 30
(D) $18 - 6\sqrt{2}$
(E) $12 - 3\sqrt{2}$

GO ON TO NEXT PAGE ►

Practice Test 3

13. There are 12 men on a basketball team, and in a game 5 of them play at any one time. If the game is one hour long and if each man plays exactly the same amount of time, how many minutes does each man play?

(A) 10
(B) 12
(C) 24
(D) 25
(E) 30

14. Which of the following expresses the circumference of a circle in terms of A, its area?

(A) $2A$
(B) $2A\sqrt{\pi}$
(C) $2\pi\sqrt{A}$
(D) $2\sqrt{\pi A}$
(E) $2\pi A$

15. What is the value of k if the line that passes through $(3, -3)$ and $(k, 5)$ has a slope of $\frac{2}{3}$?

(A) 0
(B) 6
(C) $8\frac{1}{3}$
(D) 15
(E) 18

16. If x is an odd number, what is the difference between the smallest odd number greater than $5x + 4$ and the largest odd number less than $3x + 7$?

(A) $2x$
(B) $2x - 3$
(C) $2x + 3$
(D) $8x + 7$
(E) $8x + 8$

17. The measures of the angles of a triangle are in the ratio of 1:2:3. What is the ratio of the length of the smallest side to the length of the longest side?

(A) $1:\sqrt{2}$
(B) $1:\sqrt{3}$
(C) 1:2
(D) 1:3
(E) It cannot be determined from the information given.

18. A car going 50 miles per hour set out on a 200-mile trip at 12:00 P.M. Exactly 20 minutes later, a second car left from the same place and followed the same route. How fast, in miles per hour, was the second car going if it caught up with the first car at 2:00 P.M.?

(A) 55
(B) 60
(C) 65
(D) 70
(E) 75

19. If a is inversely proportional to b and $b = 5$ when $a = 3$, what is the value of b when $a = 10$?

(A) $\frac{1}{2}$
(B) $\frac{3}{2}$
(C) 2
(D) $\frac{50}{3}$
(E) 30

20. If 12% of a equals 60% of b, then b is equal to what percent of a?

(A) 20%
(B) 25%
(C) 50%
(D) 200%
(E) 500%

IF YOU FINISH IN LESS THAN 25 MINUTES, YOU MAY CHECK YOUR WORK ON THIS SECTION ONLY. DO NOT TURN TO ANY OTHER SECTION IN THE TEST.

STOP

SECTION 3/CRITICAL READING

TIME: 25 MINUTES

24 QUESTIONS (25–48)

Directions: For each question in this section, select the best answer from among the choices given and fill in the corresponding circle on the answer sheet.

Each sentence below has one or two blanks, each blank indicating that something has been omitted. Beneath the sentence are five words or sets of words labeled A through E. Choose the word or set of words that, when inserted in the sentence, best fits the meaning of the sentence as a whole.

EXAMPLE:

Medieval kingdoms did not become constitutional republics overnight; on the contrary, the change was ----.

(A) unpopular (B) unexpected
(C) advantageous (D) sufficient (E) gradual

Ⓐ Ⓑ Ⓒ Ⓓ ●

25. The dean tried to retain control of the situation on campus, but her attempt was ---- by the board of trustees.

(A) endorsed (B) frustrated (C) disclosed
(D) witnessed (E) justified

26. The extended heat wave left many people ----, lacking their usual energy and interest in life.

(A) isolated (B) fervid (C) intemperate
(D) listless (E) nomadic

27. Disliking sudden changes in plans when she traveled abroad, Ethel refused to make any alterations to her ----.

(A) manuscript (B) itinerary (C) residence
(D) detour (E) wardrobe

28. Though Mark had reservations about many of the fraternity's policies, he diplomatically kept them to himself and allowed his fellow members to interpret his ---- as a sign of ---- on his part.

(A) complaints..reluctance
(B) silence..acquiescence
(C) arguments..pugnacity
(D) comments..inarticulateness
(E) selfishness..wisdom

29. Just as avarice is the mark of the miser, indulgence is the mark of the ----.

(A) pauper (B) philanthropist (C) coward
(D) martinet (E) glutton

30. Given the many areas of conflict still awaiting ----, the outcome of the peace talks remains ----.

(A) justification..pragmatic
(B) settlement..permanent
(C) resolution..problematic
(D) compromise..plausible
(E) arbitration..pacific

31. While some people take satisfaction from a religious or mystical explanation of human intelligence, for Bonner, the more ---- and ---- the explanation, the better she likes it.

(A) rational..materialistic
(B) logical..spiritual
(C) pragmatic..dubious
(D) theoretical..rudimentary
(E) occult..viable

32. Unfortunately, the book comes down so firmly on the nature side of the nature-nurture debate that it tends to ---- many of the subtleties of the argument, leaving the reader with a highly ---- view of the issue.

(A) carry through..lucid
(B) skim over..simplistic
(C) go beyond..dogmatic
(D) sidestep..cerebral
(E) highlight..arbitrary

GO ON TO NEXT PAGE ▶

Directions: Each of the passages below precedes two questions based on its content. Answer the questions following each passage on the basis of what is stated or implied in that passage.

Questions 33 and 34 are based on the following passage.

To students today, continental drift is a commonplace. They cheerfully talk about supercontinents that break apart or about shifts in the earth's crust as if everyone has always known that this solid earth beneath our feet is seated on large, rigid plates that float on a soft, partly molten layer of the earth's mantle. Not so. It was not quite a century ago that Alfred Wegener first proposed the theory that the components making up the supercontinent Pangaea had slowly moved thousands of miles apart over lengthy periods of geologic time.

33. In lines 1–2, "a commonplace" most nearly means

(A) a customary location
(B) a traditional rank
(C) an accepted concept
(D) a vulgar saying
(E) an inexpensive property

34. The passage's final sentence (lines 7–12) primarily serves to emphasize the

(A) definitive nature of an experiment
(B) recent origin of a theory
(C) sudden end to a controversy
(D) limited possibilities for research
(E) stubborn character of a scientist

Questions 35 and 36 are based on the following passage.

The morning after the battle of Fredericksburg, the ground before the stone wall was covered with wounded, dead, and dying Northerners. Hours passed by as soldiers from both sides listened to the cries for water and pleas for help. Finally, Richard Kirkland, a young Confederate sergeant, could bear it no more. Receiving permission from his general to help the wounded, he ventured over the wall. Under Northern fire, he reached the nearest sufferer and gave him water. As soon as they understood his intent, the enemy ceased fire, and for an hour and a half Kirkland tended the wounded unharmed.

35. The primary function of the passage is to

(A) establish that Kirkland sought his commander's approval before taking action
(B) indicate the young sergeant's eagerness to be seen as a hero
(C) dramatize the degree of suffering experienced during the Civil War
(D) depict an instance of heroism under fire
(E) analyze the military importance of the battle of Fredericksburg

36. In line 7, "bear" most nearly means

(A) carry (B) endure (C) produce
(D) conduct (E) warrant

GO ON TO NEXT PAGE ▶

Directions: The passages below are followed by questions on their content; questions following a pair of related passages may also be based on the relationship between the paired passages. Answer the questions on the basis of what is stated or implied in the passages and in any introductory material that may be provided.

Questions 37–48 are based on the following passages.

In the following passages, the novelist Virginia Woolf and a contemporary literary critic separately discuss the relationship between women and fiction.

Passage 1

The most superficial inquiry into women's writing instantly raises a host of questions. Why, we ask at once, was there no continuous writing done by women before the eighteenth century? Why did they then write almost habitually as men, and in the course of that writing produce, one after another, some of the classics of English fiction? And why did their art then, and why to some extent does their art still, take the form of fiction?

A little thought will show us that we are asking questions to which we shall get, as answer, only further fiction. The answer lies at present locked in old diaries, stuffed away in old drawers, half obliterated in the memories of the aged. It is to be found in the lives of the obscure—in those almost unlit corridors of history where the figures of generations of women are so dimly, so fitfully perceived. For very little is known about women. The history of England is the history of the male line, not of the female. Of our fathers we know always some fact, some distinction. They were soldiers or they were sailors; they filled that office or they made that law. But of our mothers, our grandmothers, our great-grandmothers, what remains? Nothing but a tradition. One was beautiful; one was red-haired; one was kissed by a Queen. We know nothing of them except their names and the dates of their marriages and the number of children they bore.

Thus, if we wish to know why at any particular time women did this or that, why they wrote nothing, why on the other hand they wrote masterpieces, it is extremely difficult to tell. Anyone who should seek among those old papers, who should turn history wrong side out and so construct a faithful picture of the daily life of the ordinary woman in Shakespeare's time, in Milton's time, in Johnson's time, would not only write a book of astonishing interest, but would furnish the critic with a weapon which he now lacks. The extraordinary woman depends on the ordinary woman. It is only when we know what were the conditions of the average woman's life—the number of her children, whether she had money of her own, if she had a room to herself, whether she had help in bringing up her family, if she had servants, whether part of the housework was her task—it is only when we can measure the way of life and the experience of life made possible to the ordinary woman that we can account for the success or failure of the extraordinary woman as writer.

Passage 2

As the works of dozens of women writers have been rescued from what E.P. Thompson calls "the enormous condescension of posterity," and considered in relation to each other, the lost continent of the female tradition has risen like Atlantis from the sea of English literature. It is now becoming clear that, contrary to Mill's theory, women have had a literature of their own all along. The woman novelist, according to Vineta Colby, was "really neither single nor anomalous," but she was also more than a "register and spokesman for her age." She was part of a tradition that had its origins before her age, and has carried on through our own.

Many literary historians have begun to reinterpret and revise the study of women writers. Ellen Moers sees women's literature as an international movement, "apart from, but hardly subordinate to the mainstream: an undercurrent, rapid and powerful. This 'movement' began in the late eighteenth century, was multinational, and produced some of the greatest literary works of two centuries, as well as most of the lucrative potboilers." Other critics are beginning to agree that when we look at women writers collectively we can see an imaginative continuum, the recurrence of certain patterns, themes, problems, and images from generation to generation.

This book is an effort to describe the female literary tradition in the English novel from the generation of the Brontes to the present day, and to show how the development of this tradition is similar to the development of any literary subculture. It is important to see the female literary tradition in these broad terms, in relation to the

GO ON TO NEXT PAGE ▶

wider evolution of women's self-awareness and to the ways any minority group finds its direction of self-expression relative to a dominant society, because we cannot show a pattern of deliberate progress and accumulation. It is true, as Ellen Moers writes, that "women studied with a special closeness the works written by their own sex"; in terms of influences, borrowings, and affinities, the tradition is strongly marked. But it is also full of holes and hiatuses, because of what Germaine Greer calls the "phenomenon of the transience of female literary fame"; "almost uninterruptedly since the Interregnum, a small group of women have enjoyed dazzling literary prestige during their own lifetimes, only to vanish without trace from the records of posterity." Thus each generation of women writers has found itself, in a sense, without a history, forced to rediscover the past anew, forging again and again the consciousness of their sex. Given this perpetual disruption, and also the self-hatred that has alienated women writers from a sense of collective identity, it does not seem possible to speak of a movement.

37. The questions in lines 2–9 chiefly serve to

(A) suggest how the author defines women's writing
(B) outline the direction of the author's research
(C) underscore how little is known about the subject
(D) divert the reader's attention from the central issue
(E) express the author's reluctance to appear dogmatic

38. In line 22, "filled" most nearly means

(A) inflated (B) blocked (C) furnished
(D) held (E) pervaded

39. Woolf's point in lines 23–29 about how little is known about women is made primarily through

(A) case histories (B) examples (C) statistics
(D) metaphors (E) repeated quotations

40. The individual women mentioned in lines 25–29 are presented primarily as instances of people who

(A) encountered royalty
(B) gave birth to children
(C) observed family traditions
(D) sought to become writers
(E) lived largely unrecorded lives

41. The "conditions" of the average woman's life to which the author refers (line 42) include all of the following EXCEPT the woman's

(A) financial circumstances
(B) medical problems
(C) maternal obligations
(D) social position
(E) housing arrangements

42. In the first paragraph of Passage 2, the author makes use of all the following techniques EXCEPT

(A) extended metaphor
(B) enumeration and classification
(C) classical allusion
(D) direct quotation
(E) comparison and contrast

43. The metaphor of the newly arisen "lost continent" (lines 55–57) is used primarily to convey

(A) the vast degree of effort involved in reinterpreting women's literature
(B) the number of works of literature that have been created by women
(C) the way forgotten literary works have resurfaced after many years
(D) the extent to which books written by women appeared unrelated
(E) the overwhelming size of the problem confronting the author

GO ON TO NEXT PAGE ►

44. In the second paragraph of Passage 2, the author's attitude toward the literary critics cited can best be described as one of

(A) irony (B) ambivalence (C) disparagement
(D) receptiveness (E) awe

45. In line 92, "closeness" most nearly means

(A) proximity in space
(B) narrow margin of victory
(C) disposition to secrecy
(D) cautiousness about expenditures
(E) minute attention to details

46. Which of the following words could best be substituted for "forging" (line 104) without substantially changing the author's meaning?

(A) counterfeiting (B) creating (C) exploring
(D) diverting (E) straining

47. It can be inferred from Passage 2 that the author considers Moers's work to be

(A) fallacious and misleading
(B) scholarly and definitive
(C) admirable but inaccurate in certain of its conclusions
(D) popular but irrelevant to mainstream female literary criticism
(E) idiosyncratic but of importance historically

48. Compared with the author of Passage 2, the author of Passage 1 is

(A) more academic and less colloquial
(B) less effusive and more detached
(C) less didactic and more dogmatic
(D) less scholarly and more descriptive
(E) more radical and less entertaining

IF YOU FINISH IN LESS THAN 25 MINUTES, YOU MAY CHECK YOUR WORK ON THIS SECTION ONLY. DO NOT TURN TO ANY OTHER SECTION IN THE TEST.

STOP

SECTION 4/MATHEMATICS

TIME: 25 MINUTES

18 QUESTIONS (21–38)

Directions:

For questions 21–28, determine which of the five choices is correct, and blacken that choice on your answer sheet. You may use any blank space on the page for your work.

NOTES:

- You may use a calculator whenever you believe it will be helpful.
- Use the diagrams provided to help you solve the problems. Unless you see the phrase
  <u>Note:</u> Figure not drawn to scale
  under a diagram, it has been drawn as accurately as possible. Unless it is stated that a figure is three dimensional, you may assume that it lies in a plane.

Reference

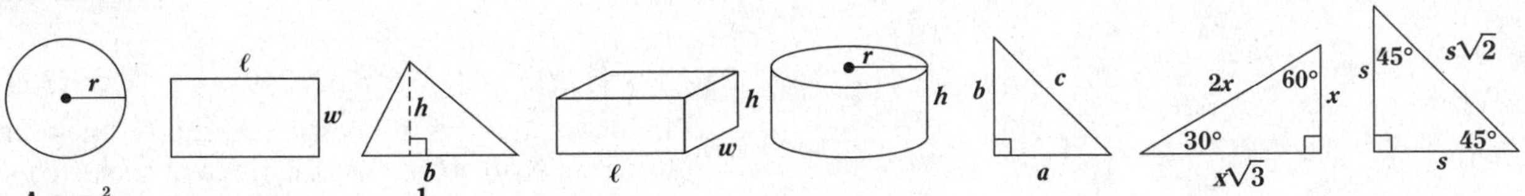

$A = \pi r^2$ $C = 2\pi r$ | $A = \ell w$ | $A = \frac{1}{2}bh$ | $V = \ell wh$ | $V = \pi r^2 h$ | $c^2 = a^2 + b^2$ | **Special Right Triangles**

Number of degrees in a circle: 360

Sum of the measures, in degrees, of the three angles of a triangle: 180

21. What is the value of $2x^2 - 4x - 3$ when $x = -5$?

(A) 27
(B) 67
(C) 73
(D) 87
(E) 117

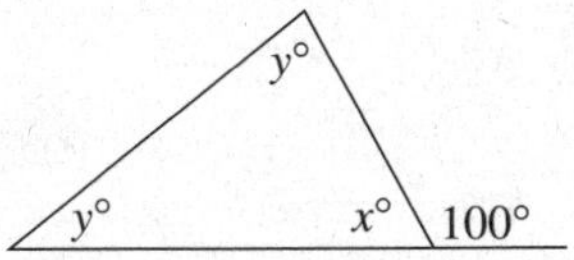

<u>Note</u>: Figure not drawn to scale

22. In the figure above, what is the value of y?

(A) 20
(B) 40
(C) 50
(D) 80
(E) It cannot be determined from the information given.

23. If $\frac{1}{b} + \frac{1}{b} + \frac{1}{b} + \frac{1}{b} = 12$, then $b =$

(A) $\frac{1}{12}$
(B) $\frac{1}{4}$
(C) $\frac{1}{3}$
(D) 3
(E) 4

24. Lucy had to unpack c cartons. After unpacking d of them, what percent of the cartons were not yet unpacked?

(A) $100(c - d)\%$
(B) $\frac{c-d}{100}\%$
(C) $\frac{c-d}{100c}\%$
(D) $\frac{100(c-d)}{d}\%$
(E) $\frac{100(c-d)}{c}\%$

GO ON TO NEXT PAGE ▶

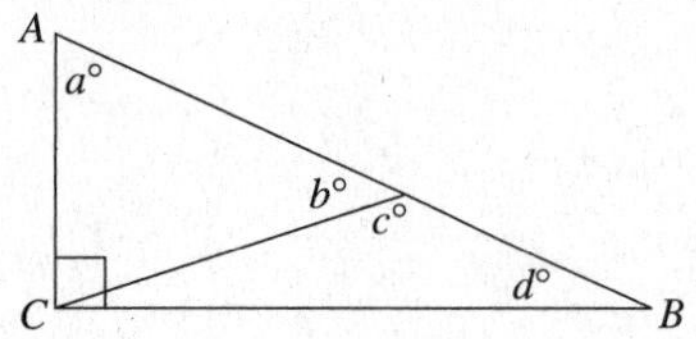

25. In the figure above, $\triangle ABC$ is a right triangle. What is the value of $a + b + c + d$?

(A) 180
(B) 240
(C) 270
(D) 300
(E) 360

26. If $\frac{1}{x} + \frac{1}{3} + \frac{1}{4} = 1$, then $x =$

(A) $\frac{5}{12}$
(B) $\frac{7}{5}$
(C) 2
(D) $\frac{12}{5}$
(E) 5

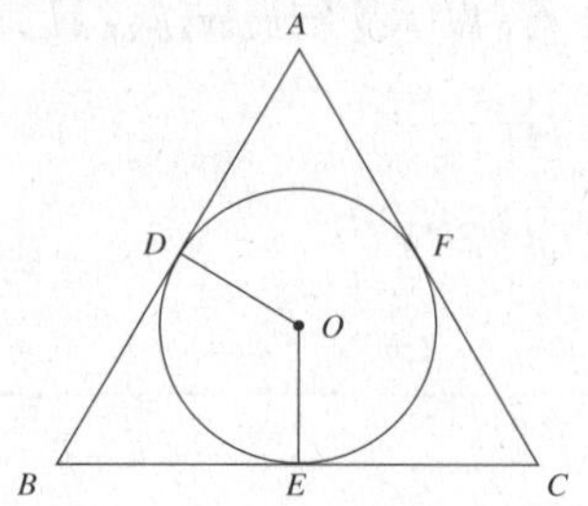

Note: Figure not drawn to scale

27. In the figure above, $AB = AC$ and the sides of triangle ABC are tangent to circle O, at points D, E, and F. If $m\angle A = 30°$, what is $m\angle DOE$?

(A) 75
(B) 90
(C) 105
(D) 120
(E) 150

28. $A = \{1, 2\}$ $B = \{2, 3\}$ $C = \{3, 4\}$

In how many ways is it possible to choose one number from each set so that the three numbers could be the lengths of the three sides of a triangle?

(A) None
(B) 1
(C) 4
(D) 6
(E) 8

GO ON TO NEXT PAGE ▶

Student-Produced Response Directions

In questions 29–38, first solve the problem, and then enter your answer on the grid provided on the answer sheet. The instructions for entering your answers follow.

- First, write your answer in the boxes at the top of the grid.
- Second, grid your answer in the columns below the boxes.
- Use the fraction bar in the first row or the decimal point in the second row to enter fractions and decimals.

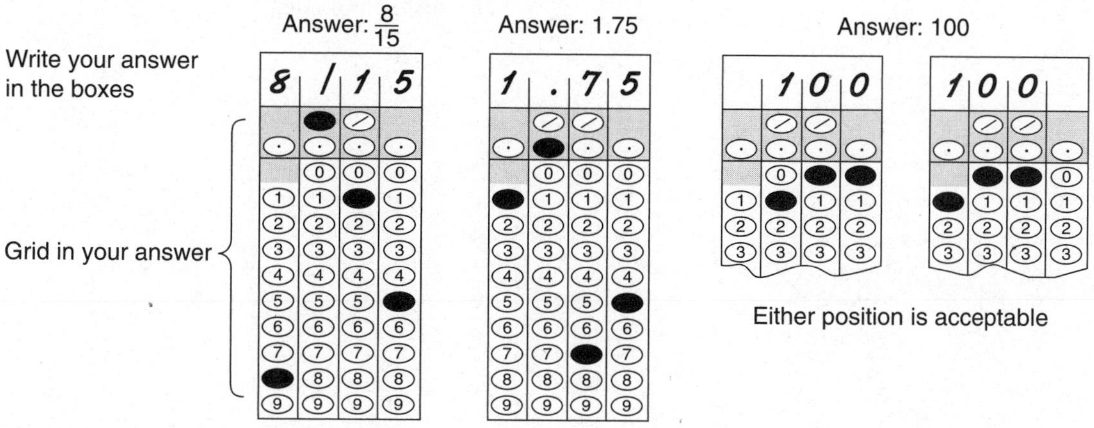

Either position is acceptable

- Grid only one space in each column.
- Entering the answer in the boxes is recommended as an aid in gridding but is not required.
- The machine scoring your exam can read only what you grid, so you **must grid-in your answers correctly to get credit.**
- If a question has more than one correct answer, grid-in only one of them.
- The grid does not have a minus sign; so no answer can be negative.
- A mixed number *must* be converted to an improper fraction or a decimal before it is gridded. Enter $1\frac{1}{4}$ as $\frac{5}{4}$ or 1.25; the machine will interpret 11/4 as $\frac{11}{4}$ and mark it wrong.
- **All decimals must be entered as accurately as possible.** Here are three acceptable ways of gridding $\frac{3}{11} = 0.272727\ldots$

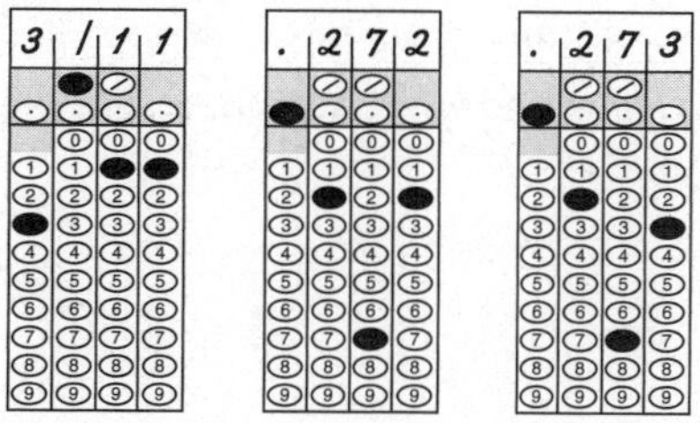

- Note that rounding to .273 is acceptable because you are using the full grid, but you would receive **no credit** for .3 or .27, because they are less accurate.

29. If $a * b = (a + b)^2 - (a - b)^2$, what is the value of $7 * 11$?

30. If $3x - 11 = 11 - 3x$, what is the value of x?

31. Jim, Kim, Ben, and Len divided $1000 as follows: Kim got twice as much as Jim, Ben got 3 times as much as Jim, and Len got $100. How much, in dollars, did Jim get?

32. If x, y, and z are different positive integers less than 10, what is the greatest possible value of $\frac{x^2 - y}{z}$?

33. A (−3, 2) and B (5, −1) are the endpoints of a diameter of a circle whose center is at (x, y). What is the value of $x + y$?

Practice Test 3

GO ON TO NEXT PAGE ▶

34. $\frac{3}{7} = 0.428571428571\ldots$, with the digits 4, 2, 8, 5, 7, 1 repeating indefinitely in that order. What digit is in the 200th place to the right of the decimal point?

35. In the addition problem below, each letter represents a different digit.

$$\begin{array}{r} AB \\ +CD \\ \hline AAA \end{array}$$

What is the value of $A + B + C + D$?

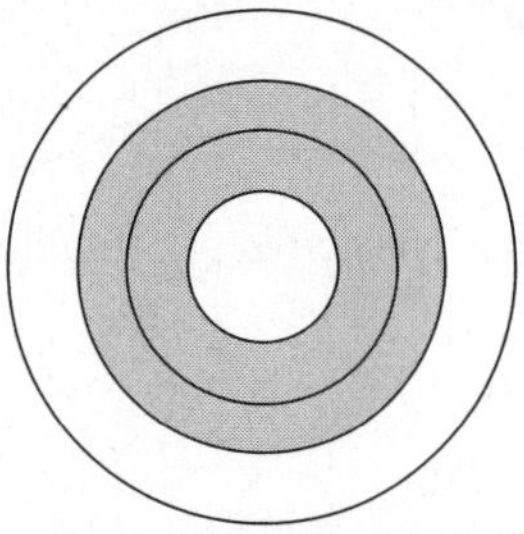

36. The figure above consists of 4 circles with the same center. The radii of the 4 circles are 1, 2, 3, and 4.

If a and b are the areas in the figure above of the shaded region and white region, respectively, what is the value of $\frac{a}{b}$?

37. In a jar containing only red and blue marbles, 40% of the marbles are red. If the average weight of a red marble is 40 grams and the average weight of a blue marble is 60 grams, what is the average weight, in grams, of all the marbles in the jar?

38. How many sides does a polygon have if the measure of each interior angle is twice the measure of each exterior angle?

IF YOU FINISH IN LESS THAN 25 MINUTES, YOU MAY CHECK YOUR WORK ON THIS SECTION ONLY. DO NOT TURN TO ANY OTHER SECTION IN THE TEST.

STOP

SECTION 5/WRITING SKILLS

TIME: 30 MINUTES

39 QUESTIONS (1–39)

Directions: For each question in this section, select the best answer from among the choices given and fill in the corresponding circle on the answer sheet.

Some or all parts of the following sentences are underlined. The first answer choice, (A), simply repeats the underlined part of the sentence. The other four choices present four alternative ways to phrase the underlined part. Select the answer that produces the most effective sentence, one that is clear and exact, and blacken the appropriate space on your answer sheet. In selecting your choice, be sure that it is standard written English and that it expresses the meaning of the original sentence.

EXAMPLE:

The first biography of author Eudora Welty came out in 1998, and she was eighty-nine years old at the time.

(A) and she was eighty-nine years old at the time
(B) at the time when she was eighty-nine
(C) upon becoming an eighty-nine year old
(D) when she was eighty-nine
(E) at the age of eighty-nine years old

Ⓐ Ⓑ Ⓒ ● Ⓔ

1. The police officer refused to permit us to enter the apartment, saying that he had orders to stop him going into the building.

(A) stop him going (B) prevent him going
(C) stop his going (D) stop us going
(E) stop our going

2. After conducting the orchestra for six concerts, Beethoven's *Ninth Symphony* was scheduled.

(A) After conducting
(B) After his conducting
(C) While conducting
(D) Although he conducted
(E) After he had conducted

3. Jackie Robinson became the first black player in major league baseball, he paved the way for black athletes to be accepted on the field.

(A) Jackie Robinson became the first black player in major league baseball, he
(B) Jackie Robinson, in becoming the first black player in major league baseball, he
(C) Jackie Robinson became the first black player in major league baseball; he
(D) Jackie Robinson, the first black player in major league baseball; he
(E) Jackie Robinson had become the first black player in major league baseball and he

4. Sitting in the Coliseum, the music couldn't hardly be heard because of the cheering and yelling of the spectators.

(A) the music couldn't hardly be heard because of
(B) the music couldn't hardly be heard due to
(C) the music could hardly be heard due to
(D) we could hardly be heard because of
(E) we could hardly hear the music because of

5. The contents of the examination came as a shock to the student, everything on it having no resemblance to what she had studied.

(A) as a shock to the student, everything on it having
(B) to the student as a shock, being that everything on it had
(C) to the student as a shock, with everything on it having
(D) as a shock to the student, everything on it has
(E) as a shock to the student; everything on it had

GO ON TO NEXT PAGE ▶

6. Across the nation, curricular changes sweeping the universities as schools reassess the knowledge that educated people should have.
   (A) curricular changes sweeping the universities as schools
   (B) curricular changes are sweeping the universities as schools
   (C) changes are sweeping the curricular since schools
   (D) curricular changes sweeping the universities causing schools to
   (E) curricular changes sweep the universities, but schools

7. If you have enjoyed these kind of programs, write to your local public television station and ask for more.
   (A) these kind of programs
   (B) those kind of programs
   (C) these kinds of programs
   (D) these kind of a program
   (E) these kind of a program

8. In her critique of the newly opened restaurant, the reviewer discussed the elaborate menu, the impressive wine list, and how the waiters functioned.
   (A) list, and how the waiters functioned
   (B) list and how the waiters functioned
   (C) list, and the excellent service
   (D) list, and even the excellent service
   (E) list, and how the waiters usually function

9. Contemporary poets are not abandoning rhyme, but some avoiding it.
   (A) but some avoiding it
   (B) but it is avoided by some of them
   (C) but it is being avoided
   (D) but some are avoiding it
   (E) but it has been being avoided by some

10. Your complaint is no different from the last customer who expected a refund.
    (A) Your complaint is no different from the last customer
    (B) Your complaint is no different from that of the last customer
    (C) Your complaint is similar to the last customer
    (D) Your complaint is no different then that of the last customer
    (E) Your complaint is the same as the last customer

11. According to the review board, many laboratory tests were ordered by the staff of the hospital that had no medical justification.
    (A) many laboratory tests were ordered by the staff of the hospital that
    (B) many laboratory tests were ordered by the staff of the hospital who
    (C) the staff of the hospital ordered many laboratory tests that
    (D) the staff of the hospital, who ordered many laboratory tests that
    (E) the ordering of many laboratory tests by the staff of the hospital which

12. Confident about the outcome, President Obama, along with his staff, are traveling to the conference.
    (A) Confident about the outcome, President Obama, along with his staff, are traveling
    (B) Confident about the outcome, President Obama's party are traveling
    (C) Confident about the outcome, President Obama, along with his staff, is traveling
    (D) With confidence about the outcome, President Obama, along with his staff, are traveling
    (E) President Obama, along with his staff, is traveling confidently about the outcome

GO ON TO NEXT PAGE ►

13. Helen Keller was blind and deaf from infancy and she learned to communicate using both sign language and speech.

(A) Helen Keller was blind and deaf from infancy and she
(B) Although blind and deaf from infancy, Helen Keller
(C) Although being blind and deaf from the time she was an infant, Helen Keller
(D) Being blind and deaf from infancy, Helen Keller
(E) Helen Keller, being blind and deaf from infancy, she

14. Standing alone beside her husband's grave, grief overwhelmed the widow and she wept inconsolably.

(A) grief overwhelmed the widow and she wept inconsolably
(B) grief overwhelmed the widow, who wept inconsolably
(C) grief overwhelmed the widow that wept inconsolably
(D) the widow, overwhelmed by grief, wept inconsolably
(E) the widow was overwhelmed by grief, she wept inconsolably

15. Survivors of a major catastrophe are likely to exhibit aberrations of behavior because of the trauma they have experienced.

(A) likely to exhibit aberrations of behavior because of the trauma they have experienced
(B) likely to exhibit aberrations of behavior because of them having experienced a trauma
(C) liable to exhibit aberrations from behavior due to the trauma they experienced
(D) liable to exhibit aberrations of behavior, the reason being that they have experienced a trauma
(E) likely for exhibiting aberrations of behavior due to the trauma they had experienced

16. Because the warranty on the defective toaster has expired, the store manager cannot do nothing about the problem.

(A) has expired, the store manager cannot do nothing about the problem
(B) has expired, the store manager cannot do anything against the problem
(C) has expired, the store manager can do nothing about the problem
(D) had expired, the store manager cannot do nothing about the problem
(E) has expired, the store manager cannot do nothing for the problem

17. In 1940, during the Battle of Britain, German bombs severely have damaged Holy Trinity Church in London, but the two bronze angels on the altar rail survived the bombardment unscathed.

(A) In 1940, during the Battle of Britain, German bombs severely have damaged Holy Trinity Church
(B) In 1940, during the Battle of Britain, German bombs severe have damaged Holy Trinity Church
(C) In 1940, during the Battle of Britain, German bombs severely damaging Holy Trinity Church
(D) During the Battle of Britain in 1940, German bombs severely have damaged Holy Trinity Church
(E) In 1940, during the Battle of Britain, German bombs severely damaged Holy Trinity Church

18. Not surprising, given the popularity of the spectacles in which they appeared, gladiators captured the public imagination.

(A) Not surprising, given the popularity of the spectacles in which they appeared
(B) Not surprising, because they were given the popularity of the spectacles in which they appeared
(C) Not surprisingly, given the popularity of the spectacles in which they appeared
(D) Not surprisingly, giving the popularity of the spectacles in which they appeared
(E) Not surprising, given the popularity of the spectacles where they appeared

GO ON TO NEXT PAGE ▶

19. Whether we admit it or not, biomedical research is currently supported on the backs of postdoctoral fellows, who make the industry possible by providing cheap labor.

(A) research is currently supported on the backs of postdoctoral fellows, who make the industry possible by providing
(B) research are currently supported on the backs of postdoctoral fellows, who make possible the industry for providing
(C) research is currently supported in back of postdoctoral fellows, who have made the industry possible by providing
(D) research is currently supported on the backs of postdoctoral fellows, with them making the industry possible by the provision of
(E) research is currently being supported on the backs of postdoctoral fellows, being that they make the industry possible by providing

20. Because the insect order Odonata, to which dragonflies belong, is not well studied, authoritative manuals on dragonflies that could be read and understood by the untrained observer were scarce until recently.

(A) belong, is not well studied, authoritative manuals on dragonflies that could be read and understood by the untrained observer were scarce until recently
(B) belong, are not well studied, authoritative manuals on dragonflies, which could be read and understood by the untrained observer were scarce until recently
(C) belong, is not well studied, until recently there were not scarcely any authoritative manuals on dragonflies that the untrained observer could read and understand
(D) belonged, was not well studied, authoritarian manuals on dragonflies that observers could have read and understood without being trained until recently were scarce
(E) belong, is not well studied, authoritative manuals on the dragonfly that could be read and understood by the untrained observer was scarcely until recently

GO ON TO NEXT PAGE ►

The sentences in this section may contain errors in grammar, usage, choice of words, or idioms. There is either just one error per sentence, or the sentence is correct. Some words or phrases are underlined and lettered; everything else in the sentence is correct.

If an underlined word or phrase is incorrect, choose that letter; if the sentence is correct, select No error. Then blacken the appropriate space on your answer sheet.

EXAMPLE:

The region has a climate so severe that [A] plants growing there [B] rarely had been [C] more than twelve inches high [D]. No error [E]

Ⓐ Ⓑ ● Ⓓ Ⓔ

21. Notice the immediate [A] affect [B] this [C] drug has on the behavior of [D] the rats in the cage. No error [E]

22. In spite of [A] official denials, news sources reported that [B] the bombs that hit Tripoli in 1986 were really [C] intended to kill [D] Muammar al-Qaddafi. No error [E]

23. Neither [A] the teacher nor her pupils were [B] enthused [C] about going on [D] the field trip. No error [E]

24. While [A] the Egyptian president Anwar El-Sadat was reviewing a military parade in 1981, a band of [B] commandos had shot [C] him and others in the vicinity [D]. No error [E]

25. Please do not be aggravated [A] by his bad manners [B] since [C] he is merely [D] trying to attract attention. No error [E]

26. Neither the opera singers or [A] the general public had seen [B] as much glitter [C] in years as they did during *Turandot*, the finale of [D] the opera season. No error [E]

27. His story about having been abducted by strange beings [A] in a spaceship was so [B] incredulous [C] that [D] no one believed him. No error [E]

28. The hot air balloon had burst as they were preparing [A] for launch [B], and the platform had broke [C] as a result [D]. No error [E]

29. Ann Landers, whose [A] name was a household word to millions of [B] readers, are [C] well-known [D] for family advice. No error [E]

Practice Test 3

GO ON TO NEXT PAGE ►

30. Child custody in surrogate mother cases is just
one of the many controversial issues that are
A B C
currently being decided upon in the courts.
D
No error
E

31. If you continue to drive so recklessly, you
A B
are likely to have a serious accident in the very
C D
near future. No error
E

32. The general, along with the members of
A
his general staff, seem to favor
B C
immediate retaliation. No error
D E

33. The rescue workers resented him criticizing their
A B
efforts because he had ignored their requests for
C
assistance up to that time. No error
D E

34. Casey Jones, who was killed in the line of duty,
A B
became a hero to fellow railroad workers and
C
was to be immortalized by a ballad. No error
D E

GO ON TO NEXT PAGE ▶

Improving Paragraphs Directions

The passage below is the unedited draft of a student's essay. Some of the essay needs to be rewritten to make the meaning clearer and more precise. Read the essay carefully.

The essay is followed by questions about changes that might improve all or part of its organization, development, sentence structure, use of language, appropriateness to the audience, or use of standard written English. Choose the answer that most clearly and effectively expresses the student's intended meaning. Indicate your choice by filling in the corresponding space on the answer sheet.

[1] Members of our community have objected to the inclusion of various pieces of art in the local art exhibit. **[2]** They say that these pieces offend community values. **[3]** The exhibit in its entirety should be presented.

[4] The reason for this is that people have varied tastes, and those who like this form of art have a right to see the complete exhibit. **[5]** An exhibit like this one gives the community a rare chance to see the latest modern art nearby, and many people have looked forward to it with great anticipation. **[6]** It would be an unfortunate blow to those people for it not to be shown.

[7] The exhibit may contain pieces of art that tend to be slightly erotic, but what is being shown that most people haven't already seen? **[8]** So, give it an R or an X rating and don't let small children in. **[9]** But how many small children voluntarily go to see an art exhibit? **[10]** The exhibit includes examples of a new style of modern art. **[11]** The paintings show crowds of nude people. **[12]** The exhibit is at the library's new art gallery. **[13]** For centuries artists have been painting and sculpting people in the nude. **[14]** Why are these works of art different? **[15]** Perhaps they are more graphic in some respects, but we live in a entirely different society than from the past. **[16]** It is strange indeed for people in this day and age to be offended by the sight of the human anatomy.

[17] If people don't agree with these pieces, they simply should just not go. **[18]** But they should not be allowed to prevent others from seeing it.

35. Taking into account the sentences that precede and follow sentence 3, which of the following is the best revision of sentence 3?

(A) On the other hand, the whole exhibit should be presented.
(B) The exhibit, however, should be presented in its entirety.
(C) The exhibit should be entirely presented regardless of what the critics say.
(D) But another point of view is that the exhibit should be presented in its entirety.
(E) Still other members also say the whole exhibit should be presented in its entirety.

36. In the context of paragraph 3, which of the following is the best revision of sentences 10, 11, and 12?

(A) Paintings on exhibit at the library showing crowds of nude people and done in a new style of modern art.
(B) The exhibit, on display at the library, includes paintings of crowds of nude people done in a new style of modern art.
(C) The exhibit includes paintings in a new style of modern art, which shows crowds of nude people at the library.
(D) The library is the site of the exhibit which shows a new style of modern art, with paintings showing crowds of nude people.
(E) The new style of modern art includes examples of paintings showing crowds of nude people on exhibit in the library.

GO ON TO NEXT PAGE ▶

37. To improve the clarity and coherence of the whole essay, where is the best place to relocate the ideas contained in sentences 10, 11, and 12?

(A) before sentence 1
(B) between sentences 1 and 2
(C) bbetween sentences 8 and 9
(D) between sentences 15 and 16
(E) after sentence 18

38. Which of the following is the best revision of the underlined segment of sentence 15 below?

Perhaps they are more graphic in some respects, but we live in a entirely different society than from the past.

(A) an entirely different society than of the past
(B) a completely different society than the past
(C) a society completely different than from past societies
(D) a society which is entirely different from the way societies have been in the past
(E) an entirely different society from that of the past

39. Which of the following revisions of sentence 17 provides the best transition between paragraphs 3 and 4?

(A) If anyone doesn't approve of these pieces, they simply should not go to the exhibit.
(B) Anyone disagreeing with the pieces in the exhibit shouldn't go to it.
(C) Anyone who disapproves of nudity in art simply shouldn't go to the exhibit.
(D) If anyone dislikes the sight of nudes in art, this show isn't for them.
(E) Don't go if you disapprove of nudity in art.

Practice Test 3

IF YOU FINISH IN LESS THAN 30 MINUTES, YOU MAY CHECK YOUR WORK ON THIS SECTION ONLY. DO NOT TURN TO ANY OTHER SECTION IN THE TEST.

STOP

Answer Key

Section 1 Critical Reading

1. A	6. E	11. A	16. D	21. C
2. B	7. C	12. E	17. B	22. D
3. E	8. B	13. E	18. B	23. E
4. D	9. C	14. A	19. B	24. B
5. D	10. C	15. D	20. D	

Section 2 Mathematics

1. B	5. C	9. C	13. D	17. C
2. D	6. D	10. D	14. D	18. B
3. B	7. B	11. C	15. D	19. B
4. D	8. E	12. B	16. A	20. A

Section 3 Critical Reading

25. B	30. C	35. D	40. E	45. E
26. D	31. A	36. B	41. B	46. B
27. B	32. D	37. C	42. B	47. C
28. B	33. C	38. D	43. C	48. D
29. E	34. B	39. B	44. D	

Section 4 Mathematics

21. B	23. C	25. C	27. C
22. C	24. E	26. D	28. C

29.
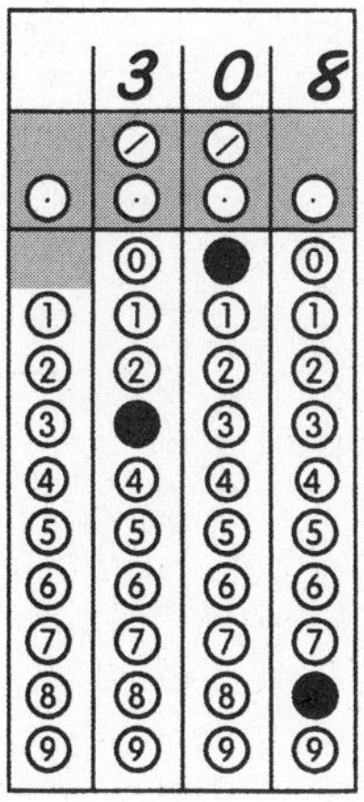

30.
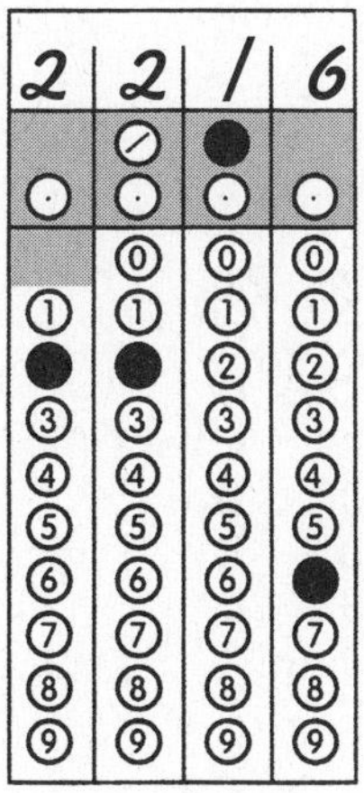

or 11/3
3.66

31.
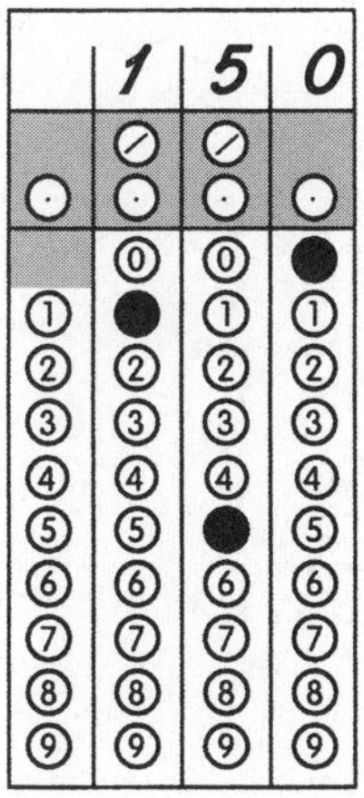

32.
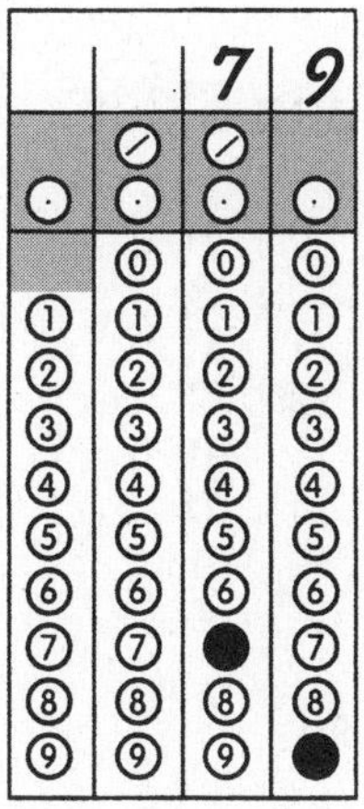

33.
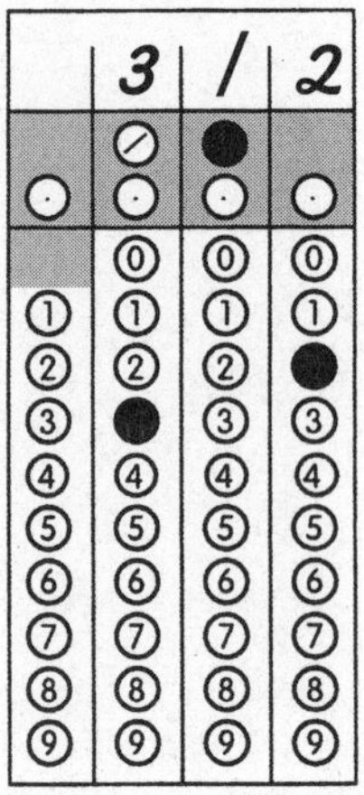

or **1.5**

34.
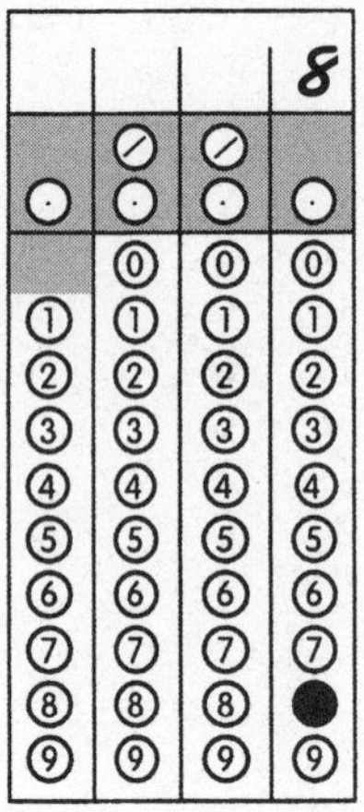

35.
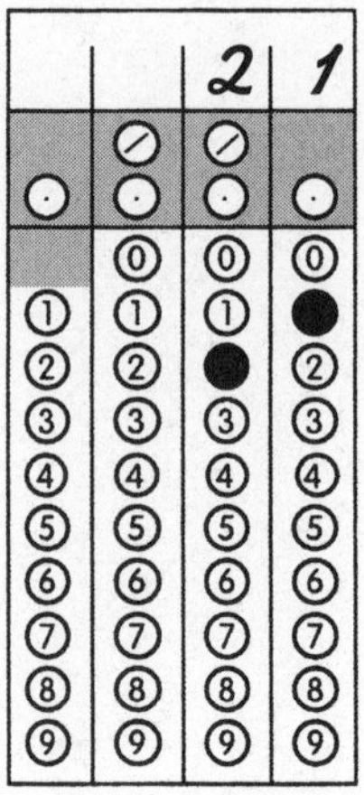

36.
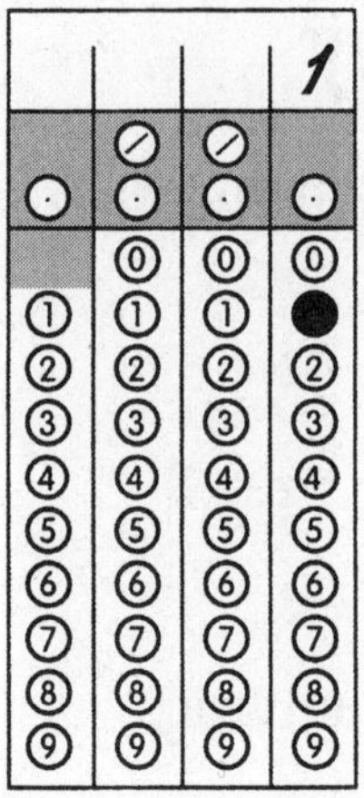

37.
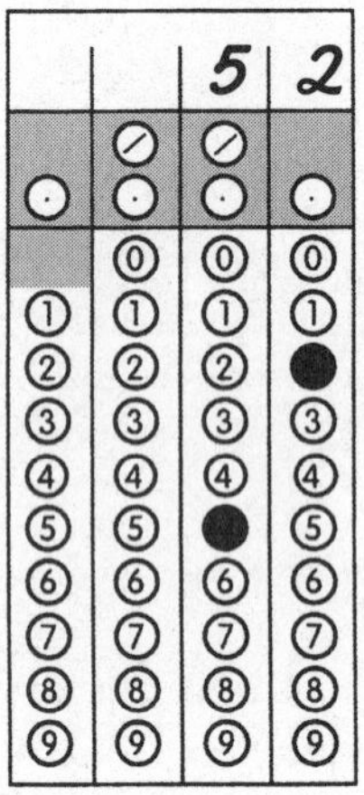

38.
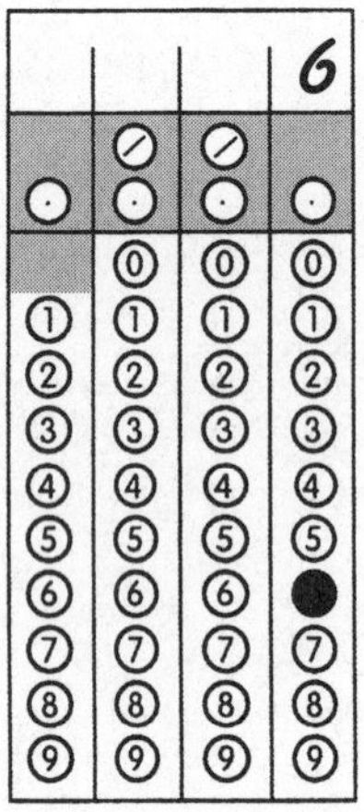

Section 5 Writing Skills

1. **E**
2. **E**
3. **C**
4. **E**
5. **E**
6. **B**
7. **C**
8. **C**
9. **D**
10. **B**
11. **C**
12. **C**
13. **B**
14. **D**
15. **A**
16. **C**
17. **E**
18. **C**
19. **A**
20. **A**
21. **B**
22. **E**
23. **C**
24. **C**
25. **A**
26. **A**
27. **C**
28. **C**
29. **C**
30. **D**
31. **E**
32. **C**
33. **A**
34. **D**
35. **D**
36. **B**
37. **A**
38. **E**
39. **C**

Practice Test 3

Scoring Chart—Practice Test 3

Critical Reading Sections			Mathematics Sections		
Section 1: 24 Questions (1–24)			**Section 2: 20 Questions (1–20)**		
Number correct	_____	(A)	Number correct	_____	(A)
Number omitted	_____	(B)	Number omitted	_____	(B)
Number incorrect	_____	(C)	Number incorrect	_____	(C)
$\frac{1}{4}$ (C)	_____	(D)	$\frac{1}{4}$ (C)	_____	(D)
(A) − (D)	_____	Raw Score I	(A) − (D)	_____	Raw Score I
Section 3: 24 Questions (25–48)			**Section 4: First 8 Questions (21–28)**		
Number correct	_____	(A)	Number correct	_____	(A)
Number omitted	_____	(B)	Number omitted	_____	(B)
Number incorrect	_____	(C)	Number incorrect	_____	(C)
$\frac{1}{4}$ (C)	_____	(D)	$\frac{1}{4}$ (C)	_____	(D)
(A) − (D)	_____	Raw Score II	(A) − (D)	_____	Raw Score II
			Section 4: Next 10 Questions (29–38)		
			Number correct	_____	Raw Score III
Total Critical Reading Raw Score			**Total Mathematics Raw Score**		
Raw Scores I + II	_____		Raw Scores I + II + III	_____	

NOTE: In each section (A) + (B) + (C) should equal the number of questions in that section.

Writing Skills Section

Section 5: 39 Questions (1–39)		
Number correct	_____	(A)
Number omitted	_____	(B)
Number incorrect	_____	(C)
$\frac{1}{4}$ (C)	_____	(D)
Writing Skills Raw Score		
(A) − (D)	_____	

Evaluation Chart

Study your score. Your raw score is an indication of your probable achievement on the PSAT/NMSQT. As a guide to the amount of work you need or want to do with this book, study the following.

Raw Score			**Self-Rating**
Critical Reading	*Mathematics*	*Writing Skills*	
42–48	35–38	33–39	Superior
37–41	30–34	28–32	Very good
32–36	25–29	23–27	Good
26–31	21–24	17–22	Above average
20–25	17–20	12–16	Average
12–19	10–16	7–11	Below average
less than 12	less than 10	less than 7	Inadequate

ANSWER EXPLANATIONS

Section 1 Critical Reading

1. **(A)** *Though* calls for a contrast. From someone with the reputation of a skilled craftsman, we expect fine work; instead, the work here is not polished but *crude*.

2. **(B)** According to the definition set off by dashes, the science of taxonomy is to classify or categorize living creatures, sorting them into groups with individual *names*.

3. **(E)** Why would fights break out in a small rookery? They would do so because there is not enough room to accommodate all the birds that need to build a nest. Because space is *limited*, each bird therefore must *vie for* (struggle or fight) its own patch of land.

4. **(D)** A person who could not support his claims for alleged cures with hard scientific data might as a consequence be called a *charlatan* (a faker or quack) by skeptics or disbelievers in his powers.

5. **(D)** It is Williams's *propensity* or liking for theatricality that causes critics to *denigrate* or belittle his plays as mere melodrama. Note how the use of *mere* and the sense of the Shakespearean quotation convey the idea that Williams's plays have been sullied or belittled.

6. **(E)** You can arrive at the correct answer by the process of elimination.

   True scientists do not jump to conclusions but methodically work their way toward them. Therefore, they are *systematic* and *deliberate*. You can eliminate Choices A and B.

   True scientists work toward their conclusions unerringly, that is, without making errors. Therefore, they are *accurate*. You can eliminate Choice C.

   True scientists are not strangers to hard work. Instead, they are *diligent* or hard-working. You can eliminate Choice D.

   Only Choice E is left. It is the correct answer. The author never characterizes true scientists as *inspired* in their approach to science.

7. **(C)** To champion a method or cause is to *espouse* (adopt or embrace) it.

8. **(B)** Unlike the author of Passage 1, the author of Passage 2 directly quotes a scientist, the naturalist Donald Culross Peattie. Thus, the author of Passage 2 makes use of *direct citation.* (Be on the lookout for quotation marks. They signal a direct quote or citation. While the author of Passage 1 refers to Boyle and Hooke by name, he does not quote them *directly.*)

9. **(C)** The author of Passage 1 wholeheartedly believes in the inductive method of reasoning, the modern scientific method advocated by Boyle and Hooke. Peattie, however, makes fun of this method and calls it plodding (poky and slow). It is therefore likely that the author of Passage 1 would respond to Peattie's mocking comments by arguing that Peattie *fails to appreciate the virtues of the inductive method sufficiently*.

10. **(C)** You can arrive at the correct answer by the process of elimination.

    Statement I is true. The passage states that the tornado's lifetime is never more than a few hours. Therefore, you can eliminate Choices B and D.

    Statement II is true. The first paragraph indicates that a fraction of the thunderstorm's tremendous energy "is concentrated into an area no more than several hundred meters in diameter." A later portion of the passage refers to the tornado's "concentrated high winds." Therefore, you can eliminate Choice A.

    Statement III is untrue. The passage indicates that tornadoes may vary markedly in size and shape. Therefore, you can eliminate Choice E.

    Only Choice C is left. It is the correct answer.

11. **(A)** The opening paragraph's concluding sentence serves as a *transition* or linking sentence connecting one part of the lengthy discussion to another. In this case, it introduces several paragraphs that describe tornadoes. The sentence is not a *concession* (acknowledgment; yielding a point in an argument). It is not an *apology* (expression of regret; formal defense). Neutral in tone, it is neither a *criticism* (serious judgment, often pointing out faults) nor a *refutation* (disproof of an argument).

Note the following icons, used throughout this book:

Time saver	Look it up; math reference fact	Helpful Hint
Educated guess	Prefixes, roots, and suffixes	Caution!
Did you notice?	Positive or negative?	Calculator use is recommended

12. **(E)** The reduced atmospheric pressure in the core region *pulls* or draws air to the base of the tornado.

13. **(E)** Paragraph three states that the "warmer and drier the inflowing air is, the greater the pressure drop must be for condensation to occur and a cloud to form." This suggests that temperature and humidity affect the tornado and that it *responds to changes in temperature and humidity*.

    Choice A is incorrect. The passage indicates that in the Northern Hemisphere a tornado's winds may be counterclockwise; it never suggests that a tornado's winds are *invariably* counterclockwise. Choice B is incorrect. Paragraph four states that a tornado's lifetime is never more than a few hours. Choice C is incorrect. The *warmer* and *drier* the air is, the greater the pressure drop has to be for the funnel cloud to form. This does not suggest that the cloud will not form if the air is cool and dry. Choice D is incorrect. A thunderstorm's cumulonimbus cloud can be more than 17 kilometers high. A tornado's funnel cloud is described as smaller than this.

14. **(A)** The author states that "if the core fills with dust, the funnel may take on a more exotic hue, such as the red of west Oklahoma clay." The hue or color of the funnel thus depends on what the soil in that region is made of.

15. **(D)** The author suggests a hypothesis (tornado noise "may result from the interaction of the concentrated high winds with the ground"). He provides a concrete example ("the red of west Oklahoma clay"). He indicates a time span ("never more than a few hours"). He uses similes ("roaring like a freight train"). He does not, however, argue a particular point of view.

16. **(D)** The author calls the industrialists and their "couldn't-lose" bankers and backers "canny boys" (shrewd fellows) and says the adults considered stories about these wheelers and dealers "inspirational to children." Clearly, she finds neither the stories nor the men inspirational: she looks on both with *irony*.

17. **(B)** In stating that she and the other children were "unthinkingly familiar" with the moguls' enormous buildings "as so much weird scenery on long drives," the author reveals that the children viewed these buildings as an accepted *backdrop to their lives*, something they saw in passing without giving it much thought.

18. **(B)** The moguls were fabulous men in being *celebrated* or famed for their wealth and philanthropy.

19. **(B)** The author's remark here can best be described as *an ironic aside*, a parenthetic comment that digresses from the theme or topic under discussion.

20. **(D)** The mother's tone in this comment is highly sardonic. Clearly, she is not someone who cares to rave or talk boastfully about her good birth and noble connections. Instead, she dismisses such people as snobs and dismisses Europe as a fit home for snobs.

21. **(C)** Beneath the lawns lie musket balls and arrowheads and bones, all relics of *Pittsburgh's buried past*. Note that in the paragraph that immediately follows this description the author cites details from Pittsburgh's history.

22. **(D)** To say that one knows something and does not know it is to state a *paradox*, an apparently self-contradictory declaration.

23. **(E)** In breaking the wilderness, the first white settlers *penetrated* the forest, bursting through the undergrowth into territory known only to the Native Americans.

24. **(B)** Summing up Pittsburgh's history, the author starts with modern big industry and works her way back in time till she concludes citing the pioneers who were the first white settlers in the region. Thus, she organizes the paragraph in *reverse chronological order*.

Section 2 Mathematics

For many problems, the explanation provides a reference to one or more **KEY FACTS** from Chapter 7. These are the mathematical facts that you need to solve that problem. If a solution refers to **KEY FACT J2**, for example, the solution depends on the second **KEY FACT** discussed in Section J of Chapter 7.

For some problems, an alternative solution, indicated by two asterisks (**), follows the first solution. When this occurs, usually one of the solutions is the direct mathematical one and the other is based on one of the tactics discussed in Chapters 6 and 7.

See page 234 for an explanation of the symbol ⇒, which is used in several answer explanations.

1. **(B)** $88 ÷ $16 per hour = 5.5 hours.

   **If you prefer, set up a ratio and cross-multiply:

$$\frac{16 \text{ dollars}}{1 \text{ hour}} = \frac{88 \text{ dollars}}{x \text{ hours}}.$$

2. **(D)** In 11 days Sarah saves \$88. If 11 days ago she had \$324, she now has \$324 + \$88 = \$412, and 11 days from now will have \$412 + \$88 = \$500.

**From 11 days ago to 11 days from now is 22 days. In 22 days Sarah saves 22 × \$8 = \$176, and \$176 + \$324 = \$500.

**Remember, even on easy questions, some of the choices are absurd. Clearly, 11 days from now Sarah will have much more money than she did 11 days ago. So the answer has to be much more than \$324. You can eliminate choices A and B and almost certainly C.

3. **(B)** The average of a and b is $\frac{a+b}{2}$, and the product of that with 7 is $7\left(\frac{a+b}{2}\right) = \frac{7a+7b}{2}$.

**It is easier and quicker to do this directly. So substitute for a and b, only if you get stuck or confused. If $a = 2$ and $b = 4$, their average is 3, and the product of 7 and their average is 21. Only Choice B is equal to 21 when $a = 2$ and $b = 4$.

4. **(D)** Let the number be x, and write the equation

$$\frac{3}{4}x = 7 + \frac{1}{6}x.$$

Multiply both sides by 12: $9x = 84 + 2x$

Subtract $2x$ from each side and divide by 7:

$$7x = 84 \Rightarrow x = 12$$

Be careful: 12 is *not* the answer. You were asked for $\frac{5}{3}$ of the number. $\frac{5}{3}(12) = 20$.

5. **(C)** By **KEY FACT K2**, the sum of the measures of two adjacent angles of a parallelogram is 180°. Therefore,

$$180 = 10x + 25x - 30 = 35x - 30,$$

which implies that $35x = 210$ and $x = 6$.

6. **(D)** There's nothing to do except check the choices, although it is often faster to start with E and work toward A.

E: $9 * 9 = \sqrt{9 + \sqrt{9}} = \sqrt{9+3} = \sqrt{12}$, which is not an integer.

D: $7 * 4 = \sqrt{7 + \sqrt{4}} = \sqrt{7+2} = \sqrt{9} = 3$, an integer. The answer is D. Once you find the answer, do not waste any time trying the other choices—they won't work.

7. **(B)** The factory produces 64 engines per day × 25 days per month × 12 months per year = 19,200 engines per year, and 96,000 ÷ 19,200 = 5.

8. **(E)** Label each angle in the diagram.

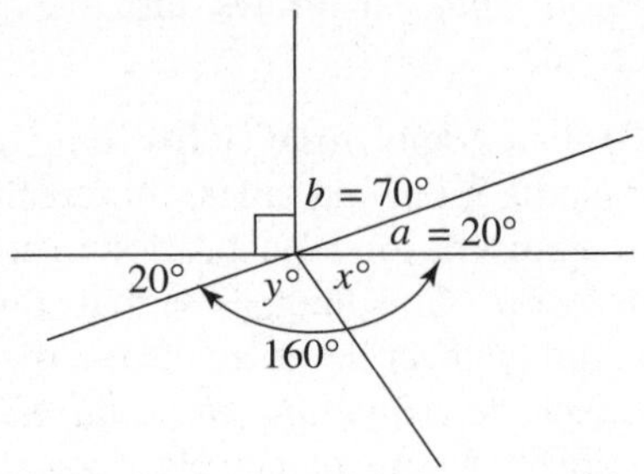

Since vertical angles are equal, $a = 20$, and so $x + y = 160$. We can see that $b = 70$, but there are no other vertical angles, and it is impossible to determine x or y from the information given.

9. **(C)** Since $x^2 - y^2 = (x - y)(x + y)$, then

$$75 = x^2 - y^2 = (x - y)(x + y) = 5(x + y).$$

Therefore, $x + y = 15$. Adding the equations

$$x + y = 15 \text{ and } x - y = 5, \text{ we get}$$
$$2x = 20 \Rightarrow x = 10 \Rightarrow y = 5.$$

Use **TACTIC 6-1: backsolve. Choice C works.

10. **(D)** If Julie had to pay 30% of the value of her inheritance in taxes, she still owned 70% of her inheritance: 70% of 40% is 28% (0.70 × 0.40 = 0.28).

Use **TACTIC 6-3. Assume the estate was worth \$100. Julie received 40% or \$40. Her tax was 30% of \$40, or \$12. She still had \$28, or 28% of the \$100 estate.

11. **(C)** The given expression (3!)(4!) = 6(24) = 144. Now, evaluate the three choices.

I: 7! = 5040, which is much too big (false).
II: 12! is even bigger (false).
III: 4! + 5! = 24 + 120 = 144 (true).
III only is true.

12. **(B)** It is given that $BE = BC$; also $BC = AD$, since they are opposite sides of a rectangle. Label each of them w, as shown in the diagram.

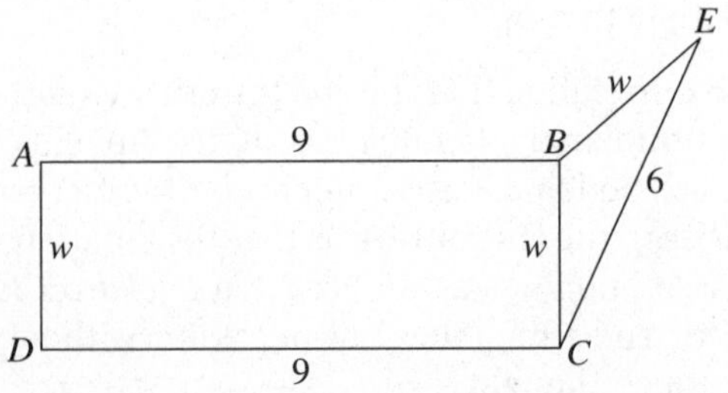

Then $R = 18 + 2w$ and $T = 6 + 2w$. So, $R - T = (18 + 2w) - (6 + 2w) = 18 - 6 = 12$.

13. **(D)** Since the game takes one hour, or 60 minutes, and there are always 5 men playing, the game consists of $5 \times 60 = 300$ player-minutes. If that is evenly divided among the 12 players, each one plays $300 \div 12 = 25$ minutes.

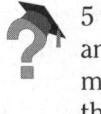

**If you get stuck, test the choices. Eliminate the choices that can't be right, and guess. If 5 men played the first 10 or 12 minutes and 5 other men played the next 10 or 12 minutes, there wouldn't be 5 men available to play the rest of the game. So 10 and 12 are much too small. Eliminate A and B. If 5 men played for 30 minutes and 5 other men played the next 30 minutes, the game would be over, and 2 men wouldn't have played at all. Eliminate E since 30 is too large. The answer must be 24 or 25.

14. **(D)** Since $A = \pi r^2$, $r^2 = \frac{A}{\pi}$ and $r = \sqrt{\frac{A}{\pi}} = \frac{\sqrt{A}}{\sqrt{\pi}}$.

The circumference, C, equals $2\pi r$. So,

$$C = 2\pi \frac{\sqrt{A}}{\sqrt{\pi}} = 2\sqrt{\pi}\sqrt{A} = 2\sqrt{\pi A}$$

**Let r, the radius of the circle, be 2. Then the circumference, C, is $2\pi r = 4\pi$ and the area, A, is $\pi r^2 = 4\pi$. Only choice D is equal to 4π when $A = 4\pi$.

15. **(D)** By **KEY FACT N4**, the slope $= \frac{y_2 - y_1}{x_2 - x_1}$.

Then $\frac{2}{3} = \frac{5-(-3)}{k-3} = \frac{8}{k-3}$.

Cross-multiply:

$$24 = 2k - 6 \Rightarrow 2k = 30 \Rightarrow k = 15.$$

**If you don't remember the formula, make a quick sketch:

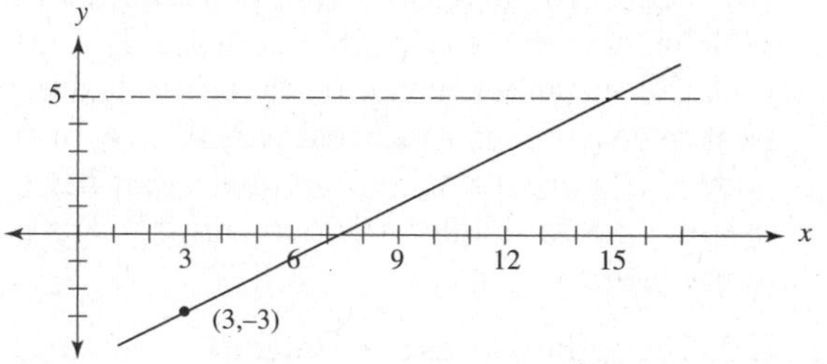

Since the slope is positive, k is greater than 3, and since the slope is less than 1, the line is going up too slowly for k to be 6 or 8. Guess 15.

16. **(A)** If x is odd, so are $5x$ and $5x + 4$. To get the smallest odd number greater than $5x + 4$, add 2: $5x + 6$. On the other hand, $3x + 7$ is even, and the largest odd number smaller than it is 1 less than $3x + 7$, namely $3x + 6$. The required difference is $(5x + 6) - (3x + 6) = 2x$.

Use **TACTIC 6-2 and let $x = 3$. The smallest odd number greater than 19 is 21; the largest odd number less than 16 is 15; and $21 - 15 = 6$.

Which answer equals 6 when $x = 3$? Only A.

17. **(C)** It's worth remembering that when the three angles of a triangle are in the ratio of 1:2:3, the triangle is a 30-60-90 right triangle. (If you don't remember that, then solve the equation $x + 2x + 3x = 180$.) In a 30-60-90 right triangle the sides are a, $a\sqrt{3}$, and $2a$; so the desired ratio is $a{:}2a = 1{:}2$.

18. **(B)** At 2:00, the first car had been going 50 miles per hour for 2 hours and so had gone 100 miles. The second car covered the same 100 miles in 1 hour and 40 minutes, or $1\frac{2}{3} = \frac{5}{3}$ hours. Therefore, its rate was $100 \div \frac{5}{3} = 100 \times \frac{3}{5} = 60$ miles per hour.

19. **(B)** Since a is inversely proportional to b, there is a constant k such that $ab = k$. (See Section 7-D.)

So $k = (3)(5) = 15$.

Therefore, $10b = 15 \Rightarrow b = \frac{15}{10} = \frac{3}{2}$.

20. **(A)** If 12% of a = 60% of b, then

$$.12a = .60b \Rightarrow 12a = 60b \Rightarrow b = \frac{12a}{50} = \frac{a}{5}.$$

So, b is $\frac{1}{5}$ or 20% of a.

**Let $b = 100$. Then, since 12% of a = 60% of b, we have $0.12a = 60$. So, $a = 60 \div 0.12 = 500$. Finally, 100 is $\frac{1}{5}$ or 20% of 500.

Section 3 Critical Reading

25. **(B)** The use of *but* indicates that the dean's attempt to keep control failed. It did so because it was *frustrated* by the board of trustees. None of the other possible actions of the board of trustees would necessarily have caused the dean's attempt to fail.

26. **(D)** To lack one's usual energy and interest in life is by definition to be *listless* (languid, spiritless). Note how the phrase following the comma serves to define the missing word.

27. **(B)** A plan for a journey is by definition an *itinerary*.

28. **(B)** Mark keeps his reservations or reluctance to go along with his fraternity's policies to himself: he says nothing. By saying nothing, he lets his fraternity brothers assume his *silence* is a sign of *acquiescence* or agreement.

29. **(E)** A *glutton* is by definition a person who eats or drinks excessively, someone who indulges his or her appetites without restraint.

30. **(C)** The phrase "given the . . ." signals cause and effect. *Because* many areas of conflict are still in need of *resolution* or settlement, we do not know what the outcome of the peace talks will be. In other words, the end result of the talks remains *problematic* (unclear and unsettled; perplexing).

31. **(A)** *While* signals a contrast. Bonner does not like religious or mystical (spiritual; not apparent to the senses) explanations of intelligence. Instead she likes *rational* (logical) and *materialistic* ones that define reality as explainable only in terms of physical matter.

32. **(D)** It would be unfortunate for a book to come down very firmly on one side of a debate if, in the process, it *skimmed over* (examined superficially or missed entirely) tricky spots in the argument and gave the reader a *simplistic*, oversimplified picture of the subject.

33. **(C)** If students talk about continental drift as if everyone has always known about the concept, then it is an *accepted concept* or commonplace.

34. **(B)** The author is denying that everyone has always known about the theory of continental drift. ("Not so.") He states that it was "not quite" a century ago that the theory was proposed. Thus, he is emphasizing the relatively *recent origin* of the theory.

35. **(D)** The passage serves simply to portray or *depict an instance of heroism under fire*.

36. **(B)** Kirkland could no longer bear or *endure* the cries of the dying.

37. **(C)** Repetition often is used rhetorically for emphasis. By asking question after question about why women's writing has taken the shape it has, the author *underscores* or emphasizes *how little is known about* a significant subject.

38. **(D)** To fill an office is to work in or *hold* that job.

39. **(B)** To make her point, Woolf gives *examples* of three women about whom little is known.

40. **(E)** "One was beautiful; one was red-haired; one was kissed by a Queen." What did these women have in common? They all led *largely unrecorded lives*: their grandchildren know only stray fragments about the history of these women's lives.

41. **(B)** You can answer this question by using the process of elimination. The author includes among the conditions of the average woman's life the question of whether she had money of her own, in other words, her *financial circumstances*. Therefore, you can eliminate Choice A. Likewise, the author wishes to know the number of the average woman's children in order to assess her *maternal obligations*. You can eliminate Choice C. In inquiring whether the average woman had servants or other household help, the author seeks information about her *social position* or rank. You can eliminate Choice D. Finally, in asking whether the average woman had a room to herself, the author seeks information about her *housing arrangements*. You can eliminate Choice E. Only Choice B is left. It is the correct answer. The author never specifically inquires about the average woman's illnesses or *medical problems*.

42. **(B)** The writer neither lists (*enumerates*) nor sorts (*classifies*) anything in the opening paragraph.

Choice A is incorrect. The writer likens the female tradition to a lost continent and develops the metaphor by describing the continent "rising . . . from the sea of English literature." Choice C is incorrect. The author refers or *alludes* to the classical legend of Atlantis. Choice D is incorrect. The author quotes Colby and Thompson. Choice E is incorrect. The author contrasts the revised view of women's literature with Mill's view.

43. **(C)** The legend of Atlantis tells of a continent that sank beneath the sea, only to rise again. The author uses the metaphor of the newly arisen lost continent to give the reader a sense of how an enormous body of *literary works written by women* has once more come to public attention, *resurfacing after many years*.

44. **(D)** The author opens the paragraph by stating that many literary critics have begun reinterpreting the study of women's literature. She then goes on to cite individual comments that support her assertion. Clearly, she is *receptive* or open to the ideas of these writers, for they and she share a common sense of the need to reinterpret their common field.

Choices A and B are incorrect. The author cites the literary critics straightforwardly, presenting their statements as evidence supporting her thesis. Choice C is incorrect. The author does not *disparage* or belittle these critics. By quoting them respectfully she implicitly acknowledges their competence. Choice E is incorrect. The author quotes the critics as acknowledged experts in the field. However, she is quite ready to disagree with their conclusions (as she disagrees with Moers's view of women's literature as an international movement). Clearly, she does not look on these critics with *awe*.

45. **(E)** To study something with a special closeness is to pay *minute attention to details*.

46. **(B)** If women writers have no history, they have to rediscover the past. In the process, they *create* or forge their consciousness of what their sex has achieved. Here *forge* is used with its meaning of *fashion* or *make*, as blacksmiths forge metal by hammering it into shape. It is in this sense that James Joyce used *forge* in *A Portrait of the Artist as a Young Man*, whose hero goes forth to "forge in the smithy of (his) soul the uncreated conscience of (his) race."

47. **(C)** The author both cites Moers's work in support of her own assertions and argues against the validity of Moers's conclusion that women's literature is an international movement. Thus, while she finds Moers's work basically *admirable* and worthy of respect, she considers it *inaccurate* in some of the conclusions it draws.

    Choice A is incorrect. The author would not cite Moers as she does in the second paragraph if she believed Moers to be wholly *misleading*. Choice B is incorrect. Since the author disagrees with at least one of Moers's conclusions, she obviously does not find Moers's work the *definitive* or final word. Choices D and E are incorrect. Neither is supported by the author's mentions of Moers.

48. **(D)** Woolf does not document her argument with extensive quotations from literary critics. Instead, she uses telling examples ("One was beautiful; one was red-haired; one was kissed by a Queen") to show how little we know about our grandmothers' actual lives. She is *less scholarly and more descriptive* in her approach to the subject.

Section 4 Mathematics

For many problems, the explanation provides a reference to one or more **KEY FACTS** from Chapter 7. These are the mathematical facts that you need to solve that problem. If a solution refers to **KEY FACT J2**, for example, the solution depends on the second **KEY FACT** discussed in Section J of Chapter 7.

For some problems, an alternative solution, indicated by two asterisks (**), follows the first solution. When this occurs, usually one of the solutions is the direct mathematical one and the other is based on one of the tactics discussed in Chapters 6 and 7.

See page 234 for an explanation of the symbol $\Rightarrow$, which is used in several answer explanations.

21. **(B)** If $x = -5$, then

$$2x^2 - 4x - 3 = 2(-5)^2 - 4(-5) - 3 = 2(25) + 20 - 3 = 67.$$

22. **(C)** Since $x + 100 = 180$, $x = 80$; also,

$$y + y + x = 180 \Rightarrow$$
$$2y + 80 = 180 \Rightarrow$$
$$2y = 100 \Rightarrow y = 50.$$

    Since by **KEY FACT J2 the measure of an exterior angle of a triangle is equal to the sum of the measures of the two opposite interior angles, $100 = y + y$. So, $y = 50$.

23. **(C)** $12 = \frac{1}{b} + \frac{1}{b} + \frac{1}{b} + \frac{1}{b} = \frac{4}{b} \Rightarrow 12b = 4$

    So, $b = \frac{4}{12} = \frac{1}{3}$.

24. **(E)** If d of the cartons were unpacked, $c - d$ were still full, so the fraction of the cartons that were not yet unpacked was $\frac{c-d}{c}$. To get the percent, multiply the fractional part by 100%: $\frac{100(c-d)}{c}\%$.

    Use **TACTIC 8-2. If Lucy had 10 cartons to unpack, then after unpacking 2 of them, 8 of the 10 (80%) still had to be unpacked. Only $\frac{100(c-d)}{c}\%$ equals 80% when $c = 10$ and $d = 2$.

25. **(C)** Since the sum of the measures of the two acute angles of a right triangle is 90°, $a + d = 90$. Also, $b + c = 180$. Therefore,

$$a + b + c + d = 90 + 180 = 270.$$

26. **(D)** First add $\frac{1}{3} + \frac{1}{4}$ and then subtract that sum from both sides:

$$\frac{1}{x} + \left(\frac{1}{3} + \frac{1}{4}\right) = \frac{1}{x} + \frac{7}{12} = 1 \Rightarrow \frac{1}{x} = \frac{5}{12}.$$

    Finally, take the reciprocal of each side (or cross-multiply): $x = \frac{12}{5}$.

27. **(C)** Since $AB = AC$, by **KEY FACT J2**, $m\angle B = m\angle C$. So, by **KEY FACT J1**,

$$30 + m\angle B + m\angle C = 180 \Rightarrow$$
$$m\angle B + m\angle C = 150 \Rightarrow m\angle B = 75.$$

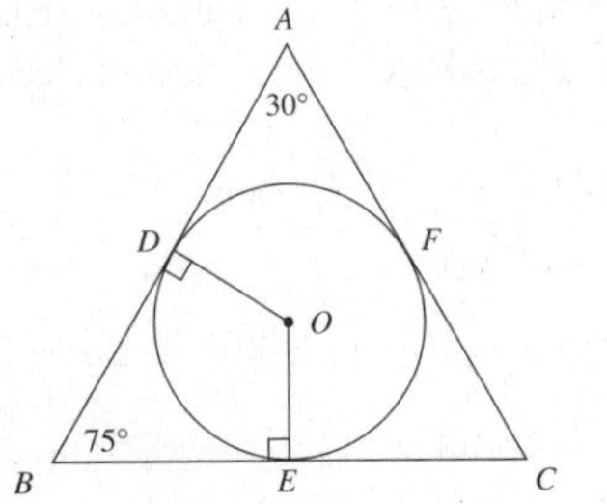

Also, since $\overline{AB}$ and $\overline{BC}$ are tangents, then, by **KEY FACT L10**, the radii $\overline{OD}$ and $\overline{OE}$ are perpendicular to $\overline{AB}$ and $\overline{BC}$, respectively, and hence form 90° angles. Finally, by **KEY FACT K1**, the sum of the four angles in quadrilateral *ODBE* is 360:

$$75 + 90 + 90 + m\angle DOE = 360 \Rightarrow$$
$$255 + m\angle DOE = 360 \Rightarrow m\angle DOE = 105.$$

28. **(C)** According to the triangle inequality **(KEY FACT J9)**, the sum of the lengths of two sides of a triangle must be greater than the length of the third. Now use **TACTIC 6-10**: systematically test each possibility. Try choosing 1 from *A*: you can't choose 2 from *B*, because 1 + 2 = 3, which is not greater than any number in *C*; you can, however, choose 3 from *B* and 3 from *C*. So one way is (1,3,3). The other ways are (2,2,3), (2,3,3), and (2,3,4), a total of 4 ways.

29. **(308)** Don't do any algebra. Just replace a and b by 7 and 11 in the original expression:

$$(7 + 11)^2 - (7 - 11)^2 =$$
$$18^2 - (-4)^2 = 324 - 16 = 308.$$

30. $\left(\mathbf{\frac{22}{6}} \textbf{ or } \mathbf{\frac{11}{3}} \textbf{ or 3.66}\right)$ Notice that the left-hand side of the equation is the negative of the right-hand side, meaning that each side is equal to 0. Therefore,

$$3x - 11 = 0 \Rightarrow 3x = 11 \Rightarrow x = \frac{11}{3}.$$

**Just solve the equation

$$3x - 11 = 11 - 3x \Rightarrow 6x = 22 \Rightarrow x = \frac{22}{6}.$$

Note that it is *not* necessary to reduce $\frac{22}{6}$. (It's not even advisable.)

31. **(150)** Since Len got \$100, the other three shared the remaining \$900. If x represents Jim's share, then Kim got $2x$ and Ben got $3x$. Then

$$900 = x + 2x + 3x = 6x \Rightarrow x = 150.$$

32. **(79)** For a fraction to be large, the numerator should be as large as possible and the denominator as small as possible. The greatest value that $x^2 - y$ could have is 80, by letting $x = 9$ and $y = 1$. Since x, y, and z are different, the least that z could be is 2, and the value of the fraction would be $\frac{80}{2}$, or 40. However, if you interchange x and y, you get 79 for the numerator $(9^2 - 2)$ and 1 for the denominator: $\frac{79}{1}$ or 79.

33. $\left(\mathbf{\frac{3}{2}} \textbf{ or 1.5}\right)$ The center of a circle is the midpoint of any diameter. Therefore, by the midpoint formula **(KEY FACT N3)**

$$(x, y) = \left(\frac{-3+5}{2}, \frac{2+(-1)}{2}\right) = \left(\frac{2}{2}, \frac{1}{2}\right) = \left(1, \frac{1}{2}\right).$$

$$\text{So } x + y = 1 + \tfrac{1}{2} = 1\tfrac{1}{2}.$$

Note: Since you cannot grid-in a mixed number, you *must* enter $1\frac{1}{2}$ as $\frac{3}{2}$ or 1.5.

34. **(8)** Since the repeating portion of this decimal number is 6 digits long, divide 200 by 6 to determine how many times the sequence 4, 2, 8, 5, 7, 1 repeats in the first 200 digits. When 200 is divided by 6, the quotient is 33.333 . . . Ignore the decimal portion. There are 33 complete repetitions, and since 33 × 6 = 198, the 198th digit ends the 33rd group and so is a 1. Then the 199th digit is 4, and the 200th digit is 2.

35. **(21)** The sum of 2 two-digit numbers must be less than 200; so $A = 1$, and the sum is 111. If $B + D$ were 1, either B or D would be 0 and the other would be 1; but $A = 1$ and each letter represents a different digit. So $B + D$ must be 11, which means that 1 is carried into the tens column. In the tens column we must add 1 (for A), the 1 we carried, and C, and the sum is 11. Then $1 + 1 + C = 11$, and $C = 9$.

So, $A = 1$, $C = 9$, and $B + D = 11$. Therefore, $A + B + C + D = 1 + 9 + 11 = 21$.

36. **(1)** Since the entire region is a circle of radius 4, its area is $\pi(4)^2 = 16\pi$. The shaded region is a circle of radius 3 minus the small white circle of radius 1; so its area is $9\pi - \pi = 8\pi$ $(a = 8\pi)$. The area of the white region can be found by subtracting the area of the shaded region (8π) from the total area (16π). So $b = 16\pi - 8\pi = 8\pi$. Finally, $\frac{a}{b} = \frac{8\pi}{8\pi} = 1$.

37. **(52)** This is a weighted average:

$$\frac{40\%(40) + 60\%(60)}{100\%} = \frac{16 + 36}{1} = 52.$$

**If you prefer, assume there are 100 marbles, 40 of which are red and 60 of which are blue:

$$\frac{40(40) + 60(60)}{100} = \frac{1600 + 3600}{100} = 52.$$

38. **(6)** Let x represent the degree measure of each exterior angle, and then $2x$ is the degree measure of each interior angle. Since the sum of the measures of an interior and exterior angle is 180°: $x + 2x = 180 \Rightarrow 3x = 180 \Rightarrow x = 60$. Since the sum of the measures of all the exterior angles of a polygon is 360°, there are $360 \div 60 = 6$ angles and, of course, 6 sides.

Section 5 Writing Skills

1. **(E)** Error in pronoun case. The noun or pronoun preceding a gerund (*going*) should be in the possessive case.

2. **(E)** Error in modification. The dangling modifier is best corrected in Choice E.

3. **(C)** Comma splice. Choices A and B are run-on sentences. Choices D and E are ungrammatical.

4. **(E)** Error in modification and double negative. Both are corrected in Choice E.

5. **(E)** Error in coordination and subordination. By changing *having* to *had* and connecting the two main clauses with a semicolon, you tighten the sentence and eliminate wordiness.

6. **(B)** Sentence fragment. Choice B expresses the author's meaning directly and concisely. All other choices are indirect, ungrammatical, or fail to retain the meaning of the original statement.

7. **(C)** Error in agreement. *Kind* should be modified by *this* or *that; kinds,* by *these* or *those.*

8. **(C)** Error in parallelism. *New, list,* and *service* are all nouns. Thus, parallel structure is retained in Choice C.

9. **(D)** This corrects the sentence fragment smoothly.

10. **(B)** Error in logical comparison. Compare *complaints* with *complaints*, not with *customers*. The faulty comparison is corrected in Choice B.

11. **(C)** Error in modification. Choice C corrects the misplaced modifier and eliminates the unnecessary use of the passive voice.

12. **(C)** Error in subject-verb agreement. The phrase *along with his staff* is not part of the subject of the sentence. The subject is *President Obama* (singular); the verb should be *is traveling* (singular).

13. **(B)** Error in coordination and subordination. The use of the subordinating conjunction *Although* and the deletion of unnecessary words strengthen this sentence.

14. **(D)** Choices A, B, and C have dangling modifiers; Choice E creates a run-on sentence.

15. **(A)** Sentence is correct.

16. **(C)** Double negative. Change *cannot do nothing* to *can do nothing.*

17. **(E)** Error in sequence of tenses. The present perfect tense (*have damaged*) refers to some unspecified time in the past. Here, however, the author is telling about something that occurred at a definite time in the past: "In 1940, during the Battle of Britain." In this context, the simple past tense (*damaged*) is correct.

18. **(C)** Adjective-adverb confusion. The adverb phrase *Not surprisingly* modifies (describes or limits) the rest of the sentence.

19. **(A)** Sentence is correct.

20. **(A)** Sentence is correct.

21. **(B)** Error in diction. *Affect* is a verb and should not be used in place of *effect*.

22. **(E)** Sentence is correct.

23. **(C)** Error in diction. There is no such verb as *enthuse*. Change *enthused* to *enthusiastic*.

24. **(C)** Error in tense. Change *had shot* to *shot*.

25. **(A)** Error in diction. Use *irritated* instead of *aggravated*.

26. **(A)** Error in idiom. Change *neither . . . or* to *neither . . . nor*.

27. **(C)** Error in diction. Change *incredulous* to *incredible.*

28. **(C)** Error in tense. Change *had broke* to *had broken*.

29. **(C)** Error in subject-verb agreement. The subject, *Ann Landers*, is singular; the verb should be singular—*is*.

30. **(D)** Error in diction. Issues are *decided* or settled. The actual choice made is what is *decided upon*. Delete *upon*.

31. **(E)** Sentence is correct.

32. **(C)** Error in subject-verb agreement. The subject, *general*, is singular; the verb should be singular—*seems*.

33. **(A)** Error in pronoun case. The possessive pronoun precedes a gerund. Change *him* to *his*.

34. **(D)** Error in tense. Change *was to be immortalized* to *was immortalized.*

35. **(D)** Choices A, B, and C abruptly state the contrasting point of view without regard to the context.

    Choice D takes the context into account and provides for a smooth progression of thought. It is the best answer.

    Choice E is confusing. It is unclear until the end of the sentence whether the *other members* support or oppose the exhibit.

36. **(B)** Choice A lacks a main verb; therefore, it is a sentence fragment.

    Choice B accurately combines the sentences. It is the best answer.

    Choice C expresses the idea in a way that the writer could not have intended.

    Choice D subordinates important ideas and emphasizes a lesser one.

    Choice E restates the idea in a manner that changes the writer's intended meaning.

37. **(A)** Choice A is the best choice because the sentences contain basic information about the topic. Readers are left in the dark unless the information appears as early as possible in the essay.

38. **(E)** Choice A contains faulty idiom; the phrase *than of the past* is nonstandard usage. Choice B contains a faulty comparison; *society* and *the past* cannot be logically compared. Choice C contains an error in idiom; the phrase *than from* is redundant. Choice D is correct but excessively wordy. Choice E is the best answer.

39. **(C)** Choice A provides a reasonable transition, but it contains an error in pronoun-antecedent agreement. The pronoun *they* is plural; its antecedent *anyone* is singular.

    Choice B contains an error in diction. One can *disapprove of* but not *disagree with* a piece of art.

    Choice C alludes to the content of the previous paragraph and is clearly and succinctly expressed. It is the best answer.

    Choice D contains an error in pronoun-antecedent agreement. The pronoun *them* is plural; the antecedent *anyone* is singular.

    Choice E is inconsistent in tone and mood with the rest of the essay.

Answer Sheet—Practice Test 4

Each mark should completely fill the appropriate space, and should be as dark as all other marks. Make all erasures complete. Traces of an erasure may be read as an answer.

Section 1 – Critical Reading

25 minutes

1 Ⓐ Ⓑ Ⓒ Ⓓ Ⓔ
2 Ⓐ Ⓑ Ⓒ Ⓓ Ⓔ
3 Ⓐ Ⓑ Ⓒ Ⓓ Ⓔ
4 Ⓐ Ⓑ Ⓒ Ⓓ Ⓔ
5 Ⓐ Ⓑ Ⓒ Ⓓ Ⓔ
6 Ⓐ Ⓑ Ⓒ Ⓓ Ⓔ
7 Ⓐ Ⓑ Ⓒ Ⓓ Ⓔ
8 Ⓐ Ⓑ Ⓒ Ⓓ Ⓔ
9 Ⓐ Ⓑ Ⓒ Ⓓ Ⓔ
10 Ⓐ Ⓑ Ⓒ Ⓓ Ⓔ
11 Ⓐ Ⓑ Ⓒ Ⓓ Ⓔ
12 Ⓐ Ⓑ Ⓒ Ⓓ Ⓔ
13 Ⓐ Ⓑ Ⓒ Ⓓ Ⓔ
14 Ⓐ Ⓑ Ⓒ Ⓓ Ⓔ
15 Ⓐ Ⓑ Ⓒ Ⓓ Ⓔ
16 Ⓐ Ⓑ Ⓒ Ⓓ Ⓔ
17 Ⓐ Ⓑ Ⓒ Ⓓ Ⓔ
18 Ⓐ Ⓑ Ⓒ Ⓓ Ⓔ
19 Ⓐ Ⓑ Ⓒ Ⓓ Ⓔ
20 Ⓐ Ⓑ Ⓒ Ⓓ Ⓔ
21 Ⓐ Ⓑ Ⓒ Ⓓ Ⓔ
22 Ⓐ Ⓑ Ⓒ Ⓓ Ⓔ
23 Ⓐ Ⓑ Ⓒ Ⓓ Ⓔ
24 Ⓐ Ⓑ Ⓒ Ⓓ Ⓔ

Section 2 – Math

25 minutes

1 Ⓐ Ⓑ Ⓒ Ⓓ Ⓔ
2 Ⓐ Ⓑ Ⓒ Ⓓ Ⓔ
3 Ⓐ Ⓑ Ⓒ Ⓓ Ⓔ
4 Ⓐ Ⓑ Ⓒ Ⓓ Ⓔ
5 Ⓐ Ⓑ Ⓒ Ⓓ Ⓔ
6 Ⓐ Ⓑ Ⓒ Ⓓ Ⓔ
7 Ⓐ Ⓑ Ⓒ Ⓓ Ⓔ
8 Ⓐ Ⓑ Ⓒ Ⓓ Ⓔ
9 Ⓐ Ⓑ Ⓒ Ⓓ Ⓔ
10 Ⓐ Ⓑ Ⓒ Ⓓ Ⓔ
11 Ⓐ Ⓑ Ⓒ Ⓓ Ⓔ
12 Ⓐ Ⓑ Ⓒ Ⓓ Ⓔ
13 Ⓐ Ⓑ Ⓒ Ⓓ Ⓔ
14 Ⓐ Ⓑ Ⓒ Ⓓ Ⓔ
15 Ⓐ Ⓑ Ⓒ Ⓓ Ⓔ
16 Ⓐ Ⓑ Ⓒ Ⓓ Ⓔ
17 Ⓐ Ⓑ Ⓒ Ⓓ Ⓔ
18 Ⓐ Ⓑ Ⓒ Ⓓ Ⓔ
19 Ⓐ Ⓑ Ⓒ Ⓓ Ⓔ
20 Ⓐ Ⓑ Ⓒ Ⓓ Ⓔ

Section 3 – Critical Reading

25 minutes

25 Ⓐ Ⓑ Ⓒ Ⓓ Ⓔ
26 Ⓐ Ⓑ Ⓒ Ⓓ Ⓔ
27 Ⓐ Ⓑ Ⓒ Ⓓ Ⓔ
28 Ⓐ Ⓑ Ⓒ Ⓓ Ⓔ
29 Ⓐ Ⓑ Ⓒ Ⓓ Ⓔ
30 Ⓐ Ⓑ Ⓒ Ⓓ Ⓔ
31 Ⓐ Ⓑ Ⓒ Ⓓ Ⓔ
32 Ⓐ Ⓑ Ⓒ Ⓓ Ⓔ
33 Ⓐ Ⓑ Ⓒ Ⓓ Ⓔ
34 Ⓐ Ⓑ Ⓒ Ⓓ Ⓔ
35 Ⓐ Ⓑ Ⓒ Ⓓ Ⓔ
36 Ⓐ Ⓑ Ⓒ Ⓓ Ⓔ
37 Ⓐ Ⓑ Ⓒ Ⓓ Ⓔ
38 Ⓐ Ⓑ Ⓒ Ⓓ Ⓔ
39 Ⓐ Ⓑ Ⓒ Ⓓ Ⓔ
40 Ⓐ Ⓑ Ⓒ Ⓓ Ⓔ
41 Ⓐ Ⓑ Ⓒ Ⓓ Ⓔ
42 Ⓐ Ⓑ Ⓒ Ⓓ Ⓔ
43 Ⓐ Ⓑ Ⓒ Ⓓ Ⓔ
44 Ⓐ Ⓑ Ⓒ Ⓓ Ⓔ
45 Ⓐ Ⓑ Ⓒ Ⓓ Ⓔ
46 Ⓐ Ⓑ Ⓒ Ⓓ Ⓔ
47 Ⓐ Ⓑ Ⓒ Ⓓ Ⓔ
48 Ⓐ Ⓑ Ⓒ Ⓓ Ⓔ

Remove answer sheet by cutting on dotted line

Section 4 – Math

25 minutes

21 Ⓐ Ⓑ Ⓒ Ⓓ Ⓔ
22 Ⓐ Ⓑ Ⓒ Ⓓ Ⓔ
23 Ⓐ Ⓑ Ⓒ Ⓓ Ⓔ
24 Ⓐ Ⓑ Ⓒ Ⓓ Ⓔ
25 Ⓐ Ⓑ Ⓒ Ⓓ Ⓔ
26 Ⓐ Ⓑ Ⓒ Ⓓ Ⓔ
27 Ⓐ Ⓑ Ⓒ Ⓓ Ⓔ
28 Ⓐ Ⓑ Ⓒ Ⓓ Ⓔ

29

	/	/	
.	.	.	.
	0	0	0
1	1	1	1
2	2	2	2
3	3	3	3
4	4	4	4
5	5	5	5
6	6	6	6
7	7	7	7
8	8	8	8
9	9	9	9

30

	/	/	
.	.	.	.
	0	0	0
1	1	1	1
2	2	2	2
3	3	3	3
4	4	4	4
5	5	5	5
6	6	6	6
7	7	7	7
8	8	8	8
9	9	9	9

31

	/	/	
.	.	.	.
	0	0	0
1	1	1	1
2	2	2	2
3	3	3	3
4	4	4	4
5	5	5	5
6	6	6	6
7	7	7	7
8	8	8	8
9	9	9	9

32

	/	/	
.	.	.	.
	0	0	0
1	1	1	1
2	2	2	2
3	3	3	3
4	4	4	4
5	5	5	5
6	6	6	6
7	7	7	7
8	8	8	8
9	9	9	9

33

	/	/	
.	.	.	.
	0	0	0
1	1	1	1
2	2	2	2
3	3	3	3
4	4	4	4
5	5	5	5
6	6	6	6
7	7	7	7
8	8	8	8
9	9	9	9

34

	/	/	
.	.	.	.
	0	0	0
1	1	1	1
2	2	2	2
3	3	3	3
4	4	4	4
5	5	5	5
6	6	6	6
7	7	7	7
8	8	8	8
9	9	9	9

35

	/	/	
.	.	.	.
	0	0	0
1	1	1	1
2	2	2	2
3	3	3	3
4	4	4	4
5	5	5	5
6	6	6	6
7	7	7	7
8	8	8	8
9	9	9	9

36

	/	/	
.	.	.	.
	0	0	0
1	1	1	1
2	2	2	2
3	3	3	3
4	4	4	4
5	5	5	5
6	6	6	6
7	7	7	7
8	8	8	8
9	9	9	9

37

	/	/	
.	.	.	.
	0	0	0
1	1	1	1
2	2	2	2
3	3	3	3
4	4	4	4
5	5	5	5
6	6	6	6
7	7	7	7
8	8	8	8
9	9	9	9

38

	/	/	
.	.	.	.
	0	0	0
1	1	1	1
2	2	2	2
3	3	3	3
4	4	4	4
5	5	5	5
6	6	6	6
7	7	7	7
8	8	8	8
9	9	9	9

Section 5 – Writing

30 minutes

1 Ⓐ Ⓑ Ⓒ Ⓓ Ⓔ
2 Ⓐ Ⓑ Ⓒ Ⓓ Ⓔ
3 Ⓐ Ⓑ Ⓒ Ⓓ Ⓔ
4 Ⓐ Ⓑ Ⓒ Ⓓ Ⓔ
5 Ⓐ Ⓑ Ⓒ Ⓓ Ⓔ
6 Ⓐ Ⓑ Ⓒ Ⓓ Ⓔ
7 Ⓐ Ⓑ Ⓒ Ⓓ Ⓔ
8 Ⓐ Ⓑ Ⓒ Ⓓ Ⓔ
9 Ⓐ Ⓑ Ⓒ Ⓓ Ⓔ
10 Ⓐ Ⓑ Ⓒ Ⓓ Ⓔ
11 Ⓐ Ⓑ Ⓒ Ⓓ Ⓔ
12 Ⓐ Ⓑ Ⓒ Ⓓ Ⓔ
13 Ⓐ Ⓑ Ⓒ Ⓓ Ⓔ
14 Ⓐ Ⓑ Ⓒ Ⓓ Ⓔ
15 Ⓐ Ⓑ Ⓒ Ⓓ Ⓔ
16 Ⓐ Ⓑ Ⓒ Ⓓ Ⓔ
17 Ⓐ Ⓑ Ⓒ Ⓓ Ⓔ
18 Ⓐ Ⓑ Ⓒ Ⓓ Ⓔ
19 Ⓐ Ⓑ Ⓒ Ⓓ Ⓔ
20 Ⓐ Ⓑ Ⓒ Ⓓ Ⓔ
21 Ⓐ Ⓑ Ⓒ Ⓓ Ⓔ
22 Ⓐ Ⓑ Ⓒ Ⓓ Ⓔ
23 Ⓐ Ⓑ Ⓒ Ⓓ Ⓔ
24 Ⓐ Ⓑ Ⓒ Ⓓ Ⓔ
25 Ⓐ Ⓑ Ⓒ Ⓓ Ⓔ
26 Ⓐ Ⓑ Ⓒ Ⓓ Ⓔ
27 Ⓐ Ⓑ Ⓒ Ⓓ Ⓔ
28 Ⓐ Ⓑ Ⓒ Ⓓ Ⓔ
29 Ⓐ Ⓑ Ⓒ Ⓓ Ⓔ
30 Ⓐ Ⓑ Ⓒ Ⓓ Ⓔ
31 Ⓐ Ⓑ Ⓒ Ⓓ Ⓔ
32 Ⓐ Ⓑ Ⓒ Ⓓ Ⓔ
33 Ⓐ Ⓑ Ⓒ Ⓓ Ⓔ
34 Ⓐ Ⓑ Ⓒ Ⓓ Ⓔ
35 Ⓐ Ⓑ Ⓒ Ⓓ Ⓔ
36 Ⓐ Ⓑ Ⓒ Ⓓ Ⓔ
37 Ⓐ Ⓑ Ⓒ Ⓓ Ⓔ
38 Ⓐ Ⓑ Ⓒ Ⓓ Ⓔ
39 Ⓐ Ⓑ Ⓒ Ⓓ Ⓔ

SECTION 1/CRITICAL READING

TIME: 25 MINUTES
24 QUESTIONS (1–24)

Directions: For each question in this section, select the best answer from among the choices given and fill in the corresponding circle on the answer sheet.

Each sentence below has one or two blanks, each blank indicating that something has been omitted. Beneath the sentence are five words or sets of words labeled A through E. Choose the word or set of words that, when inserted in the sentence, best fits the meaning of the sentence as a whole.

EXAMPLE:

Medieval kingdoms did not become constitutional republics overnight; on the contrary, the change was ----.

(A) unpopular (B) unexpected
(C) advantageous (D) sufficient (E) gradual

Ⓐ Ⓑ Ⓒ Ⓓ ●

1. The traditional French café is slowly becoming ----, a victim to the growing popularity of *le fast food.*

(A) celebrated (B) indispensable
(C) prevalent (D) extinct (E) fashionable

2. Although we expected the women's basketball coach to be ---- over the recent victory of the team, we found her surprisingly ----.

(A) ecstatic..gleeful
(B) ambivalent..devious
(C) triumphant..responsive
(D) elated..naive
(E) jubilant..disheartened

3. The debate coach suggested that he eliminate his ---- remarks in his otherwise serious speech because they were ----.

(A) bantering..inappropriate
(B) jesting..accurate
(C) solemn..irrelevant
(D) tacit..digressive
(E) perfunctory..inconsiderate

4. Many young people and adults, uncomfortable with math, feel it is a subject best ---- engineers, scientists, and that small, elite group endowed at birth with a talent for the ---- world of numbers.

(A) ignored by..abstract
(B) suited to..accessible
(C) studied by..interminable
(D) left to..esoteric
(E) avoided by..abstruse

5. Her novel published to universal acclaim, her literary gifts acknowledged by the chief figures of the Harlem Renaissance, her reputation as yet ---- by envious slights, Hurston clearly was at the ---- of her career.

(A) undamaged..ebb
(B) untarnished..zenith
(C) untainted..end
(D) blackened..mercy
(E) unmarred..whim

GO ON TO NEXT PAGE ▶

Directions: The passages below are followed by questions based on their content; questions following a pair of related passages may also be based on the relationship between the paired passages. Answer the questions on the basis of what is stated or implied in the passages and in any introductory material that may be provided.

Questions 6–9 are based on the following passages.

Passage 1

Although commonly held up as a cornerstone of American democracy, the Mayflower Compact had little impact on the growth of freedom in America. Indeed, the compact limited its signers' liberty. That was its intent. Of the *Mayflower*'s 100 emigrants, less than half were Pilgrims. The rest were "strangers," non-Pilgrims who, finding themselves hundreds of miles north of their planned destination in Virginia, believed themselves outside the bounds of governmental authority. Rather than respect the rules of the Pilgrims, these strangers wanted to go their own way. By signing the compact, both Pilgrims and non-Pilgrims agreed to accept whatever form of government was established after landing.

Passage 2

What is the Mayflower Compact? It is a social contract that established a system of government by voluntary agreement. Forty-one men of different social classes, some Pilgrims, some not, all committed to a new life in a new land, were equal signers of this remarkable document. At a time when the liberties of Englishmen were still constrained by the remains of the feudal system, this compact laid a sound foundation for the principle of government by mutual consent of the governed. Let others belittle its importance if they will. To me, the Mayflower Compact will always be a cornerstone of American democracy.

6. In line 1, "held up" most nearly means

(A) delayed (B) cited (C) accommodated
(D) waylaid (E) carried

7. The author of the Passage 1 can best be described as

(A) a debunker (B) an atheist
(C) a mythmaker (D) an elitist
(E) an authoritarian

8. Unlike the author of Passage 1, the author of Passage 2 makes use of

(A) historical data
(B) direct quotation
(C) personal voice
(D) specific details
(E) literary anecdotes

9. The author of Passage 2 would most likely argue that the opening assertion of Passage 1 (lines 1–4) was

(A) meant to be taken literally
(B) accurate and to the point
(C) unnecessarily cautious
(D) taken out of context
(E) of dubious validity

Directions: Each passage below is followed by questions based on its content. Answer the questions following each passage on the basis of what is stated or implied in that passage and in any introductory material that may be provided.

Questions 10–15 are based on the following passage.

The following passage is excerpted from a book on prominent black Americans during Franklin Delano Roosevelt's presidency.

Like her white friends Eleanor Roosevelt and Aubrey Williams, Mary Bethune believed in the fundamental commitment of the New Deal to assist the black American's struggle and in the need for blacks to assume responsibilities to help win that struggle. Unlike those of her white liberal associates, however, Bethune's ideas had evolved out of a long experience as a "race leader." Founder of a small black college in Florida, she had become widely known by 1935 as an organizer of black women's groups and as a civil and political rights activist. Deeply religious, certain of her own capabilities, she held a relatively uncluttered view of what she felt were the New Deal's and her own people's obligations to the cause of racial justice. Unafraid to speak her mind to powerful whites, including the President, or to differing black factions, she combined faith in the ultimate willingness of whites to discard their prejudice and bigotry with a strong sense of racial pride and commitment to Negro self-help.

More than her liberal white friends, Bethune argued for a strong and direct black voice in initiating and shaping government policy. She pursued this in her conversations with President Roosevelt, in numerous memoranda to Aubrey Williams, and in her administrative work as head of the National Youth Administration's Office of Negro Affairs. With the assistance of Williams, she was successful in having blacks selected to NYA posts at the national, state, and local levels. But she also wanted a black presence throughout the federal government. At the beginning of the war she joined other black leaders in demanding appointments to the Selective Service Board and to the Department of the Army; and she was instrumental in 1941 in securing Earl Dickerson's membership on the Fair Employment Practices Committee. By 1944, she was still making appeals for black representation in "all public programs, federal, state, and local," and "in policy-making posts as well as rank and file jobs."

Though recognizing the weakness in the Roosevelt administration's response to Negro needs, Mary Bethune remained in essence a black partisan champion of the New Deal during the 1930s and 1940s. Her strong advocacy of administration policies and programs was predicated on a number of factors: her assessment of the low status of black Americans during the Depression; her faith in the willingness of some liberal whites to work for the inclusion of blacks in the government's reform and recovery measures; her conviction that only massive federal aid could elevate the Negro economically; and her belief that the thirties and forties were producing a more self-aware and self- assured black population. Like a number of her white friends in government, Bethune assumed that the preservation of democracy and black people's "full integration into the benefits and the responsibilities" of American life were inextricably tied together. She was convinced that, with the help of a friendly government, a militant, aggressive "New Negro" would emerge out of the devastation of depression and war, a "New Negro" who would "save America from itself," who would lead America toward the full realization of its democratic ideas.

10. The author's primary goal in the passage is to do which of the following?

(A) criticize Mary Bethune for adhering too closely to New Deal policies
(B) argue that Mary Bethune was too optimistic in her assessment of race relations
(C) explore Mary Bethune's convictions and her influence on black progress in the Roosevelt years
(D) point out the weaknesses of the white liberal approach to black needs during Roosevelt's presidency
(E) summarize the attainments of blacks under the auspices of Roosevelt's New Deal

GO ON TO NEXT PAGE ▶

11. It can be inferred from the passage that Aubrey Williams was which of the following?

I. A man with influence in the National Youth Administration
II. A white liberal
III. A man of strong religious convictions

(A) I only
(B) II only
(C) I and II only
(D) II and III only
(E) I, II, and III

12. The author mentions Earl Dickerson (lines 36–37) primarily in order to

(A) cite an instance of Bethune's political impact
(B) contrast his career with that of Bethune
(C) introduce the subject of a subsequent paragraph
(D) provide an example of Bethune's "New Negro"
(E) show that Dickerson was a leader of his fellow blacks

13. In line 36, "instrumental" most nearly means

(A) subordinate (B) triumphant (C) musical (D) gracious (E) helpful

14. It can be inferred from the passage that Bethune believed the "New Negro" would "save America from itself" (lines 61–67) by

(A) joining the Army and helping America overthrow its Fascist enemies
(B) helping America accomplish its egalitarian ideals
(C) voting for administration antipoverty programs
(D) electing other blacks to government office
(E) expressing a belief in racial pride

15. The author uses all the following techniques in the passage EXCEPT

(A) comparison and contrast
(B) development of an extended metaphor
(C) direct quotation
(D) general statement and concrete examples
(E) repetition of central ideas

Questions 16–24 are based upon the following passage.

In this excerpt from the novel Hard Times *by Charles Dickens, the reader is introduced to Thomas Gradgrind, headmaster of a so-called model school.*

Thomas Gradgrind, sir. A man of realities. A man of facts and calculations. A man who proceeds upon the principle that two and two are four, and nothing over, and who is not to be talked into allowing for anything over. Thomas Gradgrind, sir—peremptorily Thomas—Thomas Gradgrind. With a rule and a pair of scales, and the multiplication table always in his pocket, sir, ready to weigh and measure any parcel of human nature, and tell you exactly what it comes to. It is a mere question of figures, a case of simple arithmetic. You might hope to get some other nonsensical belief into the head of George Gradgrind, or Augustus Gradgrind, or John Gradgrind, or Joseph Gradgrind (all suppositions, non-existent persons), but into the head of Thomas Gradgrind—no, sir!

Mr. Gradgrind walked homeward from the school in a state of considerable satisfaction. It was his school, and he intended it to be a model. He intended every child in it to be a model—just as the young Gradgrinds were all models.

There were five young Gradgrinds, and they were models every one. They had been lectured at from their tenderest years; coursed, like little hares. Almost as soon as they could run alone, they had been made to run to the lecture-room. The first object with which they had an association, or of which they had a remembrance, was a large blackboard with a dry Ogre chalking ghastly white figures on it.

Not that they knew, by name or nature, anything about an Ogre. Fact forbid! I only use the word to express a monster in a lecturing castle, with Heaven knows how many heads manipulated into one, taking childhood captive, and dragging it into gloomy statistical dens by the hair.

No little Gradgrind had ever seen a face in the moon; it was up in the moon before it could speak distinctly. No little Gradgrind had ever learnt the silly jingle, Twinkle, twinkle, little star; how I wonder what you are! No little Gradgrind had ever known wonder on the subject of the stars, each little Gradgrind having at five years old dissected the Great Bear like a Professor Owen, and driven Charles's Wain like a locomotive engine-driver. No little Gradgrind had ever associated a cow in a field with that famous cow with the crumpled horn who tossed the dog who worried the cat who killed the rat who ate the malt, or with that yet more famous cow who swallowed Tom Thumb: it had never heard of those celebrities, and had only been introduced to a cow as a graminivorous ruminating quadruped with several stomachs.

16. The phrase "peremptorily Thomas" in line 6 emphasizes Gradgrind's
(A) absolute insistence upon facts
(B) dislike of the name Augustus
(C) need to remind himself of the simplest details
(D) desire to be on a first-name basis with others
(E) inability to introduce himself properly

17. In line 7, "rule" most nearly means
(A) legal regulation
(B) academic custom
(C) scientific principle
(D) dominion over schoolchildren
(E) straight edge used in measuring

18. Gradgrind's mood as he marches homeward (lines 18–19) can best be characterized as one of
(A) uncertainty (B) complacency
(C) boredom (D) relief (E) cynicism

19. The author's tone in describing Thomas Gradgrind's educational methodology is
(A) openly admiring
(B) acutely concerned
(C) bitterly scornful
(D) broadly satirical
(E) warmly nostalgic

20. The passage suggests that Gradgrind rejects from his curriculum anything that is in the least
(A) analytical (B) mechanical (C) fanciful
(D) dogmatic (E) pragmatic

21. The passage is narrated from the point of view of
(A) Thomas Gradgrind
(B) an observer who does not know Gradgrind at first but who comes to know about him in the course of the passage
(C) an observer whose understanding of Gradgrind is necessarily incomplete
(D) an observer who knows all about Gradgrind's thoughts and feelings
(E) an instructor at Gradgrind's model school

22. It can be inferred from the passage that the Great Bear and Charles's Wain most likely are
(A) subjects of nursery rhymes
(B) groupings of stars
(C) zoological phenomena
(D) themes of popular songs
(E) popular toys for children

23. Which of the following axioms is closest to Gradgrind's view of education as presented in the passage?
(A) Experience keeps a dear school, but fools will learn in no other.
(B) Let early education be a sort of amusement, that you may be better able to find out the natural bent.
(C) Education is what you have left over after you have forgotten everything you have learned.
(D) A teacher who can arouse a feeling for one single good action accomplishes more than one who fills our memory with rows on rows of natural objects, classified with name and form.
(E) Modern science, as training the mind to an exact and impartial analysis of fact, is an education specially fitted to promote sound citizenship.

24. In line 52, the word "celebrities" refers to
(A) the little Gradgrinds
(B) famous professors
(C) heavenly bodies
(D) locomotive engine-drivers
(E) fictional characters

IF YOU FINISH IN LESS THAN 25 MINUTES, YOU MAY CHECK YOUR WORK ON THIS SECTION ONLY. DO NOT TURN TO ANY OTHER SECTION IN THE TEST.

STOP

SECTION 2/MATHEMATICS

TIME: 25 MINUTES

20 QUESTIONS (1–20)

Directions:

For each question in this section, determine which of the five choices is correct, and blacken that choice on your answer sheet. You may use any blank space on the page for your work.

NOTES:

- You may use a calculator whenever you believe it will be helpful.
- Use the diagrams provided to help you solve the problems. Unless you see the phrase
  Note: Figure not drawn to scale
  under a diagram, it has been drawn as accurately as possible. Unless it is stated that a figure is three dimensional, you may assume that it lies in a plane.

Reference

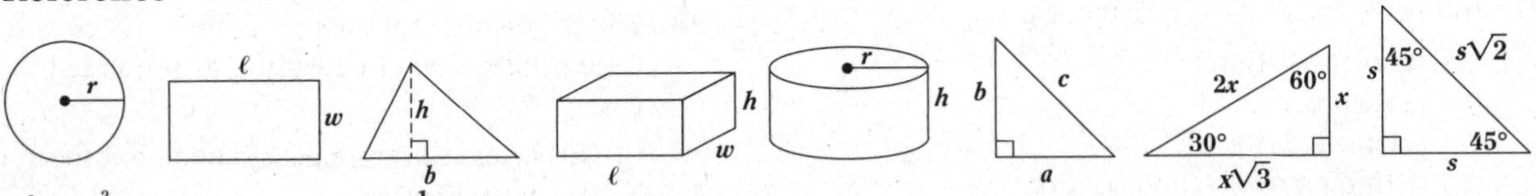

$A = \pi r^2$
$C = 2\pi r$ $\quad A = \ell w \quad A = \frac{1}{2}bh \quad V = \ell wh \quad V = \pi r^2 h \quad c^2 = a^2 + b^2$ **Special Right Triangles**

Number of degrees in a circle: 360
Sum of the measures, in degrees, of the three angles of a triangle: 180

1. What is the value of m if $(7 - 2)(7 - m) = 35$?

(A) -7
(B) -5
(C) 0
(D) 5
(E) 7

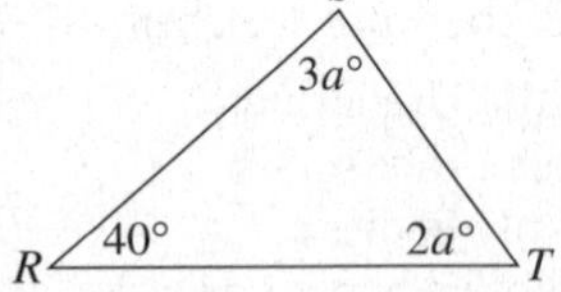

2. In the figure above, what is the value of a?

(A) 10
(B) 20
(C) 28
(D) 36
(E) 45

3. Samir studied for exactly 225 minutes. If he began studying at 10:05 A.M., at what time did he stop studying?

(A) 12:30 P.M.
(B) 1:00 P.M.
(C) 1:30 P.M.
(D) 1:50 P.M.
(E) 2:00 P.M.

4. What positive number n satisfies the equation, $(9)(9)(9)n = \frac{(27)(27)}{n}$?

(A) $\frac{1}{3}$
(B) 1
(C) 3
(D) 9
(E) 27

GO ON TO NEXT PAGE ▶

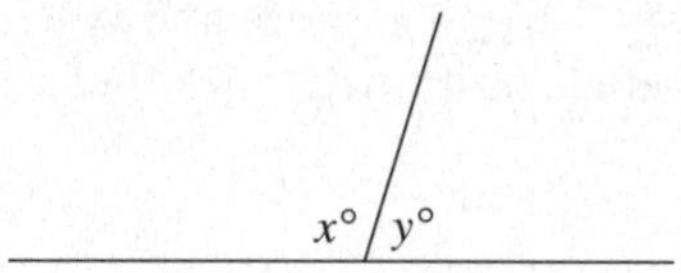

Note: Figure not drawn to scale

5. In the figure above, if x is 140 more than y, what is the value of y?

(A) 10
(B) 15
(C) 20
(D) 30
(E) 40

6. If $x^2 = 10$, what is x^6?

(A) $10\sqrt{10}$
(B) 100
(C) $100\sqrt{10}$
(D) 1000
(E) $1000\sqrt{10}$

7. If a, b, c, and d are four consecutive integers, which of the following could be their average (arithmetic mean)?

I. 99
II. 99.5
III. 100

(A) I only
(B) II only
(C) I and II only
(D) II and III only
(E) I, II, and III

8. What is the diameter of a circle whose area is A?

(A) $2\sqrt{\dfrac{A}{\pi}}$

(B) $\sqrt{\dfrac{A}{\pi}}$

(C) $\dfrac{A}{2\pi}$

(D) $\dfrac{A}{\pi}$

(E) $\dfrac{2\sqrt{A}}{\pi}$

9. The following chart lists the monthly salaries in 2010 of five people and the percent change in their salaries from 2010 to 2012.

Name	**2010 Salary**	**% change**
Ann	$4200	+6%
Ben	$4000	+11%
Dan	$3500	+25%
Ken	$5000	−12%
Len	$3200	+35%

Who had the highest salary in 2012?

(A) Ann
(B) Ben
(C) Dan
(D) Ken
(E) Len

10. If the measures of the angles of a triangle are in the ratio of 1:1:2, what is the ratio of the lengths of the sides?

(A) 1:1:2
(B) 1:1:3
(C) $1:1:\sqrt{2}$
(D) 2:2:3
(E) $1:\sqrt{3}:2$

11. A, B, and C are points with $AC = 2AB$. Which of the following could be true?

I. A, B, and C are the vertices of a right triangle.
II. A, B, and C are three of the vertices of a square.
III. A, B, and C all lie on the circumference of a circle.

(A) I only
(B) III only
(C) I and II only
(D) I and III only
(E) I, II, and III

12. Last year Ross bought two paintings. Last week he sold them for \$1200 each. He had a 20% profit on one painting and a 20% loss on the other. What was his net loss or profit?

(A) He lost exactly \$100.
(B) He lost less than \$100.
(C) He lost more than \$100.
(D) He earned less than \$100.
(E) He earned more than \$100.

13. What is the measure in degrees of the smaller angle formed by the hour hand and the minute hand of a clock at 3:30?

(A) 15
(B) 60
(C) 70
(D) 75
(E) 90

14. If m is an integer, which of the following could be true?

I. $\frac{15}{m}$ is an even integer
II. $\frac{m}{15}$ is an even integer
III. $15m$ is a prime

(A) I only
(B) II only
(C) III only
(D) I and II only
(E) II and III only

Questions 15–16 refer to the following definition.

For any integers m and n: $m*n$ represents the remainder when m is divided by n.

15. What is the value of

$$6*1 + 6*2 + 6*3 + 6*4 + 6*5 + 6*6?$$

(A) 0
(B) 3
(C) 6
(D) 9
(E) 14

16. If $a < b$, what is the maximum possible value of $a*b + b*a$?

(A) $a + b$
(B) $ab - 1$
(C) $2a - 1$
(D) $2b - 1$
(E) $a + b - 1$

17. If $x + y = 10$, $y + z = 15$, and $x + z = 17$, what is the average (arithmetic mean) of x, y, and z?

(A) 7
(B) 14
(C) 15
(D) 21
(E) It cannot be determined from the information given.

18. If x is a positive integer, which of the following CANNOT be an integer?

(A) $\sqrt{x-1}$
(B) $\sqrt{x^2-1}$
(C) $\frac{1}{x}$
(D) $\frac{x+2}{x+1}$
(E) $\frac{7}{x+1}$

19. Which of the following CANNOT be expressed as the sum of two or more consecutive positive integers?

(A) 12
(B) 13
(C) 14
(D) 15
(E) 16

20. If p painters can complete a job in d days, how long will it take q painters, all working at the same rate, to complete 25% of the job?

(A) $\frac{pd}{4q}$
(B) $\frac{q}{4pd}$
(C) $\frac{4pd}{q}$
(D) $\frac{pq}{4d}$
(E) $\frac{pqd}{4}$

IF YOU FINISH IN LESS THAN 25 MINUTES, YOU MAY CHECK YOUR WORK ON THIS SECTION ONLY. DO NOT TURN TO ANY OTHER SECTION IN THE TEST.

STOP

SECTION 3/CRITICAL READING

TIME: 25 MINUTES

24 QUESTIONS (25–48)

Directions: For each question in this section, select the best answer from among the choices given and fill in the corresponding circle on the answer sheet.

Each sentence below has one or two blanks, each blank indicating that something has been omitted. Beneath the sentence are five words or sets of words labeled A through E. Choose the word or set of words that, when inserted in the sentence, best fits the meaning of the sentence as a whole.

EXAMPLE:

Medieval kingdoms did not become constitutional republics overnight; on the contrary, the change was ----.

(A) unpopular (B) unexpected
(C) advantageous (D) sufficient (E) gradual

Ⓐ Ⓑ Ⓒ Ⓓ ●

25. Once known only to importers of exotic foreign delicacies, the kiwi fruit has been transplanted successfully to America and is now ---- a much wider market.

(A) accessible to
(B) unknown to
(C) perplexing to
(D) comparable to
(E) uncultivated by

26. Continuously looking for new ways of presenting her material, for fresh methods of capturing her students' attention, she has been ---- in the classroom.

(A) a pedant (B) a misfit (C) an innovator
(D) a stoic (E) a martinet

27. This coming trip to France should provide me with ---- test of the value of my conversational French class.

(A) an intimate (B) an uncertain
(C) a pragmatic (D) a pretentious
(E) an arbitrary

28. Allowing women a voice in tribal government did not ---- Cherokee custom, for traditional Cherokee society was matrilineal, granting women the right to own property and to divorce their husbands.

(A) violate (B) emulate (C) retrace
(D) preclude (E) fulfill

29. In a shocking instance of ---- research, one of the most influential researchers in the field of genetics reported on experiments that were never carried out and published deliberately ---- scientific papers on his nonexistent work.

(A) comprehensive..abstract
(B) theoretical..challenging
(C) erroneous..impartial
(D) derivative..authoritative
(E) fraudulent..deceptive

30. Many of the characters portrayed by Clint Eastwood are strong but ---- types, rugged men of few words.

(A) ruthless (B) equivocal (C) laconic
(D) stingy (E) vociferous

31. Like sauces, without a certain amount of spice, conversations grow ----.

(A) eloquent (B) heated (C) elaborate
(D) straightforward (E) insipid

32. Both ---- and ----, Scrooge seldom smiled and never gave away a halfpenny.

(A) sanguine..miserly
(B) acerbic..magnanimous
(C) morose..munificent
(D) crabbed..parsimonious
(E) sullen..philanthropic

GO ON TO NEXT PAGE ▶

Directions: Each of the passages below precedes two questions based on its content. Answer the questions following each passage on the basis of what is stated or implied in that passage.

Questions 33 and 34 are based on the following passage.

"The very first requirement in a hospital (is) that it should do the sick no harm." So wrote Florence Nightingale, nursing pioneer. Most people picture Nightingale as the brave "Lady with the Lamp" who journeyed to the Crimea to nurse British soldiers wounded in the war. It was after the war, however, that Nightingale came into her own as the world's most renowned authority on hospital reform. In *Notes on Hospitals*, Nightingale addressed every aspect of hospital construction and management, from replacing wooden bedsteads with iron ones, to minimizing infection by dividing hospitals into airy, self-contained pavilions.

33. Which statement best expresses the author's central point about Florence Nightingale?

(A) She deserved great praise for her work with wounded soldiers in the Crimea.
(B) She worried about the effects of infection on mortality rates.
(C) Her greatest accomplishments were in improving hospital planning and administration.
(D) She preferred airy, separate hospital units to large wards.
(E) Her change of focus to hospital administration represented a loss to the nursing profession.

34. In line 10, "addressed" most nearly means

(A) orated (B) labeled (C) set apart
(D) dealt with (E) averted

Questions 35 and 36 are based on the following passage.

Critics call Edgar Allan Poe the father of detective fiction. Whom then should we call detective fiction's mother? Agatha Christie, say some mystery readers. Dorothy Sayers, say others. Well before Christie and Sayers wrote their classic British whodunits, however, an American named Anna Katharine Green wrote a best-seller about the murder of a Fifth Avenue millionaire. *The Leavenworth Case*, which sold over 150,000 copies, marked the initial appearance of Inspector Ebenezer Gryce, the first serial detective in genre history. Today, with two novels back in print after nearly a century, Gryce's long-neglected creator is finally beginning to receive the recognition she deserves.

35. The author's purpose in writing this passage is most likely to

(A) relegate a writer to obscurity
(B) contrast the careers of Poe and Green
(C) introduce the concept of the serial detective
(D) dismiss the contributions of British authors
(E) reclaim a forgotten literary pioneer

36. In line 10, "marked" most nearly means

(A) graded (B) noticed (C) denoted
(D) branded (E) disfigured

GO ON TO NEXT PAGE ▶

Directions: The passages below are followed by questions on their content; questions following a pair of related passages may also be based on the relationship between the paired passages. Answer the questions on the basis of what is stated or implied in the passages and in any introductory material that may be provided.

Questions 37–48 are based on the following passages.

The following passages are excerpted from recent essays about flying.

Passage 1

Flying alone in an open plane is the purest experience of flight possible. That pure experience is felt at its most intense in acrobatic flying, when you are upside down, or pointed at the sky or at the earth, and moving in ways that you can only in the unsubstantial medium of the air. Acrobatic flying is a useless skill in its particulars—nobody *needs* to do a loop or a roll, not even a fighter pilot—but this skill extends your control of the plane and yourself and makes extreme actions in the sky comfortable. When you reach the top of a loop, upside down and engine at full throttle, and tilt your head back to pick up the horizon line behind you, you are as far outside instinctive human behavior as you can go—hanging in space, the sky below you and the earth above, inscribing a circle on emptiness. And then the nose drops across the horizon; your speed increases and the plane scoops through into normal flight, and you are back in the normal world, with the earth put back in its place. The going out and coming back are what makes a loop so satisfying.

After a while, that is. At first it was terrifying, like being invited to a suicide that you didn't want to commit. "This is a loop," my instructor said casually. He lowered the plane's nose to gain airspeed, and then pulled sharply up. The earth, and my stomach, fell away from me; and we were upside down, and I could feel gravity clawing at me, pulling me out into the mile of empty space between me and the ground. I grabbed at the sides of the cockpit and hung on until gravity was on my side again.

"You seemed a little nervous that time," the instructor said when the plane was right side up again. "You've got to have confidence in that seat belt, or you'll never do a decent loop. So this time, when we get on top, I want you to put both arms out of the cockpit." And I did it. It was like stepping off a bridge, but I did it, and the belt held, and the plane came round. And after that I could fly a loop. It was, as I said, satisfying.

Passage 2

The black plane dropped spinning, and flattened out spinning the other way; it began to carve the air into forms that built wildly and musically on each other and never ended. Reluctantly, I started paying attention. Rahm drew high above the world an inexhaustibly glorious line; it piled over our heads in loops and arabesques. The plane moved every way a line can move, and it controlled three dimensions, so the line carved massive and subtle slits in the air like sculptures. The plane looped the loop, seeming to arch its back like a gymnast; it stalled, dropped, and spun out of it climbing; it spiraled and knifed west on one side's wings and back east on another; it turned cartwheels, which must be physically impossible; it played with its own line like a cat with yarn. How did the pilot know where in the air he was? If he got lost, the ground would swat him.

His was pure energy and naked spirit. I have thought about it for years. Rahm's line unrolled in time. Like music, it split the bulging rim of the future along its seam. It pried out the present. We watchers waited for the split-second curve of beauty in the present to reveal itself. The human pilot, Dave Rahm, worked in the cockpit right at the plane's nose; his very body tore into the future for us and reeled it down upon us like a curling peel.

Like any fine artist, he controlled the tension of the audience's longing. You desired, unwittingly, a certain kind of roll or climb, or a return to a certain portion of the air, and he fulfilled your hope slantingly, like a poet, or evaded it until you thought you would burst, and then fulfilled it surprisingly, so you gasped and cried out.

The oddest, most exhilarating and exhausting thing was this: he never quit. The music had no periods, no rests or endings; the poetry's beautiful sentence never ended; the line had no finish; the sculptured forms piled overhead, one into another without surcease. Who could breathe, in a world where rhythm itself had no periods?

I went home and thought about Rahm's performance that night, and the next day, and the next.

I had thought I knew my way around beauty a little bit. I knew I had devoted a good part of my life to it, memorizing poetry and focusing my attention on complexity of rhythm in particular, on force, movement, repetition, and surprise, in both poetry and prose. Now I had stood among dandelions between two asphalt runways in Bellingham, Washington, and begun learning about beauty. Even the Boston Museum of Fine Arts was never more inspiring than this small northwestern airport on this time-killing Sunday afternoon in June. Nothing on earth is more gladdening than knowing we must roll up our sleeves and move back the boundaries of the humanly possible once more.

37. According to the author of Passage 1, training in acrobatic flying

(A) has only theoretical value
(B) expands a pilot's range of capabilities
(C) is an essential part of general pilot training
(D) comes naturally to most pilots
(E) should be required only of fighter pilots

38. In line 6, "medium" most nearly means

(A) midpoint
(B) appropriate occupation
(C) method of communication
(D) environment
(E) compromise

39. To "pick up the horizon line" (line 13) is to

(A) lift it higher
(B) spot it visually
(C) measure its distance
(D) choose it eagerly
(E) increase its visibility

40. Passage 1 suggests that the author's grabbing at the sides of the cockpit (lines 31–33) was

(A) instinctive (B) terrifying (C) essential
(D) habit forming (E) life threatening

41. In line 40, the word "held" most nearly means

(A) carried (B) detained (C) accommodated
(D) remained valid (E) maintained its grasp

42. By putting both arms out of the cockpit (lines 38–40), the author

(A) chooses the path of least resistance
(B) enables himself to steer the plane more freely
(C) relies totally on his seat belt to keep him safe
(D) allows himself to give full expression to his nervousness
(E) is better able to breathe deeply and relax

43. The author's use of the word "satisfying" (line 42) represents

(A) a simile (B) an understatement
(C) a fallacy (D) a euphemism
(E) a hypothesis

44. The author of Passage 2 mentions her initial reluctance to watch the stunt flying (lines 46–47) in order to

(A) demonstrate her hostility to commercial entertainment
(B) reveal her fear of such dangerous enterprises
(C) minimize her participation in aerial acrobatics
(D) indicate how captivating the demonstration was
(E) emphasize the acuteness of her perceptions

45. By fulfilling "your hope slantingly, like a poet" (line 74), the author means that

(A) the pilot flew the plane on a diagonal
(B) Rahm was a writer of popular verse
(C) the pilot had a bias against executing certain kinds of rolls
(D) Rahm refused to satisfy your expectations directly
(E) the pilot's sense of aesthetic judgment was askew

GO ON TO NEXT PAGE ▶

46. At the end of Passage 2, the author is left feeling

(A) empty in the aftermath of the stunning performance she has seen
(B) jubilant at the prospect of moving from Boston to Washington
(C) exhilarated by her awareness of new potentials for humanity
(D) glad that she has not wasted any more time memorizing poetry
(E) surprised by her response to an art form she had not previously believed possible

47. Compared with Passage 2, Passage 1 is

(A) less informative
(B) more tentative
(C) more argumentative
(D) more speculative
(E) less lyrical

48. How would the author of Passage 2 most likely react to the assessment of acrobatic flying in lines 6–11?

(A) She would consider it too utilitarian an assessment of an aesthetic experience.
(B) She would reject it as an inaccurate description of the pilot's technique.
(C) She would admire it as a poetic evocation of the pilot's art.
(D) She would criticize it as a digression from the author's main point.
(E) She would regard it as too effusive to be appropriate to its subject.

IF YOU FINISH IN LESS THAN 25 MINUTES, YOU MAY CHECK YOUR WORK ON THIS SECTION ONLY. DO NOT TURN TO ANY OTHER SECTION IN THE TEST.

STOP

SECTION 4/MATHEMATICS

TIME: 25 MINUTES

18 QUESTIONS (21–38)

Directions:

For questions 21–28, determine which of the five choices is correct, and blacken that choice on your answer sheet. You may use any blank space on the page for your work.

NOTES:

- You may use a calculator whenever you believe it will be helpful.
- Use the diagrams provided to help you solve the problems. Unless you see the phrase <u>Note:</u> Figure not drawn to scale under a diagram, it has been drawn as accurately as possible. Unless it is stated that a figure is three dimensional, you may assume that it lies in a plane.

Reference

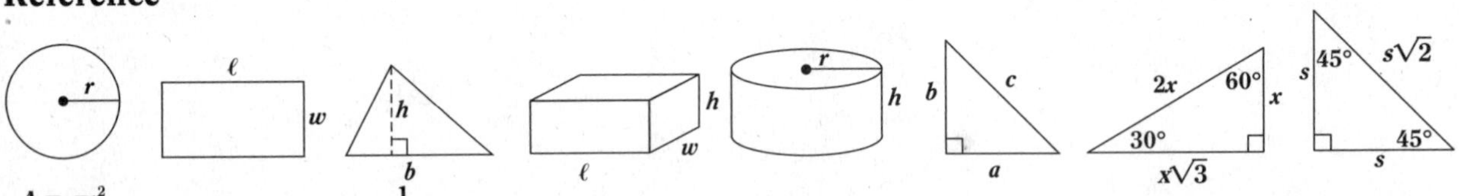

$A = \pi r^2$ $C = 2\pi r$ $A = \ell w$ $A = \frac{1}{2}bh$ $V = \ell wh$ $V = \pi r^2 h$ $c^2 = a^2 + b^2$ **Special Right Triangles**

Number of degrees in a circle: 360

Sum of the measures, in degrees, of the three angles of a triangle: 180

21. If $2x - 1 = 9$, what is $20x - 1$?

(A) 19
(B) 80
(C) 90
(D) 99
(E) 100

22. If $8 - (8 + w) = 8$, then $w =$

(A) −16
(B) −8
(C) 0
(D) 8
(E) 16

23. One positive number is $\frac{1}{5}$ of another number. If the product of the numbers is 20, what is their sum?

(A) 4
(B) 8
(C) 10
(D) 12
(E) 20

24. Mr. Riccardo wrote a number on the chalkboard. When he added 3 to the number, he got the same result as when he multiplied the number by 3. What is the number he wrote?

(A) −3
(B) 0
(C) 1.5
(D) $\sqrt{3}$
(E) 3

25. If a team played g games and lost l of them, what fraction of the games played did the team win?

(A) $\frac{l-g}{l}$

(B) $\frac{l-g}{g}$

(C) $\frac{g-l}{g}$

(D) $\frac{g}{g-l}$

(E) $\frac{g-l}{l}$

26. If Steven was born on Friday, August 13, 2010, and Daniel was born exactly 200 days later, on what day of the week was Daniel born?

(A) Monday
(B) Tuesday
(C) Friday
(D) Saturday
(E) Sunday

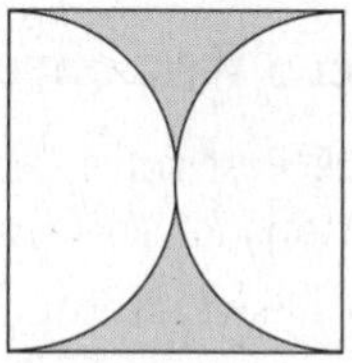

27. In the figure above, the shaded region is bounded by two semicircles and two sides of a square. If the area of the square is 20, what is the area of the shaded region?

(A) $20 - \pi$
(B) $5(4 - \pi)$
(C) 4π
(D) $\sqrt{20}(2 + \pi)$
(E) $2\sqrt{20} + 10\pi$

28. If $a - b = 10$, $b - c = 20$ and $c - d = 30$, what is the value of $a - d$?

(A) 40
(B) 50
(C) 60
(D) 80
(E) 100

Student-Produced Response Directions

In questions 29–38, first solve the problem, and then enter your answer on the grid provided on the answer sheet. The instructions for entering your answers follow.

- First, write your answer in the boxes at the top of the grid.
- Second, grid your answer in the columns below the boxes.
- Use the fraction bar in the first row or the decimal point in the second row to enter fractions and decimals.

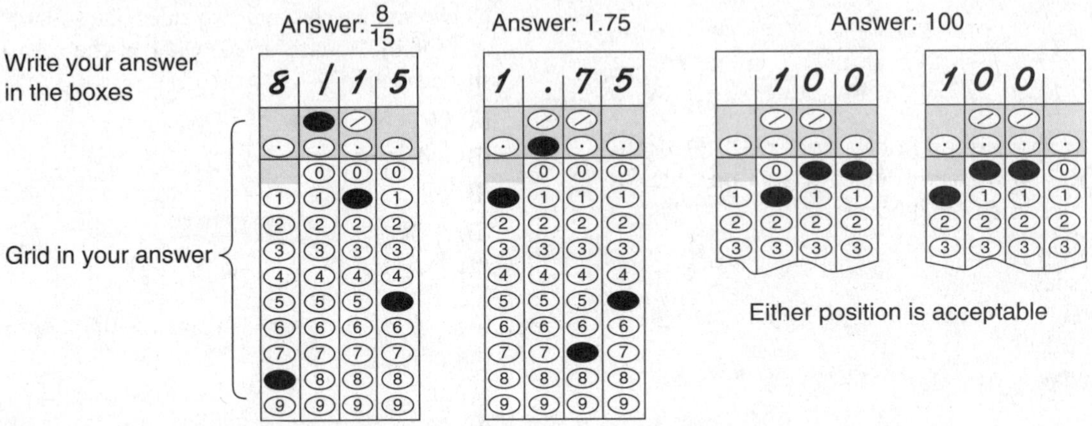

- Grid only one space in each column.
- Entering the answer in the boxes is recommended as an aid in gridding but is not required.
- The machine scoring your exam can read only what you grid, so you **must grid-in your answers correctly to get credit.**
- If a question has more than one correct answer, grid-in only one of them.
- The grid does not have a minus sign; so no answer can be negative.
- A mixed number *must* be converted to an improper fraction or a decimal before it is gridded. Enter $1\frac{1}{4}$ as $\frac{5}{4}$ or 1.25; the machine will interpret 11/4 as $\frac{11}{4}$ and mark it wrong.
- **All decimals must be entered as accurately as possible.** Here are three acceptable ways of gridding $\frac{3}{11} = 0.272727\ldots$

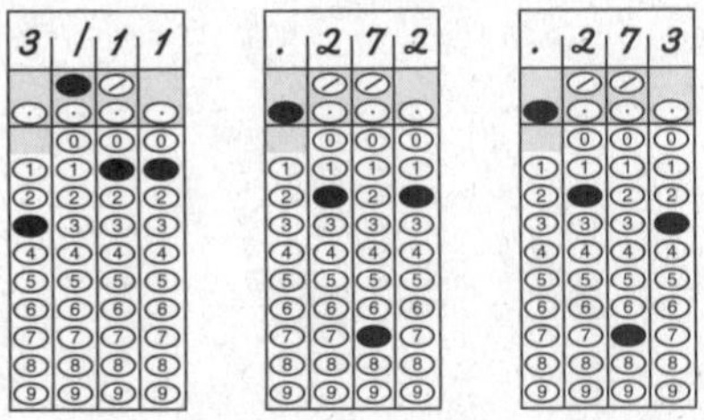

- Note that rounding to .273 is acceptable because you are using the full grid, but you would receive **no credit** for .3 or .27, because they are less accurate.

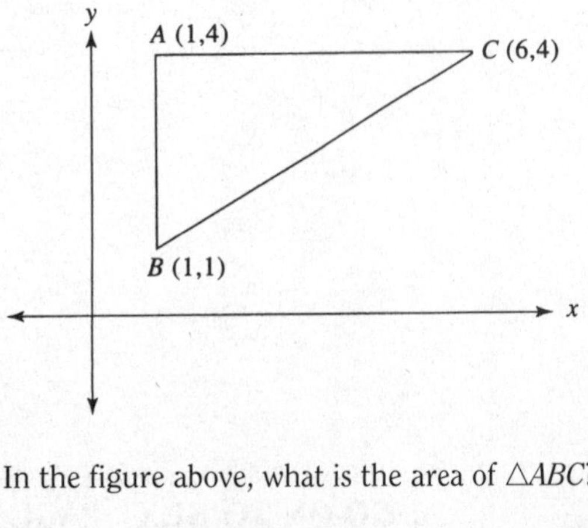

29. In the figure above, what is the area of $\triangle ABC$?

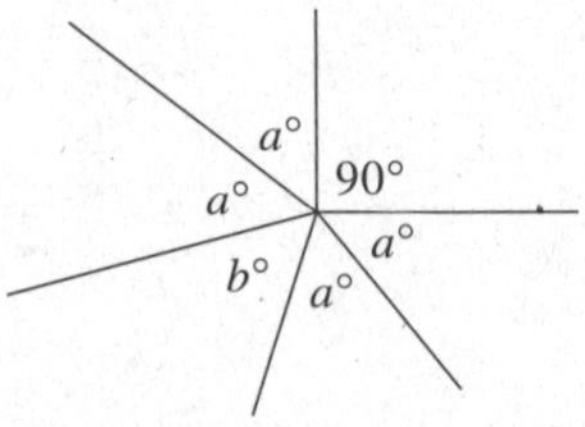

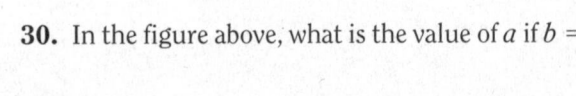

30. In the figure above, what is the value of a if $b = 60$?

GO ON TO NEXT PAGE ▶

31. If the average (arithmetic mean) of 20, 30, 40, 50 and y is 100, what is the value of y?

32. At Central High School, 40% of the members of the Spanish club are boys. How many members does the club have if 30 of the members are girls?

33. Line l passes through the points (1, 3) and (4, 7). Line m passes through (7, 5) parallel to l, and line n passes through (7, 5) perpendicular to l. What is the sum of the slopes of lines m and n?

34. The first two terms of a sequence are 1 and 2. Every other term in the sequence is the sum of the two terms immediately preceding it. For example, the third term is $1 + 2 = 3$ and the fourth term is $2 + 3 = 5$. How many of the first 100 terms are odd?

35. If $5(\sqrt{x} - 3) = 3\sqrt{x} - 5$, then $x =$

36. If 3 bangs = 2 clangs and 4 bangs = 5 tangs, then 1 clang is equal to how many tangs?

37. There are 25 students in a class, 40% of whom are girls. If the average (arithmetic mean) weight of the girls is 120 pounds and the average weight of the boys in the class is 150 pounds, what is the average weight of the children in the class?

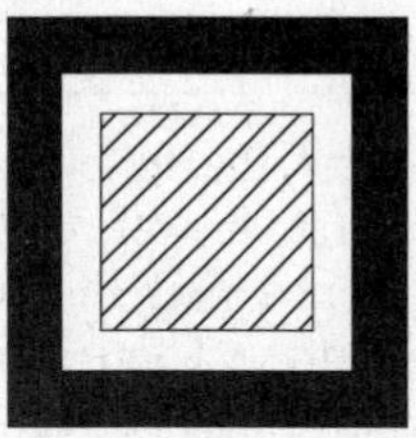

38. In the figure above, the diagonals of the three squares are 3, 4, and 5. What is the ratio of the black area to the striped area?

IF YOU FINISH IN LESS THAN 25 MINUTES, YOU MAY CHECK YOUR WORK ON THIS SECTION ONLY. DO NOT TURN TO ANY OTHER SECTION IN THE TEST.

STOP

SECTION 5/WRITING SKILLS

TIME: 30 MINUTES

39 QUESTIONS (1–39)

Directions: For each question in this section, select the best answer from among the choices given and fill in the corresponding circle on the answer sheet.

Some or all parts of the following sentences are underlined. The first answer choice, (A), simply repeats the underlined part of the sentence. The other four choices present four alternative ways to phrase the underlined part. Select the answer that produces the most effective sentence, one that is clear and exact, and blacken the appropriate space on your answer sheet. In selecting your choice, be sure that it is standard written English and that it expresses the meaning of the original sentence.

EXAMPLE:

The first biography of author Eudora Welty came out in 1998, and she was eighty-nine years old at the time.

(A) and she was eighty-nine years old at the time
(B) at the time when she was eighty-nine
(C) upon becoming an eighty-nine year old
(D) when she was eighty-nine
(E) at the age of eighty-nine years old

Ⓐ Ⓑ Ⓒ ● Ⓔ

1. Maya Angelou is almost as talented a performer as she is a poet.

(A) almost as talented a performer as she is a poet
(B) almost equally talented, whether a performer or a poet
(C) of the same talent as a performer and a poet, almost
(D) a talented poet, and almost so talented in performing
(E) talented as a poet, with almost as much talent in performing

2. The imminent historian stood in bed, recuperating from a viral infection, while his paper was being read at the convention.

(A) imminent historian stood
(B) imminent historian remained
(C) eminent historian stayed
(D) eminent historian stood
(E) eminent historian had remained

3. At the zoo, the brightly plumaged birds that fluttered overhead like tropical flowers in a breeze.

(A) birds that fluttered (B) birds fluttering
(C) birds which fluttered (D) birds fluttered
(E) birds aflutter

4. When the National Association for the Advancement of Colored People examined discrimination in the music business, its report concentrating on offstage employment opportunities.

(A) its report concentrating on offstage employment opportunities
(B) its report having concentrated on offstage employment opportunities
(C) its report concentrated on offstage employment opportunities
(D) its report concentrating in offstage employment opportunities
(E) its report concentrated in offstage employment opportunities

5. Some doctors volunteer to serve the poor in addition to their regular practices, they find healing the poor provides different insights than healing the rich.

(A) Some doctors volunteer to serve the poor in addition to their regular practices, they find
(B) Besides their regular practices, some doctors serve the poor to find
(C) In addition to running their regular practices, some doctors volunteer to serve the poor; they find that
(D) Some doctors, in volunteering to serve the poor, find
(E) Running their regular practices and serving the poor help some doctors realize that

GO ON TO NEXT PAGE ►

6. In India, Mahatma Gandhi was more than a political leader he was the enlightened one embodying the soul of the nation.

(A) political leader he was
(B) political leader; he was
(C) political leader, he was
(D) political leader which was
(E) political leader, although he was

7. Because of a teacher shortage in the math and science disciplines, educators are encouraging retired scientists and engineers to pursue a second career in teaching.

(A) Because of a teacher shortage in the math and science disciplines, educators are encouraging
(B) Educators, faced with a teacher shortage in technical disciplines have encouraged
(C) In addition to a teacher shortage in the math and science areas, educators encourage
(D) Teacher shortages in the math and science disciplines have forced educators to hire
(E) Because there is a teacher shortage in the math and science disciplines, educators encourage

8. Neither the principal or the teachers had been satisfied with the addition of a crossing guard, and wanted a traffic light installed at the street crossing.

(A) Neither the principal or the teachers had been satisfied with the addition of a crossing guard, and
(B) Neither the principal nor the teachers were satisfied with the addition of a crossing guard; they
(C) Because neither the principal or the teachers had been satisfied with the addition of a crossing guard, they
(D) As the result of the addition of a crossing guard, the principal and the teachers
(E) Neither the principal nor the teachers feels the crossing guard is sufficient; and they

9. Most of the students like to read these kind of detective stories as recreational reading.

(A) these kind of detective stories
(B) these kind of detective story
(C) this kind of detective story
(D) this kinds of detective story
(E) those kind of detective story

10. Because of his now chronic throat ailment, the tenor recently has not and apparently never will sing again.

(A) has not and apparently never will sing
(B) had not sung and apparently never would sing
(C) has not and apparently never would sing
(D) has not sung and apparently never will sing
(E) had not and apparently never will sing

11. Having the best record for attendance, the school awarded him a medal at graduation.

(A) the school awarded him a medal
(B) the school awarded a medal to him
(C) he was awarded a medal by the school
(D) a medal was awarded to him by the school
(E) a school medal was awarded to him

12. Several regulations were proposed by the president of the university that had a sexist bias, according to women students.

(A) Several regulations were proposed by the president of the university that
(B) Several regulations were proposed by the president of the university who
(C) The proposal of several regulations by the president of the university which
(D) The president of the university, who proposed several regulations that
(E) The president of the university proposed several regulations that

13. The difference between the candidates is that one is radical; the other, conservative.

(A) one is radical; the other, conservative
(B) one is radical; the other being conservative
(C) while one is radical; the other, conservative
(D) one is radical, the other, conservative
(E) one is radical, although the other is more conservative

14. Police academies, on seeing as how new recruits lack basic driving skills, are teaching recruits the basics on test fields and neighborhood streets.

(A) Police academies, on seeing as how new recruits lack basic driving skills, are teaching
(B) Since new police recruits lack basic driving skills, police academies are teaching
(C) Police academies, because new recruits are lacking basic driving skills, teach
(D) As a result of new recruits lacking basic driving skills, police academies are teaching
(E) Even though new recruits lack basic driving skills, police academies are teaching

GO ON TO NEXT PAGE ▶

15. Although the babysitter had expected the twins to protest being told to go to bed, they went to their room without scarcely a murmur.
   (A) being told to go to bed, they went to their room without scarcely a murmur
   (B) being told to go to bed, they had gone off to their room without scarcely a murmur
   (C) being told that they should go to bed, they went to their room without scarcely a murmur
   (D) being told to go to bed, however, they went to their room without scarcely a murmur
   (E) being told to go to bed, they went to their room with scarcely a murmur

16. Although hydroponics is unsuitable for growing root vegetables and trees, which require soil and space, the system is ideal for cultivating a wide variety of plants such as tomatoes and beans.
   (A) Although hydroponics is unsuitable for growing root vegetables and trees, which require
   (B) Although hydroponics being unsuitable for growing root vegetables and trees, which require
   (C) Although hydroponics is unsuitable for growing root vegetables and trees, being that they require
   (D) Although hydroponics is unsuited to grow root vegetables and trees, these require
   (E) Although hydroponics is unsuitable for growing root vegetables and trees, and they require

17. Acutely aware of how much he owed to the generosity of Mr. Fezziwig, young Ebenezer addressed his benefactor respectively.
   (A) Acutely aware of how much he owed to the generosity of Mr. Fezziwig, young Ebenezer addressed his benefactor respectively.
   (B) Being that he was acutely aware of how much he owed to the generosity of Mr. Fezziwig, young Ebenezer addressed his benefactor respectively.
   (C) Young Ebenezer was acutely aware of how much he owed to the generosity of Mr. Fezziwig, so he addressed his benefactor respectively.
   (D) Acutely aware of how much he owed to the generosity of Mr. Fezziwig, young Ebenezer addressed his benefactor respectfully.
   (E) Acutely aware of how much he owed to the generosity of Mr. Fezziwig, young Ebenezer addressed his respective benefactor.

18. Although the suspect resolutely maintained his innocence, the jury found his story entirely incredulous.
   (A) the jury found his story entirely incredulous
   (B) the jury found his entire story incredulous
   (C) his story was found by the jury to be entirely incredulous
   (D) the jury found his story entirely incredible
   (E) the jury had found his story entirely incredulous

19. Many studies of new drugs are funded by major pharmaceutical firms, which suggests the possibility of bias in their conclusions.
   (A) which suggests the possibility of bias in their conclusions
   (B) thus the possibility of bias to their conclusions is suggested
   (C) a state of affairs that suggests the possibility of bias in their conclusions
   (D) and the possibility of bias in their conclusions being suggested
   (E) this fact suggests the possibility of bias in their conclusions

20. Intended to promote safety in the workplace, the regulation stipulates that protective goggles must be worn while welding.
   (A) that protective goggles must be worn while welding
   (B) that protective goggles while welding must be worn
   (C) that, while welding, protective goggles must be worn
   (D) that one must wear protective goggles while you weld
   (E) that you must wear protective goggles when you are welding

The sentences in this section may contain errors in grammar, usage, choice of words, or idioms. There is either just one error per sentence, or the sentence is correct. Some words or phrases are underlined and lettered; everything else in the sentence is correct.

If an underlined word or phrase is incorrect, choose that letter; if the sentence is correct, select No error. Then blacken the appropriate space on your answer sheet.

EXAMPLE:

The region has a climate so severe that (A) plants growing there (B) rarely had been (C) more than twelve inches high (D). No error (E)

Ⓐ Ⓑ ● Ⓓ Ⓔ

21. As (A) some of (B) the conglomerates gain more power, the legal codes regarding (C) bankruptcy and monopoly will need (D) further consideration. No error (E)

22. In 1777, the Second Continental Congress has adopted (A) a resolution to designate (B) the design for the American flag, but (C) no flags were issued until (D) 1783. No error (E)

23. He dashed into (A) the burning building, irregardless (B) of the risk involved (C), to warn the sleeping occupants (D). No error (E)

24. According to (A) Ms. Lynch's portfolio, there (B) is little doubt that she and her staff is (C) eminently qualified (D) for the assignment. No error (E)

25. Neither the Republican members of the committee who (A) supported the proposed legislation or (B) the Democratic members who opposed it controlled a clear majority (C); the votes of the independents were (D) crucial. No error (E)

26. No one (A) can predict what (B) the affect (C) of the government investigations will be (D) on American politics in the near future. No error (E)

27. In order to (A) give adequate attention to all students, many teachers prefer (B) team teaching, which (C) divides students according to his and her (D) abilities. No error (E)

28. I was irritated by (A) you (B) coming into the room as (C) you did—shouting (D) and screaming. No error (E)

29. Just like (A) prehistoric man, some groups of (B) southwestern Indians have dwelled (C) in caves along steep, rocky (D) ledges. No error (E)

30. I find (A) that sculpture more unusual (B) than (C) any of the other sculptures exhibited during (D) this special exhibit. No error (E)

31. One (A) of the basic economic reactions is that (B) as bond prices fall, stock prices rise, (C) and an increase in interest rates (D). No error (E)

32. Some (A) of the major networks have created (B) special prepared (C) news stories about life on city streets to publicize (D) the plight of the homeless. No error (E)

33. Some women (A) have made a clear-cut choice (B) between a career and motherhood; others have been creating (C) a balance between (D) the two. No error (E)

34. The renter of the car initialed (A) the clause in the contract to indicate (B) his (C) awareness that he was liable (D) for any damage to the automobile. No error (E)

Improving Paragraphs Directions

The passage below is the unedited draft of a student's essay. Some of the essay needs to be rewritten to make the meaning clearer and more precise. Read the essay carefully.

The essay is followed by questions about changes that might improve all or part of its organization, development, sentence structure, use of language, appropriateness to the audience, or use of standard written English. Choose the answer that most clearly and effectively expresses the student's intended meaning. Indicate your choice by filling in the corresponding space on the answer sheet.

[1] For two hundred years United States citizens have taken for granted their right to life, liberty, and the pursuit of happiness. **[2]** From the experiences in the former Yugoslavia to the repressive regime in the People's Republic of China, Americans should know, however, that human rights are always in danger.

[3] During the period of the conquistadores and Spanish colonial rule of Latin America, for example. **[4]** Latin American natives were often violated and repressed by European settlers, an example of this is the fact that the land formerly owned by the native Latin Americans was taken away from them so the people lost the right to own land. **[5]** Secondly, the Latin American people were forced to work this land as slaves on their own land. **[6]** These human rights violations were overcome by the independence movements led by such freedom fighters as Bolivar and San Martin in the late 1800s.

[7] In the Soviet Union, the extremely repressive Stalinist regime after WW II violated the rights of the Russian peasants, known as kulaks. **[8]** Collectivizing their farmlands by force, their rights were violated by Stalin. **[9]** Therefore, their private possessions were lost. **[10]** Another way by which they had their human rights violated was by forcing political opponents to remain silent, to work in labor camps, or to be killed. **[11]** After Stalin's death in 1953, one of his successors, Nikita Khrushchev, attempted to denounce the Stalinist regime. **[12]** However, it took another thirty years and the collapse of the Soviet Union to bring about basic human rights in Russia.

[13] About the history of human rights violations, the Serbs in the former Yugoslavia and the leaders of Communist China should know that they can't go on forever. **[14]** Eventually, their power will be usurped, or the people will rise up to claim their God-given human rights.

35. Taking into account the sentences that precede and follow sentence 3, which of the following is the best revision of sentence 3?

(A) As an example, the time that the Spanish were expanding their empire and searching for gold.
(B) Take, for example, during the era of the conquistadores and Spanish colonial rule in Latin America.
(C) Consider, for example, the period of the conquistadores and Spanish colonial rule in Latin America.
(D) The Spanish expanded their empire into Latin America in the 16th century.
(E) For instance, the period of Spanish colonialism in Latin America, for example.

36. Which of the following is the best revision of sentence 4?

(A) The land of Latin American natives was confiscated by European settlers. In fact, the rights of the natives to own land was violated and repressed.
(B) European settlers in Latin America have seized the land and the natives had repressed the right to own property.
(C) The colonial rulers confiscated the natives' property and denied them the right to own land.
(D) Having their rights violated, the natives of Latin America had their land taken away. Then the European settlers repress their right to own any land at all.
(E) The rights of the Latin American natives were violated and repressed. For example, they took their land and they prohibited them from owning land.

GO ON TO NEXT PAGE ▶

37. In the context of paragraph 3, which is the best revision of sentences 8 and 9?

(A) Forcing them to collectivize their farmlands, Stalin confiscated their private property.
(B) One of the ways by which Stalin violated their rights was by forcing people to collectivize their farmlands, thus causing them to lose their right to hold private possessions.
(C) One way in which the kulaks had their rights violated was Stalin forcing them to collectivize their farmlands and therefore, surrender private property.
(D) Having lost the right to own private property, Stalin collectivized the kulaks' farmland.
(E) The loss of private property and the collectivization of farmland was one way by which Stalin violated their rights.

38. Considering the content of the entire essay, which revision of the underlined segment of sentence 13 below provides the best transition between paragraphs 3 and 4?

<u>About the history of human rights violations,</u> the Serbs in the former Yugoslavia and the leaders of Communist China should know that they can't go on forever.

(A) In conclusion,
(B) Finally,
(C) Last but not least,
(D) Based on the history of international agreements on human rights,
(E) If the experience of Latin America and the Soviet Union means anything,

39. On the basis of the essay as a whole, which of the following describes the writer's intention in the last paragraph?

(A) To draw a conclusion based on the evidence in the passage
(B) To prepare readers for the future
(C) To instruct readers about the past
(D) To offer solutions to the problem posed by the essay
(E) To give an example

IF YOU FINISH IN LESS THAN 30 MINUTES, YOU MAY CHECK YOUR WORK ON THIS SECTION ONLY. DO NOT TURN TO ANY OTHER SECTION IN THE TEST.

STOP

Answer Key

Section 1 Critical Reading

1. **D**	6. **B**	11. **C**	16. **A**	21. **D**
2. **E**	7. **A**	12. **A**	17. **E**	22. **B**
3. **A**	8. **C**	13. **E**	18. **B**	23. **E**
4. **D**	9. **E**	14. **B**	19. **D**	24. **E**
5. **B**	10. **C**	15. **B**	20. **C**	

Section 2 Mathematics

1. **C**	5. **C**	9. **A**	13. **D**	17. **A**
2. **C**	6. **D**	10. **C**	14. **B**	18. **D**
3. **D**	7. **B**	11. **D**	15. **B**	19. **E**
4. **B**	8. **A**	12. **A**	16. **C**	20. **A**

Section 3 Critical Reading

25. **A**	30. **C**	35. **E**	40. **A**	45. **D**
26. **C**	31. **E**	36. **C**	41. **E**	46. **C**
27. **C**	32. **D**	37. **B**	42. **C**	47. **E**
28. **A**	33. **C**	38. **D**	43. **B**	48. **A**
29. **E**	34. **D**	39. **B**	44. **D**	

Section 4 Mathematics

21. **D**	23. **D**	25. **C**	27. **B**
22. **B**	24. **C**	26. **B**	28. **C**

29.

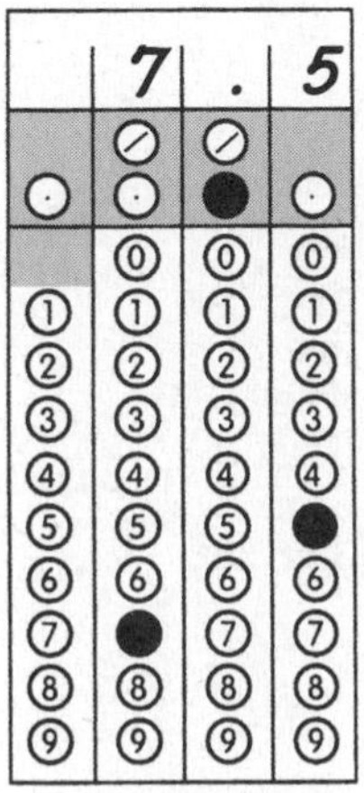

or 15/2

30.

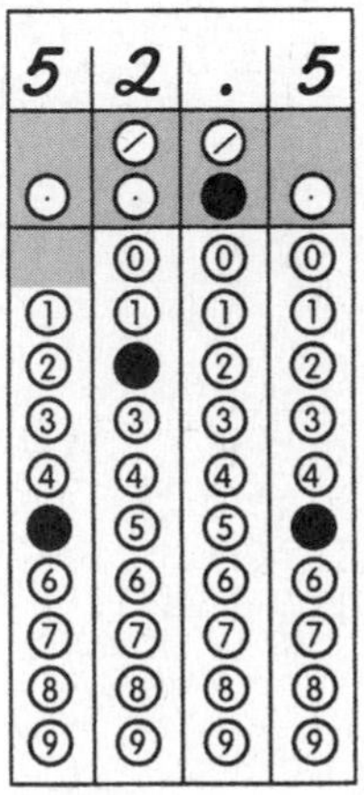

31.

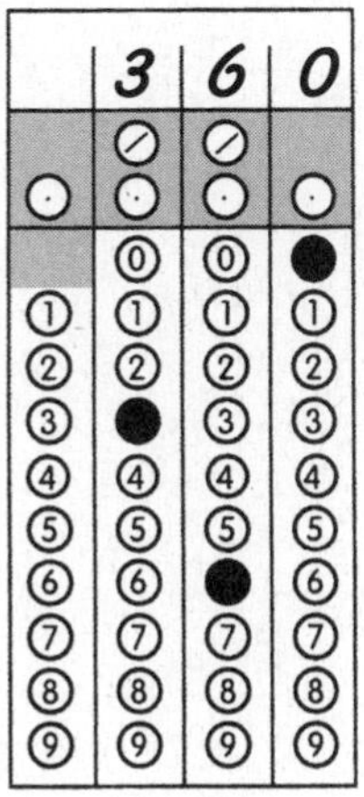

32.

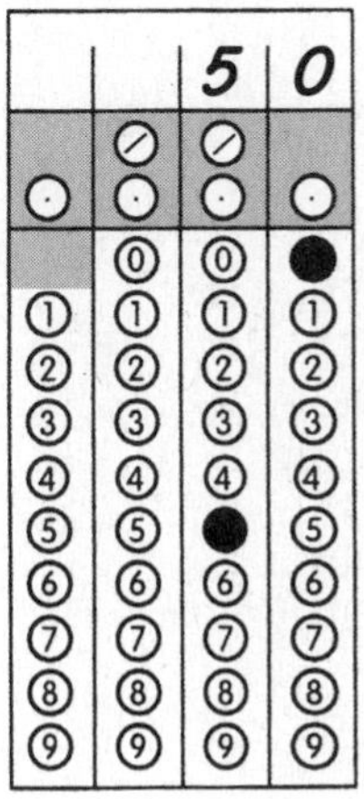

33.
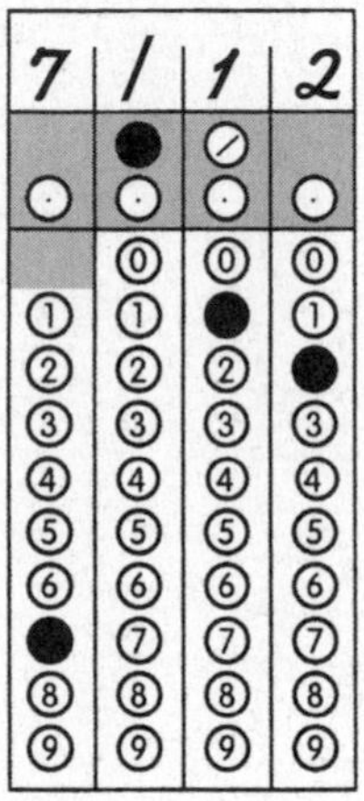

34.
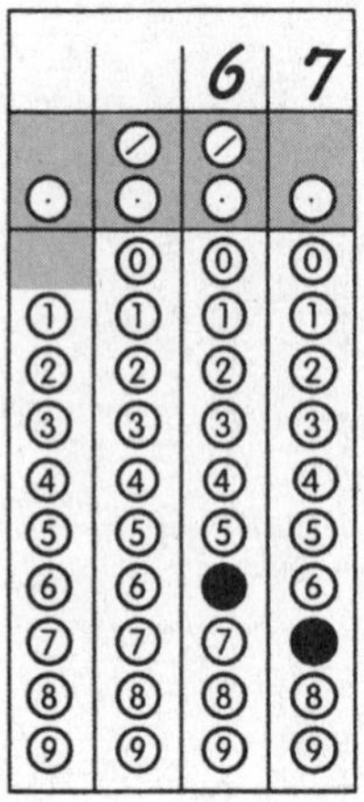

35.
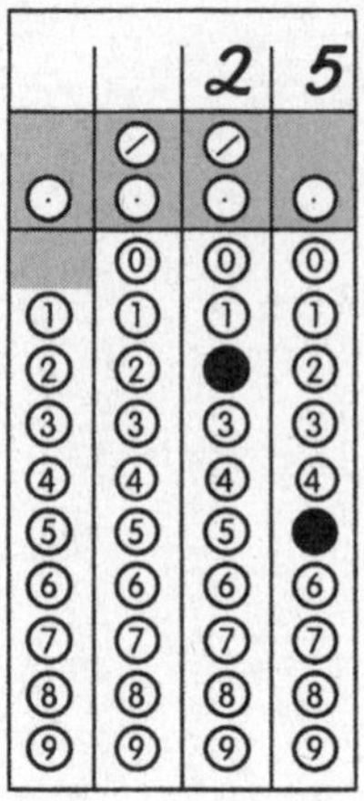

36.
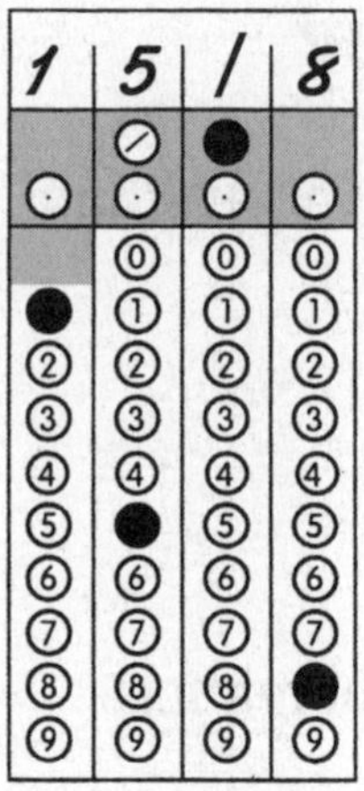

or 1.87

or 1.88

37.
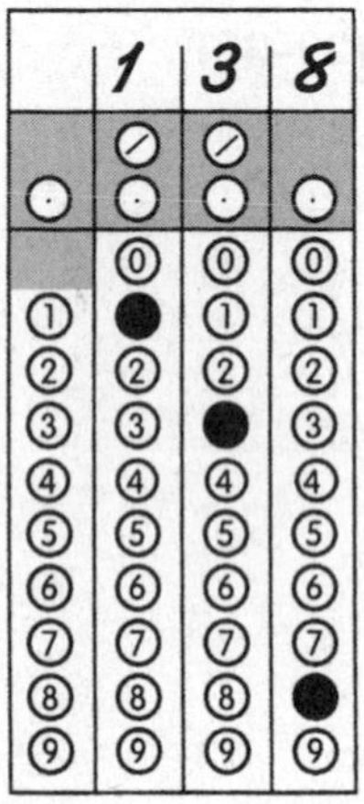

38.
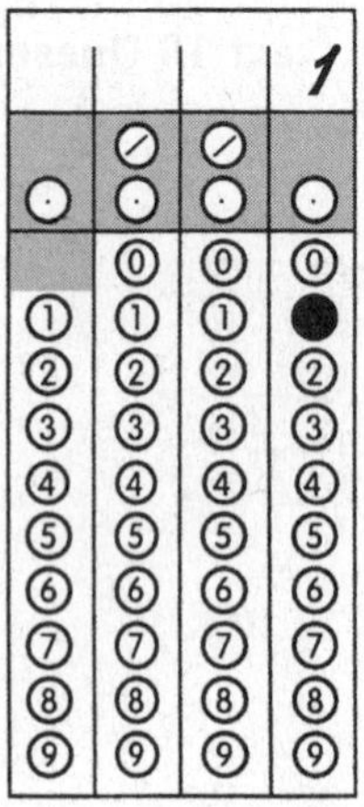

Section 5 Writing Skills

1.	**A**	9.	**C**	17.	**D**	25.	**B**	33.	**C**
2.	**C**	10.	**D**	18.	**D**	26.	**C**	34.	**E**
3.	**D**	11.	**C**	19.	**C**	27.	**D**	35.	**C**
4.	**C**	12.	**E**	20.	**E**	28.	**B**	36.	**C**
5.	**C**	13.	**A**	21.	**E**	29.	**E**	37.	**A**
6.	**B**	14.	**B**	22.	**A**	30.	**E**	38.	**E**
7.	**A**	15.	**E**	23.	**B**	31.	**D**	39.	**A**
8.	**B**	16.	**A**	24.	**C**	32.	**C**		

Scoring Chart–Practice Test 4

Critical Reading Sections		Mathematics Sections	
Section 1: 24 Questions (1–24)		**Section 2: 20 Questions (1–20)**	
Number correct	________ (A)	Number correct	________ (A)
Number omitted	________ (B)	Number omitted	________ (B)
Number incorrect	________ (C)	Number incorrect	________ (C)
$\frac{1}{4}$ (C)	________ (D)	$\frac{1}{4}$ (C)	________ (D)
(A) − (D)	________ Raw Score I	(A) − (D)	________ Raw Score I
Section 3: 24 Questions (25–48)		**Section 4: First 8 Questions (21–28)**	
Number correct	________ (A)	Number correct	________ (A)
Number omitted	________ (B)	Number omitted	________ (B)
Number incorrect	________ (C)	Number incorrect	________ (C)
$\frac{1}{4}$ (C)	________ (D)	$\frac{1}{4}$ (C)	________ (D)
(A) − (D)	________ Raw Score II	(A) − (D)	________ Raw Score II
		Section 4: Next 10 Questions (29–38)	
Total Critical Reading Raw Score		Number correct	________ Raw Score III
Raw Scores I + II	________	**Total Mathematics Raw Score**	
		Raw Scores I + II + III	________

NOTE: In each section (A) + (B) + (C) should equal the number of questions in that section.

Writing Skills Section

Section 5: 39 Questions (1–39)

Number correct	________ (A)
Number omitted	________ (B)
Number incorrect	________ (C)
$\frac{1}{4}$ (C)	________ (D)
Writing Skills Raw Score	
(A) − (D)	________

Evaluation Chart

Study your score. Your raw score is an indication of your probable achievement on the PSAT/NMSQT. As a guide to the amount of work you need or want to do with this book, study the following.

Raw Score			Self-Rating
Critical Reading	*Mathematics*	*Writing Skills*	
42–48	35–38	33–39	Superior
37–41	30–34	28–32	Very good
32–36	25–29	23–27	Good
26–31	21–24	17–22	Above average
20–25	17–20	12–16	Average
12–19	10–16	7–11	Below average
less than 12	less than 10	less than 7	Inadequate

ANSWER EXPLANATIONS

Section 1 Critical Reading

1. **(D)** Fast-food restaurants are growing more popular in France. The traditional café is therefore growing less popular (falling "victim to the growing popularity" of McBurgers) and is slowly *becoming extinct* (vanishing, disappearing; dying out).

2. **(E)** *Although* signals a contrast. You would expect the coach to be *jubilant* (extremely joyful) about her team's victory. Instead, she was *disheartened* (discouraged).

3. **(A)** *Bantering* or joking remarks are clearly *inappropriate* in a serious speech.

4. **(D)** People uncomfortable with math would be likely to think the field should be *left to* those gifted in such an *esoteric* (hard to understand; known only to a chosen few) subject.

5. **(B)** A writer whose work was universally acclaimed or applauded and whose reputation was not yet *tarnished* or stained would be at the *zenith* or high point of her career.

6. **(B)** The Pilgrims have traditionally been held up or *cited* as defenders of democracy.

7. **(A)** In challenging the traditional image of the Mayflower Compact as a cornerstone of American democracy, the author reveals himself to be a *debunker*, one who exposes false claims or attacks established beliefs.

8. **(C)** Unlike the author of Passage 1, the author of Passage 2 speaks in the first person. "To *me*," he says, "the Mayflower Compact will always be a cornerstone of American democracy." Thus, he makes use of *personal voice.*

9. **(E)** The opening sentence of Passage 1 asserts that the Mayflower Compact had little impact on the growth of freedom in America. The author of Passage 2, however, maintains that the compact "laid a sound foundation" for American democracy. Clearly, he doubts that Passage 1's opening assertion is true. In other words, he would argue that the assertion was of *dubious validity.*

10. **(C)** The entire passage examines Bethune's beliefs in the ultimate victory of racial justice and in the possibility of winning whites to her cause. In addition, it clearly shows Bethune, in her work to get her people represented in all public problems, having an impact on her people's progress.

11. **(C)** You can arrive at the correct answer by the process of elimination.
 Williams assisted Bethune in influencing the advancement of blacks within the NYA. Therefore, you can eliminate Choices B and D. The opening sentence of the first paragraph indicates Williams was one of Bethune's white friends; references to him in the second paragraph suggest he was a liberal. Therefore, you can eliminate Choice A. Nothing in the passage suggests Williams was religious. Therefore, you can eliminate Choice E. Only Choice C is left. It is the correct answer.

12. **(A)** Bethune's success in getting Dickerson's appointment is a clear example of her impact.
 Choice B is incorrect. The author is stressing how helpful Bethune was to Dickerson, not how different Bethune's career was from Dickerson's. Choice C is incorrect. Dickerson is not the subject of the paragraph that follows. Choice D is incorrect. The author brings up Bethune's belief in the "New Negro" well after he mentions her assistance to Dickerson. He draws no connection between Dickerson and the "New Negro." Choice E is incorrect. The author is making a point about Bethune, not about Dickerson.

13. **(E)** Bethune was the intermediary who helped arrange for Dickerson's new position. She was instrumental or *helpful* in gaining this end.

14. **(B)** By leading America to a "full realization of its democratic ideals," the New Negro would be *helping America accomplish its egalitarian goals*.

15. **(B)** The author compares and contrasts Bethune with her white liberal friends. The author directly quotes the wording of Bethune's 1944 appeals for black representation. The author gives concrete examples of the ways in which Bethune remained a black partisan champion of the New Deal. The author constantly reiterates the idea that Bethune

Note the following icons, used throughout this book:

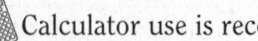

Time saver	Look it up; math reference fact	Helpful Hint
Educated guess	Prefixes, roots, and suffixes	Caution!
Did you notice?	Positive or negative?	Calculator use is recommended

had an ongoing influence on black progress during the Roosevelt years. However, the author uses figurative language only minimally and never develops an extended metaphor.

16. **(A)** Dickens implies that Gradgrind is so peremptory (absolute; dogmatic) about facts that he would insist upon the fact that his given name was, in fact, Thomas.

17. **(E)** Gradgrind carries scales and a rule in his pocket to "weigh and measure any parcel of human nature." Though Dickens plays upon several meanings of *rule* here, the word basically refers to a ruler or measuring stick.

18. **(B)** As he walks home, Gradgrind is in "a state of considerable satisfaction." He is pleased with himself and with the school he has created; his mood is clearly one of *complacency* or smugness.

19. **(D)** Dickens is poking fun at Gradgrind's teaching methods and is thus *broadly satirical* (full of ridicule).

20. **(C)** Gradgrind never introduces his pupils to nursery rhymes or to fantasy creatures such as ogres. This suggests that he rejects from his curriculum anything that is in the least *fanciful* or imaginative.

21. **(D)** Dickens has written the passage from the point of view of an omniscient narrator, *an observer who knows all about Gradgrind's thoughts and feelings.* The narrator knows all about Gradgrind's emotional state, his goals as headmaster, his manner of speech. In short, he knows Gradgrind through and through.

22. **(B)** The little Gradgrinds, having studied the Great Bear and Charles's Wain, had never "known wonder on the subject of stars." This suggests that the Great Bear and the Wain are constellations, or *groupings of stars*.

23. **(E)** Gradgrind's main idea is to fill his pupils full of *facts*, particularly facts about *science* (statistics, constellations, graminivorous quadrupeds, etc.).

24. **(E)** The famous cow with the crumpled horn ("The House That Jack Built") and the yet more famous cow who swallowed Tom Thumb in the folk tale are legendary *fictional characters* with whose celebrity the young Gradgrinds are unacquainted.

Section 2 Mathematics

For many problems, the explanation provides a reference to one or more **KEY FACTS** from Chapter 7. These are the mathematical facts that you need to solve that problem. If a solution refers to **KEY FACT J2**, for example, the solution depends on the second **KEY FACT** discussed in Section J of Chapter 7.

For some problems, an alternative solution, indicated by two asterisks (**), follows the first solution. When this occurs, usually one of the solutions is the direct mathematical one and the other is based on one of the tactics discussed in Chapters 6 and 7.

See page 234 for an explanation of the symbol $\Rightarrow$, which is used in several answer explanations.

1. **(C)** $35 = (7 - 2)(7 - m) = 5(7 - m) = 35 - 5m$. So, $5m = 0$, and, therefore, $m = 0$.

2. **(C)** Since the sum of the measures of the three angles of a triangle is 180° (**KEY FACT J1**), then

$$40 + 2a + 3a = 180 \Rightarrow 40 + 5a = 180 \Rightarrow 5a = 140 \Rightarrow a = 28.$$

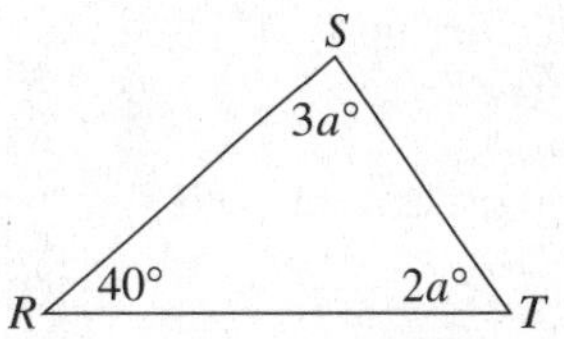

Use **TACTIC 6-6. If you trust the diagram, there are many ways to go. If a were 45, $2a$ would be 90, which is clearly wrong. Likewise, if a were 10, $2a$ would be 20, which is also way off. In fact, $\angle S$ appears to be *about* a 90° angle. So, $3a \approx 90$, which means $a \approx 30$. Choose 28.

3. **(D)** To convert 225 minutes to hours, divide by 60: the quotient is 3 and the remainder is 45. Therefore, 225 minutes from 10:05 A.M. is 3 hours and 45 minutes from 10:05 A.M., which is 1:50 P.M.

**If you divide 225 by 60 on your calculator, you get 3.75, and then you have to convert 0.75, or $\frac{3}{4}$, of an hour to 45 minutes.

4. **(B)** The easiest solution is to quickly reduce, by repeatedly dividing each side by 9:

$$(\overset{1}{\cancel{9}})(\overset{1}{\cancel{9}})(\overset{1}{\cancel{9}})n = \frac{{}^{\cancel{3}}(\overset{1}{\cancel{27}})(\overset{1}{\cancel{27}})^{\cancel{3}}}{n}. \text{ So } n = \frac{1}{n} \Rightarrow n = 1.$$

**Of course, you can rewrite the equation as $n^2 = \frac{(27)(27)}{(9)(9)(9)}$ and use your calculator: $n^2 = 1$.

Practice Test 4

5. **(C)** Since the two angles, x and y, form a straight angle, $x + y = 180$ (**KEY FACT I2**). Also, it is given that $x = y + 140$. Therefore,

$$(y + 140) + y = 180 \Rightarrow 2y + 140 = 180 \Rightarrow$$
$$2y = 40 \Rightarrow y = 20.$$

Use **TACTIC 6-1 and backsolve. Start with 20, Choice C. If $y = 20$, then
$x = 140 + 20 = 160$, and $20 + 160 = 180$;
so it works. The answer is Choice C.

6. **(D)** If $x^2 = 10$, then
$$x^6 = x^2 \cdot x^2 \cdot x^2 = 10 \times 10 \times 10 = 1000.$$

**Use your calculator: $x = \sqrt{10}$, and $(\sqrt{10})^6 = 1000$.

7. **(B)** The average of four consecutive integers is the average of the middle two and so is always 0.5 more than an integer: the average of 1, 2, 3, and 4 is 2.5; the average of 10, 11, 12, and 13 is 11.5; and the average of 98, 99, 100, and 101 is 99.5. Only II is true.

8. **(A)** The formula for the area of a circle is: $A = \pi r^2$.
Divide both sides by π: $r^2 = \dfrac{A}{\pi}$

Take the square root of each side: $r = \sqrt{\dfrac{A}{\pi}}$.

The diameter is twice the radius: $d = 2r = 2\sqrt{\dfrac{A}{\pi}}$.

**Let the radius of the circle be 1. Then, the area is π, and the diameter is 2. Which of the five choices is equal to 2 when $A = \pi$? Only $2\sqrt{\dfrac{A}{\pi}}$.

9. **(A)** Calculate each 2012 salary by multiplying each 2010 salary by (1 + the percent change). Ann had the highest 2012 salary:
$$\$4200(1.06) = \$4452.$$

10. **(C)** For some number x, the measures of the angles are x, x, and $2x$; so
$$180 = x + x + 2x = 4x \Rightarrow x = 45.$$
Therefore, the triangle is a 45-45-90 triangle, and, by **KEY FACT J5**, the ratio of the sides is $1:1:\sqrt{2}$.

11. **(D)** Draw diagrams. *A, B, C could be* the vertices of a right triangle (I is true). If *A, B, C* were the vertices of a square, then $AC = \sqrt{2}(AB)$ (II is false). *A, B, C could* all lie on a circle. In fact, the only way that three points couldn't lie on a circle would be if they all were on the same line (III is true). Statements I and III only are true.

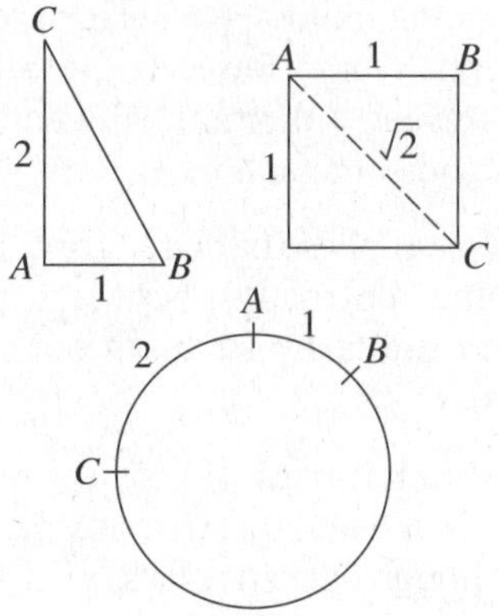

12. **(A)** On the first painting, Ross made a 20% profit; so if he bought it for x dollars and sold it for \$1200,
$1200 = x + .20x = 1.2x \Rightarrow x = 1200 \div 1.2 = 1000$.
His profit was \$200.

On the second painting, Ross lost 20%; so if he bought it for y dollars and sold it for \$1200,
$1200 = y - .20y = .80y \Rightarrow y = 1200 \div .80 = 1500$.
His loss was \$300.

In all, he lost exactly \$100.

13. **(D)** Draw a picture.

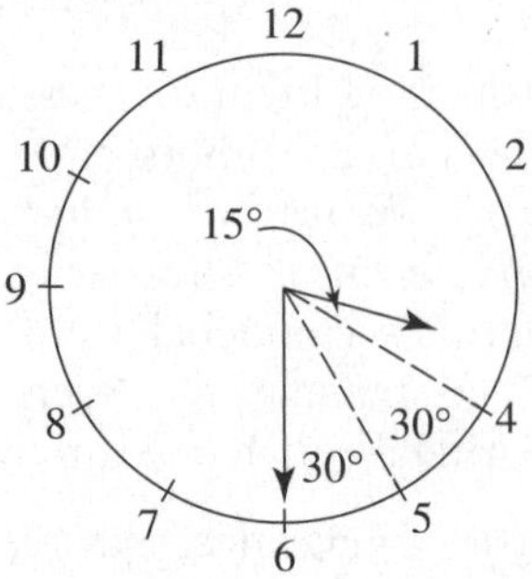

The minute hand, of course, is pointing right at 6. The hour hand, however, is *not* pointing at 3. It was pointing at 3 at 3:00, half an hour ago. The hour hand is now one-half of the way between the 3 and 4. So there are 15° between the hour hand and 4 and another 60° between 4 and 6, a total of 75°.
**If you can't figure the answer out exactly, guess. From the picture, you should see that the angle definitely measures more than 60° and less than 90°. Eliminate Choices A, B, and E.

14. **(B)** Check each statement. The only factors of 15 are ±1, ±3, ±5, and ±15. If m is any of these, $\frac{15}{m}$ is an odd integer. (I is false.) Eliminate Choices A and D. Could $\frac{m}{15}$ be an even integer? Sure, it could be *any* even integer; for example, if $m = 30$, $\frac{m}{15} = 2$; if $m = 150$, $\frac{m}{15} = 10$. (II is true.) Eliminate Choice C. Could $15m$ be prime? No, $15m$ is divisible by 15. (III is false.) II is the only true statement.

15. **(B)** Since 1, 2, 3, and 6 are each divisors of 6, the remainder is 0 when they are divided into 6. The only nonzero remainders occur when 6 is divided by 4, in which case the remainder is 2, and when 6 is divided by 5, in which case the remainder is 1. The sum of the remainders is 3.

16. **(C)** Since $a < b$, when a is divided by b, the quotient is 0 and the remainder is a; so $a*b = a$. When *any* number is divided by a, the remainder must be less than a, and so the maximum value of $b*a$ is $a - 1$. Therefore, the greatest possible value of $a*b + b*a$ is $a + (a - 1) = 2a - 1$.
Use **TACTIC 6-2: plug in numbers. Let $a = 2$ and $b = 3$. When 2 is divided by 3, the quotient is 0 and the remainder is 2:
$$2 = 0(3) + 2. \text{ So } 2*3 = 2.$$
When 3 is divided by 2, the quotient is 1 and the remainder is 1:
$$3 = 1(2) + 1. \text{ So } 3*2 = 1.$$
$2*3 + 3*2 = 2 + 1 = 3$. Which choice equals 3 when $a = 2$ and $b = 3$? Only $2a - 1$.

17. **(A)** Use **TACTIC G3**: When you have more than two equations, add them
$$x + y = 10$$
$$y + z = 15$$
$$+\ x + z = 17$$
$$2x + 2y + 2z = 42$$
Divide by 2: $x + y + z = 21$
To get the average, divide the sum by 3: $\frac{x + y + z}{3} = \frac{21}{3} = 7$
(*Note:* you *could* solve for x, y, z, but you shouldn't.)

18. **(D)** Check each choice. (A) If $x = 5$, $\sqrt{x - 1} = 2$. (B) This one is more difficult; the only possibility is $x = 1$, in which case $\sqrt{x^2 - 1} = 0$. If you don't see that immediately, keep Choice B under consideration, and test the rest. (C) If $x = 1$, $\frac{1}{x} = 1$. (D) For positive x, $\frac{x + 2}{x + 1}$ is always greater than 1 but less than 2; $\frac{x + 2}{x + 1}$ cannot be an integer—that's it. If you didn't reason that out, check Choice E. $\frac{7}{x + 1}$ is an integer if $x = 6$. You should have eliminated at least Choices A, C, and E.

19. **(E)** Any odd number is the sum of two consecutive integers: $6 + 7 = 13$ and $7 + 8 = 15$. Eliminate Choices B and D. Next try the sum of three consecutive integers: $3 + 4 + 5 = 12$. Eliminate Choice A. Now try four consecutive integers: $2 + 3 + 4 + 5 = 14$. Eliminate Choice C. The answer must be 16.

20. **(A)** If p painters can complete a job in d days, then 1 painter will take p times as long: it would take 1 painter pd days to complete the job and $\frac{1}{4}pd = \frac{pd}{4}$ days to complete 25%, or $\frac{1}{4}$, of the job. Finally, if the work is divided up among q painters it would take $\frac{pd}{4} \div q = \frac{pd}{4q}$ days.
Use **TACTIC 6-2: plug in easy-to-use numbers. If 2 painters can complete the job in 4 days, it would take them 1 day to complete 25% of the job. It would take 1 painter twice as long—2 days. Which choice is equal to 2, when $p = 2, d = 4$, and $q = 1$? Only $\frac{pd}{4q}$. Remember: Test each choice with your calculator and eliminate a choice as soon as it is clear that it is not equal to 2.

Section 3 Critical Reading

25. **(A)** Because it can now be grown successfully in America, the once-rare fruit is now *accessible* or readily available to American consumers.

26. **(C)** Someone always searching for new ways to do things is by definition *an innovator* (someone who introduces changes into the existing ways of doing things).

27. **(C)** A trip to France, with all the chances for conversing in French it would provide, would be a practical or *pragmatic* test of how much you had learned of conversational French.

28. **(A)** Since Cherokee society already granted certain rights to women, it did not break with or *violate* Cherokee custom to allow women their rights.

29. **(E)** Though scientists might be upset by *erroneous* (faulty) or *derivative* (unoriginal) work, the scientific community would be most shocked by *fraudulent* or faked research that was intentionally *deceptive* or deceitful.

30. **(C)** The key phrase "of few words" indicates that Eastwood's characters are *laconic*, untalkative types.

31. **(E)** *Insipid* (flavorless; dull and uninteresting) is a term that applies equally well to food and to conversations.

32. **(D)** Someone *crabbed* (bad-humored; harsh; morose) seldom smiles; someone *parsimonious* (stingy; miserly) never gives away money. Note how parallel structure determines word order: the first missing adjective relates to the first verb ("seldom smiled"); the second missing adjective relates to the second verb ("never gave away").

33. **(C)** The passage contrasts the image of Nightingale, the night nurse carrying a lamp as she walked the wards, with the image of Nightingale, the hospital authority. What is more, it states that Nightingale "came into her own as the world's most renowned authority on hospital reform." To come into one's own is to achieve one's potential, to become fulfilled. According to the author, Nightingale did not reach her full potential until she became a recognized authority on hospital reform. To the author, therefore, *her greatest accomplishments were in improving hospital planning and administration.*

34. **(D)** When Nightingale addressed these aspects of hospital construction and management, she *dealt with* them thoroughly and in great detail.

35. **(E)** In this passage, the author celebrates the return into print of Green's novels and makes a case for her as the mother of detective fiction. Thus, the author's purpose is most likely to *reclaim* Green, *a forgotten literary pioneer*, from a century's worth of neglect, in process restoring her reputation.

36. **(C)** The publication of *The Leavenworth Case* marked or *denoted* (signaled) the first appearance of Inspector Gryce.

37. **(B)** In extending the pilot's control of the plane and making extreme actions (loops, sudden swerves, dives, etc.) comfortable, acrobatic flying *extends a pilot's range of capabilities*.

38. **(D)** The medium of the air is the *environment* in which flying creatures function.

39. **(B)** In the course of doing a loop, you lose sight of the horizon and must tilt your head backward to catch sight of the horizon line again. Thus, to pick up the horizon line is to *spot it visually*.

40. **(A)** Earlier in the passage, the author describes the experience of doing a loop as being "as far outside instinctive human behavior as you can go." In grabbing at the sides of the cockpit during the loop, the author is reverting to *instinctive*, involuntary behavior.

    Choice B is incorrect. The experience of doing a loop was terrifying; grabbing the sides of the cockpit was not. Choice C is incorrect. It was not essential for the author to grab the sides of the cockpit; his seat belt was strong enough to keep him from falling out of the plane. Choice D is incorrect. The author did not wind up making a habit of grabbing the sides of the cockpit; he did it only that once. Choice E is incorrect. The experience of doing a loop may have seemed life threatening; grabbing the sides of the cockpit was not.

41. **(E)** In saying the belt held, the author means that it did not slip or come unfastened; instead, it *maintained its grasp*, keeping him safe.

42. **(C)** The instructor tells the author to put his arms out of the cockpit so that he can learn to have confidence in his seat belt's ability to hold him in the plane. He does so, *relying totally on his seat belt to keep him safe*.

43. **(B)** By stressing the terror that went into learning how to fly a loop, the author makes you feel that *satisfying* is an extremely mild word to describe the exhilaration of overcoming such an extreme fear and mastering such an unnatural skill. It is clearly an *understatement*.

44. **(D)** The author was not a fan of stunt flying; she was reluctant to pay attention to the aerial display. Therefore, this particular aerial display must have been unusually *captivating* to capture her attention.

45. **(D)** The author describes the audience's longing for a particular effect in the stunt-flying demonstration ("a certain kind of roll or climb, or a return to a certain portion of the air"). This is akin to a reader's longing for a particular effect in a poem—for example, a certain kind of image or rhyme or the return of an earlier refrain. Poets, however, play with their readers' expectations, sometimes varying exact end-rhymes with an occasional assonance or consonance (*slant* rhymes), as when Emily Dickinson unexpectedly rhymes *came* with *home*. Thus, in saying that Rahm "fulfilled your hope slantingly, like a poet," the author means that he *refused to satisfy your expectations directly* but gave you something unexpected instead.

46. **(C)** By "moving back the boundaries of the humanly possible" the author is talking about becoming aware *of new potentials for humanity*. This new knowledge leaves her gladdened and *exhilarated*.

47. **(E)** Passage 1 is both descriptive and informative. In recounting the story of the flying lesson, it is anecdotal. However, in comparison with Passage 2, it is not particularly poetic or *lyrical*.

48. **(A)** The author of Passage 1 talks about how useful acrobatic flying is in improving the skills of pilots. The author of Passage 2, however, looks on acrobatic flying as *an aesthetic experience*: she responds to Rahm's aerial demonstration as a new form of beauty, a performance that engages her aesthetically. Therefore, she would most likely consider the assessment of aerial flying in Passage 1 *too utilitarian* (concerned with practical usefulness) to be appropriate for an aesthetic experience.

Section 4 Mathematics

For many problems, the explanation provides a reference to one or more **KEY FACTS** from Chapter 7. These are the mathematical facts that you need to solve that problem. If a solution refers to **KEY FACT J2**, for example, the solution depends on the second **KEY FACT** discussed in Section J of Chapter 7.

For some problems, an alternative solution, indicated by two asterisks (**), follows the first solution. When this occurs, usually one of the solutions is the direct mathematical one and the other is based on one of the tactics discussed in Chapters 6 and 7.

See page 234 for an explanation of the symbol ⇒, which is used in several answer explanations.

21. **(D)** $2x - 1 = 9 \Rightarrow 2x = 10 \Rightarrow x = 5$. Then $20x = 100$ and $20x - 1 = 99$.

22. **(B)** Since $8 - (8 + w) = -w$, the equation becomes $-w = 8$. So, $w = -8$.

23. **(D)** Let the numbers be x and $\frac{1}{5}x$. Then

$$20 = x\left(\frac{1}{5}x\right) = \frac{1}{5}x^2 \Rightarrow x^2 = 100 \Rightarrow$$
$$x = 10 \text{ or } x = -10.$$

Since the numbers are positive, $x = 10$, $\frac{1}{5}x = 2$, and their sum is 12.

**You can avoid using algebra by just testing pairs of small numbers, where one number is 5 times the other: 1 and 5? No. 2 and 10? Yes.

24. **(C)** Let x be Mr. Riccardo's number.

Then $x + 3 = 3x \Rightarrow 3 = 2x \Rightarrow x = 1.5$.

Use **TACTIC 6-1 and backsolve. Start with Choice C:

$1.5 + 3 = 4.5$ and $1.5 \times 3 = 4.5$. It works.

25. **(C)** If a team lost l of the g games it played, it won the rest: $g - l$. The fraction is $\frac{g-l}{g}$.

Use **TACTIC 6-2 and choose easy-to-use numbers. If the team lost 1 of its 3 games, it lost $\frac{1}{3}$ of them and won $\frac{2}{3}$ of them. Only Choice C equals $\frac{2}{3}$ when $g = 3$ and $l = 1$.

26. **(B)** When 200 is divided by 7, the quotient is 28 and the remainder is 4. Therefore, 200 days is 4 days more than 28 weeks. Twenty-eight weeks after a Friday is again a Friday, and 4 days after that is Tuesday. (Note that it is irrelevant that the *date* was August 13, 2010; this problem concerned only the day of the week.)

27. **(B)** Since the area of the square is 20, each side is $\sqrt{20}$. The radius of each semicircle, therefore, is $\frac{\sqrt{20}}{2}$.

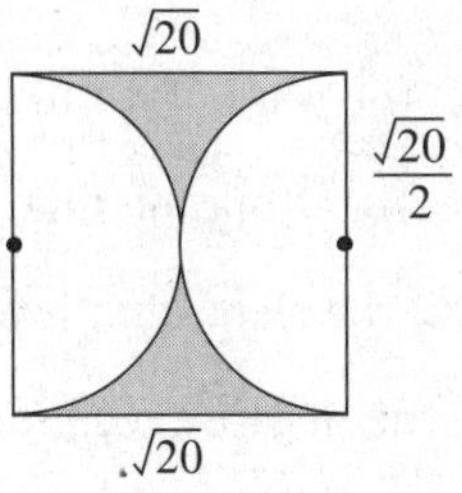

The area of the two semicircles is equal to the area of a circle of radius $\frac{\sqrt{20}}{2}$:

$$\pi\left(\frac{\sqrt{20}}{2}\right)^2 = \pi\left(\frac{20}{4}\right) = 5\pi.$$

So the area of the shaded region is

$$20 - 5\pi = 5(4 - \pi).$$

Use **TACTIC 6-6: trust the diagram and use your calculator, if necessary, to eliminate absurd answer choices. Clearly, the shaded area is less than half the area of the square, so it is surely less than 10. Approximating π by 3 and the square root of 20 by 4 or 5, we see that choices A, B, C, D, and E are about 17, 5, 12, 22, and 40, respectively. Clearly, the answer is choice B.

28. **(C)** Adding the three equations, we get immediately that $a - d = 60$.

**Pick any number for d; say $d = 10$. Then $c = 40$, $b = 60$, and $a = 70$. Finally, $70 - 10 = 60$.

29. **(7.5 or 15/2)** $\triangle ABC$ is a right triangle; its area is given by $\frac{1}{2}(AB)(AC)$. Since $\overline{AB}$ is vertical, find its length by subtracting the y-coordinates: $AB = 4 - 1 = 3$. Similarly, since $\overline{AC}$ is horizontal, find its length by subtracting the x-coordinates: $BC = 6 - 1 = 5$. Then, area of $\triangle ABC = \frac{1}{2}(3)(5) = \frac{15}{2} = 7.5$.

30. **(52.5)** Since the sum of all the angles around a point is 360° (**KEY FACT I3**),

$$90 + a + a + 60 + a + a = 360 \Rightarrow$$
$$4a + 150 = 360 \Rightarrow 4a = 210 \Rightarrow a = 52.5.$$

31. **(360°)** By **TACTIC E1**, if the average of five numbers is 100, their sum is $5 \times 100 = 500$. Since $20 + 30 + 40 + 50 = 140$, the fifth number, x, is $500 - 140 = 360$.

32. **(50)** Since 40% of the members of the club are boys, then 60% are girls. Let m be the number of members of the club.
Then $.60m = 30 \Rightarrow m = 30 \div .60 = 50$.

33. **($\frac{7}{12}$)** Use the slope formula (**KEY FACT N4**) to calculate the slope of line l: $\frac{7-3}{4-1} = \frac{4}{3}$. By **KEY FACT N6**, the slope of m is also $\frac{4}{3}$ and the slope of n is $-\frac{3}{4}$, the negative reciprocal of $\frac{4}{3}$. So the sum of the two slopes is $\frac{4}{3} + (-\frac{3}{4}) = \frac{7}{12}$.

34. **(67)** Write out enough terms of the sequence until you see a pattern.

$$1, 2, 3, 5, 8, 13, 21, 34, 55, \ldots$$

There are several patterns you might notice, but one observation is that the terms are

<u>odd, even, odd</u>, <u>odd, even, odd</u>, . . .

with the sequence <u>odd, even, odd</u> repeating indefinitely. The first 99 terms consist of 33 groups, with 2 odd numbers in each group, for a total of 66 odd numbers. The 100th number is the first number in the next group, which is odd. So there are 67 odd terms.

35. **(25)** $5(\sqrt{x} - 3) = 3\sqrt{x} - 5 \Rightarrow$

$$5\sqrt{x} - 15 = 3\sqrt{x} - 5 \Rightarrow$$
$$2\sqrt{x} - 15 = -5 \Rightarrow$$
$$2\sqrt{x} = 10 \Rightarrow \sqrt{x} = 5 \Rightarrow x = 25.$$

36. **($\frac{15}{8}$ or 1.87 or 1.88)** Use b, c, and t for "bangs," "clangs," and "tangs," respectively. Then the given equations are: $3b = 2c$ and $4b = 5t$. Multiply the first equation by 4 and the second by 3:

$$12b = 8c \text{ and } 12b = 15t$$

So

$$8c = 15t \Rightarrow c = \frac{15}{8}t$$

So

$$1 \text{ clang} = \frac{15}{8} \text{ tangs.}$$

37. **(138)** Since 40% of 25 is 10, there are 10 girls and $25 - 10 = 15$ boys in the class. The total weight of the 10 girls is $10 \times 120 = 1200$ pounds and the total weight of the 15 boys is $15 \times 150 = 2250$. Therefore, the average weight of all 25 children is

$$\frac{1200 + 2250}{25} = \frac{3450}{25} = 138.$$

38. **(1)** By **KEY FACT K9**, the area of a square whose diagonal is d is $\frac{d^2}{2}$. Since the area of the black region is the area of the large square minus the area of the middle square, the black area is:

$$\frac{1}{2}(5^2) - \frac{1}{2}(4^2) = \frac{1}{2}(25) - \frac{1}{2}(16) =$$
$$12.5 - 8 = 4.5.$$

The striped region is a square whose diagonal is 3, and so its area is $\frac{1}{2}(3^2) = \frac{1}{2}(9) = 4.5$. Therefore, the two areas are equal, and so the ratio of their areas is 1.

Section 5 Writing Skills

1. **(A)** Sentence is correct.
2. **(C)** The two errors in diction (*imminent* for *eminent* and *stood* for *stayed*) are corrected in Choice C.
3. **(D)** This corrects the sentence fragment.
4. **(C)** Choice C corrects the sentence fragment.
5. **(C)** Comma splice. Choice C corrects the run-on sentence and expresses the author's meaning directly and concisely. All other choices are indirect, ungrammatical, or do not retain the meaning of the original sentence.
6. **(B)** Choice B corrects the run-on sentence.
7. **(A)** Sentence is correct.
8. **(B)** Error in coordination and subordination. Choice B corrects the conjunction *neither* . . . *nor* (not *neither* . . . *or*) and retains the meaning of the original sentence.
9. **(C)** Error in pronoun number agreement. Use *this kind of story* or *these kinds of stories*.
10. **(D)** The omission of the correct verb form is corrected in Choice D.
11. **(C)** Error in modification. The dangling participle construction is corrected in Choice C.
12. **(E)** Error in modification and word order. Choice E corrects the misplaced modifier and eliminates the unnecessary use of the passive voice.
13. **(A)** The use of the semicolon to separate the pair of clauses is correct.
14. **(B)** Choice B expresses the author's meaning directly and concisely. All other choices are indirect, ungrammatical, or do not retain the meaning of the original sentence.

15. **(E)** Double negative. Change *without scarcely a murmur* to *with scarcely a murmur.*

16. **(A)** Sentence is correct.

17. **(D)** Error in usage. Do not confuse *respectively* (singly in the order mentioned) and *respectfully* (politely and deferentially).

18. **(D)** Error in usage. The story is *incredible* or improbable; the jurors are *incredulous* (skeptical, disbelieving).

19. **(C)** Error in relative pronoun use. Relative pronouns are noun substitutes that serve to introduce subordinate clauses. Replace *which* with *a state of affairs that*.

20. **(E)** Dangling modifier. Ask yourself who is welding. Certainly not the goggles!

21. **(E)** Sentence is correct.

22. **(A)** Error in sequence of tenses. Change *has adopted* to *adopted.*

23. **(B)** Error in diction. Change *irregardless* to *regardless*.

24. **(C)** Error in subject-verb agreement. The subject *she and her staff* is plural; the verb should be plural—*are*.

25. **(B)** Error in diction. Change *or* to *nor*.

26. **(C)** Error in diction. Change *affect* to *effect*.

27. **(D)** Error in pronoun agreement. Change *his and her* to *their*.

28. **(B)** Error in pronoun case. Change *you* to *your*.

29. **(E)** Sentence is correct.

30. **(E)** Sentence is correct.

31. **(D)** Error in parallelism. Change *an increase in interest rates* to *interest rates increase.*

32. **(C)** Adjective and adverb confusion. Change *special prepared* to *specially prepared.*

33. **(C)** Error in tense. Change *been creating* to *created.*

34. **(E)** Sentence is correct.

35. **(C)** Choice A is a sentence fragment.
 Choice B violates standard English idiom. The phrase *for example* should be followed by a noun, not by a prepositional phrase.
 Choice C is a complete sentence and serves as an appropriate topic sentence for the second paragraph. It is the best answer.
 Choice D serves neither as a good transition from the first to the second paragraph nor as an effective topic sentence for the second paragraph.
 Choice E is a sentence fragment; also the phrases *for instance* and *for example* are redundant.

36. **(C)** Choice A contains an error in subject-verb agreement. The plural subject *rights* should have a plural verb, *were*.
 Choice B shifts verb tenses from present perfect (*have seized*) to past perfect (*had repressed*). Confusion ensues.
 Choice C succinctly and accurately revises the original sentence. It is the best answer.
 Choice D is a confusion of verb tenses, which renders the sentence almost incomprehensible.
 Choice E has a severe pronoun reference problem. It is unclear to whom the pronouns *they, their,* and *them* refer.

37. **(A)** Choice A clearly and succinctly explains the fate of the kulaks. It is the best answer.
 Choice B is wordy and awkwardly expressed.
 Choice C is wordy and contains a usage error. Because *forcing* is a gerund, *Stalin* should be possessive (*Stalin's*).
 Choice D contains a dangling participle. It says that Stalin lost this right to own private property, an idea contrary to what the writer intended.
 Choice E is not accurately expressed and contains an error in subject-verb agreement. The compound subject *loss* and *collectivization* requires a plural verb.

38. **(E)** Choices A, B, and C are trite and abrupt transitions. They should be avoided.
 Choice D is not a good answer because the essay does not discuss international agreements on human rights.
 Choice E accurately and smoothly provides a link between the content of the essay and the concluding paragraph. It is the best answer.

39. **(A)** Only Choice A accurately describes the function of the last paragraph. The conclusion—that people will eventually claim their rights—grows out of the discussion in paragraphs 1, 2, and 3. Therefore, Choice A is the best answer.

After the PSAT/NMSQT

After the scores of the PSAT/NMSQT are received, you, your parents, and your guidance counselor can begin to make plans for college. Here are some Barron's reference books that will be very helpful to you.

Barron's SAT by Sharon Weiner Green and Ira K. Wolf (2012, 26th Edition). This classic includes a diagnostic test and five additional practice tests that enable you to practice under exact SAT format and test conditions; all tests have answer keys and answer explanations. Extensive review and practice is provided for each type of test question. The Critical Reading review also includes the 3500 word list, with definitions and parts of speech. The Writing review includes common grammar and usage errors. The Mathematical Reasoning review covers basic arithmetic through high school algebra and geometry. Testing tactics and strategies are featured. Two additional practice tests are provided on an optional CD-ROM.

Critical Reading Workbook for the SAT by Sharon Weiner Green (2012, 14th Edition), ***Math Workbook for the SAT*** by Lawrence Leff (2012, 5th Edition), ***Writing Workbook for the SAT*** by George Ehrenhaft (2012, 3rd Edition). These workbooks provide the detailed review you may need for specific sections of the test. Each book contains hundreds of practice questions with answers and extensive review specific to the topic.

Grammar Workbook for the SAT, ACT...and More by George Ehrenhaft (2010, 2nd Edition). This workbook provides a review of the grammatical issues you are most likely to be asked about on the SAT, ACT, and other standardized tests. You'll learn terms you need to know and how to avoid the grammar pitfalls that give almost everyone a headache. And you will learn how to write a proper exam essay. The book includes plenty of practice questions with complete answer explanations.

Hot Words for the SAT by Linda Carnevale (2010, 4th Edition). This book includes hundreds of words, grouped by concept, with definitions, sample sentences, and quizzes.

SAT 2400 by Linda Carnevale and Roselyn Teukolsky (2012, 4th Edition). Written for the student who is aiming for that perfect score, this book breaks down the toughest questions and analyzes why they are tough. Practice tests are provided for each of the three SAT sections: critical reading, writing, and math. An optional CD-ROM contains a complete practice SAT test and fifty additional practice questions.

SAT Flash Cards by Sharon Weiner Green and Ira K. Wolf (2011, 2nd Edition). This handy boxed set includes 200 math cards with 75 important math facts, strategies, and sample multiple-choice and grid-in questions; 200 grammar cards covering parts of speech, sentence construction, and more; and 100 vocabulary cards with definitions and sample sentences.

Essays That Will Get You Into College by Daniel Kaufman, Chris Dowhan, and Adrienne Dowhan (2009, 3rd Edition). More than fifty model essays that have worked for applicants, with advice, discussion, and commentary, reveal the secrets of successful essay writing.

Barron's Profiles of American Colleges (2012, 30th Edition). Profiles of more than 1,600 regionally accredited four-year American colleges and universities give the prospective student a preview of his or her relationship to a particular college—based on its facilities, outstanding features and programs, admission requirements, costs, available financial aid, extracurricular activities, programs and major offerings, degrees awarded, enrollment, religious affiliation, housing facilities, and social and honorary societies. CD-ROM included.

Index

THE FOLLOWING DOCUMENTATION APPLIES IF YOU PURCHASED
***PSAT/NMSQT, 16th Edition* with CD-ROM.**

How to Use the CD-ROM

The software is not installed on your computer; it runs directly from the CD-ROM. Barron's CD-ROM includes an "autorun" feature that automatically launches the application when the CD is inserted into the CD-ROM drive. In the unlikely event that the autorun feature is disabled, follow the manual launching instructions below.

Windows®

1. Click on the Start button and choose "My Computer" or "Computer."
2. Double-click on the CD-ROM drive, which will be named **PSAT_NMSQT.exe**.
3. Double-click **PSAT_NMSQT.exe** to launch the program.

MAC®

1. Double-click the CD-ROM icon.
2. Double-click the **PSAT_NMSQT** icon to start the program.

SYSTEM REQUIREMENTS
(Flash Player 10.2 is recommended)

Microsoft® Windows®
Processor: Intel Pentium 4 2.33GHz, Athlon 64 2800+ or faster processor (or equivalent).
Memory: 128MB of RAM.
Graphics Memory: 128MB.
Platforms:
Windows 7, Windows Vista®, Windows XP, Windows Server® 2008, Windows Server 2003.

MAC® OS X
Processor: Intel Core™ Duo 1.33GHz or faster processor.
Memory: 256MB of RAM.
Graphics Memory: 128MB.
Platforms:
Mac OS X 10.6, Mac OS X 10.5, Mac OS X 10.4 (Intel) and higher.

Linux® and Solaris™
Processor: Intel Pentium 4 2.33GHz, AMD Athlon 64 2800+ or faster processor (or equivalent).
Memory: 512MB of RAM.
Graphics Memory: 128MB.
Platforms:
Red Hat® Enterprise Linux (RHEL) 5 or later, openSUSE® 11 or later, Ubuntu 9.10 or later.
Solaris: Solaris™ 10.